THE PALI TEXT SOCIETY'S PALI-ENGLISH DICTIONARY

EDITED BY

T. W. RHYS DAVIDS,
F.B.A., D.Sc., Ph.D., L.L.D., D.Litt.
and WILLIAM STEDE, Ph.D.

GYAN

Published by

GYAN

Gyan Publishing House
5, Ansari Road
Daryaganj, New Delhi-110002
Phone: 011-47034999, 9811692060
E-mail: books@gyanbooks.com

Distribution Network
gyanbooks.com
India, USA, Canada, UK, Australia, France

ISBN : 978-81-212-4485-5 (PB)
First Published, 1921

2nd Impression 2020

Printed at: Gyan Press, Delhi.

THE PALI TEXT SOCIETY'S PALI-ENGLISH DICTIONARY

EDITED BY

T. W. RHYS DAVIDS, F.B.A., D.Sc., Ph.D., LL.D., D.Litt.
and WILLIAM STEDE, Ph.D.

PUBLISHED BY
THE PALI TEXT SOCIETY
LONDON

FOREWORD.

It is somewhat hard to realize, seeing how important and valuable the work has been, that when ROBERT CAESAR CHILDERS published, in 1872, the first volume of his Pali Dictionary, he only had at his command a few pages of the canonical Pali books. Since then, owing mainly to the persistent labours of the Pali Text Society, practically the whole of these books, amounting to between ten and twelve thousand pages, have been made available to scholars. These books had no authors. They are anthologies which gradually grew up in the community. Their composition, as to the Vinaya and the four Nikayas (with the possible exception of the supplements) was complete within about a century of the Buddha's death; and the rest belong to the following century. When scholars have leisure to collect and study the data to be found in this pre-Sanskrit literature, it will necessarily throw as much light on the history of ideas and language as the study of such names and places as are mentioned in it (quite incidentally) has already thrown upon the political divisions, social customs, and economic conditions of ancient India.

Some of these latter facts I have endeavoured to collect in my 'Buddhist India'; and perhaps the most salient discovery is the quite unexpected conclusion that, for about two centuries (both before the Buddha's birth and after his death), the paramount power in India was Kosala — a kingdom stretching from Nepal on the North to the Ganges on the South, and from the Ganges on the West to the territories of the Vajjian confederacy on the East. In this, the most powerful kingdom in India; there had naturally arisen a standard vernacular differing from the local forms of speech just as standard English differs from the local (usually county) dialects. The Pali of the canonical books is based on that standard Kosala vernacular as spoken in the 6th and 7th centuries B. C. It cannot be called the 'literary' form of that vernacular, for it was not written at all till long afterwards. That vernacular was the mother tongue of the Buddha. He was born in what is now Nepal, but was then a district under the suzerainty of Kosala and in one of the earliest Pali documents he is represented as calling himself a Kosalan.

When, about a thousand years afterwards, some pandits in Ceylon began to write in Pali, they wrote in a style strikingly different from that of the old texts. Part of that difference is no doubt due simply to a greater power of fluent expression unhampered by the necessity of constantly considering that the words composed had to be learnt by heart. When the Sinhalese used Pali, they were so familiar with the method of writing on palmleaves that the question of memorizing simply did not arise. It came up again later. But none of the works belonging to this period were intended to be learnt. They were intended to be read.

On the other hand they were for the most part reproductions of older material that had, till then, been preserved in Sinhalese. Though the Sinhalese pandits were writing in Pali, to them, of course, a dead language, they probably did their thinking in their own mother tongue. Now they had had then, for many generations, so close and intimate an intercourse with their Dravidian neighbours that Dravidian habits of speech had crept into Sinhalese. It was inevitable that some of the peculiarities of their own tongue, and especially these Dravidanisms, should have influenced their style when they wrote in Pali. It will be for future scholars to ascertain exactly how far this influence can be traced in the idioms and in the order of the arrangement of the matter of these Ceylon Pali books of the fifth and sixth centuries A. D.

There is no evidence that the Sinhalese at that time knew Sanskrit. Some centuries afterwards a few of them learnt the elements of classical Sanskrit and very proud they were of it. They introduced the Sanskrit forms of Sinhalese words when writing 'high' Sinhalese. And the authors of such works as the Dāṭhāvaṇsa, the Saddhammopayana, and the Mahābodhivaṇsa, make use of Pali words derived from Sanskrit — that is, they turned into Pali form certain Sanskrit words they found either in the Amara-koṣa, or in the course of their very limited reading, and used them as Pali. It would be very desirable to have a list of such Pali words thus derived from Sanskrit. It would not be a long one.

Here we come once more to the question of memory. From the 11th cent. onwards it became a sort of fashion to write manuals in verse, or in prose and verse, on such subjects as it was deemed expedient for novices to know. Just as the first book written in Pali in Ceylon was a chain of memoriter verses strung together by very indifferent Pali verses, so at the end we have these scarcely intelligible memoriter verses meant to be learned by heart by the pupils.

According to the traditions handed down among the Sinhalese, Pali, that is, the language used in the texts, could also be called Māgadhī. What exactly did they mean by that? They could not be referring to the Māgadhī of the Prakrit grammarians, for the latter wrote some centuries afterwards. Could they have meant the dialect spoken in Magadha at the date when they used the phrase, say, the sixth century A. D.? That could only be if they had any exact knowledge of the different vernaculars of North India at the time. For that there is no evidence, and it is in itself very improbable. What they did mean is probably simply the language used by Asoka, the king of Magadha. For their traditions also stated that the texts had been brought to them officially by Asoka's son Mahinda; and not in writing, but in the memory of Mahinda and his companions. Now we know something of the language of Asoka. We have his edicts engraved in different parts of India, differing slightly in compliance with local varieties of speech. Disregarding these local differences, what is left may be considered the language of head-quarters where these edicts were certainly drafted. This 'Māgadhī' contains none of the peculiar characteristics we associate with the Magadhī dialect. It is in fact a younger form of that standard Kosalan *lingua franca* mentioned above.

Now it is very suggestive that we hear nothing of how the king of Magadha became also king of Kosala. Had this happened quietly, by succession, the event would have scarcely altered the relation of the languages of the two kingdoms. That of the older and larger would still have retained its supremacy. So when the Scottish dynasty succeeded to the English throne, the two languages remained distinct, but English became more and more the standard.

However this may be, it has become of essential importance to have a Dictionary of a language the history of whose literature is bound up with so many delicate and interesting problems. The Pali Text Society, after long continued exertion and many cruel rebuffs and disappointments is now at last in a position to offer to scholars the first instalment of such a dictionary.

The merits and demerits of the work will be sufficiently plain even from the first fasciculus. But one or two remarks are necessary to make the position of my colleague and myself clear.

We have given throughout the Sanskrit roots corresponding to the Pali roots, and have omitted the latter. It may be objected that this is a strange method to use in a Pali dictionary, especially as the vernacular on which Pali is based had never passed through the stage of Sanskrit. That may be so; and it may not be possible, historically, that any Pali word in the canon could have been actually derived from the corresponding Sanskrit word. Nevertheless the Sanskrit form, though arisen quite independently, may throw light upon the Pali form; and as Pali roots have not yet been adequately studied in Europe, the plan adopted will probably, at least for the present, be more useful.

This work is essentially preliminary. There is a large number of words of which we do not know the derivation. There is a still larger number of which the derivation does not give the meaning, but rather the reverse. It is so in every living language. Who could guess, from the derivation, the complicated meaning of such words as 'conscience', 'emotion', 'disposition'? The derivation would be as likely to mislead as to guide. We have made much progress. No one needs now to use the one English word 'desire' as a translation of sixteen distinct Pali words, no one of which means precisely desire. Yet this was done in Vol. X of the *Sacred Books of the East* by MAX MÜLLER and FAUSBÖLL [1]). The same argument applies to as many concrete words as abstract ones. Here again we claim to have made much advance. But in either case, to wait for perfection would postpone the much needed dictionary to the Greek kalends. It has therefore been decided to proceed as rapidly as possible with the completion of this first edition, and to reserve the proceeds of the sale for the eventual issue of a second edition which shall come nearer to our ideals of what a Pali Dictionary should be.

We have to thank Mrs. STEDE for valuable help in copying out material noted in my interleaved copy of Childers, and in collating indexes published by the Society; Mrs. RHYS DAVIDS for revising certain articles on the technical terms of psychology and philosophy; and the following scholars for kindly placing at our disposal the material they had collected for the now abandoned scheme of an international Pali Dictionary:

Prof. STEN KONOW. Words beginning with *S* or *H*. (Published in *J P T S.* 1909 and 1907, revised by Prof. Dr. D. ANDERSEN).

Dr. MABEL H. BODE. *B*, *Bh* and *M*.

Prof. DUROISELLE. *K*.

Dr. W. H. D. ROUSE. *C—Ñ*.

In this connection I should wish to refer to the work of Dr. EDMOND HARDY. When he died he left a great deal of material; some of which has reached us in time to be made available. He was giving his whole time, and all his enthusiasm to

1) See Mrs. RHYS DAVIDS in *J R A S.*, 1898, p. 58.

the work, and had he lived the dictionary would probably have been finished before the war. His loss was really the beginning of the end of the international undertaking.

Anybody familiar with this sort of work will know what care and patience, what scholarly knowledge and judgment are involved in the collection of such material, in the sorting, the sifting and final arrangement of it, in the adding of cross references, in the consideration of etymological puzzles, in the comparison and correction of various or faulty readings, and in the verification of references given by others, or found in the indexes. For all this work the users of the Dictionary will have to thank my colleague, Dr. WILLIAM STEDE. It may be interesting to notice here that the total number of references to appear in this first edition of the new dictionary is estimated to be between one hundred and fifty and one hundred and sixty thousand. The Bavarian Academy has awarded to Dr. STEDE a personal grant of 3100 marks for his work on this Dictionary.

Chipstead, Surrey. July, 1921. T. W. RHYS DAVIDS.

List of Donors to the Pali Dictionary Fund down to 1 July, 1921.

		£	s.	d.
His Majesty the late King of Siam		500	0	0
Anonymous		507	7	11
Mrs. Ludwig Mond		300	0	0
Royal Asiatic Society (ten donations)		105	0	0
Victoria University of Manchester (four donations)		63	0	0
British Academy (five donations)		50	0	0
Gilbert H. Richardson, Esq. (three donations)		15	0	0
Lord Chalmers, K.C.B.		10	0	0
Mrs. Plimmer		10	0	0
F. L. Woodward, Esq. (two donations)		2	2	0
Captain Meysey Thompson		1	1	0
Mr. Kojiro Matsukata		500	0	0
Professor Charles R. Lanman		21	0	0
Professor James H. Woods		10	0	0
per Professor C. R. Lanman:				
Mr. Charles D. Burrage	($ 50 00)	12	11	3
Mr. Albert W. Ellis	(„ 25 00)	6	5	8
Mr. Charles T. Grinnell	(„ 10 00)	2	10	3
Dr. William S. Bigelow	(„ 100 00)	25	7	8
Mrs. Isabella S. Gardner	(„ 50 00)	12	13	9
Professor James R. Jewett	(„ 25 00)	6	6	11
		£ 2160	6	5

At the present prices of printing and paper the whole Dictionary is estimated to cost about £ 3500. At least £ 1000 more is therefore now urgently needed.

A.

List of the Chiefs Books consulted for Vocabulary

(with Abbreviations).

1. PALI BOOKS.

1a Canonical.

Anguttara-Nikāya 5 vols. P T S. 1885—1900 (A).
Buddha-Vaṃsa P T S. 1882 (Bu).
Cariyā-Piṭaka P T S. 1882 (Cp.).
Dhammapada P T S. 1914 (Dh).
Dhamma-Sangaṇi P T S. 1885 (Dhs).
Dīgha-Nikāya 3 vols. P T S. (D).
Iti-vuttaka P T S. 1890 (It.).
Kathā-Vatthu 2 vols. P T S. 1894, 95 (Kvu).
Khuddaka-Pāṭha P T S. 1915 (Kh).
Majjhima-Nikāya 3 vols. P T S. 1887—1902 (M).
Niddesa I Mahā° 2 vols. P T S. 1916, 17 (Nd[1]).
Niddesa II Culla° P T S. 1918 (Nd[2]).
Paṭisambhidāmagga 2 vols. P T S. 1905, 1907 (Ps).
Peta-Vatthu P T S. 1889 (Pv).
Puggala-Paññatti P T S. 1883 (Pug).
Saṃyutta-Nikāya 5 vols. P T S. 1884—1898 (S).
Sutta-Nipāta P T S. 1913 (Sn).
Thera-therīgāthā P T S. 1883 (Th 1) & (Th 2).
Udāna P T S. 1885 (Ud).
Vibhanga P T S. 1904 (Vbh).
Vimāna-Vatthu P T S. 1886 (Vv).
Vinaya-Piṭaka 5 vols. London 1879—83 (Vin).

1b Post-Canonical.

Atthasālinī, P T S. 1897 (DhsA).
Buddhadatta's Manuals, P T S. 1915 (Bdhd).
Dāṭhāvaṃsa, J P T S. 1884 (Dāvs).
Dhammapada Commentary, 4 vols. P T S. 1906—14 (DhA).
Dīpavaṃsa, London 1879 (Dpvs).
Jātaka, 6 vols. London 1877—96 (J).
Khuddaka-Pāṭha Commentary, P T S. 1915 (KhA).
Mahāvaṃsa, P T S. 1908 (Mhvs).
Mahā-Bodhi-Vaṃsa, P T S. 1891 (Mhbv).
Milindapañha, London 1880 (Miln).
Netti-Pakaraṇa, P T S. 1902 (Nett).
Pañca-gati-dīpana, J P T S. 1884 (Pgdp).
Peta-Vatthu Commentary, P T S. 1894 (PvA).
Puggala-Paññatti Commentary, J P T S. 1914 (Pug A).
Saddhammopāyana, J P T S. 1887 (Sdhp).
Sumangala-Vilāsinī, vol. I, P T S. 1886 (DA I).

Sutta-Nipāta Commentary, 2 vols. P T S. 1916—17 (SnA).
Therīgāthā Commentary, P T S. 1891 (ThA).
Vimāna-Vatthu Commentary, P T S. 1901 (VvA).
Visuddhi-Magga, 2 vols. P T S. 1920—21 (Vism).

Note. The system adopted in quotations of passages from Pali text is that proposed in J P T S. 1909, pp. 385—87, with this modification that Peta-vatthu (Pv) is quoted by canto and verse, and Culla-Niddesa (Nd[2]) by number of word in "Explanatory Matter".

2. BUDDHIST SANSKRIT.

Avadāna-śataka, ed. J. S. Speyer (Bibl. Buddhica III), 2 vols., St. Pétersbourg 1906. (Av. Ś.).

Divyâvadana, ed. Cowell & Neill, Cambridge 1886. (Divy).

Jātaka-mālā, ed. H. Kern (Haward Or. Ser. I), Boston 1891. (Jtm).

Lalita-vistara, ed. S. Lefmann, I. Halle 1902. (Lal. V.).

Mahā-vastu, ed. É. Senart, 3 vols., Paris 1882—1897.

Śikṣā-samuccaya. Ed. C. Bendall. St. Petersburg, 1902 [Śikṣ].

3. TRANSLATIONS.

Buddh. Manual of Psychological Ethics (trsl. of the Dhamma-sangaṇi) by Mrs. Rhys Davids (R. As. Soc. Trsl. Fund XII), London 1900. (*Dhs trsl.*).

Compendium of Philosophy (trsl. of the Abhidhamm' attha-sangaha) by S. Z. Aung and Mrs. Rhys Davids, P T S. Trsl. 1910. (*Cpd.*).

Dialogues of the Buddha, trsl. by T. W. and C. A. F. Rhys Davids, London I. 1899; II. 1910; III. 1921. (*Dial.*).

Expositor (trsl. of the Attha-sālinī), by Maung Tin, P T S. Trsl. 1920, 21.

Kathāvatthu trsl. ("Points of Controversy), by Aung and Mrs. Rhys Davids, P T S. Trsl. 1915. (*Kvu trsl.*).

Kindred Sayings (Saṇyutta Nikāya I), by Mrs. Rhys Davids, P T S. Trsl. 1917. (*K S.*).

Mahāvaṇsa trsl. by W. Geiger, P T S. Trsl. 1912.

Manual of a Mystic (Yogâvacara), trs. by F. L. Woodward, P T S. Trsl. 1916. (*Mystic*).

Neumann, K. E., Lieder der Mönche und Nonnen, Berlin 1899.

Psalms of the Brethren (trsl. Mrs. Rhys Davids), P T S. Trsl. 1913.
" " " Sisters (" " " "), " " 1909.

Questions of Milinda (trsl. T. W. Rhys Davids), S B E. vols. 35, 36.

Vinaya Texts (trsl. Rhys Davids & Oldenberg), " " " " 13, 17, 20.

4. GRAMMATICAL & OTHER LITERATURE; PERIODICALS, ETC.

Abhidhānappadīpikā, ed. W. Subhūti, Colombo[1] 1883. (Abhp.).

Andersen, D., A Pāli Reader, 2 pts; Copenhagen 1901, 1907.

Aufrecht, Th., Halāyudha's Abhidhāna-ratna-mālā, London 1861.

Brugmann, K., Kurze vergleichende Grammatik der indogerm. Sprachen, Strassburg 1902.

Childers, R. C., A Dictionary of the Pali Language, London 1874.

Geiger, W., Pāli Literatur und Sprache, Strassburg 1916. (Geiger, *P. Gr.*).
Grassmann, W., Wörterbuch zum Rig Veda, Leipzig 1873.
Journal of the American Oriental Society (*J A O S.*).
„ Asiatique, Paris (*J. As.*)
„ of the Pāli Text Society (*J P T S.*).
„ „ „ Royal Asiatic Society, London (*J R A S.*).
Kaccāyana-ppakaraṇa, ed. & trsl. Senart (J. As. 1871) (Kacc).
Kern, H., Toevoegselen op 't Woordenboek van Childers; 2 pts (Verhandelingen Kon. Ak. van Wetenschappen te Amsterdam N. R. XVI, 5), Amsterdam 1916. (*Toev.*).
Kuhn's Zeitschrift für vergleichende Sprachforschung (*K Z.*).
Mahāvyutpatti, ed. Mironow (Bibl. Buddhica XIII) St. Pétersbourg 1910, 11. (Mvyut).
Müller, Ed., Simplified Grammar of the Pali Language, London 1884.
Trenckner, V., Notes on the Milindapañho, in J P T S. 1908, 102 sq.
Uhlenbeck, H., Kurzgefasstes Etym. Wörterbuch d. Altindischen Sprache, Amsterdam 1898.
Walde, A., Lateinisches Etymologisches Wörterbuch, Heidelberg² 1910.
Zeitschrift der Deutschen Morgenländischen Gesellschaft, Leipzig 1847 sq. (*Z D M S.*).

B. LIST OF ABBREVIATIONS.

1. Titles of Books (the no. refers to section of A).

A	Anguttara	*1a*
Abhp	Abhidhānappadīpikā	4
Ap	Apadāna	*1a*
Av. Ś.	Avadāna-śataka	2
Bdhd	Buddhadatta	1
Brethren: see Psalms		3
Bu	Buddha-vaŋsa	*1a*
Cp	Cariyā-piṭaka	*1a*
Cpd	Compendium	3
D	Dīgha	*1a*
Dāvs	Dāṭhā-vaŋsa	*1b*
Dh	Dhammapada	*1a*
Dhs	Dhammasangaṇi	*1a*
Dhs trsl.	Atthasālinī	3
Dial.	Dialogues	3
Divy	Divyâvadāna	2
Dpvs	Dīpavaŋsa	*1b*
Halāyudha: see Aufrecht		4
It	Itivuttaka	*1a*
J	Jātaka	*1b*
J A O S.	Journal Amer. Or. Soc.	4
J As.	„ Asiatique	4
J P T S.	„ Pāli Text Soc.	4
J R A S.	„ Royal Asiatic Soc.	4
Jtm	Jātakamālā	2
Kacc	Kaccāyana	4
Kh	Khuddakapāṭha	*1a*
K S	Kindred Sayings	3
Kvu	Kathāvatthu	*1a*
K Z	Kuhn's Zeitschrift	4
Lal. V.	Lalita Vistara	2
M	Majjhima	*1a*
Mhbv	Mahābodhi-vaŋsa	*1b*
Mhvs	Mahāvaŋsa	*1b*
Miln	Milinda-pañha	*1b*
M Vastu	Mahā-vastu	2
Mvyut	Mahāvyutpatti	4
Mystic: see Manual		3
Nd¹	Mahāniddesa	*1a*
Nd²	Cullaniddesa	*1a*
Nett	Netti-pakaraṇa	*1b*
Pgdp	Pañcagati-dīpana	*1b*
Ps	Paṭisambhidā-magga	*1a*
Pug	Puggala-paññatti	*1a*
Pv	Petavatthu	*1a*
S	Saŋyutta	*1a*
S B E	Sacred Books of the East	3
Sdhp	Saddhammopāyana	*1b*
Śikṣ	Śikṣāsamuccaya	2
Sisters: see Psalms		3
Sn	Sutta-nipāta	*1a*
Th 1	Theragathā	*1a*
Th 2	Therīgatha	*1a*
Toev.	Toevoegselen	4

Ud	Udāna	1a
Vbh	Vibhanga	1a
Vin	Vinaya	1a
Vism	Visuddhi-magga	1b
Vv	Vimānavatthu	1a
ZDMG.	Zeitschrift der Deutschen Morgenländischen Gesellschaft	4

2. General & grammatical terms.

A in combn with a Title-letter (e.g. DhA) = Commentary (on Dh).
abl. ablative
abs. absolute(ly)
abstr. abstract
acc. accusative
act. active
add. addition
adj. adjective
adv. adverb
Ags. Anglo-Saxon
aor. aorist
appl. applied
art. article
attr. attribute
Av. Avesta

BB Burmese MSS
bef. before
BSk. Buddhist Sanskrit

C (& Cy) Commentary (when cited in expln of a Text passage).
caus. causative
cert. certain
coll. collective
combd, combn combined, combination
comp. comparative, comparison, composition
cons. consonant
corr. correct(ed)
correl. correlation, correlative
cp. compare
cpd. compound

dat. dative
den. denominative
der. derived, derivation
des. desiderative
dial. dialect(ical)
diff. different
dist. distinct, distinguished

E. English
e. g. for instance
encl. enclitic
ep. epithet
esp. especially
etym. etymology
exc. except
excl. exclamation, exclusive
expl. explanation, explained

f. feminine
fig. figurative(ly)
foll. following
form. formation
fr. from
freq. frequently, Frequentative
fut. future

Gall. Gallic
gen. genitive
ger. gerund
Ger. German
Goth. Gothic
Gr. Greek
gram. grammar, °atical
grd. gerundive

ibid. at the same passage
id. the same
id. p. identical passage
i. e. that is
i. g. in general
imper. imperative
impers. impersonal
impf. imperfect
Ind. Index
ind. indicative
indecl. indeclinable
indef. indefinite
inf. infinitive
instr. instrumental
interr. interrogative
intrs. intransitive
iter. iterative

Lat. Latin
l. c. loco citato
lit. literal(ly), literary
Lit. Lithuanian
loc. locative

m. masculine
med. medium (middle)

N. Name
n. noun, note
nom. nominative
Np. Name of person
Npl. „ „ place
nt. neuter
num. numeral

Obulg. Old-bulgarian
Ohg. Old-high-german
Oicel. „ -icelandic
Oir. „ -irish
onom. onomatopoetic
opp. opposed, opposite
ord. ordinal, ordinary
orig. original(ly)

P. Pāli
part. particle

pass	passive
perf.	perfect
pers.	personal
pl.	plural
pop.	popular
poss.	possessive
pot.	potential
pp.	past participle
ppr.	present „
prec.	preceding
pred.	predicative
pref.	prefix
prep.	preposition
pres.	present
pret.	preterite
Prk.	Prakrit
prob.	probably
pron.	pronoun
pt.	part
P T S.	Pāli Text Society
q. v.	quod vide (which see)
ref.	reference, referred
refl.	reflexive
rel.	relation, relative
sep.	separate(ly)
sg.	singular
Sk.	Sanskrit
sq.	and following
SS.	Singhalese MSS.
ster.	stereotype
suff.	suffix
sup.	superlative
s. v.	sub voce (under the word mentioned)
syn.	synonym(ous)
T.	Text
trans.	transitive
trsl.	translated, translation
t. t.	technical term
t. t. g.	„ „ in grammar
v.	verse
var.	variant, various
var. lect.	various reading
voc.	vocative
Wtb.	Wörterbuch

3. Typographical.

*(s)quel indicates a (reconstructed or conjectured) Indogermanic root.

*Sk means, that the Sanskrit word is constructed after the Pāli word; or as Sk. form is only found in lexicographical lists.

â: the cap over a vowel indicates that the a is the result of a syncope a + a (e. g. khuddânukhudda), whereas ā represents the proper ā, either pure or contracted with a preceding a (khīṇāsava = khīṇa + āsava).

° represents the head-word either as first (°—) or second (—°) part of a compound; sometimes also an easily supplemented part of a word.

> indicates an etymological relation or line of development between the words mentioned.

~ and ≈ means "at similar" or "at identical, parallel passages".

The meaning of all other abbreviations may easily be inferred from the context.

A-[1] the prep. ā shortened before double cons., as **akkosati** (ā + **kruś**), **akkhāti** (ā + **khyā**), **abbahati** (ā + **bṛh**). — Best to be classed here is the a- we call expletive. It represents a reduction of ā- (mostly before liquids and nasals and with single consonant instead of double). Thus **anantaka** (for **ā-nantaka** = **nantaka**) Vv.80[1]; **amajjapa** (for **ā-majjapa** = **majjapa**) J VI.328; **amāpaya** (for **ā-māpaya** = **māpaya**) J VI.518; **apassato** (= **passantassa**) J VI.552.

A-[2] (**an-** before vowels) [Vedic a-, an-; Idg. *n̥, gradation form to *ne (see na[2]); Gr. ἀ, ἀν-; Lat. *en-, in-; Goth., Ohg. & Ags. un-; Oir. an-, in-] neg. part. prefixed to (1) nouns and adjectives; (2) verbal forms, used like (1), whether *part.*, *ger.*, *grd.* or *inf.*; (3) finite verbal forms. In comp[n]. with words having originally two initial cons. the latter reappear in their assimilated form (e. g. appaṭicchavin). In meaning it equals na-, nir- and vi-. Often we find it opp. to sa-. Verbal negatives which occur in specific verb. function will be enum[d]. separately, while examples of neg. form. of (1) & (2) are given under their positive form unless the neg. involves a distinctly new concept, or if its form is likely to lead to confusion or misunderstanding. — Concerning the combining & contrasting (orig. neg.) -a- (â) in redupl. formations like **bhav-â-bhava** see **ā**[1].

A-[3] [Vedic a-; Idg. *e (loc. of pron. stem, cp. ayaṃ; orig. a deictic adv. with specific reference to the past, cp. Sk sma); Gr. ἐ-; also in Gr. ἐκεῖ, Lat. equidem, enim] the augment (sign of action in the past), prefixed to the root in *pret.*, *aor.* & *cond.* tenses; often omitted in ordinary prose. See forms under each verb; cp. also **ajja**. Identical with this a- is the a- which functions as base of some pron. forms like **ato**, **attha**, **asu** etc. (q. v.).

A-[4] the sound a (**a-kāra**) J VI.328, 552; VvA 279, 307, 311.

Aṃsa[1] [Vedic aṃsa; cp. Gr. ὦμος, Lat. umerus, Goth ams, Arm. us] (a) the shoulder AV II.110; Sn 609. **aṃse karoti** to put on the shoulder, to shoulder J I.9. (b.) a part (lit. side) (cp. °āsa in **koṭṭhāsa** and expl[n] of **aṃsa** as **koṭṭhāsa** at DA I.312, also v. l. **mettāsa** for **mettaṃsa** at It 22). — **atīt'aṃse** in former times, formerly D II.224; Th 2, 314. **mettaṃsa** sharing friendship (with) A IV.151 = It 22 = J IV.71 (In which connection Miln 402 reads **ahiṃsā**). — Disjunctive **ekena aṃsena . . . ekena aṃsena** on the one hand (side) . . . on the other, partly . . . partly A I.61. From this: **ekaṃsa** (adj.) on the one hand (only), i. e. incomplete (opp. **ubhayaṃsa**) or (as not admitting of a counterpart) definite, certain, without doubt (opp. **dvidhā**): see **ekaṃsa**. — **paccansena** according to each one's share A III.38. **puṭaṃsena** with a knapsack for provisions D I.117; A II 183; cp. DA I.288, with v. l. **puṭosena** at both passages.

-**kūṭa** "shoulder prominence", the shoulder Vin III.127; DhA III.214; IV.136; VvA 121. — **vaṭṭaka** a shoulder strap (mostly comb[d] with kāyabandhana; vv. ll. °vaddhaka, °bandhaka) Vin I.204 (T. °bandhaka); II.114 (ddh); IV.170 (ddh); Vv 33[40] (T. °bandhana, C. v. l. °vaṭṭaka); DhA III.452.

Aṃsa[2] [see next] point, corner, edge; freq. in comb[n] with **numerals**, e. g. **catur**° four-cornered, **chaḷ**°, **aṭṭh**°, **soḷas**° etc. (q. v.) all at Dhs 617 (cp. DhsA 317). In connection with a Vimāna: **āyat**° with wide or protruding capitals (of its pillars) Vv 84[15]; as part of a carriage-pole Vv 64[2] (= kubbara-phale patiṭṭhitā heṭṭhima-aṃsā VvA 265).

Aṃsi (f.) [cp. Vedic aśri, aśra, aśani; Gr. ἄκρος pointed, ἄκρις, also ὀξύς sharp: Lat. ācer sharp. Further connections in Walde Lat. Wtb. under ācer] a corner, edge (= **aṃsa**[2]) Vv 78[2] (= **aṃsa-bhāga** VvA 303).

Aṃsu [cp. Sk. aṃśu (Halāyudha) a ray of light] a thread Vin III.224. -**mālin**, sun Sāsv I.

Akaṭa (adj.) [a + kaṭa] not made, not artificial, natural; °**yūsa** natural juice Vin I.206.

Akampiyatta (nt.) [abstr. fr. akampiya, grd. of a + kampati] the condition of not being shaken, stableness Miln 354.

Akalu (cp. agalu) an ointment J IV.440 (**akaluñ candanañ ca**, v. l. BB aggalun; C. expl[s] as **kālâkaluñ ca rattacandanañ ca**, thus implying a blacking or dark ointment); VI.144 (°**candana-vilitta**; v. l. BB **aggalu**°); Miln 338 (°**tagara-tālīsaka-lohita-candana**).

Akāca (adj.) [a + kāca] pure, flawless, clear D II.244; Sn 476; J V.203.

Akācin (adj.) = akāca Vv 60[1]. Kern (Toevoegselen s. v.) proposes reading **akkācin** (= Sk. arka-arcin shining as the sun), but VvA 253 expl[s] by **niddosa**, and there is no v. l. to warrant a misreading.

Akāsiya (adj. -n.) [a + kāsika?] "not from the kāsī-country" (?); official name of certain tax-gatherers in the king's service J VI.212 (**akāsiya-sankhātā rāja-purisā** C.).

Akiccakāra (adj.) [a + kicca + kāra] 1. not doing one's duty, doing what ought not to be done A II.67; Dh 292; Miln 66; DA I.296. — 2. ineffective (of medicine) Miln 151.

Akiriya (adj.) [a + kiriya] not practical, unwise, foolish J III.530 (°**rūpa** = **akattabba-rūpa** C.); Miln 250.

Akilāsu (adj.) [a + kilāsu] not lazy, diligent, active, untiring S I.47; V.162; J I.109; Miln 382.

Akissava at S I.149 is probably faulty reading for **akiñcana**.

Akutobhaya (adj.) see **ku**°.

Akuppa (adj.) [a + kuppa, grd. of **kup**, cp. BSk. akopya M Vastu III.200] not to be shaken, immovable; sure, steadfast, safe Vin I.11 (akuppā me ceto-vimutti) = S II.239; Vin II.69; IV.214; D III.273; M I.205, 298; S II.171; A III.119, 198; Miln 361.

Akuppatā (f.) [abstr. fr. last] "state of not being shaken", surety, safety; Ep. of Nibbāna Th I, 364.

Akka [cp. Sk. arka] N. of a plant: Calotropis Gigantea, swallow-wort M I.429 (°**assa jiyā** bowstrings made from that plant).

-**nāla** a kind of dress material Vin I.306 (vv. ll. **agga**° & **akkha**°). -**vāṭa** a kind of gate to a plantation, a movable fence made of the akka plant Vin II.164 (cp. akkha-vāṭa).

Akkanta [pp. of akkamati] stepped upon, mounted on A I.8; J I.71; Miln 152; DhA I.200.

Akkandati [ā + kandati, **krand**] to lament, wail, cry S IV.206.

Akkamana (nt.) [cp. BSk. ākramaṇa Itm 31[58]] going near, approaching, stepping upon, walking to J I.62.

Akkamati [ā + kamati, **kram**] to tread upon, to approach, attack J I.7, 279; ThA 9; — to rise Vin III. 38. — ger. **akkamma** Cp. III.7[2]. — pp. **akkanta** (q. v.).

Akkuṭṭha (adj. n.) [pp. of akkosati] 1. (adj.) being reviled, scolded, railed at Sn 366 (= **dasahi akkosavatthūhi abhisatto** SnA 364); J VI.187. — 2. (nt.) reviling, scolding, swearing at; in comb[n] **akkuṭṭha-vandita** Sn 702 (= **akkosa-vandana** SnA 492) Th 2, 388 (expl[n] ThA 256 as above).

Akkula (adj.) [= ākula] confused, perplexed, agitated, frightened Ud 5 (**akkulopakkula** and **akkulapakkulika**). See **ākula**.

Akkosa [ā + **kruś** = **kruñc**, see kuñca & koñca²; to sound root kṛ, see note on gala] shouting at, abuse, insult, reproach, reviling Sn 623; Miln 8 (+ **paribhāsa**); SnA 492; ThA 256; PvA 243; DhA II.61.

-**vatthu** always as dasa a°-vatthūni 10 bases of abuse, 10 expressions of cursing J I.191; SnA 364, 467; DhA I.212; IV.2.

Akkosaka (adj.) [from last] one who abuses, scolds or reviles, + **paribhāsaka** A II.58; III.252; IV.156; V.317; PvA 251.

Akkosati [to **kruś** see akkosa] to scold, swear at, abuse, revile J I.191; II.416; III.27; DhA I 211; II.44. Often comb^d with **paribhāsati**, e. g. Vin II.296; DhA IV.2; PvA 10. — aor. **akkocchi** Dh 3; J III.212 (= **akkosi** DhA I.43. Der. wrongly fr. **krudh** by Kacc. VI.417; cp. Franke, Einh. Pāli-gramm. 37, and Geiger P. Gr. § 164). -pp. **akkuṭṭha** (q. v.).

Akkha¹ [Vedic akṣa; Av. aša; Gr. ἄξων ἅμαξα chariot with *one* axle); Lat. axis; Ohg. etc. ahsa, E. axle, to root of Lat. ago, Sk. **aj**] the axle of a wheel D II.96; S V.6; A I.112; J I.109, 192; V.155 (**akkhassa phalakaŋ yathā**; C.: **suvannaphalakaŋ viya**, i. e. shiny, like the polished surface of an axle); Miln 27 (+ **īsā** + **cakka**), 277 (**atibhārena sakaṭassa akkho bhijjati**: the axle of the cart breaks when the load is too heavy); PvA 277.

-**akkhan abbhañjati** to lubricate the axle S II.177; Miln 367.

-**chinna** one whose axle is broken; with broken axle S I.57; Miln 67. -**bhagga** with a broken axle J V.433. -**bhañjana** the breaking of the axle DhA I.375; PvA 277.

Akkha² [Vedic akṣa, prob. to akṣi & Lat. oculus, "that which has eyes" i. e. a die; cp. also Lat. ālea game at dice (fr.* asclea?)] a die D I.6 (but expl^d at DA I.86 as ball-game: **gulakīḷa**); S I.149 = A V.171 = Sn 659 (**appamatto ayaŋ kali yo akkhesu dhanaparājayo**); J I.379 (**kūṭ°** a false player, sharper, cheat) **anakkha** one who is not a gambler J V.116 (C.: **ajūtakara**). Cp. also **accha³**.

-**dassa** (cp. Sk. akṣadarśaka) one who looks at (i. e. examines) the dice, an umpire, a judge Vin III.47; Miln 114, 327, 343 (dhamma-nagare). -**dhutta** one who has the vice of gambling D II.348; III.183; M III.170; Sn 106 (+ itthidhutta & surādhutta). -**vāṭa** fence round an arena for wrestling J IV.81. (? read akka-).

Akkha³ (adj.) (—°) [to akkhi] having eyes, with eyes PvA 39 (BB. **rattakkha** with eyes red from weeping, glosson assumukha). Prob. **akkhana** is connected with **akkha**.

Akkhaka [akkha¹ + ka] the collar-bone Vin IV.213 (adhakkhakaŋ); V.216.

Akkhaṇa [a + khaṇa, BSk. akṣaṇa AvŚ I.291 = 332] wrong time, bad luck, misadventure, misfortune. There are 9 enum^d at D III.263; the usual set consists of 8; thus D III.287; VvA 193; Sdhp 4 sq. See also **khaṇa**.

-**vedhin** (adj. n.) a skilled archer, one who shoots on the moment, i. e. without losing time, expl^d as one who shoots without missing (the target) or as quickly as lightning (**akkhaṇa** = **vijju**). In var. comb^ns.; mostly as **durepātin a.** A I.284 (+ **mahato kāyassa padāletā**); II.170 sq. (id.), 202; IV.423, 425; J II.91 (expl^d as either "**avirādhita -vedhī**" or "**akkhaṇaŋ vuccati vijju**": one who takes and shoots his arrows as fast as lightning), III.322; IV.494 (C. expl^ns **aviraddha-vedhin vijju-ālokena vijjhana -samattha** p. 497). In other comb^n at J I.58 (**akkhaṇavedhin** + **vālavedhin**); V.129 (the 4 kinds of archers: a., **vālavedhin**, **saddavedhin** & **saravedhin**).

In BSk. we find aksuṇṇavedha (a Sanskritised Pāli form, cp. Mathurā kṣuṇa = Sk. kṣaṇa) at Divy 58, 100, 442 (always with dūrevedha), where MSS. however read akṣuṇa°; also at Lal. Vist. 178. See Divy Index, where trsl^n is given as "an act of throwing the spear so as to graze the mark" (Schiefner gives "Streifschuss"). — *Note.* The explanations are not satisfactory. We should expect either an etym. bearing on the meaning "hitting the centre of the target" (i. e. its "eye") (cp. E. bull's eye), in which case a direct relation to akkha = akkhi eye would not seem improbable (cp. formation ikkhana) or an etym. like "hitting without mishap", in which case the expression would be derived directly from akkhaṇa (see prec.) with the omission of the neg. an-; akkhaṇa in the meaning of "lightning" (J II.91 C.) is not supported by literary evidence.

Akkhata (adj.) [pp. of a + **kṣan**, cp. parikkhata¹] unhurt, without fault Mhvs 19, 56 (C. niddosa). — acc. **akkhataŋ** (adv.) in safety. unhurt. Only in one phrase Vv 84⁵² (**paccāgamuŋ Pāṭaliputtaŋ akkhataŋ**) & Pv IV.1¹ (**nessāmi taŋ Pāṭaliputtaŋ akkhataŋ**); see VvA 351 & PvA 272.

Akkhaya (adj.) [a + khaya, **kṣi**] not decaying, in **akkhayapaṭibhāna**, of unfailing skill in exposition Miln 3, 21.

Akkhara (adj.) [Vedic akṣara] constant, durable, lasting D III.86. As tt. for one of 4 branches of Vedic learning (D I.88) it is Phonetics which probably inculded Grammar, and is expl^d by **sikkhā** (DA I.247 = SnA 477) — pl. nt. **akkharāni** sounds, tones, words. **citt'akkhara** of a discourse (**suttanta**) having variety & beauty of words or sounds (opposed to beauty of thought) A I.72 = III.107 = S II.267. **Akkharāni** are the sauce, flavour (**vyañjana**) of poetry S I.38. To know the context of the a° the words of the texts, is characteristic of an Arahant Dh 352 (C. is ambiguous DhA IV.70). Later: **akkharaŋ** a syllable or sound PvA 280 (called **sadda** in next line); **akkharāni** an inscription J II.90; IV.7 (**likhitāni** written), 489; VI,390, 407. In Grammar: a letter Kacc. I.

-**cintaka** a grammarian or versifier KhA 17; SnA 16, 23, 321. cp. 466; PvA 120. -**pabheda** in phrase sakkharappabheda phonology & etymology D I.88 (akkharappabhedo ti sikkhā ca nirutti ca SnA 447 = DA I.247) = A III.223 = Sn p. 105. -**piṇḍa** "word-ball", i. e. sequence of words or sounds DhA IV.70 (= akkharānan sannipāto Dh 352).

Akkharikā (f.) a game (recognising syllables written in the air or on one's back). D I.7; Vin II.10; III.180. So expl^d at DA I.86. It may be translated "letter game"; but all Indian letters of that date were syllables.

Akkhāta (adj.) [pp. of akkhāti] announced, proclaimed, told, shown A I.34 (**dur°**); II 195; IV.285, 322; V.265, 283; Sn 172, 276, 595, 718.

Akkhātar one who relates, a speaker, preacher story-teller S I.11, 191; III.66; Sn 167.

Akkhāti [ā + **khyā**, Idg. *seq^u; cp. Sk. ākhyāti, Lat. inquam, Gr. ἐννέπω, Goth. saihvan, Ger. sehen etc. See also akkhi & cakkhu] to declare, announce, tell Sn 87, 172; imper. **akkhāhi** Sn 988, 1085; aor. **akkhāsi** Sn 251, 504, 1131 (= ācikkhi etc. Nd² 465); fut. **akkhissati** Pv IV.1⁶³; cond. **akkhissaŋ** Sn 997; J VI.523. — Pass. **akkhāyati** to be proclaimed, in phrase **aggaŋ a.** to be deemed chief or superior, to be first, to excel Miln 118, 182 (also in BSk. agram ākhyāyate M Vastu III.390); ger. **akkheyya** to be pronounced S I.11; It 53. — pp. **akkhāta** (q. v.). — Intensive or Frequentative is **ācikkhati**.

Akkhāna (nt.) [Sk. ākhyāna] telling stories, recitation; tale, legend D I.6 (= DA I.84: **Bhārata-Rāmāyanādi**); III.183; M I.503; III.167; Sdhp. 237. — preaching, teaching Nd¹ 91 (**dhamm°**). The 5th Veda J V.450. (**vedam akkhānapañcaman**; C: **itihāsapañcamaŋ vedacatukkaŋ**). — The spelling **ākhyāna** also occurs (q. v.).

Akkhāyika (adj.) relating, narrating J III.535; **lokakkhāyikā** kathā talk about nature-lore D I.8; Miln 316.

Akkhāyin (adj.) telling, relating, announcing S II.35; III.7; J III.105.

Akkhi (nt.) [to ***oks**, an enlarged form of ***oq**[u], cp. Sk. īkṣate, kṣaṇa, pratīka, anīka; Gr. ὄσσε, ὤψ (Κύκλωψ), ὀφθαλμός, πρόσωπον; Lat. oculus, Ags. ēowan (= E eye & wind-ow); Goth. augō. See also cakkhu & cp. akkha[2] & ikkhaṇika] the eye. M I.383 (**ubbhatehi akkhkīhi**); Sn 197, 608; J I.223, 279; V.77; VI.336; Pv II.9[26] (**akkhīni paggharanti**: shed tears, cp. PvA 123); VvA 65 (°**īni bhamanti**, my eyes swim) cp. akkhīni me dhūmāyanti DhA I.475; DhA II.26; III.196 (°**īni ummīletvā** opening the eyes); Sdhp 103, 380. — In comb[n] with sa- as **sacchi** & **sakkhi** (q. v.). As adj. (—°) **akkha**[3] (q.v.). **-añjana** eye ointment, collyrium DhA III.354. **-kūpa** the socket of the eye J IV.407. **-gaṇḍa** eye-protuberance, i. e. eye-brow (?) J VI.504 (for pamukha T.). **-gūtha** secretion from the eye PvA 198. **-gūthaka** id. Sn 197 (= dvīhi akkhicchiddehi apanita-ttaca-maŋsasadiso a°-gūthako SnA 248). **-chidda** the eye-hole SnA 248. **-dala** the eye-lid DA I.194; ThA 259; DhsA 378. **-pāta** "fall of the eye", i. e. a look, in mand° of soft looks (adj.) PvA 57. **-pūra** an eye-full, in akkhipūraŋ assuŋ (assu?) an eye full of tears J. VI.191. **-mala** dirt from the eye Pv III 5[3] (= °gūtha C.). **-roga** eye disease DhA I.9.

Akkhika[1] (—°) (adj.) having eyes, with eyes Th I.960 (añjan° with eyes anointed); DhA IV.98 (**aḍḍh°** with half an eye, i. e. stealthily); Sdhp 286 (tamb° red-eyed). **-an°** having no eyes DhA I.11.

Akkhika[2] (nt.) [cp. Sk. akṣa] the mesh of a net J I.208. **-hāraka** one who takes up a mesh (?) M I.383 (corresp. with **aṇḍahāraka**).

Akkhitta[1] see **khitta**.

Akkhitta[2] (adj.) [BSk ākṣipta Divy 363, pp. of ā + **kṣip**] hit, struck, thrown J III.255 (= **ākaḍḍhita** C.).

Akkhin (adj.) = **akkhika** J III.190 (mand° softeyed); Vv 32[3] (**tamb°** red-eyed); DhA I.11.

Akkhobbha (adj.) [a + **kṣubh**, see khobha] not to be shaken, imperturbable Miln 21.

Akkhobhana (adj) = **akkhobbha** J V.322 (= **khobhetun** na sakkhā C.).

Akkhobinī (f.) [= akkhobhiṇī] one of the highest numerals (1 followed by 42 ciphers, Childers) J V.319; VI.395.

Akhaṇḍaphulla see **khaṇḍa**.

Akhata (adj.) not dug: see **khāta**.

Akhetta barren-soil: see **khetta**. — In cpd. °**ññu** the neg. belongs to the whole: not knowing a good field (for alms) J IV.371.

Agati see gati. -°**gamana** practising a wrong course of life, evil practice, wrong doing D III.228 (4: **chanda°**, **dosa° moha° bhaya°**); A II.18 sq., J IV.402; V.98, 510; PvA 161.

Agada [Vedic agada; a + gada] medicine, drug, counter-poison J I 80 (°**harītaka**); Miln 121, 302, 319, 334; DA I.67; DhA I.215; PvA 198 (= **osadhaŋ**).

Agaru (adj.) [cp. Sk. aguru, a + garu] (a) not heavy, not troublesome, only in phrase: **sace te agaru** "if it does not inconvenience you, if you doint mind" (cp. BSk. yadi te aguru. Av. S I.94, 229; II.90) Vin. I.25; IV.17, D I.51; DhA I.39. — (b) disrespectful, irreverent (against = gen.) D I.89; Sn p. 51.

Agalu [cp. Sk. aguru, which is believed to appear in Hebr. ahālim (aloe), also in Gr. ἀλόη & ἀγάλλοχον] fragrant aloe wood, Agallochum Vv 53[1] (aggalu = VvA 237 agalugandha); VvA 158 (+ **candana**). Cp. also Av. Ś I.24, and **akalu**.

Agāra (nt.) [cp. Sk. agāra, probably with the a- of communion; Gr. ἀγείρω to collect, ἀγορά market. Cp. in meaning & etym. gaha[1]]. — 1. house or hut, usually implying the comforts of living at home as opp. to **anagāra** homelessness or the state of a homeless wanderer (mendicant). See **anagāriyā**. — Thus freq. in two phrases contrasting the state of a householder (or layman, cp. **gihin**), with that of a religious wanderer (**pabbajita**), viz. (a.) **kesamassuŋ ohāretvā kāsāyāni vatthāni acchādetvā agārasmā anagāriyaŋ pabbajati** "to shave off hair & beard, put on the yellow robes, and wander forth out of the home into the homeless state" D I.60 etc.; cp. Nd[2] 172[II]. See also S I.185 (**agārasmā anagāriyaŋ nikkhanta**); M II.55 (**agāraŋ ajjhāvasatā**); Sn 274, 805 (°**n āvasati**), and with **pabbajita** D I.89, 115, 202, 230; Pv II.13[17]. — (b.) of a "**rājā cakkavattin**" compared with a "sambuddha": **sace agāraŋ āvasati vijeyya paṭhaviŋ imaŋ adaṇḍena asatthena . . . sace ca so pabbajati agārā anagāriyaŋ vivaṭacchado sambuddho arahā bhavissati** "he will become the greatest king when he stays at home, but the greatest saint when he takes up the homeless life", the prophesy made for the infant Gotama D II.16; Sn 1002, 1003. — Further passages for **agāra** e. g. Vin I.15; D I.102 (BB. has v. l. agyâgāra, but DA I.270 expl. as dānâgāra); A I.156, 281; II.52 sq.; Dh 14, 140; J I.51, 56; III.392; Dpvs. I.36. — 2. **anagāra** (adj.) houseless, homeless; a mendicant (opp. **gahaṭṭha**) Sn 628 = Dh 404; Sn 639, 640 (+ **paribbaje**); Pv II.2[5] (= **anāvāsa** PvA 80). — (nt.) the homeless state (= **anagāriyā**) Sn 376. See also **agga**[2]. — 3. °**āgāra**: Owing to freq. occurrence of **agāra** at the end of cpds. of which the first word ends in a, we have a dozen quite familiar words ending apparently in **āgāra**. This form has been considered therefore as a proper doublet of **agāra**. This however is wrong. The long ā is simply a contraction of the short a at the end of the first part of the cpd. with the short a at the beginning of **agāra**. Of the cpds. the most common are: — **āgantuk°** reception hall for strangers or guests S IV.219; V.21. — **itth°** ladys bower S I.58, 89. — **kūṭ°** a house with a peaked roof, or with gables S II.103. 263; III.156; IV.186; V.43; A I.230; III.10, 364; IV.231; V.21. **-koṭṭh°** storehouse, granary D I.134 (cp. DA I.295); S I.89. **-tiṇ°** a house covered with grass S IV.185; A I.101. **-bhus°** threshing shed, barn A I.241. **-santh°** a council hall D I.91; II.147; S IV.182; V.453; A II.207; IV.179 sq. **-suññ°** an uninhabited shed; solitude S V.89, 157, 310 sq., 329 sq.; A I.241 (v. l. for bhusâgāra); III.353; IV.139, 392, 437; V.88, 109, 323 sq.

Agāraka (nt.) [fr. agāra] a small house, a cottage M I.450; J VI.81.

Agārika (adj.) 1. having a house, in **eka°**, **dva°** etc. D I.166 = A I 295 = II.206. — 2. a householder, layman Vin I.17. f. **agārikā** a housewife Vin I.272. See also **āgārika**.

Agārin (adj.) [fr. agāra] one who has or inhabits a house, a householder Sn 376, Th I.1009; J III.234. — f. **agārinī** a housewife Vv 52[1] (= **gehassāminī** VvA 225); Pv III.4[3] (id. PvA 194).

Agāriya = **agārika**, a layman M I.504 (°**bhūta**). — Usually in neg. **anagāriyā** (f.) the homeless state (= **anagāraŋ**) as opp. to **agāra** (q. v.) in formula **agārasmā anagariyaŋ pabbajita** (gone out from the house into the homeless state) Vin I.15; M I.16; II.55, 75; A I.49; D III.30 sq., 145 sq.; Sn 274, 1003; Pv II.13[16]; DA I.112.

Agga[1] (adj. n.) [Vedic agra; cp. Av. agrō first; Lith. agrs early] 1. (adj;) (a.) of time: the first, foremost Dpvs IV.13 (sangahaŋ first collection). See cpds. — (b.) of space: the highest, topmost, J I.52 (°sākhā). — (c.) of quality: illustrious, excellent, the best, highest, chief Vin IV.232 (**agga-m-agga**) most exellent, D II.4: S I.29 (a. sattassa Sambuddha); A II.17 = Pv IV.3^{41} (lokassa Buddho aggo [A: aggaŋ] pavuccati); It 88, 89; Sn 875 (suddhi); PvA 5. Often combd. with seṭṭha (best), e. g. D II.15; S III.83, 264. — 2. (nt.) top, point. (a.) *lit.*: the top or tip (nearly always —°); as **ār°** point of an awl Sn 625, 631; Dh 401; **kus°** tip of a blade of grass Dh 70; Sdhp 349; **tiṇ°** id PvA 241; **dum°** top of a tree J II.155; **dhaj°** of a banner S I.219; **pabbat°** of a mountain Sdhp 352; **sākh°** of a branch PvA 157; etc. — (b.) *fig.* the best part, the ideal, excellence, prominence, first place, often to be trsl. as adj. the highest, best of all etc. S II.29 (aggena aggassa patti hoti: only the best attain to the highest); Mhvs 7, 26. Usually as —°; e. g. **dum°** the best of trees, an excellent tree Vv 35^{41} (cp. VvA 161); **dhan°** plenty D III.164; **madhur°** S I.41, 161, 237; **bhav°** the best existence S III.83; **rūp°** extraordinary beauty J I.291; **lābh°** highest gain J III.127; **sambodhi-y-agga** highest wisdom Sn 693 (= sabbaññuta-ñāṇaŋ SnA 489; the best part or quality of anything, in enumn of the five "excellencies" of first-fruits (**panca aggāni**, after which the N. Pañcaggadāyaka), viz. khettaggaŋ rās° koṭṭh° kumbhi° bhojan° SnA 270. sukh° perfect bliss Sdhp 243. Thus freq. in phrase **aggaŋ akkhāyati** to deserve or receive the highest praise, to be the most excellent D I.124; S III.156, 264; A II.17 (Tathāgato); It 87 (id.); Nd[2] 517 D (appamādo); Miln 183. — 3. *Cases as adv.*: aggena (instr.) in the beginning, beginning from, from (as prep.), by (id.) Vin II.167. (aggena gaṇhāti to take from, to subtract, to find the difference; Kern Toev. s. v. unnecessarily changes aggena into agghena), 257 (yadaggena at the moment when or from, foll. by tad eva "then"; cp. agge), 294 (bhikkh° from alms); Vbh 423 (vass° by the number of years). **aggato** (abl.) in the beginning Sn 217 (+ majjhato, sesato). aggato kata taken by its worth, valued, esteemed Th 2, 386, 394. **agge** (loc) 1. at the top A II.201 (opp. mūle at the root); J IV.156 (id.); Sn 233 (phusit° with flowers at the top: supupphitaggasākhā KhA 192); J II.153 (ukkh°); III.126 (kūp°). — 2 (as prep.) from. After, since, usually in phrases yad° (foll. by tad°) from what time, since what date D I.152; II.206; & ajja-t-agge from this day, after to day D I.85; M I.528; A V.300; Sn p. 25 (cp. BSk. adyāgrena Av. Ś. II.13); at the end: bhattagge after a meal Vin II.212.

-angulī the main finger, i. e. index finger J VI.404. **āsana** main seat DA I.267. **-upaṭṭhāka** chief personal attendant D II.6. **-kārikā** first taste, sample Vin III.80. **-kulika** of an esteemed clan Pv III.5^{5} (= seṭṭh° PvA 199). **-ñña** recognized as primitive primeval, D III.225 (porāṇa +), A II.27 sq.; IV.246, Kvu 341. **-danta** one who is most excellently self-restrained (of the Buddha) Th I.354. **-dāna** a splendid gift Vin III.39. **-dvāra** main door J I.114. **-nakha** tip of the nail Vin IV.221. **-nagara** the first or most splendid of cities Vin I.229. **-nikkhitta** highly praised or famed Miln 343. **-nikkhittaka** an original depositary of the Faith Dpvs IV.5. **-pakatimant** of the highest character J V.351 (= aggasabhāva). **-patta** having attained perfection D III.48 sq. **-pasāda** the highest grace A II.34; It 87. **-piṇḍa** the best oblation or alms I.141; M I 28; II.204. **-piṇḍika** receiving the best oblations J VI.140. **-puggala** the best of men (of the Buddha) Sn 684; DhA II.39; Sdhp. 92, 558. **-purohita** chief or prime minister J VI.391. **-phala** the highest or supreme fruit (i. e. Arahantship) J I.148; Pv IV.1^{88}; PvA 230. **-bīja** having eggs from above (opp. mūla°), i. e. propagated by slips or cuttings D I.5; DA I.81. **-magga** (adj.) having reached the top of the path, i. e. Arahantship ThA 20. **-mahesī** the king's chief wife, queen-consort J I.262; III.187, 393; V.88; DhA I.199; PvA 76. **-rājā** the chief king J VI.391; Miln 27. **-vara** most meritorious, best Dpvs VI.68. **-vāda** the original doctrine (= theravāda) Dpvs IV.13. **-vādin** one who proclaims the highest good (of the Buddha) Th I, 1142.

Agga[2] (nt.) (only —°) [a contracted form of agāra] a (small) house, housing, accomodation; shelter, hut; hall. **dān°** a house of donation, i. e. a public or private house where alms are given J III.470; IV.379, 403; VI.487; PvA 121; Miln 2. **salāk°** a hut where food is distributed to the bhikkhus by tickets, a food office J I.123, VvA 75.

Aggatā (f.) [abstr. of agga] pre-eminence, prominence, superiority Kvu 556 (°ŋ gata); Dpvs IV.1 (guṇaggataŋ gatā). — (adj.) **mahaggata** of great value or superiority D I.80; III.224.

Aggatta (nt.) [abstr. of agga = Sk. agratvan] the state or condition of being the first, pre-eminence PvA 9, 89.

Aggavant (adj.) occupying the first place, of great eminence A I.70, 243.

Aggalu see agalu.

Aggaḷa & **Aggaḷā** (f.) (also occasionally with l.) [cp. Sk. argala & argalā to ***areg** to protect, ward off, secure etc., as in Ags. reced house; ***aleg** in Sk. rakṣati to protect, Gr. ἀλέξω id., Ags. ealh temple. Cp. also ***areq** in Gr. ἀρκέω = Lat. arceo, Orcus, Ohg rigil bolt.] a contrivance to fasten anything for security or obstruction: 1. a bolt or cross-bar Vin I.290; D I.89 (°ŋ ākoṭeti to knock upon the cross-bar a = kavāṭa DA I.252); A IV.359 (id.); S. IV.290; A I.101 = 137 = IV.231. (**phusit°** with fastened bolts, securely shut Th I.385 (id.); Vin IV.47; J. V.293 (°ŋ **uppīḷeti** to lift up the cross-bar. — 2. a strip of cloth for strengthening a dress etc., a gusset Vin I.290 (+ tunna), 392 (Bdhgh on MV VIII.21, 1); J I.8 (+ tunna) VI.71 (°ŋ **datvā**); Vin IV.121.

-dāna putting in a gusset J I.8. **-phalaka** the post or board, in which the cross-bar is fixed (cp. °vaṭṭi) M III.95. **-vaṭṭi** = °phalaka Vin II.120, 148. **-sūci** bolting pin M I.126.

Aggi [Vedic agni = Lat. ignis. Besides the contracted form aggi we find the diaeretic forms gini (q. v.) and aggini (see below)] fire. — 1: fire, flames, sparks; conflagration, Vin II.120 (fire in bathroom); M I.487 (anāhāro nibbuto f. gone out for lack of fuel); S IV.185, 399 (sa-upādāno jalati provided with fuel blazes); Sn 62; Dh 70 (= asaniaggi DhA III.71); J I.216 (sparks), 294 (pyre); II.102; III.55; IV.139; VvA 20 (aggimhi tāpanaŋ + udake temanaŋ). — The var. phases of lighting and extinguishing the fire are given at A IV.45: aggiŋ ujjāleti (kindle, make burn), ajjhupekkhati (look after, keep up), nibbāpeti (extinguish, put out), nikkhipati (put down, lay). Other phrases are e. g. aggiŋ jāleti (kindle) J II.44; gaṇhāti (make or take) J I.494 (cp. below b); deti (set light to) J I.294; nibbāpeti (put out) It 93; Sdhp 552. aggi nibbāyati the f. goes out S II.85; M I.487; J I.212 (udake through water); Miln 304. aggi nibbuto the f. is extinguished (cp. °nibbāna) J I.61; Miln 304. agginā dahati to burn by means of fire, to set fire to A I.136, 199; PvA 20. **udar°** the fire supposed to regulate digestion PvA 33; cp. *Dial.* II.208, note 2; **kapp'uṭṭhān°** the universal conflagration J III.185; **dāv°** a wood or jungle fire J I.212; **naḷ°** the burning of a reed J VI.100; **padīp°** fire of a lamp Miln 47. 2. the sacrificial fire: In one or two of the passages in the older texts this use of Aggi is ambiguous. It may possibly be intended to denote the personal Agni, the fire-god. But the commentators do not think so, and the Jātaka commentary, when it means Agni, has the phrase **Aggi Bhagavā** the Lord Agni, e. g. at J I.285, 494; II.44. The ancient ceremony of kindling a holy fire on the day the child is born and keeping it up throughout his life, is also referred to by that commentary e. g. J I.285; II.43. **Aggiŋ paricarati** (cp. °paricāriyā) to serve the sacred fire Vin I.31 (jaṭilā aggī paricaritukāmā); A v.263, 266; Th 2, 143 (= aggihuttan paric° ThA 136); Dh 107; J 1.494; DhA 11.232. aggiŋ juhati (cp. °homa, °hutta) to sacrifice (in)to the fire A 11.207; often combd. with aggihuttan paricarati, e.g. S 1.166; Sn p. 79. aggiŋ namati & santappeti to worship the fire A v.235. aggissa (gen.) paricāriko J VI.207 (cp. below °paricārika); aggissa adhānaŋ A IV.41. — 3. (ethical, always —°) the fire of burning, consuming, feverish sensations. Freq. in standard set of 3 fires, viz. rāg°, dos°, moh°, or the fires of lust, anger and bewilderment. The number three may possibly have been chosen with reference to the three sacrificial fires of Vedic ritual. At S IV.19; A IV.41 sq. there are 7 fires, the 4 last of which are **āhuneyy°**, **gahapat°**, **dakkhiṇeyy°**, **kaṭṭh°**. But this trinity of cardinal sins lies at the basis of Buddhist ethics, & the fire simile was more probably suggested by the number. D III.217; It 92, Vbh 368. In late books are found others: **ind°** the fire of the senses PvA 56; **dukkh°** the glow of suffering ib. 60; **bhavadukkh°** of the misery of becomings Sdhp. 552; **vippaṭisār°** burning remorse PvA 60; sok° burning grief ib. 41.

Note. The form **aggini** occurs only at Sn 668 & 670 in the meaning of "pyre", and in combn. with sama "like", viz. aggini-samaŋ jalitaŋ 668 (= samantato jalitaŋ aggiŋ Sn A 480); aggini-samāsu 670 (= aggisamāsu Sn A 481). The form agginī in phrase niccagginī can either be referred to gini (q. v.) or has to be taken as nom. of aggini (in adj. function with ī metri causa; otherwise as adj. agginiŋ), meaning looking constantly after the fire, i. e. careful, observant, alert.

-agāra (agyâgāra) a heated room or hut with a fire Vin I.24; IV.109; D I.101, 102 (as v. l. BB for agāra); M I.501; A v.234, 250. **-khandha** a great mass of fire, a huge fire, fire-brand S II.85; A IV. 128; Th 2, 351 (°samākāmā); J IV.139; VI.330; Ps I.125; Dpvs VI.37; Miln 304. **-gata** having become (like) fire Miln 302. **-ja** fire-born J v.404 (C; text aggijāta). **-ṭṭha** fire-place J v.155. **-ṭṭhāna** fire-place Vin II.120 (jantāghare, in bathroom). **-daḍḍha** consumed by fire Dh 136; Pv 1.7⁴. **-dāha** (mahā°) a holocaust A I.178. **-nikāsin** like fire J III.320 (suriya). **-nibbāna** the extinction of fire J I.212. **-pajjota** fire-light A II.140 (one of the 4 lights, viz. canda°, suriya°, a°, paññā°). **-paricaraṇa** (-ṭṭhāna) the place where the (sacrificial) fire is attended to DhA I.199. **-paricariyā** fire-worship DhA II.232; Sn A 291 (pāri°) 456. **-paricārika** one who worship the fire A v.263 (brāhmaṇa). **-sālā** a heated hall or refectory Vin I.25, 49 = II.210; I.139; II.154. **-sikhā** the crest of the fire, the flame, in simile °*ūpama*, like a flaming fire Sn 703; Dh 308 = It 43, 90 (ayoguḷa). **-hutta** (nt.) the sacrificial fire (see above 2), Vin I.33, 36 = J I.83; Vin I.246 = Sn 568 (°mukha-yañña); S I 166; Dh 392; Sn 249, p. 79; J IV.211; VI.525; ThA 136 (= aggi); DhA IV.151 (°n brāhmaṇo namati). **-huttaka** (nt.) fire-offering J VI.522 (= aggi-jūhana C.). **-hotta** = °hutta SnA 456 (v. l. BB °hutta). **-homa** fire-oblation (or perhaps sacrificing to Agni) D I.9 (= aggi-jūhana DA I.93).

Aggika (adj.) [aggi + ka] one who worships the fire Vin I.71 (jaṭilaka); D II.339 sq. (jaṭila); S I.166 (brāhmaṇa).

Aggha [see agghati] 1. price, value, worth, Miln 244; Mhvs 26, 22; 30, 76; VvA 77. — **mahaggha** (adj.) of great value J IV.138; V.414; VI.209; Pv II.1¹⁸. See also mahâraha. **appaggha** (adj.) of little value J. IV.139; V.414. — **anaggha** (nt.) pricelessness, J v.484; cattari anagghāni the four priceless things, viz. setacchatta, nisīdanapallanka, ādhāraka, pādapiṭhikā DhA III.120, 186. (adj.) priceless, invaluable J v.414; Mhvs 26, 25; DhA IV.216. — **agghena** (instr.) for the price of Vin II.52, cp. Bdhgh on p. 311, 312. — 2. an oblation made to a guest D II.240; J IV.396 = 476.

-kāraka a valuator J I.124. **-pada** valuableness J v.473 (°lakkhaṇaŋ nāma mantaŋ).

Agghaka (adj.) = aggha; worth, having the value of (—°) Mhvs 30, 77. an° priceless Mhvs 30, 72.

Agghati (intr.) [Sk. arghati, **argh** = **arh** (see arhati), cp. Gr. ἀλφή reward, ἀλφάνω to deserve] to be worth, to have the value of (acc.), to deserve J I.112 (satasahassaŋ; aḍḍhamāsakaŋ); VI.174, 367 (padarajaŋ); DhA III.35 (maṇin nâgghāma); Mhvs 32, 28. Freq. in stock phrase **kalaŋ nâgghati (nâgghantī)** soḷasiŋ not to be worth the 16th part of (cp. kala) Vin II.156; S I.233; Dh 70; Vv 20⁷ (= nânubhoti VvA 104), 43⁷; J v.284. — Caus. **agghāpeti** to value, to appraise, to have a price put on (acc.) J I.124; IV.137, 278; Miln 192; Mhvs 27, 23. Cp. agghāpanaka & agghāpaniya.

Agghanaka (adj.) (—°) [fr. *agghana, abstr. to agghati] having the value of, equal to, worth Vin IV.226; J I.61 (satasahass°), 112; DA I.80 (kahāpaṇ°); DhA III.120 (cuddasakoṭi°); Mhvs 26, 22; 34, 87. — f. **°ikā** J I.178 (satasahass°).

Agghaniya (adj.) [in function & form grd. of agghati] priceless, invaluable, beyond the reach of money Miln 192.

Agghāpanaka [fr. agghāpana to agghāpeti, Caus. of agghati] a valuator, appraiser J I.124, 125; v.276 (°ika).

Agghāpaniya (adj.) [grd. of agghāpeti, see agghati] that which is to be valued, in **°kamma** the business of a valuator J IV.137.

Agghika (nt.) (—°) [= agghiya] an oblation, decoration or salutation in the form of garlands, flowers etc., therefore meaning "string, garland" (cp. Sinhalese ägä "festoon work") Mhvs 19, 38 (**pupph°**) 34, 73 (**ratan°**) 34, 76 (**dhaj°**); Dāvs I.39 (**pupphamay°**); v.51 (**kusum°**).

Agghiya (adj. -n.) [grd. form from agghati] 1. (adj.) valuable, precious, worth J VI.265 (maṇi); DhA II.41 (ratan° of jewel's worth); Mhvs 30, 92. — 2. (nt.) a respectful oblation J v.324 = VI.516; Dpvs VI.65; VII.4.

Agha¹ (nt.) [cp. Sk. agha, of uncertain etym.] evil, grief, pain, suffering, misfortune S I 22; M I.500 (**roga gaṇḍa salla agha**); A II.128 (id.); J v.100; Th 2, 491; Sdhp 51. — adj. painful, bringing pain J VI.507 (agha-m-miga = aghakara m. C.). **-bhūta** a source of pain S III.189 (+ agha & salla).

Agha² (m. nt.) [the etym. suggested by Morris *J P T S* 1889, 200 (with ref. to M I.500, which belongs under agha¹) is untenable (to Sk. kha, as a-kha = agha, cp. Jain Prk. khaha). Neither does the pop. etym. of Bdhgh. offer any clue (= a + gha from **ghan** that which does not strike or aghaṭṭaniya is not strikeable DhsA 326, cp. Dhs. trsl. 194 & J IV.154 aghe ṭhitā = appaṭighe ākāse ṭhitā the air which does not offer any resistance). On the other hand the primary meaning is *darkness*, as seen from the phrase **lokantarikā aghā asaŋvutā andhakārā** D II.12; S v.454, and BSk. **aghasaŋvṛta** M Vastu II.240, adj. dark M Vastu I.41; II.162; Lal Vist 552] the sky, orig. the dark sky, dark space, the abyss of space D II.12; S v.45 ; Vv 16¹ (aghasi gama, loc. = vehāsaŋ gama VvA 78); J IV.154; Dhs 638 (+ aghagata); Vbh 84 (id.).

-gata going through or being in the sky or atmosphere Dhs 638, 722; Vbh 84. **-gāmin** moving through the atmosphere or space i. e. a planet S I.67 = Miln 242 (ādicco seṭṭho aghagāminaŋ).

Aghata at Th 1, 321 may be read as agha-gata or (preferably) with v. l. as aggha-gataŋ, or (with Neumann) as agghaŋ agghatânaŋ. See also Mrs. Rh. D, *Psalms of the Brethren*, p. 191.

Agghammiga [to agha¹?] a sort of wild animal J VI.247 (= aghâvaha miga) 507 (= aghakara). Cp. BSk. agharika Divy 475.

Aghavin (adj.) [to agha¹] suffering pain, being in misery Sn 694 (= dukkhita SnA 489).

Anka[1] = anga, sign, mark, brand Miln 79; °**karana** branding J IV.366, 375. See also anketi.

Anka[2] [Vedic anka book, bent etc., **anc**, cp. ankura & ankusa. Gr. ἀγκών elbow, ἄγκυρα = anchor; Lat. uncus nail; Ohg. angul = E. angle] (a.) a hook J V.322 = VI.218 (v. l. BB anga). — (b.) the lap (i. e. the bent position) or the hollow above the hips where infants are carried by Hindos mothers or nurses (**ankena vahati**) Vin II.114; D II.19 (**anke pariharati** to hold on one's lap or carry on one's hips), 20 (**nisīdāpeti** seat on one's lap); M II.97 (**ankena vahitvā**); Th 1, 299; J I.262 (**anke nisinna**); II.127, 236; VI.513; DhA I.170 (**ankena vahitvā**) PvA 17 (**nisīdāpeti**).

Ankita [pp. of anketi] marked, branded J I.231 (cakkankitā Satthu padā); II.185 (°**kaṇṇaka** with perforated ears).

Ankura [cp. Sk. ankura, to anka a bend = a tendril etc.] a shoot, a sprout (lit. or fig.) J II.105; VI.331 (Buddh °a nascent Buddha), 486; Dbs 617 (°vaṇṇa); Miln 50, 251 269; Sdhp 273; Mhvs 15, 43.

Ankusa [Vedic ankuśa; to **anc**, see anka[2]] a hook, a pole with a hook, used (1) for plucking fruit off trees, a crook J I.9 (°pacchi hook & basket); V.89 = VI.520 (pacchikbanitti°), 529 (= phalānaŋ gaṇhanatthaŋ ankusaŋ). — (2) to drive an elephant, a goad (cp patoda & tutta) Vin II.196 (+ kasā); J VI.489; ThA 173 (ovādan ankusaŋ katvā, fig. guide); Sdhp 147 (daṇḍ°). — (3) N. of a certain method of inference in Logic (naya), consisting in inferring certain mental states of a general character from respective traits where they are to be found Nett 2, 4, 127; Nett A 208; — acc° beyond the reach of the goad D II.266 (nāga). See also ankusaka.

-gayha (the art) how to grasp and handle an eleph.-driver's hook M II.94 (sippa). **-gaha** an eleph.-driver Dh 826.

Ankusaka [see anka[2], cp. ankusa] 1. a crook for plucking fruit J III.22. — 2. an eleph.-driver's hook J III.431.

-yattha a crooked stick, alpenstock, staff (of an ascetic) J II.68 (+ pacchi).

Anketi [Denom. fr. anka[1]] to mark out, brand J I.451 lakkhaṇena); II.399. — pp. **ankita**, q. v.

Ankola [dial. for ankura] a species of tree **Alangium Hexapetalum** J VI.535. Cp. next.

Ankolaka = ankola J IV.440; V.420.

Anga (nt.) [Vedic anga, **anc** cp. Lat. angulus = angle, corner etc., ungulus finger-ring = Sk. anguliya. See also anka, anguṭṭha & angula] (1) (lit.) a constituent part of the body, a limb, member; also of objects: part, member (see cpd. °sambhāra); **uttam'anga** the reproductive organ J V.197; also as "head" at ThA 209. Usually in cpds. (see below, esp. °paccanga), as **sabbanga-kalyāṇī** perfect in all limbs Pv III.3[6] (= sobhaṇa-sabbanga-paccangī PvA 189) and in redupl[n]. **anga-m-angāni** limb by limb, with all limbs (see also below anga + paccanga) Vin III.119; Vv 38[2] (°ehi naccamāna); Pv II.12[10], [13], [18] (sunakho te khādati). — (2) (fig.) a constituent part of a whole or system or collection, e. g. **uposath°** the vows of the fast J I.50; **bhavanga** the constituents or the condition of becoming (see bhava & cp. *Cpd.* 265 sq.); **bojjhanga** (q. v.). Esp. with **numerals**: cattāri angāni 4 constituents A II.79 (viz. sīla, samādhi, paññā, vimutti and rūpa, vedanā, saññā, bhava), aṭṭhangika (q. v.) magga the Path with its eight constituents or the eightfold Path (KhA 85: aṭṭh' angāni assā ti) navanga Buddha-sāsana see nava. — (3) a constituent part as characteristic, prominent or distinguishing, a mark, attribute, sign, quality D I.113 sq., 117 (**iminā p' angena** by this quality, or: in this respect, cp. below 4; DA I.281 expl[s] tena kāraṇena). In a special sense striking (abnormal) sign or mark on the body D I.9, from which a prophesy is made (: hattha-pādādisu yena kenaci evarūpena angena samannāgato dīghāyu .. hotī ti .. angasatthan = chiromantics DA I.92). Thus in comb[n]. with **samannāgata & sampanna** always meaning endowed with "good", superior, remarkable "qualities", e. g. J I.3 (sabbanga-sampanna nagaraŋ a city possessing all marks of perfection); II.207. — In enum[n]. with var. **numerals**: tīhi angehi s. A I.115; cattāri sotapannassa a- D III.227 = A IV.405 sq.; pañcanga-vippahīno (i. e. giving up the 5 hindrances, see nīvaraṇa) and pañcanga-samannāgato (i. e. endowed with the 5 good qualities, viz. the sīla-kkhandha, see kkhandha II.A d) S I.99 = A I.161; V.15, 29. Similarly the 5 attributes of a brahmin (viz. sujāta of pure birth, ajjhāyaka a student of the Vedas, abhirūpa handsome, sīlava of good conduct, paṇḍita clever) D I.119, 120. Eight qualities of a king D I.137. Ten qualities of an Arahant (cp. dasa[1] B 2) S III.83; Kh IV.10 = KhA 88; cp. M I.446 (dasah' angehi samannāgato rañño assājāniyo). — (4) (modally) part, share, interest, concern; **ajjhattikaŋ** angaŋ my own part or interest in the outside world) A I.16 sq. = S V.101 sq.; It 9. rañño angaŋ an asset or profit for the king M I.446. Thus adv. **tadanga** (see also ta° I.a) as a matter of fact, in this respect, for sure, certainly and **tadangena** by these means, through this, therefore M I.492; A IV.411; Sdhp 455, 456; iminā p' angena for that reason M II.168. — In comp[n]. with verbs **angī°** (angī°): angigata having limbs or ports, divided DA I.313; cp. samangi (-bhūta).

-jāta "the distinguishing member", i. e. sign of male or female (see above 3); membrum virile and muliebre Vin I.191 (of cows); III.20, 37, 205; J II.359; Miln 124. **-paccanga** one limb or the other, limbs great and small M I.81; J VI-20, used (a) *collectively*: the condition of perfect limbs, or adj. with perfect limbs, having all limbs Pv II.12[12] (= paripuṇṇa-sabbanga-paccangavatī PvA 158); SnA 383; DhA I.390; ThA 288; Sdhp 83 fig. rathassa angapaccangan M I.395; sabbanga-paccangāni all limbs Miln 148. — (b) *distributively* (cp. similar redupl. formations like chiddâvachidda, seṭṭhânu-seṭṭhi, khaṇḍākhaṇḍa, cuṇṇavicuṇṇa) limb after limb, one limb after the other (like angamangāni above 1), piecemeal M I.133 (°e daseyya), 366; J I.20; IV.324 (chinditvā). **-paccangatā** the condition or state of perfect limbs, i. e. a perfect body VvA 134 (suvisuddh°). **-paccangin** having all limbs (perfect) D I.34 (sabbanga-peccangī); PvA 189. **-rāga** painting or rouging the body Vin II.107 (+ mukha°). **-laṭṭhi** spront, offshoot ThA 226. **-vāta** gout Vin I.205. **-vijjā** the art of prognosticating from marks on the body, chiromantics, palmistry etc. (cp. above 3) D I.9 (see expl. at DA I.93); J I 290 (°āya cheka clever in fortune-telling); °*ânubhāva* the power of knowing the art of signs on the body J II.200; V.284; °*pāṭhaka* one who in versed in palmistry etc. J II.21, 250; V.458. **-vekalla** bodily deformity DhA II.26. **-sattha** the science of prognosticating from certain bodily marks DA I.92. **-sambhāra** the combination of parts Miln 28 = S I.135; Miln 41. **-hetuka** a species of wild birds, living in forests J VI.538.

Angaṇa[1] (nt.) [cp. Sk. angaṇa & °na; to anga?] an open space, a clearing, Vin II.218; J I.109 (= manussānan sañcaraṇa-ṭṭhāne anāvaṭe bhūmibhāge C.); II.243, 290, 357; Dāvs I.27. — **cetiy°** an open space before a Chaitya Miln 366, DA I.191, 197; VvA 254. **rāj°** the empty space before the king's palace, the royal square J I.124, 152; II.2; DhA II.45.

-ṭṭhāna a clearing (in a wood or park) J I.249, 421. **-pariyanta** the end or border of a clearing J II.200.

Angaṇa[2] [prob. to **anj**, thus a variant of añjana, q. v.]; a speck or freckle (on the face) A V.92, 94 sq. (+ raja). Usually in neg. **anangana** (adj.) free from fleck or blemish, clear, (of the mind) (opp. sângana Sn 279); D I.76; M I.24 sq.; 100 (+ raja); A II.211; Sn 517 (+ vigata-raja = anganānan abhāvā malānaŋ ca vigamā ... SnA 427), 622 = Dh 125 (= nikkilesa DhA III.34); Dh 236, 351; Pug 60; Nett 87.

Angada [cp. Sk. angada; prob. anga + da that which is given to the limbs] a bracelet J V.9, 410 (citt°, adj. with manifold bracelets).

Angadin (adj.) [to angada] wearing a bracelet J V.9.

Angāra (m. nt.) [Vedic angāra] charcoal, burning coal, embers A III.97, 380, 407; J I.73; III.54, 55; V.488; Sn 668; Sdhp 32. **kul°** the charcoal of the family, a squanderer S IV.324 (see under kula).
-**kaṭāha** a pot for holding burning coal, a charcoal pan DA I.261. -**kapalla** an earthenware pan for ashes DhA I.260; Dhs A 333; VvA 142. -**kammakara** a charcoal burner J VI.209. -**kāsu** a charcoal pit M I.74, 365; Th 2, 491; J I.233; Sn 396; ThA 288; DhA I.442; Sdhp 208. -**pacchi** a basket for ashes DhA IV.191. -**pabbata** the mountain of live embers, the glowing mount (in Niraya) A I.141; Miln 303; PvA 221 (°āropana); Sdhp 208. -**maŋsa** roast meat Mhvs 10, 16. -**masi** ashes DhA III.309. -**rāsi** a heap of burning coal J III.55.

Angāraka (adj.) [cp. Sk. angāraka] like charcoal, of red colour, N. of the planet Mars DA I.95; cp. J I.73.

Angārika a charcoal-burner J VI.206 (= angāra-kammakara p. 209).

Angārin (adj.) [to angāra] (burning) like coal, of bright-red colour, crimson Th I, 527 = J I.87 (dumā trees in full bloom).

Angika (—°) (adj.) [fr. anga] consisting of parts, — fold; only in compⁿ· with num. like aṭṭh°, duv° (see dve), catur°, pañc° etc., q. v.

Angin (adj.) limbed, having limbs or parts, — fold, see catur° & pacc° (under anga-paccangin). — f. **anginī** having sprouts or shoots (of a tree) Th 2, 297 (= ThA 226).

Anguṭṭha [cp. Sk. anguṣṭha, see etym. under anga] 1. the thumb Vin III.34; Miln 123; PvA 198. — 2. the great toe J II.92; Mhvs 35, 43.
-**pada** thumb-mark A IV.127 = S III.154. -**sineha** love drawn from the thumb, i. e. extraordinary love Pv III.5², cp. PvA 198.

Anguṭṭhaka = anguṭṭha J IV.378; V.281; pād° the great toe S V.270.

Angula [Vedic angula, lit. "limblet" see anga for etym.] 1. a finger or toe M I.395 (vank' angulaŋ karoti to bend the fingers, v. l. angulin); A III.6 (id.); J V 70 (goṇ° adj. with ox toes, explᵈ· by C. as with toes like an ox's tail; vv. ll. °anguṭṭha and °angulī). — 2. a finger as measure, i. e. a finger-breadth, an inch Vin II.294, 306 (dvangula 2 inches wide); Mhvs 19, 11 (aṭṭh°); DhA III.127 (ek°).
-**aṭṭhi** (? cp. anga-laṭṭhi) fingers (or toes) and bones DA I.93. -**anguli** fingers and toes DhA III.214. -**antarikā** the interstices between the fingers Vin III.39; Miln 180; DhA III.214.

Angulika (nt.) [= angulī] a finger J III.13 (pañc°); V.204 (vaṭṭ° = pavāḷ° ankurasadisā vaṭṭanguli p. 207). See also pañcangulika.

Angulī & **Anguli** (thus always in cpds.) (f.) [Vedic angulī & °i; see anga] a finger A IV.127; Sn 610; J III.416; IV.474; V.215 (vaṭṭ° with rounded fingers); Miln 395; DhA II.59; IV.210; SnA 229.
-**patodaka** nudging with the fingers Vin III.84 = IV.110; D I.91 = A IV.343. -**pada** finger-mark A IV.127 = S III.154. -**poṭha** snapping or cracking the fingers J V.67. -**muddikā** a signet ring Vin II.106; J IV.498; V.439, 467. -**sanghaṭṭana°** = poṭha DA I.256.

Anguleyyaka (nt.) [cp. Sk. angulīyaka that which belongs to the finger, Mhg. vingerlîn = ring; E. bracelet, Fr. bras; thimble thumb etc.] an ornament for the finger, a finger-ring J II.444 (= nikkha).

Acankama (adj.) [a + cankama] not fit for walking, not level or even Th I, 1174 (magga).

Acittaka (adj.) [a + citta² + ka] 1. without thought or intention unconscious, unintentional DhA II.42. — 2. without heart or feeling, instr. **acittakena** (adv.) heartlesely J IV.58 (C. for acetasā).

Acittikata (adj.) [a + citta² + kata; cp. cittikāra] not well thought of Miln 229.

Acira see cira & cp. nacira.

Acela (adj. -n.) [a + cela] one who is not clothed, esp. t. t. for an anti-Buddhist naked ascetic D I.161, 165; III.6, 12, 17 sq.; S I.78; J V.75.

Acelaka = acela D I.166; III 40; A I.295; II.206; III.384 (°sāvaka); J III.246; VI.229; Pug 55; DhA III.489.

Acc- 1. a + c°, e. g. accuta = a + cuta. — 2. Assimilation group of (a) ati + vowel; (b) c + cons. e. g. acci = arci.

Accagā [ati + agā] 3rd sg. pret. of ati-gacchati (q. v. for similar forms) he overcame, should or could overcome Sn 1040 (explᵈ· wrongly as pp. = atikkanta at Nd² 10 and as atīta at DhA IV.434); Dh 414.

Accankusa (adj.) [ati + ankusa] beyond the reach of the goad D II.266 (nāga).

Accatari see atitarati.

Accati [Vedic arcati, ṛc, orig. meaning to be clear & to sing i. e. to sound clear, cp. arci] to praise, honour, celebrate Dāvs V.66 (accayittha, pret.) — pp **accita**, q. v.

Accanta (adj. — & adv. °—) [ati + anta, lit. "up to the end"] 1. uninterrupted, continuous, perpetual J I.223; Miln 413; VvA 71; PvA 73, 125, 266; Sdhp 288. — 2. final, absolute, complete; adv. thoroughly S I.130 (°ŋ hataputtā' mhi); III.13 = A I.291 sq.; V.326 sq. (°niṭṭha, °yogakkhemin); Kvu 586 (°niyāmatā final assurance; cp. Kvu trsl. 340). — 3. (°—) exceedingly extremely, very much A I.145 (°sukhumāla, extremely delicate), Miln 26 (id.); Sn 794 (°suddhi = paramattha-accantasuddhi SnA 528); Th I, 692 (°ruci); Dh 162 (°dussīlya = ekanta° DhA III.153).

Accaya [from acceti, ati + i, going on or beyond; cp. Sk. atyaya] (1) (temporal) lapse, passing; passing away, end, death. Usually as instr. **accayena** after the lapse of, at the end or death of after Vin I.25; D II.127 (rattiyā a.), 154 (mam° when I shall be dead); M I.438 (temās° after 3 months); S I.69; Snp. 102 (catunnaŋ māsānaŋ), p. 110 (rattiyā); J I.253 (ekāha-dvīh°), 291 (katipāh° after a few days); PvA 47 (katipāh°), 82 (dasamās°), 145 (vassasatānaŋ). — (2) (modal) passing or getting over, overcoming, conquering, only in phrase **dur-accaya** difficult to overcome, of kāmapanka Sn 945 (= dur-atikkamanīya SnA 568), of sanga Sn 948: taṇhā Dh 336; sota It 95. — (3) (fig.) going beyond (the norm), transgression, offence Vin I.133 (thull° a grave offence), 167 (id.); II.110, 170; esp. in foll. phrases: **accayo maŋ accagamā** a fault has overcome me, i. e. has been committed by me (in confession formula) D I.85 (= abhibhavitvā pavatto has overwhelmed me DA I.236); A I.54; M I.438 (id.); **accayaŋ accayato passati** to recognise a breach of the regulation as such Vin I.315; A I.103; II.146 sq.; °ŋ **deseti** to confess the transgression S I.239; °ŋ **accayato paṭiganhāti** to accept (the confession of) the fault, i. e. to pardon the transgression, in confession-formula at D I.85 = (Vin II.192; M I.438 etc.). In the same sense accaya-paṭiggahaṇa pardon, absolution J v.380; **accayena desanaŋ paṭiganhāti** J 1.379; **accayaŋ khamati** to forgive Miln 420.

Accasara (adj.) [a form. fr. aor. accasari (ati + sṛ), influenced in meaning by analogy of ati + a + sara (smṛ). Not with Morris (J. P. T. S. 1889, 200) a corruption of accaya + sara (smṛ), thus meaning "mindful of a fault"] 1. going beyond the limits (of proper behaviour), too self-sure, overbearing, arrogant, proud S 1.239 (v. l. accayasara caused by prolepsis of foll. accaya); J IV.6 (+ atisara); DhA IV.230 (= expecting too much). — 2. going beyond the limits (of understanding), beyond grasp, transcendental (of pañha a question) M 1.304; S v.218 (v. l. SS for BB reading ajjhapara). Cp. accasārin.

Accasarā (f.) [abstr. to accasara] overbearing, pride, self-surity Vbh 358 (+ māyā). *Note.* In id. p. at Pug 23 we read acchādanā instead of accasarā.

Accasari [fr. ati + sṛ] aor 3. sg. of atisarati to go beyond the limit, to go astray J v.70.

Accasarin (adj.) = accasara 1., aspiring too high Sn 8 sq. (yo nâccasārī, opp. to na paccasārī; expld. at SnA 21 by yo nâtidhāvi, opp. na ohiyyi).

Accahasi [fr. ati + hṛ] aor 3 sg. of atiharati to bring over, to bring, to take J III.484 (= ativiya āhari C.).

Accâbhikkhaṇa (°—) [ati + abhikkhaṇa] too often J v.233 (°saŋsagga; C. expls. ativiya abhiṇha).

Accāraddha (adj. adv.) [ati + āraddha] exerting oneself, very or too much, with great exertion Vin 1.182; Th 1, 638; SnA 21.

Accāyata (adj.) [ati + āyata] too long A III.375.

Accāyika (adj.) [fr. accaya] out of time, viz. 1 irregular, extraordinary J VI.549, 553. — 2. urgent, pressing M 1.149 (karaṇiyaŋ business) II.112; J 1.338; v.17 °ŋ (nt.) hurry DhA 1.18. See also acceka.

Accāsanna (adj.) [ati + āsanna] very near, too near PvA 42 (na a. n'âtidūra neither too near nor too far, at an easy distance).

Accâhita (adj.) [ati + ahita] very cruel, very unfriendly, terrible J IV.46 = v.146 (= ati ahita C.) = VI.306 (id.).

Accāvadati [ati + āvadati; or is it = ajjhāvadati = adhi + āvadati?] to speak more or better, to surpass in talk or speech; to talk somebody down, to persuade, entice Vin IV.224, 263; S II.204 sq.; J v.433 (v. l. BB ajjhārati), 434 (v. l. BB aghācarati for ajjhācarati = ajjhāvadati?).

Acci & (in verse) **accī** (f.) [Vedic arci m. & arcis nt. & f. to ṛc, cp. accati] a ray of light, a beam, flame S IV.290 (spelt acchi), 399; A IV.103; v.9; Sn 1074 (vuccati jālasikhā Nd² 11); J v.213; Miln 40; ThA 154 (dīp°); Sdhp 250.

Accikā (f.) [fr. acci] a flame M 1.74; S II.99.

Accita [pp. of accati] honoured, praised, esteemed J VI.180.

Accimant (adj.) [fr. acci, cp. Vedic arcimant & arciṣmant] flaming, glowing, fiery; brilliant Th 1, 527; J v.266; VI.248; Vv 38⁶.

Acci-bandha (adj.) [= accibaddha?] at Vin 1.287 is expld. by Bdhgh as caturassa-kedāra-baddha ("divided into short pieces" Vin Texts II.207), i. e. with squares of irrigated fields. The vv. ll. are acca° and acchi°, and we should prefer the conjecture **acchi-baddha** "in the shape of cubes or dice", i. e. with square fields.

Accuggacchati [ati + uggacchati] to rise out (of), ger. accuggamma D II.38; A v.152 (in simile of lotus).

Accuggata (adj.) [ati + uggata] 1. very high or lofty Miln 346 (giri); VvA 197; DhA II.65. — 2. too high, i. e. too shrill or loud J VI.133 (sadda), 516 (fig. = atikuddha very angry C.).

Accuṇha (adj.) [ati + uṇha] very hot, too hot Sn 966; Nd¹ 487; DhA II.85, 87 (v. l. for abbhuṇha). See also ati-uṇha.

Accuta (adj.) [a + cuta] immoveable; everlasting, eternal; nt. °ŋ Ep. of Nibbāna (see also cuta) A IV.295, 327; Sn 204, 1086 (= nicca etc. Nd² 12); Dh 225 (= sassata DhA III.321); Sdhp 47.

Accupaṭṭhapeti at J v.124 is to be read with v.l. as apaccupaṭṭhapeti (does not indulge in or care for).

Aaccupati at J IV.250 read **accuppati**, aor. 3rd sg. of accuppatati to fall in between (lit. on to), to interfere (with two people quarelling). C. expls. atigantvā uppati. There is no need for Kern's corr. acchupati (Toev. s. v.).

Accussanna (adj.) [ati + ussanna] too full, too thick Vin II.151.

Acceka = accāyika, special; °cīvara a special robe Vin III.261; cp. Vin Texts 1.29³.

Acceti [ati + eti fr. i] 1. to pass (of time), to go by, to elapse Th 1, 145 (accayanti ahorattā). — 2. to overcome, to get over Miln 36 (dukkhaŋ). — Caus. acceti to make go on (loc.), to put on J VI.17 (sūlasmiŋ; C. āvuṇeti), but at this passage prob. to be read **appeti** (q. v.).

Accogāḷha (adj.) [ati + ogāḷha] too abundant, too plentiful (of riches), lit. plunged into A IV.282, 287, 323 sq.

Accodaka (nt.) [ati + udaka] too much water (opp. anodaka no water) DhA 1.52.

Accodara (nt.) [ati + udara] too much eating, greediness, lit. too much of a belly J IV.279 (C. ati-udara).

Accha¹ (adj.) [cp. Sk. accha, dial., to ṛc (see accati), thus "shining"; cp. Sk. ṛkṣa bald, bare and Vedic ṛkvan bright. Monier-Williams however takes it as a + cha fr. **chad**, thus "not covered, not shaded"] clear, transparent Vin 1.206 (°kañjika); D 1.76 (maṇi = tanucchavi DA 1.221), 80 (udakapatta), 84 (udaka-rahada); M 1.100; S II.281 (°patta); III.105 (id.); A 1.9; J II.100 (udaka); Vv 79¹⁰ (vāri); DA 1.113 (yāgu).

-odaka having clear water, with clear water (of lotus ponds) Vv 44¹¹; 81⁵; f. °odikā Vv 41² = 60².

Accha² [Vedic ṛkṣa = Gr. ἄρκτος, Lat. ursus, Cymr. arth] a bear Vin 1.200; A III.101; J v.197, 406, 416; Miln 23, 149. At J VI.507 accha figures as N. of an animal, but is in expln. taken in the sense of accha⁴ (acchā nāma aghammigā C.). *Note.* Another peculiar form of accha is P. ikka (q. v.).

Accha³ = akkha² (a die) see acci-bandha.

Accha⁴ (adj.) [Ved. ṛkṣa] hurtful, painful, bad DhA IV.163 (°ruja).

Acchaka = accha², a bear J v.71.

Acchati [Vedic āsyati & āste, **ās**; cp. Gr. ἧσται] 1. to sit, to sit still Vin 1.289; A II.15; It 120 (in set **carati tiṭṭhati a. sayati**, where otherwise nisinna stands for acchati); Vv 74¹ (= nisīdati VvA 298); PvA 4. — 2. to stay, remain, to leave alone Th 1, 936; J IV.306. — 3. to be, behave, live Vin II.195; D 1.102; S 1.212; Vv 11²; Pv III.3¹ (= nisīdati vasati PvA 188); Miln 88; DhA 1.424. In this sense often pleonastic for finite verb, thus aggiŋ karitvā a. (= aggiŋ karoti) D I.102; aggiŋ paricaranto a. (= aggiŋ paricarati) DA I.270; tantaŋ pasārento a. (= tantaŋ pasāreti) DhA I.424. — Pot. acche It 110; aor. acchi Vin IV.308; DhA I.424.

Acchanna (adj.) [pp. of acchādeti] covered with, clothed in, fig. steeped in (c. loc.) J III.323 (lohite a. = nimugga C.). At D I.91 **nacchanna** is for na channa (see channa²) = not fair, not suitable or proper (paṭirūpa).

Acchambhin (adj.) [a + chambhin] not frightened, undismayed, fearless Sn 42 (reading achambhin; Nd² 13 expl^s. abhīru anutrāsi etc.); J VI.322 (= nikkampa C.). See chambhin.

Accharā¹ (f.) [etym. uncertain, but certainly dialectical; Trenckner connects it with ācchurita (Notes 76); Childers compares Sk. akṣara (see akkhara); there may be a connection with akkhaṇa in akkhaṇa-vedhin (cp. BSk. acchaṭā Divy 555), or possibly a relation to ā + **tsar**, thus meaning "stealthily", although the primary meaning is "snapping, a quick sound"] the snapping of the fingers, the bringing together of the finger-tips: 1. (lit.) **accharaŋ paharati** to snap the fingers J II.447; III.191; IV.124, 126; V.314; VI.366; DhA I.38, 424. — As measure: as much as one may hold with the finger-tips, a pinch J V.385; DhA II.273 (°gahaṇamattaŋ); cp. ekacchara-matta DhA II.274. — 2. (fig.) a finger's snap, i. e. a short moment, in **ek'acchara-kkhaṇe** in one moment Miln 102, and in def. of acchariya (q. v) at DA I.43; VvA 329.

-sanghāta the snapping of the fingers as signifying a short duration of time, a moment, *°matta* momentary, only for one moment (cp. BSk. acchaṭāsanghāta Divy 142) A I.10, 34, 38; IV.396; Th 1, 405; 2, 67 (expld. at ThA 76 as ghaṭikāmattam pi khaṇaŋ angulipoṭhanamattam pi kālaŋ). **-sadda** the sound of the snapping of a finger J III.127.

Accharā² (f.) [Vedic apsaras = āpa, water + sarati, orig. water nymph] a celestial nymph M I.253 (pl. accharāyo) II.64; Th 2, 374 (= devaccharā ThA 252); J V.152 sq. (Alambusā a.) Vv 5⁵ (= devakaññā VvA 37); Vv 17²; 18¹¹ etc.; DhA III.8, 19; PvA 46 (dev°); Miln 169; Sdhp 298.

Accharika (nt. or f.?) [fr. accharā²] in °ŋ **vādeti** to make heavenly music (lit. the sounds of an accharā or heavenly nymph) A IV.265.

Acchariya (adj.-nt.) [cp. Sk. āścarya since Upanishads of uncertain etym. — The conventional etym. of Pāli grammarians connects it with accharā¹ (which is prob. correct & thus reduces Sk. āścarya to a Sanskritisation of acchariya) viz. Dhammapāla: anabhiṇha-ppavattitāya accharāpaharaṇa yoggaŋ that which happens without a moment's notice, at the snap of a finger; i. e. causally unconnected (cp. Goth. silda-leiks in similar meaning) VvA 329; and Buddhaghosa: accharā-yoggan ti acchariyaŋ accharaŋ paharituŋ yuttan ti attho DA I.43] wonderful, surprising, strange, marvellous D II.155; M I.79; III.118, 125, 144 (an°); S IV.371; A I.181; Miln 28, 253; DhA III.171; PvA 121; VvA 71 (an°). As nt. often in exclamations: how wonderful! what a marvel! J I.223, 279; IV.138; VI.94 (a. vata bho); DhA IV.51 (aho a.); VvA 103 (aho ti acchariyatthena nipāto). Thus freq. comb^d. with **abbhutaŋ** = how wonderful & strange, marvellous, beyond comprehension, e. g. D I.2, 60, 206, 210; II.8; and in phrase **acchariyā abbhutā dhammā** strange & wonderful things, i. e. wonderful signs, portents marvels, M III.118, 125; A IV.198; Miln 8; also as adj. in phrase **acchariya-abbhuta-(citta-)jātā** with their hearts full of wonder and surprise DhA IV.52; PvA 6, 50. — See also acchera & accheraka.

Acchādana (nt.) [fr. acchādeti] covering, clothing Th 1, 698; Miln 279. — fig. protection, sheltering J I.307.

Acchādanā (f.) [= prec.] covering, hiding, concealment Pug 19, 23. — *Note.* In id. p. at Vbh 358 we read accasarā for acchādanā. Is the latter merely a gloss?

Acchādeti [ā + chādeti¹, Caus. of **chad**, cp. BSk. ācchādayati jīvitena to keep alive Av. Ś, I.300; Divy 136, 137] to cover, to clothe, to put on D I.63 = It 75; J I.254; III.189; IV.318; Pug 57; Pv I.10⁵ (ger. acchādayitvāna); DA I.181 (= paridahitvā); PvA 49, 50. — fig. to envelop, to fill J VI.581 (abbhaŋ rajo acchādesi dust filled the air). — pp. **acchanna** (q. v.).

Acchi at S IV.290 is faulty spelling for acci (q. v.).

Acchijja (v. l. accheja) destroying (?) S I.127. Is the reading warranted? Cp. acchecchi.

Acchidda see chidda.

Acchindati [ā + chindati, lit. to break for oneself] to remove forcibly, to take away, rob, plunder Vin IV.247 (sayaŋ a. to appropriate); J II.422; III.179; IV.343; Miln 20; Sdhp 122. — ger. **acchinditvā** J II.422; DhA I.349; PvA 241 (sayaŋ); & **acchetvā** M I.434. Caus. II. **acchindāpeti** to induce a person to theft Vin IV.224, 247.

Acchinna (adj.) [ā + chinna, pp. of acchindati] removed, taken away, stolen, robbed Vin IV.278, 303; J II.78; IV.45; V.212.

Acchiva [*Sk. akṣiba and akṣība] a certain species of tree (Hypanthera Moringa) J VI.535.

Acchupeti [ā + chupeti, Caus. of chupati] to procure or provide a hold, to insert, to put on or in Vin I.290 (aggaḷaŋ) II.112.

Acchecchi [Sk. acchaitsīt] 3rd sg. aor. of chindati "he has cut out or broken, has destroyed" (see also chindati 3), in comb^n. with **taṇhaŋ** M I.122; S I.12, 23, 127 (so read for acchejja); IV.105, 207. It 47; A III.246, 445; DhA IV.70 (gloss acchindi, for acchidda pret. of Dh 351). The v. l. at all passages is **acchejji**, which is to be accounted for on graphological grounds, ch & j being substituted in MSS. Kern (Toevoegselen s. v.) mistakes the form & tries to explain acchejji as adj. = ati-ejin (ejā), acchecchi = ati-icchin (icchā). The syntactical construction however clearly points to an aor.

Acchejja = a + chejja not to be destroyed, indestructible, see chindati.

Acchedana (nt.) [abstr. to acchindati] robbing, plundering J VI.544.

Acchera (adj.) = acchariya wonderful, marvellous S I.181; Vv 84¹³ (comp. accheratara); Pv III.5¹ (°rūpa = acchariyasabhāva PvA 197); Sdhp 244, 398.

Accheraka (adj.) = acchera (acchariya) J I.279; Bu I.9 (pāṭihīraŋ).

Aja [Vedic aja fr. **aj** (Lat. ago to drive), cp. ajina] a he-goat, a ram D I.6, 127; A II.207; J I.241; III.278 sq.; V.241; Pug 56; PvA 80.

-eḷaka [Sk. ajaiḍaka] goats & sheep D I.5, 141; A II.42 sq., 209; J I.166; VI.110; Pug 58. As pl. °ā S I.76; It 36; J IV.363. **-pada** goat-footed M I.134. **-pāla** goatherd, in *°nigrodharukkha* (Npl.) "goatherds' Nigrodha-tree" Vin I.2 sq. Dpvs I.29 (cp. M Vastu III.302). **-pālikā** a woman goatherd Vin III.38. **-lakkhaṇa** "goat-sign", i. e. prophesying from signs on a goat etc. D I.9 (expl^d. DA I.94 as "evarūpānaŋ ajānaŋ mansaŋ khāditabbaŋ evarūpānaŋ na khāditabban ti"). **-laṇḍikā** (pl.) goats' dung, in phrase nāḷimattā a. a cup full of goats' dung (which is put down a bad minister's throat as punishment) J I.419; DhA II.70; PvA 282. **-vata** "goats' habit", a practice of certain ascetics (to live after the fashion of goats) J IV.318.

Ajaka a goat, pl. goats Vin II.154. — f. ajikā J III.278 & ajiyā J V.241.

Ajagara [aja + gara = gala fr. *gel to devour, thus "goat-eater"] a large snake (rock-snake?), Boa Constrictor J VI.507; Miln 23, 303, 364, 406; DhA III.60. Also as ajakara at J III.484 (cp. Trenckner, Notes p. 64).

Ajacca (adj.) [a + jacca] of low birth J III.19; VI.100.

Ajajjara see jajjara.

Ajaddhuka & **Ajaddhumāra** see jaddhu.

Ajamoja [Sk. ajamoda, cp. Sk. ajāji] cummin-seed VvA 186.

Ajā (f.) a she-goat J III.125; IV.251.

Ajānana (°—) (nt.) [a + jānana] not knowing, ignorance (of) J V.199 (°bhāva); VI.177 (°kāla).

Ajina (nt.) [Vedic ajina, to aja, orig. goats' skin] the hide of the black antelope, worn as a garment by ascetics D I.167; Sn 1027; J I.12, 53; IV.387; V.407. kharājina a rough skin (as garment) M I.343; S IV.118; A II.207; Sn 249 (= kharāni a°-cammāni SnA 291). dantājina? ivory (q. v.).

-**khipa** a cloak made of a network of strips of a black antelope's hide D I.167; S I.117; A I.240, 295; II.206; Vin I.306; III.34; J VI.569. -**paveṇi** a cloth of the size of a couch made from pieces of ant. skin sewn together Vin I.192; D I.7 (= ajina-cammehi mañcappamāṇena sibbitvā katā paveṇi DA I.87); A I.181. -**sāṭī** a garment of skins (= ajina-camma-sāṭī DhA IV.156) Dh 394 = J I.481 = III.85.

Ajini aor 3rd sg. jayati, q. v.

Ajiya = ajikā (see ajaka).

Ajira (nt.). [Vedic ajira to **aj**, cp. Gr. ἀγρός, Lat. ager, Goth. akrs = Ger. Acker, = E. acre] a court, a yard Mhvs 35, 3.

Ajīraka (nt.) [a + jīraka] indigestion J I.404; II.181, 291; III.213, 225.

Ajeyya[1] & **Ajjeyya** (adj.) [a + jeyya, grd. of jayati, q. v.] — (a) not to be taken by force Kh VIII.8 (cp. KhA 223). — (b) not to be overpowered, invincible Sn 288; J V.509.

Ajeyya[2] (adj.) [a + jeyya, grd. of jīyati, q. v.] not decaying, not growing old, permanent J VI.323.

Ajja & **Ajjā** (adv.) [Vedic adya & adyā, a + dyā, a° being base of demonstr. pron. (see a³) and dyā an old loc. of dyaus (see diva), thus "on this day"] to-day, now Sn 75, 153, 158, 970, 998; Dh 326; J I.279; III.425 (read bahutaŋ ajjā; not with Kern, Toev. s. v. as "food"); Pv I.11¹ (= idāni PvA 59); PvA 6, 23; Mhvs 15, 64. — Freq. in phrase **ajjatagge** (= ajjato + agge(?) or ajja-t-agge, see agga³) from this day onward, henceforth Vin I.18; D I.85; DA I.235.

-**kālaŋ** (adv.) this morning J VI.180; -**divasa** the present day Mhvs 32, 23.

Ajjatana (adj.) [cp. Sk. adyatana] referring to the day, to day's, present, modern (opp. **porāṇa**) Th I, 552; Dh 227; J II.409. — dat. ajjhatanāya for to day Vin I.17; PvA 171 & passim.

Ajjatā (f.) [abstr. fr. ajja] the present time, in **ajjatañ ca** this very day S I.83 (v. l. ajjeva).

Ajjati [Vedic arjati, **ṛj**, a variant of **arh**, see arahati] to get, procure, obtain J III.263 (?). pp. ajjita (q. v.).

Ajjava (adj.-n.) [cp. Sk. ārjava, to **ṛju**, see uju] straight, upright (usually combd. with **maddava** gentle, soft) D III.213; A I.94; II.113; III.248; Sn 250 (+ maddava), 292 (id.); J III.274; Dhs 1339; Vbh 359 (an°); SnA 292 (= ujubhāva), 317 (id.).

Ajjavatā (f.) [fr. prec.] straight forwardness, rectitude, uprightness Dhs 1339. (+ ajimhatā & avankatā).

Ajjita [pp. of ajjati] obtained Sdhp 98.

Ajjuka [*Sk. arjaka] N. of a plant, Ocimum Gratissimum Vin IV.35; DA I.81 (all MSS. have ajjaka).

Ajjukaṇṇa [*Sk. arjakarṇa] N. of a tree Pentaptera Tomentosa J VI.535 (nn).

Ajjuṇho (adv.) [haplology fr. ajja-juṇho; see juṇhā] this moonlight night Vin I.25; IV.80.

Ajjuna [Vedic arjuna, to **raj**; cp. Gr. ἀργός white, ἄργυρος silver, Lat. argentum] the tree Pentaptera Arjuna J VI.535; DhA I.105 (°rukkha).

Ajjh- Assimilation group of adhi + vowel.

Ajjhagā [adhi + agā] 3rd sg. pret. of **adhigacchati** (q. v. for similar forms) he came to, got to, found, obtained, experienced S I.12 (vimānaŋ); Sn 225 (expld. at KhA 180 by vindi paṭilabhi), 956 (ratiŋ; expld. at Nd¹ 457 by adhigacchi); It 69 (jātimaraṇaŋ); Dh 154 (taṇhānaŋ khayaŋ); Vv 32⁷ (visesaŋ attained distinction; expld. at VvA 135 by adhigata); 50²¹ (amataŋ santiŋ; expld. VvA 215 by v. l. SS adhigañchi, T. adhigacchati).

Ajjhatta (adj. -n.) [cp. Sk. adhyātma, cp. attā], that which is personal, subjective, arises from within (in contrast to anything outside, objective or impersonal); as adv. & °— interior, personal, inwardly (opp. **bahiddhā bāhira** etc. outward, outwardly); Cp. ajjhattika & see *Dhs. trsl.* 272. — D I.37 (subjective, inward, of the peace of the 2nd jhāna), 70 = A II.210; V.206 (inward happiness. a. sukkhaŋ = niyakajjhattaŋ attano santāne ti attho DA I.183 cp. DhsA 169, 338, 361); S I.70, 169; II 27 (kathaŋ kathī hoti is in inward doubt), 40 (sukhaŋ dukkhaŋ); III.180 (id.); IV.1 sg. (āyatanāni), 139, 196; V.74 (**ṭhitaŋ cittaŋ ajjhattaŋ** susaṇṭhitaŋ suvimuttaŋ a mind firm, inwardly well planted, quite set free), 110, 143, 263, 297, 390; A I.40 (rūpasaññī), 272 (kāmacchanda etc.); II.158. (sukhadukkhaŋ), 211; III.86 (cetosamatha), 92 (vūpasantacitta); IV.32 (sankhittaŋ), 57 (itthindriyaŋ), 299 (cittaŋ), 305 (rūpasaññī), 360 (cetosamatha), 437 (vūpasantacitta); V 79 sq., 335 sq. (sati); It 39 (cetosamatha inward peace), 80, 82, 94; J I.045 (chātajjhatta with hungry insides); V.338 (id.); Ps I.76 (cakkhu etc.); Dhs 161 (= attano jātaŋ DhsA 169), 204, 1044; Pug 59; Vbh 1 sq. (khandhā), 228 (sati), 327 (paññā), 342 (arūpasaññī). — adv. °ŋ inwardly, personally (in contrast-pair **ajjhattaŋ vā bahiddhā vā**; see also cpd. °bahiddhā) A I.284; II.171; IV.305; V.61; Sn 917 (= upajjhayassa vā ācariyassa vā te guṇā assū ti Nd¹ 350).

-**ārammaṇa** a subjective object of thought Dhs 1047. -**cintin** thought occupied with internal things Sn 174, 388. -**bahiddhā** inside & outside, personal-external, mutual, interacting S II.252 sq.; III.47; IV.382; Nd² 15; Dhs 1049 etc. (see also bahiddhā). -**rata** with inward joy D II.107 = S V.263 = Dh 362 = Ud 64 (+ samāhita); Th I, 981; A IV.312; DhA IV.90 (= gocar' ajjhatta-sankhātāya kammaṭṭhāna-bhāvanāya rata). -**rūpa** one's own or inner form Vin III.113 (opp. bahiddhā-rūpa & ajjh°-bah° r.). -**saññojana** an inner fetter, inward bond A I.63 sq.; Pug 22; Vbh 361. -**santi** inner peace Sn 837 (= ajjhattānaŋ rāgādīnaŋ santibhāva SnA 545; cp. Nd¹ 185). -**samuṭṭhāna** originating from within J I.207 (of biri; opp. bahiddhā°).

Ajjhattika (adj.) [ajjhatta + ika], personal, inward (cp. *Dhs trsl.* 207 & Nd^1 346: ajjhattikaŋ vuccati cittaŋ); opp. bāhira outward (q. v.). See also āyatana. — M I.62; S I.73 (°ā rakkhā na bāhirā); IV.7 sq. (āyatanāni); V.101 (anga); A I.16 (anga); II.164 (dhātuyo); III.400 (āyatanāni); V.52 (id.); It 114 (id.), 9 (anga); Kh IV. (= KhA 82); J IV.402 (bāhira-vatthuŋ ayācitvā ajjhattikassa nāmaŋ ganhati); Dhs 673, 751; Vbh 13, 67, 82 sq., 119, 131, 392 sq.

Ajjhapara S V.218: substitute v. l. **accasara** (q. v.).

Ajjhappatta (& **Ajjhapatta**) [adhi + ā + *prāpta] 1. having reached, approached, coming near to J II.450; VI.566 (p; C. attano santikaŋ patta). — 2. having fallen upon, attacked J II.59; V.198 (p; C. sampatta) — 3. attained, found, got Sn 1134 (= adhigacchi Nd^2); J III.296 (p. C. sampatta); V.158 (ajjhāpatta; C. sampatta).

Ajjhabhavi 3rd sg. aor. of **adhibhavati** to conquer, overpower, overcome S I.240 (prohib. mā vo kodho ajjhabhavi); J II.336. Cp. ajjhabhu & ajjhobhavati.

Ajjhabhāsi 3rd sg. aor. of **adhibhāseti** to address S IV.117 (gāthāhi); Kh V. = Sn p. 46 (gāthāya); PvA 56, 90.

Ajjhabhu (3rd sg. aor. of **adhibhavati** (q. v.) to overcome, conquer It 76 (dujjayaŋ a. he conquered him who is hard to conquer; v. l. ajjhabhi for ajjhabhavi). Cp. ajjhabhavi.

Ajjhayana (nt.) [adhi + **i**] study (learning by heart) of the Vedas Miln 225. See also ajjhena.

Ajjhavodahi 3rd sg. aor. of ajjhodahati [Sk. adhyavadhāti] to put down J V.365 (= odahi, ṭhapesi C.). Kern, Toev. s. v. proposes reading ajjhavādahi (= Sk. avādhāt).

Ajjhāgāre (adv.) [adhi + agāre, loc. of agāra] at home, in one's own house A I.132 = It 109; A II.70.

Ajjhācarati [adhi (or ati?) + ā + **car**] 1. to conduct oneself according to Vin II.301; M I.523; Miln 266. — 2. to flirt with (perhaps to embrace) J IV.231 (aññam-aññaŋ). pp. **ajjhāciṇṇa**. See also accāvadati & aticarati.

Ajjhācāra [to adhi (ati?) + ā + **car**] 1. minor conduct (conduct of a bhikkhu as to those minor rules not included in the Pārājika's or Saŋghādisesa's) Vin I.63 (see note in *Vin. Texts,* I.184. — 2. flirtation Vin III.128 (in the Old Cy as expl^n of avabhāsati). — 3. sexual intercourse J I.396; V.327 (°cara v. l. for ajjhāvara); Miln 127 (an°).

Ajjhāciṇṇa [pp. of ajjhācarati] habitually done Vin II.80 sq., 301.

Ajjhājīva [adhi (ati?) + ā + **jīv**] too rigorous or strenuous a livelihood M II.245 (+ adhipāṭimokkha).

Ajjhāpajjati [adhi + ā + **pad**] to commit an offence, to incur, to become guilty of (acc.) Vin IV.237. pp. **ajjhāpanna** (q. v.).

Ajjhāpatti (f.) [abstr. to ajjhāpajjati] incurring guilt Dhs 299 (an°).

Ajjhāpana^1 (nt.) [fr. Caus. II. of ajjheti] teaching of the sacred writ, instruction Miln 225.

Ajjhāpana^2 (nt.) [ā + jhāpana fr. **kṣā**] burning, conflagration J VI.311.

Ajjhāpanna [pp. of adhi + āpajjati] become guilty of offence D I.245; III.43; S II.270; A IV.277, 280; V.178, 181. an° guiltless, innocent Vin I.103; D III.46; S II.194, 269; A V.181; Miln 401. For all passages except A IV.277, 280, cp. ajjhopanna.

Ajjhāpīḷita [adhi + ā + pīḷita] harassed, overpowered, tormented PvA 180 (khuppipāsāya by hunger & thirst).

Ajjhābhava [cp. Sk. adhyābhava] eccessive power, predominance J II.357.

Ajjhābhavati [adhi + ā + **bhū**, in meaning of abhi + **bhu**] to predominate J II.357.

Ajjhāyaka [cp. Sk. adhyāyaka, cp. ajjhayana] (a brahmin) engaged in learning the Veda (**mantajjhāyaka** J VI.209; SnA 192), a scholar of the brahmanic texts, a studious, learned person D I.88, 120; III.94; A I.163; III.223; Sn 140 (°kula: thus for ajjhāyakula Fsb.); Th 1, 1171; J I.3; VI.201, 498; DA I.247.

Ajjhāruha (& °rūha) (adj.) [to adhi + ā + **ruh**] growing up over, overwhelming A III.63 sq. = S V.96; J III.399.

Ajjhārūḷha (adj.) [pp. of adhi + ā + **ruh**] grown up or high over J III.399.

Ajjhārūhati [adhi + ārohati cp. atyārohati] to rise into the air, to climb over, spread over S I.221 = Nett 173 (= ajjhottharati SA; cp. Mrs. Rh. D. *Kindred Sayings* I.285).

Ajjhāvadati see accāvadati.

Ajjhāvara [fr. adhi + ā + **var**] surrounding; waiting on, service, retinue J V.322, 324, 326, 327 (expl^d at all passages by **parisā**). Should we read ajjhācara? Cp. ajjhācāra.

Ajjhāvasatar [n. ag. to ajjhāvasati] one who inhabits D I.63 (agāraŋ).

Ajjhāvasati [adhi + ā + **vas**] to inhabit (agāraŋ a house; i. e. to be settled or live the settled life of a householder) D II.16; M I.353; Vin IV.224; J I.50; Pug 57; Miln 348. — pp. **ajjhāvuttha** (q. v.).

Ajjhāvuttha [cp. Sk. adhyuṣita; pp. of ajjhāvasati] inhabited, occupied (of a house) Vin II.210; J I.145; II.333; PvA 24 (°ghara); fig. occupied by SnA 566 (= anosita).

Ajjhāsaya [fr. adhi + ā + **śri**, orig. hanging on, leaning on, BSk. however adhyāśaya Divy 586] intention, desire, wish, disposition, bent D II.224 (adj.: intent on, practising); J I.88, 90; II.352; V.382; DhsA 314, 334; PvA 88, 116, 133 (adj. dān° intent on giving alms), 168; Sdhp 219, 518. Freq. in phrase **ajjhāsayânurūpa** according to his wish, as he wanted PvA 61, 106, 128.

Ajjhāsayatā (f.) [abstr. to ajjhāsaya] desire, longing PvA 127 (uḷār° great desire for c. loc.).

Ajjhasita [pp. of adhi + ā + **śri**] intent on, bent on Miln 361 (jhān°). Cp. ajjhosita & nissita.

Ajjhiṭṭha [pp. of ajjhesati] requested, asked, invited Vin I.113 (an° unbidden); D II.289 (Buddhaghosa and text read ajjhitta); Sn p. 218 (= ajjhesita Nd^2 16); J VI.292 (= āṇatta C.); DhA IV.100 (v. l. abhijjhiṭṭha). See also an°.

Ajjhupagacchati [adhi + upa + **gam**] to come to, to reach, obtain; to consent to, agree, submit Th 2, 474 (= sampaṭicchati ThA 285); J II.403; Miln 300; pp. **ajjhupagata** (q. v.).

Ajjhupagata [pp. of ajjhupagacchati] come to, obtained, reached A V.87, cp. 210; V.187 sq.

Ajjhupagamana (nt.) [adhi + upa + **gam**] consent, agreement, justification Vin II.97, 104.

Ajjhupaharati [adhi + upa + **hṛ**; cp. upaharati] to take (food) to oneself J II.293 (aor. ajjhupāhari = ajjhohari C.).

Ajjhupekkhati [adhi + upa + **ikṣ**; cp. BSk. adhyupekṣati] 1. to look on A I.257; Miln 275. — 2. to look on intently or with care, to oversee, to take care of A IV.45 (kaṭṭh'aggi, has to be looked after); PvA 149 (sisaŋ colaŋ vā). — 3. to look on indifferently to be indifferent, to neglect Vin II.78 = III.162, cp. J I.147; M I.155; II.223; A III.194, 435; J V.229; DhA IV.125.

Ajjhupekkhana (nt.) & °ā (f.) [abstr. from ajjhupekkhati] care, diligence, attention Ps I.16; II.119; Vbh 230 sq.; DhA IV.3.

Ajjhupekkhitar [n. ag. to ajjhupekkhati] one who looks on (carefully), one who takes care or controls, an overseer, caretaker S V.69 (sādhukaŋ), 324 (id.), 331 sq.; Vbh 227.

Ajjhupeti [cp. Sk. abhyupeti; adhi + upa + i] to go to meet, to receive J IV.440.

Ajjheti [Sk. ādhyāyati, Denom. fr. adhyāya] to be anxious about, to fret, worry Sn 948 (socati +); expl^d at Nd[1] 433 by nijjhāyati, at SnA 568 by abhijjhati (gloss BB gijjhati).

Ajjhena (nt.) [Sk. adhyayana, see also ajjhayana] study (esp. of the Vedas) M III.1; J II.327 (as v. l. to be preferred to ajjhesanā); III.114 (= japa); V.10 (pl. = vede); VI.201 = 207; Vbh 353; SnA 314 (mant°).
-kujja (°kūta v. l.?) a hypocrite, a pharisee Sn 242; cp. SnA 286.

Ajjhesati (adhi + **iṣ**; cp. BSk. adhyeṣate Divy 160] to request, ask, bid DhA IV.18; aor. **ajjhesi** Vin II.200; pp. **ajjhiṭṭha** & **ajjhesita** (q. v.), with which cp. pariyiṭṭha & °esita.

Ajjhesanā (f.) [see ajjhesati] request, entreaty Vin I.6 = D II.38 = S I.138; J II.327 (better v. l. ajjhena).

Ajjhesita [pp. of ajjhesati; cp. ajjhiṭṭha] requested, asked, bidden Nd[2] 16 (= ajjhiṭṭha).

Ajjhokāsa [adhi + okāsa] the open air, only in loc. **ajjhokāse** in the open Vin I.15; S I.212; DhA IV.100.

Ajjhogāḷha [pp. of ajjhogāhati] plunged into, immersed; having entered M I.457; S I.201; Miln 348.

Ajjhogāhati (& °gāheti) [Sk. *abhyavagāhate; adhi (= abhi) + ava + **gāh**] to plunge into, to enter, to go into D I.101 (vanaŋ), 222 (samuddaŋ); M I.359, 536; A III.75, 368; IV.356; V.133; Vin III.18; J I.7; Nd[1] 152 (ogāhati +); Miln 87 (samuddaŋ); 300 (vanaŋ). — pp. ajjhogāḷha (q. v.). Cp. pariyogāhati.

Ajjhoṭhapeti [adhi + ava + ṭhapeti, Caus. of **sthā**] to bring to PvA 148 (gāmaŋ), where we should read °ṭṭhapeti.

Ajjhotthata [pp. of ajjhottharati] spread over; covered, filled; overcome, crushed, overpowered J I.363 (ajjhottaṭa), 410; V.91 (= adhipanna); DhA I.278; PvA 55; Dāvs V.5.

Ajjhottharati [adhi + ava + **stṛ**] to cover over, spread out, spread over, cover; to submerge, flood Vin I.111; J I.61, 72, 73; Miln 296, 336; Dh I.264; Pass. °tthariyati to be overrun with (instr.), to be smothered, to be flooded A III.92 = Pug 67; aor. **ajjhotthari** VvA 48 (gāmapadeso: was flooded). pp. **ajjhotthata** (q. v.).

Ajjhopanna (?) only found in one stock phrase, viz. gathita (q. v.) mucchita ajjhopanna with ref. to selfishness, greed, bonds of craving. The reading **ajjhopanna** is the lectio difficilior, but the accredited reading **ajjhosāna** seems to be clearer and to harmonize better with the cognate ajjhosita & ajjhosāna (n.) in the same context. The confusion between the two is old-standing and hard to be accounted for. Trenckner under v. l. to M I.162 on p. 543 gives ajjhopanna as BB (= adhi-opanna). The MSS. of Nd[2] clearly show ajjhopanna as inferior reading, which may well be attributable to the very frequent SS substitution of p for s (see Nd[2] Introd. XIX.). Besides this mixture of vv. ll. with s and p there is another confusion between the vv. ll. **ajjhāpanna** and **ajjhopanna** which adds to the complication of the case. However since the evidence of a better reading between these two preponderates for ajjhopanna we may consider the o as established, and, with a little more clearness to be desired, may in the end decide for **ajjhosāna** (q. v.), which in this case would have been liable to change through analogy with ajjhāpanna, from which it took the ā and p. Cp. also ajjhosita. The foll. is a synopsis of readings as preferred or confused by the Ed. of the var. texts. — 1. **ajjhopanna** as T. reading: M I.162, 173, 369; A I.74; II.28; III.68, 242; Nd 75, 76; DA I.59; **as v. l.**: D I.245. — 2. **ajjhosāna as v. l.**: A I.74 (C. expl^s. ajjhosāya gilitvā ṭhita); Nd[2] under nissita & passim; Ud 75, 76 (ajjhosanna); DA I.59 (id.). — 3. **ajjhāpanna** as T. reading: D I.245; III.43, 46; S. II.194, 270: IV.332 (ajjhapaṇṇa); A V.178, 181; Nd[2] under nissita; Miln 401; **as v. l.**: M I.162; A III.242; Ud 75, 76.

Ajjhobhavati [adhi + ava + **bhu**, Sk. abhi°] to overcome, overpower, destroy J II.80 (aor. ajjhobhavi = adhibhavi C.).

Ajjhomaddati [adhi + ava + **mṛd**] to crush down A IV.191, 193.

Ajjhomucchita [pp. adhi + ava + **mūrch**, cp. adhimuccita] stiffened out (in a swoon), lying in a faint (?) A III.57 sq. (v. l. ajjhomuñcita or °muccita better: sarīre attached to her body, clinging to her b.).

Ajjholambati [adhi + ava + **lamb**] to hang or hold on to (acc.), to cling to S III 137; M III.164 = Nett 179, cp. Sdhp 284 & 296.

Ajjhosa = ajjhosāya, in verse only as **ajjhosa tiṭṭhati** to cleave or cling to S IV.73; Th 1, 98, 794.

Ajjhosati [adhi + ava + sayati, **sā**, to bind, pp. sita: see ajjhosita] to be bound to, to be attached, bent on; to desire, cleave to, indulge in. Fut. **ajjhosissati** (does it belong here?) M I.328 (c. acc. paṭhaviŋ, better as ajjhesati). grd. **ajjhositabba** M I.109 (+ abhinanditabba, v. l. °etabba); DhsA 5 (id.); ger. **ajjhosāya** (q. v.) pp. **ajjhosita** (q. v.).

Ajjhosāna (nt.) cleaving to (earthly joys), attachment, D II.58 sq.; III.289; M I.498 (+ abhinandana); S III.187; A I.66; II.11 (diṭṭhi°, kāma° + taṇhā). In comb^n. with (icchā) and mucchā at Nd[2] under chanda & nissita and taṇhā (see also ajjhopanna), and at Dhs 1059 of lābha, (the expl^n. at DhsA 363, 370, from as to eat, is popular etym.) Nett 23 sq. (of taṇhā).

Ajjhosāya [ger. of ajjhosati, cp. BSk. adhyavasāya tiṣṭhati Divy 37, 534] being tied to, hanging on, attached to, only in phrase **a. tiṭṭhati** (+ abhinandati, same in Divy) M I.266; S. IV.36 sq.; 60, 71 sq.; Miln 69. See also **ajjhosa.**

Ajjhosita [cp. Sk. adhyavasita, from adhi + ava + **sā**; but sita is liable to confusion with sita = Sk. śrita, also through likeness of meaning with esita; see ajjhāsita & ajjhesita] hanging on, cleaving to, being bent on, (c. loc.) S II.94 (+ mamāyita); A II.25 (diṭṭha suta muta +); Nd[1] 75, 106, 163 = Nd[2] under nissita; Th 2, 470 (asāre = taṇhāvasena abhiniviṭṭha ThA 284); Pv IV.8[4] (mayhaŋ ghare = taṇhābhinivisena abhiniviṭṭha PvA 267; v. l. BB ajjhesita, SS ajjhāsita). -**an°** S IV.213; V.319; Nd[1] 411; Miln 74 (pabbajita).

Ajjhohata [pp. of ajjhoharati] having swallowed Sdhp 610 (balisaŋ maccho viya: like a fish the fishhook).

Ajjhoharaṇa (nt.) = ajjhohāra 1. A V.324; J VI.213.

Ajjhoharaṇiya (adj.) [grd. of ajjhoharati] something fit to eat, eatable, for eating J VI.258; DhA I.284.

Ajjhoharati [Sk. abhyavaharati; adhi (= abhi) + ava + hṛ] to swallow, eat, take as food M I.245; J I.460; II.293; VI.205, 213; Miln 366; PvA 283 (aor.) -pp. ajjhohaṭa (q.v.).

Ajjhohāra [Sk. abhyavahāra] 1. taking food, swallowing, eating & drinking Vin IV.233; Miln 176, 366. — 2. N. of a fabulous fish (swallower"; cp. timingala) J V.462.

Añcati J I.417, read añchati (see next).

Añchati [in meaning = ākaḍḍhati, which latter is also the Sk. gloss (ākārṣayati) to the Jain Prk. aṇchāvei = añchati: see Morris, J. P. T. S. 1893, 60] to pull, drag, pull along, to turn on a lathe D II.291 (bhamakāro dighaŋ a., where K has note: añjanto ti pi acchanto ti pi pātho) = M I.56 (vv. ll. p. 532 acch° & añj°); Th 1, 750 (añcāmi T., v.l. aññāmi). Añchati should also be read at J I 417 for **udakaŋ añcanti** (in expl[n.] of udañcanī pulling the water up from a well, q. v.), where it corresponds to **udakaŋ ākkaḍḍhati** in the same sentence.

Añja (adv.) [orig. imper. of añjati[1]; cp. Sk. anjasā (instr.) quickly, Goth. anaks suddenly, lit. with a pull or jerk] pull on! go on! gee up! J I.192.

Añjati[1] [= Sk. ṛñjati, ṛjyati to stretch, pull along, draw out, erect; cp. Sk. ṛju straight, caus. irajyati; Gr. ὀρέγω; Lat. rego, rectus = erect. See also P. uju, añchati, ajjita, ānañja-ānejja]. See añja, añjaya, añjali, añjasa.

Añjati[2] & **Añjeti** [= Sk. añjayati, Caus. of anakti to smear etc.; cp. Sk. añji ointment, ājya butter; Lat. unguo to anoint, unguentum ointment; Ohg. ancho = Ger. Anke butter] to smear, anoint, paint S II.281; J IV.219 (akkhīni añjetvā, v. l. BB añcitvā). Caus. II. **añjāpeti** DhA I.21. — pp. **añjita** (q. v.).

Añjana (nt.) [from añjati[2]] ointment, esp. a collyrium for the eyes, made of antimony, adj. anointed, smeary; glossy, black (cp. kaṇha II. and kāla[1] note). — 1. Vin I.203 (five kinds viz. kāḷ°, ras°, sot°, geruka, kapalla); D I.7, 12; DA I.98 (khār°); 284; DhA III.354 (akkhi° eye-salve). — 2. glossy, jet-black J I.194; II.369; V.416. The reading añjana at A IV.468 is wrong, it should be corrected into thanamajjanamattaŋ. See also pacc°. In meaning collyrium box at Th 2, 413 (= añjana-nāḷi ThA 267); DhA II.25.

-**akkhiha** with anointed eyes Th 1, 960. -**upapisana** perfume to mix with ointment Vin I.203; II.112. -**cuṇṇa** aromatic powder DhsA 13. -**nāḷi** an ointment tube, collyrium box ThA 267. -**rukkha** N. of a tree ("black" tree) J I.331. -**vaṇṇa** of the colour of collyrium, i. e. shiny, glossy, dark, black D II.18 (lomāni); J I.138 (kesā), 194; II.369; PvA 258 (vana).

Añjanī (f.) [fr. añjana] a box for ointment, a collyrium pot Vin I.203, 204; II.135; IV.168; M II.65 = Th 1, 773.

Añjanisalākā (f.) a stick to put the ointment on with Vin I.203; II.135; J III.419.

Añjaya (adj.) [from añjati[1]] straight J III.12 (vv. ll. ajjava & and ājjava better?) expl[d] by C. as ujuka, akuṭila. See also ajjava. Should we assume misreading for añjasa?

Añjali [cp. Sk. añjali, fr. añjati[1]] extending, stretching forth, gesture of lifting up the hands as a token of reverence (cp. E. to "tender" one's respect), putting the ten fingers together and raising them to the head (VvA 7: dasanakha-samodhāna-samujjalaŋ añjaliŋ paggayha). Only in stock phrases (a.) **añjaliŋ paṇāmeti** to bend forth the outstretched hands Vin II.188; D I.118; Sn 352; Sn p. 79. (b.) °ŋ **paggaṇhāti** to perform the a. salutation J I.54; DhA IV.212; VvA 7, 312 (sirasmiŋ on one's head); PvA 93. (c.) °ŋ karoti id. PvA 178; cp. **katañjali** (adj.) with raised hands Sn 1023; J I.17; PvA 50, and **añjalikata** id. Pv II.12[20]. Cp. pañjali

-**kamma** respectful salutation, as above A I.123; II.180; IV.130; Vv 78[8], 83[16]; DhA I.32. -**karaṇīya** (adj.) that is worthy of being thus honoured D III.5; A II.34; III.36; IV.13 sq.; It 88.

Añjalikā (f.) [= añjali] the raising of the hands as a sign of respectful salutation Vv 1[8] (expl[d] at VvA 24 as dasanakha-samodhāna samujjalaŋ añjaliŋ sirasi paggaṇhantī guṇa-visiṭṭhānaŋ apacayānaŋ akāsiŋ).

Añjasa [Sk. āñjasa (?). Cp. ārjava = P. ajjava, see añjati[1] & añjaya] straight, straightforward (of a road) D I.235; J I.5; Th 2, 99; Vv 50[20] (cp. VvA 215); VvA 84 (= akuṭila); Mhvs 25, 5; Miln 217; Sdhp 328, 595. Cp. pañjasa.

Añjita [Sk. ankta & añjayita, pp. of añjeti] smeared, anointed J I.77 (su-añjitāni akkhīni); IV.421 (añjit'akkha).

Añña (pron.) [Vedic anya, with compar. suff. ya; Goth. anþar; Ohg. andar; formation with n analagous to those with l in Gr. ἄλλος (ἄλjος), Lat. alius (cp. alter), Goth. aljis Ags. elles = E. else. From demonstr. base *eno, see na[1] and cp. a[3]] another etc. — A. *By itself*: 1. other, not the same, different, another, somebody else (opp. oneself) Vin III.144 (aññena, scil. maggena, gacchati to take a different route); Sn 459, 789, 904; Dh 158 (opp. attānaŋ), 165; J I.151 (opp. attano); II.333 (aññaŋ vyākaroti give a diff. answer). — 2. another one, a second; nt. else, further Sn 1052 (= uttariŋ nt. Nd[2] 17); else J I.294. aññaŋ kiñci (indef.) anything else J I.151. yo añño every other, whoever else J I.256. — 3. aññe (pl.) (the) others, the rest Sn 189, 663, 911; Dh 43, 252, 355; J I.254. — B. del. *in correlation*: 1. *copulative.* añña.. añña the one .. the other (.. the third etc.); this, that & the other; some .. some Vin I.15; Miln 40; etc. — 2. *reciprocative* **añño aññaŋ, aññamaññaŋ, aññoññaŋ** one another, each other, mutually, reciprocally (in ordinary construction & declension of a noun or adj. in *sg.*; cp. Gr. ἀλλήλων, ἀλλήλους in *pl.*). (a.) **añño aññaŋ** Dh 165. (b.) **aññamañña** (cp. BSk. anyamanya M Vastu II.436), as *pron.*: n'ālaŋ aññamaññassa sukhāya vā dukkhāya vā D I.56 = S III.211. n'aññamaññassa dukkhaŋ iccheyya do not wish evil to each other Sn 148. daṇḍehi aññamaññaŋ upakkamanti (approach each other) M I.86 = Nd[2] 199. °ŋ agāravo viharati A III.247. dve janā °ŋ ghātayiŋsu (slew each other) J I.254. aññamaññaŋ hasanti J V.111; °ŋ musale hantvā J V.267. °ŋ daṇḍâbhigātena PvA 58; or *adj.*: aññamaññaŋ veraŋ bandhiŋsu (established mutual enmity) J II.353; °ŋ piyasaŋvāsaŋ vasiŋsu J II.153; aññamaññaŋ accayaŋ desetvā (their mutual mistake) DhA I.57; or *adv.* dve pi aññamaññaŋ paṭibaddha citta ahesuŋ (in love with each other) J III.188; or °—: aññamañña-paccaya mutually dependent, interrelated Ps II.49, 58. — (c.) **aññoñña** (°—) J V.251 (°nissita); Dāvs V.45 (°bhinna). — 3. *disjunctive* añña .. añña one .. the other, this one ... that one, different, different from aññaŋ jīvaŋ .. aññaŋ sarīraŋ one is the soul .. the other is the body, i. e. the soul is different from the body D I.157; M I.430; A V.193; aññā va saññā bhavissati añño attā D I.187. Thus also in phrase **aññena aññaŋ** opposite, the contrary, differently, contradictory (lit. other from that which is other) Vin II.85 (paṭicarati make counter-charges); D I.57 (vyākāsi gave the opposite or contradictory reply); Miln 171 (aññaŋ kayiramānaŋ aññena sambharati). — **anañña** (1) not another, i. e. the same, self-same, identical M I.256 (= ayaŋ). — (2) not another, i. e. alone, by oneself, oneself only Sn 65 (°posin; opp. paraŋ) = Nd 4, cp. Nd[2] 36. — (3) not another, i. e. no more, only, alone Sn p. 106 (dve va gatiyo bhavanti anaññā: and no other or no more, only two). See also under cpds.

-**ādisa** different J VI.212, °tā difference PvA 243. -**khantika** acquiescing in diff. views, following another faith (see khantika) D I.187; M I.487. **-titthiya** an adherent of another sect, a non-Buddhist.; D III.115; M I.494, 512; P II.21, 32 sq., 119; III.116 sq.; IV.51, 228; V.6, 27 sq.; A I.65, 240; II.176; IV.35 sq.; Vin I.60; J I.93; II.415. **-diṭṭhika** having diff. views (combd. with añña-khantika) D I.187; M I.487. **-neyya** (an°) not to be guided by somebody else, i. e. independent in one's views, having attained the right knowledge by oneself (opp. para°) Sn 55, 213, 364. **-mano** (an°) (adj.) not setting one's heart upon others Vv 11[5] (see VvA 58). **-vada** holding other views, an° (adj.) Dpvs IV.24. **-vādaka** one who gives a diff. account of things, one who distorts a matter, a prevaricator Vin IV.36. **-vihita** being occupied with something else, distracted, absent-minded Vin IV.269; DhA III.352, 381; °tā distraction, absent-mindedness DhA I.181. **-saraṇa** (an°) not betaking oneself to others for refuge, i. e. of independent, sure knowledge S III.42 = V.154. **-sita** dependent or relying on others Sn 825.

Aññatama (pron. adj.) [añña + superl. suff. tama; see also aññatara] one out of many, the one or the other of, a certain, any Mhvs 38, 14.

Aññatara (pron. adj.) [Sk. anyatara, añña + compar. suff. tara, cp. Lat. alter, Goth. anþar etc.] one of a certain number, a certain, somebody, some; often used (like **eka**) as indef. article "a". Very frequent, e. g. Sn 35, 210; It 103; Dh 137, 157; J I.221, 253; II.132 etc. devaññatara a certain god, i. e. any kind of god S IV.180 = A IV.461.

Aññattha (adv.) [from añña = aññatra, adv. of place, cp. kattha, ettha] somewhere or anywhere else, elsewhere (either place where or whereto) J I.291; II.154; DhsA 163; DhA I.212; III.351; PvA 45; Mhvs 4, 37; 22, 14.

Aññatra (adv.) [anya + tra, see also aññattha] elsewhere, somewhere else J V.252; Pv IV.1[62]. In compn. also = añña°, e. g. aññatra-yoga (adj.) following another discipline D I.187; M I.487. — As prep. c. abl. (and instr.) but, besides, except, e. g. a. iminā tapo-pakkamena D I.168; kiŋ karaṇīyaŋ a. dhammacariyāya S I.101; ko nu aññatra-m-ariyehi who else but the Nobles Sn 886 (= ṭhapetvā saññā-mattena SnA 555). **-kiŋ aññatra** what but, i. e. what else is the cause but, or: this is due to; but for D I.90 (vusitavā-mānī k. a. avusitattā); S I.29 (k. k. a. adassanā except from blindness); Sn 206 (id.).

Aññathatta (nt.) [aññathā + tta] 1. change, alteration S III.37; IV.40; A I.153; III.66; Kvu 227 (= jarā C, cp. *Kvu trsl.* 55 n. 2); Miln 209. — 2. difference J I.147; It 11. — 3. erroneous supposition, mistake Vin II.2; S III.91; IV.329. — 4. fickleness, change of mind, doubt, wavering, M I.448, 457 (+ domanassa); J I.33 (cittaŋ); PvA 195 (cittassa).

Aññathā (adv.) [añña + thā] in a different manner, otherwise, differently S I.24; Sn 588, 757; DhsA 163; PvA 125, 133. anaññathā without mistake Vv 44[18]; anaññatha (nt.) certainty, truth Ps II.104 (= tatha).

-**bhāva** (1) a different existence A II.10; It 9 = 94; Sn 729, 740, 752; (2) a state of difference; i. e. change, alteration, unstableness D I.36; S II.274; III.8, 16, 42; Vbh 379. **-bhāvin** based on difference S III.225 sq.; IV.23 sq., 66 sq.; an° free from difference Vin I.36.

Aññadatthu (adv.) [lit. aññad atthu let there be anything else, i. e. be it what it will, there is nothing else, all, everything, surely] part. of affirmation = surely, all-round, absolutely (ekaŋsa-vacane nipāto DA I.111) only, at any rate D I.91; II.284; Sn 828 (na h' aññadatth' atthi pasaŋsa-lābhā, expld. SnA 541 as na hi ettha pasaŋsa-lābhato añño attho atthi, cp. also Nd[1] 168); Miln 133; VvA 58; PvA 97, 114.

-**dasa** sure-seeing, seeing everything, all pervading D I.18; III.135, 185; A II.24; III.202; IV.89, 105; It 15.

Aññadā (adv.) [añña + dā, cp. kadā, tadā, yadā] at another time, else, once S IV.285; J V.12; DhA IV.125.

Aññā (f.) [Sk. ājñā, = ā + **jñā**, cp. ājānāti] knowledge, recognition, perfect knowledge, philosophic insight, knowledge par excellence, viz. Arahantship, saving knowledge, gnosis (cp. on term *Compend.* 176 n. 3 and *Psalms of Brethren* introd. XXXIII.) M I.445; S I.4 (sammad°), 24 (aññāya nibbuta); II.221; V.69, 129 (diṭṭh' eva dhamme), 133, 237; A III.82, 143, 192; V.108; It 39 sq., 53, 104; Dh 75, 96; Kh VII.11; Miln 334. — **aññaŋ vyākaroti** to manifest ones Arahantship (by a discourse or by mere exclamation) Vin I.183; S II.51 sq., 120; IV.139; V.222; J I.140; II.333. See also arahatta.

-**atthika** desirous of higher knowledge Pv IV.1[14]. **-ārādhana** the attainment of full insight M I.479. **-indriya** the faculty of perfect knowledge or of knowledge made perfect D III.219; S V.204; It 53; Pug 2; Dhs 362, 505, 552; Nett 15, 54, 60. **-citta** the thought of gnosis, the intention of gaining Arahantship S II.267; A III.437. **-paṭivedha** comprehension of insight Vin II.238. **-vimokkha** deliverance by the highest insight Sn 1105, 1107 (Nd[2] 19: vuccati arahatta-vimokkho).

Aññāṇa (nt.) [a + ñāṇa] ignorance; see ñāṇa 3 e.

Aññāṇaka (nt.) [Demin. of aññāṇa] ignorance Vin IV.144.

Aññāṇin (adj.) [a + ñāṇin] ignorant, not knowing DhA III.106.

Aññāta[1] [pp. of ājānāti, q. v.] known, recognised Sn 699. an° what is not known, in phrase anaññāta-ññassāmī' t' indriya the faculty of him (who belives): "I shall know what is not known (yet)" D III.219; S V.204; It 53; Pug 2; Dhs 296 (cp. Dhs trsl. 86); Nett 15, 54, 60, 191. **-mānin** one who prides himself in having perfect knowledge, one who imagines to be in possession of right insight A III.175 sq.; Th 1, 953.

Aññāta[2] [a + ñāta] unknown, see ñāta.

Aññātaka[1] [a + ñātaka, cp. Sk. ajñāti] he who is not a kinsman DhA I.222.

Aññātaka[2] (adj.) [Demin. of aññāta[2]] unknown, unrecognisable, only in phrase °**vesena** in unknown form, in disguise J I.14; III.116; V.102.

Aññātar [n. ag. to ājānāti] one who knows, a knower of D II.286; M I.169; S I.105 (dhammassa); Kvu 561.

Aññātāvin (adj. -n.) [from ājānāti] one who has complete insight DhsA 291.

-**indriya** (°tāv' indr.) the faculty of one whose knowledge is made perfect Dhs 555 (cp. *Dhs trsl.* 150) and same loci as under aññindriya (see aññā).

Aññātukāma (adj.) [ā + jñātuŋ + kāma] desirous of gaining right knowledge A III.192. See ājānāti.

Aññāya [ger. of ājānāti, q. v. for detail] recognising, knowing, in the conviction of S I.24; A III.41; Dh 275, 411.

Aññoñña see añña B 2 c.

Añhamāna [Sk. aśnāna, ppr. med. of aśnāti, **aś** to eat] eating, taking food; enjoying: only SS at Sn 240; all MSS at 239 have asamāna. SnA 284 expls. by āhārayamāna.

Aṭaṭa [BSk. aṭaṭa (e. g. Divy 67), prob. to **aṭ** roam about. On this notion cp. description of roaming about in Niraya at Nd[1] 405 bottom] N. of a certain purgatory or Niraya A V.173 = Sn p. 126.

Aṭanaka (adj.) [cp. Sk. aṭana, to **aṭ**] roaming about, wild J V.105 (°gāvī).

Aṭanī (f.) a support a stand inserted under the leg of a bedstead Vin IV.168; Sām. Pās. on Pāc. 14 (quoted Min.

Pāt. 86 and Vin IV.357); DhA I.234; J II.387, 425, 484 supports of a seat. Morris, J. P. T. S. 1884, 69 compares Marāthi aḍaṇī a three-legged stand. See also *Vin Texts* II.53.

Aṭala (adj.) [cp. Sk. aṭṭa & aṭṭālaka stronghold] solid, firm, strong, only in phrase **aṭaliyo upāhanā** strong sandals M II.155 (vv. ll. pataliye & agaliyo) = S I.226 (vv. ll. āṭaliyo & āṭaliko). At the latter passage Bdhgh. expl^s. gaṇangaṇ-ūpāhanā, Mrs. Rh. D. (*Kindred Sayings* I.291) trsls. "huskined shoes".

Aṭavī (f.) [Sk. aṭavī: Non-Aryan, prob. Dravidian] 1. forest, woods J I.306; II.117; III.220; DhA I.13; PvA 277. — 2. inhabitant of the forest, man of the woods, wild tribe J VI.55 (= aṭavicorā C.).
-**rakkhika** guardian of the forest J II.335. -**sankhepa** at A I.178 = III.66 is prob. faulty reading for v. l. °sankopa "inroad of savage tribes".

Aṭṭa[1] [cp. see aṭṭaka] a platform to be used as a watch-tower Vin I.140; DA I.209.

Aṭṭa[2] [cp. Sk. artha, see also attha 5 b] lawsuit, case, cause Vin IV.224; J II.2, 75; IV.129 (°ŋ vinicchināti to judge a cause), 150 (°ŋ tīreti to see a suit through); VI.336.

Aṭṭa[3] [Sk. ārta, pp. of ardati, **ṛd** to dissolve, afflict etc.; cp. Sk. ārdra (= P. adda and alla); Gr. ἄρδω to moisten, ἄρδα dirt. See also aṭṭīyati & aṭṭita] distressed, tormented, afflicted; molested, plagued, hurt Sn 694 (+ vyasanagata; SnA 489 ātura); Th 2, 439 (= aṭṭita ThA 270), 441 (= pīḷita ThA 271); J IV.293 (= ātura C.); Vv 80[9] (= aṭṭita upadduta VvA 311). Often —°: iṇaṭṭa oppressed by debt M I.463; Miln 32; chāt° tormented by hunger VvA 76; vedan° afflicted by pain Vin II.61; III.100; J I.293; sūcik° (read for sūcikaṭṭha) pained by stitch Pv III.2[3].
-**ssara** cry of distress Vin III.105; S II.255; J I.265; II.117; Miln 357; PvA 285.

Aṭṭaka [Demin. of aṭṭa[1]] a platform to be used as a watch-house on piles, or in a tree Vin I.173; II.416; III.322, 372; DA I.209.

Aṭṭāna at Vin II.106 is obscure, should it not rather be read with Bdhgh as **aṭṭhāna**? (cp. Bdhgh on p. 315).

Aṭṭāla [from aṭṭa] a watch-tower, a room at the top of a house, or above a gate (koṭṭhaka) Th 1, 863; J III.160; V.373; Miln 1, 330; DhA III.488.

Aṭṭālaka [Sk. aṭṭālaka] = aṭṭāla; J II.94, 220, 224; VI.390, 433; Miln 67, 81.

Aṭṭita (& occasionally **addita**, e. g. Pv II.6[2]; Th 2, 77, 89; Th 1, 406) [Sk. ardita, pp. of ardayati, Caus. of ardati, see aṭṭa[3]] pained, distressed, grieved, terrified Th 1, 157; J II.436; IV.85 (v. l. addhita); V.84; VvA 311; ThA 270; Mhvs 1, 25; 6, 21; Dpvs I.66; II.23; XIII.9; Sdhp 205. — See remarks of Morris J. P. T. S. 1886, 104, & 1887. 47.

Aṭṭīyati & **Aṭṭiyati** [Denom. fr. aṭṭa[3], q. v.] to be in trouble or anxiety, to be worried, to be incommodated, usually comb^d. with **harāyati**, e. g. D I.213 (+ jigucchati); S I.131; M I.423; Pv I.10[2] (= aṭṭā dukkhitā PvA 48), freq. in ppr. **aṭṭiyamāna harayāmāna** (+ jigucchamāna) Vin II.292; J I.66, 292; It 43; Nd[2] 566; Ps I.159. — Spelling sometimes addiyāmi, e. g. Th 1, 140. — pp. aṭṭita & addita.

Aṭṭiyana (nt.) [cp. Sk. ardana, to aṭṭiyati] fright, terror, amazement DhA II.179.

Aṭṭha[1] [Vedic aṣṭau, old dual, Idg. *octou, pointing to a system of counting by tetrads (see also nava); Av. ašta, Gr. ὀκτώ, Lat. octo, Goth. ahtau = Ohg. ahto, Ger. acht, E. eight] *num. card*, eight, decl. like pl. of adj. in-a.
A. The number in *objective* significance, based on natural phenomena: see cpds. °angula, °nakha, °pada, °pāda.
B. The number in *subjective* significance. — (1) As mark of respectability and honour, based on the idea of the double square: (a) in meaning "a couple" aṭṭha matakukkuṭe aṭṭha jīva-k. gahetvā (with 8 dead & 8 live cocks; eight instead of 2 because gift intended for a king) DhA I.213. sanghassa a salākabhattaŋ dāpesi VvA 75 = DhA III.104. a. piṇḍapātāni adadaŋ Vv 34[8]. a. vattha-yugāni (a double pair as offering) PvA 232, a therā PvA 32. — The highest respectability is expressed by $8 \times 8 = 64$, and in this sense is freq. applied to *gifts*, where the giver gives a higher potency of a pair (2^3). Thus a "royal" gift goes under the name of sabb-aṭṭhakaŋ dānaŋ (8 elephants, 8 horses, 8 slaves etc.) where each of 8 constituents is presented in 8 exemplars DhA II.45, 46, 71. In the same sense aṭṭh' aṭṭha kahāpaṇā (as gift) DhA II.41; aṭṭh-aṭṭhakā dibbākaññā Vv 67[3] (= catusaṭṭhi VvA 290); aṭṭhaṭṭhaka Dpvs VI.56. Quite conspicuous is the meaning of a "couple" in the phrase satt-aṭṭha 7 or 8 = a couple, e. g. sattaṭṭha divasā, a week or so J I.86; J II.101; VvA 264 (saŋvacchарā years). — (b.) used as definite *measure* of quantity & distance, where it also implies the respectability of the gift, 8 being the lowest unit of items that may be given decently. Thus freq. as aṭṭha kahāpaṇā J I.483; IV.138; VvA 76; Miln 291. — In distances: a. karīsā DhA II.80; IV.217; PvA 258; a. usabhā J IV.142. — (c.) in comb^n. with 100 and 1000 it assumes the meaning of "a great many", hundreds, thousands. Thus **aṭṭha sataŋ** 800, Sn 227. As denotation of wealt (cp. below under 18 and 80): a-°sata-sahassa-vibhava DhA IV.7. But aṭṭhasata at S IV.232 means 108 (3×36), probably also at J V.377. — **aṭṭha sahassaŋ** 8000 J V.39 (nāgā). The same meaning applies to 80 as well as to its use as unit in comb^n. with any other decimal (18, 28, 38 etc.): (α) 80 (**asīti**) a great many. Here belong the 80 smaller signs of a Mahāpurisa (see anuvyañjana), besides the 32 main signs (see dvattiŋsa) VvA 213 etc. Freq. as measure of *riches*, e. g. 80 waggon loads Pv II.7[5]; asīti-koṭivibhava DhA III.129; PvA 196; asīti hatth' ubbedho rāsi (of gold) VvA 66, etc. See further references under asīti. — (β) The foll. are examples of 8 with other decimals: 18 **aṭṭhādasa** (only M III.239: manopavicārā) & **aṭṭhārasa** (this the later form) VvA 213 (avenika-buddhadhammā: Bhagavant's qualities); as measure J VI.432 (18 hands high, of a fence); of a great mass or multitue: aṭṭhārasa koṭiyo or °koṭi, 18 koṭis J I.92 (of gold), 227; IV.378 (°dhana, riches); DhA II.43 (of people); Miln 20 (id.); a. akkhohini-sankhāsenā J VI.395. a. vatthū Vin II.204. — 28 **aṭṭhavīsati** nakkhattāni Nd[1] 382; paṭisallāṇaguṇā Miln 140. — 38 **aṭṭhatiŋsā** Miln 359 (rājaparisā). — 48 **aṭṭhacattārīsaŋ** vassāni Sn 289. — 68 **aṭṭhasaṭṭhi** Th 1, 1217 °sitā savitakkā, where id. p. at S I.187 however reads atha saṭṭhi-tasitā vitakkā); J I.64 (turiya-satasahassāni) — 98 **aṭṭhanavuti** (cp. 98 the age of Eli, 1 Sam. IV.15) Sn 311 (rogā, a higher set than the original 3 diseases, cp. navuti). — (2) As number of *symmetry* or of an intrinsic, harmonious, symmetrical set, aṭṭha denotes, like dasa (q. v.) a comprehensive unity. See esp. the cpds. for this application. °aŋsa and °angika. Closely related to nos. 2 and 4 aṭṭha is in the geometrical progression of 2. 4. 8. 16. 32. where each subsequent number shows a higher symmetry or involves a greater importance (cp. 8×8 under 1 a) — J V.409 (a. mangalena samannāgata, of Indra's chariot: with the 8 lucky signs); VvA 193 (aṭṭhahi akkhaṇehi vajjitaŋ manussabhāvaŋ: the 8 unlucky signs). In progression: J IV.3 (aṭṭha petiyo, following after 4, then foll. by 8, 16, 32); PvA 75 (a. kapparukkhā at each point of the compass, 32 in all). Further: 8 expressions of bad language DhA IV.3.
-**aŋsa** with eight edges, octagonal, octahedral, implying perfect or divine symmetry (see above B 2), of a diamond D I.76 = M III.121 (maṇi veḷuriyo a.); Miln 282 (maṇiratanaŋ subhaŋ jātimantaŋ a.) of the pillars of a heavenly palace (Vimāna) J VI.127 = 173 = Vv 78[2] (a. sukatā thambhā); Vv 84[16] (āyataŋsa = āyatā hutvā aṭṭha-soḷasa-dvattiŋsādi-aŋsavanto VvA 339). Of a ball of string Pv

IV.3[28] (gulaparimaṇḍala, cp. PvA 254). Of geometrical figures in general Dhs 617. -anga (of) eight parts, eightfold, consisting of eight ingredients or constituents (see also next and above B 2 on significance of aṭṭha in this connection), in compn. with °*upeta* characterised by the eight parts (i. e. the observance of the first eight of the commandments or vows, see sīla & cp. anga 2), of **uposatha**, the fast-day A I.215; Sn 402 (Sn A 378 expls. ekam pi divasaŋ apariccajanto aṭṭhangupetaŋ uposathaŋ upavassa); cp. aṭṭhanguposathin (adj.) Mhvs 36, 84. In BSk. always in phrase aṣṭānga-samanvāgata upavāsa, e. g. Divy 398; Sp. Av. Ś I.338, 399; also vrata Av. Ś I.170. In the same sense aṭṭhangupeta **pāṭihāriyapakkha** (q. v.) Sn 402, where Vv 15[6] has °susamāgata (expld. at VvA 72 by pāṇātipātā veramaṇī-ādihi aṭṭhah' angehi samannāgata). °*samannāgata* endowed with the eight qualities (see anga 3), of rājā, a king D I.137 sq., of brahmassara, the supreme or most excellent voice (of the Buddha) D II.211; J I.95; VvA 217. Also in Buddh. Sk. aṣṭāngopeta svara of the voice of the Buddha, e. g. Sp. Av. Ś I.149. **-angika** having eight constituents, being made up of eight (intrinsic) parts, embracing eight items (see above B 2); of the **uposatha** (as in prec. aṭṭhang' uposatha) Sn 401; of the "Eightfold Noble Path" (ariyo a. maggo). (Also in BSk. as aṣṭāngika mārga, e. g. Lal. Vist. 540, cp. aṣṭāngamārgadeśika of the Buddha, Divy 124, 265); D I.156, 157, 165; M I.118; It 18; Sn 1130 (magga uttama); Dh 191, 273; Th 2, 158, 171; Kh IV.; Vin I.10; Nd[2] 485; DA I.313; DhA III.402. **-angula** eight finger-breadths thick, eight inches thick, i. e. very thick, of double thickness J II.91 (in contrast to caturangula); Mhvs 29, 11 (with sattangula). **-aḍḍha** (v. l. aḍḍhaṭṭha) half of eight, i. e. four (°pāda) J VI.354, see also aḍḍha[1]. **-nakha** having eight nails or claws J VI.354 (: ekekasmiŋ pāde dvinnaŋ, dvinnaŋ khurānaŋ vasena C.). **-nava** eight or nine DhA III.179. **-pada** 1. a chequered board for gambling or playing drafts etc., lit. having eight squares, i. e. on each side (DA I.85: ekekāya pantiyā aṭṭha aṭṭha padāni assā ti), cp. dasapada D I.6. — 2. eightfold, folded or plaited in eight, cross-plaited (of hair) Th 1, 772 (aṭṭhāpada-katā kesā); J II.5 (°ṭṭhapana = cross-plaiting). **-padaka** a small square ($\frac{1}{8}$), i. e. a patch Vin I.297; II.150. **-pāda** an octopod, a kind of (fabulous) spider (or deer?) J V.377; VI.538; cp. Sk. aṣṭapāda = śarabha a fabulous eight-legged animal. **-mangala** having eight anspicious signs J V.409 (expld. here to mean a horse with white hair on the face, tail, mane, and breast, and above each of the four hoofs). **-vanka** with eight facets, lit. eight-crooked, i. e. polished on eight sides, of a jewel J VI.388. **-vidha** eightfold Dhs 219.

Aṭṭha[2] see attha.

Aṭṭhaka (adj.) [Sk. aṣṭaka] — 1. eightfold Vin I.196 = Ud 59 (°vaggikāni); VvA 75 = DhA III.104 (°bhatta). — 2. °ā (f.) the eight day of the lunar month (cp. aṭṭhamī), in phrase **rattīsu antar' aṭṭhakāsu** in the nights between the eighths, i. e. the 8th day before and after the full moon Vin I.31, 288 (see *Vin Texts* I.130n); M I.79; A I.136; Miln 396; J I.390. — 3. °ŋ (nt.) an octad Vv 67[2] (aṭṭh° eight octads = 64); VvA 289, 290. On sabbaṭṭhaka see aṭṭha B 1 a. See also antara.

Aṭṭhama (num. ord.) [Sk. aṣṭama, see aṭṭha[1]] the eighth Sn 107, 230 (cp. KhA 187), 437. — f. °ī the eighth day of the lunar half month (cp. aṭṭhakā) A I.144; Sn 402; Vv 16[8] (in all three pass. as pakkhassa cātuddasī pañcadasī ca aṭṭhamī); A I.142; Sn 570 (ito aṭṭhami, scil. divase, loc.).

Aṭṭhamaka = aṭṭhama the eighth. — 1. lit. Miln 291 (att° self-eighth). — 2. as tt. the eighth of eight persons who strive after the highest perfection, reckoned from the first or Arahant. Hence the eighth is he who stands on the lowest step of the Path and is called a sotāpanna (q. v.) Kvu 243—251 (cp. *Kvu trsl.* 146 sq.); Nett 19, 49, 50; Ps II.193 (+ sotāpanna).

Aṭṭhāna (nt.) [ā + ṭṭhāna] stand, post; name of the rubbing-post which, well cut & with incised rows of squares, was let into the ground of a bathing-place, serving as a rubber to people bathing Vin II.105, 106 (read aṭṭhāne with BB; cp. Vin II.315).

Aṭṭhi°[1] [= attha (aṭṭha) in compn. with **kar** & **bhū**, as freq. in Sk. and P. with i for a, like citti-kata (for citta°), angi-bhūta (for anga°); cp. the freq. combn. (with similar meaning) manasi-kata (besides manasā-k.), also upadhikaroti and others. This combn. is restricted to the pp and der. (°kata & °katvā). Other explns. by Morris J. P. T. S. 1886, 107; Windisch, M. & B. 100], in combn. with **katvā**: to make something one's attha, i. e. object, to find out the essence or profitableness or value of anything, to recognise the nature of, to realise, understand, know. Nearly always in stock phrase **aṭṭhikatvā manasikatvā** D II.204; M I.325, 445; S I.112 sq. = 189, 220; V.76; A II.116; III.163; J I.189; V.151 (: attano atthikabhāvaŋ katvā atthiko hutvā sakkaccaŋ suṇeyya C.); Ud 80 (: adhikicca, ayaŋ no attho adhigantabbo evaŋ sallakkhetvā tāya desanāya atthikā hutvā C.); Sdhp 220 (°katvāna).

Aṭṭhi[2] (nt.) [Sk. asthi = Av. asti, Gr. ὀστεον, ὀστρακον, ἀστράγαλος; Lat. os (*oss); also Gr. ὄζος branch Goth. asts] — 1. a bone A I.50; IV.129; Sn 194 (°nahāru bones & tendons); Dh 149, 150; J I.70; III.26, 184; VI.448 (°vedhin); DhA III.109 (300 bones of the human body, as also at Suśruta III.5); KhA 49; PvA 68 (°camma-nahāru), 215 (gosīs°); Sdhp 46, 103. — 2. the stone of a fruit J II.104. **-kankala** [Sk. °kankāla] a skeleton M I.364; cp. °sankhalika. **-kadali** a special kind of the plantain tree (Musa Sapientum) J V.406. **-kalyāṇa** beauty of bones DhA I.387. **-camma** bones and skin J II.339; DhA III.43; PvA 68 **-taca** id. J II.295. **-maya** made of bone Vin II.115. **-miñjā** marrow A IV.129; DhA I.181; III.361; KhA 52. **-yaka** (T. aṭṭhīyaka) bones & liver S I.206. **-sankhalikā** [B. Sk. °śakalā Sp. Av. Ś I.274 sq., see also aṭṭhika°] a chain of bones, i. e. a skeleton DhA III.479; PvA 152. **-sanghāṭa** conjunction of bones, i. e. skeleton Vism 21; DhA II.28; PvA 206. **-sañcaya** a heap of bones It 17 = Bdhd 87. **-saññā** the idea of bones (cp. aṭṭhika°) Th 1, 18. **-saṇṭhāna** a skeleton Sdhp 101.

Aṭṭhika[1] (nt.) [fr. aṭṭhi] 1. = aṭṭhi 1 a bone M III.92; J I.265, 428; VI.404; PvA 41. — 2 = aṭṭhi 2 kernel, stone DhA II.53 (tāl°); Mhvs 15, 42.

-sankhalikā a chain of bones, a skeleton A III.324 see also under kaṭaṭṭhika. **-saññā** the idea of a skeleton S V.129 sq.; A II.17; Dhs 264.

Aṭṭhika[2] at PvA 180 (sūcik°) to be read aṭṭita (q. v.) for aṭṭika.

Aṭṭhita[1] see ṭhita.

Aṭṭhita[2] [ā + ṭhita] undertaken, arrived at, looked after, considered J II.247 (= adhiṭṭhita C.).

Aṭṭhita[3] see aṭṭhika.

Aṭṭhilla at Vin II.266 is expld. by Bdhgh on p. 327 by gojanghaṭṭika, perhaps more likely = Sk. aṣṭhīlā a round pebble or stone.

Aḍḍha[1] (& addha) [etym. uncertain, Sk. ardha] one half, half; usually in compn. (see below), like diyaḍḍha $1\frac{1}{2}$ (°sata 150) PvA 155 (see as to meaning *Stede, Peta Vatthu* p. 107). *Note.* aḍḍha is never used by itself, for "half" in absolute position upaḍḍha (q. v.) is always used.

-akkhika with furtive glance ("half an eye") DhA IV.98. **-aṭṭha** half of eight, i. e. four (cp. aṭṭhaḍḍha) S II.222 (°ratana); J VI.354 (°pāda quadruped; v. l. for aṭṭhaḍḍha). **-āḷhaka** $\frac{1}{2}$ an āḷhaka (measure) DhA III.367. **-uḍḍha** [cp.

Mahāraṣṭrī form cauttha = Sk. caturtha] three and a half J I.82; IV.180; V.417, 420; DhA I.87; Mhvs 12, 53. -ocitaka half plucked off J I.120. -karīsa (-matta) half a k. in extent VvA 64 (cp. aṭṭha-karīsa). -kahāpaṇa ½ kahāpaṇa A V.83. -kāsika (or °ya) worth half a thousand kāsiyas (i. e. of Benares monetary standard) Vin I.281 (kambala, a woollen garment of that value; cp. *Vin Texts* II.195); II.150 (bimbohanāni, pillows; so read for aḍḍhakāyikāni in T.); J V.447 (a°-kāsigaṇikā for a-°kāsiya° a courtezan who charges that price, in phrase a°-k°-gaṇika viya na bahunnaŋ piyā manāpā). -kumbha a half (-filled) pitcher Sn 721. -kusi (tt. of tailoring) a short intermediate cross-seam Vin I.287. -kosa half a room, a small room J VI.81 (= a° kosantara C.). -gāvuta half a league J VI 55. -cūḷa (°vāhā vīhi) ½ a measure (of rice) Miln 102, perhaps misread for aḍḍhāḷha (āḷha = āḷhaka, cp. A III.52), a half āḷha of rice. -tiya the third (unit) less half, i. e. two and a half VvA 66 (māsā); J I.49, 206, 255 (°sata 250). Cp. next. -teyya = °tiya 2½ Vin IV.117; J II.129 (°sata); DA I.173 (v. l. BB for °tiya); DhA I.95 (°sata), 279; PvA 20 (°sahassa). -telasa [cp. BSk. ardhatrayodaśa] twelve and a half Vin I 243, 247; D II.6 (°bhikkhusatāni, cp. tayo B I b); DhA III.369. -daṇḍaka a short stick M I.87 = A I.47; II.122 = Nd² 604 = Miln 197. -duka see °ruka. -nāḷika (-matta) half a nāḷi-measure full J VI.366. -pallanka half a divan Vin II.280. -bhāga half a share, one half Vv 13⁶ (= upaḍḍhabhāga VvA 61); Pv I.11⁵. -maṇḍala semi-circle, semi circular sewing Vin I.287. -māna half a māna measure J I.468 (m. = aṭṭhannaŋ nāḷinaŋ nāmaŋ C.). -māsa half a month, a half month, a fortnight Vin III.254 (ūnak°); A V.85; J III.218; VvA 66. Freq. in acc. as adv. for a fortnight, e. g. Vin IV.117; VvA 67; PvA 55. -māsaka half a bean (as weight or measure of value, see māsaka) J I.111. -māsika half-monthly Pug 55. -muṇḍaka shaven over half the head (sign of loss of freedom) Mhvs 6, 42. -yoga a certain kind of house (usually with pāsāda) Vin I.58 = 96, 107, 139, 239, 284; II.146. Acc. to Vin T. I.174 "a gold coloured Bengal house" (Bdhgh), an interpretation which is not correct: we have to read supaṇṇa vankageha "like a Garuḷa bird's crooked wing", i. e. where the roof is bent on one side. -yojana half a yojana (in distance) J V.410; DA I.35 (in expl$^{n.}$ of addhāna-magga); DhA I.147; II.74. -rattā midnight A III.407 (°aŋ adv. at m.); Vv 81¹⁶ (°rattāyaŋ adv. = aḍḍharattiyaŋ VvA 315); J I.164 (samaye); IV.159 (id.). -ratti = °rattā VvA 255, 315 (= majjhimayāma-samaya); PvA 155. -ruka (v. l. °duka) a certain fashion of wearing the hair Vin II.134; Bdhgh expl$^{n.}$ on p. 319: aḍhadukan ti udare lomarāji-ṭhapanaŋ "leaving a stripe of hair on the stomach". -vivaṭa (dvāra) half open J V.293.

Aḍḍha² (adj.) [Sk. āḍhya fr. ṛddha pp. of **ṛdh**, ṛdhnote & ṛdhyate (see ijjhati) to thrive cp. Gr. ἄλθομαι thrive, Lat. alo to nourish. Cp. also Vedic iḍā refreshment & P. iddhi power. See also āḷhiya] rich, opulent, wealthy, well-to-do; usually in comb$^{n.}$ with **mahaddhana** & **mahābhoga** of great wealth & resources (foll. by pahūta-jātarūparajata pahūta vittūpakaraṇa etc.). Thus at D I.115, 134, 137; III.163; Pug 52; DhA I.3; VvA 322; PvA 3, 78 etc. In other comb$^{n.}$ Vv 31⁴ (°kula); Nd² 615 (Sakka = aḍḍho mahaddhano dhanavā); DA I.281 (= issara); DhA II.37 (°kula); Sdhp 270 (satasākh°), 312 (guṇ°), 540 sq. (id.), 561.

Aḍḍhaka (adj.) wealthy, rich, influential J IV.495; Pv II.8² (= mahāvibhava PvA 107).

Aḍḍhatā (f.) [abstr. to aḍḍha] riches, wealth, opulence Sdhp 316.

Aṇa [Sk. ṛṇa; see etym. under iṇa, of which aṇa is a doublet. See also āṇaṇya] debt, only in neg. **anaṇa** (adj.) free from debt Vin I.6 = S I.137, 234 = D II.39; Th 2, 364 (i. e. without a new birth); A II.69; J V.481; ThA 245.

Aṇu (adj.) [Sk. aṇu; as to etym. see Walde Lat. Wtb. under ulna. See also āṇi] small, minute, atomic, subtle (opp. thūla, q. v.) D I.223; S I.136; V.96 (°bīja); Sn 299 (aṇuto aṇuŋ gradually); J III.12 (= appamattaka); IV.203; Dhs 230, 617 (= kisa); ThA 173; Miln 361. *Note* aṇu is freq. spelt anu, thus usually in cpd. °matta.

-**thūla** (aṇuŋthūla) fine and coarse, small & large Dh 31 (= mahantañ ca khuddakañ ca DhA I.282), 409 = Sn 633; J IV.192; DhA IV.184. -**matta** of small size, atomic, least Sn 431; Vbh 244, 247 (cp. M III.134; A II.22); Dpvs IV.20. The spelling is **anumatta** at D I.63 = It 118; Dh 284; DA I.181; Sdhp 347. -**sahagata** accompanied by a minimum of, i. e. residuum Kvu 81, cp. Kvu trsl. 66 n. 3.

Aṇuka (adj.) = aṇu Sn 146, KhA 246.

Aṇḍa (nt.) [Etym. unknown. Cp. Sk. aṇḍa] 1. an egg Vin III.3; S II.258; M I.104; A IV.125 sq. — 2. (pl.) the testicles Vin III.106. — 3. (in camm°) a water-bag J I.249 (see Morris J. P. T. S. 1884, 69).

-**kosa** shell of eggs Vin III.3 = M .104; A IV.126, 176. -**cheda(ka)** one who castrates, a gelder J IV.364, 366. -**ja** 1. born from eggs S III.241 (of snakes); M I.73; J II.53 = V.85; Miln 267. — 2. a bird J. V.189. -**bhārin** bearing his testicles S II.258 = Vin III.100. -**sambhava** the product of an egg, i. e. a bird Th 1, 599. -**hāraka** one who takes or exstirpates the testicles M I.383.

Aṇḍaka¹ (nt.) = aṇḍa, egg DhA I.60; III.137 (sakuṇ°).

Aṇḍaka² (adj.) [Sk.? prob. an inorganic form; the diaeresis of caṇḍaka into c° aṇḍaka seems very plausible. As to meaning cp. DhsA 396 and see *Dhs trsl.* 349, also Morris J. P. T. S. 1893, 6, who, not satisfactorily, tries to establish a relation to **ard**, as in aṭṭa³] only used of vācā, speech: harsh, rough, insolent M I.286; A V.265, 283, 293 (gloss kaṇṭakā); J III.260; Dhs 1343, cp. DhsA 396.

Aṇṇa (food, cereal). See passages under aparaṇṇa & pubbaṇṇa.

Aṇṇava (nt.) [Sk. arṇa & arṇava to ṛ, ṛṇoti to move, Idg. ***er** to be in quick motion, cp. Gr. ὄρνυμι; Lat. orior; Goth. rinnan = E. run; Ohg. runs, river, flow.] 1. a great flood (= ogha), the sea or ocean (often as mah°, cp. BSk. mahārṇava, e. g. Jtm 31¹⁵) M I.134; S I.214; IV.157 (mahā udak°); Sn 173 (fig. for saŋsāra see SnA 214), 183, 184; J I.119 (°kucchi), 227 (id.); V.159 (mah°); Mhvs 5, 60; 19, 16 (mah°). — 2. a stream, river J III. 521; V.255.

Aṇha [Sk. ahna, day, see ahan] day, only as —° in apar°, pubb°, majjh°, sāy°, q. v.

Atakkaka (adj.) [a + takka²] not mixed with buttermilk J VI.21.

Ataccha (nt.) [a + taccha²] falsehood, untruth D I.3; J VI.207.

Ati (indecl.) [Sk. ati = Gr. ἔτι moreover, yet, and; Lat. et and, Goth. iþ; also connected with Gr. ἀτάρ but, Lat. at but (= over, outside) Goth. aþþan] adv. and prep. of direction (forward motion), in primary meaning "on, and further", then "up to and beyond". I. in abstr. position **adverbially** (only as ttg.): in excess, extremely, very (cp. II.3) J VI.133 (ati uggata C. = accuggata T.), 307 (ati ahitaŋ C. = accāhitaŋ T.).

II. as **prefix**, meaning. — 1. on to, up to, towards, until); as far as: accanta up to the end; aticchati to go further, pass on; atipāta "falling on to"; attack slaying; atimāpeti to put damage on to, i. e. to destroy. — 2. over, beyond, past, by, trans-; with verbs: (a.) trs. atikkamati to pass beyond, surpass; atimaññati to put one's "manas" over, to despise; atirocati to surpass in splendour. (b.) intr. atikkanta passed by; atikkama traversing; aticca transgressing; atīta past, gone beyond. — Also with verbal derivations: accaya lapse, also sin, transgression ("going over"); atireka remainder, left over; atisaya overflow, abundance; atisāra stepping over, sin. — 3. exceedingly, in a high or excessive degree either very (much) or too (much); in nominal compn. (a), rarely also in verbal compn. see (b). — (a) with nouns & adj.: °āsanna too near; °uttama the very highest; °udaka too much water; °khippa too soon; °dāna excessive alms giving; °dāruṇa very cruel; °dīgha extremely long; °dūra too near; deva a super-god °pago too early; °bālha too much; °bhāra a too heavy load; °manāpa very lovely; °manohara very charming; °mahant too great; °vikāla very inconvenient; °vela a very long time; °sambādha too tight, etc. etc. — (b.) with verb: atibhuñjati to eat excessively.

III. A peculiar use of ati is its' function in *reduplication-compounds*, expressing "and, adding further, and so on, even more, etc." like that of the other comparing or contrasting prefixes a (ā), anu, ava, paṭi, vi (e. g. khaṇḍâkhaṇḍa, seṭṭhânuseṭṭhi, chiddâvacchidda, angapaccanga, cuṇṇavicuṇṇa). In this function it is however restricted to comparatively few expressions and has not by far the wide range of ā (q. v.), the only phrases being the foll. viz. **cakkâticakkaŋ mañcâtimañcaŋ bandhati** to heap carts upon carts, couches upon couches (in order to see a procession) Vin IV.360 (Bdhgh); J II.331; IV.81; DhA IV.61. **-devâtideva** god upon god, god and more than a god (see atideva); **mānâtimāna** all kinds of conceit; **vankâtivanka** crooked all over J I.160. — IV. Semantically **ati** is closely related to **abhi**, so that in consequence of dialectical variation we frequently find ati in Pāli, where the corresp. expression in later Sk. shows abhi. See e. g. the foll. cases for comparison: accuṇha ati-jāta, °pīḷita °brūheti, °vassati, °vāyati, °veṭheti.

Note The contracted (assimilation-) form of ati before vowels is **acc-** (q. v.). See also for adv. use atiriva, ativiya, atīva.

Ati-ambila (adj.) [ati + ambila] too sour DhA II.85.

Ati-arahant [ati + arahant] a super-Arahant, one who surpasses even other Arahants Miln 277.

Ati-issara (adj.) very powerful (?) J V.441 (°bhesajja, medicin).

Ati-uṇha (adj.) too hot PvA 37 (°ātapa glow). See also accuṇha (which is the usual form).

Ati-uttama (adj.) by far the best or highest VvA 80.

Ati-udaka too much water, excess of water DhA I.52.

Ati-ussura (adj.) only in loc. °e (adv.) too soon after sunrise, too early VvA 65 (laddhabhattatā eating too early).

Ati-eti [ati + i] to go past or beyond, see ger. **aticca** and pp. **atīta.**

Atikata (pp.) more than done to, i. e. retaliated; paid back in an excessive degree A I.62.

Atikaddhati [ati + kaḍḍhati] to pull too hard, to labour, trouble, drudge Vin III.17.

Atikaṇha (adj.) [ati + kaṇha] too black Vin IV.7.

Atikaruṇa (adj.) [ati + karuṇa] very pitiful, extremely miserable J I.202; IV.142; VI.53.

Atikassa (ger.) [fr. atikassati ati + kṛṣ; Sk. atikṛṣya] pulling (right) through J V.173 (rajjuŋ, a rope, through the nostrils; v. l. BB. anti°).

Atikāla [ati + kāla] in instr. **atikālena** adv. in very good time very early Vin I.70 (+ atidivā).

Atikkanta [pp. of atikamati] passed beyond, passed by, gone by, elapsed; passed over, passing beyond, surpassing J II.128 (tīṇi saŋvaccharāni); DhA III.133 (tayo vaye passed beyond the 3 ages of life); PvA 55 (māse °e after the lapse of a month), 74 (kati divasā °ā how many days have passed).

-mānusaka superhuman It 100; Pug 60; cp. BSk. atikrānta-mānuṣyaka M Vastu III.321.

Atikkantikā (f.) [Der. abstr. fr. prec.] transgressing, overstepping the bounds (of good behaviour), lawlessness Miln 122.

Atikkama [Sk. atikrama] going over or further, passing beyond, traversing; fig. overcoming of, overstepping, failing against, transgression Dh 191; Dhs 299; PvA 154 (katipayayojan°), 159 (°caraṇa sinful mode of life); Miln 158 (dur° hard to overcome); Sdhp 64.

Atikkamaṇaka (adj.) [atikkamaṇa + ka] exceeding J I.153.

Atikkamati [ati + kamati] (1) to go beyond, to pass over, to cross, to pass by. (2) to overcome, to conquer, to surpass, to be superior to. — J IV.141; Dh 221 (Pot. °eyya, overcome); PvA 67 (maggena: passes by). grd. **atikkamanīya** to be overcome D II.13 (an°); SnA 568 (dur°). ger. atikkamma D II.12 (surpassing); It 51 (māradheyyaŋ, passing over), cp. vv. ll. under adhigayha; and **atikkamitva** going beyond, overcoming, transcending (J IV.139 (samuddaŋ); Pug 17; J I.162 (raṭṭhaŋ having left). Often to be trsl. as adv. "beyond", e. g. pare beyond others PvA 15; Vasabhagāmaŋ beyond the village of V. PvA 168. — pp. **atikkanta** (q. v.).

Atikkameti [Caus. of atikkamati] to make pass, to cause to pass over J I.151.

Atikkhippaŋ (adv.) [ati + khippa] too soon Vin II.284.

Atikhaṇa (nt.) [ati + khaṇa(na)] too much digging J II.296.

Atikhāta (nt.) = prec. J II.296.

Atikhiṇa (adj.) [ati + khīṇa] in cāpâtikhīṇa broken bow (?) Dh 156 (expld. at DhA III.132 as cāpāto atikhīṇa cāpā vinimmutta).

Atiga (—°) (adj.) [ati + ga] going over, overcoming, surmounting, getting over Sn 250 (sanga°); Dh 370 (id.); Sn 795 (sīma°, cp. Nd¹ 99), 1096 (ogha°); Nd¹ 100 (= atikkanta); Nd² 180 (id.).

Atigacchati [ati + gacchati] to go over, i. e. to overcome, surmount, conquer, get the better of, only in pret. (aor.) 3rd sg. **accagā** (q. v. and see gacchati 3) Sn 1040; Dh 414 and **accagamā** (see gacchati 2) Vin II.192; D I.85; S II.205; DA I.236 (= abhibhavitvā pavatta). Also 3rd pl. accaguŋ It 93, 95.

Atigāḷeti [ati + gāḷeti, Caus. of galati, cp. Sk. vi-gālayati] to destroy, make perish, waste away J VI.211 (= atigālayati vināseti C. p. 215). Perhaps reading should be atigāḷheti (see atigāḷhita.

Atigāḷha (adj.) [ati + gāḷha 1] very tight or close, intensive J I.62. Cp. atigāḷhita.

Atigāḷhita [pp. of atigāḷheti, Denom. fr. atigāḷha; cp. Sk. atigāhate to overcome] oppressed, harmed, overcome, defeated, destroyed J V.401 (= atipīḷita C.).

Atighora (adj.) [ati + ghora] very terrible or fierce Sdhp 285.

Aticaraṇa (nt.) [fr. aticarati] transgression PvA 159.

Aticarati [ati + carati] 1. to go about, to roam about Pv II.12[15]; PvA 57. — 2. to transgress, to commit adultery J I.496. Cp. next.

Aticaritar [n. ag. of. aticarati] one who transgresses, esp. a woman who commits adultery A II.61 (all MSS. read aticaritvā); IV.66 (T. aticarittā).

Aticariyā (f.) [ati + cariyā] transgression, sin, adultery D III.190.

Aticāra [from aticarati] transgression Vv 15[8] (= aticca cāra VvA 72).

Aticārin (adj. n.) [from aticarati] transgressing, sinning, esp. as f. aticārinī an adultress S II.259; IV.242; D III.190; A III.261; Pv II.12[14]; PvA 151 (v. l. BB), 152; VvA 110.

Aticitra (adj.) [ati + citra] very splendid, brilliant, quite exceptional Miln 28.

Aticca (grd.) [ger. of ati + eti, ati + i] 1. passing beyond, traversing, overcoming, surmounting Sn 519, 529, 531. Used adverbially = beyond, in access, more than usual, exceedingly Sn 373, 804 (= vassasataŋ atikkamitvā Nd[1] 120). — 2. failing, transgressing, sinning, esp. committing adultery J V,424; VvA 72,

Aticchati [*Sk. ati-ṛcchati, ati + ṛ, cp. aṇṇava] to go on, only occurring in imper. aticchatha (bhante) "please go on, Sir", asking a bhikkhu to seek alms elsewhere, thus refusing a gift in a civil way. [The interpretation given by Trenckner, as quoted by Childers, is from ati + iṣ "go and beg further on". (Tr. Notes 65) but this would entail a meaning like "desire in excess", since iṣ does not convey the notion of movement] J III.462; DhA IV.98 (T. aticcha, vv. ll. °atha); VvA 101; Miln 8. — Caus. **aticchāpeti** to make go on, to ask to go further J III.462. — Cp. icchatā.

Aticchatta [ati + chatta] a "super"-sunshade, a sunshade of extraordinary size & colours DhsA 2.

Atitāta (adj.) [ati + jāta, perhaps ati in sense of abhi, cp. abhijāta] well-born, well behaved, gentlemanly It 14 (opp. **avajāta**).

Atitarati [ati + tarati] to pass over, cross, go beyond aor. accatari S IV.157 = It 57 (°āri).

Atituccha (adj.) [ati + tuccha] very, or quite empty Sdhp 430.

Atituṭṭhi (f.) [ati + tuṭṭhi] extreme joy J I.207.

Atitula (adj.) [ati + tula] beyond compare, incomparable Th 1, 831 = Sn 561 (= tulaŋ atito nirupamo ti attho SnA 455).

Atitta (adj.) [a + titta] dissatisfied, unsatisfied J I.440; Dh 48.

Atittha (nt.) [a + tittha] "that which is not a fording-place". i. e. not the right way, manner or time; as °— wrongly in the wrong way J I.343; IV.379; VI.241; DhA III.347; DA I.38.

Atithi [Sk. atithi of **at = at**, see aṭati; orig. the wanderer, cp. Vedic atithin wandering] a guest, stranger, newcomer D I.117 (= āgantuka-navaka pāhuṇaka DA I.288); A II.68; III.45, 260; J IV.31, 274; V.388; Kh VIII.7 (= n' atthi assa ṭhiti yamhi vā tamhi vā divase āgacchatī ti atithi KhA 222); VvA 24 (= āgantuka).

Atidāna (nt.) [ati + dāna] too generous giving, an excessive gift of alms Miln 277; PvA 129, 130.

Atidāruṇa (adj.) [Sk. atidāruṇa, ati + dāruṇa] very cruel, extremely fierce Pv III.7[3].

Atidiṭṭhi (f.) [ati + diṭṭhi] higher doctrine, super knowledge (?) Vin I.63 = II.4 (+ adhisīla; should we read **adhi-diṭṭhi**?)

Atidivā (adv.) [ati + divā] late in the day, in the afternoon Vin I.70 (+ **atikālena**); S I.200; A III.117.

Atidisati [ati + disati] to give further explanation, to explain in detail Miln. 304.

Atidīgha (adj.) [ati + dīgha] too long, extremely long J IV. 165; Pv II.10[2]; VvA 103 (opp. atirassa).

Atidukkha [ati + dukkha] great evil, exceedingly painful excessive suffering PvA 65; Sdhp 95. In atidukkhavāca PvA 15 ati belongs to the whole cpd., i. e. of very hurtful speech.

Atidūra (adj.) [ati + dūra] very or too far Vin I.46; J II.154; Pv II.9[65] = DhA III.220 (vv. ll. suvidūre); PvA 42 (opp. accāsanna).

Atideva [ati + deva] a super god, god above gods, usually Ep. of the Buddha S I.141; Th 1, 489; Nd[2] 307 (cp. adhi°); Miln 277. atidevadeva id. Miln 203, 209. **devâtideva** god over the gods (of the Buddha) Nd[2] 307 a.

Atidhamati [ati + dhamati] to beat a drum too hard J I.283; pp. **atidhanta** ibid.

Atidhātatā [ati + dhāta + ta] oversatiation J II.193.

Atidhāvati [ati + dhāvati 1] to run past, to outstrip or get ahead of S III.103; IV.230; M III.19; It 43; Miln 136; SnA 21.

Atidhonacārin [ati + dhonacārin] indulging too much in the use of the "dhonas", i. e. the four requisites of the bhikkhu, or transgressing the proper use or normal application of the requisites (expl[n.] at DhA III.344, cp. dhona) Dh 240 = Nett 129.

Atināmeti [BSk. atināmayati, e. g. Divy 82, 443; ati + nāmeti] to pass time A I.206; Miln 345.

Atiniggaṇhāti [ati + niggaṇhāti] to rebuke too much J VI.417.

Atinīcaka (adj.) [ati + nīcaka] too low, only in phrase **cakkavāḷaŋ atisambādhaŋ Brahmaloko atinīcako** the World is too narrow and Heaven too low (to comprehend the merit of a person, as sign of exceeding merit) DhA I.310; III.310 = VvA 68.

Atineti [ati + neti] to bring up to, to fetch, to provide with Vin II.180 (udakaŋ).

Atipaṇḍita (adj. [ati + paṇḍita] too clever DhA IV.38.

Atipaṇḍitatā (f.) [abstr. of atipaṇḍita] too much cleverness DhA II.29.

Atipadāna (nt.) [ati + pa + dāna] too much alms-giving Pv II.943 (= atidāna PvA 130).

Atipapañca [ati + p.] too great a delay, excessive tarrying J I.64; II.93.

Atipariccāga [ati + pariccāga] excess in liberality DhA III.11.

Atipassati [ati + passati; cp. Sk. anupaśyati] to look for, catch sight of, discover M III.132 (nāgaŋ).

Atipāta [ati + **pat**] attack, only in phrase **pāṇâtipāta** destruction of life, slaying, killing, murder D I.4 (pāṇātipātā veramaṇī, refraining from killing, the first of the dasasīla or decalogue); DA I.69 (= pāṇavadha, pāṇaghāta); Sn 242; Kh II. cp. KhA 26; PvA 28, 33 etc.

Atipātin (adj. -n.) one who attacks or destroys Sn 248; J VI.449 (in war nāgakkhandh° = hatthikkhande khaggena chinditvā C.); PvA 27 (pāṇ°).

Atipāteti [Denom. fr. atipāta] to destroy S V.453; Dh 246 (v. l. for atimāpeti, q. v.). Cp. paripāteti.

Atipīṇita (adj.) [ati + pīṇita] too much beloved, too dear, too lovely DhA V.70.

Atipīḷita [ati + pīḷita, cp. Sk. abhipīḍita] pressed against, oppressed, harassed, vexed J v.401 (= atigāḷhita).

Atippago (adv.) [cp. Sk. atiprage] too early, usually elliptical = it is too early (with inf. carituŋ etc.) D I.178; M I.84; A IV.35.

Atibaddha [pp. of atibandhati; cp. Sk. anubaddha] tied to, coupled J I.192 = Vin IV.5.

Atibandhati [ati + bandhati; cp. Sk. anubandhati] to tie close to, to harness on, to couple J I.191 sq. — pp. atibaddha q. v.

Atibahala (adj.) [ati + bahala] very thick J VI.365.

Atibāḷha (adj.) [ati + bāḷha] very great or strong PvA 178; nt. adv. °ŋ too much D I.93, 95; M I.253.

Atibāheti [ati + bāheti, Caus. to **bṛh**[1]; cp. Sk. ābṛhati] to drive away, to pull out J IV.366 (= abbāheti).

Atibrahmā [ati + brahmā] a greater Brahma, a super-god Miln 277; DhA II.60 (Brahmuṇā a. greater than B.).

Atibrūheti [ati + brūheti, **bṛh**[2], but by C. taken incorrectly to **brū**; cp. Sk. abhi-bṛṇhayati] to shout out, roar, cry J V.361 (= mahāsaddaŋ nicchāreti).

Atibhagini-putta [ati + bh.-p.] a very dear nephew J I.223.

Atibhāra [ati + bhāra] too heavy a load Miln 277 (°ena sakaṭassa akkho bhijjati).

Atibhārita (adj.) [ati + bhārita] too heavily weighed, overloaded Vin IV.47.

Atibhāriya (adj.) too serious DhA I.70.

Atibhuñjati [ati + bhuñjati] to eat too much, to overeat Miln 153.

Atibhutta (nt.) [ati + bhutta] overeating Miln 135.

Atibhoti [ati + bhavati, cp. Sk. atibhavati & abhibhavati] to excel, overcome, to get the better of, to deceive J I.163 (= ajjhottharati vañceti C.).

Atimaññati [Sk. atimanyate; ati + **man**] to despise, slighten, neglect Sn 148 (= KhA 247 atikkamitvā maññati); Dh 365, 366; J II.347; Pv I.7[6] (°issaŋ, v. l. °asiŋ = atikkamitvā avamaññiŋ PvA 37); PvA 36; Sdhp 609.

Atimaññanā (f.) [abstr. to prec., cp. atimāna] arrogance, contempt, neglect Miln 122.

Atimanāpa (adj.) [ati + manāpa] very lovely PvA 77 (+ abhirūpa).

Atimanorama (adj.) [ati + manorama] very charming J I.60.

Atimanohara (adj.) [ati + manohara] very charming PvA 46.

Atimanda(ka) (adj.) [ati + manda] too slow, too weak Sdhp 204, 273, 488.

Atimamāyati [ati + mamāyati, cp. Sk. atimamāyate in diff. meaning = envy] to favour too much, to spoil or fondle J II.316.

Atimahant (adj.) [ati + mahant] very or too great J I.221; PvA 75.

Atimāpeti [ati + māpeti, Caus. of **mī**, mināte, orig. meaning "to do damage to"] to injure, destroy, kill; only in the stock phrase pāṇaŋ atimāpeti (with v. l. atipāteti) to destroy life, to kill D I.52 (v. l. °pāteti) = DA I.159 (: pāṇaŋ hanati pi parehi hanāpeti either to kill or incite others to murder); M I.404, 516; S IV.343; A III.205 (correct T. reading atimāteti; v. l. pāteti); Dh 246 (v. l. °pāteti) = DhA III.356 (: parassa jīvitindriyaŋ upacchindati).

Atimāna [Sk. atimāna, ati + māna] high opinion (of oneself), pride, arrogance, conceit, M I.363; Sn 853 (see expl[n.] at Nd[1] 233), 942, 968; J VI.235; Nd[1] 490; Miln 289. Cp. atimaññanā.

Atimānin (adj.) [fr. atimāna] D II.45 (thaddha +); Sn 143 (an°) 244; KhA 236.

Atimukhara (adj.) [ati + mukhara] very talkative, a chatterbox J I.418; DhA II.70. **atimukharatā** (f. abstr.) ibid.

Atimuttaka [Sk. atimuktaka] N. of a plant, Gaertnera Racemosa Vin II.256 = M I.32; Miln 338.

Atimuduka (adj.) [ati + muduka] very soft, mild or feeble J I.262.

Atiyakkha (ati + yakkha] a sorcerer, wizard, fortuneteller J VI.502 (C.: bhūtavijjā ikkhaṇika).

Atiyācaka (adj.) [ati + yācaka] one who asks too much Vin III 147.

Atiyācanā (f.) [ati + yācanā] asking or begging too much Vin III.147.

Atirattiŋ (adv.) [ati + ratti; cp. atidivā] late in the night, at midnight J I.436 (opp. atipabhāte).

Atirassa (adj.) [ati + rassa] too short (opp. **atidīgha**) Vin IV.7; J VI.457; VvA 103.

Atirājā [ati + rājā] a higher king, the greatest king. more than a king DhA II.60; Miln 277.

Atiriccati [ati + riccati, see ritta] to be left over, to remain Sdhp 23, 126.

Atiritta (adj.) [pp. of ati + **ric**, see ritta] left over, only as neg. **an°** applied to food, i.e. food which is not the leavings of a meal, fresh food Vin I.213 sq, 238; II.301; IV.82 sq., 85.

Atiriva (ati-r-iva) see **ativiya**.

Atireka (adj.) [Sk. atireka, ati + **ric**, rinakti; see ritta] surplus, too much; exceeding, excessive, in a high degree; extra Vin I.255; J I.72 (°padasata), 109; 441 (in higher positions); Miln 216; DhsA 2; DhA II.98.
-**cīvara** an extra robe Vin I.289. -**pāda** exceeding the worth of a pāda, more than a pāda, Vin III.47.

Atirekatā (f.) [abstr. to prec.] excessiveness, surplus, excess Kvu 607.

Atirocati [ati + **ruc**] to shine magnificently (trs.) to outshine, to surpass in splendour D II 208; Dh 59; Pv II.9[58]; Miln 336 (+ **virocati**); DhA I.446 (= atikkamitvā **virocati**); III.219; PvA 139 (= ativiya **virocati**).

Ativankin (adj.) [ati + vankin] very crooked J I.160 (vankātivankin crooked all over; cp. ati III.).

Ativaṇṇati [ati + vaṇṇati] to surpass, excel D II.267.

Ativatta [pp. of ativattati: Sk. ativṛtta] passed beyond, surpassed, overcome (act. & pass.), conquered Sn 1133 (bhava°); Nd[2] 21 (= atikkanta, vītivatta); J V.84 (bhaya°); Miln 146, 154.

Ativattati [ati + **vṛt**, Sk. ativartate] to pass, pass over, go beyond; to overcome, get over; conquer Vin II.237 (samuddo velaŋ n°); S II.92 (saŋsāraŋ); IV.158 (id.) It 9 (saŋsāraŋ) = A II.10 = Nd[2] 172[a]; Th I, 412; J I.58, 280; IV.134; VI.113, 114; PvA 276. — pp. **ativatta** (q. v.).

Ativattar[1] [Sk. *ativaktṛ, n. ag. to ati-vacati; cp. ativākya] one who insults or offends J V.266 (isīnaŋ ativattāro = dharusavācāhi atikkamitvā vattāro C.).

Ativattar[2] [Sk. *ativartṛ, n. ag. to ati-vattati] one who overcomes or is to be overcome Sn 785 (svātivattā = durativattā duttarā duppatarā Nd[1] 76).

Ativasa (adj.) [ati + vasa fr. vaś] being under somebody's rule, dependent upon (c. gen.) Dh 74 (= vase vattati DhA II.79).

Ativassati [ati + vassati, cp. Sk. abhivarṣati] to rain down on, upon or into Th 1, 447 = Vin II.240.

Ativākya (nt.) [ati + **vac**, cp. Sk. ativāda, fr. ati + **vad**] abuse, blame, reproach Dh 320, 321 (= aṭṭha-anariya-vohāra-vasena pavattaŋ vītikkama-vacanaŋ DhA IV.3); J VI.508.

Ativāta [ati + vāta] too much wind, a wind which is too strong, a gale, storm Miln 277.

Ativāyati [ati + vāyati] to fill (excessively) with an odour or perfume, to satiate, permeate, pervade Miln 333 (+ vāyati; cp. abhivāyati ibid 385).

Ativāha [fr. ati + **vah**, cp. Sk. ativahati & abhivāha] carrying, carrying over; a conveyance; one who conveys, i. e. a conductor, guide Th 1, 616 (said of sīla, good character); J V.433. — Cp. ativāhika.

Ativāhika [fr. ativāha] one who belongs to a conveyance, one who conveys or guides, a conductor (of a caravan) J V.471, 472 (°purisa).

Ativikāla (adj.) [ati + vikāla] at a very inconvenient time, much too exete D I 108 (= suṭṭhu vikāla DA I.277).

Ativijjhati [Sk. atividhyati, ati + **vyadh**] to pierce, to enter into (fig.), to see through, only in phrase **paññāya ativijjha** (ger.) **passati** to recognise in all details M I.480; S V.226; A II.178.

Ativiya (adv.) [Sk. atīva] = ati + iva, orig. "much-like" like an excess = excessive-ly. There are three forms of this expression, viz. (1) ati + iva in contraction **atīva** (q. v.); — (2) ati + iva with epenthetic r: **atiriva** D II.264 (v. l. SS. atīva); Sn 679, 680, 683; SnA 486; — (3) ati + viya (the doublet of iva) = **ativiya** J I.61, 263; DhA II.71 (a. upakāra of great service); PvA 22, 56, 139.

Ativisā (f.) [Sk. ativiṣā] N. of a plant Vin I.201; IV.35.

Ativissaṭṭha (adj.) [ati + vissaṭṭha] too abundant, in °vākya one who talks too much, a chatterbox J V.204.

Ativissāsika (adj.) [ati + vissāsika] very, or too confidential J I.86.

Ativissuta (adj.) [ati + vissuta] very famous, renowned Sdhp 473.

Ativeṭheti [ati + **veṣṭ**, cp. Sk. abhiveṣṭate] to wrap over, to cover, to enclose; to press, oppress, stifle Vin II.101; J V.452 (-ativiya veṭheti piḷeti C.).

Atiyela (adj.) [ati + vela] excessive (of time); nt. adv. °ŋ a very long time; excessively D I.19 (= atikālaŋ aticiran ti attho DA I.113); M I.122; Sn 973 (see expl^n. at Nd[1] 504); J III.103 = Nd[1] 504.

Atilīna (adj.) [ati + līna] too much attached to worldly matters S V.263.

Atilūkha (adj.) [ati + lūkha] too wretched, very miserable Sdhp 409.

Atiloma (adj.) [ati + loma] too hairy, having too much hair J VI.457 (opp. aloma).

Atisañcara (°cāra?) [ati + sañcāra] wandering about too much Miln 277.

Atisaṇha (adj.) [ati + saṇha] too subtle DhA III.326.

Atisanta (adj.) [ati + santa[1]] extremely peaceful Sdhp 496.

Atisambādha (adj.) [ati + sambādha] too tight, crowded or narrow DhA I.310; III.310 = VvA 68; cp. atinīcaka. — f. abstr. **atisambādhatā** the state of being too narrow J I.7.

Atisaya [cp. Sk. atiśaya, fr. ati + **śī**] superiority, distinction, excellence, abundance VvA 135 (= visesa); PvA 86; Dāvs II.62.

Atisayati [ati + **śī**] to surpass, excel; ger. **atisayitvā** Miln 336 (+ atikkamitvā).

Atisara (adj.) [fr. atisarati; cp. accasara] transgressing, sinning J IV.6; cp. atisāra.

Atisarati [ati + **sṛ**] to go too far, to go beyond the limit, to overstep, transgress, aor. accasari (q. v.) Sn 8 sq. (opp. paccasari; C. atidhāvi); J V.70 and **atisari** J IV.6. — ger. **atisitvā** (for *atisaritvā) D I.222; S IV.94; A I.145; V.226, 256; Sn 908 (= Nd[1] 324 atikkamitvā etc.).

Atisāyaŋ (adv.) [ati + sāyaŋ] very late, late in the evening J V.94.

Atisāra [fr. ati + **sṛ**, see atisarati. Cp. Sk. atisāra in diff. meaning but BSk. atisāra (sâtisāra) in the same meaning) going too far, overstepping the limit, trespassing, false step, slip, danger Vin I.55 (**sâtisāra**), 326 (id.); S I.74; M III.237; Sn 889 (atisāraŋ diṭṭhiyo = diṭṭhigatāni Nd[1] 297; going beyond the proper limits of the right faith), J V.221 (dhamm°), 379; DhA I.182; DhsA 28. See also **atisara**.

Atisithila (adj.) [ati + sithila] very loose, shaky or weak A III.375.

Atisīta (adj.) [ati + sīta] too cold DhA II.85.

Atisītala (adj.) [ati + sītala] very cold J III.55.

Atihaṭṭha (adj.) [ati + haṭṭha] very pleased Sdhp 323.

Atiharati [ati + **hṛ**] to carry over, to bring over, bring, draw over Vin II.209; IV.264; S I.89; J I.292; V.347. — Caus. **atiharāpeti** to cause to bring over, bring in, reap, collect, harvest Vin II.181; III.18; Miln 66; DhA IV.77. — See also **atihita**.

Atihita [ati + **hṛ**, pp. of atiharati, hita unusual for hata, perhaps through analogy with Sk. abhi + **dhā**] brought over (from the field into the house), harvested, borne home Th 1, 381 (vīhi).

Atihīna (adj.) [ati + hīna] very poor or destitute A IV.282, 287; 323 (opp. **accogāḷha**).

Atihīḷeti [ati + **hīḍ**] to despise J IV.331 (= atimaññati C.).

Atīta (adj.-n.) [Sk. atīta, ati + ita, pp. of **i**. Cp. accaya & ati eti] 1. (temporal) past, gone by (cp. accaya 1) (a) adj. **atītaŋ addhānaŋ** in the time which is past S III.86; A IV.219; V.32. — Pv II.12[12] (atītānaŋ, scil. attabhāvānaŋ, pariyanto na dissati); khaṇâtīta with the right moment past Dh 315 = Sn 333; atītayobbana he who is past youth or whose youth is past Sn 110. — (b) nt. the past: atīte (loc.) once upon a time J I.98 etc. **atītaŋ āhari** he told (a tale of) the past, i. e. a Jātaka J I.213, 218, 221 etc. — S I.5 (atītaŋ nânusocati); A III.400 (a. eko anto); Sn 851, 1112. In this sense very frequently comb^d. with or opposed to **anāgata** the future & **paccuppanna** the present, e. g. atītânāgate in past & future S II.58; Sn 373; J VI.364. Or all three in ster. comb^n. atīt°-anāgata-paccuppanna (this the usual order) D III.100, 135; S II.26, 110, 252; III.19, 47, 187; IV.4 sq.; 151 sq.; A I.264 sq., 284; II.171, 202; III.151; V.33; It 53; Nd[2] 22; but also occasionally atīta paccuppanna anāgata,

e. g. PvA 100. — 2. (modal) passed out of, having overcome or surmounted, gone over, free from (cp. accaya 2) S I.97 (maraṇaŋ an° not free from death), 121 (sabba-vera-bhaya°); A II.21; III.346 (sabbasaŋyojana°); Sn 373 (kappa°), 598 (khaya°, of the moon = ūnabhāvaŋ atīta Sn A 463); Th 1, 413 (c. abl.) — 3. (id.) overstepping, having transgressed or neglected (cp. accaya 3) Dh 176 (dhammaŋ).

-aŋsa the past (= atīta koṭṭhāse, atikkantabhavesū ti attho ThA 233) D II.222; III.275; Th 2, 314. -ārammaṇa state of mind arising out of the past Dhs 1041.

Atīradassin (adj.-n.) [a + tīra + dassin] not seeing the shore J I.46; VI.440; also as **atīradassanī** (f.) J V.75 (**nāvā**). Cp. D I 222.

Atīva (indecl.) [ati + iva, see also ativiya] very much, exceedingly J II.413; Mhvs 33, 2 etc.

Ato (adv.) [Sk. ataḥ] hence, now, therefore S I.15; M I.498; Miln 87; J V.398 (= tato C.).

Atoṇa [etym.?] a class of jugglers or acrobats(?) Miln 191.

Atta[1] [ā + d + ta; that is, pp. of ādadāti with the base form reduced to **d.** Idg *d-to; cp. Sk. ātta] that which has been taken up, assumed. **Atta-daṇḍa,** he who has taken a stick in hand, a violent person, S I.236; IV.117; Sn 630, 935; Dh 406. **Attañjaha,** rejecting what had been assumed, Sn 790. Attaŋ pahāya Sn 800. The opp. is **niratta,** that which has not been assumed, has been thrown off, rejected. The Arahant has neither atta nor niratta (Sn 787, 858, 919), neither assumption nor rejection, he keeps an open mind on all speculative theories. See Nd I.82, 90, 107, 352; II.271; SnA 523; DhA IV.180 for the traditional exegesis. As legal t. t. **attādānaŋ ādīyati** is to take upon oneself the conduct, before the Chapter, of a legal point already raised. Vin II.247 (quoted V.91).

Atta[2] see attan.

Atta[3] [Sk. akta, pp. of añjati] see upatta.

Attan (m.) & **atta** (the latter is the form used in compn.) [Vedic ātman, not to Gr. ἄνεμος = Lat. animus, but to Gr. ἀτμός steam, Ohg. ātum breath, Ags. aeþm]. — I. *Inflection.* (1) of *attan-* (n. stem); the foll. cases are the most freq.: acc. **attānaŋ** D I.13, 185; S I.24; Sn 132, 451. — gen. dat. **attano** Sn 334, 592 etc., also as abl. A III.337 (attano ca parato ca as regards himself and others). — instr. abl. **attanā** S I.24; Sn 132, 451; DhA II.75; PvA 15, 214 etc. On use of attanā see below III.1 C. — loc. **attani** S V.177; A I.149 (attanī metri causa); II.52 (anattani); III.181; M I.138; Sn 666, 756, 784; Vbh 376 (an°). — (2) of *atta-* (a-stem) we find the foll. cases: acc. **attaŋ** Dh 379. — instr. **attena** S IV.54. — abl. **attato** S I.188; Ps I.143; II.48; Vbh 336.

Meanings. I. The soul as postulated in the animistic theories held in N India in the 6th and 7th cent. B. C. It is described in the Upanishads as a small creature, in shape like a man, dwelling in ordinary times in the heart. It escapes from the body in sleep or trance; when it returns to the body life and motion reappear. It escapes from the body at death, then continues to carry on an everlasting life of its own. For numerous other details see Rh. D. *Theory of Soul in the Upanishads J R A S* 1899. *Bt. India* 251—255. Buddhism repudiated all such theories, thus differing from other religions. Sixteen such theories about the soul D I.31. Seven other theories D I.34. Three others D I.186/7. A 'soul' according to general belief was some thing permanent, unchangeable, not affected by sorrow S IV.54 = Kvu 67; Vin I.14; M I.138. See also M I.233; III.265, 271; S II.17, 109; III.135; A I.284; II.164, 171; V.188; S IV.400. Cp. ātuman, tuma, puggala, jīva, satta, pāṇa and nāma-rūpa.

2. Oneself, himself, yourself. Nom. attā, very rare. S I.71, 169; III 120; A I.57, 149 (you yourself know whether that is true or false. Cp. Manu VIII.84. Here attā comes very near to the European idea of conscience. But conscience as a unity or entity is not accepted by Buddhism) Sn 284; Dh 166, 380; Miln 54 (the image, outward appearance, of oneself). Acc. **attānaŋ** S I.44 (would not give for himself, as a slave) A I.89; Sn 709. Acc. attaŋ Dh 379. Abl. **attato** as oneself S I.188; Ps I.143; II.48; Vbh 336. Loc. **attani** A I.149; III.181; Sn 666, 784. Instr. **attanā** S I.57 = Dh 66; S I.75; II.68; A I.53; III.211; IV.405; Dh 165. On one's own account, spontaneously S IV.307; V.354; A I.297; II.99, 218; III.81; J I.156; PvA 15, 20. In composition with numerals **atta-dutiya** himself and one other D II.147; °catuttha with himself as fourth M I.393; A III.36; °pañcama Dpvs VIII.2; °sattama J I.233; °aṭṭhama VvA 149 (as atta-n-aṭṭhama Vv 34[13]), & °aṭṭhamaka Miln 291.

anattā (n. and predicative adj.) not a soul, without a soul. Most freq. in combn. with dukkha & anicca — (1) as noun: S III.141 (°anupassin); IV.49; V.345 (°saññin); A II.52 = Ps II.80 (anattani anattā; opp. to anattani attā, the opinion of the micchādiṭṭhigatā sattā); Dh 279; Ps II.37, 45 sq. (°anupassanā), 106 (yaŋ aniccañ ca dukkhañ ca taŋ anattā); DhA III. 406 (°lakkhaṇa). — (2) as adj. (pred.): S IV.152 sq.; S IV.166; S IV.130 sq., 148 sq.; Vin I.13 = S III.66 = Nd[2] 680 Q 1; S III.20 sq.; 178 sq., 196 sq.; sabbe dhammā anattā Vin V.86; S III.133; IV.28, 401.

-**attha** one's own profit or interest Sn 75; Nd[2] 23; J IV.56, 96; otherwise as atta-d-attha, e.g. Sn 284. -**atthiya** looking after one's own needs Th 1, 1097. -**âdhipaka** master of oneself, self-mastered A I.150. -**adhipateyya** self-dependence, self-reliance, independence A I.147. -**âdhīna** independent D I.72. -**ânudiṭṭhi** speculation about souls S III.185; IV.148; A III.447; Sn 1119; Ps I.143; Vbh 368; Miln 146. -**ânuyogin** one who concentrates his attention on himself Dh 209; DhA III.275. -**ânuvāda** blaming oneself A II.121; Vbh 376. -**uññā** self-humiliation Vbh 353 (+ att-avaññā). -**uddesa** relation to oneself Vin III.149 (= attano atthāya), also °ika ibid. 144. -**kata** self-made S I.134 (opp. para°). -**kāma** love of self A II.21; adj. a lover of "soul", one who cares for his own soul S I.75. -**kāra** individual self, fixed individuality, oneself (cp. ahaŋkāra) D I.53 (opp. para°); A III 337 (id.) DA I.160; as nt. at J V.401 in the sense of service (self-doing", slavery) (attakārāni karonti bhattusu). -**kilamatha** self-mortification D III.113; S IV.330; V.421; M III.230. -**garahin** self-censuring Sn 778. -**gutta** self-guarded Dh 379. -**gutti** watchfulness as regards one's self, self-care A II.72. -**ghañña** self-destruction Dh 164. -**ja** proceeding from oneself Dh 161 (pāpa). -**ñū** knowing oneself A IV.113, cp. D III.252. -**(n)tapa** self-mortifying, self-vexing D III.232 = A II.205 (opp. paran°); M I.341, 411; II.159; Pug 55, 56. -**daṇḍa** see atta[1]. -**danta** self-restrained, self-controlled Dh 104, 322. -**diṭṭhi** speculation concerning the nature of the soul Nd[1] 107; SnA 523, 527. -**dīpa** relying on oneself, independent, founded on oneself (+ attasaraṇa, opp. añña°) D II.100 = III.42; V.154; Sn 501 (= attano guṇe eva attano dīpaŋ katvā SnA 416). -**paccakkha** only in instr. °ena by or with his own presence, i. e. himself J V.119. -**paccakkhika** eye-witness J V.119. -**paccatthika** hostile to oneself Vin II.94, 96. -**paṭilābha** acquisition of a personality D I.195 (tayo: oḷārika, manomaya, arūpa). -**paritāpana** self-chastisement, mortification D III.232 = A II.205; M I.341; PvA 18, 30. -**parittā** charm (protection) for oneself Vin II.110. -**paribhava** disrespect for one's own person Vbh 353. -**bhāva** one's own nature (1) person, personality, individuality, living creature; form, appearance [cp. *Dhs trsl.* LXXI and BSk. **ātmabhāva** body Divy 70, 73 (°pratilambha), 230; Sp. Av. Ś I.162 (pratilambha), 167, 171] Vin II.238 (living beings, forms); S V.442 (bodily appearance); A I.279 (oḷārika a substantial creature); II.17 (creature); DhA II.64, 69 (appearance); SnA 132 (personality). — (2) life, rebirth A I.134 sq.; III.412;

DhA II.68; PvA 8, 15, 166 (atītā °ā former lives). °ŋ pavatteti to lead a life, to live PvA 29, 181. Thus in cpd. **paṭilābha** assumption of an existence, becoming reborn as an individual Vin II.185; III.105; D III.231; M III.46; S II.255, 272, 283; III.144; A II.159, 188; III.122 sq. — (3) character, quality of heart Sn 388 (= citta SnA 374); J I.61. **-rūpa** "of the form of self", self-like only in instr. °ena as adv. by oneself, on one's own account, for the sake of oneself S IV.97; A II.120. **-vadha** self-destruction S II.241; A II.73. **-vāda** theory of (a persistent) soul D III.230; M I.66; D II.58; S II.3, 245 sq.; III.103, 165, 203; IV.1 sq., 43 sq., 153 sq.; Ps I.156 sq.; Vbh 136, 375. For var. points of an "attavādic" doctrine see Index to Saŋyutta Nikāya. **-vyābādha** personal harm or distress self-suffering, one's own disaster (opp. para°) M I 369; S IV.339 = A I.157; A II.179. **-vetana** supporting oneself, earning one's own living Sn 24. **-sañcetanā** self-perception, self-consciousness (opp. para°) D III.231; A II.159. **-sambhava** originating from one's self S I.70; A IV.312; Dh 161 (pāpa); Th 1, 260. **-sambhūta** arisen from oneself Sn 272. **-sammāpaṇidhi** thorough pursuit or development of one's personality A II.32; Sn 260, cp. KhA 132. **-saraṇa** see °dīpa. **-sukha** happiness of oneself, self-success Dpvs I.66, cp. II.11. **-hita** personal welfare one's own good (opp. para°) D II.233; A II.95 sq. **-hetu** for one's own sake, out of self-consideration Sn 122; Dh 328.

Attaniya (adj.) [from attā] belonging to the soul, having a soul, of the nature of soul, soul-lika; usually nt. anything of the nature of soul M I.138 = Kvu 67; M I.297; II.263; S III.77 (yaŋ kho anattaniyaŋ whatever has no soul), 127; IV.54 = Nd^2 680 F; S IV.82 = III.33 = Nd^2 680 Q 3; S IV.168; V.6; Nd^2 680 D. Cp. *Dhs trsl.* XXXV ff.

Attamana [atta^1 + mano, having an up raised mind. Bdhgh's explⁿ. is saka-mano DA I.255 = attā + mano. He applies the same explⁿ. to attamanatā (at Dhs 9, see Dhs trsl. 12) = attano manatā mentality of one's self] delighted, pleased, enraptured D I.3, 90 (an°); II.14; A III.337, 343; IV.344; Sn 45 = Dh 328 (= upaṭṭhita-satt DhA IV.29); Sn 995; Nd^2 24 (= tuṭṭha-mano haṭṭha-mano etc.); Vv 1^4; Pug 33 (an°); Miln 18; DA I.52; DhA I.89 (an°-dhātuka displeased); PvA 23, 132; VvA 21 (where Dhpāla gives two explns, either tuṭṭhamano or sakamano).

Attamanatā (f.) [abstr. to prec.] satisfaction, joy, pleasure, transport of mind M I.114; A I.276; IV.62; Pug 18 (an°); Dhs 9, 86, 418 (an°); PvA 132; VvA 67 (an°).

Attāṇa (adj.) [a + tāṇa] without shelter or protection J I.229; Miln 148, 325; ThA 285.

Attha^1 (also **aṭṭha**, esp. in combns mentioned under 3) (m. & nt.) [Vedic artha from ṛ, arti & ṛṇoti to reach, attain or to proceed (to or from), thus originally result (or cause), profit, attainment. Cp. semantically Fr. chose, Lat. causa] **1.** interest, advantage, gain; (moral) good, blessing, welfare; profit, prosperity, well-being M I.111 (atthassa ninnetar, of the Buddha, bringer of good); S IV.94 (id.); S I.34 (attano a. one's own welfare), 55 (id.) 86, 102, 126 = A II.46 (atthassa patti); S I.162 (attano ca parassa ca); II.222 (id.); IV.347 (°ŋ bhañjati destroy the good or welfare, always with musāvādena by lying, cp. attha-bhañjanaka); A I.61 (°ŋ anubhoti to fare well, to have a (good) result); III.364 (samparāyika a. profit in the future life); A V.223 sq. (anattho ca attho ca detriment & profit); It 44 (v. l. attā better); Sn 37, 58 (= Nd^2 26, where the six kinds of advantages are enumd. as att° par° ubhay°, i. e. advantage, resulting for oneself, for others, for both; diṭṭhadhammik° samparāyik° param° gain for this life, for a future life, and highest gain of all, i. e. Arahantship); Sn 331 (ko attho supitena what good is it to sleep = na hi sakkā supantena koci attho papuṇituŋ SnA 338; cp. ko attho supinena te Pv II.6^1); PvA 30 (atthaŋ sādheti does good, results in good, 69 (samparāyikena atthena). — dat. **atthāya** for the good, for the benefit of (gen.); to advantage, often combd. with hitāya sukhāya, e. g. D III.211 sq.; It 79. — Kh VIII.1 (to my benefit); Pv I.4^3 (= upakārāya PvA 18), II.12^9 (to great advantage). See also below 6.

Sometimes in a more concrete meaning = riches, wealth, e. g. J I.256 (= vaḍḍhiŋ C.); III.394 (id.); Pv IV.1^4 (= dhanaŋ PvA 219). — Often as —°: att°, one's own welfare, usually combd. with par° and **ubhay°** (see above) S II.29; V.121; A I.158, 216; III.63 sq.; IV.134; Sn 75 (att-aṭṭha, v. l. attha Nd^2), 284 (atta-d-attha); **uttam°** the highest gain, the very best thing Dh 386 (= arahatta DhA IV.142); Sn 324 (= arahatta SnA 332); **param°** id. Nd^2 26; **sad°** one's own weal D II.141; M I.4; S II.29; V.145; A I.144; **sāttha** (adj.) connected with advantage, beneficial, profitable (of the Dhamma; or should we take it as "with the meaning, in spirit"? see sāttha) D I.62; S V.352; A II.147; III.152; Nd^2 316. — **2.** need, want (c. instr.), use (for = instr.) S I.37 (°jāta when need has arisen, in need); J I.254; III.126, 281; IV.1; DhA I.398 (n' atthi eteh' attho I have no use for them); VvA 250; PvA 24 (yāvadattha, adj. as much as is needed, sufficient = anappaka). — **3.** sense, meaning, import (of a word), denotation, signification. In this application attha is always spelt aṭṭha in cpds. aṭṭh-uppatti and aṭṭha-kathā (see below). On term see also *Cpd.* 4. — S III.93 (atthaŋ vibhajati explain the sense); A I.23 (id.), 60 (nīt° primary meaning, literal meaning; neyy° secondary or inferred meaning); II.189 (°ŋ ācikkhati to interpret); Sn 126 (°ŋ pucchita asked the (correct) sense, the lit. meaning), 251 (°ŋ akkhāti); Th 1, 374; attho paramo the highest sense, the ultimate sense or intrinsic meaning It 98, cp. *Cpd.* 6, 81, 223; Miln 28 (paramatthato in the absolute sense); Miln 18 (atthato according to its meaning, opp. vyañjanato by letter, orthographically); DhA II.82; III.175; KhA 81 (pad° meaning of a word); SnA 91 (id.); PvA 15 (°ŋ vadati to explain, interpret), 16, 19 (hitatthadhammatā "fitness of the best sense", i. e. practical application), 71. Very frequent in Commentary style at the conclusion of an explained passage as **ti attho** "this is the meaning", thus it is meant, this is the sense, e. g. DA I.65; DhA IV.140, 141; PvA 33, etc. — Contrasted with **dhamma** in the combn. attho ca dhammo ca it (attha) refers to the (primary, natural) meaning of the word, while dhamma relates to the (interpreted) meaning of the text, to its bearing on the norm and conduct; or one might say they represent the theoretical and practical side of the text (pāḷi) to be discussed, the "letter" and the "spirit". Thus at A I.69; V.222, 254; Sn 326 (= bhāsitatthañ ca pāḷidhammañ ca SnA 333); It 84 (duṭṭho atthaŋ na jānāti dhammaŋ na passati: he realises neither the meaning nor the importance); Dh 363 (= bhāsitatthañ c' eva desanādhammañ ca); J II.353; VI.368; Nd^2 386 (meaning & proper nature); Pv III.9^6 (but expld. by PvA 211 as hita = benefit, good, thus referring it to above 1). For the same use see cpds. °dhamma, °paṭisambhidā, esp. in adv. use (see under 6) Sn 430 (yen' atthena for which purpose), 508 (kena atthena v. l. BB for T attanā), J I.411 (atthaŋ vā kāraṇaŋ vā reason and cause); DhA II.95 (+ kāraṇa(; PvA 11 (ayaŋ h' ettha attho this is the reason why). — **5.** (in very wide application, covering the same ground as Lat. res & Fr. chose): (a) matter, affair, thing, often untranslatable and simply to be given as "this" or "that" S II.36 (ekena-padena sabbo attho vutto the whole matter is said with one word); J I.151 (taŋ atthaŋ the matter); II.160 (imaŋ a. this); VI.289 (taŋ atthaŋ pakāsento); PvA 6 (taŋ atthaŋ pucchi asked it), 11 (visajjeti explains it), 29 (vuttaŋ atthaŋ what had been said), 82 (id.). — (b) affair, cause, case (cp. aṭṭa^2 and Lat. causa) Dh 256, 331; Miln 47 (kassa atthaŋ dhāresi whose cause do you support, with whom do you agree?). See also **alamattha**. — **6.** Adv. use of oblique cases in the sense of a prep.: (a) dat. **atthāya** for the sake of, in order to, for J I.254 dhan° atthāya for wealth, kim° what for, why?), 279; II.133; III.54; DhA II.82; PvA 55, 75, 78. — (b) acc. atthaŋ on account of, in order to, often instead of an infinitive or with another inf. substitute J I.279 (kim°); III.53 (id.); I.253; II.128; Dpvs VI.79; DhA I.397; PvA 32 (dassan° in order to see), 78, 167, etc. — (c) abl. atthā J III.518 (pitu atthā = atthāya C.). — (d) loc. atthe instead of, for VvA 10; PvA 33; etc.

anattha (m. & nt.) 1. unprofitable situation or condition, mischief, harm, misery, misfortune S I.103; II.196 (anatthāya saŋvattati); A IV.96 (°ŋ adhipajjati) It 84 (°janano doso ill-will brings discomfort); J I.63, 196; Pug 37; Dhs 1060, 1231; Sdhp 87; DA I.52 (anatthajanano kodho, cp. It 83 and Nd² 420 Q²); DhA II.73; PvA 13, 61, 114, 199. — 2. (= attha 3) incorrect sense, false meaning, as adj. senseless (and therefore unprofitable, no good, irrelevant) A V.222, 254 (adhammo ca); Dh 100 (= aniyyānad°īpaka DhA II.208); Sn 126 (expld. at SnA 180 as ahitaŋ).

-akkhāyin showing what is profitable D III.187. **-attha** riches J VI.290 (= atthabhūtaŋ atthaŋ C.). **-antara** difference between the (two) meanings Miln 158. At Th 1, 374, Oldenberg's reading, but the v. l. (also C. reading) atthandhara is much better = he who knows the (correct) meaning, esp. as it corresponds with dhamma-dhara (q. v.). **-abhisamaya** grasp of the proficient S I.87 (see abhisamaya). **-uddhāra** synopsis or abstract of contents ("matter") of the Vinaya Dpvs V.37. **-upaparikkhā** investigation of meaning, (+ dhamma-savanna) M III.175; A III.381 sq.; IV.221; V.126. **-uppatti** (aṭṭh°) sense, meaning, explanation, interpretation J I.89; DA I.242; KhA 216; VvA 197, 203 (cp. pāḷito) PvA 2, 6, 78; etc. **-kāma** (adj.) (a) well-wishing, a well-wisher, friend, one who is interested in the welfare of others (cp. Sk. arthakāma, e. g. Bhagavadgīta II.5: gurūn arthakāman) S I.140, 144, 197; A III.143; D III.164 (bahuno janassa a., + hitakāmo); J I.241; Pv IV.3⁸¹; Pv A 25; SnA 287 (an°). — (b) one who is interested in his own gain or good, either in good or bad sense (= greedy) S I.44; PvA 112. — **-kathā** (aṭṭha°) exposition of the sense, explanation, commentary J V.38, 170; PvA 1, 71, etc. freq. in N. of Com. **-kara** beneficial, useful Vin III.149; Miln 321. **-karaṇa** the business of trying a case, holding court, giving judgment (v. l. aṭṭa°) D II.20; S I.74 (judgment hall?). **-kavi** a didactic poet (see kavi) A II.230. **-kāmin** = °kāma, well-wishing Sn 986 (devatā atthakāminī). **-kāraṇā** (abl.) for the sake of gain D III.186. **-kusala** clever in finding out what is good or profitable Sn 143 (= atthacheka KhA 236). **-cara** doing good, busy in the interest of others, obliging S I.23 (narānaŋ = "working out man's salvation"). **-caraka** (adj.) one who devotes himself to being useful to others, doing good, one who renders service to others, e. g. an attendant, messenger, agent etc. D I.107 (= hitakāraka DA I.276); J II.87; III.326; IV.230; VI.369. **-cariyā** useful conduct or behaviour D III.152, 190, 232; A II.32, 248; IV.219, 364. **-ññu** one who knows what is useful or who knows the (plain or correct) meaning of something (+ dhammaññū) D III.252; A III.148; IV.113 sq. **-dassin** intent upon the (moral) good Sn 385 (= hitânupassin SnA 373). **-dassimant** one who examines a cause (cp. Sk. arthadarśika) J VI.286 (but expld. by C. as "saṇha-sukhuma-pañña" of deep insight, one who has a fine and minute knowledge). **-desanā** interpretation, exegesis Miln 21 (dhamm°). **-dhamma** "reason and morality", see above n⁰. 3. °*anusāsaka* one who advises regarding the meaning and application of the Law, a professor of moral philosophy J II.105; DhA II.71. **-pada** a profitable saying, a word of good sense, text, motto A II.189; III.356; Dh 100. **-paṭisambhidā** knowledge of the meaning (of words) combd. with dhamma° of the text or spirit (see above n⁰. 3) Ps I.132; II.150; Vbh 293 sq. **-paṭisaŋvedin** experiencing good D III.241 (+ dhamma°); A I.151; III.21. **-baddha** expecting some good from (c. loc.) Sn 382. **-bhañjanaka** breaking the welfare of, hurting DhA III.356 (paresaŋ of others, by means of telling lies, musāvādena). **-majjha** of beautiful waist J V.170 (= sumajjhā C.; reading must be faulty, there is hardly any connection with attha; v. l. atta). **-rasa** sweetness (or substance, essence) of meaning (+ dhamma°, vimutti°) Nd² 466; Ps II.88, 89. **-vasa** "dependence on the sense", reasonableness, reason, consequence, cause D II.285; M I.464; II.120; III.150; S II.202; III.93; IV.303; V.224: A I.61, 77, 98; II.240; III.72, 169, 237; Dh 289 (= kāraṇa DhA III.435); It 89; Sn 297; Ud 14. **-vasika** sensible It 89; Miln 406. **-vasin** bent on (one's) aim or purpose Th 1, 539. **-vādin** one who speaks good, i. e. whose words are doing good or who speaks only useful speech, always in combn. with kāla° bhūta° dhamma° D I.4; III.175; A I.204; II.22, 209; Pug 58; DA I.76 (expld. as "one who speaks for the sake of reaping blessings here and hereafter"). **-saŋvaṇṇanā** explanation, exegesis PvA 1. **-saŋhita** connected with good, bringing good, profitable, useful, salutary D I.189; S II.223; IV.330; V.417; A III.196 sq., 244; Sn 722 (= hitena saŋhitaŋ SnA 500); Pug 58. **-sandassana** determination of meaning, definition Ps I.105. **-siddhi** profit, advantage, benefit J I.402; PvA 63.

Attha² (nt.) [Vedic asta, of uncertain etym.] home, primarily as place of rest & shelter, but in P. phraselogy abstracted from the "going home", i. e. setting of the sun, as disappearance, going out of existence, annihilation, extinction. Only in acc. and as °— in foll phrases: **atthangacchati** to disappear, to go out of existence, to vanish Dh 226 (= vināsaŋ natthibhāvaŋ gacchati DhA III.324), 384 (= parikkhayaŋ gacchati); pp. **atthangata** gone home, gone to rest, gone, disappeared; of the sun (= set): J I.175 (atthangate suriye at sunset); PvA 55 (id.) 216 (anatthangate s. before sunset) fig. Sn 472 (atthagata). 475 (id.); 1075 (= niruddha ucchinna vinaṭṭha anupādi-sesāya nibbāna-dhātuyā nibbuta); It 58; Dhs 1038; Vbh 195. **-atthagatatta** (nt. abstr.) disappearance SnA 409. **-atthangama** (atthagama passim) annihilation, disappearance; opposed to samudaya (coming into existence) and synonymous with nirodha (destruction) D I.34, 37, 183; S IV.327; A III.326; Ps II.4, 6, 39; Pug 52; Dhs 165, 265, 501, 579; Vbh 105. **-atthagamana** (nt.) setting (of the sun) J I.101 (suriyass' atthagamanā at sunset) DA I.95 (= ogamana). — **attha-gāmin**, in phrase uday° atthagāmin leading to birth and death (of paññā): see udaya. **-atthaŋ paleti** = atthangacchati (fig.) Sn 1074 (= atthangameti nirujjhati Nd² 28). — Also **atthamita** (pp. of i) set (of the sun) in phrase anatthamite suriye before sunset (with anatthangamite as v. l. at both pass.) DhA I.86; III.127. — Cp. also abbhattha.

Attha³ pres. 2nd pl. of atthi (q. v.).

Atthata [pp. of attharati] spread, covered, spread over with (—°) Vin I.265; IV.287; V.172 (also °an); A III.50; PvA 141.

Atthatta (nt.) [abstr. fr. attha¹] reason, cause; only in abl. atthattā according to the sense, by reason of, on account of PvA 189 (—°).

Atthara [fr. attharati] a rug (for horses, elephants etc.) D I.7.

Attharaka [= atthara] a covering J I.9; DA I.87. — f. °**ikā** a layer J I.9; V.280.

Attharaṇa (nt.) [fr. attharati] a covering, carpet, cover, rug Vin II.291; A II.56; III.53; Mhvs 3, 20; 15, 40; 25, 102; ThA 22.

Attharati [ā + stṛ] to spread, to cover, to spread out; stretch, lay out Vin I.254; V.172; J I.199; V.113; VI.428; Dh I.272. — pp. atthata (q. v.). — Caus. **attharāpeti** to caused to be spread J V.110; Mhvs 3, 20; 29, 7; 34, 69.

Atthavant (adj.) [cp. Sk. arthavant] full of benefit S I.30; Th 1, 740; Miln 172.

Atthāra [cp. Sk. āstāra, fr. attharati] spreading out Vin V.172 (see kaṭhina). **atthāraka** same ibid.; Vin II.87 (covering).

Atthi [Sk. asti, 1st sg. asmi; Gr. εἰμί-ἐστί; Lat. sum-est; Goth. im-ist; Ags. eom-is E. am-is] to be, to exist. — Pres. Ind. 1st sg. **asmi** Sn 1120, 1143; J I.151; III.55, and **amhi** M I.429; Sn 694; J II.153; Pv I.10²; II.8². — 2nd sg. **asi** Sn 420; J II.160 ('si); III.278; Vv 32⁴; PvA 4. — 3rd sg. **atthi** Sn 377, 672, 884; J I.278. Often used for 3rd pl. (= santi), e. g. J I.280; II.2; III.55. — 1st pl. **asma** [Sk. smaḥ] Sn 594, 595; asmase Sn 595, and **amha** Sn 570; J II.128. 2nd pl. **attha** J II.128; PvA 39, 74 (āgat' attha you *have* come). — 3rd pl. **santi** Sn 1077; Nd¹ 637 (= saŋvijjanti atthi upalabbhanti); J II.353; PvA 7, 22. — Imper. **atthu** Sn 340; J I.59; III.26. — Pot. 1st sg. **siyā** [Sk. syām] Pv II.8⁸, and **assaŋ** [Cond. used as Pot.] Sn 1120; Pv I.12⁵ (= bhaveyyaŋ PvA 64). — 2nd sg. **siyā** [Sk. syāḥ] Pv II.8¹. — 3rd sg. **siyā** [Sk. syāt] D II.154; Sn 325, 1092; Nd² 105 (= jāneyya, nibbatteyya); J I.262; PvA 13, and **assa** D I.135, 196; II.154; A V.194; Sn 49, 143; Dh 124, 260; Pv II.3²⁴; 9²⁴. — 1st pl. **assu** PvA 27. — 3rd pl. **assu** [cp. Sk. syuḥ] Sn 532; Dh 74; Pv IV.1³⁶ (= bhaveyyuŋ PvA 231). — Aor. 1st sg. **āsiŋ** [Sk. āsaŋ] Sn 284; Pv I.2¹ (= ahosiŋ PvA 10); II.3⁴ (= ahosiŋ PvA 83). — 3rd sg. **āsi** [Sk. āsīt] Sn 994. — 3rd **āsuŋ** [cp. Sk. Perf. āsuḥ] Pv II.3²¹, 13³ (ti pi pāṭho for su). — Ppr. ***sat** only in loc. **sati** (as loc. abs.) Dh 146; J I.150, 263, **santa** Sn 105; Nd² 635; J I.150 (loc. evaŋ sante in this case); III.26, and **samāna** (q. v.) J I.266; IV.138. **-bhāva** state of being, existence, being J I.222, 290; II.415; DhA II.5; IV.217 (atthibhāva vā natthibhāva vā whether there is or not).

Atthika (adj.) [cp. Sk. arthika] 1. (to attha¹) profitable, good, proper. In this meaning the MSS show a variance of spelling either **atthika** or **aṭṭhika** or **aṭṭhita**; in all cases atthika should be preferred D I.55 (°vāda); M II.212 (aṭṭhita); A III.219 sq. (idaŋ atthikaŋ this is suitable, of good avail; T aṭṭhitaŋ, vv. ll. as above); Sn 1058 (aṭṭhita; Nd² 20 also aṭṭhita, which at this pass. shows a confusion between aṭṭha and a-ṭhita); J V.151 (in def. of aṭṭhikatvā q. v.); Pug 69, 70 (T aṭṭhika, aṭṭhita SS; expld. by Pug A V.4 by kalyāṇāya). — 2. (to attha¹ 2) desirous of (—°), wanting, seeking for, in need of (c. instr.) A II.199 (uday° desirous of increase); Sn 333, 460, 487 (puññ°), 987 (dhan° greedy for wealth); J I.263 (rajj° coveting a kingdom); V.19; Pv II.2²⁸ (bhojan° in need of food); IV.1¹ (kāraṇ°), 1²¹ (khiḍḍ° for play), 1⁶³ (puññ°); PvA 95 (sasena a. wanting a rabbit), 120; DA I.70 (atthikā those who like to). **-anatthika** one who does not care for, or is not satisfied with (c. instr.) J V.460; PvA 20; of no good Th 1, 956 ("of little zeal" Mrs. Rh. D.).
-bhāva (a) usefulness, profitableness Pug A V.4. (b) state of need, distress PvA 120.

Atthikavant (adj.) [atthika + vant] one who wants something, one who is on a certain errand D I.90 (atthikaŋ assa atthī ti DA I.255).

Atthitā (f.) [f. abstr. fr. atthi cp. atthibhāva] state of being, existence, being, reality M I.486; S II.17 (°añ c' eva natthitañ ca to be and not to be); III.135; J V.110 (kassaci atthitaŋ vā natthitaŋ vā jānāhi see if there is anybody or not); DhsA 394. — Often in abl. **atthitāya** by reason of, on account of, this being so DhA III.344 (idam-atthitāya under this condition) PvA 94, 97, 143.

Atthin (adj.) (—°) [Vedic arthin] desirous, wanting anything; see mant°, vād°.

Atthiya (adj.) (—°) [= atthika] having a purpose or end S III.189 (kim° for what purpose?); A V.1 sq. (id.), 311 sq.; Th 1, 1097 (att° having one's purpose in oneself), 1274; Sn 354 (yad atthiyaŋ on account of what).

Atra (adv.) [Sk. atra] here; atra atra here & there J I.414 = IV.5 (in expln. of atriccha).

Atraja (adj.) [Sk. *ātma-ja, corrupted form for attaja (see attā) through analogy with Sk. atra "here". This form occurs only in J and similar sources, i. e. popular lore] born from oneself, one's own, appl. to sons, of which there are 4 kinds enumd., viz. atraja khettaja, dinnaka, antevāsika p. Nd² 448. — J I.135; III.103 = Nd¹ 504; J III.181; V.465; VI.20; Mhvs 4, 12; 13, 4; 36, 57.

Atriccha (adj.) [the popular etym. suggested at JA IV.4 is atra atra icchamāna desiring here & there; but see atricchā] very covetous, greedy, wanting too much J I.414 = IV.4; III.206.

Atricchā (f.) [Sk. *atṛptyā, a + tṛpt + yā, influenced by Desid. titṛpsati, so that atricchā phonetically rather corresponds to a form *a.-tṛpsyā (cch = psy, cp. P. chāta Sk. psāta). For the simple Sk. tṛpti see titti (from tappati²). According to Kern, but phonetically hardly justifiable it is Sk. aticcha = ati + icchā "too much desire", with r in dissolution of geminated tt, like atraja for attaja. See also atriccha adj. and cp. *J P T S.* 1884, 69] great desire, greed, excessive longing, insatiability J IV.5, 327.

Atricchatā (f.) [see atricchā] excessive lust J. III.222.

Atha (indecl.) [Sk. atha, cp. atho] copulative & adversative part. 1. after positive clauses, in enumerations, in the beginning & continuation of a story: and, and also, or; and then, now D II.2; III.152, 199 (athâparaŋ etad avoca); M I.435; Sn 1006, 1007, 1017; Sn p. 126 (athâparaŋ etad avoca: and further, something else); Dh 69, 119, 377; J II.158; Pv II.6⁴; PvA 3, 8 (atha na and not), 70. — 2. after negative clauses: but M I.430; Sn 990, 1047; Dh 85, 136, 387; PvA 68. Often combd. with other part., e. g. **atha kho** (pos. & neg.) now, and then; but, rather, moreover Vin I.1; D I.141, 167, 174; A V.195; PvA 79, 221, 251. na-atha kho na neither-nor PvA 28. **atha kho pana** and yet D I.139. **atha ca pana** on the other hand J I.279. **atha vā** or (after prec. ca), nor (after prec. na) Sn 134; Dh 140, 271; Pv I.4¹; II.1⁴. **athā vā pi** Sn 917, 921.

Athabbaṇa [Vedic atharvan; as regards etym. see Walde, Lat. Wtb. under ater] (1) the Atharva Veda DA I.247 = SnA 447 (°veda). — (2) one who is familiar with the (magic formulas of the) Atharvaveda J VI.490 (sâlhabbaṇa = sahatthivejja, with the elephant-healer or doctor). See also āthabbaṇa.

Atho (indecl.) [Sk. atho, atha + u] copulative and adversative part.: and, also, and further, likewise, nay S I.106; Sn 43, 155, 647; Dh 151, 234, 423; J I.83; II.185; IV.495; It 106; Kh VIII.7; Pv IV.3¹⁵; PvA 251 (atho ti nipātamattaŋ avadhāraṇ-atthe vā). Also combd. with other part., like **atho pi** Sn 222, 537, 985; Pv II.3²⁰; KhA 166.

Ada (adj.) (—°) [to **ad**, see adeti, cp. °ga, °tha, °da etc.] eating S IV.195 (kiṭṭhâda eating corn); J II.439 (vantâda = vantakhādaka C.).

Adaka (adj.) = ada J V.91 (purisâdaka man-eater).

Adana (nt.) [from adeti] eating, food J V.374 (v.l. modana).

Adasaka (adj.) see dasā.

Adāsa [prob. = adaŋsa, from ḍasati to bite, cp. dāṭhā tooth; lit meaning "toothless" or "not biting"] a kind of bird J IV.466.

Adiṭṭhā [a + diṭṭhā, ger. of *dassati] not seeing, without seeing J IV.192 (T. adaṭṭhā, v. l. BB na diṭṭhā, C. adisvā); V.219.

Adinna (pp.) [a + dinna] that which is not given, freq. in phrase **adinn' ādāna** (BSk. adattādāna Divy 302) seizing or grasping that which is not given to one, i. e. stealing, is the 2nd of the ten qualifications of bad character or sīla (dasa-sīla see sīla II.). Vin I.83 (°ā veramaṇī); D I.4 (= parassa haraṇaŋ theyyaŋ corikā ti vuttaŋ hoti DA I.71); III.68 sq., 82, 92, 181 sq.; M I.361; It 63; Kh II., cp. KhA 26. — **adinnādāyin** he who takes what is not given, a thief; stealing, thieving (cp. BSk. adattādāyika Divy 301, 418) Vin I.85; D I.138; Sdhp 78.

Adu (or ādu) (indecl.) [perhaps identical with aduŋ, nt. of pron. asu] part. of affirmation: even, yea, nay; always in emphatic exclamations Vv 62[2] (= udāhu VvA 258; v. l. SS. ādu) = Pv IV.3[17] (ādu) = DhA I.31 (T. ādu, v. l. adu); Vv 63[1] (v. l. ādu); J V.330 (T. ādu, C. adu; expld. on p. 331 fantastically as aduñ ca aduñ ca kammaŋ karohī ti). See also **ādu.**

Aduŋ nt. of pron. **asu.**

Adūsaka (adj.) [a + dūsaka] innocent J V.143 (= niraparādha C.); VI.84, 552. f. **adūsikā** Sn 312.

Adūsiya = adūsaka J V.220 (= anaparādha C.).

Adeti [Sk. ādayati, Caus. of atti, **ad** to eat, 1st sg. admi = Gr. ἔδω, Lat. edo; Goth. itan = Ohg. ezzan = E. eat] to eat. Pres. ind. **ademi** etc. J V.31, 92, 197, 496; VI.106. pot. **adeyya** J V.107, 392, 493.

Adda[1] [cp. Sk. ārdraka] ginger J I.244 (°singivera).

Adda[2] & **Addā** 3rd sg. aor. of *dassati; see *dassati 2. a.

Adda[3] (adj.) [Sk. ārdra, from ṛdati or ardati to melt, cp. Gr. ἄρδω to moisten, ἄρδα dirt; see also alla] wet, moist, slippery J IV.353; VI.309; Miln 346.

-āvalepana "smeared with moisture", i. e. shiny, glittering S IV.187 (kūṭāgāra); M I.86 = Nd[2] 99[6] (upakāriyo). See also addha[2].

Addakkhi 3rd sg. aor. of *dassati; see *dassati 1 b.

Addasā 3rd sg. aor. of *dassati; see *dassati 2 a.

Addā & **Addāyanā** at Vbh 371 in def. of anādariya is either faulty writing, or dial. form or pop. etym. for ādā and ādāyana; see ādariya.

Addāyate [v. denom. fr. adda] to be or get wet, fig. to be attached to J IV.351. See also allīyati.

Addi [Sk. ardri] a mountain Dāvs II.13.

Addita (pp.) [see aṭṭita which is the more correct spelling] afflicted, smarted, oppressed J I.21; II.407; III.261; IV.295; V.53, 268; Th 1, 406; Mhvs 1, 25; PvA 260; Sdhp 37, 281.

Addha[1] (num.) [= aḍḍha, q. v.] one half, half (°—) D I.166 (°māsika); A II.160 (°māsa); J I.59 (°**yojana**); III. 189 (°māsa).

Addha[2] (adj.) [= adda[3], Sk. ārdra] soiled, wet; fig. attached to, intoxicated with (cp. sineha) M II.223 (na anaddhabhūtaŋ attānaŋ dukkhena addhabhāveti he dirties the impure self with ill); S III.1 (addhabhūto kāyo impure body); J VI.548 (°nakha with dirty nails, C. pūtinakha).

Addhan (in cpds. **addha**°) [Vedic adhvan, orig. meaning "stretch, length", both of space & time. — Cases: *nom.* addhā, *gen. dat.* addhuno, *instr.* addhunā, *acc.* addhānaŋ, *loc.* addhani; *pl.* addhā. See also addhāna] 1. (of space) a path, road, also journey (see cpds. & derivations); only in *one* ster. phrase J IV.384 = V.137 (**pathaddhuno paṇṇarase va cando**, gen. for loc. °addhani, on his course, in his orbit; expld. at IV.384 by ākāsa-patha-sankhātassa addhuno majjhe ṭhito and at V.137 by pathaddhagato addha-pathe gaganamajjhe ṭhito); Pv III.3[1] (**pathaddhani** paṇṇarase va cando; loc. same meaning as prec., expld. at PvA 188 by attano pathabhūte addhani gaganatala-magge). This phrase (pathaddhan) however is expld. by Kern (Toev. s. v. pathaddu) as "gone half-way", i. e. on full-moon-day. He rejects the expln. of C. — 2. (of time) a stretch of time, an interval of time, a period, also a lifetime (see cpds.); only in *two* standard applications viz. (a) as mode of time (past, present & future) in **tayo addhā** three divisions of time (atīta, anāgata, paccuppanna) D III.216; It 53, 70. (b) in phrase **dīghaŋ addhānaŋ** (acc.) a very long time A II.1, 10 (dīghaŋ **addhānaŋ** saŋsāraŋ); Sn 740 (dīghaŋ addhāna saŋsāra); Dh 207 (dīghaŋ addhāna socati); J I.137. gen. dīghassa addhuno PvA 148 (gatattā because a long time has elapsed), instr. dīghena addhunā S I.78; A II.118; PvA 28.

-āyu duration of life A II.66 (dīghaŋ °ŋ a long lifetime. **-gata** one who has gone the road or traversed the space or span of life, an old man [cp. BSk. adhvagata M Vastu II.150], always combd. with **vayo anuppatto,** sometimes in ster. formula with **jiṇṇa** & **mahallaka** Vin II.188; D I.48 (cp. DA I.143); M I.82; Sn pp. 50, 92; PvA 149. **-gū** [Vedic adhvaga] a wayfarer, traveller, journeyman Th 255 = S I.212 (but the latter has panthagu, v. l. addhagū); J III.95 (v. l. patthagu = panthagu); Dh 302.

Addhā (adv.) [Vedic addhā, cp. Av. azdā certainty] part. of affirmation and emphasis: certainly, for sure, really, truly D I.143; J I.19 (a. ahaŋ Buddho bhavissāmi) 66 (a. tvaŋ Buddho bhavissasi), 203, 279: III.340; V.307, 410 (C. expln. differs) Sn 47, 1057; Nd[2] 30 = Ps II.21 (ekaŋsa-vacanaŋ nissaŋsaya-vacanaŋ etc.) addhā hi J IV. 399; Pv IV.1[52].

Addhaneyya (adj.) = adhaniya 2, lasting J V.507 (an°).

Addhaniya (adj.) [fr. addhan] 1. belonging to the road' fit for travelling (of the travelling season) Th 1, 529. — 2. belonging to a (long) time, lasting a long geriod, lasting, enduring D III.211; J I.393 (an°) VI.71. See also addhaneyya.

Addhariya [Vedic adhvaryu fr. adhvara sacrifice] a sacrificing priest. N. of a class of Brahmins D I.237 (brāhmaṇa).

Addhāna (nt.) [orig. the acc. of **addhan,** taken as nt. from phrase dīghaŋ addhānaŋ. It occurs only in acc. which may always be taken as acc. of addhan; thus the assumption of a special form addhāna would be superfluous, were it not for later forms like addhāne (loc.) Miln 126; PvA 75 v.l. BB, and for cpds.] same meaning as **addhan,** but as simplex only used with reference to time (i. e. a long time, cp. VvA 117 addhānaŋ = ciraŋ). Usually in phrase **atītaŋ** (anāgataŋ etc.) **addhānaŋ** in the past (future etc.), e. g. D I.200; S I.140: A V.32; Miln 126 (anāgatamaddhāne for °aŋ); PvA 75 (v. l. addhāne). **dīghaŋ addhānaŋ** Pv I.10[5]. Also in phrase **addhānaŋ āpādeti** to make out the length of time or period, i. e. to live out one's lifetime S IV.110; J II.293 (= jīvitaddhānaŋ āpādi āyuŋ vindi C).

-daratha exhaustion from travelling DA I.287. **-magga** a (proper) road for journeying, a long road between two towns, high road D I.1, 73, 79; M I.276 (kantār°); DA I.35 (interpreted as "addhayojanaŋ gacchissāmī ti bhuñjitabban ti ādi vacanato addha-yojanam pi addhāna maggo hoti", thus taken to addha "half", from counting by ½ miles); VvA 40, 292. Cp. also antarāmagga. **-parissama** "fatigue of the road", i. e. fatigue from travelling VvA 305. **-vemattatā** difference of time or period Miln 285 (+ āyuvemattatā).

Addhika [fr. addhan] a wanderer, wayfarer, traveller DA I.298 (= pathāvin), 270; PvA 78, 127 (°jana people travelling). Often comb^{d.} with kapaṇa beggar, tramp, as **kapaṇaddhikā** (pl.) tramps and travellers (in which connection also as °iddhika, q. v.), e. g. J I.6 (v. l. °iddhika 262; DhA II.26.

Addhita at Pv II.6² is to be corrected to **aṭṭita** (sic v. l. BB).

Addhin (adj.) (—°) [fr. addhan] belonging to the road or travelling, one who is on the road, a traveller, in gataddhin one who has performed his journey (= addhagata) Dh 90.

Addhuva see **dhuva**.

Adrūbhaka see **dubbha**.

Advejjhatā see **dvejjhatā**.

Adha° in cpds. like adhagga see under adho.

Adhamma see **dhamma**.

Adhama (adj.) [Vedic adhama = Lat. infimus, superl. of adho, q. v.] the lowest (lit. & fig.), the vilest, worst Sn 12 (narâdhama), 135 (vasalâdhama); Dh 78 (purisa°); J III.151 (miga°); V.394 (uttamâdhama), 437 (id.), 397; Sdhp 387.

Adhara (adj.) [Vedic adhara, compar. of adho] the lower J III.26 (adharoṭṭha the l. lip).

Adhi [Vedic adhi; base of demonstr. pron. a° + suffix-dhi, corresponding in form to Gr. ἔν-θα "on this" = here, cp. ὅθι where, in meaning equal to adv. of direction Gr. δέ (toward) = Ohg. zuo, E. to].

A. Prep. and pref. of direction & place: (a) as direction denoting a movement towards a definite end or goal = up to, over, toward, to, on (see C 1 a). — (b) as place where (prep. c. loc. or abs.) = on top of, above, over, in; in addition to. Often simply deictic "here" (e. g.) ajjhatta = adhi + ātman "this self here" (see C 1 b).

B. adhi is freq. as modification pref., i. e. in loose comp^{n.} with n. or v. and as first part of a double prefix-cpd., like ajjhā° (adhi + ā), adhippa° (adhi + pra), but never occurs as a fixed base, i. e. as 2nd part of a pref.-cpd., like ā in paccā° (prati + ā), paryā° (pari + ā) or **ava** in paryava° (pari + ava) or **ud** in abhyud° (abhi + ud), samud° (sam + ud). As such (i. e. modification) it is usually intensifying, meaning "over above, in addition, quite, par excellence, super"-(adhideva a super-god, cp. ati-deva), but very often has lost this power & become meaningless (like E. up in "shut up, fill up, join up etc), esp. in double pref.-cpds. (ajjhāvasati "to dwell here-in" = āvasati "to dwell in, to inhabit") (see C 2). — In the expl^{ns} of P. Commentators adhi is often (sometimes far-fetchedly) interpreted by abhibhū "overpowering" see e. g. C. on adhiṭṭhāti & adhiṭṭhita; and by virtue of this intens. meaning we find a close relationship between the prefixes **ati, adhi** and **abhi**, all interchanging dialectically so that P. adhi often represents Sk. ati or abhi; thus adhi > ati in adhikusala, °kodhita, °jeguccha, °brahmā; adhi > abhi in adhippatthita, °pāteti, °ppāya, °ppeta, °bādheti, °bhū, °vāha. Cp. also ati IV.

C. The main applications of adhi are the foll.: 1. *primary meaning* (in verbs & verb derivations): either direction in which or place where, depending on the meaning of the verb determinate, either lit. or fig. — (a) *where to*: adhiyita (adhi + ita) "gone on to or into" = studied; ajjhesita (adhi + esita) "wished for"; °kata "put to" i. e. commissioned; °kāra commission; °gacchati "to go on to & reach it" = obtain; °gama attainment; °gaṇhāti to overtake = surpass, °peta (adhi + pra + ita) "gone in to" = meant, understood; °pāya sense meaning, intention; °bhāsati to speak to = address; °mutta intent upon; °vacana "saying in addition" = attribute, metaphor, cp. Fr. sur-nom; °vāsāna assent, °vāseti to dwell in, give in = consent. — (b) *where*: °tiṭṭhati (°ṭṭhāti) to stand by = look after, perform; °ṭṭhāna place where; °vasati to inhabit; °sayana "lying in", inhabiting. — 2. *secondary meaning* (as emphatic modification): (a) with nouns or adjectives: adhi-jeguccha very detestable; °matta "in an extreme measure", °pa supreme lord; °pacca lordship; °paññā higher, additional wisdom; °vara the very best; °sīla thorough character or morality. — (b) with verbs (in double pref.-cpds.); **adhi + ava**: ajjhogāheti plunge into; ajjhoṭhapeti to bring down to (its destination); °otthata covered completely; °oharati to swallow right down. **adhi + ā**: ajjhappatta having reached (the end); ajjhapīḷita quite overwhelmed; °āvuttha inhabited; °ārūhati grown up over; °āsaya desire, wish (cp. Ger. n. Anliegen & v. daranliegen). **adhi + upa**: ajjhupagacchati to reach, obtain; °upeti to receive; °upekkhati "to look all along over" = to superintend **adhi + pra**: adhippattheti to long for, to desire.

Note. The contracted (assimilation-)form of adhi before vowels is **ajjh-** (q. v.).

Adhika (adj.) [fr. adhi; cp. Sk. adhika] exceeding, extraordinary, superior, Pug 35; VvA 80 (= anadhivara, visiṭṭha); DA I.141, 222; Dpvs V.32 (an°); DhA III.238; KhA 193 (= anuttara); Sdhp 337, 447. — compar. **adhikatara** DhA II.7; III.176; nt. °ŋ as adv. extraordinarily PvA 86 (= adhimattaŋ). In comb^{n.} with *numerals* adhika has the meaning of "in addition, with an additional, plus" (cp. ādi + ādika, with which it is evidently confounded, adhika being constructed in the same way as ādika, i. e. preceding the noun-determination), e. g. catunahutâdhikāni dve yojana-sahassāni 2000 + 94 (= 294 000) J I.25; sattamāsâdhikāni sattavassāni 7 years and 7 months J V.319; paññāsâdhikāni pañca vassa-satani 500 + 50 (= 550) PvA 152. See also **sâdhika**.

Adhikata (adj.) [adhi + kata; cp. Sk. adhikṛta] 1. commissioned with, an overseer, Pv II.9²¹ (dāne adhikata = ṭhapita PvA 124). — 2. caused by Miln 67 (kamma°). — 3. affected by something, i. e. confused, puzzled, in doubt Miln 144 (+ vimātijāta).

Adhikaraṇa (nt.) [adhi + karaṇa] 1. attendance, supervision, management of affairs, administration PvA 209. — 2. relation, reference, reason, cause, consequence D II.59 (—°: in consequence of); S II.41; V.19. Esp. acc. °ŋ as adv. (—°) in consequence of, for the sake of, because of, from M I.410 (rūpâdhikaraṇaŋ); S IV.339 (rāga°); Miln 281 (mudda° for the sake of the royal seal, orig. in attendance on the r. s.). Kimâdhikaraṇaŋ why, on account of what J IV.4 (= kiŋkāraṇaŋ) yatvâdhikaraṇaŋ (yat + adhi°) by reason of what, since, because (used as conj.) D I.70 = A I.113 = II.16 = D III.225. — 3. case, question, cause, subject of discussion, dispute. There are 4 sorts of a. enum^{d.} at var. passages, viz. **vivāda° anuvāda° āpatta° kicca°** "questions of dispute, of censure, of misconduct, of duties" Vin II.88; III.164; IV.126, 238; M II.247. — Often ref.: Vin II.74; S IV.63 = V.346 (dhamma° a question of the Dh.); A I.53 (case), 79; II.239 (vūpasanta); V.71, 72; Pug 20, 55; DhA IV.2 (°ssa uppamassa vūpasama), adhikaraṇaŋ karoti to raise a dispute M I.122 °ŋ vūpasameti to settle a question or difficulty Vin II.261. **-kāraka** one who causes dispute discussions or dissent Vin IV.230 (f. °ikā); A III.252. **-samatha** the settlings of questions that have arisen. There are seven rules for settling cases enum^{d.} at D III.254; M II.247; A I.99; IV.144.

Adhikaraṇika [fr. adhikaraṇa] one who has to do with the settling of disputes or questions, a judge A V.164, 167.

Adhikaraṇī (f.) [to adhikaraṇa 1, orig. meaning "serving, that which serves, i. e. instrument"] a smith's anvil J III.285; Dāvs III.16 sq.; DhsA 263.

Adhikāra [cp. Sk. adhikāra] attendance, service, administration, supervision, management, help Vin I.55; J I.56;

VI.251; Miln 60, 115, 165; PvA 124 (dāna°; cp. Pv II.9²¹); DhA II.41.

Adhikārika (adj.) (—°) [to adhikāra] serving as, referring to Vin III.274 (Bdhgh).

Adhikuṭṭanā (f.) [adhi + koṭṭanā or koṭṭana] an executioner's block Th 2, 58; cp. ThA 65 (v. l. kuḍḍanā, should prob. be read koṭṭana); ThA 287.

Adhikusala (adj.) [adhi + kusala] in °ā dhammā "items of higher righteousness" D III.145.

Adhikodhita (adj.) [adhi + kodhita] very angry J V.117.

Adhigacchati [adhi + gacchati] to get to, to come into possession of, to acquire, attain, find; fig. to understand D I.229 (vivesaŋ) M I.140 (anvesaŋ n' âdhigacchanti do not find); S I.22 (Nibbānaŋ); II.278 (id.); A I.162 (id.); Dh 187, 365; It 82 (santiŋ); Th 2, 51; Pug 30, 31; Pv I.7⁴ (nibbutiŋ = labhati PvA 37); III.7¹⁰ (amataŋ padaŋ). opt. **adhigaccheyya** D I.224 (kusalaŋ dhammaŋ); M I.114 (madhu-piṇḍikaŋ); Dh 61 and **adhigacche** Dh 368. ger. °gantvā D I.224; J I.45 (ānisaŋse); and °gamma Pv I.11⁹ (= vinditvā paṭilabhitvā PvA 60). grd. °gantabba It 104 (nibbāna). cond. °gacchissaŋ Sn 446. 1st aor. 3 sg. **ajjhagā** Sn 225 (= vindi paṭilabhi KhA 180); Dh 154; Vv 32⁷; 3 pl. **ajjhagū** J I.256 (vyasanaŋ) & ajjhāgamuŋ S I.12. 2nd aor. 3 sg. **adhigacchi** Nd¹ 457. — pp. **adhigata** (q. v.).

Adhigaṇhāti [adhi + gaṇhāti] to surpass, excel S I.87 = DA I.32; D III.146; S IV.275; A III.33; It 19. Ger. **adhigayha** Pv II.9⁶² = DhA III.219 (v. l. BB at both pass. atikkamma); & **adhiggahetvā** It 20. — pp. **adhiggahīta** (q. v.).

Adhigata [pp. of adhigacchati] got into possession of, conquered, attained, found J I.374; VvA 135.

Adhigatavant (adj.-n.) [fr. adhigata] one who has found or obtained VvA 296 (Nibbānaŋ).

Adhigama [fr. adhigacchati] attainment, acquisition; also fig. knowledge, information, study (the latter mainly in Miln) D III.255; S II.139; A II.148; IV.22, 332; V.194; J I.406; Nett 91; Miln 133, 215, 358, 362, 388; PvA 207.

Adhigameti [adhi + gameti, Caus. of gacchati] to make obtain, to procure PvA 30.

Adhiggahīta [pp. of adhigaṇhāti] excelled, surpassed; overpowered, taken by (instr.), possessed J III.427 (= anuggahīta C.); V.102; VI.525 = 574; It 103; Miln 188, 189; Sdhp 98.

Adhiciṇṇa only at S III.12, where v. l. is **aviciṇṇa**, which is to be preferred. See viciṇṇa.

Adhicitta (nt.) [adhi + citta] "higher thought", meditation, contemplation, usually in combⁿ. with **adhisīla** and **adhipaññā** Vin 170; D III.219; M I.451; A I.254, 256; Nd¹ 39 = Nd² 689 (°sikkhā); Dh 185 (= aṭṭha-samāpatti-sankhāta adhika-citta DhA III.238).

Adhiceto (adj.) [adhi + ceto] lofty-minded, entranced Th 1, 68 = Ud 43 = Vin IV.54 = DhA III.384.

Adhicca¹ [ger. of adhi + eti, see adhīyati] learning, studying, learning by heart J III.218, 327 = IV.301; IV.184 (vede = adhīyitvā C.), 477 (sajjhāyitvā C.); VI.213; Miln 164.

Adhicca² (°—) [Sk. *adhṛtya, a + *dhicca, ger. of **dhṛ**, cp. dhāra, dhāraṇa 3, dhāreti 4] unsupported, uncaused, fortuitous, without cause or reason; in foll. phrases: °**āpattika** guilty without intention M I.443; °**uppatti** spontaneous origin DhsA 238; °**laddha** obtained without being asked for, unexpectedly Vv 84²² = J V.171 = VI 315 (explᵈ. at J V.171 by ahetunā, at VI.316 by akāraṇena) °samuppanna arisen without a cause, spontaneous, unconditioned D I.28 = Ud 69; D III.33, 138; S II.223 (sukhadukkhaŋ); A III.440 (id.); Ps I.155; DA I.118 (= akāraṇa°).

Adhicca³ (adj.) [= adhicca 2 in adj. function, influenced by, homonym abhabba] without a cause (for assumption), unreasonable, unlikely S V.457.

Adhijeguccha (nt.) [adhi + jeguccha] intense scrupulous regard (for others) D I.174, 176.

Adhiṭṭhaka (adj.) (—°) [fr. adhiṭṭhāti] bent on, given to, addicted to J V.427 (surā°).

Adhiṭṭhāti (adhiṭṭhahati) [Sk. adhitiṣṭhati, adhi + **sthā**] 1. to stand on J III.278 (ger. °āya); DhA IV.183 (ger. °hitvā); fig. to insist on Th 1, 1131 (aor. °āhi). — 2. to concentrate or fix one's attention on (c. acc.), to direct one's thoughts to, to make up one's mind, to wish Vin I.115 (inf. °ṭhātuŋ), 297 (id.), 125 (grd. °ṭhātabba) J I.80 (aor. °ahi); III.278; IV.134 (v. l. ati° C. explˢ. abhibhavitvā tiṭṭhati); DhA I.34; IV.201 (ger. °hitvā); PvA 23 (aor. °ṭhāsi) 171 (id.), 75 (ger. °hitvā). On adhiṭṭheyya see *Cpd.* 209, n. 2; 219, n. 1. — 3. to undertake, practice, perform, look after, to celebrate S II.17; A I.115 sq.; J I.50; PvA 209 (ger. °ṭhāya). — pp. adhiṭṭhita (q. v.).

Adhiṭṭhāna (nt.) [fr. adhi + **sthā**] 1. decision, resolution, self-determination, will (cp. on this meaning *Cpd.* 62) D III.229 (where 4 are enumᵈ., viz. paññā°, sacca° cāga° upasama°); J I.23; V.174; Ps I.108; II.171 sq., 207; DhsA 166 (cp. *Dhs. trsl.* 44). — 2. mentioned in bad sense with **abhinivesa** and **anusaya**, obstinacy, prejudice and bias M I.136; III.31, 240; S II.17; III.10, 135, 194. — As adj. (—°) applying oneself to, bent on A III.363. — 3. looking after, management, direction, power Miln 309 (devānaŋ); PvA 141 (so read for adhitaṭṭhāna). [adiṭṭhāna as PvA 89, used as explanatory for āvāsa, should perhaps be read **adhiṭṭhāna** in the sense of fixed, permanent, abode].

Adhiṭṭhāyaka (adj.) (—°) superintending, watching, looking after, in **kamma°** Mhvs 5, 175; 30, 98; **kammanta°** DhA I.393.

Adhiṭṭhita (adj.) [pp. of adhiṭṭhāti] 1. standing on (c. loc.), esp. with the idea of standing above, towering over Vv 63³⁰ (hemarathe a. = sakalaŋ ṭhānaŋ abhibhavitvā ṭhita VvA 269). — (a) looked after, managed, undertaken, governed Vin I.57; S V.278 (sv'âdhiṭṭhita); PvA 141 (kammanta). — (b) undertaking, bent on (c. acc.) Sn 820 (ekacariyaŋ).

Adhideva [adhi + deva] a superior or supreme god, above the gods M II.132; A IV.304; Sn 1148; Nd² 307ᵇ, 422 a. Cp. atideva.

Adhipa [Sk. adhipa, abbrev. of adhipati] ruler, lord, master J II.369; III.324; V.393; Pv II.8⁶ (jan° king); Dāvs III.52; VvA 314.

Adhipaka (adj.) (—°) [fr. prec.] mastering, ruling or governed, influenced by (cp. adhipati) A I.150 (atta° loka° dhamma°).

Adhipajjati [adhi + pajjati] to come to, reach, attain A IV.96 (anatthaŋ); pp. **adhipanna**.

Adhipaññā (f.) [adhi + paññā] higher wisdom or knowledge, insight (cp. jhāna & paññā); usually in combⁿ. with adhicitta & adhisīla Vin I.70; D I.174; III.219 (°sikkhā); A I.240; II.92 sq., 239; III.106 sq., 327; IV.360; Nd¹ 39 (id.); Ps I.20, 25 sq., 45 sq., 169; II.11, 244; Pug 61.

Adhipatati [adhi + patati] to fly past, vanish J IV.111 (= ativiya patati sīghaŋ atikkamati C.). — Caus. **adhipāteti** (q. v.) in diff. meaning. Cp also adhipāta.

Adhipatana (nt.) [fr. adhipatati] attack, pressing ThA 271.

Adhipati (n.-adj.) [adhi + pati, cp. adhipa] 1. ruler, master J IV.223; Vv 81[1]; Miln 388; DhA 1.36 (= seṭṭha). — 2. ruling over, governing, predominant; ruled or governed by Vbh 216 sq. (chandaŋ adhipatiŋ katvā making energy predominant); DhsA 125, 126 (atta° autonomous, loka° heteronomous, influenced by society). See also *Dhs. trsl.* 20 & *Cpd.* 60.

Adhipateyya (nt.) A 1.147; III 33 = S IV.275 is probably misreading for ādhipateyya.

Adhipatthita [pp. adhi + pattheti, cp. Sk. abhi + arthayati] desired, wished, begged for D 1.120.

Adhipanna [cp. Sk. abhipanna, adhi + **pad**] gone into, affected with, seized by (—°), a victim of (c. loc.) S 1.72, Th 2, 345 (kāmesu); Sn 1123 (taṇhā° = taṇhānugata Nd[2] 32); Dh 288; J III.38, 369; IV.396; V.91, 379 (= dosena ajjhotthaṭa); VI.27.

Adhipāṭimokkha (nt.) [adhi + pāṭimokkha] the higher, moral, code Vin V.1 (pāṭim° +); M II.245 (+ ajjhājīva).

Adhipāta[1] [adhipāteti] splitting, breaking, only in phrase **muddhā**° head-splitting Sn 988 sq., 1004, 1025 (v. l. Nd[2] °vipāta).

Adhipāta[2] [from adhipatati = Sk. atipatati, to fly past, flit] a moth Sn 964. Expl[d]. at Nd[1] 484 as "adhipātikā ti tā uppatitvā khādanti taŋkāraṇā a. vuccanti"; Ud 72 (expl[d]. by C. as salabhā).

Adhipatikā (f.) [fr. adhipāta[2]] a moth, a mosquito Nd[1] 484 (see adhipāta[2]).

Adhipāteti [Caus. fr. adhipatati, cp. Sk. abhipātayati & P. atipāteti] to break, split J IV.337 (= chindati). At Ud 8 prob. to be read **adhibādheti** (v. l. avibādeti. T. adhipāteti).

Adhippagharati [adhi + ppa + gharati] to flow, to trickle ThA 284.

Adhippāgā 3 sg. aor. of adhippagacchati to go to J V.59.

Adhippāya [adhi + ppa + **i**; Sk. abhiprāya] 1. intention, wish desire S 1.124; V.108; A II.81; III.363 (bhoga°); V.65; J 1.79, 83; Sdhp 62. As adj. (—°) desiring PvA 226 (hass° in play = khiḍḍatthika). — 2. sense, meaning, conclusion, inference (cp. adhigama) Miln 148; PvA 8, 16, 48, 131 (the moral of a story). -adhippāyena (instr.) in the way of, like PvA 215 (kiḷ for fun).

Adhippāyosa [adhi + pāyosa] distinction, difference, peculiarity, special meaning M 146; S III.66; IV.208; A 1.267; IV.158; V.48 sq.

Adhippeta [Sk. abhipreta, adhi + ppa + **i**, lit. gone into, gone for; cp. adhippāya] 1. desired, approved of, agreeable D 1.120; II.236; VvA 312, 315. — 2. meant, understood, intended as J III.263; PvA 9, 80, 120, 164.

Adhippetatta (nt.) [abstr. fr. adhippeta] the fact of being meant or understood as, in abl. °ā with reference to, as is to be understood of VvA 13; PvA 52.

Adhibādheti [adhi + bādheti, cp. Sk. abhibādhayati] to vex, oppress, gore (to death) Ud 8 (T. adhipāteti, v. l. avibādeti).

Adhibrahmā [adhi + Brahmā, cp. atibrahmā] a superior Brahmā, higher than Brahmā M II.132.

Adhibhavati [adhi + bhavati, cp. Sk. & P. abhibhavati] to overcome, overpower, surpass S IV.185 sq. (cp. adhibhū); A V.248, 282 (°bhoti); J II.336; V.30. — aor. **adhibhavi** J II.80. 3. pl. **adhibhaŋsu** S IV.185. See also ajjhabhavi & ajjhabhū. pp. **adhibhūta** (q. v.).

Adhibhāsati [adhi + bhāsati] to address, to speak to; aor. **ajjhabhāsi** Vin II.195; S 1.103; IV.117; Sn p. 87; PvA 56, 90.

Adhibhū (adj.) (—°) [fr. adhi + **bhū**, cp. adhibhavati & Sk. adhibhū] overpowering, having power over; master, conqueror, lord S IV.186 (anadhibhū not mastering. For **adhibhūta** the v. l. abhi° is to be preferred as more usual in this connection, see abhibhū); Sn 684 (miga°; v. l. abhi°).

Adhibhūta [cp. adhibhū & adhibhūta] overpowered S IV.186.

Adhimatta (adj.) [adhi + matta of **mā**] extreme, exceeding, extraordinary; nt. adv. °ŋ extremely M 1.152, 243; S IV. 160; A II.150; IV.241; J 1.92; Pug 15; Miln 146, 189, 274, 290; Pv II.3[6] (= adhikataraŋ PvA 86); DhA II.85; cp. PvA 281.

Adhimattata (nt.) [abstr. fr. prec.] preponderance A II.150; DhsA 324 (cp. *Dhs. trsl.* 200).

Adhimana (n.-adj.) [adhi + mano] (n.) attention, direction of mind, concentration Sn 692 (adhimanasā bhavātha). — (adj.) directing one's mind upon, intent (on) J IV.433 (= pasannacitta); V.29 (an°; v. l. °māna).

Adhimāna [adhi + māna] undue estimate of oneself M II.252; A V.162 sq.

Adhimānika (adj.) [fr. adhimāna] having undue confidence in oneself, conceited A V 162, 169, 317; DhA III.111.

Adhimuccati [Pass. of adhi + **muc**] 1. to be drawn to, feel attached to or inclined towards, to indulge in (c. loc.) S III.225; IV.185; A IV.24, 145 sq., 460; V.17; Pug 63. — 2. to become settled, to make up one's mind as to (with loc.), to become clear about Vin 1.209 (aor. °mucci); D 1.106; S 1.116 (pot. °mucceyya); It 43; DA 1.275. — 3. to take courage, to have faith Sn 559; Miln 234; DA 1.214, 316; J IV.272; V.103; DhH 1.196; III.258; IV.170. — 4. of a spirit, to possess, to enter into a body, with loc. of the body. A late idiom for the older anvāvisati. J IV.172; V.103, 429; DhA 1.196; III.258; IV.170. — pp. adhimuccita and **adhimutta**. — Caus. **adhimoceti** to incline to (trs.); to direct upon (with loc.) S V.409 (cittaŋ devesu a.).

Adhimuccana (nt.) [fr. adhi + **muc**] making up one's mind, confidence DhsA 133, 190.

Adhimuccita & **Adhimucchita** (pp.) [either adhi + **muc** or **mūrch**; it would seem more probable to connect it with the former (cp. adhimuccati) and consider all vv. ll. °mucchita as spurious; but in view of the credit of several passages we have to assume a regular analogy-form °mucchita, cp. mucchati and see also *JPTS* 1886, 109] drawn towards, attached to, infatuated, indulging in (with loc.) M II.223 (an°); S 1.113; Th 1, 732 (v. l. °muccita), 923 (cch), 1175; J II.437 (cch); III.242; V.255 (kāmesu °mucchita, v. l. °muccita). Cp. ajjhomucchita.

Adhimuccitar [n. ag. of adhimuccati] one who determines for something, easily trusting, giving credence A III.165 (v. l. °mucchitā).

Adhimutta (adj.) [pp. of adhimuccati, cp. BSk. adhimukta. Av. Ś 1.8, 112; Divy 49, 302 etc.] intent upon (—° or with loc. or acc.), applying oneself to, keen on, inclined to, given to Vin 1.183; A V.34, 38; Dh 226; Sn 1071, 1149 (°citta); Nd[2] 33; J 1.370 (dān°) Pug 26; PvA 134 (dān°).

Adhimutti (f.) [adhi + mutti] resolve, intention, disposition D 1.174; A V.36; Ps 1.124; Miln 161, 169; Vbh 340, 341; DA 1.44, 103; Sdhp 378.

Adhimuttika (adj.) [= adhimutta] inclined to, attached to, bent on S II.154, 158; It 70; Vbh 339 sq. + tā (f.) inclination D I.2.

Adhimokkha [fr. adhi + **muc**] firm resolve, determination, decision M III.25 sq.; Vbh 165 sq., 425; DhsA 145, 264. See *Dhs. trsl.* 5; *Cpd.* 17, 40, 95.

Adhiyita see adhīyati.

Adhiroha [fr. adhi + **ruh**] ascent, ascending; in **dur°** hard to ascend Miln 322.

Adhivacana (nt.) [adhi + vacana] designation, term, attribute, metaphor, metaphorical expression D II.62; M I.113, 144, 460; A II.70, 124; III.310; IV.89, 285, 340; It 15, 114; Sn p. 218; J I.117; Nd² 34 = Dhs 1306 (= nāma sankhā paññatti etc.); Vbh 6; PvA 63. See on term *Dhs. trsl.* 340.
-**patha** "process of synonymous nomenclature" (Mrs. Rh. D.) D II.68; S III.71; Dhs 1306; DhsA 51.

Adhivattati [adhi + vattati] to come on, proceed, issue, result S I.101; A II.32.

Adhivattha (adj.) [pp. of adhivasati] inhabiting, living in (c. loc.) Vin I.28; S I.197; J I.223; II.385; III.327; PvA 17. The form **adhivuttha** occurs at J VI.370.

Adhivara (adj.) [adhi + vara] superb, excellent, surpassing Vv 16³ (an° unsurpassed, unrivalled; VvA 80 = adhika, visiṭṭha).

Adhivāsa [fr. adhi + **vas**] endurance, forbearance, holding out; only as adj. in **dur°** difficult to hold out Th I, 111.

Adhivāsaka (& °**ika**) (adj.) [fr. adhivāsa] willing, agreeable, enduring, patient Vin IV.130; M I.10, 526; A II.118; III.163; V.132; J III.369 (an°); IV.11, 77.

Adhivāsana (nt.) [fr. adhi + **vas**] 1 assent A III.31; DhA I.33. — 2. forbearance, endurance M I.10; J II.237; III.263; IV.307; V.174.

Adhivāsanatā (f.) [abstr. fr. adhivāsana] patience, endurance, Dhs 1342; Vbh 360 (an°).

Adhivāseti [Caus. of adhivasat., cp. BSk. adhivāsayati in meaning of 3] 1. to wait for (c. acc.) J I.254; II.352; III.277. — 2. to have patience, bear, endure (c. acc.) D II.128, 157; J I.46; III.281 (pahāre); IV.279, 407; V.51, 200; VvA 336, 337. — 3. to consent, agree, give in Vin I.17; D I.109 (cp. DA I.277); S IV.76; DhA I.33; PvA 17, 20, 75 and freq. passim. — Caus. **adhivāsāpeti** to cause to wait J I.254.

Adhivāha [fr. adhi + **vah**; cp. Sk. abhivahati] a carrier, bearer, adj. bringing S IV.70 (dukkha°); A I.6; Th I, 494.

Adhivāhana (nt.-adj.) [fr. adhi + **vah**] carrying, bringing, bearing Sn 79; f. °ī Th I, 519.

Adhivimuttatta (nt.) = adhivimokkhatta & adhimutti, i. e. propensity, the fact of being inclined or given to J V.254 (T. kāmādhivimuttita, v. l. °muttata).

Adhivimokkhatta (nt.) = adhimokkha; being inclined to DhsA 261.

Adhivutti (f.) [adhi + vutti, fr. adhi + **vac**, cp. Sk. abhivadati] expression, saying, opinion; only in tt. **adhivutti-pada** (v. l. **adhimutti-p.** at all passages) D I.13 (expl^d. by adhivacana-pada DA I.103); M II.228; A V.36.

Adhivuttha see **adhivattha.**

Adhisayana (nt.-adj.) [fr. adhiseti] lying on or in, inhabiting PvA 80 (mañcaŋ).

Adhisayita [pp. of adhiseti] sat on, addled (of eggs) Vin III.3; S III.153.

Adhisīla (nt.) [adhi + sīla] higher morality, usually in threefold set of **adhicitta-sikkha, adhipaññā° adhisīla°** Vin I.70; D I.174; III.219; A III.133; IV.25; DhA I.334; PvA 207. See also adhicitta, sikkhā & sīla.

Adhiseti [adhi + **seti**] to lie on, sit on, live in, to follow, pursue Dh 41; Sn 671 (= gacchati C.) — pp. **adhisayita.**

Adhīna (adj.) (—°) [cp. Sk. adhīna] subject, dependent D I.72 (atta° & para°); J IV.112; DA I.217; also written **ādhīna** J V.350. See also under para.

Adhīyati & adhiyati [Med. of adhi + **i**, 1st sg. adhīye taken as base in Pāli] to study, lit. to approach (cp. adhigacchati); to learn by heart (the Vedas & other Sacred Books) Vin I.270; S I.202 (dhammapadāni); J IV.184 (adhīyitvā), 496 (adhīyamāna); VI.458; DhA III.446 (adhīyassu). — ger. **adhīyitvā** J IV.75; **adhiyānaŋ** J V.450 (= sajjhāyitvā C.) & **adhicca**: see adhicca 2; pp. **adhiyita** D I.96.

Adhunā (adv.) [Vedic adhunā] just now, quite recently D II.208; Vin II.185 (kālakata); Miln 155; Dāvs II.94.
-**āgata** a new comer M I.457; J II.105. -**âbhisitta** newly or just anointed D II.227. -**uppanna** just arisen D II.208, 221.

Adhura (nt.) [a + dhura, see dhura 2] irresponsibility, indifference to oblihations J IV.241.

Adho (adv.) [Vedic adhaḥ; compar. adharaḥ = Lat. inferus, Goth. undar, E. under, Ind. *n̥dher-; superl. adhamaḥ = Lat. infimus] below, usually comb^d. or contrasted with **uddhaŋ** "above" and **tiriyaŋ** "across", describing the 3 dimensions. — **uddhaŋ** and **adho** above and below, marking zenith & nadir. Thus with uddhaŋ and the 4 bearings **(disā)** and intermediate points **(anudisā)** at S I.122; III.124; A IV.167; with uddhaŋ & tiriyaŋ at Sn 150, 537, 1055, 1068. Expl^d. at KhA 248 by heṭṭhā and in detail (dogmatically & speculatively) at Nd² 155. For further ref. see uddhaŋ. The comp^n. form of adho before vowels is adh°.
-**akkhaka** beneath the collar-bone Vin IV.213. -**agga** with the points downward (of the upper row of teeth) J V.156 (+ uddh° expl^d. by uparima-danta C.). -**kata** turned down, or upside down J I.20; VI.298. -**gata** gone by, past. Adv. °ŋ since (cp. uddhaŋ adv. later or after) J VI.187 (ito māsaŋ adhogataŋ since one month ago). -**gala** (so read for T. udho°) down the throat PvA 104. -**mukha** head forward, face downward, bent over, upturned Vin II.78; M I.132, 234: Vv 16¹ (= heṭṭhā mukha VvA 78). -**bhāga** the lower part (of the body) M I.473; DhA I.148. -**virecana** action of a purgative (opp. uddha° of an emetic) D I.12; DA I.98 (= adho dosānaŋ nīharaṇaŋ); DhsA 404. -**sākhaŋ** (+ uddhamūlaŋ) branches down (& roots up, i. e. uprooted) DhA I.75. -**sira** (adj.) head downward J IV.194. -**siraŋ** (adv.) with bowed head (cp. avaŋsiraŋ) J VI.298 (= siraŋ adhokatvā heṭṭhāmukho C.). -**sīsa** (adj.) head first, headlong J I.233; V.472 (°ka).

An- form of the neg. prefix a-before vowels. For negatives beginning with an° see the positive.

Ana- negative prefix, contained in **anappameyya,** (Th I, 1089), **anamatagga** & **anabhava.** See *Vinaya Texts* II.113.

Anajjhiṭṭha (adj.) [an + ajjhiṭṭha] uncalled, unbidden, unasked Vin I.113; Pv I.12³ (T. anabbhita, v. l. anijjhiṭṭha; J III.165 has **anavhāta;** Th 2, 129 **ayācita;** PvA 64 expl^s. by anavhāta).

Anabhāva [ana + bhāva] the utter cessation of becoming. In the oldest Pali only in adj. form anabhāvaŋ kata or gata. This again found only in a string of four adjectives together expressing the most utter destruction. They are used at Vin III.3 of bad qualities, at S II.63 of certain wrong opinions, at M I.487; S IV.62 = V.527 of the khandas, at M I.331 of the Mental Intoxications (Āsavas), at A IV.73 of certain tastes, of a bad kamma A I.135, of evil passions A I.137, 184, 218; II.214 of pride A II.41, of craving A II.249, of the bonds A IV.8. In the supplement to the Dīgha (D III.326) and in the Iti-vuttaka (p. 115) a later idiom, anabhāvaŋ gameti, cause to perish, is used of evil thoughts. Bdhgh (quoted Vin III.267) reports as v. l. anubhāva. Cp. Nd I.90; and Nd² under pahīna.

Anabbhita (adj.) [an + abbhita] not restored, not to be restored Vin IV.242; Pv I.12³ (where reading prob. faulty & due to a gloss; the id. p. at Th 2, 129 has ayācita & at J III.165 **anavhāta**; PvA 64 expls. by anavhāta, v. l. anabbhita).

Anabhuṇṇatatā (f.) [an + abbhuṇṇata + tā] the state of not being erect, i. e. hanging down J v.156.

Anabhijjhā (f.) [an + abhijjhā] absence of covetousness or desire D III.229, 269; Dhs 32, 35, 277.

Anabhijjhālū (adj.) [an + abhijjhālū] not greedy or covetous D III.82; Pug 40.

Anabhijjhita (adj.) [an + abhijjhita] not desired Sn 40 (cp. Nd² 38); Vv 47⁴ (= na abhikankhita VvA 201).

Anabhinandati etc. see abhi° etc.

Anabhirata (adj.) [an + abhirata] not taking delight in J I.61 (naccādisu).

Anabhirati (f.) [an + abhirati] not delighting in, dissatisfaction, discontent D I.17 (+ paritassanā); III.289; J III. 395; DA I.111.

Anabhiraddha (adj.) [an + abhiraddha] in anger Vin IV.236.

Anabhiraddhi (f.) [an + abhiraddhi] anger, wrath D I.3 (= kopass'etaŋ adhivacanaŋ DA I.52).

Anabhisambhuṇamāna (adj.) [ppr. med. of an + abhisambhuṇāti] not obtaining, unable to get or keep up D I.101 (= asampāpuṇanto avisahamāno vā DA I.268).

Anamatagga (adj.) [ana (= a neg.) + mata (fr. **man**) + aggā (pl.). So Dhammapāla (avidit-agga ThA 289); Ñāṇakitti in Ṭīkā on DhsA 11; Trenckner, *Notes* 64; Oldenberg, *Vin. Texts* II.114. Childers takes it as an + amata + agga, and Jacobi (*Erzähl.* 33 and 89) and Pischel (*Gram.* § 251) as a + namat (fr. **nam**) + agga. It is Sanskritized at Divy 197 by anavarāgra, doubtless by some mistake. Weber, *Ind. Str.* III.150 suggests an + āmrta, which does not suit the context at all]. Ep. of Saṃsāra "whose beginning and end are alike unthinkable", i. e., without beginning or end. Found in two passages of the Canon: S II.178, 187 sq. = III.149, 151 = v.226, 441 (quoted Kvu 29, called Anamatagga-pariyāya at DhA II.268) and Th 2, 495, 6. Later references are Nd² 664; PvA 166; DhA I.11; II.13, 32; Sdhp 505. [Cp. anāmata and amatagga, and cp. the English idiom "world without end". The meaning can best be seen, not from the derivation (which is uncertain), but from the examples quoted above from the Saṃyutta. According to the Yoga, on the contrary (see e. g., Woods, *Yoga-system of Patañjali*, 119), it is a possible, and indeed a necessary quality of the Yogī, to understand the beginning and end of Saṃsāra].

Anamha (adj.) [according to Morris *J P T S* 1884, 70 = ana-mha "unlaughing" with ana = an (cp. anabhāva & anamatagga) and mha from **smi**, cp. vimhayati = Sk. vismayati] being in consternation or distress, crying J III. 223 (°kāle = ārodana-kāle C.).

Anaya [a + naya] misfortune, distress Miln 277, usually combd. with **vyasana** (as also in BSk, e. g. Jtm 215) Vin II.199; S IV.159; A v.156; Miln 292; VvA 327; Sdhp 362.

Anariya (adj.) [an + ariya, see also anāriya] not Aryan, ignoble, low Vin I.10; D III.232 (°vohāra, 3 sets of 4; the same at Vin v.125); Sn 664, 782 (°dhamma); Pug 13. — See ariya.

Anala (adj.) [an + ala] 1. not sufficient, not enough; unable, impossible, unmanageable M I.455; J II.326 = IV. 471. — 2. dissatisfied, insatiate J v.63 (= atitta C.). — 3. °ŋ **kata** dissatisfied, satiated, S I.15 (kāmesu).

Anavaya (adj.) [derivation doubtful. See Trenckner *Pali Misc.* 65] not lacking, complete in (loc.), fulfilling D I.88 (= anūna paripūra-kārin DA I.248); A III.152 (= samatta paripuṇṇa AA quoted by Tr. on Miln 10).

Anavosita (adj.) [an + avosita; or ana + avosita = avusita?] unfulfilled, undone Th 1, 101.

Anasana (nt.) [an + asana, cp. Sk. an-aśana] not eating, fasting, hunger D III.75 & in same context at Sn 311 (= khudā SnA 324).

Anasitvāna [ger. of an + aśati] without eating, fasting J IV.371.

Anasuyyaŋ [Sk. anasūyan, ppr. of an + asūyati] not grumbling J III.27 (v. l. for anusuyyaŋ T.).

Anasuropa [an + asuropa] absence of abruptness Dhs 1341.

Anasūyaka (adj.) [Sk. anasūyaka, cp. usūya not grumbling, not envious J II.192.

Anassaka (adj.) either an-assaka or a-nassaka (q. v.).

Anassana (nt.) [a + nassana, **naś**; cp. Sk. naśana] imperishableness, freedom from waste J IV.168.

Anassāvin (adj.) [an + assāvin; cp. assāva + āsava] not intoxicated, not enjoying or finding pleasure in Sn 853 (sātiyesu a. = sātavatthusa kāmaguṇesu taṇhasanthavavirahita SnA 549).

Anassāsika (adj.) [an + assāsa + ika; cp. Sk. āśvāsana & BSk. anāśvāsika Divy 207] not consoling, discouraging, not comforting M I.514; S II.191.

Anassuŋ 1st sq, pret. of anusūyati (= Sk. anvaśruvaŋ) I have heard M I.393.

Anāgata (adj.) [an + āgata] not come yet, i. e. future. On usual combn. with **atīta**: see this. D III.100 sq., 134 sq., 220, 275; M III.188 sq.; S I.5; II.283; A III.100 sq., 400; Sn 318, 373, 851; It 53; J IV.159; VI.364; Dhs 1039, 1416.

Anāgamana (nt.) [an + āgamana] not coming, not returning J I 203, 264.

Anāgāmitā (f.) [anāgāmin + tā] the state or condition of an Anāgāmin S v.129, 181, 285; A III.82; v.108, 300 sq.; Sn p. 140 = A III.143; It 1 sq., 39, 40.

Anāgāmin (adj.-n.) [an + āgāmin] one who does not return, a Never-Returner, as tt. designating one who has attained the 3rd stage out of four in the breaking of the bonds (Saŋyojanas) which keep a man back from Arahantship. So near is the Anāgāmin to the goal, that after death he will be reborn in one of the highest heaven and there obtain Arahantship, never returning to rebirth as a man. But in the oldest passages referring to these 4 stages, the description of the third does not use the word anāgāmin (D I.156; II.92; III.107; M II.146) and anāgāmin does not mean the breaking of bonds, but the cultivation of certain specified good mental habits (S III.168, the anatta doctrine; S v.200–2, the five Indriyas; A I.64; I.200, cultivation of good qualities, II 163; v.86, 171 = S 149). We have only two cases in the canon of any living persons being called anāgāmin. Those are at S v.177 and 178. The word there means one who has broken the lower five of the ten bonds, & the individuals named are laymen. At D II.92 nine others, of whom eight are laymen, are declared after their death to have reached the third stage (as above) during life, but they are not called anāgāmins. At It 96 there are only 3 stages, the worldling, the Anāgāmin, and the Arahant; and the Saŋyojanas are not referred to. It is probable that already in the Nikāya period the older, wider meaning was falling into disuse. The Abhidhamma books seem to refer only to the Saŋyojana explanation; the commentaries, so far as we know them, ignore any other. See Ps II.194; *Kv. Tr.* 74; *Dhs. Tr.* 302 n; *Cp.* 69. -**phala** fruition of the state of an Anāgāmin; always in combn. sotāpatti° sakadāgāmi° anāgāmi° arahatta° Vin I.293; II.240; IV.29; D I.229; II.227, 255; S III.168; V.411; A I.23, 44; III.272 sq.; IV.204, 276, 372 sq. -**magga** the path of one who does not return (in rebirths) Nd² 569b.

Anāgāra & **Anāgāriyā** see agāra & agāriyā.

Anāghāta [an + āghāta] freedom from anger or ill-will Vin II.249.

Anācāra [an + ācāra] misconduct, immorality J II.133; III. 276; adj. **anācārin** Pug 57.

Anājāniya (adj.) [an + ājāniya] of inferior race, not of good blood M I.367.

Anādara [an + ādara] (a) (m) disrespect PvA 257. — (b.) (adj.) disrespectful Sn 247 (= ādaravirahita SnA 290).

Anādaratā (f.) [abstr. fr. anādara] want of consideration, in expln. of dovacassatā at Dhs 1325 = Vbh 359 = Pug 30 (where reading is **anādariyatā**).

Anādariya (nt.) [fr. anādara] disregard, disrespect Vin I.176; IV.113 (where expld. in extenso); Dhs 1325 = Pug 20 = Vbh 359.

Anādā [ger. of an + ādiyati] without taking up or on to oneself Vin IV.120 (= anādiyitvā C.).

Anādāna (adj.) [an + ādāna] free from attachment (opp. sādāna) A II.10 = It 9 = 109 = Nd² 172a; Sn 620, 741, 1094; Nd² 41 (where as nt. = taṇha); Dh 352 (= khandhādisu niggabaṇa DhA IV.70), 396, 406, 421.

Anāditvā [ger. of an + ādiyati] not taking up, not heeding J IV.352 (v. l. for T. anādiyitvā).

Anādiyitvā [ger. of an + ādiyati, Sk. anādāya] without assuming or taking up, not heeding Vin IV.120; J IV.352; DhA I.41. See also ādiyati.

Anānu- represents the metrically lengthened from of ananu- (an + anu), as found e. g. in the foll. cpds.: °**tappaŋ** (ppr.) not regretting J V.492; °**puṭṭha** questioned Sn 782 (= apucchita SnA 521); °**yāyin** not following or not defiled by evil Sn 1071 (expld. at Nd² 42 by both avedhamāna (?) avigacchamāna & by arajjamāna adussamāna); °**loma** not fit or suitable D II.273 (v. l. anu°).

Anāpāthagata (adj.) [an + āpātha + gata] not fallen into the way of (the hunter), escaped him M I.174.

Anāpāda (adj.) [an + āpāda] unmarried (of a woman) J IV.178 (āpāda = apādāna C.; aññehi akata-pariggahā).

Anāpucchā see āpucchati.

Anābādha (adj.) [an + ābādha] safe and sound VvA 351.

Anāmata (adj.) [an + amata the ā being due to metrical lengthening] not affected by death, immortal J II.56 (= asusāna-ṭṭhāna C.); DhA II.99.

Anāmanta (°—) [an + āmanta] without asking or being asked; in °**kata** unasked, unpermitted, uninvited J VI.226; °**cāra** living uninvited Vin V.132; A III.259.

Anāmaya (adj.) [an + āmaya] free from illness, not decaying, healthy Vv 15¹⁰ (= aroga VvA 74), 17¹.

Anāmasita (adj.) [an + āmasita, pp. of āmassati] not touched, virgin- VvA 113 (°khetta).

Anāmassa (adj.) [grd. of an + āmassati, Sk. āmaśya] not to be touched J II 360 (C. anāmāsitabba).

Anāyatana (nt.) [an + āyatana] nonexertion, not exerting oneself, sluggishness, indolence J V.121 (°sīla = dussīla C.).

Anāyasa (adj.) [an + āya + sa, or should we read anāyāsa?] void of means, unluckly, unfortunate Vv 84⁵ (= natthi ettha āyo sukhan ti anāyasaŋ VvA 335).

Anāyāsa (adj.) [an + āyāsa] free from trouble or sorrow, peaceful Th I, 1008.

Anārambha [an + ārambha] that which is without moil and toil Sn 745 (= nibbāna SnA 507).

Anārādhaka (adj.) [an + ārādhaka] one who fails, unsuccessful Vin I.70.

Anāriya (adj.) [doublet of anariya] not Aryan, ignoble, Sn 815 (v. l. SS. anariya).

Anālamba (adj.) [an + ālamba] without support (from above), unsuspended, not held Sn 173 (+ appatiṭṭha; expld. at SnA 214 by heṭṭhā patiṭṭhâbhāvena upari ālambhāvena ca gambhīra).

Anālaya [an + ālaya] aversion, doing away with Vin I.10 (taṇhāya).

Anāḷhiya & **Anāḷhika** (adj.) [an + āḷhiya, Sk. āḍhya, see also addha²] not rich, poor, miserable, destitute, usually combd. with daḷidda M I.450; II.178 (v. l. BB. anāḷiya); A III.352 sq. (vv. ll. BB. anāḷhika), 384; J V.96.

Anāvaṭa (°—) [an + āvaṭa] not shut; in °**dvāratā** (f.) not closing the door against another, accessibility, openhand edness D III.191.

Anāvattin (adj.-n.) [an + āvattin] one who does not return, almost syn. with anāgāmin in phrase **anāvatti-dhamma**, one who is not destined to shift or return from one birth to another, D I.156 (cp. DA I.313); III.132; Pug 16 sq., 62.

Anāvasūraŋ (adv.) [an + ava + sūra = suriya, with ava lengthened to āva in verse] as long as the sun does not set, before sun-down J V.56 (= anatthaṅgata-suriyaŋ C.) cp. Sk. utsūra.

Anāvāsa (adj.-n.) [an + āvāsa] uninhabited, an uninhabited place Vin II.22, 33; J II.77.

Anāvikata etc. see āvikata.

Anāvila (adj.) [an + āvila] undisturbed, unstained, clean, pure D I.84 (= nikkaddama DA I.226); III.269, 270; Sn 637 (= nikkilesa SnA 469 = DhA IV.192); Th 2, 369 (āvilacitta +); Dh 82, 413; ThA 251; Sdhp 479.

Anāvuttha (adj.) [an + āvuttha, pp. of āvasati] not dwelt in D .II30.

Anāsaka (adj.) [an + āsaka] fasting, not taking food S IV.118. f. °**ā** [cp. Sk. anāśaka nt.] fasting, abstaining from food Dh 141 (= bhatta-paṭikkhepa DhA III.77).

Anāsakatta (nt.) [abstr. of anāsaka] fasting Sn 249 (= abhojana SnA 292).

Anāsava (adj.) [an + āsava] free from the 4 intoxications (see āsava) Vin II.148 = 164; D III.112; Sn 1105, 1133; Dh 94, 126, 386; Nd² 44; It 75; Pug 27, Dhs 1101, 1451; Vbh 426; Th I, 100; Pv II.6¹⁵; VvA 9. See āsava and cp. nirāsava.

Anāsasāna (adj.) [an + āsasāna] not longing after anything Sn 369 (SnA 365 however reads anāsayāna & has anāsasāna as v. l. Cp. also vv. ll. to āsasāna. Expl^{d} by kañci rūpâdi-dhammaŋ nâsiŋsati SnA 365.

Anāhāra (adj.) [an + āhāra] being without food M I.487; Sn 985.

Anikkaḍḍhanā (f.) [a + nikkaḍḍhanā] not throwing out or expelling J III.22.

Anikkasāva (adj.) [a + nikkasāva, cp. nikasāva] not free from impurity, impure, stained Dh 9 = Th 1, 969 = J II.198 = V.50; DhA I.82 (= rāgâdihi kasāvehi sakasāva).

Anikhāta (adj.) [a + nikhāta, pp. of nikhanati] not dug into, not dug down, not deep J VI.109 (°kūla; C. agambhīrā).

Anigha see nigha[1] and īgha.

Anicchā (f.) [an + icchā] dispassion S V.6; adj. °a without desires, not desiring Sn 707.

Aniñjana (nt.) [an + iñjana] immobility, steadfastness Ps I.15.

Aniñjita (adj.) [an + iñjita] immoveable, undisturbed, unshaken Th 1, 386.

Aniṭṭhangata see niṭṭhā[2].

Aniṭṭhita see niṭṭhita.

Anitthi (f.) [an + itthi] a woman lacking the characteristics of womanhood, a woman ceasing to be a woman, "non-woman" J II.126 (comp^{d} with anadī a river without water; interpreted by ucchiṭṭh-itthi).

Anindi- [the comp^{n} form of nindā] in °ḷocana (with) faultless eyes J VI.265.

Anindita (adj.) [a + nindita] blameless, faultless J IV.106 (°angin of blameless body or limbs).

Anibbisaŋ [ppr. of nibbisati, q. v.] not finding Th 1, 78 = Dh 153 (= taŋ ñāṇaŋ avindanto DhA III.128).

Animisa (adj.) [Ved. animeṣa, cp. nimisati] not winking, waking, watchful Dāvs V.26 (nayana).

Aniyata (adj.) [a + niyata] not settled, uncertain, doubtful Vin I.112; II.287; D III.217.

Aniyamita (adj.) [pp. of a + niyameti] indefinite (as tt. g.) VvA 231.

Anila [from **an**, cp. Sk. aniti to breathe, cp. Gr. ἄνεμος wind; Lat. animus breath, soul, mind] wind J IV.119 (°patha air, sky); Miln 181; VvA 237; Sdhp 594.

Anirākata (adj.) [a + nirākata] see nirankaroti.

Anissara (adj.) [an + issara] without a personal creator Th 1, 713.

Anissukin (adj.) [an + issukin, see also an-ussukin] not hard, not greedy, generous D III.47 (+ amaccharin; v. l. anussukin); SnA 569 (see under niṭṭhurin).

Anīka (nt.) [Ved. anīka face, front, army to Idg. *og̃ (see), cp. Gr. ὄμμα eye, Lat. oculus, see also Sk. pratīka and P. akkhi] army, array, troops (orig. "front", i. e. of the battle-array) Vin IV.107 (where expl^{d} in detail); Sn 623 (bala° strong in arms, with strong array i. e. of khanti, which precedes; cp. SnA 467).

-agga a splendid army Sn 421 (= balakāya senāmukha SnA 384). -ṭṭha a sentinel, royal guard D III.64, 148; J V.100; VI.15 ("men on horseback", horseguard); Miln 234, 264. -dassana troop-inspection D I.6 (aṇīka° at DA I.85, q. v. interpretation); Vin IV.107 (senābyūha +).

Anīgha see nigha[1] and cp. īgha.

Anīti (f.) [an + īti] safety, soundness, sound condition, health A IV.238; Miln 323 (abl. °ito).

Anītika (adj.) [fr. anīti] free from injury or harm, healthy, secure Vin II.79 = 124 (+ anupaddava); III.162; S IV.371; Sn 1137 (īti vuccanti kilesā etc. Nd^{2} 48); Miln 304.

Anītiha (adj.) [an + ītiha, the latter a cpd. der. fr. iti + ha = saying so and so, cp. itihāsa & itihītihaŋ] not such and such, not based on hearsay (itiha), not guesswork or (mere) talk A II.26; Th 1, 331 (cp. M I.520); Sn 1053 (= Nd^{2} 49, 151); J I.456; Nett 166 (cp. It 28).

Anu[1] (indecl.) [Vedic anu, Av. anu; Gr. ἄνω to ἄνα along, up; Av. ana, Goth. ana, Ohg. ana, Ags. on, Ger. an, Lat. an (in anhelare etc.)] prep. & pref. — A. As *prep.* anu is only found occasionally, and here its old (vedic) function with *acc.* is superseded by the *loc.* — Traces of use w. *acc.* may be seen in expressions of time like **anu pañcāhaŋ** by 5 days, i. e. after (every) 5 days (cp. ved. anu dyūn day by day); a. **vassaŋ** for one year or yearly; a. saŋvaccharaŋ id. — (b) More freq. w. *loc.* (= alongside, with, by) a. **tīre** by the bank S IV.177; **pathe** by the way J V.302; **pariveṇiyaŋ** in every cell Vin I.80; **magge** along the road J V.201; **vāte** with the wind J II.382.

B. As *pref.*: (a) *General character.* anu is freq. as modifying (directional) element with well-defined meaning ("along"), as such also as 1st component of pref.-cpds., e. g. anu + ā (anvā°), anu + pra (anuppa°), + pari, + vi, + saŋ. — As base, i. e. 2nd part of a pref.-cpd. it is rare and only found in comb^{n} sam-anu°. The prefix saŋ is its nearest relation as modifying pref. The opp. of anu is paṭi and both are often found in one cpd. (cp. °loma, °vāta). (b) *Meanings.* I. With verbs of *motion*: "along towards". — (a) the motion viewed from the front backward = after, behind; esp. with verbs denoting to go, follow etc. E. g. °aya going after, connexion; °āgacch° follow, °kkamati follow, °dhāvati run after, °patta received, °parivattati move about after, °bandhati run after, °bala rear-guard, °bhāsati speak after, repeat, °vāda speaking after, blame, °vicarati roam about °viloketi look round after (survey), °saŋcarati proceed around etc. — (b) the motion viewed from the back forward = for, towards an aim, on to, over to, forward. Esp. in double pref.-cpds. (esp. with °ppa°), e. g. anu-ādisati design for, dedicate °kankhin longing for, °cintana care for, °tiṭṭhati look after, °padinna given over to, °pavecchati hand over, °paviṭṭha entered into, °pasaŋkamati go up to, °rodati cry for, °socati mourn for. — II. With verbs denoting a *state* or *condition*: (a) *literal*: along, at, to, combined with. Often resembling E. be- or Ger. be-, also Lat. ad- and con-. Thus often transitiving or simply emphatic. E. g. °kampā *com*-passion, °kiṇṇa be-set, °gaṇhāti take pity *on*, °gāyati be-singen, °jagghati laugh at, belaugh, °ddaya pity with, °masati touch *at*, °yuñjati order along, °yoga devotion *to*, °rakkhati be-guard, °litta be-smeared or *an*-ointed, °vitakheti reflect over, °sara con-sequential; etc. — (b) *applied*: according to, in conformity with. E. g. °kūla being to will, °chavika befitting, °ñāta permitted, *al*-lowed, °mati *con*-sent, *a*-greement, °madati ap-preciate, °rūpa = con-form, °vattin acting according to, °ssavana by hearsay, °sāsati ad-vise, com-mand etc. — III. (a) (fig.) following after = second to, secondary, supplementy, inferior minor after-, smaller; e. g. °dhamma lesser morality, °pabbajā discipleship, °pavattaka ruling after, °bhāga after-share, °majjha mediocre, °yāgin assisting in sacrifice, °vyañjana smaller marks, etc.; cp. paṭi in same sense. — (b) *distributive* (cp. A. a.) each, every, one by one, (one after one): °disā in each direction, °pañcāhaŋ every 5 days, °pubba one after the other. — IV. As one of the contrasting (-comparative) prefixes (see remarks on ati & cp. ā[3]) anu often occurs in reduplicative cpds. after the style of khuddânukhuddaka "small and still smaller", i. e. all sorts of small items or whatever is small or insignificant. More freq. comb^{ns} are the foll.: (q. v. under each heading) padânupadaŋ, pubbânupubbaka, ponkhânuponkhaŋ, buddhânubuddha, vādânuvāda, seṭṭhânuseṭṭhi. — V. As regards *dialectical differences* in meanings of prefixes, anu is freq. found in Pāli where the Sk. variant presents apa (for ava), abhi or ava. For P. anu = Sk. (Ved.) apa see anuddhasta; = Sk. abhi see anu-gijjhati, °brūheti, °sandahati; = Sk. ava see anu-kantati, °kassati^2, °kiṇṇa, °gāhati, °bujjhati °bodha, °lokin, °vajja.

Note (a) anu in comp^n is always contracted to °ânu°, never elided like adhi = 'dhi or abhi = 'bhi. The rigid character of this rule accounts for forms isolated out of this sort of cpds. (like mahânubhāva), like ānupubbikathā (fr. *pubbānupubba°), ānubhāva etc. We find ānu also in comb^n. with an- under the influence of metre. — (b) the assimilation (contracted) form of anu before vowels is **anv°**.

Anu^2 (adj.) subtile; freq. spelling for aṇu, e. g. D I.223; Sdhp 271, 346 (anuŋ thūlaŋ). See aṇu.

Anukankhin (adj.) [fr. anu + **kānkṣ**] striving after, longing for J v.499 (piya°).

Anukantati [anu + kantati^2] to cut Dh 311 (hatthaŋ = phāleti DhA III.484).

Anukampaka & °ika (adj.) [fr. anukampati] kind of heart, merciful, compassionate, full of pity (—° or c. loc.) D III.187; S I.105 (loka°), 197; v.157; A IV.265 sq.; It 66 (sabba-bhūta°); Pv I.3^3 (= kāruṇika PvA 16), 5^3 (= atthakāma, hitesin PvA 25), 8^6; II.1^4 (= anuggaṇhataka PvA 69), 2^1; ThA 174; PvA 196 (satthā sattesu a.).

Anukampati [anu + kampati] to have pity on, to commiserate, to pity, to sympathise with (c. acc.) S I.82, 206; v.189. Imper. **anukampa** Pv II.1^6 (= anuddayaŋ karohi PvA 70) & **anukampassu** Pv III.2^8 (= anugganha PvA 181). Med. ppr. **anukampamāna** Sn 37 (= anupekkhamāna anugayhamāna Nd^2 50); PvA 35 (taŋ), 62 (pitaraŋ), 104. — pp. **anukampita** (q. v.).

Anukampana (nt.) [fr. last] compassion, pity PvA 16, 88.

Anukampā (f.) [abstr. fr. anukampati] compassion, pity, mercy D I.204; M I.161; II.113; S I.206; II.274 (loka°); IV.323; v.259 sq.; A I.64, 92; II.159; III.49; IV.139; Pug 35. — Often in abl. **anukampāya** out of pity, for the sake of D III.211 (loka° ont of compassion for all mankind, + atthaya hitāya); J III.280; PvA 47, 147.

Anukampita (adj.) [pp. of anukampati] compassioned, gratified, remembered, having done a good deed (of mercy) Pv III.2^{30}.

Anukampin (adj.) [cp. anukampaka] compassionate, anxious for, commiserating. Only in foll. phrases: **hita°** full of solicitude for the welfare of S v.86; Sn 693; Pv III.7^6. **sabbapāṇa-bhūta-hita°** id. S IV.314; A II.210; III.92; IV.249; Pug 57, 68. **sabba-bhūta°** S I.25, 110; A II.9; It 102.

Anukaroti [anu + **kṛ**] to imitate, "to do after" A I.212; J I.491; II.162; DhA IV.197. — ppr. **anukabbaŋ** Vin II.201 (mamâ°). — Med. **anukubbati** S I.19 = J IV.65. — See also anukubba. On **anvakāsi** see anukassati 2.

Anukassati [anu + kassati, **kṛṣ**] 1. [Sk. anukarṣati] to draw after, to repeat, recite, quote D II.255 (silokaŋ). — 2. [Sk. ava-karṣati] to draw or take of, to remove, throw down, Th I, 869 (aor. **anvakāsi** = khipi, chaḍḍesi C.).

Anukāma (adj.) [anu + kāma] responding to love, loving in return J II.157.

Anukāra [cp. anukaroti] imitation Dpvs v.39.

Anukārin (adj.) imitating Dāvs v.32.

Anukiṇṇa [pp. of anu + kirati] strewn with, beset with, dotted all over Pv IV.12^1 (bhamara-gaṇa°).

Anukubba (adj.) (—°) [= Sk. anukurvat, ppr. of anukaroti] "doing correspondingly" giving back, retaliating J II.205 (kicca°).

Anukubbati see **anukaroti**.

Anukula freq. spelling for **anukūla**.

Anukulaka (adj.) = anukula Sdhp 242 (iccha° according to wish).

Anukūla (adj.) [anu + kūla, opp. paṭikūla] favourable, agreeable, suitable, pleasant VvA 280; spelt anukula at Sdhp 297, 312.

-bhava complaisance, willingness VvA 71. **-yañña** a propitiative sacrifice D I.144 (expl^d. at DA I.302 as anukula° = sacrifice for the propagation of the clan).

Anukkaṇṭhati [an + ukkaṇṭhati] not to be sorry or not to lack anything, in ppr. °**anto** J v.10; and pp. °**ita** without regret or in plenty PvA 13.

Anukkaṇṭhana (nt.) [an + ukkaṇṭhana] having no lack anything, being contented or happy J VI.4.

Anukkama [to anukkamati] 1. order, turn, succession, going along; only in instr. **anukkamena** gradually, in due course or succession J I.157, 262, 290; VvA 157; PvA 5, 14, 35 etc. — 2. that which keeps an animal in (regular) step, i. e. a bridle M I.446; Sn 622 (sandānaŋ saha°).

Anukkamati [anu + **kram**] 1. to follow, go along (a path = acc.) A v.195; It 80 (maggaŋ). — 2. to advance (not with Morris *JPTS.* 1886, 111 as "abandon") S I.24, Th I, 194.

Anukkhipati [anu + khipati] to throw out Cp. XI.6 (vaṭṭaŋ).

Anukkhepa [anu + khepa, see anukkhipati] compensation Vin I.285.

Anukhaṇati [anu + khaṇati] to dig after or further J v.233.

Anukhuddaka (adj.) [anu + khuddaka] in cpd. **khudda°** whatever there is of minor things, all less important items Vin II.287 = D II.154 = Miln 142; Miln 144.

Anuga (—°) (adj.-suff.) [fr. anu + **gam**] following or followed by, going after, undergoing, being in or under, standing under the influence of Sn 332 (**vasa°** in the power of), 791 (**ejā°** = abhibhūta Sn 527), 1095 (Māra-**vasa°** = abhibhuyya viharanti Nd^2 507); It 91 (**ejā°**); J III.224 (**vasa°** = vasavattin C.); Mhvs 7, 3.

Anugacchati [anu + gacchati] to go after, to follow, to go or fall into (w. acc.) KhA 223; PvA 141 (°gacchanto); aor. °gamāsi Vin I.16, & **anvagā** Mhvs 7, 10; 3rd pl. **anvagū** Sn 586 (vasaŋ = vasaŋ gata SnA 461). Pass. **anugammati**, ppr. anugammamāna accompanied or followed by, surrounded, adorned with J I.53; v.370. — pp. **anugata** (q. v.).

Anugata (adj.) [pp. of anugacchati] gone after, accompanied by, come to; following; fig. fallen or gone into, affected with (—°), being a victim of, suffering M I.16; D III.85, 173 (parisā); A II.185 (sota°, v. l. anudhata); J II.292 (samudda°); v.369; Nd^2 32 (taṇhā°); PvA 102 (nāmaŋ mayhaŋ a. has been given to me), 133 (kammaphala°).

Anugati (f.) (—°) [fr. anu + **gam**] following, being in the train of, falling under, adherence to, dependence on S I.104 (vas° being in the power). Usually in cpd. **diṭṭhânugati** a sign (lit. belonging to) of speculation Vin II.108; S II.203; Pug 33; DhA IV.39.

Anugama [fr. anu + **gam**] following after, only as adj. in dur° difficult to be followed J IV.65.

Anugāmika (adj.) going along with, following, accompanying; resulting from, consequential on Kh VIII.8 (**nidhi**, a treasure acc. a man to the next world); J IV.280 (°**nidhi**); Miln 159 (parisā); PvA 132, 253 (danaŋ nāma °aŋ nidānan ti).

Anugāmin (adj.) [fr. anugacchati] following, attending on; an attendant, follower SnA 453 (= anuyutta).

Anugāyati [anu + gāyati] to sing after or to, recite (a magic formula or hymn) praise, celebrate D I.104, 238; Sn 1131 (anugāyissaŋ); Miln 120.

Anugāhati [anu + gāhati] to plunge into, to enter (acc.) Sdhp 611.

Anugijjhati [anu + gijjhati] to be greedy after, to covet Sn 769 (cp. Nd[1] 12); J III.207; IV.4 (= giddhā gathitā hutvā alliyanti C.). pp. °**giddhā** (q. v.). Cp. abhigijjhati.

Anugiddha [pp. of anugijjhati] greedy after, hankering after, desiring, coveting Sn 86 (anânu°), 144, 952; Th 1, 580.

Anugganha (adj.) [cp. anuggaha] compassionate, ready to help PvA 42 °sila.

Anugganhataka (adj.) [= anugganha] compassionate, commiserating, helping PvA 69 (= anukampaka).

Anugganhana (nt.) anuggaha[1] DhsA 403.

Anu(g)ganhāti [anu + ganhāti] to have pity on, to feel sorry for, to help, give protection T I.53 (vācaŋ; cp. DA I.169: sārato aganhanto); J II.74; Nd[2] 50 (ppr. med. °gaynamāna = anukampamāna); Pug 36; PvA 181 (imper. **anugganha** = anukampassu). pp. **anuggahīta** (q. v.).

Anuggaha [anu + **grah**] "taking up", compassion, love for, kindness, assistance, help, favour, benefit S II.11; III.109; IV.104; V.162; A I.92, 114; II.145; IV.167; V.70; It 12, 98; J I.151; V.150; Pug 25; PvA 145; ThA 104.

Anuggaha[2] (adj.) [an + uggaha] not taking up Sn 912 (= na gaṇhāti Nd[1] 330).

Anuggahīta (& °ita) [pp. of anugganhāti] commiserated, made happy, satisfied M I.457; S II.274; III.91; IV.263; A III.172; J III.428.

Anuggāhaka (adj.) [fr. anuggaha] helping assisting S III.5; V.162; Miln 354 (nt. = help).

Anugghāṭeti [an + ugghāṭeti] not to unfasten or open (a door) Miln 371 (kavāṭaŋ).

Anugghāta [an + ugghāta] not shaking, a steady walk J VI.253.

Anugghātin (adj.) [fr. last] not shaking, not jerking, J VI.252; Vv 5[3] (read °ī for i); VvA 36.

Anughāyati [anu + ghāyati[1]] to smell, snuff, sniff up Miln 343 (gandhaŋ).

Anucankamati [anu + cankamati] to follow (along) after, to go after D I.235; M I.227; Th 1, 481, 1044; Caus. °āpeti M I.253, cp. Lal. Vist. 147, 3; M Vastu I.350.

Anucankamana (nt.) [fr. anucankamati] sidewalk J I.7.

Anucarati [anu + cariti] to more along, to follow; to practice; pp. **anuciṇṇa** & **anucarita** (q. v.)

Anucarita (—°) [pp. of anucarati] connected with, accompanied by, pervaded with D I.16, 21 (vīmaŋsa° = anuvicarita DA I.106); M I.68 (id.); Miln 226.

Anuciṇṇa (pp.) [pp. of anucarati] 1. pursuing, following out, practising, doing; having attained or practised Vin II.203 = It 86 (pamādaŋ); J I 20 (v.126); Th 1, 236; 2, 206; Dpvs IV.9. — 2. adorned with, accompanied by, connected with J IV.286.

Anucintana (nt.) [fr. anucinteti] thinking, upon, intention, care for PvA 164.

Anucinteti [anu + cinteti] to think upon, to meditate, consider S I.203 (v. l. for anuvicinteti).

Anuccangin see **anujjangin**.

Anucchavika (& °ya) (adj.) [anu + chavi + ka] "according to one's skin", befitting, suitable, proper, pleasing, fit for, J I.58, 62, 126, 218; II.5; IV.137, 138; Miln 358; DhA I.203, 390; II.55, 56; VvA 68, 78; PvA 13, 26 (= kappiya), 66, 81, 286. anucchaviya at Vin II.7 (an°); III.120 (id. + ananulomika); Miln 13.

Anucchiṭṭha (adj.) [see ucchiṭṭha] (food) that is not thrown away or left over; untouched, clean (food) J III.257; DhA II.3 (vv. ll. anucciṭṭha).

Anujānāti [anu + jānāti] 1. to give permission, grant, allow Vin IV.225; A II.197; Pv IV.1[61]; PvA 55, 79, 142. — 2. to advise, prescribe Vin I.83; II.301; Sn 982. — grd. **anuññeyya** that which is allowed A II.197; pp. **anuññāta** (q. v.) Caus. **anujānāpeti** J I.156.

Anujagghati [anu + jagghati] to laugh at, deride, mock D I.91; DA I.258 (cp. sañjagghati ibid 256).

Anujavati [anu + javati] to run after, to hasten after, to follow J VI.452 (= anubandhati).

Anujāta (adj.) [anu + jāta] "born after" i. e. after the image of, resembling, taking after; esp. said of a son (putta), resembling his father, a worthy son It 64 (atijāta +, opp. avajāta); Th 1, 827 (fig. following the example of), 1279; J VI.380; DhA I.129; Dāvs II.66.

Anujīvati [anu + jīvati] to live after, i. e. like (acc.), to live for or on, subsist by J IV.271 (= upajīvati, tassânubhāvena jīvitaŋ laddhaŋ (C.). — pp. **anujīvata** (q. v.).

Anujīvita (nt.) [pp. of anujīvati] living (after), living, livelihood, subsistence, life Sn 836 (= jīvitaŋ SnA 545).

Anujīvin (adj.-n.) [fr. anujīvati] living upon, another, dependent; a follower, a dependant A I.152; III.44; J III 485; Dāvs V.43.

Anujju (adj.) [an + ujju] not straight, crooked, bent, in cpds. °**angin** (anujjangin) with (evenly) bent limbs, i. e. with perfect limbs, graceful f. °ī Ep. of a beautiful woman J V.40 (= kañcana-sannibha-sarīrā C.); VI.500 (T. anuccangī, C. aninditā agarahitangī); °**gāmin** going crooked i. e. snake J IV.330; °**bhūta** not upright (fig. of citta) J V.293.

Anujjuka = anujju J III.318.

Anujjhāna (nt.) [anu + jhāna] meditation, reflection, introspection Miln 352 (°bahula).

Anuññāta (adj.) [pp. of anujānāti] permitted, allowed; sanctioned, given leave, ordained D I.88; J I.92; II.353, 416; Pv I.12[3] (na. a. = ananuññāta at id. p. Th 2, 129 expl[d.] at PvA 64 by ananumata); Pug 28; DA I.247 248, 267; PvA 12, 81.

Anuññātatta (nt.) [abstr. to anuññāta] being permitted, permission J II.353.

Anuṭṭhaka (adj.) [fr. an + uṭṭhahati] not rising, not rousing oneself, inactive, lazy Th 1, 1033.

Anuṭṭhahati [anu + ṭhahati = °ṭhāti, see °tiṭṭhati] to carry out, look after, practise do J v.121. — pp. **anuṭṭhita** (q. v.).

Anuṭṭhahāna (adj.) [ppr. of an + uṭṭhahati] one who does not rouse himself, not getting up, inactive Dh 280 (= anuṭṭhahanto avāyāmanto DhA III.409).

Anuṭṭhātar [n. ag. to an + uṭṭhahati] one without energy or zeal Sn 96 (niddāsīlin sabhāsīlin +) SnA 169 (= viriya-tejavirahita).

Anuṭṭhāna (nt.) [an + uṭṭhāna] "the not getting up", inactivity, want of energy Dh 241 (sarīra-paṭijagganaŋ akaronto DhA III.347).

Anuṭṭhita [pp. of anuṭṭhati = anutiṭṭhati] practising, effecting or effected, come to, experienced, done D II.103; S IV. 200; A III.290 sq.; IV.300; J II.61; Miln 198; PvA 132 (cp. anugata).

Anuṭṭhubhati [formally Sk. anuṣṭobhati, but in meaning = *anuṣṭīvati; anu + ṭṭhubhati, the etym. of which see under niṭṭhubhati] to lick up with one's saliva DA I.138.

Anuṭṭhurin v. l. at SnA 569, see **niṭṭhurin.**

Anuḍasati [anu + ḍasati] to bite J VI.192.

Anuḍahati [anu + ḍahati] to burn over again, burn thoroughly, fig. to destroy, consume J II.330; VI.423. Pass. °ḍayhati J v.426. — Also spelt °dahati, e. g. at S IV. 190 = v.53; Th 2, 488.

Anuḍahana (nt.) [fr. anuḍahati] conflagration, burning up, consumption J v.271; ThA 287 (d).

Anuṇṇata (adj.) [uṇṇata] not raised, not elated, not haughty, humble Sn 702 (care = uddhaccaŋ nâpajjeyya SnA 492).

Anutappati [anu + tappati[1]; Sk. anutapyate, Pass. of anutapati] to be sorry for, to regret, repent, feel remorse J I.113; IV.358; v.492 (ppr. an-anutappaŋ); Dh 67, 314; Pv II.9[42]; DhA II.40. grd. **anutappa** to be regretted A I.22, 77; III.294, and **anutāpiya** A III.46 (an°).

Anutāpa [fr. anu + **tāpa**] anguish, remorse, conscience Vv 40[5] (= vippaṭisāra VvA 180); DhsA 384.

Anutāpin (adj.) [fr. anutāpa] repenting, regretting Th 2, 57, 190; VvA 115.

Anutāpiya grd. of anutappati, q. v.

Anutāḷeti [anu + taḷeti] to beat J II.280.

Anutiṭṭhati [anu + tiṭṭhati see also anuṭṭhahati] to look after, to manage, carry on J v.113 (= anugacchati); PvA 78.

Anutīre (adv.) [anu + tīre, loc. of tīra] along side or near the bank (of a river) Sn 18 (= tīra-samīpe SnA 28). Cp. anu A b.

Anuttara (adj.) [an + uttara] "nothing higher", without a superior, incomparable, second to none, unsurpassed, excellent, preeminent Sn 234 (= adhikassa kassaci abhāvato KhA 193), 1003; Dh 23, 55 (= asadisa appaṭibhāga DhA I.423); Pv IV.3[52] (dhamma); Dhs 1294; DA I.129; PvA 1, 5, 6, 18, etc.

Anuttariya (nt.) [abstr. fr. anuttara] preeminence, superiority, excellency; highest ideal, greatest good. They are mentioned as sets of 3 (viz. **dassana°, paṭipadā°, vimutti°**) at D III.219, or of 6 (viz. **dassana°, savana°, lābha°, sikkhā°, pāricariyā°, anussata°**) at D III.250, 281; A I.22; III.284, 325 sq., 452; Ps I.5. Cp. M I.235; A v.37. See also ānuttariya.

Anuttāna (adj.) [an + uttāna] not (lying) open, not exposed; fig. unexplained, unclear J VI.247.

Anutthunā (f.) [fr. anutthunāti] wailing, crying, lamenting Nd[1] 167 (= vācāpalāpa vippalāpa etc.).

Anutthunāti [anu + thunati (thunāti); anu + **stan**] to wail, moan, deplore, lament, bewail D III.86; Sn 827 (cp. Nd[1] 167); Dh 156; J III.115; v.346, 479; DhA III.133; PvA 60 (wrongly applied for ghāyati, of the fire of conscience).

Anutrāsin (adj.) [an + utrāsin] not terrified, at ease Th 1, 864.

Anuthera [anu + thera] an inferior Thera, one who comes next to the elder Vin II.212 (**therânutherā** Th. & next in age).

Anudadāti [anu + dadāti] to concede, grant, admit, fut. **anudassati** Miln 276, 375.

Anudayati (to sympathise with) see under **anuddā.**

Anudassita [pp. of anudasseti] manifested Miln 119.

Anudahati see anuḍahati.

Anudiṭṭha [pp. of anudisati] pointed out, appointed, dedicated, *nt.* consecration, dedication J v.393 (anudiṭṭha = asukassa nāma dassatī ti C.); Pv I.10[1] (= uddiṭṭha PvA 50).

Anudiṭṭhi (f.) [anu + diṭṭhi] an "after-view", sceptical view, speculation, heresy D I.12; M II.228; S III.45 sq.; Th 1, 754; Miln 325; DA I.103. **attânudiṭṭhi** (q. v.) a soul-speculation.

Anudisati [anu + disati] to point out, direct, bid, address PvA 99 (aor. anudesi + anvesi). — pp. **anudiṭṭha** (q. v.).

Anudisā (f.) [anu + disā] an intermediate point of the compass, often collectively for the usual 4 intermediate points D I.222; S I.122; III.124.

Anudīpeti [anu + dīpeti] to explain Miln 227 (dhammâdhammaŋ).

Anudūta [anu + dūta] a person sent with another, a travelling companion Vin II.19, 295; DhA II.76, 78.

Anudeva see **anvadeva.**

Anuddayatā (f.) [abstr. to anuddayā] sympathy with (—°) compassion, kindness, favour, usually as **par°** kindness to or sympathy with other people S II.218; v.169 (T. anudayatā); A III.184; It 72; Vbh 356.

Anuddayā (& anudayā) (f.) [anu + dayā] compassion, pity, mercy, care Vin II.196; S I.204; II.199; IV.323; A II.176; III.189; Pug 35 (anukampā); J I.147, 186, 214; PvA 70, 88, 181 (= anukampā). In compn **anudaya°** e. g. **°sampanna** full of mercy J I.151, 262; PvA 66.

Anuddā (f.) [contracted form of anuddayā] = **anuddayā** Dhs 1056, where also the other abstr. formations **anuddāyanā** & **anuddāyitattaŋ** "care, forbearance & consideration"; DhsA 362 (anudayatī ti anuddā).

Anuddhaŋseti [anu + dhaŋseti] to spoil, corrupt, degrade Vin IV.148 (expln. here in slightly diff. meaning = codeti vā codāpeti vā to reprove, scold, bring down); It 42. Usually in ster. phrase **rāgo cittaŋ a.** lust degrades the heart Vin III.111; M I.26; S I.186; A I.266; II.126; III. 393 sq. — pp. **anuddhasta** (q. v.).

Anuddhata (adj.) [an + uddhata] not puffed up, not proud, unconceited calm, subdued Sn 850 (= uddhacca-virahita SnA 549, cp. anuṇṇata); It 30; Dh 363 (= nibbutacitta DhA IV.93); Vv 64[8]; Pug 59.

Anuddharin (adj.) [an + uddharin] not proud Sn 952 (= anussukin SnA 569) see **niṭṭhurin.**

Anuddhasta (adj.) [anu + dhasta, pp. of anuddhaŋseti, cp. Sk. apadhvasta] spoilt, corrupt, degraded M I.462 (citta); A II.126 (id.).

Anudhamma [anu + dhamma] 1. in compⁿ· with dhamma as **dhammânudhamma** to be judged as a redupl. cpd. after the manner of cpds. mentioned under anu IV. & meaning "the Law in all its parts, the dhamma and what belongs to it, the Law in its fullness". For instances see dhamma C. IV. Freq. in phrase dh°-ânudh°-**paṭipanna** "one who masters the completeness of the Dh.", e. g. S II.18; III.163; It 81; Ps II.189. — 2. conformity or accordance with the Law, lawfulness, relation, essence, consistency, truth; in phrase **dhammassa** (c') **ânudhammaŋ vyākaroti** to explain the truth of the Dh. Vin I.234; D I.161; M I.368, 482; S II.33; III.6; IV.51; V.7. See further M III.30; Sn 963 (cp. Nd¹ 481 for exegesis). Also in cpd. °cārin living according to the Dhamma, living in truth S II.81, 108; A II.8; Dh 20 (cp. DhA I.158); Vv 31⁷; Sn 69 (see Nd² 51).

Anudhammatā (f.) [abstr. to anudhamma) lawfulness, conformity to the Dhamma A II.46; Ps I.35, 36.

Anudhāreti [anu + dhāreti] to hold up DA I.61 (chattaŋ), cp. J I.53, dhariyamāna.

Anudhāvati [anu + dhāvati] to run after, to chase, follow, persecute, pursue M I.474; S I.9; Dh 85; Th I, 1174; Miln 253, 372.

Anudhāvin (adj.-n.) [fr. anudhāvati] one who runs after S I.9, 117.

Anunadī(-tire) along the bank of the river S IV.177 should be read anu nadītire (= anu prep. c. loc.; see under anu A).

Anunamati [anu + namati] to incline, bend (intrs.), give way Miln 372 (of a bow).

Anunaya [fr. anuneti] "leading along", friendliness, courtesy, falling in with, fawning D III.254 (°saŋyojana); A IV.7 sq. (id.) M I.191; Dhs 1059; Vbh 145; Nett 79; combᵈ· w. opp. **paṭigha** (repugnance) at Miln 44, 122, 322.

Anunayana (nt.) [fr. anuneti] fawning DhsA 362.

Anunāsika (adj.) [anu + nāsā + ika] nasal; as tt. g. the sound ŋ; in °lopa apocope of the nasal ŋ VvA 114, 253, 275, 333.

Anunīta (adj.) [pp. of anuneti] led, induced S IV.71; Sn 781.

Anunetar [n. ag. fr. anuneti] one who reconciles or conciliates Ps II.194 (netā vinetā anunetā).

Anuneti [anu + neti] to conciliate, appease, win over, flatter S I.232 (ppr. anunayamāna); pp. **anunīta** (q. v.).

Anupa see anūpa.

Anupakampati [anu + pakampati] to shake, move, to be unsteady Th I, 191 = Ud 41.

Anupakkama [an + upakkama] not attacking, instr. °ena not by attack (from external enemies) Vin II.195.

Anupakkuṭṭha (adj.) [an + upak°] blameless, irreproachable D I.113; Vin IV.160; Sn p. 115; DA I.281.

Anupakkhandati [anu + pa + khandati] to push oneself forward, to encroach on D I.122 (= anupavisati DA I.290); ger. **anupakhajja** pushing oneself in, intruding Vin II.88 (= antopavisati), 213; IV.43 (= anupavisati); M I.151, 469; S III.113; Vism 18.

Anupakhajjati [den. fr. anupakhajja, ger. of anupakkhandati] to encroach, intrude Vin V.163.

Anupagacchati [anu + pa + gacchati] to go or return into (c. acc.) D I.55 (anupeti +).

Anupaghāta [an + upaghāta] not hurting Dh 185 (anūpa° metri causa; expldᵈ· by anupahananañ c'eva anupaghātanañ ca DhA III.238).

Anupacita (adj.) [anu + pa + cita, pp. of anupacināti] heaped up, accumulated ThA 56.

Anupacināti [an + upacināti] not to observe or notice J V.339 (= anoloketi C.; v. l. anapaviṇāti).

Anupajagghati [anu + pa + jagghati] to laugh at, to deride, mock over A I.198 (v. l. anusaŋ°).

Anupajjati [anu + **pad**] to follow, accompany J IV.304. — pp. anupanna (q. v.).

Anupañcāhaŋ (adv.) [anu + pañcā + ahaŋ] every five days PvA 139 (+ anudasāhaŋ).

Anupaññatti (f.) [anu + paññatti] a supplementary regulation or order Vin II.286; V.2 sq.

Anupaṭipāṭi (f.) [anu + paṭipāṭi] succession; as adv. in order, successively DA I.277 (kathā = anupubbikathā); DhA III.340 (anupaṭipāṭiyā = anupubbena); Vism 244.

Anupaṭṭhita (adj.) [anu + pa + ṭhita] setting out after, following, attacking J V.452.

Anupatati [anu + patati] 1. to follow, go after, J VI.555 anupatiyāsi Subj.). — 2. to fall upon, to befall, attack Vin III.106 = M I.364; S I.23 (read °patanti for °patatanti) = Dh 221 (dukkhā); Th I, 41 = 1167 (of lightning). — pp. **anupatita** (q. v.). Cp. also **anupāta** & **anupātin**.

Anupatita [pp. of anupatati] "befallen", affected with, oppressed by (—°) S II.173 (dukkha°); III.69 (id.); Sn 334 (pamāda°).

Anupatitatta (nt.) [abstr. of anupatita] the fact of being attacked by, being a victim of (—°) SnA 339.

Anupatta (anuppatta) [pp. of anupāpuṇāti; cp. Sk. anuprāpta] (having) attained, received, got to (c. acc.), reached D I.87—111; II 2; It 38; Sn 027, 635; Dh 386, 403; Pv IV.1⁶⁶; PvA 59 (dukkhaŋ), 242. In phrase **addhagata vayo-anuppatta** having reached old age, e. g. Vin II.188; D I.48; Sn pp. 50, 92; PvA 149.

Anupatti (anuppatti) (f.) [anu + patti] attainment, accomplishment, wish, desire (fulfilled), ideal S I.46, 52.

Anupathe at J V.302 should be read as anu pathe by the way at the wayside; anu to be taken as prep. c. loc. (see anu A). C. explⁿˢ· as janghamagga-mahāmaggānaŋ antare.

Anupada [cp. Sk. anupadaŋ adv., anu + pada] 1. the "afterfoot", i. e. second foot a verse, also a mode of reciting, where the second foot is recited without the first one Vin IV.15 (cp. 355); Miln 340 (anupadena anupadaŋ katheti). — 2. (adj.) (following) on foot, at every, step, continuous, repeated, in °dhamma-vipassanā uninterrupted contemplation M III.25; °vaṇṇanā word-by-word explanation DhsA 168. As nt. adv. °ŋ close behind, immediately after (c. gen.) J II.230 (tassânupadaŋ agamāsi); VI.422. Esp. freq. in combⁿ· **padânupadaŋ** (adv.) foot after foot, i. e. in the footsteps, immediately behind J III. 504; VI.555; DhA I.69; II.38.

Anupadātar (anuppadātar) [n. ag. of anupadeti] one who gives, or one who sets forth, effects, designs D I.4 (cp. DA I.74); A II.209.

Anupadāna (anuppadāna) (nt.) [anu + pa + dāna, cp. anupadeti] giving, administering, furnishing, the giving of (—°) D I.12 (cp. DA I.98; both read anuppādāna); J III.205; Miln 315.

Anupadinna (anuppadinna) [pp. of anupadeti] given, handed over, furnished, dedicated Pv 1.5[12].

Anupadeti (anuppadeti) [anu + pa + dadāti] to give out, give as a present, hand over; to design, set forth, undertake S III.131 (Pot. anuppadajjuŋ); M I.416 (Pot. anupadajjeyya, see dadāti 1.3); Miln 210 (°deti). fut. °dassati (see dadāti 1.1); D III.92; S IV.303 (v. l. SS for T. anusarissati); A III.43; Sn 983. ger. °datvā SnA 35. inf. °dātuŋ A I.117. pp. °dinna (q. v.).

Anupaddava (adj.) [an + upaddava] free from danger, uninjured, safe Vin II.79 = 124 (+ anītika); III.162; Dh 338; DhA IV.48; PvA 250 (expl[n] for siva).

Anupadhāreti [an + upadhār°] to disregard, to heed not, to neglect DhA IV.197; VvA 260.

Anupadhika (adj.) [an + upadhi + ka] free from attachment (see upadhi) Vin I 36 (anupadhika); D. III 112 (anupadhika opp. to sa-upadhika); Sn 1057 (anūpadhika T., but Nd[2] anūpadhika. with ū for u metri causa).

Anupanna, [pp. of anupajjati] gone into, reached, attained Sn 764 (māradheyya°).

Anupabandhati (anuppa°) [anu + pa + bandhati] to follow immediately, to be incessant, to keep on (without stopping), to continue Miln 132. — Caus. °āpeti ibid.

Anupabandhanatā (anuppa°) (f.) [abstr. to prec.] non-stopping, not ceasing Miln 132.

Anupabandhanā (anuppa°) (f.) [abstr. fr. anupabandhati] continuance, incessance, Pug 18 = Vbh 357 (in exegesis of upanāha).

Anupabbajjā (f.) [anu + pabbajjā, cp. BSk. anupravrajati Divy 61] giving up wordly life in imitation of another S V.97 = It 107.

Anupaya (adj.) [an + upaya] unattached, "aloof" S I.181 (akankha apiha +).

Anuparigacchati [anu + pari + gacchati] to walk round and round, to go round about (c. acc.) Vin III.119; S I.75 (ger. °gamma); Sn 447 (aor. °pariyagā = parito parito agamāsi Sn A 393); J IV.267.

Anuparidhāvati [anu + pari + dhāvati] to run up & down or to move round & round (cp. anuparivattati) S. III.150 (khīlan).

Anupariyāti [anu + pari + yāti] to go round about, to go about, to wander or travel all over (c. acc.) Vin II.111; S I.102, 124; Th 1, 1235 (°pariyeti), 1250 (id. to search); Pv III.3[4] (= anuvicarati); Miln 38; PvA 92 (°yāyitvā, ger.) 217.

Anupariyāya (adj) [adjectivised ger. of anupariyāti] going round, encircling, in °patha the path leading or going round the city D II.83 = S IV 194 = A V.195; A IV.107.

Anuparivattati [anu + pari + vṛt] to go or move round, viz. 1. to deal with, be engaged in, perform, worship Vin III.307 (ādiccaŋ); D I.240; PvA 97. — 2. to meet Miln 204 (Devadatto ca Bodhisatto ca ekato anuparivattanti). — 3. to move round & round, move on and on, keep on rolling (c. acc.), evolve S. III.150 (anuparidhāvati +) Miln 253 (anudhāvati + kāyan).

Anuparivatti (f.) (—°) [anu + parivatti] dealing with, occupation, connection with S III.16.

Anuparivāreti [anu + pari + vāreti] to surround, stand by, attend on (c. acc.) Vin I.338; M I.153; DhA I.55.

Anuparivenịyaŋ [anu + parivenịyaŋ = loc. of pariveṇi] should be written anu pariveṇiyaŋ ("in every cell, cell by cell"), anu here functioning as prep. c. loc. (see anu A) Vin I.80, 106.

Anuparisakkati [anu + pari + sakkati] to move round, to be occupied with, take an interest in (c. acc.) S IV.312 (v.l. °vattati).

Anuparisakkana (nt.) [fr. anuparisakkati] dealing with, interest in S IV.312 (v.l. °vattana).

Anupariharati [anu + pari + harati] to surround, enfold, embrace M I.306.

Anupalitta (adj.) [an + upalitta] unsmeared, unstained, free from taint M I.319, 386 (in verse): as °ūpalitta in verse of Sn & Dh: Sn 211 (= lepānaŋ abhāvā SnA 261), 392, 468, 790, 845; Dh 353.

Anupavajja (adj.) [grd. of an + upavadati] blameless, without fault Miln 391.

Anupavattaka (anuppa°) (adj.) to anupavatteti] one who succeeds (another) King or Ruler in the ruling of an empire (cakkaŋ) Miln 342, 362; SnA 454. See also **anuvattaka.**

Anupavatteti (anuppa°) [anu + pa + vatteti, fr. **vṛt**] to keep moving on after, to continue rolling, with **cakkaŋ** to wield suppreme power after, i.e. in succession or imitation of a predecessor S I.191; Miln 362. See also **anuvatteti.**

Anupavāda [an + upavāda] not blaming or finding fault, abstaining from grumbling or abuse Dh 185 (anūpa° in metre; expl[d] at DhA III.238 as anupavādanañ c'eva anupavādāpanañ ca "not scolding as well as not inciting others to grumbling"); adj. °**vādaka** Pug 60, & °**vādin** M I.360.

Anupaviṭṭha (anuppa°) [pp. of anupavisati] entered, gone or got into, fallen into (c. acc.) Miln 270, 318 sq., 409 (coming for shelter); PvA 97, 152 (Gangānadiŋ a. nadī: flowing into the G.).

Anupaviṭṭhatā (f.) [abstr. to anupaviṭṭha] the fact of having entered Miln 257.

Anupavisati [anu + pa + visati] to go into, to enter Dh I.290; VvA 42 (= ogāhati). — pp. °**paviṭṭha** (q.v.) — Caus. °**paveseti** (q.v.).

Anupavecchati (anuppa°) [see under pavecchati] to give, give over to, offer up, present, supply Vin I.221 (°pavacchati); D I.74 (= pavesati DA I.218); II.78; M I.446; III.133; A II.64; III.26 (v.l. °vacch°); J V.394; Sn 208 (v.l. °vacch°); SnA 256 (= anupavesati); PvA 28.

Anupaveseti [anu + pa + **vis**, cp. BSk. anupraveśayati Divy 238] to make enter, to give over, to supply SnA 256 (= °pavecchati).

Anupasankamati[1] [anu + pa + saŋkamati] to go along up to (c. acc.) PvA 179.

Anupasankamati[2] [an + upasank°] not to go to, not to approach DhA II.30 (+ apayirupāsati).

Anupasanṭhapanā (f.) [an + upasanṭhapanā] not stopping, incessance, continuance Pug 18 (but id. p. at Vbh 357 has anusansandanā instead); cp. **anupabandhanā.**

Anupassaka (adj.) [fr. anupassati] observing, viewing, contemplating Th 1, 420.

Anupassati [anu + passati] to look at, contemplate, observe Sn 477; Ps I.57, 187; Sn A 505.

Anupassanā (f.) [abstr. of anupassati, cf. Sk. anudarśana] looking at, viewing, contemplating, consideration, realisation S v.178 sq., Sn p. 140; Ps I.10, 20, 96; II.37, 41 sq., 67 sq.; Vbh 194. See **anicca°**, **anatta°**, **dukkha°**.

Anupassin (—°) (adj.) [fr. anupassati] viewing, observing, realising S II.84 sq., V.294 sq., 311 sq., 345, Dh 7, 253; Sn 255, 728; Ps I.191 sq.; Vbh 193 sq., 236; Sdhp 411.

Anupahata[1] [anu + pa + hata, pp. of anu + pa + **han**] thrown up, blown up Miln 274.

Anupahata[2] (adj.) [an + upahata] not destroyed, not spoilt DhA II.33 (°jivhapasāda).

Anupāta [of anupatati] attack in speech, contest, reproach A I.161.

Anupātin (adj.) [fr. anupāta] 1. following, indulging in J III.523 (khaṇa°). — 2. attacking, hurting J v.399.

Anupādaŋ (adv.) [anu + pāda] at the foot Vism 182 (opp. **anusīsaŋ** at the head).

Anupādā [ger. of an + upādiyati = anupādāya] **anupādāniya**, **anupādāya**, **anupādiyāna**, **anupādiyitvā** see **upādiyati**.

Anupādāna & **Anupādi** see **upādāna** & **upādi**.

Anupāpita [pp. of anupāpeti] having been lead to or made to reach, attained, found Miln 252.

Anupāpuṇāti (anuppā°) [anu + pāpuṇāti] to reach, attain, get to, find S I.105; ger. **anuppatvāna** Pv II.9[24] (= °pāpuṇitvā PvA 123). — pp. **anupatta** (q. v.). — Caus. **anupāpeti** (q. v.).

Anupāpeti [Caus. of anupāpuṇāti] to make reach or attain, to lead to, to give or make find J VI.88; Cp. XI. 4 (aor. **anupāpayi**); Miln 276. — pp. **anupāpita** (q. v.).

Anupāya [an + upāya] wrong means J I.256; Sdhp 405.

Anupāyāsa see **upāyāsa**.

Anupālaka (adj.) [anu + pālaka] guarding, preserving Sdhp 474.

Anupālana (nt.) [fr. anupāleti] maintenance, guarding, keeping Dpvs III.2.

Anupāleti [anu + pāleti] to safeguard, warrant, maintain Miln 160 (santatiŋ).

Anupāhana (adj.) [an + upāhana] without shoes J VI.552.

Anupiya (anuppiya) (adj.) [anu + piya] flattering, plessant, nt. pleasantness, flattery, in °**bhāṇin** one who flatters D III.185; J II.390; V.360; and °**bhāṇitar** id. Vbh 352.

Anupīḷaŋ at PvA 161 is to be read **anuppīḷan** (q. v.).

Anupucchati [anu + pucchati] to ask or inquire after (c. acc.) Sn 432, 1113. — pp. **anupuṭṭha** (q. v.).

Anupuṭṭha [pp. of anupucchati] asked Sn 782 (= pucchita SnA 521).

Anupubba (adj.) [anu + pubba] following in one's turn, successive, gradual, by and by, regular Vin II.237 (mahāsamuddo a°-ninno etc.); D I.184; Sn 511; J V.155 (regularly formed, of ūrū). Cases adverbially: **anupubbena** (instr.) by and by, in course of time, later, gradually Vin I.83; Dh 239 (= anupaṭipāṭiyā DhA III.340); Pug 41, 64; J II.2, 105; III.127; Miln 22; PvA 19. **anupubbaso** (abl. cp. Sk. anupūrvaśaḥ) in regular order Sn 1000. — In compn. both anupubba° & anupubbi° (q. v.).

-kāraṇa gradual performance, graded practice M I.446. **-nirodha** successive passing away, fading away in regular succession, i. e. in due course. The nine stages of this process are the same as those mentioned under °vihāra, & are enumd. as such at D III.266, 290; A IV.409, 456; Ps I.35. **-vihāra** a state of gradually ascending stages, by means of which the highest aim of meditation & trance is attained, viz. complete cessation of all consciousness. These are 9 stages, consisting of the 4 jhānas, the 4 āyatanāni & as the crowning phrase "saññā-vedayita-nirodha" (see jhāna[1]). Enumd. as such in var. places, esp. at the foll.: D II.156; III.265, 290; A IV.410; Nd[2] under jhāna; Ps I.5; Miln 176. **-sikkhā** regular instruction or study (dhammavinaye) M I.479; III.1 (+ °kiriyā °paṭipadā).

Anupubbaka (adj.) = anupubba, in cpd. **pubbânupubbaka** all in succession or in turn, one by one (on nature of this kind of cpd. see anu B IV.) Vin I.20 (°ānaŋ kulānaŋ puttā the sons of each clan, one by one).

Anupubbata (nt.) [fr. anupubba] acting in turn, gradatioo, succession Vv 64[14] (= anukūla kiriyā i. e. as it pleases VvA 280) cp. ānupubbatā.

Anupubbi-kathā (f.) [anupubba + kathā, formation like dhammi-kathā] a gradual instruction, graduated sermon, regulated exposition of the ever higher values of four subjects (dāna-kathā, sīla°, sagga°, magga°) i. e. charity, righteousness, the heavens, and the Path. Bdhgh. explains the term as anupubbikathā nāma dānânantaraŋ sīlaŋ sīlânantaro saggo saggânantaro maggo ti etesaŋ dīpana-kathā" (DA I.277). Vin I.15, 18; II.156, 192; D I.110; II.41; M I.379; J I.8; VvA 66, 197, 208; DA I.308; DhA I.6; Miln 228. — The spelling is frequently **ānupubbikathā** (as to lengthening of anu see anu Note (a)), e. g. at D I.110; II.41; M I.379; J I.8; Miln 228.

Anupekkhati [anu + pekkhati] 1. to concentrate oneself on, to look carefully A III.23. — 2. to consider, to show consideration for, Nd[2] 50 (ppr. °amāna = anukampamāna). — Caus. **anupekkheti** to cause some one to consider carefully Vin II.73.

Anupekkhanatā (f.) [abstr. fr. anupekkhana, see anupekkhati] concentration (of thought) Dhs 8, 85, 284, 372.

Anupeti [anu + pa + **i**] to go into D I.55 (+ anupagacchati) S III.207; DA I.165.

Anupeseti [anu + pa + **iṣ**] to send forth after Miln 36.

Anuposathikaŋ see anvaddhamāsaŋ.

Anuposiya (adj.) [grd. of anu + **puṣ**] to be nourished or fostered Sdhp 318.

Anuppa° in all combns. of anu + ppa see under headings **anupa°**.

Anuppadajjuŋ (S III.131) see **anupadeti**.

Anuppanna (°uppāda, °uppādeti) see **uppanna** etc.

Anuppīḷa (adj.) [an + uppīḷa] not molested, not oppressed (by robbers etc.) not ruined, free from harm J III.443; v.378; VvA 351; PvA 161.

Anupharaṇa (nt.) [anu + pharaṇa] flashing through, pervading Miln 148.

Anuphusīyati [anu + phusīyati, cp. Sk. pruṣāyati, Caus. of **pruṣ**] to sprinkle, moisten, make wet J v.242 (himaŋ; C. pateyya).

Anubajjhati at PvA 56 is faulty reading for **anubandhati** (q. v.).

Anubaddha [pp. of anubandhati] following, standing behind (piṭṭhito) D I.1, 226.

Anubandha [anu + **bandh**] bondage M III.170; It 91.

Anubandhati [anu + bandhati] to follow, run after, pursue J I.195; II.230; VI.452 (= anujavati); PvA 56 (substitute for anubajjhanti!), 103, 155. aor. °bandhi J II.154, 353; III.504; PvA 260 (= anvāgacchi). ger. °bandhitvā J I.254. grd. °bandhitabba M I.106. — pp. anubaddha (q. v.).

Anubandhana (nt.) [fr. anubandhati] that which connects or follows, connection, consequence J VI.526 (°dukkha).

Anubala (nt.) [anu + bala] rear-guard, retinue, suite, in °ŋ bhavati to accompany or follow somebody Miln 125.

Anubujjhati [anu + bujjhati, Med. of **budh**, cp. Sk. avabudhyate] to remember, recollect J III.387 (with **avabujjhati** in prec. verse).

Anubujjhana (nt.) [fr. anubujjhati] awakening, recognition Ps I.18 (bujjhana +).

Anubuddha [pp. of anu + bodhati] 1. awakened (act. & pass.), recognised, conceived, seen, known D II.123 (°ā ime dhammā); S I.137 (dhammo vimalen' ânubuddho) II.203; IV.188; A II.1; III.14; IV.105; SnA 431. In phrase **buddhânubuddha** (as to nature of cpd. see anu B IV.) either "fully awakened (enlightened)" or "wakened hy by the wake" (Mrs. Rh. D.) Th 1, 679 = 1246. — 2. a lesser Buddha, inferior than the Buddha DA I.40. Cp. **buddhânubuddha**.

Anubodha [anu + **budh**] awakening; perception, recognition, understanding S I.126 (?) = A V.46 (anubodhiŋ as aor. of anubodhati?); Pug 21; Miln 233. Freq. in compⁿ. **ananubodha** (adj.) not understanding, not knowing the truth S II.92; III.261; V.431; A II.1; IV.105; Dhs 390, 1061; VvA 321 (= anavabodha) and **duranubodha** (adj.) hard to understand, difficult to known D I.12, 22; S I.136.

Anubodhati [anu + **budh**] to wake up, to realise, perceive, understand; aor. anubodhiŋ A V.46 (?) = S I.126 (anubodhaŋ). — Caus. °**bodheti** to awaken, fig. to make see to instruct J VI.139 (°ayamāna) — pp. **anubuddha** (q. v.).

Anubodhana (nt.) [fr. anubodhati] awakening, understanding, recognition Ps I.18 (bodhana +).

Anubbajati [anu + **vraj**] to go along, wander, follow, tread (a path) J IV.399 (maggaŋ = pabbajati C.).

Anubbata (adj.) [Vedic anuvrata, anu + vata] subject to the will of another, obedient, faithful, devoted J III.521; VI.557.

Anubbillāvitatta see ubbill°.

Anubyañjana see anuvyañjana.

Anubrūhita [qq. of anubrūheti] strengthened with (—°), full of Ps I.167.

Anubrūheti [brūheti] to do very much or often, to practice, frequent, to be fond of (c. acc.), foster S I.178 (anubrūhaye); M III.187 (id., so read for manu°), Th 2, 163 (°ehi); Cp. III.1² (saŋvegaŋ anubrūhayiŋ aor.); J III.191 (suññāgāraŋ). Often in phrase **vivekaŋ anubrūheti** to devote oneself to detachment or solitude, e.g. J I.9 (inf. °brūhetuŋ); III.31 (°brūhessāmi), Dh 75 (°brūhaye = °brūheyya vaḍḍheyya DhA II.103). — pp. **anubrūhita** (q.v.) Cp. also **brūhana**.

Anubhaṇanā (f.) [anu + bhaṇana] talking to, admonition, scolding Vin II.88 (anuvadanā +).

Anubhavati & **Anubhoti** [anu + bhavati] to come to or by, to undergo, suffer (feel), get, undertake, partake in, experience D I.129; II.12 (°bhonti); M II.204; A I.61 (atthaŋ °bhoti to have a good result); J VI.97 (°bhoma); Pv I.10¹¹ (°bhonti vipākaŋ); PvA 52 (°issati = vedissati); Sdhf 290. Esp. freq. with **dukkhaŋ** to suffer pain, e.g. PvA I.11¹⁰ (°bhonti); PvA 43, 68, 79 etc. (cp. anubhavana). — ppr. med. °**bhavamāna** J I.50; aor. °**bhavi** PvA 75 (sampattiŋ); ger. °**bhavitvā** J IV.1; PvA 4 (sampattiŋ), 67 (dukkhaŋ), 73 (sampattiŋ); grd. °**bhaviyāna** (in order to receive) Pv II.8⁶ (= anubbavitvā PvA 109). — Pass. **anubhūyati** & °**bhavīyati** to be undergone or being experienced; ppr. °**bhūyamāna** PvA 8, 159 (mayā a. = anubhūta), 214 (attanā by him) & °**bhavīyamāna** PvA 33 (dukkhaŋ). — pp. **anubhūta** (q.v.).

Anubhavana (nt.) [fr. anubhavati] experiencing, suffering; sensation or physical sensibility (cf. *Cpd.* 229, 232¹) Nett 28 (iṭṭhâniṭṭh-ânubhavana-lakkhaṇā vedanā "feeling is characterised by the experiencing of what is pleasant and unpleasant"); Miln 60 (vedayita-lakkhaṇā vedanā anubhavana-lakkhaṇā ca); PvA 152 (kamma-vipāka°). Esp. in combⁿ. with **dukkha°** suffering painful sensations, e.g. at J IV.3; Miln 181; DhA IV.75; PvA 52.

Anubhāga [anu + bhāga] a secondary or inferior part, (after-)share, what is left over Vin II.167.

Anubhāyati [anu + bhāyati] to be afraid of J VI.302 (kissa nv' ânubhāyissaŋ, so read for kissânu°).

Anubhāva [fr. anubhavati] orig. meaning "experience, concomitance" and found only in cpds. as —°, in meaning "experiencing the sensation of or belonging to, experience of, accordance with", e. g. mahā° sensation of greatness, rājā° s. belonging to a king, what is in accordance with kingship, i. e. majesty. Through preponderance of expressions of distinction there arises the meaning of anubhāva as "power, majesty, greatness, splendour etc." & as such it was separated from the 1st component and taken as **ānubhāva** with ā instead of a, since the compositional character had obliterated the character of the a. As such (ānubhāva abs.) found only in later language. — (1) **anubhāva** (—°): **mahānubhāva** (of) great majestat, eminence, power S I.146 sq.; II.274; IV.323; Sn p. 93; Pv II.1¹²; PvA 76. **deva°** of divine power or majesty D II.12; **devatā°** id. J I.168; **dibba°** id. PvA 71, 110. **rājā°** kingly splendour, pomp D I.49; J IV 247; PvA 279 etc. **-anubhāvena** (instr. —°) in accordance with, by means of J II.200 (angavijjā°); PvA 53 (iddh°), 77 (kamma°), 148 (id.), 162 (rāja°), 184 (dāna°), 186 (puñña°). **yatbânubhāvaŋ** (adv.) in accordance with (me), as much as (9 can). after ability, according to power S I.31; Vv 1⁵ (= yathābalaŋ VvA 25). — (2) **ānubhāva** majesty power, magnificence, glory, splendour J V.10, 456; Pv II.8¹¹; VvA 14; PvA 43, 122, 272. See also ānu°.

Anubhāvatā (f.) [= anubhāva + tā] majesty, power S I.156 (mahā°).

Anubhāsati [anu + bhāsati] to speak after, to repeat D I.104; Miln 345; DA I.273.

Anubhūta [pp. of anubhavati] (having or being) experienced, suffered, enjoyed PvA II.12¹⁸. nt. suffering, experience J I.254; Miln 78, 80.

Anubhūyamānatta (nt.) [abstr. fr. ppr. Pass. of anubhavati] the fact of having to undergo, experiencing PvA 103.

Anuma (-dassika) see **anoma°**.

Anumagge at J V.201 should be read **anu magge** along the road, by the way; anu here used as prep. c. loc. (see anu A b).

Anumajjati [anu + majjati] 1. to strike along, to stroke, to touch DA I.276 (= anumasati). — 2. to beat, thresh, fig. to thresh out J VI.548; Miln 90. — Pass. **anumajjīyati** Miln 275 (cp. p. 428).

Anumajjana (nt.) [abstr. fr. anumajjati] threshing out, pounding up (*Dhs. trsl.* 11), always used with ref. to the term **vicāra** (q.v.) Miln 62; DhsA 114; DA I.63, 122.

Anumajjha (adj.) [anu + majjha] mediocre, without going to extremes J IV.192; V.387.

Anumaññati [anu + maññati] to assent, approve, give leave Th 1, 72. — pp. **anumata** (q. v.).

Anumata [pp. of anumaññati] approved of, given consent to, finding approval, given leave D I.99 (= anuññāta DA I.267); J V.399 (= muta); Miln 185, 212, 231, 275; PvA 64 (= anuññāta).

Anumati (f.) [from anumaññati] consent, permission, agreement, assent, approval Vin II.294, 301, 306; D. I.137, 143; Dpvs IV.47, Cf. V.18; DA I.297; VvA 17, PvA 114.

Anumatta see aṇu°.

Anumasati [anu + masati] to touch D I.106 (= anumajjati DA I.276).

Anumāna [fr. anu + **man**] inference Miln 330 (naya +), 372, 413; Sdhp 74.

Anumitta [anu + mitta] a secondary friend, a follower. acquaintance J V.77.

Anumināti [cf. Sk. anumāti, anu + mināti from **mi**, Sk. minoti, with confusion of roots **mā** & **mi**] to observe, draw an inference M I.97; PvA 227 (°anto + nayaŋ nento). See also anumīyati.

Anumīyati [Sk. anumīyate, Pass. of anu + **mā**, measure, in sense of Med.] to observe, conclude or infer from S III.36. Cp. anumināti.

Anumodaka (adj.) [fr. anumodati] one who enjoys, one who is glad of or thankful for (c. acc.) Vin V.172; PvA 122; Sdhf 512.

Anumodati [anu + modati] to find satisfaction in (acc.), to rejoice in, be thankful for (c. acc.), appreciate, benefit from, to be pleased, to enjoy Vin II.212 (bhattagge a. to say grace after a meal); S II.54; A III.50 (°modanīya); IV.411; Dh 177 (ppr. °modamāna); It 78; Pv II.9[19] (dānaŋ °modamāna = enjoying, gladly receiving); I,5[4] (anumodare = are pleased; pitisomanassajātā honti PvA 27); J II.112; PvA 19, 46, 81, 201) imper. **modāhi**); Sdhp. 501 sq. — pp. **anumodita** (q. v.).

Anumodana (nt.) [fr. anumodati] "according to taste", i.e. satisfaction, thanks, esp. after a meal or after receiving gifts = to say grace or benediction, blessing, thanksgiving. In latter sense with **dadāti** (give thanks for = loc.), karoti (= Lat. gratias agere) or **vacati** (say or tell thanks): °ŋ datvā PvA 89; °ŋ katvā J I.91; DhA III.170, 172; VvA 118; PvA 17, 47; °ŋ **vatvā** VvA 40 (pānīyadāne for the gift of water), 295, 306 etc. °ŋ **karoti** also "to do a favour" PvA 275. Cp. further DhA I.198 (°gāthā verses expressing thanks, benediction); II.97 (Satthāraŋ °ŋ yācinsu asked his blessing), PvA 23 (°atthaŋ in order to thank), 26 (id.), 121, 141 (katabhatta°), 142; Sdhp 213, 218, 516.

Anumodita [pp. of anumodati] enjoyed, rejoiced in PvA 77.

Anummatta (adj.) [an + ummatta] not out of mind, sane, of sound mind Miln 122; Sdhp 205.

Anuyanta at A V.22 is doubtful reading (v.l. **anuyutta**). The meaning is either "inferior to, dependent on, a subject of, a vassal" or "attending on". The explanation may compare Sk. anuyātaŋ attendance [anu + **yā**, cp. anuyāyin] or Sk. yantṛ ruler [**yam**], in which latter case anu-yantṛ would be "an inferior ruler" and P. yanta would represent the n. a.g. yantā as a-stem. The v. l. is perhaps preferable as long as other passages with anuyanta are not found (see **anuyutta** 2).

Anuyāgin (adj.) [fr. anu + **yaj**] offering after the example of another D I.142.

Anuyāta [pp. of anuyāti] gone through or after, followed, pursued S II.105 (magga); A V.236; It 29: Miln 217.

Anuyāti (& **anuyāyati**) [anu + **yā**] 1. to go after, to follow J VI.49 (fut. °yissati), 499 (yāyantaŋ anuyāyati = anugacchati C). — 2. to go along by, to go over, to visit Miln 391 (°yāyati). — pp. **anuyāta** (q. v.). See also anusaŋyāyati.

Anuyāyin (adj.) [cp. Sk. anuyāyin, anu + **yā**] going after, following, subject to (gen.) Sn 1017 (anânuyāyin); J VI.309; Miln 284.

Anuyuñjanā (f.) (& °yuñjana nt.) [abstr. fr. anuyuñjati] application or devotion to (—°) Miln 178; VvA 346 (anuyujjanaŋ wrong spelling?)

Anuyuñjati [anu + yuñjati] 1. to practice, give oneself up to (acc.), attend, pursue S I.25, 122 (°yuñjan "in loving self-devotion" Mrs. Rh. D.); III.154; IV.104, 175; Dh 26 (pamādaŋ = **pavatteti** DhA I.257), 247 (surāmeraya-pānaŋ = **sevati** bahulīkaroti DhA III.356); PvA 61 (kammaṭṭhānaŋ). — 2. to ask a question, to call to account, take to task Vin II.79; Vv 33[5]; ppr. Pass. °**yuñjiyamāna** PvA 192. — pp. **anuyutta** (q. v.). — Caus. **anuyojeti** "to put to", to address, admonish, exhort DhA IV.20.

Anuyutta [pp. of anuyuñjati] 1. applying oneself to, dealing with, practising, given to, intent upon D I.166, 167; III. 232 = A II 205 (attaparitāpan' ânuyogaŋ a.); S III.153; IV.104; Sn 663 (lobhaguṇe), 814 (methunaŋ = samāyutta SnA 536), 972 (jhān°); Pug 55; PvA 163 (jāgariya°), 206. — 2. following, attending on; an attendant, inferior, vassal, in expression **khattiya** or **rājā anuyutta** a prince royal or a smaller king (see khattiya 3 b) A V.22 (v l. for T. anuyanta, q. v.); Sn 553 (= **anugāmin, sevaka** SnA 453).

Anuyoga [Sk. anuyoga, fr. anu + **yuj**] 1. application, devotion to (—°), execution, practice of (—°); often comb[d]. with anuyutta in phrase °**anuyogaŋ anuyutta** = practising, e. g. Vin I.190 (maṇḍan' ânuyogaŋ anuyutta); D III.113 (attakilamath' ânuyogaŋ a.); A II.205 (attaparitāpan' ânuyogaŋ a.). — As adj. (—°) doing, given to, practising (cp. anuyutta). D I.5; III.107; M I.385; S I.182; III.239; IV.330; V.320; A I.14; III.249; IV.460 sq.; V. 17 sq., 205; J I.90 (padhān' ânuyogakiccaŋ); Vv 84[38] (dhamma°); Miln 348; DA I. 78, 104. — 2. invitation, appeal, question (cp. anuyuñjati 2) Miln 10 (ācariyassa °ŋ datvā).

Anuyogavant (adj.) [anuyoga + vant] applying oneself to, full of application or zeal, devoted PvA 207.

Anuyogin (adj.) [fr. anuyoga] applying oneself to, devoted to (—°) Dh 209 (atta° given to oneself, self-concentrated).

Anurakkhaka (adj.) [fr. anurakkhati, cp. °rakkhin] preserving, keeping up J IV.192 (vaŋsa°); VI.1 (id.).

Anurakkhaṇa (nt.) & °ā (f.) [abstr. fr. anurakkhati] guarding, protection preservation D III.225 sq.; A II.16 sq.; J I.133; Rug 12; Dpvs IV.24 (adj.); VvA 32 (citta°); Sdhp 449.

Anurakkhati [anu + rakkhati] to guard, watch over (acc.), preserve, protect, shield Sn 149; Dh 327; J I.46; Pug 12. — ppr. med.° **rakkhamāna(ka)** as adj. Sdhp 621.

Anurakkhā (f.) [= anurakkhaṇā] guarding, protection, preservation S IV.323 (anuddayā a. anukampā).

Anurakkhin (adj.) [fr. anurakkhati] guarding, preserving, keeping J V.24.

Anurakkhiya (adj.) [f. anurakkhati] in **dur**° difficult to guard Vin III.149.

Anurañjita [pp. of anu + rañjeti, Caus. of **rañj**] illumined, brightened, beautified Bu I.45 (byāmapabhā° by the shine of the halo); VvA 4 (saññhātapa° for saññhāpabhā°).

Anuratta (adj.) pp. of anu + **rañj**] attached or devoted to, fond of, faithful Th 2, 446 (bhattāraŋ); J I.297; Miln 146.

Anuravati [anu + ravati] to resound, to sound after, linger (of sound) Miln 63.

Anuravanā (f.) [abstr. fr. anuravati] lingering of the sound, resounding Miln 63.

Anuraho (adv.) [anu + raho] in secret, face to face, private M I.27.

Anurujjhati [Sk. anurudhyate, Pass. of anu + **rudh**] to conform oneself to, have a regard for, approve, to be pleased A IV.158; Dhs A 362. — pp. **anuruddha** (q. v.).

Anuruddha [pp. of anurujjhati] enggaged in, devoted to; compliant or complied with, pleased S IV.71, (anānuruddha).

Anurūpa (adj.) [anu + rūpa] suitable, adequate, seeming, fit, worthy; adapted to, corresponding, conform with (—°) J I.91; VI.366 (tad°); PvA 61 (ajjhāsaya° according to his wish), 128 (id.) 78, 122, 130, 155; etc. Cp. also **paṭirūpa** in same meaning.

Anurodati [anu + rodati] to cry after, cry for J III.166 = Pv I.12[1] (dārako candaŋ a.).

Anurodha [fr. anu + **rudh**] compliance, consideration satisfaction (opp. **virodha**) S I.111; IV.210; Sn 362; Dhs 1059; Vbh 145; DhsA 362.

Anulapanā (f.) [anu + lapanā, **lap**] scolding, blame, accusation Vin II.88 (spelt anullapanā; comb[d.] with anuvadana & anubhaṇanā).

Anulitta (adj.) [cp. Sk. anulipta, pp. of anulimpati] anointed, besmeared J I.266; PvA 211.

Anulimpati [anu + limpati] to anoint, besmear, Miln 394 (°limpitabba). Caus. °**limpeti** in same meaning Miln 169, and °**lepeti** Milm 169 (grd. °**lepanīya** to be treated with ointment). — pp. **anulitta** (q. v.).

Anulimpana (nt.) [fr. anulimpati] anointing Miln 353, 394.

Anulepa [fr. anu + **lip**] anointing Miln 152.

Anulokin (adj.) [fr. anu + loketi, cp. Sk. & P. avalokin & anuviloketi] looking (up) at, seeing (—°) M I.147 (sīsa°).

Anuloma (adj.) [Sk. anu + loma] "with the hair or grain", i. e. in natural order, suitable, fit, adapted to, adaptable, straight forward D II.273 (anānuloma, q. v.) S IV.401; Ps II.67, 70; DhA II.208. — nt. direct order, state of fitting in, adaptation Miln 148.

-**ñāṇa** insight of adaptation (cp. *Cpd.* 66, 68) DhA II.208. -**paṭiloma** in regular order & reverse, forward & backward (Ep. of paṭiccasamuppāda, also in BSk.) Vin I.1; A IV.448.

Anulomika (& °ya) (adj.) [fr. anuloma] suitable, fit, agreeable; in proper order, adapted to (—°) Vin II.7 (an°); III.120 (an° = ananucchaviya); IV.239; A I.106; III.116 sq.; It 103 (sāmaññassa°); Sn 385 (pabbajita°); KhA 243 (ananulomiya); DhsA 25; Sdhp 65.

Anulometi [v. denom. fr. anuloma] to conform to, to be in accordance with Miln 372.

Anuḷāratta (nt.) [abstr. fr. an + uḷāra] smallness, littleness, insignificance VvA 24.

Anuvajja (adj.) [grd. of anu + vadati, cp. anuvāda & Sk. avavadya] to be blamed, censurable, worthy of reproach Sn p. 78 (an° = anuvādavimutta SnA 396).

Anuvattaka (adj.) [fr. anuvatteti] 1. = **anupavattaka** (q. v.) Th I, 1014 (cakka°). — 2. following, siding in with (—°) Vin IV.218 (ukkhittânuvattikā f.).

Anuvattati [Sk. anuvartati, anu + vattati] 1. to follow, imitate, follow one's example (c. acc.), to be obedient D II.244; Vin II.309 (Bdhgh.); IV.218; J I.125, 300; DA I.288; PvA 19. — 2. to practice, execute Pv IV. 7[12]. — Caus. °**vatteti** (q. v.).

Anuvattana (nt.) [abstr. fr. anuvattati] complying with, conformity with (—°), compliance, observance, obedience J I.367 (dhamma°); V.78.

Anuvattin (adj.) [fr. anuvattati] following, acting according to or in conformity with (—°), obedient J II.348 (f. °inī); III.319 (id.); Dh 86 (dhamma°); Vv 15[5] (vasa° = anukūlabhāvena vattana sīla VvA 71); DhA II.161.

Anuvatteti [anu + vatteti] = **anupavatteti** (q. v.) Th I, 826 (dhammacakkaŋ: "after his example turn the wheel" Mrs. Rh. D.).

Anuvadati [Sk. ava°; anu + vadati] to blame, censure, reproach Vin II.80, 88. — grd. **anuvajja** (q. v.).

Anuvadanā (f.) [fr. anuvadati] blaming, blame, censure Vin II.88 (anuvāda +).

Anuvasati [anu + vasati] to live with somebody, to dwell, inhabit J II.421. Caus. °**vāseti** to pass, spend (time) J VI.296. — pp. °**vuttha** (q. v.).

Anuvassaŋ (adv.) [anu + vassa] for one rainy season; every rainy season or year, i. e. annually C. on Th I, 24.

Anuvassika (adj.) [fr. anuvassaŋ] one who has (just) passed one rainy season Th I, 24 ("scarce have the rains gone by" Mrs. Rh. D.; see *trsl.* p. 29 n. 2).

Anuvāceti [anu + Caus. of **vac**] to say after, to repeat (words), to recite or make recite after or again D I.104 (= tehi aññesaŋ vācitaŋ anuvācenti DA I.273); Miln 345. Cp. anubhāseti.

Anuvāta[1] [anu + **vā** to blow] a forward wind, the wind that blows from behind, a favourable wind; °ŋ adv. with the wind, in the direction of the wind (opp. **paṭivātaŋ**). A I.226 (°paṭivātaŋ); Sdhp 425 (paṭivāta°). In anuvāte (anu + vāte) at J II.382 "with the wind, facing te w., in front of the wind" anu is to be taken as prep. c. loc. & to be separated from vāte (see anu A b.).

Anuvāta[2] [anu + **vā** to weave (?) in analogy to vāta from **vā** to blow] only in connection with the making of the bhikkhus garment (**cīvara**) "weaving on, supplementary weaving, or along the seam", i. e. hem, seam, binding Vin I.254, 297; II.177; IV.121 (aggaḷa +); PvA 73 (anuvāte appabhonte since the binding was insufficient).

Anuvada [fr. anuvadati, cp. Sk. anuvāda in meaning of "repetition"] 1. blaming, censure, admonition Vin II.5, 32; A II.121 (atta°, para°); Vbh 376. — 2. in comb[n.] **vādânuvāda**: talk and lesser or additional talk, i. e. "small talk" (see anu B IV.) D I.161; M I.368.

-**adhikaraṇa** a question or case of censure Vin II.88 sq.; III.164 (one of the 4 adhikaraṇāni, q. v.).

Anuvāsana (nt.) [fr. anuvāseti] an oily enema, an injection Miln 353.

Anuvāseti [anu + vāseti, Caus. of vāsa[3] odour, perfume] to treat with fragrant oil, i. e. to make an injection or give an enema of salubrious oil Miln 169; grd. °**vāsanīya** ibid.; pp. °**vāsita** Miln 214.

Anuvikkhitta (adj.) [anu + vi + khitta, pp. of anu + vikkhipati] dispersed over S V.277 sq. (+ anuvisaṭa).

Anuvigaṇeti [anu + vi + gaṇeti] to take care of, regard, heed, consider Th I, 109.

Anuvicarati [anu + vi + carati] to wander about, stroll roam through, explore D I.235; J II.128; III.188; PvA 189 (= anupariyāti). — Caus. °**vicāreti** to think over (lit. to make one's mind wander over), to meditate, ponder (cp. anuvicinteti); always combd. with **anuvitakketi** (q. v.) A I.264 (cetasā), III.178 (dhammaŋ cetasā a.). — pp. **anuvicarita** (q. v.).

Anuvicarita [pp. of anuvicāreti] reflected, pondered over, thought out S III.203 (manasā); DA I.106 (= **anucarita**).

Anuvicāra [anu + vicāra, cf. anuvicāreti] meditation, reflexion, thought Dhs 85 (= **vicāra**).

Anuvicinaka [fr. anu + viciṇāti] one who examines, an examiner Miln 365.

Anuvicinteti [anu + vi + cinteti] to think or ponder over, to meditate D II.203; S I 203 (yoniso °cintaya, imper. "marshall thy thoughts in ordered governance" Mrs. Rh. D.; v. l. anucintaya); Th 1, 747; Dh 364; It 82 (dhammaŋ °ayaŋ); J III.396; IV 227; V.223 (dhammaŋ °cintayanto).

Anuvicca [ger. of anuvijjati, for the regular from **anuvijja** prob. through influence of anu + **i** (anu-v-icca for anvicca), cf. anveti & adhicca; & see anuvijjati] having known or found out, knowing well or thoroughly, testing, finding out M I.301, 361 (v. l. °**vijja**); A II.3, 84; V.88; Dh 229 (= jānitvā DhA III.329); Sn 530 (= anuviditvā SnA 431); J I.459 (= jānitvā C.); III.426; Pug. 49.
-**kāra** a thorough investigation, examination, test Vin I.236 (here spelt **anuvijja**) = M I.379 (= °viditvā C.) = A IV.185.

Anuvijjaka [fr. anuvijja, ger. of anuvijjati] one who finds out, an examiner Vin V.161.

Anuvijjati [anu + vid, with fusion of Vedic vetti to know, and Pass. of vindati to find (= vidyate)] to know thoroughly, to find out, to trace, to come to know; inf. °**vijjituŋ** J III.506; ger. °**viditvā** Sn A 431, also °**vijja** & **vicca** (see both under anuvicca); grd. **anuvejja** not to be known, unfathomable, unknowable M I.140 (Tathāgato ananuvejjo). — Caus. **anuvijjāpeti** to make some one find out J V.162. — pp. **anuvidita** (q. v.).

Anuvijjhati [anu + **vyadh**] 1. to pierce or be pierced, to be struck or hurt with (instr.) J VI.439 — 2. to be affected with, to fall into, to incur DhA III.380 (aparādhaŋ). — pp. **anuviddha** (q. v.).

Anuvitakketi [anu + vi + takketi] to reflect, think, ponder over, usually combd with **anuvicāreti** D I.119; III.242; S V.67 = It 107 (anussarati +); A III.383.

Anuvidita [pp. of anuvijjati] found out, recognised; one who has found out or knows well Sn 528, 530 (= anubuddha Sn A 431). Same in B.Sk., e.g. M Vastu III.398.

Anuviddha (adj.) [pp. of anuvijjhati] pierced, intertwined or set with (—°) VvA 278.

Anuvidhīyati [cf. Sk. anuvidhīyate & adj. anuvidhāyin; Pass. of anu + vi + **dhā**, cf. vidahati] to act in conformity with, to follow (instruction) M II.105 = Th 1, 875; S IV.199; J II.98; III.357.

Anuvidhiyanā (f.) [abstr. fr. aouvidhīyati] acting according to, conformity with M I.43.

Anuviloketi [anu + vi + loketi; B.Sk. anuvilokayati] to look round at, look over, survey, muster M I.339; Sn p. 140; J I.53; Miln 7 (lakaŋ), 21 (parisaŋ), 230.

Anuvivaṭṭa [anu + vivaṭṭa] an "after-evolution", devolution; as part of a bhikkhu's dress: a sub-vivaṭṭa (q. v.) Vin I.287 (**vivaṭṭa** +).

Anuvisaṭa (anu + visaṭa, pp. of anu + vi + **sṛ**] spread over S V.277 sq.; J IV.102.

Anuvuttha [pp. of anuvasati, cf. Sk. anūṣita] living with, staying, dwelling J II.42 (cira°); V.445 (id.).

Anuvejja (adj.) in an° see **anuvijjati**.

Anuvyañjana & **anubyañjana** (e. g. Vin IV.15; J I.12) (nt.) [anu + vyañjana] accompanying (i. e. secondary) attribute, minor or inferior characteristic, supplementary or additional sign or mark (cf. mahāpurisa-lakkhaṇa) Vin I.65 (abl. anuvyañjanaso "in detail"); M III.126; S IV.168; A IV.279 (abl.); V.73 sq.; Pug 24, 58; Miln 339; VvA 315; DhsA 400.
-**gāhin** taking up or occupying oneself with details, taken up with lesser or inferior marks D I.70 (cf. M Vastu III.52); III.225; S IV.104; A I.113; II.16, 152 sq.; Dhs 1345 (cf. *Dhs trsl.* 351).

Anusaŋyāyati [anu + saŋ + yāyati] to traverse; to go up to, surround, visit (acc.) M I.209 (Bhagavantaŋ °itvā), J IV.214 (v.l. anuyāyitvā). See also **anuyāti** and **anusaññāti**.

Anusaŋvacchara (adj.) [anu + saŋv°] yearly DhA I.388 (nakkhattaŋ). Usually nt. °ŋ as adv. yearly, every year J I.68; V.99. On use of anu in this combn. see anu A a.

Anusañcarati [anu + saŋ + carati] to walk along, to go round about, to visit M I.279; S V.53, 301; J I.202; III.502; PvA 279 (nagaraŋ). — pp. **anusañcarita** (q. v.).

Anusañcarita [pp. of anusañcarati] frequented, visited, resorted to Miln 387.

Anusañceteti [anu + saŋ + ceteti] to set ones mind on, concentrate, think over, meditate Pug 12.

Anusaññāti [either anu + saŋ + **jñā** (jānāti) or (preferably) = anusaŋyāti as short form of anusaŋyāyati, like anuyāti > anuyāyati of anu + saŋ + **yā**, cf. Sk. anusaŋyāti in same meaning] to go to, to visit, inspect, control; ppr. med. °**saññāyamāna** Vin III.43 (kammante); inf. °**saññātuŋ** A I.68. (janapade).

Anusaṭa [Sk. anusṛta, pp. of anu + **sṛ**] sprinkled with (—°), bestrewn, scattered Vv 5³ (paduma° magga = vippakiṇṇa VvA 36).

Anusatthar [n. ag. to anu + **śās**, cf. Sk. anuśāsitṛ & P. satthar] instructor, adviser J IV.178 (ācariya +). Cp. anusāsaka.

Anusatthi (f.) [Sk. anuśāsti, anu + **śās**, cp. anusāsana] admonition, rule instruction J I.241; Miln 98, 172, 186 (dhamma°), 225, 227, 347.

Anusandati [Vedic anusyandati, anu + **syad**] to stream along after, to follow, to be connected with. Thus to be read at Miln 63 for anusandahati (anuravati +; of sound), while at A IV.47 the reading is to be corrected to **anusandahati**.

Anusandahati [anu + saŋ + **dhā**, cf. Vedic abhi + saŋ + dhā] to direct upon, to apply to A IV.47 sq. (cittaŋ samāpattiyā; so to be read with v. l. for anusandati); Miln 63 (but here prob. to be read as **anusandati, q.v.**).

Anusandhanatā (f.) [= anusandhi] application, adjusting Dhs 8 (citassa).

Anusandhi (f.) [fr. anu + saŋ + **dhā**] connection, (logical) conclusion, application DA I.122 (where 3 kinds are enumd., viz. pucchā°, ajjhāsayā°, yathā°); Nett 14 (pucchato; Hard., in Index "complete cessation"?1). Esp. freq. in (Jātaka) phrase **anusandhiŋ ghateti** "to form the connection", to draw the conclusion, to show the application of the story or point out its maxim J I.106; 308; DhA II.40, 47; etc.

Anusampavankatā (f.) [anu + saŋ + pavankatā; is reading correct?] disputing, quarelling (?) Vin II.88 (under anuvād-âdhikaraṇa).

Anusaya [anu + śī, seti Sk. anuśaya has a diff. meaning] (see Kvu trsl. 234 n. 2 and Cpd. 172 n. 2). Bent, bias, proclivity, the persistance of a dormant or latent disposition, predisposition, tendency. Always in bad sense. In the oldest texts the word usually occurs absolutely, without mention of the cause or direction of the bias. So Sn. 14 = 369, 545; M. III.31; S. III.130, IV.33, V.28 236; A. I.44; II.157; III.74, 246, 443. Or in the triplet obstinacy, prejudice and bias (**adhiṭṭhānâbhinivesânusayā**) S. II.17; III.10, 135, 161; A. V.III. Occusionally a source of the bias il mentioned. Thns pride at S. I.188; II.252 ff., 275; III.80, 103, 169, 253; IV.41, 197; A I.132, IV.70 doubt at M. I.483 — ignorance lust and hatred at S IV.205, M III.285. At D III.254, 282; S V.60; and A IV.9. we have a list of seven anusaya's, the above fine and delusion and craving for rebirth. Hence-forward these lists govern the connotation of the word; but it would be wrong to put that connotation back into the earlier passages. Later refereuses are Ps I.26, 70 ff., 123, 130, 195; II.36, 84, 94, 158; Pug 21; Vbh 340, 383, 356; Kvu 405 ff. Dpvs I.42.

Anusayita [pp. of anuseti, anu + śī] dormant, only in combn. **dīgharatta°** latent so long Th I, 768; Sn 355, 649. Cp. anusaya & anusayin.

Anusayin (adj.) [fr. anusaya] D II.283 (me dīgharatta°), 'for me, so long obsessed (with doubts)'. The reading is uncertain.

Anusarati [anu + sṛ] to follow, conform oneself to S IV. 303 (phalaŋ anusarissati BB, but balaŋ anupadassati SS perhaps to be preferred). — Caus. **anusāreti** to bring together with, to send up to or against Miln 36 (aññamaññaŋ a. anupeseti).

Anusavati at S II.54 (āsavā na a.; v. l. anusayanti) & IV. 188 (akusalā dhammā na a.; v. l. anuseti) should preferably be read anusayati: see anuseti 2.

Anusahagata (adj.) having a residium, accompanied by a minimum of.. S III.130; Kvu 81, see aṇu°.

Anusāyika (adj.) [fr. anusaya] attached to one, i. e. inherent, chronic (of disease) M II.70 (ābādha, v. l. BB anussāyika); DhA I.431 (roga).

Anusāra [fr. anu + sṛ] "going along with", following, conformity. Only in obl. eases (—°) **anusārena** (instr.) in consequence of, in accordance with, according to J I.8; PvA 187 (tad), 227; and **anusārato** (abl.) id. Sdhp 91.

Anusārin (—°) (adj.) [fr. anu + sarati] following, striving after, acting in accordance with, living up to or after. Freq. in formula **dhammânusārin saddhânusārin** living in conformity with the Norm & the Faith D III.254; M I.142, 479; S III.225; V.200 sq.; A I.74; IV.10; Pug 15. — Cp. also S I.15 (bhavasota°); IV.128 (id.); J VI.444 (paṇḍitassa° = veyyāvaccakara C.); Sdhp 528 (attha°).

Anusāreti see anusarati.

Anusāsaka [fr. anusāsati] adviser, instructor, counsellor J II.105; Miln 186, 217, 264. Cp. anusatthar.

Anusāsati [Vedic anuśāsati, anu + sās] 1. to advise, admonish, instruct in or give advice upon (c. acc.) to exhort to Vin I.83; D I.135; II.154; Dh 77, 159 (aññaŋ); J VI.368; cp. I.10³; Pv II.6⁸; PvA 148. — grd. **anusāsiya** Vin I.59; and **°sāsitabba** DhA III.99. — Pass °**sāsiyati** Vin II.200; Miln 186. — 2. to rule, govern (acc.) administer to (dat.) S I.236 = Sn 1002 (paṭhaviŋ dhammena-m-anusāsati, of a Cakkavattin); J II.2; VI.517 (rajjassa = rajjaŋ C., i. e. take care of) DA I.246 (read °sāsantena); PvA 161 (rajjaŋ). — pp. **anusiṭṭha** (q. v.); cp. anusatthar, anusatthi & ovadati.

Anusāsana (nt.) [Vedic anuśāsana, fr. anu + śās] advice, instruction, admonition D III.107; A I.292 (°pāṭihāriya, cp. anusāsanī); Miln 359.

Anusāsanī (f.) [fr. anusāsati, cp. anusāsana] instruction, teaching, commandment, order S V.108; A II.147; III.87; V.24 sq., 49, 338; J V.113; Th 2, 172, 180; Pv III.7⁶; ThA 162; VvA 19, 80, 81.

-**pāṭihāriya** (anusāsani°) the miracle of teaching, the wonder worked by the commandments (of the Buddha) Vin II.200; D I.212, 214; III.220; A I.170; V.327; J III.323; Ps II.227 sq.

Anusikkhati [Vedic anuśikṣati; anu + Desid. of śak] to learn of somebody (gen.); to follow one's example, to imitate Vin II.201 (ppr. med. °amāna); S I.235; A IV. 282, 286, 323; Sn 294 (vattaŋ, cp. RV III.59, 2 : vratena śikṣati), 934; J I.89; II.98; III.315; V.334; VI.62; Th I, 963; Miln 61. — Caus **anusikkhāpeti** to teach [= Sk. anuśikṣayati] Miln 352.

Anusikkhin (adj.) [fr. anusikhati] studying, learning M I. 100; Dh 226 (ahoratta° = divā ca rattiñ ca tisso sikkhā sikkhamāna DhA III.324).

Anusiṭṭha (Vedic anuśiṣṭa, pp. of anusāsati] instructed, admonished, advised; ordered, commanded M II.96; J I.226; Pv II.8¹¹; Miln 284, 349.

Anusibbati [anu + sibbati, **siv** to sew] to interweave Vin III.336 (introd. to Sam. Pās.).

Anusuṇāti [anu + **śru**] to hear; pret. **anassuŋ** [Sk. anvaśruvaŋ] I heard M I.333.

Anusumbhati [anu + sumbhati (sobhati); **śubh** or (Vedic) **śumbh**] to adorn, embellish, prepare J VI.76.

Anusuyyaŋ [cp. Sk. anasūyaŋ] reading at J III.27, see anasuyyaŋ.

Anusuyyaka (adj.) [an + usuyyaka] not envious, not jealous Sn 325 (= usuyyāvigamena a. SnA 332); J II.192 (v. l. anussuyyaka); V.112.

Anuseṭṭhi [anu + seṭṭhi] 1. an under-seṭṭhi (banker, merchant) J V.384 (see anu B III. a.). — 2. in redupl. cpd. seṭṭhânuseṭṭhi (see anu B IV) "bankers & lesser bankers", i. e. all kinds of well-to-do families J VI.331.

Anuseti [anu + seti. cp. Sk. anuśayate or° śete, from śī] to "lie down with", i. e. (1) trs. to dwell on, harp on (an idea) S II.65; III.36; IV.208. — 2. (of the idea) to obsess, to fill the mind persistently, to lie dormant & be continually cropping up. M I.40, 108, 433; S II.54 (so read with SS for anusavanti) IV.188; A I.283; III.246; Pug 32, 48. — pp. **anusayita** (q. v.).

Anusocati [anu + socati] to mourn for, to bewail Sn 851 (atītaŋ na a.; cp. Nd¹ 222); Pv I.12⁷; II.6⁸; PvA 95.

Anusocana (nt.) [abstr. fr. anusocati] bewailing, mourning PvA 65.

Anusota° [anu + sota, in °ŋ as adv. or acc. to expln. under anu A a.] in **anusotaŋ** (adv.) along the stream or current, down-stream A II.12; J I.70 (opp. **paṭisotaŋ** against the stream); PvA 169 (Gangāya a. āgacchanto).

-**gāmin** "one who follows the stream", i. e. giving way to ones inclinations, following ones will A II.5, 6 (opp. paṭi°); Sn. 319 (= sotaŋ anugacchanto Sn A 330); Pug 62.

Anussati (f.) [Sk. anusmṛti, fr. anu + **smṛ**, cp. sati] remembrance, recollection, thinking of, mindfulness. A late list of subjects to be kept in mind comprises *six* **anussati-ṭṭhānāni**, viz. **Buddha°, Dhamma°, Sangha°, sīla°, cāga°, devatā°**, i. e. proper attention to the Buddha, the Doctrines, the Church, to morality, charity, the gods. Thus at D III.250, 280 (cp. A I.211); A III.284, 312 sq., 452; V.329 sq.; Ps I.28. Expanded to 10 subjects (the above plus **ānāpāna-sati, maraṇa-sati, kāyagatā-sati, upasamânussati**) at A I.30, 42 (cp. Lal. Vist 34). For other references see D I.81; S V.67 = It 107 (anussaraṇa at latter pass.); A III.284, 325, 452. Ps I.48, 95, 186; Pug 25, 60; Dhs 14, 23, 1350 (anussati here to be corr. to asati, see *Dhs. trsl.* 351); Sdhp. 225, 231, 482. See also anuttariya (anussat-ânuttariya).

Anussada (adj.) [an + ussada without haughtiness Sn 624 (vv. ll. anusaddha & anussuda; Sn A 467 expl^n. by taṇhā ussadâbhāva) = Dh 400 (which pass. has **anussuta**; v.l. K.B. anussada; DhA IV.165 expl^s. with taṇhā-ussāvâbhāva, vv. ll. °ussada°); It 97 (vv. ll. anussata & anussara).

Anussaraṇa (nt.) [abstr. to anussarati] remembrance, memory, recollection It 107 (= anussati at id. p. S V.67); PvA 25, 29.

Anussarati [Vedic anusmarati, anu + **smṛ**] to remember, recollect, have memory of (acc.), bear in mind; be aware of D II.8, 53, 54 (jātito etc.); S III.86 sq. (pubbenivāsaŋ); V.67 (dhammaŋ a. anuvitakketi), 303 (kappasahassaŋ); A I.25, 164 (pubbenivāsaŋ), 207 (Tathāgataŋ, Dhammaŋ etc.); III.285 (id.), 323 (nivāsaŋ), 418; V.34, 38, 132, 199, 336 (kalyāṇamitte); It 82 (dhammaŋ), 98 (pubbenivāsaŋ); J I.167; II.111; Dh 364; Pv I.5⁹; Pug 60; Sdhp 580, 587; DA I.257; KhA 213; DhA II.84; IV.95; PvA 29, 53, 69, 79, 107. — pp. **anussarita** (see anussaritar). — Caus **anussarāpeti** to remind someone, to call to mind J II.147.

Anussaritar [n. ag. to anussarita, pp. of anussarati] one who recollects or remembers S V.197, 225 (saritar +); A V.25, 28.

Anussava [anu + sava fr. **śru**, cp. Vedic śravas nt.] hearsay, report, tradition M I.520; II.211; S II.115; IV.138; A I.26; J I.158 (with ref. to part. kira = anussav'atthe nipāto; so also at VvA 322, cf. anussavana); II.396, 430 (id.); IV.441; instr. °ena from hearsay, by report A II.191 (cf. itihītihaŋ).

Anussavana (nt.) [anu + savana fr. **śru**] = anussava PvA 103 (kira-saddo anussavane, from hearsay).

Anussavika (adj.) [fr. anussava] "belonging to hearsay", traditional; one who is familiar with tradition or who learns from hearsay M I.520; II.211. Cp. anussutika.

Anussāvaka [fr. anussāveti] one who proclaims or announces, a speaker (of a kammavācā) Vin I.74.

Anussāvana (nt.) & °ā (f.) [fr. anussāveti] a proclamation Vin I.317, 340; V.170, 186, 202 sq.

Anussāvita [pp. of anussāveti] proclaimed, announced Vin I.103.

Anussāveti [anu + sāveti, Caus. of **śru**, cp. B.Sk. anuśrāvayati "to proclaim aloud the guilt of a criminal" AvŚ. I.102; II.182] to cause to be heard or sound; to proclaim, utter speak out Vin I.103 (°ssāviyamāna ppr. Pass.); II.48 (saddaŋ a.). — pp. **anussāvita**.

Anussuka (adj.) [an + ussuka] free from greed Dh 199; cf. anussukin v. l. D III.47, also anissukin and apalāsin.

Anussukita [an + ussuk°] VvA 74 & **anussukin** Pug 23 = **anussuka**.

Anussuta¹ (adj.) [an + ussuta, ud + **sṛ**] free from lust Dh 400 (= ussāvâbhāvena anussuta C.). See also **anussada**.

Anussuta² [anu + suta, pp. of **śru**] heard of; only in cpd. ananussuta unheard of S II.9; Pug 14.

Anussutika (adj.) [fr. anu + **śru**, cp. anussavika] according to tradition or report, one who goes by or learns from hearsay DA I.106, 107.

Anussuyyaka see **anusuyyaka**.

Anuhasati [anu + hasati] to laugh at, to ridicule DA I.256.

Anuhīrati [for °hariyati, anu + **hṛ**] to be held up over, ppr. **anuhīramāna** D II.15 (vv. ll. v. l. anubhiram°; glosses B. K. anudhāriyam°, cp. Trenckner, *Notes* 79).

Anūna (adj.) [Vedic anūna, an + **ūna**] not lacking, entire, complete, without deficiency J VI 273; Dpvs V.52; Miln 226; DA I.248 (+ paripūra, expl^d by anavaya).

Anūnaka = anūna Dpvs IV.34.

Anūnatā (f.) [abstr. fr. anūna] completeness Cp. III.6¹¹.

Anūpa (adj.) [Vedic anūpa, anu + ap: see āpa, orig. alongside of water] watery, moist; watery land, lowland J. IV.358 (anopa T; anupa C. p. 359), 381 (°khetta); Miln 129 (°khetta).

Anūpghāta [metrically for anupa°] not killing, not murdering. Dh 185 (= anupahananañ c'eva anupaghātanañ ca DhA III.238).

Anūpadhika for anu° in metre Sn 1057, see **upadhi**.

Anūpanāhin (adj.) [an + upanāhin, with ū metri causa] not bearing ill-will, not angry with J IV.463.

Anūpama at It 122 is metric reading for **anupama** (see upama).

Anūpalitta (adj.) [an + upalitta, with ū in metre] free from taint, unstained, unsmeared Sn 211, 392, 468, 790, 845; Dh 353; cf. Nd¹ 90 and DhA IV.72.

Anūpavāda [an + upavāda, with metrically lengthened u] not grumbling, not finding fault Dh 185 (= anupavādanañ c' eva anupavadāpanañ ca DhA III.238).

Anūhata (adj.) [pp. of an + ūhaññati, ud + **han**] not rooted out, not removed or destroyed Th 1, 223 = Nd² 97⁴; Dh 338 (= asamucchinna DhA IV.48).

Aneka (adj.) (usually °—) [an = eka] not one, i. e. many, various; countless, numberless It 99 (saŋvaṭṭakappā countless aeons); Sn 688 (°sākha); Dh 153 (°jātisāra); J IV.2; VI.366.
-**pariyāyena** (instr.) in many ways Vin I.16; Sn p. 15. -**rūpa** various, manifold Sn 1049, 1079, 1082; Nd² 54 (= anekavidha). -**vidha** manifold Nd² 54; DA I.103. -**vihita** various, manifold D I.12, 13, 178; It 98; Pug 55; DA I.103 (= anekavidha).

Anekaŋsā (f.) [an + ekaŋsā] doubt Nd² 1.

Anekaŋsikatā (f.) [abstr. fr. anekaŋsa + kata] uncertainty, doubtfulness Miln 93.

Aneja (adj.) [an + ejā] free from desires or lust D II.157; Sn 920, 1043, 1101, 1112; It 91 (opp. ejânuga Nd¹ 353 = Nd² 55; Dh 414 (= taṇhāya abhāvena DhA IV. 194), 422; Pv IV.1³⁵ (nittaṇha PvA 230).

Anedha (adj.) [an + edha] without fuel J IV.26 (= anindhana).

Aneḷa (adj.) [an + eḷa = ena, see neḷa & cp. BSk. eḍa (mūka); Vedic anena] faultless, pure; only in foll. cpds.: °gala free from the dripping or oozing of impurity (thus expld. at DA I.282, viz. elagalana-virahita), but more likely in lit. meaning "having a pure or clear throat" or, of vācā speech: "clearly enunciated" (thus Mrs. Rh. D. at *Kindred Sayings* I.241) Vin I.197 = D I.114 = S I.189; A II.51, 97; III.114. 195. Cp. also M Vastu III. 322. — °**mūga** same as prec. "having a clear throat", i. e. not dumb, fig. clever, skilled D III.265; Sn 70 (= alālāmukha SnA 124), cp. Nd² 259.

Aneḷaka (adj.) [cp. BSk. aneḍaka, e. g. Av. Ś. I.187, 243; M Vastu I.339; III.322] = aneḷa, pure, clear M II.5; J VI.529.

Anesanā (f.) [an + esanā] impropriety S II.194; J II.86; IV.381; Miln 343, 401; DA I.169; DhA IV.34; Sdhp 392, 427.

Ano- is a frequent form of compn. **an-ava**, see **ava**.

Anoka (nt.) [an + oka] houselessness, a houseless state, fig freedom from worldliness or attachment to life, singleness S V.24 = A V.232 = Dh 87 (okā anokaŋ āgamma). — adj. homeless, free from attachment S I.176; Dh 87 (= **anālaya** DhA II.162); Sn 966 (adj.: expld at Nd¹ 487 by abhisankhāra-sahagatassa viññāṇassa okāsaŋ na karoti, & at SnA 573 by abhisankhāra-viññān' ādinaŋ anokāsabhūta).

-**sārin** living in a houseless state, fig. being free from wordly attachment S III.10 = Nd¹ 197; Sn 628 (= **anālaya-cārin** SnA 468); Ud 32; Dh 404 (v. l. anokka°); DhA IV.174 (= **anālaya-cārin**); Miln 386.

Anogha in anogha-tiṇṇa see **ogha**.

Anojaka = **anojā** Vv 35⁴ (= VvA 161, where classed with yodhikā bandhujīvakā).

Anojagghati at D I.91 is v. l. for **anujagghati**.

Anojā (f.) [*Sk. anujā] a kind of shrub or tree with red flowers J VI.536 (korandaka +); usually in cpd. **anoja-puppha** the a. flower, used for wreaths etc. J I.9 (°dāma, a garland of a flowers); VI.227 (id.); DhA II.116 (°cangoṭaka).

Anottappa (nt.) [an + ottappa] recklessness, hardness D III.212; It 34 (ahirika +); Pug 20; Dhs 365. Cp. anottāpin.

Anottāpin & **Anottappin** (adj.) [fr. anottappa] not afraid of sin, bold, reckless, shameless D III.252, 282 (pp; ahirika); Sn 133 (p; ahirika +); It 27, 115 (anātāpin anottappin, vv. ll. anottāpin); Pug *20*, 24.

Anodaka (adj.) [an + udaka] without water, dry J I.307; DhA I.52; Sdhp 443.

Anodissaka (adj.) [an + odissa + ka] unrestricted, without exception, general, universal; only in cpd. °**vasena** universally, thoroughly (with ref. to mettā) J I.81; II 146; VvA 97 (in general; opp. **odissaka-vasena**). See also Mrs. Rh. D. *Psalms of the Brethren* p. 5 n. 1.

Anonamati [an + onamati] not to bend, to be inflexible, in foll. expressions: **anonamaka** (nt.) not stooping DhA II.136; **anonamanto** (ppr.) not bending D II.17 = III. 143; **anonami-daṇḍa** (for anonamiya°) an inflexible stick Miln 238 (anoṇami° T, but anonami° vv. ll., see Miln 427).

Anopa see **anūpa**.

Anoma (adj.) (only °—) [an + oma] not inferior, superior, perfect, supreme, in foll. cpds.

-**guṇa** supreme virtue DA I.288. -**dassika** of superior beauty Vv 20⁷, VvA 103 (both as v. l.; T. anuma°); Vv 43⁷. -**dassin** one who has supreme knowledge; of unexcelled wisdom (Name of a Buddha) J I.228. -**nāma** of perfect name S I.33 ("by name the Peerless" Mrs. Rh. D.), 235; Sn 153, 177 (cp. SnA 200). -**nikkama** of perfect energy Vv 64²¹ (= paripuṇṇa-viriyatāya a. VvA 284). -**pañña** of lofty or supreme wisdom (Ep. of the Buddha) Sn 343. 352 (= mahāpañña SnA 347); Th 2, 522 (= paripuṇṇa-pañña ThA 296), DhA I.31. -**vaṇṇa** of excellent colour Sn 686 J VI.202. -**viriya** of supreme exertion or energy Sn 353.

Anomajjati [anu + ava + majjati, **mṛj**] to rub along over, to stroke, only in phrase **gattāni pāṇinā a.** to rub over one's limbs with the hand M I.80, 509; S V.216.

Anorapāra (adj.) [an + ora + pāra] having (a shore) neither on this side nor beyond Miln 319.

Anoramati [an + ava + **ram**] not to stop, to continue J III.487; DhA III.9 (ger. °itvā continually).

Anovassa (nt.) [an + ovassa; cp. Sk. anavavarṣana] absence of rain, drought J V.317 (v. l. BB for anvāvassa T.; q. v.).

Anovassaka (adj.) [an + ovassaka] sheltered from the rain, dry Vin II.211; IV.272; J I.172; II.50; III.73; DhA II. 263; ThA 188.

Anosita (adj.) [an + ava + sita, pp. of **sā**] not inhabited (by), not accessible (to) Sn 937 (= anajjhositaŋ Nd¹ 441; jarādihi anajjhāvutthaŋ ṭhānaŋ SnA 566).

Anta¹ [Vedic anta; Goth. andeis = Ohg. anti = E. end; cp. also Lat. antiae forehead (: E. antler), and the prep. anti opposite, antika near = Lat. ante; Gr. ἀντί & ἄντα opposite; Goth., Ags. and; Ger. ant-; orig. the opposite (i. e. what stands against or faces the starting-point)]. 1. end, finish, goal S IV.368 (of Nibbāna): Sn 467; J II.159. **antaŋ karoti** to make an end (of) Sn 283. 512; Dh 275, cp. antakara, °kiriyā. — loc. **ante** at the end of, immediately after J I.203 (vijay°). — 2. limit, border, edge Vin I.47; Dh 305 (van°); J III.188. — 3. side: see ekamantaŋ (on one side, aside). — 4. opposite side, opposite, counterpart; pl. parts, contrasts, extremes; thus also used as "constituent, principle" (in **tayo** & **cattāro antā**; or does it belong to anta² 2. in this meaning? Cp. ekantaŋ extremely, under anta²): **dve antā** (two extremes) Vin I.10; S II.17; III.135. **ubho antā** (both sides) Vin I.10; S II.17; J I.8; Nd¹ 109. **eko, dutiyo anto** (contrasts) Nd¹ 52. As tayo antā or principles (?), viz. sakkāya, s.-samudaya, s.-nirodha D III.216, cp. A III. 401; as **cattāro**, viz. the 3 mentioned plus s.-nirodha-gāmini-paṭipadā at S III.157. Interpreted by Morris as "goal" (*J P T S.* 1894, 70). — Often pleonastically, to be expld as a "pars pro toto" figure, like **kammanta** (q. v.) the end of the work, i. e. the whole work (cp. E. sea-*side*, country-*side*); **vananta** the border of the wood = the woods Dh 305; Pv II.3¹⁰ (expld by vana PvA 86; same use in BSk., vanānta e. g. at Jtm VI.21; cp. also **grāmânta** Av. Ś. I.210); **suttanta** (q. v.), etc. Cp. ākāsanta J VI.89 & the pleonastic use of patha. -**ananta** (n.) no end, infinitude; (adj.) endless, corresponds either to Sk. anta or antya, see anta².

-**ânanta** end & no end, or finite and endless, D I.22; DA I.115. -**ânantika** (holding views of, or talking about) finiteness and infinitude D I.22 (see expln. at DA I.115); S III.214, 258 sq.; Ps I.155. -**kara** putting an end to, (n.) a deliverer, saviour; usually in phrase dukkhass'a. (of the Buddha) M I.48, 531; A II.2; III.400 sq.; Th 1, 195; It 18; Sn 32, 337. 539; Pug 71. In other combn. A II.163 (vijjāy'); Sn 1148 (pañhān'). —-**kiriyā** putting an end to, ending, relief, extirpation; always used with ref. to dukkha S IV.93; It 89; Sn 454, 725; DhA IV.45. -**gata** = antagū Nd² 436 (+ koṭigata). -**gāhikā** (f.), viz. diṭṭhi, is an attribute of micchādiṭṭhi, i. e. heretical doctrine. The meaning of anta in this combn. is not quite clear: either "holding (wrong) principles (goals, Morris)", viz. the 3 as specified above 4 under tayo antā (thus Morris *J P T S.* 1884, 70), or "taking extreme sides, i. e. extremist", or "wrong, opposite (= antya, see anta²)" (thus Kern, *Toev.* s. v.) Vin I.172; D III.45, 48 (an°); S I.154; A I.154; II.240; III.130; Ps I.151 sq. -**gū** one who has gone to the end, one who has gone through or overcome (dukkha) A IV.254, 258, 262; Sn 401 (= vaṭṭa-dukkhassa antagata); 539. **-ruddhi** at J VI.8 is doubtful reading (antaruci?). **-vaṭṭi** rimmed circumference J III.159. **-saññin** being conscious of an end (of the world) D I.22, cp. DA I.115.

Anta[2] (adj.) [Vedic antya] **1.** having an end, belonging to the end; only in neg. **ananta** endless, infinite, boundless (opp. **antavant**); which may be taken as equal to anta[1] (corresp. with Sk. anta (adj.) or antya; also in doublet anañca, see ākās'ānañca and viññāŋ'ānañca); D I.23, 34 = D III.224, 262 sq.; Sn 468 (°pañña); Dh 179, 180 (°gocara having an unlimited range of mental vision, cp. DhA III.197); J I.178. — **2.** extreme, last, worst J II.440 (C. hīna, lāmaka); see also anta[1] 4. — acc. as adv. in **ekantaŋ** extremely, very much, "utterly" Dh 228 etc. See eka.

Anta[3] (nt.) [Vedic āntra, contr. fr. antara inner = Lat. interus, Gr. ἔντερα intestines] the lower intestine, bowels, mesentery It 89; J I.66, 260 (°vaddhi-maŋsa etc.); Vism 258; DhA I.80.

-gaṇṭhi twisting of the bowels, lit. "a knot in the intestines" Vin I.275 (°ābādha). **-guṇa** [see guṇa[2] = gula[1]] the intestinal tract, the bowels S II.270; A IV.132; Kh III. = Miln 26; Vism 42; KhA 57. **-mukha** the anus J IV.402. **-vaṭṭi** = °guṇa Vism 258.

Antaka [Vedic antaka] being at the end, or making an end, Ep. of Death or Māra Vin I.21; S I.72; Th 2, 59 (expl[d] by ThA 65 as lāmaka va Māra, thus taken = anta[2]); Dh 48 (= maraṇa-sankhāto antako DhA II.366), 288 (= maraṇa DhA III.434).

Antamaso (adv.) [orig. abl. of antama, *Sk. antamaśaḥ; cp. BSk. antaśaḥ as same formation fr. anta, in same meaning ("even") Av. Ś. I.314; Divy 161] even Vin III. 260; IV.123; D I.168; M III.127; A V.195; J II.129; DA I.170; SnA 35; VvA 155.

Antara (adj.) [Vedic antara, cp. Gr. ἔντερα = Sk. antra (see anta[3]), Lat. interus fr. prep. inter. See also ante & anto]. Primary meanings are "inside" and "in between"; as adj. "inner"; in prep. use & in cpds. "inside, in between". Further development of meaning is with a view of contrasting the (two) sides of the inside relation, i. e. having a space between, different from; thus nt. **antaraŋ** difference.

I. (*Adj.-n*) **1.** (a) inner, having or being inside It 83 (tayo antarā malā three inward stains); esp. as —° in cpds. **āmis°** with greed inside, greedy, selfish Vin I.303; **dos°** with anger inside, i. e. angry Vin II.249; D III.237; M I.123; PvA 78 (so read for des°). Abl. **antarato** from within It 83. (b) in between, distant; dvādasa yojan' antaraŋ ṭhānaŋ PvA 139 139. — **2.** In noun-function (nt.): (a). *spatial*: the *inside* (of) Vv 36[1] (pītantara a yellow cloak or inside garment = pītavaṇṇa uttariya VvA 116); Dāvs I.10 (dīp' antara-vāsin living on the island); DhA I.358 (kaṇṇa-chidd° the inside of the ear; VvA 50 (kacch° inner room or apartment). Therefore also "space in between", *break* J V.352 (= chidda C.), & *obstacle*, hindrance, i. g. what stands in between: see cpds. and antara-dhāyati (for antaraŋ dhāyati). — (b). *temporal*: an interval of time, hence time in general, & also a specified time, i. e. occasion. As *interval* in Buddhantaraŋ the time between the death of one Buddha and the appearance of another, PvA 10, 14, 21, 47, 191 etc. As *time*: It 121 (etasmiŋ antare in that time or at this occasion); Pv I.10[11] (dīghaŋ antaraŋ = dīghaŋ kālaŋ PvA 52); PvA 5 (etasmiŋ antare at this time, just then). As *occasion*: J V.287; Pug 55 (eḷaka-m-antaraŋ occasion of getting rain). S I.20, quoted DA I.34, (mañ ca tañ ca kiŋ antaraŋ what is there between me and you?) C. expl[s.] kiŋ kāraṇā. M[rs.] Rh. D. in *trsl[n]*. p. 256 "of me if is and thee (this talk) — now why is this"; J VI.8 (assa antaraŋ na passiŋsu they did not see a diff. in him). — **3** Phrases: **antaraŋ karoti** (a) to keep away from or at a distance (trs. and intrs.), to hold aloof, lit. "to make a space in between" M III.14; J. IV.2 (°katvā leaving behind); Pug A 231 (ummāraŋ a. katvā staying away from a threshold); also adverbially: dasa yojanāni a. katvā at a distance of 10 y. PvA 139. — (b.) to remove, destroy J VI.56 (v. l. BB. antarāyaŋ karoti).

II. *In prep. use* (°—) with acc. (direction) or loc. (rest): inside (of), in the midst of, between, during (cp. III. use of cases). (a.) w. acc.: antaragharaŋ paviṭṭha gone into the house Miln 11. — (b.) w. loc.: antaraghare nisīdanti (inside the house) Vin II.213; °dīpake in the centre of the island J I.240; °dvāre in the door J V.231; °magge on the road (cp. antarāmagge) PvA 109; °bhatte in phrase ekasmiŋ yeva a. during one meal J I 19 = DhA I.249; °bhattasmiŋ id. DhA IV.12; °vīthiyaŋ in the middle of the road PvA 96. °satthīsu between the thighs Vin II.161 (has antarā satthīnaŋ) = J I.218.

III. *Adverbial use of cases*, instr. **antarena** in between D I.56; S IV.59, 73; J I.393; PvA 13 (kāl° in a little while, na kālantarena ib. 19). Often in comb[n]. **antarantarena** (c. gen.) right in between (lit. in between the space of) DhA I.63, 358. — loc. **antare** in, inside of, in between (—° or c. gen. KhA 81 (sutt° in the Sutta); DhA III.416 (mama a.); PvA 56, 63 (rukkh°). Also as **antarantare** right inside, right in the middle of (c. gen.) KhA 57; DhA I.59 (vanasaṇḍassa a.). — abl. **antarā** (see also sep. article of antarā) in comb[n.] **antarantarā** from time to time, occasionally; successively time after time Sn p. 107; DhA II.86; IV.191; PvA 272.

IV. **anantara** (adj.) having or leaving nothing in between i. e. immediately following, incessant, next, adjoining J IV.139; Miln 382 (solid; DhA I.397; PvA 63 (tadantaraŋ immediately hereafter), 92 (immed. preceding), 97 (next in caste). See also abbhantara.

-atīta gone past in the meantime J II.243. **-kappa** an intermediary kappa (q. v.) D I 54. **-kāraṇa** a cause of impediment, hindrance, obstacle Pug A 231. **-cakka** "the intermediate round", i. e. in astrology all that belongs to the intermediate points of the compass Miln 178. **-cara** one who goes in between or inside, i. e. a robber S IV.173. **-bāhira** (adj.) inside & outside J I.125. **-bhogika** one who has power (wealth, influence) inside the kings dominion or under the king, a subordinate chieftain (cp. antara-raṭṭha) Vin III.47 **-raṭṭha** an intermediate kingdom, rulership of a subordinate prince J V.135. **-vāsa** an interregnum Dpvs V.80. **-vāsaka** "inner or intermediate garment", one of the 3 robes of a Buddhist bhikkhu (viz. the saṅghāṭi, uttarāsanga & a.) Vin I.94, 289; II.272. Cf. next. **-sāṭaka** an inner or lower garment [cp. Sk. antarīya id.], under garment, i. e. the one between the outer one & the body VvA 166 (q. v.).

Antaraŋsa [B.Sk. antarāŋsa; antara + aŋsa] "in between the shoulders", i. e. the chest J V.173 = VI.171 (phrase **lohitakkho vihat' antaraŋso**).

Antaraṭṭhaka (adj.) [antara + aṭṭhaka] only in phrases **rattisu antaraṭṭhakāsu** and **antaraṭṭhake hima-pāta-samaye** (in which antara functions as prep. c. loc., according to antara II. b.) i. e. in the nights (& in the time of the falling of snow) between the eighths (i. e. the eighth day before & after the full moon: see aṭṭhaka[2]). First phrase at Vin I.31, 288; III 31; second at M I.79 (cp. p. 536 where Trenckner divides anta-raṭṭhaka); A I.136 (in nom.); J I.390; Miln 396.

Antaradhāna (nt.) [fr. antaradhāyati] disappearance A I.58 (saddhammassa); II.147; III.176 sq.; Miln 133; Dhs 645, 738, 871. Cp. °dhāyana.

Antaradhāyati [antara + dhāyati] to disappear Sn 449 (°dhāyatha 3rd sg. med.); Vv 81[28] (id.); J I.119 = DhA I.248; DhA IV.191 (ppr. °dhāyamāna & aor. dhāyi) PvA 152, 217, (°dhāyi), 245; VvA 48. — ppr. **antarahita** (q. v.). — Caus. **antaradhāpeti** to cause to disappear, to destroy J I.147; II.415; PvA 123.

Antaradhāyana (nt.) [fr. antaradhāyati] disappearance DhA IV.191. (v. l. °adhāna).

Antarayati [cp. denom. fr. antara] to go or step in between, ger. **antaritvā** (= antarayitvā) J I.218.

Antarahita (adj.) [pp. of antaradhāyati] 1. disappeared, gone, left D I.222. M I.487. Miln 18. PvA 245. — 2 in phrase **anantarahitāya bhūmiyā** (loc) on the bare soil (lit. on the ground with nothing put in between it & the person lying down, i. e. on an uncovered or unobstructed ground) Vin I.47; II.209; M II.57.

Antarā (adv.) [abl. or adv. formation fr. antara; Vedic antarā.] *prep.* (c. gen. acc. or loc.), *pref.* (°—) and *adv.* "in between" (of space & time), midway, inside; during, meanwhile, between. On interpretation of term see DA I.34 sq. — (1). (prep.) c. acc. (of the two points compared as termini; cp. B.Sk. antarā ca Divy 94 etc.) D I.1 (antarā ca Rājagahaŋ antarā ca Nāḷandaŋ between R. and N.). — c. gen. & loc. Vin II.161 (satthīnaŋ between the thighs, where id. p. at J I.218 has antara-satthīsu); A II.245 (satthīnaŋ. but v. l. satthimhi). — (2) (adv.) meanwhile Sn 291, 694; It 85; Dh 237. — occasionally Miln 251. — (3). (pref.) see cpds.
-**kathā** "in between talk, talk for pastime, chance conversation, D II.1, 8, 9; S I.79; IV.281; A III.167; Sn p. 115; DA I.49 and freq. passim. -**gacchati** to come in between, to prevent J VI.295. -**parinibbāyin** an Anāgāmin who passes away in the middle of his term of life in some particular heaven D III.237; A I.233; Pug 16. -**magge** (loc.) on the road, on the way J I.253; Miln 16; DhA II.21; III.337; PvA 151, 258, 269, 273 (cp. antara°). -**maraṇa** premature death DhA I.409; PvA 136. -**muttaka** one who is released in the meantime Vin II.167.

Antarāpaṇa (nt.) [antarā + paṇa "in between the shopping or trading"] place where the trading goes on, bazaar J I.55; VI.52; Miln 1, 330; DhA I.181.

Antarāya[1] [antara + aya from i, lit. "coming in between"] obstacle, hindrance, impediment to (—°); prevention, bar; danger, accident to (—). There are 10 dangers (to or from) enumd. at Vin I.112, 169 etc., viz. **rāja°, cora°, aggi°, udaka°, manussa°, amanussa°, vāḷa°, siriŋsapa°, jīvita°, brakmacariya°**. In B.Sk. 7 at Divy 544, viz. rājā-caura-manuṣy-amanuṣya-vyāḍ-agny-udakaŋ. — D I.3, 25, 26; A III.243, 306; IV.320; Sn 691, 692; Dh 286 (= jīvit° DhA III.431); J I.62, 128; KhA 181; DhA II 52; VvA 1 = PvA 1 (hat° removing the obstacles) -**antarāyaŋ karoti** to keep away from, hinder, hold back, prevent, destroy Vin I.15; J VI.171; Vism 120; PvA 20.
-**kara** one who causes impediments or bars the way, an obstructor D I.227; S I.34; A I.161; Pv IV.3[22].

Antarāya[2] (adv.) [dat. of antara or formation fr. antara + ger. of i?) in the meantime Sn 1120 (cp Nd[2] 58) = antarā Sn A 603.

Antarāyika (adj.) [fr. antarāya] causing an obstacle, forming an impediment Vin I.94 = II.272; M I.130; S II.226; ThA 288.

Antarāyikin (adj.-n.) [cp. antarāyika] one who meets with an obstacle, finding difficulties Vin IV.280 (an° = asati antarāye).

Antarāḷa (nt.) [Sk antarāla] interior, interval Dāvs I.52; III.53 (nabh°).

Antarika (adj.) [fr. antara] "being in between", i. e. — 1. intermediate, next, following: see an°. — 2. distant, lying in between PvA 173 (aneka-yojan° ṭhāna). See also f. antarikā. — 3. inside: see antarikā. -**anantarika** with no interval, succeeding, immediately following, next Vin II.165, 212 (ān°); IV.234.

Antarikā (f.) [abstr. fr. antarika] "what lies in between or near", i. e. — 1. the inside of Vin IV.272 (bhājan°). — 2. the neighbourhood, region of (—°), sphere, compass Vin III.39 (ur°, angul°); J I.265 (yakkhassa sīm° inside the yś sphere of influence). — 3. interval, interstice Vin II.116 (sutt° in lace); A I.124 (vijj° the interval of lightning).

Antalikkha (nt.) [Vedic antarikṣa = antari-kṣa (**kṣi**), lit. situated in between sky and earth] the atmosphere or air D II.15; A III.239; IV.199; Sn 222, 688; Dh 127 = Miln 150 = PvA 104; Pv I.3[1] (= vehāyasa-saññita a. PvA 14); KhA 166.
-**ga** going through the air A I.215. -**cara** walking through the air Vin I.21; D I.17; S I.111; J V.267; DA I.110.

Antavant (ādj.) [anta[1] + °vant] having an end, finite D I.22, 31, 187; Ps I.151 sq.; 157; Dhs 1099, 1117, 1175; Miln 145. -**anantavant** endless, infinite A V.193 (loka). See also loka.

Anti (indecl.) [Vedic anti = Lat ante, Gr. ἀντί, Goth. and; Ags. and-, Ger. ant-, ent-] adv. & prep. c. gen.: opposite, near J V.399 (tav' antiŋ āgatā, read as tav' anti-m-āgatā; C. santikaŋ), 400, 404; VI.565 (sāmikass' anti = antike C.). — Cp. **antika**.

Antika (adj.-n.) —1. [der fr. anti] near KhA 217; nt. neighbourhood Kh VIII.1. (odak°); J VI.565 (antike loc. = anti near). — 2. [der fr. anta = Sk. antya] being at the end, final, finished, over S I.130 (purisā etad-antikā, v. l. SS antiyā: men are (to me) at the end for that, i. e. men do not exist any more for me, for the purpose of begetting sons.

Antima (adj.) [Cp. superl. of anta] last, final (used almost exclusively with ref. to the last & final reincarnation; thus in combn. with **deha** & **sarīra**, the last body) D II.15; Dh 351; It 50 (antimaŋ dehaŋ dhāreti), 53 (id.); Vv 5[12]; Sn 478 (sarīraŋ antimaŋ dhāreti) 502; Miln 122, 148; VvA 106 (sarīr' antima-dhārin); Sdhp 278.
-**dehadhara** one who wears his last body It 101 (˘dhāra T, °dhara v. l.); VvA 163. -**dhārin** = prec. S I.14, 53 (+ khīṇāsava); II.278; It 32, 40; Sn 471. -**vatthu** "the last thing", i. e. the extreme, final or worst (sin) Vin I. 121, 135, 167, 320. -**sarīra** the last body; (adj.) having ones last rebirth S I.210 (Buddho a°-sarīro); A II.37; Sn 624; Dh 352, 400; DhA IV.166 (= koṭiyaŋ ṭhito attabhāvo).

Ante° (pref.) [Sk. antaḥ, with change of -aḥ to -e, instead of the usual -o, prob. through interpreting it as loc. of anta] near, inside, within; only in foll. cpds.: °**pura** (nt.) "inner town", the king's palace, esp. its inner apartments, i. e. harem [Sk. antaḥpura, cp. also P. antopura] Vin I.75, 269; A V.81; J II.125; IV.472; Miln 1; PvA 23, 81, 280; °**purikā** harem woman DhsA 403; °**vāsika** one who lives in, i. e. lodges or lives with his master or teacher, a pupil Vin I.60; III.25; S I.180; IV.136; J I. 166; II 278; III.83, 463; PvA 12; VvA 138; °**vāsin** = °vāsika Vin III.66; D I.1, 45, 74, 78, 88, 108, 157; M III.116; DA I.36.

Anto (indecl.) [Sk. antaḥ; Av antarə Lat. inter, Oir. etar between, Ohg. untar; Idg. *entar, compar. of *en (in) = inner, inside] prep. inside, either c. acc. denoting direction = into, or c. loc. denoting place where = in. As prefix (°—) in, within, inside, inner (see cpds.) (1.) prep. *c. acc.* anto nivesanaŋ gata gone into the house J I.158; anto jālaŋ pavisati go into the net DhA III.175; anto gāmaŋ pavisati to go into the village DhA II.273; anto nagaraŋ pavisati DhA II.89; PvA 47. — (2) *c. loc.* anto gabbhe J II.182; gāme DhA II.52; gehe DhA II.84; nadiyaŋ J VI.278; nivesane J II.323; vasse in the rainy season J IV.242; vimānasmiŋ Pv I.10[1]; sattāhe inside of a week PvA 55.

-koṭisanthāra "house of the Golden Pavement" J IV.113. -gadha (°gata? Kern *Toev.*) in phrase °*hetu*, by inner reason or by reason of its intensity PvA 10; VvA 12. -jana "the inside people", i. e. people belonging to the house, the family (= Lat. familia) D III.61 (opp. to servants); A I.152; J VI.301; DA I.300. -jāla the inside of the net, the net DhA IV.41. -jālikata "in-netted", gone into the net D I.45; DA I.127. -nijjhāna inner conflagration PvA 18. -nimugga altogether immersed D I.75; A III.26. -parisoka inner grief Ps I.38. -pura = antepura J I.262. -mano "turning ones mind inside", thoughtful, melancholy Vin III.19. -bhavika being inside Miln 95. -rukkhatā being among trees J I.7. -vasati to inhabit, live within S IV.136. -vaḷañjanaka (parijana) indoor-people J V.118. -vassa the rainy season (lit. the interval of the r. s.) VvA 66. -vihāra the inside of the V. DhA I.50 (°âbhimukhī turning towards etc.), -samorodha barricading within Dhs 1157 (so read for anta°, cp. *Dhs. trsl.* 311). -soka inner grief Ps I.38.

Andu [cp. Sk. andu, andū & anduka] a chain, fetter Vin I.108 = III.249 (tiṇ°); D I.245; J I 21 (°ghara prison-house); DhA IV.54 (°bandhana).

Andha (adj.) [Vedic andha, Lat. andabata (see Walde, Lat. Wtb. s. v.), other etym. doubtful] 1. (lit.) blind, blinded, blindfolded J I.216 (dhūm°); Pv IV.1[48]; PvA 3. — dark, dull, blinding M III.151 (°andhaŋ adv. dulled); Sn 669 (Ep. of timisa, like Vedic andhaŋ tamaḥ); DhA II.49 (°vana dark forest). — 2. (fig.) mentally blinded, dull of mind, foolish, not seeing D I.191 (+ acakkhuka), 239 (°veṇi, reading & meaning uncertain); A I.128; Th 2, 394 (= bāla ThA 258). See cpds. °karaṇa, °kāra, °bāla, °bhūta.

-ākula blinded, foolish Vv 84[9] (= paññācakkhuno abhāvena VvA 337). -karaṇa blinding, making blind, causing bewilderment (fig.), confusing It 82 (+ acakkhukaraṇa); Miln 113 (pañha, + gambhira). -kāra blindness (lit. & fig), darkness, dullness, bewilderment Vin I.16; D II.12; A I.56; II.54; III.233; J III.188; Th 1, 1034; Dh 146; Sn 763; Vv 21[4] (= avijj° VvA 106); Pug 30; Dhs 617; DA I.228; VvA 51, 53, 116, 161; PvA 6; Sdhp 14, 280. -tamo deep darkness (lit. & fig.) S V.443; It 84 (v. l.; T. andhaŋ tamaŋ); J VI.247. -bāla blinded by folly, foolish, dull of mind, silly J I.246, 262; VI.337; DhA II.43, 89; III.179; VvA 67; PvA 4, 264. -bhūta blinded (fig.), mentally blind, not knowing, ignorant S IV.21; A II.72; J VI.139 (spelled °bhuta); Dh 59, 174 (= paññā-cakkhuno abhāvena DhA III.175). -vesa "blind form", disguise J III.418.

Andhaka [fr. andha] "blind fly", i. e. dark or yellow fly or gad-fly Sn 20 (= kāṇa-makhhikānaŋ adhivacanaŋ SnA 33).

Anna (nt.) [Vedic anna, orig. pp. of adati to eat] "eating", food, esp. boiled rice, but includes all that is eaten as food, viz. odana, kummāsa, sattu, maccha, maŋsa (rice, gruel, flour, fish, meat) Nd[1] 372 = 495. Anna is spelt aṇṇa in combns apar' aṇṇa and pubb' aṇṇa. Under dhañña (Nd[2] 314) are distinguished 2 kinds, viz. raw, natural cereals (pubb' aṇṇaŋ: sāli, vīhi, yava, godhūma, kangu, varaka, kudrūsaka) and boiled, prepared food (apar' aṇṇaŋ: sūpeyya curry). SnA 378 (on Sn 403) expls. anna by yāgubhattâdi. — D I.7; A I.107, 132; II.70, 85, 203; Sn 82, 240, 403, 924; J III.190; Pug 51; Sdhp 106, 214.

-āpa food & water Sdhp 100. -da giving food Sn 297. -pāna food & water, eating & drinking, to eat & to drink Sn 485, 487; Pv I.5[2], 8[2]; KhA 207, 209; PvA 7, 8, 30, 31, 43.

Annaya in dur° see anvaya.

Anvakāsi 3rd sg. aor. of anukassati 2: drew out, removed, threw down Th 1, 869 (= khipi, chaḍḍesi C.).

Anvakkhara (adj.) [anu + akkhara] "according to the syllable", syll. after syll., also a mode of reciting by syllables Vin IV.15, cp. 355. Cp. anupadaŋ.

Anvagā 3rd sg. aor. of anugacchati Mhvs 7, 10. Also in assim. form annagā J V.258.

Anvagū 3rd pl. aor. of anugacchati S I.39; Sn 586.

Anvaḍḍhamāsaŋ (adv.) [anu + aḍḍha + māsa] every fortnight, twice a month M II.8; Vin IV.315 (= anuposathikaŋ); DhA I.162; II.25.

Anvattha (adj.) [anu + attha] according to the sense, answering to the matter, having sense ThA 6 (°saññābhāva).

Anvadeva (adv.) [anva-d-eva with euphonic d.; like samma-d-eva corresponding to Sk. anvag-eva] behind, after, later D I.172; M III.172; S V.1 (spelt anudeva); A I.11; V. 214; It 34.

Anvaya (n.-adj.) [Vedic anvaya in diff. meaning; fr. anu + i, see anveti & anvāya] 1. (n.) conformity, accordance D II. 83 = III.100; M 5, 69 (dhamm° logical conclusion of); S II.58; D 3, 226 (anvaye ñāṇaŋ); Pv II.11[3] (tassa kammassa anvāya, v. l. BB anvaya & anvāya; accordingly, according to = paccayā PvA 147); PvA 228 (anvayato, adv. in accordance). — 2. (adj.) following, having the same course, behaving according to, consequential, in conformity with (—°) D I.46 (tad°); M I.238 (kāyo citt° acting in conformity to the mind, obeying the mind); Sn 254 (an° inconsistent); It 79 (tass°). — dur° spelt durannaya conforming with difficulty, hard to manage or to find out Dh 92 (gati = na sakkā paññāpetuŋ DhA II.173); Sn 243, 251 (= duviññāpaya SnA 287 dunneyya ibid. 293).

Anvayatā (f.) [abstr. to anvaya] conformity, accordance M I.500 (kāy° giving in to the body).

Anvahaŋ (adv.) [anu + aha] every day, daily Dāvs IV.8.

Anvāgacchati [anu + ā + gacchati] 1. to go along after, to follow, run after, pursue; aor. anvāgacchi Pv IV.5[6] (= anubandhi PvA 260). — 2. to come back again J I.454 (ger. °gantvāna). — pp. anvāgata (q. v.).

Anvāgata [pp. of anvāgacchati] having pursued, attained; endowed with Th 1, 63; J IV.385; V.4.

Anvādisati [anu + ā + disati] to advise, dedicate, assign; imper. °disāhi Pv II.2[6] (= uddissa dehi PvA 80); III.2[8] (= ādisa PvA 181).

Anvādhika (adj.) [derivation uncertain] a tailoring term. Only at Vin I.297. Rendered (*Vinaya Texts* II.232) by 'half and half'; that is a patchwork, half of new material, half of old. Bdhgh's note (see the text, p. 392) adds that the new material must be cut up.

Anvāmaddati [anu + ā + maddati] to squeeze, wring J III. 481 (galakaŋ anvāmaddi wrung his neck; vv. ll. anvānumaṭṭi & anvāvamaddi; C. gīvaŋ maddi).

Anvāya [ger. of anveti; cp. anvaya] undergoing, experiencing, attaining; as prep. (c. acc.) in consequence of, through, after D I.13 (ātappaŋ by means of self-sacrifice), 97 (saŋvāsaŋ as a result of their cohabitation); J I.56 (buddhiŋ), 127 (piyasaŋvāsaŋ), 148 (gabbhaparipākaŋ). Often in phrase vuddhiŋ anvāya growing up, e. g. J I.278; III. 126; DhA II.87.

Anvāyika (adj.-n.) [fr. anvāya] following; one who follows, a companion D III.169; Nd[2] 59; J III.348.

Anvārohati [anu + ā + rohati] to go up to, visit, ascend J IV.465 (aor. anvāruhi).

Anvāvassa at J v.317 should be read with v. l. BB as anovassa absence of rain.

Anvāviṭṭha [pp. of anvāvisati] possessed (by evil spirits) S I.114.

Anvāvisati [anu + ā + visati] to go into, to take possession of, to visit M I.326; S I.67; Miln 156. — pp. **anvāviṭṭha** (q. v.). Cp. adhimuccati.

Anvāsatta [pp. of anu + ā + **sañj**, cp. anusatta = Sk. anusakta] clung on to, befallen by (instr.), attached to A IV.356 (v. l. anvāhata), cp. Ud 35 (anvāsanna q. v.). See also foll.

Anvāsattatā (f.) [abstr. fr. anvāsatta] being attacked by, falling a prey to (instr.), attachment to DhA I.287 (in same context as anvāsatta A IV.356 & anvāsanna Ud 35).

Anvāsanna [pp. of anu + ā + **sad**] endowed with, possessed of, attacked by, Ud 35 (doubtfull; v. l. ajjhāpanna), = A IV.356 which has **anvāsatta**.

Anvāssavati [anu + ā + savati, **sru**] to stream into, to attack, befall D I.70; A III.99; Pug 20, 58.

Anvāhata [pp. of anu + ā + **han**] struck, beaten; perplexed Dh 39 (°cetasa).

Anvāhiṇḍati [anu + ā + hiṇḍati] to wander to (acc.) A IV.374, 376 [BSk. same, e. g. Divy 68 etc.].

Anveti [cp. anu + eti, from **i**] to follow, approach, go with Sn 1103 (= anugacchati anvāyiko hoti Nd² 59); Dh 1 (= kāyikaŋ ... dukkhaŋ anugacchati DhA I.24), 2, 71, 124; perhaps at Pv II.6²⁰ (with v. l. BB at PvA 99) for **anvesi** (see anvesati; expl^{d.} by anudesi = was anxious for, helped, instructed).

Anvesa [from next] seeking, searching, investigation, M I.140 (°ŋ n'âdhigacchanti do not find).

Anvesati [anu + esati] to look, for search, seek S I.112 (ppr. anvesaŋ = pariyesamāna C.); Cp III.11⁷ (ppr. anvesanto). — aor. **anvesi** [Sk. anveṣi fr. icchati] Pv II.6²⁰ (? perhaps better with v. l. PvA 99 as anventi of anveti).

Anvesin [anu-esin] (adj.) striving after, seeking, wishing for Sn 965 (kusala°).

Anha [Vedic ahan] see pubbanha, majjhanha, sāyanha. Cp. aha.

Apa° [Vedic apa; Idg. *apo = Gr. ἀπό, Av. apa, Lat. ab from *ap (cp. aperio); Goth. af, Ger. ab, Ags. E. of. — A compar. form fr. apa is apara "further away"] Well-defined directional prefix, meaning "away from, off". Usually as base-prefix (except with ā), & very seldom in comp^{n.} with other modifying prefixes (like sam, abhi etc.). — 1. **apa** = Vedic **apa** (Idg. *apo): apeti to go away = Gr. ἄπειμι, Lat. abeo, Goth. afiddja; apeta gone away, rid; °kaḍḍhati to draw away, remove; °kamati walk away; °gacchati go away; °nidhāti put away (= ἀποτίθημι, abdo); °nudati push away; °neti lead away; °vattati turn away (= āverto); °sakkati step aside; °harati take away. — 2. **apa** = Vedic **ava** (Idg. *aue; see ava for details). There exists a widespread confusion between the two preps. apa & ava, favoured both by semantic (apa = away, ava = down, cp. E. off) & phonetic affinity (p softened to b, esp. in BB Mss., & then to v, as b > v is frequent, e. g. bya° > vya° etc.). Thus we find in Pāli apa where Vedic and later literary Sk. have ava in the foll. instances: apakanti, °kassati, °kirati, °gata, °cāra, °jhāyati, °thaṭa, °dāna, °dhāreti, °nata, °nāmeti, °nīta, °lekhana, °loketi, °vadati.

Apakaḍḍhati [apa + kaḍḍhati, cp. Sk. apa-karṣati] to draw away, take off, remove D I.180; III.127; DhA II.86. — Caus. **apakaḍḍhāpeti** J I.342; IV.415; Miln 34. — Cp. **apakassati**; & see pakattheti.

Apakata [pp. of apakaroti] put off, done away, in ājīvik' âpakata being without a living M I.463 (the usual phrase being °apagata); Miln 279 (id.). At It 89 the reading of same phrase is ājīvikā pakatā (v. l. ā° vakatā).

Apakataññū (adj.) [a + pa + kataññu] ungrateful Vin II.199.

Apakantati [apa + kantati, Sk. ava + kṛntati] to cut off Th 2, 217 (gale = gīvaŋ chindati ThA 178; Kern, *Toev.* corrects to kabale a.).

Apakaroti [apa + karoti, cp. Sk. apakaroti & apakṛta in same meaning] to throw away, put off; hurt, offend, slight; possibly in reading T. **apakiritūna** at Th 2, 447 (q. v.). — pp. **apakata** (q. v.). Cp. apakāra.

Apakassati [Sk. apa- & ava-karṣati, cp. apakaḍḍhati] to throw away, remove Sn 281 (v.l. BB & SnA ava°; expl^{d.} by niddhamati & nikkaḍḍhati SnA 311). -ger. **apakassa** Sn II.198 = Miln 389. See also **apakāsati**.

Apakāra & **°ka** [cf. Sk. apakāra & apakaroti] injury, mischief; one who injures or offends DhA III.63; Sdhp 283.

Apakāsati at Vin II.204 is to be read as **apakassati** and interpreted as "draw away, distract, bring about a split or dissension (of the Sangha)". The v. l. on p. 325 justifies the correction (apakassati) as well as Bdhgh's expl^{n.} "parisaŋ ākaḍḍhanti". — Cp. A III.145 & see **avapakāsati**. The reading at the id. p. at A v.74 is **avakassati** (comb^{d.} w. vavakassati, where Vin II.204 has avapakāsati), which is much to be preferred (see vavakassati).

Apakiritūna at Th 2, 447 T (reading of C. is abhi°) is explained ThA 271 to mean apakiritvā chaḍḍetvā throwing away, slighting, offending. The correct etym = Sk. avakirati (ava + **kṛ²** to strew, cast out) in sense "to cast off, reject", to which also belongs kirāta in meaning "cast off" i. e. man of a so-called low tribe. See also avakirati 2.

Apakkamati [cp. Sk. apakramati, apa + **kram**] to go away, depart, go to one side J III.27; Sdhp 294. — aor. **apakkami** Pv IV.7⁵; ger. **apakkamitvā** PvA 43, 124, & **apakkamma** Pv II.9²⁸.

Apagacchati [apa + **gam**] to go away, turn aside DhA I.401 (°gantvā). — pp. **apagata** (q. v.).

Apagata [pp. of apagacchati] 1. gone, gone away from (c. abl.), removed; deceased, departed It 112; PvA 39, 63 (= peta), 64 (= gata). — 2. (°—) freq. as prefix, meaning without, lit. having lost, removed from; free from Vin II.129 (°gabbhā having lost her foetus, having a miscarriage); J I.61 (°vattha without clothes); PvA 38 (°soka free from grief), 47 (°lajja not shy), 219 (°viññāṇa without feeling). — Cp. **apakata**.

Apagabbha (adj.) [a + pa + gabbha] not entering another womb, i. e. not destined to another rebirth Vin III.3.

Apagama [Sk. apagama] going away, disappearance Sdhp 508.

Apanga (apāṅga) [Sk. apāṅga] the outer corner of the eye J III.419 (asitâpangin black-eyed); IV.219 (bahi°). Spelt **avanga** at Vin II.267, where the phrase avangaŋ karoti, i. e. expl^{d.} by Bdhgh. ibid p. 327 as "avangadese adhomukhaŋ lekhaŋ karonti". According to Kern, *Toev.* 20, Bdhgh's explⁿ is not quite correct, since avanga stands here in the meaning of "a coloured mark upon the body" (cp. PW. apāṅga).

Apacaya [fr. apa + **ci**] falling off, diminution (opp. ācaya gathering, heaping up), unmaking, esp. loss (of wordliness), decrease (of possibility of rebirth Vin II.2 = III.21 = IV.213; cp. J III.342; S II.95 (kāyassa ācayo pi apacayo pi); A IV.280 = Vin II.259 (opp. ācaya); J III.342 (sekho °ena na tappati); Vbh 106, 319, 326, 330.

-gāmin going towards decrease, "making for the undoing of rebirth" (*Dhs trsl.* 82) A v.243, 277; Dhs 277, 339, 505, 1014; Vbh 12, 16 sq.; Nett 87 (cp. Kvu 156).

Apacāyati [fr. apa—**ci**, cp. cināti & cayati, with diff. meaning in Sk.; better expl^d. perhaps as denom. fr. *apacāya in meaning of apacāyana, cp. apacita] to honour, respect, pay reverence D I.91 (pūjeti +); J III.82. — Pot. apace (for apaceyya, may be taken to apacināti 2) A IV.245; ThA 72 (here to apacināti 1). — pp. apacita (q. v.).

Apacāyana (nt.) [abstr. fr. apa + **cāy**, which is itself a der. fr. **ci**, cināti] honouring, honour, worship, reverence J I.220; V.326; DA I.256 (°kamma); VvA 24 (°ŋ karoti = añjalikaŋ karoti); PvA 104 (°kara, adj.), 128 (+ pāricariya).

Apacāyika (adj.) [fr. *apacāya, cp. B.Sk. apacāyaka MVastu I.198; Divy 293] honouring, respecting J IV.94 (vaddha°, cp. vaddhâpacāyin); Pv II.7 [8] (jeṭṭha°); IV.3[24] (id.). In B.Sk. the corresp. phrase is jyeṣṭhâpacayaka.

Apacāyin (adj.) [fr. *apacāya; cp. apacāyika] honouring, paying homage, revering Sn 325 (vaddha° = vaddhānaŋ apaciti karaṇena SnA 332) = Dh 109; J I.47, 132, 201; II.299; V.325; Miln 206; Sdhp 549.

Apacara [fr. apa + **car**, cp. Sk. apa & abhi-carati] falling off, fault, wrong doing J VI.375.

Apacita [pp. of apacayati or apacināti] honoured, worshipped, esteemed Th 1, 186; J II.169; IV.75; Vv 5[10] (= pūjita VvA 39); 35[11] (cp. VvA 164); Miln 21.

Apaciti (f.) [Vedic apaciti in diff. meaning, viz. expiation] honour, respect, esteem, reverence Th 1, 589; J I.220; II.435; III.82; IV.308; VI.88; Miln 180, 234 (°ŋ karoti), 377 (pūjana +); SnA 332 (°karaṇa). Cp. apacāyana.

Apacināti [apa + cināti] 1. [in meaning of Sk. apacīyate cp. P. upaciyyati Pass. of upacināti] to get rid of, do away with, (cp. apacaya), diminish, make less S III.89 (opp. ācināti); Th 1, 807; J IV.172 (apacineth' eva kāmāni = viddhaŋseyyatha C.). Here belong prob. aor. 3rd pl. **apaciyiŋsu** (to be read for upacciŋsu) at J VI. 187 (akkhīni a. "the eyes gave out") and Pot. pres. apace ThA 72 (on v.40). — 2. [= apacayati] to honour, esteem; observe, guard Vin I.264 (apacinayamāna cīvaraŋ (?) v. l apacitiyamāna; trsl. guarding his claim is, *Vin Texts*); M I.324 (see detail under apaviṇāti) Th 1, 186 (grd. apacineyya to be honoured); J V.339 (anapacinanto for T. anupacinanto, v. l. anapavinati). — pp. apacita (q.v.).

Apacca [Vedic apatya nt.; der. fr. apa] offspring, child D I.90 (bandhupāda° cp. muṇḍaka), 103 (id.); S I.69 (an°) Sn 991; DA I.254.

Apaccakkha (adj.) [a + paṭi + akkha] unseen; in instr. f. apaccakkhāya as adv. without being seen, not by direct evidence Miln 46 sq.

Apacchapurima (adj.) [a + paccha + purima] "neither after nor before", i. e. at the same time, simultaneous J III.295.

Apajaha (adj.) [a + pajaha] not giving up, greedy, miserly A III.76 (v. l. apānuta; C. expl^s. (a)vaḍḍhinissita mānatthaddha).

Apajita (nt.) [pp. of apa + **ji**] defeat Dh. 105.

Apajjhāyati [apa + jhāyati[1]; cp. Sk. abhi-dhyāyati] to muse, meditate, ponder, consider M I.334 (nijjhāyati +); III.14 (id.).

Apaññaka (adj.) = apañña, ignorant Dpvs VI.29.

Apaṭṭhapeti [Caus. fr. apa-tiṭṭhati, cp. Sk. apa + **sthā** to stand aloof] to put aside, leave out, neglect J IV.308; V.236.

Apaṇṇaka (adj.) [a + paṇṇaka; see paṇṇaka; Weber Ind. Str. III.150 & Kuhn, Beitr. p. 53 take it as *a-praśna-ka] certain, true, absolute M I.401, 411; A V.85, 294, 296; J I.104 (where expl^d as **ekaŋsika aviruddha niyyānika**).

Apaṇṇakatā (f.) [abstr. of apaṇṇaka] certainty, absoluteness S IV.351 sq.

Apatacchika only in khārāpatācch° (q. v.) a kind of torture.

Apattha[1] (adj.) [Sk. apāsta, pp. of apa + **as**[2]] thrown away Dh 149 (= chaḍḍita DhA III.112).

Apattha[2] 2nd pl. pret. of pāpuṇāti (q. v.).

Apatthaṭa = avatthaṭa covered Th 1, 759.

Apatthita & **Apatthiya** see **pattheti.**

Apadāna (nt.) 1. [= Sk. apadāna] removing, breaking off, D III.88. — 2. [= Sk. avadāna cp. ovāda] advice, admonition, instruction, morals Vin II.4 (an° not taking advice), 7 (id.) M I.96; A V.337 sq. (saddhā°) Th 1, 47. — 3. legend, life history. In the title Mahāpadāna suttanta it refers to the 7 Buddhas. In the title Apadānaŋ, that is 'the stories', it refers almost exclusively to Arahants. The other, (older), connotation seems to have afterwards died out. See *Dialogues* II.3. — Cp. also pariyāpadāna.

Apadisa [fr. apa + **dis**'] reference, testimony, witness DhA II.39.

Apadisati [apa + disati] to call to witness, to refer to, to quote Vin III.159; J I.215; III.234; IV.203; Miln 270; DhA II.39; Nett 93.

Apadesa [cp. Sk. apadeśa] 1. reason, cause, argument M I.287 (an°). — 2. statement, designation PvA 8. — 3. pretext J III.60; IV.13; PvA 154. Thus also **apadesaka** J VI.179.

Apadhāreti [Caus. of apa + **dhṛ**, cp. Sk. ava-dhārayati, but also BSk. apadhārayati Divy 231] to observe, request, ask ThA 16.

Apanata [pp. of apanamati] "bent away", drawn aside, in ster. comb^n. **abhinata** + **apanata** ("strained forth & strained aside" Mrs Rh. D. *Kindred S.* p. 39) M I.386; S I.28.

Apanamati [semantically doubtful] to go away Sn 1102 (apanamissati, v. l. apalām° & apagam°; expl^d at Nd[2] 60 by vajissati pakkhamissati etc. — pp. **apanata** (q. v.) — Caus. apanāmeti.

Apanāmeti [Caus. fr. apanamati] 1. to take away, remove M I.96 = A I.198 (kathaŋ bahiddhā a. carry outside); Kh VIII.4 (= aññaŋ ṭhānaŋ gameti KhA 220). — 2. [= Sk. ava-namati] to bend down, lower, put down Vin II.208 (chattaŋ); S I.226 (id.); J II.287 (id., v. l. apanetvā); D I.126 (hatthaŋ, for salute).

Apanidahati (& apanidheti) [apa + ni + **dhā**, cp. Vedic apadhā hiding-place; Sk. apadadhāti = Gr. ἀποτίθημι = Lat. abdo "do away"] to hide, conceal Vin IV.123 (°dheti, °dheyya, °dhessati); PvA 215 (°dhāya ger.). — pp. **apanihita.** — Caus. **apanidhāpeti** to induce somebody to conceal Vin IV.123.

Apanihita [pp. of apanidahati] concealed, in abstr. °**ttaŋ** (nt.) hiding, concealing, theft PvA 216.

Apanīta [Sk. apanīta, pp. of apa + nī, see apaneti & cp. also onīta = apanīta] taken away or off. removed, dispelled PvA 39.

Apanudati & **Apanudeti** [apa + **nud**, cp. Vedic apanudati & Caus. Sk. apanodayati] to push or drive away, remove, dispel; pres. **apanudeti** Miln 38. aor. **apānudi** Pv I.8[6] (= apanesi PvA 41); II.3[14] (= avahari aggahesi PvA 86); Dāvs I.8. ger. **apanujja** D II.223. See also der. **apanudana.**

Apanudana & **Apanūdana** (nt.) [Sk. apanodana, fr. apanudati] taking or driving away, removal Vin II.148 = J I.94 (dukkha°); Sn 252 (id.); PvA 114 (id.).

Apanuditar [n. ag. fr. apanudati, Sk. apanoditṛ] remover, dispeller D III.148.

Apaneti [apa + **nī**] to lead away, take or put away, remove J I.62, 138; II.4, 155 (aor. apānayi) III.26; Miln 188, 259, 413; PvA 41, 74, 198 (= harati) Sdhp 63. Pass. **apanīyati** S I.176. — pp. **apanīta** (q. v.).

Apapibati [apa + pibati] to drink from something J III.126 (aor. apāpāsi).

Apabbūhati & **Apabyūhati** [apa + vi + **ūh**] to push off, remove, scrape away A III.187 (apaviyūhitvā, vv. ll. °bbūhitvā); J I.265 (paŋsuŋ). — Caus. °**byūhāpeti** to make remove or brush J IV.349 (paŋsuŋ).

Apabyāma see **apavyāma**.

Apamāra [Sk. apasmāra] epilepsy Vin I.93. Cp. **apasmāra**.

Apamārika (adj.) [cp. Sk. apasmārin] epileptic Vin IV.8, 10, 11.

Apayāti [Sk. apayāti, apa + **yā**] to go away J VI.183 (apāyāti metri causa; expl[d.] by C. as apagacchati palāyati). — Caus. **apayāpeti** [Sk. apayāpayati] to make go, drive away, dismiss M III.176; S II.119.

Apayāna (nt.) [Sk. apayāna, fr. apayāti] going away, retreat D I.9 (opp. upa°); DA I.95.

Apara (adj.) [Vedic apara, der. fr. apa with compar. suffix -ra = Idg. *aporos "further away, second"; cp. Gr. ἀπωτέρω farther, Lat. aprilis the second month (after March, i. e. April). Goth. afar = after] another, i. e. additional, following, next, second (with pron. inflexion, i. e. nom. pl. apare) D III.190 (°pajā another, i. e. future generation); Sn 791, 1089 (n'); J I.59 (aparaŋ divasaŋ on some day following); III.51 (apare tayo sahāyā "other friends three", i. e. three friends, cp. similarly Fr. nous autres Français); IV.3 (dīpa); PvA 81 (°divase on another day), 226; with other part. like aparo pi D III 128. — nt. **aparaŋ** what follows i. e. future state, consequence; future Vin I.35 (nâparaŋ nothing more); Sn 1092 (much the same as punabbhava, cp. Nd[2] 61). Cases adverbially; **aparaŋ** (acc.) further, besides, also J I.256; III.278; often with other part. like **athâparaŋ** & further, moreover Sn 974; and **puna c' aparaŋ** It 100; Miln 418 (so read for puna ca paraŋ) and passim; **aparam pi** Vism 9. — **aparena** in future D III.201. — Repeated (reduplicative formation) **aparâparaŋ** (local) to & fro J I.265, 278; PvA 198; (temporal) again and again, off & on J II.377; Miln 132 VvA 271; PvA 176 (= punappunaŋ).

-**anta** (aparanta) = aparaŋ, with anta in same function as in cpds. vananta (see anta[1] 5): (a.) further away, westward J V.471; Miln 292 (janapada). (b.) future D I.30 (°kappika, cp. DA I.118); M II.228 (°ânudiṭṭhi thought of the future); S III 46 (id.). -**âpariya** (fr. aparâpara) ever-following, successive, continuou, everlasting; used with ref. to kamma J V.126; Miln 108. -**bhāga** the future, lit. a later part of time, only in loc. aparabhāge at a future date, later on J I.34, 262; IV.1; VvA 66.

Aparajju (adv.) [Sk. apare-dyus] on the foll. day Vin II.167; S I.186; Miln 48.

Aparajjhati [Sk. aparādhyate, apa + **rādh**] to sin or offend against (c. loc.) Vin II.78 = III.161; J V.68; VI.367; Miln 189; PvA 263. — pp. **aparaddha** & **aparādhita** (q. v.).

Aparaṇṇa (nt.) [apara + aṇṇa = anna] "the other kind of cereal", prepared or cooked cereals, pulse etc. Opp. to pubbaṇṇa the unprepared or raw corn (= āmakadhañña Vin IV.265; Vin III.151 (pubb° +); IV.265, 267; A IV. 108, 112 (tila-mugga-māsā°; opp. sāli-yavaka etc.); Nd[1] 314 (aparaṇṇaŋ nāma sūpeyyaŋ); J V.406 (°jā = hareṇukā, pea); Miln 106 (pubbaṇṇa°). See also dhañña & harita.

Aparaddha [pp. of aparajjhati] missed (c. acc.), gone wrong, failed, sinned (against = loc.) D I.91, 103, 180; S I.103 (suddhimaggaŋ); Th 1, 78; Sn 891 (suddhiŋ = viraddha khalita Nd[1] 300); PvA 195.

Aparapaccaya (adj.) [a + para + paccaya] not dependent or relying on others Vin I.12 (vesārajja-ppatta +); D I.110 (id.); M II 41; M I.491; S III.83; DA I.278 (= nâssa paro paccayo).

Aparājita (adj.) [Vedic aparājita; a + parājita] unconquered Sn 269; J I.71, 165.

Aparādha [fr. apa + **rādh**] sin, fault, offence, guilt J I.264 (nir°); III.394; IV.495; VvA 69; PvA 87, 116.

Aparādhika (adj.) [fr. aparādha, cp. Sk. aparādhin] guilty, offending, criminal J II.117 (vāja°); Miln 149 (issara°), 189 (aparādhikatā).

Aparādhita [pp. of aparādheti, Caus. of apa + **rādh**; cp. aparaddha] transgressed, sinned, failing J V.26 (so read for aparādh' ito).

Aparāyin (adj.) [a + parāyin, cp. parāyana] having no support J III.386 (f. °ī; C. appatiṭṭhā appaṭisaraṇā).

Apalāpin see **apalāsin** [Sk. apalāpin "denying, concealing" different].

Apalāḷeti [apa + lāḷeti] to draw over to Vin I.85.

Apalāyin (adj.) [a + palāyin] not running away, steadfast, brave, fearless Nd[2] 13 (abhīru anutrāsin apalāyin as expl[n.] of acchambhin and vīra); J IV.296; V.4 (where C. gives variant "**apalāpinī** ti pi pāṭho", which latter has v. l. **apalāsinī** & is expl[d.] by C. as palāpa-rahite anavajjasarīre p. 5). See also apalāsin.

Apalāsin (adj.) [apaḷāsin; but spelling altogether uncertain. There seems to exist a confusion between the forms apalāyin, apalāpin & apalāsin, owing to freq. miswriting of s, y, p in MSS. (cp. Nd[2] introd. p. XIX.). We should be inclined to give apalāsin, as the lectio difficilior, the preference. The expl[n.] at Pug 22 as "yassa puggalassa ayaŋ paḷāso pahīno ayaŋ vuccati puggalo apaḷāsī" does not help us to clear up the etym. nor the vv. ll.] either "not neglectful, pure, clean" (= apalāpin fr. palāsa chaff, cp. apalāyin at J V.4), or "not selfish, not hard, generous" (as inferred from comb[n.] with amakkhin & amaccharin), or "brave, fearless, energetic" (= apalāyin) D III 47, cp. Pug 22. See **palāsin**.

Apalibuddha & **Apalibodha** [a + palibuddha, pp. of pari + **bṛh**, see palibujjhati] unobstructed, unhindered, free J III. 381 (°bodha); Miln 388; DhA III.198.

Apalekhana (nt.) [apa + lekhana from **likh** in meaning of **lih**, corresponding to Sk. ava-lehana] licking off, in cpd. **hatthâpalekhana** "hand-licking" (i. e. licking one's hand after a meal, the practice of certain ascetics) M I 77 (with v. l. hatthâvalekhana M I.535; Trenckner compares BSk. hastapralehaka Lal. Vist. 312 & hastâvalehaka ibid. 323), 412; Pug 55 (expl[d.] at Pug A 231 as hatthe piṇḍamhe niṭṭhite jivhāya hatthaŋ apalekhati).

Apalekhati [apa + lekhati in meaning of Sk. avalihati] to lick off Pug A 231 (hatthaŋ).

Apalepa in "so 'palepa patito jarāgharo" at Th 2, 270 is to be read as "so palepa°". Morris's interpret. *JPTS.* 1886, 126 therefore superfluous.

Apalokana (nt.) [fr. apaloketi] permission, leave, in °**kamma** proposal of a resolution, obtaining leave (see kamma 1.3) Vin II.89; IV.152

Apalokita [pp. of apaloketi; Sk. avalokita] 1. asked permission, consulted S III.5. — 2. (nt.) permission, consent, M I.337 (Nāgâpalokitaŋ apalokesi). — 3. (nt.) an Ep. of Nibbāna S IV.370.

Apalokin (adj.) [Sk. avalokin] "looking before oneself", looking at, cautious Miln 398.

Apaloketi [BSk. ava-lokayati] 1. to look ahead, to look before, to be cautious, to look after M I.557 (v. l. for apaciṇāti, where J V.339 C. has avaloketi); Miln 398. — 2. to look up to, to obtain permission from (acc.), to get leave, to give notice of Vin III.10, 11; IV.226 (anapaloketvā = anāpucchā), 267 (+ āpucchitvā); M I.337; S III.95 (bhikkhusaṅghaŋ anapaloketvā without informing the Saṅgha); J VI.298 (vājānaŋ); DhA I.67. — pp. **apalokita** (q. v.). See also apalokana & °lokin.

Apavagga [Sk. apavarga] completion, end, final delivery, Nibbāna; in phrase **saggâpavagga** Dāvs II.62; III.75.

Apavattati [apa + **vṛt**, cp. Lat. āverto] to turn away or aside, to go away J IV.347 (v. l. apasakkati).

Apavadati [apa + vadati] to reproach, reprove, reject, despise D I.122 (= paṭikkhipati DA I.290); S V.118 (+ paṭikkosati).

Apavahati [apa + vahati] to carry or drive away; Caus. **apavāheti** to remove, give up Miln 324 (kaddamaŋ).

Apaviṭṭha at Pv III 8² is to be read **apaviddha** (q. v.).

Apaviṇāti is probably misreading for **apaciṇāti** (see apac° 2). As v. l. at J V.339 (anapavinanto) for T. anupacinanto (expl^d. by avaloketi C.). Other vv. ll. are anuvi° & apavi°; meaning "not paying attention". The positive form we find as **apavīṇati** "to take care of, to pay attention to" (c. acc.) at M I.324, where Trenckner unwarrantedly assumes a special root **veṇ** (see Notes p. 78¹), but the vv. ll. to this passage (see M. I.557) with apavīṇāti and apacinati confirm the reading apaciṇāti, as does the gloss apaloketi.

Apaviddha [pp. of apavijjhati, Vedic apa + **vyadh**] thrown away, rejected, discarded, removed S I.202; III.143; Sn 200 (susānasmiŋ = **chaḍḍita** SnA 250); Th 1, 635 = Dh 292 (= **chaḍḍita** DhA III.452); Pv III.8² (susānasmiŋ; so read for T. apaviṭṭha); J I.255; III.426; VI.90 (= **chaḍḍita** C.). Sdhp 366.

Apaviyūhati see **appabbūhati**.

Apavīṇati see **apaviṇāti** (= apaciṇāti).

Apavyāma [apa + vyāma] disrespect, neglect, in phrase **apayvāmato** (apaby°) **karoti** to treat disrespectfully, to insult, defile S I.226 (v. l. abyāmato; C. expl^s. apabyāmato karitvā abyāmato katvā); Kvu 472 (vv. ll. asabyākato, abyāto, apabyāto; *Kvu trsl.* 270 n. 1 remarks: "B. trsl.: abyāsakato. The Burmese scholar U. Pandi, suggests we should read apabyākato, by which he understands blasphemously"; it is here comb^d. with **niṭṭhubhati**, as at DhA II.36); DhA II.36 ("want of forbearance" Ed.; doubtful reading; vv. ll. appabyāyakamma & apasāma). For further detail see **apasavya**.

Apasakkati [apa + sakkati] to go away, to go aside J IV.347 (v. l. for apavattati); VvA 101; PvA 265 (aor. °sakki = apakkami).

Apasavya (adj.) [apa + savya] right (i. e. not left), contrary Ud 50 (T. has niṭṭhubhitvā abyāmato karitvā; vv. ll. are apabhyāmāto, abhyāmato & C. apasabyāmato), where C. expl^s. apasabyāmato karitvā by apasabyaŋ katvā, "which latter corresponds in form but not in meaning to Sk. apasavyaŋ karoti to go on the right side" (Morris *J P T S.* 1886, 127). — See **apavyāma**.

Apasāda [fr. apa + **sad**] putting down, blame, disparagement M III.230.

Apasādita [pp. of apasādeti] blamed, reproached, disparaged S II.219; SnA 541.

Apasādeti [Caus. of apa + **sad**] 1. to refuse, decline Vin IV.213, 263; J V.417 (= uyyojeti). — 2. to depreciate, blame, disparage Vin III.101; M III.230 (opp. ussādeti); DA I.160. — pp. **apasādita** (q. v.).

Apasmāra [Sk. apasmāra, lit. want of memory, apa + **smṛ**] epilepsy, convulsion, fit J IV.84. Cp. apamāra.

Apassanto etc. see **passati**.

Apassaya [cp. Sk. apāśraya, fr. apasseti] 1. support, rest ThA 258. — 2. bed, bolster, mattress, in **kaṇṭak°** a mattress of thorns, a bolster filled with thorns (as cushion for ascetics) M I.78; J I 493; III.235. -**sâppassaya** with a head rest J IV.299.

-**pīṭhaka** a chair with a head-rest J III.235.

Apassayika (adj.) [fr. apassaya; cp. Sk. apāśrayin —°] reclining on, in **kaṇṭaka°** one who lies on a bed of thorns (see kaṇṭaka) M I.78; J IV.299 (v. l. kaṇḍikesayika); Pug 55.

Apassita [pp. of apasseti] 1. leaning against J II.69 (tālamūlaŋ = nissāya ṭhita C.). — 2. depending on, trusting in (c. acc. or loc.) Vv 10¹ (parâgāraŋ = nissita VvA 101); J IV.25 (balamhi = balanissita). See also avassita.

Apasseti [Sk. apāśrayati, apa + ā + **śri**] to lean against, have a support in (acc.), to depend on. — 1. (lit.) lean against Vin II.175 (bhitti apassetabbo the wall to be used as a head-rest). — 2. (fig.) mostly in ger. **apassāya** dependent upon, depending on, trusting in (loc. or acc. or —°) Vin III.38; J I.214; PvA 189. — pp. **apassita** (q. v.). — See also avasseti.

Apassena (nt.) [fr. apasseti] a rest, support, dependence M III.127 (°ka); D III.224 (cattāri apassenāni); as adj. **caturâpassena** one who has the fourfold support viz. saṅkhāy' ekaŋ paṭisevati, adhivāseti, parivajjeti, vinodeti A V.30.

-**phalaka** (cp. Morris *J P T S.* 1884, 71) a bolster-slab, head-rest Vin I.48; II.175, 209.

Apahattar [n. ag. to apaharati] one who takes away or removes, destroyer M I 447 = Kvu 528.

Apahara [Sk. apahāra, fr. apaharati] taking away, stealing, robbing J II.34.

Apaharaṇa (nt.) = apahara Miln 195.

Apaharati [apa + **hṛ**] to take away, remove, captivate, rob J III.315 (aor. apahārayiŋ); Miln 413; DA I.38.

Apākaṭatā (f.) [a + pākaṭa + tā] unfitness Miln 232 (v. l. apākatatta perhaps better).

Apākatika (adj.) [a + pākata + ika] not in proper or natural shape, out of order, disturbed DhA II.7. Cp. **appakāra**.

Apācīna (adj.) [Vedic apācīna; cp. apācaḥ & apāka, western; to Lat. opācus, orig. turned away (from the east or the sun) i. e. opposite, dark] westerly, backward, below S III.84; It 120 (apācīnaŋ used as adv. and taking here the place of adho in comb^n. with uddhaŋ tiriyaŋ; the reading is a conjecture of Windisch's, the vv. ll. are apācinaŋ; apācini, apāci & apāminaŋ, C. expl^s. by heṭṭhā).

Apāṭuka (adj.) [a + pāṭu + ka (?), acc. to Morris *J P T S.* 1893, 7 der. fr. apaṭu not sharp, blunt, uncouth. This is hardly correct. See pātur] not open, sly, insidious Th 1, 940 (as v. l. for T. avāṭuka, trsl. by Mrs. Rh. D. as "unscrupulous", by Neumann as "ohne Redlichkeit"). Context suggests a meaning similar to the preceding nekatika, i. e. fraudulent. See also next.

Apāṭubha (adj.) [a + pāṭu + bha (?), at the only passage changed by Morris *J P T S.* 1893, 7 to apāṭuka but without reason] = apāṭuka, i. e. sly, fraudulent J IV.184 (in context with nekatika; C. expls. apāṭubhāva dhanuppāda-virahita, in which latter virahita does not fit in; the pass. seems corrupt).

Apāda (?) [apa + ā + **dā**] giving away in marriage J IV. 179 (in expln. of anāpāda unmarried; reading should prob. be āpāda = pariggaha).

Apādaka (adj.) [a + pāda + ka] not having feet, footless, creeping, Ep. of snakes & fishes Vin II.110 = J II.146 (where see expln.). Spelt **apada(ka)** at It 87 (v. l. apāda).

Apāna (nt.) breathing out, respiration (so Ch.; no ref. in P. Canon?) On Prāṇa & Apāna see G. W. Brown in J. Am. Or. Soc. 39, 1919 pp. 104—112. See ānāpāna.

Apānakatta (nt.) [a + pānaka + ttaŋ] "waterless state", living without drinking water J V.243.

Apāpaka (adj.) [a + pāpaka] guiltless, innocent f. °**ikā** Vv 31^4; 32^6.

Apāpata (adj.) [apa + ā + pata] falling down into (c. acc.) J IV.234 (aggiŋ).

Apāpurana (nt.) [fr. apāpurati] a key (to a door) Vin I.80; III 119; M III.127. See also avāpuraṇa.

Apāpurati & **Apāpuṇati** [Sk. apāvṛṇoti, apa + ā + **vṛ**, but Vedic only apa-vṛṇoti corresponding to Lat. aperio = *apa-uerio. On form see Trenckner, *Notes* 63] to open (a door) Vin I.5 (apāpur' etaŋ Amatassa dvāraŋ: imper.; where id. p. S I.137 has avāpur°, T., but v. l. apāpur°); Vv 64^{27} (apāpuranto Amatassa dvāraŋ, expld. at VvA 284 by vivaranto); It 80 (apāvuṇanti A. dv. as T. conj.; with v. l. apānuṃanti, apāpurenti & apāpuranti). — pp. apāruta (q. v.). — Pass. **apāpurīyati** [cp. BSk. apāvurīyati M Vastu II.158] to be opened M III.184 (v. l. avā°); J I.63 (avā°); Th 2, 494 (apāpuṇitvā). See also avāpurati.

Apabhata [pp. of apa + ā + **bhṛ** cp. Vedic apa-bharati, but Lat. aufero to ava°] taken away, stolen J III.54.

Apāya [Sk. apāya, fr. apa + **i**, cp. apeti] "going away" viz. — 1. separation, loss Dh 211 (piya° = viyoga DhA III.276). — 2. loss (of property) D III.181, 182; A II. 166; IV.283; J III.387 (atth°). — 3. leakage, out flow (of water) D I.74; A II.166; IV.287. — 4. lapse, falling away (in conduct) D I.100. — 5. a transient state of loss and woe after death. Four such states are specified purgatory (niraya), rebirth as an animal, or as a ghost, or as a Titan (Asura). Analogous expressions are **vinipāta** & **duggati**. All combined at D I.82; III.111; A I.55; It 12, 73; Nd^2 under kāya; & freq. elsewhere. — apāya-duggativinipāta as attr. of saŋsāra S II.92, 232; IV.158, 313; V.342; opp. to khīṇâpāya-duggati-vinipāta of an Arahant A IV.405; V.182 sq. — See also foll. pass.: M III.25 (anapāya); Sn 231; Th 2, 63; J IV.299; Pug 51; VvA 118 (opp. sugati); PvA 103; Sdhp 43, 75 & cp. niraya, duggati, vinipāta.

-**gāmin** going te ruin or leading to a state of suffering DhA III.175; cp. °gamanīya id. Ps. I.94, °gamanīyatā J IV.499. -**mukha** "facing ruin", leading to destruction (= vināsa-mukha DA I.268), usually as nt. „cause of ruin" D I.101 (cattāri apāya mukhāni); III.181, 182 (cha bhogānaŋ a° -mukhāni, i. e. causes of the loss of one's possessions); A II.166; IV.283, 287. -**samudda** the ocean of distress DhA III.432. -**sahāya** a spendthrift companion D III.185.

Apāyika (adj.) [also as **āpāyika** (q. v.); fr. apāya] belonging to the apāyas or states of misery D I.103; III.6, 9, 12; It 42; PvA 60 (dukkha).

Apāyin (adj.) [fr. apāya] going away J I.163 (aḍḍharattāv'apāyin = aḍḍharatte apāyin C.). -an° not going away, i. e. constantly following (chāyā anapāyinī, the shadow) Dh 2; Th I, 1041; Miln 72.

Apāra (nt.) [a + pāra] 1. the near bank of a river J III.230 (+ atiṇṇaŋ, C. paratīraŋ atiṇṇaŋ). — 2. (fig.) not the further shore (of life), the world here, i.e. (opp. pāraŋ = Nibbāna) Sn 1129, 1130; Nd^2 62; Dh 385 (expld. as bāhirāni cha āyatanāni DhA IV.141). See pāra & cp. avara.

Apāraṇeyya (adj.) [grd. of paraneti + a°] that which cannot be achieved, unattainable J VI.36 (= apāpetabba).

Apāruta [Sk. apāvṛta, pp. of apāpurati] open (of a door) Vin I.7 = M I.169 (apārutā tesaŋ Amatassa dvārā); D I.136 (= vivaṭa-dvāra DA I.297); J I.264 (°dvāra).

Apālamba ["a Vedic term for the hinder part of a carriage" Morris *JPTS.* 1886, 128; the "Vedic" unidentified] a mechanism to stop a chariot, a safe guard "to prevent warriors from falling out" (C.) S I.33 (Mrs Rh. D. trsl. "leaning board"); J VI.252 (v. l. upā°; Kern trsl. "remhout", i. e. brake).

Apāhata [pp. of apa + **hṛ**] driven off or back, refuted, refused Sn 826 (°smiŋ = apasādite vade SnA 541).

Api (indecl.) [Sk. api & pi; Idg. *epi *pi *opi; cp. Gr. ἔπι on to, ὄπι (ὄπισθεν behind, ὀπίσσω back = close at one's heels); Lat. ob. in certain functions; Goth. iftuma. — The assimil. form before vorvels is app° (= Sk. apy°). See further details under pi.] both prep. & conj., orig. meaning "close by", then as prep. "towards, to, on to, on" and as adv. "later, and, moreover". — 1 (prep. & pref.) (a) prep. c. loc.: **api ratte** later on in the night (q. v.) — (b) pref.: **apidhāna** putting on to; **apiḷahati** bind on to, apihita (= Gr. ἐπίθετος, epithet) put on to, (q. v.). — 2. (conj. & part.). (a) in affirmative sentences meaning primarily "moreover, further, and then, even": — (α) (single) *prothetic*: api dibbesu kāmesu even in heavenly joys Dh 187; ko disvā na pasīdeyya api kaṇhābhijātiko even an unfortunate-born Sn 563 api yojanāni gacchāma, even for leagues we go Pv IV.10^7 (= anekāni yojanāni pi g. PvA 270. *Epithetic* (more freq. in the form **pi**): muhuttam api even a little while Dh 106, 107; aham api daṭṭhukāmo I also wish to see Sn 685. Out of prothetic use (= even = even if) develops the conditional meaning of "if", as in api sakkuṇemu (and then we may = if we may) J V.24 (c. = api nāma sakkuṇeyyāma; see further under β app'eva nāma). — **api-api** in correlation corresponds to Lat. et-et Sk ca-ca, meaning both ... and, and ... as well as, & is esp. freq. in combn. **app' ekacce ... app' ekacce** (and) some ... and others, i. e. some ... others [*not* with Kern *Toev.* s. v. to **appa**!], e. g. at D I.118; Th 2, 216; VvA 208, etc. -**app' ekadā** "morever once" = sometimes Vin IV.178; S I.162; IV.111; J I.67; DhA III.303, etc. — (β) (in combn with other emphatic or executive particles) **api ca** further, and also, moreover D I.96; Miln 25, 47. -**api ca kho** moreover, and yet, still, all the same It 89 (+ pana v. l.); Miln 20, 239. -**api ca kho pana** all the same, never mind, nevertheless J I.253. -**api ssu** so much so Vin II.76. -**app' eva nāma** (with pot.) (either) surely, indeed, yes, I reckon, (or) I presume, it is likely that, perhaps Vin I.16 (surely); II.85 (id.); cp. pi D I.205 (sve pi upasaŋkameyyāma tomorrow I shall surely come along), 226 (siyā thus shall it be); M I.460 = It 89 (moreover, indeed); J I.168 (surely) Vin II.262 (perhaps) J V.421 (id., piyavācaŋ labheyyāma). — (b) in interrog.-dubit. sentences as part. of interrog. (w. indic. or pot.) corresponding to Lat. nonne, i e. awaiting an affirmative answer ("not, not then"): api yasaŋ kulaputtaŋ passeyya do you not see ... Vin I.16; api samaṇa balivadde addasā have you not then seen ... S I.115; api kiñci labhāmase shall we then not get anything? J III.26; api me pitaraŋ passatha do you then not see my father? PvA 38. — Also combd. with other interr. part. e. g. **api nu** J. II.415.

Apitika (adj.) [a + pitika] fatherless J V.251.

Apithīyati [for apidhīyati; api + **dhā**] Pass. of apidahati to be obstructed, covered, barred, obscured J II.158. See also **pithīyati.**

Apidahati [api + **dhā**, cp. Gr. ἐπιτίθημι] to put on (see api I b), to cover up, obstruct, J V.60 (inf. apidhetuŋ). pp. apihita, Pass. apithīyati, Der. apidhāna (q. v.).

Apidhāna (nt.) [Vedic apidhāna in same meaning] cover, lid Vin I.203, 204; II.122. See apidahati.

Apiratte [read api ratte, see api I a] later in the night J VI.560.

Apilāpana (nt.) [fr. api + **lap**] counting up, repetition [Kern, *Toev*, s.v. gives der. fr. a + plāvana] Nett 15, 28, 54; Miln 37.

Apilāpanatā (f.) in the pass. at Dhs 14 = Nd^2 628 is evidently meant to be taken as a + pilāpana + tā (fr. pilavati, **plu**), but whether the der. & interpret. of Dhs A is correct, we are unable to say. On general principles it looks like popular etym. Mrs. Rh. D. translates (p. 16) "opposite of superficiality" (lit "not floating"); see her detailed note *Dhs trsl.* 16.

Apilāpeti [api + **lap**] "to talk close by", i. e. to count up, recite, or: talk idly, boast of Miln 37 (sāpatheyyaŋ).

Apiḷandha (adj.) at Vv 36^1 should be read as **apiḷaddha** (= Sk. apinaddha) pp. of apiḷandhati (apiḷandhati) "adorned with", or (with v. l. SS) as **apiḷandhana**; VvA 167 expls. by analankata, mistaking the **a** of api for a negation.

Apiḷandhana (nt.) [fr. apiḷandhati, also in shorter (& more usual) form **piḷandhana**, q. v.] that which is tied on, i.e. band, ornament, apparel, parure Vv 64^{10}, 64^{18} (expld. inacurately at VvA 279 by; a-kāro nipātamattaŋ, piḷandhanaŋ = ābhāraṇaŋ); J VI.472 (c. pilandhituŋ pi ayuttaŋ?).

Apiḷahati & **Apiḷandhati** [Sk. apinahyati, on n : ḷ see note on gala, & cp. guṇa : guḷa, veṇu : veḷu etc. On ndh for yh see avanandhati] to tie on, fasten, bind together; to adorn oneself with (acc.) J V.400 (ger. apiḷayha = piḷandhitvā C.) — Cp. apiḷandhana & pp apiladdha.

Apiha (adj.) [apihālu? a + piha, uncertain origin, see next. Morris *J.P.T.S.* 1886 takes it as a + spṛha] "unhankering" (Mrs Rh. D.) S I 181 (+ akankha; v. l. BB asita).

Apihālu (adj.) [a + pihālu, analysed by Fausböll Sn. Gloss. p. 229 as a-spṛhayālu, but Bdhgh evidently different (see below)] not hankering, free from craving, not greedy S I.187 = Th I, 1218 (akuhako nipako apihālu); Sn 852 (+ amaccharin, expl^d. at SnA 549 as apihana-sīlo, patthanātaṇhāya rahito ti vuttaŋ hoti, thus perhaps taking it as a + pi (= api) + hana (fr. **dhā**, cp. pidahati & pihita); cp. also Nd^2 227).

Apihita [pp. of apidahati] covered J IV.4.

Apuccaṇḍatā (f.) [a + pūti + aṇḍa + tā] "not being a rotten egg," i. e. normal state, healthy birth, soundness M I.357.

Apuccha (adj.) [a + pucchā] "not a question", i. e. not to be asked Miln 316.

Apekkha (adj.) [= apekkhā] waiting for, looking for S I.122 (otāra°).

Apekkhati I. [Sk. apīkṣate, apa + **īkṣ**] to desire, long for, look for, expect Sn 435 (kāme n'āpekkhate cittaŋ), 773 (ppr. apekkhamāna); J IV.226 (id.); Dhs A 365. anapekkhamāna paying no attention to (acc.) Sn 59; J V.359. — 2. [Sk. avikṣate, ava + **īkṣ**; see avekkhati] to consider, refer to, look at, ger. apekkhitvā (cp. Sk. avikṣya) with reference to VvA 13. — pp. **apekkhita** (q. v.).

Apekkhavant (adj.) [fr. apekkhā] full of longing or desire, longing, craving Vin IV.214; S III.16; Th I, 558; J V.453 (= sataṇha); Sn A 76.

Apekkhā & **Apekhā** (f.) [Sk. apekṣā, fr. apa + **īkṣ**. The spelling is either kkh or kh, they are both used promiscuously, a tendency towards kh prevailing, as in upekhā, sekha] attention, regard, affection for (loc.); desire, longing for (c. loc.) S I.77; III.132; V.409 (mātā-pitusu); Vin IV.214; Sn 38 (= vuccati taṇhā etc. Nd^2 65; = taṇhā sineha SnA 76); J I.9, 141; Th I, 558; Dh 345 (puttesu dāresu ca = taṇhā DhA IV.56); Dhs 1059, 1136 (= ālayakaraṇa-vasena apekkhatī ti apekkhā Dhs A 365, cp. *Dhs trsl.* 279). Freq. as adj. (—°or in comb^n. with sa° and an°), viz. Vin III.90 (visuddha°); S I.122 (otara°); **sa°** A III.258, 433; IV·60 sq.; an° without consideration, regardless, indifferent S V.164; A III.252, 347, 434; Sn 200 (anapekkhā honti ñātayo); J I 9. Cp. anapekkhin & apekkhavant; also B.Sk. avekṣatā.

Apekkhita [pp. of apekkhati] taken care of, looked after, considered J VI.142, 149 (= olokita C.).

Apekkhin (adj.) [Sk. apekṣin, but B.Sk. avekṣin, e.g. Jtm 215; fr apa + **īkṣ**] considering, regarding, expecting, looking for; usually neg. an° indifferent (against) = loc.) S I.16, 77; II.281; III.19, 87; Sn 166 (kāmesu), 823 (id.), 857; Dh 346. Cp. apekkhavant.

Apeta (adj.) [pp. of apeti] gone away; (med.) freed of, rid of, deprived of (instr., abl. or °—) Dh 9 (damasaccena); PvA 35 (dukkhato); usually °— in sense of "without, -less", e. g. apeta-kaddama free from mud, stainless Dh 95; °vattha without dress J V.16; °viññāṇa without feeling, senseless Dh 41; Th 2, 468; °viññāṇattaŋ senselessness, lack of feeling PvA 63.

Apetatta (nt.) [abstr. to apeta] absence (of) PvA 92.

Apeti [apa + **i**, cp. Gr. ἄπειμι, Lat. abeo, Goth. af-iddja] to go away, to disappear D I.180 (upeti pi apeti pi); J I.292; Sn 1143 (= n' apagacchanti na vijahanti Nd^2 66). — pp. apeta (q. v.).

Apetteyyatā (f.) [a + petteyyatā, abstr. fr. *paitrya fatherly] in comb^n. with **amatteyyatā** irreverence against father and mother D III.70 (cp. Dh 332 & DhA IV.34).

Apeyya (adj.) [a + peyya, grd. of **pā**] not to be drunk, not drinkable J VI.205 (sāgara).

Apesiya (nt.) [? of uncertain origin] a means of barring a door Vin II.154 (Bdhgh. expl^{ns} on p. 321: apesī ti dīghadārumhi khāṇuke pavesetvā kaṇḍaka-sākhāhi vinandhitvā kataŋ dvāra-ṭṭhakanakaŋ).

Apesiyamāna (adj.) [ppr. fr. a + peseti (q. v.)] not being in service Vin II.177.

App' in app' ekacce etc. see api.

Appa (adj.) [Vedic alpa, cp. Gr. ἀλαπάζω (λαπάζω) to empty (to make little), ἀλαπαδνός weak; Lith. alpnas weak, alpstù to faint] small, little, insignificant, often in the sense of "very little = (next to) nothing" (so in most cpds.); thus expl^d. at VvA 334 as equivalent to a *negative* part. (see appodaka) D I.61 (opp. mahant, DA I.170 = parittaka); Sn 713, 775, 805, 896 (= appaka, omaka, thoka, lamaka, jatukka, parittaka Nd^1 306); Dh 174; J I.262; Pug 39. — nt. **appaŋ** a little, a small portion, a trifle; pl. appāni small things, trifles A II.26 = It 102; A II.138; Dh 20 (= thokaŋ eka-vagga-dvi-vagga-mattam pi DhA I.158), 224 (°smiŋ yācito asked for little), 259. -**aggha** of little value (opp. mahaggha priceless) J I.9; Pug 33; DhA IV.184. -**assāda** [BSk. alpâsvāda, cp. Divy 224 = Dh 186: alpa + ā + **svād**] of little taste or enjoyment, affording little pleasure (always used of kāmā) Vin II.25 = M I.130 = A III.97 = Nd^2 71; Sn 61; Dh

186 (= supina-sadisatāya paritta-sukha DhA III 240); Th 2, 358 (= ThA 244): J II.313; Vism 124. -ātanka little (or no) illness, freedom from illness, good health (= appābādha with which often combd.) [BSk. alpātanka & alpātankatā] D I.204 (+ appābādha); III.166; A III.65, 103; Miln 14. **-ābādha** same as appātanka (q.v.) D I.204; III.166, 237; M II.125; A I.25; II.88; III.30, 65 sq., 103, 153; Pv IV.1[44]; °**ābādhatā** id. [cp. BSk. alpābādhatā good health] A I.38. **-āyuka** short lived D I.18; PvA 103, also as °**āyukin** Vv 41[6]. **-āhāra** taking little or no food, fasting M II.5; Sn 165 (= ekāsana-bhojitāya ca parimita-bhojitāya ca SnA 207), also as °**āhāratā** M I.245; II.5. **-odaka** having little or no water, dry Sn 777 (macche va appodake khīṇasote = parittodake Nd¹ 50); Vv 84[3] (+ appabhakkha; expld. at VvA 334 as "appa-saddo h' ettha abhāvattho appiccho appanigghoso ti ādisu viya"); J I.70; DhA IV.12. **-kasira** in instr. °kasirena with little or no difficulty D I.251; S V.51; Th 1, 16. **-kicca** having few duties, free from obligations, free from care Sn 144 (= appaŋ kiccaŋ assā ti KhA 241). **-gandha** not smelling or having a bad smell Miln 252 (opp. sugandha). **-ṭṭha** "standing in little"; i. e. connected with little trouble D I.143; A I.169. **-thāmaka** having little or no strength, weak S IV.206. **-dassa** having little knowledge or wisdom Sn 1134 (see Nd² 69; expld. by paritta-pañña SnA 605). **-nigghosa** with little sound, quiet, still, soundless (cp. VvA 334, as quoted above under °odaka) A V.15 (+ appasadda); Sn 338; Nd¹ 377; Miln 371. **-pañña**, of little wisdom J II.166; III.223, 263. **-puñña** of little merit M II.5. **-puññatā** having little merit, unworthiness Pv IV.10[1]. **-phalatā** bringing little fruit PvA 139. **-bhakkha** having little or nothing to eat Vv 84[3]. **-bhoga** having little wealth, i. e. poor, indigent Sn 114 (= sannicitānaŋ ca bhogānaŋ āyamukhassa ca abhāvato SnA 173). **-maññati** to consider as small, to underrate: see separately. **-matta** little, slight, mean, (usually as °ka; not to be confounded with appamatta²) A III.275; J I.242; also meaning "contented with little" (of the bhikkhu) It 103 = A II.27; f. °ā trifle, smallness, insignificance D I.91; DA I.55. **-mattaka** small, insignificant, trifling, nt. a trifle (cp. °matta) Vin I, 213; II.177 (°vissajjaka the distributor of little things, cp. A III.275 & Vin IV.38, 155); D I.3 (= appamattā etassā ti appamattakaŋ DA I.55); J I.167; III.12 (= aṇu); PvA 262. **-middha** "little slothful", i. e. diligent, alert Miln 412. **-rajakkha** having little or no obtuseness D II.37; M I.169; Sdhp 519. **-ssaka** having little of one's own, possessing little A I.261; II.203. **-sattha** having few or no companions, lonely, alone Dh 123. **-sadda** free from noise, quiet M II.2, 23, 30; A V.15; Sn 925 (= appanigghosa Nd¹ 377); Pug 35; Miln 371. **-siddhika** bringing little success or welfare, dangerous J IV.4 (= mandasiddhi vināsabahula C.); VI.34 (samuddo a. bahu-antarāyiko). **-ssuta** possessing small knowledge, ignorant, uneducated D I.93 (opp. bahussuta); III.252, 282; S IV.242; It 59; Dh 152; Pug 20, 62; Dhs 1327. **-harita** having little or no grass S I.169; Sn p. 15 (= paritta-harita-tiṇa SnA 154).

Appaka (adj.) [appa + ka] little, small, trifling; pl. few. nt. °ŋ adv. a little D II.4; A V.232 sq., 253 sq.; Sn 909 (opp. bahu); Dh 85 (appakā = thokā na bahū DhA II.160); Pv I.10² (= paritta PvA 48); II.9[39]; Pug 62; PvA 6, 60 (= paritta). f. **appikā** J I.228. — instr. **appakena** by little, i. e. easily DA I.256. **-anappaka** not little, i. e. much, considerable, great; pl. many S IV.46; Dh 144; Pv I.11[1] (= bahū PvA 58); PvA 24, 25 (read anappake pi for T. °appakeci; so also KhA 208).

Appakāra (adj.) [a + pakāra] not of natural form, of bad appearance, ugly, deformed J V.69 (= sarīrappakāra-rahita dussaṇṭhāna C.). Cp. apākatika.

Appakiṇṇa [appa + kiṇṇa, although in formation also = a + pakiṇṇa] little or not crowded, not overheaped A V.15 (C. anākiṇṇa).

Appagabbha (adj.) [a + pagabbha] unobtrusive, free from boldness, modest S II.198 = Miln 389, Sn 144, 852 (cp. Nd¹ 228 & KhA 232); Dh 245.

Appaccaya [a + paccaya] 1. (n.) discontent, dissatisfaction, dejection, sulkiness D I.3 (= appatītā honti tena atuṭṭhā asomanassitā ti appacayo: domanass' etaŋ adhivacanaŋ DA I.52); III.159; M I.442; A I.79, 124, 187; II 203; III.181 sq.; IV.168, 193; J II.277; Sn p. 92 (kapa + dosa + appacaya); Vv 83[31] (= domanassaŋ VvA 343); SnA 423 (= appatītaŋ domanassaŋ). — 2. (adj.) unconditioned Dhs 1084, 1437.

Appaṭi° [a + paṭi°] see in general under **paṭi°**.

Appaṭikārika (adj.) [a + paṭikārika] "not providing against", i. e. not making good, not making amends for, destructive J V.418 (spelling here & in C. appati°).

Appaṭikopeti [a + paṭikopeti] not to disturb, shake or break (fig.) J V.173 (uposathaŋ).

Appaṭikkhippa (adj.) [a + paṭikkhippa, grd. of paṭikkhipati] not to be refused J II.370.

Appaṭigandhika & °**iya** (adj.) [a + paṭi + gandha + ika] not smelling disagreeable, i. e. with beautiful smell, scented, odorous J V.405 (°ika, but C. °iya; expld. by sugandhena udakena samannāgata); VI.518; Pv II.1[20]; III.2[26].

Appaṭigha (adj.) [a + paṭigha] (a) not forming an obstacle, not injuring, unobstructive Sn 42 (see expld. at Nd² 239; SnA 88 expls. "katthaci satte vā sankhāre vā bhayena na paṭihaññati ti a."). — (b) psychol. t. t. appld. to rūpa: not reacting or impinging (opp. sappaṭigha) D III.217; Dhs 660, 756, 1090, 1443.

Appaṭicchavi (adj.) at Pv II.1[13] is faulty reading for **sampatitacchavi** (v. l.).

Appaṭibhāga (adj.) [a + paṭibhāga] not having a counterpart, unequalled, incomparable DhA I.423 (= anuttara).

Appaṭibhāṇa (adj.) [a + paṭibhāṇa] not answering back, bewildered, cowed down Vin III.162; A III.57; °**ŋ karoti** to intimidate, bewilder J V.238, 369.

Appaṭima (adj.) [a + paṭima fr. prep. paṭi but cp. Vedic apratimāna fr. prati + **mā**] matchless, incomparable, invaluable Th 1, 614; Miln 239.

Appaṭivattiya (adj.) [a + paṭi + vattiya = vṛtya, grd. of **vṛt**] (a) not to be rolled back Sn 554 (of dhammacakka, may however be taken in meaning of b.). — (b) irresistable J II.245 (sīhanada). *Note.* The spelling with ṭ is only found as v. l. at J II.245; otherwise as t.

Appaṭivāṇa (nt.) [a + paṭivāṇa, for °vrāṇa, the guṇa-form of **vṛ**, cp. Sk. prativāraṇa] non-obstruction, not hindering, not opposing or contradicting A I.50; III.41; V.93 sq.; adj. J I.326; Th 2, 55.

Appaṭivāṇitā (f.) [abstr. from (ap)paṭivāṇa] not being hindered, non-obstruction, free effort; only in phrase "**asantuṭṭhitā ca kusalesu dhammesu appaṭivāṇitā ca padhānasmiŋ**" (discontent with good states and the not shrinking back in the struggle Dhs trsl. 358) A I.50, 95 = D III.214 = Dhs 1367.

Appaṭivāṇī (f.) [almost identical w. appaṭivāṇitā, only used in diff. phrase] non-hindrance, non-restriction, free action, inpulsive effort; only in stock phrase **chando vāyāmo ussāho ussoḷhī appaṭivāṇī** S II.132; V.440; A II.93, 195; III.307 sq.; IV.320; Nd² under chanda C. [cp. similarly Divy 654].

Appaṭivāṇīya (adj.) [grd. of a + paṭi + **vṛ**; cp. BSk. aprativāṇiḥ Divy 655; M Vastu III.343] not to be obstructed, irresistible S I.212 (appld. to Nibbāna; Mrs. Rh. D. *Kindred S.* p. 274 trsls. "that source from whence there is no turning back").

Appaṭividdha (adj.) [a + paṭi + viddha] "not shot through" i. e. unhurt J VI.446.

Appaṭivibhatta (°bhogin) (adj.) [a + paṭi + vibhatta] (not eating) without sharing with others (with omission of another negative: see Trenckner, Miln p. 429, where also Bdhgh's expln.) A III.289; Miln 373; cp. Miln trsl. II.292.

Appaṭivekkhiya [ger. of a + paṭi + avekkhati] not observing or noticing J IV.4 (= apaccavekkhitvā anavekkhitvā C.).

Appaṭisankhā (f.) [a + paṭisankhā] want of judgment Pug 21 = Dhs 1346.

Appaṭisandhika (and °iya) (adj.) [a + paṭisandhi + ka (ya)] 1. what cannot be put together again, unmendable, irreparable (°iya) Pv I.12⁹ (= puna pākatiko na hoti PvA 66) = J III.167 (= paṭipākatiko kātuŋ na sakkā C.). — 2. incapable of reunion, not subject to reunion, i. e. to rebirth J V.100 (°bhāva).

Appaṭisama (adj.) [a + paṭi = sama; cp. BSk. apratisama M Vastu I.104] not having it's equal, incomparable J I.94 (Baddha-sirī).

Appaṭissavatā (f.) [a + paṭissavatā] want of deference Pug 20 = Dhs 1325.

Appaṇihita (adj.) [a + paṇihita] aimless, not bent on anything, free from desire, usually as nt. aimlessness, combd. w. animittaŋ Vin III.92, 93 = IV.25; Dhs 351, 508, 556. See on term *Cpd.* 67; *Dhs trsl.* 93, 143 & cp. paṇihita.

Appatiṭṭha (adj.) [a + patiṭṭha] 1. not standing still S I.1. — 2. without a footing or ground to stand on, bottomless Sn 173.

Appatissa (& appaṭissa) (adj.) [a + paṭi + śru] not docile, rebellious, always in combn. with agārava A II.20; III.7 sq., 14 sq., 247, 439. Appatissa-vāsa an unruly state, anarchy J II.352. See also **paṭissā**.

Appatīta (adj.) [a + patīta, of prati + i, Sk. pratīta] dissatisfied, displeased, disappointed (cp. appaccaya) J V.103 (at this passage preferably to be read with v. l. as appatika = without husband, C. expls. assāmika), 155 (cp. C. on p. 156); DA I.52; SnA 423.

Appaduṭṭha (adj.) [a + paduṭṭha] not corrupt, faultless, of good behaviour Sn 662 (= padosâbhāvena a. SnA 478); Dh 137 (= niraparādha DhA III.70).

Appadhaŋsa (adj.) [= appadhaŋsiya, Sk. apradhvaŋsya] not to be destroyed J IV.344 (v. l. duppadhaŋsa).

Appadhaŋsika (& °iya) (adj.) [grd. of a + padhaŋseti] not to be violated or destroyed, inconquerable, indestructable D III.175 (°ika, v. l. °iya); J III.159 (°iya); VvA 208 (°iya); PvA 117 (°iya). Cp. **appadhaŋsa**.

Appadhaŋsita (adj.) [pp. of a + padhaŋseti] not violated, unhurt, not offended Vin IV.229.

Appanā (f.) [cp. Sk. arpaṇa, abstr. fr. appeti = arpayati from of ṛ, to fix, turn, direct one's mind; see appeti] application (of mind), ecstasy, fixing of thought on an object, conception (as psychol. t. t.) J II.61 (°patta); Miln 62 (of vitakka); Dhs 7, 21, 298; Vism 144 (°samādhi); DhsA 55, 142 (def. by Bdhg. as "ekaggaŋ cittaŋ ārammaṇe appeti"), 214 (°jhāna). See on term *Cpd.* pp. 56 sq., 68, 129, 215; *Dhs trsl.* XXVIII, 10, 53, 82, 347.

Appabhoti (Appahoti) see pahoti.

Appamaññati [appa + maññati] to think little of, to underrate, despise Dh 121 (= avajānāti DhA III.16; v. l. avapamaññati).

Appamaññā (f.) [a + pamaññā, abstr. fr. pamāṇa = Sk. *pramāṇya] boundlessness, infinitude, as psych. t. t. appld. in later books to the four varieties of philanthropy, viz. mettā karuṇā muditā upekkhā i. e. love, pity, sympathy, desinterestedness, and as such enumd. at D III.223 (q. v. for detailed ref. as to var. passages); Ps I.84; Vbh 272 sq.; DhsA 195. By itself at Sn 507 (= mettajjhāna-sankhātā a. SnA 417). See for further expln. *Dhs trsl.* p. 66 and mettā.

Appamatta¹ (adj.) [appa + matta] see appa.

Appamatta² (adj.) [a + pamatta, pp. of pamadati] not negligent, i. e. diligent, careful, heedful, vigilant, alert, zealous M I.391—92; S I.4; Sn 223 (cp. KhA 169), 507, 779 (cp. Nd¹ 59); Dh 22 (cp. DhA I.229); Th 2, 338 = upaṭṭhitasati Th A 239).

Appamāda [a + pamāda] thoughtfulness, carefulness, conscientiousness, watchfulness, vigilance, earnestness, zeal D I.13 (: a. vuccati satiyā avippavāso DA I.104); III.30, 104 sq., 112, 244, 248, 272; M I.477 (°phala); S I.25, 86, 158, 214; II.29, 132; IV.78 (°vihārin), 97, 125, 252 sq.; V.30 sq. (°sampadā), 41 sq., 91, 135, 240, 250, 308, 350; A I.16, 50. (°adhigata); III.330, 364, 449; IV.28 (°gāravatā) 120 (°ŋ garu-karoti); V.21, 126 (kusalesu dhammesu); Sn 184, 264, 334 (= sati-avippavāsa-sankhāta a. SnA 339); It 16 (°ŋ pasaŋsanti puññakiriyāsu paṇḍitā), 74 (°vihārin); Dh 57 (°vihārin, cp. DhA I.434); 327 (°rata = satiyā avippavāse abhirata DhA IV.26); Dāvs II. 35; KhA 142.

Appamāṇa (freq. spelled appamāna) (adj.) [a + pamāṇa] 1. "without measure", immeasurable, endless, boundless, unlimited, unrestricted all-permeating S IV.186 (°cetaso); A II.73; V.63; Sn 507 (mettaŋ cittaŋ bhāvayaŋ appamāṇaŋ = anavasesa-pharaṇena SnA 417; cp. appamaññā); It 21 (mettā), 78; J II.61; Ps II.126 sq.; Vbh 16, 24, 49, 62, 326 sq.; Dhs 182, 1021, 1024, 1405; DhsA 45, 196 (°gocara, cp. anantagocara). See also on term *Dhs trsl.* 60. — 2. "without difference", irrelevant, in general (in commentary style) J I.165; II.323.

Appameyya (adj.) [a + pameyya = Sk. aprameya, grd. of a + pra + mā] immeasurable, infinite, boundless M I.386; S V.400; A I.266; Th 1, 1089 (an°); Pug 35; Miln 331; Sdhp 338.

Appavattā (f.) [a + pavattā] the state of not going on, the stop (to all that), the non-continuance (of all that) Th 1, 767; Miln 326.

Appasāda see pasāda.

Appassāda see appa.

Appahīna (adj.) [a + pahīna, pp. of pahāyati] not given up, not renounced M I.386; It 56, 57; Nd² 70 D¹; Pug 12, 18.

Appāṇaka (adj.) [a + pāṇa + ka] breathless, i. e. (1) holding one's breath in a form of ecstatic meditation (jhāna) M I.243; J I.67 [cp. BSk. āsphānaka Lal. V.314, 324; M Vastu II.124; should the Pāli form be taken as *a + prāṇaka?]. (2) not holding anything breathing, i. e. inanimate, lifeless, not containing life Sn p. 15 (of water).

Appikā (f.) of appaka.

Appiccha (adj.) [appa + iccha from iṣ, cp. icchā] desiring little or nothing, easily satisfied, unassuming, contented, unpretentious S I.63, 65; A III.432; IV.2, 218 sq., 229; V.124 sq., 130, 154, 167; Sn 628, 707; Dh 404; Pv IV.7³; Pug 70.

Appicchatā (f.) [abstr. fr. prec.] contentment, being satisfied with little, unostentatiousness Vin III.21; D III.115; M I.13; S II 202, 208 sq.; A I.12, 16 sq.; III.219 sq., 448; IV.218, 280 (opp. mahicchatā); Miln 242; SnA 494 (catubbidhā, viz. paccaya-dhutanga-pariyatti-adhigama-vasena); PvA 73. As one of the 5 dhutanga-dhammā at Vism 81.

Appita (adj.) [pp. of appeti, cp. BSk. arpita, e. g. prītyarpitaŋ cakṣuḥ Jtm 31[69]] 1. fixed, applied, concentrated (mind) Miln 415 (mānasa) Sdhp 233 (citta). — 2. brought to, put to, fixed on J VI.78 (maraṇamukhe); **visappita** (an arrow to which) poison (is) applied, so read for visap(p)īta at J V.36 & Vism 303.

Appiya & **Appiyatā** see **piya** etc.

Appekadā (adv.) see api 2 a[2].

Appeti [Vedic arpayati, Caus. of **ṛ**, ṛṇoti & ṛcchati (cp. icchati[2]), Idg. ***ar** (to insert or put together, cp. also ***er** under aṇṇava) to which belong Sk. ara spoke of a wheel; Gr. ἀραρίσκω to put together, ἅρμα chariot, ἄρθρον limb, ἀρετή virtue; Lat. arma = E. arms (i. e. weapon), artus fixed, tight, also limb, ars = art. For further connections see aṇṇava] 1. **(*er)** to move forward, rush on, run into (of river) Vin II.238; Miln 70. — 2. **(*ar)** to fit in, fix, apply, insert, put on to (lit. & fig.) Vin II.136, 137; J III.34 (nimba-sūlasmiŋ to impale, C. āvuṇāti); VI.17 (T. sūlasmiŋ acceti, vv. ll. abbeti = appeti & upeti, C. āvuṇati); Miln 62 (dāruŋ sandbismiŋ); VvA 110 (saññāṇaŋ). Cp. Trenckner, *Notes* 64 n. 19, who defends reading abbeti at T. passages.

Appesakkha (adj.) [acc. to Childers = Sk. *alpa + īśa + ākhya, the latter fr. ā + **khyā** "being called lord of little"; Trenckner on Miln 65 (see p. 422) says: "appesakkha & mahesakkha are traditionally expld. appaparivāra & mahāparivāra, the former, I suppose, from appe & sakkha (Sk. sākhya), the latter an imitation of it". Thus the etym. would be "having little association or friendship" and resemble the term appasattha. The BSk. forms are alpeśākhya & maheśākhya, e. g. at Av. Ś II. 153; Divy 243] of little power, weak, impotent S II.229; Miln 65; Sdhp 89.

Appoti [the contracted form of āpnoti, usually pāpuṇāti, fr. **āp**] to attain, reach, get Vism 350 (in etym. of āpo).

Appodaka see **appa**.

Appossukka (adj.) [appa + ussuka, Sk. alpotsuka, e. g. Lal. V. 509; Divy 41, 57, 86, 159. It is not necessary to assume a hypothetic form of *autsukya as der. fr. ussuka] unconcerned, living at ease, careless", not bothering", keeping still, inactive Vin II.188; M III.175, 176; S I 202 (in stock phrase **appossukka tuṇhībhūta sankasāya** "living at ease, given to silence, resigned" Mrs. Rh. D. *Dhs trsl.* 258, see also *JPTS.* 1909, 22); II. 177 (id.); IV.178 (id.); Th 2, 457 (= nirussukka ThA 282); Sn 43 (= abyāvaṭa anapekkha Nd[2] 72); Dh 330 (= nirālaya DhA IV.31); J I.197; IV.71; Miln 371 (a. tiṭṭhati to keep still); DA I.264.

Appossukkatā (f.) [abstr. fr. prec.] inaction, reluctance, carelessness, indifference Vin I.5; D II.36; Miln 232; DhA II.15.

Apphuta (& apphuṭa) [Sk. *ā-sphṛta for a-sphārita pp. of **sphar**, cp. phurati; phuṭa & also phusati] untouched, unpervaded, not penetrated D I.74 = M I.276 (pītisukhena).

Apphoṭā (f.) [fr. appoṭeti to blossom] N. of a kind of Jasmine J VI.336.

Apphoṭita [pp. of apphoṭeti] baving snapped one's fingers or clapped one's hands J II 311 (°kāle).

Apphoṭeti [ā + phoṭeti, **sphuṭ**] to snap the fingers or clap the hands (as sign of pleasure) Miln 13, 20, pp. **apphoṭhita**.

Aphusa [Sk. *aspṛśya, a + grd. of phusati to touch] not to be touched Miln 157 (trsl. unchangeable by other circumstances; Tr. on p. 425 remarks "aphusāni kiriyāni seems wrong, at any rate it is unintelligible to me").

Apheggukа (adj.) [a + pheggu + ka] not weak, i. e strong J III.318.

Abaddha [a + baddha] not tied, unbound, unfettered Sn 39 (v. l. and Nd[2] abandha; expld. by rajju-bandhan' ādisu yena kenaci abaddha SnA 83).

Abandha (n.-adj.) [a + bandha] not tied to, not a follower or victim of It 56 (mārassa; v. l. abaddha).

Abandhana (adj.) [a + bandhana] without fetters or bonds, unfettered, untrammelled Sn 948, cp. Nd[1] 433.

Ababa [of uncertain origin, prob. onomatopoetic]. N. of a cert. Purgatory, enumd. with many other similar names at A V.173 = Sn p. 126 (cp. aṭaṭa, abbuda & also Av. Ś I.4, 10 & see for further expln. of term SnA 476 sq.

Abala (adj.) [a + bala] not strong, weak, feeble Sn 1120 (= dubbala, appabala, appathāma Nd[2] 73); Dh 29 (°assa a weak horse = dubbalassa DhA I.262; opp. sīghassa a quick horse).

Abbaje T. reading at A II.39, evidently interpreted by ed. as ā + vraje, pot. of ā + **vraj** to go to, come to (cp. pabbajati), but is preferably with v. l. SS to be read aṇḍaje (corresponding with vihangama in prec. line).

Abbaṇa (adj.) [a + vaṇa, Sk. avraṇa] without wounds Dh 124.

Abbata (n.-adj.) [a + vata, Sk. avrata] (a) (nt.) that which is not "vata" i. e. moral obligation, breaking of the moral obligation Sn 839 (asīlata +); Nd[1] 188 (v. l. SS abhabbata; expld. again as a-vatta). SnA 545 (= dhutangavataŋ vinā). — (b) (adj.) one who offends against the moral obligation, lawless Dh 264 (= sīlavatena ca dhutavatena ca virahita DhA III.391; vv. ll. k. adhūta & abhūta; B. abbhuta, C. abbuta).

Abbaya in uday° at Miln 393 stands for **avyaya**.

Abbahati (& **abbuhati**) [the first more freq. for pres., the second often in aor. forms; Sk. ābṛhati, ā + **bṛh**[1], pp. bṛḍha (see abbūḷha)] to draw off, pull out (a sting or dart); imper. pres. abbaha Th 1, 404; J II.95 (v. l. BB appuha = abbuha; C. expls. by uddharatha). — aor. **abbahi** J V.198 (v. l. BB abbuhi), abbahī (metri causa) J III.390 (v. l. BB dhabbuḷi = abbuḷhi) = Pv I.8[6] (which reads T. abbūḷha, but PvA 41 expls. nīhari) = DhA I.30 (vv. ll. sabbahi, sabbamhi; gloss K. B abbūḷhaŋ) = Vv 83[9] (T. abbuḷhi; v. l. BB abbuḷhaŋ, SS avyahi; VvA 327 expls. as uddhari), & **abbubi** A III.55 (v. l. abbahi, C. abbahī ti nīhari), see also vv. ll. under abbabi. — ger. **abbuyha** Sn 939 (= abbuhitvā uddharitvā Nd[1] 419; v. . SS abbuyhitvā; SnA 567 reads **avyuyha** & expls. by uddharitvā); S I.121 (taṇhaŋ); III.26 (id.; but spelt abbhuyha). — pp. **abbuḷha** (q. v.). — Caus. **abbāheti** [Sk. ābarhayati] to pull out, drag out J IV.364 (satthaŋ abbāhayanti; v. l. abbhā°); DhA II.249 (asiŋ). ger. **abbāhitvā** (= °hetvā) Vin II 201 (bhisa-muḷālaŋ) with v. l. BB aggahetvā, SS abbūhitvā, cp. Vin I.214 (vv. ll. aggahitvā & abbāhitvā). pp. **abbūḷhita** (q. v.).

Abbāhana (nt.) [abstr. fr. abbahati] pulling out (of a sting) DhA III.404 (sic. T.; v. l. abbūhana; Fausböll aḍahana; glosses C. aṭṭhangata & aṭṭhangika, K. nibbāpana). See also **abbuḷhana** and **abbhāhana**.

Abbuda (nt.) [etym. unknown, orig. meaning "swelling", the Sk. form arbuda seems to be a trsl. of P. abbuda] 1. the foetus in the 1st & 2nd months after conception, the 2nd of the five prenatal stages of development, viz. **kalala, abbuda, pesi, ghana, pasākha** Nd[1] 120; Miln 40; Vism 236. — 2. a tumour, canker, sore Vin III.294, 307 (only in Samantapāsādikā; both times as sāsanassa a). — 3. a very high numeral, appld. exclusively to the denotation of a vast period of suffering in Purgatory; in this sense used as adj. of Niraya (abbudo nirayo the "vast-period" hell, cp. nirabbuda). S I.149 = A II.3 (chattiṇsati pañca ca abbudāni); S I.152 = A V.173 = Sn p. 126 (cp. SnA 476: abbudo nāma koci pacceka-nirayo n' atthi, Avicimhi yeva abbuda-gaṇanāya paccanokāso pana abbudo nirayo ti vutto; see also *Kindred Sayings* p. 190); J III.360 (sataŋ ninnahuta-sahassānaŋ ekaŋ abbudaŋ). — 4. a term used for "hell" in the riddle S I.43 (kiŋsu lokasmiŋ abbudaŋ "who are they who make a hell on earth" Mrs. Rh. D. The answer is "thieves"; so we can scarcely take it in meaning of 2 or 3. The C. has vināsa-karaṇaŋ.

Abbuḷhati (?) & **Abbuhati** see abbahati.

Abbuḷhana (nt.) [fr. abbahati = abbuhati (abbuḷhati)] the pulling out (of a sting), in phrase taṇhā-sallassa abbuḷhanaŋ as one of the 12 acchievements of a Mahesi Nd[1] 343 = Nd[2] 503 (eds. of Nd[1] have abbūhana, v. l. SS abbussāna; ed. of Nd[2] abbuḷhana, v. l. SS abbahana, BB abbuhana). Cp. abbāhana.

Abbūḷha (adj.) [Sk. ābṛḍha, pp. of a + **bṛh**[1], see abbahati] drawn out, pulled (of a sting or dart), fig. removed, destroyed. Most freq. in combn. °salla with the sting removed, having the sting (of craving thirst, taṇhā) pulled out D II.283 (v. l. SS asammūḷha); Sn 593, 779 (= abbūḷhita-salla Nd[1] 59; rāgâdi-sallānaŋ abbūḷhattā a. SnA 518); J III.390 = Vv 83[10] = Pv I.8[1] = DhA I.30. — In other connection: M I 139 = A III.84 (°esika = taṇhā pabīnā; see esikā); Th I, 321; KhA 153 (°soka).

Abbūḷhatta (nt.) [abstr. of abbūḷha] pulling out, removal, destroying SnA 518.

Abbūḷhita (& abbūhitta at J III.541) [pp. of abbāheti Caus. of abbābati] pulled out, removed, destroyed Nd[1] 59 (abbūḷhita-sallo + uddhaṭa° etc. for abbūḷha); J III.541 (uncertain reading; v. l. BB appahita, SS abyūhita; C. expls. puppbakaŋ ṭhapitaŋ appaggharakaŋ kataŋ; should we explain as ā + vi + **ūh** and read abyūhita?).

Abbeti [Trenckner, Notes 64 n. 19] at J III.34 & VI.17 is probably a mistake in MSS for appeti.

Abbokiṇṇa I. [= abbhokiṇṇa, abhi + ava + kiṇṇa, cp. abhikiṇṇa] filled M I.387 (paripuṇṇa +); DhA IV.182 (pañca jātisatāni a.). — 2. [seems to be misunderstood for abbocchinna, a + vi + ava + chinna] uninterrupted, constant, as °ŋ adv. in combn. with **satataŋ samitaŋ** A IV.13 = 145; Kvu 401 (v. l. abbhokiṇṇa), cp. also *Kvu trsl.* 231 n. I (abbokiṇṇa undiluted?); Vbh 320. — 3. doubtful spelling at Vin III.271 (Bdhgh on Pārāj. III.I, 3).

Abbocchinna see abbokiṇṇa 2 and abbhochinna.

Abbohārika (adj.) [a + vi + ava + hārika of voharati] not of legal or conventional status, i. e. — (a) negligible, not to be decided Vin III.91, 112 (see also *Kvu trsl.* 361 n. 4). — (b) uncommon, extraordinary J III.309 (v. l. BB abbho°); V.271, 286 (Kern: ineffective).

Abbha (nt.) [Vedic abhra nt. & later Sk. abhra m. "dark cloud"; Idg. *m̥bhro, cp. Gr. ἀφρός scum, froth, Lat. imber rain; also Sk. ambha water, Gr. ὄμβρος rain, Oir ambu water]. A (dense & dark) cloud, a cloudy mass A II.53 = Vin II.295 = Miln 273 in list of to things that obscure moon- & sunshine, viz. **abbhaŋ mahikā** (mahiyā A) **dhūmarajo** (megho Miln), **Rāhu**. This list is referred to at SnA 487 & VvA 134. S I.101 (°sama pabbata a mountain like a thunder-cloud); J VI.581 (abbhaŋ rajo acchādesi); Pv IV.3[9] (nil° = nīla-megha PvA 251). As f. **abbhā** at Dhs 617 & DhsA 317 (used in sense of adj. "dull"; DhsA expls. by valāhaka); perhaps also in **abbhāmatta**. **-kūṭa** the point or summit of a storm-cloud Th I, 1064; J VI.249, 250; Vv I[1] (= valāhaka-sikhara VvA 12). **-ghana** a mass of clouds, a thick cloud It 64; Sn 348 (cp. SnA 348). **-paṭala** a mass of clouds DhsA 239. **-mutta** free from clouds Sn 687 (also as abbhāmutta Dh 382). **-saŋvilāpa** thundering S IV.289.

Abbhakkhāti [abhi + ā + **khyā**, cp. Sk. ākhyāti] to speak against to accuse, slander D I·161 = A I.161 (an-abbhakkhātu-kāma); IV.182 (id.); J IV.377. Cp. Intens. **abbhācikkhati.**

Abbhakkhāna (nt.) [fr. abbhakkhāti] accusation, slander, calumny D III.248, 250; M I.130; III.207; A III.290 sq.; Dh 139 (cp. DhA III.70).

Abbhacchādita [pp. of abhi + ā + chādeti] covered (with) Th I, 1068.

Abbhañjati [abhi + añj] to anoint; to oil, to lubricate M I.343 (sappi-telena); S IV.177; Pug 56; DhA III.311 = VvA 68 (sata-pāka-telena). Caus. abbhañjeti same J I.438 (telena °etvā); V.376 (sata-pāka-telena °ayiŋsu); Caus. II. abbhanjāpeti to cause to anoint J III.372.

Abbhañjana (nt.) [fr. abbhañjati] anointing, lubricating, oiling; unction, unguent Vin I 205; III.79; Miln 367 (akkhassa a.); Vism 264; VvA 295.

Abbhatika (adj.) [ā + bhata + ika, **bhṛ**] brought (to), procured, got, J VI.291.

Abbhatikkanta [pp. of abhi + ati + **kram**, cp. atikkanta] one who has thoroughly, left behind J V.376.

Abbhatīta [pp. of abhi + ati + **i**, cp. atīta & atikkanta] emphatic of atīta in all meanings, viz. I passed, gone by S II.183 (+ atikkanta); nt. °ŋ what is gone or over, the past J III.169. — 2. passed away, dead M I.465; S IV.398; Th I, 242, 1035. — 3. transgressed, overstepped, neglected J III.541 (saŋyama).

Abbhattha (nt.) [abhi + attha[2] in acc. abhi + atthaŋ, abhi in function of "towards" = homeward, as under abhi I.I a; cp. Vedic abhi sadhasthaŋ to the seat R. V. IX. 21. 3] = attha[2], only in phrase **abbhattaŋ gacchati** "to go towards home", i. e. setting; fig. to disappear, vanish, M I.115, 119; III.25; A IV.32; Miln 305; pp. abbhattangata "set", gone, disappeared Dhs 1038 (atthangata +); Kvu 576.

Abbhatthatā (f.) [abstr. fr. abbhatta] "going towards setting", disappearance, death J V.469.

Abbhanumodati [abhi + anu + modati] to be much pleased at to show great appreciation of Vin I.196; D I.143, 190; S IV.224; Miln 29, 210; DhA IV.102 (v. l. °ānu°).

Abbhanumodana (nt.) (& °ā f.) [fr. abbhanumodati] being pleased, satisfaction, thanksgiving DA I.227; VvA 52 (°ānu°); Sdhp 218.

Abbhantara (adj.) [abhi + antara; abhi here in directive function = towards the inside, in there, with-in, cp. abhi I.I a] = antara, i. e. internal, inner, being within or between; nt. °ŋ the inner part, interior, interval (also as °—) Vin I.III (satt° with interval of seven); A IV.16 (opp. bāhira); Dh 394 (id.); Th I, 757 (°āpassaya lying inside); J III.395 (°amba the inside of the Mango); Miln 30 (°e vāyo jivo), 262, 281 (bāhir-abbhantara dhana); DhA II.74 (adj. c. gen. being among; v. l. abbhantare). — Cases used adverbially: instr. **abbhantarena** in the meantime, in between DhA II.59. loc. **abbhantare** in the midst of, inside of, within (c. gen. or —°) J I.262 (rañño), 280 (tuyhaŋ); DhA II.64 (v. l. antare), 92 (sattavass°); PvA 48 (= anto).

Abbhantarika (adj.-n.) [fr. abbhantara, cp. Sk. abhyantara in same meaning] intimate friend, confidant, "chum" J I.86 (+ ativissāsika), 337 ("insider", opp. bāhiraka).

Abbhantarima (adj.) [superl. formation fr. abbhantara in contrasting function] internal, inner (opp. **bāhirima**) Vin III.149; J V.38.

Abbhākuṭika (adj.) [a + bhākuṭi + ka; Sk. bhrakuṭi frown] not frowning, genial Vin III.181 (but here spelt bhākuṭik-abhākuṭika); D I.116, cp. DA I.287; DhA IV.8 (as v.l.; T. has abbhokuṭika).

Abbhāgata [abhi + ā + gata] having arrived or come; (m.) a guest, stranger Vv I[5] (= abhi-āgata, āgantuka VvA 24).

Abbhāgamana (nt.) [abhi + ā + gamana; cp. Sk. abhyāgama] coming arrival, approach Vin IV.221.

Abbhāghāta [abhi + āghāta] slaughtering-place Vin III.151 (+ āghāta).

Abbhācikkhati [Intens. of abbhākkhāti] to accuse, slander, calumniate D I.161; III.248, 250; M I.130, 368, 482; III.207; A I.161.

Abbhāna (nt.) [abhi + āyana of ā + **yā (I)**] coming back, rehabilitation of a bhikkhu who has undergone a penance for an expiable offence Vin I.49 (°āraha), 53 (id.), 143, 327; II.33, 40, 162; A I.99. — Cp. **abbheti.**

Abbhāmatta (adj.) [abbhā + matta (?) according to the Pāli Com.; but more likely = Vedic abhva huge, enormous, monstrous, with ā metri causa. On abhva (a + **bhū** what is contradictory to anything that is) cp. abbhuta & abbhuŋ, and see Walde, Lat. Wtb. under dubius] monstrous, dreadful, enormous, "of the size of a large cloud" (thus C. on S I.205 & J III.309) S I.205 = Th I, 652 (v.l. abbha° & abbhāmutta) = J III.309 (v.l. °mutta).

Abbhāhata [abhi + ā + hata, pp. of **han**] struck, attacked, afflicted S I.40 (maccunā); Th I, 448; Sn 581; J VI.26, 440; Vism 31, 232; DA I.140, 147; DhA IV.25.

Abbhāhana (nt.) [either = abbāhana or āvāhana] in **udaka°** the pulling up or drawing up of water Vin II.318 (Bdhgh. on Cullavagga V.16, 2, corresponding to udaka-vāhana on p. 122).

Abbhita [pp. of abbheti] **1.** come back, rehabilitated, reinstated Vin III.186 = IV.242 (an°). — **2.** uncertain reading at Pv I.12[3] in sense of "called" (an° uncalled), where id. p. at J III.165 reads anavhāta & at Th 2, 129 ayācita.

Abbhu [a + **bhū** most likely = Vedic abhva and P. abbhuŋ, see also abbhāmatta] unprofitableness, idleness, nonsense J V.295 (= abhūti avaḍḍhi C.).

Abbhuŋ (interj.) [Vedic abhvaŋ, nt. of abhva, see expl[d]. under abbhamatta. Not quite correct Morris *J P T S.* 1889, 201: abbhuŋ = ā + bhuk; cp also abbhuta] alas! terrible, dreadful, awful (excl. of fright & shock) Vin II. 115 (Bdhgh. expl[s]. as "utrāsa-vacanam-etaŋ"); M I.448. — See also **abbhu** & **abbhuta.**

Abbhukkiraṇa (nt.) [abhi + ud + **kṛ**] drawing out, pulling, in daṇḍa-sattha° drawing a stick or sword Nd[2] 576[4] (cp. abbhokkiraṇa). Or is it **abbhuttīraṇa** (cp. uttiṇṇa outlet).

Abbhukkirati [abhi + ud + kirati] to sprinkle over, to rinse (with water) D II.172 (cakkaratanaŋ; neither with Morris *J P T S.* 1886, 131 "give up", nor with trsl. of J II.311 "roll along"); J V.390; PvA 75. Cp. **abbhokkirati.**

Abbhuggacchati [abhi + ud + gacchati] to go forth, go out, rise into D I.112, 127; A III.252 (kitti-saddo a.); Pug 36. ger. °**gantvā** J I.88 (ākāsaŋ), 202; DhA IV.198. aor. °**gañchi** M I.126 (kittisaddo); J I.93. — pp. **abbhuggata.**

Abbhuggata [pp. of abbhuggacchati] gone forth, gone out, risen D I.88 (kitti-saddo a., cp. DhA I.146: sadevakaŋ lokaŋ ajjhottharitvā uggato), 107 (saddo); Sn p. 103 (kittisaddo).

Abbhuggamana (nt.-adj.) [fr. abbhuggacchati] going out over, rising over (c. acc.) PvA 65 (candaŋ nabhaŋ abbhuggamanaŋ; so read for T. abbhuggamānaŋ).

Abbhujjalana (nt.) [abhi + ud + jalana, from **jval**] breathing out fire, i. e. carrying fire in one's mouth (by means of a charm) D I.11 (= mantena mukhato aggi-jala-nībaraṇaŋ DA I.97).

Abbhuṭṭhāti (°ṭṭhahati) [abhi + ud + **sthā**] to get up to, proceed to, D I.105 (cankamaŋ).

Abbhuṇṇata [pp. of abbhunnamati] standing up, held up, erect J V.156 (in **abbhuṇṇatatā** state of being erect, stiffness), 197 (°unnata; v.l. abbhantara, is reading correct?).

Abbhuṇha (adj.) [abhi + uṇha] (a) very hot DhA II.87 (v.l. accuṇha). (b) quite hot, still warm (of milk) DhA II.67.

Abbhuta[1] (adj. nt.) [*Sk. adbhuta which appears to be constructed from the Pāli & offers like its companion *āścarya (acchariya abbhuta see below) serious difficulties as to etym. The most probable solution is that P. abbhuta is a secondary adj.-formation from abbhuŋ which in itself is nt. of abbha = Vedic abhva (see etym. under abbhāmatta and cp. abbhu, abbhuŋ & *J P T S.* 1889, 201). In meaning abbhuta is identical with Vedic abhva contrary to what usually happens, i. e. striking, abnormal, gruesome, horrible etc.; & that its significance as a + **bhū** ("unreal?") is felt in the background is also evident from the traditional etym. of the Pāli Commentators (see below). See also acchariya] terrifying, astonishing; strange, exceptional, puzzling, extraordinary, marvellous, supernormal. Described as a term of surprise & consternation (vimhay' āvahass' adhivacanaŋ DA I.43 & VvA 329) & expl[d]. as "something that is not" or "has not been before", viz. abhūtaŋ ThA 233; abhūta-pubbatāya abbhutaŋ VvA 191, 329; abhūta-pubbaŋ DA I.43. — **1.** (adj.) wonderful, marvellous etc. Sn 681 (kiŋ °ŋ, comb[d]. with lomahaŋsana); J IV.355 (id.); Th 2, 316 (abbhutaŋ vata vācaŋ bhāsasi = acchariyaŋ ThA 233); Vv 44[9] (°dassaneyya); Sdhp 345, 496. — **2.** (nt.) the wonderful, a wonder, marvel S IV.371, also in °dhamma (see Cpd.). Very freq. in comb[n]. with **acchariyaŋ** and a part. of exclamation, viz. **acchariyaŋ bho abbhutaŋ bho** wonderful indeed & beyond comprehension, strange & stupefying D I.206; acch. vata bho abbh. **vata bho** D I.60; acch. bhante abbh. A II.50; aho acch. aho abbh. J I.88; acch. vata abbh. vata Vv 83[16]. — Thus also in phrase **acchariyā abbhutā dhammā** wonderful & extraordinary signs or things M III.118, 125; A II.130; IV.198; Miln 8; and in **acchariya-abbhuta-citta-jāta** dumbfounded & surprised J I.88; DhA IV.52; PvA 6, 50.

-dhamma mysterious phenomenon, something wonderful, supernormal; designation of one of the nine angas or divisions of the Buddhist Scriptures (see nava B 2) Vin III.8; M I.133; A II.103; III.86, 177; Pug 43; Miln 344; PvA 2, etc.

Abbhuta[2] (nt.) [= abbhuta[1] in the sense of invoking strange powers in gambling, thus being under direct spell of the "unknown"] a bet, a wager, only in phrase **abbhutaŋ** karoti (sahassena) to make a bet or to bet (a thousand, i. e. kahāpaṇa's or pieces of money) Vin III.138; IV.5; J I.191; V.427; VI.192; PvA 151; & in phrase pañcahi sahassehi abbhutaŋ hotu J VI.193

Abbhudāharati [abhi + ud + ā + harati] to bring towards, to fetch, to begin or introduce (a conversation) M II.132.

Abbhudīreti [abhi + ud + īreti] to raise the voice, to utter Th 2, 402; DA I.61; Sdhp 514.

Abbhudeti [abhi + ud + eti] to go out over, to rise A II.50, 51 (opp. atthaŋ eti, of the sun). — ppr. **abbhuddayaŋ** Vv 64[11] (= abhi-uggacchanto VvA 280; abbhusayaŋ ti pi pāṭho).

Abbhuddhunāti [abhi + ud + dhunāti] to shake very much Vv 64[9] (= adhikaŋ uddhunāti VvA 278).

Abbhunnadita [pp. of abhi + ud + nadati] resounding, resonant Th 1, 1065).

Abbhunnamati [abhi + ud + namati] to, spring up, burst forth D II.164. — pp. **abbhunnata** (& °unnata), q. v. — Caus. abbhunnāmeti to stiffen, straighten out, hold up, erect D I.120 (kāyaŋ one's body); A II.245 (id.); D I.126 (patodalaṭṭhiŋ; opp. apanāmeti to bend down).

Abbhuyyāta [pp. of abbhuyyāti] marched against, attacked Vin I.342; M II.124.

Abbhuyyāti [abhi + up + yāti of yā] to go against, to go against, to march (an army) against, to attack S I.82 (aor °uyyāsi). — pp. abbhuyyāta (q. v.).

Abbhusūyaka (adj.) [abhi + usūyā + ka] zealous, showing zeal, endeavouring in (—°) Pgdp 101.

Abbhussakati & °usukkati [abhi + ud + ṣvaṣk, see sakkati] to go out over, rise above (acc.), ascend, freq. in phrase ādicco nabhaŋ abbhussakkamāno M I.317 = S III.156 = It 20. — See also S I.65; V.44; A I.242 (same simile); V.22 (id.).

Abbhussahanatā (f.) [abstr. fr. abhi + *utsahana, cp. ussāha] instigation, incitement Vin II.88.

Abbhusseti [abhi + ud + seti of śī] to rise; v. l. at Vv 64[17] according to VvA 280: abbhuddayaŋ (see abbhudeti) abbhussayan ti pi pāṭho.

Abbheti [abhi + ā + i] to rehabilitate a bhikkhu who has been suspended for breach of rules Vin II.7 (abbhento), 33 (abbheyya); III.112 (abbheti), 186 = IV.242 (abbhetabba) — pp. **abbhita** (q. v.). See also abbhāna.

Abbhokāsa [abhi + avakāsa] the open air, an open & unsheltered space D I.63 (= alagganatthena a. viya DA I.180), 71 (= acchanna DA I.210), 89; M III.132; A II.210; III.92; IV.437, V.65; Sn p. 139 (°e nissinna sitting in the open) J I.29, 215; Pug 57.

Abbhokāsika (adj.) [fr. abbhokāsa] belonging to the open air, one who lives in the open, the practice of certain ascetics. D I.167; M I.282; A III.220; Vin V.131, 193; J IV.8 (+ nesajjika); Pug 69; Miln 20, 342. (One of the 13 Dhutaŋgas). See also Nd[1] 188; Nd[2] 587.

-**anga** the practice or system of the "campers-out" Nd[1] 558 (so read for abbhokāsi-kankhā, cp. Nd[1] 188).

Abbhokiṇṇa [pp. of abbhokirati] see abbokiṇṇa.

Abbhokirati [abhi + ava + kirati] to sprinkle over, to cover, bedeck Vv 5[9] (= abhi-okirati abhippakirati), 35[11] (v. l. abbhuk°). Cp. **abbhukkirati** & **abbhokkiraṇa** — pp. **abbhokiṇṇa** see under **abbokiṇṇa**.

Abbhokuṭika spelling at DhA IV.8 for abbhākuṭika.

Abbhokkiraṇa (nt.) [fr. abbhokirati] in naṭānaŋ a. "turnings of dancers" DA I.84 in expl[n.] of sobha-nagarakaŋ of D I.6.

Abbhocchinna (besides abbocch°, q. v. under **abbokiṇṇa**[2]) [a + vi + ava + chinna] not cut off, uninterrupted, continuous J I.470 (v. l. abbo°); VI.254, 373; Cp. I.6[3]; Miln 72; Vism 362 (bb), 391 (bb).

Abbhohārika see abbo°.

Aby° see **avy°**.

Abhabba (adj.) [a + bhavya. The Sk. abhavya has a different meaning] impossible, not likely, unable D III.13 sq., 19, 26 sq., 133; It 106, 117; Sn 231 (see KhA 189); Dh 32; J I 116; Pug 13.

-**ṭṭhāna** a (moral) impossibility of which there are 9 enum[d.] among things that are not likely to be found in an Arahant's character: see D III.133 & 235 (where the five first only are given as a set).

Abhabbatā (f.) [abstr. fr. abhabba] an impossibility, unlikelihood Sn 232, cp. KhA 191.

Abhaya (adj.) [a + bhaya] free from fear or danger, fearless, safe Dh 258. — nt. abhayaŋ confidence, safety Dh 317, cp. DhA III.491. For further ref[s.] see **bhaya**.

Abhi- [prefix, Vedic abhi, which represents both Idg *m̥bhi, as in Gr. ἀμφί around, Lat. ambi, amb round about, Oir. imb, Gall. ambi, Ohg. umbi, Ags. ymb, cp. also Vedic (Pāli) abhitaḥ on both sides; and Idg. *obhi, as in Lat. ob towards, against (cp. obsess, obstruct), Goth. bi, Ohg. Ags. bī = E. be-.

I. *Meaning.* — 1. The primary meaning of abhi is that of taking possession and mastering, as contained in E. coming *by* and *over*-coming, thus literally having the function of (*a*) facing and aggressing = towards, against, on to, at (see II. 1, *a*); and (*b*) mastering = over, along over, out over, on top of (see II. 1, *b*). 2. Out of this is developed the fig. meaning of increasing, i. e., an intensifying of the action implied in the verb (see III. 1). Next to saŋ- it is the most frequent modification prefix in the meaning of "very much, greatly" as the first part of a double-prefix cpd. (see III. 2), and therefore often seemingly superfluous, i. e., weakened in meaning, where the second part already denotes intensity as in abhi-vi-ji (side by side with vi-ji), abhi-ā-kkhā (side by side with ā-kkhā), abhi-anu-mud (side by side with anu-mud). In these latter cases abhi shows a purely deictic character corresponding to Ger. her-bei-kommen (for bei-kommen), E. fill up (for fill); e. g., abhhatikkanta (= ati ° C.), abbhatīta ("vorbei gegangen"), abbhantara ("with-in", b-innen or "in here"), abbhudāharati, abhipūreti ("fill up"), etc. (see also II. 1, *c*).

II. *Lit. Meaning.* — 1. As single pref.: (*a*) against, to, on to, at-, viz., abbhatthangata gone towards home, abhighāta striking at, °jjhā think at, °mana thinking on, °mukha facing, turned towards, °yāti at-tack, °rūhati ascend, °lāsa long for, °vadati ad-dress, °sapati ac-curse, °hata hit at. (*b*) out, over, all around: abbhudeti go out over, °kamati exceed, °jāti off-spring, °jānāti know all over, °bhavati overcome, °vaḍḍhati increase, °vuṭṭha poured out or over, °sandeti make over-flow, °siñcati sprinkle over. (*c*) abhi has the function of transitivising intrs. verbs after the manner of E. be- (con-) and Ger. er-, thus resembling in meaning a simple Caus. formation, like the foll.: abhigajjati thunder on, °jānāti "er-kennen" °jāyati be-get, °tthaneti = °gajjati, °nadati "er tönen", °nandati approve of (cp. anerkennen), °passati con-template, °ramati indulge in, °ropeti honour, °vaḍḍha increased, °saddahati believe in. — 2. As base in comp[n.] (2nd part of cpd.) abhi occurs only in comb[n.] **sam-abhi** (which is, however, of late occurrence and a peculiarity of later texts, and is still more freq. in BSk.: see under sam-).

III. *Fig. Meaning* (intensifying). — 1. A single pref.: abhikiṇṇa strewn all over, °jalati shine forth, °jighacchati be very hungry, °tatta much exhausted, °tāpa very hot, °toseti pleuse greatly, °nava quite fresh, °nipuṇa very clever, °nīla of a deep black, °manāpa very pleasant, °mangaly very lucky, °yobbana full youth, °rati great liking, °ratta deep red, °ruci intense satisfaction, °rūpa very handsome (= adhika-rūpa C.), °sambuddha wide and fully-awake, cp. abbhuddhunāti to shake greatly (= adhikaŋuddh° C.). — As 1st part of a prep.-cpd. (as modification-pref.) in foll. combinations: abhi-ud (abbhud-) °ati, °anu, °ava, °ā, °ni, °ppa, °vi, °saŋ. See all these s. v. and note that the contraction (assimilation before vowel) form of abhi is abbh°. — On its relation to pari, see pari°, to ava see ava°.

IV. *Dialectical Variation.* — There are dial. variations in the use and meanings of abhi. Vedic abhi besides corresponding to abhi in P. is represented also by ati°, adhi° and anu°, since all are similar in meaning, and psychologically easily fused and confused (cp. meanings: abhi = on to, towards; ati = up to and beyond; adhi = up to, towards, over; anu = along towards). For all the foll. verbs we find in Pāli one or other of these three prefixes. So ati in °jāti, °pīḷita, °brūheti, °vassati, °vāyati, °veṭheti; also as vv. ll. with abhi-kīrati, °pavassati, °roceti, cp. atikkanta-abhi° (Sk. abhikrānta); adhi in °patthita, °pāteti, °ppāya, °ppeta, °bādheti, °bhū, °vāha (vice versa P. abhi-ropeti compared with Sk. adhiropayati); anu in °gijjhati, °brūheti, °sandahati.

Abhikankhati [abhi + kankhati] to desire after, long for, wish for S I.140, 198 (Nibbānaŋ); J II.428; IV.10, 241; VvA 38, 283; ThA 244. — pp. **abhikankhita.** Cp. BSk. abhikāṅkṣati, e. g. Jtm. p. 221.

Abhikankhanatā (f.) [abhi + kankhana + tā] wishing, longing, desire DA I.242.

Abhikankhita [pp. of abhikankhati] desired, wished, longed for VvA 201 (= abhijjhita).

Abhikankhin (adj.) cp. wishing for, desirous of (—°) Th 2, 360 (sītibhāva°).

Abhikiṇṇa [pp. of abhikirati] **1.** strewn over with (—°), adorned, covered filled Pv II.11^2 (puppha°). — **2.** overwhelmed, overcome, crushed by (—°) It 89 (dukkh°; vv. ll. dukkhâtiṇṇa & otiṇṇa) = A I.147 (which reads dukkhotiṇṇa). See also avatiṇṇa.

Abhikirati — **1.** [Sk. abhikirati] to sprinkle or cover over: see **abhikiṇṇa 1.** — **2.** [Sk. avakirati, cp. apakiritūna] to overwhelm, destroy, put out, throw away, crush S I.54; Th 1, 598; 2, 447 (ger. °kiritūna, reading of C. for T. apa°, expl^d. by chaḍḍetvā); Dh 25 (°kīrati metri causa; dīpaŋ abhikīrati = viddhaŋseti vikirati DhA I.255; v. l. atikirati); J IV.121 (°kīrati; dīpaŋ = viddhaŋseti C.); VI.541 (nandiyo m^3 abhikīrare = abhikiranti abhikkamanti C.); DhA I.255 (inf. °kirituŋ). — pp. **abhikiṇṇa** see abhikiṇṇa 2.

Abhikīḷati [abhi + kīḷati] to play (a game), to sport Miln 359 (kīḷaŋ).

Abhikūjita [abhi + kūjita, pp. of **kūj**] resounding (with the song of birds) Pv II.12^3 (cakkavāka°; so read for kujita). Cp. **abhinikūjita.**

Abhikkanta (adj.-n.) [pp. of abhikkamati, in sense of Sk. and also P. atikkanta] (*a*) (*adj.*) lit. gone forward, gone out, gone beyond. According to the traditional expl^n. preserved by Bdhgh. & Dhp (see e. g. DA I.227 = KhA 114 = VvA 52) it is used in 4 applications: abhikkantasaddo khaya (+ pabbaniya KhA) sundar°-âbhirūpa-abbhanumodanesu dissati. These are: **1.** (lit.) gone away, passed, gone out, departed (+ nikkhanta, meaning khaya "wane"), in phrase abhikkantāya rattiyā at the waning of the night Vin I.26; D II.220; M I.142. **2.** excellent, supreme (= sundara) Sn 1118 (°dassāvin having the most exellent knowledge = aggadassāvin etc. Nd^2 76); usually in compar °tara (+ paṇitatara) D I.62, 74, 216; A II.101; III.350 sq.; V.140, 207 sq.; DA I.171 (= atimanāpatara). **3.** pleasing, superb, extremely wonderful, as exclamation °ŋ repeated with bho (bhante), showing appreciation (= abbhânumodana) D I.85, 110, 234; Sn p. 15, 24, etc. freq. **4.** surpassing, beautiful (always with °vaṇṇa = abhirūpa) Vin I.26; D II.220; M I.142; Pv II.1^{10} = Vv 9^1 (= atimanāpa abhirūpa PvA 71); KhA 115 (= abhirūpachavin). — (*b*) (*nt.*) **abhikkantaŋ** (comb^d. with and opp. to paṭikkantaŋ) going forward (and backward), approach (and receding) D I.70 (= gamaṇa + nivattana DA I.183); Vin III.181; A II.104, 106 sq.; VvA 6.

Abhikkama going forward, approach, going out Pv IV.1^2 (opp. paṭikkama going back); DhA III.124 (°paṭikkama).

Abhikkamati [Vedic abhikramati, abhi + kamati] to go forward, to proceed, approach D I.50 (= abhimukho kamati, gacchati, pavisati DA I.151); II.147, 256 (abhikkāmuŋ aor.); DhA III.124 (evaŋ °itabbaŋ evaŋ paṭikkamitabbaŋ thus to approach & thus to withdraw). — pp. **abhikkanta** (q. v.).

Abhikkhaṇa^1 (nt.) [fr. abhikkhanati] digging up of the ground M I.143.

Abhikkhaṇa^2 (nt.) [abhi + *ikkhaṇa from **īkṣ,** cp. Sk. abhikṣṇa of which the contracted form is P. **abhiṇhaŋ**] only as acc. adv. °ŋ constantly, repeated, often Vv 24^{12} (= abhiṇhaŋ VvA 116); Pv II.8^4 (= abhiṇhaŋ bahuso PvA 107); Pug 31; DhA II.91.

Abhikkhaṇati [abhi + khaṇati] to dig up M I.142.

Abhikkhipati [abhi + khipati] to throw Dāvs III.60; cp. abhinikkhipati ibid. 12.

Abhigajjati [abhi + gajjati from **garj,** sound-root, cp. P. gaggara] (a) to roar, shout, thunder, to shout or roar at (c. acc.) Sn 831 (shouting or railing = gajjanto uggajjanto Nd^1 172); ger. **abhigajjiya** thunderin. Cp. III.10^8. — (b) hum, chatter, twitter (of birds); see **abhigajjin.**

Abhigajjin (adj.) [fr. abhigajjati] warbling, singing, chattering Th 1, 1108, 1136.

Abhigamanīya (adj.) [grd. of abhigacchati] to be approached, accessible PvA 9.

Abhigijjhati [abhi + gijjhati] **1.** to be greedy for, to crave for, show delight in (c. loc.) Sn 1039 (kāmesu, cp. Nd^2 77). — **2.** to envy (acc.) S I.15 (aññam-aññaŋ).

Abhigīta [pp. of abhigāyati, cp. gīta] **1.** sung for. Only in one phrase, gāthābhigītaŋ, that which is gained by singing or chanting verses (Ger. "ersungen") S I.173 = Sn 81 = Miln 228. See SnA 151. — **2.** resounding with, filled with song (of birds) J VI.272 (= abhiruda).

Abhighāta [Sk. abhighāta, abhi + ghāta] (a) striking, slaying, killing PvA 58 (daṇḍa°), 283 (sakkhara°). — (b) impact, contact DhsA 312 (rūpa° etc.).

Abhicetasika (adj.) [abhi + ceto + ika] dependent on the clearest consciousness. On the spelling see ābhic^c (of jhāna) M I.33, 356; III.11; S II.278; A II.23; V.132. (Spelt. ābhi° at M I.33; A III.114; Vin V.136). See *Dial.* III.108.

Abhiceteti [abhi + ceteti] to intend, devise, have in mind J IV.310 (manasā pāpaŋ).

Abhicchanna (adj.) [abhi + channa] covered with, bedecked or adorned with (—°) J II.48 (hema-jāla°, v. l. abhisañchanna), 370 (id.); Sn 772 (= ucchanna āvuṭa etc. Nd^1 24, cp. Nd^2 365).

Abhicchita (adj.) [abhi + icchita, cp. Sk. abhīpsita] desired J VI.445 (so read for **abhijjhita**).

Abhijacca (adj.) [Sk. ābhijātya; abhi + jacca] of noble birth J V.120.

Abhijaneti occasional spelling for **abhijāneti.**

Abhijappati [abhi + jappati] to wish for, strive after, pray for S I.143 (read asmâbhijappanti & cp. *Kindred Sayings* p. 180) = J III.359 (= namati pattheti piheti C.); Sn 923, 1046 (+ āsiŋsati thometi; Nd^2 79 = jappati & same under icchati). Cp. in meaning **abhigijjhati.**

Abhijappana (nt.) [doubtful whether to jappati or to japati to mumble, to which belongs jappana in kaṇṇa° DA I.97] in hattha° casting a spell to make the victim throw up or wring his hands D I.11; DA I.97.

Abhijappā (f.) [abstr. fr. abhijappati, cp. jappā] praying for, wishing, desire, longing Dhs 1059 = Nd^2 taṇhā II.; Dhs 1136.

Abhijappin (adj.) [fr. abhijappati] praying for, desiring A III.353 (kāma-lābha°).

Abhijalati [abhi + jalati] to shine forth, ppr. °anto resplendent PvA 189.

Abhijavati [abhi + javati] to be eager, active Sn 668.

Abhijāta (adj.) [abi + jāta] of noble birth, well-born, S I.69; Vv 29³; Miln 359 (°kulakulīna belonging to a family of high or noble birth).

Abhijāti (f.) [abhi + jāti] 1. Species. Only as t. t. in use by certain non-Buddhist teachers. They divided mankind into six species, each named after a colour D I.53, 54; A III.383 ff. (quoted DA I.162) gives details of each species. Two of them, the black and the white, are interpreted in a Buddhist sense at D III.250, M II.222, and Netti 158. This interpretation (but not the theory of the six species) has been widely adopted by subsequent Hindu writers. — 2. Rebirth, descent, Miln 226.

Abhijātika (adj.) [fr. abhijāti] belonging to ones birth or race, born of, being by birth; only in cpd. kaṇhâbhijātika of dark birth, that is, low in the social scale D III.251 = A III.348; Sn 563 = Th 1, 833; cp. J P T S. 1893, 11; in sense of "evil disposed or of bad character" at J V.87 (= kāḷaka-sabhāva C.).

Abhijātitā (f.) [abstr. fr. abhijāti] the fact of being born, descendency VvA 216.

Abhijāna (nt. or m?) [Sk. abhijñāna] recognition, remembrance, recollection Miln 78. See also **abhiññā**.

Abhijānāti [abhi + **jñā**, cp. jānāti & abhiññā] to know by experience, to know fully or thoroughly, to recognise, know of (c. acc.), to be conscious or aware of D I.143; S II.58, 105, 219, 278; III.59, 91; IV.50, 324, 399; V.52, 176, 282, 299; Sn 1117 (diṭṭhiŋ Gotamassa na a.); J IV.142; Pv II.7¹⁰ = II.10³ (n'âbhijānāmi bhuttaŋ vā pītaŋ); Sdhp 550; etc. — Pot. **abhijāneyya** Nd² 78ᵃ, & **abhijaññā** Sn 917, 1059 (= jāneyyāsi SnA 592); aor **abhaññāsi** Sn p. 16. — ppr. **abhijānaŋ** S IV.19, 89; Sn 788 (= °jānanto C.), 1114 (= °jānants Nd² 78ᵇ) **abhijānitva** DhA IV.233; **abhiññāya** S IV.16; V.392; Sn 534 (sabbadhammaŋ), 743 (jātikkhayaŋ), 1115, 1148; It 91 (dhammaŋ); Dh 166 (atta-d-atthaŋ); freq. in phrase **sayaŋ abhiññaya** from personal knowledge or self-experience It 97 (v.l. abhiññā); Dh 353; and **abhiññā** [short form, like ādā for ādāya, cp. upādā] in phrase **sayaŋ abhiññā** D I.31 (+ sacchikatvā); S II.217; It 97 (v.l. for °abhiññāya), in **abhiññā-vosita** perfected by highest knowledge S I.167 = 175 = Dh 423 ("master of supernormal lore" Mrs Rh. D. in kindred S. p. 208; cp. also DhA IV.233); It 47 = 61 = 81, and perhaps also in phrase sabbaŋ **abhiññāpariññeyya** S IV.29. — grd. **abhiññeyya** S IV.29; Sn 558 (°ŋ abhiññātaŋ known is the knowable); Nd² s.v.; DhA IV.233. — pp. **abhiññāta** (q. v.).

Abhijāyati [abhi + jāyati, Pass. of **jan**, but in sense of a Caus. = janeti] to beget, produce, effect, attain, in phrase akaṇhaŋ asukkaŋ Nibbānaŋ a. D III.251; A III.384 sq. At Sn 214 abhijāyati means "to behave, to be", cp. SnA 265 (abhijāyati = bhavati).

Abhijigiŋsati [abhi + jigiŋsati] to wish to overcome, to covet J VI.193 (= jinituŋ icchati C). Burmese scribes spell °jigīsati; Th 1, 743 ("cheat"? Mrs Rh. D.; "vernichten" Neumann). See also **abhijeti**, and nijigiŋsanatā.

Abhijighacchati [abhi + jighacchati] to be very hungry PvA 271.

Abhijīvanika (adj.) [abhi + jīvana + ika] belonging to ones livehood, forming ones living Vin I.187 (sippa).

Abhijīhanā (f.) [abhi + jīhanā of **jeh** to open ones mouth] strenuousness, exertion, strong endeavour J VI.373 (viriyakaraṇa C.).

Abhijeti [abhi + jayati] to win, acquire, conquer J VI.273 (ābhi° metri causā).

Abhijoteti [abhi + joteti] to make clear, explain, illuminate J V.339.

Abhijjanaka (adj.) [a + bhijjana + ka, from bhijja, grd. of **bhid**] not to be broken, not to be moved or changed, uninfluenced J II.170; DhA III.189.

Abhijjamāna (adj.) [ppr. passive of a + **bhid**, see bhindati] that which is not being broken up or divided. In the stock description of the varieties of the lower Iddhi the phrase **udake pi abhijjamāne gacchati** is doubtful. The principal passages are D I.78, 212; III.112, 281; M I.34, 494; II.18; A I.170, 255; III.17; V.199; S II 121; V.264. In about half of these passages the reading is abhijjamāno. The various readings show that the MSS also are equally divided on this point. Bdgb. (Vism 396) reads °māne, and explains it, relying on Ps II.208, as that sort of water in which a man does not sink. Pv III.1¹ has the same idiom. Dhammapāla's note on that (PvA 169) is corrupt. At D I.78 the Colombo ed. 1904, reads **abhejjamāne** and tr. 'not dividing (the water)'; at D I.212 it reads **abhijjamāno** and tr. 'not sinking (in the water)'.

Abhijjhā (f.) [fr. abhi + **dhyā** (jhāyati¹), cp. Sk. abhidhyāna], covetousness, in meaning almost identical with **lobha** (cp. *Dhs. trsl.* 22) D I.70, 71 (°āya cittaŋ parisodheti he cleanses his heart from coveting; abhijjhāya = abl.; cp. DA I.211 = abhijjhāto); M I.347 (id.); D III.49, 71 sq., 172, 230, 269; S IV.73, 104, 188, 322 (adj. vigat'âbhijjha), 343 (°āyavipāka); A I.280; III.92; V.251 sq.; It 118; Nd¹ 98 (as one of the 4 kāya-gantha, q. v.); Nd² taṇhā II.¹; Pug 20, 59; Dhs 1136 (°kāyagantha); Vbh 195, 244 (vigat'âbhijjha), 362, 364, 391; Nett 13; DhA I.23; PvA 103, 282; Sdhp 56, 69. — Often comb^d with °**domanassa** covetousness & discontent, e. g. at D III.58, 77, 141, 221, 276; M I.340; III.2; A I.39, 296; II.16, 152; IV.300 sq., 457 sq.; V.348, 351; Vbh 105, 193 sq. -**anabhijjhā** absence of covetousness Dhs 35, 62. — See also anupassin, gantha, domanassa, sīla.

Abhijjhātar see **abhijjhitar**.

Abhijjhāti [cp. abhidyāti, abhi + jhāyati¹; see also **abhijjhāyati**] to wish for (acc.), long for, covet S V.74 (so read for abhijjhati); ger. abhijjhāya J VI 174 (= patthetvā C.). — pp. **abhijjhita**.

Abhijjhāyati [Sk. abhidhyāyati, abhi + jhāyati¹; see also **abhijjhāti**] to wish for, covet (c. acc.). Sn 301 (aor. abhijjhāyiŋsu = abhipatthayamāna jhāyiŋsu Sn A 320).

Abhijjhālū (& °u) (adj.) [cp. jhāyin from jhāyati¹; abhijjhālu with °ālu for °āgu which in its turn is for āyin. The B.Sk. form is abhidyālu, e. g. Divy 301, a curious reconstruction] covetous D I.139; III.82; S II.168; III.93; A I.298; II.30, 59, 220 (an° + avyapannacitto sammādiṭṭhiko at conclusion of sīla); V.92 sq., 163, 286 sq.; It 90, 91; Pug 39, 40.

Abhijjhiṭṭa v. l. at DhA IV.101 for **ajjhiṭṭha**.

Abhijjhita [pp. of abhijjhāti] coveted, J. VI.445; usually neg. an° not coveted, Vin I.287; Sn 40 (= anabhipatthita Sn A 85; cp. Nd² 38); Vv 47⁴ (= na abhikankhita VvA 201).

Abhijjhitar [n. ag. fr. abhijjhita in med. function] one who covets M I.287 (T. abhijjhātar, v. l. °itar) = A V.265 (T. °itar, v. l. °atar).

Abhiñña (adj.) (usually —°) [Sk. abhijña] knowing, possessed of knowledge, esp. higher or supernormal knowledge (abhiññā), intelligent; thus in **chalabhiñña** one who possesses the 6 abhiññās Vin III.88; **dandh°** of sluggish intellect D III.106; A II.149; V.63 (opp. khipp°); **mah°** of great insight S II.139. — Compar. **abhiññatara** S V.159 (read bhiyyo 'bhiññataro).

Abhiññatā (f.) [fr. abhiññā] in cpd. **mahā°** state or condition of great intelligence or supernormal knowledge S IV.263; V.175, 298 sq.

Abhiññā[1] (f.) [fr. abhi + **jñā**, see jānāti]. Rare in the older texts. It appears in two contexts. Firstly, certain conditions are said to conduce (inter alia) to serenity, to special knowledge (**abhiññā**), to special wisdom, and to Nibbāna. These conditions precedent are the Path (S V.421 = Vin I.10 = S IV.331), the Path + best knowledge and full emancipation (A V.238), the Four Applications of Mindfulness (S V.179) and the Four Steps to Iddhi (S. V.255). The contrary is three times stated; wrong-doing, priestly superstitions, and vain speculation do not conduce to abhiññā and the rest (D III.131; A III 325 sq. and V.216). Secondly, we find a list of what might now be called psychic powers. It gives us 1, Iddhi (cp. levitation); 2, the Heavenly Ear (cp. clairaudience); 3, knowing others' thoughts (cp. thought-reading); 4, recollecting one's previous births; 5, knowing other people's rebirths; 6, certainty of emancipation already attained (cp. final assurance). This list occurs only at D III.281 as a list of abhiññās. It stands there in a sort of index of principal subjects appended at the end of the Dīgha, and belongs therefore to the very close of the Nikāya period. But it is based on older material. Descriptions of each of the six, not called abhiññā's, and interspersed by expository sentences or paragraphs, are found at D I.89 sq. (*trsl. Dial.* I.89 sq.); M I.34 (see *Buddh. Suttas*, 210 sq.); A I.255, 258 = III.17, 280 = IV.421. At S I.191; Vin II.16; Pug 14, we have the adj. **chaḷabhiññā** ("endowed with the 6 Apperceptions"). At S II.216 we have five, and at S V.282, 290 six abhiññā's mentioned in glosses to the text. And at S II.217, 222 a bhikkhu claims the 6 powers. See also M II.11; III.96. It is from these passages that the list at D III. has been made up, and called abhiññā's.

Afterwards the use of the word becomes stereotyped. In the Old Commentaries (in the Canon), in the later ones (of the 5th cent. A.D.), and in medieval and modern Pāli, abhiññā, nine times out ten, means just the powers given in this list. Here and there we find glimpses of the older, wider meaning of special, supernormal power of apperception and knowledge to be acquired by long training in life and thought. See Nd[1] 108, 328 (expln. of ñāṇa); Nd[2] s. v. and No. 466; Ps I.35; II.156, 189; Vbh 228, 334; Pug 14; Nett 19, 20; Miln 342; Vism 373; Mhvs XIX.20; DA I.175; DhA II.49; IV.30; Sdhp 228, 470, 482. See also the discussion in the *Cpd.* 60 sp., 224 sq. For the phrase sayaṃ abhiññā sacchikatvā and abhiññā-vosita see abhijānāti. The late phrase yath' abhiññaṃ means 'as you please, according to liking, as you like', J V.365 (= yathādhippāyaṃ yathārucim C.). For abhiññā in the use of an adj. (°abhiñña) see **abhiñña.**

Abhiññā[2] ger. of abhijānāti.

Abhiññāta [pp. of abhijānāti] 1. known, recognised Sn 588 (abhiññeyyaṃ °ṇ). — 2. (well)-known, distinguished D I.89 (°kolañña = pākaṭa-kulaja DA I.252), 235; Sn p. 115.

Abhiññeyya grd. of abhijānāti.

Abhiṭhāna (nt.) [abhi + ṭhāna, cp. abhitiṭṭhati; lit. that which stands out above others] a great or deadly crime. Only at Sn 231 = Kh VI.10 (quoted Kvu 109). Six are there mentioned, & are explained (KhA 189) as "matricide, parricide, killing an Arahant, causing schisms, wounding a Buddha, following other teachers". For other relations & suggestions see *Dhs trsl.* 267. — See also ānantarika.

Abhiṇhaṃ (adv.) [contracted form of abhikkhaṇaṃ] repeatedly, continuous, often M I.442 (°āpattika a habitual offender), 446 (°kāraṇa continuous practice); Sn 335 (°saṃvāsa continuous living together); J I.190; Pug 32; DhA II.239; VvA 116 (= abhikkhaṇa), 207, 332; PvA 107 (= abhikkhaṇaṃ). Cp. **abhiṇhaso.**

Abhiṇhaso (adv.) [adv. case fr. abhiṇha; cp. bahuso = Sk. bahuśaḥ] always, ever S I.194; Th I, 25; Sn 559, 560, 998.

Abhitakketi [abhi + takketi] to search for Dāvs V.4.

Abhitatta [pp. of abhi + tapati] scorched (by heat), dried up, exhausted, in phrases uṇha° Vin II.220; Miln 97, and ghamma° S II.110, 118; Sn 1014; J II.223; VvA 40; PvA 114.

Abhitāpa [abhi + tāpa] extreme heat, glow; adj. very hot Vin III.83 (sīsa° sunstroke); M I.507 (mahā° very hot); Miln 67 (mahābhitāpatara much hotter); Pv IV.1[8] (mahā°, of niraya).

Abhitāḷita [abhi + tāḷita fr. tāḷeti] hammered to pieces, beaten, struck Vism 231 (muggara°).

Abhitiṭṭhati [abhi + tiṭṭhati] to stand out supreme, to excel, surpass D II.261; J VI.474 (abhiṭṭhāya = abhibhavitvā C.).

Abhitunna (tuṇṇa) [not as Morris, *J.P.T.S.* 1886, 135, suggested fr. abhi + **tud,** but acc. to Kern, *Toev.* p. 4 fr. abhi + **tūrv.** (Cp. turati & tarati[2] and Ved. turvati). Thus the correct spelling is °**tuṇṇa** = Sk. abhitūrṇa. The latter occurs as v. l. under the disguise of (sok-)âbituṇḍa for °abhituṇṇa at M. Vastu III.2]. Overwhelmed, overcome, overpowered S II.20; Ps I.129 (dukkha°), 164; J I.407; 509 (°tuṇṇa); II.399, 401; III.23 (soka°); IV.330; V.268; Sdhp 281.

Abhito (indecl.) adv. case fr. prep. abhi etym.]. — 1. round about, on both sides J VI.535 (= ubhayapassesu C.), 539. — 2. near, in the presence of Vv 64[1] (= samīpe VvA 275).

Abhitoseti [abhi + toseti] to please thoroughly, to satisfy, gratify Sn 709 (= atīva toseti Sn A 496).

Abhitthaneti [abhi + thaneti] to roar, to thunder J I.330, 332 = Cp. III.10[7].

Abhittharati [abhi + tarati[2], evidently wrong for abhittarati] to make haste Dh 116 (= turitaturitaṃ sīghasīghaṃ karoti DhA III.4).

Abhitthavati [abhi + thavati] to praise J I.89; III.531; Dāvs III.23; DhA I.77; PvA 22; cp. **abhitthunati.**

Abhitthavana (nt.) [fr. prec.] praise Th A 74.

Abhitthunati [abhi + thunati; cp. abhitthavati] to praise J I.17 (aor abhitthuniṃsu); cp. thunati 2. — pp. °**tthuta** DhA I.88.

Abhida[1] (adj.) as attr. of sun & moon at M II.34, 35 is doubtful in reading & meaning; vv. ll. abhidosa & abhidesa, Neumann *trsl.* "unbeschränkt". The context seems to require a meaning like "full, powerful" or unbroken, unrestricted (abhijja or abhīta "fearless"?") or does abhida represent Vedic abhidyu heavenly?

Abhida[2] Only in the difficult old verse D II.107 (= S V.263 = A IV.312 = Nd 64 = Nett 60 = Divy 203). Aorist 3rd sg. fr. bhindati he broke.

Abhidassana (nt.) [abhi + dassana] sight, appearance, show J VI.193.

Abhideyya in sabba° at PvA 78 is with v. l. BB to be read sabbapātheyyaṃ.

Abhidosa (°—) the evening before, last night; °kālakata M I.170 = J I.81; °gata gone last night J VI.386 (= hiyyo paṭhama-yāme C.).

Abhidosika belonging to last night (of gruel) Vin III.15; Miln 291. See ābhi°.

Abhiddavati [abhi + **dru,** cp. dava²] to rush on, to assail Mhvs 6, 5; Dāvs III.47.

Abhidhamati [abhi + dhamati, cp. Sk. abhi° & api-dhamati] blow on or at A I.257.

Abhidhamma [abhi + dhamma] the "special Dhamma," i. e., 1. theory of the doctrine, the doctrine classified, the doctrine pure and simple (without any admixture of literary grace or of personalities, or of anecdotes, or of arguments ad personam), Vin I.64, 68; III.144; IV.344. Coupled with abhivinaya, D III.267; M I.272. — 2. (only in the Chronicles and Commentaries) name of the Third Piṭaka, the third group of the canonical books. Dpvs V.37; PvA 140. See the detailed discussion at DA I.15, 18 sq. [As the word abhidhamma standing alone is not found in Sn or S or A, and only once or twice in the Dialogues, it probably came into use only towards the end of the period in which the 4 great Nikāyas grew up.] -kathā discourse on philosophical or psychological matters, M I.214, 218; A III.106, 392. See dhammakathā.

Abhidhammika see ābhidhammika.

Abhidhara (adj.) [abhi + dhara] firm, bold, in °māna firm-minded Dh p. 81 (acc. to Morris *J.P.T.S.* 1886, 135; not verified).

Abhidhāyin (adj.) [abhi + dhāyin fr. **dhā**]" putting on", designing, calling, meaning Pgdp 98.

Abhidhāreti [abhi + dhāreti] to hold aloft J I.34 = Bu IV.1.

Abhidhāvati [abhi + dhāvati] to run towards, to rush about, rush on, hasten Vin II.195; S I.209; J II.217; III.83; DhA IV.23.

Abhidhāvin (adj.) fr. abhidhāvati] "pouring in", rushing on, running J VI.559.

Abhinata [pp. of abhi + namati] bent, (strained, fig. bent on pleasure M I.386 (+ apanata); S I.28 (id.; Mrs. Rh. D. "strained forth", cp. *Kindred S* I.39). See also **apanata.**

Abhinadati [abhi + nadati] to resound, to be full of noise J VI.531. Cp. abhinādita.

Abhinandati [abhi + nandati] to rejoice at, find pleasure in (acc.), approve of, be pleased or delighted with (acc.) D I.46 (bhāsitaŋ), 55 (id.), 158, 223; M I.109, 458; S I.32 (annaŋ), 57, 14, (cakkhuŋ, rūpe etc.); A IV.411; Th 1, 1006; Dh 75, 219; Sn 1054, 1057, 1111; Nd² 82; Miln 25; DA I.160; DhA III.194 (aor. abhinandi, opp. paṭikkosi) VvA 65 (vacanaŋ). — pp. **abhinandita** (q. v.). — Often in combn. with **abhivadati** (q. v.).

Abhinandana (nt.) & °ā (f.) [fr. abhinandati, cp. **nandanā**], pleasure, delight, enjoyment D I.244; M I.498; J IV.397.

Abhinandita [pp. of abhinandati] only in an° not enjoyed, not (being) an object of pleasure S IV.213 = It 38; S V. 319.

Abhinandin (adj.) [fr. abhinandati, cp. **nandin**] rejoicing at, finding pleasure in (loc. or —°), enjoying A II.54 (piyarūpa); esp. freq. in phrase (taṇhā) tatratatr'âbhinandinī finding its pleasure in this or that [cp. B.Sk. tṛṣṇā tatra-tatr'âbhinandinī M Vastu III.332] Vin I.10; S V.421; Ps II.147; Nett 72, etc.

Abhinamati [abhi + namati] to bend. — pp. **abhinata** (q.v.).

Abhinaya [abhi + naya] a dramatic representation VvA 209 (sākhā°).

Abhinava (adj.) [abhi + nava] quite young, new or fresh Vin III.337; J II.143 (devaputta), 435 (so read for accuṇha in expln of paccaggha; v.v. ll. abbhuṇha & abbiṇha); ThA 201 (°yobbana = abhiyobbana); PvA 40 (°saṇṭhāna), 87 (= paccaggha) 155.

Abhinādita [pp. of abhinādeti, Caus. of abhi + **nad**; see **nadati**] resounding with (—°), filled with the noise (or song) of (birds) J VI.530 (= abhinadanto C.); PvA 157 (= abhiruda).

Abhinikūjita (adj.) [abhi + nikūjita] resounding with, full of the noise of (birds) J V.232 (of the barking of a dog), 304 (of the cuckoo); so read for °kuñjita T.). Cp. **abhikūjita.**

Abhinikkhamati [abhi + nikkhamati] to go forth from (abl.), go out, issue Dhs A 91; esp. fig. to leave the household life, to retire from the world Sn 64 (= gehā abhinikkhamitvā kāsāya-vattho hutvā Sn A 117).

Abhinikkhamana (nt.) [abhi + nikkhamana] departure, going away, esp. the going out into monastic life, retirement, renunciation. Usually as **mahā°** the great renunciation J I.61; PvA 19.

Abhinikkhipati [abhi + nikkhipati] to lay down, put down Davs III.12, 60.

Abhiniggaṇhanā (f.) [abstr. fr. abhiniggaṇhāti] holding back Vin III.121 (+ abhinippīḷanā).

Abhiniggaṇhāti [abhi + niggaṇhāti] to hold back, restrain, prevent, prohibit; always in combn. with **abhinippīḷeti** M I.120; A V.230. — Cp. **abhiniggaṇhanā.**

Abhinindriya [vv. ll. at all passages for **ahīnindriya**] doubtful meaning. The other is expld by Bdhgh at DA I.120 as paripuṇṇ°; and at 222 as avikal-indriya not defective, perfect sense-organ. He must have read ahīn°. Abhi-n-indriya could only be expld as "with supersense-organs", i. e. with organs of supernormal thought or perception, thus coming near in meaning to **abhiññindriya**; We should read ahīn° throughout D I.34, 77, 186, 195. II.13; M II.18; III.121; Nd² under pucchā⁶ (only ahīn°).

Abhininnāmeti [abhi + ninnāmeti cp. BSk. abhinirṇāmayati Lal. V. 439] to bend towards, to turn or direct to D I.76 (cittaŋ ñāṇa-dassanāya); M I.234; S I.123; IV.178; Pug 60.

Abhinipajjati [abhi + nipajjati] to lie down on Vin IV.273 (+ abhinisīdati); A IV.188 (in = acc. + abhinisīdati); Pug 67 (id.).

Abhinipatati [abhi + nipatati] to rush on (to) J II.8.

Abhinipāta (-matta) destroying, hurting (?) at Vbh 321 is expld. by āpātha-matta [cp. Divy 125 śastrâbhinipāta splitting open or cutting with a knife].

Abhinipātana (nt.) [fr. abhi-ni-pāteti] in daṇḍa-sattha° attacking with stick or knife Nd² 576⁴.

Abhinipātin (adj.) [abhi + nipātin] falling on to (—°) J II.7.

Abhinipuṇa (adj.) [abhi + nipuṇa] very thorough, very clever D III.167.

Abhinippajjati [abhi + nippajjati] to be produced, accrue, get, come (to) M I.86 (bhogā abhinipphajjanti: sic) = Nd² 99 (has n'âbhinippajjanti). — Cp. **abhinipphādeti.**

Abhinippata at J VI.36 is to be read **abhinippanna** (so v. l. BB.).

Abhinippatta at Dhs 1035, 1036 is to be read **abhinibbatta.**

Abhinippanna (& °nipphanna) [abhi + nippanna, pp. of °nippajjati] produced, effected, accomplished D II.223 (siloka); J VI.36 (so read for abhinippata); Miln 8 (pph.).

Abhinippīḷanā (f.) [abstr. to abhinippīḷeti, cp. nippīḷana] pressing, squeezing, taking hold of Vin III.121 (+ abhiniggaṇhanā).

Abhinippīḷeti [abhi + nippīḷeti] to squeeze, crush, subdue Vism 399; often in combn. with **abhiniggaṇhāti** M I. 120; A V.230.

Abhinipphatti (f.) [abhi + nipphatti] production, effecting D II.283 (v. l. °nibbatti).

Abhinipphādeti [abhi + nipphādeti] to bring into existence, produce, effect, work, perform D I.78 (bhājana-vikatiṇ); Vin II.183 (iddhiṇ); S V.156, 255; Miln 39.

Abhinibbatta [abhi + nibbatta, pp. of abhinibbattati] reproduced, reborn A IV.40, 401; Nd[2] 256 (nibbatta abhi° pātubhūta); Dhs 1035, 1036 (so read for° nippatta); VvA 9 (puññ'ānubhāva° by the power of merit).

Abhinibbattati [abhi + nibbattati] to become, to be reproduced, to result Pug 51. — pp. **abhinibbatta.** — Cp. B.Sk. wrongly abhinivartate].

Abhinibbatti (f.) [abhi + nibbatti] becoming, birth, rebirth, D I.229; II.283 (v. l. for abhinipphatti) S II.65 (punabbhava°), 101 (id.); IV.14, 215; A V.121; PvA 35.

Abhinibbatteti [abhi + nibbatteti, caus. of °nibbattati] to produce, cause, cause to become S III.152; A V.47; Nd[2] under jāneti.

Abhinibbijjati [either Med. fr. nibbindati of **vid** for *nirvidyate (see nibbindati B), or secondary formation fr. ger. nibbijja. Reading however not beyond all doubt] to be disgusted with, to avoid, shun, turn away from Sn 281 (T. abhinibbijjayātha, v. l. BB° nibbijjiyātha & °nibbajjiyātha, SnA expls. by vivajjeyyātha mā bhajeyyātha; v. l. BB. abhinippajjiyā) = A IV.172 (T. abhinibbajjayātha, vv. ll. °nibbajjeyyātha & °nibbijjayātha); ger. **abhinibbijja** Th 2, 84.

Abhinibbijjhati [abhi + nibbijjhati] to break quite through (of the chick coming through the shell of the egg) Vin III.3; M I.104 = S III.153 (read° nibbijjheyyun for nibbijjeyyun — Cp. *Buddh. Suttas* 233, 234.

Abhinibbidā (f.) [abhi + nibbidā; confused with abhinibbhidā] disgust with the world, taedium Nett 61 (taken as abhinibbhidā, according to expln. as "padālanā-paññatti avijj'aṇḍa-kosānaṇ"), 98 (so MSS, but C. abhinibbidhā).

Abhinibbuta (adj.) [abhi + nibbuta] perfectly cooled, calmed, serene, esp. in two phrases, viz. diṭṭha **dhamm' âbhinibbuta** A I.142 = M III.187; Sn 1087; Nd[2] 83, and **abhinibbutatta** of cooled mind Sn 343 (= apariḍayhamāna-citta SnA 347), 456, 469, 783. Also at Sdhp. 35.

Abhinibbhidā (f.) [this the better, although not correct spelling; there exists a confusion with **abhinibbidā**, therefore spelling also **abhinibbidhā** (Vin III.4, C. on Nett 98). To abhinibbijjhati, cp. B.Sk. abhinirbheda M Vastu I.272, which is wrongly referred to **bhid** instead of **vyadh.**] the successful breaking through (like the chick through the shell of the egg), coming into (proper) life Vin III 4; M I.104; 357; Nett 98 (C. reading). See also **abhinibbidā.**

Abhinimantanatā (f.) [abstr. to abhinimanteti] speaking to, adressing, invitation M I.331.

Abhinimanteti [abhi + nimanteti] to invite to (c. instr.), to offer to D I.61 (āsanena).

Abhinimmadana (nt.) [abhi + nimmadana] crushing, subduing, levelling out M III.132; A IV.189 sq.

Abhinimmita [abhi + nimmita, pp. of abhinimmināti] created. (by magic) Vv 16[1] (pañca rathā satā; cp. VvA 79).

Abhinimmināti [abhi + nimmināti, cp. BSk. abhinirmāti Jtm 32; abhinirminoti Divy 251; abhinirmimīte Divy 166] to create (by magic), produce, shape, make S III.152 (rūpaṇ); A I.279 (oḷārikaṇ attabhāvaṇ); Nd[2] under pucchā[6] (rūpaṇ manomayaṇ); VvA 16 (mahantaṇ hatthi-rāja-vaṇṇaṇ). — pp. **abhinimmita** (q. v.).

Abhiniropana (nt.) & **ā** (f.) [fr. abhiniropeti] fixing one's mind upon, application of the mind Ps I.16, 21, 30, 69, 75, 90; Vbh 87; Dhs 7, 21, 298 (cp. *Dhs trsl.* II.19). See also **abhiropana.**

Abhiniropeti [abhi + niropeti] to implant, fix into (one's mind), inculcate Nett 33.

Abhinivajjeti [abhi + nivajjeti] to avoid, get rid of D III. 113; M I.119, 364, 402; S V.119, 295, 318; A III.169 sq.; It 81.

Abhinivassati [abhi + ni + vassati fr. **vṛṣ**] lit. to pour out in abundance, fig. to produce in plenty. Cp I.10[3] (kalyāṇe good deeds).

Abhiniviṭṭha (adj.) [abhi + niviṭṭha, pp. of abhi-nivisati] "settled in", attached to, clinging on Nd[2] 152 (gahita parāmaṭṭha a.); PvA 267 (= ajjhāsita Pv IV.8[4]).

Abhinivisati [abhi + nivisati] to cling to, adhere to, be attached to Nd[1] 308, 309 (parāmasati +). — pp. **abhiniviṭṭha**; cp. also **abhinivesa.**

Abhinivesa [abhi + nivesa, see nivesa[2] & cp. nivesana] "settling in", i. e. wishing for, tendency towards (—°), inclination, adherence; as adj. liking, loving, being given or inclined to D III.230; M I.136, 251; S II.17; III.10, 13, 135, 161, 186 (saṇyojana° IV.50; A III.363 (paṭhavī°, adj.); Nd[2] 227 (gāha parāmasa +); Pug 22; Vbh 145; Dhs 381, 1003, 1099; Nett 28; PvA 252 (micchā°), 267 (taṇhā°); Sdhp 71. — Often combd. with **adhiṭṭhāna** e. g. S II.17; Nd[2] 176, and in phrase **idaṇ-sacc' âbhinivesa** adherence to one's dogmas, as one of the 4 Ties: see kāyagantha and cp. *Cpd.* 171 n. 5.

Abhinisīdati [abhi + nisīdati] to sit down by or on (acc.), always combd. with **abhinipajjati** Vin III.29; IV.273; A V.188; Pug 67.

Abhinissaṭa (pp.) [abhi + nissaṭa] escaped Th 1, 1089.

Abhinihata (pp.) [abhi + nihata] oppressed. crushed, slain J IV.4.

Abhinīta (pp.) [pp. of abhi-neti] led to, brought to, obliged by (—°) M I.463 = Miln 32 (rājā & cora°); M I.282; S III.93; Th 1, 350 = 435 (vātaroga° "foredone with cramping pains" Mrs. Rh. D.); Pug 29; Miln 362.

Abhinīla (adj.) [abhi + nīla] very black, deep black, only with ref. to the eyes, in phrase **°netta** with deep-black eyes D II.18; III.144, 167 sq. [cp. Sp. Av. Ś I.367 & 370 abhinīla-padma-netra]; Th 2, 257 (nettā ahesuṇ abbhinīla-m-āyatā).

Abhinīhanati [abhi + nis + **han,** cp. Sk. nirhanti] to drive away, put away, destroy, remove, avoid M I.119 (in phrase āṇiṇ a. abhinīharati abhinivajjeti).

Abhinīharati [abhi + nīharati] 1. to take out, throw out M I.119 (see abhinīhanati). — 2. to direct to, to apply to (orig. to isolate? Is reading correct?) in phrase **ñāṇadassanāya cittaṇ abhinīharati abhininnāmeti** D I.76 (= tanninnaṇ tapponaṇ karoti DA I.220, 224; v. l. abhini°) Cp. the latter phrase also in BSk. as abhijñābhinirhāra Av. Ś II.3 (see ref. & note Index p. 221); and the pp. abhinirhṛta (ṛddhiḥ) in Divy 48, 49 to obtain? Ind.), 264 (take to burial), 542.

Abhinīhāra [abhi + nihāra, to abhinīharati; cp. BSk. sarīr' bhinirhāra taking (the body) out to burial, lit. meaning, see note on abhinīharati] being bent on ("downward force" *Dhs trsl.* 242), i. e. taking oneself out to, way of acting, (proper) behaviour, endeavour, resolve, aspiration S III.267 sq. (°kusala); A II.189; III.311; IV.34 (°kusala); J I.14 (Buddhabhāvāya a. resolve to become a Buddha), 15 (Buddhattāya); Ps I.61 sq.; II.121; Nett 26; Miln 216; DhA I.392; II.82 (kata°).

Abhipattika (adj.) [fr. abhipatti] one who has attained, attaining (—°), getting possession of S I.200 (devakañña°).

Abhipatthita (pp.) [fr. abhipattheti] hoped, wished, longed for Miln 383; SnA 85.

Abhipattheti [abhi + pattheti] to hope for, long for, wish for Kh VIII.10; SnA 320; DhA I.30. — pp. **abhipatthita** (q. v.).

Abhipassati [abhi + passati] to have regard for, look for, strive after A I.147 (Nibbānaŋ); III.75; Sn 896 (khema°), 1070 (rattamahā°) Nd[1] 308; Nd[2] 428; J VI.370.

Abhipāteti [abhi + pāteti] to make fall, to bring to fall, to throw J II.91 (kaṇḍaŋ).

Abhipāruta (adj.) [abhi + pāruta, pp. of abhipārupati] dressed Miln 222.

Abhipāleti [abhi + pāleti] to protect Vv 84[21], cp. VvA 341.

Abhipīḷita (pp.) [fr. abhipīḷeti] crushed, squeezed Sdhp 278, 279.

Abhipīḷeti [abhi + pīḷeti] to crush, squeeze Miln 166. — pp. **abhipīḷita** (q. v.).

Abhipucchati [abhi + pucchati] Sk. abhipṛcchati] to ask J IV.18.

Abhipūreti [abhi + pūreti] to fill (up) Miln 238; Dāvs III. 60 (paŋsūhi).

Abhippakiṇṇa [pp. of abhippakirati] completely strewn (with) J I.62.

Abhippakirati [abhi + pakirati] to strew over, to cover (completely) D II.137 (pupphāni Tathāgatassa sarīraŋ okiranti ajjhokiranti a.); VvA 38 (for abbhokirati Vv 5[9]). — pp. **abhippakiṇṇa** (q. v.).

Abhippamodati [abhi + pamodati] to rejoice (intrs.); to please, satisfy (trs, c. acc.) M I.425; S V.312, 330; A V.112; J III 530; Ps I.95, 176, 190.

Abhippalambati [abhi + palambati] to hang down M III. 164 (olambati ajjholambati a.).

Abhippavassati [abhi + pavassati] to shed rain upon, to pour down; intrs. to rain, to pour, fall. Usually in phrase mahāmegho abhippavassati a great cloud bursts Miln 8, 13, 36, 304; PvA 132 (v. l. ati°); intrs. Miln 18 (pupphāni °iŋsu poured down). — pp. **abhippavuṭṭha.**

Abhippavuṭṭha (pp.) [fr. abhippavassati] having rained, poured, fallen; trs. S V.51 (bandhanāni meghena °āni) = A V.127; intrs. M II.117 (mahāmegho °o there has been a cloudburst).

Abhippasanna (adj.) [pp. of abhippasīdati, cp. BSk. abhiprasanna] finding one's peace in (c. loc.), trusting in, having faith in, believing in, devoted to (loc.) Vin III.43; D I.211 (Bhagavati) S I.134; IV.319; V.225, 378; A III. 237, 270, 326 sq.; Sn p. 104 (brāhmaṇesu); PvA 54 (sāsand), 142 (id.). Cp. **vippasanna** in same meaning.

Abhippasāda [abhi + pasāda, cp. BSk. abhiprasāda Av. Ś 12 (cittasyu°) & vippasāda] faith, belief, reliance, trust Dhs 12 ("sense of assurance" *trsl.*, + saddhā), 25, 96, 288; PvA 223.

Abhippasādeti [Caus. of abhippasīdati, cp. BSk. abhiprasādayati Divy 68, 85, pp. abhiprasādita-manāḥ Jtm 213, 220] to establish one's faith in (loc.), to be reconciled with, to propitiate Th 1, 1173 = Vv 21[2] (manaŋ arahantamhi = cittaŋ pasādeti VvA 105).

Abhippāsāreti [abhi + pasāreti, cp. BSk. abhiprasārayati Divy 389] to stretch out Vin I.179 (pāde).

Abhippasīdati [abhi + pasīdati] to have faith in D I.211 (fut. °issati). — pp. **abhippasanna**; Caus. **abhippasādeti.**

Abhippaharaṇa (nt.) [abhi + paharaṇa] attacking, fighting, as adj. *f.* °aṇī fighting, Ep. of Mārassa senā, the army of M. Sn 439 (kaṇhassa° the fighting army of k. = samaṇabrāhmaṇānaŋ nippothanī antarāyakārī SnA 390).

Abhibyāpeti [abhi + vyāpeti, cp. Sk. vyāpnoti, vi + **āp**] to pervade Miln 251.

Abhibhakkhayati [abhi + bhakkhayati] to eat (of animals) Vin II.201 (bhinko paṅkaŋ a.).

Abhibhava [fr. abhibhavati] defeat, humiliation SnA 436.

Abhibhavati [abhi + bhavati] to overcome, master, be Lord over, vanguish, conquer S I.18, 32, 121 (maraṇaŋ); IV. 71 (rāgadose), 117 (kodhaŋ), 246, 249 (sāmikaŋ); J I.56, 280; PvA 94 (= balīyati, vaḍḍhati). — fut. **abhihessati** see abhihāreti 4. — ger. **abhibhuyya** Vin I.294; Dh 328; It 41 (māraŋ sasenaŋ); Sn 45, 72 (°cārin), 1097, Nd[2] 85 (= abhibhavitvā ajjhottharitvā pariyādiyitvā); and **abhibhavitvā** PvA 113 (= pasayha), 136. — grd. **abhibhavanīya** to be overcome PvA 57. — Pass. ppr. **abhibhūyamāna** being overcome (by) PvA 80, 103. — pp. **abhibhūta** (q. v.).

Abhibhavana (nt.) [fr. abhibhavati] overcoming, vanquishing, mastering S II.210 (v. l. BB abhipatthana).

Abhibhavanīyatā (f.) [abstr. fr. abhibhavanīya, grd. of abhibhavati] as an° invincibility PvA 117.

Abhibhāyatana (nt.) [abhibhū + āyatana] position of a master or lord, station of mastery. The traditional account of these gives 8 stations or stages of mastery over the senses (see *Dial.* II.118; *Exp.* I.252), detailed identically at all the foll. passages, viz. D II.110; III.260 (& 287); M II.13; A I.40; IV.305, 348; V.61. Mentioned only at S IV.77 (6 stations); Ps I.5; Nd[2] 466 (as an accomplishment of the Bhagavant); Dhs 247.

Abhibhāsana (nt.) [abhi + bhāsana fr. **bhās**] enlightenment or delight ("light & delight" trsl.) Th 1, 613 (= tosana C.).

Abhibhū (n.-adj.) [Vedic abhibhū, fr. abhi + **bhū**, cp. abhibhavati] overcoming, conquering, vanquishing, having power over, a Lord or Master of (—°) D III.29; S II. 284; Sn 211 (sabba°), 545 (Māra°, cp. Mārasena-pamaddana 561), 642. — Often in phrase abhibhū anabhibhūta aññadatthudasa vasavattin, i. e. unvanquished Lord of all D I 18; III.135 = Nd[2] 276; A II.24; IV.94; It 122; cp. DA I.111 (= abhibhavitvā ṭhito jeṭṭhako' ham asmīti).

Abhibhūta [pp of abhibhavati] overpowered, overwhelmed, vanquished D I.121; S I.137 (jāti-jarā°); II.228 (lābhasakkāra-silokena); A I.202 (pāpakehi dhammehi); J I.189; PvA 14, 41 (= pareta), 60 (= upagata), 68, 77, 80 (= pareta). Often neg. an° unconquered, e. g. Sn 934; Nd[1] 400; & see phrase under abhibhū.

Abhimangala (adj.) [abhi + mangala] (very) fortunate, lucky, anspicious, in °sammatā (of Visākhā) "benedicted", blessed Vin III.187 = DhA I.409. Opp. avamangala.

Abhimaṇḍita (pp. —°) [abhi + maṇḍita] adorned, embellished, beautified Miln 361; Sdhp 17.

Abhimata (adj.) [BSk. abhimata, e. g. Jtm 211; pp. of abhimanyate] desired, wished for; agreeable, pleasant C. on Th 1, 91.

Abhimatthati (°eti) & °mantheti [abhi + **math** or **manth,** cp. nimmatheti] 1. to cleave, cut; to crush, destroy M I.243 (sikharena muddhānaŋ °mantheti); S I.127; Dh 161 (v. l. °nth°); J IV.457 (matthako sikharena °matthiyamāno); DhA III.152 (= kantati viddhaŋseti). — 2. to rub, to produce by friction (esp. fire, aggiŋ; cp. Vedic agniŋ nirmanthati) M I.240.

Abhimaddati [Sk. abhimardati & °mṛdnāti; abhi + **mṛd**] to crush S I.102; A I.198; Sdhp 288.

Abhimana (adj.) [abhi + mano, BSk. abhimana, e. g. M Vastu III.259] having one's mind turned on, thinking of or on (c. acc.) Th 1, 1122; J VI.451.

Abhimanāpa (adj.) [abhi + manāpa] very pleasing VvA 53 (where id. p. at PvA 71 has **atimanāpa**).

Abhimantheti see **abhimatthati.**

Abhimāra [cp. Sk. abhimara slaughter] a bandit, bravo, robber J II.199; DA I.152.

Abhimukha (adj.) [abhi + mukha] facing, turned towards, approaching J II.3 (°ā ahesuŋ met each other). Usually —° turned to, going to, inclined towards D I.50 (puratthа°); J I.203 (devaloka°), 223 (varaṇa-rukkha°); II.3 (nagara°), 416 (Jetavana°); DhA I.170 (tad°); II.89 (nagara°); PvA 3 (kāma°, opp. vimukha), 74 (uyyāna°). — nt. °ŋ adv. to, towards J I.263 (matta-vāraṇe); PvA 4 (āghātana°, may here be taken as pred. adj.); DhA III.310 (uttara°).

Abhiyācati [abhi + yācati] to ask, beg, entreat Sn 1101, cp. Nd² 86.

Abhiyāti [Vedic abhiyāti in same meaning; abhi + **yā**] to go against (in a hostile manner, to attack (c. acc.) S I.216 (aor. abhiyaŋsu, v. l. SS abhijiyiŋsu); DhA III.310 (aor. abhiyāsi as v. l. for T. reading pāyāsi; the id. p. VvA 68 reads pāyāsi with v. l. upāyāsi).

Abhiyujjhati [abhi + yujjhati from **yudh**] to contend, quarrel with J I.342.

Abhiyuñjati [abhi + **yuj**] to accuse, charge; intrs. fall to one's share Vin III.50; IV.304.

Abhiyoga [cp. abhiyuñjati] practice, observance Dāvs IV.7.

Abhiyogin (adj.) [fr. abhiyoga] applying oneself to, practised. skilled (an augur, sooth sayer) D III.168.

Abhiyobbana (nt.) [abhi + yobbana] much youthfulness, early or tender youth Th 2, 258 (= abhinavayobbanakāla ThA 211).

Abhirakkhati [abhi + rakkhati] to guard, protect J VI.589 (= pāleti C.). Cp. parirakkhati.

Abhirakkhā (f.) [fr. abhirakkhati] protection, guard J I.204 (= ārakkhā 203).

Abhirata (adj.) (—°) [pp. of abhiramati] fond of, indulging in, finding delight in A IV.224 (nekkhamma°); V.175 (id.), Sn 86 (nibbāna°), 275 (vihesa°), 276 (kalaha°); J V.382 (dāna°); PvA 54 (puññakamma°), 61 (satibhavana°), 105 (dānādipuñña°).

Abhiratatta (nt.) [abstr. fr. abhirata] the fact of being fond of, delighting in (—°) J V.254 (kāma°).

Abhirati (f.) [fr. abhi + **ram**] delight or pleasure in (loc. or —°) S I.185; IV.260; A V.122; Dh 88. -an° displeasure, discontent, distaste Vin II.110; D I.17 (+ paritassanā); S I.185; V.132; A III.259; IV.50; V.72 sq., 122; J III.395; DA I.111; PvA 187.

Abhiratta (adj.) [abhi + ratta] very red J V.156; fig. very much excited or affected with (—°) Sn 891 (sandiṭṭhirāgena a.).

Abhiraddha (adj.) [pp. of abhi + **rādh**] propitiated, satisfied A IV.185 (+ attamana).

Abhiraddhi (f.) [fr. abhiraddha] only in neg. **an°** displeasure, dislike, discontent A I.79; DA I.52 (= kopass' etaŋ adhivacanaŋ).

Abhiramati [abhi + **ram**] to sport, enjoy oneself, find pleasure in or with (c. loc.), to indulge in love Sn 718, 1085; J I.192; III.189, 393; DhA I.119; PvA 3, 61, 145. — ppr. act. **abhiranto** only as nt. °ŋ in adv. phrase yathâbhirantaŋ after one's liking, as much as he pleases, after one's heart's content Vin I.34; M I.170; Sn 53. — ppr. med. **abhiramamāna** J III.188, PvA 162. — pp. **abhirata** (q. v.). — 2nd Caus. **abhiramāpeti** (q. v.).

Abhiramana (nt.) [fr. abhiramati] sporting, dallying, amusing oneself PvA 16.

Abhiramāpana (nt.) [fr. abhiramāpeti, Caus² of abhiramati] causing pleasure to (acc.), being a source of pleasure, making happy M III.132 (gāmante).

Abhiramāpeti [Caus. II. fr. abhiramati] 1. to induce to sport, to cause one to take pleasure J III.393. — 2. to delight, amuse, divert J I.61. — Cp. **abhiramāpana.**

Abhiravati [abhi + ravati] to shout out Bu II.90 = J I.18 (v.99).

Abhirādhita [pp. of abhirādheti] having succeeded in, fallen to one's share, attained Th 1, 259.

Abhirādhin (adj.) (—°) [fr. abhirādheti] pleasing, giving pleasure, satisfaction J IV.274 (mitta° = ārādhento tosento C.).

Abhirādheti [abhi + rādheti] to please, satisfy, make happy J I.421; DA I.52. — aor. (pret.) **abhirādhayi** Vv 31⁸ (= abhirādhesi VvA 130); Vv 64²³ (gloss for abhirocayi VvA 282); J I.421; III.386 (= paritosesi C.). — pp. **abhirādhita.**

Abhiruci (f.) [Sk. abhiruci, fr. abhi + **ruc**] delight, longing, pleasure, satisfaction PvA 168 (= ajjhāsaya).

Abhirucita (adj.) [pp. fr. abhi + **ruc**] pleasing, agreeable, liked J I.402; DhA I.45.

Abhiruda (adj. —°) [Sk. abhiruta] resounding with (the cries of animals, esp. the song of birds), full of the sound of (birds) Th 1, 1062 (kuñjara°), 1113 (mayūra-koñca°); J IV.466 (adāsakunta°); V.304 (mayūra-koñca°); VI.172 (id., = upagīta C.), 272 (sakunta°; = abhigīta C.), 483 (mayūra-koñca°), 539; Pv II.12³ (haŋsa-koñca°; = abhinādita PvA 157). — The form abhiruta occurs at Th 1, 49.

Abhirūpa (adj.) [abhi + rūpa] of perfect form, (very), handsome, beautiful, lovely Sn 410 (= dassanīya' angapeccanga SnA 383); J I.207; Pug 52; DA I.281 (= aññehi manussehi adhikarūpa); VvA 53; PvA 61 (= abhikkanta). Occurs in the idiomatic phrase denoting the characteristics of true beauty **abhirūpa dassanīya pāsādika** (+ paramāya vaṇṇa-pokkharatāya samannāgata), e. g. Vin I.268; D I.47, 114, 120; S II.279; A II.86, 203; Nd² 659; Pug 66; DhA I.281 (compar.); PvA 46.

Abhirūḷha [pp. of abhirūhati] mounted, gone up to, ascended J V.217; DhA I.103.

Abhirūhati (abhiruhati) [abhi + **ruh**] to ascend, mount, climb; to go on or in to (c. acc.) Dh 321; Th 1, 271; J I.259; II.388; III.220; IV.138 (nāvaŋ); VI.272 (peculiar aor. °rucchi with ābhi metri causa; = abhirūhi C.); DA I.253. — ger. **abhiruyha** J III.189; PvA 75, 152 (as v. l.; T. has °ruyhitva), 271 (nāvaŋ), & **abhirūhitvā** J I.50 (pabbataŋ) II.128.

Abhirūhana (nt.) [BSk. °rūhana, e. g. M Vastu II.289] climbing, ascending, climb Miln 356.

Abhiroceti [abhi + roceti, Caus. of **ruc**] 1. to like, to find delight in (acc.), to desire, long for J III.192; V.222 (= roceti); Vv 64[23] (vataŋ abhirocayi = abhirocesi ruccitvā pūresi ti attho; abhirādhayī ti pi pāṭho; sādhesi nipphādesī ti attho VvA 282). — 2. to please, satisfy, entertain, gladden Vv 64[24] (but VvA 292: abhibhavitvā vijjotati, thus to no. 3). — 3. v. l. for **atiroceti** (to surpass in splendour) at Vv 81[12], cp. also no. 2.

Abhiropana (nt.) [fr. abhiropeti] concentration of mind, attention (seems restricted to Ps II. only) Ps II.82 (v. l. abhiniropana), 84, 93, 115 (buddhi°), 142 (°virāga), 145 (°vimutti), 216 (°abhisamaya). See also **abhiniropana.**

Abhiropeti [abhi + ropeti, cp. Sk. adhiropayati, Caus. of **ruh**] to fix one's mind on, to pay attention, to show reverence, to honour Vv 37[7] (aor. °ropayi = ropesi VvA 169), 37[10] (id.; = pūjaŋ kāresi VvA 172), 60[4] (= pūjesi VvA 253); Dāvs V.19.

Abhilakkhita (adj.) [Sk. abhilakṣita in diff. meaning; pp. of abhi + **lakṣ**] fixed, designed, inaugurated, marked by auspices J IV.1; DA 1.18.

Abhilakkhitatta (nt.) [abstr. fr. abhilakkhita] having signs or marks, being characterised, characteristics DhsA 62.

Abhilanghati [abhi + langhati] to ascend, rise, travel or pass over (of the moon traversing the sky) J III.364; VI.221.

Abhilambati [abhi + lambati] to hang down over (c. acc.) M III.164 = Nett 179 (+ ajjholambati); J V.70 (papātaŋ), 269 (Vetaraṇiŋ). — pp. **abhilambita** (q. v.).

Abhilambita (adj.) [pp. of abhilambati] hanging down J V.407 (nīladuma°).

Abhilāpa [fr. abhi + **lap**] talk, phrasing, expression Sn 49 (vācābhilāpa making phrases, talking, idle or objectionable speech = tiracchānakathā Nd² 561); It 89 (? reading abhilāpāyaŋ uncertain, vv. ll. abhipāyaŋ abhipāpāyaŋ, abhisāpāyaŋ, abhisapāyaŋ, atisappāyaŋ. The corresp. passage S III.93 reads abhisapayaŋ: curse, and C. on It 89 expl[s.] abhilāpo ti akkoso, see *Brethren* 376 n. 1); Dhs 1306 = Nd² 34 (as exegesis or paraphrase of adhivacana, comb[d.] with vyañjana & trsl. by Mrs. Rh. D. as "a distinctive mark of discourse"); DA 1.20, 23, 281; DhsA 51.

Abhilāsa [Sk. abhilāṣa, abhi + **laṣ**] desire, wish, longing PvA 154.

Abhilekheti [Caus. of abhi + **likh**] to cause to be inscribed Dāvs V.67 (cāritta-lekhaŋ °lekhayi).

Abhilepana (nt.) [abhi + lepana] "smearing over", stain, pollution Sn 1032, 1033 = Nett 10, 11 (see Nd² 88 = laggana "sticking to", bandhana, upakkilesa).

Abhivagga [abhi + vagga] great mass (?), superior force (?), only in phrase °**ena omaddati** to crush with sup. force or overpower M 1.87 = Nd² 199[6].

Abhivañcana (nt.) [abhi + **vañc**] deceit, fraud Dāvs III.64.

Abhivaṭṭa [pp. of abhivassati, see also abhivuṭṭha] rained upon Dh 335 (gloss °vuṭṭha; cp. DhA IV.45); Miln 176, 197, 286. — *Note.* Andersen *P. R.* prefers reading abhivaḍḍha at Dh 335 "the abounding Bīrana grass").

Abhivaḍḍhati [Vedic abhivardhati, abhi + **vṛdh**] 1. to increase (intrs.) D 1.113, 195 (opp. hāyati); M II.225; A III.46 (bhogā a.); Dh 24; Miln 374; PvA 8, 133; Sdhp 288, 523. — 2. to grow over or beyond, to outgrow J III.399 (vanaspatiŋ). — pp. **abhivuḍḍha** & °**vuddha** (q. v.).

Abhivaḍḍhana (adj.-nt.) [fr. abhivaḍḍhati] increasing (trs.), augmenting; f. °ī Sdhp 68.

Abhivaḍḍhi (f.) [cp. Sk. abhivṛddhi, fr. abhi + **vṛdh**] increase, growth Miln 94. — See also **abhivuḍḍhi.**

Abhivaṇṇita [pp. of abhivaṇṇeti] praised Dpvs 1.4.

Abhivaṇṇeti [abhi + vaṇṇeti] to praise Sdhp 588 (°ayi). — pp. **abhivaṇṇita.**

Abhivadati [abhi + vadati] 1. to speak out, declare, promise J 1.83 = Vin 1.36; J VI.220. — 2. to speak (kindly) to, to welcome, salute, greet. In this sense always comb[d] with **abhinandati**, e. g. at M 1.109, 266, 458; S III.14; IV.36 sq.; Miln 69. — Caus. **abhivādeti.**

Abhivandati [abhi + vandati] to salute respectfully, to honour, greet; grd. °**vandanīya** Miln 227.

Abhivassaka (adj.) [fr. abhivassati] raining, fig. shedding, pouring out, yielding VvA 38 (puppha°).

Abhivassati [abhi + vassati from **vṛṣ**] to rain, shed rain, pour; fig. rain down, pour out, shed D III.160 (abhivassaŋ metri causa); A III.34; Th 1, 985; J 1.18 (V.100; pupphā a. stream down); cp. III.10[6]; Miln 132, 411. — pp. **abhivaṭṭa** & **abhivuṭṭha** (q. v.). — Caus. II. **abhivassāpeti** to cause (the sky to) rain Miln 132.

Abhivassin (adj.) = **abhivassaka** It 64, 65 (sabbattha°).

Abhivādana (nt.) [fr. abhivādeti] respectful greeting, salutation, giving welcome, showing respect or devotion A II.180; IV.130, 276; J 1.81, 82, 218; Dh 109 (°sīlin of devout character, cp. DhA II.239); VvA 24; Sdhp 549 (°sīla).

Abhivādeti [Caus. of abhivadati] to salute, greet, welcome, honour Vin II.208 sq.; D 1.61; A III.223; IV.173; Vv 1[5] (abhivādayiŋ aor. = abhivādanaŋ kāresiŋ vandiŋ VvA 24); Miln 162. Often in comb[n] with **padakkhiṇaŋ karoti** in sense of to bid goodbye, to say adieu, farewell, e. g. D 1.89, 125, 225; Sn 1010. — Caus. II. **abhivādāpeti** to cause some one to salute, to make welcome Vin II.208 (°etabba).

Abhivāyati [abhi + vāyati; cp. Sk. abhivāti] to blow through, to pervade Miln 385.

Abhivāreti [abhi + vāreti, Caus. of **vṛ**] to hold back, refuse, deny J V.325 (= nivāreti C.).

Abhivāheti [abhi + vāheti, Caus. of **vah**] to remove, to put away Bu X.5.

Abhivijayati (& **vijināti**) [abhi + vijayati] to overpower, to conquer. Of °jayati the ger. °**jiya** at D 1.89, 134; II.16. Of °jināti the pres. 3rd pl. °**jinanti** at Miln 39; the ger. °**jinitvā** at M 1.253; Pug 66.

Abhiviññāpeti [abhi + viññāpeti] to turn somebody's mind on (c. acc.), to induce somebody (dat.) to (acc.) Vin III.18 (purāṇadutiyikāya methunaŋ dhammaŋ abhiviññāpesi).

Abhivitarati [abhi + vitarati] "to go down to", i. e. give in, to pay heed, observe Vin 1.134 and in ster. expl[n.] of sañcicca at Vin II.91; III.73, 112; IV.290.

Abhivinaya [abhi + vinaya] higher discipline, the refinements of discipline or Vinaya; comb[d.] with abhidhamma, e. g. D III.267; M 1.472; also with vinaya Vin V.1 sq.

Abhivindati [abhi + vindati] to find, get, obtain Sn 460 (= labhati adhigacchati SnA 405).

Abhivisiṭṭha (adj.) [abhi + visiṭṭha] most excellent, very distinguished DA 1.99, 313.

Abhivissajjati [abhi + vissajjati] to send out, send forth, deal out, give D III.160.

Abhivissattha [abhi + vissattha, pp. of abhivissasati, Sk. abhiviśvasta] confided in, taken into confidence M II.52 (v. l. °visaṭṭha).

Abhivuṭṭha [pp. of abhivassati, see also abhivaṭṭa] poured out or over, shed out (of water or rain) Th 1, 1065; Dh 335 (gloss); PvA 29.

Abhivuḍḍha [pp. of abhivaḍḍhati, see also °vuddha] increased, enriched PvA 150.

Abhivuddha [pp. of abhivaḍḍhati, see also °vuḍḍha] grown up Miln 361.

Abhivuddhi (f.) [Sk. abhivṛddhi, see also abhivaḍḍhi] increase, growth, prosperity Miln 34.

Abhiveṭheti: Kern's (*Toev.* s. v.) proposed reading at J v.452 for ati°, which however does not agree with C. expln. on p. 454.

Abhivedeti [abhi + Caus. of **vid**] 1. to make known, to communicate Dāvs v.2, 11. — 2. to know J vi.175 (= jānāti C.).

Abhivihacca [ger. of abhi + vihanati] having destroyed, removed or expelled; only in one simile of the sun driving darkness away at M 1.317 = S iii 156; v.44 = It 20.

Abhivyāpeti see **abhibyāpeti.**

Abhisaŋvisati [abhi + saŋvisati]. Only in **abhisaŋvisseyya-gattaŋ** (or-bhastaŋ or-santuŋ) Th 2, 466 a compound of doubtful derivation and meaning. Mrs. Rh. D., following Dhammapāla (p. 283) 'a bag of skin with carrion filled'.

Abhisaŋsati [Vedic abhiśaŋsati, abhi + **śaŋs**] to execrate, revile, lay a curse on J v.174 (°saŋsittha 3rd sg. pret. med. = paribhāsi C.) — aor. **abhisasi** J vi.187, 505, 522 (= akkosi C.), 563 (id.). — pp. **abhisattha.** Cp. also **abhisiŋsati.**

Abhisaŋsanā (f.) [? abhisaŋsati] is doubtful reading at Vv 64[10]; meaning "neighing" (of horses) VvA 272, 279.

Abhisankhata (adj.) [abhi + sankhata, pp. of abhisankharoti] prepared, fixed, made up, arranged, done M 1.350; A ii.43; v.343; J 1.50; Nd[1] 186 (kappita +); PvA 7, 8.

Abhisankharoti (& °**khāreti** in Pot.) [abhi + sankharoti] to prepare, do, perform, work, get up Vin 1.16 (iddh' âbhisankhāraŋ °khāreyya); D 1.184 (id.); S ii.40; iii.87, 92; iv.132, 290; v.449; A 1.201; Sn 984 (ger. °itvā: having got up this curse, cp. SnA 582); PvA 56 (iddh' âbhisaŋkhāraŋ), 172 (id.), 212 (id.). — pp. **abhisankhata** (q. v.).

Abhisankhāra [abhi + sankhāra] 1. putting forth, performance, doing, working, practice: only in two combns., viz. (a) gamiya° (or gamika°) a heathenisch practice Vin 1.233; A iv.180, & (b) **iddha**° (= iddhi°) working of supernormal powers Vin 1.16; D 1.106; S iii.92; iv.289; v.270; Sn p. 107; PvA 56, 172, 212. — 2. preparation, store, accumulation (of kamma, merit or demerit), substratum, state (see for detail sankhāra) S iii.58 (an°); Nd[1] 334, 442; Nd[2] s. v.; Vbh 135 (puñña° etc.), 340; DhsA 357 (°viññāna "storing intellect" *Dhs trsl.* 262).

Abhisankhārika (adj.) [fr. abhisankhāra] what belongs to or is done by the sankhāras; accumulated by or accumulating merit, having special (meritorious) effect (or specially prepared?) Vin ii.77 = iii.160; Sdhp 309 (sa °paccaya).

Abhisankhipati [abhi + sankhipati] to throw together, heap together, concentrate Vbh 1 sq., 82 sq., 216 sq., 400; Miln 46.

Abhisanga [fr. abhi + sañj, cp. abhiśajjati & Sk. abhisanga] 1. sticking to, cleaving to, adherence to J v.6; Nett 110, 112; DhsA 129 (°hetukaŋ dukkhaŋ) 249 (°rasa).

Abhisangin (adj.) [fr. abhisanga] cleaving to (—°) Sdhp 566.

Abhisajjati [abhi + **sañj**; cp. abhisanga] to be in ill temper, to be angry, to curse, imprecate (in meaning of abhisanga 2) D 1.91 (= kodha-vasena laggati DA 1.257); iii.159; J iii.120 (+ kuppati); iv.22 (abhisajji kuppi vyāpajji, cp. BSk. abhiṣajyate kupyati vyāpadyate. Av. Ś 1.286); v.175 (= kopeti C.); Dh 408 (abhisaje Pot. = kujjhāpana-vasena laggapeyya DhA iv.182); Pug 30, 36. — See also abhisajjana & abhisajjanā.

Abhisajjana (nt.-adj.) [abstr. fr. abhisajjati in meaning of abhisanga 2] only as adv. f. °**nī** Ep. of vācā scolding, abusing, cursing A v.265 (para°). Cp. next.

Abhisajjanā (f) [abstr. fr. abhisajjati, cp. abhisajjana] at Sn 49 evidently means "scolding, cursing, being in bad temper" (cp. abhisajjati), as its combn. with vāc' âbhilāpa indicates, but is expld. both by Nd[2] & Bdhgh. as "sticking to, cleaving, craving, desire" (= taṇhā), after the meaning of abhisanga. See Nd[2] 89 & 107; SnA 98 (sineha-vasena), cp. also the compromise-expln by Bdhgh. of abhisajjati as kodha-vasena laggati (DA 1.257).

Abhisañcināti (& °cayati) [abhi + sañcināti] to accumulate, collect (merit) Vv 47[6] (Pot. °sañceyyaŋ = °sañcineyyaŋ VvA 202).

Abhisañcetayita [pp. of abhisañceteti] raised into consciousness, thought out, intended, planned M 1.350; S ii. 65; iv.132; A v.343.

Abhisañceteti [abhi + sañceteti or °cinteti] to bring to consciousness, think out, devise, plan S ii.82. — pp. **abhisañcetayita** (q. v.).

Abhisaññā (f.). Only in the compound **abhi-saññā-nirodha** D 1.179, 184. The prefix abhi qualifies, not saññā, but the whole compound, which means 'trance'. It is an expression used, not by Buddhists, but by certain wanderers. See **saññā-vedayita-nirodha.**

Abhisaññūhati [abhi + saññūhati, i. e. saŋ-ni-ūhati] to heap up, concentrate Vbh 1, 2, 82 sq.; 216 sq., 400; Miln 46. Cp. **abhisankhipati.**

Abhisaṭa [pp. of abhisarati, abhi + **sṛ** to flow] 1. (med.) streamed forth, come together J vi.56 (= sannipatita C.). — 2. (pass.) approached, visited Vin 1.268.

Abhisatta [pp. of abhisapati, cp. Sk. abhiśapta, fr. abhi + **śap**] cursed, accursed, railed at, reviled J iii.460; v.71; SnA 364 (= akkuṭṭha); VvA 335.

Abhisattha [pp. of abhisaŋsati] cursed, accursed Th 1, 118 "old age falls on her as if it had been cursed upon her" (that is, laid upon her by: a curse). Morris *JPTS.* 1886, 145 gives the commentator's equivalents, "commanded, worked by a charm". This is a curious idiom. Any European would say that the woman herself, not the old age, was accursed. But the whole verse is a riddle and Kern's translation (*Toev.* s. v.) 'hurried up' seems to us impossible.

Abhisaddahati [abhi + saddahati, cp. Sk. abhiśraddadhāti, e. g. Divy 17, 337] to have faith in, believe in (c. acc.), believe S v.226; Th 1, 785; Pv iv.1[13], 1[25] (°saddaheyya = patiñeyya PvA 226); Nett 11; Miln 258; PvA 26; Dāvs iii.58.

Abhisantāpeti [abhi + santāpeti, Caus. of santapati] to burn out, scorch, destroy M 1.121.

Abhisanda [abhi + sanda of **syad,** cp. BSk. abhisyanda, e. g. M Vastu ii.276] outflow, overflow, yield, issue, result; only in foll. phrases: **cattāro puññ' âbhisandā kusal' âbhisandā** (yields in merit) S v.391 sq.; A ii.54 sq.; iii.51, 337; vi.245, & **kamm' âbhisanda** result of kamma Miln 276. — Cp. **abhisandana.**

Abhisandana (nt.) [= abhisanda] result, outcome, consequence Ps 1.17 (sukhassa).

Abhisandahati [abhi + sandahati of saŋ + **dhā**] to put together, to make ready Th 1, 151; ger. **abhisandhāya** in sense of a prep. = on account of, because of J II.386 (= paṭicca C.).

Abhisandeti [abhi + sandeti, Caus. of **syad**] to make overflow, to make full, fill, pervade D I.73, 74.

Abhisanna (adj.) [pp. of abhisandati = abhi + **syand**, cp. Sk. abhisanna] overflowing, filled with (—°), full Vin I. 279 (°kāya a body full of humours, cp. II.119 & Miln 134); J I.17 (v.88; pītiyā); Miln 112 (duggandha°).

Abhisapati [abhi + sapati, of **śap**] to execrate, curse, accurse Vin IV.276; J IV.389; V.87; DhA I.42. — pp. abhisatta.

Abhisapana (nt.) [fr. abhisapati] cursing, curse PvA 144 (so read for abhisampanna).

Abhisamaya [abhi + samaya, from sam + **i**, cp. abhisameti & sameti; BSk. abhisamaya, e. g. Divy 200, 654] "coming by completely", insight into, comprehension, realization, clear understanding, grasp, penetration. See on term *Kvu trsl.* 381 sq. — Esp. in full phrases: **attha°** grasp of what is proficient S I.87 = A III.49 = It 17, cp. A II.46; **ariyasaccānaŋ** a. full understanding of the 4 noble truths S V.415, 440, 441 [cp. Divy 654: anabhisamitānāŋ caturnāŋ āryasatyānāŋ a.]; Sn 758 (sacca° = sacc' âvabodha SnA 509); Miln 214 (catusacc°); Sdhp 467 (catusacc°), 525 (saccānaŋ); **dhamm' âbhisamaya** full grasp of the Dhamma, quasi conversion [cp. dharm' âbhisamaya Divy 200] S II.134; Miln 20, 350; VvA 219; PvA 9 etc. frequent; **sammā-mān' âbhisamaya** full understanding of false pride in ster. phrase" acchecchi (for acchejji) taṇhaŋ, vivattayi saññojanaŋ sammāmānâbhisamayā antam akāsi dukkhassa" at S IV.205, 207, 399; A III.246, 444; It 47; cp. māna° S I.188 = Th 2, 20 (tato mānâbhisamayā upasanto carissasi, trsl. by Mrs. Rh. D. in *K. S.* 239 "hath the mind mastered vain imaginings, then mayst thou go thy ways calm and serene"); Sn 342 (expl^d. by mānassa abhisamayo khayo vayo pahānaŋ SnA 344). Also in foll. passages: S II.5 (paññāya), 104 (id.), 133 sq. (Abhisamaya Saŋyutta); Sn 737 (phassa°, expl^d. ad sensum but not at verbum by phassa-nirodha SnA 509); Ps II.215; Pug 41; Vv 16^10 (= saccapaṭivedha VvA 85); DA I.32; DhA I.109; VvA 73 (bhāvana°), 84 (sacchikiriya°); Dpvs I.31. **-anabhisamaya** not grasping correctly, insufficient understanding, taken up wrongly S III.260; Pug 21; Dhs 390, 1061, 1162 (Mrs. Rh. D. trsl^s. "lack of coordination").

Abhisamāgacchati [abhi + sam + āgacchati, cp. in meaning adhigacchati] to come to (understand) completely, to grasp fully, to master KhA 236 (for abhisamecca Sn 143).

Abhisamācārika (adj.) [abhi + samācārika, to samācāra] belonging to the practice of the lesser ethics; to be practiced; belonging to or what is the least to be expected of good conduct, proper. Of **sikkhā** Vin V.181; A II.243 sq.; of **dhamma** M I.469; A III.14 sq.; 422.

Abhisamikkhati (& °ekkhati), [abhi + sam + **īks**, cp. samikkhati] to behold, see, regard, notice J. IV.19 (2nd sg. med. °samekkhase = olokesi C.). — ger. **°samikkha** & **°samekkha** [B.Sk. °samikṣya, e.g. Jtm. p. 28, 30 etc.] J V.340 (°samikkha, v. l. sañcikkha = passitvā C.); 393, 394 (= disvā C.).

Abhisameta [pp. of abhisameti, fr. abhi + sam + **i**, taken as caus. formation, against the regular form Sk.P. samita & B.Sk. abhisamita] completely grasped or realised, understood, mastered S V.128 (dhamma a.), 440 (anabhisametāni cattāri ariyasaccāni, cp. Divy 654 anabhisamitāni c.a.); A IV.384 (appattaŋ asacchikataŋ +).

Abhisametāvin (adj.) [possess. adj. -formation, equalling a n. ag. form., pp. abhisameta] commanding full understanding or penetration, posessing complete insight (of the truth) Vin III.189; S II.133; V.458 sq.

Abhisameti [abhi + sameti, sam + **i**; in inflexion base is taken partly as ordinary & partly as causative, e. g. aor. °samiŋsu & °samesuŋ, pp. sameta: Sk. samita. Cp. B.Sk. abhisamayati, either caus. or denom. formation, Divy 617: caturāryasatyāni a.] to come by, to attain, to realise, grasp, understand (cp. adhigacchati) Miln 214 (catusaccâbhisamayaŋ abhisameti). Freq. in comb^n. **abhisambujjhati, abhisameti**; **abhisambujjhitvā abhisametvā**, e. g. S II.25; III.139; Kvu 321. — fut. **°samessati** S V.441. — aor. **°samiŋsu** Miln 350; **°samesuŋ** S V.415. — ger. **°samecca** (for °icca under influence of °sametvā as caus. form.; Trenckner's expl^n. *Notes* 56^4 is unnecessary & hardly justifiable) S V.438 (an° by not thoroughly understanding); A V.50 (samm'attha° through complete realisation of what is proficient); Sn 143 (= abhisamāgantvā KhA 236); and **°sametvā** S II.25; III.139. — pp. **abhisameta** (q.v.).

Abhisampanna at PvA 144 is wrong reading for v. l. abhisapana (curse).

Abhisamparāya [abhi + samparāya] future lot, fate, state after death, future condition of rebirth; usually in foll. phrases: **kā gati ko abhisamparāyo** (as hendiadys) 'what fate in the world-to-come', D II.91; Vin I.293; S IV.59, 63; V.346, 356, 369; DhA I.221. — **evaŋ-gatika evanabhisamparāya** (adj.) "leading to such & such a rebirth, such & such a future state" D I.16, 24, 32, 33 etc. (= evaŋ-vidhā paralokā ti DA I.108). **-abhisamparāyaŋ** (acc. as adv.) in future, after death A I.48; II.197; III.347; IV.104; Pv III.5^10 (= punabbhave PvA 200). — **diṭṭhe c'eva dhamme abhisamparāyañ ca** "in this world and in the world to come" A II.61; Pug 38; Miln 162; PvA 195 etc. (see also diṭṭha). — Used absolutely at PvA 122 (= fate).

Abhisambujjhati [abhi + sambujjhati] to become wide-awake, to awake to the highest knowledge, to gain the highest wisdom (sammāsambodhiŋ) D III.135; It 121. aor. **°sambujjhi** S V.433; PvA 19. In comb^n. **abhisambujjhati abhisameti**, e. g. S. II.25; III.139. — ppr. med. **°sambudhāna**; pp. **°sambuddha** — Caus. **°sambodheti** to make awake, to awaken, to enlighten; pp. **°bodhita.**

Abhisambujjhana (nt.) = abhisambodhi J I.59.

Abhisambuddha [pp. of abhisambujjhati] (a) (pass.) realised, perfectly understood D III.273; S IV.331; It 121. an° not understood M I.71, 92, 114, 163, 240. — (l.) (med.) one who has come to the realisation of the highest wisdom, fully-awakened, attained Buddhahood, realising, enlightened (in or as to = acc.) Vin I.1; D II.4; M I.6 (sammāsambodhiŋ); S I 68, 138, 139 & passim PvA 94, 99.

Abhisambuddhatta (nt.) [abstr. fr. abhisambuddha] thorough realisation, perfect understanding S V.433.

Abhisambudhāna (adj.) [formation of a ppr. med. fr. pp. abhsam + **budh** instead of abhisam + **bujjh°**] awaking, realising, knowing, understanding Dh 46 (= bujjhanto jānanto ti attho DhA I.337).

Abhisambodhi (f.) [abhi + sambodhi] the highest enlightenment J I.14 (parama°). Cp. abhisambujjhana and (sammā-) sambodhi.

Abhisambodhita (adj.) [pp. of abhisambodheti, Caus. of abhi + sambujjhati] awakened to the highest wisdom PvA 137 (Bhagavā).

Abhisambhava [fr. abhisambhavati] only in **dur°** hard to overcome or get over, hard to obtain or reach, troublesome S V.454; A V.202; Sn 429, 701; J V.269, VI.139, 439.

Abhisambhavati (°bhoti) [abhi + sambhavati] "to come up to", i. e. to be able to (get or stand or overcome); to attain, reach, to bear A IV.241; Th 1, 436; Nd^1 471,

485; J III.140; V.150, 417; VI.292, 293, 507 (fut. med. °sambhossaŋ = sahissāmi adhivāsessāmi C.); Ps II.193. — ger. °bhutvā Th 1, 1057 & °bhavitvā Sn 52 (cp. Nd² 85). — aor. °bhosi D II.232. — grd. °bhavanīya D II.210; Ps II.193. — See also **abhisambhuṇāti**.

Abhisambhuṇāti [considered to be a bastard form of abhisambhavati, but probably of diff. origin & etym.; also in Bh. Sk. freq.] to be able (to get or reach); only in neg. ppr. **anabhisambhuṇanto** unable D I.101 (= asampāpuṇanto avisahamāno vā DA I.268); Nd¹ 77, 312.

Abhsambhū (adj.) [fr. abhi + sam + **bhū**] getting, attaining (?) D II.255 (lomahaŋsa°).

Abhisambhūta [pp. of abhisambhavati] attained, got Sdhp 556.

Abhisammati [abhi + **śam**, Sk. abhiśamyati] to cease, stop; trs. (Caus.) to allay, pacify, still J VI.420 (pp. abhisammanto for °sammento? Reading uncertain).

Abhisara [fr. abhi + sarati, of **sṛ** to go] retinue J V.373.

Abhisallekhika (adj.) [abhi + sallekha + ika] austere, stern, only in f. °ā (scil. kathā) A III.117 sq.; IV.352, 357; V.67.

Abhisavati (better °ssavati?) [abhi + savati, of **sru**] to flow towards or into J VI.359 (najjo Gangaŋ a.).

Abhisasi aor. of **abhisaŋsati** (q. v.).

Abhisādheti [abhi + sādheti] to carry out, arrange; to get; procure, attain J VI.180; Miln 264.

Abhisāpa [abhisapati] a curse, anathema S III.93 = It 89 (which letter reads abhilāpa and It A expl^s. by akkosa: see vv. ll. under abhilāpa & cp. *Brethren* 376 n. 1.); Th 1, 118.

Abhisāriyā (f.) [Sk. abhisārikā, fr. abhi + **sṛ**] a woman who goes to meet her lover J III.139.

Abhisāreti [abhi + sāreti, Caus. of abhisarati] to approach, to persecute J VI.377.

Abhisiŋsati [= abhisaŋsati, abhi + **śaŋs**. As to Sk. **śaŋs** > P. **siŋs** cp. āsiŋsati, as to meaning cp. nature of prayer as a solemn rite to the "infernals", cp. im-precare], to utter a solemn wish, Vv 81^18 (aor. °sīsi. v. l. °sisi. VvA 316 expl^s. by icchi sampaticchi).

Abhisiñcati [abhi + siñcati fr. **sic** to sprinkle; see also āsiñcati & ava°, Vedic only ā°] to sprinkle over, fig. to anoint (King), to consecrate A I.107 (Khattiy' âbhisekena) J I.399 (fig. °itvā ger. II.409 (id.); VI.161 (id.); Nd¹ 298; Miln 336 (amatena lokaŋ abhisiñci Bhagavā); PvA 144 (read abhisiñci cimillik añ ca . . .) — Pass. abhisiñcati Miln 359. — pp. **abhisitta**. — Caus. **abhiseceti**.

Abhisitta [pp. of abhisañcati, Sk. °sikta] 1. sprinkled over, anointed Sn 889 (manasā, cp. N¹ 298); Miln 336 (amatena loka a). — 2. consecrated (King), inaugurated (more freq. in this conn. is avasitta), Vin III.44; A I.107 (Khattiyo Khattiyehi Khattiy' âbhisekena a.); II.87 (v.l. for avasitta, also an°).

Abhiseka [fr. abhi + **sic**, cp. Sk. abhiṣeka] anointing, consecration, inauguration (as king) A I.107 (cp. abhisitta); II.87 read abhisek' -anabhisitto; J II.104, 352; DhA I.350; PvA 74. Gr. ābhisekika.

Abhisecana (nt.) = abhiseka, viz. (a) ablution, washing off Th 2, 239 & 245 (udaka°). — (b) consecration J II.353.

Abhiseceti [caus. of abhisiñcati] to cause to be sprinkled or inaugurated J V.26. (imper. abhisecayassu).

Abhisevanā (f.) [abhi + sevana fr. **sev**] pursuit, indulgence in (—°) Sdhp 210 (pāpakamma°).

Abhissara (adj.) [abhi + issara] only neg. an° in formula atāṇo loko anabhissaro "without a Lord or protector" M II.68 (v.l. °abhisaro); Ps I.126 (v.l. id.).

Abhihansati [abhi + haŋsati fr. **hṛṣ**] 1. (trs.) to gladden, please, satisfy S IV.190 (abhihaṭṭhuŋ); A V.350 (id.). — 2. (intr.) to find delight in (c. acc.), to enjoy S V.74 (rūpaŋ manāpaŋ); A IV.419 sq. (T. reads °hiŋsamāna jhānaŋ v.l. °hisamāna).

Abhihaṭa [pp. of abhiharati] brought, offered, presented, fetched D I.166 = Pug 55 (= puretaraŋ gahetvā āhatan bhikkhaŋ Pug A 231); DhA II.79.

Abhihaṭṭhuŋ [ger. of abhiharati]. Only in praise abhihaṭṭhuŋ pavāreti, to offer having fetched up. M. I.224; A V.350, 352; S IV.190; V.53, 300. See note in *Vinaya Texts* II.440.

Abhihata [pp. of abhihanati] hit, struck PvA 55.

Abhihanati (& °hanti) [abhi + **han**] 1. to strike, hit PvA 258. — 2. to overpower kill. destroy J V.174 (inf. °hantu for T. hantuŋ). — pp. **abhihata** (q. v.).

Abhiharati [abhi + harati, cp. Sk. abhyāharati & Vedic āharati & ābharati] — 1. to bring (to), to offer, fetch D III.170; J I.54, 157; III.537; IV.421; Dh I.272. — 2. to curse, revile, abuse [cp. Sk. anuvyāharati & abhivyā°] A I.198. — Pass. **abhihariyati** VvA 172 (for abhiharati of Vv 37^10; corresp. with ābhata VvA 172). — pp. **abhihaṭa** (q.v.). — Caus. **abhihāreti** 1. to cause to be brought, to gain, to acquire D II.188 = 192 = 195 Th 1, 637; J IV.421 (abhihārayaŋ with gloss abhibhārayin). — 2. to betake oneself to, to visit, take to, go to Sn 414 (Paṇḍavaŋ °hāresi = āruhi Sn A 383), 708 (vanantaŋ abhihāraye = vanaŋ gaccheyya SnA 495); Th 2, 146 (aor. °hārayiŋ; uyyānaŋ = upanesi ThA 138). — 3. to put on (mail), only in fut. **abhihessati** J IV.92 (kavacaŋ; C. expl^s. wrongly by °hanissati bhindissati so evidently taking it as abhibhavissati). — 4. At J VI.27 kiŋ yobbanena ciṇṇena yaŋ jarā **abhihessati** the latter is fut of **abhibhavati** (for °bhavissati) as indicated by gloss **abhibhuyyati**.

Abhihāra [fr. abhiharati] bringing, offering, gift S I.82; Sn 710; J I.81 (āsanā).

Abhihiŋsati spurious reading at A IV.419 for °**haŋsati** (q.v.).

Abhihiŋsanā (& °ŋ) [for abhihesanā cp. P. hesā = Sk. hreṣā, & hesitaŋ] neighing Vv 64^10 = VvA 279 (gloss abhihesana). See in detail under **abhisaŋsanā**.

Abhihita S I.50. Read abhigīta with SS. So also for abhihita on p. 51. 'So enchanted was I by the Buddha's rune'. The godlet abscribes a magic potency to the couplet.

Abhihesana see **abhihiŋsanā**.

Abhihessati see **abhihāreti** 3 & 4.

Abhīta (adj.) [a + bhīta] fearless J VI.193. See also **abhida** 1.

Abhīruka (adj.) [a + bhīru + ka] fearless DA I.250.

Abhumma (adj.) [a + bhumma] groundless, unfounded, unsubstantial, J V.178; VI.495.

Abhūta (adj.) [a + bhūta] not real, false, not true, usually as nt. °ŋ falsehood, lie, deceit Sn 387; It 37; instr. **abhūtena** falsely D I.161.

-**vādin** one who speaks falsely or tells lies Sn 661 = Dh 306 = It 42; expl^d. as "ariy' ûpavāda-vasena alika -vādin" SnA 478; as "tucchena paraŋ abhācikkhanto" DhA III.477.

Abhejja (adj.) [grd. of a + **bhid**, cp. Sk. abhedya] not to be split or divided, not to be drawn away or caused to be dissented, inalienable Sn 255 (mitto abhejjo parehi); J I.263 (varasūra . . .) III.318 (°rūpa of strong character =

abhijja-hadaya); Pug 30 (= acchejja Pug A 212); Miln 160 (°parisā); Sdhp 312 (+ appadusiya); Pgdp 97 (°parivāra).

Amacca [Vedic amātya (only in meaning "companion"), adj. formation fr. amā, an adverbial loc.-gen. of pron. 1st person, Sk. ahaŋ = Idg. *emo (cp. Sk. m-ama), meaning "(those) of me or with me", i. e. those who are in my house] 1. friend, companion, fellow-worker, helper, esp. one who gives his advice, a bosom-friend It 73; J VI. 512 (sahajātā amaccā); Pv II.6^{20} (a °— paricārikā well-advising friends as company or around him). Freq. in comb$^{n.}$ with mitta as **mitt' âmaccā**, friends & colleagues D III.189—90; S 1 90 = A II.67; PvA 29; or with **ñāti** (ñāti-sālohitā intimate friends & near-relations), mittâmaccā ñātisālohitā Vin II.126; Sn p. 104 (= mittā ca kammakarā ca SnA 447); mittā vā amaccā vā ñāti vā sālohitā vā A I.222; PvA 28; amaccā ñāti-sanghā ca A I.152. — 2. Especially a king's intimate friend, king's favourite, confidant J I.262; PvA 73 (°kula), 74 (amaccā ca purohito ca), 81 (sabba-kammika amacca), 93; and his special adviser or privy councillor, as such distinguished from the official ministers (purohita, mahāmatta, pārisajja); usually comb$^{d.}$ with **pārisajjā** (pl.) viz. D I.136 (= piya-sahāyaka DA I.297, but cp. the foll. expl$^{n.}$ of pārisajjā as "sesā āṇatti-karā"); Vin I.348; D III.64 (amaccā pārisajjā gaṇaka-mahāmattā); A I.142 (catunnaŋ mahārājānaŋ a. pārisajjā). See on the question of ministers in general Fick, *Sociale Gliederung* p. 93, 164 & Banerjea, *Public Administration in Ancient India* pp. 106—120.

Amajja [etym.?] a bud J V.416 (= makula C.).

Amajjapāyaka [a + majja + pāyaka, cp. Sk. amadyapa] one who abstains from intoxicants, a teetotaler J II.192.

Amata^{1} (nt.) [a + mata = mṛta pp. of **mṛ**, Vedic amṛta = Gr. ἀ-μ(β)ροτ-ο & ἀμβροσία = Lat. im-mort-a(lis] 1. The drink of the gods, ambrosia, water of immortality, (cp. BSk. amṛta-varṣa "rain of Ambrosia" Jtm 221). — 2. A general conception of a state of durability & non-change, a state of security i. e. where there is not any more rebirth or re-death. So Bdhgh at KhA 180 (on Sn 225) "na jāyati na jīyati na mīyati ti amatan ti vuccati", or at DhA I.228 "ajātattā na jiyyati na miyyati tasmā amatan ti vuccati". — Vin I.7 = M I.169 (apārutā tesaŋ amatassa dvārā); Vin I.39; D II.39, 217, 241; S I.32 (= rāgado-samoha-khayo), 193; III.2 (°ena abhisitta "sprinkled with A."); IV.94 (°assa dātā), 370; V.402 (°assa patti); A I.45 sq.; III.451; IV.455; V.226 sq., 256 sq. (°assa dātā); J I.4 (V.25); IV.378, 386; V.456 (°mahā-nibbāna); Sn 204, 225, 228 (= nibbāna KhA 185); Th 1, 310 (= agada antidote); It 46 = 62 (as dhātu), 80 (°assa dvāra); Dh 114, 374 (= amata-mahā-nibbāna DhA IV.110); Miln 258 (°dhura savanûpaga), 319 (agado amataŋ & nibbānaŋ âmataŋ), 336 (amatena lokaŋ abhisiñci Bhagavā), 346 (dhamm' âmataŋ); DA I.217 (°nibbāna); DhA I.87 (°ŋ pāyeti); Dāvs II.34; V.31; Sdhp 1, 209, 530, 571.
-ogadha diving into the ambrosia (of Nibbāna) S V. 41, 54, 181, 220, 232; A III.79, 304; IV.46 sq., 317, 387; V.105 sq.; Sn 635; Th 1, 179, 748; Dh 411 (= amataŋ nibbānaŋ ogahetvā DhA IV.186); Vv 50^{20}. **-osadha** the medicine of Ambrosia, ambrosial medicine Miln 247. **-gāmin** going or leading to the ambrosia (of Nibbāna) S I.123; IV.370; V.8; A III.329; Th 2, 222. **-dasa** one who sees Amata or Nibbāna Th 1, 336. **-dundubhi** the drum of the Immortal (Nibbāna) M I.171 = Vin I.8 (has °dudrabhi). **-dvāra** the door to Nibbāna M I.353; S I. 137 = Vin I.5; S II.43, 45, 58, 80; A V.346. **-dhātu** the element of Ambrosia or Nibbāna A III.356. **-patta** having attained to Ambrosia A IV.455. **-pada** the region or place of Ambrosia S I.212 ("Bourne Ambrosial" *trsl$^{n.}$* p. 274); II.280; Dh 21 (= amatassa adhigama-upāyo vuttaŋ hoti DhA I.228). **-phala** ambrosial fruit S I.173 = Sn 80. **-magga** the path to Ambrosia DhA I.94.

Amata^{2} (adj.) [see amata^{1}] belonging to Amṛta = ambrosial Sn 452 = S I.189 (amatā vācā = amata-sadisā sādubhāvena SnA 399: "ambrosial"), 960 (gacchati amataŋ disaŋ = nibbānaŋ, taŋ hi amatan ti tathā niddisitabbato disā cā ti SnA 572). Perhaps also at It 46 = 62 (amataŋ dhātuŋ = ambrosial state or Amṛta as dhātu).

Amatabbāka (?) at VvA 111, acc. to Hardy (Index) "a precious stone of dark blue colour".

Amattaññū (adj.) [a + matta + °ñu = Sk. amātrajña] not knowing any bounds (in the taking of food), intemperate, immoderate It 23 (bhojanamhi); Dh 7 (id.); Pug 21.

Amattaññutā (f.) [abstr. to prec.] immoderation (in food) D III.213; It 23 (bhojane); Pug 21; Dhs 1346 (bhojane); DhsA 402.

Amatteyyatā (f.) [from matteyyatā] irreverence towards one's mother D III.70, 71.

Amanussa [a + manussa] a being which is not human, a fairy demon, ghost, god, spirit, yakkha Vin I.277; D I. 116; S I.91, J I.99; Dhs 617; Miln 207; DhsA 319; DhA I.13 (°pariggahīta haunted); PvA 216. — Cp. amānusa.

Amanussika (adj.) [fr. amanussa] belonging to or caused by a spirit Vin I.202, 203 (°âbādha being possessed by a demon).

Amama (adj.) [a + mama, gen. of ahaŋ, pron. 1st person, lit. "not (saying: this is) of me"] not egotistical, unselfish Sn 220 (+ subbata), 777; J IV.372 (+ nirāsaya); VI.259 (= mamāyana-taṇhā-rahita C.); Pv IV.1^{34} (= mamaŋkāra-virahita PvA 230); Mhvs 1, 66, comb$^{d.}$ with **nirāsa** (free from longing), at Sn 469 = 494; Ud 32; J IV.303; VI.259.

Amara (adj.) [a + mara from **mṛ**] not mortal, not subject to death Th 1, 276; Sn 249 (= amara-bhāva-patthanatāya pavatta-kāya-kilesa SnA 291); J V.80 (= amaraṇa-sabhāva), 218; Dāvs V.62.

Amaratta (nt.) [abstr. fr. amara] immortality J V.223 (= devatta C.).

Amarā (?) a kind of slippery fish, an eel (?) Only in expression **amarā-vikkhepika** eel-wobbler, one who practices eel-wriggling, fr. °vikkhepa "oscillation like the a. fish". In English idiom "a man who sits on the fence" D I.24; M I.521; Ps I.155. The expl$^{n.}$ given by Bdhgh at DA I.115 is "amarā nāma maccha-jāti, sā ummujjana-nimmujjan ādi vasena . . gahetuŋ na sakkoti" etc. This meaning is not beyond doubt, but Kern's expl^{n} *Toev.* 71 does not help to clear it up.

Amala (adj.) [a + mala] without stain or fault J V.4; Sdhp 246, 591, 596.

Amassuka (adj.) [a + massu + ka] beardless J II.175.

Amājāta (adj.) [amā + jāta; amā adv. "at home", Vedic amā, see under amacca] born in the house, of a slave J I.226 (dāsa, so read for āmajāta, an old mistake, expl$^{d.}$ by C. forcibly as "āma ahaŋ vo dāsī ti"!). See also āmāya.

Amātika (adj.) [a + mātika from mātā] without a mother, motherless J V.251.

Amānusa (adj.) [Vedic amānuṣa, usually of demons, but also of gods; a + mānusa, cp. amanussa] non- or super-human, unhuman, demonic, peculiar to a non-human (Peta or Yakkha) Pv II.12^{20} (kāma); IV.1^{87} (as n.); IV.3^{6} (gandha, of Petas). — f. °ī Dh 373 (rati = dibbā rati DhA IV.110); Pv III.7^{9} (ratti, love).

Amāmaka (adj.) [a + mama + ka, cp. amama] "not of me" i. e. not belonging to my party, not siding with me DhA I.66.

Amāya (adj.) [a + māyā] not deceiving, open, honest Sn 941 (see Nd^{1} 422: māyā vuccati vañcanikā cariyā). Cp. next.

Amāyāvin (adj.) [a + māyāvin, cp. amāya] without guile, not deceiving, honest D III.47 (asaṭha +), 55 (id.), 237; DhA I.69 (asaṭhena a.).

Amitābha (adj.) [a + mita (pp. of **mā**) + ā + **bhā**] of boundless or immeasurable splendour Sdhp 255.

Amitta [Vedic amitra; a + mitta] one who is not friend, an enemy D III.185; It 83; Sn 561 (= paccatthika SnA 455); Dh 66, 207; J VI.274 (°tāpana harassing the enemies).

Amilātatā (f.) [a + milāta + tā] the condition of not being withered J V.156.

Amu° base of demonstr. pron. "that", see **asu.**

Amucchita (adj.) [a + mucchita] not infatuated (lit. not stupified or bewildered), not greedy; only in phrase agathita amucchita anajjhāpanna (or anajjhopanna) D III.46; M I.369; S II.194. See ajjhopanna.

Amutta (adj.) [a + mutta] not released, not free from (c. abl.) It 93 (mārabandhanā).

Amutra (adv.) [pron. base amu + tra] in that place, there; in another state of existence D I.4, 14, 184; It 99.

Amūḷha-vinaya "acquittal on the ground of restored sanity" (Childers) Vin I.325 (IX.6, 2); II.81 (IV.5), 99 (IV.14, 27); IV.207, 351; M II.248.

Amoha (adj.) [a + moha, cp. Sk. amogha] not dull. As n. absence of stupidity or delusion D III.214; Pug 25. — The form **amogha** occurs at J VI.26 in the meaning of "efficacious, auspicious" (said of ratyā nights).

Amba [Derivation unknown. Not found in pre-Buddhist literature. The Sk. is āmra. Probably non-Aryan], the Mango tree, Mangifera Indica D I.46, 53, 235; J II.105, 160; Vv 79[10]; Pug 45; Miln 46; PvA 153, 187.
-aṭṭhi the kernel or stone of the m. fruit DhA III.207, 208. **-ārāma** a garden of mangoes, mango grove Vv 79[5]; VvA 305. **-kañjika** mango gruel Vv 33[31] (= ambilakañjika VvA 147). **-pakka** a (ripe) mango fruit J II.104, 394; DhA III.207. **-panta** a border of mango trees VvA 198. **-pānaka** a drink made from mangoes DhA III.207. **-piṇḍi** a bunch of mangoes J III.53; DhA III.207. **-pesikā** the peel, rind, of the m. fruit Vin II.109. **-potaka** a mango sprout DhA III.206 sq. **-phala** a m. fruit PvA 273, 274. **-rukkha** a m. tree DhA III.207; VvA 198. **-vana** a m. grove or wood D II.126; J I.139; VvA 305. **-siñcaka** one who waters the mangoes, a tender or keeper of mangoes Vv 79[1].

Ambaka[1] (adj.) [= ambakā?] "womanish" (?), inferior, silly, stupid, of narrow intellect. Occurs only with reference to a woman, in combn. with bālā A III.349 (v. l. amma°) = V.139 (where spelt **ambhaka** with v. l. appaka° and gloss andhaka); V.150 (spelt **ambbaka** perhaps in diff. meaning).
-maddarī see next.

Ambaka[2] [demin. of amba] a little mango, only in °maddarī a kind of bird [etym. uncertain] A I.188.

Ambakā (f.) [Sk. ambikā demin. of ambī mother, wife, see P. amma & cp. also Sk. ambālikā f.] mother, good wife, used as a general endearing term for a woman Vin I.232 = D II.97 (here in play of words with Ambapālī expld. by Bdhgh at Vin I.385 as ambakā ti itthiyikā).

Ambara[1] (nt.) [Vedic ambara circumference, horizon] the sky, Dāvs I.38; IV.51; V.32. — *Note.* At J V.390 we have to read muraja-ālambara, and not mura-jāla-ambara.

Ambara[2] (m.-nt.) [etym. = ambara[1] (?) or more likely a distortion of kambala; for the latter speaks the combn. rattambara = ratta-kambala. — The word would thus be due to an erroneous syllable division rattak-ambala (= ambara) instead of ratta-kambala] some sort of cloth and an (upper) garment made of it (cp. kambala) Vv 53[1] (ratt° = uttariya VvA 236).

Ambala at J II.246 (°koṭṭhaka-āsana-sālā) for ambara[1](?) or for ambaka[2] (?), or should we read kambala° ?.

Ambāṭaka the hog-plum, Spondias Mangifera (a kind of mango) Vin II.17 (°vana); DA I.271 (°rukkha).

Ambila (adj.) [Sk. ambla = Lat. amarus] sour, acid; one of the 6 rasas or tastes, viz. a., lavaṇa, tittaka, kaṭuka, kasāya, madhura (see under rasa): thus at Miln 56. Another enumeration at Nd[2] 540 & Dhs 629. — J I.242 (°anambila), 505 (loṇ°); II.394 (loṇ°); DA I.270 (°yāgu sour gruel); DhA II.85 (ati-ambila, with accuṇha & atisīta).

Ambu (nt.) [Vedic ambu & ambhas = Gr. ὄμβρος, Lat. imber rain; cp. also Sk. abhra rain-cloud & Gr. ἀφρός scum: see P. abbha] water J V.6; Nd[1] 202 (a. vuccati udakaŋ); Dāvs II.16. — Cp. **ambha.**
-cārin "living in the water", a fish Sn 62 (= maccha Nd[2] 91). **-sevāla** a water-plant Th I, 113.

Ambuja (m. & nt.) [ambu + ja of **jan**] "water-born", i. e. 1. (m.) a fish S I.52. — 2. (nt.) a lotus Sn 845 (= paduma Nd[1] 202); Dāvs V.46; Sdhp 360.

Ambuda [ambu + da fr. **dā**] "water-giver", a cloud Dāvs V.32; Sdhp 270, 275.

Ambha & **Ambho** (nt.) [see ambu] water, sea Dāvs IV.54.

Ambhaka see **ambaka.**

Ambho (indecl.) [fr. haŋ + bho, see bho, orig. "hallo you there"] part. of exclamation, employed: 1. to draw attention = look here, hey! hallo! Vin III.73 (= ālapan' âdhivacana); J II.3; PvA 62. — 2. to mark reproach & anger = you silly, you rascal D I.194; It 114; J I.174 (v. l. amho), 254; Miln 48.

Amma (indecl.) [voc. of ammā] endearing term, used (1) by children in addressing their mother = mammy, mother dear D I.93; J II.133; IV.1, 281 (amma tāta uṭṭhetha daddy mammy, get up!); DhA II.87; PvA 73, 74. — (2) in general when addressing a woman familiarly = good woman, my (good) lady, dear, thus to a woman J I.292; PvA 63; DhA II.44; to a girl PvA 6; to a daughter DhA II.48; III.172. — Cp. **ambakā.**

Ammaṇa (nt.) [of uncertain etym.; Sk. armaṇa is Sanskritised Pāli. See on form & meaning Childers s. v. and Kern, *Toev.* p. 72] 1. a trough J V.297; VI.381 (bhatt°). — 2. a certain measure of capacity J I.62; II.436 (taṇḍul°). — As °ka at J II.117 (v. l. ampaṇaka); DA I.84.

Ammā (f.) [onomat. from child language; Sk. ambā, cp. Gr. ἀμμάς mother, Oisl. amma "granny", Ohg. amma "mammy", nurse; also Lat. amita father's sister & amāre to love] mother J III.392 (gen. ammāya). — Voc. amma (see sep.).

Amha & **Amhan** (nt.) [Sk. aśman, see also asama?] a stone Sn 443 (instr. amhanā, but SnA 392 reads asmanā = pāsāṇena).
-maya made of stone, hard Dh 161 (= pāsāṇa° DhA III.151).

Amha, Amhi see **atthi.**

Amhā (f.) [etym. uncertain; Morris *J P T S.* 1889, 201 too vague] a cow (?) A I.229. The C. says nothing.

Amhākaŋ, Amhe see **ahaŋ.**

Amho = ambho J I.174 (v. l.).

Aya[1] see **ayo.**

Aya[2] (fr. **i**, go) 1. income, in **aya-potthaka** receipt book J I.2. — 2. inlet (for water, **aya-mukha**) D I.74; A II. 166, IV.287.

Ayaŋ (pron.) [Sk. ayaŋ etc., pron. base Idg. *i (cp. Sk. iba), f. *ī. Cp. Gr. ἰν, μιν; Lat. is (f. ea, nt. id); Goth is, nt. ita; Ohg. er (= he), nt. ez (= it); Lith. jis (he), f. ji (she).] demonstr. pron. "this, he"; f. ayaŋ; nt. idaŋ & imaŋ "this, it" etc. This pron. combines in its inflection two stems, viz. **as°** (ayaŋ in nom. m. & f.) & **im°** (id° in nom. nt.).

I. Forms. A. (*sg.*) *nom.* m. ayaŋ Sn 235; J I.168. 279; f. ayaŋ [Sk. iyaŋ] Kh VII.12; J II.128, 133; nt. idaŋ Sn 224; J III.53; & imaŋ Miln 46. *acc.* m. imaŋ J II.160; f. imaŋ [Sk. imāŋ] Sn 545, 1002; J I.280. *gen. dat.* m. imassa J I.222, 279 & assa Sn 234, 1100; Kh VII.12 (dat.); J II.158; f. imissā J I.179 & assā [Sk. asyāḥ] J I.290; DhA III.172. *instr.* m. nt. iminā J I.279; PvA 80 & (peculiarly or perhaps for amunā) aminā Sn 137; f. imāya [Sk. anayā] J I.267. The instr. anena [Sk. anena] is not proved in Pāli. *abl.* asmā Sn 185; Dh 220; & imasmā (not proved). *loc.* m. nt. imasmiŋ Kh III.; J II. 159 & asmiŋ Sn 634; Dh 242; f. imissā PvA 79 (or imissaŋ?) & imāyaŋ (no ref.). — B. (*pl.*) *nom.* m. ime J I.221; Pv I.8[3]; f. imā [Sk. imāḥ] Sn 897 & imāyo Sn 1122; nt. imāni [= Sk.] Vin I.84. *acc.* m. ime [Sk. imān] J I.266; II.416; f. imā [Sk. imāḥ] Sn 429; J II.160. *gen.* imesaŋ J II.160 & esaŋ [Sk. eṣāŋ] M II.86, & esānaŋ M II.154; III.259; f. also āsaŋ J I.302 (= etāsaŋ C.) & imāsaŋ. *instr.* m. nt imehi J VI.364; f. imāhi. *loc.* m. nt. imesu [Sk. eṣu] J I.307.

II. *Meanings* (1) ayaŋ refers to *what is immediately in front* of the speaker (the subject in question) or before his eyes or in his present time & situation, thus often to be trsld. by "before our eyes", "the present", "this here", "just this" (& not the other) (opp. para), viz. atthi imasmiŋ kāye "in this our visible body" Kh III.; yath' âyaŋ padīpo "like this lamp here" Sn 235; ayaŋ dakkhiṇā dinnā "the gift which is just given before our eyes" Kh VII.12; ime pādā imaŋ sīsaŋ ayaŋ kāyo Pv I.8[3]; asmiŋ loke paramhi ca "in this world & the other" Sn 634, asmā lokā paraŋ lokaŋ kathaŋ pecca na socati Sn 185; cp. also Dh 220, 410; J I.168; III.53. — (2) It refers to *what immediately precedes* the present of the speaker, or to what has just been mentioned in the sentence; viz. yaŋ kiñci vittaŋ . . . idam pi Buddhe ratanaŋ "whatever . . . that" Sn 224; ime divase these days (just gone) J II.416; cp. also Vin I.84; Sn 429; J II.128, 160. — (3) It refers to *what immediately follows* either in time or in thought or in connection: dve ime antā "these are the two extremes, viz." Vin I.10; ayaŋ eva ariyo maggo "this then is the way" ibid.; cp. J I.280. — (4) With a touch of (often sarcastic) characterisation it establishes a *closer personal relation* between the speaker & the object in question & is to be trsld. by "like that, such (like), that there, yonder, yon", e. g. imassa vānarindassa "of that fellow, the monkey" J I.279; cp J I. 222, 307; II 160 (imesaŋ sattānaŋ "creatures like us"). So also repeated as ayañ ca ayañ ca "this and this", "so and so" J II.3; idañ c' idañ ca "such & such a thing" J II.5. — (5) In combn with a pron. rel. it expresses either a *generalisation* (whoever, whatever) or a *specialisation* (= that is to say, what there is of, i. e. Ger. und zwar), e. g. yâyaŋ taṇhā Vin I.10; yo ca ayaŋ . . . yo ca ayaŋ "I mean this . . . and I mean" ibid.; ye kec' ime Sn 381; yadidaŋ "i. e." Miln 25; yatha-y-idaŋ "in order that" (w. pot.) Sn 1092. See also seyyathīdaŋ. — (6) The gen. of all genders functions in general as a *possessive pron.* of the 3rd = his, her, its (lit. of him etc.) and thus resembles the use of tassa, e. g. āsava' ssa na vijjanti "his are no intoxications" Sn 1100; sīlaŋ assā bhindāpessāmi "I shall cause her character to be defamed" J I.290; assa bhariyā "his wife" J II.158 etc. freq.

Ayana (nt.) [Vedic ayana, fr. **i**] (a) "going", road. — (b) going to, goal S V.167 (ekāyano maggo leading to one goal, a direct way), 185 (id.); DA I.313; Dāvs IV.40. — See also eka°.

Ayasa (nt.) [a + yasa, cp. Sk. ayaśaḥ] ill repute, disgrace Miln 139, 272; Dāvs I.8.

Ayira (& **Ayyira**) (n.-adj.) [Vedic ārya, Metathesis for ariya as diaeretic form of ārya, of which the contracted (assimilation) form is ayya. See also ariya] (n.) ariyan, nobleman, gentleman (opp. servant); (adj.) arīyan, wellborn, belonging to the ruling race, noble, aristocratic, gentlemanly J V.257; Vv 39[6]. — f. **ayirā** lady, mistress (of a servant) J II.349 (v. l. oyyakā); voc. ayire my lady J V.138 (= ayye C.).

Ayiraka = ayira; cp. ariyaka & ayyaka; D III.190 (v. l. BB yy); J II.313.

Ayo & **Aya** (nt.) [Sk. ayaḥ nt. iron & ore, Idg. *ajes-, cp. Av. ayah, Lat. aes, Goth. aiz, Ohg. ēr (= Ger. Erz.), Ags. ār (= E. ore).] iron. The *nom.* **ayo** found only in set of 5 metals forming an alloy of gold (jātarūpa), viz. **ayo**, **loha** (copper), **tipu** (tin), **sīsa** (lead), **sajjha** (silver) A III.16 = S V.92; of obl. cases only the *instr.* **ayasā** occurs Dh 240 (= ayato DhA III.344); Pv I.10[13] (paṭikujjita, of Niraya). — Iron is the material used κατ' ἐξοχήν in the outfit & construction of Purgatory or Niraya (see niraya & Avīci & cp. Vism 56 sq.). — In compn. both **ayo°** & **aya°** occur as bases.

I. **ayo°**: -**kapāla** an iron pot A IV.70 (v. l. °guhala); Nd[2] 304 III. D 2 (of Niraya). -**kūṭa** an iron hammer PvA 284. -**khīla** an iron stake S V.444; M III.183 = Nd[2] 304 III. C; SnA 479. -**guḷa** an iron ball S V.283; Dh 308; It 43 = 90; Th 2, 489; DA I.84. -**ghana** an iron club Ud 93; VvA 20. -**ghara** an iron house J IV.492. -**paṭala** an iron roof or ceiling (of Niraya) PvA 52. -**pākāra** an iron fence Pv I.10[13] = Nd[2] 304 III. D I. -**maya** made of iron Sn 669 (kūṭa); J IV.492 (nāvā); Pv I.10[14] (bhūmi of N.); PvA 43, 52. -**muggara** an iron club PvA 55. -**sanku** an iron spike S IV.168; Sn 667.

II. **aya°**: -**kapāla** = ayo° DhA I.148 (v. l. ayo°). -**kāra** a worker in iron Miln 331. -**kūṭa** = ayo° J I.108; DhA II.69 (v. l.). -**nangala** an iron plough DhA I.223; III.67. -**paṭṭaka** an iron plate or sheet (cp. loha°) J V.359. -**paṭhavi** an iron floor (of Avīci) DhA I.148. -**sanghāṭaka** an iron (door) post DhA IV.104. -**sūla** an iron stake Sn 667; DhA I.148.

Ayojjha (adj.) [Sk. ayodhya] not to be conquered or subdued M II.24.

Ayya (n.-adj.) [contracted form for the diaeretic ariya (q. v. for etym.). See also ayira] (a) (n.) gentleman, sire, lord, master J III.167 = PvA 65; DhA I.8 (ayyā pl. the worthy gentlemen, the worthies), 13 (amhākaŋ ayyo our worthy Sir); II.95. — (b) (adj.) worthy, gentlemanly, honourable Vin II.191; DhA II.94 sq. — The *voc.* is used as a polite form of address (cp. Ger. "Sie" and E. address "Esq.") like E. Sir, milord or simply "you" with the implication of a pluralis majestatis; thus voc. proper **ayya** J I.221, 279, 308; pl. nom. as voc. **ayyā** in addressing several J II.128, 415; nom. sg. as voc. (for all genders & numbers) **ayyo** Vin II.215; J III.126, 127. — f. **ayyā** lady, mistress M II.96 (= mother of a prince); DhA I.398; voc. **ayye** my lady J V.138.

-**putta** lit. son of an Ariyan, i. e. an aristocratic (young) man gentleman (cp. in meaning kulaputta); thus (a) son of my master (lit.) said by a servant J III.167; (b) lord, master, "governor" J I.62 (by a servant); DA I.257 (= sāmi, opp. dāsi-putta); PvA 145 (by a wife to her husband); DhA II.110; (c) prince (see *W. Z. K. M.* XII., 1898, 75 sq. & *Epigraphia Indica* III.137 sq.) J VI.146.

Ayyaka [demin. of ayya] grandfather, (so also BSk., e. g. M Vastu II.426; III.264) J III.155; IV.146; VI.196; Pv I.8[4]; Miln 284. ayyaka-payyakā grandfather & great grandfather, forefathers, ancestors J I.2; PvA 107 (= pitāmahā). — f. **ayyakā** grandmother, granny Vin II.169; S I.97; J II.349 (here used for "lady", as v. l. BB); & **ayyikā** Th 2, 159; Vism 379.

Ara [Vedic ara fr. **ṛ**, ṛṇoti; see etym. under appeti & cp. more esp. Lat. artus limb, Gr. ἅρμα chariot, also P. aṇṇava] the spoke of a wheel D II.17 (sahass° âra adj. with thousand spokes), cp. Miln 285; J IV.209; VI.261; Miln 238; DhA II.142; VvA 106 (in allegorical etym. of arahant = saŋsāra-cakkassa arānaŋ hatattā "breaker of the spokes of the wheel of transmigration") = PvA 7 (has saŋsāra-vaṭṭassa); VvA 277.

Arakkhiya (adj.) [a + rakkhiya, grd. of rakkhati] not to be guarded, viz. (1) impossible to watch (said of women folk) J II.326 (a. nāma itthiyo); III.90 (mātugāmo nāma a.). — (2) unnecessary to be guarded Vin II.194 (Tathāgatā).

Arakkheyya (adj.) [in form = arakkhiya] only in nt. "that which does not need to be guarded against", what one does not need to heed, superfluous to beware of A IV.82 (cattāri Tathāgatassa a° āni). — 3 arakkheyyāni are enum[d.] at D III.217 (but as ārakkh°, which is also given by Childers).

Araghaṭṭa [Sk. araghaṭṭaka (so Halāyudha, see Aufrecht p. 138), dialect.] a wheel for raising water from a well Bdgh. on cakkavaṭṭaka at CV V.16, 2 (Vin II.318). So read for T. arahatta-ghaṭi-yanta acc to Morris, *J P T S.* 1885, 30; cp. also *Vin. Texts* III.112. — The 2rd part of the cpd. is doubtful; Morris & Aufrecht compare the modern Hindi form arhaṭ or rahaṭ "a well-wheel".

Araja (adj.) [a + raja] free from dust or impurity S IV.218 (of the wind); Vv 53[6] (= apagata-raja VvA 236).

Arañña (nt.) [Vedic araṇya; from araṇa, remote, + ya. In the Rig V. araṇya still means remoteness (opp. to amā, at home). In the Ath V. it has come to mean wilderness or forest. Connected with ārād and āre, remote, far from]. forest D I.71; M I.16; III.104; S I.4, 7, 29, 181, 203 (mahā); A I.60 (°vanapatthāni); II.252; III.135, 138; Sn 39, 53, 119; Dh 99, 329, 330; It 90; Vv 56[1]; Ps I.176. [The commentators, give a wider meaning to the word. Thus the O. C. (Vin III.46, quoted Vism 72 & SnA 83) says every place, except a village and the approach thereto, is arañña. See also Vin III.51; DA I.209; PvA 73; VvA 249; J I.149, 215; II.138; V.70].
-**āyatana** a forest haunt Vin II.201; S II.269; J I.173; VvA 301; PvA 54, 78, 141. -**kuṭikā** a hut in the forest, a forest lodge S I.61; III.116; IV.116, 380; DhA IV.31 (as v. l.; T. has °kuṭi). -**gata** gone into the forest (as loneliness) M I.323; A III.353; V.109 sq., 207, 323 sq. -**ṭhāna** a place in the forest J I.253. -**vāsa** a dwelling in the forest, a hermitage J I.90. -**vihāra** living in (the) loneliness (of the forest) A III.343 sq.

Araññaka (& Āraññaka) (adj.) [arañña + ka] belonging to solitude or to the forest, living in the forest, fond of solitude, living as hermits (bhikkhu) M I.214 (ā°), 469; III.89; S II.187, 202 (v. l. ā°), 208 sq.; 281; A III.343, 391; IV.291, 344, 435; V.10. See also āraññaka.

Araññakatta (nt.) [abstr. fr. araññaka] the habit of one who lives in the forest, indulgence in solitude & sequestration, a hermit's practice, seclusion S II.202, 208 sq. See also āraññakatta.

Araṇa[1] (adj.-n.) [Vedic araṇa fr. *ara $\sqrt{ṛ}$, which as abl. ārā is used as adv. far from, cp. P. ārakā. Orig. meaning "removed from, remote, far". See also arañña] I. (adj.) living in solitude, far from the madding crowd M III.237 (°vibhanga-sutta); S I.44, 45; J I.340 (tittha° ?).

Araṇa[2] (nt.) [a + raṇa] quietude, peace Nett 55 (+ tāṇa), 176 (or as adj. = peaceful) ThA 134 (+ saraṇa); Vbh 19 sq. (opp. **saraṇa**). See saraṇa[2].

-**vihārin** (or araṇā-vihārin) [to be most likely taken as araṇā°, abl. of araṇa in function of ārakā, i. e. adv. far from, away; the spelling araṇa would refer it to araṇa[2]. As regards meaning the P. Commentators expl[n.] it as opp. of raṇa fight, battle, i. e. peacefullness, friendliness & see in it a syn. of metta. Thus Dhammapāla at PvA 230 expl[s.] it as "mettā-vihārin", & in this meaning it is found freq. in BSk. e. g. Divy 401; Av. Ś II.131 (q. v. for further ref. under note 3); M Vastu I.165; II.292. Cp. also the epithet of the Buddhas raṇañjaha] one who lives in seclusion, an anchoret, hermit; hence a harmless, peaceful person A I.24; Th 2, 358, 360; Pv IV.1[33] (= PvA 230); ThA 244. Cp. *Dhs trsl.* 336.

Araṇi & °**ī** (f.) [Vedic araṇī & araṇi fr. **ṛ**] wood for kindling fire by attrition, only in foll. cpds.: °**potaka** small firewood, all that is needed for producing fire, chiefly drill sticks Miln 53; °**sahita** (nt.) same Vin II.217; J I. 212 (ī); V.46 (ī); DhA II.246; °**mathana** rubbing of firewood J VI.209. — *Note.* The reading at PvA 211 araṇiyehi devehi sadi-savaṇṇa is surely a misreading (v. l. BB ariyehi).

Arati (f.) [a + rati] dislike, discontent, aversion Sn 270, 436, 642, 938; Dh 418 (= ukkaṇṭhitattaŋ DhA IV.225); Th 2, 339 (= ukkaṇṭhi ThA 239); Sdhp 476.

Aravinda [ara + vinda (?) Halāyudha gives as Sk. aravinda nt.] a lotus, Nymphaea Nelumbo Dāvs V.62.

Araha (adj.) (—°) [Vedic arha of **arh**] I. worthy of, deserving, entitled to, worth Dh 195 (pūjā°); Pv II.8[6] (dakkhiṇā°); VvA 23 (daṇḍa° deserving punishment). Freq. in cpd. **mahâraha** [Sk. mahârgha] worth much, of great value, costly, dear J I.50, 58; III.83, etc. (see mahant). — 2. fit for, apt for, suitable PvA 26 (paribhoga° fit for eating).

Arahati [Vedic arhati, etym. uncertain but cp. agghati] to be worthy of, to deserve, to merit (= Lat. debeo) Sn 431, 552 (rājā arahasi bhavituŋ); J I.262; Dh 9, 10, 230; Pv III.6[6]. — ppr. arahant (q. v.). Cp. also adj. **araha.**

Arahatta[1] (nt.) [abstr. formation fr. arahat°, 2nd base of arahant in comp[n.]: see arahant IV.2] the state or condition of an Arahant, i. e. perfection in the Buddhist sense = Nibbāna (S IV.151) final & absolute emancipation, Arahantship, the attainment of the last & highest stage of the Path (see magga & anāgāmin). This is not restricted by age or sex or calling. There is one instance in the Canon of a child having attained Arahantship at the age of 7. One or two others occur in the Comy ThA 64 (Selā); PvA 53 (Sankicca). Many women Arahants are mentioned by name in the oldest texts. About 400 men Arahants are known. Most of them were bhikkhus, but A III.451 gives the names of more than a score lay Arahants (cp. D II.93 = S V.360, and the references in *Dial.* III.5 n[4]). — Arahattaŋ is defined at S IV.252 as rāga-kkhaya, dosa°, moha°. Descriptions of this state are to be found in the formulae expressing the feelings of an Arahant (see arahant II.). Vin II.254; D III.10, 11, 255; A III.34, 421, 430; V.209; Pug 73; Nett 15, 82; DA I.180, 188, 191; DhA II 95; IV.193; PvA 14. — *Phrases:* **arahattaŋ sacchikaroti** to experience Arahantship Vin II.74; D I.229; **arahattaŋ pāpuṇāti** to attain or reach Arahantship (usually in aor. pāpuṇi) J II.229 ThA 64; DhA II.49 (saha paṭisambhidāhi) 93 (id.); PvA 53, 54, 61, 233 & freq. elsewhere; cp. arahattāya paṭipanna D III.255; A I.120; IV.292 sq., 372 sq.
-**gahaṇa** attainment of Arahantship DhA I.8. -**patta** (& **patti**) one who has attained Ar. S I.196; V.273; A II.157; III.376; IV.235. -**phala** the fruit of Ar. Vin I.39, 41, 293; III.93; D III.227, 277; S III.168; V.44; A I.23, 45; III.272; IV.276; Dhs 1017; Vbh 326. -**magga** the Path of Ar. S I.78; A III.391; DA I.224. -**vimokkha** the emancipation of Ar. Nd[2] 19.

Arahatta[2] in °**ghaṭi** see **araghaṭṭa.**

Arahant (adj.-n.) [Vedic arhant, ppr. of arhati (see arahati), meaning deserving, worthy]. Before Buddhism used as honorific title of high officials like the English 'His Worship'; at the rise of Buddhism applied popularly to all ascetics (*Dial.* III.3—6). Adopted by the Buddhists as t. t. for one who has attained the Summum Bonum of religious aspiration (Nibbāna).

I. *Cases* nom. sg. **arahaŋ** Vin I.9; D I.49; M I.245, 280; S I.169; see also formula C. under II., & **arahā** Vin I.8, 25, 26; II.110, 161; D III.255; It 95; Kh IV.; gen. **arahato** S IV.175; Sn 590; instr. **arahatā** S III.168; DA I.43; acc. **arahantaŋ** D III.10; Dh 420; Sn 644; Loc. **arahantamhi** Vv 21[2]. — nom. pl. **arahanto** Vin I.19; IV.112; S I.78, 235; II.220; IV.123; gen. **arahataŋ** Vin III.1; S I.214; Sn 186; It 112; Pv I.11[12]. Other cases are of rare occurrence.

II. *Formulae.* Arahantship finds its expression in freq. occurring formulae, of which the standard ones are the foll.: **A. khīṇā jāti vusitaŋ brahmacariyaŋ kataŋ karaṇīyaŋ nâparaŋ itthattāya** "destroyed is (re-) birth, lived is a chaste life, (of a student) done is what had to be done, after this present life there in no beyond". Vin I.14, 35, 183; D I.84, 177, 203; M I.139; II.39; S I. 140; II.51, 82, 95, 120, 245; III.21, 45, 55, 68, 71, 90, 94, 195, 223; IV.2, 20, 35, 45, 86, 107, 151, 383; V.72, 90, 144, 222; A I.165; II.211; III.93; IV.88, 179, 302; V.155, 162; Sn p. 16; Pug 61, etc. — **B. eko vūpakaṭṭho appamatto ātāpī pahitatto** 'alone, secluded, earnest, zealous, master of himself' D I.177; II.153 & continued with A: S I.140, 161; II.21; III.36, 74; IV.64; V.144, 166; A I.282; II.249; III.70, 217, 301, 376; IV. 235. — **C. arahaŋ khīṇāsavo vusitavā katakaraṇīyo ohitabhāro anupatta-sadattho parikkhīṇa-bhava-saññojano sammad-aññā vimutto**: D III.83, 97; M I.4, 236; S I.71; III.161, 193; IV.125; V.145, 205, 273, 302; A I.144; III.359, 376; IV.362, 369, 371 sq., It 38. — **D. ñāṇañ ca pana me dassanaŋ udapādi akuppā me ceto-vimutti ayaŋ antimā jāti natthi dāni punabbhavo** "there arose in me insight, the emancipation of my heart became unshake able, this is my last birth, there is now no rebirth for me: S II.171; III.28; IV.8; V.204; A I.259; IV.56, 305, 448.

III. *Other passages* (selected) Vin I.8 (arahā sītibhūto nibbuto), 9 (arahaŋ Tathāgato Sammāsambuddho), 19 (ekādasa loke arahanto), 20 (ekasaṭṭhi id.). 25 sq.; II. 110, 161; III.1; IV.112 (te arahanto udake kīḷanti); D I.49 (Bhagavā arahaŋ), 144; III.10, 255: M I.245 (Gotamo na pi kālaŋ karoti: arahaŋ samaṇo Gotamo), 280; S I.9, 26, 50 (Tathāgato), 78, 140, 161, 169, 175, 178 (+ sītibhūta), 208, 214, 235 (khīṇāsavā arahanto); III. 160 (arahā tissā?), 168; IV.123, 175, 260, 393; V.159 sq., 164, 200 sq.; A I.22 (Sammāsambuddho), 27, 109, 266; II.134; III.376, 391, 439; IV.364, 394; V.120; Sn 186, 590, 644, 1003; It 95 (+ khīṇāsava), 112; Kh IV. (dasahi angehi samannāgato arahā ti vuccati: see KhA 88); Vv 21[2]; I.217; Dh 164, 420 (khīṇāsava +); Ps II.3, 19, 194, 203 sq.; Pug 37, 73; Vbh 324, 336, 422; Pv I.1[1] (khettūpamā arahanto), 11[12]; IV.1[32].

IV. In compn. & der. we find two bases, viz. (1) **arahanta°** in **°ghāta** the killing or murder of an Arahant (considered as one of the six deadly crimes): see abhiṭhāna; **°ghātaka** the murderer of the A.: Vin I.89, 136, 168, 320; **°magga** (arahatta°?) the path of an A.: D I. 144. — (2) **arahat°** in (arahad-)**dhaja** the flag or banner of an A.: J I.65.

V. See further details & passages under anāgāmin, khīṇa, buddha. On the relationship of Buddha and Arahant see *Dial.* II.1—3; III.6. For riddles or word-play on the form arahant see M I.280; A IV.145; DA I.146 = VvA 105, 6 = PvA 7; DhA IV.228; DhsA 349.

Arāti [a + rāti, cp. Sk. arāti] an enemy Dāvs IV.1.

Ari [Ved. ari; fr. ṛ] an enemy. — The word is used in exegesis & word expln., thus in etym. of arahant (see ref. under arahant v.); of bhūri Ps II.197. — Otherwise in late language only, e. g. Sdhp 493 (°bhūta). See also arindama & aribhāseti.

Ariñcamāna [ppr. med. of P. riñcati for ricyati] not leaving behind, not giving up, i. e. pursuing earnestly Sn 69 (jhānaŋ = ajáhamana SnA 123, cp. Nd[2] 94).

Ariṭṭha[1] (adj.) [a + riṭṭha = Vedic ariṣṭa, pp of a + **riṣ** to hurt or be hurt] unhurt Sdhp 279.

Ariṭṭha[2] [Sk. ariṣṭa, N. of a tree] a kind of spiritous liquor Vin IV.110.

Ariṭṭhaka (adj.) [fr. ariṭṭha] (a) unhurt; perfect DA I,94 (°ŋ ñāṇaŋ). — (b) [fr. ariṭṭha in meaning of "soap-berry plant"?] in phrase mahā ariṭṭhako maṇi S I.104 "a great mass of soap stone" (cp. Rh. D. in *J. R. A. S.* 1895, 893 sq.), "a shaped block of steatite" (Mrs. Rh. D. in *K. S* 130).

Aritta (nt.) [Vedic aritra, Idg. *ere to row (Sk. ṛ to move); cf. Gr. ἐρέσσω to row, ἐρετμός rudder, Lat. remus, Ohg. ruodar = rudder; Ags. rōwan = E. row] a rudder. Usually in combn. with **piya** (phiya) oar, as piyārittaŋ (phiy°) oar & rudder, thus at S I.103 (T. piya°, v. l. phiya°); A II.201 (piya°); J IV.164 (T. piya°, v.l. phiya°); Sn 321 (piya +; SnA 330 phiya = dabbi-padara, aritta = veḷudaṇḍa). DhsA 149.

Arindama [Sk. arindama, ariŋ + dama of **dam**] a tamer of enemies victor, conqueror Pv IV.3[15] (= arīnaŋ damanasīla PvA 251); Sdhp 276.

Aribhāseti [= ariŋ bhāseti] to denounce, lit. to call an enemy J IV.285.

Ariya (adj.-n.) [Vedic ārya, of uncertain etym. The other Pāli forms are ayira & ayya] 1. (*racial*) Aryan D II.87. — 2. (*social*) noble, distinguished, of high birth. — 3. (*ethical*) in accord with the customs and ideals of the Aryan clans, held in esteem by Aryans, generally approved. Hence: right, good, ideal. [The early Buddhists had no such ideas as we cover with the words Buddhist and Indian. Ariya does not exactly mean either. But it often comes very near to what they would have considered the best in each]. — (*adj.*): D I.70 = (°ena sīlakkhandhena samannāgata fitted out with our standard morality); III.64 (cakkavatti-vatta), 246 (diṭṭhi); M I.139 (pannaddhaja); II.103 (ariyāya jātiyā jāto, become of the Aryan lineage); S II.273 (tuṇhībhāva); IV.250 (vaddhi), 287 (dhamma); V.82 (bojjhangā), 166 (satipaṭṭhānā), 222 (vimutti), 228 (ñāṇa), 255 (iddhipādā), 421 (maggo), 435 (saccāni), 467 (paññā-cakkhu); A I.71 (parisā); II.36 (ñāya); III.451 (ñāṇa); IV.153 (tuṇhībhāva); V.206 (sīlakkhandha); It 35 (paññā), 47 (bhikkhu sammaddaso); Sn 177 (patha = aṭṭhangiko maggo SnA 216); Dh 236 (bhūmi), 270; Ps II.212 (iddhi). **-alamariya** fully or thoroughly good D I.163 = III.82 = A IV.363; **nâlamariya** not at all good, object, ignoble ibid. — (*m.*) Vin I.197 (na ramati pāpe); D I.37 = (yaŋ taŋ ariyā ācikkhanti upekkhako satimā etc.: see 3rd. jhāna), 245; III.111 (°ānaŋ anupavādaka one who defames the noble); M I.17, 280 (sottiyo ariyo arahaŋ); S I.225 (°ānaŋ upavādaka); II.123 (id.); IV.53 (°assa vinayo), 95 (id.); A I.256 (°ānaŋ upavādaka); III.19, 252 (id.); IV.145 (dele! see arihatatta); V.68, 145 sq., 200, 317; It 21, 108 Dh 22, 164, 207; J III.354 = Miln 230; M I.7, 1 (ariyānaŋ adassāvin: "not recognising the Noble Ones PvA 26, 146; DhA II.99; Sdhp 444 (°ānaŋ vaŋsa). — **anariya** (*adj.* & *n.*) not Ariyan, ignoble, undignified, low, common, uncultured A I.81; Sn 664 (= asappurisa SnA 479; DhsA 353); J II.281 (= dussīla pāpadhamma C.); V.48 (°rūpa shameless), 87; DhA IV.3. — See also ñāṇa, magga, sacca, sāvaka.

-āvakāsa appearing noble J V.87. — **uposatha** the ideal feast day (as one of 3) A I.205 sq., 212. — **kanta** loved by the Best D III.227. — **gaṇā** (pl.) troops of worthies

J VI.50 (= brāhmaṇa-gaṇā, te kira tāda ariyâcārā ahesuŋ, tena te evam āha C.). — **garahin** casting blame on the righteous Sn 660. — **citta** a noble heart. — **traja** a true descendant of the Noble ones Dpvs V.92. — **dasa** having the ideal (or best) belief It 93 = 94. — **dhana** sublime treasure; always as sattavidha° sevenfold, viz. saddhā°, sīla°, hiri°, ottappa°, suta°, cāga°, paññā° "faith, a moral life, modesty, fear of evil, learning, self-denial, wisdom" ThA 240; VvA 113; DA II.34. — **dhamma** the national customs of the Argans (= ariyānaŋ eso dhammo Nd¹ 71, 72) M I.1, 7, 135; A II.69; V.145 sq., 241, 274; Sn 783; Dhs 1003. — **puggala** an (ethically) model person, Ps I.167; Vin V.117; ThA 206. — **magga** the Aryan Path. — **vaŋsa** the (fourfold) noble family, i. e. of recluses content with the 4 requisites D III.224 = A II.27 = Ps I.84 = Nd² 141; cp. A III.146. — **vattin** leading a noble life, of good conduct J III.443. — **vatā** at Th 1, 334 should be read °vattā (nom. sg. of vattar, vac) "speaking noble words". — **vāsa** the most excellent state of mind, habitual disposition, constant practice. Ten such at D III.269, 291 = A V.29 (Passage recommended to all Buddhists by Asoka in the Bhabra Edict). — **vihāra** the best practice S V.326. — **vohāra** noble or honorable practice. There are four, abstinence from lying, from slander, from harsh language, from frivolous talk. They are otherwise known as the 4 vaci-kammantā & represent sīla nos. 4—7. See D III.232; A II.246; Vin V.125. — **sangha** the communion of the Nobles ones PvA 1. — **sacca**, a standard truth, an established fact, D I.189, II.90, 304 sq.; III *277*; M I.62, 184; III.248; S V.415 sq. = Vin I.10, 230. It 17; Sn 229, 230, 267; Dh 190; DhA III.246; KhA 81, 151, 185, 187; ThA 178, 282, 291; VvA 73. — **sāvaka** a disciple of the noble ones (= ariyānaŋ santike sutattā a. SnA 166). M I.8, 46, 91, 181, 323; II.262; III.134, 228, 272; It 75; Sn 90; Miln 339; DhA I.5, (opp. putthujjana). — **sīlin** of unblemished conduct, practising virtue D I.115 (= sīlaŋ ariyaŋ uttamaŋ parisuddhaŋ DA I.286); M II.167.

When the commentators, many centuries afterwards, began to write Pali in S. India & Ceylon, far from the ancient seat of the Aryan clans, the racial sense of the word **ariya** was scarcely, if at all, present to their minds. Dhammapāla especially was probably a non-Aryan, and certainly lived in a Dravidian environment. The then current similar popular etmologies of **ariya** and **arahant** (cp. next article) also assisted the confusion in their minds. They sometimes therefore erroneously identify the two words and explain Aryans as meaning Arahants (DhA I.230; SnA 537; PvA 60). In other ways also they misrepresented the old texts by ignoring the racial force of the word. Thus at J V.48 the text, speaking of a hunter belonging to one of the aboriginal tribes, calls him anariya-rūpa. The C. explains this as "shameless", but what the text has, is simply that he looked like a non-Aryan. (cp 'frank' in English)..

Arīhatatta in phrase "arīhattā ariyo hoti" at A IV.145 is wrong reading for arīnaŋ hatattā. The whole phrase is inserted by mistake from a gloss explaining arahā in the foll. sentence "ārakattā kilesānaŋ arīnaŋ hatattā ... arahā hoti", and is to be deleted (omitted also by SS).

Aru (nt.) [Vedic aruḥ, unknown etym.] a wound, a sore, only in cpds.: °**kāya** a heap of sores M II.64 = Dh 147 = Th 1, 769 (= navannaŋ vaṇamukhānaŋ vasena arubhūta kāya DhA III.109 = VvA 77); °**gatta** (adj.) with wounds in the body M I.506 (+ pakka-gatta); Miln 357 (id); °**pakka** decaying with sores S IV.198 (°āni gattāni); °**bhūta** consisting of wounds, a mass of wounds VvA 77 = DhA III.109.

Aruka = aru; only in cpd. °**ûpamacitto** (adj.) having a heart like a sore (of a man in anger A I.124 = Pug 30 (expl^d at Pug A 212 as purāṇa-vaṇa-sadisa-citto "an old wound" i. e. continually breaking open).

Aruṇa [Vedic aruṇa (adj.) of the colour of fire, i. e. ruddy, nt. the dawn; of Idg. ***ereu** as in Sk. aruṣa reddish, Av. aurušа white, also Sk ravi sun; an enlarged from of Idg. ***reu** as in Sk. rudhira, rohita red (bloody; see etym. under rohita), Gr. ἐρυθρός, Lat. ruber.] the sun Vin II.68; IV.245; J II.154; V.403; VI.330; Dpvs I.56; DA I.30. — a. uggacchati the sun rises J I.108; VvA 75, & see cpds.

-**ugga** sunrise Vin IV.272; S V.29, 78, 101, 442 (at all Saŋyutta pass. the v.l. SS is aruṇagga); Vism 49. -**uggamana** sunrise (opp. oggamanna). Vin III.196, 204, 264; IV.86, 166, 230, 244; DhA I.165; II.6; PvA 109. -**utu** the occasion of the sun (-rise) DhA I.165. -**vaṇṇa** of the colour of the sun, reddish, yellowish, golden Vism 123; DhA II.3 = PvA 216. -**sadisa** (vaṇṇa) like the sun (in colour) PvA 211 (gloss for suriyavaṇṇa).

Arubheda the Rigveda ThA 206.

Arūpa (adj.) [a + rūpa] without form or body, incorporeal, D I.195 sq.; III.240; Sn 755; It 62; Sdhp 228, 463, 480. See details under rūpa.

-**âvacara** the realm or world of Formlessness, Dhs 1281—1285; Ps I.83 sq., 101. -**kāyika** belonging to the group of formless beings Miln 317 (devā). -**ṭhāyin** standing in or being founded on the Formless It 62. -**taṇhā** "thirst" for the Formless D III.216. -**dhātu** the element or sphere of the Incoporeal (as one of the 3 dhātus rūpa°, arūpa°, nirodha°; see dhātu) D III.215, 275; It 45. -**bhava** formless existence D III.216. -**loka** the world of the Formless, Sdhp 494. -**saññin** not having the idea of form D II.110; III.260; *Exp.* I.252.

Arūpin (adj.) [a + rūpin] = arūpa; D I.31 (arūpī attā hoti: see DA I.119), 195; III.111, 139; It 87 (rūpino va arūpino va sattā).

Are (indecl.) [onomat. Cp. Sk. lalallā, Gr. λαλέω, Lat. lallo = E. lull, Ger. lallen & without redupl. Ags. holā, Ger. halloh, E. lo. An abbrev. form of are is re. Cf. also alālā] exclam. of astonishment & excitement: he! hallo! I say!, implying an imprecation: Away with you (with voc.) J I.225 (dāsiputta-ceṭaka); IV.391 (duṭṭha-caṇḍāla); DA I.265 (= re); VvA 68 (dubbinī), 217 („how in the world").

Ala¹ freq. spelling for **aḷa**.

Ala² (adj.) [alaŋ adv. as adj.] enough, only in neg. **anala** insufficient, impossible M I.455; J II.326 = IV.471.

Alaŋ (indecl.) [Vedic araŋ. In meaning 1. **alaŋ** is the expanded continuation of Vedic araŋ, an adv. acc. of ara (adj.) suitable; fitly, aptly rightly fr. **ṛ** Cp. aṇṇava, appeti, ara. In meaning 2. **alaŋ** is the same as are] emphatic particle 1. in **affirmative** sentences: part. of assurance & emphasis = for sure, very much (so), indeed, truly. *Note.* In connection with a dat. or an infin. the latter only apparently depend upon alaŋ, in reality they belong to the syntax of the whole sentence (as dat. or inf. absolute). It is customary however (since the practice of the Pāli grammarians) to regard them as interdependent and interpret the construction as "fit for, proper" (= yuttaŋ Pāli Com.), which meaning easily arises ont of the connotation of alaŋ, e.g. alam eva kātuŋ to be sure, this is to be done = this is proper to be done. In this sense (c. dat.) it may also be comp^d. with Vedic araŋ c. dat. — (a) (abs.) only in comb^n. with dat. or inf. (see c. & Note above). — (b.) (°—) see cpds. — (c.) with *dat.* or *infin.*: alaŋ antarāyāya for certain an obstaele M I.130 (opp. nâlaŋ not at all); alaŋ te vippaṭisārāya you ought to feel sorry for it Vin II.250; alaŋ vacanāya one says rightly S II.18; alaŋ hitāya untold happiness DhA II.41. — ito ce pi so bhavaŋ Gotamo yojana-sate viharati alam eva ..... upasankamituŋ even if he were 100 miles from here, (surely) even so (i. e. it is fit or proper even then) one must go to him D I.117 (expl^d. at DA I.288 by yuttam eva = it is proper); alam eva kātuŋ kalyāṇaŋ indeed one must do good = it is appropriate to do good Pv II.9[23] (= yuttaŋ PvA 122); alaŋ puññāni kātave "come, let us do meritorious works" Vv 44[15] (= yuttaŋ VvA 191). — 2. in *negative* or prohibitive sentences: part. of disapprobation reproach & warning; enough! have done with! fie! stop! alas! (etc. see are). — (a) (abs.) enough: nâlaŋ thutuŋ it is not enough to praise Sn 217; te pi na honti me alaŋ they are not enough for me Pv I.6[3]. — (b) with *voc.*: alaŋ Devadatta mā te rucci sanghabhedo "look out D. or take care D. that you do not split up the community" Vin II.198; alaŋ Vakkali kin te iminā pūtikāyena diṭṭhena ... S III.120. — (c) enough of (with *instr.*): alaŋ ettakena enough of this, so much of that Miln 18; alam me Buddhena enough for me of the Buddha = I am tired of the B. DhA II.34.

-attha (adj.) "quite the thing", truly good, very profitable, useful D II.231; M II.69 (so read for alamatta); A II.180; Th 1, 252; J I.401 (so read for °atta). **-ariya** truly genuine, right noble, honourable indeed, only in °ñāṇa-dassana [cp. BSk. alamārya-jñāna-darśana Lal v.309, 509] Vin I.9; A III.64, 430; v.88; J I.389 (cp. ariya). **-kammaniya** (quite or thoroughly) suitable Vin III.187. **-pateyya**: see the latter. **-vacanīyā** (f.) a woman who has to be addressed with "alaŋ" (i. e. "fie"), which means that she ceases to be the wife of a man & returns into her parental home Vin III.144, cp. 274 (Bdhgh's. expln.). **-samakkhātar** one who makes sufficiently clear It 107. **-sājīva** one who is thoroughly fit to associate with his fellow A III.81. **-sāṭaka** "curse-coat", one who curses his waist-coat (alaŋ sāṭaka!) because of his having eaten too much it will not fit; an over-eater; one of the 5 kinds of gluttons or improper eaters as enumd. at DhA IV.16 = DhsA 404.

Alakkhika (& **īka**) (adj.) [a + lakkhika] unfortunate unhappy, of bad luck Vin III.23; J III.259.

Alakkhī (f.) [a + lakkhi] bad luck, misfortune Th 1, 1123.

Alagadda [Der. unknown. In late Sk. alagarda is a water-snake] a kind of snake M I.133 = DA I.21; DhA IV. 132 (°camma, so read for T. alla-camma, vv. ll. alanda° & alandu°).

Alagga (adj.) [pp. of laggati] not stuck or attached Nd² 107 (also **alaggita**); **alaggamāna** (ppr.) id. DhA III.298.

Alaggana (nt.) [a + laggana] not hanging on anything, not being suspended DA I.180.

Alaŋkata [pp. of alankaroti] 1. "made too much", made much of, done up, adorned, fitted out Dh 142 (= vatthâbharaṇa-paṭimaṇḍita DhA III.83); Pv II.3[6]; Vv I[1]; J III.392; IV.60. — 2. "done enough" (see alaŋ, use with instr.), only neg. **analankata** in meaning "insatiate" S I.15 (kāmesu).

Alaŋkaraṇa (nt.) [alaŋ + karaṇa, fr. alankaroti] doing up, fitting out, ornamentation J I.60.

Alaŋkaraṇaka (adj.) [fr. alankaraṇa] adorning, embellishing, decorating DhA I.410.

Alaŋkaroti [alaŋ + karoti, Vedic araṅkaroti] to make much of i. e. to adorn, embellish, decorate J I.60; III.189; VI. 368. ger. °karitvā DhA I.410; PvA 74. — pp. **alankata**. — Caus. **alankārāpeti** to cause to be adorned J I.52.

Alaŋkāra [fr. alankaroti, cp. Vedic araṅkṛti] "getting up" i. e. fitting out, ornament, decoration; esp. trinkets, ornaments D III.190; A III.239; 263 sq.; J VI.368; PvA 23, 46, 70 (—° adj. adorned with), 74; Sdhp 249.

Alattaka [Sk. alaktaka] lac, a red animal dye J IV.114 (°pāṭala); DhA II.174; IV.197.

Alanda & **Alandu** see alagadda.

Alamba (adj.) [a + lamba] not hanging down, not drooping, short J V.302; VI.3 (°tthaniyo not flabby: of a woman's breasts cp. alamb' ordhva-stanī Suśruta I.371).

Alasa (adj.) [a + lasa] idle, lazy, slack, slothful, languid S I.44, 217; Sn 96 (= jāti-alaso SnA 170); J IV.30; Dh 280 (= mahā-alaso DhA III.410). Opp. **analasa** vigorous, energetic S I.44; D III.190 (dakka +); Vin IV.211; Nd² 141 (id.).

Alasatā (f.) [abstr. fr. alasa] sloth, laziness; only in neg. analasatā zeal, industry VvA 229.

Alassa (nt.) at S I.43 is spurious spelling for **ālassa** idleness, sloth; v. l. BB ālasya.

Alāta (nt.) [Sk. alāta, related to Lat. altāre altar, adoleo to burn] a firebrand A II.95 (chava° a burning corpse, see chava); J I.68; Pug 36; DhA III.442.

Alāpu (nt.) [= alābu, with p for b: see Trenckner *Notes* 62[16]] a gourd, pumpkin Dh 149 (= DhA III.112; vv. ll. alābu & alābbu).

Alābu [Sk. alābū f.] a long white gourd, Cucurbita Lagenaris M I.80 (tittaka°), 315 (id.); PvA 47 (id.); DhsA 405. — See also **alāpu**.

Alābhaka [a + labhaka] not getting, loss, detriment Vin III.77.

Alālā (indecl.) [a + lālā interjection fr. sound root *lal, see etym. under are] "not saying lā lā" i. e. not babbling, not dumb, in °**mukha** not (deaf &) dumb SnA 124 (= aneḷamūga of Sn 70).

Alika (adj.) [Sk. alīka] contrary, false, untrue S I.189; J III.198; VI.361; Miln 26, 99. — nt. °ŋ a lie, falsehood Dh 264.

-vādin one who tells a lie, a liar Dh 223 = VvA 69 (has alīka°); J II.4; SnA 478 (for abhūta-vādin Sn 661).

Alīnatā (f.) [abstr. of alīna] open mindedness, prudence, sincerity J I.366.

Aluḷita (adj.) [a + luḷita, pp. of **lul**] unmoved, undisturbed Miln 383.

Aloṇika (adj.) [a + loṇika] not salted J III.409; VvA 184.

Aloma (adj.) [a + loma] not hairy (upon the body) J VI.457.

Alola (adj.) [a + lola] undisturbed, not distracted (by desires), not wavering: of firm resolution, concentrated Sn 65 (= nillolupa Nd² 98; = rasavisesesu anākula SnA 118).

Alla (adj.) (only °—) [Vedic ārdra, to Gr. ἄρδω moisten, ἄρδα dirt] — 1. moist, wet M III.94 (°mattikā-puñja a heap of moist clay; may be taken in meaning 2). — 2. fresh (opp. stale), new; freshly plucked, gathered or caught, viz. °**kusamuṭṭhi** freshly plucked grass A V.234 = 249; °**gomaya** fresh dung A V.234; DhA I.377; °**camma** living skin Vism 195; °**tiṇa** fresh grass DA I.77; PvA 40; °**dārūni** green sticks J I.318; °**madhu** fresh honey DhA II.197; °**maŋsa-sarīra** a body of living flesh DhA II.51 = IV.166; °**rasa** fresh-tasting DhA II.155; °**rohita-maccha** fresh fish J III.333. — 3. wet = with connotation of clean (through being washed), freshly washed, °**kesa** with clean hair PvA 82 (sīsaŋ nahātvā allakesa); usually combd. with **allavattha** with clean clothes (in an ablution; often as a sign of mourning) Ud 14, 91; DhA IV.220; or with odāta vattha (id.) J III.425. °**pāṇi** with clean hand Pv II.9[9] (= dhota-pāṇi PvA 116). [For **analla-gatta** at S I.183 better read, with ibid 169, **an-allīna-gatta**. For alla-camma at Dhp A IV.132. **alagadda-camma**, with the v.l., is preferable].

Allāpa [Sk. ālāpa; ā + lāpa] conversation, talk; only in cpd. °**sallāpa** conversation (lit. talking to & pro or together) J I.189; Miln 15; VvA 96; PvA 86.

Allika (?) [either from alla = allikaŋ nt. in meaning defilement, getting soiled by (—°), or from allīyati = alliyakaŋ, a der. fr. ger. alliya clinging to, sticking to. The whole word is doubtful.] only in cpd. (kāma-) **sukh' allik'ânuyoga** given to the attachment to sensual joys Vin I.10; D III.113, 130; S IV.330; V.421; Nett 110.

Allīna [pp. of allīyati; Sk. ālīna] (a) sticking to, adhering or adhered to, clinging M I.80; A V.187; Nd² under nissita (in form asita allina upagata). — (b.) soiled by (—°), dirtied A II.201. **-anallīna** "to which nothing sticks", i. e. pure, undefiled, clean S I.169 (id. p. on p. 183 reads analla: see **alla**). Cp. ālaya.

Allīyati [ā + līyati, **lī**, līyate, layate] to cling to, stick to, adhere to (in both senses, good or bad); to covet. — (a) lit. kesā sīsaŋ allīyiŋsu the hair stuck to the head J I.64; khaggo lomesu allīyi the sword stuck in the hair J I.273. — (b) fig. to covet, desire etc.: in idiomatic phrase **allīyati** (S III.190 v.l.; T. ālayati) **kelāyati vanāyati** (S III.190 v.l.; T. manāyati; M I.260 T. dhanāyati, but v.l. p. 552 vanāyati) mamāyati "to caress dearly & be extremely jealous of" (c. acc.) at M I.260 & S III.190. — J IV.5; V.154 (allīyituŋ, v.l. illīyituŋ); DhsA 364 (vanati bhajati a); pp. allīna — Caus. **alliyāpeti** [cp. Sk. ālāpayati, but B.Sk. allīpeti M Vastu III.144; pp. allīpita ibid. I.311; III.408; pass. allīpīyate III.127.] to make stick, to to bring near to (c. acc. or loc.) J II.325 (hatthiŋ mahābhittiyan alliyāpetvā); IV.392 (sīsena sīsaŋ alliyāpetvā).

Aḷa [etym. unknown] 1. the claw of a crab M I.234; S I.123; J I.223, 505 (°chinno kakkaṭako; T. spells ala°); II.342; III.295; — 2. the nails (of finger or toe) (?) in °**chinna** one whose nails are cut off Vin I.91.

Aḷāra (adj.) [Is it the same as uḷāra?] only used with ref. to the eyelashes, & usually expld. by **visāla**, i.e. extended, wide, but also by **bahala**, i.e. thick. The meaning & etym. is as yet uncertain. Kern, (*Toev.* s.v.) transls. by "bent, crooked, arched". °**akkhin** with wide eyes (eyelashes?) J I.306 (= visāla-netta C.); °**pamha** with thick eye-lashes Vv 35¹ (= bahala-saŋyata-pakhuma C.; v.l. °pamukha); °**bhamuka** having thick eyebrows or °lashes J VI.503 (so read for °pamukha; C. expls by visāl-akkhigaṇḍa). Cp. āḷāra.

Aḷhaka in udak' aḷhaka VvA 155 read **āḷhaka**.

Ava° (prefix) I. *Relation between ava & o.* Phonetically the difference between ava & o is this, that **ava** is the older form, whereas **o** represents a later development. Historically the case is often reversed — that is, the form in o was in use first & the form in ava was built up, sometimes quite independently, long afterwards. **Okaḍḍhati, okappati, okappanā, okassati, okāra, okantati, okkamati, ogacchati, odāta** and others may be used as examples. The difference in many cases has given rise to a differentiation of meaning, like E. ripe: rife, quash: squash; Ger. Knabe: Knappe etc. (see below B 2). — A. The old Pāli form of the prefix is **o**. In same cases however a Vedic form in ava has been preserved by virtue of its archaic character. In words forming the 2nd part of a cpd. we have ava, while the absolute form of the same word has o. See e.g. avakāsa (—°) > okāsa (°—); avacara > ocaraka; avatata; avadāta; avabhāsa; avasāna. — B. 1. the proportion in the words before us (early and later) is that **o** alone is found in 65°/₀ of all cases, **ava** alone in 24°/₀, and **ava** as well as **o** in 11°/₀. The proportion of forms in **ava** increases as the books or passages become later. Restricted to the older literature (the 4 Nikāyas) are the foll. forms with o: okiri, okkanti, okkamati, okkhipati, ogacchati, ossajati. — (1) The Pāli form (o°) shows a differentiation in meaning against the later Sanskrit forms (ava°). See the foll.:

avakappanā harnessing: okappanā confidence;
avakkanti (not Sk.): okkanti appearance;
avakkhitta thrown down: okkhitta subdued;
avacara sphere of motion: ocaraka spy;
avatiṇṇa descended: otiṇṇa affected with love;
avaharati to move down, put off: oharati to steal.

(2) In certain secondary verb-formations, arisen on Pāli grounds, the form o° is used almost exclusively pointing thus to a clearly marked dialectical development of Pāli. Among these formations are *Deminutives* in °ka usually; the *Gerund* & the *Infinitive* usually; the *Causatives* throughout.

II. *Ava as prefix* .[P. ava = Vedic ava & occasionally o; Av. ava; Lat. au- (aufero = avabharati, aufugio etc.); Obg. u-; Oir. ō, ua. See further relations in Walde, Lat. Wtb. under au]. — *Meaning*. (Rest:) lower, low (opp. ut°, see e. g. uccâvaca high & low, and below III. c), expld. as **heṭṭhā** (DhA IV.54 under avaŋ) or **adho** (ibid. 153; SnA 290). — (Motion:) down, downward, away (down), off; e.g. avasūra sun-down; adv. avaŋ (q. v., opp. uddhaŋ). — (a) *lit. away from, off*: ava-kantati to cut off; °gana away from the crowd; °chindati cut off; °yīyati fall off; °bhāsati shine out, effulge; °muñcati take off; °siṭṭha left over. — *down, out, over*: °kirati pour down or out over; °khitta thrown down; °gacchati go down; °gāheti dip down; °tarati descend; °patita fallen down; °sajjati emit; °siñcati pour out over; °sīdati sink down. — (b) *fig. down* in connection with verbs of emotion (cp. Lat. de- in despico to despise, lit. look down on), see ava-jānāti, °bhūta, °mānita, °vajja, °hasati. — *away from*, i. e. the opposite of, as equivalent to a negation and often taking the place of the neg. prefix a° (an°), e.g. in avajaya (= ajaya), °jāta, °mangala (= a°), °pakkhin, °patta.

Affinities of ava. — (a) **apa.** There exists an exceedingly frequent interchange of forms with apa° and ava°, the historical relation of which has not yet been thoroughly investigated. For a comparison of the two the BSk. forms are indispensable, and often afford a clue as to the nature of the word in question. See on this **apa 2** and cp. the foll. words under ava: avakata, °karoti, °khalita, °anga, ottappa, avattha, °nīta, °dāna, °pivati, °rundhati, °lekhati, °vadati, °varaka, °sakkati, avassaya, avasseti, °hita, avāpurīyati, avekkhati. — (b) **abhi.** The similarity between abhi & ava is seen from a comparison of meaning abhi II. b and ava II. a. The two prefixes are practically synonymous in the foll. words: °kankhati, °kamati, °kiṇṇa, °khipati, °maddati, °rata, °lambati, °lekheti, °lepana, °siñcati. — (c) The contrary of ava is **ut** (cp. above II.2). Among the freq. contrast-pairs showing the two, like E. up & down, are the foll. ukkaŋsâvakaŋsa, uggaman-oggamana, uccâvaca, ullangheti-olangheti, ullittâvalitta; ogilituŋ-uggilituŋ, onaman-unnamana. Two other combns. founded on the same principle (of intensifying contrast) are chiddâvacchidda and ava° in contrast with vi° in olambavilamba, olugga-vilugga.

Avaŋ (adv.) [Vedic avāk & avāŋ] the prep. ava in adv. use, down, downward; in C. often expld. by **adho.** Rarely absolute, the only passage found so far being Sn 685 (avaŋ sari he went down, v. l. avasari, expld. by otari SnA 486). Opp. uddhaŋ (above, up high). Freq. in cpd. **avaŋsira** (adj.) head downward (+ uddhaŋpāda feet up), a position characteristic of beings in Niraya (Purgatory), e.g. S I.48; Sn 248 (patanti sattā nirayaŋ avaŋsirā = adhogata-sīsā SnA 290); Vv 52²³ (of Revatī, + uddhaŋpāda); Pv IV.1⁴⁶; J I.233 (+ uddhapāda); IV.103 (nirayaŋ vajanti yathā adhammo patito avaŋsiro); Nd¹ 404 (uddhaŋpāda +); DhA IV.153 (gloss adhosira). — On avaŋ° cp. further avakkāra, avākaroti, avekkhipati.

Avakaŋsa [fr. ava-karṣati; on ŋs: *rṣ cp. haŋsati: harṣati] dragging down, detraction, abasement, in cpd. **ukkaŋsâvak°** lifting up & pulling down, raising and lowering, rise & fall D I.54.

Avakankhati (—°) [ava + kankhati; cp. Sk. anu-kāṅkṣati] to wish for, strive after S IV.57 (n'); J IV.371 (n'); V 340 (n'), 348 (n' = na pattheti C).

Avakaḍḍhati [ava + kaḍḍhati, cp. avakassati & apakassati] Nett 4 (avakaḍḍhayitvā). Pass. **avakaḍḍhati** J IV.415 (hadayaŋ me a. my heart is weighed down = sokena avakaḍḍhīyati C; v.l. avakassati). — pp. **avakaḍḍhita.**

Avakaḍḍhita [pp. of avakaḍḍhati] pulled down, dragged away DhA III.195.

Avakata = apakata, v.l. at It 89.

Avakanta [for *avakatta, Sk. avakṛtta; pp. of avakantati, see kanta²] cut, cut open, cut off J IV.251 (galak' âvakantaŋ).

Avakantati & **okantati** (okk°) [cp. Sk. avakṛntati, ava + kantati, cp. also apakantati] to cut off, cut out, cut away, carve — (ava:) J IV.155. — pp. **avakanta** & **avakantita.**

Avakantita [pp. of avakantati] cut out PvA 213.

Avakappanā & **okappanā** (f.) [ava + kappanā] preparation, fixing up, esp. harnessing J VI.408.

Avakaroti [Sk. apakaroti, cp. P. apa°] „to put down", to despise, throw away; only in der. avakāra & avakārin. — pp. **avakata** (q. v.). — See also avākaroti & cp. avakirati 2.

Avakassati & **okassati** [cp. Sk. avakarṣati, ava + kṛṣ; see also apakassati & avakaḍḍhati] to drag down, to draw or pull away, distract, remove. — A V.74 = Vin II.204 (+ vavakassati).

Avakārakaŋ (adv.) [fr. avakāra] throwing away, scattering about Vin II.214.

Avakārin (adj.) (—°) [fr. avakāra] despising, degrading, neglecting Vbh 393 sq. (an°).

Avakāsa & **okāsa** [ava + **kāś** to shine, cp. Sk. avakāśa] 1. "appearance": akkhuddâvakāso dassanāya not little (or inferior) to behold (of appearance) D I.114; ariyāvakāsa appearing noble or having the app. of an Aryan J V.87; katâvakāsa put into appearance Vv 22⁹. — 2. "opportunity": kata° given leave D I.276 Sn 1030; anavakāsakārin not giving occasion Miln 383. — **anavakāsa** not having a chance or opportunity (to happen), impossible; always in stcr. phrase aṭṭhānaŋ etaŋ anavakāso Vin II.199; A I.26; V.169; Pug 11, 12; PvA 28.

Avakirati & **okirati** [ava + kirati] 1. to pour down on, to pour out over; aor. avakiri PvA 86; ger. °kiritvā J V.144. — 2. to cast out, reject, throw out; aor. avākiri Vv 30⁵ = 48⁵ (v.l. °kari; VvA 126 expl^s by chaḍḍesi vināsesi). — Pass. **avakirīyati** Pv III.1¹⁰ (= chaḍḍīyati PvA 174); grd. °kiriya (see sep.). See also apakiritūna. pp. **okiṇṇa.**

Avakiriya [grd of avakirati] to be cast out or thrown away; rejectable, low, contemptible J V.143 (taken by C. as ger. = avakiritvā).

Avakujja (adj.) [ava + kujja, cp. B.Sk. avakubja M Vastu I.29, avakubjaka ibid. 213; II.412] face downward, head first, prone, bent over (opp. ukkujja & uttāna) J I.13 = Bu II.52; J V.295; VI.40; Pv IV.10⁸; PvA 178.
-**pañña** (adj.) one whose reason is turned upside down (like an upturned pot, i.e. empty) A I.130; Pug 31 (= adhomukha-pañña Pug A 214).

Avakkanta (—°) [pp. of last] entered by, beset with, overwhelmed by (instr.) S III.69 (dukkha°, sukha° and an°).

Avakkanti (f.) [fr. avakkamati] entry, appearance, coming down into, opportunity for rebirth S II.66 (nāmarūpassa); III.46 (pañcannaŋ indriyānaŋ); Pug 13 (= okkanti nibbatti pātubhāvo Pug A 184); Kvu 142 (nāmarūpassa); Miln 123 (gabbhassa).

Avakkama [fr. avakkamati] entering, appearance J V.330 (gabbhassa).

Avakkamati & okkamati [ava + kamati fr. **kram**] to approach. to enter, go into or near to, to fall into, appear in, only in ger. (poetically) avakamma J III.480 (v.l. apa°).

Avakkāra [Sk. avaskara faeces, fr. avaŋ + karoti] throwing away, refuse, sweepings; only in cpd. °pātī a bowl for refuse, slop basin, ash-bin Vin I.157, 352; II.216; M I.207; DhA I.305.

Avakkhalita [pp. of avakkhaleti, Caus. of **kṣal**] washed off, taken away from, detracted DA I.66 (v.l. apa°).

Avakkhitta & **okkhitta** [pp. of avakkhipati] 1. [= Sk. avakṣipta] thrown down, flung down, cast down, dropped; thrown out, rejected. (avā:) M I.296 (ujjhita +); DA I.281 (an°), 289 (piṇḍa); PvA 174 (piṇḍa). 2. [= Sk. utkṣipta?] thrown off, gained, produced, got (cp. uppādita), in phrase sed' âvakkhitta gained by sweat A II.67; III.45.

Avakkhipati & **okkhipati** [ava + khipati; cp. Sk. avakṣipati] to throw down or out, cast down, drop; fig. usually appl^d to the eyes = to cast down, hence transferred to the other senses and used in meaning of "to keep under, to restrain, to have control over" (cp. also avakkhāyati), aor. °khipi DA I.268 (bhusaŋ, v.l. avakkhasi).

Avakkhipana (nt.) [fr. avakkhipati] throwing down, putting down J I.163.

Avagacchati [ava + gacchati] to come to, approach, visit (cp. Vedic avagacchati) PvA 87.

Avagaṇḍa (-kāraka) (adj.) [ava + gaṇḍa°] "making a swelling", i. e. puffing out the cheeks, stuffing the cheeks, full (when eating); only nt. °ŋ as adv. after the manner or in the way of stuffing etc. Vin II.214; IV.196.

Avagata [pp. of avagacchati] at PvA 222 is uncertain reading; the meaning is „known, understood" (aññāta Pv IV.1¹¹); perhaps we should read āvikata or adhigata (so v.l. BB).

Avagāhati & **ogāhati** [ava + gāhati] to plunge or enter into, to be absorbed in (acc. & loc.) Vism 678; (vipassanāvīdhiŋ) Sdhp 370, 383.

Avaguṇṭhana (adj.) (—°) [fr. oguṇṭheti] covering Sdhp 314.

Avaggaha [Sk. avagraha] hindrance, impediment, used at DA I.95 as syn. for drought (dubbhikkhā).

Avanga see apanga.

Avaca (adj.) [der. fr. ava after the analogy of ucca > ut] low, only in comb^n. uccâvacā (pl.) high and low, see ucca. KvuA 38.

Avacana (nt.) [a + vacana] "non-word", i. e. the wrong word or expression J I.410.

Avacara (—°) (n.—adj.) [ava + **car**, also BSk. avacara in same sense, e.g. antaḥpurâvacarā the inmates of the harem Jtm 210] (a) (adj.) living in or with, moving in D I.206 (santika° one who stays near, a companion); fig. dealing or familiar with, at home in A II.189 (atakka°); IV.314 (parisā°); J I.60 (tāḷa° one conversant with music, a musician, see tāḷa¹); II.95 (sangāma°); Miln 44 (id. and yoga°). — (b) (n.) sphere (of moving or activity), realm, plane (of temporal existence); only as t.t. in **kāmâvacara rupâvacara arūpâvacara** or the 3 realms of sense-desires, form and non-form: **kāma°** D I.34 (°deva); Dbs 431 (as adj.); **rūpa°** Pug 37; **arūpa°** Pug 38; Ps I.83, 84, 101; Dhs A 387; PvA 138, 163; to be omitted in Dhs 1268, 1278.

Avacaraka & **ocaraka** (adj.—n.) [fr. avacara] 1. only in cpd. kāmâvacarika as adj. to kāmâvacara, belonging to the sphere of sense experiencies, Sdhp. 254. — 2. Late form of ocaraka, spy, only in C. on Th 1, 315 ff. quoted in *Brethren* 189, n 3. Occurs in BSk (Divy 127).

Avacaraṇa (nt.) [fr. avacarati 1] being familiar with, dealing with, occupation J II.95.

Avacuttha 2nd pret. of **vac**, in prohib form mā evaŋ avacuttha do not speak thus J VI.72; DhA IV.228.

Avacchidda (—°) (adj.) [ava + chidda] perforated, only in redupl. (intensive) cpd. **chiddâvacchidda** perforated all over, nothing but holes J III.491; DhA I.122. 284, 319. Cp. chidda-vicchidda.

Avacchedaka (—°) (adj) [ava + cheda + ka] cutting off, as nt. °ŋ adv. in phrase kabaḷâvacchedakaŋ after the manner of cutting off mouthfuls (of food) Vin II.214; IV.196; cp. āsāvacchedika whose hope or longing has been cut off or destroyed Vin I. 259.

Avajaya [ava + jaya, cp. apajita] defeat DhA II.228 (v.l. for T. ajaya).

Avajāta (adj.) [ava + jāta; cp. B.Sk. avajāta in meaning misborn, miscarriage] low-born, of low or base birth, fig. of low character (opp. abhijāta) Sn 664 (= buddhassa avajātaputta SnA 479); It 63; Miln 359.

Avajānāti [ava + **jñā**] 1. to deny Vin II.85; A III.164 = Pug 65. — 2. (later) to despise DhA III.16; PvA 175 (grd. °jānitabba) — Of short stem-form **ñā** are found the foll: grd. avaññeyya PvA 175, and with o°: grd. oññātabba PvA 195; pp. **avañāta**, besides **avaññāta**.

Avajīyati [ava + jīyati; Sk. avajīryate] to be diminished, to be lost, be undone J I.313 (jitaŋ a; v.l. avajīy°); Dh 179 (jitaŋ a = dujjitaŋ hoti DhA III.197).

Avajja (adj.) [Sk. avadya, seemigly a + vadya, but in reality a der. fr. ava. According to Childers = Sk. avarjya from **vraj**, thus meaning "not to be shunned, not forbidden". This interpretⁿ is justified by context of Dh 318, 319. The P. commentator refers it to ava + **vad** (for *ava-vadya) in sense of to blame, cp. apavadati] low, inferior, blamable, bad, deprecable Dh 318, 319; Dhs 1160. More fig. in neg. form **anavajja** blameless, faultless D I.70 (= anindita DA I.183); A II.26 = It 102; Sn 47 (°bhojin carrying on a blameless mode of livelihood, see Nd² 39), 263 (= anindita agarahita KhA 140): Ps II.116, 170; Pug 30, 41, 58; Sdhp 436. Opp. **sāvajja**.

Avajjatā (f.) [abstr. to prec.), only neg. an° blamelessnses, faultlessness Pug 25, 41; Dhs 1349.

Avajjha (adj.) [grd of a + vadhati, Sk. vadhya, **vadh**] not to be killed or destroyed, inviolable Sn 288; J V.49; VI.132.

Avañcana (adj.) [a + vañcana from **vañc**] not (even) tottering, i.e. unfit for any motion (esp. walking), said of crippled feet J I.214 = Cp III.9¹⁰.

Avañña (adj.) [to avaññā] despised, despicable Pv III.1¹³ (= avaññeyya avajānitabba PvA 175).

Avaññatti (f.) [ava + ñatti = Sk. *avajñapti, fr. ava + **jñā**] only as neg. an° the fact of not being despised, inferior or surpassed, egotism, pride, arrogance It 72; Vbh 350, 356; °**kāma** (adj.) wishing not to be surpassed, unwilling to be second, wanting to be praised A II.240; IV.1 sq.

Avaññā (f.) [Sk. avajñā, fr. ava + **jñā**] contempt, disregard, disrespect J I.257 (°ya).

Avaññāta (adj.) [pp. of avajānāti] despised, treated with contempt PvA 135 (an°); Sdhp 88, 90.

Avataŋsaka (= vaṭ°) see *Vin Texts* II.347.

Avaṭṭhāna (nt.) [Sk. avasthāna] position, standing place J I.508; PvA 286.

Avaṭṭhita (ad.) [Sk. avasthita, ava + ṭhita] "standing down" = standing up, firm, fixed, settled, lasting Th 1, 1140. Usually neg. an° unsettled, unsteady; not lasting, changeable Dh 38 (°citta; cp. DhA 1.308 cittaŋ thāvaraŋ natthi); PvA 87 (= na sassata not lasting for ever).

Avaṭṭhitatā (f.) [abstr. fr. prec.] steadiness, only as neg. an° unsteadiness, fickleness ThA 259.

Avaṭṭhiti (f.) [Sk. avasthiti] (firm) position, posture, steadfastness S V.228; Dhs 11, 570.

Avaḍḍhi (f.) [a + vaḍḍhi] "non-growth", decay DhA III.335; C on A III.76 (cp. apajaha).

Avaṇṭa (adj.) [a + vaṇṭa] without a stalk J V.155.

Avaṇṇa [a + vaṇṇa] blame, reproach, fault D I.1 (= dosā nindā DA I.37); It 67; Pug 48, 59.

Avaṇṇanīya (adj.) [grd. of a + vaṇṇeti] indescribable J V.282.

Avataŋsa see **vataŋsaka**.

Avatata & **otata** [ava + tata, pp. of **tan**] stretched over, covered, spread over with Vv 64³ (—°); VvA 276 (= chādita).

Avatiṭṭhati [ava + tiṭṭhati] to abide, linger, stand still. D I.251 = S IV.322 = A V.299 (tatra°); S I.25 (v.l. otiṭṭhati); Th. 1, 21; J II.62; IV.208 (aor. avaṭṭhāsi). — pp. **avaṭṭhita** (q. v.).

Avatiṇṇa & **otiṇṇa** [pp. of starati] fallen into, affected with (—°), as **ava**° rare late or poetical form of **o**°, e. g. J V.98 (issâ°). See **otiṇṇa**.

Avattha¹ [der. uncertain] aimless (of cārikā, a bhikkhu's wandering, going on tour) A III.171 (C. avavatthika).

Avattha² [Sk. apāsta, apa + āsta, pp. of **as**²] thrown away J V.302 (= chaḍḍita C.).

Avattharaṇa (nt.) [fr. avattharati] setting in array, deploying (of an army) J II.104 (of a robber-band), 336.

Avattharati [ava + tharati, **stṛ**] to strew, cover over or up J I.74 (°amāna ppr.), 255 (°itvā ger.); IV.84; Dāvs I.38. — pp. otthaṭa Cp. pariy°.

Avatthāraṇa (nt.) = avattharaṇa DA I.274.

Avatthu (&° ka) (adj.) [a + vatthu] groundless, unfounded (fig) Vin II.241; J I.440 (°kaŋ vacanaŋ). For lit meaning see **vatthu**.

Avadāta (= odāta) Dāvs III.14 (metri causa).

Avadāna see **apadāna**.

Avadāniya (adj.) [fr. avadāna cutting off; ava + **dā**² to cut] stingy, niggardly Sn 774 (= Nd¹ 36 which explˢ. as follows: avaŋ gacchanti ti pi avadāniyā; maccharino pi vuccanti avadāniyā; buddhānaŋ vacanaŋ n'ādiyantī ti avadāniyā. Sn A 516 condenses this explⁿ. into the foll.: avangamanatāya maccharitāya buddhâdīnaŋ vacanaŋ anādiyanatāya ca avadāniyā).

Avadāpana (cleansing): see **vodāpana**.

Avadāpeti (to deal out) only BSk pary° Divy 202.

Avadāyati [denom. fr. avadā in same meaning as anuddā, to **dā**¹: see dayati²] to have pity on, to feel sorry for J IV.178 (bhūtānaŋ nâvadāyissaŋ, gloss n'ânukampiyaŋ).

Avadīyati [Sk. avadīryati, ava + **dṛ**¹, dṛṇāti, see etym. under darī] to burst, split open J VI.183 (= bhijjati C.) see also **uddīyati**,

Avadehaka (—°) (adj.) [ava + deha + ka but more likely direct fr. ava + **dih**] in the idiom **udarāvadehakaŋ bhuñjati**, to eat ones fill M I.102; Th 1, 935. Vism 33 has udarāvadehaka-bhojana, a heavy meal.

Avadhāraṇa (nt.) [Cp. Sk. avadhāraṇa, fr. ava + **dhṛ**] calling attention to, affirmation, emphasis; as t.t. used by C's in explanation of evaŋ at DA I.27; and of kho at PvA 11, 18.

Avadhi 3 sg. aor. of **vadhati**. — At DhA II.73 avadhi = odhi.

Avanata see avaṇata.

Avanati (—°) (f.) [fr. avanamati] stooping, bending, bowing down, humiliation Miln 387 (unnat'âvanati).

Avani (f.) [Vedic avani] bed or course of a river; earth, ground Dāvs IV.5.

Avapakāsati [ava + pa + kāsati = kassati, fr. **kṛṣ**] is a doubtful comp[d]. of kassati, the comb[d]. ava + pa occurring only in this word. In all likelihood it is a distortion of **vavakassati** (vi + ava + kassati), supplementing the ordinary **apakassati**. See meaning & further discussion under apakāsati — Vin II.204 (apakāsati +; v.l. avapakassati; Bdhgh. in expl[n]. on p. 325 has apapakāsati which seems, to imply (a)vavakassati); A III.145 sq. (avapakāsituŋ).

Avapatta see opatta.

Avapāyin (—°) (adj.) [cp. avapivati] coming for a drink, drinking J I.163.

Avapivati [ava + **pā**, cp. apapibati] to drink from J I.163.

Avabujjhati (—°) [Cp. BSk. avabudhyate] to understand A IV.66 = It 83 (n'avabujjhati); A IV.98 (id.) J I.378 = III.387 (interchanging with anubujjhati at the latter pass).

Avabodha [ava + bodha] perception, understanding, full knowledge Sn A 509 (sacca°). — Neg. **an°** not awakened to the truth Vv 82[6] (= ananubodha VvA 319).

Avabodhati (—°) [cp. Sk. avabodhati] to realise, perceive, pay attention to J III.151 nâva°).

Avabhāsa [later form of obhāsa] Only in cpd. **gambhīrāvabhāso** D II.55, looking deep. Same cpd. at A II.105 = Pug 46 has obhāsa.

Avabhāsaka (—°) (adj.) [fr. avabhāsa] shining, shedding light on, illuminating Sdhp 14.

Avabhāsita (—°) [late form of obhāsita] shining with, resplendent Sdhp 590.

Avabhuñjati [ava + bhuñjati] to eat, to eat up J III.272 (inf. °bhottuŋ), 273.

Avabhūta (adj.) [ava + bhūta, pp. of ava + **bhū**] "come down", despised, low, unworthy M II.210.

Avamangala (adj.) [ava + mangala, ava here in privative function] of bad omen, unlucky, infaustus (opp. abhimangala); nt. bad luck, ill omen J I.372, 402; II.197; VI.10, 424; DhA III.123; PvA 261. Cf. next.

Avamaññati [Sk. avamanyate] to slight, to disregard, despise DhA I.170; PvA 37, 175; Sdhp 271. — pp. Caus. **avamānita.**

Avamangalla (adj.) [fr. avamangala] of bad omen, nt. anything importune, unlucky J I.446.

Avamāna & omāna [fr. ava + **man**, think] disregard, disrespect, contempt J II.386; III.423; V.384. Cp. next.

Avamānana (nt.) [fr. avamāna] = avamāna J I.22.

Avamāneti [Caus. of avamaññati] to despise J V.246. — pp. **avamānita** PvA 36.

Avaya only in neg. **anavaya.**

Avayava [Der[n] uncertain. Cp. mediaeval Sk. avayava] limb, member, constituent, part VvA 53 (sarīra° = gattā). 168, 201, 276; PvA 211 (sarīra° = gattā), 251 (mūl° the fibres of the root). As t. t. g. at SnA 397. In the commentaries **avayava** is often used where **aṅga** would have been used in the older texts.

Avarajjhati (—°) [ava + rajjhati of **rādh**, cp. Sk. avarādhyate] to neglect, fail, spurn Th 1, 167; J IV.428 (v.l. °rujjh°).

Avaruddha [fr. avarundhati] 1. Doubtful reading at Vin IV.181, apparently meaning 'in revolt, out of hand' (of slaves) — 2. [late form of oruddha] restrained Sdhp. 592.

Avaruddhaka [avruddha + ka] subdued, expelled, banished J VI.575; Dpvs I.21 (Np).

Avaruddhati [Sk. aparundhati; ava + ruddhati of **rudh**] to expel, remove, banish J VI.505 (= nīharati C.), 515. See also **avarundhati.**

Avarundhati [ava + rundhati. Only referred to by Dhp. in his Cy (ThA 271) on oruddha] to put under restraint, to put into one's harem as subsidiary wife.

Avalambati [= **olambati**]. Only in late verse. To hang down. Pv II.1[18]; 10[2]. Ger. avalamba (for °bya) Pv III.3[5]; cp. olubbha.

Avalitta (—°) [Sk. avalipta, pp. of ava-limpati] besmeared; in cpd. **ullittâvalitta** "smeared up & down" i.e. plastered inside & outside A I.101.

Avalekhati [ava + lekhati, **likh**, Sk. avalikhati] to scrape off Vin II.221 (v. l. apa°).

Avalekhana[1] (nt.) [fr. avalekhati] (a) scraping, scraping off Vin II.141 (°pidhara), 221 (°kaṭṭha). (b) scratching in, writing down J IV.402, (°sattha a chisel for engraving letters).

Avalekhana[2] (nt.) v. l. for **apalekhana.**

Avalepana (—°) (nt.) [fr. ava + **lip**] smearing, daubing, plastering M I.385 (pīta°); Sn 194 (kāyo taca-maŋs' âvalepano the body plastered with skin & flesh).

Avasa (adj.) [a + vasa] powerless Sdhp 290.

Avasaṭa & **Osaṭa** [Sk. apasṛta, cp. also samavasṛta, pp. of ava + **sṛ**] withdrawn, gone away; one who has left a community & gone over to another sect, a renegade Vin IV.216, 217 (= titthāyatanaŋ saŋkata).

Avasarati [ava + **sṛ**] to go down, to go away (to) Sn 685 (v. l. BB. T. avaŋsari).

Avasāna (—°) [for **osāna**] (nt.) stopping ceasing; end, finish, conclusion J I.87 (bhattakicc-âvasāne at the end of the meal); PvA 76 (id.).

Avasāya [fr. avaseti] stopping, end, finish Th 2, 12 (= avasānaŋ niṭṭhānaŋ ThA 19). But the id. p. at Dhp 218 has anakkhāte.

Avasiñcanaka (—°) (adj.) [fr. osiñcati] pouring over (act. & med.), overflowing J I.400 (an°).

Avasiṭṭha (sic & not osiṭṭha) [pp. of avasissati, Sk. avaśiṣṭa] left, remaining, over S II.133; J I.138; V.339; VvA 66, pl. avasiṭṭhā all who are left, the others PvA 165 (janā).

Avasiṭṭhaka (adj.) [fr. avasiṭṭha] remaining, left J III.311.

Avasitta (—°) [pp. of osiñcati] besprinkled, anointed, consecrated, only in phrase **rājā khattiyo muddhâvasitto** of a properly consecrated king (see also khattiya) D I. 69; II.227; III.64; Pug 56; DA I.182 (T. muddhâvassita, v. l. °abhisitta); etc. — See also **abhisitta.**

Avasin (adj.-n.) [a + vasin fr. **vaś**] not having control over oneself, D II.275.

Avasissati [Sk. avaśiṣyate, Pass. of ava + **śis**; but expld. by Kern, *Toev.* s. v. as fut of avasīdati] to be left over, to remain, in phrase yaŋ pamāṇa-kataŋ kammaŋ na taŋ tatrâvasissati D I.251; A V.299 = S IV.322; J II.61 (see expln. on p. 62). Also in the phrases **taco ca nahārū ca aṭṭhi ca avasissatu sarīre upasussatu maŋsa-lohitaŋ** M I.481; A I.50; S II.28, and **sarīrāni avasissanti** S II. 83. With the latter phrases cp. **avasussati.**

Avasī metri causa for avasi, a + vasi, aor. of **vas**[4] to stop, stay, rest J V.66 (mā avasī).

Avasussati [Sk. *ava-śuṣyati of **śuṣ**] to dry up, to wither; in later quotations of the old **kāmaŋ taco ca nahāru ca aṭṭhi ca avasussatu** (upasussatu sarire maŋsalohitaŋ) J I.71, 110; Sdhp 46. It is a later spelling for the older avasissatu see Trenckner (M I.569). — fut. **avasucchati** (= Sk. *°śokṣyati, fut. of Intens.) J VI.550 (v. l. BB °sussati; C. avasucchissati).

Avasūra [ava + sūra; ava here in function of *avaŋs see ava II] sundown, sunset, acc. °ŋ as adv. at or with sundown J V.56 (anāvasūraŋ metrically).

Avasesa[1] [Sk. avaśeṣa, fr. ava + **śiṣ**, cp. avasissati] remainder, remaining part; only in cpds. **an°** (adj.) without any remainder, i. e. fully, completely M I.220 = A V.347 (°dohin); A I.20 sq., 88; Sn 146; Pug 17; Dhs 363, 553; SnA 417 (°pharaṇa); PvA 71 (°ato, adv. altogether, not leaving anything out); & **sâvasesa** leaving something over, having something left A I.20 sq., 88; Pv III.5[5] (jīvita° having still a little life left).

Avasesa[2] (adj.) [see prec.] remaining, left Sn 694 (āyu avaseso); J III.19; Vbh 107 (taṇhā ca avasesā ca kilesā); PvA 19 (avasesā ca ñātakā the rest of the relatives), 21 (avasesā parisā), 201 (aṭṭhi-tacamatt' âvasesa-sarīra with a body on which nothing but skin & bones were left), 206 (aṭṭhi-saṅghātamatt' âvasesa-sarīra). — nt. (as pred.) °ŋ what is left PvA 52 (app' avasesaŋ); KhA 245 (n' atthi tesaŋ avasesaŋ).

Avasesaka (adj.) [fr. avasesa[2]] being left, overflowing, additional, more J I.400 (an°); Dpvs IV.45.

Avassa (adj.) [a + **vaś**] against one's will, inevitable J I. 19 (°bhāvin); V.319 (°gāmitā). Usually as nt. °ŋ adv. inevitably (cp. BSk. avaśyaŋ Divy 347; Av. Ś I.209 etc.) J III.271; DA I.263; Sdhp 293.

Avassakaŋ (adv.) [see avassa] inevitably Dpvs IX.13.

Avassajati & **ossajati** [ava + **sṛj**, perhaps ud + **sṛj** = Sk. utsṛjati, although the usual Vedic form is avasṛjati. The form ossajati puzzled the BSk. writers in their sanskritisation apotsṛjati = apa + ut + **sṛj** Divy 203] to let loose, let go, send off, give up, dismiss, release (ava): J IV.425; V.487 (aor. avassaji read for avissaji).

Avassana (nt.) [a + vassana, Sk. vāśana of **vāś** to bleat] not bleating J IV.251.

Avassaya [Sk. *avāśraya for the usual apāśraya, see P. apassaya!] support, help, protection, refuge J I.211; II. 197; IV.167; Miln 160; DhA II.267; IV.198; PvA 5, 113.

Avassava [ava + sava, Sk. °srava fr. **sru** to flow] outflow, effect, only neg. **anassava** no further effect Vin II.89; M I.93; II.246; A III.334 sp.

Avasseti [ava + ā + **śri**, for the usual *apāśrayati; see apasseti] to lean against, to depend on, find shelter in (loc.) J II.80 (aor. avassayiŋ = vāsaŋ kappesiŋ C.). — pp. **avassita.**

Avassāvana (nt.) [fr. ava + Caus. of **sru** to flow] straining, filtering (?) J II.288.

Avassita [for apassita, Sk. apaśrita] depending on, dealing with J V.375. See apassita.

Avassuta (adj.) [Sk. *avasruta, pp. of ava + **sru**, cp. avassava] 1. (lit.) flowing out or down, oozing, leaking J IV. 20. — 2. (fig.) (cp. **anvāssava** & **āsava**) filled with desire, lustful (opp. **anavassuta**, q. v.) Vin II.236; S IV.70, 184 (an°); A I.261, 262 (an°); II.240; IV.128, 201; Sn 63 (an°); Pug 27, 36; Dpvs II.5 (T. reads **avassita**). — Neg. **anavassuta**: 1. not leaking, without a leak J IV.20 (nāvā = udaka-pavesan' âbhāvena a. C.). — 2. free from leakage, i. e. from lust or moral intoxication Dh 39 (°citta); Sn 63 (see expld. in detail at Nd[2] 40); SnA 116 (= kilesa-anvāssava-virahita).

Avahaṭa [pp. of avaharati] taken away, stolen Miln 46, 47.

Avaharaṇa (—°) [fr. avaharati in both meanings] taking away, removal; theft PvA 47 (sāṭaka°), 92 (soka°).

Avaharati & **oharati** [ava + **hṛ**] to steal J I.384; PvA 47 (avahari vatthaŋ), 86 (id., = apānudi). — pp. **avahaṭa** (q. v.).

Avahasati [ava + **has**] to laugh at, deride, mock J V.111 (aññamaññaŋ); PvA 178. — aor. **avahasi** J IV.413.

Avahāra [fr. avaharati] taking, acquiring, acquisition Vin V.129 (pañca avahārā, viz. theyya°, pasayha°, parikappa°, paṭicchanna°, kusa°).

Avahīyati [for ohīyati] to be left behind, to stay behind J V.340.

Avāgata [ava + ā + gacchati] only in phrase dhammā avāgat-amhā, we are fallen from righteousness, J V.82. (C. explains apāgata).

Avākaroti [either ava + ā + karoti or avaŋ + karoti, the latter more probable. It is not necessary to take it with Kern, *Toev.* s. v. as Sk. apākṛnoti, apa + ā + **kṛ**] 1. to revoke, undo, rescind, not fulfill, spoil, destroy J III.339 (avākayirā = avakareyya chindeyya C.); V.495, 500; VI. 280. — 2. to give back, restore J VI.577 (= deti C.).

Avākirati wrong by Hardy VvA Index for **avakirati** (q. v.).

Avāṭuka see **apāṭuka.**

Avāpuraṇa (nt.) [same as apāpuraṇa] a key S III.132; A IV.374.

Avāpurati [same as apāpurati] to open (a door) J I.63; VI.373.

Avāvaṭa (adj.) [a + vāvaṭa] unobstructed, unhindered, free. Of a woman, not married J V.213 (= apetâvaraṇā, which read for °bharaṇā, apariggahitā C.).

Avikampamāna (adj.) [a + vi + kampamāna, ppr. med. of **kamp**] not hesitating, not wavering, not doubting J IV.310 (= anosakkamāna C.; Kern takes it at this passage as a + vikalpamāna, see *Toev.* s.v., but unnecessarily); VI.176 (= nirāsanka C.); J VI.273.

Avikampin (adj.) [fr. a + vi + **kamp**] unmoved, not shaking, steady Vv 50[22] (= acala VvA 215).

Avikopin (adj.) [a + vikopin; fr. vi + **kup**] not agitated, not moving, unshaken, undisturbed J VI.226 (acchejja +).

Avikkhepa [a + vikkhepa] calmness, balance, equanimity D III.213; A I.83; Ps I.94; II.228; Dhs 11, 15, 570.

Avicāreti [a + vicāreti] not to examine VvA 336.

Aviccaŋ at J v.434 read **aviviccaŋ** [a + viviccaŋ] i. e. not secretly, openly.

Avijānaŋ [a + vijānaŋ] not knowing, ignorant Dh 38, 60; It 103.

Avijjā (f.) [Sk. avidyā; fr. a + **vid**] ignorance; the main root of evil and of continual rebirth (see paṭicca-samuppāda, cp. S II.6, 9, 12; Sn p. 141 & many other passages). See on term *Cpd.* 83 n. 3, 187 sq., 262 sq. & for further detail **vijjā**. avijjā is termed an **anusaya** (D III.254, 282; S IV.205, 208 sq., 212); it is one of the **āsavā** (Vin III.4; D I.84; III.216; It 49; Dhs 1100, 1109), of the **oghā** (D III.230, 276; Dhs 390, 1061, 1162), of the **nīvaraṇāni** (S II.23; A I.223; It 8; Dhs 1162, 1486), of the **saŋyojanāni** (D III.254; Dhs 1131, 1460). See for various characterisatons the foll. passages: Vin I.1; III.3; D III.212, 230, 234, 274; M I.54, 67, 144; S II.4, 26, 263; III.47, 162; IV.256; V.52; A I.8, 285; II.132, 158, 247; III.84 sq., 414; IV.228; It 34 (yā kāc' imā duggatiyo asmiŋ loke paramhi ca avijjāmūlakā sabbā icchā-lobha-sammussayā), 57, 81; Sn 199, 277, 729 (jāti-maraṇa-saŋsāraŋ ye vajanti punapunaŋ ... avijjāy'eva sā gati), 730, 1026, 1033 (avijjāya nivuto loko); Dh 243; Nd² 99; Pug 21; Dhs 390, 1061, 1162; DhA III.350; IV.161 (°paligha).

Aviññāṇaka (adj.) [a + viññāṇa + ka] senseless, without feeling or consciousness, unfeeling DhA I.6 (saviññāṇaka +).

Aviññū (adj.) = **aviddasu**.

Avitakka (adj.) [a + vitakka] free from thought D III.219, 274; Th 2, 75 ("where reasonings cease" trsl.); Dhs 161 ("free from the working of conception" trsl.), 504 etc.

Avidūra (adj.) [a + vidūra] not far, near; usually in loc. °e as adv. near Sn. 147.

Aviddasu (adj.) [a + viddasu] ignorant, foolish Sn 762 (= bāla Sn A 509); Dh 268 = Nd² 514 (= aviññū DhA III.395); PvA 18 (so read for avindasu).

Avināsaka (°ika) (adj.) [a + vināsa + ka] not causing destruction A III.38 (°ika); J v.116 (= anāsaka C.).

Avināsana (adj.) [a + vināsana] imperishable Dpvs IV.16.

Avinicchayaññū (adj.) [a + vinicchaya + ññū] not knowing how to decide J v.367.

Avinibbhujaŋ (adj.) [ppr. of a + vinibbhujati] unable to distinguish or to know J v.121 (= atīrento C.).

Avinibbhoga (ad.) [a + vinibbhoga] not to be distinguished, indistinct J III.428 (°sadda).

Avipariṇāma [a + viparināma] absence of change, steadfastness, endurance D I.18; III.31, 33 (°dhamma); DA I.113 (= jarā-vasena vipariṇāmassa abhāvato).

Avippaṭisāra [a + vippaṭisāra] absence of regret or remorse A III.46.

Avippavāsa (adj.-n.) [a + vippavāsa] thoughtfulness, mindfulness, attention; adj. not neglectful, mindful, attentive, eager Vin v.216; Sn 1142 (cp. Nd² 101: anussatiyā bhāvento); DA I.104 (appamādo vuccati satiyā avippavāso); DhA IV.26 (appamāda = satiyā avippavāsa).

Aviruddha (adj.) [a + viruddha] not contrary, unobstructed, free, without difficulties Dh 406; Sn 365, 704, 854.

Avirūḷhi (f.) [a + virūḷhi] absence or cesssation of growth Sn 235; DhA I.245 (°dhamma).

Avirodha [a + virodha] absence of obstruction, gentleness M II.105 = Th 1, 875.

Avirodhana (nt.) = avirodha J III.320, 412; v.378.

Avivāda [a + vivāda] absence of contesting or disputing, agreement, harmony D III.245; Sn 896 (°bhūma SnA 557 or °bhumma Nd¹ 308, expl^d. as Nibbāna).

Avisaŋvādaka (adj.) [a + visaŋvada + ka] not deceiving, not lying D I.4; III.170; Pug 57; DA I.73.

Avisaŋvādanatā (f.) [abstr. fr. a + visaŋvāda] honesty, faithfulness, uprightness D III.190.

Avisaŋvādeti [a + visaŋ + Caus. of **vad**] to keep one's word, to be honest, to be true J v.124.

Avisaggatā (f.) [a + visaggatā, v.l. viy°, thus as a + viyagga, Sk. vyagra = ākula] state of being undisturbed, harmony, balance J VI.224 (C. avisaggata). Cp. avyagga.

Avisare at J v.117 according to Kern, *Toev.* s.v. corrupted from avisaye, i.e. towards a wrong or unworthy object [a + visaya, loc], C. differently: avisare = avisaritvā atikkamitvā; v.l. **adhisare**.

Avisāhaṭa (adj.) [a + visāhaṭa] imperturbed Dhs 15, 24, 287, 570. (°mānasata).

Avissaji at J VI.79 is with Kern, *Toev.* s. v. better to be read **avassaji** (see avassajati).

Avissajjiya (adj.) [grd. of a + vissajjati] not to be given away, inalienable (cp. avebhangiya) Vin I.305 (°ika for °iya); II.170 (five such objects in detail); v.216 (+ avebh°); J VI.568.

Avissāsaniya (adj.) [a + visāsana + iya, ika] not to be trusted, untrustworthy J III.474.

Aviha [of uncertain etym.] the world of the Aviha's, i.e. the 12th of the 16 Brahmā-words, cd. *Kindred Sayings* 48 n. 3; *Cpd.* 139. — S I.35, 60; A I.279; Pug 17.

Avihiŋsa (Avihesa) (f.) [a + vihiŋsā] absence of cruelty, mercy, humanity, friendliness, love D III.213, 215, 240 (avihesā); Sn 292 (= sakaruṇabhāva SnA 318); It 82 (°vitakka).

Aviheṭhaka (adj.) [a + viheṭhaka] not harassing, not hurting D III.166 (but cp. SnA 318 **avihesaka** in same context); Miln 219.

Avī° in general see **vī°**.

Avīci [B.Sk. avīci a + vīci (?) no intermission, or no pleasure (?), unknown, but very likely popular etym.] 1. **avīci-niraya**, one of the (great) hells (see **niraya**), described in vivid colours at many passages of the Pali canon, e.g. at Vin II.203 = It 86; Nd¹ 18, 347, 405 = Nd² 304 III o; Ps I.83; Dhs 1281; J I.71, 96; III.182; IV.159; DhA I.148; PvA 52; SnA 290; Sdhp 37, 194; Pgdp 5 sq.; etc etc. — 2. disintegration, decay Vism 449 (a. jarā nāma).

Avekalla (°—) adj.) [a + vekalla] without deficiency, in °**buddhi** complete knowledge J VI.297.

Avekkhati [B.Sk. avikṣate. The regular Pāli form however is apekkhati, to which the BSk. av° corresponds] to look at, to consider, to see It 33 (v.l. ap°); Dh 28, 50, J IV.6; DhA I.259 (= passati).

Avekkhipati [avaŋ + khipati, avaŋ here in form **ave** corresp. to avaḥ, cp. pure for puraḥ etc.] to jump, hop, lit. to throw (a foot) down J IV.251 (= pacchimapāde khipati C.).

Avecca (adv.) [Uusually taken as ava + ger. of **i** (°itya), cp. adhicca & abhisamecca, but by P. grammarians as a + vecca. The form is not sufficiently cleared semantically; B.Sk. avetya, e.g. Itm. 210, is a Sanskritisation of the P. form] certainly, definitely, absolutely, perfectly, expl^d.

by Bdhgh. as acala (on D II.217), or as paññāya ajjhogahetvā (on Sn 229); by Dhp. as apara-paccaya-bhāvena (on Pv IV.1[28]). — Usually in phrase **Buddhe Dhamme Sanghe avecca-pasāda** perfect faith in the B., the Dhamma & the Sangha, e.g. at M I.47; S II.69; IV.271 sq., 304; V.344, 405; A I.222; II.56; III.212, 332, 451; IV.406; V.183; further at Ps I.161 (°pasanna); Sn 229 (yo ariyasaccāni avecca passati); Pv IV.1[28].

Avedha (adj.) [a + vedha, grd. of **vidh (vyadh)** to pierce, Sk. avedhya] not to be hurt or disturbed, inviolable, unshakable, imperturbable Sn 322 (°dhamma = akampanasabhāva SnA 331).

Avebhangika (adj.) [fr. a + vi + bhanga] not to be divided or distributed Vin I.305. Cp. next.

Avebhangiya (nt.) [= avebhangika] that which is not to be divided, an inalienable possession; 5 such objects enumd. at Vin II.171, which are the same as under avissajjiya (q. v.); V.129.

Avera (adj.) [a + vera] peaceable, mild, friendly Sn 150 (= veravirahita KhA 248); Sdhp 338. — °ŋ (nt.) friendliness, kindness D I.247 (°citta); Dh 5 (= khantimetta DhA I 51).

Averin (adj.—n.) = avera Dh 197, 258.

Avosita [reading uncertain, cp. avyosita] only in neg. an° unfulfilled, undone Th I, 101.

Avyagga (ad) [a + vyagga, Sc. vyagra] not bewildered, not confused S V.66. Cp. **avisaggatā**.

Avyattatā (f.) [abstr. fr. avyatta] state or condition of not being manifest or visible, concealment, hiding DhA II.38.

Avyatha (adj.) [a + vyatha, cp. Sk. vyathā misfortune] not miserable, fortunate J III.466 (= akilamāna C.).

Avyaya [a + vyaya] absence of loss or change, safety D I.72 (instr. °ena safely); Miln 393 (as abbaya T.).

Avyāpajjha[1] (abyābajjha) (nt.) [a + vyāpajjha or bajjha, a confusion between the roots **bādh** or **pad**] (act.) kindness of heart; (pass.) freedom from suffering (Ep. of Nibbāna) Vin I.183 (avyāpajjh'ādhimutta); It 31 (abyābojjh'ārāma).

Avyāpajjha[2] (abyābajjha) adj.) [either a + *vyāpadya or more likely a + *vyābādhya] free from oppression or injury; not hurting, kind D II.242 (avera +), 276; M I.90; It 16 = 52 (sukhaŋ); Miln 410 (avera +).

Avyāpanna (adj.) [a + vyāpanna] free from desire to injure, free from malice, friendly, benevolent D III.82,83 (°citta); A II.220 (id.); Pug 68 (id.). — Same in B.Sk. e.g. Divy 105, 302.

Avyāpāda [a + vyāpāda] absence of desire to injure, freedom from malice D III.215, 229, 240; It 82 (all MSS. have aby°); Dhs 33, 36, 277, 313, 1056.

Avyāyata (adj.) [a + vyāyata of **yam**] at random, without discrimination, careless J I.496 (= avyatta C.).

Avyāyika (adj.) [fr. avyaya] not liable to loss or change, imperishable J V.508 (= avigacchanaka C.).

Avyāvaṭa (adj.) [a + vyāvaṭa = Sk vyāpṛta] not occupied, i. e. careless, neglectful, not worrying Vin III.136; Nd[2] 72 (abyāvaṭa for appossukka Sn 43); J III.65; VI.188. Miln 177 (abyā°).

Avyāseka (adj.) [a + vy + āseka] untouched, unimpaired D I.182 (°sukha = kilesa vyāseka-virahitattā avyāseka DA I.183); Pug 59.

Avyāharati [a + vy + āharati] not to bring or procure J V.80.

Avyosita (adj.) [a + vyosita, Sk. vyavasita] not having reached perfection, imperfect Th I, 784 (aby°).

Avhaya [fr. avhayati; cp. Sk. āhvaya "betting"] calling, name; adj. (—°) called, having the name of Sn 684 (isi°), 686 (Asit°), 689 (kanhasiri°), 1133 (Sacc°, cp. Nd[2] 624).

Avhayati & **Avheti** [Sk. āhvayati, ā + **hū** or **hvā**] — 1. to call upon, invoke, appeal to D I.244 (avhayāma imper.); PvA 164. — 2. to call, call up, summon M I.17; J II.10, 252 (= pakkosati); V.220 (avhayesi); VI.18, 192, 273 (avhettha pret.); Vv 33[1] (avheti). — 3. to give a name, to call, to address SnA 487 (= āmanteti ālapati). — pp. avhāta (q. v.).

Avhāta [pp. of avhayati] called, summoned J III.165 = (an° = anāhuta ayācita) = Pv I.12[3], cp. PvA 64. The id. p. at Th 2, 129 reads **ayācita**.

Avhāna (nt.) [fr. avhayati, Sk. āhvāna in diff. meaning] — 1. begging, calling, asking Sn 710; Vism 68 (°ānabhinandanā). — 2. addressing, naming SnA 605 (= nāma).

Avhāyana (nt) [cp. Sk. āhvayana] calling to, asking, invocation, imploration D I.11 (Sir-avhāyane, v. l. avhayana; expld. at DA I.97 with reading Sirivhāyana as "ehi Siri mayhaŋ sire patiṭṭhāhi ti evaŋ sire Siriyā avhayanaŋ"), 244, 245 (v. l. avhāna).

Avhāyika (adj.) [fr. avhaya] calling, giving a name; (m.) one who gives a name J I.401 = III.234.

Asa (adj.) [for asaŋ = asanto, a + santo, ppr. of **as** in meaning "good"] bad J IV.435 = VI.235 (sataŋ vā asaŋ, acc. sg. with v. l. santaŋ . . ., expld. by sappurisaŋ vā asappurisaŋ vā C.); V.448 (n. pl. f. asā expld. by asatiyo lāmikā C.; cp. p. 446 V.319).

Asaŋvata (adj.) [pp. of + saŋvuṇāti, cp. saŋvuta] unrestricted, open J VI.306.

Asaŋvara [a + saŋvāra] absence of closing or restraint, no control Dhs 1345.

Asaŋvāsa (adj.) [a + saŋvāsa] deprived of co-residence, expelled from the community Vin IV.213, 214.

Asaŋvindaŋ [ppr. a + saŋvindati] not finding, not knowing Th I, 717.

Asaŋvuta (adj.) [pp. of a + saŋvuṇāti, cp. saŋvata] not restrained Dhs 1345, 1347.

Asaŋsaṭṭha (adj.) [a + saŋsaṭṭha] not mixed or mixing, not associating, not given to society M I.214; S I.63; Sn 628 = Dh 404 (= dassana-savana-samullāpa paribhogakāya-saŋsaggānaŋ abhāvena SnA 469 = DhA IV.173).

Asaŋhārima (adj.) = asaŋhāriya (?) Vin IV.272.

Asaŋhāriya (adj.) [grd. of a + saŋharati] not to be destroyed or shattered It 77; Th I, 372; Nd[2] 110.

Asaŋhīra (adj.) [= asaŋhāriya of saŋ + **hṛ**] immovable, unconquerable, irrefutable Vin II.96; S I.193; A IV.141; V.71; Sn 1149 (as Ep. of Nibbāna, cp. Nd[2] 110); J I. 62; IV.283 (°citta unfaltering); Dpvs IV.12.

Asakka (adj.) [a + sakka; Sk. aśakya] impossible J V. 362 (°rūpa).

Asakkuṇeyya (adj.) [grd. of a + sakkoti] impossible, unable to J I.55; KhA 185 and passim.

Asakkhara (adj.) [a + sakkhara] not stony, free from gravel or stones, smooth J V.168; DhA III.401 (opp. sasakkhara).

Asakyadhītā (f.) [a + sakyadhītā] not a true Buddhist nun Vin IV.214.

Asagguṇa [a + sagguṇa] bad quality, vice Sdhp 382 (°bhāvin, the a° belongs to the whole cpd.).

Asankita & °iya (adj.) [a + sankita, pp. of **śank**] not hesitating, not afraid, not anxious, firm, bold J I.334 (°iya); V.241; Sdhp 435, 541.

Asankuppa (adj.) [a + sankuppa, grd. of **kup**] not to be shaken; immovable, steady, safe (Ep. of Nibbāna) Sn 1149 (cp. Nd² 106); Th 1, 649.

Asankusaka (adj.) [a + sankusaka, which is distorted from Sk. sankasuka splitting, crumbling, see Kern, *Toev.* p. 18] not contrary J VI.297 (°vattin, C. appaṭilomavattin, cp. J trsl^n. VI.143).

Asankheyya (adj.) [a + sankheyya, grd. of saŋ-**khyā**] incalculable, innumerable, nt. an immense period A II.142; Miln 232 (cattāri a.), 289 DhA I.5, 83, 104.

Asanga (adj.) [a + sanga] not sticking to anything, free from attachment, unattached Th 2, 396 (°mānasa, = anāsattacitta ThA 259); Miln 343. Cp. next.

Asangita (adj.) [fr. asanga, a + sangita, or should we read asangika?] not sticking or stuck, unimpeded, free, quick J V.409.

Asacca (adj.) [a + sacca] not true, false J V.399.

Asajjamāna (adj.) [ppr. med. of a + sajjati, **sañj**] not clinging, not stuck, unattached Sn 38, 71 (cp. Nd² 107); Dh 221 (nāmarūpasmiŋ a. = alaggamana DhA III.298).

Asajjittho 2nd sg. pret. med. of **sajjati** to stick or cling to, to hesitate J I.376. See **sajjati.**

Asajjhaya [a + sajjhāya] non-repetition Dh 241 (cp. DhA III.347).

Asañña (adj.) [a + saññā] unconscious, °**sattā** unconscious beings N. of a class of Devas D I.28 (cp. DA I.118 and BSk. asaŋjñika-sattvāḥ Divy 505).

Asaññata (adj.) [a + saññata, pp. of saŋ + **yam**] unrestrained, intemperate, lacking self-control It 43 = 90 = Sn 662 = Dh 307.

Asaññin (adj.) [a + saññin] unconscious D I.54 (°gabbhā, cp. DA I.163); III.111, 140, 263; It 87; Sn 874.

Asaṭha (adj.) [a + saṭha] without guile, not fraudulent, honest D III.47, 55, 237; DhA I.69.

Asaṇṭhita (adj.) [a + saṇṭhita] not composed, unsettled, fickle It 62, 94.

Asat (Asanto) [a + sat, ppr. of asti] not being, not being good, i. e. bad, not genuine (cp. asa); freq., e. g. Sn 94, 131, 881, 950; Dh 73, 77, 367; It 69 (asanto nirayaŋ nenti). See also **asaddhamma.**

***Asati** (& **Asanāti** q. v.) [Sk. aśnāti, **aś** to partake of, to eat or drink cp. aŋśa share, part] to eat; imper. asnātu J V 376; fut. **asissāmi** Th 1, 223; Sn 970. — ppr. med. **asamāna** J V.59; Sn 239. ger. **asitvā** Miln 167; & **asitvāna** J IV.371 (an°). pp. asita (q. v.). See also the spurious forms **asmiye** & **añhati** (añhamāna Sn 240), also **āsita**¹.

Asatiyā (adv.) [instr. of a + sati] heedlessly, unintentionally J III.486.

Asatta (adj.) [pp. of a + sajjati] not clinging or attached, free from attachment Sn 1059; Dh 419; Nd² 107, 108; DhA IV.228.

Asattha (n. adj.) [a + sattha] absence of a sword or knife, without a knife, usually combd. with **adaṇḍa** in var. phrases: see under **daṇḍa.** Also at Th 1, 757 (+ avaṇa).

Asadisa (adj.) [a + sadisa] incomparable, not having its like DhA II.89; III.120 (°dāna).

Asaddha (adj.) [a + saddha] not believing, without faith D III.252, 282.

Asaddhamma [a + sat + dhamma, cp. asat & BSk. asaddharma] evil condition, sin, esp. sexual intercourse; usually mentioned as a set of several sins, viz. as 3 at It 85; as 4 at A II.47; as 7 at D III.252, 282; as 8 at Vin II.202.

Asana¹ (nt.) [Vedic aśan(m)] stone, rock J II.91; V.131.

Asana² (nt.) [cp. Sk. aśana of **aś**, cp. asati] eating, food; adj. eating J I.472 (ghatâsana Ep. of the fire; V.64 (id.). Usually in neg. form **anasana** fasting, famine, hunger Sn 311 (= khudā SnA 324); DA I.139. See also **nirasana.**

Asana³ (nt.) [Sk. asana] the tree Pentaptera Tomentosa J I.40 (as Bodhi-tree of Gotama); II.91; V.420; VI.530.

Asana⁴ (nt.) [cp. Sk. asanā, to asyati to hurl, throw] an arrow M I.82 = S I.62. Cp. **asanī.**

Asanāti [see **asati**] to eat, to consume (food) J I.472; V.64; VI.14 (Fsb. note: read asnāti; C. paribhuñjati).

Asanī (f.) [Vedic aśani in same meaning; with Sk. aśri corner, caturaśra four cornered (see assa), to Lat. ācer pointed, sharp, Gr. ἄκρος pointed, Ags. egl sting, Ohg. ekka corner, point. Connected with this is Sk. aśan (see **asana**¹). Cp. also aŋsa & asama²] orig. a sharp stone as hurling-weapon thence in mythol. Indra's thunderbolt, thunder-clap, lightning J I.71, 167; II.154; III.323; Miln 277; VvA 83.

-**aggi** the fire of thunder, i. e. lightning or fire caused by lightning DhA III.71. -**pāta** the falling of the thunderbolt, thunderclap, lightning DA I.280 (or should we read asannipāta?); PvA 45. -**vicakka** same as °pāta (?) S II. 229 (= lābha-sakkāra-silokassa adhivacana); D III.44, 47.

Asantasaŋ & °**anto** (adj.) [ppr. of a + santasati] fearless, not afraid Sn 71, 74; J IV.101; VI.306; Nd² 109.

Asantāsin (adj.) [a + santāsin, cp. asantāsaŋ] fearless, not trembling, not afraid Sn 850; Dh 351; Nd² 109; DhA IV.70.

Asantuṭṭha [pp. of a + santussati] not contented with, greedy, insatiate, unhappy Sn 108. Cp. next.

Asantuṭṭhitā (f.) [abstr. fr. asantuṭṭhita = asantuṭṭha] dissatisfaction, discontentment D III.214 (so read for tutth°) = A I.95.

Asanthava [a + santhava] dissociation, separation from society, seclusion Sn 207.

Asandhitā (f.) [a + sandhi + tā] absence of joints, disconnected state J VI.16.

Asannata (adj.) [a + sannata] not bent or bending Sdhp 417.

Asapatta (adj.-n.) [a + sapatta = Sk. sapatna] (act.) without enmity, friendly (med.) having no enemy or foe, secure, peaceful D II.276; Sn 150 (= vigata-paccatthika, mettavihārin KhA 249); Th 2, 512.

Asapattī (f.) [a + sapattī] without co-wife or rival in marriage S IV.249.

Asappurisa [a + sappurisa, cp. asat] a low, bad or unworthy man M III.37; SnA 479 (= anariya Sn 664).

Asabala (adj.) [a + sabala] unspotted D II.80 = III.245.

Asabbha (adj.) [a + sabbha, i. e. *sabhya cp. sabhā & in meaning court: courteous, hof: höflich etc.] not belonging to the assembly-room, not consistent with good manners, impolite, vile, low, of base character J III.527 (mātugāma); Dh 77 = J III.367 = Th 1, 994; Miln 221; DhA I.256; ThA 246 (akkhi). Cp. next. — *Note.* Both sabbha and sabbhin occur only in the negative form.

Asabbhin = asabbha J I.494, more freq. in cpds. as asabbhi°, e. g.

-kāraṇa a low or sinful act Miln 280. **-rūpa** low, common J VI.386 (= asādhu-jātika, lāmaka), 387 (= asabbhijātika), 414 (= apaṇḍita-jātika). Cp. prec.

***Asabha** [Sk. ṛṣabha] see usabha.

Asama[1] (adj.) [a + sama] unequal, incomparable J I.40 (+ appaṭipuggala); Sdhp 578 (+ atula). Esp. freq. in cpd. **°dhura** lit. carrying more than an equal burden, of incomparable strength, very steadfast or resolute Sn 694 (= asama-viriya SnA 489); J I.193; VI.259, 330.

Asama[2] (nt.) [the diaeretic form of Sk. aśman hurling stone, of which the contracted form is amha (q. v.); connected with Lat. ocris "mons confragosus"; Gr. ἄκμων anvil; Lith. akmû stone, see also **asana**[1] (Sk. aśan stone for throwing) and **asani**] stone, rock DA I.270, 271 (°muṭṭhika having a hammer of stone; v. l. BB. ayamuṭṭhika); SnA 392 (instr. asmanā).

Asamaggiya (nt.) [abstr. fr. a + samagga] lack of concord, disharmony J VI.516 (so read for asāmaggiya).

Asamaṇa at Pug 27 is to be read **assamaṇa** (q. v.).

Asamapekkhana (nt.) & °ā (f.) [fr. a + sam + apekkhati] lack of consideration S III.261; Dhs 390, 1061, 1162.

Asamāhita (adj.) [a + samāhita] not composed, uncontrolled, not firm It 113 (opp. susamāhita); Dh 110, 111; Pug 35.

Asamijjhanaka (adj.) [a + samijjhana + ka] unsuccessful, without result, fruitless; f. **°ikā** J III.252.

Asamiddhi (f.) [a + samiddhi] misfortune, lack of success J VI.584.

Asamosaraṇa (nt.) [a + samosaraṇa] not coming together, not meeting, separation J V.233.

Asampakampiya (adj.) [grd. of a + sampakampeti] not to be shaken, not to be moved Sn 229 (= kampetuŋ vā cāletuŋ vā asakkuṇeyyo KhA 185).

Asampajañña (nt.) [a + sampajañña] lack of intelligence D III.213; Dhs 390, 1061, 1162, 1351.

Asampāyanto [ppr. of a + sampāyati] unable to solve or explain Sn p. 92.

Asambādha (adj.) [a + sambādha] unobstructed Sn 150 (= sambādha-virahita KhA 248); J I.80; ThA 293.

Asammodiya (nt.) [a + sammodiya] disagreement, dissension J VI.517 (= asamaggiya C.).

Asammosa [a + sammosa cp. B.Sk. asammoṣadharman Ep. of the Buddha; Divy 49 etc] absence of confusion D III.221 = Dhs 1366.

Asayaŋvasin (adj.) [a + sayaŋ + vasiŋ] not under one's own control, i. e. dependent D II.262; J I.337.

Asayha (adj.) [a + sayha, grd. of **sah** = Sk. asahya] impossible, insuperable J VI.337. Usually in cpd. **°sāhin** conquering the unconquerable, doing the impossible, achieving what has not been achieved before Th 1, 536, Pv II.9[22] (Angīrasa); It 32.

Asahana (nt.-adj.) [a + sahana] not enduring, non-endurance, inability J III.20; PvA 17.

Asahāya (adj.) [a + sahāya] one who is without friends; who is dependent on himself Miln 225.

Asā see āsa.

Asāta (adj.) [a + sāta, Sk. aśāta, Kern's interpretation & etymology of asāta at *Toev.* s.v. p. 90 is improbable] disagreeable Vin I.78 (asātā vedanā, cp. asātā vedanā M Vastu I 5); Sn 867; J I.288, 410; II.105; Dhs 152, 1343.

Asādhāraṇa (adj.) [a + sādhāraṇa cp. asādhāraṇa Divy 561] not general, not shared, uncommon, unique Vin III.35; Kh VIII.9; J I.58, 78; Miln 285; DA I.71; Sdhp 589, 592.

Asāmapāka (adj.) [a + sāma + pāka] one who does not cook (a meal) for himself (a practice of ascetics) DA I.270.

Asāra (n. adj.) [a + sāra] that which is not substance, worthlessness; adj. worthless, vain, idle Sn 937 (= asāra nissāra sārâpagata Nd[1] 409); Dh 11, 12 (cp. DhA I.114 for interpretation).

Asāraka (adj.) [a + sāraka] unessential, worthless, sapless, rotten Th 1, 260; J II.163 = DhA I.144.

Asāraddha (adj.) [a + sāraddha] not excited, cool A I.148 = It 119 (passaddho kāyo a.; v. l. assāraddha).

Asāhasa (nt.) [a + sāhasa] absence of violence, meekness, peaceableness D III.147 (asāhase rata fond of peace); acc. as adv. asāhasaŋ without violence, not arbitrarily J III.319; instr. **asāhasena** id. J VI.280; Dh 257 (= amusāvādena DhA III.382).

Asi [Vedic asi, Av. aŋhū Lat. ensis] a sword, a large knife D I.77 (= DA I.222); M II.99; A I.48 = (asinā sīsaŋ chindante); IV.97 (asinā hanti attānaŋ); J IV.118 (asi sunisito), 184; V.45 (here meaning "sickle"), 475 (asiñ ca me maññasi, probably faulty for either "āsiñ ca me" or "āsiñcam me"); Vism 201 (ñāṇâsi the sword of knowledge); PvA 253 (asinā pahaṭa).

-camma sword & shield Vin II.192; A III.93; J VI.449. **-tharu** the hilt of a sword DhA IV.66. **-nakha** having nails like swords Pgdp 29. **-patta** having sword-like leaves, with swords (knives) for leaves (of the sword-leaf-wood in Niraya, a late feature in the descriptions of Purgatory in Indian speculative Theology, see e. g. Mārk-aṇḍeya-purāṇa XII.24 sq.; Mhbhārata XII.321; Manu IV.90; XII. 75; Scherman, *Visionsliteratur* pp. 23 sq.) J VI.250 (°niraya); PvA 221 (°vana); Sdhp 194. **-pāsa** having swords for snares (a class of deities) Miln 191. **-māla** "sword-dirt", i.e. rust on a sword, a rusty sword or knife, in °ŋ karoti or kāreti "to do the rusty sword trick", a kind of torture J III.178 (+ sīsaŋ chindāpeti); Dāvs III.35. **-lakkhaṇa** "sword-sign", i. e. (fortune-telling from) marks on a sword D I.9; J I.455. **-loma** having swords for hair S II.257, cp. Vin III.106. **-sūna** slaughter-house (so also B.Sk. asisūnā Divy 10, 15; see further detail under "kāma"similes) Vin II.26; M I.130, 143; A III 97. **-sūla** a sword-blade Th 2, 488 (expld. at ThA 287 by adhikuṭṭanatthena, i. e. with reference to the executioner's block, cp. also sattisūla).

Asika (adj.) (—°) [asi + ka] having a sword, with a sword in phrase **ukkhitt'asika** with drawn sword, M I.377; J I.393.

Asita[1] [Sk. aśita, pp. of *asati, Sk. aśnāti] having eaten, eating; (nt.) that which is eaten or enjoyed, food M I.57; A III.30, 32 (°pīta-khāyita etc.); PvA 25 (id.); J VI.555 °(āsana having enjoyed one's food, satisfied). Cp. **āsita**[1].

Asita[2] (adj.) [a + sita pp. of ***śri**, Sk. aśrita] not clinging to, unattached, independent, free (from wrong desires) D II.261 (°âtiga); M I.386; Th 1, 38, 1242 (see Mrs Rh. D. in *Brethren* 404 note 2); J II.247; It 97; Sn 251, 519, 593, 686 (Asitavhaya, called the Asita i. e. the Unattached; cp. SnA 487), 698 (id.), 717, 957, 1065 (cp. Nd[2] 111 & nissaya).

Asita[3] (adj.) [Sk. asita; Idg. *ās, cp. Lat. āreo to be dry, i. e. burnt up; Gr. ἄζω to dry; orig. meaning burnt, hence of burnt, i. e. black colour (of ashes)] black-blue, black M II.180 (°vyābhangī); A III.5 (id.); Th 2, 480 (= indanīla ThA 286); J III.419 (°āpangin black-eyed); V. 302; Dāvs I.45.

Asīti (num.) [Sk. aśīti] 80 (on symbolical meaning & freq. application see aṭṭha[1] B 1 c, where also most of the ref's. In addition we mention the foll.:) J I.233 (°hattha 80 hands, i.e. 80 cubits deep); III.174 (°sahassa-vāraṇa-parivuta); VI.20 (vassasahassāni); Miln 23 (asītiyā bhikkhusahassehi saddhiŋ); Vism 46 (satakoṭiyo) DhA I.14, 19 (mahātherā); II.25 (°koṭi-vibhava). Cp. āsītika.

Asu (pron.) [Sk. asau (m.), adas (nt.); base amu° in oblique cases & derivation, e.g. adv. amutra (q.v.)] pron. demonstr. "that", that one, usually comb[d]. with yo (yaŋ), e.g. asu yo so puriso M I.366; yaŋ aduŋ khettaŋ S IV.315. — nom. sg. m. **asu** S IV.195; Miln 242; f. asu J V.396 (asū metri causā); nt. **aduŋ** M I.364, 483; A I.250. Of oblique cases e. g. **amunā** (instr.) A I.250. Cp. also next.

Asuka (pron.-adj.) [asu + ka] such a one, this or that, a certain Vin III.87; J I.148; PvA 29, 30, 35, 109, 122 (°ŋ gatiŋ gata).

Asuci (adj.) [a + suci] not clean, impure, unclean Sn 75 (°manussā, see Nd[2] 112); Pug 27, 36; Sdhp 378, 603.

Asucīka (nt.) [abstr. fr. asuci] impurity, unclean living, defilement Sn 243 (°missita = asucibhāva-missita SnA 286.

Asubha (adj.) [a + subha] impure, unpleasant, bad, ugly, nasty; nt. °ŋ nastiness, impurity. Cp. on term and the Asubha-meditation, as well as on the 10 asubhas or offensive objects *Dhs. trsl.* 70 and *Cpd.* 121 n. 6. — S IV.111 (asubhato manasikaroti); V.320; Sn 341; Sdhp 368. **-subhâsubha** pleasant unpleasant, good & bad Sn 633; J III. 243; Miln 136.

-ânupassin realising or intuitising the corruptness (of the body) It 80, 81; DhA I.76. **-kathā** talk about impurity Vin III.68. **-kammaṭṭhāna** reflection on impurity DhA III.425. **-nimitta** sign of the unclean i. e. idea of impurity Vism 77. **-bhāvanā** contemplation of the impurity (of the body) Vin III.68. **-saññā** idea of impurity D III.253, 283, 289, 291. **-saññin** having an idea of or realising the impurity (of the body) It 93.

Asura [Vedic asura in more comprehensive meaning; connected with Av. ahurō Lord, ahurō mazdā°; perhaps to Av. anhuš & Lat. erus master] a fallen angel, a Titan; pl. **asurā** the Titans, a class of mythological beings. Dhpāla at PvA 272 & the C. on J V.186 define them as kāḷakañjaka-bhedā asurā. The are classed with other similar inferior deities, e. g. with garuḷā, nāgā, yakkhā at Miln 117; with supaṇṇā, gandhabbā, yakkhā at DA I.51. — The fight between Gods & Titans is also reflected in the oldest books of the Pāli Canon and occurs in identical description at the foll. passages under the title of **devâsura-sangāma**: D II.285; S I.222 (cp. 216 sq.), IV.201 sq., V.447; M I.253; A IV.432. — Rebirth as an Asura is considered as one of the four umhappy rebirths or evil fates after death (apāyā; viz. niraya, tiracchāna-yoni, petā or pettivisaya, asurā), e. g. at It 93; J V.186; Pv IV.11[1], see also apāya. — Other passages in general: S I.216 sq. (fight of Devas & Asuras); IV.203; A II.91; IV.198 sq., 206; Sn 681; Nd[1] 89, 92, 448; DhA I.264 (°kaññā); Sdhp 366, 436.

-inda Chief or king of the Titans. Several Asuras are accredited with the rôle of leaders, most commonly Vepacitti (S I.222; IV.201 sq.) and Rāhu (A II.17, 53; III.243). Besides these we find Pahārāda (gloss Mahābhadda) at A IV.197. **-kāya** the body or assembly of the asuras A I.143; J V.186; ThA 285. **-parivāra** a retinue of Asuras A II.91. **-rakkhasā** Asuras and Rakkhasas (Rakṣasas) Sn 310 (defined by Bdhgh at SnA 323 as pabbata-pāda-nivāsino dānava-yakkha-saññitā).

Asuropa [probably a haplological contraction of asura-ropa. On various suggestions as to etym. & meaning see Morris's discussion at *JPTS.* 1893, 8 sq. The word is found as āsulopa in the Asoka inscriptions] anger, malice, hatred; abruptness, want of forbearance Pug 18 = Vbh 357; Dhs 418, 1060, 1115, 1341 (an°); DhsA 396.

Asussūsaŋ [ppr. of a + susūsati, Desid. of **śru**, cp. Sk. śuśrūṣati] not wishing to hear or listen, disobedient J V.121.

Asūyaka see **anasūyaka.**

Asūra (adj.) [a + sura[1]] — 1. not brave, not valiant, cowardly Sn 439. — 2. uncouth, stupid J VI.292 (cp. Kern. *Toev.* p. 48).

Asekha (& Asekkha) (adj. n.) [a + sekha] not requiring to be trained, adept, perfect, m. one who is no longer a learner, an expert; very often meaning an Arahant (cp. B.Sk. aśaikṣa occurring only in phrase śaikṣâśaikṣāḥ those in training & the adepts, e.g. Divy 261, 337; Av. Ś I.269, 335; II.144) Vin I.62 sq.; III.24; S I.99; D III.218, 219; It 51 (asekho sīlakkhandho; v. l. asekkha); Pug 14 (= arahant); Dhs 584, 1017, 1401; Kvu 303 sq.

-muni the perfectly Wise DhA III.321. **-bala** the power of an Arahant, enum[d]. in a set of 10 at Ps II.173, cp. 176.

Asecanaka (adj.) [a + secana + ka, fr. **sic** to sprinkle, cp. B.Sk. asecanaka-darśana in same meaning e g. Divy 23, 226, 334] unmixed, un adulterated, i. e. with full and unimpaired properties, delicious, sublime, lovely M I.114; S I.213 (a. ojava "that elixir that no infusion needs" Mrs Rh. D.) = Th 2, 55 (expl[d]. as anāsittakaŋ pakatiyā °va mahārasaŋ at ThA 61) = Th 2, 196 (= anāsittakaŋ ojavantaŋ sabhāva-madhuraŋ ThA 168); S V.321; A III. 237 sq. Miln 405.

Asevanā (f.) [a + sevanā] not practising, abstinence from Sn 259 (= abhajanā apayirupāsanā KhA 124).

Asesa (adj.) [a + sesa] not leaving a remnant, without a remainder, **all**, entire, complete Sn 2 sq., 351, 355, 500, 1037 (= sabba Nd[2] 113). As °— (adv.) entirely, fully, completely Sn p. 141 (°virāga-nirodha); Miln 212 (°vacana inclusive statement).

Asesita (adj.) [pp. of a + Caus. of **śiṣ**, see seseti & sissati] leaving nothing over, having nothing left, entire, whole, all J III.153.

Asoka[1] (adj.) [a + soka, cp. Sk. aśoka] free from sorrow Sn 268 (= nissoka abbūḷha-soka-salla KhA 153); Dh 412; Th 2, 512.

Asoka[2] [Sk. aśoka] the Asoka tree, Jonesia Asoka J V.188; Vv 35[4], 35[9] (°rukkha); Vism 625 (°ankura); VvA 173 (°rukkha).

Asoṇḍa (adj.) [a + soṇḍa] not being a drunkard, abstaining from drink J V.116. — f. asoṇḍī A III.38.

Asotata (nt.) [abstr. a + sota + ta, having no ears, being earless J VI.16.

Asnāti [Sk. aśnāti to eat, to take food; the regular Pāli forms are asati (as base) and asanāti] to eat; imper. asnātu J V.376.

Asman (nt.) [Vedic aśman; the usual P. forms are amha and asama[2]] stone, rock; only in instr. **asmanā** SnA 362.

Asmasati [spurious form for the usual assasati = Sk. āśvasati] to trust, to rely on J V.56 (Pot. asmase).

Asmi (I am) see **atthi.**

Asmimāna [asmi + māna] the pride that says "I am", pride of self, egotism (same in B.Sk. e.g. Divy 210, 314) Vin I.3; D III.273; M I.139, 425; A III.85; Ps I.26; Kvu 212; DhA I.237. Cp. ahaŋ asmi.

Asmiye 1 sg. ind. pres. med. of **aś** to eat, in sense of a fut. "I shall eat" J V.397, 405 (C. bhuñjissāmi). The form is to be expld. as denom. formn. fr. -āśa food, = aŋsiyati and with metathesis **asmiyati.** See also **añhati** which would correspond either to *aŋśyati or aśnāti (see **asati**).

Assa[1] [for aŋsa[1], q. v. for etym.] shoulder; in cpd. **assapuṭa** shoulder-bag, knapsack i. e. a bag containing provisions, instr. **assupuṭena** with provisions. Later exegesis has interpreted this as a bag full of ashes, and vv. ll. as well as Commentators take assa = bhasma ashes (thus also Morris *JPTS.* 1893, 10 without being able to give an etymology). The word was already misunderstood by Bdhgh. when he explained the Dīgha passage by bhasmapuṭena, sīse chārikaŋ okiritvā ti attho DA 1.267. After all it is the same as **puṭaŋsa** (see under aŋsa[1]). — D 1 98, cp. A II.242 (v. l. bhasma°); DA 1.267 (v. l. bhassa°).

Assa[2] [for aŋsa[2] = Sk. aśra point, corner, cp. Sk. aśri, Gr. ἄκρος & ὀξύς sharp, Lat. acer] corner, point; occurs only in cpd. **caturassa** four-cornered, quadrangular, regular (of symmetrical form, Vin II.316; J IV.46, 492; Pv II.1[19]. Perhaps also at Th 2, 229 (see under assa[3]). Occurs also in form **caturaŋsa** under catur).

Assa[3] [Vedic aśva, cp. Av. aspō; Gr. ἵππος, dial. ἴκκος; Lat. equus; Oir. ech; Gall. epo-; Cymr. ep, Goth. aíhva; Os. ehu; Ags. eoh] a horse; often mentioned alongside of and combd. with **hatthi** (elephant) Vin III.6 (pañcamattehi assa-satehi), 52 (enumd. under catuppadā, quadrupeds, with hatthi oṭṭha goṇa gadrabha & pasuka); A II.207; V.271; Sn 769 (gavâssa). At Th II.229 the commentary explains **caturassa** as 'four in hand'; but the context shows that the more usual sense of caturassa (see assa[2]) was probably what the poet meant; Dh 94, 143, 144 (bhadra, a good horse), 380 (id.); Vv 20[3] (+ assatarī); VvA 78; DhA 1.392 (hatthi-assâdayo); Sdhp 367 (duṭṭh°). **-ājānīya** [cp. BSk. aśvājāneya Divy 509, 511] a thoroughbred horse, a blood horse A 1.77, 244; II.113 sq., 250 sq.; III.248, 282 sq.; IV.188, 397; V.166, 323; PvA 216. See also **ājāniya**. **-âroha** one who climbs on a horse, a rider on horseback, N. of an occupation "cavalry" D 1.51 (+ hatthâroha; expld. at DA 1.156 by sabbe pi assācariya-assavejja-assabhaṇḍādayo). **-kaṇṇa** N. of a tree, Vatica Robusta, lit. "horse-ear" (cp. similarly Goth. aíhva-tundi the thornbush, lit. horse-tooth) J II.161; IV.209; VI.528. **-khalunka** an inferior horse ("shaker"), opp. sadassa. A 1.287 = IV.397. **-tthara** a horse cover, a horse blanket Vin 1.192; D 1.7. **-damma** a horse to be tamed, a fierce horse, a stallion A II.112; °*sārathi* a horse trainer A II. 112, 114; V.323 sq.; DhA IV.4. **-potaka** the young of a horse, a foal or colt J II.288. **-bandha** a groom J II. 98; V.449; DhA 1.392. **-bhaṇḍa** (for °bandha? or should we read °paṇḍaka?) a groom or horse-trainer, a trader in horses Vin 1.85 (see on form of word Kern, *Toev.* p. 35). **-bhaṇḍaka** horse-trappings J II.113. **-maṇḍala** circus Vism 308, cp. M 1.446. **-maṇḍalika** exercising-ground Vin III.6. **-medha** N. of a sacrifice: the horse-sacrifice [Vedic aśvamedha as Np.] S 1.76 (v. l. sassa°); It 21 (+ purisamedha); Sn 303. **-yuddha** a horse-fight D 1.7. **-rūpaka** a figure of a horse, a toy horse DhA II.69 (+ hatthi-rūpaka). **-lakkhaṇa** (earning fees by judging) the marks on a horse D 1.9. **-laṇḍa** horse-manure, horse-dung DhA IV.156 (hatthi-laṇḍa +). **-vāṇija** a horse-dealer Vin III.6. **-sadassa** a noble steed of the horse kind A 1.289 = IV.397 (in comparison with purisa°).

Assa[4] is gen. dat. sg. of **ayaŋ**, this.

Assa[5] 3. sg. Pot. of asmi (see **atthi**).

Assaka[1] (—°) [assa[3] + ka] with a horse, having a horse; an° without a horse J VI.515 (+ arathaka).

Assaka[2] (adj.) [a + saka; Sk. asvaka] not having one's own, poor, destitute M 1.450; II.68; A III.352; Ps 1 126 (v. l. asaka).

Assatara [Vedic aśvatara, aśva + compar. suffix tara in function of "a kind of", thus lit. a kind of horse, cp. Lat. matertera a kind of mother. i. e. aunt] a mule Dh 322 = DhA 1.213; DhA IV.4 (= vaḷavāya gadrabhena jāta); J IV.464 (kambojake assatare sudante: imported from Cambodia); VI.342. — f. **assatarī** a she-mule Vin II.188; S 1.154; II.241; A II.73; Miln 166. — **assatarī-ratha** a chariot drawn by she-mules Vv 20[3], 20[8] (T. assatarī ratā) = 43[8]; Pv 1.11[1] (= assatariyutta ratha PvA 56); J VI.355.

Assattha[1] [Vedic aśvattha, expld. in *KZ* 1.467 as aśvâ-ttha dial. for aśva-stha "standing place for horses, which etym. is problematic; it is likely that the Sk. word is borrowed from a local dialect.] the holy fig-tree, Ficus Religiosa; the tree under which the Buddha attained enlightenment, i. e. the Bo tree Vin IV.35; D II.4 (sammā-sambuddho assatthassa mūle abhisambuddho); S V.96; J 1.16 (V.75, in word-play with assattha[2] of V.79).

Assattha[2] [pp. of assasati; cp. BSk. āśvasta Av. Ś 1.210] encouraged, comforted A IV.184 (v. l. as gloss assāsaka); Ps 1.131 (loka an°; v. l. assaka); J 1.16 (V.79 cp. assattha[1]); VI.309 (= laddhassasa C.), 566.

Assaddha (adj.) [a + saddhā] without faith, unbelieving, Sn 663; Pug 13, 20; Dhs 1327; DhA II.187.

Assaddhiya (nt.) [a + saddhiya, in form, but not in meaning a grd. of saddahati, for which usually saddheyya; cp. Sk. aśradheyya incredible] disbelief S 1.25; A III.421; V.113 sq., 146, 148 sq., 158, 161; Vbh 371; DA 1.235; Sdhp 80.

Assama [ā + **śram**] a hermitage (of a brahmin ascetic esp. a jaṭila) Vin 1.24 = IV.108; 1.26, 246; III.147; Sn 979; Sn p. 104, 111; J 1.315 (°pada) V.75 (id.) 321. VI.76 (°pada). The word is not found anywhere in the Canon in the technical sense of the later Sanskrit law books, where "the 4 āśramas" is used as a t. t. for the four stages in the life of a brahmin priest (not of a brahmin by birth). See *Dial.* 1.211—217.

Assamaṇa [a + samaṇa] not a true Samaṇa Vin 1.96; Sn 282; Pug 27 (so read for asamaṇa); Pug A 207. — f. **assamaṇī** Vin IV.214.

Assaya [ā + sayati, **śri**] resting place, shelter, refuge, seat DA 1.67 (puññ°). Cp. BSk. rājāśraya Jtm 31[58]; aśraya also in meaning "body": see Av. Ś. 1.175 & Index II.223.

Assava (adj.) [ā + suṇāti, **śru**] loyal D 1.137; Sn 22, 23, 32; J IV.98; VI.49; Miln 254; an° inattentive, not docile DhA 1.7.

Assavati [ā + **sru**] to flow J II.276 (= paggharati C.). Cp. also āsavati.

Assavanatā (f.) [abstr. fr. assavana] not listening to, inattention M 1.168.

Assavanīya (adj.) [a + savanīya] not pleasant to hear Sdhp 82.

Assasati [ā + **śvas**, on semantical inversion of ā & pa see under **ā**[1] 3] 1. to breathe, to breathe out, to exhale, J 1 163; VI.305 (gloss assāsento passāsento susu ti saddaŋ karonto); Vism 272. Usually in combn. with **passasati** to inhale, i. e. to breathe in & out, D II.291 = M 1.56, cp. M 1.425; J II.53, cp. V.36. — 2. to breathe freely or quietly, to feel relieved, to be comforted, to have courage S IV.43; J IV.93 assasitvāna ger. = vissamitvā c.); VI.190 (assāsa imper., with mā soci); med. assase J IV.57 (C. for asmase T.; expld. by vissase), 111 (°itvā). — 3. to enter by the breath, to bewitch, enchant, take possession J IV.495 (= assāsa-vātena upahanati āvisati C.). — Caus. **assāseti**. — pp. **assattha**[2]. See also assāsa-passāsa.

Assāda [ā + sādiyati, **svad**] taste, sweetness, enjoyment, satisfaction D I.22 (vedanānaŋ samudaya atthangama assāda etc.); M I.85; S II.84 sq. (°ānupassin), 170 sq.; III.27 sq. (ko rūpassa assādo), 62, 102; IV.8 sq., 220; V.193, 203 sq.; A I.50 (°ānupassin), 258, 260; II.10; III.447 (°diṭṭhi) J I.508; IV.113, Sn 448; Ps I.139 sq., (°diṭṭhi), 157; cp. I.10[11]; Pv IV.6[2] (kām°); Vbh 368 (°diṭṭhi); Nett 27 sq.; Miln 388; Vism 76 (paviveka-ras°); Sdhp 37, 51. See also appassāda under **appa**.

Assādanā (f.) [cp. assāda] sweetness, taste, enjoyment S I 124; Sn 447 (= sādubhāva SnA 393).

Assādeti [Denom. fr. assāda] to taste S II.227 (lābha-sakkāra-silokaŋ); Vism 73 (paviveka-sukha-rasaŋ); DhA I.318.

Assāraddha v. l. at It 111 for asāraddha.

Assāvin (adj.) [ā + **sru**] only in **an°** not enjoying or finding pleasure, not intoxicated Sn 853 (sātiyesu a. = sāta-vatthusa kāmaguṇesu taṇhā-santhava-virahita SnA 549). See also **āsava**.

Assāsa [Sk. āśvāsa, ā + **śvas**] 1. (lit.) breathing, esp. breathing out (so Vism 272), exhalation, opp. to **passāsa** inhalation, with which often comb[d.] or contrasted; thus as cpd. **assāsa-passāsa** meaning breathing (in & out), sign of life, process of breathing, breath D II.157 = S I.159 = Th 1, 905; D III.266; M I.243; S I.106; IV.293; V.330, 336; A IV.409; V.135; J II.146; VI.82; Miln 31, 85; Vism 116, 197. — assāsa in contrast with passāsa at Ps I.95, 164 sq., 182 sq. — 2. (fig.) breathing easily, freely or quietly, relief, comfort, consolation, confidence M I.64; S II.50 (dhamma-vinaye); IV.254 (param-assāsa-ppatta); A I.192; III.297 sq. (dhamma-vinaye); IV.185; J VI.309 (see assattha[2]); Miln 354; PvA 104 (°matta only a little breathing space); Sdhp 299 (param°), 313.

Assāsaka (adj. n.) [fr. assāsa] 1. (cp. assāsa 1) having breath, breathing, in **an°** not able to draw breath Vin III.84; IV.111. — 2. (cp. assāsa[2]) (m. & nt.) that which gives comfort & relief, confidence, expectancy J I.84; VI. 150. Cp. next.

Assāsika (adj.) [fr. assāsa in meaning of assāsa 2, cp. assāsaka 2] only in neg. **an°** not able to afford comfort, giving no comfort or security M I.514; III.30; J II.298 (= aññaŋ assāsetuŋ asamatthatāya na assāsika). Cp. BSk. anāśvāsika in ster. phrase anitya adhruva anāśvāsika vipariṇāmadharman Divy 207; Av. Ś. 139, 144; whereas the corresp. Pāli equivalent runs anicca addhuva asassata (= appāyuka) vipariṇāma-dhamma thus inviting the conjecture that BSk. āśvāsika is somehow destorted out of P. asassata.

Assāsin (adj.) [Sk. āśvāsin] reviving, cheering up, consoled, happy S IV.43 (an°).

Assāseti [Caus. of assasati] to console, soothe, calm, comfort, satisfy J VI.190, 512; DhA I.13.

Assita (adj.) [Sk. aśrita. ā + pp. of **śri**] dependent on, relying, supported by (acc.); abiding, living in or on D II.255 (tad°); Vv 50[10] (sīho va guhaŋ a.): Th 1, 149 (janaŋ ev' assito jano); Sdhp 401.

Assirī (adj.) [a + siri] without splendour, having lost its brightness, in **assirī viya khāyati** Nett 62 = Ud 79 (which latter has sassar' iva, cp. C. on passage l. c.).

Assu[1] (nt.) [Vedic aśru, Av. asrū, Lith aszarà, with etym. not definitely clear: see Walde, *Lat. Wtb.* under lacrima] a tear Vin I.87 (assūni pavatteti to shed tears); S II.282 (id.); Dh 74; Th 2, 496 (cp. ThA 289); KhA 65; DhA I.12 (°puṇṇa-netta with eyes full of tears); II.98; PvA 125.
-dhārā a shower of tears DhA IV.15 (pavatteti to shed). **-mukha** (adj.) with tearful face [cp. BSk. aśrumukha e. g. Jtm 31[76]] D I.115, 141; Dh 67; Pug 56; DA I.284; PvA 39. **-mocana** shedding of tears PvA 18.

Assu[2] is 3rd pl. pot. of **atthi**.

Assu[3] (indecl.) [Sk. sma] expletive part. also used in emphatic sense of "surely, yes, indeed" Sn 231 (according to Fausböll, but preferably with P. T. S. ed. as tayas su for tay' assu, cp. KhA 188); Vv 32[4] (assa v. l. SS) = VvA 135 (assū ti nipāta-mattaŋ). Perhaps we ought to take this assu[3] together with the foll. assu[4] as a modification of ssu (see **su**[2]). Cp. āsu.

Assu[4] part. for Sk svid (and sma?) see under **su**[2]. According to this view Fausbölls reading ken' assu at Sn 1032 is to be emended to kena ssu.

Assuka (nt.) [assu[1] + ka] a tear Vin II.289; Sn 691; Pv IV.5[3].

Assutavant (adj.) [a + sutavant] one who has not heard, ignorant M I.1, 8, 135; Dhs 1003, 1217, cp. Dhs trsl. 258.

Aha[1] (indecl.) [cp. Sk. aha & P. aho; Germ. aha; Lat. ehem etc.] exclamation of surprise, consternation, pain etc. "oh! alas! woe!". Perhaps to be seen in cpd. °**kāmā** miserable pleasures lit. "woe to these pleasures!") gloss at ThA 292 for T. kāmakāmā of Th 2, 506 (expl[d.] by C. as "ahā ti lāmaka-pariyāyo"). See also **ahaha**.

Aha[2] (—°) & **Aho** (°—) (nt.) [Vedic ahan & ahas] a day. (1) °**aha** only in foll. cpds. & cases: *instr.* ekâhena in one day J VI. 366; *loc.* tadahe on that (same) day PvA 46; *acc.* katipâhaŋ (for) some or several days J I.152 etc. (kattpâha); sattāhaŋ seven days, a week Vin I.1; D II. 14; J IV.2, and freq.; anvahaŋ daily Dāvs IV.8. — The initial **a** of **ahaŋ** (*acc.*) is elided after l, which often appears lengthened: kati 'haŋ how many days? S I.7; ekâha-dvī 'haŋ one or two days J I.292; dvīha-tī 'han two or three days J II.103; VvA 45; ekâha-dvī 'h' accayena after the lapse of one or two days J I.253. — A doublet of aha is **anha** (through metathesis from ahan), which only occurs in phrases **pubbanho** & **sāyanha** (q. v.); an adj. der. fr. aha is °**ahika**: see pañcâhika (consisting of 5 days). — (2) **aho**° in cpd. **ahoratta** (m. & nt.) [cp. BSk. ahorātraŋ Av. Ś. I.209] & **ahoratti** (f.) day & night, occurring mostly in oblique cases and adverbially in *acc.* **ahorattaŋ**: M I.417 (°ānusikkhin); Dh 226 (id.; expl[d.] by divā ca rattiñ ca tisso sikkhā sikkhamāna DhA III. 324); Th 1, 145 (ahorattā accayanti); J IV.108 (°ānaŋ accaye); Pv II.13[1] (°ŋ); Miln 82 (ena). — **ahorattiŋ** Dh 387; J VI.313 (v. l. BB for T. aho va rattiŋ).

Ahaŋ (pron.) [Vedic ahaŋ = Av. azəm; Gr. ἐγώ(ν); Lat. ego; Goth. ik, Ags. ic, Ohg. ih etc.] pron. of 1st person "I". — nom. sg. **ahaŋ** S III.235; A IV.53; Dh 222, 320; Sn 172, 192, 685, 989, 1054, 1143; J I.61; II.159. — In pregnant sense (my ego, myself, I as the one & only, i. e. egotistically) in foll. phrases: yaŋ vadanti mama . . na te ahaŋ S I.116, 123; ahaŋ asmi "I am" (cp. ahaŋkāra below) S I.129; III.46, 128 sq.; IV.203; A II.212, 215 sq.; Vism 13; ahaŋ pure ti "I am the first" Vv 84[50] (= ahamahaŋkārā ti VvA 351). — gen. dat. **mayhaŋ** Sn 431, 479; J I.279; II.160, **mama** S I.115; Sn 22, 23, 341, 997; J II.159, & **mamaŋ** S I.116; Sn 253 (= mama C.), 694, 982. — instr. **mayā** Sn 135, 336, 557, 982; J I.222, 279. — acc. **maŋ** Sn 356, 366, 425, 936; J II. 159; III.26, & **mamaŋ** J III.55, 394. — loc. **mayi** Sn 559; J III 188. The enclitic form the sg. is me, & functions in diff. cases, as gen. (Sn 983; J II.159), acc. (Sn 982), instr. (J I.138, 222), & abl. — Pl. nom. **mayaŋ** (we) Sn 31, 91, 167, 999; J II.159; VI.365, **amhe** J II. 129, & **vayaŋ** (q. v.). — gen. **amhākaŋ** J I.221; II.159 & **asmākaŋ** Sn p. 106. — acc. **amhe** J I.222; II.415 & **asme** J III.359. — instr. **amhehi** J I.150; II.417 & **asmābhi** ThA 153 (Ap. 132). — loc. **amhesu** J I.222. — The enclitic form for the pl. is no (for acc. dat & gen.): see under **vayaŋ**.
-kāra selfishness, egotism, arrogance (see also mamaŋkāra) M III.18, 32; S II.253; III.80, 136, 169 sq.; IV.41, 197, 202; A I.132 sq.; III.444; Ud 70; Nett 127, and freq. passim.

Ahaha [onomat. after exclamation ahahā: see aha¹] 1. exclamation of woe J III.450 (ahahā in metre). — 2. (nt.) N. of a certain division of Purgatory (Niraya), lit. oh woe! A V.173 = Sn p. 126.

Ahāsa [a + hāsa, cp. Sk. ahāsa & aharṣa] absence of exultancy, modesty J III.466 (= an-ubbillāvitattaŋ C.).

Ahāsi 3rd sg. aor. of **harati** (q. v.).

Ahi [Vedic ahi, with Av. aži perhaps to Lat. anguis etc., see Walde *Lat. Wtb.* s. v.] a snake Vin II.109; D I.77; S IV.198; A III.306 sq.; IV.320; V.289; Nd¹ 484; Vism 345 (+ kukkura etc.); VvA 100; PvA 144.
-kuṇapa the carcase of a snake Vin III.68 = M I.73 = A IV.377. **-gāha** a snake catcher or trainer J VI.192. **-guṇṭhika** (? reading uncertain, we find as vv. ll. °guṇḍika, °guṇṭika & °kuṇḍika; the BSk. paraphrase is °tuṇḍika Divy 497. In view of this uncertainty we are unable to pronounce a safe etymology; it is in all probability a dialectical, may be Non-Aryan, word. See also under kuṇḍika & guṇṭhika & cp. Morris in *J P T S.* 1886, 153) a snake charmer J I.370 (°guṇḍ°); II.267; III.348 (°guṇḍ°); IV.456 (T. °guṇṭ; v. l. BB °kuṇḍ°) 308 (T. °kuṇḍ°, v. l. SS °guṇṭh°), 456 (T. °guṇṭ°; v. l. BB °kuṇḍ°); VI.171 (T. °guṇḍ°; v. l. BB °kuṇḍ°); Miln 23, 305. **-chattaka** (nt.) "a snake's parasol", a mushroom D III.87; J II.95; Ud 81 (C. on VIII.5, 1). **-tuṇḍika** = °guṇṭhika Vism 304, 500. **-peta** a Peta in form of a snake DhA II.63. **-mekhalā** "snake-girdle", i. e. outfit or appearance of a snake DhA I.139. **-vātaka** (-roga) N. of a certain disease ("snake-wind-sickness") Vin I.78; J II.79; IV.200; DhA I.169, 187, 231; III.437. **-vijjā** "snake-craft", i. e. fortune-telling or sorcery by means of snakes D I.9 (= sappa-daṭṭha-tikicchana-vijjā c' eva sapp' avhāyana-vijjā ca "the art of healing snake bites as well as the invocation of snakes (for magic purposes)" DA I.93).

Ahiŋsaka (adj.) [fr. ahiŋsā] not injuring others, harmless, humane, S I.165; Th 1, 879; Dh 225; J IV.447.

Ahiŋsā (f.) [a + hiŋsā] not hurting, humanity, kindness D III.147; A I.151; Dh 261, 270; J IV.71; Miln 402.

Ahita (adj.-n.) [a + hita] not good or friendly, harmful, bad; unkindliness D III.246; Dh 163; Sn 665, 692; Miln 199 (°kāma).

Ahirika & **Ahirīka** (adj.) [fr. a + hirī] shameless, unscrupulous D III.212, 252, 282; A II.219; Dh 244; Sn 133 (°īka); It 27 (°īka); Pug 19 (also nt. unscrupulousness); Dhs 365; Nett 39, 126; DhA III.352.

Ahīnindriya see discussed under **abhinindriya.**

Ahuvāsiŋ 1st sg. pret. of hoti (q. v.) I was Vv 82⁶ (= ahosiŋ VvA 321).

Ahuhāliya (nt.) [onomat.] a hoarse & loud laugh J III.223 (= danta-vidaŋsaka-mahā-hasita C.).

Ahe (indecl.) [= aho, cp. aha¹] exclamation of surprise or bewilderment: alas! woe etc., perhaps in cpd. **ahevana** a dense forest (lit. oh! this forest, alas! the forest (i. e. how big it is) J V.63 (uttamāhevanandaho, if reading is correct, which is not beyond doubt. C. on p. 64 expl^s. as "ahevanaŋ vuccati vanasaṇḍo").

Aho (indecl.) [Sk. aho, for etym. see **aha¹**] exclamation of surprise, astonishment or consternation: yea, indeed, well; I say! for sure! VvA 103 (aho ti acchariy' atthena nipāto); J I.88 (aho acchariyaŋ aho abbhutaŋ), 140. Usually comb^d. with similar emphatic particles, e. g. aho vata DhA II.85; PvA 131 (= sādhu vata); aho vata re D I. 107; Pv II.9⁴⁵. Cp. **ahe.**

Ahosi-kamma (nt.) an act or thought whose kamma has no longer any potential force: *Cpd.* 145. At p. 45 ahosikakamma is said to be a kamma inhibited by a more powerful one. See Buddhaghosa in Vism. Chap. XIX.

LIST OF CORRECTIONS.

p. 15, col. 2, l. 21 fr. b. read symmetry for summetry.
p. 45, col. 2, l. 22 fr. t. read anūpaghāta for anūpghāta.
p. 19, col. 2, l. 9 fr. t. read atidūra for atidura.
p. 54, col. 2, l. 22 fr. t. read vowels for vorvels.

THE PALI TEXT SOCIETY'S PALI-ENGLISH DICTIONARY

EDITED BY

T. W. RHYS DAVIDS F.B.A. D.Sc. Ph.D. LL.D. D.Litt.

and WILLIAM STEDE Ph.D.

Part II (Ā—O)

PUBLISHED BY
THE PALI TEXT SOCIETY
LONDON

First published - - - 1922
Reprinted - - - - 1948
Reprinted - - - - 1952

Ā[1] (indecl.) [Vedic ā, prep. with acc., loc., abl., meaning "to, towards", & also "from". Orig. an emphatic-deictic part. (Idg. *ē) = Gr. ἦ surely, really; Ohg. -ā etc., increment of a (Idg. *e), as in Sk. a-sau; Gr. ἐκεῖ (cp. a[3]), see Brugmann, *Kurze Vergl. Gr.* 464, 465] a frequent prefix, used as well-defined simple base-prefix (with root-derivations), but not as modification (i. e. first part of a double prefix cpd. like sam-ā-dhi) except in one case ā-ni-saŋsa (which is doubtful & of diff. origin, viz. from combn. āsaŋsa-nisaŋsa, see below 3[b]). It denotes either *touch* (contact) or a personal (close) relation to the object (ā ti anussaraṇ' atthe nipāto PvA 165), or the *aim* of the action expressed in the verb. — (1.) As *prep.* c. abl. only in J in meaning "up to, until, about, near" J VI.192 (ā sahassehi = yāva s. C.), prob. a late development. As *pref.* in meaning "forth, out, to, towards, at, on" in foll. applications: — (a) *aim* in general or *touch* in particular (lit.), e. g. ākaḍḍhati pull to, along or up; °kāsa shining forth; °koṭeti knock *at*; °gacchati go towards; °camati rinse over; °neti bring towards, *ad*-duce; °bhā shining forth; °bhujati bend in; °masati touch at; °yata stretched out; °rabhati *at*-tempt; °rohana a-scending; °laya hanging on; °loketi look at; °vattati ad-vert; °vahati bring to; °vāsa dwelling at; °sādeti touch; °sīdati sit by; °hanati strike at. — (b) in *reflexive* function: close relation to *subject* or person actively concerned, e. g. ādāti take on or up (to oneself); °dāsa looking at, mirror; °dhāra support; °nandati rejoice; °nisaŋsa subjective gain; °bādha being affected; °modita pleased; °rakkha guarding; °rādhita satisfied; °rāma (personal) delight in; °lingati embrace (to oneself); °hāra taking to (oneself). — (c) in *transitive* function: close relation to the *object* passively concerned, e. g. āghātana killing; °carati indulge in; °cikkhati point out, explain; °jīva living on; °ṇāpeti give an order to somebody; °disati point out to some one; °bhindati cut; °manteti ad-dress; °yācati pray to; °roceti speak to; siñcati besprinkle; °sevati indulge in. — (d) out of meaning (a) develops that of an intensive-frequentative prefix in sense of "all-round, completely, very much", e. g. ākiṇṇa strewn all over; °kula mixed up; °dhuta moved about; °rāva shouting out or very much; °luḷati move about; °hiṇḍati roam about. — 2. *Affinities.* Closely related in meaning and often interchanging are the foll. prep. (prefixes): anu (°bhati), abhi (°saŋsati), pa (°tapati), paṭi (°kankhati) in meaning 1 a—c; and vi (°kirati, °ghāta, °cameti, °lepa, °lopa), sam (°tapati, °dassati) in meaning 1 d. See also 3[b]. — 3. *Combinations*: (a) Intensifying combns. of other modifying prefixes with ā as base: anu + ā (anvā-gacchati, °disati, °maddati, °rohati, °visati, °sanna, °hata), paṭi + ā (paccā-janati, °ttharati, °dāti, °savati), pari + ā (pariyā-ñāta, °dāti, °pajjati, °harati), sam + ā (samā-disati, °dāna, °dhi, °pajjati, °rabhati). — (b) Contrast-combns. with other pref. in a double cpd. of noun, adj. or verb (cp. above 2) in meaning of "up & down, in & out, to & fro"; ā + **ni**: āvedhika-nibbedhika, āsaŋsa-nisaŋsa (contracted to ānisaŋsa), āsevita-nisevita; ā + **pa**: assasati-passasati (where both terms are semantically alike; in exegesis however they have been differentiated in a way which looks like a distortion of the original meaning, viz. assasati is taken as "breathing *out*", passasati as "breathing *in*": see Vism 271), assāsa-passāsa, āmodita-pamodita, āhuna-pāhuna, āhuneyya-pāhuneyya; ā + **paccā**: ākoṭita-paccākoṭita; ā + **pari**: ākaḍḍhana-parikaḍḍhana, āsankita-parisankita; ā + **vi**: ālokita-vilokita, āvāha-vivāha, āveṭhana-viniveṭhana; a + **sam**: allāpa-sallāpa: ā + **samā**: āciṇṇa-samāciṇṇa. — 4. Before double consonants ā is shortened to a and words containing ā in this form are to be found under a°, e. g. akkamaṇa, akkhitta, acchādeti, aññāta, appoṭeti, allāpa, assāda.

Ā°[2] guṇa or increment of a° in connection with such suffixes as -ya, -iya, -itta. So in āyasakya fr. ayasaka; āruppa from arūpa; ārogya fr. aroga; ālasiya fr. alasa; ādhipacca fr. adhipati; ābhidosika fr. abhidosa etc.

Ā°[3] of various other origins (guṇa e. g. of ṛ or lengthening of ordinary root a°), rare, as ālinda (for alinda), āsabha (fr. usabha).

Ā°[4] infix in repetition-cpds. denoting accumulation or variety (by contrast with the opposite, cp. ā[1] 3[b]), constitutes a guṇa- or increment-form of neg. pref. a (see a[2]), as in foll.: **phalâphala** all sorts of fruit (lit. what is fruit & not fruit) freq. in Jātakas, e. g. I.416; II.160; III.127; IV.220, 307, 449; V.313; VI.520; **kāraṇâkāraṇāni** all sorts of duties J VI.333; DhA I.385; **khaṇḍâkhaṇḍa** pêle-mêle J I.114; III.256; **gaṇḍâgaṇḍa** a mass of boils DhA III.297; **cirâciraŋ** continually Vin IV.261; **bhavâbhava** all kinds of existences Sn 801, cp. Nd[1] 109; Nd[2] 664; Th I, 784 (°esu = mahant-âmahantesu bh. C., see *Brethren* 305); **rūpârūpa** the whole aggregate ThA 285; etc.

Ākankhati [ā + **kānkṣ**, cp. **kankhati**] to wish for, think of, desire; intend, plan, design Vin II.244 (°amāna); D I.78, 176; S I.46; Sn 569 (°amāna); Sn p. 102 (= icchati SnA 436); DhA I.29; SnA 229; VvA 149; PvA 229.

Ākankhā f. [fr. ā + **kānkṣ**] longing, wish; as adj. at Th I, 1030.

Ākaḍḍhati [ā + kaḍḍhati] to pull along, pull to (oneself), drag or draw out, pull up Vin II.325 (Bdhgh. for apakassati, see under apakāsati); IV.219; J I.172, 192, 417; Miln 102, 135; ThA 117 (°eti); VvA 226; PvA 68. — Pass. **ākaḍḍhiyati** J II.122 (°amāna-locana with eyes drawn away or attracted); Miln 102; Vism 163; VvA 207 (°amāna-hadaya with torn heart). — pp. **ākaḍḍhita**.

Ākaḍḍhana (nt.) [fr. ākaḍḍhati] drawing away or to, pulling out, distraction VvA 212 (°parikaḍḍhana pulling about); DhsA 363; Miln 154 (°parikaḍḍhana), 352. — As f. Vin III.121.

Ākaḍḍhita [pp. of akaḍḍheti] pulled out, dragged along; upset, overthrown J III.256 (= akkhitta[2]).

Ākantana (?) a possible reading, for the dūrakantana of the text at Th I, 1123, for which we might read dūrākantana.

Ākappa [cp. Sk. ākalpa ā + kappa] 1. attire, appearance, Vin I.44 (an°) = II.213; J I.505. — 2. deportment Dhs 713 (ā° gamanādi-ākāro DhsA 321).
-sampanna, suitably attired, well dressed, A III.78; J IV.542; **an°** sampanna, ill dressed, J I.420.

Ākampita [pp. of ākampeti, Caus. of ā + **kamp**] shaking, trembling Miln 154 (°hadaya).

Ākara [cp. Sk. ākara] a mine, usually in cpd. **ratan-ākara** a mine of jewels Th I, 1049; J II.414; VI. 459; Dpvs I.18. — Cp. also Miln 356; VvA 13.

Ākassati [ā + kassati] to draw along, draw after, plough, cultivate Nd[1] 428.

Ākāra [a + karoti, **kṛ**] "the (way of) making", i. e. (1) state, condition J I.237 (avasan° condition of inhabitability); II.154 (patan° state of falling, labile equilibrium), cp. paṇṇ°. — (2) property, quality, attribute D I.76 (anāvila sabb°-sampanna endowed with all good qualities, of a jewel); II.157 (°varûpeta); J II.352 (sabb° paripuṇṇa altogether perfect in qualities). — (3) sign, appearance, form, D I.175; J I.266 (chātak° sign of hunger); Miln 24 (°ena by the sign of..); VvA 27 (therassa ā. form of the Th.); PvA 90, 283 (rañño ā. the king's person); Sdhp 363. — (4) way, mode, manner, sa-ākāra in all their modes D I.13 = 82 = III.111; J I.266 (āgaman° the mode of his coming). Esp. in instr. sg. & pl. with *num.* or *pron.* (in this way, in two ways etc.): chah'ākārehi in a sixfold manner Nd[2] 680 (cp. kāraṇehi in same sense); Nett 73, 74 (dvādasah'ākārehi); Vism 613 (navah'ākārehi indriyāni tikkhāni bhavanti); PvA 64 (yen'ākārena āgato ten'ākārena gato as he came so he went), 99 (id.). — (5) reason, ground, account D I.138, 139; Nett 4, 8 sq., 38; DhA I.14; KhA 100 (in expln. of evaŋ). In this meaning freq. with **dass** (dasseti, dassana, nidassana etc.) in commentary style "what is meant by", the (statement of) reason why or of, notion, idea PvA 26 (dātabb°-dassana), 27 (thoman°-dassana), 75 (kāruññ°ŋ dassesi), 121 (pucchan°-nidassanaŋ what has been asked); SnA 135 (°nidassana).

-parivitakka study of conditions, careful consideration, examination of reasons S II.115; IV.138; A II.191 = Nd[2] 151.

Ākāraka (nt.) [ākāra + ka] appearance; reason, manner (cp. ākāra[4]) J I.269 (ākārakena = kāraṇena C.).

Ākāravant (adj.) [fr. ākāra] having a reason, reasonable, founded M I.401 (saddhā).

Ākāsa[1] [Sk. ākāśa fr. ā + **kāś**, lit. shining forth, i. e. the illuminated space] air, sky, atmosphere; space. On the concept see *Cpd.* 5, 16, 226. On a fanciful etym. of ākāsa (fr. ā + kassati of **kṛṣ**) at DhsA 325 see *Dhs trsl.* 194. — D I.55 (°ŋ indriyāni sankamanti the sense-faculties pass into space); III.224, 253, 262, 265; S III.207; IV.218; V.49, 264; J I.253; II.353; III.52, 188; IV.154; VI.126; Sn 944, 1065; Nd[1] 428; Pv II.1[18]; SnA 110, 152; PvA 93; Sdhp 42, 464. -ākāsena gacchati to go through the air PvA 75 (āgacch°), 103, 105, 162; °ena carati id. J II.103; °e gacchati id. PvA 65 (cando). — Formula "**ananto ākāso**" freq.; e. g. at D I.183; A II.184; IV. 40, 410 sq.; V.345.

-anta "the end of the sky", the sky, the air (on °anta see anta[1] 4) J VI.89. **-ānañca** (or **ânañca**) the infinity of space, in cpd. °āyatana the sphere or plane of the infinity of space, the "space-infinity-plane", the sphere of unbounded space. The consciousness of this sphere forms the first one of the 4 (or 6) higher attainments or recognitions of the mind, standing beyond the fourth jhāna, viz. (1) ākās°, (2) viññāŋ'ānañc-āyatana (3) ākiñcaññ°, (4) n'eva saññânâsaññ°, (5) nirodha, (6) phala. — D I.34, 183; II.70, 112, 156; III.224, 262 sq.; M I.40, 159; III. 27, 44; S V.119; Ps I.36; Dhs 205, 501, 579, 1418; Nett 26, 39; Vism 326, 340, 453; DA I.120 (see Nd[2] under ākāsa; Dhs 265 sq.; *Dhs trsl.* 71). As classed with jhāna see also Nd[2] 672 (sādhu-vihārin). **-kasiṇa** one of the kasiṇ'āyatanas (see under kasiṇa) D III.268; A I.41. **-gangā** N. of the celestial river J I.95; III.344. **-gamana** going through the air (as a trick of elephants) Miln 201. **-cārika** walking through the air J II.103. **-cārin** = °cārika VvA 6. **-ṭṭha** living in the sky (of devatā) Bu I.29; Miln 181, 285; KhA 120; SnA 476. **-tala** upper story, terrace on the top of a palace SnA 87. **-dhātu** the element of space D III.247; M I 423; III.31; A I.176; III.34; Dhs 638.

Ākāsa[2] (nt.?) a game, playing chess 'in the air' (*sans voir*) Vin II.10 = D I.6 (= aṭṭhapada-dasapadesu viya ākāse yeva kīḷanaŋ DA I.85).

Ākāsaka (adj.) [ākāsa + ka] being in or belonging to the air or sky J VI.124.

Ākāsati [fr. ākāsa[1]] to shine J VI.89.

Ākiñcañña (nt.) [abstr. fr. akiñcana] state of having nothing, absence of (any) possessions; nothingness (the latter as philosophical t. t.; cp. below °āyatana & see *Dhs trsl.* 74). — Sn 976, 1070, 1115 (°sambhava, cp. Nd[2] 116); Th 2, 341 (= akiñcanabhāva ThA 240; trsl. "cherish no wordly wishes whatsoëer"); Nd[2] 115, see ākāsa; Miln 342.

-āyatana realm or sphere of nothingness (cp. ākāsa°) D I.35, 184; II.156; III.224, 253, 262 sq.; M I.41, 165; II.254, 263; III.28, 44, S IV.217; A I.268; IV.40, 401; Ps I.36; Nett 26, 39; Vism 333. See also jhāna & vimokkha.

Ākiṇṇa [pp. of ākirati] 1. strewn over, beset with, crowded, full of, dense, rich in (°—) Vin III.130 (°loma with dense hair); S I.204 (°kammanta "in motley tasks engaged"); IV.37 (gāmanto ā. bhikkhūhi etc.); A III.104 (°vihāro); IV.4; V.15 (an° C. for appakiṇṇa); Sn 408 (°varalakkhaṇa = **vipula**-varalakkh° SnA 383); Pv II.12[4] (nānā-dijagaṇ° = āyutta PvA 157); Pug 31; PvA 32 (= parikiṇṇa); Sdhp 595. — Freq. in idiomatic phrase describing a flourishing city "iddha phīta bahujana ākiṇṇa-manussa", e. g. D I.211; II.147 (°yakkha for °manussa; full of yakkhas, i. e. under their protection); A III.215; cp. Miln 2 (°jana-manussa). — 2. (uncertain whether to be taken as above 1 or as equal to avakiṇṇa fr. avakirati 2) dejected, base, vile, ruthless S I.205 = J III.309 = 539 = SnA 383. At *K. S.* 261, Mrs. Rh. D. translates "ruthless" & quotes C. as implying twofold exegesis of (a) impure, and (b) hard, ruthless. It is interesting to notice that Bdhgh. explains the same verse differently at SnA 383, viz. by **vipula**°, as above under Sn 408, & takes ākiṇṇaludda as vipulaludda, i. e. beset with cruelty, very or intensely cruel, thus referring it to ākiṇṇa 1.

Ākirati [ā + kirati] to strew over, scatter, sprinkle, disperse, fill, heap Sn 665; Dh 313; Pv II.4[9] (dānaŋ vipulaŋ ākiri = vippakirati PvA 92); Miln 175, 238, 323 (imper. ākirāhi); Sn 383. — pp. ākiṇṇa.

Ākiritatta (nt.) [ākirita + tta; abstr. fr. ākirita, pp. of ākirati Caus.] the fact or state of being filled or heaped with Miln 173 (sakataŋ dhaññassa ā).

Ākilāyati v. l. at KhA 66 for āgilāyati.

Ākucca (or °ā?) [etym. unknown, prob. non-Aryan] an iguana J VI.538 (C. godhā; gloss amatt'ākuccā).

Ākurati [onomat. to sound-root ***kur** = ***kor** as in Lat. cornix, corvus etc. See gala note 2 B and cp. kukkuṭa kokila, khaṭa etc., all words expressing a rasping noise in the throat. The attempts at etym. by Trenckner (Miln p. 425 as Denom. of ākula) & Morris (*J P T S.* 1886, 154 as contr. Denom. of ankura "intumescence", thus meaning "to swell") are hardly correct] to be hoarse Miln 152 (kaṇṭho ākurati).

Ākula (adj.) [ā + ***kul** of which Sk.-P. kula, to Idg *quel to turn round, cp. also cakka & carati; lit. meaning "revolving quickly", & so "confused"] entangled, confused, upset, twisted, bewildered J I.123 (salākaggaŋ °ŋ karoti to upset or disturb); Vv 84[9] (andha°); PvA 287 (an° clear). Often reduplicated as **ākulākula** thoroughly confused Miln 117, 220; PvA 56; **ākula-pākula** Ud 5 (so read for akkula-pakkula); **ākula-samākula** J VI.270. — On phrase **tantākula-jātā gulā-guṇṭhika-jātā** see **guḷā**.

Ākulaka (adj.) [fr. ākula] entangled D II.55 (tant° for the usual tantākula, as given under guḷā).

Ākulanīya (adj.) [grd. of ā + *kulāyati, Denom. of kula] in an° not to be confounded or upset PvA 118.

Ākuli (-puppha) at KhA 60 (milāta°) read (according to Index p. 870) as milāta-**bakula**-puppha. Vism 260 (id. p.) however reads ākuli-puppha "tangle-flower" (?), cp. Ud 5, gāthā 7 bakkula, which is preferably to be read as pākula.

Ākoṭana[1] (nt.) [fr. ākoṭeti] beating on, knocking M I.385; Miln 63, 306; DhsA 144.

Ākoṭana[2] (adj.) [= ākoṭana[1]] beating, driving, inciting, urging J VI.253 (f. ākoṭanī of paññā, expld. by "nivāraṇa-patoda-laṭṭhi viya paññā koṭinī hoti" p. 254).

Ākoṭita [pp. of ākoṭeti] — 1. beaten, touched, knocked against J I.303; Miln 62 (of a gong). — 2. pressed, beaten down (tight), flattened, in phrase ākoṭita-paccākoṭita flattened & pressed all round (of the cīvara) S II. 281; DhA I.37.

Ākoṭeti [a + koṭṭeti, Sk. kuṭṭayati; BSk. ākoṭayati e.g. Divy 117 dvāraŋ trir ā°, Cowell "break" (?); Av.Ś. Index p. 222 s. v.] — 1. to beat down, pound, stamp J I.264. — 2. to beat, knock, thrash Vin II.217; J II.274; PvA 55 (aññamaññaŋ); Sdhp 159. — 3. Esp. with ref. to knocking at the door, in phrases aggaḷaŋ koṭeti to beat on the bolt D I.89; A IV.359; V.65; DA I.252 (cp. aggaḷa); dvāraŋ ā. J V.217; DhA II.145; or simply ākoṭeti Vv 81[11] (ākoṭayitvāna = appoṭetvā VvA 316). — 4. (intrs.) to knock against anything J I.239. — pp. ākoṭita (q. v.). Caus. II. ākoṭapeti J III.361.

Ākhu [Vedic ākhu, fr. ā + **khan**, lit. the digger in, i. e. a mole; but given as rat or mouse by Halāyudha] a mouse or rat Pgdp 10.

Āgacchati [ā + gacchati, **gam**] to come to or towards, approach, go back, arive etc.

I. *Forms* (same arrangement as under gacchati): (1) √**gacch**: *pres.* āgacchati D I.161; J II.153; Pv IV.1[51]; *fut.* āgacchissati J III.53; *aor.* āgacchi Pv II.13[3]; PvA 64. — (2) √**gam**: *aor.* āgamāsi PvA 81, āgamā D I.108; J III.128, and pl. āgamiŋsu J I.118; *fut.* āgamissati VvA 3; PvA 122; *ger.* āgamma (q. v.) & āgantvā J I.151; Miln 14; *Caus.* āgameti (q. v.). — (3) √**gā**: *aor.* āgā Sn 841; Pv I.12[3] (= āgacchi PvA 64). — pp. āgata (q. v.).

II. *Meanings*: (1) to come to, approach, arrive D I.108; Pv I.11[3]; II.13[3]; Miln 14; to return, to come back (cp. āgata) PvA 81, 122. — (2) to come into, to result, deserve (cp. āgama[2]) D I.161 (gārayhaŋ ṭhānaŋ deserve blame, come to be blamed); Pv IV.1[51] (get to, be a profit to = upakappati PvA 241). — (3) to come by, to come out to (be understood as), to refer or be referred to, to be meant or understood (cp. āgata 3 & āgama 3) J I.118 (tīṇi piṭakāni āgamiŋsu); SnA 321; VvA 3. See also **āgamma.**

Āgata [pp. of āgacchati] (1) come, arrived Miln 18 (°kāraṇa the reason of his coming); VvA 78 (°ṭṭhāna); PvA 81 (kiŋ āgat'attha why have you come here) come by, got attained (°—) A II.110 = Pug 48 (°visa); Mhvs XIV. 28 (°phala = anāgānuphala) -āgat'āgatā (pl.) people coming & going, passers by, all comers PvA 39, 78, 129; VvA 190 (Ep. of saṅgha). -sv'āgata "wel-come", greeted, hailed; nt. welcome, hail Th 2, 337; Pv IV.3[16], opp. **durāgata** not liked, unwelcome, A II.117, 143, 153; III. 163; Th 2, 337. — (2) come down, handed down (by memory, said of texts) D I.88; DhA II.35; KhA 229; VvA 30; āgatāgamo, one to whom the āgama, or the āgamas, have been handed down, Vin I.127, 337; II 8; IV.158; A II.147; Miln 19, 21. — (3) **anāgata** not come yet, i. e. future; usually in comb[n.] with atīta (past) & paccuppanna (present): see **atīta** and **anāgata.**

Āgati (f.) [ā + gati] coming, coming back, return S III.53; J II.172. Usually opp. to **gati** going away. Used in special sense of rebirth and re-death in the course of saŋsāra. Thus in āgati gati cuti upapatti D I.162; A III.54 sq., 60 sq., 74; cp. also S II.67; Pv II.9[23] (gatiŋ āgatiŋ vā).

Āgada (m.) & **Āgadana** (nt.) [ā + **gad** to speak] a word; talk, speech DA I.66 (= vacana).

Āgantar [N. ag. fr. āgacchati] one who is coming or going to come A I.63; II.159; It 4, 95 (nom. āgantā only one MS, all others āgantvā). an° A I.64; II.160.

Āgantu (adj.) [Sk. āgantu] — 1. occasional, incidental J VI.358. — 2. an occasional arrival, a new comer, stranger J VI.529 (= āgantuka-jana C.); ThA 16.

Āgantuka (adj.-n.) [āgantu + ka; cp. BSk. āgantuka in same meaning as P. viz. āgantukā bhikṣavaḥ Av. Ś I.87, 286; Divy 50] — 1. coming, arriving, new comer, guest, stranger, esp. a newly arrived bhikkhu; a visitor (opp. gamika one who goes away) Vin I.132, 167; II.170; III. 65, 181; IV.24, A I.10; III.41, 366; J VI.333; Ud 25; DhA II.54, 74; VvA 24; PvA 54. — 2. adventitious, incidental (= āgantu[1]) Miln 304 (of megha & roga). — 3. accessory, superimposed, added Vism 195.

-**bhatta** food given to a guest, meal for a visitor Vin I.292 (opp. gamika°); II.16.

Āgama [fr. ā + **gam**] — 1. coming, approach, result, D I.53 (āgamanaŋ pavattatī ti DA I.160; cp. Sdhp 249 dukkh°). — 2. that which one goes by, resource, reference, source of reference, text, Scripture, Canon; thus a designation of (?) the Pātimokkha, Vin II.95 = 249, or of the Four Nikāyas, DA I.1, 2 (dīgh°). A def. at Vism 442 runs "antamaso opamma-vagga-mattassa pi buddhavacanassa pariyāpuṇanaŋ". See also āgata 2, for phrase **āgat'āgama**, handed down in the Canon, Vin *loc. cit.* **Svāgamo**, versed in the doctrine, Pv IV.1[33] (sv° = suṭṭhu āgat'āgamo, PvA 230); Miln 215. BSk. in same use and meaning, e. g. Divy 17, 333, āgamāni = the Four Nikāyas. — 3. rule practice, discipline, obedience, Sn 834 (āgamā parivitakkaŋ), cp. Davs V.22 (takk°, discipline of right thought) Sdhp 224 (āgamato, in obedience to). — 4. meaning, understanding, KhA 107 (vaṇṇ°). — 5. repayment (of a debt) J. VI.245. — 6. as gram. tt. "augment", a consonant or syllable added or inserted SnA 23 (sa-kār'āgama).

Āgamana (nt.) [fr. āgacchati, Sk. same] oncoming, arrival, approach A III.172; DA I.160; PvA 4, 81; Sdhp 224, 356. an° not coming or returning J I.203, 264.

Āgameti [caus of agacchati] to cause somebody or something to come to one, i. e. (1) to wait, to stay Vin II. 166, 182, 212; D I.112, 113; S IV.291; PvA 4, 55. — (2) to wait for, to welcome Vin II.128 (ppr. āgamayamāna); M I.161 (id.) J I.69 (id. + kālaŋ).

Āgamma (adv.) [orig. ger. of āgacchati, q. v. under I.2 for form & under II.3 for meaning. BSk. āgamya in meaning after the Pāli form, e. g. Divy 95, 405 (with gen.); Av. Ś I 85, 210 etc.; M Vastu I.243, 313]. With reference to (c. acc.), owing to, relating to; by means of, thanks to. In meaning nearly synonymous with ārabbha, sandhāya & paṭicca (see *A. S.* 318 s. v.) D I.229; It 71; J I.50; VI 424; Kh VIII.14 (= nissāya KhA 229); PvA 5, 21 etc.

Āgāmitā found only in neg. form anāgāmitā.

Āgāmin (adj. n.) [ā + gāmin] returning, one who returns, esp. one who returns to another form of life in saŋsāra (cp. āgati), one who is liable to rebirth A I.63; II.159; It 95. See **anāgāmin.**

Āgāra (—°) see agāra.

Āgāraka & °ika (adj.-n.) (—°) [cp. BSk. āgārika Divy 275, & agārika] belonging to the house, viz. (1) having control over the house, keeping, surveying, in cpds. **koṭṭh°** possessor or keeper of a storehouse Vin I.209; **bandhan°** prison-keeper A II.207; **bhaṇḍ°** keeper of wares, treasurer PvA 2 (see also bhaṇḍ°). — (2) being in the house, sharing (the house), companion S III.190 (paŋsv° playmate).

Āgāḷha (adj.) (ā + gāḷha 1; cp. Sk. samāgāḍhaŋ] strong, hard, harsh, rough (of speech), usually in instr. as adv. **āgāḷhena** roughly, harshly A I.283, 295; Pug 32 (so to be read for agāḷhena, although Pug A 215 has a°, but expl[s.] by atigāḷhena vacanena); instr. f. **āgāḷhāya** Vin V. 122 (ceteyya; Bdhgh. on p. 230 reads āgaḷāya and expl[s.]

by daḷhabhāvāya). See also Nett 77 (āgāḷhā paṭipadā a rough path), 95 (id.; v. l. agāḷhā).

Āgilāyati [ā + gilāyati; Sk. glāyati, cp. gilāna] to be wearied, exhausted or tired, to ache, to become weak or faint Vin II.200; D III.209; M I.354; S IV.184; KhA 66 (hadayaŋ ā.). Cp. **āyamati.**

Āgu (nt.) [for Vedic āgas nt.] guilt, offence, S I.123; A III.346; Sn 522 = Nd² 337 (in expln. of nāga as āguŋ na karotī ti nāgo); Nd¹ 201. *Note.* A reconstructed **āgas** is found at Sdhp 294 in cpd. akatāgasa not having committed sin.
 -cārin one who does evil, D II.339; M II.88; III.163; S II.100, 128; A II.240; Miln 110.

Āghāta [Sk. āghāta only in lit. meaning of striking, killing, but cp. BSk. āghāta in meaning "hurtfulness" at M Vastu I.79; Av. Ś II.129; cp. ghāta & ghāteti] anger, ill-will, hatred, malice D I.3, 31; III.72 sq.; S I.179; J I.113; Dhs 1060, 1231; Vbh 167, 362, 389; Miln 136; Vism 306; DA I.52; VvA 67; PvA 178. **-anāghāta** freedom from ill will Vin II.249; A V.80.
 -paṭivinaya repression of ill-will; the usual enumn. of ā-° paṭivinayā comprises *nine*, for which see D III.262, 289; Vin V.137; A IV.408; besides this there are sets of *five* at A III.185 sq.; SnA 10, 11, and one of *ten* at Vin V.138. **-vatthu** occasion of ill-will; closely connected with °paṭivinaya & like that enumd. in sets of *nine* (Vin V.137; A IV.408; Ps I.130; J III.291, 404; V.149; Vbh 389; Nett 23; SnA 12), and of *ten* (Vin V.138; A V. 150; Ps I.130; Vbh 391).

Āghātana (nt.) [ā + ghāta(na), cp. āghata which has changed its meaning] — 1. slaying, striking, destroying, killing Th 1, 418, 711; death D I.31 (= maraṇa DA I.119). — 2. shambles, slaughter-house Vin I.182 (gav°); A IV.138; J VI.113. — 3. place of execution Vin III.151; J I.326, 439; III.59; Miln 110; DhA IV.52; PvA 4, 5.

Āghāteti [Denom. fr. āghāta, in form = ā + ghāteti, but diff. in meaning] only in phrase **cittaŋ** a. (with loc.) to incite one's heart to hatred against, to obdurate one's heart Sdhp. 126 = S I.151 = A V.172.

Ācamati [ā + **cam**] to take in water, to resorb, to rinse J III.297; Miln 152, 262 (+ dhamati). — Caus. I. **ācameti** (a) to purge, rinse one's mouth Vin II.142; M II. 112; A III.337; Pv IV.1⁵³ (ācamayitvā = mukhaŋ vikkhāletvā PvA 241); Miln 152 (°ayamāna). — (b) to wash off, clean oneself after evacuation Vin II.221. — Caus. II. **ācamāpeti** to cause somebody to rinse himself J VI.8.

Ācamana (nt.) [ā + camana of **cam**] rinsing, washing with water, used (a) for the mouth D I.12 (= udakena mukhasiddhi-karaṇa DA I.98); (b) after evacuation J III 486.
 -kumbhī water-pitcher used for rinsing Vin I.49, 52; II.142, 210, 222. **-pādukā** slippers worn when rinsing Vin I.190; II.142, 222. **-sarāvaka** a saucer for rinsing Vin II.142, 221.

Ācamā (f.) [fr. ā + **cam**] absorption, resorption Nd¹ 429 (on Sn 945, which both in T. and in SnA reads **ājava**; expld. by taṇhā in Nidd.). *Note.* Index to SnA (Pj III) has **ācāma.**

Ācaya [ā + caya] heaping up, accumulation, collection, mass (opp. **apacaya**). See on term *Dhs trsl.* 195 & *Cpd.* 251, 252. — S II.94 (kāyassa ācayo pi apacayo pi); A IV.280 = Vin II.259 (opp. apacaya); Dhs 642, 685; Vbh 319, 326, 330; Vism 449; DhA II.25.
 -gāmin making for piling up (of rebirth) A V.243, 276; Dhs 584, 1013, 1397; Kvu 357.

Ācarati [ā + carati] — 1. to practice, perform, indulge in Vin I.56; II.118; Sn 327 (ācare dhamma-sandosa-vādaŋ), 401; Miln 171, 257 (pāpaŋ). Cp. pp. **ācarita** in BSk. e. g. Av. Ś I.124, 153, 213 in same meaning. — pp. **āciṇṇa.** — 2. to step upon, pass through J V.153.

Ācarin (adj.-n.) [fr. ā + **car**] teaching, f. **ācarinī** a female teacher Vin IV.227 (in contrast to gaṇa & in same sense as ācariya m. at Vin IV.130), 317 (id.).

Ācariya [fr. ā + **car**] a teacher (almost syn. with **upajjhāya**) Vin I.60, 61, 119 (°upajjhāya); II.231; IV.130 (gaṇo vā ācariyo a meeting of the bhikkhus or a single teacher, cp. f. ācarinī); D I.103, 116 (gaṇ°) 238 (sattamâcariya-mahāyuga seventh age of great teachers); III.189 sq.; M III.115; S I.68 (gaṇ°), 177; IV.176 (yogg°); A I.132 (pubb°); Sn 595; Nd¹ 350 (upajjhāya vā āc°); J II.100, 411; IV.91; V.501; Pv IV.3²³, 3⁵¹ (= ācāra-samācāra-sikkhāpaka PvA 252); Miln 201, 262 (master goldsmith?); Vism 99 sq.; KhA 12, 155; SnA 422; VvA 138. — For contracted form of ācariya see **ācera.**
 -kula the clan of the teacher A II.112. **-dhana** a teacher's fee S I.177; A V.347. **-pācariya** teacher upon teacher, lit. "teacher & teacher's teacher" (see ā¹ 3ᵇ) D I.94, 114, 115, 238; S IV.306, 308; DA I.286; SnA 452 (= ācariyo c'eva ācariya-ācariyo ca). **-bhariyā** the teacher's fee J V.457; VI.178; DhA I.253. **-muṭṭhi** "the teacher's fist" i. e. close-fistedness in teaching, keeping things back, D II.100; S V.153; J II.221, 250; Miln 144; SnA 180, 368. **-vaŋsa** the line of the teachers Miln 148. **-vatta** serving the teacher, service to the t. DhA I.92. **-vāda** traditional teaching; later as heterodox teaching, sectarian teaching (opp. theravāda orthodox doctrine) Miln 148; Dpvs V.30; Mhbv 96.

Ācariyaka [ācariya + ka, diff. from Sk. ācariyaka nt. art of teaching] a teacher Vin I.249; III.25, 41; D I.88, 119, 187; II.112; M I.514; II.32; S V.261; A II.170; IV. 310. See also **sācariyaka.**

Ācāma [Sk. ācāma] the scum or foam of boiling rice D I.166; M I.78; A I.295; J II.289; Pug 55; VvA 99 sq.; DhA III.325 (°kuṇḍaka).

Ācāmeti [for ācameti? cp. Sk. ācāmayati, Caus. of ā + **cam**] at M II.112 in imper. **ācāmehi** be pleased or be thanked(?); perhaps the reading is incorrect.

Ācāra [ā + **car**] way of behaving, conduct, practice, esp. right conduct, good manners; adj. (—°) practising, indulging in, or of such & such a conduct. — Sn 280 (pāpa°); J I.106 (vipassana°); II.280 (°ariya); VI.52 (ariya°); SnA 157; PvA 12 (sila°), 36, 67, 252; Sdhp 441. **-an°** bad behaviour Vin II.118 (°ŋ ācarati indulge in bad habits); DhA II.201 (°kiriyā). Cp. sam°.
 -kusala versed in good manners Dh 376 (cp. DhA IV.111). **-gocara** pasturing in good conduct; i. e. practice of right behaviour D I.63 = It 118; M I.33; S V.187; A I.63 sq.; II.14, 39; III.113, 155, 262; IV.140, 172, 352; V.71 sq., 89, 133, 198; Vbh 244, 246 (cp. Miln 368, 370, quot. Vin III.185); Vism I.8. **-vipatti** failure of morality, a slip in good conduct Vin I.171.

Ācārin (adj. n.) [fr. ācāra] of good conduct, one who behaves well A I.211 (anācārī viratā l. 4 fr. bottom is better read as ācārī virato, in accordance with v. l.).

Ācikkhaka (adj. n.) [ā + cikkha + ka of cikkhati] one who tells or shows DhA I.71.

Ācikkhati [Freq. of ā + khyā, i. e. akkhāti] to tell, relate, show, describe, explain D I.110; A II 189 (atthaŋ ā to interpret); Pug 59; DhA I.14; SnA 155; PvA 121, 164 (describe). — imper. pres. **ācikkha** Sn 1097 (= brūhi Nd² 119 & 455); Pv I.10⁹; II.8¹; and **ācikkhāhi** DhA II.27. — aor. **ācikkhi** PvA 6, 58, 61, 83. — ācikkhati often occurs in stock phrase ācikkhati deseti paññāpeti paṭṭhapeti vivarati etc., e. g. Nd¹ 271; Nd² 465; Vism 163. — attānaŋ ā. to disclose one's identity PvA 89, 100. — pp. ācikkhita (q. v.). — Caus. II. ācikkhāpeti to cause somebody to tell DhA II.27.

Ācikkhana (adj.-nt.) [ā + cikkhana of cikkhati] telling, announcing J III.444; PvA 121.

Ācikkhita [pp. of acikkhati] shown, described, told PvA 154 (°magga), 203 (an° = anakkhāta).

Ācikkhitar [n. ag. fr. ācikkhati] one who tells or shows DhA II.107 (for pavattar).

Āciṇa [pp. of ācināti? or is it distorted from āciṇṇa?] accumulated; practised, performed Dh 121 (pāpaŋ = pāpaŋ āciṇanto karonto DhA III.16). It may also be spelt ācina.

Āciṇṇa [ā + ciṇṇa, pp. of ācarati] practiced, performed, (habitually) indulged in M I.372 (kamma, cp. Miln 226 and the expln. of āciṇṇaka kamma as "chronic karma" at *Cpd.* 144); S IV.419; A V.74 sq.; J I.81; DA I.91 (for aviciṇṇa at D I.8), 275; Vism 269; DhA I.37 (°samāciṇṇa thoroughly fulfilled); VvA 108; PvA 54; Sdhp 90.
-kappa ordinance or rule of right conduct or customary practice (?) Vin I.79; II.301; Dpvs IV.47; cp. V.18.

Ācita [pp. of ācināti] accumulated, collected, covered, furnished or endowed with J VI.250 (= nicita); Vv 41¹; DhsA 310. See also āciṇa.

Ācināti [ā + cināti] to heap up, accumulate S III.89 (v. l. ācinati); IV.73 (ppr. ācinato dukkhaŋ); DhsA 44. — pp. ācita & āciṇa (ācina). — Pass. ācīyati (q. v.).

Ācīyati (& **Āceyyati**) [Pass. of ācināti, cp. cīyati] to be heaped up, to increase, to grow; ppr. āceyyamāna J V.6 (= ācīyanto vaḍḍhanto C.).

Ācera is the contracted form of ācariya; only found in the *Jātakas*, e. g. J IV.248; VI.563.

Ācela in kañcanācela-bhūsita "adorned with golden clothes" Pv II.12⁷ stands for cela°.

Ājañña is the contracted form of ājāniya.

Ājava see ācamā.

Ājāna (adj.) [ā + jāna from **jñā**] understandable, only in cpd. durājāna hard to understand S IV.127; Sn 145, 162; J I.295, 300.

Ājānana (nt.) [ā + jānana, cp. Sk. ajñāna] learning, knowing, understanding; knowledge J I.181 (°sabhāva of the character of knowing, fit to learn); PvA 225.

Ājānāti [ā + jānāti] to understand, to know, to learn D I.189; Sn 1064 (°amāna = vijānamāna Nd² 120). As aññāti at Vism 200. — pp. aññāta. Cp. also āṇāpeti.

Ājāniya (**ājānīya**) (adj. n.) [cp. BSk. ājāneya & Sk. ājāti birth, good birth. Instead of its correct derivation from ā + **jan** (to be born, i. e. well-born) it is by Bdhgh. connected with ā + **jñā** (to learn, i. e. to be trained). See for these popular etym. e. g. J I.181: sārathissa cittarucitaŋ kāraṇaŋ ājānana-sabhāvo ājañño, and DhA IV.4: yaŋ assadamma-sārathi kāraṇaŋ kāreti tassa khippaŋ jānana-samatthā ājāniyā. — The contracted form of the word is **ājañña**] of good race or breed; almost exclusively used to denote a thoroughbred horse (cp. assājāniya under assa³). (a) ājāniya (the more common & younger Pāli form): Sn 462, 528, 532; J I.178, 194; Dpvs IV.26; DhA I.402; III.49; IV.4; VvA 78; PvA 216. — (b) ājānīya: M I.445; A V.323; Dh 322 = Nd² 475. — (c) ājañña = (mostly in poetry): Sn 300 = 304; J I.181; Pv IV.1⁵⁴; purisājañña "a steed of man", i. e. a man of noble race) S III.91 = Th 1, 1084 = Sn 544 = VvA 9; A V.325. -anājāniya of inferior birth M I.367.
-susu the young of a noble horse, a noble foal M I. 445 (°ūpamo dhamma-pariyāyo).

Ājānīyatā (f.) [abstr. fr. ājāniya] good breed PvA 214.

Ājira [= ajira with lengthened initial a] a courtyard Mhvs 35, 3.

Ājīva [ā + jīva; Sk. ājīva] livelihood, mode of living, living, subsistence, D I.54; A III.124 (parisuddha°); Sn 407 (°ŋ = parisodhayi = micchājīvaŋ hitvā sammājīvaŋ eva pavattayi SnA 382), 617; Pug 51; Vbh 107, 235; Miln 229 (bhinna°); Vism 306 (id.); DhsA 390; Sdhp 342, 375, 392. Esp. freq. in the contrast pair sammā-ājīva & micchā-ā° right mode & wrong mode of gaining a living, e. g. at S II.168 sq.; III.239; V 9; A I.271; II 53, 240, 270; IV.82; Vbh 105, 246. See also magga (ariyaṭṭhaṅgika).
-pārisuddhi purity or propriety of livelihood Miln 336; Vism 22 sq., 44; DhA IV.111. -vipatti failure in method of gaining a living A I.270. -sampadā perfection of (right) livelihood A I.271; DA I.235.

Ājīvaka (& °ika) [ājīva + ka, orig. "one finding his living" (scil. in a peculiar way); cp. BSk. ājīvika Divy 393, 427] an ascetic, one of the numerous sects of non-buddhist ascetics. On their austerities, practice & way of living see esp. DhA II.55 sq. and on the whole question Barua, B. M. *The Ājīvikas*, Univ. of Calcutta 1920. — (a) ājīvika: Vin I.291; II.284; IV.74, 91; M I.31, 483; S I. 217; A III.276, 384; J I.81, 257, 390. — (b) ājīvika: Vin I.8; Sn 381 (v. l. BB. °aka).
-sāvaka a hearer or lay disciple of the ājīvaka ascetics Vin II 130, 165; A I.217.

Ājīvika (nt.) (or **ajivikā** f.?) [fr. ajīva] sustenance of life, livelihood, living Vbh 379 (°bhaya) Miln 196 (id.); PvA 274, and in phrase ājīvik'āpakata being deprived of a livelihood, without a living M I.463 = S III.93 (T. reads jīvikā pakatā) = It 89 (reads ājīvikā pakatā) = Miln 279.

Ājīvin (adj.-n.) [fr. ājīva] having one's livelihood, finding one's subsistence, living, leading a life of (—°) D III.64; A V.190 (lūkha°).

Āṭa [etym.? Cp. Sk. āṭi Turdus Ginginianus, see Aufrecht, Halāyudha p. 148] a kind of bird J VI.539 (= dabbimukha C.).

Āṭaviya is to be read for aṭaviyo (q. v.) at J VI.55 [= Sk. āṭavika].

Āṭhapanā (f.) at Pug 18 & v. l. at Vbh 357 is to be read aṭṭhapanā (so T. at Vbh 357).

Āṇañja see ānejja.

Āṇaṇya see ānaṇya.

Āṇatti (f.) [ā + ñatti (cp. āṇāpeti), Caus. of **jñā**] order, command, ordinance, injunction Vin I.62; KhA 29; PvA 260; Sdhp 59, 354.

Āṇattika (adj.) [āṇatti + ka] belonging to an ordinance or command, of the nature of an injunction KhA 29.

Āṇā (f.) [Sk. ājñā, ā + **jñā**] order, command, authority Miln 253; DA I.289; KhA 179, 180, 194; PvA 217; Sdhp 347, 576. rāj'āṇā the king's command or authority J I.433; III.351; PvA 242. āṇaŋ deti to give an order J I.398; °ŋ pavatteti to issue an order Miln 189, cp. āṇāpavatti J III.504; IV.145.

Āṇāpaka (adj. n.) [fr. āṇāpeti] 1. (adj.) giving an order Vism 303. — 2. (n.) one who gives or calls out orders, a town-crier, an announcer of the orders (of an authority) Miln 147.

Āṇāpana (nt.) [abstr. fr. āṇāpeti] ordering or being, ordered, command, order PvA 135.

Āṇāpeti [ā + ñāpeti, Caus. of ā + jānāti fr. **jñā**, cp. Sk. ājñāpayati] to give an order, to enjoin, command (with acc. of person) J III.351; Miln 147; DhA II.82; VvA 68 (dāsiyo), 69; PvA 4, 39, 81.

Āṇi (Vedic āṇi to aṇu fine, thin, flexible, in formation an *n*-enlargement of Idg. *olenā, cp. Ohg. lun, Ger. lünse, Ags. lynes = E. linch, further related to Lat. ulna elbow, Gr. ὠλένη, Ohg. elina, Ags. eln = E. el-bow. See Walde, *Lat. Wtb.* under ulna & lacertus]. — 1. the pin of a wheel-axle, a linch-pin M I.119; S II.266, 267; A II.32; Sn 654; J VI.253, 432; SnA 243; KhA 45, 50. — 2. a peg, pin, bolt, stop (at a door) M I.119; S II 266 (drum stick); J IV.30; VI.432, 460; Th 1, 744; Dh I.39. — 3. (fig.) (°—) peg-like (or secured by a peg, of a door), small, little in °**colaka** a small (piece of) rag Vin II.271, cp. I.205 (vaṇabandhana-colaka); °**dvāra** Th 1, 355; C. khuddaka-dvāra, quoted at *Brethren* 200, trsl. by Mrs. Rh. D. as "the towngate's sallyport" by Neumann as "Gestöck" (fastening, enclosure) āṇi-gaṇṭhik'āhato ayopatto at Vism 108; DA I.199 is apparently a sort of brush made of four or fire small pieces of flexible wood.

Ātanka [etym. uncertain; Sk. ātanka] illness, sickness, disease M I.437; S III.1; Sn 966 (°phassa, cp. Nd[1] 486). Freq. in cpd. **appātanka** freedom from illness, health (cp. appābādha) D I.204; III.166; A III.65, 103; Miln 14. — f. abstr. **appātankatā** M I.124.

Ātankin (adj.) [fr. ātanka] sick, ill J V.84 (= gilāna C.).

Ātata [fr. ā + tan, pp. tata; lit. stretched, covered over] generic name for drums covered with leather on one side Dpvs XIV.14; VvA 37 (q. v. for enumn. of musical instruments), 96.

Ātatta [ā + tatta[1], pp. of ā-tapati] heated, burnt, scorched, dry J V.69 (°rūpa = sukkha-sarīra C.).

Ātapa [ā + tapa] — 1. sun-heat Sn 52; J I.336; Dhs 617; Dpvs I.57; VvA 54; PvA 58. — 2. glow, heat (in general) Pv I.7[4]; Sdhp 396. — 3. (fig.) (cp. tapa[2]) ardour, zeal, exertion PvA 98 (viriyā-tapa; perhaps better to be read °ātāpa q. v.). Cp. ātappa.
-**vāraṇa** "warding off the sun-heat", i. e. a parasol, sun-shade Dāvs I.28; V.35.

Ātapatā (f.) [abstr. of ātapa] glowing or burning state, heat Sdhp 122.

Ātapati [ā + **tap**] to burn J III.447.

Ātappa (nt.) [Sk. *ātāpya, fr. ātāpa] ardour, zeal, exertion D I.13; III.30 sq., 104 sq., 238 sq.; M III.210; S II.132, 196 sq.; A I.153; III.249; IV.460 sq.; V.17 sq.; Sn 1062 (= ussāha ussoḷhi thāma etc. Nd[2] 122); J III.447; Nd[1] 378; Vbh 194 (= vāyāma); DA I.104.

Ātāpa [ā + tāpa fr. **tap**; cp. tāpeti] glow, heat; fig. ardour, keen endeavour, or perhaps better "torturing, mortification" Miln 313 (cittassa ātāpo paritāpo); PvA 98 (viriya°). Cp. ātappa & ātāpana.

Ātāpana (nt.) [ā + tāpana] tormenting, torture, mortification M I.78; A I.296 (°paritāpana); II.207 (id.); Pug 55 (id.); Vism 3 (id.).

Ātāpin (adj.) [fr. ātāpa, cp. BSk. ātāpin Av. Ś I.233; II. 194 = Divy 37; 618] ardent, zealous, strenuous, active D III.58, 76 sq., 141 (+ sampajāna), 221, 276; M I.22, 56, 116, 207, 349; II.11; III.89, 128, 156; S I 13, 117 sq., 140, 165; II.21, 136 sq.; III.73 sq.; IV.37, 48, 54, 218; V.165, 187, 213; A II.13 sq.; III 38, 100 sq.; IV. 29, 177 sq., 266 sq., 300, 457 sq.; V.343 sq.; Sn 926; Nd[1] 378; It 41, 42; Vbh 193 sq.; Miln 34, 366; Vism 3 (= viriyavā); DhA I.120; SnA 157, 503. — Freq. in the formula of Arahantship "eko vūpakaṭṭho appamatto ātāpī pahitatto": see arahant II. B. See also satipaṭṭhāna. — Opp. **anātāpin** S II.195 sq.; A II.13; It 27 (+ anottappin).

Ātāpeti [ā + tāpeti] to burn, scorch; fig. to torment, inflict pain, torture M I.341 (+ paritāpeti); S IV.337; Miln 314, 315.

Ātitheyya (nt.) [fr. ati + theyya] great theft (?) A I.93; IV. 63 sq. (v. l. ati° which is perhaps to be preferred).

Ātu [dialectical] father M I.449 (cp. Trenckner's note on p. 567: the text no doubt purports to make the woman speak a sort of patois).

Ātuman [Vedic ātman, diaeretic form for the usual contracted attan; only found in poetry. Cp. also the shortened form tuman] self. nom. sg. **ātumo** Pv IV.5[2] (= sabhāvo PvA 259), **ātumā** Nd[1] 69 (ātumā vuccati attā), 296 (id.), & **ātumāno** Nd[1] 351; acc. **ātumānaŋ** Sn 782 (= attānaŋ SnA 521), 888, 918; loc. **ātume** Pv II.13[11] (= attani C.).

Ātura (adj.) [Sk. ātura, cp. BSk. ātura, e. g. Jtm 31[10]] ill, sick, diseased; miserable, affected S III.1 (°kāya); A I. 250; Sn 331; Vv 83[14] (°rūpa = abhitunna-kāya VvA 328); J I.197 (°anna "food of the miserable", i. e. last meal of one going to be killed; C. expls. as maraṇa-bhojana), 211 (°citta); II.420 (°anna, as above); III.201; V.90, 433; VI.248; Miln 139, 168; DhA I.31 (°rūpa); PvA 160, 161; VvA 77; Sdhp 507. Used by Commentators as syn. of aṭṭo, e. g. at J IV.293; SnA 489 -**anātura** healthy, well, in good condition S III.1; Dh 198.

Āthabbaṇa (nt.) [= athabbaṇa, q. v.] the Atharva Veda as a code of magic working formulas, witchcraft, sorcery Sn 927 (v. l. ath°, see interpreted at Nd[1] 381; expld. as āthabbaṇika-manta-ppayoga at SnA 564).

Āthabbaṇika (adj. n.) [fr. athabbana] one conversant with magic, wonder-worker, medicine-man Nd[1] 381; SnA 564.

Ādapeti [Caus. of ādāti] to cause one to take, to accept, agree to M II.104; S I.132.

Ādara [Sk. ādara, prob. ā + dara, cp. semantically Ger. ehrfurcht awe] consideration of, esteem, regard, respect, reverence, honour J V.493; SnA 290; DA I.30; DhsA 61; VvA 36, 61, 101, 321; PvA 121, 123, 135, 278; Sdhp 2, 21, 207, 560. -**anādara** lack of reverence, disregard, disrespect; (adj.) disrespectful S I.96; Vin IV.218; Sn 247 (= ādara-virahita SnA 290; DA I.284; VvA 219; PvA 3, 5, 54, 67, 257.

Ādaratā (f.) [abstr. fr. ādara] = ādara, in neg. **an°** want of consideration J IV.229; Dhs 1325 = Vbh 359 (in expln. of dovacassatā).

Ādariya (nt.) [abstr. fr. ādara] showing respect of honour; neg. **an°** disregard, disrespect Vin II.220; A V.146, 148; Pug 20; Vbh 371; miln 266.

Ādava [ā + dava[2]?] is gloss at VvA 216 for maddava Vv 51[24]; meaning: excitement, adj. exciting. The passage in VvA is somewhat corrupt, & therefore unclear.

Ādahati[1] [ā + dahati[1]] to put down, put on, settle, fix Vism 289 (samaŋ ā. = samādahati). Cp. sam° and ādhiyati.

Ādahati[2] [ā + dahati[2]] to set fire to, to burn J VI.201, 203.

Ādā [ger. of ādāti from reduced base *da of dadāti 1b] taking up, taking to oneself Vin IV.120 (= anādiyitvā C.; cp. the usual form ādāya).

Ādāti (Ādadāti) [ā + dadāti of dadāti base 1 dā] to take up, accept, appropriate, grasp, seize; grd. **ādātabba** Vin I.50; inf. **ādātuŋ** D III.133 (adinnaŋ theyyasankhātaŋ ā.). — ger. **ādā** & **ādāya** (see sep.); grd. **ādeyya**, Caus. **ādapeti** (q. v.). — See also **ādiyati** & **ādeti**.

Ādāna (nt.) [ād + āna, or directly from ā + **dā**, base 1 of dadāti] taking up, getting, grasping, seizing; fig. appropriating, clinging to the world, seizing on (worldly objects). (1) (lit.) taking (food), pasturing M III.133; J V.371 (& °esana). — (2) getting, acquiring, taking, seizing S II.94; A IV.400 (daṇḍ°); PvA 27 (phal°); esp. freq. in adinn° seizing what is not given, i. e. theft: see under adinna. — (3) (fig.) attachment, clinging A V.233, 253 (°paṭinissagga); Dh 89 (id.; cp. DhA II.163); Sn 1103 (°taṇhā), 1104 (°satta); Nd[1] 98 (°gantha); Nd[2] 123, 124. -an° free from attachment S I.236 (sādānesu anādāno "not laying hold mong them that grip" trsl.); A II.10; It 109; J IV.354; Miln 342; DhA IV.70 (= khandhādisu niggahaṇo). Cp. upa°, pari°.

Ādāya [ger. of ādāti, either from base 1 of dadāti (dā) or base 2 (dāy). See also ādiya] having received or taken, taking up, seizing on, receiving; freq. used in the sense of a prep. "with" (c. acc.) Sn 120, 247, 452; J V.13; Vbh 245; DhA II.74; SnA 139; PvA 10, 13, 38, 61 etc. — At Vin I.70 the form ādāya is used as a noun f. ādāyā in meaning of "a casually taken up belief" (tassa ādāyassa vaṇṇe bhaṇati). Cp. upa°, pari°.

Ādāyin (adj.-n.) [fr. ā + dadāti base 2, cp. ādāya] taking up, grasping, receiving; one who takes, seizes or appropriates D I.4 (dinn°); A III.80; V.137 (sār°); DA I.72.

Ādāsa [Sk. ādarśa, ā + **dṛś**, P. dass, of dassati[1] 2] a mirror Vin II.107; D I.7, 11 (°pañha mirror-questioning, cp. DA I.97: "ādāse devataŋ otaretvā pañha-pucchanaŋ"), 80; II.93 (dhamma'-ādāsaŋ nāma dhamma-pariyāyaŋ desessāmi); S V.357 (id.); A V.92, 97 sq., 103; J I.504; Dhs 617 (°maṇḍala); Vism 591 (in simile); KhA 50 (°daṇḍa) 237; DhA I.226.

-tala the surface of the mirror, in similes at Vism 450, 456, 489.

Ādāsaka = ādāsa Th 2, 411.

Ādi [Sk. ādi, etym. uncertain] — 1. (m.) starting-point beginning Sn 358 (acc. ādiŋ = kāraṇaŋ SnA 351); Dh 375 (nom. ādi); Miln 10 (ādimhi); J VI.567 (abl. ādito from the beginning). For use as nt. see below 2 b. — 2. (adj. & adv.) (a) (°—) beginning, initially, first, principal, chief: see cpds. — (b) (°—) beginning with, being the first (of a series which either is supposed to be familiar in its constituents to the reader or hearer or is immediately intelligible from the context), i. e. and so on, so forth (cp. adhika); e. g. rukkha-gumb-ādayo (acc. pl.) trees, jungle etc. J I.150; amba-panas' ādīhi rukkehi sampanno (and similar kinds of fruit) J I.278; amba-labuj'ādīnaŋ phalānaŋ anto J II.159; asi-satti-dhami-ādīni āvudhāni (weapons, such as sword, knife, bow & the like) J I.150; kasi-gorakkh' ādīni karonte manusse J II.128; . . . ti ādinā nayena in this and similar ways J I.81; PvA 30. Absolute as nt. pl. **ādīnī** with ti (evaŋ) (ādīni), closing a quotation, meaning "this and such like", e. g. at J II.128, 416 (ti ādīni viravitvā). — In phrase **ādiŋ katvā** meaning "putting (him, her, it) first", i.e. beginning with, from . . . on, from . . . down (c. acc.) e. g. DhA I.393 (rājānaŋ ādiŋ K. from the king down); PvA 20 (vihāraŋ ādikatvā), 21 (pañcavaggiye ādiŋ K.).

-kammika [cp. BSk. ādikarmaka Divy 544] a beginner Vin III.116; IV.100; Miln 59; Vism 241; DhsA 187. **-kalyāṇa** in phrase ādikalyāṇa majjhe-kalyāṇa pariyosāna-kalyāṇa of the Dhamma, "beautiful in the beginning, the middle & the end" see references under dhamma C. 3 and cp. DA I.175 (= ādimhi kalyāṇa etc.); SnA 444; abstr. **°kalyāṇatā** Vism 4. **-pubbangama** original Dpvs IV.26. **-brahmacariyaka** belonging to the principles or fundaments of moral life D I.189; III.284; M I.431; II.125, 211; III. 192; S II.75, 223; IV.91; V.417, 438; f. *°ikā* Vin I.64, 68; A I.231 sq. **-majjhapariyosāna** beginning, middle & end Miln 10; cp. above ādikalyāṇa.

Ādika (adj.) [ādi + ka] from the beginning, initial (see adhika); instr. **ādikena** in the beginning, at once, at the same time M I.395, 479; II.213; S II.224; J VI.567. Cp. ādiya[3].

Ādicca [Vedic āditya] the sun S I.15, 47; II.284; III.156; V.44, 101; A I.242; V.22, 263, 266 sq.; It 85; Sn 550, 569, 1097 ("ādicco vuccati suriyo" Nd[2] 125); DhA IV. 143; Sdhp 14, 17, 40.

-upaṭṭhānā sun-worship D I.11 (= jīvikatthāya ādicca-paricariyā DA I.97); J II.72 (°jātaka; ādiccaŋ upatiṭṭhati p. 73 = suriyaŋ namassamāno tiṭṭhati C.). **-patha** the path of the sun, i. e. the sky, the heavens Dh 175 (= ākāsa DhA III.177). **-bandhu** "kinsman of the sun", Ep. of the Buddha Vin II.296; S I.186, 192; A II.54; Sn 54, 915, 1128; Nd[1] 341; Nd[2] 125b; Vv 42[5], 78[10]; VvA 116.

Ādiṇṇa [Sk. ādīrṇa, pp. of ā + **dṛ**, see ādiyati[2]] broken, split open S IV.193 (= sipātikā with burst pod); cp. M I.306.

Ādiṇṇata (nt.) [abstr. fr. ādiṇṇa] state of being broken or split Ps I.49.

Āditta [ā + ditta[1], Sk. ādīpta, pp. of ā + **dīp**] set on fire, blazing, burning Vin I.34; Kv 209 (sabbaŋ ādittaŋ); S III.71; IV.19, 108; A IV.320 (°cela); Sn 591; J IV.391; Pv I.8[5] (= paditta jalita PvA 41); Kvu 209; DA I.264; PvA 149; Sdhp 599.

-pariyāya the discourse or sermon on the fire (lit. being in flames) S IV.168 sq.; Vin I.34; DhA I.88.

Ādina only at D I.115 (T. reading ādīna, but v. l. S id. ādina, B p. abhinna) in phrase ādina-khattiya-kula primordial. See note in *Dial.* I.148.

Ādiya[1] (adj.) grd. of admi, **ad,** Sk. ādya] edible, eatable A III.45 (bhojanāni).

Ādiya[2] in °mukha is uncertain reading at A III.164 sq. (vv. ll. ādeyya° & ādheyya), meaning perhaps "grasp-mouth", i. e. gossip; thus equal to ger. of ādiyati[1]. Perhaps to be taken to ādiyati[2]. The same phrase occurs at Pug 65 (T. ādheyya°, C. has v. l. ādheyya°) where Pug A 248 expl[ns.] "ādito dheyyamukho, paṭhama-vacanasmiŋ yeva ṭhapita-mukho ti attho" (sticking to one's word?). See **ādheyya**.

Ādiya[3] = ādika, instr. **ādiyena** in the beginning J VI.567 (= ādikena C.).

Ādiya[4] ger. of ādiyati.

Ādiyati [ā + diyati, med. pass. base of dadāti[4], viz. di° & dī°; see also ādati & ādeti] to take up; take to oneself, seize on, grasp, appropriate, fig. take notice of, take to heart, heed. — pres. **ādiyati** A III.46; Sn 119, 156, 633, 785, Nd[1] 67; Nd[2] 123, 124; J III.296: V.367. — pot. **ādiye** Sn 400; imper. **ādiya** M III.133 (so read for adissa?). — aor. **ādiyi** D III.65; A III.209, **ādiyāsi** Pv IV.1[48] (sayaŋ daṇḍaŋ ā. = acchinditvā gaṇhasi PvA 241), & **ādapayi** (Caus. formation fr. ādāti?) to take heed S I.132 (v. l. ādiyi, trsl. "put this into thy mind"). — ger. **ādiyitvā** Vin IV.120 (= ādā); J II.224 (C. for ādiya T.); III.104; IV.352 (an° not heeding; v. l. anāditvā, cp. anādiyanto not attending J III.196); DhA III.32 (id.); PvA

13 (T. anādayitva not heeding), 212 (vacanaŋ anādiyitvā not paying attention to his word), ādiya S III.26 (v. l. an° for anādiya); J II.223 (= ādiyitvā C.); see also ādiya^2, & ādīya S III.26 (an°). See also upādiyati & pariyādiyati.

Ādiyati [ā + diyati, Sk. ādīryate, Pass. of **dṛ** to split: see etym. under **darī**] to split, go asunder, break Ps I.49. — pp. ādiṇṇa. See also **avadīyati**. Cp. also upādiṇṇa.

Ādiyanatā (f.) [abstr. formation ādiyana (fr. ādiya ger. of ādiyati) + ta] in **an°** the fact of not taking up or heeding SnA 516.

Ādisati [ā + disati] (a) to announce, tell, point out, refer to. — (b) to dedicate (a gift, dakkhiṇaŋ or dānaŋ). — pres. ind. ādisati D I.213 = A I.170 (tell or read one's character); Sn 1112 (atitaŋ); Nd^1 382 (nakkhattaŋ set the horoscope); Miln 294 (dānaŋ); pot. ādiseyya Th 2, 307 (dakkhiṇaŋ); Pv IV.1^{30} (id. = uddiseyya PvA 228), & ādise Vin I.229 = D II.88 (dakkhiṇaŋ); imper. ādisa PvA 49. — fut. ādissati Th 2, 308 (dakkhiṇaŋ) PvA 88 (id.). — aor. ādisi Pv II.2^8; PvA 46 (dakkhiṇaŋ); pl. ādisiŋsu ibid. 53 (id.) & ādisuŋ Pv I.10^6 (id.). — ger. ādissa Vin III.127; Sn 1018; Pv II.1^6 (dānaŋ), & **ādisitvāna** Th 2, 311. — grd. ādissa (adj.) to be told or shown M I.12.

Ādiso (adv.) [orig. abl. of ādi, formed with °saḥ] from the beginning, i. e. thoroughly, absolutely D I.180; M III.208.

Ādissa at M III.133 is an imper. pres. meaning "take", & should probably better be read **ādiya** (in correspondsion with ādāna). It is not grd. of ādisati, which its form might suggest.

Ādīna at D I.115 & S V.74 (vv. ll. ādina, & abhinna) see ādina. See **diṇṇa**.

Ādīnava [ā + dīna + va (nt.), a substantivised adj., orig. meaning "full of wretchedness", cp. BSk. ādīnava M Vastu III.297 (misery); Divy 329] disadvantage, danger (in or through = loc.) D I.38 (vedanānaŋ assādañ ca ādīnavañ ca etc.), 213 (iddhi-pāṭihāriye M I.318; S I.9 (ettha bhīyo); II.170 sq. (dhātūnaŋ); III.27, 62, 102 (rūpassa etc.); IV.7, 168; A I.57 (akaraṇīye kayiramāne) 258 (ko loke assādo); III.250 sq.; 267 sq. (duccarite), 270 (puggala-ppasāde); IV.439 sq.; V.81; J I.146; IV.2; It 9 = A II.10 = Nd^2 172^a; Sn 36, 50 (cp. Nd^2 127), 69, 424, 732; Th 2, 17 (kāye ā. = dosa ThA 23), 485 (kāmesu ā. = dosa ThA 287); Pv III.10^7 (= dosa PvA 214); IV.6^1 (= dosa PvA 263); Ps I.192 sq.; II.9, 10; PvA 12, 208. — There are several sets of sources of evil or danger, viz. five **dussīlassa sīla-vipattiyā ā.** at D II.85 = III.235 = A III.252; five **akkhantiyā ā.** at Vbh 378; six of six each at D III.182 sq. — In phrase **kāmānaŋ ā. okāro sankileso** D I.110, 148; M I.115; Nett 42; DhA 16.

-ânupassin realising the danger or evil of S II.85 (upādāniyesu dhammesu) abstr. °ânupassanā Vism 647 sq., 695. **-dassāvin** same as °ânupassin D I.245 (an°); A V.178 (id.); D III.46; S II.194, 269; A III.146; V.181 sq.; Nd^2 141. **-pariyesanā** search for danger in (—°) S II.171; III.29; IV.8 sq. **-saññā** consciousness of danger D I.79; III.253, 283; A III.79.

Ādīpanīya (adj.) [grd. of ā + dīpeti] to be explained Miln 270.

Ādīpita [pp. of ādīpeti, ā + caus. of **dīp**, cp. dīpeti] ablaze, in flames S I.31 (loka; v. l. ādittaka) 108; J V.366; DhA III 32 (v. l. āditta).

Ādu (indecl.) [see also **adu**] emphatic (adversative) part. (1) of affirmation & emphasis: but, indeed, rather J III. 499 = VI.443; V.180; VI.552. — (2) as 2nd component of a disjunctive question, mostly in corresponsion udāhu ... ādu (= kiŋ ... udāhu SnA 350), viz. is it so ... or" Th I, 1274 = Sn 354; Pv IV.3^{11} = DhA I.31; J V.384; VI.382; without udāhu at J V.460 (adu). The close connection with udāhu suggesto an expl$^{n.}$ of ādu as a somehow distorted abbreviation of udāhu.

Ādeti [ā + deti, base^2 of dadāti (day^6 & de°), cp. also ādiyati] to take, receive, get Sn 121 (= gaṇhāti SnA 179), 954 (= upādiyati gaṇhāti Nd^1 444); cp. I.4^3; J III. 103, 296; V.366 (= gaṇhāti C.; cp. ādiyati on p. 367); Miln 336.

Ādeyya (adj.) [grd. of ādāti (q. v.)] to be taken up, acceptable, pleasant, welcome, only in phrase °vacana welcome or acceptable speech, glad words Vin II.158; J VI.243; Miln 110; ThA 42.

Ādeva, Ādevanā [ā + **div.** devati] lamenting, deploring, crying etc. in ster. phrase (explaining parideva or pariddava) ādevo **paridevo ādevanā** pari° **ādevitattaŋ** pari° Nd^1 370 = Nd^2 416 = Ps I.38.

Ādesa [fr. ādisati, cp. Sk. ādeśa] information, pointing out; as tt. g. characteristic, determination, substitute, e. g. kutonidānā is at SnA 303 said to equal kiŋ-nidānā, the to of kuto (abl.) equalling or being substituted for the acc. case: paccatta-vacanassa to-ādeso veditabbo.

Ādesanā (f.) [ā + desanā] pointing out, guessing, prophesy; only in phrase °**pāṭihāriya** trick or marvellous ability of mind-reading or guessing other peoples character Vin II. 200; D I.212, 213; III.220; A I.170, 292; V.327; Ps II. 227. For pāṭihāriya is subsiituted °vidhā (lit. variety of, i. e. act or performance etc.) at D III.103.

Ādhāna (nt.) [ā + dhāna] — 1. putting up, putting down, placing, laying A IV.41 (aggissa ādhānaŋ, v. l. of 6 MSS ādānaŋ). — 2. receptacle M I.414 (udak°), cp. ādheyya. — 3. enclosure, hedge Miln 220 (kaṇṭak° thorny brake, see under kaṇṭaka).

-gāhin holding one's own place, i. e. obstinate (?), reading uncertain & interchanging with ādāna, only in one ster. phrase, viz. sandiṭṭhi-parāmāsin ādhāna-gāhin duppaṭinissaggin Vin II.89; M I.43, 96; A III.335 (v. l. ādāna°, C. expl^s by daḷhagāhin); D III.247 (adhāna°).

Ādhāra [ā + dhāra] — 1. a container, receptacle, basin, lit. holder A III.27; J VI.257. — 2. "holding up", i. e. support, basis, prop. esp. a (round) stool or stand for the alms-bowl (patta) Vin II.113 (an° patto); M III.95; S V.21; J V.202. — fig. S V.20 (an° without a support, cittaŋ); Vism 8, 444. — 3. (tt. g.) name for the loc. case ("resting on") Sn 211.

Ādhāraka (m. & nt.) [ā + dhāraka, or simply ādhāra + ka] — 1. a stool or stand (as ādhāra^2) (always m., except at J I.33 where °āni pl. nt.) J I.33; DhA III.290 = VvA 220; DhA III.120 = 186 (one of the four priceless things of a Tathāgata, viz.: setacchattaŋ, nisīdanapallanko, ādhārako pādapīṭhaŋ). — 2. a reading desk, pulpit J III.235; IV.299.

Ādhāraṇatā (f.) [ā + dhāraṇatā] concentration, attention, mindfulness SnA 290 (+ daḷhīkaraṇa), 398 (id.).

Ādhārita [pp. of ā + dhāreti, cp. dhāreti^1] supported, held up Miln 68.

Ādhāvati [ā + dhavati^1] to run towards a goal, to run after M I.265 (where id. p. S II.26 has upadh°); DA I. 39. Freq. in comb$^{n.}$ **ādhāvati paridhāvati** to run about, e. g. J I.127, 134, 158; II.68.

Ādhāvana (nt.) [fr. ādhāvati] onrush, violent motion Miln 135.

Ādhipacca (& **Ādhipateyya**) (nt.) [fr. adhi + pati + ya "being over-lord"; see also adhipateyya] supreme rule, lordship, sovereignty, power S V.342 (issariy°); A I.62 (id.), 147, 212; II.205 (id.); III.33, 76; IV.252 sg.; Pv II.9^{50} (one of the ṭhānas, cp. ṭhāna II.2b; see also D III.

146, where spelt ādhipateyya; expld. by issariya at PvA 137); J I.57; Dāvs v.17; VvA 126 (gehe ā = issariya). The three (att°, lok°, dhamm°) at Vism 14.

Ādhuta [ā + dhuta¹] shaken, moved (by the wind, i. e. fanned Vv 39⁴ (v. l. adhuta which is perhaps to be preferred, i. e. not shaken, cp. vātadhutaŋ Dāvs v.49; VvA 178 expls. by saṇikaŋ vidhūpayamāna, i. e. gently fanned).

Ādheyya (adj.) [grd. of ā + dadhāti cp. ādhāna²] to be deposited (in one's head & heart Pug A), to be heeded, to be appropriated [in latter meaning easily mixed with ādheyya, cp. vv. ll. under ādiya²]; nt. depository (= ādhātabbatā ṭhapetabbatā Pug A 217) Pug 34 (°ŋ gacchati is deposited); Miln 359 (sabbe tass' ādheyya² honti they all become deposited in him, i. e. his deposits or his property).
-mukha see ādiya².

Ānaka [Sk. ānaka, cp. Morris *J P T S.* 1893, 10] a kind of kettledrum, beaten only at one end S II.266; J II. 344; Dpvs XVI.14.

Ānañca see ākāsa° and viññāṇa°.

Ānañja see ānejja.

Ānaṇya (nt.) [Sk. ānṛṇya, so also BSk. e. g. Jtm 31¹⁸; from a + ṛṇa, P. iṇa but also aṇa in composition, thus an-aṇa as base of ânaṇya] freedom from debt D I.73; A III.354 (Ep. of Nibbāna, cp. anaṇa); Nd¹ 160; Vism 44; DA I.3.

Ānadati [ā + nadati] to trumpet (of elephants) J IV.233.

Ānana (nt.) [Vedic āna, later Sk. ānana from **an** to breathe] the mouth; adj. (—°) having a mouth Sdhp 103; Pgdp 63 (vikaṭ°).

Ānantarika (& °ya) [fr. an + antara + ika] without an interval, immediately following, successive Vin I.321; II. 212; Pug 13; Dhs 1291.
-kamma "conduct that finds retribution without delay" (*Kvu trsl.* 275 n. 2) Vin II.193; J I.45; Kvu 480; Miln 25 (cp. *Dhs trsl.* 267); Vism 177 (as prohibiting practice of kammaṭṭhāna).

Ānanda [Vedic ānanda, fr. ā + **nand,** cp. BSk. ānandī joy Divy 37] joy, pleasure, bliss, delight D I.3; Sn 679, 687; J I.207 (°maccha Leviathan); VI.589 (°bheri festive drum); DA I 53 (= pītiyā etaŋ adhivacanaŋ).

Ānandati [ā + nandati] to be pleased or delighted J VI. 589 (aor. ānandi in T. reading ānandi vittā, expld. by C. as nanditthā was pleased; we should however read ānandi-cittā with gladdened heart). See also **ānandiya.**

Ānandin (adj.) [fr. ā + **nand**] joyful, friendly Th I, 555; J IV.226.

Ānandiya (adj.-) [grd. of ānandati] enjoyable, nt. joy, feast J VI.589 (°ŋ acarati to celebrate the feast = ānanda-chaṇa C.).

Ānandī (f.) [ā + nandī, cp. ānanda] joy, happiness in cpd. ānandi-citta J VI.589 (so read probably for ānandi vitta: see ānandati).

Ānaya (adj.) [ā + naya] to be brought, in **suvānaya** easy to bring S I.124 = J I.80.

Ānayati see **āneti.**

Ānāpāna (nt.) [āna + apāna, cpds. of **an** to breathe] inhaled & exhaled breath, inspiration & respiration S V.132, 311 sq.; J I.58; Ps I.162 (°kathā); usually in cpd. °sati concentration by in-breathing & out-breathing (cp. *Man. of Mystic* 70) M I.425 (cp. D II.291); III.82; Vin III.70; A I.30; It 80; Ps I.166, 172, 185 (°samādhi); Nd² 466 B (id.); Miln 332; Vism 111, 197, 266 sq.; SnA 165. See detail under sati.

Ānāpeti see āneti.

Ānāmeti [ā + nāmeti, Caus. of namati, which is usually spelt nameti] to make bend, to bend, to bring toward or under J V.154 (doubtful reading fut ānāmayissasi. v. l. ānayissati, C. ānessasi = lead to).

Ānisaŋsa [ā + ni + saŋsa, BSk. distorted to anuśaŋsa] praise i. e. that which is commendable, profit, merit, advantage, good result, blessing in or from (c. loc.). — There are *five* ānisaŋsā sīlavato sīla-sampadāya or blessings which accrue to the virtuous enumd. at D II.86, viz. **bhogakkhandha** great wealth, **kittisadda** good report, **visārada** self-confidence, **asammūlho kālaŋ karoti** an untroubled death, **saggaŋ lokaŋ uppajjati** a happy state after death. — D I.110, 143; III.132 (four), 236 (five); M I.204; S I.46, 52; III.8, 93 (mahā°); V.69 (seven), 73, 129, 133, 237 (seven), 267, 276; A I.58 (karaṇīye kariyamāne); II.26, 185, 239, 243 (sikkhā°); III.41 (dāne), 248 (dhammasavane), 250 (yāguyā), 251 (upaṭṭhita-satissa), 253 sq. (sīlavato sīlasampadāya etc., as above), 267 (sucarite), 441; IV.150 (mettāya ceto-vimuttiyā), 361 (dhammasavane), 439 sq. (nekkhamme avitakke nippītike), 442, 443 sq. (ākās'ānañcāyatane); V.1, 106 (mahā°), 311; It 28, 29, 40 (sikkhā°); Sn 256 (phala°), 784, 952; J I.9, 94; V.491 (v. l. ann°); Nd¹ 73, 104, 441; Kvu 400; Miln 198; VvA 6, 113; PvA 9 (dāna°) 12, 64 (= phala), 208, 221 (= guṇa); Sdhp 263. — *Eleven* ānisaŋsas of *mettā* (cp. Ps II.130) are given in detail at Vism 311—314; on another *eight* see pp. 644 sq.

Ānisada (nt.) [a + **sad**] "sit down", bottom, behind M I. 80 = 245; J III.435 (gloss asata) Vism 251 = KhA 45 (°ttaca), 252 (°maŋsa).

Ānuttariya (nt.) [see also anuttariya which as —° probably represents ānutt°] incomparableness, excellency, supreme ideal D III.102 sq.; A V.37.

Ānīta [pp. of āneti] fetched, brought (here), brought back adduced J I.291; III.127; IV.1.

Ānupuṭṭha metri causa for **anupuṭṭha** (q. v.).

Ānupubba (nt.) [abstr. fr. anupubba] rule, regularity, order Th I, 727 (cp. M Vastu II.224 ānupubbā).

Ānupubbatā (f.) (or °ta nt.?) [fr. last] succession; only in tt. g. padânu-pubbatā word sequence, in expln. of iti Nd¹ 140; Nd² 137 (v. l. °ka).

Ānupubbikathā [for anupubbi° representing its isolated composition form, cp. ānubhāva & see also anupubbi°] regulated exposition, graduated sermon D I.110; II.41 sq.; M I.379; J I.8; Miln 228; DA I.277, 308; DhA IV.199.

Ānubhāva [the dissociated composition form of anubhāva, q. v. for details. Only in later language] greatness, magnificence, majesty, splendour J I.69 (mahanto); II.102 (of a jewel) V.491; DhA II.58.

Ānejja and **Ānañja** [abstr. fr. an + *añja or *ejja = *ijja. The Sanskritised equivalent would be *iñjya or *iṅgya of **ing** to stir, move, with a peculiar substitution of ***ang** in Pāli, referring it to a base with ṛ (probably Sk. **ṛj**, ṛñjati) in analogy to a form like Sk. ṛṇa = Pāli aṇa & iṇa, both a & i representing Sk. ṛ. The form añja would thus correspond to a Sk. *aññya (*aṅgya). The third P. form ān-eñja is a direct (later, and probably re-instituted) formation from Sk. iñjya, which in an interesting way became in BSk. re-sanskritised to āñijya (which on the other hand may represent āñejja & thus give the latter the feature of a later, but more specifically Pāli form).

The editions of P. Texts show a great variance of spelling, based on MSS. vacillation, in part also due to confusion of derivation] immovability, imperturbability, impassibility. The word is *n.* but occurs as *adj.* at Vin III. 109 (ānañja samādhi, with which cp. BSk. āniñjya śāntiḥ at Av. Ś I.199. — The term usually occurs in cpd. ānejja-ppatta (adj.) immovable lit. having attained impassibility, expl[d.] by Bdhgh. at Vin III.267 (on Pār. I.1, 6) as acala, niccala, i. e. motionless. This cpd. is indicated below by (p.) after the reference. — The various spellings of the word are as follows: — 1. ānejja D I.76 (v. l. ānañja-p.) A II.184 (p.); III.93 (p.), 100 (p.), 377 sq. (p.); Nd² 471 (v. l. aneja, ānañja) = Vbh 137 (āneñja); Nd² 569ª (v. l. ānañja), 601 (v. l. anejja & aneñja); Pug 60 (p.); DA I.219 (v. l. BB āneñja). — 2. ānañja Vin III.4 (p.) (v. l. ānañca°, anañja°, ānañja°; Bdhgh. ānejja° p. 267), 109; Ud 27 (samādhi, adj. v. l. ānañca); DhA IV.46. See also below cpd. °kāraṇa. — A peculiarity of Trenckner's spelling is āṇañja at M II.229 (v. l. aṇañja, aneñja, āneñja), 253, 254. — 3. āneñja S II.82 (v. l. āṇañje, or is it āṇeñja?); D III.217 (°âbhisankhāra of imperturbable character, remaining static, cp. *Kvu trsl.* 358); Nd¹ 90 (id.), 206, 442; Ps II.206; Vbh 135, 340; Vism 377 (p.), 386 (sixteen° fold), 571; Nett 87, 99. — See also iñjati.

-kāraṇa trick of immovability, i. e. pretending to be dead (done by an elephant, but see differently Morris *J P T S.* 1886, 154) J I.415; II.325 (v. l. āṇañja, āneñca, ānañca); IV.308; V.273, 310.

Āneñjatā (f.) [fr. āneñja] steadfastness Vism 330, 386.

Āneti [ā + neti] to bring, to bring towards, to fetch, procure, convey, bring back Sn 110; PvA 54, 92. pot. 1st pl. ānema (or imper. 2nd pl. **ānetha** M I.371. fut. **ānayissati** S I.124; Pv II.6⁵; J III.173; V.154 (v. l.), & **ānessati** J V.154. inf. **ānayituŋ** Pv II 6¹⁰, ger. **ānetvā** PvA 42, 74. aor. **ānesi** PvA 3, & **ānayi** Pv I.7¹ (sapatiŋ). — pp. **ānīta** (q. v.). — Med. pass. **ānīyati** & **āniyyati** D II.245 (āniyyataŋ imper. shall be brought); M I. 371 (ppr. ānīyamāna). — Caus. II. **ānāpeti** to cause to be fetched J III.391; V.225.

Āpa & **Āpo** (nt.) [Vedic ap & āp, f. sg. apā, pl. āpaḥ, later Sk. also āpaḥ nt. — Idg. ***ap** & ***ab,** primarily to Lith. ùpé water, Old Prussian ape river, Gr. Ἀπία N. of the Peloponnesus; further (as ***ab**) to Lat. amnis river, Sk. abda cloud, & perhaps ambu water] water; philosophically t. t. for cohesion, representative of one of the 4 great elements (cp. mahābhūta), viz. paṭhavī, āpo, tejo, vāyo: see *Cpd.* 268 & *Dhs trsl.* 201, also below °dhātu. — D II.259; M I.327; S II.103; III.54, 207; A IV.312, 375; Sn 307, 391 (°ŋ), 392 (loc. ape), 437 (id.); J IV.8 (paṭhavi-āpa-tejo°); Dhs 652; Miln 363 (gen. āpassa, with paṭhavī etc.); Sdhp 100.

-kasiṇa the water-device, i. e. meditation by (the element of) water (cp. *Mystic* 75 n.) D III.268; J I.313; Dhs 203; Vism 170; DhA I 312; III.214. **-dhātu** the fluid element, the essential element in water, i. e element of cohesion (see *Cpd.* 155 n. 2; *Mystic* 9 n. 2; *Dhs trsl.* 201, 242) D III.228, 247; M I.187, 422: Dhs 652; Nett 74. See also **dhātu. -rasa** the taste of water A I.32; SnA 6. **-sama** resembling water M I.423.

Āpakā (f.) [= āpagā] river J V.452; VI.518.

Āpagā (f.) [āpa + ga of **gam**] a river Th 1, 309; Sn 319; J V.454; Dāvs I.52; VvA 41.

Āpajjati [Sk. āpadyate, ā + **pad**] to get into, to meet with (acc.); to undergo; to make, produce, exhibit Vin II.126 (saŋvaraŋ); D I.222 (pariyeṭṭhiŋ); It 113 (vuddhiŋ); J I.73; Pug 20, 33 (diṭṭh'ânugatiŋ); PvA 29 (ppr. āpajjanto); DhA II.71. — pot. **āpajjeyya** D I.119 (musāvādaŋ). — aor. āpajji J V.349; PvA 124 (sankocaŋ) & āpādi S I.37; A II.34; It 85; J II.293; 3rd pl. āpādu D II.273. — ger. **āpajjitva** PvA 22 (saŋvegaŋ), 151. — pp. **āpanna** (q. v.). — Caus. **āpādeti** (q. v.). — *Note.* The reading **āpajja** in āpajja naŋ It 86 is uncertain (vv. ll. āsajja & ālajja). The id. p. at Vin II.203 (CV. VII.4, 8) has āsajjanaŋ, for which Bdhgh, on p. 325 has āpajjanaŋ. Cp. pariyāpajjati.

Āpaṇa [Sk. āpaṇa, a **paṇ**] a bazaar, shop Vin I.140; J I.55; V.445; Pv II.3²²; Miln 2, 341; SnA 440; DhA I. 317; II.89; VvA 157; PvA 88, 333 (phal° fruit shop), 215.

Āpaṇika [fr. āpaṇa] a shopkeeper, tradesman J I.124; Miln 344; VvA 157; DhA II.89.

Āpatacchika at J VI.17 is C. reading for apatacchika in **khārâpat°** (q. v.).

Āpatati [ā + patati] to fall on to, to rush on to J V.349 (= upadhāvati C.); VI.451 (= āgacchati C.); Miln 371.

Āpatti (f.) [Sk. āpatti, fr. ā + **pad,** cp. apajjati & BSk. āpatti, e. g, Divy 330] an ecclesiastical offence (cp. *Kvu trsl.* 362 n. 1), Vin I.103 (°khandha), 164 (°ŋ paṭikaroti), 322 (°ŋ passati), 354 (avasesā & anavasesā); II.2 sq. (°ŋ ropeti), 59, 60 (°pariyanta), 88 (°adhikaraṇa), 259 (°ŋ paṭikaroti); IV.344; D III.212 (°kusalatā); A I.84 (id.), 87; II.240 (°bhaya); Dhs 1330 sq. (cp. *Dhs trsl.* 346). — **anāpatti** Vin III.35.

Āpattika (adj.) [āpatti + ka, cp. BSk. āpattika Divy 303] guilty of an offence M I.443; Vin IV.224. **an°** Vin I.127.

Āpatha in micchāpatha, dvedhāpatha as classified in Vbh Ind. p. 441 should be grouped under **patha** as micchā°, dvedhā°.

Āpathaka in °jjhāyin Nd² 342² is read **āpādaka°** at Nd¹ 226, and āpātaka° at Vism 26.

Āpadā (f.) [Sk. āpad, fr. ā + **pad,** cp. āpajjati & BSk. āpad, e. g. in āpadgata Jtm 31³³] accident, misfortune, distress, D III.190; A II.68 (loc. pl. āpadāsu), 187; III. 45; IV.31; Th 1, 371; J IV.163 (āpadatthā, a difficult form; vv. ll. T. aparattā, āpadatvā, C. aparatthā; expl[d.] by āpadāya); V.340 (loc. āpade), 368; PvA 130 (quot.); Sdhp 312, 554. *Note.* For the contracted form in loc. pl. āpāsu (= ***āpatsu**) see ***āpā.**

Āpanna [pp. of āpajjati] — 1. entered upon, fallen into, possessed of, having done Vin I.164 (āpattiŋ ā.); III.90; D I.4 (dayāpanna merciful); Nd² 32 (taṇhāya). — 2. unfortunate, miserable J I.19 (V.124). Cp. pari°.

***Āpā** (& ***Āvā**) (f.) [for āpadā, q. v.] misery, misfortune J II.317 (loc. pl. āpāsu, v. l. avāsu, C. āpadāsu); III.12 (BB āvāsu); V.82 (avāgata gone into misery, v. l. apagata, C. apagata parihīna), 445 (loc. āvāsu, v. l. avāsu, C. āpadāsu), 448 (āvāsu kiccesu; v. l. apassu, read āpāsu). *Note.* Since ***āpā** only occurs in loc. pl., the form āpāsu is to be regarded as a direct contraction of Sk. **āpatsu.**

Āpāṇa [ā + pāṇa] life, lit. breathing, only in cpd. **°koṭi** the end of life Miln 397; Dāvs III.93; adj. **-koṭika** M II.120; Vism 10.

Āpādaka (adj.-n.) [fr. ā + **pad**] — 1. (adj.) producing, leading to (—°) VvA 4 (abhiññ° catuttha-jjhāna). — 2. (n.) one who takes care of a child, a protector, guardian A I.62 = 132 = It 110 (+ posaka). — f. **āpādikā** a nurse, foster-mother Vin II.289 (+ posikā).

Āpādā (f.) [short for āpādikā] a nursing woman, in **an°** not nursing, unmarried J IV.178.

Āpādi aor. of **āpajjati** (q. v.).

Āpādeti [Caus. of āpajjati] to produce, make out, bring, bring into M I.78; III.248; S IV.110 (addhānaŋ to live one's life, cp. addhānaŋ āpādi J II.293 = jīvit'addhānaŋ āpādi āyuŋ vindi C.); SnA 466. — Cp. pari°.

Āpātha [etym.? Trenckner, Miln p. 428 says: "I suspect ā. to be corrupted from āpāta (cp. āpatati), under an impression that it is allied to patha; but it is scarcely ever written so"] sphere, range, focus, field (of consciousness or perception; cp. *Dhs trsl.* 199), appearance A II.67; J I.336; Vbh 321; Miln 298; Vism 21, 548; DA I.228; DhsA 308, 333; VvA 232 (°kāla); DhA IV.85; Sdhp 356. Usually in phrase āpāthaŋ gacchati to come into focus, to become clear, to appear M I.190; S IV.160, or °ŋ āgacchati Vin I.184; A III.377 sq.; IV.404; Vism 125. Cp. °gata below. -gata come into the sphere of, appearing, visible M I.174 = Nd[2] jhāna (an° unapproached); PvA 23 (āpāthaŋ gata). -gatatta abstr. fr. last: appearance Vism 617.

Āpāthaka (adj.) [fr. āpātha] belonging to the (perceptual) sphere of, visible, in °nisādin lying down visible D III.44, 47. Cp. āpathaka.

Āpāna (nt.) [fr. ā + pā] drinking; drinking party, banquet; banqueting-hall, drinking-hall J I.52 (°maṇḍala); V.292 (°bhūmi); Vism 399 (id.); DhA I.213 (id., rañño).

Āpānaka (adj.) [āpāna + ka] drinking, one who is in the habit of drinking D I.167.

Āpānīya (adj.) [fr. āpāna, ā + pā] drinkable, fit for drinking or drinking with, in °kaŋsa drinking-bowl, goblet M I. 316; S II.110.

Āpāyika (adj.-n.) [fr. apāya] one suffering in an apāya or state of misery after death Vin II.202 = It 85 (v. l. ap°); Vin II.205; D I.103; A I.265; It 42; Vism 16; PvA 60.

Āpiyati [fr. ṛ, cp. appāyati & appeti] to be in motion (in etym. of āpo) Vism 364.

Āpucchati [ā + pucchati] to enquire after, look for, ask, esp. to ask permission or leave; aor. āpucchi J I.140; PvA 110; grd. āpucchitabba DhA I.6; ger. āpucchitvā Vin IV.267 (apaloketvā +); Miln 29; PvA 111; āpucchitūna (cp. Geiger § 211) Th 2, 426; āpuccha Th 2, 416, & āpucchā [= āpṛcchya, cp. Vedic ācyā for ācya], only in neg. form an° without asking Vin II.211, 219; IV.165, 226 (= anapaloketvā); DhA I.81. — pp. āpucchita Vin IV.272.

Āpūrati [a + pūrati] to be filled, to become full, to increase J III.154 (cando ā. = pūrati C.); IV.26, 99, 100.

Āpeti [Caus. of **āp,** see appoti & pāpuṇāti] to cause to reach or obtain J VI.46. Cp. vy°.

Āphusati [ā + phusati] to feel, realise, attain to, reach; aor. āphusi Vv 16[9] (= adhigacchi VvA 84).

Ābaddha [pp. of ābandhati] tied, bound, bound up DA I. 127; fig. bound to, attached to, in love with DhA I.88; PvA 82 (Tissāya °sineha); Sdhp 372 (sineh, °hadaya).

Ābandhaka (adj.) [ā + **bandh,** cp. Sk. ābandha tie, bond] (being) tied to (loc.) PvA 169 (sīse).

Ābandhati (ā + bandhati, Sk. ābadhnāti, **bandh**] to bind to, tie, fasten on to, hold fast; fig. to tie to, to attach to, J IV.132, 289; V.319, 338, 359. — pp. ābaddha.

Ābandhana (nt.) [fr. ā + **bandh**] — 1. tie, bond DA I. 181 = Pug A 236 (°atthena ñāti yeva ñāti-parivaṭṭo). — 2. tying, binding Vism 351 (°lakkhaṇa, of āpodhātu). — 3. reins (?) or harness (on a chariot) J V.319 (but cp. C. expl[n]. "hatthi-assa-rathesu ābandhitabbāni bhaṇḍakāni", thus taking it as ā + bhaṇḍa + na, i. e. wares, loads etc.). With this cp. Sk. ābandha, according to Halāyudha 2, 420 a thong of leather which fastens the oxen to the yoke of a plough.

Ābādha [ā + **bādh** to oppress, Vedic ābādha oppression] affliction, illness, disease Vin IV.261; D I.72; II.13; A I.121; III.94, 143; IV.333, 415 sq., 440; Dh 138; Pug 28; Vism 41 (udara-vāta°) 95; VvA 351 (an° safe & sound); SnA 476; Sdhp 85. — A list of ābādhas or illnesses, as classified on grounds of aetiology, runs as follows: pitta-samuṭṭhānā, semha°, vāta°, sannipātikā, utu-pariṇāmajā, visama-parihārajā, opakkamikā, kammavipākajā (after Nd[2] 304[I C.], recurring with slight variations at S IV.230; A II.87; III.131; V.110; Nd[1] 17, 47; Miln 112, cp. 135). — Another list of illnesses mentioned in the *Vinaya* is given in *Index* to Vin II., p. 351. — Five ābādhas at Vin I. 71, viz. kuṭṭhaŋ gaṇḍo kilāso soso apamāro said to be raging in Magadha cp. p. 93. — Three ābādhas at D III.75, viz. icchā anasanaŋ jarā, cp. Sn 311. — See also cpd. appābādha (health) under appa.

Ābādhika (adj.-n.) [fr. ābādha] affected with illness, a sick person A III.189, 238; Nd[1] 160; Miln 302; DA 212; DhA I.31; PvA 271. — f. **ābādhikinī** a sick woman A II.144.

Ābādhita [pp. of ābādheti, Caus. of ā + bādh] afflicted, oppressed, molested Th 1, 185.

Ābādheti [ā + Caus. of **bādh,** cp. ābādha] to oppress, vex, annoy, harass S IV.329.

Ābila (adj.) [Sk. āvila; see also P. āvila] turbid, disturbed, soiled J V.90.

Ābhata [pp. of ā + bharati from **bhṛ**] brought (there or here), carried, conveyed, taken D I.142; S I.65; A II.83 (for yathābhūtaŋ?); Pv III.5[4] (ratt° = rattiyaŋ ā. PvA 199); DhA II.57, 81; IV.89; VvA 65.

Ābhataka (adj.) = ābhata; DA I.205 (v. l. ābhata).

Ābharaṇa (nt.) [Sk. ābharaṇa, ā + **bhṛ**] that which is taken up or put on, viz. ornament, decoration, trinkets D I. 104; Vv 80[2]; J III.11, 31; DhA III.83; VvA 187.

Ābharati [ā + **bhṛ**] to bring, to carry; ger. ābhatvā J IV.351.

Ābhassara (adj.-n) [etym. uncertain; one suggested in *Cpd.* 138 n. 4 is ā + *__bha__ + **sar,** i. e. from whose bodies are emitted rays like lightning, more probably a comb[n]. of ābhā + **svar** (to shine, be bright), i. e. shining in splendour] shining, brilliant, radiant, N. of a class of gods in the Brahma heavens "the radiant gods", usually referred to as the representatives of supreme love (pīti & mettā); thus at D I.17; Dh 200; It 15; DhA III.258 (°loka). In another context at Vism 414 sq.

Ābhā (f.) [Sk. ābhā, fr. ā + **bhā,** see ābhāti] shine, splendour, lustre, light D II.12; M III.147 (adj. —°); S II.150 (°dhātu); A II.130, 139; III.34; Mhvs XI.11; VvA 234 (of a Vimāna, v. l. pabhā); DhA IV.191; Sdhp 286.

Ābhāti [ā + **bhā**] to shine, shine forth, radiate Dh 387 (= virocati DhA IV.144); J V.204. See also **ābheti.**

Ābhāveti [ā + bhāveti] to cultivate, pursue Pv II.13[19] (mettacittaŋ; gloss & v. l. abhāvetvā; expl[d]. as vaḍḍhetvā brūhetvā PvA 168).

Ābhāsa [Sk. ābhāsa, fr. ā + bhās] splendour, light, appearance M II.215; III.215.

Ābhicetasika (adj.) See abhicetasika. This spelling, with guṇa of the first syllable, is probably more correct; but the short a is the more frequent.

Ābhidosika (adj.) [abhidos + ika] belonging to the evening before, of last night Vin III.15 (of food; stale); M I.170 (°kālakata died last night); Miln 291.

Ābhidhammika (adj.) [abhidhamma + ika] belonging to the specialised Dhamma, versed in or studying the Abhidhamma Miln 17, 341; Vism 93. As abhi° atKhA 151; J IV.219.

Ābhindati [ā + bhindati] to split, cut, strike (with an axe) S IV.160 (v. l. a°).

Ābhisekika (adj.) [fr. abhiseka] belonging to the consecration (of a king) Vin V.129.

Ābhujati [ā + bhujati, **bhuj**[1]] to bend, bend towards or in, contract; usually in phrase **pallankaŋ** ā° "to bend in the round lap" or "bend in hookwise", to sit cross-legged (as a devotee with straightened back), e. g. at Vin I.24; D I.71; M I.56 (v. l. ābhuñjitvā), 219; A III. 320; Pug 68; Ps I.176; J I.71, 213; Miln 289; DA I. 58, 210. In other connection J I.18 (v.101; of the ocean "to recede"); Miln 253 (kāyaŋ).

Ābhujana (nt.) [fr. abhujati] crouching, bending, turning in, in phrase pallank'ābhujana sitting cross-legged J I 17 (v.91); PvA 219.

Ābhujī (f.) [lit. the one that bends, prob. a poetic metaphor] N. of a tree, the Bhūrja or Bhojpatr J V.195 (= bhūjapatta-vana C.), 405 (= bhūjapatta C.).

Ābhuñjati [ā + **bhuj**[2], Sk. bhunakti] to enjoy, partake of, take in, feel, experience J IV.456 (bhoge; Rh. D. "hold in its hood"?); DhsA 333.

Ābhuñjana (nt.) [fr. ābhuñjati] partaking of, enjoying, experiencing DhsA 333.

Ābheti [*ābhayati = ābhāti, q. v.] to shine Pv II.12[6] (ppr. °entī); Vv 8[2] (°antī, v. l. °entī; = obhāsentī VvA 50).

Ābhoga [fr. ābhuñjati, **bhuj**[2] to enjoy etc. The translators of Kvu derive it from **bhuj**[1] to bend etc. (*Kvu trsl.* 221 n. 4) which however is hardly correct, cp. the similar meaning of gocara "pasturing", fig. perception etc.] ideation, idea, thought D I.37 (= manasikāro samannāhāro DA I.122; cp. semantically āhāra = ābhoga, food); Vbh 320; Miln 97; Vism 164, 325, 354; Dāvs 62; KhA 42 (°paccavekkhana), 43 (id.) 68.

Āma[1] (indecl.) [a specific Pāli formation representing either amma (q. v.) or a gradation of pron. base amu° "that" (see asu), thus deictic-emphatic exclam[n.] Cp. also BSk. āma e. g. Av. Ś I.36] affirmative part. "yes, indeed, certainly" D I.192 sq. (as v. l. BB.; T. has āmo); J I.115, 226 (in C. expl[n.] of T. amā-jāta which is to be read for āmajāta); II.92; V.448; Miln 11, 19, 253; DhA I.10, 34; II.39, 44; VvA 69; PvA 12, 22, 56, 61, 75, 93 etc.

Āma[2] (adj.) [Vedic āma = Gr. ὠμός, connected with Lat. amārus. The more common P. form is **āmaka** (q v.)] raw, viz. (a) unbaked (of an earthen vessel), unfinished Sn 443; (b) uncooked (of flesh), nt. raw flesh, only in foll. cpds.: °**gandha** "smell of raw flesh", verminous odour, a smell attributed in particular to rotting corpses (cp. similarly BSk. āmagandha M Vastu III.214) D II.242 sq.; A I.280; Sn 241, 242 (= vissagandha kuṇapagandha SnA 286), 248, 251; Dhs 625; and °**giddha** greedy after flesh (used as bait) J VI.416 (= āmasankhāta āmisa C.).

Āmaka (adj.) [= āma[2]] raw, uncooked D I.5 = Pug 58 (°maŋsa raw flesh); M I.80 (titta-kalābu āmaka-cchinno). -**dhañña** "raw" grain, corn in its natural, unprepared state D I.5 = Pug 58 (see DA I.78 for definition); Vin IV.264; V.135. -**sāka** raw vegetables Vism 70. -**susāna** "cemetery of raw flesh" charnelgrove (cp. āmagandha under ama[2]), i. e. fetid smelling cremation ground J I.264, 489; IV.45 sq.; VI.10; DhA I.176; VvA 76; PvA 196.

Āmaṭṭha [Sk. āmṛṣṭa, pp. of āmasati; cp. āmasita] touched, handled J I.98 (an°); DA I.107 (= parāmaṭṭha); Sdhp 333.

Āmaṇḍaliya [ā + maṇḍala + iya] a formation resembling a circle, in phrase °ŋ **karoti** to form a ring (of people) or a circle, to stand closely together M I 225 (cp. Sk. āmaṇḍalikaroti).

Āmata in anāmata at J II.56 is metric for **amata**.

Āmattikā (f.) [ā + mattikā] earthenware, crockery; in °**āpaṇa** a crockery shop, chandler's shop Vin IV.243.

Āmaddana (nt.) [ā + maddana of **mṛd**] crushing VvA 311.

Āmanta (adj.-adv.) [either ger. of āmanteti (q. v.) or root der. fr. ā + **mant,** cp. āmantaṇā] asking or asked, invited, only as an° without being asked, unasked, uninvited Vin I.254 (°cāra); A III.259 (id.).

Āmantana (nt.) & °nā (f., also °ṇā) [from āmanteti] addressing, calling; invitation, greeting Sn 40 (cp. Nd[2] 128); °**vacana** the address-form of speech i. e. the vocative case (cp. Sk. āmantritaŋ id.) SnA 435; KhA 167.

Āmantanaka (adj.-n.) [fr. āmantaṇa] addressing, speaking to, conversing; f. °ikā interlocutor, companion, favourite queen Vv 18[8] (= allāpa-sallāpa-yoggā kiḷanakāle vā tena (i. e. Sakkena) āmantetabbā VvA 96).

Āmantaṇīya (adj.) [grd. of āmanteti] to be addressed J IV.371.

Āmantita [pp. of āmanteti] addressed, called, invited Pv II.3[13] (= nimantita PvA 86).

Āmanteti [denom. of ā + *mantra] to call, address, speak to, invite, consult J VI.265; DA I.297; SnA 487 (= ālapati & avhayati); PvA 75, 80, 127. — aor. **āmantesi** D II.16; Sn p. 78 (= ālapi SnA 394) & in poetry **āmantayi** Sn 997; Pv II.2[7]; 3[1] (perhaps better with v. l. SS samantayi). — ger. **āmanta** (= Sk. *āmantrya) J III.209, 315 (= āmantayitvā C.), 329; IV.111; V.233; VI.511. — pp. **āmantita** (q. v.). — Caus. II. **āmantāpeti** to invite to come, to cause to be called, to send for D I.134 (v. l. āmanteti); Miln 149.

Āmaya [etym.? cp. Sk. āmaya] affliction, illness, misery; only as **an°** (adj) not afflicted, not decaying, healthy, well (cp. BSk. nirāmaya Aśvaghoṣa II.9) Vin I.294; Vv 15[10] (= aroga VvA 74); 17[7]; 36[9]; J III.260, 528; IV. 427; VI.23. Positive only very late, e. g. Sdhp 397.

Āmalaka [cp. Sk. āmalaka] emblic myrobalan, Phyllanthus Emblica Vin I.201, 278; II.149 (°vaṇṭika pīṭha); S I.150; A V.170; Sn p. 125 (°matti); J IV.363; V.380 (as v. l. for T. āmala); Miln 11; DhA I.319; VvA 7.

Āmalakī (f.) āmalaka Vin I.30; M I.456 (°vana).

Āmasati [ā + masati fr. **mṛś**] to touch (upon), to handle, to lay hold on Vin II.221; III.48 (kumbhiŋ); J III.319 (id.); A V.263, 266; J IV.67; Ps II.209; Miln 306; SnA 400; DhsA 302; VvA 17. — aor. **āmasi** J II.360; ger. **āmasitvā** Vin III.140 (udakapattaŋ) J II.330; grd. **āmassa** J II.360 (an°) and **āmasitabba** id. (C.). — pp. **āmaṭṭha** & **āmasita** (q. v.).

Āmasana (nt.) [fr. āmasati] touching, handling; touch Vin IV.214. Cp. III.118; Miln 127, 306; DA I.78.

Āmasita [pp. of āmasati] touched, taken hold of, occupied VvA 113 (an° khetta virgin land).

Āmāya (adj.) [to be considered either a der. from amā (see amājāta in same meaning) or to be spelt amāya which metri causa may be written ā°] "born in the house" (cp. semantically Gr. ἐνδογενής > indigenous), inborn, being by birth, in cpd. °**dāsa** (dāsī) a born slave, a slave by birth J VI.117 (= gehadāsiyā kucchismiŋ jātadasī C.), 285 (= dāsassa dāsiyā kucchimhi jātadāsā).

Āmāsaya [āma² + āsaya, cp. Sk. āmāśaya & āmāśraya] receptacle of undigested food, i.e. the stomach Vism 260; KhA 59. Opp. pakkāsaya.

Āmilāka (nt.?) [etym.?] a woollen cover into which a floral pattern is woven DA 1.87.

Āmisa (nt.) [der. fr. āma raw, q. v. for etym. — Vedic āmis (m.); later Sk. āmiṣa (nt.), both in lit. & fig. meaning] — 1. originally raw meat; hence prevailing notion of "raw, unprepared, uncultivated"; thus °**khāra** raw lye Vin I. 206. — 2. "fleshy, of the flesh" (as opposed to mind or spirit), hence material, physical; generally in opposition to **dhamma** (see dhamma B 1. a. and also next no.), thus at M I.12 (°dāyāda); It 101 (id.); A I.91 = It 98 (°dāna material gifts opp. to spiritual ones); Dhs 1344 (°paṭisanthāra hospitality towards bodily needs, cp. *Dhs trsl.* 350). — 3. food, esp. palatable food (cp. E. sweetmeat); food for enjoyment, dainties Vin II.269 sq.; J II.6; Miln 413 (lok°); DA 1.83 (°sannidhi). — 4. bait S I.67; IV.158; J IV.57, 219; VI.416; DA I.270. — 5. gain, reward, money, douceur, gratuity, "tip" PvA 36, 46; esp. in phrase °**kiñcikkha-hetu** for the sake of some (little) gain S II.234; A I.128; V.265, 283 sq., 293 sq.; Pug 29; Pv II.8³ (= kiñci āmisaŋ patthento PvA 107); Miln 93; VvA 241 (= bhogahetu). — 6. enjoyment Pv II.8² (= kāmāmise-laggacitto PvA 107). — 7. greed, desire, lust Vin I.303 (°antara out of greed, selfish, opp. mettacitto); A III.144 (id.), 184 (id.); I.73 (°garu parisā); J V.91 (°cakkhu); Ps II.238 (mār°). See also cpds. with nir° and sa°.

Āmuñcati [ā + **muc**] to put on, take up; to be attached to, cling to DhsA 305. — pp. **āmutta** (q. v.).

Āmutta [Sk. āmukta, pp. of ā + **muc**, cp. also BSk. āmukta jewel Divy 2, 3 etc., a meaning which might also be seen in the later Pāli passages, e. g. at PvA 134. Semantically cp. ābharaṇa] having put on, clothed in, dressed with, adorned with (always °—) D I.104 (°mālābharaṇa); Vin II.156 = Vv 20⁸ (°maṇi-kuṇḍala); S I.211; J IV.460; V. 155; VI.492; Vv 72¹ (= paṭimukka); 80² (°hatthābharaṇa); Pv II.9¹⁰ (°maṇikuṇḍala) J IV.183; VvA 182.

Āmeṇḍita (or **Ameḍita**) [Sk. āmreḍita fram ā + **mreḍ**, dialectical] — 1. (nt.) sympathy in °ŋ karoti to show sympathy (? so Morris *JPTS.* 1887, 106) DA I.228 = SnA 155 (v. l. at DA āmeḍita).

Āmo = āma D I.192, 3.

Āmoda [Sk. āmoda, fr. ā + **mud**] that which pleases; fragrance, perfume Dāvs V.51.

Āmodanā (f.) [fr. ā + **mud**] rejoicing Dhs 86, 285.

Āmodamāna (adj.) [ppr. med. of āmodeti] rejoicing, glad S I.100 (v. l. anu°) = It 66; Vv 64⁸ (= pamodamāna VvA 278); J V.45.

Āmodita [pp. fr. āmodeti] pleased, satisfied, glad J I.17 (V.80); V.45 (°pamodita highly pleased); Miln 346.

Āmodeti [Sk. āmodayati, Caus. of ā + **mud**] to please, gladden, satisfy Th 1, 649 (cittaŋ); J V.34. — pp. **āmodita** (q. v.).

Āya [Sk. āya; ā + **i**] 1. coming in, entrance M III 93. — 2. tax J V.113. — 3. income, earning, profit, gain (opp. **vaya** loss) A IV.282 = 323; Sn 978; J I.228; KhA 38 (in expl$^{n.}$ of kāya), 82 (in etym. of āyatana); PvA 130. — 4. (āyā f.?) a lucky dice ("the incomer") J VI.281.

-**kammika** a treasurer DhA I.184. -**kusala** clever in earnings Nett 20. -**kosalla** proficiency in money making D III.220 (one of the three kosallas); Vbh 325. -**pariccāga** expediture of one's income PvA 8. -**mukha** (lit.) entrance, inflow, going in D I.74 (= āgamana-magga DA I.78); M II.15; A II.166; (fig.) revenue income, money SnA 173.

Āyata [Sk. āyata, pp. of ā + **yam**, cp. āyamati] — 1. (adj.) outstretched, extended, long, in length (with numeral) D III.73 (ñātikkhaya, prolonged or heavy?); M I.178 (dighato ā°; tiriyañ ca vitthata); J I.77, 273 (tettiŋs²-angul'āyato khaggo); III.438; Vv 84¹⁵ (°aŋsa; cp. expl$^{n.}$ at VvA 339); SnA 447; DhsA 48; PvA 152 (dāṭhā fangs; lomā hair), 185 (°vaṭṭa); Sdhp 257. — 2. (n.) a bow J III.438.

-**agga** having its point (end) stretched forward, i. e. in the future (see āyati) It 15, 52. -**paṇhin** having long eye-lashes (one of the signs of a Mahāpurisa) D II.17 = III.143. -**pamha** a long eye-lash Th 2, 384 (= dīghapakhuma ThA 250).

Āyataka (adj.) [= āyata] — 1. long, extended, prolonged, kept up, lasting Vin II.108 (gītassara); A III.251 (id.); J I.362. — 2. sudden, abrupt, instr. °ena abruptly Vin II.237.

Āyatana (nt.) [Sk. āyatana, not found in the Vedas; but freq. in BSk. From ā + **yam**, cp. āyata. The pl. is āyatanā at S IV.70. — For full definition of term as seen by the Pāli Commentators see Bdhgh's expl^{n} at DA I. 124, 125, with which cp. the popular etym. at KhA 82: "āyassa vā tananato āyatassa vā saŋsāradukkhassa nayanato āyatanāni" and at Vism 527 "āye tanoti āyatañ ca nayatī ti ā."] — 1. stretch, extent, reach, compass, region; sphere, locus, place, spot; position, occasion (corresponding to Bdhgh's definition at DA I.124 as "samosaraṇa") D III.241, 279 (vimutti°); S II.41, 269; IV.217; V.119 sq., 318 sq.; A III.141 (ariya°); V.61 (abhibh°, q. v.) Sn 406 (rajass° "haunt of passion" = rāgādi-rajassa uppatti-deso SnA 381); J I.80 (raj°). Freq. in phrase **arañña°** a lonely spot, a spot in the forest J I.173; VvA 301; PvA 42, 54. — 2. exertion, doing, working, practice, performance (comprising Bdhgh's definition at DA I.124 as paññatti), usually —°, viz. **kamm°** Nd¹ 505; Vbh 324, 353; **kasiṇ°** A V.46 sq., 60; Ps I.28; **titth°** A I.173, 175; Vbh 145, 367; **sipp°** (art, craft) D I.51; Nd² 505; Vbh 324, 353; cp. **an°** non-exertion, indolence, sluggishness J V.121. — 3. sphere of perception or sense in general, object of thought, sense-organ & object; relation, order. — *Cpd.* p. 183 says rightly: "āyatana cannot be rendered by a single English word to cover both sense-organs (the mind being regarded as 6th sense) and sense objects". — These āyatanāni (relations, functions, reciprocalities) are thus divided into two groups, inner (ajjhattikāni) and outer (bāhirāni), and comprise the foll.: (a) ajjhatt°: 1. **cakkhu** eye, 2. **sota** ear, 3. **ghāna** nose, 4. **jivhā** tongue, 5. **kāya** body, 6. **mano** mind; (b) bāh°: 1. **rūpa** visible object, 2. **sadda** sound, 3. **gandha** odour, 4. **rasa** taste, 5. **phoṭṭhabba** tangible object, 6. **dhamma** cognizable object. — For details as regards connotation & application see *Dhs trsl.* introduction li sq. *Cpd.* 90 n. 2; 254 sq. — Approximately covering this meaning (3) is Bdhgh's definition of āyatana at DA I.124 as sañjāti and as kāraṇa (origin & cause, i. e. mutually occasioning & conditioning relations or adaptations). See also Nd² under rūpa for further classifications. — For the above mentioned *12* āyatanāni see the foll. passages: D II.302 sq.; III.102, 243; A III.400; V.52; Sn 373 (cp. SnA 366); Ps I.7, 22, 101, 137; II. 181, 225, 230; Dhs 1335; Vbh 401 sq.; Nett 57, 82; Vism 481; ThA 49, 285. Of these *6* are mentioned at S I.113, II.3; IV.100, 174 sq.; It 114; Vbh 135 sq., 294; Nett 13, 28, 30; Vism 565 sq. Other sets of *10* at Nett 69; of *4* at D II.112, 156; of *2* at D II.69. — Here also belongs ākās' ānañc' āyatana, ākiñcañ° etc. (see under ākāsa etc. and s. v.), e. g. at D I.34 sq., 183; A IV.451 sq.; Vbh 172, 189, 262 sq.; Vism 324 sq. — Unclassified passages: M I.61; II.233; III.32, 216, 273; S I.196; II.6, 8, 24, 72 sq.; III.228; IV.98; V.426; A I.113, 163, 225; III.17, 27, 82, 426; IV.146, 426; V.30, 321, 351, 359;

Nd¹ 109, 133, 171, 340; J I.381 (paripuṇṇa°); Vbh 412 sq. (id.).
-uppāda birth of the āyatanas (see above 3) Vin I.185. -kusala skilled in the ā. M III.63. -kusalatā skill in the spheres (of sense) D III.212; Dhs 1335. -ṭṭha founded in the sense-organs Ps I.132; II.121.

Āyatanika (adj.) [fr. āyatana] belonging to the sphere of (some special sense, see āyatana 3) S IV.126 (phass° niraya & sagga).

Āyati (f.) [fr. ā + **yam**, cp. Sk. āyati] "stretching forth", extension, length (of time), future. Only (?) in acc. āyatiŋ (adv.) in future Vin II.89, 185; III.3; Sn 49; It 115 (T. reads āyati but cp. p. 94 where T. āyatiŋ, v. l. āyati); J I.89; V.431; DA I 236.

Āyatika (adj.) [fr. last] future S I.142.

Āyatikā (f.) [of āyataka] a tube, waterpipe Vin II.123.

Āyatta [Sk. āyatta, pp. of ā + **yat**]. — 1. striving, active, ready, exerted J V.395 (°mana = ussukkamana C.). — 2. striven after, pursued J I.341. — 3. dependent on Vism 310 (assāsa-passāsa°); Nett 194; Sdhp 477, 605.

Āyanā (f.) [?] at DhsA 259 and Vism 26 is a grammarian's construction, abstracted from f. abstr. words ending in °āyanā, e. g. kankhā > kankhāyanā, of which the correct expl^n. is a derivation fr. caus.-formation kankhāyati > kankhāy + a + nā. What the idea of Bdhgh. was in propounding his expl^n. is hard to say, perhaps he related it to **i** and understood it to be the same as **āyāna**.

Āyamati [ā + **yam**] to stretch, extend, stretch out, draw out Miln 176, usually in ster. phrase **piṭṭhi** me **āgilāyati** tam **ahaŋ āyamissāmi** "my back feels weak, I will stretch it" Vin II.200; D III.209; M I.354; S IV.184; J I.491. — Besides this in commentaries e. g. J III.489 (mukhaŋ āyamituŋ).

Āyasa (adj.) [Sk. āyasa, of ayas iron] made of iron S II. 182; A III.58; Dh 345; J IV.416; V.81; Vv 84⁵ (an°? cp. the rather strange expl^n. at VvA 335).

Āyasakya (nt.) dishonour, disgrace, bad repute A IV.96; J V.17; VvA 110; usually in phrase °ŋ **pāpuṇāti** to fall into disgrace Th 1, 292; J II.33 = 271; III.514. [Bdhgh. on A IV.96 explains it as ayasaka + ya with guṇa of the initial, cp. ārogya].

Āyasmant (adj.) [Sk. āyuṣmant, the P. form showing assimilation of u to a] lit. old, i. e. venerable; used, either as adj. or absolute as a respectful appellation of a bhikkhu of some standing (cp. the semantically identical **thera**). It occurs usually in nom. **āyāsma** and is expl^d. in Nd by typical formula "piya-vacanaŋ garu°, sagārava-sappatiss-âdhivacanaŋ", e. g. Nd¹ 140, 445; Nd² 130 on var. Sn loci (e. g. 814, 1032, 1040, 1061, 1096). — Freq. in all texts, of later passages see SnA 158; PvA 53, 54, 63, 78. — See also **āvuso**.

Āyāga [ā + yāga of **yaj**] sacrificial fee, gift; (m.) recipient of a sacrifice or gift (deyyadhamma) Sn 486 (= deyyadhammānaŋ adhiṭṭhāna-bhūta SnA 412); Th 1, 566; J VI. 205 (°vatthu worthy object of sacrificial fees).

Āyācaka (adj.-n.) [fr. ā + **yāc**] one who begs or prays, petitioner Miln 129.

Āyācati [ā + **yāc**, cp. Buddh. Sk. āyācate Divy I.] — 1. to request, beg, implore, pray to (acc.) Vin III.127; D I.240; PvA 160. — 2. to make a vow, to vow, promise A I. 88; J I.169 = V.472; I.260; II.117. — pp. āyācita (q. v.).

Āyācana (nt.) [fr. āyācati] — 1. asking, adhortation, addressing (t. t. g. in expl^n. of imperative) SnA 43, 176, 412. — 2. a vow, prayer A I.88; III.47; J I.169 = V.472.

Āyācita [pp. of āyācati] vowed, promised J I.169 (°bhatta-jātaka, N.).

Āyāta [pp. of āyāt.; cp. BSk. āyāta in same meaning at Jtm 210] gone to, undertaken Sdhp 407.

Āyāti [ā + yāti of **yā**] to come on or here, to come near, approach, get into S I.240; Sn 669; Sn p. 116 (= gacchati SnA 463); J IV.410; Pv II.12¹² (= āgacchati PvA 158); DhA I.93 (imper. āyāma let us go). — pp. **āyāta**.

Āyāna (nt.) [fr. ā + **yā** to go] coming, arrival: see **āyanā**.

Āyāma [fr. ā + **yam**, see āyamati] — 1. (lit.) stretching, stretching out, extension Vin I.349 = J III.488 (mukh°). — 2. (appl.) usually as linear measure: extension, length (often comb^d. with and contrasted to **vitthāra** breadth or width & **ubbedha** height), as n. (esp. in abl. āyāmato & instr. āyāmena in length) or as adj. (—°): J I.7, 49 (°ato tīṇi yojanasatāni, vitthārato aḍḍhatiyāni); III.389; Miln 17 (ratanaŋ soḷasahatthaŋ āyāmena aṭṭhahatthaŋ vitthārena), 282 (ratanaŋ catuhatth'āyāmaŋ); Vism 205 (+ vitth°); Khb 133 (+ vitthāra & parikkhepa); VvA 188 (soḷasa-yojan°), 199 (°vitthārehi), 221 (°ato + vitth°); PvA 77 (+ vitth°), 113 (id. + ubbedha); DhA I.17 (saṭṭhi-yojan°).

Āyāsa [cp. Sk. āyāsa, etym.?] trouble, sorrow, only neg. an° (adj.) peaceful, free from trouble A IV.98; Th 1, 1008.

Āyu (nt.) [Vedic āyus; Av. āyu, gradation form of same root as Gr. αἰών "aeon", αἰέν always; Lat. aevum, Goth. aiws. Ohg. ēwa, in always; Ger. ewig eternal; Ags. āē eternity, ā always (cp. ever and aye)] life, vitality, duration of life, longevity D III.68, 69, 73, 77; S III.143 (usmā ca); IV.294; A I.155; II.63, 66 (addh°); III.47; IV.76, 139; Sn 694, 1019; It 89; J I.197 (dīgh°); Vv 55⁵ (cp. VvA 247 with its definition of divine life as comprising 30 600 000 years); Vism 229 (length of man's āyu = 100 years); Dhs 19, 82, 295, 644, 716; Sdhp 234, 239, 258. — Long or divine life, dibbaŋ āyu is one of the 10 attributes of ādhipateyya or majesty (see **ṭhāna**), thus at Vin I.294; D III.146; S IV.275 sq.; A I.115; III. 33; IV.242, 396; Pv II.9⁵⁹ (= jīvitaŋ PvA 136).
-ūhā see āyūhā. -kappa duration of life Miln 141; DhA I.250. -khaya decay of life (cp. jīvita-kkhaya) D I.17 (cp. DA I.110); III.29. -pamāṇa span or measure of life time D II.3; A I.213, 267; II.126 sq.; IV.138, 252 sq., 261; V.172; Pug 16; Vbh 422 sq.; SnA 476. -pariyanta end of life It 99; Vism 422. -sankhaya exhaustion of life or lifetime Dpvs V.102. -sankhāra (usually pl. °ā) constituent of life, conditions or properties resulting in life, vital principle D II.106; M I.295 sq.; S II.266; A IV.311 sq.; Ud 64; J IV.215; Miln 285; Vism 292; DhA I.129; PvA 210. Cp. BSk. āyuḥ-saŋskāra Divy 203.

Āyuka (—°) (adj.) [fr. āyu] — 1. being of life; having a life or age A IV.396 (niyat°); VvA 196 (yāvatāyukā dibbasampatti divine bliss lasting for a lifetime). Esp. freq. in comb^n. with **dīgha** (long) and **appa** (short) as dīghāyuka A IV.240; PvA 27; appāyuka A IV.247; PvA 103; both at Vism 422. In phrase vīsati-vassasahass'āyukesu manussesu at the time when men lived 20 000 years D II.5—12 (see Table at *Dial.* II.6); DhA II.9; PvA 135; dasa-vassasahass'āyukesu manussesu (10 000 years) PvA 73; cattāḷisa° DhA I.103; catusaṭṭhi-kapp'āyukā subhakiṇhā Vism 422.

Āyukin (adj.) [fr. āyu] = āyuka; in appāyukin short lived Vv 41⁶.

Āyuta (adj.) [Sk. ayuta, pp. of ā + **yu**, yuvati] — 1. connected with, endowed, furnished with Th 1, 753 (dve pannaras'āyuta due to twice fifteen); Sn 301 (nārī-varagaṇ° = °saŋyutta SnA 320); Pv II.12⁴ (nānā-saragaṇ° = °yutta PvA 157). — 2. seized, conquered, in **dur°** hard to conquer, invincible J VI.271 (= paccatthikehi durāsada C.).

Āyutta [Sk. āyukta; pp. of ā + **yuj**] — 1. yoked, to connected with, full of Pv I.10^{14} (tejas'āyuta T., but PvA 52 reads °āyutta and explns. as samāyutta); PvA 157 (= ākiṇṇa of Pv II.12^{4}). — 2. intent upon, devoted to S I.67.

Āyuttaka (adj.-n.) [āyutta + ka] one who is devoted to or entrusted with, a trustee, agent, superintendent, overseer J I.230 (°vesa); IV.492; DhA I.101, 103, 180.

Āyudha is the Vedic form of the common Pāli form **āvudha** weapon, and occurs only spuriously at D I.9 (v. l. āvudha).

Āyuvant (adj.) [fr. āyu] advanced in years, old, of age Th I, 234.

Āyusmant (adj.) [Sk. āyuṣmant; see also the regular P. form āyasmant] having life or vitality PvA 63 (āyusmā-viññāṇa feeling or sense of vitality; is reading correct?).

Āyussa (adj.) [Sk. *āyuṣya] connected with life, bringing (long) life A III.145 dhamma).

Āyūhaka (adj.) [fr. āyūhati] keen, eager, active Miln 207 (+ viriyavā).

Āyūhati [ā + y + ūhati with euphonic y, fr. Vedic ūhati, **ūh**^{1}, a gradation of **vah** (see etym. under vahati). Kern's etym. on *Toev.* 99 = āyodhati is to be doubted, more acceptable is Morris' expln. at *JPTS.* 1885, 58 sq, although contradictory in part.] lit. to push on or forward, aim at, go for, i. e. (1) to endeavour, strain, exert oneself S I.1 (ppr. anāyūhaŋ unstriving), 48; J VI.35 (= viriyaŋ karoti C.), 283 (= vāyamati C.). — (2) to be keen on (w. acc.), to cultivate, pursue, do Sn 210 (= karoti SnA 258); Miln 108 (kammaŋ āyūhitvā), 214 (kammaŋ āyūhi), 326 (maggaŋ). — pp. **āyūhita** (q. v.).

Āyūhana (adj.-nt.) [fr. āyūhati] — 1. endeavouring, striving, Ps I.10 sq., 32, 52; II.218; Vism 103, 212, 462, 579. f. āyūhanī Dhs 1059 ("she who toils" trsl.) = Vbh 361 = Nd^{2} taṇhā I. (has āyūhanā). — 2. furtherance, pursuit DA I.64 (bhavassa).

Āyūhā f. [āyu + ūhā] life, lifetime, only in **°pariyosāna** at the end of (his) life PvA 136, 162; VvA 319.

Āyūhāpeti [Caus. II. fr. āyūhati] to cause somebody to toil or strive after DhsA 364.

Āyūhita [*Sk. ā + ūhita, pp. of **ūh**] busy, eager, active Miln 181.

Āyoga [Sk. āyoga, of ā + **yuj**; cp. āyutta] — 1. binding, bandage Vin II.135; Vv 33^{41}; VvA 142 (°paṭṭa). — 2. yoke Dhs 1061 (avijj°), 1162. — 3. ornament, decoration Nd^{1} 226; J III.447 (°vatta, for v. l. °vanta?). — 4. occupation, devotion to, pursuit, exertion D I.187; Dh 185 (= payoga-karaṇa DhA III.238). — 5. (t.t.) obligation, guarantee (?) SnA 179. — Cp. sam°.

Ārakatta (nt.) [*ārakāt + tvaŋ] warding off, keeping away, holding aloof, being far from (c. gen.); occurring only in pop. etym. of arahant at A IV.145; DhA IV.228; DA I.146 = VvA 105, 106 = PvA 7; cp. DhsA 349.

Ārakā (adv.) [Sk. ārāt & ārakāt, abl. form. fr. *āraka, see ārā^{2}] far off, far from, away from, also used as prep. c. abl. and as adj. pl. keeping away from, removed, far Vin II.239 = A IV.202 (sanghamhā); D I.99, 102 (adj.) 167; M I.280 (adj.) S II.99; IV.43 sq.; A I.281; It 91; J I.272; III.525; V.451; Miln 243; VvA 72, 73 (adj. + viratā).

Ārakkha [ā + rakkha] watch, guard, protection, care D II.59; III.289; S IV.97, 175, 195; A II.120; III.38; IV. 266, 270, 281 (°sampadā), 322 (id.), 400; V.29 sq.; J I.203; II.326; IV.29 (°purisa); V.212 (°ṭṭhāna, i. e. harem), 374 (°parivāra); Pug 21 (an°), 24; Miln 154; Vism 19 (°gocara preventive behaviour, cautiousness); SnA 476 (°devatā); KhA 120 (id.), 169; DhA II.146; PvA 195; Sdhp 357, 365.

Ārakkhika [fr. ārakkha] a guard, watchman J IV.29.

Ārakkheyya see arakkheyya.

Āragga (nt.) [ārā + agga; Sk. ārāgra of ārā an awl, a prick] the point of an awl, the head of certain arrows, having the shape of an awl, or an arrow of that kind (see Halayudha p. 151) A I.65; Sn 625, 631; Dh 401, 407; Vism 306; DhA II.51; IV.181.

Āracayāracayā [ā + racayā a ger. or abl. form. fr. ā + ***rac**, in usual Sk. meaning "to produce", but here as a sound-root for slashing noise, in reduplication for sake of intensification. Altogether problematic] by means of hammering, slashing or beating (like beating a hide) Sn 673 (gloss ārajayārajayā fr. ā + ***rañj** or ***raj**). — SnA 481 explns. the passage as follows: ārajayārajayā; i. e. yathā manussā allacammaŋ bhūmiyaŋ pattharitvā khīlehi ākoṭenti, evaŋ ākoṭetvā pharasūhi phāḷetvā ekam ekaŋ koṭiŋ chinditvā vihananti, chinnachinnakoṭi punappuna samuṭṭhāti; āracayāracayā ti pi pāṭho, āviñjitvā (v. l. BB. āvijjhitvā) āviñjitvā ti attho. — Cp. **ārañjita**.

Āraññaka (adj.) [fr. arañña + ka] belonging to solitude or the forest, sequestered; living in the forest, fond of seclusion, living as hermits (bhikkhū). Freq. spelt araññaka (q. v.). — Vin I.92 (bhikkhū); II.32, 197, 217 (bh.), 265 (bh.); M I.214; A III.100 sq., 219; IV.21; V.66; J III.174 (v. l. BB. a°); Miln 342; DhA II.94 (vihāra).

Āraññakatta (nt.) [abstr. fr. āraññaka, see also araññakatta] the habit of sequestration or living in solitude M I.214; III.40; A I.38.

Āraññika (adj.) = āraññaka Vin III.15; A I.24; Pug 69; Vism 61, 71 (where defined); Miln 341.

Ārañjita [in form = Sk. *ārañjita, ā + pp. of rañjayati, Caus. of **rañj** or **raj**, but in meaning different. Perhaps to **rac** (as *racita) to furnish with, prepare, or better still to be regarded as an idiomatic Pāli form of sound-root ***rac** (see āracayā°) mixed with **rañj**, of which we find another example in the double spelling of āracayā (& ārajayā) q. v.] furrowed, cut open, dug up, slashed, torn (perhaps also "beaten") M I.178 (hatthipadaŋ dantehi ārañjitaŋ an elephant-track bearing the marks of tusks, i. e. occasional slashes or furrows).

Ārata [Sk. ārata, pp. of ā + **ram**, cp. ārati] leaving off, keeping away from, abstaining J IV.372 (= virata); Nd^{2} 591 (+ virata paṭivirata).

Ārati (f.) [Sk. ārati, ā + **ram**] leaving off, abstinence Vv 63^{9} (= paṭivirati VvA 263); in exegetical style occurring in typ. combn. with virati paṭivirati veramaṇī, e. g. at Nd^{2} 462; Dhs 299.

Āratta (nt.?) [Sk. cp. ārakta, pp. of ā + **raj**] time, period (orig. affected, tinted with), only in cpd. **vassāratta** the rainy season, lent J IV.444; Dāvs II.74.

Āraddha (adj.) [pp. of ā + **rabh**] begun, started, bent on, undertaking, holding on to, resolved, firm A I.148 (āraddhaŋ me viriyaŋ It 30; PvA 73 (ṭhapetun began to place), 212 (gantuŋ). Cp. **ārādhaka** I.

-**citta** concentrated of mind, decided, settled D I.176; M I.414; S II.21; Sn p. 102; SnA 436. Cp. ārādheti I. -**viriya** (adj.) strenuous, energetic, resolute Vin I.182; D III.252, 268, 282, 285; A I.24; Sn 68, 344; It 71 (opp. hīna-viriya); Nd^{2} 131; Ps I.171; ThA 95. Cp. **viriyārambha**; f. abstr. *°viriyatā* M I.19.

Ārabbha (indecl.) [ger. of ārabhati^{2} in abs. function; cp. Sk. ārabhya meaning since, from] — 1. beginning, undertaking etc., in cpd. °**vatthu** occasion for making an effort, concern, duty, obligation D III.256 = A IV.334 (eight such occasions enumd). — 2. (prep. with acc.) lit. beginning with, taking (into consideration), referring to, concerning, with reference to, about D I.180; A II.27 = It 103 (senāsanaŋ ā.); Sn 972 (upekhaŋ; v. l. ārambha; C. uppādetvā); Pv I.4[1] (pubbe pete ā.); DhA I.3; II.37; PvA 3 (seṭṭhiputta-petaŋ ā.), 16, and passim.

Ārabhati[1] [not with Morris *J P T S.* 1889, 202 fr. **rabh** and identical with arabhati[2], but with Kern, *Toev.* s. v. identical with Sk. ālabhate, ā + **labh** meaning to seize the sacrificial animal in order to kill it; cp. nirārambha] to kill, destroy M I.371 (pāṇaŋ).

Ārabhati[2] & **Ārabbhati** [ā + rabhati, Sk. ārabhati & arambhati, a + **rabb**] to begin, start, undertake, attempt S I.156 (ārabbhatha "bestir yourselves") = Miln 245 = Th 1, 256 (bh.); Pug 64 (bh.); viriyaŋ ārabhati to make an effort, to exert oneself (cp. ārambha) A IV.334. — aor. **ārabhi** DhA II.38 & **ārabbhi** PvA 35. — ger. ārabbha, see sep. — pp. **āraddha** (q. v.).

Ārambha [Sk. ārambha in meaning "beginning", fr ā + **rabh** (rambh) cp. ārabhati] — 1. attempt, effort, inception of energy (cp. *Dhs trsl.* 15 & *K. S.* p. 318 giving C. def. as kicca, karaṇīya, attha, i. e. 1. undertaking & duty, 2. object) S I.76 (mah°); V.66, 104 sq. (°dhātu); III.338 (id.), 166 (°ja; T. arabbhaja, v. l. ārambhaja to be preferred) = Pug 64; Miln 244; Net 41; DhsA 145. -**viriyārambha** (cp. āraddha-viriya) zeal, resolution, energy Vin II.197; S IV.175; A I.12, 16. — 2. support, ground, object, thing Nett 70 sq., 107; an° unsupported, independent Sn 743 (= nibbāna SnA 507). Cp. also nirambha, upārambha, sārambha.

Ārammaṇa (nt.) [cp. Sk. ālambana, **lamb,** but in meaning confounded with **rambh** (see rabhati)] primary meaning "foundation", from this applied in the foll. senses: (1) support, help, footing, expedient, anything to be depended upon as a means of achieving what is desired, i. e. basis of operation, chance Sn 1069 (= ālambana, nissaya, upanissaya Nd[2] 132); Pv I.4[1] (yaŋ kiñc' ārammaṇaŋ katvā); ārammaṇaŋ labhati (+ otāraŋ labhati) to get the chance S II.268; IV.185. — (2) condition, ground, cause, means, esp. a cause of desire or clinging to life, pl. °ā causes of rebirth (interpreted by taṇhā at Nd[1] 429), lust Sn 474 (= paccayā SnA 410), 945 (= Nd[1] 429); KhA 23; DhA I.288 (sappāy°); PvA 279. — (3) a basis for the working of the mind & intellect; i. e. sense-object, object of thought or consciousness, the outward constituent in the relation of subject & object, object in general. In this meaning of "relation" it is closely connected with **āyatana** (see āyatana[3]), so that it sometimes takes its place, it is also similar to **visaya.** *Cpd.* 3 distinguishes a 5 fold object, viz. citta, cetasika, pasāda- & sukhuma-rūpa, paññatti, nibbāna. See on term especially *Cpd.* 3, 14; *Dhs trsl.* XLI. & 209. — A I.82 sq.; IV.385; Sn 506; Ps I.57 sq., 84 (four ā.); II.97, 118, 143; Dhs 1 (dhamm° object of ideation), 180, 584, 1186 et passim; Vbh 12, 79, 92, 319, 332 (four); Nett 191 (six); Vism 87 sq., 375 (°sankantika), 430 sq. (in var. sets with ref. to var. objects), 533; DhsA 48, 127; VvA 11, 38. — rūpārammaṇa lit. dependence on form, i. e. object of sight, visible form, especially striking appearance, visibility, sight D III.228; S III.53; A I.82; J I.304; II.439, 442; PvA 265. — ārammaṇaŋ karoti to make it an object (of intellection or intention), to make it one's concern (cp. Pv I.4[1], above 1). — ārammaṇa-**kusala** clever in the objects (of meditation) S III.266; ā°-**paccayatā** relation of presentation (i. e. of subj. & obj.) Nett 80. — (4) (—°) (adj.) being supported by, depending on, centred in, concentrated upon PvA 8 (nissay°), 98 (ek°); VvA 119 (buddh° pīti rapture centred in the Buddha).

Āraha (adj.) metri causa for **araha** deserving J VI.164.

Ārā[1] (f.) [Sk. ārâ; *ēl "pointed", as in Ohg. āla = Ger. ahle, Ags. ǣl = E awl; Oicel. alr] an awl; see cp. āragga. Perhaps a der. of ārā is āḷakā (q. v.).

Ārā[2] (indecl.) [Vedic ārād, abl. as adv.; orig. a root der. fr. *ara remoteness, as in Sk. araṇa foreign & araṇya solitude q. v. under araṇa[1] and arañña] far from, remote (from) (adv. as well as prep. with abl.) Sn 156 (pamādamhā), 736; Dh 253 (āsavakkhayā; DhA III.377 expls. by dūragata); J II.449 (jhānabhūmiyā; = dūre ṭhita C.); V.78 (saŋyame; = dūrato C.). See also ārakā.
-**cāra** [in this combn. by Kern, *Toev.* s. v. unecessarily expld. as ārā = ārya; cp. similar phrases under ārakā] a life remote (from evil) A IV.389. -**cārin** living far from evil leading a virtuous life D I.4; M I.179; III.33; A III.216, 348; IV.249; V.138, 205; DA I.72 (= abrahmacariyato dūra-cārin).

Ārādhaka (adj.-n.) [fr. ā + **rādh**] 1. [perhaps for *āraddhaka because of analogy to āraddha of ā + **rabh**] successful, accomplishing or accomplished, undertaking, eager Vin I.70 (an° one who fails); M I.491; II.197 = A I.69 = Miln 243; S V.19; A V.329 (in correlation with āraddhaviriya). — 2. pleasing, propitiating Miln 227; VvA 220 (°ikā f.).

Ārādhana (nt.) & °ā (f.) (either fr. ā + **rādh** or ā + **rabh,** cp. ārādhaka] satisfying, accomplishing; satisfaction, accomplishment D II.287 (opp. virādhanā failure); M I.479; II.199; A V.211 sq.; J IV.427.

Ārādhanīya (adj.) [grd. fr. ārādheti] to be attained, to be won; successful Vin I.70 (an°); J II.233 (dur°).

Ārādhita [pp. of ārādheti; Sk. ārādhita, but BSk. ārāgita, e. g. Divy 131, 233] pleased Sdhp 510.

Ārādheti [Caus. of ā + **rādh,** in meaning 2 confused with ārabhati. In BSk. strangely distorted to ārāgayati; freq. in Divy as well as Av. Ś] — 1. to please, win favour, propitiate, convince J I.337 (dārake), 421, 452; II.72 (manusse); IV.274 (for abhirādheti T.); Vism 73 (ārādhayanto Nāthassa vana-vāsena mānasaŋ); DhA II.71; Dāvs III.93 (ārādhayi sabbajanaŋ); Miln 352. In older literature only in phrase **cittaŋ ārādheti** to please one's heart, to gladden, win over, propitiate D I.118 sq., 175 (but cp. āraddha-citta to ārabhati); M I.85, 341; S II.107; V.109; J II.372; Miln 25. — 2. to attain, accomplish, fulfill, succeed S V.23 (maggaŋ), 82, 180, 294; It III. (v. l. ārām°); Sn 488 = 509. Cp. ārādhaka 1. — pp. **ārādhita** (q. v.). — See also parābhetvā.

Ārāma [Sk. ārāma, ā + **ram**] — 1. pleasure, fondness of (—°), delight, always as adj. (—°) delighting in, enjoying, finding pleasure in (usually combd. with rata, e. g. dhammārāma dhammarata finding delight in the Dh.) S I.235; IV.389 sq. (bhav°, upādān°); A I.35, 37, 130; II.28 (bhāvan°); It 82 (dhamm°); Sn 327 (id.; expld. by SnA 333 as rati and "dhamme ārāmo assā ti"); Pug 53 (samagg°); Vbh 351. — 2. a pleasure-ground, park, garden (lit. sport, sporting); classified at Vin III.49 as pupph° and phal° a park with flowers or with fruit (i. e. orchard), def. at DhA III.246 as Veḷuvana-Jīvak' ambavan' ādayo, i. e. the park of Veḷuvana, or the park belonging to Jīvaka or mango-groves in general. Therefore: (a) (in general) · park, resort for pastime etc. Vin II.109; D I.106; Dh 188; Vv 79[5] (amb° garden of mangoes); VvA 305 (id.); Pv II.7[8] (pl. ārāmāni = ārām' ūpavanāni PvA 102). — (b) (in special) a private park, given to the Buddha or the Sangha for the benefit of the bhikkhus, where they meet & hold discussions about sacred & secular matters; a place of recreation and meditation, a meeting place for religious gatherings. Amongst the many ārāmas given to the bhikkhus the most renowned is that of Anāthapiṇḍika (Jetavana; see J I.92—94) D I.178; Vin IV.69; others more frequently mentioned are e. g.

the park of Ambapālī (Vin I.233); of Mallikā (D I.178), etc. — Vin I.39, 140, 283, 291; II.170; III.6, 45, 162; IV.85; A II.176; Dpvs V.18.

-pāla keeper of a park or orchard, gardener Vin II. 109; VvA 288. **-ropa, -ropana** planter, planting of pleasure-groves S I.33; PvA 151. **-vatthu** the site of an Ārāma Vin I.140; II. 170; III.50, 90.

Ārāmakinī (f.) see ārāmika.

Ārāmatā (f.) [abstr. fr. ārāma 1] pleasure, satisfaction A II.28; III.116; Vbh 381; Miln 233.

Ārāmika (adj.) [fr. ārāma] 1. (to ārāma 1) finding delight in, fond of (c. gen.) (or servant in general?) Miln 6 (sanghassa trsl. at the service of the order). — 2. (to ārāma 2) belonging to an Ārāma, one who shares the congregation, an attendant of the Ārāma Vin I.207 sq.; II.177 (& °pesaka), 211; III.24; IV.40; V.204; A II.78 (°samaṇuddesa); III.109 (id.), 275 (°pesaka); J I.38 (°kicca) Vism 74 (°samaṇuddesa). — f. ārāmakinī a female attendant or visitor of an Ārāma Vin I.208.

Ārāva [cp. Sk. ārāva, fr. ā + **ru**] cry, sound, noise Dāvs IV.46.

Āraha (nt.) only in pl. gihīnaŋ ārahānī, things proper to laymen, D III.163.

Āriya in anāriya at Sn 815 is metric for anariya (q. v.).

Āruṇṇa (nt.) [orig. pp of ā + **rud**] weeping, crying, lamenting Miln 357.

Āruppa (adj.) [fr. arūpa as ā (= a²) — *rūpya] formless, incorporeal; nt. formless existence D III.275; M I.410, cp. 472; III.163; S I.131 (°ṭṭhāyin); II.123; A IV.316; It 61; Sn 754; J I.406; Dhs 1385 (cp. trsl. 57); Vism 338; DA I.224; SnA 488, 508; Sdhp 5, 10; the four: Vism 111, 326 sq.

Āruhati [ā + **ruh**] to climb, ascend, go up or on to Sn 1014 (aor. āruhaŋ); Sdhp 188; ger. āruhitvā Sn 321 & āruyha J VI.452; Sn 139 (v. l. abhiruyha); It 71. — Caus. āropeti (q. v.).

Ārūgya see ārogya.

Ārūḷha [pp. of āruhati] — 1. ascended, mounted, gone up-gone on to IV.137; J VI.452 (T. āruḷha); Vism 135 (nek, khamma-paṭipadaŋ an°); VvA 64 (magga°); PvA 47 (°nāva), 56 (hatthi°). — 2. come about, effected, made, done PvA 2, 144 (cp. BSk. pratijñām ārūḍha having taken a vow Divy 26). — 3. (of an ornament) put on (to), arrayed J VI.153, 488.

Ārūha see āroha.

Ārogatā (f.) [abstr. fr. a + roga + tā] freedom from illness, health Miln 341.

Ārogya (nt.) [abstr. fr. aroga, i. e. ā (= a²) + roga + ya] absence of illness, health D I.11; III.220 (°mada), 235 (°sampadā); M I.451 (T. ārūgya, v. l. ārogya), 508, 509; S II.109; A I.146 (°mada); II.143; III.72; V.135 sq.; Sn 749, 257 = Dh 204 = J III.196; Nd¹ 160; Vism 77 (°mada pride of health); PvA 129, 198; Sdhp 234.

Ārocāpana (nt.) [fr. ārocāpeti, Caus. of āroceti] announcement DhA II.167.

Ārocāpeti (Caus. II. of āroceti) to make some one announce, to let somebody know, usually in phrase **kālaŋ ā.** Sn p. 111; J I.115, 125; DhA II.89; PvA 141.

Ārocita [pp. of āroceti] announced, called Vin II.213 (kāla).

Āroceti [ā + roceti, Caus. of **ruc**; cp. BSk. ārocayati Sp. Av. Ś I.9 etc.] to relate, to tell, announce, speak to, address D I.109, 224; Pv II.8⁹ (aor. ārocayi); PvA 4, 13 (aññamaññaŋ anārocetvā not speaking to each other), 81, 274 & freq. passim. — pp. ārocita; Caus. II. ārocāpeti (q. v.).

Ārodana (nt.) [fr. ā + **rud**, cp. āruṇṇa] crying, lamenting A III.268 sq.; J I.34; DhA I.184; II.100.

Āropana (nt.) [fr. āropeti] "putting on to", impaling Miln 197 (sūl°), 290 (id.).

Āropita [pp. of āropeti] — 1. produced, come forward, set up PvA 2. — 2. effected, made S III.12; PvA 92, 257. — 3. put on (to a stake), impaled PvA 220 (= āvuta).

Āropeti [Caus. of āruhati]. — 1. to make ascend, to lead up to (w. acc.) PvA 76 (pāsādaŋ), 160 (id.) — 2 to put on, take up to (w. acc. or loc.) Pv II.9² (yakkhaŋ yānaŋ āropayitvāna); PvA 62 (sarīraŋ citakaŋ ā.), 100 (bhaṇḍaŋ sakaṭesu ā.). — 3. to put on, commit to the care of, entrust, give over to (w. loc.) J I.227; PvA 154 (rajjaŋ amaccesu ā.). — 4. to bring about, get ready, make PvA 73, 257 (sangahaŋ ā. make a collection); SnA 51, 142. — 5. to exhibit, tell, show, give S I.160 (ovadaŋ); Miln 176 (dosaŋ); DhA II.75 (id.) — 6. vādaŋ āropeti to refute a person, to get the better of (gen.) Vin I.60; M II.122; S I.160. — pp. āropita (q. v.).

Āroha (—°) [fr. ā + **ruh**] — 1. climbing up, growth, increase, extent, in cpd. °**pariṇāha** length & circumference S II.206; A I.288; II.250; IV.397; V.19; J III.192; V. 299; VI.20; Vbh 345 (°māna + pariṇāha-māna); SnA 382. — 2. one who has climbed up, mounted on, a rider, usually in cpd. ass° & **hatth°** horse-rider & elephant-rider S IV.310; A II.166 = III.162 (T. ārūha); IV.107; DhsA 305. — 3. outfit, possession (or increase, as 1?) Sn 420 (vaṇṇ°).

Ārohaṇa (nt.) [fr. ā + **ruh**] climbing, ascending; ascent J I.70; VI.488; Miln 352; Vism 244; PvA 74.

Ālaka-manda [ālaya°?] at Vin II.152 is of uncertain reading and meaning ("open to view"? or "not having pegs" = āḷaka?) vv. ll. āḷakamanta & ālakamandāra; Bdhgh on p. 321 expl^ns. āḷakamandā ti ekangaṇā manussâbhikiṇṇā, i. e. full of a crowd of people, Ch. quotes ālakamandā as "the city of Kuvera" (cp. Sk. alakā).

Ālaggeti [ā + Caus. of **lag**] to (make) hang on to (loc.), to stick on, fasten to Vin II.110 (pattaŋ veḷagge ālaggetvā).

Ālapati [ā + lapati] to address S I.177, 212; J V.201; SnA 42, 347, 383, 394 (= āmantayi of Sn 997), 487 (— avhayati); PvA 11, 13, 33, 69.

Ālapana (nt.) & °ā (f.) [fr. ā + **lap**] talking to, addressing, conversation Vin III.73 (with ref. to exclam. "ambho"); J V.253 (°ā); Vism 23 (°ā); SnA 396; PvA 131 (re ti ā.).

Ālapanatā (f.) [abstr. fr. ālapana] speaking to, conversing with, conversation M I.331) (an°).

Ālamba [Sk. ālamba, ā + **lamb**] anything to hang on, support S I.53 (an° without support); Sn 173 (id. + appatiṭṭha); J III.396; Miln 343; Sdhp 245, 463.

Ālambati [ā + **lamb**] to hang on to or up, to take hold of, to fasten to Vin I.28, J I.57; VI.192; Vv 84⁴⁸; ThA 34. — **ālambeti** id. VvA 32.

Ālambana (adj.-nt.) [fr. ā + **lamb**, cp. ālamba] (adj.) hanging down from, hanging up J III.396; IV.457; SnA 214. — (nt.) support, balustrade (or screen?) Vin II.117, 152 (°bāha) Miln 126.

Ālambara & **Āḷambara** (nt.) [Sk. āḍambara] a drum Vin I.15 (l); J II.344 (l); V.390 (l); Vv 54¹⁸ (l).

Ālaya (m. & nt.) [cp. Sk. ālaya, ā + **lī**, līyate, cp. allīna & allīyati, also nirālaya] — 1. orig. roosting place, perch, i. e. abode settling place, house J 1.10 (geh°); Miln 213; DhA II.162 (an° = anoka), 170 (= oka). — 2. "hanging on", attachment, desire, clinging, lust S 1.136 = Vin 1.4 (°rāma "devoted to the things to which it clings" K. S.); Vin III.20, 111; S IV.372 (an°); V.421 sq. (id.); A II. 34, 131 (°rāma); III.35; It 88; Sn 177 (kām° = kāmesu taṇhā-diṭṭhi-vasena duvidho ālayo SnA 216), 535 (+ āsavāni), 635; Nett 121, 123 (°samugghāta); Vism 293 (id.), 497; Miln 203 (Buddh °ŋ akāsi?); DhA 1.121; IV.186 (= taṇhā); SnA 468 (= anoka of Sn 366). — 3. pretence, pretext, feint [cp. BSk. ālaya M Vastu III.314] J 1.157 (gilān°), 438; III.533 (mat°); IV.37 (gabbhinī); VI 20, 262 (gilān°).

Ālayati see allīyati.

Ālassa (nt.) [Der. fr. alasa] sloth, idleness, laziness S 1.43; D III.182; A IV.59; V.136; Sdhp 567. Spelling also ālasya S 1.43 (v. l. BB); Vbh 352; Miln 289, and ālasiya J 1.427; DA 1.310; DhA 1.299; VvA 43.

Ālāna & **Āḷāna** (nt.) [for ānāhana with substitution of l for n (cp. apilandhana for apinandh° and contraction of °āhana to °āna originally meaning "tying to" then the thing to which anything is tied] a peg, stake, post, esp. one to which an elephant is tied J 1.415; IV.308; DhA 1.126 (!) where all MSS. have āḷāhana, perhaps correctly.

Āli[1] (m. or f.? [Sk. āḷi] a certain kind of fish J V.405.

Āli[2] & **Āḷi** (f.) [Sk. ālī] a dike, embankment Vin II.256; M III.96; A II.166 (°pabbheda); III.28; J 1.336; III.533, 334.

Ālika in saccālika at S IV.306 is sacc'alika distortion of truth, falsehood S IV.306.

Ālikhati [ā + likhati] to draw, delineate, copy in writing or drawing J 1.71; Miln 51.

Āliṅga [ā + ling] a small drum J V.156 (suvaṇṇ°-tala).

Āliṅgati [ā + **ling**] to embrace, enfold D 1.230; III.73; J 1.281; IV.21, 316, 438; V.8; Miln 7; DhA 1.101 : VvA 260.

Ālitta [pp. of ālimpati; Sk. ālipta] besmeared, stained Th 1, 737.

Ālinda (& **Āḷinda**) [Sk. alinda] a terrace or verandah before the house-door Vin 1.248; II.153; D 1.89; M II.119; S. IV.290 (!); A V.65 (!); J VI.429; DA 1.252; DhA 1. 26; IV.196; SnA 55 (°ka-vāsin; v. l. alindaka); Mhvs 35, 3. As ālindaka at J III.283.

Ālippati Pass. of ālimpeti (q. v.).

Ālimpana (nt.) [for āḷimp° = Sk. ādīpana, see ālimpeti[2]] conflagration, burning, flame Miln 43.

Ālimpita [pp. of ālimpeti[2]] ignited, lit. A IV.102 (v. l. ālepita).

Ālimpeti[1] [Sk. ālimpayati or ālepayati, ā + **lip** or **limp**] to smear, anoint Vin II.107; S IV.177 (vaṇaŋ). — Caus. II. ālimpāpeti Vin IV.316. — Pass. ālimpīyati Miln 74 & ālippati DhA IV.166 (v. l. for lippati). — pp. ālitta (q. v.).

Ālimpeti[2] [for Sk. ādipayati, with change of d to l over ḷ and substitution of limp for lip after analogy of roots in °mp, like lup > lump, lip > limp] to kindle, ignite, set fire to Vin II.138 (dayo ālimpetabbo); III.58; D II.163 (citakaŋ); A 1.257; DhA 1.177 (āvāsaŋ read āvāpaŋ), 225; PvA 62 (kaṭṭhāni). — pp. ālimpita (q. v.).

Ālu (nt.) [Sk. ālu & °ka; cognate with Lat. ālum & alium, see Walde Lat. Wtb. under alium] a bulbous plant, Radix Globosa Esculenta or Amorphophallus (Kern), Arum Campanulatum (Hardy) J IV.371 = VI.578; IV.373.

Āluka[1] = ālu J IV.46 (C. for ālupa).

Āluka[2] (adj.) [etym.?] susceptible of, longing for, affected with (—°) Vin 1.288 (sīt°); DA 1.198 (id.); J II.278 (taṇh° greedy).

Ālupa (nt.) [etym.? Kern, *Toev.* s. v. suggests ālu-a > ālu-va > ālupa] = āluka the edible root of Amorphophallus Campanulatus J IV.46 (= āluka-kaṇḍa C.).

Ālumpakāra [reading not sure, to ālumpati or ālopa] breaking off, falling off (?) or forming into bits (?) DhA II.55 (°gūtha).

Ālumpati [ā + **lup** or **lump**, cp. ālopa] to pull out, break off M 1.324.

Āluḷa (adj. [fr. ā + **lul**] being in motion, confusion or agitation, disturbed, agitated J VI.431.

Āluḷati [ā + **lul**; Sk. ālolati, cp. also P. āloḷeti] to move here & there, ppr. med. āluḷamāna agitated, whirling about DhA IV.47 (T. ālūl°; v. l. āḷul°) confuse DhsA 375. Caus. āluḷeti to set in motion, agitate, confound J II.9, 33. — pp. āluḷita (q. v.).

Āluḷita [pp. of āluḷeti] agitated, confused J II.101; Miln 397 (+ khalita).

Ālepa [cp. Sk. ālepa, of ā + **lip**] ointment, salve, liniment Vin 1.274; Miln 74; DhsA 249.

Ālepana (nt.) [fr. ā + **lip**] anointing, application of salve D 1.7 (mukkh°).

Āloka [ā + **lok**, Sk. āloka] seeing, sight (obj. & subj.), i. e. — 1. sight, view, look S IV.128 = Sn 763; A III. 236 (āloke nikkhitta laid before one's eye). **anāloka** without sight, blind Miln 296 (andha +). — 2. light A 1. 164 (tamo vigato ā. uppanno) = It 100 (vihato); A II. 139 (four lights, i.e. canda°, suriya°, agg°, paññ°, of the moon, sun, fire & wisdom); J II 34; Dhs 617 (opp. andhakāra); VvA 51 (dīp°). — 3. (clear) sight, power of observation, intuition, in comb^n. with vijjā knowledge D II.33 = S II.7 = 105, cp. Ps II.150 sq. (obhāsaṭṭhena, S A. on II.7). — 4. splendour VvA 53; DvA 71.

-**kara** making light, bringing light, n. light-bringer It 108. -**karaṇa** making light, illumining It 108. -**da** giving light or insight Th 1, 3. -**dassana** seeing light, i.e. perceiving Th 1, 422. -**pharaṇa** diffusing light or diffusion of light Vbh 334; Nett 89. -**bahula** good in sight, fig. full of foresight A III.432. -**bhūta** light J VI 459. -**saññā** consciousness or faculty of sight or perception D III.223; A II.45; III.93 -**saññin** conscious of sight, i. e. susceptible to sight or insight D III.49; M III.3; A II 211; III.92, 323; IV.437; V.207; Pug 69. -**sandhi** "break for the light", a slit to look through, an opening, a crack or casement Vin 1.48 = II.209 = 218; II.172; III.65; IV.47; J IV.310; PvA 24.

Ālokana (nt.) [fr. ā + **lok**] looking at, regarding DA 1.194.

Ālokita (nt.) [pp. of āloketi] looking before, looking at, looking forward (opp. vilokitaŋ looking behind or backward), always in comb^n. **ālokita-vilokita** in ster. phrase at D 1.70 = e. g. A II.104, 106, 210; Pug 44, 45, 50; Vism 19; VvA 6; DA 1.193 (ālokitaŋ purato pekkhanaŋ vil° anudisā p.).

Āloketar [n. ag. to āloketi] one who looks forward or before, a beholder DA 1.194 (opp. viloketar).

Āloketi [Sk. ālokayati, ā + **lok**] to look before, look at, regard, see DA 1.193, 194. — pp. ālokita (q. v.).

Ālopa [ā + **lup,** cp. ālumpati; BSk. ālopa, e.g. Av. Ś I.173, 341; Divy 290, 481] a piece (cut off), a bit (of food) morsel, esp. bits of food gathered by bhikkhus D I.5 = A V.206; III.176; A II 209; III.304; IV.318; Th 1, 1055; It 18; Pv II.1[7]; Pug 58; Miln 231, 406; Vism 106; DA I.80 (= vilopa-karaṇaŋ).

Ālopati [ālopeti? ā + lopeti, Caus. of ālumpati] to break in, plunder, violate Th 1, 743.

Ālopika (adj.) [ālopa + ika] getting or having, or consisting of pieces (of food) A I.295; II.206; Pug 55.

Āloḷa [fr. ā + **luḷ,** cp. āluḷati & āloḷeti] confusion, uproar, agitation DhA I.38.

Āloḷī (f.) [a + **luḷ**] that which is stirred up, mud, in cpd. sītāloḷī mud or loam from the furrow adhering to the plough Vin I.206.

Āloḷeti [Caus. of āluḷati, cp. āluḷeti] to confuse, mix, shake together, jumble S I.175; J II.272, 363; IV.333; VI.331; Vism 105.

Āḷaka (or °ā f.) [Dimin of aḷa (?) or of ārā 1 (?). See Morris *JPTS.* 1886, 158] — 1. a thorn, sting, dart, spike, used either as arrow-straightener Miln 418; DhA I.288; or (perhaps also for piece of bone, fishbone) in making up a comb VvA 349 (°sandhāpana = comb; how Hardy got the meaning of "alum" in Ind. to VvA is incomprehensible). — 2 a peg, spike, stake or post (to tie an elephant to, cp. ālāna). Cp. II,1[3].

Āḷamba = āḷambara Vv 18[9] = 50[24]. See **āḷambara.**

Āḷavaka (& °ika) (adj.-n.) [= āṭavika] dwelling in forests, a forest-dweller S II.235. As Np. at Vism 208.

Āḷādvāraka (adj.) at J V.81, 82 is corrupt & should with v. l. perhaps better be read **advāraka** without doors. Cp. Kern, *Toev.* 29 (ālāraka?). J V.81 has āḷāraka only.

Āḷāra (adj.) [= aḷāra or uḷāra or = Sk. arāla?] thick, massed, dense or crooked, arched (?), only in cpd. °**pamha** with thick eyelashes Vv 64[11] (= gopakhuma VvA 279); Pv III.3[6] (= vellita-dīgha-nīla-pamukha). Cp. alāra.

Āḷārika & °**iya** (adj.-n.) [Sk. ārālika, of uncertain etym.] a cook D I.51 (= bhattakāraka DA I.157); J V.296 (= bhattakāraka C.); 307; VI.276 (°iya, C. °ika = sūpika); Miln 331.

Āḷāhana (nt.) [fr. ā + **ḍah** or **dah,** see dahati] a place of cremation, cemetery D I.55; J I.287 (here meaning the funereal fire) 402; III.505; Pv II.12[2]; Vism 76; Miln 350; DA I.166; DhA I.26; III.276; PvA 92, 161, 163 (= sarīrassa daḍḍha-ṭṭhāna). — *Note.* For āḷāhana in meaning "peg, stake" see ālāna.

Āḷika at A III.352, 384 (an°) is preferably to be read āḷhika, see **āḷhaka.**

Āḷha (nt.) = **āḷhaka**; only at A III.52 (udak°), where perhaps better with v. l. to be read as **āḷhaka.** The id. p. at A II.55 has ālhaka only.

Āḷhaka (m. & nt.) [Sk. āḍhaka, fr. *āḍha probably meaning "grain"] a certain measure of capacity, originally for grain; in older texts usually applied to a liquid measure (udaka°). Its size is given by Bdhgh. at SnA 476 as follows: "cattāro patthā āḷhakāni doṇaŋ etc." — udakāḷhaka S V.400; A II.55 = III.337; VvA 155. — In other connections at J I.419 (aḍḍh°); III.541 (mitaŋ āḷhakena = dhañña-māpaka-kammaŋ kataŋ C.); Miln 229 (patt°); DhA III.367 (aḍḍh°).

-**thālikā** a bowl of the capacity of an āḷhaka Vin I.240; A III.369; DhA III.370 (v. l. bhatta-thālikā).

Āḷhiya (& **āḷhika**) (adj.) [fr. *āḷha, Sk. āḍhya, orig. possessing grain, rich in grain, i. e. wealth; semantically cp. dhañña[2]] rich, happy, fortunate; only in neg. **anāḷhiya** poor, unlucky, miserable M I.450; II.178 (+ daḷidda); A III.352 sq. (so read with v. l. BB. °āḷhika for T. °āḷika; combd. with daḷidda; v. l. SS. anaddhika); J V.96, 97 (+ daḷidda; C. na āḷhika).

Āvajati [ā + vajati, **vraj**] — 1. to go into, to or towards J III.434; IV.49, 107. — 2. to return, come back J V.24, 479.

Āvajjati [not with Senart M Vastu 377 = ava + **dhyā,** but = Sk. āvṛṇakti ā + **vṛj,** with pres. act. āvajjeti = Sk. āvarjayati] — 1. to reflect upon, notice, take in, advert to, catch (a sound), listen J I.81; II.423; V.3; Miln 106. — 2. to remove, upset (a vessel), pour out Vin I.286 (kumbhiŋ); J II.102 (gloss āsiñcati). — Caus **āvajjeti** (q. v.).

Āvajjana (nt.) [fr. āvajjati, cp. BSk. āvarjana in diff. meaning] turning to, paying attention, apprehending, adverting the mind. — See discussion of term at *Cpd.* 85, 227 (the C. derive āvajjana fr. āvaṭṭeti to turn towards, this confusion being due to close resemblance of jj and ṭṭ in writing); also *Kvu trsl.* 221 n. 4 (on Kvu 380 which has āvaṭṭanā), 282 n. 2 (on Kvu 491 āvaṭṭanā). — Ps II.5, 120; J II.243; Vbh 320; Miln 102 sq.; Vism 432; DA I.271.

Āvajjita [pp. of āvajjeti cp. BSk. āvarjita, e.g. Divy 171; Itm 221] bent, turned to, inclined; noticed, observed Miln 297; Vism 432 (citta); Sdhp 433.

Āvajjitatta (nt.) [abstr. fr. āvajjita] inclination of mind, observation, paying attention Ps II.27 sq.

Āvajjeti [Caus. of āvajjati] 1. to turn over, incline, bend M III.96; J IV.56 (so read for āvijjhanto); DA I.10 (kāyaŋ). — 2. to incline (the mind); observe, reflect, muse, think, heed, listen for. According to *Cpd.* 227 often paraphrased in C. by pariṇāmeti. — J I.69, 74, 81, 89, 108, 200; Miln 297; DhA II.96; PvA 181 (= manasikaroti). — 3. to cause to yield A III.27 (perhaps better āvaṭṭ°). — pp. **āvajjita** (q. v.).

Āvaṭa [Sk. āvṛta, pp. of ā + **vṛ**] covered, veiled, shut off against, prohibited D I.97, 246; M I.381 (°dvāra); J VI.267. -**anāvaṭa** uncovered, unveiled, exposed, open D I.137 (°dvāra); III.191 (°dvāratā); S I.55; J V.213; Pv III.6[4]; Miln 283. Cp. **āvuta**[2] & vy°.

Āvaṭṭa (adj.-n.) [Sk. āvarta, ā + **vṛt**] — 1. turning round, winding, twisting M I.382; S I.32 (dvi-r-ā° turning twice) J II.217; SnA 439 (°gangā). — 2. turned, brought round, changed, enticed M I.381; DhA II.153. — 3. an eddy, whirlpool, vortex M I.460 = A II.123 (°bhaya); Miln 122, 196, 377. — 4. circumference J V.337; Dāvs V.24; DhA III 184.

Āvaṭṭati [= āvattati] in phrase ā. vivaṭṭati to turn forward & backward Vism 504.

Āvaṭṭana (nt.) [fr. ā + **vṛt,** cp. āvaṭṭa 2 and āvaṭṭanin] turning, twisting; enticement, snare, temptation J III.494; DhA II.153.

Āvaṭṭanā (f.) [most likely for āvajjana. q. v. & see also *Kvu trsl.* 221, 282] turning to (of the mind), adverting, apprehending Kvu 380, 491.

Āvaṭṭanin (adj.) [fr. āvaṭṭana] turning (away or towards), changing, tempting, enticing M I.375, 381; A II.190; J II.330 = IV.471; DA I.250. — Cp. etymologically the same, but semantically diff. āvattanin.

Āvaṭṭin (adj.-n.) [fr. āvaṭṭa instead of āvaṭṭana] only at M I.91 in neg. an° not enticed by (loc.), i. e. kāmesu. — Cp. āvattin.

Āvaṭṭeti [ā + vaṭṭeti, Caus. of **vṛt,** cp. BSk. āvartayati to employ spells Divy 438] to turn round, entice, change, convert, bring or win over M I.375, 381, 383, 505; A III.27; DA I.272.

Āvatta[1] (adj.) [pp. of āvattati] gone away to, fallen back to, in phrase hīnāy'āvatta (see same phrase under āvattati) M I.460; S II.50; J I.206.

Āvatta[2] (nt.) [Sk. āvarta, of ā + **vṛt,** cp. āvaṭṭa[winding, turn, bent J I.70 (in a river); Nett 81 (v.l. āvaṭṭa?), 105 (°hārasampāta).

Āvattaka (adj.) [āvatta + ka] turning, in **dakkhiṇ°** turning to the right, dextrorsal D II.18; cp. dakkhiṇâvatta at DA I.259.

Āvattati [ā + vattati, of **vṛt**] to turn round, come to, go back, go away to, turn to; only in phrase **hīnāya āvattati** to turn to "the low", i. e. to give up orders & return to the world Vin I.17; M I.460; S II.231; IV.191; Sn p. 92 (= osakkati SnA 423); Ud 21; Pug 66; Miln 246. — pp. āvatta (q. v.). Cp. āvaṭṭati.

Āvattana (adj.-nt.) [Sk. āvartana] turning; turn, return Nett 113; Miln 251.

Āvattanin (adj.) [fr. āvattana] turning round or back Th I, 16 (cp. **āvaṭṭanin**).

Āvattin (adj.-n.) [fr. āvatta, cp. āvaṭṭin in diff. meaning] returning, coming back, one who returns, in spec. meaning of one who comes back in transmigration, syn. with āgāmin (an°), only in neg. **anāvattin** not returning, a non-returner, with **°dhamma** not liable to return at D I. 156; III.132; S V.346, 357, 376, 406; M I.91; DA I.313.

Āvatthika (adj.) [ā + vatthika] befitting, original, inherent (one of the 4 kinds of nomenclature) Vism 210 = KhA 107.

Āvapati [a + **vap**] to give away to offer, to deposit as a pledge Miln 279.

Āvapana (nt.) [fr. āvapati] sowing, dispersing, offering depositing, scattering J I.321.

Āvara (adj.) [fr. ā + **vṛ**] obstructing, keeping off from J V.325 (so to be read in ariya-magg-âvara).

Āvaraṇa (adj.-n.) [fr. ā + **vṛ,** cp. āvarati; BSk. āvaraṇa in pañc' āvaraṇāni Divy 378] shutting off, barring out, withstanding; nt. hindrance, obstruction, bar Vin I.84 (°ŋ karoti to prohibit, hinder); II.262 (id.); D I.246 (syn. of pañca nivaraṇāni); S V.93 sq.; A III.63; J I.78 (an°); V.412 (nadiŋ °ena bandhāpeti to obstruct or dam off the river); Sn 66 (pahāya pañc' āvaraṇāni cetaso, cp. Nd[2] 379), 1005 (an°-dassāviṇ); Ps I.131 sq.; II.158 (an°); Pug 13; Dhs 1059, 1136; Vbh 341, 342; Miln 21 (dur° hard to withstand or oppose). — dant° "screen of the teeth", lip J IV.188; VI.590.

Āvaraṇatā (f) [abstr. fr. āvaraṇa] keeping away from, withholding from A III 436.

Āvaraṇīya (adj.) [grd. fr. āvarati], only neg. **an°** not to be obstructed, impossible to obstruct M III.3; Miln 157.

Āvarati [ā + **vṛ,** cp. āvuṇāti] to shut out from (abl.), hold back from, refuse, withhold, obstruct M I.380 (dvāraŋ); Sn 922 (pot. °aye, cp. Nd[1] 368); DA I.235 (dvāraŋ); Dpvs I.38. — pp. **āvaṭa** and **āvuta**[2] (q. v.).

Āvalī (f.) [cp. Sk. āvalī & see valī] a row, range J V.69; DA I.140.

Āvasati [ā + **vas**] to live at or in, to inhabit, reside, stay M II.72; S I.42; Sn 43, 805, 1134; Nd[1] 123, 127; Nd[2] 133; J VI.317. — pp. **āvuttha** (q. v.).

Āvasatha [Sk āvasatha, fr. ā + **vas**] dwelling-place, habitation; abode, house, dwelling Vin I 226 (°āgāra resting-house); IV.304 (= kavāṭabaddha); S I.94, 229; IV.329; Sn 287, 672; J IV.396; VI.425; Pug 51; Miln 279.

Āvaha (adj.) (—°) [fr. ā + **vah**] bringing, going, causing Pv II.9[24] (sukh°); Vv 22[11] (id); Dāvs II.37; PvA 86 (upakār°), 116 (anatth°); Sdhp 15, 98, 206.

Āvahati [ā + vahati] to bring, cause, entail, give S I.42 = Sn 181, 182 (āvahāti sukhaŋ metri causā); J III.169; V. 80; Sn 823; Nd[1] 302; PvA 6. — Pass. āvuyhati VvA 237 (ppr. °amāna).

Āvahana (adj) (—°) [= āvaha] bringing, causing Th I, 519; Sn 256.

Āvahanaka (adj.-nt) [= āvahana] one who brings VvA 114 (sukhassa).

Āva (misery, misfortune) see **avā.**

Āvāṭa [etym.?] a hole dug in the ground, a pit, a well D I.142 (yaññ°); J I.99, 264; II 406; III.286; IV 46 (caturassa); VI.10; DhA I.223; VvA 63; PvA 225.

Āvāpa [if correct, fr. ā + **vā**[2] to blow with caus. p. — Cp. *JRAS.* 1898, 750 sp.] a potter's furnace DhA I.177 (read for āvāsa?), 178.

Āvāra [Sk. āvāra, fr. ā + **vṛ**] warding off, protection, guard J VI 432 (yanta-yutta°, does it mean "cover, shield"?). — For cpd. khandh'āvāra see **khandha.**

Āvāreti [Sk. āvārayati, ā + Caus. of **vṛ**] to ward off, hold back, bar, S IV 298; Nett 99.

Āvāsa [Sk. āvāsa; ā + **vas**] sojourn, stay, dwelling, living; dwelling-place, residence Vin I.92; D III.234; S IV.91; A II 68, 168; III.46, 262; Sn 406; Dh 73 (cp. DhA II.77); Nd[1] 128; J VI.105; Dhs 1122; Pug, 15, 19, 57; KhA 40; DhA I.177 (āvāsaŋ ālimpeti: read āvāpaŋ); PvA 13, 14, 36; VvA 113; Sdhp 247. **-anāvāsa** (n. & adj.) uninhabited, without a home; an uninhabited place A IV.345; J II.77; Pv II.3[33]; PvA 80 (= anāgāra); VvA 46. **-kappa** the practice of (holding Uposatha in different) residence (within the same boundary) Vin II.294, 300, 306; Dpvs IV.47, cp. V.18. **-palibodha** the obstruction of having a home (in set of 10 Palibodhas) KhA 39; cp. Vism 90 sq. **-sappāyatā** suitability of residence Vism 127.

Āvāsika (adj.) [āvāsa + ika] living in, residing at home, being in (constant or fixed) residence, usually appl[d.] to bhikkhus (opp. āgantuka) Vin I.128 sq.; II.15, 170; III. 65; V.203 sq.; M I.473; A I.236; III.261 sq., 366; J IV.310; Pv IV.8[4] (= nibaddha-vasanaka PvA 267).

Āvāha [ā + **vah**] taking in marriage, lit. carrying away to oneself, marriage D I.99; J VI.363; SnA 273, 448; DhA IV.7. Often in cpd. **ā° vivāha(ka)** lit. leading to (one's home) & leading away (from the bride's home), wedding feast D III.183 (°ka); J I.452; VvA 109, 157 (v. l. °ka).

Āvāhana (nt.) [ā + vahana, of **vah**] — 1. = āvāha, i. e. marriage, taking a wife D I.11 (= āvāha-karaṇa DA I. 96). — 2. "getting up, bringing together", i. e. a mass, a group or formation, in senā° a contingent of an army J IV.91.

Āvi (adv.) [Sk. āviḥ, to Gr. ἀίω to hear, Lat. audio (fr. *auizdiō) to hear] clear, manifest, evident; openly, before one's eyes, in full view. Only in phrase **āvi vā raho** openly or secret A V.350, 353; Pv II.7[10] = DhA IV.21

(āvī v. l.), expl$^{d.}$ at PvA 103 by pakāsanaŋ paresaŋ pākaṭavasana. Otherwise in foll. cpds. (with **kar** & **bhū**): °**kamma** making clear, evidence, explanation Vin II.88; III.24; Pug 19, 23; °karoti to make clear, show, explain D III.121; Sn 84, 85, 349; J V.457; Pug 57; VvA 79, 150; °bhavati (°bhoti) to become visible or evident, to be explained, to get clear J I.136; Vism 287 (fnt. āvibhavissati); DhA II.51, 82; **bhāva** appearance, manifestation D I.78; A III.17; J II.50, 111; Vism 390 sq. (revelation, opp. tirobhāva). Cp. pātur.

Āvijjhati (āviñjati, āviñchati) [ā + vijjhati of **vyadh** to pierce; thus recognised by Morris *J P T S.* 1884, 72, against Trenckner, *Notes* 59 (to **piñj**) & Hardy Nett. *Ind.* = vicchāy] — 1. to encircle, encompass, comprise, go round, usually in ger. āvijjhitvā (w. acc.) used as prep. round about, near J I.153 (khettaŋ), 170 (pokkharaṇiŋ); DA I.245 (nagaraŋ bahi āvijjhitvā round the outer circle of the town). Ordinarily = go round (acc.) at J IV.59 (chārika-puñjaŋ). — 2. [as in lit. Sk.] to swing round, brandish, twirl, whirl round Vin III.127 (daṇḍaŋ āviñji); M III.141 (matthena āviñjati to churn); J I.313; V.291 (cakkaŋ, of a potter's wheel); SnA 481 (T. āviñj°, v. l. āvijjh°; see āracaya°); DhA II.277 (āviñchamāna T.; v. l. āsiñciy°, āvajiy°, āgañch°). — 3. to resort to, go to, approach, incline to S IV.199 (T. āviñch°; v. l. avicch° & āviñj°); Nett 13. — 4. to arrange, set in order J II.406. — 5. to pull (?) A IV.86 (kaṇṇasotani āvijjeyyāsi, v.l. āvijj°, āviñj°, āvicc°, āviñch°; cp. Trenckner, *Notes* 59 āviñjati "to pull"). — pp. **āviddha** (q. v.).

Āvijjhana (so for āviñchana & āviñjana) (adj.-n.) [fr. āvijjhati, lit. piercing through, i. e. revolving axis] — 1. (= āvijjhati 2) swinging round, hanging loose, spinning in **āvijjhana-rajju** a loose, rope, esp. in mythology the swinging or whirling rope by which Sakka holds the world's wheel or axis, in the latter sense at DhA II.143 (T. āviñch° (v. l. āvijj°) = III.97, 98 (where āviñjanaṭṭhāna for °rajju). Otherwise a rope used in connection with the opening & shutting of a door (pulling rope?) Vin II.120, 148; J V.298, 299 (T. āviñj°, v. l. āvicch° & āvij°). — 2. (cp. āvijjhati 3) going to, approach, contact with DhsA 312 (°rasa, T. āviñj°, v. l. āviñch°; or is it "encompassing"? = āvijjhati 1?): Vism 444 (āviñjanarasa). — 3. (cp. āvijjhati 5) pulling, drawing along Vin III.121 (= ākaḍḍhanā nāma).

Āvijjhanaka (nt.) [fr. āvijjhati in meaning 2] whirling round, that which spins round, the whirling-round wheel (or pole) of the world (cp. the potter's wheel), the world-axis DhA II.146 (T. āviñch°).

Āviddha [pp. of āvijjhati 2, cp. BSk. āviddha in meaning curved, crooked Av. S I.87 Lal. V. 207] whirling or spinning round, revolving; swung round, set into whirling motion J IV.6 (cakkaŋ = kumbhakāra-cakkam iva bhamati C.); V.291. What does an-āviddha at PvA 135 mean?

Āvila (adj.) [is it a haplological contraction from ā + vi + **lul** to roll about?] stirred up, agitated, disturbed, stained, soiled, dirty A I.9; III.233; J V.16, 90 (ābila); Nd^1 488 (+ luḷita). 489; ThA 251; DA I.226. More frequent as **anāvila** undisturbed, clean, pure, serene D I.76; S III. 83; IV.118; A I.9; III.236; Sn 160; Dh 82, 413; J III. 157; Miln 34; VvA 29, 30; ThA 251.

Āvilati [fr. āvila or is it a direct contraction of ā + vi + lulati?] to whirl round, to be agitated, to be in motion Miln 259 (+ luḷati).

Āvilatta (nt.) [abstr. fr. āvila] confusion, disturbance, agitation Sn 967; Nd^1 488.

Āvisati [ā + **viś**] to approach, to enter Vin IV.334; Sn 936 (aor. āvisi); J IV.410, 496; Vism 42.

Āvuṇāti [in form = *avṛnoti, ā + **vṛ**, cp. āvarati, but in meaning = *āvayati, ā + **vā** to weave, thus a confusion of the two roots, the latter being merged into the former] to string upon, to fix on to (c. loc.), to impale J I.430; III.35; V.145; VI.105. — Caus. II. āvuṇāpeti J III.218 (sūle). — pp. āvuta^1 (q. v.), whereas the other pp. āvaṭa is the true derivative of ā + **vṛ**.

Āvuta [pp. of āvuṇāti in meaning of Sk. āvayati, the corresponding Sk. form being ā + uta = ota] — 1. strung upon, tied on, fixed on to D I.76 (suttaŋ); II.13 (id.); A I.286 (tantāvutaŋ web); J III.52 (valliyā); VI.346 (suttakena); DA I.94 (°sutta). — 2. impaled, stuck on (sūle on the pale) J I.430; III.35; V.497; VI.105; PvA 217, 220.

Āvuta^2 = **Āvaṭa** (see āvuṇāti & āvuta^1) covered, obstructed, hindered It 8 (mohena); also in phrase **āvuta nivuta ophuta** etc. Nd^1 24 (t) = Nd^2 365 = DA I.59.

Āvuttha [pp. of āvasati] inhabited D II.50 (an°); S I.33.

Āvudha (nt.) [Vedic āyudha, fr. ā + **yudh** to fight] an instrument to fight with, a weapon, stick etc. D III 219; M II.100; A IV.107, 110; Sn 1008; J I.150; II.110; III. 467; IV.160, 283, 437; Nd^2 on Sn 72; Miln 8, 339; DhA II.2; IV.207; SnA 225, 466 (°jīvika = issattha). See also **āyudha**.

Āvuyhamāna ppr. of āvuyhati (Pass. of āvahati), being conveyed or brought VvA 237 (reading uncertain).

Āvuso (voc. pl. m.) [a contracted form of āyusmanto pl. of āyusman, of which the regular Pāli form is āyasmant, with v for y as frequently in Pāli, e. g. āvudha for āyudha] friend, a form of polite address "friend, brother, Sir", usually in conversation between bhikkhus. The grammatical construction is with the pl. of the verb, like bhavaŋ and bhavanto. — Vin II.302; D I.151, 157; II.8; SnA 227; DhA I.9; II.93; PvA 12, 13, 38, 208.

Āveṭhana (nt.) [ā + veṭhana, **veṣṭ**] rolling up, winding up or round, fig. explanation Miln 28 (+ nibbeṭhana, lit. rolling up and rolling down, ravelling & unravelling), 231 (°viniveṭhana).

Āveṭhita [pp. of āveṭheti, ā + **veṣṭ**, cp. āvedhikā] turned round, slung round or over J IV.383 sq. (v. l. āvedhita & āveḷita, C. expl$^{s.}$ by parivattita).

Āveṇi (adj.) (—°) [according to Trenckner, *Notes* 75 fr. ā + vinā "Sine quā non", but very doubtful] special, peculiar, separate Vin II.204 (°uposatha etc.); J I.490 (°sangha-kammāni).

Āveṇika (adj.) [fr. āveṇi; cp. BSk. āveṇika Av. Ś I.14, 108; Divy 2, 182, 268, 302] special, extraordinary, exceptional S IV.239; A V.74 sq.; Vism 268; VvA 112 (°bhāva peculiarity, specialty), KhA 23, 35.

Āveṇiya (adj.) = **āveṇika** Vin I.71; J IV.358; VI.128.

Āvedha [cp. Sk. āviddha, ā + pp. of **vyadh**] piercing, hole, wound J II.276 (v. l. aveddha; C. = viddha-ṭṭhāne vaṇa).

Āvedhika (adj. f. scil. paññā) [ā + vedhaka of āvedha, **vyadh**, but confused with āveṭh° of ā + **veṣṭ**, cp. āveṭhana & nibbedhaka] piercing, penetrating; or ravelling, turning, rolling up or round (cp. āvijjhati which is derived from ā + **vyadh**, but takes its meaning from āveṭheti), discrimination, thinking over J II.9 (+ nibbedhikā, v. l. for both ṭh).

Āveḷa (adj. & °ā f.) [not with Müller *P. Gr.* 10, 30, 37 = Sk. āpīḍa, but fr. ā + **veṣṭh** to wind or turn round, which in P. is represented by āveṭheti as well as āvijjhati; ḷ then standing for either ḍh (ṭh) or dh (āvedha, q. v.). There may have been an analogy influence through **vell** to move to and fro, cp. āveḷita. Müller refers to āveḷā rightly the late dial. (Prk.) āmela] — 1. turning round, swinging round; diffusion, radiation; protuberance, with reference to the rays of the Buddha at J I.12, 95, 501. — 2. (f.) a garland or other ornament slung round & worn over the head Vv 36[2] (kañcan°; = āveḷa-pilandhana VvA 167). See āveḷin.

Āvellita (l?) [pp. of ā + **vell**, cp. āveḷa & BSk. āviddha curved, crooked Av. Ś I.87, Lal. V. 207] turned round, wound, curved J VI.354 (°singika with curved horns, v. l. āvellita).

Āveḷin (adj.) [fr. āveḷā] wearing garlands or other head-ornaments, usually in f. °inī J V.409 (= kaṇṇālankārehi yuttā C.); Vv 30[2] (voc. āvelini, but at id. p. 48[2] āveline), 32[3]; VvA 125 (on Vv 30[2] expl[s]. as ratana-maya-pupph°-āveḷavatī).

Āvesana (nt.) [fr. āvisati] entrance; workshop; living-place, house Vin II 117 (°vitthaka, meaning?); M II 53; Pv II.9[15].

Āsa[1] contr.-form of aŋsa in cpd. **koṭṭhāsa** part., portion etc.: see aŋsa[1]. Can we compare BSk. āsapātrī (see next).

Āsa[2] [Sk. āśa] food, only in cpd. **pātarāsa** morning food, breakfast Sn 387 (pāto asitabbo ti pātar-āso piṇḍapātass' etaŋ nāmaŋ SnA 374); DhA IV.211; see further ref. under pātar; and **pacchā-āsa** aftermath S I.74. Can we compare BSk. āsa-pātrī (vessel) Divy 246? Der. fr. āsa is **āsaka** with abstr. ending āsakattaŋ "eating", food, in nānā° various food or na + anāsak°) Sn 249. See also **nirāsa**, which may be taken either as nir + *āśa or nir + *āśā.

Āsa[3] the adj. form of āsā (f.), wish, hope. See under **āsā**.

Āsa[4] archaic 3rd sg. perf. of atthi to be, only in cpd. **itihāsa** = iti ha āsa "thus it has been".

Āsaŋsa (adj.) [of *āśaŋsā, see next] hoping, expecting something, longing for A I.108 = Pug 27 (expl[d]. by Pug A 208 as "so hi arahattaŋ āsaŋsati pattheti ti āsaŋso"); SnA 321, 336. Cp. nir°.

Āsaŋsati [for the usual āsiŋsati, ā + **śaŋs**] to expect, hope for, wish Pug A 208 (= pattheti). See also **āsamāna**.

Āsaŋsā (f.) [from ā + śaŋs] wish, desire, expectation, hope J IV.92. — Cp. **nirāsaŋsa**.

Āsaŋsuka (adj.) [fr. āsaŋsā] full of expectation, longing, hankering after, Th 2, 273 (= āsiŋsanaka ThA 217; trsl. "cadging").

Āsaka (adj.) [of āsa[2]] belonging to food, having food, only in neg. an° fasting S IV.118; Dh 141 (f. ā fasting = bhatta-paṭikkhepa DhA III.77); J V.17; VI.63.

Āsakatta (nt.) [abstr. fr. āsaka] having food, feeding, in an° fasting Sn 249 (= abhojana SnA 292).

Āsankati [ā + **śank**] to be doubtful or afraid, to suspect, distrust, J I.151 (pret. āsankittha), 163 (aor. āsanki); II. 203; SnA 298. — pp. **āsankita** (q v.),

Āsankā (f) [Sk. āśankā fr. ā + **śank**] fear, apprehension, doubt, suspicion J I.338; II.383; III.533; VI.350, 370; DhA III.485; VvA 110. — Cp. **sāsanka** & **nirāsanka**.

Āsankita (adj.) [pp. of āsankati] suspected, in fear, afraid, apprehensive, doubtful (obj. & subj.) Miln 173, 372 (°parisankita full of apprehension and suspicion); DhA I.223; VvA 110. — Cp. **ussankita** & **parisankita**.

Āsankin (—°) (adj) [fr. āsankā] fearing, anxious, apprehensive Sn 255 (bhedā°); J III.192 (id.).

Āsanga [ā + sanga fr. **sañj** to hang on, cp. Sk. āsanga & āsakti] — 1. adhering, clinging to, attachment, pursuit J IV.11. — 2. that which hangs on (the body), clothing, garment, dress; adj. dressed or clothed in (—°); usually in cpd. **uttarāsanga** a loose (hanging) outer robe e. g. Vin I.289; S IV.290; PvA 73; VvA 33 (suddh°), 51 (id.).

Āsangin (adj.) [fr. āsanga] hanging on, attached to J IV 11.

Āsajja (indecl.) [ger. of āsādeti, Caus. of āsīdati, ā + **sad**; Sk. āsādya] — 1. sitting on, going to, approaching; allocated, belonging to; sometimes merely as prep. acc. "near" (cp. āsanna) Sn 418 (āsajja naŋ upāvisi he came up near to him), 448 (kāko va selaŋ ā. nibbijjāpema Gotamaŋ); J II.95; VI.194; Miln 271. — 2. put on to (lit. sitting or sticking on), hitting, striking S I.127 (khaṇuŋ va urasā ā. nibbijjapetha Gotamā "ye've thrust as 't were your breast against a stake. Disgusted, come ye hence from Gotama" *trsl.* p. 159; C. expl[s]. by paharitvā, which comes near the usual paraphrase ghaṭṭetvā) — 3. knocking against or "giving one a setting-to", insulting, offending, assailing D I.107 (ā. ā. avocāsi = ghaṭṭetvā DA I.276); A III.373 (tādisaŋ bhikkhuŋ ā.); J V.267 (isiŋ ā. Gotamaŋ; C. p. 272 āsādetvā); Pv IV.7[10] (isiŋ ā. = āsādetvā PvA 266). — 4. "sitting on", i. e. attending constantly to, persevering, energetically, with energy or emphasis, willingly, spontaneonsly M I.250; D III.258 = A IV.236 (dānaŋ deti); Vv 10[6] (dānaŋ adāsiŋ; cp. VvA 55 samāgantvā). See āsada, āsādeti, āsīdeti, āsajjana.

Āsajjana (nt.) [fr. āsajja in meaning of no. 3] "knocking against", setting on, insult, offence Vin II.203 (°ŋ Tathāgataŋ an insult to the T.; quoted as such at VvA 55, where two meanings of ā. are given, corresponding to āsajja 1 & 3, viz. samāgama & ghaṭṭana, the latter in this quot.) = It 86 (so to be read with v. l.; T. has āpajja naŋ); S I.114 (apuññaŋ pasavi Māro āsajjanaŋ Tathāgataŋ; trsl. "in seeking the T. to assail"); J V.208.

Āsati [from **as**] to sit DA I.208; h. sg. āsi S I.130. — pp. āsīna (q. v.).

Āsatta[1] [pp. of ā + **sañj**] (a) lit. hanging on, in phrase kaṇṭhe āsatto kuṇapo a corpse hanging round one's neck M I.120; J I.5. — (b) fig. attached to, clinging to J I. 377 (+ satta lagga); ThA 259 (an°).

Āsatta[2] [pp. of ā + **śap**] accursed, cursed J V.446 (an°).

Āsatti (f.) [ā + **sañj**] attachment, hanging on (w. loc.), dependence, clinging Vin II.156 = A I.138; S I.212; Sn 777 (bhavesu); Nd[1] 51, 221; Nett 12, 128. — Cp. **nirāsattin**.

Āsada [ā + **sad**; cp. āsajja & āsādeti] — 1. approach, dealing with, business with (acc.), concern, affair, means of acting or getting Vin II.195 = J V.336 (mā kuñjara nāgam āsado); M I.326 (metaŋ āsado = mā etaŋ āsado do not meddle with this, lit., be not this any affair); J I 414 (cakkaŋ āsado you have to do with the wheel; interpreted as adj. in meaning patto = finding, getting); VI.528 (interpreted as ankusa a hook, i. e. means of getting something). — 2. (as adj.) in phrase **durāsada** hard to sit on, i. e. hard to get at, unapproachable, difficult to attack or manage or conquer Sn p. 107 (cp. SnA 451); J VI.272; Vv 50[16] (= anupagamanīyato kenaci pi anāsādanīyato ca durāsado VvA 213); Miln 21; Dpvs V.21; VI.38; Sdhp 384.

Āsana (nt.) [from āsati] sitting, sitting down; a seat, throne M I.469; Vin I.272 (= pallankassa okāsa); S I.46 (ek° sitting alone, a solitary seat); A III.389 (an° without a seat); Sn 338, 718, 810, 981; Nd[1] 131; J IV.435 (āsan' ûdaka-dāyin giving seat & drink); V.403 (id.); VI.413;

DhA II.31 (dhamm° the preacher's seat or throne); SnA 401; PvA 16, 23, 141.
-âbhihara gift or distinction of the seat J I.81. -ûpagata endowed with a seat, sitting down Sn 708 (= nisinna SnA 495). -paññāpaka one who appoints seats Vin II.305. -paṭikkhitta one who rejects all seats, or objects to sitting down D I.167; A I.296; II.206; Pug 55. -sālā a hall with seating accommodation Vism 69; DhA II. 65; IV.46.

Āsanaka (nt.) [āsana + ka] a small seat Vv 1⁵.

Āsanika (adj.) [fr. āsana] having a seat; in ek° sitting by oneself Vism 69.

Āsandi (f.) [fr. ā + **sad**] an extra long chair, a deck-chair Vin I.192; II.142, 163, 169, 170; D I.7 (= pamāṇâtikkant' āsanaŋ DA I.86), 55 = M I.515 = S III.307 (used as a bier) A I.181; J I.108. See note at *Dial.* I.11.

Āsandikā (f.) fr. āsandi] a small chair or tabouret Vin II. 149; KhA 44.

Āsanna (adj.) [pp. of ā + **sad**, see āsīdati] near (cp. āsajja¹), opp. dūra J II.154; DhA II 91; PvA 42, 243.

Āsappanā (fr.) [fr. + **sṛp**] lit. "creeping on to", doubt, mistrust, always combd. with **parisappanā** Nd³ 1; Dhs 1004 (trsl. "evasion", cp. *Dhs trsl.* p 116), 1118, 1235; DA I.69.

Āsabha [the guṇa- and compn. form of usabha, corresponding to Sk. ārṣabha > ṛṣabha, see usabha] (in compn.) a bull, peculiar to a bull, bull-like, fig. a man of strong & eminent qualities, a hero or great man, a leader, thus in tār° Sn 687; nar° Sn 684, 696; āsabha-camma bull's hide J VI. 453 (v. l. usabha°).
-ṭṭhāna (as āsabhaṇṭhāna) "bull's place", first place, distinguished position, leadership M I.69; S II.27; A II.8 (C. seṭṭha-ṭṭhāna uttama-ṭṭhāna); III.9; V.33 sq.; DA I. 31; KhA 104.

Āsabhin (adj) [fr. āsabha] bull-like, becoming to a bull, lordly, majestic, imposing, bold; only in phrase °ŋ vācaŋ bhāsati "speak the lordly word" D II.15, 82; M III.123 J I.53; DA I.91; cp. Dāvs I.28 (nicchārayi vācaŋ āsabhiŋ).

Āsamāna (adj.) [ppr. of āsaŋsati or āsiŋsati, for the usual earlier āsasāna] wishing, desiring, hoping, expecting Vv 84⁶ (kiŋ a = kiŋ paccāsiŋ santo VvA 336); Pv IV.1²⁴ (= āsiŋsamāna patthayamana PvA 226).

Āsaya [ā + **śī**, cp. in similar meaning & derivation anusaya. The semantically related Sk. āśraya from ā + **śri** is in P. represented by assaya. Cp. also BSk. āśayataḥ intentionally, in earnest Divy 281; Av. Ś II 161] — 1. abode, haunt, receptacle; dependence on, refuge, support, condition S I.38; Vin III.151; J II.99; Miln 257; VvA 60; PvA 210; jal° river VvA 47; Pgdp 80; adj. depending on, living in (—°) Miln 317; Nd¹ 362 (bil°, dak° etc.). See also āmāsaya, pakkāsaya. — 2. (fig.) inclination, intention, will, hope; often combd. & compared with **anusaya** (inclination, hankering, disposition), e. g. at Ps I. 133; II.158; Vbh 340; Vism 140 (°posana); PvA 197.— SnA 182 (°vipatti), 314 (°suddhi), KhA 103 (°sampatti). Cp. nirāsaya. — 3. outflow, excretion Pv III.5³ (gabbh° = gabbha-mala PvA 198); Vism 344.

Āsayati [ā + **śī**; lit. "lie on", cp. Ger. anliegen & Sk. āśaya = Ger. Angelegenheit] to wish, desire, hope, intend J IV.291 (grd. āsāyana, gloss esamāna). See āsaya.

Āsava [fr. ā + **sru**, would corresp. to a Sk. *āsrava, cp. Sk. āsrāva. The BSk. āśrava is a (wrong) sankritisation of the Pāli āsava, cp. Divy 391 & kṣīṇāśrava] that which flows (out or on to) outflow & influx. 1. spirit, the intoxicating extract or secretion of a tree or flower, O. C. in Vin IV.110 (four kinds); B. on D III.182 (five kinds) DhsA 48; KhA 26; J IV.222; VI.9. — 2. discharge from a sore, A I.124, 127 = Pug 30. — 3. in psychology, t.t. for certain specified ideas which intoxicate the mind (bemuddle it, befoozle it, so that it cannot rise to higher things). Freedom from the "Āsavas" constitutes Arahantship, & the fight for the extinction of these āsavas forms one of the main duties of man. On the difficulty of translating the term see *Cpd.* 227. See also discussion of term āsava (= āsavantī ti āsavā) at DhsA 48 (cp. *Expositor* pp. 63 sq.). See also *Cpd.* 227 sq., & especially *Dhs trsl.* 291 sq. — The 4 āsavas are **kām°**, **bhav°**, **diṭṭh°**, **avijj°**, i. e. sensuality, rebirth (lust of life), speculation and ignorance. — They are mentioned as such at D II.81, 84, 91, 94, 98, 123, 126; A I.165 sq., 196; II.211; III.93, 414; IV.79; Ps I.94, 117; Dhs 1099, 1448; Nd² 134; Nett 31, 114 sq. — The set of 3, which is probably older (kāma°, bhava°, avijjā°) occurs at M I 55; A I.165; III.414; S IV.256; V.56, 189; It 49; Vbh 364. For other connections see Vin I.14 (anupādāya āsavehi cittāni vimucciŋsu), 17, 20, 182; II.202; III.5 (°samudaya, °nirodha etc.); D I.83, 167; III.78, 108, 130, 220, 223, 230, 240, 283; M I.7 sq., 23, 35, 76, 219, 279, 445 (°ṭhāniya); II.22; III.72, 277; S II.187 sq. (°ehi cittaŋ vimucci); III.45 (id.); IV.107 (id.), 20; V.8, 28, 410; A I.85 sq. (vaḍḍhanti), 98, 165 (°samudaya, °nirodha etc.), 187; II.154 (°ehi cittaŋ vimuttaŋ), 196; III.21, 93 (°samudaya, °nirodha etc.), 245, 387 sq., 410, 414; IV.13, 146 (°pariyādāna end of the ā.), 161 (°vighāta-pariḷāha); V.70, 237; Th 2, 4, 99, 101 (pahāsi āsave sabbe); Sn 162, 374, 535 (pl. āsavāni), 546, 749, 915, 1100; Dh 93, 253, 292; Nd¹ 331 (pubb°); Vbh 42, 64, 426; Pug 11, 13, 27, 30 sq.; Miln 419; DhsA 48; ThA 94, 173; KhA 26; DA I 224; Sdhp 1; Pgdp 65 (piyāsava-surā, meaning?).
Referring specially to the *extinction* (**khaya**) of the āsavas & to Arahantship following as a result are the foll. passages: (1) **āsavānaŋ khaya** D I.156; S II 29, 214; III 57, 96 sq, 152 sq.; IV.105, 175; V.92, 203, 220, 271, 284; A I.107 sq., 123 sq., 232 sq., 273, 291; II.6, 36, 44 sq., 149 sq., 214; III 69, 114, 131, 202, 306, 319 sq.; IV 83 sq., 119, 140 sq., 314 sq.; V.10 sq., 36, 69, 94 sq, 105, 132, 174 sq, 343 sq.; It 49; Pug 27, 62; Vbh 334, 344; Vism 9; DA I.224; cp. °parikkhaya A V 343 sq. See also arahatta formula C. — (2) **khīṇāsava** (adj.) one whose Āsavas are destroyed (see khīṇa) S I.13, 48, 53, 146; II 83, 239; III.199, 128, 178; IV.217; A I 77, 109, 241, 266; IV.120, 224, 370 sq.; V.40, 253 sq; Ps II 173; cp. parikkhīṇā āsavā A IV.418, 434, 451 sq.; āsavakhīṇa Sn 370. — (3) **anāsava** (adj.) one who is free from the āsavas, an Arahant Vin II 148 = 164; D III.112; S I 130; II 214, 222; III.83; IV.128; A I.81, 107 sq, 123 sq., 273, 291; II.6, 36, 87, 146; III.19, 29, 114, 166; IV.98, 140 sq., 314 sq., 400; A V.10 sq, 36, 242, 340; Sn 1105, 1133; Dh 94, 126, 386; Th I.100; It 75; Nd² 44; Pv II.6¹⁵; Pug 27; Vbh 426; Dhs 1101, 1451; VvA 9. Cp. **nirāsava** ThA 148. — Opp. **sāsava** S III 47; V.232; A I.81; V 242; Dhs 990; Nett 10; Vism 13, 438.

Āsavati [ā + **sru**, cp. Sk. āsravati; its doublet is assavati] to flow towards, come to, occur, happen Nett 116.

Āsasāna [either grd. for *āsaŋsāna or contracted form of ppr. med. of āsaŋsati (= āsiŋsati) for *asaŋsamāna] hoping, wishing, desiring, longing for Sn 369 (an°; SnA 365 however reads āsayāna), 1090; Th 2, 528; J IV.18 (= āsiŋsanto C.), 381; V.391 (= āsiŋsanto C.). See anāsasāna, āsaŋsati, āsamāna & āsayāna.

Āsā (f.) [cp. Sk. āśaḥ f.] expectation, hope, wish, longing, desire; adj. **āsa** (—°) longing for, anticipating, desirous of Vin I 255 (°avacchedika hope-destroying), 259; D II. 206; III.88; M III.138 (āsaŋ karoti); A I 86 (dve āsā), 107 (vigat-āso one whose longings have gone); Sn 474,

634, 794, 864; J I.267, 285; V.401; VI.452 (°chinna = chinnāsa C.); Nd¹ 99, 261, 213 sq; Vv 37¹³ (perhaps better to be read with v. l. SS ahaŋ, cp. VvA 172); Pug 27 (vigat° = arahattāsāya vigatattā vigatāso Pug A 208); Dhs 1059 (+ āsiŋsanā etc.), 1136; PvA 22 (chinn° disappointed), 29 (°ābhibhūta), 105; Dāvs V 13; Sdhp 78, 111, 498, 609.

Āsāṭikā (f.) [cp. Marāṭhi āsāḍi] a fly's egg, a nit M I.220 sq.; A V.347 sq., 351, 359; Nett 59; J III.176.

Āsādeti [Caus. of āsīdati, ā + **sad**; cp. āsajja & āsanna] — 1. to lay hand on, to touch, strike; fig. the offend, assail, insult M I.371; J I.481; V.197; aor. **āsādesi** Th 1, 280 (mā ā. Tathāgate); ger. **āsādetvā** J V.272; Miln 100, 205 (°ayitvā); PvA 266 (isiŋ), **āsādiya** J V.154 (āsādiya metri causa; isiŋ, cp. āsajja³), & **āsajja** (q. v.); infin. **āsāduŋ** J V.154 & **āsādituŋ** ibid.; grd. **āsādanīya** Miln 205; VvA 213 (an°). — 2. to come near to (c. acc.), approach, get J III.206 (khuracakkaŋ).

Āsāḷhā & **Āsāḷhī** (f.) [Sk. āṣāḍha] N. of a month (June–July) and of a Nakkhatta; only in compⁿ. as Āsaḷha° & Āsaḷhi°, viz. °nakkhatta J I.50; SnA 208; °puṇṇamā J I.63; DhA I.87; SnA 199; VvA 66; PvA 137; °māsa SnA 378 (= vassūpanāyikāya purimabhāge A.); VvA 307 (= gimhānaŋ pacchimo māso).

Āsāvatī (f.) N. of a creeper (growing at the celestial grove Cittalatā) J III.250, 251.

Āsāsati [cp. Sk. āśāsati & āśāsti, ā + **śās**] to pray for, expect, hope; confounded with **śaŋs** in āsaŋsati & āsiŋsati (q. v.) & their derivations. — pp. **āsiṭṭha** (q. v.).

Āsi & **Āsiŋ** 3ʳᵈ & 1ˢᵗ sg. aor. of **atthi** (q. v.).

Āsiŋsaka (adj.) [fr. ā + siŋsati, cp. āsaŋsā] wishing, aspiring after, praying for Miln 342.

Āsiŋsati [Sk. āśaŋsati, ā + **śaŋs**, cp. also **śās** & āsāsati, further abhisaŋsati, abhisiŋsati & āsaŋsati] to hope for, wish, pray for (lit. praise for the sake of gain), desire, (w. acc.) S I.34, 62; Sn 779, 1044, 1046 (see Nd² 135); J I.267; III.251; IV.18; V.435; VI.43; Nd¹ 60; Mhvs 30, 100; VvA 337; PvA 226 (ppr. āsiŋsamāna for āsamāna, q. v.).

Āsiŋsanaka (adj.) [fr. āsiŋsanā] hoping for something, lit. praising somebody for the sake of gain, cadging ThA 217 (for āsaŋsuka Th 2, 273).

Āsiŋsanā (f.) [abstr. fr. ā + **śaŋs**, cp. āsiŋsati] desire, wish, craving J V.28; Dhs 1059, 1136 (+ āsiŋsitatta). As āsīsanā at Nett 53.

Āsiŋsaniya (adj.) [grd. of āsiŋsati] to be wished for, desirable Miln 2 (°ratana).

Āsikkhita [pp. of ā + **śiks**, Sk. āśikṣita] schooled, instructed PvA 67, 68.

Āsiñcati [ā + **sic**, cp. abhisiñcati & avasiñcati] to sprinkle, besprinkle Vin I.44; II.208; J IV.376; Vv 79⁶ (= siñcati VvA 307); PvA 41 (udakena), 104, 213 (ger. °itvā). — pp. **āsitta** (q. v.). Cp. vy°.

Āsiṭṭha [pp. of āsāsati, Sk. āśiṣṭa] wished or longed for PvA 104.

***Āsita**¹ [= asita¹?] "having eaten", but probably **māsita** (pp. of **mṛś** to touch, cp. Sk. mṛśita, which is ordinarily in massita), since it only occurs in combⁿˢ. where m precedes, viz. J II.446 (dumapakkani-m-asita, where C. reading is māsita & explⁿ. khāditvā asita (v. l. āsita) dhāta); Miln 302 (visam-āsita affected with poison = visamāsita). Cp. also the form **māsi(n)** touching, eating at J VI.354 (tiṇa°, expld. by C. as khādaka). — āsita at J V.70 is very doubtful, v. l. āsina & asita; C. expls. by dhāta suhita p. 73.

***Āsita**² [registered as such with meaning "performed" by Hardy in Index] at VvA 276 is better read with v. l. SS **bhāsita** (-vādana etc.).

Āsitta [pp. of āsiñcati, Sk. āsikta] sprinkled, poured out, anointed J V.87; Pug 31; Miln 286; DhsA 307; DhA I.10; VvA 69.

Āsittaka (adj.) [āsitta + ka] mixed, mingled, adulterated Vin II.123 (°ūpadhāna "decorated divan"?); ThA 61, 168 (an° for asecanaka, q. v.).

Āsītika (adj.) [fr. asīta] 80 years old M II.124; J III.395; SnA 172.

Āsītikā (f.) [etym.? Cp. BSk. āsītakī Lal. V. 319] a certain plant M I.80 = 245 (°paṅba).

Āsīdati [cp. Sk. āsīdati, ā + **sad**] — 1. to come together, lit. to sit by D I.248 (v. l. BB ādisitvā for āsīditvā, to be preferred?). — 2. to come or go near, to approach (w. acc.), to get (to) A III.69 (āsīvisaŋ), 373 (na sādhurūpaŋ āsīde, should perhaps be read without the na); J IV.56. — 3. to knock against, insult, offend attack J V. 267 (Pot. āsīde = pharusa-vacanehe kāyakammena vā ghaṭṭento upagaccheyya C.). — pp. **āsanna** (q. v.). See also āsajja, āsajjana, āsada & Caus. āsādeti.

Āsīna (adj.) [pp. of **ās**, see āsati] sitting S I.195 = Nd² 136; Sn 1105, 1136; Dh 227, 386; J I.390; III.95; V. 340; VI.297; Dāvs II.17.

Āsīyati [etym. doubtful; Trenckner Miln p. 422 = ā + **śyā** to freeze or dry up, but taken by him in meaning to thaw, to warm oneself; Müller, *P. Gr.* 40 same with meaning "cool oneself"; Morris' *J P T S.* 1884, 72 as ā + **śrā** or **śrī** to become ripe, come to perfection, evidently at fault because of **śrā** etc. not found in Sk. More likely as a Pass. formation to be referred to ā + **śī** as in āsaya, i. e. to abide etc.] to have one's home, one's abode or support in (loc.), to live in, thrive by means of, to depend on Miln 75 (kaddame jāyati udake āsīyati i. e. the lotus is born in the mud and is supported or thrives by means of the water).

Āsīvisa Derivation uncertain. The BSk. āśīviṣa (e. g. Jtm 31⁶¹) is a Sanskritisation of the Pali. To suppose this to come from ahi + visa (snake's poison) would give a wrong meaning, and leave unexplained the change from ahi to āsi] a snake Vin IV.108; S IV.172; A II.110; III. 69; J I.245; II.274; IV.30, 496; V.82, 267; Pug 48; Vism 470 (in comp.); DhA I.139; II.8, 38; SnA 334, 458, 465; VvA 308.

Āsīsanā see **āsiŋsanā**.

Āsu expletive particle = **assu**³ J V.241 (v. l. assu; nipātamattaŋ Cp. 243).

Āsuŋ 3ʳᵈ pl. aor. of **atthi**.

Āsumbhati (& **Āsumhati**) [ā + **śumbh** to glide] to bring to fall, throw down or round, sling round Vin IV.263, 265; Vv 50¹¹ (°itvāna); J III.435 (aor. āsumhi, gloss khipi).

Āsevati [ā + **sev**] to frequent, visit; to practise, pursue, indulge, enjoy A I.10; Sn 73 (cp. Nd² 94); Ps II.93 (maggaŋ). — pp. **āsevita**.

Āsevana (nt.) & āsevanā (f.) [fr. āsevati] — 1. practice, pursuit, indulgence in Vin II.117; PvA 45. — 2. succession, repetition Dhs 1367; Kvu 510 (cp. *trsl.* 294, 362); Vism 538.

Āsevita [pp. of āsevati] frequented, indulged, practised, enjoyed J I.21 (v.141; āsevita-nisevita); II.60; Sdhp 93, 237.

Āha [Vedic āha, orig. perfect of **ah** to speak, meaning "he began to speak", thus in meaning of pres. "he says"] a perfect in meaning of pret. & pres. "he says or he said", he spoke, also spoke to somebody (w. acc.), as at J I.197 (cullalohitaŋ āha). Usually in 3rd person, very rarely used of 2nd person, as at Sn 839, 840 (= kathesi bhaṇasi Nd 188, 191). — 3rd sg. **āha** Vin II.191; Sn 790 (= bhaṇati Nd¹ 87), 888; J I.280; III.53 and freq. passim; 3rd pl. **āhu** Sn 87, 181; Dh 345; J I.59; SnA 377, and **āhaŋsu** J I.222; III.278 and freq.

Āhacca¹ ger. of **āhanati**.

Āhacca² (adj.) [grd. of āharati, corresponding to a Sk. *āhṛtya] 1. (cp. āharati¹) to be removed, removable, in °**pādaka-pīṭha** & °**mañca** a collapsible bed or chair, i e. whose legs or feet can be put on & taken away at pleasure (by drawing out a pin) Vin II.149 (cp. *Vin Texts* III.164 n. 5); IV.40, 46 (def. as "ange vijjhitvā ṭhito hoti" it stands by means of a perforated limb), 168, 169. — 2. (cp. āharati²) reciting, repeating, or to be quoted, recitation (of the Scriptures); by authority or by tradition M III.139; DhsA 9, & in cpds. °**pada** a text quoted from Scripture), tradition Miln 148 (°ena by reference to the text of the Scriptures); °**vacana** a saying of the Scriptures, a traditional or proverbial saying Nett 21 (in def. of suttaŋ).

Āhaṭa [pp. of āharati] brought, carried, obtained Vin I.121; III.53; D II.180 (spelt āhata); J III.512 (gloss ānīta); Dāvs I.58.

Āhata [pp. of āhanati] struck, beaten, stamped; afflicted, affected with (—°) Vin IV.236 = D III.238 (kupito anattamano āhata-citto); Vin I.75, 76; S I.170 (tilak°, so read for tilakā-hata, affected with freckles, C. kāḷa-setādi vaṇṇehi tilakehi āhatagatta, *K. S* p. 318); J III 456; Sdhp 187, 401.

Āhataka [fr. āhata] "one who is beaten", a slave, a worker (of low grade) Vin IV.224 (in def. of kammakāra, as bhaṭaka + ā).

Āhanati [ā + **han**] to beat, strike, press against, touch ppr. **āhananto** Miln 21 (dhamma-bheriŋ); Dāvs IV.50. — ger. **āhacca** touching M I 493; J I.330; VI 2, 200; Sn 716 = uppīḷetva SnA 498; Vism 420. — pp. **āhata** (q. v.).

Āhanana (nt.) [fr. ā + **han**] beating, striking, coming into touch, "impinging" Vism 142 (+ pariyāhanana, in def. of vitakka) = DhsA 114 (cp. *Expos.* 151); Vism 515 (id.).

Āharaṇa (adj.-n.) [fr. āharati] to be taken; taking away; only in phrase acorāharaṇo nidhi a treasure not to be taken by thieves Miln 320; Kh VIII.9; KhA 224; Sdhp 589.

Āharaṇaka [āharaṇa + ka] one who has to take or bring, a messenger J II.199; III.328.

Āharati [ā + **hṛ**] — 1. to take, take up, take hold of, take out, take away M I.429 (sallaŋ); S I 121; III.123; J I.40 (ger. āharitvā "with"), 293 (te hattaŋ); Nd² 540ᶜ (puttamaŋsaŋ, read āhāreyya?); Pv II.3¹⁰; DA I.186, 188. — 2. to bring, bring down, fetch D II.245; J IV 159 (nāvaŋ; v. l. āhāhitvā); V.466; VvA 63 (bhattaŋ); PvA 75. — 3. to get, acquire, bring upon oneself J V.433 (padosaŋ); DhA II.89. — 4. to bring on to, put into (w. loc.); fig. & intrs. to hold on to, put oneself to, touch, resort to M I.395 (kaṭhalaŋ mukhe ā.; also inf. āhattuŋ); Th 1, 1156 (pāpacitte ā.; Mrs. Rh. D. *Brethren* ver. 1156, not as "accost" p. 419, *n.*). — 5. to assault, strike, offend (for pāhari?) Th 1, 1173. — 6. (fig) to take up, fall or go back on (w. acc.), recite, quote, repeat (usually with desanaŋ & dasseti of an instructive story or sermon or homily) J III 383 (desanaŋ), 401; V.462 (vatthuŋ āharitvā dassesi told a story for example); SnA 376; PvA 38, 39 (atītaŋ), 42, 66, 99 (dhamma-desanaŋ). See also **payirudāharati**. — pp. **āhaṭa** (q. v.). — Caus. II **āhārapeti** to cause to be brought or fetched; to wish to take, to call or ask for J III.88, 342; V.466; PvA 215.

Āharima (adj.) [fr. āharati] "fetching", fascinating. captivating, charming Vin IV.299; Th 2, 299; ThA 227; VvA 14, 15, 77.

Āhariya [grd. of āharati] one who is to bring something J III.328.

Āhavana & **Āhavanīya** see under āhuneyya.

Āhāra [fr. ā + **hṛ**, lit. taking up or on to oneself] feeding, support, food, nutriment (lit & fig.). The term is used comprehensively and the usual enumⁿ. comprises four kinds of nutriment, viz. (1) kabaḷinkāra āhāro (bodily nutriment, either oḷāriko gross, solid, or sukhumo fine), (2) phassāhāro n. of contact, (3) manosañcetanā° n. of volition (= cetanā S. A. on II.11 f.), (4) viññāṇ° of consciousness. Thus at M I.261; D III.228, 276; Dhs 71—73; Vism 341. Another definition of Dhammapāla's refers it to the fourfold tasting as asita (eaten), pīta (drunk), khāyita (chewed), sāyita (tasted) food PvA 25. A synonym with mūla, hetu, etc. for cause, Yamaka, I.3; Yam. A (*J P T S.*, 1910—12) 54. See on term also *Dhs trsl.* 30. — Vin I.84; D I.166; S I.172; II.11, 13, 98 sq. (the 4 kinds, in detail); III 54 (sa°); V.64, 391; A III.51 (sukhass°), 79, 142 sq., 192 sq.; IV.49, 108; V.52 (the four), 108, 113 (avijjāya etc.), 116 (bhavataṇhāya), 269 sq. (nerayikānaŋ etc.); Sn 78, 165, 707, 747; Nd¹ 25; Ps I.22 (the four) 122 (id.), 55, 76 sq; Kvu 508; Pug 21, 55; Vbh 2, 13, 72, 89, 320, 383, 401 sq. (the four); Dhs 58, 121, 358, 646; Nett 31, 114, 124; DhsA 153, 401; DhA I.183 (°ŋ pacchindati to bring up food, to vomit); II 87; VvA 118; PvA 14, 35, 112, 148 (utu° physical nutriment); Sdhp 100, 395, 406; A V.136 gives ten āhāra opposed to ten paripanthā. -an° without food, unfed M I.487 (aggi); S III.126; V.105; Sn 985.

-**ūpahāra** consumption of food, feeding, eating Vin III. 136. -**ṭhitika** subsisting or living on food D III.211, 273; A V.50, 55; Ps I.5, 122. -**pariggaha** taking up or acquirement of food Miln 244 or is it "restraint or abstinence in food"? Same combⁿ. at Miln 313. -**maya** "food-like", feeding stuff, food J III.523. -**lolatā** greed after food SnA 35. -**samudaya** origin of nutriment S III.59.

Āhāratthaŋ [āhāra + tta] the state of being food. In the idiom āhārattaŋ pharati; Vin I.199, of medicine, 'to penetrate into food-ness', to come under the category of food; Miln 152, of poison, to turn into food. [According to Oldenberg (Vin I.381) his MSS read about equally °attaŋ and °atthaŋ. Trenckner prints °atthaŋ, and records no variant (see p. 425)].

Āhāreti [Denom. fr. āhāra] to take food, eat, feed on S II.13; III.240; IV.104; A I.114, 295; II.40, 145, 206; IV. 167; Nd² 540ᶜ (āhāraŋ & puttamaŋsaŋ cp. S II.98).

Āhika (—°) (adj.) [der. fr. aha²] only in pañcāhika every five days (cp. pañcāhaŋ & sattāhaŋ) M III.157.

Āhiṇḍati [ā + **hiṇḍ**, cp. BSk. āhiṇḍate Divy 165 etc.] to wander about, to roam, to be on an errand, to be engaged in (w. acc.) Vin I 203 (senāsana-cārikaŋ), 217; II. 132 (na sakkoti vinā daṇḍena āhiṇḍituŋ); IV.62; J I.48, 108, 239; Nd² 540ᴴ; Pv III.2²⁰ (= vicarati PvA 185); Vism 38, 284 (aṭaviŋ); VvA 238 (tattha tattha); PvA 143.

Āhita [pp. of ā + **dhā**] put up, heaped; provided with fuel (of a fire), blazing Sn 18 (gini = ābhato jalito vā SnA 28). See sam°.

Āhu 3rd pl. of āha (q. v.).

Āhuti (f.) [Vedic āhuti, ā + **hu**] oblation, sacrifice; veneration, adoration M III 167; S I.141; Th 1, 566 (°inaŋ paṭiggaho recipient of sacrificial gifts); J I.15; V.70 (id.); Vv 64[33] (paramâhutiŋ gato deserving the highest adoration); Sn 249, 458; Kvu 530; SnA 175; VvA 285.

Āhuna = āhuti, in āhuna-pāhuna giving oblations and sacrificing VvA 155; by itself at Vism 219.

Āhuneyya (adj.) [a grd. form. fr. ā + **hu**, cp. āhuti] sacrificial, worthy of offerings or of sacrifice, venerable, adorable, worshipful D III.5, 217 (aggi); A II.56, 70 (sāhuneyyaka), 145 sq. (id.); IV.13, 41 (aggi); It 88 (+ pāhuneyya); Vv 64[33] (cp. VvA 285). See def. at Vism 219 where expld. by "āhavanīya" and "āhavanaŋ arahati" deserving of offerings.

Āhundarika (adj.) [doubtful or āhuṇḍ°?] according to Morris *JPTS.* 1884, 73 "crowded up, blocked up, impassable" Vin I.79; IV.297; Vism 413 (°ŋ andha-tamaŋ).

I.

I in i-kāra the letter or sound i SnA 12 (°lopa), 508 (id.).

Ikka [Sk. ṛkṣa, of which the regular representation is P. accha[2]] a bear J VI.538 (= accha C.).

Ikkāsa (?) [uncertain as regard meaning & etym.] at Vin II.151 (+ kasāva) is trsl. by "slime of trees", according to Bdhgh's expln. on p. 321 (to C. V. VI.3, 1), who however reads **nikkāsa.**

Ikkhaṇa (nt.) [fr. **īkṣ**] seeing Vism 16.

Ikkhaṇika [fr. **ikṣ** to look or see, cp. akkhi] a fortuneteller Vin III.107; S II.260; J I.456, 457; VI.504.

Ikkhati [fr. **īkṣ**] to look J V 153; ThA 147; DhsA 172.

Ingita (nt.) [pp. of ingati = iñjati] movement, gesture, sign J II.195, 408; VI.368, 459.

Ingha (indecl.) [Sk. anga prob. after P. ingha (or añja, q. v.); fr. iñjati, cp. *JPTS.* 1883, 84] part. of exhortation, lit. "get a move on", come on, go on, look here, Sn 83, 189, 862, 875 = 1052; J V.148; Pv IV.5[1]; Vv 53[9] (= codan'atthe nipāto VvA 237); VvA 47; DhA IV.62.

Inghāḷa [according to Morris *JPTS.* 1884, 74 = angāra, cp. Marāthī ingala live coal] coal, embers, in inghāḷakhu Th 2, 386 a pit of glowing embers (= angāra-kāsu ThA 256). The whole cpd. is doubtful.

Icc' see iti.

Iccha (—°) (adj.) [the adj. form of icchā] wishing, longing, having desires, only in pāp° having evil desires S I.50; II.156; an° without desires S I.61, 204; Sn 707; app° id. Sn 628, 707.

Icchaka (—°) (adj.) [fr. iccha] wishing, desirous, only in nt. adv. **yad-icchikaŋ** (and **yen°**) after one's wish or liking M III.97; A III.28.

Icchati[1] [Sk. icchati, **iṣ**, cp. Av. isaiti, Obulg. iskati, Ohg. eiscōn, Ags. āscian = E. ask; all of same meaning "seek, wish"] to wish, desire, ask for (c. acc.), expect S I.210 (dhammaŋ sotuŋ .i.); Sn 127, 345, 512, 813, 836; Dh 162, 291; Nd[1] 3, 138, 164; Nd[2] s. v.; Pv II.6[3]; Pug 19; Miln 269, 327; SnA 16, 23, 321; KhA 17; PvA 20, 71, 74; Pot. icche Dh 84; Sn 835 Pv II.6[6] & **iccheyya** D II.2, 10; Sn 35; Dh 73, 88; ppr. **icchaŋ** Sn 826, 831, 937; Dh 334 (phalaŋ) aor. **icchi** PvA 31. — grd. **icchitabba** PvA 8. — pp. **iṭṭha** & **icchita** (q. v.). — *Note.* In prep.-cpds. the root **iṣ**[2] (icchati) is confused with root **iṣ**[1] (iṣati, esati) with pp. both °iṭṭha and °isita. Thus ajjhesati, pp. ajjhiṭṭha & ajjhesita; anvesati (Sk. anvicchati); pariyesati (Sk. paricchati), pp. pariyiṭṭha & pariyesita.

Icchati[2] [Sk. ṛcchati of ṛ, concerning which see appeti] see **aticchati** & cp. **icchatā.**

Icchatā (—°) (f.) [abstr. fr. icchā] wishfulness, wishing: only in **aticchatā** too great wish for, covetousness, greed Vbh 350 (cp. aticchati, which is probably the primary basis of the word); **mah°** & **pāp°** Vbh 351, 370.

Icchana (nt.) [fr. **iṣ**[2], cp. Sk. īpsana] desiring, wish J IV. 5; VI.244.

Icchā (f.) [fr. icchati, **iṣ**[2]] wish, longing, desire D II.243; III.75; S I.40 (°dhūpāyito loko), 44 (naraŋ parikassati); A II.143; IV.293 sq.; 325 sq.; V.40, 42 sq.; Sn 773, 872; Dh 74, 264 (°lobha-samāpanna); Nd[1] 29, 30; Pug 19; Dhs 1059, 1136; Vbh 101, 357, 361, 370; Nett 18, 23, 24; Asl. 363; DhsA 250 (read icchā for issā? See Dhs trsl. 100); SnA 108; PvA 65, 155; Sdhp 242, 320. **-âvacara** moving in desires M I.27 (pāpaka); Nett 27. **-âvatiṇṇa** affected with desire, overcome by covetousness Sn 306. **-pakata** same Vin I.97; A III.119, 191, 219 sq.; Pug 69; Miln 357; Vism 24 (where Bdhgh however takes it as "icchāya apakata" and puts apakata = upadduta). **-vinaya** discipline of one's wishes D III.252, A IV.15; V.165 sq.

Icchita [pp. of icchati] wished, desired, longed for J I.208; DhsA 364; PvA 3, 53, 64 (read anicchita for anijjhiṭṭha, which may be a contamination of icchita & iṭṭha), 113, 127 (twice).

Ijjhati [Vedic ṛdhyate & ṛdhnoti; Gr. ἄλθομαι to thrive, Lat. alo to nourish, also Vedic iḍā refreshment & P. iddhi power] to have a good result, turn out a blessing. succeed, prosper, be successful S I.175 ("work effectively" trsl.; = samijjhati mahapphalaŋ hoti C.); IV.303; Sn 461, 485; J V.393; Pv II.1[11]; II.9[13] (= samijjhati PvA 120); Pot. ijjhe Sn 458, 459; pret. ijjhittha (= Sk. ṛdhyiṣṭha) Vv 20[6] (= nippajjittha mahapphalo ahuvattha VvA 103). — pp. iddha. See also aḍḍha[2] & aḍḍhaka. Cp. sam°.

Ijjhana (nt.) & °ā (f.) [fr. ijjhati] success, carrying out successfully Ps I.17 sq., 74, 181; II.125, 143 sq., 161, 174; Vbh 217 sq.; Vism 266, 383 (°aṭṭhena iddhi); DhsA 91, 118, 237.

Iñjanā (f.) & °aŋ (nt.) [fr. **iñj**, see iñjati] shaking, movement, motion Sn 193 (= calanā phandanā SnA 245); Nett 88 (= phandanā C.). an° immobility, steadfastness Ps I.15; II.118.

Iñjita [pp. of iñjati] shaken, moved Th 1, 386 (an°). Usually as nt. **iñjitaŋ** shaking, turning about, movement, vacillation M I.454; S I.109; IV.202; A II.45; Sn 750, 1040

Iñjati [Vedic ṛñjati (cp. P. ajjati). Also found as ingati (so Veda), and as **ang** in Sk. anga = P. añja & ingha & Vedic pali-angati to turn about. See also ānejja & añjati[1]] to shake, move, turn about, stir D I.56; S I.107, 132, 181 (aniñjamāna ppr. med. "impassive"); III.211; Th 1, 42; 2, 231; Nd[2] s. v. (+ calati vedhati); Vism 377; DA I.167. — pp. **iñjita** (q. v.).

(pl. iñjitā), 1048 (see Nd² 140); Dh 255; Vbh 390. — On the 7 iñjitas see *JPTS.* 1884, 58.

Iñjitatta (nt.) [abstr. fr. iñjita nt.] state of vacillation, wavering, motion S v.315 (kāyassa).

Iṭṭha (adj.) [pp. of icchati] pleasing, welcome, agreeable, pleasant, often in the idiomatic group **iṭṭha kanta manāpa** (of objects pleasing to the senses) D I.245; II.192; M 185; S IV.60, 158, 235 sq.; V.22, 60, 147; A II.66 sq.; V.135 (dasa, dhammā etc., ten objects affording pleasure); Sn 759; It 15; Vbh 2, 100, 337. — Alone as nt. meaning welfare, good state, pleasure, happiness at Sn 154 (+ aniṭṭha); Nett 28 (+ aniṭṭha); Vism 167 (id.); PvA 116 (= bhadraŋ), 140. **-aniṭṭha** unpleasant, disagreeable PvA 32, 52, 60, 116. — See also pariy°, in which iṭṭha stands for eṭṭha.

Iṭṭhakā (Itthakā) (f.) [BSk. iṣṭakā, e. g. Divy 221; from the Idg. root ***idh** > ***aidh** to burn, cp. Sk. idhma firewood, inddhe to kindle (**idh** or **indh**), edhaḥ fuel; Gr. αἴθω burn, αἶθος fire-brand; Lat. aedes, aestas & aestus; more especially Av. ištya tile, brick] — 1. a burnt brick, a tile Vin II 121 (°pākara a brick wall, distinguished fr. silāpakāra & dāru°); J III.435, 446 (pākār'iṭṭhikā read °aṭṭhakā); V.213 (rattiṭṭhikā); Vism 355 (°dārugomaya); PvA 4 (°cuṇṇa-makkhita-sīsa the head rubbed with brick-powder, i. e. plaster; a ceremony performed on one to be executed, cp. Mṛcchakaṭika x.5 piṣṭa-cūrṇ'âvakīrṇaśca puruṣo 'haŋ paśūkṛtaḥ with striking equation iṣṭaka > piṣṭa). — 2. pl. (as suvaṇṇa°) gold or gilt tiles used for covering a cetiya or tope DhA III.29, 61; VvA 157.

Iṭṭhi° in °khagga-dhāra at J VI.223 should be read **iddha.**

Iṇa (nt.) [Sk. ṛṇa, see also P. an-aṇa] debt D I.71, 73; A III.352; V.324 (enumd. with baddha, jāni & kali); Sn 120; J I.307; II.388, 423; III.66; IV.184 (iṇagga for nagga?); 256; V.253 (where enumd. as one of the 4 paribhogas, viz. theyya°, iṇa°, dāya°, sāmi°); VI.69, 193; Miln 375; PvA 273, 276. iṇaŋ gaṇhāti to borrow money or take up a loan Vism 556; SnA 289; PvA 3. — iṇaŋ **muñcati** to discharge a debt J IV.280; V.238; °ŋ **sodheti** same PvA 276; **labhati** same PvA 3.

-apagama absence of debt ThA 245. **-gāhaka** a borrower Miln 364. **-ghāta** stricken by debt Sn 246 (= iṇaŋ gahetvā tassa appadānena iṇaghāta). **-ṭṭha** (with iṇaṭṭa as v. l. at all passages, see aṭṭa) fallen into or being in debt M I.463 = S III.93 = It 89 = Miln 279. **-paṇṇa** promissory note J I.230; IV.256. **-mokkha** release from debt J IV.280; V.239. **-sādhaka** negotiator of a loan Miln 365.

Iṇāyika [fr. iṇa] one connected with a debt, viz. (1) a creditor S I.170; J IV.159, 256; VI.178; ThA 271 see also dhanika); PvA 3. — (2) a debtor Vin I.76; Nd 160.

Ita [pp. of eti, **i**] gone, only in cpd. **dur-ita** gone badly, as nt. evil, wrong Dāvs I.61; otherwise in compn. with prep., as peta, vita etc.

Itara¹ (adj.) [Ved. itara = Lat. iterum a second time; compar. of pron. base ***i**, as in ayaŋ, etaŋ, iti etc.] other, second, next; different Dh 85, 104, 222; J II.3; III.26; IV.4; PvA 13, 14, 42, 83, 117. In repetition cpd. **itarītara** one or the other, whatsoever, any Sn 42; J V.425; Nd² 141; Miln 395; KhA 145, 147; acc. **itarītaraŋ** & instr. **itarītarena** used as adv. of one kind or another, in every way, anyhow [cp. BSk. itaretara M Vastu III. 348 and see Wackernagel *Altind. Gram.* II. Ś 121 c.] J VI 448 (°ŋ); Dh 331 (°ena); Vv 84¹ (text reads itritarena, v. l. itaritarena, expld. by itaritaraŋ VvA 333).

Itara² (adj.) freq. spelling for **ittara** (q. v.).

Iti (ti) (indecl.) [Vedic iti, of pron. base ***i**, cp. Sk. itthaŋ thus, itthā here, there; Av. iþa so; Lat. ita & item thus. Cp. also P. ettha; lit. "here, there (now), then"] emphatic-deictic particle "thus". Occurs in both forms iti & ti, the former in higher style (poetry), the latter more familiar in conversational prose. The function of "iti" is expld. by the old Pāli C. in a conventional phrase, looking upon it more as a "filling" particle than trying to define its meaning viz. "iti ti padasandhi padasaŋsaggo padapāripurī akkharasamavāyo etc." Nd¹ 123 = Nd² 137. The same expln also for iti' haŋ (see below IV.) — I. As *deictic adv.* "thus, in this way" (Vism 423 iti = evaŋ) pointing to something either just mentioned or about to be mentioned: (a) referring to what precedes Sn 253 (n'eso maman ti iti naŋ vijaññā), 805; It 123 (ito devā... taŋ namassanti); Dh 74 (iti bālassa sankappo thus think the foolish), 286 (iti bālo vicinteti); Vv 79¹⁰ (= evaŋ VvA 307); VvA 5. — (b) referring to what follows D I.63 (iti paṭisañcikkhati); A I.205 (id.) — II. As *emphatic part.* pointing out or marking off a statement either as not one's own (reported) or as the definite contents of (one's own or other's) thoughts. On the whole untranslatable (unless written as quotation marks), often only setting off a statement as emphatic, where we would either underline the word or phrase in question, or print it in italics, or put it in quot. marks (e. g. bālo ti vuccati Dh 63 = bālo vuccati). — 1. in direct speech (as given by writer or narrator). e. g. sādhu bhante Kassapa lābhataŋ esā janatā dassanāyā ti. Tena hi Sīha tvaŋ yeva Bhagavato ārocehī ti. Evaŋ bhante ti kho Sīho.... D I.151. — 2. in indirect speech: (a) as statement of a fact "so it is that" (cp. E. "viz.", Ger. "und zwar"), mostly untranslated Kh IV. (arahā ti pavuccati); J I.253 (tasmā pesanaka-corā t' eva vuccanti); III.51 (tayo sahāyā ahesuŋ makkato sigālo uddo ti); PvA 112 (ankuro pañca-sakaṭasatehi... aññataro pi brāhmaṇo pañca-sakaṭasatehī ti dve janā sakata-sahassehi... paṭipannā). — (b) as statement of a thought "like this", "I think", so, thus Sn 61 ("sango eso" iti ñatvā knowing "this is defilement"), 253 ("neso maman" ti iti naŋ vijaññā), 783 ("iti' han" ti), 1094 (etaŋ dīpaŋ anāparaŋ **Nibbānaŋ** iti naŋ brūmi I call this N.), 1130 (aparā pāraŋ gaccheyya tasmā "Parāyanaŋ" iti). — III. *Peculiarities of spelling.* (1) in combn. with other part. iti is elided & contracted as follows: icc' eva, t' eva, etc. — (2) final a, i, u preceding ti are lengthened to ā, ī, ū, e. g. mā evaŋ akattbā ti DhA I.7; kati dhurānī ti ibid: dve yeva dhurāni bhikkhū ti ibid — IV. *Combinations* with other emphatic particles: + **eva** thus indeed, in truth, really; as icc' eva Pv I 11⁹ (= evam eva PvA 59); t' eva J I.253; Miln 114; tv' eva J I.203; II.2. **-iti kira** thus now, perhaps, I should say D I.228, 229, 240. **-iti kho** thus, therefore D I.98, 103; III.135. **iti vā** and so on(?), thus and such (similar cases) Nd¹ 13 = Nd² 420 A¹. **-iti ha** thus surely, indeed Sn 934, 1084 (see below under itihītihaŋ; cp. SnA Index 669: itiha? and itikirā); It 76; DA I.247, as iti haŋ at Sn 783 (same expln. at Nd¹ 71 as for iti). **-kin ti** how J II.159.

-kirā (f.) [a substantivised iti kira] hearsay, lit. "so I guess" or "I have heard" A I.189 = II.191 sq. = Nd² 151. Cp. itiha. **-bhava** becoming so & so (opp. abhava not becoming) Vin II.184 (°ābhava); D I.8 (ip = iti bhavo iti abhavo DA I.91); A II.248; It 109 (id.); syn. with itthabhava (q. v.). **-vāda** "speaking so & so", talk, gossip M I.133; S V.73; A II.26; It III.35. **-vuttaka** (nt.) [a noun formation fr. iti vuttaŋ] "so it has been said", (book of) quotations, "Logia", N. of the fourth book of the Khuddaka-nikāya, named thus because every sutta begins with vuttaŋ h' etaŋ Bhagavatā "thus has the Buddha said" (see khuddaka and navanga) Vin III.8; M I.133; A II.7, 103; III.86, 177, 361 sq.; Pug 43, 62; KhA 12. Kern, *Toev.* s. v. compares the interesting BSk. distortion itivṛttaŋ. **-hāsa** [= iti ha āsa, preserving the Vedic form āsa, 3rd sg. perf. of atthi] "thus indeed it has been", legendary love, oral tradition, history; usually mentioned as a branch of brahmanic learning, in phrase itihāsa-pañca-mānaŋ padako veyyākaraṇo etc. D I 88 = (see DA I.247); A I.163; III.223; Sn 447, 1020.

Cp. also M Vastu I.556. **-hītiha** [itiha + itiha] "so & so" talk, gossip, oral tradition belief by hearsay etc. (cp. itikirā & anītiha. Nd² spells itihītiha) M I 520; S I.154; Sn 1084; Nd² 151.

Ito (indecl.) [Vedic itaḥ, abl.-adv. formation fr. pron. base *i, cp. iti, ayaŋ etc.] adv. of succession or motion in space & time "from here". "from now". (1) with ref. to **space**: (a) from here, from this, often implying the present existence (in opp. to the "other" world) It 77; Sn 271 (°ja. °nidāna caused or founded in or by this existence = attabhāvaŋ sandhāy' āha SnA 303), 774 (cutāse), 870 (°nidāna), 1062 (from this source, i. e. from me), 1101; Pv I.5¹ (ito dinnaŋ what is given in this world); I.6² (i. e. manussalokato PvA 33); I.12³ (= idhalokato PvA 64); Nett 93 (ito bahiddhā); PvA 46 (ito dukkhato mutti). — (b) here (with implication of movement), in phrases ito c' ito here and there PvA 4. 6; and ito vā etto vā here & there DhA II.80. — (2) with ref. to **time**: from here, from now, hence (in chronological records with num. ord. or card., with ref. either to past or future). (a) referring to the *past*, since D II.2 (ito so ekanavuto kappo 91 kappas ago): Sn 570 (ito aṭṭhame, scil. divase & days ago SnA 457; T. reads aṭṭhami); VvA 319 (ito kira tiŋsa-kappa-sahasse); PvA 19 (dvā navuti kappe 92 kappas ago), 21 (id.), 78 (pañcamāya jātiyā in the fifth previous re-birth). — (b) referring to the *future*, i. e. henceforth, in future, from now e. g. ito sattame divase in a week VvA 138; ito paraŋ further, after this SnA 160, 178, 412, 549; PvA 83; ito paṭṭhāya from now on, henceforward J I.63 (ito dāni p.); PvA 41.

Ittara (sometimes spelt **itara**) (adj.) [Vedic itvara in meaning "going", going along, hence developed meaning "passing"; fr. **I**] — 1. passing, changeable, short, temporary, brief, unstable M I.318 (opp. dīgharattaŋ); A II.187; J I 393; III.83 (°dassana = khaṇika° C.), IV.112 (°vāsa temporary abode); Pv I 11¹¹ (= na cira-kāla-ṭṭhāyin anicca vipariṇāma-dhamma PvA 60); DA I.195; PvA 60 (= paritta khaṇika). — 2. small, inferior, poor, unreliable, mean M II.47 (°jacca of inferior birth); A II.34; Sn 757 (= paritta paccupaṭṭhāna SnA 509); Miln 93, 114 (°pañña of small wisdom). This meaning (2) also in BSk. itvara, e. g. Divy 317 (dāna).

Ittaratā (f.) [fr. ittara] changeableness Miln 93 (of a woman).

Ittha (indecl.) [the regular representative of Vedic itthā here, there, but preserved only in cpds. while the Pāli form is **ettha**] here, in this world (or "thus, in such a way), only in cpd. °**bhāv' aññathā-bhāva** such an (i. e. earthly) existence and one of another kind, or existence here (in this life) and in another form" (cp. itibhāva & itthatta) Sn 729, 740 = 752; It 9 (v. l. itthi° for iti°) = A II.10 = Nd² 172ª; It 94 (v. l. ittha°). There is likely to have been a confusion between ittha = Sk. itthā & itthaŋ = Sk. itthaŋ (see next).

Itthaŋ (indecl.) [adv. fr. pron. base °i, as also iti in same meaning] thus, in this way D I.53, 213; Dāvs IV.35; V.18. **-nāma** (itthan°) having such as name, called thus, so-called Vin I.56; IV.136; J I.297; Miln 115; DhA II.98. **-bhūta** being thus, of this kind, modal, only in cpd. °*lakkhaṇa* or °*ākhyāna* the sign or case of modality, i. e. the ablative ease SnA 441; VvA 162, 174; PvA 150.

Itthatta¹ (nt.) [ittha + *tvaŋ, abstr. fr. ittha. The curious BSk. distortion of this word is icchatta M Vastu 417] being here (in this world), in the present state of becoming, this (earthly) state (not "thusness" or "life as we conceive it", as Mrs. Rh. D. in *K. S.* I.177; although a confusion between ittha & itthaŋ seems to exist, see ittha); "life in these conditions" *K. S.* II.17; expld. by itthabhāva C. on S I.140 (see *K. S.* 318). — See also freq. formula A of arahatta. — D I.18, 84; A I.63; II.82, 159, 203; Sn 158; Dhs 633; Pug 70, 71; DA I.112.

Itthatta² (nt.) [itthi + *tvaŋ abstr. fr. itthi] state or condition of femininity, womanhood, muliebrity Dhs 633 (= itthi-sabhāva DhsA 321).

Itthi & Itthī (f.) [Vedic strı, Av. strī woman, perhaps with Sk. sātuḥ uterus fr. Idg. °sī to sow or produce, Lat. sero, Goth. saian, Obg. sěen, Ags. sāwan etc., cp. also Cymr. hil progeny, Oir. sīl seed; see J. Schmidt, *K. Z.* XXV.29. The regular representative of Vedic strī is P. **thī**, which only occurs rarely (in poetry & compⁿ.) see thī] woman, female; also (usually as —°) wife. Opp. purisa man (see e. g. for contrast of itthi and purisa J V.72, 398; Nett 93; DhA I.390; PvA 153). — S I.33 (nibbānass' eva santike), 42, 125 (majjhim°, mah°), 185; A I.28, 138; II.115, 209; III.68, 90, 156; IV.196 (purisaŋ bandhati); Sn 112, 769 (nom. pl. thiyo = itthi-saññikā thiyo SnA 513); J I.286 (itthi doso), 300 (gen. pl. itthīnaŋ); II.415 (nom. pl. thiyo); V.397 (thi-ghātaka), 398 (gen. dat. itthiyā), V.425 (nom pl. itthiyo); Vbh 336, 337; DA I.147; PvA 5, 44, 46, 67, 154 (amanuss° of petis); Sdhp 64, 79. — **anitthi** a woman lacking the characteristics of womanhood, an unfaithful wife J II.126 (= ucchiṭṭh° C.); kul'-itthi a wife of good descent Vin II.10; A III.76; IV.16, 19; dahar° a young wife J I.291; dur° a poor woman J IV.38. — Some general characterisations of womanhood: 10 kinds of women enumᵈ. at Vin III.139 = A V.264 = VvA 72, viz. mātu-rakkhitā, pitu°, mātāpitu°, bhātu°, bhaginī°, ñāti°, gotta°, dhamma°, sarakkhā, saparidaṇḍā; see Vin III.139 for explⁿ. — S I.38 (malaŋ brahmacariyassa), 43 (id.); J I.287 (itthiyo nāma āsā lāmikā pacchimikā); IV. 222 (itthiyo papāto akkhāto; pamattaŋ pamathenti); V. 425 (sīho yathā ... tath' itthiyo); women as goods for sale S I.43 (bhaṇḍānaŋ uttamaŋ); DhA I.390 (itthiyo vikkiṇiya bhaṇḍaŋ).

-agāra (-āgāra) as **itthāgāra** women's apartment, seraglio Vin I.72; IV.158; S I.58, 89; J I.90; also coll. for women-folk, women (cp. Ger. frauenzimmer) D II.249; J V.188. **-indriya** the female principle or sex, femininity (opp. puris' indriya) S V.204; A IV.57 sq.; Vism 447, 492; Dhs 585, 633, 653 et passim. **-kathā** talk about women D I.7 (cp. DA I.90). **-kāma** the craving for a woman S IV.343. **-kutta** a woman's behaviour, woman's wiles, charming behaviour, coquetry A IV.57 = Dhs 633; J I.296, 433; II.127, 329; IV.219, 472; DhA IV.197. **-ghātaka** a woman-killer J V. 398. **-dhana** wife's treasure, dowry Vin III.16. **-dhutta** a rogue in the matter of women, one who indulges in women Sn 106; J III.260; PvA 5. **-nimitta** characteristic of a woman Dhs 633, 713, 836. **-pariggaha** a woman's company, a woman Nd¹ 11. **-bhāva** existence as woman, womanhood S I.129; Th 2, 216 (referring to a yakkhinī, cp. ThA 178; Dhs 633; PvA 168. **-rūpa** womanly beauty A I.1; III.68; Th 2, 294. **-lakkhaṇa** fortune-telling regarding a woman D I.9 (cp. DhA I.94, + purisa°); J VI. 135. **-linga** "sign of a woman", feminine quality, female sex Vism 184; Dhs 633, 713, 836; DhsA 321 sq. **-sadda** the sound (or word) "woman" DhA I.15. **-soṇḍī** a woman addicted to drink Sn 112.

Itthikā (f.) [fr. itthi] a woman Vin III.16; D II.14; J I. 336; Vv 18¹; Sdhp 79. As adj. **itthika** in **bahutthika** having many women, plentiful in women Vin II.256 (kulāni bahuttikāni appapurisakāni rich in women & lacking in men); S II.264 (id. and **appitthikāni**).

Ida & Idaŋ (indecl.) [nt. of ayaŋ (idaŋ) in function of a deictic part.] emphatic demonstr. adv. in local, temporal & modal function, as (1) in this, here: **idappaccayatā** having its foundation in this. i. e. causally connected, by way of cause Vin I.5 = S I.136; D I.185; Dhs 1004, 1061; Vbh 340, 362, 365; Vism 518; etc. — (2) now, then which idha is more freq.) D II.267, 270, almost syn. (for with kira. — (3) just (this), even so, only: **idam-atthika** just sufficient, proper, right Th I, 984 (civara); Pug 69 (read so for °matthika, see Pug A 250); as **idam-atthitā** "being satisfied with what is sufficient" at Vism 81;

expl^d. as **atthika-bhāva** at Pug A 250. **idaŋsaccâbhinivesa** inclination to say: only this is the truth, i. e. inclination to dogmatise, one of the four kāya-ganthā, viz. abhijjhā, byāpāda, sīlabbata-parāmāsa, idaŋ° (see Dhs 1135 & Dhs trsl. 304); D III.230; S V.59; Nd¹ 98; Nett 115 sq.

Idāni (indecl.) [Vedic idānīŋ] now Dh 235, 237; KhA 247.

Iddha¹ [pp. of iddhe to **idh** or **indh**, cp. indhana & idhuma] in flames, burning, flaming bright, clear J VI.223 (°khaggadharā balī; so read for T. iṭṭhi-khagga°); Dpvs VI.42.

Iddha² [pp. of ijjhati; cp. Sk. ṛddha] (a) prosperous, opulent, wealthy D I.211 (in idiomatic phrase iddha phīta bahujana, of a prosperous town); A III.215 (id.); J VI.227, 361 (= issara C.), 517; Dāvs I.11. — (b) successful, satisfactory, sufficient Vin I.212 (bhattaŋ); IV.313 (ovādo).

Iddhi [Vedic ṛddhi from **ardh**, to prosper; Pali ijjhati]. There is no single word in English for Iddhi, as the idea is unknown in Europe. The main sense seems to be 'potency'. — 1. Pre-Buddhistic; the Iddhi of a layman. The four Iddhis of a king are personal beauty, long life, good health, and popularity (D II.177; M III.176, cp. J III.454 for a later set). The Iddhi of a rich young noble is 1. The use of a beautiful garden, 2. of soft and pleasant clothing. 3. of different houses for the different seasons, 4. of good food, A I.145. At M I.152 the Iddhi of a hunter, is the craft and skill with which he captures game; but at p. 155 other game have an Iddhi of their own by which they outwit the hunter. The Iddhi, the power of a confederation of clans, is referred to at D II.72. It is by the Iddhi they possess that birds are able to fly (Dhp 175). — 2. Psychic powers. including most of those claimed for modern mediums (see under Abhiññā). Ten such are given in a stock paragraph. They are the power to project mind-made images of oneself; to become invisible; to pass through solid things, such as a wall; to penetrate solid ground as if it were water; to walk on water; to fly through the air; to touch sun and moon; to ascend into the highest heavens (D I 77, 212; II.87, 213; III.112, 281; S II.121; V.264, 303; A I 170, 255; III.17, 28, 82, 425; V.199; Ps I III; II.207; Vism 378 sq., 384; DA I.122). For other such powers see S I.144; IV.290; V.263; A III.340. — 3. The Buddhist theory of Iddhi. At D I.213 the Buddha is represented as saying: 'It is because I see danger in the practice of these mystic wonders that I loathe and abhor and am ashamed thereof'. The mystic wonder that he himself believed in and advocated (p. 214) was the wonder of education. What education was meant in the case of Iddhi, we learn from M I.33; A III.425, and from the four bases of Iddhi, the **Iddhipādā**. They are the making determination in respect of concentration on purpose, on will, on thoughts & on investigation (D II.212; M I.103; A I.39, 297; II.256; III. 82; Ps I.III; II 154, 164, 205; Vbh 216). It was an offence against the regulations of the Saŋgha for a Bhikkhu to display before the laity these psychic powers beyond the capacity of ordinary men (Vin II.112). And falsely to claim the possession of such powers involved expulsion from the Order (Vin III.91). The psychic powers of Iddhi were looked upon as inferior (as the Iddhi of an unconverted man seeking his own profit), compared to the higher Iddhi, the Ariyan Iddhi (D III.112; A I.93; Vin II.183). There is no valid evidence that any one of the ten Iddhis in the above list actually took place. A few instances are given, but all are in texts more than a century later than the recorded wonder. And now for nearly two thousand years we have no further instances. Various points on Iddhi discussed at *Dial.* I.272, 3; *Cpd.* 60 ff.; *Expositor* 121. Also at Kvu 55; Ps II.150; Vism XII; DhA I.91; J I.47, 360.

-ânubhāva (iddhânu°) power or majesty of thaumaturgy Vin 31, 209. 240; III.67; S I 147; IV.290; PvA 53. **-âbhisankhāra** (iddhâbhi°) exercise of any of the psychic powers Vin I.16, 17, 25; D I.106; S III.92; IV.289; V.270; Sn p. 107; PvA 57, 172 212. **-pāṭihāriya** a wonder of psychic power Vin I.25, 28, 180, 209; II.76, 112, 200; D I.211, 212; III.3, 4, 9, 12 sq., 27; S IV.290; A I.170, 292; Ps II.227. **-pāda** constituent or basis of psychic power Vin II.240; D II.103, 115 sq., 120; III.77, 102, 127, 221; M II.11; III.296; S I.116, 132; III.96, 153; IV.360; V.254, 255, 259 sq., 264 sq., 269 sq., 275, 285; A IV.128 sq., 203, 463; V.175; Nd¹ 14. 45 (°dhīra), 340 (°pucchā); Nd¹ s. v.; Ps I.17, 21, 84; II.56, 85 sq., 120, 166, 174; Ud 62; Dhs 358, 528, 552; Nett 16, 31, 83; DhsA 237; DhA III.177; IV.32. **-bala** the power of working wonders VvA 4; PvA 171. **-yāna** the carriage (fig.) of psychic faculties Miln 276. **-vikubbanā** the practice of psychic powers Vism 373 sq. **-vidhā** kinds of iddhi D I.77, 212; II.213; III.112, 281; S II.121; V.264 sq, 303; A I.170 sq.; 255; III.17, 28, 82 sq., 425 sq.; V.199; Ps I.III; II.207; Vism 384; DA I.222. **-visaya** range or extent of psychic power Vin III.67; Nett 23.

Iddhika¹ (—°) (adj.) the compn. form of addhika in cpd. **kapaṇ-iddhika** tramps & wayfarers (see kapaṇa), e. g. at J I.6; IV.15; PvA 78.

Iddhika² (—°) (adj.) [iddhi + ka] possessed of power, only in cpd. **mah-iddhika** of great power, always comb^d. with **mah-ânubhāva**, e. g. at Vin I.31; II.193; III.101; S II. 155; M I.34; Th 1, 429. As **mahiddhiya** at J V.149. See **mahiddhika**.

Iddhimant (adj.) [fr. iddhi] — 1. (lit.) successful, proficient, only in neg. an° unfortunate, miserable, poor J VI.361. — 2. (fig.) possessing psychic powers Vin III.67; IV.108; A I.23, 25; II.185; III.340; IV.312; Sn 179; Nett 23; Sdhp 32, 472.

Idha (indecl.) [Sk. iha, adv. of space fr. pron. base *i (cp. ayaŋ, iti etc.), cp. Lat. ihi, Gr. ἰθα-γενής, Av. ida] here, in this place, in this connection, now; esp. in this world or present existence Sn 1038, 1056, 1065; It 99 (idh' ûpapanna reborn in this existence); Dh 5, 15, 267, 343, 392; Nd¹ 40, 109, 156; Nd² 145, 146; SnA 147; PvA 45, 60, 71. **-idhaloka** this world, the world of men Sn 1043 (= manussaloka Nd² 552 c); PvA 64; in this religion, Vbh 245. On diff. meanings of idha see DhsA 348.

Idhuma [Sk. idhma, see etym. under iṭṭhakā] fire-wood — Tela-kaṭāha-gāthā, p. 53, *J P T S.* 1884.

Inda [Vedic indra, most likely to same root as **indu** moon, viz. *Idg. ***eid** to shine, cp. Lat. idūs middle of month (after the full moon), Oir. ēsce moon. Jacobi in *K. Z.* XXXI.316 sq. connects Indra with Lat. neriosus strong & Nero). — 1. The Vedic god Indra D I.244; II.261, 274; Sn 310, 316, 679, 1024; Nd I.177. — 2. lord, chief, king. Sakko devānaŋ indo D I.216, 217; II.221, 275; S I.219. Vepacitti asurindo S I 221 ff. manussinda, S I.69, manujinda, Sn 553, narinda, Sn 863, all of the Buddha, 'chief of men'; cp. Vism 491. [Europeans have found a strange difficulty in understanding the real relation of Sakka to Indra. The few references to Indra in the Nikāyas should be classed with the other fragments of Vedic mythology to be found in them. Sakka belongs only to the Buddhist mythology then being built up. He is not only quite different from Indra, but is the direct contrary of that blustering, drunken, god of war. See the passages collected in *Dial.* II.294—298. The idiom sa-Indā devā, D II.261, 274; A V.325, means 'the gods about Indra, Indras retinue', this being a Vedic story. But **Devā Tāvatiŋsā sahindakā** means the T. gods together with their leader (D II.208—212; S III.90; cp. Vv 30¹) this being a Buddhist story].

-aggi (ind' aggi) Indra's fire, i. e. lightning PvA 56. **-gajjita** (nt.) Indra's thunder Miln 22. **-jāla** deception DA I.85. **-jālika** a juggler, conjurer Miln 331. **-dhanu** the rainbow DA I.40. **-bhavana** the realm of Indra Nd¹ 448 (cp. Tāvatiŋsa-bhavana). **-liṅga** the characteristic of Indra Vism 491. **-sāla** N. of tree J IV.92.

Indaka [dimin. fr. inda] — 1. Np. (see Dict. of names), e.g. at Pv II.9[51]; PvA 136 sq. — 2. (—°) see inda 2.

Indakhīla [inda + khīla, cp. BSk. indrakīla Divy 250, 365, 544; Av. Ś I.109, 223]. "Indra's post"; the post, stake or column of Indra, at or before the city gate; also a large slab of stone let into the ground at the entrance of a house D II.254 (°ŋ ūhacca, cp. DhA II.181); Vin IV.160 (expld. ibid. as sayani-gharassa ummāro, i.e. threshold); S V.444 (ayokhīlo +); Dh 95 (°ūpama, cp. DhA II.181); Th 1, 663; J I.89; Miln 364; Vism 72, 466; SnA 201; DA I.209 (nikkhamitvā bahi °ā); DhA II.180 (°sadisaŋ Sāriputtassa cittaŋ), 181 (nagara-dvāre nikhataŋ °ŋ).

Indagū see hindagū.

Indagopaka [inda + gopaka, cp. Vedic indragopā having Indra as protector] a sort of insect ("cochineal, a red beetle", Böhtlingk), observed to come out of the ground after rain Th 1, 13; Vin III.42; J IV.258; V.168; DhA I.20; *Brethren* p. 18, *n.*

Indanīla [inda + nīla "Indra's blue"] a sapphire J I.80; Miln 118; VvA 111 (+ mahānīla).

Indavāruṇī (f.) [inda + vāruṇa] the Coloquintida plant J IV.8 (°ka-rukkha).

Indīvara (nt.) [etym.?] the blue water lily, Nymphaea Stellata or Cassia Fistula J V.92 (°ī-samā ratti); VI.536; Vv 45[1] (= uddālaka-puppha VvA 197).

Indriya (nt.) [Vedic indriya adj. only in meaning "belonging to Indra"; nt. strength, might (cp. inda), but in specific Pāli sense "belonging to the ruler", i.e. governing, ruling nt. governing, ruling or controlling principle] A. *On term:* Indriya is one of the most comprehensive & important categories of Buddhist psychological philosophy & ethics, meaning "controlling principle, directive force, élan, δύναμις", in the foll. applications: (a) with reference to sense-perceptibility "faculty, function", often wrongly interpreted as "organ"; (b) w. ref. to objective aspects of form and matter "kind, characteristic, determinating principle, sign, mark" (cp. woman-hood, hood = Goth. haidus "kind, form"); (c) w. ref. to moods of sensation and (d) to moral powers or motives controlling action, "principle, controlling" force; (e) w. ref. to cognition & insight "category". — Definitions of indriya among others at DhsA 119; cp. *Expositor* 157; *Dhs trsl.* LVII; *Cpd.* 228, 229.

B. *Classifications and groups* of indriyāni. An exhaustive list comprises the indriyāni enumd under A a—e, thus establishing a canonical scheme of 22 Controlling Powers (bāvīsati indriyāni), running thus at Vbh 122 sq. (see trsl. at *Cpd.* 175, 176); and discussed in detail at Vism 491 sq. (*a. sensorial*) (1) **cakkh-undriya** ("the eye which is a power", Cpd. 228) the eye or (personal potentiality of) vision, (2) **sot-indriya** the ear or hearing, (3) **ghān°** nose or smell, (4) **jivh°** tongue or taste, (5) **kāy°** body-sensibility, (6) **man°**) mind; (*b. material*) (7) **itth°** female sex or femininity, (8) **puris°** male sex or masculinity, (9) **jīvit°** life or vitality; (*c. sensational*) (10) **sukh°** pleasure, (11) **dukkh°** pain, (12) **somanass°** joy, (13) **domanass°** grief, (14) **upekh°** hedonic indifference (*d. moral*) (15) **saddh°** faith, (16) **viriy°** energy, (17) **sat°** mindfulness, (18) **samādh°** concentration, (19) **paññ°** reason; (*e. cognitional*) (20) **anaññāta-ñassāmīt°** the thought "I shall come to know the unknown", (21) **aññ°** (= aññā) gnosis, (22) **aññātā-v°** one who knows. — Jīvitindriya (no. 9) is in some redactions placed before itth° (no. 7), e.g. at Ps I.7, 137. — From this list are detached several groups, mentioned frequently and in various connections, no. 6 manas (mano, man-indriya) wavering in its function, being either included under (a) or (more frequently) omitted, so that the first set (a) is marked off as pañc' indriyāni, the 6th being silently included (see below). This uncertainty regarding manas deserves to be noted. The foll. groups may be mentioned here viz. 19 (nos. 1—19) at Ps I.137; 10 (pañca rūpīni & pañca arūpīni) at Nett 69; three groups of five (nos. 1—5, 10—14, 15—19) at D III.239, cp. 278; four (group d without paññā, i.e. nos. 15—18) at A II.141; three (saddh°, samādh°, paññ°, i.e. nos. 15, 18, 19) at A I. 118 sq. Under aṭṭhavidhaŋ indriya-rūpaŋ (*Cpd.* 159) or rūpaŋ as indriyaŋ "form which is faculty" Dhs 661 (cp. *trsl.* p. 204) are understood the 5 sensitives (nos. 1—5), the 2 sex-states (nos. 7, 8) and the vital force (no. 9), i.e. groups a & b of enumn.; discussed & defined in detail at Dhs 709—717, 971—973. — It is often to be guessed from the context only, which of the sets of 5 indriyāni (usually either group a or d) is meant. These detached groups are classed as below under C. f. — *Note.* This system of 22 indriyāni reflects a revised & more elaborate form of the 25 (or 23) categories of the Sānkhya philosophy, with its 10 elements, 10 indriyāni & the isolated position of manas.

C. *Material in detail* (grouped according to A a—e) (a) *sensorial*: (mentioned or referred to as set of 5 viz B. nos. 1—5): M I.295: S III.46 (pañcannaŋ °ānaŋ avakkanti), 225; IV.168; A II.151 (as set of 6, viz. B. nos. 1—6): M I.9; S IV.176; V.74, 205, 230; A I.113; II.16, 39, 152; III.99, 163, 387 sq.; V.348. Specially referring to restraint & control of the senses in foll. phrases: indriyāni saŋvutāni S II.231, 271; IV.112; pañcasu °esu saŋvuto Sn 340 (= lakkhaṇato pana chaṭṭhaŋ pi vuttaŋ yeva hoti, i.e. the 6th as manas included, SnA 343); °esu susaŋvutā Th 2, 196 (= mana-chaṭṭhesu i° suṭṭhu saŋvutā ThA 168) indriyesu guttadvāra & guttadvāratā D III.107; S II.218; IV.103, 112, 175; A I.25, 94, 113; II.39; III.70, 138, 173, 199, 449 sq.; IV.25, 166; V.134; It 23, 24; Nd[1] 14; Vbh 248, 360; DA I.182 (= manachaṭṭesu indriyesu pihita-dvāro hoti), i. vippasannāni S II. 275; III.2, 235; IV.294; V.301; A I.181; III.380. °ānaŋ samatā (v. l. samatha) A III.375 sq. (see also f. below) °āni bhāvitāni Sn 516 (= cakkh' ādīni cha i. SnA 426); Nd[2] 475 B[6]. — Various: S I.26 (rakkhati), 48 (°ūpasame rato); IV.40, 140 (°sampanna); V.216, 217 sq. (independent in function, mano as referee); Ps I.190 (man°); Vbh 13 (rūpa), 341 (mud° & tikkh°) 384 (ahīn°). — (b) *physical*: (above B 7—9) all three: S V.204; Vism 447; itthi° & purisa° A IV.57; Vbh 122, 415 sq.; puris° A III.404; jīvit° Vbh 123, 137; Vism 230 (°upaccheda = maraṇa). See also under itthi, jīvita & purisa. — (c) *sensational* (above B 10—14): S V.207 sq. (see Cpd. 111 & cp. p. 15), 211 sq.; Vbh 15, 71; Nett 88. — (d) *moral* (above B 15—19): S III.96, 153; IV.36, 365 sq.; V.193 sq., 202, 219 (corresponding to pañcabalāni), 220 sq. (and amata), 223 sq. (their culture brings assurance of no rebirth), 227 sq. (paññā the chief one), 235, 237 (sevenfold fruit of), A IV.125 sq., 203, 225; V.56, 175; Ps II.49, 51 sq., 86; Nd[1] 14; Nd[2] 628 (sat° + satibala); Kvu 589; Vbh 341; Nett 15, 28, 47, 54. Often in standard combn. with satipaṭṭhāna, sammappadhāna, iddhipāda, indriya, bala, bojjhanga, magga (see Nd[2] s. v. p. 263) D II.120; Vin III. 93; Ps II.166 & passim. As set of 4 indriyāni (nos. 16—19) at Nett 83. — (e) *cognitional* (above B 20—22) D III.219 = S V.204 (as peculiar to Arahantship); It 53; Ps I.115; II.30. — (f) *collectively*, either two or more of groups a—e, also var. peculiar uses: personal; esp. physical faculties S I.61 (pākat°), 204 (id.); III.207 (ākāsaŋ °āni sankamanti); IV.294 (vipari-bhinnāni); A III.441 (°ānaŋ avekallatā). magic power A IV.264 sq. (okkhipati °āni). indriyānaŋ paripāko (moral or physical) over-ripeness of faculties S II.2, 42; A V.203; Nd[2] 252 (in def. of jarā); Vbh 137. moral forces Vin I.183 (°ānaŋ samatā, + viriyānaŋ s. as sign of Arahant); II.240 (pañc°). principle of life ekindriyaŋ jīvaŋ Vin III.156; Miln 259 heart or seat of feeling in phrase °āni paricāreti to satisfy one's heart PvA 16, 58, 77. obligation, duty, vow in phrase °āni bhinditvā breaking one's vow J II.274; IV.190.

D. *Unclassified material* D I 77 (ahīn°); III 239 (domanass° & somanass°) M I.437 (vemattatā), 453 (id.); II. 11, 106; III.296; S III.225; V.209 (dukkh°, domanass°); A I.39, 42 sq., 297; II.38 (sant°), 149 sq.; III.277, 282;

Ps I.16, 21, 88, 180; II.1 sq., 13, 84, 119, 132, 143, 145, 110, 223; Nd[1] 45 (°dhīra), 171 (°kusala), 341 (pucchā); Dhs 58, 121, 528, 556 (dukkh°), 560, 6r4. 736; Nett 18 (sotāpannassa), 28 (°vavatthāna), 162 (lok'uttara); Vism 350 (°vekallatā); Sdhp 280, 342, 364, 371, 449, 473.

E. *As adj.* (—°) having one's senses, mind or heart as such & such S I.138 (tikkh° & mud°); III.93 (pākat°); V.269 (id.); A I.70 (id.) & passim (id.); A I.70 (saŋvut°) 266 (id.), 236 (gutt°); II.6 (samāhit°); Sn 214 (susamāhit° his senses well-composed); PvA 70 (pīṇit° joyful or gladdened of heart).

F. *Some compounds*: **-gutta** one who restrains & watches his senses S I.154; Dh 375. **-gutti** keeping watch over the senses, self-restraint DhA IV.111. [a] **paropariya,** [b] **paropariyatta** & [c] **paropariyatti** (°ñāṇa) (knowledge of) what goes on in the senses and intentions of others [a] J I.78; [b] A V 34, 38; [b] Ps I.121 sq., 133 sq.; II.158, 175; [b] Vbh 340, 342; [c] S V.205; [c] Nett 101. See remark under paropariya. **-bhāvanā** cultivation of the (five, see above C[d]) moral qualities Vin I.294 (+ balabhāvanā); M III.298. **-saŋvara** restraint or subjugation of the senses D II.281; M I.269, 346; S I.54; A III.360; IV.99; V.113 sq., 136, 206; Nd[1] 483; Nett 27, 121 sq.; Vism 20 sq.

Indhana (nt.) [Vedic indhana, of **idh** or **indh** to kindle, cp. iddha[1]] firewood, fuel J IV.27 (adj. an° without fuel, aggi); V.447; ThA 256; VvA 335; Sdhp 608. Cp. idhuma.

Ibbha (adj.) [Ved. ibhya belonging to the servants] menial; a retainer, in the phrase **muṇḍakā samaṇakā ibbhā kaṇhā** (kiṇhā) **bandhupādâpaccā** D I.90 (v.l. SS imbha; T. kiṇhā, v. l. kaṇhā), 91, 103; M I.334 (kiṇhā, v.l. kaṇhā). Also at J VI.214. Expl[d.] by Bdhgh. as gahapatika at DA I.254, (also at J VI.215).

Iriṇa (nt.) [Vedic iriṇa, on etym. see Walde, *Lat. Wtb.* under rarus] barren soil, desert J VI.560 (= niroja C.). Cp. iriṇa.

Iriyati [fr. **īr** to set in motion, to stir, Sk. īrte, but pres. formation influenced by iriyā & also by Sk. iyarti of **ṛ** (see acchati & icchati[2]); cp. Caus. īrayati (= P. ireti), pp. īrṇa & īrita. See also issā] to move, to wander about, stir; fig. to move, behave, show a certain way of deportment M I.74, 75; S I.53 (dukkhaŋ aticca iriyati); IV.71; A III.451; V.41; Sn 947, 1063, 1097; Th I.276; J III.498 (= viharati); Nd[1] 431; Nd[2] 147 (= carati etc.); Vism 16; DA I.70.

Iriyanā (f.) [fr. iriyati] way of moving on, progress, Dhs 19, 82, 295, 380, 441, 716.

Iriyā (f.) [cp. from iriyati, BSk. īryā Divy 485] movement, posture, deportment M I.81; Sn 1038 (= cariyā vatti vihāro Nd[2] 148); It 31; Vism 145 (+ vutti pālana yapana).

-patha way of deportment; mode of movement; good behaviour. There are 4 iriyāpathas or postures, viz. walking, standing, sitting, lying down (see Ps II.225 & DA I.183). Cp. BSk. īryāpatha Divy 37. — Vin I.39; It.146 (°sampanna); M I.71 (chinn° a cripple); S V.78 (cattāro i.); Sn 385; Nd[1] 225, 226; Nd[2] s. v.; J I.22 (of a lion), 66, 506; Miln 17; Vism 104, 128, 290, 396; DhA I.9; IV.17; VvA 6; PvA 141; Sdhp 604.

Irubbeda the Rig-veda Dpvs V.62 (iruveda); Miln 178; DA I.247; SnA 447.

Illiyā (f.) [fr. illī, cp. Sk. *ilikā] = illī J V.259; VI.50.

Illī (f.) [cp. Vedic ilībiśa Np. of a demon] a sort of weapon, a short one-edged sword J V.259.

Illīyituŋ v. l. for allīyituŋ at J V.154.

Iva (indecl.) [Vedic iva & va] part. of comparison: like, as Dh 1, 2, 7, 8, 287, 334; J I.295; SnA 12 (= opamma-vacanaŋ). Elided to 'va, diaeretic-metathetic form **viya** (q. v.).

Isi [Vedic ṛṣi fr. **ṛṣ**. — Voc. ise Sn 1025; pl. npm. isayo, gen. isinaŋ S II.280 & isīnaŋ S I.192; etc. inst. isibhi Th I, 1065] — I. a holy man, one gifted with special powers of insight & inspiration, an anchoret, a Seer, Sage, Saint, "Master" D I.96 (kaṇho isi ahosi); S I.33, 35, 65, 128, 191, 192, 226 sq., 236 (ācāro isīnaŋ); II.280 (dhammo isinaŋ dhajo); A II.24, 51; Vin IV.15 = 22 (°bhāsito dhammo); It 123; Sn 284, 458, 979, 689, 691, 1008, 1025, 1043, 1044, 1116 (dev° divine Seer), 1126, Nd[2] 149 (isi-nāmakā ye keci isi-pabbajjaŋ pabbajitā ājīvikā nigaṇṭhā jaṭilā tāpasā); Dh 281; J I.17 (v.90: isayo n' atthi me samā of Buddha); J V.140 (°gaṇa), 266, 267 (isi Gotamo); Pv II.6[14] (= yama-niyam' ādīnaŋ esanatthena isayo PvA 98); II.13[3] (= jhān' ādīnaŋ guṇānaŋ esanatthena isi PvA 163); IV.7[3] (= asekkhānaŋ sīlakkhandh' ādīnaŋ esanatthena isiŋ PvA 265); Miln 19 (°vāta) 248 (°bhattika); DA I.266 (gen isino); Sdhp 200, 384. See also mahesi. — 2. (in *brahmanic* tradition) the ten (divinely) inspired singers or composers of the Vedic hymns (brāhmaṇānaŋ pubbakā isayo mantānaŋ kattāro pavattāro), whose names are given at D I.104 = 238 = A III.224 = IV.61 as follows: Aṭṭhaka, Vāmaka, Vāmadeva, Vessāmitta, Yamataggi (Yamadaggi), Angirasa, Bharadvāja, Vāseṭṭha, Kassapa, Bhagu.

-nisabha the first (lit. "bull") among Saints, Ep. of the Buddha Sn 698; Vv 16[7] (cp. VvA 82). **-pabbajjā** the (holy) life of an anchoret Vism 123; DhA I.105; IV.55; PvA 162. **-vāta** the wind of a Saint Miln 19; Vism 18. **-sattama** the 7th of the great Sages (i.e. Gotama Buddha, as 7th in the sequence of Vipassin, Sikhin, Vessabhu, Kakusandha, Koṇāgamana & Kassapa Buddhas) M I.386; S I.192; Sn 356; Th I, 1240 (= Bhagavā isi ca sattamo ca uttamaṭṭhena SnA 351); Vv 21[1] (= buddha-isinaŋ Vipassi-ādīnaŋ sattamo VvA 105).

Isikā (**isīkā**) (f.) [Sk. iṣīkā] a reed D I.77, cp. DA I.222; J VI.67 (isikā).

Isitta (nt.) [abstr. fr. isi] rishi-ship D I.104 (= isi-bhāva DA I.274).

Issati [denom. fr. issā, Av. arəṣyeiti to be jealous, Gr. ἔρατai to desire; connected also with Sk. arṣati fr. **ṛṣ** to flow, Lat. erro; & Sk. irasyati to be angry = Gr. Ἄρης God of war, ἄρη; Ags. eorsian to be angry] to bear ill-will, to be angry, to envy J III.7; ppr. med. issamānaka Sdhp 89, f. °ikā A II.203. — pp. **issita** (q. v.).

Issattha (nt. m.) [cp. Sk. iṣvastra nt. bow, fr. iṣu (= P. usu) an arrow + **as** to throw. Cp. P. issāsa. — Bdhgh. in a strange way dissects it as "usuñ ca satthañ cā ti vuttaŋ hoti" (i. e. isu arrow + sattha sword, knife) SnA 466] — I. (nt.) archery (as means of livelihood & occupation) M I.85; III.1; S I.100 (so read with v. l.; T. has issatta, C. expl[ns.] by usu-sippaŋ *K. S.* p. 318); Sn 617 (°ŋ upajīvati = āvudha jīvikaŋ SnA 466); J VI.81; Sdhp 390. — 2. (m.) an archer Miln 250, 305, 352, 418.

Issatthaka [issattha + ka] an archer Miln 419.

Issara [Vedic īśvara, from **īś** to have power, cp. also P. īsa] lord, ruler, master, chief A IV.90; Sn 552; J I.89 (°jana), 100, 283 (°bheri); IV.132 (°jana); Pv IV.6[1] (°mada); Miln 253 (an° without a ruler); DhsA 141; DA I.111; PvA 31 (gehassa issarā); Sdhp 348, 431. — 2. creative deity, Brahmā, D III.28; M II.222 = A I.173; Vism 598.

Issariya [fr. issara] rulership, mastership, supremacy, dominion (Syn. ādhipacca) D III.190; S I.43, 100 (°mada); V.342 (issariy-âdhipacca); A I.62 (°ādhipacca); II.205, 249; III.38; IV.263; Sn 112; Dh 73; Ud 18; Ps II.171, 176; J I.156; V.443; DhA II.73; VvA 126 (for ādhipacca) PvA 42, 117, 137 (for ādhipacca); Sdhp 418, 583.

Issariyatā (f.) [fr. issariya] mastership, lordship Sdhp 422.

Issā[1] (f.) [Sk. īrṣyā to Sk. irin forceful, irasyati to be angry, Lat. īra anger, Gr. Ἄρης God of war; Ags. eorsian to e angry. See also issati] jealousy, anger, envy, ill-will

D II.277 (°macchariya); III.44 (id.); M I.15; S II.260; A I.95, 105 (°mala), 299; II 203; IV.8 (°saññojana), 148, 349, 465; V.42 sq., 156, 310; Sn 110; J V.90 (°âvatiṇṇa); Pv II.37; Vv 15^5; Pug 19, 23; Vbh 380, 391; Dhs 1121, 1131, 1460; Vism 470 (def.); PvA 24, 46, 87; DhA II.76; Miln 155; Sdhp 313. 510.
-pakata overcome by envy, of an envious nature S II.260; Miln 155; PvA 31. See remarks under apakata & pakata.

Issā^2 (f.) [cp. Sk. ṛśya-mṛga] in **issammiga** (= issāmiga) J V.410, & **issāmiga** J V.431, a species of antelope, cp. J V.425 **issāsinga** the antlers of this antelope.

Issāyanā (& **Issāyitatta**) [abstr. formations fr. issā] = issā Pug 19, 23; Dhs 1121; Vism 470.

Issāsa [Sk. iṣvāsa, see issattha] an archer Vin IV.124; M III.1; A IV.423 (issāso vā issās' antevāsī vā); J II.87; IV.494; Miln 232; DA I.156.

Issāsin [Sk. iṣvāsa in meaning "bow" + in] an archer, lit. one having a bow J IV.494 (= issāsa C.).

Issita [pp. of **īrṣ** (see issati); Sk. īrṣita] being envied or scolded, giving offence or causing anger J V.44.

Issukin (adj.) [fr. issā, Sk. īrṣyu + ka + in] envious, jealous Vin II.89 (+ maccharin); D III 45, 246; M I.43, 96; S IV.241; A III.140, 335; IV.2; Dh 262; J III.259; Pv. II.3^4; Pug 19, 23; DhA III.389; PvA 174. See also an°.

Iha (indecl.) [Sk. iha; form iha is rare in Pāli, the usual form is idha (q. v.)] adv. of place "here" Sn 460.

I.

Īgha (?) [doubtful as to origin & etym. since only found in cpd. anīgha & abs. only in exegetical literature. If genuine, it should belong to **ṛgh** Sk. ṛghāyati to tremble, rage etc. See discussed under nigha^1] confusion, rage, badness SnA 590 (in expl^n of anigha). Usually as **an°** (or anigha), e. g. J III.343 (= niddukkha C.); V.343.

Īti & **Ītī** (f.) [Sk. īti, of doubtful origin] ill, calamity, plague, distress, often comb$^{b.}$ with & substituted for upaddava, cp. BSk. ītay' opadrava (attack of plague) Divy 119. — Sn 51; J I.27 (V.189); V.401 = upaddava; Nd^1 381; Nd^2 48, 636 (+ upaddava = santāpa); Miln 152, 247, 418. -anīti sound condition, health, safety A IV.238; Miln 323.

Ītika (adj.) [fr. īti] connected or affected with ill or harm, only in neg. **an°**.

Ītiha a doublet of itiha, only found in neg. **an°**.

Īdisa (adj.) [Sk. īdṛś, I + **dṛś**, lit. so-looking] such like, such DhsA 400 (f. °ī); PvA 50, (id.) 51.

Īriṇa (nt.) [= iriṇa, q. v. & cp. Sk. īriṇa] barren soil, desert D I.248; A V.156 sq.; J V.70 (= sukkha-kantāra C.); VI.560; VvA 334.

Īrita [pp. of īreti, Caus. of **īr**, see iriyati] — 1. set in motion, stirred, moved, shaken Vv 39^4 (vāt'erita moved by the wind); J I.32 (id.); Vv 64^{20} (haday'erita); Pv II.12^3 (malut'erita); PvA 156 (has erita for ī°); VvA 177 (= calita). — 2. uttered, proclaimed, said Dāvs V.12.

Īsa [fr. **īś** to have power, perf. īśe = Goth. aih; cp. Sk. īśvara = P. issara, & BSk. īśa, e. g. Jtm 31^{81}] lord, owner, ruler J IV.209 (of a black lion = kāḷa-sīha C.); VvA 168. f. īsī see mahesī a chief queen. Cp. also **mahesakkha**.

Īsaka [dimin. of īsā] a pole J II.152; VI.456 (°agga the top of a pole).

Īsakaŋ (adv.) [nt. of īsaka] a little, slightly, easily M I. 450; J I.77; VI.456; DA I.252, 310; VvA 36; Vism 136, 137, 231, īsakam pi even a little Vism 106; Sdhp 586.

Īsā (f.) [Vedic īṣā] the pole of a plough or of a carriage S I.104 (naṅgal' īsā read with v. l. for naṅgala-sīsā T.), 172, 224 (°mukha): A IV.191 (rath°); Sn 77; J I.203 (°mukha); IV.209; Ud 42; Miln 27; SnA 146; VvA 269 (°mūlaŋ = rathassa uro).
-danta having teeth (tusks) as long as a plough-pole (of an elephant) Vin I.352; M I.414; Vv 20^9 = 43^9 (= ratha-īsā-sadisa-danto); J VI.490 = 515.

Īsāka (adj.) [fr. īsā] having a pole (said of a carriage) J VI.252.

Īhati [Vedic **īh**, cp. Av. īzā ardour, eagerness, āziš greed] to endeavour, attempt, strive after Vin III.268 (Bdhgh.) J VI.518 (cp. Kern, *Toev.* p. 112); DA I.139; VvA 35.

Īhā (f.) [fr. **īh**] exertion, endeavour, activity, only in adj. nir-īha void of activity Miln 413.

U.

U the sound or syllable u, expl$^{d.}$ by Bdhgh at Vism 495 as expressing origin (= ud).

Ukkaŋsa [fr. ud + **kṛṣ** see ukkassati] exaltation, excellence, superiority (opp. avakkaŋsa) D I.54 (ukkaŋs-âvakkaŋsa = hāyana-vaḍḍhana DA I.165); M I.518; Vism 563 (id.); VvA 146 (°gata excellent), 335 (instr. ukkaŋsena par excellence, exceedingly) PvA 228 (°vasena, with ref. to devatās; v. l. SS okk°).

Ukkaŋsaka (adj.) [fr. ukkaŋsa] raising, exalting (oneself), extolling M I.19 (att°; opp. para-vambhin); J II.152. Cp. **sāmukkaŋsika.**

Ukkaŋsati [ud + **kṛṣ**, karsati, lit draw or up, raise] to exalt, praise M I.498; J IV.108. — pp. **ukkaṭṭha.** — **ukkaŋseti** in same meaning M I.402 sq. (attānaŋ u. paraŋ vambheti); A II.27; Fd^2 141.

Ukkaŋsanā (f.) [abstr. of ukkaŋsati] raising, extolling, exaltation, in att° self-exaltation, self-praise M I.402 (opp. para-vambhanā); Nd^2 505 (id.).

Ukkaṭṭha (adj.) [pp. of ukkaŋsati] — 1. exalted, high, prominent, glorious, excellent, most freq. opp. to **hīna**, in phrase hīna-m-ukkaṭṭha-majjhime Vin IV.7; J I.20 (V.129), 22 (V.143); III.218 (= uttama C.). In other comb$^{n.}$ at Vism 64 (u. majjhima mudu referring to the 3 grades of the Dhutangas); SnA 160 (dvipadā sabba sattānaŋ ukkaṭṭhā); VvA 105 (superl. ukkaṭṭhatama with ref. to Gotama as the most exalted of the 7 Rishis); Sdhp 506 (opp. lāmaka). — 2. large, comprehensive, great, in ukkaṭṭho patto a bowl of great capacity (as diff. from majjhima & omaka p.) Vin IV.243 (= uk. nāma patto aḍḍhālhak' odanaŋ gaṇhāti catu-bhāgaŋ khādanaŋ vā tadūpiyaŋ vā byañjanaŋ). — 3. detailed, exhaustive, specialised Vism 37 (ati-ukkaṭṭha-desanā); also in phrase °vasena in detail SnA 181. — 4. arrogant, insolent J v. 16. — 5. used as nom at J I.387 in meaning „battle, conflict". — an° Vism 64 (°cīvara).

-niddesa exhaustive exposition, special designation, term par excellence DhsA 70; VvA 231; PvA 7. -pariccheda comprehensive connotation SnA 229, 231, 376.

Ukkaṭṭhatā (f.) [abstr. fr. ukkaṭṭha] superiority, eminence, exalted state J IV.303 (opp. hīnatā).

Ukkaṭṭhita [for ukkaṭhita, ud + pp. of **kvath,** see kaṭhati & kuthati] boiled up, boiling, seething A III.231 & 234 (udapatto agginā santatto ukkaṭṭhito, v. l. ukkuṭṭhito); J IV.118 (v. l. pakkudhita = pakkuṭhita, as gloss).

Ukkaṇṭhati [fr. ud + **kaṇṭh** in secondary meaning of kaṇṭha neck, lit. to stretch one's neck for anything; i. e. long for, be hungry after etc.] to long for, to be dissatisfied, to fret J I.386 (°māna); III.143 (°itvā); IV.3, 160; V.10 (anukkhaṇṭhanto); DhsA 407; PvA 162 (mā ukkaṇṭhi, v. l. ukkaṇhi, so read for T. mā khuṇḍali). — pp. ukkaṇṭhita (q. v.). Cp. pari°.

Ukkaṇṭhanā (f.) [fr. ukkaṇṭhati] emotion, commotion D II.239.

Ukkaṇṭhā (f.) [fr. ukkaṇṭh°] longing, desire; distress, regret Nett 88; PvA 55 (spelt kkh), 60, 145, 152.

Ukkaṇṭhi (f.) [fr. ukkaṇṭh°] longing, dissatisfaction ThA 239 (= arati).

Ukkaṇṭhikā (f.) [abstr. fr. ukkaṇṭhita] = ukkaṇṭhi, i. e. longing, state of distress, pain J III.643.

Ukkaṇṭhita [pp. of ukkaṇṭhati] dissatisfied, regretting, longing, fretting J I.196; II.92, 115; III.185; Miln 281; DhA IV.66, 225; PvA 13 (an°), 55, 187.

Ukkaṇṇa (adj.) [ud + kaṇṇa] having the ears erect (?) J VI.559.

Ukkaṇṇaka (ad.) [ut + kaṇṇa + ka lit. "with ears out" or is it ukkaṇḍaka?] a certain disease (? mange) of jackals, S II.230, 271; S. A. 'the fur falls off from the whole body'.

Ukkantati [ud + kantati] to cut out, tear out, skin Vin I.217 (°itva); J I.164; IV.210 (v. l. for okk°); V.10 (ger. ukkacca); Pv III.9[4] (ukkantvā, v. l. BB ukkacca); PvA 210 (v. l. SS ni°), 211 (= chinditvā).

Ukkapiṇḍaka [etymology unknown] only in pl.; vermin, Vin I 211 = 239. See comment at *Vin. Texts* II.70.

Ukkantikaŋ (nt. adv.), in jhān° & kasiṇ°, after the method of stepping away from or skipping Vism 374.

Ukkamati (or okk° which is v. l. at all passages quoted) [ud + kamati from **kram**] to step aside, step out from (w. abl.), depart from A III.301 (maggā); J III.531; IV. 101 (maggā); Ud 13 (id.); DA I.185 (id.). Caus. **ukkāmeti**; Caus. II. ukkamāpeti J II.3.

Ukkamana (nt.) [fr. ukkamati] stepping away from Vism 374.

Ukkala in phrase ukkala-vassa-bhañña S III.73 = A II.31 = Kvu 141 is trsld. as "the folk of Ukkala, Lenten speakers of old" (see *Kvu trsl.* 95 with n. 2). Another interpretation is ukkalāvassa°, i. e. ukkalā + avassa° [*avaśya°], one who speaks of, or like, a porter (ukkala = Sk utkala porter, one who carries a load) and bondsman M III.78 reads Okkalā (v. l. Ukkalā)-Vassa-Bhaññā, all as N. pr.

Ukkalāpa see **uklāpa.**

Ukkalissati [= ukkilissati? ud + kilissati] to become depraved, to revoke (?) Miln 143.

Ukkā (f.) [Vedic ulkā & ulkuṣī, cp. Gr. ἔλλαξ (= λαμπρῶς torch Hesychius), Fελχάνος (= Volcanus); Lat. Volcanus, Oir. Olcān, Idg. *u̯lq to be fiery] 1. firebrand, glow of fire, torch D I.49, 108; S II.264; Th 2, 488 (°ūpama); J I.34 (dhamm-okkā); II.401; IV.291; V.322; Vism 428; ThA 287; DA I.148; DhA I.42, 205; PvA 154. Esp. as tiṇ° firebrand of dry grass M I.128, 365; Nd[2] 40[1c]; DhA I.126; Sdhp 573. — 2. a furnace or forge of a smith A I.310, 257; J VI.437; see also below °mukha. — 3. a meteor: see below °pāta.

-dhāra a torch-bearer Sn 335; It 108; Miln 1. -pāta "falling of a firebrand", a meteor D I.10 (= ākāsato ukkānaŋ patanaŋ DA I.95); J I.374; VI.476; Miln 178. -mukha the opening or receiver of a furnace, a goldsmith's smelting pot A I.257; J VI.217 (= kammār'uddhana C.), 574; Sn 686; DhA II.250.

Ukkācanā (f.) [fr. ukkāceti, ud + ***kāc,** see ukkācita] enlightening, clearing up, instruction Vbh 352 (in def. of lapanā, v. l. °kāpanā). *Note* Kern, *Toev.* s. v. compares Vism p. 115 & Sk. uddīpana in same sense. Def. at Vism 27 (= uddīpanā).

Ukkācita [pp. either to ***kāc** to shine or to kāceti denom. fr. kāca[1]] enlightened, made bright (fig.) or cleaned, cleared up A I.72, 286 (°vinīta parisā enlightened & trained).

Ukkāceti [according to Morris *J P T S.* 1884, 112 a denom. fr. kāca[2] a carrying pole, although the idea of a bucket is somewhat removed from that of a pole] to bale out water, to empty by means of buckets J II.70 (v. l. ussiñcati).

Ukkāmeti [Caus. of ukkamati] to cause to step aside J VI.11.

Ukkāra [fr. ud + **kṛ** "do out"] dung, excrement J IV.485, otherwise only in cpd. **ukkāra-bhūmi** dung-hill J I.5, 146 (so read for ukkar°), II.40; III.16, 75, 377; IV.72, 305; Vism 196 (°ūpama kuṇapa); DhA III.208. Cp. **uccāra.**

Ukkāsikā (f.?) [doubtful] at Vin II.106 is not clear. Vin Texts III.68 leave it untranslated. Bdhgh's expln. is vaṭṭavaṭṭi (paṭṭa°? a leaf? Cp. S III.141), prob. = vaṭṭi (Sk. varti a kind of pad). See details given by Morris *J P T S.* 1887, 113, who trsls. "rubber, a kind of pad or roll of cotton with which the delicate bather could rub himself without too much friction".

Ukkāsati [ud + kāsati of **kas** to cough] to "ahem"! to cough, to clear one's throat Vin II.222; IV.16; M II.4; A V.65; aor. ukkāsi J I.161, 217. — pp. **ukkāsita.**

Ukkāsita [pp. of ukkāsati] coughed, clearing one's throat, coughed out, hawking D I.89; Bu I.52 (+ khipita) — °sadda the noise of clearing the throat D I.50; J I.119; DhA I.250 (+ khipita°).

Ukkiṇṇa [pp. of ud + **kṛ** dig[2]] dug up or out D I.105; J IV.106; Miln 330; DA I.274 (= khāta).

Ukkiledeti [Caus. of ud + **klid,** see kilijjati] to take the dirt out, to clean out DA I.255 (dosaŋ); SnA 274 (rāgaŋ; v. l. BB. uggileti).

Ukkujja (adj.) [ud + kujja] set up, upright, opp. either nikkujja or avakujja A I.131; S V.89 (ukkujj'āvakujja); Pug 32 (= uparimukho ṭhapito C. 214).

Ukkujjati (°eti) [Denom. fr. ukkujja] to bend up, turn up, set upright Vin I.181; II.126 (pattaŋ), 269 (bhikkhuŋ); mostly in phrase nikkujjitaŋ ukkujjeyya "(like) one might raise up one who has fallen" D I.85, 110; II.132, 152; Sn p. 15 (= uparimukhaŋ karoti DA I.228 = SnA 155).

Ukkujjana (nt.) [fr. ukkujjati] raising up, setting up again Vin II.126 (patt°).

Ukkuṭika [fr. ud + *kuṭ = *kuñc, as in kuṭila & kuñcita; lit. "bending up". The BSk. form is ukkuṭuka, e. g. Av. S I.315] a special manner of squatting. The soles of the feet are firmly on the ground, the man sinks down, the

heels slightly rising as he does so, until the thighs rest on the calves, and the hams are about six inches or more from the ground. Then with elbows on knees he balances himself. Few Europeans can adopt this posture, & none (save miners) can maintain it with comfort, as the calf muscles upset the balance. Indians find it easy, & when the palms of the hands are also held together upwards, it indicates submission. See *Dial.* I.231 n. 4. — Vin I.45 (°ŋ nisīdati); III.228; A I.296; II.206; Pug 55; Vism 62, 104, 105 (quot. fr. Papañca Sūdanī) 426; DhA I.201, 217; II.61 (as posture of humility); III.195; IV.223.
-padhāna [in BSk. distorted to utkuṭuka-prahāṇa Divy 339 = Dh 141] exertion when squatting (an ascetic habit) D I 167; M I.78, 515; A I.296; II.206; J I.493; III.235; IV.299; Dh 141 (= ukkuṭika-bhāvena āraddha-viriyo DhA III.78).

Ukkuṭṭhi (f.) [fr. ud + **kruś**, cp. ***kruñc** as in P. kuñca & Sk. krośati] shouting out, acclamation J II.367; VI.41; Bu I.35; Miln 21; Vism 245; DhA II.43; VvA 132 (°sadda).

Ukkusa [see ukkuṭṭhi & cp. BSk. utkrośa watchman (?) Divy 453] an osprey J IV.291 (°rājā), 392.

Ukkūla (adj.) [ud + kūla] sloping up, steep, high (opp. vikkūla) A I.35 sq.; Vism 153 (nadī); SnA 42. Cp. utkūla-nikūla-sama Lal. V. 340.

Ukkoṭana (nt.) [fr. ud + ***kuṭ** to be crooked or to deceive, cp. kujja & kuṭila crooked] crookedness, perverting justice, taking bribes to get people into unlawful possessions (Bdhgh.) D I.5; III.176; S V.473; A II.209, V.206; DA I.79 = Pug A 240 ("assāmike sāmike kātuŋ lañcagahanaŋ").

Ukkoṭanaka (adj.) [fr. ukkoṭana] belonging to the perversion of justice Vin II.94.

Ukkoṭeti [denom. fr. *ukkoṭ-ana] to disturb what is settled, to open up again a legal question that has been adjudged, Vin II.94, 303; IV.126; J II.387; DA I.5.

Ukkhali (°lī) (f.) [der. fr. Vedic ukha & ukhā pot, boiler; related to Lat. aulla (fr. *auxla); Goth. auhns oven] a pot in which to boil rice (& other food) J I.68, 235; V.389, 471; Pug 33; Vism 346 (°mukhavaṭṭi), 356 (°kapāla, in comp.); DhA I.136; II.5; III.371; IV.130; Pug A 231; VvA 100. Cp. next.

Ukkhalikā (f.) = **ukkhali**. Th 2, 23 (= bhatta-pacana-bhājanaŋ ThA 29); DhA IV.98 (°kāla); DhsA 376.

Ukkhā (?) [can it be compared with Vedic ukṣan ?] in ukkhā-sataŋ dānaŋ, given at various times of the day (meaning = ἑκατόμβη ?) S II.264 (v. l. ukkā). Or is it to be read ukhāsataŋ d. i. e. consisting of 100 pots (of rice = mahā-danaŋ ?). S A: paṇītabhojana-bharitānaŋ mahā-ukkhalīnaŋ sataŋ dānaŋ. Cp. ukhā cooking vessel ThA 71 (Ap. V.38). Kern, *Toev.* under ukkhā trsl. "zeker muntstuck", i. e. kind of gift.

Ukkhita [pp. of **ukṣ** sprinkle] besmeared, besprinkled J IV.331 (ruhir°, so read for °rakkhita). Cp. **okkhita**.

Ukkhitta [pp. of ukkhipati] taken up, lifted up, t.t. of the canon law "suspended" Vin IV.218; J III.487.
-°āsika with drawn sword M I.377; S IV.173; J I.393; DhsA 329; Vism 230 (vadhaka), 479. **-paligha** having the obstacles removed M I.139; A III.84; Dh 398 = Sn 622 (= ayijjā-palighassa ukkhittatāya u. SnA 467 = DhA IV.161). — **sira** with uplifted head Vism 162.

Ukkhittaka (adj.-n.) [fr. ukkhitta] a bhikkhu who has been suspended Vin I.97, 121; II.61, 173, 213.

Ukkhipati [ut + khipati, **kṣip**]. To hold up, to take up J I.213; IV.391; VI.350; Vism 4 (satthaŋ); PvA 265. At t. t. of canon law, to suspend (a bhikkhu for breach of rules) Vin IV.309; Pug 33. **-ukkhipiyati** to be suspended Vin II.61. Caus. II. **ukkhipāpeti** to cause to be supported J I.52; II.15, 38; III.285, 436. — pp. **ukkhitta**, ger. ukkhipitvā as adv. "upright" Vism 126.

Ukkhipana (nt.) [fr. ud + **kṣip**] 1. pushing upwards J I.163. — 2. throwing up, sneering Vism 29 (vācāya).

Ukkheṭita [pp. of ud + **kheṭ** or ***kheḷ**, see kheḷa] spit out, thrown off, in phrase moho (rāgo etc) catto vanto mutto pahīno paṭinissaṭṭho u. Vin III.97 = IV.27.

Ukkhepa (adj.-n.) [fr. ud + **kṣip**] (adj.) throwing away DhA IV.59 (°dāya a throw-away donation, tip). — (m.) lifting up raising J I.394 (cel°); VI.508; DA I.273; **dur°** hard to lift or raise Sdhp 347.

Ukkhepaka (adj.) [fr. ukkhepa] throwing (up); °ŋ (acc.) in the manner of throwing Vin II.214 = IV.195 (piṇḍ°).

Ukkhepana (nt.) [fr. ud + **kṣip**] suspension J III.487.

Ukkhepanā (f.) [= last] throwing up, provocation, sneering Vbh 352 = Vism 23, expl^d. at p. 29.

Ukkhepaniya (adj.) [ukkhepana + iya, cp. BSk. utkṣepanīyaŋ karma Divy 329] referring to the suspension (of a bhikkhu), **°kamma** act or resolution of suspension Vin I.49, 53, 98, 143, 168; II.27, 226, 230, 298: A I.99.

Uklāpa (ukkalāpa) (adj.) [cp. Sk. ut-kalāpayati to let go] — 1. deserted J II.275 (ukkalāpa T.; vv. ll. uklāpa & ullāpa). — 2. dirtied, soiled Vin II.154, 208, 222; Vism 128; DhA III.168 (ukkalāpa).

Ugga[1] (adj.) [Vedic ugra, from ukṣati, weak base of **vakṣ** as in vakṣana, vakṣayati = Gr. ἀϝέξω, Goth. wahsjan "to wax", also Lat. augeo & P. oja] mighty, huge, strong, fierce, grave, m. a mighty or great person, noble lord D I 103; S I.51 = VvA 116 (uggateja "the fiery heat"); J IV.496; V.452 (°teja); VI.490 (+ rājaputtā, expl^d. with etymologising effort as uggatā paññatā by C.); Miln 331; DhA II.57 (°tapa); Sdhp 286 (°daṇḍa), 304 (id.). — Cp. sam°. As Np. at Vism 233 & J I.94.
-putta a nobleman, mighty lord S I.185 ("high born warrior" trsl.); J VI.353 (= amacca-putta C.); Th I, 1210.

Ugga[2] = uggamana, in aruṇ-ugga sunrise Vin II.272.

Uggacchati [ud + **gam**] to rise, get up out of (lit. & fig.) Th I, 181; aruṇe uggacchante at sunrise VvA 75; Pv IV.8; Vism 43, ger. **uggañchitvāna** Miln 376. — pp. uggata (q. v.).

Uggajjati [ud + gajjati] to shout out Nd[1] 172.

Uggaṇhāti [ud + **gṛh**, see ganhāti] to take up, acquire, learn [cp. BSk. udgṛhṇāti in same sense, e. g. Divy 18, 77 etc.] Sn 912 (uggahananta = uggahaṇanti = uggaṇhanti SnA 561); imper. **uggaṇha** J II.30 (sippaŋ) & **uggaṇhāhi** Miln 10 (mantāni); ger. **uggayha** Sn 832, 845; Nd[1] 173. — Caus. **uggaheti** in same meaning Sdhp 520; aor. **uggahesi** Pv III.5[4] (nakkhatta-yogan = akari PvA 198); ger. **uggahetvā** J V.282, VvA 98 (vipassanā-kammaṭṭhānaŋ); infin. **uggahetuŋ** VvA 138 (sippaŋ to study a craft). — Caus. II. **uggaṇhāpeti** to instruct J V.217; VI.353. — pp. **uggahita** (q. v.). See also **uggahāyati**. — A peculiar ppr. med. is **uggāhamāna** going or wanting to learn DA I 32 (cp. **uggāhaka**).

Uggata [pp. of uggacchati] come out, risen; high, lofty, exalted J IV.213 (suriya), 296 (°atta), 490; V.244; Pv IV.1[4] (°atta one who has risen = uggata-sabbhāva samiddha PvA 220); VvA 217 (°mānasa); DA I.248; PvA 68 (°phāsuka with ribs come out or showing, i. e. emaciated, for upphāsulika). Cp. acc°.

Uggatta in all Pv. readings is to be read **uttatta°**, thus at Pv III.3[2]; PvA 10, 188.

Uggaṭṭhana at J VI.590 means a kind of ornament or trinket, it should prob. be read ugghaṭṭana [fr. ghaṭṭeti] lit. "tinkling", i. e. a bangle.

Uggama [fr. ud + **gam**; Sk. udgama] rising up Sdhp 594.

Uggamana (°na) (nt.) [fr. ud + **gam**] going up, rising; rise (of sun & stars) D I.10, 240; S II.268 (suriy°); J IV.321 (an°), 388; Pv II 9[41] (suriy°); DA I.95 (= udayana); DhA I.165 (aruṇ°); II.6 (id.); VvA 326 (oggaman°); PvA 109 (aruṇ°). Cp. ugga[2] & uggama.

Uggaha (adj.) (—°) [fr. ud + **gṛh**, see gaṇhāti] — 1. taking up, acquiring, learning Vism 96 (ācariy°), 99 (°paripucchā); 277 (kananaṭṭhānassa). — 2. noticing, taking notice, perception (as opp. to manasikāra) Vism 125, 241 sq. neg. an° Sn 912 (= gaṇhāti Nd[1] 330). Cp. **dhanuggaha**.

Uggahaṇa (nt.) [fr. uggaṇhāti] learning, taking up, studying PvA 3 (sipp°). As **uggaṇhana** at Vism 277.

Uggahāyati [poetic form of uggaheti (see uggaṇhāti), but according to Kern, *Toev.* s. v. representing Ved. udgṛbhāyati] to take hold of, to take up Sn 791 (= gaṇhāti Nd[1] 91). — ger. uggahāya Sn 837.

Uggahita [pp. of uggaṇhāti] taken up, taken, acquired Vin I.212; J III.168 (°sippa, adj.), 325; IV.220; VI 76; Vism 241. The metric form is **uggahīta** at Sn 795, 833, 1098; Nd[1] 175 = Nd[2] 152 (= gahita parāmaṭṭha).

Uggahetar [n. ag. to ugganhāti, Caus. uggaheti] one who takes up, acquires or learns A IV.196.

Uggāra [ud + **gṛ** or ***gḷ** to swallow, see gala & gilati; lit. to swallow up] spitting out, vomiting, ejection Vism 54; DA I.41; KhA 61.

Uggāhaka (adj.-n.) [fr. ud + **gṛh**, see uggaṇhāti] one who is eager to learn J V.148 [cp. M Vastu III.373 ogrāhaka in same context].

Uggāhamāna see uggaṇhāti.

Uggirati[1] [Sk. udgirati, ud + **gṛ**[2]; but BSk. udgirati in meaning to sing, chant, utter, formation fr. **gṛ**[2] instead of **gṛ**, pres. gṛṇāti; in giraṃ udgirati Jtm 31[26]. — The by-form oggirati is uggilati with interchange of ḷ and ṛ, roots *gṛ & *gḷ, see gala & gilati] to vomit up ("swallow up") to spit out Ud 14 (uggiritvāna); DA I.41 (uggāraṃ uggiranto). Cp. BSk. prodgīrṇa cast out Divy 589.

Uggirati[2] [cp. Sk. udgurate, ud + **gur**] to lift up, carry Vin IV.147 = DhA III 50 (talasattikaṃ expl[d]. by uccāreti); J I.150 (āvudhāni); VI.460, 472. Cp. sam°.

Uggilati = uggirati[1], i. e. to spit out (opp. ogilati) M I.393; S IV.323; J III 529; Miln 5; PvA 283.

Uggīva (nt.) [ud + gīva] a neckband to hold a basket hanging down J VI.562 (uggīvañ c'āpi aṃsato = aṃsakūṭe pacchi-lagganakaṃ C.).

Ugghaṃseti [ud + **ghṛṣ**, see ghaṃsati[1]] to rub Vin II.106. — pp. **ugghaṭṭha** (q. v.).

Ugghaṭita (adj.) [pp. of ud + ghaṭati; cp. BSk. udghaṭaka skilled Divy 3, 26 and phrase at M Vastu III.260 udghaṭitajña] striving, exerting oneself; keen, eager in cpd. °ññū of quick understanding A II.135; Pug 41; Nett 7—9, 125; DA I.291.

Ugghaṭeti [ud + ghaṭati] to open, reveal (? so Hardy in Index to Nett) Nett 9; **ugghaṭiyati** & **ugghaṭanā** ibid.

Ugghaṭṭa (Ugghaṭṭha?) [should be pp. of ugghaṃsati = Sk. udghṛṣṭa, see ghaṃsati[1], but taken by Bdhgh. either as pp. of or an adj. der. fr. ghaṭṭ, see ghaṭṭeti] knocked, crushed, rubbed against, only in phrase **ughaṭṭa-pāda** foot-sore Sn 980 (= maggakkamaṇena ghaṭṭa-pādatala etc. SnA 582); J IV.20 (ṭṭh; expl[d]. by unha-vālukāya ghaṭṭapāda); V.69 (= raj'okiṇṇa-pāda C. not to the point).

Uggharati [ud + **kṣar**] to ooze Th 1, 394 = DhA III.117.

Ugghaṭana (nt.?) [fr. ugghāṭeti] that which can be removed, in °kiṭikā a curtain to be drawn aside Vin II.153 (cp. Vin Texts III.174, 176). Ch. s. v. gives "rope & bucket of a well" as meaning (kavāṭaṃ anugghāṭeti). Cp. ugghāṭana.

Ugghāṭita [pp. of ugghāṭeti] opened Miln 55; DhA I.134.

Ugghāṭeti [for ugghaṭṭeti, ud + ghaṭṭ but BSk. udghāṭayati Divy 130] to remove, take away, unfasten, abolish, put an end to Vin II.148 (tālāni), 208 (ghaṭikaṃ); IV.37; J II.31; VI.68; Miln 140 (bhava-paṭisandhiṃ), 371; Vism 374. — Caus. II. ugghāṭāpeti to have opened J V.381.

Ugghāta [ud + ghāta] shaking, jolting; jolt, jerk Vin II. 276 (yān°); J VI.253 (an°); DhA III.283 (yān°).

Ugghāti (f.) [fr. ud + ghāta] — 1. shaking, shock VvA 36. — 2. striking, conquering; victory, comb[d]. with **nighāti** Sn 828; Nd[1] 167; SnA 541; Nett 110 (T. reads ugghāta°).

Ugghātita [pp. of ugghāteti, denom. fr. udghāta] struck, killed A III.68.

Ugghosanā (f.) [abstr. fr. ugghoseti, cp. ghosanā] proclamation DA I.310.

Ugghoseti [ud + ghoseti] to shout out, announce, proclaim J I.75; DhA II.94; PvA 127.

Ucca (adj.) [For udya, adj. formation from prep. ud above, up] high (opp. avaca low) D I.194; M II.213; A V.82 (°ṭhāniyaṃ nīce ṭhāne ṭhapeti puts on a low place which ought to be placed high); Pv IV.7[4] (uccaṃ paggayha lifting high up = uccataraṃ katvā PvA 265); Pug 52, 58; DA I.135; PvA 176.

-**âvaca** high and low, various, manifold Vin I.70, 203; J IV.115, 363 (= mahaggha-samaggha C. p. 366); Sn 703, 714, 792, 959; Dh 83; Nd[1] 93, 467; Vv 12[1] (= vividha VvA 60); 31[1]. -**kulīnatā** high birth A III.48 (cp. uccā°).

Uccaka (adj.) [fr. ucca] high Vin II.149 (āsandikā a kind of high chair).

Uccatta (nt.) [fr. ucca = Sk. uccatvaṃ] height J III.318.

Uccaya [fr. ud + **ci**, see cināti; Sk. uccaya] heaping up, heap, pile, accumulation Dh 115, 191, 192; Vv 47[11]; 82[1] (= cetiya VvA 321); KhA III.5, 9; DhsA 41 (pāpassa). -**siluccaya** a mountain Th 1, 692; J I.29 (V.209); VI.272, 278; Dāvs V.63.

Uccā (°—) (adv.) [cp. Sk. uccā, instr. sg. of uccaṃ, cp. paścā behind, as well as uccaiḥ instr. pl. — In BSk. we find ucca° (uccakulīna Av. Ś III.117) as well as uccaṃ (uccaṃgama Divy 476). It is in all cases restricted to cpds.] high (lit. & fig.), raised, in foll. cpds.

-**kaṇerukā** a tall female elephant M I.178. -**kāḷārikā** id. M I.178 (v. l. °kāḷārikā to be preferred). -**kula** a high, noble family Pv III.1[10] (= uccā khattiya-kul-âdino PvA 176). -**kulīnatā** birth in a high-class family, high rank M III.37; VvA 32. -**sadda** a loud noise D I.143, 178; A III.30. -**sayana** a high bed (+ mahāsayana) Vin I. 192; D I.5, 7; cp. DA I.78.

Uccāra [Ud + **car**] discharge, excrement, faeces Vin III.36 (°ṃ gacchati to go to stool); IV.265, 266 (uccāro nāma gūtho vuccati); DhA II.56 (°karaṇa defecation); uccāra-passāva faeces & urine D I.70; M I.83; J I.5; II.19.

Uccāraṇā (f.) [fr. uccāreti] lifting up, raising Vin III.121.

Uccārita [pp. of uccāreti] — 1. uttered, let out PvA 280 (akkharāni). — 2. lifted, raised ThA 255.

Uccāreti [ud + cāreti, Caus. of **car**] to lift up, raise aloft Vin III.81; IV.147 = DhA III.50; M I.135. — pp. uccārita (q. v.).

Uccālinga [etym.?] a maw-worm Vin III.38, 112; J II.146.

Uccināti [ud + cināti] to select, choose, search, gather, pick out or up Vin I.73; II.285 (aor. uccini); J IV.9; Pv III.2^4 (nantake = gavesana-vasena gahetvāna PvA 185); Dpvs IV.2.

Ucchanga [Sk. utsanga, ts > cch like Sk. utsahate > BSk. ucchahate see ussahati] the hip, the lap Vin I.225; M I. 366; A I.130 (°pañña); J I.5, 308; II.412; III.22; IV.38, 151; Pug 31; Vism 279; DhA II.72.

Ucchādana (nt.) [ut + **sād,** Caus. of **sad,** sīdati, cp. ussada] rubbing the limbs, anointing the body with perfumes shampooing D I.7, 76; at the latter passage in comb^n. anicc°-**dhamma,** of the body, meaning "erosion, decay", and comb^d. with **parimaddana** abrasion (see about detail of meaning *Dial.* I.87); thus in same formula at M I. 500; S IV.83; J I.146 & passim; A I.62; II.70 (+ nahāpana); IV.54, 386; It 111; Th 2, 89 (nahāpan°); Miln 241 (°parimaddana) 315 (+ nahāpana); DA I.88.

Ucchādeti [fr. ut + **sād,** see ucchādana] to rub the body with perfumes J VI.298; Miln 241 (+ parimaddati nahāpeti); DA I.88.

Ucchiṭṭha [pp. of ud + **śiṣ**] left, left over, rejected, thrown out; impure, vile Vin II.115 (°odakaŋ); IV.266 (id.); J II.83 (bhattaŋ ucchiṭṭhaŋ akatvā), 126 (°nadī impure; also itthi outcast), 363; IV.386 (°ŋ piṇḍaŋ), 388; VI.508; Miln 315; DhA I.52; II.85; III.208; PvA 80 (= chaḍḍita), 173 (°bhattaŋ). At J IV.433 read ucch° for **uccitṭha.** -an° not touched or thrown away (of food) J III.257; DhA II.3. — See also **uttiṭṭha** & **ucchepaka.**

Ucchiṭṭhaka (fr. ucchiṭṭha) = ucchiṭṭha J IV.386; VI.63, 509.

Ucchindati [ud + **chid,** see chindati] to break up, destroy, annihilate S V.432 (bhavataṇhaŋ); A IV.17 (fut ucchecchāmi to be read with v. l. for T. ucchejjissāmi); Sn 2 (pret. udacchida), 208 (ger. ucchijja); J V.383; Dh 285. — Pass. ucchijjati to be destroyed or annihilated, to cease to exist S IV.309; J V.242, 467; Miln 192; PvA 63, 130 (= na pavattati), 253 (= natthi). — pp. **ucchinna** (q. v.).

Ucchinna [pp. of ucchindati] broken up, destroyed S III. 10; A V.32; Sn 746. Cp. sam°.

Ucchu [Sk. cp. Vedic Np. Ikṣvāku fr. ikṣu] sugar-cane Vin IV.35; A III.76; IV.279; Miln 46; DhA IV.199 (°ūnaŋ yanta sugar-cane mill), PvA 257, 260; VvA 124.

-**agga** (ucch°) top of s. c. Vism 172. -**khaṇḍikā** a bit of sugar-cane Vv 33^{26}. -**khādana** eating s.c. Vism 70. -**khetta** sugar-cane field J I.339; VvA 256. -**gaṇṭhikā** a kind of sugar-cane, Batatas Paniculata J I.339; VI.114 (so read for °ghaṭika). -**pāla** watchman of s.-c. VvA 256. -**pīḷana,** cane-pressing, Asl. 274. -**puṭa** sugar-cane basket J IV.363. -**bīja** seed of s.-c. A I.32; V.213. -**yantra** a sugar-mill J I.339. -**rasa** s.-c. juice Vin I.246; Vism 489; VvA 180. -**vāta,** Asl. 274. -**sālā,** Asl. 274.

Uccheda [fr. ud + **chid, chind,** see ucchindati & cp. cheda] breaking up, disintegration, perishing (of the soul) Vin III.2 (either after this life, or after kāmadeva life, or after brahmadeva life) D I.34, 55; S IV.323; Nd^1 324; Miln 413; Nett 95, 112, 160; DA I.120.

-**diṭṭhi** the doctrine of the annihilation (of the soul), as opp. to sassata- or atta-diṭṭhi (the continuance of the soul after death) S II.20; III.99, 110 sq; Ps I.150, 158; Nd^1 248 (opp. sassati°); Dhs 1317; Nett 40, 127; SnA 523 (opp. atta°). -**vāda** (adj.) one who professes the doctrine of annihilation (ucchedadiṭṭhi) Vin I.235; III.2; D I.34, 55; S II.18; IV.401; A IV.174, 182 sq.; Nd^1 282; Pug 38. -**vādin** = °vāda Nett 111; J V.244.

Ucchedana (adj.) [fr. ud + **chid**] cutting off, destroying; f. °**anī** J V.16 (surā).

Ucchedin (adj.) an adherent of the ucchedavāda J V.241.

Ucchepaka (nt.) [= ucchiṭṭhaka in sense of ucchiṭṭhabhatta] leavings of food M II.7 (v. l. uccepaka with cc for cch as ucciṭṭha: ucchiṭṭha). The passage is to be read ucchepake va te ratā. A diff. connotation would be implied by taking ucchepaka = uñchā, as Neumann does (Majjhima trsl.^{2} II.682).

Uju & **Ujju** (adj.) [Vedic ṛju, also ṛjyati, irajyate to stretch out: cp. Gr. ὀρέγω to stretch; Lat. rego to govern; Goth. ufrakjan to straighten up; Ohg. recchen = Ger. recken = E. reach; Oir. rēn span. See also P. ajjava] straight, direct; straightforward, honest, upright D III.150 [T. ujja), 352 (do.) 422, 550; VP 18^1 (= sabba-jimha-vanka-kuṭilabhāv'āpagama-hetutāya u. VvA 96); Pug 59; Vbh 244 (ujuŋ kāyaŋ paṇidhāya); Vism 219 (uju avanka akuṭila); DA I.210 (id.); KhA 236; DhA I.288 (cittaŋ ujuŋ akuṭilaŋ nibbisevanaŋ karoti); VvA 281 (°koṭi-vanka); PvA 123 (an°).

-**angin** (ujjangin) having straight limbs, neg. an° not having straight limbs, i. e. pliable, skilful, nimble, graceful J V.40 (= kañcana-sannibha-sarīra C.); VI.500 (T. anuccangin = anindita-agarahitangin C.). -**gata** walking straight, of upright life M I.46; A III.285 sq. (°citta); V.290 sq.; Sn 350 (ujju°), 477 (id.); Dh 108 (ujju°, see DhA II.234 for interpretation). -**gāmin,** neg. an° going crooked, a snake J IV.330. -**cittatā** straightness, unwieldiness of heart Vbh 350. -**diṭṭhitā** the fact of having a straightforward view or theory (of life) Miln 257. -**paṭipanna** living uprightly D I.192; S IV.304; V.343; Vism 219. -**magga** the straight road D I.235; Vin V.149; It 104; J I.344; VI.252; DhA II.192. -**bhāva** straightness, uprightness SnA 292, 317; PvA 51. -**bhūta** straight, upright S I.100, 170; II.279; V.384, 404; A II.57; IV.292; J I.94; V.293 (an°); Vv 34^{23} (see VvA 155); Pv I.10^{10} (= citta-jimha-vanka-kuṭila-bhāva-karānaŋ kilesānaŋ abhāvena ujubhāvappatta PvA 51). -**vaŋsa** straight lineage, direct descendency J V.251. -**vāta** a soft wind Miln 283. -**vipaccanīka** in direct opposition D I.1; M I.402; DA I.38.

Ujuka & **Ujjuka** (adj.) [uju + ka] straight, direct, upright M I.124; S I.33 (ujuko so maggo, the road to Nibbāna), 260 (citta); IV.298; V.143, 165; J I.163; V.297 (opp. khujja); DhA I.18 (°magga); Sdhp 321. -**anujjuka** crooked, not straight S IV.299; J III.318.

Ujukatā (f.) [abstr. fr. ujuka] straightness, rectitude Dhs 50, 51 (kāyassa, cittassa); Vism 436 sq.

Ujutā (f.) [abstr. of uju] straight(forward)ness, rectitude Dhs 50, 51.

Ujjagghati [ud + jagghati] to laugh at, deride, mock, make fun of Vin III.128; Th 2, 74 (spelt jjh = hasati ThA 78); A III.91 (ujjh°, v. l. ujj°) = Pug 67 (= pāṇiŋ paharitvā mahāhasitaŋ hasati Pug A 249).

Ujjangala [ud + jangala] hard, barren soil; a very sandy and deserted place D II.146 (°nagaraka, trsl. "town in the midst of a jungle", cp. *Dial.* II.161); J I.391; Vv 85^5 (= ukkaŋsena jangala i. e. exceedingly dusty or sandy, dry); Pv II.9^{10} (spelt ujjhangala, expl^d. by ativiya-thaddhabhūmibhāga at PvA 139); Vism 107. Also in BSk. ujjangala, e. g. M Vastu II.207.

Ujjala (adj.) [ud + **jval,** see jalati] blazing, flashing; bright, beautiful J I.220; Dāvs II.63.

Ujjalati [ud + jalati, **jval**] to blaze up, shine forth Vin I.31; VvA 161 (+ jotati). — Caus. **ujjāleti** to make shine, to kindle Vin I.31; Miln 259; Vism 428; ThA 69 (Ap. V.14, read dīpān ujjālayiŋ); VvA 51 (padīpaŋ).

Ujjava (adj.) [ud + java] "running up", in cpd. ujjav-ujjava a certain term in the art of spinning or weaving Vin IV.

300, expl[d]. by "yattakaŋ patthena (patthana?) añcitaŋ hoti tasmi takkamhi vedhite".

Ujjavati [ud + javati] to go up-stream Vin II.301.

Ujjavanikāya instr. fem. of ujjavanaka used as adv. [ud + javanaka, q. v.] up-stream, lit "running up" Vin II.290; IV.65 (in expl[n]. of uddhaŋgāmin, opp. ojavanikāya).

Ujjahati [ud + jahati] to give up, let go; imper. ujjaha S I.188; Th 2, 19; Sn 342.

Ujju & **Ujjuka** see **uju** & **ujuka**.

Ujjota [ud + *jot of jotati, Sk. u dyotate] light, lustre J I.183 (°kara); Miln 321.

Ujjotita [pp. of ujjoteti, ud + joteti] illumined Dāvs V.53.

Ujjhaggati see ujjagghati.

Ujjhaggikā (f.) [fr. ujjagghati, spelling varies] loud laughter Vin II.213, cp. IV.187.

Ujjhatī [Sk. ujjhati, **ujjh**] — 1. to forsake, leave, give up J VI.138; Dāvs II.86. — 2. to sweep or brush away J VI.296. — pp. **ujjhita** (q. v.).

Ujjhatti (f.) [fr. ud + jhāyati[1], corresponding to a Sk. *ud-dhyāti] irritation, discontent A IV.223, 467 (v. l. ujj°); cp. **ujjhāna**.

Ujjhāna (nt.) [ud + jhāna[1] or jhāna[2]?] — 1. taking offence, captiousness Dh 253 (= paresaŋ randha-gavesitāya DhA III.377); Miln 352 (an°-bahula). — 2. complaining, wailing J IV.287.
-saññin, -saññika irritable S I.23; Th 1, 958; Vin II.214, cp. IV.194; Dpvs II.6; DhA III.376 (°saññitā irritability).

Ujjhāpana (nt.) [fr. ud + jhāyati[1] or jhāyati[2] to burn, to which jhāpeti to bring to ruin etc.? cp. ujjhāna] stirring up, provoking J V.91 (devat°), 94 (°kamma).

Ujjhāpanaka (adj.) [fr. ujjhāpana] one who stirs up another to discontent Vin IV.38.

Ujjhāpeti [Caus. of ujjhāyati] to harass, vex, irritate M I. 126; S I.209 ("give occasion for offence"); Vin IV.38 (cp. p. 356); J V.286; PvA 266.

Ujjhāyati [ud + jhāyati[1] or perhaps more likely jhāyati[2] to burn, fig. to be consumed. According to Müller P. G. pp. 12 & 42 = Sk. ava-**dhyā**, but that is doubtful phonetically as well as semantically] to be irritated, to be annoyed or offended, to get angry, grumble; often in phrase **ujjhāyati khīyati vipāceti** expressing great annoyance Vin I.53, 62, 73; II.207; IV.226; S I.232 & passim. — S I.232 (mā ujjhāyittha); J II.15; DhA II.20; aor. ujjhāyi J I.475; DhA II.88, inf. ujjhātuŋ J II.355. — Caus. **ujjhāpeti** (q. v.).

Ujjhita [pp. of ujjhati] destitute, forsaken; thrown out, cast away M I.296 (+ avakkhitta); Th 1, 315 (itthi); 2, 386 (cp. ThA 256 vātakkhitto viya yo koci dahano); Dh 58 (= chaḍḍita of sweepings DhA I.445); J III.499; V.302; VI.51.

Uñcha & **Uñchā** (f.) [Sk. uñcha & unchana, to **uñch**. Neumann's etym. uñchā = E. ounce, Ger. unze (Majjhima trsl.[2] II.682) is incorrect, see Walde *Lat. Wtb.* under uncia] anything gathered for sustenance, gleaning S II. 281; A I.36; III.66 sq., 104; Vin III.87; Sn 977; Th 2, 329, 349; J III.389; IV.23, 28, 434, 471 (°ya, dat. = phalâphal'atthāya C.); ThA 235, 242. Cp. samuñchaka.
-cariyā wandering for, or on search for gleaning, J II.272; III.37, 515; V.3; DA I.270; VvA 103; ThA 208. **-cārika** (adj.) going about after gleanings, one of 8 kinds of tāpasā SnA 295 (cp. DA I.270, 271). **-patta** the gleaning-bowl, in phrase uñchāpattāgate rato "fond of that which has come into the gl. b." Th 1, 155 = Pv IV.7[3] (= uñchena bhikkhācāreṇa laddhe pattagate āhāre rato PvA 265; trsl[d]. in Psalms of Brethren "contented with whatever fills the bowl"). aññāt°, marked off as discarded (goods) S II.281, so S A.

Uñchati [fr. **uñch**] to gather for sustenance, seek (alms), glean Vism 60 (= gavesati).

Uññā (f.) [= avaññā (?) from ava + **jñā**, or after uññātabba?] contempt Vin IV.241; Vbh 353 sq. (att°).

Uññātabba (adj.) [grd. fr. ava + **jñā** (?)] to be despised, contemptible, only in stock-phrase "daharo na uṇṇātabbo na paribhotabbo" S I.69; Sn p. 93; SnA 424 (= na avajānitabbo, na nīcaŋ katvā jānitabbo ti). In same connection at J V.63 mā naŋ daharo [ti] uññāsi (v. l. maññāsi) apucchitvāna (v. l. ā°).

Uṭṭitvā at Vin II.131 is doubtful reading (see p. 318, v. l. uḍḍhetvā), and should perhaps be read uḍḍetvā (= oḍḍetva, see uḍḍeti), meaning "putting into a sling, tying or binding up".

Uṭṭepaka one who scares away (or catches?) crows (kāk°) Vin I.79 (vv. ll. uṭṭhe°, uḍḍe°, uḍe°). See remarks on **uṭṭepeti**.

Uṭṭepeti in phrase kāke u. "to scare crows away" (or to catch them in snares?) at Vin I.79. Reading doubtful & should probably be read uḍḍepeti (? Caus. of uḍḍeti = oḍḍeti, or of uḍḍeti to make fly away). The vv. ll. given to this passage are uṭṭeceti, upaṭṭhāpeti, uḍḍoyeti. See also **uṭṭepaka**.

Uṭṭhapana see vo°.

Uṭṭhahati & **Uṭṭhāti** [ud + **sthā** see tiṭṭhati & uttiṭṭhati] to rise, stand up, get up, to arise, to be produced, to rouse or exert oneself, to be active, pres. **uṭṭhahati** Pug 51. — pot. **uṭṭhaheyya** S I.217; as imper. uttiṭṭhe Dh 168 (expl[d]. by uttiṭṭhitvā paresaŋ gharadvāre ṭhatvā DhA III.165, cp. Vin Texts I.152). — imper. 2nd pl. uṭṭhahatha Sn 331; 2nd sg. uṭṭhehi Pv II.6[1]; J IV.433. — ppr. **uṭṭhahanto** M I.86; S I.217; J I.476. — aor. **uṭṭhahi** J I.117; PvA 75. — ger. **uṭṭhahitvā** PvA 4, 43, 55, 152, & **uṭṭhāya** Sn 401. — inf. **uṭṭhātuŋ** J I.187. — *Note.* When uṭṭh° follows a word ending in a vowel, and without a pause in the sense, a v is generally prefixed for euphony, e. g. gabbho vuṭṭhāsi an embryo was produced or arose Vin II.278; āsanā vuṭṭhāya arising from his seat, Vism 126. See also under vuṭṭhahati. — pp. **uṭṭhita**; Caus. **uṭṭhāpeti**. — Cp. **pariyuṭṭhāti**.

Uṭṭhahāna [ppr. of uṭṭhahati] exerting oneself, rousing oneself; an° sluggish, lazy Dh 280 (= ayāyāmanto DhA III. 409); cp. anuṭṭhahaŋ S I.217.

Uṭṭhātar [n. ag. of ut + **ṣthā**, see uṭṭhahati] one who gets up or rouses himself, one who shows energy S I.214; A IV.285, 288, 322; Sn 187; J VI.297. **-an°** one who is without energy S I.217; Sn 96.

Uṭṭhāna (nt.) [fr. ut + **ṣthā**] — 1. rising, rise, getting up, standing (opp. sayana & nisīdana lying or sitting down) D II.134 (sīha-seyyaŋ kappesi uṭṭhāna-saññaŋ manasikaritvā); Dh 280 (°kāla); J I.392 (an°-seyyā a bed from which one cannot get up); Vism 73 (aruṇ-uṭṭhāna-velā time of sunrise) DhA I.17. — 2. rise, origin, occasion or opportunity for; as adj. (—°) producing J I.47 (kapp°); VI.459; Miln 326 (dhaññ° khettaŋ atthi). — 3. "rousing", exertion, energy, zeal, activity, manly vigour, industry, often syn. with viriya M I.86; A I.94; II.135 (°phala); III.45 (°viriya), 311; IV.281 (°sampadā); It 66 (°adhigataŋ dhanaŋ earned by industry); Pv IV.3[24]; Pug 51 (°phala); Miln 344, 416; ThA 267 (°viriya); PvA 129 (+ viriya). **-an°** want of energy, sluggishness A IV.195; Dh 241. — *Note.* The form vuṭṭhāna appears for uṭṭh° after a vowel under the same conditions as vuṭṭhahati for uṭṭhahati (q. v.) gabbha-vuṭṭhānaŋ J I.114. See also **vuṭṭh°**, and cp. pariy°.

Uṭṭhānaka (—°) (adj.) [fr. uṭṭhāna] — 1. giving rise to yielding (revenue), producing J I.377, 420 (satasahass°); III. 229 (id.); V.44 (id.). Cp. uṭṭhāyika. — 2. energetic J VI.246.

Uṭṭhānavant (adj.) [uṭṭhāna + vant] strenuous, active Dh 24.

Uṭṭhāpeti [Caus. II. of uṭṭhahati] — 1. to make rise only in phrase **aruṇaŋ** (suriyaŋ) **u.** to let the sun rise, i. e. wait for sunrise or to go on till sunrise J I.318; VI.330; Vism 71, 73 (aruṇaŋ). — 2. to raise J VI.32 (paṭhaviŋ). — 3. to fit up J VI.445 (nāvaŋ). — 4. to exalt, praise DA I.256. — 5. to turn a person out DhA IV.69. — See also **vuṭṭhāpeti.**

Uṭṭhāyaka (adj.) [adj. formation fr. uṭṭhāya, ger. of uṭṭhahati] "getting-up-ish", i. e. ready to get up, quick, alert, active, industrious; f. °ikā Th 2, 413 (= uṭṭhāna-viriya-sampannā ThA 267; v. l. uṭṭhāhikā).

Uṭṭhāyika (adj.) [= uṭṭhānaka] yielding, producing J II.403 (satasahass°).

Uṭṭhāyin (adj.) [adj. form. fr. uṭṭhāya, cp. uṭṭhāyaka] getting up D I.60 (pubb° + pacchā-nipātin rising early & lying down late).

Uṭṭhāhaka (adj.) [for uṭṭhāyaka after analogy of gāhaka etc.] = uṭṭhāyaka J V.448; f. °ikā A III.38 (v. l. °āyikā); IV.266 sq.

Uṭṭhita [pp. of uṭṭhahati] — 1. risen, got up Pv II.9[41] (kāl°); Vism 73. — 2. arisen, produced J I.36; Miln 155. — 3. striving, exerting oneself, active J II.61; Dh 168; Miln 213. -an° S II.264; Ps I.172. — Cp. pariy°. — *Note.* The form is **vuṭṭhita** when following upon a vowel see **vuṭṭhita** & **uṭṭhahati,** e. g. paṭisallāṇā vuṭṭhito arisen from the seclusion D II.9; pāto vuṭṭhito risen early PvA 128.

Uḍḍayhana (nt.) [fr. uḍḍayhati, see uddahati] burning up, conflagration Pug 13 (°velā = jhāyana-kālo Pug A 187); KhA 181 (T. uḍḍahanavelā v. l. preferable uḍḍayh°).

Uḍḍahati [ud + ḍahati] to burn up (intrs.) KhA 181 (uḍḍaheyya with v. l. uḍḍayheyya, the latter preferable). Usually in Pass. **uḍḍayhati** to be burnt, to burn up (intrs.) S III.149, 150 (v. l. for ḍayhati); J III.22 (udayhate); V.194. fut. uḍḍayhissati J I.48.

Uḍḍita [pp. of uḍḍeti[2]] ensnared (?), bound, tied up S I.40 (= taṇhāya ullanghita C.; trsl[d.] "the world is all strung up").

Uḍḍeti[1] [ud + ḍeti to fly. The etym. is doubtful, Müller P. Gr. 99 identifies uḍḍeti[1] & uḍḍeti[2] both as causatives to **ḍī.** Of uḍḍeti[2] two forms exist, uḍḍ° & oḍḍ°, the latter of which may be a variant of the former, but with specialisation of meaning ("lay snares"), it may be a cpd. with ava° instead of ud°. It is extremely doubtful whether uḍḍeti[2] belongs here, we should rather separate it & refer it to another root, probably **lī,** layate (as in allīna, nilīyati etc.), to stick to, adhere, fasten etc. The change l > ḍ is a freq. Pāli phenomenon. Another Caus. II. of the same root **(ḍī?)** is uṭṭepeti] to fly up M I.364 (kāko maŋsapesiŋ ādāya uḍḍayeyya; vv. ll. ubbaḍaheyya, uyya, dayeyya); J V.256, 368. 417.

Uḍḍeti[2] [see discussion under uḍḍeti[1]] (a) to bind up, tie up to, string up Vin II.131 (so read for uṭṭitvā, v. l. uḍḍhetvā). — (b) to throw away, reject PvA 256 (+ chaḍḍayāmi gloss). — pp. **uḍḍita.**

Uḍḍha (—°) (num. ord.) [the apocope form of catuttha = uttha, dialectically reduced to uḍḍha under the influence of the preceding aḍḍha] the fourth, only in cpd. **aḍḍh-uḍḍha** "half of the fourth unit", i. e. three & a half (cp. diyaḍḍha 1½ and aḍḍha-teyya 2½) J V.417 sq. (°āni itthisahassāni); Mhvs XII.53.

Uṇṇa (nt.) & **Uṇṇā** (f.) [Sk. ūrṇa & ūrṇā; Sat. lāna wool; Goth. wulla; Ohg. wolla = E. wool; Lith. vilna; Cymr. gwlan (= E. flannel); Gr. λῆνος, also οὖλος = Lat. vellus (fleece) = Ags. wil-mod] — 1. wool A III.37 = IV.265 (+ kappāsā cotton); J II.147; SnA 263 (paṭṭ°). — 2. hair between the eyebrows Sn 1022, & in stock phrase, describing one of the 32 signs of a Mahāpurisa, bhamuk'antare jātā uṇṇā odātā etc. D II.18 = III.144 = 170 = SnA 285. Also at Vism 552 in jāti-uṇṇāya.

-ja in uṇṇaja mukha J VI.218, meaning "rounded, swelling"? (C. expl[s.] by kañcan'ādāso viya paripuṇṇaŋ mukhaŋ). -nābhi (either uṇṇa° or uṇṇā, cp. Vedic ūrṇavābhi, ūrṇa + vābhi from Idg. ***uebh** to weave as in Lat. vespa = wasp, of which shorter root in Sk. **vā**) a spider, lit. "wool- i. e. thread-weaver", only in comb[n.] with sarabū & mūsikā at Vin II.110 = A II.73 = J II.147 (= makkaṭaka C.).

Uṇṇata (adj.) [pp. of uṇṇamati, Sk. unnata] raised, high, fig. haughty (opp. oṇata) A II.86; Sn 702 (an° care = uddhaccaŋ n'āpajjeyya SnA 492); Pug 52 (= ucca uggata Pug A 229). Cp. **unnata.**

Uṇṇati (f.) [fr. uṇṇamati] haughtiness Sn 830; Md[1] 158, 170; Dhs 1116, 1233. Cp. **unnati.**

Uṇṇama [fr. uṇṇamati] loftiness, height, haughtiness Dhs 1116, 1233. Cp. **unnama.**

Uṇṇamati [ud + **nam**] to rise up, to be raised, to straighten up, to be haughty or conceited Sn 366, 829, 928; Nd[1] 169; J VI.346 inf. uṇṇametave Sn 206. Cp. **unnamati.**

Uṇṇī (f.) [Sk. aurṇī fr. aurṇa woollen, der. of ūrṇa] a woollen dress Vin II.108.

Uṇha (adj.-n.) [adj. uṣṇā f. to oṣati to burn, pp. uṣṭa burnt, Sk. uṣṇa = Lat. ustus; cp. Gr. εὔω, Lat. uro to burn, Ags. ysla glowing cinders, Lith. usnis nettle] hot, as adj. only in phrase **uṇhaŋ lohitaŋ chaḍḍeti** to spill hot blood, i. e. to kill oneself DhA I.95; otherwise in cpds.; abs. only as nt. "heat" & always in contrast to sītaŋ "cold" Vin II.117 (sītena pi uṇhena pi); D II.15 (opp. sīta); M I.85; A I.145 = 170 = J V.417 (sītaŋ vā uṇhaŋ vā tiṇaŋ vā rajo vā ussāvo vā); Sn 52, 966 (acc.°); Nd[1] 486 = Nd[2] 677 (same as under sīta); J I.17 (v 93); Miln 410 (megho uṇhaŋ nibbāpeti); PvA 37 (ati°).

-ākāra appearance of heat, often in phrase (Sakkassa) paṇḍu-kambala-sil'āsanaŋ uṇhākāraŋ dassesi, of Sakka's throne showing an appearance of heat as a sign of some extraordinary event happening in the world, e. g. J.I.330; V.92; DhA I.17, and passim. -odaka hot water VvA 68. -kalla glowing-hot embers or ashes J II.94 (so read for °kalala); IV.389 (°vassa, rain of hot ashes, v. l. °kukkuḷavassa). -kāla hot weather Vin II.209.

Uṇhatta (nt.) [abstr. fr. uṇha] hot state, heat Vism 171.

Uṇhīsa [Sk. uṣṇīṣa] a turban D I.7; II.19 = III.145 (°sīsa cp. *Dial.* II.16); J II.88; Miln 330; DA I.89; DhsA 198.

Ut(t)aṇḍa see uddaṇḍa.

Utu (m. & nt.) [Vedic ṛtu special or proper time, with adj. ṛta straight, right, rite, ṛti manner to Lat. ars "art", Gr. δαμαρ(τ), further Lat. rītus (rite), Ags. rīm number; of ***ar** to fit in, adjust etc. q. v. under appeti] — 1. (lit.) (a) (good or proper) time, season: aruṇa-utu occasion or time of the sun(-rise) DhA I.165; utuŋ gaṇhāti to watch for the right time (in horoscopic practice), to prognosticate ibid. sarīraŋ utuŋ gaṇhāpeti "to cause the body to take season", i. e. to refresh the body by cool, sleep, washing etc. J III.527; DA I.252. — (b) yearly change, time of the year, season Vism 128. There are usually three seasons mentioned, viz. the hot, rainy and wintry season or **gimha**, **vassa** & **hemanta** A IV.138; SnA 317. Six seasons (in connection with nakkhatta) at J V.330 & VI.524. Often utu is to be understood, as in hemantikena (scil. utunā) in the wintry season S V.51. — (c) the menses SnA 317; J V.330 (utusinātāya read utusi nhātāya; utusi loc., as expld. by C. pupphe uppanne utumhi nahātāya). — 2. (applied in a philosophical sense: one of the five fold cosmic order, physical change, physical law of causation (opp. kamma), physical order: see Asl. 272 f.; Dialogues, II, 8, *n.*; *Kvu trsln.* 207; cp. Mrs. Rh. D. Buddhism, p. 119 f., *Cpd.* 161, *Dhs trsln.* introd. XVII; & cp. cpds. So in connection with kamma at Vism 451, 614; J VI.105 (kamma-paccayena utunā samuṭṭhitā Veraraṇī); perhaps also at Miln 410 (megha ututo samuṭṭhahitvā).

-āhāra physical nutriment (cp. *Dhs trsln.* 174) PvA 148. **-ûpasevanā** seasonable activity, pursuit (of activities) according to the seasons, observance of the seasons Sn 249 (= gimhe ātapa-ṭṭhāna-sevanā vasse rukkha-mūla-sevanā hemante jalappavesa-sevanā SnA 291). **-kāla** seasonable, favourable time (of the year) Vin I.299; II.173. **-ja** produced by the seasons or by physical change Miln 268 (kamma°, hetu°, utu°); Vism 451. **-nibbatta** coming to existence through physical causes Miln 268. **-pamāṇa** measure of the season, i. e. the exact season Vin I.95. **-pariṇāma** change (adversity) of the season (as cause of disease) S IV.230; A II.87; III.131; V.110; Miln 112, 304; Vism 31. **-parissaya** danger or risk of the seasons A III.388. **-pubba** festival on the eve of each of the (6) seasons J VI.524. **-vāra** time of the season, °vārena °vārena according to the turn of the season J I.58. **-vikāra** change of season Vism 262. **-veramaṇī** abstinence during the time of menstruation Sn 291 (cp. SnA 317). **-saŋvacchara** the year or cycle of the seasons, pl. °ā the seasons D III.85 = A II.75; S V.442. The phrase utusaŋvaccharāni at Pv II.9[15] is by Dhammapāla taken as a bahuvrīhi cpd., viz. cycles of seasons & of years, i. e. vasanta-gimh'ādike bahū utū ca citta-saŋvacchar'adi bahūni saŋvaccharāni ca PvA 135. Similarly at J V.330 (with Cy). **-sappāya** suitable to the season, seasonable DhA 327. **-samaya** time of the menses SnA 317.

Utuka (—°) (adj.) [utu + ka] seasonable, only in cpd. **sabbotuka** belonging to all seasons, perennial D II.179; Pv IV.12[2] (= pupphupaga-rukkhādīhi sabbesu utūsu sukkhāvaha PvA 275); Sdhp 248.

Utunī (f.) [formed fr. utu like bhikkhunī fr. bhikkhu] a menstruating woman Vin III.18; IV.303; S IV.239; A III. 221, 229; Miln 127. an° A III.221, 226.

Utta [pp. of **vac**, Sk. ukta; for which the usual form is vutta only as **dur°** speaking badly or spoken of badly, i. e. of bad repute A II.117, 143; III.163; Kh VIII.2; KhA 218.

Uttaṇḍāla (adj.) [ud + taṇḍula] "grainy", i. e. having too many rice grains (of rice gruel), too thick or solid (opp. **atikilinna** too thin or liquid) J I.340; III.383 (id.); IV.44 (id.).

Uttatta [ud + tatta[1], pp. of ud + **tap**, Sk. uttapta] heated; of metals: molten, refined; shining, splendid, pure J VI. 574 (hemaŋ uttattaŋ agginā); Vv 84[11]; Pv III.3[2] (°rūpa, so read for uggata°, reading correct at PvA 188 °singī); PvA 10 (°kanaka, T. uggatta°); Mhbv 25 (id.).

Uttanta [= utrasta, is reading correct? frightened, faint Vin III.84. See **uttasta** & **utrasta**.

Uttama (adj.) [superl. of ud°, to which compar. is uttara. See etym. under ud°] "ut-most", highest, greatest, best Sn 1054 (dhammaŋ uttamaŋ the highest ideal = Nibbāna, for which seṭṭhaŋ Sn 1064; cp. Nd[2] 317); Dh 56; Nd[1] 211; Nd[2] 502 (in paraphrase of mahā combd. with pavara); KhA 124; DhA I.430: PvA 1, 50. — **dum-uttama** a splendid tree Vv 39[3]; nar° the best of men Sn 1021 (= narāsabha of 996); pur° the most magnificent town Sn 1012; puris° the noblest man Th 1, 629, 1084; nt. **uttamaŋ** the highest ideal, i. e. Arahantship J I.96.

-anga the best or most important limb or part of the body, viz. (a) the head Vin II 256 = M I.32 = A IV.278 (in phrase uttamange sirasmiŋ); J II.163; also in cpd. °*bhūta* the hair of the head Th 2, 253 (= kesa-kalāpa ThA 209, 210) & °*ruha* id. J I.138 = VI.96 (= kesā C.); (b) the eye J IV.403; (c) the penis J V.197. **-attha** the highest gain or good (i. e. Arahantship SnA 332) Sn 324; Dh 386, 403; DhA IV.142; ThA 160. **-adhama** most contemptible J V.394, 437. **-guṇā** (pl.) loftiest virtues J I.96. **-purisa** It 97 & **-porisa** the greatest man (= mahāpurisa) Dh 97 (see DhA II.188). **-bhāva** the highest condition, state or place DhA II.188 (°ŋ patto = puris'uttamo).

Uttamatā (f.) [abstr. fr. uttama] highest amount, climax, limit DA I.169 (for paramatā).

Uttara[1] (adj.) compar. of ud°, q. v. for etym.; the superl. is uttama] — 1. higher, high, superior, upper, only in cpds., J II.420 (musal° with the club on top of him? Cy not clear, perhaps to uttara[2]); see also below. — 2. northern (with disā region or point of compass) D I.153; M I.123; S I.224; PvA 75. uttarāmukha (for uttaraŋmukha) turning north, facing north Sn 1010. — 3. subsequent, following, second (°—) J I.63 (°āsāḷha-nakkhatta). — 4. over, beyond (—°): aṭṭh'utara-sata eight over a hundred, i. e. 108; DhA I.388. — **sa-uttara** having something above or higher, having a superior i. e. inferior D I.80 (citta), II.299; M I.59; S V.265; Vbh 324 (paññā); Dhs 1292, 1596; DhsA 50. — **anuttara** without a superior, unrivalled, unparalleled D I.40; S I.124; II.278; III.84; Sn 179. See also under **annuttara**.

-attharaṇa upper cover J VI.253. **-âbhimukha** facing North D II.15. **-āsanga** an upper robe Vin I.289; II. 126; S I.81; IV.290; A I.67, 145; II.146; DhA I.218; PvA 73; VvA 33 = 51. **-itara** something higher, superior D I.45, 156, 174; S I.81; J I.364; DhA II.60; IV.4. **-oṭṭha** the upper lip (opp. adhar°) J II.420; III.26; IV. 184. **-chada** a cover, coverlet, awning (sa° a carpet with awnings or canopy above it) D I.7; A I.181; III.50. **-chadana** = °chada D II.187; DhA I.87. **-dvāra** the northern gate J VI.364. **-dhamma** the higher norm of the world (lok°), higher righteousness D II.188 (paṭividdha-lok'uttara-dhammatāya uttama-bhāvaŋ patta). **-pāsaka** the (upper) lintel (of a door) Vin II.120 = 148. **-pubba** north-eastern J VI.518. **-sse** (v. l. °suve) on the day after tomorrow A I.240.

Uttara[2] (adj.) [fr. uttarati] crossing over, to be crossed, in **dur°** difficult to cross or to get out of S I.197 (not duruttamo); Miln 158; and in cpd. °setu one who is going to cross a bridge Miln 194 (cp. uttāra-setu).

Uttaraṇa (nt.) [fr. uttarati] bringing or moving out, saving, delivery Th 1, 418; J I.195. In BSk. uttaraṇa only in sense of crossing, overcoming, e. g. Jtm 31 [8] (°setu). — Cp. uttara.

Uttarati [ud + tarati[1]] — 1. to come out of (water) Vin II.221 (opp. otarati); J I.108 (id.). — 2. to go over, to flow over (of water), to boil over Miln 117, 118, 132, 260, 277. — 3. to cross over, to go beyond M I.135; aor. **udatāri** Sn 471 (oghaŋ). — 4. to go over, to overspread J V.204 (ger. uttariyāna = avattharitvā C.). — pp. **otiṇṇa** (q. v.). — Caus. **uttareti** (q. v.).

Uttari (°—) & **Uttariŋ** (adv.) [compn. form of uttara, cp. angi-bhūta uttani-karoti etc.] out, over, beyond; additional, moreover, further, besides. — (1) **uttariŋ**: D I.71; M I.83; III.148; S IV.15; Sn 796 (uttariŋ kurute = uttariŋ karoti Nd[2] 102, i. e. to do more than anything, to do best, to esteem especially); J II.23; III.324; Miln 10 (ito uttariŋ anything beyond this, any more) DhA IV.109 (bhāveti to cultivate especially; see vuttari); VvA 152. — uttariŋ appaṭivijjhanto not going further in comprehension, i. e. reaching the highest degree of comprehension, Vism 314, referring to Ps II.131, which is quoted at Miln 198, as the last of the 11 blessings of mettā. — (2) **uttari°** in foll. cpds.

-karaṇīya an additional duty, higher obligation S II. 99; III.168; A V.157 = 164, It 118. **-bhanga** an extra portion, tit-bit, dainties, additional or after-meal bits Vin II.214; III.160; IV.259; J II.419; DhA I.214 sa-uttari-bhanga together with dainty bits J I.186, cp. 196 (yāgu). **-bhangika** serving as dainties J I.196. **-manussa** beyond the power of men, superhuman, in cpd. *°dhamma* an order which is above man, extraordinary condition, transcendental norm, adj. of a transcendental character, miraculous, overwhelming Vin I.209; II.112; III.105; IV.24; D I 211; III.3, 12, 18; M I.68; II.200; S IV.290, 300, 337; A III.430; V.88; DhA III.480. **-sāṭaka** a further, i. e. upper or outer garment, cloak, mantle J II.246; DhA IV.200; PvA 48, 49 (= uttarīyaŋ).

Uttarika (adj.) [fr. uttara] transcending, superior, superhuman Nett 50.

Uttariya (nt.) [abstr. fr. uttara; uttara + ya = Sk. *uttarya] — 1. state of being higher. Cp. III.3[5]; neg. an° state of being unsurpassed (lit. with nothing higher), pre-eminence; see **annuttariya**. — 2. an answer, rejoinder DhA I.44 (karaṇ°-karaṇa).

Uttarīya (nt.) [fr. uttara] an outer garment, cloak Pv 10[3] (= uparivasanaŋ uparihāraŋ uttarisāṭakaŋ PvA 49); Dāvs III.30; ThA 253.

Uttasati[1] [identical in form with next] only in Caus. **uttāseti** to impale, q. v.

Uttasati[2] [ut + tasati[2]] — 1. to frighten J I.47 (v.267). — to be alarmed or terrified Vin I.74 (ubbijjati u. palāyati); III.145 (id.); J II.384; VI.79; ppr. uttasaŋ Th I, 86; & uttasanto Pv II.2[3]. — See utrasati. Caus. **uttāseti** (q. v.). — pp. **uttasta** & **utrasta** (q. v.). Cp. also **uttanta.**

Uttasana (adj.-nt.) [fr. ud + **tras**, cp. uttāsana] frightening, fear J I.414 (v. l. for uttasta).

Uttasta [pp. of uttasati[2]; usual form utrasta (q. v.)] frightened, terrified, faint-hearted J I.414 (°bhikkhu; v. l. uttasana°).

Uttāna (adj.) [fr. ut + **tan,** see tanoti & tanta] — 1. streched out (flat), lying on one's back, supine Vin I.271 (mañcake uttānaŋ nipajjāpetvā making her lie back on the couch); II.215; J I.205; Pv IV.10[8] (opp. avakujja); PvA 178 (id.), 265. — 2. clear, manifest, open, evident [cp. BSk. uttāna in same sense at Av. Ś II.106] D I.116; S II.28 (dhammo uttāno vivaṭo pakāsito): J II.168 (= pākaṭa); V.460; PvA 66, 89, 140, 168. — **anuttāna** unclear, not explained J VI.247. — The cpd. form (°—) of uttāna in combn. with **kṛ** & **bhū** is uttānī° (q. v.). — 3. superficial, "flat", shallow A I.70 (parisa); Pug 46.

-mukha "clear mouthed", speaking plainly, easily understood D I.116 (see DA I.287); DhA IV.8. **-seyyaka** "lying on one's back", i. e. an infant M I.432; A III.6; Th I, 935; Miln 40; Vism 97 (°dāraka).

Uttānaka (adj.) [fr. uttāna] — 1. (= uttāna[1]) lying on one's back J VI.38 (°ŋ pātetvā); DhA I.184. — 2. (= uttāna[2]) clear, open D II 55; M I.340 = DhA I.173.

Uttānī (°—) [the compn. form of uttāna in cpds. with **kṛ** & **bhū** cp BSk. uttānī-karoti M Vastu III.408; uttānī-kṛta Av. Ś I.287; II.151] open, manifest etc., in **°kamma** (uttānī°) declaration, exposition, manifestation S V.443; Pug 19; Vbh 259, 358; Nett 5, 8, 9, 38. — **°karaṇa** id. SnA 445. — **°karoti** to make clear or open, to declare, show up, confess (a sin) Vin I.103; S II.25, 154; III.132, 139; IV.166; V.261; A I.286; III.361 sq.

Uttāpeti [Caus. of uttapati] to heat, to cause pain, torment J VI.161.

Uttāra [fr. ud + **tṛ** as in uttarati] crossing, passing over, °setu a bridge for crossing (a river) S IV.174 = M I.134; cp. uttara[2].

Uttārita [pp. of uttāreti] pulled out, brought or moved out J I.194.

Uttāritatta (nt.) [abstr. fr. uttārita] the fact of having or being brought or moved out J I.195.

Uttāreti [Caus. of uttarati] to make come out, to move or pull out J I.194; SnA 349. — pp. **uttārita** (q. v.).

Uttāsa [Sk. uttrāsa, fr. ud + **tras**] terror, fear, fright D III.148; S V.386; Miln 170; PvA 180.

Uttāsana (nt.) [fr. uttāseti[2]] impalement J II.444; SnA 61 (sūle).

Uttāsavant (adj.) [uttāsa + vant] showing fear or fright, fearful S III.16 sq.

Uttāsita [pp. of uttāseti[2]] impaled Pv IV.1[6] (= āvuta āropita VvA 220); J I.499; IV.29.

Uttāseti[1] [Caus of uttasati, ud + **tras,** of which **taŋs** is uttāseti[2] is a variant] to frighten, terrify J I.230, 385; II.117.

Uttāseti[2] [cp. Sk. uttaŋsayati in meaning to adorn with a wreath ud + **taŋs** to shake, a variation of **tars** to shake, tremble] to impale A I.48; J I.230, 326; II.443; III.34; IV.29. — pp. **uttāsita** (q. v.). Cp. uttāsana.

Uttiṭṭha [= ucchiṭṭha? Cp. ucchepaka. By Pāli Cys. referred to uṭṭhahati "alms which one stands up for, or expects"] left over, thrown out Vin I.44 (°patta); Th I, 1057 (°piṇḍa); 2, 348 (°piṇḍa = vivaṭadvāre ghare ghare patiṭṭhitvā labhanaka-piṇḍa ThA 242); J IV.380 (°piṇḍa; C. similarly as at ThA; not to the point); 386 (°piṇḍa = ucchiṭṭhaka piṇḍa C.); Miln 213, 214.

Uttiṭṭhe see **uṭṭhahati.**

Uttiṇa (adj.) [ud + tiṇa] in uttiṇaŋ karoti to take the straw off, lit. to make off-straw; to deprive of the roof M II.53. Cp. next.

Uttiṇṇa [pp. of uttarati] drawn out, pulled out, nt. outlet, passage J II.72 (paṇṇasālāya uttiṇṇāni karoti make entrances in the hut). Or should it be **uttiṇa**?

Utrasta [pp. of uttasati, also cp. uttasta] frightened, terrified, alarmed Vin II.184; S I.53, 54 (an°); Sn 986; Miln 23; DhA II.6 (°mānasa); PvA 243 (°citta), 250 (°sabhāva).

Utrāsa [= uttāsa] terror J II.8 (citt°).

Utrāsin (adj.) [fr. *Sk. uttrāsa = P. uttāsa] terrified, frightened, fearful, anxious S I.99, 219. — Usually neg. an° in phrase abhīru anutrāsin apalāyin without fear, steadfast & not running away S I.99; Th I, 864; Nd[2] 13; J IV.296; V.4; Miln 339. See also apalāyin.

Ud- [Vedic ud-; Goth. ūt = Ohg. ūz = E. out, Oir. ud-; cp. Lat. ūsque "from-unto" & Gr. ὕστερος = Sk. uttara] prefix in verbal & nominal combn. One half of all the words beginning with u° are combns. with ud°, which in compn. appears modified according to the rules of assimilation as prevailing in Pāli. — I. *Original meaning* "out in an upward direction", out of, forth; like ummujjati to rise up out of (water), ujjalati to blaze up high; udeti to come out of & go up; ukkaṇṭha stretching one's neck out high (cp. Ger. "empor"); uggilati to "swallow up", i. e. spit out. — The opposites of ud- are represented by either **ava** or **o°** (see under II. & IV. & cp. ucc-âvaca;

uddhambhāgiya: orambhāgiya), ni (see below) or vi (as udaya: vi-aya or vaya). — II. Hence develop 2 clearly defined meanings, viz. (1) out, out of, away from —: °aṇha ("day-out"); °agga ("top-out"); °āgacchati; °ikkhati look out for, expect; °kantati tear out; °khitta thrown off; °khipati pick out; °gacchati come out; °gamana rising (opp. o°); °gajjati shout out; °gilati (opp. o°); °ghoseti shout out; °cināti pick out; °chiṭṭha thrown out; °jagghati laugh at, cp. Ger. aus-lachen °tatta smelted out; °tāna stretched out; °dāleti tear out; °dhaṭa lifted out, drawn out; °disati point out to; °drīyati pull out; °pajjati to be produced; °patti & °pāda coming out, origin, birth; °paṭipatiyā out of reach; °paḷāseti sound out; °phāsulika "ribs out"; etc. etc. — (2) up (high) or high up, upwards, on to (cp. ucca high, uttara higher) —: °kujja erect (opp. ava°); °kūla sloping up (opp. vi°); °khipati throw-up, °gaṇhāti take up; °chindati cut up; °javati go up-stream, °javana id. (opp. o°); uññā pride; °ṭhāna "standing up"; °ṭhita got up; °tarati come out, go up (opp. o°); °nata raised up, high (opp. o°); °nama e-levation; °nāmin raised (opp. ni°); °patati fly up; etc. etc. — III. More specialised meanings (from elliptical or figurative use) are: (1) ud° = without, "ex-", e.g. unuangala "out-plough" = without a plough; uppabbajita an ex-bhikkhu. — (2) ud° = off, i.e. out of the way, wrong, e.g. uppatha a wrong road, ummagga id. — (3) ud° = out of the ordinary, i.e. exceedingly, e.g. ujjangala extremely dusty; uppaṇḍuka very pale; uppoṭheti to beat hard. — IV. Dialectical variations & combinations. — (1) Owing to semantic affinity we often find an interchange between ud° and ava° (cp. E. break up = break down, grind up or down, tie up or down), according to different points of view. This wavering between the two prefixes was favoured by the fact that o always had shown an unstable tendency & had often been substituted for or replaced by ū, which in its place was reduced to u before a double consonant, thus doing away with the diff. between ū & u or o & u. For comparison see the foll.: ukkamati & okk°; uññā: avaññā; uddīyati: odd°; uḍḍeyya: oḍḍ°; uppīḷeti: opīḷ°; etc., & cp. abbhokirati > abbhukkirati. — (2) the most freq. comb^ns. that ud° enters into are those with the intensifying prefixes abhi° and sam°; see e.g. abhi + ud (= abbhud°) + gacchati, °jalati; °ṭhāti; °namati etc.; sam + ud + eti; °kamati; °chindati; °tejeti; °pajjati etc.

Uda[1] (indecl.) [Sk. uta & u, with Lat. aut (or), Gr. αὖτι (again), αὐτάρ (but, or), Goth. auk = Ger. auch to pron. base ava° yonder, cp. ava II.] disjunctive part. "or"; either singly, as at Sn 455, 955, 1090; J v.478 (v. l. udāhu); Nd[1] 445 (expl^d. as "padasandhi" with same formula as iti, q. v.); Pv II.12[16] (kāyena uda cetasā); or comb^d. with other synonymous particles, as **uda va** at Sn 193, 842, 1075; It 82 = 117 (caraŋ vā yadi vā titthaŋ nisinno uda vā sayaŋ walking or standing, sitting or lying down); KhA 191. — See also **udāhu**.

Uda[2] (°—) [Vedic udan (nt.), also later uda (but only °—), commonly udaka, q. v.] water, wave. In cpds. sometimes the older form udan° is preserved (like udañjala, udaññavant), but generally it has been substituted by the later uda° (see under udakaccha, udakanti, udakumbha, udapatta, udapāna, udabindu).

Udaka (nt.) [Vedic udaka, uda + ka (see uda[2]), of Idg. *ued, *ud, fuller form *eued (as in Sk. odati, odman flood, odana gruel, q. v.); cp. Sk. unatti, undati to water, udra = Av. udra = Ags. otor = E. otter ("water-animal"); Gr. ὕδωρ water ("hydro"), ὕδρα hydra ("water-animal"); Lat. unda wave; Goth. watō = Ohg. wazzar = E. water; Obulg. voda water, vydra otter] water Vin II.120, 213; D II.15 (°assa dhārā gushes or showers of w.); Dh 80, 145; J I.212; Pv I.5[1]; Pug 31, 32; Miln 318; VvA 20 (udake temanaŋ aggimhe tāpanaŋ); DhA I.289; DhA III. 176, 256; PvA 39, 70. — Syn. ambu, ela, jala etc. — The comp^n. form (—°) is either ûdaka (āsanûdaka-dāyin J IV.435) or °odaka (pādodaka water for the feet PvA 78). odaka occurs also in abs. form (q. v.), cp. also oka. Bdgh.'s kaŋ = udakaŋ, tena dāritaŋ: kandaraŋ ti is a false etymology; DA I.209.

-aṇṇava water-flood M I.134. -āyatika a water-pipe Vin II.123. -āḷhaka a certain measure of water, an āḷhaka of w. S V.400; A II.55 = III.337; VvA 155. -ûpama resembling water, like water A IV.11 (puggala). -ogāhana plunging into water J III.235. -ogha a water flood VvA 48. -orohaka descending into water, bathing; N. of a class of ascetics, lit. "bather" M I.281; S IV.312; A V. 263. -orohaṇa plunging into water, taking a bath, bathing D I.167; S I.182; A I.296; II.206; J IV.299; Pug 55. -kalaha the "water dispute" DhA III.256. -kāka a water crow J II.441. -kicca libation of water, lit. water-performance; cleansing, washing D II.15. -kīḷā sporting in the w. J VI.420. -gahaṇasāṭaka bathing-gown J V.477. -ghaṭa a water pitcher PvA 66. -cāṭi a water jar DhA I.52. -ṭṭhāna a stand for water Vin II.120. -tumba a water vessel J II.441; DA I.202; DhA II.193. -telaka an oily preparation mixed with water Vin II.107. -dantapoṇa water for rinsing the mouth & tooth-cleaner Vin III.51; IV.90, 92, 233; J IV.69. -daha a lake (of water) D I.45. -doṇikā a water-tub or trough Vin II.220. -dhārā a shower of water Ps I.125; J IV.351. -niddhamana a water spout or drain Vin II.120, 123; DhA II.37. -nibbāhana an aquaduct Miln 295. -paṭiggaha receiving or accepting water Vin II.213. -patta a waterbowl Vin II. 107; D I.80; S III.105. -puñchanī a towel Vin II.122. -posita fed or nourished by water VvA 173. -phusita a drop of water S II.135. -bindu a drop of w. It 84 (v. l. for udabindu); PvA 99. -bubbula a w. bubble A IV.137; Vism 109, 479 (in comp.). -bhasta devoid of water ThA 212 (for anodaka Th 2, 265). -maṇika a water-pot Vin I.227; M I.354; A III.27; Miln 28; DhA I.79. -mallaka a cup for w. A I.250. -rakkhasa a water-sprite DhA III.74. -rahada a lake (of w.) D I.74, 84; A I.9; II.105; III.25; Sn 467; Pug 47. -rūha a water plant Vv 35[6]. -lekhā writing on w. A I.283 = Pug 32 (in simile °ûpama like writing on w.; cp. Pug A 215). -vāra "waterturn", i.e. fetching water DhA I.49. -vāraka bucket S II.118. -vāha a flow of water, flowing w. J VI.162. -vāhaka rise or swelling (lit. carrying or pulling along (of water), overflowing, flood A I.178. -vāhana pulling up water Vin II.122 (°rajju). -sadda sound of water Dhs 621. -sarāvaka a saucer for w. Vin II.120. -sāṭaka = sāṭikā J II 13. -sāṭikā "water-cloak", a bathing-mantle Vin I. 74 = II.272; IV.279 (= yāya nivattha nhāyati C.); DhA II.61 (T. °sātaka). -suddhika ablution with water (after passing urine) Vin IV.262 (= mutta-karaṇassa dhovanā C.).

Udakaccha [uda + kaccha] watery soil, swamp J V.137.

Udakanti [uda + kanti] descent into the water S II.179 = 187.

Udakumbha [uda + kumbha] a water jug J I 20; Dh 121, 122; Pv I.12[9].

Udagga (adj.) [ud + agga, lit. "out-top", cp. Sk. udagra] topmost, high, lofty Th I, 110; fig. elated, exalted, exultant, joyful, happy D I.110 (°citta); Sn 689 (+ sumana), 1028 (id.); Pv IV.1[58] (attamana +); IV.5[8] (haṭṭha +); Miln 248; DhA II.42 (haṭṭha-pahaṭṭha udagg-udagga in high glee & jubilant), Vism 346 (id.); Sdhp 323. See also der. odagya.

Udaggatā (f.) [abstr. fr. udagga] exaltation, jubilation, glee Sdhp 298.

Udaggi° in udaggihuttaŋ [= ud + aggi + hutta, cp. Vedic agnihotra] the fire prepared (for sacrifice) J V 396 (= uda-aggihuttaŋ C. wrongly), lit. "the sacrifice (being) out"

Udangaṇa (nt.) [ud + angaṇa[1]; Kern unnecessarily changes it to uttankana "a place for digging for water" see *Toev.* p. 96] an open place J I.109.

Udacchida 3rd sg. praet of ucchindati to break up Sn 2, 3 (°ā metri causa).

Udañcana (nt.) [fr. ud + **añc,** see añchati] a bucket for drawing water out of a well DhA I.94.

Udañcanin (adj.-n.) [ud + añcanin to **añc** see añchati] draining, pulling up water f. °ī a bucket or pail J I. 417 (f. °ī).

Udañjala [udan + jala see uda²] in °ŋ kīḷati a water-game: playing with drops of water (?) Vin III.118 (Bdhgh.: udañjalan ti udaka-cikkhallo vuccati p. 274).

Udaññavant (adj.) [udan = uda(ka) + vant] rich in water, well-watered J V.405 (= udaka-sampanna C.).

Udaṇha [ud + aṇha] day-break, dawn, sunrise J V.155.

Udatāri 3rd sg aor. of **uttarati** to cross over Sn 471 (oghaŋ).

Udatta (adj.) [Sk. udātta] elevated, high, lofty, clever Nett 7, 118, 123 (= uḷārapañña C.).

Udadhi [uda + **dhi,** lit. water-container] the sea, ocean S I.67; It 86; Sn 720; J V.326; VI.526; ThA 289; VvA 155 ("udakaŋ ettha dhīyatī ti udadhi"); Sdhp 322, 577.

Udapatta¹ [uda for ud, and **patta,** pp. of pat, for patita? Kern, *Toev.* s. v. takes it as *udak-prāpta, risen, flying up, sprung up J III.484 (= uppatita C.); V.71 (= uṭṭhita C.).

Udapatta² [uda + patta; Sk. udapātra] a bowl of water, a water-jug, ewer M I.100; S V.121; A III.230 sq., 236; V.92, 94, 97 sq.

Udapādi 3rd sg. aor. of **uppajjati** to arise, originate, become D I.110, 180, 185; S II.273; It 52, 99; SnA 346, 462.

Udapāna [uda + pāna lit. "(place for) drinking water"; cp. opāna, which in the incorrect opinion of Pāli Commentators represents a contracted udapāna] a well, a cistern Vin I.139; II 122; M I.80; A IV.171; J III.216; Ud 78; Pv II.7⁸; II.9²⁵; Miln 411; Vism 244 (in simile); DA I.298; VvA 40; PvA 78.

Udappatta see udapatta.

Udabindu [uda + bindu] a drop of water M I 78; Sn 812; Dh 121, 122, 336; It 84 (v. l. udaka°); Nd¹ 135; SnA 114; DhA II.51.

Udabbhadhi aor. 3rd sg. of **ubbadhati** [ud + **vadh**] to destroy, kill Sn 4 (= ucchindanto vadhati SnA 18).

Udabbahe 3rd sg. Pot. of ubbahati [ud + **bṛh**¹, see also abbahati] to draw out, tear out, remove Th I, 158; Sn 583 (= ubbaheyya dhāreyya (?) SnA 460); J II.223 (= udabbaheyya C.); VI.587 (= hareyya C.); aor. **udabbahi** Vin IV.5.

Udaya [fr. ud + **i,** cp. udeti] rise, growth; increment, increase; income, revenue, interest A II.199; Ps I.34; Vv 84⁷ (dhan'atthika uddayaŋ patthayāna = ānisaŋsaŋ atirekalābhaŋ VvA 336); 84⁵²; DhA II.270; PvA 146 (ulār° vipāka), 273 (°bhūtāni pañca kahāpaṇa-satāni labhitvā, with interest); Sdhp 40, 230, 258. — See also **uddaya.**
-**attha** rise and fall, birth & death (to attha²) M I.356; S V.197 sq., 395; A III.152 sq.; IV.111, 289, 352; V.15, 25. -**atthika** desirous of increase, interest or wealth (cp. above Vv 84⁷ dhan'atthika) A II.199. -**bbaya** (ud-aya + vy-aya) increase & decrease, rise & fall, birth & death, up & down D III.223; S I.46 = 52 (lokassa); III.130; A II.90; III.32; IV.32; It 120; Vism 287; Ps I.54; ThA 90. -**vyaya** = °bbaya S IV.140; A II.15 (khandhānaŋ); Dh 113, 374 (khandhānan, see DhA IV.110).

Udayaŋ & **Udayanto** ppr. of udeti (q. v.).

Udayana (nt.) [fr. ud + **i**] going up, rise DA I.95.

Udara (nt.) [Vedic udara; Av. udara belly; Gr. ὕστερος = Lat. uterus belly, womb; Lith. védaras stomach, See also Walde, *Lat. Wtb.* under vensica] — 1. the belly, stomach D II.266; Sn 78, 604, 609, 716; J I.146, 164, 265; Miln 213; PvA 283; KhA 57, 58; DhA I.47 (pregnant); Sdhp 102. — 2. cavity, interior, inside Dāvs I.56 (mandir-odare). -**ūnūdara** with empty belly Th I, 982; Miln 406, 407; cp. ūna.
-**aggi** the fire of the belly or stomach (i. e. of digestion) KhA 59; SnA 462; PvA 33; -**âvadehakaŋ** (adv.) bhuñjati to eat to fill the stomach, eat to satiety, to be gluttonous M I.102; A V.18; Th I, 935; Vism 33. -**paṭala** the mucous membrane of the stomach Vism 359 (= sarīr'-abbhantara 261); SnA 248; KhA 55, 61. -**pūra** stomach-filling Vism 108. -**vaṭṭi** "belly-sack", belly Vin III.39, 117; Vism 262 where KhA reads ud. paṭala). -**vāta** the wind of the belly, stomach-ache 9J I.33, 433; Vism 41 (°ābādha); DhA IV.129.

Udariya (nt.) [fr. udara] the stomach Kh III. (cp. KhA 57); Vism 258, 358. Cp. **sodariya.**

Udassaye 2nd sg. pot. of ud + assayati [ā + **śri,** cp. assaya] J V.26 (meaning to instal, raise?), expld. by C. as ussayāpesi (?) Reading may be faulty for udāsase (?).

Udahāraka [uda + hāraka] a water-carrier J II.80.

Udahāriya (adj.) [fr. udahāra fetching of water, uda + **hṛ**] going for water Vv 50⁹.

Udāgacchati [ud + ā + gacchati] to come to completion DA I.288. Cp. sam°.

Udāna (nt.) [fr. ud + **an** to breathe] — 1. "breathing out", exulting cry, i. e. an utterance, mostly in metrical form, inspired by a particularly intense emotion, whether it be joyful or sorrowful (cp. K. S. p. 29 n. 2) D I.50, 92; S I.20, 27, 82, 160; A I.67; J I.76; Pug 43, 62; Nett 174; PvA 67; Sdhp 514. — The utterance of such an inspired thought is usually introduced with the standing phrase "**imaŋ udānaŋ udānesi**" i. e. breathed forth this solemn utterance [Cp. BSk. udānaŋ udānayati Divy 99 etc.], e. g. at Vin I.2 sq., 12, 230, 353; D I.47; II.107 (udāna of triumph); S III.55; Mhvs XIX.29; DA I.140; Ud. I passim; SnA 354 ("the familiar quotation about the sakyas"). Occasionally (later) we find other phrases, as e. g. udānaŋ pavatti J I.61; abhāsi Vin IV.54; kathesi J VI. 38. — 2. one of the angas or categories of the Buddhist Scriptures: see under **nava** & **anga.** — Cp. vodāna.

Udānita [pp. of udāneti] uttered, breathed forth, said DhA IV.55.

Udāneti [denom. f. udāna, cp. BSk. udānayati] to breathe out or forth, usually in phrase udānaŋ udānesi: see under udāna¹. Absolutely only at J III.218.

Udāpatvā at J V.255 is uncertain reading (v. l. udapatvā, C. explns. reading udapatvā by uppatitvā = flying up), perhaps we should read udapatta flew up, pret. of ud + **pat** = Sk. *udapaptat (so Kern, *Toev.* s. v.).

Udāyati at DA I.266 (udāyissati fut.) is hardly correct; D I.96 has here udriyissati (q. v.), which belongs to darati to break, tear etc., udāyati could only belong to dāyāti meaning to cut, mow, reap. but not to split etc. DA I.266 explns. udāyissati with bhijjhissati. The difficulty is removed by reading udrīyissati. To v. l. undriyati cp. °undriya for °uddaya (dukkh° for dukkhudraya see **udraya).** We find udāyati once more at Vism 156 in expln. of ekodi, where it is evidently meant for udeti (Caus. = uṭṭhapeti).

Udāra (adj.) [Sk. udāra, of which the usual P. form is ulāra (q. v.). Cp. BSk. audāra & audārika.] raised, sublime, noble, excellent Dāvs III.4 (samussit-odāra-sitātapattaŋ); DA I.50 (°issariya); Sdhp 429, 591.

Udāvatta [pp. of udāvattate, ud + ā vattati] retired, desisting J v.158 (= udāvattitva nivattitva C.).

Udāsīna (adj.) [ud + āsīna, pp. of **ās** to sit; lit. sit apart, be indifferent] indifferent, passive, neutral DhsA 129.

Udāhaṭa [pp. of udāharati] uttered, spoken; called, quoted Pug 41.

Udāharaṇa (nt.) [fr. udāharati] example, instance J III.401 (°ŋ āharitvā dassento), 510; Miln 345; SnA 445; VvA 297.

Udāharati [ud + ā + **hṛ**] to utter, recite, speak. Sn 389; J III.289; DA I.140 (see udāhāra). — pp. **udāhaṭa** (q. v.). Cp. pariy°.

Udāhāra [fr. udāharati] utterance, speech DA I.140 (°ŋ udāhari = udānaŋ udānesi); Pug A 223.

Udāhu (indecl.) [uta + āho, cp. P. uda & aho und Sk. utāro] disjunctive-adversative particle "or", in direct questions D I 157; II.8; Sn 599, 875, 885; J I.20, 83; VvA 258 (= ādu); PvA 33, 51; Miln 10. — The first part of the question is often introduced with **kiŋ**, while **udāhu** follows in the second (disjunctive) part, e. g. kin nakkhattaŋ kīḷissasi udāhu bhatiŋ karissasi VvA 63; kiŋ amhehi saddhiŋ āgamissasi udāhu pacchā will you come with us or later? DhA II.96: See under kiŋ. — Often combd. with other expletive particles, e. g. udāhu ve Sn 1075, 1077; udāhu no Sn 347; eva . . . no udāhu (so . . . or not) D I.152; (ayaŋ) nu kho — udāhu (ayaŋ) is it (this) — (this) Vism 313.

Udi (or udī) is artificial adj. formn. fr. udeti, meaning "rising, excelling", in expln. of ekodi at Vism 156 (udāyatī ti udi uṭṭhapetī ti attho).

Udikkhati [ud + **īkṣ**, Sk. udīkṣate] — 1. to look at, to survey, to perceive Vin I.25 (udiccare, 3sd. pl. pres. med.); J v.71, 296; Vv 81[21] (aor. udikkhisaŋ = ullokesiŋ VvA 316); Dāvs II 109; Sdhp 308. — 2. to look out for, to expect J I.344; VvA 118. — 3. to envy Miln 338.

Udikkhitar [n. ag. of udikkhati] one who looks for or after D III 167.

Udicca (adj.) [apparently an adjectivised ger. of udeti but distorted from & in meaning = Sk. udañc, f. udīcī northern, the north] "rising", used in a geographical sense of the N. W. country, i. e. north-westerly, of north-western origin (cp. *Brethren* 79, *Miln trsln.* II.45 n. 1) J I.140, 324, 343, 373; Miln 236. — See also **uddiya**.

Udiccare 3sd. pl. pres. med. of udikkhati (q. v.).

Udita[1] [pp. of ud—**i**, see udeti] risen, high, elevated Miln 222; (°odita); Dāvs IV.42; Sdhp 14 (of the sun) 442 (°odita).

Udita[2] [pp. of **vad**, see vadati] spoken, proclaimed, uttered Vuttodaya 2 (quoted by Childers in Khuddaka-pāṭha ed. 1869, p. 22).

Udīraṇa (nt.) [fr. udīreti] utterance, saying J v.237; Dhs 637, 720; Miln 145.

Udīrita [pp. of udīreti] uttered J III.339; v.394 = 407.

Udīretī [ud + īreti, cp. in meaning īrita] — 1. to set in motion, stir up, cause J III.441 (dukkhaŋ udīraye Pot. = udīreyya C.); v.395 (kalahaŋ to begin a quarrel). — 2. to utter, proclaim, speak, say S I.190; Sn 632 (pot. °raye = bhāseyya SnA 468); Dh 408 (giraŋ udīraye = bhāseyya DhA IV.182); J v.78 (vākyaŋ); Pass. **udīyati** (uddiyyati = Sk. udīryate) Th I, 1232 (nigghoso).

Udu (adj.) [= *ṛtu? cp. utu & uju] straight, upright, in °mano straight-minded D III.167, 168 (= uju° in v. l. and expln. by C.).

Udukkhala (m. & nt.) [Sk. ulūkhalā] a mortar Vin I.202 (+ musala pestle); J I.502; II.428; v.49; II.161, 335; Ud 69 (m; + musaḷa); DhA II.131 (°sālā); Vism 354 (in comp.). The relation between **udukkhala** and **musala** is seen best from the description of eating at Vism 344 and DA I.200, where the lower teeth play the rôle of **ud.**, the upper teeth act as **m.**, while the tongue takes the part of a hand. On this passage & other connections as well as etym. see Morris *J P T S.* 1893, 37.

Udukkhalikā (f.) [fr. udukkhala] part of a door (threshold?) Vin II.148 (+ uttara-pasaka lintel of a door).

Udumbara [Sk. udumbara] the glomerous fig tree, Ficus Glomerata D II.4; Vin IV 35; A IV 283 (°khādika), 283 (id.), 324 (id.); Sn 5; DhA I.284; SnA 19; KhA 46, 56; VvA 213. Cp. **odumbara.**

Udeti (ud + eti of **i** to go] to go out or up, to rise (of the sun), to come out, to increase Asl. 169; Vism 156 (eko udetī ti ekodi); J II.33; III.324; ppr. udayaŋ It 85 (ādicco), & udayanto PvA 154 (udayante suriye = sole surgente). — pp. udita (see udita[1]). Cp. udicca & udi.

Udda[1] [Vedic udra, to uda[2] water, lit. living in water; Cp. Gr. ὕδρος "hydra"; Ohg. ottar = Ags. otor = E. otter; Lith. ûdra = Obulg. vydra otter] an aquatic animal, the otter (?) Childers s. v. doubts the identity of this creature with the regular otter, since it lives in the jungle. Is it a beaver? — Vin I.186 (°camma otter-skin, used for sandals); Cp. I.10[2] (°pota); J III.51 sq., 335. The names of two otters at J III.333 are Gambhīra-cārin and Anutīra-cārin.

Udda[2] [for uda[2]?] water, in passage amakkhito uddena, amakkhito semhena, a. ruhirena i. e. not stained by any kind of (dirty) fluid D II.14; M III.122.

Uddaṇḍa [ud + daṇḍa] a kind of building (or hut), in which the sticks stand out (?) Nd[1] 226 = Nd[2] 97[6] (uṭanda) = Vism 25 (v. l. BB uṭṭanda).

Uddaya[1] [a (metric?) variant of udaya] gain, advantage, profit Vv 84[7] (see udaya); J v.39 (satt°-mahāpaduma of profit to beings?).

Uddaya[2] in compounds **dukkh°** and **sukh°**. see **udraya.**

Uddalomī [= udda + lomin beaver-hair-y?] a woollen coverlet with a fringe at each end D I.7 (= ubhato dasaŋ uṇṇā-may' attharaṇaŋ; keci ubhato uggata-pupphaŋ ti vadanti DA I.87); A I.181. See however uddha-lomin under **uddhaŋ.**

Uddassetī [ud + dasseti, Caus. of dassati[1]] to show, reveal, point out, order, inform, instruct D II.321 sq.; M I.480 (read uddassessāmi for conjectured reading uddisissāmi?); II.60 (v. l. uddiset°) A IV.66.

Uddāna (nt.) [fr. ud + **dā**, dayati to bind: see under dāma] a *group* of Suttas, used throughout the Vinaya Piṭaka, with ref. to each Khandhaka, in the Saŋyutta, the Anguttara and other books (cp. Miln 407) for each group of about ten Suttas (cp. DhsA 27). The Uddāna gives, in a sort of doggerel verse, at the end of each group, the titles of the Suttas in the group. It may then be roughly rendered "summary". If all the Uddānas were collected together, they would form a table of contents to the whole work. — Otherwise the word has only been found used of *fishes* "macchuddāna" (so J II.425; DhA II.132). It then means a group of fish placed apart for for sale in one lot. Perhaps a *set* or a *batch* would meet the case.

Uddāpa [*udvāpa] foundation of a wall, in stock phrase **daḷh°** etc. D III.101; S v.194 = also at J VI.276 (= pākāra-vatthu C.). Kern, *Toev.* s. v. refers it to Sk. ud-vapati to dig out, and translates "moat, ditch". The meaning "wall" or "mound" however harmonises quite well with the der. fr. "digging", cp. E. dike > Ger. Teich. See also **uddāma** 2.

Uddāpavant (adj.) [fr. uddāpa] having a wall or embankment S II.106 (v. l. uddhā°); C. expls. as āpato uggatattā J IV.536 (so read with v. l. for T. uddhā pavatta; C. expls. as tīra-mariyādā-bandhana).

Uddāma [fr. ud + **dā** as in uddāna, see dāma] 1. (adj.) "out of bounds", unrestrained, restless Dāvs V.56 (°sāgara). — 2. (n.) wall, enclosure (either as "binding in", protecting or as equivalent of uddāpa fr. ud + **vam** "to throw up" in sense of to throw up earth, to dig a mound = udvapati) in phrase aṭṭāla-uddāma-parikhādīni watchtowers, enceintes, moats etc. DhA III.488.

Uddāraka [?] some wild animal J V.416 (reading uncertain, expln. ditto).

Uddāla = uddālaka, only as Np. J IV.298 sq.

Uddālaka [fr. ud + **dal**, see dalati] the Uddāla tree, Cassia Fistula (also known as indīvara), or Cordia Myxa, lit. "uprooter" Vv 6[1] (= vātaghātako yo rājarukkho ti pi vuccati VvA 43); J IV.301 (°rukkha), 440; V.199 (= vātaghātaka C.), 405; VI.530 (so read for uddh°); VvA 197 (°puppha = indīvara); PvA 169.

Uddālanaka (adj.) [fr. uddālana > ud + dāleti] referring to destruction or vandalism, tearing out Vin IV.169.

Uddāleti [ud + dāleti, Caus. of **dal**, see dalati] to tear out or off Vin IV.170; S IV.178.

Uddiṭṭha [pp. of uddisati] — 1. pointed out, appointed, set out, put forth, proposed, put down, codified M I.480 (pañha); Sn p. 91 (id. = uddesa-matten' eva vutta, na vibhangena SnA 422); SnA 372. — 2. appointed, dedicated J V.393 (an °ŋ pupphaŋ = asukassa nāma dassāmī ti); PvA 50; KhA 138.

Uddiya (adj.) [Sk. udīcya?] northern, northwestern (i. e. Nepalese) J IV.352 (°kambala) in expln. of uddiyāna [Sk. udīcīna?]. See **udicca** & cp. Morris in *J P T S.* 1889, 202, and last not least Lüders in *K. Z.* 1920 (vol. 49), 233 sq. The word is not sufficiently cleared up yet.

Uddisati [ud + disati] — 1. to propose, point out, appoint, allot Dh 353, cp. DhA IV.72; Miln 94 (satihāraŋ); fut. uddisissati M I.480 (ex conj., is probably to be changed to uddassessati, q. v.). — 2. to specify PvA 22 (aor. uddisi), 25 (= nīyādeti, dadāti), 27. — Pass. **uddissati** to show oneself, to be seen Pv III.2[12], and **uddissiyati** PvA 46. — pp. **uddiṭṭha** (q. v.). — Caus. II. **uddisāpeti** (q. v.). — ger. **uddissa** (q. v.).

Uddisāpeti [Caus. II. of uddisati] — 1. to make recite Vin I.47 = II.224; IV.290. — 2. to dedicate PvA 35 (v. l. ādisati).

Udissa (indecl.) [orig. ger. of uddisati] — 1. indicating, with signs or indications J III.354 = Miln 230. — 2. prep w. acc.: (a) (lit.) pointing to, tending towards, towards, to PvA 250 Suraṭṭha-visayaŋ). — (b) (appld.) with reference to, on account of, for, concerning PvA 8 (pete), 17 (= ārabbha), 49 (ratanattayaŋ), 70 (maŋ), 146.
-kata allotted to, specified as, meant for (cp. odissa & odissaka) Vin I.237 (maŋsa); II.163; D I.166 = A I.295 = Pug 55 (viz. bhikkhā); M I.77; KhA 222; J II.262, 263 (bhatta).

Uddissana (nt.) [fr. uddissa] dedication PvA 27, 80.

Uddīpanā (f.) [fr. ud + dīpeti] explanation, reasoning, argument Vism 27 (for ukkācanā).

Uddīyati, Uddīyana etc. see udrī°.

Uddeka [Sk. udreka, ud + **ric**] vomit, spouting out, eruption Vism 261 (where id. p. at KhA 61 reads uggāra); °ŋ dadāti to vomit Vin I.277.

Uddekanika (adj.) [uddeka + ana + ika] spouting, ejecting M II.39 (maṇika; perhaps better to be read with v. l. as udañjanika = udañcanika fit for drawing up water).

Uddesa [fr. uddisati] — 1. pointing out, setting forth, proposition, exposition, indication, programme M III.223 (u. uddiṭṭha), 239; S IV.299; SnA 422. — 2. explanation S V.110 sq.; **sa-uddesa** (adj.) with (the necessary) expln., point by point, in detail, D I.13, 81; III.111; A III.418; It 99; Nd[2] 617[1]. — 3. **samaṇuddesa** one marked as a Samaṇa, a novice (cp. sāmaṇera) D I.151; M III.128; A IV.343; uddesa-bhatta special or specified food Vin I.58 = 96, cp. II.175, propounding, recitation, repetition Vin I.50 = II.228 (uddesena paripucchāya ovādena by recitation, questioning & advice); II.219 (°ŋ dadāti to hold a recitation + paripucchaŋ d); A IV.114 (+ paripucchā); V.50 sq. (pañho, u. veyyākaraṇaŋ); Nd[2] 385[2] (+ paripucchā); J I.116; Miln 257 (+ paripucchā). **ek'udesa** a single repetition Vin III.47; A III.67, 180; Miln 10, 18.

Uddesaka (adj.) [fr. uddesa] assigning, defining, determining, in bhatt° one who sorts out the food VvA 92.

Uddesika (adj. nt.) [fr. uddesa] — 1. indicating, referring to, respecting, defining; (nt.) indication, definition D II.100 (mam °bhikkhusangho); Miln 159 (id.); KhA 29. — Esp. as —° in phrase **aṭṭha-vass'** uddesika-kāla the time referring to (or indicating) the 8th year, i. e. at the age of 8 PvA 67; soḷasa-vass° M I.88; J I.456; VvA 259. In the same application **padesika** (q. v.). — 2. memorial J IV.228 (cetiya).

Uddehaka (adj.) [fr. ud + **dih**, see deha] "bubbling up", only adv. °ŋ in cpd. **pheṇ°** (paccamāna) boiling) under production of scum (foam) M III.167; A I.141; J III.46; Miln 357.

Uddosita [Derivation uncertain. Cp. Müller *P. Gr.* 42] shed, stable (?) Vin I.140; II.278; III.200; IV.223.

Uddha (adj.) [possibly a combn. of aḍḍha[2] & uddhaŋ; or should we read aḍḍh° or vuḍḍh°?] in phrase **uddhehi vatthehi** in rich, lofty clothes J IV.154 (of a devatā; passage may be corrupt).

Uddhaŋ (& **Uddha°**) (indecl.) [nt. of adj. *uddha = Sk. ūrdhva high; to Idg. ***ared**(h) as in Lat. arduus steep, or ***ured** as in Sk. vardhate to raise, Gr. ὀρθός straight] high up, on top, above (adv. & prep.). — On uddhaŋ in spatial, temporal, ethical & psychological application see in detail Nd[2] 155. — I. (*adv.*). — A. (of *space*) up, aloft, on top, above (opp. adho) Vin III.121; KhA 248 (= upari). — In contrast with adho (above > below) D I.23, 153, 251; Vism 176 (u. adho tiriyaŋ expld.); DA I.98 (see also adho). — Esp. with ref. to the points of the compass as "in zenith" (opp. adho "in nadir"), e. g. at D I.222 ("straight up"); It 120; J I.20. — B. (of *time*) in future, ahead, hence Sn 894; Nd[1] 303 (u. vuccati anāgataŋ). — II. (*prep.* with abl. & instr.). — A. (of *space*) in phrase uddhaŋ pādatalā adho kesamatthakā (above the soles & below the scalp) D II.293, 294; III.104; A III.323; V.109. — B. (of *time*) after, hence Pv I.10[12] (u. catūhi māsehi after 4 months = catunnaŋ māsānaŋ upari PvA 52); PvA 147 (sattahi vassa satehi u., meaning here 700 years **ago**, cp. **ito** in similar application, meaning both past & future), 148 (sattāhato u. after a week; uttari v. l. BB.). — In cpds. uddha° & uddhaŋ° (see below). The reading udhogalaŋ at PvA 104 is to corrected to adho°. — III. *Note* (cp. Trenckner, *Notes* 60). In certain cases we find **ubbhaŋ** for uddhaŋ. Notice the foll.: ubbhaŋ yojanaŋ uggato J V.269; ubbhaṭṭhako hoti "standing erect" D I.167; M I.78; ubbhamukhu "mouth (face) upwards", turned upwards S III.238; Miln 122.

(1) uddha° in: -gāmin going upwards S v.370 sq. -cchiddaka (-vātapānā) (windows) having openings above DhA I.211. -pāda heels upwards either with *adhosira* (head down) A IV.133, or *avansira* Vv 52[25] (v. l.); J I. 233. -mukha turned upwards, adv. °ā upwards or backwards (of a river) Miln 295 (Gangā u. sandati; in same context ubbha° Miln 122). -lomin "having hair on the upper side", a kind of couch or bed (or rug on a couch) Vin I.192 = II.163, 169. So is prob. to be read for uddalomī (q. v.). -virecana action of an emetic (lit. throwing up) (opp. adho-virecana of a purgative) D I.12 (= uddhaŋ dosānaŋ niharaṇaŋ DA I.98); DhA III.126; SnA 86. -suddha clean on top Vin II.152. — (2) uddhaŋ° in: -āghātanika an after-deather, a teacher who maintains that the soul exists after death D I.31, cp. DA I.119. -pāda feet up (& head down) Vv 52[25] (v. l. uddha°). -bhāgiya belonging to the upper part (opp. oram°): see saŋyojana. -virecana v. l. BB. at SnA 86 for uddha°. -sara(ŋ) (adv.) with raised or lofty voice, lit. "sounding high" Sn 901, see Nd[1] 315. -sota (adj.) one who is going upwards in the stream of life [cp. BSk. ūrdhvasrotaḥ Mahāvy § 46] D III.237; S v.69, 201, 205, 237, 285, 314, 378; A I.233; II.134; IV.14 sq., 73 sq., 146, 380; v.120; Dh 218; Th II.12; Pug 17; Nett 190; DhA III.289; lit. up-stream at J III.371.

Uddhaŋsati [ud + dhaŋsati, in lit. meaning of **dhvaŋs**, see dhaŋsati] to fly out or up (of dust) Vv 78[4] na tatth' uddhaŋsati rajo; expl[d.] by uggacchati VvA 304. — pp. uddhasta (q. v.).

Uddhagga (adj.) [uddha + agga] — 1. standing on end (lit. with raised point), bristling, of the hair of a Mahāpurisa D II.18 = III.144, 154. — 2. prominent, conspicuous J IV.345 (°rājin having prominent stripes, of a lion). — 3. pointing upwards (of the lower teeth, opp. adhagga point-downwards) J v.156 (= heṭṭhima-danta C.). — 4. lofty, beneficial (of gifts) A II.68 (dakkhiṇā); III.46 (id.) see also **uddhaggika**.

Uddhaggika (adj.) [cp. uddhagga) aiming at or resulting in a lofty end, promoting spiritual welfare, beneficial (of gifts) D I.51 = III.66; S I.90; A III.259; DA I.158.

Uddhacca (nt.) [substantivised ger. of ud-dharati, ud + **dhṛ**, cp. uddhaṭa & uddhata. The BSk. auddhatya shows a strange distortion. BSk. uddhava seems to be also a substitute for uddhacca] over-balancing, agitation, excitement, distraction, flurry (see on meaning *Dialogues* I.82; *Dhs trsl[n.]* 119; *Cpd.* 18, 45, 83). A I.256, 282; III.375, 421, 449; IV.87; v.142, 145, 148; D III.234; S v.277 sq.; DhSA 260; SnA 492 (in sense of "haughtiness"? for Sn 702 uṇṇata); Nd[1] 220, 501; Ps I.81, 83; II.9, 97 sq.; 119, 142, 145, 169, 176; Pug 18, 59; Dhs 427, 429 (cittassa), 1159, 1229, 1426, 1482; Vbh 168, 369, 372, 377; Vism 137, 469 (= uddhata-bhāva); Sdhp 459. Together with **kukkucca** "flurry or worry" u. is enum[d.] as the 4th of the 5th nīvaraṇa's and as the 9th of the 10 saŋyojana's (q. v.), e. g. at D I.71, 246; III 49, 234, 269, 278; S I.99; A I.3; III.16; v.30; Nd[2] 379; Dhs 1486.

Uddhaja (adj.) [uddhaŋ + ja] upright, honest M I.386 (v. l. for pannadhaja).

Uddhaṭa [pp. of uddharati[2]; see also uddhata, uddhita & uddhacca] — 1. pulled out J II.26. — 2. pulled out, destroyed, extirpated, in phrase° **dāṭha** with its fangs removed (of a snake) J I.505; II.259; VI.6. — 3. cut off or out Miln 231 (uddhaṭ-uddhaṭe ālope whenever a piece is cut off). — 4. drawn out, lifted out, raised J I.143; sass°kāle at the time of lifting the corn; v.49 (°paŋsu). Cp. uddhaṭa-bīja castrated J II.237.

Uddhata [pp. of uddharati[1]; as to its relation to uddhaṭa see remarks under uddhacca]. — 1. lifted up, raised, risen, high (of the sun, only in this special phrase u. aruṇo) Vin II.236; Ud 27 (vv. ll. uggata & uddhasta). — 2. unbalanced, disturbed, agitated, shaken S I.61 (+ unnaḷa "muddled in mind & puffed up" trsl.), 204 (id.) v.112 (līnaŋ cittaŋ uddhataŋ c.), 114 = Vism 133, 269; A II.23; III.391; v.93 sq., 142, 163; It 72; Th 2, 77 (so read with v. l., T. has uddhaṭa; ThA 80 expl[ns.] as nān' ārammaṇe vikkhitta-citta asamāhita); Nd[2] 433 (+ avūpasanta-citto); Pug 35 (= uddhaccena samannāgata Pug A 217). -an° well balanced, not shaken, calm, subdued M I.470; A II.211; v.93 sq., 104; Sn 850 (= uddhaccavirahita SnA 549); Dh 363 (= nibbutacitto DhA IV.93); J v.203; Vv 64[8]. — See also ubbhata.

Uddhana (nt.) [*ud-dhvana, fr. ud + **dhvan** instead of **dhmā**, for uddhamana (*uddhmāna Sk.), see dhamati] an oven J I.33, 68, 71, 346; II.133, 277; III.178, 425; v.385, 471; II.218 (kammār°), 574; Sn p. 105; Miln 118, 257; Vism 171, 254; DhA I.52, 224; II.3; III.219 (°panti); IV.176.

Uddhamma [ud + dhamma] false doctrine Dpvs v.19.

Uddharaṇa (nt) [abstr. fr. uddharati] — 1. taking up, lifting, raising Miln 307 (sass°-samaya the time of gathering the corn; to uddharati 1. but cp. in same meaning uddhaṭa from uddharati 2). DA I.192. — 2. pulling or drawing out (cp. uddharati 2) Vin III.29. See also ubbahati[2].

Uddharati [ud + dharate of **dhṛ**] — 1. (in this meaning confused with ubbharati from **bṛh**, cp. interchange of ddh & bbh in uddha: ubbha, possibly also with **bṛh**: see abbahati and cp. ubbahati[1]). (a) to raise, rise, lift up; hence: to raise too much, overbalance, shake etc.: see pp. uddhata (*udbhṛta) & cp. uddhacca & uddharaṇa. — (b) to take up, lift, to remove, take away D I.135 (baliŋ uddhareyya raise a tax); M I.306 (hīyaŋ); J I.193 (aor. poet. udaddhari = uddharitvā kaḍḍhitvā pavaṭṭesi C.); VvA 157. — Caus. **uddharāpeti** Vin II.180, 181; J VI.95. — 2. to pull out, draw out (syn. with abbahati, q. v. for comparison) D I. 77 (ahiŋ karaṇḍā uddhareyya, further on ahi k. ubbhato) PvA 115 (= abbahati); imper. uddharatha J II.95 (for abbaha); Dh 327 (attānaŋ duggā); aor. uddhari J III.190 (aṅkena); cond. uddhare Th 1, 756; ger. uddharitvā D I.234; Nd[1] 419; SnA 567; DhA IV.26; PvA 139, & (poet.) uddhatvā J IV.406 (cakkhūni. so read for T. laddhatvāñ cakkhūni = akkhīni uddharitvā C.). — pp. **uddhaṭa** & **ubbhata**.

Uddharin in an° Sn 952 see under **niṭṭhurin**.

Uddhasetā see uddhasta.

Uddhasta [pp. of uddhaŋseti, see dhaŋsati & cp. anuddhaŋseti] attacked, perhaps "spoilt" (smothered!) in comb[n.] with pariyonaddha (covered) at A I.202 (T. uddhaseta, expl[d.] by upari dhaŋsita C.); II.211 (vv. ll. uddhasota for °etā & uddhaŋso). — Registered with **an°** as anuddhasta in Index vol. to A, should however be read as **anuddhasta** (q. v.). Cp. also **viddhasta**.

Uddhāra (& **ubbhāra** in Vin.; e. g. II.255, cp. 256 where ubbhata unterchanges with uddhāra) [fr. uddharati[1]] — 1. taking away, withdrawal, suspension, in **kaṭhin°** (q. v.) Vin I.255 sq.; III.262; IV.287; v.177 sq. — 2. a tax, levy, debt, in phrase °ŋ **sodheti** (so read for sādheti loc. cit.) to clear up a debt J II.341; III.106; IV.45, 247. **uddhāra-sodhana** (v. l. sādh°) the clearance of a debt J II.341. — 3. synopsis or abstract Dpvs v.37 (atth° of the meaning of the Vin.); SnA 237 (atth° + pad°).

Uddhālaka at J VI.530 is to be read **uddālaka**.

Uddhita [a by-form of uddhaṭa] pulled out, destroyed, extirpated, removed J VI.237 (°pphala = uddhaṭa-bīja C.).

Uddhunāti [ud + **dhunāti**] to shake VvA 279.

Uddhumāta (adj.) [pp. of uddhumāyati] swollen, bloated, risen (of flour) A I.140; Sn 200 (of a corpse); SnA 100 sq., 171; DA I.114. Cp. next.

Uddhumātaka (adj.) [prec. + ka] swollen, bloated, puffed up M I.88 (of a corpse; + vinīlaka); Vism 178, 193 (id.); J I.164 (udaraŋ °ŋ katvā), 420 (°nimitta appearance of being blown up); Miln 332; DhA I.307. See also subha & asubha.
-**saññā** the idea of a bloated corpse A II.17; Dhs 263; Miln 331; cp. *Dhs trsl*ⁿ. 69.

Uddhumātatta (nt.) [abstr. fr. uddhumāta] swollen condition Vism 178.

Uddhumāyati [ud + **dhmā**, see dhamati & remarks on uddhacca] to be blown up, to swell up, rise; aor. °āyi J III.26; VvA 76; ger. °ājitvā J II.18; DhA I.126. — pp. uddhumāta & °āyita (q. v.).

Uddhumāyana (nt.) [fr. uddhumāyati] puffing, blowing or swelling up J IV.37.

Uddhumāyika (adj.) [cp. uddhumāyita] like blowing or swelling up, of blown-up appearance M I.142 sq.

Uddhumāyita [pp. of uddhumāyati] swollen, bloated, puffed up VvA 218.

Udrabhati [? doubtful in form & etym.] to eat M I.306 (upacikā bījaŋ na udrabheyyuŋ; vv. ll. on p. 555: udrah°, udah°, udāh°, uddhah°, uṭṭhah°; udraheyyun ti khādeyyuŋ C. (udrabhāsane dhātum)). — *Note.* The Dhātupāṭha, 212, and the Dhātu-mañjūsā, 311, explain udrabha by adane, eating.

Udraya (& **Uddaya**) (—°) [perhaps a bastard form of uddaya = udaya yielding etc. The BSk. usually renders P. **dd** by **dr.** If so, then equal to adaya & uddaya[1]] coming forth, result, consequence. Usually in foll. two phrases: **dukkh°** (yielding pain) & **sukh°** (giving pleasure); e. g. as **dukkh°** at M I 415; J IV.398; V.119 (v. l. °indriya); Pv I.11[10] (so read for T. °andriya, cp. undriyati as v. l. for udāyati); Ps II.79 (kammaŋ); as **sukh°** at J V.389 (v. l. °indriya); DhA II.47 (°uddaya). Both dukkh° & sukh° at Ps I.80. Besides these in foll. combⁿˢ.: kaṭuk° causing bitterness J V.241; sa° with (good or evil) consequences S II.29; M I.271.

Udrīyati (& **Uddīyati**) [cp. Sk. ud dīryate, Pass of ud + **dṛ**, dṛṇōti, and P. darati & dalati; see also avadīyati which may be a Sanskritised uddīyati for uddīyati] to burst, split open, break, fall to pieces Vin I.148 (vihāro udriyati); II 174 (id); IV.254 (i); D I.96 (°iyissati = bhijjhissati DA I.96, so read for udāyati); S I 113, 119.

Udrīyana & **Uddīyana** (nt.) [fr. udrīyati] breaking or splitting open, bursting J I.72; DhA II 7 (°sadda), 100 (paṭhavī-uddīyana-sadda; vv. ll. uddri°, udri°).

Undura [etym ?] a rat Vin I.209; II.148, 152; III.151; J I.120; Miln 23, 363. Spelt undūra at Vism 62.

Unna [pp. of **ud,** unatti & undati, see udaka] in phrase pīti-vegen'unna "bubbling up with the excitement of joy", overflowing with joy Mhvs 19, 29 (expl^d. by uggatacitta i. e. lofty, exalted C.). — It may however be better & more in keeping with Pāli word-formation as well as with meaning & interpretation to explain the word as ud + na, taking °na as abs. (base)-form of **nam,** thus lit. "bent up", i. e. raised, high, in meaning of unnata. Cp. the exactly similar formation, use & meaning of ninna = ninnata. Thus unna > ninna would correspond to unnata > ninnata.

Unnaka [etym.?] a species of perfume J VI 537 (gloss kuṭantaja).

Unnangala (adj.) [ud + nangala, on meaning of ud in this case see ud] in phrase °ŋ karoti, according to Morris, *JPTS.* 1887, 120 "to make an up-ploughing, to turn up etc.", but more aptly with C. on J VI.328 to make "out-plough" (*not* "up-plough") in sense of out-of-work, i. e. to make the people put their ploughs (or work in general) away and prepare for a festival; to take a holiday. A typical "Jātaka"-phrase; J I.228; II.296, 367; III. 129, 414; IV.355; VI.328; DhA III.10.

Unnata [pp. of unnamati. Besides this form we find **uṇṇata** in fig. special meaning, q. v.] raised, high, lofty, in high situation (opp. oṇata) Pv IV.6[6] (= sāmin PvA 262); J I.71; II 369; VI 487; Miln 146, 387; DA I.45 See also unnaḷa.

Unnati (f) [fr. unnamati; cp. uṇṇati] rising, lifting up, elevation Miln 387 (°avanati).

Unnadati [ud + nadati] to resound, shout out, roar J I.110; II 90; III.271, 325; Miln 18; aor. **unnadi** J I 74; Miln 13. — Caus. **unnādeti** (q. v.).

Unnama [fr ud + **nam**; cp. also uṇṇama in fig. meaning] rising ground, elevation, plateau Kh VII.7 = Pv I.5[1] (= thala unnata-padesa PvA 29); Miln 349; DA I.154.

Unnamati [ud + namati, see uṇṇamati in fig. meaning] to rise up, ascend Miln 117 (oṇamati +); Vism 306. — Caus. unnāmeti (q. v.). — pp. **unnata** & **uṇṇata** (q. v.).

Unnala & **Unnaḷa** (adj.) [Bdhgh. has ud + nala; but it is either a dissimilated form for *ullala (n > l change freq., cp. P. nangala > lāngala; nalāṭa > lalāṭa) from ud + **lal** to sport, thus meaning "sporting, sporty, wild" etc.; or (still more likely) with Kern, *Toev.* s. v. a dial. form of unnata P. uṇṇata, although the P. Commentators never thought of that. Cp. with this the BSk. unnata in same stock phrase uddhata unnata capala M Vastu I.305, and the Marathic Prk. mula = Sk. mṛta, Pischel, *Gr.* § 244. To these may be added P. celakedu > cetakedu J VI.538] showing off, insolent, arrogant, proud, haughty, in phrase **uddhata unnaḷa capala** M I.32; S I.61 = 204 (trsl^d. as "muddled in mind, puffed up, vain", expl^d. as uggata-nala uddhaṭa-tuccha-māna K. S. 318); A I.70, 266; II.26; III 199, 355, 391; It 113 (+ asamāhita); Dh 292 (+ pamatta; expl^d. as "māna-naḷaŋ ukkhipitvā caraṇena unnala" DhA III.452); Th 1, 634; Pug 35 (= uggata-naḷo tuccha-mānaŋ ukkhipitvā ti attho PugA 217).

Unnahanā (f.) [ud + **nah,** see nayhati] flattering, tying or pushing oneself on to somebody, begging Vism 27.

Unnāda [fr. ud + **nad**] shout, shouting J II 405.

Unnādin (adj.) [fr. ud + **nad**] shouting out; resounding, noisy, loud, tumultuous Vin III.336; D I.95, 143, 178; J II.216.

Unnādeti [Caus. of unnadati] to make resound J I.408 (paṭhaviŋ); II.34.

Unnāmin (adj) [ud + **nam** in Caus. form] raising or rising; in combⁿ. with **ninnāmin** raised & bent, high & low A IV.237 (of cultivated land).

Unnāmeti (uṇṇ°) [Caus. of unnamati] to raise DhsA 5; written **uṇṇameti** (with a for ā before mutes & liquids) at Sn 206 (inf. uṇṇametave).

Upa — [Vedic upa; Av. upa on, up; Gr. ὑπό under, ὑπέρ over; Lat. sub fr. *(e)ks-upo; Goth. uf under & on; Ohg. ūf = Ags. up = E. up; Oir. fo under. See also upari] prefix denoting nearness or close touch (cp. similarly ā), usually with the idea of approach from below or rest on top, on, upon, up, by. — In compⁿ. a upa is always contracted to **ūpa,** e. g. devūpaṭṭhāna, lokūpaga, puññūpatthambhita. — Meanings: (1) (Rest): on upon, up —: °kiṇṇa covered over; °jīvati live on (cp. anu°); °tthambhita propped up, sup-ported; °cita heaped up, ac-cumulated; °dhāreti hold or take up; °nata bent on; °nissaya foundation; °nissita depending on etc. — (2) (Aim): (out) up to (the speaker or hearer); cp. the meanings developed out of this as "higher, above" in upara, upari, upama = Lat. superus, supremus E. g. °kaḍḍhati drag on to; °kappati come to, accrue; °kappana ad-ministering; °kāra service to; °kkhata administered; °gacchati go to, ap-proach (cp. upâtigacchati); °disati ad-vise; °dhāvati run up to; °nadati to sound out; °nikkhamati come out up to; °nisevita gone on to or after; °neti bring on to; etc. — (3) (Nearness): close by, close to, near, "ad-"; e. g. °kaṇṇaka close to the ear; °cāra ap-plication; °ṭṭhāna at-tending; ṭṭhita ap-proached; °tiṭṭhati stand by, look after; °dduta urged; °nāmeti place close to; °nibandhati tie close to; °nisīdati sit close to or down by. — (4) (Intensive use): quite, altogether, "up"; e. g. °antika quite near; °chindati cut up. — (5) (Diminutive use as in Lat. subabsurdus; Gr. ὑπόλευκος whitish; Oir. fo-dord; Cymr. go-durdd murmur): nearly, about, somewhat, a little, secondary, by —, miniature, made after the style of, e. g. °aḍḍha about half; °kacchaka like a little hollow; °kaṇḍakin (= °paṇḍukin? whitish); °deva a minor god; °nibha somewhat similar to; °nīla bluish; upapurohita minor priest; uparajja viceroyalty; upalohitaka, uparopa; °vana a little forest. etc. *Note*. The nearest semantic affinity of upa is ā°.

Upaka (—°) [for °upaga] found only in combn. **kulûpaka** where second k stands for g. through assimilation with first k. Only with ref. to a bhikkhu = one who frequents a certain family (for the purpose of getting alms), a family friend, associate Vin I.192, 208; III.84; S II.200 sq.; A III.258 sq.; Nd² 385¹; Pv III.8⁵; PvA 266. — f **kulûpikā** (bhikkhunī) Vin II.268; IV.66. — Sporadic in gayhûpaka (for °ûpaga) at J IV.219.

Upakaccha (°—) [upa + kacchā²] only in combn. with °antare lit. "in between the hips or loins or arm-pits", in 3 phrases (cp. Kern, *Toev.* II.140 s. v.), viz. upakacchantare **katvā** taking (it) between the legs J I.63, 425, **khipitvā** throwing (it) into the armpits J V.211 & **ṭhapetvā** id. J V.46.

Upakacchaka [upa + kacchā + ka, cp. Sk. upakakṣa in diff. meaning] (1) [= upa + kaccha¹ + ka] like an enclosure, adj. in the form of a hollow or a shelter J I.158. (2) [= upa + kacchā² + ka] like the armpit, a hollow, usually the armpit, but occasionally it seems to be applied to the hip or waist Vin III.39; IV.260 (pudendum muliebre); Miln 293; J V.437 (= kaccha²).

Upakaṭṭha (adj.) [pp. of upa + **karś** to draw up or near to] approaching, near J IV.213 (yāva upakaṭṭha-majjhantikā till nearly noon). Usually in foll. two phrases: **upakaṭṭhe kāle** when the time was near, i. e. at the approach of meal-time Vin IV.175; VvA 6, 294; and **upakaṭṭhāya vassûpanāyikāya** as Lent was approaching Vin I.253; PvA 42; VvA 44. Cp. vûpakaṭṭha. — loc. upakaṭṭhe as adv. or prep. "near, in the neighbourhood of" Nd² 639 (= santike); Dāvs V.41 (so read for upakaṇṭhe).

Upakaḍḍhati [upa + kaḍḍhati, cp. upakaṭṭha] to drag or pull on to (w. dat.), or down to D I.180 (+ apakaḍḍhati); III.127 (id.); M I.365; S I.49; II.99; Dh 311 (nirayāya = niraye nibbattapeti DhA III.484).

Upakaṇṭha at Dāvs V.41 is to be corrected to upakaṭṭha.

Upakaṇḍakin (Pv II.1¹³) see under **uppaṇḍukin**.

Upakaṇṇa (°—) [upa + kaṇṇa] lit. (spot) near the ear, only in oblique cases or in der. °ka (q. v.) Th I, 200 (upakaṇṇamhi close to the ear, under the ear).

Upakaṇṇaka (adj.) [upa + kaṇṇa + ka) by the ear, being at or on the ear of somebody, only in loc. as adv. upakaṇṇake secretly Vin I.237; II.99; IV.20, 271; S I.86; A III.57; SnA 186; and in cpd. °**jappin** one who whispers into the ear (of another), spreader of reports A III. 136. Cp. kaṇṇajappaka & kaṇṇajappana.

Upakappati [upa + kappati] intrs.) to be beneficial to (w. dat.), to serve, to accrue S I.85; Pv I.4⁴ (= nippajjati PvA 19); I.5¹ (petānaṃ); I.10⁴ (= viniyujjati PvA 49); J V.350; PvA 8, 29 (petānaṃ), 27 (id.), 241; Sdhp 501, 504.

Upakappana (nt.) [fr. upakappati] profit PvA 29 (dān°), 49 (an°).

Upakappanaka (adj.) [fr. upakappana] profitable J I.398; DhA II.133.

Upakaraṇa (nt.) [fr. upa + **kṛ**] help, service, support; means of existence, livelihood D II.340; A II.86; J I.7; PvA 60 (commodities), 133 (°manussa, adj. suitable, fit); Sdhp 69. In general any instrument or means of achieving a purpose, viz. apparatus of a ship J IV.165; **tunnavaya°** a weaver's outfit J II.364; **dabb°** fit to be used as wood Vism 120; **dān°** materials for a gift PvA 105 (so read & cp. upakkhaṭa); **nahān°** bathing requisites VvA 248; **vitt°** luxuries A V.264 sq., 283, 290 sq.; PvA 71.

Upakaroti [upa + karoti] to do a service, serve, help, support Th 2, 89 (aor. upakāsiṃ = anugaṇhiṃ santappesiṃ ThA 88). — pp. **upakkhaṭa** (q. v.).

Upakāra [fr. upa + **kṛ**, cp. upakaraṇa] service, help, benefit, obligation, favour D III.187 sq.; VvA 68; PvA 8, 18 (°āya hoti is good for); Sdhp 283, 447, 530. — **bahûpakāra** (adj.) of great help, very serviceable or helpful S IV.295; PvA 114. upakāraṃ karoti to do a favour, to oblige PvA 42, 88, 159 (kata); katûpakāra one to whom a service has been rendered PvA 116.
-**āvaha** useful, serviceable. doing good PvA 86.

Upakāraka (adj.) [fr. upakāra] serviceable, helping, effective J V.99; Vism 534. — f. **upakārikā** 1. [benefactress, helper J III.437. — 2. fortification (strengthening of the defence) on a city wall D I.105, see DA I.274 & cp. parikkhāra. — 3. (philosophy) = cause (that which is an aid in the persistence or happening of any given thing) **Tikapaṭṭhāna** I.11.

Upakārin (adj.-n.) [fr. upakāra; cp. ASk. upakārin Jtm. 31⁴²] a benefactor M I.86; J III.11; DA I.187; Sdhp 540, 546.

Upakiṇṇa [pp. of upakirati] strewn over with (—°), covered Vv 35¹ (rucak°, so read for rājak°; expld by okiṇṇa VvA 160).

Upakiriyā (f.) [fr. upa + **kṛ**] implement, ornament J V.408.

Upakūjati [upa + kūjati] to sing to (of birds) J IV.296 (kūjantaṃ u. = replies w. song to the singing). — pp. **upakūjita** (q. v.).

Upakūjita (—°) [pp. of upakūjati] resounding, filled with the hum or song of (birds) J IV.359; PvA 154.

Upakūla [upa + kūla] embankment, a river's bank, riverside J VI.26 (rukkh'ûpakūlaje the trees sprung up at its bank).

Upakūlita [derivation uncertain] used of the nose in old age Th 2, 258 (jarāya **paṭisedhikā viya** says the commentary. Morris *JPTS.* 1884, 74 trsls. obstructed; Mrs. Rh. D. in "*Sisters*" takes it for upakūḷita and trsls. seared and shrivelled. So also Ed. Müller *JRAS.* 1919. 538. This is probably right; but Oldenberg, Pischel and Hardy all read **upakūlita**.

Upakūḷita [pp. of **kūḍ**, a variant of **kuth**, kvathati] singed, boiled, roasted J I.405 ("half-roasted" = aḍḍhajjhāmaka C.). See also **upakūsita**.

Upakūsita at J II.134 is perhaps faulty for °kūḷita, which is suggested by C. expln. "kukkule jhāmo" and also by v. l. °kuṭhita (for kuṭṭhita boiled, sweltering, hot). The variant (gloss) °kūjita may have the same origin, viz. °kūḷita, was however interpreted (v. l. BB.) by °kupita (meaning "shaken, disturbed by fire").

Upakka see uppakka.

Upakkanta [pp. of upakkamati] 1. attacked by (—°) Miln 112. — 2. attacking, intriguing or plotting against (loc.) DA I.140.

Upakkama [fr. upa + **kram**] (1) lit. (a) going to, nearing, approach (—°) VvA 72. — (b) attack Vin II.195; Miln 157; DA I.69, 71. — (2) applied (a) in general: doing, acting, undertaking, act S I.152 = Sn p. 126. — (b) in special: ways, means, i. e. either good of helpful means, expedient, remedy Sn 575; Miln 151, 152; or bad or unfair means, treachery, plotting Th 1, 143; J IV.115 (punishment); Miln 135, 176.

Upakkamati [upa + kamati of **kram**] to go on to, i. e. (1) to attack M I.86 = Ud 71. — (2) to undertake Vin III.110, 111. — (3) to begin Vin IV.316; DA I.318.

Upakkamana (nt.) [fr. upa + **kram**] going near to, attacking J IV.12.

Upakkitaka [fr. upa + **krī** to buy] a buyer, hawker, dealer comb^d. with bhataka DhA I.119 = Ud 23 (C. expl^s. by "yo kahāpaṇâdihi kiñci kināti so upakkitako ti vuccati"); Ps II.196 (? T. upakkhittaka).

Upakkiliṭṭha [pp. of upa + **klid** or **kliś**, cp. kilesa & next] soiled, stained, depraved, impure S I.179; A I.207 (citta); Vism 13.

Upakkilesa [fr. upa + **kliś**] anything that spoils or obstructs, a minor stain, impurity, defilement, depravity, Vin II.295 (cp. SnA 487 & VvA 134 & see abbha); M I.36, 91; D III.42 sq., 49 sq., 201; S V.92 sq. (pañca cittassa upakkilesā), 108, 115; A I.10 (āgantuka), 207 (cittassa), 253 (oḷārika etc.); II.53 (candima-suriyānaŋ samaṇa-brāhmaṇānaŋ), 67; III.16 (jātarūpassa, cittassa), 386 sq.; IV.177 (vigatā); V.195; Ps I.164 (eighteen); Pug 60; Dhs 1059, 1136; Nett 86 sq., 94, 114 sq.; Sdhp 216, 225 (as upaklesa). Ten stains at Vism 633.

Upakkuṭṭha [pp. of upakkosati] blamed, reproached, censured, faulty D I.113 (an°); Sn p. 115 (id.); J III.523; DA I.211.

Upakkosa [fr. upa + **kruś**] censure, reproach J VI.489.

Upakkosati [upa + kosati] to scold, reprove, blame D I. 161; J III.436, 523; IV.81, 317, 409.

Upakkhaṭa & °ta [pp. of upakaroti] done as a favour or service, given, prepared, administered D I.127 (= sajjita DA I.294); Pv II.8⁴ (=sajjita PvA 107); J VI.139; Miln 156.

Upakkhalati [upa + khalati] to stumble, trip D II.250; M II.209; A III.101; J III.433.

Upakkhalana (nt.) [fr. prec.] stumbling, tripping Vism 500.

Upakkhittaka at Ps II.196 see upakk°.

Upakhandha [upa + khandha] lit. upper (side of the) trunk, back, shoulder J IV.210 (= khandha C.).

Upaga (always as °ûpaga) (adj.) [upa + ga] — 1. going to, getting to, reaching, in phrases kāy°, S II.24; ākās'ānañc' āyatan° etc. Ps I.84; kāy° S II.24; brahmalok° Pv II.13¹⁹; yathākamm° D I.82. — 2. coming into, experiencing, having, as vikappan° according to option Vin IV.283; phal° bearing fruit, & pupph° having flowers, in flower PvA 275. — 3. attached to, belonging to, being at J I.51 (hatth°); VvA 12 (id. + pādûpaga). — 4. in phrase gayh° lit. "accessible to the grip", acquisition of property, theft J IV.219 (T. gayhûpaka); Miln 325; DhA II.29; PvA 4.

Upagacchati [upa + gacchati] — 1. to come to, go to, approach, flow to (of water) D II.12; PvA 12 (vasanaṭṭhānaŋ), 29, 32 (vāsaŋ) 132; ger. °**gantvā** PvA 70 (attano santikaŋ), & °**gamma** S II.17, 20. — 2. to undergo, go (in) to, to begin, undertake Sn 152 (diṭṭhiŋ anupagamma); J I.106 (vassaŋ); PvA 42 (id.); J I.200; niddaŋ upagacchati to drop off into sleep PvA 43 (aor. upagacchi, MSS. °gañchi), 105, 128. — pp. **upagata** (q. v.).

Upagaṇhanā (f.) [abstr. of upa + **gṛh**] taking up, keeping up. meditating Miln 37.

Upagaṇhāti [upa + gaṇhāti] to take up (for meditation) Miln 38.

Upagata [pp. of upagacchati] — 1. gone to, come, approached (intrs.) Sn 708 (āsan° = nisinna SnA 495); PvA 77 (santikaŋ), 78, 79 (petalokaŋ), 123. — 2. undergoing, coming or come under, overpowered, suffering Nd² under asita (= ajjhupagata in same conn. at A V.187); Pv I.11¹⁰ (khuppipās°); PvA 60 (= abhibhūta).

Upagamana (nt.) [fr. upa + **gam**] approaching, going or coming to, undergoing, undertaking Vin II.97 (+ ajjhupag°); Nett 27; Vism 600; PvA 42 (vass°).

Upagamanaka (adj.) [fr. upagamana] going to, one who goes to (with acc.) PvA 168 (= °upaga).

Upagaḷita [pp. of upagaḷati] flowing out, spat or slobbered out J V.471 (°khelo; v. l. paggharita).

Upagāmin (adj.) [fr. upa + **gam**, cp. °upaga] going to, undergoing, experiencing A II.6 (jāti jar°).

Upagūhati [upa + gūhati] to embrace J I.346, 349; II.424; III.437; V.157, 328, 384. — ger. **upaguyha** J VI.300.

Upagghāta [pp. of next] scented, smelled, kissed J VI.543 (C. sīsamhi upasinghita).

Upagghāyati [upa + **ghrā**, see ghāyati¹] to smell at, in sense of "to kiss" J V.328 (also inf. upagghātuŋ).

Upaghaṭṭita [pp. of upaghaṭṭeti] knocked or knocking against J I.26 (v.179).

Upaghāta [fr. upa + **(g)han**, cp. ghāta] hurting, injuring, injury M III.237; S II.218; IV.323 sq.; A III.173; Th 1, 583; Miln 274, 307, 347; DA I.273. an° not hurting others, kindness Dh 185.

Upaghātana (nt.) [fr. upaghāta] hurting DhA III.237 (an°).

Upaghātika (adj.) [fr. upaghāta] injuring, offending Vin II.13.

Upaghātin (adj.) [fr. upaghāta] hurting, injuring J III.523.

Upacaya [fr. upa + **ci**, cp. caya & ācaya] heaping up, gathering, accumulation, heap. As t.t. with ref. to kamma "conservation", with ref. to body & form "integration". (See discussion & defin. at *Cpd.* 253; *Dhs trsl.* 195). — D I.76 (= odana = kummās'ûpacayo, see under kāya); Dhs 582, 642 (rūpassa u. = āyatanānaŋ ācayo), 864; Vbh 147, 151 sq.; Kvu 520; Nett 113; Vism 449; DA I.220; PvA 198 (but v. l. paccayassa preferable).

Upacarati [upa + carati] to deal with, handle, use J VI. 180. — pp. **upaciṇṇa** & **upacarita** (q. v.).

Upacarita [pp. of upacarati] practised, served, enacted, performed Miln 359, 360.

Upacāra [fr. upa + **car**] — 1. approach, access Vin II.120, 152; IV.304; J I.83, 172; DhsA 328 (phal°). — 2. habit, practice, conduct Vin II.20 (dassan°); SnA 140 (id.); J III.280. — 3. way, means application, use of (esp. of spells etc.) J III.280 (mantassa); VI.180; Miln 153, 154 (dur° an evil spell); VvA 127 (gram. t.t. kāraṇ°). — 4. entrance, access, i. e. immediate vicinity or neighbourhood of (—°) J IV.182 (nagar[c]); usually as **gām°** Vin I.109; III.46; IV.230; KhA 77; SnA 83, 179. — 5. attention, attendance Vin IV.272; J VI.180; Miln 154. — 6. civility, polite behaviour J II.56; VI.102. — 7. On upacāra as philos. t.t. and its relation to **appanā** see *Dhs trsln.* 53, 54; *Cpd.* 55; *Mystic* p. XI. Thus used of **samādhi** (neighbourhood-, or access-concentration, distinguishing it from appanā-samādhi) at Vism 85, 126, 144 and passim.

Upacikā (f.) [connected with Sk. upadikā, although the relation is not quite clear. Attempts at explns. by Trencker *Notes* 62 (*utpādikā > upatikā > upacikā) & Kern, *Toev.* p. 102 (upacikā = Vedic upajīka, this fr. upajihikā for °dihikā, vv. ll. upadehihā & upadīkā). It may however be a direct der. from upa + **ci**, thus meaning "making heaps, a builder"] the termite or white ant Vin II.113, 148, 152; III.151; M I.306; J III.320; IV.331; Miln 363, 392; Vism 62; DhA II.25; III.15.

Upaciṇṇa [pp. of upacarati] used, frequented, known (as value) J VI.180.

Upacita [pp. of upacināti] — 1. heaped up, accumulated, collected, produced (usually of puñña merit, & kamma karma) Sn 697; KhA 132; SnA 492; VvA 7, 271, 342; PvA 30, 150. — 2. built up, conserved (of the body) Miln 232; DA I.220.

Upacitatta (nt.) [abstr. fr. upacita] storing up, accumulation Dhs 431.

Upacināti [upa + **ci**] — 1. to collect, heap up, accumulate (puññaŋ or pāpaŋ) VvA 254; PvA 8, 241. — 2. to concentrate, pay attention Th 1, 199 (C. upacetuŋ for ocetuŋ T.); J V.339 (= oloketi). — Pass. **upaciyyati** Th 1, 807. — pp. **upacita** (q. v.).

Upacca = **uppacca** (q. v.) "flying up" (= uppatitvā PvA 103) at Th 2, 248 (= ThA 205, where v. l. and gloss upecca & upacca, expld. by upanetvā), as well as at Pv II.7[11] (= PvA 103 where readg upaccha; & gloss upacca & upecca).

Upaccagā [upa + ati + agā of **gam**] 3rd sg. pret. of upātigacchati (q. v.) to escape, pass, go by; to overcome Sn 333 (mā upaccagā = mā atikkami SnA 339) = Th 2, 5 (= mā atikkami ThA 12); Sn 636, 641, 827 (= accagā atikkanta Nd[1] 167); Dh 315, 412, 417 (= atikkanta DhA IV.225); Bu II.43. — pl. **upaccaguŋ** S I.35; A III.311.

Upaccati (?) in phrase "akkhīni upacciŋsu" at J VI.187 is probably faulty for **apaciyiŋsu** aor. of apaciyyati, Pass. of apacināti (cp. upaciyyati > upacināti) "the eyes failed", lost power, went bad; cp. apacaya falling off, diminution. If not this reading we should suggest **upacchijjiŋsu** from upacchindati "were destroyed", which however is not quite the sense wanted.

Upacchindati [upa + chindati] to break up or off, to destroy, interrupt, to stop Sn 972 (pot. °chinde); J IV. 127; Nd[1] 502; ThA 267; PvA 31 (kulavaŋso upacchijji aor. pass.); Vism 164, 676 (bhavangaŋ).

Upacchinna [pp. of upacchindati] cut off, interrupted J I. 477; Miln 306.

Upacchubhati [upa + chubhati from **kṣubh** or **chubh**, see chuddha, khobha, nicchubhati, nicchodeti] to throw at M I.364 (vv. ll. °chumbh°, °cubh°).

Upaccheda [fr. upa + **chid**] breaking or cutting off, destruction, stoppage, interruption M I.245, 327 (pāṇ° murder); J I.67; Miln 134 (paveṇ° break of tradition) PvA 82 (kulavaŋs°); DhA I.152 (āhār °ŋ karoti to prevent fr. taking food); DA I.136, 159.

Upacchedaka (adj.-n.) [fr. upaccheda] destroying, breaking off, stopping, interrupting J I.418 (vacan°); IV.357; DA I.69 (jīvit' indriy°); VvA 72 (id.).

Upajānāti [upa + jānāti] to learn, acquire or have knowledge of (w. gen. or instr.), to know Vin I.272 (saŋyamassa); II.181 (gharāvās'atthena); A I.50 (dvinnaŋ dhammānaŋ upaññāsiŋ). — fut. **upaññissati** (& **upaññassati** Sn 716) Sn 701, 716 (= upaññayissati kathayissati SnA 498); J V.215. — pp. **upaññāta** (q. v.).

Upajīvati [upa + jīvati] to live on (w. acc.), to depend on, to live by somebody, to be supported by (acc.) D I.228; S I.217; Sn 612 sq.; Th 1, 943; J III.309, 338; IV.271 (= anujīvati); Pv II.9[50] (Ankuraŋ u. ti taŋ nissāya jīvanti PvA 134); Miln 231.

Upajīvika (adj.) [= upajīvin] Sdhp 501 (see next).

Upajīvin (—°) (adj.-n.) [fr. upa + **jīv**] living on, subsisting by A II.135 (phal°); Sn 217 (para-datt°), J I.227 (vohār°); IV.380; Pug 51; Miln 160 (Satth°); VvA 141 (sipp°). f. upajīvinī in rūp° (itthi) a woman earning her living by her beauty (i. e. a courtesan) Miln 122; PvA 46; cp. kiliṭṭha-kamm° gaṇikā PvA 195.

Upajūta (nt.) [upa + jūta] stake at game J VI.192.

Upajjha see next.

Upajjhāya [Vedic upādhyāya, upa + adhi + **i**, lit. "one who is gone close up to"] a spiritual teacher or preceptor, master. Often combd. with **ācariya** e. g. Vin I. 119; Nd[1] 350; the ācariya being only the deputy or substitute of the upajjhāya. Vin I.45, 53, 62, 120; IV. 130; S I.185; A II.66, 78; III.69; Sn 346; DhA II.93; PvA 55, 60, 230. — A short form of upajjhāya is **upajjha**, found in the Vinaya, e. g. at Vin I.94; III.35; with f. **upajjhā** Vin IV.326.

Upaññāta [pp. of upajānāti] found out, learnt, known Vin I.40; J V.325, 368; A I.61.

Upaṭṭita [upa + aṭṭita, from **ard**, see aṭṭita] pained, terrified; overcome, overwhelmed J VI.82 (visavegena).

Upaṭṭhapeti & **°ṭṭhāpeti** [Caus. II. of upaṭṭhahati] 1. to provide, procure, get ready, put forth, give Vin II.210; D II.19; M I.429; J I.266; IV.2; V.218; Pug 59, 68; Miln 15, 257, 366 (pānīyaŋ paribhojanīyaŋ), 397; DA I.270; Sdhp 356. — 2. to cause to be present Vin I.45; S I.170; Pv IV.1[70]. — 3. to cause to be waited on or to be nursed A V.72 (gilānaŋ upaṭṭhātuŋ vā upaṭṭhāpetuŋ vā). — 4. to keep (a servant) for hire Vin II.267. — 5. to ordain Vin I.62, 83.

Upaṭṭhahati & **°ṭṭhāti** [upa + **sthā**, cp. upatiṭṭhati] 1 (trs.) to stand near or at hand (with acc.), to wait on, attend on, serve, minister, to care for, look after, nurse (in sickness) Vin I.50, 302; IV.326; M III.25; S I.167; A III.94; V.72; Sn 82 = 481 (imper. °ṭṭhahassu); J I.67 (ppr. °ṭṭhahamāna), 262 (ppr. °ṭṭhahanto); IV.131; V.396; Dpvs II.16; PvA 19, 20. — aor. **upaṭṭhahi** PvA 14, 42, 82. — inf. **upaṭṭhātuŋ** A V.72; PvA 20. — ger. **upaṭṭhahitvā** PvA 76. — grd. **upaṭṭhātabba** Vin I.302; PvA 20. — pp. **upaṭṭhita** (q. v.). — 2. (intrs.) to stand out or forth, to appear, to arise, occur, to be present M I.104 sq.; A IV.32; J IV.203 (mante anupaṭṭhahante since the spell did not occur to him); V.207; Miln 64; ThA 258. — aor. **upaṭṭhāsi** J I.61; IV.3; PvA 42. — Caus. I. **upaṭṭheti**; Caus. II. **upaṭṭhapeti** & **°ṭṭhāpeti** (q. v.). — Pass. **upaṭṭhīyati** J IV.131 (ppr. °ṭṭhiyamāna), & **upaṭṭhahīyati** A III.94 (ppr. °ṭṭhahiyamāna).

Upaṭṭhāka [fr. upa + **sthā**, cp. BSk. upasthāka M Vastu I.251, and upasthāyaka Divy 426; Av. Ś. I.214; II.85, 112.] a servitor, personal attendant, servant, "famulus". Ānanda was the last u. of Gotama Buddha (see D I.206; Th 1, 1041 f.; ThA in *Brethren* loc. cit.; Vin I.179 (Sāgato u.), 194; II.186; III.66; IV.47; D I.150 (Nāgita); S III.113; A I.121; III.31, 189; J I 15, 100 (a merchant's); II.416; Pug 28; DhA II.93; VvA 149; PvA 211. — agg°

main follower, chief attendant D II.6; gilān° an attendant in sickness, nurse Vin I.303; A I.26; sangh° one who looks after the community of Bhikkhus Vin I.216; A I.26; III.39. — **dupaṭṭhāka** & **supaṭṭhāka** a bad (& good) attendant Vin I.302.

-kula a family entertaining (or ministering to) a thera or a bhikkhu, a family devoted to the service of (gen.) Vin I.83 (Sāriputtassa), 213; III.62, 66, 67; IV.283, 286; VvA 120.

Upaṭṭhāna (nt.) [fr. upa + **sthā**] — 1. attendance, waiting on, looking after, service, care, ministering A I.151, 225; Sn 138; J I.226, 237, 291; II.101; IV.138; VI.351. Ps I.107; II.7 sq., 28, 230; PvA 104, 145 (paccekabuddhassa), 176; VvA 75 (ther°); Sdhp 560. — 2. worship, (divine) service D III.188 sq. (°ŋ gacchati); PvA 122. **Buddh°** attendance on a Buddha PvA 93; ThA 18. — 3. a state room J III.257.

-sambhāra means of catering, provisions PvA 20. **-sālā** hall for attendance, assembly room, chapel [cp. BSk. upasthāna-śālā Divy 207] Vin I.49, 139; II.153, 208; III. 70 (at Vesālī); IV.15, 42; D II.119 (at Vesālī); S II.280; V.321; A II.51, 197; III.298; DhA I.37, 38; III.413.

Upaṭṭhāpana (nt.) [fr. upa + **sthā**] attendance, service Vin IV. 291.

Upaṭṭhita [pp. of upaṭṭhahati or upatiṭṭhāti, cp. BSk. upasthita Divy 281, 342] — 1. furnished provided, served, got ready, honoured with Sn 295 (°asmiŋ yaññasmiŋ); J V.173 (annene pānena); Pv I.5² (= sajjita paṭiyatta PvA 25); II.98 (= payirupāsita PvA 116); PvA 132. — 2. come, come about, appeared, arrived; present, existing Sn 130 (bhattakāle upaṭṭhite when mealtime has come), 898; Dh 235; Miln 274; PvA 124 (dānakāle °e). — 3. standing up (ready), keeping in readiness M I.77; A II.206; Sn 708 (= ṭhito C.); Pv II.9⁵³ (ready for service, serving, waiting upon cp. PvA 135.

-sati with ready attention, one whose attention is fixed, concentrated Vin I.63; D III.252, 282; S IV.186; A III. 251; Pug 35.

Upaṭṭheti [Caus. of upaṭṭhahati] to make serve or attend; sakkaccaŋ u (with acc.) to bestow respect (upon) Vin IV.275. fut. °essati Vin IV.291. to place, fix (parimukhaŋ satiŋ upaṭṭhapetvā) Vibh. 244.

Upaḍayhati [upa + ḍayhati] to be burnt up Miln 277.

Upaḍḍha (adj.-nt.) [upa + aḍḍha, used abs. whereas aḍḍha only in compⁿ., cp. also BSk. upārdha Divy 86, 144, 514; AvS I.211, 240] half Vin I.281 (°kāsina); II.200 (°āsana); J III.11 (°rajja); Vism 320 (°gāma); DhA I.15, 205 (°uposathakamma); II.85; KhA 239 (°gāthā); SnA 298; VvA 38, 61, 120; PvA 209, 276.

Upatappati [upa + tappati¹)] to be vexed or tormented J V.90; DhsA 42.

Upatāpa [fr. upa + **tap**] vexation, trouble Vism 166.

Upatāpana (nt.) [upa + tāpana] vexation, tormenting, torture J IV.13; ThA 243.

Upatāpika (adj.) [fr. upatāpa] causing pain, molesting J II.224.

Upatāpeti [upa + tāpeti] to cause pain, to vex, torment, harass J II.178, 224; IV.11; DhsA 42 (vibādhati +).

Upatiṭṭhati [upa + **sthā**, cp. upaṭṭhahati, °ṭṭhāti etc.] lit. "to stand by", to look after, to worship Pv III.1¹⁸; J II.73 (ādiccaŋ = namassamāno tiṭṭhati C.); Miln 231 (ger. °tiṭṭhitvā); J V.173 (°tiṭṭhate). pp. **upaṭṭhita** (q. v.).

Upatta [upa + akta, pp. of **añj**] smeared, spread over M I.343; J I.399.

Upatthaddha [upa + thaddha, pp. of upatthambhati] — 1. stiff Vin III.37 (angāni). — 2. supported or held up by, resting on, founded on, relying on Th 1, 1058, 1194; 2, 72 (yobbanena); J I.47 (v. 267: mettābalena); V. 121, 301; Kvu 251 (cakkhu dhamm° "when it is the medium of an idea"); Nett 117; Miln 110 (kāruñña-bal°).

Upatthambha [fr. upa + **stambh**] — 1. a support, prop, stay Miln 355, 415, 417; Sdhp 565. — 2. relief, ease Vin III.112. — 3. encouragement J V.270; DhA I.279.

Upatthambhaka (adj. nt.) [fr. upatthambha) holding up, supporting, sustaining DhsA 153.

Upatthambhana (nt.) = upatthambha Miln 36; J I.447; DA I.124; ThA 258; Vism 279.

Upatthambhita [pp. of upatthambheti] propped up, supported, sustained J I.107; Miln 36; DA I 234; PvA 117 (puñña-phal°), 148 (utu-āhārehi u.).

Upatthambheti [upa + thambheti, Caus. of thambhati] to make firm, shore up, support, prop up J I.127 [ppr. °ayamāna), 447; DA I.113; DhA III.73 (°ayamāna ppr.). — pp. **upatthambhita**.

Upatthara [fr. upa + **stṛ**] a (floor) covering, carpet, rug D I.103 (rath°); J II.126 (pabbat°); II.534.

Upatheyya [for upadheyya, see Trenckner, *Notes* 62¹⁶] a cushion J VI.490, 513.

Upadaŋsitar [n. ag. fr. upadaŋseti] one who shows Pug 49 (where upadhaŋsita is to be corrected to upad°, as already pointed out by Morris *J P T S.* 1887, 126. The word seems to be a crux to commentators, philologists, and translators, like upadaŋseti. Kern, *Toev.* s. v. keeps to the reading upah°, tries to connect it with Sk. dharṣati & trslˢ. "one who confirms". The Pug A leaves the word unexplained).

Upadaŋseti [= upadasseti with °aŋs° for °ass° like dhaŋseti = Sk. dharṣayati, haŋsa = harṣa etc. only in poetical passages] to cause to appear, to manifest M II.120; S I. 64, 65 (of gods, to become resplendent, to show divers colour-tones); A II.84 = III.139 = 264 = Pug 49 (to show pleasure); Th 1.335, to bring forth (a goad, and so incite, urge on); Vin IV.309.

Upadasseti (upa + dasseti, Caus. of **drś**, cp. also upadaŋseti] to make manifest, to show Miln 276, 316, 347.

Upadahati [upa + dahati¹] to put down, supply, furnish, put on; give, cause, make Vin IV.149; D II.135 (vippaṭisāraŋ); A I.203 (dukkhaŋ); Miln 109, 139, 164, 286, 383. grd. pass. **°dahātabba** to be given or caused Vin II.250 = A III.197 (vippaṭisāra). Cp. upadhi.

Upadāyaka (adj.) (—°) [fr. upa + **dā**] giving, bestowing Sdhp 319.

Upadiṭṭha [pp. of upadisati] pointed out, put forth, specified Miln 144 (pañha).

Upadisati [upa + disati] to point out, show, advise, specify J V. 457 (sippaŋ); Miln 21 (dhamma-maggaŋ). — pp. **upadiṭṭha** (q. v.).

Upadissati [upa + dissati] to be seen (open), to be shown up, to be found out or discovered Sn 140 (pres. upadissare = °nti SnA 192).

Upadeva [upa + deva, on use of upa in this meaning see upa 5] a secondary, lesser, minor god PvA 136.

Upadesa [fr. upadisati] pointing out, indication, instruction, advice PvA 26 (tadupadesena read for tadupād°; KhA 208 differs at id. p.); KhA 100; Sdhp 227.

Upaddava [upa + dava² of **dru**] lit. rushing on; accident, misfortune, distress, oppression S II.210; A I.101; Sn 51; Dh 338 (an°); DhA I.16; Sdhp 267, 398.

Upaddavati [fr. upa + **dru**] to annoy, trouble DA I.213. — pp. **upadduta** (q. v.).

Upadduta [pp. of upaddavati] overrun, oppressed, annoyed, overcome, distressed Vin II.170; III.144, 283; S II.210; IV.29; J I.26, 61, 339; II.102; IV.324, 494; Pv II.10[8]; Vism 24 (= apakata); Miln 279; VvA 311 (aṭṭita +); PvA 61. an° unmolested PvA 195; anupaddutatta state of not being molested VvA 95.

Upadhaŋsitar & **Upadhaŋseti** at Pug 49 is to be read upad° (q. v.).

Upadhāna (adj. nt.) [fr. upa + **dhā**, cp. upadahati] "putting under", i. e. (1) a pillow, cushion D I.7; S II.267 = Miln 366 (kaḷingar°); S III.145; A I.137, 181; III.50; J IV.201; V.506 (tamb° = ratt° C.); (2) imposing, giving, causing Dh 291 dukkh°).

Upadhāneti [f. upa + **dhā**] to suppose, think, reflect DhA I.239 (should be corrected to **upadhāreti**).

Upadhāraṇā (nt.) [fr. upa + **dhṛ**) "receptacle", milk-pail D II.192; A IV.393; J VI.503. See kaŋs°. Kern, *Toev.* I. 142 proposes corruption fr. kaŋs'ūpadohana, which latter however does not occur in Pali.

Upadhāraṇā (f) [cp. upadhāraṇa] calculation VvA 7.

Upadhārita [pp. of upadhāreti] considered, reflected upon Dh I.28; sūpadh° Miln 10; dūpadh° Vin IV.275.

Upadhāreti (Caus. of upa + **dhṛ**, cp. dhāreti 3] 1. "to hold or take up" (cp. semantically Lat. teneo = E. tenet), to reason out, conclude, reflect, surmise, know as such & such, realise J I.338; DhA I.28, 41; II.15, 20, 37, 96; IV.197 (an°); VvA 48, 200 (an°), 234, 260 (an°), 324; PvA 119 (for jānāti). — 2. to look out for (acc.) J III. 65; VI.2.

Upadhāvati [upa + dhāvati 1] to run up to or after, fall upon, surround Vin II.207; IV.260 (pp. °dhāvita); S I.185; S II.26 (aparantaŋ); Th 1, 1209; Miln 209; VvA 256; PvA 154, 168, 173 (for padhāvitā).

Upadhi [fr. upa + **dhā**, cp. upadahati & BSk. upadhi Divy 50, 224, 534] 1. putting down or under, foundation, basis, ground, substratum (of rebirth) S I.117, 124, 134, 186; A II.24 (°saṅkhaya); III.382 (id.); IV.150 (°kkhaya); It 21, 69; Sn 364, 728 (upadhi-nidānā dukkha = vaṭṭa-dukkhaŋ SnA 505), 789, 992; Nd[1] 27, 141; Nd[2] 157; Vbh 338; Nett 29; DhA IV.33. — (2) clinging to rebirth (as impeding spiritual progress), attachment (almost syn. with kilesa or taṇhā, cp. nirupadhi & anupadhi); S A. = pañcakkhandhā, S II.108. At M I 162 (cp. Sn 33 = S I.6 = I.107) wife and children, flocks and herds, silver and gold are called **upadhayo**. **upadhi** is the root of sorrow ib. 45; S II.108; Sn 728 = 1930 = Th I.152 and the rejection of all upadhis is Nibbāna D II.36. (cp. S I.136; III.133; V.226; A I.80; M I.107 = II.93; Vin I.5, 36 = J I.83 = Mvst II.444; It 46, 62).; D III.112 calls that which has **upadhi** ignoble (= non-Aryan). At S I.117 = Divy 224 upadhi is called a bond (saṅgo). Cp. opadhika. — The upadhis were later systematized into a set of 10, which are given at Nd[2] 157 as follows: 5 taṇh' upadhis (taṇhā, diṭṭhi, kilesa, kamma, duccarita), āhār-upadhi, paṭigh°, catasso upādinnā dhātuyo u. (viz. kāma, diṭṭhi, sīlabbata, attavāda; see D III.230), cha ajjhattikāni āyatanāni u., cha viññāṇa-kāyā u. Another modified classification see at *Brethren* p. 398.

Upadhika (Upadhīka) (adj.) (—°) [fr. upadhi] having a substratum, showing attachment to rebirth, only in cpds. an° free from clinging Vin I.36; Sn 1057, & **nir°** id. S I.141.

Upadheyya (nt.) [cp. upadhāna] a cushion J VI.490 (for upatheyya, q. v.).

Upanaccati [upa + naccati] to perform a dance D II.268.

Upanata [pp. of upanamati] inclined, bent, prone PvA 190.

Upanadati [upa + nadati] to resound (with song) Pv III.3[4] (= vikūjati PvA 189).

Upanandha [pp. of upanayhati, see naddha & nandhati] scorned, grumbled at Vin II.118.

Upanandhati [a secondary der. fr. upanandha, pp. of upanayhati] to bear enmity towards, to grumble at (with loc.); aor. **upanandhi** Vin II.118 (tasmiŋ); IV.83; Mhvs 36, 117.

Upanamati [upa + namati] to be bent on, strive after J III 324 (= upagacchati C.). — pp. **upanata**; Caus. **upanāmeti** (q. v.).

Upanayana (nt.) [fr. upa + **nī**; cp. naya & nayana] tt. for the minor premiss, subsumption (see *Kvu trsl.* 11) Miln 154; Nett 63; DhsA 329 (so read with v. l. for °najana).

Upanayhati [upa + nayhati] — 1. to come into touch with It 68 = J IV.435 (pūtimacchaŋ kusaggena, cp DhA I.45). — 2. to bear enmity towards (loc.), to grudge, scorn Dh 3, 4. — pp. **upanandha** (for °naddha). — See also **upanandhati**.

Upanayhanā (f.) & °**nayhitatta** (nt.) are syn. for **upanāha** (grudge, ill-will) in exegesis at Pug 18 = 22, whereas id. p. at Vbh 357 reads upanahanā upanahitattaŋ (with v. l. upanayihanā & upanayihitattaŋ).

Upanāmita [pp. of upanāmeti] brought up to, placed against D II.134.

Upanāmeti [Caus. of upanamati] 1. to bend over to, to place against or close to, to approach, bring near D II. 134; S I.207; Th 1, 1055; Sn p. 48 (= attano kāyaŋ Bhagavato upanāmeti); J I.62; V.215; SnA 151. — 2. to offer, to present J IV.386; II.5; Miln 210, 373; PvA 274. — pp. **upanāmita** (q. v.). [cp. BSk. upanāmayati to hand over Divy 13, 14, 22].

Upanāyika (—°) (adj.) [fr. upa + **nī**] — 1. referring to, belonging to in cpd. **att°** ref. to oneself Vin III.91; Vism 27. — 2. beginning, in phrase **vass'ūpanāyikā** (f.) the approach of the rainy season, period for entering on Lent (cp. BSk. varṣopanāyikā Divy 18, 489 & see also upakaṭṭha and vassa) Vin I.253; A I.51 (divided into 2 parts, first & second, or purimikā & pacchimikā); J III.332; DA I.8; DhA I.203; III.438; VvA 44; PvA 42.

Upanāha [fr. upa + **nah**, see upanayhati, same in BSk.; e. g. at M Vastu II.56.] ill-will, grudge, enmity M I.15; A I.91, 95, 299; IV.148, 349, 456; V.39, 41 sq., 209, 310; Pug 18 = Vbh 357 (pubbakālaŋ kodho aparakālaŋ upanāho Miln 289.

Upanāhin (adj.-n.) [fr. upanāha] one who bears ill-will, grudging, grumbling, finding fault Vin II.89; M I.95; D III.45; S II.206; IV.241; A III.260, 334; V.123, 156; Sn 116; Th 1, 502; J III.260 (kodhana +); Pug 18; Vbh 357. — Opp. an° not being angry (loc.) D III.47; S II. 207; IV.244; A V.124 sq.; J IV.463.

Upanikkhamati [upa + nikkhamati] to go out, to come out (up to somebody) Th 2, 37; 169; J III 244; Pv I. 10[1] (aor. °nikkhami; imper. °nikkhamassu).

Upanikkhitta [upa + n°] laid down (secretly), placed by or on top S V.457; J VI.390; Miln 80. — m. a spy J VI.394 (°purisa).

Upanikkhittaka [= prec.] a spy J VI 409 (°manussa), 431 (id.), 450 (id.).

Upanikkhipati (upa + n°] to deposit near, to lay up Vin I.312; S II.136 sq ; Miln 78, 80; Nett 21, 22; DA I. 125. — pp. **upanikkhitta** (q. v.).

Upanikkhipana (nt.) [fr. °nikkhipati] putting down (near somebody), putting in the way, trap Vin III.77.

Upanikkhepa [fr. upa + nis + **kṣip**] "putting near", depositing; — 1. appl[d]. to the course of memory, association of ideas Miln 78, 80; cp. °nikkhepana S II.276. — 2. deposit, pledge J VI.192, 193 (= upajūta).

Upanighaŋsati [upa + ni + ghaŋsati[1]] to rub up against, to crush (close) up to DhA I.58.

Upanijjhāna (nt.) [upa + nijjhāna[1]] meditation, reflection, consideration only in two phrases: ārammaṇa° & lakkhaṇa°, with ref. to jhāna J V.251; DhA I.230; III.276; VvA 38, 213. Cp. **nijjhāyana.**

Upanijjhāyati [upa + nijjhāyati] to meditate upon, consider, look at, reflect on Vin I.193 ("covet"); II 269; III. 118; D I.20; A IV.55; Miln 124; Vism 418. — pp. **upanijjhāyita** (q. v.).

Upanijjhāyana [for °nijjhāna] meditation, reflection Miln 127; Vism 418.

Upanijjhāyita [pp. of °nijjhāyati] considered, looked at, thought over or about Sn p. 147 (= diṭṭha, ālokita SnA 508).

Upanidhā (f.) [abstracted from upanidhāya or direct formation fr. upa + ni + **dhā**?] comparison Nd[2] 158 (= upamā; should we read upanidhāya?).

Upanidhāya (indecl.) [ger. of upa + nidahati of **dhā**] comparing in comparison, as prep. w. acc. "compared with" M I.374; III.177 (Himavantaŋ pabbatarājānaŋ); S II.133 (mahāpaṭhaviŋ), 262; V.457 (Sineru-pabbata-rājānaŋ); A III.181 sq.; IV.253 sq. (dibbasukhaŋ); Th 1, 496 (kammaŋ); J II.93; DA I.29, 59, 283.

Upanidhi (f.) [upa + ni + **dhā**, cp. nidhi] — 1. deposit, pledge Vin III.51. — 2. comparison, in phrase **upanidhiŋ na upeti** "does not come into comparison, cannot be compared with" M III.177; S II.263; V.457 (so read for upanidhaŋ); Ud 23.

Upanipajjati [upa + ni + **pad**] to lie down close to or on top of (acc.) Vism 269; J V.231.

Upanibajjhati see **upanibandhati.**

Upanibaddha [pp. of °nibandhati] — 1. tied on to Miln 253, 254. — 2. closely connected with, close to Vin III. 308 (Samanta Pāsādikā). — 3. attached to DA I.128.

Upanibandha [upa + ni + **bandh**] 1. close connection, dependence Vism 19 (°gocara). — 2. (adj. —°) connected with, dependent on Vism 235 (jīvitaŋ assāsa-passāsa° etc).

Upanibandhati [upa + n°) to tie close to, to bind on to, attach M III.132; Miln 254, 412. — Pass. **upanibajjhati** to be attached to Sn 218. — pp. **°nibaddha** (q. v.).

Upanibandhana (adj. nt.) [upa + n°] (adj.) closely connected with D I.46; DA I.128; (nt.) tie, fetter, leash Miln 253.

Upanibbatta [upa + nibbatta] come out, produced DA I.247.

Upanibha (adj. [upa + nibha] somewhat like (—°) M I. 58 = A III.324 (sankha-vaṇṇa°); J I.207 (= sadisa C.); V.302 (tāla°).

Upanivattati [upa + n°] to return Sn 712; J IV.417; V.126.

Upanisā (f.) [if = Vedic upaniṣad, it would be fr. upa + ni + **sad,** but if, what is more likely, a contracted form of upanissaya, it would be fr. upa + ni + **śri.** The history of this word has yet to be written, cp. Kern, *Toev.* s. v. & Divy 530 svopaniṣad] — 1. cause, means D II. 217, 259; M III.71 (samādhiŋ sa-upanisaŋ); S II.30—32 (S A. = kāraṇa, paccaya); V.25; A I.198; III.20, 200 sq., 360; IV.99, 336, 351; V.4 sq., 313 sq.; Sn 322 (= upanissaya SnA 331); p. 140 (= kāraṇa, payojana SnA 503); Dh 75 (cp. DhA II.102 aññā nibbānagāminī paṭipadā). — 2. likeness, counterfeit [= Sk. upaniṣad = aupamye Pāṇini I.4, 79] J VI.470 (= paṭirūpaka C.).

Upanisīdati [upa + nisīdati of **sad**] to sit close to or down by D I.95; A IV.10; J II.347; Pv IV.1[63] (ger. °sajja = °sīditvā PvA 242); Vism 269.

Upanisevati [upa + n°] to pursue, follow, go up after, cling to (acc.) M I.306. — pp. **upanisevita** (q. v.).

Upanisevana (adj.) [fr. upanisevati] going close after, following J V.399 [f. °ī.).

Upanisevita [pp. of upanisevati] gone on to, furnished with, sticking or clinging to, full of J V.302 (kakka°).

Upanissaya [upa + ni°] basis, reliance, support, foundation, assurance, certainty; esp. sufficing condition or qualification for Arahantship (see long article in Childers s. v.); no 9 in the 24 paccayas, Tikapatthāna, Tikapaṭṭhāna I.1, a term only found in the Paṭṭhāna, the Jātaka & later exegetical literature J I.78, 508; IV.96; VI.70; Nett 80; Vism 19 (°gocara), 535 (°paccaya); DhsA 315 (id.); DhA II.33; VvA 98; PvA 38 (sotāpatti-phalassa), 55 (°sampatti); Sdhp 265, 320.

Upanissayati [upa + ni°] to depend or rely on (acc.) Miln 240 (attānaŋ). — ger. **°nissāya** (q. v.); — pp. **°nissita** (q. v.).

Upanissāya (adv.) [ger. of upanissayati, cp. nissayati in same use & meaning) near, close by (with acc.); depending on, by means of (acc) M II.3; S II.269; Sn 867 (taŋ), 901 (tāpa°), 978, PvA 9 (Rājagahaŋ), 67 (id.); VvA 63 (Rājagaha-seṭṭhiŋ "with"). Cp. BSk. upaniśritya also a ger. formation, in same meaning, e. g. at Divy 54, 207, 505.

Upanissita [upa + ni°] dependent or relying on Sn 877; Nd[1] 283, Miln 245.

Upanīta [pp. of upaneti] 1. brought up to or into (mostly —°) Th 2, 498; Sn 677 (niraye), 774 (dukkha°), 898 (bhava°); J III.45 (thūṇa°); IV.271 (dukkh°); Nd[1] 38; Dh 237 (°yaya = atikkantavayo DhA III.337, advanced in age); Pv IV.1[10] (dukkha° made to suffer). **an°** Sn 846. — 2. offered, presented J I 88; PvA 274, 286. — 3. brought to conclusion, brought to an end (of life) J V.375 (= maraṇa-santikaŋ u. C.). — 4. bringing up (for trial), charging M I.251 (vacanapatha, cp. upanīya).

Upanīya (°īyya, °eyya) [ger. of upaneti] "bringing up" (for trial), charging, accusing D I.107 (vadati, cp. DA I. 276); A I.172 (°vācā); cp. upanīta 3.

Upanīla (adj.) [upa + nīla] somewhat dark-blue J V.168.

Upaneti [upa + neti] to bring up to, conduce, adduce; to present, give J I.200; Miln 396; DA I.276; PvA 39, 43, 49, 53, 74. — Pass. **upanīyati** (°nīyyati) — 1. to be brought (up to) J IV.398; ppr. °nīyamāna J I.200; PvA 5. — 2. to be brought to conclusion, or to and end (of life) M II.68; S I.2. — 3. to be carried along or away A I.155. — pp. **upanīta** (q. v.). — ger. upanīya (q. v.).

Upanti (adv.) [upa + anti] near, before, in presence of J IV.337.

Upantika (adj.) [upa + antika] nt. acc. °ŋ near J IV.337; V.58 (with gen.); VI.418 (so read for °ā); loc. °e near or quite near Pv II.9[15] (= samīpe gehassa PvA 120).

Upapacciyati see **uppaccati.**

Upapajjati [doubtful whether a legitimate form as upa + **pad** or a diaeretic form of uppajjati = ud + **pad.** In this case all passages ought to go under the latter. Trenckner however (*Notes* 77) defends upa° & considers in many cases upp° a substitution for upa. The diaeresis may be due to metre, as nearly all forms are found in poetry. The v. l. upp° is apparently frequent; but it is almost impossible to distinguish between upap° and upp° in the

Sinhalese writing, and either the scribe or the reader may mistake one for the other] to get to, be reborn in (acc.); to originate, rise Vin III.20 (nirayaŋ); A III.415; V.292 sq.; Sn 584; It 13 (nirayaŋ), 14 (sugatiŋ; v.l. upp°), 67 (saggaŋ lokaŋ; v.l. upp°); 43 = Dh 307 (nirayaŋ); Dh 126, 140; Pv I.10[1] (v.l. BB. udapajjatha = uppajja PvA 50); Pug 16, 51, 60; Nett 37, 99, cp. Kvu 611 sq. — pp. upapannā (q.v.). — Caus. **upapādeti** & pp. **upapādita** (q.v.).

Upapatti [fr. upa + **pad**, cp. uppatti] — 1. birth, rebirth, (lit. attainment) M I.82; S III.53; IV.398; A V. 289 sq.; Sn 139, 643, 836; Dh 419 (sattānaŋ); in var. specifications as: deva° rebirth among gods PvA 6, 81; devaloka° A I.115; kāma° existence in the sensuous universe D III.218; It 94; arūpa° in the formless spheres Vbh 172, 267, 296; rūpa°, in the world of form Vbh 171 sq., 263 sq.; 299; niraya° in Purgatory PvA 53. — 2. occasion, opportunity (lit. "coming to"); object for, in dāna° objects suitable for gifts A IV.239 (where 8 enumd., see dāna).
-deva a god by birth (or rebirth) VvA 18; also given as uppatti-deva, e.g. at KhA 123. See detail under **deva**.

Upapattika (—°) (adj.) [fr. upapatti] belonging to a birth or rebirth; in peta° born as a Peta PvA 119. — Cp. **upapātika**.

Upapanna [pp. of upapajjati] — 1. (—°) possessed of, having attained, being furnished with Sn 68 (thāma-bala), 212, 322, 1077 (ñāṇa°, cp. Nd² 266ᵇ and uppanna-ñāṇa). — 2. reborn, come to existence in (with acc.) S I.35 (Avihaŋ, expld. by C. not quite to the point as "nipphattivasena upagata", i.e. gone to A, on account of their perfection. Should we read uppanna?) A V.68.

Upaparikkhaṇa (nt.) = upaparikkhā VvA 232.

Upaparikkhati [upa + pari + **īkṣ**; cp. BSk. upaparīkṣate Divy 5, 230] to investigate, ascertain, test, examine M I.133, 292, 443; S II.216; III.42, 140; IV.174; J I.489; II.400; V.235; Miln 91, 293; Dāvs V.27; Sdhp 539; PvA 60 (paññāya u. = ñatvā), 140 (= viceyya).

Upaparikkhā (f.) [fr. upaparikkhati, cp. BSk. upaparīkṣā Divy 3 etc.] investigation, examination Vin III.314; M II.175 (attha°); A III.381 sq.; IV.221; V.126; Dhs 16, 20, 292; Pug 25; Nett 8, 42; DA I.171.

Upaparikkhin (adj.) [fr. upaparikkhati] investigating, reflecting, testing S III.61; A IV.221 sq., 296, 328. Cp. BSk. upaparīkṣaka Divy 212.

Upapāta = upapatti [but der. fr. **pat** (cp. uppāda¹ = ud + **pat** but uppāda² = ud + **pad**) with the meaning of the casual & unusual] rebirth Vin III.4; S IV.59 (cut°); Pug 50.

Upapātika (adj.) [fr. upapāta but evidently mixed with uppāda¹ and uppāda², cp. upapajjati, upapatti & BSk. upapāduka Av. S II.94, 95; Divy 523] = opapātika i.e. rebirth without parents, as a deva DA on D III.107; ThA 207.

Upapādita [pp. of upapādeti, Caus. of upapajjati] accomplished J II.236.

Upapādeti [Caus. of upapajjati] to execute, perform J V.346.

Upapāramī (f.) [upa + pāramī, cp. upa 5] minor perfection Bu I.77 (opp. paramattha-pāramī); DhA I.84.

Upapisana [upa + **piṣ**] grinding, powder, in añjan° powdered ointment (for the eyes) Vin I.203; II.112.

Upapurohita [upa + purohita, see upa 5] a minor or assistant priest J IV.304.

Upapīḷa at D I.135 read uppīḷa (q.v.).

Upapphusati [upa + phusati, of **spṛś**] to touch; aor. upapphusi J V.417, 420.

Upaplavati [upa + plavati, cp. uppilavati] to swim or float to (acc.), in uncertain reading as aor. **upaplaviŋ** at Sn 1145 (dīpā dīpaŋ upaplaviŋ floated from land to land; vv. ll. at SnA 606 uppalaviŋ & upallaviŋ; all MSS. of Nd² p. 54 & no. 160 write upallaviŋ). Perhaps we should better read **uppalaviŋ** (or upallaviŋ) as diaeretic form for *upplaviŋ, aor. of **uppilavati** (or uplavati), q. v. Expld. at Nd² 160 by samupallaviŋ.

Upabbajati [upa + **vraj**] to go to, resort to, visit Th 1, 1052; J IV.270, 295; V.495 (= upagacchati C.); VI.43.

Upabbūḷha see sam°.

Upabrūhaṇa (nt.) [fr. upa + **bṛh**², cp. BSk. upabṛṇhita Jtm 31⁰⁵] expansion, increase, augmentation Vism 145; DhsA 117.

Upabhuñjaka (adj.) [fr. next] one who eats or enjoys Vism 555.

Upabhuñjati [upa + **bhuj**] to enjoy J III.495; V.350 (inf. °bhottuŋ). — grd. **upabhogga**. — pp. **upabhuttu** (q.v.).

Upabhutta [pp. of upabhuñjati] enjoyed Dāvs III.65.

Upabhoga [fr. upa + **bhuj** cp. upabhuñjati] enjoyment, profit Vin IV.267; J II.431; IV.219 (v.l. paribhoga); VI. 361; Miln 201, 403; PvA 49, 220 (°paribhoga); DhA IV.7 (id.); Sdhp 268, 341, 547.

Upabhogin (adj.) [fr. upabhuñjati] enjoying Miln 267.

Upabhogga (adj.) [Sk. upabhogya, grd. of upabhuñjati] to be enjoyed, enjoyable Miln 201.

Upama (adj.) [compar.-superl. formation fr. upa, cp. Lat. summus fr. *(s)ub-mo] "coming quite or nearly up to", i.e. like, similar, equal D I.239 (andha-veṇ°); M I.432 (taruṇ° a young looking fellow); A IV.11 udak° puggala a man like water); Pv I.1¹ (khett° like a well cultivated field; = sadisa PvA 7); PvA 2, 8 etc. — *Note.* ūpama metri causa see ū° and cp. opamma & upamā.

Upamā (f.) [f. of upama in abstract meaning] likeness, simile, parable, example (cp. formula introducing u. S II. 114; M I.148); Sn 705 (cp. Dh 129, 130), 1137 (= upanidhā sadisaŋ paṭibhāgo Nd² 158); It 114; Vism 341, 478, 512, 582 sq., 591 sq.; PvA 29, 112 (dheu°); SnA 329, 384; Sdhp 29, 44, 259.
-**vacana** expression of comparison (usually applied to part. evaŋ) SnA 13, 472; KhA 185, 195, 208, 212; PvA 25.

Upamāna (nt.) [fr. upa + **mā**] comparison, the 2nd part of the comparison J V.341; VvA 13.

Upamānita [pp. of caus. upa + **mā**] measured out, likened, like, comparable Th 2, 382 (= sadisa ThA 255).

Upameti [upa + **mā**] to measure one thing by another, to compare J VI.252; Vism 314 (°metvā, read °netvā?).

Upameyya (adj.) [grd. of upa + **mā**] to be compared, that which is to be likened or compared, the 1st part of a comparison VvA 13.

Upaya [fr. upa + **i**, cp. upāya] approach, undertaking, taking up; clinging to, attachment, only as adj. (—°) in an° (anūpaya metri causā) not going near, aloof, unattached S I.141, 181; II.284; Sn 786, 787, 897 (cp. SnA 558); and in **rūpûpaya** (vv. ll. rūpupaya & rūpupāya) "clinging to form" (etc.) S III.53 = Nd¹ 25 = Nd² 570 (+ rup'ārammaṇa).

Upayācati [upa + yācati] to beg, entreat, pray to J VI. 150 (divyaŋ).

Upayācitaka (nt.) [of adj. upa + yācita + ka; pp. of yācati] begging, asking, praying, propitiation J VI.150 (= devatānaŋ āyācana).

Upayāti [upa + yāti of **yā**] to go to, to approach S I.76; II.118 (also Caus. °yāpeti); Dpvs VI.69; Sdhp 579.

Upayāna (nt.) [fr. upa + **yā**, cp. BSk. upayāna Jtm 31[63]] nearing, approach, arrival D I.10; DA I.94.

Upayānaka [fr. upayāna] a crab J VI.530.

Upayuñjati [upa + **yuj**] to combine, connect with; to use, apply; ppr. med. **upayujjamāna** VvA 245 (preferably be read as °bhuñjamāna, with reference to enjoying drink & food).

Upayoga [fr. upa + **yuj**] connection, combination; employment, application J VI.432 (nagare upayogaŋ netvā for use in the town? v. l. upabhogaŋ). Usually in cpd. °vacana as tt. g. meaning either combined or condensed expression, ellipsis SnA 386; KhA 236; PvA 73, 135; or the *acc.* case, which is frequently substituted for the foll. cases: sāmi-vacana SnA 127; PvA 102; bhumma° SnA 140; KhA 116; karaṇa° SnA 148; sampadāna° J V.214; SnA 317; itthambhūta° SnA 441; nissakka° J V.498.

Uparacita [pp. of upa + **rac**] formed ThA 211; Sdhp 616.

Uparajja (nt.) [upa + rajja, cp. uparaja] viceroyalty A III. 154 (v. l. opa°); J I.511; IV.176; DA I.134.

Uparata [pp. of uparamati] having ceased, desisting from (—°), restraining oneself (cp. orata) Vin I.245 (ratt-ûparata abstaining from food at night = ratti-bhojanato uparata DA I.77); D I.5 (id.); M I.319 (bhaya°); Sn 914 (= virata etc. Nd[1] 337); Miln 96, 307; DhsA 403 (vihiŋs°).

Uparati (f.) [fr. upa + **ram**] ceasing, resting; cessation M I.10; S IV.104; Miln 274.

Uparamati [upa + **ram**] to cease, desist, to be quiet J III. 489; V.391 (v. l. for upāramati, also in C.); Miln 152.

Uparamā (f.) [cp. lit. Sk. uparama, to uparamati] cessation Miln 41, 44 (an°).

Uparava [fr. upa + **ru**] noise J II.2.

Uparājā [upa + rājā; see upa 5] a secondary or deputy king, a viceroy J I.504; II.316; DhA I.392.

Upari (indecl.) [Vedic upari, der. fr. upa, Idg. *uper(i); Gr. ὑπέρ, Lat. s-uper; Goth. ufar, Ohg. ubir = Ger. über E. over; Oir. for] over, above (prep. & prefix) 1. (adv.) on top, above (opp. adho below) Vin IV.46 (opp. heṭṭhā); J VI.432; KhA 248 (= uddhaŋ; opp. adho); SnA 392 (abhimukho u. gacchati explaining paccuggacchati of Sn 442); PvA 11 (heṭṭhā manussa-saṇṭhānaŋ upari sūkara-s°), 47 (upari chattaŋ dhāriyamāna), 145 (sabbattha upari upon everything). — 2. (prep. w. gen) with ref. either to *space* = on top of, on, upon, as in kassa upari sāpo patissati on whom shall the curse fall? DhA I 41; attano u. patati falls upon himself PvA 45; etissā upari kodho anger on her, i. e. against her VvA 68; or to *time* = on top of, after, later, as in catunnaŋ māsānaŋ upari after 4 months PvA 52 (= uddhaŋ catūhi māsehi of Pv I.10[12]); sattannaŋ vassa-satānaŋ upari after 700 years PvA 144. — 3. (adv. in compn., meaning "upper, higher, on the upper or top side", or "on top of", if the phrase is in loc. case. See below.

-cara walking in the air, suspended, flying J III.454. **-pāsāda** the upper story of a palace, loc. on the terrace D I.112 (loc.); PvA 105, 279. **-piṭṭhi** top side, platform Vin II 207 (loc). **-bhaddaka** N. of a tree [either Sk. bhadraka Pinus Deodara, or bhadra Nauclea Cadamba, after Kern, *Toev.* s. v.] J VI.269. **-bhāga** the upper part; used in instr., loc. or aor. in sense of "above, over, beyond" J IV.232 (instr.). **-bhāva** higher state or condition M I.45 (opp. adh°). **-mukha** face upwards DA I. 228; Pug A 214. **-vasana** upper garment PvA 49. **-vāta** higher than the wind, loc. on the wind J II.11; or in °*passe* (loc.) on the upper (wind-) side DhA II.17. **-visāla** extended on top, i. e. of great width, very wide J III.207. **-vehāsa** high in the air (°—), in °*kuṭī* a lofty or open air chamber, or a room in the upper story of the Vihāra Vin IV.46 (what the C. means by expln. majjhimassa purisassa asīsa-ghaṭṭā "not knocking against the head of a middle-(sized) man" is not quite clear). **-sacca** higher truth PvA 66 (so read for upari sacca).

Upariṭṭha (adj.) [superl. formation fr. upari in analogy to seṭṭha] highest, topmost, most excellent Th I, 910. Cp. next.

Upariṭṭhima (adj.) [double-superl. formation after analogy of seṭṭha, pacchima & heṭṭhima: heṭṭhā] = upariṭṭha & uparima Dhs 1016, 1300, 1401; Pug 16, 17 (saññojanāni = uddhaŋbhāgiya-saññojanāni Pug A 198).

Uparima (adj.) [upari + ma, superl. formation] uppermost, above, overhead D III.189 (disā); Nett 88. Cp. upariṭṭhima.

Upariya (adv.) [fr. upari] above, on top, in compd. **heṭṭh°** below and above Vism 1.

Uparujjhati [Sk. uparudhyate, Pass. of uparundhati] to be stopped, broken, annihilated, destroyed D I.223; Th I, 145; It 106; Sn 724, 1036, 1110; Nd[2] 159 (= nirujjhati vūpasammati atthangacchati); Miln 151; Sdhp 280. — pp. **uparuddha.**

Uparuddha [pp. of uparujjhati] stopped, ceased Miln 151 (°jīvita).

Uparundhati [upa + **rudh**] to break up, hinder, stop, keep in check M I.243; J I.358; Th I, 143, 1117; Sn 118, 916 (pot. uparundhe, but uparuddhe Nd[1] 346 = uparuddheyya etc.); Miln 151, 245, 313. — ger. **uparundhiya** Th I, 525; Sn 751; aor. **uparundhi** J IV.133; PvA 271. — Pass. **uparujjhati** (q. v.).

Uparūḷha [upa + rūḷha, pp. of **ruh**] grown again, recovered J IV.408 (cakkhu).

Uparocati [upa + **ruc**] to please (intrs.) J VI.64.

Uparodati [upa + **rud**] 1. to lament J VI.551 (fut °rucchati) — 2. to sing in a whining tone J V.304.

Uparodha [fr. upa + **rudh**] obstacle; breaking up, destruction, end J III.210, 252; Pv IV.1[6]; Miln 245, 313.

Uparodhana (nt.) [fr. upa + **rudh**] breaking up, destruction Sn 732, 761.

Uparodheti [Caus of uparundhati] to cause to break up; to hinder, stop; destroy Vin III.73.

Uparopa [upa + ropa, cp. upa 5] "little plant", sapling Vin II.154. See also next.

Uparopaka = uparopa, sapling J II 345; IV.359.

Upala [Lit. Sk. upala, etym. uncertain] a stone Dāvs III.87.

Upalakkhaṇā (f.) & °aŋ (nt) [upa + lakkhaṇa] discrimination S III.261 (an°); Dhs 16, 20, 292, 1057; Pug 25; VvA 240.

Upalakkheti [upa + **lakṣay**] to distinguish, discriminate Vism 172.

Upaladdha [pp. of upalabhati] acquired, got, found J VI. 211 (°bāla; v. l. paluddha°); Sdhp 4, 386.

Upaladdhi (f.) [fr. upa + **labh**] acquisition; knowledge Miln 268; VvA 279.

Upalabhati [upa + **labh**] to receive, get, obtain to find, made out Miln 124 (kāraṇaŋ); usually in Pass. upalabbhati to be found or got, to be known; to exist M I.138 (an°); S I.135; IV.384; Sn 858; Pv II.11[1] (= paccanubhavīyati PvA 146); Kvu 1, 2; Miln 25; PvA 87.

Upalāpana (nt.) [fr. upa + **lap**] talking over or down, persuasion; diplomacy, humbug D II.76; Miln 115, 117.

Upalāpeti [Caus. of upa + **lap**] to persuade, coax, prevail upon, talk over, cajole Vin I.119; III.21; J II.266; III.265; IV.215; PvA 36, 46, 276.

Upalāḷita [pp. of upalāḷeti] caressed, coaxed Sdhp 301.

Upalāḷeti [Caus. of upa + **lal**; cp. BSk. upalāḍayati Divy 114, 503]. — 1. to caress, coax, fondle, win over J II. 267; Vism 300; Sdhp 375. — 2. to boast of, exult in J II.151. — pp. upalāḷita (q. v.).

Upaḷāseti [upa + Caus. of **las**] to sound forth, to (make) sound (a bugle) D II.337 (for uppaḷāseti? q. v.).

Upalikkhati [upa + **likh**] to scratch, scrape, wound A III. 94 sq. (= vijjhati C.).

Upalitta [pp. of upalimpati] smeared with (—°), stained, tainted Th 2, 467 (cp. ThA 284; T. reads apalitta); Pug 56. Usually neg. an° free from taint, undefiled M I.319, 386; Miln 318; metri causa **anūpalitta** S I.141; 284; Sn 211, 392, 468, 790, 845; Dh 353 (cp. DhA IV.7).

Upalippati [Pass. of upalimpati] to be defiled; to stick to, hang on to Sn 547, 812; J III.66 (= allīyatt C.); Miln 250, 337.

Upalimpati [upa + **lip**] to smear, defile D II.18; Vin III. 312; J I.178; IV.435; Miln 154. — Pass. **upalippati**, pp. **upalitta** (q. v.).

Upalepa [fr. upa + **lip**] defilement J IV.435.

Upalohitaka (adj. [upa + lohita + ka, see upa 5] reddish J III.21 (= rattavaṇṇa C.).

Upallaviŋ Sn 1145 see **upaplavati.**

Upavajja (adj.) [grd. of upavadati] blameworthy S IV.59, 60; A II.242. an° blameless, without fault S IV.57 sq; A IV.82; Miln 391.

Upavajjatā (f.) [abstr. fr. upavajja] blameworthiness S IV. 59 (an°).

Upavaṇṇeti [upa + vaṇṇeti] to describe fully Sdhp 487.

Upavattati [upa + **vṛt**] to come to pass, to take place J VI.58.

Upavadati [upa + **vad**] to tell (secretly) against, to tell tales; to insult, blame D I.90; S III.125 (attā sīlato na upav.); A II.121 (id.); V.88; J II.196; PvA 13.

Upavana (nt.) [upa + vana, see upa 5] a kind of wood, miniature wood, park J IV.431; V.249; Miln 1; VvA 170 (= vana), 344; ThA 201; PvA 102 (ārām°), 177 (mahā°).

Upavasati [upa + vasiti]. — 1. to dwell in or at J III.113; DA I.139. — 2. to live (trs.); to observe, keep (a holy day); only in phrase **uposathaŋ upavasati** to observe the fast day S I.208; A I.142, 144, 205; Sn 402 (ger. upavassa); J III.444; SnA 199; PvA 209. — pp. **upavuttha** (q. v.). See also uposatha.

Upavāda [fr. upa + **vad**] insulting, railing; blaming, finding fault Nd[1] 386; PvA 269; **an°** (adj.) not grumbling or abusing Dh 185 (anūpa° metri causa).

Upavādaka (adj.) [fr. upavāda] blaming, finding fault, speaking evil of (gen.), generally in phrase **ariyānaŋ u.** insulting the gentle Vin III.5; A I.256; III.19; IV.178; V.68; It 58, 99. — an° Ps I.115; Pug 60.

Upavādin (adj. [fr. upavāda] = upavādaka; in **ariy°** S I. 225; II.124; V.266; Pv IV.3[30]. **an°** M I.360.

Upavāyati [upa + vāyati] to blow on or towards somebody M I.424; A IV.46; Th 1, 544; Pv III.6[6]; Miln 97.

Upavāsa [fr. upa + **vas**, see upavasati] keeping a prescribed day, fasting, self-denial, abstaining from enjoyments [Same as **uposatha**; used extensively in BSk. in meaning of uposatha, e. g. at Av. Ś I.338, 339; Divy 398 in phrase aṣṭānga-samanvāgataŋ upavāsaŋ upavasati] A V.40 (? uncertain; vv. ll. upāsaka, ovāpavāssa, yopavāsa); J VI.508; SnA 199 (in expl[n]. of uposatha).

Upavāsita (adj.) (upa + vāsita] perfumed PvA 164 (for gandha-samerita).

Upavāhana (nt.) [upa + vāhana] carrying away, washing away Sn 391 (saṅghāṭi-raj-ūpa° = paŋsu-malādino saṅghāṭirajassa dhovanaŋ SnA 375).

Upavicāra [upa + vicāra; cp. BSk. upavicāra Divy 19, trsl[d]. on p. 704 in Notes by "perplexed by doubts" (?)] applying (ones mind), to, discrimination D III.245 (domanass°); M III.239; S IV.232 (somanass° etc.); A III.363 sq.; V.134; Ps I.17; Dh 8, 85, 284; Vbh 381.

Upavijaññā (f.) (adj.) [grd. formation of upa + vi + **jan**, cp. Sk. vijanya] about to bring forth a child, nearing childbirth M I.384; Th 2, 218; Ud 13; Dāvs III.38; ThA 197.

Upavisati [upa + visati] to come near, to approach a person J IV.408; V.377; aor. **upāvisi** Sn 415, 418 (āsajja upāvisi = samīpaŋ gantvā nisīdi SnA 384).

Upavīṇa [upa + vīṇā] the neck of a lute S IV. 197; Miln 53.

Upavīta [?] covered (?) at VvA 8 in phrase "vettalatādīhi upavītaŋ āsanaŋ" should prob. be read **upanīta** (vv. ll. uparivīta & upajita); or could it be pp. of upavīyati (woven with)?

Upavīyati [Pass. of upa + **vā**[2] to weave] te be woven J VI.26.

Upavuttha [pp. of upavasati] celebrated, kept (of a fastday) A I.211 (uposatha); Sn 403 (uposatha). Cp. **uposatha.**

Upavhyati [upa + ā + **hū**, cp. avhayati for *ahvayati] to invoke, call upon D II.259; S I.168.

Upasaŋvasati [upa + saŋ + **vas**] to live with somebody, to associate with (acc.) J I.152.

Upasaṇharaṇa (nt.) [fr. upasaṇharati] drawing together, bringing up to, comparison Vism 232 sq.; J V.186.

Upasaṇharati [upa + saŋ + **hṛ**] — 1. to collect, bring together, heap up, gather Miln 132. — 2. to dispose, arrange, concentrate, collect, focus Vin IV.220 (kāyaŋ); M I.436 (cittaŋ), 468 (cittaŋ tathattāya); S V.213 sq. (id.); DhsA 309 (cakkhuŋ). — 3. to take hold of, take care of, provide, serve, look after Miln 232.

Upasaṇhāra [fr. upa + saŋ + **hṛ**] taking hold of, taking up, possession, in **devat°** being seized or possessed by a god Miln 298.

Upasaṇhita (adj.) [pp. of upa + saŋ + **dhā**] accompanied by, furnished or connected with (-°) D I.152; M I.37, 119 (chand°); S II.220 (kusal°); IV.60 (kām°), 79 (id.); Sn 341 (rāg°), 1132 (giraŋ vaṇṇ° = vaṇṇena upetaŋ Nd[2]); Th 1, 970; J I.6; II.134, 172; V.361.

Upasankamati [upa + saŋ + **kram**, cp. BSk. upasankramati Av. Ś. I.209] — 1. to go up to (with acc.), to approach, come near; freq. in stock phrase "yena (Pokkharasādissa parivesanā) ten' upasankami, upasankamitvā paññatte āsane nisīdi", e. g. Vin I.270; D I.109; II.1, and passim. — aor. °sankami Pv. II.2[10]; SnA 130, 140; KhA 116; PvA 88; ger. °sankamitvā SnA 140; PvA 6, 12, 19, 20, 88; °sankamma Sn 166, 418, 460, 980, 986; inf. °sankamituŋ PvA 79. —. 2. to attend on (as a physician), to treat Miln 169, 233, 353; DA I.7.

Upasankamana (nt.) [fr. upasankamati] going near, approach M II.176; S V.67 = It 107; PvA 232.

Upasankheyya (adj.) [grd of upa + sankharoti] to be prepared, produced or contracted Sn 849 (= °sankhātabba SnA 549; cp. Nd[1] 213.

Upasagga [Sk upasarga, of upa + **sṛj**] — 1. attack, trouble, danger Vin I.33; A I.101; Th 2, 353; Dh 139 (where spelt upassaga, cp. DhA III.70); Miln 418. — 2. (tt. g.) prefix, preposition J II.67 (saŋ), 126 (apa); III.121 (ni, pa); DA I.245 (adhi); KhA 101 (sa° and an°); PvA 88 (atthe nipāto a particle put in metri causa, explⁿ· of handa); DhsA 163, 405.

Upasagga [follows here!].

Upasaṇṭhapanā (f.) [fr. upa + saṇṭhapeti] stopping, causing to cease, settling Pug 18 (see also an°).

Upasanta [pp. of upa + **śam**, cp. upasammati] calmed, composed, tranquil, at pease M I.125; S I.83, 162; A III. 394; Sn 848, 919, 1087, 1099; Nd[1] 210, 352, 434; Nd[2] 161; Dh 201, 378; Miln 394; DhA III.260; IV.114; PvA 132 (= santa).

Upasama [Sk. upaśama, upa + **śam**] calm, quiet, appeasement, allaying, assuagement, tranquillizing Vin I.10 = S IV.331 = V.421 (in freq. phrase upasamāya abhiññāya sambodhāya nibbānāya saŋvattati; see nibbāna III.7); D I.50; III.130 sq., 136 sq., 229 (as one of the 4 objects of adhiṭṭhāna, viz. paññā° sacca° cāga° upasama°); M I. 67; III.246; S I.30, 34 (sīlena), 46 citta-v-ūpasama), 48, 55; II.223, 277; III.86 (sankhārānaŋ . . . v-ūpasamo) D II. 157; S I.158 (see vūpasama and sankhāra); (ariyaŋ maggaŋ dukkh°-gāminaŋ); IV.62, 331; V.65 (avūpasama), 179, 234 (°gāmin), 378 sq.; A I.3 (avūpasama), 30, 42; II.14 (vitakk°); III.325 sq.; V.216, 238 sq.; Sn 257, 724, 735, 737; It 18 (dukkh°) 83; Dh 205; Nd[1] 351; J I.97; Ps I.95; Miln 170, 248; Vism 197 (°ânussati); Sdhp 587. Cp. vi° (vū°).

Upasamati [upa + **śam** in trs. meaning for usual sammati in intrs. meaning] to appease, calm, allay, assuage Sn 919; Th 1, 50 (pot. upasama = upasameyya nibbāpeyya Nd[1] 352). — pp. **upasanta** q. v.).

Upasamāna (nt.) = upasama Th 1, 421; Sdhp 335 (dukkh°).

Upasampajjati [upa + sampajjati] to attain, enter on, acquire, take upon oneself usually in ger. **upasampajja** M I.89: S III.8; A IV.13; V.69; Dhs 160 (see DhsA 167); DA I.313; SnA 158. — pp. **upasampanna** (q. v.).

Upasampadā (f.) [fr. upa + saŋ + **pad**] — 1. taking, acquiring; obtaining, taking upon oneself, undertaking D II.49; M I.93; A III.65; Dh 183 (cp. DhA III.236); Nett 44 (kusalassa). — 2. (in special sense) taking up the bhikkhuship, higher ordination, admission to the privileges of recognized bhikkhus [cp. BSk. upasampad & °padā Divy 21, 281 etc.] Vin I.12, 20, 95, 146 and passim; III.15; IV.52; D I.176, 177, 202; S I.161; A IV.276 sq. & passim; DhA II.61 (pabbajjā +); PvA 54 (laddh° one who has received ordination), 179 (id.).

Upasampanna [pp. of upasampajjati] obtained, got, received; in special sense of having attained the recognition of bhikkhuship, ordained [cp. BSk. upasampanna Divy 281] S I.161; A V.70; Vin III.24; IV.52, 130; Miln 13.

Upasampādeti [Denom. fr. upasampadā] 1. to attain to, obtain, produce DhsA 167 (= nipphādeti). — 2. to admit to bhikkhuship, to ordain Vin IV.130, 226, 317 (= vuṭṭhāpeti); grd. °etabba Vin I.64 sq.; IV.48; A V.72.

Upasamphassati [upa + sam + **spṛś**] to embrace J V.297.

Upasammati [Sk. upaśāmyati, upa + **śam** in intrs. function] to grow calm, to cease, to be settled or composed, to be appeased S I.62, 221; Dh 100 sq.

Upasavyāna (nt.?) [?] "a robe worn over the left shoulder" (Hardy, Index to ed.) VvA 166 (v. l. upavasavya).

Upasiŋsaka (adj.) [fr. upa + siŋsati = **śaŋs**, cp. āsiŋsaka] striving after, longing or wishing for Miln 393 (āhār°; Morris *J P T S.* 1884, 75 proposes reading upasinghaka).

Upasinghaka (adj.) [fr. upa + **singh**] sniffing after J II. 339; III.144; Miln 393 (? see upasiŋsaka).

Upasinghati [upa + **singh**] — 1. to sniff at S I.204 (padumaŋ); I.455; J II.339, 408; VI.336. — 2. to sniff up Vin I.279. — Caus. **°āyati** to touch gently KhA 136. Caus. II. **°āpeti** to touch lightly, to stroke J IV.407.

Upasinghita [pp. of upasinghati] scented, smelled at (loc.) J VI.543 (sīsaŋhi; C. for upagghāta).

Upasussati [upa + sussati] to dry up M I.481; Sn 433; J I.71.

Upasecana (nt.) [fr. upa + **sic**] sprinkling over, i. e. sauce Th 1, 842; J II.422; III.144; IV.371 (maŋs°); VI.24. See also nandi° & maŋsa°.

Upaseniyā (f.) [Sk. upa + either śayanika of śayana, or śayanīya of **śī**] (a girl) who likes to be always near (her mother), a pet, darling, fondling J VI.64 (=mātaraŋ upagantvā sayanika C.).

Upasevati [upa + **sev**] — 1. to practice, frequent, pursue Miln 355. — 2. to serve, honour, Sn 318 (°amāna). — pp. **upasevita** (q. v.).

Upasevanā (f.) [abstr. fr. upasevati] serving, pursuing, following, service, honouring, pursuit S III.53 = Nd[1] 25 = Nd[2] 570 (nand° pleasure-seeking); It 68 (bāl° & dhīr°); Sn 249 (utu° observance of the seasons); Miln 351.

Upasevita [pp. of upasevati] visited, frequented PvA 147 (for sevita).

Upasevin (adj.) (—°) [fr upasevati] pursuing, following, going after A III.136 (vyatta°); Miln 264 (rāj°); DhA III.482 (para-dār°).

Upasobhati [upa + **śubh**] to appear beautiful, to shine forth Th 1, 1080. — Caus. **°sobheti** to make beautiful, embellish, adorn Vv 52[6]; J V.132; PvA 153. — pp. **upasobhita** (q. v.).

Upasobhita [pp. of upasobheti] embellished, beautified, adorned PvA 153, 187; Sdhp 593.

Upassagga see **upasagga**.

Upassaṭṭha [Sk. upasṛṣṭa, pp. of upa + **sṛj**] "thrown upon", overcome, visited, afflicted, ruined, oppressed S IV.29; A III.226 (udak°); J I.61; II.239.

Upassaya [fr. upa + **śri**, cp. assaya & missaya] abode, resting home. dwelling, asylum S I.32, 33; Vv 68[4]; Miln 160. Esp. freq. as **bhikkhuni°** or **bhikkhun°** a nunnery Vin II.259; IV.265, 292; S II.215; J I.147, 428; Miln 124.

Upassāsa [upa + assāsa; upa + ā + **śvas**] breathing J I.160.

Upassuti (f.) [fr. upa + **śru**] listening to, attention S II. 75; IV.91; J V.100; Miln 92.

Upassutika (adj.) [fr. upassuti] one who listens, an eaves-dropper J V.81.

Upahacca (°—) [ger. of upahanti] — 1. spoiling, impairing, defiling J V.267 (manaŋ) — 2. reducing, cutting short; only in phrase **upahacca-parinibbāyin** "coming to extinction after reducing the time of rebirths (or after having almost reached the destruction of life") S V.70, 201 sq.; A I.233 sq.; IV.380; Pug 17 (upagantvā kālakiriyaŋ āyukkhayassa āsane ṭhatvā ti attho Pug A 199); Nett 190. — The term is not quite clear; there seems to have existed very early confusion with upapacca > upapajja > uppajja, as indicated by BSk. upapadya-parinirvāyin, and by remarks of C. on Kvu 268, as quoted at *Kvu trsl*[n]. 158, 159.

Upahaññati [Pass. of upahanti] to be spoilt or injured Sn 584; J IV.14; Miln 26.

Upahata [pp. of upahanti] injured, spoilt; destroyed D I.86 (phrase khata + upahata); S I.238 (na sûpahata "not easily put out" trsl.); II 227; A I.161; Dh 134; J VI. 515; Miln 223, 302; DhA II.33 (an°).

Upahattar [Sk. *upahartṛ, n. ag. of upa + **hṛ**] a bringer (of) M I.447 sq.

Upahanti (& °hanati J I.454) [upa + **han**] to impair, injure; to reduce, cut short; to destroy, only in ger. **upahacca**; pp. upahata & Pass. **upahaññati** (q. v.).

Upaharaṇa (nt.) [fr. upa + **hṛ**] — 1. presentation; luxury J I.231. — 2. taking, seizing J VI.198.

Upaharati [upa + **hṛ**] to bring, offer, present A II.87; III. 33; Dh I.301, 302; J V.477.

Upahāra [fr. upa + **hṛ**] bringing forward, present, offering, gift Vin III.136 (āhār°) A II.87; III.33; V.66 (mett°); J I.47; IV.455; VI.117; DA I.97.

Upahiŋsati [upa + **hiŋs**] to injure, hurt Vin II.203; J IV.156.

Upāgacchati [upa + ā + **gam**] to come to, arrive at, reach, obtain, usually aor. upāgañchi Cp I 10[10], pl. upāgañchuŋ Sn 1126; or upāgami Sn 426, 685, pl. upāgamuŋ Sn 302, 1126. Besides in pres. imper. upāgaccha PvA 64 (so read for upagaccha). — pp. **upāgata**.

Upāgata [pp. of upāgacchati] come to, having reached or attained Sn 1016; PvA 117 (yakkhattaŋ); Sdhp 280.

Upāta [according to Kern, *Toev.* s. v. = Sk. upātta, pp of upa + ā + **dā** "taken up"; after Morris *J P T S.* 1884, 75 = uppāta "flying up"] thrown up, cast up, raised (of dust) Th 1, 675.

Upâtigacchati [upa + ati + gacchati] to "go out over", to surpass, overcome, only in 3rd sg. pret. **upaccagā** Sn 333, 636, 641, 827; Th 1, 181; 2, 4; J I.258; VI.182; & 3rd pl. **upaccaguŋ** S I.35; A III.311; J III.201.

Upâtidhāvati [upa + ā + dhāvati] to run on or in to Ud 72.

Upâtipanna [pp. of upâtipajjati, upa + ā + **pad**] fallen into, a prey to (with loc.) Sn 495 (= nipanna with gloss adhimutta SnA 415).

Upâtivatta [pp. of upâtivattati] gone beyond, escaped from, free from (with acc.) S I.143; A II.15; Sn 55, 474, 520, 907; J III.7, 360; Nd[1] 322 = Nd[2] 163. Cp. BSk. upātivṛtta in same sense at M Vastu III.281.

Upâtivattati [upa + ati + vattati] to go beyond, overstep M I.327; Sn 712 (v. l. for upanivattati); Nett 49. — pp. **upâtivatta** (q. v.).

Upādā (adv.) [shortened ger. of upādiyati for the usual upādāya in specialised meaning] lit. "taking up", i. e. subsisting on something else, not original, secondary, derived (of rūpa form) Dhs 877, 960, 1210; Vism 275, 444 (24 fold); DhsA 215, 299, 333, cp. *Dhs trsl*[n]. 127, 197. — Usually (and this is the earlier use of upādā) as neg. **anupādā** (for anupādāya) in meaning "not taking up any more (fuel, so as to keep the fire of rebirth alive)", not clinging to love of the world, or the kilesas q. v., having no more tendency to becoming; in phrases **a. parinibbānaŋ** "unsupported emancipation" M I.148; S IV.48; V.29; DhA I.286 etc.; **a. vimokkho** mental release A V.64 (A A: catuhi upādānehi agahetvā cittassa vimokkho; arahattass'etaŋ nāmaŋ); Vin V.164; Ps II.45 sq.; **a. vimutto** D I.17 (= kiñci dhammaŋ anupādiyitvā vimutto DA I.109); cp. M III.227 (paritassanā).

Upādāna (nt.) [fr. upa + ā + **dā**] — (lit. that (material) substratum by means of which an active process is kept alive or going), fuel, supply, provision; adj. (—°) supported by, drawing one's existence from S I.69; II 85 (aggikkhandho °assa pariyādānā by means of taking up fuel); V.284 (vāt°); J III.342 sa-upādāna (adj.) provided with fuel S IV.399; anupādāna without fuel DhA II.163. — 2. (appl[d].) "drawing upon", grasping, holding on, grip, attachment; adj. (—°) finding one's support by or in, clinging to, taking up, nourished by. See on term *Dhs trsl*[n]. 323 & *Cpd.* 171. They are classified as 4 upādānāni or four Graspings viz. kām°, diṭṭh°, sīlabbat°, attavād° or the graspings arising from sense-desires, speculation, belief in rites, belief in the soul-theory D II.58; III.230; M I.51, 66; S II.3; V 59; Dhs 1213; Ps I.129; II.46, 47; Vbh 375; Nett 48; Vism 569. — For upādāna in var. connections see the foll. passages: D I.25; II.31, 33, 56; III.278; M I.66, 136 (attavād°) 266; S II.14, 17, 30, 85; III.10, 13 sq., 101, 135, 167, 191; IV.32, 87 sq., 102 (taṇissitaŋ viññāṇaŋ tadupādānaŋ), 390, 400 (= taṇhā); A IV.69; V.111 (upāy°); Sn 170, 358, 546; Ps I.51 sq., 193; II.45 sq, 113; Vbh 18, 30, 67, 79, 119, 132; Dhs 1059, 1136, 1213, 1536 sq.; Nett 28 sq., 41 sq., 114 sq.; DhA IV.194. — **sa°** full of attachment (to life) M I.65; Vin III.111; S IV.102; **an°** unattached, not showing attachment to existence S IV.399; Vin III.111; Th 1, 840; Miln 32; DA I.98.

-kkhandha, usually as pañc' upādāna-kkhandhā the factors of the "fivefold clinging to existence" [cp. BSk. pañc' u°-skandhāḥ Av. Ś II.168[1] & note] D II.35, 301 sq.; III.223, 286; M I.61, 144, 185; III.15, 30, 114, 295; Ps II.109 sq.; Vbh 101; Vism 505 (khandha-pañcaka). See for detail khandha II.B 2. **-kkhaya** extinction or disappearance of attachment S II.54; A III.376 sq.; Sn 475, 743; It 75. **-nidāna** the ground of upādāna; adj. founded on or caused by attachment Ps II.111; Vbh 135 sq. **-nirodha** destruction of "grasping" Vin I.1 (in formula of paṭicca-samuppāda); S II.7; III.14; A I.177. **-paccaya** = °nidāna S II.5; III 94; Sn 507, 742.

Upādāniya (adj.) [fr. upādāna, for *upādānika > °aka] belonging to or connected with upādāna, sensual, (inclined to) grasping; material (of rūpa), derived. See on term *Dhs trsl*[n]. 203, 322. — S II.84; III.47; IV.89, 108; Dhs 584, 1219, 1538; Vbh 12 sq., 30, 56, 119, 125, 319, 326.

Upādāya (adv.) [ger. of upādiyati] — 1. (as prep. with acc.) lit. "taking it up" (as such & such), i. e. (a) out of, as, for; in phrase anukampaŋ upādāya out of pity or mercy D I.204; PvA 61, 141, 164. — (b) compared with, alongside of, with reference to, according to D I.205 (kālañ ca samayañ ca acc. to time & convenience); DhA I.391; VvA 65 (paŋsucuṇṇaŋ); PvA 268 (manussalokaŋ). The same use of upādāya is found in BSk., e. g. at Divy 25, 359, 413; Av. Ś I.255. — 2. (in same meaning & application as upādā, i. e. in neg. form first & then in positive abstraction from the latter) as philosophical term "hanging on to", i. e. derived, secondary (with rūpa) Vbh 12, 67 etc.; Nd[1] 266. Usually as **anupādāya** "not clinging to", without any (further) clinging (to rebirth), emancipated, unconditioned, free [cp. BSk. paritt-anupādāya free from the world Divy 655], freq. in phrase a. nibbuta completely emancipated S II.279; A I.162; IV. 290; besides in foll. pass.: Vin I.14 (a. cittaŋ vimuccati) 182 (id.); S II.187 sq.; IV.20, 107; V.317; Dh 89 = S V.24 (ādānapaṭi-nisagge a. ye ratā); Dh 414; Sn 363; It 94 (+ aparitassato).

Upādi° [the compⁿ-from of upādāna, derived fr. upādā in analogy to nouns in °a & °ā which change their a to i in compⁿ. with **kr** & **bhū**; otherwise a n. formation fr. **dā** analogous to °dhi fr. **dhā** in upadhi] = upādāna, but in more concrete meaning of "stuff of life", substratum of being, khandha; only in combⁿ. with °sesa (adj.) having some fuel of life (= khandhas or substratum) left, i. e. still dependent (on existence), not free, materially determined S V.129, 181; A III.143; It 40; Vism 509. More frequently neg. **an-upādi-sesa** (nibbāna, nibbānadhātu or parinibbāna, cp. similarly BSk. anupādi-vimukti M Vastu I.69) completely emancipated, free, without any (material) substratum Vin II.239 (nibbāna-dhātu); D III.135; M I.148 (parinibbāna); A II.120; IV.75 sq., 202, 313; J I.28, 55; Sn 876; It 39, 121 (nibbāna-dhātu); Ps. I.101; Vism 509; DhA IV.108 (nibbāna); VvA 164, 165. Opp. **sa-upādisesa** A IV.75 sq., 378 sq.; Sn 354 (opp. nibbāyi); Vism 509; Nett 92. See further ref. under nibbāna & parinibbāna.

Upādiṇṇa [for °ādinna with substitution of ṇṇ for nn owing to wrong derivation as pp. from ādiyati² instead of ādiyati¹] grasped at, laid hold of; or "the issue of grasping", i. e. material, derived, secondary (cp. upādā), see def. at *Dhs trslⁿ.* 201, 324. — Dhs 585, 877, 1211, 1534; Vbh 2 sq., 326, 433; Vism 349, 451; an° Vin III.113; Dhs 585, 991, 1212, 1535.

Upādiṇṇaka (adj.) = upādiṇṇa DhsA 311, 315, 378; Vism 398.

Upādiyati [upa + ā + **dā**, see ādiyati¹] to take hold of, to grasp, cling to, show attachment (to the world), cp. upādāna D II.292; M I.56, 67; S II.14; III.73, 94, 135; IV. 168 (na kiñci loke u. = parinibbāyati); Sn 752, 1103, 1104; Nd¹ 444 (= ādeti); Nd² 164. ppr. **upādiyaŋ** S IV. 24 = 65 (an°); — ppr. med. **upādiyamāna** S III.73; SnA 409, & **upādiyāna** (°ādiyāno) Sn 470; Dh 20. — ger. **upādāya** in lit. meaning "taking up" J I.30; Miln 184, 338, 341; for specialised meaning & use as prep. see separately as also **upādā** and **upādiyitvā** VvA 209; DA I.109 (an°); DhA IV.194 (an°). — pp. **upādiṇṇa** (q. v.).

Upādhi [fr. upa + ā + **dhā**] 1. cushion J VI.253. — 2. supplement, ornament (?), in °ratha "the chariot with the outfit", expld. by C. as the royal chariot with the golden slipper J VI.22.

Upādhiya [fr. upāhi] being furnished with a cushion J VI. 252 (adj.).

Upāya [fr. upa + **i**, cp. upaya] approach; fig. way, means, expedient, stratagem S III.53 sq., 58; D III.220 (°kosalla); Sn 321 (°ññū); J I.256; Nd² 570 (for upaya); PvA 20, 31, 39, 45, 104, 161; Sdhp 10, 12, 350, 385. — Cases adverbially; instr. **upāyena** by artifice or means of a trick PvA 93; yena kenaci u. PvA 113. — abl. **upāyaso** by some means, somehow J III.443; V.401 (= upāyena C.). — **anupāya** wrong means J I.256; Sdhp 405; without going near, without having a propensity for S I.181; M III.25. **-kusala** clever in resource J I.98; Nett 20; SnA 274.

Upāyatta (nt.) [abstr. fr. upāya] a means of (—°) VvA 84 (paṭipajjan°).

Upāyana (nt.) [fr. upa + **i**, cp. upāya] going to (in special sense), enterprise, offering, tribute, present J V.347; VI. 327; Miln 155, 171, 241; Sdhp 616, 619.

Upāyāsa [upa + āyāsa, cp. BSk. upāyāsa Divy 210, 314.] (a kind of) trouble, turbulence, tribulation, unrest, disturbance, unsettled condition M I.8, 144, 368; III.237; A I.144, 177, 203 (sa°); II.123, 203; III.3, 97, 429; Sn 542; It 89 = A I.147 = M I.460; J II.277 (°bahula); IV.22 (id.); Pug 30, 36; Vbh 247; Nett 29; Miln 69; Vism 504 (def.); DA I.121. — **anupāyāsa** peacefulness, composure, serenity, sincerity D III.159; A III.429; Ps I 11 sq.

Upāramati [upa + ā + **ram**] to cease, to desist J V.391, 498.

Upāraddha [pp. of upārambhati] blamed, reprimanded, reproved A V 230.

Upārambha [Sk. upārambha, upa + ālambhate] — 1. reproof, reproach, censure M I.134, 432; S III.73; V.73; A I.199; II.181; III.175; IV.25; Vbh 372. — 2. (adj.) ill-disposed, hostile Th 1, 360 sq.; DA I.21, 263.

Upārambhati [Sk. upālambhate, upa + ā + **labh**] to blame, reprimand, reproach M I.432, 433. — pp. **upāraddha** (q. v.).

Upālāpeti at PvA 276 read **upalāpeti** (q. v.).

Upāvisi 3rd sg. aor. of **upavisati** (q. v.).

Upāsaka [fr. upa + **ās**, cp. upāsati] a devout or faithful layman, a lay devotee Vin I.4, 16 (tevāciko u.), 37, 139, 195 sq.; II.125; III.6, 92; IV.14, 109; D I.85; II.105, 113; III.134, 148, 153, 168, 172 sq., 264; M I.29, 467, 490; S V.395, 410; A I.56 sq.; II.132 (°parisā); III 206 (°caṇḍāla, °ratana); IV.220 sq. (kittāvatā hoti); Sn 376, 384; J I.83; Pv I 10⁴; Vbh 248 (°sikkhā); DA I.234; PvA 36, 38, 54, 61, 207. — f. **upāsikā** Vin I.18, 141, 216; III.39; IV.21, 79; D III.124, 148, 172, 264; M I.29, 467, 491; S II 235 sq.; A I.88; II.132; V.287 sq.; Miln 383; PvA 151, 160.

Upāsakatta (nt.) [abstr. fr. upāsaka] state of being a believing layman or a lay follower of the Buddha Vin I.37; S IV,301; Vv 84²¹.

Upāsati [upa + **ās**] lit. "to sit close by", to go after, attend, follow, serve, honour, worship D II.287; A I.162; J V. 339, 371 (= upagacchati C.); Miln 418 (lakkhe upāseti fix his attention on the target). — 3rd pl. pres. med. **upāsare** A I.162; J IV.417 (= upāyanti C.). Cp. **payirupāsati**. — pp. **upāsita** & **upāsīna** (q. v.). See also upāsaka, upāsana¹.

Upāsana¹ (nt.) [fr. upāsati] attendance, service, honour S I.46 (samaṇ°); Th 1, 239; Miln 115. Cp. payir°.

Upāsana² (nt.) [fr. upāsati] — 1. archery J VI.448; usually in phrase **katûpāsana** skilled in archery M I.82; S II. 266; A II.48; J IV.211; Mhvs 24, 1. — Miln 232 (°ŋ sikkhitvā). — 2. practice Miln 419. — 3. in °sālā gymnasium, training ground Miln 352.

Upāsikā see **upāsaka**; cp. payir°.

Upāsita [pp. of upāsati] honoured, served, attended S I 133, cp. Nd² 165; Th 1, 179.

Upāsīna [pp. of upāsati] sitting near or close to J V.336.

Upāhata [upa + āhata] struck, afflicted, hurt J I.414.

Upāhanā (f.) [with metathesis for upānahā = Sk. upānah f. or upānaha m.; but cp. BSk. upānaha nt. Divy 6] a shoe, sandal Vin I.185; II.118, 207 (adj. sa-upāhana), 208; S I.226; J IV.173, 223; Pv II.4⁹; Nd² 226; KhA 45; DhA I.381 (chatt °ŋ as nt? v. l. °nā); PvA 127, 186. — **upāhanaŋ** (or upāhanā) **ārohati** to put on sandals J IV. 16; VI. 524; opp. omuñcati take off Vin II.207, 208; J III.415; IV.16. — *Note.* An older form **upānad°** (for upānadh = Sk. upānah) is seen by Kern in pānadûpama J II.223, which is read by him as upānadûpama (v. l. upāhan-upama). See *Toev.* s. v. upānad.

Upiya [ger. of upeti] undergoing, going into, metri causa as ūpiya (—?) and opiya, viz. hadayasmiŋ opiya S I 199 = Th 1, 119; senûpiya J v.96 (v. l. senopiya; C. sayanûpagata). In **tadûpiya** the 2nd part upiya represents an adj. upaka fr. upa (see ta I. a), thus found at Miln 9.

Upekkhaka (adj.) [fr. upekkhā] disinterested, resigned, stoical Vin III.4; D I.37, 183; III.113, 222, 245, 269, 281: S V.295 sq., 318; A III.169 sq., 279; V.30; Sn 515, 855, 912; It 81; Nd¹ 241, 330; Pug 50, 59; Dhs 163; DhsA 172.

Upekkhati [upa + **īkṣ**] to look on, to be disinterested or indifferent Sn 911; Nd¹ 328; J VI.294.

Upekkhanā (f.) [abstr. fr. upa + **īkṣ**] is commentator's paraphrase for upekkhā (q. v.) Nd¹ 501 = Nd² 166; Vbh 230.

Upekkhavant (adj.) = upekkhaka J V.403.

Upekkhā & **Upekhā** (f.) [fr. upa + **īkṣ**, cp. BSk. upekṣā Divy 483; Jtm 211. On spelling upekhā for upekkhā see Müller P. Gr. 16] "looking on", hedonic neutrality or indifference, zero point between joy & sorrow (Cpd. 66); disinterestedness, neutral feeling, equanimity. Sometimes equivalent to adukkham-asukha-vedanā "feeling which is neither pain nor pleasure". See detailed discussion of term at *Cpd.* 229—232, & cp. *Dhs trsln.* 39. — Ten kinds of upekkhā are enumd. at DhsA 172 (cp. *Dhs trsln.* 48; Hardy, *Man. Buddhism* 505). — D I 38 (°sati-parisuddhi purity of mindfulness which comes of disinterestedness cp. Vin III.4; Dhs 165 & Dhs trsln. 50), 251; II.279 (twofold); III.50, 78, 106, 224 sq., 239, 245 (six °upavicāras), 252, 282; M I.79, 364; III 219; S IV.71, 114 sq., V.209 sq. (°indriya); A I 42; 81 (°sukha), 256 (°nimitta); III.185, 291 (°cetovimutti); IV.47 sq., 70 sq., 300, 443; V.301, 360; Sn 67, 73, 972, 1107, (°satisaŋsuddha); Nd¹ 501 = Nd² 166; Ps I.8, 36, 60, 167, 177; Pug 59 (°sati); Nett 25, 97 (°dhātu), 121 sq.; Vbh 12, 15 (°indriya), 54 (id.), 69, 85 (°dhātu), 228, 324, 326 (°sambojjhanga), 381 (°upavicāra); Dhs 150, 153, 165, 262, 556, 1001, 1278, 1582; Vism 134 (°sambojjhanga, 5 conditions of), 148 (°ânubrūhanā), 160 (def. & tenfold), 317 (°bhāvanā), 319 (°brahmavihāra), 325 (°vihārin), 461; SnA 128; Sdhp 461.

Upeta [pp. of upeti] furnished with, endowed with, possessed of Sn 402, 463, 700, 722; Dh 10, 280; Nd² s. v., Th 1, 789; Pv I.7⁶ (bal°); II 7¹² (phal°, v. l. preferable °upaga), IV.1³⁴ (ariyaŋ aṭṭhangavaraŋ upetaŋ = aṭṭhahi angehi upetaŋ yuttaŋ PvA 243); Vism 18 (+ sam°, upagata, samupagata etc); PvA 7. — *Note.* The BSk. usually has samanvāgata for upeta (see aṭṭhanga).

Upeti [upa + **i**] to go to (with acc.), come to, approach, undergo, attain D I.55 (paṭhavi-kāyaŋ an-upeti does not go into an earthly body), 180; M I.486 (na upeti, as answer: "does not meet the question"); S III.93; It 89; Sn 209, (na sankhaŋ "cannot be reckoned as") 749, 911, 1074; 728 (dukkhaŋ), 897; Sn 404 (deve); Nd¹ 63; Nd² 167; Dh 151, 306, 342; Sn 318; J IV.309 (maraṇaŋ upeti to die), 312 (id.), 463 (id.); V.212 (v. l. opeti, q. v.); Th 1, 17 (gabbhaŋ); Pv II.3³⁴ (saggaŋ upehi ṭhānaŋ); IV. 3⁵² (saraṇaŋ buddhaŋ dhammaŋ); Nett 66; fut. **upessaŋ** Sn 29; 2nd sg. upehisi Dh 238, 348. — ger. **upecca** Vv 33⁷; S I.209 = Nett 131; VvA 146 (realising = upagantvā cetetvā vā); PvA 103 (gloss for uppacca flying up); see also upiya & uppacca. — pp. **upeta**.

Upocita [pp. of upa + ava + **ci**] heaped up, abounding, comfortable J IV.471.

Uposatha [Vedic upavasatha, the eve of the Soma sacrifice, day of preparation]. At the time of the rise of Buddhism the word had come to mean the day preceding four stages of the moon's waxing and waning, viz. 1st, 8th, 15th, 23d nights of the lunar month that is to say, a weekly sacred day, a Sabbath. These days were utilized by the pre-Buddhistic reforming communities for the expounding of their views, Vin I.101. The Buddhists adopted this practice and on the 15th day of the half-month held a chapter of the Order to expound their dhamma, *ib.* 102. They also utilized one or other of these Up. days for the recitation of the Pāṭimokkha (pāṭimokkhuddesa), *ibid.* On Up. days laymen take upon themselves the Up. vows, that is to say, the eight Sīlas, during the day. See Sīla. The day in the middle of the month is called cātudassiko or pannarasiko according as the month is shorter or longer. The reckoning is not by the month (māsa), but by the half-month (pakkha), so the twenty-third day is simply aṭṭhamī, the same as the eighth day. There is an accasional Up. called sāmaggi-uposatho, "reconciliation-Up.", which is held when a quarrel among the fraternity has been made up, the gen. confession forming as it were a seal to the reconciliation (Vin V.123; Mah. 42). — Vin I.111, 112, 175, 177: II.5, 32, 204, 276; III.164, 169; D III. 60, 61, 145, 147; A I.205 sq. (3 uposathas: gopālaka°, nigaṇṭha°, ariya°), 208 (dhamm°), 211 (devatā°); IV.248 (aṭṭhanga-samannāgata), 258 sq. (id.), 276, 388 (navah angehi upavuttha); V.83; Sn 153 (pannaraso u); Vbh 422; Vism 227 (°sutta = A I.206 sq.); Sdhp 439; DA I.139; SnA 199; VvA 71, 109; PvA 66, 201. — The hall or chapel in the monastery in which the Pāṭimokkha is recited is called **uposathaggaŋ** (Vin III.66), or °agāraŋ (Vin I.107; DhA II.49). The Up. service is called °kamma (Vin I.102; V.142; J I.232; III.342, 444; DhA I.205). **uposathaŋ karoti** to hold the Up. service (Vin I.107, 175, 177; J I.425). Keeping the Sabbath (by laymen) is called **uposathaŋ upavasati** (A I.142, 144, 205, 208; IV.248; see upavasati), or uposathavāsaŋ vasati (J V.177). The ceremony of a layman taking upon himself the eight sīlas is called uposathaŋ samādiyati (see sīlaŋ & samādiyati); uposatha-sīla observance of the Up. (VvA 71). The Up. day or Sabbath is also called uposatha-divasa (J III.52).

Uposathika (adj.) [fr. uposatha] — 1. belonging to the Uposatha in phrase anuposathikaŋ (adv.) on every U., i. e. every fortnight Vin IV.315. — 2. observing the Sabbath, fasting (cp. BSk. uposadhika M Vastu II.9); Vin I 58; IV. 75, 78; J III.52; Vism 66 (bhatta); DhA I.205.

Uposathin (adj.) [fr. upusatha] = uposathika, fasting Mhvs 17, 6.

Uppakitaka indexed at Ud III.2 wrongly for **upakkitaka** (q. v.).

Uppakka (adj.) [fr. ud + **pac**, cp. Sk. pakva & see also uppaccati] — 1. "boiled out", scorched, seared, dried or shrivelled up; in phrase itthiŋ uppakkaŋ okilinin okiriniŋ Vin III.107 = S II.260; expld. by Bdhgh. Vin III.273 as "kharena agginā pakkasarira". — 2. "boiled up", swollen (of eyes through crying) J VI.10.

Uppacca [ger. of uppatati] flying up Th 2, 248 (see under upacca)); S I.209 (v. l. BB. upecca, C. uppatitvā pi sakuṇo viya) = Pv II.7¹⁷ (= uppatitvā PvA 103) = DhA IV.21 (gloss uppatitvā) = Nett 131 (upecca)

Uppaccati [ud + paccati, Pass. of **pac**] in ppr. **uppacciyamāna** (so read for upapacciyamāna, as suggested by v. l. BB. uppajj°) "being boiled out", i. e. dried or shrivelled up (cp. uppakka 1) J IV.327. Not with Morris *J P T S.* 1887, 129 "being tormented", nor with Kern, *Toev.* under upapacc° as ppr. to **pṛc** (*upapṛcyamāna) "dicht opgesloten", a meaning foreign to this root.

Upajjati [ud + pajjati of **pad**] to come out, to arise, to be produced, to be born or reborn, to come into existence D I.180; Sn 584; Pv II.1¹¹ (= nibbattati PvA 71); PvA 8 (nibbattati +), 9, 20, 129 (= pātubhavati); DA I.165. — Pass. **uppajjiyati** Vin I.50. — ppr. uppajjanto PvA 5, 21; fut. °pajjissati PvA 5 (bhummadevesu, corresp. with niraye nibbattissati ibid.(, 67 (niraye); aor. uppajji PvA 21, 50, 66; & udapādi (q. v.) Vin III.4; J I.81; ger. °pajjitvā D II.157 = S I.6, 158 = II.193 = J I.392 = Th 1, 1159; & uppajja J IV.24. — Caus. **uppādeti** (q. v.). — pp. **uppanna** (q. v.). See also **upapajjati** and **upapanna**.

Uppajjana (adj.-nt.) [fr. uppajjati] coming into existence; birth, rebirth PvA 9 (°vasena), 33 (id.).

Uppajjanaka (adj.) [fr. uppajjana] (belonging to) coming into existence, i. e. arising suddenly or without apparent cause, in °bhaṇḍa a treasure trove J III.150.

Uppajjitar [n. ag. fr. uppajjati] one who produces or is reborn in (with acc.) D I.143 (saggaŋ etc.).

Uppaṭipāṭiyā [abl. of uppaṭipāṭi, ud + paṭipāṭi] lit. "out of reach", i. e. in a distance J I.89; or impossible Vism 96 (ekapañho pi n. āgato nâhosi not one question was impossible to be understood). As tt. g. "with reference to the preceding", supra Vism 272; SnA 124, 128; DhsA 135 (T. °paṭipāṭika).

Uppaṇḍanā (f.) [abstr. fr. ut + **paṇḍ** or unknown etym.] ridiculing, mocking Miln 357; Vism 29; PugA 250 (°kathā).

Uppaṇḍuppaṇḍukajāta (adj.) [redupl. intens. formation; ud + paṇḍu + ka + jāta; paṇḍu yellowish. The word is evidently a corruption of something else, perhaps upapaṇṇḍuka upa in meaning of "somewhat like", cp. upanīla, upanibha etc. and reading at Pv II.1[13] upakaṇḍakin. The latter may itself be a corruption, but is expl[d.] at PvA 72 by upakaṇḍaka-jāta "shrivelled up all over, nothing but pieces (?)". The trsl[n.] is thus doubtful; the BSk. is the P. form retranslated into utpāṇḍuka Divy 334, 463, and trsl[d.] "very pale"] "having become very pale" (?), or "somewhat pale" (?), with dubbaṇṇa in Khp, A 234, and in a stock phrase of three different settings, viz. (1) kiso lūkho dubbaṇṇo upp° dhamani-santhata-gatto Vin I.276; III.19, 110, M II.121; distorted to BSk. bhīto utp°. kṛśāluko durbalako mlānako at Divy 334. — (2) kiso upp°. J VI. 71; DhA IV.66. — (3) upp° dhamanisanth° J I.346; II.92; V.95; DhA I.367. Besides in a doubtful passage at Pv II.1[13] (upakaṇḍakin, v. l. uppaṇḍ° BB.), expl[d.] at PvA 72 "upakaṇḍakajāta", vv. ll. uppaṇḍaka° and uppaṇḍupaṇḍuka°.

Uppaṇḍeti [ut + **paṇḍ**, of uncertain origin] to ridicule, mock, to deride, make fun of Vin I.216, 272, 293; IV. 278; A III.91 = Pug 67 (ūhasati ullapati +); J V.288, 300; DhA II.29; III.41; PvA 175 (avamaññati +). — *Note.* The BSk. utprāsayati at Divy 17 represents the P. uppaṇḍeti & must somehow be a corruption of the latter (vv. ll. at Divy 17 are utprāśayati, utprāṇayati & utprāśrayati).

Uppatati [ud + patati] to fly or rise up into the air; to spring upwards, jump up; 3rd sg. pret. **udapatta** [Sk. *udapaptat] J III.484 (so read for °patto, & change si to pi); ger. **uppatitvā** J III.484; IV.213; PvA 103, 215; and uppacca (q. v.). — pp. **uppatita** (q. v.).

Uppatita [pp. of uppatati] jumped up, arisen, come about Sn 1 (= uddhamukhaŋ patitaŋ gataŋ SnA 4), 591; Dh 222 (= uppanna DhA III.301); Th 1, 371.

Uppatti (f.) [Vedic utpatti, ud + **pad**] coming forth, product, genesis, origin, rebirth, occasion A II.133 (°paṭilābhikāni saŋyojanāni); Vbh 137 (°bhava), 411; cp. *Compendium*, 262 f. (khaṇa); Miln 127 (°divasa); Vism 571 sq. (°bhava, 9 fold: kāma° etc.); SnA 46, 159, 241, 254, 312, 445; PvA 144, 215. On uppatti deva see deva and upapatti. — See also atthuppatti, dānuppatti.

Uppatha [Sk. utpatha, ud + patha] a wrong road or course D I.10 (°gamana, of planets); S I.38, 43; J V.453; VI. 235; DhA III.356 (°cāra).

Uppanna [pp. of uppajjati] born, reborn, arisen, produced, D I.192 (lokaŋ u. born into the world); Vin III.4; Sn 55 °ñāṇa; see Nd[2] 168), 998; J I.99; Pv II.2[2] (pettivisayaŋ); Dhs 1035, 1416; Vbh 12, 17, 50, 319; 327; DhA III. 301; PvA 21 (petesu), 33, 144, 155. — **anuppanna** not arisen M II.11; not of good class D I.97 (see DA I.267).

Uppabbajati [ud + pabbajati] to leave the Order DhA I. 68; PvA 55. — pp. **°pabbajita.** — Caus. **uppabbājeti** to turn out of the Order J IV.219; DhA IV.195. — Caus. II. **uppabbajāpeti** to induce some one to leave the Order J IV.304.

Uppabbajita [ud + pabbajita] one who has left the community of bhikkhus, an ex-bhikkhu VvA 319; DhA I.311.

Uppala [Sk. utpala, uncertain etym.] the (blue) lotus; a waterlily. The 7 kinds of lotuses, mentioned at J V.37 are: nīla-ratta-set-uppala, ratta-seta-paduma, seta-kumuda, kalla-hāra. — D I.75; II.19; Vin III.33 (°gandha); J II. 443; Dh 55; Vv 32[2]; 35[4]; Pv II.1[20]; III.10[5]; DhA I.384 (nīl°); III.394 (id.); ThA 254, 255; VvA 132, 161. — What is meant by **uppala-patta** (lotus-leaf?) at Vin IV. 261?

Uppalaka [uppala + ka] "lotus-like", N. of a hell (cp. BSk. utpala at Divy 67 etc.) A V.173. See also puṇḍarika.

Uppalin (adj.-n.) [fr. uppala] having lotuses rich in l., only in f. **uppalinī** a lotus-pond D I.75; II.38; S I.138; A III. 26; Vv 32[2]; DA I.219.

Uppaḷāseti [ud + pra + **las**, cp. Sk. samullāsayati in same meaning] to sound out or forth, to make sound Miln 21 (dhamma-sankhaŋ). Reading at D II.337 is **upaḷāseti** in same meaning.

Uppāṭaka [fr. ud + **paṭ** in meaning of "biting, stinging"] an insect, vermin S I.170 (santhāro °ehi sañchanno "a siesta-couch covered by vermin swarm" trsl[d.] p. 215 & note).

Uppāṭana (nt.) [fr. ud + **paṭ**] pulling out, uprooting, destroying, skinning J I.454; II.283; VI.238; Miln 166; PvA 46 (kes°); Sdhp 140 (camm°). Cp. sam°.

Uppāṭanaka (adj.) [fr. uppāṭana] pulling up, tearing out, uprooting J I.303 (°vāta); IV.333 (id.).

Uppāṭeti [Sk. utpāṭayati, Caus. of ud + **paṭ** to split, cp. also BSk. utpāṭayati nidhānaŋ to dig out a treasure Av. Ś I.294] to split, tear asunder; root out, remove, destroy Vin II.151 (chaviŋ to skin); M II.110 (attānaŋ); Th 2, 396 (ger. uppāṭiyā = °pāṭetvā ThA 259); J I.281 (bījāni); IV.162, 382; VI.109 (= luñcati); Miln 86; DhA III.206. — Caus. **uppāṭāpeti** in pp. **uppāṭāpita** caused to be torn off DhA III.208. See also **upphāleti.**

Uppāda[1] [Sk. utpāta, ud + **pat**] flying up, jump; a sudden & unusual event, portent, omen D I.9 (v. l. uppāta) = Vism 30 (T. uppāta, v. l. uppāda) Sn 360; J I.374; VI. 475; Miln 178.

Uppāda[2] [Sk. utpāda, ud + **pad**] coming into existence, appearance, birth Vin I.185; D I.185; S III.39 (+ vaya); IV.14; V.30; A I.152 (+ vaya), 286, 296; II.248 (taṇh°); III.123 (citt° state of consciousness); IV.65 (id.); Dh 182, 194; J I.59, 107 (sat°); Vbh 303 (citt°), 375 (taṇh°); PvA 10; ThA 282. — **anuppāda** either "not coming into existence" D III.270, M I.60; A I.286, 296; II.214, 249; III.84 sq.; Ps I.59, 66; Dhs 1367; or "not ripe" D I.12.

Uppādaka (adj.) (—°) [fr. uppāda[2]] producing, generating PvA 13 (dukkh°). f. °ikā DhA IV.109 (jhān°).

Uppādana (nt.) [fr. uppada[2]] making, generating, causing PvA 71 (anubal° read for anubalappadāna?) 114.

Uppādin (adj.) [fr. uppāda[2]] having an origin, arising, bound to arise Dhs 1037, 1416; Vbh 17, 50, 74, 92 and passim; DhsA 45.

Uppādetar [n. ag. fr. uppādeti] one who produces, causes or brings into existence, creator, producer M I.79; S I. 191; III.66; V.351; Miln 217.

Uppādeti [Caus. of uppajjati, ud + **pad**] — 1. to give rise to, to produce, put forth, show, evince, make D I.135; M I.162, 185; Pug 25; PvA 4, 16, 19, 59; Sdhp 539. **cittaŋ u.** to give a (temporary) thought to (with loc.) J I.81; Miln 85; DhA II.89; PvA 3. — 2. to get, obtain, find J IV.2; Miln 140; DhA I.90; PvA 121. — 3. in **lohitaŋ u.** to draw (blood) Miln 214.

Uppilavati (& **Uplavati**) [Sk. utplavati, ud + **plu,** cp. utplutya jumping up, rising Sp. Av. Ś I.209] — 1. to emerge (out of water), to rise, float S IV.313 (uplava imper.); Miln 80, 379; VvA 47 (uplavitvā, v. l. uppalavitvā); DA I.256 (v. l. upari lavati). — 2. to jump up, frisk about, to be elated or buoyant J II.97 (cp. Morris *J P T S.* 1887, 139); Miln 370. — See also upaplavati, uplāpeti & ubbillāvita etc.

Uppīḷa (adj.) [ud + **pīḍ**] oppressing or oppressed: **an°** free from oppression, not hurt or destroyed D I.135 (opp. sa-uppīḷa; T. upapīḷa but v. l. upp°); J III.443; V.378; PvA 161.

Uppīḷita [pp. of uppīḷeti] pressed J VI.3.

Uppīḷeti [ud + **pīḍ** for ava + **pīḍ,** cp. uplāpeti = opilāpeti, & opīḷeti] — 1. to press (down) on to, to hold (tight) to (with acc.), to cover up or close M I.539 (piṭṭhi-pāṇiŋ hanukena); J I 483 (hatthena akkhīni); II.245 (hatthikumbhe mukhaŋ); V.293 (aggalaŋ); ThA 188. — 2. to stampede VvA 83 (paṭhaviŋ).

Uppoṭheti [ud + poṭheti] to beat PvA 4.

Upplavana at DhA I.309 remains to be explained, T. faulty.

Upphāleti [Caus. of ud + **phal**] to cut, rip or split open Vin I.276 (udara-cchaviŋ upphāletvā; v. l. uppāṭetvā, perhaps preferable).

Upphāsulika (adj.) [ud + phāsulikā for phāsukikā = phāsukā a rib] "with ribs out", i. e. with ribs showing, emaciated, thin, "skinny" Pv II.1[1] (= uggata-phāsuka PvA 68); IV.10[1] (MSS. uppā°); ThA 133 (spelt uppa°).

Uplāpeti [Sk. avaplāvayati, Caus. of ava + **plu,** with substitution of ud for ava; see also uppilavati] to immerse M I.135 (vv. ll. upal° & opil°); J IV.162 (fig. put into the shade, overpower; v. l. upal°). See also **opilāpeti** & **ubbillāvita.**

Ubbaṭuma (adj.) [ud + *vṛti (of **vṛt**) + ma (for mā > mant); cp. Sk. udvṛtta & vṛtimant] going out of its direction, going wrong (or upset?), in phrase **ubbaṭumaŋ rathaŋ karoti** to put a cart out of its direction A IV. 191, 193.

Ubbaṭṭeti [Caus. of ud + **vṛt,** as doublet of ubbatteti, cp. BSk. udvartayati Divy 12, 36] to anoint, give perfumes (to a guest), to shampoo J I.87 (gandhacuṇṇena), 238 (id.); V.89, 438.

Ubbaṭṭhaka misprint in Pug Index as well as at Pug A 233 for **ubbhaṭṭhaka** (q. v.).

Ubbattati [ud + **vṛt**] to go upwards, to rise, swell J VI. 486 (sāgaro ubbatti). See also next.

Ubbatteti [Caus. of ud + **vṛt,** of which doublet is ubbaṭṭeti; cp. also ubbaṭuma] — 1. to tear out J I.199; Miln 101 (sadevake loke ubbattiyante); DhA I.5 (hadayamaŋsaŋ), 75 (rukkhaŋ). — 2. to cause to swell or rise J III.361 (Gangāsotaŋ); IV.161 (samuddaŋ). — 3. (intrs.) to go out of direction, or in the wrong direction Vism 327 (neva ubbaṭṭati na vivaṭṭati; v. l. uppaṭṭati); DhA III.155.

Ubbadhati [ud + vadhati] to kill, destroy Sn 4 (praet. udabbadhi = ucchindanto vadheti SnA 18).

Ubbandhati [ud + bandhati] to hang up, strangle Vin III. 73 (rajjuyā); J I.504 (id.); III.345; Th 2, 80; Vism 501; VvA 139, 207 (ubbandhitu-kāmā in the intention of hanging herself).

Ubbarī (f.) [Sk. urvarā, Av. urvara plant] fertile soil, sown field; fig. woman, wife J VI 473 (= orodha C.).

Ubbasati see **ubbisati.**

Ubbaha (adj.) (—°) [fr. ud + **vṛh,** i. e. to ubbahati[1]] only in cpd. dur° hard to pull out, difficult to remove Th I, 124, 495 = 1053.

Ubbahati[1] [ud + **bṛh** or **vṛh,** see also uddharati] to pull out, take away, destroy Sn 583 (udabbahe pot. = ubbaheyya dhāreyya SnA 460); Th I, 158; J II.223 (udabbahe = udabbaheyya C.); IV.462 (ubbahe); VI.587 (= hareyya C.).

Ubbahati[2] [ud + vahati, although possibly same as ubbahati[1], in meaning of uddharati, which has taken up meanings of *udbharati, as well as of *udbṛhati and *udvahati] to carry away, take away, lift (the corn after cutting); only in Caus. II. ubbahāpeti to have the corn harvested Vin II 180 = A I.241. — Here belong uddhaṭa and uddharaṇa. Cp. also pavāḷha.

Ubbāḷha [adj. pp. of ud + bāhati = **vāh** or more likely of ud + **bādh**] oppressed, troubled, harassed, annoyed, vexed Vin I.148, 353; II.119; IV.308; J I.300; Vism 182 (kuṇapa-gandhena); DhA I.343.

Ubbāsīyati [Pass. of ubbāseti, ud + **vas**] "to be dis-inhabited", i. e. to be abandoned by the inhabitants Mhvs 6, 22 (= chaḍḍiyati C.). — Cp. ubbisati.

Ubbāhana (nt.) [fr. ubbahati[2]] carrying, lifting, in °samattha fit for carrying, i. e. a beast of burden, of an elephant J VI.448.

Ubbāhikā (f.) [orig. f. of ubbāhika, adj. fr. ubbāheti in abstr. use] a method of deciding on the expulsion of a bhikkhu, always in instr. **ubbāhikāya** "by means of a referendum", the settlement of a dispute being laid in the hands of certain chosen brethren (see *Vin Texts* III.49 sq.) Vin II.95, 97, 305; V.139, 197; A V.41; Mhvs 4, 46.

Ubbāheti [hardly to be decided whether fr. ud + **vāh** (to press, urge), or **bṛh** or **bādh**; cp. uddharati 2] to oppress, vex, hinder, incommodate J V.417 sq.

Ubbigga [Sk. udvigna, pp. of ud + **vij**] agitated, flurried, anxious Vin II.184; S I.53; Th I, 408; J I.486; III.313; Miln 23, 236, 340 (an°); Vism 54 (satat°); DhA II.27; ThA 267; Sdhp 8, 77.

Ubbijjati [Pass. of ud + **vij**] to be agitated, frightened or afraid Vin I.74 (u. uttasati palāyati); III.145 (id.); S I. 228 (aor. ubbijji); Miln 149 (tasati +), 286 (+ saŋviji); Vism 58. — Caus. **ubbejeti** (q. v.). — pp. **ubbigga** (q. v.).

Ubbijjanā (f.) [abstr. fr. ubbijjati] agitation, uneasiness DA I.111. Cp. ubbega.

Ubbinaya (adj.) [ud + vinaya] being outside the Vinaya, ex- or un-Vinaya, wrong Vinaya Vin II.307; Dpvs V.19.

Ubbilāpa (v. l. uppilāva, which is prob. the correct reading] joyous state of mind, elation Ud 37. See next.

Ubbilāvita (according to the very plausible expl[n]. given by Morris *J P T S.* 1887, 137 sq. for uppilāpita, pp. of uppilāpeti = uplāpeti < uplāveti, as expl[d]. under uppilavati, ud + **plu**; with ll for l after cases like Sk. ālīyate > P. allīyati, ālāpa > allāpa etc., and bb for pp as in vanibbaka = Sk. vanīpaka (*vanipp°)] happy, elated, buoyant, Itt.

frisky; only in cpds. °atta rejoicing, exultancy, elation of mind D I.3, 37; J III 466; Miln 183; DA I.53, 122; and °ākāra id. DhA I.237. At Vism 158 "cetaso ubbilāvitaŋ" stands for ubbilāvitattaŋ, with v. l. BB uppilāvitaŋ. Cp. J V.114 (ubbilāvita-cittatā).

Ubbilla [either a secondary formation fr. ubbilāvita, or representing uppilava (uppilāva) for upplava, ud + **plu,** as discussed under ubbilāvita.[1] The BSk. word udvilya Lal. V. 351, 357, or audvilya Divy 82 is an artificial reconstruction from the Pāli, after the equation of Sk. dvādaśa > dial. P. bārasa, whereas the original Sk. dv. is in regular P. represented by dd, as in *dvīpa > dīpa, *udvāpa > uddāpa. Müller's construction ubbilla > *udvela rests on the same grounds, see P. Gr. 12.] elation, elated state of mind M III.159; °bhāva id. DA I.122; Sdhp 167. See next.

Ubbisati [better reading v. l. ubbasati, ud + **vas]** "to be out home", to live away from home J II.76. — See also **ubbāsīyati.** — pp. **ubbisita** (°kāle) ibid.

Ubbūḷhavant see **uruḷhavant.**

Ubbega [Sk. udvega, fr. ud + **vij**] excitement, fright, anguish D III.148; later, also transport, rapture, in cpd. (°pīti); Vism 143; DhsA 124; PugA 226.

Ubbegin (adj.) [fr. ubbega] full of anguish or fear J III. 313 (= ubbegavant C.).

Ubbejanīya (adj.) [fr. ubbejeti] agitating, causing anxiety J I.323, 504.

Ubbejitar & **Ubbejetar** [n. ag. fr. ubbejeti] a terrifier, a terror to A II.109 (°etar); IV.189 (id.); Pug 47, 48 (= ghaṭṭetvā vijjhitvā ubbegappattaŋ karotī ti PugA 226).

Ubbejeti [Caus. of ud + **vij**] to set into agitation, terrify, frighten Miln 388 (°jayitabba grd.); PugA 226.

Ubbeṭhana (nt.) [fr. ud + **veṣṭ**] an envelope, wrap J VI.508.

Ubbedha [ud + vedha of **vyadh**] height, only as measure, contrasted with **āyāma** length, & **vitthāra** width J I.29 (v.219; asīti-hatth°), 203 (yojana-sahass°); VvA 33 (yojana°), 66 (asīti-hatth°), 158 (hattha-sat°), 188 (soḷasa-yojan°), 221, 339; PvA 113. See also pabbedha.

Ubbedhati [ud + vedhati = Sk. vyathate] to be moved, to shake (intrs.), quiver, quake J VI.437 (= kampati C.).

Ubbhaŋ (& **Ubbha°**) (indecl.) [a doublet of uddhaŋ, see uddhaŋ III.] up, over, above, on top J V.269 (ubbhaŋ yojanaŋ uggata); in cpds. like **ubbhakkhakaŋ** above the collar bone Vin IV.213; **ubbhajānumaṇḍalaŋ** above the knee Vin IV.213; **ubbhamukha** upwards S III.238; Miln 122.

Ubbhaṭṭhaka (adj.) [ubbha + ṭha + ka of **sthā**, prob. contracted fr. ubbhaṭṭhitaka] standing erect or upright D I.167; M I.78, 92, 167, 282, 308; A I.296; II.206; Pug 55 (ubb°; = uddhaŋ ṭhitaka PugA 233).

Ubbhaṇḍita [pp. of ubbhaṇḍeti, ud + ***bhaṇḍ,** cp. bhāṇḍa] bundled up, fixed up, wrapped up, full Vin I.287.

Ubbhata [pp. of uddharati with bbh for ddh as in ubbhaŋ for uddhaŋ; cp. ubbahati and see also the doublet uddhaṭa] drawn out, pulled out, brought out, thrown out or up, withdrawn Vin I.256 (kaṭhina, cp. uddhāra & ubbhāra); III.196 (id.); D I.77 (cp. uddharati); M I.383 (ubbhatehi akkhīhi); Dh 34 (okamokata u. = *okamokataḥ u.); J I.268; PvA 163.

Ubbhava [ud + bhava] birth, origination, production Pgdp 91 (dānassa phal°). Cp. BSk. udbhāvanā Divy 184 (guṇ°) 492 (id.).

Ubbhāra = uddhāra (suspension, withdrawal, removal) Vin I.255, 300; V.136, 175; cp. *Vin Texts* I.19; II.157.

Ubbhijjati [ud + **bhid**] to burst upwards, to spring up out of the ground, to well up; to sprout D I.74 = M III. 93 = III.26; J I.18 (v.104); Dh 339 (ger. ubbhijja = uppajjitvā DhA IV.49); DA I.218. — pp. **ubbhinna.**

Ubbhida[1] (nt.) [Sk. udbhida] kitchen salt Vin I.202, cp. *Vin Texts* II.48.

Ubbhida[2] (adj.) [fr. ud + **bhid**] breaking or bursting forth, in cpd. °**odaka** "whose waters well up", or "spring water" D I.74; M I.276; DA I.218.

Ubbhinna [pp. of ubbhijjati] springing up, welling up Dh I.218.

Ubbhujati [ud + **bhuj**] to bend up, to lift up (forcibly), ger. °itvā in meaning of "forcibly" Vin II.222; III.40.

***Ubha** see **ubho**; cp. ubhato & ubhaya.

Ubhato (adv.) [abl. of *ubha, to which ubhaya & ubho] both, twofold, in both (or two) ways, on both sides; usually °—, as °**bhāgavimutta** one who is emancipated in two ways D II.71; *Dialogues* II.70, *n.* 1; M I.477 (cp. 385 °vimaṭṭha); S I.191; A I.73; IV.10, 77; Pug 14, 73; Nett 190; °**byañjanaka** (vyañj°) having the characteristics of both sexes, hermaphrodite Vin I.89, 136, 168; III.28; V. 222; °**sangha** twofold Sangha, viz. bhikkhu° & bhikkhunī Vin II.255; IV.52, 242, 287; Mhvs 32[34]. — See further Vin II.287 (°vinaye); D I.7 (°lohitaka, cp. DA I.87); M I.57 (°mukha tied up at both ends), 129 (°daṇḍaka-kakaca a saw with teeth on both sides), 393 (koṭiko pañho; S IV.323 (id.).

Ubhaya (adj.) [*ubha + ya, see ubho] both, twofold Sn 547, 628, 712, 1106, 1107, 801 (°ante); Nd[1] 109 (°ante); J I.52; PvA 11, 24, 35, 51. — nt. °ŋ as adv. in combn. with ca c'ûbhayaŋ following after 2nd. part of comprehension) "and both" for both-and; and also, alike, as well Dh 404 (gahaṭṭhehi anāgārehi c'ûbhayaŋ with householders and houseless alike); Pv I.6[9]. — *Note.* The form ubhayo at Pv II.3[10] is to be regarded as fem. pl. of ubho (= duve PvA 86).

-**aŋsa** lit. both shoulders or both parts, i. e. completely, thoroughly, all round (°—) in °bhāvita thoroughly trained D I.154 (cp. DA I.312 ubhaya-koṭṭhāsāya bhāvito).

Ubhayattha [adv.) [Sk. ubhayatra, fr. ubhaya] in both places, in both cases Vin I.107; A III.64; Dh 15—17; DhA I.29 (°ettha), 30; PvA 130.

Ubho (adj.) [Sk. ubhau, an old remnant of a dual form in Pāli; cp. Gr. ἄμφω both, Lat. ambo, Lith. abū, Goth. bai, Obg. beide = E. both. To prep.-adv. *amb, *ambi; see abhi & cp. also vīsati] both; nom. acc. ubho S I.87 = A III.48 = It 16; It 43 = Sn 661 = Dh 306; Sn 220, 543, 597; Dh 74, 256, 269; 412; Nd[1] 109; Pv I.7[6]; J I.223; II.3; PvA 13, 82 (tā ubho). — **ubhantaŋ** both ends, both sides Sn 1042 (see Nd[2] 169; Sn A 588 expls. by ubho ante). — gen. **ubhinnaŋ** S I.162; II. 222; J II.3; instr. **ubhohi** (hatthehi) Vin II.256; J IV.142; loc. **ubhosu** Sn 778 (antesu); J I.264 (passesu; PvA 94 (hatthesu). — *Note.* The form **ubhayo** at Pv II.3[10] is to be regarded as a nom. fem. (= duve PvA 86).

Ummagga [ud + magga, lit. "off-track"] — 1. an underground watercourse, a conduit, main M I.171; A II.189; J VI.426, 432; SnA 50 ("ummaggo paññā pavuccati"); DhA I.252 (°cora); II.37 (v. l. umanga); IV.104; PvA 44 (read with v. l. SS kummagga). — 2. a side track, a wrong way, devious way S I.193 (v. l. °manga) = Th 1, 1242; S IV.195; A IV.191.

Ummanga [ud + manga (?) or for ummagga, q. v. for vv. ll.] "out luck", i. e. unlucky; or "one who has gone off the right path" Vin V.144.

Ummatta (adj.) [ud + matta of **mad**] out of one's mind, mad S V.447 (+ viceta); J V.386; Miln 122; Sdhp 88;

PvA 40 (°puggala read with v. l. SS for dummati puggala). Cp. next & **ummāda**.
-rūpa like mad, madly, insane Pv I.8[1]; II.6[3] (where J III.156 has santaramāna).

Ummattaka (adj.) = ummatta; Vin I.123, 321; II.60, 80; III.27, 33; A IV.248; Vism 260 (reason for); Miln 277; PvA 38, 39, 93 (°vesa appearance of a madman), 95. — f. **ummattikā** Vin IV.259, 265; ThA 111.

Ummaddeti [ud + maddeti, Caus. of **mṛd**] to rub something on (acc.) Vin II.107 = 266 (mukhaŋ).

Ummasati [ud + masati of **mṛs**.] to touch, take hold of, lift up Vin III.121. Cp. next.

Ummasanā (f.) [abstr. fr. ummasati] lifting up Vin III.121 (= uddhaŋ uccāraṇā).

Ummā (f.) [cp. Sk. umā] flax, only in cpd. °**puppha** the (azure) flower of flax M II.13 = A V.61 (v. l. dammā°, ummāta°); D II.260; Th 1, 1068; DhsA 13. Also (m.) N. of a gem Miln 118.

Ummāda [ud + māda] madness, distraction, mental aberration S I.126 (°ŋ pāpuṇeyya citta-vikkhepaŋ vā); A II.80; III.119; V.169; Pug 69; PvA 6 (°patta frantic, out of mind), 94 (°vāta), 162 (°patta).

Ummādanā (f.) (or °aŋ nt.) [abstr. fr. ummāda] maddening Sn 399 (+ mohanaŋ = paraloke ummādanaŋ idhaloke mohanaŋ SnA 377); ThA 2, 357 (cp. ThA 243).

Ummāra [according to Müller P. Gr. = Sk. udumbara (?)] — 1. a threshold Vin IV.160 (= indakhīla); Th 2, 410; J I. 62; III.101; Vism 425; DhA I.350. — 2. a curb-stone J VI.11. — 3. as **uttar°** (the upper threshold) the lintel J I.111; DhA II.5 (v. l. upari°). — 4. window-sash or sill J I.347; IV.356.

Ummi (& **Ummī**) (f.) [for the usual ūmi, cp. similar double forms of bhummi > bhūmi] a wave Th 1, 681; Miln 346.

Ummisati [ud + misati] to open one's eyes J III.96 (opp. nimisati; v. l. ummisati for °mīḷ° ?).

Ummihati [ud + **mih**] to urinate Vin I.78 (ūhanati +).

Ummīleti [Caus. of ud + **mīl**; opp. ni(m)mīleti] to open one's eyes J I.439; II.195; IV.457; VI.185; Miln 179, 357, 394; Vism 185, 186; DhA II.28 (opp. ni°); VvA 205, 314.

Ummuka (nt.) [Sk. ulmuka perhaps to Lat. adoleo, cp. also alāta firebrand; see Walde, Lat. Wtb. s. v. adoleo] a fire brand Vin IV.265; S IV.92 (T. ummukka meaning "loosened"?); J II.69 v. l. °kk), 404 (kk); III.356.

Ummujjati [ud + **majj**] to emerge, rise up (out of water) Vin I.180; S IV.312; A IV.11 sq; J II.149, 284; III.507; IV.139; Pug 71; Miln 118; DA I.37, 127; PvA 113.

Ummujjana (nt.) [fr. ummujjati] emerging Vism 175 (+ nimmojjana); DA I.115.

Ummujjamānaka (adj.) [ummujjamāna, ppr. med. of ummujjati, + ka] emerging A II.182.

Ummujjā (f.) [fr. ummujjati] emerging, jumping out of (water), only in phrase **ummujja-nimujjaŋ karoti** to emerge & dive D I.78; M I.69; A I.170; J IV.139; Nett 110; Vism 395 (= Ps II.208).

Ummūla (adj.) [ud + mūla] "roots-out", with roots showing, laying bare the roots J I.249 (°ŋ karoti); Sdhp 452.

Ummūlaka (adj.) [= ummūla] uprooting, laying bare the roots J I.303 (vāta).

Ummūleti [Caus. fr. ummūla] to uproot, to root out J I.329.

Umhayati [Sk. *ut-smayate, ud + **smi**] to laugh out loud J II.131 (= hasitaŋ karoti); III.44; IV.197; V.299 (°amāna = hasamāna C.). Caus. **umhāpeti** J V.297.

Uyyassu (imper. 3[rd.] sg.) is v. l. BB. and C. reading at J VI.145, 146 for dayassu, fly; probably for (i) yassu of **yā** to go.

Uyyāti [ud + **yā**] to go out, to go away J II.3, 4 (imper. uyyāhi); IV.101. — Caus. **uyyāpeti** to cause to go away, to bring or take out S IV.312.

Uyyāna (nt.) [Sk. udyāna, fr. ud + **yā**] a park, pleasure grove, a (royal) garden J I.120, 149; II.104; IV.213; V.95; VI.333; PvA 6, 74, 76; VvA 7; Sdhp 7.
-kīḷā amusement in the park, sports DhA I.220; IV.3. **-pāla** overseer of parks, head gardener, park keeper J II. 105, 191; IV.264. **-bhūmi** garden ground, pleasure ground J I.58; Vv 64[10]; Pv II.12[9]; DA I.235.

Uyyānavant (adj.) [fr. uyyāna] full of pleasure gardens Pv III.3[6].

Uyyāma [Sk. udyama, ud + **yam**; P. uyyāma with ā for a, as niyāma > niyama; cp. BSk. udyama Jtm 210] exertion, effort, endeavour Dhs 13, 22, 289, 571; DhsA 146.

Uyyuñjati [ud + **yuj**] to go away, depart, leave one's house Dh 91 (cp. DhA II.170). — pp. **uyyutta**. — Caus. **uyyojeti** (q. v.).

Uyyuta (adj.) [ud + yuta] striving, busy (in a good or bad cause) Sn 247, 248; J V.95.

Uyyutta [pp. of uyyuñjati] striving, active, zealous, energetic J I.232.

Uyyoga [fr. ud + **yuj**] departure, approach of death Dh 236 (cp. DhA III.335).

Uyyojana (nt.) [fr. uyyojeti] inciting, instigation A IV.233.

Uyyojita [pp. of uyyojeti] instigated Miln 228; PvA 105.

Uyyojeti [Caus. of uyyuñjati] — 1. to instigate Vin IV.235; J III.265. — 2. to dismiss, take leave of (acc.), send off, let go Vin I.179; A III.75; J I.119 (bhikkhu-sanghaŋ), 293; III.188; V.217; VI.72; Vism 91; DhA I.14, 15, 398; II.44; VvA 179; PvA 93. — pp. **uyyojita** (q. v.).

Uyyodhika (nt.) [fr. ud + **yudh**] a plan of combat, sham fight Vin IV.107; D I.6; A V.65; DA I.85.

Ura (m. nt.) & **Uro** (nt.) [Sk. uras] — 1. the breast, chest. — Cases after the nt. s.-declension are instr. **urasā** Th 1, 27; Sn 609; & loc. **urasi** Sn 255; J III.148; IV. 118, also **urasiŋ** J III.386 (= urasmiŋ C.). Other cases of nt. a-stem, e. g. instr. urena J III.90; PvA 75; loc. ure D I.135; J I.156, 433, 447; PvA 62 (ure jāta; cp. orasa). — Vin II.105 (contrasted with piṭṭhi back); IV.129; J IV.3; V.159, 202; Nd² 659; Pv IV.10[8]; DhA III.175; DA I.254; DhsA 321; PvA 62, 66. — **uraŋ deti** (with loc.) to put oneself on to something with one's chest, fig. to apply oneself to J I.367, 401, 408; III.139, 455; IV.219; V.118, 278. — 2. (appl[d.]) the base of a carriage pole Vv 63[28] (= īsāmūla VvA 269).
-ga going on the chest, creeping, i. e. a snake S I.69; Sn 1, 604; J I 7; IV.330; VI.208; Vv 80[8]; Pv I.12[1] (= urena gacchati ti urago sappass' etaŋ adhivacanaŋ PvA 63); PvA 61, 67. **-cakka** an iron wheel (put on the chest), as an instrument of torture in Niraya J I.363, 414. **-cchada** "breast cover", breast plate (for ornament) Vin II.10; J IV.3; V.215, 409; VI.480; ThA 253. **-ttāḷi** beating one's breast (as a sign of mourning & sorrow) M I.86, 136; A II.188; III.54, 416; IV.293; PvA 39. **-tthala** the breast A II.174.

Urabbha [Sk. urabhra, with uiā & uraṇa to be compared with Gr. ἀρήν wether, cp. Hom. εἶρος wool; Lat. vervex;

Ags. waru = E. ware (orig. sheepskins) = Ger. ware. Here also belongs P. urāṇī] a ram D I.127; A I.251 sq.; II.207; IV.41 sq.; J V 241; Pug 56; DA I.294; DhA II.6. See also **orabbhika.**

Urāṇī (f.) [or uraṇī?, f. of uraṇa, see urabbha] an ewe J V.241 (= urāṇikā C.); v. l. uraṇī & uraṇikā.

Uru (adj.) [cp. Av. ravah space; Gr. εὐρύς wide; Lat. rūs free or wide space, field; Idg. *ru, *uer wide, to which also Goth. rūms space = Ags. rūm, E. room, Ger. raum] wide, large; excellent, eminent J V.89; Miln 354; Sdhp 345, 592. — pl. **urū** sands, soil J V.303.

Urundā (f.) [ura + undā?] freedom of the chest, free breathing, relief D II.269 (v. l. uruddhā perhaps preferable, for ura + uddharaṇa lifting or raising the chest).

Urūḷhava (adj.) [doubtful, prob. for urūḷhavant, with affix vant to a pp. formed with ud°. The word is taken by Kern, *Toev.* s. v. as ud-ūḷha of **vah** (with d for r). The well accredited (and older) variant **ubbuḷhavā** is expld. (see Kern, s. v.) as pp. of ud + **bṛh**², cp. upabrūhana. Perhaps we have to consider this as the legitimate form urūḷhava as its corruption. Morris, *J P T S.* 1887, 141 takes urūḷhavā as ud + rūḷha, pp. of **ruh** (with r. for rr = dr), thus "overgrown"] large, bulky, immense; great, big, strong. Only in one stock phrase "nāgo isādanto urūḷhavo" Vv 20⁹, 43⁹; J VI.488; of which variant n. I. ubbuḷhavā M I.414 = 450. The word is expld. at J VI.488 by "ubbāhana-samattha"; at VvA 104 (pl. urūḷhavā) by "thāmajava-parakkamehi byūhanto (v. l. brahmanto) mahantaŋ yuddha-kiccaŋ vahituŋ samatthā ti attho". The BSk. **udviddha** (Divy 7) may possibly be a corruption of ubbūḷha.

Ulati is a commentator's invention; said to be = **gacchati** to go Vism 60 (in definition of paŋsu-kūla; paŋsu viya kucchita-bhāvaŋ ulatī ti paŋsu-kūlaŋ).

Ulūka [Sk. ulūka; cp. Lat. ulucus & ulula owl, ululāre to howl, Ger. uhu; onomat. ***ul,** as in Gr. ὀλολύζω, Sk. ululi, Lith. ulūti] an owl Vin I.186 (°camma, sandals of owl's skin); III.34; A V.289 sq.; J II.208, 352 (as king of the birds); Miln 403; DhA I.50 (kāka° crows & owls). **-pakkha** owls' wings (used as dress) Vin I.305; D I.167. **-pakkhika** dress of owls' wings, or owl feathers A I.241, 296; II.206; Pug 55 (= ulūka-pattāni ganthetvā kata-nivāsanaŋ Pug A 233).

Ullanghati [ud + **langh,** cp. BSk. prollanghya transgressing (= pra + ullangh°) Divy 596] to leap up J III.222 (udakato °itvā). — Caus. **ullangheti** to make jump up (always with olangheti, i. e. to make dance up & down) Vin III.121; J V.434; DhA IV.197. — pp. **ullanghita** (q v.).

Ullanghanā (f.) [abstr. fr. ud + **langh**] jumping up, lifting up, raising Vin III.121; J IV.5 (°samattha?).

Ullanghita [pp. of ullangheti] being jumped on, set on C. on S I.40 (see *K. S.* I.318) (for uḍḍita = taṇhāya ullanghita).

Ullapati [ud + lapati] to call out, to talk to, lay claim to Vin I.97; III.105; Pug 67 (= katheti Pug A 249).

Ullapana (nt.) & °ā (f.) [fr. ullapati] calling out, enticing, laying claim to Vin III.101; Th 2, 357; Miln 127; ThA 243. — **ullapanā** = uddhaŋ katvā lapanā Vism 27.

Ullahaka (adj.) [?] only in acc. nt. ullahakaŋ used adverbially, in cpd. **dant°** after the manner of rubbing the teeth, by means of grinding the teeth M III.167. Seems to be a ἅπαξ λεγομένον.

Ullāpa is v. l. for uklāpa (q. v.).

Ullikhana (nt.) [fr. ud + **likh**] combing, scratching VvA 349; ThA 267.

Ullikhita [pp. of ud + **likh**] scratched, combed Vin I.254; J II.92 (aḍḍhullikhitehi kesehi); Ud 22 (id. with upaḍḍh° for aḍḍh°); VvA 197.

Ullingeti [Denom. of ud + linga] to exhibit, show as a characteristic Vism 492.

Ullitta [pp. of ud + **lip**] smeared; only in combn. **ullittâvalitta** smeared up & down, i. e. smeared all round Vin II.117; M II.8; A I.101, 137; IV.231; Th I, 737.

Ullumpati [ud + **lup,** cp. BSk. ullumpati Mahāvy § 268] to take up, to help (with acc.), to save Vin II.277; D I.249.

Ullumpana (nt.) [fr. ullumpati] saving, helping; in phrase °sabhāva-saṇṭhita of a helping disposition, full of mercy DA I.177; PvA 35. Same as **ullopana** (q. v.).

Ullulita [pp. of ulloleti] waved, shaken (by the wind); waving J VI.536.

Ulloka [ud + lok°] doubtful in its meaning; occurs at Vin I.48 = II.209 as ullokā paṭhamaŋ ohāreti, trsl. *Vin Texts* by "a cloth to remove cobwebs", but better by Andersen, *Pāli Reader* as "as soon as it is seen"; at Vin II.151 the translators give "a cloth placed under the bedstead to keep the stuffing from coming out". See on term Morris *J P T S.* 1885, 31. — In cpd. ulloka-paduma at J VI.432 it may mean "bright lotus" (lit. to be looked at). See ulloketi.

Ullokaka (adj.) [fr. ulloketi] looking on (to), looking out; in phrase **mukh°** looking into a person's face; i. e. cheerful, winning; or "of bright face", with a winning smile D I.60; DA I.59, 168; PvA 219 (°ika for °aka).

Ullokita [pp. of ulloketi] looked at, looked on J I.253; DA I 193.

Ulloketi [ud + lok°, cp. loka, āloka & viloka] to look on to, look for, await J I.232 (ākāsaŋ), 253; II.221, 434; DA I.153, 168; VvA 316. — pp. **ullokita** (q. v.).

Ullopana (nt.) = **ullumpana** DhA I.309 (T. faulty; see remarks ad locum).

Ullola [fr. ud + **lul**] — I. a wave J III.228; VI.394. — 2. commotion, unrest J IV.306, 476.

Ullolanā (f.) [fr. ulloleti] wavering, loitering (in expectation of something), greed ThA 243.

Ulloleti [denom. fr. ullola] to stroll or hang about, to wait for, expect ThA 243. — pp. **ullulita.**

Uḷāra (adj.) [Vedic udāra, BSk. audāra] great, eminent, excellent, superb, lofty, noble, rich. — Dhammapāla at VvA 10—11 distinguishes 3 meanings: tīhi atthehi uḷāraŋ; paṇītaŋ (excellent), seṭṭhaŋ (best), mahantaŋ (great) Vin III.41 (°bhoga); D I.96; M III.38 (°bhogatā); S V.159; Sn 53, 58, 301; Nd² 170; J I.399; V.95; Vv I¹; 84²⁶; Pv I.5¹² (= hita samiddha PvA 30); VvA 18 (°pabhāva = mahānubhāva); ThA 173, 280; PvA 5, 6, 7, 8, 25, 30, 43, 58 and passim; Sdhp 26, 260, 416. — Der. **oḷārika** (q. v.).

Uḷāratā (f.) = **uḷāratta** Sdhp 254.

Uḷāratta (nt.) [abstr. fr. uḷāra] greatness etc.; only neg. an° smallness, insignificance, inferiority VvA 24.

Uḷu [Sk. uḍu, dialectical?] a lunar mansion Miln 178.

Uḷunka [dial.?] a ladle, a spoon Vin I.286; J I.120, 157; III.461; Miln 8; DhA I.425; II.3, 20; IV.75, 123.

Uḷumpa [dial.?] a raft, a float Vin I.230; III 63 (°ŋ bandhati); J IV.2; DhA II.120.

Uviṭṭa [= viṭṭha, pp. of **viś**, with prefixed u] having entered, come in D II.274 (v. l. BK. upa°).

Usabha[1] [Vedic ṛṣabha; Av. aršan male, Gr. ἄρσην, ἄρρην masculine, to Idg. *eres & *rēs to wet, sprinkle (with semen), as also in Sk. rasa juice, rasā wet, liquid, Lat. rōs dew. A parallel root *ueres in Sk. varṣa rain, Gr. ἕρση dew; Sk. vṛṣan & vṛṣabha bull] a bull; often fig. as symbol of manliness and strength (cp. nisabha) D I.6 (°yuddha bull-fight), 9 (°lakkhaṇa signs on a b.), 127; Vin III.39 (puris° "bull of a man", a very strong man); A I.188; II.207; IV.41 sq., 376; V.347, 350; Sn 26 sq., 416, 646, 684; Dh 422; J I.28 (V.203; °kkhandha broad-shouldered), 336; V.99 (bharatūsabha); VI.136; Pug 56; Vism 153 (°camma, in simile); DhA I.396; SnA 226, 333; KhA 144; PvA 163; VvA 85. — The compn. forms of usabha are **āsabha, isabha** (in nisabha) & **esabha** (q. v.). The relations between usabha, vasabha & nisabha are discussed at SnA 40.

Usabha[2] (nt.) [= usabha[1], in special application (?)] a certain measure of length, consisting of 20 yaṭṭhis (see yaṭṭhi) or 140 cubits J I.64 (eight), 70 (id.); II.91; IV.17 (one), 142 (eight); DhA I.108 (°mattaŋ).

Usā (f.) [doubtful] (a certain) food J VI.80.

Usīra (m. & nt.) [Sk. uśīra] the fragrant root of Andropogon Muricatum (cp. bīraṇa) Vin I.201; II.130 (°mayā vijanī); S II.88 (°nāḷi); A II.199 (id.); Dh 337; J V.39; Th I, 402 (°attho).

Usu (m. & f.) Sk. iṣu] an arrow Vin III.106 (°loma); D I.9; M I.86; III.133; S I.127; A II.117; III.162; J IV.416; VI.79, 248, 454; Miln 331, 339; SnA 466; PvA 155.
-kāra an arrow-maker, fletcher M II.105; Dh 80, 145; Th I, 29; J II.275; VI.66; DhA I.288.

Usumā (f.) [the diaeretic form of Sk. uṣman, of which the direct equivalent is P. usmā (q. v.)] heat J I.31 (= uṇha III.55), 243; II.433; Vism 172 (usuma-vaṭṭi-sadisa); DA I.186; DhA I.225; II.20.

Usuyyaka (adj.) [fr. usuyyā] envious, jealous Vin II.190; Sn 318, 325; J II.192 (v.l. asuyy°); V.114. — *Note.* The long vowel form **usūyaka** occurs in cpd. **abbhusūyaka** (q. v.). Spelling ussuyikā occurs at Vv 33[21] (see VvA 147).

Usuyyati & **Usūyati** [Sk. asūyati; fr. usuyā envy] to be jealous or envious, to envy (with acc.) Vin I.242; J III. 27 (ppr. an-usuyyaŋ); Pv II.3[20] (maŋ usūyasi = mayhaŋ issaŋ karosi PvA 87).

Usuyyanā (f.) & **Usuyyitatta** (nt.) are exegetical abstr. formations of **usuyyā** (q. v.). Dhs 1121; Pug 19.

Usuyyā & **Usūyā** (f.) [Sk. asūyā] envy, jealousy, detraction S I.127 (ū); Sn 245 (u); J II.193 (ū); III.99 (ū; v. l. ussuyyā); Miln 402 (ū); Dhs 1121 (u); VvA 71 (u); SnA 332 (u).

Usmā (f.) [see usumā] heat D II.335, 338; M I.295; S II. III.143; IV.215, 294; V.212; Dhs 964; DA I.310. — In combn. with °kata it appears as **usmī°**, e. g. at M I 132, 258.
-gata heated, belonging to heat Dhs 964; as tt. one who mortifies or chastises himself, an ascetic J V.209 (= samaṇateja C.; cp. BSk. uṣṇagata & uṣmagata Divy 166, 240, 271, 469, & see Kern's mistakes at *Toev.* s. v.).

Ussa (adj.) [der. fr. ud = *ud-s(y)a, in analogy to oma fr. ava; but taken by Kern, *Toev.* s. v. as an abbreviated ussada] superior, higher (opp. oma inferior) A III.359; Sn 860 (= Nd[1] 251 with spelling ossa), 954.

Ussakkati[1] [ud + **sṛp**, see sakkati] to creep out or up to, to rise A III.241 sq.; Miln 260.

Ussakkati[2] [by-form of ussukkati] to endeavour Vism 437; VvA 95 (Caus. II. ussakkāpesi), 214.

Ussankita (adj.) [pp. of ud + **śank**] = ussankin A III.128; DhA III.485 (+ pari°; cp. ā°).

Ussankin (adj.) [fr. ud + **śank**] distrustful, fearful, anxious Vin II.192.

Ussankha (adj.) [ud + sankha] with ankles midway (?) in °pāda the 7th of the characteristics of a Mahāpurisa D II.17; III.143, 154; DA explains: the ankles are not over the heels, but midway in the length of the foot.

Ussajjati [ud + **sṛj**, cp. BSk. protsṛjati Divy 587] to dismiss, set free, take off, hurl A IV.191.

Ussaṭa [pp. of ud + sarati of **sṛ**, cp. saṭa for *sūta] run away M II.65.

Ussada [most likely to ud + **syad**; see ussanna]: this word is beset with difficulties, the phrase satt-ussada is applied in all kinds of meanings, evidently the result of an original application & meaning having become obliterated. satt° is taken as *sapta (seven) as well as *sattva (being), ussada as prominence, protuberance, fulness, arrogance. The meanings may be tabulated as follows: (1) prominence (cp. Sk. utsedha), used in characterisation of the Nirayas, as "projecting, prominent hells", ussadanirayā (but see also below 4) J I.174; IV.3, 422 (pallankaŋ, v. l. caturassaŋ, with four corners); V.266. — adj. prominent ThA 13 (tej-ussadehi ariyamaggadhammehi, or as below 4?). — 2. protuberance, bump, swelling J IV.188; also in phrase **sattussada** having 7 protuberances, a qualification of the Mahāpurisa D III.151 (viz. on both hands, feet, shoulders, and on his back). — 3. rubbing in, anointing, ointment; adj. anointed with (—°), in candan° J III.139; IV.60; Th I, 267; Vv 53[1]; DhA I.28; VvA 237. — 4. a crowd adj. full of (—°) in phrase **sattussada** crowded with (human beings) D I.87 (cp. DA I.245: aneka-satta-samākiṇṇa; but in same sense BSk. **sapt-otsada** Divy 620, 621); Pv IV.1[8] (of Niraya = full of beings, expld. by sattehi ussanna uparūpari nicita PvA 221. — 5. qualification, characteristic, mark, attribute, in **catussada** "having the four qualifications (of a good village)" J IV.309 (viz. plenty of people, corn, wood and water C.). The phrase is evidently shaped after D I.87 (under 4). As "preponderant quality, characteristic" we find **ussada** used at Vism 103 (cf. Asl. 267) in combns. lobh°, dos°, moh°, alobh° etc. (quoted from the "Ussadakittana"), and similarly at VvA 19 in Dhammapāla's definition of **manussa** (lobh'ādīhi alobh'ādīhi sahitassa manassa ussannatāya manussā), viz. sattā manussa-jātikā tesu lobh'ādayo alobh'ādayo ca **ussadā**. — 6. (metaph.) self-elevation, arrogance, conceit, haughtiness Vin I.3; Sn 515, 624 (an° = taṇhā-ussada-abhāvena SnA 467), 783 (expld. by Nd[1] 72 under formula **sattussada**; i. e. showing 7 bad qualities, viz. rāga, dosa, moha etc.), 855. — See also **ussādana, ussādeti** etc.

Ussadaka (adj.) [fr. ussada 4] over-full, overflowing A III.231, 234 (°jāta, of a kettle, with vv. ll. ussuraka° & ussuka°).

Ussanna (adj.) [pp. of ud + **syad**, cp. abhisanna] — 1. overflowing, heaped up, crowded; extensive, abundant, preponderant, excessive, full of (°—) Vin I.285 (cīvaraŋ u. overstocked; II.270 (āmisaŋ too abundant); III.286; Th 2, 444 (= upacita ThA 271); J I.48, 145 °kusala-mūla); DhA I.26 (id.); (lobho etc.) Asl. 267; Miln 223 (id.); J I.336 (kāla, fulfilled); III.418; IV.140; Pv III.5[1] (°puñña, cp. PvA 197); PvA 71 (°pabbā thick glow). Cp. accussanna. — 2. anointed VvA 237. — 3. spread out, wide DhA II.67 (mahāpathavī u.), 72 (id.).

Ussannatā (f.) [abstr. fr. ussanna] accumulation, fulness, plenty Kvu 467 (where *Kvu trsln.* p. 275 gives ussadattā); VvA 18, 19.

Ussaya in °**vādika** Vin IV.224 is a variant of **usuyya°** "using envious language, quarrelsome". — Another ussaya [fr. ud + **śri**, cp. Sk. ucchrita, P. ussita & ussāpeti] meaning "accumulation" is found in cpd. **samussaya** only.

Ussayāpeti see **udassaye.**

Ussarati [ud + sarati of **sṛ**] to run out, run away J I.434 (imper. ussaratha); V.437. — pp. **ussaṭa** (q. v.). — Caus. **ussāreti** (q. v.).

Ussava [Sk. utsava] feast, making merry, holiday Vin III. 249; J I.475; II.13, 248; VvA 7, 109 (°divasa).

Ussahati [ud + **sah**, cp. BSk. utsaha Jtm 215; utsahetavya Divy 494; utsahana Divy 490; ucchahate for utsahate Av. Ś II.21] to be able, to be fit for, to dare, venture Vin I.47, 83; II.208; III.17; D I.135; S IV.308, 310; Miln 242; VvA 100. — Caus. **ussāheti** (see pp. **ussāhita**).

Ussāda [fr. ussādeti] throwing up on DA I.122.

Ussādana (nt.) [to ussādeti, cp. ussādita] — 1. overflowing, piling up, abundance M III.230 (opp. apasādana). — 2. (probably confused with ussāraṇa) tumult, uproar, confusion A III.91, 92 (v. l. ussāraṇa) = Pug 66 (= hatthi-assarathâdīnaŋ c'eva balakāyassa ca uccāsadda-mahāsaddo Pug A 249).

Ussādita [fr. ussādeti, BSk. ucchāyita Divy 76, 77, 466]. [See ussāpita & ussārita under ussāpeti & ussāreti. There exists in Pāli as well as in BSk. a confusion of different roots to express the notion of raising, rising, lifting & unfolding, viz. **sṛ, syad, śri, sad, chad.** (See ussada, ucchādana, ussādeti, ussāpeti, ussāreti)].

Ussādiyati [Pass. med. of ussādeti, cp. ussada 4] to be in abundance, to be over Vin II.167.

Ussādeti [denom. fr. ussada 1] — 1. to dismiss D III.128 [for ussāreti¹] — 2. to raise, cause to rise up on, haul up, pile up M I.135; III.230; A IV.198, 201; Miln 187, 250. — Pass. **ussādiyati** (q. v.). — pp. **ussādita** (q. v.).

Ussāpana (nt.) [fr. ussāpeti] lifting up, raising, erecting, unfolding (of a flag or banner) A IV.41; Nd² 503 (dhamma-dhajassa).

Ussāpita [pp. of ussāpeti, cp. ussādita] lifted, raised, unfurled Miln 328 (dhamma-dhaja); J II.219.

Ussāpeti [Caus. of ud + **śri**, cp. BSk. ucchrāpayati Av. S I.384, 386, 387; II.2] to lift up, erect, raise, exalt Vin II.195; A IV.43; J II.219; IV.16; V.95 (chattaŋ); PvA 75 (id.); Miln 21; DhA I.3; III 118 (kaṭṭhāni). — pp. **ussāpita** & **ussita** (q. v.). See also **usseti.**

Ussāraṇa (nt.) [fr. ussāreti] procession, going or running about, tumult DhA II.7 (so read for ossāraṇā). Cp. **ussādana.**

Ussārita [pp. of ussāreti²] lifted out or up Vism 63 (samudda-vīcīhi thale ussārita; v. l. ussādita).

Ussāreti¹ [Caus. of ussarati] to cause to move back, to cause to go away or to recede Vin I.32, 46 (here a student, when folding up his master's robe, has to make the corners move back a hand's breadth each time. Then the crease or fold will change and not tend to wear through), 276; II.237 (here the reading ussādeti may be preferred); J I.419; IV.349; V.347. — Caus. II. **ussārāpeti** J II.290.

Ussāreti² [= ussādeti] to cause to raise aloft (of a flag), to lift J V.319 (= ussāpeti). — pp. **ussārita.**

Ussāva¹ [either = Sk. avaśyāya, or to ud + **sru**] hoarfrost, dew D II.19; J IV.120; V.417; °**bindu** a dew drop A IV.137; Pv IV.1⁶; SnA 458; in comparisons: Vism 231, 633.

Ussāva² [fr. ud + **sru**] outflow, taint, stain (cp. āsava) DhA IV.165 (taṇhā°; v. l. ussada, to ussada 6).

Ussāvana (nt.) [= ussāpana] proclamation (of a building as legal store house); in °**antika** within the proclaimed limit Vin I.239.

Ussāsa see **nirussāsa.**

Ussāha [Sk. utsāha & utsaha, see ussahati] strength, power, energy; endeavour, good-will M II.174; S V.440; A I. 147; II.93, 195; III.75, 307; IV.320; V.93 sq.; Miln 323, 329 (dhiti +) Vism 330; Sdhp 49, 223, 535, 619; SnA 50; DhA III.394; PvA 31, 106, 166; VvA 32, 48. — In exegetical literature often comb^d. with the quâsi synonym **ussoḷhi** e. g. at Nd² s. v.; Dhs 13, 22, 289, 571.

Ussāhana (f.) [fr. ussahati, cp. BSk. utsahana Divy 490] = ussāha Nett 8.

Ussāhita [pp. of ussāheti, Caus. of ussahati] determined, incited, encouraged, urged J I.329; VvA 109; PvA 201. Cp. sam°.

Ussiñcati [ud + **sic**] to bale out, exhaust J I.450; II.70; IV.16; Miln 261.

Ussiñcana (nt.) [fr. ussiñcati] drying, baling out, raising water, exhausting J I.417.

Ussita [Sk. ucchrita, pp. of ud + **sri**, see ussāpeti] erected, high S V.228; Th 1, 424 (pannaddhaja); J V.386; Vv 84¹⁸; VvA 339. Cp. sam°.

Ussīsaka (nt.) [ud + sīsa + ka] the head of a bed, a pillow for the head J I.266; II.410, 443; IV.154; V.99; VI.32, 37, 56; DhA I.184 (°passe, opp. pāda-passe).

Ussuka (adj.) [Sk. utsuka, also BSk. e. g. Jtm 31⁶⁸] — 1. endeavouring, zealous, eager, active S I.15 (an° inactive); A IV.266; Sn 298. — 2. greedy, longing for Dh 199 (an°).

Ussukita (adj.) = **ussukin**; only neg. **an°** free from greed VvA 74.

Ussukin (adj.) [fr. ussuka] greedy, longing; only neg. **an°** Pug 23.

Ussukka (nt.) [*utsukya fr. ussuka; cp. BSk. utsukya Divy 601 and autsukya Av. Ś I.85] zeal, energy, endeavour, hard work, eagerness Vin I.50; S IV.288, 291, 302; Nd² s. v. Nett 29; VvA 147; PvA 5, 135; Vism 90 (āpajjati); 644 (°ppahānaŋ). — Cp. **appossukka.**

Ussukkatā (f.) = **ussukka** A V.195.

Ussukkati [denom. fr. ussukka] to endeavour D I.230. — Caus. II. **ussukkāpeti** to practice eagerly, to indulge in, to perform VvA 95, 98, 243. See also **ussakkati.**

Ussuta (adj.) [pp. of ud + **sru**, cp. avassuta] defiled, lustful (cp. āsava), only neg. **an°** free from defilement Dh 400.

Ussuyā, Ussuyaka, uss.

Ussussati [ud + sussati of **śuṣ**] to dry up (intrs.) S I.126; III.149 (mahāsamuddo u.); Sn 985; J VI.195.

Ussūra (adj) [ut + sūra] "sun-out", the sun being out; i. e. after sunrise or after noon, adverbially in °**bhatta** eating after mid-day, unpunctual meals A III.260, and °**seyyā** sleep after sunrise, sleeping late D III.184; DhA II.227. Besides as loc. adv. **ussūre** the sun having been up (for a long time), i. e. at evening Vin I 293; IV.77; J II.286, also in ati-ussūre too long after sunrise VvA 65; DhA III.305.

Usseti [ud + **śri**] to erect, raise, stand up J IV 302; aor. ussesi J VI.203. — Caus. **ussāpeti**; pp. **ussita** & **ussāpita** (q. v.).

Usseneti [denom. fr. ussena = ussayana, ud + **śri** (?)] to draw on to oneself, to be friendly S III.89 (v. l. ussi°);

A II.214 sq. (opp. paṭisseneti); Ps II.167 (ussi°); Kvu I. 93 (reading ussineti + visineti). See also paṭiseneti.

Usseḷheti (?) Vin II.10 (for ussoḷh° ?); cp. ussoḷhikāya.

Ussota (adj.) [ud + sota] nt. ussotaŋ as adv. "up-stream" Miln 117.

Ussoḷhi (f.) [a by-form of ussāha fr. ud + **sah**, pp. *soḍha dialectical] exertion M I.103; S II.132; V.440; A II. 93, 195; III.307; IV.320; V.93 sq. Often combd. with ussāha (q. v.).

Ussoḷhikā (f.) [adj. of ussoḷhi] belonging to exertion, only in instr. as adv. ussoḷhikāya "in the way of exertion", i. e. ardently, keenly, eagerly S I.170 (naccati)

Uhunkara [onomat. uhu + kara, see under ulūka] an owl (lit. "uhu"-maker) J VI.538 (= ulūka C.).

Ū.

Ūkā (f.) [Sk. yūkā, prob. dialectical] a louse J I.453; II. 324; III.393; V.298; Miln 11; Vism 445; DhsA 307, 319; DhA III.342; VvA 86.

Ūtagītaŋ at J I.290 in phrase "jimaŋ ūtagītaŋ gāyanto" read "imaŋ jūtagītaŋ g."

Ūna (adj.) [Vedic ūna; cp. Av. ūna, Gr. εὔνις, Lat. vānus, Goth. wans, Ags. won = E. want] wanting, deficient, less M II.73; J V.330; DhA I.77; DhA IV.210. Mostly adverbially with numerals = one less, but one, minus (one or two); usually with **eka** (as ekūna one less, e. g. ekūna-aṭṭhasataŋ (799) J I.57; ekūna-pañcasate KhA 91, ekūna-vīsati (19) Vism 287; eken'ūnesu pañcasu attabhāvasatesu (499) J I.167; also with eka in instr. as eken'ūnapañcasatāni (deficient by one) Vin II.285; KhA 91; sometimes without eka, e. g. ūnapañcasatāni (499) Vin III.284; ūnavīsati (19) Vin IV.130, 148. With "two" less: dvīhi ūnaŋ sahassaŋ (998) J I.255. — **anūna** not deficient, complete PvA 285 (= paripuṇṇa).
-udara (ūnudara, ūnūdara, ūnodara) an empty stomach, adj. of empty stomach; °udara J II.293; VI.295; °ūdara J VI.258; Miln 406; odara Sn 707; DhA I.170. **-bhāva** depletion, deficiency SnA 463 (v. l. hānabhāva).

Ūnaka (adj.) [ūna + ka] deficient, wanting, lacking Vin III.81, 254; IV.263; Sn 721; Miln 310, 311, (°satta-vassika one who is not yet 7 years old), 414; DhA I.79.

Ūnatta (nt.) [abstr. fr. ūna] depletion, deficiency Vin II. 239; J V.450.

Ūpāya at DhA II.93 stands for upāya.

Ūpiya see **upiya** & **opiya**.

Ūmika [f. ūmi] wave Miln 197 (°vanka waterfall, cataract).

Ūmī & **Ūmi** (f.) [Sk. ūrmi, fr. Idg. *uel (see nibbāna I.2); cp. Gr. ἐλύω in wind, ἕλιξ wound; Lat. volvo to roll; Ags. wylm wave; Ohg. wallan; also Sk. ulva, varutra, valaya, vallī, vṛṇoti. See details in Walde, Lat. Wtb. under volvo] a wave M I.460 (°bhaya); S IV.157; V.123 (°jāta); A III.232 sq. (id.); Sn 920; J II.216; III.262; IV.141; Miln 260 (°jāta). — *Note*. A parallel form of ūmī is **ummī**.

Ūru [Vedic ūru; cp. Lat. vārus bow-legged, of Idg. *uā, to which also Ohg. wado = Ger. wade calf of leg] the thigh Sn 610; Vin II.105 (in contrast with bāha); III. 106; J I.277; II.275, 443; III.82; V.89, 155; Nd² 659 (so read for uru); Vv 64[13]; DA I.135 = Vin II.190.
-aṭṭhi(ka) the thigh bone M I.58; III.92; J I.428 (ūraṭṭhika); KhA 49, 50 (ūraṭṭhi). **-(k)khambha** stiffening or rigidity of the thigh, paralysis of the leg (as symptom of fright) M I.237; J V.23.

Ūsa [Sk. ūṣa] salt-ground; saline substance, always combd. with khāra S III.131 (°gandha); A I.209.

Ūsara (adj.) [Sk. ūṣara, fr. ūṣa] saline S IV.315; A IV.237; DhsA 243. — nt. °ŋ a spot with saline soil PvA 139 (gloss for ujjhangala).

Ūha see vy°, sam°.

Ūhacca[1] (indecl.) [ger. of ūharati, ud + **hṛ** (or ava + **hṛ**, cp. ohacca & oharati) for uddharati I & 2] — I. lifting up, raising or rising J III.206. — 2. pulling out, taking away, removing D II.254 (cp. DhA II.181); S I.27 (v. l. for ohacca); Sn 1119 (= uddharitvā uppāṭayitvā Nd² 171).

Ūhacca[2] (indecl.) [ger. of ūhanati[2] = ūhadati] soiling by defecation, defecating J II.71 (= vaccaŋ katvā C.).

Ūhaññati [Pass. of ūhanati[1]] to be soiled; to be disturbed aor. ūhaññi Vin I.48; M I.116; aor. also ūhani M I.243.

Ūhata[1] [pp. of ud + **hṛ** or **dhṛ** thus for uddhaṭa as well as uddhata] — I. lifted, risen, raised Vin III.70; J V.403. — 2. taken out, pulled out, destroyed Th I, 223 = Nd² 97[4]; Th I, 514; Dh 338 (= ucchinna DhA IV.48). — 3. soiled with excrements Vin II.222.

Ūhata[2] [pp. of ūhanati[1]] disturbed M I.116.

Ūhadati [for ūhanati[2] (?) or formed secondarily fr. ūhacca or ohacca?] to defecate J II.355; DhA II.181 (so read with v. l. for T. ūhadayati).

Ūhana (nt.) [fr. ūhanati ?] reasoning, consideration, examination Miln 32 ("comprehension" trsl.; as characteristic of manasikāra); Vism 142 = DhsA 114 ("prescinding" trsl.; as characteristic of vitakka).

Ūhanati[1] [ud + han] to disturb, shake up; defile, soil M I.243; J II.73. — Pass. aor. ūhani: see **ūhaññati**. — pp. **ūhata**[2] (q. v.). Cp. sam°.

Ūhanati[2] [either ud + **han** or ava + **han**, cp. ohanati] I. to cut off, discharge, emit, defecate Vin I.78; III.227. — 2. [prob. for ūharati, cp. ūhacca[1]] to lift up, to take away M I.117 (opp. odahati). Cp. ohana in bimb-ohana. — ger. **ūhacca**[2] (q. v.).

Ūharati [for uddharati] only in forms of ger. **ūhacca**[1] and pp. **ūhata**[1] (q. v.).

Ūhasati [either ud or ava + **has**, cp. avahasati] to laugh at, deride, mock A III.91; J V.452 (+ pahasati); Pug 67 (= avahasati Pug A 249).

Ūhasana (nt.) [fr. ūhasati] laughing, mocking Miln 127.

Ūhā (f.) [etym.?] life, only in cpd. āyūha lifetime PvA 136, 162 (°pariyosāna). — As N. of a river at Miln 70. — Cp. BSk. ūhá in ūhāpoha Av. Ś I.209, 235.

E.

Eka (adj.-num.) [Vedic eka, i. e. e-ka to Idg. *oi as in Av. aēva, Gr. οἶος one, alone; and also with diff. suffix in Lat. ū-nus, cp. Gr. οἰνός (one on the dice), Goth. etc. ains = E. one] one. Eka follows the pron. declension, i. e. nom. pl. is eke (e. g. Sn 43, 294, 780 etc.) — 1. "one" as number, either with or without contrast to two or more; often also "single" opp. to nānā various, many (q. v.). Very frequent by itself as well as with other numerals, ekangula one thumb Mhvs 29, 11; DhA III. 127; ekapasse in one quarter DhA II.52; ekamaccha a single fish J I.222. In enumeration: eka dve pañca dasa DhA I.24. With other numerals: eka-tiŋsa (31) D II.2; °saṭṭhi (61) Vin I.20; °navuti (91) DhA I.97; °sata (101) DhA II.14. Cp. use of "one less" in ekūna (see under cpds. & ūna). — 2. (as predicative and adj.) one, by oneself, one only, alone, solitary A III.67 (ek-uddesa); J I.59 (ekadivasena on the one day only, i. e. on the same day); Dh 395; Sn 35, 1136 (see Nd² 172ᵃ), ekaŋ ekaŋ one by one S I 104 (devo ekaŋ ekaŋ phusāyati rains drop by drop), cp. ekameka. — 3. a certain one, some one, some; adj. in function of an indefinite article = a, one (definite or indefinite): ekasmiŋ samaye once upon a time J I.306; ekena upāyena by some means J III.393; ekaŋ kulaŋ gantuŋ to a certain clan (corresp. with asuka) DhA I.45; ekadivasaŋ one day J I.58; III.26; PvA 67. Cp. Sn 1069 (see Nd² 172ᵇ). — All these three categories are found represented in freq. cpds., of which the foll. are but a small selection.

-akkhi see °pokkhara. -agga calm, tranquil (of persons just converted), collected [cp. Buddh. Sk. ekāgra Jtm 31¹⁰] S IV.125; A I.70, 266; II.14, 29; III.175 (°citta), 391; Sn 341; J I.88; Nett 28, cp. Miln 139. -aggatā concentration; capacity to individualise; contemplation, tranquillity of mind (see on term *Cpd.* 16, 178³, 237, 240) S V.21, 197, 269 (cittassa); A I.36; IV.40; Dhs 11 (cittassa); Vism 84. -anga a part, division, something belonging to J III.308; Ud 69. -angaṇa one (clear) space J II.357. -āgārika a thief, robber D I.52, 166; A I.154, 295; II.206; III.129; Nd¹ 416; Nd² 304 III.A. DA I.159 (= ekam eva gharaŋ parivāretvā vilumpanaŋ DA I.159). -āyana leading to one goal, direct way or "leading to the goal as the one & only way (magga) M I.63; S V.167, 185. -ārakkha having one protector or guardian D III.269; A V.29 sq. -ālopika = ekāgārika D I.166; A I.295; II.206. -āsana sitting or living alone M I.437; Sn 718; Dh 305; J V.397; Miln 342; Vism 60 (expld. with reference to eating, viz. ekāsane bhojanaŋ ekāsanaŋ, perhaps comparing āsana with asana². The foll. °āsanika is ibid. expld. as "taŋ sīlam assā ti ekāsaniko"). -āsanika one who keeps to himself Miln 20, 216; Vism 69. -âha one day M I.88; usually in cpd. ekâhadvîhaŋ one or two days J I.255; DhA I.391. -âhika of or for one day D I.166. -uttarika(-nikāya) is another title for Anguttarika-nikāya Miln 392. -ūna one less, minus one, usually as 1st part of a numeral cpd., like °*vīsati* (20—1 = 19) DhA I.4; °*paññāsa* (49) J III.220; °*saṭṭhi* (59) DhA III.412; °*pañcasatā* (499) DhA II.204. See ūna. -eka one by one, each, severally, one to each D II.18 (°loma); III.144 (id.), 157; J I.222; DhA I.101 (ekekassa no ekekaŋ māsaŋ one month for each of us); II.114; VvA 256; PvA 42, 43. -ghana compact, solid, hard Dh 81. -cara wandering or living alone, solitary S I.16; Sn 166, 451; Dh 37. -cariyā walking alone, solitude Dh 61; Sn 820. -cārin = °cara Miln 105. -cittakkhaṇika of the duration of *one* thought Vism 138. -cintin "thinking one thing (only)", simple Miln 92. -thūpa (all) in one heap, mixed up, together J V.17 (= sūkarapotakā viya C.). -doṇikā(-nāvā) a trough-shaped canoe with an outrigger J VI.305. -paṭalika having a single sole (of sandals, upāhanā) Vism 125. -paṭṭa single cloth (cp. dupaṭṭa) Vism 109. -padika(-magga) a small (lit. for one foot) foot-path J I.315; V.491. -pala one carat worth (see pala) Vism 339. -passayika is to be read ek'apassayika (see under apa°). -pahārena all at once Vism 418; DhsA 333. -piṭaka knowing *one* Piṭaka Vism 62. -puttika having only one son KhA 237. -purisika (itthi) (a woman) true to one man J I.290. -pokkhara a sort of drum J VI.21, 580 (C. explns. by ek-akkhi-bherī). -bījin having only one (more) seed, i. e. destined to be reborn only once S V.205; A I.233; IV.380; Nett 189. -bhattika having one meal a day A I.212; III.216; J I.91. -bhattakinī a woman true to one husband J III.63. -rajja sole sovereignty Dh 178; PvA 74. -rājā universal king J I.47 (of the Sun). -vāciya a single remark or objection J II.353. -vāraŋ once J I.292; °vārena id. DhA I.10. -sadisa fully alike or resembling, identical J I.291. -sama equal J VI.261. -sāṭa & sāṭaka having a single vestment, a "one-rober" S I.78 (°ka); Ud 65.

Ekaŋsa¹ (adj.) [eka + aŋsa¹] belonging to one shoulder, on or with one shoulder; only in phrase ekaŋsaŋ uttarāsangaŋ karoti to arrange the upper robe over one shoulder (the left) Vin I.46; II.188 & passim.

Ekaŋsa² [eka + aŋsa¹ or better aŋsa²] "one part or point", i. e. one-pointedness, definiteness; affirmation, certainty, absoluteness D I.153; A II.46; Sn 427, 1027; J III.224 (ekaŋsatthe nipāto for "nūna"); SnA 414 (°vacana for "taggha"). — Opp. an° Miln 225. — instr. ekaŋsena as adv. for certain, absolutely, definitely, inevitably D I.122, 161, 162; M I.393; S IV.326; A V.190; J I.150; III. 224; PvA 11.

Ekaŋsika (adj.) [fr. ekaŋsa²] certain D I.189, 191; an° uncertain, indefinite D I.191.

Ekaŋsikatā (f.) [abstr. fr. ekaŋsika] as neg. an° indefiniteness Miln 93.

Ekaka (adj.) [eka + ka] single, alone, solitary Vin II.212; J I.255; II.234; IV.2. — f. ekikā Vin IV.229; J I.307; III.139.

Ekacca (adj.) [der. fr. eka with suffix *tya, implying likeness or comparison, lit. "one-like", cp. E. one-like = one-ly = only] one, certain, definite D I.162; A I.8; often in pl. ekacce some, a few D I.118; A V.194; Th 2, 216; J II. 129; III.126. See also app° under api.

Ekaccika (adj.) [fr. ekacca] single, not doubled (of cloth, opp. to diguṇa) J V.216 (°vasana = eka-paṭṭa-nivattha).

Ekacciya (adj.) = ekacca S I.199; J IV.259; acc. as adv. °ŋ once, single Vin I.289 (cp. *Vin Texts* II.212).

Ekajjhaŋ (adv.) [fr. eka, cp. literary Sk. aikadhyaŋ, but BSk. ekadhyaŋ M Vastu I.304] in the same place, in conjunction, together Miln 144 (karoti), KhA 167; SnA 38.

Ekato (adv.) [abl. formation fr. eka, cp. Sk. ekataḥ] — 1. on the one side (opp. on the other) J III.51; IV.141. — 2. together J II.415; III.57 (vasanto), 52 (sannipatanti), 391; IV.390; DhA I.18. ekato *karoti* to put together, to collect VvA 3. ekato *hutvā* "coming to one", agreeing DhA I.102, cp. ekato ahesuŋ J I.201.

Ekatta (nt.) [abstr. fr. eka] — 1. unity D I.31. — 2. loneliness, solitude, separation Sn 718; Th 1, 49; Miln 162; J VI.64; VvA 202 (= ekibhāva).

Ekattatā (f.) [fr. ekatta] unity, combination, unification, concentration Nett 4, 72 sq., 107 sq.

Ekadatthu (adv.) [eka-d-atthu, cp. aññadatthu] once, definitely, specially J III.105 (= ekaŋsena C.).

Ekadā (adv.) [fr. eka] once, at the same time, at one time, once upon a time S I.162; Sn 198; DhA II.41; Miln 213.

Ekanta (adj.) [Sk. ekānta] one-sided, on one end, with one top, topmost (°—) usually in function of an adv. as °—, meaning "absolutely, extremely, extraordinary, quite" etc. — 1. (lit.) at one end, only in °lomin a woollen coverlet with a fringe at one end D I.7 (= ekato dasaŋ uṇṇāmay' attharaṇaŋ keci ekato uggata-pupphan ti vadanti DA I.87); Vin I.192; II.163, 169; A I.181. — 2. (fig.) extremely, very much, in freq. combns; e. g. °kāḷaka A III.406; IV.11; °gata S V.225; A III.326; °dukkha M I.74; S II.173; III.70 (+ sukha); A V.289; °dussīlya DhA III.153; °nibbidā A III.83; IV.143; °paripuṇṇa S II.219; V.204; °manāpa S IV.238; °sukha A II.231; III.409; °sukhin DA I.119 etc.

Ekantarika (adj.) [eka + antarika] with one in between, alternate J IV.195, °bhāvena (instr. adv.) in alternation, alternately Vism 374; ekantarikāya (adv.) with intervals Vism 244.

Ekamantaŋ (adv.) [eka + anta, acc. in adv. function, cp. BSk. ekamante M Vastu I.35] on one side, apart, aside Vin I.47, 94 = II.272; D I.106; Sn p. 13 (expld. at SnA 140 as follows: bhāvana-puŋsaka-niddeso, ek'okāsaŋ ekapassan ti vuttaŋ hoti, bhummatthe vā upayogavacanaŋ); Sn 580, 1009, 1017; J I.291; II.102, 111; SnA 314, 456. — Also in loc. ekamante on one side DhA I.40.

Ekameka (adj.) [eka-m-eka, cp. BSk. ekameka M Vastu III.358] one by one, each A V.173; Vv 78[2].

Ekavidha (adj.) [eka + vidha] of one kind, single, simple Vism 514; adv. ekavidhā singly, simply Vism 528.

Ekaso (adv.) [Sk. ekaśaḥ] singly, one by one J III.224 (an°).

Ekākiya (adj.) alone, solitary Th 1, 541; Miln 398.

Ekādasa (num.) [Sk. ekādaśa] eleven Vin I.19. — num. ord. ekādasama the eleventh Sn 111, 113.

Ekānika (adj.) = ekākiya; instr. ekānikena as adv. "by oneself" Miln 402.

Ekikā see **ekaka**.

Ekībhāva [eka + bhāva, with ī for a in compn. with **bhū**] being alone, loneliness, solitude D III 245; M II.250; A III.289; V.89, 164; Vism 34; SnA 92, 93; DhA II.103; VvA 202; DA I.253, 309.

Ekodi (adj.) [most likely eka + odi for odhi, see avadhi[2] & cp. avadahati, avadahana, lit. of one attention, limited to one point. Thus also suggested by Morris *J P T S.* 1885, 32 sq. The word was Sanskritised into ekoti, e.g. at M Vastu III.212, 213; Lal. Vist. 147, 439] concentrated, attentive, fixed A III.354; Nd[1] 478. Usually in compn. with **kṛ** & **bhū** (which points however to a form ekoda° with the regular change of a to i in connection with these roots!), as ekodi-karoti to concentrate M I.116; S IV.263; °bhavati to become settled S IV.196; V.144; °bhūta concentrated Sn 975; °bhāva concentration, fixing one's mind on one point D I.37; III.78, 131; A I.254; III.24; Vism 156 (expl. as eko udeti); Dhs 161 (cp. *Dhs trsln.* 46); DhsA 169; Nett 89.

Ejā (f.) [to **iñj**, q. v. and see ānejja. There is also a Sk. root **ej** to stir, move] motion, turbulence, distraction, seduction, craving S IV.64; Sn 791; It 91; Nd[1] 91, 353; Dhs 1059 (cp. *Dhs trsln.* 277); VvA 232. — **aneja** (adj.) unmoved, undisturbed, calm, passionless S I.27, 141, 159; III.83; IV.64; A II.15; Nd[1] 353; VvA 107.

Eṭṭha [pp. of ā + **iṣ**] see pariy°; do. °eṭṭhi.

Eṭṭhi (f.) [fr. eṭṭha, ā + **iṣ**, cp. Sk. eṣṭi] desire, wish, in combn. with gaveṭṭhi pariyeṭṭhi etc. Vbh 353 = Vism 23, 29 etc.

Eṇi (f.) [etym.? dial.] a kind of antelope, only two foll. cpds.: °**jangha** "limbed like the antelope" (one of the physical characteristics of the Superman) D II.17; III.143, 156; M II.136; S I.16; Sn 165; °**miga** the eṇi deer J V.416; SnA 207, 217.

Eṇeyya D III.157; J VI.537 sq., & **Eṇeyyaka** A I.48; II.122; J V.155 Nd[2] 604 = eṇi.

Etad (pron. adj.) [Vedic etad, of pron. base *e; see Walde, *Lat. Wtb.* under equidem] demonstr. pron. "this", with on the whole the same meaning and function as tad, only more definite and emphatic. Declined like tad. *Cases*: nt. sg. etad (poetical-archaic form) A II.17; Sn 274, 430, 822, 1087; J I.61, 279; & etaŋ (the usual form) Sn 51, 207, 1036, 1115; J II.159; pl. etāni Sn 52; J II.159. — m. sg. esa Sn 81, 416, 1052; J I.279; II.159; Miln 18; DhA I.18; & eso Sn 61, 312, 393; J VI.336; pl. ete Sn 188, 760; J I.223. — f. sg. esā Sn 80, 451; J I.307; pl. etā Sn 297, 897; J II.129. — Oblique cases: gen. dat. etassa J II.159; f. etissā J III.280; instr. etena Sn 655; J I.222; pl. loc. etesu Sn 248, 339, 1055; f. etāsu Sn 607. Other cases regular & frequent.

Etarahi (adv.) [Sk. etarhi, cp. tarahi & carahi] now, at present D I.29, 151, 179, 200; II.3; J I.215 (opp. tadā); III.82; VI.364 (instead of paccuppanna).

Etādisa (adj.) [etad + disa, of **dṛś**, cp. Sk. etādṛśa] such, such like, of this kind D II.157; Sn 588, 681, 836; Pv I.9[4]; IV.1[86] (= edisa yathā-vutta-rūpa PvA 243); PvA 11.71.

Eti [P. eti represents Sk. eti as well as ā-eti, i.e. to go and to come (here); with Sk. eti cp. Av. aeiti, Gr. εἶσι, Lat. eo, it; Goth. iddja went, Obulg. iti, Oir. etha] to go, go to, reach; often (= ā + eti) to come back, return Sn 364, 376, 666 (come); J VI.365 (return); ppr. **ento** J III.433 (acc. suriyaŋ atthaŋ entaŋ the setting sun); imper. 2nd sg. ehi only in meaning "come" (see separately), 3rd etu D I.60; 2nd pl. etha D I.211; Sn 997; J II.129; DhA I.95 (in admission formula "etha bhikkhavo", come ye [and be] bhikkhus! See ehi bhikkhu). — fut. essati J VI.190, 365, & ehiti J II.153; 2nd sg. ehisi Dh 236, 369. — pp. **ita** (q. v.).

Etta (adv.) [= Sk. atra, see also ettha] there, here Pv I.5[6] (sic; cp. KhA 254 note).

Ettaka (adj.) [etta + ka, contrasting-comparative function, cp. tattaka] so much, this much, according to context referring either to deficiency or abundance, thus developing 2 meanings, viz. (1) just as much (& no more), only so little, all this, just this, such a small number, a little; pl. so few, just so many D I.117 (opp. aparimāṇa), 124; A IV.114; Nd[2] 304 III. (ettakena na tussati is not satisfied with this much); Vv 79[12] (cp. VvA 307); Miln 10, 18 (alaŋ ettakena enough of this much); DhA I.90 (enough, this much), 93, 399 (pl. ettakā); II.54 (only one), 174 sq.; VvA 233 (a little), 323. — ettakaŋ kālaŋ a short time (but see also under 2) J I.34; DhA II.20. — (2) ever so much (and not less), so much, pl. so many, ever so many, so & so many, such a lot A III.337; J I.207 (pl. ettakā), 375 (nt. ettakaŋ); III.80 (id.), 94 (°ŋ dhanaŋ such great wealth); Miln 37 (pl.); DhA I.392, 396 (pl. f. ettikā), 397, 398; II.14, 89 (pl.), 241 (pl. so many); VvA 65 (dhanaŋ). — ettakaŋ kālaŋ for some time, such a long time (see also above, under 1) DhA II.62, 81; III.318; VvA 330.

Ettato (adv.) [with double suffix for *atra-taḥ] from here, therefore S I.185.

Ettāvatā (adv.) [fr. etta = ettaka, cp. kittāvatā: kittaka] so far, to that extent, even by this much D I.205, 207; S II.17; Sn 478; Vv 55[6] (cp. VvA 248); Pv IV.1[61]; Miln 14; DA I.80; SnA 4; PvA 243.

Etto (adv.) [in analogy to ito fr. *et°, as ito fr. *it°] orig. abl. of etad; from this, from it, thence, hence, out of here Sn 448, 875; J I.223 (opp. ito), V.498; Pv I.1[1]; II.10[4]; DhA II.80 (ito vā etto vā here & there); PvA 103.

Ettha (adv.) [= Sk. atra, cp. etta] here, in this place; also temporal "now", & modal "in this case, in this matter" D II.12; S V.375; Dh 174; Sn 61, 171, 424, 441, 502, 1037, & freq. passim.

Edisa (adj.) [Sk. īdṛśa] such like, such Vv 37[3]; PvA 69, 243.

Edisaka = edisa Sn 313.

Edha [Sk. edhaḥ, cp. idhma, inddhe; Gr. αἶθος, αἴθω, Lat. aedes, Ohg. eit, Ags. ād funeral pile, etc. See idhuma & iṭṭhaka] fuel, fire etc. Only in adj. neg. an° without fuel J IV.26.

Edhati [**edh**, cp. iddhati] to prosper, succeed in, increase S I.217 (sukhaŋ); Sn 298; Dh 193; J I.223; III.151. — sukh'edhita at Vin III.13 is better read as sukhe ṭhita, as at J VI.219.

Ena (pron.) [fr. pron. base *ĕ, cp. e-ka; to this cp. in form & meaning Lat. ūnus, Gr. οἰνός, Ohg. ein, Oir. ōin] only used in acc. enaŋ (taŋ enaŋ) "him, this one, the same" Sn 583, 981, 1114; Dh 118, 313; J III.395; Nd[2] 304 III. B. See also **naŋ**.

Eraka[1] (adj.) [fr. ereti] driving away, moving J IV.20 (°vāta); °vattika a certain kind of torture M I.87 = A I.47 = II.122 = Nd[2] 604 = Miln 197.

Eraka[2] (nt.) [fr. ereti] Typha-grass J IV.88. As eragu (?) a kind of grass used for making coverlets Vin I.196 (eraka Bdhgh. on D I.166).

Eraṇḍa [dial. ?] the castor oil plant Nd[2] 680 II.; J II.440. Cp. **elaṇḍa**.

Erāvaṇa N. of Indra's elephant Sn 379; Vv 44[13]; VvA 15.

Erita [pp. of ereti] moved, shaken, driven J IV.424; Vv 39[4], 42[4]; Th 1, 104, Pv II.12[3]; Vism 172 (+ samerita), 342 (vāt° moved by the wind). Cp. **īrita**.

Ereti [= īreti (q. v.) Caus. of **īr**, Sk. īrayati] to move, set into motion, raise (one's voice) M I.21; Sn 350 (eraya imper.); Th 1, 209 (eraye); J IV.478. — pp. **erita** (q.v.).

Ela (nt.) [?] salt (?) or water (?) in **elambiya** (= el'ambu-ja) born in (salt) water Sn 845 (= ela-saññaka ambumhi jāta); Nd[1] 202 (elaŋ vuccati udakaŋ).

Elaṇḍa = eraṇḍa (?) M I.124.

Elambaraka [?] N. of a creeping vine J VI.536.

Elāluka (Eḷāluka) (nt.) [etym. ?] a kind of cucumber (?) Vv 33[29]; J I.205; V.37; DhA I.278.

Eḷa (nt.) [Sk. enas] in eḷamūga deaf & dumb A II.252; III.436; IV.226; Miln 20, 251 (cp. *Miln trsl.* II.71). A rather strange use and expln. of eḷamūga (with ref. to a snake "spitting") we find at J III.347, where it is expld. as "eḷa-paggharantena mukhena eḷamūgaŋ" i. e. called eḷamūga because of the saliva (foam ?) dripping from its mouth, v. l. elamukha. — Cp. **neḷa** & **aneḷa**.

Eḷaka[1] [?] a threshold (see Morris, *JPTS.* 1887, 146) Vin II.149 (°pādaka-pītha, why not "having feet resembling those of a ram"? Cp. *Vin Texts* III.165 "a chair raised on a pedestal"); D I.166; A I.295; II.206. The word & its meaning seems uncertain.

Eḷaka[2] [Sk. eḍaka] a ram, a wild goat Sn 309; Vism 500 (in simile); J I.166; Pug A 233 (= urabbha). — f. **eḷakā** S II.228, elikā Th 2, 438, eḷikī J III.481.

Eḷagala see aneḷa

Eḷagalā (f.) [dial. ?] the plant Cassia Tora (cp. Sk. eḍagaja the ringworm-shrub, Cassia Alata, after Halāyudha), J III. 222 (= kambojī C.).

'agga in kāmāmis° at PvA 107 is to be read kāmā-e lagga°.

Eva (adv.) [Vedic eva] emphatic part "so, even, just"; very freq. in all contexts & combns. — 1. **eva** J I.61 (ajj'eva this veryday), 278 (tath'eva likewise); II.113 (ahaŋ e. just I), 154 (ekam e. just one), 160 (attano e. his very own). — 2. eva often appears with prothetic (sandhi-)y as **yeva**, most frequently after i and e, but also after the other vowels and ŋ, cp. J I.293, 307; II.110, 128, 129, 159; IV.3; VI.363. — 3. After ŋ eva also takes the form of ñeva, mostly with assimilation of ŋ to ñ, viz. tañ ñeva J I.223; tasmiñ ñeva J I.139; ahañ ñeva Miln 40. — 4. After long vowels eva is often shortened to va (q. v.).

-rūpa (1) such, like that Sn 279, 280; It 108; J II. 352, etc. — (2) of such form, beauty or virtue J I.294; III.128, etc.

Evaŋ (adv.) [Vedic evaŋ] so, thus, in this way, either referring to what precedes or what follows, e. g. (1) thus (as mentioned expld. at Vism 528 as "niddiṭṭha-naya-nidassana") D I.193 (evaŋ sante this being being so), 195 (id.); Vin II.194 (evaŋ bhante, yes); J I.222; Pv II.13[12] evaŋ etaŋ, just so). — (2) thus (as follows) M I. 483 (evaŋ me sutaŋ "thus have I heard"). — Often combd. with similar emphatic part., as evam eva kho "in just the same way" (in final conclusions) D I.104, 199, 228, 237, 239; in older form evaŋ byā kho (= evam iva kho) Vin II.26; IV.134 = DA I.27; evam evaŋ "just so" D I.51; Sn 1115; evaŋ kho D I.113; evam pi Sn 1134; evaŋ su D I.104; etc. etc.

-diṭṭhin holding such a view M I.484. **-nāma** having that name M I.429.

Esa[1] see etad.

Esa[2] (adj.) = esin Sn 286.

Esati [ā + **iṣ**[1] with confusion of **iṣ**[1] and **iṣ**[2], icchati, see also ajjhesati, anvesati, pariyesati] to seek, search, strive for Sn 592 (esāno ppr. med.), 919; Dh 131.

Esanā (f.) [fr. esati] desire, longing, wih D III.216, 270; M I.79; S V.54, 139; A I.93; II.41; V.31; VvA 83; PvA 98, 163, 265. See also **anesanā**, **isi** & **pariy°**.

Esanī (f.) [fr. **iṣ**] a surgeon's probe M II.256.

Esabha (—°) a by-form of **usabha** (p. v.), in cpd. rathesabha.

Esika (nt.) & **Esikā**[1] (f.) [a by-form of isikā] a pillar, post A IV.106, 109. Freq. in cpd. **°ṭṭhāyin** as stable as a pillar D I.14; S III.202, 211, 217; DA I.105.

Esikā[2] desire, see **abbūḷha**.

Esin (adj.) [Sk. eṣin, of **iṣ**] seeking, wishing, desiring S II.11 (sambhav°); J I.87 (phal°); IV.26 (dukkham°); Pv II.9[21] (gharam); PvA 132.

Ehi [imper. of eti] come, come here Sn 165; J II 159; VI. 367; DhA I.49. In the later language part. of exhortation = Gr. ἄγε, Lat. age, "come on" DhA II.91; PvA 201 (+ tāva = ἄγε δή). **ehipassika** (adj.) [ehi + passa + ika] of the Dhamma, that which invites every man to come to see for himself, open to all, expld. at Vism 216 as "ehi, passa imaŋ dhamman ti evaŋ pavattaŋ ehi-passa-vidhaŋ arahatī ti", D II.217; III.5, 227; S I.9; IV.41, 272; V.343; A I.158; II.198. **ehibhadantika** one who accepts an invitation D I.166; M I.342; II.161; A I.295; II.206. **ehi bhikkhu** "come bhikkhu!" the oldest formula of admission to the order Vin I.12; III.24; DhA I.87; J I.82; f. ehi **bhikkhunī** Vin IV.214 pl. etha bhikkhavo DhA I.95. **ehibhikkhu-pabbajjā** initiation into Bhikkhuship SnA 456. **ehibhikkhubhāva** state of being invited to join the Sangha, admission to the Order J I.82, 86; DhA II.32; SnA 456. **ehisāgata-(& svāgata-)vādin** a man of courtesy (lit. one who habitually says: "come you are welcome") D I.116; Vin II.11; III.181.

O.

O Initial o in Pali may represent a Vedic o or a Vedic au (see ojas, ogha, etc.). Or it may be guṇa of u (see oḷārika, opakammika, etc.). But it is usually a prefix representing Vedic ava. The form in o is the regular use in old Pali; there are only two or three cases where ava, for metrical or other reasons, introduced. In post-canonical Pali the form in ava is the regular one. For new formations we believe there is no exception to this rule. But the old form in o has in a few cases, survived. Though o; standing alone, is derived from ava, yet compounds with o are almost invariably older than the corresponding compounds with ava (see note on ogamana).

Oka (nt.) [Vedic okas (nt.), fr. **uc** to like, thus orig. "comfort", hence place of comfort, sheltered place, habitation. The indigenous interpretation connects oka partly with okāsa = fig. room (for rising), chance, occasion (thus Nd[1] 487 on Sn 966: see anoka; SnA 573 ibid.; SnA 547: see anoka; SnA 573 ibid.; SnA 547: see below), partly with udaka (as contraction): see below on Dh 34. Geiger (*P. Gr.* § 20) considers oka to be a direct contraction of udaka (via *udᵃka, *utka, *ukka, *okka). The customary synomym for oka (both lit. & fig.) is ālaya] resting place, shelter, resort; house, dwelling; fig. (this meaning according to later commentators prevailing in anoka, liking, fondness, attachment to (worldly things) S III.9 = Sn 844 (okam pahāya; oka here is expld. at SnA 547 by rūpa-vatth' ādi-viññaṇass' okāso); S V.24 = A V. 232 = Dh 87 (okā anokam āgamma); Dh 34 (oka-m-okata ubbhato, i. e. oka-m-okato from this & that abode, from all places, thus taken as okato, whereas Bdhgh. takes it as okasya okato and interprets the first oka as contracted form of udaka, water, which happens to fit in with the sense required at this passage, but is not warranted otherwise excpt by Bdhgh's quotation "okapuṇṇehi cīvarehī ti ettha udakaŋ". This quot. is taken from Vin I.253, which must be regarded as a corrupt passage cp. remarks of Bdhgh. on p. 387: oghapuṇṇehī ti pi pāṭho. The rest of his interpretation at DhA I.289 runs: "okaŋ okaŋ pahāya aniketa-sārī ti ettha ālayo, idha (i. e. at Dh 34) ubhayam pi labbhati okamokato udaka-sankhātā ālayā ti attho", i. e. from the water's abode. Bdhgh's expln. is of course problematic); Dh 91 (okam okaŋ jahanti "they leave whatever shelter they have", expld. by ālaya DhA II.170).

-**cara** (f. °carikā J VI.416; °cārikā M I.117) living in the house (said of animals), i. e. tame (cp. same etym. of "tame" = Lat. domus, domesticus). The passage M I. 117, 118 has caused confusion by oka being taken as "water". But from the context as well as from C. on J VI.416 it is clear that here a tame animal is meant by means of which other wild ones are caught. The passage at M I.117 runs "odaheyya okacaraŋ ṭhapeyya okacārikaŋ" i. e. he puts down a male decoy and places a female (to entice the others), opp. "uhaneyya o. nāseyya o." i. e. takes away the male & kills the female. -**(ñ)jaha** giving up the house (and its comfort), renouncing (the world), giving up attachment Sn 1101 (= ālayaŋjahaŋ SnA 598; cp. Nd[2] 176 with v. l. oghaŋjaha). -**anoka** houseless, homeless, comfortless, renouncing, free from attachment: see separately.

Okaḍḍhati [o + kaḍḍhati] to drag away, remove Th 2, 444. See also ava°.

Okantati (okkant°) [o + kantati, cp. also apakantati] to cut off, cut out, cut away, carve; pres. **okantati** M I. 129; Pv III.10² (= ava° PvA 213); ger. **okantitvā** J I. 154 (migaŋ o. after carving the deer); PvA 192 (piṭṭhimaŋsāni), & **okacca** J IV.210 (T. okkacca, v. l. BB ukk°; C. expls. by okkantitvā). — pp. **avakanta** & **avakantita**.

Okappati [o + kappati] to preface, arrange, make ready, settle on, feel confident, put (trust) in Vin IV.4; Ps II.19 (= saddahati ibid. 21); Miln 150, 234; DA I.243.

Okappanā (f.) [o + kappanā] fixing one's mind (on), settling in, putting (trust) in, confidence Dhs 12, 25, 96, 288; Nett 15, 19, 28; Vbh 170.

Okappeti [o + kappeti] to fix one's mind on, to put one's trust in M I.11; Miln 234 (okappessati).

Okampeti [o + Caus. of **kamp**] to shake, to wag, only in phrase sīsaŋ okampeti to shake one's head M I.108, 171; S I.118.

Okassati [o + kassati, see also apakassati & avakaḍḍhati] to drag down, draw or pull away, distract, remove. Only in ger. **okassa**, always combd. with pasayha "removing by force" D II.74 (T. okk°); A IV.16 (T. okk°, v. l. ok°), 65 (id.); Miln 210. Also in Caus. **okasseti** to pull out, draw out Th 2, 116 (vaṭṭiŋ = dīpavaṭṭiŋ ākaḍḍheti ThA 117). [MSS. often spell okk°].

Okāra [o + kāra fr. karoti, BSk. okāra, e. g. M Vastu III. 357] only in stock phrase kāmānaŋ ādīnavo okāro sankileso D I.110, 148 (= lāmaka-bhāva DA I 277); M I.115, 379, 405 sq.; II.145; A IV.186; Nett 42 (v. l. vokāra); DhA I.6, 67. The exact meaning is uncertain. Etymologically it would be degradation. But Bdhgh. prefers folly, vanity, and this suits the context better.

Okāsa [ava + **kāś** to shine] — 1. lit. "visibility", (visible) space as geometrical term, open space, atmosphere, air as space D I.34 (ananto okāso); Vism 184 (with disā & paricchedа), 243 (id.); PvA 14 (okāsaŋ pharitvā permeating the atmosphere). This meaning is more pronounced in **ākāsa**. — 2. "visibility", i. e. appearance, as adj. looking like, appearing. This meaning closely resembles & often passes over into meaning 3, e. g. katokāsa kamma when the k. makes its appearance = when its chance or opportunity arises PvA 63; okāsaŋ deti to give one's appearance, i. e. to let any one see, to be seen by (dat.) PvA 19. — 3. occasion, chance, opportunity, permission, consent, leave A I.253; IV.449; J IV.413 (vātassa o. natthi the wind has no access); SnA 547. — In this meaning freq. in combn. with foll. verbs: (a) okāsaŋ **karoti** to give permission, to admit, allow; to give a chance or opportunity, freq. with pañhassa veyyā-karaṇāya (to ask a question), e. g. D I 51, 205; M II.142; S IV 57. — Vin I.114, 170; Nd[1] 487; PvA 222. — Caus. °ŋ karoti Vin II.5, 6, 276; Caus. II. °ŋ kārāpeti Vin I.114, 170. — katokāsa given permission (to speak), admitted in audience, granted leave Sn 1031; VvA 65 (raññā); anokāsakata without having got permission Vin I.114. — (b) okāsaŋ **yācati** to ask permission M II.123. — (c) okāsaŋ **deti** to give permission, to consent, give room J II.3; VvA 138. — (d) with **bhū**: anokāsa-bhāva want of opportunity Sdhp 15; anokāsa-bhūta not giving (lit. becoming) an opportunity SnA 573. Elliptically for o. detha *Yogāvacara's Man.* 4 etc.

-**âdhigama** finding an opportunity D II.214 sq.; A IV. 449. -**kamma** giving opportunity or permission Sn p. 94 (°kata allowed); Pv IV.1¹¹ (°ŋ karoti to give permission). -**matta** permission Sn p. 94. -**loka** the visible world (= manussa-loka) Vism 205; VvA 29.

Okāsati [ava + **kāś**] to be visible; Caus. **okāseti** to make visible, let appear, show S IV.290.

Okiṇṇa [pp. of okirati; BSk. avakīrṇa Divy 282; Jtm 31⁹²] strewn over, beset by, covered with, full of J V.74, 370; PvA 86, 189 (= otata of Pv III.3³).

Okiraṇa [o + kiraṇa] casting out (see the later avakirati²), only as adj.-f. **okiriṇī** (okiliṇī through dialect. variation) a cast-out woman (cast-out on acct of some cutaneous disease), in double combn. okilinī okirinī (perhaps only the latter should be written) Vin III.107 = S II.260 (in play of words with avakirati[1]). Bdhgh's allegorical expln. at Vin III.273 puts okilinī = kilinnasarīrā, okiriṇī = aṅgāraparikiṇṇa. Cp. kirāta.

Okirati [o + kirati] — 1. to pour down on, pour out over M I.79; aor. okiri Vin III.107 = S II.260; Pv II.3[8]; PvA 82. — 2. to cast-out, reject, throw out: see **okiraṇa**. — pp. **okiṇṇa** (q. v.). — Caus. II. **okirāpeti** to cause to pour out or to sprinkle over Vism 74 (vālikaŋ).

Okilinī see okiraṇa.

Okoṭimaka (adj.) [o + koṭi + mant + ka. Ava in BSk., in formula durvarṇa durdaśśana avakoṭimaka Sp. Av. Ś I. 280. Kern (note on above passage) problematically refers it to Sk. avakūṭara = vairūpya (Pāṇini V.2, 30). The Commentary on S I.237 explns. by mahodara (fat-bellied) as well as lakuṇṭaka (dwarf); Pug A 227 expls. by lakuṇṭaka only] lit. "having the top lowered", with the head squashed in or down, i. e. of compressed & bulging out stature; misshapen, deformed, of ugly shape (Mrs. Rh. D. trsls hunchback at S I.94, pot-bellied at S I.237; Warren, *Buddhism* p. 426 trsls. decrepit). It occurs only in one stock phrase, viz. **dubbaṇṇa dud-das(s)ika okoṭimaka** "of bad complexion, of ugly appearance and dwarfed" at Vin II.90 = S I.94 = A I.107 = II.85 = III.285 sq. = Pug 51. The same also at M III.169; S I.237; II.279; Ud 76.

Okkanta [pp. of okkamati] coming on, approaching, taking place D II.12; Miln 299 (middhe okkante). See also avakkanta S II.174; III.46.

Okkanti (f.) [fr. okkamati] entry (lit. descent), appearance, coming to be. Usually in stock phrase **jāti sañjāti o. nibbatti** M III.249; S II.3; III.225; Nd[2] 257; Pug A 184. Also in gabbh° entry into the womb DA I.130.

Okkantika (adj.) [fr. okkanti] coming into existence again and again, recurring. Only as epithet of pīti, joy. The opposite is khaṇika, momentary Vism 143 = DhsA 115 (*Expositor* 153 trsls. "flooding").

Okkandika [**kand** or **kram**?] at J II.448 is doubtful, v. l. **okkantika**. It is used adverbially: **okkandikaŋ kīḷati** to sport (loudly or joyfully). C. explns. as "migo viya okkandi-katvā kīḷati"; in the way of roaring (?) or frisking about (?), like a deer.

Okkamati [o + kamati fr. **kram**] lit. to enter, go down into, fall into. fig. to come on, to develop, to appear in (of a subjective state). It is strange that this important word has been so much misunderstood, for the English idiom is the same. We say 'he went to sleep', without meaning that he went anywhere. So we may twist it round and say that 'sleep overcame him', without meaning any struggle. The two phrases mean exactly the same — an internal change, or developement, culminating in sleep. So in Pali **niddā okkami** sleep fell upon him, Vin I.15; **niddaŋ okkami** he fell on sleep, asleep, DhA I.9; PvA 47. At It 76 we hear that a dullness developed (dubbaṇṇiyaŋ okkami) on the body of a god, he lost his radiance. At D II.12; M III.119 a god, on his rebirth, entered his new mother's womb (kucchiŋ okkami). At D II 63 occurs the question 'if consciousness were not to develop in the womb?' (viññāṇaŋ na okkamissatha) S V.283 'abiding in the sense of bliss' (sukha-saññaŋ okkamitvā). See also Pug 13 = 28 (niyāma okk°, 'he enters on the Path'). — Caus. **okkāmeti** to make enter, to bring to S IV.312 (saggaŋ). — pp. **okkanta**. See also avakkamati.

Okkamana (nt.) [fr. okkamati] entering into, approaching, reaching M III.6; A III.108 (entering the path); also in phrase nibbānassa okkamanāya A IV.111 sq., cp. 230 sq.

Okkala see **ukkala**.

Okkassa see okkassati.

Okkhāyati [ava + khāyati, corresp. to Sk. kṣeti fr. **kṣi** to lie] to lie low, to be restrained (in this sense evidently confounded with avakkhipati) S IV.144 sq. (cakkhuŋ etc. okkhāyati).

Okkhāyika (adj.) [fr. ava + khāyin fr. **kṣi**, cp. avakkhāyati; Kern, *Toev.* s. v. suggests relation to BSk. avakhāta of **khan**, and compares Lal. V. 319] low-lying, deep, remote, only in one phrase, viz. udaka-tarakā gambhīragatā okkhāyikā M I.80, 245.

Okkhita [pp. of ava + ukkhati, Sk. avokṣita, fr. **ukṣ** to sprinkle] besprinkled, bestrewn with (—°) Th 2, 145 (candan° = candanânulitta ThA 137); J V.72 (so in v. l. T. reads okkita; C. explns. by okiṇṇa parikkita parivārita).

Okkhitta [pp. of okkhipati] thrown down, flung down, cast down, dropped; thrown out, rejected; only in phrase **okkhitta-cakkhu**, with down-cast eyes, i. e. turning the eyes away from any objectionable sight which might impair the morale of the bhikkhu; thus meaning "with eyes under control Sn 63, 411, 972; Nd[1] 498; Nd[2] 177; Pv IV.3[44] (v. l. ukkh°); VvA 6. — For further use & meaning. See **avakkhitta**.

Okkhipati [ava + khipati; Sk. avakṣipati] to throw down or out, cast down, drop; fig. usually appld. to the eyes = cast down, hence transferred to the other senses and used in meaning "keep under, restrain, to have control over" (cp. also avakkhāyati); aor. °khipi A IV.264 (indriyāni); ger. °khipitvā Vin IV.18 (id.). — pp. **avakkhitta** & **okkhitta** (q. v.).

Ogacchati [ava + gacchati] to go down, sink down, recede; of sun & moon: to set D I.240 (opp. uggacchati); A IV. 101 (udakāni og.). See also **ava°**.

Ogaṇa (adj.) [Vedic ogaṇa with dial. o for ava] separated from the troop or crowd, standing alone, Vin I.80; J IV. 432 = (gaṇaŋ ohīna C.).

Ogadha (—°) (adj.) [Sk. avagāḍha; P. form with shortened a, fr. ava + **gāh**, see gādba[1] & gāhati] immersed, merging into, diving or plunging into. Only in two main phrases, viz. **Amatogadha** & **Nibbānogadha** diving into N. — Besides these only in jagat'ogadha steeped in the world S I.186.

Ogamana (nt.) [o + gam + ana; Sk. avagamana. That word is rather more than a thousand years later than the Pāli one. It would be ridiculous were one to suppose that the P. could be derived from the Sk. On the other hand the Sk. cannot be derived from the P. for it was formed at a time & place when & where P. was unknown, just as the Pali was formed at a time & place when & where Sk. was unknown. The two words are quite independent. They have no connection with one another except that they are examples of a rule of word-formation common to the two languages] going down, setting (of sun & moon), always in contrast to **uggamana** (rising), therefore freq. v. l. ogg° D I.10, 68; DA I.95 (= atthaogamana); VvA 326.

Ogahana (nt.) [o + gahana fr. gāhati; Sk. avagāhana; concerning shortening of ā cp. avagadha] submersion, ducking, bathing; fig. for bathing-place Sn 214 (= manussānaŋ nahāna-tittha SnA 265). See also **avagāhana**.

Ogādha[1] (adj.) [Sk. avagāḍha; ava + gādha[2]] immersed, entered; firm, firmly footed or grounded in (—°), spelt **ogāḷha** Miln 1 (abhidhamma-vinay°). Cp. BSk. avagādhaśrāddha of deep faith Divy 268. Cp. pariyogāḷha.

Ogādha[2] (nt.) [ava + gādha[2]] a firm place, firm ground, only in cpd. **ogādhappatta** having gained a sure footing A III.297 sq.

Ogāha [fr. o + **gah**] diving into; only in cpd. pariy°.

Ogāhati (ogāheti) [Sk. avagāhate; ava + gāhati] to plunge or enter into, to be absorbed in (w. acc. or loc.). Pv II. 12[11]; Vv 6[1] (= anupavisati VvA 42), 39[2] (sālavanaŋ o. = pavisati VvA 177). ogāheti PvA 155 (pokkharaṇiŋ); ger. ogāhetvā M III.175 (T. ogah°; v. l. ogāhitvā); PvA 287 (lokanāthassa sāsanaŋ, v. l. °itvā). See also ava°.

Ogāhana (nt.) [fr. ogāhati] plunging into (—°) PvA 158.

Ogilati [o + gilati] to swallow down (opp. uggilati) M I. 393 (inf. ogilituŋ) Miln 5 (id.).

Oguṇṭhita [pp. of oguṇṭheti, cp. BSk. avaguṇṭhita, e. g. Jtm 30] covered or dressed (with) Vin II.207; PvA 86 (v. l. okuṇṭhita).

Oguṇṭheti [o + guṇṭheti] to cover, veil over, hide S IV.122 (ger. oguṇṭhitvā sīsaŋ, perhaps better read as oguṇṭhitā; v. l. SS. okuṇṭhitū). — pp. **oguṇṭhita** (q. v.).

Ogumpheti [ava + Denom. of gumpha garland] to string together, wind round, adorn with wreaths, cover, dress Vin I.194 (Pass. ogumphiyanti; vv. ll. ogumbhiyanti, ogubbiy°, ogummīy°, okumpiy°); II.142 (ogumphetvā).

Oggata [pp. of avagacchati: spelling gg on acct. of contrast with uggata, cp. avagamana. Müller *P. Gr.* 43 unwarrantedly puts oggata = apagata] gone down, set (of the sun) Vin IV.55 (oggate suriye = atthangate s.), 268 (id. = ratt' andhakāre); Th I, 477 (anoggatasmiŋ suriyasmiŋ).

Ogha [Vedic ogha and augha; BSk. ogha, e. g. Divy 95 caturogh' ottīrṇa, Jtm 215 mahaugha. Etym. uncertain]. 1. (rare in the old texts) a flood of water VvA 48 (udak' ogha); usually as **mahogha** a great flood Dh 47; Vism 512; VvA 110; DhA II.274 = ThA 175. — 2. (always in sg.) the flood of ignorance and vain desires which sweep a man down, away from the security of emancipation. To him who has "crossed the flood", **oghatiṇṇo**, are ascribed all, or nearly all, the mental and moral qualifications of the Arahant. For details see Sn 173, 219, 471, 495, 1059, 1064, 1070, 1082; A II.200 sq. Less often we have details of what the flood consists of. Thus **kāmogha** the fl. of lusts A III.69 (cp. Dhs 1095, where o. is one of the many names of **taṇhā**, craving, thirst). In the popular old riddle at S I.3 and Th I, 15, 633 (included also in the Dhp. Anthology, 370) the "flood" is 15 states of mind (the 5 bonds which impede a man on his entrance upon the Aryan Path, the 5 which impede him in his progress towards the end of the Path, and 5 other bonds: lust, ill temper, stupidity, conceit, and vain speculation). Five **Oghas** referred to at S I.126 are possibly these last. Sn 945 says that the flood is **gedha** greed, and the **avijjogha** of Pug 21 may perhaps belong here. As means of crossing the flood we have the Path S I.193 (°assa nittharaṇatthaŋ); IV.257; V.59; It III. (°assa nittharaṇatthāya); faith S I.214 = Sn 184 = Miln 36; mindfulness S V.168, 186; the island Dh 25; and the dyke Th I.7 = Sn 4 (cp. D II.89). 3. Towards the close of the Nikāya period we find, for the first time, the use of the word in the pl., and the mention of 4 **Oghas** identical with the 4 **Āsavas** (mental Intoxicants). See D III.230, 276; S IV.175, 257; V.59, 292, 309; Nd[1] 57, 159; Nd[2] 178. When the oghas had been thus grouped and classified in the livery, as it were, of a more popular simile, the older use of the word fell off, a tendency arose to think only of 4 oghas, and of these only as a name or phase of the 4 āsavas. So the Abhidhamma books (Dhs 1151; Vbh 25 sq., 43, 65, 77, 129; Comp. Phil. 171). The Netti follows this (31, 114–24). Grouped in combn. āsavagantha-ogha-yoga-agati-taṇh'upādāna at Vism 211. The later history of the word has yet to be investigated. But it may be already stated that the 5th cent. commentators persist in the error of explaining the old word ogha, used in the singular, as referring to the 4 Āsavas; and they extend the old simile in other ways. Dhammapāla of Kāñcipura twice uses the word in the sense of flood of water (VvA 48, 110, see above 1).

-**átiga** one who has overcome the flood Sn 1096 (cp. Nd[2] 180). -**tiṇṇa** id. S I.3, 142; Sn 178, 823, 1082, 1101, 1145; Dh 370 (= cattāro oghe tiṇṇa DhA IV.109); Vv 64[28] (= catunnaŋ oghānaŋ saŋsāra-mah'oghassa taritattā o. VvA 284); 82[7]; Nd[1] 159; Nd[2] 179.

Oghana (nt.) watering, flooding (?) M I.306 (v. l. ogha).

Oghanīya (adj.) [fr. ogha(na)] that which can be engulfed by floods (metaph.) Dhs 584 (cp. *Dhs trsl.* 308); Vbh 12, 25 & passim; DhsA 49.

Ocaraka [fr. ocarati] in special meaning of one who makes himself at home or familiar with, an investigator, informant, scout, spy (ocarakā ti carapurisā C. on Ud 66). — Thus also in BSk. as avacaraka one who furnishes information Divy 127; an adaptation from the Pāli. — Vin III.47, 52; M I.129 = 189 (corā ocarakā, for carā?); S I.79 (purisā carā (v. l. corā) ocarakā (okacarā v. l. SS) janapadaŋ ocaritvā etc.; cp. *K. S.* p. 106 n. 1) = Ud 66 (reads corā o.).

Ocarati [o + carati] to be after something, to go into, to search, reconnoitre, investigate, pry Vin III.52 (ger. °itvā); M I 502 (ocarati); S I.79 (°itvā: so read for T. ocaritā; C. explns. by vīmaŋsitvā taŋ taŋ pavattiŋ ñatvā). — pp. **ociṇṇa**.

Ociṇṇa [pp. of ocarati] gone into, investigated, scouted, explored S I.79 = Ud 66 (reads otiṇṇa).

Ocita [o + cita, pp. of ocināti[1]] gathered, picked off J III. 22; IV.135, 156; Sdhp 387.

Ocināti (ocinati) — 1. [= Sk. avacinoti, ava + **ci**[1]] to gather, pluck, pick off DhA I.366; also in pp. **ocita**. — 2. [= Sk. avacinoti or °ciketi ava + **ci**[2], cp. apacināti[2]] to disregard, disrespect, treat with contempt; pres. ocināyati (for ocināti metri causa) J VI.4 (= avajānāti C.).

Ocīraka see **odīraka**.

Occhindati [o + chindati] to cut off, sever J II.388 (maggaŋ occhindati & occhindamāna to bar the way; v. l. BB. ochijjati), 404.

Ojavant (adj.) [fr. ojā; Vedic ojasvant in diff. meaning: powerful] possessing strengthening qualities, giving strength M I.480; S I.212 (so read for ovajaŋ; phrase ojavaŋ asecanakaŋ of Nibbāna, trsld. "elixir"); Th 2, 196 (id. = ojavantaŋ ThA 168); A III.260 (an° of food, i. e. not nourishing DhA I.106.

Ojavantatā (f.) [abstr. fr. ajavant] richness in sap, strength giving (nourishing) quality J I.68 (of milk).

Ojahāti [o + jahati] to give up, leave, leave behind, renounce, ger. **ohāya** D I.115 (ñāti-sanghaŋ & hirañña-suvaṇṇaŋ); M II.166 (id.); J V.340 (= chaḍḍetvā C.); PvA 93 (maŋ). — Pass. **avahīyati** & **ohīyati**, pp. **ohīna** (q. v.). — See also **ohanati**.

Ojā (f.) [Vedic ojas nt., also BSk. oja nt. Divy 105; fr. ***aug** to increase, as in Lat. auges, augustus & auxilium, Goth. aukan (augment), Ags. ēacian; cp. also Gr. ἀέξω, Sk. ukṣati & vakṣana increase] strength, but only in meaning of strength-giving, nutritive essence (appld. to food) M I.245; S II.87; V.162 (dhamm'); A III.396; J I.68; Dhs 646, 740, 875; Miln 156; DhA II.154 (paṭhav°). See also def. at Vism 450 (referring to kabaliṅkār'āhāra. The compn. form is oja, e. g. ojadāna J V.243; ojaṭṭhamaka (rūpa) Vism 341.

Ojināti [Sk. avajayati, ava + **ji**] to conquer, vanquish, subdue J VI.222 (ojināmase).

Oñāta [pp. o + jānāti, see also avañāta] despised Miln 191, 229, 288.

Oṭṭha[1] [Vedic oṣṭha, idg. *ō (u) s; Av. aosta lip; Lat. ōs mouth = Sk. āḥ; Ags. ōr margin] the lip A IV.131; Sn 608; J II.264; III.26 (adhar° & uttar° lower & upper lip), 278; V.156; DhA I.212; III.163; IV.1; VvA 11; PvA 260. Cp. **bimboṭṭha.**

Oṭṭha[2] [Vedic uṣṭra, f. uṣṭrī, buffalo = Ohg. Ags. ūr, Lat. urus bison, aurochs. In cl. Sk. it means a camel]. It is mentioned in two lists of domestic animals, Vin III.52; Miln 32. At J III.385 a story is told of an oṭṭhī-vyādhi who fought gallantly in the wars, and was afterwards used to drag a dung-cart. Morris, *J P T S.* 1887, 150 suggests elephant.

Oṭṭhubhati [cp. Sk. avaṣṭhīvati] to spit out M I.79, 127.

Oḍḍita [pp. of oḍḍeti] thrown out, laid (of a snare) J I. 183; II.443; V.341; ThA 243.

Oḍḍeti [for uḍḍeti (?). See further under uḍḍeti] to throw out (a net), to lay snares A I.33 = J II.37, 153; III.184 and passim; ThA 243. — pp. oḍḍita (q. v.).

Oḍḍha [better spelling **oḍha**, pp. of ā + **vah**] carried away, appropriated, only in cpd. **sah-oḍhā** corā thieves with their plunder Vism 180 (cp. Sk. sahoḍha Manu IX.270).

Oṇata [pp. of oṇamati] bent down, low, inclined. Usually of social rank or grade, comb[d.] with & opp. to **uṇṇata,** i. e. raised & degraded, lofty and low A II.86 = Pug 52 (= nīca lāmaka Pug A 229); Pv IV.6[6]; Miln 387; DA I.45; PvA 29.

Oṇamati [o + namati] (instr.) to incline, bend down to, bow to (dat.) Miln 220, 234 (oṇamati & oṇamissati), 400; DA I.112. Caus. **oṇāmeti** M II.137 (kāyaŋ). — pp. **oṇata** & Caus. **oṇamita.**

Oṇamana (nt.) [fr. oṇamati] bending down, inclining, bowing down to Miln 234.

Oṇamita [pp. of onameti, Caus. of **nam**] having bowed down, bowing down Miln 234.

Oṇi (m. or f.) [cp. Vedic oṇi charge, or a kind of Soma vessel] charge, only in cpd. **oṇi-rakkha** a keeper of entrusted wares, bailee Vin III.47, 53 (= āhaṭaŋ bhaṇḍaŋ gopento).

Oṇīta see onīta.

Oṇojana (nt.) [fr. oṇojeti, Sk. avanejana] washing off, cleaning, washing one's hands Vin II.31 (Bdhgh. refers it to fig. meaning onojeti[2] by explaining as "vissajjana" gift, presentation).

Oṇojeti (with vowel assimilation o > e for oṇejeti = ava + nejeti, Sk. °nejayati fr. **nij.** Kern, *Toev.* II.138, complementary to remarks s. v. on p. 5 expl[ns.] as assimil. onuj° > onij°, like anu° BSk. ani° (ānisaŋsa ānuśaŋsā), the further process being onoj° for unuj°. The etym. remains however doubtful] — 1. to cause to wash off, to wash, cleanse: see oṇojana. — 2. (fig.) to give as a present, dedicate (with the rite of washing one's hands, i. e. a clean gift) Vin I.39; IV.156; A IV.210 = 214 (oṇojesi aor.); Miln 236.

Otata [o + tata, pp. of **tan**] stretched over, covered, spread over with; Dh 162 (v. l. otthata); Miln 307 (+ vitata); DhA III.153 (= pariyonandhitvā ṭhita). See also **avatata** & **sam-otata.**

Otaraṇa (adj.) [fr. otarati] going down, descending Nett 1, 2, 4, 107.

Otarati [o + tarati] to descend, to go down to (c. acc.), to be take oneself to, ppr. **otaranto** Vin II.221. — aor. otari SnA 486 (for avaŋsari); DhA I.19 (cankamanaŋ); PvA 47 (nāvāya mahāsamuddaŋ), 75. — inf. **otarituŋ** Pug 65, 75 (sangamaŋ). — ger. otaritvā PvA 94 (pāsādā from the palace), 140 (devalokato). — Caus. II. **otarāpeti** to cause to descend, to bring down to J VI.345. — pp. **otiṇṇa.** — Caus. I. **otāreti.** Opp. **uttarati.**

Otallaka (adj.) [of uncertain etym. perhaps *avatāryaka from ava + **tṛ,** or from uttāḷa?] clothed in rags, poor, indigent J IV.380 (= lāmaka olamba-vilamba-nantaka-dharo C.).

Otāpaka (adj.) [fr. otāpeti] drying or dried (in the sun), with ref. to food SnA 35 (parivāsika-bhattaŋ bhuñjati hatth'otāpakaŋ khādati).

Otāpeti [o + tāpeti] to dry in the sun Vin II.113; IV.281; Miln 371 (kummo udakato nikkhamitvā kāyaŋ o. fig. applied to mānasa).

Otāra [fr. otarati, BSk. avatāra. The Sk. avatāra is centuries later and means 'incarnation'] — 1. descent to, i. e. approach to, access, fig. chance, opportunity **otāraŋ labhati.** Only in the Māra myth. e, the tempter, 'gets his chance' to tempt the Buddha or the disciples, M I. 334; S I.122; IV.178, 185; DhA III.121. (avatāraŋ labhati, Divy 144, 145) ot° **adhigacchati,** to find a chance, Sn 446. [Fausböll here translates 'defect'. This is fair as exegesis. Every moral or intellectual defect gives the enemy a chance. But otāra does not mean defect]. **Ot° gavesati** to seek an opportunity, DhA III.21. **Otārāpekkha,** watching for a chance, S I.122. At one passage, A III. 67 = 259, it is said that constant association leads to agreement, agreement to trust, and trust to otāra. The Com. has nothing. 'Carelessness' would suit the context. o. gavesati to look for an opportunity DhA III.21, and otāraŋ labhati to get a chance S I.122; IV.178, 185; M I.334; DhA III.21 (gloss okāra & okāsa); cp. avatāraŋ labhati Divy 144, 145 etc. — 2. access, fig. inclination to, being at home with, approach, familiarity (cp. otiṇṇa and avacara adj.) A III.67, 259. — 3. (influenced by ocarati[2] and ociṇṇa) being after something, spying, finding out; hence: fault, blame, defect, flaw Sn 446 (= randha vivara SnA 393); also in phrase **otārāpekkha** spying faults S I.122 (which may be taken to meaning 1, but meaning 3 is accredited by BSk. avatāraprekṣin Divy 322), Mrs. Rh. D. translates the latter passage by "watching for access".

Otāreti [Caus. of otarati] to cause to come down, to bring down, take down J I.426; IV.402; Nett 21, 22; DhA II.81.

Otiṇṇa [pp. of otarati; the form ava° only found in poetry as —° e. g. issâvatiṇṇa J V.98; dukkha°, soka° etc. see below 2] — 1. (med.) gone down, descended PvA 104 (uddho-galaŋ na otiṇṇaŋ not gone down further than the throat). — 2. (pass.) beset by (cp. avatāra 2), affected with, a victim of, approached by M I.460 = A II.123 (dukkh' otiṇṇa) = It 89 (as v. l.; T. has dukkhâbhikiṇṇa, which is either gloss or wrong reading for dukkhâvatiṇṇa); M II.10; S I.123 (sokâva°), 137 (id.); Sn 306 (icchâvatiṇṇa affected with desire), 939 (sallena otiṇṇo = pierced by an arrow, expl[d.] by Nd[1] 414 as "sallena viddho phuṭṭho"); J V.98 (issâva° = issāya otiṇṇa C.). — 3. (in special sense) affected with love, enamoured, clinging to, fallen in love with Vin III.128 (= sāratto apekkhavā paṭibaddha-citto); A III.67, 259 (°citta); SnA 322 (id.). — *Note.* otiṇṇa at S V.162 should with v. l. SS be deleted. See also **avatiṇṇa.**

Ottappa (nt.) [fr. tappati[1] + **ud,** would corresp. to a Sk. form *auttapya fr. ut-tapya to be regretted, tormented by remorse. The BSk. form is a wrong adaptation of the Pāli form, taking o° for apa°, viz. apatrapya M Vastu III. 53 and apatrapā ibid. I.463. Müller, *P. Gr.* & Fausböll, Sutta Nipāta Index were both misled by the BSk. form, as also recently Kern, *Toev.* s. v.] fear of exile, shrinking back from doing wrong, remorse. See on term and its distinction from hiri (shame) *Dhs trsl.* 20, also DhsA 124, 126; Vism 8, 9 and the definition at SnA 181. Ottappa generally goes with hiri as one of the 7 noble treasures (see ariya-dhanā). Hiri-ottappa It 36; J I.129; hir-ottappa at M I.271; S II.220; V.1; A II.78; IV.99, 151; V.214; It 34; J I.127, 206; VvA 23. See also hiri. — Further passages: D III.212; M I.356; S II.196, 206, 208; V.89; A I.50, 83, 95; III.4 sq., 352; IV.11; V.123 sq.; Pug 71; Dhs 147, 277; Nett 39. — **anottappa** (nt.) lack of conscience, unscrupulousness, disregard of morality A I.50, 83, 95; III.421; V.146, 214; Vbh 341, 359, 370, 391; as adj. It 34 (ahirika +).

-gāravatā respect for conscience, A III.331; IV.29. **-dhana** the treasure of (moral) self-control D III.163, 251, 282; VvA 113. **-bala** the power of a (good) conscience D III.253; Ps II.169, 176; Dhs 31, 102 (trl$^{n.}$ power of the fear of blame).

Ottappati [ut + tappati[1]] to feel a sense of guilt, to be conscious or afraid of evil S I.154; Ps II.169, 176; Pug 20, 21; Dhs 31; Miln 171.

Ottappin & **Ottāpin** (adj.) [fr. ottappa] afraid of wrong, conscientious, scrupulous (a) ottappin D III.252, 282; It 28, 119. — (b) ottāpin M I.43 sq.; S II.159 sq., 196, 207; IV.243 sq.; A II.13 sq.; III.3 sq., 112; IV.1 sq.; V.123, 146. **Anottappin** bold, reckless, unscrupulous Pug 20 (+ ahirika). **anottāpin** at S II.159 sq., 195, 206; IV. 240 sq.; Sn 133 (ahirika +).

Otthaṭa [pp. of ottharati] — 1. spread over, veiled, hidden by (—°) Miln 299 (mahik° suriya the sun hidden by a fog). — 2. strewn over (with) Sdhp 246 (—°).

Otthata = **Otthaṭa**, v. l. at Dh 162 for **otata**.

Ottharaka (nt.) [fr. of tharati] a kind of strainer, a filter Vin II.119.

Ottharaṇa (nt.) [fr. ottharati] spreading over, veiling Miln 299 (mahik°).

Ottharati [o + tharati, Sk. root **str**] to spread over, spread out, cover Miln 121 (opp. patikkamati, of water). See also **avattharati.**

Odaka (nt.) [comp$^{n.}$ form of udaka] water; abs. only at J III.282. — an° without water, dried up Th 2, 265 (= udaka-bhasta ThA 212). Cp. comb$^{n.}$ sītodaka, e. g. M I. 376. See udaka.

-antika — 1. neighbourhood of the water, a place near the water (see antika[1]) Kh VIII.1, 3 (gambhīre udakantike, which Childers, *Kh. trsl$^{n.}$* p. 30, interprets "a deep pit"; see also KhA 217 sq.). — 2. "water at the end", i. e. final ablution (see antika[2]), in spec. sense the ablution following upon the sexual act Vin III.21; cp. **odak-antikatā** (f. abstr.) final ablution, cleansing J II.126.

Odagya (nt.) [der. fr. udagga] exultation, elation Nd[1] 3 ≟ Nd[2] 446 = Dhs 9, 86, 285, 373; DhsA 143 (= udaggasabhāva a "topmost" condition).

Odana (m. & nt.) [Sk. odana, to Idg. ***ud**, from which also udaka, q. v. for full etym.] boiled (milk-)rice, gruel Vin II.214 (m.); D I.76, 105; S I.82 (nāḷik°); DhA IV. 17 (id.); A III.49; IV.231; Sn 18; J III.425 (til° m.); Dhs 646, 740, 875; PvA 73; VvA 98; Sdhp 113. Comb$^{d.}$ with kummāsa (sour milk) in phrase o-k-upa-caya a heap of boiled rice and sour milk, of the body (see kāya I.); also at M I.247.

Odanika [fr. odana] a cook J III.49.

Odaniya (adj.) [fr. odana, cp. Sk. odanika] belonging to rice-gruel, made of rice-gruel Vin III.59 (°ghara a rice-kitchen); VvA 73 (°surā rice-liquor).

Odapattakinī (f.) (adj.) [f. of uda + pattaka + in, i. e. having a bowl of water, Ep. of bhariyā a wife, viz. the wife in the quality of providing the house with water. Thus in enum$^{n.}$ of the 10 kinds of wives (& women in general) at Vin III.140 (expl$^{d.}$ by udakapattaŋ āmasitvā vāseti) = VvA 73.

Odapattiyā at Cp. II.4[8] = last.

Odarika & °ya (adj.) [fr. udara] living for one's belly, voracious, gluttonous Miln 357; J VI.208 (°ya); Th I, 101.

Odarikatta (nt.) [fr. odarika] stomach-filling M I.461; Vism 71.

Odahati [o + dahati, fr. **dhā**] — 1. to put down, to put in, supply M I.117 (okacaraŋ, see under oka); II.216 (agad'angāraŋ vaṇa-mukhe odaheyya); Th I, 774 (migavo pāsaŋ odahi the hunter set a snare; Morris, *J P T S.* 1884, 76 suggests change of reading to aḍḍayi, hardly justified); J III.201 (visaŋ odahi araññe), 272 (passaŋ o. to turn one's flanks towards, dat.); Miln 156 (kāye ojaŋ odahissāma supply the body with strength). — 2. (fig.) to apply, in phrase sotaŋ odahati to listen D I.230; Dāvs V.68. — pp. **ohita.**

Odahana (nt.) [fr. odahati] — 1. putting down, applying, application M I.216; heaping up, storing DhA III.118. — 2. putting in, fig. attention, devotion Nett 29.

Odāta (adj.) [Derivation unknown. The Sk. is avadāta, ava + dāta, pp. of hypothetical **dā**[4] to clean, purify] clean, white, prominently applied to the dress as a sign of distinction (white), or special purity at festivities, ablutions & sacrificial functions D II.18 (uṇṇā, of the Buddha); III.268; A III.239; IV.94, 263, 306, 349; V.62; Dhs 617 = (in enum$^{n.}$ of colours); DA I.219; VvA 111. See also **ava°.**

-kasiṇa meditation on the white (colour) Vism 174. **-vaṇṇa** of white colour, white M II.14; Dhs 247. **-vattha** a white dress; adj. wearing a white dress, dressed in white D I.7, 76, 104; J III.425 (+ alla-kesa). **-vasana** dressed in white (of householders or laymen as opposed to the yellow dress of the bhikkhus) D I.211; III.118, 124 sq., 210; M I.491, II.23; A I.73; III.384; IV.217 [cp. BSk. avadāta-vasana Divy 160].

Odātaka (adj.) [fr. odāta] white, clean, dressed in white S II.284 (v. l. SS odāta); Th I, 965 (dhaja).

Odissa (adv.) [ger. of o + disati = Sk. diśati, cp. uddissa] only in neg. **anodissa** without a purpose, indefinitely (?) Miln 156 (should we read anudissa?).

Odissaka (adj.) [fr. odissa] only in adv. expression **odissaka-vasena** definitely, in special, specifically (opp. to anodissaka-vasena in general, universally) J I.82; II.146; VvA 97. See also **anodissaka** & **odhiso.**

Odīraka in odīrakajāta S IV.193 should with v. l. be read **ocīraka** [= ava + cira + ka] "with its bark off", stripped of its bark.

Odumbara (adj.) [fr. udumbara] belonging to the Udumbara tree Vv 50[16]; cp. VvA 213.

Odhasta [Sk. avadhvasta, pp. of ava + dhvaŋsati: see dhaŋsati] fallen down, scattered M I.124 = S IV.176 (°patoda; S reads odhasata but has v. l. odhasta).

Odhānīya (nt.) [fr. avadhāna, ava + **dhā**, cp. Gr. ἀποθήκη, see odahati] a place for putting something down or into, a receptacle Vin I.204 (salāk°, vy. ll. and gloss on p. 381 as follows: salākaṭṭhāniya A, salākātaniya C, salākadhāraya B, salāk'odhāniyan ti yattha salākaŋ odahanti taŋ D E). — Cp. samodhāneti.

Odhi [from odahati, Sk. avadhi, fr. ava + **dhā**] putting down, fixing, i. e. boundary, limit, extent DhA II.80

(jaṇṇu-mattena odhinā to the extent of the knee, i. e. kneedeep); IV.204 (id.). — **odhiso** (adv.) limited, specifically Vbh 246; Nett 12; Vism 309. Opp. **anodhi** M III. 219 (°jina), also in **anodhiso** (adv.) unlimited, universal, general Ps II. 130, cp. anodissaka (odissaka); also as **anodhikatvā** without limit or distinction, absolutely Kvu 208, and **odhisodhiso** "piecemeal" Kvu 103 (cp. *Kvu trsln.* 76², 127¹).
-**sunka** "extent of toll", stake J VI.279 (= sunkhakoṭṭhāsaŋ C.).

Odhika (adj.) [fr. odhi] "according to limit", i. e. all kinds of, various, in phrase yathodhikāni kāmāni Sn 60, cp. Nd² 526; J V.392 (id.).

Odhunāti [o + dhunāti] to shake off M I.229; S III.155; A III.365 (+ niddhunāti); Pv IV.3²⁴ (v. l. BB ophun°, SS otu°) = PvA 256; Vin II.317 (Bdhgh. in expln. of ogumphetvā of CV. V.11, 6; p. 117); Miln 399 (+ vidhunāti).

Onaddha [pp. of onandhati] bound, tied; put over, covered Vin II.150, 270 sq. (°mañca, °pīṭha); M II.64; Dh 146 (andhakārena); Sdhp 182. See also **onayhati.**

Onandhati [o + nandhati, a secondary pres. form constructed from naddha after bandhati > baddha; see also apiḷandhati] to bind, fasten; to cover up Vin II.150 (inf. onandhituŋ); Miln 261.

Onamaka (adj.) [fr. onamati] bending down, stooping DhA II.136 (an°).

Onamati [o + namati] to bend down (instr.), stoop D II. 17 (anonamanto ppr. not bending); III.143 (id.); Vv 39³ (onamitvā ger.). — pp. **oṇata.**

Onamana (nt.) [abstr. fr. onamati] in compn. with °unnamana lowering & raising, bending down & up DhA I.17.

Onayhati [ava + nayhati] to tie down, to cover over, envelop, shroud DhsA 378 (megho ākāsaŋ o.) — pp. **onaddha.**

Onāha [fr. ava + **nah,** cp. onaddha & onayhati] drawing over, covering, shrouding D I.246 (spelt onaha); Miln 300; Dhs 1157 (= megho viya ākāsaŋ kāyaŋ onayhati).

Onīta [in form = Sk. avanīta, but semantically = apanīta. Thus also BSk. apanīta, pp. of apa + **nī,** see apaneti] only found in one ster. phrase, viz. **onīta-patta-pāṇi** "having removed (or removing) his hand from the bowl", a phrase causing constructional difficulties & sometimes taken in glosses as "onitta°" (fr. **nij**), i. e. having washed (bowl and hands after the meal). The Cs. expln. as onīto pattato pāṇi yeva, i. e. "the hand is taken away from the bowl". The spelling is frequently oṇīta, probably through BB sources. See on term also Trenckner, *Notes* 66²⁴ & cp. apa-nīta-pātra at M Vastu III.142. The expression is always combd. with bhuttāvin "having eaten" and occurs very frequently, e. g. at Vin II.147; D I.109 (= DA I. 277, q. v. for the 2 explns. mentioned above M II.50, 93; S V.384; A II.63; Sn p. 111 (= pattato onītapāṇi, apanītahattha SnA 456); VvA 118; PvA 278.

Oneti, prob. for **apaneti,** see **apaneti** & pp. **onīta.**

Onojeti see **oṇojeti.**

Opakkamika (adj.) [fr. upakkama] characterising a sensation of pain: attacking suddenly, spasmodic, acute; always in connection with **ābādha** or **vedanā** M I.92, 241; S IV. 230 = A II.87 = III.131 = V.110 = Nd² 304¹ᶜ = Miln 112.

Opakkhin (adj.) [o + pakkhin. adj. fr. pakkha wing, cp. similarly avapatta] "with wings off", i. e. having one's wings clipped, powerless A I.188 (°ŋ karoti to deprive of one's wings or strength; so read for T. opapakkhiŋ karoti).

Opaguyha see **opavayha.**

Opatati [o + **pat**] to fall or fly down (on), to fall over (w. acc.) J II.228 (lokāmisaŋ °anto); VI.561 (°itvā ger.); Miln 368, 396. — pp. **opatita.**

Opatita [pp. of opatati] falling (down) PvA 29 (udaka; v. l. ovuḷhita, opalahita; context reads at PvA 29 mahāsobbhehi opatitena udakena, but id. p. at KhA 213 reads mahāsobbha-sannipātehi).

Opatta (adj.) [o + patta, Sk. avapattra] with leaves fallen off, leafless (of trees) J III.495 (opatta = avapatta nippatta patita-patta C.).

Opadhika (adj.) [fr. upadhi. BSk. after the P., aupadhika Divy 542] forming a substratum for rebirth (always with ref. to puñña, merit). Not with Morris, *J P T S.* 1885, 38 as "exceedingly great"; the correct interpretation is given by Dhpāla at VvA 154 as "atta-bhāva-janaka paṭisandhi-pavatti-vipāka-dāyaka". — S I.233 = A IV.292 = Vv 34²¹; It 20 (v. l. osadhika), 78.

Opanayika (adj.) [fr. upaneti, upa + **nī**] leading to (Nibbāna) S IV.41 sq., 272, 339; V.343; A I.158; II.198; D III.5; Vism 217.

Opapakkhi in phrase **°ŋ karoti** at A I.188 read **opakkhiŋ** karoti to deprive of one's wings, to render powerless.

Opapaccayika (adj.) [= opapātika] having the characteristic of being born without parents, as deva Nett 28 (upādāna).

Opapātika (adj.) [fr. upapatti; the BSk. form is a curious distortion of the P. form, viz. aupapāduka Av. Ś II.89; Divy 300, 627, 649] arisen or reborn without visible cause (i. e. without parents), spontaneous rebirth (*Kvu trsl.* 283²), apparitional rebirth (*Cpd.* 165⁴, q. v.) D I.27, 55, 156; III.132, 230 (°yoni), 265; M I.34, 73, 287, 401 sq., 436 sq., 465 sq.; II.52; III.22, 80, 247; S III.206, 240 sq., 246 sq.; IV.348; V.346, 357 sq., 406; A I.232, 245, 269; II.5, 89, 186; IV.12, 226, 399, 423 sq.; V. 265 sq., 286 sq., 343 sq.; Pug 16, 62, 63; Vbh 412 sq.; Miln 267; Vism 552 sq., 559; DA I.165, 313. The C. on M I.34 explns. by "sesa-yoni-paṭikkhepa-vacanaŋ etaŋ". See also Pug. A I, § 40.

Opapātin (adj.) = opapātika, in phrase opapātiyā (for opapātiniyā?) iddhiyā at S V 282 (so read for T. opapāti ha?) is doubtful reading & perhaps best to be omitted altogether.

Opama at J I.89 & Sdhp 93 (anopama) stands for ūpama, which metri causā for **upama.**

Opamma (nt.) [fr. upama; cp. Sk. aupamya] likeness, simile, comparison, metaphor M I.378; Vin V.164; Miln 1, 70, 330; Vism 117, 622; ThA 290.

Oparajja viceroyalty is v. l. for **uparajja.** Thus at M II. 76; A III.154.

Opavayha (adj. n.) [fr. upavayha, grd. of upavahati] fit for riding, suitable as conveyance, state-elephant (of the elephant of the king) S V.351 = Nett 136 (v. l. opaguyha; C. explns. by ārohana-yogga); J II.20 (SS opavuyha); IV. 91 (v. l. °guyha); VI.488 (T. opavuyha, v. l. opaguyha; gajuttama opavayha = rāja-vāhana C.); DA I.147 (ārohana-yogga opavuyha, v. l. °guyha); VvA 316 (T. opaguyha to be corrected to °vayha).

Opasamika (adj.) [fr. upa + sama + ika; cp. BSk. aupaśamika Av. Ś II.107; M Vastu II.41] leading to quiet, allaying, quieting; Ep. of Dhamma D III.264 sq.; A II.132.

Opasāyika (adj.) [fr. upasaya, upa + **śī**] being near at hand or at one's bidding (?) M I.328.

Opāṭeti [ava + Caus. of **paṭ,** Sk. avapāṭayati] to tear as under, unravel, open Vin II.150 (chaviŋ opāṭetvā).

Opāta [o + pāta fr. patati to fall. Vedic avapāta] — 1. falling or flying down, downfall, descent J v: 561. — 2. a pitfall J I.143; DhA IV.211.

Opāteti [o + Caus. of **pat**] to make fall, to destroy (cp. atipāteti), i. e. 1. to break, to interrupt, in kathaŋ opāteti to interrupt a conversation M II.10, 122, 168; A III.137, 392 sq.; Sn p. 107. — 2. to drop, to omit (a syllable) Vin IV.15.

Opāna (nt.) [o + pāna fr. pivati. Vedic avapāna. The P. Commentators however take o as a contracted form of udaka, e. g. Bdhgh. at DA I.298 = udapāna]. Only in phrase **opāna-bhūta** (adj.) a man who has become a welling spring as it were, for the satisfaction of all men's wants; expld. as "khata-pokkharaṇī viya hutvā" DA I. 298 = J V.174. — Vin I.236; D I.137; M I.379; A IV. 185; Vv 65[4]; Pv IV.1[60]; J III.142; IV.34; V.172; Vbh 247; Miln 411; Vism 18; VvA 286; DA I 177, 298.

Opārambha (adj.) [fr. upārambha] acting as a support, supporting, helpful M II.113.

Opiya is metric for **upiya** [upa + ger. of **i**] undergoing, going into S I.199 = Th 1, 119 (nibbānaŋ hadayasmiŋ opiya; Mrs. Rh. D. trsls. "suffering N. in thy heart to sink", SA. hadayasmiŋ pakkhipitvā.

Opilavati [Sk. avaplavati, ava + **plu**] to be immersed, to sink down S II.224. — Caus. **opilāpeti** (see sep.).

Opilāpita [pp. of opilāpeti] immersed into (loc.), gutted with water, drenched J I.212, 214.

Opilāpeti [Caus. of opilavati, cp. Sk. avaplāvayati] to immerse, to dip in or down, to drop (into = loc.) Vin I. 157 = 225 = S I.169 (C.: nimujjapeti, see *K. S.* 318); M I.207 = III.157; DhA III.3 (°āpetvā; so read with vv. ll. for opiḷetvā); J III.282. — pp. **opilāpita**.

Opiḷeti in "bhattaŋ pacchiyaŋ opiḷetvā" at DhA II.3 is with v. l. to be read opilāpetvā (gloss odahitvā), i. e. dropping the food into the basket.

Opuñchati is uncertain reading for opuñjeti.

Opuñchana or **Opañjana** (nt.) [fr. opuñjeti] heaping up, covering over; a heap, layer DhA III.296.

Opuñjeti or °ati [o + puñjeti Denom. of puñja, heap] to heap up, make a heap, cover over with (Morris, *JPTS.* 1887, 153 trsls. "cleanse") Vin II.176 (opuñjati bhattaŋ); J IV.377 (opuñchetvā T., but v. l. opuñjetvā; gloss upalimpitvā); DhA III.296 (opuñchitvā, gloss sammajjitvā). — Caus. **opuñjāpeti** in same meaning "to smear" Vin III.16 (opuñjāpetvā; v. l. opuñchāpetvā).

Opunāti also as **opuṇāti** (Dh) [o + punāti fr. **pū**] to winnow, sift; fig. lay bare, expose Dh 252 (= bhusaŋ opuṇanto viya DhA III.375); SnA 312. — Caus. **opunāpeti** [cp. BSk. opunāpeti M Vastu III.178] to cause to sift A I.242; J I.447.

Opuppha [o + puppha] bud, young flower J VI.497 (vv. ll. p. 498 opaṇṇa & opatta).

Opeti [unless we here deal with a very old misspelling for oseti we have to consider it a secondary derivation from opiya in Caus. sense, i e. Caus. fr. upa + **i**. Trenckner, *Notes* 77, 78 offers an etym. of ā + vapati, thus **opiya** would be *āvupiya, a risky conclusion, which besides being discrepant in meaning (āvapati = to distribute) necessitates der. of opiya fr. opati (*āvapati) instead of vice versā. There is no other instance of *āva being contracted to o. Trenckner then puts opiya = ūpiya in tadūpiya ("conform with this", see ta° I[a]), which is however a direct derivation from upa = upaka, upiya, of which a superl. formation is upamā ("likeness"). Trenckner's expln. of ūpiya as der. fr. ā + **vap** does not fit in with its meaning] to make go into (c. loc.), to deposit, receive (syn. with osāpeti) S I.236 (SA na.. pakkhipanti) = Th 2, 283 = J V.252 (T. upeti); in which Th 2, 283 has oseti (ThA 216, with expln. of oseti = ṭhapeti on p. 219). — aor. opl J IV.457 (ukkhipi gloss); VI.185 (= pakkhipi gloss). — ger. **opitvā** (opetvā?) J IV.457 (gloss khipetvā).

Ophuṭa [a difficult, but legitimate form arisen out of analogy, fusing ava-vuta (= Sk. vṛta from **vṛ**; opp. *apāvuta = P. apāruta) and ava-phuṭa (Sk. sphuṭa from **sphuṭ**). We should probably read ovuta in all instances] covered, obstructed; always in combn. **āvuta nivuta ophuṭa** (oputa, ovuta) D I.246 (T. ophuta, vv. ll. ophuṭa & opuṭa); M III.131 (T. ovuṭa); Nd[1] 24 ovuṭa, v. l. SS ophuṭa); Nd[2] 365 (ophuṭa, v. l. BB oputa; SS ovuta); DA I.59 (o muta); SnA 596 (oputa = pariyo-naddha); Miln 161 (ovut.).

Obandhati [o + bandhati] to bind, to tie on to Vin I .116 (obandhitvā ger.).

Obhagga [o + bhagga, pp. of **bhañj**, Sk. avabhagna] broken down, broken up, broken S V 96 (°vibhagga); A IV.435 (obhagg'obhagga); DhA I.58 (id.); J I.55 (°sarira).

Obhañjati [o + **bhañj**] to fold up, bend over, crease (a garment); only Caus. II. obhañjāpeti J I.499 (dhovāpeti +). See also pp. obhagga.

Obhata [pp. of obharati] having taken away or off, only in cpd. °cumbaṭā with the "cumbaṭa" taken off, descriptive of a woman in her habit of carrying vessels on her head (on the cumbaṭa stand) Vin III.140 = VvA 73 (Hardy: "a woman with a circlet of cloth on her head"?).

Obharati [ava + bharati, cp. Sk. avabharati = Lat. aufero] to carry away or off, to take off. — pp. **obhata**.

Obhāsa [from obhāsati] shine, splendour, light, lustre, effulgence; appearance. In clairvoyant language also "aura" (see *Cpd.* 214[1] with C. expln. "rays emitted from the body on account of insight") — D I.220 (effulgence of light); M III.120, 157; A II 130, 139; IV.302; It 108 (obhāsakara); Ps I.114, 119 (paññā°); II.100, 150 sq., 159, 162; Vism 28, 41; PvA 276 (ŋ pharati to emit a radiance); Sdhp 325. With **nimitta** and **parikathā** at Vism 23; SnA 497. See also **avabhāsa**.

Obhāsati[1] [o + bhāsati from **bhās**, cp. Sk. avabhāsati] to shine, to be splendid Pv I.2[1] (= pabhāseti vijjoteti PvA 10). — Caus. **obhāseti** to make radiant or resplendent, to illumine, to fill with light or splendour. — pres. **obhāseti** Pv III.1[15] (= joteti PvA 176); Miln 336; ppr. **obbhāsayanto** Pv I.11[1] (= vijjotamāna PvA 56) & **obhāsento** Pv II.1[10] (= jotanto ekālokaŋ karonto PvA 71); ger. **obhāsetvā** S I.66; Kh V. = Sn p. 46; KhA 116 (= ābhāya pharitvā ekobhāsaŋ karitvā). — pp. **avabhāsita**.

Obhāsati[2] [ava + bhāsati fr. **bhāṣ**; Sk. apabhāṣati] to speak to (inopportunely), to rail at, offend, abuse Vin II.262; III 128.

Obhāsana (nt.-adj.) [fr. obhāsa, cp. Sk. avabhāsana] shining VvA 276 (Hardy: "speaking to someone").

Obhoga [o + bhoga from **bhuj** to bend] bending, winding, curve, the fold of a robe Vin I.46 (obhoge kāyabandhanaŋ kātabbaŋ).

Oma (adj.) [Vedic avama, superl. formation fr. ava] lower (in position & rank), inferior, low; pl. omā A III.359 (in contrast with ussā superiors); Sn 860 (ussā samā omā superiors, equals, inferiors), 954; SnA 347 (= paritta lāmaka). — More freq. in neg. form anoma not inferior, i. e. excellent.

Omaka (adj.) [oma + ka] lower in rank, inferior; low, insignificant Nd[1] 306 (appaka +); J II.142; DhA I.203.

Omaṭṭha [pp. of omasati] touched S I.13 = 53 = Th 1, 39.

Omaddati [o + maddati from **mṛd,** BSk. avamardati Jtm 31[33]] — 1. to rub J VI.262 (sarīraŋ omaddanto); Miln 220. — 2. to crush, oppress M I 87 = Nd[2] 199[6] (abhivaggena); J II.95.

Omasati [o + mas = Sk. **mṛṣ**] — 1. (lit.) to touch J V. 446. — 2. (fig.) to touch a person, to reproach, insult Vin IV.4 sq. — pp. **omaṭṭha.**

Omasanā (f.) [fr. omasati] touching, touch Vin III.121 (= heṭṭhā oropanā).

Omāna[1] [fr. o + **man,** think. The Sk. avamāna is later] disregard, disrespect, contempt DhA II.52 (+ atimāna). Cp. foll. & see also **avamāna.**

Omāna[2] [at J II.443 we read **ucce sakuṇa omāna** meaning 'Oh bird, flying high'. With the present material we see no satisfactory solution of this puzzle. There is a Burmese correction which is at variance with the commentary] "flying", the v. l. BB is **ḍemāna** (fr. **ḍī**). C. expl[ns.] by caramāna gacchamāna. Müller, *P. Gr.* 99 proposes to read ḍemāna for omāna.

Omissaka (adj.) [o + missaka] mixed, miscellaneous, various J V.37; VI.224 (°parisā). Cp. vo°.

Omukka (adj.) [fr. + **muc**] cast off, second hand Vin I.187.

Omuñcati [o + **muc**] to take off, loosen, release; unfasten, undo, doff D I.126 (veṭhanaŋ as form of salute); J II.326; VI.73 (sāṭakaŋ); Vism 338; PvA 63 (tacaŋ); VvA 75 (ābharaṇāni). — Caus. **omuñcāpeti** to cause to take off Vin I.273. — pp. **omutta.**

Omutta [pp. of omuñcati] released, freed, discharged, taken off It 56 (read omutt'assa Mārapāso for T. omukkassa m.).

Omutteti [Sk. avamūtrayati, Denom. fr. mūtra, urine] to discharge urine, pass water M I.79, 127.

Oyācati [o + **yāc,** opp. āyācati] to wish ill, to curse, imprecate Vin III.137.

Ora (adj.) [compar. formation fr. ava; Vedic avara] below, inferior, posterior. Usually as nt. **oraŋ** the below, the near side, this world Sn 15; VvA 42 (orato abl. from this side). — Cases adverbially: acc. **oraŋ** (with abl.) on this side of, below, under, within M III.142; Sn 804 (oraŋ vassasatā); Pv IV.3[35] (oraŋ chahi māsehi in less than 6 months or after 6 months; id. p. at Pv I.10[12] has uddhaŋ); PvA 154 (dahato); instr. **orena** J. V.72; abl. **orato** on this side Miln 210.

-pāra the below and the above, the lower & higher worlds Sn 1 (see SnA 13 = Nd[2] 422[b] and cp. paroparaŋ); Miln 319 (samuddo anorapāro, boundless ocean). **-pure** (avarapure) below the fortress M I.68 (bahinagare +). **-mattaka** belonging only to this world, mundane; hence: trifling, insignificant, little, evanescent Vin II.85, 203 = It 85; D I 3; M I.449; A IV.22; V.157, 164; Vbh 247; Nett 62; DhA I 203; DA I.55.

Oraka (adj.) [ora + ka] inferior, posterior Vin I.19; II. 159; M II.47; Sn 692 (= paritta SnA 489; cp. omaka); J I.381.

Orata [o + rata, pp. of ramati] — 1. delighted, satisfied, pleased Miln 210 (cp. abhirata). — 2. desisting, abstaining from, restraining oneself VvA 72 (= virato; cp. uparata).

Orabbhika [fr. urabbha. The Sk. aurabhrika is later & differs in meaning one who kills sheep, a butcher (of sheep) M I 343, 412; S II.256; A I.251; II.207 = Pug 56; III.303; Th 2, 242 (= urabbhaghātaka ThA 204); J V.270 VI.111 (and their punishment in Niraya); Pug A 244 (urabbhā vuccanti eḷakā; urabbhe hanatī ti orabbhiko).

Oramati [Denom. fr. ora instead of orameti] to stay or be on this side, i. e. to stand still, to get no further J I.492 (oramituŋ na icchi), 498 (oramāma na pārema). *Note.* This form may also be expl[d.] & taken as imper. of ava + ramati (cp. avarata 2), i. e. let us desist, let us give up, (i. e. we shall not get through to the other side). **-anoramati** (neg.) see sep. — On the whole question see also Morris, *J P T S.* 1887, 154 sq.

Oramāpeti (Caus. II. of oramati] to make someone desist from J V.474 (manussa-maŋsā).

Orambhāgiya (adj.) [ora + bhāga + iya; BSk. avarabhāgīya, c. g. Divy 533] being a share of the lower, i. e. this world, belonging to the kāma world, Ep. of the 5 saŋyojanāni (see also saŋyojana) D I.156; III.107, 108, 132; M I.432; It 114; Pug 22; Nett 14; SnA 13; DA I.313. — *Note.* A curious form of this word is found at Th 2, 166 orambhāga-manīya, with gloss (ThA 158) oraŋ āgamanīya. Probably the bh should be deleted.

Oravitar [ora + n. ag. of vitarati?] doubtful reading at A V.149, meaning concerned with worldly things (?). The vv. ll. are oramitā, oravikā, oramato, oravī.

Orasa (adj.) [Fr. ura, uras breast Vedic aurasa] belonging to one's own breast, self-begotten, legitimate; innate, natural, own M II.84; III.29; S II.221 (Bhagavato putto o. mukhato jāto); III.83; J III.272; Vv 50[22]; ThA 236; KhA 248; PvA 62 (urejāta +).

Orima [superl. formation fr. ora, equivalent to avama] the lower or lowest, the one on this side, this (opp. yonder); only in comb[n.] **orima-tīra** the shore on this side, the near shore (opp. pāra° and pārima° the far side) D I.244; S IV.175 (sakkāyass' adhivacanaŋ) = SnA 24; Dhs 597; Vism 512 (°tīra-mah'ogha); DhA II.99.

Oruddha [fr. orundhati. In meaning equalling Sk. aparuddha as well as ava°] — 1. kept back, restrained, subdued A III.393. — 2. imprisoned J IV.4. See also ava°.

Orundhati [cp. Sk. avarundhate] to get, attain, take for a wife. — ger. **orundhiya** J IV.480. — aor. **oruddha** Th 2, 445. — pp. **oruddha.** See also avarundhati.

Orodha [fr. orundhati; Sk. avarodha] obstruction; confinement, harem, seraglio Vin II.290; IV.261 (rāj' orodhā harem-lady, concubine); J IV.393, 404.

Oropaṇa (nt.) [abstr. fr. oropeti] taking down, removal, cutting off (hair), in **kes' oropaṇa** hair-cutting DhA II. 53 (T. has at one place orohaṇa, v. l. oropaṇa).

Oropeti [Caus. fr. orohati; BSk. avaropayati] to take down, bring down, deprive of, lay aside, take away, cut off (hair) VvA 64 (bhattabhājanaŋ oropeti) — ger. **oropayitvā** Sn 44 (= nikkhipitvā paṭippassambhayitvā Nd[2] 181; apanetvā SnA 91); J VI.211 (kesamassuŋ).

Orohaṇa (nt.) [abstr. fr. orahati] descent, in udak'orohanānuyoga practice of descending in to the water (i. e. bathing) Pug 55; J I.193; Miln 350.

Orohati [o + rohati] to descend, climb down D II.21; M III.131; J I.50; Miln 395; PvA 14. — Caus. **oropeti** (q. v.).

Olaggeti [Caus. of o + **lag**] to make stick to, to put on, hold fast, restrain M II 178; A III.384 (vv. ll. oloketi, olabheti, oketi); Th 1, 355.

Olagga [Sk. avalagna, pp. of avalagati] restrained, checked Th 1, 356.

Olanghanā (f.) [fr. **olangheti**] bending down Vin III.121 (= heṭṭhā onamanā).

Olangheti [Caus. of ava + **langh**] to make jump down, in phrase **ullangheti olangheti** to make dance up & down J v.434 = DhA iv.197 (the latter has T. ullaggheti ol°; but v. l. ullangheti ol°).

Olamba (adj.) [fr. ava + **lamb**] hanging down Vin iii.49; J iv.380 (°vilamba).

Olambaka (adj.-n.) [see **olambati**] — 1. (adj.) hanging down VvA 32 (°dāma). — 2. (n.) (a) support, walking stick J iv.40 (hatth°). — (b) plumb-line J vi.392.

Olambati & **avalambati** [ava + **lamb**] to hang down, hang on, to be supported by, rest on. The form in o is the older. Pres. avalambare Pv ii.1[18] (= olambamānā tiṭṭhanti PvA 77); ii.10[2] (= olambanti PvA 142); olambati M iii.164 (+ ajjholambati); J i.194; PvA 46. — ger. avalamba (for °bya) Pv iii.3[5] (= olambitva PvA 189) & **olambetvā** J iii.218. See also **olubbha**.

Olambanaka [fr. olambati] an armchair, lit. a chair with supports Vin ii.142.

Olikhati [o + **likh**, cp. Sk. apalikhati] to scrape off, cut off, shave off (hair) A iii.295 (veṇiŋ olikhituŋ); Th 1, 169 (kese olikhissaŋ); 2, 88.

Oligalla [of unknown etym.: prob. Non-Aryan, cp. BSk. oḍigalla Saddh. P. chap. vi.] a dirty pool near a village M iii.168; S v.361; A i.161; iii.389; Miln 220; Vism 343.

Oliyati [o + līyate from **lī**] to stick, stick fast, adhere, cling to It 43; Nett 174. — pp **olīna** (see avalīna).

Olīna [pp. of oliyate] adhering, sticking or clinging to (worldliness), infatuated M i.200 (°vuttika); J vi.569 (anolīna-mānasa); Vbh 350 (°vuttikā); Miln 393 (an°).

Olīyanā [fr. oliyati] adhering, infatuation Ps i.157; Dhs 1156, 1236.

Olugga [pp. of olujjati] breaking off, falling to pieces, rotting away M i.80, 245 (olugga-vilugga), 450 (id.); Vism 107 (id.).

Olujjati [Sk. avarujyate, Pass. of ava + **ruj**] to break off, go to wreck, fall away S ii.218 (v. l. ull°). — pp. **olugga**.

Olubbha [assimil. form of olumbha which in all likelihood for olambya, ger. of olambati. The form presents difficulties. See also Morris, *J P T S.* 1887, 156] holding on to, leaning on, supporting oneself by (with acc.); most frequently in phrase **daṇḍaŋ olubbha** leaning on a stick, e. g. M i.108 (= daṇḍaŋ olambitvā C.; see M i 539); A iii.298; Th 2, 27 (= ālambitvā); VvA 105. In other connections: S i.118; iii.129; J i.265 (āvāṭa-mukha-vaṭṭiyaŋ); vi.40 (hatthe); DhA ii.57 (passaŋ; gloss olambi); VvA 217, 219.

Olumpeti [o + Caus. of **lup**] to strip off, seize, pick, pluck Vin i.278 (bhesajjan olumpetvā, vv.ll. ulumpetvā, oḷump°, odametvā).

Olokana (nt.) [see oloketi] looking, looking at, sight Sdhp 479 (mukhass°).

Olokanaka (adj.-n.) [fr. oloketi] window Vin ii.267 (olokanakena olokenti, adv.).

Oloketi [BSk. avalokayati or apaloketi] to look at, to look down or over to, to examine, contemplate, inspect, consider J i.85, 108 (nakkhattaŋ); Pv ii.9[64]; DhA i.10, 12, 25, 26; ii.96 (v. l. for T. voloketi); iii.296; PvA 4, 5, 74, 124.

Oḷāra at PvA 110 is with v. l. BB to be read **uḷāra**.

Oḷārika (adj.) [fr. uḷāra] gross, coarse, material, ample (see on term *Dhs trsl.* 208 & *Cpd.* 159 n. 4) D i.37, 186 sq. (attā) 195, 197, 199; M i.48, 139, 247; ii.230; iii.16, 299; S ii.275 (vihāra); iii.47 (opp. sukhuma); iv.382 (id.); v.259 sq.; A iv.309 sq. (nimittaŋ obhāso); J i.67; Dhs 585, 675, 889; Vbh 1, 13, 379; Vism 155 (°anga), 274 sq. (with ref. to breathing), 450.

Oḷumpika (adj.) [Deriv. unknown, BSk. olumpika and oḍumpika M Vastu iii.113, 443. In the Śvet-Upan. we find the form **uḍupa** a skiff.] Sen. Kacc 390 belonging to a skiff (no ref. in Pāli Canon?); cp. BSk. olumpika M Vastu iii. 113 & oḍumpika ibid. 443.

Ovaja at S i.212 read **ojava**.

Ovaṭa [o + vaṭa, pp. of **vṛ**, another form of ovuta = ophuta, q. v.] obstructed, prevented Vin ii.255 = iv.52 = A iv.277 (v. l. ovāda); also an° ibid.

Ovaṭṭika (nt.) [fr. ava + **vṛt**] — 1. girdle, waistband M ii.47; J iii.285 (v. l. ovaddhi°); Vism 312; DhA ii.37; iv.206; DA i.218 (Morris, *J P T S.* 1887, 156: a kind of bag). — 2. a bracelet Vin ii.106 (= valayaŋ C.). — 3. a patch, patching (°karaṇa), darning (?) Vin i.254 (vv. ll. ovaṭṭiya°, ovadhita° ovadhīya°); J ii.197 (v.l. ovaddhi°). See also **ovaddheyya** (ava°).

Ovadati [o + vadati. The Sk. avavadati is some centuries later and is diff. in meaning] to give advice, to admonish, exhort, instruct, usually combd. with **anusāsati**. — pres. ovadati Vin iv.52 sq.; DhA i.11, 13; imper. ovadatu M iii.267. — pot. **avadeyya** Vin iv.52 (= aṭṭhahi garudhammehi ovadati); Sn 1051 (= anusāseyya). — aor. ovadi DhA i.397. — inf. **ovadituŋ** Vin i.59 (+ anusāsituŋ). — grd. **ovaditabba** Vin ii.5; and **ovadiya** (see sep.). — Pass. **avadiyati**; ppr. **°iyamāna** Pug 64 (+ anusāsiyamāna).

Ovadiya (adj.) [grd. of ovadati] who or what can be advised, advisable Vin i.59 (+ anusāsiya); Vv 84[36] (= ovāda-vasena vattabbaŋ VvA 345).

Ovaddheyya a process to be carried out with the kaṭhina robes. The meaning is obscure Vin i.254. See the note at *Vin. Texts* ii.154; Vin i.254 is not clear (see cxpln. by C. on p. 388). The vv. ll. are ovadeyya° ovadheyya° ovaṭṭheyya°.

Ovamati [o + **vam**] to throw up, vomit Ud 78.

Ovaraka (nt.) [Deriv. uncertain. The Sk. apavaraka is some centuries later. The Sk. apavaraka forbidden or secret room, Halāyudha "lying-in chamber"] an inner room Vin i.217; M i.253; J i.391 (jāto varake T. to be read as jāt'ovarake i.e. the inner chamber where he was born, thus also at VvA 158); Vism 90, 431; VvA 304 (= gabbha).

Ovariyāna [ger. of o + **vṛ**] forbidding, obstructing, holding back, preventing Th 2, 367 (v. l. ovadiyāna, thus also ThA 250 explained "maŋ gacchantiŋ avaditvā gamanaŋ nisedhetvā".

Ovassa & **°ka** see **anovassa(ka)**.

Ovassati [o + vassati] to rain down on, to make wet. — Pass. **ovassati** to become wet through rain Vin ii.121.

Ovahati [o + vahati] to carry down. — Pass. **ovuyhati** It 114 (ind. & pot. ovuyheyya).

Ovāda [BSk. avavāda in same sense as P.] advice, instruction, admonition, exhortation Vin i.50 = ii.228; ii.255 = iv.52; D i.137 (°paṭikara, function of a king); J iii.256 (anovādakara one who cannot be helped by advice, cp. ovadaka); Nett 91, 92; DhA i.13, 398 (dasavidha o.); VvA 345. — ovādaŋ **deti** to give advice PvA 11, 12, 15, 89, 100 etc.; ovādaŋ **gaṇhāti** to take or accept advice J i.159.

Ovādaka (adj.-n.) [fr. ovāda; cp. BSk. avavādaka in same meaning, e. g. Divy 48, 254, 385] admonishing (act.) or being admonished (pass.); giving or taking advice; a spiritual instructor or adviser M I.145; A I.25; S V.67 = It 107. — **anovādaka** one who cannot or does not want to be advised, incorrigible J I.159; III.256, 304; V.314.

Ovādin (adj.-n.) [fr. ovāda] = ovādaka M I.360 (anovādin).

Ovijjhati [ava + **vyadh**] to pierce through Vism 304.

Ovuta see ophuta.

Ovuyhati [Pass. of ovahati] to be carried down (a river) It 114.

Osakkati [o + sakkati fr. P. **sakk** = *Sk. **ṣvaṣk,** cp. Māgadhī osakkai; but sometimes confused with **sṛp,** cp. P. osappati & Sk. apasarpati] to draw back, move back D I.230; J IV.348 (for apavattati C.); V.295 (an-osakkitvā). See also Trenckner, *Notes* p. 60.

Osajjati [o + **sṛj**] to emit, evacuate PvA 268 (vaccaŋ excrement, + ohanati). — pp. **osaṭṭha.**

Osaṭa [pp. of o + **sṛ**] having withdrawn to (acc.), gone to or into, undergone, visited M I.176, 469 (padasamācāro sangha-majjhe o.); III.2 (Rājagahaŋ vass'āvāsaŋ o.); Miln 24 (sākacchā osaṭā bahū). See also **avasaṭa.**

Osaṇheti [o + saṇheti, denom. fr. saṇha] to make smooth, to smooth out, comb or brush down (hair) Vin II.107 (kese); J IV.219 (id.).

Osadha (nt.) [Vedic auṣadha] see osadhī.

Osadhika v. l. It 20 for **opadhika.**

Osadhikā (f.) [fr. osadha] remedy, esp. poultice, fomentation J IV.361.

Osadhī (f.) [Vedic avaṣa + dhī: bearer of balm, comfort, refreshment]. There is no difference in meaning between osadha and osadhī; both mean equally any medicine, whether of herbs or other ingredients. Cp. e. g. A IV.100 (bījagāma-bhūtagāmā .. osadhi-tiṇavanappatayo) Pv II.6[10], with Sn 296 (gāvo ... yāsa jāyanti osadhā); D I.12, cp. DA I.98; Pv III.5[3]; PvA 86; J IV.31; VI.331 (? trsl[n.] medicinal *herb*). Figuratively, 'balm of salvation' (amatosadha) Miln 247. Osadhi-tārakā, star of healing. The only thing we know about this star is its white brilliance, S I.65; It 20 = A V.62; Vv 9[2]; Pv II.1[10]; cp. PvA 71; Vism 412. Childers calls it Venus, but gives no evidence; other translators render it 'morning star'. According to Hindu mythology the lord of medicine is the moon (osadhīśa), not any particular star.

Osanna (adj.) [o + pp. of **syad** to move on] given out, exhausted, weak Miln 250 (°viriya).

Osappati [o + **sṛp** to creep] to draw back, give way J VI.190 (osappissati; gloss apīyati).

Osaraka (adj.) [fr. osarati, osaraṇa & osaṭa] of the nature of a resort, fit for resorting to, over-hanging eaves, affording shelter Vin II.153. See also **osāraka.**

Osaraṇa (nt.) [fr. avasarati] — 1. return to, going into (acc.) visiting J I.154 (gāmantaŋ °kāle). — 2. withdrawal, distraction, drawing or moving away, heresy Sn 538 (= ogahanāni titthāni, diṭṭhiyo ti attho SnA 434).

Osarati [o + **sṛ,** blow to go away to recede to, to visit M I.176 (gāmaŋ etc.); II.122. — pp. **osaṭa.** See also **avasarati.**

Osāna (nt.) [fr. osāpeti] stopping, ceasing; end, finish, conclusion S V.79 (read paṭikkamosāna), 177, 344; Sn 938 (see Nd[1] 412): osāna-gāthā the concluding stanza J IV. 373; PvA 15, 30 etc. See also **avasāna** & **pariy°.**

Osāpeti [With Morris, *JPTS.* 1887, 158 Caus. of ava + **sā,** Sk. avasāyayati (cp. P. avaseti, oseti), but by MSS. & Pāli grammarians taken as Caus. of **sṛ:** sarāpeti contracted to sāpeti, thus ultimately the same as Sk. sārayati = P. sāreti (thus vv. ll.). Not with Trenckner, *Notes* 78 and Müller *P. Gr.* 42. Caus. of ā + **viś** to sling] to put forth, bring to an end, settle, put down, fix, decide S I.81 (fut. osāpayissāmi; vv. ll. oyayiss° and obhāyiss° = Ud 66 (T. otarissāmi? vv. ll. obhāyiss°, otāy° & osāy°; C. paṭipajjissāmi karissāmi); J I.25 (osāpeti, v. l. obhāseti); Nd[1] 412 (in expl[n.] of osāna); VvA 77 (agghaŋ o. to fix a price; vv. ll. ohāpeti & onarāpeti) = DhA III.108 (v. l. osāreti). Cp. **osāreti.**

Osāraka [fr. osarati] shelter, outhouse J III.446. See also osaraka.

Osāraṇā (f.) [fr. osāreti 3] — 1. restoration, rehabilitation reinstatement (of a bhikkhu after exclusion from the Sangha) Vin I.322; Miln 344. — 2. procession (?) (perhaps reading should be ussāraṇā) DhA II.1 (T. oss°).

Osārita [pp. of osāreti 3] restored, rehabilitated Vin IV.138.

Osāreti [Caus. of o + **sṛ** to flow] — 1. (with v. l. osāpeti, reading osāreti is uncertain) to stow away, deposit, put in, put away (see also opeti) J VI.52, 67 (pattaŋ thavikāya o.). — 2. to bring out, expound, propound, explain Miln 13 (abhidhammapiṭikaŋ), 203 (kāraṇaŋ), 349 (lekhaŋ to compose a letter). — 3. (t.t.) to restore a bhikkhu who has undergone penance Vin I.96, 322, 340; IV.53 (osārehi ayyā ti vuccamāno osāreti). — Pass. osāriyati Vin II.61; pp. **osārita** (cp. **osāraṇā**).

Osiñcati [o + siñcati] — 1. to pour out or down over, to besprinkle Vin II.262; M I.87 (telena); Pv I.8[5] (ppr. osiñcaŋ = āsiñcanto PvA 41). — 2. to scoop out, empty, drain (water) J V.450 (osinciyā, pot. = osiñceyya C.). — pp. **avasitta** & **ositta.**

Osita [pp. of ava + **sā**] inhabited (by), accessible (to) Sn 937 (an°). Cp. vy°.

Ositta [pp. of osiñcati] sprinkled, besprinkled J V.400. See also avasitta.

Osīdati [fr. o + **sad**] to settle down, to sink, run aground (of ships) S IV.314 (osīda bho sappi-tela); Miln 277 (nāvā osīdati). — ger. osīditvā J II.293. — Caus. II. osīdāpeti J IV.139 (nāvaŋ).

Osīdana (nt.) [fr. osīdati] sinking DhsA 363.

Ossa see ussa.

Ossakk° see osakk°.

Ossagga [fr. ossajati] relaxation, in cpd. sati-ossagga (for which more common sati-vossagga) relaxation of memory, inattention, thoughtlessness DhA III.163 (for pamāda Dh 167). See **vossagga.**

Ossajati [o + **sṛj** send off] to let loose, let go, send off, give up, dismiss, release D II.106 (aor. ossaji); Sn 270 = S I.207; Th I, 321; J IV.260. — pp. **ossaṭṭha.** See also **avassajati.**

Osajjana (nt.) [fr. ossajati] release, dismissal, sending off DA I.130.

Ossaṭṭha [pp. of ossajati] let loose, released, given up, thrown down D II.106; S III.241; J I.64; IV.460 (= nissaṭṭha).

Ossanna [pp. of osīdati for osanna, ss after ussanna] sunk, low down, deficient, lacking J I.336 (opp. ussanna). Hardly to be derived from ava + **syad.**

Ossavana (nt) [fr. ava + **sru**] outflow, running water M I.189 (v. l. ossāvana & osavana). Cp. **avassava.**

Ohana only in cpd. bimb'ohana, see under **bimba.**

Ohanati [ava + **han,** but prob. a new formation from Pass. avahīyati of **hā,** taking it to **han** instead of the latter] to defecate, to empty the bowels PvA 268 (+ osajjati).

Oharaṇa (nt.) [fr. oharati] lit. "taking away", leading astray, side-track, deviating path J VI.525 (C.: gamana-magga). Cp. avaharaṇa.

Oharati [o + **hṛ** take] — 1. to take away, take down, take off S I.27 (ger. ohacca, v. l. ūhacca); Pv II.6[6] (imper. ohara = ohārehi PvA 95); DhA IV.56 (see ohārin). See also ava°. — Caus. I. **ohāreti** (see avahārati); Caus. II. **oharāpeti** in meaning of oharati to take down, to cut or shave off (hair) J VI.52 (kesamassuŋ); DhA II.53 (cp. oropeti). — pp. **avahaṭa.**

Ohāya ger. of **ojahāti.**

Ohāra see **avahāra** & cp. **vohāra.**

Ohāraṇa (nt.) [fr. ohāreti, cp. avaharaṇa] taking down, cutting off (hair) J I.64 (kesa-massu°).

Ohārin (adj.-n.) [fr. avaharati] dragging down, weighty, heavy Dh 346 (= avaharati heṭṭhā harati ti DhA IV.56).

Ohāreti [Caus. of oharati] — 1. to give up, leave behind, renounce (cp. ojahāti) Sn 64 (= oropeti Nd[2] 183). — 2. to take down (see oharati 1) Vin I.48; PvA 95. — 3. to cut down, shave off (hair; see oharāpeti under oharati) It 75 (kesamassuŋ hair & beard, v. l. ohāyāpetvā); Pug 56 (id.).

Ohita [pp. of odahati; BSk. avahita (Jtm 210 e. g.) as well as apahita (Lal. V. 552 e. g.)] — 1. put down into, deposited Dh 150. — 2. put down, laid down, taken off, relieved of, in phrase **ohitabhāro** (arahaŋ) (a Saint) who has laid down the burden: see arahatta III. C.; cp. °khandha-bhāra DhA IV.168. — 3. put down in, hidden, put away in (—°) Sn 1022 = (kos'ohita). — 4. (fig.) put down to, applied to, in **ohita-sota** listening, attentive, intent upon (cp. sotaŋ odahati to listen) usually in phrase ohitasoto dhammaŋ suṇāti; M I.480; III.201; S V.96; A IV.391; Vism 300 (+ aṭṭhiŋ katvā).

Ohiyyaka (adj.-n.) [fr. ohīyati, avahiyyati] one who is left behind (in the house as a guard) Vin III.208; IV.94; S I.185 (vihārapāla).

Ohīna [pp. of ojahāti] having left behind J IV.432 (gaṇaŋ).

Ohīyati (ohiyyati) [ava + hīyati, Pass. of **ha,** see avajahāti] — 1. to be left behind, to stay behind J V.340 (avahīyati = ohiyyati C.). — 2. to stay behind, to fall out (in order to urinate or defecate); ger. **ohījitvā** Vin IV.229; DhA II.21 (cp. ohanati). See also **ohiyyaka.**

Ohīḷanā (f.) [ava + hīḷanā, of **hīḍ**] scorning, scornfulness Vbh 353 (+ ohīḷattaŋ).

LIST OF CORRECTIONS.

To part I:

p. X. before Mahāvaŋsa . . . . . . , Khuddhasikkhā. *J P T S.* 1883 (Khus).
„ Netti . . . . , Mūlasikkhā, *J P T S.* 1883 (Mūls).
„ XI. after Visuddhi . . . . . , Yogāvacara's Manual, *P T S.* 1896 (Yog).
for Haward read Harvard.
to Mahāvastu . . . . . . add (Mvst).
under 3 add Neumann, Die Reden Gotamo Buddha's (Mittlere Sammlung), vols. I.—III.² 1921
for Anug read S. Z. Aung.
to Questions of . . . . add (Miln).
to Vinaya Texts . . . add (Vin T.).
„ 4 „ Brāhmaṇa (Br.).
add Śatapatha-Brāhmaṇa (trsl. J. Eggeling) S B E. vols. (Śat. Br.).
„ Dhātupāṭha & Dhātumañjūsā, ed. Andersen & Smith, Copenhagen 1921 (Dhtp, Dhtm).
„ XII. „ B. 1. add B R. Böhtlingk and Roth.
„ Dhtm Dhātumañjūsa . . . . . 4.
Dhtp Dhātupāṭha . . . . . . 4.
„ XIII. „ 2 „ cond. conditional.
„ 1 col. 1, l. 25 read ā⁴ for ā².
„ 6 „ 2, „ 22 „ "part or interest (opp. bāhiraŋ the interest in the outside world)".
„ 11 „ 2, 3, „ excessive for ecc°.
„ 14 „ 2, 28 „ believes „ belives.
„ 15 „ 2, to p. 17, col. 1 headlines read Aṭṭha, Aḍḍha for Attha, Addha.
„ 19 „ 1, 6, read adulteress for adultress.
„ 21 „ 1, 26 „ late for exete.
„ 24 „ 1, transfer °kāma to precede-kāmin.
„ 2, 25 read phraseology for phraselogy.
„ 26 „ 2, 41 „ period for geriod.
p. 32 „ 2, 10 „ unlucky for unluckly.
„ 33 „ 2, 11, fr. b. read supplementary for supplementy.
„ 35 „ 1, 5, „ „ move for more.
„ 38 „ 1, 30, read worldly for wordly & 67 for 97.
„ 2, 24 „ supreme „ suppreme.
„ 42 „ 1, 1, fr. b. dele *in*.
„ 2, 36 read facing *the* wind.
„ 43 „ 2, line 46 read connected for nonnected.
„ 44 „ 1, „ 2 „ quarrelling „ quarelling.
„ 1, „ 39 „ residuum „ residium.
„ 47 „ 2, „ 11 fr. b. read Trenckner for Trenckener.
„ 48 „ 1, under Antarā read -gacchati for -gattchati.
„ 52 „ 1, „ Apapibati read J II.126 for III.126.
„ 1, line 16, fr. b. read continuous for continuou.
„ 56 „ 2, „ 8, „ „ impulsive „ in°.
„ 57 „ 1, „ 19, „ „ indestructible for °able.
„ 59 „ 1, „ 14, read achievements for acch°.
„ 70 „ 1, „ 19, fr. b. read heathenish for °isch.
„ 71 „ 1, „ 2, „ „ possessing „ posess°.
„ 72 „ 1, „ 11, read Abhisambhū for Absambhū.
„ 77 „ 2, Aribhāseti correct to Pari° according to Fausböll (J v. corr.).
„ 2, l. 9 read spirituous for spiritous.
„ 81 „ 2, „ 3 fr. b. read experiences.
„ 82 „ 2, under Avadāta read metri for matri.
„ 89 „ 1, after Asita³ put in new article **Asita⁴** (m. nt.) [fr. asi] a sickle J III.129; v.46.
„ 1, l. 35 read intuiting for intuitising.
„ 91 „ 1, „ 16 „ intoxicated for intoricated.

A number of minor printer's errors, like omitting an occasional spiritus, or putting ` as accent for ', as well as c for e, n for u & vice versa in familiar words, are not mentioned as they will be easily found out & corrected by the reader.

THE PALI TEXT SOCIETY'S PALI-ENGLISH DICTIONARY

EDITED BY

T. W. RHYS DAVIDS F.B.A. D.Sc. Ph.D. LL.D. D.Litt.

and WILLIAM STEDE Ph.D.

Part III (K—Cit)

PUBLISHED BY
THE PALI TEXT SOCIETY
LONDON

First published - - - 1922
Reprinted - - - - 1947
Reprinted - - - - 1952

K.

Ka° (pron. interr.) [Sk. kaḥ, Idg. *quo besides *qui (see ki° & kiŋ) & *quu (see ku°). Cp. Av. ka-; Gr. πῇ, πῶς, ποῖος, etc.; Lat. quī; Oir. co-te; Cymr. pa; Goth. hvas, Ags. hwā (=E. who), Ohg. hwër] who? — m. ko, f. kā (nt. kiŋ, q. v.); follows regular decl. of an a-theme with some formations fr. ki°, which base is otherwise restricted to the nt. — From ka° also nt. pl. kāni (Sn 324, 961) & some adv. forms like kathaŋ, kadā, kahaŋ, etc. — 1. (*a*) ka°: nom. m. ko Sn 173, 765, 1024; J I.279; Dh 146; f. kā J VI.364; PvA 41; gen. sg. kassa Miln 25; instr. kena; abl. kasmā (nt.) as adv. "why" Sn 883, 885; PvA 4, 13, 63, etc. — (*b*) ki° (m. & f.; nt. see kiŋ): gen. sg. kissa Dh 237; J II.104. **ko-nāmo** (of) what name Miln 14; DhA II.92, occurs besides kin-nāmo Miln 15. —**kvattho** what (is the) use Vv 50[10] stands for ko attho. — All cases are freq. emphasized by addition of the affirm. part. nu & su, e. g. ko su'dha tarati oghaŋ (who then or who possibly) Sn 173; kena ssu nivuto loko "by what then is the world obstructed?" Sn 1032; kasmā nu saccāni vadanti . . . Sn 885. — 2. In *indef.* meaning comb[d] with -ci (Sk. cid: see under ca 1 and ci°): koci, kāci, etc., whoever, some (usually with neg. **na koci**, etc., equalling "not anybody"), nt. **kiñci** (q. v.); e. g. mā jātu koci lokasmiŋ pāpiccho It 85; no yāti koci loke Dh 179; n'âhaŋ bhatako 'smi kassaci Sn 25; na hi nassati kassaci kammaŋ "nobody's trace of action is lost" Sn 666; kassaci kiñci na (deti) (he gives) nothing to anybody VvA 322; PvA 45. — In *Sandhi* the orig. d of cid is restored, e. g. app' eva nāma kocid eva puriso idh' agaccheyya, "would that some man or other would come here!" PvA 153. — Also in *correl.* with *rel.* pron. ya (see details under ya°): yo hi koci gorakkhaŋ upajīvati kassako so na brāhmaṇo (whoever—he) Sn 612. See also kad°.

Kaŋsa [cp. Sk. kaŋsa; of uncertain etym., perhaps of Babylonian origin, cp. hirañña] 1. bronze Miln 2; magnified by late commentators occasionally into silver or gold. Thus J VI.504 (silver) and J I.338; IV.107; VI.509 (gold), considered more suitable to a fairy king. — 2. a bronze gong Dh 134 (DhA III.58). — 3. a bronze dish J I.336; āpānīya° a bronze drinking cup, goblet M. I.316. — 4. a "bronze," i. e. a bronze coin worth 4 kahāpaṇas Vin IV.255, 256. See Rhys Davids, *Coins and Measures* §§ 12, 22. — "Golden bronze" in a fairy tale at Vv 5[4] is explained by Dhammapāla VvA 36 as "bells." — It is doubtful whether *brass* was known in the Ganges valley when the earlier books were composed; but kaŋsa may have meant *metal* as opposed to earthenware. See the compounds.

-**upadahārana** (n. a.) metal milk-pail (?) in phrase: dhenusahassāni dukūla-sandanāni (?) kaŋsūpadhāraṇāni D II.192; A IV.393; J VI.503 (expl[d] at 504). Kern (*Toev.* p. 142) proposes correction to kaŋs'ûpadohana (=Sk. kāŋsy'opodohana), i.e. giving milk to the extent of a metal pailful. -**kaṇṭaka** metal thorns, bits of sharp metal, nails J V.102 (cp. sakaṇṭaka) -**kūṭa** cheating with false or spurious metal D I.5 (=DA I.79: selling brass plates for gold ones). -**tāla** bronze gong DhA I.389; DhsA 319 (°tāḷa); VvA 161 or cymbals J VI.277, 411. -**thāla** metal dish, as distinguished from earthenware D I.74 (in simile of dakkho nahāpako=A III.25) cp. DA I. 217; Vism 283 (in simile); DhA III.57 (: a gong); DA I.217; DhA IV.67=J III.224; reading at Miln 62 to be °tāla (see *J.P.T.S.* 1886, 122). -**pattharika** a dealer in bronze ware Vin II.135. -**pāti** & **pātī** a bronze bowl, usually for food: M I.25; A IV.393; Sn 14; PvA 274. -**pūra** full of metal J IV.107. -**bhaṇḍa** brass ware Vin II.135. -**bhājana** a bronze vessel Vism 142 (in simile). -**maya** made of bronze Vin I.190; II.112; -**mallaka** metal dish, e. g. of gold J III.21. -**loha** bronze Miln 267.

Kaŋsati=kassati, see ava°.

Kakaca [onomat. to sound root kṛ, cp. note on gala; Sk. krakaca] a saw Th 1, 445; J IV.30; V.52; VI.261; DA I.212; in simile °-ūpama ovāda M I.129. Another simile of the saw (a man sawing a tree) is found at Ps I.171, quoted & referred to at Vism 280, 281.

-**khaṇḍa** fragment or bit of saw J I.321. -**danta** tooth of a saw, DA I.37 (kakaca-danta-pantiyaŋ kīḷamāna).

Kakaṇṭaka, the chameleon J I.442, 487; II.63; VI.346; VvA 258.

Kaku [Brh. kakud, cp. kākud hollow, curvature, Lat. cacumen, & cumulus] a peak, summit, projecting corner S I.100 (where satakkatu in Text has to be corrected to satakkaku: megho thanayaŋ vijjumālī satakkaku. Com. expl[n] sikhara, kūṭa) A III.34 (=AA 620~kūṭa). Cp. satakkaku & Morris, *J.P.T.S.* 1891-93, 5.

Kakuṭa a dove, pigeon, only in cpds.:

-**pāda** dove-footed (i. e. having beautiful feet) DhA I.119; f. pādī appl. to Apsaras, J II.93; DhA I.119; Miln 169.

Kakutthaka see ku°.

Kakudha [cp. Sk. kakuda, and kaku above] 1. the hump on the shoulders of an Indian bull J II.225; J VI.340. — 2. a cock's comb: see sisa kakudha. — 3. a king's symbol or emblem (nt.) J V.264. There are 5 such insignia regis, regalia: s. kakudha-bhaṇḍa. — 4. a tree, the Terminalia Arjuna, Vin I.28; J VI.519; kakudha-rukkha DhA IV.153. *Note.* On pakudha as twin-form of ka° see Trenckner, *J.P.T.S.* 1908, 108.

-**phala** the fruit of the kakudha tree Mhvs XI.14, where it is also said to be a kind of pearl; see mutta. -**bhaṇḍa** ensign of royalty J I.53; IV.151; V.289 (=sakāyura). The 5 regalia (as mentioned at J V.264) are vāḷavījanī, uṇhīsa, khagga, chatta, pādukā: the fan, diadem, sword, canopy, slippers. — pañcavidha-k° PvA 74.

Kakka[1] [cp. Sk. kalka, also kalanka & kalusa] a sediment deposited by oily substances, when ground; a paste Vin I.205 (tila°), 255. Three kinds enumerated at J. VI.232: sāsapa° (mustard-paste), mattika° (fragrant earth-paste, cp. Fuller's earth), tila° (sesamum paste). At DA I.88, a fourth paste is given as haliddi°, used before the application of face powder (poudre de riz, mukha-cuṇṇa). Cp kakku.

Kakka[2] [cp. Sk. karka) a kind of gem; a precious stone of yellowish colour VvA 111.

Kakkaṭa a large deer (?) J VI.538 (expl[d] as mahāmiga).

Kakkaṭaka [cp. Sk. karkaṭa, karkara "hard," kankata "mail"; cp. Gr. καρκίνος & Lat. cancer; also B. Sk. kakkaṭaka hook] a crab S I.123; M I.234; J I.222; Vv 54[6] (VvA 243, 245); DhA III.299 (mama . . . kakkaṭakassa viya akkhīni nikkhamiṃsu, as a sign of being in love). Cp. kakkhaḷa.
 -**nala** a kind of sea-reed of reddish colour, J IV.141; also a name for coral, ibid. -**magga** fissures in canals; frequented by crabs, DhsA 270. -**yantaka** a ladder with hooks at one end for fastening it to a wall, Mhvs IX.17. -**rasa** a flavour made from crabs, crab-curry, VvA 243.

Kakkara [onomat. cp. Sk. kṛkavāku cock, Gr. κέρκαξ, κερκίς, Lat. querquedula, partridge; sound-root kṛ, see note on gala] a jungle cock used as a decoy J II.162, purāṇa°, II.161; cp. dīpaka[1] & see Kern, *Toev.* p. 118: K°-Jātaka, N° 209.

Kakkaratā (f.) roughness, harshness, deceitfulness, Pug 19, 23.

Kakkariya (nt.) harshness, Pug 19, 23.

Kakkaru a kind of creeper (°jātāni = valliphalāni) J VI.536.

Kakkasa (adj.) [Sk. karkaśa to root kṛ as in kakkaṭaka] rough, hard, harsh, esp. of speech (vācā para-kaṭukā Dhs 1343), M I.286 = Dhs 1343; A V.265 = 283, 293; DhsA 396. —akakkasa: smooth Sn 632; J III.282; V.203, 206, 405, 406 (cp. *J.P.T.S.* 1891-93, 13); akakkasaṅga, with smooth limbs, handsome, J V.204.

Kakkassa roughness Sn 328, Miln 252.

Kakkārika (and °uka) [fr. karkaru] a kind of cucumber Vv 33[28] = eḷāluka VvA 347.

Kakkāru (Sk. karkāru, connected with karkaṭaka] 1. a pumpkin-gourd, the Beninkasa Cerifera J VI.536: kakkārujātāni = valliphalāni (reading kakkaru to be corr.). — 2. a heavenly flower J III.87, 88 = dibbapuppha

Kakkāreti [*kaṭ-kāreti to make kaṭ, see note on gala for sound-root kṛ & cp. khaṭakhaṭa] to make the sound kak, to half choke J II.105.

Kakku [cp. kakka = kalka] a powder for the face, slightly adhesive, used by ladies, J V.302 where 5 kinds are enum[d]: sāsapa°, loṇa°, mattika°, tila°, haliddi°.

Kakkoṭaka (?) KhA 38, spelt takk° at Vism 258.

Kakkola see takkola.

Kakkhaḷa [kakkhaṭa, cp. Sk. karkara = P. kakkaṭaka] 1. rough, hard, harsh (lit. & fig.) Dhs 648 (opp. muduka Dhs 962 (rūpaṃ paṭhavīdhātu: kakkhaḷaṃ kharagataṃ kakkhaḷattaṃ kakkhaḷabhāvo); Vism 349 (= thaddha), 591, 592 (°lakkhaṇa); DhA II.95; IV.104; Miln 67, 112; PvA 243 (= asaddha, akkosakāraka, opp. muduka); VvA 138 (= pharusa). — 2. cruel, fierce, pitiless J I.187, 266; II.204; IV.162, 427. Akakkhaḷa not hard or harsh, smooth, pleasant DhsA 397. -°**vacata**, kind speech, ibid. (= apharusa °vācatā mudu°).
 -**kathā** hard speech, cruel words J VI.561. -**kamma** cruelty, atrocity J III.481. -**bhāva** rigidity Dhs 962 (see kakkhaḷa) MA 21: harshness, cruelty J III.480. a° absence of hardness or rigidity DhsA 151.

Kakkhaḷatā (f.) [abstr. fr. prec.] hardness, rigidity, Dhs 859; Vbh 82; J V.167; DhsA 166.—akakkhaḷatā absence of roughness, pleasantness Dhs 44, 45, 324, 640, 728, 859; DhsA 151; VvA 214 (= saṇha).

Kakkhaḷatta (nt.) hardness, roughness, harshness Vin II.86; Vbh 82; Vism 365; cp. M.Vastu I.166: kakkhaṭatva.

Kakkhaḷiya hardness, rigidity, roughness, Vbh 350.

Kanka [Sk. kanka, to sound-root kṇ, cp. kinkiṇī & see note on gala] a heron M I.364, 429; J V.475.
 -**patta** a heron's plume J V.475.

Kankata [= kaṃ or kiṃ + kṛta, to kiṇi, "the tinklings"] elephant's trappings VvA 104 (= kappa).

Kankaṇa (nt.) [to same root as kanka] a bracelet, ornament for the wrist Th 2, 259 (= ThA 211).

Kankala [Sk. kankāla & cp. śṛnkhala (as kaṇṇa > śṛnga), orig. meaning "chain"] skeleton; only in cpd. **atthi°**. Aṭṭhikankal' ūpamā kāmā Vin II.25; M I.130, 364; J V.210; Th 1, 1150 (°kuṭika): aṭṭhikankalasannibha Th 2, 488 (= ThA 287; cp. Morris, *J.P.T.S.* 1885, 75): aṭṭhikankala aṭṭhi-puñja aṭṭhi-rāsi S II.185 = It 17 (but in the verses on same page: puggalass' aṭṭhisañcayo). Cp. aṭṭhisankhalikā PvA 152; aṭṭhika sankhalikā J I.433; aṭṭhi-sanghāṭa Th 1, 60.

Kankuṭṭhaka [cp. Sk. kankuṣṭha] a kind of soil or mould, of a golden or silver colour Mhvs 32. 6 (see note on p. 355).

Kankhati [Sk. **kānkṣ** cp. **śank**, Lat. cunctor] 1. with loc.: to be uncertain, unsettled, to doubt (syn. **vicikicchati**, with which always combined). **Kankhati vicikicchati** dvīsu mahāpurisa-**lakkhaṇesu** D I.106 is in doubt and perplexity about (Bgh's gloss, patthanaṃ uppādati DA I.275, is more edifying than exact.) = Sn 107; na kankhati na vicikicchati S II.17 = III.135; kankheyya vicikiccheyya S II.50, 54; III.122; V.225 (corr. khankheyya!) 226; same with Satthari kankheyya dhamme° sanghe° sikkhāya° A IV.460 = V.17 = M I.101 = Dhs 1004; cp. Dhs. 1118. — 2. with acc.: to expect, to wait for, to look forward to. **Kālaṃ** k. to abide one's time, to wait for death S I.65 (appiccho sorato danto k. k. bhāvito (so read for bhatiko) sudanto); Sn 516 (id..with bhāvito sadanto); It 69 (id. bhāvitatto).—J V.411 (= icchati); VI.229 (= oloketi). pp. **kankhita** S III.99; Sn 540; (+ vicikicchita); inf. **kankhituṃ** S IV.350 = 399 (+ vicikicchituṃ).

Kankhana (nt.) doubting, doubt, hesitation MA 97; DhsA 259.

Kankhanīya [grd. of kankhati] to be doubted S IV.399.

Kankhā (f.) [cp. Sk. kānkṣā] 1. doubt, uncertainty S I.181; III.203 (dukkhe k. etc.; cp. Nd[2] 1); Sn 541, 1149; °ṃ vinayati Sn 58, 559, 1025; k. pahīyati Ps II.62; comb[d] with **vimati**: D I.105; III.116; S IV.327; V.161; A II.79, 160, 185; DA I.274; with vicikicchā: S IV.350; Dhs. 425. Defined as = kankhāyanā & kankhāyitatta Nd[2]1; Dhs 425 (under vicikicchā). 3 doubts enum[d] at D III.217; 4 in passages with vimati (see above); 7 at Dhs 1004; 8 at Nd[2] 1 & Dhs 1118; 16 at M I.8 & Vism 518. — 2. as adj. doubting, doubtful, in **akankha** one who has overcome all doubt, one who possesses right knowledge (vijjā), in comb[ns] akankha apiha anupaya S I.181; akhila a. Sn 477, 1059; Nd[2]1; cp. vitiṇṇa° Sn 514; avitiṇṇa° Sn 249, 318, 320 (= ajānaṃ); nikkankha S II.84 (+ nibbicikiccha). — 3. expectation SA 183. — On connotation of k. in general see *Dhs trsl.* p. 115 n[1].
 -**cchida** removing or destroying doubt Sn 87. -**cchedana** the removal of d. J I.98; IV.69. -**ṭṭhāniya** founded on d., doubtful (dhammā) D III.285; A IV.152, 154; V.16; AA 689. -**dhamma** a doubting state of mind, doubt D II.149; S IV.350. -**vitaraṇa** overcoming of doubt Miln 233; DhsA 352, °*visuddhi* complete purification in consequence of the removal of all doubt D III.288; M I.147; Ud 60; Vism 523; Bdhd 116 sq. -**samangin** affected with doubts, having doubts DhsA 259.

Kankhāyati [Denom. fr. kankhā] to doubt, pp. **Kankhayita** Sn 1021.

Kankhāyanā (f.) + **kankhāyitatta** (nt.) doubting and hesitation, doubtfulness, Nd² 1; Dhs 425, 1004, 1118; DhsA 259.

Kankhin (adj.) [Sk. kānkṣin] 1. doubting, wavering, undecided, irresolute D II.241; Sn 1148; Nd² 185; comb^d with vecikicchin S III.99; M I.18; A II.174; Sn 510. — 2. longing for Pgdp 106 (mokkha°). — akankhin not doubting, confident, sure (cp. akankha) D II.241; A II.175.

Kangu (f.) [derivation unknown, prob. non-Aryan, cp. Sk. kangu] the panic seed, *Panicum Italicum;* millet, used as food by the poor (cp. piyangu); mentioned as one of the seven kinds of grains (see dhañña) at Vin IV.264; DA I.78. — Miln 267; Mbvs 32, 30.
-piṭṭha millet flour, in °*maya* made of m. meal J VI.581. -bhatta a dish of (boiled) millet meal Vism 418 (in simile).

Kaca [Sk. kaca, cp. kāñcī and Latin cingo, cicatrix] the hair (of the head), in °*kalāpa* a mass of hair, tresses Dāvs IV.51.

Kacavara [to kaca ?] 1. sweepings, dust, rubbish (usually in comb^n with chaḍḍeti and sammajjati) J I.292; III.163; IV.300; Vism 70; DA I.7; DhA I.52; SnA 311. — 2. rags, old clothes SA 283 (= pilotikā).
-chaḍḍana throwing out sweepings, in °*pacchi* a dust basket, a bin J I.290. -chaḍḍanaka a dust pan J I.161 (+ muṭṭhi-sammujjani). -chaḍḍani a dust pan DhA III.7 (sammajjani +). -chaḍḍikā (dāsī) a maid for sweeping dust, a cinderella DhA IV.210.

Kacci & **kaccid** (indecl.) [Sk. kaccid = kad + cid, see kad°] indef. interrog. particle expressing doubt or suspense, equivalent to Gr. *ἄν*, Lat. ne, num, nonne: then perhaps; I doubt whether, I hope, I am not sure, etc., Vin I.158, 350; D I.50 (k. maŋ na vañcesi I hope you do not deceive me), 106; S III.120, 125; Sn. 335, 354, p. 87; J I.103, 279; V.373; DhA II.39 (k. tumhe gatā "have you not gone," answer: āma "yes"); PvA 27 (k. tan dānaŋ upakappati does that gift really benefit the dead ?), 178 (k. vo piṇḍapāto laddho have you received any alms ?). Cp. kin. — Often comb^d with other indef. particles, e. g. kacci nu Vin I.41; J III.236; VI.542; k. nu kho "perhaps" (Ger. etwa, doch nicht) J I.279; k. pana J I.103. — When followed by nu or su the original d reappears according to rules of Sandhi: kaccinnu J II.133; V.174, 348; VI. 23; kaccissu Sn 1045, 1079 (see Nd² 186).

Kaccikāra a kind of large shrub, the Caesalpina Digyna J VI.535 (should we write with BB kacchi° ?).

Kaccha¹ (nt.) [cp. Sk. kaccha, prob. dial.] 1. marshy land, marshes; long grass, rush, reed S I.52 (te hi sotthiŋ gamissanti kacche vāmakase magā), 78 (parūḷha k-nakha-lomā with nails and hair like long-grown grass, cp. same at J III.315 & Sdhp 104); J V.23 (carāmi kacchāni vanāni ca); VI.100 (parūḷha-kacchā tagarā); Sn 20 (kacche rūḷhatiṇe caranti gāvo); SnA 33 (pabbata° opp. to nadī°, mountain, & river marshes). Kern (*Toev.* II.139) doubts the genuineness of the phrase parūḷha°. — 2. an arrow (made of reed) M I.429 (kaṇḍo . . . yen' amhi viddho yadi vā kacchaŋ yadi vā ropiman ti).

Kaccha² (adj.) [ger. of **kath**] fit to be spoken of A I.197 (Com. = kathetuŋ yutta). akaccha ibid.

Kacchaka¹ a kind of fig-tree DA I.81. — 2. the tree Cedrela Toona Vin IV.35; S V.96; Vism 183.

Kacchati¹ Pass. of katheti (ppr. kacchamāna A III.181). — 2. Pass. of karoti.

Kacchantara (nt.) [see kacchā²] 1. interior, dwelling, apartment VvA 50 (= nivesa). — 2. the armpit: see upa°.

Kacchapa [Sk. kacchapa, dial. fr. *kaśyapa, orig. Ep of kumma, like magga of paṭipadā] a tortoise, turtle S IV.177 (kummo kacchapo); in simile of the blind turtle (kāṇo k.) M III.169 = S V.455; Th 2, 500 (cp. *J.P.T.S.* 1907, 73, 174).—f. kacchapinī a female t. Miln 67.
-lakkhaṇa "tortoise-sign," i. e. fortune-telling on the ground of a tortoise being found in a painting or an ornament; a superstition included in the list of tiracchāna-vijjā D I.9≈; DA I.94. -loma "tortoise-hair," i. e. an impossibility, absurdity J III.477, cp. sasavisāṇa; *maya* made of t. hair J III.478.

Kacchapaka see hattha°.

Kacchapuṭa [see kaccha¹] reed-basket, sling-basket, pingo, in -vāṇija a trader, hawker, pedlar J I.111.

Kacchā¹ (f.) [derivation unknown, cp. Sk. kakṣā, Lat. cohus, incohare & see details under gaha¹] 1. enclosure, denoting both the enclosing and the enclosed, i. e. wall or room: see kacchantara.—2. an ornament for head & neck (of an elephant), veilings, ribbon Vv 21⁸ = 69⁸ (= gīveyyaka VvA); J IV.395 (kacchaŋ nāgānaŋ bandhatha gīveyyaŋ paṭimuñcatha). 3. belt, loin- or waist-cloth (cp. next) Vin II.319; J V.306 (= saŋvelli); Miln 36; DhA I.389.

Kacchā² (f.) & **kaccha** (m. nt.) [Derivation unknown, cp. Sk. kakṣa & kakṣā, Lat. coxa, Ohg. hahsa]; the armpit Vin I.15 (addasa . . . kacche vīṇaŋ . . . aññissā kacche ālambaraŋ); S I.122 = Sn 449 (sokaparetassa vīṇā kacchā abhassatha); It 76 (kacchehi sedā muccanti: sweat drops from their armpits); J V.434 = DhA IV.197 (thanaŋ dasseti k°ŋ dass° nābhiŋ dass°); J V.435 (thanāni k° āni ca dassayantī; expl^d on p. 437 by upakacchaka); VI.578. The phrase parūḷha-kaccha-nakhaloma means "with long-grown finger-nails and long hair in the armpit," e. g. S I.78.
-loma (kaccha°) hair growing in the armpit Miln 163 (should probably be read parūḷha-k.-nakha-l., as above).

Kacchikāra see kacci°.

Kacchu [Derivation uncertain, cp. Sk. kacchu, dial. for kharju: perhaps connected with khajjati, eating, biting] 1. the plant Carpopogon pruriens, the fruit of which causes itch when applied to the skin DhA III.297 (mahā° -phalāni). — 2. itch, scab, a cutaneous disease, usually in phrase kacchuyā khajjati "to be eaten by itch" (cp. E. itch > eat) Vin I.202, 296; J V.207; Pv II.3¹¹ (cp. kapi°); Vism 345; DhA I.299.
-cuṇṇa the powdered fruit of Carpopogon pruriens, causing itch DhA III.297. -piḷakā scab & boils J V.207.

Kajjala [Sk. kajjala, dial. fr. kad + jala, from jalati, **jval**, orig. burning badly or dimly, a dirty burn] lamp-black or soot, used as a collyrium Vin II.50 (read k. for kapalla, cp. *J.P.T.S.* 1887, 167).

Kajjopakkamaka a kind of gem Miln 118 (vajira k. phussarāga lohitanka).

Kañcaka a kind of tree (dāsima°) J VI.536 (expl^d as "dve rukkhajātiyo"). BB have koñcaka.

Kañcana (nt.) [Derivation uncertain, cp. Sk. kāñcana, either from khacati (shine = the shining metal, cp. kāca (glass) & Sk. **kāś**), or from kanaka gold, cp. Gr. *κνηκός* (yellow). P. kañcana is poetical] gold A III.346 = Th 1, 691 (muttaŋ selā va k.); Th 2, 266 (k° ssa phalakaŋ va); VvA 4, 9 (= jātarūpa). Esp. freq. in cpds. = of or like gold.
-agghika a golden garland Bu X. 26. -agghiya id. Bu V.29. -āveḷā id. J VI.49; Vv 36²; Pv II.12⁷ (thus

for °ācela); III.9³; PvA 157. **-kadalikkhaṇḍa** a g. bunch of bananas J VI.13. **-thūpa** a gilt stupa DhA III.483; IV.120. **-patimā** a gilt or golden image or statue J VI.553; VvA 168. **-paṭṭa** a g. turban or coronet J VI.217. **-patta** a g. dish J V.377. **-pallanka** a gilt palanquin J I.204. **-bimba** the golden bimba fruit Vv 36⁸ (but expl^d at VvA 168 by majjita-k-paṭimā-sadisa "like a polished golden statue"). **-bubbula** a gilt ornament in form of a ball Mhvs 34, 74. **-rūpa** a g. figure J III.93. **-latā** g. strings surrounding the royal drum J VI.589. **-vaṇṇa** of g. colour, gilt, shining, bright J V.342 (=paṇḍara). **-velli** a g. robe, girdle or waist cloth J V.398 (but expl^d as "k-rūpaka-sadisa-sarīra "having a body like a g. statue"), cp. J V.306, where velli is expl^d by kacchā, girdle. **-sannibha** like g., golden-coloured (cp. k-vaṇṇa and Sk. kanaka-varṇa Sp. Av. Ś. I.121, 135, etc.), in phrase *°taca* "with golden-coloured skin," Ep. of the Buddha and one of the 32 signs of a great man (mahāpurisa-lakkhaṇa) D II.17; III.143, 159; M II.136; Miln 75; attr. of a devatā Vv 30², 32²; VvA 284; of a bhikkhu Sn 551=Th I. 821. **-sūci** a gold pin, a hair-pin of gold J VI.242.

Kañcanaka (adj.) golden J IV.379 (°daṇḍa).

Kañcuka [from **kañc** (kac) to bind, cp. Gr. κάκαλα fetter, Sk. kañcuka] I. a closely fitting jacket, a bodice Vin I.306=II.267; A I.145; DhA III.295 (paṭa°ŋ paṭimuñcitvā dressed in a close bodice); PvA 63 (urago tacaŋ kañcukaŋ omuñcanto viya). — 2. the slough of a snake (cp. I) DA I.222. — 3. armour, coat of mail J V.128 (sannāha°); DA I.157 (of leather); Dāvs V.14. — 4. a case, covering, encasement; of one pagoda incasing another: Mhvs I.42.

Kañjaka N. of a class of Titans PvA 272 (kāla-k°-bhedā Asurā; should we read khañjaka? Cp. Hardy, *Manual of Buddhism* 59).

Kañjika (nt.) [Sk. kāñjika] sour rice-gruel J I.238 (udaka°); Vv 33³⁷ (amba°), 43⁵ (=yāgu VvA 186); DhA I.78, 288; VvA 99 (ācāma-k°-loṇudaka as expl° of loṇa-sovīraka "salty fluid, i. e. the scum of sour gruel"). Cp. next.

Kañjiya (nt.)=kañjika; J III.145 (ambila°); VI.365 (°āpaṇa); DhA II.3; IV.164.
-tela a thick substance rising as a scum on rice-gruel, used in straightening arrows DhA I.288.

Kaññā (f.) [from kanīna young, compar. kanīyah, superl. kaniṣṭha; orig. "newly sprung" from ***qen**, cp. Gr. καινός, Vedic kanyā, Lat. re-cen(t)s, Ags. hindema "novissimus." See also kaniṭṭha] a young (unmarried) woman, maiden, girl Pv I.11¹. — As emblem of beauty in simile khattiya-kaññā vā . . . pannarasa-vassuddesikā vā solasa-vassuddesikā vā . . . M I.88; in comb^n khattiya-kaññā, brāhmaṇa-k°, etc. A II.205; IV.128; Kisāgotamī nāma khattiya-k° J I.60; deva° a celestial nymph J I.61.
-dāna giving away of a girl in marriage Pgdp 85.

Kaṭa¹ [Sk. kaṭa from kṛṇatti: to do wicker-work, roll up, plait; ***gert**, cp. Gr. κάρταλος, Lat. cratis=E. crate, Goth. haurds, E. hurdle] a mat: see cpds. & kaṭallaka.
-sara a reed: Saccharum Sara, used as medicine DhsA 78. **-sāra** (DhA I.268) & **sāraka** a mat for sitting or lying on, made of the stalks of the screw-pine, Pandanus Furcatus J VI.474; V.97; DA I.137; DhA II.183

Kaṭa² another form of kaṭi (hip), only used in cpds.:
-aṭṭhika the hip-bone D II.296=M I.58, 89=M III.92 (as v.l.). *Note.* kaṭiṭṭhika at M III.92 and as v.l. at D II.296. **-sāṭaka** a loin-cloth J IV.248.

Kaṭa³=kata [pp. of karoti] in meaning of "original," good (cp. sat); as nt. "the lucky die" in phrase kaṭaggaha (see below). Also in comb^n with su° & duk° for sukata & dukkata (e. g. Vin II.289; DhA III.486; IV.150), and in meaning of "bad, evil" in kaṭana. Cp. also kali.
-ggaha "he who throws the lucky die," one who is lucky, fortunate, in phrase "ubhayattha k." lucky in both worlds, i. e. here & beyond Th I, 462; J IV.322 (=jayaggaha victorious C.); cp. Morris in *J.P.T.S.* 1887, 159. Also in "ubhayam ettha k." S IV.351 sq. — Opposed to **kali** the unlucky die, in phrase kaliŋ gaṇhāti to have bad luck J VI.206 (kaliggaha=parājayasaŋkhāta, i. e. one who is defeated, as opp. to kaṭaggaha=jayasankhāta), 228, 282.

Kaṭaka (m. nt.) anything circular, a ring, a wheel (thus in kara° Vin II.122); a bracelet PvA 134.

Kaṭakañcukatā see kaṭu°.

Kaṭakaṭāyati=taṭataṭāyati to crush, grind, creak, snap PugA. I.34; VvA 121 (as v.l.); Vism 264. Cp. also karakarā.

Kaṭacchu [cp. on etym. Morris in *J.P.T.S.* 1887, 163] a ladle, a spoon; expl^d by uḷunka DhA IV.75, 123; by dabbi PvA 135. Used for butter VvA 68, otherwise for cooked food in general, esp. rice gruel. — Vin II.216; J I.454; III.277.
-gāha "holding on to one's spoon," i. e. disinclination to give food, niggardliness, stinginess DhsA 376, cp. Dhs trsl. 300 n². **-gāhika** "spoon in hand," serving with ladles (in the distribution of food at the Mahādāna) PvA 135. **-parissāvana** a perforated ladle Vin II.118. **-bhikkhā** "ladle-begging," i. e. the food given with a ladle to a bhikkhu when he calls at a house on his begging tour Th I, 934; Miln 9; DhA IV.123; as representing a small gift to one individual, opposed to the Mahādanā Pv II.9⁶⁷; as an individual meal contrasted with public feeding (salāka-bhatta) DhA I.379. **-matta** (**bhatta**) "only a spoonful of rice" Miln 8; DhA IV.75.

Kaṭacchuka (adj.) relating to spoons Vin II.233.

Kaṭana (nt.) [from kaṭa, pp. of karoti] an evil deed A IV.172 (v.l.=AA 744 kaṭanaŋ vuccati pāpakammaŋ).

Kaṭallaka [to kaṭa¹] a puppet (pagliaccio), a marionette with some contrivance to make it dance J V.16 (dāru°, expl^d by dārumaya-yanta-rūpaka).

Kaṭasī (f.) [prob. a contamination of kaṭa + sīva(thikā), charnel-house, under influence of foll. va(ḍḍh°), cp. Sk. kaṭa (?) a corpse] a cemetery; only in phrase **kaṭasiŋ vaḍḍheti** "to increase the cemetery, referring to dying and being buried repeatedly in the course of numerous rebirths, expl^d by susāna & āḷāhana ThA 291. —vaḍḍhenti kaṭasiŋ ghoraŋ ādiyanti punabbhavaŋ Vin II.296=A II.54=Th I, 456 (where ācinanti (?) for ādiy°), 575; Th 2, 502. Also in cpds. **°vaḍḍhana** J I.146; Ud 72=Nett 174; **°vaḍḍhita** S II.178 sq.=Nd² 664.

Kaṭākaṭa see kata I.3.

Kaṭāha (m. nt.) [Sk. kaṭāha] a pot [in older texts only as —°]. — I. pot, vessel, vase, receptacle. **udaka°** Vin II.122; **ghaṭi°** Vin II.115; **loha°** Vin II.170. **ayo°** (in simile "diva-santatte ayokaṭāhe") M I.453=A IV.138; **gūtha°** Vin IV.265; **tumba°** (a gourd used as receptacle for food) Vin II.114; **alābu°** DhsA 405. — Uncompounded only at Dpvs 92 (°ka); Mhvs 17, 47; 18, 24. — 2. anything shaped like a pot, as the skull: **sīsa°** D II.297=M I.58; Miln 197.

Kaṭi [Sk. kaṭi, ***(s)quel**; orig. bending, curvature, cp. Gr. σκέλος hip, Lat. scelus crooked deed, Ger. scheel squint] hip, waist Vin III.22, 112; Nd² 659; J IV.32; Miln 418. In cpds. also **kaṭa** (q. v.).

-thālaka a cert. bone on the small of the back J VI.509. -padesa the buttocks J III.37. -pamāṇa (adj.) as far as the waist J VI.593. -pariyosāna the end of the hips, the bottom J II.275. -puthulaka (adj.) with broad hips, having beautiful hips J V.303 (in expl^n of soṇī puthulā). -bhāga the waist J III.373. -bhāra a burden carried on the hip (also a way of carrying children) Vin II.137; III.49. -sandhi the joint of the hip Miln 418, Vism 185. -samohita (adj.) fastened or clinging to the waist J V.206. -sutta a belt, girdle (as ornament) PvA 134. -suttaka a string or cord around the waist to fasten the loin-cloth Vin II.271; also an ornamental waist-band, girdle Vin II.107 (see *Vin. Texts* III.69, 142, 348).

Kaṭuka (adj.) [Sk. kaṭu(ka), from *(s)qner to cut; cp. Sk. kṛṇoti (kṛntati), Lat. caro "cutlet." — k. is almost exclusively poetical; usually expl^d in prose by aniṭṭha, tikhiṇa, ghora (of niraya); often comb^d with khara, opp. madhura, e. g. PvA 119] sharp, bitter, acid, severe. — 1. severe, sharp (fig.), of dukkha, vedanā, kāmā, etc. M I.10 = A II.143; J VI.115; Th 2, 451 (= ThA 281); SA 56. — painful, terrible, frightful (-appl^d to the fruits of evil actions and to the sufferings in Niraya: see kammapphala & niraya) J III.519; Pv I.10^2, 11^1; IV.1^8, 7^6. — bitter, or perhaps pungent of taste DhS 291; Miln 65, 112; J III.201. — 2. (nt.) pungency, acidity, bitterness D II.349 = J I.380; Th 2, 503 (pañca°); J VI.509. — *Note.* Is k. to be written instead of kadukkha at VvA 316, where it explains maraṇa? Cp. J III.201: tesaŋ taŋ kaṭukaŋ āsi, maraṇaŋ ten' upāgamuŋ.

-udraya causing bitterness or pain J V.241, cp. dukkhudraya J V.119. -odaka a bitter draught Sdhp 159. -pabhedana (adj.) having a pungent juice exuding from the temples, said of an elephant in rut Dh 324 (= tikhiṇamada DhA IV.13). -pphala a kind of perfume made of the berry of an aromatic plant J II.416 = DhA III.475 (kappūra-k°-ādīni), cp. Sk. kakkolaka. — (adj.) of bitter fruit J II.106 (of the mango); S I.57 = J III.291 = Dh 66 (of kamma); Pv I.11^{10} (id.). -bhaṇḍa (sg. & pl.) spices. There are 4 enum^d at J III.86: hingujīraka, singiveraka, marica, pipphali; 3 at VvA 186 (as tikaṭuka, cp. kaṭula): ajamoja, hingujīraka, lasuṇa; PvA 135; DhA II.131. -bhāva stinginess DhsA 376. -rohiṇī the black hellebore Vin I.201 (as medicine). -vipāka (adj.) having a bitter result (of pāpa) Miln 206; compar. °tara S II.128. -sāsana a harsh command J VI.498.

Kaṭukañcukatā (f.) [der. by Bdhgh. as kaṭuka + añcuka (añc), a popular etymology (DhsA 376). At Dhs 1122 and as v.l. K in Vbh we have the spelling **kaṭakancukatā** (for kaṭakuñcakatā?), on which and °kuñcaka see Morris, *J.P.T.S.* 1887, 159 sq. and *Dhs. trsl.* 300 n^2. — Morris' derivation is kaṭa (**kar**) + kañcuka + tā (kañcuka = kuñcaka to **kuñc**, to contract), thus a der^n fr. kañcuka "bodice" and meaning "being tightened in by a bodice," i. e. tightness. Although the reading kaṭukañc° is the established reading, the var. lect. **kaṭakuñc°** is probably etym. correct, semantically undoubtedly better. It has undergone dissimilatory vowel-metathesis under influence of popular analogy with kaṭuka. With kuñcikatā cp. the similar expression derived from the same root: **kuṇali-mukha**, of a stingy person Pv II.9^{28}, which is expl^d by "sanku citaŋ mukhaŋ akāsi" (see kuñcita)] closeness, tightness, close-fistedness, niggardliness. Expl^d as "the shrinking up of the heart," which prevents the flow or manifestation of generosity. It occurs only in the stock phrase "vevicchaŋ kadariyaŋ k. aggahitattaŋ cittassa" in **macchariya**-passage at Nd^2 614 = Dhs 1122 = Pug 19, 23 = Vbh 357, 371; and in the macchariya expl^n at Vism 470.

Kaṭukatta (nt.) pungency, acidity, bitterness Miln 56, 63.

Kaṭumikā (f.) [from karoti; see Sk. kṛtrima & kuṭṭima; also kutta & kutti] artificiality, outward help, suggestion, appl^d to sati Miln 78, 79 (cp. *Miln trsl.* I.121 n and MVastu I.477).

Kaṭula (adj.) [Sk. kaṭura] containing pungent substances (generally three: tekaṭula) Vin I.210 (yāgu), cp. tikaṭuka.

Kaṭuviya (adj.) [kaṭu viya?] impure, defiled, in °kata A I.280.

Kaṭerukkha a kind of creeper J VI.536 (perhaps read as next).

Kaṭeruha a flowering plant J VI.537 (= pupphagaccha). Cp. kaseruka.

Kaṭṭha^1 [Sk. kṛṣṭa, pp. of kasati, cp. kiṭṭha] ploughed, tilled Sn 80; Miln 255; PvA 45, 62. -a° untilled, unprepared Anvs 27. -su° well-ploughed A I.229; Miln 255.

Kaṭṭha^2 (adj.) [Sk. kaṣṭa] bad, useless: see kaṭṭhaka^2. Only in cpds.; perhaps also in pakaṭṭhaka.

-anga pithless, sapless, of no value (of trees) J II.163 = DhA I.144. -mukha "with the injurious mouth," a kind of snake DhsA 300.

Kaṭṭha^3 (nt.) [Brh. kāṣṭha, cp. Ohg. holz] 1. a piece of wood, esp. a stick used as fuel, chips, firewood S I.168 = Sn 462; M I.234 (+ kaṭhala); PvA 256 (+ tiṇa). In phrase "sattussada sa-tiṇa-kaṭṭh' odaka sa-dhañña" (densely populated with good supply of grass, firewood, water, and corn) in ster. description of a prosperous place (cp. Xenophon's πόλις οἰκουμένη εὐδαίμων καὶ μεγάλη D I.87, 111, etc.). Both sg. (coll.) & pl. as "sticks" D II.341, esp. in phrase **kaṭṭhaŋ** phāleti to chop sticks Vin I.31; Sn p. 104; J II.144; Pv II.9^{51} (= PvA 135), or k°ŋ pāteti (phāteti = phāleti? See pāteti) M I.21. Frequent also in similes: M I.241 = II.93 = III.95 (alla k.); M III.242 = S II.97 = IV.215 = V.212 (dve k.); A III.6 (+ kaṭhala); IV.72 (+ tiṇa); I.124 = Pug 30, 36 (+ kaṭhala). — 2. a piece of stick used for building huts (wattle and daub) M I.190. — 3. a stick, in **avalekhana°** (for scraping) Vin II.141, 221, and in **danta°** a tooth-pick VvA 63, etc. (see danta). — 4. (adj.) in cpds. = of wood, wooden.

-aggi wood-fire, natural fire A IV.41, 45, enumerated last among the 7 fires. -atthaŋ for the purpose of fuel, in phrase k. pharati to serve as fuel A II.95 = S III.93 = It 90 = J I.482. -atthara a mat made of twigs (cp. kaṭasāra) J V.197, also as -attharika (& °kā) J VI.21; DhA I.135; f. at J I.9; IV.329; VI.57. -kalingara chips and chaff DhA III.122 (cp. k-khaṇḍa). -khaṇḍa a piece of wood, splinter, chip, suggesting something useless, trifling DhA I.321 (as expl^n of niratthaŋ va kalingaraŋ); ThA 284 (as expl^n of chuṭṭho kalingaraŋ viya). -tāla a wooden key Vin II.148 (cp. *Vin. Texts* III.162). -tāḷa a w. gong DhsA 319. -tumba a w. vessel Vin I.205. -pādukā a wooden shoe, clog Vin I.188. -puñja a heap of w. A IV.72; J II.327. -phālaka wood-cutter Vism 413. -bhatin a wood-cutter Dpvs 20, 28, where given as a nickname of King Tissa. -mañcaka a wooden bed Miln 366. -maya wooden Vin I.203; J I.289 = V.435. -rūpa (& °ka) a w. figure, doll J I.287. -vāha a cartload of fire-wood S II.84. -vāhana riding on a faggot J I.136. -vipalāvita drifting wood J I.326. -hatthin a w. elephant, built by order of King Caṇḍapajjota to decoy King Udena (cp. the horse of Troy) DhA I.193. -hāraka (f. °ikā) gathering fire-wood, an occupation of poor people M I.79; S I.180; J I.134; II.412; IV. 148; V.417; Miln 331; Vism 120; VvA 173. -hārin = °hāraka Vin III.41; J I.133 (title of J no. 7, referred to at DhA I.349).

Kaṭṭhaka^1 (m. nt.) [to kaṭṭha^3] a kind of reed Dh 164; DhA III.156 (= velu-sankhāta-kaṭṭha).

Kaṭṭhaka^2 (m. pl.) [to kaṭṭha^2] a kind of fairy D II.261

Kaṭṭhissa (nt.) [Sk. ?] a silken coverlet embroidered with gems D I.7 = Vin I.192 = II.163; DA I.87 = AA 445.

Kaṭhati [Sk. kvathati; cp. Goth. hvaþo scum, hvaþjan to seethe. The Dhātumañjūsā (no. 132, ed. Andersen & Smith) comments on **kaṭh** with "sosāna-pākesu." See also kuthati] 1. to boil, to stew Bdhgh on Vin I.205, see *Vin. Texts* II.57 n¹, where pp. is given as kuthita. Similarly Th 2, 504 (cp. *Sisters* 174 n⁴, but cp. *Mil. trs.* II.271 "distressed"; E. Müller, *J.R.A.S.* 1910, 539). — 2. to be scorched, pp. **kaṭhita** (= hot) Miln 323, 325, 357, 397. — The pp. occurs as °kaṭṭhita & °kuṭṭhita in cpds uk° pa° (q. v.). See also kuṭṭhita.

Kaṭhala [Sk. kaṭhara (°la, °lla, °lya: all found in Av. Ś and Divy), to kṛṇāti; cp. khāṭi] gravel, pebble, potsherd J III.225; V.417; VvA 157; comb^d with **sakkhara** at D I.84 = A I.9, and in simile at A I.253. As f. comb^d with **kaṭṭha** at A I.124 = Pug 30, 36; A III.6; as m. in same comb^n at Vism 261.

Kaṭhalaka gravel, potsherd J III.227; Miln 34.

Kaṭhina (adj.-n.) [Sk. kaṭhina & kaṭhora with dial. ṭh for rth; cp. Gr. κρατύς, κρατερός strong, κράτος strength; Goth. hardus = Ags. heard = E. hard. Cp. also Sk. kṛtsna = P. kasiṇa]. 1. (adj.) hard, firm, stiff. Cp. II.2; Dhs 44, 45 (where also der. f. abstr. akaṭhinatā absence of rigidity, comb^d with akakkhalatā, cp. DhsA 151 **akaṭhina-bhāva**); PvA 152 (°dāṭha).—(fig.) hard, harsh, cruel J I.295 = V.448 (= thaddha-hadaya); adv. °ŋ fiercely, violently Miln 273, 274.—2. (nt.) the cotton cloth which was annually supplied by the laity to the bhikkhus for the purpose of making robes Vin I.253 sq.; also a wooden frame used by the bh. in sewing their robes Vin. II.115-117. — On the k. robe see Vin. I.298 sq.; III.196 sq., 203 sq., 261 sq.; IV.74, 100, 245 sq., 286 sq.; V.15, 88, 119, 172 sq.; 218. Cp. *Vin. Texts* I.18; II.148; III.92.

-attharaṇa the dedication of the k. cloth Vin I.266, see next. **-atthāra** the spreading out, i. e. dedication of the k. cloth by the people to the community of bhikkhus. On rules concerning this distribution and description of the ceremony see Vin I.254 sq.; Bu IX.7; cp. Vin V.128 sq., 205 **-uddhāra** the withdrawal or suspension of the five privileges accorded to a bhikkhu at the k. ceremony Vin I.255, 259; III.262; IV.287, 288; V.177-179, cp. next & *Vin. Texts* II.157, 234, 235. **-ubbhāra** = °uddhāra, in kaṭhinassa ubbhārāya "for the suspension of the k. privileges" Vin I.255. **-khandhaka** the chapter or section treating of k., the 7th of the Mahāvagga of the Vinaya Vin II.253-267. **-cīvara** a k. robe made of k. cloth Bu IX.7. **-dussa** the k. cloth Vin I.254. **-maṇḍapa** a shed in which the bhikkhus stitched their k. cloth into robes Vin II.117. **-rajju** string used to fix the k. cloth on to the frame Vin II.116. **-sālā** = °maṇḍapa Vin II.116.

Kaṭhinaka (adj.) referring to the kaṭhina cloth Vin V.61, 114.

Kaḍḍhati [dialect. form supposed to equal Sk. karṣati, cp. Prk. kaḍḍhai to pull, tear, khaḍḍā pit, dug-out. See also Bloomfield, *J.A.O.S.* XIV. 1921 p. 465.] 1. to draw out, drag, pull, tug J I.193, 225, 265, 273 (khaggaŋ k. to draw the sword). — 2. to draw in, suck up (udakaŋ) J IV.141. — 3. to draw a line, to scratch J. I.78, 111, 123; VI.56 (lekhaŋ).

Kaḍḍhana (nt.). 1. pulling, drawing Miln 231. — 2. refusing, rejecting, renunciation, appl. to the self-denial of missionary theras following Gotama Buddha's example Mhvs 12, 55.

Kaḍḍhanaka (adj.) pulling, dragging J V.260.

Kaṇa [Derivation uncertain, possibly connected with kana; positive of kanīyān = small; Vedic kaṇa] the fine red powder between the husk and the grain of rice, husk-powder D I.9 (°homa), expl^d at DA I.93 by kuṇḍaka. — (adj.) made of husk-powder or of finely broken rice, of cakes J I.423 (k-pūva = kuṇḍakena pakka-pūva). —**akaṇa** (adj.) free from the coating of red powder, characteristic of the best rice Mhvs 5, 30; Anvs 27 (akaṇaŋ karoti to whiten the rice). Cp. kākaṇa.

-bhakkha eating husk-powder, a practice of cert. ascetics D I.166 = M I.78 = A I.241≈.

Kaṇaya [Derivation unknown, cp. Sk. kaṇaya = kaṇapa] a sort of spear, lance J I.273; II.364 (like a spear, of a bird's beak); Miln 339.

-agga the point of a spear J I.329 (like . . ., of a beak).

Kaṇavīra [Sk. karavīra] Nerium odorum, oleander, the flower of which is frequently used in the garland worn by criminals when led to the place of execution (cp. Rouse, *J. trsl.* IV.119 and Mṛcchakaṭika X. beginning: diṇṇa-kalavīla-dāme. See also under kaṇṭha) Vism 183 (n); DhsA 317; SnA 283; VvA 177; cp. next.

Kaṇavera = kaṇavīra J III.61; IV.191; V.420; VI.406.

Kaṇājaka (nt.) a porridge of broken rice, eaten together with sour gruel (bilanga-dutiya; always in this comb° except at J V.230) Vin II.77 (cp. *Vin. Texts* III.9); S I.90, 91; A I.145; IV.392; J I.228; III.299; DhA III.10; IV.77; VvA 222, 298 (corr. bilanka; Hardy at VvA Index p. 364 expl. as "a certain weight"(?)).

-bhatta a meal of k. porridge J V.230.

Kaṇikā (f.) [cp. kaṇa] 1. a small particle of broken rice (opp. taṇḍula a full grain) J VI.341, 366 (°āhi pūvaŋ pacitvā). 2. a small spot, a freckle, mole, in a° (adj.) having no moles D I.80, and sa° with moles D. I.80 (cp. DA I.223).

Kaṇikāra (m. nt.) & **kaṇṇikāra** J IV.440; V.420; the difference stated at J. V.422 is kaṇi° = mahāpupdhā kaṇṇi° = khuddakapupphā) [Sk. karṇikāra]—1. (m.) the tree Pterospermum acerifolium J. I.40; V.295; VI.269, 537. — 2. (nt.) its (yellow) flower (k-puppha), taken metaphorically as typical emblem of yellow and of brightness. Thus in similes at D. II.111 (= pīta) = M II.14 (ṇṇ) = A V.61 (ṇṇ); DhA I.388; of the yellow robes (kāsāyāni) J II.25; with ref. to the blood of the heart Vism 256; = golden VvA 65; DhA II.250 (v. l. ṇṇ).

-makula a k. bud J. II.83.

Kaṇerika (nt.) a helmet (?) J VI.397.

Kaṇeru (m. f.) [Derivation uncertain, just possibly connected with kara, trunk. Sanskrit has kareṇu, but the medieval vocabularies give also kaṇeru] a young elephant J II.342; IV.49; V.39, 50, 416; VI.497; DhA I.196 (v. l.) kareṇukā) — f. °kā M I.178. — See also **kareṇu**.

Kaṇṭa (cp. next) a thorn Miln 351.

Kaṇṭaka [From kantati* to cut. Brh. kaṇṭaka. Spelt also kaṇṭhaka] 1. a thorn Sn 845; Vin I.188; J V.102; VI.105 (in description of the Vetaraṇī); cp. kusa°. — 2. any instrument with a sharp point Sdhp 201. — 3. a bone, fish-bone J I.222; in **piṭṭhi°** a bone of the spine D II.297≈ (see kaṭaṭṭhi); M I.80 = 245; Vism 271; Sdhp 102. — 4. (fig.) an obstacle, hindrance, nuisance ("thorn in my side"); Kvu 572; enemy, infestor; a dacoit, thief, robber D I.135 (sa° and a°, of the country as infested with dacoits or free from them, cp. DA I.296); J. I.186 (paṭikaṇṭaka, enemy); V.450; Th 1, 946; DhA I.177 (akkhimhi); VvA 301. — 5. (fig.) anything sharp, thorny, causing pain: of kāmā (passions) S IV.189, 195, 198; Ud 24; Kvu 202; cp. sa°. — Thus grouped, like saŋyojanāni, into 10 obstacles to perfection (dasa k.) A V.134; as "bringing much trouble" J IV.117. Often in standing phrase khāṇu-kaṇṭaka stumbling and obstruction A I.35; SnA 334. As abstr. kaṇṭakattaŋ hindrance at Vism 269 (sadda°). —akaṇṭaka 1. free from thorns J II.118; V.260. — 2. (fig.) free from thieves, quiet, peaceful D I.135; also not difficult, easy, happy, bringing blessings (of the right path) A V.135; Vv 18[7]; VvA 96. —sakaṇṭaka 1. having bones (of food) J IV.192, 193. — 2. (fig.) beset with thieves, dangerous D I.135; thorny, i. e. painful, miserable (of duggati and kāmā) S IV.195; Th 2, 352; J V.260. — Cp. also kaṇḍaka and nikkaṇṭaka.

-āpacita covered with thorns J VI.249 (cp. °ācita); -āpassaya (= kaṇṭak' apāśraya) a bed made of an outstretched skin, under which are placed thorns or iron spikes; to lie or stand on such is a practice of certain naked ascetics D I.167 = M I.78≈. -āpassayika (adj. to prec.) "bed-of-thorns-man" D I.167≈. At J I.493 the reading is k-āpassaya, at III.74 k-apassaya; at III.235 the reading is kaṇṭhaka-seyyaŋ kappetha (should it be k-āpassaye seyyaŋ k° ?); D I.167 reads kaṇṭhakā-passayika. -ācita covered with thorns J V.167. -ādhāna a thorny brake, a thorny hedge M I.10 (k-dhāna; for dhāna = ṭhāna see dhāna & cp. rāja-dhānī); A I.35; Miln 220. -kasā a thorny whip used for punishment and torture J III.41. -gahana a thorny thicket or jungle S II.228. -gumba a th. bush J I.208. -latā a th. creeper, the Capparis Zeilanica J V.175. -vaṭṭa a thorny brake or hedge M I.448.

Kaṇṭaki (*f.*) in cpd. °vāṭa a thorny fence (cactus hedge?) Vin II.154.

Kaṇṭha [*quent from *quelt, primarily neck, cp. Lat. collus "the turner." Syn. with k. is gīvā, primarily throat, Brh. kaṇṭha] 1. throat A IV.131; J V.448; Miln 152 (kaṇṭho ākurati, is hoarse); PvA 280 (akkharāni mahatā kaṇṭhena uccaritāni). The throat of Petas is narrow and parched with thirst: PvA 99 (k-oṭṭha-tālūnaŋ tassita), 180 (sūci° like a needle's eye, cp. sūcicchidda. v. l. sūcikaṭṭha "whose bones are like needles"), 260 (visukkha-k-ṭṭha-jivhā). — 2. neck Vin I.15; Dh 307 (kāsāva°); Vv 64[17] (expl[d] at VvA 280 by gīvūpagasīsūpagādi-ābharaṇāni). Esp. in loc. kaṇṭhe round the neck, with ref. to var. things tied round, e. g. kuṇapaŋ k. āsattaŋ A IV.377; kuṇapaŋ k. baddhaŋ J I.5; k. mālā J I.166, 192; k. bandhanti vaḍḍhanaŋ J III.226; with the wreath of karavīra flowers (q. v.) on a criminal ready for execution: rattavaṇṇa-virala-mālāya bandhakaṇṭha PvA 4 (cp. AvŚ I.102; II.182: karavīra-mālābaddha [sakta II.182]-kaṇṭheguṇa).

-kūpa the cavity of the throat Mhbv 137. -ja produced in the throat, i. e. guttural Sāsv 150. -suttaka an ornamental string or string of beads worn round the neck Vin II.106.

Kaṇṭhaka[1] thorn, see kaṇṭaka

Kaṇṭhaka[2] N. of Gotama's horse, on which he left his father's palace Mhbv 25; spelt kanthaka at J I.54, 62 sq.

Kaṇḍa (m. nt.) [perhaps as *kaldno fr. *kalad to break, cp. Gr. κλαδαρός, Lat. clades, etc., Sk. kāṇḍa. See also khagga and khaṇḍa] 1. the portion of a stalk or cane between one knot and another; the whole stalk or shaft; the shaft of an arrow, an arrow in general M I.429 (two kinds of arrows: kaccha & ropima, cp. kaṇḍa-cittaka); J I.150; II.91; III.273; V.39; Miln 44, 73; Mhvs 25, 89. As arrow also in the "Tell" story of Culladhanuggaha at J III.220 & DhA IV.66. — 2. a section, portion or paragraph of a book DA I.12; Pgdp 161. — 3. a small portion, a bit or lump DhA I.134 (pūva°); Mhvs 17, 35. — 4. kaṇḍaŋ (adv.) a portion of time, for a while, a little Pgdp 36. — See also khaṇḍa, with which it is often confounded. Der. upa-kaṇḍakin (adj.) (thin) like a stalk or arrow Pv. II.1[13] (of a Petī).

-gamana the going of an arrow, i. e. the distance covered by an arrow in flight, a bow-shot J II.334; cp. kaṇḍu. -cittaka (Sk. kāṇḍa-citraka) an excellent arrow A. II.202. -nāḷi a quiver J III.220. -pahāra an arrow-shot, arrow-wound Miln 16 (ekena k-paharena dve mahākāyā padālitā "two birds killed with one stone"), 73. -vāraṇa (adj.) warding off arrows, appl. to a shield J VI.592 (nt.); a shield J IV.366.

Kaṇḍaka = kaṇṭaka Vin II.318 (Bdhgh.); A III.383; Bu XIII.29. —akaṇḍaka free from thieves, safe, secure PvA 161.

Kaṇḍarā (f.) sinew, tendon Vin I.91, 322 (in cpd. kaṇḍara-cchinna one whose tendons (of the feet) have been cut); Kvu 23, 31; Vism 253, 254 (where KhA 49 reads miñja).

Kaṇḍita at J I.155 is misprint; read: kaṇḍam assa atthi ti kaṇḍī taŋ kaṇḍinaŋ.

Kaṇḍin (adj.) having a shaft inserted, appl. to the head of an arrow (salla) J I.155; (m.) an archer ibid.

Kaṇḍu[1] (f.) [perhaps from *kanad to bite, scratch; cp. Sk. kandara, Gr. κναδάλλω to bite, κνώδων, κνώδαλον, etc., Sk. kaṇḍu m. & f.] the itch, itching, itchy feeling, desire to scratch Vin I.202, 296; J. V.198; Vism 345. kaṇḍuŋ karoti to make or cause to itch J V.198; vineti to allay the itch, to scratch J V.199.—(fig.) worldly attachment, irritation caused by the lusts, in "kaṇḍuŋ saŋhanti" (as result of jhāna) A IV. 437.

-uppala a kind of lotus-blossom Dāvs IV.48; -paṭicchādi an "itch-cloth," i. e. a covering allowed to the bhikkhus when suffering from itch or other cutaneous disease Vin I.296, 297; IV.171, 172. -rogin (adj.) suffering from the itch Khus 105.

Kaṇḍu°[2] [= kaṇḍa in comp[n]] an arrow-shot (as measure), in sahassa-kaṇḍu sata-bheṇḍu Th I, 164 = J II.334 (but the latter: sata-bhedo), expl[d] at Th I, 164[n] by sahassakaṇḍo sahassa [sata ?]-bhūmako and at J II.334 by sahassa-kaṇḍubbedho ti pāsādo satabhūmiko ahosi; in preceding lines the expression used is "sahassa-kaṇḍagamanaŋ uccaŋ."

Kaṇḍuka the itch, itchy feeling, irritation J V.198.

Kaṇḍuvati (kandūvati) [Denom. fr. kaṇḍu. Sk. kandūyati] 1. to itch, to be itchy, to be irritated, to suffer from itch Vin I.205; II.121; J V.198 (kaṇḍuvāyati); DhA III.297 (kaṇḍūvantī). — 2. to scratch, rub, scrape A. II.207; J VI.413; Pug 56.

Kaṇḍuvana (nt.) [fr. kaṇḍūvati] 1. itching, itchy feeling DhA I.440; cp. Dhātumañjūsā no. 416 kaṇḍūvana.— 2. scratching, scraping M I.508; J II.249 (appl. to bad music).

Kaṇḍusa (nt) a strip of cloth used to mark the kaṭhina robe, in °karaṇa Vin I.254, and °ka ibid. 290.

Kaṇḍūyana (nt.) [See kaṇḍuvana] the itch J V.69.

Kaṇḍolikā (f.) a wicker-basket or stand Vin II.114, 143 (see *Vin. Texts* III.86).

Kaṇṇa [Vedic karṇa, orig. not associated with hearing, therefore not used to signify the sense (sota is used instead; cp. akkhi > cakkhu), but as "projection" to *ker, from which also Sk. śṛṅga horn. Cp. Gr. κόρυς helmet; Lat. cornu & cervus = E. corner, horn & hart. Further related Sk. aśri (caturaśraḥ four-cornered), śaṣkuli auditory passage; Lat. ācer = Gr. ἄκρις, ἄκανος, ὀξύς; Ger. ecke; also Sk. śūla & P. koṇa] 1. a corner, an angle Vin I.48, 286; J I.73; III.42; V.38; VI.519; PvA 74; DhA II.178; Dāvs II.111. —cīvara° the edge of the garment Vism 389. Freq. in cpd. catu° (catukkaṇṇa) four-cornered, square, as Ep. of Niraya Nd[2] 304[III]. = Pv I.10[13] (expl[d] by catu-koṇa).

Also of cloth Vin II.228; J I.426; IV.250. — 2. the ear Sn 608; J I.146, 194; DhA I.390 (dasā°). Freq. in phrase **kaṇṇaŋ** chindati (to cut off the ear) as punishment, e. g. A I.47. — loc. **kaṇṇe** in the ear, i. e. in a low tone, in a whisper DhA I.166. — 3. the tip of a spoon J. I.347. —**assakaṇṇa** N. of a tree (see under assa[3]).

-**alankāra** an ornament for the ear J V.409. -**āyata** (mutta) (a pearl) inserted in the lobe of the ear J II. 275, 276. -**kita** (should it be kaṇha° ? cp. paŋsukita, malaggakita; kita=kata) spoiled, rusty, blunt Vin II.115 (of needles); dirty, mouldy Vin I.48 (of a floor); II.209 (of walls); stained, soiled Vin IV.281 (of robes). -**gūthaka** the cerumen, wax, of the ear, Vin II.134; Sn 197= J I.146. -**cālana** shaking the ears J III.99. -**cūḷa** the root of the ear J VI.488; as °cūlikā at J II.276; Vism 255; DhA IV.13. -**chidda** (nt.) the orifice of the ear, the outer auditory passage (cp. sūci-chidda eye of the needle) Vin III.39; J II.244, 261. -**chinna** one whose ears are cut off Vin I.322; Kvu 31. -**cheda** cutting or tearing off of the ear Miln 197, 290. -**jappaka** one who whispers into the ear, one who tells secretly, also a gossip Vin II.98; **sa°** whispered into the ear, appl. to a method of taking votes ibid. Cp. upakaṇṇakajappin. -**jappana** whispering into the ear D I.11; DA I.97. -**tela** anointing the ear with medicinal oil D I.12 (expl[d] at DA I.98, where reading is °telanaŋ). -**nāsa** ear & nose J II.117; Miln 5 (°chinna). -**patta** the lobe of the ear J V.463. As °panta at ThA 211. -**pāli**=°patta Th 2, 259 (expl[d] by °panta). -**piṭṭhī** the upper part or top of the ear DhA I.394. -**puccha** the "tail" or flap of the ear Sdhp 168. -**bila** orifice of the ear Vism 195. -**bheri** a sort of drum. Cp. IX.24. -**mala** "ear-dirt," ear-wax, in *°haraṇī*, an instrument for removing the wax from the ear Vin II.135. -**mālā** a garland from corner to corner (of a temple) Dāvs II.111. -**muṇḍa** I. (adj.) one whose ears have been shorn or clipped Pv II.12[18] (of the dog of Hell, cp. PvA 152 chinnakaṇṇa). — 2. (°ka) "with blunt corners," N. of the first one of the fabulous 7 Great Lakes (satta-mahā-sarā) in the Himavant, enum[d] at J V.415; Vism 416; DA I.164. -**mūla** the root of the ear, the ear in gen. J I.335; III.124; loc. fig in a low tone DhA I.173; near, near by DhA II.8 (mama k.). -**roga** a disease of the ear DhsA 340. -**vallī** the lobe of the ear Mhvs 25, 94. -**vijjhana** perforating the ear, *°mangala* the ceremony of ear-piercing DhA II.87; cp. mangala. -**vedha** (cp. prec.) ear-piercing, a quasi religious ceremony on children J V.167. -**sakkhali** & °**ikā** the orifice or auditory passage of the ear DhA I.148; DhsA 334, in which latter passage *°ikaŋ paharati* means to impinge on the ear (said of the wind); *°ikaŋ bhindati* (=bhindanto viya paharati) to break the ear (with unpleasant words) DhA II.178 (T. sankhaliŋ, v. l. sakkhaliŋ). -**sankhali** a small chain attached to the ear with a small ornament suspended from it J V.438. -**sandhovika** washing the ears A V.202. -**sukha** I. (adj.) pleasant to the ear, agreeable D I.4=M I.179, 268 =A II.209≈; Miln I; DA I.75=DhsA 397; — 2. (nt.) pleasant speech J II.187; V.167; opp. kaṇṇa-sūla. -**sutta** an ornamental string hanging from the ear Vin II.143. -**suttaka** a string from corner to corner, a clothes-line Vin I.286. -**sūla** I. a piercing pain (lit. stake) in the ear, ear-ache VvA 243. — 2. what is disagreeable to hear, harsh speech DhsA 397 (opp. °sukha).

-**sota** the auditory passage, the ear (+ nāsika-sotāni, as **ubho** sotāni, i. e. heṭṭhā & uparimā) D I.106=Sn 108; A IV.86; J II.359; Miln 286, 357; DhA II.72.

Kaṇṇaka (& °**ika**) (adj.) [fr. kaṇṇa] having corners or ears (-°); f. °ikā Vin II.137; J II.185. —**kāḷa-kaṇṇika** see under kāḷa.

Kaṇṇavant (adj.) [fr. kaṇṇa] having an (open) ear, i. e. clever, sharp J II.261 (=kaṇṇachiddaŋ pana na kassaci n'atthi C.).

Kaṇṇikā (f.) [cp. kaṇṇaka & Sk. karṇikā] I. an ornament for the ear, in °lakkhaṇa: see below. — 2. the pericarp of a lotus J I.152, 183; V.416; Miln 361; Vism 124 (paduma°); VvA 43. — 3. the corner of the upper story of a palace or pagoda, house-top J I.201; III.146, 318, 431, 472; DhA I.77 (kūṭāgāra°); DA I.43; VvA 304; Bdhd 92. — 4. a sheaf in the form of a pinnacle DhA I.98. — In cpds. kaṇṇika°.

-**baddha** bound into a sheaf; fig. of objects of thoughts DhA I.304. -**maṇḍala** part of the roof of a house J. III.317; DhA III.66; VI.178. -**rukkha** a tree or log. used to form the top of a house J I.201=DhA I.269. -**lakkhaṇa** the art of telling fortune by marks on ornaments of the ear, or of the house-top D I.9 (=pilandhana-k° pi geha-k° pi vasena DA I.94).

Kaṇṇikāra see kaṇikāra.

Kaṇha (adj.) [cp. Vedic kṛṣṇa, Lith. kérszas] dark, black, as attr. of darkness, opposed to light, syn. with kāḷa (q. v. for etym.); opp. sukka. In general it is hard to separate the lit. and fig. meanings, an ethical implication is to be found in nearly all cases (except I.). The contrast with sukka (brightness) goes through all applications, with ref. to light as well as quality. — I. Of the sense of sight: **k-sukka** dark & bright (about black & white see nīla & seta), forming one system of colour-sensations (the colourless, as distinguished from the red-green and yellow-blue systems). As such enum[d] in connection with quasi definition of vision, together with nīla, pīta, lohita, mañjeṭṭha at D II.328=M I.509 sq. =II.201 (see also mañjeṭṭha). — II. (objective). I. of dark (black), poisonous snakes: **kaṇhā** (f.) J II.215 (=kāḷa-sappa C); °**sappa** J I.336; III.269, 347; V.446; Vism 664 (in simile); Miln 149; PvA 62; °**sīsā** with black heads A III.241 (kimī). — 2. of (an abundance of) smooth, dark (=shiny) hair (cp. in meaning E. gloom: gloss=black: shiny), as Ep. of King Vasudeva Pv II.6[1], syn. with Kesavā (the Hairy, cp. Ἀπόλλων Οὐλαῖος Samson, etc., see also siniddha-, nīla-, kāla-kesa). **sukaṇha-sīsa** with very dark hair J V.205, also as **sukaṇha-kaṇha-sīsa** J V.202 (cp. susukāḷa). °**jaṭi** an ascetic with dark & glossy hair J VI.507, cp. V.205 sukaṇhajaṭila. °**añjana** glossy polish J V.155 (expl[d] as sukhumakaṇha-lom' ācitattā). — 3. of the black trail of fire in °**vattanin** (cp. Vedic kṛṣṇa-vartaniŋ agniŋ R.V. VIII.23, 19) S I.69=J III.140 (cp. III.9); J V.63. — 4. of the black (fertile) soil of Avanti "kaṇh-uttara" black on the surface Vin I.195. — III. (Applied). I. °**pakkha** the dark (moonless) half of the month, during which the spirits of the departed suffer and the powers of darkness prevail PvA 135, cp. Pv III.6[4], see also pakkha[1] 3. — 2. attr. of all dark powers and anything belonging to their sphere, e. g. of Māra Sn 355, 439 (=Namuci); of demons, goblins (pisācā) D I.93 with ref. to the "black-born" ancestor of the Kaṇhāyanas (cp. Dh I.263 kāḷa-vaṇṇa), cp. also kāḷa in °sunakha, the Dog of Purgatory PvA 152. — 3. of a dark, i. e. miserable, unfortunate birth, or social condition D III.81 sq. (brāhmano va sukko vaṇṇo, kaṇho añño vaṇṇo). °**abhijāti** a special species of men according to the doctrine of Gosāla DA I.162; A III.383 sq. °**abhijātika** "of black birth," of low social grade D III.251=A. III.384; Sn 563; cp. Th I, 833 and *J.P.T.S.* 1893, II; in the sense of "evil disposition" at J V.87 (expl[d] as kāḷaka-sabhāva). — 4. of dark, evil actions or qualities: °**dhamma** A V.232=Dh 87; D III.82; Sn 967; Pug 30; Miln 200, 337; °**paṭipadā** J I.105, and °**magga** the evil way A V.244, 278; °**bhāvakara** causing a low (re-)birth J IV.9 (+ pāpa-kammāni), and in same context as dhamma comb[d] with °**sukka** at A IV. 33; Sn 526 (where kaṇhā° for kaṇha°); Miln 37; °**kamma** "black action" M I.39; °**vipāka** black result, 4 kinds of actions and 4 results, viz. kaṇha°, sukka°, kaṇha-sukka°, akaṇha-asukka° D

III.230=M I.389 sq.=A II.230 sq.; Nett 232. akaṇha 1. not dark, i. e. light, in °netta with bright eyes, Ep. of King Pingala-netta J II.242 in contrast with Māra (although pingala-cakkhu is also Ep. of Māra or his representatives, cp. J V.42; Pv II.4[1]). — 2. not evil, i. e. good A II.230, 231. —atikaṇha very dark Vin IV.7; sukaṇha id. see above II.2.

Kata (& sometimes **kaṭa**) [pp. of karoti] done, worked, made. Extremely rare as v. trs. in the common meaning of E. make, Ger. machen, or Fr. faire (see the cognate **kapp** and **jan**, also uppajjati & vissajjati); its proper sphere of application is either ethical (as pāpaŋ, kusalaŋ, kammaŋ: cp. II.1 b) or in such combinations, where its original meaning of "built, prepared, worked out" is still preserved (cp. I.1 a nagara, and 2 a).

I. As verb-determinant (predicative). — 1. in verbal function (Pass.) with nominal determination "done, made" (a) in predicative (epithetic) position: Dh 17 (pāpaŋ me kataŋ evil has been done by me), 68 (tañ ca kammaŋ kataŋ), 150 (aṭṭhīnaŋ nagaraŋ kataŋ a city built of bones, of the body), 173 (yassa pāpaŋ kataŋ kammaŋ). — (b) in absolute (prothetic) position, often with expression of the agent in instr. D I.84=177=M I.40=Sn p. 16 (in formula kataŋ karaṇīyaŋ, etc., done is what had to be done, cp. arahant II.A.); Vin III.72 (kataŋ mayā kalyāṇaŋ akataŋ mayā pāpaŋ); Pv I.5[5] (amhākaŋ katā pūjā done to us is homage). — So also in composition (°-), e. g. (nahāpakehi) °parikammatā the preparations (being) finished (by the barbers) J VI.145; (tena) °paricaya the acquaintance made (with him) VvA 24; PvA 4; (tattha) °paricayatā the acquaintance (with that spot) VvA 331; (tesaŋ) °pubba done before D II.75=A IV.17; (kena) J VI.575; °matta (made) drunk Th 1, 199; (cira) °saŋsagga having (long) been in contact with, familiar J III.63 (and a°). 2. in adj. (med-passive) function (kaṭa & kata); either passive: made, or made of; done by=being like, consisting of; or medio-reflexive: one who has done, having done; also "with" (i. e. this or that action done). — (a) *in pregnant meaning*: prepared, cultivated, trained, skilled; kat-ākaṭa prepared & natural Vin I.206 (of yūsa); akaṭa natural ibid., not cultivated (of soil) Vin I.48= II.209; DA I.78, 98; untrained J III.57, 58.—°atta self-possessed, disciplined J IV.291; °indiya trained in his senses Th 1, 725; °ūpāsana skilled, esp. in archery M I.82; S I.62; A II.48=IV.429; S I.99; J IV.211; Miln 352, °kamma practised, skilled J V.243; of a servant S I.205 (read āse for ase), of a thief A III.102 (cp. below II.1 a); °phaṇa having (i. e. with) its hood erected, of a snake J VI.166; °buddhi of trained mind, clever J III.58; a° ibid.; °mallaka of made-up teeth, an artificial back-scratcher Vin II.316; a° not artificially made, the genuine article Vin II.106; °yogga trained serviceable S I.99; a° useless S I.98. °rūpa done naturally, spontaneously J V.317 (expl[d] by °jāniya; °sabhāva); °veṇī having (i. e. with) the hair done up into a chignon J V.431; °hattha (one) who has exercised his hands, dexterous, skilful, esp. in archery M I.82; S I.62, 98; II.266; A II.48; J IV.211,; V.41; VI.448; Miln 353; DhA I.358; a° unskilled, awkward S I.98; su° well-trained J V 41 (cp. °upāsana), °hatthika an artificial or toy-elephant J VI.551. — (b) *in ordinary meaning*: made or done; °kamma the deed done (in a former existence) J I.167; VvA 252; PvA 10; °piṭṭha made of flour (dough) PvA 16 (of a doll); °bhāva the performance or happening of J III.400; Mhbv 33; °**sanketa** (one who has made an agreement) J V.436 — (c) *with adverbial determination* (su°, du°; cp. dūrato, puro, atta, sayaŋ, & II.2 c): sukata well laid out, of a road J VI.293, well built, of a cart Sn 300=304; J IV.395, well done, i. e. good A I.102 (°kamma-kārin doing good works). -**dukkata** badly made, of a robe Vin IV.279 (t), badly done, i. e. evil A I.102 (°kamma kārin); **sukata-dukkata** good & evil (°kammāni deeds) D I.27= 55=S IV.351; Miln 5, 25. 3. as noun (nt.) kataŋ that which has been done, the deed. — (a) *absolute*: J III.26 (katassa appaṭikāraka not reciprocating the deed); V.434 (kataŋ anukaroti he imitates what has been done) **kat-ākataŋ** what has been done & left undone Vin IV.211; katāni akatāni ca deeds done & not done Dh 50. — (b) *with adv. determination* (su°, du°): sukataŋ goodness (in moral sense) Sn 240; Dh 314; dukkataŋ badness Vin I.76; II.106; Dh 314; dukkata-kārin doing wrong Sn 664

II. As noun-determinant (attributive) in composition (var. applications & meanings). — 1. *As 1st pt. of comp[d]*: Impersonal, denoting the result or finishing of that which is implied in the object with ref. to the act or state resulting, i. e. "so and so made or done"; or personal, denoting the person affected by or concerned with the act. The lit. translation would be "having become one who has done" (act.: see a), or "to whom has been done" (pass.: see b). — (a) *medio-active*. *Temporal*: the action being done, i. e. "after." The noun-determinates usually bear a relation to *time*, especially to meal-times, as **kat-anna-kicca** having finished his meal Dāvs I.59; °bhatta-kicca after the meal J IV.123; PvA 93; °purebhatta-kicca having finished the duties of the morning DA I.45 sq.; SnA 131 sq.; °pātarāsa breakfast J I.227; DhA I.117, a° before br. A IV.64; °pātarāsa-bhatta id. J VI.349; °ānumodana after thanking (for the meal) J I.304; °bhatt'ānumodana after expressing satisfaction with the meal PvA 141. In the same application: **kat-okāsa** having made its appearance, of kamma Vv 32[9] (cp. VvA 113); PvA 63; °kamma(-cora) (a thief) who has just "done the deed," i. e. committed a theft J III.34; Vism 180 (katakammā corā & akata° thieves who have finished their "job" & those who have not); DhA II.38 (corehi katakammaŋ the job done by the th.), cp. above I.2 a; °kāla "done their time," deceased, of Petas J III.164 (pete kālakate); PvA 29, cp. kāla; °cīvara after finishing his robe Vin I.255, 265; °pac-cuggamana having gone forth to meet J III. 93. °paṇi-dhāna from the moment of his making an earnest resolve (to become a Buddha) VvA 3; °pariyosita finished, ready, i. e. after the end was made VvA 250; °buddha-kicca after he had done the obligations of a Buddha VvA 165, 319; DA I.2; °maraṇa after dying, i. e. dead PvA 29; °massu-kamma after having his beard done J V.309 (see note to II.1 b). — *Qualitative*: with ethical import, the state resulting out of action, i. e. of such habit, or "like, of such character." The qualification is either made by kamma, deed, work, or kicca, what can be or ought to be done, or any other specified action, as °pāpa-kamma one who has done wrong DhA I.360 (& a°); °karaṇīya one who has done all that could be done, one who is in the state of perfection (an Arahant), in formula arahaŋ khīṇ'āsavo vusitavā ohitabhāro (cp. above I.1 b & arahant II.A) M I.4, 235; It 38; Miln 138; °kicca having performed his obligations, perfected, Ep. of an Arahant, usually in comb[n] with anāsava S I.47, 178; Dh 386; Pv II.6[18]; Th 2, 337, as adj.: kata-kiccāni hi arahato indriyāni Nett 20; °kiccatā the perfection of Arahantship Miln 339. — With other determinations: -**āgasa** one who has done evil Sdhp 294. -**ādhikāra** having exerted oneself, one who strives after the right path J I.56; Miln 115. -**āparādha** guilty, a transgressor J III.42. -**ābhinihāra** (one) who has formed the resolution (to become a Buddha) J. I.2; DhA I.135. -**ābhinivesa** (one) who studies intently, or one who has made a strong determination J I.110 (& a°). -**ussāha** energetic Sdhp 127. -**kalyāṇa** in passage kata-kalyāṇo kata-kusalo kata-bhīruttāṇo akata-pāpo akata-luddho (luddo) [: °thaddho It] akata-kibbiso having done good, of good character, etc. A II.174=Vin III.72=It 25=DhsA 383; PvA 174; also Pass. to whom something good has been done J I.137; III.12; Pv II.9[6]; akata-kalyāṇa a man of bad actions It 25; Pv II.7⁶. **-kibbisa** a guilty person M I.39; Vin III.72 (a°), of beings tormented in Purgatory Pv IV.7⁷; PvA 59. **-kusala** a good man: see °kalyāṇa. **-thaddha** hard-hearted, unfeeling, cruel: see °kalyāṇa. **-nissama** untiring, valiant, bold J V.243. **-parappavāda** practised in disputing with others DA I.117. **-pāpa** an evil-doer It 25; Pv II.7⁸ (+ akata-kalyāṇa); PvA 5; a°: see °kalyāṇa. **-puñña** one who has done good deeds, a good man D II.144; Dh 16, 18, 220; Pv III.5²; Miln 129; PvA 5, 176; a° one who has not done good (in previous lives) Miln 250; VvA 94. **-puññatā** the fact of having done good deeds D III.276 (pubbe in former births); A II.31; Sn 260, cp. KhA 132, 230; J II.114. **-bahukāra** having done much favour, obliging Dāvs IV.39. **-bhīruttāṇa** one who has offered protection to the fearful: see °kalyāṇa. **-bhūmikamma** one who has laid the ground-work (of sanctification) Miln 352. **-ludda** cruel M III.165; a° gentle Nett 180; cp °kalyāṇa. **-vināsaka** (one) who has caused ruin J I.467. **-vissāsa** trusting, confiding J I.389. **-ssama** painstaking, taking trouble Sdhp 277 (and a°). — (b) *medio-passive:* The state as result of an action, which affected the person concerned with the action (reflexive or passive), or "possessed of, afflicted or affected with." In this application it is simply periphrastic for the ordinary Passive. — *Note.* In the case of the noun being incapable of functioning as verb (when primary), the object in question is specified by °kamma or °kicca, both of which are then only supplementary to the initial kata°, e. g. kata-massu-kamma "having had the beard (-doing) done," as diff. fr. secondary nouns (i. e. verb-derivations), e. g. kat-âbhiseka "having had the anointing done." — In this application: °citta-kamma decorated, variegated DhA I.192; °daṇḍa-kamma afflicted with punishment (=daṇḍāyita punished) Vin I.76; °massu-kamma with trimmed beard, after the beard-trimming J V.309 (cp. J III.11 & karaṇa). — Various combinations: **katañjalin** with raised hands, as a token of veneration or supplication Sn 1023; Th 2, 482; J I.17=Bu 24, 27; PvA 50, 141; VvA 78. **-attha** one who has received benefits J I.378. **-ânuggaha** assisted, aided J II.449; VvA 102. **-âbhiseka** anointed, consecrated Mhvs 26, 6. **-ûpakāra** assisted, befriended J I.378; PvA 116. **-okāsa** one who has been given permission, received into audience, or permitted to speak Vin I.7; D II.39, 277; Sn 1030, 1031 (°âva°); J V.140; VI.341; Miln 95. **-jātihingulika** done up, adorned with pure vermilion J III.303. **-nāmadheyya** having received a name, called J V.492. **-paṭisanthāra** having been received kindly J VI.160; DhA I.80. **-pariggaha** being taken to wife, married to (instr.) PvA 161 (& a°). **-paritta** one on whom a protective spell has been worked, charm-protected Miln 152. **-bhaddaka** one to whom good has been done PvA 116. **-sakkāra** honoured, revered J V.353; Mhvs 9, 8 (su°). **-sangaha** one who has taken part in the redaction of the Scriptures Mhvs 5, 106. **-sannāha** clad in armour DhA I.358. **-sikkha** (having been) trained Miln 353. — 2. *As 2ⁿᵈ pt. of cpd.:* Denoting the performance of the verbal notion with ref. to the object affected by it, i. e. simply a Passive of the verb implied in the determinant, with emphasis of the verb-notion: "made so & so, used as, reduced to" (garukata=garavita). — (a) with *nouns* (see s. v.) e. g., anabhāva-kata, kavi°, kāla-vaṇṇa° (reduced to a black colour) Vin I.48=II.209, tāl'âvatthu°, pamāṇa°, bahuli°, yāni°, sankhār'-ûpekkhā°, etc. — (b) with *adjectives*, e. g. garu°, bahu°. — (c) with *adverbial* substitutes, e. g. atta°, para° (paraŋ°), sacchi°, sayaŋ, etc.

Kataka (nt.) [fr. kantati²] a scrubber, used after a bath Vin II.129, 143; cp. *Vin. Texts* II.318.

Kataññu (adj.) [cp. Sk. kṛtajña] lit. knowing, i. e. acknowledging what has been done (to one), i. e. grateful often in combⁿ with **katavedin** grateful and mindful of benefits S II. 272; A I.87=Pug 26; Vv 81²⁷; Sdhp 509, 524. **akataññu** 1. ungrateful S I.225; J III.26 (=kata-guṇaŋ ajānanto C.), 474; IV.124; PvA 116; Bdhd 81. — 2. (separate akata-ññu) knowing the Uncreated, i. e. knowing Nibbāna Dh 97, 383; DhA II.188; IV.139. — akataññu-rūpa (& °sambhava) of ungrateful nature J IV.98, 99.

Kataññutā (f.) [abstr. fr. last] gratefulness (defined at KhA 144 as katassa jānanatā) Sn 265; J I.122 (T. °nā, v. l. °tā); III.25; Pv II.9⁷; VvA 63; Sdhp 497, 540. In combⁿ with **kataveditā** S II.272; A I.61; II.226, 229. kataññū-kataveditā J III.492. **-akataññutā** ungratefulness, in comb° with **akataveditā** A I.61; III.273; J V.419; as one of the 4 offences deserving of Niraya A II.226.

Katatta (nt.) [abstr. fr. kata, cp. Sk. kṛtatvaŋ] the doing of, performance of, only in abl. katattā D II.2.3, A I.56; J III.128; Dhs 431, 654; SnA 356; DhA III.154; IV. 142. Used adverbially in meaning of "owing to, on account of" Miln 275; DhsA 262; Mhvs 3, 40. **-akatattā** through non-performance of, in absence or in default of A. I.56; PvA 69, 154.

Katana (nt.) [fr. kata] a bad deed, injuring, doing evil (cp. kaṭana) J IV.42 (yam me akkhāsi . . . katanaŋ kataŋ), cp. Morris in *J.P.T.S.* 1893, 15.

Katama (adj.) [cp. Vedic katama, interr. pron. with formation of num. ord., in function=katara, cp. antama>antara, Lat. dextimus>dexter] which, which one (of two or more) Vin II.89; M I.7; J I.172; Miln 309; PvA 27. In some cases merely emphatic for ko, e. g. Vin I.30 (katamena maggena āgato ?); D I.197 (katamo so atta-paṭilābho ?); J I.97; Sn 995; Miln 51. — instr. katamena (scil. maggena) adv. by which way, how ? Miln 57, 58.

Katara (adj.) [Vedic katara, interr. pron. with formation of num. ord., cp. Gr. πότερος, Lat. uter] which one (of a certain number, usually of two) J I.4; PvA 119. Often only emphatic for ko, e. g. J. I.298 (kataraŋ upaddavaŋ na kareyya), and used uninflected in cpds., as katara-geha J III.9; °gandhaŋ J VI.336; °divasaŋ J II.251; °nagarato (from what city) DhA I.390; °nāma (kataraŋnāma, adj.) (of what name) ibid. —**katarasmiŋ** magge in which way, how ? J IV.110.

Katavedin (adj.) [kata + vedin, see kataññu] mindful, grateful S I.225; Pug 26; J I.424; II.26.

Kataveditā (f.) [abstr. fr. last] gratefulness: see **kataññutā**.

Katāvin (adj.-n.) [secondary formation fr. kata] one who has done (what could be done), used like **katakicca** to denote one who has attained Arahantship S I.14; Miln 264.

Kati (indecl.) [interr. pron.; used like Lat. quot. Already Vedic.] how many ? Vin I.83 (k. sikkhāpadāni), 155; S I.3 (°sangâtiga having overcome how many attachments ?), 70; Sn 83, 960, 1018; Ps II.72; Miln 78; DhA I.7, 188; PvA 74.

Katikā (f.) [to katheti or karoti ?] 1. agreement, contract, pact Vin I.153 (T. kātikā), 309; J VI.71; Miln 171, 360. — 2. talking, conversation, talk (adhammikā k., cp. kathikā & kathā) J II.449. —**katikaŋ** karoti to make an arrangement or agreement Vin III.104, 220, 230; J. I.81; IV.267; DhA I.91; VvA 46. In cpds. **katika°**, e. g. **°vatta** observance of an agreement, **°ŋ** karoti to be faithful to a pact Dh I.8; **°ŋ** bhindati to break an agreement J VI.541; **°saṇṭhāna** the entering of an agreement Vin II.76, 208; III.160.

Katipaya (adj.) [cp. Sk. katipaya] some, several, a few (in cpds. or in *pl.*) J I.230, 487; III.280, 419; IV.125; V.162; Pv II.9³³ (=appake only a few); DhA I.94 (very few); PvA 46. In *sg.* little, insignificant Vv 53[20] (=appikā f.). °vāre a few times, a few turns J v.132; vi.52; PvA 135; Mhbv 3.

Katipāhan (adv.) [katipaya + ahan, contracted, see aha[2]] (for) a few days Vin iii.14; J i.152, 298, 466; ii.38; iii.48; iv.147; Mhvs 7, 38; PvA 145, 161; VvA 222. katipāhena (instr.) within a few days Mhvs 17, 41; DhA i.344; PvA 13, 161. katipāh'accayena after (the lapse of) a few days J i.245; DhA i.175; PvA 47.

Katima [num. ord. fr. kati], f. **katimī** in k. pakkhassa which (of many other) day of the half-month Vin i.117.

Kativassa (adj.) [kati + vassa] 1. (having) how many years, how old? J v.331. — 2. (having had) how many rainy seasons (in the bhikkhu's career) of how many years' seniority? Vin i.86; Ud 59; Miln 28; DhA i.37.

Katividha (adj.) [kati + vidha, for Vedic katidhā] of how many kinds Vism 84.

Kate (adv.) [loc. of kata] for the sake of, on behalf of; with acc. maŋ k. J iv.14; with gen. maŋsassa k. J v.500.

Katta [pp. of kantati[2]; cp. Sk. kṛtta] is represented in Pali by kanta[3]; katta being found only in cpd. pari°.

Kattabba (adj.) [grd. of karoti] 1. to be done, to be made or performed; that which might or could be done Dh 53; J i.77, 267; v.362. — 2. (nt.) that which is to be done, obligation, duty Th 1, 330; J ii.154; v.402; DhA i.211. —**akattabba** (adj.) not to be done J iii.131; v.147; (nt.) that which ought not to be done J v.402. **kattabb' âkattabba** to be done and not to be done J i.387. **kattabba-yuttaka** 1. (adj.) fit or proper to be done DhA i.13. — 2. (nt.) duty, obligation J iii.9; vi.164; DhA i.180; (the last) duties towards the deceased J i.431. — Cp. **kātabba**.

Kattabbaka (nt.) [fr. last] task, duty Th 1, 330.

Kattabbatā (f.) [fr. kattabba] fitness, duty, that which is to be done J ii. 179 (iti-°āya because I had to do it thus).

Kattar [n. ag. fr. karoti, cp. Sk. kartṛ] one who makes or creates, a maker, doer; in foll. construction. I. *Dependent.* Either in verb-function with acc., as n. agent to all phrases with karoti e. g. pañhaŋ karoti to put a question, pañhaŋ kattā one who puts a question; or in n. function with gen., e. g. mantānaŋ kattāro the authors of the Mantas, or in cpd. rāja-kattāro makers of kings. — II. *Dependent.* as n. **kattā** the doer: kattā hoti no bhāsitā he is a man of action, and not of words. — 1. (indef.) one who does anything (with acc.) A i.103; ii.67; v.347, 350 sq.; (with gen.) J i.378; iii.136 (one who does evil, in same meaning at iii.26, C. akataññū, cp. *J.P.T.S.* 1893, 15: not to **krt**!); iv.98 (expl[d] as kata by C); v.258; Miln 25, 296; Bdhd 85 sq. — 2. an author, maker, creator D i.18 (of Brahmā: issaro, k., nimmātā), 104 (mantānaŋ); A ii.102; Dh i.111. — 3. an officer of a king, the king's messenger J v.220 (=225); vi.259, 268, 302, 313, 492. *Note.* At J v.225 & vi.302 the voc. is katte (of a-decl.), cp. also nom. °katta for °kattā in salla-katta. — 4. as t.t.g. N. of the instr. case VvA 97; Kacc 136, 143, 277.

Kattara (adj.) (only°-) [cp. Sk. kṛtvan (?), in diff. meaning] °daṇḍa a walking-stick or staff (of an ascetic) Vin i.188; ii.76=208 sq.; iii.160; J i.9; v.132; vi.52, 56, 520; Vism 91, 125, 181. °yaṭṭhi=prec. J ii.441; DA i.207; iii.140. °ratha an old (?) chariot J iii.299. °suppa a winnowing basket Vin i.269=DhA i.174 (°e pakkhipitvā sankāra-kūṭe chaḍḍehi).

Kattari & °ī (f.) [to kantati[2]] scissors, shears J iii.298, with ref. to the "shears" of a crab, "as with scissors"; cp. *Vin. Texts* iii.138 (see next).

Kattarikā (f.) [fr. last] scissors, or a knife Vin ii.134; J. i.223.

Kattikā (f.) (& °kattika) [cp. Sk. kṛttikā f. pl. the Pleiades & BSk. karthika] N. of a month (Oct.-Nov.), during which the full moon is near the constellation of Pleiades. It is the last month of the rainy season, terminating on the full moon day of Kattikā (kattika-puṇṇamā). This season is divided into 5 months: Āsāḷha, Sāvaṇa, Bhaddara (Poṭṭhapāda), Assayuja, Kattikā; the month Assayuja is also called pubba-kattikā, whereas the fifth, K., is also known as pacchima-kattikā; both are comprised in the term **k.-dvemāsika.** Bhikkhus retiring for the first 3 months of the Vassa (rainy season) are **kattika-temāsikā**, if they include the 4th, they are **k.-cātumāsikā.** The full moon of Assayuja is termed **k.-temāsinī** that of Kattika is **k.-cātumāsinī.** See Vinaya passages & cp. nakkhatta. — Nett 143 (kattiko, v. l. kattikā).

-**cātumāsinī** see above Vin iii.263. -**coraka** a thief who in the month of K., after the distribution of robes, attacks bhikkhus Vin iii.262. -**chaṇa** a festival held at the end of Lent on the full moon of pubba-kattikā, and coinciding with the Pavāraṇā J i.433; ii.372; v.212 sq.; Mhvs 17, 17. -**temāsi**(-**puṇṇamā**) (the full moon) of pubbakattikā Vin iii.261; Mhvs 17, 1 (°puṇṇamāsi). -**māsa** the month K. J ii.372; Mhvs 12, 2 (kattike māse). -**sukkapakkha** the bright fortnight of K. Mhvs 17, 64.

Kattu° 1. base of inf. kattuŋ (of karoti), in compd[s] °kamyatā willingness to do something Vbh 208; Vism 320, 385; DhA iii.289; °kāma desirous to do Vin ii.226. °kāmatā desire to do or to perform Vism 466; VvA 43. — 2. base of **kattar** in comp[n].

Kattha (adv.) [der. fr. interr. base ka° (kad[2]), whereas Sk. kutra is der. fr. base ku°, cp. kuttha] where? where to, whither? Vin i.83, 107; ii.76; D i.223; Sn 487, 1036; J iii.76; Pv ii.9[16]; DhA i.3. —**k.** nu kho where then, where I wonder? D i.215 sq., PvA 22 (with Pot.) -**katthaci**(d) (indef.) anywhere, at some place or other J i.137; v.468; wherever, in whatever place Miln 366; PvA 284; KhA 247; J iii.229; iv.9, 45; as katthacid eva J. iv. 92; PvA 173. Sometimes doubled katthaci katthaci in whatsoever place J iv.341. -**na k.** nowhere M. i.424; Miln 77; VvA 14.

-**ṭhita** fig. in what condition or state? D ii.241 (corresp. with ettha); J iv.110. -**vāsa** in what residence? Sn 412. -**vāsika** residing where? J ii.128, 273.

Katthati [cp. Sk. katthate, etym. unexpl[d]] to boast Sn 783 (ppr. med. akatthamāna). Cp. pavikatthita.

Katthitar (n. ag. fr. katthati] a boaster Sn 930.

Katthin (adj.) [fr. **katth**] boasting A v.157 (+ vikatthin).

Katthu (?) a jackal, in °soṇā j. & dogs J vi.538 (for koṭṭhu°).

Kathaŋ (adv.) [cp. Vedic kathaŋ & kathā] dubit. interr. part. 1. how; with ind. pres. PvA 6 (k. puriso paṭilabhati), or with fut. & cond. J i.222; ii.159 (k. tattha gamissāmi); vi.500; PvA 54 (na dassāmi) — 2. why, for what reason? J iii.81; v.506. Combined with -**ca** Vin i.114; ii.83. -**carahi** D ii.192. -**nu** & -**nu kho** Vin ii.26, J iii.99; iv. 339; Nd[2] 189, see also evaŋ nu kho. -**pana** D ii.163. -**su** Nd[2] 189. -**hi** J iv.339; DhA i.432. -**hi nāma** Vin i.45; ii.105; iii.137; iv.300; all in the same meaning; -**ci** (kathañci) scarcely, with difficulty Th 1, 456.

-**katha** "saying how? how?" i. e. doubt, uncertainty, unsettled mind (cp. kaṅkhā); expl. as vicikicchā dukkhe kankhā Nd[2] 190; D ii.282; Sn 500, 866, 1063, 1088; DhA iv.194; as adj. and at end of cpd. °-katha, e. g. vigata° (in phrase tiṇṇa-vicikiccha . . . vesārajjappatta) D i.110=Vin i.12; tiṇṇa° (+ visalla) Sn 17, 86, 367. k-k-salla "the arrow of doubt" D ii.283

(vicikicchā +). -**kathin** having doubts, unsettled, uncertain D II.287; M I.8; Nd² 191; DhsA 352; a° free from doubt, Ep. of Arahant (expl^d DA I.211: "not saying how and how is this?"); M I.108; It 49; Sn 534, 635, 868, 1064; in phrases tiṇṇa-vicikiccho viharati akathankathī kusalesu dhammesu D I.71 = Pug 59, jhāyī anejo a° Dh 414 (: DhA IV.194) = Sn 638. -**kara** (adj.) how acting, what doing? k. ahaŋ no nirayam pateyyaŋ ("τί ποιῶν μακάριος ἔσομαι") J IV.339; Sn 376; J IV.75; V.148. -**jīvin** leading what kind of life? Sn 181. -**dassin** holding what views? Sn 848 (see °sīla). -**pakāra** of what kind Vin I.358; Sn 241 (:ka-thappakāra). -**paṭipanna** going what way, i. e. how acting? D II.277, 279, 281. -**bhāvita** how cultivated or practised? S V.119. -**bhūta** "how being," of what sort, what like D II.139, 158; -**rūpa** of what kind? M I.218; A I.249; III.35; J III.525. -**vaṇṇa** of what appearance, what like? D II.244. -**vidha** what sort of? J V.95, 146; DhsA 305. -**sameta** how constituted? Sn 873. -**sīla** of what character or conduct? how in his morality? Sn 848 (kathaŋdassī kathaŋsīlo upasanto ti vuccati).

Kathana (nt.) [fr. **kath**, see katheti] 1. conversing, talking J I.299; III.459; VI.340. — 2. telling i. e. answering, solving (a question) J V.66 (pañha°).—3. preaching DhA I.7. — 4. reciting, narrating Kacc. 130. Cp. kathita. —**akathana** not talking or telling J I.420; VI.424; not speaking fr. anger J IV.108; DhA I.440.

-**ākāra**, in °ŋ karoti to enter into conversation with J VI.413. -**samattha** able to speak (of the tongue) J III.459; able to talk or converse with (saddhiŋ) J VI.340. -**sīla** (one) in the habit of talking, garrulous J I.299; a° J I.420.

Kathala (potsherd) spelling at Vism 261 for kaṭhala.

Kathalī (metri causâ) = next, in the Uddāna at Vin II.234

Kathalika (nt.) [der. uncertain], always in comb^n pād'-odaka pāda-pīṭha pāda-k°: either a *cloth* to wipe the feet with after washing them, or a *footstool* Vin I.9, 47; II.22 sq., 210, 216. At VvA 8 however with pāda-pīṭha expl^d as a footstool (pāda-ṭhapana-yoggaŋ dāru-khaṇḍaŋ āsanaŋ). Bdhgh (on CV II.1.1) expl^d pāda-pīṭha as a stool to put the washed foot on, pāda-katha-lika as a stool to put the unwashed foot on, or a cloth to rub the feet with (ghaŋsana).

Kathā (f.) [fr. **kath** to tell or talk, see katheti; nearest synonym is **lap**, cp. vāc' âbhilāpa & sallāpa] 1. talk, talking, conversation A I.130; PvA 39. So in antarā° D I.179; Sn p. 107, 115; cp. sallāpa. Also in tirac-chāna° low, common speech, comprising 28 kinds of conversational talk a bhikkhu should not indulge in, enum^d in full at D I.7 = 178 = III.36 & passim (e. g. S V.419: corr. suddha° to yuddha° !; A V.128 = Nd² 192); ref. to at A III.256; V.185; J I.58; Pug 35. Similarly in **gāma**° Sn 922; **viggāhikā k.** A IV.87; Sn 930. Ten good themes of conversation (kathā-vatthūni) are enum^d at M III.113 = A III.117 = IV.357 = V.67; Miln 344; similarly **dhammī kathā** A II.51; IV.307; V.192; Sn 325; **pavattanī k.** A I.151; yutta kathāyaŋ Sn 826; **sammo-danīyā k.** in salutation formula s°ŋ k°ŋ sāraṇiyaŋ viti-sāretvā D I.52, 108, etc.; A V.185; Sn 419, pp. 86, 93, 107, 116. — 2. speech, sermon, discourse, lecture Vin I.203, 290 (°ŋ karoti to discuss); A III.174; IV. 358. Freq. in **anupubbi**° a sermon in regular succession, graduated sermon, discussing the 4 points of the ladder of "holiness," viz. dānakathā, sīla°, sagga°, magga° (see anupubba) Vin I.15; A III.184; IV.186, 209, 213; DhA I.6; VvA 66. — 3. a (longer) story, often with **vitthāra**° an account in detail, e. g. PvA 19. **bāhira**° profane story KhA 48. — 4. word, words, advice: °ŋ gaṇhāti to accept an advice J II.173; III.424. — 5. explanation, exposition, in **aṭṭha**° (q. v.), cp. gati° Ps II.72. — 6. discussion, in °vatthu (see below) Mhvs 5, 138. -**dukkathā** harmful conversation or idle talk A III. 181; opp. su° A III.182. -**kathaŋ vaḍḍheti** "to in-crease the talk," to dispute sharply J I.404; V.412. °ŋ **samuṭṭhāpeti** to start a conversation J I.119 IV. 73. — At the end of cpds. (as adj.) °**kathā** e. g. chinna° Sn 711; ṭhita° DA I.73; madhura° J III.342; VI.255.

-**âbhiññāṇa** recollection due to speech Miln 78, 79. -**ojja** (k°-udya, to **vad**) a dispute, quarrel Sn 825, 828. -**dhamma** a topic of conversation DA I.43. -**nigghosa** the sound of praise, flattery J II.350. -**pavatti** the course of a conversation J I.119; DhA I.249; Mhbv 61. -**pābhata** subject of a conversation, story J I.252, 364. -**bāhulla** abundance of talk, loquacity A IV.87. -**magga** narrative, account, history J I.2. -**rasa** the sweetness of (this) speech Miln 345. -**vatthu** 1. subject of a discourse or discussion, argument M I.372; II.127, 132. There are 10 enum^d at A IV.352, 357 (see kathā) and at Vism 19 as qualities of a kalyāṇa-mitta, referred to at A V.67, 129; Vism 127; DhA IV.30. Three are given at D III.220 = A I.197. °*kusala* well up in the subjects of discussion VvA 354. — 2. N. of the fifth book of the Abhidhamma Piṭaka, the seven constituents of which are enum^d at var. places (e. g. DA I.17; Mhbv 94, where Xvu takes the 3rd place), see also *J.P.T.S.* 1882, 1888, 1896. -**samuṭṭhāna** the arising of a discussion Mhvs 5, 138. -**samuṭṭhāpana** starting a conversation J I.119; III.278; DhA I.250. -**sampayoga** conversational inter-course A I.197. -**sallāpa** talk, conversation Vin I.77; D I.89 sq., 107 sq.; II.150; M I.178; A II.197; V.188; Ud 40; J II.283; Miln 31; DA I.276 (expl^d as kathana-paṭikathana); DhA II.91 (°ŋ karoti); VvA 153.

Kathāpeti Caus. II. of katheti (q. v.).

Kathika (adj.) (—°) [fr. kathā, cp. Sk. kathaka] relating, speaking, conversing about, expounding, in cpds. **citta**° Th 2, 449 (cp. citra-kathin); (a) tiracchāna° A IV.153; **dhamma**° J I.148; III.342; IV.2 (°thera); VI.255 (mahā°); as *noun* a preacher, speaker, expounder A III.174; Mhvs 14, 64 (mahā°).

Kathikā (f.) [fr. last ?] agreement Dpvs 19, 22; see **katikā**.

Kathita [pp. of katheti, cp. Sk. kathita] said, spoken, related J II.310; IV.73; V.493. su° well said or told J. IV.73. As nt. with instr. J IV.72 (tena kathitaŋ the discourse (given) by him).

Kathin (adj.) (—°) [cp. kathika] speaking; one who speaks, a speaker, preacher J I.148 (dhamma-kathikesu citra-kathī); Miln 90, 348 (°seṭṭha best of speakers). See also kathaŋ-kathin.

Katheti (v. den. fr. kathā, cp. Sk. kathayate] aor. kathesi, inf. kathetuŋ & kathetave (Vin I.359); Pass. **kathīyati** & katheti (Miln 22, cp. Trenckner, *Notes* 122); ppr. Pass. **kathiyamāna** & **kacchamāna** (A. III.181); **grd. kathetabba, kathanīya** & **kaccha**, — 1. to speak, say, tell, relate (in detail: vitthārato PvA 77). mā kathesi (= mā bhaṇi) do not speak PvA 16. — to tell (a story): J. I.2; IV.137; PvA 12, 13. — 2. to converse with J. VI.413; PvA 86 (= āmantayi). — 3. to report, to inform J V.460. — 4. to recite DhA I.166. — 5. to expound, explain, preach J I.30; Miln 131; DhA I.88; Nd² s. v. — 6. to speak about (with acc.) Vin II.168. — 7. to refer to J I.307. — 8. to answer or solve (a question) J I.165; V.66. — Caus II. **kathāpeti** to make say Mhvs 24, 4 (aor. kathāpayi); DhA II.35; KhA 118.

Kad° [old form of interr. pron. nt., equal to **kiŋ**; cp. (Vedic) kad in kadarthaŋ = kiŋarthaŋ to what purpose] orig. "what?" used adverbially; then indef. "any kind of," as (na) kac(-cana) "not at all"; kac-cid "any kind of; is it anything? what then?" Mostly used in disparaging sense of showing inferiority, contempt, or defectiveness, and equal to kā° (in denoting badness or smallness, e. g. kākanika, kāpurisa, see also kantāra & kappaṭa), kiṃ°, ku.° For relation of ku > ka cp. kutra > kattha & kadā.

-anna bad food Kacc 178. -asana id. Kacc 178. -dukkha (?) great evil (=death) VvA 316 (expl[d] as maraṇa, cp. kaṭuka).

Kadamba (cp. Sk. kadamba] the kadamba tree, Nauclea cordifolia (with orange-coloured, fragrant blossoms) J. VI.535, 539; Vism 206; DhA I.309 (°puppha); Mhvs 25, 48 (id.).

Kadara (adj.) miserable J II.136 (expl[d] as lūkha, kasira).

Kadariya (adj.) [cp. Sk. kadarya, kad + arya ?] mean, miserly, stingy, selfish; usually expl[d] by thaddhamaccharī (PvA 102; DhA III.189, 313), and mentioned with maccharī, freq. also with paribhāsaka S I.34, 96; A II.59; IV.79 sq.; Dh 177, 223; J V.273; Sn 663; Vv 29[5]. As cause of Peta birth freq. in Pv., e. g. I.9[3]; II.7[7]; IV.1[46]; PvA 25, 99, 236. — (nt.) avarice, stinginess, selfishness, grouped under macchariya Dhs 1122; Sn 362 (with kodha).

Kadariyatā (f.) [abstr. fr. last] stinginess, niggardliness D II.243; Miln 180; PvA 45.

Kadala (nt.) the plantain tree Kacc 335.

Kadalī[1] (f.) [Sk. kadalī] — 1. the plantain, Musa sapientium. Owing to the softness and unsubstantiality of its trunk it is used as a frequent symbol of unsubstantiality, transitoriness and worthlessness. As the plantain or banana plant always dies down after producing fruit, is destroyed as it were by its own fruit, it is used as a simile for a bad man destroyed by the fruit of his own deeds: S I.154 = Vin II.188 = S II.241 = A II.73 = DhA III.156; cp. Miln 166; — as an image of unsubstantiality, Cp. III.2[4]. The tree is used as ornament on great festivals: J I.11; VI.590 (in simile), 592; VvA 31. — 2. a flag, banner, i. e. plantain leaves having the appearance of banners (-dhaja) J V.195; VI.412. In cpds. kadali°.

-khandha the trunk of the plantain tree, often in similes as symbol of worthlessness, e. g. M I.233 = S III.141 = IV.167; Vism 479; Nd[2] 680 A[II].; J VI.442; as symbol of smoothness and beauty of limbs VvA 280; -taru the plantain tree Dāvs V.49; -toraṇa a triumphal arch made of pl. stems and leaves Mhbv 169; -patta a pl. leaf used as an improvised plate to eat from J V.4; DhA I.59; -phala the fruit of the plantain J V.37.

Kadalī[2] (f.) a kind of deer, an antelope only in °miga J V.406, 416; VI.539; DA I.87; and °pavara-pacc.-attharaṇa (nt.) the hide of the k. deer, used as a rug or cover D I.7 = A I.181 = Vin I.192 = II.163, 169; sim. D. II.187; (adj.) (of pallanka) A I.137 = III.50 = IV.394.

Kadā (indecl.) [Vedic kadā. Cp. tadā, sadā in Pali, and perhaps Latin quando]. interr. adv. when ? (very often foll. by fut.) Th 1, 1091-1106; J II.212; VI. 46; DhA I.33; PvA 2. — Comb[d] with -ssu J V.103, 215; VI.49 sq. -ci [cid] indef. — 1. at some time A IV.101. — 2. sometimes J I.98; PvA 271. — 3. once upon a time Dāvs I.30. — 4. perhaps, may be J I.297; VI.364. + eva: kadācideva VvA 213; -kadāci kadāci from time to time, every now and then J I.216; IV. 120; DhsA 238; PvA 253. -kadāci karahaci at some time or other, at times A I.179; Miln 73; DhA III.362. -na kadāci at no time, never S I.66; J V.434; VI.363; same with mā k° J VI.310; Mhvs 25, 113; cp. kudācana. —kadāc-uppattika (adj.) happening only sometimes, occasional Miln 114.

Kaddama [Derivation unknown. Sk. kardama] mud, mire, filth Nd[2] 374 (=panka); J I.100; III.220 (written kadamo in verse and kaddemo in gloss); VI.240, 390; PvA 189 (=panka), 215; compared with moral impurities J III.290 & Miln 35. a° free from mud or dirt, clean Vin II.201, of a lake J III.289; fig. pure of character J III.290. kaddamīkata made muddy or dirty, defiled J VI.59 (kilesehi).

-odaka muddy water Vin II.262; Vism 127. -parikhā a moat filled with mud, as a defence J VI. 390; -bahula (adj.) muddy, full of mud DhA I.333;

Kanaka (nt.) [cp. Sk. kanaka; Gr. κνῆκος yellow; Ags. hunig = E. honey. See also kañcana] gold, usually as uttatta° molten gold; said of the colour of the skin Bu I.59; Pv III.3[2]; J V.416; PvA 10 suvaṇṇa).

-agga gold-crested J V.156; -chavin of golden complexion J VI.13; -taca (adj.) id. J V.393; -pabhā golden splendour Bu XXIII.23; -vimāna a fairy palace of gold VvA 6; PvA 47, 53; -sikharī a golden peak, in °rājā king of the golden peaks (i. e. Himālayas): Dāvs IV.30.

Kaniṭṭha (adj.) [Sk. kaniṣṭha; compar. & superl.; see kaññā] younger, youngest, younger born Vin III.146 (isi the younger); J II.6; PvA 42, 54; esp. the younger brother (opp. jeṭṭha, °ka) J I.132; DhA I.6, 13; Mhvs. 9, 7; PvA 19, 55. Comb[d] with jeṭṭhaka the elder & younger brothers J I.253; sabba- k. the very youngest J I.395. f. kaniṭṭhā the youngest daughter DhA I.396. — fig. later, lesser, inferior, in °phala the lesser fruit (of sanctification) Pv IV.1[88]. —akaniṭṭha "not the smaller" i. e. the greatest, highest; in akaniṭṭhagāmin going to the highest gods (cp. parinibbāyin) S V.237 = 285, etc. °bhavana the abode of the highest gods J. III.487.

Kaniṭṭhaka (adj.) younger (opp. jeṭṭha) A IV.93 = J II.348; DhA I.152; the younger brother Mhvs 5, 33, 8, 10; 35, 49; 36, 116; -°ikā and °akā a younger sister, Mhvs I, 49; Pv I.11[6] (better read for kaniṭṭhā).

Kaniṭṭhatta (nt.) the more recent and therefore lower, less developed state (of sanctification) DhA I.152.

Kaniṭṭhī (f.) a younger sister Mhvs 7, 67.

Kaniya (adj.) [compar. of kan°, Sk. kanīyaṃs] younger, less, inferior Kacc 122 (only as a grammarian's construction, not in the living language where it had coalesced with *kanyā = kaññā).

Kanta[1] [Sk. kānta, pp. of kāmeti] — 1. (adj.) in special sense an attribute of worldly pleasure (cp. kāma, kāmaguṇā): pleasant, lovely, enjoyable; freq. in form. iṭṭhā kantā manāpā, referring to the pleasures of the senses S I.245; II.192; IV.60, 158, 235 sq.; V.22, 60, 147; A II.66 sq.; M I.85; Sn 759; It 15; Vbh 2, 100, 337; bāla° (lovely in the opinion of the ignorant) Sn 399. — D II.265 III.227 (ariya°); J III.264; V.447; with ref. to the fruit of action as giving pleasure: °phala Kvu 35, 211, PvA 277 (hatthi-) k° pleasing to elephants; of manta DhA I.163; of vīnā J VI.255, 262; DhA I.163. — 2. beloved by, favourite of, charming J VI.255, 262; DhA I.163. — 3. (n.) the beloved one, the husband J VI.370 (wrongly written kan tena); of a precious stone Miln 118; Sdhp 608, cp. suriya°, canda°—kantā (f.) the beloved one, the wife J V.295; kantena (instr.) agreeably, with kind words A II.213; J V.486 (where porisādassa kante should be read as porisādassak' ante). —a° undesired, disagreeable, unpleasant, in same form as kanta, e. g. D II.192; in other comb[n] J V.295; Vbh 100; Nett 180; PvA 193. —akantena with unpleasant words A II.213. —kantatara compar. J III.260.

-bhāva the state of being pleasant DA I.76; VvA 323.

Kanta[2] [pp. of kantati[2], Sk. kṛtta. kanta is analogy-form. after pres. kantati, regularly we should expect katta. See also avakanta. It may be simply misreading for katta, cp. kern, *Toev.* under parikanta.] cut, cut out or off Th 2, 223 (°salla = samucchinna-rāg'-ādi-salla ThA 179) cp. katta & pari°.

Kantati^1 [Sk. kṛṇatti, *qert, cp. kata, & Lat. cratis, crassus, E. crate] to plait, twist, spin, esp. suttaŋ (thread) Vin IV.300; PvA 75; DhA III.273; kappāsaŋ A III.295. Cp. pari°.

Kantati^2 [Sk. kṛntati; *(s)qert, to cut; cp. Gr. κείρω, to shear; Lat. caro, cena; Ohg. sceran, E. shear; see also kaṭu] to cut, cut off J II.53 (: as nik° in gloss, where it should be mūlāni kant°); III.185; VI.154, DhA III.152 (+ viddhaŋseti).

Kantāra (adj. n.) [perhaps from kad-tarati, difficult to cross, Sk. (?) kāntāra] difficult to pass, scil. magga, a difficult road, waste land, wilderness, expl^d as nirudaka īriṇa VvA 334 (on Vv 84^3), comb^d with maru° PvA 99 and marukantāramagga PvA 112; opp. khemantabhūmi. Usually 5 kinds of wilds are enumerated: cora°, vāla°, nirudaka°, amanussa°, appabhakkha° J I.99; SA 324; 4 kinds at Nd^2 630: cora°, vāla° dubhikkha° nirudaka°. The term is used both lit. & fig. (of the wilds of ignorance, false doctrine, or of difficulties, hardship). As the seat of demons (Petas and Yakkhas) freq. in Pv (see above), also J I.395. As diṭṭhi° in pass. diṭṭhi-gata, etc. M I.8, 486, Pug 22 (on diṭṭhi vipatti).
-addhāna a road in the wilderness, a dangerous path (fig.)Th 1, 95~D I.73=M I.276; -paṭipanna a wanderer through the wilderness, i. e. a forester J III.537. -magga a difficult road (cp. kummagga) J II.294 (lit.); in simile: S II.118. -mukha the entrance to a desert J I.99.

Kantāriya (adj.) [from kantāra] (one) living in or belonging to the desert, the guardian of a wilderness, applied to a Yakkha Vv 84^{21} (=VvA 341).

Kantika^1 (adj.) [to kantat^1] spinning PvA 75 (sutta° itthiyo).

Kantika^2=kanta^1 in a° unpleasant, disgusting Pv III.4^1 (=PvA 193).

Kantita^1 [Sk. kṛtta, pp. of kantati^1] spun, (sutta) Vin IV.300.

Kantita^2 (adj.) Sk. kṛtta pp. of kantati^2] cut off, severed Miln 240.

Kanda [Sk. kanda] a tuberous root, a bulb, tuber, as radish, etc. J I.273; IV.373; VI.516; VvA 335; °mūla bulbs and roots (°phala) D I.101; a bulbous root J V.202.

Kandati [Sk. krandati to *q(e)lem; cp. Gr. καλέω, κέλαδος, Lat. clamor, calare, calendae, Ohg. hellan to shout] to cry, wail, weep, lament, bewail Dh 371; Vv 83^{12}; J VI.166; Miln 11, 148; freq. of Petas: PvA 43, 160, 262 (cp. rodati). — In kāmaguṇā pass. urattāḷiŋ k. M. I.86=Nd^2 s. v.; A III.54 (urattāḷi for °iŋ v. l.); in phrase bāhā paggayha k° Vin I.237; II.284; J V.267.

Kandana (nt.) [Sk. krandana] crying, lamenting PvA 262

Kandara [Sk. kandara] — 1. a cave, grotto, generally. on the slope or at the foot of a mountain Vin II.76, 146; used as a dwelling-place Th 1, 602; J I.205; III.172. — 2. a glen, defile, gully D I.71=A II.210=Pug 59; A IV.437; Miln 36; expl^d at DA I.209 (as a mountainous part broken by the water of a river; the etym. is a popular one, viz. " kaŋ vuccati udakaŋ; tena dāritaŋ "). k-padarasākhā A I.243=II.240; PvA 29.

Kandala N. of a plant with white flowers J IV.442. —makuḷa knob (?) of k. plant Vism 253 (as in description of sinews).

Kandaḷa N. of esculent water lily, having an enormous bulb D I.264.

Kandita (adj.) [pp. of kandati] weeping, lamenting Dāvs IV.46; a° not weeping J III.58. (n. nt.) crying, lamentation J III.57; Miln 148.

Kanna (adj.) [Sk. skanna] trickling down J V.445.

Kannāma=kinnāma J VI.126.

Kapaṇa (adj. n.) [Sk. kṛpaṇa from **kṛp** wail, cp. Lat. crepo; Ags. hraefn=E. raven. Cp. also Sk. kṛcchra] — 1. poor, miserable, wretched; a beggar; freq. expl^d by varāka, duggata, dīna and daḷidda; very often classed with low-caste people, as caṇḍālā Pv. III.1^{13} & pesakārā (Ud 4). Sn 818 J I.312, 321; III.199; Pv II.9^{14}; III.1^{13}, IV.5^2; DA I.298; DhA I.233; Th A 178. — 2. small, short, insignificant A I.213; Bdhd 84. (f.) °ā a miserable woman J IV.285; -°an (adv.) pitifully, piteously, with verbs of weeping, etc. J III.295; V.499; VI.143; a° not poor J III.199; —ati° very miserable Pgdp 74. Der. °tā wretchedness Sdhp 315.
-addhikā pl. often with °ādi, which means samaṇabrāhmaṇa-k°-vaṇibbaka-yācakā (e. g. D I.137; PvA 78) beggars and wayfarers, tramps J I.6, 262, DhA I.105, 188 (written k°-andhika); see also DA I.298 and kapaṇikā; -iddhikā pl. (probably miswriting for °addh°, cp. Trenckner, *J.P.T.S.* 1908, 130) D I.137; It 65; DA I.298; -itthī a poor woman J III.448; -jīvikā in °aŋ kappeti to make a poor livelihood J I.312; -bhāva the state of being miserable PvA 274; -manussa a wretched fellow, a beggar Vism·343; -laddhaka obtained in pain, said of children J VI.150, cp. kiccha laddhaka; -visikhā the street or quarter of the poor, the slums Ud 4; -vuttin leading a poor life PvA 175.

Kapaṇikā (f.) a (mentally) miserable woman Th 2, 219; ThA 178; cp. kapaṇā; also as kapaṇiyā J VI.93.

Kapalla at Vin I.203, is an error for kajjala, lamp-black, used in preparation of a collyrium (cp. *J.P.T.S.* 1887, 167).

Kapalla (nt.) [Sk kapāla; orig. skull, bowl, cp. kapola & Lat. caput, capula, capillus, Goth. haubi, E. head]— 1. a bowl in form of a skull, or the shell of reptiles; see kapāla.— 2. an earthenware pan used to carry ashes J I.8; VI.66, 75; DhA I.288. — 3. a frying pan (see cpds. & cp. aṅgāra-kapalla) Sn 672. -kapalla is only a variant of kapāla.
-pāti an earthen pot, a pan J I.347=Dh A I.371; -pūva a pancake J I.345; DhA I.367; VvA 123; Mhvs 35, 67.

Kapallaka — 1. a small earthen bowl J VI.59; DhA I.224. — 2. a frying pan J I.346.

Kapāla (nt.) [Sk. kapāla, see kapalla] — 1. a tortoise- or turtle-shell S I.7=Miln 371; S IV.179; as ornament at DA I.89. — 2. the skull, cp. kaṭāha in sīsakaṭāha. — 3. a frying pan (usually as ayo°, of iron, e. g. A IV.70; Nd^2 304^{III}; VvA 335) J II.352; Vv 84^6; DhA I.148 (v. l. °kapalla); Bdhd 100 (in simile). — 4. a begging bowl, used by certain ascetics S IV.190; V.53, 301; A I.36; III.225; J I.89; PvA 3. — 5. a potsherd J II.301.
-ābhata the food collected in a bowl A I.36; -khaṇḍa a bit of potsherd J II.301; -hattha " with a bowl in his hand," begging, or a beggar, Th 1, 1118; J I.89; III.32; V.468; PvA 3.

Kapālaka — 1. a small vessel, bowl J I.425. — 2. a beggar's bowl J I.235; DhA II.26.

Kapāsa=kappāsa, q. v. Dāvs II.39.

Kapi [Sk. kapi, original designation of a brownish colour, cp. kapila & kapota] a monkey (freq. in similes) Sn 791; Th 2, 1080; J I.170; III.148, cp. kavi.
-kacchu the plant Mucuna pruritus Pv II.3^{10}; °*phala* its fruit PvA 86; -citta " having a monkey's mind," capricious, fickle J III.148=525; -naccanā Npl., Pv IV.1^{37}; -niddā " monkey-sleep," dozing Miln 300.

Kapiñjala [Derivation unknown. Sk. kapiñjala] a wild bird, possibly the francolin partridge Kvu 268; J VI.538 (B.B. kapiñjara).

Kapiṭhana the tree Thespesia populneoides Vin IV. 35.

Kapiṭṭha and °ttha — 1. the tree Feronia elephantum, the wood-apple tree J VI.534; Vism 183 (°ka); Mhvs 29, 11; — 2. °ŋ (nt.) the wood apple Miln 189; — 3. the position of the hand when the fingers are slightly and loosely bent in J I.237; kapitthaka S V.96.

Kapitthana=kapiṭhana J II.445; VI.529, 550, 553; v. l. at Vism 183 for °itthaka.

Kapila (adj.) [Sk. kapila, cp. kapi] brown, tawny, reddish, of hair & beard VvA 222; °ā f. a brown cow DhA IV.153.

Kapisīsa [Sk. kapiśīrṣa] the lintel of a door D II.143 (cp. Rh.D. *Buddh. Suttas* p. 95 n[1]) -°ka the cavity in a door-post for receiving the bolt Vin II.120, 148 (cp. *Vin. Texts* II.106 n[3]).

Kapota [Sk. kapota, greyish blue, cp. kapi] — 1. (m.) a pigeon, a dove J I.243; Miln 403; — 2. (f.) °i a female pigeon PvA 47; °ka (f. °ikā Miln 365) a small pigeon J I.244.

-pāda (of the colour) of a pigeon's foot J I.9.

Kapola [Sk. kapola, cp. kapalla, orig. meaning "hollow"] the cheek Vism 263, 362; DhA I.194.

Kappa (adj. n.) [Sk. kalpa, see kappeti for etym. & formation] anything made with a definite object in view, prepared, arranged; or that which is fit, suitable, proper. See also DhA I.103 & KhA 115 for var. meanings. —I *Literal Meaning*.— 1. (adj.) fitting, suitable, proper (cp. °tā) (=kappiya) in kappākappesu kusalo Th 1, 251, °kovido Mhvs 15, 16; Sn 911; as juice Miln 161.— (—°) made as, like, resembling Vin I.290 (ahata°); Sn 35 (khaggavisāṇa°); hetu° acting as cause to Sn 16; Miln 105; —a° incomparable Mhvs 14, 65; — 2. (nt.) a fitting, i. e. harness or trapping (cp. kappana) Vv 20[8] (VvA 104); — a small black dot or smudge (kappa-bindu) imprinted on a new robe to make it lawful Vin I.255; IV.227, 286: also fig. a making-up (of a trick): lesa° DA I.103; VvA 348. — II. *Applied Meaning*.— 1. (qualitative) ordinance, precept, rule; practice, manner Vin II.294, 301 (:kappati singiloṇa-kappo "fit is the rule concerning . . ."); cp. Mhvs 4, 9; one of the chaḷanga, the 6 disciplines of Vedic interpretation, VvA 265; — 2. (temporal) a "fixed" time, time with ref. to individual and cosmic life. As āyu at DA I.103 (cp.kappaŋ); as a cycle of time=saŋsāra at Sn 521, 535, 860 (na eti kappaŋ); as a measure of time: an age of the world Vin III.109; Miln 108; Sdhp 256, 257; PvA 21; It 17=Bdhd 87=S II.185. There are 3 principal cycles or aeons: mahā°, asankheyya°, antara°; each mahā° consists of 4 asankheyya-kappas, viz. saŋvaṭṭa° saŋvaṭṭaṭṭhāyi° vivaṭṭa° vivaṭṭaṭṭhāyi° A II.142; often abbreviated to saŋvaṭṭa-vivaṭṭa° D I.14; It 15; freq. in formula ekampijātiŋ, etc. Vin III.4=D III.51, 111= It 99. On pubbanta° & aparanta°, past & future kappas see D I.12 sq. paṭhama-kappe at the beginning of the world, once upon a time (cp. atīte) J I.207. When kappa stands by itself, a Mahā-kappa is understood: DA I.162. A whole, complete kappa is designated by kevala° Sn pp. 18=46~125; Sn 517; also dīgha° S II.181; Sdhp 257. For *similes* as to the enormous length of a kappa see S II.181 & DA I.164=PvA 254. — acc. kappaŋ adv.: for a long time D II.103=115= Ud 62, quot. at DA I.103; Vin II.198; It 17; Miln 108; mayi āyukappaŋ J I.119, cp. Miln 141. Cp. **sankappa**.

-**atīta** one who has gone beyond time, an Arahant Sn 373. **avasesaŋ** (acc.) for the rest of the kappa, in kappaŋ vā k-āvasesaŋ vā D II.117=A IV.309=Ud 62; Miln 140: -**āyuka** (one) whose life extends over a kappa Mhvs V.87; -**uṭṭhāna** arising at or belonging to the (end of a) **kappa**: -*aggi* the fire which destroys the Universe J II.397; III.185; IV.498; V.336; VI.554; Vism 304; -*kāla* the time of the end of the world J V.244; -uṭṭhāna (by itself) the end of the world J I.4=Vism 415; -**kata** on which a kappa, i. e. smudge, has been made, ref. to the cīvara of a bhikkhu (see above) Vin I.255; IV.227, 286; DA I.103; -(ñ)**jaha** (one) who has left time behind, free from saŋsāra, an Arahant Sn 1101 (but expl[d] at Nd[2] s. v., see also DA I.103 as free from dve kappā: diṭṭhi° taṇha°). -**jāla** the consumption of the kappa by fire, the end of a kappa Dpvs I.61. -**ṭṭha** staying there for a kappa, i. e. in purgatory in āpāyiko nerayiko + atekiccho, said of Devadatta Vin II.202, 206; A III.402 ~IV.160; It 11~85. -**ṭṭhāyin** lasting a whole cycle, of a vimāna Th 1, 1190. -**ṭṭhika** enduring for an aeon: kibbisa (of Devadatta) Vin II.198=204; (cp. *Vin. Texts* III.254) sālarukkha J V.416; see also ṭhitakappiŋ Pug 13. -**ṭṭhitika** id. DhA I.50 (vera); Miln 108 (kammaŋ). ("sabbe pi magga-samangino puggalā ṭhita kappino.") -**ṭṭhiya**-=prec. A V.75; J I.172, 213; V.33; Miln 109, 214. °**rukkha** the tree that lasts for a kappa, ref. to the cittapāṭalī, the pied trumpet-tree in the abode of the Asuras J I.202; -**nibbatta** originated at the beginning of the k. (appl. to the flames of purgatory) J V.272; -**parivaṭṭa** the evolution of a k; the end of the world Dpvs I.59; -pādapa=°rukkha Mhbv 2; -**rukkha** a wishing tree, magical tree, fulfilling all wishes; sometimes fig. J VI.117, 594; Vism 206; PvA 75, 176, 121; VvA 32 (where comb[d] with cintāmaṇi); DhA IV.208; -latā a creeper like the kapparukkha VvA 12; -**vināsaka** (scil. aggi): the fire consuming the world at the end of a k. Vism 414 sq.; (mahāmegho) DhA III.362; -**samaṇa** an ascetic acc. to precepts, an earnest ascetic J VI.60 (cp. samaṇa-kappa); -**halāhala** "the k-uproar," the uproar near the end of a kalpa J I.47.

Kappaka [fr. **kḷp**, kappeti] a barber, hairdresser, also attendant to the king; his other function (of preparing baths) is expressed in the term nahāpaka (Pv II.9[37]) or nahāpita (°ā ?) (DA I.157) Vin. I.344; II.182; D I.51 (=DA I.157, in list of various occupations); J I.60, 137; III.315; Pv II.9[37]; III.1[6] (where expl. by nahāpita in the meaning of "bathed," cp. expl. ad I.10[6]) DhA I.85 (°vesa disguise of a barber), 342 (pasādhana° one who arranges the dress, etc., hairdresser).

-**jātika** belonging to or reborn in the barber class, in this sense representing a low. "black" birth PvA 176.

Kappaṭa [kad-paṭa=ku-paṭa] a dirty, old rag, torn garment (of a bhikkhu) Th 1.199.

Kappatā (f.) [abstr. fr. kappa] fitness, suitability DA I.207.

Kappati [Pass. of kappeti, cp. Sk. kalpyate] to be fit, seeming, proper, with dat. of person D II.162; Vin II.263, 294; III.36; Th 1.488; Mhvs 4, 11; 15, 16.

Kappana (nt.) [fr. kappeti, cp. Sk. kalpana] the act of preparing, fixing; that which is fixed, arranged, performed. 1. kappanā (f.) the fixing of a horse's harness, harnessing, saddling J I.62; — 2. (nt.) (—°) procuring, making: jīvika°; a livelihood J III.32; putting into order; danta° J I.321; — 3. (adj.) (—°) trimmed, arranged with: nānāratana° VvA 35.

Kappara [cp. Sk. kūrpara] the elbow Vin III.121=IV.221; J I.293; 297; DhA I.48, 394; VvA 206.

Kappāsa [cp. Sk. karpāsa] 1. the silk-cotton tree J III.286; VI.336. — 2. cotton D II.141; A III.295; S V.284; J I.350; VI.41; comb. w. uṇṇa A III.37=IV.265=268.

-**aṭṭhi** a cotton seed DhA III.71; -**paṭala** the film of the cotton seed Vism 446; Bdhd 66; -**picu** cotton S V.284; J V.110, 343; VI.184; -**maya** made of cotton PvA 77.

Kappāsika (adj.) made of cotton D II.188, cp. A IV.394; D II.351; Vin I.58=97=281; J VI.590; Pv II.1[17]. (nt.) cotton stuff Miln 267.

-**paṇṇa** the leaf of the cotton tree, used medicinally

Vin I.201; -sukhuma fine, delicate cotton stuff D II.188; A IV.394; Miln 105.

Kappāsī (f.) [=kappāsa] cotton J VI.537; PvA 146.

Kappika (—°) (adj.) [fr. kappa] 1. belonging to a kappa, in paṭhama° -kāla the time of the first Age DA I.247; Vbh 412 (of manussā); VvA 19 (of Manu); without the kāla (id.) at J I.222; as noun the men of the first Age J II.352. — 2. In cpds. . . . pubbanta° and aparanta° the ika° belongs to the whole cpd. D I.39 sq.; DA I.103. See also kappiya 2.

Kappita [pp. of kappeti] 1. prepared, arranged, i. e. harnessed D I.49; J VI.268; i. e. plaited DA I.274; i. e. trimmed: °kesamassu "with hair & beard trimmed" D II.325; S IV.343; J V.173. 350; VI.268; Vv 73[1]. — 2. getting procuring; as °jīvika a living J V.270; made ready, drawn up (in battle array) D II.189; — 3. decorated with, adorned with Sdhp 247. -su° well prepared, beautifully harnessed or trimmed Vv 60[1].

Kappin (adj.) [fr. kappa] 1. (cp. kappa II.1[a]) getting, procuring, acquiring (pañña°) Sn 1090; — 2. (cp. kappa II.1[b]) having a kappa (as duration), lasting a Cycle Pu 13; in Mahā° enduring a Mahākappa DA I.164=PvA 254.

Kappiya (adj.) [fr. kappa] 1. (cp. kappa II.1[a]) according to rule, right, suitable, fitting, proper, appropriate (PvA 26=anucchavika paṭirūpa) J I.392; DA I.9; PvA 25, 141. —a° not right, not proper, unlawful Vin I.45, 211; II.118; III.20; (nt) that which is proper A I.84; Dhs 1160; —a° ibid; -kappiyâkappiya (nt) that which is proper and that which is not J I.316; DA I.78. — 2. (cp. kappa II.1[b]) connected with time, subject to kappa, i. e. temporal, of time, subject to saŋsāra; of devamanussā Sn 521; na+of the Muni Sn 914. In another sense ("belonging to an Age") in cpd. paṭhama °-kāla the time of the first Age J II.352. —a° delivered from time, free from saŋsāra, Ep. of an Arahant Sn 860; cp. Miln 49, 50. See also kappika.

-**ânuloma** (nt.) accordance with the rule Nett 192. -**kāraka** "one who makes it befitting," i. e. who by offering anything to a Bhikkhu, makes it legally acceptable Vin I.206; -**kuṭi** (f.) a building outside the Vihāra, wherein allowable articles were stored, a kind of warehouse Vin I.139; II.159; -**dāraka** a boy given to the Bhikkhus to work for them in the Vihāra DA I.78 (v. l. BB °kāraka); -**bhaṇḍa** utensils allowable to the Bhikkhus J I.41; DhA I.412. a° thing unauthorised Vin. II.169; a list of such forbidden articles is found at Vin I.192; -**bhūmi** (f.) a plot of ground set apart for storing (allowable) provisions Vin I.239 (cp. °kuṭi); -**lesa** [cp. Sk. kalpya] guile appropriate to one's own purpose VvA 348; -**saññin** (a) imagining as lawful (that which is not) A I.84; a° opp. ibid. -°tā the imagining as lawful (that which is not) appl. to kukkucca Dhs 1160; a° opp. ibid.

Kappu (nt.)=kappa in the dialect used by Makkhali Gosāla, presumably the dialect of Vesāli, D I.54; DA I.164 (a Burmese MS. reads kappi, and so do Pv IV.3[33]; PvA 254).

Kappūra (m. & nt.) [cp. Sk. karpūra] camphor: (a) the plant J VI.537. — (b) the resinous exudation, the prepared odoriferant substance (cp. kaṭukapphala) J II.416=DhA III.475; Miln 382; Dāvs V.50.

Kappeti [Der. from kappa, cp. Sk. kṛpa shape, form; *qu̥rep caus. from. fr. *qu̥er=Sk. **kr**, karoti to shape, to make, cp. karoti] to cause to fit, to create, build, construct, arrange, prepare, order.

I. *lit.* 1. in special sense: to prepare, get done, i. e. harness: J I.62; plait DA I.274, an offering (yaññaŋ) Sn 1043; i. e. to trim etc. M II.155; J III.223; Mhvs 25, 64. 2, generally (to be translated according to the meaning of accompanying noun), to make, get up, carry on etc. (=Fr. passer), viz. iriyāpathaŋ to keep one's composure Th I.570; J V.262; Bdhd 33; **jīvitaŋ**: to lead one's life PvA 3, 4, 13; divāvihāraŋ to take the noonday rest Mhvs 19, 79; **nisajjaŋ** to sit down Vin III.191; vāsaŋ, saŋvāsaŋ to make one's abode D II.88; Sn 283; PvA 36, 47; saŋvāsaŋ to have (sexual) intercourse with J III.448; Mhvs 5, 212; PvA 6; seyyaŋ: to lie down, to make one's bed Pug 55 etc. (acelaka-passage=D I.166).

II. *fig.* 1. in special sense: to construct or form an opinion, to conjecture, to think Sn 799; DA I.103; — 2. generally: to ordain, prescribe, determine J V.238 (=say vidahati) — Caus. II. kappāpeti to cause to be made in all senses of kappeti; e. g. Vin II.134 (massuŋ k. to get one's beard done); J V.262 (hatthiyānāni k. to harness the elephant-cars); DA I.147 (pañca hatthinikā-satāni k. harness the 500 elephants). Pass. kappīyati in ppr. kappiyamāna getting harnessed J I.62.

Kabara (adj.) [cp. Sk. kabara] variegated, spotted, striped; mixed, intermingled; in patches Vism 190. Of a cow (°gāvī) DhA I.71 (°go-rūpa) ibid. 99; of a calf (°vaccha) J V.106; of a dog (°vaṇṇa=sabala q. v.) J VI.107; of leprosy J V.69; of the shade of trees (°cchāya, opp. sanda°) M I.75; J IV.152; DhA I.375.

-**kucchi** having a belly striped with many colours, of a monster J I.273; -**kuṭṭha** a kind of leprosy J V.69; -**maṇi** the cat's eye, a precious stone, also called masāragalla, but also an emerald; both are prob. varieties of the cat's eye VvA 167, 304.

Kabala (m., nt.) [cp. Sk. kavala BSk. kavaḍa Divy 290 (+ālopa), 298, 470] a small piece (=ālopa PvA 70), a mouthful, always appl. to food, either solid (i. e. as much as is made into a ball with the fingers when eating), or liquid Vin II.214; It 18=J III.409; IV.93; Dh 324; Miln 180, 400; Bdhd 69; DhA II.65; PvA 39; Mhvs 19, 74. Kabale kabale on every morsel J I.68; Miln 231; -**sakabala** appl. to the mouth, with the mouth full of food Vin II.214; IV. 195; — Sometimes written kabaḷa.

-**âvacchedaka** choosing portions of a mouthful, nibbling at a morsel Vin II.214; IV.196.

Kabalinkāra (adj.) [kabala in compⁿ form kabalī° before **kr** & **bhū**; kabalin for kabalī°] always in combⁿ with āhāra, food "made into a ball," i. e. eatable, material food, as one of the 4 kinds of food (see stock phrase k° āhāro oḷāriko vā sukhumo vā . . . at M I.48= S II.11, 98=D III.228, 276; Bdhd 135) Dhs 585, 646 (where fully described), 816; Miln 245; Vism 236, 341, 450, 616; Bdhd 69, 74; DA I.120. Written kabalīkāra nearly always in Burmese, and sometimes in Singh. MSS.; s. also Nett 114-118.

-**āhāra-bhakkha** (of attā, soul) feeding on material food D I.34, 186, 195; -bhakkha, same A III.192=V.336 (appl. to the kāmâvacara devas); DA I.120.

Kabaḷikā (f.) [cp. Sk. kavalikā] a bandage, a piece of cloth put over a sore or wound Vin I.205 (cp. *Vin. Texts* II.58 n[4]).

Kabba (nt.) [cp. Sk. kāvya] a poem, poetical composition, song, ballad in °ŋ **karoti** to compose a song J VI.410; -**karaṇa** making poems DA I.95; and -**kāra** a poet Kh 21; J VI.410.

Kabya=kabba in cpds. °**âlankāra** composing in beautiful verse, a beautiful poem in °ŋ bandhati, to compose a poem ibid.; and -**kāraka** a poet, ibid.

Kama [fr. **kram**, cp. Vedic krama (—°) step, in uru°, BSk. krama reprieve, Divy 505] — 1. (nt.) going, proceeding, course, step, way, manner, e. g. sabbatth'âvihatakkama "having a course on all sides unobstructed" Sdhp 425; vaḍḍhana° process of development Bdhd 96 paṭiloma° (going) the opposite way Bdhd 106; cp. also

Bdhd 107, 111. a fivefold kama or process (of development or division), succession, is given at Vism 476 with uppattik°, pahāna°, paṭipattik°, bhūmik°, desanāk°, where they are illustrated by examples. Threefold applied to upādāna at Vism 570 (viz. uppattik°, pahānak°, desanāk°) — 2. oblique cases (late and technical) "by way of going," i. e. in order or in due course, in succession: kamato Vism 476, 483, 497; Bdhd 70, 103; kamena by & by, gradually Mhvs. 3, 33; 5, 136; 13, 6; Dāvs 1.30; SnA 455; Bdhd 88; yathākkamaŋ Bdhd 96. — 3. (adj.) (—°) having a certain way of going: catukkama walking on all fours (= catuppāda) Pv 1.11[8].

Kamana a step, stepping, gait J v.155, in expl[n] J v.156 taken to be ppr. med. — See san°.

Kamati [kram, Dhtp. expl[d] by padavikkhepe; ppr. med. kamamāna S 1.33; Sn 176; Intens. cankamati.] to walk. (I) lit. 1. c. loc. to walk, travel, go through: dibbe pathe Sn 176; ariye pathe S 1.33; ākāse D 1.212 = M 1 69 = A III.17; — 2. c. acc. to go or get to, to enter M II.18; J VI.107; Pv 1.1[2] (saggaŋ) — (II) fig. 1. to succeed, have effect, to affect M 1.186; J v.198; Miln 198; — 2. to plunge into, to enter into A II.144; — 3. impers. to come to (c. dat) S IV.283.

Kamaṇḍalu (m., nt.) [etym. uncertain] the waterpot with long spout used by non-Buddhist ascetics S 1.167; J II.73 (= kuṇḍikā); IV.362, 370; VI.86, 525, 570; Sn p. 80; DhA III.448—adj. **kamaṇḍaluka** [read kā° ?] "with the waterpot" A v.263 (brāhmaṇā pacchābhūmakā k.).

Kamatthaŋ (adv.) [kaŋ atthaŋ] for what purpose, why? J III.398 (= kimatthaŋ).

Kamanīya (adj.) [grd of kāmayati] (a) desirable, beautiful, lovely J v.155, 156; Miln 11; (b) pleasant, sweet (-sounding) D II.171; J 1.96. — As nt. a desirable object S 1.22.

Kamala (nt.) a lotus, freq. comb[d] with kuvalaya; or with uppala J 1.146; DA 1.40, expl[d] as vārikiñjakkha PvA 77. 1. lotus, the lotus flower, Nelumbium J 1.146; DA 1.40; Mhbv 3; Sdhp 325; VvA 43, 181, 191; PvA 23, 77; — At J 1.119, 149 a better reading is obtained by corr. kambala to kamala, at J 1.178 however kamb° should be retained.— 2. a kind of grass, of which sandals were made Vin. 1.190 (s. *Vin. Texts* II.23 n.) — 3. f. **kamalā** a graceful woman J v.160: **-komalakarā** (f.) (of a woman) having lotus-like (soft) hands Mhbv 29; **-dala** a lotus leaf Vism 465; Mhbv 3; Bdhd 19; DhsA 127; VvA 35, 38. — **-pādukā** sandals of k. grass Vin 1.190.

Kamalin (adj.) [fr. kamala] rich in lotus, covered with lotuses (of a pond) in kamalinī-kāmuka "the lover of lotuses," Ep. of the Sun Mhbv. 3 (v. l. °sāmika perhaps to be preferred).

Kampa (—°) [fr. kamp] trembling, shaking; tremor DA 1.130 (paṭhavi°); Sdhp 401; a° (adj.) not trembling, unshaken; calm, tranquil Sdhp 594; Mhvs 15, 175.

Kampaka (adj.) [fr. kampa] shaking, one who shakes or causes to tremble Miln 343 (paṭhavi°).

Kampati [kamp to shake Dhtp. 186: calane; p. pres. kampanto, kampaŋ, kampamāna; aor. akampi; caus. kampeti; p. pres. kampetan Dpvs XVII.51; ger. kampayitvāna D II.108; J v.178] — to shake, tremble, waver Kh 6; J 1.23; Sn 268 (expl. KhA 153: calati, vedhati); Bdhd 84;—Cp. anu°, pa°, vi°, sam°.—**kampamāna** (adj.) trembling J III.161; agitated, troubled (°citta) J II.337; a° not trembling, unhesitating, steadfast J VI. 293.

Kampana [fr. kamp] 1. adj. causing to shake DhA 1.84, trembling Kacc 271; 2. (nt) (a) an earthquake J 1.26 47; (b) tremor (of feelings) J III.163.

-rasa (adj.) "whose essence is to tremble," said of doubt (vicikicchā) DhsA 259.

Kampin (adj.) [fr. kampa] see vi°.

Kampiya (adj.) [grd. of kampati] in a° not to be shaken, immovable, strong Th 2, 195; Miln 386; (nt.) firmness, said of the 5 moral powers (balāni) DA 1.64.

Kampurī (va.) at Th 2, 262 is to be corr. into kambu-r-iva (see Morris, *J.P.T.S.* 1884, 76).

Kambala (m., nt.) [cp. Sk. kambala] 1. woollen stuff, woollen blanket or garment. From J IV.353 it appears that it was a product of the north, probably Nepal (cp. *J.P.T.S.* 1889, 203); enum[d] as one of the 6 kinds of cīvaras, together w. koseyya & **kappāsika** at Vin 1.58 = 96, also at A IV.394 (s. °sukhuma); freq. preceded by **ratta** (e. g. DA 1.40. Cp. also ambara[2] and ambala), which shows that it was commonly dyed red; also as **paṇḍu** Sn 689; Bdhd 1. — Some woollen garments (aḍḍhakāsika) were not allowed for Bhikkhus: Vin 1.281; II.174; see further J 1.43, 178, 322; IV.138; Miln 17, 88, 105; DhA 1.226; II.89 sq. 2. a garment: two kinds of hair-(blankets, i. e.) garments viz. **kesa°** and **vāla°** mentioned Vin 1.305 = D 1.167 = A 1.240, 295. — 3. woollen thread Vin 1.190 (expl[d] by uṇṇā) (cp. *Vin. Texts* II.23); J VI.340; — 4. a tribe of Nāgas J VI.165.

-kañcuka a (red) woollen covering thrown over a temple, as an ornament Mhvs 34, 74; **-kūṭāgāra** a bamboo structure covered with (red) woollen cloth, used as funeral pile DhA 1.69; **-pādukā** woollen slippers Vin 1.190; **-puñja** a heap of blankets J 1.149; **-maddana** dyeing the rug Vin 1.254 (cp. *Vin. Texts* II.154); **-ratana** a precious rug of wool J IV.138; Miln 17 (16 ft. long & 18 ft. wide); **-vaṇṇa** (adj.) of the colour of woollen fabric, i. e. red J v.359 (°maŋsa); **-silāsana** (paṇḍu°) a stone-seat, covered with a white k. blanket, forming the throne of Sakka DhA 1.17; **-sukhuma** fine, delicate woollen stuff D II.188 = A IV.394; Miln 105; **-sutta** a woollen thread J VI.340.

Kambalin (adj.) [fr. kambala] having a woollen garment D 1.55; II.150.

Kambalīya (nt.) [fr. kambala] (a sort of) woollen garment Pv II.1[17] (cp. PvA 77).

Kambu [cp. Sk. kambu, Halāyudha = śankha; Dhtp. saŋvaraṇe] 1. a conch, a shell: saṇha-kambu-r-iva . . . sobhate su gīvā Th 2, 262 (for kampurī'va); s. cpds. — 2. a ring or bracelet (made of shells or perhaps gold: see Kern, *Toev. s.* v.) J IV.18, 466 (+ kāyūra); Pv II.12[7], III.9[3] (= PvA 157, sankhavalaya) Vv 36[2] (= VvA 167 hatth'ālankāra), worn on the wrist, while the kāyūra is worn on the upper part of the arm (bhujālankāra ibid.); — 3. a golden ring, given as second meaning at VvA 167, so also expl. at J IV.18, 130; J v.400.

-gīva (adj.) having a neck shaped like a shell, i. e. in spirals, having lines or folds, considered as lucky J IV.130 (= suvaṇṇālingasadisagīvo), cp. above 1; **-tala** the base or lower part of a shell, viz. the spiral part, fig. the lines of the neck J v.155 (°ābhāsā gīvā, expl[d] on p. 156 as suvaṇṇālingatala-sannibhā); also the (polished) surface of a shell, used as simile for smoothness J v.204, 207; **-pariharaka** a wristlet or bracelet VvA 167.

Kambussa [fr. preceding] gold or golden ornament (bracelet) J v.260, 261 (: kambussaŋ vuccati suvaṇṇaŋ).

Kambojaka (adj.) coming fr. Kamboja J IV.464 (assatara).

Kambojā (f.) N of a country J v.446 (°ka raṭṭha); Pv II.91 (etc.); Vism 332, 334, 336.

Kamboji (m., nt.) [meaning & etym. unexpl[d]] the plant Cassia tora or alata J III.223 (°gumba=eḷagalā-gumba; vv. ll. kammoja° & tampo° [for kambo°]).

Kamma (nt.) [Vedic karman, work esp. sacrificial process. For ending °man=Idg. *men cp. Sk. dhāman=Gr. δῆμα, Sk. nāman=Lat nomen] the doing, deed, work; orig. meaning (see karoti) either building (cp. Lit. kùrti, Opr. kūra to build) or weaving, plaiting (still in mālākamma and latā° "the intertwining of garlands and creepers"; also in kamma-kara possibly orig. employed in weaving, i. e. serving); cp. Lat. texo, to weave=Sk. takṣan builder, artisan, & Ger. wirken, orig. weben. Grammatically karman has in Pāli almost altogether passed into the -a decl., the cons. forms for instr. & abl. kammā and kammanā gen. dat. kammuno, are rare. The nom. pl. is both kammā and kammāni.

I. *Crude meaning.* 1. (lit.) Acting in a special sense, i. e. office, *occupation*, doing, action, profession. Two kinds are given at Vin IV.6, viz. low (hīna) & high (ukkaṭṭha) professions. To the former belong the kammāni of a koṭṭhaka and a pupphacchaḍḍaka, to the latter belong vāṇijjā and gorakkhā.—Kamma as a profession or business is regarded as a hindrance to the religious life, & is counted among the ten obstacles (see paḷibodha). In this sense it is at Vism 94 expl[d] by navakamma (see below 2a).—**kassa°** ploughing, occupation of a ploughman Vism 284; **kumbhakāra°** profession of a potter J VI.372; tunna° weaving Vism 122; PvA 161. **purohita°** office of a high-priest (=abstr. n. porohiccaŋ) SnA 466; **vāṇija°** trade Sāsv. 40.—**kammanā** by profession Sn 650, 651; **kammāni** (pl.) occupations Sn 263=Kh v.6 (anavajjāni k.=anākulā kammantā Sn 262). **parcsaŋ** k°ŋ katvā doing other people's work=being a servant VvA 299; sa° pasutā bent upon their own occupations D I.135, cp. attano k°- kubbānaŋ Dh 217. **kamma-karaṇa-sālā** work-room (here: weaving shed) PvA 120.

2. Acting in general, *action*, deed, doing (nearly always —°) (a) (active) act, deed, job, often to be rendered by the special verb befitting the special action, like civara° mending the cloak VvA 250; **uposatha°** observing the Sabbath Vbh 422; **nava°** making new, renovating, repairing, patching Vin II.119, 159 (°karoti to make repairs); J I.92: Vism 94, adj. navakammika one occupied with repairs Vin II.15; S I.179; **patthita°** the desired action (i. e. sexual intercourse) DhA II.49; **kammaŋ karoti** to be active or in working, to act: **nāgo pādehi k.k.** the elephant works with his feet M I.414; **kata°** the job done by the thieves DhA II.38 (corehi), as adj. **kata°** cora (& akata °cora) a thief who has finished his deed (& one who has not) Vism 180, also in special sense: occasion for action or work, i. e. *necessity*, purpose: ukkāya kammaŋ n'atthi, the torch does not work, is no good Vism 428. (b) (passive) the act of being done (—°), anything done (in its result), *work*, often as collect. abstr. (to be trsl[d]. by E. ending -ing): **apaccakkha°** not being aware, deception Vbh 85; **daḷhī°** strengthening, increase Vbh 357, Vism 122; **citta°** variegated work, **mālā°** garlands, **latā°** creeper (-work) Vism 108; **nāma°** naming Bdhd 83; **pañhā°** questioning, "questionnaire" Vism 6. — So in *definitions* **niṭṭhuriya°**=niṭṭhuriya Vbh 357; **nimitta°**= nimitta, **obhāsa°**=obhāsa (apparition > appearing) Vbh 353. — (c) (intrs.) making, getting, act, *process* (-°). Often trsl. as abstr. n. with ending -ion or -ment, e. g. **okāsa°** opportunity of speaking, giving an audience Sn p. 94; **pātu°** making clear, manifestation DhA IV.198 **anāvi°**, **anuttāni°** concealment Vbh 358; **kata°** (adj.) one who has done the act or process, gone through the experience SnA 355; **añjali°**, **sāmīci°** veneration, honouring (in formula with nipaccakāra abhivādana paccuṭṭhāna) D III.83 (≈Vin II.162, 255); A I.123; II.180; J. I.218, 219.

3. (Specialised) an "act" in an ecclesiastical sense; proceedings, ceremony, performed by a lawfully constituted chapter of bhikkhus Vin I.49, 53, 144, 318; II.70, 93; V.220 sq.; Khus *J.P.T.S.* 1883, 101. At these formal functions a motion is put before the assembly and the announcement of it is called the ñatti Vin I.56, after which the bhikkhus are asked whether they approve of the motion or not. If this question is put once, it is a ñattidutiyakamma Vin II.89; if put three times, a ñatticatuttha° Vin I.56 (cp. *Vin. Texts* I.169 n[2]). There are 6 kinds of official acts the Sangha can perform: see Vin I.317 sq.; for the rules about the validity of these ecclesiastical functions see Vin I.312-333 (cp. *Vin T.* II.256-285). The most important ecclesiastical acts are: apalokanakamma, ukkhepanīya° uposatha° tajjaniya° tassapāpiyyasikā° nissaya°, patiññākaraṇīya°, paṭipucchākaraṇīya° paṭisāraṇiya° pabbājaniya°, sammukhākaraṇīya°. — In this sense: **kammaŋ karoti** (w. gen.) to take proceedings against Vin I.49, 143, 317; II.83, 260; **kammaŋ garahati** to find fault with proceedings gone through Vin II.5; **kammaŋ paṭippassambheti** to revoke official proceedings against a bhikkhu Vin III.145.

4. In cpds.:— **-adhiṭṭhāyaka** superintendent of work, inspector Mhvs 5, 174; 30, 98; **-ādhipateyya** one whose supremacy is action Miln 288; **-ārambha** commencement of an undertaking Mhvs 28, 21; **-āraha** (a) entitled to take part in the performance of an "act" Vin IV.153; V.221; **-ārāma** (a) delighting in activity D II.77; A IV.22; It 71, 79; **-ārāmatā** taking pleasure in (worldly) activity D II.78=A IV.22, cp. Vbh 381; A III.116, 173, 293 sq., 330, 449; IV.22 sq., 331; V.163; It 71; **āvadāna** a tale of heroic deeds J VI.295; **-kara** or **°kāra**: used indiscriminately. 1. (adj.) doing work, or active, in puriso dāso+pubbuṭṭhāyī "willing to work" D 1.60 et sim. (=DA I.168: analaso). A I.145; II.67; Vv 75[4]; 2. (n.) a workman, a servant (a weaver?) usually in form dāsā ti vā pessā ti vā kammakarā ti vā Vin I.243; D I.141=Pug 56 (also °kārā); A II.208; III.77, 172; Th 2, 340; J I.57. Also as dāsā pessā k°kārā A III.37=IV.265, 393, and dāsā k° kārā Vin I.240, 272; II.154; D III.191; S I.92:—a handyman J I.239; Miln 378; (f) **-ī** a female servant Vin II.267; °kāra Vin IV.224, kārī Dhs A98=VvA 73 (appl. to a wife); **-karaṇa** 1. working, labour, service J III.219; PvA 120; DA I.168; 2. the effects of karma J I.146; **-karanā** and kāraṇā see below; **-kāma** liking work, industrious; a° lazy A IV.93=J II.348; **-kāraka** a workman, a servant DA I.8; Mhvs 30, 42; Nd[2] 427; a sailor J IV.139; **-garu** bent on work Miln 288; **-ccheda** the interruption of work J I.149; 246; III.270; **-jāta** sort of action J V.24 (=kammam eva); **-dhura** (m. nt.) draught-work J I.196; **-dheyya** work to be performed, duty A IV.285=325; cp. J VI.297; **-dhoreyya** "fit to bear the burden of action" Miln 288 (cp. *Mil. trsl.* II.140); **-niketavā** having action as one's house or temple ibid.; **-nipphādana** accomplishing the business J VI.162; **-ppatta** entitled to take part in an eccles. act Vin I.318; V.221; **-bahula** abounding in action (appl. to the world of men) Miln 7; **-mūla** the price of the transaction Miln 334; **-rata** delighting in business D II.78; It 71; **-vatthu** objects, items of an act Vin V.116; **-vācā** the text or word of an official Act. These texts form some of the oldest literature and are embodied in the Vinaya (cp. Vin I.317 sq.; III.174, 176; IV.153, etc.). The number of officially recognized k° is eleven, see *J.P.T.S.* 1882, 1888, 1896, 1907; k°ŋ karoti to carry out an official Act Mhvs 5, 207; DhsA 399; -°ŋ anussāveti to proclaim a k°, to put a resolution to a chapter of bhikkhus Vin I.317; **-vossagga** difference of occupation J VI.216; **-sajja** (a) "ready for action," i. e. for battle J V.232; **-sādutā** "agreeableness to work" DhsA 151 (cp. kammaññatā & kamyatā); **-sāmin** "a master in action," an active man Miln 288; **-sippī** an artisan VvA 278; **-sīla** one whose habit it is

to work, energetic, persevering Miln 288, a° indolent, lazy J VI.245; a°-ttaŋ indolence, laziness Mhvs 23, 21; -hīna devoid of occupation, inactive Miln 288.

II. *Applied* (*pregnant*) *meaning*: doing, acting with ref. to both deed and doer. It is impossible to draw a clear line between the source of the act (i. e. the acting subject, the actor) and the act (either the object or phenomenon acted, produced, i. e. the deed as objective phenomenon, or the process of acting, i. e. the deed as subjective phenomenon). Since the latter (the act) is to be judged by its consequences, its effects, its manifestation always assumes a quality (in its most obvious characteristics either good or bad or indifferent), and since the act reflects on the actor, this quality is also attached to him. This is the popular, psychological view, and so it is expressed in language, although reason attributes goodness and badness to the actor first, and then to the act. In the expression of language there is no difference between: 1. the deed as such and the doer in character: anything done (as good or bad) has a corresponding source; 2. the performance of the single act and the habit of acting: anything done tends to be repeated; 3. the deed with ref. both to its cause and its effect: anything done is caused and is in itself the cause of something else. As meanings of kamma we therefore have to distinguish the foll. different sides of a "deed," viz.

1. the deed as expressing the doer's will, i. e. qualified deed, good or bad; 2. the repeated deed as expression of the doer's habit = his character; 3. the deed as having consequences for the doer, as such a source qualified according to good and evil; as deed done accumulated and forming a deposit of the doer's merit and demerit (his "karma"). Thus pāpakamma = a bad deed, one who has done a bad deed, one who has a bad character, the potential effect of a bad deed = bad karma. The context alone decides which of these meanings is the one intended by the speaker or writer.

Concerning the analysis of the various semantic developments the following practical distinctions can be made: 1. Objective action, characterized by time: as past = done, meaning *deed* (with kata); or future = to be done, meaning *duty* (with kātabba). 2. Subjective action, characterized by quality, as reflecting on the agent. 3. Interaction of act and agent: (a) in subjective relation, cause and effect as action and reaction on the individual (individual "karma," appearing in his life, either here or beyond), characterized as regards action (having results) and as regards actor (having to cope with these results): (b) in objective relation, i. e. abstracted from the individual and generalized as Principle, or cause and effect as Norm of Happening (universal "karma," appearing in Saŋsāra, as driving power of the world), characterized (a) as cause, (b) as consequence, (c) as cause-consequence in the principle of retribution (talio), (d) as restricted to time.

1. (Objective): with ref. to the Past: kiŋ kammaŋ akāsi nārī what (deed) has this woman done? Pv I.9²; tassā katakammaŋ pucchi he asked what had been done by her PvA 37, 83, etc. — with ref. to the Future: k. kātabbaŋ hoti I have an obligation, under 8 kusītavatthūni D III.255 = A IV.332; cattāri kammāni kattā hoti "he performs the 4 obligations" (of gahapati) A II.67.

2. (Subjective) (a) doing in general, acting, action, deed; var. kinds of doings enum. under micchājīva D I.12 (santikamma, paṇidhi°, etc.); tassa kammassa katattā through (the performance of) that deed D III.156; dukkaraŋ kamma-kubbataŋ he who of those who act, acts badly S I.19; abhabbo taŋ kammaŋ kātum incapable of doing that deed S III.225; sañcetanika k. deed done intentionally M III.207; A V.292 sq.; pamāṇakataŋ k. D I.251 = S IV.322. kataraŋ k°ŋ karonto ahaŋ nirayaŋ na gaccheyyaŋ? how (i. e. what doing) shall I not go to Niraya? J IV.340; yaŋ kiñci sithilaŋ k°ŋ . . . na taŋ hoti mahapphalaŋ . . . S I.49 = Dh 312 = Th I, 277; kadariya° a stingy action PvA 25; k. classed with sippa, vijjā-caraṇa D III.156; kāni k°āni sammā-niviṭṭha established slightly in what doings? Sn 324; (b) Repeated action in general, constituting a person's habit of acting or character (cp. kata II.I. a.), action as reflecting on the agent or bearing his characteristics; disposition, character. Esp. in phrase kammena samannāgata "endowed with the quality of acting in such and such a manner, being of such and such character": tīhi dhammehi samannāgato niraye nikkhitto "endowed with (these) three qualites a man will go to N." A I.292 sq.; asucinā kāya-k°ena sam° asucimanussā "bad people are those who are of bad ways (or character)" Nd² 112; anavajja kāya-k° sam° A II.69 (cp. A IV.364); kāya-kamma-vacī-kammena sam° kusalena (pabbajita) "a bhikkhu of good character in deed and speech" D I.63; kāya . . . (etc.) -k°sam° bāla (and opp. paṇḍita) A II.252 (cp. A I.102, 104); visamena kāya (etc.) -k° sam° A I.154 = III.129; sāvajjena kāya (etc.) -k° sam° A II.135 — kammaŋ vijjā ca dhammo ca sīlaŋ jīvitam uttamaŋ, etena maccā sujjhanti, na gottena dhanena vā S I.34 = 55; M III.262, quoted at Vism 3, where k. is grouped with vipassanā, jhāna, sīla, satipaṭṭhāna as main ideals of virtue; kammanā by character, as opp. to jaccā or jātiyā, by birth: Sn 136; 164; 599; nihīna° manussā (of bad, wretched character) Sn 661; manāpena bahulaŋ kāya (etc.) -kammena A II.87 = III.33, 131; and esp. with mettā, as enum. under aparihāniyā and sārāṇiyā dhammā D II.80; A III.288; mettena kāya-(etc.)-kammena D II.144; III.191; A V.350 sq. (c) Particular actions, as manifested in various ways, by various channels of activity (k°-dvārā), expressions of personality, as by deed, word and thought (kāyena, vācāya, manasā). Kamma κατ' ἐξοχήν means action by hand (body) in formula vacasā manasā kammanā ca Sn 330, 365; later specified by kāya-kamma, for which kāya-kammanta in some sense (q. v.), and complementing vacī-k° mano-k°; so in foll. combns: citte arakkhite kāya-k° pi arakkhitaŋ hoti (vacī° mano°) A I.261 sq.; yaŋ nu kho ahaŋ idaŋ kāyena k° kattukāmo idaŋ me kāya-k° attabyādhāya pi saŋvatteyya . . . "whatever deed I am going to do with my hands (I have to consider:) is this deed, done by my hands, likely to bring me evil?" M I.415; kāya-(vacī- etc.) kamma, which to perform & to leave (sevitabbaŋ and a°) A I.110 = III.150; as anulomika° A I.106; sabbaŋ kāya-k° (vacī° mano°) Buddhassa ñāṇānuparivattati "all manifestation of deed (word & thought) are within the knowledge of Buddha" Nd² 235; yaŋ lobhapakataŋ kammaŋ karoti kāyena vā vācāya vā manasā vā tassa vipākaŋ anubhoti . . . Nett 37; kin nu kāyena v° m° dukkaṭaŋ kataŋ what evil have you done by body, word or thought? Pv II.1⁸ and freq.; ekūna-tiŋsa kāya-kammāni Bdhd 49. (d) Deeds characterized as *evil* (pāpa-kammāni, pāpāni k°, pāpakāni k°; pāpakamma adj., cp. pāpa-kammanta adj.). pāpakamma: n'atthi loke raho nāma p° pakubbato "there is no hiding (-place) in this world for him who does evil" A I.149; so p°-o dummedho jānaŋ dukkaṭaŋ attano . . . "he, afflicted with (the result of) evil-doing . . ." A III.354; p°-ŋ pavaḍḍhento ibid.; yaŋ p°-ŋ kataŋ sabban taŋ idha vedanīyaŋ "whatever wrong I have done I have to suffer for" A V.301; pabbajitvāna kāyena p°-ŋ vivajjayi "avoid evil-acting" Sn 407; nissaŋsayaŋ p°-ŋ . . . "undoubtedly there is some evil deed (the cause of this) i. e. some evil karma Pv IV.16¹.—pāpaŋ kammaŋ: appamattikam pi p° k° kataŋ taŋ enaŋ nirayaŋ upaneti "even a small sin brings man to N." A I.249, tayā v'etaŋ p° k° kataŋ tvañ ñeva etassa vipākaŋ paṭisaŋvedissasi "you yourself have done this sin you yourself shall feel its consequences" M III.180 = A I.139, na hi p° kataŋ k° sajju khīraŋ va muccati Dh 71 = Nett 161; yassa p° kataŋ k° kusalena pithīyati

so imaŋ lokaŋ pabhāseti "he will shine in this world who covers an evil deed with a good one" M II.104=Dh 173=Th 1, 872; p°-ssa k°-ssa samatikkamo "the overcoming of evil karma" S IV.320; p°ssa k°ssa kiriyāya "in the performance of evil" M 1.372; p°āni k°āni karaŋ bālo na bujjhati "he, like a fool, awaketh not, doing sinful deeds" Dh 136=Th 1, 146; pāpā p°ehi k°ehi nirayaŋ upapajjare "sinners by virtue of evil deeds go to N." Dh 307; te ca p°esu k°esu abhiṇhaṃ upadissare Sn 140. **-pāpakāni kammāni:** p°ānaŋ k°ānaŋ hetu coraŋ rājāno gāhetvā vividhā kamma-kāraṇā kārenti "for his evil deeds the kings seize the thief and have him punished" A 1.48; ye loke p°āni k° karonti te vividhā kamma-kāraṇā kariyanti "those who do evil deeds in this world, are punished with various punishments" M III.186=A 1.142; k°ŋ karoti p°ŋ kāyena vācā uda cetasā vā Sn 232 (=kh 190); similarly Sn 127; karontā p°ŋ k°ŋ yaŋ hoti kaṭukapphalaŋ, "doing evil which is of bitter fruit" Dh 66=S 1.57=Nett 131; k°ehi p°ehi Sn 215.—*In the same sense:* na taŋ k°ŋ kataŋ sādhu yaŋ katvā anutappati "not well done is that deed for which he feels remorse" S 1.57=Dh 67=Nett 132; āveni-kammāni karonti (with ref. to sangha-bheda) A v.74; adhammika-kammāni A 1.74; asuci-k°āni (as suggested by 5 and attributes: asuci, duggandha, etc.) A III.269; sāvajja-kammāni (as deserving Niraya) (opp. avajja > sagga) A II.237; kammāni ānantarikāni deeds which have an immediate effect; there are five, enum[d] at Vbh 378.—(e) deeds characterized as *good* or meritorious (**kusala, bhaddaka,** etc.) taŋ k°ŋ katvā kusalaŋ sukhudrayaŋ D III.157; puñña-kammo of meritorious (character) S 1.143; kusalehi k°ehi vippayuttā carati viññāṇa-cariyā Ps 1.80; kusalassa k°ssa katattā Vbh 173 sq.; 266 sq.; 297 sq.; kusala-k°-paccayāni Bdhd 12; puñña-kamma, merit, comp[d] with kapparukkha in its rewarding power VvA 32 (cp. puññânubhāva-nissandena "in consequence of their being affected with merit" PvA 58)—Cp. also cpds.: kamma-kilesa, k°-ṭṭhāna, k°-patha; k°lakkhaṇa k°-samādāna.

3. (Interaction) A. in subjective relation; (a) character of interaction as regards action; action or deed as having results: **phala** and **vipāka** (fruit and maturing); both expressions being used either singly or jointly, either °—or independ[t]; **phala:** tassa mayhaŋ atīte katassa kammassa phalaŋ "the fruit of a deed done by me in former times" ThA 270; Vv 47[6] (=VvA 202); desanā . . . k-phalaŋ paccakkhakāriṇī "an instruction demonstrating the fruit of action" PvA 1; similarly PvA 2; cp. also ibid. 26, 49, 52, 82 (v. l. for kammabala). **vipāka:** yassa k°ssa vipākena . . . niraye pacceyyāsi . . . "through the ripening of whatever deed will you be matured (i. e. tortured) in N." M II.104; tassa k°ssa vipākena saggaŋ lokaŋ uppajji "by the result of that deed he went to Heaven" S 1.92; II.255; k-vipāka-kovida "well aware of the fruit of action," i. e. of retribution Sn 653; kissa k-vipākena "through the result of what (action)" Pv 1.6[8]; inunā asubhena k-vipākena Nett 160; k-vipāka with ref. to avyākata-dhammā: Vbh 182; with ref. to jhāna ibid. 268, 281; with ref. to dukkha ibid. 106; k-vipāka-ja produced by the maturing of (some evil) action, as one kind of ābādha, illness: A v.110=Nd[2] 304[1]; same as result of good action, as one kind of iddhi (supernatural power) Ps II.174; -vipāka (adj.). asakkaccakatānaŋ kammānaŋ vipāko the reaper of careless deeds A IV.393; der. vepakka (adj.) in dukkha-vepakka resulting in pain Sn 537. — **-phala + vipāka:** freq. in form. sukaṭa dukkhaṭānaŋ kammānaŋ phalaŋ vipāko: D 1.55=III.264=M 1.401=S IV.348=A 1.268=IV.226=v.265, 286 sq.; cp. *J.P.T.S.* 1883, 8; nissanda-phala-bhūto vipāko ThA 270; tiṇṇaŋ k°ānaŋ phalaŋ, tiṇṇaŋ k-ānaŋ vipāko D II.186 — (b) the effect of the deed on the doer: the consequences fall upon the doer, in the majority of cases expressed as punishment or affliction: yathā yathâyaŋ puriso kammaŋ karoti tathā tathā taŋ paṭisaŋvedissati "in whichever way this man does a deed, in the same way he will experience it (in its effect)" A 1.249; na vijjati so jagati-ppadeso yathā ṭhito muñceyya pāpa-kammā "there is no place in the world where you could escape the consequences of evil-doing" Dh 127=Miln 150=PvA 104, cp. Divy 532; so the action is represented as vedaniya, to be felt; in various combinations: in this world or the future state, as good or bad, as much or little A IV.382; the agent is represented as the inheritor, possessor, of (the results of) his action in the old formula: kammassakā sattā k-dāyādā k-yonī k-bandhū . . . yaŋ k°ŋ karonti kalyānaŋ vā pāpakaŋ vā tassa dāyādā bhavanti M III.203=A III.72 sq.=186=v.88~288 sq. (see also cpds.). The punishment is expressed by **kamma-karaṇa** (or °kāraṇa), "being done back with the deed," or the reaction of the deed, in phrase kamma-karaṇaŋ kāreti or kārāpeti "he causes the reaction of the deed to take place" and pass. kamma-karaṇā kariyati he is afflicted with the reaction, i. e. the punishment of his doing. The 5 main punishments in Niraya see under kāraṇaŋ, the usual punishments (beating with whips, etc.) are enumerated passim, e. g. M III.164, 181, and Nd[2] 604. [As regards form and meaning Morris *J.P.T.S.* 1884, 76 and 1893, 15 proposes kāraṇā f. "pain, punishment," fr. **kṛ** to tear or injure, "the pains of karma, or torture"; Prof. Duroiselle follows him, but with no special reason: the derivation as nt. causative-abstr. fr. karoti presents no difficulty.]—ye kira bho pāpakāni k°-āni karonti te diṭṭh' eva dhamme evarūpā vividhā k-kāraṇā kariyanti, kim anga pana parattha! "Those who, as you know, do evil are punished with various tortures even in this world, how much more then in the world to come!" M III.181; M III.186=A 1.142; sim. **k°-kāraṇāni kārenti** (v. l. better than text-reading) S IV.344; Sdhp 7; Nd[2] on dukkha. As k-karaṇaŋ saŋvidahiŋsu J II.398; kamma-kāraṇa-ppatta one who undergoes punishment Vism 500. See also examples under 2d and M 1.87; A 1.47; J v.429; Miln 197.

B. in objective relation: universal karma, law of cause and consequence.—(a) karma as cause of existence (see also d, purāṇa° and pubbe kataŋ k°): compared to the fruitful soil (khetta), as substratum of all existence in kāma, rūpa, arūpa dhātu A 1.223 (kāma-dhātu-vepakkañ ce kammaŋ nâbhavissa api nu kho kāmabhavo paññāyethā ti? No h'etaŋ . . . iti kho kammaŋ khettaŋ . . .); as one of the 6 causes or substrata of existence A III.410; kammanā vattati loko kammanā vattati pajā "by means of karma the world goes on, mankind goes on" Sn 654; kamma-paccayā through karma PvA 25 (=Kh 207); k°ŋ kilesā hetu saŋsārassa "k. and passions are the cause of saŋsāra (renewed existence)" Nett 113; see on k. as principle: Ps II.78; 79 (ch. VII., kamma-kathā) M 1.372 sq.; Nett. 161; 180-182; k. as 3 fold: Bdhd 117; as 4 fold M III.215; and as cause in general Vism 600 (where enum[d] as one of the 4 paccaya's or stays of rūpa, viz. k., citta, utu, āhāra); Bdhd 63, 57, 116, 134 sq.; Vbh 366; Miln 40 sq. as a factor in the five-fold order (dhammatā or niyama) of the cosmos: k°-niyama DA. on D II, 12; DhsA. 272; Cp. cpds.: kammaja (resulting from karma) Bdhd 68, 72, 75; °-vātā, birth-pains i. e. the winds resulting from karma (caliŋsu) DhA 1.165; DhA II.262; k°-nimitta Bdhd 11, 57, 62; k°-sambhava Bdhd 66; k°-samuṭṭhāna Vism 600; Bdhd 67, 72; see further cpds. below.—(b) karma as result or consequence. There are 3 kamma-nidānāni, factors producing karma and its effect: lobha, dosa, moha, as such (tīṇi nidānāni kammānaŋ samudayāya, 3 causes of the arising of karma) described A 1.134=263=III.338=Nd[2] 517; so also A v.86; 262; Vbh 208. With the cessation of these 3 the factor of karma ceases: lobha-kkhayā kamma-nidāna-saŋkhayo A v.262. There are 3 other nidānāni as atīte anāgate paccuppanne chanda A 1.264.

and 3 others as producing or inciting existence (called here kamma-bhava, consequential existence) are puñña, apuñña, ānejja (merit, demerit and immovability) Vbh 137=Nd^2 471. — (c) karma as cause-consequence: its manifestation consists in essential likeness between deed and result, cause and effect: like for like "as the cause, so the result." Karma in this special sense is Retribution or Retaliation; a law, the working of which cannot be escaped (cp. Dh 127, as quoted above 3 A (b), and Pv II.7^{17}: sace taŋ pāpakaŋ kammaŋ karissatha karotha vā, na vo dukkhā pamutt' atthi) — na hi nassati kassaci kammaŋ "nobody's (trace, result of) action is ever lost" Sn 666; puññâpuñña-kammassa nissandena kanaka vimāne ekikā hutvā nibbatti "through the consequence of both merit and demerit" PvA 47; cp. VvA 14; yatth' assa attabhāvo nibbattati tattha taŋ k°ŋ vipaccati "wherever a man comes to be born, there ripens his action" A I.134; — correspondence between "light" and "dark" deeds and their respective consequence are 4 fold: kaṇha-kamma > kaṇha vipāka, sukka°, kaṇha-sukka, akaṇha-asukka: D III.230=M I.389=A II.230 sq.; so sakena kammena nirayaŋ upapajjati Nd^2 304^{III}; k°-ânubhâva -ukkhitta "thrown, set into motion, by the power of k." PvA 78; sucarita-k-ânubhavâvanibbattāni vimānāni "created by the power of their result of good conduct" VvA 1^{27}; k-ânubhāvena by the working of k. PvA 77; k°-vega-ukkhittā (same) PvA 284; yathā kamm-ûpaga "undergoing the respective consequences (of former deeds) affected with respective karma: see cpds., and cp. yathā kammaŋ gato gone (into a new existence) according to his karma J I.153 & freq.; see cpds.; k-sarikkhatā "the karma-likeness," the correspondence of cause and consequence: taŋ k-s°ŋ vibhāventaŋ suvaṇṇamayaŋ ahosi "this, manifesting the karma-correspondence, was golden" VvA 6; so also **k-sarikkhaka,** in accordance with their deed, retributionary, of kamma-phalaŋ, the result of action: tassa kamma-sarikkhakaŋ kammaphalaŋ hoti "for her the fruit of action became like action," i. e. the consequence was according to her deed. PvA 206; 284; 258; as nt.: k-s°ŋ pan'assa udapādi "the retribution for him has come" DhA I.128; J III.203; cp. also Miln 40 sq.; 65 sq.; 108. — (d) The working and exhaustion of karma, its building up by new karma (nava°) and its destruction by expiration of old karma (purāṇa). The final annihilation of all result (°kkhaya) constitutes Arahantship. nava > purāṇa-kamma: as aparipakka, not ripe, and paropakka, ripe D I.54=S III.212; as pañca-kammuno satāni, etc. ibid.; kāyo . . . purāṇaŋ k°ŋ abhisankhataŋ ("our body is an accumulation of former karma") S II.65=Nd^2 680 D; see also A II.197; Pv IV.7^1; PvA 1, 45; Nett 179; and with simile of the snake stripping its slough (porāṇassa k°ssa parikkhīṇattā . . . santo yathā kammaŋ gacchati) PvA 63. — k°-nirodha or °kkhaya: so . . . na tāva kālaŋ karoti yāva na taŋ pāpakammaŋ vyanti hoti "He does not die so long as the evil karma is unexhausted" A I.141≈; nava-purāṇāni k°āni desissāmi k°-nirodhaŋ k°-nirodha-gāminiñ ca paṭipadaŋ "the new and the old karma I shall demonstrate to you, the destruction of k. and the way which leads to the destruction of k." S IV.132∼A III.410; . . . navânaŋ k°ânaŋ akaraṇā setughātaŋ; iti k-kkhayā dukkhakkhayo . . . (end of misery through the end of karma) A I.220=M II.214; same Ps I.55-57; cp. also A I.263; Nd^2 411 (expl. as kamma-parāyaṇa vipāka-p°: "gone beyond karma and its results," i. e. having attained Nibbāna). See also the foll. cpds.: k°-âbhisankhāsa, °āvaraṇa, °kkhaya, °nibandhana.

-âdhikata ruled by karma, Miln 67, 68; °ena by the influence of k. ibid. **-âdhiggahita** gripped by karma Miln 188, 189; **-ânurūpa** (adj.) (of vipāka) according to one's karma J III.160; DA I.37; **-âbhisankhāra** (3 B) accumulation of k. Nd^2 116, 283, 506. **-âbhisanda** in °ena in consequence of k. Miln 276, cp. *J.P.T.S.* 1886, 146; **-âraha** see I.; **-âyatana** 1. work Vbh 324, cp. Miln 78; 2. action=kamma J III.542; cp. J IV.451, 452. **-âyūhana** the heaping up of k. Vism 530; DhsA 267, 268; cp. k°ŋ āyūhi Miln 214 and *J.P.T.S.* 1885, 58. **-āvaraṇa** the obstruction caused by k. A III.436=Pug 13=Vbh 341 (in defin. of sattā abhabbā: kammâvaraṇena samannāgatā, kiles°, vipāk° . .), Kvu 341; Miln 154, 155; Vism 177 (=ānantariya-kamma); **-ûpaga** in yatha kamm-ûpage satte: the beings as undergoing (the consequences of) their respective kamma (3B) in form. cavamāne upapajjamāne hīne paṇīte suvaṇṇe dubbaṇṇe sugate duggate . . . pajānāti (or passati) Vin III.5=D I.82=S II.122 (214)=V.266=A IV.178=V.13 (35, 200, 340)=Vbh 344; abbreviated in M III.178; Nett. 178; see also similar Sn 587; Bdhd 111; **-upacaya** accumulation of k. Kvu A. 156; **-kathā** exposition of k.; chapter in Ps II.98; **-kāma** (adj.) desirous of good karma Th 2, 275; PvA 174; a° opp.= inactive, indolent A IV.92, PvA 174; **-kiriyā-dassana** (adj.) understanding the workings of k. J I.45; **-kiliṭṭha** bad, evil k. Dh 15 (=DhA I.129, expl. kiliṭṭha-k°); **-kilesa** (2) depravity of action, bad works, there are 4 enum^d at D III.181=J III.321, as the non-performance of sīla 1-4 (see sīla), equal to pāpa-kāya-k°; **-kkhaya** (3 B) the termination, exhaustion of the influence of k.; its destruction: sabba-k°-kkhayaŋ patto vimutto upadhi-sankhaye S I.134; as brought about by neutral, indifferent kamma: D III.230=A II.230 sq.; M I.93, DhsA 89; **-ja** (3 B) produced by k. J I.52; as one mode of the origin of disease Miln 135; Nd^2 304^1; appl^d. to all existence Miln 271; Vism 624 (kammajaŋ āyatana-dvāra-vasena pākaṭaŋ hoti); appl^d to rūpa Vism 451, 614; appl. to pains of childbirth (°vātā) J I.52, DhA I.165; a° not caused by k., of ākāsa and nibbāna Miln 268, 271; **-ṭṭhāna** (2) 1. a branch of industry or occupation, profession, said of diff. occupations as farmer, trader, householder and mendicant M II.197; A V.83. 2. occasion or ground for (contemplating) kamma (see ṭhāna II.2. c.), kamma-subject, a technical term referring to the instruments of meditation, esp. objects used by meditation to realize impermanence. These exercises ("stations of exercise" *Expos.* 224) are highly valued as leading to Arahantship DhA I.8 (yāva arahattaŋ kamma-ṭṭhānaŋ kathesi), 96; PvA 98 (catu-sacca-kamma-ṭṭhāna-bhāvanā meditation on the 4 truths and the objects of meditation). Freq. in phrase kammaṭṭhāne anuyutto (or anuyoga-vasena) na cirass'eva arahattaŋ pāpuṇi: J III.36; Sāsv 49; see also J I.7, 97, 182, 303, 414; Sdhp 493. These subjects of meditation are given as 38 at DhsA 168 (cp. *Cpd.* 202), as 32 (dvattiŋs' ākāra-k°) at Vism 240 sq., as 40 at Vism 110 sq. (in detail); as pañca-sandhika at Vism 277; some of them are mentioned at J I.116; DhA I.221, 336; IV.90; -°ŋ *anuyuñjati* to give oneself up to meditation Sāsv 151; PvA 61; -°ŋ *uggaṇhāti* to accept from his teacher a particular instrument of meditation Vism 277 sq. (also °assa uggaho & uggaṇhana); KhA 40; DhA I.9, 262; IV.106; PvA 42; -°ŋ *katheti* to teach a pupil how to meditate on one of the k° DhA I.8, 248, 336; PvA 61; -°ŋ *adāsi* DhA IV.106; °*gaṇhāti* J III.246; Vism 89; °*ācikkhana* instruction in a formula of exercise DhsA 246; °*dāyaka* the giver of a k-ṭṭh° object, the spiritual adviser and teacher, who must be a kalyāṇamitta (q. v.), one who has entered the Path; Vism 89; Bdhd 89, 91, cp. Vism 241; **-ṭṭhānika** a person practising kammaṭṭhāna Vism 97, 187, 189; DhA I.335; **-tappana** the being depressed on acct. of one's (bad) karma DhA I.150. — **-dāyāda** (3 A (b) and cp. °ssaka) the inheritor of k., i. e. inheriting the consequences of one's own deeds M I.390; Miln 65=DhsA 66; **-dvāra** "the door of action," i. e. the medium by which action is manifested (by kāya, vacī, mano) (s. 2b) J IV.14; KvuA 135; DhsA 82; Bdhd 8; **-dhāraya** name of a class of noun-compounds Kacc 166; **-nānatta** manifoldness of k. DhsA 64 (also -nānākaraṇa ib.); -nibandhana (3 B) bound to k. (: rathass'āṇī va yāyato, as the linchpin to the cart) Sn 654; -nibbatta (3 B) produced through k. Miln 268; DhsA 361; -nimitta the sign, token of k. DhsA 411; -nirodha the destruction of k. [see 3 B (d)]; -paccaya the ground, basis of karma Vism 538; KvuA 101; °paccayena by means of k. J VI.105, Vism 538; (adj.) J V.271, DhsA 304; -paṭisaraṇa (a) having k. as a place of refuge or as a protector J VI.102; Miln 65; cp. DhsA 66; -paṭibāḷha strong by k. Miln 301; -pathā (2 b) pl. the ways of acting (=sīla q. v.), divided into kusala (meritorious, good) and akusala (demeritorious, evil) and classified according to the 3 manifestations into 3 kāya°, 4 vācī°, 3 mano°, altogether 10; so at Vin V.138, S II.168, A V.57, 268; as kus° and akus° at D III.71, 269, 290; as 7 only at S II.167; as akus° only at A V.54, 266; Vbh 391; Nett 43; Bdhd 129, 131; °ppatta having acquired the 10 items of (good) action Sdhp 56, 57. -phala [3 A (a)] the fruit of k., the result of (formerly) performed actions J I.350; VvA 39, PvA 1, 26, 52; °-*upajivin* 1. living on the fruit of one's labour (ad I) J IV.160; — 2. living according to the result of former deeds A II.135; -bandhu having k. as one's relative, i. e. closely tied to one's karma (see °ssaka) Th 1, 496; cp. J VI.100, etc. -bala the power of k. J VI.108; PvA 82. -bhava [3 B (b)] karmic existence, existence through karma Vbh 137; DhsA 37; -bhūmi 1. the place of work J III.411; 2. the ground of actions, i. e. the field of meritorious deeds Miln 229; -mūla (good) k. as a price (for long life, etc.) Miln 333, 334, 341; -mūlaka produced by k. Miln 134; -yoni having k. for matrix, i. e. as the cause of rebirth Miln 65; DhsA 66. -lakkhaṇa having k. as distinctive characteristic A I.102; AA 370; -vagga name of section in Nipāta IV of Anguttara (Nos. 232-238) A II.230 sq.; -vavaṭṭhāna the continuance of k. DhsA 85; -vāda (a) holding to the view of (the power and efficacy of) k. S II.33 sq.; A I.287 (+kiriyavāda, viriyavāda); -vādin believing in k. D I.115; Vin I.71; J VI.60; -vipāka [3 A (a)] the ripening of k., the result of one's actions (see above) Vbh 106, 182, 268, 281; as one of the four mysteries (acinteyyāni) of Buddhism at Miln 189. —°*ja* produced as a result of k.: D II.20; Mhbv 78; Ps II.174, 213; Miln 135; Vism 382 (appl^{d} to iddhi); concerning disease as not produced by k., see A V.110; Miln 134, 135; AA 433, 556. -visuddhi meritorious karma Dh 16 (=Dh I.132); -visesa variety or difference of k. DhsA 313; -vega the impetus of k. PvA 284; -sacca (adj.) having its reality only in k.; said of loka, the world A II.232. -samādāna (2) the acquisition of ways of acting, one's character, or the incurring of karma, either as micchādiṭṭhi° (of wrong views) or sammādiṭṭhi (conforming to the right doctrine), so in yathākamm-ûpaga passage (q. v.): D III.96; M I.70; III.178, 179; four such qualities or kinds of karma enum. at Nett 98; of Buddha's knowledge as regards the quality of a man's character: S V.304; A III.417 sq.; Ps II.174; Vbh 338; -samārambha [3 B (a)] having its beginning in k.; said of loka, the world of men; with °*ṭṭhāyin*: lasting as long as the origin (cause) of k. exists A II.232; -samuṭṭhāna [3 B (a)] rising from k. Miln 127; DhsA 82; Kvu 100; -sambhava produced by k. Miln 127; -sarikkhaka [see above 3 B (c)] similar or like in consequence to the deed done DhA III.334 (°vipāka). -sarikkhatā (do.) the likeness between deed and result; -sahāya "companion to the deed," said of thought DhsA 323; -socana sorrowing for one's (bad) deeds DhA I.128. -(s)saka [3 A (b), q. v.] (a) one whose karma is his own property, possessed of his own k. M III.203, etc. (in phrase k., kamma-dāyāda, kamma-bandhu, etc.; cp. Vism 301); J IV.128; Miln 65; DA I.37=who goes according to his own karma (attano k°ānurūpaŋ gatiŋ gacchanti, n'eva pitā puttassa kammena gacchati, na putto pitu kammena . . .); der. °*tā* the fact that every being has his very own karma A III.186; Dhs 1366; Vbh 324; °ta as adj.; qualifying ñāṇa, i. e. the knowledge of the individual, specific nature of karma Dhs 1366, Vbh 328.

Kammaka (adj.) [fr. kamma] connected with, depend^{t} on karma Miln 137 (a°).

Kammanīya, °iya & kammañña (adj.) "workable," fit for work, dexterous, ready, wieldy. Often of citta "with active mind" in formula vigatūpakkilesa mudubhūta k° ṭhita ānejjappatta D I.76, etc.=M I.22= Pug 68; S III.232; V.92, 233; A I.9; DhA I.289; Bdhd 101, expl^{d} at Vism 377 (°iya). Further of citta (muduñ ca kammaññañ ca pabhassarañ ca) A I.257 (reads °iyañ)=Vism 247; of upekhā and sati Nd^{2} 661, cp. Bdhd 104; of kāya & citta Bdhd 121. Said of a lute=workable, ready for playing A III.375=Vin I.182. Of the body A IV.335. — a° not ready, sluggish A IV.333; Vism 146. — kammañña-bhāva the state of being workable, readiness, of kāya Dhs 46, of vedanā, etc., Dhs 326, of citta DhsA 130, see next; a° unworkable condition DhsA 130.

Kammaññatā (f.) [abstr. fr. prec.] workableness, adaptability, readiness, appl. to the wood of the sandal tree (in simile) A I.9; said of kāya and citta in connection with kammaññattaŋ k°bhāvo k°mudutā: Dhs 46, 47=326=641=730; cp. Dhs 585; similar Bdhd 16, 20, 71; DhsA 130, 151 (=kammasādutā) a° unworkableness, inertness, unwieldiness, sluggishness Miln 300; Nett 86, 108, cp. Dhs 1156, 1236; DhsA 255; expl^{d} as cittagelaññaŋ DhsA 377; as cetaso līnattaŋ Vbh 373.

Kammanta [Sk. karmānta; kamma+anta, cp. anta ^{1}4.] 1. doing, acting, working; work, business, occupation, profession. paṭicchanna° of secret acting Sn 127= Vbh 357; as being punished in Niraya A I.60; S IV.180; as occupation esp. in pl. kammantā: S V.45=135; DhA I.42 (kammantā nappavattanti, no business proceeds, all occupations are at a standstill); anākula° Sn 262=Kh V.5; abbhantarā k° uṇṇā ti vā, kappāsā ti vā as housework, falling to the share of the wife A III.37=IV.365; khetta° occupation in the field A III.77; see also D I.71; M III.7; S I.204; Miln 9, 33; and below; as place of occupation: Sn p. 13, PvA 62. Phrases: °ŋ adhiṭṭhāti to look after the business A I.115; PvA 141; jahati give up the occupation S IV.324; PvA 133; °ŋ payojeti to do or carry on business D I.71; II.175; III.66, 95; A III.57; °ŋ pavatteti to set a business on foot PvA 42 (and vicāreti: PvA 93); °ŋ saŋvidahati to provide with work A IV.269=272. Mhvs VI.16. — 2. deed, action in ethical sense= kamma, character, etc., Kh 136 (k°=kamma); pāpa° doing wrong Pv IV.8^{1}; IV.16^{1}, J VI.104 (opp. puñña°); as specified by kāya° vacī °mano° A V.292 sq.; VvA 130 (in parisuddha-kāya-kammantatā); dhammikā k°ā M II.191; ākiṇṇa-k° (evam-) of such character S I.204; kurūra-k° (adj.) of cruel character A III.383=Pug 56 (in def. of puggalo orabbhiko); sammā° of right doing, opp. micchā°, as constituting one element of character as pertaining to "Magga" (: q. v.) D II.216; S II.168; V.1; A III.411; Bdhd 135; expl. as kāya-kamma (=sīla 1-3) at S V.9=Vbh 105; Vbh 235; as kāya-duccaritehi ārati virati . . . Vbh 106.

-ādhiṭṭhāyika superintendent of work DhA I.393; -ṭṭhāna: 1. the spot where the ceremonies of the Ploughing Festival take place J I.57; 2. the common ground of a village, a village bazaar J IV.306; -dāsa a farm-servant J I.468; -bheri the drum announcing the (taking up of) business DhA III.100; -vipatti "failure of action," evil-doing A I.270 opp. -sampadā "perfection of action, right-doing" A I.271; -saŋvidhāna the providing of work D III.191 (one of the 5 duties of the gahapati).

Kammantika (adj.) [fr. kammanta] 1. a business manager J I.227. — 2. a labourer, artisan, assistant J I.377.

Kammāra [Vedic karmāra] a smith, a worker in metals generally D II.126, A V.263; a silversmith Sn 962= Dh 239; J I.223; a goldsmith J III.281; V.282. The smiths in old India do not seem to be divided into black-, gold- and silver-smiths, but seem to have been able to work equally well in iron, gold, and silver, as can be seen e. g. from J III.282 and VvA 250, where the smith is the maker of a needle. They were constituted into a guild, and some of them were well-to-do as appears from what is said of Cunda at D II.126; owing to their usefulness they were held in great esteem by the people and king alike J III.281.
-**uddhana** a smith's furnace, a forge J VI.218; -**kula** a smithy M I.25; **kūṭa** a smith's hammer Vism 254; -**gaggarī** a smith's bellows S I.106; J VI.165; Vism 287 (in comparison); -**putta** "son of a smith," i. e. a smith by birth and trade D II.126; A V.263; as goldsmith J VI.237, Sn 48 (Nd² ad loc.: k° vuccati suvaṇṇakāro); -**bhaṇḍu** (bhaṇḍ. cp. Sk. bhāṇḍika a barber) a smith with a bald head Vin I.76; -**sālā** a smithy Vism 413; Mhvs 5, 31.

Kammāsa [Vedic kalmāṣa, which may be referred, with kalana, kaluṣa, kalanka and Gr. κελαινός to *qel, fr. which also Sk. kāla black-blue, Gr. κηλάς, κηλίς; Lat. cālīgo & callidus] 1. variegated, spotted, blemished J V.69 (°vaṇṇa), said of the spotted appearance of leprosy. — fig. inconsistent, varying A II.187. — 2. (nt.) inconsistency, blemish, blot A IV.55; Vism 51. — a° not spotted, i. e. unblemished, pure, said of moral conduct D II.80; A II.52; III.36, 572; VI.54, 192; Bdhd 89.
-**kārin** in a° not acting inconsistently A II.187; cp. ibid. 243. -**pāda** 1. (a) having speckled feet J V.475; (b) (m) one who has speckled feet, i. e. an ogre; also N. of a Yakkha J V.503, 511 (cp. *J.P.T.S.* 1909, 236 sq.).

Kammika (adj.-n.) [fr. kamma] 1. (-°) one who does or looks after; one whose occupation is of such & such a character: **āya**° revenue-overseer, treasurer DhA I.184; sabba° (always with ref. to *amacca*, the king's minister) one who does everything, the king's confidant Vism 130; PvA 81. — On term ādi° beginner (e. g. Vism 241) see *Cpd.* 53, 129 n.2. — 2. a merchant, trader, in jalapatha° and thalapatha° by sea & by land J I.121. — 3. a superintendent, overseer, manager J II.305 (executioner of an order); VI.294; Mhvs 30, 31. — 4. one connected with the execution of an ecclesiastical Act Vin II.5 (cp. p. 22); Bdhd 106.

Kammin (adj.) (—°) [fr. kamma, cp. kammaka] doing, performing, practising J VI.105; Sdhp 196, 292.

Kamya (adj.) (—°) [fr. **kām**] wishing for, desiring DhsA 365 (sādhu°; v. l. °kāma); kamyā, abl. in the desire for, see next.

Kamyā (—°) in abl. function (of kamyā f. for kamyāya or kamya adj. ?) in the desire for: S I.143=J III.361 (expl^d by kāmatāya); Sn 854, 929.

Kamyatā (—°) & **kammatā** (Nd) [fr. **kām**] wish, desire, longing for, striving after; with inf. or equivalent: kathetu° VvA 18; muñcitu° (+ paṭisankhā) Ps 1.60, 65; Bdhd 123; asotu°, adaṭṭhu° and adassana° Vbh 372. Esp. in definitions, as of *chanda*: kattu° Vbh 208; Bdhd 20; of *jappā*: puñcikatā sādhu° Vbh 351; 361=Dhs 1059; Nd² s. v. taṇhā^n (: has the better reading mucchañci katā asādhu°; v. l. pucchañci°; both Vbh and Dhs have sādu in text which should be corrected to asādhu°; see detail under puñcikatā); of *māna*; **ketu**° Nd² 505; Dhs 1116=1233; Vbh 350 sq.; Bdhd 24; of lapanā: pāṭu° (v. l. cāṭu°) Vbh 246= 352. — As abl. (=kamyā) in dassana° S I.193=Th I, 1241; Sn 121 (expl. as icchāya SnA 179). Cp. kammaññatā & kamma-sādutā.

Kaya [fr. **krī**] purchase, buying A III.226 (+ vi°).
-(**a**)**kkaya**, buying & selling Pv I.5⁴ (see also Kh VII.6 and note). -**vikkaya** (kraya vikraya) buying & selling, trade in °paṭivirata D I.5=A II.209=V.205= Pug 58; D I.64; S V.473; Sn 929; J V.243; Khus 114; DhA I.78; PvA 29 (=KhA 212).

Kayati [**krī**, perhaps connected with **kṛ**] to buy; Inf. ketuŋ J III.282; cp. kiṇāti.

Kayika [fr. **krī**, cp. BSk. krayika Divy 505] a buyer, trader, dealer Miln 334.

Kayin a buyer J VI.110.

Kara [fr. **kṛ**] 1. (adj.) (—°) producing, causing, forming, making, doing, e. g. anta° putting an end to; pabhaŋ causing splendour; pāpa° doing evil; divā° & divasa the day-maker, i. e. the sun; kaṇhabhāva° causing a "black" existence (of pāpakamma) J IV.9; padasandhi° forming a hiatus PvA 52; vacana°, etc. — 2. (m) "the maker," i. e. the hand Mhvs 5, 255-256; 30, 67. -**atikaraŋ** (adv.) doing too much, going too far J I.431; -**dukkara** (a) difficult to do, not easy, hard, arduous S I.7; IV.260; A I.286; IV.31, 135; V.202; + durabhisambhavo Sn 429 701; Ud. 61; (n. nt.) something difficult, a difficult task A I.286 (cp. IV.31); J I.395; Miln 121, dukkara-kārikā "doing of a hard task," exertion, austerity M I.93; Nd² 262ᵇ. -**sukara** easy to do S I.9; II.181; Dh 163; Ud 61; na sukaraŋ w. inf. it is not easy to . . . D I.250; A III.52, 184; IV.334.
-**kaṭaka** (m. nt.) a hand-wheel, i. e. a pulley by which to draw up a bucket of water Vin II.122; cp. *Vin. Texts* III.112; -**ja** "born of kamma" in *karaja-kāya* the body sprung from action, an expression always used in a contemptible manner, therefore=the impure, vile, low body A V.300; J I.5; Vism 287, 404; DA I.113, 217, 221; DhA I.10; III.420; DhsA 403. *karaja-rūpa* Vism 326. -**tala** the palm of the hand Mhbv 6, 34; -**mara** "one who ought to die from the hand (of the enemy)," but who, when captured, was spared and employed as slave; a slave J III.147, 361; IV.220; DhA III.487; -*°ān . ī* a woman taken in a raid, but subsequently taken to wife; one of the 10 kinds of wives (see itthi) Vin III.140 (=dhajāhaṭā); -*gāhan ganhāti* to make prisoner J I.355; III.361; -**mita** "to be measured with (two) hands," in °majjhā, a woman of slender waist J V.219; VI.457.

Karaka¹ [Etymology unknown. The Sanskrit is also karaka, and the medieval koṣas give as meaning, besides drinking vessel, also a coco-nut shell used as such (with which may be compared Lat. carīna, nutshell, keel of a boat; and Gr. κάρυα, nut.) It is scarcely possible that this could have been the original meaning. The coconut was not cultivated, perhaps not even known, in Kosala at the date of the rise of Pali and Buddhism] 1. Water-pot, drinking-vessel (= : pānīya-bhājana PvA 251). It is one of the seven requisites of a samaṇa Vin II.302. It is called **dhammakaraka** there, and at II. 118, 177. This means "regulation waterpot" as it was provided with a strainer (parissavana) to prevent injury to living things. See also Miln 68; Pv III.2²⁴; PvA 185. — 2. hail (also karakā) J IV. 167; Miln 38; Mhvs XII. 9.
-**vassa** a shower of hail, hail-storm J IV.167; Miln 38, 308; DhA I.360.

Karakarā (for kaṭakaṭā, q. v.) (adv.) by way of gnashing or grinding the teeth (cp. Sk. dantān kaṭakaṭāpya), i. e. severely (of biting) J III.203 (passage ought to be read as karakarā nikhāditvā).

Karañja [cp. Sk. karañja, accord. to Aufrecht, Halāyudha p. 176 the Dalbergia arborea] the tree Pongamia glabra, used medicinally Vin I.201 ; J VI.518, 519.

Karaṇa [fr. kṛ, cp. Vedic karaṇa] 1. adj. (f. ī) (—°) doing, making, causing, producing ; as cakkhu° ñāṇa° (leading to clear knowledge) S IV.331 ; V.97 ; It 83 ; and acakkhu° etc. S V.97 ; nāthā °ā dhammā A V.23 (cp. V.89) and thera° A II.22 ; dubbaṇṇa° S V.217 ; see also D I.245 ; M. I.15 ; S V.96, 115 ; A IV.94 ; V.268 ; Miln 289. — 2. (nt.) (—°) the making, producing of ; the doing, performance of (=kamma), as bali° offering of food =bali kamma) PvA 81 ; gabbha° Sn 927 ; pānujja° Sn 256. 3. (abs.) (a) the doing up, preparing J V.400, VI.270 (of a building : the construction) (b) the doing, performance of, as pāṇātipātassa k° and ak° (" commission and omission ") ; DhA I.214 ; means of action J III.92. (c) ttg. the instrumental case (with or without °*vacana*) PvA 33 ; VvA 25, 53, 162, 174. -°atthe in the sense of, with the meaning of the instrumental case J III.98 ; V.444 ; PvA 35 ; VvA 304 ; DhsA 48 ; Kacc 157. — 4. (—°) state, condition ; in noun-abstract function= °ttaŋ (cp. kamma I.2) as nānā° (=nānattaŋ) difference M II.128 ; S IV.294 ; Bdhd 94 ; kasi° ploughing PvA 66 ; kattabba° (=kattabbattaŋ) " what is to be done," i. e. duty PvA 30 ; pūjā° veneration PvA 30. sakkāra° reverence, devotion SnA 284.

Note : in massu° and kamma° some grammarians have tried to derive k° from a root kṛ, to hurt, cut, torture (see Morris *J.P.T.S.* 1893, 15), which is however quite unnecessary [see kamma 3 A (b), kata[n] 1 (b)]. Karaṇa here stands for kamma, as clearly indicated by semantic grounds as well as by J VI.270 where it explains kappita-kesa-massu, and J III.114=V.309 where massu-kamma takes the place of °karaṇa, so also DA I.137. a° Negative in all meanings of the positive, i. e. the non-performing J I.131 ; V.222 ; Nett 81 ; PvA 59 ; DhsA 127 ; non-undertaking (of business) J I.229 ; non-commission M I.93 ; abstaining from Dhs 299. Cpd. -uttariya (nt.) angry rejoinder, vehement defence DhA I.44.

Karaṇīya [grd. of karoti] 1. adj. (a) that ought to be, must or should be done, to be done, to be made (=kātabbaŋ karaṇārahaŋ KhA 236) Vin I.58 ; D I.3, cp. Miln 183 ; A V.210 ; DA I.7. Often —° in the sense of " doing, making," as yathā kāma° S II.226 ; cp. IV.91, 159 ; " having business " bahu° D II.76 ; A III.116 ; S II.215 ; anukampa° PvA 61. — (b) done, in the sense of undoing, i. e. overcome, undone D II.76 cp. *Dial.* II.81 n. — 2. (m.) one who has still something left to perform (for the attainment of Arahantship, a sekha J III.23. — 3. (nt.) (a) what ought to be done, duty, obligation ; affairs, business D I.85 ; II.68, 74 cp. A IV.16 ; M I.271 ; S III.168 ; IV.281 cp. Vin III.12 ; Vin I.139 ; A I.58 ; Sn 143 ; Sn p. 32 (yaŋ te karaṇīyaŋ taŋ karohi " do what you have to do ") ; — °ŋ tīreti to conclude a business Vin II.158 ; J V.298. Kataŋ °ŋ done is what was to be done, I have done my task, in freq. formula " khīṇā jāti vusitaŋ brahmacariyaŋ . . ." to mark the attainment of Arahantship D I.84 ; II.68=153 ; Th 2, 223 ; Vin I.14 ; Sn p. 16 ; DA I.226, etc. See Arahant II.C. — There are 3 duties each of a samaṇa, farmer and householder enumerated at A I.229 ; 3 of a bhikkhu A I.230 ; — (b) use, need (with instr.) : appamādena k° S IV.125 ; cetanāya k° A V.2, 312 ; cp. Miln 5, 78. **akaraṇīya** 1. (adj.) (a) what ought not to be done, prohibited A I.58 ; III.208=DA I.235. — (b) incapable of being done (c. gen.) It 18. — (c) improper, not befitting (c. gen.) Vin I.45=216=III.20 ; PvA 64. — (d) not to be " done," i. e. not to be overcome or defeated D II.76 ; A IV.113 ; — (e) having nothing to do Vin I.154. — 2. (nt.) a forbidden matter, prohibition Vin II.278 — sa° 1. having business, busy Vin I.155 ; — 2. one who has still something to do (in sense of above 2) D II.143 ; Th 1, 1045 ; DA I.9.

Karaṇīyatā (f.) [abstr. fr. prec.] the fact that something has to be performed, an obligation Vin II.89, 93 ; sa° being left with something to do Miln 140.

Karaṇḍa (m. nt.) [cp. Sk. karaṇḍa, °ka, °ikā. The Dhātumañjūsā expl[s] k. by " bhājanatthe "] 1. a basket or box of wicker-work Mhvs 31, 98 ; Dāvs V.60 ; DhA III.18 ; — 2. the cast skin, slough of a serpent D I.77 (=DA I.222 ahi-kañcuka) cp. *Dial.* I.88.

Karaṇḍaka [fr. last] a box, basket, casket, as dussa° M I.215=S V.71=A IV.230 (in simile) ; S III.131 ; V.351 cp. Pug 34 ; J I 96 ; III.527 ; V.473 (here to be changed into koraṇḍaka) ; DA I.222 (viliva°) ; SnA 11.

Karamanda [etym. ?] a shrub Vism 183 (+kanavīra).

Karati[1] [cp. Sk. kṛntati] to cut, injure, hurt ; in " karato kārayato chindato chedāpayato . . ." D I.52=M I.516 ; S III.208.

Karati[2] (°tī) (f.) a superior kind of bean, the Dolichos catjang J VI.536 (=rājamāsa).

Karabha the trunk of an elephant ; in **karabhoru** (k°+ūru) (a woman) with beautiful thighs Mhbv 29.

Karamara see Kara.

Karaḷa (karala) a wisp of grass (tiṇa°) DhA III.38 ; DhsA 272.

Karavī [cp. Sk. kala-kaṇṭha cuckoo, & kalavinka sparrow] the Indian cuckoo J VI.539.

Karavīka same J V.204, 416 ; Vv 36[4] ; Vism 112, 206 ; VvA 166, 219.

-**bhāṇin** speaking like the cuckoo, i. e. with a clear and melodious voice, one of the mahāpurisa-lakkhaṇas D II.20=III.144=173=M II.137, etc. ; cp. *Dial.* II.17 n. and BSk. kalaviṅka-manojna-bhāṣin Sp. Av.Ś I.371 (Index p. 225, where references to Lalitavist. are given).

Karavīya (°iya)=prec. J VI.538.

Karavīra [cp. Sk. karavīra] 1. the oleander, Nerium odorum. Its flower was used especially in garlands worn by delinquents (see kaṇṭha) — 2. a kind of grass J IV.92. -**patta** a kind of arrow M I.429.

Karahi (Sk. karhi, when ? kar=loc. of pron. st. *quo= Lat. cur why, Goth. hvar, E. where), only in **karaha-ci** (karhi cid) at some time, generally preceded by **kadāci** D I.17 ; II.139 ; M I.177, 454 ; A I.179 ; IV.101 ; Miln 73, 76.

Karin (adj.) [fr. kara] " one who has a hand," an elephant (cp. hatthin) Mhvs 24, 34 ; 25, 68 ; Dāvs IV.2. In cpds. kari.

-**gajjita** the cry of the elephant, an elephant's trumpeting Dāvs V.56 ; -**vara** an excellent elephant Mhbv 4, 143 ; Dāvs IV.2.

Kari-paribandha (adj.) [=karīsa-paribaddha] bound up in filth, full of filth, disgusting ; Ep. of the body Th 1, 1152. Kari here is abbrev. of karīsa[2] (see note ad loc.).

Karīsa[1] (nt.) a square measure of land, being that space on which a karīsa of seed can be sown (Tamil karisa), see Rhys Davids, *Ancient Coins and Measures of Ceylon*, p. 18 ; J I.94, 212 ; IV.233, 276 ; VvA 64.

Karīsa[2] (nt.) [cp. Sk. karīṣa, to chṛṇatti to vomit, cp. Lat. -cerda in mūscerda, sūcerda] refuse, filth, excrement, dung D II.293 ; J I.5 ; Vism 259, 358 (in detail) ; PvA 87, 258 ; KhA 59 ; mutta° urine and fæces A I.139 ; Sn 835.

-**magga** the anus J IV.327 ; -**vāca** (nt.) a cesspool J III.263 (=gūthakūpa) ; -**vāyin**, f. °inī diffusing an odour of excrement PvA 87.

Karuṇā (f.) [cp. Vedic karuṇa nt. (holy) action; Sk. karuṇā, fr. **kṛ**. As adj. karuṇa see under 3.] pity, compassion. Karuṇā is one of the 4 qualities of character significant of a human being who has attained enfranchisement of heart (ceto-vimutti) in the 4 sentiments, viz. mettā k.° upekhā muditā Freq. found in this formula with °sahagatena cetasā. The first two qualities are complementary, and SnA 128 (on Sn 73) explains k° as "ahita-dukkh-âpanaya-kāmatā," the desire of removing bane and sorrow (from one's fellowmen), whilst mettā is expl. as "hita-sukh-ûpanaya-kāmatā," the desire of bringing (to one's fellow-men) that which is welfare and good. Other definitions are "paradukkhe sati sādhūnaŋ hadayakampanaŋ karotī ti" Bdhd 21; "sattesu k° karuṇāyanā karuṇāyitattaŋ karuṇā cetovimutti" as expl. of avihiŋsa dhātu Vbh 87; paradukkhāsahana-rasā Vism 318. K°-sahagatena cetasā denotes the exalted state of compassion for all beings (all that is encompassed in the sphere of one's good influence: see cātuddisa "extending over the 4, i. e. all, directions): D I.251; III.78, 50, 224; S IV.296, 322, 351; V.115; A I.183, 196; II.129, 184; III.225; V.300, 345; J II.129; Nd[2] on Sn 73; Vbh 273, 280; Dhs 1258. The def. of karuṇā at Vism 318 runs "paradukkhe sati sādhūnaŋ hadaya-kampanaŋ karoti." Frequently referred to as an ideal of contemplation (in conn. w. bhāvanā & jhāna), so in "karuṇaŋ cetovimuttiŋ bhāveti" S V.119; A I.38; V.360; in k° cetovimutti bhāvitā bahulī katā, etc. D III.248; A III.291; IV.300; in k°-sahagataŋ saddhindriyaŋ A I.42; unspecified S V.131; A III.185; Nett 121, 124; Ps I.8; k°+mettā Nett 25; k°+muditā Bdhd 16 sq., 26 sq., 29; ananta k° pañña as Ep. of Buddha Bdhd 1; karuṇaŋ dūrato katvā, without mercy, of the Yamadūtā, messengers of Death Sdhp 287; mahā° great compassion Ps I.126, 133; -°samāpatti a 'gest,' feat of great compassion: in which Buddha is represented when rising and surveying the world to look for beings to be worthy of his mercy and help D II.237; Ps. I, 126 f. DhA I.26, 367; PvA 61, 195; — 3. As adj. only in cpds. (e. g. °vācā merciful speech; neg. akaruṇa merciless Mhbv 85, & ati° very merciful J IV.142) and as adv. karuṇaŋ pitifully, piteously, mournfully, in k° paridevati J VI.498, 513, 551; Cp. IX.54; also in abl. karuṇā J VI.466. —See also kāruñña.

-**âdhimutta** intent upon compassion D II.241, 242; -**ânuvattin** following the dictates of mercy Dāvs III.46; -**guṇaja** originating in the quality of compassion Sdhp 570; -**jala** water of c., shower of mercy Miln 22; Mhbv 16; -**jhāna** meditation on pity, ecstasy of c. D II.237-39; -**ṭṭhāniya** worthy of c. PvA 72; -**para** one who is highest in compassion, compassionate Sdhp 112, 345; -**bala** the power of c. Mhvs 15, 61, 130; Sdhp 577; -**brahmavihāra** divine state of pity Vism 319. -**bhāvanā** consideration or cultivation of pity Vism 314 sq. -**rasa** the sweetness of c. Mhbv 16; -**vihāra** (a heart) in the state of c. Vism 324 (& adj. °vihārin); DA I.33; -**sāgara** an ocean of mercy Mhbv 7; -**sītala** "cool with c." + hadaya, whose heart is tempered with mercy Sdhp 33; DA I.1.

Karuṇāyati [v. den. fr. karuṇā; cp. BSk. karuṇāyati Divy 105] to feel pity for, to have compassion on Sn 1065 (°āyamāna; expl. by Nd[2] as anuddayamāno anurakkh° anuggaṇh° anukamp°); Vbh 273; Vism 314. *Der.* °āyanā compassionateness Vbh 87=273 (and °āyitattaŋ ibid.).

Karumbhaka a species of rice-plant of a ruddy colour Miln 252 (see *Mil. trsl.* II.73).

Karumhā (pl.) a class of Devas D II.260.

Kareṇu [metathesis for kaṇeru, q. v., cp. Sk. kareṇu] elephant, in cpd. -**lolita** resounding with the noise made by elephants, of a forest Th 2, 273.

Kareṇukā (f.) [fr. kareṇu) a female elephant J II.343; DhA I.196 (v. l. for kaṇeru).

Kareri in Childers the tree Capparis trifoliata, but see *Brethren*, p. 363, n. 2: musk-rose tree or "karer"; Th 1, 1062; Ud 31; J V.405; VI.534.

Karoṭi[1] (f.) 1. a basin, cup, bowl, dish J I.243; II.363; III.225; IV.67; V.289, 290. — 2. the skull (cp. kaḷopi. On the form cp. *Dial.* I.227 n.) J VI.592.

Karoṭi[2] (m.) a class of genii that formed one of the 5 guards of the devas against the asuras J I.204, associated with the nāgas (cp. Divy 218; and Morris, *J.P.T.S.* 1893, 22). As N. of Supaṇṇas (a kind of Garuḍas) expl[d] as "tesaŋ karoṭi nāma pānabhojanaŋ" by C. on J I.204. Kern, *Toev.* s. v. compares BSk. karoṭapāṇayah a class of Yakṣas MVastu I.30.

Karoṭika [fr. karoṭi[1])] 1. a bowl, basin J IV.68; DhA II.131 (sappi°). — 2. the skull J VI.592; where it may be a helmet in the form of a skull.

Karoṭiya=karoṭika 2, J VI.593.

Karoti v. irreg. [Sk. karoti, *qụer to form, to build (or plait, weave? see kamma), cp. kar-man, Lith. kùrti to build, O.Tr. cruth form; Lat. corpus, with p- addition, as Sk. kṛpa, **kḷp**=**kṛp**. Derived are kalpa>kappa, kalpate>kappeti]. Of the endless variety of forms given by grammarians only the foll. are bona fide and borne out by passages from our texts (when bracketed, found in gram. works only): I. *Act.* 1. Ind. Pres. karomi, etc. Sn 78, 216, 512, 666=Dh 306=It 42; Opt. kare Dh 42, 43, pl. (kareyyāma) kareyyātha Sn p. 101; or (sing.) kareyya (freq.), kareyyāsi PvA 11; kareyya Sn 920, 923; kuriyā (=Sk. kuryāt) J VI.206; Ppr. karan Dh 136, or karonto (f. karontī) Dh 16, 116. — 2. Impf. (akara, etc.).— 3. Aor. (akaŋ) akariŋ, etc., 3rd sing. akāsi Sn 343, 537, 2nd pl. akattha Pv I.11[2]; PvA 45, 75; 3rd pl. akariŋsu; akaŋsu Sn 882; PvA 74; without augment kari DhA II.59. Prohibitive mā(a)kāsi Sn 339, 1068, etc. — 4. Imper. karohi Sn p. 32; 1062; karotha Sn 223; KhA 168. — 5. Fut. karissāmi, etc.; kassāmi Pv IV.1[39]; kāsaŋ J IV.286; VI.36; kāhāmi (in sense of I *will* do, I am determined to do, usually w. puññaŋ & kusalaŋ poetical only) Pv II.11[3]; Vv 33[102]; 2nd sing. kāhasi Sn 427, 428; Dh 154; 1st pl. kāhāma Pv IV.10[11]. — 6. Inf. kātuŋ PvA 4, 61, 69, 115, Kh VI.10, etc.; kattuŋ VvA 13; kātave Mhvs 35, 29; Vv 44[18] (=kātuŋ); kātuye Th 2, 418. — 7. Pp. kata, see sep. — 8. Ger. katvā Sn 127, 661, 705, etc.; katvāna (poet.) Sn 89, 269, Pv I.1[3]; karitvā see IV. II. *Med.* 1. Ind. pres. (kubbe, etc.) 3rd sing. kubbati Sn 168, 811; 3rd pl. kubbanti Sn 794; or 3rd sing. kurute Sn 94, 796, 819; It. 67; Opt. (kubbe, etc.) 2nd pl. kubbetha Sn 702, 719, 917; It 87; or 3rd sing. kayirā Sn 728=1051; S I.24; Dh 53, 117; kayirātha (always expl. by kareyya) Dh 25, 117; It 13; Pv I.11[11]; KhA 224; kubbaye Sn 943. — Ppr. (kurumāna, kubbāno, karāno) (a)kubbaŋ Sn 844, 913; (a)kubbanto It 86; f. (vi)kubbantī Vv 11[2]; (a)kubbamāna Sn 777, 778, 897; (vi)kubbamāna Vv 33[1]. — 2. Impf. (akariŋ, 2nd sing. akarase, etc.) 3rd sing. akubbatha Pv II.13[18]; 1st pl. akaramhase J III.26, °a DhA I.145. — 3. Aor. (none) — 4. Imper. (2nd sing. kurussu, 3rd sing. kurutaŋ, 2nd pl. kuruvho) 3rd sing. kurutaŋ (=Sk. kurutāŋ) J VI.288. — 5. Fut. (none). III. *Pass.* 1. Ind. pres. (karīyati, etc.) kayirati Dh 292=Th 1, 635; KhA 168; and kīrati Th 1, 143. Ppr. (karīyamāna, kayira°). — 2. Fut. kariyissati Vin I.107. — 3. Grd. karaṇiya (q. v.), (kayya) kātabba DhA I.338. IV. *Caus.* I. (Denom. to kāra) kārayati=kāreti, in origin. meaning of build, construct, and fig. perform, exercise, rule, wield (rajjaŋ): kārehi PvA 81 (of huts), kārayissāmi Pv II.6[4] (of doll); kāressaŋ J V.297 (do.), akārayi Pv II.13[10]; akārayuŋ Mhvs IV.3; akāresi Mhvs 23, 85;

kāretuŋ PvA 74; kārayamāna VvA 9 (of chair); kāretvā (nāmaŋ) PvA 162; karitvā Sn 444 (vasiŋ) 674; 680 (vittiŋ); p. 97 (uttarāsangaŋ). V. *Caus.* II. Kārāpeti S I.179; PvA 20; Aor. kārāpesi he had (= caused to be) erected, constructed Vin II.159; fut. kārāpessāmi Mhvs 20, 9; ger. kārāpetvā PvA 123; grd. kārapetabba Vin II.134.

Meanings of karoti: 1. to build, erect Mhvs 19, 36; 20, 9 (Caus.). — 2. to act, perform, make, do Vin I.155; J I.24; II.153 (tathā karomi yathā na . . . I prevent, cp. Lat. facio ne . . .); III.297; Pv I.8[8] = II.6[19]; Mhvs 3, 1; 7, 22; — 3. to produce DhA I.172; — 4. to write, compose J VI.410; PvA 287; — 5. to put on, dress Vin II.277; J I.9; — 6. to impose (a punishment) Mhvs 4, 14; — 7. to turn into (with loc. or two acc.) J II.32; Mhvs 9, 27; — 8. to use as (with two acc.) J I.113; II.24; — 9. to bring into (with loc.) J V.454 — 10. to place (with loc.) J V.274; (with acc. of the person) Dh 162. It is very often used periphrastically, where the trslⁿ would simply employ the noun as verb, e. g. kathaŋ k° D II.98; kodhaŋ k° and kopaŋ k° to be angry J IV.22; VI.257; cayaŋ k° to hoard up; corikaŋ k° to steal Vin I.75; taṇhaŋ k° (c. loc.) to desire J I.5; sītaŋ k° to cool D II.129. — It is often compᵈ with nouns or adjectives with a change of final vowel to ī (i) uttāni° to make clear D II.105; pākaṭī°, bahulī°, muṭṭhī°, etc. (q. v.). Cp. the same process in conn. with bhavati. — The meanings of karoti are varied according to the word with which it is connected; it would be impossible and unnecessary to give an exhaustive list of all its various shades. Only a few illustrations may suffice: aŋse k° to place on one's shoulder J I.9; antarāyaŋ k° to prevent J I.232; ādiŋ k° (c. acc.) to begin with; nimittaŋ k° to give a hint D II.103; pātarāsaŋ k° to breakfast; mānasaŋ k° to make up one's mind; mahaŋ k° to hold a festival D II.165; massuŋ k° to trim the beard DhA I.253; musāvādaŋ k° to tell a lie J VI.401; rajjaŋ k° to reign S I.218; vase k° to bring into one's power J I.79; sandhiŋ k° to make an agreement Mhvs 16; sinehaŋ k° to become fond of J I.190. — Similarly, cpᵈ with adverbs: alaŋ k° to make much of, i. e. to adorn, embellish; dūrato k° to keep at a distance, i. e. keep free from PvA 17; Sdhp 287; purak k° (purakkharoti) to place before, i. e. to honour Pv III.7[1]. — Note phrase kiŋ karissati what difference does it make? (Cp. Ger. was macht's) D I.120; or what about . . . J I.152.

Kalakala (adj.) [cp. Sk. kala] any indistinct and confused noise Mhbv 23 (of the tramping of an army); in -mukhara sounding confusedly (of the ocean) ibid. 18. Cp. karakarā.

Kalati [**kal**, kālayati] to utter an (indistinct) sound: pp. kalita Th I, 22.

Kalanda [cp. Sk. karaṇḍa piece of wood ?] heap, stack (like a heap of wood ? cp. kaliṅgara) Miln 292 (sīsa°).

Kalandaka 1. a squirrel Miln 368; — 2. an (ornamental) cloth or mat, spread as a seat J VI.224; -nivāpa N. of a locality in Veḷuvana, near Rājagaha, where oblations had been made to squirrels D II.116; Vin I.137; II.105, 290, etc.

Kalabha [cp. Sk. kalabha] the young of an elephant: see **hatthi°** and cp. **kalāra**

Kalamba (nt.) [cp. Sk. kalamba menispermum calumba, kalambī convolvulus repens] N. of a certain herb or plant (Convolv. repens ?); may be a bulb or radish J IV.46 (= tālakanda), cp. p. 371, 373 (where C explˢ by tāla-kanda; gloss BB however gives latā-tanta); VI.578. See also kadamba & kaḷimba.

-rukkha the Cadamba tree J VI.290.

Kalambaka = kalamba, the C. tree J VI.535.

Kalambukā (f.) = kalambaka D III.87 (vv. ll. kaladukā, kalabakā) the trslⁿ (*Dial.* III.84) has "bamboo."

Kalala (m. nt.) 1. mud J I.12, 73; Miln 125, 324, 346; Mhbv 150; PvA 215 (= kaddama); DhA III.61; IV.25. — su° "well-muddied" i. e. having soft soil (of a field) Miln 255. — 2. the residue of sesamum oil (tela°), used for embalming J II.155. — 3. in Embryology: the "soil," the placenta S I.206 = Kvu II.494; Miln 125. Also the first stage in the formation of the fœtus (of which the first 4 during the first month are k., abbuda, pesi, ghana, after which the stages are counted by months 1-5 & 10; see Vism 236; Nd[1] 120; & cp. Miln 40). — 4. the fœtus, appl. to an egg, i. e. the yolk Miln 49. — In cpds with kar & bhū the form is kalalī°.

-gata (a) fallen into the mud Miln 325; -gahaṇa "mud thicket," dense mud at the bottom of rivers or lakes J I.329; -**kata** made muddy, disturbed Vv 84[31] (VvA 343); -bhūta = prec., A I.9, cp. J II.100; A III.233; Miln 35; -makkhita soiled with mud DhA III.61.

Kalasa (nt.) [cp. Vedic kalaśa] 1. a pot, waterpot, dish, jar M III.141; J IV.384; Dāvs IV.49; PvA 162. — 2. the female breasts (likened to a jar) Mhbv 2, 22.

Kalaha [cp. Sk. kalaha, fr. **kal**] quarrel, dispute, fight A I.170; IV.196, 401; Sn 862, 863 (+ vivāda); J I.483; Nd[2] 427; DhA III.256 (udaka° about the water); IV.219; Sdhp 135. °ŋ udīreti to quarrel J V.395; karoti id. J I.191, 404; PvA 13; vaḍḍheti to increase the tumult, noise J V.412; DhA III.255. — a° harmony, accord, agreement S I.224; mahā° a serious quarrel, a row J IV.88.

-**Abhirata** delighting in quarrels, quarrelsome Sn 276, Th I, 958. -ŋkara picking up a quarrel J VI.45; -**karaṇa** quarrelling, fighting J V.413; -**kāraka** (f.-ī) quarrelsome, pugnacious A IV.196; Vin I.328; II.1; -**kāraṇa** the cause or reason of a dispute J III.151; VI.336; -jāta "to whom a quarrel has arisen," quarrelling, disputing A I.70; Vin I.341; II.86, 261; Ud 67; J III.149; -**pavaḍḍhanī** growth or increase of quarrels, prolongation of strife (under 6 evils arising from intemperance) D III.182 = DhsA 380; -**vaḍḍhana** (nt.) inciting & incitement to quarrel J V.393, 394; -sadda brawl, dispute J VI.336.

Kalā [Vedic kalā *squel, to Lat scalpo, Gr. σκάλλω, Ohg scolla, scilling, scala. The Dhtp. (no 613) explˢ kala by "saṅkhyāne."] 1. a small fraction of a whole, generally the 16th part; the 16th part of the moon's disk; often the 16th part again subdivided into 16 parts and so on: one infinitesimal part (see VvA 103; DhA II.63), in this sense in the expression kalaŋ nâgghati soḷasiŋ "not worth an infinitesimal portion of" = very much inferior to S I.19; III.156 = V.44 = It 20; A I.166, 213; IV.252; Ud 11; Dh 70; Vv 43[7]; DhA II.63 (= koṭṭhāsa) DhA IV.74. — 2. an art, a trick (lit. part, turn) J I.163.—kalaŋ upeti to be divided or separated Miln 106; DhA I.119; see sakala. — In cpd. with bhū as kalī -bhavati to be divided, broken up J I.467 (= bhijjati). Cp. vikala.

Kalāpa [cp. Sk. kalāpa] 1. anything that comprises a number of things of the same kind; a bundle, bunch: sheaf; a row, multitude; usually of grass, bamboo- or sugar-canes, sometimes of hair and feathers S IV.290 (tiṇa°); J I.158 (do.); 25 (naḷa°), 51 (mālā°), 100 (uppala-kumuda°); V.39 (usīra°); Miln 33; PvA 257, 260 (ucchu°), 272 (veḷu°); 46 (kesā), 142 (mora-piñja°) — 2. a quiver Vin II.192; It 68; J VI.236; Miln 418; PvA 154, 169. — 3. in philosophy: a group of qualities, pertaining to the material body (cp. rūpa°) Vism 364 (dasadhamma°) 626 (phassa-pañcamakā dhammā); Bdhd 77 (rūpa°), 78, 120.

-agga (nt.) "the first (of the) bunch," the first (sheaves) of a crop, given away as alms DhA I.98.

-sammasanā grasping (characteristics) by groups Vism 287, 606, 626 sq.

Kalāpaka 1. a band, string (of pearls) Vin II.315; Mhvs 30, 67. — 2. a bundle, group J I.239.

Kalāpin (adj.) [fr. kalāpa] having a quiver J VI.49 (acc. pl. °ine). f. kalāpinī a bundle, sheaf (yava°) S IV.201; II.114 (naḷa°).

Kalābuka (nt.) [cp. Sk. kalāpaka] a girdle, made of several strings or bands plaited together Vin II.136, 144, 319;

Kalāya a kind of pea, the chick-pea M I.245 (kaḷāya); S I.150; A V.170; Sn p. 124; J II.75 (= varaka, the bean Phaseolus trilobus, and kālarāja-māsa); J III.370; DhA I.319. Its size may be gathered from its relation to other fruits in ascending scale at A V.170 = S I.150 = Sn p. 124 (where the size of an ever-increasing boil is described). It is larger than a kidney bean (mugga) and smaller than the kernel of the jujube (kolaṭṭhi).
-matta of the size of a chick-pea S I.150; A V.170; Sn p. 124 (I); J III.370; DhA I.319.

Kalāyati [Denom. fr. kalā] to have a measure, to outstrip J I.163 (taken here as " trick, deceive ").

Kalāra in hatthi° at Ud 41, expl^d in C by potaka, but cp. the same passage at DhA I.58 which reads kalabha, undoubtedly better. Cp. kaḷārikā.

Kali (m.) [cp. Sk. kali] 1. the unlucky die (see akkha); " the dice were seeds of a tree called the vibhitaka . . . An extra seed was called the kali " (*Dial.* II.368 n.) D II.349; J I.380; Dh I.252 (= DhA III.375); at J VI.228, 282, 357 it is opposed to kaṭa, q. v. — 2. (= kaliggaha) an unlucky throw at dice, bad luck, symbolically as a piece of bad luck in a general worldly sense or bad quality, demerit, sin (in moral sense) kaliŋ vicināti " gathers up demerit " Sn 658; appamatto kali . . . akkhesu dhanaparājayo . . . mahantataro kali yo sugatesu manam padosaye S I.149 = A II.3 = V.171, 174 = Sn 659 = Nett 132; cp. M III.170; A V.324; Dh 202 (= DhA III.261 aparādha). — 3. the last of the 4 ages of the world (see °yuga). — 4. sinful, a sinner Sn 664 (= pāpaka). — 5. saliva, spittle, froth (cp. kheḷa) Th 2, 458, 501; J V.134.
-(g)gaha the unlucky throw at dice, the losing throw; symbolically bad luck, evil consequence in worldly & moral sense (ubhayattha k° faring badly in both worlds) M I.403 = 406; III.170 (in simile). See kaṭaggaha; -devatā (m. pl.) the devotees of kali, the followers of the goddess kali Miln 191 (see *Miln trsl.* I.266 n.); -(p)piya one who is fond of cheating at dice, a gambler Pgdp 68; -yuga (nt.) one of the 4 (or 8) ages of the world, the age of vice, misery and bad luck; it is the age in which we are Sāsv 4, 44, Vinl 281; -sāsana (nt.) in °ŋ āropeti to find fault with others Vin VI.93, 360.

Kalingara (m. nt.) (BB I) [cp. Sk. kaḍankara & kaḍangara, on which in sense of " log " see Kern, *Toev.* s. v. kalingara] 1. a log, a piece of wood M I.449, 451; S II.268; DhA III.315; often in sense of something useless, or a trifle (comb^d with kaṭṭha q. v.) Dh 41; DhA I.321 (= kaṭṭhakhaṇḍa, a chip) Th 2, 468 (id.) as kaṭṭhakalingarāni DhA II.142. — 2. a plank, viz. a step in a staircase, in sopāna° Vin II.128, cp. sopāna-kaḷevara.
-ûpadhāna a wooden block used for putting one's head on when sleeping S II.267; Miln 366; -kaṇḍa a wooden arrow J III.273 (acittaŋ k°: without feeling)

Kalingu (m. nt.) [cp. Sk. kalinga & kalingaka] the Laurus camphora, the Indian laurel J VI.537.

Kalita [pp. of kalati] sounding indistinctly Th 2, 22.

Kalusa [cp. Sk. kaluṣa] muddy, dirty, impure; in °bhāva the state of being turbid, impure, obscured (of the mind) DA I.275.

Kalevara see kaḷebara.

Kalya see kalla; -rūpa pleased, glad Sn 680, 683; a° not pleased Sn 691.

Kalyatā (f.) 1. the state of being sound, able, pliant J II.12. — 2. pleasantness, agreeableness, readiness, in a° opp. (appl^d to citta) Dhs 1156; DhsA 377 (= gilānabhāva).

Kalyāṇa (& kallāṇa) [Vedic kalyāṇa] 1. (adj.) beautiful, charming; auspicious, helpful, morally good. Syn. bhaddaka PvA 9, 116) and kusala (S II.118; PvA 9, 122); opp. pāpa (S I.83; M I.43; PvA 101, 116 and under °mitta). kata° = katûpakāra PvA 116 Appl^d to dhamma in phrase ādi° majjhe° pariyosāne° D I.62 and ≈; S V.152; Sn p. 103; VvA 87; Vism 213 sq. (in var. applications); etc. — As m one who observes the sīlapadaŋ (opp. pāpa, who violates it) A II.222, cp. k°-mittā = sīlâdihi adhikā SnA 341. — S IV.303; V.2, 29, 78; A III.77; IV.361; Vin II.8, 95; J I.4; Miln 297; -kata° (opp. kata-pāpa) of good, virtuous character, in phrase k° katakusala, etc. It 25, etc. (see kata II.1 a). k° of kitti (-sadda) D I.49 (= DA I.146 seṭṭha); S IV.374; V.352; of jhāna (tividha°) Bdhd 96, 98, 99; of mittā, friends in general (see also cpd.) Dh 78 (na bhaje pāpake mitte . . . bhajetha m° kalyāṇe), 116, 375 (= suddhājīvin); Sn 338. — 2. (nt.) (a) a good or useful thing, good things Vin I.117; A III.109; cp. bhadraŋ. — (b) goodness, virtue, merit, meritorious action J V.49 (kalyāṇā here nt. nom. in sense of pl.; cp. Vedic nt.), 492; — °ŋ karoti to perform good deeds S I.72; A I.138 sq.; Vin I.73; PvA 122. — (c) kindness, good service J I.378; III.12 (= upakāra), 68 (°ŋ karoti). — (d) beauty, attraction, perfection; enum^d as 5 kalyāni, viz. kesa°, maŋsa°, aṭṭhi°, chavi°, vaya° i. e. beauty of hair, flesh, teeth, skin, youth J I.394; DhA I.387.
-ajjhāsaya the wish or intention to do good DhA I.9; — -âdhimuttika disposed towards virtue, bent on goodness S II.154, 158; It 70, 78; Vbh 341; -kāma desiring what is good A III.109; -kārin (a) doing good, virtuous (opp. pāpa°) S I.227, cp. J II.202 = III.158; DhsA 390; (m.) who has rendered a service J VI.182; -carita walking in goodness, practising virtue Vbh 341; -jātika one whose nature is pleasantness, agreeable J III.82; -dassana looking nice, lovely, handsome Sn 551 = Th 1, 821 (+ kañcanasannibhattaca); -dhamma (1) of virtuous character, of good conduct, virtuous Vin I.73; III.133; S V.352; Pug 26; It 96; Pv IV.1[55]; Miln 129; DhA I.380; J II.65 (= sundara°), PvA 230 (= sundara-sīla); sīlavā + k° (of bhikkhu, etc.) M I.334; S IV.303; PvA 13. — k°ena k°atara perfectly good or virtuous A II.224. — (2) the Good Doctrine DhA I.7. -°tā the state of having a virtuous character A II.36; -pañña " wise in goodness " possessed of true wisdom Th 1, 506; It 97; -paṭipadā the path of goodness or virtue, consisting of dāna, uposathakamma & dasakusalakammapathā J III.342; -paṭibhāṇa of happy retort, of good reply A III.58, cp. Miln 3; -pāpaka good and bad J V.238; VI.225; Kvu 45; (nt.) goodness and evil J V.493; -pīti one who delights in what is good Sn 969; -bhattika having good, nice food Vin II.77; III.160 (of a householder); -mitta 1. a good companion, a virtuous friend, an honest, pure friend; at Pug 24 he is said to " have faith, be virtuous, learned, liberal and wise "; M I.43 (opp. pāpa°); S I.83, 87 (do.); A IV.30, 357; Pug 37, 41; J III.197; Bdhd 90; a° not a virtuous friend DhsA 247. — 2. as t.t. a spiritual guide, spiritual adviser. The Buddha is the spiritual friend par excellence, but any other Arahant can act as such S V.3; Vism 89, 98, 121; cp. kammaṭṭhāna-dāyaka. -mittatā friendship with the good and virtuous, association with the virtuous S I.87; such friendship is of immense help for the attainment of the Path and Perfection S V.3, 32; it is the sign that the bhikkhu will realize the 7

bojjhangas S v.78=101; A I.16, 83, it is one of the 7 things conducive to the welfare of a bhikkhu D III.212; A IV.29, 282; Th 2, 213; It 10; Dhs 1328=Pug 24; Vism 107. — a° not having a virtuous friend and good adviser DhsA 247. -rūpa beautiful, handsome J III.82; v.204; -vākkaraṇa, usually comb. with °vāca, of pleasant conversation, of good address or enunciation, reciting clearly D I.93, 115; A II.97; III.114, 263; IV.279; Vin II.139; Miln 21; DA I.263 (=madhura-vacana); a° not pronouncing or reciting clearly D I.94, 122; -°tā the fact of being of good and pleasing address A I.38; -vāca, usually in form. k° k°-vākkaraṇo poriyā vācāya samannāgato D I.114; A II.97; III.114, 195, 263; IV.279; Vin II.139; DA I.282; -sadda a lucky word or speech J II.64; -sampavanka a good companion A IV.357 (in phrase k°-mitta k°-sahāya k°-s°); Pug 37; -°tā companionship with a virtuous friend S I.87. -sahāya a good, virtuous companion A IV.284; 357; Pug 37; cp. prec., -°tā=prec. S I.87; -sīla practising virtue, of good conduct, virtuous Th 1, 1008; It 96.

Kalyāṇaka (adj.) [fr. last] good, virtuous DA I.226; DhsA 32.

Kalyāṇatā (f.) [abstr. fr. kalyāṇa] beauty, goodness, virtuousness Vism 4 (ādi); k°-**kusala** clever, experienced in what is good Nett 20.

Kalyāṇin (adj.) [fr. kalyāṇa] (a) beautiful, handsome Vv IV.^{5}; — (b) auspicious, lucky, good, proper J v.124; Ud 59; — (c) f. [cp.-I Vedic kalyāṇī] a beautiful woman, a belle, usually in janapada° D I.193=M II.40; S II.234; J I.394; v.154.

Kalla^1 & **Kalya** (adj.) [cp. Sk. kalya] 1. well, healthy, sound Vin I.291. — 2. clever, able, dexterous Miln 48, 87. — 3. ready, prepared J II.12, cp. -citta. — 4. fit, proper, right S II.13 (pañha). — nt. kallaŋ it is proper, befitting (with inf. or inf.-substitute): vacanāya proper to say D I.168, 169; A I.144; abhinandituŋ D II.69; -kallaŋ nu [kho] is it proper? M III.19; S IV.346; Miln 25. — a° 1. not well, unfit Th 2, 439, cp. ThA 270. — 2. unbecoming, unbefitting D II.68; J v.394.
-kāya sound (in body), refreshed Vin I.291; -kusala of sound skill (cp. kallita) S III.265; -citta of ready, amenable mind, in form. k°, mudu-citta, vinīvaraṇa°, udagga°, etc. D I.110=148=II.41=A IV.209=Vin I.16=II.156; VvA 53, 286; Vv 50^{19} (=kammaniya-citta "her mind was prepared for, responsive to the teaching of the dhamma"); PvA 38. -cittatā the preparedness of the mind (to receive the truth) J II.12 (cp citta-kalyatā); -rūpa 1. of beautiful appearance Th I, 212, — 2. pleased, joyful (kalya°) Sn 680, 683, 691; -sarīra having a sound body, healthy J II.51; a°-tā not being sound in body, ill-health VvA 243.

Kalla^2 (m. nt.) ashes J III.94 (for kalala), also in °-**vassa** a shower of ashes J IV.389.

Kallaka (adj.) [fr. last] in a° unwell, indisposed Vin III.62; J III.464; DhsA 377.

Kallatā (f.) see kalyatā; -a° unreadiness, unpreparedness, indisposition (of citta), in expl° of thīna Nd^2 290= Dhs 1156=1236=Nett 86; DhsA 378; Nett 26. The reading in Nd^2 is akalyāṇatā, in Dhs akalyatā; follows akammaññatā.

Kallahāra [cp. Sk. kahlāra, the P. form to be expl^d as a diaeretic inversion kalhāra > kallahāra] the white esculent water lily J v.37; Dpvs XVI.19.

Kallita (nt.) [fr. kalla] pleasantness, agreeableness S III.270, 273 (samādhismiŋ -°kusala); A III.311; IV.34 (id.).

Kallola [cp. Sk. kallola] a billow, in -°mālā a series of billows Dāvs IV.44.

Kaḷāya=kalāya.

Kaḷāra (adj.) [cp. Sk. karāla projecting (of teeth), whereas kaḍāra means tawny] always referring to teeth: with long, protruding teeth, of Petas (cp. attr. of the dog of the "Underworld" PvA 152: tikhiṇâyatakaṭhina-dāṭho and the figure of the witch in fairy-tales) J v.91 (=nikkhantadanto); VI.548 (=sūkara-dāṭhehi samannāgato p. 549); Pv II.4^1 (=k°-danto PvA 90).

Kaḷārikā (f.) [fr. last, lit. with protruding teeth] a kind of large (female) elephant M I. 178 (so read with v. l. for kāḷ°). Cp. kalāra.

Kaḷingara=kalingara.

Kaḷimb(h)aka (cp. kaḍamba, kalamba) a mark used to keep the interstices between the threads of the kaṭhina even, when being woven Vin II.116, 317 (v. l. kaḷimpaka).

Kaḷīra the top sprout of a plant or tree, esp. of the bamboo and cert. palm trees (e. g. coco-nut tree) which is edible Sn 38 (vaŋsa°=veḷugumba Nd^2 556 and p. 58); Th 1, 72; J I.74, cp. III.179; VI.26; Miln 201 (vaŋsa°); Vism 255 (vaŋsa°-cakkalaka, so read for kalira°; KhA 50 at id. passage reads kaḷīra-daṇḍa).
-(c)chejja (nt.) "the cutting off of the sprout," a kind of torture Miln 193, cp. *Miln. trsl.* I.270 and kadalīccheda.

Kaḷebara (: kale° and kalevara) (m. & nt.) [cp. BSk. kaḍebara Av. Ś. II.26] 1. the body S I.62=A II.48;=IV.429 =M I.82; J II.437, III.96, 244; Vism 49, 230. — 2. a dead body, corpse, carcass; often in description of death: khandhānaŋ bhedo k°assa nikkhepo, D II.355= M. I.49=Vbh 137; Th 2, 467; J III.180, 511; v.459; Mhvs 20^{10}; 37^{81}; PvA 80. Cp. kuṇapa. — 3. the step in a flight of stairs M II.92, cp. kalingara.

Kaḷopī (=khaḷopi) f. 1. a vessel, basin, pot: see cpds. — 2. a basket, crate (=pacchi ThA 219; J v.252) M I.77, 342; S I.236=Th 2, 283 (where osenti is to be corr. to openti); J v.252. — On the form of the word (=karoṭi ?) see Trenckner *J.P.T.S.* 1908, 109 and Davids, *Dial.* I.227. kaḷopī (as khaḷopī) is expl^d at Pug A p. 231 as "ukkhalī, pacchi vā."
-mukha the brim of a pan or cooking vessel D I.166 =M I.77=342=A I.295=II.206 (kumbhi-m°+kaḷopi-m°); -hattha with a vessel or basket in his hand A IV.376.

Kavaca (nt.) [cp. Sk. kavaca] a mail, a coat of mail, armour D II.107=Ud 64 (appl^d to existence); Th 1, 614 (of sīla); J IV.92, 296; Miln 199, 257; Vism 73.
-jālikā a mail-coat Miln 199.

Kavandha (m. nt.) [cp. Sk. kavandha & kabandha] 1. the (headless) trunk of the body, endowed with the power of motion Vin III.107; cp. S II.260 (asīsaka°); Miln 292; DhA I.314. — 2. a headless dwarf, whose head has been crushed down into his body J v.424, 427 (cp. the story of Dhanu, the Rākṣasa who was punished by having his head and thighs forced into his body, Raghuvaŋsa XII.57).

Kavāṭa (m. nt.) 1. the panels of the door, the door proper, not the aperture Vin II.114, 120, 207, 208 (see Vin II.148 for the description of a door) IV.269, 304 (°baddha =āvasatha); J I.19; Nd^2 235^{1d}; Vism 28 (°koṇa door-corner). — 2. dvāra° a door-post J I.63; II.334; PvA 280. — 3. a window Mhvs IX.17; — °ŋ paṇāmeti to open the door Vin II.114, 120, 207; °ŋ ākoṭeti to knock at the door D I.88 (=Dh I.252); Vin II.208. — **akavāṭaka** (adj.) having no doors, doorless Vin II.148, 154 (v. l. for akkavāta Text).

-piṭṭha the panels and posts of a door; the door and the door-posts Vin I.47, 48=II.208, 218; -baddha "door-bound," closed, secure Vin IV.292 (see also above).

Kavāṭaka=kavāṭa Vin II.148; DA I.62 (nivaraṇa°).

Kavi [Vedic kavi] a poet S I.38; II.267; Dāvs I.10; four classes enum^d at A II.230 & DA I.95, viz. 1. cintā° an original p. 2. suta° one who puts into verse what he has heard. 3. attha° a didactic p. 4. paṭibhāṇa° an improvisor.
-kata composed by poets S II.267; A I.72.

Kavya [cp. Vedic kavya wise; sacrificer] poetry; ballad, ode (cp. kabba) J VI.213, 216.
-kāra a poet J VI.216.

Kaviṭṭha [cp. kapittha] the elephant-apple tree, Feronia elephantum J V.38 (°vana).

Kasaka see kassaka.

Kasaṭa (metathesis of sakaṭa, cp. Trenckner, Miln p. 423) 1. (adj.) bad, nasty; bitter, acrid; insipid, disgusting A I.72; J II.96; 159. — 2. (m.) (a) fault, vice, defect M I.281; Ps II.87. — (b) leavings, dregs VvA 288 (v. l. sakaṭa). — (c) something bitter or nasty J II.96; V.18. — (d) bitter juice J II.105 (nimba°). — sa° faulty, wrong, bitter to eat, unpalatable Miln 119.
-ôdaka insipid, tasteless water J II.97.

Kasati [kṛṣ or karṣ] to till, to plough S I.172, 173=Sn 80; Th I.531; J I.57; II.165; VI.365. — kassate (3rd sing. med.) Th I. 530. — pp. kattha (q. v.) Caus. II. **kasāpeti** Miln 66, 82; DhA I.224.

Kasana (nt.) ploughing, tilling J IV.167; VI.328, 364; Vism 384 (+vapana sowing).

Kasambu [Derivation uncertain] anything worthless, rubbish, filth, impurity; fig. low passions S I.166; Sn 281=Miln 414=A IV.172; Vism 258 (maŋsa°), 259 (parama°).
-jāta one whose nature is impurity, in comb. brahmacāripaṭiñño antopūti avassuto k° S IV.181; A II.240; IV.128, 201; Vin II.236; Pug 27, 34, 36; Vism 57 (+avassuta pāpa). °ka-jāta ibid. in vv. ll.

Kasā (f.) [Vedic kaśā] a whip Vin I.99 (in Uddāna); M I.87, etc.; Dh 143; Miln 197. — **-kasāhi tāḷeti** to whip, lash, flog as punishment for malefactors here, as well as in Niraya (see kamma-karaṇā) M I.87=A I.47=II.122, etc.; PvA 4 (of a thief scourged on his way to the place of execution); DhA II.39 (id.).
-niviṭṭha touched by the whip, whipped Dh 144 (=DhA III.86); -pahāra a stroke with the whip, a lash J III.178; -hata struck with the whip, scourged Vin I.75; 91=322; Sdhp 147.

Kasāya and **Kasāva** [Derivation uncertain. The word first appears in the late Vedic form **kaṣāya**, a decoction, distillation, essence; used fig^y of evil. The old Pali form is kasāva] 1. a kind of paste or gum used in colouring walls Vin II.151. — 2. an astringent decoction extracted from plants Vin I.207; 277; J V.198. — 3. (of taste), astringent DhS 629; Miln 65; DhA II.31. — 4. (of colour) reddish-yellow, orange coloured Vin I.277. — 5. (ethical) the fundamental faults (rāga, dosa, moha) A I.112; Dh 10; Vbh 368. -a° faultless, flawless, in akasāvattaŋ being without defect A I.112 (of a wheel, with -sa° ibid.); -sa° faulty DhA I.82; -mahā° wicked J IV.387. In cpds. both forms, viz. (kasāya)-yoga an astringent remedy J V.198 (kasāva° ibid.); -rasa reddish-yellow dye J II.198; (kasāva)-ôdaka an astringent decoction Vin I.205; -gandha having a pungent smell Vin I.277; -rasa having an astringent taste ibid.; -vaṇṇa of reddish-yellow colour ibid.

Kasāyatta (nt.) [abstr. fr. kasāya] astringency Miln 56.

Kasi and **Kasī** (f.) [fr. kasāti] tilling, ploughing; agriculture, cultivation M II.198; S I.172, 173=Sn 76 sq.; Vin IV.6; Pv I.5[6] (k°, gorakkha, vaṇijjā); PvA 7; Sdhp 390 (k°, vaṇijjā); VvA 63. — °ŋ **kasati** to plough, to till the land J I.277; Vism 284.
-kamma the act or occupation of ploughing, agriculture J II.165, 300; III.270. -karaṇa ploughing, tilling of the field PvA 66; -khetta a place for cultivation, a field PvA 8 (kasī°); -gorakkha agriculture and cattle breeding D I.135; -bhaṇḍa ploughing implements DhA I.307.

Kasiṇa[1] [Vedic kṛtsna] (adj.) entire, whole J IV.111, 112.

Kasiṇa[2] [Deriv. uncertain] (nt.) one of the aids to **kammaṭṭhāna** the practice by means of which mystic meditation (bhāvanā, jhāna) may be attained. They are fully described at A V.46 sq., 60; usually enumerated as *ten* [sāvakā dasa k° -āyatanāni bhāventi]: paṭhavī°, āpo°, tejo°, vāyo°, nīla°, pīta°, lohita°, odāta°, ākāsa°, viññāṇa°—that is, earth, water, fire, air; blue, yellow, red, white; space, intellection (or perhaps consciousness) M II.14; D III.268, 290; Nett 89, 112; Dhs 202; Ps I.6, 95; cp. *Manual* 49-52; Bdhd 4, 90 sq., 95 sq. — For the last two (ākāsa° and viññāṇa°) we find in later sources āloka° and (paricchinn') ākāsa° Vism 110; cp. *Dhs trsl.* 43 n. 4, 57 n. 2; *Cpd.* 54, 202. — Eight (the above omitting the last two) are given at Ps I.49, 143, 149. — See further J I.313; III.519; DhsA 186 sq. There are 14 manners of practising the kasiṇas (of which the first nine are: k°-ânulomaŋ; k°-paṭilomaŋ; k°-ânupaṭilomaŋ; jhānânulomaŋ; jh°-paṭi°; jh°-ânupaṭi°; jh°-ukkantikaŋ; k° ukk°; jh°-k°-ukk°) Vism 374; cp. Bdhd 5, 101 sq., 104, 152. — *Nine* qualities or properties of (paṭhavi-) kasiṇa are enum^d at Vism 117. — Each k. is *fivefold*, according to uddhaŋ, adho, tiriyaŋ, advayaŋ, appamāṇaŋ; M II.15, etc. — **kasiṇaŋ oloketi** to fix one's gaze on the particular kasiṇa chosen J V.314; °ŋ **samannāharati** to concentrate one's mind on the k. J III.519.
-āyatana the base or object of a kasiṇa exercise (see above as 10 such objects) D III.268; M II.14; Ps I.28, etc.; -ārammaṇa=°āyatana Vism 427 (three, viz. tejo°, odāta°, āloka°). -kamma the k. practice J I.141; IV.306; V.162, 193. -jhāna the k. meditation DhsA 413. -dosa fault of the k. object Vism 117, 123 (the 4 faults of paṭhavī-kasiṇa being confusion of the 4 colours). -parikamma the preliminary, preparatory rites to the exercise of a kasiṇa meditation, such as preparing the frame, repeating the necessary formulas, etc. J I.8, 245; III.13 526; DhsA 187; -°ŋ katheti to give instructions in these preparations J III.369; °ŋ karoti to perform the k-preparations J IV.117; V.132, 427; VI.68; -maṇḍala a board or stone or piece of ground divided by depressions to be used as a mechanical aid to jhāna exercise. In each division of the maṇḍala a sample of a kasiṇa was put. Several of these stone maṇḍalas have been found in the ruins at Anurādhapura. Cp. *Cpd.* 54 f. 202 f. J III.501; DhA IV.208. -samāpatti attainment in respect of the k. exercise Nd[2] 466[8] (ten such).

Kasita (pp. of kasati) ploughed, tilled Anvs 44; -a° untilled ibid. 27, 44. — Cp. vi°.

Kasira (adj.) [Probably fr. Vedic kṛcchra, the deriv. of which is uncertain] miserable, painful, troubled, wretched A IV.283; Sn 574; J II.136; IV.113=VI.17; Pv IV.1[21] (=PvA 229 dukkha). — adv. kasirā (abl.) with difficulty J V.435; -kasirena (instr.) D I.251; M I.104; S I.94; Vin I.195; J I.338; III.513. -a° without pain, easy, comfortable J VI.224 (=niddukkha); -lābhin obtaining without difficulty (f° inī A IV.342) in formula

akicchalābhī akasiralābhī etc. M I.33; S II.278; A I.184; II.23, 36; IV.106; Ud 36; Pug 11, 12.
-ābhata amassed with toil and difficulty (of wealth) J V.435; -vuttika finding it hard to get a livelihood A I.107 = Pug 51.

Kaseruka [etym. connected with Sk. kaseru backbone ?] a plant, shrub SnA 284 (v. l. kaŋsīruka for kiŋsuka ?). See also **kaṭeruha.**

Kassaka [fr. kasati] a husbandman, cultivator, peasant, farmer, ploughman D I.61 (k° gahapatiko kārakārako rāsi-vaḍḍhako); A I.241; A. I.229, 239 (the three duties of a farmer); S I.172 = Sn 76; III.155 (v. l. for T. kasaka); IV. 314; Vin IV.108; Bdhd 96; DA I.170; often in *similes,* e. g. Pv I.1[1]; II.9[68] (likeness to the doer of good works); Vism 152, 284, 320. -vaṇṇa (under) the disguise of a peasant S I.115 (of Māra).

Kassati [kṛṣ] see ava°, anu° (aor. anvakāsi), pari°; otherwise **kasati**; cp. also **kissati.**

Kassāma fut. of karoti.

Kahaŋ [cp. Vedic kuha; for a: u cp. kad°.] interr. adv. where ? whither ? Vin I.217; D I.151; Sn p. 106; J II.7; III.76; V.440. — k-nu kho where then ? D I.92; II.143, 263.

Kahāpaṇa [doubtful as regards etym.; the (later) Sk. kārṣāpaṇa looks like an adaptation of a dial. form] 1. A square copper coin M II.163; A I.250; V.83 sq.; Vin II.294; III. 238; DhsA 280 (at this passage included under rajataŋ, silver, together with loha-māsaka, dāru-māsaka and jatu-māsaka); S I.82; A I.250; Vin II.294; IV.249; J I.478, 483; II.388; Mhvs 30[14]. The extant specimens in our museums weigh about ⅝ of a penny, and the purchasing power of a k. in our earliest records seems to have been about a florin. — Frequent numbers as denoting a gift, a remuneration or alms, are 100,000 (J II.96); 18 koṭis (J I.92); 1,000 (J II.277, 431; V.128, 217; PvA 153, 161); 700 (J III.343); 100 (DhA III.239); 80 (PvA 102); 10 or 20 (DhA IV.226); 8 (which is considered, socially, almost the lowest sum J IV.138; I.483). A nominal fine of 1 k. (= a farthing) Miln 193. — ekaŋ k° pi not a single farthing J I.2; similarly eka-kahāpaṇen' eva Vism 312. — Various qualities of a kahāpaṇa are referred to by Bdhgh in similes at Vism 437 and 515. *Black* kahāpaṇas are mentioned at DhA III.254. — See Rh. Davids, *Ancient Measures of Ceylon; Buddh. India,* pp. 100-102, fig. 24; *Miln trsl.* I.239.
-gabbha a closet for storing money, a safe DhA IV.104; -vassa a shower of money Dh 186 (= DhA III.240).

Kahāpaṇaka (nt.) N. of a torture which consisted in cutting off small pieces of flesh, the size of a kahāpaṇa, all over the body, with sharp razors M I.87 = A I.47, II.122; cp. Miln 97, 290, 358.

Kā (indecl.) interj. imitating the crow's cry: **kā kā** J IV.72.

Kā° in composition, is assimilated (and contracted) form of kad°, as kāpuppha, kāpurisa.

Kāka [onomat., cp. Sk. kāka; for other onomat. relatives see note on gala] the crow; freq. in similes: S I.124 = Sn 448; J I.164. Its thievish ways are described at DhA III.352; said to have ten bad qualities A V.149; J I.342; III.126; kākā vā kulalā vā Vin IV.40. — As bird (of the dead) frequenting places of interment and cremation, often with other carcass-eating animals (sigāla, gijjha) Sn 201; PvA 198 (= dhanka); cp. kākoḷa. — In cpds. often used derisively. — f. **kākī** J II.39, 150; III.431.
-āmasaka "touching as much as a crow," attr. of a person not enjoying his meals DhA IV.16; DhsA 404; -uṭṭepaka a crow-scarer, a boy under fifteen, employed as such in the monastery grounds Vin I.79 cp. 371. -opamā the simile of the crow DhA II.75. -orava "crow-cawing," appl[d] to angry and confused words Vin I.239, cp. IV.82; -ōlūka crows and owls J II.351; DhA I.50; Mhbv 15; -guyha (tall) enough to hide a crow (of young corn, yava) J II.174; cp. *J. trsl.* II.122; -nīḷa a crow's nest J II.365; -paññā "crow-wisdom," i. e. foolishness which leads to ruin through greed J V.255, 258; cp. VI.358; -paṭṭanaka a deserted village, inhabited only by crows J VI. 456; -pāda crow's foot or footmark Vism 179 (as pattern); -peyya "(so full) that a crow can easily drink of it," full to the brim, overflowing, of a pond: samatittika k° "with even banks and drinkable for crows" (i. e. with the water on a level with the land) D I.244; S II.134 (do.); D II.89; M I.435; A III.27; J. II.174; Ud 90; cp. note to *J. trsl.* II.122; PvA 202. See also peyya. -bhatta "a crow's meal," i. e. remnants left from a meal thrown out for the crows J II.149; -vaṇṇa "crow-coloured" N. of a king Mhvs 22[11]; -vassa the cry of a crow Vin II.17; -sīsa the head of a crow J II.351; as adj.: having a crow's head, appl[d] to a fabulous flying horse D II.174; cp. J II.129; -sūra a "crow-hero," appl. to a shameless, unconscientious fellow Dh 244; DhA III.352; -ssaraka (having a voice) sounding like a crow Vin I.115.

Kākacchati [derived by Fausböll fr. **kās,** to cough; by Trenckner fr. **krath;** by Childers & E. Müller fr. **kath;** should it not rather be a den. fr. kakaca a saw ?] to snore Vin IV.355; A III.299; J I.61, 160 (= ghuru-ghurûpassāsa; cp. DA I.42 ghurû-ghurûpassāsī); I.318; VI.57; Miln 85; Vism 311.

Kākaṇa (nt.) [kā (for kad°) + kaṇa = less than a particle] a coin of very small value Sdhp 514.

Kākaṇikā (f.) = prec. J I.120, 419; VI.346; DA I.212; DhA I.391; VvA 77 = DhA III.108. From the latter passages its monetary value in the opinion of the Commentator may be guessed at as being ⅛ of a kahāpaṇa; it occurs here in a descending line where each succeeding coin marks half the value of the preceding one, viz., kahāpaṇa, aḍḍha, pāda, māsaka, **kākaṇikā,** upon which follows mudhā "for nothing."
-agghanaka "not even a farthing's worth," worth next to nothing J VI.346.

Kākola and **Kākoḷa** [Onomat. The Lit. Sk. has the same form] a raven, esp. in his quality as bird of prey, feeding on carrion (cp. kāka) J III.246 (= vanakāka); V.268, 270 (gijjha k° ā ca ayomukhā . . . khādanti naraŋ kibbisa-kārinaŋ); VI.566.
-gaṇā (pl.) flocks of ravens Sn 675; VV52[15] (= VvA 227).

Kāca[1] [Der. unknown. The word first occurs in the Śat Br. & may well be non-Aryan] a glass-like substance made of siliceous clay; crystal Vin I.190; II.112 (cp. Divy 503, kācamaṇi rock-crystal). — a° not of glass or quartz, i. e. pure, clear, flawless, appl. to precious stones D II.244 = J II.418 (= akakkasa) Sn 476. In the same sense also MVastu I.164.
-ambha (nt.) red crystal J VI.268 (= rattamaṇi); -maya made of crystal, crystalline Vin I.190; II.112.

Kāca[2] [cp. Sk. kāca & kāja] a pingo, a yoke, a carrying-pole, usually made of bamboo, at both ends of which baskets are hung (double pingo). Besides this there is a single pingo (ekato-kājo) with only one basket and "middle" p. (antarā°) with two bearers and the basket suspended in the middle Vin II.137; J I.154; V.13, 293, 295 sq., 320, 345; PvA 168
-daṇḍaka the pole of a pingo DA I.41.

Kācanā (f.) [fr. kāca[2]] balancing like carrying on a kāca, fig. deliberation, pondering Vbh 352 = Vism 27.

Kācin (adj.) [fr. kāca[1]], only neg. a° free from quartz, free from grit, flawless Vv 60[1] (=niddosa VvA 253).

Kāja =kāca[2], i. e. carrying-pole M III.148; J I.9; III.325; V.200; Dpvs XII 3; Mhvs 5, 24; DhA IV.232.
-koṭi the end of a carrying-pole J I.9; V.200. -hāraka a pingo-bearer DhA IV.128.

Kāṭa-koṭacikā [kāṭa + koṭacikā] a low term of abuse, "pudendum virile & muliebre" Vin IV.7 (Buddhagh IV.354: kātan ti purisa-nimittaŋ); cp. Morris, *J.P.T.S.* 1884, 1889.

Kāṇa (adj.) [cp. Sk. kāṇa] blind, usually of one eye, occasionally of both (see PugA 227) S I.94; Vin II.90 = A I.107 = II.85 = Pug 51 (in expl[n] of tamaparāyaṇa purisa); Th 2, 438; J I.222 (one-eyed); VI.74 (of both eyes); DhA III.71.
-kaccha Np. Sdhp 44; -kacchapa "the blind turtle" in the well-known parable of a man's chances of human rebirth after a state of punishment Th 2, 500 (=ThA 290); Miln 204; DhsA 60; cp. M III.169 = S V.455.

Kātabba (adj. -n.) (grd. of karoti) that which ought to, can or must be done (see karoti) J I.264, etc. Also as kattabba PvA 30.

Kātuŋ and **Kātu°** (in comp[n] with kāma) inf. of karoti.
-kāma desirous of doing or making, etc. Mhvs 37[34] (a°). PvA 115; -kāmatā the desire to do, etc. J IV.253; V.364. See also kattu° in same comb[ns]

Kātuye is Vedic inf. of karoti Th 2, 418 (in ThA 268 taken as kātuŋ ayye!)

Kādamba [cp. Sk. kādamba] a kind of goose with grey wings J V.420; VvA 163.

Kādambaka made of Kadamba wood; also °ya for °ka; both at J V.320.

Kānana (nt.) [cp. Sk. kānana] a glade in the forest, a grove, wood Sn 1134 (=Nd[2] s. v. vanasaṇḍa); Th 2, 254 (=ThA 210 upavana); J VI.557; Sdhp 574.

Kānāmā f. of konāma of what name? what is her (or your) name? Vin II.272, 273; J VI.338.

Kāpilanī patron. f. of Kapila; the lady of the Kapila clan Th 2, 65.

Kāpilavatthava (adj.) of or from Kapilavatthu, belonging to K. D II.165, 256; S IV.182.

Kāpurisa [kad + purisa] a low, vile, contemptible man, a wretch Vin II.188; D III.279; S I.91, 154; II.241; V.204; Th 1, 124, 495; J II.42; VI.437; Pv II.9[30] (PvA 125 = lāmaka°); sometimes denoting one who has not entered the Path A III.24; Th 2, 189.

Kāpotaka (adj.) [fr. kapota] pigeon-coloured, grey, of a dull white, said of the bones of a skeleton D I.55; Dh 149 (=DhA III.112).

Kāpotikā (f.) [of doubtful origin, fr. kapota, but probably popular etym., one may compare Sk. kāpiśāyana, a sort of spirituous liquor Halāyudha 2, 175, which expresses a diff. notion, i. e. fr. kapi] a kind of intoxicating drink, of a reddish colour (like pigeons' feet) Vin IV.109, cp. J I.360 (surā).

Kāma (m. nt.) [Dhtp (603) & Dhtm (843) paraphrase by "icchāyaŋ," cp. Vedic kāma, **kam** = Idg. ***qā**] to desire, cp. Lat. carus, Goth. hōrs, E whore. — 1. *Objective*: pleasantness, pleasure-giving, an object of sensual enjoyment; — 2. subjective: (*a*) enjoyment, pleasure on occasion of sense, (*b*) sense-desire. Buddhist commentators express 1 and 2 by kāmiyatī ti kāmo, and kametī ti kāmo *Cpd.* 81, *n.* 2. Kāma as sense-desire and enjoyment *plus* objects of the same is a collective name for all but the very higher or refined conditions of life. The kāma-bhava or -loka (worlds of sense-desire) includes 4 of the 5 modes (gati's) of existence and part of the fifth or deva-loka. See Bhava. The term is not found analyzed till the later books of the Canon are consulted, thus, Nd[1] 1 distinguishes (1) vatthukāmā: desires relating to a base, i. e. physical organ or external object, and (2) kilesakāmā: desire considered subjectively. So also Nd[2] 202, quoted DhA II.162; III.240; and very often as ubho kāmā. A more logical definition is given by Dhammapāla on Vv 1[1] (VvA 11). He classifies as follows: 1. manāpiyā rūpādi-visayā. — 2. chandarāga. — 3. sabbasmiŋ lobha. — 4. gāmadhamma. — 5. hitacchanda. — 6. seribhāva, i. e. k. concerned with (1) pleasant objects, (2) impulsive desire, (3) greed for anything, (4) sexual lust, (5) effort to do good, (6) self-determination.

In all enumerations of obstacles to perfection, or of general divisions and definitions of mental conditions, kāma occupies the leading position. It is the first of the five obstacles (nīvaraṇāni), the three esanās (longings), the four upādānas (attachments), the four oghas (floods of worldly turbulence), the four āsavas (intoxicants of mind), the three taṇhās, the four yogas; and k. stands first on the list of the six factors of existence: kāmā, vedanā, saññā, āsavā, kamma, dukkha, which are discussed at A III.410 sq. as regards their origin, difference, consequences, destruction and remedy. — Kāma is most frequently connected with rāga (passion), with chanda (impulse) and gedha (greed), all expressing the active, clinging, and impulsive character of desire. — The foll. is the list of synonyms given at various places for kāma-cchanda: (1) chanda, impulse; (2) rāga, excitement; (3) nandī, enjoyment; (4) taṇhā, thirst; (5) sineha, love; (6) pipāsā, thirst; (7) pariḷāha, consuming passion; (8) gedha, greed; (9) mucchā, swoon, or confused state of mind; (10) ajjhosāna, hanging on, or attachment Nd[1]. At Nd[2] 200; Dhs 1097 (omitting No. 8), cp. DhsA 370; similarly at Vism 569 (omitting Nos. 6 and 8), cp. Dhs 1214; Vbh 375. This set of 10 characteristics is followed by kām-ogha, kāma-yoga, kām-upādāna at Nd[2] 200, cp. Vism 141 (kām-ogha, °āsava, °upādāna). Similarly at D III.238: kāme avigata-rāga, °chanda, °pema, °pipāsa, °pariḷāha, °taṇha. See also kāma-chanda below under cpds. In connection with synonyms it may be noticed that most of the verbs used in a kāma-context are verbs the primary meaning of which is "adhering to" or "grasping," hence, attachment; viz. esanā (**iṣ** to Lat ira), upādāna (upa + ā + **dā** taking up), taṇhā (**tṛṣ**, Lat. torreo = thirst) pipāsā (the wish to drink), sineha (**snih**, Lat. nix = melting), etc. — On the other hand, the reaction of the passions on the subject is expressed by khajjati "to be eaten up" pariḍayhati "to be burnt," etc. The foll. passage also illustrates the various synonymic expressions: kāme paribhuñjati, kāma-majjhe vasati, kāma-pariḷāhena pariḍayhati, kāma-vitakkehi khajjati, kāma-pariyesanāyā ussukko, A I.68; cp. M I.463; III.129. Under this aspect kāma is essentially an evil, but to the popular view it is one of the indispensable attributes of bliss and happiness to be enjoyed as a reward of virtue in this world (mānussa-kāmā) as well as in the next (dibbā kāmā). See kāmā-vacara about the various stages of next-world happiness. Numerous examples are to be found in Pv and Vv, where a standing Ep. of the Blest is sabbakāma-samiddha "fully equipped with all objects of pleasure," e. g. Pv I.10[5]; PvA 46. The other-world pleasures are greater than the earthly ones: S V.409; but to the Wise even these are unsatisfactory, since they still are signs of, and lead to, rebirth (kāmūpapatti, It 94): api dibbesu kāmesu ratiŋ so nādhigacchati Dh 187; rāgaŋ vinayetha mānusesu dibbesu kāmesu cāpi bhikkhu Sn 361, see also It 94. — Kāma as sensual pleasure finds its most marked application in the sphere of the sexual: kāmesu micchācārin, transgressing in lusts, sinning in the lusts of the flesh, or violating the third rule of conduct equivalent to abrahmacariyā, inchastity (see sīla) Pug 38, 39; It 63, etc. itthi-kāmehi paricāreti "he enjoys himself with the charms of woman" S IV.343. Kāmesu brahmacariyavā practising chastity Sn 1041. Kāmatthā for sexual amusement A III.229.

Redemption from kāma is to be effected by self-control (*saŋyama*) and meditation (*jhāna*), by knowledge, right effort and renunciation. "To give up passion" as a practice of him who wishes to enter on the Path is expressed by: kāmānaŋ pahānaŋ, kāma-saññānaŋ pariññā, kāma-pipāsānaŋ-paṭivinayo, kāma-vitakkānaŋ samugghāto kāma-pariḷāhānaŋ vūpasamo Vin III.111; -kāmesu (ca) *appaṭibaddhacitto* "uddhaŋsoto" ti vuccati: he whose mind is not in the bonds of desire is called "one who is above the stream" Dh 218; cp. Th 2, 12; — tasmā jantu sadā sato kāmāni parivajjaye Sn 771; — yo kāme parivajjeti Sn 768 = Nett 69. — nikkhamma gharā *panujja* kāme Sn 359; — ye ca kāme pariññāya caranti akutobhayā te ve pāragatā loke ye pattā āsavakkhayaŋ A III.69. — Kāmānaŋ *pariññaŋ* paññāpeti Gotamo M I.84; cp. A V.64; kāme *pajahati*: S I.12 = 31; Sn 704; kāmānaŋ vippahāna S I.47; — ye kāme hitvā agihā caranti Sn 464; — kāmā nirujjhanti (through jhāna) A IV.410; kāme panudati Dh 383 = S I.15 (context broken), cp. kāma-sukhaŋ analaŋkaritvā Sn 59; — kāmesu anapekkhin Sn 166 = Ś I.16 (abbrev.); S II.281; Sn 857; — cp. rāgaŋ vinayetha . . . Sn 361. vivicc' eva kāmehi, aloof from sensuous joys is the prescription for all Jhāna-exercise.

Applications of these expressions:—kāmesu palāḷita A III.5; kāmesu mucchita S I.74; kāmālaye asatta S I.33; kāmesu kathaŋ nameyya S I.117; kāmesu anikīḷitāvin S I.9 (cp. kela); kittassa munino carato kāmesu anapekhino oghatiṇṇassa pihayanti kāmesu *gathitā* pajā Sn 823 (gadhitā Nd[1]); — kāmesu asaññata Sn 243; — yo na lippati kāmesu tam ahaŋ brūmi brāhmaṇaŋ Dh 401; — Muni santivādo agiddho kāme ca loke ca anūpalitto Sn 845; kāmesu *giddha* D III.107; Sn 774; kāmesu gedhaŋ āpajjati S I.73; — na so *rajjati* kāmesu Sn 161; — kāmānaŋ *vasam* upāgamum Sn 315 (= kāmānaŋ āsattataŋ pāpuniŋsu SnA 325); kāme *parivajjeti* Sn 768, kāme *anugijjhati* Sn 769.

Character of Kāmā. The pleasures of the senses are evanescent, transient (sabbe kāmā aniccā, etc. A II.177), and of no real taste (appāsādā); they do not give permanent satisfaction; the happiness which they yield is only a deception, or a dream, from which the dreamer awakens with sorrow and regret. Therefore the Buddha says "Even though the pleasure is great, the regret is greater: ādīnavo ettha bhiyyo" (see k-sukha). Thus kāmā as kālikā (needing time) S I.9, 117; aniccā (transitory) S I.22; kāmā citrā madhurā "pleasures are manifold and sweet" (i. e. tasty) Sn 50; but also appassādā bahudukkhā bahupāyāsā: quot. M I.91; see Nd[2] 71. Another passage with var. descriptions and comparisons of kāma, beginning with app' assādā dukkhā kāmā is found at J IV.118. -atittaŋ yeva kāmesu antako kurute vasaŋ Dh 48; — na kahāpaṇa-vassena titti kāmesu vijjati appasādā dukkhā kāmā iti viññāya paṇḍito "not for showers of coins is satisfaction to be found in pleasures—of no taste and full of misery are pleasures: thus say the wise and they understand" Dh 186; cp. M I.130; Vin II.25 (cp. Divy 224). — Kāmato jāyatī *soko* kāmato jāyatī *bhayaŋ* kāmato vippamuttassa n'atthi soko kuto bhayan ti "of pleasure is born sorrow, of pleasure is born fear" Dh 215. — Kāmānam adhivacanāni, attributes of kāma are: bhaya, dukkha, roga, gaṇḍa, salla, sanga, panka, gabbha A IV.289; Nd[2] p. 62 on Sn 51; same, except salla & gabbha: A III.310. The misery of such pleasures is painted in vivid colours in the Buddha's discourse on pains of pleasures M I.85 and parallel passages (see e. g. Nd[2] 199), how kāma is the cause of egoism, avarice, quarrels between kings, nations, families, how it leads to warfare, murder, lasciviousness, torture and madness. Kāmānaŋ ādīnavo (the danger of passions) M I.85 sq. = Nd[2] 199, quot. SnA 114 (on Sn 61); as one of the five anupubbikathās: K° ādīnavaŋ okāraŋ saŋkilesaŋ A IV.186, 209, 439; — they are the leaders in the army of Māra: kāmā te paṭhamā senā Sn 436; — yo evamvādī . . . n'atthi kāmesu doso ti so kāmesu pātavyataŋ āpajjati A I.266 = M I.305 sq.

Similes.—In the foll. passage (following on appassādā bahudukkhā, etc.) the pleasures of the senses are likened to: (1) aṭṭhi-kankhala, a chain of bones; — (2) maŋsapesa, a piece of (decaying) flesh; — (3) tiṇ'-ukkā, a torch of grass; (4) angāra-kāsu, a pit of glowing cinders; — (5) supina, a dream; (6) yācita, beggings; — (7) rukkha-phala, the fruit of a tree; — (8) asi-sūna, a slaughter-house; — (9) satti-sūla, a sharp stake; — (10) sappa-sira, a snake's head, i. e. the bite of a snake at Vin II.25; M I.130; A III.97 (where aṭṭhi-sankhala); Nd[2] 71 (leaving out No. 10). Out of this list are taken single quotations of No. 4 at D III.283; A IV.224 = V.175; No. 5 at DhA III.240; No. 8 at M I.144; No. 9 at S I.128 = Th 2, 58 & 141 (with khandhānaŋ for khandhāsaŋ); No. 10 as āsīvisa (poisonous fangs of a snake) yesu mucchitā bālā Th 2, 451, and several at many other places of the Canon.

Cases used adverbially:—kāmaŋ acc. as adv. (*a*) yathā kāmaŋ according to inclination, at will, as much as one chooses S I.227; J I.203; PvA 63, 113, 176; yena kāmaŋ wherever he likes, just as he pleases A IV.194; Vv I.1[1] (= icchānurūpaŋ VvA 11) — (b) willingly, gladly, let it be that, usually with imper. S I.222; J I.233; III.147; IV.273; VvA 95; kāmaŋ taco nahāru ca aṭṭhi ca avasissatu (avasussatu in J) sarīre upasussatu maŋsa-lohitaŋ "willingly shall skin, sinews and bone remain, whilst flesh and blood shall wither in the body" M I.481; A I.50; S II.28; J I.71, 110; -kāmasā (instr.) in same sense J IV.320; VI.181; -kāmena (instr.) do. J V.222, 226; -kāmā for the love of, longing after (often with hi) J III.466; IV.285, 365; V.294; VI.563, 589; cp. Mhv III.18, 467. -akāmā unwillingly D I.94; J VI.506; involuntarily J V.237.

°kāma (adj.) desiring, striving after, fond of, pursuing, in kāma-kāma pleasure-loving Sn 239 (kāme kāmayanto SnA 284); Dh 83 (cp. on this passage Morris, *J.P.T.S.* 1893, 39-41); same expl[n] as prec. at DhA II.156; Th 2, 506. — atthakāma well-wishing, desirous of good, benevolent J I.241; V.504 (anukampakā +); *sic lege* for attakāmarūpā, M I.205, III,155, cf. S i.44 with ib. 75; A II.21; Pv IV.3[61]; VvA 11 (in quotation); PvA 25, 112; mānakāma proud S I.4; lābhakāma fond of taking; grasping, selfish A II.240; dūsetu° desiring to molest Vin IV.212; dhamma° Sn 92; pasaŋsa° Sn 825. So frequently in comb. w. inf., meaning, willing to, wishing to, going to, desirous of: jīvitu°, amaritu°, dātu°, daṭṭhu°, dassana°, kātu°, pattu°, netu°, gantu°, bhojetu°, etc. -sakāma (-adj.) willing J V.295. -akāma 1. not desiring, i. e. unwilling: M II.181; mayhaŋ akāmāya against my wish (= mama anicchantiyā) Pv II.10[7], J V.121, 183, etc. 2. without desire, desireless, passionless Sn 445. -nikkāma same Sn 1131.

-agga (nt.) the greatest pleasure, intense enjoyment M II.43; Vv 16[3] (= VvA 79, attributed to the Paranimmita-vasavattino-devā); -aggi the fire of passion J V.487; -ajjhosāna (nt.) attachment to lust and desire, No. 10 in kāmacchanda series (see above); -ādhikaraṇa having its cause in desire M I.85; S I.74; -ādhimutta, bent upon the enjoyment of sensual pleasures A III.168; J VI.159; -ānusārin pursuing worldly pleasures J II.117; -andha blinded by passion Ud 76 = Th 1, 297; -ābhibhū overcoming passions, Ep. of the Buddha D II.274; -ābhimukha bent upon lust, voluptuous PvA 3; -āvacara "having its province in kāma," belonging to the realm of sensuous pleasures. This term applies to the eleven grades of beings who are still under the influence of sensual desires and pleasures, as well as to all thoughts and conditions arising in this sphere of sensuous experience D I.34 (of the soul, expl^d DA 120 : cha k°-devapariyāpanna); J I.47; Dhs 1, 431; Ps 1, 84, 85, 101; Vbh 324; Vism 88, 372, 452 (rūpa°, arūpa°, lokuttara), 493 (of indriyas); 574; PvA 138. *-kamma* an action causing rebirth in the six kāma-worlds Dhs 414, 418, 431; *-devatā* PvA 138 (+brahmādevatā) and *-devā* the gods of the pleasure-heavens J I.47; V.5; VI.99; Vism 392; or of the kāmâvacara-devaloka J VI.586, *-bhūmi* and *-loka* the plane or world of kāma Ps I.83; J VI.99; see also avacara; -âvacaraka belonging to the realm of kāma J VI.99; Sdhp 254 (°ika); -assāda the relish of sensual pleasures PvA 262; DA I.89, 311; -ātura affected by passion, love-sick J III.170; -ārāma pleasure-loving A IV.438 (gihī k-bhogī, °ratā, °sammuditā); -ālya, the abode of sensual pleasure (i. e. kāma-loka) S I.33=Sn 177; Sn 306; -āvaṭṭa the whirlpool of sensuality J II.330; -āsava the intoxication of passion, sensuality, lusts; def. as kāmesu kāma-chando, etc. (see above k-chando) Vbh 364, 374; Dhs 1097; as the first of four impurities, viz. k°, bhava°, diṭṭhi°, avijjā° at Vin III.5 (the detachment from which constitutes Arahantship); Vbh 373; Dhs 1096, 1448; as three (prec. without diṭṭhi°) at It 49; Vbh 364; cp. D I.84; II.81; III.216; M I.7; -itthi a pleasure-woman, a concubine Vin I.36; J I.83; V.490; VI.220; -upabhoga the enjoyment of pleasures VvA 79; -upādāna clinging to sensuality, arising from taṇhā, as k° diṭṭhi° sīlabbata°, attavāda° D III.230; M I.51; Vbh 136, 375; Vism 569; -ûpapatti existence or rebirth in the sensuous universe. These are three: (1) Paccupaṭṭhita-kāmā (including mankind, four lowest devalokas, Asuras, Petas and animals), (2) Nimmāna-ratino devā, (3) Paranimmita-vasavattino devā D III.218; It 94. -ûpasaṇhita endowed with pleasantness: in formula rūpā (saddā, etc.) iṭṭhā kantā manāpā piyarūpā k° rajaniyā "forms (sounds, etc.=any object of sense), desirable, lovely, agreeable, pleasant, endowed with pleasantness, prompting desires" D I.245=M I.85; 504; D II.265; M III.267; VvA 127. -esanā the craving for pleasure. There are three esanās: kāma°, bhava°, brahmacariya° D III.216 270; A II.42; Vbh 366; It 48; S V.54; -ogha the flood of sensual desires A III.69; D III.230, 276; Vbh 375; Vism 141; DhsA 166; Nd² 178 (viz. kām°, bhav°, diṭṭh°, avijj°). -kaṇṭaka the sting of lust Ud 27; -kara the fulfilment of one's desires J V.370 (=kāmakiriyā) -karaṇiya in yathā° pāpimato the puppet of the wicked (lit. one with whom one can do as one likes) M I.173; It 56; -kalala the mud of passions J III.293; -kāra the fulfilment of desires Sn 351=Th 1, 1271; -kārin acting according to one's own inclination Th 1. 971; or acting willingly DA I.71; -koṭṭhāsa a constituent of sensual pleasure (=kāmaguṇa) J III.382; V.149; DA I.121; PvA 205; -kopa the fury of passion Th 1, 671; -gavesin, pleasure-seeking Dh 99=Th 1, 992. -gijjha J I.210 and -giddha greedy for pleasure, craving for love J III.432; V.256; VI.245; -giddhimā, same J VI.525. -giddhin f. °inī same Mhvs VI.3. -guṇā (pl.) always as pañca: the five strands of sensual pleasures, viz., the pleasures which are to be enjoyed by means of the five senses; collectively all sensual pleasures. Def. as cakkhuviññeyyā rūpā, etc. A III.411; D I.245; II.271; III.131, 234; Nd² s. v.; Ps I.129; as manāpiyehi rūpādībi pañcahi kāma-koṭṭhāsehi bandhanehi vā DA I.121, where it is also divided into two groups: mānusakā and dibbā. As constituents of kāmarāga at Nett 28; as vana (desire) Nett 81. — In the popular view they are also to be enjoyed in "heaven": saggaṇ lokaṇ upapajjissāmi tattha dibbehi pañcahi k-guṇehi samappito samangibhūto paricāressāmī ti Vin III.72; mentioned as pleasures in Nandana S I.5; M I.505; A III.40, IV.118; in various other connections S IV.202; Vv 30⁷; Pv III.7¹ (°ehi sobhasi; expl. PvA 205 by kāma-koṭṭhāsehi); PvA 58 (paricārenti); cp. also kāma-kāmin. As the highest joys of this earth they are the share of men of good fortune, like kings, etc. (mānusakā k° guṇā) S V.409; A V.272, but the same passage with "dibbehi pañcahi k°-guṇehi samappita . . ." also refers to earthly pleasures, e. g. S I.79, 80 (of kings); S V.342 (of a Cakkavatti); A II.125; IV.55, 239; V.203; of the soul D I.36; Vbh 379; other passages simply quoting k-g° as worldly pleasures are e. g. S I.16=Sn 171; S I.92; IV.196, 326; A III.69 (itthirūpasmiṇ); D I.60, 104; Sdhp 261. In the estimation of the early Buddhists, however, this bundle of pleasures is to be banned from the thought of every earnest striver after perfection: their critique of the kāmaguṇā begins with "pañc' ime bhikkhave kāmaguṇā . . ." and is found at various places, e. g. in full at M I.85=Nd² s. v.; M I.454; II.42; III.114; quoted at M I.92; A III.411; IV.415, 430, 449, 458. Other expressions voicing the same view are: gedho pañcannaṇ k°-guṇānaṇ adhivacanaṇ A III.312 sq.; asisūnā . . . adhivac° M I.144; nivāpo . . . adhivac° M. I.155; sâvaṭṭo . . . adhivac° It 114. In connection w. rata & giddha PvA 3; pahīna M III.295; gathita & mucchita M I.173; mā te kāmaguṇe bhamassu cittaṇ "Let not thy heart roam in the fivefold pleasures" Dh 371; cittassa vossaggo Vbh 370; asantuṭṭha Vbh 350. See also Sn 50, 51, 171, 284, 337. -guṇika consisting of fivefold desire, appl. to rāga S II.99; J IV.220; Dhs A.371; -gedha a craving for pleasure S I.100; ThA 225; -cāgin he who has abandoned lusts Sn 719. -citta impure thought J II.214; -chanda excitement of sensual pleasure, grouped as the first of the series of five obstacles (pañca nīvaraṇāni) D I.156, 246; III.234, 278; A I.231; IV.457; A I.134=Sn 1106; S I.99; V.64; Bdhd 72, 96, 130; Nd² 200, 420A. Also as the first in the series of ten fetters (saṇyojanāni) which are given above (p. 31) as synonyms of kāma. Enumerated under 1-10 at Nd² 200 as eight in order: 1, 2, 3, 4, 5, 7, 9, 10 (omitting pipāsā and gedha) Vbh 364; Dhs 1114, 1153; Nd² ad chandarāga and bhavachanda; in order: 2, 3, 5, 9, 6, 7, 10, 4 at A II.10; — as nine (like above, omitting gedha) at Vbh 374; Dhs 1097; — as five in order: 1, 5, 9, 6, 7, (cp. above passage A II.10) at M I.241; — as four in order: 1, 5, 9, 7 at S IV.188; — as six nīvaraṇas (5 + avijjā) at Dhs 1170, 1486. See also D I.246; III.234, 269; Ps I.103, 108; II.22, 26, 44, 169; Vism 141; Sdhp 459; -jāla the net of desires Th 1, 355; -taṇhā thirst after sensual pleasures; the first of the three taṇhās, viz. kāma°, bhava°, vibhava° D III.216, 275; It 50; Vbh 365 (where defined as kāmadhātupaṭisaṇyutto rāgo); Dhs 1059, 1136 (cp. taṇhā: jappāpassage); as the three taṇhā, viz. ponobbhavikā, nandirāga-sahagatā, tatratatr' âbhinandinī at Vin I.10=Vbh 101; as k-taṇhāhi khajjamāno k-pariḷāhena pariḍayhamāno M I.504. See also D II.308; S I.131; A II.11; Th 2, 140; J II.311; V.451; Miln 318. -da granting desires, bestowing objects of pleasure and delight; Ep. of Yakkhas and of Vessantara (cp. the good fairy) J VI.498, 525; Mhvs 19, 9; as sabba° Pv II.13⁸; -dada=prec. Pv II.9¹⁸; PvA 112; J VI.508; of a stone Miln 243, 252; of Nibbāna Miln 321; Kh VIII.10: esa devamanussānaṇ sabbakāmadado nidhi "this is the treasure which gives all pleasures to gods and men"; -dukkha the pain of sensual pleasures J IV.118; -duha granting wishes, like a cow giving milk J V.33; VI.214; f° duhā the cow of plenty J IV.20; -dhātu "element of desire." i. e. 1. the world of desire, that sphere of existence in which beings are still in the bonds of sensuality, extending from the Avici-niraya to the heaven of the Paranimmita-vasavatti-devas S II.151; Th 1, 181; also 2. sensual pleasures, desires, of which there are six dhātus, viz. kāma°, vyāpāda, vihiṇsā°, nekkhamma°, avyāpāda°, avihiṇsā°, Vbh 86; Nett 97; D III.215=Vbh 363 (as the first three=akusaladhātus); Vbh 404. See also D III.275; Th 1, 378; J V.454; Vism 486 (cp.

Vbh 86). **-nandī** sensual delight (cp. °chanda) A II.11; Dhs 1114, etc. **-nidānaŋ** acc. adv. as the consequence of passion, through passion, M 1.85, etc. (in kāmaguṇā passage); **-nissaraṇa** deliverance from passion, the extinction of passion It 61 (as three nissaraṇiyā dhātuyo), cp. A III.245; **-nissita** depending on craving Miln 11; **-nīta** led by desire J II.214, 215; **-panka** the mire of lusts Sn 945; Th 2, 354; J V.186, 256; VI.230, 505; Mhbv 3; **-paṭisandhi-sukhin** finding happiness in the association with desire M III.230; **-pariḷāha** the flame or the fever of passion M 1.242, 508; S IV.188; A 1.68 (pariḍayhati, khajjati, etc.); A II.11; Vin III.20; Nd² 374 (comᵈ with °palibodha); DhA II.2; see also kāmacchanda passage. **-pāla** the guardian of wishes, i. e. benefactor J V.221; **-pipāsā** thirst for sensuality M 1.242; A II.11, and under k°-chanda; **-bandha** Ud 93, and **-bandhana** the bonds of desire J VI.28, also in the sense of k°-guṇā, q. v.; **-bhava** a state of existence dominated by pleasures. It is the second kind of existence, the first being caused by kamma Vbh 137. It rests on the effect of kamma, which is manifested in the kāma-dhātu A 1.223. It is the first form of the 3 bhavas, viz. kāma°, rūpa°, arūpa° Vin 1.36; D III.216; A. IV.402; Vism 572. Emancipation from this existence is the first condition to the attainment of Arahantship: kāmabhave asatta akiñcana Sn 176, 1059, 1091 (expl. SnA 215: tividhe bhave alaggana); Bdhd 61. *°parikkhīṇa* one who has overcome the desire-existence Dh 415=Sn 639. **-bhoga** enjoyment of sensual pleasures, gratification of desires S 1.74 (sāratta -°esu giddhā kāmesu mucchitā); Th 2, 464; It 94 (-°esu paṇḍito who discriminates in worldly pleasures); J II.65; **-bhogin** enjoying the pleasures of the senses Vin 1.203, 287; II.136, 149; D III.124, 125; Miln 243, 350, as Ep. of the kāmûpapatti-beings It 94; as ten kinds A V.177; as bringing evil, being blameworthy S 1.78; cp. A IV.281, 438; S IV.333 sq.; A III.351; Th 2, 480; J III.154. ye keci kāmesu asaññatā janā avītarāgā idha k-bhogino (etc.) A II.6, cp. II.17. kāmabhogī kām'ārāmo kāmarato kāma-sammudita A IV.439; *-°seyyā* sleeping at ease, way of lying down, the second of the four ways of sleeping (kāmabhogiseyyā vāmena passena) A II.244; **-bhojin** =°bhogin Ud 65; **-magga** the path of sensuous pleasures J V.67; **-matta** intoxicated with sensuous pleasures J VI.231; **-mucchā** sensual stupor or languor S IV.189; A II.11; Dhs 1114, etc. (see kāmacchanda); **-yoga** application to sensuous enjoyment, one of the four yogas, viz. kāma°, bhava°, diṭṭhi°, avijjā° (cp. āsavā) A II.10; only the first two, at It 95; cp. D III.230, 276; S V.59; DhsA 166; **-rata** delighting in pleasures J V.255; **-rati** amorous enjoyment (as arati) Th 2, 58 and 141; J 1.211; III.396; IV.107. -n'atthi nissaraṇaŋ loke kiŋ vivekena kāhasi bhuñjassu k-ratiyo māhu pacchânutāpinī S 1.128. mā pamādam anuyuñjetha, mā kāmaratisanthavaŋ appamatto hi jhāyanto pappoti paramaŋ sukhan S 1.25=Dh 27=Th 1, 884; **-rasa** the taste of love J II.329; III.170; V.451; **-rāga** sensual passion, lust. This term embraces the kāmaguṇā & the three rāgas: Dhs 1131, 1460; Nett 28; M 1.433 sq.; D III.254, 282; S 1.22=A III.411; S 1.13, 53; III.155; Th 2, 68, 77; PvA 6; see also k-chanda passage. Relinquishing this desire befits the Saint: Sn 139 (°ŋ virājetvā brahmalokûpago). As k-rāgavyāpāda Dhs 362; SnA 205; **-rūpa** a form assumed at will VvA 80, or a form which enjoys the pleasures of heaven Vbh 426; **-lāpin** talking as one likes D 1.91 (=DA 1.257 yadicchaka-bhāṇin); **-lābha** the grasping of pleasures, in °abhijappin A III.353; **-loka** the world of pleasures=kāmâvacara, q. v. Sdhp 233, 261; **-vaṇṇin** assuming any form at will, Protean J II.255=III.409=Vv 33¹⁰¹; J V.157; Vv 16³; VvA 80, 143, 146; **-vasika** under the influence of passions J II.215; **-vitakka** a thought concerning some sensuous pleasure, one of the three evil thoughts (kāma° vyāpāda° vihiŋsā°) D III.215, 226; M 1.114; A 1.68; J 1.63; III.18, 375; IV.490; VI.29; It 82, 115; Vbh 362; Miln 310; **-vega** the impulse of lust J VI.268; **-sagga** the heaven of sensuous beings, there are six q. v. under sagga J 1.105; II.130; III.258; IV.490; VI.29, 432; at all these passages only referred to, not enumᵈ; cp. k-âvacara; **-sankappa-bahula** full of aspirations after pleasure A III.145, 259; D III.215; **-sanga** attachment to passion Ud 75; **-saññā** lustful idea or thought: one of the three akusala-saññās (as vitakka) D 1.182; III.215; M II.262; S 1.126; Vbh 363; Th 1, 1039; virata k āya S 1.53=Sn 175; **-saññojana** the obstacle or hindrance formed by pleasures; °âtiga Ep. of Arahant, free of the fetters of lust A III.373 (+kāmarāgaŋ virājetvā); **-sineha** love of pleasures Dhs 1097 (also as °sneha M 1.241; S IV.188; A II.10); see k-chanda; **-sukha** happiness or welfare arising from (sensual) pleasure, worldly happiness, valued as mīḷha°, puthujjana°, anariya°, and not worth pursuit: see kāmaguṇā, which passage closes: yaŋ ime pañca k-guṇe paṭicca uppajjati sukhaŋ somanassaŋ idaŋ vuccati k-sukhaŋ A IV.415; S IV.225; varying with . . . somanassaŋ ayaŋ kāmānaŋ assādo M 1.85, 92, etc. — As kāma° and nekkhamma° A 1.80; as renounced by the Saint: anapekkhino k° ŋ pahāya Dh 346=S 1.77; M III.230; Sn 59 (see Nd² s. v.). See also S IV.208; M II.43; Th 2, 483; Vv 6¹⁷; J II.140; III.396; V.428; *kāmasukhallik'ânuyoga* attachment to worldly enjoyment S IV.330; V.421; Vin 1.10; D III.113; Nett 110; Vism 5, 32; **-sutta** N. of the first sutta of the Aṭṭhakavagga of Sn; **-seṭṭhā** (pl.) a class of devas D II.258; **-sevanā** pursuit of, indulgence in, sensuous pleasure J II.180; III.464; **-sevin** adj. to prec. J IV.118; **-hetu** having craving as a cause: in ādīnava-section, foll. on kāmaguṇā M 1.86, etc., of wealth S 1.74; **-hetuka** caused by passion Th 2, 355=ThA 243; J V.220, 225.

Kāmaka (adj.) [fr. kāma] only —° in neg. **akāmaka** unwilling, undesirous D 1.115; M 1.163; Vin III.13; J IV.31; cp. **kāmuka**.

Kāmaṇḍaluka (adj.) having a kamaṇḍalu (q. v.) S IV.312 cp. A V.263.

Kāmatā (f.) [abstr. fr. kāma] desire, longing, with noun: viveka° . . . to be alone PvA 43; anattha° J IV.14; with inf. PvA 65 (gahetu°); J III.362 (vināsetu°); Mhvs 5, 260; DhA 1.91.

Kāmin (adj.) [fr. kāma] 1. having kāma, i. e. enjoying pleasure, gratifying one's own desires in **kāma-kāmin** realizing all wishes; attr. of beings in one of the Sugatis, the blissful states, of Yakkhas, Devas or Devaññataras (Pv 1.3³=PvA 16), as a reward for former merit; usually in combⁿ with bhuñjāmi paribhogavant (Pv IV.3⁴⁶) or as "nandino devalokasmiŋ modanti k-kāmino" A II.62=It 112; Th 1, 242; J III.154; Pv II.1¹⁸; Pv III.1¹⁶ (expl. "as enjoying after their hearts' content all pleasures they can wish for"). — 2. giving kāma, i. e. benevolent, fulfilling people's wishes; **satisfying** their desires, in **atthakāmini** devatā Sn 986. — **akāmakāmin** passionless, dispassionate Sn 1096, syn. of vītataṇhā without desire (cp. Nd² 4).

Kāmuka (adj. -n.) [cp. Sk. kāmuka] desiring, loving, fond of; a sweetheart, lover J V.306; Mhbv 3.

Kāmeti [den. fr. kāma] to desire, to crave, 1. to crave for any object of pleasure: Th 1, 93; J III.154; IV.167; V.480; — 2. to desire a woman, to be in love with D 1.241; M II.40; J II.226; V.425; VI.307, 326, etc. — pp. **kāmita** in kāmita-vatthu the desired object PvA 119; VvA 122; grd. **kāmitabba** to be desired, desirable PvA 16 (v. l. for kañña, better), 73; VvA 127; and **kāmetabba** J. V.156 (=kamanīya); ppr. (kāmaŋ) **kāmayamānassa** Sn 766 (=icchamānassa, etc., Nd¹); J VI.172=Nett 69.

Kāya [der. probably fr. ci, cinoti to heap up, cp. nikāya heaping up, accumulation or collection; Sk. kāya] group, heap, collection, aggregate, body. — Definitions and synonyms. — SnA 31 gives the foll. synonyms and similes of kāya: kuṭi, guhā (Sn 772), deha, sandeha (Dh 148 = Th 1, 20), nāvā (Dh 369), ratha (S IV.292), dhaja, vammika (M I.144), kuṭikā (Th 1, 1); and at KhA 38 the foll. def.: kāye ti sarīre, sarīraŋ hi asuci-sañcayato kucchitānaŋ vā kesādīnaŋ āyabhūtato kāyo ti vuccati. . . . It is equivalent to deha: S I.27; PvA 10; to sarīra KhA 38; PvA 63, to nikāya (deva°) D III.264; and cp. formula of jāti: sattānaŋ tamhi tamhi sattanikāye jāti . . . Nd² 257.

Literal meaning.—1. mahājana-kāya a collection of people, a crowd S IV.191; V.170; VvA 78; —bala° a great crowd Sn p. 105; DhA I.193, 398. — 2. group or division: satta kāyā akaṭā, etc. (seven eternal groups or principles) D I.56 = M I.517 = S III.211 (in Pakudha Kaccāyana's theory); with reference to groups of sensations or sense-organs, as vedanā-kāya, sañña°, viññāṇa°, phassa°, etc. S III.60, 61; D III.243, 244; taṇhā° D III.244; appl. to hatthi°, ratha°, patti°, groups of elephants, carriages or soldiers S I.72. — A good idea of the extensive meaning of kāya may be gathered from the classification of the 7 kāyas at J II.91, viz. camma°, dāru°, loha°, ayo°, vāluka°, udaka°, phalaka°, or "bodies" (great masses, substances) of skin, wood, copper, iron, sand, water, and planks. — Var. other combns: Asura° A I.143; D III.7; Ābhassara° ("world of radiance") D I.17 = III.29, 84; Deva° S I.27, 30; D III.264 (°nikāya); dibbā kāyā A I.143; Tāvatiŋsa° D III.15.

Applied meaning.—I. Kāya under the *physical* aspect is an aggregate of a multiplicity of elements which finally can be reduced to the four "great" elements, viz. earth, water, fire, and air (D I.55). This "heap," in the valuation of the Wise (muni), shares with all other objects the qualities of such elements, and is therefore regarded as contemptible, as something which one has to get rid of, as a source of impurity. It is subject to time and change, it is built up and kept alive by cravings, and with death it is disintegrated into the elements. But the kamma which determined the appearance of this physical body has naturally been renewed and assumes a new form. II. Kāya under the *psychological* aspect is the seat of sensation (Dhs §§ 613-16), and represents the fundamental organ of touch which underlies all other sensation. Developed only in later thought DhsA. 311 cf. Mrs. Rhys Davids, *Bud. Psy. Ethics* lvi. ff.; *Bud. Psy.* 143, 185 f.

I. (*Physical*).—(a) Understanding of the body is attained through *introspection* (sati). In the group of the four *sati-paṭṭhānas*, the foundations of introspection, the recognition of the true character of "body" comes first (see Vbh 193). The standing formula of this recognition is kāye kāyânupassī . . . contemplating body as an accumulation, on which follows the description of this aggregate: "he sees that the body is clothed in skin, full of all kinds of dirty matter, and that in this body there are hair, nails, teeth," etc (the enumeration of the 32 ākāras, as given Kh III.). The conclusions drawn from this meditation give a man the right attitude. The formula occurs frequently, both in full and abridged, e. g. D II.293, 294; III.104, 141; A III.323 = V.109; S IV.111 = V.278; Vbh 193 f. 194; Nett 83, 123; with slight variation: kāye asubhânupassī . . . A III.142 sq.; V.109 (under asubhasaññā); It 81; cp. kāye aniccânupassī S IV.211; and kāyagatā sati. — This accumulation is described in another formula with: ayaŋ . . . kāyo rūpī cātum(m)ahābhūtiko mātā-pettika-sambhavo odana-kummās' upacayo, etc. "this body has form (i. e. is material, visible), is born from mother and father, is a heap of gruel and sour milk, is subject to constant dressing and tending, to breaking up and decay," etc., with inferences D I.55 = S III.207; S II.94; IV.194; V.282, 370; D I.76, 209; M I.144, 500; II.17; A IV.386 = S IV.83.

(b) *Various qualities and functions* of the material body. As trunk of the body (opposed to pakkhā and sīsa) S II.231; also at Pv I.8³; as depending on nourishment (āhāra-ṭṭhitika, etc.) S V.64; A II.145 (with taṇhā, māna, methuna); as needing attention: see 'parihārika. As saviññāṇaka, having consciousness A IV.53 = S II.252 = S III.80, 103, 136, 169; cp. āyu usmā ca viññāṇaŋ yadā kāyaŋ jahant' imaŋ S III.143. As in need of breathing assāsa-passāsa S V.330, 336; as tired, fatigued (kilanta-kāya) kilanta-kāyā kilanta-cittā te devā tamhā kāyā cavanti "tired in body, tired in mind these gods fall out of this assembly" (D I.20; III.32 ≈); in other connection PvA 43; see also kilanta. kāyo kilanto D III.255 sq.; = A IV.332; S V.317; M I.116; jiṇṇassa me . . . kāyo na paleti Sn 1144; ātura-kāyo S III.1 (cittaŋ anāturaŋ); paripuṇṇa-k° suruci sujāto, etc., with a perfect body (of the Buddha) Sn 548 = Th 1, 818; cp. mahā-k° (of Brahmins) Sn 298. The body of a Buddha is said to be endowed with the 32 signs of a great man: Bhagavato kāye dvattiŋsa mahāpurisa-lakkhaṇāni . . . Sn p. 107, cp. 549. The Tathāgata is said to be dhamma-kāyo "author and speaker of Doctrine," in the same sense Brahma-kāyo "the best body" (i. e. of Doctrine) D III.84 (*Dial.* iii. 81).

(c) *Valuation of physical body.* From the contemplating of its true character (kāyânupassī) follows its estimation as a transient, decaying, and repulsive object. — kāye anicc' ânupassī S IV.211 (and vay' ânupassī, nirodh' ânupassī), so also asubhânupassī It 81; kāyañ ca bhindantaŋ ñatvā It 69; evaŋdhammo (i. e. a heap of changing elements) A III.324; aciraŋ vat' ayaŋ kāyo paṭhaviŋ adhisessati chuddho apetaviññāṇo niratthaŋ va kaliṅgaraŋ Dh 41. pittaŋ semhañ ca vamati kāyamhā Sn 198. As bahu-dukkho bahu-ādīnavo A V.109; as anicca dukkha, etc. M I.500; II.17; kāyena aṭṭiyamānā harayamānā S IV.62; V.320; dissati imassa kāyassa ācayo pi apacayo pi ādānam pi nikkhepanam pi S II.94. — This body is eaten by crows and vultures after its death: S V.370. Represented as pūti° foul S I.131; III.120. — Bdhgh. at Vism 240 defines kāya as "catu-mahābhūtika pūti-kāya" (cp. similar passages on p. 367: patthaddho bhavati kāyo, pūtiko bhavati kāyo).

(d) *Similes.*—Out of the great number of epithets (adhivacanāni) and comparisons only a few can be mentioned (cp. above under def. & syn.): The body is compared to an abscess (gaṇḍa) S IV.83 = A IV.386; a city (nagara) S IV.194; a cart (ratha) S IV.292; an ant-hill (vammīka) M I.144; all in reference to its consisting of the four fundamental elements, cp. also: pheṇ' ûpamaŋ kāyaŋ imaŋ viditvā "knowing that the body is like froth" Dh 46; kumbh' ûpamaŋ kāyaŋ imaŋ viditvā nagar' ûpamaŋ cittaŋ idaŋ ṭhapetvā Dh 40: the body is as fragile as a water-pot.

(e) *Dissolution* of the body is expressed in the standard phrase: kāyassa bhedā param maraṇā . . ., i. e. after death . . . upon which usually follows the mention of one of the gatis, the destinies which the new kāya has to experience, e. g. D I.82, 107, 143, 162, 245, 247, 252; III.96, 97, 146, 181, 235; M I.22; S I.94; III.241; Dh 140; It 12, 14; J I.152; PvA 27, etc., etc. Cp. also IV.

II. (*Psychological*).—As the seat of feeling, kāya is the fifth in the enumeration of the senses (āyatanāni). It is ajjhattika as sense (i. e. subjective) and its object is the tangible (phoṭṭhabba). The contact between subject and object consists either in touching (phusitvā) or in sensing (viññeyya). The formulas vary, but are in essence the same all through, e. g. kāya-viññeyyā phoṭṭhabbā D I.245; kāyena phoṭṭhabbaŋ phusitvā D III.226, 250, 269; M I.33; II.42; S IV.104, 112; kāyena phusitvā A V.11; kāyo c' eva phoṭṭhabbā ca D III.102. Best to be grouped here is an application of kāya in the sense of the self as experiencing a great joy;

the whole being, the "inner sense," or heart. This realization of intense happiness (such as it is while it lasts), pīti-sukha, is the result of the four stages of meditation, and as such it is always mentioned after the jhānas in the formula: so imaŋ eva kāyaŋ vivekajena pīti-sukhena abhisandeti . . . "His very body does he so pervade with the joy and ease born of detachment from worldliness" D I.73 sq.=M I.277; A II.41, etc. — A similar context is that in which kāya is represented as passaddha, calmed down, i. e. in a state which is free from worldly attachment (vivekaja). This "peace" of the body (may be translated as "my senses, my spirits" in this connection) flows out of the peace of the mind and this is born out of the joy accompanying complete satisfaction (pamuditā) in attaining the desired end. The formula is pamnditassa pīti jāyati pītimanassa kāyo passambhati, passaddhakāyo sukhaŋ vedeti, sukhino cittaŋ samādhiyati D III.241, 288; S IV.351; M I.37; A III.21, 285; IV.176; V.3, 333; Vbh 227. — Similarly: pamuditāya pīti jāyati, pītimanāya kāyo p°, passadhakāyā sukhaŋ ved° Vin I.294 (cp. *Vin. Texts* II.224: "all my frame will be at peace," or "individuality"; see note) passaddhakāya-sankhāra mentioned at A V.29 sq. is one of the ten ariya-vāsā, the noblest conditions. A qnasi-analogy between kāya and kāma is apparent from a number of other passages: kāya-chando -°sneho -°anvayatā pahīyati M I.500; ajjhattañ ca bahiddha ca kāye chandaŋ virājaye Sn 203; kāye avigata-rāgo hoti (kāme, rūpe) D III.238=A III.249; madhurakajāto viya kāyo S III.106; A III.69.

III. (*Ethical*).—Kāya is one of the three channels by which a man's personality is connected with his environment & by which his character is judged, viz. action, the three being kāya, vacī (vāca) and manas. These three kammantas, activities or agents, form the three subdivisions of the sīla, the rules of conduct. Kāya is the first and most conspicuous agent, or the principle of action κατ' ἐξοχήν, character in its pregnant sense.

Kāya as one of a triad.—Its usual combination is in the formula mentioned, and as such found in the whole of the Pāli Canon. But there is also another combination, found only in the older texts, viz. kayenā vācāya uda cetasā: yañ ca karoti kāyena vācāya uda cetasā taŋ hi tassa sakaŋ hoti tañ ca ādāya gacchati S I.93 yo dhammacārī kāyena vācāya uda cetasā idh eva nam pasaŋsanti pacca sagge pamodati S I.102. — So also at A I.63; Sn 232. Besides in formula arakkhitena kāyena a° vācāya a° cittena S II.231=271; IV.112. — With su- and duccarita the combⁿ is extremely frequent, e. g. S I.71, 72; M I.22, etc., etc. In other comb. we have kāya- (v°., m.°) kamma, moneyya, soceyya, etc. — k°. v°. m°. hiŋsati S I.165; saŋsappati A V.289 sq.; kāye (v°. m°.) sati kāya-sañcetanā-hetu uppajjati S II.39 sq.; The variations of k- in the ethics of the Dhamma under this view of k°. v°. m°. are manifold, all based on the fundamental distinctions between good and bad, all being the raison d'être of kamma: yaŋ . . . etarahi kammaŋ karoti kāyena v. m. idaŋ vuccati navakammaŋ S IV.132. — Passages with reference to good works are e. g. D III.245; A I.151; V.302 sq.; (see also Kamma II.2 b. c.). — With reference to evil: S III.241, 247; A I.201; kin nu kāyena vācāyā manasā dukkaṭaŋ kataŋ Pv II.1³ and passim. Assutavā puthujjano tīhi ṭhānehi micchā paṭipajjati kāyena v. m. S II.151; pāpaŋ na kayirā vacasā manasā kāyena vā kiñcana sabbaloke S I.12=31; yassa kāyena vācāya manasā n'atthi dukkaṭaŋ saŋvutaŋ tīhi ṭhānehi, tam ahaŋ brūmi brāhmaṇaŋ Dh 391=Nett 183. Kāyena saŋvaro sādhu sādhu vācāya saŋvaro manasā saŋvaro sādhu sādhu sabbattha saŋvaro Dh 361=S I.73=Miln 399; ye ca kāyena v. m. ca susaŋvutā na te Māravasānugā, na te Mārassa paccagū S I.104; vācānurakkhī manasā susaŋvuto kāyena ca akusalaŋ na kayirā Dh 281=Nett 183.

Kāya as one of a dyad: vācā and kāya: S I.172 (°gutta) M I.461 (rakkhita and a°); Pv I.2² (°saññatā and opp.); Vism 28 (k°-vacī-kamma); PvA 98.

Kāya alone as a collective expression for the three: A I.54; Dh 259, 391; Sn 206, 407; kāye avītarāgo M I.101; A III.249; IV.461 sq.; °-samācāra S V.354; kāyaŋ paṇidhāya Ps I.175; Vbh 244=252; bhāvita° and a° M I.239; A I.250; III.106 sq., cp.: kāya-ppakopaŋ rakkheyya, kāyena saŋvuto siyā kāyaduccaritaŋ hitvā, kāyena sucaritaŋ care Dh 231. Ahiŋsakā ye munayo niccaŋ kāyena saŋvutā Dh 225.

Kāya in combⁿ with citta: ṭhito va kāyo hoti ṭhitaŋ cittaŋ . . . S V.74; anikaṭṭha-kāyo nikaṭṭha-citto A II.137; sāraddha-kāyo sankiliṭṭha-citto A V.93=95=97; bhāvita-kāyo, °sīlo, °citto, °pañño S IV.111; A IV.111; V.42 sq. Apakassa kāyaŋ apakassa cittaŋ S II.198. Kāya-citta-passaddhi, etc. Dhs §§ 29-51. In these six couples (or yugalas) later Abhidhamma distinguished kāya as=the cetasikas (mental properties, or the vedanā, saññā and sankhārā khandhas), body being excluded. Cpd. 96. See also combⁿ kilanta-kāya, kilanta-citta under kilamati.

IV. (*Various*).—Kāyena (i. e. "visibly") aññamaññaŋ passituŋ A II.61; as nānatta° and ekatta° at A IV.39 =Nd² 570. The relation between *rūpa-kāya* (=cātumahābhūtika), and *nāma-kāya*, the mental compound (=vedanā saññā, etc.) is discussed at Nett 77, 78, and Ps I.183 sq., see also S II.24. K. is anattā, i. e. k. has no soul A V.109; S IV.166. n'āyaŋ kāyo tumhākaŋ n'āpi paresaŋ, purāṇaŋ idaŋ kammaŋ . . . "neither is this body yours, nor anyone else's: it is (the appearance of) former karma" S II.64, 65=Nd² 680. Dissamānena kāyena and upaḍḍha-dissamānena S I.156. — *Manomaya*-kāya a body made by the mind (cp. VvA 10 and DA I.110, 120, 222) according to Bdhgh only at the time of jhāna S V.282 sq.; manomaya pīti-bhakkha sayaŋpabha D I.17=VvA 10; manomayaŋ kāyaŋ abhinimmināya . . . D I.77; m° sabbanga-paccangī D I.34, 77, 186, 195. — Under the control of psychic powers (*iddhi*): kāyena va saŋvatteti he does as he likes with his body, i. e. he walks on water, is ubiquitous, etc. (yāva brahmalokā pi: even up to heaven) S V.265=D I.78=A I.170: see also S V.283, 284. — In the various stages of *Saŋsāra*; kāyaŋ nikkhipati he lays down his (old) body S IV.60, 400; cp. S III.241 (ossaṭṭha-kāya); referring to continuous change of body during day and night (of a Petī) Pv II.12¹¹.

-anga a limb of the body, kāy'angaŋ vāc'angaŋ vā na kopenti: they remain motionless and speechless (ref. to the bhikkhus begging) J III.354; DhsA 93, 240; -ānupassin in combⁿ kāye kāyānupassī "realizing in the body an aggregate" D II.94, 100, 291 sq.; D III.58, 77, 141, 221, 276; M I.56; A I.39, 296; II.256; III.449; IV.300, 457 sq.; S IV.211; V.9, 75, 298, 329 sq.; Vbh 193 sq.; 236; see also above. Der.: °anupassanā Ps. I.178, 184; II.152, 163, 232; °passita Nett. 123; -āyatana the sense of touch D III.243, 280, 290; Dhs 585, 613, 653, 783;—indriya same D III.239; Dhs 585, 613, 972; -ujjukatā straightness of body (+citta°, of thought) Dhs 53, 277, 330; Vism 466; Bdhd 16, 20. -ûpaga going to a (new) body S II.24; -kamma "bodily action," deed performed by the body in contradistinction to deeds by speech or thought (see above) D I.250; III.191, 245, 279; M I.415; III.206; A I.104; III.6, 9, 141 sq.; V.289; Th 2, 277; Ps II.195; Dhs 981, 1006; Vbh 208, 321, 366; Pug 41; Bdhd 69; DhsA 68, 77, 344. -kammaññatā wieldiness, alertness of the bodily senses included under nāmakāya Dhs 46, 277, 326. -kammanta=°kamma, in comb. °*sampatti* and °*sandosa* A V.292, 294, 297; M I.17. -kali "the misfortune of having a body"=this miserable body Th 2, 458, 501; ThA 282, 291; -kasāva bodily impurity or depravity A I.112; -gata "relating to the body," always combined with sati in the same sense as °anupassin (see above) S I.188; M. III.92; A I.44; Sn 340 (cp. SnA 343); Th 1, 468, 1225; J I.394; Dh 293 = Nett 39; Dh 299; Miln 248, 336, 393; Vism 111, 197, 240 sq. -gantha bodily tie or fetter (binding one to saŋsāra), of which there are four: abhijjhā, byāpāda, sīlabbata-parāmāsa, idaŋ-saccâbhinivesa D III.230 = S V.59 = Dhs 1135 = Vbh 374; cp. Mrs. Rh. D., *Dhs. trsl.* p. 304; —gandha spelling for °gantha at Nett 115-119; -gutta one who guards his body, i. e. controls his action (+vacīgutta) S I.172 = Sn 74; -gutti the care or protection of the body Vin I.295; J II.162; -citta body and mind: °*ābādha* physical and mental disease J IV.166; see other comb^{ns} above; -ḍāha fever Vin I.214; -tapana chastisement of body, curbing one's material desires, asceticism PvA 98. -thāma physical strength J III.114; -daratha bodily distress J V.397; VI.295; -daḷha bodily vigour Vin II.76, 313; -dukkha bodily pain (+ceto°) M III.288; -duccarita misconduct by the body, evil deeds done through the instrumentality of the body (cp. °kamma) D III.52, 96, 111, 214; A I.48; Dh 231; It 54, 58; Dhs 300, 1305; Bdhd 16, 20; -duṭṭhulla unchastity Th 1, 114; -dvāra the channel or outlet of bodily senses J I.276; IV.14; VvA 73; DhA IV.85; Bdhd 69; -dhātu the "element" of body, i. e. the faculty of touch, sensibility Dhs 613; Kvu 12; -pakopa blameworthy conduct, misbehaviour (+vacī°, mano°) Dh 231 = DhA 330; -pacālaka (nt.) shaking or swaying the body, "swaggering" Vin II.213; -paṭibaddha 1. adj. (of the breath), dependent on, or connected with the body S IV.293; attached or bound to the body J III.377; V.254; 2. m. an article of dress worn on the body Vin III.123, IV.214; -payoga the instrumentality or use of the body DA I.72 = DhsA 98; -pariyantika limited by the body, said of *vedanā*, sensation S V.320 = A II.198; -parihārika tending or protecting the body D I.71 = A II.209 = Pug 58; Vism 65 (cīvara); DA I.207; -pasāda clearness of the sense of touch or sense in general DhsA 306; Bdhd 62, 66, 74; cp. *Dhs. trsl.* p. 173^n, 198^n; -passaddhi serenity or quietude of the senses S IV.125 (cp. IV.351 and above); V.66, 104; Dhs 40, 277, 320; DhsA 130; Bdhd 16, 19, 29; -pāgabbhiya "body-forwardness" immodesty, lasciviousness, gener. said of women J II.32; V.449; -pāgabbhiniya same J I.288; -pāguññatā good condition of the mental faculties, fitness of sense, opp. kāyagelañña, apathy Dhs 46, 277, 326; Vism 466; Bdhd 16, 20, 157; -phandita (nt.) bodily activity J III.25; -baddha fastened to the body, appl. to robes DA I.207; -bandhana a girdle or waistband Vin I.46, 51; II.118, 135, 177, 213, 266; M I.237; -bala physical strength PvA 30; -bhāvanā meditation or training with regard to action D III.219; M I.237; cp. Miln 85; -macchera "body-selfishness," pampering the body Th 1, 1033; -mudutā pliability of sense = °kammaññatā Dhs 41, 277, 324; Bdhd 16, 20, 157; -muni a sage with regard to action It 56; -moneyya the true wisdom regarding the use of the body as an instrument of action It 56, 67; D III.220; A I.273; Nd^2 514; -ratha the "carriage-like" body J VI.253; -lahutā buoyancy of sense = °muduta, same loci; -vanka crookedness of action A I.112; -vikāra change of position of the body J III.354; -vijambhana alertness DhA IV.113; -viññatti intimation by body, i. e. merely by one's appearance, appl. chiefly to the begging bhikkhu Dhs 585, 636, 654, 844; DhsA 82, 301; Miln 229, 230; Vism 448; Bdhd 69, 70; -viññāṇa consciousness by means of touch, sensory consciousness D III.243; Dhs 556, 585, 651, 685, 790; Miln 59; Vbh 180; °*dhātu* element of touch-consciousness Dhs 560; Vbh 88; Kvu 12; -viññeyya to be perceived by the sense of touch (+phoṭṭhabba, see above) D I.245; II.281; III.234; M I.85, 144; Dhs 589, 967, 1095; Vbh 14; Kvu 210; Miln 270; -vipphandana throbbing of the body, bodily suffusion, appl^d to °*vinnatti* Bdhd 69, 70; DhsA 323; -viveka seclusion of the body, hermitism J I.289; DhsA 165; -vūpakāsa = °viveka D III.285 (+citta° "singleness" of heart); -veyyāvacca menial duties J I.12; °*kara* a servant J II.334; -veyyāvaṭika same J VI.418; Sn p. 104; DhA I.27; °*kamma* id. J V.317 (= veyyāvacca) DhsA 160; -saŋsagga bodily contact, sexual intercourse Vin III.121, 190; J VI.566; -sakkhin he who has realized and gained the final truth concerning the body (cp. °anupassin) D III.105, 254; M I.478 = Pug 14, 29; M II.113; III.45; A I.74; 118; IV.10, 451; V.23; Ps II.52, 62; Nett 190; Kvu 58; Vism 93, 387. -sankhāra the material aggregate, substratum of body Vin III.71; S II.40; III.125; IV.293; A I.122; II.158, 231; Ps I.184, 186; Vism 530. -sangaha control of body (+citta°) Nett 91; -sañcetanā (-hetu) ground (for the rise of), material, i. e. impure thoughts A II.157; Vism 530 (+vacī°, mano°). -samācāra (good) conduct as regards one's actions D II.279 (+vacī°) M I.272 sq.; II.113; III.45; S V.354; A III.186 sq. -sampīḷana crushing the body (of dukkha) Nett 29; -samphassa the sense of touch (see āyatana) D III.243; S V.351; Dhs 585, 616, 651, 684; °ja arisen through touch or sensibility D III.244; Dhs 445, 558; -sucarita good conduct in action, as one of the three °kammāni (vacī°, mano°) D III.52, 96, 111, 169, 215; It 55, 59, 99, Dhs 1306; -suci purity of body, i. e. of action (+vacī°, ceto°) A I.273; It 55; -soceyya purification of body (+vacī°, mano°) D III.219; A I.271; V 264, 266; It 55.

Kāyika (adj.) [fr. kāya] 1. belonging to the body, i. e. felt by the body (experienced by the senses), or resulting from the body, i. e. done by the body (= acted as opposed to spoken or thought). sukhaŋ physical happiness (opp. cetasika°) S V.209; A I.81; dukkhaŋ D II.306; M I.302 (opp. cetasikaŋ); kāyikaŋ (sc. dhammaŋ) sikkhati to teach the conduct of body (opp. vācasikaŋ) Vin II.248. In comb. with vācasika also at S I.190; Pug 21; Vism 18 (of anācara); PvA 119 (of saŋyama, control) Shhp 55; Bdhd 26, 134; referring to diff. kinds of amusements Nd^2 219 = SnA 86. 2. -° (of devas) belonging to the company of—: ° D I.220; gandhabba° PvA 119.

Kāyūra & **Kāyura** [see also keyūra, which is the only form in Sk.] 1. an ornamental bracket or ring worn on the upper arm (bāh'ālankāra Pv; bhuj° Vv) or neck (gīvāya pilandhana J III.437); a bracelet or necklace Vin II.106; J III.437; IV.92; Pv III.9^3; Vv 36^2. — 2. adj. as sakāyura raṭṭha having the insignia "regis" J V.289 = 486.

Kāyūrin (adj.) [fr. last] wearing bracelets Pv III.9^1.

Kār—secondary root of karoti, in denom. and intensive function in kāra, kāraka, kāraṇa, kārin, kāreti and their derivations.

Kāra [fr. kar-, cp. Vedic kāra song of praise, which is, however, derived fr. **kṛ** = **kir** to praise; also Vedic °kāra in brāhma°, fr. **kṛ**] 1. abs. (a) deed, service, act of mercy or worship, homage: kāra-paṇṇaka J VI.24 (vegetable as oblation); appako pi kato kāro devûpapattiŋ āvahati "even a small gift of mercy brings about rebirth among the gods" PvA 6. -kāraka one who performs a religious duty D I.61 (= DA I.170). (b) doing, manner, way: yena kārena akattha tena k° pavattamānaŋ phalaŋ "as you have done so will be the fruit" PvA 45. — 2. (-°) (a) the production or application of, i. e. the state or quality of . . .: atta° one's own state = ahaŋ kāra, individuality; para° the personality of others A III.337; citti° reflection, thought PvA 26; see e. g. andha° darkness, sak° homage, etc. — balakkārena forcibly PvA 68. — (b) as ttg. the item, i. e. particle, letter, sound or word, e. g. ma-kāra the letter m PvA 52; ca-kāra the particle ca PvA 15; sa-kāra the sound sa SnA 23. — (c) (adj. -n.) [cp. kara] one who does, handles or deals with: ayakāra iron-smith Miln 331.

Kārā (f.) [cp. Sk. kārā] confinement, captivity, jail, in °bhedaka cora a thief who has broken out of jail Vin I.75.

Kāraka (usually -°) the doer (of): Vin II.221 (capu-capu°); sāsana° he who does according to (my) advice Sn 445; Bdhd 85 sq.; — f. kārikā: veyyāvacca° a servant PvA 65 (text reads °tā); as *n.* the performance of (-°), service: dukkara-kārikā the performance of evil deeds S I.103; Th 2, 413 (=ThA 267). -agga-kārikā first test, sample Vin III.80.

Kāraṇa (nt.) [in meaning 1 represented in later Sk. by kāraṇā f., in meaning 2 = Sk. kāraṇa nt., equivalent to prakṛti, natural form, constituent, reason, cause]. 1. —(a) a deed, action, performance, esp. an act imposed or inflicted .pon somebody by a higher authority (by the king as representative of justice or by kamma: M III.181; see kamma II 3.A b.) as an ordeal, a feat or punishment: a labour or task in the sense of the 12 labours of Heracles or the labours of Hades. kāraṇaŋ kārāpeti "he makes somebody perform the task." Pass. kāraṇaŋ or kāraṇā kariyati. Thus as a set of *five* tasks or purgatory obligations under the name of pañcavidha-bandhana "the group of five" (not, as Warren *trsl.* p. 257 "inflict on him the torture called the fivefold pinion"), a means of punishment in Niraya (q. v. under pañca). Not primarily torture (Rh. Davids, *Miln trsl.* I.254, and others with wrong derivation from kṛntati). At DhA III.70 these punishments are comprehended under the term dasa-dukkhakāraṇāni (the *ten* punishments in misery); the meaning "punishment" also at J IV.87 (tantarajjukaŋ k°ŋ katvā), whereas at J VI.416 k. is directly paraphrased by "maraṇa," as much as "killing." Often spelt karaṇa, q. v.; the spelling **kāraṇā** (as f.) at Miln 185 seems to be a later spelling for kāraṇaŋ. See karaṇa for further reference. — Kiŋ kāraṇaŋ ajja kāressati "what task will he impose on me to-day?" A V.324; as pañcavidhabandhana K° A I.141, PvA 251, Nd² 304[III]. — As adj. °kāraṇa in dāruṇa° "being obliged to go through the dreadful trial" PvA 221. — (b) duty obligation, in kāraṇ' ākāraṇā (pl.) duties great and small DhA I.385. Cp. also kāraṇaŋ karoti to try M I.444. — (c) a trick (i. e. a duty imposed by a higher authority through training) J II.325 (ānañja°); Miln 201 (ākāsa-gamana°). 2. — (a) acting, action as (material) cause: k°-bhūta being the cause of . . . PvA 15; —(b) (intellectual) cause, reason Miln 150; DhA I.389; esp. as -°: arodana° the reason for not crying PvA 63; asocana° same, ibid. 62; āgamana° the reason for coming (here) ibid. 81, 106. = pariyatti, DhA. 36. = attha, SA on I.215, SnA. I.238—instr. kāraṇena by necessity, needs PvA 195; tena k° therefore ibid. 40 — abl. kāraṇā by means of, through, by (=hetu or nissāya) PvA 27; imasmā k° therefore PvA 40; kāraṇaṭṭhā (expl. as attha-kāraṇā Nd²) for the purpose of some object or advantage Sn 75; opp. nikkāraṇā from unselfishness ibid.—sakāraṇa (adj.) with good reason (of vacana) PvA 109.

Kāraṇika [der. fr. prec.] the meaning ought to be "one who is under a certain obligation" or "one who dispenses certain obligations." In usu° S II.257 however used simply in the sense of making: arrow-maker, fletcher. Perhaps the reading should be °kāraka.

Kāraṇḍava[1] [of uncertain etym., cp. karaṇḍa] chaff, offal, sweepings, fig. dirt, impurity: yava° A IV.169 (chaff); samaṇa° ibid. — In passage kāraṇḍavaŋ niddhamatha, kasambuŋ apakassatha A IV.172 = Sn 281 = Miln 414 trsl[d] by Rh. Davids *Miln trsl.* II.303 "get rid of filth, put aside rubbish from you," expl. SnA 311 by kacavara (q. v.). Rh. D's note[3] loc. cit. is to be modified according to the parallel passages just given.

Kāraṇḍava[2] [cp. Sk. kāraṇḍava] a sort of duck Vv 35[8] (expl[d] as also by Halāyudha 2, 99 by kādamba, black goose).

Kārāpaka [fr. kārāpeti] a schemer, inventor J VI.333.

Kārāpaṇa see kāreti.

Kārāpita [pp. of kārāpeti, Caus. of karoti] made to do J VI.374.

Kārikā see kāraka

Kāritā = kārikā (performance); see pāripūri°.

Kārin (-°) (adj.) doing: yathāvādī tathākārī "as he says so he does" D III.135, Sn 357; see for examples the various cpds. as kamma°, kibbisa°, khaṇḍa°, chidda°, dukkaṭa°, dvaya°, paccakkha°, pubba°, sakkacca°, sampajāna°, etc.

Kāriya (adj.) [grd of kāreti, Caus. of karoti] to be done, neg. akāriya to be undone, (not) to be made good It 18.

Kāruñña (nt.) [fr. karuṇa] compassion (usually with anudayā and anukampā) S II.199; A III.189; Vism 300; PvA 75; Sdhp 509.

Kāruññatā (f.) compassionateness S I.138.

Kāruṇika (adj.) [fr. karuṇa] compassionate, merciful Pv II.1[13]; PvA 16; Bdhd 49; often with mahā°: of great mercy Sdhp 330, 557; so of the Buddha: mahākāruṇika nātha "the Saviour of great mercy" in introductory stanzas to Pv and Vv.

Kāreti (Causative of karoti), to construct, to build, etc.; pp. kārita; der. -kārāpaṇa the construction of (vihāra°) DhA I.416. For details see karoti IV.; see also kārāpaka & kārāpita.

Kāla (and **Kāḷa**) — *Preliminary.* 1. dark (syn. kaṇha, which cp. for meaning and applications), black, blue-black, misty, cloudy. Its proper sphere of application is the dark as opposed to light, and it is therefore characteristic of all phenomena or beings belonging to the realm of darkness, as the night, the new moon, death, ghosts, etc. — There are two etymologies suggestible, both of which may have been blended since Indo-Aryan times: (a) kāla = Sk. kāla, blue-black, kālī black cloud from ***qāl** (with which conn. ***qel** in kalanka, spot, kalusa dirty, kammāsa speckled, Gr. κελαινός, Mhg. hilwe mist) = Lat. cālidus spot, Gr. κηλίς spot, and κηλάς dark cloud; cp. Lat. cāligo mist, fog, darkness. — (b) see below, under note. — Hence. **2.** the morning mist, or darkness preceding light, daybreak, morning (cp. E. morning = Goth. maúrgins twilight, Sk. marka eclipse, darkness; and also gloaming = gleaming = twilight), then: time in general, esp. a fixed time, a point from or to which to reckon, i. e. term or terminus (a quo or ad quem). — *Note.* The definition of colour-expressions is extremely difficult. To a primitive colour-sense the principal difference worthy of notation is that between dark and light, or dull and bright, which in their expressions, however, are represented as complements for which the same word may be used in either sense of the complementary part (dark for light and vice versa, cp. E. gleam > gloom). All we can say is that kāla belongs to the group of expressions for *dark* which may be represented simultaneously by black, blue, or brown. That on the other hand, black, when polished or smooth, supplies also the notion of "shining" is evidenced by kāḷa and kaṇha as well, as e. g. by ***skei** in Sk. chāyā = Gr. σκιά shadow as against Ags. hǣven "blue" (E. heaven) and Ohg. skīnan, E. to shine and sky. The psychological value of a colour depends on its light-reflecting (or light-absorbing) quality. A bright black appears lighter (reflects more light) than a dull grey, therefore a polished (añjana) black (=sukāḷa) may readily be called "brilliant." In the same way kāla, combined with other colour-words of *black* connotation does not need to mean "black," but may mean simply a kind of black, i. e. brown. This depends on the semasiological contrast or equation of the passage in question. Cp. Sk. śyāma (dark-grey) and śyāva (brown) under kāsāya. That the notion of the speckled or variegated colour belongs to the sphere of black, is psychologically simple (: dark specks against a light ground, cp. kammāsa), and is also shown by the *second etymology of kāla*=Sk. śāra, mottled, speckled=Lat. cærulus, black-blue and perhaps cælum " the blue " (cp. heaven)=Gr. κηρύλος the blue ice-bird. (On k>s cp. kaṇṇa>śṛṅga, kilamati>śramati, kilissati>ślis°, etc.) The usual spelling of kāla as kāḷa indicates a connection of the l with the r of śāra. — The definition of kāla as jhām' angārasadisa is conventional and is used both by Bdhgh. and Dhpāla: DhsA 317 and PvA 90.

1. **Kāḷa,** dark, black, etc., in enum^n^ of colours Vv 22¹ (see VvA 111). na kāḷo samaṇo Gotamo, na pi sāmo: mangura-cchavi samaṇo G. " The ascetic Gotamo is neither black nor brown: he is of a golden skin " M I.246; similarly as kāḷī vā sāmā vā mangura-cchavī vā of a kalyāṇī, a beautiful woman at D I.193=M. II.40; kāḷa-sāma at Vin IV.120 is to be taken as dark-grey. — Of the dark half of the month: see °pakkha, or as the new moon: āgame kāḷe " on the next new moon day " Vin I.176. — of Petas: Pv II.4¹ (kāḷī f.); PvA 56¹ (°rūpa); of the dog of Yama (°sunakha) PvA 151. — In other conn^n^: kāḷavaṇṇa-bhūmi dark-brown (i. e. fertile) soil Vin I.48=II.209.

-añjana black collyrium Vin I.203; **-ānusārī** black, (polished ?) Anusāri (" a kind of dark, fragrant sandal wood " *Vin. Texts* II.51) Vin I.203; S III.156=V.44=A V.22; **-ayasa** black (dark) iron (to distinguish it from bronze, Rh. D., *Miln trsl.* II.364; cp. blacksmith>silversmith) Miln 414, 415; **-kañjaka** a kind of Asuras, Titans D III.7; J V.187; PvA 272; **-kaṇṇī** " black-eared," as an unlucky quality. Cp. III.6¹¹; J I.239; IV.189; V.134, 211; VI.347; DhA I.307; II.26; the vision of the " black-eared " is a bad omen, which spoils the luck of a hunter, e. g. at DhA III.31 (referring here to the sight of a bhikkhu); as " witch " PvA 272; DhA III.38, 181; as k-k. sakuṇa, a bird of ill omen J II.153; **-kaṇṇika**=prec.; **-kabara** spotted, freckled J VI.540; **-kesa** (adj.) with glossy or shiny hair, by itself (kāḷa-kesa) rare, e. g. at J VI.578; usually in cpd. *susukāḷa-kesa* " having an over-abundance of brilliant hair " said of Gotama. This was afterwards applied figuratively in the description of his parting from home, rising to a new life, as it were, possessed of the full strength and vigour of his manhood (as the rising Sun). Cp. the Shamash-Saga, which attributes to the Sun a wealth of shiny, glossy (=polished, dark) hair (=rays), and kāḷa in this connection is to be interpreted just as kaṇha (q. v.) in similar combinations (e. g. as Kṛṣṇa Hṛṣīkesa or Kesavā). On this feature of the Sun-god and various expressions of it see ample material in Palmer, *The Samson Saga* pp. 33-46. — The double application of su° does not offer any difficulty, sukāḷa is felt as a simplex in the same way as εὐπλοκαμός or duh° in comb^ns^ like sudubbala PvA 149, sudullabha VvA 20. Bdhgh. already interprets the cpd. in this way (DA I.284=suṭṭhu-k°, añjana-vaṇṇa k° va hutvā; cp. kaṇh-añjana J V.155). Cp. also siniddha-nīla-mudu-kuñcita-keso J I.89, and sukaṇhakaṇha J V.202. — susukāḷakesa of others than the Buddha: M II.66. Modern editors and lexicographers see in susu° the Sk. śiśu young of an animal, cub, overlooking the semantical difficulty involved by taking it as a separate word. This mistake has been applied to the compound at all the passages where it is found, and so we find the reading susu kāḷakeso at M I.82=A II.22=J II.57; M I.163=A I.68=S I.9, 117; also in Childer's (relying on Burnouf), or even susū k° at S IV.111; the only passages showing the right reading susu-k° are D I.115, M I.463. Konow under susu *J.P.T.S.* 1909, 212 has both. **-kokila** the black (brown) cuckoo VvA 57; **-jallika** (kāḷi° for kāḷa°) having black drops or specks (of dirt) A I.253; **-daṇḍa** a black staff, Sdhp 287 (attr. to the messengers of Yama, cp. Yama as having a black stick at Śat. Br. xi. 6, 1, 7 and 13); **-pakkha** the dark side, i. e. moonless fortnight of the month A II.18; -° *cātuddasī* the 14th day of the dark fortnight PvA 55; -° *ratti* a moonless night VvA 167; (opp. dosina I.) **-meyya** a sort of bird J VI.539; **-loṇa** black (dark) salt Vin I.202 (Bdhgh. pakati-loṇa, natural salt); **-loha** " black metal," iron ore Miln 267; **-valli** a kind of creeper Vism 36, 183. **-sīha** a special kind of lion J IV.208. **-sutta** a black thread or wire, a carpenter's measuring line J II.405; Miln 413; also N. of a Purgatory (nivaya) J V.266. See Morris *J.P.T.S.* 1884, 76-78; **-hatthin** " black elephant," an instrument of torture in Avīci Sdhp 195.

2. **Kāla** time, etc. (a) *Morning*: kāle early Pv II.9⁴¹ (=pāto PvA 128), kālassa in the morning (gen. of time), early VvA 256. Cp. paccūsa-kāle at dawn DhA III.242. Opposed to evening or night in kālena in the morning Pv I.6³ (opp. sāyaṃ). Kāle juṇhe by day and by night Nd² 631. — (b) *time in general*: gacchante gacchante kāle in course of time DhA I.319; evaṃ gacchante kāle as time went on PvA 54, 75, 127, etc. —kālaṃ for a time Vin I.176 (spelt kāḷaṃ); kañci kālaṃ some time yet VvA 288; ettakaṃ kālaṃ for a long time PvA 102.—kālena kālaṃ (1) from time to time PvA 151; VvA 255, 276; — (2) continuously, constantly A IV. 45; Pug 11 (+samayena samayaṃ); D I.74 (: but expl^d^ at DA I.218 by kāle kāle in the sense of " every fortnight or every ten days "). kāle in (all) time, always (cp. *aiti*) Sn 73 (expl. in Nd² by niccakāle under sadā; but at SnA 128 by phāsu-kālena " in good time "); **-kāle kāle** from time to time, or repeatedly VvA 352. See also cira°, sabba°. — (c) *Time in special*, either (1) appointed time, date, fixed time, or (2) suitable time, proper time, good time, opportunity. Cp. Gr. καιρός and ὥρα; or (3) time of death, death. — (1) *Mealtime:* PvA 25; VvA 6; esp. in phrase kālo bho Gotamo, niṭṭhitaṃ bhattaṃ " it is time, Gotama, the meal is ready " D I.119=226; Sn p. 111; and in kālaṃ āroceti or ārocāpeti he announces the time (for dinner) D I.109, 226; Sn p. 111; PvA 22, 141; VvA 173. *-date*: kālato from the date or day of . . ., e. g. diṭṭha° paṭṭhāya " from the day that she first saw her " VvA 206; gihi° paṭṭhāya " from the day of being a layman " PvA 13. (2) proper time, *right time*: also season, as in utu° favourable time (of the year) Vin I.299; II.173; kālaṃ jānāti " he knows the proper time " A IV.114; as cattāro kālā, four opportunities A II.140; yassa kālaṃ maññasi for what you think it is time (to go), i. e. goodbye D I.106, 189, etc. The 3 times of the cycle of existence are given at Vism 578 as past, present, and future. —kāla° (adj.) in (due) time, timely Vism 229 (°maraṇa timely death). — Opp. **akāla** (it is the) wrong time or inopportune D I.205; akāla-cārin going (begging) at the improper time Sn 386. akālamegha a cloud arising unexpectedly (at the wrong time) Miln 144. —kāle at the proper time, with vikāle (opp.) Vin I.199, 200; J II.133; Sn 386. **akāle** in the wrong season VvA 288. kālena in proper time, at the right moment A II.140; Sn 326, 387 (=yutta kālena SnA 374); Pv I.5³ (=ṭhitakālena PvA 26); Pug 50; It 42; KhA 144 (=khaṇena samayena). Cp. vikāla. (3) The day, as appointed by fate or kamma, point of time (for death, cp. Vism 236), the "last hour," cp. ἦμαρ, illa dies. So in the meaning of *death* appl^d^ not only to this earthly existence, but to all others (peta°, deva°, etc.) as well, in phrase **kālaṃ karoti** " he does his time=he has fulfilled his time " Vin III.80; Sn 343, DhA I.70; and frequently elsewhere; cp. -kata, -kiriyā. — As death in kālaṃ kankhati to await the appointed time S I.187; Sn 516 (cp. kankhati) and in der^n^ kālika. — Other examples for this use of kāla see under bhatta°, yañña°, vappa°.

-antara interval, period: kālantarena in a little while PvA 13; na kālantare at once PvA 19; **-kata** (adj.) dead Sn 586, 590; in comb^n^ petā kālakatā " the Petas who have fulfilled their (earthly) time Sn 807; Pv I.5⁷; I.12¹. Also as **kālankata** Pv II.7⁹; Vv 80⁹; Vism 296.

-kiriyā death (often comb^d with maraṇa) M II.108; A I.22, 77, 261 (as bhaddikā, cp. A III.293); IV.320; Sn 694; Pv I.10[12] (of a Petī who has come to the end of her existence); DhA II.36; IV.77. -gata=°kata PvA 29, 40. -ññū knowing the proper time for . . . (c. dat. or loc.) Sn 325; described at A IV.113 sq.; as one of the five qualities of a rājā cakkavattī (viz. atthaññū, dhamma°, matta°, k°, parisa°) A III.148; one of the seven qual. of a sappurisa, a good man (=prec.+atta°, puggala°) D III.252, 283; as quality of the Tathāgata D III.134=Nd[2] 276; Pug 50. -ññutā n. abstr. to prec. A II.101; -(p)pavedana announcement of death(-time) Th I, 563=J I.118=Vism 389=DhA I.248. -bhojana in a° eating at the improper time S V.470; -vādin speaking at the proper time, in formula kāla° bhūta° attha° dhamma° vinaya° under sīla No. 7: D I.4; III.175; DA I.76; A II.22, 209; Pug 58; -vipassin considering the right moment, taking the opportunity It 41. -sataŋ (°sahassaŋ, etc.) a hundred (thousand, etc.) times Vism 243.

Kālika (adj.) [fr. kāla 2] belonging to time, in time, as sabba-kālika always in time, cp. Gr. ὡραῖος Vv 39[2]; with time, i. e. gradual, slowly, delayed S I.117=Nd[2] 645; usually neg. **akālika** 1. not delayed, immediate, in this world, comb. with sandiṭṭhika S II.58; S I.117=IV.41=339=V.343;—2. subject to time, i. e. temporal, vanishing PvA 87;—3. unusual, out of season Miln 114 (cp. akāla). — See also tāva-kālika.

Kālīya a kind of (shiny) sandal wood; so to be read for tālīsa at Vin I.203 (see note on p. 381).

Kālusiya (and **Kālussiya**) (nt.) [der. fr. kalusa, stained, dirty see cognates under kammāsa and kāla] darkness, obscurity DA I.95; PvA 124 (cakkhu°); fig. (dosa°) VvA 30.

Kāḷa see kāla 1.

Kāḷaka (adj.) [fr. kāḷa] black, stained; in enumeration of colours at Dhs 617 (of rūpa) with nīla, pītaka, lohitaka, odāta, k°, mañjeṭṭha; of a robe A II.241; f. kāḷikā VvA 103;—(nt.) a black spot, a stain, also a black grain in the rice, in apagata° without a speck or stain (of a clean robe) D I.110=A IV.186=210=213; vicita° (of rice) "with the black grains removed" D I.105; A IV.231; Miln 16; vigata° (same) A III.49. — A black spot (of hair) J V.197 (=kaṇha-r-iva). — Fig. of character DhA IV.172.

Kāḷārika see kaḷārika.

Kāveyya (nt.) [grd. fr. kāvyate fr. kavi poet cp. Sk. kāvya] 1. poetry, the making of poems, poetry as business: one of the forbidden occupations D I.11 (=DA I.95 kabba-karaṇa)—2. poetry, song, poem (of suttanta) A I.72=III.107.

-matta intoxicated with poetry, musing, dreaming S I.110, 196.

Kāsa[1] [cp. Sk. kāśa] a kind of reed, Saccharum spontaneum S III.137.

Kāsa[2] [cp. Sk. kāsa] cough; in list of diseases under ābādhā A V.110=Nd[2] 304[1].

Kāsāya and **Kāsāva** (adj.) [Sk. kāṣāya from the Pāli; kāsāya prob. fr. Sk. śyāma or śyāva brown=Pāli sāma, with kā=kad, a kind of, thus meaning a kind of brown, i. e. yellow. See further under sāma and cp. kāla] 1. **Kāsāya** as attr. of **vatthāni**, the yellow robes of the Buddhist mendicant, in phrase kāsāyāni v° acchādetvā agārasmā anagāriyaŋ pabbajitvā, describing the taking up of the "homeless state" D I.60, 61, 63, 115; M II.67; A I.107; II.208; IV.118, 274, 280; Pug 57; Nd[2] 172. °vattha (adj.) with yellow robes Sn 64; cp. °*nivattha* J III.179 (dressed in yellow, of the executioner: see Fick, *Soziale Gliederung* p. 104 & cp. kāsāya-nivāsana J III.41; kāsāviya J IV.447); PvA 20; °vāsin dressed in yellow Sn 487. — 2. Kāsāva (vattha) the yellow robe (*never* in above formula) Vin I.287; S IV.190=V.53=301; Dh 9, 10=Th 1, 969, 970=J II.198=V.50; Miln 11. °kaṇṭhā (pl.) the "yellow necks" those whose necks are dressed in yellow Dh 307 (=DhA III.480)=It 43; °pajjota glittering with yellow robes Vbh 247; Miln 19.

Kāsāvaka [fr. kāsāva] a yellow robe DhA II.86.

Kāsāviya [fr. kāsāva] one who is dressed in yellow, esp. of the royal executioner (cp. kāsāya-vattha) J IV.447 (=cora-ghātaka C.).

Kāsika (adj.) [cp. Sk. kāśika & in a diff. sense aḍḍha-kāsika] belonging to the Kāsī country, or to Benares; in °uttama (scil. vattha) an upper garment made of Benares cloth Pv I.10[8]; J VI.49 (where to be read kāsik' uttama for kāsi-kuttama). °vattha Benares muslin A I.248; III.50; Pug 34; Miln 2; DhA I.417; Vism 115.

Kāsu [cp. Sk. karṣū, fr. kṛṣ] a hole; only in cpd. angāra-kāsu a cinderhole, a fire-pit, usually understood as a pit of glowing cinders J I.232. Mostly found in similes, e. g. S IV.56, 188; Sn 396; Sdhp. 208; and in kāmā angārakās' ūpamā metaphor A IV.224=V.175; see also kāma.

Ki° 2nd. stem of interr. pron. (cp. ka° ku°); 1. in oblique cases of ko (kaḥ), as gen. kissa, loc. kismiŋ & kiŋhi. — 2. in nt. **kiŋ** what? (cp. Gr. τί, Lat. quid; ending -m besides -d in kad, as Lat. quom, tum besides quod, id). — 3. in primary derivations, as kittaka, kīva (=Sk. kiyant) which stands in same relation to *qui as Lat. quantus to *quo; and in secondary derivations from kiŋ, as kiñci, kiñcakkha, kīdisa, etc.

Kin [nt. of rel. pron. ka] 1. as *nt. subst.* what? sotānaŋ kiŋ nivāraṇaŋ what is the obstruction? Sn 1032; **kiŋ** tava patthanāya what is it about your wish, i. e. what good is your wish? VvA 226; kim idaŋ this is what, that is why, therefore, PvA 11; often with su in dubitative question: kiŋ sū' dha vittaŋ purisassa seṭṭhaŋ what, then, is the best treasure of man in this world? Sn 181; or with nu: kiŋ nu kho what is it then (in series evaŋ nu kho, na nu kho, kathaŋ nu kho) Nd[2] 186. — Gen. **kissa** of what? Pv I.9[1]; II.9[40] (=kīdisassa) and in kissa hetu on the ground of what i. e. why? Sn 1131; Pv II.8[1] (=kiŋ nimittaŋ). — Instr. kena by what or how is it that: kena ssu nivuto loko Sn 1032. — Acc. **kiŋ**: kiŋ kāhasi what will you do? Sn 428; kiŋ āgamma kiŋ ārabbha on what grounds & for what reason? D I.13, 14, etc.; kiŋ nissita to what purpose Sn 1043. — Loc., **kismiŋ** in what or what about: kismiŋ vivādo "what is the quarrel about?" D I.237; or kimhi, e. g. kimhi sikkhamāno in what instructed? D II.241 (corresponds to ettha=in this). The ŋ of kiŋ in Sandhi is either elided or contracted or undergoes the usual Sandhi changes; ki ha=kiŋ ha KhA 78, kissa=kiŋ assa Sn 1032; kīdisa (q. v.)=kiŋ disa; kiñci (see below)=kiŋ cid; kiŋ va a little: see kittaka. — 2. as *interr. particle*, introducing a question=Lat. nonne, Gr. ἄν: kiŋ idāni pi dinne te labheyyuŋ? "Will they receive that which is given now?" PvA 22. So as disjunctive particle in comb. with udāhu (whether—or): kiŋ-udāhu what (about this) . . . or is it (otherwise), is it so . . . or is it not so? (cp. πότερον—ἤ, Lat. utrum-an): kim imasmiŋ attabhāve pitaraŋ pucchasi udāhu atīte? "do you enquire about your father in this existence, or in a past one?" PvA 38; kiŋ nakkhattaŋ kīḷissasi udāhu bhatiŋ karissasi? "Will you take a holiday or will you work?" VvA 63. — Very often modified and intensified by other exhortative particles: kiŋ aññatra (with abl.) unless (by), except for Sn 206 (see aññatra) kin nu kho why, but why, why in the world? D II.131; J II.159; DhA

II.91. As kimo in kimo nu why then? J III.373; v.479 (=kim eva); kimu Sdhp 137; kim pana=nonne: kim pana bhante addasa? "Have you not seen?" D II.132; kim pana tvaŋ maññasi what then do you think=do you not think then, that? . . . J I.171; kim anga how much more or less, i. e. far more, or far less Miln 274 as kim anga pana why then? M III.181; Miln 23; Vism 233; kin ti how then? D II.74; kin ti te sutaŋ have you not heard? D I.104; kintikaro=kathankaro q. v.; kiñca (cp. kiñcâpi under kiñci)=num-que, nonne; is it not that, rather J I.135 (expl[d] in c. by garahatte ca anuggahatthe nipāto). — kiñci in comb. with yaŋ or yad: whatever; in other comb[n] positive: some, neg.: na kiñci nothing; yad atthi kiñci whatever there is of . . . Sn 231; n'atthi kiñci there is nothing: see under atthi and kiñcana; kiñci n'atthi loke there is nothing in this world . . . Sn 1122. — kiñcâpi whatever, however much: kiñcâpi te tattha yatā caranti "however much they endeavour in this" Sn 1080; J I.147; It 114; KhA 187, 190. Same as disjunctive conjunction with foll. pana: (=Lat. quamvis) kiñcâpi hi . . . pana although . . . yet DhA I.391; kiñcâpi with pot. . . . atha kho although—yet; it may be that—but S I.72. — 3. In composition (°-) often implying doubt, uncertainty ("what is it, that is so & so?"), or expressing strangeness (: doubtful likeness), e. g. kinnara a kind of man (but not sure about it), a half-man; kimpakka odd-looking or doubtful (poisonous) fruit: kimpurisa a strange man (doubtful whether man or beast); cp. kiŋsuka.

-akkhāyin preaching what? in conn. with kiŋ vādin saying what? i. e. holding what views? A I.62; -atthaŋ for what purpose J I.279. -atthiya to what purpose J IV.239; Miln 19; VvA 230; to any purpose, of any use S V.171; -abhiñña having what name? J VI.126. -kara doing whatever (his duty), a servant, in k°-patissāvin an obedient servant D I.61 (cp. expl[n] at DA I.168) A III.37; IV.265 sq.; ThA 252; -karaṇīya business, occupation A III.113, 116, 258; V.24, 90, 338; -kāraṇā (abl. of kāraṇa) by reason of what, i. e. why? PvA 25; -kusalagavesin striving after that which is good M I.163=240; -jacca of what caste? Sn p. 80; -nāma of what name? Miln 15, 17; DhA III.397 (both konāma and kiŋnāma). -pakka strange or unknown (doubtful) fruit, in °*rukkha* a tree with odd fruit (i. e. poisonous fruit, cp. Rām. II.66, 6; Kern, *Toev.* s. v. takes it to be Strychnos nux vomica) J I.368. -purisa 1. a wild man of the woods J IV.254; VI.272, 497. — 2. =kinnara (q. v.) A I.77; J V.42, 416. f. kimpurisī J V.215, 216. -phala=°pakka, in °*rukkha* a tree with unknown (poisonous) fruit J I.271. -rukkha what kind of tree J V.203. -vādin holding what view? A I.62; -samācāra (a) of what conduct, in comb. with; -sīla of what character Sn 324 (=SnA 331).

Kiŋsuka [kiŋ+su+ka] N. of a tree (creeper), lit. "whatever-like," or "what do you call it," i. e. strange tree (see kiŋ su & kiŋ 3), pop. name for the Butea frondosa S IV.193 (parable of the k.); J II.265 (°opama-jātaka); V.405; VI.536. Perhaps v. l. at SnA 284.

-puppha the (red) flower of the k. tree Vism 252. -vaṇṇa of the colour of the k. (flower) J I.73 (angārā ashes).

Kikita (?) dense, thick (?) SS at S IV.289 (for kuṭṭhita), said of the heat.

Kikī [onomat. to sound-root **kṛ** (see note on gala), cp. Sk. kṛka-vāku cock, after the cry of the bird] 1. (m.) the blue jay (J II.350 k. sakuṇo). — 2. (f.) a hen (or the female of the jay?), in simile fr. the Apadāna of a hen watching her egg Vism 36 (aṇḍaŋ anurakkhamānā); J III.375 (rakkhati); cp. SnA 317 (kikī sakuṇikā aṇḍassa upari seti).

Kinkaṇika (m. nt.) [=kinkiṇika] a small bell J IV.362; VvA 12.

Kinkiṇika (m. nt.) [onomat. formation fr. sound part. kiṇi, see note on gala] a small bell J IV.259, 413; (suvaṇṇa°); Vv 78[1] (=kinkiṇi VvA 303); Vin III.42 (kinkiṇikā saddo).

-jāla a net or fringe of tinkling bells D II.183; J I.32; DhA I.274.

Kicca (nt.) [grd. of karoti=Sk. kṛtya] 1. (adj.) that which ought to be done, that which is to be performed; nt. something to do DhA I.15. Def[d] as kātabban ti kiccaŋ, kiñcid eva karaṇīyan ti KhA 218; kattabaŋ karaṇiyaŋ DhA III.452. — 2. (nt.) (a) duty, obligation, service, attention; ceremony, performance. The sg. is used collectively as pl. — adj. (—°) one who is under an obligation, etc., or to whom an obligation, etc., is due A II.67; Dh 276, 293; J III.26; DhA I.5. — kattabbak°-karaṇa "the performance of incumbent duties" PvA 30; idaŋ me kiccaŋ akāsi "he has done me this service" PvA 29. — In special sense of the duties to the dead: ahaŋ tava pitu °ŋ karomi "I will do the last duty to your father" PvA 274. — a° that which is not (his) duty A II.67; Dh 292, 293. — (b) (as philos. term) function; rasa (essence) is either kicca r°- or sampatti r, function or property. *Cpd.* 13, 213, n. l.; Vism 162 (parivyatta° quite conspicuous f.), 264 (abbhañjana° f. of lucubrating), 338, 493 (indriyānaŋ kiccaŋ), 547 (tad-ārammaṇa°, bhavanga°, cuti°, etc.); kiccavasena by way of f. Abhdh.-sangaha v.8, cp. *Dhs. trsl.* 132 (with ref. to DhsA 264); kiccato Vism 581. —appa° having few or no duties Sn 144 (cp. KhA 241. —ārāmika° duties of the Ārāma J I.38. —udaka° water-performance, ablution D II.15. —kata° one who has performed his duties or mission, i. e. an Arahant Sn 1105; Vv 53[1] (cp. VvA 231. —bahu° having many obligations, being very busy A III.116 sq. —bhatta° meal DA I.45 sq.; PvA 76; freq. in formula kata° (see kata), cp. kat-anna-kicca Dāvs I.59. —mata° funeral rites PvA 274. —sarīra° the duties of the body, i. e. funeral rites PvA 74). — *Note.* In comp[n] with kud° kicca appears as kuk-kucca (q. v.).

-**ākiccā** pl. (kicca+kicca, see Trenckner, Notes *J.P.T.S.* 1908, 127; cp. ṭhānāṭhāna, bhavābhava maggāmagga, phalāphala, etc.) duties of all kinds, various duties: ativasā assu kiccākiccesu "they shall serve me in all duties" Dh 74 (DhA II.78=khuddakamahantesu karaṇīyesu "in small and great duties"); °esu yuttapayutto māṇavo (cp. a maid "of all work") VvA 298; °esu ussukā endeavouring to do all duties Sn 298 (but expl[d] at SnA 319 as "zeal in what is to be done and what is not to be done," taken as kicca+akicca cp. akicca); -**ādhikaraṇa** settlement of the agenda at formal meetings of a chapter Vin II.89=III.164; III.168; V.101 sq.; 150 sq.; See *Vin Texts* III.45; -**kara** doing one's duty S I.91; Sn 676; -**karaṇīyāni** pl.=kiccākicca, various duties A IV.87; -**kārin**=kiccakara A III.443.

Kiccayatā (f.) [abstr. fr. last] duty Vin II.89 (k° karaṇīyatā); Miln 42.

Kiccha [see kasira] 1. (adj.) (a) distressed, in difficulty, poor, miserable, painful: kicchā vatâyaŋ idha vutti yaŋ jano passati kibbisakārī (miserable is the life of one who does wrong) Sn 676=parihīnattha, in poverty PvA 220 (kicco=kiccho). — (b) difficult to obtain, hard, troublesome Dh 182 (kiccho manussapaṭilābho, DhA 235=dullabho). — 2. (nt.) distress, misery, pain, suffering: kicchaŋ āpanno loko D II.30; S II.5; °ŋ vā so nigacchati "he gets into difficulties (i. e. becomes poor)" J V.330 (=dukkhaŋ nigacchati); Vism 314; DhA I.80. — Oblique cases used adverbially: instr. kicchena with difficulty J I.147, 191 (paṭijaggita); V.331 (id.) abl. kicchā id. J V.330. — **akiccha** (°-) without

difficulty, easily, in phrase akiccha-lābhin taking or sharing willingly (+ kasira-lābhin) M I.33, 354 = S II.278 = A II.23, 36; A III.31, 114.
-patta fallen into misery Pv III.5[4] (= PvA 199 dukkhappatta) -vuttin living in misery, poor Pv II.9[14] (= dukkhajīvita).

Kicchati [v. denom. fr. kiccha, cp. Sk. kṛcchrāyate] to be troubled, to be wearied, to suffer Th I, 962 (w. acc. of obj.); usually with kilamati: k° kāyo kilamati Th I, 1073. Used in a play of words with vicikicchati by Bdhgh at Dhs.[A] 354 as "ārammaṇaŋ nicchetuŋ asakkonto kicchati kilamati" and at Bdhd. 25 (on vicikicchā) as sabhāvaŋ vicinanto etāya kicchati kilamati.

Kiñcana (adj.-nt.) [kiŋ + cana, equal to kiŋ + ci, indef. pron.] only in neg. sentences: something, anything. From the freq. context in the older texts it has assumed the moral implication of something that sticks or adheres to the character of a man, and which he must get rid of, if he wants to attain to a higher moral condition. — Def. as the 3 impurities of character (rāga, dosa, moha) at D III.217; M I.298; S IV.297; Vbh 368; Nd[2] 206[b] (adding māna, diṭṭhi, kilesa, duccarita); as obstruction (palibujjhana), consisting in rāga, etc. at DhA III.258 (on Dh 200). Khīṇa-saŋsāro na c'atthi kiñcanaŋ "he has destroyed saŋsāra and there is no obstruction (for him)" Th I, 306. n'āhaŋ kassaci kiñcanaŋ tasmiŋ na ca mama katthaci kiñcanaŋ n'atthi "I am not part of anything (i. e. associated with anything), and herein for me there is no attachment to anything" A II.177.— akiñcana (adj.) having nothing Miln 220. — In special sense "being without a moral stain," def. at Nd[2] 5 as not having the above (3 or 7) impurities. Thus freq. an attribute of an Arahant: "yassa pure ca pacchā ca majjhe ca n'atthi kiñcanaŋ akiñcanaŋ anādānaŋ tam ahaŋ brūmi brāhmaṇan" Dh 421 = Sn 645, cf. Th I. 537; kāme akiñcano "not attached to kāma" as Ep. of a khīṇāsava A V.232 sq. = 253 sq. Often comb[d] with anādāna: Dh 421; Sn 620, 645, 1094.—Akiñcano kāmabhave asatto "having nothing and not attached to the world of rebirths" Vin I.36; Sn 176, 1059; —akiñcanaŋ nânupatanti dukkhā "ill does not befall him who has nothing" S I.23. — sakiñcana (adj.) full of worldly attachment Sn 620 = DA 246.

Kiñcikkha (nt.) [E. Müller *P. Gr.* p. 35 expl[s] kiñcid + ka] a trifle, a small thing: yaŋ vā taŋ vā appamattakaŋ Sn 121; 131; PugA 210 (III.4). āmisa-kiñcikkha-hetu "for the sake of a little gain" A I.128 = Pug 29; at Pv II.8[3] as āmisa-kiñci-hetu (but all vv. ll. B. have °kiñcakkha°) "for some food" (expl[d] at PvA 107: kiñci āmisaŋ patthento); —katā kiñcikkhabāvanā at S IV.118 is evidently corrupt (v. l. °bhādhanā for bādhanā ?).
-kamyatā in the desire for some little thing Sn 121 (cp. SnA 179: appamattake kismiñcid eva icchāya).

Kiñjakkha (m. nt.) [cp. Sk. kiñjalka & remarks at Aufrecht *Halāyudha* p. 186] a filament, esp. of the lotus S III.130; J I.66, 183; V.39; Vv 22[1]; -vāri° Pv II.1[20] (= kesara PvA 77) in comb[n] with kesara VvA 12, 111, 175.

Kiṭaka [doubtful] only at Pv I.9[2,4] of clothes which are changed into missā kiṭakā, which is expl. at PvA 44 by kiṭakasadisāni lohapaṭṭasadisāni bhavanti "they become like (hot) copper plates."

Kiṭika at Vin II.153 of ālinda, a verandah, said to be saŋsaraṇa° ugghāṭana° (a movable screen or a curtain that can be drawn aside) *Vin Texts* III.174, 176.

Kiṭṭha [cp. Sk. kṛṣṭa **kṛṣ**] growing corn, the crop on the ground, a cornfield A III.393 (in simile), cp. S IV.195.
-āda eating corn A III.393. -ārakkha the guardian of the cornfield S IV.196. -sambādha "when the corn is thick," in °*samaye* near harvest-time M I.115 (in simile); J I.143 (sassa-samaye +), 338.

Kiṇakiṇāyati [= kinkiṇāyati, denom. fr. kinkiṇi, small bell] to tinkle; also spelt kiṇikiṇāyati J III.315. See also kilikilāyati and cp. Sk. kiṭikiṭāyati to grind (one's teeth) & Prk. kiḍikiḍiya (chattering) Weber, *Bhagavatī* p. 289; also BSk. kaṭakaṭāyati Tal. Vist. 251. See taṭataṭayati & note on gala.

Kiṇāti [**krī** Vedic kriṇāti] to buy Vism 318; pot. kiṇe J V.375; ger. kiṇitvā M I.384; J I.92, 94; inf. kiṇituŋ J III.282.

Kiṇi (indecl.) a part., expressing the sound of a small bell: "tink" DhA I.339 (v. l. kiri; see also kili and note on gala).

Kiṇṇa[1] [cp. Sk. kiṇva] ferment, yeast; Vin II.116; VvA 73.

Kiṇṇa[2] [pp. of kirati] strewn, scattered, covered; only in comp[n] with prefixes: ā°, o°, ud°, upa°, pari°, saŋ°; see also appa°.

Kiṇha (adj.) [see kaṇha; DA I.254 kiṇhā ti kaṇhā, kāḷakā ti attho] black; in the stock phrase muṇḍakā samaṇakā ibbhā k° bandhupādâpaccā D I.90 = 116; S IV.117; M I.334; II.177; in a moral sense = bad, wicked, with nâlam-ariyā dhammā D I.163.

Kita [pp. of **kṛ**, with i for a, cp. kiraṇa for karaṇa. The Dhtp. expl[d] by nivāsane] 1. adorned: mālā° adorned with garlands Vin III.249. — 2. soiled, only in cpds. kaṇṇa° said of a wall, also of the ground at Vin I.48 = II.209; and paŋsu°, soiled with dust Vin II.101, 174.

Kitava & kitavā [= kaṭavā ? cp. kaṭa] one who plays false; a cheat; adj. deceitful S I.24; J V.116; 117 (a°); -kitavā at Dh 252 (= DhA III.375) in comb[t] with saṭha also at J VI.228, where the connection with kaṭa is evident: kaṭaŋ Aḷāto gaṇhāti kitavā sikkhito yathā = like one who is skilled in having the kaṭa, the lucky die. Expl[d] at DhA III.375 as taken from fowling: kitavāya attabhāvaŋ paṭicchādeti "he hides himself by means of a pretence" (behind sham branches).

Kittaka (pron. interr.) [fr. kīva, cp. ettaka & BSk. kettaka (MVastu I.50); see Trenckner, *Notes* p. 134] how much? how great? nt. as adv.: to what extent? pl.: how many? Vin I.297; k°ŋ antovassaŋ avasiṭṭhaŋ "how much of the rainy season is left?" VvA 66; kittakā pana vo bhante parivāra-bhikkhū? "How many bhikkhus are in your retinue?" J I.32. — As indef.: a little; kittakaŋ jīvissāmi, J V.505; kittakaŋ addhānaŋ a short time VvA 117 (= kiŋva ciraŋ).

Kittana (nt.) [f. kitteti] praise PvA 31, 107.

Kittāvatā (adv.) to what extent? how far? in what respect? K° nu kho mahāpurisa hoti "in what respect is a man a great man?" Nd[2] 502 B; k° nu kho paññavā ti vuccati? M I.292.

Kitti & Kittī f. [Vedic kīrti, ***qer**: cp. Gr. καρκαίρω, Ohg. hruod, hruom = Ger. ruhm; ***qār**: cp. Sk. kāru poet; Gr. κῆρυξ herald, Lat. carmen hymn of praise. — The expl[ns] of Dhtp (579) & Dhtm (812) are *saŋsadde & saŋsaddane*] fame, renown, glory, honour, yaso ca kitti ca S I.25; kittiñ ca sukhañ ca S I.187; yaso kitti sukhañ ca A II.32 yaso kitti ca "fame and renown" Sn 817 (= Nd[1] 147, where appl. to the religious perfection attained by a samaṇa); Sn 185 (in the same sense); VvA 68 (bāhira°-bhāva becoming known outside); yaso kitti Sdhp 234.
-sadda the sound of fame, praise, renown (thutighosa DA I.146) esp. appl[d] to the Buddha, whose fame is heralded before him: Bhagavantaŋ Gotamaŋ evaŋ

kalyāṇo k°-saddo abbhuggato "the high reputation went forth over the world, concerning the Venerable Gotama": (such is this Exalted One, Arahant, etc.) D I.49, 87, 115, 116, 236; S IV.323, 374; V.352; A I.57, 180; III.30, 39, 58, 253, 267; IV.80; etc. The same with reference to others: Miln 284. Appl^d to the good reputation of a man (of a kalyāṇamitta) at Pug 37; the opposite is pāpako kittisaddo, bad reputation: A I.126; III.269; Pug 36; -vaṇṇa praise, in °hara receiving or deserving praise D III.191; cp. °bhatā Nd[1] 147.

Kittika (adj.) [fr. kitti] famous VvA 200.

Kittita (pp. of kitteti] told Bdhd 124; su° well told Sn 1057.

Kittima (adj.) [cp. Sk. kṛtimā, der. fr. kṛti, karoti, in sense of kata I.2 (a) made up, artificial; clever, skilful ThA 227; DhA 391 (of nāma); VvA 275 (of ratha: cleverly constructed)]. Cp. also kutta, — f. kittimā at J III.70; VI.508 is according to Kern, *Toev.* s. v. a misspelling for tittima.

Kitteti [v. den. fr. kitti] 1. to praise, extol PvA 124, 162; — 2. to proclaim, announce, relate, tell; ppr. kittento praising PvA 159. — *fut.* kittayissati in sense of aor. Vv 34[5] (=katheti VvA 151). -kittayissāmi I shall relate Sn 1053, 1132. *grd:* kittanīya to be praised PvA 9. — *aor.* akittayi Sn 875, 921. — pp. kittita.

Kinnara [kiŋ + nara, lit. what-man, see kiŋ 3] a little bird with a head like a man's] J IV.106, 254, 438, V.47, 456; Mil 267. Canda kinnara Np. J I.91, VI.283, VI.74. — f. kinnarā Np. of a queen J V. 437 sq., and kinnarī Th 2, 381 (cp. ThA 255), J II.121 (matta-kinnarī viya), 230; IV.432 sq. Cp. kimpurisa.

Kinnāma see under kiŋ.

Kipillikā (f.) & **Kipillaka** (nt.) [Cp. Sk. pipīlikā, see Trenckner, *Notes*, p. 108] an ant Sn 602 (kuntha°); DhA I.360; J IV.142 (kuntha°); V.39 (tamba°-°āni); Miln 272. — **kipillaka** J I.487 (v. l. BB. for pillaka); IV.375 (tamba°-puṭa); DhA IV.134 (v. l. SS. for T. pillaka). — Cp. kuntha & pipīlikā.

Kibbisa (nt.) [Ved. kilbiṣa, according to Grassmann to ***kil** as in kilāsa, thus originally "stain, dirt." Buddh. Sk. kilviṣa classed with aparādha at Mvyntp. 245 No. 903] wrongdoing, demerit, fault, usually with °ŋ karoti to do wrong Sn 246; Sdhp, 204; J III.135 or °ŋ pasavati A V.75; Vin II.198. -kata° (adj.) having done wrong in akata-kalyāṇo, etc. A II.174 and ≈(see kalyāṇa and kata II.1 a); M I.39; Pv IV.7[7]; PvA 59. -kāraka[1] = next J III.14; -kārin, doing wrong Sn 665 sq.; PvA 58.

Kibbisaka = kibbisa Sdhp 290.

Kimi m. [Vedic kṛmi] a worm, vermin: setā kimī kaṇhasīsā A III.241; Miln 272; DA I.199; — As animal of death and putrefaction M I.507; J I.146; Sn 201; esp. with ref. to the punishment of Petas: Pv I.3[1]; Th 2, 439; PvA 192; Sdhp 603. As glow-worm M II.34, 41 (with khajjopanaka); sālaka° a very minute insect Miln 312. In similes: Th 1, 1175 (kimī va milhasallitto); Vism 500, 598. In cpd. kimi-kula the worm kind (genus worm) Miln 100; Vism 235; °gaṇa crowd of worms Vism 314.

Kimina (adj.) [from kimi] covered with worms J V.270.

Kira (& **Kila**) [Vedic kila] adv. 1. emphatic: really, truly, surely. (Gr. δή) — 2. presumptive (with pres. or fut.): I should think one would expect. — 3. narrative (with aor.): now, then, you know (Gr. δέ, Lat. at, G. aber). — kira in continuous story is what "iti" is in direct or indirect speech. It connects new points in a narrative with something preceding, either as expected or guessed. It is aoristic in character (cp. Sk. sma). In questions it is dubitative, while in ordinary statements it gives the appearance of probability, rather than certainty, to the sentence. Therefore the definitions of commentators: "people say" or "I have heard": kira-saddo *anussavane*: "kira refers to a report by hearsay" PvA 103; kira-saddo *anussav'atthe* J I.158; VvA 322 are conventional and one-sided, and in both cases do not give the meaning required at the specified passages. The same holds good for J I.158 & II.430 (kirā ti anussavatthe nipāto). — 1. mahantaŋ kira Bārāṇasirajjaŋ "the kingdom of B. is truly great" J I.126; attā hi kira duddamo "self is difficult to subdue, we know" Dh 159; amoghaŋ kira me puṭṭhaŋ Sn 356. — na kira surely not Sn 840; J I.158. — 2. esā kira Visākhā nāma "that I presume is the Visākhā" (of whom we have heard) DhA I.399; petā hi kira jānanti "the petas, I should say, will know" Pv II.7[10]; evaŋ kira Uttare? "I suppose this is so, Uttarā" VvA 69. evaŋ kira saggaŋ gamissatha "thus you will surely go to Heaven" Vv 82[8]; "I hear" DhA I.392. — 3. atīte kira with aor. once upon a time . . . PvA 46, etc.; so kira pubbe . . . akāsi, at one time, you know, he had made . . . J I.125; sā kira dāsi adāsi now the maid gave her . . . PvA 46; cp. J I.195, etc.

Kiraṇa (nt.) 1. [fr. kṛ, karoti to do] an occupation, place of work, workshop J IV.223. Cp. kita & kittima. — 2. [fr. kṛ, kirati to scatter, cp. pp. kiṇṇa] scattering, effusion (of sun rays), effulgence VvA 169, 199.

Kirati [kīr] to scatter, strew; not found in simples, only in cpds. apa°, abbhuk°, abhi°, ava° (o°), pari°, vi°. See also pp. **kiṇṇa**[2].

Kirāta (& **kirāṭa**) [prob. dial.] a man of a tribe of junglemen, classed with dwarfs among the attendants of a chief DA I.148. See on the Kirāta as a mountain tribe Zimmer, *Altindisches Leben* p. 34. Cp. also apakiritūna & okirati[2], okiraṇa. — A secondary meaning of kirāṭa is that of a fraudulent merchant, a cheat (see kirāsa & kerāṭika).

Kirāsa (adj.) [a by-form of kirāṭa] false, fraudulent J IV.223 (= kerāṭika).

Kiriyati [Pass. of kīrati or karoti] to be affected or moved Vism. 318.

Kiriya, **Kiriyā** & **Kriyā** [abstr. fr. karoti] 1. (n.) — (a) (—°) action, performance, deed; the doing = fulfilment; cp. °karaṇa, anta°, making an end of, putting a stop to (dukkhassa) S III.149; IV.93; Sn 454, 725; —kāla° "fulfilment of one's time" i. e. death S III.122; Pv I.10[12]; Sn 694; Pug 17; kusala° performance of good actions S I.101; V.456; dāna° the bestowing of gifts PvA 123; pāpa° commission of sin Pug 19 = 23; puñña° the performance of good works S I.87 = 89 = A III.48; a° PvA 54 mangala° celebration of a festival PvA 86; massu-kiriyā the dressing of the beard J III.314 (cp. m-karaṇa and kappanā); sacchi° realization, see s. v. -akiriyā the non-performance of, omission, abstaining from (a° akaraṇa = veramaṇī) J III.530; Vbh 285. — (b) an act in a special sense = promise, vow, dedication, intention, pledge: PvA 18; justice: Miln 171; kiriyaŋ bhindati to break one's vow Miln 206. — (c) philosophically: action ineffective as to result, non-causative, an action which ends in itself (Mrs. Rh. D. in *Dhs. trsl.* xciii.), inoperative (see *Cpd.* 19). In this sense it is grouped with kamma (cp. for relation kamma: kiriyā = Ger. sache: ursache). Thus is the theory of Makkhali: n'atthi kammaŋ, n'atthi kiriyaŋ n'atthi viriyan ti = there is no karma, no after-effect and no vigour in this world A I.286 (different at D I.53); n'atthi kiriyā it does not matter M I.405. — 2. (adj.) (a) making no difference, indefinite; of no result, as def. of avyākatā dhammā Vbh 106, 182 = 302 = Dhs 566 and 989 (manodhātu kiriyā neva kusalā nâkusalā na ca kammavipākā: indifferent, neither good nor bad and having no fruit of kamma), same of jhāna Vbh 268 = 281; DhsA 388. — (b) indecisive, in akiriyaŋ vyākaroti to give an indecisive answer, to reply evasively D I.53 and≈

-pada (ttg.) the verb (i. e. that which supplies the action) VvA 315; -vāda (adj.) promulgating the (view of a) consequence of action, believing in merit and demerit, usually comb^d with kammavāda (q. v.) also °vādin: D I.115 (of Gotama) A I.62; Vin I.71; a°-denying the difference between merit & demerit A IV.174 = Vin I.234; 242, Vin III.2; A IV.180 sq.; S III.73. (+natthikavāda); -vādin adj. to prec. A I.62; -hetu being a cause of discrimination Dhs 1424 sq.

Kiriyatā (f.) [abstr. fr. last] the performance of (—°), state of, etc. See sakkacca°, sacchi°, sātacca°.

Kiriṭin (adj.) enveloped, adorned Pv III.9¹ (= veṭhitasīsa).

Kila see kili (the sound click).

Kilañjā (f.) a mat of fibre or rushes, matting Vism 327; also a screen, a fascine, hurdle, faggots; a crate, crating: tassa gandhabbaŋ kilañjā-kaṇḍūvanaŋ viya hutvā . . . J II.249; "his music was like the scraping of a mat"; suvaṇṇa-kilañjā a gilt mat J IV.212. As a fascine, used in making a road: DhA I.442. as a screen (comb^d with chatta, fan) PvA 127; as faggots: J I.158; Miln 287; as a crate or basket, used by distillers: M I.228 = 374 (soṇḍikā-kilañjā) (cp. the trsl^n under soṇḍa in *J.P.T.S.* 1909); to which is likened the hood of a snake: S I.106 (snake = māra).

Kilanta [pp. of kilamati] tired, exhausted, weary, either with **°kāya** tired in body PvA 43; VvA 65 (indicating the falling asleep); or °citta tired in mind D I.20 = III.32 (paduṭṭhacitta+, of the waning of the gods); or both **°kāya-citta** Pv III.2³; opp. akilanta-kāya-citta alert, vigorous; with sound body and mind.

Kilama [spelt klama, fr. **klam**] fatigue J V.397 (= kilanta-bhāva).

Kilamati [Sk. klamati, a variation of śramati **srī** from **sri** to lean, cp. kilanta, as "sleepy," and Lat. clīnāre, clemens. To k > ś cp. kaṇṇa > śṛnga, kilissati > śliṣyati, etc. The Dhtp (222) & Dhtm (316) paraphrase **kilam** by *gilāne*.] 1. to go short of, to be in want of (instr.) DhA II.79; na piṇḍakena kilamati does not go short of food Vin II.15. 87; IV.23 sq. — 2. to weary, to be wearied, tired, fatigued; to be in trouble or in misery PvA 215 (to be incommodated) 277 (be in distress); fut. kilamissāmi PvA 76. Cp. pari°. — pp. **kilanta.**

Kilamatha [fr. **klam**, in formation cp. samatha] tiredness, fatigue, exhaustion M I.168; A II.199; S I.136; as kāya°, citta° S V.128; as daratha° A III.238; PvA 23; as niddā° A II.48, 50.

Kilamita [pp. of kilameti] worn out, tired, fatigued Pv II.8³.

Kilameti [denom. fr. kilama] to be tired or fatigued J I.115; ppr. kilamayanto D I.52. — pp. **kilamita.**

Kilāsa [cp. Sk. kilāsa] a cutaneous disease, perhaps leprosy, enum^d under the var. diseases (ābādhā) together with kuṭṭha gaṇḍa k° sosa Vin II.271; A V.110; Nd² 304¹.

Kilāsika & **°iya** (adj.) [fr. last] afflicted with a cutaneous disease, a leper, in same comb^n as kilāsa, Vin I.93; Kvu 31 (°iya).

Kilāsu [fr. **sram**, cp. kilamatha. E Müller *P. Gr.* 38 = glāsnu, **glā**, cp. gilāna] exhausted, tired of (c. dat. or inf.) Vin III.8; a° untiring in (c. dat. or acc.) S I.47; V.162; J I.109; Miln 382.

Kili (sometimes **kila**) [onomat. fr. sound-root **kḷ**] 1. indecl. the sound "click," of the noise of a trap when shutting J I.243; II.363, 397 (as "kili"). — Also repeated "kilikili ti" click, click J I.70. — 2. as n. f. tinkling, clicking, ticking (cp. kiṇi), in kiliŋ karoti to tinkle J V.203.

Kilikilāyati [denom. fr. kili with reduplication] to tinkle J V.206; (freq. fr. kili or den. fr. kilikilā; cp. kilakilā "shouting for joy" AvŚ I.48 and in cpd. hāhākāra-kilakilā "shouting hā-hā and hail-hail" ibid. I.67 MVastu III.312 and Divy 459). See also kiṇakiṇāyati. *Note.*—**Kil** is one of the variations of the sound-imitating *q^el*, which otherwise appears as *q^al*, *q^ul* in Gr. κελ-αδος, L. cal-are, Ohg. hell-an (cp. Sk. krandati ?) also Gr. κλάζω, L. clango, Goth. hlahjan ("laugh") and in Sk kolāhala, kokila, cp. cuculus (cuckoo) and perhaps Sk. ululī, ulūka (owl), Gr. ὀλολύζω, L. ululare. See also the cognate *q^er* under kitti.

Kilijjati [med-pass. of **kilid** = Sk. **klid**, to be wet. prob. = **śliṣ** to stick to, and confounded with **svid**, cp. also kelana & khela. The meaning "to get wet, to be soiled" only in pp. kilinna. — The Dhtm (199), however, expl^s k. by parideva lament, to be in trouble, which is not quite in harmony with the meaning; it is more likely that in P. we have a confusion between **klid** & **kliś** in a meaning which differs from Sk.] to become heated, to get into a state of inflammation, to fester (of wounds) Vin I.205 (vaṇo kilijjittha festered); Sn 671 (gloss for kilissati, expl^d at SnA 481 by pūti hoti). — pp. kilinna. See also **ukkiledeti** (to clean out a stain, to "disinfect").

Kiliṭṭha [pp of kilissati] 1. soiled, stained, impure; of gatta, limbs J I.129; of cīvara, cloak Bdhd 92; of vattha, clothes DhA II.261; of pāvāra-puppha, mango blossom KhA 58 = Vism 258. — 2. unclean, lustful (morally) bad, in **°kamma** dirty pursuit, i. e. cohabitation J IV.190; PvA 195 (of a gaṇikā); together with **kuthita** Miln 250.

Kilinna [pp. of kilijjati] 1. wet, usually with saliva and perspiration Vin III.37; J I.61 (lālā°), 164 (kheḷa°); DA I.284 (assu°); VvA 67 (seda°). — 2. The other meaning of **kilid** (to get inflamed) is to be found in kilinna-sarīra (adj.) with an inflamed body (i. e. suffering from a skin-disease), which is Bdhgh's expl° of okilinī: see under **okiraṇa.**

Kilissati [Sk. kliśyati = **kliś** or **śliṣ** to adhere, cp. P. kheḷa and silesuma or semha, Sk. śleṣma, slime. Same root as Gr. λείμαξ snail; Ags. slīm slime. Another, specifically Pāli, meaning is that of going bad, being vexed, with ref. to a *heated* state. This lies at the bottom of the Dhtp. (445) & Dhtm. (686) expl^n by *upatāpe*.] 1. to get wet, soiled or stained, to dirty oneself, be impure It 76 (of clothes, in the passing away of a deva); Th 1, 954 (kilisissanti, for kilissanti); Ps I.130. Kilisseyya Dh 158 (expl^d as nindaŋ labhati) to do wrong. Cp. pari°.

Kilissana (nt.) getting dirty, staining J I.8.

Kilesa (and **klesa**) [from kilissati] 1. stain, soil, impurity, fig. affliction; in a moral sense, depravity, lust. Its occurrence in the Piṭakas is rare; in later works, very frequent, where it is approx. tantamount to our terms lower, or unregenerate nature, sinful desires, vices, passions.

1. Kilesa as obstacle (see °āvaraṇa, °-sampayutta, °-vippayutta, °pahāna) Ps I.33; Sdhp 455; bhikkhu

bhinnakileso "one whose passions are broken up" Vbh 246, PvA 51; upasanta kileso "one whose passions are calmed" PvA 230; no ce pi jātu puriso kilese vāto yathā abbhaghanaŋ vihāne Sn 348; pariyodapeyya attānaŋ cittaklesehi paṇḍito S v.24 = A v.232, 253 = Dh 88. 2. Occurs in such combinations as kilesā ca khandhā ca abhisankhārā ca Nd² 487; kilesa + khandha: Ps I.69-72; II.36, 140; cp. Vbh 44, 68; kilesa + saŋsāra PvA 7; kammaŋ kilesā hetu saŋsārassa Nett 113, cp. 191. — 3. kilesa also occurs in a series explanatory of taṇhā, in the stereotype combⁿ of t., diṭṭhi, kilesa "clinging to existence, false ideas and lust" (see Nd² s. v. taṇhā v.). — 4. In the same function it stands with rāga, viz. rāga dosa moha kilesa, i. e. sensuality, bewilderment and lust (see Nd² s. v. rāga II.), cp. Dhs 982, 1006. — The grouping as dasa kilesa-vatthūni is: lobha dosa moha māna diṭṭhi vicikicchā thinaŋ uddhaccaŋ ahirikaŋ anottappaŋ Dhs 1548 = Vbh 341; Vism 683; mentioned at Ps I.130. — These with the exception of the last two, are also grouped as aṭṭha k°-vatthūni at Vbh 385.—As three kilesas (past, present and future) at Ps II.217. — 5. The giving up of kilesa is one of the four essentials of perfection: the recognition of evil, the removal of its source (which is kilesa), the meditation on the Path, and the realization of the extinction of evil (see Nd² s. v. dukkha II.). Kilesa in this connection interchanges with samudaya, as denoting the *origin* of evil; cp. samudayo kilesā Nett 191.

-āvaraṇa the obstacle of lust Vbh 342 = Pug 13; Vism 177; °āvaraṇatā id. A III.436; **-kkhaya** the destruction of lust Bdhd 81; -paripantha danger of lust J VI.57; -pahāna the giving up of worldly lust Vin III.92 sq., IV.25; Bdhd 129, 131; -puñja the heap of lusts; consisting of ten qualities, viz. the four āhārā (etc. four of each:), vipallāsā, upādānāni, yogā, gandhā, āsavā, oghā, sallā, viññāṇaṭṭhitiyo, agatigamanāni. Nett 113, 114; 116 sq. -bhūmi the substratum or essence of lust Nett 2, 192; there are four mentioned at Nett 161: anusaya°, pariyuṭṭhāna°, saŋyojana°, upādāna°; **-māra** death which is the consequence of sinful desire DhA I.317 (in expl. of Māra); **-vatthūni** (pl.) the (10) divisions of kilesa (see above) Dhs 1229, 1548; Vism 20. -vinaya the discipline of lust Nett 22; **-vippayutta** free from lust (dhamma principles, to which belongs Nibbāna) Dhs 1555; -sampayutta connected or affected with lust Dhs 1554 (as 12 principles); Vbh 18 = 30 = 44 = 56, 68, 80, 96, 120, 323.

Kileseti [v. den. fr. kilesa] to become soiled or stained (fig.): indriyāni kilesenti Sdhp. 364.

Kiloma [= next ?] at J III.49 taken as syn. of loma, hair and used in sense of pharusa, shaggy, rough (in kiloma maŋsakhaṇḍa as simile for kiloma-vācā).

Kilomaka [= Sk. kloman, the right lung, cp. Greek πλεύμων, Lat. pulmo] the pleura M I.185 = Kh III, Nett 77 = Vbh 193; J IV.292; Miln 26. Discussed in detail at Vism 257, 357.

Kisa (adj.) [Sk. kṛśa, perhaps to Lat. gracilis, slim] lean, haggard, emaciated, opp. thūla fat (VvA 103). As Ep. of ascetics Sn 165, Dh 395 = Th 1, 243; esp. as Ep. of petas: Pv II.1¹³; Sn 426, 585; Sdhp 101; Miln 303. For phrase kisa-dhamani-santhata see the latter.

Kisaka = kisa Vin I.36 = J I.83; f. kisikā Th 2, 27.

Kissati [den. fr. kisa] 1. to get thin, to become exhausted, to waste, weary, worry J VI.495 (pret. mā kisittha = C. mā kisā bhava). — 2. [Pass. of kassati, **kṛṣ**] see pari°.

Kissava in neg. akissava at S I.149 is doubtful in origin and meaning. The trslⁿ gives "without wisdom." Should we read akittima or akiñcana, as we suggested under a°, although this latter does not quite agree with the sense required ?

Kīṭa (nt.) [cp. Sk. kīṭa] a general term for insect DhA I.187; usually in combⁿ with paṭanga, beetle (moth ?) M III.168 (with puḷava); Sn 602; J VI.208; Miln 272 (°vaṇṇa); PvA 67; Vism 115. **kīṭa** at J v.373 means a kind of shield (= cāṭipāla ? c.), the reading should prob. be kheṭa.

Kīṭaka (nt.) one or all kinds of insects Vin I.188.

Kīta [pp. of kiṇāti] bought J I.224 (°dāsa a bought slave) II.185.

Kīdisa (interr. adj.) [cp. Sk. kīdṛś = kiŋ dṛśa] what like ? of what kind ? which ? (cp. tādisa) Sn 836, 1089 (= kiŋ saṇṭhita Nd²; Pv II.6³; PvA 50, 51; VvA 76). — As Np. S IV.193. — See also Kīrisa.

Kīra [cp. Sk. kīra] a parrot Abhp 640 (cp. cirīṭi).

Kīrisa = kīdisa Th 2, 385 (cp. ThA 256).

Kīla = a pin, a stake, see Khīla.

Kīḷati [Sk. krīḍati] to play, sport, enjoy or amuse oneself Vin IV.112 (udake k. sport in the water); Pv II.1²¹ (= indriyāni paricarāmi PvA 77) D II.196; J v.38; Th 2, 147; PvA 16, 67, 77, 189; — c. acc. to celebrate: nakkhattaŋ J I.50; VvA 63; PvA 73; ThA 137; chaṇaŋ DhA III.100. — pp. kīḷita. Caus. II. **kīḷāpeti** to make play, to train J II.267 (sappaŋ to train or tame a snake).

Kīḷanaka [fr. kiḷati] a plaything, a toy Th 2, 384 (with ref. to the moon).

Kīḷanā (f.) [fr. same) playing, sport, amusement Nett 18; PvA 67; DhA III.461 (nakkhatta° celebration).

Kīḷā f. [fr. **krīḍ**, cp. Sk. krīḍā] play, sport, enjoyment; udakakiḷaŋ kiḷanti enjoying herself on the water PvA 189. — uyyāna° amusement in the park DhA I.220; IV. 3; nakkhatta-kiḷaŋ kiḷati to celebrate a festival (i. e. the full moon when standing in a certain Nakkhatta) VvA 109, ThA 137; sāla-kiḷā sport in the sāla woods J v.38; kiḷādhippāyena in play, for fun PvA 215; — Cp. kiḷikā.

-goḷa a ball to play with Vism 254. **-goḷaka** id. Vism 256 (cp. KhA 53); ThA 255; -pasuta bent on play J I.58; -bhaṇḍaka (nt.) toy Miln 229 (= kiḷāpanaka M I.266); -maṇḍala play-circle, children's games, playground J VI.332; DhA III.146; -sālā playhouse J VI.332.

Kīḷāpanaka 1. (nt.) a plaything, toy M I.266, 384; a list given at A v.203. — 2. (adj.) one who makes play J IV.308 (sappa° a snake-trainer, cp. sappaŋ kiḷāpeti J II.267).

Kīḷikā (f.) play, sport, amusement; always —°, like kumāra° D II.196; uyyāna° (sport in the garden) J III.275; IV.23, 390; udaka° ThA 186.

Kīḷita [pp. of kiḷati] played or having played, playing, sporting; celebrated (of a festival) A IV.55 (hasitalapita°); PvA 76 (sādhu°). —(nt.) amusement, sport, celebration M I.229 (kiḷita-jātaŋ kiḷati). Cp. sahapaŋsu°°; see also keḷi & khiḍḍā.

Kīvant & **Kīva** (interr. adj. and adv.) [Sk. kiyant and kīvant; formed fr. interr. stem ki] how great ? how much ? how many ? and in later language how ? (cp. rel. yāva). As indef.: Kīvanto tattha bheravā "however great the terrors" Sn 959. — Kīva kaṭuka how painful ? PvA 226; k°-ciraŋ how long ? Pj and Sn 1004; k°-dīghaŋ same Sn p. 126; k° dūre how far ? Miln 16; DhA I.386; k°-mahantaŋ how big ? DhA I.29; VvA 325; k° bahuŋ how much ? DhA IV.193.

Kīvatika (interr. adj.) [fr. last] of number: how much ? how many ? Kīvatikā bhikkhū how many Bhikkhus ? Vin I.117.

Ku (kud- and kum-) 3rd stem of interrog. pron. ka (on form and meaning cp. kad; =Lat.* quu in (qu)ubi, like katara < (qu)uter; cp. also Vedic kū how? Sk. kutra, kutaḥ, kuha, kva) where? when? whither? whence? As adv. in cpds. in disparaging sense of "what of"? i. e. nothing of, bad, wrong, little, e. g. kum-magga wrong path: kuk-kucca = kud-kicca doing wrong, troubling about little = worry. —kuŋ at PvA 57 (in expl. of kuñjara) is interpreted as paṭhavi.

1. **Kuto** where from? whence? Dh 62; k°bhayaŋ whence i. e. why fear? Dh 212 sq.; Sn 271, 862; Pv II.6^9; how? J VI.330; with nu whence or why then? Sn 1049 (=kacci ssu Nd^2 s. v.). kut-ettha = kuto ettha J. I.53. -na kuto from nowhere Sn 35, 919; a-kuto id. in akutobhaya "with nothing to fear from anywhere" i. e. with no reason for fear S I.192; Th 1, 510; Th II, 333; Sn 50: (modāmi akutobhayo); Pv II.1^{21} (id.); kuto-ja arisen from where? Sn 270; -°nidāna having its foundation or origin in what? Sn 270, 864 sq.

2. **Kudā** at what time, when? (cp. kadā) Pug 27; indef. kudācanaŋ: at any time, na k° never Sn 221 (expl. by soḷasim pi kalaŋ SnA 277); Dh 5, 210; Bdhd 125; gamanena na pattabbo lokass' anto k° "by walking, the end of the world can never be reached" S I.62.

3. **Kuva, kva**, where? Sn 970 (kuvaŋ & kuva) indef. kvaci anywhere; with na: nowhere; yassa n'atthi upamā kvaci "of whom (i. e. of Gotama) there is no likeness anywhere" Sn 1137; cp. 218, 395; expl^d by Nd^2 like kuhiñci. kuvaŋ at D III.183.

4. **Kutha** (kudha) where? J V.485 (= kuhiŋ).

5. **Kuhiŋ** (= kuhaŋ, cp. Sk. kuha) where? whither? Often with fut.: k° bhikkhu gamissati Sn 411; ko gacchasi where are you going? Pv II.8^1; tvaŋ ettakaŋ divasaŋ k° gatā where have you been all these days? PvA 6; 13; 42; indef. kuhiñci, anywhere, with na k°: nowhere, or: not in anything, in: n'atthi taṇhā k° loke "he has no desire for anything in this world" Sn 496, 783, 1048 see Nd on 783 & 1048 = kimhici; Dh 180.

Kukutthaka (v. l. BB. kukkuṭhaka) a kind of bird J VI.539. Kern (*Toev.* s. v.) takes it to be Sk. kukkutaka, phasianus gallus.

Kukku [cp. Sk. kiṣku?] a measure of length S V.445 = A IV.404, and in kukkukata Vin I.255 = V.172 (cp. however *Vin. Texts* I.154. on Bdhgh's note = temporary).

Kukkuka [fr. kukku] "of the kukku-measure," to be measured by a kukku. Of a stone-pillar, 16 k's high S V.445 = A IV.404. — akukkuka-jāta of enormous height (of a tree) M I.233 = S III.141 (text: akukkajāta) = IV.167; A II.200 (text: akukkuccakajāta). Kern (*Toev.* s. v. kukka) takes it to mean "grown crooked," a° the opposite.

Kukkucca [kud-kicca] 1. bad doing, misconduct, bad character. Def. kucchitaŋ kataŋ kukataŋ tassa bhāvo kukkuccaŋ Vism 470 & Bdhd 24; — Various explanations in Nd^2 on Sn 1106 = Dhs 1160, in its literal sense it is bad behaviour with hands and feet (hattha-pada°) J I.119 = DA I.42 (in comb^n with ukkāsita & khipitasadda); hattha° alone J II.142. — 2. remorse, scruple, worry. In this sense often with vippaṭissāra; and in conn. w. uddhacca it is the fourth of the five nīvaraṇas (q. v.) Vin I.49; IV.70; D I.246; S I.99; M I.437; A I.134 = Sn 1106; A I.282; Sn 925; Nd^2 379; DhA III.483; IV.88; Sdhp 459; Bdhd 96. — na kiñci k°ŋ na koci vippaṭissāreti "has nobody any remorse?" S III.120 = IV.46. The dispelling of scrupulousness is one of the duties and virtues of a muni: k°ŋ vinodetuŋ A V.72; k. pahāya D I.71 = A II.210 = Pug 59; chinnakukkucca (adj.) free from remorse M I.108; khīṇāsava k°-vūpasanta S I.167 = Sn 82. — akukkucca (adj.) free from worry, having no remorse Sn 850. Kukkuccaŋ kurute (c. gen.) to be scrupulous about J I.377; karoŋsu DhA IV.88; cp. kukkuccaŋ āpajjati (expl. by saṅkati) J III.66.

Kukkuccaka (adj.) conscientious (too) scrupulous, "faithful in little" J I.376; VvA. 319.

Kukkuccāyati [denom. fr. kukkucca] to feel remorse, to worry A I.85; Pug 26. Der. are kukkuccāyanā and °āyitatta = kukkucca in def. at Dhs 1160 = Nd^2 s. v

Kukkucciya = kukkucca Sn 972.

Kukkuṭa (Sk. kurkuṭa & kukkuṭa; onomatopoetic = Lat. cucurio, Ger. kikeriki) a cock Miln 363; J IV.58; VvA 163; f. kukkuṭī a hen DhA I.48; ThA 255; in simile M I.104 = 357 = A IV.125 sq., 176 sq. (cp. °potako).

-aṇḍa (kukkuṭ°) a hen's egg Vism 261. -patta the wing of a cock A IV.47. -potaka a chicken, in simile M I.104 = 357 = A IV.126 = 176. -yuddha a cock fight D I.6; -lakkhaṇa divining by means of a cock D I.9; -sampātika a shower of hot ashes (cock as symbol of fire) A I.159 = D III.75, cp. Divy 316 and see Morris, *J.P.T.S.* 1885, 38; -sūkarā (pl.) cocks and pigs D I.5 = A II.209 = Pug 58; D I.141; A II.42 sq.; It 36.

Kukkura [Sk. kurkura, or is it ku-krura? Cp. kurūra) a dog, usually of a fierce character, a hound A III.389; V.271; J I.175 sq.; 189; Pv III.7^9; Sdhp 90. In similes: S IV.198; M I.364; A IV.377. — f. kukkurinī Miln 67.

-vatika (adj.) imitating a dog, cynic M I.387 (+ dukkara kāraka; also as k°-vata, °sīla, °citta, °ākappa); D III.6, 7; Nett 99 (+ govatika; -saṅgha a pack of hounds A III.75.

Kukkuḷa [taken as variant of kukkuṭa by Morris, *J.P.T.S.* 1885, 39; occurs also in BSk. as Name of a Purgatory, e. g. MVastu I.6; III.369, 455. The classical Sk. form is kukūla] hot ashes, embers S III.177; J II.134; Kvu 208, cf. trans. 127; with ref. to Purgatory S I.209; J V.143 (°nāma Niraya); Sdhp 194; Pgdp 24.

-vassa a shower of hot ashes J I.73; IV.389 (v. l.).

Kukkusa 1. the red powder of rice husks Vin II.280 (see Bdgh II.328: kukkusaŋ mattikaŋ = kuṇḍakañ c'eva mattikañ ca). — 2. (adj.) variegated, spotted J VI.539 (= kaḷakabara 540; v. l. B. ukkusa).

Kuṅkuma (nt.) [cp. Sk. kuṅkuma] saffron Miln 382; Vism 241.

Kuṅkumin (adj.) fidgety J V.435.

Kuṅkumiya (nt.) noise, tumult J V.437 (= kolāhala).

Kucchi (f.) [Sk. kukṣiḥ, cp. kośa] a cavity, esp. the belly (Vism 101) or the womb; aṇṇava° the interior of the ocean I.119, 227; J V.416; jāla° the hollow of the net J I.210. As womb frequent, e. g. mātu° J I.149; DA I.224; PvA 19, 63, 111, 195; as pregnant womb containing gabbha J I.50; II.2; VI.482; DhA II.261

-ḍāha enteric fever DhA I.182; -parihārika sustaining, feeding the belly D I.71 = Pug 58; -roga abdominal trouble J I.243; -vikāra disturbance of the bowels Vin I.301; -vitthambhana steadying the action of the bowels (digestion) Dhs 646 = 740 = 875.

Kucchita [Sk. kutsita, pp. of **kutsāy**] contemptible, vile, bad, only in Com^s VvA 215; in def. of kāya KhA 38; in def. of kusala DhsA 39; VvA 169; in def. of kukkucca Vism 470; in def. of paŋsu-kūla Vism 60.

Kucchimant (adj.) [fr. kucchi] pregnant J V.181.

Kujati [or kujjati? see kujja] in kujantā dīnalocanā Sdhp 160: to be bent, crooked, humpbacked?

Kujana (adj.) [fr. kujati] only neg. a° not going crooked, in ratho akujano nāma S I.33.

Kujja (adj.) [Sk. kubja, humpbacked; √qub, Lat. cubare, Gr. κυφός, Mhg. hogger. humpback] lit. "bent," as nt. kujjaŋ in ajjhena-kujjaŋ Sn 242 crookedness, deceit, fraud (cp. SnA 286 kūṭa?). Cp. kujati & khujja, see also ava°, uk°, nik°, paṭi°, pali°.

Kujjhati [cp. Vedic krunhyate, fr. **krudh**] to be angry with (dat.) A I.283 = Pug 32, 48; Vism 306; mā kujjhittha kujjhataŋ, "don't be angry" S I.240; mā kujjhi J III.22; na kujjheyya Dh. 224; ger. kujjhitvā PvA 117, grd. kujjhitabba Pv IV.1.[11]

Kujjhana (adj.) [fr. kujjhati] angry = kodhana VvA 71; Pug A 215 (°bhāva). Kujjhanā (f.) anger, irritation, together with kujjhitattaŋ in defn of kodha Dhs 1060 = Pug 18, 22.

Kujjhāpana (nt.) [Caus. formation fr. kujjhati] being angry at DhA IV.182.

Kuñca (nt.) [kruñc, cp. Sk. krośati, Pali koñca, Lat. crocio, cornix, corvus; Gr. κρώζω, κραυγή; all of crowing noise; from sound-root **kṛ**, see note on gala] a crowing or trumpeting noise (in compounds only). —kāra cackling (of a hen) ThA 255; -nāda trumpeting (of an elephant) J III.114.

Kuñcikā (f.) a key, Bdhgh on C.V. V.29, 2 (Vin II.319) cp. tāla Vin II.148; Vism 251 (°kosaka a case for a key); DA I.200, 207, 252; DhA II.143.

Kuñcita (adj.) [pp. of **kuñc** or **kruñc**; cp. Sk. kruñcati, to be crooked, Lat. crux, Ohg. hrukki, also Sk. kuñcita bent] bent, crooked J I.89 (°kesa with wavy hair); V.202 (°agga: kaṇṇesu lambanti ca kuñcitaggā: expld on p. 204 by sīhakuṇḍale sandhāya vadati, evidently taking kuñcita as a sort of earring); of Petas, Sdhp 102.

Kuñja (m.) a hollow, a glen, dell, used by Dhpāla in expln of kuñjara at VvA 35 (kuñjaro ti kuñje giritale ramati) and PvA 57 (kuŋ pathaviŋ jīrayati kuñjo suvāraŋ aticarati kuñjaro ti). -nadī° a river glen DA I.209.

Kuñjara (m.) [Deriv. unknown. The sound is not unlike an elephant's trumpeting & need not be Aryan, which has hasti. The Sk. of the epics & fables uses both h° and k°] an elephant Vin II.195; M I.229, 375; S I.157; Dh 322, 324, 327; J V.336; Vv 5[1]; Pv I.11[3]; DhA IV.4; ThA 252; Miln 245. -deva° chief of the gods, Ep. of Sakka Vv 47[7]; J V.158.
-vara a state elephant VvA 181. -sālā an elephant's stable DhA IV.203.

Kuṭa a pitcher Vv 50[9]; J I.120; DhA II.19, 261; III.18. Kuṭa is to be read at J I.145 for kūṭa (antokuṭe padīpo viya; cp. ghaṭa). *Note.* Kuṭa at DhsA 263 stands for kūṭa[3] sledge-hammer.

Kuṭaka a cheat Pgdp 12; read kūṭaka So also in gāma kuṭaka S II.258.

Kuṭaja a kind of root (Wrightia antidysenterica or Nericum antidysentericum), used as a medicine Vin I.201 (cp. Vin. Texts II.45).

Kuṭaṭi see paṭi° and cp. kūṭa[1], koṭṭeti & in diff. sense kuṭṭa[1].

Kuṭava (v. l. S. kū°; B. kulāvaka) a nest J III.74; v. l. at DhA II.23 (for kuṭikā).

Kuṭikā (f.) from kuṭī [B. Sk. kuṭikā Av.Ś. II.156] a little hut, usually made of sticks, grass and clay, poetical of an abode of a bhikkhu Vin III.35, 41, 42 = VvA 10; PvA 42, 81; DhA II.23. Cp. also tiṇa°, dāru°; arañña° a hut in the woods S I.61; III.116; IV.380. Often fig. for body (see kāya). Th I, I.—As adj. -°, e. g. aṭṭhakuṭiko gāmo a village of 8 huts Dh I.313.

Kuṭimbika (also kuṭumbika) a man of property, a landlord, the head of a family, J I.68, 126, 169, 225; II.423; PvA 31, 38, 73, 82. Kuṭumbiya-putta Np. Vism 48.

Kuṭila (adj.) bent, crooked (cp. **kuj** and **kuc**, Morris *J.P.T.S.* 1893, 15) J III.112 (= jimha); Miln 297 (°saŋkuṭila), 418 (of an arrow); nt. a bend, a crook Miln 351. -a° straight Vv 16[7] (-magga).
-bhāva crookedness of character Vism 466; PvA 51; VvA 84. -a° uprightness Bdhd 20.

Kuṭilatā (f.) [fr. kuṭila] crookedness, falseness, in a°, uprightness of character Dhs 50, 51; DhA I.173.

Kuṭī (kuṭi°) (f.) any single-roomed abode, a hut, cabin, cot, shed Vin III.144 (on vehāsa-kuṭī see vehāsa & Vin IV.46); Sn 18, 19; Pv II.2[8]; VvA 188, 256 (cīvara°, a cloak as tent). See also kappiya°, gandha°, paṇṇa°, vacca°.
-kāra the making of a hut, in *°sikkhāpada*, a rule regarding the method of building a hut J II.282; III.78, 351; -dūsaka (a) destroying a hut or nest DhA II. 23; -purisa a "hut man," a peasant Miln 147.

Kuṭukuñcaka see kaṭukañcuka.

Kuṭumba (nt.) family property & estates J I.122, 225; rāja° (and °kuṭumbaka) the king's property J I.369, 439. -kuṭumbaŋ saṇṭhapeti to set up an establishment J I.225; II.423; III.376.

Kuṭumbika see kuṭimbika.

Kuṭṭa[1] [cp. koṭṭeti, **kuṭ** to crush, which is expld by Dhtp (90, 555) & Dhtm (115, 781) together with **koṭṭ** by chedana; it is there taken together with **kuṭ** of kūṭa[1], which is expld as koṭilla] powder. Sāsapa° mustard powder Vin I.205; II.151 (at the latter passage to be read for °kuḍḍa, cp. *Vin Texts* III.171), 205.

Kuṭṭa[2] [of doubtful origin & form, cp. var. BSk. forms koṭṭa-rājā, koṭa° & koḍḍa°, e. g. MVastu I.231] only found in cpds. °dārūni sticks in a wattle & daub wall Vism 354, and in kuṭṭa-rājā subordinate prince, possibly kuḍḍa° a wattle and daub prince S III.156 (v. l. kuḍḍa°); = V.44 (v. l. kujja°); cp. kuḍḍa° J V.102 sq., where expl. pāpa-rājā, with vv. ll. kuta and kūṭa. See also khujja and khuddaka-rājā.

Kuṭṭha[1] (nt.) (cp. **kuṣ**; Sk. kuṣṭhā f.) leprosy J V.69, 72, 89; VI.196, 383; Vism 35 (+gaṇḍa); DA I.260, 261, 272. The disease described at DhA 161 sq. is probably leprosy. Cp. kilāsa. On var. kinds of leprosy see J V.69, IV.196.

Kuṭṭha[2] a kind of fragrant plant (Costus speciosus) or spice J VI.537.

Kuṭṭhita hot, sweltering (of uṇha) S IV.289 (v. l. kikita); molten (of tamba, cp. uttatta) Pgdp 33. See also kaṭhati kuthati, ukkaṭṭhita & pakkuṭṭhita.

Kuṭṭhin a leper M I.506 (in simile); Th I, 1054; J V.413; VI.196; Ud 49; DhA III.255.

Kuṭṭhilikā the pericarp or envelope of a seed (phala°) VvA 344 (= sipāṭikā).

Kuṭhārī (f.) [cp. Sk. kuṭhāra, axe = Lat. culter, knife from *(s)qer, to cut, in Lat. caro, etc]. An axe, a hatchet Vin III.144; S IV.160, 167; M I.233 = S III.141; A. I.141; II.201; IV.171; J I.431; DhA III.59; PvA 277. Purisassa hi jātassa kuthārī jāyate mukhe "when man is born, together with him is born an axe in his mouth (to cut evil speech)" S I.149 – Sn 657 = A V.174.

Kuḍumalaka [for kusuma°] an opening bud A IV.117, 119.

Kuḍḍa [to **kṣud** to grind, cp. cuṇṇa] a wall built of wattle and daub, in °nagaraka "a little wattle and daub town" D II.146, 169 (cp. Rh.D. on this in Buddh. Suttas p. 99). Three such kinds of simply-built walls are mentioned at Vin IV.266, viz. iṭṭhakā° of tiles, silā°

of stone, dāru° of wood. The expl[n] of kuḍḍa at Vism 394 is "geha-bhittiyā etam adhivacanaŋ." Kuḍḍa-rājā see under kuṭṭa). Also in tirokuḍḍaŋ outside the wall M I.34 = II.18; A IV.55; Vism 394, and tirokuḍḍesu Kh VIII[1] = Pv I.5[1]. — parakuḍḍaŋ nissāya J II.431 (near another man's wall) is doubtful; vv. ll. S. kuḍḍhaŋ. B. kuṭaŋ and kuṭṭaŋ. (kuḍḍa-) pāda the lower part of a lath and plaster wall Vin II.152. *Note.* Kuḍḍa at Vin II.151 is to be read kuṭṭa.

Kuḍḍa-mūla a sort of root Vin III.15.

Kuḍḍaka in eka° and dvi° having single or double walls J I.92.

Kuṇa (adj.) [cp. kuṇi lame from *qer, to bend = Gr. κυλλός crooked and lame, Lat. curvus & coluber snake] distorted, bent, crooked, lame Pv II.9[26] (v. l. kuṇḍa; cp. PvA 123. kuṇita paṭikuṇita an-ujubhūta); DhA III.71 (kāṇa° blind and lame).

Kuṇapa [der. fr. kuṇa? ch. Sk. kuṇapa] a corpse, carcase, Vin III.68 = M I.73 = A IV.377 (ahi°, kukkura°, manussa° pūti°); A IV.198 sq.; Sn 205; J I.61, 146; PvA 15. Kaṇṭhe āsatto kuṇapo a corpse hanging round one's neck M I.120; J I.5; also Vin III.68≈. — The abovementioned list of corpses (ahi°, etc.) is amplified at Vism 343 as follows: hatthi°, assa°, go°, mahiŋsa°, manussa°, ahi°, kukkura°. Cp. kaḷebara.

-gandha smell of a rotting corpse SnA 286; PvA 32.

Kuṇalin in kuṇalikata and kuṇalīmukha contracted, contorted Pv II.9 [26.28] (Hardy, but Minayeff and Hardy's S.S. Kuṇḍalī°), expl[d] PvA 123 by mukhavikārena vikuṇitaŋ (or vikucitaŋ SS.) sakuṇitaŋ (better: saṅkucitaŋ) (cp. Sk. **kuc** or **kuñc** to shrink).

Kuṇāla N. of a bird (the Indian cuckoo) J V.214 sq. (kuṇāla-jātaka). Kuṇāla-daha "cuckoo-lake," N. of one of the seven great lakes in the Himavant Vism 416.

Kuṇālaka [fr. kuṇāla] the cuckoo J V.406 (=kokila).

Kuṇi (adj.) deformed, paralysed (orig. bent, crooked, cp. kuṇa) only of the arm, acc. to Pug A IV.19 either of one or both arms (hands) J I.353 (expl. kuṇṭhahattha) = DhA I.376; Pug 51 (kāṇa, kuṇi, khañja); see khañja.

Kuṇita (or kuṇika) = kuṇa PvA 123, 125 (or should it be kucita?). Cp. paṭi°.

Kuṇṭha [cp. kuṇa and kuṇḍa] 1. bent, lame; blunt (of a sword) DhA I.311 (°kuddāla); Pug A I.34 (of asi, opp. tikkhina); °tiṇa a kind of grass Vism 353. — 2. a cripple J II.117.

Kuṇṭhita [a variant of guṇṭhita, as also found in cpd. palikuṇṭhita] Pv II.3[8] and **kuṇḍita** S I.197, both in phrase paŋsu°, according to Hardy, PvA p. 302 to be corrected to guṇṭhita covered with dust (see guṇṭheti). The v. l. at both places is °kuṭṭhita. Also found as paŋsukuṇṭhita at J VI.559 (=°makkhita C; v. l. B B. kuṇḍita).

Kuṇḍa (a) bent, crooked DA I.296 (°daṇḍaka); PvA 181.

Kuṇḍaka the red powder of rice husks (cp. kukkusa) Vin II.151; 280; J II.289 (text has kuṇḍadaka) = DhA III.325 (ibid. as ācāma°). Also used as toilet powder: DhA II.261 (kuṇḍakena sarīraŋ makkhetvā). —sakuṇḍaka (-bhatta) (a meal) with husk powder-cake J V.383.

-angārapūva pancake of rice powder DhA III.324; -kucchi in °sindhavapotaka "the rice- (cake-) belly colt" J II.288; -khādaka (a) eating rice-powder J II.288; (cp. DhA III.325); -dhūma, lit. smoke of red rice powder, Ep. of the blood J III.542; -pūva cake of husk-powder J I.422 sq.; -muṭṭhi a handful of rice-powder VvA 5; DhA I.425; -yāgu husk-powder gruel J II.288.

Kuṇḍala [cp. kuṇḍa, orig. bending, i. e. winding] a ring esp. earring A I.254 = III.16; J IV.358 (su° with beautiful earrings); DhA I.25. Frequent as maṇi°, a jewelled earring Vin II.156; S I.77; M I.366; Pv II.9[60]; sīha° or sīhamukha° an earring with a jewel called "lion's mouth" J V.205 (=kuñcita), 438. In sāgara° it means the ocean belt Miln 220 = J III.32 (where expl. as sāgaramajjhe dīpavasena ṭhitattā tassa kuṇḍalabhūtaŋ). Cp. also rajju° a rope as belt VvA 212. —kuṇḍalavatta turning, twisting round D II.18 (of the hair of a Mahāpurisa).

Kuṇḍalin[1] (adj.) [fr. kuṇḍala] wearing earrings S IV.343; J V.136; VI.478. su° Vv 73[1]. Cp. Maṭṭha° Np. DhA I.25; Pv II.5.

Kuṇḍalin[2] in kuṇḍali-kata contorted Pv II.9[27]. See kuṇalin and cp. Morris, *J.P.T.S.* 1893, 14.

Kuṇḍi (f.) [=kuṇḍikā] a pail or pot, in phrase kuṇḍipaddhana giving a pailful of milk J VI.504 (Kern, *Toev.* s. v. compares phrase Sk. kāŋsy'ôpadohana & proposes reading **kuṇḍ' opadohana**. See also kaŋsupadhāraṇa).

Kuṇḍika [cp. kuṇḍa] bending, in ahi-kuṇḍika (?) a snake charmer (lit. bender) J IV.308 (v. l. S. guṇṭhika) see ahi; and catu-kuṇḍika bent as regards his four limbs, i. e. walking on all fours M I.79; Pv III.2[4] (expl. at PvA 181).

Kuṇḍikā (f.) a water-pot J I.8, 9, II.73 (=kamaṇḍalu), 317; V.390; DhA I.92 (cp. kuṭa).

Kutuka (adj.) eager, in sakutuka eagerness Dāvs IV.41.

Kutumbaka (-puppha) N. of a flower J I.60.

Kutūhala (m. nt.) tumult, excitement; Dāvs V.22; DhA III.194 (v. l. kot°). a° (adj.) unperturbed, not shamming J I.387 (expl. by avikiṇṇa-vaco of straight speech). See also kotūhala.

-mangala a festivity, ceremony, Nd[2] in expl. of anekarūpena Sn 1079, 1082; -sālā a hall for recreation, a common room D I.179 = S IV.398 = M II.2, cp. Divy 143.

Kuto see under **ku°**.

Kutta (nt.) [Der. fr. kattā = Sk. kṛtṛ as kṛttra = P. kutta, cp. Sk. kṛtrima artificial = P. kuttima, in caus. — pass. sense = kappita of **kḷp**)] "being made up." 1. Work. The beginning of things was the work of Brahmā. The use of kutta implies that the work was so easy as to be nearer play than work, and to have been carried out in a mood of graceful sport. D III.28. — 2. behaviour, i. e. charming behaviour, coquetry J II.329, comb[d] with līḷā (graceful carriage) J I.296, 433; and with vilāsa (charming behaviour) J II.127; IV.219, 472; itthi° and purisa° A IV.57 = Dhs 633 (expl. at DhsA 321 by kiriyā). — As adj. in kuttavāla, well arranged, plaited tails D I.105 (expl[d] at DA I.274 as kappita-vāla; cp. kappita).

Kuttaka [der. fr. kutta, that which is made up or "woven," with orig. meaning of karoti to weave ?] 1. nt. a woollen carpet (DA I.87 = as used for dancing-women), together with kaṭṭhissa and koseyya in list of forbidden articles of bedding D I.7 = A I.181 = Vin I.192 = II.163. — 2. adj. "made up," pretending, in samaṇa-k° a sham ascetic Vin III.68-71.

Kuttama in kāsi-kuttama J VI.49 should be read as kāsik'-uttama.

Kutti (f.) [cp. kutta] arrangement, fitting, trapping, harnessing Vin II.108 (sara°: accuracy in sound, harmony); J III.314 (massu° beard-dressing, expl[d] by massu-kiriyā. Here corresponding to Sk *kḷpti !); IV.352 (hattha°, elephant trappings, cp. kappanā); V.215 (=karaṇa, cp. Sk. kalpa).

Kutthaka S I.66 should be replaced by v. l. koṭṭhaka.

Kutha see under ku°.

Kuthati [Sk. kvathati cp. kaṭhati, kaṭhita, kuṭṭhita, ukkaṭṭhita & upakūḷita^{2}] to cook, to boil: **kuthanto** (ppr) boiling (putrid, foul? So Kern, *Toev*, s. v.) J VI.105 (of Vetaraṇī, cp. kuṭṭhita).—pp. **kuthita.**

Kuthana (nt.) [fr. **kvath**=kuth] digestion Vism 345.

Kuthita [pp. of kuthati] 1. boiled, cooked Th 2, 504; KhA 62; Vism 259=KhA 58. Cp. vikkuthita.— 2. digested Vism 345.—3. fig. tormented, distressed (perhaps: rotten, foul, cp. kilijjati=pūti hoti) Miln 250 (+kiliṭṭha).—Cp. *Vin. Texts* II.57 on Bdhgh's note to MV VI.14, 5.

Kudaṇḍaka a throng J III.204.

Kudassu (kud-assu) interj. to be sure, surely (c. fut.) A I.107; Nett 87; SnA 103.

Kudā see under ku°.

Kudāra (ku-dāra) a bad wife Pv IV.1^{47}.

Kudārikā at Pv IV.1^{47} & PvA 240 is spelling for kuṭhārikā.

Kudiṭṭhi (f.) [ku+diṭṭhi] wrong belief Sdhp 86.

Kuddāla a spade or a hoe (kanda-mūla-phalagahaṇ'-atthaŋ DA I.269) Vin III.144; J V.45; DhA IV.218. Often in comb^{n} **kuddāla-piṭaka** "hoe and basket" D I.101; S II.88; V.53; A I.204; II.199; J I.225, 336.

Kuddālaka=prec. DhA I.266.

Kuddha (adj.) [pp. of kujjhati] angry A IV.96 (and akkuddha IV.93); Pv I.7^{7}; J II.352, 353; VI.517; DhA II.44. Nom. pl. kuddhāse It 2=7.

Kudrūsa a kind of grain Miln 267; also as **kudrūsaka** Vin IV.264; D III.71; Nd^{2} 314; DA I.78; DhsA 331.

Kunta [cp. Sk. kunta lance ?] a kind of bird, otherwise called adāsa J IV. 466.

Kuntanī (f.) a curlew (koñca), used as homing bird J III.134.

Kuntha, only in comb^{n} **kuntha-kipillaka** (or °ikā) a sort of ant J I.439; IV.142; Sn 602 (°ikā); Vism 408; KhA 189. Cp. kimi.

Kunda (nt.) the jasmine Dāvs V.28.

Kunnadī (f.) (kuŋ-nadī) a small river, a rivulet S I.109; II.32, 118; A IV.100; J III.221; Vism 231, 416; DA I.58.

Kupatha (kuŋ+patha) wrong path (cp. kummagga) Miln 390.

Kupita (adj.) [pp. of kuppati]—1. shaken, disturbed Th 2, 504 (by fire=ThA 292); J III.344 (°indriya).— 2. offended, angry D III.238=M I.101=A IV.460= V.18; M. I.27; A III.196 sq.; Pv I.6^{7}. Often comb^{n} with **anattamana** "angry and displeased" Vin II.189; D I.3, 90 (=DA I.255 kuddha).—As nt. **kupitaŋ** disturbance, in **paccanta°** a disturbance on the borderland J III.497; Miln 314; PvA 20.

Kuppa (adj.) [ger. of kuppati] shaking, unsteady, movable; A III.128 (°dhammo, unsteady, of a pāpabhikkhu); Sn 784; of a **kamma**: a proceeding that can be quashed Vin II.71 (also a°). *nt.* kuppaŋ anger Vin II.133 (karissāmi I shall pretend to be angry).—**akuppa** (adj.) and **akuppaŋ** (nt.) steadfast, not to be shaken, an Ep. of arahant and nibbāna (cp. asankuppa); akuppa-dhammo Pug 11 (see akuppa). Akuppaŋ as freedom from anger at Vin II.251.

Kuppati [Sk. kupyate, ***qup** to be agitated, to shake= Lat. cupio, cupidus, "to crave with agitation," cp. semantically Lat. tremere>Fr. craindre] to shake, to quiver, to be agitated, to be disturbed, to be angry.— aor. kuppi, pp. kupita, ger. kuppa, caus. kopeti A III.101; Sn. 826, 854; Pug 11, 12, 30. Of the wind Miln 135; of childbirth udaravāto kuppi (or kupita) J II.393, 433; paccanto kuppi the border land was disturbed J IV.446 (cp. kupita).

Kuppila [?] a kind of flower J VI.218 (C: mantālaka-makula).

Kubbati^{2} etc. see karoti II.

Kubbanaka [fr. kuŋ-vana] brushwood or a small, and therefore unproductive, wood Sn 1134 (expl. Nd^{2} by rittavanaka appabhakkha appodaka).

Kubbara the pole of a carriage A IV.191, 193; VvA 269, 271, 275. ratha° S I.109, Vv 64^{2} (=vedikā VvA). Der. (vividha-) kubbaratā VvA 276.

Kumati wrong thought, wrong view (cp. kudiṭṭhi) Bdhd 137.

Kumāra [Vedic kumāra] a young boy, son Sn 685 sq. (kuhiŋ kumāro aham api daṭṭhukāmo: w. ref. to the child Gotama); Pv III.5^{2}; PvA 39, 41 (=māṇava); daharo kumāro M II.24, 44.—a son of (-°) rāja° PvA 163; khattiya°, brāhmaṇa° Bdhd 84; deva° J III.392 yakkha° Bdhd 84.

-**kīḷā** the amusement of a boy J I.137; -**pañhā** questions suitable for a boy Kh III.; -**lakkhaṇa** divination by means of a young male child (+kumāri°) D I.9.

Kumāraka 1. m. a young boy, a youngster, kumārakā vā kumāriyo boys and girls S III.190. 2. nt. °ŋ a childish thing A III.114.—f. °**ikā** a young girl, a virgin J I.290, 411; II.180; IV.219 (thulla°); VI.64; DhA III.171.

-**vāda** speech like a young boy's; S II.219.

Kumārī (f.) a young girl Vin II.10; V.129 (thulla°); A III.76; J III.395 (daharī k°); Pug 66 (itthī vā k° vā).

-**pañha** obtaining oracular answers from a girl supposed to be possessed by a spirit D I.11 (cp. DA I.97).

Kumina (nt.) a fish net Vin III.63; Th 1, 297; J II.238; ThA 243.

Kumuda (nt.) 1. the *white* lotus Dh 285; Vv 35^{4} (=VvA 161); J V.37 (seta°); Vism 174; DA I.139.—2. a high numeral, in vīsati kumudā nirayā A V.173=Sn p. 126.

-**naḷa** a lotus-stalk J I.223; -**patta** (-vaṇṇa) (having the colour of) white lotus petals J I.58 (Ep. of sindhavā, steeds); -**bhaṇḍikā** a kind of corn Miln 292; -**vaṇṇa** (adj.) of the colour of white lotus (sindhavā) PvA 74. -**vana** a mass of white lotuses J V 37.

Kumbha [for etym. s. kūpa and cp. Low Ger. kump or kumme, a round pot] 1. a round jar, waterpot (=kulālabhājana earthenware DhA I.317), frequent in similes, either as illustrating fragility or emptiness and fullness: A I.130, 131=Pug 32; A V.337; S II.83; Miln 414. As uda° waterpot Dh 121; J I.20; Pv I.12^{2}. —2. one of the frontal globes of an elephant Vin II.195 (hatthissa); VvA 182 (°ālankārā ornaments for these).

-**ūpama** resembling a jar, of kāya Dh 40 (=DhA I.317); of var. kinds of puggalā A II.104=Pug 45. -**kāra** 1. a potter; enumerated with other occupations and trades at D I.51=Miln 331. Vin IV.7. In similes, generally referring to his skill D I.78=M II.18; Vism 142, 376; Sn 577; DhA I.39 (°sālā). rāja° the king's potter J I.121. — 2. a bird (Phasianus gallus? Hardy) VvA 163. — Cpds. : °*antevāsin* the potter's apprentice D I.78 = M II.18 ; -°*nivesana* the dwelling of a potter Vin I.342, 344 ; S III.119 ; °*pāka* the potter's oven S II.83 ; A IV.102 ; °-*putta* son of a potter (cp. *Dial.* I.100), a potter Vin III.41 sq. ; -kārikā a large earthen vessel (used as a hut to live in, Bdhgh) Vin II.143, cp. *Vin. Texts* III.156 ; -ṭṭhāna-kathā gossip at the well D I.8 = D III.36 = A V.128 = S V.419, expl^d. at DA I.90 by udaka-ṭṭhānakathā, with variant udakatittha-kathā ti pi vuccati kumbha-dāsi-kathā vā ; -thūṇa a sort of drum D I.6 (expl. at DA I.84 : caturassara-ammanakatāḷaŋ kumbhasaddan ti pi eke) ; D III.183 ; J V.506 (pāṇissaraŋ +). -°*ika* one who plays that kind of drum Vin IV.285 = 302 ; -tthenaka of cora, a thief, " who steals by means of a pot " (i. e. lights his candle under a pot (?) Bdhgh on Vin II.256, cp. *Vin. Texts* III.325 " robber burglars ") only in simile Vin II.256 = S II.264 = A IV.278 ; -dāsi a slave girl who brings the water from the well D I.168 ; Miln 331 ; DhA I.401 (udakatitthato k° viya ānītā). -dūhana milking into the pitchers, giving a pail of milk (of gāvo, cows) Sn 309. Cp. kuṇḍi. -bhāramatta as much as a pot can hold J V.46 ; -matta of the size of a pot, in kumbha-mattarahassangā mahodarā yakkhā, explⁿ. of kum-bhaṇḍā J III.147.

Kumbhaṇḍa I. m. a class of fairies or genii grouped with Yakkhas, Rakkhasas and Asuras S II.258 (k° puriso vehāsaŋ gacchanto) ; J I.204 ; III.147 (with def.) ; Miln 267 ; DhA I.280 ; Pgdp 60. — 2. nt. a kind of gourd J I.411 (lābu°) ; V.37 ; (elāḷuka-lābuka°) ; DA I.73 = DhA I.309 (placed on the back of a horse, as symbol of instability) ; the same as f. kumbhaṇḍī Vism 183 (lābu +).

Kumbhī (f.) a large round pot (often comb^d with kaḷopī,) Vin I.49, 52, 286 ; II.142, 210 ; Th 2, 283. loha° a copper (also as lohamaya k° Sn 670), in °pakkhepana, one of the ordeals in Niraya PvA 221. Also a name for one of the Nirayas (see lohakumbhī). Cp. nidhi°.

-mukha the rim of a pot (always with kaḷopi-mukha) D I.166 and ≈ (see kaḷopī) ; Vism 328.

Kumbhīla (kuŋ + bhīra ?) a crocodile (of the Ganges) J I.216, 278 ; DhA I.201 ; III.362.

-bhaya the fear of the crocodile, in enumeration of several objects causing fear, at M I.459 sq. = A II.123 sq. ; Miln 196 = Nd² on bhaya. — Th 2, 502 ; -rājā the king of the crocodiles J II.159.

Kumbhīlaka [fr. kumbhīla] a kind of bird (" little crocodile ") J IV.347.

Kumma [Vedic kūrma] a tortoise S IV.177 (+ kacchapa) ; M I.143 ; J V.489 ; Miln 363, 408 (here as land-tortoise : cittaka-dhara°).

Kummagga (and kumagga) [kuŋ + magga] a wrong path (lit. and fig.) Miln 390 (+ kupatha) ; fig. (= micchā-patha) Dhs 381, 1003 ; Pug 22. Kummaggaŋ paṭi-pajjati to lose one's way, to go astray. lit. Pv IV.3⁵ ; PvA 44 (v. l. SS.) ; fig. Sn 736 ; It 117 ; Th 2, 245.

Kummāsa [Vedic kulmāṣa] junket, usually with odana, boiled rice. In formula of kāya (cātummahābhūtika etc., see kāya) D I.76 = M II.17 and ≈ ; in enum. of material food (kabaḷinkārāhāra) Dhs 646, 740, 875. — Vin III.15 ; J I.228 ; Vv 14⁶ (= VvA 62 yava°), VvA 98 (odana°). In combⁿ with pūva (cake) DhA I.367 ; PvA 244.

Kummiga (kuŋ + miga) a small or insignificant animal Miln 346.

Kuyyaka a kind of flower J I.60 (°puppha).

Kuraṇḍaka [cp. Sk. kuraṇṭaka blossom of a species of Amaranth] a shrub and its flower Vism 183 (see also kuravaka & koraṇḍaka). °leṇa Npl. Vism 38.

Kurara an osprey J IV.295, 397 (= ukkusa) ; V.416 ; VI.539 (= seta°).

Kuravaka [= Sk. kuraṇṭaka Halāyudha, cp. kuraṇḍaka] N. of a tree, in ratta° J I.39 (= bimbijāla the red Amaranth tree).

Kurunga [deriv. unknown. The corresponding Sk. forms are kulunga and kulanga] a kind of antelope, in -miga the antelope deer J I.173 (k°-jātaka) ; II.153 (do.).

Kuruṭṭharū (v. l. kururū) D II.242.

Kurundī N. of one of the lost SS commentaries on the Vinaya, used by Buddhaghosa (cp. *Vin. Texts* I.258 ; II.14).

Kuruvindaka vermillion in *cuṇṇa*, a bath-powder made from k. J III.282 ; and °suttī a string of beads covered with this powder Vin II.106 (cp. Bdhgh Vin II.315 ; *Vin. Texts* III.67).

Kurūra (adj.) [Sk. krūra, cp. Lat. cruor thick blood, Gr. κρέας (raw) flesh, Sk. kraviḥ ; Ohg. hrō, E. raw] bloody, raw, cruel, in °kammanta following a cruel (bloody) occupation (as hunting, fishing, bird killing, etc.) A III.383 = Pug 56 (expld. Pug A 233 by dāruṇa°, also at PvA 181).

Kurūrin = kurūra Pv III.2³.

Kula (nt ; but poetic pl. kulā Pv II.9⁴³ [Idg. *qṷel (revolve) ; see under kaṇṭha, cakka and carati] I. clan, a high social grade, " good family," cp. Gr. (doric) φυά, Goth. kuni. A collection of cognates and agnates, in sense of Ohg. sippa, clan ; " house " in sense of line or descent (cp. House of Bourbon, Homeric γενέη). Bdhgh at Vism 91 distinguishes 2 kinds of kulāni, viz. ñāti-kulaŋ & upaṭṭhāka-kulaŋ. — I. A II.249 (on welfare and ill-luck of clans) ; Sn 144 ; 711 ; It 109 sq. (sabrahma-kāni, etc.) ; Dh 193. — brāhmaṇa° a Brahmanic family A V.249 ; J IV.411, etc. ; vāṇija° the household of a trader J III.82 ; kassaka° id. of a farmer J II.109 ; purāṇaseṭṭhi° of a banker J VI.364 ; upaṭṭhāka° (Sāri-puttassa) a family who devoted themselves to the service of S. Vin I.83 ; sindhava° VvA 280. — uccākula of high descent Pv III.1¹⁶, opp. nica° of mean birth Sn 411 (cp. °kulīno) ; viz. caṇḍālakula, nesāda°, veṇa°, etc. M II.152 = A I.107 = II.85 = III.385 = Pug 51 ; sadisa° a descent of equal standing PvA 82 ; kula-rūpa-sam-panna endowed with " race " and beauty PvA 3, 280. — 2. household, in the sense of house ; kulāni people DhA I.388 ; parakulesu among other people Dh 73 ; parakule do. VvA 66 ; kule kule appaṭibaddhacitto not in love with a particular family Sn 65 ; cp. kule gaṇe āvāse (asatto or similar terms) Nd² on taṇhā IV. — devakula temple J II.411 ; rāja° the king's household, palace J I.290 ; III.277 ; VI.368 ; kulāni bahutthikāni (= bahuitthikāni, bahukitthi° A IV.278) appapurisāni " communities in which there are many women but few men " Vin II.256 = S II.264 = A IV.278 ; ñāti-kulā (my) home Vv 37¹⁰ (: pitugehaŋ sandhāya VvA 171).

-angāra " the charcoal of the family " i. e. one who brings a family to ruin, said of a squanderer S IV.324 (text kulangāroti : but vv. ll. show ti as superfluous) ; printed kulanguro (for kul-ankuro ? v. l. kulangāro) kulapacchimako (should it be kulapacchijjako ? cp. vv. ll. at J IV.69) dhanavināsako J VI.380. Also in kulapacchimako kulagaro pāpadhammo J IV.69. Both these refer to an avajāta putta. Cp. also kulassa angārabhūta DhA III.350 ; Sn A 192 (of a dujjāto putto). and kulagandhana ; -itthi a wife of good descent, together with kuladhītā, °kumāri, °suṇhā, °dāsī at Vin II.10; A III.76; Vism 18. -ûpaka (also read as °upaka, °ûpaga; °upaga; for ûpaga, see Trenckner, P.M. 62, n. 16; cp. kulopaka Divy 307) frequenting a family, dependent on a (or one & the same) family (for alms, etc.); a friend, an associate. Freq. in formula kulûpako hoti bahukāni kulāni upasankamati, e. g. Vin III.131, 135; IV.20. — Vin I.192, 208; III.84, 237; V.132; S II.200 sq.; A III.136, 258 sq.; Pv III.8^5; Vism 28; DA I.142 (rāja°); PvA 266. f. *kulûpikā* (bhikkhunī) Vin II.268; IV.66; -gandhana at It 64 and kule gandhina at J IV.34 occur in the same sense and context as kulangāra in J.-passages on avajāta-putta. The It-MSS. either explain k- gandhana by kulacchedaka or have vv. ll. kuladhaŋsana and kusajantuno. Should it be read as kulaṅgāraka? Cp. gandhina; -geha clanhouse, i. e. father's house DhA I.49. -tanti in kulatanti-kulapaveṇi-rakkhako anujāto putto "one who keeps up the line & tradition of the family" J VI.380; -dattika (and °dattiya) given by the family or clan J III.221 (°sāmika); IV.146 (where DhA I.346 reads °santaka). 189 (°kambala); VI.348 (pati). -dāsī a female slave in a respectable family Vin II.10; VvA 196; -dūsaka one who brings a family into bad repute Sn 89; DhA II.109; -dvāra the door of a family Sn 288; -dhītā the daughter of a respectable family Vin II.10; DhA III.172; VvA 6; PvA 112; -pasāda the favour received by a family, °ka one who enjoys this favour A I.25, cp. SnA 165, opp. of kuladūsaka; -putta a clansman, a (young) man of good family, fils de famille, cp. Low Ger. haussohn; a gentleman, man of good birth. As 2nd characteristic of a Brahmin (with sujāto as 1st) in formula at D I.93, 94≈; Vin I.15, 43, 185, 288, 350; M I.85≈(in kāmānaŋ ādīnavo passage), 192, 210, 463; A II.249; J I.82; VI.71; It 89; VvA 128; PvA 12, 29; -macchariya selfishness concerning one's family, touchiness about his clan D III.234 (in list of 5 kinds of selfishness); also to be read at Dhs 1122 for kusala°; -vaŋsa lineage, progeny M II.181; A III.43; IV.61; DA I.256; expressions for the keeping up of the lineage or its neglect are: °ṭhapana D III 189; PvA 5; nassati or nāseti J IV.69; VvA 149; upacchindati PvA 31, 82; -santaka belonging to one's family, property of the clan J I.52; DhA I.346 (where J IV.146 reads °dattika).

Kulanka -pādaka "buttresses of timber" (*Vin. Texts* III.174) Vin II.152 (cp. Bdhgh. p. 321 and also Morris, *J.P.T.S.* 1884, 78).

Kulattha a kind of vetch M I.245 (°yūsa): Miln 267; Vism 256 (°yūsa).

Kulala a vulture, hawk, falcon, either in comb^{n} with kāka or gijjha, or both. Kāka + k° Vin IV.40; Sn 675 (=SnA 250); gijjha + k° PvA 198; gijjhā kākā k° Vin III.106; kākā k° gijjhā M I.58; cp. gijjho kanko kulalo M I.364, 429.

Kulāla a potter; only in -cakka a potter's wheel J I.63; -bhājana a potter's vessel DhA I.316; PvA 274.

Kulāva I. waste (?) Vin II.292: na kulāvaŋ gamenti "don't let anything go to waste." Reading doubtful. — 2. a cert. bird J VI.538.

Kulāvaka (nt.) a nest D I.91 (=DA I.257 nivāsaṭṭhanaŋ); S I.8; S I.224 = J I.203 (a brood of birds = supaṇṇapotakā); J III.74 (v. l. BB), 431; VI.344; DhA II.22.

Kulika (adj.) [fr. kula] belonging to a family, in agga^{c} coming from a very good family PvA 199.

Kuḷika (?) in kata°-kalāpaka a bundle of beads? Bdhgh Vin II.315 (C.V. V.1, 3) in expl^{n} of kuruvindaka-sutti.

Kulinka a bird J III.541 (=sakuṇika 542) Cp. kulunka.

Kulin = kulika, in akulino rājāno ignoble kings Anvs. introd. (see *J.P.T.S.* 1886 p. 35^6, where akuliro which is conjectured as akulino by Andersen, Pāli Reader, p. 102^4).

Kulīna = prec. in abhijāta-kula-kulīna descendant of a recognized clan Miln 359 (of a king); uccā° of noble birth, in uccākulīnatā descent from a high family S I.87; M III.37; VvA 32; nīca° of mean birth Sn 462.

Kulīra a crab, in kulīra-pādaka "a crab-footer," i. e. a (sort of) bedstead Vin II.149; IV. 40 (kulira), cp. Bdhgh on latter passage at Vin IV.357 (kuḷira° and kuḷiya°): a bedstead with curved or carved legs; esp. when carved to represent animal's feet (*Vin. Texts* III.164).

Kulīraka a crab J VI.539 (= kakkaṭaka 540).

Kulunka a cert. small bird J III.478. Cp. kulinka.

Kulla^1 a raft (of basket-work) (orig. meaning "hollow shaft," cp. Sk. kulya, bone; Lat. caulis stalk, Gr. καυλός, Ohg. hol, E. hollow) Vin I.230; D II.89 (kullaŋ bandhati); M I.134 (kullūpama dhamma).

Kulla^2 (adj.) [fr. kula, Sk. kaula & kaulya, *kulya] belonging to the family J IV.34 (°vatta family custom).

Kullaka crate, basket work, a kind of raft, a little basket J VI.64.

-vihāra (adj.) the state of being like one who has found a raft (?) Vin II.304 (cp. Bdhgh uttānavihāra ibid. p. 330, and *Vin. Texts* III.404: an easy life). More correct is Kern's expl^{n} (*Toev.* s. v.) which puts kullaka in this comb^{n} = kulla^2 (Sk. kauyla), thus meaning well-bred, of good family, gentlemanly. -saṇṭhāna consisting of stalks bound together, like a raft J II.406-408 (not correct Morris, *J.P.T.S.* 1884, 78). Cp. Kern, *Toev.* I.154.

Kuva(ŋ) see ku-.

Kuvalaya the (blue) water-lily, lotus, usually comb^{d} with kamala, q. v. Vv 35^4; DA I.50; VvA 161, 181; PvA 23, 77.

Kuvilāra = kovilāra J V.69 (v. l. B. ko°).

Kusa I. the kusa grass (Poa cynosuroides) DhA III 484: tikhiṇadhāraŋ tiṇaŋ antamaso tālapaṇṇam pi; Dh 311; J I.190 (= tiṇa); IV.140. — 2. a blade of grass used as a mark or a lot: pātite kuse "when the lot has been cast" Vin I.299; kusaŋ sankāmetvā "having passed the lot on" Vin III.58.

-agga the point of a blade of grass PvA 254 = DA I.164; Sdhp 349; kusaggena bhuñjati or pivati to eat or drink only (as little as) with a blade of grass Dh 70; VvA 73 (cp. Udānavarga p. 105); -kaṇṭhaka = prec. Pv III.2^{28}; -cīra a garment of grass Vin I.305 = D I.167 = A I.240, 295 = II.206 = Pug 55; -pāta the casting of a kusa lot Vin I.285; -muṭṭhi a handful of grass A V.234 = 249.

Kusaka = prec. Vv 35^5 (= VvA 162).

Kusala (adj.) [cp. Sk. kuśala] I. (adj.) clever, skilful, expert; good, right, meritorious M I.226; Dh 44; J I.222. Esp. appl. in moral sense (= puñña), whereas akusala is practically equivalent to pāpa. ekam pi ce pāṇaŋ aduṭṭhacitto mettāyati kusalo tena hoti It 21; sappañño paṇḍito kusalo naro Sn 591, cp. 523; Pv I.3^3 (= nipuṇa). With kamma = a meritorious action, in kammaŋ katvā kusalaŋ D III.157; Vv III.2^7; Pv I.10^{11} see cpds. — ācāra-k° good in conduct Dh 376; parappavāda° skilled in disputation Dpvs IV.19; magga° (and opp. amagga°) one who is an expert as regards the Path (lit. & fig.) S III.108; samāpatti, etc. A V.156 sq.; sāhttaka-payoge k° skilled in the art of throwing potsherds PvA 282. — In derivation k. is expl[d] by Dhpāla & Bdhgh by kucchita and salana, viz. kucchita-sala-uādi atthena kusalaŋ VvA 169; kucchite pāpadhamme salayanti calayanti kappenti viddhaŋsenti ti kusalā DhsA 39; where four alternative derivations are given (cp Mrs. Rh. D., *Dhs. trsl.* p. lxxxii). — 2. (nt.) a good thing, good deeds, virtue, merit, good consciousness (citta omitted; cp. DhsA 162, 200, etc.): yassa pāpaŋ kataŋ kammaŋ kusalena pithiyati, so imaŋ lokaŋ pabhāseti "he makes this world shine, who covers an evil deed with a good one" M II.104=Dh 173=Th 1, 872; sukhañ ca k. pucchi (fitness) Sn 981; Vv 30[1] (=ārogyaŋ); D I.24; J VI.367; Pv I.1[3] (=puñña); PvA 75; Miln 25. — In special sense as ten kusalāni equivalent to the dasasīlaŋ (cp. sīla) M I.47; A V.241, 274. All good qualities (dhammā) which constitute right and meritorious conduct are comprised in the phrase -kusala-dhammā Sn 1039, 1078, expld. in extenso Nd[2] s. v. See also cpd. °dhamma. — Kusalaŋ karoti to do what is good and righteous, i. e. kāyena, vācāya, manasā It 78; cp. Dh 53; sabba-pāpassa akaraṇaŋ kusalassa upasampadā sacittapariyodapanaŋ etaŋ Buddhānusāsanaŋ D II.49=Dh 183; cp. Nett 43, 81, 171, 186. Kusalaŋ bhāveti to pursue righteousness (together with akusalaŋ pajahati to give up wrong habits) A I.58; IV.109 sq.; It 9. — **akusala** adj.: improper, wrong, bad; nt.: demerit, evil deed D I.37, 163; bālo+akusalo Sn 879, 887; =pāpa PvA 60, cp. pāpasuto akatakusalo ib. 6. kusalaŋ & akusalaŋ are discussed in detail (with ref. to rūpâvacara° fivefold, to arūpâvacara° & lokuttara° fourfold, to kāmâvacara° eight & twelvefold) at Vism 452-454. — **kusalâkusala** good and bad M I.489; S V.91; Miln 25; Nett 161, 192; Dhs 1124 sq. — **sukusala** (dhammānaŋ) highly skilled D I.180 (cp. M. II.31).

-**anuesin** striving after righteousness Sn 965; cp. kinkusalānuesin D II.151 and kinkusalagavesin M I.163 sq.; -**abhisanda** overflow of merit (+puñña°) A II.54 sq.; III.51; 337; -**kamma** meritorious action, right conduct A I.104; 292 sq.; Ps I.85; II.72 sq.; PvA 9, 26; -**cittā** (pl.) good thoughts Vbh 169-173, 184, 285 sq., 294 sq.; -**cetanā** right volition Vbh 135; -**dhammā** (pl.) (all) points of righteousness, good qualities of character S II.206; M I.98; A IV.11 sq.; V.90 sq.; 123 sq.; Pug 68, 71; Vbh 105; Ps I.101, 132; II.15, 230; VvA 74, 127; -**pakkha** "the side of virtue," all that belongs to good character M III.77 (and a°) with adj. °pakkhika S V.91; -**macchariya** Dhs 1122 is to be corrected to kula° instead of kusala° (meanness as regards family) cp. Nd[2] on veviccha; -**mūla** the basis or root of goodness or merit; there are three: alobha, adosa, amoha M I.47, 489=A I.203=Nett 183; D III.214; Dhs 32, 313, 981; Vbh 169 sq., 210; Nett 126. Cp. °paccaya Vbh 169; °ropanā Nett 50; -**vitakka** good reasoning, of which there are three: nekkhamma°, avyāpāda°, avihiŋsā° D III.215; It 82; Nett 126; -**vipāka** being a fruit of good kamma Dhs 454; Vism 454 (twofold, viz. ahetuka & sahetuka). -**vedanā** good, pure feeling Vbh 3 sq.; cp. °saññā and °sankhārā Vbh 6 sq.; Nett 126 (three °saññā, same as under °vitakkā); -**sīla** good, proper conduct of life M II.25 sq.; adj. °sīlin D I.115 (=DA I.286).

Kusalatā [fem. abstr. fr. kusala] (only -°) skill, cleverness, accomplishment; good quality. — lakkhaṇa° skill in interpreting special signs VvA 138; aparicita° neglect in acquiring good qualities PvA 67. For foll. cp. Mrs. Rh. D. *Dhs. trsl.* pp. 345-348; āpatti° skill as to what is an offence; samāpatti° in the Attainments; dhātu° in the Elements; manasikāra° proficiency in attention; āyatana° skill in the spheres; paṭiccasamuppāda° skill in conditioned Genesis; ṭhāna° and aṭṭhāna° skill in affirming (negating) causal conjuncture: all at D III.212 and Dhs 1329-1338; cp. A I.84, 94.

Kusi (nt.) one of the four cross seams of the robe of a bhikkhu Vin I.287; II.177; and aḍḍha° intermediate cross seam ibid. See Bdhgh's note in *Vin. Texts* II.208.

Kusīta (adj.) [Sk. kusīda; cp. kosajja] indolent, inert, inactive. Expl. by kāma-vitakkādīhi vitakkehi vītināmanakapuggalo DhA II.260; by nibbiriyo DhA III.410; by alaso PvA 175. Often comb[d] with **hīna-viriya**, devoid of zeal; It 27, 116; Dh 7, 112, 280; Miln 300, 396. Also equivalent to alasa Dh 112; comb[d] with dussīla Miln 300, 396; with duppañña D III.252=282; A II.227, 230; III.7, 183, 433. — In other connections: M I.43, 471; A III.7 sq., 127; V.95, 146, 153, 329 sq.; S II.29, 159, 206; It 71, 102; J IV.131 (nibbiriya+); Vism 132; DhA I.69. The eight kusīta-vatthūni, occasions of indolence, are enumerated at A IV.332; D III.255; Vbh 385. — **akusīta** alert, mindful, careful Sn 68 (+alīnacitto); Nd[2] s. v.; Sdhp 391.

Kusītatā (f.) [abstr. fr. kusīta] in a° alertness, brightness, keenness VvA 138.

Kusuma (nt.) any flower J III.394 (°dāma); V.37; PvA 157 (=puppha); VvA 42; Dpvs I.4; Sdhp 246, 595; Dāvs V.51 (°agghika), fig. vimutti° the flower of emancipation Th 1, 100; Miln 399.

Kusumita (adj.) in flower, blooming VvA 160, 162.

Kusumbha (nt.) the safflower, Carthamus tinctorius, used for dying red J V.211 (°rattavattha); VI.264 (do); Khus IV.2.

Kussubbha and **kussobbha** (nt.) [Sk. kuśvabhra] a small pond, usually comb[d] with kunnadī and appl[d] in similes: S II.32=A I.243=V.114; S II.118; V.47, 63, 395; A II.140; IV.100; Sn 720; PvA 29; DA I.58.

Kuha (adj.) [Sk. kuha; *qeudh to conceal, cp. Gr. κεύθω; Ags hȳdan, E. hide] deceitful, fraudulent, false, in phrase kuhā thaddhā lapā singī A II.26=Th 1, 959=It 113. — **akuha** honest, upright M I.386; Sn 957; Miln 352.

Kuhaka [der. fr. prec.] deceitful, cheating; a cheat, a fraud, comb[d] with **lapaka** D I.8; A III.111. — A V.159 sq.; Sn 984, 987; J I.375 (°tāpasa); DhA IV.152 (°brāhmaṇa); IV.153 (°cora); Miln 310, 357; PvA 13; DA I.91.

Kuhanā (f.) [abstr. fr. adj. kuhana=kuhaka] 1. deceit, fraud, hypocrisy, usually in comb[n] kuhana-lapana "deceit and talking-over"=deceitful talk D I.8; A III.430; DA I.92; Miln 383; Nd[2] on avajja. — M I.465=It 28, 29; S IV.118; A V.159 sq.; Vism 23; Vbh 352; Sdhp 375. — 2. menacing SnA 582. — Opp. akuhaka Sn 852. — Var. commentator's derivations are **kuhāyanā** (fr. kuhanā) and **kuhitattaŋ** (fr. kuheti), to be found at Vism 26.

-**vatthūni** (pl.) cases or opportunities of deceit, three of which are discussed at Nd[2] on nikkuha, mentioned also at Vism 24; DA I.91 & SnA 107.

Kuhara (nt.) (der. fr. kuha) a hole, a cavity; lit. a hiding-place Dāvs I.62.

Kuhiŋ see under ku°.

Kuhilikā (pl.) kuhali flowers Attanugaluvaŋsa 216.

Kuhīyati only in pahaŋsīyati+k° "he exults and rejoices" at Miln 326 (cp. *Miln trsl.* II.220, where printed kuhūyati).

Kuheti [v. denom. fr. kuha] to deceive DA 91; ger. kuhitvā deceiving J VI.212.

Kūjati [**kuj**, expl[d] with **guj** at Dhtp 78 by "avyatte sadde"] to sing (of birds; cp. vikūjati) J II.439; IV.296; Dāvs V.51. — pp. **kūjita** see abhi°, upa°.

Kūṭa[1] (nt.) [Dhtp 472 & Dhtm 526 expl. **kuṭ** of kūṭa[1] by koṭille (koṭilye), cp. Sk. kūṭa trap, cp. Gr. παλεύω to trap birds] a trap, a snare; fig. falsehood, deceit. As trap J I.143 (kūṭapāsādi); IV.416 (expl[n] paṭicchannapāsa). As deceit, cheating in formula tulā° kaṇsa° māna° "cheating with weight, coin and measure" (DA I.78=vañcana) D I.5=III.176=S V.473=M I.180 =A II.209; V.205=Pug 58. māna° PvA 278. — As adj. false, deceitful, cheating, see cpds. — *Note*. kūṭe J I.145 ought to be read kuṭe (antokuṭe padīpo viya, cp. ghaṭa).

-aṭṭa a false suit, in °kāra a false suitor J II.2; DhA I.353; -jaṭila a fraudulent ascetic J I.375; DhA I.40; -māna false measure PvA 191; -vāṇija a false-trader Pv III.4[2]; PvA 191; -vinicchayikatā a lie (false discrimination) PvA 210. -vedin lier, calumniator J IV.177.

Kūṭa[2] (m. nt.) [Vedic kūṭa horn, bone of the forehead, prominence, point, ***qele** to jut forth, be prominent; cp. Lat. celsus, collis, columen; Gr. κολωνός κολοφών; Ags. holm, E. hill] — (a) prominence, top (cp. koṭi), in abbha° ridge of the cloud Vv I.[1] (=sikhara); aṇsa° shoulder, clavicle, VvA 121, 123 pabbata° mountain peak Vin II.193; J I.73. Cp. koṭa. — (b) the top of a house, roof, pinnacle A I.261; Vv 78[4] (=kaṇṇikā VvA 304); gaha° Dh 154; PvA 55. Cp. also kūṭāgāra. — (c) a heap, an accumulation, in sankāra° dust-heap M II.7; PvA 144. — (d) the topmost point, in phrase desanāya kūṭaṇ gahetvā or desanā kūṭaṇ gaṇhanto "leading up to the climax of the instruction" J I.275, 393, 401; V.151; VI.478; VvA 243. Cp. arahattena kūṭaṇ gaṇhanto J I.114; arahattaphalena k. gaṇhiṇ ThA 99.

-anga the shoulder Vv 15[8] (=VvA 123). -āgāra (nt.) a building with a peaked roof or pinnacles, possibly gabled; or with an upper storey Vin I.268; S II.103= V.218; III.156; IV.186; V.43, 75, 228; A I.101, 261; III.10, 364; IV.231; V.21; Pv III.1[7]; 2[21]; Vv 8[2] (=ratanamayakaṇṇikāya bandhaketuvanto VvA 50); VvA 6 (upari°, with upper storey) v. l. kuṭṭhāgāra; PvA 282 (°dhaja with a flag on the summit); DhA IV.186. In cpds.: -° *matta* as big as an upper chamber J I.273; Miln 67; -°*sālā* a pavilion (see description of Maṇḍalamāḷa at DA I.43) Vin III.15, 68, 87; IV.75; D I.150; S II.103=V.218; IV.186. -(n)gama going towards the point (of the roof), converging to the summit S II.263= III.156=V.43; -ṭṭha standing erect, straight, immovable, in phrase vañjha k° esikaṭṭhāyin D I.14=56= S III.211=M I.517 (expl. DA I.105 by pabbatakūṭaṇ viya ṭhita); -poṇa at Vism 268 is to be read °goṇa: see kūṭa[4].

Kūṭa[3] (nt.) [***qolā** to beat; cp. Lat. clava; Gr. κλάω, κόλος, and also Sk. khaḍga; Lat. clades, procello; Gr. κλαδαρός. The expl[n] of **kuṭ**[3] at Dhtp 557 & Dhtm 783 is "āko ṭane"] a hammer, usually as aya° an iron sledgehammer J I.108; or ayo° PvA 284; ayomaya° Sn 669; kammāra° Vism 254.

Kūṭa[4] (adj.) [Sk. kūṭa, not horned; ***(s)qer** to cut, mutilate, curtail, cp. Lat. caro, curtus; also Sk. kṛdhu maimed. The expl[n] of **kuṭ** as "chede," or "chedane" (cutting) at Dhtp 90, 555; Dhtm 115, 526, 781 may refer to this kūṭa. See also kuṭṭa] without horns, i. e. harmless, of goṇa a draught bullock Vin IV.5=J I.192 (in play of words with kūṭa deceitful J. trsl. misses the point & translates "rascal"). These maimed oxen (cows & calves) are represented as practically useless & sluggish in similes at Vism 268, 269: kūṭa-goṇa- (so read for °poṇa)-yutta-ratha a cart to which such a bullock is harnessed (uppathaṇ dhāvati runs the wrong way); kūṭa-dhenuyā khīraṇ pivitvā kūṭa-vaccho, etc., such a calf lies still at the post. — Kūṭa-danta as Np. should prob. belong here, thus meaning "ox-tooth" (derisively) (D I.127; Vism 208), with which may be compared danta-kūṭa (see under danta).

Kūṭeyya (nt.) [der. fr. *kūṭya of kūṭa[1], cp. in formation sāṭheyya] fraud, deceit, in comb[n] with sāṭheyya & vankeyya M I.340; A V.167.

Kūpa (m.) [Vedic kūpa, orig. curvature viz. (a) interior = cavity, cp. Lat. cupa, Gr. κύπελλον cup; also Gr. κύμβη, Sk. kumbha; — (b) exterior=heap, cp. Ags. hēap, Ohg. heap, Sk. kūpa mast]. 1. a pit, a cavity: akkhi° the socket of the eye M I.80, 245; DhsA 306; gūtha° a cesspool D II.324; Sn 279; Pv II.3[18]; Pug 36; miḷha° a pit for evacuations Pgdp 23, 24; **loma°** the root of the hair, a pore of the skin DA I.57; Vism 262, 360; also in na loma-kūpamattaṇ pi not even a hair-root J I.31; III.55; vacca°=gūtha° Vin II.141, 222. As a tank or a well: J VI.213; VvA 305. — 2. the mast of a boat J III.126; Miln 363, 378. See next.

-khaṇa one who digs a pit J VI.213. -tala the floor of a pit Vism 362.

Kūpaka=kūpa 1. Vism 361 (akkhi°), 362 (naditīra°), 449 (id.); =kūpa. 2. J II.112; IV.17.

Kūla (nt.) [Dhtp 271: kūla āvaraṇe] a slope, a bank, an embankment. Usually of rivers: S I.143=J III.361; A I.162; Sn 977; J I.227; Miln 36: udapāna° the facing of a well Vin II.122; vaccakūpassa k° the sides of a cesspool Vin II.141. See also paṇsu°, & cp. uk°, upa°, paṭi°.

Kūra (nt.) in sukkha° boiled rice (?) Vin IV.86; DhA II.171.

Keka [?] N. of a tree J V.405. Kern, *Toev.* s. v. suggests misreading for koka Phœnix sylvestris.

Keṭubha [deriv. unknown] expl[d] by Buddhaghosa DA I. 247 as "the science which assists the officiating priests by laying down rules for the rites, or by leaving them to their discretion" (so Trenckner, *J.P.T.S.* 1908, 116). In short, the ritual; the kalpa as it is called as one of the vedangas. Only in a stock list of the subject a learned Brahmin is supposed to have mastered D I.88; A I.163, 166; Sn 1020; Miln 10, 178. So in BSk; AvŚ II.19; Divy 619.

Keṭubhin [deriv. unknown] MA 152 (on M I.32) has "trained deceivers (sikkhitā kerātikā); very deceitful, false all through"; III.6=A III.199.

Ketaka [etym. uncertain] N. of a flower J IV.482.

Ketana sign etc., see saṇ°.

Ketu [Vedic ketu, *(s)qait, clear; cp. Lat. caelum (=*caidlom), Ohg heitar, heit; Goth. haidus; E. -hood, orig. appearance, form, like] — 1. ray, beam of light, splendour, effulgence Th 1, 64; which is a riddle on the various meanings of ketu. — 2. flag, banner, sign, perhaps as token of splendour Th 1, 64. **dhamma-k°** having the Doctrine as his banner A I.109=III.149; **dhūma-k°** having smoke as its splendour, of fire, J IV.26; VvA 161 in expl[n] of dhūmasikha.

-kamyatā desire for prominence, self-advertisement (perhaps vainglory, arrogance) Vism 469; Dhs 1116 (Dhs A. trs. 479), 1233=Nd[2] 505; Nd[1] on Sn 829 (=uṇṇama); — **mālā** "garland of rays" VvA 323.

Ketuṇ see kayati.

Ketuvant (adj.) [fr. ketu] having flags, adorned with flags VvA 50.

Kedāra (m. nt.) an irrigated field, prepared for ploughing, arable land in its first stage of cultivation: kedāre pāyetvā karissāma "we shall till the fields after watering them" J I.215; as square-shaped (i. e. marked out as an allotment) Vin I.391 (caturassa°; Bdhgh on MV VIII.12, 1); J III.255 (catukkaṇṇa°); surrounded by a trench, denoting the boundary (-mariyādā) DhA

III.6. — J IV.167; V.35; PvA 7 (=khetta). The spelling is sometimes ketāra (J III.255 v. l.) see Trenckner, *J.P.T.S.* 1908, 112. *Note.* The prefix ke- suggests an obsolete noun of the meaning "water," as also in kebuka, ke-vaṭṭa; perhaps Sk. kṣvid, kṣvedate, to be wet, ooze? ke would then be k(h)ed, and kedara=ked+dṛ, bursting forth of water=inundation; kebuka =kedvu(d)ka (udaka); kevaṭṭa=ked+vṛ, moving on the water, fisherman; (cp. AvŚ Index Kaivarta: name of an officer on board a trading vessel).

-koṭi top or corner-point of a field Vism 180.

Kebuka [on ke- see note to prec.] water J VI.38 (=42: k. vuccati udakaŋ). As nadī a river at J III.91, where Seruma at similar passage p. 189.

Keyūra (nt.) a bracelet, bangle DhA II.220 (v. l. kāyura).

Keyūrin (adj.) wearing a bracelet PvA 211 (=kāyūrin).

Keyya (ger. of kayati) for sale J VI.180 (=vikkiṇitabba).

Kerāṭika (adj.) [fr. kirāṭa] deceitful, false, hypocritic J I.461 (expl^d by biḷāra); IV.220; IV.223 (=kirāsa); MA 152; DhA III.389 (=saṭha). — a° honest, frank J V.117 (=akitava, ajūtakara).

Kerāṭiya=prec. J III.260 (°lakkhaṇa); MA 152.

Kelisā at Th I, 1010 is to be corrected into keḷiyo (see keḷi[2]).

Keḷanā (f.) [fr. kilissati? or is it khelana?] desire, greed, usually shown in fondness for articles of personal adornment: thus "selfishness" Vbh 351=DA I.286 (+paṭikeḷanā). In this passage it is given as a rather doubtful expl^n of cāpalla, which would connect it with **kṣvel** to jump, or **khel** to swing, oscillate, waver, cp. expl^n Dhtp 278 kela khela=calane. Another passage is Nd[2] 585, where it is comb^d with parikeḷanā and acts as syn. of vibhūsanā.

Keḷāyati [Denom. fr. **kḷ** in meaning "to amuse oneself with," i. e. take a pride in. Always comb^d with mamāyati. BSk. same meaning (to be fond of): śālikṣetrāṇi k. gopāyati Divy 631. Morris, *J.P.T.S.* 1893, 16 puts it (wrongly?) to **kel** to quiver: see also keḷanā] to adorn oneself with (acc.), to fondle, treasure, take pride in (gen.) M I.260 (allīyati kelāyati dhanāyati mamāyati, where dhanāyati is to be read as vanāyati as shown by v. l. S. III.190 & M I.552); S III.190 (id.); Miln 73. — pp. keḷāyita.

Keḷāyana (nt.) [fr. keḷāyati, cp. kelanā & keḷi] playfulness, unsettledness Vism 134 (opp. majjhatta), 317.

Keḷāyita [pp. of keḷāyati] desired, fondled, made much of J IV.198 (expl^d with the ster. phrase kelāyati mamāyati pattheti piheti icchatī ti attho).

Keḷāsa (cp. Sk. kailāsa] N. of a mountain Bdhd 138.

Keḷi[1] (f.) [fr. **krīḍ** to play, sport: see kiḷati] 1. play, amusement, sport PvA 265 (=khiḍḍā); parihāsa° merry play, fun J I.116. — 2. playing at dice, gambling, in °maṇḍala "circle of the game," draught-board; °ŋ bhindati to break the board, i. e. to throw the die over the edge so as to make the throw invalid (cp. Cunningham, *Stupa of Bharhut*, plate 45) J I.379.

Keḷi[2] (f.) [either fr. **kil** as in kilijjati & kilissati, or fr. **kel**, as given under kelanā] the meaning is not quite defined, it may be taken as "attachment, lust, desire," or "selfishness, deceit" (cp. kerāṭika & kilissati), or "unsettledness, wavering." — keḷi-sīla of unsettled character, unreliable, deceitful PvA 241. °sīlaka id. J II.447. — pañca citta-keḷiyo=pañca nivaraṇāni (kāmacchanda etc.), the gratifications of the heart Th I, 1010 (corr. kelisā to keḷiyo!). — citta-keḷiŋ kiḷantā bahuŋ pāpakammaŋ katvā enjoying themselves (wrongly) to their heart's content J III.43. Cp. kāmesu a-ni-kīḷitāvin unstained by desires S I.9, 117.

Kevaṭṭa [on ke- see kedāra] fisherman D I.45 (in simile of dakkhō k°) A III.31=342, cp. IV.91; Ud 24 sq.; J I.210; DhA II.132; IV.41; PvA 178 (°gāma, in which to be reborn, is punishment, fishermen being considered outcast); cp. J VI.399 N. of a brahmin minister, also D I.411 N. of Kevaḍḍha (?).

-dvāra N. of one of the gates of Benares, and a village near by Vv 19[7]; VvA 97.

Kevala (adj.-adv.) [cp. Lat. caelebs=*caivilo-b° to live by oneself, i. e. to live in celibacy, perhaps also, Goth. hails, Ohg. heil, E. whole] expression of the concept of unity and totality: only, alone; whole, complete; adv. altogether or only — 1. °ṛ (adv.) (a) only=just: k. tvaŋ amhākaŋ vacanaŋ karohi "do all we tell you" PvA 4; — only=but, with this difference: VvA 203, 249; — k. . . . vippalapati he only talks PvA 93; — and yet: "sakkā nu kiñci adatvā k. sagge nibbattituŋ?" is it possible not to give anything, and yet go to heaven? kevalaŋ mano-pasāda-mattena only by purity of mind DhA I.33; kevalaŋ vacchake balava-piyacittatāya simply by the strong love towards the baby-calf Vism 313; (b) alone: k. araññaŋ gamissāmi VvA 260; — exclusive Miln 247. — na k. . . . atha kho not only . . . but also VvA 227. — 2. whole, entire Sn p. 108; Cp. I.10[19]; Pv II.6[3] (=sakala PvA 95); Vism 528 (=asammissa, sakala); Pv II.6[3] (=sakala PvA 95). — k.>akevala entire>deficient M I.326. °ŋ entirely, thoroughly, all round: k° obhāsenti VvA 282.

-kappa a whole kappa Sn pp. 18, 45, 125; KhA 115; VvA 124, 255. -paripuṇṇa fulfilled in its entirety (sakala DA I.177) of the Doctrine; expl^d also at Nett 10.

Kevalin (adj.) [fr. kevala] one who is fully accomplished, an Arahant; often with mahesi and uttamapurisa. Def^n sabbaguṇa-paripuṇṇa sabba-yoga-visaŋyutta Sn A 153. — ye suvimuttā te kevalino ye kevalino vaṭṭaŋ tesaŋ natthi paññāpanāya S III.59 sq., i. e. "those who are thoroughly emancipated, these are the accomplished . . ."; kevalīnaŋ mahesiŋ khīṇ' āsavaŋ Sn 82=S I.167; — k. vusitavā uttamapuriso Nd[2] on tiṇṇa=A V.16. — with gen.: brahmacariyassa k. "perfected in morality" A II.23. — As Ep. of "brāhmaṇa" Sn 519=Nd[2] s. v.; of dhammacakka A II.9; see also Sn 490, 595. — akevalin not accomplished, not perfected Sn 878, 891.

Kesa [Vedic keśa; cp. kesara hair, mane=Lat. caesaries, hair of the head, Ags. heord=E. hair] the hair of the head S I.115 (haṭa-haṭa-k°, with dishevelled hair); A I.138 (palita-kesa with grey hair; also at J I.59); Sn 456 (nivutta°). 608; Th I, 169; J I.59, 138; III.393; Miln 26; KhA 42; Vism 353 (in detail). The wearing of long hair was forbidden to the Bhikkhus: Vin II.107 sq.; 133 (cp. kesa-massu); — dark (glossy) hair is a distinction of beauty: susukāla-keso (of Gotama) D I.115; cp. kaṇha and kalyāṇa; PvA 26. — The hair of Petas is long and dishevelled PvA 56; Sdhp 103; it is the only cover of their nakedness: kesehi paṭicchanna "covered only with my hair" Pv I.10[2]. — kesesu gahetvā to take by the hair (in Niraya) D I.234; — kesaŋ oropeti to have one's hair cut Vin II.133.

-oropaṇa(-satthaka) (a) hair-cutting (knife), i. e. a razor DhA I.431; -ohāraka one who cuts the hair, a barber Vism 413. -kambala a hair blanket (according to Bdhgh human hair) D I.167=A I.240, 295=II.206=Vin I.305=M I.78=Pug 55; A I.286. -kambalin wearing a hair **blanket** (of Ajita) D I.55. -kalāpā (pl.) (atimanohara°) beautiful tresses PvA 46; -kalyāṇa beauty of hair DhA I.387; -kārika hairdresser Vv 17[5]; -dhātu the hair-relic (of the Buddha) J I.81; -nivāsin covered only with hair of Petas (: keseh' eva paṭicchādita-kopīnā) Pv III.1[6]. °massu hair and beard; kappita-k°-m° (adj.) with h. and b. dressed D I.104; A IV.94; J VI.268. Esp. freq. in form kesa-massuŋ ohāretvā kāsāyāni vatthāni acchādetvā agārasmā anagāriyaŋ pabbajati "to shave off hair & beard, dress in yellow robes and leave the home for the homeless state," i. e. renounce the world and take up the life of a Wanderer D I.60, 115; III.60, 64, 76; A I.107; III.386; It 75; Pug 57; similarly A II.207 = Pug 56. -sobha the splendour or beauty of the hair PvA 46. -hattha a tuft of hair PvA 157; VvA 167.

Kesayati see kisa.

Kesara[1] a mane, in -sīha a maned lion J II.244; SnA 127.

Kesara[2] [fr. kesa] filament of flowers, hairy structures of plants esp. of the lotus; usually of kiñjakkha PvA 77; VvA 12; 111; — sa-kesarehi padumapattehi lotus-leaves with their hairs VvA 32; nicula-k° fibres of the Nicula tree VvA 134.
-bhāra a sort of fan (cp. vāladhi and cāmara) VvA 278.

Kesarin [fr. kesara[1]] having a mane, of a lion, also name of a battle-array (°saŋgāmo) Dpvs I.7; cp. AvŚ I.56.

Kesava [fr. last] of rich hair, of beautiful hair. Ep. of King Vāsudeva (cp. kaṇha) Pv II.6[2].

Kesika (adj.) [fr. kesa] hairy, of mangoes Miln 334.

Ko see ka.

Koka[1] [not = Sk. koka, cuckoo] a wolf J VI.525; Nd[1] 13 = Nd[2] 420; Miln 267 = J V.416. °vighāsa remainder of a wolf's meal Vin III.58.

Koka[2] [cp. Sk. koka] N. of a tree, Phœnix sylvestris: see keka.

Kokanada (nt.) [cp. Sk. kokanada] the (red) lotus A III.239 = J I.116.

Kokāsika the red lotus in °jāta "like the red lotus," said of the flower of the Pāricchattaka tree A IV.118.

Kokila [cp. Sk. koka a kind of goose, also cuckoo, with derivation kokila cuckoo; cp. Gr. κόκκυξ, Lat. cuculus, E. cuckoo] the Indian cuckoo. Two kinds mentioned at VvA 57: kāla° and phussa° black and speckled k. — As citra° at J V.416. — Vv 11[1], 58[8]; VvA 132, 163.

Koca [fr. kuc] see saŋ°.

Koci see ka.

Koccha[1] (nt.) some kind of seat or settee, made of bark, grass or rushes Vin II.149; IV.40 (where the foll def. is given: kocchaŋ nāma vāka-mayaŋ vā usīra-mayaŋ vā muñjamayaŋ vā babbaja-mayaŋ vā anto saŋveṭhetvā baddhaŋ hoti. Cp. *Vin. Texts* I.34; III.165); J V.407. Also in list of 16 obstructions (palibodhā) at Miln 11.

Koccha[2] (nt.) a comb (for hair-dressing) Vin II.107; Vv 84[16] (= VvA 349); Th 2, 254, 411 (= ThA 267).
-kāra a comb-maker Miln 331 (not in corresp. list of vocations at D I.51).

Koja mail armour J IV.296 (= kavaca).

Kojava a rug or cover with long hair, a fleecy counterpane Vin I.281; DhA I 177; III.297 (pāvāra°); Dāvs V.30. Often in expl[n] of goṇaka (q. v.) as dīgha-lomaka mahākojava DA I.86; PvA 157.

Koñca[1] [cp. Sk. krauñca & kruñc] the heron, often in comb[n] with mayūra (peacock): Th I, 1113; Vv 11[1], 35[8]; J V.304; VI.272; or with haŋsa Pv II.12[3]. — Expl[d] as sārasa VvA 57; jiṇṇa° an old heron Dh 155.

Koñca[2] = abbr. of koñca-nāda, trumpeting, in koñcaŋ karoti to trumpet (of elephants) Vin III.109; J VI.497.
-nāda the trumpeting of an elephant ("the heron's cry") [not with Morris, *J.P.T.S.* 1887, 163 sq. to **kruñc.** (meaning to bend, cp. Lat. crux, E. ridge), but prob. a contamination of krośa, fr. **krus** to crow, and kuñja = kuñjara, elephant (q. v.). Partly suggested at Divy 251; see also expl[n] at VvA 35, where this connection is quite evident.] J I.50; Miln 76 (in etymol. play with koñca); VvA 35. -rāva = prec. DhA IV.70. -vādikā a kind of bird J VI.538.

Koṭa [fr. kūṭa[2]] belonging to a peak, in cpd. °pabbata "peak-mountain," Npl. Vism 127 (write as K°), 292.

Koṭacikā pudendum muliebre, in conn. with kāṭa as a vile term of abuse Vin IV.7 (Bdhgh. koṭacikā ti itthinimittaŋ . . . hīno nāma akkoso).

Koṭi (f.) [cp. Sk. koṭi & kūṭa[2]] the end—(a) *of space*: the extreme part, top, summit, point (cp. anta to which it is opposed at J VI.371): dhanu-koṭiŋ nissāya "through the (curved) end of my bow," i. e. by means of hunting J II.200; aṭṭhi-koṭi the tip of the bone J III.26; cāpa° a bow VvA 261; vema° the part of a loom that is moved DhA III.175; khetta° the top (end) of the field SnA 150; cankamana° the far end of the cloister J IV.30; PvA 79. — (b) *of time*: a division of time, with reference either to the past or the future, in pubba° the past (cp. pubbanta), also as purima°; and pacchima° the future (cp. aparanta). These expressions are used only of saŋsara: saŋsārassa purima koṭi na paññāyati "the first end, i. e. the beginning of S. is not known" Nd[2] 664; DhsA 11; of pacchimā koṭi ibid. — anamatagg' āyaŋ saŋsāro, pubba° na paññāyati S's end and beginning are unthinkable, its starting-point is not known (to beings obstructed by ignorance) S II.178 = III.149 = Nd[2] 664 = Kvu 29 = PvA 166; cp. Bdhd 118 (p.k. na ñāyati). — koṭiyaŋ ṭhito bhāvo "my existence in the past" J I.167. — (c) *of number*: the "end" of the scale, i. e. extremely high, as numeral representing approximately the figure a hundred thousand (cp. Kirfel, *Kosmographie*. p. 336). It follows on sata-sahassāni Nd[2] 664, and is often increased by sata° or sahassa°, esp. in records of wealth (dhana) Sn 677; J I.227, 230, 345 = DhA I.367 (asīti°-vibhavo); J I.478; PvA 3, 96; cp. also koṭisatā arahanto Miln 6, 18. — kahāpaṇa-koṭi-santhārena "for the price (lit. by the spreading out) of a 100,000 kahāpanas" Vin II.159 = J I.94 (ref. to the buying of Jetavana by Anāthapiṇḍika).
-gata "gone to the end," having reached the end, i. e. perfection, nibbāna. Nd[2] 436; -ppatta = prec. Nd[2] 436; as "extreme" J I.67. -simbalī N. of a tree (in Avīci) Sdhp 194.

Koṭika (adj.) [fr. koṭi] I. having a point or a top, with ref. to the human teeth as eka°, dvi°, ti°, catu°, or teeth with one, two, etc., points Vism 251. — 2. having an end or climax SA on pariyanta (see *KS*. p. 320); āpāna° lasting till the end of life Miln 397; Vism 10. — 3. referring to (both) ends (of saŋsāra), in ubhato° pañhā questions regarding past & future M I.393 sq.

Koṭin (adj.) [fr. koṭi] aiming for an end or goal J VI.254 (cp. ākoṭana[2]).

Koṭilla (nt.) [fr. kuṭila] crookedness Dhtm 526; Abhp 859. As koṭilya at Dhtp 472.

Koṭumbara (nt.) [cp. BSk. kauṭumba Divy 559] a kind of cloth J VI.47 (coming from the kingdom of k.), 500 (spelt kodumb°). -°ka k.-stuffs Miln 2.

Koṭṭa (?) breaking, asi-k° note on Vin IV.363 (for asikoṭṭha Vin IV.171 ?); °aṭṭhi at Vism 254 read koṭṭh°.

Koṭṭana [fr. koṭṭeti] 1. grinding, crushing, pounding (grains) J I.475; °pacan' ādi pounding and cooking, etc. DhA II.261. — 2. hammering or cutting (?) in dāru° J II.18; VI.86 (maŋsa°, here "beating," T. spells ṭṭh). Cp. adhikuṭṭanā.

Koṭṭita (pp. of koṭṭeti] beaten down, made even Vism 254, 255.

Koṭṭima a floor of pounded stones, or is it cloth? Dāvs IV.47.

Koṭṭeti [cp. Sk. kuṭ & kuṭṭa[1]. Expl[d] one-sidedly by Dhtp (91 & 556) as "chedane" which is found only in 3 and adhikuṭṭanā. The meaning "beat" is attributed by Dhtp (557) & Dhtm (783) to root **kuṭ**[3] (see kūṭa[3]) by expl[n] "akoṭane." Cp. also kūṭa[4]; ākoṭeti & paṭikoṭeti]—1. to beat, smash, crush, pound J I.478; VI.366 (spelt ṭṭh); DhA I.25 (suvaṇṇaŋ) 165. — 2. to make even (the gronnd or floor) Vin II.291 (in making floors); J VI.332. — 3. to cut, kill SnA 178 (=hanti of Sn 121); DhA I.70 (pharasunā). — pp. **koṭṭita**. — Caus. **koṭṭāpeti** to cause to beat, to massage Vin II.266; J IV.37 (ṭṭ the only v. l. B.; T. has ṭṭh).

Koṭṭha[1] (m. nt.) [Sk. koṣṭha abdomen, any cavity for holding food, cp. kuṣṭa groin, and also Gr. κύτος cavity, κύσθος pudendum muliebre, κύστις bladder = E. cyst, chest; Lat. cunnus pudendum, Ger. hode testicle] anything hollow and closed in (Cp. gabbha for both meanings) as — 1. the stomach or abdomen Miln 265, Vism 357; Sdhp 257. — 2. a closet, a monk's cell, a storeroom, M I.332; Th 2, 283 (?)=ThA, 219; J II.168. — 3. a sheath, in asi° Vin IV.171.

-aṭṭhi a stomach bone or bone of the abdomen Vism 254, 255. **-abbhantara** the intestinal canal Miln 67; **-āgāra** (nt.) storehouse, granary, treasury: in conn. with kosa (q. v.) in formula paripuṇṇa-kosa-koṭṭhāgāra (adj.) D I.134, expl[d] at DA I.295 as threefold, viz. dhana° dhañña° vattha°, treasury, granary, warehouse; PvA 126, 133; **-āgārika** a storehouse-keeper, one who hoards up wealth Vin I.209; DhA I.101; **-āsa** [=koṭṭha + aŋsa] share, division, part; °koṭṭhāsa (adj.) divided into, consisting of. K. is a prose word only and in all Com. passages is used to explain bhāga: J I.254; 266; VI.368; Miln 324; DhA IV.; 108 (=pada), 154; PvA 58, 111, 205 (kāma°=kāmaguṇā); VvA 62; anekena k°-ena infinitely PvA 221.

Koṭṭha[2] a bird J VI.539 (woodpecker ?).

Koṭṭha[3] [cp. Sk. kuṭṭha] N. of a plant, Costus speciosus (?) J V.420.

Koṭṭhaka[1] (nt.) "a kind of koṭṭha," the stronghold over a gateway, used as a store-room for various things, a chamber, treasury, granary Vin II.153, 210; for the purpose of keeping water in it Vin II.121=142; 220; treasury J I.230; II.168; — store-room J II.246; koṭthake pāturahosi appeared at the gateway, i. e. arrived at the mansion Vin I.291.; — **udaka-k** a bath-room, bath cabinet Vin I.205 (cp. Bdhgh's expl[n] at *Vin. Texts* II.57); so also **nahāna-k**° and **piṭṭhi-k**°, bath-room behind a hermitage J III.71; DhA II.19; a gateway, Vin II.77; usually in cpd. **dvāra-k**° "door cavity," i. e. room over the gate: gharaŋ satta-dvāra-koṭṭhaka-paṭimaṇḍitaŋ "a mansion adorned with seven gateways" J I.227=230, 290; VvA 322. dvāra-koṭṭhakesu āsanāni paṭṭhapenti "they spread mats in the gateways" VvA 6; esp. with bahi: bahi-dvārakoṭṭhakā nikkhāmetvā "leading him out in front of the gateway" A IV.206; °e thita or nisinna standing or sitting in front of the gateway S I.77; M I.161, 382; A III.30. — bala-k. a line of infantry J I.179. — koṭṭhaka-kamma or the occupation connected with a storehouse (or bathroom ?) is mentioned as an example of a low occupation at Vin IV.6; Kern, *Toev.* s. v. "someone who sweeps away dirt."

Koṭṭhaka[2] [cp. Sk. koyaṣṭika] the paddy-bird, as **rukkha**° J III.25; II.163 (v. l. ṭṭ).

Koṭṭhu see kotthu.

Koṭṭheti at J II.424 the v. l. khobheti (nāvaŋ) should be substituted. See also koṭṭeti.

Koṇa [cp. Sk. koṇa & also P. kaṇṇa] 1. a corner Vin II.137; catu°=catu-kaṇṇa PvA 52; —°racchā cross-roads PvA 24. — 2. a bow for a musical instrument Miln 53.

Koṇṭa (v. l. B. koṇḍa) (?) a man of dirty habits J II.209, 210, 212.

Koṇṭha a cripple J II.118.

Koṇḍa-damaka (?) [cp. kuṇḍa] J IV.389; also as v. l. B at J II.209.

Koṇḍañña a well-known gotta J II.360.

Kotūhala (nt.) [on formation cp. kolāhala; see also kutūhala] excitement, tumult, festival, fair Dāvs II.80; esp. in °mangalaŋ paccāgacchati he visits the fair or show of . . . M I.265; A. III.439; °mangalika celebrating feasts, festive A III.206; J I.373; Miln 94 (cp. *Miln trsl.* I.143[n]: the native commentator refers it to erroneous views and discipline called kotūhala and mangalika) — (b) adj.: kotuhala excited, eager for, desirous of Miln 4; DhA I.330.

-sadda shout of excitement Miln 301.

Kotthali (koṭṭhali ?) a sack (?) Vin III.189=IV.269.

Kotthu [koṭṭhu J only: cp. Sk. kroṣṭu, of **kruś**] a jackal D III.25, 26; M I.334; Nd[1] 149 (spelt koṭṭhu); J VI.537 (°sunā: expl[d] by sigāla-sunakhā, katthu-soṇā ti pi pāṭho). **kotthuka** (and koṭṭhuka)=prec. S I.66 (where text has kutthaka) J II.108; Miln 23.

Kodaṇḍa (nt.) [cp. Sk. kodaṇḍa] a cross-bow M I.429 (opp. to cāpa); Miln 351 (dhanu and k°). °**ka** same J IV.433 (expl[d] by dhanu).

Kodumbara see koṭumbara.

Kodha [Vedic krodha fr. **krudh**, cp. kujjhati] anger. Nearest synonyms are **āghāta** (Dhs. 1060=Nd[2] 576, both expositions also of dosa), upanāha (always in chain rāga, dosa, moha, kodha, upanāha) and dhūma (cp. θυμός, Mhg. toûm=anger). As pair k. and upanāha A I.91, 95; in sequence kodha upanāha makkha palāsa, etc. Nd[2] rāga I.; Vbh 357 sq.; Vism 53, 107, 306; in formula abhijjhā byāpāda k. upanāha M I.36; A I.299=IV.148; cp. A IV.456=V.209; V.39, 49 sq., 310, 361. As equivalent of āghāta Dhs 1060=Nd[2] 576, cp. Pug 18. In other comb[n]: with mada and thambha Sn 245; **kadariya** Sn 362; pesuniya Sn 928; mosavajja Sn 866, 868 (cp. S I.169). Other passages, e. g. A I.283; S I.240; Sn 537 (lobha°); Pv II.3[7]; Dh I.52 (anattha-janano kodho); PvA 55, 222. — kodha is one of the obstacles to Arahantship, and freedom from kodha is one of the fundamental virtues of a well-balanced mind. — mā vo kodho ajjhabhavi "let not anger get the better of you" S I.240; māno hi te brāhmaṇa khāribhāro kodho dhūmo bhasmani mosavajjaŋ, etc. "anger is the smoke (smouldering) in the ashes" S I.169=Nd[2] 576. — kodhaŋ chetvā cutting off anger S I.41=47=161=237; kodhaŋ jahe vippajaheyya mānaŋ "give up anger, renounce conceit" J I.23 25=Dh 221; kodhaŋ pajahanti vipassino: "the wise give up anger" It 2=7; panuṇṇa-kodha (adj.) one who has driven out anger Sn 469; akkodhena jine kodhaŋ conquer anger by meekness Dh 223=J II.4= VvA 69. Yo ye uppatitaŋ kodhaŋ rathaŋ bhantaŋ va dhāraye tam ahaŋ sārathiŋ brūmi — "He who restrains rising anger as he would a drifting cart, him I call a waggoner" Dh 222, cp. Sn 1. — **akkodha** freedom from anger, meekness, conciliation M 1.44; S 1.240 (with avihiṇsā tenderness, kindness); A 1.95; Dh 223 = J 11.4 = VvA 69.

-**âtimāna** anger and conceit Sn 968. -**upāyāsa** companionship or association with anger, the state of being pervaded with anger (opp. akkodh°) M 1.360, 363; often compared with phenomena of nature suggesting swelling up, viz. "uddhumāyika" kodhupāyāsassa adhivacanaṇ M 1.144; "sa-ummī" It 114; "sobbho papāto" S 111.109; -**garu** "having respect for" i. e. pursuing anger (opp. saddhammagaru) A 11.46 sq., 84; -**paññāṇa** (adj.) knowing the true nature of anger Sn 96 (cp. SnA 170); -**bhakkha** feeding on, i. e. fostering anger, Ep. of a Yakkha S 1.238; -**vinaya** the discipline or control of anger A 1.91; v.165, 167 (comb[d] with upanāha vinaya).

Kodhana (adj.) [fr. kodha] having anger, angry, uncontrolled]; usually in comb[n] with **upanāhin**, e. g. Vin 11.89; D 111.45, 246; A v.156, cp. Sn 116; S 11.206; Pug 18. — k° kodhābhibhūta A iv.94 sq.; k° kodhavinayassa na vaṇṇavādī A v.165. — Used of caṇḍa PvA 83. — Cp. S iv.240; M 1.42 sq., 95 sq.; PvA 82. — akkodhana friendly, well-disposed, loving D 111.159; S 11.207; iv.243; M 1.42 sq., 95 sq.; Sn 19, 624, 850, 941; Vv 15[5]; VvA 69.

Konta a pennant, standard (cp. kunta) J vi.454; DA 1.244; SnA 317.

Kontimant at J vi.454 is expl[d] by camma-kāra, thus "worker in leather (-shields or armour)," with der. fr. konta ("satthitāya kontāya likhattā . . ."), but reading and meaning are uncertain.

Kopa [fr. **kup**] ill-temper, anger, grudge Vin 11.184 = Sn 6; Dhs 1060; with appaccaya (mistrust) M 1.27; almost exclusively in phrase kopañ ca dosañ ca appaccayañ ca pātukaroti (pātvakāsi) "he shows forth ill-temper, malice and mistrust" (of a "codita" bhikkhu) D 111.159; S iv.305; M 1.96 sq., 250, 442; A 1.124, 187; 11.203; 111.181 sq.; iv.168, 193; J 1.301; Sn p. 92. — akopa (adj.) friendly, without hatred, composed Sn 499.

-**antara** (adj.) one who is under the power of ill-temper S 1.24.

Kopaneyya (adj.) [fr. kopa] apt to arouse anger J vi.257.

Kopīna (nt.) [cp. Sk. kaupīna] a loin-cloth J v.404; Pv 11.3[23]; PvA 172; Sdhp 106.

-**niddaṇsanin** "one who removes the loin-cloth," i. e. shameless, impure D 111.183.

Kopeti [caus. of kuppati] to set into agitation, to shake, to disturb: rājadhamme akopetvā not disturbing the royal rules PvA 161; J 11.366 = DhA iv.88; kammaṇ kopetuṇ Vin iv.153 to find fault with a lawful decision; kāyangaṇ na kopeti not to move a limb of the body: see kāya. Cp. paṭi°, pari°, vi°, saṇ°.

Komala see kamala; Mhbv 29.

Komāra [fr. kumāra] (adj.) juvenile, belonging to a youth or maiden: f. komārī a virgin A iv.210.

-**pati** husband of a girl-wife J 11.120. -**brahmacariyā** (°ṇ carati) to practise the vow of chastity or virginity A 111.224; ThA 99. -**bhacca** Np. "master of the k°-science," i. e. of the medical treatment of infants (see note on Vin 1.269 at *Vin. Texts* 11.174). As such it is the cognomen of Jīvaka D 1.47 (as Komārabhacca DA 1.132); Vin 1.71; J 1.116; cp. Sdhp 351.

Komāraka (and °ika) = prec. A 1.261; J 11.180 (dhamma virginity); of a young tree S iv.160. —f. °ikā J 111.266.

Komudī (f.) [fr. kumuda the white waterlily, cp. Sk. kaumudī] moonlight; the full-moon day in the month Kattika, usually in phrase **komudī catumāsinī** Vin 1.155, 176, sq.; D 1.47 (expl[d] at DA 1.139 as: tadā kira kumudāni supupphitāni honti) or in phrase komudiyā puṇṇamāya DhA 111.461.

Koraka (m. nt.) [cp. Sk. koraka] 1. a bud J 11.265. — 2. a sheath J 111.282.

Korakita (adj.) [fr. koraka] full of buds VvA 288.

Korajika (adj.) [fr. ku+**raj** or **rañj**, cp. rāga] affected, excitable, infatuated Nd[1] 226 = Nd[2] 342 (v. l. kocaraka) = Vism 26 (v. l. korañjika).

Koraṇḍaka [= kuraṇḍaka] a shrub and its flower J v.473 (°dāma, so read for karaṇḍaka), vi.536; as Npl. in Koraṇḍaka-vihāra Vism 91.

Korabya [Sk. kauravya] Np. as cognomen: the descendant of Kuru J 11.371 (of Dhanañjaya).

Koriyā (f.) a hen v. l. (ti vā pāḷi) at Th 2, 381 for turiyā. See also ThA 255 (= kuñcakārakukkuṭī).

Kola (m. nt.) [Halāyudha 11.71 gives kola in meaning of "hog," corrupted fr. kroḍa] the jujube fruit M 1.80; A 111.49 (sampanna-kolakaṇ sūkaramaṇsa "pork with jujube"); J 111.22 (= badara); vi.578.

-**mattiyo** (pl.) of the size of a j. fruit, always comb. w. kolaṭṭhi-mattiyo, of boils A v.170 = Sn p. 125, cp. S 1.150; -**rukkha** the j. tree SnA 356; DA 1.262; -**sampāka** cooked with (the juice of) jujube Vv 43[5] (= VvA 186).

Kolankola [der. fr. kula] going from kula to kula (clan to clan) in saṇsāra: A 1.233 = Pug 16; S v.205; Nett 189, cp. A iv.381; A v.120.

Kolañña (adj.) [fr. kula] born of (good) family (cp. kulaja); as -°, belonging to the family of . . . D 1.89; DA 1.252; Miln 256. —**khīṇa-kolañña** (adj.) one who has come down in the world Vin 1.86.

Kolaṭṭhi the kernel of the jujube, only in cpd. °**mattiyo** (pl.) S 1.150 = A v.170 = Sn p. 125 (with kolamattiyo), and °mattā Th 2, 498 = ThA 289; DhA 1.319.

Kolaputti at A 1.38 is composition form of **kulaputta**, and is to be combined with the foll. -**vaṇṇa-pokkharatā**, i. e. light colour as becoming a man of good family. Kern, *Toev.* s. v. quite unnecessarily interprets it as "heron-colour," comparing Sk. kolapuccha heron. A similar passage at Nd[1] 80 = Nd[2] 505 reads kolaputtikena vā vaṇṇapokkharatāya vā, thus taking kolaputtikaṇ as nt, meaning a man of good virtue. The A passage may be corrupt and should then be read °puttikaṇ.

Kolamba (and koḷamba VvA) a pot or vessel in general. In Vin always together with **ghaṭa**, pitcher: Vin 1.208, 213, 225, 286; J 1.33; DA 1.58; VvA 36.

Kolāhala (nt.) (cp. also halāhala) shouting, uproar, excitement about (-°), tumult, foreboding, warning about something, hailing. There are 5 kolāhalāni enum[d] at KhA 120 sq. viz. **kappa°** (the announcement of the end of the world, cp. Vism 415 sq.), **cakkavatti°** (of a world-king), **buddha°** (of a Buddha), **mangala°** (that a Buddha will pronounce the "εὐαγγέλιον"), **moneyya°** (that a monk will enquire of the Lord after the highest wisdom, cp. SnA 490). One may compare the 3 (mahā-)halāhalāni given at J 1.48 as kappa-halāhala, buddha° and cakkavatti°, eka-kolāhalaṇ *one* uproar J iv.404; vi.586; DhA 11.96. See also Vin 11.165, 275, 280; J v.437; DhA 1.190; PvA 4; VvA 132.

Koliya (adj.) [fr. kola] of the fruit of the jujube tree J 111.22, but wrongly expl[d] as kula-dattika ph. = given by a man of (good) family.

Koḷiniyā (f.) well-bred, of good family J 11.348 (BB koleyyaka).

Koleyyaka (adj.) of good breed, noble, appl[d] to dogs J I.175; IV.437. Cp. koliniyā, and Divy 165: kolika-gadrabha a donkey of good breed.

Koḷāpa (and kolāpa) (adj.) 1. dry, sapless; always appl[d] to wood, freq. in similes S IV.161, 185; M I.242; III.95; J III.495; Miln 151; DhA II.51; IV.166. — 2. hollow tree Nd² 40; SnA 355 (where Weber, *Ind. Streifen* V.1862, p. 429 suggests reading koṭara = Sk. koṭara hollow tree; unwarranted).

Koḷikā (or kolika?) (f.) adj. = kolaka, appl. to boils, in piḷikoḷikā (itthi) having boils of jujube size Th 2, 395 (expl. at ThA 259: akkhidalesu nibbattanakā pīḷikā vuccati).

Kovida (adj.) [ku + vid.] one who is in the possession of right wisdom, with ref. either to dhamma, magga, or ariyasaccāni, closely related to medhāvin and paṇḍita. S I.146, 194, 196 (ceto-pariyāya°); A II.46; M I.1, 7, 135, 300, 310, 433; Dh 403 = Sn 627; Sn 484 (jāti-maraṇa°), 653 (kammavipāka°); Pv I.11[12]; Vv 15[9] (= VvA 73), 63[30] (= VvA 269); Miln 344; Sdhp 350. —akovida ignorant of true wisdom (dhammassa) S I.162; Sn 763; S IV.287 = Nd² on attānudiṭṭhi.

Koviḷāra [cp. Sk. kovidāra] a sort of ebony, Bauhinia variegata; a tree in the devaloka (pāricchattaka koviḷāra: k-blossom, called p. VvA 174) A IV.117 sq.; Sn 44; J IV.29; Vv 38[1]; DhA I.270.

-puppha the flower of the K. tree SnA 354 (where the limbs of one afflicted with leprosy are compared with this flower).

Kosa[1] (m. nt.) [cp. Sk. kośa and koṣa, cavity, box vessel, cp. Goth. hūs, E. house; related also kukṣi = P. kucchi] any cavity or enclosure containing anything, viz. 1. a store-room or storehouse, treasury or granary A IV.95 (rāja°); Sn 525; J IV.409 (= wealth, stores); J VI.81 (aḍḍhakosa only half a house) in cpd. -° koṭṭhāgāra, expl[d] at DA I.295 as koso vuccati bhaṇḍāgāraṃ. Four kinds are mentioned: hatthī°, assā°, rathā°, raṭṭhaṃ°. — 2. a sheath, in khura° Vism 251, paṇṇa° KhA 46. — 3. a vessel or bowl for food: see kosaka. — 4. a cocoon, see -°kāraka; — 5. the membranous cover of the male sexual organ, the praeputium J V.197. The Com. expl[s] by sarīra-saṅkhāta k°. See cpd. kosohita. — Cp. also kosī.

-ārakkha the keeper of the king's treasury (or granary) A III.57; -ohita ensheathed, in phrase kosohita vatthaguyha "having the pudendum in a bag." Only in the brahmin cosmogonic myth of the superman (mahā-purisa) D III.143, 161. Applied as to this item, to the Buddha D I.106 (in the C[y] DA I.275, correct the misprint kesa into kosa) D II.17; Sn 1022 pp. 106, 107; Miln 167. For the myth see *Dial* III.132-136. -kāraka the "cocoon-maker," i. e. the silk-worm, Vin III.224; Vism 251. -koṭṭhāgāra "treasury and granary" usually in phrase paripuṇṇa -k -k (adj.) "with stores of treasures and other wealth" Vin I.342; D I.134; S I.89; Miln 2; & passim.

Kosa[2] at VvA 349 is marked by Hardy, Index and trsl[d] by scar or pock. It should be corrected to kesa, on evidence of corresp. passage in ThA 267 (cp. koccha).

Kosaka [fr. kosa] 1. a sheath for a needle J III.282; — 2. a bowl, container, or vessel for food J I.349 (v. l. kesaka); M II.6, 7, (-°āhāra adj. living on a bowl-full of food; also aḍḍha°) Vism 263. — 3. case for a key (kuñcikā°) Vism 251.

Kosajja (nt.) [From kusīta] idleness, sloth, indolence, expl[d] at Vbh 369. — Vin II.2; S V.277-280; A I.11, 16; II.218; III.375, 421; V.146 sq.; 159 sq.; A IV.195 = Dh 241; Miln 351; Vism 132; Nett 127; DhA III.347; IV.85; DhsA 146; SnA 21.

Kosamattha = ka + samattha "who is able," i. e. able, fit DA I.27.

Kosalla (nt.) [der. fr. kusala] proficiency. There are 3 kinds mentioned at D III.220, Vbh 325 & Vism 439 sq., viz. āya°, apāya° and upāya°; at Dhs 16 = 20 = 292 = 555 = Nd². ad paññā it is classed between paṇḍicca and nepuñña. See also Pug 25; Vism 128 sq. (appanā°), 241 sq. (uggaha° & manasikāra°), 248 (bojjhanga°); PvA 63, 99 (upāya°).

Kosātakī (f.) [cp. Sk. kośātakī] a kind of creeper Vv 47[4]; Vism 256, 260, 359; VvA 200; -bīja the seed of the k. A I.32 = V.212.

Kosika = kosiya, an owl J V.120.

Kosiya an owl J II.353, cp. Np. Kosiyāyana J I.496. Biḷārakosika (and °kosiya) J IV.69.

Kosī (f.) a sheath D I.77 = M II.17.

Koseyya [der. fr. kosa, cp. Sk. kauśeya silk-cloth and P. kosa-kāraka] silk; silken material Vin I.58 = Miln 267; Vin I.192, 281; II.163, 169; D I.7. cp. A I.181 (see DA I.87); A IV.394; Pv II.1[17]; J I.43; VI.47.

-pāvāra a silk garment Vin I.281; -vattha a silk garment DhA I.395.

Kohañña (nt.) [fr. kuhana] hypocrisy, deceit J II.72; III.268; IV.304; DhA I.141.

Kvaṇ (indecl.) is together with kuṇ registered as a part. of sound ("sadde") at Dhtp 118 & Dhtm 173.

Kh.

Kha syllable & ending, functioning also as root, meaning "void, empty" or as n. meaning "space"; expld. by Bdhgh with ref. to dukkha as "khaŋ saddo pana tucche; tucchaŋ hi ākāsaŋ khan ti vuccati" Vism 494. — In meaning "space, sky" in cpd. khaga "sky-goer" (cp. viha-ga of same meaning), i. e. bird Abhp 624; Bdhd 56.

Khagga [Sk. khaḍga; perhaps to Lat. clades and gladius; cp. also kūṭa³] 1. a sword (often with dhanu, bow) at D I.7 (Dh I.89 = asi) as one of the forbidden articles of ornament (cp. BSk. khaḍga-maṇi Divy 147, one of the royal insignia); — khaggaŋ bhandati to gird on one's sword PvA 154. khaggaŋ sannayhati id. DhA III.75; °gāhaka a sword-bearer Miln 114; °tala sword-blade Mhvs 25, 90. — 2. a rhinoceros J v.406 (= gavaja), 416; VI.277 (°miga), 538. In cpd. °visāṇā (cp. BSk. khaḍgaviṣāṇa Divy 294 = Sn 36) the horn of a rh. (: khagga-visāṇaŋ nāma khagga-miga-singaŋ SnA 65) Sn 35 sq. (N. of Sutta); Nd² 217 (khagga-visāṇa-kappa "like the horn of the rh." Ep. of a Paccekabuddha, (cp. Divy 294, 582), also at Vism 234.

Khacita [pp. of **khac** as root expl^d at Dhtm. 518 by "bandhana"] inlaid, adorned with, usually with jewels e. g. VvA 14, 277; maṇi-muttādi khacitī ghaṇṭā "bells inlaid with jewels, pearls, etc." VvA 36; of a fan inlaid with ivory (danta-khacita) Vin III.287 (Sam. Pās.). Suvaṇṇa-khacita-gajak' attharaṇā "elephants' trappings interwoven with gold" VvA 104; of a chair, inlaid with pearls J I.41; of a canopy embroidered with golden stars J I.57.

Khajja (adj.-nt.) [grd. of khajjati] to be eaten or chewed, eatable, solid food, usually in cpd. -bhojja solid and other food, divided into 4 kinds, viz. asita, pīta, khāyita, sāyita Pv I.5² (= PvA 25) J I.58; Miln 2. -bhājaka a distributor of food (an office falling to the lot of a senior bhikkhu) Vin II.176 (= v.204); III. 38, 155.

Khajjaka (adj.) [fr. last] eatable, i. e. solid food (as °bhojjanāni opposed to yāgu PvA 23); (nt.) J I.186 (of 18 kinds, opp. yāgu); I.235 (id.); Miln 294. -°bhājaka = prec.

Khajjati (= khādiyati, Pass. of khādati; Dhtm 93 bhakkhaṇa) 1. to be eaten, chewed, eaten up, as by animals: upacikāhi Vin II.113; suṇakhehi Pv III.7⁸; pulavehi J III.177; cp. Pv IV.5² (cut in two) — 2. to be itchy, to be irritated by itch (cp. E. "itch" = Intens. of "eat") J v.198 (kh° kanduvāyati); Pv II.3⁹ (kacchuyā kh°) — 3. to be devoured (fig.), to be consumed, to be a victim of: kāmataṇhāhi M I.504; rūpena S III.87, 88 (khajjaniya-pariyāya, quoted Vism 479). — ppr. **khajjamāna** Pv II.1⁶ (consumed by hunger & thirst).

Khajjara caterpillar Pgdp 48.

Khajjopakana [cp. Sk. khadyota] the fire-fly M II.34 = 41; J II.415; VI.330, 441; DhA III.178; also **khajjūpanaka** Vism 412 (in simile). See Trenckner *J.P.T.S.* 1908, 59 & 79.

Khañja (adj.) [cp. Sk. khañja, Dhtp 81: khañja gativekalye] lame (either on *one* foot or *both*: PugA 227) Vin II.90 = A I.107 = II.85 = Pug 51 (comb. with kāṇa and kuṇi); Th 2, 438 (+ kāṇa); DhA I.376 (+ kuṇi).

Khañjati [fr. khañja] to be lame Pv III.2²⁸.

Khañjana (nt.) hobbling, walking lame PvA 185.

Khaṭakhaṭa (khāṭ-kata, making khāṭ; cp. kakkāreti) the noise of hawking or clearing one's throat: -sadda Vin I.88; DhA III.330; cp. khakkhaṭa (v. l. khaṭkhaṭa) Divy 518 = utkāśanaśabda.

Khaṭopikā (f.) [perhaps connected with Sk khaṭvā? uncertain] couch, bedstead M I.450, 451 (vv. ll. ka°, khajj°).

Khaṇa¹ (m.) [Derivation unknown. It has been suggested that khaṇa and the Sk. kshaṇa are derived from īkshaṇa (seeing) by process of contraction. This seems very forced; and both words are, in all probability, other than the word from which this hypothesis would derive them.] 1. Sdhp 584; khaṇo ve mā upaccagā "let not the slightest time be wasted" Sn 333 = Dh 315; cf. Th. II.5 (cp. khaṇātita); n' atthi so kh° vā layo vā muhutto vā yaŋ (nadī) āramati "there is no moment, no inkling, no particle of time that the river stops flowing" A IV.137 (as simile of eternal flow of happening, of unbroken continuity of change); Vism 238 (jīvita°), 473; (khaṇa-vasena uppād'-ādi-khaṇa-ttaya, viz. uppāda, ṭhiti, bhanga, cp. p. 431); J IV.128; aṭṭha-kkhaṇa-vinimmutto kh° paramadullabho: one opportunity out of eight, very difficult to be obtained Sdhp 4, 16; cp. 45, 46. — 2. moment as coincidence of two events: "at the same moment," esp. in phrase taŋ **khaṇaŋ yeva** "all at once," simultaneously, with which syn. ṭhānaso J I.167, 253; III.276, PvA 19; PvA 27, 35; tasmiŋ khaṇe J II.154; PvA 67; Sdhp 17. — 3. the moment as something expected or appointed (cp. *καιρός*), therefore the *right* moment, or the proper time. So with ref. to birth, rebirth, fruit of action, attainment of Arahantship, presence on earth of a Buddha, etc., in cpds.: cuti-kkhaṇo Bdhd 106; paṭisandhi° Ps II.72 sq.; Bdhd 59, 77, 78; uppatti° Vbh 411 sq.; sotāpattimagga° Ps II.3; phala° Ps I.26, Bdhd 80; nikanti° Ps II.72 sq.; upacāra° Bdhd 94; citta° id. 38, 95. -khaṇe khaṇe from time to time Dn 239 (= okāse okāse DhA III.340, but cp. *Comp.* 161, n. 5). Buddhuppāda°, Th II.A, 12. akkhaṇa see sep. Also akkhaṇavedhin. -akkhaṇe at the wrong time, inopportune Pv IV.1⁴⁰ (= akāle). On kh. laya, muhutta cp. *Points of Contr.* 296, n. 5.

-**ātīta** having missed the opportunity Sn 333 = Dh 315 (= DhA III.489); -**ññū** knowing, realizing the opportunity Sn 325 (cp. SnA 333). -paccuppanna arisen at the moment or momentarily Vism 431 (one of the 3 kinds of paccuppanna: kh°., santati°, addhā°). -paritta small as a moment Vism 238.

Khaṇa² [fr. **khaṇ**] digging J II.296. Cp. atikhaṇa.

Khaṇati [fr. khan or khaṇ; Dhtp 179: anadāraṇe] 1. to dig (? better "destroy"; cp. Kern *Toev.* s. v.), dig out.

uproot Dh 247, 337; Sn p. 101; J II.205; IV.371, 373; Sdhp 394. Also khanati & cp. abhikkhaṇati, palikkhaṇati. — 2. [=Sk. kṣaṇati] to destroy Vin II.26 (attānaŋ); M I.132 (id.). — pp. **khata** & **khāta** (cp. palikkhata).

Khaṇana (nt.) [fr. **khaṇ**] digging Miln 351 (pokkharaṇi°).

Khaṇika (adj.) [fr. khaṇa] unstable, momentary, temporary, evanescent, changeable; usually syn. with ittara, e. g. J I.393; III.83; PvA 60. — Vism 626 (khaṇikato from the standpoint of the momentary). Khaṇikā pīti "momentary joy" is one of the 5 kinds of joy, viz. khuddikā, khaṇikā, okkantikā, ubbegā, pharaṇā (see pīti) Vism 143, DhsA 115.

-**citta** temporary or momentary thought Vism 289. -**maraṇa** sudden death Vism 229. -**vassa** momentary, i. e. sudden rain (-shower) J VI.486.

Khaṇikatta (nt.) [fr. khaṇika] evanescence, momentariness Vism 301.

Khaṇḍa [freq. spelt kaṇḍa (q. v.). Cp. Sk. khaṇḍa; expl[d] at Dhtp 105 as "chedana"] 1. (adj.) broken, usually of teeth; Th 2, 260 (=ThA 211); Miln 342; Vism 51. — 2. (m. nt.) a broken piece, a bit, camma° a strip of hide Vin II.122; coḷa° a bit of cloth PvA 70; pilotika° bits of rags PvA 171; pūva° a bit of cake J III.276; — **akhaṇḍa** unbroken, entire, whole, in -kārin (sikkhāya) fulfilling or practising the whole of (the commandments) Pv IV.3[43] and °sīla observing fully the sīla-precepts Vv 113; cp. Vism 51 & Bdhh 89.

-**ākhaṇḍa** (redupl.-iter. formation with distributive function) piece by piece, nothing but pieces, broken up into bits Vism 115. -**ākhaṇḍika** piece by piece, consisting of nothing but bits, in kh °ŋ **chindati** to break up into fragments A I.204 (of māluvālatā); II.199 (of thūṇā); S II.88 (of rukkha); cp. Vin III.43 (dārūni °ŋ chedāpetvā); J V.231 (°ŋ katvā). -**danta** having broken teeth, as sign of old age in phrase kh° palitakesa, etc. "with broken teeth and grey hair" A I.138 and ≃; J I.59, 79 (id.). -**phulla** [Bdhgh on Vin II.160; khaṇḍa =bhinn'okāso, phulla=phalit' okāso.] broken and shattered portions; °ŋ paṭisankharoti to repair dilapidations Vin II.160 (=navakammaŋ karoti) 286; III.287; A III.263; cp. same expression at Divy 22. a° unbroken and unimpaired fig. of sīla, the rule of conduct in its entirety, with nothing detracted Vv 83[16]=Pv IV.1[76] (cp. akhaṇḍasīla)=DhA I.32.

Khaṇḍati to break, DhA IV.14; pp. **khaṇḍita** broken, PvA 158 (-kaṇṇo=chinnakaṇṇo).

Khaṇḍikā (f.) [fr. khaṇḍa] a broken bit, a stick, in ucchu° Vv 33[28] (=ucchu-yaṭṭhi DhA III.315).

Khaṇḍicca (nt.) the state of being broken (of teeth), having broken teeth, in phrase kh° pālicca, etc., as signs of old age (see above) M I.49=D II.305; A III.196; Dhs 644=736=869; DhA III.123; in similar connection Vism 449.

Khaṇḍeti [v. denom. fr. khaṇḍa] to renounce, to remit, in vetanaŋ °etvā J III.188.

Khata[1] [pp. of khanati] 1. dug up, uprooted, fig. one whose foundation (of salvation) has been cut off; in comb[n] with **upahata** D I.86 (=DA I.237); khataŋ upahataŋ attānaŋ pariharati "he keeps himself uprooted and half-dead" i. e. he continues to lead a life of false ideas A I.105=II.4; opp. akkhataŋ anupahataŋ, etc. A I.89.

Khata[2] [pp. of **kṣan**, to wound] hurt, wounded; pādo kh° hoti sakalikāya "he grazed his foot" S I.27=Miln 134, 179. — **akkhata** unmolested, unhurt Vv 84[52] (=anupadduta VvA 351). See also parikkhata.

Khataka [fr. khata[2]] damage, injury VvA 206, **khatakaŋ** dāsiyā deti "she did harm to the servant, she struck the s." Or is it khalikaŋ? (cp. khaleti); the passage is corrupt.

Khatta (nt.) [Sk. kṣatra, to **kṣi**, cp. Gr. κτάομαι, κτῆμα, possession] rule, power, possession; only in cpds.:

-**dhamma** the law of ruling, political science J V.490 (is it khattu°=khattā°?) -**vijjā** polity D I.9, condemned as a practice of heretics. Bdhgh at DA I.93 explains it as nīti-sattha, political science (=°dhamma). See Rh. D. *Dialogues* I.18. -**vijjavādin** a person who inculcates Macchiavellian tricks J V.228 (paraphrased: mātāpitaro pi māretvā attano va attho kāmetabbo ti "even at the expense of killing father and mother is wealth to be desired for oneself"), so also J V.240; -**vijjācariya** one who practises kh- °vijjā ibid.; -**vida** (so read for °vidha)=°vijja (adj.) a tricky person, ibid. (v. l. °vijja, better). Cp. Sk. kṣātra-vidya.

Khattar [Sk. kṣattṛ fr. kṣatra] attendant, companion, charioteer, the king's minister and adviser (Lat. satelles "satellite" has been compared for etym.) D I.112 (=DA I.280, kh° vuccati pucchita-pucchita-pañhaŋ vyākaraṇa-samattho mahāmatto: "kh° is called the King's minister who is able to answer all his questions"); Buddhaghosa evidently connects it with katheti, to speak, respond=katthā; gādhaŋ k° A II.107=Pug 43 v. l. for kattā (cp. Pug A 225).

Khattiya [der. fr. khatta=kṣatra "having possessions"; Sk. kṣatriya] pl. nom. also khattiyāse J III.441. A shortened form is khatya J VI.397. — f. khattiyā A III.226-229, khattī D. I.193, and khattiyī. A member of one of the clans or tribes recognised as of Aryan descent. To be such was to belong to the highest social rank. The question of such social divisions in the Buddha's time is discussed in *Dialogues* I.97-107; and it is there shown that whenever they are referred to in lists the khattiyas always come first. **Khattiyo** seṭṭho jane tasmiŋ D I.199=II.97=M I.358=S I.153, II.284. This favourite verse is put into the mouth of a god; and he adds that whoever is perfect in wisdom and righteousness is the best of all. On the social prestige of the khattiyas see further M II.150-157; III.169; A II.86; S I.71, 93; Vin IV.6-10. On the religious side of the question D III.82; 93; M I.149, 177; II.84; S I.98. Wealth does not come into consideration at all. Only a very small percentage of the khattiyas were wealthy in the opinion of that time and place. Such are referred to at S I.15. All kings and chieftains were khattiyas D I.69, 136; III.44, 46, 61; A I.100; III.299; IV.259. Khattiyas are called rājāno Dhp 294, quoted Netti 165.

-**ābhiseka** the inauguration of a king A I.107, 108 (of the crown-prince)=A II.87; -**kaññā** a maid of khattiya birth J I.60; III.394; -**kula** a khattiya clan, a princely house, Vin II.161 (w. ref. to Gotama's descent); III.80; -**parisā** the assembly of the khattiyas; as one of the four parisās (kh°, brāhmaṇa°, gahapati°, samaṇa) at Vin I.227; A II.133; as the first one of the eight (1-4 as above, Cātummahārājika°, Tāvatiŋsa°, Māra°, Brahma°) at M I.72=D III.260; -**mahāsāla** "the wealthy khattiya" (see above II.1) D III.258, etc.; -**māyā** "the magic of the noble" DhA I.166; -**vaŋsa** aristocratic descent DA I.267; -**sukhumāla** a tender, youthful prince (of the Tathāgata: buddha°, kh°) DhA I.5.

Khattiyī (f.) a female khattiya, in series brāhmaṇī kh° vessī suddī caṇḍālī nesādī veṇī rathakārī pukkusī A III.229; similarly M II.33, 40.

°**Khattuŋ** [Sk. °kṛtvah, cp. °kad] in comp[n] with numerals "times": dvikkhattuŋ, tikkhattuŋ, etc.; twice, three times, etc.

Khadira [Sk. khadira; Gr. κίσσαρος, ivy; Lat. hedera, ivy] the tree Acacia catechu, in cpds. -angārā (pl.) embers of (burnt) acacia-wood J I.232; PvA 152; -ghaṭikā a piece of a.-wood J IV.88; -tthambha a post of a.-wood DhA III.206; -patta a bowl made of a.-wood J V.389; -vana a forest of acacias J II.162; -sūla an impaling stake of a.-wood J IV.29.

Khanati see khaṇati.

Khanitti (f.) [to **khan**, cp. Sk. khanitra] a spade or hoe Vin I.270; J VI.520 = V.89 (+ ankusa).

Khantar [n. agent of khanti] possessed of meekness or gentleness; docile, manageable. Said of an elephant A II.116 = III.161 sq.

Khanti & **Khantī** f. [Sk. kṣānti] patience, forbearance, forgiveness. Def. at Dhs 1341: khantī khamanatā adhivāsanatā acaṇḍikkaŋ anasuropo attamanatā cittassa. Most frequent combinations: with mettā (love) (see below); -titikkhā (forbearance): khantī paramaŋ tapo titikkhā nibbānaŋ paramaŋ vadanti Buddhā Dh 184 = D II.49 = Vism 295; khantiyā bhiyyo na vijjati, S I.226; cp. DhA III.237: titikkhā-sankhātā khantī; -avihiŋsā (tolerance): kh°, avihiŋsā, mettatā, anudayatā, S V.169; -akodhana (forbearing, gentle) VvA 71; -soraccaŋ (docility, tractableness) D III.213 = A I.94; also with maddava (gentleness) and s. as quality of a well-bred horse A III.248, cp. A II.113 and khantā; -sovaccassatā (kind speech) Sn 266 (cp. KhA 148). See also cpds. — Khanti is one of the ten paramitās J I.22, 23: cp. A III.254, 255. — In other connections: khantiyā upasamena upeta S I.30; ativissuto Sdhp 473; anulomikāya kh°iyā samannāgata (being of gentle and forbearing disposition) A III.437, 441; Ps II.236 sq.; Vbh 340. See also A III.372; Sn 189, 292, 897, 944. — In scholastic language frequent in combination diṭṭhi khanti ruci, in def. of idha (Vbh 245), tattha (Nd²), diṭṭhi (Nd²), cp. Nd² 151 and Vbh 325 sq. — **akkhanti** intolerance Vin IV.241 (= kopa): Vbh 360 (in def as opp. of khanti Dhs 1341, q. v. above), 378.

-bala (nt.) the force of forbearance; (adj.) one whose strength is patience: . . . aduṭṭho yo titikkhati khantībalaŋ balānikaŋ tam ahaŋ brūmi brāhmaṇaŋ Dh 399 = Sn 623; — DhA IV.164; Ps II.171, 176; -mettā forbearing love, in phrase kh° -mettānuddaya-sampanna (adj.) one whose character is compassion and loving forbearance J I.151, 262; PvA 66 (+ yuttakāra); VvA 71 (in explⁿ of akodhana); -suñña (nt.) the void of khanti Ps II.183; -soracca (nt.) gentleness and forbearance S I.100, 222; A II.68; J III.487; DhA I.56; °e niviṭṭha "established in forbearance and meekness" A III.46 = D III.61.

Khantika (adj.) [fr. prec.] acquiescing in-, of such and such a belief, in añña° belonging to another faith, combᵈ with aññadiṭṭhika and aññarucika D I.187; M I.487.

Khandati [**skand**] to jump, only in cpd. pakkhandati; given as root khand at Dhtm 196 with meaning "pakkhandana."

Khandha [Sk. skandha] — I. *Crude meaning*: bulk, massiveness (gross) substance. A. esp. used (a) of an elephant: the bulk of the body, i. e. its back S I.95; vāraṇassa J III.392; hatthi-khandha-vara-gata on the back of the state elephant J I.325; PvA 75. Also with ref. to an elephant (hatthināga) sañjāta° "to whom has grown bulk — a large back" Sn 53, expl. SnA 103 by susaṇṭhitakkhandho "well endowed with bulk." — (b) of a person: the shoulder or back: nangalaŋ khandhe karitvā S I.115 appl. to Māra; Vism 100; DhA IV.168 (ohita°-bhāra the load lifted off his shoulder). — — (c) of a tree: the trunk. rukkhassa PvA 114, also as rukkha° J I.324; tāla° the stem of a palm PvA 56; nigrodhassa khandhaja (see cpds.) S I.207 = Sn 272; mūlaŋ atikkamma kh° ŋ sāraŋ pariyesitabbaŋ "one must go beyond the root and search the trunk for sweetness" S IV.94. — (d) as t.t. in exegetical literature: section, chapter, lit. material as collected into uniform bulk; freq. in postscripts to Texts and Commentaries. See also khandhaka. — B. More general as denoting bulk (-°); e. g. aggi° a great mass of fire M II.34, 41; J IV.139; udaka° a mass of water (i. e. ocean) A III.336; S IV.179; J I.324; PvA 62; puñña° a great accumulation of merit A III.336 = S V.400; bhoga° a store of wealth A V.84; J I.6; maṇi° an extraordinarily large jewel (possessing magic power) J II.102 sq. —

II. *Applied meaning*.—A. (-°) the body of, a collection of, mass, or parts of; in collective sense "all that is comprised under"; forming the substance of. — (a) dukkha° all that is comprised under "dukkha," all that goes to make up or forms the substance, the idea of "ill." Most prominent in phrase kevalassa dukkhakkhandhassa samudaya and nirodha (the origin & destruction of all that is suffering) with ref. to the paṭicca-samuppāda, the chain of causal existence (q. v.) Vin I.1; S II.95; III.14; A I.177; V. 184 & passim. Similarly: samudaya Vbh 135 sq. nirodha Nett 64; antakiriyā A I.147; vyādhimaraṇatunnānaŋ dukkhakkhandhaŋ vyapānudi Th 2, 162. — (b) lobha° dosa° moha° the three ingredients or integrations of greed, suffering and bewilderment, lit. "the big bulk or mass of greed" (see also under padāleti), S V.88 (nibbijjhati through the satta bojjhangā). — (c) vayo° a division of age, part of age, as threefold: purima°, majjhima°, pacchima° Nd² in def. of sadā. — (d) sīla (etc.) kh° the 3 (or 5) groups or parts which constitute the factors of right living (dhamma), viz. (1) sīla° the group dealing with the practice of morality; (2) samādhi° that dealing with the development of concentration; (3) paññā° that dealing with the development of true wisdom. They are also known under the terms of sīla-sampadā, citta°, paññā° D I.172 sq.; see sīla. — D I.206; Nett 64 sq.; 126. tīhi dhammehi samannāgato "possessed of the three qualities," viz. sīla-kkhandhesu, etc. It 51; cp. A I.291; V.326. tīhi khandhehi . . . aṭṭhangiko maggo sangahito M I.301; sīlakkhandhaŋ, etc. paripūreti "to fulfil the sīla-group" A I.125; II.20, III.15 sq. These 3 are completed to a set of 5 by (4) vimutti° the group dealing with the attainment of emancipation and (5) vimutti-ñāṇa-dassana °the group dealing with the realization of the achievement of emancipation. As 1-4 only at D III.229 (misprint puñña for paññā); cp. A I.125. As 5 at S I.99 = A I.162; S V.162; A III.134, 271; V.16 (all loc. = S I.99); It 107, 108; Nd² under sīla.

B. (absolute) in individual sense: constituent element, factor, substantiality. More especially as khandhā (pl.) the elements or substrata of sensory existence, sensorial aggregates which condition the appearance of life in any form. Their character according to quality and value of life and body is evanescent, fraught with ills & leading to rebirth. Paraphrased by Bdhgh. as rāsi, heap, e. g. Asl. 141; Vibh A 1 f.; cf. *B. Psy.* 42. 1. Unspecified. They are usually enumerated in the foll. stereotyped set of 5: rūpa° (material qualities), vedanā (feeling), saññā (perception), sankhārā (coefficients of consciousness), viññāṇa (consciousness). For further ref. see rūpa; cp. also Mrs. Rh. D. *Dhs trsl.* pp. 40-56. They are enumerated in a different order at S I.112, viz. rūpaŋ vedayitaŋ saññaŋ viññāṇaŋ yañ ca sankhataŋ n' eso 'ham asmi. Detailed discussions as to their nature see e. g. S III.101 (= Vbh 1-61); S III.47; III.86. As being comprised in each of the dhātus, viz. kāma° rūpa° arūpa-dhātu Vbh 404 sq.

(a) *As factors of existence* (cp. bhava). Their rôle as such is illustrated by the famous simile: "yathā hi angasambhārā hoti saddo ratho iti evaŋ khandhesu santesu hoti satto ti sammuti" "just as it is by the condition precedent of the co-existence of its various parts, that the word 'chariot' is used, just so it is that when the skandhas are there, we talk of a 'being'" (Rh. D.) (cp. Hardy, *Man. Buddh.* p. 425) S I.135 = Miln 28. Their connotation "khandha" is discussed at S III.101 = M III.16: "kittāvatā nu kho khandhānaŋ khandhâdhivacanaŋ? rūpaŋ (etc.) atītânāgatapaccuppannaŋ ajjhattaŋ vā bahiddhā vā oḷārikaŋ," etc.: i.e. material qualities are equivalent terms for the kh. What causes the manifestation of each kh.? cattāro mahābhūtā . . . paccayo rūpa-khandhassa paññāpanāya; phasso . . . vedanā°, saññā°, sankhārā°, etc.; nāmarūpaŋ . . . viññāṇa°: the material elements are the cause of rūpa, touch is that of vedanā, saññā, sankhārā, name and shape that of viññāṇa (S III.101); cp. M I.138 sq., 234 sq. On the same principle rests their division in: rūpa-kāyo rūpakkhandho nāmakāyo cattāro arūpino khandhā "the material body forms the material factor (of existence), the individualized body the 4 immaterial factors" Nett 41; the rūpakkhandha only is kāmadhātu-pariyāpanno: Vbh 409; the 4 arūpino kh° discussed at Ps II.74, also at Vbh 230, 407 sq. (grouped with what is apariyāpanna) — Being the "substantial" factors of existence, birth & death depend on the khandhas. They appear in every new conjuncture of individuality concerning their function in this paṭisandhi-kkhaṇe; see Ps II.72-76. Thus the var. phases of life in transmigration are defined as — (jāti:) ya tesaŋ tesaŋ sattānaŋ tamhi tamhi satta-nikāye jāti sañjāti okkanti abhinibbatti khandhānaŋ pātubhāvo āyatanānaŋ paṭilābho Nd² on Sn 1052; cp. jāti dvīhi khandhehi sangahitā ti VvA 29; khandhānaŋ pātubhāvo jāti S II.3; Nett 29; khandhānaŋ nibbatti jāti Vism 199. — (maraṇaŋ:) yā tesaŋ tesaŋ sattānaŋ . . . cuti cavanatā bhedo antaradhānaŋ maccu maraṇaŋ kālakiriyā khandhānaŋ bhedo kalevarassa nikkhepo M I.49 = Vbh 137 = S II.3, 42. — vivaṭṭa-kkhandha (adj.) one whose khandhas have revolved (passed away), i. e. dead S I.121 = III.123. — kh°anaŋ udaya-vyaya (or udayabbaya) the rising and passing of the kh., transmigration Dh 374 = Th 1, 23, 379 = It 120 = KhA 82; Ps 1.54 sq. — (b) *Their relation to attachment and craving* (kāma): sattisūlûpamā kāmā khandhānaŋ adhikuṭṭanā S I.128 = Th 2, 58, 141 (ThA 65: natthi tesaŋ adhik° ?); craving is their cause & soil: hetupaṭicca sambhūtā kh. S I.134; the 4 arūpino kh. are based on lobha, dosa, moha Vbh 208. — (c) *their annihilation*: the kh. remain as long as the knowledge of their true character is not attained, i. e. of their cause & removal: yaŋ rūpaŋ, etc. . . . n' etaŋ mama n' eso 'haŋ asmi na m' eso attā ti; evaŋ etaŋ yathābhūtaŋ sammappaññāya passati; evaŋ kho jānato passato . . . ahankāramamankāra-mānânusayā na honti ti S III.103; -pañca-kkhandhe pariññāya S III.83; pañca-kkhandhā pariññātā tiṭṭhanti chinnamūlakā Th 2, 106. See also S I.134. — (d) *their relation to dhātu* (the physical elements) and *āyatana* (the elements of sense-perception) is close, since they are all dependent on sensory experience. The 5 khandhas are frequently mentioned with the 18 dhātuyo & the 12 āyatanāni: khandhā ca dh° cha ca āyatanā ime hetuŋ paṭicca sambhūtā hetubhangā nirujjhare S I.134; kh°-dh°-āyatanaŋ sankhataŋ jātimūlaŋ Th 2, 472; dhammaŋ adesesi khandh'-āyatana-dhātuyo Th 2, 43 (cp. ThA 49). Enumerated under sabba-dhammā Ps I.101 = II.230; under dhammā (states) Dhs 121, as lokuttara-kkhandhā, etc. Dhs 358, 528, 552. — khandhānaŋ khandhaṭṭho abhiññeyyo, dhātūnaŋ dhātuṭṭho, etc. Ps I.17; cp. I.132; II.121, 157. In def. of kāmâvacarā bhūmi Ps 1.83. In def. of dukkha and its recognition Nett 57. In def. of arahanto khīṇāsavā Nd² on sankhāta-dhammā ("kh. sankhātā," etc.), on tiṇṇa ("khandha- (etc.) pariyante thitā"), & passim. — (e) *their valuation* & their bearing on the "soul"-conception is described in the terms of na mama (na tumhākaŋ), anattā, aniccaŋ and dukkhaŋ (cp. upādānakkh° infra and rūpa): rūpaŋ (etc.) . . . aniccaŋ, dukkhaŋ, n' eso 'ham asmi, n 'eso me attā "material qualities (etc. kh. 2-5) are evanescent, bad, I am not this body, this body is not my soul" Vin I.14 = S IV.382. n' eso 'ham asmi na m' eso attā S I.112; III.103, 130 & passim; cp. kāyo na tumhākaŋ (anattā rūpaŋ) S II.65; Nd² 680; and rūpaŋ na tumhākaŋ S III.33 M I.140 = Nd² 680. — rūpaŋ, etc. as anattā: Vin I.13; S III.78, 132-134; A I.284 = II.171; 202; cp. S III.101; Vin I.14. — as aniccaŋ: S III.41, 52, 102, 122, 132 sq., 181 sq., 195 sq., 202-224, 227; A IV.147 (aniccânupassī dukkhânupassī); anicca dukkha roga, etc., Ps II.238 sq.; Vbh 324. — 2. Specified as panc' upādāna-kkhandhā the factors of the fivefold clinging to existence. Defined & discussed in detail (rūpûpadāna-kkhandha, etc.) S III.47; 86-88; also Vin I.10; S III.127 sq. Specified S III.58 III.100 = M III.16; S III.114, 158 sq.; V.52, 60; A IV.458; Vism 443 sq. (in ch. xiv: Khandha-niddesa), 611 sq. (judged aniccato, etc.). — Mentioned as a set exemplifying the number 5: Kh III.; Ps I.22, 122. Enumerated in var. connections S I.112; D III.233; M I.190; A V.52; Kh IV. (expl^d KhA 82 = A V.52); Miln 12 (var. references concerning the discussion of the kh. in the Abhidhamma). — What is said of the khandhas alone—see above 1 (a)-(e)—is equally applied to them in connection with upādāna. — (a) As regards their *origin* they are characterized as chandamūlakā "rooted in desire, or in wilful desire" S III.100; cp. yo kho . . . pañcas' upādānakkhandhesu chandarāgo taŋ tattha upādānaŋ ti M I.300, 511. Therefore the foll. attributes are characteristic: kummo pañcann' etaŋ upād° ānaŋ adhivacanaŋ M I.144; bhārā have pañcakkh°ā S III.26; pañcavadhakā paccatthikā pañcann' . . . adhivacanaŋ S IV.174; pañc' upād° . . . sakkāyo vutto M I.299 = S IV.259. — (b) their contemplation leads to the recognition of their character as *dukkha, anicca, anattā*: na kiñci attānaŋ vā attaniyaŋ vā pañcasu upādānakkhandhesu S III.128; rogato, etc. . . . manasikātabbā pañc° S III.167; pañcasu upād°esu aniccânupassī "realizing the evanescence in the 5 aggregates of attachment" A V.109; same with udayavyayânupassī S III.130; A II.45, 90; III.32; IV.153; and dhammânupassī M I.61. Out of which realization follows their gradual destruction: pañc' . . . khandhānaŋ samudayo atthangamo assādo, etc. S III.31, 160 sq.; A II.45, 90; IV.153; Nd² under sankhārā. That they occupy a prominent position as determinants of dukkha is evident from their rôle in the exposition of dukkha as the first one of the noble truths: sankhittena pañc'upādānakkhandhā pi dukkhā "in short, the 5 kh. are associated with pain" Vin I.10 = M I.48 = A I.177 = S V.421; Ps I.37, 39; Vbh 101 & passim; cp. katamaŋ dukkham ariyasaccaŋ? pañc'upād° ā tissa vacanīyaŋ, seyyathīdaŋ . . . S III.158 = V.425; khandhādisā dukkhā Dh 202 (& expl. DhA III.261). — 3. Separately mentioned: khandhā as tayo arūpino kh° (ved°, sañña°, sankh°) DhA I.22; viññāṇa-kh° (the skandha of discriminative consciousness) in Def. of manas: manindriyaŋ viññāṇaŋ viññ°-khandho tajjā manoviññāṇadhātu Nd² on Sn 1142 = Dhs 68.

-âdhivacana having kh. as attribute (see above) S III.101 = M III.16; -āvāra a camp, either (1) fortified (with niveseti) or (2) not (with bandhāpeti), esp. in the latter meaning w. ref. to a halting place of a caravan (= khandhāvāra ?) (1) J IV. 151; V.162; DhA I.193, 199.— (2) J I.101, 332; PvA 113; DhA II.79. Said of a hermitage J V.35. — fig. in sīla-khandhāvāraŋ bandhitvā "to settle in the camp of good conduct" DA I.244; -ja (adj.-n.) sprung from the trunk (of the tree), i. e. a growth or parasite S I.207 = Sn 272, expl. at SnA 304; khandhesu jātā khandha-jā, pārohānam etaŋ adhivacanaŋ. -niddesa disquisition about the khandhas Vism (ch. xiv esp.) 482, 485, 492, 509, 558, 589. -paṭipāṭi succession of khandhas Vism 411 sq. -paritta protective spell as regards the khandhas (as N. of a

Suttanta) Vism 414. -bīja "trunk seed" as one kind of var. seeds, with mūla° phaḷu° agga° bīja° at Vin v.132, & D 1.5, expl[d] DA 1.81: nāma assattho nigrodho pilakkho udumbaro kacchako kapitthano ti evam-ādi. -rasa taste of the stem, one of various tastes, as mūla° khandha° taca° patta° puppha°, etc. Dhs 629 = Nd² 540. -loka the world of sensory aggregates, with dhātu- and āyatanaloka Ps 1.122. -vibhanga division dealing with the khandhas (i. e. Vibh. 1 sq.) Miln 12. -santāna duration of the khandhas Vism 414.

Khandhaka [fr. khandha] division, chapter, esp. in the Vinaya (at end of each division we find usually the postscript: so & so khandhakaŋ niṭṭhitaŋ "here ends the chapter of . . ."); in cpd. °vatta, i. e. duties or observances specified in the v. khandha or chapter of the Vinaya which deals with these duties Vism 12, 101 (cp. Vin II.231). 188.

Khandhiman (adj.) having a (big) trunk, of a tree A III.43.

Khama (adj.) [fr. **kṣam**] (a) patient, forgiving. (b) enduring, bearing, hardened to (frost & heat, e. g.), fit for. — (a) kh. belongs to the lovable attributes of a bhikkhu (kh. rūpānaŋ, saddānaŋ, etc.; indulgent as regards sights, sounds, etc.) A III.113 = 138; the same applied to the king's horse A III.282. Khamā paṭipadā the way of gentleness (and opp. akkhamā), viz. akkosantaŋ na paccakosati "not to shout back at him who shouts at you" A II.152 sq.; cp. Nett 77; classified under the four paṭipadā at D III.229. In combn. w. vacana of meek, gentle speech, in vattā vacana° a speaker of good & meek words S I.63; II.282; Miln 380; cp. suvaco khamo A v.24 sq., forgiving: Miln 207.— (b) khamo sītassa uṇhassa, etc., enduring frost & heat A III.389 = v.132; addhāna° padhāna° (fit for) A III.30; ranga°, anuyoga°, vimajjana° M I.385. — **akkhama** (adj.) impatient, intolerant, in comb[n] dubbaca dovacassa karaṇehi dhammehi samannāgata S II.204 sq. = A II.147 sq. With ref. to rūpa, saddā, etc. (see also above), of an elephant A III.156 sq. — D III.229; Sdhp 95.

Khamati [Dhtp 218: sahane, cp. Sk. kṣamate, perhaps to Lat. humus, cp. Sk. kṣāh, kṣāman soil; Gr. χθών, χαμαι] 1. to be patient, to endure, to forgive (acc. of object and gen. of person): n' āhaŋ bhayā khamāmi Vepacittino (not do I forgive V. out of fear) S I.221, 222; aparādhaŋ kh. to forgive a fault J III.394. khamatha forgive DhA II.254; khamatha me pardon me Miln 13; DhA I.40. — 2. (impers.) to be fit, to seem good; esp. in phrase yathā te khameyya "as may seem good to you; if you please" D I.60, 108; M I.487. sabbaŋ me na khamati "I do not approve of" M I.497 sq.; na khamati "it is not right" D II.67. — 3. to be fit for, to indulge in, to approve of, in nijjhānaŋ khamanti M I.133, 480; cp. diṭṭhi-nijjhāna-kkhanti M I.480 & A I.189. — ppr. med. khamamāna Vin I.281 (uppaḍḍhakāsinaŋ kh°) fit for, allowing of, worth, cp. Bdhgh. note *Vin Texts* I.195. — grd. khamanīya to be allayed, becoming better (of a disease) Vin I.204; D II.99. — caus. khamāpeti to pacify, to ask one's pardon, to apologize (to = acc.) J I.267; PvA 123, 195; DhA I.38, 39; II.75, 254. — to ask permission or leave (i. e. to say good-bye) DhA I.14.

Khamana (nt.) long-suffering Miln 351; bearing, suffering Sdhp 202; and a° intolerance Bdhd 24.

Khamanatā (f.) forbearance and a° intolerance, harshness both as syn. of khanti & akkhanti Dhs 1342, Vbh 360.

Khamā (f.) [fr. ksam] (a) patience, endurance. (b) the earth (cp. chamā & see khamati) J IV.8 (v. l. B. chamāya).

Khamāpanā (f.) [abstr. fr. khamāpeti, Caus. of khamati] asking for pardon J IV.389.

Khambha [Sk. khambha & sthambha] 1. prop, support, in °kata "making a prop," i. e. with his arms akimbo Vin II.213 = IV.188. — 2. obstruction, stiffening, paralysis, in ūru° "stiffening of the thigh" M I.237 (through pain); J v.23 (through fear). See also chambheti & thambha.

Khambheti [Caus. fr. prec. — Sk. **skambh**, skabhnāti] 1. to prop, to support Th 2, 28 (but expl. at ThA 35 by vi°, obstruct) — 2. to obstruct, to put out, in pp. khambhita (= vi°) Nd² 220, where it explains khitta. — ger. khambhiya: see vi°.

Khaya [Sk. kṣaya to **kṣi**, kṣiṇoti & ksiṇāti; cp. Lat. situs withering, Gr. φθίσις, φθίνω, φθίω wasting. See also khepeti under khipati] waste, destruction, consumption; decay, ruin, loss; of the passing away of night VvA 52; mostly in applied meaning with ref. to the extinction of passions & such elements as condition, life, & rebirth, e. g. āsavānaŋ kh. It 103 sq., esp. in formula āsavānaŋ khayā anāsavaŋ cetovimuttiŋ upasampajja A I.107 = 221 = D III.78, 108, 132 = It 100 and passim. — rāgassa, dosassa, mohassa kh. M I.5; A I.299, cp. rāga°, dosa°, moha°, A I.159; dosa° S III.160, 191; IV.250. — taṇhānaŋ kh. Dh 154; sankhārānaŋ kh. Dh. 383; sabbamaññitānaŋ, etc. M I.486; āyu°, puñña° Vism 502. — yo dukkhassa pajānāti idh' eva khayaŋ attano Sn 626 = Dh 402; khayaŋ virāgaŋ amataŋ paṇītaŋ Sn 225. — In exegesis of rūpassa aniccatā: rūpassa khayo vayo bhedo Dhs 645 = 738 = 872. — See also khīṇa and the foll. cpds. s. v.: āyu°, upadhi°, upādāna°, jāti°, jīvita°, taṇha°, dukkha°, puñña°, bhava°, loka°, saŋyojana, sabbadhamma°, samudda°.

-**ātīta** (a) gone beyond, recovered from the waning period (of chanda, the moon = the new moon) Sn 598; -**ānupassin** (a) realizing the fact of decay A IV.146 sq. = v.359 (+ vayânupassin); -**ñāṇa** knowledge of the fact of decay M II.38 = Pug 60; in the same sense khaye ñāṇa Nett 15, 54, 59, 127, 191, cp. kvu 230 sq.; -**dhamma** the law of decay A III.54; Ps I.53, 76, 78.

Khara¹ [cp. Sk. khara] 1. (adj.) rough, hard, sharp; painful D II.127 (ābādha); J III.26 (vedanā) Miln 26 (+ sakkhara-kaṭhala-vālikā), PvA 152 (loma, shaggy hair; cp. Np. Khara-loma-yakkha Vism 208). — °ka = khara rough, stony PvA 265 (= thaṇḍila). — 2. (m.) a donkey, a mule, in -putta, nickname of a horse J III.278. — 3. a saw J II.230 (= kakaca C.); VI.261.

-**ājina** a rough skin, as garment of an ascetic Sn 249 (= kharāni ajina-cammāni Sn A 291); Pug 56; -**gata** of rough constitution Dhs 962; also as khari-gata M I.185; Vism 349 (= pharusa). -**mukha** a conch J VI.580. -**ssara** of rough sound S II.128.

Khara² [Sk. kṣara] water J III.282.

Kharatta (nt.) [fr. khara] roughness A I.54; PvA 90 (in expl[n] of pharusa).

Khala [cp. Sk. khala] 1. corn ready for threshing, the threshing floor Nd² 587, Vism 120; DA I.203 (khalaŋ sodheti). — 2. threshing, mash, in ekamaŋsa-khalaŋ karoti "to reduce to one mash of flesh" D I.52 = M I.377 (+ maŋsa-puñja; DA I.160 = maŋsa-rāsi).

-**agga** the best corn for threshing DhA I.98; IV.98; -**kāla** the time for threshing DhA IV.98; -**bhaṇḍ'agga** the best agricultural implement for threshing DhA I.98; IV.98; -**bhaṇḍa-kāla** the time for the application of the latter DhA IV.98; -**maṇḍala** a threshing-floor Vism 123; DhA I.266 (°matta, as large as . . .).

Khalanka in -pāda at J VI.3 should probably be read kalanka° (q. v.).

Khalati [Dhtp 260: kampane; Dhtm 375: sañcalane; cp. Sk. skhalati, cp. Gr. σφάλλω to bring to fall, to fail] to stumble; ger. khalitvā Th 1, 45; Miln 187; pp. khalita q. v. Cp. upa°, pa°.

Khali a paste Vin II.321 (:Bdhgh. on C.V. VI.3, 1 for madda).

Khalika (or khalikā f.) a dice-board, in khalikāya kīḷanti to play at dice (see illustr. in Rh. D. *Buddh. India* p. 77) Vin II.10; cp. D I.6 (in enumⁿ of various amusements; expl. at DA I.85 by jūta-khalika pāsaka-kīḷanaŋ). See also kali.

Khalita[1] [Sk. khalati=Lat. calvus, bald; cp. khallāṭa] bald-headed A I.138 (+vilūna); Th 2, 255 (=vilūnakesa ThA 210).

Khalita[2] [pp. med. of khalati, cp. Dhtp 611; Dhtm 406 khala=soceyye] (adj. & n.) 1. faltering, stumbling, wrong-doing, failure A I.198; Nd[1] 300; Th 2, 261; DhA III.196 (of the voice; ThA 211=pakkhalita); J I.78; Miln 94, 408. — 2. disturbed, treated badly J VI. 375. — **akhalita** undisturbed Th 1, 512.

Khalu [indecl., usually contracted to kho, q. v.] either *positive*: indeed, surely, truly D I.87; Sn p. 103; J IV.391 (as khaḷu); Mhvs VII.17; or *negative*: indeed not Vism 60 (=paṭisedhan' atthe nipāto). -pacchābhattika (adj.)=na p°: a person who refuses food offered to him after the normal time Vin V.131=193; Pug 69; Vism 61. See Com. quot. by Childers, p. 310.

Khalunka [adj. fr. khala in caus. sense of khaleti, to shake. In formation=khalanga > khalanka > khalunka, cp. kulūpaka for kulūpaga] only applᵈ to a horse=shaking, a shaker, racer (esp. as java A I.287), fig. of purisa at Anguttara passages. Described as bold and hard to manage A IV.190 sq.; as a horse which cannot be trusted and is inferior to an ājānīya (a thoroughbred) A V.166. Three kinds at A I.287 sq.=IV.397 sq. In expl. of vaḷavā (mare) at J I.180=sindhavakule ajāto khalunk'asso; as vaḷavā khaḷunkā J I.184. — Der. **khalunkatā** in a°, not shaking, steadiness VvA 278.

Khaleti [Sk. kṣālayati of **kṣal** ?] lit. to wash (cp. pakkhāleti), slang for "to treat badly," "to give a rubbing" or thrashing (exact meaning problematic); only at J IV.205=382: gale gahetvā khalayātha jammaŋ "take the rascal by the throat and thrash him" (Com. khalayātha khalikāraŋ (i. e. a "rub," kind of punishment) pāpetvā niddhamatha=give him a thrashing & throw him out. v. l. at both passages is galayātha).

Khallaka in baddhā upāhanāyo shoes with heel-coverings (?) Vin I.186 (see Bdhgh. note on it *Vin Texts* II.15). — Also as **khalla**-baddhādibhedaŋ upāhanaŋ at PvA 127 in explⁿ of upāhana. Kern (*Toev.* s. v.) sees in it a kind of stuff or material.

Khallāṭa [Sk. khalvāṭa, cp. khalita] bald, in -sīsa a bald head DhA I.309. Der. **khallāṭiya** baldness, in khallāṭiyapetī the bald-headed Petī PvA 46 (where spelled khalātiya) and 67.

Khallika only at S V.421; cp. S IV.330 (Dhammacakka-p-Sutta). It is a misreading. Read with Oldenberg, Vin I.10, kāmesu **kāmasukhallikānuyoga** (devotion to the passions, to the pleasures of sense). See **kāmasukha** and **allika**.

Khaḷopī [and khalopi, also kalopī, q. v. Cp. Trenckner *Notes*, p. 60, possibly=karoṭi] a pot, usually with kumbhī: D I.167 (-mukha+kumbhi-mukha); Pug 55; Miln 107.

Khāṇu [also often spelled **khānu**; prob.=Sk. sthāṇu, corrupted in etym. with khaṇati, cp. Trenckner, *Notes* 58, n. 6] a stump (of a tree), a stake. Often used in description of uneven roads; together with **kaṇṭaka**, thorns A I.35; III.389; Vism 261 (°paharaṇ' aggi), 342 (°magga); SnA 334. — jhāma° a burnt stump (as characteristic of kālaka) S IV.193. — nikhāta° an uprooted trunk DA I.73. Khāṇu-kondañña N. of a Thera Vism 380; DhA II.254.

Khāṇuka=khāṇu S V.379 (avihata°): J II.18, 154; V.45 (loha-daṇḍa-kh° pins & stakes of brass); Miln 187 (mūle vā khāṇuke vā . . . khalitvā stumbling over roots & stumps); Vism 381=DhA II.254 (with ref. to the name of Khāṇu-kondañña who by robbers was mistaken for a tree stump); VvA 338 (in a road=sankuka).

Khāta (adj.) [Sk. khāta; pp. of **khan**] dug DA I.274 (=ukkiṇṇa), a° not dug Miln 351 (°taḷāka). Cp. **atikhāta** J II.296.

Khāda (nt.) eating, in -kāraṇa the reason of eating . . . PvA 37.

Khādaka (adj.) eating (nt.) Vism 479; eating, living on (adj. -°), an eater J IV.307; PvA 44; lohita -maŋsa° (of Yakkhas) J I.133, 266; camma° J I.176; gūtha° (of a Peta) PvA 266.

Khādati [Dhtp 155 "khāda bhakkhane"; cp. Sk. khādati, cp. Gr. κνώδων the barbed hook of a javelin, i. e. "the biter"; Lith. kándu to bite] to chew, bite, eat, devour (=Ger. fressen); to destroy. — *Pres.* Dh 240; J I.152 (sassāni); III.26; Pv I.6^3 (puttāni, of a Petī); I.9^4. — kaṭṭhaŋ kh° to use a toothpick J I.80, 282, — dante kh° to gnash the teeth J I.161. — santakaŋ kh° to consume one's property DhsA 135. — of beasts, e. g. Sn 201, 675. — *Pot.* khādeyya J III.26. — *Imper.* khāda J I.150 (maŋsaŋ); II.128 (khādaniyaŋ); VI.367. (pūvaŋ); PvA 39, 78. — *Part. pres.* khādanto J I.61; III.276. — *Fut.* khādissati J I.221; II.129. — *Aor.* khādiŋsu PvA 20. — *Pass. ppr.* khādiyamāna (cp. khajjati) PvA 69 (taṇhāya) (expl. of khajjamāna). — *Inf.* khādituŋ J I.222; II.153; DhA IV.226. — *Ger.* khāditvā J I.266, 278 (phalāni); PvA 5, 32 (devour); poetical khādiyā J V.464 (=khāditvā). — *Grd.* khāditabba J III.52, and khādaniya (q .v.). — *Pp.* **khādita** (q. v.). Cp. pali°.

Khādana (nt.) the act of eating (or being eaten) PvA 158. — adj. f. khādanī the eater Dpvs 238; khādana at J II.405 is to be read as ni° (q. v.). Cp. vi°.

Khādaniya [grd. of khādati; also as khādanīya] hard or solid food, opp. to and freq. combᵈ with **bhojaniya** (q. v.). So at D II.127; J I.90, 235; III.127; Sn. p 110; Miln 9, 11. — Also in combⁿ anna, pāna, kh° Sn 924; II.4^9. By itself J III.276. — piṭṭha° pastry Vin I.248.

Khādā (f.) food, in rāja° royal food Sn 831 (rājakhādāya puṭṭho=rājakhādanīyena rājabhojanīyena posito Nd[1] 171; where printed °khadāya throughout).

Khādāpana [fr. khādāpeti] causing to be eaten (kind of punishment) Miln 197 (sunakhehi).

Khādāpeti (Caus. II. of khādati] to make eat J III.370; VI.335.

Khādika=khādaka, in aññamañña° S V.456.

Khādita (adj.) [pp. med. & pass. of khādati] eaten, or having eaten, eaten up, consumed J I.223; II.154; PvA 5. — A twin form of **khādita** is **khāyita**, formed prob. on analogy of sāyita, with which freq. combined (cp., however, Trenckner P.M. 57), e. g. Pug 59; Vism 258; PvA 25. Used as the poetical form Pv I.12^{11} (expl. PvA 158=khādita). — Der. **khāditatta** (nt.) the fact of being eaten J I.176.
— **ṭṭhāna** the eating place, place of feeding J V.447.

Khādin, f. khādinī=khādaka PvA 31.

Khāyati [pass.=Sk. khyāyate, **khyā**] to seem to be, to appear like (viya) J I.279; aor. khāyiŋsu J I.61; ppr. med. **khāyamāna** J IV. 140; PvA 251. Cp. pakkhāyati.

Khāyita see khādita; cp. avakkhāyika.

Khāra [Sk. kṣāra, pungent, saline, sharp to **kṣā**, kṣāyati to burn, cp. Gr. ξηρός, dry; Lat. serenus, dry, clear, seresco to dry] any alkaline substance, potash, lye. In comb^n with ūsa (salt earth) at S III.131 (-gandha); A I.209. — Used as a caustic Pv III.10^2; Sdhp 281. See also chārikā.

-**āpatacchika** a means of torturing, in enum^n of var. tortures (under vividha-kamma-kāraṇā kārenti) M I.87 = A I.48 = II.122 = Nd^2 604; J VI.17 (v. l. °ṭicch°; C. has āpatacchika, v. l. paṭicchaka); Vism 500; Miln 197. Both A & Nd have v. l. kharāpaṭicchaka; -**odaka** an alkaline solution Vism 264, 420; DhA I.189; PvA 213; cp. khārodikā nadī (in Niraya) Sdhp 194.

Khāraka (adj.) [fr. khāra] sharp or dry, said of the buds of the Pāricchattaka A IV.117 sq.

Khārī (f.) [and khāri-] a certain measure of capacity (esp. of grain, see below khārika). It is used of the eight requisites of an ascetic, and often in conn. with his yoke (kāja): " a khārī-load."

-**kāja** Vin I.33 (cp. *Vin Texts* I.132); J V.204. -**bhaṇḍa** DhA III.243 (:kahaŋ te kh-bh° ko pabbajita parikkhāro); -**bhāra** a shoulder-yoke S I.169; J III.83; -**vidha** = °kāja S I.78 = Ud 65; D I.101. At Ud and D passages it is read vividha, but DA I.269 makes it clear: khārī ti araṇi-kamaṇḍalu-sūcādayo tāpasa-parikkhārā; vidho ti kāco, tasmā khāribharitaŋ kācam ādāyā ti attho. As Kern (*Toev.* s. v.) points out, °vidha is a distortion of vivadha, which is synonymous with kāja.

Khārika[1] [adj. to khāra] alkaline, in enum^n of tastes (cp. rasa) at S III 87; Dhs 629 and ≈.

Khārika[2] [adj. of khārī] of the khārī measure, in vīsati° kosalako tilavāho A V.173 = Sn p. 126.

Khāleti Caus. of khalati: see khaleti & vikkhāleti.

Khāhinti at Th 2, 509 is to be read kāhinti (= karissanti ThA 293).

Khiḍḍā [Vedic krīḍā, cp. kīḷati] play, amusement, pleasure usually comb^d with rati, enjoyment. Var. degrees of pleasures (bāla°, etc.) mentioned at A V.203; var. kinds of amusement enumerated at Nd^2 219; as expounded at D I.6 under jūta-pamādaṭṭhāna. Generally divided into kāyikā & vācasikā khiḍḍā (Nd^2; SnA 86). Expl. as kīḷanā SnA 86, as hassādhippāya (means of mirth) PvA 226; sahāyakādīhi keḷi PvA 265. Cp. Sn 926; Pv IV.1^{21}.

-**dasaka** " the decad of play," i. e. the second 10 years of man's life, fr. 11-20 years of age Vism 619. -**padosika** corrupted by pleasures D I.19, 20 = DA I.113 (v. l. padūsika); -**rati** play & enjoyment Sn 41, 59; Vv 16^{12}, 32^7; Pv IV.7^2; Vism 619.

Khitta [pp. of **khip**, to throw Dhtp 479; peraṇe] thrown; cast, overthrown Dh 34; rajo paṭivātaŋ kh°, dirt thrown against the wind S I.13, 164 = Sn 662 = Dh 125 = J III.203; ratti-khittā sarā arrows shot in the night Dh 304 = Nett 11; acchi vātavegena khittā a flame overthrown by the power of the wind, blown out Sn 1074 (expl^d Nd^2 220 by ukkhittā nuṇṇā, khambhitā); in interpret. of khetta PvA 7 said of sowing: khittaŋ vuttaŋ bījaŋ. — **akkhitta** not upset, not deranged, undisturbed, in qualities required of a brahmin w. ref. to his genealogy: yāva sattamā pitāmahāyugā akkhitto D I.113 = Sn p. 115, etc. Cp. vi°.

-**citta** (a) one whose mind is thrown over, upset, unhinged, usually comb^d with ummattaka, out of one's mind Vin I.131, 321; II.64, etc.; Sdhp 88. Cp. citta-kkhepa.

Khipa (nt.) [fr. **kṣip**] a throw, anything thrown over, as ajina° a cloak of antelope hide D I.167 and ≈; or thrown out, as a fishing net (= kumina) eel-basket A I.33 = 287; Th 2, 357 (= ThA 243). Cp. khippa & vikkhepika.

Khipati [Vedic kṣipati] to throw, to cast, to throw out or forth, to upset Sn p. 32 (cittaŋ); J I.223 (sīsaŋ), 290 (pāsake); II.3 (daḷhaŋ daḷhassa: to pit force against force) — aor. khipi S IV.2, 3 (khuracakkaŋ); PvA 87 (= atthāresi). — *ger.* khipitvā J I.202. — *1st caus.* khepeti (perhaps to **kṣi**, see khaya) to throw in, to put in, to spend (of time): dīgham addhānaŋ khepetvā J I.137; Th 2, 168 (khepeti jātisaŋsāraŋ = pariyosāpeti ThA 159); DhA I.102 (dvenavuti-kappe khepesuŋ); āyuŋ khepehi spend (the rest of) your life PvA 148; ger. khepayitvāna (saŋsāraŋ) Pv IV.3^{32} (= khepetvā PvA 254). In this sense Trenckner (P. M. 76) takes it as corresponding to Sk. kṣāpayati of **kṣi** = to cause to waste. See also khepana. — *2nd caus.* khipāpeti to cause to be thrown J I.202; IV.139 (jalaŋ). Cp also khepa.

Khipana (nt.) the act of throwing or the state of being thrown J I.290 (pasaka- k°).

Khipanā (f.) [fr. khipati] throwing up, provocation, mockery, slander Miln 357; Vbh 352; cp. Vism 29.

Khipita (nt.) [pp. of khipati = that which is thrown out; acc. to Trenckner *Notes* p. 75 for khupita fr. **kṣu** to sneeze; possibly a contamination of the two] sneezing, expectoration Pv II.2^3 (expl. PvA 80: mukhato nikkhantamala); DhA I.314 (°roga + kāsa, coughing).

-**sadda** the sound of expectorations D I.50; DhA I.250.

Khippa (adj.): [Vedic kṣipra to **kṣip**] 1. quick, lit. in the way of throwing (cp. " like a shot ") Sn 350 (of vacana = lahu SnA). — 2. a sort of fishing net or eel-basket (cp. khipa & Sk. kṣepaṇī) S I.74. — nt. adv. khippaŋ quickly A II.118 = III.164; Sn 413, 682, 998; Dh 65, 137, 236, 289; J IV.142; Pv II.8^4, 9^2, 12^{21}, Pug 32. — Compar. khippatara Sn p. 126.

-**abhiññā** quick intuition (opp. dandh°) D III.106; Dhs 177; Nett 7, 24, 50, 77, 112 sq.; 123 sq.; Vism 138.

Khippati [fr. **kṣip**] to ill-treat, in ppr. khippamāna Vv 84^{44}, expl^d at VvA 348 by vambhento, pīḷanto.

Khila (m. nt.) [cp. Sk. khila] waste or fallow land A III.248; fig. barrenness of mind, mental obstruction. There are five ceto-khilā enum^d in detail at M I.101 = A IV.460 = D III.238 (see under ceto); mentioned A V.17; SnA 262. As three khilā, viz. rāga, dosa, moha at S V.57; also with other qualities at Nd^2 9. In comb^n with paligha S I.27 (chetvā kh° ŋ); khilaŋ pabhindati to break up the fallowness (of one's heart) S I.193; III.134; Sn 973.— **akhila** (adj.) not fallow, unobstructed, open-hearted: cittaŋ susamāhitaŋ . . . akhilaŋ sabbabhūtesu D II.261; S IV.118; in comb^n with anāsava Sn 212; with akankha Sn 477, 1059; with vivattacchada Sn 1147; cp. vigatakhila Sn 19.

Khiḷa [cp. Sk. kiṇa] hard skin, callosity J V.204 (v. l. kiṇa).

Khīṇa [pp. of khīyati, Pass. to khayati] destroyed, exhausted, removed, wasted, gone; in cpds. °- often to be translated " without." It is mostly applied to the destruction of the passions (āsavā) & demerit (kamma). Khīṇā jāti " destroyed is the possibility of rebirth," in freq. occurring formula " kh. j. vusitaŋ brahmacariyaŋ kataŋ karaṇīyaŋ nāparaŋ itthattāya," denoting the attainment of Arahantship. (See arahant II, formula A) Vin I. 35; D I.84, 177, 203; M II.39; Sn p. 16; Pug 61 etc. See expl^n at DA I.225 = SnA 138. — khīṇaŋ mayhaŋ kammaŋ J IV.3, similarly khīṇaŋ purāṇaŋ navaŋ natthi sambhavaŋ Sn 235 (khīṇa = samucchinna KhA 194); pāpakamme khīṇe PvA 105. āsavakhīṇa one whose cravings are destroyed Sn 370, cp. 162.

-āsava (adj.) whose mind is free from the four mental obsessions, Ep. of an Arahant Vin I.183; M I. 145; II.43; III.30; D III.97, 133, 235; It 95; Sn 82, 471, 539, 644; Dh 89, 420; PvA 7 (=arahanto); cp. BSk kṣīṇāśrava Divy 542. — The seven powers of a kh.° (khīṇāsava-balāni) discussed at D III.283; Ps I.35; ten powers at Ps II.173, 176; cp. Vism 144 (where a kh. walks through the air). -punabbhava one in whom the conditions of another existence have been destroyed (=khīṇāsava) Sn 514, 656; -bīja one who is without the seed (of renewed existence) (=prec.) Sn 235 (=ucchinna-bīja KhA 194); -maccha without fish (of a lake) Dh 155; -vyappatha without the way of (evil) speech (vyapp°=vācāya patho; expl. SnA 204 as na pharusavāco) Sn 158; -sota with the stream gone, i. e. without water, in macche appodake kh° Sn 777.

Khīṇatta (nt.) DA I.225 & khīṇatā (f.) DhA IV.228, the fact of being destroyed.

Khīya [cp. khīyati[2]] in -dhammaŋ āpajjati to fall into a state of mental depression Vin IV.151, 154; A III.269; IV.374. See also remarks by Kern, *Toev.* s. v.

Khīyati [Sk. kṣīyate, pass. to khayati] to be exhausted, to waste away, to become dejected, to fall away from Vin IV.152; J I.290 (dhana); Pv II.9[42]; 11[2]; Ps I.94, 96; II.31 (āsavā); Bdhd 80. — ppr. khīyamāna Sn 434; Bdhd 19. aor. khīyi D III.93; grd. khīyitabba ibid. see also khāya and khīyanaka. In phrase "ujjhāyati khīyati vipāceti it seems to correspond to jhāyati[2] [Sk. kṣāyati] and the meaning is "to become chafed or heated, to become vexed, angry; to take offence"; as evidenced by the comb[n] with quâsi-synonyms ujjhāyati & vipāceti, both referring to a heated state, fig. for anger (cp. kilissati). Thus at Vin II.259 & passim. See ujjhāyati for further refs.

Khīyanaka (a) [der. fr. khīya] in comb[n] with pācittiya a "falling away" offence (legal term denoting the falling away from a consent once given) (see khīya) Vin II.94, 100; IV.38.

Khīra (nt.) [Sk. kṣīra] milk, milky fluid, milky juice Vin I.243; II.301; M I.343 sq.=A II.207=Pug 56; A II.95 (in simile with dadhi, navanīta, sappi, sappi-maṇḍa)=D I.201; DhA I.98; enum[d] with dadhi, etc., as one constituent of material food (kabaḷinkāro āhāro) at Dhs 646=740=875; — J IV.138 (mātu kh°); 140; Dh 71=Nett 161; Miln 41; PvA 198 (=sneha, milky juice); VvA 75; DhA I.98 (nirudaka kh°, milk without water). —duddha-khīra one who has milked Sn 18.

-ôdaka (nt.) milk-water or milk & water lit. J II.104, 106; fig. in simile khīrodakībhūtā for a samaggā parisā "a congregation at harmony as milk and water blend" A I.70; S IV.225=M I.207, 398=A III.67, 104; -odana (nt.) milk-rice (boiled) Vv33[24] (=VvA 147). -gandha the smell of milk J VI.357. -ghaṭa a pot of milk Miln 48; -paka drinking milk; sucking (of a calf: vaccho mātari kh°) Dh 284 (v. l. khīra-pāna); DhA III.424; -paṇṇin (m.) N. of a tree the leaves of which contain a milky sap, Calotropis gigantea M I.429; -matta having had his fill of milk, happy (of a babe) S I.108; -mūla the price of milk; money with which to buy milk DhA IV.217; -sâmin master of the milk (+dhīrasâmin) Bdhd 62.

Khīranikā (f.) a milk-giving cow S I.174.

Khīla [Sk. kīla & khīla] a stake, post, bolt, peg Vin II.116 (khīlaŋ nikhanitvā digging in or erecting a post); S III.150 (kh° vā thambha vā); IV.200 (daḷha° a strong post, Ep. of satī); Mhvs 29, 49. — ayo° an iron stake A I.141; S V.444; Nd[2] 304[III]; Sn 28 (nikhāta, erected); SnA 479. Cp. inda°.

ṭṭhāyi-ṭhita standing like a post (of a stubborn horse) A IV.192, 194.

Khīlaka (adj.) having sticks or stumps (as obstacles), in a° unobstructed J V.203 (=akāca nikkaṇṭaka 206).

Khīḷana [der. fr. khīḷeti] scorn Miln 357.

Khīḷeti [to kīḷ or to khila ?] to scorn, deride, only in comb[n] hīḷita khīḷita garahita (pp.) Miln 229, 288; cp. khīlana.

Khu (-°) is doubtful second part of inghāḷa° (q. v.).

Khuŋseti [kruś ? Dhtp 625: akkosane; cp. Müller *P.G.* 52 to scold, to curse, to be angry at, to have spite against D I.90, DA I.256 (=ghaṭṭeti); Vin IV.7; SnA 357; DhA IV.38. — pp. khuŋsita DhA II.75.

Khujja (adj.) [either Sk kubja, of which khujja would be the older form (cp. Walde, *Lat. Etym. Wtb.* s. v. cubitum), or Sk. kṣudra (?) (so Müller, *P.G.* p. 52). See also the variant kujja & cp. kuṭṭa[2]] 1. humpbacked J V.426 (+piṭhasappī); DA I.148 (in comb[n] with vāmana & kirāta); f. DhA I.194, 226. — 2. small, inferior, in kh°-rājā a smaller, subordinate king Sdhp 453.

Khuṇḍali at PvA 162 (mā kh.) is to be read ukkaṇṭhi.

Khudā [Sk. kṣudh & kṣudhā, also BSk. kṣud in kṣuttarṣa hunger & thirst Jtm p. 30] hunger Sn 52 (+pipāsā: Nd[2] s. v. kh° vuccati chātako), 966; Pv I.6[4] (=jighacchā) II.1[5] (+taṇhā), 2[4]; PvA 72. See khuppipāsā.

Khudda (adj.) [Vedic kṣudra] small, inferior, low; trifling, insignificant; na khuddaŋ samācare kiñci "he shall not pursue anything trifling" Sn 145 (=lāmakaŋ KhA 243); kh° ca bālaŋ Sn 318. Opp. to strong Vv 32[10] (of migā=balavasena nihīnā VvA 136).

-ânukhuddaka, in °āni sikkhāpadāni the minor observances of discipline, the lesser & minor precepts Vin II.287=D II. 154; Vin IV.143; A I.233; cp. Divy 465; -âvakāsa in akhuddâvakāso dassanāya not appearing inferior, one of the attributes of a well-bred brahmin (with brahmavaṇṇī) D I.114, 120, etc. -desa, in °issara ruler of a small district Sdhp 348.

Khuddaka=khudda; usually in cpds. In sequence khuddaka-majjhima-mahā Vism 100. Of smaller sections or subdivisions of canonical books Vin V.145 sq. (with ref. to the paññattis), see also below. -catuppade kh° ca mahallake Sn 603. Khuddaka (m.) the little one, Miln 40 (mātā °assa).

-nadī=kunnadī, a small river PvA 154; -nikāya name of a collection of canonical books, mostly short (the fifth of the five Nikāyas) comprising the foll. 15 books: Khuddaka-Pāṭha, Dhammapada, Udāna, Itivuttaka, Sutta-Nipāta, Vimāna-Vatthu, Peta-Vatthu, Thera and Therī Gāthā, Jātaka (verses only), Niddesa, Paṭisambhidāmagga, Apadāna, Buddha-Vaŋsa, Cariyā-Piṭaka. The name Kh-N. is taken from the fact that it is a collection of short books—short, that is, as compared with the Four Nikāyas. Anvs (*J.P.T.S.* 1886) p. 35; Gvns (*J.P.T.S.* 1886) p. 57; PvA 2, etc. -pāṭha N. of the first book in the Khuddaka Nikāya; -mañcaka a small or low bed J I.167; -rājā an inferior king J V.37 (+mahārājā); SnA 121; cp. khujja & kuṭṭa; -vagguli (f.) a small singing bird DhA III.223; -vatthuka belonging to or having smaller sections Vin V.114.

Khuppipāsā [cp. khudā] hunger & thirst: °āya miyamāno M I.85. Personified as belonging to the army of Māra Sn 436=Nd[2] on visenikatvā. To be tormented by hunger & thirst is the special lot of the *Petas*: Pv I.11[10]; II.2[2], PvA 10, 32, 37, 58, etc.; Vism 501; Sdhp 9, 101, 507.

Khubhati see saŋ° & khobha. The root is given at Dhtp 206 & 435 as "khubha=sañcalane."

Khura[1] [Vedic khura] the hoof of an animal Vv 64[10] (of a horse=turagānaŋ khuranipāta, the clattering of a horse's hoof VvA 279), cp. Sk. kṣura, a monkey's claw Sp. AvS I.236.

Khura² [Vedic kṣura, to **kṣṇu**, kṣṇoti to whet, kṣṇotra whetstone; cp. Gr. χναύω scrape, ξύω shave, Lat. novacula razor. The Pali Dhtp (486) gives as meanings "chedana & vilekhana"] a razor Vin II.134; S IV.169 (tiṇha a sharp r.) DhA II.257.
-agga the hall of tonsure PvA 53; -appa a kind of arrow D I.96; M I.429 (+vekaṇḍa); Vism 381. -kosa razor-sheath Vism 251, 255. -cakka a wheel, sharp as a razor J IV.3; -dhāra 1. carrying razors, said of the Vetaraṇī whose waters are like razors Sn 674 (+tiṇhadhāra); J V.269; Vism 163. — 2. the haft of a razor, or its case Sn 716 (°ūpama); Vism 500; DhA II.257; -nāsa having a nose like a razor J IV.139; -pariyanta a disk as sharp as a razor, a butcher-knife D I.52 (=DA I.160; khura-nemi khura-sadisa-pariyanta), cp. °cakka; -māla N. of an ocean, in °samudda J IV.137; -mālī (f.)= prec. ibid.; -muṇḍa close-shaven Vin I.344; VvA 207. Khuramuṇḍaŋ karoti to shave closely D I.98; S IV.344= A II.241; -bhaṇḍa the outfit of a barber, viz. khura, khura-silā, khura-sipāṭikā, namataka Vin I.249, II.134. cp. *Vin. Texts* III.138; -silā a whetstone Vin II.134; -sipāṭikā a powder prepared with s. gum to prevent razors from rusting Vin II.134.

Kheṭa [cp. Sk. kheṭaka] a shield: see kiṭa.

Khetta (nt.) [Vedic kṣetra, to **kṣi**, kṣeti, kṣiti, dwelling-place, Gr. κτίζω, Lat. situs founded, situated, E. site; cp. also Sk. kṣema "being settled," composure. See also khattiya. Dhammapāla connects khetta with **kṣip** & **trā** in his explⁿ at PvA 7: khittaŋ vuttaŋ bījaŋ tāyati . . . ti khettaŋ] 1. (lit.) a field, a plot of land, arable land, a site, D I.231; S I.134 (bījaŋ khette virūhati; in simile); three kinds of fields at S IV.315, viz. agga°, majjhima°, hīna° (in simile); A I.229=239; IV.237 (do.); Sn 524; J I.153 (sāli-yava°); Pv II.9[68]=DhA III.220 (khette bījaŋ ropitaŋ); Miln 47; PvA 62; DhA I.98. Often as a mark of wealth=possession, e. g. D III.93 in defⁿ of khattiya: khettānaŋ patī ti khattiya., In the same sense connected with vatthu (field & farm cp. Haus und Hof), to denote objects of trade, etc. D I.5 (expl^d at DA I.78: khetta nāma yasmiŋ pubbaṇṇaŋ rūhati, vatthu nāma yasmiŋ aparaṇṇaŋ rūhati, "kh. is where the first crop grows and v. where the second." A similar explⁿ at Nd¹ 248, where *khetta* is divided into sāli°, vīhi, mugga°, māsa°, yava°, godhūma°, tila°, i. e. the pubbaṇṇāni, and *vatthu* expl^d ghara°, koṭṭhaka°, pure°, pacchā°, ārāma°, vihāra° without ref. to aṇṇa.) S II.41; Sn 769. Together with other earthly possessions as wealth (hirañña, suvaṇṇa) Sn 858; Nd² on lepa, gahaṭṭha, etc. As example in definition of visible objects Dhs 597; Vbh 71 sq. — Kasi° a tilled field, a field ready to bear Pv I.1², cp. PvA 8; jāti° "a region in which a Buddha may be born" (Hardy, after Childers s. khetta) PvA 138. Cp. the threefold division of a Buddha-kkhetta at Vism 414, viz. jāti°, āṇā°, visaya°. — 2. fig. (of kamma) the soil of merit, the deposit of good deeds, which, like a fertile field, bears fruit to the advantage of the "giver" of gifts or the "doer" of good works. See dakkhiṇeyya°, puñña° (see detailed explⁿ at Vism 220; khetta here= virūhana-ṭṭhāna), brahma°. — A I.162, 223 (kammaŋ, khettaŋ, viññāṇaŋ bījaŋ); IV.237; It 98; VvA 113.— akhetta barren soil A III.384 (akhettaññu not finding a good soil); IV.418 (do.); PvA 137. Sukhetta a good soil, fertile land S I.21; PvA 137; opp. **dukkhetta** S V.379.
-ūpama to be likened to a (fruitful) field, Ep. of an Arahant Pv I.1¹; -kammanta work in the field A III.77; -gata turned into a field, of puññakamma "good work becoming a field of merit" PvA 136, 191; -gopaka a field watcher J III.52; -ja "born on one's land," one of the 4 kinds of sons Nd¹ 247; Nd² 448; J I.135. -jina one unsurpassed in the possession of a "field" Sn 523, 524; -pāla one who guards a field J III.54; -mahantatā the supremeness of the field (of merit) VvA 108; -rakkhaka the guardian of a field J II.110; -vatthu possession of land & goods (see above) D III.164; S V.473=A II.209; A V.137; Pug 58; PvA 3; -sampatti the successful attainment of a field of (merit) PvA 198; VvA 102; see VvA 30, 32 on the three sampattis, viz. khetta°, citta°, payoga°; -sāmika the owner of the field Miln 47; VvA 311. -sodhana the cleaning of the field (before it is ploughed) DhA III.284.

Kheda (adj.) [Sk. kheda fatigue, khedati; perhaps to Lat. caedo] subject to fatigue, tired VvA 276. — As noun "fatigue" at Vism 71.

Khepa [cp. khipati] (-°) throwing, casting, Sdhp 42. Usually in citta-kkhepa loss of mind, perplexity Dh 138. Cp. vi°, saŋ°.

Khepana [cp. khepeti] -° the passing of, appl^d to time: āyu° VvA 311.

Khepita [pp. of khepeti] destroyed, brought to waste, annihilated, khepitatta (nt.) the fact of being destroyed, destruction, annihilation, DhA II.163 (kilesavaṭṭassa kh.).

Khepeti see khipati.

Khema [Vedic kṣema to **ksi**, cp. khetta] 1. (adj.) full of peace, safe; tranquil, calm D I.73 (of a country); S I.123 (of the path leading to the ambrosial, i. e. Nibbāna) I.189=Sn 454 (of vācā nibbānapattiyā); M I.227 (vivaṭaŋ amatadvāraŋ khemaŋ nibbānapattiyā "opened is the door to the Immortal, leading to peace, for the attainment of Nibbāna") A III.354 (of ñāṇa) It 32; Sn 268 (=abhaya, nirupaddava KhA 153); Dh 189 sq.; Pv IV.3³ (of a road=nibbhaya PvA 250); VvA 85. — 2. (nt.) shelter, place of security, tranquillity, home of peace, the Serene (Ep. of Nibbāna). In general: D I.11 (peace, opp. bhaya); Sn 896 (+avivādabhūmi); 953. — In particular of Nibbāna: S IV.371; A IV.455; Vv 53[20] (amataŋ khemaŋ); Ps I.59. See also yoga. Abl. khemato, from the standpoint of the Serene S II.109; Sn 414, 1098; Nd² s. v. (+tāṇato, etc.).
-atta one who is at peace (+viratta) S I.112 (=khemībhūtaŋ assabhāvaŋ SA). -anta security, in °bhūmi a peaceful country (opp. kantāra), a paradise (as Ep. of Nibbāna) D I.73; Nd² on Satthā; Vism 303. -ṭṭhāna the place of shelter, the home of tranquillity Th 2, 350 (=Nibbāna ThA 242); -ṭṭhita peaceful, appeased, unmolested D I.135; -dassin looking upon the Serene Sn 809; -ppatta having attained tranquillity (=abhayappatta, vesārajjappatta) M I.72=A II.9.

Khemin (adj.) one who enjoys security or peace S III.13; Sn 145 (=abhaya KhA 244); Dh 258.

Kheḷa [Sk. kheṭa, cp. kṣveḍa and śleṣma, P. silesuma. See also **kilid** & **kilis**, cp. ukkheṭita. On root kheḷa see keḷanā; it is given by Dhtp 279 in meaning "calana." The latter (kheḷa) has of course nothing to do with kheḷa] phlegm, saliva, foam; usually with singhāṇikā mucus, sometimes in the sense of perspiration, sweat A I.34; IV.137; Sn 196 (+singh°); Kh II.=Miln 26 (cp. Vism 263 in detail, & KhA 66); J I.61; IV.23; VI.367; Vism 259, 343 (+singhāṇikā), 362; DhA III.181; IV.20, 170; Pv II.2³ as food for Petas, cp. Av.S. I.279 (kheḷamūtropajīvinī; II.113: kheṭavadutsṛjya); PvA 80 (=niṭṭhubhana).
-kilinna wet with exudation J I.164; **-mallaka** a spitting box, a cuspidor Vin I.48; II.175, 209 sq.; -singhāṇikā phlegm & mucus DhA I.50.

Kheḷākapa (Vin) & **kheḷāsika** (DhA) an abusive term "eating phlegm" (?) [Muller, *P.G.* 30=kheṭātmaka] Vin II.188, cp. *Vin. Texts* III.239; °vāda the use of the term "phlegm-eater," calling one by this name Vin II.189; DhA 140.

Kho [before vowels often khv'; contr. of khalu=Sk. khalu] an enclitic particle of affirmation & emphasis: indeed, really, surely; in narration: then, now (cp. kira); in question: then, perhaps, really. Def. as adhikār' antara-nidassan' atthe nipāto KhA 113; as avadhāraṇaŋ (affirmative particle) PvA 11, 18. — A few of its uses are as foll.: abhabbo kho Vin I.17; pasādā kho D II.155. After pron.: mayhaŋ kho J I.279; ete kho Vin I.10; idaŋ kho ibid.; so ca kho J I.51; yo kho M I.428; — After a negation: na kho indeed not J II.111; no ca khv' āssa A V.195; mā kho J I.253; — Often comb[d] with pana: na sakkhā kho pana "is it then not possible" J I.151; api ca kho pana J I.253; siyā kho pana D II.154; — Following other particles, esp. in aoristic narration: atha kho (extremely frequent); tatra kho; tâpi kho; api ca kho; evaŋ bhante ti kho; evaŋ byā kho Vin IV.134; Dh I.27, etc. — In interr. sentences it often follows nu: kin nu kho J I.279; atthi nu kho J III.52; kahan nu kho J I.255.

Khobha (m.) [cp. Vedic **kṣubh** kṣobhayati, to shake=Goth. skiuban Ger. schieben, to push, E. shove] shaking, shock Vism 31, 157; khobhaŋ karoti to shake VvA 35, 36, 278; khobha-karaṇa shaking up, disturbance Vism 474. See also akkhobbha.

Khoma [cp. Vedic kṣauma] adj. flaxen; nt. a linen cloth, linen garment, usually comb[d] with **kappāsika** Vin I.58, 96, 281; A IV.394; V.234=249 (°yuga); J VI.47, 500; Pv II.1[17]; DhA I.417.

-pilotikā a linen cloth Vin I.296.

G.

°Ga [fr. **gam**] adj., only as ending: going. See e. g. atiga, anuga, antalikkha°, ura°, pāra°, majjha°, samīpa°, hattha°. It also appears as °*gu*, e. g. in addha°, anta°, paṭṭha°, pāra°, veda°. — dugga (m. & nt.) a difficult road Dh 327 = Miln 379; Pv II.7^{6} (= duggamana-ṭṭhāna PvA 102); II.9^{25}; J II.385.

Gagana (nt.) the sky (with reference to sidereal motions); usually of the *moon:* g° majjhe puṇṇacando viya J I.149, 212; g° tale canda-maṇḍalaŋ J III.365; cando g° majjhe ṭhito J V.137; cando gagane viya sobhati Vism 58; g° tale candaŋ viya DhA I.372; g° tale puṇṇa-canda "the full-moon in the expanse of the heavens" VvA 3; g° talamagga the (moon's) course in the sky PvA 188; etc. Of the *sun:* suriyo ākāse antalikkhe gaganapathe gacchati Nd^{2} on Sn 1097. *Unspecified:* J I.57; Vism 176 (°tal-âbhimukhaŋ).

Gaggara [Vedic gargara throat, whirlpool. ***gṷer** to sling down, to whirl, cp. Gr. βάραθρον, Lat. gurges, gurgulio, Ohg. querechela "kehle"] 1. roaring, only in f. gaggarī a blacksmith's bellows: kammāra°, in simile M I.243; S I.106; Vism 287. — 2. (nt.) cackling, cawing, in haŋsa° the sound of geese J V.96 (expl. by haŋsa-madhurassara). Gaggarā as N. of a lake at Vism 208. — See note on gala.

Gaggaraka [fr. gaggara] a whirlpool, eddy J V.405; according to Kern *Toev.* s. v. a sort of fish (Sk. gargaraka, Pimelodus Gagora); as gaggalaka at Miln 197.

Gaggarāyati [v. den. fr. prec.; cp. gurgulio: gurges, E. gargle & gurgle] to whirl, roar, bellow, of the waves of the Gangā Miln 3. — cp. galagalāyati.

Gaccha [not = Sk. kaccha, grass-land, as Morris, *J.P.T.S.* 1893, 16. The passage J III.287 stands with gaccha; v. l. kaccha for gaccha at A IV.74; g° for k° at Sn 20] a shrub, a bush, usually together with latā, creeper & rukkha, tree, e. g. Nd^{2} 235, 1^{d}; J I.73; Miln 268; Vism 182 (described on p. 183). With dāya, wood A IV.74. puppha° a flowering shrub J I.120; khuddaka°-vana a wood of small shrubs J V.37. — PvA 274; VvA 301 (-gumba, brushwood, underwood); DhA I.171 (-po-thana-ṭṭhāna); IV.78 (-mūla).

Gacchati [Vedic gacchati, a desiderative (future) formation from ***gṷem** "I am intent upon going," i. e. I go, with the foll. bases. — (1) Future-present ***gṷemskéti** > *gaścati > Sk. gacchati = Gr. βάσκω (to βαίνω). In meaning cp. i, Sk. emi, Gr. εἶμι "I shall go" & in form also Sk. pṛcchāti = Lat. porsco "I want to know." Vedic icchati "to desire." — (2) Present ***gṷemio** = Sk. gamati = Gr. βαίνω, Lat. venio, Goth. qiman, Ohg. koman, E. come; and non-present formations as Osk. kúmbened, Sk. gata = Lat. ventus; gantu = (ad) ventus. — (3) ***gṷā**, which is correlated to ***stā**, in Pret. Sk. ágām, Gr. ἔβην, cp. βῆμα]. These three formations are represented in Pāli as follows (1) gacch°, in pres. gacchati; imper. gaccha & gacchāhi; pot. gacche (Dh 46, 224) & gaccheyya; p.pres. gacchanto, med. gacchamāna; fut (2nd) gacchissati; aor. agacchi (VvA 307; v. l. agañchi). — (2) gam° in three variations; viz. (a) *gam°*, in pres. caus. gameti; fut. gamissati; aor. 3 sg. agamā (Sn 408, 976; Vv 79^{7}; Mhvs VII.9), agamāsi & gami (Pv II.8^{6}) 1. pl. agamiŋhase (Pv II.3^{10}), pl. agamuŋ (Sn 290), agamaŋsu & gamiŋsu; prohib. mā gami; ger. gamya (J V.31); grd. gamanīya (KhA 223). See also der. gama, gamana, gāmika, gāmin. — (b) *gan°*, in aor. agañchi (on this form see Trenckner, *Notes*, p. 71 sq. — In n'āgañchi J III.190 it belongs to ā + gam); pres.-aor gañchisi (Sn 665); inf. gantuŋ; ger. gantvā; grd. gantabba. See also der. gantar. — (c) *ga°*, in pp. gata. See also ga, gati, gatta. — 3. gā°, in pret. agā (Pv II.3^{22}), 3rd pl. aor. agū (= Sk. °uḥ), in ajjhagū, anvagū (q. v.).

Meanings and Use: 1. to go, to be in motion, to move, to go on (opp. to stand still, tiṭṭhati). Freq. in comb^{n} with tiṭṭhati nisīdati seyyaŋ kappeti "to go, to stand, sit down & lie down," to denote all positions and every kind of behaviour; Nd^{2} s. v. gacchati. — evaŋ kāle gacchante, as time went on J III.52, or evaŋ g° kāle (PvA 54, 75) or gacchante gacchante kāle DhA I.319; gacchati = paleti PvA 56; vemakoṭi gantvā pahari (whilst moving) DhA III.176. — 2. to go, to walk (opp. to run, dhāvati) DhA I.389. — 3. to go away, to go out, to go forth (opp. to stay, or to come āgacchati): agamāsi he went Pv II.8^{6}; yo maŋ icchati anvetu yo vā n' icchati gacchatu "who wants me may come, who does not may go" Sn 564; āgacchantānañ ca gacchantānañ ca pamāṇaŋ n' atthi "there was no end of all who came & went" J II.133; gacchāma "let us go" J I.263; gaccha dāni go away now! J II.160; gaccha re muṇḍaka Vism 343; gacchāhi go then! J I.151, 222; mā gami do not go away! J IV.2; pl. mā gamittha J I.263; gacchanto on his way J I.255, 278; agamaŋsu they went away J IV.3; gantukāma anxious to go J I.222, 292; kattha gamissasi where are you going? (opp. agacchasi) DhA III.173; kahaŋ gacchissatha id. J II.128; kuhiŋ gamissati where is he going? Sn 411, 412. — 4. with acc. or substitute: to go to, to have access to, to arrive or get at (with the aim of the movement or the object of the intention); hence fig. to come to know, to experience, to realize. — (a) with *acc.* of direction: Rājagahaŋ gami he went to R. Pv II.8^{6}; Devadaha-nagaraŋ gantuŋ J I.52; gacchām' ahaŋ Kusinārāŋ I shall go to K. D II.128; Suvaṇṇabhūmiŋ gacchanti they intended to go ("were going") to S. J III.188; migavaŋ g. to go hunting J I.149; janapadaŋ gamissāma J II.129; paradāraŋ g. to approach another man's wife Dh 246. — (b) with *adverbs* of direction or purpose (atthāya): santikaŋ (or santike) gacchati to go near a person (in gen.), pitu s. gacchāma DhA III.172; devāna santike gacche Dh 224 santikaŋ also J I.152; II.159, etc. Kathaŋ tattha gamissāmi how shall I get there? J I.159; II.159; tattha agamāsi he went there J II.160. dukkhānubhavanatthāya gacchamānā "going away for the purpose of undergoing suffering" J IV.3; vohāratthāya gacchāmi I am going out (= fut.) on business J II.133. — Similarly (fig.) in foll. expressions (cp. "to go to Heaven," etc. = to live or experience a heavenly life, cp. next): Nirayaŋ gamissati J VI.368; saggaŋ lokaŋ g. J I.152; gacche pāram apārato Sn 1129, in this sense interpreted at Nd² 223 as adhigacchati phusati sacchikaroti, to experience. — Sometimes with *double acc.*: Bhagavantaŋ saraṇaŋ gacchāmi "I entrust myself to Bh." Vin I.16. — Cp. also phrases as atthangacchati to go home, to set, to disappear; antarā-gacchati to come between, to obstruct. — 5. *to go* as a stronger expression for *to be*, i. e. to behave, to have existence, to fare (cp. Ger. es geht gut, Fr. cela *va* bien = it *is* good). Here belongs gati "existence," as mode of existing, element, sphere of being, and out of this use is developed the periphrastic use of *gam°*, which places it on the same level with the verb "to be" (see b). — (a) sugatiŋ gamissasi you will go to the state of well-being, i. e. Heaven Vin II.195; It 77; opp. duggatiŋ gacchanti Dh 317-319; maggaŋ na jānanti yena gacchanti subbatā (which will fall to their share) Sn 441; gamissanti yattha gantvā na socare "they will go where one sorrows not" Sn 445; Vv 51⁴; yan ca karoti . . . tañ ca ādāya gacchati "whatever a man does that he will take with him" S I.93. — (b) *periphrastic* (w. ger. of governing verb): nagaraŋ pattharitvā gaccheyya "would spread through the town" J I.62; pariṇāmaŋ gaccheyya "could be digested" D II.127; sīhacammaŋ ādāya agamaŋsu "they took the lion's skin away with them" J II.110; itthiŋ pahāya gamissati shall leave the woman alone J VI.348; sve gahetvā gamissāmi "I shall come for it tomorrow" Miln 48.

Gaja [Sk. gaja] an elephant J IV.494; Miln 2, 346; DhsA 295 (applᵈ to a kind of thought).
-potaka the young of an elephant PvA 152; -rājā the king of the elephants Miln 346.

Gajaka = gaja, in gajakattharaṇa an elephant's cover VvA 104.

Gajjati [Sk. garjati, cp. gargara & jarā roaring, cp. uggajjati Dhtp 76: gajja sadde] to roar, to thunder, usually of clouds. Of the earth: Dāvs V.29; of a man (using harsh speech) J I.226; II.412 (mā gajji); Nd¹ 172 (= abhi°); J IV.25. — Caus. gajjayati, ger. gajjayitvā (megho g° thanayitvā (megho g° thanayitvā pavassati) It 66.

Gajjitar [n. agent fr. prec.] one who thunders, of a man in comparison with a cloud A II.102 = Pug 42.

Gaṇa [Vedic gaṇa; *ger to comprise, hold, or come together, cp. Gr. ἀγείρω to collect, ἀγορά meeting, Lat. grex, flock, Sk. jarante "conveniunt" (see Wackernagel, *Altind. Gr.* I.193). Another form of this root is **grem** in Sk. grāma, Lat. gremium; see under gāma]—1. (a) in special sense: a meeting or a chapter of (two or three) bhikkhus, a company (opposed both to sangha, the order & puggala, the individual) Vin I.58, 74, 195, 197; II.170, 171; IV.130, 216, 226, 231, 283, 310, 316, 317; V.123, 167. — (b) in general: a crowd, a multitude, a great many. See cpds. — 2. as -°: a collection of, viz., of gods, men, animals or things; a multitude, mass; flock, herd; host, group, cluster. — (a) deva° J I.203; DhA III.441; PvA 140 (°parivuta); pisāca° S I.33; tidasa° Sn 679. — (b) amacca° suite of ministers J I.264; ariya° troup of worthies J VI.50; naranari° crowds of men & women Miln 2; dāsi° a crowd of servants J II.127; tāpasa° a group of ascetics J I.140 (°parivuta); bhikkhu° J I.212 (°parivuta). — (c) dvija° J I.152; dija° Pv II.12⁴; sakuṇa°, of birds J I.207; II.352; go°, of cows A I.229; V.347, 359; J II.128; kākola°, of ravens Sn 675; bhamarā°, of bees J I.52; miga° of beasts J I.150. — (d) taru° a cluster of trees PvA 154; tāra°, a host of stars A I.215; Pv II.9⁶⁷; with ref. to the books of the Canon: Suttantika° & Ābhidhammika° Vism 93.
-ācariya "a teacher of a crowd," i. e. a t. who has (many) followers. Always in phrase sanghī ca gaṇī ca gaṇācariyo ca, and always with ref. either to Gotama: D I.116; M II.3; or to the 6 chief sectarian leaders, as Pūraṇa Kassapa, etc.: D I.47, 163; S I.68; IV.398; M I.198, 227, 233; II.2; Sn p. 91; cp. DA I.143. In general: Miln 4. -ārāma (adj.) & -ārāmatā in phrase gaṇārāmo gaṇarato gaṇārāmataŋ anuyutto: a lover of the crowd A III.422 sq.; M III.110 = Nd² on Sn 54. -gaṇin the leader of many, Ep. of Bhagavā Nd² 307. -(ŋ)gaṇupāhanā (pl.) shoes with many linings Vin I.185, 187; cp. *Vin. Texts* II.14. See also Bdhgh. on aṭaliyo (q. v. under aṭala). -pūraka (adj.) one who completes the quorum (of a bhikkhus chapter) Vin I.143 sq.; -bandhana in °ena dānaŋ datvā to give by co-operation, to give jointly DhA II.160; -bhojana food prepared as a joint meal Vin II.196; IV. 71; V.128, 135, 205; -magga in °ena gaṇetuŋ to count by way of batches Vin I.117; -vassika (adj.) through a great many years Sn 279; -sanganika (adj.) coming into contact with one another DhA I.162.

Gaṇaka [fr. **gaṇ**, to comprise in the sense of to count up] a counter, one skilled in counting familiar with arithmetic; an accountant, overseer or calculator. Enumᵈ as an occupation together with muddika at D I.51 (expl. DA I.157 by acchidda-pāṭhaka); also with muddika and sankhāyika S IV.376; as an office at the king's court (together with amaccā as gaṇaka-mahāmatta = a ministerial treasurer) D III.64, and in same context D III.148, 153, 169, 171, 177; as overseer Vin III.43; as accountant Miln 79, 293; VvA 66.

Gaṇakī (f.) = gaṇikā Vin III.135-136, in purāṇa° a woman who was formerly a courtesan, & as adj. gaṇakī-dhītā the daughter of a courtesan.

Gaṇanā (f.) counting, i. e. 1. counting up, arithmetic, number J I.29; Vism 278 sq.; Miln 79; VvA 194. — 2. counting, census, statistics; Tikap. 94; J I.35; Miln 4 (senā °ŋ kāretvā); DhA I.11, 34. — 3. the art of counting, arithmetics as a study & a profession, forbidden to the bhikkhus Vin I.77 = IV.129 (°ŋ sikkhati to study ar.); D I.11 (expl. DA I.95 by acchiddaka-gaṇanā); M I.85; III.1 (°ājīva); DA I.157. -gaṇana-patha (time-) reckoning, period of time Miln 20, 116.

Gaṇikā¹ (f.) "one who belongs to the crowd," a harlot, a courtesan (cp. gaṇakī) Vin I.231 (Ambapālī) 268, (do.); II.277 (Aḍḍhakāsī); Ud 71; Miln 122; DhA III.104; VvA 75 (Sirimā); PvA 195, 199. — Customs of a gaṇikā J IV.249; V.134. — Cp. saŋ°.

Gaṇikā² (f.) = gaṇanā, arithmetic Miln 3.

Gaṇin¹ (adj.) one who has a host of followers, Ep. of a teacher who has a large attendance of disciples; usually in standing combⁿ sanghī gaṇī gaṇācariyo (see above). Also in foll.: Sn 955, 957; Dpvs IV.8 (mahāgaṇī), 14 (therā gaṇī); gaṇī-bhūtā (pl.) in crowds, combᵈ with sanghā sanghī D I.112, explᵈ at DA I.280: pubbe nagarassa anto agaṇā bahi nikkhamitvā gaṇa-sampannā ti. See also paccekagaṇin.

Gaṇin² a large species of deer J V.406 (= gokaṇṇa).

Gaṇeti [denom. to gaṇa Dhtp 574: sankhyāne] 1. to count, to reckon, to do sums Dh 19; J VI.334; Miln 79, 293; pp. gaṇita Sn 677; pass. gaṇīyati Sdhp 434; inf. (vedic) gaṇetuye Bw. IV.28; caus. gaṇāpeti M III.1. — 2. to regard, to take notice of, to consider, to care for J I.300; IV.267.

Gaṇṭhi (m.) [Vedic granthi, to **grem** to comprise, hold together, cp. Lat. gremium, Sk. gaṇa & grāma, see also gantha] 1. a knot, a tie, a knot or joint in a stalk (of a plant) J I.172; DA I.163; DhA I.321 (°jātaŋ what has be come knotty or hard); -diṭṭhi-gaṇṭhi the tangle of false doctrine VvA 297; anta-gaṇṭh-ābādha entanglement of intestines Vin I.275. — 2. a (wooden) block Vin II.110 (of sandal wood).

-ṭṭhāna (for gaṇṭhikaṭṭhāna ?) the place of the block (i. e. of execution) J III.538 ; (reads gaṇṭhi-gaṇṭi-ṭṭhāna) ; Vism 248. — bhedaka, in °cora " the thief who breaks the block " (or rope, knot ?) DhA II.30.

Gaṇṭhikā (f.) (freq. spelled gaṇḍikā, q. v.) = gaṇṭhi, viz. 1. a knot, a tie DA I.199 (catu-pañca-gaṇṭhik'āhata patta a bowl with 4 or 5 knots, similarly āṇi-gaṇṭhik'-āhata ayopatta Vism 108 ; but see āṇi) ; DhA I.335 (°jāta = gaṇṭhijāta knotty part), 394. — 2. a block (or is it knot?) Vin II.136 (? + pāsaka ; cp. *Vin. Texts* III.144) ; V.140. Esp. in phrase gaṇṭhikaŋ paṭimuñcitvā Vin I.46 = II.213, 215, trsl[d] at *Vin. Texts* III.286 " fasten the block on (to the robe) " but at I.155 " tie the knots." Also in dhamma-gaṇṭhikā a block for execution J I.150 (v. l. gaṇḍikā). — 3. N. of a plant PvA 127. — ucchu-gaṇṭhikā sugar cane : see ucchu.

-kāsāva a yellow robe which was to be tied (or which had a block ?) J IV.446.

Gaṇḍa [a variation of gaṇṭha (-i), in both meanings of (1) swelling, knot, protuberance, and (2) the interstice between two knots or the whole of the knotty object, i. e. stem, stalk]—1. a swelling, esp. as a disease, an abscess, a boil. Freq. in similes with ref. to kāma and kāya. Mentioned with similar cutaneous diseases under kilāsa (q. v. for loci). As Ep. of kāya S IV.83 = A IV.386, of kāmī A III.310, IV.289 ; Nd[2] on Sn 51 ; also Th 2, 491 (= dukkhatā sulaya ThA 288) ; S IV.64 (= ejā) ; Sn 51, 61 (v. l. for gaḷa) ; J I.293 ; Vism 360 (°pilakā) ; DhA III.297 (gaṇḍ-ā-gaṇḍajāta, covered with all kinds of boils) ; IV.175 ; PvA 55. Cp. Av. S II.168[1]. — 2. a stalk, a shaft, in N. of a plant -°tindu-rukkha J V.99, and in der. gaṇḍikā & gaṇḍī, cp. also Av. S II.133[12]. — 3. = gaṇḍuppāda in cpd. gaṇḍamattikā clay mixed with earth-worms Vin II.151 (cp. Bdhgh. gaṇḍuppāda-gūtha-mattikā clay mixed with excrement of earthworms *Vin. Texts* III.172).

-uppāda (lit. producing upheavals, cp. a mole) an earth-worm, classed as a very low creature with kīṭā & puḷavā at M III.168 ; J V.210 (°pāṇa) ; DhA III.361 (°yoni) ; SnA 317.

Gaṇḍaka (adj.) having boils Sdhp 103.

Gaṇḍikā (f.) [a-n. formation from gaṇḍa or gaṇṭha, see also gaṇṭhikā]—1. a stalk, a shaft (cp. gaṇḍi) J I.474 ; DhsA 319 (of the branches of trees : g°-ākoṭana-sadda). — 2. a lump, a block of wood (more freq. spelling gaṇṭhikā, q. v.). — 3. N. of a plant Vv 35[4] (= bandhu-jīvaka VvA 161).

-ādhāna the putting on of a shaft or stem, as a bolt or bar Vin II.172 ; cp. *Vin. Texts* III.213 and gaṇḍī ; also ghaṭikā[2].

Gaṇḍin [adj. fr. gaṇḍa]—1. having swellings, in ure gaṇḍī (f.) with swellings on the chest, i. e. breasts J V.159, 202 (thane sandhāyâha 205). — 2. having boils, being afflicted with a glandular disease (with kuṭṭhin & kilāsin) Kvu 31.

Gaṇḍī (f.) [= gaṇḍikā in meaning 1 ; prob. = Sk. ghaṇṭā in meaning 2]—1. a shaft or stalk, used as a bar J I.237. —2. a gong DhA I.291 (gaṇḍiŋ paharati to beat the g.) ; II.54, 244 ; gaṇḍiŋ ākoṭetvā KhA 251. Cp. AvS I.258, 264, 272 ; II.87, 95 & Divy 335, 336. Also in gaṇḍi-saññā " sign with the gong " J IV.306. — 3. the executioner's block (= gaṇḍikā or gaṇṭhikā) J III.41.

Gaṇḍamba N. of the tree, under which Gotama Buddha performed the double miracle ; with ref. to this freq. in phrase gaṇḍamba-rukkha-mūle yamakapāṭihāriyaŋ katvā J I.77 ; IV.263 sq. ; DA I.57 ; PvA 137 ; Miln 349 ; Dāvs V.54. Also at DhA III.207 in play of words with amba-rukkha.

Gaṇḍusa [cp. Sk. gaṇḍūṣa] a mouthful J I.249 (khīra°).

Gaṇhati & **Gaṇhāti** [Vedic grah (grabh), gṛhṇāti pp. gṛhīta to grasp. *gher to hold, hold in, contain ; cp. Gr. χόρτος enclosure, Lat. hortus, co-hors (homestead) ; Goth. gards (house) ; Ohg. gart ; E. yard & garden. To this belong Vedic gṛha (house) in P. gaha°, gihin, geha, ghara, & also Vedic harati to seize, hasta hand]. The forms of the verb are from three bases, viz. (1) gaṇha- (Sk. gṛhṇā-) ; *Pres.* : ind. gaṇhāti (gaṇhāsi PvA 87), pot. gaṇheyya, imper. gaṇha (J I.159 ; PvA 49 = handa) & gaṇhāhi (J I.279). *Fut.* gaṇhissati ; Aor gaṇhi. Inf. gaṇhituŋ (J III.281). Ger. gaṇhitvā. Caus. gaṇhāpeti & gāhāpeti. — 2. gahe- (Sk. gṛhī-) : Fut. gahessati. Aor. aggahesi (Sn 847 ; J I.52). Inf. gahetuŋ (J I.190, 222). Ger. gahetvā & gahetvāna (poet.) (Sn 309 ; Pv II.3). — 3. gah- (Sk. gṛh-) : Aor. aggahi. Ger. gayha & gahāya (Sn 791). Pass. gayhati. Pp. gahita & gahīta. Cp. gaha, gahaṇa, gāha.

Meanings : to take, take up ; take hold of ; grasp, seize ; assume ; e. g. ovādaŋ g. to take advice J I.159 ; khaggaŋ to seize the sword J I.254-255 ; gocaraŋ to take food J III.275 ; jane to seize people J I.253 ; dhanaŋ to grasp the treasure J I.255 ; nagaraŋ to occupy the city J I.202 ; pāde gāḷhaŋ gahetvā holding her feet tight J I.255 ; macche to catch fish J III.52 ; mantaŋ to use a charm J III.280 ; rajjaŋ to seize the kingdom J I.263 ; II.102 ; sākhaŋ to take hold of a branch Sn 791 ; J I.52. Very often as a phrase to be translated by a single word, as : nāmato g. to enumerate PvA 18 ; paṭisandhiŋ g. to be born J I.149 ; maraṇaŋ g. to die J I.151 ; mūlena g. to buy J III.126, vacanaŋ g. to obey J III.276 (in neg.). The ger. gahetvā is very often simply to be translated as " with," e. g. tidaṇḍaŋ gahetvā caranto J II.317 ; satta bhikkhū gahetvā agamāsi VvA 149.

Caus. gaṇhāpeti to cause to be seized, to procure, to have taken : phalāni J II.105 ; rājānaŋ J I.264. Cp. gāhāpeti.

Gata [pp. of gacchati in medio-reflexive function] gone, in all meanings of gacchati (q. v.) viz. 1. literal : gone away, arrived at, directed to (c. acc.), opp. ṭhita : gate ṭhite nisinne (loc. abs.) when going, standing, sitting down (cp. gacchati 1) D I.70 ; opp. āgata : yassa maggaŋ na jānāsi āgatassa gatassa vā Sn 582 (cp. gati 2). Also periphrastic (= gacchati 5 b) : aṭṭhi paritvā gataŋ " the bone fell down " J III.26. Very often gata stands in the sense of a finite verb (= aor. gacchi or agamāsi) : yo ca Buddhaŋ . . . saraṇaŋ gato (cp. gacchati 4) Dh 190 ; attano vasanaṭ-ṭhānaŋ gato he went to his domicile J I.280 ; II.160 ; nāvā Aggimālaŋ gatā the ship went to Aggimālā J IV.139. — 2. in applied meaning : gone in a certain way, i. e. affected, behaved, fared, fated, being in or having come into a state or condition. So in sugata & duggata (see below) and as 2nd part of cpds. in gen., viz. *gone* ; atthaŋ° gone home, set ; addha° done with the journey (cp. gat-addhin) ; *gone into* : taṇhā° fallen a victim to thirst, tama° obscured, raho°, secluded, vyasana° fallen into misery ; *having reached* : anta° arrived at the goal (in this sense often comb[d] with patta : antagata anta-patta Nd[2], 436, 612), koṭi° perfected, parinibbāna° having ceased to exist, vijjā° having attained (right) knowledge ; *connected with, referring to, concerning* : kāya° relating to the body (kāyagatā sati, e. g. Vism 111, 197, 240 sq.) ; diṭṭhi° being of a (wrong) view ; saṅkhāra°, etc. — Sometimes gata is replaced by kata and vice versa : anabhāvaŋkata > anabhāvaŋ gacchati ; kālagata > kalakata (q. v.).

agata not gone to, not frequented : °ŋ disaŋ (of Nibbāna) Dh 323 ; purisantaraŋ °ŋ mātugāmaŋ " a maid who has not been with a man " J I.290.

sugata of happy, blessed existence, fortunate ; one who has attained the realm of bliss (= sugatiŋ gata, see gati), blessed. As np. a common Ep. of the Buddha : Vin I.35 ; III.1 ; D I.49 ; S I.192 ; A II.147 et passim (see Sugata). — D I.83 ; Sn 227 (see expl. KhA 183).

duggata of miserable existence, poor, unhappy, ill-fated, gone to the realm of misery (duggatiŋ gata PvA 33, see gati) Pv I.6[2]; II.3[17]; duggata-bhāva (poverty) J VI.366; duggat-itthi (miserable, poor) J I.290; parama-duggatāni kulāni clans in utmost misery (poverty) PvA 176.—Compar. duggatatara DhA I.427; II.135.

-atta (fr. attā) self-perfected, perfect D I.57 (expl. by koṭippatta-citto DA I:168); cp. paramāya satiyā ca gatiyā ca dhitiyā ca samannāgata M I.82; **-addhin** (adj. of addhan) one who has completed his journey (cp. addhagata) Dh 90; **-kāle** (in gata-gata-kāle) whenever he went J III.188; **-ṭṭhāna** place of existence PvA 38; =gamana in āgata-ṭṭhānaŋ vā: coming and going (lit. state of going) J III.188; **-yobbana** (adj.) past youth, of old age A I.138; Sn 98=124.

Gataka a messenger J I.86.

Gatatta I.=Sk. gat-ātman (see prec.). — 2.=Sk. gatatvaŋ the fact of having gone KhA 183.

Gati (f.) [fr. gacchati; cp. Gr. βάσις, Lat. (in-) ventio, Goth. (ga-)qumþs] I. going, going away, (opp. āgati coming) (both gati & āgati usually in pregnant sense of No. 2. See āgati); direction, course, career. Freq. of the two careers of a Mahāpurisa (viz. either a Cakkavatti or a Buddha) D II.16=Sn p. 106; Sn 1001, or of a gihī arahattaŋ patto Miln 264, with ref. to the distinction of the child Gotama J I.56. — phassâyatanānaŋ gati (course or direction) A II.161; jagato gati (id.) A II.15, 17; sakuntānaŋ g. the course, flight of birds Dh 92=Th I, 92. — Opp. āgati Pv II.9[22]. -tassā gatiŋ jānāti "he knows her going away, i. e. where she has gone" PvA 6. — 2. going away, passing on (=cuti, opp. upapatti coming into another existence); course, esp after death, destiny, as regards another (future) existence A I.112; D II.91; M I.388 (tassa kā gati ko abhisamparāyo? what is his rebirth and what his destiny?); in combn āgati vā gati vā (=cutûpapatti), rebirth & death M I.328, 334. In defn of saŋsāra expld as gati bhavâbhava cuti upapatti=one existence after the other Nd[2] 664; as gati upapatti paṭisandhi Nd[2] on dhātu (also as puna-gati rebirth). — The Arahant as being beyond Saŋsāra is also beyond gati: yassa gatiŋ na jānanti devā gandhabba-mānusā Dh 420=Sn 644; yesaŋ gati n' atthi Sn 499; and Nibbāna coincides with release from the *gatis*: gativippamokkhaŋ parinibbānaŋ SnA 368. — attā hi attano gati "everybody is (the maker of) his own future life" Dh 380; esā maccharino gati "this is the fate of the selfish" Pv III.1[14]; sabbagatī te ijjhantu "all fate be a success to you" J V.393; gato so tassa yā **gati** "he has gone where he had to go (after death)" Pv I.12[2]. — 3. behaviour, state or condition of life, sphere of existence, element, especially characterized as sugati & duggati, a happy or an unhappy existence. gati migānaŋ pavanaŋ, ākāso pakkhīnaŋ gati, vibhavo gati dhammānaŋ, nibbānaŋ arahato gati: the wood is the sphere of the beasts, the air of the birds, decay is the state of (all) things, Nibbāna the sphere of the Arahant Vin V.149=SnA 346; apuññalābho ca gatī ca pāpikā Dh 310; duggati J I.28; avijjāy' eva gati the quality of ignorance Sn 729; paramāya gatiyā samannāgato of perfect behaviour M I.82; see also defn at Vism 237. — 4. one of the five realms of existence of sentient beings (=loka), divided into the two categories of sugati (=Sagga, realm of bliss) & duggati (=Yamaloka, apāya, realm of misery). These gatis are given in the foll. order: (1) niraya purgatory, (2) tiracchānayoni the brute creation, (3) pittivisaya the ghost world, (4) manussā (m-loka) human beings, (5) devā gods: M I.73; D III.234; A IV.459; Nd[2] 550; cp. S V.474-77; Vism 552. They are described in detail in the Pañcagatidīpana (ed. L. Feer, *J.P.T.S.* 1884, 152 sq.; trsl. by the same in *Annales du Musée Guimet* V. 514-528) under Naraka-kaṇḍa, Tiracchāna°, Peta°, Manussa°, Deva°. Of these Nos. 1-3 are considered duggatis, whilst Nos. 4 and 5 are sugati. In later sources we find 6 divisions, viz. 1-3 as above, (4) asurā, (5) manussā, (6) devā, of which 1-4 are comprised under apāyā (conditions of suffering, q. v.) or duggatiyo (see Pv IV.11, cp. PvA 103). These six also at D III.264. — lokassa gatiŋ pajānāti Bhagavā Sn 377 (gati=nirayādipañcappabhedaŋ SnA 368). The first two gatis are said to be the fate of the micchādiṭṭhino D I.228, dve niṭṭhā DA I.249 (q. v. for var. appl. of gati) as well as the dussīlā (A I.60), whilst the last two are the share of the sīlavanto (A. I.60).

-gata gone its course (of a legal enquiry, vinicchaya) Vin II.85 (cp. *Vin Texts* III.26); J II.I.

agati I. no course, no access, in agati tava tattha: there you have no access S I.115. — 2 =duggati, wrong course. agatigamana a wrong course of life D III.133; A I.72; II.18 sq.; III.274 sq.; J V.510; PvA 161. Technically the four agati-gamanāni are: chanda° dosa° moha° bhaya° D III.228 (see also under chanda).

sugati (sometimes suggati after duggati e. g. J VI.224) a happy existence; a realm of bliss; the devaloka. Cp. sugatin. Usually with gacchati (sugatiŋ) & gata "gone to Heaven" Vin II.195; D II.202; It 77; PvA 65. In combn w. sagga loka (sugatiŋ, etc. uppajjati) D I.143; A I.97; J I.152. parammaraṇā sugati pāṭikankhā It 24; suggatiŋ gata Dh 18; sugati pāpehi kammehi sulabhā na hoti "bliss is not gained by evil" PvA 87; =sugga & dibbaṭṭhāna PvA 89; sugati-parāyana sure of rebirth in a realm of bliss, *ib.*

duggati a miserable existence; a realm of misery (see above gati 4). Usually with gacchati (duggatiŋ gata, reborn in a miserable state) or uppajjati D I.82; A I.97, 138 (+vinipātaŋ nirayaŋ); II.123; III.3; IV.364; Dh 17; Sn 141; SnA 192 (=dukkhappatti); PvA 87. Sakakammāni nayanti duggatiŋ, one's own deeds lead to rebirth in misery, Dh 240; with ref. to a Peta existence: Pv I.6[2]; II.1[6]; 1[13]; 3[17]. Cp. duggata.

-Gatika (adj.) I. going to, staying with, in bhikkhu° a person living with the bhikkhus Vin I.148. — 2. leading to; yaŋ° what they lead to (of the 5 indriyas) S V.230. — 3. having a certain gati, leading to one of the four kinds of rebirth: evaŋ° D I.16 (w. ref. to one of the first 3 gatis: DA I.108); niyata° whose destiny is certain (w. ref. to sugati) and aniyata° whose destiny is uncertain (w. ref. to a duggati) DhA III.173.

-Gatin (adj.=gatika) I. going, i. e. having a certain course: sabbā nadī vankagatī "every river flows crooked" J I.289. — 2. having a certain gati, fated, destined, esp. in su° & dug°: samparāye suggatī going to a happy existence after death Vin II.162=J I.219; saggaŋ sugatino yanti "those who have a happy fate (because of leading a good life) go to one of the Heavens" Dh 126.

Gatimant (adj.) of (perfect) behaviour, going right, clever (cp. gatatta under gata, & gati 3) M I.82.

Gatta (nt.) [Vedic gātra] the body, pl. gattāni the limbs. — As body: Vin I.47; S I.169=183 (analla° with pure bodies; anallina° at 169, but v. l. analla°); A I.138; Sn 673 (samacchida° with bodies cut up); Pv I.11[2] (bhinna-pabhinna°, id.); PvA 56 (=sarīra); 68. — As limbs: S IV.198 (arupakkāni festering with sores); M I.506 (id.); M I.80=246; J I.61 (lālākilinna°); Sn 1001 (honti gattesu mahāpurisalakkhaṇā), 1017, 1019; Pv III.9[1] (=sarîrâvayavā PvA 211); Miln 357 (arupakkāni).

Gathita (adj.) [pp. of ganthati to tie, cp. gantha, knot; Sk. grathita] tied, bound, fettered; enslaved, bound to, greedy for, intoxicated with (c. loc.). When abs. always in combn w. paribhuñjati and w. ref. to some object of desire (bhoga, lābha, kāmaguṇe). Usually in standing phrase gathita mucchita ajjhāpanna (ajjhopanna) "full of greed & blind desire." In this connection it is frequently (by B MSS.) spelt gadhita, and the editors of S, A, & Miln have put that in the text throughout. With mucchita & ajjhāpanna: D I.245; III.43; M I.162, 173; S II.270; IV.332; A V.178, 181 Nd² on nissita C. —c. loc.: J IV.371 (gharesu); DA I.59 (kāmaguṇesu). In other connections: ādānaganthaŋ gathitaŋ visajja Sn 794 (cp. Nd¹ 98); yāni loke gathitāni na tesu pasuto siyā Sn 940. — J IV.5 (=giddha); V.274 (gedhita for pagiddha); PvA 262 (gadhita as explⁿ of giddha)—agathita (agadhita) not fettered (by desire) without desire, free from the ties of craving (+m°, a°) S II.194, 269; A V.181; Miln 401 (trsl. Rh.D. II.339: "without craving, without faintness, without sinking").

Gada speech, sentence Dh I.66, DA I.66 f.; and on D III.135 (§ 28); **gada** at S II.230 (v. l.) in phrase diṭṭhagadena sallena is to be read diddhagadena s.

Gaddula (and gaddūla) a leather strap S III.150; J II.246; II.2°4; fig. in taṇhā-gaddūla "the leash of thirst," Nd² on jappā (taṇhā)=Dhs 1059=Vbh 361, cp. DhsA 367.

Gaddūhana (nt.) [Derivation unknown; Sk. dadrūghna] a small measure of space & time M III.127; S II.264 (°mattam pi, SA "pulling just once the cow's teat"); A IV.395; Miln 110. See Trenckner P.M. 59, 60; Rh. D. *J.R.A.S.* 1903, 375.

Gaddha [Vedic gṛdha; see gijjha] a vulture; in gaddhabādhipubbo, of the bhikkhu Ariṭṭha, who had been a vulture trainer in a former life Vin II.25=IV.218=M I.130; see also *Vin. Texts* II.377.

Gadrabha [Vedic gardabha., Lat. burdo, a mule; see Walde *Lat. Wtb.*, s. v.] an ass, donkey Vin V.129; M I.334; A I.229; J II.109, 110; V.453; DA I.163. — f. gadrabhī J II.340.

-**bhāraka** a donkey load J II.109; DhA I.123; -**bhāva** the fact of being an ass J II.110; -**rava** (& -**rāva**) the braying of an ass ibid. & Vism 415.

Gadhita see gathita.

Gantar [n. agent of gacchati in the sense of a periphrastic future] "goer" in gantā hoti he will go, he is in the habit of going, combᵈ w. sotā hantā khantā, of the king's elephant A II.116=III.161; v. l. for gatā at M II.155.

Gantha (in BB often misspelt gandha) [fr. ganthati]—1. a bond, fetter, trammel; always fig. and usually referring to and enumᵈ as the four bodily ties, or knots (kāya°, see under kāya): S V.59=Dhs 1135; D III.230; Nd¹ 98; DhA III.276; 4 kāyaganthā, viz., abhijjhā, byāpāda, sīlabbataparāmasa, idaŋsaccābhinivesa; thus Nd¹ 98; Vism 683. In other conn. Sn 347, 798, 847, 857, 912; Nd² on jappā (taṇhā); Dh 211; Ps I.129; Dhs 1059, 1472; Vbh 18, 24, 55, 65, 77, 117, 120; Nett 31, 54, 114, 124 (gandha); Sdhp 616. — chinna° (adj.) one who has cut the ties (of bad desires, binding him to the body). Combⁿ w. anigha nirāsa S I.12 (°gandha), 23; w. asita anāsava Sn 219. Cp. pahīnamānassa na santi ganthā S I.14. See also ādāna°; cp. ganthaniya. — 2. [only in late Pali, and in Sk.] composition, text, book (not with ref. to books as tied together, but to books as composed, put together. See gantheti 2).

-**dhura** the burden of the books, i. e. of studying the Scriptures, explᵈ as one who knows by heart one, two, or all Nikāyas. Always combᵈ w. vipassanādhuraŋ, the burden of contemplation DhA I.8; IV.37; -**pamocana** the state of being released from, freed from the fetters of the "body" always w. ref. to Nibbāna S I.210; A II.24; It 104, cp. 122; -**pahīna** (adj.) connected with or referring to the ganthas Dhs 1480; opp. vi° Dhs 1482.

Ganthati & **Gantheti** [Vedic grath, granth, grathnāti, to *grem, cp. Lat. gremium; see also ganṭhi gathita, gantha] 1. to tie, knot, bind, fasten together: kathaŋ mittāni ganthati "how does he bind friends" S I.214=Sn 185; mālaŋ ganthamāna tying a garland Vv 38¹ (ganthento VvA 173). Of medicines: to mix, to prepare J IV.361. — pp. ganthita tied, bound, fettered: catūhi ganthehi g° Ps I.129; — grd. ganthaniya to be tied or tending to act as a tie (of "body"); expl. as ārammaṇa-karaṇa-vasena ganthehi ganthitabba DhsA 69; dhammā g° ā ("states that tend to be, are liable to be ties" *Buddh. Ps.* p. 305; *Expositor* 64) Dhs 1141; 1478. In combⁿ saññojaniya g° oghaniya (of rūpa) Dhs 584=Vbh 12; of rūpa-kkhandha Vbh 65, of dasāyatanā ib. 77, dasindriyā ib. I.29, saccā g° and ag° (=gantha-sampayutta & vippayuttā) ib. 117. — 2. to put together, to compose: mante ganthetvā (v. l. gandhitvā) Sn 302, 306.

Ganthika (adj.) [fr. gantha 2] hard-studying DhA I.156 (bhikkhu; cp. gantha-dhura).

Gandha [Vedic gandha, from **ghrā**, ghrāti to smell, ghrāṇa smell, & see P. ghāna. Possibly conn. w. Lat. fragro=E. fragrant] smell, viz.—1. odour, smell, scent in gen. J III.189; Dh 54-56=Miln 333; Dhs 605 under ghānāyatanāni); āma° smell of raw flesh A I.280; D II.242; Sn 241 sq; maccha° the scent of fish J III.52; muttakarīsa° the smell of fæces and urine A III.158; catujāti° four kinds of scent J I.265; PvA 127; dibba-g°-puppha a flower of heavenly odour J I.289. — 2. odour, smell in particular: enumerated as mūla°, sāra°, puppha°, etc., S III.156=V.44=A V.22; Dhs 625 (under ghandāyatanāni, sphere of odours). Specified as māla°, sāra°, puppha° under tīṇi gandhajātāni A I.255; — puppha° Dh 54=A I.226. — 3. smell as olfactory sensation, belonging to the sphere (āyatanāni) of sense-impressions and sensory objects & enum. in set of the 12 ajjhatta-bāhirāni āyatanāni (see under rūpa) with **ghānena** gandhaŋ ghāyitvā "sensing smell by means of the olfactory organ" D III.102; 244=250=269=Nd² on rūpa; M III.55, 267; S IV.71; Vin I.35; Defined at Vism 447. Also as gandhā ghānaviññeyya under kāmaguṇā M II.42; D III.234, etc. In series of 10 attributes of physical quality (-rūpa, etc.) as characteristic of devas D III.146; Pv II.9⁶⁸; as sāra°, pheggu°, taca°, etc. (nine qualities in all) in definition of Gandhabba-kāyikā devā S III.250 sq. — In the same sense & similar connections: vaṇṇa-g°-ras'ūpeto Dh 49; J II.106; gandhānaŋ khamo & akkhamo (of king's elephant) A III.158 sq.; itthi°, purisa° A I.1, 2; III.68; in combⁿ w. other four senses Sn 387, 759, 974. — 4. perfume, prepared odorific substance used as a toilet requisite, either in form of an unguent or a powder. Abstinence from the use of kallæsthetics is stated in the Sīlas (D I.8) as characteristic of certain Wanderers and Brahmins. Here gandha is mentioned together with mālā (flowers, garlands): D I.5=Kh II; D I.7 (°kathā); Vin II.123; Sn 401; J I.50, 291; PvA 62. The use of scented ointment (-vilepana & ālepa, see cpds.) is allowed to the Buddhist bhikkhus (Vin I.206); and the giving of this, together with other commodities, is included in the second part of the deyyadhamma (the list of meritorious gifts to the Sangha), under Nos. 5-14 (anna-pāna-vattha-yāna-mālā-gandhā-vilepana-seyy-āvasatha-padīpeyya): S III.252; Nd² 523=It 65. Out of this enumeration: g°-m°-v°-Pv II.3¹⁸; chatta-g°-m°-upāhanā Pv II.4²; II.9³⁶; m°-g°-v° kappūra-kaṭukapphalāni J II.416. — The application of scented ointment (gandhena or gandhehi vilimpati) is customary after a bath, e. g. PvA 50 (on Pv I.10⁶); J I.254, 265; III.277. Var. kinds of perfumes or scented substances are given as g°-dhūpa-cuṇṇa-kappūra (incense, powder, camphor) J I.290; vāsa-cuṇṇa-dhūpanādi g° KhA 37. See also cpds.

duggandha a disagreeable smell Dhs 625; °ŋ vāyati to emit a nasty odour PvA 14; as adj. having a bad smell, putrid Sn 205; PvA 15 (=pūtigandha), f. -ā: duggandhā pūti vāyasi "you emit a bad odour")

Pv I.6¹ (=aniṭṭha°). -sugandha an agreeable smell Dhs 625; as adj. of pleasant smell J III.277; Sdhp. 246. -āpaṇa a perfumery shop J I.290; °ika perfume seller Miln 344; -āyatana an olfactory sense-relation, belonging to the six bāhirāni āyatanāni, the objective sensations D III.243, 290; Dhs 585, 625, 655; -ārammaṇa bearing on smell, having smell as its object Dhs 147, 157, 365, 410, 556, 608; -ālepa (nt.) anointing with perfumes Vin I.206; -āsā "hunger for odours," craving for olfactory sensations Dhs 1059; -odaka scented water J I.50; II.106; III.189; -karaṇḍaka a perfume-box S III.131; V.351; Pug 34; -kuṭī (f.) a perfumed cabin, name of a room or hut occupied by the Buddha, esp. that made for him by Anāthapiṇḍika in Jetavana (J I.92). Gotamassa g° J II.416, cp. Av. S II.40¹; DhA IV.203, 206; -cuṇṇa scented (bath-) powder J III.277; -jāta (nt.) odour, perfume ("consisting of smell"). Three kinds at A I.225 (māla°, sāra°, puppha°); enum. as candanādi DhA I.423; in defin. of gandha DA I.77; — Dh 55; -taṇhā thirst or craving for odours (cp. g°-āsā) Dhs 1059=Nd² on jappā; -tela scented oil (for a lamp) J I.61; II.104; DhA I.205; -tthena a perfume-thief S I.204; -dhātu the (sensory) element of smell Dhs 585; 625, 707 (in conn. w. °āyatana); -pañcangulika see sep.; -sañcetanā the olfactory sensation; together with °saññā perception of odours D III.244; A IV.147; V.359; -sannidhi the storing up of scented unguents D I.6 (=DA I.82).

Gandhana see gandhina.

Gandhabba [Vedic gandharva] I. a musician, a singer J II.249 sq.; III.188; VvA 36, 137. — 2. a Gandharva or heavenly musician, as a class (see °kāyika) belonging to the demigods who inhabit the Cātummahārājika realm D II.212; A II.39 (as birds); IV.200 (with asurā & nāgā), 204, 207; cp. S III.250 sq.; also said to preside over child-conception: M I.265 sq.; Miln 123 sq.

-kāyika belonging to the company of the G. S III.250 sq.; PvA 119; -mānusā (pl.) G. & men Dh 420=Sn 644; -hatthaka "a G.-hand," i. e. a wooden instrument in the shape of a bird's claw with which the body was rubbed in bathing Vin II.106, see *Vin. Texts* III.67.

Gandhabbā (f.) music, song J II.254; VvA 139; Miln 3; °ŋ karoti to make music J II.249; III.188.

Gandhāra (adj.) belonging to the Gandhāra country (Kandahar) f. gandhārī in gandhārī vijjā N. of a magical charm D I.213; at J IV.498 it renders one invisible.

Gandhika (and °uja Pv II.1²⁰; II.12¹)—I. having perfume, fragrant, scentful, J I.266 (su°); Pv II.1²⁰ (=surabhigandha); II.12¹ (sogandhiya); VvA 58 (read gandhikāgandhikehi).—2. dealing in perfume, a perfumer Miln 262 (cp. gandhin 2).

Gandhin (adj.) I. having a scent of, smelling of (-°), i. e. candana° of sandal wood J III.190; gūtha of° fæces Pv II.3¹⁵ (=karīsavāyinī PvA). — 2. dealing with scents, a perfumer PvA 127 (=māgadha; cp. gandhika 2).

Gandhina in kule antimagandhina J IV.34 (expl. by sabbapacchimaka) and *gandhana* in kula-gandhana Jt 64 see under kula°.

Gabbita (adj.) proud, arrogant J II.340 (°bhāva=issariya); III.264 (°sabhāva=dittasabhāva); Sum. V. on D III.153 (=avamata).

Gabbha [Vedic garbha, either to *gelbh, as in Lat. galba, Goth. kalbo, Ohg. kalba, E. calf, or *gue bh, as in Gr. δελφύς womb, ἀδελφός sharing the womb, brother, δέλφαξ young pig; cp. *gelt in Goth. kilþei womb, Ags. cild, Ger. kind, E. child. Meaning: a cavity, a hollow, or, seen from its outside, a swelling] I. interior, cavity (loc. gabbhe in the midst of: angāra° J III.55); an inner room, private chamber, bedroom, cell. Of a Vihāra: Vin II.303; III.119; IV.45; VvA 188; 220; — J I.90 (siri° royal chamber); III.276; Vv 78⁶ (=ovaraka VvA 304); DhA I.397; Miln 10, 295. See also anto°. — 2. the swelling of the (pregnant) womb, the womb (cp. kucchi). °ŋ upeti to be born Dh 325=Th I, 17=Nett 34, 129; °ŋ upapajjati to be born again Dh 126; gabbhā gabbhaŋ . . . dukkaŋ nigacchanti from womb to womb (i. e. from birth to birth) Sn 278; gabbhato paṭṭhāya from the time of birth J I.290, 293. As a symbol of defilement g. is an ep. of kāma A IV.289, etc. — 3. the contents of the womb, i. e. the embryo, fœtus: dasa māse °ŋ kucchinā pariharitvā having nourished the fœtus in the womb for 10 months D II 14; dibbā gabbhā D I.229; on g. as contained in kucchi, fœtus in utero, see J I.50 (kucchimhi patiṭṭhito) 134; II.2; IV.482; M I.265; Miln 123 (gabbhassa avakkanti); DhA I.3, 47; II.261. — Pv I.6⁷; PvA 31; gabbho vuṭṭhāsi the child was delivered Vin II.278; itthi-gabbho & purisa° female & male child J I.51; gabbhaŋ pāteti to destroy the fœtus Vin II.268; apagatagabbhā (adj.) having had a miscarriage Vin II.129; mūḷha-gabbhā id. M II.102 (+visatā°); paripuṇṇa-gabbhā ready to be delivered J I.52; PvA 86; saññi° a conscious fœtus D I.54=M I.518=S III.212; sannisinna-gabbhā having conceived Vin II.278.

-avakkanti (gabbhe okkanti Nd² 304¹) conception D III.103, 231; Vism 499, 500 (°okkanti); this is followed by gabbhe ṭhiti & gabbhe vuṭṭhāna, see Nd²; -āsaya the impurities of childbirth Pv III.5³ (=°mala); -karaṇa effecting a conception Sn 927; -gata leaving the womb, in putte gabbhagate when the child was born PvA 112; -dvāra the door of the bed-chamber J I.62; -parihāra "the protection of the embryo," a ceremony performed when a woman became pregnant J II.2; DhA I.4; -pātana the destruction of the embryo, abortion, an abortive preparation Vin III.83 sq., Pv I.6⁶ (akariŋ); PvA 31 (dāpesi); DhA I.47 (°bhesajja); -mala the uncleanness of delivery, i. e. all accompanying dirty matter PvA 80, 173 (as food for Petas), 198; DhA IV.215; -vīsa in ahañc' amhi gabbhavīso "I am 20 years, counting from my conception" Vin I.93; -vuṭṭhāna (nt.) childbirth, delivery J I.52; DhA I.399; II.261; -seyyā (f.) the womb; only in expressions relating to reincarnation, as: na punar eti (or upeti) gabbhaseyyaŋ "he does not go into another womb," of an Arahant Sn 29, 152, 535; Vv 53²⁴; and gabbhaseyyaka (adj.) one who enters another womb Vbh 413 sq.; Vism 272, 559, 560; Bdhd 77, 78.

Gabbhara (nt.) [Derivation uncertain. Cp. Sk. gahvara] a cavern Sn 416 (giri°); Vv 63⁵ (giri°).

Gabbhinī (adj. f.) pregnant, enceinte Vin II.268; S III.202; J I.151, 290; IV.37; Pv I.6⁶; PvA 31, 82; VvA 110 (-bhāva); in combⁿ g° pāyamānā purisantaragatā (pregnant, lactating & having had sex. intercourse) A I.295=II.206=M I.77, 238, 307, 342=Pug 55; with utunī anutunī (menstruating & having ceased to menstruate) A III.226 sq.

°Gama I. adj. going, able to go; going to, leading to; in vihangama going in the air Sn 221, 606; Th I.1108; J I.216 (cp. gamana); aghasi° id. Vv 16¹ (=vehāsaŋ° VvA 78); nabhasi° going on clouds Sn 687; nibbāna° leading to N. S V.11; dūraŋ° going far, hadayaŋ° going to one's heart, q. v. — 2. m. course, going to; in atthaŋ° going home, going to rest, etc., q. v.

Gamana I. (nt.) the fact or the state of going, movement, journey, walk; (-°) striving for, the leading of, pursuit A II.48 sq. (gamanena na pattabbo lokass' anto=one cannot walk to the end of the world); Dh 178 (saggassa going to heaven); Sn 40, 691, cp. vāraŋ°; J I.62; 216 (in expl. of vihaŋgama: (ākāse) gamanato pakkhī vihaŋ gamā ti vuccanti); 295; PvA 57. — pahiṇa° going on messages D I.5, etc.; agati° wrong pursuit, °ŋ gacchati to pursue a wrong walk of life A II.18; PvA 161; magga°

tramping, being on the road PvA 43; saraṇa° finding shelter (in the Dhamma) PvA 49.—2. (adj.) (-°) going or leading to, conducive to: nibbāna° maggo the Path leading to Nibbāna S I.186; Dh 289; duggati° magga the road to misery Th 2, 355; duggamana-ṭṭhānā (pl.) inaccessible places PvA 102 (in expl. of duggā).
-antarāya an obstacle to one's departure J I.62; -āgamana going & coming, rise and set Vv 83[6] (=ogamanuggamana VvA 326); DhA I.80 (°kāle); °sampanna senāsana a dwelling or lodging fit for going and coming, i. e. easily accessible A V.15; J I.85; °ŋ karoti to go to and fro VvA 139. -kamma going away DhA II.81. -kāraṇa a reason for or a means to going, in °ŋ karoti to try to go J I.2; -bhāva the state of having gone away J II.133; -magga (pleonastic) the way J I.202; 279; -vaṇṇa the praise of his course or journey J I.87.

Gamaniya (adj.; grd to **gam**) I. as grd. to gacchati: (a place where one) ought to go; in a° not to be gone to (+ṭhāna) VvA 72.—2. as grd. to gameti: in bhogā pahāya gamaniyā (riches that have) to be given up (by leaving) Kh VIII.8 (see expl. as KhA 223); PvA 87 (=kālikā, transient).

Gamika (and gamiya J I.87) (adj.) going away, setting out for a journey (opp. āgantuka coming back) appl. to bhikkhus only: Vin I.292 (° bhatta food for outgoing bh.); II.170 (āgantuka°), 211, 265; V.196; J VI.333 (āgantuka°). See also under abhisankhāra. Cp. Av Ś I.87; Divy 50.

Gamina (adj.) being on a "gati," only at Sn 587 in "aññe pi passe gamine yathākamm' ûpage nare."

Gameti [caus. of gacchati] to make go, to send, to set into motion, to cause to go It 115 (anabhāvaŋ to destroy), see under gacchati.

Gambhīra (adj.) [Vedic gambhīra & gabhīra] deep, profound, unfathomable, well founded, hard to perceive, difficult. — (a) lit. of lakes: Dh 83; Pv II.1[19] (=agādha); Pug 46; of a road (full of swamps) J I.196. — (b) fig. of knowledge & wisdom: dhammo g. duddaso . . . M I.487; S I.136; Tathāgato g. appameyyo duppariyogāho M I.487; parisā g. (opp. uttāna, shallow, superficial, thoughtless) A I.70; g. ṭhāna w. ref. jhāna, etc. Ps II.21; saddhamma g. Sdhp. 530; g. gūḷha nipuṇa Nd 342; lokanātho nipuṇo g. PvA 1; also w. nipuṇa J VI.355; Miln 234; Bdhd. 118, 137; — (nt.) the deep; deep ground, i. e. secure foundation Sn 173; Kh VIII.1, 3 (see KhA 217).
-avabhāsa (adj.) having the appearance of depth or profundity, D II.55; S II.36; Pug 46 (+uttāna), cp. Pug A 226; -pañña one whose wisdom is profound Sn 176, 230; 627=Dh 403 (+medhāvin) cp. DhA IV.169 & see Ps II.192 for detailed explanation; -sita resting on depth (of soil), well-founded A IV.237.

Gambhīratā (f.) [abstr. fr. prec.] depth DhA I.92.

Gamma (adj.) [fr. gāma. Vedic gramya] of or belonging to the village, common, pagan (cp. Fr. villain), always comb[d] with hīna, low & pagan Vin I.10 and ≈ (anta, standard of life); A III.325 (dassana, view); D III.130 (sukhallikānuyoga, hedonist) Sdhp 254. Cp. pothujjanika.

Gayha (adj.) [grd. of gayhati; Vedic grāhya] to be taken, to be seized, as nt. the grip, in gayhūpaga (adj.) for being taken up, for common use SnA 283. — (nt.) that which comes into one's grasp, movable property, acquisition of property DhA II.29; III.119; PvA 4. As gayhūpakaŋ at J IV.219.

Gayhaka (adj.=gayha) one who is to be taken (prisoner), in °niyyamāna id. S I.143=J III.361 (expl. as karamaragāhaŋ gahetvā niyyamāna; cp. karamara).

Gayhati [Pass. to gaṇhāti] to get seized, to be taken (see gaṇhāti); p.pres. gayhamāna being caught DhA III.175 (°ka). — grd. gayha.

Garahaka (adj.) finding fault with, rebuking; in paṭhavī° āpa°, etc., comb[d] w. paṭhavī-jigucchaka, etc. (disgusted w. the great elements) M I.327.

Garahaṇa (nt.) reproof VvA 16, as f. °ṇā at Vism 29.

Garahati [Vedic garhati Dhtp 340 nindāyaŋ] to reproach, to blame, scold, censure, find fault with: agarahiyam mā garahittha "do not blame the blameless" S I.240; D I.161 (tapaŋ to reject, disapprove of); D III.92, 93 (aor. garahi, grd. garahitabba); Sn 313, 665; Miln 222 (+jigucchanti); PvA 125, 126; Sdhp. 382. — pp. garahita blameworthy Dh 30 (pamādo); Sn 313; J V.453; Miln 288 (dasa puggalā g.). agarahita blameless, faultless PvA 89 (=anindita, 131). — See also gārayha & cp. vi°.

Garahā (f.) blame, reproach D I.135 "stating an example," see DA I.296; D III.92, 93; Sn 141; J I.10 (garahapaṭicchādanabhāva preventing all occasion for finding fault); 132 (garaha-bhaya-bhīta for fear of blame), 135 (garahatthe as a blame); Nett 184.

Garahin (adj.) blaming, censuring Sn 660 (ariya°), 778 (atta°), 913 (anatta°); Miln 380 (pāpa°).

Garu [Vedic guru; Gr. βαρύς, Lat. gravis & brutus, Goth. kaûrus] I. adj. (a) lit. heavy, opp. lahu light, appl[d] to bhāra, a load S III.26; J I.196 (=bhārika); VI.420; DhA I.48; Sdhp 494 (rūpagarubhāra the heavy load of "form"). Compar. garutara (as against Sk. garīyaŋ) PvA 191. — (b) fig. important, to be esteemed, valued or valuable A III.110 sq. (piya manāpa g. bhavanīya); c. gen. or -° bent on (often in sequence °garu, °ninna, °poṇa, etc., e. g. Vism 135); pursuing, paying homage to, reverent; (or) esteemed by, honoured, venerated: Satthugaru esteeming the Lord; Dhamma°, Sanghe g. A III.331=IV.28 sq.; dosa° S I.24; kodha°, saddhamma° (pursuing, fostering) A II.46 sq.=84 sq.; Sdhp I (sabba-loka° worshipped by all the world); Dpvs IV.12. — agaru (c. gen.) irreverent towards Sn p. 51 (Gotamassa). Cp. garuka, gārava; also agaru & agalu. — 2. N. a venerable person, a teacher: garunaŋ dassanāya & sakāsaŋ Sn 325, 326 (v. l. garūnaŋ to be preferred, so also SnA 332, 333); garūnaŋ dārā It 36. — garukaroti (for garuŋ k°) to esteem, respect, honour; usually in series sakkaroti g° māneti pūjeti Vin II.162; M I.31; D I.91; A III.76; IV.276; Nd[2] 334 (on namati), 530 (on yasassin); PvA 54. Expl. at DA I.256 by gāravaŋ karoti. — garukātabba worthy of esteem PvA 9. — garukāra (sakkāra g. mānana vandana) esteem, honour, regard Pug 19=Dhs 1121. — See also guru.
-upanissita (adj.) depending on a teacher, one being taught Ps II.202; -ṭṭhāniya one who takes the place of a teacher A III.21, 393; Nett 8; Vism 344. -dhamma a rule to be observed. There are 8 chief rules enum. at Vin II.255=A IV.276, 280; see also Vin IV.51, 315; V.136. Taken in the sense of a violation of these rules Vin I.49=II.226; I.52, 143, 144; II.279; -nissaya in °ŋ gaṇhāti to take up dependency on a teacher, i. e. to consider oneself a pupil Vin II.303; -saŋvasa association with a teacher Nd[2] 235 4[c]; Miln 408.

Garuka [from garu] somewhat heavy.—I. lit. J I.134 (of the womb in pregnancy); Dh 310; Miln 102. Usually coupled & contrasted with lahuka, light: in def. of sense of touch Dhs 648; similarly w. sithila, dhanita, dīgha, rassa Miln 344; DA I.177 (in expl. of dasavidha vyañjana). — 2. fig. (a) heavy, grave, serious esp. appl[d] to — āpatti, breach of regulations, offence (opp. lahuka) Vin V.115, 130, 145, 153; Dh 138 (ābādha, illness); appl[d] to kamma at Vism 601 (one of the four kinds); nt. as adv. considerably Miln 92 (°ŋ parinamati). —

(b) important, venerable, worthy of reverence Th 2, 368 (Satthu sāsana=garukātabba ThA 251); Miln 140. — (c) -° "heavy on," bent on, attaching importance to: nahāna° fond of bathing Vin I.196; tadattha° engaged in (jhāna) Nd² 264; kamma° attributing importance to k. Nd² 411; saddhamma° revering the Doctrine Sdhp. 520. Nibbāna-garuka Vism 117 (+N-ādhimutta & N-pabbhāra).

-āpatti a grievous offence, see above. As terasa g-°ino at Miln 310.

Garutta (nt.) the fact of being honoured or considered worthy of esteem, honourableness A v.164 sq.

Garuḷa [Derivation uncertain. Sk. garuḍa, Lat. volucer winged, volo to fly]. N. of a mythical bird, a harpy Ps II.196=Nd² 235, 3 q.; Vism 206; VvA 9 (=suvaṇṇa); DhA I.144.

Gala [*gel to devour, to swallow=Lat. gula, Ohg. kela, cp. Sk. gala jalukā, and *g̥el, as Gr. δέλεαρ, cp. also Sk. girati, gilati Dhtp 262 gives as meaning of **gal** "adana." This root **gal** also occurs at Vism 410 in fanciful def. of "puggala"; the meaning here is not exactly sure (to cry, shout ?)] the throat J I.216, 264, III.26; IV.494; I.194 (a dewlap); PvA 11, 104.

-agga the top of the throat Sdhp 379; -ajjhoharaniya able to be swallowed (of solid food) Dhs 646, 740, 875; -ggaha taking by the throat, throttling D I.144 (+daṇḍa-pahāra); -nāḷī the larynx DhA I.253; II.257; -ppamāṇa (adj.) going up to the neck J I.264 (āvāṭa); -pariyosāṇa forming the end of the throat J III.126; -ppavedhaka (nt.) pain in the throat M I.371; -mūla the bottom of the throat PvA 283. -vāṭaka the bottom (?) of the throat (œsophagus ?) Vism 185, 258.

Note.—gala with many other words containing a guttural+liquid element belongs to the onomatopoetic roots k̥l g̥l (k̥r g̥r), usually reduplicated (iterative), the main applications of which are the following:

1. The (sounding) throat in designation of *swallowing*, mostly with a dark (guttural) vowel: gulp, belch, gargle, gurgle.

2. The sound produced by the throat (voice) or *sound in general*, particularly of noises or sounds either inarticulate, confused & indefinable or natural sounds striking enough *per se* to form a sufficient means of recognition (i. e. name) of the animal which utters this sound (cuckoo, e. g.). To be divided into:

A. palatal group ("light" sounds): squeak, yell giggle, etc., applied to —(*a*) Animate Nature: the cackling, crowing noise of Palmipeds & related birds, reminding of laughter (heron, hen, cock; cp. P. koñca, Lat. gallus) — (*b*) Inanimate Nature: the grinding, nibbling, trickling, dripping, fizzing noises or sounds (P. galati, etc.).

B. guttural group ("dark" sounds): groan, growl, howl, etc., appl^d to — (*a*) Animate N.: the snorting, grunting noise of the Pachyderms & related quadrupeds (elephant, op. P. koñca, kuñjara; pig, boar) — (*b*) Inanimate N.: the roaring, crashing, thundering noises (P. gaḷagaḷāyati, ghurughurāyati).

3. The sound as indicating *motion* (produced by motion):

A. palatal group ("sharp" sounds, characteristic of *quick* motion: whizz, spin, whirl): P. gaggaraka whirlpool, Gr. κερκίς spindle, bobbin.

B. guttural group ("dull" sounds, characteristic of *slow* and heavy motion: roll, thud, thunder). Sometimes with elimination of the sound-element appl^d to swelling & fullness, as in "bulge" or Gr. σφαραγέω (be full).

These three categories are not always kept clearly separate, so that often a palatal group shifts into the sphere of a guttural one & vice versa. — The formation of k̥l g̥l roots is by no means an extinct process, nor is it restricted to any special branch of a linguistic family, as examples show. The main roots of Idg. origin are the foll. which are all represented in Pāli — (the categories are marked acc. to the foregoing scheme 1, 2A, 2B, 3): **kal** (2A): κλάζω, clango, Goth. hlahjan laugh; **kār** (2 A): κῆρυξ. Sk. kāru (cp. P. kitti), cārmen; **kel** (2 A): κέλαδος, calo (cp. P. kandati), Ohg. hellan; **ker** (2 A^a): καρκαίρω, κόρκορος=querquedula=kakkara (partridge); **kol** (2 B): cuculus, kokila (a); kolāhala and halāhala (b); **kor** (2 B^a): cornix (cp. P. kāka), corvus=crow=raven; Sk. krośati; P. koñca. — **g̥el** (1) Lat. gula, glutio, δέλεαρ; **g̥er**: (1) βόρος, βιβρώσκω, Lat. voro, Sk. girati, Ohg. querka; (3) βάραθρον (whirlpool) Sk. gargara: **gel** (1) Sk. gilati, Ohg. kela — **gal** (2 A): gallus (a) gloria (*b*); **gar** (2 A^b): γῆρυς, garrulus, Ohg. kara: **gel** (2 A): χελιδών (a) hirrio (to whine), Ohg. gellan (b): **ger**: (1) γαργαρίζω (gargle) Sk. gharghara (gurgling). (2 A^a) γέρανος = crane, Ger. krāhen, Lat. gracillo (cackle); (2 B^a) Ohg. kerran (grunt), Sk. gr̥ṇāti (sing); (2 A^b) Sk. jarate (rustle); **gur** (2 B^a): γρύζω=grundio=grunt; Lat. gurgulio; Sk. ghurghura.

With special reference to Pāli formations the foll. list shows a few sound roots which are further discussed in the Dictionary s. v. Closely connected with Idg. k̥l g̥l is the Pāli cerebral ṭ, ṭh, ḷ, r̥, so that roots with these sounds have to be classed in a mutual relation with the liquids. In most cases graphic representation varies between both (cp. gala & gaḷa) — **kil** (kiṇ) (2 A^b): kiki (cp. Sk. kr̥ka°), kilikilāyati & kinkiṇāyati (tinkle), kili (click), kinkaṇika (bell); **kur** (2 B): ākurati to hawk, to be hoarse; **khaṭ** (1) khaṭakhaṭa (hawking), kākacchati (snore); (2 A^a) kukkuṭa (cock); **gal** (1) gala (throat) uggilati (vomit); (2 A^b) galati (trickle): (2 B^a) Pk. galagajjiya (roar) & guluguliya (bellow); (2 B^b) gaḷagaḷāyati (roar); **gar** (2 A); gaggara (roar & cackle, cp. Sk. gargara to 3); (2 B); gaggarāyati (roar); (3) gaggaraka (whirlpool); **ghar** (1) Sk. gharghara (gurgling); (2 A^b) gharati (trickle), Sk. ghargharikā (bell); (2 B^b) ghurughurāyati (grunt). — See also kakaca, kanka, kankaṇa, cakora (cankora), cakkavaka, jagghati, ciṭiciṭāyati, taṭataṭayati, timingala, papphāsa.

Galaka (nt.) throat J III.481; IV.251.

Gaḷa [same as gala, see note on prec.] 1. a drop, i. e. a fall: see gaḷāgaḷa.—2. a swelling, a boil (=gaṇḍa) J IV.494 (mattā gajā bhinnagaḷā elephants in rut, with the temple-swellings broken; expl. p. 497 by madaṃ gaḷantā); Sn 61 (? v. l. gaṇḍa). — 3. a hook, a fish-hook Sn 61 (?), expl. at SnA 114 by ākaḍḍhanavasena baḷiso.

gaḷāgaḷaṃ gacchati to go from drop to drop, i. e. from fall to fall, w. ref. to the gatis J v.453 (expl. by apāyaṃ gacchati).

Gaḷagaḷāyati [=gaggarāyati, see note on gala] to roar, to crash, to thunder; deve gaḷagaḷāyate (loc. abs.) in a thunderstorm, usually as deve vassante deve g° amidst rain and heavy thunder D II.132; S I.106; A v.114 sq. (gala°); Th 1, 189; Miln 116 (gaganaṃ ravati galag°); KhA 163 (mahāmegha). — Gangā galagalantī the roaring Gangā Miln 122 (cp. halāhalasadda ibid.).

Gaḷati (and galati) [Sk. galati, cp. Ohg. quellan to well up, to flow out; see note on gala and cp. also jala water] 1. to drip, flow, trickle (trs. & intr.) Vin I.204 (**natthu** g.); M I.336 (sīsaṃ lohitena gaḷati); J IV.497 (madaṃ); IV.3 (lohitaṃ g.); V.472 (do. v. l. paggharati); Pv IV.5³ (assukāni g.). — 2. to rain Th 1, 524 (deve gaḷantamhi in a shower of rain. Cp. gala-gaḷāyati). — 3. to drop down, to fall DhA II.146 (suriyo majjhaṭṭhānato galito). — Cp. pari°.

Gaḷayati [denom. to gaḷa in sense of gaḷati 1] to drip, to drop, in assukāni g. to shed tears Sn 691.

Gaḷita rough, in a° smooth J v.203, 206 (+mudu & akakkasa); vi.64.

Gaḷocī (f.). N. of a shrub (Cocculus cordifolius); in gaḷocilatā DhA iii.110; a creeper. Cp. pūtilatā.

Gava° base of the N. go, a bull, cow, used in cpds. See gāv°, go.
-**āghātana** slaughtering of cows Vin i.182; -**assa** cows & horses Vin v.350; D i.5~; Sn 769; -**caṇḍa** fierce towards cows Pug 47; -**pāna** milky rice pudding J i.33; -(°m)**pati** "lord of cows," a bull Sn 26, 27 (usabha).

Gavacchita furnished with netting (?) (Hardy in Index) VvA 276, of a carriage (=suvaṇṇajālavitata).

Gavaja see gavaya.

Gavaya (and gavaja) a species of ox, the gayal [Sk. gavaya, cp. gavala, buffalo] J v.406. (°ja=khagga); Miln 149; DhsA 331.

Gavi a tree-like creeper, in -pphala the fruit of a g. Sn 239 (=rukkhavalliphala SnA).

°Gavesaka (adj. fr. next) looking for, seeking J i.176 (kāraṇa°); ii.3 (aguṇa°).

Gavesati [gava+esati. Vedic gaveṣate. Origin. to search after cows. Dhtp 298=maggana tracking] to seek, to search for, to wish for, strive after Dh 146 (gavessatha), 153; Th i, 183; Nd² 2, 70, 427; J i.4, 61; Miln 326; PvA 187, 202 (aor. gavesi=vicini); Bdhd 53. In Nd² always in combⁿ esati gavesati pariyesati.

Gavesana search for PvA 185.

Gavesin (adj.) seeking, looking for, striving after (usually -°) D i.95 (tāṇa°, etc.); Dh 99 (kāma°), 245 (suci°), 355 (pāra°); Nd² 503 (in expl. of mahesi, with esin & pariyesin); Bdhd 59.

Gassetuŋ at DhsA 324 is to be corrected into dassetuŋ.

Gaha¹ [see under gaṇhāti] a house, usually in cpds. (see below). J iii.396 (=the layman's life; Com. geha).
-**kāraka** a house-builder, metaph. of taṇhā (cp. kāya as geha) Dh 153, 154=Th i, 183, 184; DhA iii.128; -**kūṭa** the peak of a house, the ridge-pole, metaph. of ignorance Dh 154 (=kaṇṇika-maṇḍala DhA 128), replacing thūṇirā (pillar) at Th i, 184 in corresp. passage (=kaṇṇikā Com.); -**ṭṭha** a householder, one who leads the life of a layman (opp. anagāra, pabbajita or paribbājaka) Vin i.115 (sagahaṭṭhā parisā an assembly in which laymen were present); S i.201; A iii.114, 116, 258; It. 112 (gharaŋ esino gahaṭṭhā) Dh 404=Sn 628; Sn 43 (gharaŋ āvasanto, see Nd² 226 for explanation), 90, 134 (paribbājaŋ gahaṭṭhaŋ vā) 398, 487; Sdhp 375. -°*vatta* a layman's rule of conduct Sn 393 (=agāriyā paṭipadā SnA 376) -°*ka* belonging to a layman; acting as a layman or in the quality of a l. A ii.35 (kinkaraṇiyāni), iii.296 (brahmacariyā); -**pati** see sep.

Gaha² [Sk. graha, gaṇhāti, q. v. for etym.] "seizer," seizing, grasping, a demon, any being or object having a hold upon man. So at S i.208 where Sānu is "seized" by an epileptic fit (see note in *K.S.* i.267, 268). Used of dosa (anger) Dh 251 (exemplified at DhA iii.362 by ajagara° the grip of a boa, kumbhila° of a crocodile, yakkha° of a demon). sagaha having crocodiles, full of c. (of the ocean) (+sarakkhasa) It 57. Cp. gahaṇa & saŋ°.

Gahaṇa [fr. gaṇhāti] (adj.) seizing, taking; acquiring; (n.) seizure, grasp, hold, acquisition Vism 114 (in detail). Usually -°: nāma°-divase on the day on which a child gets its name (lit. acquiring a name) J i.199, 262; arahatta° DhA i.8; dussa° DhA ii.87; maccha° J iv.139; hattha° J i.294; byanjana°-lakkhaṇa Nett 27. gahaṇatthāya in order to get . . J i.279; ii.352.—amhākaŋ g° sugahaṇaŋ we have a tight grip J i.222, 223.

Gahaṇī (f.) the "seizer," a supposed organ of the body dealing with digestion and gestation. Sama-vepākiniyā g° iyā samannāgata "endowed with good digestion" D ii.177=iii.166. Same phrase at Av Ś i.168, 172. Cp. Vedic graha. *B. Psy.* 59, 67.
Gahaṇika in phrase saŋsuddha-gahaṇika coming from a clean womb, of pure descent, in the enum. of the indispensable good qualities of a brahmin or a noble D i.113, 115, 137 (gahaṇi expl. as kucchi DA i.281); A i.163, iii.154, 223; Sn p. 115. J i.2; duṭṭha-gahaṇika having a bad digestion Vin i.206.

Gahana [Sk. gahana, cp. also ghana] 1. adj. deep, thick, impervious, only in a° clear, unobstructed, free from obstacles Vv 18⁷ (akanataka+); Miln 160 (gahanaŋ a° kataŋ the thicket is cleared). — 2. nt. an impenetrable place, a thicket jungle, tangle. — (a) 18 gahanāni at J v.46; usually appl. to grass: tiṇa° A i.153=iii.128 (+rukkha°); Miln 369; adj. tiṇagahanā obstructed with grass (of vihārā) Vin ii.138; — S i.199 (rukkhamūla°); J i.7, 158; PvA 5 (pabbata°), 43; VvA 230 (vana°). — (b) fig. imperviousness, entanglement, obstruction, appl. to diṭṭhi, the jungle of wrong views or heresy (usually combᵈ w. diṭṭhi—kantāra, the wilderness of d., see diṭṭhi) M i.8, 485; Pug 22; DA i.108. Of rāga°, moha°, etc., and kilesa° Nd² 630 (in expl. of Satthā; rāgagahanaŋ tāreti); DhA iv.156 (on Dh 394); VvA 96.—manussa° M i.340.
-**ṭṭhāna** a lair in the jungle J i.150, 253.

Gahapati [gaha+pati. Vedic gṛhapati, where pati is still felt in its original meaning of "lord," "master," implying dignity, power & auspiciousness. Cp. Sk. dampati=dominus=δεσπότης; and pati in P. senāpati commander-in-chief, Sk. jāspati householder, Lat. hospes, Obulg. gospoda=potestas, Goth. brūþ-faþs, bride-groom, hunda-faþs=senāpati. See details under pati.] the possessor of a house, the head of the household, pater familias (freq.+seṭṭhi). — 1. In formulas: (a) as regards social standing, wealth & clanship: a man of private (i. e. not official) life, classed w. khattiyā & brāhmaṇā in kh°-mahāsālā, wealthy Nobles, brahm°-mahāsālā, do. Brahmins, gah°-m° well-to-do gentry S i.71; Nd² 135; DhA i.388. — kh°-kula, br°-kula, g°-kula the kh°, etc. clans: Vin ii.161; J i.218. kh°, amaccā, br°, g.° D i.136. — (b) as regards education & mode of life ranking with kh°, br°, g.° and samaṇā Vin i.227; A i.66; Nd² 235, see also cpd. -paṇḍita.— 2. Other applications: freq. in combⁿ brāhmaṇa-gahapatikā priests & yeomen: see gahapatika. In combⁿ w. gahapatiputta (cp. kulaputta) it comprises the members of the g. rank, clansmen of the (middle) class, and implies a tinge of "respectable people" esp. in addresses. So used by the Buddha in enumerating the people as gahapati vā gah°-putto vā aññatarasmiŋ vā kule paccājāto D i.62; M i.344. gahapatī ca gahapatāniyo householders and their wives A ii.57. In sg. the voc. gahapati may be rendered by "Sir" (Miln 17 e. g. and freq.), & in pl. gahapatayo by "Sirs" (e. g. Vin i.227; M i.401; A ii.57). — As regards occupation all resp. businesses are within the sphere of the g., most frequently mentioned as such are seṭṭhino (see below) & cp. seṭṭhi° Vin i.16, but also kassaka, farmer A i.229, 239 sq.; and dārukammika, carpenter A iii.391. Var. duties of a g. enum. at A i.229, 239. —The wealth & comfortably-living position of a g. is evident from an expression like kalyāṇa-bhattiko g. a man accustomed to good food Vin ii.77=iii.160. — f. gahapatānī Vin iii.211, 213 sq., 259 (always w. gahapati); DhA i.376; pl. gahapatāniyo see above. — *Note*. The gen. sg. of gahapati is °ino (J i.92) as well as -issa (Vin i.16; D iii.36). — 3. Single cases of gahapatis, where g. almost assumes the function of a title are Anāthapiṇḍika g. Vin ii.158 sq.; S i.56; ii.68; A ii.65; J i.92; PvA 16; Meṇḍaka g. Vin i.240 sq.; Citta S iv.281 sq.; Nakulapitā S ii.1 sq.; Potaliya M i.359; Sandhāna D iii.36 sq.; Hāliddikānī S ii.9. — See next.

-'aggi the sacred fire to be maintained by a householder, interpreted by the Buddha as the care to be bestowed on one's children & servants A IV.45; see enum. under aggī at A IV.41; D III.217; -cīvara the robe of a householder (i. e. a layman's robe) Vin I.280 sq.; °dhara wearing the householder's (private man's) robe (of a bhikkhu) M I.31; A III.391 sq.; -necayika (always with brāhmaṇa-mahāsālā) a business man of substance D I.136; III.16 sq.; -paṇḍita a learned householder. Cp. above 1 (b), together w. khattiya°, etc. M I.176, 396; w. samaṇa-brāhmaṇa° Miln 5; -parisā a company of gahapatis (together w. khattiya°, etc., see above) Vin I.227; M I.72; D III.260; -putta a member of a g. clan D I.62, 211; M I.344; S III.48, 112; PvA 22; -mahāsāla a householder of private means (cp. above 1 a) usually in comb^n with khattiya°, etc. D III.258; S I.71; IV.292; A II.86; IV.239; -ratana the "householder-gem" one of the seven fairy jewels of the mythical overlord. He is a wizard treasure-finder (see ratana) D II.16, 176; Sn p. 106. Cp. Rh.D. *Dialogues etc.* II.206.

Gahapatika (adj.-n.) belonging to the rank or grade of a householder, a member of the gentry, a man of private means (see gahapati) D I.61 (expl. as gehassa pati ekageha-matte jeṭṭhaka DA I.171); Nd^2 342; PvA 39. Often in comb^n w. khattiya & brāhmaṇa: A I.66; D III.44, 46, 61; & often in contrast to brāhmaṇa only: brāhmaṇa-gahapatika Brahmins & Privates (priests & laymen, Rh.D. *Buddh. S.* p. 258) M I.400; A I.110; It III.; J I.83, 152, 267; PvA 22. — paṇṇika g° "owner of a house of leaves" as nickname of a fruiterer J III.21; of an ascetic J IV.446.

Gahita (and gahīta Dh 311) (adj.) [pp. of gaṇhāti] seized taken, grasped D I.16; DA I.107 (=ādinna, pavattita); J I.61; IV.2; PvA 43 (v. l. for text gaṇhita). — nt. a grasp, grip DhA III.175; — gahitakaŋ karoti to accept VvA 260. -duggahīta (always °*gahīta*) hard to grasp M I.132 sq.; A II.147, 168; III.178; Dh 311; J VI.307 sq.; sugahita (sic) easy to get J I.222.

-bhāva (cittassa) the state of being held (back), holding back, preventing to act (generously) DhsA 370 (in expl^n of aggahitattaŋ cittassa Dhs 1122 see under ā°).

Gāthaka [demin. of gāthā] = gāthā, in ekaŋ me gāhi gāthakaŋ "sing to me only one little verse" J III.507.

Gāthā (f.) [Vedic gāthā, on der^n see gāyate] a verse, stanza, line of poetry, usually referring to an Anuṭṭhubbaŋ or a Tuṭṭhubbaŋ, & called a catuppādā gāthā, a stanza (śloka) of four half-lines A II.178; J IV.395. Def. as akkhara-padaniya-mita-ganthita-vacanaŋ at KhA 117. For a riddle on the word see S I.38. As a style of composition it is one of the nine Angas or divisions of the Canon (see navanga Satthu sāsana). Pl. gāthā Sn 429; J II.160; gāthāyo Vin I.5, 349; D II.157. gāthāya ajjhābhāsati to address with a verse Vin I.36, 38; Kh v. intr. — gāthāhi anumodati to thank with (these) lines Vin I.222, 230, 246, 294, etc. — gāthāyo giyamāna uttering the lines Vin I.38. — anantaragāthā the foll. stanza J IV.142; Sn 251; J I.280; Dh 102 (°sataŋ).

-abhigīta gained by verses S I.167 = Sn 81, 480 (gāthāyo bhāsitvā laddhaŋ Com. cp. Ger. "ersungen"). -āvasāne after the stanza has been ended DhA III.171; -jānanaka one who knows verses Anvs. p. 35; -dvaya (nt.) a pair of stanzas J III.395 sq.; PvA 29, 40; -pada a half line of a gāthā Dh 101; KhA 123; -sukhattaŋ in order to have a well-sounding line, metri causā, PvA 33.

Gādha^1 [Sk. gāḷha pp. of **gāh**, see gāhati] depth; a hole, a dugout A II.107 = Pug 43 (cp. PugA 225); Sdhp 394 (°ŋ khaṇati). Cp. gāḷha^2.

Gādha^2 [Sk. gāḷha firm Dhtp 167 "patiṭṭhāyaŋ" cp. also Sk. gādha, fordable & see gāḷha^1] adj. passable, fordable, in a° unfathomable, deep PvA 77 (= gambhīra). nt. a ford, a firm stand, firm ground, a safe place: gambhīre °ŋ vindati A V.202. °ŋ esati to seek the terra firma S I.127; similarly: °ŋ labhati to gain firm footing S I.47; °ŋ ajjhagā S IV.206; °ŋ labhate J VI.440 (= patiṭṭhā). Cp. o°, paṭi°.

Gādhati [v. der. fr. gādha^2] to stand fast, to be on firm ground, to have a firm footing: āpo ca paṭhavī ca tejo vāyo na gādhati "the four elements have no footing" D I.223 = S I.15; — Dhamma-Vinaye gādhati "to stand fast in the Doctrine & Discipline" S III.59 sq.

Gāma [Vedic grāma, heap, collection, parish; ***grem** to comprise; Lat. gremium; Ags. crammian (E. cram), Obulg. gramada (village community) Ohg. chram; cp. ***ger** in Gr. ἀγείρω, ἀγορά, Lat. grex.] a collection of houses, a hamlet (cp. Ger. gemeinde), a habitable place (opp. arañña: gāme vā yadi vāraññe Sn 119), a parish or village having boundaries & distinct from the surrounding country (gāmo ca gāmupacāro ca Vin I.109, 110; III.46). In size varying, but usually small & distinguished from nigama, a market-town. It is the smallest in the list of settlements making up a "state" (raṭṭhaŋ). See definition & description at Vin III.46, 200. It is the source of support for the bhikkhus, and the phrase gāmaŋ piṇḍāya carati "to visit the parish for alms" is extremely frequent. — 1. a village as such: Vin I.46; Ārāmika°, Pilinda° Vin I.28, 29 (as Ārāmikagāmaka & Pilinda-gāmaka at Vin III.249); Sakyānaŋ gāme janapade Lumbineyye Sn 683; Uruvela° Pv II.13^{18}; gāmo nātikālena pavisitabbo M I.469; °ŋ raṭṭhañ ca bhuñjati Sn 619, 711; gāme tiṇsa kulāni honti J I.199; — Sn 386, 929, 978; J II.153; VI.366; Dh 47, 49; Dhs 697 (suñño g.); PvA 73 (gāme amaccakula); 67 (gāmassa dvārasamīpena). — gāmā gāmaŋ from hamlet to hamlet M II.20; Sn 180 (with nagā nagaŋ; expl. SnA 216 as devagāmā devagāmaŋ), 192 (with purā puraŋ); Pv II.13^{18}. In the same sense gāmena gāmaŋ Nd^2 177 (with nigamena n°, nagarena n°., raṭṭhena r°., janapadena j°.). — 2. grouped with nigama, a market-town: gāmanigamo sevitabbo or asevitabbo A IV.365 sq., cp. V.101 (w. janapadapadeso); — Vin III.25, 184 (°ŋ vā nigamaŋ vā upanissāya); IV.93 (piṇḍāya pavisati); gāmassa vā nigamassa vā avidūre D I.237; M I.488; gāme vā nigame vā Pug 66. — 3. as a geographical-political unit in the constitution of a kingdom, enum^d in two sets: (a) gāma-nigama-rājadhāniyo Vin III.89; A III.108; Nd^2 271^{III}; Pv II.13^{18}; DhA I 90. — (b) gāma-nigama-nagara-raṭṭha-janapada Nd^2 177, 304^{III} (°bandhana), 305 (°kathā); with the foll. variations: g. nigama nagara M II.33-40; g. nigama janapada Sn 995; Vism 152; gāmāni nigamāni ca Sn 118 (expl^d by SnA 178: ettha ca saddena nagarāni ti pi vattabbaŋ). — See also dvāra°; paccanta°; bīja°; bhūta°; mātu°.

-anta the neighbourhood of a village, its border, the village itself, in °*nāyaka* leading to the village A III.189; °*vihārin* (= āraññaka) living near a v. M I.31, 473; A III.391 (w. nemantanika and gahapati-cīvara-dhara); — Sn 710; -antara the (interior of the) village, only in t. t. gāmantaraŋ gacchati to go into the v. Vin II.300, & in °*kappa* the "village-trip-licence" (*Vin. Texts* III.398) ib. 294, 300; cp. IV.64, 65; V.210; -ūpacāra the outskirts of a v. Vin I.109, 110; defined at Vin III.46, 200; -kathā village-talk, gossip about v.-affairs. Included in the list of foolish talks (+ nigama°, nagara°, janapada°) D I.7 (see expl^n at DA I.90); Sn 922. See kathā; -kamma that which is to be done to, or in a village, in °ŋ karoti to make a place habitable J I.199; -kūṭa "the village-fraud," a sycophant S II.258; J IV.177 (= kūṭavedin); -goṇā (pl.) the village cattle J I.194; -ghāta those who sack villages, a marauder, dacoit (of corā thieves) D I.135; S II.188; -ghātaka (corā) = °ghāta S IV.173; Miln 20; Vism 484; nt. village plundering J I.200. -jana the people of the v. Miln 47; -ṭṭhāna in purāṇa° a ruined village J II.102; -dārakā (pl.) the youngsters of the v. J III.275; f. -dārikā the girls of the v. PvA 67; -dvaya, in °vāsika living in (these) two vs. PvA 77; -dvāra the v. gates, the entrance to the v. Vin III.52; J II.110, 301; cp. PvA 67; -dhamma doings with women-folk (cp. mātugāma), vile conduct D I.4≈(+methuna) A I.211; J II.180 (=vasaladhamma); VvA 11; DA I.72 (=gāma-vāsīnaŋ dhamma?); -poddava (v. l. kāmapudava) a sham-pooer (? *Vin. Texts* III.66; Bdhgh explains: kāmapudavā ti chavi-rāga-maṇḍanânuyuttā nāgarikamanussā; gāmaŋ podavā ti pi pādho es' ev' attho, Vin II.315) Vin II.105; -bhojaka the village headman J I.199; DhA I.69; -majjhe in the midst of the v. J I.199; VI.332; -vara an excellent v. S I.97; J I.138; -vāsin the inhabitant of a v. J II.110; V.107; DA I.72; -saññā the thought of a v. M III.104; -samīpe near a v. J I.254; -sahassa a thousand parishes (80,000 under the rule of King Bimbisāra) Vin I.179; -sāmanta in the neighbourhood of a v., near a v. D I.101; (+mgama°) -sīmā the boundary of the parish Vin I.110 (+nigama°); -sūkara a village pig J III.393.

Gāmaka 1. =gāma Vin I.208; J I.199 (Macala°), 253; IV.431 (cora°); PvA 67 (Iṭṭhakāvatī and Dīgharājī); DhA II.25 (dvāra°). — 2. a villager J V.107 (=gāma-vāsin).

-āvāsa an abode in a village PvA 12; VvA 291.

Gāmaṇika=gāmaṇi S I.61; A III.76 (pūga°).

Gāmaṇī (m.) the head of a company, a chief, a village headman Vin II.296 (Maṇicūḷaka). Title of the G.-Saŋyutta (Book VIII. of the Saḷāyatana-Vagga) S IV.305 sq.; & of the G.-Jātaka J I.136, 137. —S IV.306 (Talapuṭa naṭa°), 308 (yodhājīvo g.), 310 (hatthāroho g.), 312 (Asibandhakaputta), 330 (Rāsiya).

Gāmaṇḍala "the round of the ox," like the oxen driven round & round the threshing-floor Th 1, 1143. — Cp. gomaṇḍala (s.v. go).

Gāmika 1. [to gāma] a governor of a village, overseer of a parish Vin I.179; A III.76, 78, 300 (in series w. raṭṭhika pettanika, senāpatika, pūgagamaṇika). — 2. [to gam] adj. going wandering, travelling (-°) J II.112.

°Gāmin (adj.) [from gacchati, gam] f. °iṇī, in composition °gāmi°. — (a) going, walking, lit.: sīgha° walking quickly Sn 381; — (b) leading to, making for, usually with magga or paṭipadā (gāmi-l), either lit. Pāṭaliputta-gāmi-magga the road to P. Miln 17; or fig. of ways & means connected w. one of the "gatis," as apāya° DhA III.175. udaya° paṭipadā S V.361; nibbāna° dhamma Sn 233; amata-gāmi-magga S V.8; udayattha-gāmiṇī paññā A V.15; dukkhanirodha° paṭipadā Vin I.10; cp. ācaya° Dhs 584, 1013. *Acc.* °gāminaŋ: khemaŋ Amata° M I.508; brahmacariyaŋ: nibbān' ogadha° It 28, 29; dukkhûpasama° maggaŋ Sn 724=Dh 191; niraya° maggaŋ Sn 277, ThA 243. Or °gāmiŋ: Sn 233, 381.

Gāmeyya (adj.) belonging to a village in sa° of the same v., a clansman S I.36=60 (+sakhā).

Gāyaka [fr. next] a singer PvA 3 (naṭaka°).

Gāyati [Vedic gai, gāyate] to sing, to recite, often comb[d] w. naccati to dance; ppr. gāyanto, gāyamāna & gīyamāna (Vin I.38); imper. gāhi (J III.507); fut. gāyissati; grd. gāyitabba. Vin II.108 (dhammaŋ). 196 (gāthaŋ); Sn 682 (g° ca vādayanti ca); J I.290 (gītaŋ); III.507 (naccitvā gāyitvā); Vism 121 (aor. gāyi); PvA 151. Cp. gatha, gita, geyya.

Gāyana (nt.) singing VvA 315 (naccana+).

Gārayha (adj.) [grd. of garahati] contemptible, low Vin III.186; IV.176 sq.; 242; V.149; M I.403; A II.241 (kammaŋ pādaŋ gārayhaŋ mosallaŋ); Sn 141; Nett 52; SnA 192. a° not to be blamed J VI.200 (spelt aggarayha).

Gārava (m. and [later] nt.) [cp. Sk. gaurava, fr. garu] reverence, respect, esteem; with loc. respect for, reverence towards; in the set of six venerable objects: Buddhe [Satthari], Dhamme, Sanghe, sikkhāya, appamāde, paṭisanthāre Vin V.92=D III.244. As 7 gāravā (the 6+samādhi) in adj. a° and sa° at A IV.84 (see below). D III.284; Sn 265; Vism 464 (atta° & para°). Expl[d] KhA 144 by garubhāvo; often in comb[n] with bahumāna PvA 135 (=pūjā), sañjāta-g°-bahumāna (adj.) PvA 50; VvA 205. Instr. gāravena out of respect, respectfully D II.155; J I.465. Appl[d] to the terms of address bhante & bhaddante PvA 33, 121, & āyasmā (see cpd. °adhivacana). —agārava (m. nt.) disrespect Vin V.92 (six: as above); J I.217; PvA 54. — As *adj.* in sagārava and agārava full of reverence toward (with loc.) & disrespectful; D III.244 (six g.); A IV.84 (seven); M I.469; comb[d] with appatissa & sappatissa (obedient) A III.7 sq., 14 sq., 247, 340. Also in tibba-gārava full of keen respect (Satthu-garu Dhamma-garu Sanghe ca tibba-gārava, etc.) A III.331=IV.28 sq.

-âdhivacana a title of respect, a reverential address Nd² 466 (with ref. to Bhagavā), cp. sagārava sappatissâdhivacana Nd² 130 (āyasmā).

Gāravatā [Der. fr. gārava] reverence, respect, in Satthu°, Dhamma°, etc. A III.330 sq., 423 sq.; IV.29 (ottappa°).

Gāḷha (adj.) [cp. Sk. gāḍha] 1. [cp. gādha¹] strong, tight, close; thick. In phrase pacchābāhaŋ g° bandhanaŋ bandhati to pinion the arms tightly D I.245; A II.241; J I.264; PvA 4. Of an illness (gāḷhena rogâtankena phuṭṭha) A II.174 sq.; appl[d] to poison smeared on an arrow M I.429. — gāḷhaŋ & gāḷhakaŋ (adv.) tightly J I.265, 291. — agāḷha (? prob. to be read āgāḷha) (of vacana, speech, comb[d] with pharusa) strong (?) Pug 32 (expl[d] by Com. atigāḷha thaddha), cp. 2. and gaḷita. — 2. [cp. gādha¹] deep J I.155 (°vedhin, piercing); Miln 370 (ogāhati). Cp. ajjhogāḷha, atigāḷha, ogāḷha, nigāḷhita, pagāḷha.

Gāvī (f.) [see go] gen. sg. gāviyā (Pug 56=A II.207); nom. pl. gāviyo (SnA 323; VvA 308); gen. pl. gāvīnaŋ DhA I.396; SnA 323; VvA 308). — A cow Vin I.193; A IV.418; J I.50; Ud 8, 49; Vism 525 (in simile); DhA II.35; VvA 200.

Gāvuta (nt.) [cp. Vedic gavyūti pasture land, district] a linear measure, a quarter of a yojana=80 usabhas, a little less than two miles, a league J I.57, 59; II.209; Vism 118; DhA I.396.

Gāvutika (adj.) reaching a gāvuta in extent DA I.284.

Gāvo see go.

Gāha [fr. gaṇhāti] 1. (n.) seizing, seizure, grip (cp. gaha): canda° suriya° an eclipse (lit. the moon, etc., being seized by a demon) D I.10 (=DA I.95: Rāhu candaŋ gaṇhāti). Esp. appl[d] to the sphere of the mind obsession, being possessed (by a thought), an idea, opinion, view, usually as a preconceived idea, a wrong view, misconception. So in def[n] of diṭṭhi (wrong views) with paṭiggāha & abhinivesa Nd² 271[III] (on lepa); Pug 22; Dhs 381 (=obsession like the grip of a crocodile DhsA 253), 1003; Vbh 145, 358. In the same formula as vipariyesa ggāha (wrong view), cp. viparīta° VvA 331 (see diṭṭhi). As doubt & error in anekaŋ sa+g° in def[n] of kankhā & vicikicchā Nd² 1; Vbh 168; ekaŋsa° & apaṇṇaka° certainty, right thought J I.97. — gāhaŋ vissajjeti to give up a preconceived idea J II.387. — 2. (adj.) act. holding: rasmi° holding the reins Dh 222, dabbi° holding the spoons Pv II.9[53] (=gāhaka PvA 135). - - (b) med.-pass. taken: jīvagāha taken alive, in °ŋ gaheti to take (prisoner) alive S I.84, karamaragāhaŋ gaheti same J III.361 (see kara).

Gāhaka (adj.) f. gāhikā holding (-°) chatta° Sn 688; Davs II.119; kataccha° PvA 135; cāmarī° J VI.218. Cp. saŋ°.

Gāhati [Sk. gāhate but Dhtp 349=viloḷana] to immerse, to penetrate, to plunge into: see gādha & gāḷha; cp. also avagadha ajjhogāhati, ogāhati, pagāhati.

Gāhana (nt.) [fr. last] submersion, see avagāhana, avagāhati & avagāhana.

Gāhavant in ekaŋsa-gāhavatī nibbici kicchā "doubtlessness consisting in certainty" VvA 85 in expl° of ekaŋsika.

Gāhāpaka [fr. gāhāpeti] one who is made to take up, a receiver Vin II.177 (patta°).

Gāhāpeti [caus. of gaṇhāti] to cause to take; to cause to be seized or fetched; to remove. Aor, gāhāpesi J I.53; II.37; gāhāpayi Pv IV.1[42]. — Ger. gāhāpetvā J I.166; II.127; III.281; DhA I.62 (patta-cīvaraŋ). With double acc. mahājanaŋ kathaŋ g° made people believe your words J II.416; cetake kasā g. made the servants seize their whips J III.281. Cp. gaṇhāpeti.

Gāhi Imper. pres. of gāyati J III.507.

Gāhika (-°)=gahin, see anta°.

Gāhin (adj.) (-°) grasping, taking up, striving after, ādhāna° D III.247; udaka° J I.5; piya° Dh 209; nimitta° anubyañjana°, etc.

Gāheti [v. denom. fr. gāha] to understand, to account for DA I.117.

Gingamaka (v. l. BB kinkamaka) a sort of ornament J VI.590.

Gijjha [Vedic gṛdhra, cp. gijjhati] 1. (m.) a vulture. Classed with kāka, crow & kulala, hawk M I.88; (kākā +), 364 (in simile, with kankā & kulatā) 429 (do.); Sn 201 (kākā +); PvA 198 (+ kulalā). It occurs also in the form gaddha. — 2. (adj.) greedy, desirous of (-°): kāma° J I.210 (cp. giddha); cp. paṭi°.
-kūṭa "Vulture's Peak" Np. of a hill near Rājagaha Vin II.193; DhA I.140; PvA 10 and passim. **-potaka** the young of a vulture Vism 537 (in simile).

Gijjhati [Sk. gṛdhyati, to Lat. gradior ?] to desire, to long for, to wish: pp. gaddha & giddha. Cp. abhi°, pali°. — pp. (Pass.) gijjhita Th 2, 152 (=paccāsiŋsita ThA).

Giñjakā (f.) a brick, in °āvasatha a house of bricks, as N pl. "the Brick Hall" D I.91; Vin I.232; M I.205.

Giddha (adj.) [pp. of gijjhati] greedy; greedy for, hankering after (with loc.) S I.74 (+ kāmesu mucchita); II.227; A II.2; III.68; Sn 243 (rasesu), 774 (kāmesu); 809; Pv IV.6[2] (sukhe); PvA 3 (+ rata) (=gadhita), 271 (āhāre=hungry; cp. giddhin). In series with similar terms of desire: giddha gathita (or gadhita) mucchita ajjhopanna Nd[2] 369 (nissita); SnA 286. Cp. gathita. — agiddha without greed, desireless, controlled It 92 (+ vītagedha); Sn 210 (do), 845. Cp. pa°.

Giddhi (f.) [cp. Sk. gṛdhyā or gṛdhnutā] greed, usually in cpds.: °māna greed & conceit Sn 328, °lobha g. & desire M I.360, 362 (also a° and giddhilobhin); J V.343. Der. giddhikatā (f. abstr.=Sk. gṛdhnutā) greed Vbh 351 (v. l. gedhi°).

Giddhin (adj. fr. prec.) greedy, usually -° greedy for, desirous after Pv IV.10[7] (āhāra°) f. giddhinī: gāvī vaccha° Vin I.193; S IV.181. Cp. also paligedhin.

Giddhimā (adj. fr. giddhi) greedy, full of greed J V.464 (rasa°).

Gini (poet.) [Vedic agni; this the aphetic form, arisen in a comb[n] like mahāgni=mahā-gini, as against the usual assimilation aggi] fire A III.347 (mahāgini); Sn 18, 19 (āhito > nibbuto: made > extinguished); J IV.26. —
Note. The occurrence of two phonetic representatives of one Vedic form (one by diæresis & one by contraction) is common in words containing a liquid or nasal element (l. r. n; cp. note on gala), e. g. supina & soppa (Sk. svapna), abhikkhaṇa and abhiṇha (abhīkṣṇa), silesuma & semha (śleṣman) gaḷagaḷa & gaggara (gargara), etc.

Gimha [Vedic grīṣma] I. (sg.) heat, in special application to the atmosphere: hot part (of the day or year), hot season, summer; a summer month. Always used in loc. as a designation of time. 1. of the day: VvA 40 (°samaye; v. l. gimhānamāse). — 2. of summer: usually in comb[n] w. and in contrast to hemanta winter: hemanta-gimhisu in w. & s. Dh 286 (cp. gimhika for °isu). Miln 274; Dpvs 1.55; Vism 231 (°ābhitatta worn out by the heat); Sdhp 275 (°kāle). In enum[n] w. other seasons: vasse hemante gimhe Nd[2] 631 (sadā); vasanta gimhādika utū PvA 135. — 3. of a summer month: paṭhamasmiŋ gimhe Sn 233 (see KhA 192 for expl[n]) — II. (pl.) gimhā the hot months, the season of summer, in °naŋ pacchime māse, in the last month of summer M I.79; S III.141; V.50, 321; Vv 79[6] (=āsāḷhimāse VvA 307).

Gimhāna (adj. -n.) [orig. gen. pl. of gimhā=gimhānaŋ, fr. comb[n] gimhāna(ŋ) māse, in a month of summer] of summer, summerly, the summer season A IV.138 (+ hemanta & vassa); Sn 233 (gimhānamāse); VvA 40 (v. l.). On terms for seasons in gen. cp. *Miln trsl.* II.113.

Gimhika (adj. fr. gimha) summerly, relating to the summer, for the summer Vin I.15; D II.21 (+ vassika & hemantika).

Girā [Vedic gir & gēr, song; gṛṇāti to praise, announce gūrti praise=Lat. grates "grace"; to *ger or *gṇer, see note on gala] utterance (orig. song, important utterance, still felt as such in older Pāli, therefore mostly poetical), speech, words D III.174; Sn 350, 632, 690, 1132; Dh 408; Th 2, 316, 402; Vv 50[18] (=vācā VvA); Dhs 637, 720; DhsA 93; DA I.61 (aṭṭhangupetaŋ giraŋ). J II.134.

Giri [Vedic giri, Obulg. gora mountain] a mountain; as a rule only in cpds, by itself (poetical) only at Vism 206 (in enum[n] of the 7 large mountains).
-agga mountain top, in giraggasamajja N. of a festival celebrated yearly at Rājagaha, orig. a festival on the mountain top (cp. *Dial.* I.8 & *Vin. Texts* III.71). Vin II.107, 150; IV.85, 267; J III.538; DhA I.89. The BSk. version is girivaggu-samāgama AvŚ II.24; **-kannikā** (f.) N. of a plant (Clitoria ternatea) Vism 173; DhA I.383 (v. l. kaṇṇikā cp. Sk. °karnī;) **-gabbhara**=°guhā Sn 416; **-guhā** a mountain cleft, a rift, a gorge; always in formula pabbata kandara g°, therefore almost equivalent to kandara, a grotto or cave Vin II.146; D I.71=M I.269, 274, 346, 440=A II.210=Pug 59 (as giriŋ guhaŋ); A IV.437; expl. at DA I.210: dvinnaŋ pabbatānaŋ antaraŋ ekasmiŋ yeva vā ummagga-sadisaŋ mahā-vivaraŋ; **-bbaja** (nt.) [Etym. uncertain, according to Morris *J.P.T.S.* 1884, 79 to vaja "a pen," cp. Marāthī vraja "a station of cowherds," Hindi vraja "a cow-pen"; the Vedic giribhraj° (RV. X.68. 1) "aus Bergen hervorbrechend" (Roth) suggests relation to **bhraj**, to break=**bhañj**=Lat. frango]=°guhā, a mountain cave or gorge, serving as shelter & hiding place J III.479 (trsl. by Morris loc. cit. a hill-run, a cattle-run on the hills); V.260 (sīhassa, a lion's abode) expl[d] as kañcanaguhā ibid. (for kandara-guhā ? cp. Kern, *Toev.* p. 130). S II.185. Also N. for Rājagaha Sn 408; Dpvs V.5; in its Sk. form Girivraja, which Beal, *Buddh. Records* II.149 expl[s] as "the hill-surrounded." cp. ib. II.158 (=Chin. Shan-Shing), 161; see also Cunningham, *Ancient Geogr.* 462. It does not occur in the Avadānas; **-rājā** king of the mountains, of Mount Sineru Miln 21, 224; **-sikhara** mountain top, peak VvA 4; (kañcana°, shining).

Giriyā (pl.) in dhamma° & brahma°, a name of certain theatrical entertainers Miln 191.

Gilati [Vedic girati & gilati Dhtp 488: adane; cp. gala throat, Ohg. kela, E. gullet; see note on gala] to swallow, to devour: mā Rāhu gilī caraŋ antalikkhe S I.51 = VvA 116; mā gilī lohagulaŋ Dh 371; — J III.338; Miln 106. —pp. gilita: gilitabaḷisa having swallowed the hook S IV.159. Cp. ud°, o°, pari°; — Caus. gilāpeti to make swallow J III.338.

Gilana (nt.) [fr. gilati] devouring, swallowing Miln 101.

Gilāna (adj.) [Sk. glāna, **glā** to fade, wither, be exhausted, expl[d] suitably by "hāsa-kkhaya" at Dhtp 439] sick, ill Vin I.51, 53, 61, 92, 142 sq., 176, 302 sq.; II.165, 227 sq.; IV.88, etc.; S V.80, 81 (bāḷha° very ill); A I.120 = Pug 27; A III.38, 143 sq.; IV.333; V.72 sq.; J I.150; II.395; III.392; PvA 14; VvA 76.
-ālaya pretence of illness J VI.262. -upaṭṭhāka (f. -ī) one who attends to the sick Vin I.92, 121 sq.; 142 sq.; 161, 303, A I.26; III.143 sq.; -°*bhatta* food for the attendant or nurse Vin I.292 sq.; -upaṭṭhāna tending or nursing the sick D III.191; -paccaya support or help for the sick PvA 144; usually with °*bhesajja* medicine for the sick in freq. formula of cīvarapiṇḍapāta° (the requisites of the bhikkhu): see cīvara; -pucchaka one who asks (i. e. enquires after) the sick Vin IV.88 = 115, 118; -bhatta food for the sick Vin I.142 sq.; 292 sq.; 303; Vism 66. -bhesajja medicine Vin I.292 sq.; -sālā a hall for the sick, hospital S IV.210; A III.142; Vism 259.

Gilānaka (adj.) 1. ill (= gilāna) A III.142; — 2. fit for an illness (bhesajja medicine) Miln 74.

Gilāyati: see āgilāyati.

Giha [= gaha] only in agiha (adj.) houseless, homeless (= pabbajita, a Wanderer); poet. for anagāra Sn 456, 464, 487, 497.

Gihin (adj.-n.) [fr. gaha, cp. gaha & geha; Sk. gṛhin] a householder, one who leads a domestic life, a layman (opp. pabbajita & paribbājaka). Gen. sg. gihissa (D III.147, 167) & gihino (D III.174); n. pl. gihī; in *cpds.* gihī° & gihi° (usually the latter). gihī agāraŋ ajjhāvasantā A I.49; gihī odātavasanā (clad in white robes as distinguished fr. kasāva-vasanā the yellow-robed i. e. bhikkhus) D I.211; III.117, 124, 210; M I.340; III.261; A I.74. — Contrasted with pabbajitā: A I.69; D III.147, 167, 179. gihī dhaññena dhanena vaḍḍhati D III.165. — Other passages in general: S II.120, 269; III.11; IV.180, 300 sq.; A II.65; 69 (kāmabhogī); IV.438 (do.); D III.124 (do.); A III.211 (sambodhiparāyano); IV.345 sq.; D III.167 sq.; 171 sq.; 176, 192; Sn 220, 221, 404; Dh 74; Miln 19, 264; DhA I.16 (gihīniyāma); Sdhp 376, 426; PvA 13 (gihīkālato paṭṭhāya from the time of our laymanship); DhA II.49 (id.).
-kicca a layman's or householder's duties Pv IV.1[42] (= kuṭumba-kiccāni PvA 240); -dhamma a layman's duty A III.41; -parisā a congregation of laymen S I.111; M I.373; A III.184; -bandhanāni (pl.) a layman's fetters Sn 44 (= Nd[2] 228 puttā ca dāsī dāsā ca, etc.); -byañjanāni (pl.) characteristics of a layman, or of a man of the world (w. ref. to articles of dress & ornament) Sn 44, 64 (= Nd[2] 229); Miln 11; -bhūta as a householder D II.196; -bhoga riches of a worldly man S III.93; It 90; -liṅga characteristic of a layman DhA II.61. -saŋsagga association with laymen A III.116, 258; -saŋyojana the impediments of a householder (cp. °bandhanāni) M I.483; -sukha the welfare of a g. A I.80.

Gīta [pp. of gāyati] 1. (pp.) sung, recited, solemnly proclaimed, enunciated: mantapadaŋ gītaŋ pavuttaŋ D I.104 (cp. gira). — 2. (nt.) singing, a song; grouped under vācasikā khiḍḍā, musical pastimes at Nd[2] 219; SnA 86. Usually comb[d] with nacca, dancing: A I.261; Vv81[10] as naca gītādi J I.61; VvA 131; referring to nacca-gīta-vādita, dancing with singing & instrumental accompaniment D III.183 (under samajja, kinds of festivities); Vv 32[4]. Same with visūkadassana, pantomimic show at D I.5 ≈ (cp. DA I.77; KhA 36).
-rava sound of song Mhvs VII.30; -sadda id. J IV.3; Dhs 621; DhA I.15; -ssara id. Vin II.108; A III.251; J III.188.

Gītaka (nt.) & gītikā (f.) a little song J III.507.

Gīvā (f.) [Sk. grīvā, to *guer to swallow, as signifying throat: see note on gala for etym.] the neck Sn 609; J I.74 (°ŋ pasāreti to stretch forth), 167 (pasārita°), 207, 222, 265; III.52; VvA 27 (mayūra°), 157; DA I.296 (°āya kuṇḍa-daṇḍaka-bandhana, as exhibition & punishment): similarly in the sense of "life" (hinting at decapitation) J II.300 (°ŋ karissāmi "I shall go for his neck"); IV.431 = V.23. — Syn. kaṇṭha the primary meaning of which is neck, whereas gīvā orig. throat.

Gīveyyaka (nt.) [cp. Sk. graiveyaka] necklace, an ornament for the neck (orig. "something belonging to the neck," cp. necklet, bracelet, etc.) Vin I.287; A I.254 sq. (= Vism 247, where gīveyya only); 257; III.16; J IV.395 (gīveyya only); V.297; VI.590; VvA 104.

Guggula [?] a kind of perfume J VI.537.

Gucch° in jigucchati (Des. of **gup** = Sk. jugupsate) to detest, see s. v.

Guñjā (f.) a plant (Abrus precatorius); the redness of its berries is referred to in similes; DhA IV.133 (°vaṇṇāni akkhīni). See also jiñjuka.

Guṇa[1] [Non-Aryan ?] 1. a string, a cord — (a) of a robe, etc., in (kāya-bandhanaŋ) saguṇaŋ katvā to make tight by tying with a knot Vin I.46 (*Vin. Texts:* "laying the garments on top of each other," wrongly construed); II.213 (trsln. "folding his garments"); cp. guṇaka. — (b) of musical instruments Vin I.182 = A III.375 (vīṇā). — (c) of a bow, in aguṇa stringless J V.433 (dhanu).— 2. (a strand of a rope as) constituent part, ingredient, component, element; with numerals it equals -fold, e. g. pañca kāmaguṇā the 5 strands of kāma, or 5-fold craving (see kāma); ekaguṇaŋ once, diguṇaŋ twice Sn 714; diguṇaŋ nivāpaŋ pacitvā cooking a double meal VvA 63; catugguṇa fourfold, of a saṅghāṭi D II.128; S II.221, cp. Rhys Davids, *Dialogues* II.145. aṭṭhaguṇa (hirañña) Th. 2, 153; aneka-bhāgena guṇena seyyo many times or infinitely better Pv IV.1[9]; sataguṇena sahassa° 100 and 1,000 times PvA 41; asaṅkheyyena guṇena infinitely, inconceivably Miln 106; sataguṇaŋ sahassaguṇaŋ Vism 126. — 3. (a part as) quality, esp. good quality, advantage, merit J I.266; II.112; III.55, 82. — lobha° Sn 663; sādhu° Sn 678; sīla° J I.213; II.112; Buddha° J II.111; pabbajita° J I.59.
-aggatā state of having the best qualities, superiority Dpos IV.1. -aḍḍha rich in virtue Sdhp 312, 561. -upeta in khuppipāsāhi guṇūpeto as PvA 10 is to be read khuppipās' âbhibhūto peto. -kathā "tale of virtue," praise J I.307; II.2. -kittana telling one's praises PvA 107, 120. -guṇika in phrase tantākulajāta g-g-jāta at S IV.158, see under guḷā-guṇṭhika.

Guṇa[2] [for which often guḷa with common substitution of ḷ for ṇ, partly due to dissimilation, as mālāguḷa > mālāguṇa; cp. Sk. guṇikā tumour: guḷa and gaḷa, veḷu: veṇu, and note on gala] a ball, a cluster, a chain (?), in anta° the intestines; M I.185-, Kh II., cp. KhA 57 for expln. — mālāguṇa a garland or chain (cluster) of flowers Dh 53 (but °guḷa at J I.73, 74). See guḷa[3].

Guṇa[3] [Derivation unknown. Cp. Sk. ghuna] a woodworm J III.431 (°pāṇaka).

Guṇaka (adj.) [to guḷa^1, cp. guḷika ?] having a knot at the end, thickened at the top (with ref. to kāyabandha, see guṇa 1a) Vin II.136, cp. *Vin. Texts* II.143.

Guṇavant (adj.) [to guṇa^1] possessed of good qualities, virtuous Pv II.9^{71} (=jhān' ādiguṇa-yutta); PvA 62 (mahā°).

Guṇi (f.) [of adj. guṇin, having guṇas or guḷas, i. e. strings or knots] a kind of armour J VI.449 (g. vuccatc kavacaŋ C.); see Kern, *Toev.* p. 132.

Guṇṭhika (in meaning=guṇṭhita) one who is covered with or wrapped up in, only in ahi° a snake-trainer (like a Laocoon). See details under ahi or J II.267; III.348 (text: °guṇḍika); J IV.308 (ahi-kuṇḍika, v. l. SS guṇṭhika); IV.456 (text °guṇṭika; v. l. BB °kuṇḍika). Also in guḷā-guṇṭhika (q. v.).

Guṇṭhima covered over (?), see pāli°.

Guṇṭheti [cp. Sk. guṇṭhayati Dhtp (563) & Dhtm (793) give both roots **guṇṭh** & **guṇḍ** as syn. of **veṭh**] to cover, to veil, to hide: pp. guṇṭhita in paŋsu° covered with dust Pv II.3^5 (in Hardy's conjecture for kuṇṭhita, q. v.). Also in cpd. **paliguṇṭhita** obstructed, entangled Sn 131 (mohena) where v. l. BB kuṇṭhita. Cp. o°.

Guṇḍika see guṇṭhika.

Gutta [Sk. gupta, pp. of **gup** in med.-pass. sense, cp. gopeti).— I. as pp. guarded, protected. — (a) lit. nagaraŋ guttaŋ a well-guarded city Dh 315=Th 1, 653, 1005; Devinda° protected by the Lord of gods Vv 30^8. — (b) fig. (med.) guarded, watchful, constrained; guarded in, watchful as regards . . . (with loc.) S IV.70 (agutta & sugutta, with danta, rakkhita); A III.6 (atta° self-controlled); Sn 250 (sotesu gutto+vijitindriyo), 971 (id.+yatacārin); Dh 36 (cittaŋ). — II. as n. agent (=Sk. goptṛ, cp. kata in kāla-kata=kālaŋ kartṛ) one who guards or observes, a guardian, in Dhammassa gutta Dh 257, observer of the Norm (expl. DhA III.282: dhammojapaññāya samannāgata), cp. dhammagutta S I.222.

-indriya one whose senses are guarded; with well-guarded senses Sn 63 (+rakkhita-mānasāno; expl. SnA: chassu indriyesu gopitindriyo); Nd^2 230; Vv 50^{16}; Pv IV.1^{32}; -dvāra "with guarded doors" always in comb^n with indriyesu g-d. having the doors of the senses guarded, practising self-control D I.63≈(expl^d DA I.182 by pihita-dvāro), 70; S II.218; IV.103, 112, 119 sq., 175; Sn 413 (+susaŋvuta); Pug 24. Cp. foll.; -dvāratā (f. abstr. to prec.) in indriyesu g° self constraint, control over (the doors of) one's senses, always comb^d with bhojane mattaññutā (moderation in taking food) D III.213; It 24; Pug 20, 24; Dhs 1347; PvA 163. Opp. a° lack of sense-control D III.213; It 23; Dhs 1345.

Gutti (f.) [Vedic gupti] protection, defence, guard; watchfulness. — (a) lit. of a city A IV.106 sq. — (b) fig. of the senses in indriyānaŋ gutti Dh 375; Pug 24 (+gopanā); Dhs 1348; Sdhp 341 (agutti); Vin IV.305; A II.72 (atta°); also in pl.: guttīsu ussuka keen in the practice of watchfulness D III.148.

Guttika [fr. last] a guardian, one who keeps watch over, in nagara° the town-watchman, the chief-constable PvA 4; Miln 345.

Gumpha see ogumpheti.

Gumba [Sk. gulma, ***glem** to ***gel**, to be thick, to conglomerate, cp. Lat. glomus (ball), globus, etc. See guḷa] 1. a troop, a heap, cluster, swarm. Of soldiers: Vin I.345; of fish (maccha°) D I.84=M I.279=II.22=A I.9. — 2. a thicket, a bush, jungle; the lair of an animal in a thicket (sayana° J IV.256) S III.6 (eḷagalā°); J III.52 (nivāsa°, vasana°); VvA 301 (gaccha° underwood); J I.149, 167, II.19; III.55; IV.438; VvA 63, 66. Cp. pagumba=gumba, in vana° Sn 233 (see KhA 192). veḷu° Th 1.919.— Acc. gumbaŋ (adv.) thickly, in masses balled together Miln 117 (of clouds).

-antara thicket VvA 233.

Gumbiya (adj.) [fr. gumba] one of the troop (of soldiers) Vin I.345.

Guyha [ger. of **guh**=Vedic guhya] 1. adj. to be hidden, hidden in °bhaṇḍaka the hidden part (of the body) DhA IV.197.— 2. (nt.) that which is hidden; lit. in vattha° hidden by the dress, i. e. the pudendum D I.106; Sn 1022, etc. (see vattha). fig. a secret Miln 92; guyhaŋ pariguyhati to keep a secret A IV.31; Nd^2 510.

Guru (adj.-n.) [a younger form of garu (q. v.); Sk. guru] venerable, reverend, a teacher VvA 229, 230 (°dakkhiṇā a teacher's fee); PvA 3 (°janā venerable persons); Sdhp 227 (°ûpadesa), 417.

Guḷa^1 [Sk. guḍa and gulī ball, guṭikā pill, guṇikā tumour; to ***gleu** to make into a ball, to conglomerate. Cp. Sk. glauḥ ball; Gr. γλουτός; Ohg. chliuwa; Ger. kugel, kloss; E. clot, cleat; also ***gel** with same meaning: Sk. gulma tumour, gilāyu glandular swelling; cp. Lat. glomus, globus; Ger. klamm; E. clamp, clump. A root **guḷ** is given by Dhtp 576, 77 in meaning of "mokkha"] a ball, in cpds. sutta° a ball of string (=Ohg. chliuwa) D I.54=; M III.95; PvA 145; ayo° an iron globe Dh 308; DA I.84; loha° of copper Dh 371; sela° a rockball, i. e. a heavy stone-ball J I.147.

-kīḷā play at ball DhA I.178; III.455; IV.124. -parimaṇḍala the circumference of a ball, or (adj.) round, globular, like a ball PvA 253.

Guḷa^2 (Non-Aryan ?] sugar, molasses Vin I.210, 224 sq., 245. — saguḷa sugared, sweet, or "with molasses" J VI.324 (saguḷāni, i. e. saguḷa-pūve pancakes).

-āsava sugar-juice VvA 73. -**odaka** s. -water Vin I.226. -**karaṇa** a sugar factory ibid. 210. -**pūvaka** sweet cake Mhvs 10. 3. -**phāṇita** molasses VvA 179.

Guḷa^3 [for guṇa^2, due to distance dissimilation in maṇiguṇa and mālāguṇa>maṇigula and mālāgula; cp. similarly in meaning and form Ohg. chliuwa>Ger. knäuel] a cluster, a chain (?), in maṇi° a cluster of jewels, always in simile with ref. to sparkling eyes "maniguḷa-sadisāni akkhini" J I.149; III.126, 184 (v. l. BB °guḷika); IV.256 (v. l. id.); mālā° a cluster, a chain of flowers, a garland J I.73, 54; puppha° id. Dh. 172, 233.

Guḷā (f.) [to guḷa^1] a swelling, pimple, pustule, blight, in cpd. guḷā-guṇṭhika-jāta D II.55, which is also to be read at A II.211 (in spite of Morris, prelim. remarks to A II.4, whose trsln. is otherwise correct)=guḷā-guṇṭhita covered with swellings (i. e. blight); cp. similar expression at DhA III.297 gaṇḍāgaṇḍa (-jāta) "having become covered all over with pustules (i. e. rash)." All readings at corresp. passages are to be corrected accordingly, viz., S II.92 (guḷigandhika°); IV.158 (guṇaguṇika°); the reading at Dpvs XII.32, also v. l. SS at A II.211, is as quoted above and the whole phrase runs: tantākulajātā guḷāguṇṭhikajātā "entangled like a ball of string and covered with blight."

Guḷika (adj.) [to guḷa^3=guṇa, cp. also guṇaka] like a chain, or having a chain, (nt. & f.) a cluster, a chain in maṇi° a string of jewels, a pearl necklace J III.184 (v. l. BB for °guḷa); IV.256; Vism 285 (+muttā-guḷikā).

Guḷikā (f.) [to guḷa^1; cp. Sk. guṭikā pill, guṇikā tumour] a little ball S V.462 (satta-kolaṭṭhi-mattiyo guḷikā, pl.); Th 2, 498 (kolaṭṭhimatta g° balls of the size of a jujube), cp. ThA 289.

Guhanā (f. abstr. to gūhati) hiding, concealing, keeping secret Vbh 358 (+pariguhanā). Also as gūhanā, q. v.

Guhā (f.) [Vedic guhā, **guh**, gūhati to hide (q. v.) Dhtp 337: saŋvaraṇa] a hiding place, a cave, cavern (cp. kandara & see giriguhā); fig. the heart (in °āsaya). According to Bdhgh. (on Vin I.58, see *Vin. Texts* I.174) "a hut of bricks, or in a rock, or of wood." Vin I.58, 96, 107, 239, 284; II.146; III.155; IV.48 (cp. sattapaṇṇi-guhā); Sn 772, 958; J II.418; VI.574; Vv 50[16].
-āsaya hiding in the heart; or the shelter of the heart A IV.98 (maccupāso+); J V.367 (id.); Dh 37 (cittaŋ; see DhA I.304).

Gū (-°) [fr. **gam**, cp. °ga] going, having gone (through), being skilled or perfected in. See addha°, anta°, chanda°, dhamma°, paṭṭha°, pāra, veda°.

Gūtha [Sk. gūtha; probably to Lat. bubino, see Walde, *Lat. Wtb.* s. v.] excrements, fæces, dung. As food for Petas frequently mentioned in Pv; (cp. Stede, *Peta Vatthu* 24 sq.), as a decoction of dung also used for medicinal purposes (Vin I.206 e. g.). Often comb[d] with mutta (urine): Pv I.9[1]; PvA 45, 78; DA I.198.
-kaṭāha an iron pot for defecation Vin IV.265. -kalala dung & mire J III.393; -kīḷana playing with excrements Vism 531. -kūpa a privy (cp. karīsa) M I.74; Sn 279; Pv II.3[16]; Pug 36; J VI.370; Vism 54. -khādaka living on fæces J II.211 (°pāṇaka) PvA 266; -gata having turned to dung It 90; -gandhin smelling of excrements Pv II.3[15]; -ṭṭhāna a place for excrementation Th I, 1153; -naraka=foll. Vism 501; -niraya the mire-purgatory VvA 226; Sdhp 194; -pāṇa an insect living on excrement (=°khādakapāṇa) J II.209, 212; -bhakkha feeding on stercus M III.168; PvA 192; DhA II.61; -bhānin of foul speech A I.128; Pug 29 (Kern, *Toev.* s. v. corrects into kūṭa° ?).

Gūthaka "a sort of gūtha," excretion, secretion, rheum, in akkhi° and kaṇṇa° (of eye & ear) Sn 197 (cp. SnA 248; Vism 345 sq.).

Gūḷha & gūḷhaka (adj.) [pp. of gūhati] hidden, secret Vin II.98 (gūḷha-ko salākagāho).

Gūhati [Sk. gūhati, pp. gūḍha; see guyha, guhā, etc.] to hide, to conceal. See paṭi°, pari°. — Caus. gūhayati Sdhp 189 (gūhayaŋ ppr.). Cp. gūḷha.

Gūhana (nt.) hiding, concealment Sdhp 65 (laddhi°-citta).

Gūhanā (f.) [abstr. fr. gūhati]=gūhanā (q. v.) Pug 19. Cp. pari°.

Geṇḍuka a ball for playing. The SS spelling is in all places **bheṇḍuka**, which has been taken into the text by the editors of J. and DhsA. The misspelling is due to a misreading of Singhalese bh. > g; cp. spelling parābhetvā for parāgetvā. — bheṇḍukena kīḷi J IV.30; bhūmiyaŋ pahata-bheṇḍuka (striking against the ground) J IV.30; Vism 143 (pahaṭa-citra°)=DhsA 116 (where wrongly pahaṭṭha-citta-bhenduka); J V.196 (citra-bh°); DhA III.364.

Gedha[1] [Vedic gṛdhyā, cp. gijjhati] greed. Its connection with craving and worldly attachment is often referred to. Kāmesu g° S I.73; Sn 152; A III.312 sq. (gedho: pañcann' etaŋ kāmaguṇānaŋ adhivacanaŋ). gedha-taṇhā S I.15 (v. l. kodha°); Sn 65, 945, 1098; Th 2, 352; Nd[2] 231; Dhs 1059 (under lobha), 1136; Nett 18; DhA I.366; PvA 107. -agedhatā freedom from greed Miln 276. — See also gedhi & paligedha.

Gedha[2] [=geha ? Kern] a cave A I.154=III.128 (the latter passage has rodha, cp. v. l. under gedhi).

Gedhi [Sk. gṛdhi, cp. gedha] greed, desire, jealousy, envy: gedhiŋ karoti (c. loc.) to be desirous after M I.330. -gedhikata in °citta (adj.) jealous, envious, ibid. As gedhikatā (f.) vanity, greed, conceit Nd[2] 585 (v. l. rodhigatā).

Gedhita [pp. of gijjhati] greedy, in gedhita-mano greedy-minded Pv II.8[2]; as nt. greed, in der. gedhitatta (syn. of gedhikatā) Nd[2] 585.

Geyya (nt.) [grd. of gāyati, Sk. geya] a certain style of Buddhist literature consisting of mixed prose & verse. It is only found in the ster. enum of the Scriptures in their ninefold division, beginning suttaŋ geyyaŋ veyyākaraṇaŋ. See under navanga.

Geruka (nt.) & **gerukā** (f.) [Sk. gairika] yellow ochre (Bdhgh suvaṇṇa° cp. Sk. kañcana° & svarṇa°), red chalk used as colouring Vin I.203; II.151; A I.210; Miln 133 (°cuṇṇa). Freq. in °parikamma a coating of red chalk, red colouring Vin II.117, 151, 172; °parikammakata "coated with red colouring" Vin I.48; II.218.

Gelañña (nt.) [n-abstr. fr. gilāna] sickness, illness D II.99; A I.219; III.298; IV.333 sq.; Vism 321, 466, 478.

Geha (nt.) [Sk. geha=gṛha, to **gṛh**, gaṇhāti; cp. gaha, gihin, ghara; see also gedha[2]] a dwelling, hut, house; the household J I.145, 266, 290; II.18, 103, 110, 155 VI.367; Vism 593; PvA 22, 62, 73, 82; fig. of kāya (body) Th I, 184=Dh 154. — Appl[d] to a cowshed at Miln 396.
-angana the open space in front of the house VvA 6; -jana (sg. collective) the members of the household, the servants PvA 16, 62, 93; -jhāpana incendiarism Vism 326. -ṭṭhāna a place for a dwelling DhA III.307; -dvāra the house door PvA 61; -nissita (adj.) concerning the house, connected with (the house and) worldly life Sn 280 (pāpiccha); It 117 (vitakka); cp. °sita; -patana the falling of the house J III.118. -pavesana (-mangala) (the ceremony of) entering a new hut DhA III.307; -piṭṭhi the back of the house PvA 78; -rakkhika keeping (in the) house, staying at home VvA 76 (dārakā); -vigata (nt.) the resources of the house, worldly means, riches Th 2, 327 (=upakaraṇa ThA 234); -sita (*śrita)=°nissita, connected with worldly life (opp. nekkhamma, renunciation). Of chandā & vitakkā (pl.) M I.123; domanassa & somanassa (grief & pleasure) S IV.232=Miln 45; Vbh 381; DhsA 194; dhammā, etc. S IV.71; Vbh 380; Nett 53.

Go (m.-f.) [Vedic go, Lat. bos, Gr. βοῦς, Ohg. chuo, Ags. cū=E. cow] a cow, an ox, bull, pl. cattle. For f. cp. gāvī; see also gava° for cpds. — Sg. nom. go (Sn 580, also in composition, cp. aja-go-mahisādi PvA 80=pasū); gen. gavassa (M I.429); instr. gavena, gāvena; acc. gavaŋ, gāvaŋ; abl. gavamhā, gavā (D I.201=A II.95=Pug 69); loc. gavamhi, gāvimhi (SnA 323), gave (Sn 310). — Pl. nom. gāvo (D I.141; M I.225; A I.205; II.42 sq.; Sn 20, 296, 307; J I.295); gen. gonaŋ A II.75 (cp. Vedic gonām), gavaŋ (J IV.172, cp. gavaŋ pati), gunnaŋ (A I.229, II.75; V.271; J I.194; III.112; IV.223); instr. gohi (Sn 33); acc. gāvo (M I.225; A I.205; Sn 304; Dh 19, 135); abl. gohi; loc. gosu, gavesu. — See also gava, gavesati, goṇa.
-kaṇṭaka the hoof of an ox, in °hatā bhūmi, trampled by the feet of cattle Vin I.195; A I.136 (cp. *Vin. Texts* II.34); -kaṇṇa a large species of deer J V.406 (=gaṇin), 416 (khagga+); DhsA 331 (gavaya+); cp. next; -kāṇā (f.) =gokaṇṇa D III.38=53; -kula (nt.) a cow pen, a station of cattle S IV.289; -gaṇa a herd of cattle M I.220; A I.229; J II.127; DhA I.175; VvA 311; -ghaŋsikā a cow-hide (?) Vin II.117 (cp. *Vin. Texts* III.98); -ghātaka one who kills cows, a butcher D II.294 (in simile); M I.58, 244, 364 (°sūnā, slaughter-house); S II.255; IV.56; A III.302, 380; J V.270; Vism 348 (in simile). -cara I. *Lit.* A (noun-m.) pasture, lit. "a cow's grazing," search after food; fodder, food, subsistence (a) of animals: J I.221; III.26; Dh 135 (daṇḍena gopālo gāvo pāceti gocaraŋ: with a stick the cowherd drives the cattle to pasture). Sīho gocarāya pakkamati "the lion goes forth for his hunt" A II.33=

III.121; gocarāya gacchati to go feeding, to graze Sn 39; J I.243; gocare carati to go feeding, to feed J I.242.— (b) metaph. of persons, esp. the bhikkhu: pucchitabba gocara (and agocara) "enquiries have to be made concerning the fitness or otherwise of his pasturage (i. e. the houses in which he begs for food)" Vin II.208; samaṇo gocarato nivatto an ascetic returned from his "grazing" Pv IV.1[42]: Similarly at Vism 127, where a suitable g.-gama ranks as one of the 7 desiderata for one intent on meditation. — **B.** (adj.) (-°) feeding on or in, living in; metaph. dealing with, mixing with. vana° living in the woods Pv II.6[5]; vāri° (in water) Sn 605; jala° (id.) J II.158 (opp. thala°). Vesiyā° (etc.) associating with v. Vin I.70. — II. *Applied*. **A.** (noun—m. or nt.) a "field" (of sense perception, etc.), sphere, object; -° food for, an object of (a) *psychologically*: indriyānaŋ nānāgocarāni various spheres of sense-perception S v.218; sense-object (=ārammaṇaŋ) Ps I.180; II.97; 150 sq.; DhsA 314, 315 (sampatta° physical contact with an object, gandha° smell-contact, i. e. sensation); indriya° Sdhp 365. — (b) *ethically*: ariyānaŋ gocare ratā "finding delight in the pasture of the good," walking in the ways of the good Dh 22; vimokho yesaŋ gocaro "whose pasture is liberty" Dh 92=Th 1, 92. Esp. in phrase ācāra-gocara-sampanna "pasturing in the field of good conduct" D I.63=It 118; M I.33; S v.187; It. 96; analysed as Dvandva cpd. at Vbh 246, 247, but cp. pāpācāra-gocara Sn 280, 282. This phrase (ācāra-gocara) is also discussed in detail at Vism 19, where 3 kinds of gocarā are distinguished, viz. upanissaya°, ārakkha°, upanibandha°. So also in contrast w. **agocara**, an unfit pasture, or an unfit, i. e. bad, sphere of life, in gocare & agocare carati to move iṇ a congenial or uncongenial sphere A III.389; IV.345 sq.; D III.58=77; S v.147; Vbh 246, 247 (expl. w. vesiyā° etc., cp. above=having bad associations). — **B** (adj.) -°: belonging to, dependent on, falling to the share of: eta° dependent on this M I.319; sattasaddhamma°, moving in the sphere of the seven golden rules S III.83; rūpa° to be perceived by sight J I.396; Nibbāna° belonging to N. Sdhp 467. -°*kusala* (adj.) skilled in (finding proper) food; clever in right living -° behaving properly in, exercising properly M I.220=A v.347 (of a cowherd driving out his cattle); S III.266 sq. (samādhi°); A III.311 (do.) v.352 sq. (w. ref. to cattāro satipaṭṭhānā); -°*gahaṇa* the taking of food, feeding J I.242; -°*gāma* a village for the supply of food (for the bhikkhus) PvA 12, 42; -°*ṭṭhāna* pasturage J III.52; -°*pasuta* intent on feeding J III.26; -°*bhūmi* pasturage, a common DhA III.60; -°*visaya* (the sphere of) an object of sense S v.218; Vbh 319; -**caraṇa** pasturing J VI.335; -**ṭṭha** (nt.) [Sk. goṣṭha to **sthā** to stand; cp. Lat. stabulum, stable; super-stes; Goth. awistr] a cow-stable, cow-pen M I.79; J IV.223; -**pa** [Sk. gopa, cp. gopati] a cowherd, herdsman Sn 18; Dh 19; J IV.364 (a robber); Vism 166 (in simile); DhA 157, f. gopī Sn 22, 32; -**pakhuma** (adj.) having eyelashes like a heifer D II.18; III.144, 167 sq.; VvA 162, 279 (=āḷārapamha); -**pada** a cow's footprint, a puddle A III.188; IV.102; Miln 287; also °padaka A III.188 v. l.; DA I.283; -**pariṇāyaka** leader of the cows, Ep. of a bull (gopitā+) M I.220, 225; -**pāla** a cowherd (usually as °ka) Dh 135; -**pālaka**=prec. Vin I.152, 243 sq.; M I.79, 115 sq., 220=A v.347; M I.333; S IV.181; A I.205 (-°uposatha); Miln 18, 48; Vism 279 (in comparison); DhA III.59; -**pitā** "father (protector) of the cows"=gavaŋ pati, Ep. of a bull M I.220 (+°pariṇāyaka); -**pī** f. of gopa, q. v.; -**pura** (nt.) [Sk. gopura] the gate of a city J VI.433; Miln 1, 67, 330; Bdhd 138; -**balivadda** in °nayena; in the expression gobalivadda (black-cattle-bull) i. e. by an accumulation of words VvA 258; -**bhatta** cows' fodder J IV.67; -**maṇḍala** ox-beat, ox-round, cp. III.15[1] (as gā°), quoted J I.47 (cp. assa-m°); SnA 39; also in phrase °paribbūḷha Sn 301 (expl[d] by SnA 320 as goyūthehi parikiṇṇa); J VI.27; at M I.79 however it means the cowherds or peasants (see note M I.536: gopāladārakā or gāmadārakā to v. l. gāmaṇḍala) cp. gāmaṇḍala; -**maya** (m. nt.) cowdung M I.79; A I.209, 295; v.234, 250, 263 sq.; Nett 23; DhA I.377. -°*pāṇaka* a coprophagan, dor beetle J II.156; -°*piṇḍa* a lump of cowdung J I.242; -°*bhakkha* eating cowdung D I.166≈; -**māyu** a jackal Pgdp 49; -**mutta** (and °ka) a precious stone of light red colour VvA III; DhsA 151; -**medaka**=gomuttaka VvA 111.; -**medha** a cow sacrifice, in °yañña SnA 323; -**yūtha** a herd of cows SnA 322; DhA I.323; -**rakkhā** (f.) cow-keeping, tending cattle, usually comb[d] with kasī, agriculturing M I.85; Pv I.5[8]; J I.338; II.128; given as a superior profession (ukkaṭṭha-kamma) Vin IV.6. -**ravaka** the bellowing of a cow M I.225; -**rasa** (usually pl.) produce of the cow, enum[d] in set of five, viz. khīra, dadhi, takka, navanīta, sappi (milk, cream, buttermilk, butter, ghee) Vin I.244; DhA I.158, 323, 397; VvA 147; SnA 322; -**rūpa** (collect.) cattle J I.194; IV.173; Miln 396 (bull); -**lakkhaṇa** fortune telling from cows D I.9≈; -**vaccha** (khīra° & takka°) Vism 23. -**vatika** [Sk. govratin] one who lives after the mode of cows, of bovine practices M I.837; Nett 99 (cp. govata DhsA 355, and *Dhs. trsl.* p. 261); -**vikattana** (and °vikantana; Sk. vikṛntana) a butcher's knife M I.244, 449; A III.380 Sdhp 381 (vikatta only); -**vittaka** one whose wealth is cattle J I.191; -**vinda** the supt. of cowherds A III.373; -**sappi** ghee from cow's milk Vin III.251; DhsA 320; -**sālā** cow-stable A I.188; -**singa** a cow's horn Vism 254. -**sita** mixed with milk VvA 179; -**sīla**=govatika DhsA 355; -**sīsa** (nt.) an excellent kind of sandal wood PvA 215 (cp. Sp. AvS I.67, 68, 109); -**hanuka** the jaw bone of a cow, in °ena koṭṭāpeti (koṭṭh° J) to massage with a cow's jaw bone Vin II.266, J IV.188; v.303.

Goṭaviya (goṭavisa Text) v. l. J VI.225, part of a boat, the poop (expl. ib. p. 226 by nāvāya pacchimabandho).

Goṭhaphala a medicinal seed [Sk. gotravṛkṣa? Kern] Vin I.201.

Goṇa[1] [The Sanskrit goṇa, according to B. R., is derived from the Pali] an ox, a bullock S IV.195 sq.; J I.194; IV.67; Pv I.8[2]; PvA 39, 40; VvA 63 (for ploughing); DA I.163; DhA III.60. -°sira wild ox J VI. 538(=araññagoṇaka).

Goṇa[2]=goṇaka[2], in °santhata (of a pallanka), covered with a woollen rug Vv 81[8]; Pv III.1[17]; (text saṇṭhita; v. l. BB goṇakatthata, cp. next).

Goṇaka[1] [goṇa[1]] a kind of ox, a wild bull J VI.538 (**arañña**°).

Goṇaka[2] [Sk. BSk. goṇika, cp. Pischel, *Beitr.* III.236; also spelled gonaka] a woollen cover with long fleece (DA I.86: dīghalomako mahākojavo; caturaṅgulādhikāni kira tassa lomāni) D I.7≈; S III.144; J v.506; Pv II.12[8]; Th 2, 378 (+tūlika); ThA 253 (=dīgha-lomakāḷakojava). -°atthata spread w. a goṇaka-cover A I.137=III.50=IV.394; cp. IV.94, 231 (always of a **pallanka**), See also goṇa[2].

Goṇisādika an ox-stall Vin I.240; cp. *Vin. Texts* II.121. As gonisādi Vin III.46.

Gotta (nt.) [Vedic gotra, to go] ancestry, lineage. There is no word in English for gotta. It includes all those descended, or supposed to be descended, from a common ancestor. A gotta name is always distinguished from the personal name, the name drawn from place of origin or residence, or from occupation, and lastly from the nick-name. It probably means agnate rather than cognate. About a score of gotta names are known. They are all assigned to the Buddha's time. See also Rh. D. *Dialogues* I.27, 195 sq. —jāti gotta lakkhaṇa Sn 1004; gotta salakkhaṇa Sn 1018; Ādiccā nāma gottena, Sākiyā nāma jātiyā Sn 423; jāti gotta kula

J II.3; jātiyā gottena bhogena sadisa "equal in rank, lineage & wealth" DhA II.218. — evaŋ-gotta (adj.) belonging to such & such an ancestry M I.429; II.20, 33; kathaŋ° of what lineage, or: what is your family name? D I.92; nānā° (pl.) of various families Pv II.9[16]. — With nāma (name & lineage, or nomen et cognomen): nāma-gottaŋ Vin I.93; II.239; D I.92 (expl. at DA I.257: paññatti-vasena nāmaŋ paveṇi-vasena gottaŋ: the name for recognition, the surname for lineage); Sn 648; Vv 84[45] (with nāma & nāmadheyya; expl. at VvA 348-349: nāmadheyya, as Tisso, Phusso, etc.; gotta, as Bhaggavo Bhāradvājo, etc.). — gottena by the ancestral name: Vin I.93; D II.154; Sn 1019; Dh 393; **gottato** same J I.56. Examples: Ambaṭṭha Kaṇhāyana-gottena D I.92; Vipassī Koṇḍañño g°; Kakusandho Kassapo g°; Bhagavā Gotamo g° D II.3; Nāgito Kassapo g° DA I.310; Vasudevo Kaṇho g° PvA 94.

-thaddha conceited as regards descent (+jāti° & dhana°) Sn 104; **-pañha** question after one's family name Sn 456; **-paṭisārin** (adj.) relying on lineage D I.99 (cp. *Dialogues* I.122); A V.327 sq.; **-bandhava** connected by family ties (ñāti°+) Nd[2] 455; **-rakkhita** protected by a (good) name Sn 315; VvA 72; **-vāda** talk over lineage, boasting as regards descent D I.99.

Gottā [n. ag. to gopeti=Sk. goptṛ] f. gotti protectress J V.329.

Gotrabhū [gotṛ=gottṛ, Sk. goptṛ to **gup**+bhū] "become of the lineage"; a technical term used from the end of the Nikāya period to designate one, whether layman or bhikkhu, who, as converted, was no longer of the worldlings (puthujjanā), but of the Ariyas, having Nibbāna as his aim. It occurs in a supplementary Sutta in the Majjhima (Vol. III. 256), and in another, found in two versions, at the end of the Anguttara (A IV.373 and V.23). Defined at Pug 12, 13 & Vism 138· amplified at Ps I.66-68, frequent in P (Tikap. 154 sq., 165, 324 etc.), mentioned at VvA 155. On the use of gotrabhū in medieval psychology see Aung, in *Compendium*, 66-68. Comp. the use of upanissaya at J I.235. —°ñāṇa, PPA 184; Vism 673. Ā° Vism 683.

Godhaka a kind of bird J VI.358.

Godharaṇī (f.-adj.) being able to be paired (of a young cow), or being with calf (?) Sn 26.

Godhā[1] (f.) [Sk. godhā] iguana, a large kind of lizard Vin I.215-16 (°mukha); D I.9≈(°lakkhaṇa, cp. DA I.94); J II.118; III.52; 538; DhA III.420. As godha (m.) at J V.489. Dimin. golikā at J II.147.

Godhā[2] (f.) string of a lute J VI.580 (cp. RV. 8, 58, 9).

Godhūma wheat (usually mentioned with yava, spelt) Miln 267; DA I.163; SnA 323. See dhañña.

Gopaka a guardian, watchman DA I.148; cp. khetta°.

Gopanā (f.) protecting, protection, care, watchfulness (cp. gutti) Pug 24 (+gutti) Dhs 1348; Miln 8, 243.

Gopānasī (f.) a beam supporting the framework of a roof, shaped **Λ**; fig. of old people, bent by age (see °vanka). Vin III.65, 81; S II.263; III.156; V.43, 228; M I.80; A I.261; III.364; V.21; Vism 320; DhA II.190; VvA 188.

-gaṇā (pl.) a collection of beams, the rafters Vv 78[4]; **-bhogga** (-sama) bent like a rafter (nārī) J III.395; **-vanka** (gopānasi°) as crooked as a rafter (of old people, cp. BSk. gopānasī-vakra AvŚ II.25[n5]) S I.117; M I.88; A I.138.

Gopita (adj.) [pp. of gopeti] protected, guarded, watched (lit. & fig.) J VI.367; Miln 345; SnA 116 (°indriya= guttindriya); Sdhp 398.

Gopeti [Sk. gopayati, **gup**; cp. gutta, gottā] to watch, guard, pot. gopetha Dh 315; — pp. gopita (q. v.).

Gopphaka [Dem. of goppha=Sk. gulpha] the ankle Vin IV.112; A IV.102; J V.472; DhA II.80, 214; SnA II.230.

Gomika [Sk. gomin] an owner of cows S I.6=Sn 33, 34.

Golikā see godhā[1].

Golomika (adj.) [inverted diæretic form fr. Sk. gulma=P. gumba viz. *golmika>*glomika>golomika] like a cluster; in phrase massuŋ **golomikaŋ kārāpeti** "to have the beard trimmed into a ball- or cluster-shape" Vin II.134. Bdhgh's expl[n] "like a goat's beard" (cp. *Vin. Texts* III.138) is based on pop. etym. go+loma+ika "cow-hair-like," the discrepancy being that go does *not* mean *goat*.

Golaka a ball ThA 255 (kiḷā°).

Gh.

°Gha (adj.-suffix to **ghan**) killing, destroying, see hanati. — iṇagha at Sn 246 is v. l. SS for iṇaghāta. Cp. paṭi° & see also ghana² & ghāta.

Ghaṃsati¹ [Sk. gharṣati, ***ghṛṣ** to ***gher** to rub or grind, cp. Gr. χέραδος, χερμάς, χρίω, enlarged in Lat. frendo= Ags. grindan to grind] to rub, crush, grind, S II.238; J I.190 (=ghasituṃ ? to next ?) 216; VI.331. — Caus. ghaṃsāpeti to rub against, to allow to be rubbed or crushed Vin II.266. Cp. upani°, pari°, & pahaṃsati¹. — Pass. ghaṃsīyati (ghaṃsiyati) to rub (intr.), to be rubbed Vin I.204; II.112.

Ghaṃsati² [=haṃsati for Sk. harṣati, see hassati] to be pleased, to rejoice J IV.56 (v. l. ghasati). Cp. pahaṃsati².

Ghaṃsana rubbing, in pāda-gh°ī a towel for rubbing the feet Vin II.130.

Ghaṃsikā in go°, cow-hide (?) see go.

Ghaccā (f.) [fr. hanati, **han** and **ghan**] destruction (usually -°) D III.67 (mūla°); J I.176 (sakuṇa°).

Ghañña (adj.-n.) [fr. Sk. ghana to **han**, cp. ghānya & hatya] killing, destroying (-°) see atta°.

Ghaṭa¹ [Non-Aryan ?] a hollow vessel, a bowl, vase, pitcher. Used for holding water, as well as for other purposes, which are given under pānīya° paribhojana° vacca° at Vin I.157=352=M I.207. In the Vinaya freq. comb^d with kolamba, also a deep vessel: I.209, 213, 225, 286. — As water-pitcher: J I.52, 93 (puṇṇa°), 166; VvA 118, 207, 244 (°satena nhāto viya); PvA 66 (udaka°), 179 (pānīya°), 282. — In general: S IV.196. For holding a light (in formula antoghaṭe padīpo viya upanissayo pajjalati) J I.235 (cp. kuṭa), PvA 38. Used as a drum J VI.277 (=kumbhathūna); as bhadda° Sdhp 319, 329.

-pamāṇa (adj.) of the size of a large pot J II.104; PvA 55.

Ghaṭa² (m. & f.) [Sk. ghaṭā; conn. with ganthati to bind together] multitude, heap, crowd, dense mass, i. e. thicket, cluster. itthi° a crowd of women J IV.316; maccha° a swarm of fish J II.227; vana° dense forest J II.385; IV.56; V.502; VI.11, 519, 564; brahma° company of brahmins J VI.99.

Ghaṭaka [Dem. of prec.] 1. a small jar (?) Vin II.129, 130 (comb^d w. kataka & sammajjanī); cp. *Vin. Texts* III.130. — 2. the capital of a pillar J I.32 (cp. kumbha).

Ghaṭati [Sk. ghaṭate, to **granth**, cp. ganthati. The Dhtp gives two roots **ghaṭ**, of which one is expl^d by "ghāṭane" (No. 554), the other by "īhāyaṃ," i. e. from exertion (No. 98)] to apply oneself to, to exert oneself, to strive; usually in formula uṭṭhahati gh° vāyamati M I.86; S I.267 (yamati for vāy°); Pug 51; or yuñjati gh° vāy° J IV.131. — Sdhp 426, 450.

Ghaṭana see Ghaṭṭana.

Ghaṭikā¹ (f.) [to ghaṭa¹] a small bowl, used for begging alms Th 2, 422 (=ThA 269: bhikkhā-kapāla).

Ghaṭikā² (f.) [to ghaṭa², orig. meaning "knot," cp. gantha & ganṭhi, also gaṇḍa] 1. a small stick, a piece of a branch, a twig J I.331; IV.87 (khadira°); VI.331; Th 2, 499 (=khaṇḍa ThA 290). upadhānaghaṭikā J III.179 (belonging to the outfit of an executioner); pāsa° J II.253 is a sort of magic stick or die (=pāsaka) — 2. a game of sticks ("tip-cat" sticks *Miln trsl.* II.32). D I.6≈(DA I.85: ghaṭikā ti vuccati dīgha-daṇḍakena rassa daṇḍaka-paharaṇa kīḷā, tip-cat); Vin II.10; III.181; M I.266; A V.203; Miln 229. — 3. a stack of twigs S II.178, 4; (a stick used as) a bolt Vin II.120, 208; III.119; usually as sūci° a needle-shaped stick Vin II.237 (cp. *Vin. Texts* III.106); S IV.290; Ud 52; J I.346. Cp. gaṇḍikādhāna.

Ghaṭita [pp. of ghaṭeti] connected, combined Vism 192.

Ghaṭī (f.) [to ghaṭa¹] a jar DhA I.426. In cpds. also ghaṭi°. -odana rice boiled in a jar DhA I.426; **-kaṭāha** a water pot, or rather a bowl for gathering alms (cp. ghaṭikā¹) Vin II.115 (=ghaṭi-kapāla Bdhgh); -kāra a potter DhA I.380; Np. of a kumbhakāra S I.35, 60; M II.45 sq. (=°suttanta, mentioned as such at DhA III.251); J I.43.

Ghaṭīyati [Pass. of ghaṭeti] 1. to be connected or continued DhA 1.46 (paveṇī na gh.), 174. — 2. to be obstructed Nd² 102 (=virujjhati, paṭihaññati).

Ghaṭeti [Denom. fr. ghaṭa², cp. gantheti] to join, to connect, to unite J I.139; freq. in anusandhiṃ ghaṭetvā adding the connection (between one rebirth & another) J I.220, 308.

Ghaṭṭa see araghaṭṭa; meaning "rubbed, knocked against" in phrase ghaṭṭa-pāda-tala SnA 582 (for **ugghaṭṭha**); also at Vin IV.46 in def. of vehāsa-kuṭī (a cell or hut with air, i. e., spacious, airy) as majjhimassa purisassa a-sīsa-ghaṭṭā "so that a man of medium height does not knock his head (against the ceiling)"; of uncertain meaning ("beating"?) at J I.454 (v. l. for T. **ghoṭa**).

Ghaṭṭana (nt.) [Sk. ghaṭana, to **granth**, cp. **gantha**] 1. combining, putting together, combination, composition, J I.220; PA. 312, etc. — 2. striking, fig. insulting (ghaṭṭana=āsajjana) VvA 55. To meaning "strike" cp. saṃghaṭṭana.

Ghaṭṭeti [Sk. ghaṭṭayati] to strike, beat, knock against, touch; fig. to offend, mock, object to. (a) lit. M II.4 (jannukena; text reads ghatteti, v. l. ghaṭeti); Sn 48 (=saṃ° Nd² 233); J I.218; Pv IV.10⁹ (=paṭihaṃsati PvA 271); DA I.256 (=khuṃseti); DhA I.251. — (b) fig. A III.343; Sn 847 (cp. Nd¹ 208); Vism 18. — pp. ghaṭṭita Pug 30, 36; psychologically ghaṭṭayati=ruppati. B or S III.86. — Pass. ghaṭīyati (q.v.).—Cp. āsajja and ugghāṭeti.

Ghaṇṭā (f.) a small bell (cp. kinkanikā) J IV.215; VvA 36, 37, 279 (khuddaka°). As ghaṇṭī at Vism 181.

Ghata (nt.) [Vedic ghṛta, **ghṛ** to sprinkle, moisten] clarified butter VvA 326; Miln 41; Sdhp 201 (-bindu). With ref. to the sacrificial fire (fire as eating ghee, or being sprinkled w. ghee) ghatāsana; J I.472; V.64, 446; Pv I.8⁵ (ghatasitta).

Ghana[1] [Vedic ghana, cp. Gr. εὐθηνής ?] (a) (adj.) solid, compact, massive; dense, thick; in eka° of one solid mass (of sela, rock) Vin I.185=Dh 81=Th 1, 643=Miln 386; A III.378, cp. ghanasela-pabbata DhA I.74. —gh. paŋsu J I.264, paṭhavī (solid ground) J I.74; PvA 75; palāsa (foliage) PvA 113; buddharasmiyo J I.12; °maŋsa solid, pure flesh DhA I.80; °sāṭaka (thick cloth) J I.292; °sañchanna (thickly covered) PvA 258; °suvaṇṇakoṭṭima DhA IV.135; abbha° a thick cloud Sn 348 (cp. SnA 348). — (b) (m.) the fœtus at a certain stage (the last before birth & the 4th in the enum. of the foll. stages: kalala, abbuda, pesī, gh.) S I.206; J IV.496; Miln 40; Vism 236. The latter meaning is semantically to be explained as "swelling" & to be compared with Gr. βρύω to swell and ἔμβρυον=embryo (the gravid uterus).

Ghana[2] [Vedic ghana to hanti (ghanti, cp. ghātayati), *guhen "strike," cp. Gr. θείνω, φόνος, Lat. of-fendo, Ags. guð, Ohg. gundea] a club, a stick, a hammer; in ayo° an iron club VvA 20. Also coll. term for a musical instrument played by striking, as cymbal, tambourine, etc. VvA 37.

Ghanika [to ghana[1] in meaning of "cloud" (Sk.)] a class of devas (cloud-gods ?) Miln 191.

Ghamma [Vedic gharma=Gr. θερμός, Lat. formus, Ohg. etc. warm; to *guher "warm," cp. Sk. ghṛṇoti, hara; Gr. θέρος, etc.] heat; hot season, summer. Either in loc. ghamme J IV.172 (=gimha-kāle); Pv IV.5[3] & ghammani ("in summer" or "by the heat") S I.143=J III.360 (sampareta overcome by heat); Sn 353; J IV.239; V. 3.—Or. in cpd. with °abhitatta (ghammâbhitatta, overpowered by heat) M I.74; D II.266; A III.187 sq.; Sn 1014 (cp. 353 ghammatatta); Miln 318; VvA 40; PvA 114.

Ghara[1] (nt.; pl. °ā Dh 241, 302) [cp. gaha & geha] a house A II.68; Sn 43 (gahaṭṭhā gharaŋ āvasantā), 337 (abl. gharā), 889 (id. gharamhā); J I.290 (id. gharato); IV.2, 364, 492 (ayo°); Pug 57; Miln 47. Combd with vatthu PvA 3, 17. — sūcighara a needle-case VvA 251.
-ājira house-yard Vism 144 (where Dhs A 116 in id. passage reads gharadvāra). -āvāsa the household life (as contrasted with the life of a mendicant) Vin II.180 (gharāvāsatthaŋ); A II.208; M I.179, 240, 267, 344; Sn 406 (cp. S V.350); J I.61; PvA 61; -kapoṭa [Sk. gṛhakapota] the house-pigeon Miln 364, 403; -golikā house or domestic lizard J II.147. -dāsī a female house-slave Pv II.3[21]; -dvāra a house-door J IV.142; Dhs A 116; PvA 93; -bandhana the bonds of the house, i. e. the establishing of marriage DhA I.4; -mukha an opening in the house, the front of the house Nd[2] 177; -mesin one who looks after the house, a pater familias, householder Sn 188; It 112 (gahaṭṭha+); J VI.575; -sandhi a cleft or crevice in the house PvA 24; -sūkara a tame, domestic pig DhA IV.16.

Ghara[2] [a drink (cp. gala) & garala poison] (°-); in -°dinnakābādha sickness in consequence of a poisonous drink (expl. as suffering fr. the results of sorcery) Vin I.206 (cp. *Vin. Texts* II.60); -visa poison Pug 48; DhA II.38; -sappa a poisonous snake DhA II.256.

Gharaṇī (f.) [fr. ghara[1]] a house-wife Vin I.271; S I.201; Pv III.1[9] (=ghara-sāminī PvA 174); DhA III.209.

Ghasa (adj.-n.) eating, an eater; in mahagghasa a big eater A V.149 (of the crow); Dh 325; Miln 288.

Ghasati [Vedic grasati & *ghasti, pp. grasta, cp. Gr. γράω to gnaw, γράστις fodder, Lat. gramen grass] to eat J III.210; ppr. ghasamāna Vin II.201; Th 1, 749. — Cp. ghasa, ghasta & ghāsa. See also jaddhu. Desid. jighacchati.

Ghasta [pp. of ghasati=Sk. grasta] only in vanka° having eaten or swallowed the hook (cp. grasta-vanka) D II.266 (v-g° va ambujo); J VI.113.

Ghāṭa see saŋ°; ghāṭana see ghaṭati.

Ghāta (usually -°) [Sk. ghāta & ghātana; to **han** (ghan), strike, kill; see etym. under ghana[2] & hanti] killing, murdering; slaughter, destruction, robbery D I.135 (gāma°, etc. village robbery); setu° the pulling down of a bridge (fig.) Vin I.59, etc. (see setu); pantha° highway robbery, brigandage, "waylaying" J I.253. — Th 2, 474, 493 (=samugghāta Com.); Sn 246 (ina°); VvA 72 (pāṇa°+pāṇa-vadha & °atipāta). Cp. next & vi°; saŋ°.

Ghātaka (adj.-°) murdering, destroying, slaughtering Vin I.89 (arahanta°), 136 (id.), 168 (id.); II.194 (manussa°); IV.260 (tala°) J IV.366 (gāma° corā robbers infesting the village); V.397 (thi°=itthi°); Pug 56 (maccha°). — As noun: (m.) one who slays, an executioner: go° a bull-slaughterer M I.244, etc. (see go); cora° an executioner or hangman J III.41; Pug 56; PvA 5. — (nt.) brigandage, robbery, slaughtering: gāmaghātakaŋ karoti J I.200.

Ghātikā (f. abstr. to ghātaka) murder J I.176 sq.

Ghātita (adj.) [pp. of ghāteti] killed, destroyed ThA 289; also in Der. ghātitatta (nt.) the fact of having killed J I.167. Cp. ugghātita.

Ghātin (adj.-n.) killing; a murderer J I.168 (pāṇa°); VI.67 (ghātimhi=ghātake).

Ghātimant (adj.) able to strike, able to pierce (of a needle), in ghana° going through hard material easily J III.282.

Ghāteti [Denom. fr. ghāta, cp. Sk. ghātayati to **han**] to kill, slay, slaughter It 22 (yo na hanti na ghāteti); Dh 129, 405; J I.255; Mhvs VII.35, 36. — aor. aghātayi J I.254; ger. ghātetvā J I.166. — Caus. ghātāpeti to have somebody killed J IV.124. — Cp. ghacca, ghātita, āghāteti.

Ghāna (nt.) [Sk. ghrāṇa to **ghrā**, see ghāyati. On n for ṇ cp. Trenckner, *Notes*, p. 81] the nose; usually in its function as organ of smell=sense of smell (either in phrase ghānena gandhaŋ ghāyati: to smell an odour by means of the nose; or in ghana-viññeyyā gandhā: odours which are sensed by the nose). In the enum. of the senses gh. is always mentioned in the 3rd place (after cakkhu & sota, eye & ear); see under rūpa. In this connection: Vin I.34; D I.21, 245; III.102, 244 sq.; S I.115; M I.112, 191; II.42; Dh 360; Pug 20; Miln 270; Vism 444 sq. (with defn). — In other connections: Pv II.2[4] (ghāna-chinna, one whose nose is cut off).
-āyatana the organ of smell D III.243, 280; Dhs 585, 605, 608; -indriya the sense of smell D III.239; Dhs 585 etc. (as above); -dhātu the element of smell Dhs. as above; -viññāṇa perception of smell Dhs 443, 608, 628; -samphassa contact with the sense of smell S I.115; D III. & Dhs as above.

Ghāyati[1] [Sk. ghrāti & jighrati, to **ghrā**, cp. gandha] to smell, always with gandhaŋ; ger. ghātvā S IV.71, 74 or ghāyitvā J I.210 (jālagandhaŋ); III.52 (macchagandhaŋ); Miln 347. Cp. sāyati & upagghāyati.

Ghāyati[2] [a variant of jhāyati] to be consumed, to be tormented by thirst Pv I.11[10] (ghāyire=ghāyanti PvA 60; v. l. BB jhāyire & jhāynati) Miln 397.

Ghāsa [Vedic ghāsa, fr. ghasati, q. v. cp. Lat. gramen=grass] grass for fodder, pasturing: food J I.511 (°ŋ kurute); PvA 173 (°atthāya gacchati "go feeding"). Mostly in: -esana search for food (=gocara) S I.141; Sn 711. — Cp. vi°.
-chada (chāda & chādana) food & clothing, i. e. tending, fostering, good care (=posana) (act.) or being well looked after, well provided (pass.); chada: Pug 51; chāda: J I.94; A I.107; II.85; III.385; chādana: D I.60; M I.360; VvA 23, 137; -hāraka one who fetches the fodder (food) Th 1, 910.

Ghāsana (nt.)=ghāsa; in -°ṭṭhāna pasture (=gocara) VvA 218.

Ghuṭṭha [Sk. ghuṣṭha, pp. **ghuṣ**, see ghoseti & cp. saŋ°] proclaimed, announced; renowned J I.50 (of festival); 425 (nakkhattaŋ); II.248 (ussava); Pv II.8[2] (dūra° of wide renown, world-famed of Bārāṇasī); DhA III.100 (chaṇe ghuṭṭhe when the fair was opened).

Ghuru-ghuru onomat. expression of snoring & grunting noise [gṛ-gṛ to ***gel** or ***ger**, see note on gala] in **-passāsa** (& °in) snoring & breathing heavily, panting, snorting & puffing S I.115 (of Māra); J I.160 (of sleeping bhikkhus, gh° kākacchamānā breathing loud & snoring). Cp. next.

Ghurughurāyati [Denom. fr. prec.] to snore J III.538; DhA I.307. Cp. Prk. ghurughuranti varāhā (grunting hogs) & ghurukkanti vagghā (roaring tigers).

Ghoṭaka [cp. Sk. ghoṭaka, Halāyudha 2, 281] a (bad) horse J VI.452.

Ghota is read at J I.454, probably for ghaṭṭa; meaning is "striking, stroke," comb[d] with kasā, whip.

Ghora (adj.) [Vedic ghora, orig. meaning, wailing, howling, lamenting, to ***gher**, ***ger**, see note on gala & cp. ghuru. A root **ghur** is given by Dhtp 487 in meaning of "bhīma," i. e. horrible. — Rel. to Goth. gaurs, sad; Ohg. gōrag, miserable; & perhaps Lat. funus, funeral. See Walde, *Lat. Wtb.* s. v.] terrible, frightful, awful Vin II.147. Freq. as attr. of niraya (syn. with **dāruṇa**; PvA 87, 159, 206) Pv I.10[12]; IV.1[8]. Of an oath (sapatha) Pv I.6[8]; II.12[16]. — ghorassara of a terrible cry (Ep. of an ass) Miln 363, 365.

Ghosa [Vedic ghoṣa to **ghus**] 1. shout, sound, utterance Vin II.115 ("Buddha" -ghosa); M I.294; A I.87, 228; Sn p. 106; Sn 696, 698; Dhs 637, 720 (+ghosa-kamma). — 2. shouting, howling, wailing (of Petas) Pv III.3[4]; IV.3[6], 3[38].

-pamāṇa to be measured (or judged) by one's reputation A II.71=Pug 53; also as **pamāṇika** DhA III.114 (in same context).

Ghosaka (adj.) sounding, proclaiming, shouting out (-°), in dhamma° praising the Law J II.286; Satthu guṇa° sounding the praise of the Master DhA III.114. As n. Name of a deva (Gh. devaputta) DhA I.173.

Ghosanā (f.) fame, renown, praise, in Māra° J I.71.

Ghosavant (adj.) full of sound, roaring J III.189.

Ghosita 1. [pp. of ghoseti] proclaimed, renowned, PvA 107 (=ghuṭṭha); VvA 31 (nakkhattaŋ). As Npl. Ghositārāma DhA I.53, 161, 208. — 2. [n. ag.=ghositṛ, cp. ghosaka] one who proclaims, advocates, or heralds; in Np. Ghositaseṭṭhi DhA I.187.

Ghoseti [Denom. of ghosa, cp. Sk. ghoṣayati, caus. to **ghuṣ**] to proclaim, announce; cry aloud, wail, shout J II.112; III.52; Pv II.9[37] (=uggh°); IV.6[3]; pp. ghosita & ghuṭṭha (q. v.). — Caus. ghosāpeti to have proclaimed J I.71.

C.

Ca (indef. enclitic particle) [Vedic ca adv. to rel. pron. *quo, idg. *que=Gr. τε, Lat. que, Goth. -h. Cp. ka, ki, ku] 1. *Indefinite* (after demonstr. pron. in the sense of kiŋ=what about? or how is it? cp. kiŋ)=ever, whoever, what-ever, etc. [Sk. kaśca, Gr. ὅς τε, Lat. quisque, Goth. hvazuh] so ca whoever (see below 3), tañ ca pan' amhākaŋ ruccati tena c' amhā attamanā M I.93; yañ ca kho . . . ceteti yañ ca pakappeti . . . whatever he thinks, whatever he intends . . . S II.65. As a rule the Pali form corresp. to Sk. kaśca is *kascid=koci, & ci (cid) is the regular P. representative of the indefinite ca (cp. cana & api). — 2. *Copulative or disjunctive* according to the general context being positive or negative. (a) copulative: and, then, now: tadā ca now then, and then (in historical exposition) J III.188. Most frequent in connecting two or three words, usually placed after the second, but also after the third: atthaŋ anatthañ ca Dh 256; pubbāparāni ca Dh 352; alaŋ etehi ambehi jambūhi panasehi ca J II.160. — In the same sense added to each link of the chain as ca-ca (cp. Sk. ca-ca, Gr. τε τε, Lat. que que; also mixed with constituents of similar pairs as api-ca, cp. τε-καί): tuyhañ ca tassā ca to you and her (orig. this or whatever to you, whatever to her)=to you as well as to her J I.151. Often with the first member emphasized by eva: c' eva, as well as: hasi c' eva rodi ca he laughed as well as cried J I.167; maŋsena c' eva phalāphalena ca with flesh as well as with all kinds of fruit J III.127; subhaddako c' eva supesalo ca J III.82; c' eva apace padūse pi ca waste and even defile ThA 72 (Ap V.40). — (b) disjunctive: but (esp. after a negation): yo ca but who Th I. 401; yadā ca but when (cp. tadā ca) J III.128. In conditional clauses (cp. 3) combd with sace=but if, on the other hand: sace agāraŋ ajjhāvasati . . . sace ca pabbajati agārā Sn 1003. With neg. na ca=but not: mahati vata te bondi, na ca paññā tadūpikā (but your wisdom is not in the same proportion) J II.160. — 3. *Conditional:* if [=Vedic ced, Lat. absque] D I.186, 207; II.36, 57 (jāti ca not va); M I.91; S III.66 (rūpañ ca attā abhavissa); A I.58; V.87; J II.110 (ciram pi kho khadeyya yavaŋ . . . ravamāno ca dūsayi: "he might have eaten a long time, if he had not come to harm by his cry," or "but"); IV.487; V.185, 216 (Sakko ca me varaŋ dajjā so ca labbhetha me varo: "if S. will give me a wish, that wish will be granted," or: "whatever wish he will allow, that one will be fulfilled"); VI.206, 208. — na ca (at the beginning of an interrog. phrase)= if not S I.190 (ahaŋ ca kho . . . pavāremi, na ca me Bhagavā kiñci garahati: if the Bh. will not blame me). For BSk. ca=ced see AvŚ II.189, n. 9.

Cakita (adj.) [Sk. cakita, **cak**] disturbed; afraid, timid Dāvs IV.35, 46.

Cakora [Sk. cakora to **kol** (kor), see note on gala] the francolin partridge (Perdix rufa) J V.416; Vv 35[8]; VvA 163. See also cankora.

Cakka (nt.) [Vedic cakra, redupl. formation fr. ***quel** to turn round (cp. P. kaṇṭha>Lat. collus & see also note on gala)=that which is (continuously) turning, i. e. wheel, or abstr. the shape or periphery of it, i. e. circle. **Cakra**=Gr. κύκλος, **Ags.** hveohl, hveol=wheel. The unredupl. form in Sk. carati (versatur), Gr. πέλομαι, πολεύω, πόλος (pole); Lat. colo, incolo; Obulg. kolo wheel, Oisl. hvel] I. *Crude meaning:* 1. a wheel (of a carriage) Dh 1; PvA 65 (ratha°); Miln 27. — 2. a discus used as a missile weapon J I.74; Pgdp 36; cp. khura° a razor as an instr. of torture. — 3. a disc, a circle: heṭṭhāpādatalesu cakkāni jātāni, forming the 2nd characteristic mark of a Mahāpurisa D II.17= III.143; D III.149. — J II.331; Miln 51. — 4. an array of troops (under tayo vyūhā: paduma° cakka° sakaṭa°) J II.404=IV.343. — II. *Applied meaning:* 1. (a wheel as component part of a carriage, or one of a duad or tetrad=) collection, set, part; succession; sphere, region, cycle Vin I.330 (cp. *Vin. Texts* II.281); III.96; iriyāpatha° the 4 ways of behaviour, the various positions (standing, walking, sitting, lying down) DA I.249; Sdhp 604. sā°, miga° the sphere or region of dogs & wild animals Miln 178; cakkena (instr.) in succession PvA 111. cakkaŋ kātabbaŋ, or bandhitabbaŋ freq. in Yam. and Paṭṭh. "The cycle of formulated words is to be here repeated." — 2. (like the four wheels constituting the moving power of a carriage=) a vehicle, instrument, means & ways; attribute, quality; state, condition, esp. good condition (fit instrumentality), catucakka an instr. of four, a lucky tetrad, a fourwheeler of the body as expressing itself in the four kinds of deportment, iriyāpathas A II.32; S I.16, 63 (catucakkaŋ). In this sense generalized as a happy state, consisting of "4 blessings": patirūpadesa-vāsa, sappurisûpassaya, atta-sammāpaṇidhi, pubbe-kata-puññatā A II.32; J V.114; mentioned at Ps I.84. Cp. also Sn 554 sq.; 684. Esp. pronounced in the two phrases dhamma-cakka (the wheel of the Doctrine, i. e. the symbol of conquering efficacy, or happiness implicated in the D.) and brahma-c° the best wheel, the supreme instrument, the noblest quality. Both with pavatteti to start & keep up (like starting & guiding a carriage), to set rolling, to originate, to make universally known. dhamma° e. g. S I.191; A I.23, 101; II.34, 120; III.151; IV.313; Sn 556 sq.; 693; J III.412; Ps II.159 sq.; PvA 67 (see dhamma). brahma° M I.71; S II.27; A II.9, 24; III.9, 417; V.33; Vbh 317 sq.; 344 (see brahma). Cp. cakkavattin (below). — Cp. vi°.

-chinna (udaka) (water of a well) the wheel of which is broken Ud 83; -bhañjanin one who destroys a state of welfare & good J V.112 (patirūpadesavāsādino kusala-cakkassa bhañjanī C.); -bheda breaking peace or concord, sowing discord Vin II.198; III.171; -yuga a pair of wheels Vv 83[2]; -ratana the treasure of the wheel, that is of the sun (cp. Rh. D. *Buddh. Suttas* p. 252; *Dialogues* II.197, 102) D II.172; III.59 sq., 75; J I.63; II.311; DA I.249. See also cakkavattin; **-vaṭṭaka** (nt.) a scoop-wheel (a wheel revolving over a well with a string of earthen pots going down empty & coming up full, after dredger fashion) Vin II.122; -vattin (cp. dhammacakkaŋ pavatteti above) he who sets rolling the Wheel, a just & faithful king (rājā hoti c. dhammiko dhammarājā cāturanto Sn p. 106, in corresp. pass. v. 1002 as vijeyya paṭhaviŋ imaŋ adaṇḍena asatthena dhammena-m-anusāsati). A definition is given by

Bdhgh. at DA I.249. — Three sorts of c. are later distinguished: a cakkavāḷa-c° a universal king, or cātu-ranta-c° (ruling over four great continents Sn p. 106; KhA 227), a dīpa-c° (ruling over one), a padesa-c° (ruling over part of one) Usually in phrase rājā cakkavattin: D I.88; III.156; IV.302; V.44, 99, 342; D II.16, 172; III.59 sq., 75, 142 sq.; M III.65; A I.76, 109 sq.; II.37, 133, 245; III.147 sq, 365; IV.89, 105; V.22; Kh VIII.12 (°sukha); J I.51; II.395; IV.119; Vbh 336; PvA 117; VvA 18; Sdhp 238, 453; DhA II.135 (°siri). -°gabbha Vism 126; -°rajjaŋ kāresi J II.311; **-viddha** (nt.) a particular form of shooting J V.130; **-samārūḷha** (adj.) having mounted the wheels, i. e. their carts (of janapadā) A I.178; III.66, 104.

Cakkalaka [fr. cakka] a disc or tuft (?) Vism 255 (kaḷīra°, where KhA 50 reads in same context kaḷīra-daṇḍa).

Cakkali (f.) drapery Vin II.174.

Cakkalikā a window blind, curtain Vin II.148.

Cakkavāka [Vedic cakravāka, cp. kṛkavāku, to sound root kṛ, see note on gala] the ruddy goose (Anas Casarca) J III.520; IV.70 sq. (N. of J No. 451); Pv II.12[3]; Miln 364, 401; — f. cakkavākī J III.524; VI.189=501.

Cakkavāḷa (m. & nt.) a circle, a sphere, esp. a mythical range of mountains supposed to encircle the world; pl. worlds or spheres J I.53, 203; VI.330; Vism 205 (its extent), 207, 367, 421; DhsA 297; DhA II. 15; III.438; in the trope "cakkavāḷaŋ atisambādhaŋ brahmaloko atinīco" (= the whole world cannot hold it) to express immensity DhA I.310; VvA 68.

-gabbha the interior of the C. sphere J IV.119; DA I.284; **-pabbata** (nt.) the C. mountains, "world's end" J III.32; VI.272; **-rajja** (nt.) the whole world, strictly speaking the whole region of a sphere J II.392.

Cakkhu (nt.) [Vedic cakṣuḥ, etym. not clear, as redupl. perhaps to **īkṣ**, akṣa eye, kṣaṇa moment, or as intens. to **cit**, cp. cinteti, & see Walde, *Lat. Wtb.* under inquam] the eye (nom. sg. cakkhuŋ Vin I.34; S I.115; M III.136, etc.). — I. *The eye as organ of sense*—(a) psychologically: cakkhunā rūpaŋ disvā "seeing visible object (shape) with the eye" (Nd² on rūpa q. v.) is the defin. of this first & most important of the senses (cp. Pv II.6¹ dakkhiṇa c. = the most valuable thing): the psychology of sight is discussed at DA I.194 sq., and more fully at Dhs 597 sq. (see DhsA 306 sq; *Dhs trsl.* 173 sq.); cp. cakkhunā puriso ālokati rūpagatāni Nd² 234. In any enumeration of the senses cakkhu heads the list, e. g. Vin I.34; D I.21; II.308, 336 sq.; III.102, 225, 244 sq.; 269; Nett 28.—See rūpa. Also combd. with sota: M I.318; III.264; A I.281.— cakkhusmiŋ haññati rūpehi S IV.201; hata° A I.129. passāmi naŋ manasā cakkhunā va "I see him with my mind as with my eye" Sn 1142.—\ in I.184; S I.32, 199; IV.123; Dh 360; J IV.137; DA I.183; Nett 191. Vism 444 sq. As adj. (-°) seeing, having or catching sight of: eka° (dvi°) one-eyed (two°) A I.128 sq.; āmisa° seeing an object of sensual enjoyment S II.226; IV.159; J V.91 (= kilesalola). acakkhu blind A III.250, 256; Ps I.129. — (b) ethically: as a "sense" belonging to what is called "body" (kāya) it shares all the qualities of the latter (see kāya), & is to be regarded as an instr. only, i. e. the person must not value it by itself or identify himself with it. Subduing the senses means in the first place acquiring control over one's eyes (cp. okkhitta cakkhu, with down-cast eyes Sn 63, 411, 972; Pv IV.3⁴⁴; & indriyesu guttadvāra; °indriya). In this connection the foll. passages may be mentioned: Vin I.34; D I.70; S IV.123; II.244 (aniccaŋ, etc.); III.255 (do.) IV.81, 128 (na tumhākaŋ); Ps I.132 (aniccaṭṭhaŋ). Numerous others see under rūpa. — II. *The eye as the most important channel of mental acquiring*, as faculty of perception & apperception; insight, knowledge (cp. veda, οἶδα to vid, to see). In connection with ñāṇa (γνῶσις) it refers to the apperception of the truth (see dhamma-cakkhu): intuition and recognition, which means perfect understanding (cp. the use of the phrase jānāti passati "to know and to see" = to understand clearly). See e. g. S II.7-11, 105; IV.233; V.179; 258; 422 sq. Most frequently as dhamma° "the eye of the truth," said of the attainment of that right knowledge which leads to Arahantship, in phrase virajaŋ vitamalaŋ dh-cakkhuŋ uppajjati Vin I.16; D I.86, 110; S II.134 sq.; IV.47; 107; V.467; A IV.186; Ps II.150 sq.; 162; Miln 16. Similarly paññā°, It 52; ariya° M I.510. — III. *The eye as the instr. of supersensuous perception*, "clear" sight, clairvoyance. This is the gift of favoured beings whose senses are more highly developed than those of others, and who through right cognition have acquired the two "eyes" or visionary faculties, termed **dibba-cakkhu** & **buddha-cakkhu** It 52; D II.38 resp. They are most completely described at Nd² 235 (under cakkhumā), & the foll. categories of the range of application of cakkhu are set forth: 1. **maŋsa-cakkhu**: the physical eye which is said to be exceptionally powerful & sensitive. See Kv III.7 (trans. p. 149 ff.). Vism 428 (maŋsa° 2 ñāṇa°).—2. **dibba-°**: the deva-eye, the eye of a seer, all-pervading, & seeing all that proceeds in hidden worlds.— 3. **paññā°**: the eye of wisdom; he who knows all that can be known (jānaŋ passaŋ recognizing & seeing, i. e. of perfect understanding; cakkhubhūta ñāṇa° dhamma° brahma°). — 4. **buddha°**: the eye of a Buddha or of complete intuition, i. e. of a person who "sees the heart of man," of a being realizing the moral state of other beings and determined to help them on the Path to Right Knowledge. — 5. **samanta°**: (a summary account of Nos. 1-4, & in all Scripture-passages a standing Ep. of Gotama Buddha, see below), the eye of all round knowledge, the eye of a Tathāgata, of a being perfected in all wisdom. — Out of these are mentioned & discussed singly or in sets: (Nos. 1-5): DhsA 306; SnA 351; (Nos. 1-3:) It 52 = Kvu 251 sg. (It 52 = Kvu 254); (dibba:) Vin I.8, 288; II.183; III.5; D I.82, 162; III. 52, III, 281; M I.213; S I.144, 196; II.122, 213, 276; IV.240; V.266, 305; A I.165, 256, 281 sq.; III.19, 29, 418; IV.85, 141, 178, 291; V.13, 35, 68, 200, 211, 340; J III.346; Ps I.114; II.175; Vbh 344; PvA 5. — (paññā°:) S IV.292; V.467; A I.35; DhA III.174, 175. — (buddha°:) Vin I.6; S I.138; Ps II.33; PvA 61. — (samanta°:) S I.137 = Nd² 235⁴; Sn 345, 378, 1063, 1069, 1090, 1133; Ps II.31 = Nd² 235⁵.

-āyatana (either cakkh' or cakkhv°) the organ or sense of sight D III.243, 280, 290; Dhs 585, 653; **-indriya** (cakkhundriya) the organ of eye, faculty of vision D I.70; III.225, 239; A I.113; Dhs 585, 597, 661, 830, 971; Vism 7; **-karaṇa** (always in combⁿ w. ñāṇa-karaṇa) producing (right) insight (and knowledge) It 82 (of kusala-vitakkā); f. °ī S IV.331 (of majjhimā paṭipadā); Ps II.147; **-dada** one who gives the eye (of understanding) Th I, 3; **-dhātu** the element of vision Dhs 597, 703, 817. **-patha** the range of vision; sight J I.65 = DhA I.173; J I.146; IV.189, 378, 403 (= cakkhūnaŋ etaŋ nāmaŋ C.); VvA 119; **-bhūta** (+ ñāṇa°) (adj.) one who has become the possessor of right understanding S II.255; IV.94; A V.226 sq. **-lola** greed (or greedy) with the eye Nd² 177; **-viññāṇa** consciousness by means of visual perception, visual cognition Vin I.34; D II.308, 310; III.243; Dhs 433, 556, 585, 589, 620; cp. Mrs. Rh. D. *Buddh. Psych. Eth.* p. 177; *Miln trsl.* I.80, 89; **-viññeyya** (adj.) (i e. rūpā) to be apperceived by the sense of sight Vin I.184; D II.281; III.234; Dhs 589, 967, 1095; **-samphassa** contact with the sense of vision (usually with °ja: sprung from visual contact) (of vedanā, feelings) Vin I.34; D II.308 sq.; III.243; Ps I.5, 40, 136.

Cakkhuka (adj.) having eyes, seeing (-°), in dibba° A I.23, 148 (see cakkhu III.²) and a° blind D I.191; S III.140; Nd 67.

Cakkhumant (adj.) [cakkhu + mant] having eyes, being gifted with sight; of clear sight, intuition or wisdom; possessing knowledge (cp. samantacakkhu) D I.76 (one who knows, i. e. a connoisseur); cakkhumanto rūpāni dakkhinti "those who have eyes to see shall see" (of the Buddha) D I.85, 110, etc. — Vin I.16; S I.27; A I.116, 124; IV.106; Dh 273; It 108, 115; DA I.221; DhA III.403; IV.85. — Esp. as Ep. of the Buddha: the All-wise S I.121, 134, 159, 210; Sn 31, 160, 992, 1028, 1110, 1128; Vv 12⁵ (=pañcahi cakkhūhi cakkhumā Buddh Bhagavā VvA 60, cp. cakkhu III.); Vv 81²⁷.

Cakkhula (adj.) [=cakkhuka] in visama° squint-eyed, squinting J I.353; VI.548.

Cakkhussa (adj.) [Vedic cakṣuṣya] pleasing to or good for the eyes (opp. a°) Vin II.137, 148.

Cankama [Sk. cankrama & cankramā, fr. cankamati] (a) walking up & down S IV.104. — (b) the place where one is walking, esp. a terraced walk, cloister Vin I.15, 182; II.220; D I.105; S I.212; A I.114; 183; III.29; IV.87; J I.17; II.273; V.132 (cp. kattaradaṇḍa-passages).

Cankamati [Intens. of kamati, to **kram**=Sk. cankramīti; cp. kamati] to walk about, to walk up & down Vin I.15, 182; II.193, 220; IV.18; S I.107, 212; PvA 105. — Caus. cankamāpeti J III.9.

Cankamana (nt.) [fr. cankamati] 1. walking up & down S II.282; DhA I.10. — 2. a cloister walk (=cankama) VvA 188. Usually °-: Vin I.139 (°sālā); J III.85; IV.329; PvA 79 (°koṭi the far end of the cloister).

Cankamika (adj.) [fr. cankama] one who has the habit of walking about Miln 216 (ṭhāna° standing & walking).

Cankora [cp. cakora] the Greek partridge Vv 35⁸ (cp. VvA 163); J VI.538.

Cangavāra [cp. Tamil canguvaḍa a dhoney, Anglo-Ind. ḍoni, a canoe hollowed from a log, see also doṇi] a hollow vessel, a bowl, cask M I.142; J V.186 (in similes). As °ka Miln 365 (trsl. Miln II.278 by "straining cloth"). — Cp. cañcu "a box" Divy 131.

Cangoṭaka [cp. cangavāra] a casket, a box J I.65; IV.257; V.110, 303; VI.369, 534; DhA II.116; III.101; VvA 33, 158; Mhvs IV.106; Anvs p. 35 Vism 173.

Caccara (nt.) [Sk. catvara, cp. Trenckner, *Notes*, p. 56] a quadrangular place, a square, courtyard; a place where four roads meet, a cross-road Vin III.151; IV.271; Miln 1 (+catukkasinghāṭaka), 330 (do.); J I.425 (°raccha).

Caja (adj.) giving up, to be given up; in cpd. duc° hard to give up A III.50; J V.8. Cp. cāga.

Cajati [Sk. tyajate, **tyaj**=Gr. σοβέω to scare away] 1. to let loose, to emit, to discharge A II.33; J II.342 (mutta karīsaŋ) fig. to utter (a speech) J V.362. — 2. to abandon, to give up, sacrifice (with loc. of person to whom: Asuresu pāṇaŋ S I.224=J I.203) Dh 290; J II.205; III.211; V.464; VI.570. — pp. catta, q. v. — grd. caja [Sk. tyajya] q. v.

Cañcala (adj.) [Intens. of **cal**=car, to move, with n instead of r in reduplication, cp. Sk. cañcūryate=carcariti, cañcala (=*carcara), Gr. γαργαλίζω & γαγγαλίζω to tickle; see also note on gala & cp. cankamati] moving to & fro, trembling, unsteady J IV.498 (=calācala); Sdhp 317, 598.

Caṭula (adj.) [Sk. catura] clever, skilled Mhbv 148. See catura.

Caṇḍa (adj.) [Sk. caṇḍa] fierce, violent; quick-tempered, uncontrolled, passionate Vin II.194 (hatthī); D. I.90 (=māna-nissita-kopa-yutta DA I.256); S I.176; II.242; A II.109=Pug 47 (sakagava°); J I.450; II.210, 349; Vism 343, 279 (°sota, fierce current), (°hatthi); DhA IV.9 (goṇa) 104; Sdhp 41, 590, 598. — f. caṇḍī M I.126; J II.443; III.259; Pv II.3⁴ (=kodhanā PvA 83). — Compar. caṇḍatara S II.242. — In cpds. caṇḍi°, see caṇḍikata & caṇḍitta.

Caṇḍaka (adj.)=caṇḍa; f. caṇḍikā Pv II.3⁵. & caṇḍiyā J III.259 (=kodhanā).

Caṇḍikata (adj.) [cp. caṇḍa] angry Vin IV.310.

Caṇḍikka (nt.) [*caṇḍikya, of caṇḍika > caṇḍaka] ferocity, anger, churlishness Nd² 313, 576, Dhs 418, 1060, 1115, 1231; Vbh 357; DhA II.227. Cp. caṇḍitta.

Caṇḍitta (nt.) anger Dhs 418; Pug 18=22. Cp. caṇḍikka.

Caṇḍāla [Vedic caṇḍāla] a man of a certain low tribe, one of the low classes, an outcaste; grouped with others under nīcā kulā (low-born clans) as caṇḍālā nesādā veṇā rathakārā pukkusā at A I.107=II.85=Pug 51. As caṇḍāla-pukkusā with the four recognized grades of society (see jāti & khattiya) at A I.162. — Vin IV.6; M II.152; S V.168 sq. (°vaŋsa); A III.214, 228 (brāhmaṇa°); IV.376; J IV.303; PvA 175; Miln 200. — f. caṇḍālī A III.226; Pv III.1¹³; DhA II.25. See also pukkusa.

Caṇḍāla (nt.) a kind of amusement or trick D I.6≈(=ayo-gulakīḷā play with an iron ball DA I.84).

Catukka[1] (nt.) [fr. catu=*catuka > *catukyaŋ] 1. a tetrad, a set of four, consisting of four parts: °pañcaka-jjhānā (pl.) the fourfold & the fivefold system of meditation DhsA 168; see cpds. — 2. a place where four roads meet J VI.389; Miln 330 (see also below); esp. in phrase catukke catukke kasāhi tāḷeti (or is it "in sets of four"? See Morris, *J.P.T.S.* 1884, 79) J I.326; II.123; DhA IV.52. — 3. a square (in a village) Miln 1, 365; J II.194; V.459; DhA 317.

-bhatta a meal for four bhikkhus Vin II.77; III.160; -magga the 4 fold path Nett 113; -yañña (usually sabba catukka°) a sacrifice consisting of (all) the four parts J III.44, 45; PvA 280; cp. J I.335. (Or is it the "cross-road sacrifice"?)

Catukka[2] [origin. "consisting only of one quarter"?] empty, shallow, little Nd² 415 (°pañña, with omaka-pañña, lāmaka-p°); J IV.441 (nadī=tuccha Com.).

Catuttha (num. ord.) [Vedic caturthá, Idg. ***queturtó**=Gr. τέτρατος, Lat. quartus, Ohg. fiordo] the fourth Sn 97, 99, 450; J III.55; VI.367; °ŋ (adv.) for the fourth time DhA III.174. — f. catutthī Sn 436; Vism 338.—See also (*s.v.* Aḍḍha) aḍḍhuḍḍha.

-bhatta food eaten only every fourth day J V.424. -magga "the fourth Path," of Arahantship DhA I.309; -mana (?) (nt.) name of the tongue, in so far as it forms the fourth vatthu (beside eyes, ears, nose) according to the gloss: J V.155; extremely doubtful.

Catur, catu° in composition [Vedic catvārah (m.) catvāri (nt.) fr. *quetuor, *quetur = Gr. τέτταρες (hom. πίσυρες), Lat. quattuor, Goth. fidwōr, Ohg. fior, Ags fēower, E. four; catasras (f.) fr. *qu(e)tru, cp. tisrás. Also as adv. catur fr. *quetrus=Lat. quater & quadru°] base of numeral four; 1. As *num. adj.* nom. & acc. m. cattāro (Dh 109; J III.51) and caturo (Sn 84, 188), f. catasso (Sn 1122), nt. cattāri (Sn. 227); gen. m. catunnaŋ (Sn p. 102), [f. catassannaŋ]; instr. catubbhi (Sn 229), catūhi (Sn 231) & catuhi; loc. catūsu (J I.262) & catusu. — 2. As *num. adv.*, catu° catur° in cpds. catuddasa (14), also through elision & reduction cuddasa PvA 55, 283, etc., cp. also cātuddasī. Catuvīsati (24) Sn 457; catusaṭṭhi (64) J I.50; II.193; PvA 74; caturāsīti (84) usually with vassa-sahassāni J I.137; II.311; Pv IV.7⁷; DhA II.58; PvA 9, 31, 254, etc. See also cattārīsa (40).

-(r)aŋsa (=caturassa, having four edges, four-edged Dhs 617; PvA 189 (read °sobhitāya); -(r)anga (consisting of) four limbs or divisions, fourfold M I.77; J I.390; II.190, 192; VI.169 (uposatha, cp. aṭṭhanga); Dpvs I.6; Sdhp 64; -(r)angika=prec. Dhs 147, 157, 397; KhA 85; Sdhp 58; -(r)angin (adj.) comprising four parts, f. °inī, of an army consisting of elephants, chariots, cavalry & infantry D II.190; J II.102, 104; Vism 146;

SnA 225, 353; DhA IV.144; cp. J VI.275; -(r)angula (adj.) measuring 4 fingers, 4 fingers broad or wide, Vin I.46; S II.178; J VI.534; Th I, 1137; Vism 124. -(r)angulika = prec. Th 2, 498 (= ThA, 290); -(r)anta see cātur°; -(r)assa [catur + assa²] four-cornered, quadrangular, regular Vin II.310 (Bdhgh); J IV.46 (āvāṭa) 492 (sālā); V.49; Pv II.1¹⁹. Cp. caturaŋsa & next; -(r)assara (see last) with 4 sharp sides (of a hammer; °muggara) DhA I.126; -(r)âdhiṭṭhāna (adj.) one who has taken the four resolutions (see adhiṭṭhāna) M III.239; -(r)âpassena (adj.) endowed with the four apassena: lit.: reclining on four A V.29, 30; D III.269, 270; -ussada (catussada) full of four, endowed with 4 things, rich in four attributes J IV.309 (expld. p. 311 as having plenty of people, grain, wood & water); IV.422 = 461 "with four pillows" (p. 422 has caturassada for caturussada, which latter is also to be preferred to catussada, unless this is a haplology). In the same connection occurs satt-ussada (full of people) D I.111 e. g. & Pv IV.1⁸ (see satta). The formation "cattussada" has probably been influenced by "sattussada"; -(k)kaṇṇa (& °ka) (a) with 4 corners Vin II.137; J III.255. — (b) "between four ears," i. e. secret, of manta (counsel) J VI.391; -(k)kama walking with four (feet), quadruped Vv 64⁸; Pv I.11³; -kuṇḍika on all fours M I.79; A III.188; D III.6; Pv III.2⁷ (cp. PvA 181); -koṇa four cornered, crossed, in °*raccha* cross road PvA 24; -(k)khandha the four khandhas, viz. feeling, perception, synthesis & intellect (see khandha) DhsA 345; -(g)guṇa fourfold, quadruple D II.135; S I 27; J I.213; VvA 186; Sdhp 40; -cakka with four wheels S I.16 = 63 (said of the human body, see under cakka); -jāta of four sorts, viz. gandha (perfume) having four ingredients ThA 72 (see next) -jāti of four kinds J I.265, V.79; (gandha). These 4 ingredients of perfume are saffron, jasmine, Turkish (tarukkha) & Greek incense (yavana); -jātiya (& °jātika) in °gandha prec. J III.291; IV.377; PvA 127; Miln 354; J I.178 (°ka); -(d)disā (pl.) the 4 quarters of the globe S I.167 = Sn p. 79; D I.251; may also be taken for abl. sg. as adv.: in the 4 quarters Vin I.16, cp. acc. catuddisaŋ D II.12; -(d)dīpika covering the 4 continents, of megha (a cloud) DhA II.95; -dvāra with 4 gates, of a house D I.102 (= DA I.270); of Avīciniraya It 86; J IV.3; Pv I.10¹³; cp. Catudvāra Jātaka (No. 439; J IV.1 sq.); -nahuta ninety-four J I.25; VI.486; -paccaya the four requisites (see paccaya) J III.273. °*santosa* contentment with °DhA IV.111; -paṇṇasa fifty-four DhA I.4; -(p)patha a fourways J IV.460; -(p)pada [Sk. caturpād, Gr. τετράπους, Lat. quadrupes] a quadruped Vin II.110; S I.6; A V.21; Sn 603, 964; It 87; J I.152; III.82; -parivaṭṭa (cp. aṭṭha °adhideva-ñāṇadassana A IV.304) fourfold circle S III.59 sq. (pañcupādānakkhandhe). -parisā (f.) the fourfold assembly, scil. of male & female bhikkhus & upāsakas (cp. parisā) PvA 11; -pala fourfold Vism 339. -(p)pādaka (adj.) consisting of 4 padas, i. e. a sloka; f. °ikā (gāthā) a complete stanza or sloka Anvs p. 35; -pārisuddhasīla (nt.) the four precepts of purity J III.291; DhA IV.111; -(b)bidha (catur + vidha) fourfold ThA 74; -(b)bipallāsa (catur + vipallāsa) the fourfold change (cp. Nett 85) Th + I, 1143; SnA 46; -byūha (catur + vyūha) arranged in 4 arrays (of hāra) Nett 3, 105; -bhāga the 4th part, a quarter Dh 108; -bhūmika having 4 stories or stages (of citta or dhamma) DhA I.21; IV.72; DhsA 344, 345; cp. Vism 493 (of indriya); -madhura (nt.) sweetness (syrup) of 4 (ingredients) DA I.136; ThA 68; -mahāpatha a crossing on a high-road Vism 235. -mahābhūtika consisting of the four great elements DhsA 403; -(m)mahārājika: see cātum°; -māsa 4 months, a season PvA 96; Dpvs I.24, 37 (cā°); see under māsa; -sacca the four truths or facts (see ariyasacca) DhA III.386; Miln 334; (*s*)*sāla* (nt.) [catur + sāla] a square formed by 4 houses, in phrase catuhi gabbhehi paṭimaṇḍitaŋ catussālaŋ kāretvā VvA 220; DhA III.291; -'ha (catuha & catūha) 4 days; catuhena within 4 days S II.191; catūhapañcāha 4 or 5 days Vin IV.280. — See also cpds. with cātu°.

Catura [Deriv. uncertain. Perhaps from **tvar** to move, that is quickly. Sk. catura] clever, skilled, shrewd J III.266; VI.25. — Der. f. abstr. caturatā cleverness Vbh 351 (= cāturiya).

Caturiya at Vv 41² is to be read ca turiya, etc. Otherwise see cāturiya.

Catta [pp. of cajati] given up, sacrificed A II.41; III.50; Th I, 209 (°vaṇṇa who has lost fame); J II.336; IV.195; V.41 (°jīvita).

Cattatta (nt.) [fr. catta] the fact of giving up, abandonment, resignation Vbh 254 sq.; DhsA 381.

Cattārīsa (& cattāḷīsa) [Sk. catvāriŋśat] forty S II.85; Sn p. 87; It 99~. Usually cattāḷīsa J I.58; V.433; DhA I.41; II.9. 93.

-danta having 40 teeth (one of the characteristics of a Mahāpurisa) D II.18; III.144, 172.

Cattārīsaka (adj.) having forty M III.77.

Cadika at Miln 197 (ūmikavankacadika) prob. for °madika.

Cana (-°) [Vedic cana fr. rel. pron. ***quo** + demonstr. pron. *no, cp. anā, nānā; Gr. νή; Lat. -ne in quandone = P. kudācana. cana = Goth. hun, Ohg. gin, Ger. ir-gen-d. Cp. ci] indef. particle "like, as if," added to rel. or interrog. pronouns, as kiñcana anything, kudācana at any time, etc. Cp. ca & ci.

Canaŋ = cana; and then, if Vin III.121 (cp. ca 3); or should it be separated at this passage into ca naŋ?

Canda [Vedic candra from ***(s)quend** to be light or glowing, cp. candana sandal (incense) wood, Gr. κάνδαρος cinder; Lat. candeo, candidus, incendo; Cymr. cann white; E. candid, candle, incense, cinder] the moon (i. e. the shiner) S I.196; II.206; M II.104; A I.227; II.139 sq.; III.34; Dh 413; Sn 465, 569, 1016; J III.52; VI.232; Pv I.12⁷; II.6⁶; Vv 64⁷ (maṇi° a shiny jewel, or a moonlike jewel, see VvA 278, v. l. °sanda). -puṇṇa° the full moon J I.149, 267; V.215; °*mukha* with a face like a full moon (of the Buddha) DhA III.171. Canda is extremely frequent in similes & comparisons: see list in *J.P.T.S.* 1907, 85 sq. In enumerations of heavenly bodies or divine beings Canda always precedes Suriya (the Sun), e. g. D II.259; A I.215; II.139; Nd² 308 (under Devatā). Cp. candimant. On quâsi mythol. etym. see Vism 418.

-kanta a gem Miln 118; -(g)gāha a moon-eclipse (lit. seizure, i. e. by Rāhu) D I.10 (cp. DA I.95); **-maṇḍala** the moon's disc, the shiny disc, i. e. the moon A I.283; J I.253; III.55; IV.378; V.123; Dhs 617; Vism 216 (in compar.); PvA 65; -suriyā (pl.) sun & moon J IV.61.

Candaka = canda VvA 278 (maṇi°); Sdhp 92 (mayūra° the eye in a peacock's tail).

Candatta (nt.) [abstr. fr. canda] in cpd. paripuṇṇa° state or condition of the full moon SnA 502.

Candana (m. & nt.) [Deriv. unknown. Possibly non-Aryan; but see under canda, Sk. candana] sandal (tree, wood or unguent, also perfume) Vin I.203; A I.9, 145, 226; III.237; Dh 54; J V.420 (tree, m.); Miln 382; DhA I.422; IV.189 (°pūjā); VvA 158 (agalu° with aloe & sandal); PvA 76. — Kāsika° sandal from Kāsī A III.391; IV.281; Miln 243, 348; ratta° red s. J IV.442; lohita° id. A V.22; J I.37; hari° yellow s. J I.146.

-ussada covered with sandal perfumes Th I, 267; Pv III.9¹ (= candanasārānulitto PvA 211); -gaṇṭhi (or better gaṇḍi; see the latter) a block of sandal wood Vin II.110; -gandhin having a scent of sandal J III.190; -vilepana sandal unguent J IV.3. -sāra choice sandal (wood or perfume) Vv 52³, J I.53, 340.

Candanikā (f.) a pool at the entrance of a village (usually, but not necessarily dirty: see Vin II.122 & cp. candanapanka Av.Ś I.221, see also PW sub candana²) S V.361; M I.11, 73, 448; A I.161; Th I, 567; J V.15; Miln 220; Vism 264, 343, 359; Sdhp 132.

Candimā (m. or f. ?) [Sk. candramas m. & candrimā f., cp. pūrṇimā; a cpd. of canda+ mā, cp. māsa. The Pāli form, however, is based on a supposed derivation fr. canda+ mant, like bhagavā, and is most likely m. On this formation cp. Lat. lumen = Sk. rukmān luminous, shiny] the moon. By itself only in similes at Dh 208, 387 (at end of pada) & in " abbhā mutto va candimā " M II.104 = Dh 172 = Th 1, 871; Dh 382 = Th 1, 873; Ps 1.175. — Otherwise only in comb^{n} with suriya, moon & sun, D 1.240; II.12; III.85 sq., 90, 112; S III.266; v.264 sq.; D 1.227; II.53, 130; v.59; Vv 30; J II.213; Miln 191; Vism 153. Also in cpd. candimāpabhā the light of the moon (thus BB, whereas SS read at all passages candiyā° or candiya-pabhā) S III.156 = v.44 = It 20.

Capala (adj.) [Sk. capala cp. cāpa bow; from ***qep** to shake or quiver, see Walde *Lat. Wtb.* under caperro] moving to & fro, wavering, trembling, unsteady, fickle S 1.204; v.269; M 1.470 (and a° steady); A III.199, 355, 391; Dh 33; Pug 35; J 1.295; II.360. At J VI.548 it means one who lets the saliva flow out of his mouth (expl^{d} by paggharita-lāla " trickle-spit ").

Capalatā (f.) [fr. last] fickleness, unsteadiness Miln 93, 251; Pgdp 47, 64. At Nd^{2} 585 as capalanā+ cāpalyaṃ with gedhikatā, meaning greed, desire (cp. capala at J VI.548).

Capu (or capucapu) a sound made when smacking one's lips Vin II.214 (capucapukāraka adj.), 221; IV.197.

Cappeti [Sk. carvayati Dhtp 295 gives root **cabb** in meaning " adana "] to chew Bdhgh on Vin II.115. Cp. jappati.

Camati (& cameti) [**cam**, to sip; but given at Dhtm 552 in meaning " adana," eating] to rinse, only in cpd. ācamati (ācameti).

Camara [Deriv. unknown, probably non-Aryan. Sk. camara] 1. the Yak ox (Bos grunniens) J 1.149; III.18, 375; v.416; Miln 365. — f. -ī J 1.20; Sdhp 621. — In cpds. camarī° J IV.256. — 2. a kind of antelope (-ī) J VI.537.

-**vījanī** (f.) a chowry (the bushy tail of the Yak made into a brush to drive away flies) Vin II.130. This is one of the royal ensigns (see kakudhabhaṇḍa & cp. vāla-vījanī).

Camasa [Vedic camasa, a cup] a ladle or spoon for sacrificing into the sacred fire J VI.528^{24} = 529^{4} (unite ca with masa, cp. 529^{9} and n. 4: aggijuhana-kaṭacchu-sankhātimasañca [for camasañ ca] v. l. B^{d}). Cp. Kern, *Toevoegselen* s. v.

Camu (f.) [Both derivation and exact meaning uncertain. The Vedic camū is a peculiar vessel into wh. the Soma flows from the press. In late Pali & Sk. it means a kind of small army, perhaps a division drawn up more or less in the shape of the Vedic vessel] an army J II.22; °nātha a general Mhvs °pati id. Dāvs 1.3.

Campa = campaka J VI.151.

Campaka the Champaka tree (Michelia champaka) having fragrant white & yellow flowers J v.420; VI.269; Miln 338; DA 1.280; Vism 514 (°rukkha, in simile); DhA 1.384; VvA 194.

Campā (f.) N. of a town (Bhagulpore) & a river D 1.111; DA 1.279; J IV.454.

Campeyya N. of a Nāgarāja J IV.454 (= °jātaka, No. 506); Vism 304.

Campeyyaka (adj.) belonging to Campā Vin v.114; J VI.269 (here: a Champaka-like tree).

Camma (nt.) [Vedic carman, cp. Lat. corium hide or leather, cortex bark, scortum hide; Ohg. herdo; Ags. heorða = E. hide; also Sk. kṛtti; Ohg. scirm (shield); E. skin; from ***sqer** to cut, skin (cp. kaṭu) = the cut-off hide, cp. Gr. δέρω: δέρμα] 1. skin, hide, leather Vin 1.192 (sīha° vyaggha° dīpi°), 196 (eḷaka° aja° miga°); A IV.393 (sīha° dīpi°); PvA 157 (kadalimiga° as rug); J II.110 (sīha°); III.82, 184; Miln 53; Sdhp 140. It is supposed to be subcutaneous (under chavi as tegument), & next to the bone: chaviṃ chindetvā cammaṃ chindati S II.238 = A IV.129; freq. in expr. like aṭṭhi-camma-nahāru-matta (skin & bones) PvA 68, see under nahāru; camma-maṃsa-nahāru PvA 80. — 2. a shield Vin II.192 (asi° sword & shield); M 1.86; A III.93; J v.373; VI.580.

-**aṇḍa** a water-skin J 1.250; -**kāra** a worker in leather, a tanner Vin IV.7; Miln 331; a harness-maker J v.45; a waggon-builder and general artisan J IV.174 (= rathakāra); also as -**kārin** PvA 175 (= rathakārin); -**khaṇḍa** an animal's skin, used as a rug Miln 366; Vism 99; skin used as a water-vessel (see khaṇḍa) Vin II.122; Ps 1.176; -**ghaṭaka** a water-skin J II.345; -**naddha** (nt.) a drum Bu 1.31; -**pasibbaka** a sack, made of skin or leather ThA 283; J VI.431, 432 (as v. l.); -**bandha** a leather strap Vin 1.194; -**bhastā** (f.) a sack J v.45; -**māluka** a leather bag J VI.431, 432; -**yodhin** a soldier in cuirass D 1.51 ≈ (in list of var. occupations; DA 1.157: cammakañcukaṃ pavisitvā); A IV.107, 110; -**varatta** (f.) a leather thong J II.153; -**vāsin** one who wears the skin (of a black antelope), i. e. a hermit J VI.528; -**sāṭaka** an ascetic wearing clothes of skin J III.82 (nāma paribbājaka).

Cammaka a skin Bu II.52.

Caya [from cināti] piling, heaping; collection, mass Vin II.117; DhsA 44; in building: a layer Vin II.122, 152. As -° one who heaps up, a collector, hoarder M 1.452 (nikkha°, khetta°, etc.). See also ā°, apa°, upa°.

Cara (n-adj.) [from **car**, carati] 1. the act of going about, walking; one who walks or lives (usually -°): oka° living in water M 1.117; J VI.416; antara° S IV.173; eka° solitary Sn 166; saddhiṃ° a companion Sn 45; anattha° J v.433; jala° Dāvs IV.38. See also cāreti & gocara. — Instr. carasā (adv.) walking M 1.449. — cara-vāda " going about talk," gossip, idle talk S III.12; v.419. — sucara easy, duccara difficult Vin III.26. — 2. one who is sent on a message, a secret emissary, a spy S 1.79. Also as carapurisa J II.404; IV.343; VI.469; DhA 1.193. — *Note.*—cara-purāya at A v.133 should be changed into v. l. SS paramparāya.

Caraka 1. = cara^{2} (a messenger) J VI.369 (attha°); adj. walking through: sabbalokaṃ° J v.395. — 2. any animal S 1.106; PvA 153 (vana°).

Caraṇa (nt.) [of a deer, called pañca-hattha " having 5 hands," i. e. the mouth and the 4 feet] 1. walking about, grazing, feeding VvA 308 (°ṭṭhāna). — 2. the foot Vin IV.212; J v.431. — 3. acting, behaviour, good conduct, freq. in comb^{n} with vijjā, e. g. A II.163; v.327; Dh 144; Vism 202 (in detail); PvA 1, etc. — D III.97, 156; Sn 410, 462, 536; Miln 24. sampanna-caraṇa (adj.) accomplished in right behaviour S 1.153, 166; Sn 1126; Pv II.13^{8}. — Cp. sañ°.

Caraṇavant (adj.) one of good conduct (= sampanna-caraṇa) Sn 533, 536.

Carati [Vedic carati, ***quel** to move, turn, turn round (cp. kaṇṭha & kula) = Lat. colo (incolo), Gr. πέλομαι, πόλος (also αἰπόλος goat-herd & βουκόλος cowherd = gocara); also P. cakka, q. v. A doublet of **car** is **cal**, see calati. Dhtp 243 expl^{d} **car** by " gati-bhakkhanesu "] to move about, to " live and move," to behave, to be. — *Imper.* act. cara (J 1.152), carā (metri causa, J III.393); — imper. med. carassu (Sn 696), pl. carāmase (= exhortative, Sn 32); — *ppr.* caranto (J 1.152; PvA 14) & caraṃ (Sn 151; Dh 61, 305; It 117); med. caramāna (Vin 1.83; Pv 1.10^{10}; PvA 160); — *pot.* careyya (Sn 45, 386, 1065; Dh 142, 328) & care (Sn 35; Dh 49, 168, 329; It 120); — *fut.* carissati (M 1.428); — *aor.* sg. 1st

acariŋ (S III.29), acārisaŋ (Pv III.9[5]), 3rd acari (Sn 344), acāri (Sn 354; Dh 326); cari (J II.133). — pl. 3rd acariŋsu (Sn 809), acārisuŋ (Sn 284); cariŋsu (Sn 289), acaruŋ (Sn 289), acāruŋ (J VI.114); — *inf.* carituŋ (caritu-kāma J II.103); — *ger.* caritvā (J I.50) & caritvāna (Sn 816); — *pp.* ciṇṇa (q. v.) — *Caus.* cāreti (= Denom. of cara), pp. carita. 2nd caus. carāpeti (q. v.). — See also cara, caraṇa, cariyā, cāraka, cārikā, cārin.

Meaning: 1. Lit. (a) to move about, to walk, travel, etc.; almost synon. with gacchati in contrast to tiṭṭhati to stand still; cp. phrase carañ vā yadi vā tiṭṭhaŋ nisinno udāhu sayaŋ It 117 (walking, standing, sitting, reclining; the four iriyāpathā); care tiṭṭhe acche saye It 120; tiṭṭhaŋ caraŋ nisinno vā sayāno vā Sn 151. — Defined as "catūhi iriyāpathehi vicarati" (i. e. more generally applied as "behaviour," irrespective of position) DhA II.36. Expl. constantly by series viharati iriyati vattati pāleti yapeti yāpeti Nd[2] 237. — carāmi loke I move about (= I live) in the world Sn 25, 455; agiho c. I lead a homeless life Sn 456, 464; eko c. he keeps to himself Sn 35, 956; Dh 305, 329; sato c. he is mindful Sn 1054, 1085; gocaraŋ gaṇhanto c. to walk about grazing (see below) J III.275; gavesanto c. to look for J I.61. — (b) With definition of a purpose: piṇḍāya c. to go for alms (gāmaŋ to the village) Sn 386; bhikkhāya c. id. J III.82. — With acc. (in etymol. constr.) to undertake, set out for, undergo, or simply to perform, to do. Either with c. cārikaŋ to wander about, to travel: Vin I.83; S I.305 (applied: "walk ye a walk"); Sn 92; Dh 326; PvA 14 (janapada-cārikaŋ), 160 (pabbata-c° wandering over the mountains); or with cāraŋ: piṇḍa-c.° carati to perform the begging-round Sn 414; or with caritaŋ: duccaritaŋ c. to lead a bad life Sn 665 (see carita). Also with acc. of similar meaning, as esanaŋ c. to beg Th 1, 123; vadhaŋ c. to kill Th 1, 138; dukkhaŋ c. to undergo pain S I.210. — (c) In pregnant sense: to go out for food, to graze (as gocaraŋ c. to pasture, see gocara). Appl. to cows: caranti gāvo Sn 20; J III.479; or to the bhikkhu: Pv I.10[10] (bh. caramāno = bhikkhāya c. PvA 51); Sn 386 (vikāle na c. buddhā: the Buddhas do not graze at the wrong time). — 2. Appl[d] meaning: (a) abs. to behave, conduct oneself Sn 1080; J VI.114; Miln 25 (kāmesu micchā c. to commit immorality). — (b) with obj. to practise, exercise, lead a life: brahmacariyaŋ c. to lead a life of purity Vin I.17; Sn 289, 566, 1128; dhammañ c. to walk in righteousness J I.152; sucaritaŋ c. to act rightly, duccaritaŋ c. to act perversely S I.94; Dh 231.

Carahi (adv.) [Sk. tarhi; with change t > c due to analogy with °ci (°cid) in comb[n] with interr.] then, therefore, now, esp. after interr. pron.: ko carahi jānāti who then knows? Sn 990; kathañ carahi jānemu how then shall we know? Sn 999; kiñ c. A V.194. — Vin I.36; II.292; Sn 988; J III.312; Miln 25; DA I.289.

Carāpeti [Caus. II. of carati] to cause to move, to make go J I.267 (bheriŋ c. to have the drum beaten); PvA 75 (do.); DhA I.398 (to circulate). As cārāpeti J V.510 (bheriŋ).

Carita [pp. of cāreti, see cara & carati] 1. (adj.) going, moving, being like, behaving (-°) J VI.313; Miln 92 (rāgac° = ratta): Vism 105, 114 (rāga°, dosa°, moha°, etc.). — 2. (nt.) action, behaviour, living Dh 330 (ekassa c. living alone); Ps I.124; Miln 178. See also carati 1[b], 2[b]. Esp. freq. with su° and duc°: good, right, proper or (nt.) good action, right conduct & the opposite; e. g. sucarita Dh 168, 231; PvA 12, 71, 120; duccarita A I.146; II.85, 141; III.267, 352; D III 111, 214; Dh 169, Sn 665; Pv 1.9[4] (°ŋ caritvā), etc. See also kāya° vacī° mano° under kāya.

Caritaka (nt.) conduct (= carita[2]) Th 1, 36.

Caritar [n. agent to cāreti, cp. carita] walking, performing (c. acc.) M I.77.

Carima (adj.) [Vedic carama, Gr. τέλος end, πάλαι a long time (ago)] subsequent, last (opp. pubba) Th 2, 203; It 18; J V.120. — **acarima** not later (apubba ac° simultaneously) D I.185; M III.65; Pug. 13.

-**bhava** the last rebirth (in Saŋsāra, with ref. to Arahantship) ThA 260, cp. caramabhavika in Divy (freq.) & next.

Carimaka (adj.) last (= carima) M I.426; Nd[2] 569[b] (°viññāṇassa nirodha, the destruction of the last conscious state, of the death of an Arahant); Vism 291.

Cariya (nt.) & cariyā (f.) [from **car**, carati] (mostly -°) conduct, behaviour, state of, life of. Three cariyās at Ps I.79; six at Vism 101; eight at Ps II.19 sq., 225 & four sets of eight in detail at Nd[2] 237[b]. Very freq. in dhamma° & brahma°, a good walk of life, proper conduct, chastity — eka° living alone Sn 820; unchā° begging J II.272; III.37; bhikkhā° a life of begging Sn 700; nagga° nakedness Dh 141. — See also carati 2[b]. In cpds. cariyā°.

-**piṭaka** the last book in the Khuddaka-nikāya; -**manussa** a spy, an outpost J III.361 (v. l. cārika°).

Cala (adj.) [see calati] moving, quivering; unsteady, fickle, transient S IV.68 (dhammā calā c' eva vyayā ca aniccā, etc.); J II.299; III.381; V.345; Miln 93, 418; Sdhp 430, 494. -**acala** steadfast, immovable S I.232; J I.71 (ṭṭhāna); Vv 51[4] (°ṭṭhāna = Ep. of Nibbāna); acalaŋ sukhaŋ (= Nibbāna) Th 2, 350; cp. **niccala** motionless DhA III.38.

-**ācala** [intens. redupl.] moving to & fro, in constant motion, unsteady J IV.494, 498 (= cañcala); Miln 92; (cp. Divy 180, 281); -**kkaku** having a quivering hump J III.380 IV.330 (= calamānakakudha or calakakudha).

Calaka[1] (m.) a camp marshal, adjutant D I.51≈(in list of various occupations); A IV.107 sq.

Calaka[2] (nt.) [perhaps from **carv** to chew; but Sk. carvana, chewing, is not found in the specific sense of P. calaka. Cp. ucchiṭṭha and cuṇṇa] a piece of meat thrown away after having been chewed Vin II.115; IV.266 (= vighāsa); VvA 222 (°aṭṭhikāni meat-remnants & bones).

Calati [Dhtp 251 kampana, to shake. Perhaps connected with **car**, carati] to move, stir, be agitated, tremble, be confused, waver S I.107; Sn 752; J I.303 (kileso cali); III.188 (macchā c.) Miln 260. — ppr. med. calamāna J IV.331. — Esp. freq. in expression kammaja-vātā caliŋsu the labour-pains began to stir J I.52; VI.485. — pp. calita (q. v.). — caus. **caleti** to shake S I.109.

Calana (adj. & nt.) shaking, trembling, vibrating; excitement J III.188; DhsA 72. — f. **calanī** (quick, + **laṅghī**) a kind of antelope J VI.537.

Calita (adj.) [pp. of calati] wavering, unsteady Miln 93, 251; Vism 113; VvA 177. — (nt.) Sn p. 146.

Cavati [Vedic cyavate from **cyu** = Gr. σεύω; cp. Lat. cieo, cio, sollicitus, Gr. κίω, κινέω, Goth. haitan = Ohg. heizan] to move, get into motion, shift, to fall away, decease, esp. to pass from one state of existence into another D I.14 (sañsaranti c° upapajjanti, cp. DA I.105); Kh VIII.4 (= KhA 220: apeti vigacchati acetano pi samāno puññakkhaya-vasena aññaŋ ṭhānaŋ gacchati); It 99 = Nd[2] 235[2] (satte cavamāne upapajjamāne); It 77 (devo deva-kāyā c. "the god falls from the assembly of gods"), Sn 1073 for bhavetha (= Nd[2] 238;) PvA 10. Caus. cāveti: inf. cāvetuŋ S I.128 sq., 134 (°kāma.) — pp. cuta (q. v.), see also cuti.

Cavana (nt.) [from cavati] shifting, moving, passing away, only in °**dhamma** doomed to fall, destined to decease D I.18, 19; III.31, 33; M I.326; It 76; J IV.484; VI.482 (°dhammatā).

Cavanatā (f.) state of shifting, removal S II.3≈(cuti+); M I.49 (id.).

Cāga [from cajati, to give up, Vedic **tyaj**. Cp. Sk. tyāga] (a) abandoning, giving up, renunciation Vin I.10; S III.13, 26, 158; M I.486; A I.299. More freq. as: (b) liberality, generosity, munificence (n.) generous, munificent (adj.): sīlasampanno saddho purisapuggalo sabbe maccharino loke cāgena atirocati "he who is virtuous & religious excels all stingy people in generosity" A III.34. In freq. combns e. g. sacca dama dhiti c. Sn 188=S I.215; sacca dama c. khanti Sn 189=S I.215; mutta° (adj.) liberal, munificent, S V.351=392. °paribhāvita citta "a heart bent on giving" S V.369. In this sense cāga forms one of the (3, 4, 5 or 7) noble treasures of a man (cp. the Catholic treasure of grace & see °dhana below), viz. (as 5) saddhā, sīla, suta, cāga, paññā (faith, virtue, right knowledge, liberality, wisdom) S I.232; A I.210; III.80=S IV.250; M III.99; D III.164, 165; cp. A I.152=III.44; (as 4: the last minus suta) S V.395; A II.62 (sama°); (as 3) saddhā, sīla, cāga J II.112; (as 7) ajjhesanā, tapo, sīla, sacca, cāga, sati, mati J II.327; cp. śīla-śruta-tyāga Itm 31[1]. — PvA 30, 120; Sdhp 214, 323. See also anussati & anussarati.

-adhiṭṭhāna the resolution of generosity, as one of the 4: paññā°, sacca°, c°., upasama° D III.229; **-anussati** generosity A I.30; V.331; D III.250, 280; Vism 197; **-kathā** talk about munificence A III.181; **-dhana** the treasure of the good gift, as one of the 7 riches or blessings, the ariya-dhanāni, viz. saddhā, sīla, hiri, ottappa, suta, c., paññā D III.163, 251.; A IV.5; VvA 113; as one of 5 (see above) A III.53; **-sampadā** (& sampanna) the blessing of (or blessed with) the virtue of munificence A I.62; II.66; III.53; IV.221, etc.

Cāgavant (adj.) generous A III.183; IV.217, 220; Pug 24.

Cāgin (adj.) giving up, sacrificing, resigning Sn 719 (kāma°).

Cāṭi (f.) [cp. Hindī cāṭā] 1. a jar, vessel, pot J I.199; 302 (pānīya°); III.277 (madhu° honey jar); DhA I.394 (tela° oil tank); VvA 76 (sālibhatta° holding a meal of rice).— 2. a measure of capacity J II.404; IV.343. — 3. a large vessel of the tank type used for living in Vin I.153.

-pañjara a cage made of, or of the form of a large earthen jar, wherein a man could lie in ambush J V.372, 385; **-pāla** (nt.) an earthenware shield (?) J V.373 (=kīṭa).

Cāṭu [cp. cāru] pleasant, polite in °kammatā politeness, flattery Miln 370 (cp. Sk. cāṭukāra); cāṭu-kamyatā Vbh 246; Vism 17, 23, 27; KhA 236.

Cātur° (and cātu°) [see catur] consisting of four. Only in cpds. viz.

-(r)anta (adj.) "of our ends," i. e. covering or belonging to the 4 points of the compass, all-encircling. Ep. of the earth: J II.343 (paṭhavī); IV.309 (mahī) -(n-m.) one who rules over the 4 points; i. e. over the whole world (of a Cakkavattin) D I.88 (cp. DA I.249); II.16; Sn 552. See also Sp. AvS II.111, n. 2; **-kummāsa** sour gruel with four ingredients VvA 308; **-(d)dasī** (f.) [to catuddasa fourteen] the 14th day of the lunar half month A I.141. PvA 55; VvA 71, 99, 129. With pañcadasī, aṭṭhamī & pāṭihāriyapakkha at Sn 402; Vv 15[3]. °dasika belonging to the 14th day at Vin IV.315; **-(d)disa** (adj.) belonging to, or comprising the four quarters, appld to a man of humanitarian mind Sn 42 ("showing universal love," see Nd[2] 239); cp. RV X.136. Esp. appld to the bhikkhu-sangha "the universal congregation of bhikkhus" Vin I 305; II.147; D I.145; J I.93; Pv II.2[8]; III.2[14] (expld PvA 185 by catūhi disāhi āgata-bhikkhu-sangha). Cp. AvŚ I.266; II.109; **-(d)dīpa** of four continents: rājā Th 2, 486; cp. M Vastu I.108, 114; **-(d)dīpaka** sweeping over the whole earth (of a storm) Vin I.290, cp. J IV.314 & AvŚ I.258; **-(b)bedā** (pl.) the four Vedas Miln 3; **-māsin** of 4 months; f. °inī Vin I.155; D I.47; M III.79; DA I.139, cp. komudī; **-(m)mahāpatha** the place where 4 roads cross, a cross-road D I.102, 194=243; M I.124; III.91; cp. catu°. **-(m)mahābhūtika** consisting of the 4 great elements (of kāya) D I.34, 55, 186, 195; S II.94 sq.; Miln 379; cp. Av.Ś II.191 & Sk. cāturbhautika; **-(m)mahārājikā** (pl.) (sc. devā) the retinue of the Four Kings, inhabiting the lowest of the 6 devalokas Vin I.12; III.18; D I.215; Nd[2] 307 (under devā); J II.311 (deva-loka); **-yāma** (saṃvara) fourfold restraint (see yāma) D I.57, 58 (cp. DA I.167); III.48 sq.; S I.66; M I.377; Vism 416. Cp. *Dial.* I.75 n[1].

Cāturiya (nt.) [cp. catura+iya] skill, cleverness, shrewdness J III.267; VI.410; ThA, 227; Vbh 551; Vism 104; Dāvs V.30.

Cāpa (m. nt.) [Sk. cāpa, from *qēp tremble, cp. capala wavering, quivering] a bow M I.429 (opposed to kodaṇḍa); Dh 156 (°ātikhīṇa shot from the bow, cp. DhA III.132), 320 (abl. cāpāto metri causa); J IV.272; V.400; Miln 105 (daḷha°), 352.

-koṭi the end of a bow VvA 261; **nāḷi** (f.) a bow-case J II.88; **-lasuṇa** (nt.) a kind of garlic Vin IV.259.

Cāpalla (nt.) [Der. fr. capala, Sk. cāpalya] fickleness D I.115 (=DA I.286). Also as cāpalya M I.470; Vbh 351; Vism 106.

Cāmara (nt.) [from camara] a chowrie, the tail of bos grunniens used as a whisk Sn 688; Vv 64[3]; J VI.510; VvA 271, 276. Cpd. cāmarī-gāhaka J VI.218 (anka) a hook holding the whisk.

Cāmīkara (nt.). [Deriv. unknown. Sk. cāmīkara] gold VvA 12, 13, 166.

Cāyati [fr. **ci**] to honour, only in cpd. -apacāyati (q. v.). The Dhtp (237) defines the root **cāy** by pūjā.

Cāra [fr. **car** carati to move about] motion, walking, going; doing, behaviour, action, process Miln 162 (+vihāra); Dhs 8=85 (=vicāra); DhsA 167. Usually -° (n. & adj.): kāma° going at will J IV.261; pamāda° a slothful life J I.9; piṇḍa° alms-begging Sn 414, 708; sabbaratti° wandering all night S I.201; samavattha° A III.257. See also carati 1[b].

-vihāra doing & behaving, i. e. good conduct J II.232; Dpvs. VI.38; cp. Miln 162 (above).

Cāraka (cārika) (adj.) wandering about, living, going, behaving, always -°, like ākāsa°, niketa°, pure° (see pubbangama), vana°, — f. cārikā journey, wandering, esp. as cārikaṃ carati to go on alms-pilgrimage (see carati 1[b]) Vin I.83; J I.82; II.286; Dh 326; Miln 14, 22; °ṃ pakkamati to set out wandering J I.87; Miln 16. — S I.199; M I.117; A III.257; DA I.239 sq. (in detail on two cārikā); VvA 165; EnA 295 (unchā°).

Cāraṇa (adj.) = cāraka Sn 162 (saṃsuddha°).

Cāraṇika v.v. vāraṇika Th I.1129? a little play, masque, cp. Sk cāraṇa & Mrs. Rh. D. *Pss of the Brethren*, 419.

Cāritta (nt.) [From **car**] practice, proceeding, manner of acting, conduct J I.90, 367; II.277 (loka°); V.285 (vanka°); Miln 133; VvA 31. — cārittaṃ āpajjati to mix with, to call on, to have intercourse with (c loc.) M I.470; S II.270 (kulesu); M I.287 = III.46 (kāmesu); J III.46 (rakkhita-gopitesu).

-vāritta manner of acting & avoiding J III.195, cp. Th I, 591; Vism 10. See on their mutual relation Vism 11; **-sīla** code of morality VvA 37.

Cārin (only -°) (adj.) walking, living, experiencing; behaving, acting, practising. (a) lit. asanga° S I.199; akāla° Sn 386; ambu° Sn 62; vihangapatha° Sdhp 241; sapadāna° M I.30; Sn 65; pariyanta° Sn 904. — (b) fig. anudhamma° Sn 69; āgu° A II.240; A III.163; dhamma° Miln 19; brahma° Sn 695; manāpa° Vv 31[4]; yata° Sn 971; sama° Miln 19. See all s. v. & cp. caṭu.

Cāru (adj.) [Vedic cāru & cāyu to *qe-*qā, as in kāma, Lat. carus, etc., see under kāma] charming, desirable, pleasant, beautiful J VI.481; Miln 201; Sdhp 428, 512; VvA 36 (=vaggu), sucāru S I.181; Pv II.12[12] (=suṭṭhu-manorama).
-**dassana** lovely to behold Sn 548; J VI.449 (expl. on p. 450 as: cāru vuccati suvaṇṇaŋ=suvaṇṇadassana); VI.579; f. -ī Pv III.6[14].

Cāreti [Denom. fr. cara; cp. carati] to set going, to pasture, feed, preserve: indriyāni c. to feast one's senses (cp. Ger. "augenweide") PvA 58; khantiŋ c. to feed meekness DA I.277; olambakaŋ cārento drooping J I.174; Pass. ppr. cāriyamāna being handed round J IV.2 (not vā°)—pp. carita. — Cp. vi°.

Cāla [From calati] shaking, a shock, only in bhūmi° earthquake.

Cālanī (f.) [to cālana of calaka²] a pestle, a mortar Vin I.202 (in cuṇṇa° & dussa°, cp. saṇha).

Cāleti [caus. of calati] to move, to shake J V.40; to scatter J I.71 (tiṇāni); to sift Vin I.202.

Cāvanā (f.) moving, shifting, disappearance Vin III.112 (ṭhānato); Sdhp 61 (id.).

Cāveti [caus. of cavati] to bring to fall, move, drive away; disturb, distract A IV.343 (samādhimhā); J 1.60 (inf. cāvetu-kāma); II.329 (jhānā, abl.). Aor. acāvayi (prohib.) Sn 442 (ṭhānā).

Ci (cid in Sandhi) [Vedic cid nom. nt. to interr. base *qu̯i (as in Gr. τίς, Lat. quis, Goth. hvi-leiks, see ki°, cp. ka°, ku°), = Gr. τι(δ), Lat. quid & quid(d)em, Av. ciṯ (cp. tad, yad, kad beside taŋ, yaŋ, kiŋ)] indef. interr. particle (always -°), in koci (=Sk. kaścid) whoever, kiñci (kincid-eva) whatever, kadāci at some time or any time, etc. (q. v.), see also ca, cana, ce.

Cikicchati [Sk. cikitsati, Desid. of cit, cinteti. Cp. vicikicchā], usually tikicchati to reflect, think over, intend, aim at. Pp. cikicchita KhA 188 (in explⁿ of vicikicchita q. v.).

Cikkhati (cikkhanā, etc.) [Freq. of khyā. Dhtp 19: cikkh= vacane] to tell, to announce: see ā° & paṭisaŋ°.

Cikkhalla (nt.) [Sk. cikkaṇa & cikkala, slippery+ya] mud, mire, swamp; often with udaka°. Vin I.253; II.120, 159, 291; III.41; A III.394; J I.196; Miln 286, 311, 397; PvA 102, 189, 215. — (adj.) Vin II.221; IV.312; Pv IV.1[16]; Miln 286.

Cikkhallavant (adj.) muddy PvA 225.

Cikkhassati [Desid. of kṣar = Sk. cikṣariṣati] to wish to drop, to ooze out Miln 152 (°ssanto), see Kern. *Toev.* II.139 & Morris, *J.P.T.S.* 1884, 87.

Cingulaka (& °ika) (m. nt.) 1. a kind of plant Sn 239 (=kaṇavīra-pupphasaṇṭhāna-sīsa SnA 283). — 2. a toy windmill, made of palm-leaves, etc. (DA 1.86: tāla-paṇṇādīhi kataŋ vātappahārena paribbhamana-cakkaŋ) Vin II.10; D I.6 M I.266; A V.203; Miln 229.

Cingulāyati [Denom. fr. cingula] to twirl round, to revolve like a windmill A I.112.

Ciccitāyati [onomat. cp. ciṭiciṭāyati] to hiss, fizz, sizzle (always combᵈ with ciṭiciṭāyati) Vin I.225; S I.169; Sn p. 15; Pug 36; Miln 258 sq.

Ciccitāyana (nt.) fizzing Vism 408 (°sadda).

Ciñcā (f.) [Sk. ciñcā & tintiḍikā] the tamarind tree J V.38 (°vana), SnA 78.

Ciṭi-ciṭi [redupl. interj.] fizz' DA I.137.

Ciṭiciṭāyati see ciccitāyati; Vin I.225; cp. Divy 606.

Ciṇṇa [pp. of carati] travelled over, resorted to, made a habit of; done, performed, practised J III.541; Miln 360. — su° well performed, accomplished S I.42=214=Sn 181; Pv III.5[6]. — Cp. ā°, pari°, vi°.
-**ṭṭhāna** the place where one is wont to go J II.159; -**mānatta** one who performs the Mānatta Vin IV.242; -**vasin** one who has reached mastership in (c. loc.) ThA 74; Vism 154, 158, 164, 169, 331 sq., 376; der. -**vāsibhāva** DhsA 167 (read vasī°).

Ciṇṇatta (nt.) [Der. fr. ciṇṇa] custom, habit Miln 57, 105.

Cita [pp. of cināti] heaped; lined or faced with (cp. citaka²) pokkharaṇiyo iṭṭhakāhi citā D II.178, cp. Vin II.123.
-antaraŋsa "one whose shoulder-hole is heaped up," one who has the shoulders well filled out (Ep. of a Mahāpurisa) D II.18; III.144, 164.

Citaka & **Citakā** (f.) [from ci, cināti to heap up].— 1. a heap, a pile, esp. a funeral pile; a tumulus D II.163; cp. II.10[11]. J I.255; V.488; VI.559, 576; DA I.6; DhA I.69; II.240; VvA 234; PvA 39. — 2. (adj.) inlaid: suvaṇṇa°, with gold J VI.218 (=°khacita).

Citi (f.) [From ci, cināti, to heap up] a heap, made of bricks J VI.204 (city-avayata-piṭṭhikā). See also cetiya.

Cittaka (nt.) [to citta¹] a sectarian mark on the forehead in °dhara-kumma a tortoise bearing this mark, a land-tortoise Miln 364, 408, cp. *Miln trsl.* II.352.

Citta¹ & **Citra** (adj.) [to cetati; *(s)qait to shine, to be bright, cp. Sk. citra, Sk. P. ketu, Av. ciþrō, Lat. caelum, Ags. hador, Ohg. heitar, see also citta²] variegated, manifold, beautiful; tasty, sweet, spiced (of cakes), J IV.30 (geṇḍuka); Dh 171 (rājaratha); Vv 47[9]; Pv II.11[2] (aneka°); IV.3[13] (pūvā=madhurā PvA 251). **Citta** (nt.) painting Th I, 674. — Sn 50 (kāmā=Nd² 240 nānāvaṇṇā), 251 (gāthā); J V.196 (geṇḍuka), 241 VI.218. — sucitta gaily coloured or dressed S I.226 (b); Dh 151 (rājaratha); Pv I.10[9] (vimāna).
-**akkhara** (adj.) with beautiful vowels S II.267 (Cp. °vyañjana); -**attharaka** a variegated carpet DA I.256; -**āgāra** a painted house, i. e. furnished with pictures; a picture gallery Vin III.298; -**upāhana** a gaily coloured sandal D I.7≈; -**kata** adorned, dressed up M II.64= Dh 147=Th I, 769; DhA III.109 (=vicitta); -**katha** (adj.) =next S I.199 (+bahussuta); -**kathin** a brilliant speaker, a wise speaker, an orator, preacher. Freq. combᵈ w. bahussuta (of wide knowledge, learned), e. g. paṇḍita . . . medhāvin kalyāṇapaṭibhāna S IV.375, samaṇa bahussuta c. uḷāra Vv 84[26]. — A III.58; J I.148; Miln I, 21; -**kathika**=°kathin A I.24; Th 2, 449 (+bahussuta), explᵈ at ThA 281 by cittadhammakatha; -**kamma** decoration, ornamentation, painting J IV.408; VI.333; Miln 278; Vism 306; PvA 147; DhsA 334; (m.) a painter J VI.481; -**kāra** a painter, a decorator (cp. rajaka) S II.101=III.152; Th 2, 255; J VI.333; -**chatta** at J VI.540 to be changed into °patta; -**patta** (adj.) having variegated wings J VI.540, 590; -**pāṭalī** (f.) N. of a plant (the "pied" trumpet-flower) in the world of Asuras J I.202; DhA I.280; -**pekhuna** having coloured wings J I.207; VI.539; -**bimba** (-mukhi) (a woman whose face is) like a painted image J V.452 (cp cittakata); -**miga** the spotted antelope J VI.538; -**rūpa** (nt.) a wonder, something wonderful J VI.512; as adv. °ŋ (to citta²?) easily Vin II.78=III.161; IV.177, 232; -**latā** the plant Rubia Munjista J VI.278; °*vana* the R.M. grove, one of Indra's gardens [Sk. caitraratha] J I.52, 104; II.188; VI.590, etc.; -**vitāna** a bright canopy DhA IV.14; -**vyañjana** (adj.) with beautiful consonants (cp. °akkhara) S II.267 A I.73=III.107; -**sāṇī** variegated cloth J II.290; DhA IV.14; -**sālā** a painted room or picture gallery DA I.253; -**sibbana** with fine sewing; a cover of various embroidery Sn 304= J IV.395; J VI.218.

Citta² (nt.) [Sk. citta, orig. pp. of cinteti, **cit**, cp. yutta > yuñjati, mutta > muñcati. On etym. from **cit**, see cinteti].

I. *Meaning*: the heart (psychologically), i. e. the centre & focus of man's emotional nature as well as that intellectual element which inheres in & accompanies its manifestations; i. e. thought. In this wise citta denotes both the agent & that which is enacted (see kamma II. introd.), for in Indian Psychology citta is the seat & organ of thought (cetasā cinteti; cp. Gr. φρήν, although on the whole it corresponds more to the Homeric θυμός). As in the verb (cinteti) there are two stems closely allied and almost inseparable in meaning (see § III.), viz. cit & cet (citta & cetas); cp. ye should restrain, curb, subdue citta by ceto, M I.120, 242 (cp. attanā coday' attānaŋ Dhp 379 f.); cetasā cittaŋ samannesati S I.194 (cp. cetasā cittaŋ samannesati S I.194). In their general use there is no distinction to be made between the two (see § III.). — The meaning of citta is best understood when explaining it by expressions familiar to us, as: with all my heart; heart and soul; I have no heart to do it; blessed are the pure in heart; singleness of heart (cp. ekagga); all of which emphasize the emotional & conative side or "thought" more than its mental & rational side (for which see manas & viññāṇa). It may therefore be rendered by intention, impulse, design; mood, disposition, state of mind, reaction to impressions. It is only in later scholastic lgg. that we are justified in applying the term "thought" in its technical sense. It needs to be pointed out, as complementary to this view, that citta nearly always occurs in the singular (= heart), & out of 150 cases in the Nikāyas only 3 times in the plural (= thoughts). The substantiality of citta (cetas) is also evident from its connection with kamma (heart as source of action), kāma & the senses in general. — On the whole subject see Mrs. Rh. D. *Buddh. Psych. Eth.* introd. & *Bud. Psy.* ch. II.

II. *Cases of citta* (cetas), their relation & frequency (enum^d for gram. purposes). — The paradigma is (numbers denoting %, not including cpds.): Nom. cittaŋ; Gen. (Dat.) cetaso (44) & cittassa (9); Instr. cetasā (42) & cittena (3); Loc. citte (2) & cittamhi (2). — Nom. cittaŋ (see below). Gen. cittassa only (of older passages) in c° upakkileso S III.232; V.92; A I.207; c° damatho Dh 35 & c° vasena M I.214; III.156. Instr. cittena only in S I. viz. cittena nīyati loko p. 39; upakkiliṭṭha° p. 179; asallīnena c° p. 159. Loc. citte only as loc. abs. in samāhite citte (see below) & in citte vyāpanne kāyakammam pi v. hoti A I.162; cittamhi only S I.129 & cittasmiŋ only S I.132. — Plural only in Nom. cittāni in one phrase: āsavehi cittāni (vi) muccinsu "they purified their hearts from intoxications" Vin I.35; S III.132; IV.20; Sn p. 149; besides this in scholastic works = thoughts, e. g. Vbh 403 (satta cittāni).

III. *Citta & cetas* in promiscuous application. There is no cogent evidence of a clear separation of their respective fields of meaning; a few cases indicate the rôle of cetas as seat of citta, whereas most of them show no distinction. There are cpds. having both citta° & ceto° in identical meanings (see e. g. citta-samādhi & ceto°), others show a preference for either one or the other, as ceto is preferred in ceto-khila & ceto-vimutti (but: vimutta-citta), whereas citta is restricted to comb^n w. upakkilesa, etc. The foll. sentences will illustrate this. Vivaṭena cetasā sappabhāsaŋ cittaŋ bhāveti "with open heart he contemplates a radiant thought" S V.263 = D III.223 = A IV.86; cetasā cittaŋ samannesati vippamuttaŋ "with his heart he scrutinizes their pure mind" S I.194; vigatābhijjhena cetasā is followed by abhijjāya cittaŋ parisodheti D III.49; anupārambhacitto bhabbo cetaso vikkhepaŋ pahātuŋ A V.149; cetaso vūpasamo foll. by vūpasanta-citto A I.4; samāhite citte foll. by ceto-samādhi D I.13≈; cittaŋ paduṭṭhaŋ foll. by ceto-padosa A I.8; cp. It. 12, 13; cetaso tato cittaŋ nivāraye "a desire of his heart he shall exclude from this" S IV.195.

IV. *Citta in its relation to other terms* referring to mental processes.

1. citta ≈ hadaya, the heart as incorporating man's personality: hadayaŋ phaleyya, cittavikkhepaŋ pāpuṇeyya (break his heart, upset his reason) S I.126; cittaŋ te khipissāmi hadayan te phālessāmi id. S I.207, 214; Sn p. 32; kāmarāgena cittaŋ me pariḍayhati S I.188 > nibbāpehi me hadaya-pariḷāhaŋ Miln 318 ("my heart is on fire"); cp. abhinibbutatto Sn 343 = apariḍayhamāna-citto SnA 347; cittaŋ adhiṭṭhahati to set one's heart on, to wish DhA I.327.

2. c. as *mental status*, contrasted to (a) *physical* status: citta > kāya, e. g. kilanta° weary in body & mind D I.20 = III.32; ātura° S III.2-5; nikaṭṭha° A II.137; ṭhita° steadfast in body & soul (cp. ṭhitatta) S V.74; °passaddhi quiet of body & soul S V.66. The Commentators distinguish those six pairs of the saṅkhārākkhandha, or the cetasikas: citta-kāya-passaddhi, -lahutā, etc. as quiet, buoyancy, etc., of (a) the viññāṇakkhandha (consciousness), (b) the other 3 mental khandhas, making up the nāma-kāya (DhsA 150 on Dhs. 62: *Compendium of Phil.* 96, *n.* 3); passaddha° D III.241, 288. — (b) *intellectual* status: citta > manas & viññāṇa (mind > thought & understanding). These three constitute the invisible energizer of the body, alias mind in its manifestations: yañ ca vuccati cittan ti vā mano ti vā viññāṇan ti vā: (α) ayaŋ attā nicco dhuvo, etc., D I.21; (β) tatr' assutavā puthujjano n' ālaŋ nibbinditυŋ, etc. S II.94; (γ) taŋ rattiyā ca divasassa ca añña-d-eva uppajjati aññaŋ nirujjhati S II.95, cf. ThA. i on 125. — Under ādesanā-pāṭihāriya (thought reading): evam pi te mano ittham pi te mano iti pi te cittaŋ (thus is your thought & thus your mind, i. e. habit of thinking) D I.213 = III.103; A I.170. — niccaŋ idaŋ c. niccaŋ idaŋ mano S I.53; cittena niyyati loko "by thoughts the world is led" S I.39 = A II.177 (cp. KS 55); apatiṭṭhita-citto ādina-manaso avyāpanna-cetaso S V.74; vyāpanna-citto paduṭṭha-manasan-kappo S III.93; paduṭṭha-citto = paduṭṭha-manaso PvA 34, 43.

3. c. as *emotional habitus*: (a) *active* = intention, contrasted or compared with: (α) will, c. as one of the four samādhis, viz. chanda, viriya, c., vīmaŋsā D III.77; S V.268; Vbh 288. — (β) action, c. as the source of kamma: citte vyāpanne kāyakammam pi vyāpannaŋ hoti "when the intention is evil, the deed is evil as well" A I.262; cittaŋ appamāṇaŋ . . . yaŋ kiñci pamāṇakataŋ kammaŋ, etc. A V.299. — Esp. in contrast to kāya & vācā, in triad kāyena vācāya cittena (in deed & speech & will otherwise as k. v. manasā, see under kāya III.) S II.231, 271 = IV.112. Similarly taŋ vācaŋ appahāya (cittaŋ°, diṭṭhiŋ°) S IV.319 = D III.13, 15; & under the constituents of the dakkhiṇeyya-sampatti as khetta-sampatti, citta°, payoga° (the recipient of the gift, the good-will, the means) VvA 30, 32. — (b) *passive* = mood, feelings, emotion, ranging with kāya & paññā under the (3) bhāvanā D III.219; S IV.111; A III.106; cp. M I.237; Nett 91; classed with kāya vedanā dhammā under the (4) satipaṭṭhānas D II.95, 100, 299 sq.; S V.114, etc. (see kāya cpds.). As part of the sīlakkhandha (with sīla ethics, paññā understanding) in adhisīla, etc. Vin V.181; Ps II.243; Vbh 325; cp. tisso sampadā, scil. sīla, citta, diṭṭhi (see sīla & cp. cetanā, cetasika) A I.269. — citta & paññā are frequently grouped together, e. g. S I.13 = 165; D III.269; Th I.125 sq. As feeling citta is contrasted with intellection in the group saññā c. diṭṭhi A II.52; Ps II.80; Vbh 376.

4. *Definitions of citta* (direct or implied): cittan ti viññāṇaŋ bhūmikavatthu-ārammaṇa-kiriyādi-cittatāya pan' etaŋ cittan ti vuttaŋ DhA I.228; cittan ti mano mānasaŋ KhA 153; cittaŋ manoviññāṇaŋ ti cittassa etaŋ vevacanaŋ Nett 54. yaŋ cittaŋ mano mānasaŋ hadayaŋ paṇḍaraŋ, etc. Dhs 6 = 111 (same for def. of

manindriya, under § 17; see *Buddh. Psych.*). As rūpâvacara citta at Vism 376.

V. *Citta in its range of semantical applications:* (1) *heart*, will, intention, etc. (see I.).

(a) heart as general status of sensory-emotional being; its relation to the senses (indriyāni). A steadfast & constrained heart is the sign of healthy emotional equilibrium, this presupposes the control over the senses; samādahaŋsu cittaŋ attano ujukaŋ akaŋsu, sārathī va nettāni gahetvā indriyāni rakkhanti paṇḍitā S I.26; ujugato-citto ariyasāvako A III.285; ṭhita c. S I.159≈; A III.377=IV.404 (+ānejjappatta); c. na kampati Sn 268; na vikampate S IV.71; opp. capalaŋ c. Dh 33; khitta° a heart unbalanced A II.52 (+visaññin); opp.: avikkhitta° A V.149; PvA 26; c. rakkhitaŋ mahato atthāya saŋvattati a guarded heart turns to great profit A I.7; similarly: c. dantaŋ, guttaŋ, saŋvutaŋ ibid. — cittaŋ rakkhetha medhāvī cittaŋ guttaŋ sukhāvahaŋ Dh 36; cakkhundriyaŋ asaŋvutassa viharato cittaŋ vyāsiñcati . . . rūpesu S IV.78; ye cittaŋ saññamessanti mokkhanti Mārabandhanā "from the fetters of Māra those are released who control their heart" Dh 37; pāpā cittaŋ nivāraye Dh 116; bhikkhuno c. kulesu na sajjati, gayhati, bajjhati S II.198 (cp. Schiller: "Nicht an die Güter hänge dein *Herz*").

(b) Contact with kāma & rāga: a lustful, worldly, craving heart. — (α) *kāmā:* kāmā mathenti cittaŋ Sn 50; S IV.210; kāmarāgena ḍayhāmi S I.188; kāme nâpekkhate cittaŋ Sn 435; mā te kāmaguṇe bhamassu cittaŋ Dh 371; manussakehi kāmehi cittaŋ vuṭṭhapetvā S V.409; na uḷāresu kāmaguṇesu bhogāya cittaŋ namati A IV.392; S I.92; kāmāsavā pi cittaŋ vimuccati A II.211, etc.; kāmesu c. na pakkhandati na ppasīdati na santiṭṭhati (my h. does not leap, sit or stand in cravings) D III.239; kāmesu tibbasārāgo vyāpannacitto S III.93; kāmāmise laggacitto (divide thus!) PvA 107. — (β) *rāgā:* rāgo cittaŋ anuddhaŋseti (defilement harasses his heart) S I.185; II.231=271; A II.126; III.393; rāga-pariyuṭṭhitaŋ c. hoti A III.285; sārattacitto S IV.73; viratta° S IV.74; Sn 235; PvA 168. — (γ) *various:* paṭibaddha — c. (fettered in the bonds of °) A IV.60; Sn 37, 65; PvA 46, 151, etc. — pariyādinna° (grasping, greedy), usually comb^d w. lābhena abhibhūta: S II.226, 228; IV.125; A IV.160; D III.249. — upakkiliṭṭha° (etc.) (defiled) S I.179; III.151, 232 sq.; V.92 (kāmacchando cittassa upakkileso); A I.207; V.93 sq. — otiṇṇa° fallen in love A III.67; SnA 322

(c) A heart, composed, concentrated, settled, self-controlled, mastered, constrained. — (α) c. pasīdati (pasanna-°c) (a heart full of grace, settled in faith) S I.98; A I.207; III.248; Sn 434; pasanna°: A IV.209, 213; Sn 316, 403, 690, cp. c. pakkhandati pasīdati S III.133; A III.245; also vippasanna°: S V.144; Sn 506; cp. vippasannena cetasā Pv I.10^{10} — (β) c. santiṭṭhati in set s. sannisīdati, ekodihoti, samādhiyati (cp. cetaso ekodibhāva) S II.273; IV.263; A II.94, 157. — (γ) c. samādhiyati (samāhita-c°, cp. ceto-samadhi quiescence) D I.13=III.30, 108; S I.120, 129, 188; IV.78=351; A I.164; II.211; III.17, 280; IV.177; Vbh 227; Vism 376, etc.—(δ) supatiṭṭhita-c° always in formula catūsu satipaṭṭhānesu-s-c°: S III.93; V.154; 301; D III.101; A V.195. — (ε) susaṇṭhita c. S V.74. — vasībhūta c. S I.132; A I.165. — danta c. Dh 35. — (d) "with purpose of heart," a heart set on, striving after, endeavouring, etc. — (α) cittaŋ namati (inclines his h. on, with dat: appossukkatāya S I.137); nekkhamma-ninna S III.233; viveka° D III.283; A IV.233; V.175. — (β) cittaŋ padahati (pa+dhā: προ-τίθητι) in phrase chandaŋ janeti vāyamati viriyaŋ ārabbhati c° ŋ paggaṇhāti padahati D III.221; A II.15=IV.462; S V.269; Nd^2 97; Nett 18. In the same sense pa-ni-dahati (in paṇidhi, paṇihita bent down on) (cp. ceto-paṇidhi) S I.133 (tattha) IV.309 (dup°); V.157; Dh 42=Ud 39; Dh 43 (sammā°).

(e) *An evil heart* ("out of heart proceed evil thoughts" Mk. 7, 21) — (α) paduṭṭha-c° (cp. ceto-padosa) D I.20= III.32; A I.8 (opp. pasanna-c°); IV.92; It 12, 13; Pv A 33, 43, etc. — (β) vyāpanna-c°: citte vyāpanne kāyakammam pi vyāpannaŋ hoti A I.262. Opp. a°: S IV.322; A II.220. — (γ) samoha-c° (+sarāga, etc.) D I.79; II.299; III.281; Vism 410, & passim.

(f) "*blessed are the pure in heart*," a pure, clean, purified (cp. Ger. geläutert), emancipated, free, detached heart. (α) mutta-c°, vimutta-c°, etc. (cp. cetaso vimokkho, ceto-vimutti, muttena cetasā), āsavehi cittāni mucciŋsu S III.132, etc.; vi° Sn p. 149. — vimutta: S I.28 (+subhāvita), 29, 46=52; III.45 (+viratta), 90; IV.236 (rāgā); Sn 23 (+sudanta); Nd^2 587. — suvimutta: S I.126, 141, 233; IV.164; A III.245; V.29; Sn 975 (+satimā). — (β) cittaŋ parisodheti M I.347; A II.211; S IV.104. — (γ) alīna c. (unstained) S I.159; A V.149; Sn 68; 717; Nd^2 97 (cp. cetaso līnatta).

(g) *good-will*, a loving thought, kindliness, tender-heartedness, love ("love the Lord with all your heart"). — (α) metta-c° usually in phrase mettacittaŋ bhāveti "to nourish the heart with loving thought," to produce good-will D I.167; S II.264; A I.10; V.81; Sn 507 (cp. mettā-sahagatena cetasā). — (β) bhāvita-c° "keep thy heart with all diligence" (Prov. 4, 23) S I.188 (+susamāhita); IV.294; V.369 (saddhā-paribhāvita); A I.6 (+bahulīkata, etc.); Sn 134 (=S I.188); Dh 89=S V.29; PvA 139.

(h) *a heart calmed*, allayed, passionless (santa° upasanta°) D III.49; S I.141; Sn 746.

(i) *a wieldy heart*, a heart ready & prepared for truth, an open & receptive mind: kalla°, mudu°, udagga°, pasanna° A IV.186; kalla° PvA 38 (sanctified); lahu° S I.201; udagga° Sn 689, 1028; S I.190 (+mudita); mudu° PvA 54.

(k) *Various phrases*. Abbhuta-cittajātā "while wonder filled their hearts" S I.178; evaŋcitto "in this state of mind" S II.199; Sn 985; cittam me Gotamo jānāti (G. knows my heart) S I.178; theyya-citto intending to steal Vin III.58; āraddha-citto of determined mind M I.414; S II.21, cp. 107; Sn p. 102; aññācittaŋ upaṭṭhāpeti S II.267; nānā° of varying mind J I.295; nihīnacitto low-minded PvA 107; nikaṭṭha° A II.137; āhata° A IV.460=V.18; supahata° S I.238 (cp. Miln 26); visankhāragata° Dh 154; sampanna° Sn 164; vibbhanta° S I.61=A I.70=II.30=III.391.

(2) *thought:* mā pāpakaŋ akusalaŋ cittaŋ cinteyyātha (do not think any evil thought) S V.418; na cittamattam pi (not even one thought) PvA 3; mama cittaŋ bhaveyya (I should think) PvA 40. For further instances see Dhs & Vbh Indexes & cp. cpds. See also remarks above (under I.). Citta likened to a monkey Vism 425.

-âdhipati the influence of thought (adj. °pateyya) Nett 16; Dhs 269, 359; DhsA 213. Commentators define c. here as javanacittuppāda, our "thought" in its specialized sense. *Compendium of Phil.* 177, n. 2. **-ânuparivattin** consecutive to thought Dhs 671, 772, 1522; **-ânupassanā** the critique of heart, adj. °ânupassin D II.299; III.221, 281; M I.59 & passim (cp. kāy°); **-āvila** disturbance of mind Nd^2 576 (°karaṇa); **-ujjukatā** rectitude of mind Dhs 51, 277, etc.; **-uppāda** the rise of a thought, i. e. intention, desire as theyya °ŋ uppādesi he had the intention to steal (a thought of theft) Vin III.56; — M I.43; III.45; J II.374; **-ekaggatā** "one-pointedness of mind," concentration Nett 15, 16; Vism 84, 137, 158; DhA III.425; ThA 75; cp. ekagga-citto A III.175; **-kali** a witch of a heart, a witch-like heart Th I, 356; **-kallatā** readiness of heart, preparedness of mind VvA 330; **-kilesa** stain of h. Dh 88 (DhA II.162=pañca nīvaraṇā); **-keḷisā** pastime of the mind Th I, 1010; **-kkhepa** derangement of the mind, madness Vin V.189=193 (ummāda+); A III.219 (ummāda+); DhA III.70 (=ummāda); PvA 39; Dh 138; cp. °vikkhepa; **-cetasika** belonging to heart & thought, i. e. mental state, thought, mind D I.213; Dhs 1022 (-dhammā, Mrs. Rh. D.: emotional, perceptual & synthetic states as well as those of intellect applied to sense-impressions), 1282; Ps 1.84; Miln 87; Vism 61, 84, 129, 337; -dubbhaka a rogue of a heart, a rogue-like heart Th 1, 214; -pakopana shaking or upsetting the mind It 84 (dosa); -pamaddin crushing the h. Th 2, 357 (=ThA 243; v. l. pamāthin & pamādin); -pariyāya the ways (i. e. behaviour) of the h. A v.160 (cp. ceto-paricca); -passaddhi calm of h., serenity of mind (cp. kāya°) S v.66; Dhs 62; -bhāvanā cultivation of the h. M III.149; -mala stain of h. PvA 17; -mudutā plasticity of mind (or thought) Dhs 62, 277, 325; -rucita after the heart's liking J 1.207; -rūpaŋ according to intention, as much as expected Vin 1.222; II.78; III.161; IV.177, 232; -lahutā buoyancy of thought Dhs 62, 323, 1283; Vism 465; -vikkhepa (cp. °kkhepa) madness S 1.126 (+ ummāda); Nett 27; Vism 34; -vippayutta disconnected with thought Dhs 1192, 1515; -visaŋsaṭṭha detached fr. thought Dhs 1194, 1517; -vūpasama allayment of one's h. S 1.46; -sankilesa (adj.) with impure heart (opp. c.-vodāna) S III.151; -saññatti conviction Miln 256; -santāpa "heart-burn," sorrow PvA 18 (=soka); -samādhi (cp. ceto-samādhi) concentration of mind, collectedness of thought, self-possession S IV.350; V.269; Vbh 218; -samodhāna adjustment, calming of thoughts ThA 45; -sampīḷana (adj.) h.-crushing (cp. °pamaddin & °pakopana) Nett 29 (domanassa). -sahabhū arising together with thought Dhs 670, 769, 1520. -hetuka (adj.) caused by thought Dhs 667, 767.

Citta[3] [cp. Sk. caitra, the first month of the year: March-April, orig. N. of the star Spica (in Virgo); see E. Plunket, *Ancient Calendars*, etc., pp. 134 sq., 171 sq.] N. of the month Chaitra PvA 135. Cp. Citra-māsa KhA 192.

CORRIGENDA.

TO PART I.

Page x, *under* 1*a add*: **Dukapaṭṭhāna**, P.T.S. 1906 (Dukp).

Tikapaṭṭhāna, 3 vols. P.T.S. 1921-23 (Tikp).

" 1*b* " **Papañca Sūdanī**, pt. I., P.T.S. 1922 (MA).

" xii, " 4 " Kirfel, W. Kosmographie der Inder Bonn & Leipzig 1920.

" B1 " Dukp = Dukapaṭṭhāna . . . 1*a*.

Tikp = Tikapaṭṭhāna . . . 1*a*.

Paṭṭh = Paṭṭhāna: see Duka° & Tika° . . . 1*a*.

" 42, column 2, *read* **Anuvāda** *for* **Anuvada**.

" 73, " 2, *under* Amassuka *read* J II.185 *for* 175.

" 86, " 1, " Avyāpajjha[1] *read* It 31 (abyābajjh') *for* abyābojjh'.

" 88, " 2, " Asi *read* (*under* cpds.): -māla (-kamma) sword-garland (-torture) J III.178; Davs III.35. Preferable to interpretation "sword-dirt"; see māla (mālā).

TO PART II.

Page 115, column 1, *after* Āsana *insert* Āsana[2] (?) eating Vism 116 (visam°, cp. visam-āsita Miln 302). See, however, māsana.

TO PART III.

Page 17, column 1, *exchange respective position of articles* Kamati *and* Kamaṇḍalu; *also write* Kamana *as* Kamaṇa.

" 24, " 1, *under* Karaṇa, in Note, *read passage as follows*: Karaṇa here . . . as by J VI.270, where it expls. kappitakesa-massu and J v. 309 & DhA 1.253, where massukamma takes the place of °karaṇa; and J III.314, where it is represented by massu-kutti (C.: massukiriya). Cp. also DA 1.137.

" 27, " 2, " Kalyāṇa *read* 5 kalyāṇāni *for* kalyāni.

TO PART IV.

Page 67, *for* kheḷākapa *read* kheḷāpaka . . . cp. āpaka. ? spittle-dribbler; cp. our 'windbag.'

CORRIGENDA

FURTHER CORRIGENDA TO PART I.

Page 22, column 2, *transfer* atta-kāma *to* attha°

,, 23, ,, 1, *under* attaniya *read* soul-likē *for* soul-lika.

,, 26, ,, 1, *under* adda³ *correct* Nd² 99⁶ *to* Nd² 199⁶, *and add*: The reading **allâvalepana** occurs at Nd² 40 (=S IV.187), & is perhaps to be preferred. The meaning is better to be given as "newly plastered."

,, 41, ,, 2, *under* anurakkhaṇa *read* Pug *for* Rug.

,, 79, ,, 2, *under* alla 2 *insert*: allâvalepana, *see* adda³.

TO PART II.

Page 93 should have heading **Ā** at top of page.

,, 98, column 1, *under* āṇi, last line, *read* five *for* fire.

,, 102, ,, 2, *under* āpaṇa *read* ā+ **paṇ**.

,, 103, ,, 1, *under* āpiyati *read* ṛ *for* ṇ.

,, 103, ,, 2, *under* ābhata *delete* "for yathābhūtaŋ," & *insert ref.* A II.71; It 12, 14 *with phrase* "yathābhataŋ as he has been reared (cp. J V.330[173] evaŋ kicchā bhaṭo)."

,, 103, ,, 2, *under* ābhāsa *delete* ref. M II.215.

,, 139, ,, 2, *under* upakārin *transfer* ref. M I.86 (= Nd² 199⁶) to art. upakārikā *in meani* "fortification."

THE PALI TEXT SOCIETY'S PALI-ENGLISH DICTIONARY

EDITED BY

T. W. RHYS DAVIDS F.B.A. D.Sc. Ph.D. LL.D. D.Litt.

and WILLIAM STEDE Ph.D.

Part IV (Cit—No)

PUBLISHED BY
THE PALI TEXT SOCIETY
LONDON

First published - - -	1923
Reprinted - - - -	1948
Reprinted - - - -	1952

Cittaka[a] & **Citraka**[b] 1. (adj.)[a] coloured J IV.464. — 2. (m.)[b] the spotted antelope J VI.538. — 3. (nt.) a (coloured) mark (on the forehead) Miln 408 (°dhara-kumma). — f. cittakā a counterpane of many colours (DA I.86 cittikā: vāna [read nāna°] citra-uṇṇā-may' attharaṇaŋ) Vin I.192; II.163, 169; D I.7; A I.181 ~.

Cittaka[2]: see **acittaka.**

Cittatara, compar. of citta[1], more various, more varied. S III.151 sq. — a punning passage, thus: by the procedure (caraṇa) of mind (in the past) the present mind (citta) is still more varied. Cp. SA in loco: Asl. 66: Expositor 88.

Cittatā [f. abstr. to citta[1]] SA on S III. 151 sq. (bhūmicittatāya dvāracittatāya ārammaṇacittatāya kammanānatta).

Cittatā [f. abstr. to citta[2]] "being of such a heart or mind," state of mind, character S III.152; IV.142 (vimutta°); V.158 (id.); A V.145 sq. (upārambha°); Vbh 372 (id.); Vbh 359 (amudu°); PvA 13 (visuddhi°, noble character); paṭibaddha° (in love with) PvA 145, 147, 270. In S III.152 *l* cittitā q. v.

Cittatta (n.) = cittatā S V.158.

Citti (f.) [fr. **cit,** cp. citta, cintā, cinteti, formation like mutti > muc, sitti > sic] "giving thought or heart" only in comb[n] w. **kar:** cittikaroti to honour, to esteem Ger. cittikatvā M III.24; A III.172; Pv II.9[55] (cittiŋ k. = pūjetvā PvA 135); Dpvs I.2; — acittikatvā M III.22; A IV.392. — pp. **cittikata** thought (much) of Vin IV.6 (& a°); Vbh 2.

Cittikāra [see citti] respect, consideration VvA 178 (garu°), 242; PvA 26; Vbh 371 (a°); Vism 123 (citti°), 188.

Cittita [pp. of citteti, Denom. fr. citta[1]] painted, variegated, varied, coloured or resplendent with (-°) S III.152 (*sic l.* for cittatā>. So SA, which, on p. 151, reads citten' eva cittitaŋ for cintitaŋ. Th I, 736; 2, 390 (su°); Vv 36[7]; 40[2].

Citra = citta[3], the month Chaitra, KhA 192 (°māsa).

Cināti [Sk. cinoti & cayati, **ci,** to which also **kāya,** q. v. See also caya, cita] to heap up, to collect, to accumulate. Inf. cinituŋ Vin II.152; pp. cita (q. v.). Pass. ciyati J V.7. Caus. cināpeti to construct, to build J VI.204; Miln 81. — *Note* cināti at J II.302 (to weave) is to be corr. to vināti (see Kern, *Toev.* s. v.). — Cp. ā°, pa°, vi°. — *Note.* cināti also occurs as cinati in pa°.

Cintaka (adj.) [cp. cintin] one who thinks out or invents, in **akkhara°** the grammarian PvA 120, **nīti°** the law-giver ib. 130; cp. Divy 212, 451, "overseer."

Cintana (nt.) = cintā Th 1, 695; Miln 233.

Cintanaka (adj.) thoughtful, considerate J I.222.

Cintā [to **cit,** cinteti] "the act of thinking" (cp. citti), thought S I.57; Pug 25; Dhs 16, 20, 292; Sdhp 165, 216. — loka° thinking over the world, philosophy S V.447; A II.80.

-kavi "thought-poetry," i. e. original poetry (see kavi) A II.230; **-maṇi** the jewel of thought, the true philosopher's stone VvA 32; N. of a science J III.504; **-maya** consisting of pure thought, metaphysical D III.219; J IV.270; Vbh 324; Nett 8, 50, 60 (°mayin, of paññā); Vism 439 (id.).

Cintita [pp. of cinteti, cp. also cintaka] (a) (adj.) thought out, invented, devised S I.137 (dhammo asuddho samalehi c.); III.151 (caraṇaŋ nāma cittaŋ citten' eva c.); Pv II.6[13] (mantaŋ brahma°, expl. PvA 97 by kathitaŋ). — (b) (nt.) a thought, intention, in duc° & su° (bad & good) A I.102; ThA 76; **-matta** as much a, a thought, loc. cintita-matte (yeva) at the mere thought: just as he thought it DhA I.326 (= cintita kkhaṇe in the moment of thinking it, p. 329).

Cintin [adj. to cintā] only -°: thinking of, having one's thoughts on A I.102 (duccintita° & su°), Sn 174 (ajjhatta°; v. l. B. °saññin) 388; J III.306 = IV.453 = V.176 = V.478; Miln 92.

Cinteti & ceteti [Sk. cetati to appear, perceive, & cintayati to think, **cit** (see citta[2]) in two forms: (a) Act, base with nasal infix cint (cp. muñc, yuñj, siñc, etc.); (b) Med. base (denom.) with guṇa cet (cp. moc, yoj, sec, etc. & the analogous formations of **chid,** chind, ched under chindati) to * **(s)qait:** see citta[1], with which further cp. cakṣu, cikita, ciketi, cikitsati, & in meaning passati (he sees = he knows), Gr. οἶδα = vidi, E. view = thought, Ger. anschauung] — Forms: (a) **cint:** pres. cinteti, pot. cinteyya; ppr. cintento & cintayanto (Sn 834); — aor. cintesi, 3rd pl. cintesuŋ (J I.149), acintayuŋ (Sn 258); — ger. cintetvā (J I.279) & cintiya (Mhvs VII.17, 32); — grd. cinteyya & cintetabba; pp. cintita (q. v.). Cp. also cintana, cintin. — (b) **cet:** pres. ceteti & cetayati (S I.121), pot. cetaye (Pv II.9[7] = cinteyya PvA 116); ppr. cetayāna (J V.339); fut. cetessati (Vin III.19); — aor. acetayi (Pv I.6[6] = cetesi PvA 34); — ger cecca (Vin III.112; IV.290); also cicca: see sañ°. — grd. cetabba (for *cetetabba only at J IV.157, v. l. ceteyya, expl. by cintetabba); — pp. cetayita (q. v.). Cp. also cetanā.

Note. The relation in the use of the two forms is that **cet** is the older & less understood form, since it is usually expl[d] by **cint,** whereas **cint** is never expl[d] by **cet** & therefore appears to be the more frequent & familiar form.

Meaning: (a) (*intr.*) to think, to reflect, to be of opinion. Grouped with (phuṭṭho) vedeti, ceteti, sañjānāti he has the feeling, the awareness (of the feeling), the consciousness S IV.68. Its seat is freq. mentioned with manasā (in the heart), viz. manasā diṭṭhigatāni cintayanto Sn 834; na pāpaŋ manasā pi cetaye Pv II.9[7]; J I.279; PvA 13 (he thought it over), ib. (evaŋ c. you think so); Sdhp 289 (īdisaŋ c. id.) Mhvs VII.18, 32; Miln 233 (cintayati), 406 (cintayitabba). — Prohibitive: **mā cintayi** don't think about it, don't worry, don't be afraid, never mind J I.50, 292, 424; III.289; VI.176; pl. mā cintayittha J I.457; IV.414; VI.344; Vism 426; DhA I.12; III.196; also mā cintesi J III.535. — (b) (*with acc.*) to ponder, think over, imagine, think out, design, scheme, intend, plan. In this sense grouped with (ceteti) pakappeti anuseti to intend, to start to perform, to carry out S II.65. maraṇaŋ ākankhati cetayati (ponders over) S I.121; acinteyyāni na cintetabbāni A II.80; cetabba-rūpa (a fit object of thought, a good thought) J IV.157 (= cintetabba); loka-cintaŋ c. S V.447; ajjhattarūpe, etc. ceteti Vin III.113; mangalāni acintayuŋ Sn 258; diṭṭhigatāni cintayanto Sn 834; kiŋ cintesi J I.221; sokavinayan'-upāyaŋ c. to devise a means of dispelling the grief PvA 39. — Esp. with pāpaŋ & pāpakaŋ to intend evil, to have ill-will against (c. dat.): mā pāpakaŋ akusalaŋ cittaŋ cinteyyātha S V.418; na p. cetaye manasā pi Pv II.9[7] (= cinteyya, piheyya PvA 116); p. na cintetabba PvA 114; tassā p. acetayi Pv I.6[6] (= cetesi PvA 34); kiŋ amhākaŋ cintesi what do you intend against us? J I.211. — (c) (*with dat.*) (restricted to ceteti) to set one's heart on, to think upon, strive after, desire: āgatipunabbhavāya c. to desire a future rebirth S IV.201; vimokkhāya c. to strive after emancipation S III.121; attavyābādhāya c. M III.23 = A I.157 = S IV.339; pabbajjāya c. It 75; rakkhāya me tvaŋ vihito . . . udāhu me cetayase vadhāya J III.146 — acinteyya that which must not or cannot be thought A II.80 (cattāri °āni four reflections to be avoided); VvA 323 (a. buddhānubhāva unimaginable majesty of a B.).

Cipiṭa (adj.) [pp. to **cip** (?) see next: cp. Sk. cipiṭa grain flattened after boiling] pressed flat, flattened VvA 222. To be read also at J VI.185 for vippita.

Cippiyamāna [ppr. Pass. of **cip,** see cipiṭa] crushed flat (Rh. D.; cp. also Kern *Toev.*) Miln 261.

Cimilikā (f.) see cilimikā Vin II.150; IV.40; Cp. *Vin. Texts* III.167; *J.P.T.S.* 1885, 39.

Cira (adj.) [Vedic. cira, perhaps to *queịe to rest, cp. Lat. quiēs, civis; Goth. hveila; Ohg. wīlōn; E. while] long (of time), usually in cpds. & as adv. Either **ciraŋ** (acc.) for a long time Sn 678, 730, 1029; Dh 248; Kh VII.5; J II.110; IV.3; Pv II.3^{33} or **cirena** (instr.) after a long time Vin IV.86; DhsA 239; or **cirāya** (dat.) for long Dh 342. cirassa (gen.) see cirassaŋ. — **cirataraŋ** (compar.) for a (comparatively) long time, rather long A III.58; Pv II.8^{7}. **cir-â-ciraŋ** continually Vin IV.261; J V.233. — **acira** not long (ago) lately, newly: °arahat-tappatta S I.196; °pabbajita S I.185; °parinibbute Bhagavati shortly after the death of the Bhagavant D I.204, etc.; Sn p. 59.

-**kālaŋ** (adv.) a long time freq. e. g. PvA 19, 45, 60, 109; -**ṭṭhitika** perpetual, lasting long A IV.339 (opp. pariyāpajjati); Vv 80^{1}; Pug 32, 33; Vism 37, 175; DA I.3. -**dikkhita** (not °dakkhita) having long since been initiated S I.226=J V.138 (=cirapabbajita); -**nivāsin** dwelling (there) for a long time S II.227; -**paṭika** [cp. Sk. ciraŋ prati] long since, adj. constr. in conformity w. the subject Vin I.33; D II.270= S III.120; -**pabbajita** having long since become a wanderer A III.114; Sn p. 92; DA I.143; -**ppavāsin** (adj.) long absent Dh 219 (=cirappavuttha DhA III.293). -**rattaŋ** (adv.) for a long time Sn 665, 670; J IV.371; and -**rattāya** id. J II.340; Pv I.9^{4}.

Cirassaŋ (adv.) [origin. gen. of cira=cirasya] at last Vin II.195; D I.179; S I.142; J II.439; III.315; IV.446 (read cirassa passāmi); V.328; Th 1, 868; ThA 217; PvA 60. — **na cirass' eva** shortly after D III.11; J IV.2; DhA III.176; PvA 32. — **sucirass' eva** after a very long while S I.193.

Cirāyati [Sk. cirayati, v. denom. fr. cira] to be long, to tarry, to delay, DhA I.16; VvA 64, 208; cp. ciraŋ karoti id. J II.443.

Ciriṭa [Sk. ciri, cp. kīra] a parrot J V.202 (in comp^{n} ciriti°).

Cilimikā (f.) [Der. fr. cīra] as cimilikā at Vin II.150; IV.40 a kind of cloth or carpeting, made from palm-leaves, bark, etc. Also at PvA 144 (doubtful ready).

Cillaka [kilaka or khīlaka, q. v.] a peg, post, pillar, in dāruka° Th 2, 390 (cp. ThA 257). Not with Kern (*Toev.*) "a wooden puppet," as der. fr. citta.^{1}

Cinaka (m. nt.) a kind of bean Sn 239 (=aṭavi-pabbata-padesu āropita-jāta-cina-mugga SnA 283); J V.405.

Cīnapiṭṭha (nt.) red lead DA I.40; DhsA 14.

Cīyati [Pass. of cināti] to be gathered, to be heaped up Sn 428 (cīyate pahūtaŋ puññaŋ). See also ā°.

Cīra (nt.) [Sk. cīra, cp. cīvara] 1. bark, fibre D I.167 (kusa°, vāka°, phalaka°); Vin III.34; A I.295; Pug 55. — a bark dress Vin I.305; J VI.500 (cp. cīraka). — 2. a strip (orig. of bark), in suvaṇṇa°-khacita gold-brocaded VvA 280 (see also next). Cp. ocīraka (under odīraka).

Cīraka [cp. cīra] 1. bark (see cpds.) — 2. a strip, in suvaṇṇa° gold brocade (dress) J V.197.

-**vāsika** (nt.) bark-dress (a punishment) M I.87= A I.48=Miln 197.

Cīriya (adj.) [fr. cīra] like or of bark, in cpd. **dāru°** (as Np.) "wood-barker" DhA II.35.

Cīrīḷikā (f) [cp. Sk. cīrī & jhillikā a cricket, cirilli a sort of large fish] a cricket A III.397 (v. l. cīrikā). Cp. on word-formation pipilikā & Mod. Gr. τσίτσικος cricket.

Cīvara (nt.) [*Sk. cīvara, prob.=cīra, appl^{d} orig. to a dress of bark] the (upper) robe of a Buddhist mendicant. C. is the first one of the set of 4 standard requisites of a wandering bhikkhu, viz. c°, piṇḍapāta alms-bowl, senāsana lodging, a place to sleep at, gilāna-**paccaya-bhesajja-parikkhāra** medicinal appliances for use in sickness. Thus mentioned passim e. g. Vin III.89, 99, 211; IV.154 sq.; D I.61; M II.102; A I.49; Nd^{2} s. v.; It 111. In abbreviated form Sn 339; PvA 7; Sdhp 393. In starting on his begging round the bhikkhu goes patta-cīvaraŋ ādāya, that is literally 'taking his bowl & robe.' But this is an elliptical idiom meaning 'putting on his outer robe and taking his bowl.' A bhikkhu never goes into a village without wearing all his robes, he never takes them, or any one of the three, with him. Each of the three is simply an oblong piece of cloth (usually cotton cloth). On the mode of wearing these three robes see the note at *Dialogues* II.145. — Vin III.11; D II.85; Sn p. 21; PvA 10, 13 & passim. The sewing of the robe was a festival for the laity (see under kaṭhina). There are 6 kinds of cloth mentioned for its manufacture, viz. khoma, kappāsika, koseyya, kambala, sāṇa, bhanga Vin. I.58=96=281 (cp. °dussa). Two kinds of robes are distinguished: one of the gahapatika (layman) a white one, and the other that of the bhikkhu, the c. proper, called paŋsukūlaŋ c. "the dust-heap robe" Vin V.117 (cp. gahapati). — On cīvara in general & also on special ordinances concerning its making, wearing & handling see Vin I.46, 49 sq., 196, 198, 253 sq., 285, 287 sq., 306=II.267 (of var. colours); II.115 sq. (sibbati to sew the c.); III.45, 58 (theft of a c.), 195-223, 254-266; IV.59-62, 120-123, 173, 279 sq., 283 (six kinds). — A III.108 (cīvare kalyāṇakāma); V.100, 206; Vism 62; It 103; PvA 185. — **Sīse cīvaraŋ karoti** to drape the outer robe over the head Vin II.207, 217; **°ŋ khandhe karoti** to drape it over the back Vin II.208, 217; **°ŋ nikkhipati** to lay it down or put it away Vin I.47 sq.; II.152, 224; III.198, 203, 263; **°ŋ saŋharati** to fold it up Vin I.46. — Var. expressions referring to the use of the robe: **atireka°** an extra robe Vin III.195; **acceka°** id. Vin III.260 sq.; **kāla°** (& akāla°) a robe given at (and outside) the specified time Vin III.202 sq.; IV.284, 287; **gahapati°** a layman's r. Vin III.169, 171; **ti°** the three robes, viz. sanghāṭī, uttarāsanga, antaravāsaka Vin I.288, 289; III.11, 195, 198 sq.; V.142; adj. tecīvarika wearing 3 rs. Vin V.193; **dubbala°** (as adj.) with a worn-out c. Vin III.254; IV.59, 154, 286; **paŋsukūla°** the dust-heap robe PvA 141; **sa°-bhatta** food given with a robe Vin IV.77; **lūkha°** (adj.) having a coarse robe Vin I.109 (+duccola), III.263 (id.); A I.25; **vihāra°** a robe to be used in the monastery Vin III.212.

-**kaṇṇa** the lappet of a monk's robe DhA III.420; VvA 76=DhA III.106, cp. cīvarakarṇaka Av.Ś II.184, & °ika Divy 239, 341, 350. -**kamma** (nt.) robe-making Vin II.218; III.60, 240; IV.118, 151; A V.328 sq.; DhA III.342; PvA 73, 145. -**kāra** (-samaya) (the time of) sewing the robes Vin III.256 sq. -**kāla** (-samaya) the right time for accepting robes Vin III.261; IV.286, 287; -**dāna** (-samaya) (the time for) giving robes Vin IV.77, 99; -**dussa** clothing-material Vin IV.279, 280; -**nidāhaka** putting on the c. Vin I.284; -**paṭiggāhaka** the receiver of a robe Vin I.283; II.176; V.205; A III.274 sq.; -**paṭivisa** a portion of the c. Vin I.263, 285, 301; -**palibodha** an obstacle to the valid performance of the kathina ceremony arising from a set of robes being due to a particular person [a technical term of the canon law. See *Vinaya Texts* II.149, 157, 169]. It is one of the two kaṭhinassa palibodhā (c. & āvāsa°) Vin I.265; V.117, cp. 178; -**paviveka** (nt.) the seclusion of the robe, i. e. of a non-Buddhist with two other pavivekāni (piṇḍapāta° & senāsana°) at A I.240; -**bhanga** the distribution of robes Vin IV.284; -**bhatta** robes & a meal (given to the bh.) Vin III.265; -**bhājaka** one who deals out the robes Vin I.285; II.176; V.205; A III.274 sq. (cp. °paṭiggāhaka); -**bhisī** a robe rolled up like a pillow Vin I.287 sq.; -**rajju** (f.) a rope for (hanging up) the robes; in the Vinaya always comb^{d} with °vaŋsa (see below); -**lūkha** (adj.) one who is poorly dressed Pug 53; -**vaŋsa** a bamboo peg for hanging up a robe (cp. °rajju) Vin I.47, 286; II.117,

121, 152, 153, 209, 222; III.59; J I.9; DhA III.342; -sankamanīya (nt.) a robe that ought to be handed over (to its legal owner) Vin IV.282; 283.

Cuṇṇa [Sk. cūrṇa, pp. of carvati, to chew, to *sqer to cut, break up, as in Lat. caro, Sk. kṛṇāti (cp. kaṭu); cp. Lit. kirwis axe, Lat. scrūpus sharp stone, scrupulus, scortum. See also calaka[2] & cp. Sk. kṣunna of **kṣud** to grind, to which prob. P. kuḍḍa] 1. pp. broken up, powdered; only in cpd. °vicuṇṇa crushed to bits, smashed up, piecemeal J I.73; II.120, 159, 216; III.74. — 2. (nt.) (a) any hard substance ground into a powder; dust, sand J I.216; VvA 65 (paŋsu°); Pv III.3[3] (suvaṇṇa° gold-dust; PvA 189=vālikā); DA I.245 (id.); DhsA 12. — (b) esp. "chunam" (Anglo-Ind.) i. e. a plaster, of which quicklime & sand are the chief ingredients & which is largely used in building, but also applied to the skin as a sort of soap-powder in bathing. Often comb[d] with mattikā clay, in distinction of which c. is for delicate use (tender skin), whereas m. for rougher purposes (see Vin I.202); cuṇṇāni bhesajjāni an application of c. Vin I.202. — Vin I.47=52; II.220, 224 sq.; A I.208; III.25; J V.89. cuṇṇa-tela-vālaṇḍupaka Vism 142 (where Asl 115 reads cuṇṇaŋ vā telaŋ vā leḍḍūpaka). — nahāniya° D I.74=M III.92; PvA 46; na- hāna° J II.403, 404. — gandha -cuṇṇa aromatic (bath) powder J I.87, 290; III.276; candana° id. Miln 13, 18. — iṭṭhaka° plaster (which is rubbed on the head of one to be executed) PvA 4, cp. Mṛcchakaṭika X, beginning (stanza 5) "piṣṭa-cūrṇâvakīrṇaśca puruṣo 'haŋ paśukṛtaḥ."

-cālanī a mortar for the preparation of chunam Vin I.202; -piṇḍa a lump of ch. Vin III.260; IV.154 sq.

Cuṇṇaka (adj.) [fr. cuṇṇa] (a) a preparation of chunam, paint (for the face, mukha°) D I.7; M II.64=Th 1, 771; J V.302. — (b) powder: cuṇṇakajātāni reduced to powder M III.92 (aṭṭhikāni). — f. °ikā in cuṇṇikamaŋsa mince meat J I.243.

Cuṇṇeti [Denom. of cuṇṇa] to grind to powder, to crush; to powder or paint w. chunam Vin II.107 (mukhaŋ); J IV.457. — ppr. pass cuṇṇiyamāna being ground J VI.185.

Cuta [pp. of cavati; Sk. cyuta] 1. (adj.) shifted, disappeared, deceased, passed from one existence to another Vin IV.216; Sn 774, 899; It 19, 99; J I.139, 205; Pug 17. — -accuta permanent, not under the sway of Death, Ep. of Nibbāna Dh 225. — 2. (n.) in cpd. cutûpapāta disappearance & reappearance, transmigration, Saŋsāra (see cuti) S II.67 (āgatigatiyā sati c° hoti); A III.420; IV.178; DhA I.259; usually in phrase sattānaŋ cutûpapāta-ñāṇa the discerning of the saŋsāra of beings D I.82=M I.248; D III.111. As cutuppāta at A II.183. Cp. jātisaŋsāra-ñāṇa.

Cuti (f.) [cp. Sk. cyuti, to cavati] vanishing, passing away, decease, shifting out of existence (opp. upapatti, cp also gati & āgati) D I.162; S II.3=42; III.53; M I.49; Sn 643; Dh 419; J I.19, 434; Vism 292, 460, 554; DhA IV.228.

Cudita (adj.) [pp. of codati] being urged, receiving blame, being reproved Vin I.173; II.250; II.250, 251; M I.95 sq.; A III.196 sq. -°ka id. Vin V.115, 158, 161, 164.

Cuddasa [contracted fr. catuddasa, Sk. caturdaśa, cp. catur] fourteen J I.71; VI.8; Miln 12; DhA III.120, 186.

Cunda an artist who works in ivory J VI.261 (Com: dantakāra); Miln 331.

Cundakāra a turner J VI.339.

Cumbaṭa (nt.) [cp. Prk. cumbhala] (a) a coil; a pad of cloth, a pillow J I.53 (dukūla°); II.21 (id.); VvA 73. — (b) a wreath J III.87. Cp. next.

Cumbaṭaka (nt.) cumbaṭa, viz. (a) a pillow DhA I.139; VvA 33, 165.—(b) a wreath J IV.231 (puppha°); SnA 137; DhA I.72 (mālā°).

Cumbati [Sk. cumbati. Dhtp 197 defines as "vadanasaŋyoge"] to kiss J II.193; V.328; VI.291, 344; VvA 260. Cp. pari°.

Culla & cūḷa (adj.) [Sk. kṣulla=kṣudra (P. khudda, see khuddaka), with c: k=cuṇṇa: kṣud] small, minor (opp. mahā great, major), often in conn. with names & titles of books, e. g. c° Anāthapiṇḍika=A jr. J II.287, cp. Anglo-Indian chota sahib the younger gentleman (Hind. chhota=culla); or Culla-vagga, the minor section (Vin II.) as subordinate to Mahā-vagga (Vin I.), Culla-niddesa the minor exposition (following upon Mahā-niddesa); culla-sīla the simple precepts of ethics (opp. mahā° the detailed sīla) D I.5, etc. Otherwise only in cpds.:

-angulī little finger DhA II.86. -ûpaṭṭhāka a "lesser" follower, i. e. a personal attendant (of a thera) J I.108 (cūḷ°); II.325 (cull°; DhA I.135; II.260; cūḷ); -pitā an uncle ("lesser" father=sort of father, cp. Lat. matertera, patruus, Ger. Vetter=father jun.) J II.5; III.456 (v. l. petteyya); PvA 107; DhA I.221 (cūḷa°).

Cullāsīti [=caturāsīti] eighty-four J VI.226 (mahākappe as duration of Saŋsāra); PvA 254 (id.). Also as cūḷāsīti q. v.

Cūlikā (f.) [Sk. cūlikā, cp. cūḍā]=cūḷa; kaṇṇa° the root of the ear J II.276; Vism 249, 255; DhA IV.13 (of an elephant). °baddha S II.182; *KS* II.122. See also cūḷā.

Cūḷa [Sk. cūḍa & cūlikā] 1. swelling, protuberance; root, knot, crest. As kaṇṇa-cūḷa the root of an elephant's ear J VI.488. aḍḍha-cūḷa a measure (see aḍḍha). See also cūlikā. — 2. (adj.) see culla.

Cūḷaka (adj.) [fr. cūḷā] having a cūḷa or top-knot; pañca° with five top-knots J V.250 (of a boy).

Cūḷanikā (f.) [Der. fr. culla, q. v.] only in phrase sahassī cūḷanikā lokadhātu "the system of the 1,000 lesser worlds" (distinguished from the dvi-sahassī majjhimakā & the ti-sahassī mahāsahassī lokadhātu) A I.227; Nd[2] 235, 2[b].

Cūḷā (f.) [Vedic cūḍā. to cūḍa]=cūḷa, usually in sense of crest only, esp. denoting the lock of hair left on the crown of the head when the rest of the head is shaved (cp. Anglo-Indian chuḍā & Gujarāti chotali) J I.64, 462; V.153, 249 (pañcacūḷā kumārā); DhA I.294; as mark of distinction of a king J III.211; V.187; of a servant J VI.135. — a cock's comb J II.410; III.265.

-maṇi (m.) a jewel worn in a crest or diadem, a jewelled crest J I.65; II.122; V.441.

Cūḷāsīti for cullāsīti at Th 2, 51.

Ce [Vedic ced; ce=Lat. que in absque, ne-c, etc., Goth. h in ni-h. see also ca 3] conditional particle "if," constructed either with Indicative (ito ce pi yojanasate viharati even if he lived 100 y. from here D I.117) or Conditional (tatra ce tumhe assatha kupitā D I.3), or Potential (passe ce vipulaŋ sukhaŋ Dh 290). — Always enclitic (like Lat. que) & as a rule placed after the emphasized word at the beginning of the sentence: puññañ ce puriso kayirā Dh 118; brāhmaṇo ce tvaŋ brūsi Sn 457. Usually added to pronouns or pron. adverbs: ahañ ce va kho pana ceteyyaŋ D I.185; ettha ce te mano atthi S I.116, or comb[d] with other particles, as noce, yañce, sace (q. v.). Freq. also in comb[n] with other indef. interrog. or emphatic particles, as ce va kho pana if then, if now: ahañ ce va kho pana pañhaŋ puccheyyaŋ D I.117; ahañ ce va kho pana abhivādeyyaŋ D I.125; api (pi) ce even if: api ce vassasataŋ jīve māṇavo Sn 589.

Cecca=cicca (equal to sañcicca), ger. of cinteti, corresp. to either *cetya [cet] or *cintya [cint]; only in ster. def. jānanto sañjānanto cecca abhivitaritvā Vin II.91; III.73, 112; IV.290.

Ceta a servant, a boy J III.478. See next.

Ceṭaka a servant, a slave, a (bad) fellow Vin IV.66; J II.176 = DhA IV.92 (duṭṭha° miserable fellow); III.281; IV.82 (bhātika-ceṭakā rascals of brothers); V.385; Miln 222.

Cetaka a decoy-bird (Com. dīpaka-tittira, exciting partridge) J III.357.

Cetakedu a kind of bird J VI.538. See also cela°.

Cetanaka (adj.) [see cetanā] connected with a thought or intention J VI.304; usually in a° without a thought, unintentional J II.375; VI.178; Vbh 419.

Cetanā [f. abstr. fr. **cet,** see cinteti] state of ceto in action, thinking as active thought, intention, purpose, will. Defined as action (kamma: A iii.415; cp. KV. VIII.9, § 38 untraced quotation; cp. A V.292). Often comb^{d} w. patthanā & paṇidhi (wish & aspiration), e. g. S II.99, 154; A I.32, 224; V 212; Nd^{2} 112 (in def. of asucimanussā, people of ignoble action: asuciyā cetanāya, patthanāya, paṇidhinā samannāgatā). Also classed with these in a larger group in KV., e. g. 343, 380. — Comb^{d} w. vedanā saññā c. citta phassa manasikāra in def. of nāmakāya (opp. rūpakāya) S II.3 (without citta), Ps I.183 (do.); Nett 77, 78. — Enum^{d} under the four blessings of vatthu, paccaya, c., guṇātireka (-sampadā) & def. as "cetanāya somanassa-sahagata-ñāṇa-sampayutta-bhāvo" at DhA III.94. — C. is opposed to cetasika (i. e. ceto) in its determination of the 7 items of good conduct (see sīla) which refers to actions of the body (or are *wilful,* called cetanākamma Nett 43, 96; otherwise distinguished as kāya- & yacīkammantā A V.292 sq.), whereas the 3 last items (sīla 8-10) refer to the behaviour of the mind (cetasika-kamma Nett., mano-kammanta A), viz. the shrinking back from covetousness, malice, & wrong views. — Vin III.112; S III.60; A II.232 (kaṇhassa kammassa pahānāya cetanā: intention to give up wrong-doing); VvA 72 (vadhaka-cetanā wilful murder); maraṇa-cetanā intention of death DhA I.20; āhār' āsā cetanā intention consisting in desire for food Vism 537. — PvA 8, 30 (pariccāga° intention to give); Pug 12; Miln 94; Sdhp 52, 72. — In scholastic lgg. often expl^{d} as cetanā sañcetanā sañcetayitatta (viz. state or behaviour of volition) Dhs 5; Vbh 285. — Cp. Dhs 58 (+ citta); Vbh 401 (id.); Vbh 40, 403; Vism 463 (cetayatī ti cetanā; abhisandahatī ti attho).

Cetayita [pp. of ceteti, see cinteti] intended A V.187; Miln 62.

Cetasa[1] N. of a tree, perhaps the yellow Myrobalan J V.420.

Cetasa[2] (adj.) [orig. the gen. of ceto used as nominative] only in -°: sucetasa of a good mind, good-hearted S I.4 = 29, 46 = 52; paraphrased by Buddhaghosa as sundaracetasa; pāpa° of a wicked mind, evil-minded S I.70 = 98; a° without mind S I.198; sabba° all-hearted, with all one's mind or heart, in phrase aṭṭhikatvā manasikatvā sabbacetaso samannāharitva ohitasoto (of one paying careful & proper attention) S I.112 sq. = 189, 220; A II.116; III.163, 402; IV.167. The editors have often misunderstood the phrase & we freq. find vv. ll. with sabbaŋ cetaso & sabbaŋ cetasā, — appamāṇa° S IV.186; avyāpanna° S V.74.

Cetasika (adj.) belonging to ceto, mental (opp. kāyika physical). Kāyikaŋ sukhaŋ > cetasikaŋ s. A I.81; S V. 209; kāyikā darathā > c. d. M III.287, 288; c. dukkhaŋ D II 306; A I.157; c. roga J III.337. c. kamma is sīla 8-10 (see under cetanā) Nett 43. — As n. comb^{d} with citta it is to be taken as supplementing it, viz. mind & all that belongs to it, mind and mental properties, adjuncts, co efficients (cp. vitakka-vicāra & such cpds. as phalâphala, bhavâbhava) D I.213; see also citta. Occurring in the Nikāyas in sg. only, it came to be used in pl. and, as an ultimate category, the 52 cetasikas, with citta as bare consciousness, practically superseded in mental analysis, the 5 khandha-category. See *Cpd.* p. I and pt. II. Mrs. Rh. D., *Bud. Psy.* 6, 148, 175. -°cetasikā dhammā Ps I.84; Vbh 421; Dhs 3, 18, etc. (cp. *Dhs. trsl.* pp. 6, 148).

Cetaso gen. sg. of ceto, functioning as gen. to citta (see citta & ceto).

Cetāpana (nt.) [see cetāpeti; cp. BSk. cetanika] barter Vin III.216, see also *Vin. Texts* I.22 & Kacc. 322.

Cetāpeti [Caus. of *cetati to **ci,** collect; see also Kern, *Toev.* s. v.] to get in exchange, to barter, buy Vin III.216 (expl^{d} by parivatteti), 237; IV.250.

Cetiya (nt.) [cp. from **ci,** to heap up, cp. citi, cināti] 1. a tumulus, sepulchral monument, cairn, M I.20; Dh 188; J I.237; VI.173; SnA 194 (dhātu-gharaŋ katvā cetiyaŋ patiṭṭhāpesuŋ); KhA 221; DhA III.29 (dhātu°); IV. 64; VvA 142; Sdhp 428, 430. Pre-Buddhistic cetiyas mentioned by name are Aggāḷava° Vin II.172; S I.185; Sn p. 59; DhA III.170; Ānanda° D II.123, 126; Udena° D II.102, 118; III.9; DhA III.246; Gotama (ka)° ibid.; Cāpāla° D II.102, 118; S V.250; Ma- kuṭa-bandhana° D II.160; Bahuputta° D II.102, 118; III.10; S II.220; A IV.16; Sattambaka° D II.102, 118; Sārandada D II.118, 175; A III.167; Supatiṭṭha° Vin I.35.

-**aṅgaṇa** the open space round a Cetiya Miln 366; Vism 144, 188, 392; DA I.191, 197; VvA 254. -**vandanā** Cetiya worship Vism 299.

Ceteti see cinteti.

Ceto (nt.) [Sk. cetas] = citta, q. v. for detail concerning derivation, inflexion & meaning. Cp. also cinteti. — Only the gen. cetaso & the instr. cetasā are in use; besides these there is an adj. cetaso, der. from nom. base cetas. Another adj.-form is the inflected nom. ceto, occurring only in **viceto** S V.447 (+ ummatto, out of mind).

I. **Ceto** in its relation to similar terms: (a) with **kāya** & **vācā**: kāyena vācāya cetasā (with hand, speech & heart) Sn 232; Kh IX. kāya (vācā°, ceto°) -**muni** a saint in action, speech & thought A I.273 = Nd^{2} 514. In this phrase the Nd has mano° for ceto°, which is also a v. l. at A-passage. — (b) with **paññā** (see citta IV. b) in ceto-vimutti, paññā-vimutti (see below IV.). — (c) with samādhi, pīti, sukha, etc.: see °pharaṇatā below.

II. **Cetaso** (gen.) (a) *heart.* c° upakkilesa (stain of h.) D III.49, 101; S V.93. Vinatta (attachment) S V.64. appasāda (unfaith) S I.179; ekodibhāva (singleness) D III.78; S IV.236 (see 2nd jhāna); āvaraṇāni (hindrances) S 66. — vimokkha (redemption) S I.159. santi (tranquillity) Sn 584, 593. vūpasama (id.) A I.4; S V.65. vinibandha (freedom) D III.238 = A III.249; IV.461 sq. — (b) *mind.* c° vikkhepa (disturbance) A III.448; V.149: uttrāsa (fear) Vbh 367. abhiniropanā (application) Dhs 7.—(c) *thought.* in c° parivitakko udapādi "there arose a reflection in me (gen.)" S I.139; II.273; III.96, 103.

III. **Cetasā** (instr.) — (a) *heart.* mettā-sahagatena c. (with a h. full of love) freq. in phrase ekaŋ disaŋ pharitvā, etc. e. g. D I.186, III.78, 223; S IV.296; A I.183; II.129; IV.390; V.299, 344; Vbh 272. ujubhūtena (upright) S II.279; A I.63; vivaṭena (open) D III.223 = S V.263; A IV.86. macchera-mala-pariyuṭṭhitena (in which has arisen the dirt of selfishness) S IV.240; A II.58. santim pappuyya c. S I.212. taṇhādhipateyyena (standing under the sway of thirst) S III.103. — vippasannena (devout) S I.32 = 57, 100; Dh 79; Pv I.10^{10}. muttena A IV.244. vimariyādi-katena S III.31. vigatâbhijjhena D III.49. pathavī-āpo etc.-samena A IV.375 sq. ākāsasamena A III.315 sq. sabba° S II.220. abhijjhā-sahagatena A I.206. satārakkhena D III.269; A V.30. — migabhūtena cetasā, with the heart of a wild creature M I.450. —acetasā without feeling, heartlessly J IV.52, 57. — (b) *mind*: in two phrases, viz. (*a*) c. anuvitakketi anuvicāreti "to ponder & think over in one's mind" D III.242; A I.264; III.178; — (*β*) c. pajānāti (or manasikaroti) "to know in one's mind," in the foll. expressions: para-sattānaŋ para-puggalānaŋ cetasā ceto-paricca pajānāti "he knows in his mind the ways of thought (the state of heart) of other beings" (see ceto-paricca & °pariyāya) M II.19; S II.121, 213; V.265; A I.255=III.17=280. puggalaŋ paduṭṭha-cittaŋ evaŋ c° ceto-paricca p. It 12, cp. 13. Arahanto . . . Bhagavanto c° cetoparicca viditā D III.100. para-cittapariyāya kusalo evaŋ c° ceto-paricca manasikaroti A V.160. Bhagavā [brāhmaṇassa] c° ceto-parivitakkaŋ aññāya "perceiving in his mind the thought of [the b.]" S I.178; D III.6; A III.374; Miln 10.

IV. *Cpds.* -**khila** fallowness, waste of heart or mind, usually as pañca c-khilā, viz. arising from doubt in the Master, the Norm, the Community, or the Teaching, or from anger against one's fellow-disciples D III.237, 278; M I.101; A III.248=IV.460=V.17; J III.291; Vbh 377; Vism 211. -**paṇidhi** resolution, intention, aspiration Vv 47[12] (=cittassa samma-d-eva ṭhapanaŋ VvA 203); Miln 129; -**padosa** corruption of the h., wickedness, A I.8; It 12, 13 (opp. pasāda): -**paricca** "as regards the heart," i. e. state of heart, ways of thought, character, mind (=pariyāya) in °ñāṇa Th 2, 71=227 (expl[d] at ThA 76, 197 by cetopariyañāṇa) see phrase cetasā c-p. above (III. b.); -**pariyāya** the ways of the heart (=paricca), in para-ceto-pariyāya-kusalo "an expert in the ways of others' hearts" A V.160; c.-p-kovido en-compassing the heart of others S I.146, 194=Th I, 1248; I.196=Th I, 1262. Also with syncope: °**pariya-ñāṇa** D I.79; III.100; Vism 431; DA I.223. -**parivi-takka** reflecting, reasoning S I.103, 178; -**pharaṇatā** the breaking forth or the effulgence of heart, as one of five ideals to be pursued, viz. samādhi, pīti-pharaṇatā, sukha°, ceto°, āloka° D III.278; -**vasippatta** mastery over one's h. A II.6, 36, 185; IV.312; M I.377; Vism 382; Miln 82, 85; -**vimutti** emancipation of h. (always w. paññā-vimutti), which follows out of the destruction of the intoxications of the heart (āsavānaŋ khayā anāsavā c.-v.) Vin I.11 (akuppā); D I.156, 167, 251; III.78, 108, 248 (muditā); S II.265 (mettā); M I.197 (akuppā), 205, 296; III.145 (appamāṇā, mahaggatā); A I.124; II.6, 36; III.84; Sn 725, 727=It 106; It 20 (mettā), 75, 97; Pug 27, 62; Vbh 86 (mettā) Nett 81 (virāgā); DA I.313 (=cittavimutti); -**vivaraṇa** setting the h. free A IV.352; V.67. See also arahant II D. -**samatha** calm of h. Th 2, 118; -**samādhi** concentration of mind (=citta-samādhi DA I.104) D I.13; III. 30; S IV.297; A II.54; III.51; -**samphassa** contact with thought Dhs 3.

Cela (nt.) [Derivation unknown. Cp. Sk. cela] cloth, esp clothes worn, garment, dress A I.206; Pv II.12[7] (kañ-canā° for kañcana°); III.9[3] (for veḷa); dhāti° baby's napkin J III.539. In simile of one whose clothes are on fire (āditta°+ādittasīsa) S V.440; A II.93; III.307; IV.320 — *acela* a naked ascetic D I.161, 165≈; J V.75; VI.222.

-**aṇḍaka** (v. l. aṇḍuka) a loincloth M I.150; -**ukkhepa** waving of garments (as sign of applause), usually with sādhukāra J I.54; II.253; III.285; V.67; DhA II.43; SnA II.225; VvA 132, 140; -**paṭṭikā** (not °pattika) a bandage of cloth, a turban Vin II.128 (Bdhgh. cela-sandhara); M II.93; DhA III.136; -**vitāna** an awning J I.178; II.289; IV.378; Mhbv 122; Vism 108.

Celaka 1. one who is clothed; acelaka without clothes D I.166; M I.77. — 2. a standard-bearer [cp. Sk. ceḍaka P. ceṭa & in meaning E. knight > Ger. knecht; knave > knabe, knappe] D I.51; DA I.156; A IV. 107, 110; Miln 331.

Celakedu=cetakedu J VI.538.

Celāpaka=celāvaka J V.418.

Celāvaka [cp. Sk. chilla ?] a kind of bird J VI.358 (Com. celabaka; is it celā bakā ?); J V.416. See also celāpaka.

Cokkha (adj.) [Cp. Sk. cokṣa] clean J III.21; °bhāva cleanliness M I.39 (=visuddhibhāva; to be read for T mokkha° ? See Trenckner's note on p. 530).

Coca (nt.) [Both derivation & meaning uncertain. The word is certainly not Aryan. See the note at *Vinaya Texts* II.132] the cocoa-nut or banana, or cinnamon J V.420 (°vana); -°pāna a sweet drink of banana or cocoa-nut milk Vin I.246.

Codaka (adj.) [to codeti] one who rebukes; exhorting, reproving Vin I.173; II 248 sq.; V.158, 159 etc.; S I.63; M I.95 sq.; D III.236; A I.53; III.196; IV.193 sq.; DA I.40.

Codanā (f.) [see codeti] reproof, exhortation D I.230; III.218; A III.352; Vin V.158, 159; Vism 276. — As ttg. in codan' atthe nipāto an exhortative particle J VI.211 (for ingha); VvA 237 (id.); PvA 88 v. l. (for handa).

Codita [pp. of codeti, q. v.] urged, exhorted, incited; questioned Sn 819; J VI.256; Pv II.9[66]; Vv 16[1]; PvA 152: Sdhp 309.

Codetar [n. ag. to codeti] one who reproves, one who exacts blame, etc. Vin V.184.

Codeti [Vedic codati & codayati, from **cud**] aor. acodayi (J V.112), inf. codetuŋ, grd. codetabba; Pass. cujjati & codiyati; pp. cudita & codita (q. v.): Caus. codāpeti (Vin. III.165) to urge, incite, exhort; to reprove, repri-mand, to call forth, to question; in spec. sense to demand payment of a debt (J VI.69 iṇaŋ codetvā; 245; Sn 120 iṇaŋ cujjamāna being pressed to pay up; PvA 3 iṇayikehi codiyamāna) D I.230; Vin I.43 (āpattiyā c. to reprove for an offence), 114, 170 sq., 322 sq.; II.2 sq., 80 sq.; III.164, etc.; J V.112; Dh 379; PvA 39, 74.

Copana (nt.) [**cup**, copati to stir, rel. to **kup**, see kuppati] moving, stirring DhA IV.85; DhsA 92, 240, 323.

Cora [**cur**, corayati to steal; Dhtp 530=theyye] a thief, a robber Vin I.74, 75, 88, 149; S II.100, 128=A II.240; S II.188 (gāmaghāta, etc.); IV.173; M II.74=Th I, 786; A I.48; II.121 sq.; IV.92, 278; Sn 135, 616, 652; J I.264 (°rājā, the robber king); II.104; III.84; Miln 20; Vism 180 (sah' oḍḍha c.), 314 (in simile), 489 (rāja-puris' ānubandha°, in comparison), 569 (andhakāre corassa hattha-pasāraṇaŋ viya); DhA II.30; PvA 3, 54, 274. — **mahā°** a great robber Vin III.89; D III.203; A I.153; III.128; IV.339; Miln 185. — Often used in similes: see *J.P.T.S.* 1907, 87.

-**aṭavi** wood of robbers Vism 190. — **upaddava** an attack from robbers J I.267; -**kathā** talk about thieves (one of the forbidden pastimes, see kathā) D I.7=Vin I.188≈; -**ghātaka** an executioner A II.207, J III.178; IV.447; V.303; PvA 5.

Coraka [cp. Sk. coraka] a plant used for the preparation of perfume J VI.537.

Corikā f. thieving, theft Vin I.208; J III.508; Miln 158; PvA 4, 86, 192; VvA 72 (=theyyā).

Corī (f.) a female thief Vin IV.276; J II.363; (adj.) thievish, deceitful J I.295. — **dāraka°** a female kidnapper J VI.337.

Corovassikaŋ at Nd[2] 40 (p. 85) read corovassikaŋ (as S IV.185).

Cola (& coḷa) [Cp. Sk. coḍa] a piece of cloth, a rag S I.34; J IV.380; Miln 169; PvA 73; Sdhp 396. -**bhisi** a mat spread with a piece of cloth (as a seat) Vin IV.40. — **duccola** clad in rags, badly dressed Vin I.109; III.263.

Colaka (& coḷaka)=cola Vin I.48, 296; II.113, 151, 174, 208, 225; Pv II.1[7]; Miln 53 (bark for tinder ?); DhA II.173.

Ch.

Cha & **Chaḷ** (cha in composition effects gemination of consonant, e. g. chabbīsati = cha + vīsati, chabbaṇṇa = cha + vaṇṇa, chaḷ only before vowels in compⁿ: chaḷanga, chaḷ-abhiññā) [Vedic ṣaṣ & ṣaṭ (ṣaḍ = chaḷ), Gr. ἕξ, Lat. sex, Goth. saihs] the number six.

Cases: nom. cha, gen. channaŋ, instr. chahi (& chambhī (?) J IV.310, which should be chambhi & prob. chabbhi = ṣaḍbhiḥ; see also chambhī), loc. chasu (& chassu), num. ord. chaṭṭha the sixth. Cp. also saṭṭhi (60) soḷasa (16). Six is applied whenever a "major set" is concerned (see 2), as in the foll.: 6 munis are distinguished at Nd² 514 (in pairs of 3: see muni); 6 bhikkhus as a "clique" (see chabaggiya, cp. the Vestal virgins in Rome, 6 in number); 6 are the sciences of the Veda (see chaḷanga); there are 6 buddha-dhammā (Nd² 466); 6 viññāṇakāyā (see upadhi); 6 senses & sense-organs (see āyatana) — cha dānasālā J I.282; oraŋ chahi māsehi kālakiriyā bhavissati (I shall die in 6 months, i. e. not just yet, but very soon, after the "next" moon) Pv IV.3³⁶. Six bodily faults J I.394 (viz. too long, too short, too thin, too fat, too black, too white). Six thousand Gandhabbas J II.334.

-aŋsa six-cornered Dhs 617. -anga the set of six Vedāngas, disciplines of Vedic science, viz. 1. kappa, 2. vyākaraṇā, 3. nirutti, 4. sikkhā, 5. chando (viciti), 6. jotisattha (thus enumᵈ at VvA 265; at PvA 97 in sequence 4, 1, 3, 2, 6, 5): D III.269; Vv 63¹⁶; Pv II.6¹³; Miln 178, 236. With ref. to the upekkhās, one is called the "one of six parts" (chaḷ-ang' upekkhā) Vism 160. -abhiññā the 6 branches of higher knowledge Vin II.161; Pug 14. See abhiññā. -âsīti eighty-six [i. e. twice that many in all directions; psychologically 6 × 80 = 6 × (4 × 2)¹⁰], of people: an immense number, millions Pv II.13⁷; of Petas PvA 212; of sufferings in Niraya Pv III.10⁶. -âhaŋ for six days J III.471. -kaṇṇa heard by six ears, i. e. public (opp. catukaṇṇa) J VI.392. -tiŋsa(ti) thirty-six A II.3; It 15; Dh 339; DhA III.211, 22; (°yojana-parimaṇḍala); IV.48. -danta having six tusks, in °*daha* N. of one of the Great Lakes of the Himavant (satta-mahā-sarā), lit. lake of the elephant with 6 tusks, cp. cha-visāṇa Vism 416. -dvārika entering through six doors (i. e. the senses) DhA IV.221 (taṇhā). -dhātura (= dhātuya) consisting of six elements M III.239. -pañca (chappañca) six or five Miln 292. -phass' āyatana having six seats of contact (i. e. the outer senses) M III.239; Th 1, 755; PvA 52; cp. Sn 169. -baṇṇa (= vaṇṇa) consisting of six colours (of raŋsi, rays) J V.40; DhA I.249; II.41; IV.99. -baggiya (= vaggiya) forming a group of six, a set of (sinful) Bhikkhus taken as exemplification of trespassing the rules of the Vinaya (cp. Oldenberg, *Buddha* ⁷384). Their names are Assaji, Punabhasu, Paṇḍuka, Lohitaka, Mettiya, Bhummajaka Vin II.1, 77, and passim; J II.387; DhA III.330. -bassāni (= vassāni) six years J I.85; DhA III.195. -bidha (= vidha) sixfold Vism 184. -bisāṇa (= visāṇa) having six (i. e. a "major set") of tusks (of pre-eminent elephants) J V.42 (Nāgarājā), 48 (kuñjara), cp. chaddanta. — bīsati (= vīsati) twenty-six DhA IV.233 (devalokā).

Chakana & **Chakaṇa** (nt.) [Vedic śakṛt & śakan, Gr. κόπρος: Sk. chagana is later, see Trenckner. *Notes* 62 n. 16] the dung of animals Vin I.202; J III.386 (ṇ); V.286; VI.392 (ṇ).

Chakaṇatī (f.) = chakana Nd² 199.

Chakala [cp. Sk. chagala, from chāga heifer] a he-goat J VI.237; °ka ibid. & Vin III.166. — f. chakalī J VI.559.

Chakka (nt.) [fr. cha] set of six Vism 242 (meda° & mutta°).

Chakkhattuŋ (adv.) [Sk. ṣaṭkṛtvas] six times D II.198; DhA III.196.

Chaṭṭha the sixth Sn 171, 437; DhA III.200; SnA 364. Also as chaṭṭhama Sn 101, 103; J III.280.

Chaḍḍaka (adj.) throwing away, removing, in **puppha**° a flower-rubbish remover (see pukkusa) Th 1, 620; Vism 194; — f. chaḍḍikā see kacavara°.

Chaḍḍana (nt.) throwing away, rejecting J I.290; Dhtp 571. —ī (f.) a shovel, dust-pan DhA III.7. See kacavara°.

Chaḍḍita [pp. of chaḍḍeti] thrown out, vomited; cast away, rejected, left behind S III.143; J I.91, 478; Pv II.2³ (= ucchiṭṭhaŋ vantan ti attho PvA 80); VvA 100; PvA 78, 185.

Chaḍḍeti [Vedic chardayati & chṛṇatti to vomit; cp. also avaskara excrements & karīsa dung. From *sqer to eliminate, separate, throw out (Gr. κρίνω, Lat. ex-(s)cerno), cp. Gr. σκῶς, Lat. mus(s)cerda, Ags. scearn] to spit out, to vomit, throw away; abandon, leave, reject Vin 214 sq.; IV.265; M I.207; S I.169 (chaṭṭehi wrongly for chaḍḍehi) = Sn p. 15; J I.61, 254, 265, 292; V.427; Pug 33; DhA I.95 (uṇhaŋ lohitaŋ ch. to kill oneself); II.101; III.171; VvA 126; PvA 43, 63, 174, 211; 255; Miln 15. — ger. chaḍḍūna Th 2, 469 (= chaḍḍetvā ThA 284); grd. chaḍḍetabba Vin I.48; J II.2; chaḍḍanīya Miln 252; chaḍḍiya (to be set aside) M I.12 sq. — Pass. chaḍḍīyati PvA 174. — Caus. chaḍḍāpeti to cause to be vomited, to cast off, to evacuate, to cause to be deserted Vin IV.265; J I.137; IV.139; VI.185, 534; Vism 182. — pp. chaḍḍita (q. v.). — See also kacavara°

Chaṇa a festival J I.423, 489 (surā°), 499; II.48 (mangala°), 143, III.287, 446, 538; IV.115 (surā°); V.212; VI.221; 399 (°bheri); DhA III. 100 (surā°), 443 (°vesa); IV.195; VvA 173.

Chaṇaka [= akkhaṇa? Kern; cp. Sk. *ākhaṇa] the Chaṇaka plant Miln 352; cp. akkhaṇa.

Chatta¹ (nt.) [late Vedic chattra = *chad-tra, covering to **chad**, see chādati] a sunshade ("parasol" would be misleading. The handle of a chatta is affixed at the circumference, not at the centre as it is in a parasol), a canopy Vin I.152; II.114; D I.7≈; II.15 (seta°, under which Gotama is seated); J I.267 (seta°); IV.16;

v.383; vi.370; Sn 688, 689; Miln 355; DhA I.380 sq.; DA I.89; PvA 47. — Esp. as seta° the royal canopy, one of the 5 insignia regis (setachatta-pamukhaŋ pañcavidhaŋ rāja-kakudhabhaṇḍaŋ PvA 74), see kakudhabhaṇḍa. J vi.4, 223, 389; °ŋ ussāpeti to unfold the r. canopy PvA 75; DhA I.161, 167. See also paṇṇa°.

-daṇḍa the handle of a sunshade DhA III.212; -nāḷi the tube or shaft (of reeds or bamboo) used for the making of sunshades M II.116; -mangala the coronation festival J III.407; DhA III.307; VvA 66.

Chatta[2] [cp. Sk. chātra, one who carries his master's sunshade] a pupil, a student J II.428.

Chattaka (m. nt.) 1. a sun-shade J vi.252; Th 2, 23 (= ThA 29 as nickname of sun-shade makers). See also paṇṇa°. — 2. ahi° "snake's sun-shade," N. for a mushroom: toadstool D III.87; J II.95; a mushroom, toadstool J II.95.

Chattiŋsakkhattuŋ (adv.) thirty-six times It 15.

Chada [cp. chādeti **chad** = saŋvarane Dhtp 586] anything that covers, protects or hides, viz. a cover, an awning D I.7≈ (sa-uttara° but °chadana at D II.194); — a veil, in phrase vivaṭacchada "with the veil lifted" thus spelt only at Nd[2] 242, 593, DhA I.106 (vivattha°, v. l. vaṭṭa°) & DA I.251 (vivatta°), otherwise °chadda; — shelter, clothing in phrase ghāsacchada Pug 51 (see ghāsa & cp. chāda); — a hedge J vi.60; — a wing Th 1, 1108 (citra°).

Chadana (nt.) [Vedic chad] = chada, viz. *lit.* 1. a cover, covering J I.376; v.241. — 2. a thatch, a roof Vin II.154 (various kinds), 195; J II.281; DhA II.65 (°piṭṭha); IV.104 (°assa udaka-patana-ṭṭhāna), 178; PvA 55. — 3. a leaf, foliage J I.87; Th 1, 527. — 4. hair J v.202. — *fig.* pretence, camouflage, counterfeiting Sn 89 (= paṭirūpaŋ katvā SnA 164); Dhs 1059 = Vbh 361 = Nd[2] 271[II]. Dhs reads chandanaŋ & Vbh chādanaŋ.

-iṭṭhikā a tile DhA IV.203.

Chadda (nt.) [Dhtp 590 & Dhtm 820 expl[n] a root **chadd** by "vamane," thus evidently taking it as an equivalent of **chaḍḍ**] = chada, only in phrase vivattacchadda (or vivaṭa°) D I.89; Sn 372, 378, 1003, 1147; DA I.251. Nd[2] however & DA read °chada expl. by vivaṭa-rāga-dosamoha-chadana SnA 365.

Chaddhā [Sk. saṭśah] sixfold Miln 2.

Chanda [cp. Vedic and Sk. chanda, and **skandh** to jump]. 1. impulse, excitement; intention, resolution, will; desire for, wish for, delight in (c. loc.). Expl[d] at Vism 466 as "kattu-kāmatāy" adhivacanaŋ; by Dhtp 587 & Dhtm 821 as **chand** = icchāyaŋ. — A. As *virtue*: dhammapadesu ch. striving after righteousness S I.202; tibba° ardent desire, zeal A I.229; IV.15; kusaladhamma° A III.441. Often comb[d] with other good qualities, e. g. ch. vāyāma ussāha ussoḷhi A IV.320; ch. viriya citta vīmaŋsā in set of samādhis (cp. iddhipāda) D III.77 (see below), & in cpd. °ādhipateyya. — kusalānaŋ dhammānaŋ uppādāya chandaŋ janeti vāyamati viriyaŋ ārabhati, etc., see citta v. 1 d*β*. — M II.174; A I.174 (ch. vā vāyāmo vā); III.50 (chandasā instr.); Sn 1026 (+ viriya); Vv 24[12] (= kusala° VvA 116); J vi.72; DhA I.14. — B. As *vice*: (a) kinds & character of ch. — With similar expressions: (kāya-) ch. sneha anvayatā M I.500. — ch. dosa moha bhaya D III.182; Nd[2] 337[2] (See also below chandāgati). Its nearest analogue in this sense is rāga (lust), e. g. ch. rāga dosa paṭigha D I.25 (cp. DA I.116); rūpesu uppajjati ch. vā rāgo S IV.195. See below °rāga. In this bad sense it is nearly the same as kāma (see kāma & kāmachanda: sensual desire, cp. DhsA 370, Vism 466 & Mrs. Rh. D. in *Dhs trsl.* 292) & the comb[n] kāmachanda is only an enlarged term of kāma. Kāye chanda "delight in the body" M I.500; Sn 203. bhave ch. (pleasure in existence) Th 2, 14 (cp. bhavachanda); lokasmiŋ ch. (hankering after the world) Sn 866; methunasmiŋ (sexual desire) Sn 835 (expl. by ch. vā rāgo vā peman Nd[1] 181). — Ch. in this quality is one of the roots of misery: cittass' upakkileso S III.232 sq.; v.92; mūlaŋ dukkhassa J IV.328 sq. — Other passages illustrating ch. are e. g. vyāpāda° & vihiŋsā° S II.151; rūpa-dhātuyā° S III.10; IV.72; yaŋ aniccaŋ, etc. . . . tattha° S III.122, 177; IV.145 sq.; asmī ti ch. S III.130; atilīno ch. S v.277 sq., cp. also D II.277. — (b) the emancipation from ch. as necessary for the attainment of Arahantship: — vigata° (free from excitement) and a° S I.111; III.7, 107, 190; IV.387; A II.173 sq.; D III.238; ettha chandaŋ virājetvā Sn 171 = S I.16. Kāye chandaŋ virājaye Sn 203. (a)vīta° A IV.461 sq. °ŋ vineti S I.22, 197; °ŋ vinodeti S I.186; ch. suppaṭivinīta S II.283. na tamhi °ŋ kayirātha Dh 117. — 2. (in the monastic law) consent, declaration of consent (to an official act: kamma) by an absentee Vin I.121, 122. dhammikānaŋ kammānaŋ chandaŋ datvā having given (his) consent to valid proceedings Vin IV.151, 152; cp. °dāyaka II.94. — *Note.* The commentaries follow the canonical usage of the word without adding any precision to its connotation. See Nd[2] s. v.; DhsA 370; DhA I.14, J vi.72, VvA 77.

-âgati in °gamana the wrong way (of behaviour, consisting) in excitement, one of the four agatigamanāni, viz. ch°, dosa°, moha°, bhaya° D III.133, 228; Vbh 376 (see above); -âdhipateyya (adj.) standing under the dominant influence of impulse Dhs 269, 359, 529; Vbh 288 (+ viriya°, citta°, vīmaŋsā°); -ânunīta led according to one's own desire S IV.71; Sn 781; -âraha (adj.) fit to give one's consent Vin II.93; v.221; -ja sprung from desire (dukkha) S I.22; -nānatta the diversity or various ways of impulse or desire S II.143 sq.; D III.289; Vbh 425; -pahāna the giving up of wrong desire S v.273; -mūlaka (adj.) having its root in excitement A IV.339; v.107; -rāga exciting desire (cp. kāmachanda) D II.58, 60; III.289; S I.198; II.283; III. 232 sq. (cakkhusmiŋ, etc.); IV.7 sq. 164 (Bhagavato ch-r. n' atthi), 233; A I.264 (atīte ch-r-ṭṭhāniyā dhammā); II.71; III.73; Nd[2] 413; DhA I.334; -samādhi the (right) concentration of good effort, classed under the 4 iddhipādā with viriya°; citta° vīmaŋsā° D III.77; S v.268; A I.39; Vbh 216 sq.; Nett 15; -sampadā the blessing of zeal S v.30.

Chandaka a voluntary collection (of alms for the Sangha), usually as °ŋ saŋharati to make a vol. coll. Vin IV.250; J I.422; II.45, 85 (saŋharitvā v. l. BB; text sankaḍḍhitvā), 196, 248; III.288 (nava°, a new kind of donation); Cp. BSk. chandaka-bhikṣaṇa AvŚ vol. II.227.

Chandatā (f.) [see chanda] (strong) impulse, will, desrre Nd[2] 394; Vbh 350, 370.

Chandavantatā (f.) [abstr. to adj. chandavant, chanda + vant] = chandatā VvA 319.

Chandasā (f.) [see chando] metrics, prosody Miln 3.

Chandika (adj.) [see chanda] having zeal, endeavouring usually as a° without (right) effort, & always comb[d] w. anādara & assaddha Pug 13; Vbh 341; PvA 54 (v. l.), 175.

Chandikata (adj.) & **chandikatā** (f.) (with) right effort, zealous, zeal (adj.) Th 1, 1029 (chandi°) (n.) Vbh 208.

Chando (nt.) [Vedic chandas, from **skandh**, cp. in meaning Sk. pada; Gr. ἴαμβος] metre, metrics, prosody, esp. applied to the Vedas Vin II.139 (chandaso buddhavacanaŋ āropeti to recite in metrical form, or acc. to Bdhgh. in the dialect of the Vedas cp. *Vin. Texts* III.150); S I.38; Sn 568 (Sāvittī chandaso mukhaŋ: the best of Vedic metres).

-viciti prosody VvA 265 (enum[d] as one of the 6 disciplines dealing with the Vedas: see chaḷanga).

Channa[1] [pp. of **chad**, see chādeti[1]] 1. covered J IV. 293 (vāri°); VI.432 (padara°, ceiling); ThA 257. — 2. thatched (of a hut) Sn 18. — 3. concealed, hidden, secret J II.58; IV.58. — nt. channaŋ a secret place Vin IV.220.

Channa[2] [pp. to **chad** (chand), chandayati, see chādeti[2]] fit, suitable, proper Vin II.124 (+paṭirūpa); III.128; D I.91 (+paṭirūpa); S I.9; M I.360; J III.315; V.307; VI.572; Pv II.12[15] (=yutta PvA 159).

Chapaka name of a low-class tribe Vin IV.203 (=caṇḍāla Bdhgh. on Sekh. 69 at Vin IV.364), f. °ī ib.

Chappañca [cha+pañca] six or five Miln 292.

Chab° see under cha.

Chamā (f.) [from **kṣam**, cp. khamati. It remains doubtful how the Dhtm (553, 555) came to define the root **cham** (=kṣam) as 1. hīḷane and 2. adane] the earth; only in oblique cases, used as adv. *Instr.* chamā on the ground, to the ground (=ved. kṣamā) M I.387; D III.6; J III.232; IV.285; VI.89, 528; Vv 41[4] (VvA 183; bhūmiyaŋ); Th 2, 17; 112 (ThA 116: chamāyaŋ); Pv IV.5[3] (PvA 260: bhūmiyaŋ). — *loc.* chamāyaŋ Vin I.118; A I.215; Sn 401; Vism 18; ThA 116; chamāya Vin II.214.

Chambhati [see chambheti] to be frightened DhA IV.52 (+vedhati).

Chambhita [pp. of chambheti]. Only in der. chambhitatta (nt.) the state of being stiff, paralysis, stupefaction, consternation, always comb[d] with other expressions of fear, viz. uttāsa S V.386; bhaya J I.345 (where spelled chambhittaŋ); II.336 (where wrongly expl[d] by sarīracalanaŋ), freq. in phrase **bhaya ch. lomahaŋsa** (fear, stupefaction & horripilation (" gooseflesh ") Vin II.156; S I.104; 118; 219; D I.49 (expl[d] at DA I.50 wrongly by sakala-sarīra calanaŋ); Nd[2] 470; Miln 23; Vbh 367; Vism 187. — In other connections at Nd[2] I (=Dhs 425, 1118, where thambhitatta instead of ch°); Dhs 965 (on which see *Dhs trsl.* 242).

Chambhin (adj.) [see chambheti] immovable, rigid; terrified, paralysed with fear S I.219; M I.19; J IV.310 (v. l. jambhī, here with ref. to one who is bound (stiff) with ropes (pāsasatehi chambhī) which is however taken by com. as instr. of cha & expl[d] by chasu thānesu, viz. on 4 limbs, body & neck; cp. cha). — acchambhin firm, steady, undismayed S I.220; Sn 42; J I.71. — See chambheti & chambhita.

Chambheti [cp. Sk. skabhnāti & stabhnāti, **skambh**, and P. khambha, thambha & khambheti] to be firm or rigid, fig. to be stiff with fear, paralysed: see chambhin & chambhitatta. Cp. ūrukhambha (under khambha[2]).

Challi [Sk. challi] bark, bast DhA II.165; Bdhgh on MV. VIII.29.

Chava [Derivation doubtful. Vedic śava] 1. a corpse Vin II.115 (°sīsassa patta a bowl made out of a skull). See cpds. — 2. (adj.) vile, low, miserable, wretched Vin II.112, 188; S I.66; M I.374; A II.57; J IV.263.

-aṭṭhika bones of a corpes, a skeleton C III.15, 1 (?); **-âlāta** a torch from a pyre S III.93=A II.95=It 90=J I.482; Vism 54, 299 (°ûpama). **-kuṭikā** a charnelhouse, morgue, Vin I.152; **-dāhaka** one who (officially) burns the dead, an " undertaker " Vin I.152; DhA I.68 (f. °ikā); Vism 230; Miln 331. **-dussa** a miserable garment D I.166≈A I.240; II.206. **-sarīra** a corpse Vism 178 sq. **-sitta** a water pot (see above 1) Th 1, 127.

Chavaka 1. a corpse J V.449. — 2. wretched Miln 156, 200; (°caṇḍāla, see expl[n] at J V.450).

Chavi (f.) [*(s)qeu to cover. Vedic chavi, skunāti; cp. Gr. σκῦλον; Lat. ob-scurus; Ohg. skūra (Nhg. scheuer); Ags sceo>E. sky also Goth. skōlıs>E. shoe] the (outer, thin) skin, tegument S II.256; A IV.129; Sn 194; J II.92. Distinguished from camma, the hide (under-skin, corium) S II.238 (see camma); also in comb[n] ch-cammamaŋsa Vism 235; DhA IV.56.

-kalyāṇa beauty of complexion, one of the 5 beauties (see kalyāṇa 2d) DhA I.387; **-dos'-ābādha** a skin disease, cutaneous irritation Vin I.206; **-roga** skin disease DhA III.295; **-vaṇṇa** the colour of the skin, the complexion, esp. beautiful compl., beauty Vin I.8; J III.126; DhA IV.72; PvA 14 (vaṇṇadhātu), 70, 71 (=vaṇṇa).

Chāta (adj.) [cp. Sk. psāta from **bhas** (*bhsā), Gr. ψώχω; see Walde, *Lat. Wtb.* under sabulum & cp. bhasman, probably Non-Aryan] hungry J I.338; II.301; V.69; Pv II.1[13] (=bubhukkhita, khudāya abhibhūta PvA 72) II.9[36] (jighacchita PvA 126); PvA 62; VvA 76; Miln 253; Mhvs VII.24. Cp. pari°.

-ajjhatta with hungry insides J I.345; II.203; V.338, 359; DhA I.125; DhA I.367 (chātak'); III.33, 40. **-kāla** time of being hungry.

Chātaka [fr. prec.] 1. adj. hungry J I.245, 266. — 2. (nt.) hunger, famine J I.266; II.124, 149. 367; VI.487; DhA I.170.

Chātatā [f. abstr. fr. chāta] hunger (lit. hungriness) DhA I.170.

Chādana (nt.) [to chādeti] covering, clothing, often comb[d] with ghāsa° food & clothing (q. v.) J II.79 (vattha°); Pv I.10[7] (bhojana°); II.1[7] (vattha°); PvA 50 (=vattha); DhA IV.7. — As adj. J VI.354 (of the thatch of a house).

Chādanā (f.) [fr. chādeti] covering, concealment Pug 19, 23. Cp. pari°.

Chādi (f.) [chādeti[1]] shade J IV.351.

Chādiya (nt.) covering (of a house or hut), thatch, straw, hay (for eating) J VI.354 (=gehacchādana-tiṇa).

Chādeti[1] [Caus. of **chad**, Sk. chādayati] (a) to cover, to conceal Vin II.211 (Pass. chādīyati); Sn 1022 (mukhaŋ jivhāya ch.); Dh 252; Pv III.4[3]. — (b) (of sound) to penetrate, to fill J II.253; VI.195. — pp. channa[1] (q. v.).

Chādeti[2] [for chandeti, cp. Sk. chandati & chadayati; to **khyā** ?] (a) to seem good, to please, to give pleasure S II.110; A III.54; DhA III.285 (bhattaŋ me na ch.). — (b) to be pleased with, to delight in, to approve of (c acc.) esp. in phrase bhattaŋ chādeti to appreciate the meal Vin II.138; D I.72 (=rucceyya); V.31 (chādayamāna), 33 (chādamana), 463; Th 2, 409; Pv I.11[8] (nacchādimhamhase), pp. channa[2].

Chāpa & **°ka** [Sk. śāva] the young of an animal M I.384 (°ka); S II.269 (bhinka°); J I.460; II.439 (sakuṇa°); Miln 402; -f. chāpī J VI.192 (maṇḍūka°).

Chāyā (f.) [Vedic chāyā, light & shade, ***skei** (cp. **(s)qait** in ketu), cp. Sk. śyāva; Gr. σκιά & σκοιός; Goth. skeinan. See note on kāla, vol. II, p. 38[2]] shade, shadow S I.72, 93; M II.235; III.164; A II.114; Sn 1014; Dh 2; J II.302; IV.304; V.445; Miln 90, 298; DhA I.35; PvA 12, 32, 45, 81, etc. — Yakkhas have none; J V.34; VI.337. chāyā is frequent in similes: see *J.P.T.S.* 1907, 87.

Chārikā (f.) [Cp. kṣāyati to burn, kṣāra burning; Gr. ξηρός dry, Lat. serenus dry, clear. See also khāra & bhasma.] Ashes Vin I.210; II.220; D II.164=Ud 93; A I.209; IV.103; J III.447; IV.88; V.144; DhA I.256; II.68; VvA 67; PvA 80 (chārikangāra).

Chiggaḷa [cp. chidda] a hole, in eka°-yuga M III.169≈; tāḷa° key hole S IV.290; Vism 394.

Chida (always -°) (adj.) breaking, cutting, destroying M I.386; S I.191 = Th I, 1234; Th I, 521; 1143; Sn 87 (kankha°) 491, 1021, 1101 (taṇha°); VvA 82 (id.).

Chidda [cp. Ohg. scetar. For suffix °ra, cp. rudhira, etc. Vedic **chid**+ra. Cp. Sk. chidra] 1. (adj.) having rents or fissures, perforated S IV.316; J I.419; (fig.) faulty, defective, Vin I.290. — 2. (nt.) a cutting, slit, hole, aperture, S I.43; J I.170 (eka°), 172, 419, 503; II.244, 261; (kaṇṇa°); Vism 171, 172 (bhitti°), 174 (tāḷa°); SnA 248 (akkhi°); DhA III.42; VvA 100 (bhitti°); PvA 180 (kaṇṇa°), 253 (read chidde for chinde); fig. a fault, defect, flaw Dh 229 (acchidda-vutti faultless conduct) Miln 94.

-**āvachidda** full of breaches and holes J III.491; Vism 252; DhA I.122, 284 (cp. °vichidda); III.151. -**kārin** inconsistent A II.187; -**vichidda** = °āvachidda J I.419; V.163 (sarīraŋ chiddavichiddaŋ karoti to perforate a body).

Chiddaka (adj.) having holes or meshes (of a net) D I.45.

Chiddatā (f.) perforation, being perforated J I.419.

Chiddavant (adj.) having faults, full of defects M I.272.

Chindati [Vedic **chid** in 3 forms viz. 1. (Perf.) base chid; 2. Act. (pres.) base w. nasal infix. chind; 3. Med. (denom). base w. guṇa ched. Cp. the analagous formations of **cit** under cinteti. — Idg.* **sk(h)eid**, Gr. σχίζω (E. schism); Lat. scindo (E. scissors); Ohg. scizan; Ags. scitan; cp. also Goth. skaidan, Ohg. sceidan. Root **chid** is defined at Dhtp 382, 406 as "dvedhā-karaṇa"] to cut off, to destroy, to remove, both *lit.* (bandhanaŋ, pāsaŋ, pasibbakaŋ, jīvaŋ, gīvaŋ, sīsaŋ, hatthapāde, etc.) and *fig.* (taṇhaŋ, mohaŋ, āsavā, saŋyojanāni, vicikicchaŋ, vanathaŋ, etc.) Freq. in similes: see *J.P.T.S.* 1907, 88. — *Forms*: (1) **chid**: aor. acchidā Sn 357, as acchidaŋ M II.35, acchidda Dh 351 (cp. agamā); Pass. pres. **chijjati** (Sk. chidyate) Dh 284; It 70; J I.167; Th I, 1055 = Miln 395; Miln 40; aor. chijji J III.181 (dvidhā ch. broke in two). — fut. chijjissati J I.336; — ger. chijjitvā J I.202; IV.120; — pp. chijjita J III.389; see also chida, chidda, chinna. — (2) **chind**: Act. pres. chindati S I.149 = A V.174 = Sn 657; PvA 4, 114; VvA 123; — imper. chinda Sn 346; J II.153; chindatha Dh 283; — pot. chinde Dh 370; — ppr. chindamāna J I.70, 233. — fut. chindissati DhA II.258. — aor. acchindi Vin I.88 & chindi J I.140. — ger. chinditvā J I.222, 254, 326; II.155. — inf. chindituŋ Vin I.206; PvA 253. — grd. chindiya J II.139 (duc°). — Caus. chindāpeti J II.104, 106; Vism 190 (rājāno core ch.). — (3) **ched**: fut. checchati (Sk. chetsyati) M I.434; Dh 350; Miln 391. — aor. acchecchi (Sk. acchaitsīt) S I.12; A II.249; Sn 355 = Th I,1275; J VI.261. acchejji (v. l. of acchecchi) is read at S IV.205, 207, 399; V.441; A III.246, 444; It 47. — inf. chetuŋ J IV.208; Pv IV.3[28], & chettuŋ Sn 28. — ger. chetvā Sn 66, 545, 622; Dh 283, 369; J I.255; Nd² 245, & chetvāna Sn 44; Dh 346; J III.396. — grd. chetabba Vin II.110, & chejja (often comb[d] w. bhejja, torture & maiming, as punishments) Vin III.47 (+bh°); J V.444 (id.) VI.536; Miln 83, 359. Also chejja in neg. achejja S VI.220. — Caus. chedeti Vin I.50, & chedāpeti ib.; J IV.154. See also cheda, chedana.

Chindanaka (adj.) [fr. chindati] breaking, see pari°.

Chinna [pp. of chindati] cut off, destroyed Vin I.71 (acchinna-kesa with unshaven hair); M I.430; D II.8 (°papañca); J I.255; II.155; IV.138; Dh 338; Pv I.11² (v. l. for bhinna), 11⁶; DhA IV.48. Very often in punishments of decapitation (sīsa°) or mutilation (hatthapāda°, etc.) e. g. Vin I.91; III.28; Pv II.2⁴ (ghāna-sīsa°); Miln 5. Cp. sañ°. As first part of cpd., chinna° very frequently is to be rendered by "without," e. g.

-**āsa** without hope J II.230; PvA 22, 174; -**iriyāpatha** unable to walk, i. e. a cripple Vin I.91; -**kaṇṇa** without ears PvA 151; -**gantha** untrammelled, unfettered Sn 219; -**pilotika** with torn rags, or without rags S II.28; PvA 171 (+bhinna°); -**bhatta** without food i. e. famished, starved J I.84; V.382; DhA III.106 = VvA 76; -**saŋsaya** without doubt Sn 1112; It 96, 97, 123; Nd² 244. -**sāṭaka** a torn garment Vism 51.

Chinnaka (adj.) [fr. chinna] cut; a° uncut (of cloth) Vin I.297.

Chinnikā (f.) deceitful, fraudulent, sly, only in comb[n] w. dhuttā (dhuttikā) & only appl[d] to women Vin III.128; IV.61; J II.114; Miln 122.

Chuddha [Sk. kṣubdha (?) **kṣubh**, perhaps better **ṣṭiv**, pp. ṣṭyūta (see niṭṭhubhati), cp. Pischel, *Prk. Gr.* §§ 66, 120, & Trenckner *Notes* p. 75. See also khipita] thrown away, removed, rejected, contemptible Dh 41 = Th 2, 468 (spelled chuṭṭha); J V.302.

Chupati [Dhtp 480 = samphasse] to touch Vin I.191; III.37, 121; J IV.82; VI.166; Vism 249; DhA I.166 (mā chupi). — pp. chupita.

Chupana (nt.) touching Vin III.121; J VI.387.

Chupita [pp. of chupati] touched Vin III.37; J VI.218.

Chubhati given as root **chubh** (for **kṣubh**) with def. "nicchubhe" at Dhtm 550. See khobha.

Churikā (f.) [Sk. kṣurikā to kṣura see khura, cp. chārikā > khara] a knife, a dagger, kreese Th 2, 302; J III.370; Miln 339; cp. *Miln trsln.* II.227; ThA 227; DhA III.19.

Churita: see vi°.

Cheka (adj.) 1. clever, skilful, shrewd; skilled in (c. loc.) Vin II.96; M I.509; J I.290 (anga-vijjāya); II.161, 403; V.216, 366 (°pāpaka good & bad); VI.294 (id.); Miln 293; DA I.90; VvA 36, 215; DhA I.178. — 2. genuine Vism 437 (opp. kūṭa).

Chekatā (f.) [cheka+tā] skill VvA 131.

Chejja 1. see chindati. — 2. one of the 7 notes in the gamut VvA 139.

Cheta an animal living in mountain cliffs, a sort of leopard S I.198.

Chettar [Sk. chettṛ, n-agent to chindati] cutter, destroyer Sn 343; J VI.226.

Cheda [see chindati] cutting, destruction, loss Sn 367 (°bandhana); J I.419; 485; sīsa° decapitation DhA II.204; PvA 5; aṇḍa° castration J IV.364; — bhatta °ŋ karoti to put on short rations J I.156. pada° separation of words SnA 150. -°**gāmin** (adj.) liable to break, fragile A II.81; J V.453. — Cp. vi°.

Chedaka (adj.) [fr. cheda] cutting; in aṇḍa° one who castrates J IV.366.

Chedana (nt.) [see chindati] cutting, severing, destroying D I.5; (= DA I.80 hattha°-ādi); III.176; Vin II.133; A II.209; V.206; S IV.169 (nakha°); V.473; Miln 86; Vism 102 (°vadha-bandana, etc.).

Chedanaka 1. (adj.) one who tears or cuts off PvA 7. — 2. (nt.) the process of getting cut (a cert. penance for offences: in comb[n] with āpattiyo & pācittiyaŋ) Vin II.307; IV.168, 170, 171, 279; V.133, 146 (cha ch. āpattiyo).

Cheppā (f.) [Sk. śépa] tail Vin I.191; III.21.

J.

Ja (-°) [adj.-suffix from **jan**, see janati; cp. °ga; gacchati] born, produced, sprung or arisen from. Freq. in cpds.: atta°, ito°, eka°, kuto°, khandha°, jala°, daratha°, dāru°, di°, puthuj°, pubba°, yoni°, vāri°, saha°, sineha°.

Jagat (nt.) [Vedic jagat, intens. of **gam**, see gacchati] the world, the earth A II.15, 17 (jagato gati); S I.186 (jagatogadha plunged into the world).

Jagatī (f.) [see jagat] only in cpds. as jagati°: -ppadesa a spot in the world Dh 127=PvA 104; -ruha earth grown, i. e. a tree J I.216.

Jagga (nt.) [jaggati+ya] wakefulness S I.111.

Jaggati (=jāgarati, Dhtp 22 gives **jagg** as root in meaning "niddā-khaya."] (a) to watch, to lie awake J V.269. — (b) to watch over, i. e. to tend, to nourish, rear, bring up J I.148 (dārakaŋ), 245 (āsīvisaŋ).

Jaggana (nt.) [from jaggati] watching, tending, bringing up J I.148 (dāraka°).

Jagganatā (to jāgarati] watchfulness J I.10.

Jagghati [Intens. to sound-root **ghar.** for *jaghrati. See note on gala. Kern compares Ved. jakṣati, Intens. of hasati (*Toev.* under anujagghati); Dhtp 31 **jaggh**= hasane] to laugh, to deride J III.223; V.436; VI.522. — pp. jagghita J VI.522. See also anu°, pa°.

Jagghitā (f.) laughter J III.226.

Jaghana (nt.) [Vedic jaghana, cp. Gr. κοχώνη; see janghā] the loins, the buttocks Vin II.266; J V.203.

Jaṅgala (nt.) a rough, sandy & waterless place, jungle A V.21; J IV.71; VvA 338. Cp. ujjangala.

Janghā (f.) [Vedic janghā; cp. Av. zanga, ankle; Goth. gaggan, to go; Ags. gang, walk. From ***ghengh** to walk; see also jaghana] the leg, usually the lower leg (from knee to ankle) D II.17≈(S I.16=Sn 165 (eṇi°); Sn 610; J II.240; V.42; VI.34; ThA 212). In cpds. jangha° (except in janghā-vihāra).
-ummagga a tunnel fit for walking J VI.428; -pesanika adj. going messages on foot Vin III.185; J II.82; Miln 370 (°iya); Vism 17. -**bala(ŋ)** (nissāya) by means of his leg (lit. by the strength of, cp. Fr. à force de); -magga a footpath J II.251; V.203; VvA 194. -vihāra the state of walking about (like a wanderer), usually in phrase °ŋ anucankamati anuvicarati D I.235; M I.108; Sn p. 105, p. 115; or °ŋ carati PvA 73. — A I.136; J II.272; IV.7, 74; DhA III.141.

Jangheyyaka (nt.) [see janghā] lit. "belonging to the knees"; the kneepiece of a robe Vin I.287.

Jacca (adj.) [jāti+tya] of birth, by birth (usually -°) M II.47 (ittara° of inferior birth); Sn p. 80 (kiŋ° of what birth, i. e. of what social standing); J I.342 (hīna° of low birth): Sdhp 416 (id.) J V.257 (nihīna°); Miln 189 (sama° of equal rank).
-andha (adj.) blind from birth Ud 62 sq. (Jaccandhavagga VI.4); J I.45, 76; IV.192; Vbh 412 sq.; in similes at Vism 544, 596.

Jaccā instr. of jāti.

Jajjara [From intensive of jarati] withered, feeble with age Th 2, 270; J I.5, 59 (jarā°); ThA 212; PvA 63 (°bhāva, state of being old) — a° not fading (cp. amata & ajarāmara), of Nibbāna S IV.369.

Jajjarita [pp. of intens. of **jar** see jarati] weakened DhA I.7.

Jañña (adj.) [=janya, cp. jātya; see kula & koleyyaka] of (good) birth, excellent, noble, charming, beautiful M I.30 (jaññajañña, cp. p. 528); J II.417 (=manāpa sādhu). a° J II.436.

Jaṭa a handle, only in vāsi° (h. of a razor) Vin IV.168; S III.154=A IV.127.

Jaṭā (f.) [B.Sk. jaṭā] tangle, braid, plaiting, esp. (a) the matted hair as worn by ascetics (see jaṭila) Sn 249; Dh 241, 393; J I.12 (ajina+); II.272. — (b) the tangled branches of trees J I.64. — (c) (fig.) (the tangle of) desire, lust S I.13=165.
-aṇḍuva (=°andu ?) a chain of braided hair, a matted topknot S I.117; -**ājina** braided hair & an antelope's hide (worn by ascetics) Sn 1010 (°dhara), cp. above J I.12; -dharaṇa the wearing of matted hair M I.282.

Jaṭita [pp. of **jaṭ**, to which also jaṭā; Dhtp 95: sanghāte] entangled S I.13; Miln 102, 390; Vism 1 (etym.).

Jaṭin one who wears a jaṭā, an ascetic Sn 689; f. -**inī** J VI.555.

Jaṭila [BSk. jaṭila] one who wears a jaṭā, i. e. a braid of hair, or who has his hair matted, an ascetic. Enum[d] amongst other 'religious' as ājīvikā nigaṇṭhā j. paribbājakā Nd[1] 308; ājīvikā nig° j. tāpasā Nd[2] 149, 513; — Vin I.24=IV.108; I.38 (purāṇa° who had previously been j.)=VvA 13=PvA 22; S I.78; Sn p. 103, 104 (Keṇiya j.); J I.15; II.382; Ud 6; Dpvs I.38.

Jaṭilaka=jaṭila M I.282; A III.276; Miln 202; Vism 382.

Jaṭhara (m. nt.) [Vedic jaṭhara, to ***gelt**=***gelbh** (see gabbha), cp. Goth. kilþei uterus, Ags. cild=E. child] the belly Miln 175.

Jaṇṇu(ka) [cp. jānu & jannu] the knee D II.160; J VI.332; SnA II.230; DhA I.80 (°ka); II.57 (id.), 80; IV.204; VvA 206 (jaṇṇu-kappara).

Jatu [Sk. jatu; cp. Lat. bitumen pitch; Ags. cwidu, resin, Ohg. quiti glue] lac. As medicine Vin I.201. °maṭṭhaka a decking with lac, used by women to prevent conception Vin IV.261; consisting of either jatu, kaṭṭha (wood), piṭṭha (flour), or mattikā (clay).

Jattu (nt.) [Vedic jatru] the collar-bone DhA II.55 (gloss: aŋsakūṭa); Dāvs IV.49.

Jaddhu [for jaddhuŋ, inf. to **jakṣ** (P. jaggh), corresp. to Sk. jagdhi eating food; intens. of ghasati] only in composition as a° not eating, abstaining from food. °**ka** one who fasts M I.245; °**māra** death by starvation J VI.63 (=anāsaka-maraṇa; Fsb. has note: read ajuṭṭha° ?); °**mārika** A IV.287 (v. l. ajeṭṭha°).

Jana [***genē**: see janati. Cp. Gr. γένος, γόνος; Lat. genus = Fr. gens, to which also similar in meaning] a creature, living being: (a) sg. an individual, a creature, person, man Sn 121, 676, 807, 1023 (sabba everybody). Usually collectively: people, they, one (= Fr. on), with pl. of verb Dh 249 (dadanti); often as mahājana the people, the crowd S I.115; J I.167, 294; PvA 6; lokamahājana = loka DhA III.175; or as bahu(j)jana many people, the many A I.68; Dh 320; DhA III.175. See also puthujjana. — (b) pl. men, persons, people, beings: nānā° various living beings Sn 1102 (expl^d at Nd² 248 as khattiyā brāhmaṇā vessā suddā gahaṭṭhā pabbajitā devā manussā.) dve janā J I.151; II.105; tayo j. J I.63; III.52; keci janā some people PvA 20. See also Sn 243, 598, 1077, 1121.

-**ādhipa** a king of men J II.369; -**inda** = prec. J III.280, 294; -**esabha** the leader of men, the best of all people Dh 255; -**kāya** a body or group of people J I.28; DhA I.33 (dve j.: micchā & sammā-diṭṭhikā); Dpvs I.40; -**pada** country see sep.; -**majjhe** (loc.) before (all) the people J I.294; Th 2, 394; -**vāda** people's talk, gossip Sn 973.

Janaka [to janati] 1. producing, production Vism 369; adj. (-°) producing: pasāda° Mhvs I.4 (= °kāraka); a species of karma Vism 601; *Cpd.* 144 (A.1). — 2. n. f. °ikā genetrix, mother J I.16; Dhs 1059≈(where it represents another jānikā, viz. deception, as shown by syn. māyā & B.Sk. janikā Lal. V. 541; Kern, *Toev.* p. 41).

Janatā (f.) [from janati] a collection of people (" mankind "), congregation, gathering; people, folk D I.151 (= DA I.310, correct jananā), 206; Vin II.128 = M II.93 (pacchimā); A I.61 (id.); III.251 (id.); It 33; J IV.110; Pv III.5⁷ (= janasamūha upāsakagaṇa PvA 200).

Janati¹ [Sk. janati (trs.) & jāyate (intrs.); ***gene** & ***gnē** to (be able to) produce; Gr. γίγνομαι (γένεσις) γνωτός = jāta = (g)nātus; Lat. gigno, natura, natio; Goth. knōþs & kunþs; Cymr. geni, Ags. cennan, Ohg. kind, etc.] only in Caus. janeti [Sk. janayati] often spelled jāneti (cp. jaleti: jāleti) & Pass. (intrs.) jāyati to bring forth, produce, cause, syn. sañjaneti nibbatteti abhinibbatteti Nd² s. v. (cp. karoti). ussāhaŋ j. to put forth exertion J II.407 (see chanda); (saŋ)vegaŋ j. to stir up emotion (aspiration) J III.184; PvA 32; Mhvs I.4; dukkhaŋ j. to cause discomfort PvA 63. — Aor. janayi Th 2, 162 (Māyā j. Gotamaŋ: she bore). — Pp. janita produced PvA 1. — See also jantu jamma, jāta, jāti, ñāti, etc.

Janati² to make a sound J VI.64 (= sanati saddaŋ karoti).

Janana (adj.) [to janati] producing, causing (-°) It 84 (anattha° dosa); J IV.141; Dpvs I.2; DhsA 258; Dhtp 428. — f. jananī PvA 1 (saŋvega° desanā); = mother (cp. janettī) J IV.175; PvA 79. *Note.* jananā DA I.310 is misprint for janatā.

Janapada [jana + pada, the latter in function of collective noun-abstract: see pada 3] inhabited country, the country (opp. town or market-place), the continent; politically: a province, district, county D I.136 (opp. nigama); II.349; A I.160, 178; Sn 422, 683, 995, 1102; J I.258; II.3 (opp. nagara), 139, 300; PvA 20, 32, 111 (province). See also gāma. The 16 provinces of Buddhist India are comprised in the soḷasa mahā-janapadā (Miln 350) enum^d at A I.213 = IV.252 sq. = Nd² 247 (on Sn 1102) as follows: Angā, Magadhā (+ Kālingā, Nd²) Kāsī, Kosalā, Vajjī, Mallā, Cetī (Cetiyā A IV.), Vaŋsā (Vangā A I.), Kurū, Pañcālā, Majjā (Macchā A), Sūrasenā, Assakā, Avantī, Yonā (Gandhārā A), Kambojā. Cp. Rhys Davids, *B. India* p. 23.

-**kathā** talk or gossip about the province D I.7≈; -**kalyāṇī** a country-beauty, i. e. the most beautiful girl in the province D I.193 (see kalyāṇa); -**cārikā** tramping the country PvA 14; -**tthāvariya** stableness, security, of the realm, in °patta, one who has attained a secure state of his realm, of a Cakkavattin D I.88; II.16; Sn p. 106; -**padesa** a rural district A IV.366; V.101.

Janavati (?) A IV.172.

Janitta (nt.) [**jan** + tra. cp. Gr. γενέτειρα] birthplace J II.80.

Janetti (f.) [f. to janitṛ = γενέτωρ = genitor, cp. genetrix. The Sk. form is janitri. On e:i cp. petti°: pitri°] mother D II.7 sq.; M III.248; A IV.276; J I.48; II.381; IV.48.

Jantāghara [acc. to Abhp. 214 = aggisālā, a room in which a fire is kept (viz. for the purpose of a steam bath, i. e. a hot room, cp. in meaning Mhg. kemenate = Lat. caminata, Ger. stube = E. stove; Low Ger. pesel (room) = Lat. pensile (bath) etc.) Etym. uncertain. Bühler *KZ* 25, p. 325 = yantra-gṛha (oil-mill ?); E. Hardy (*D. Lit. Ƶtg.* 1902, p. 339) = jentāka (hot dry bath), cp. *Vin. Texts* I.157; III.103. In all probability it is a distorted form (by dissimilation or analogy), perhaps of *jhānt-āgāra, to **jhā** to burn = Sk. kṣā, jhānti heat or heating (= Sk. kṣāti) + āgāra, which latter received the aspiration of the first part (= āghāra), both being reduced in length of vowels = jant-āghara]—1. a (hot) room for bathing purposes, a sitzbath Vin I.47, 139; II.119, 220 sq., 280; III.55; M III.126; J II.25, 144; Vism 18; Dpvs VIII.45. — 2. living room J I.449.

Janti at DA I.296 in jantiyā (for D I.135 jāniyā) = hāni, abandonment, giving up, payment, fine [prob. = jahanti, to jahāti]. But see jāni.

Jantu¹ [Vedic jantu, see janati] a creature, living being, man, person S I.48; A IV.227; Sn 586, 773 sq., 808, 1103; Nd² 249 (= satta, nara, puggala); Dh 105, 176, 341, 395; J I.202; II.415; V.495; Pv II.9⁴⁹ (= sattanikāya, people, a crowd PvA 134).

Jantu² a grass Vin I.196.

Jannu [cp. jaṇṇu(ka) & jānu] the knee DhA I.394. -°**ka** D II.17≈(in marks of a Mahāpurisa, v. l. ṇṇ); J IV.165; DhA I.48.

Japa (& jappa vv. ll.) [fr. japati] 1. muttering, mumbling, recitation A III.56 = J III.205 (+ manta); Sn 328 (jappa) (= niratthaka-kathā SnA 334). — 2. studying J III.114 (= ajjhena).

Jap(p)aka (adj.) whispering, see kaṇṇa.°

Japati (& jappati Dhtp 189, also japp 190 — vacane; sound-root **jap**) to mumble, whisper, utter, recite J IV.204; Pv II.6¹ (= vippalapati PvA 94); PvA 97; ppr. jappaŋ S I.166 (palāpaŋ); J IV.75. See jaḷa, japana; also pari°.

Japana (sic. DA I.97, otherwise jappana) whispering, mumbling (see japati), in **kaṇṇa**°. See also pari°.

Jappati [*not*, as customary, to **jalp**, Sk. jalpati (= japati), but in the meaning of desire, etc., for cappati to **capp**, as in cappeti = Sk, carvayati to chew, suck, be hungry (q. v.) cp. also calaka] to hunger for, to desire, yearn, long for, (c. acc.) Sn 771 (kāme), 839 (bhavaŋ), 899, 902; Nd² 79 (= pajappati), — pp. jappita Sn 902. See also jappā, jappanā, etc., also abhijjappati & pa°.

Jappanā = jappā Sn 945; Dhs 1059≈. Cp. pa°.

Jappā (f.) [to jappati] desire, lust, greed, attachment, hunger (cp. Nd² on taṇhā) S I.123 (bhava-lobha°); Sn 1033; Nd² 250; Nett 12; Dhs 279, 1059.

Jambāla [Sk. jambāla] mud; adj. jambālin muddy, as n. jambālī (f.) a dirty pool (at entrance to village) A II.166.

Jambu (f.) [Sk. jambu] the rose-apple tree, Eugenia Jambolana J II.160; V.6; Vv 6^{7}; 44^{13}, 164. — As adj. f. jambī sarcastically "rose-apple-maid," appl^{d} to a gardener's daughter J III.22.
-dīpa the country of the rose-apples i. e. India J I.263; VvA 18; Miln 27, etc. -nada see jambonada; -pakka the fruit of Eugenia jambolana, the rose-apple (of black or dark colour) Vism 409; -pesī the rind of the r.-a. fruit J V.465; -rukkha the r.-a. tree DhA III.211; -saṇḍa rose-apple grove (=°dīpa, N. for India) Sn 552 = Th I, 822.

Jambuka [Sk. jambuka, to **jambh** ?] a jackal J II.107; III.223.

Jambonada [Sk. jāmbūnada; belonging to or coming from the Jambu river (?)] a special sort of gold (in its unwelded state); also spelled **jambunada** (J IV.105; VvA 13, 340) A I.181; II.8, 29; Vv 84^{17}. Cp. jātarūpa.

Jambhati [cp. Vedic jehate, Dhtp 208 & Dhtm 298 define **jambh** as "gatta-vināma," i. e. bending the body] to yawn, to arouse oneself, to rise, go forth (of a lion) J VI.40.

Jambhanā (f.) [to jambhati] arousing, activity, alertness Vbh 352.

Jamma (adj.) [Vedic *jālma (?), dialectical ?] miserable, wretched, contemptible J II.110; III.99 (=lāmaka); f. -ī S V.217; Dh 335, 336 (of taṇhā); J II.428; V.421; DhA IV.44 (=lāmakā).

Jamman(a) (nt.) [to janati] birth, descent, rank Sn 1018.

Jaya [see jayati] vanquishing, overcoming, victory D I.10; Sn 681; J II.406; opp. parājaya Vism 401.
-ggaha the lucky die J IV.322 (=kaṭaggaha, q. v.); -parājaya victory & defeat Dh 201; -pāna the drink of victory, carousing, wassail; °ŋ pivati DhA I.193; -sumana "victory's joy," N. of a plant (cp. jātisumana) Vism 174; DhA I.17, 383.

Jayati (jeti, jināti) [Sk. jayati, ji to have power, to conquer, cp. jaya=βία; trans. of which the intrans. is jīnāti to lose power, to become old (see jīrati)] to conquer, surpass; to pillage, rob, to overpower, to defeat. — Pres. [jayati] jeti J II.3; jināti Sn 439; Dh 354; J I.289; IV.71. — Pot. jeyya Com. on Dh 103; jine Dh 103 = J II.4 = VvA 69; 3rd pl. jineyyuŋ S I.221 (opp. parājeyyuŋ). — Ppr. jayaŋ Dh 201. — Fut. jessati Vv 33^{2}; jayissati ib.; jinissati J II.183. — Aor. jini J I.313; II.404; ajini Dh 3; pl. jiniŋsu S I.221 (opp. parājiŋsu), 224 (opp. parājiŋsu, with v. l. °jiniŋsu); A IV.432 (opp. °jiyiŋsu, with v. l. °jiniŋsu). Also aor. ajesi DhA I.44 (=ajini). — Proh. (mā) jiyi J IV.107. — Ger. jetvā Sn 439; jetvāna It 76. — Inf. jinituŋ J VI.193; VvA 69. — Grd. jeyya Sn 288 (a°); jinitabba VvA 69 (v. l. jetabba). — *Pass.* jīyati (see parā°), jīyati is also Pass. to jarati — *Caus.* 1. jayāpeti to wish victory to, to hail (as a respectful greeting to a king) J II.213, 369, 375; IV.403. — 2. jāpayati to cause to rob, to incite, to plunder M I.231; It 22 = J IV.71 (v. l. hāpayati) = Miln 402; J VI.108 (to annul); Miln 227. — Des. jigiŋsati (q. v.). — pp. jina & jita (q. v.).

Jayā f. [Vedic jāyā] wife only in cpd. jayampatikā, the lady of the house and her husband, the two heads of the household. That the wife should be put first might seem suggestive of the matriarchate, but the expression means just simply "the pair of them," and the context has never anything to do with the matriarchate. — husband & wife, a married couple S II.98; J I.347; IV.70, of birds. See also jāyampatikā.

Jara (adj.) (°-) [See jarati] old, decayed (in disparaging sense), wretched, miserable; **-ûdapānaŋ** a spoilt well J IV.387; **-gava** = °goṇa Pv I.8^{1}; **-goṇa** [cp. Sk. jaradgava] a decrepit, old bull J II.135; **-sakka** "the old S" J IV.389; **-sālā** a tumble-down shed PvA 78.

Jaratā (f.) [see jarati] old age Dhs 644 ≈ (rūpassa j. decay of form); Vism 449.

Jarati [Vedic jarati & jīryati, ***gerā** to crush, to pound, overcome (cp. jayati); as intrs. to become brittle, to be consumed, to decay, cp. Lat. granum, Goth kaúrn, E. etc. corn] to suffer destruction or decay, to become old, in two roots, viz. 1. **jar** [jarati] in Caus. **jarayati** to destroy, to bring to ruin J V.501 = VI.375. — 2. **jīr** [Sk. jīryati] see jīyati, jīrati, jīrayati, jīrāpeti. — Pp. jiṇṇa. — Cp. also jara, jarā, jajjara, jīraṇatā.

Jarā (f.) & (older) jaras (nt.) [of the latter only the instr. jarasā in use: Sn 804, 1123 (=jarāya Nd^{2} 249). — Sk. jarā & jaraḥ to ***gerā**: see jarati; cp. Gr. γῆρας, γέρας, γραῦς old age, etc. See also jīraṇa(tā)] decay, decrepitude, old age Vin I.10, 34; A I.51, 138 (as Death's messenger); V.144 sq. (bhabbo jaraŋ pahātuŋ); Sn 311 (cp. D III.75); J I.59; Th 2, 252 sq.; Vism 502 (def. as twofold & discussed in its valuation as dukkha). Defined as "yā tesaŋ sattānaŋ tamhi tamhi sattanikāye jarā jīraṇatā khaṇḍiccaŋ pāliccaŋ valittacatā āyuno saŋhāni indriyānaŋ paripāko" D II.305 = M I.49 = S II.2 = Nd^{2} 252 = Dhs 644, cp. *Dhs. trsl.* p. 195. — Frequently comb^{d} with maraṇa (maccu, etc.) "decay & death" (see under jāti as to formulas): °maraṇa, D II.31 sq.; M I.49; Sn 575; °maccu Sn 581, 1092, 1094. **ajarāmara** not subject to decay & death (cp. ajajjara) Th II, 512; Pv II.6^{11}; Vv 63^{11}; J III.515.
-ghara the house of age (adj.) like a decayed house Th 2, 270 (=jiṇṇagharasadisa ThA 213). -jajjara feeble with age J I.59; -jiṇṇa decrepit with age PvA 148; -dhamma subject to growing old A I.138, 145; II.172, 247; III.54 sq., 71 sq.; -patta old J III.394; IV.403; -bhaya fear of old age A I.179; II.121; -vāta the wind of age DhA IV.25. -sutta the Suttanta on old age, N. of Sutta Niyāta IV.6 (p. 157 sq.; beginning with "appaŋ vata jīvitaŋ idaŋ"), quoted at DhA III.320.

Jala (nt.) [Sk. jala, conn. with gala drop (?), prob. dialectical; cp. udaka] water Sn 845; J I.222; III.188; IV.137.
-gocara living in the water J II.158. -ja born or sprung from w. J IV.333; V.445; VvA 42; -da "giving water," rain-cloud Dāvs V.32; -dhara [cp. jalandhara rain-cloud] the sea Miln 117; -dhi = prec. Dāvs V.38.

Jalati [Sk. jvalati, with jvarati to be hot or feverish, to **jval** to burn (Dhtp 264: dittiyaŋ), cp. Ohg. kol=coal; Celt. gûal] to burn, to shine D 3, 188; M I.487; J I.62; II.380; IV.69; It 86; Vv 46^{2}; VvA 107; Miln 223, 343. — *Caus.* jaleti & jāleti (cp. janeti: jāneti) to set on fire, light, kindle S I.169; J II.104; Miln 47. — Pp. jalita. Intens. daddaḷhati (q. v.). Cp. ujjāleti.

Jalana (n.-adj.) [Sk. jvalana] burning Pgdp 16.

Jalābu [Sk. jarāyu, slough & placenta, to **jar** see jarati, originally that which decays (=decidua); cp. Gr. γῆρας slough. As to meanings cp. gabbha] 1. the womb S III.240. — 2. the embryo J IV.38. — 3. the placenta J II.38.
-ja born from a womb, viviparous M I.73; D III.230; J II.53 = V.85.

Jalita (adj.) [pp. to jalati] set on fire, burning, shining, bright, splendid Sn 396, 668, 686; Vv 21^{6} (=jalanto jotanto VvA 107); Pv I.10^{14} (burning floor of Niraya); II.1^{12} (°ânubhāva: shining majesty); PvA 41 (=āditta burning); ThA 292.

Jalūpikā (f.) [Sk. *jalūkikā = jalūkā & (pop. etym.) jalankā (sprung fr. water), borrowed fr. Npers. zalū (? Uhlenbeck); cp. Gr. βδέλλα leech, Celt. gel; perhaps to gal in the sense of suck (?)] a leech Miln 407 (v. l. jalopikā).

Jalogi (nt. ?) toddy (i. e. juice extracted from the palmyra, the date or the cocoa palm) Vin II.294 (pātuŋ the drinking of j.), 301, 307; Mhvs 4, 10.

Jalla[1] (nt.) [*jalya to jala or gal] moisture, (wet) dirt, perspiration (mostly as seda° or in cpd. rajo°, q. v.) Sn 249 (=rajojalla SnA 291); J VI.578 (sweat under the armpits=jallikā Com.).

Jalla[2] [prob.=jhalla, see Kern, *Toevoegselen* s. v.] athlete, acrobat J VI.271.

Jallikā (f.) [demin. of jalla] a drop (of perspiration), dirt in seda°, etc. A I.253 (kāli°); Sn 198=J I.146; VI.578.

Jaḷa (adj.) [Sk. jaḍa] dull, slow, stupid D III.265 (a°); A II.252; Pug 13; Miln 251; DA I.290.

Java [Sk. java, to javati] 1. (n.) speed S II.266; V.227; M I.446; A II.113; III.248; Sn 221; J II.290; IV.2. Often comb[d] with thāma, in phrase thāmajava-sampanna endowed with strength & swiftness J I.62; VvA 104; PvA 4; Miln 4. — javena (instr.) speedily J II.377. — 2. (adj.) swift, quick J III.25; VI.244 (mano°, as quick as thought); Vv 16 (=vegavanto VvA 78); VvA 6 (sīgha°).
-cchinna without alacrity, slow, stupid (opp. sīgha-java) DhA I.262; -sampanna full of swiftness, nimbleness, or alacrity A I.244 sq.; II.250 sq.

Javati Vedic ju javate intr. to hurry, junāti trs. to incite, urge to run, hurry, hasten S I.33; J IV.213; Dāvs V.24; DhsA 265, pp. jūta.

Javana (nt.) 1. alacrity, readiness; impulse, shock Ps I.80 sq.; Vism 22; DhsA 265 (cp. *Dhs trsl.* pp. 132, 156); DA I.194. Usually in cpd. javana-pañña (adj.) of alert intellection of swift understanding together with hāsa-pañña (hāsu° at M III.25; J IV.136) & puthu° tikkha° S V.376, 377; Nd[2] 235. 3[u]. Also in cpds. °paññā Ps II.185 sq.; °paññatā A I.45; °paññattaŋ S V.413. — 2. The twelfth stage in the function (kicca) of an act of perception (or vīthicitta): the stage of full perception, or apperception. *Vism* ch. XIV. (e. g. p. 459); *Abhdhs.* pt. iii, § 6 (kiccaŋ); *Comp.* pp. 29, 115, 245. In this connection javana is taken in its equally fundamental sense of "going" (not "swiftness"), and the "going" is understood as intellectual movement.

Javanaka=java 2 (adj.) VvA 78.

Jaha (adj.) (-°) [to jahati] leaving behind, giving up, see attaŋ°, okaŋ°, kappaŋ°, raṇaŋ°, sabbaŋ°, etc (S I.52; It 58; Sn 790, 1101, etc.); duj° hard to give up Th 1, 495.

Jahati & jahāti [Vedic root hā. Cp. *ghē(i) & ghī to be devoid (of), Gr. χῆρος void of, χήρα widow, χώρα open space (cp. Sk. vihāya=ākāsa), χωρίζω separate; Lat. her-es; Sk. jihīte to go forth=Ohg. gēn, gān, Ags. gan=go; also Sk. hāni want=Goth. gaidw. cp. Gr. χατίζω] to leave, abandon, lose; give up, renounce, forsake. Ster. expl[n] at Nd[2] 255 (and passim): pajahati vinodeti byantikaroti anabhāvaŋ gameti. Lit. as well as fig.; esp. w. ref. to kāma, dosa & other evil qualities. — Pres. jahāti Sn 1, 506 (dosaŋ), 589; Dh 91; imper. jahassu Sn 1121 (rūpaŋ); pot. jahe It 34; Dh 221; J IV.58, & jaheyya Sn 362; It 115; J I.153; IV.58. — Fut. jahissāmi J III.279; IV.420; V.465; in verse: hassāmi J IV.420; V.465. — Ger. hitvā (very frequent) Sn 284, 328; Dh 29, 88, etc.; hitvāna (Sn 60), jahitvā & jahetvā (Sn 500). — Inf. jahituŋ J I.138. — Pp. jahita Sn 231; Kh 9; Miln 261. — *Pass.* hāyati S II.224; Sn 817; Miln 297, hāyate J V.488 & hīyati J II.65; Sn 944 (hīyamāna), cp. hāyare J II.327; pp. hīna (q. v.). — *Caus.* hāpeti (q. v.). See also hāni, hāyin, jaha.

Jahitikā (f.) [See jahati] (a woman) who has been jilted, or rejected, or repudiated J I.148.

Jāgara (adj.) [fr. jāgarti] waking, watchful, careful, vigilant S I.3; A II.13=It 116; M II.31; It 41; Miln 300. — bahu° wide awake, well aware, cautious Sn 972 (cp. rakkhita-mānasāno in same context v. 63); Dh 29.

Jāgaraṇa (nt.) [der. fr. jāgara] a means for waking or keeping awake Miln 301.

Jāgaratā (f.) [cp. Sk. jāgaraṇa] watchfulness, vigilance S I.3.

Jāgarati [Sk. jāgarti to be awake (redupl. perf. for jājarti) *ger & gerēi; cp. Lat expergiscor (*exprogriscor); Gr. ἐγείρω, perf. ἐγρήγορα (for *ἐγήγορα). Def. at Dhtp 254 by niddā-khaya] to be awake, to be watchful, to be on the alert (cp. guttadvāra) Dh 60 (dīghā jāgarato rattī), 226; It 41; Miln 300. — pp. jāgarita (q. v.).

Jāgarita (nt.) [pp. of jāgarti] waking, vigil It 41; Pug 59.

Jāgariyā (f.) [BSk. M Vastu jāgarikā] keeping awake, watchfulness, vigilance, esp. in the sense of being cautious of the dangers that are likely to befall one who strives after perfection. Therefore freq. in comb[n] "indriyesu guttadvāro bhojane mattaññū jāgariyaŋ anuyutto" (anuyuñjati: to apply oneself to or being devoted to vigilance), e. g. S II.218; M I.32, 273, 354 sq., 471; A I.113 sq.; II.40. — Also in °ŋ bhajati to pursue watchfulness (bhajetha keep vigil) It 42; Sn 926 (niddaŋ na bahulīkareyya j°ŋ bhajeyya ātāpī). — S IV.104; M I.273, 355; Miln 388.
-ânuyoga application or practice of watchfulness Nd[1] 484.

Jāta [pp. of janati (janeti), cp. Lat. (g)nātus, Goth. kunds; also Gr. (κασί-) γνητός, Ohg. knabo] 1. As adj.-noun: (a) born, grown, arisen, produced (=nibbatta pātubhūta Nd[2] 256) Sn 576 (jātānaŋ maccānaŋ niccaŋ maraṇato bhayaŋ); jātena maccena kattabbaŋ kusalaŋ bahuŋ Dh 53=Miln 333; yakkhinī jātâsi (born a G.) J VI.337; rukkho j. J I.222; latā jātā Dh 340; gāmanissandhena jātāni sūpeyya-paṇṇāni Vism 250. — (n.) he who or that which is born: jātassa maraṇaŋ hoti Sn 742; jātassa jarā paññāyissati J I.59; jātaŋ+bhūtaŋ (opp. ajātaŋ abhūtaŋ) It 37. — (b) "genuine," i.e. natural, true, good, sound (cp. kata, bhuta, taccha & opp. ajāta like akata, abhūta): see cpds. — 2. As predicate, often in sense of a finite verb (cp. gata): born, grown (or was born, grew); become; occurred, happened Sn 683 (Bodhisatto hitasukhatāya jāto); bhayaŋ jātaŋ (arose) Sn 207; vivādā jātā Sn 828; ekadivase j. (were born on the same day) J III.391; aphāsukaŋ jātaŋ (has occurred J I.291. — So in loc. abs. jāte (jātamhi) "when . . . has arisen, when there is . . .." e. g. atthamhi Vin I.350=M III.154=Dh 331; vādamhi Sn 832; oghe Sn 1092; kahāpaṇesu jātesu J I.121. — 3. °jāta (nt.) characteristic; pada° pedal character S I.86; aṅga° the sexual organ Vin I.191; as adj. having become . . . (=bhūta); being like or behaving as, of the kind of . . ., sometimes to be rendered by an adj. or a pp. implied in the noun: cuṇṇakajātāni aṭṭhikāni (=cuṇṇayitāni) M III.92; jālakajāta in bud A IV.117; chandajāta=chandika Sn 767; sujāta Sn 548 (well-born, i. e. auspicious, blessed, happy); pītisomanassa° joyful & glad Sn p. 94; J I.60, etc.; gandhajāta a kind of perfume (see gandha). Often untranslatable: lābhappatto jāto J III.126; vināsa-ppaccayo jāto J I.256. — 4. a Jātaka or Buddhist birth story DhA I.34.
-āmaṇḍa the (wild) castor oil plant VvA 10; -ovaraka the inner chamber where he was born VvA 158;

J I.391 (so read for jāto varake). -kamma the (soothsaying) ceremony connected w. birth, in °ŋ karoti to set the horoscope PvA 198 (=nakkhatta-yogaŋ uggaṇhāti); -divasa the day of birth, birthday J III.391; IV.38; -mangala birth festival, i. e. the feast held on the birth of a child DhA II.86; -rūpa "sterling," pure metal, i. e. gold (in its natural state, before worked, cp. jambonada). In its relation to suvaṇṇa (worked gold) it is stated to be suvaṇṇavaṇṇo (i. e. the bright-coloured metal: VvA 9; DhA IV.32: suvaṇṇo jātarūpo); at DA I.78 it is expl[d] by suvaṇṇa only & at Vin III.238 it is said to be the colour of the Buddha: j. Satthu-vaṇṇa. At A I.253 it is represented as the material for the suvaṇṇakāra (the "white"-smith as opp. to "black"-smith). — Comb[d] w. *hirañña* Pv II.7[5]; very freq. w. *rajata* (silver), in the prohibition of accepting gold & silver (D I.5)≈ as well as in other connections, e. g. Vin I.245; II.294 sq.; S I.71, 95; IV.326 (the moral dangers of "money": yassa jātarūpa-rajataŋ kappati pañca pi tassa kāmaguṇā kappanti); V.353, 407; Dhs 617. — Other passages illustr. the use & valuation of j. are S II.234 (°paripūra); V.92 (upakkilesā); A I.210 (id.); III.16 (id.); — S I.93, 117; M I.38; A I.215; III.38; IV.199, 281; V.290; J II.296; IV.102; -veda [cp. Vedic jātaveda=Agni] fire S I.168; Sn 462 (kaṭṭhā jāyati j.) Ud 93; J I.214; II.326= IV.471; V.326; VI.204, 578; Vism 171; DA I.226; DhA I.44 (nirindhana, without fuel); -ssara a natural pond or lake Vin I.111; J I.470; II.57.

Jātaka[1] (nt.) [jāta+ka, belonging to, connected with what has happened] 1. a birth story as found in the earlier books. This is always the story of a previous birth of the Buddha as a wise man of old. In this sense it occurs as the name of one of the 9 categories or varieties of literary composition (M I.133; A II.7, 103, 108; Vin III.8; Pug 43. See navanga).—2. the story of any previous birth of the Buddha, esp. as an animal. In this sense the word is not found in the 4 Nikāyas, but it occurs on the Bharhut Tope (say, end of 3rd cent. B.C.), and is frequent in the Jātaka book. — 3. the name of a book in the Pāli canon, containing the verses of 547 such stories. The text of this book has not yet been edited. See Rh. Davids' *Buddhist India*, 189-209, and *Buddh. Birth Stories*, introd., for history of the Jātaka literature. — jātakaŋ niṭṭhapeti to wind up a Jātaka tale J VI.363; jātakaŋ samodhāneti to apply a Jātaka to the incident J I.106; DhA I.82. — *Note*. The form jāta in the sense of jātaka occurs at DhA I.34.

-atthavaṇṇanā the commentary on the Jātaka book, ed. by V. Fausböll, 6 vols. with Index vol. by D. Andersen, London, 1877 sq.; -bhāṇaka a repeater of the J. book Miln 341.

Jātaka[2] (m.) [jāta+ka, belonging to what has been born] a son J I.239; IV.138.

Jātatta (nt.) [abstr. fr. jāta] the fact of being born or of having grown or arisen Vism 250; DhA I.241.

Jāti (f.) [see janati & cp. Gr. γενεά, γένεσις; Lat. gens; Goth. kind-ins]. — Instr. jātiyā (Sn 423) & jaccā (D II.8; J III.395; Dh 393); abl. jātiyā (S I.88) & jātito (by descent: D II.8); loc. jātiyaŋ (PvA 10) & jātiyā (PvA 78). — 1. birth, rebirth, possibility of rebirth, "future life" as disposition to be born again, "former life" as cause of this life. Defined (cp. the corresp. expl[n] of jarā) as: yā tesaŋ tesaŋ sattanaŋ tamhi tamhi satta-nikāye jāti sañjāti okkanti abhinibbatti khandhānaŋ pātubhāvo āyatanānaŋ paṭilābho D II.305 =S II.3=Nd[2] 257. — Jāti is a condition precedent of age, sickness & death, and is fraught with sorrow, pain & disappointment. It is itself the final outcome of a kamma, resting on avijjā, performed in anterior births; & forms thus the concluding link in the chain of the Paṭicca-samuppāda. Under the first aspect it is enum[d] in various formulæ, either in full or abbreviated (see Nd[2] 258), viz. (a) as (1) jāti, (2) jarā, (3) vyādhi, (4) maraṇa, (5) sokaparidevadukkhadomanass' upāyāsa in the dukkhaŋ ariyasaccaŋ (the noble truth of what is misfortune) Vin I.10; A I.176; III.416; °dhamma destined to be born, etc. M I.161 sq., 173; — A V.216; Nd[2] 258, 304, 630, etc., in var. connections (referring to some dukkha). — (b) as Nos. 1-4: Nd[2] 254, 494b; J I.168, etc. — (c) as Nos. 1, 2, 4 (the standard quotation, implying the whole series 1-5): S V.224; A V.144; jātipaccayā jarāmaraṇaŋ Vin I.1; D II.31, 57, etc.; °ika A II.11, 173; °iya M I.280; Nd[2] 40. — (d) to this is sometimes added (as summing up) saŋsāra: Nd[2] 282[1]; cp. kicchaŋ loko āpanno jāyati ca jīyati ca mīyati ca cavati ca uppajjati ca D II.30. — (e) as Nos. 1+4: pahīna-jātimaraṇa (adj.) (=free from life & death, i. e. saŋsāra) A I.162; °bhayassa pāraga A II.15; °kovida Sn 484; atāri °ŋ asesaŋ Sn 355 (cp. 500); °assa pāraga Sn 32. — (f)=e+saŋsāra (cp. d): sattā gacchanti saŋsāraŋ jātimaraṇagāmino A II.12=52; jātimaraṇasaŋsāraŋ ye vajanti punappunaŋ . . . avijjāy' eva sā gati Sn 729. — (g) as Nos. 1+2, which implies the whole series: atāri so jātijaraŋ A I.133= Sn 1048; jātijar' ūpaga Sn 725=It 106; saŋyojanaŋ jātijarāya chetvā It 42; — Sn 1052, 1060; Dh 238, 348; cp. jāti ādinā nihīna PvA 198. — *Other phrases & applications:* Various rebirths are seen by one who has perfect insight into all happening & remembers his former existences (D I.81; III.50; A I.164; M II.20). Arahantship implies the impossibility of a future rebirth: see formula khīṇā jāti (M I.139; Sn p. 16, etc.) and arahant II.A: jātiyā parimuccati S I.88; jātiŋ bhabbo pahātuŋ A V.144 sq. — antimā jāti the last rebirth D II.15 (cp. carima); purimā j. a former existence PvA 1; atītajātiyaŋ in a former life (=pure) PvA 10. On jāti as dukkha see Vism 498-501. — 2. descent, race, rank, genealogy (cp. φυή, genus), often comb[d] w. gotta. Two grades of descent are enum[d] at Vin IV.6 as hīnā jāti (low birth), consisting of Candāla, Veṇa, Nesāda, Rathakāra & Pukkusa; and ukkaṭṭhā j. (superior birth), comprising Khattiyas & Brāhmaṇas. — The var. meanings of jāti are given by Bdhgh at Vism 498, 499 in the foll. classification (with examples) bhava, nikāya, sankhata-lakkhaṇa, paṭisandhi, pasūti, kula, ariya-sīla. — Kiŋ hi jāti karissati? What difference makes his parentage? D I.121; jāti-rājāno kings of birth, genuine kings J I.338; na naŋ jāti nivāresi brahmalok' ūpapattiyā Sn 139; jātiŋ akkhāhi tell me the rank of his father & mother Sn 421, 1004; cp. 462; na jaccā vasalo hoti Sn 136; 142; id. w. brāhmaṇo Sn 650; with nāma & gotta in the description of a man jātiyā nāmena gottena, etc. Vin IV.6; jātito nāmato gottato by descent, personal & family name D II.8; cp. jāti-gotta-kula J II.3. See also j.-vāda. — 3. a sort of, kind of (cp. jāta 3): catujātigandha four kinds of scent J I.265; II.291. — 4. (jāti°) by (mere) birth or nature, natural (opp. artificial); or genuine, pure, excellent (opp. adulterated, inferior), cp. jāta 1 (b): in cpds., like °maṇi, °vīṇā, etc.

-kkhaya the destruction of the chance of being reborn S V.168; A I.167; Sn 209, 517, 743; Dh 423. -khetta the realm of rebirth PvA 138 (=dasa cakkavāḷasahassāni); -thaddha conceited, proud of birth Sn 104 (+dhanatthaddha, gotta°: proud of wealth & name); -thera a Th. by rank D III.218; -nirodha the extermination of (the cause of) rebirth Vin I.1≈; -pabhava the origin or root of existence Sn 728; -puppha nutmeg J VI.367; -bhaya the fear of rebirth A II.121; -bhūmi natural ground, in °bhūmaka, °bhūmika, °bhūmiya living on nat. gr. (vassaŋ vasati) M I.145; A III.366; -maṇi a genuine precious stone J II.417; -maya constituting birth, being like birth ThA 285; -vāda reputation of birth, character of descent, parentage. The 1st of the 5 characteristics constituting a "well-bred" brahmin: yāva sattamā pitāmahāyugā akkhitto anupakkuṭṭho jātivādena "of unblemished parentage back to the 7th generation" D I.120, etc. (=DA I.281); A I.166; III.152, 223; Sn 315, 596. Cp. gotta-vāda (e. g. D I.99); -vibhanga a characteristic of birth, a distinction in descent Sn 600; -vīṇā a first-class lute J II.249; -sampanna endowed with (pure) birth (in phrase khattiyo muddhâvasitto j.°) A III.152; -sambhava the origin of birth A I.142; III.311; J I.168; -sambheda difference of rank DhA I.166; -saŋsāra the cycle of transmigration, the saŋsāra of rebirths (see above I d. f.): pahīna left behind, overcome (by an Arahant) M I.139; A III.84, 86; °ŋ khepetvā id. Th 2, 168; vitiṇṇo j.° n' atthi tassa punabbhavo Sn 746; -sindhava a well-bred horse J II.97; -ssara the remembrance of (former) births (°ñāṇa) J I.167; IV.29; DhA II.27; IV.51; cp. cutûpapāta-ñāṇa); -hingulaka (& hingulikā) natural vermilion J V.67; VvA 4, 168, 324.

Jātika (-°) (adj.) I. being like, being of, having, etc. (see jāta 3): duppañña° & sappañña° M I.225; dabba° A I.254; mukhara° Sn 275; viññū° Sn 294; māna° J I.88. — 2. descended from, being of rank, belonging to the class of: maṇḍana° M II.19; aviheṭhaka° Miln 219; samāna° (of equal rank) DhA I.390; veṇa° (belonging to the bamboo-workers) PvA 175.

Jātimant (adj.) [jāti+ mant] of good birth, having natural or genuine qualities, noble, excellent Sn 420 (vaṇṇārohena sampanno jātimā viya khattiyo); J I.342 (jātimanta-kulaputtā). Of a precious stone: maṇi veḷuriyo subho j.° D I.76=M II.17; DA I.221; Miln 215. Sometimes in this spelling for jutimant Sn 1136= Nd^2 259 (expl^d by paṇḍita paññavā). — ajātima not of good birth J VI.356 (opp. sujātimant ibid.).

Jātu (indecl.) [Vedic jātu, particle of affirmation. Perhaps for jānātu one would know, cp. Gr. οἶμαι, Lat. credo, P. maññe. But BR. and Fausböll make it a contraction of jāyatu "it might happen." Neither of these derivations is satisfactory] surely, undoubtedly (ekaŋsavacanaŋ SnA 348) usually in negative (& interrog.) sentences as na jātu, not at all, never (cp. also sādhu); mā jātu Vin II.203; Sn 152, 348 (no ce hi jātu); J I.293, 374; IV.261; V.503. Na jātucca at J VI.60 is apparently for na jātu ca.

Jāna (adj.) [to jñā, see jānāti] knowing or knowable, understandable J III.24 (=jānamāna). dujjāna difficult to understand D I.170, 187; M I.487; II.43. su° recognizable, intelligible Pv IV.1^{35} (=suviññeyya PvA 230). Cp. ājāna.

Jānana (nt.) [fr. jñā] knowledge, cognizance, recognition; intelligence, learning, skill J I.145 (attānaŋ -°kālato paṭṭhāya from the time of self-recognition), 200 (-°manta knowledge of a spell, a spell known by: tumhākaŋ) II.221; SnA 330; DhA II.73 (°sabhāva= ñatta); DA I.86 (akkhara°); Vism 391 (°atthāya in order to know), 436 (=pajānana). Cp. ājānana. — ajānana not knowing (°-) J V.199; VI.177; not known J I.32 (°sippa).

Jānanaka (adj.) [Sk. *jñānaka, cp. jānana & Sk. jānaka (c. gen.) expert Av Ś II.119, 120, as n. ib. I.216] knowing DhsA 394.

Jānanatā (f.) [abstr. fr. jānana] the fact of knowing, knowledge KhA 144.

Jānapada (adj.-n.) [fr. janapada] belonging to the country, living in the c.; pl. country-folk (opp. negamā townsfolk) D I.136, 142; M II.74; J II.287, 388; DA I.297 (=janapada-vāsin).

Jānāti [Vedic jña, jānāti *genē & *gnē, cp. Gr. γιγνώσκω, γνωτός, γνῶσις; Lat. nosco, notus, (i)gnarus (cp. E. i-gnorant); Goth. kunnan; Ohg. kennan, Ags. cnāwan=E. know] to know.

I. *Forms:* The 2 Vedic roots jān° & jñā° are represented in P. by jān° & ñā° (ña°) 1. **jān**: pres. jānāti; pot. jāneyya (Sn 781) & jaññā (A IV.366; Sn 116, 775; Dh 157, 352; J II.346; IV.478) 2nd sg. jāneyyāsi (M. I.487; J I.288), 1st pl. jāniyāma (Sn 873) & (archaic) jānemu (Sn 76, 599; Vv 83^{11}); — imper. jānāhi (Sn 596, 1026; Pv II.9^{12}), 3rd. sg. jānātu (It 28); — ppr. jānanto & jānaŋ (D I.192; A I.128; Sn 722), ppr. med. jānamāna (J I.168); — fut. jānissāti (J II.342; VI.364); — aor. ajāni (Sn 536) & jāni (J I.125, 269), 3rd pl. jāniŋsu (J II.105; VvA 113); — ger. jānitvā (J I.293; III.276); inf. jānituŋ (J I.125). Caus. jānāpeti (see below IV.2). — 2. **ñā**: fut. ñassati (D I.165); — aor. aññāsi (J I.271) & ñāsi (Sn 471), 3rd pl. aññaŋsu (Vv 22^4). — ger. ñatvā (freq.); — grd. ñeyya A II.135 (see below) & ñātabba (PvA 133); — inf. ñātuŋ (freq.) — pp. ñāta (q. v.). — Pass. ñāyati to be called or named (Miln 25).

II. *Cognate Forms:* Nd^2 s. v. explains jānāti by passati dakkhati adhigacchati vindati paṭilabhati, & ñatvā (No. 267) by jānitvā tulayitvā tirayitva vibhāvayitvā vibhūtaŋ katvā (very freq.) The 1st expl^n is also applied to abhijānāti, & the 2nd to passitvā, viditaŋ katvā, abhiññāya & disvā. The use of the emphatic phrase jānāti passati is very frequent. Yaŋ tvaŋ na jānāsi na passasi taŋ tvaŋ icchasi kāmesi? Whom you know not neither have seen, is it she that you love and long for? D I.193; Bhagavā jānaŋ jānāti passaŋ passati cakkhubhūto ñāṇabhūto M I.111; similarly A IV.153 sq. See further D I.2, 40, 84, 157 sq., 165, 192 sq., 238 sq.; A I.128; III.338; V.226; Sn 908; Nd^2 35, 413, 517; Vism 200.

III. *Meaning:* (1) *Intrs.* to know, to have or gain knowledge, to be experienced, to be aware, to find out: mayam pi kho na jānāma surely, even we do not know D I.216; te kho evaŋ jāneyyaŋ they ought to know ib.; jānantā nāma n' āhesuŋ "nobody knew" J III.188; jānāhi find out J I.184; kālantarena jānissatha you will see in time PvA 13; ajānanto unawares, unsuspecting I.223; ajānamāna id. Pv II.3^{14}. — 2. *Trs.* to know, recognize, be familiar with (usually c. acc., but also with gen.: J I.337; II.243), to have knowledge of, experience, find; to infer, conclude, distinguish, state, define: yaŋ ahaŋ jānāmi taŋ tvaŋ jānāsi D I.88; aham p' etaŋ na jānāmi Sn 989; jānanti taŋ yakkhabhūtā Pv IV.1^{35}; paccakkhato ñatvā finding out personally J I.262; III.168; cittam me Gotamo jānāti S I.178; jānāti maŋ Bhagavā S I.116; kathaŋ jānemu taŋ mayaŋ? How shall we know (or identify) him? Vv 83^{11}; yathā jānemu brāhmaṇaŋ so that we may know what a b. is Sn 599; yath' āhaŋ jāneyyaŋ vasalaŋ Sn p. 21; ajānanto ignorant PvA 4; annapānaŋ ajānanto (being without bread & water) PvA 169; ittaraŋ ittarato ñatvā inferring the trifling from the trifle Pv I.11^{11}; ingha me uṇh' odakaŋ jānāhi find me some hot water S I.174; seyyaŋ jānāhi Vin IV.16; phalaŋ pāpassa jānamāna (having experienced) J I.168; mantaŋ j. (to be in possession of a charm) J I.253; maggaŋ na j. Sn 441; pamāṇaŋ ajānitvā (knowing no measure) PvA 130. — 3. With double acc.: to recognize as, to see in, take for, identify as, etc. (cp. Caus.): petaŋ maŋ jānāhi "see in me a Peta" Pv II.9^{12} (=upadhārehi PvA 119); bhadd' itthiyā ti maŋ aññaŋsu (they knew me as=they called me) Vv 22^4.

IV. *Various:* 1. Grd. ñeyya as nt.=knowledge (cp. ñāṇa): yāvatakaŋ ñeyyaŋ tāvatakaŋ ñāṇaŋ (knowledge coincides with the knowable, or: his knowledge is in proportion to the k., i. e. he knows all) Nd^2 235^{2m}; ñāṇaŋ atikkamitvā ñeyyapatho n' atthi "beyond knowledge there is no way of knowledge" ib.; ñeyyasāgara the ocean of knowledge PvA 1. — 2. Caus. jānāpeti to make known, to inform, or (with attānaŋ) to identify, to reveal oneself J I.107 (att. ajānāpetvā); VI.363; Vism 92 (att.); PvA 149 (att.); DhA II.62.

Jāni[1] (f.) [from jahati, confused in meaning with jayati. See jahati & cp. janti] deprivation, loss, confiscation of property; plundering robbery; using force, ill-treatment D I.135=A I.201 (vadhena vā bandhena vā jāniyā vā); S I.66 (hatajānisu); J I.55 (v. l. jāti), 212 (mahājānikara a great robber); IV.72 (dhana,° v. l. hāni); Dh 138 (=DhA III.70 dhanassa jāni, v. l. hāni).

Jāni[2] (f.) wife, in jānipatayo (pl.) wife & husband (cp. jāyā(m)pati) A II.59 sq.

Jānu (nt.) [Vedic jānu=Gr. γόνυ, Lat. genu, Goth., Ohg., etc. kniu, E. knee] (also as jaṇṇu(ka), q.v.) the knee J II.311; IV.41; VI.471; DA I.254.
-maṇḍala the knee-cap, the knee A I.67; II.21; III.241 sq.; PvA 179.

Jānuka (nt.)=jānu A IV.102.

Jāpayati Caus. of jayati.

Jāmātar (& jāmāta J IV.219) [Vedic jāmātar. Deriv. uncertain. BR. take it as jā+mātar, the builder up of the family, supposing the case where there is no son and the husband goes to live in the wife's family, a bīna marriage. More likely fr. ldg ***gem**, to marry. Cp. Gr. γαμέω; γαμβρός, Lat. gener] daughter's husband, son-in-law Th 2, 422 (=ThA 269 duhitu pati); J II.63; V.442.

Jāyati (jāyate) [from **jan**, see janati] to be born, to be produced, to arise, to be reborn. Pres. 3rd pl. jāyare J III.459; IV.53; Miln 337; ppr. jāyanto Sn 208; aor. jāyi J III.391; inf. jātum J I.374. — jāyati (loko), **jīyati, miyati** one is born, gets old, dies D. II.30; Vism 235. Kaṭṭhā jāyati jātavedo out of fire-wood is born the fire Sn 462. — Vin II.95=305; Sn 114, 296, 657; Dh 58, 193, 212, 282; Pv III.1[14] (are reborn as). Cp. vi°.

Jāyampatikā (pl.) [see jayampatikā & cp. jāyāpatī] wife & husband VvA 286.

Jāyā (f.) [from **jan**] wife Vin II.259=264; J IV.285.
-patī (pl.) husband & wife PvA 159; Dāvs V.2.

Jāyikā f. (cp. jāyā) wife M I.451.

Jāra [Vedic jāra] a paramour, adulterer J I.293; II.309. f. °t adulteress Vin II.259, 268; III.83

Jāla[1] (nt.) [Vedic jāla, prob. from **jaṭ** to plait, make a tangle cp. jaṭita & jaṭā; on l:ṭ cp. phulla: sphuṭa; cāru: cāṭu; cela: ceṭa] a net, netting, entanglement (lit. or fig.): snare, deception (=māyā). — A *Lit.* Nd[2] 260 (=suttajāla, a plaiting of threads); SnA 115, 263 (=suttamaya) D I.45 (anto-jālikata caught in a net); Sn 62, 71, 213, 669; J I.52; VI.139. — kinkiṇika° a row of bells D II.183; muttā° a net of pearls J I.9; VvA 40; loha° PvA 153; hema° Vv 35; a fowler's net Dh 174; a spider's web Dh 347; nets for hair J VI.188; pabbata° a chain of mountains J II.399; sirā° network of veins J V.69; PvA 68. — Freq. in similes: see *J.P.T.S.* 1907, 90. — B. *Fig.* Very often appl[d] to the snares of Māra: S I.48 (maccuno); Sn 357 (id.); DhA III.175 (Māra°); Sn 527 (deception); taṇhā° the snare of worldly thirst (cp. °tanhā) M I.271; Th I, 306; SnA 351; kāma° Th I, 355; moha° S III.83; mohasama Dh 251; diṭṭhi° the fallacies of heresy D I.46; J VI.220; ñāṇa° the net of knowledge VvA 63; DhA III.171. bhumma° (vijjā) "earthly net," i.e. gift of clearsight extending over the earth SnA 353.
-akkhi a mesh of a net J I.208; **-taṇhā** the net of thirst Dhs 1059, 1136; DhsA 307; **-pūpa** a "net-cake"? DhA I.319; **-hatthapāda** (adj.) having net-like hands & feet (one of the 32 marks of a Mahāpurisa) prob. with reference to long nails D II.17 (see *Dial.* II.14, note 3), cp. jālitambanakhehi Vv 81[16] (expl[d] at VvA 315: jālavantehi abhilohita-nakkehi. Tena jāli (v. l. jāla-) hatthataŋ mahāpurisa-lakkhaṇaŋ tambana-khataŋ anuvyañjanañ ca dasseti).

Jāla[2] [Sk. jvāla, from jalati] glow, blaze J V.326; PvA 52 (=tejas), 154 (raŋsi°); Miln 357; Vism 419 (kappa-vināsaka°).
-roruva N. of one of the two Roruva hells ("blazes") J V.271; -sikhā a glowing crest i. e. a flame Nd[2] 11 (=acci).

Jālaka (nt.) [jāla[1]+ka] 1. a net J VI.536; Dāvs V.51. — 2. a bud A IV.117 sq. (°jāta in bud). — f. jālikā chain armour Miln 199.

Jālā (f.) [see jāla[2]] a flame J I.216, 322; Miln 148, 357.

Jālin (adj.-n.) "having a net," ensnaring, deceptive: (a) lit. a fisherman J II.178. — (b) fig. usually in f. °inī of tanhā (ensnarer, witch) S I.107=Dh 180; A II.211; Th I, 162, 908; Dhs 1059; Vism 1; DhsA 363; cp. M Vastu I.166; III.92.

Jāleti [caus. of jalati. See also jaleti] to cause to burn, to light, kindle J II.104; IV.290; V.32.

-Ji (adj.-suffix) [From jayati to conquer] winning, victorious: sangāma° victorious in fight, in sangāmaj' uttama "greatest of conquerors" Dh 103; sabba° S IV.83.

Jigacchā (f.) see jighaccā.

Jigiŋsaka (adj.) [see next] one who wishes to gain, desirous of, pursuing Sn 690.

Jigiŋsati [Desid. of ji, jayati. On etym. see also Kern. *Toev.* p. 44] to desire, to wish to acquire, to covet; Sn 700; J II.285; III.172 (v. l. BB. jigissaŋ); IV.406 (v. l. SS. jihiŋ°, BB. jigī°); V.372; VI.268. As jigīsati Th I, 1110.

Jigiŋsanatā (f.) [n. abstr. fr. jigiŋsati] desire for, covetousness Vbh 353 (v. l. BB. nijigīsanatā); cp. Vism. 29

Jigucchaka (adj.) one who dislikes or disapproves of M I.327 (paṭhavī°, āpa° etc.) Miln 343.

Jigucchati [Desid. of **gup**] to shun, avoid, loathe, detest, to be disgusted with or horrified at (c. instr.) D I.213 (iddhi-pāṭihāriyena aṭṭiyāmi harāyāmi j.): A IV.174 (kāyaduccaritena); Sn 215 (kammehi pāpakehi; SnA 266=hiriyati); J II.287; Pug. 36. — ppr. jigucchamāna It 43; grd. jigucchitabba A I.126; pp. jigucchita Sn 901. — See also jegucchа, jegucchin.

Jigucchana (nt.) dislike, contempt, disgust Vism 159; PvA 120.

Jigucchā (f.) disgust for, detestation, avoidance, shunning: tapo° (detesting asceticism) D I.174; S I.67; A II.200; jigucchabībhaccha-dassana detestable & fearful-looking PvA 56. *Note.* A diff. spelling, digucchā, occurs at DhsA 210.

Jighacchati [Desid. to ghasati, eat] to have a desire to eat, to be hungry D II.266; pp. jighacchita DhA II.145.

Jighacchā (f.) [from jighacchati] appetite, hunger, often comb[d] with pipāsā, desire to drink, thirst, e. g. S I.18; A II.143, 153; Miln 304. — M I.13, 114; 364; III.1369 A III.163; Dh 203 (j. paramā rogā); J II.445; III.19; (°abhibhūta=chāta); Miln 204, 304; Sdhp 118, 388. Cp. khudā & chāta. *Note.* A diff. spelling as dighacchā occurs at A II.117.

Jiñjuka the Gunja shrub (Abrus precatorius) J IV.333 (akkhīni j. °phalasadisāni, cp. in same application guñjā); V.156 (j. °phalasannibha); DhA I.177 (°gumba).

Jiṇṇa [pp. of jarati] 1. decayed, broken up, frail, decrepit, old: vuḍḍha mahallaka andhagata vayo-anupatta Nd[2] 261; jarājiṇṇatāya jiṇṇa DA I.283. — Vin II.189; D I.114; M II.48 sq., 66; A II.249; IV.173; Sn 1 (urago va jiṇṇaŋ tacaŋ jahāti); Pv I.12[1] (same simile); Sn 1120, 1144; J I.58; III.22 (-pilotikā worn-out rags); Dh 155, 260; Pv II.11[4] (jarājiṇṇa PvA 147); Pug 33; Vism 119 (°vihārā), 356 (°sandamānikā), 357 (°koṭṭha); ThA 213 (-ghara a tumble-down house); PvA 40 (-goṇa=jaraggava), 55 (of a roof). Cp. °tara J IV.108. — 2. digested J II.362

Jiṇṇaka (adj.) =jiṇṇa Sn 98, 124; J IV.178, 366; Sdhp 299 (sālā).

Jiṇṇatā (f.) [cp. jiṇṇa, jaratā & jīraṇatā] decrepitude DA I.283 (jarā°).

Jita [pp. of jayati, conquer] conquered, subdued, mastered: (nt.) victory. jitā me pāpakā dhammā Vin I.8; — Dh 40, 104 (attā jitaŋ seyyo for attā jito seyyo see DhA II.228), 105, 179; Vv 64[27] (jitindriya one whose senses are mastered, cp. guttindriya). — Cp. vi°.

Jitatta (nt.) [n. abstr. of jita] mastery, conquest VvA 284.

Jina [pp. med. of jayati] conquering, victorious, often of the Buddha, "Victor": jitā me pāpakā dhammā tasmâhaŋ Upaka jino ti Vin I.8=M I.171; Vin V.217; Sn 379, 697, 989, 996. magga° conqueror of the Path Sn 84 sq.; saŋsuddha° (id.) Sn 372. Cp khetta°. In other connections: Pv IV.3[33]; Th 2, 419 (jin' amhase rūpinaŋ Lacchiŋ expl[d] at ThA 268 as jinā amhase jinā vat' amha rūpavatiŋ Siriŋ).

-cakka the Buddha's reign, rule, authority J IV.100; -putta disciple of the B. Miln 177; -bhūmi the ground or footing of a conqueror PvA 254; -sāsana the doctrine of the B. Dpvs IV.3, 10.

Jināti=jayati (jeti). See also vi°.

Jimha (adj.) [Vedic jihma] crooked, oblique, slant, fig. dishonest, false (cp. vanka, opp. uju) M I.31 (+vanka); A V.289, 290; J I.290 (spelled jima); III.111=V.222; VI.66; Vism 219 (ajimha=uju); PvA 51 (citta° vanka . . .; opp. uju). Cp. kuṭila.

Jimhatā (f.) [n. abstr. to jimha] crookedness, deceit (opp. ujutā) Dhs 50, 51 (+vankatā); Vbh 359.

Jimheyya (nt.) [from jimha] crookedness, deceit, fraud M I.340 (sāṭheyyāni kūṭeyyāni vankeyyāni j.°); A IV.189 (id.) V.167.

Jiyā (f.) [Vedic jyā=Gr. βιός bow, cp. also Lat. filum thread] a bow string M I.429 (five kinds); J II.88; III.323; Vism 150; DA I.207. -kāra bowstring-maker Miln 331.

Jivhā (f.) [Vedic jihvā, cp. Lat. lingua (older dingua); Goth. tuggo; Ohg. zunga; E. tongue] the tongue. — (a) physically: Vin I.34; A IV.131; Sn 673, 716; Dh 65, 360; J II.306; PvA 99 (of Petas: visukkha-kanthaṭṭha j.), 152. — Of the tongue of the mahāpurusha which could touch his ears & cover his forehead: Sn 1022; p. 108; & pahūta-jivhatā the characteristic of possessing a prominent tongue (as the 27th of the 32 Mahāpurisa-lakkhaṇāni) D I.106=Sn p. 107; D II.18. -dujjivha (adj.) having a bad tongue (of a poisonous snake) A III.260. — (b) psychologically: the sense of taste. It follows after ghāna (smell) as the 4th sense in the enum[n] of sense-organs (jivhāya rasaŋ sāyati Nd[2] under rūpa; jivhā-viññeyya rasa D I.245; II.281; M II.42) Vin I.34; D III.102, 226; M I.191; Vism 444.

-agga the tip of the tongue A III.109; IV.137; DhA II.33. -āyatana the organ of taste D III.243, 280, 290; Dhs 585, 609, 653; -indriya the sense of taste D III.239; Dhs 585, 609, 972; -nittaddana (corr. to -nitthaddhana) tying the tongue by means of a spell D I.11 (cp. DA I.96); -viññāṇa the cognition of taste M I.112; D III.243; Dhs 556, 612, 632; -samphassa contact with the sense of taste S I.115; D III.243; Dhs 585, 632, 787.

Jīna [pp. of jīyati] diminished, wasted, deprived of (with acc. or abl.) having lost; with acc.: J III.153, 223, 335; V.99 (atthaŋ: robbed of their possessions; Com. parihīna vinaṭṭha). — with abl., J V.401 (read jīnā dhanā).

Jīyati [Pass. of ji, cp. Sk. jyāti & jīryate] to become diminished, to be deprived, to lose (cp. jayati, jāni); to decay; to become old (cp. jarati, jiṇṇa) jīyasi J V.100; jīyanti J III.336 (dhanā); jiyittha S I.54; J I.468; mā jīyi do not be deprived of (ratiŋ) J IV.107. Koci kvaci na jīyati mīyati (cp. jāyati) D II.30; cakkhūni jīyare the eyes will become powerless J VI.528 (=jīyissanti); grd. jeyya: see ajeyya[2]. Cp. parijīyati. Sometimes spelt jiyy°: jiyyati J VI.150; jiyyāma J II.75 (we lose=parihāyāma). Pp. jīna, q. v.

Jīraka[1] [Vedic jīra, lively, alert, cp. jīvati & Gr. διερός, Lat. viridis] digestion, in ajīrakena by want or lack of digestion J II.181. See ajīraka.

Jīraka[2] cummin-seed Miln 63; J I.244; II.363; VvA 186.

Jīraṇa (nt.) [fr. jīr] decaying, getting old Dhtp 252.

Jīraṇatā (f.) [n. abstr. of jīr=jar, see jarati; cp. jarā & jiṇṇatā] the state of being decayed or aged, old age, decay, decrepitude M I.49; S II.2; Nd[2] 252=Dhs 644; PvA 149.

Jīrati & Jīrayati [Caus. of jarati] 1. to destroy, bring to ruin, injure, hurt Vin I.237 (jīrati); J V.501 (v. l. BB. for jarayetha, Com. vināseyya)=VI.375; PvA 57. — 2. (cp. jīyati) to get old A III.54 (jarā-dhammaŋ mā jīri "old age may not get old," or "the law of decay may not work"); Vism 235 (where id. p. D II.30 reads jīyati); DhA I.11 (cakkhūni jīranti). — 3. (intrs.) to be digested Vism 101.

Jīreti & Jīrāpeti [Verbal formation from jīra[1]] to work out, to digest J I.238, 274 (jīreti); DhA I.171. Appl. to bhati, wages: bhatiŋ ajīrāpetva not working off the w. J II.309, 381; jīrāpeti as "destroy" at ThA 269 in expl° of nijjareti (+vināpeti).

Jīva[1] (adj.-n.) [Sk. jīva, Idg. *g[u]ṭuos=Gr. βίος, Lat. vīvus, Goth. quius, Ohg. queck, E. quick, Lith. gývas] 1. the soul. Sabbe jīvā all the souls, enum[d] with sattā pāṇā bhūta in the dialect used by the followers of Gosāla D I.53(=DA I.161 jīvasaññī). "taŋ jīvaŋ taŋ sarīraŋ udāhu aññaŋ j. aññaŋ s." (is the body the soul, or is the body one thing and the soul another?) see D I.157, 188; II.333, 336, 339; S IV.392 sq.; M I.157, 426 sq.; A II.41. — Also in this sense at Miln 30, 54, 86. — Vin IV.34; S III.215, 258 sq.; IV.286; V.418; A V.31, 186, 193. — 2. life, in yāvajīvaŋ as long as life lasts, for life, during (his) lifetime D III.133; Vin I.201; Dh 64; J II.155; PvA 76.

-gāhaŋ (adv.) taken alive, in phrase j.° gaṇhāti or gaṇhāpeti S I.84; J I.180; II.404; cp. karamara; -loka the animate creation J III.394; -sūla "life-pale," a stake for execution J II.443; -sokin (=sokajīvin) leading a life of sorrow J VI.509.

Jīva[2] (nt.) the note of the jīvaka bird Sum. V. on D III.201.

Jīvaka (adj.)=jīva, in bandhu° N. of a plant VvA 43. — f. °ikā q. v.

Jīvaŋ-jīvaka (m. onom.) name of a bird, a sort of pheasant (or partridge?), which utters a note sounding like jīvaŋ jīva D III.201; J V.406, 416; VI.276, 538 [Fausböll reads jīvajīvaka in all the Jātaka passages. Speyer AvŚ II.227 has jīvañjīvaka]. With this cp. the Jain phrase jīvaŋjīveṇa gacchaī jīvaŋjīveṇaŋ ciṭṭhaī, Weber Bhagavatī pp. 289, 290, with doubtful interpretation ("living he goes with life"? or "he goes like the j. bird"?).

Jīvati [Vedic jīvati, cp. jinoti (jinvati); Dhtp 282: pāṇadhāraṇe *g̃ᵘeiō = Gr. βίομαι & ζώω, ζῆν; Lat. vivo: Goth. ga-quiunan; Mhg. quicken, cp. E. quicken] to live, be alive, live by, subsist on (c. instr. or nissāya). Imper. pres. jīva Sn 427, very freq. with ciraŋ live long . . ., as a salutation & thanksgiving. ciraŋ jīva J VI.337; c. jīvāhi Sn 1029; Pv II.3³³; c. jīvantu Pv I.5⁵; — pot. jīve Sn 440, 589; Dh 110; — ppr. jīvaŋ Sn 427, 432; — ppr. med. jīvamāna J I.307; PvA 39; — inf. jīvituŋ J I.263; Dh 123. — Sn 84 sq., 613 sq., 804; Dh 197; J III.26; IV.137; VI.183 (jīvare); PvA 111.

Jīvana (nt.) living, means of subsistence, livelihood PvA 161. Spelt jīvāna (v. l. jivino) (adj.) at J III.353 (yācana°).

Jīvamānaka (adj.) [ppr. med. of jīvati + ka] living, alive Vism 194.

Jīvikā (f.) [abstr. fr. jīvaka] living, livelihood S III.93; A V.87, 210; J IV.459; Miln 122; SnA 466. Freq. in combⁿ °ŋ kappeti to find or get one's living: J II.209; PvA 40, etc.; °kappaka finding one's livelihood (c. ger. by) J II.167. Cp. next.

Jīvita (nt.) [Vedic jīvita, orig. pp. of jīvati "that which is lived," cp. same formation in Lat. vīta = *vivita; Gr. βιότη living, sustenace, & δίαιτα, "diet"] (individual) life, lifetime, span of life; living, livelihood (cp. jīvikā) Vin II.191; S I.42; IV.169, 213; M II.73 (appaŋ); A I.155, 255; III.72; IV.136 (appakaŋ parittaŋ); Sn 181, 440, 574, 577, 931, 1077; Dh 110, 111, 130; J I.222; Pv I.11¹¹ (ittaraŋ); II.6⁷ (vijahati); Dhs 19, 295; Vism 235, 236; Ps II.245; PvA 40. — jīvitā voropeti to deprive of life, to kill Vin III.73; D III.235; M II.99; A III.146, 436; IV.370 sq.; PvA 67.
-āsā the desire for life A I.86; -indriya the faculty of life, vitality Vin III.73; S V.204; Kvu 8, 10; Miln 56; Dhs 19; Vism 32, 230 (°upaccheda destruction of life), 447 (def.); DhA II.356 (°ŋ upacchindati to destroy life); VvA 72; -kkhaya the dissolution of life, i. e. death J I.222; PvA 95, 111; -dāna "the gift of life," saving or sparing life J I.167; II.154; -nikanti desire for life A IV.48; -parikkhārā (pl.) the requisites of life M I.104 sq.; A III.120; V.211; -pariyādāna the cessation or consummation of life D I.46 (= DA I.128); S II.83; A IV.13; -pariyosāna the end of life, i. e. death J I.256; PvA 73; -mada the pride of life, enumᵈ under the 3 madā; viz. ārogya, yobbana, j.: of health, youth, life D III.220; A I.146; III.72; -rūpa (adj.) living (lifelike) J II.190; -sankhaya = °khaya Sn 74; Dh 331; Nd² 262 (= °pariyosāna); -hetu (adv.) on the ground of life, for the sake of life A IV.201, 270

Jīvin (adj.) (usually -°) living, leading a life (of . . .) S I.42, 61; Sn 88, 181; Dh 164; PvA 27. Cp. dīgha°, dhamma°.

Juṇhā (f.) [Sk. jyotsnā, see also P. dosinā] moonlight, a moonlit night, the bright fortnight of the month (opp. kālapakkha) Vin I.138, 176, J I.165; IV.498 (°pakkha).

Juti (f.) [Sk. jyuti & dyuti, to dyotate, see jotati] splendour, brightness, effulgence, light J II.353; PvA 122, 137, 198. The spelling juti at M I.328 (in combⁿ gati + juti) seems to be faulty for cuti (so as v. l. given on p. 557).
-dhara (jutin°) carrying or showing light, shining, resplendent, brilliant S I.121; J II.353; DhA I.432.

Jutika (adj.) (-°) having light, in mahā° of great splendour D II.272; A I.206; IV.248.

Jutimatā (f.) [fr. jutimant] splendour, brightness, prominence J I.4; V.405

Jutimant (adj.) [fr. juti] brilliant, bright; usually fig. as prominent in wisdom: "bright," distinguished, a great light (in this sense often as v. l. to jātimant) D II.256 (i); S V.24; Dh 89 (= DhA II.163 ñāṇajutiyā jotetvā); Sn 508; Pv IV.1³⁵ (= PvA 230 ñāṇajutiyā jutimā).

Jutimantatā (f.) [fr. jutimant] splendour SnA 453.

Juhati [Sk. juhoti, *gheu(d); cp. Gr. χέω, χύτρα, χῦλος; Lat. fundo; Goth. giutan, Ohg. giozan] to pour (into the fire), to sacrifice, offer; to give, dedicate A II.207 (aggiŋ); Sn 1046 (= Nd² 263 deti cīvaraŋ, etc.); 428 (aggihuttaŋ jūhato), p. 79 (aggiŋ); Pug 56; fut. juhissati S I.166 (aggiŋ). — pp. huta; see also hava, havi, homa.

Juhana (nt.) [fr. juhati] offering, sacrifice D I.12, J II.43.

Jūta (nt.) [Sk. dyūta pp. of div, dīvyati, P. dibbati to play at dice] gambling, playing at dice D I.7 (°ppamādaṭṭhāna cp. DA I.85); III.182, 186 (id.); J I.290; III.198; VI.281; DhA II.228. °ŋ kīḷati to play at d. J I.289; III.187. — See also dūta².
-gīta a verse sung at playing dice (for luck) J I.289, 293; -maṇḍala dice board (= phalaka J I.290) J I.293. -sālā gambling hall J VI.281.

Je (part.) exclamation: oh! ah! now then! Vin I.232, 292 (gaccha je); M I.126; VvA 187, 207; DhA IV.105.

Jeguccha (adj.) & jegucchiya (J II.437) [sec. der. fr. jigucchā] contemptible, loathsome, detestable J IV.305; Vism 250; Th I, 1056; PvA 78, 192 (asuci +). Cp. pari°. — a° not despised Sn 852; Th I, 961.

Jegucchitā (f.) [see jigucchita] avoidance, detestation, disgust Vin I.234; M I.30; A IV.182 sq.

Jegucchin (adj.) one who detests or avoids (usually -°) M I.77; (parama°), 78 A IV.174, 182 sq., 188 sq., Miln 352 (pāpa°).

Jeṭṭha (adj.) [compar.-superl. formation of jyā power, Gr. βία, from ji in jināti & jayati "stronger than others," used as superl. (& compar.) to vuḍḍha old—elder, eldest. The compar. *jeyya is a grammarian's construction, see remarks on kaniṭṭha] better (than others), best, first, supreme; first-born; elder brother or sister, elder, eldest D II.15 (aggo jeṭṭho seṭṭho = the first, foremost & best of all); A I.108; II.87; III.152; IV.175; J I.138 (°putta); II.101 (°bhātā), 128 (°yakkhinī); IV.137.
-apacāyin, in phrase kule-j.-apacāyin paying due respect to the clan-elders D III.72, 74; S V.468; Vism 415; DhA I.265. Same for °apacāyikā (f.) honour to . . . Nd² 294, & °apacāyitar D III.70, 71, 145, 169. -māsa N. of a month SnA 359.

Jeṭṭhaka = jeṭṭha J I.253; II.101 (°tāpasa); III.281 (°kammāra: head of the silversmith's guild); IV.137, 161; V.282; Pv I.11³ (putta = pubbaja PvA 57); DhA III.237 (°sīla); IV.111 (id.); PvA 36 (°bhariyā), 42 (°pesakāra head of the weaver's guild), 47 (°vāṇija), 75.

Jeti see jayati.

Jevanīya (nt.) a kind of (missile) weapon A IV.107 = 110 (combᵈ with āvudha & salāka; vv. ll. vedhanika, jeganikā, jevanika).

Jotaka (adj.) [from juti] illuminating, making light; explaining J II.420; Dpvs XIV.50; Miln 343 (= lamplighter). — f. °ikā explanation, commentary, N. of several Commentaries, e. g. the Paramatthajotikā on the Sutta Nipāta (KhA 11); cp. the similar expression dīpanī (Paramatthadīpanī on Th 2; Vv & Pv.). — Jotika Np. DhA I.385 (Jotiya); Vism 233, 382.

Jotati [Sk. dyotate to shine, *deiā; cp. Gr. δέαται shine, δῆλος clear; also Sk. dī in dīpyate; Lat. dies. Dhtp 120 gives jut in meaning "ditti," i. e. light] to shine, be splendid J I.53; VI.100, 509; PvA 71 (jotanti = obhāsenti).

Jotana (nt.) & jotanā (f.) [cp. Sk. dyotana] illumination, explanation J VI.542 ; Ps II.112 ; VvA 17 (°nā).

Joti (m. nt.) [Sk. jyotis (cp. dyuti) nt. to dyotate, see jotati] 1. light, splendour, radiance S I.93 ; A II.85 ; Vv 16². — 2. a star : see cpds. — 3. fire S I.169 ; Th 1, 415 ; J IV.206 ; sajotibhūta set on fire S II.260 ; A III.407 sq. ; J I.232.

-parāyaṇa (adj.) attaining to light or glory S I.93 ; A II.85 ; D III.233 ; Pug 51 ; -pāvaka a brilliant fire Vv 16² (expl. VvA 79 : candima-suriya-nakkhatta-tāraka-rūpānaŋ sādhāraṇa-nāmaŋ) ; -pāsāṇa a burning glass made of a crystal DhA IV.209 ; -mālikā a certain torture (setting the body on fire : making a fiery garland) M I.87 = A I.47 = II.122 = Nd¹ 154 = Nd² 604 = Miln 197 ; -rasa a certain jewel (wishing stone) VvA 111, 339 ; DhA I.198 ; Miln 118 ; -sattha the science of the stars, astronomy : one of the 6 Vedic disciplines : see chaḷanga, cp. jotisā.

Jotimant (adj.) [joti + mant, cp. also P. jutimant] luminous, endowed with light or splendour, bright, excellent (in knowledge) Sn 348 (= paññājoti-sampanna SnA 348).

Jotisā (f.) [= Sk. jyotiṣa (nt.)] astronomy Miln 3.

Joteti [Caus. of jotati] (a) trs. to cause to shine, illuminate, make clear, explain A II.51 = J V.509 (bhāsaye jotaye dhammaŋ ; Gloss J V.510 katheyya for joteyya = jotaye) It 108 ; J II.208 ; PvA 18. — (b) intrs. to shine DhA II.163 (ñāṇajutiyā jotetvā) ; pp. jotita resplendent PvA 53.

Jh.

Jhatta [pp. of jhāpeti; cp. ñatta>*jñāpayati] set on fire, consumed, dried up (w. hunger or thirst: parched) comb^d w. chāta J II.83; VI.347.

Jhatvā see jhāpeti.

Jhasa (?) a window or opening in general J II.334.

Jhāna[1] (nt.) [from jhāyati,[1] BSk. dhyāna. The (popular etym-) expl^n of jhāna is given by Bdhgh at Vism 150 as follows: "ārammaṇ' ûpanijjhānato paccanīka-jhāpanato vā jhānaŋ," i.e. called jh. from meditation on objects & from burning up anything adverse] literally meditation. But it never means vaguely meditation. It is the technical term for a special religious experience, reached in a certain order of mental states. It was originally divided into four such states. These may be summarized: 1. The mystic, with his mind free from sensuous and worldly ideas, concentrates his thoughts on some special subject (for instance, the impermanence of all things). This he thinks out by attention to the facts, and by reasoning. 2. Then uplifted above attention & reasoning, he experiences joy & ease both of body and mind. 3. Then the bliss passes away, & he becomes suffused with a sense of ease, and 4. he becomes aware of pure lucidity of mind & equanimity of heart. The whole really forms one series of mental states, & the stages might have been fixed at other points in the series. So the Dhamma-saŋgani makes a second list of five stages, by calling, in the second jhāna, the fading away of observation one stage, & the giving up of sustained thinking another stage (Dhs 167-175). And the Vibhaŋga calls the first jhāna the **pañcaŋgika-jhāna** because it, by itself, can be divided into five parts (Vbh 267). The state of mind left after the experience of the four jhānas is described as follows at D I.76: "with his heart thus serene, made pure, translucent, cultured, void of evil, supple, ready to act, firm and imperturbable." It will be seen that there is no suggestion of trance, but rather of an enhanced vitality. In the descriptions of the crises in the religious experiences of Christian saints and mystics, expressions similar to those used in the jhānas are frequent (see F. Heiler *Die Buddhistische Versenkung*, 1918). Laymen could pass through the four jhānas (S IV.301). The jhānas are only a means, not the end. To imagine that experiencing them was equivalent to Arahantship (and was therefore the end aimed at) is condemned (D I.37 ff.) as a deadly heresy. In late Pali we find the phrase **arūpajjhānā**. This is merely a new name for the last four of the eight Vimokkhā, which culminate in trance. It was because they made this the aim of their teaching that Gotama rejected the doctrines of his two teachers, Āḷāra-Kālāma & Uddaka-Rāmaputta (M I.164 f.). — The jhānas are discussed in extenso & in various combinations as regards theory & practice at: D I.34 sq.; 73 sq.; S II.210 sq.; IV.217 sq., 263 sq.; V.213 sq.; M I.276 sq., 350 sq., 454 sq.; A I.53, 163; II.126; III.394 sq.; IV.409 sq.; V.157 sq.; Vin III.4; Nd² on Sn 1119 & s.v.; Ps I.97 sq.; II.169 sq.; Vbh 257 sq.; 263 sq.; 279 sq.; Vism 88, 415.—They are frequently mentioned either as a set, or singly, when often the set is implied (as in the case of the 4th jh.). Mentioned as jh. 1-4 e. g. at Vin I.104: II.161 (foll. by sotāpanna, etc.); D II.156, 186; III.78, 131, 222: S II.278 (nikāmalābhin); A II.36 (id.); III.354; S IV.299; V.307 sq., M I.21, 41, 159, 203, 247, 398, 521; II.15, 37; Sn 69, 156, 985; Dh 372; J I.139; VvA 38; PvA 163. — Separately: the 1st: A IV.422; V.135; M I.246, 294; Miln 289; 1st-3rd: A III.323; M I.181; 1st & 2nd: M II.28; 4th: A II.41; III.325; V.31; D III.270; VvA 4. — See also Mrs. Rh. D. *Buddh. Psych.* (Quest Series) p. 107 sq.; *Dhs. trsl.* p. 52 sq.; Index to Saŋyutta N. for more refs.; also Kasiṇa.

-anuyutta applying oneself to meditation Sn 972; -anga a constituent of meditation (with ref. to the 4 jhānas) Vism 190. -kīḷā sporting in the exercise of meditation J III.45. -pasuta id. (+dhīra) Sn 709; Dh 181 (cp. DhA III.226); -rata fond of meditation S I.53, 122; IV.117; It 40; Sn 212, 503, 1009; Vv 50[16]; VvA 38; -vimokkha emancipation reached through jhāna A III.417; V.34; -sahagata accompanied by jh. (of paññābala) A I.42.

Jhāna[2] (nt.) [from jhāyati²] conflagration, fire D III.94; J I.347.

Jhānika (adj.) [fr. jhāna¹] belonging to the (4) meditations Vism 111.

Jhāpaka (adj.) one who sets fire to (cp. jhāpeti), an incendiary J III.71.

Jhāpana (nt.) setting fire to, consumption by fire, in sarīra°-kicca cremation VvA 76.

Jhāpita [pp. jhāpeti] set on fire Miln 47; Vism 76 (°kāla time of cremation).

Jhāpeti [Caus. of jhāyati²] 1. to set fire to, to burn, to cook Vin IV.265; J I.255, 294; DhA II.66; PvA 62. — 2. to destroy, to bring to ruin, to kill (see Kern, *Toev.*, p. 37 sq.) J III.441 (=ḍahati pīḷeti); VvA 38 (=jhāyati¹, connected w. jhāna: to destroy by means of jhāna); inf. jhāpetuŋ J VI.300 (+ghātetuŋ hantuŋ); ger. **jhatvā** S I.19 (reads chetvā, vv. ll. ghatvā & jhatvā)=J IV.67 (T. jhatvā, v. l. chetvā; expl^d by kilametvā); S I.41 (v. l. for T. chetvā, Bdhgh says "jhatvā ti vadhitvā"); J II.262 (+hantvā vadhitvā; expl^d by kilametvā); VI.299 (+vadhitvā); also jhatvāna J IV.57 (=hantvā). — pp. jhatta & jhāpita.

Jhāma (adj.-n.) [jhāyati²] burning, on fire, conflagration, in °**khetta** charcoal-burner's field J I.238; II.92; °**angāra** a burning cinder PvA 90. By itself: J I.405; DhA II.67.

Jhāmaka N. of a plant J VI.537; also in °bhatta (?) J II.288.

Jhāyaka (adj.) one who makes a fire D III.94.

Jhāyati[1] [Sk. dhyāyati, **dhī**; with dhīra, dhīḥ from didheti shine, perceive; cp. Goth. filu-deisei cunning, & in meaning cinteti>citta¹] to meditate, contemplate, think upon, brood over (c. acc.): search for, hunt after D II.237 (jhānaŋ); S I.25, 57; A V.323 sq. (+pa,° ni,° ava°); Sn 165, 221, 425, 709, 818 (=Nd¹ 149 pa°, ni°, ava°); Dh 27, 371, 395; J I.67, 410; Vv 50[12]; Pv IV.16[6]; Miln 66; SnA 320 (aor. jhāyiŋsu thought of). — pp. jhāyita.

Jhāyati[2] [Sk. kṣāyati to burn, **kṣāy** & **kṣī**, cp. khara & chārikā] to burn, to be on fire: fig. to be consumed, to waste away, to dry up D I.50 (=jāleti DA I.151); III.94 (to make a fire); J I.61, 62; Pv I.11[10] (jhāyare v. l. BB. for ghāyire); Miln 47; PvA 33 (=pariḍayhati); — aor. jhāyi DhA II.240 sq. — (fig.) Dh 155; J VI.189. — Caus. jhāpeti. — Cp. khīyati².

Jhāyana[1] (nt.) [der. fr. jhāyati¹] meditating, in °sīla the practice of meditation (cp. Sk. dhyānayoga) VvA 38.

Jhāyana[2] (nt.) [fr. jhāyati²] cremation, burning Pug A 187.

Jhāyin (adj.) [see jhāyati¹ & jhāna] pondering over (c. acc.) intent on: meditative, self-concentrated, engaged in jhāna-practice Vin II.75; S I.46=52; II.284; M I.334; A I.24; III.355; IV.426; V.156, 325 sq.; Sn 85 (magga°), 638, 719, 1009, 1105; It 71, 74, 112; J IV.7; Dh 23, 110, 387 (reminding of jhāyati², cp. DhA IV.144); Nd² 264; Vv 5[8]; Pv IV.1[32]; Vbh 342. Nd¹ 226=Nd² 342²=Vism 26 (āpādaka°).

N.

Ñatta (nt.) [nomen agentis from jānāti] the intellectual faculty, intelligence Dh 72 (=DhA II.73: jānanasabhāva).

Ñatti (f.) [Sk. jñapti, from jñāpayati, caus of **jñā**] announcement, declaration, esp. as t. t. a motion or resolution put at a kammavācā (proceedings at a meeting of the chapter. The usual formula is " esā ñatti; suṇātu me bhante sangho ": Vin I.340; III.150, 173, 228; — °ŋ ṭhapeti to propose a resolution Vin IV.152. — Vin V.142, 217 (na c' āpi ñatti nac a pana kammavācā). This resolution is also called a ñattikamma: Vin II.89; IV.152; V.116; A I.99. Two kinds are distinguished, viz. that at which the voting follows directly upon the motion, i. e. a ñatti-dutiya-kamma, & that at which the motion is put 3 times, & is then followed (as 4th item) by the decision, i. e. a ñ-catuttha-kamma. Both kinds are discussed at Vin I.56, 317 sq.; II.89; III.156; IV.152; & passim. Cp. Divy 356: jñapticaturtha. Cp. āṇatti, viññatti.

Ñatvā etc.: see jānāti.

Ñāṇa (nt.) [from jānāti. See also jānana. ***genē**, as in Gr. γνῶ-σις (cp. gnostic), γνώμη; Lat. (co)gnitio; Goth. kunþi; Ogh. kunst; E. knowledge] knowledge, intelligence, insight, conviction, recognition. opp. aññāṇa & avijjā, lack of k. or ignorance. — 1. *Ñāṇa in the theory of cognition:* it occurs in intensive couple-compounds with terms of sight as cakkhu (eye) & dassana (sight, view), e. g. in cakkhu-karaṇa ñāṇa-karaṇa " opening our eyes & thus producing knowledge " i. e. giving us the eye of knowledge (a mental eye) (see cakkhu, jānāti passati, & cpd. °karaṇa): Bhagavā jānaŋ jānāti passaŋ passati cakkhu-bhūto ñāṇa-bhūto (=he is one perfected in knowledge) M I.111=Nd^2 235^{3h}; natthi hetu natthi paccayo ñāṇāya dassanāya ahetu apaccayo ñāṇaŋ dassanaŋ hoti " through seeing & knowing," i. e. on grounds of definite knowledge arises the sure conviction that where there is no cause there is no consequence S V.126. Cp. also the relation of diṭṭhi to ñāṇa. This implies that all things visible are knowable as well as that all our knowledge is based on empirical grounds; yāvatakaŋ ñeyyaŋ tāvatakaŋ ñāṇaŋ Nd^2 235^{3m}; yaŋ ñāṇaŋ taŋ dassanaŋ, yaŋ dassanaŋ taŋ ñāṇaŋ Vin III.91; ñāṇa+dassana (i. e. full vision) as one of the characteristics of Arahantship: see arahant II.D. Cp. BSk. jñānadarśana, e. g. AvŚ I.210. — 2. *Scope and character of ñāṇa:* ñ. as faculty of understanding is included in paññā (cp. wisdom=perfected knowledge). The latter signifies the spiritual wisdom which embraces the fundamental truths of morality & conviction (such as aniccaŋ anattā dukkhaŋ: Miln 42); whereas ñ. is relative to common experience (see Nd^2 235^3 under cakkhumā, & on rel. of p. & ñ. Ps I.59 sq.; 118 sq.; II.189 sq.). — Perception (saññā) is necessary to the forming of ñāṇa, it precedes it (D I.185); as sure knowledge ñ. is preferable to saddhā (S IV.298); at Vin III.91 the definition of ñ. is given with tisso vijjā (3 kinds of knowledge); they are specified at Nd^2 266 as aṭṭhasamāpatti-ñāṇa (consisting in the 8 attainments, viz. jhāna & its 4 succeeding developments), pañc' abhiññā° (the 5 higher knowledges, see paññā & abhi°), micchā° (false k. or heresy). Three degrees of k. are distinguished at DA I.100, viz. sāvaka-pāramī-ñāṇa, paccekabuddha°, sabbaññuta° (highest k. of a relig. student, k. of a wise man, & omniscience). Four objects of k. (as objects of truth or sammādiṭṭhi) are enum^d as dhamme ñāṇaŋ, anvaye ñ., paricchede ñ., sammuti ñ. at D III.226, 277; other four as dukkhe ñ. (dukkha-) samudaye ñ., nirodhe ñ., magge ñ. (i. e. the knowledge of the paṭicca-samuppāda) at D III.227; Ps I.118; Vbh 235 (=sammādiṭṭhi). Right knowledge (or truth) is contrasted with false k. (micchā-ñāṇa=micchādiṭṭhi): S V.384; M II.29; A II.222; V.327; Vbh 392. — 3. *Ñāṇa in application:* (a) Vin I.35; D II.155 (opp. pasāda); S I.129 (cittamhi susamāhite ñāṇamhi vuttamānamhi); II.60 (jātipaccayā jarāmaraṇan ti ñ.: see ñ-vatthu); A I.219 (on precedence of either samādhi or ñ.); Sn 378, 789, 987 (muddhani ñāṇaŋ tassa na vijjati), 1078 (diṭṭhi, suti, ñ.: doctrine, revelation, personal knowledge, i. e. intelligence; differently expl. at Nd^2 266), 1113; Pv III.5^1 (Sugatassa ñ. is asādhāraṇaŋ) Ps I.194 sq.; II.244; Vbh 306 sq. (ñ-vibhanga), 328 sq. (kammassakataŋ ñ.); Nett 15 sq.; 161 (+ñeyya), 191 (id.). — (b) ñāṇaŋ hoti or uppajjati knowledge comes to (him) i. e. to reason, to arrive at a conclusion (with iti=that . . .) S II.124=III.28 (uppajjati); D III.278 (id.); A II.211 ≈; IV.75; V.195; S III.154. See also arahant II.D. — (c) Var. attributes of ñ.: anuttariya A V.37; aparapaccayā (k. of the non-effect of causation through lack of cause) S II.17, 78; III.135; V.179, 422 sq. (=sammādiṭṭhi), same as ahetu-ñāṇa S V.126; asādhāraṇa (incomparable, uncommon k.) A III.441; PvA 197; akuppa D III.273; ariya A III.451; pariyodāta S I.198; bhiyyosomatta S III.112; yathā bhūtaŋ (proper, definite, right k.) (concerning kāya, etc.) S V.144; A III.420; V.37. — (d) knowledge of, about or concerning, consisting in or belonging to, is expressed either by loc. or -° (equal to subj. or obj. gen.). — (α) *with loc.:* anuppāde ñ. D III.214, 274; anvaye D III.226, 277; kāye D III.274; khaye D III.214, 220 (āsavānaŋ; cp. M I.23, 183, 348; II.38), 275; S II.30; Nett 15; cutûpapāte D III.111, 220; dukkhe (etc.) D III.227; S II.4; V.8, 430; dhamme D III.226; S II.58; nibbāne S II.124 (cp. IV.86). — (β) *as* -°: anāvaraṇa DA I.100; ariya S I.228; A III.451; khanti Ps I.106; jātissara J I.167; cutûpapāta M I.22, 183, 347; II.38, etc.; ceto-pariya D III.100, & °pariyāya S V.160; dibbacakkhu Ps I.114; dhammaṭṭhiti S II.60, 124; Ps I.50; nibbidā Ps I.195; pubbe-nivāsânusati M I.22, 248, 347; II.38, etc.; Buddha° Nd^2 235^3; Ps I.133; II.31, 195; DA I.100; sabbaññuta Ps I.131 sq.; DA I.99 sq.; PvA 197; sekha S II.43, 58, 80, & asekha S III.83. — (e) aññāṇa wrong k., false view, ignorance, untruth S I.181; II.92; III.258 sq.; V.126; A II.11; Sn 347, 839; Ps I.80; Pug 21; Dhs 390, 1061; see avijjā & micchādiṭṭhi.

-indriya the faculty of cognition or understanding Dhs 157; -ûpapanna endowed with k. Sn 1077 (=Nd^2 266^b °upeta); -karaṇa (adj.) giving (right) understanding, enlightening, in comb^n w. cakkhukaraṇa (giving (in)-sight, cp. " your eyes shall be opened and ye shall be knowing good and evil " Gen. 3^5): kusalavitakkā anandha-karaṇā cakkhu° ñāṇa° It 82; f. -ī (of majjhimā-paṭipadā) S IV.331; -cakkhu the eye of k. PvA 166; -jāla the net of k., in phrase ñāṇajālassa anto paviṭṭha coming within the net, i. e. into the range of one's intelligence or mental eye (clear sight) DhA I.26; II.37, 58, 96; III.171, 193; IV.61; VvA 63; -dassana "knowing and seeing," "clear sight," i. e. perfect knowledge; having a vision of truth, i. e. recognition of truth, philosophy, (right) theory of life, all-comprising knowledge. Defined as tisso vijjā (see above 2) at Vin IV.26; fully discussed at DA I.220, cp. also def. at Ps II.244. — Vin II.178 (parisuddha°; + ājīva, dhammadesanā, veyyākaraṇa); III.90 sq.; V.164, 197; D I.76≈(following after the jhānas as the first step of paññā, see paññā-sampadā); III.134, 222 (°paṭilābha), 288 (°visuddhi); M I.195 sq.; 202 sq., 482; II.9, 31; Nett 17, 18, 28; see also vimutti°; -dassin one who possesses perfect k. Sn 478; -patha the path of k. Sn 868; -phusanā experience, gaining of k. DhA I.230; -bandhu an associate or friend of k. Sn 911; -bhūta in combⁿ w. cakkhubhūta, having become seeing & knowing, i. e. being wise S II.255; IV.94; A V.226 sq.; -vatthūni (pl.) the objects or items of (right) knowledge which means k. of the paṭiccasamuppāda or causal connection of phenomena. As 44 (i. e. 4 × 11, all constituents except avijjā, in analogy to the 4 parts of the ariyasaccāni) S II.56 sq., as 77 (7 × 11) S II.59 sq.; discussed in extenso at Vbh 306-344 (called ñāṇavatthu); -vāda talk about (the attainment of supreme) knowledge D III.13 sq.; A V.42 sq.; -vippayutta disconnected with k. Dhs 147, 157, 270; -vimokkha emancipation through k. Ps II.36, 42; -visesa distinction of k., superior k. PvA 196; -sampayutta associated with k. Dhs I, 147, 157, etc.; Vbh 169 sq., 184, 285 sq., 414 sq.

Ñāṇika (adj.) in pañca° having five truths (of samādhi) D III.278.

Ñāṇin (adj.) knowing, one who is possessed of (right) knowledge S II.169; A II.89 (sammā°); IV.340. —aññāṇin not knowing, unaware VvA 76.

Ñāta [pp. of jānāti = Gr. γνωτός, Lat. (g)notus; ajñāta (P. aññāta) = ἄγνωτος = ignotus] known, well-known; experienced, brought to knowledge, realized. In Nd[2] s. v. constantly expl. by tulita tirita vibhūta vibhāvita which series is also used as explⁿ of diṭṭha & vidita A V.195; J I.266; Sn 343 (+ yasassin); Miln 21 (id.). — aññāta not known, unknown Vin I.209; M I.430; S II.281; DhA I.208.

Ñātaka [for *ñātika from ñāti] a relation, relative, kinsman Vin II.194; M II.67; Dh 43; Sn 263 (= KhA 140: ñāyante amhākaŋ ime ti ñātakā), 296, 579; Pv II.1[4] (Minayeff, but Hardy °ika); PvA 19, 21, 31, 62, 69; DA I.90.

Ñāti [see janati; cp. Sk. jñāti, Gr. γνωτός, Lat. cognatus, Goth. knoþs] a relation, relative (= mātito pitito ca sambandhā PvA 25; = bandhū PvA 86; specialized as °sālohitā, see below). Pl. ñātayo (Pv I.4[3]; KhA 209, 214) and ñātī (M II.73; KhA 210, cp. 213; acc. also ñātī Pv I.6[7]); Sn 141; Dh 139, 204, 288; J II.353; Pv I.5[3], 12[2]; II.3[13], 6[7]. — Discussed in detail with regard to its being one of the 10 paḷibodhā at Vism 94.

-kathā (boastful) talk about relatives D I.7≈ (cp. DA I.90); -gata coming into (the ties of) relationship J VI.307 (°gataka ib. 308); -ghara the paternal home J I.52; -dhamma the duties of relatives Pv I.5[12]; (= ñātīhi ñātīnaŋ kattabba-karaṇaŋ PvA 30); -parivatta the circle of relations D I.61; M I.267; Pug 57≈; -peta a deceased relation Pv I.5[4]; -majjhagata (adj.) in the midst of one's relations Pug 29; -mittā (pl.) friends & relatives Dh 219; J III.396; Pv I.12[6]; -vyasana misfortune of relatives (opp. °sampada) D III.235; enum as one of the general misfortunes under dukkha (see Nd[2] 304F); -sangha the congregation of kinsmen, the clan A I.152; Sn 589; -sālohitā a relation by blood (contrasted with friendship: mittāmaccā Sn p. 104), often with ref. to the deceased: petā ñ-sālohitā the spirits of deceased blood-relations M I.33; A V.132, 269; PvA 27, 28; -sineha the affection of relationship PvA 29; -hetusampatti a blessing received through the kinsmen PvA 27.

Ñāpeti [Caus. of jānāti, cp. also ñatti] to make known, to explain, to announce J II.133. Cp. jānāpeti & āṇāpeti.

Ñāya [Sk. nyāya = ni + i] 1. method, truth, system, *later* = logic: °gantha book on logic Dāvs III.41. — 2. fitness, right manner, propriety, right conduct, often appl^d to the "right path" (ariyamagga = ariyañāya Vin I.10) D III.120; S V.19, 141, 167 sq., 185; A II.95; IV.426; V.194; Dh I.249; ariya ñ. S II.68; V.387; = the causal law S V.388; = kalyāṇa-kusala-dhammatā A II.36; used in apposition with dhamma and kusala D II.151; M II.181, 197; is replaced herein by sacca S I.240; = Nibbāna at Vism 219, 524; ñ.-paṭipanna walking in the right path S V.343; A II.56; III.212, 286; V.183.

-Ññū (-ññū) (adj.-suffix) [Sk. -jña, from jānāti, *gn: cp. P. gū > Sk. ga] knowing, recognizing, acknowledging, in ughaṭita°, kata°, kāla°, khaṇa°, matta°, ratta°, vara°, vipacita°, veda°, sabba°, etc. (q. v.)—fem. abstr. °ññutā in same combinations.

Ṭ.

Ṭan (?) (adv.) part of sound J I.287 (ṭan ti saddo).

Ṭh.

°Ṭha (°ṭṭha) (adj.-suffix) [from tiṭṭhati] standing, as opposed to either lying down or moving; located, being based on, founded on (e. g. appa° based on little D I.143): see kappa° (lasting a k.), kūṭa° (immovable), gaha° (founding a house, householder), dhamma°, nava°, vehāsa° (=vihan-ga). — (n.) a stand i. e. a place for: goṭṭha a stable.

Ṭhapana (nt.) 1. setting up, placing, founding; establishment, arrangement, position Vin v.114; J I.99 (aggha° fixing prices); Miln 352 (pāda°); DA I.294; (=vidhārite); PvA 5 (kulavaŋsa°). — 2. letting alone, omission, suspension, in pāṭimokkha° Vin II.241.

Ṭhapanā (f.) 1. arrangement DA I.294. — 2. application of mind, attention Pug 18, Vism 278 (=appanā).

Ṭhapita [pp. of ṭhapeti] 1. placed, put down; set up, arranged, often simply pleonastic for finite verb (=being): saŋharitvā ṭh. being folded up J I.265 (cp. similar use of gahetvā c. ger.): mukkhe ṭh. J VI.366; °sankāra (dustheap) PvA 82; pariccajane ṭh. appointed for the distribution of gifts PvA 124. — 2. suspended, left over, set aside Vin II.242 (pāṭimokkha).

Ṭhapeti [Caus. of tiṭṭhati] to place, set up, fix, arrange, establish; appoint to (c. loc.); to place aside, save, put by, leave out Vin II.32 (pavāraṇaŋ), 191 (ucce & nīce ṭhāne to place high or low), 276 (pavāraṇaŋ); v.193 (uposathaŋ), 196 (give advice); D I.120 (leaving out, discarding); Dh 40 (cittaŋ ṭh. make firm) J I.62, 138, 223, 293 (except); II.132 (puttaṭṭhāne ṭh. as daughter); J II.159; VI.365 (putting by); VvA 63 (kasiŋ ṭhapetvā except ploughing); PvA 4, 20 (varaŋ ṭhapetvā denying a wish), 39, 114 (setting up); Miln 13 (ṭhapetvā setting aside, leaving till later). — inf. ṭhapetuŋ Vin II.194; PvA 73 (saŋharitvā ṭh. to fold up: cp. ṭhapita); grd. ṭhapetabba J II.352 (rājaṭṭhāne); PvA 97; & ṭhapanīya (in pañha ṭh. a question to be left standing over, i. e. not to be asked) D III.229. — ger. ṭhapetvā (leaving out, setting aside, excepting) also used as prep. c. acc. (before or after the noun): with the omission of, besides, except D I.105 (th. dve); J I.179 (maŋ but for me), 294 (tumhe ṭh.); II.154 (ekaŋ vaddhaŋ ṭh.); IV.142 (ṭh. maŋ); VvA 100 (th. ekaŋ itthiŋ); PvA 93 (ṭh. maŋ). Cp. BSk. sthāpayitvā "except" AvŚ II.111. — Caus. ṭhapāpeti to cause to be set up; to have erected, to put up J I.266; DhA II.191.

Ṭhāna (ṭṭhāna) (nt.) [Vedic sthāna, **sthā**, see tiṭṭhati; cp. Sk. sthāman Gr. σταθμός, Lat. stamen] — I. *Connotation.* As one of the 4 iriyāpathā (behaviours) 1. contrasted (a) as standing position with sitting or reclining; (b) as rest with motion; 2. by itself without particular characterization as location.

II. *Meanings*—(1) *Literal:* place, region, locality, abode, part (-° of, or belonging to)—(a) cattāri ṭhānāni dassanīyāni four places (in the career of Buddha) to be visited D II.140=A II.120; vāse ṭhāne gamane Sn 40 (expl. by SnA 85 as mahā-upaṭṭhāna-sankhāte ṭhāne, but may be referred to I. 1 (b)); ṭhānā cāveti to remove from one's place Sn 442; J IV.138; PvA 55 (spot of the body). — (b) kumbha° (the "locality of the pitcher," i. e. the well) q. v.; arañña° (part of the forest) J I.253; PvA 32; nivāsana° (abode) PvA 76; phāsuka° J II.103; PvA 13; vasana° J I.150, 278; VvA 66; virūhana° (place for the growing of . . .) PvA 7; vihāra (place of his sojourn) PvA 22; saka° (his own abode) J II.129; PvA 66. — (c) In this meaning it approaches the metaphorical sense of "condition, state" (see 2 & cp. gati) in: dibbāni ṭhānāni heavenly regions S I.21; tidivaŋ S I.96; saggaŋ ṭh. a happy condition Pv I.1[3]; pitu gata° the place where my father went (after death) PvA 38; Yamassa ṭh.=pettivasaya PvA 59. — (d) In its pregnant sense in comb[n] with accuta & acala it represents the connotation I. 1 (b), i. e. perdurance, constancy, i. e. Nibbāna Vv 51[4]; Dh 225. — 2. *Applied meanings*— (a) state, condition; also -° (in sg.) as collective-abstract suffix in the sense of being, behaviour (corresponding to E. ending hood, ion, or ing), where it resembles abstr. formations in °tā & °ttaŋ (Sk. tā & tvaŋ), as lahuṭṭhāna=lahutā & collect. formations in °ti (Sk. daśati ten-hood; devatāti godhead, sarvatāti=P. sabbattaŋ comprehensiveness; cp. also Lat. civitātem, juventūtem). — S I.129 (condition) II.27 (asabha°)=M I.69; S III.57 (atasitāyaŋ fearless state): A II.118 sq. (four conditions); Dh 137 (dasannaŋ aññataraŋ th.° nigacchati he undergoes one of the foll. ten conditions, i. e. items of affliction, expl[d] at DhA III.70 with kāraṇa "labours"), 309 (states=dukkhakāraṇāni DhA III.482, conditions of suffering or ordeals); hattha-pāsāraṇa-ṭṭhāna condition of outstretched hands DhA I.298; loc. ṭhāne (-°) when required, at the occasion of . . . DhA I.89 (hasitabba°, saŋvega°, dātuŋ yutta°); pubbe nibbatta -ṭṭhānato paṭṭhāya "since the state (or the time) of his former birth" PvA 100. — vibhūsanaṭṭhāna ornamentation, decoration, things for adornment D I.5; Sn 59 (DA I.77 superficially: ṭhānaŋ vuccati kāraṇaŋ; SnA 112 simply vibhūsā eva v-ṭṭhānaŋ); jūta-pamāda° (gambling & intoxication) D I.6≈ (cp. expl. at KhA 26); gata° & āgata° (her) going & coming J III.188; — pariccāga° distribution of gifts PvA 124. — (b) (part=) attribute, quality, degree: aggasāvaka° (degrees of discipleship) VvA 2; esp. in set of 10 attributes, viz. rūpa (etc. 1-5), āyu, vaṇṇa, sukha, yasa, ādhipateyya D III.146; S IV.275; Pv II.9[58], also collectively [see (a)] as dasaṭṭhānaŋ S I.193; out of these are mentioned as 4 attributes āyu, vaṇṇa, sukha, bala at Vv 32[7]; other ten at A V.129 (pāsaŋsāni). — (c) (counter-part=) object (-° for), thing; item, point; pl. grounds, ways, respects. With a numeral often=a (five)fold collection of . . . S IV.249 sq. (5 objects or things, cp. Ger. fünferlei); A III.54 sq. (id.), 60 sq., 71 sq.; etehi tīhi ṭhānehi on these 3 grounds Dh 224; manussā tīhi ṭhānehi bahuŋ puññaŋ pasavanti: kāyena vācāya manasā (in 3 ways, qualities or properties) A 151 sq.; cp. II.119 sq. (=saŋvutaŋ tīhi ṭhānehi Dh 391); catuhi ṭhānehi in Com. equals catuhi ākārehi or kāraṇehi pāmujjakaraṇaŋ th. (object) Sn 256; ekaccesu ṭhānesu sameti ekaccesu na sameti "I agree in certain points, but not in others" D I.162; kankhaniya° doubtful point S IV.350, 399; — n' atthi aññaŋ ṭhānaŋ no other means, nothing else DhA II.90; agamanīya° something not to be done, not allowed VvA 72; cp. also kamma°. — (d) (standpoint=) ground for (assumption) reason, supposition, principle, esp. a sound conclusion, logic, reasonableness (opp. a° see 4): garayhaŋ th. āgacchati "he advocates a faulty principle" D I.161;

catuhi ṭh. paññāpeti (four arguments) S III.116; IV.380; ṭhāna-kusala accomplished in sound reasoning S III.61 sq. (satta°); A II.170 sq. Also with aṭṭhāna-kusala: see below 4.

III. *Adverbial use of some cases* acc. ṭhānaŋ: ettakaŋ ṭh. even a little bit DhA I.389. — abl. ṭhānaso: in combn w. hetuso with reason & cause, causally conditioned [see 2 (d)] S V.304; A III.417; V.33; Nett 94 (ñāṇa); abs. without moving (see I. 1 (b) & cp. Lat. statim) i. e. without an interval or a cause (of change), at once, immediately, spontaneously, impromptu (cp. cpd.° uppatti) S I.193; V.50, 321, 381; Pv I.4⁴ (=khaṇaŋ yeva PvA 19). — loc. ṭhāne instead = like, as dhītu ṭhāne ṭhapesi he treats her like a daughter VvA 209; puttaṭṭhāne as a son J II.132.

IV. *Contrasted with negation of term* (ṭhāna & aṭṭhāna). The meanings in this category are restricted to those mentioned above under 1 [esp. 1 (c)] & 2 (d), viz. the relations of place > not place (or wrong place, also as proper time & wrong time), i. e. somewhere > nowhere, and of possibility > impossibility (truth > falsehood). (a) ṭhānaŋ upagacchati (pathaviyā) to find a (resting) place on the ground, to stay on the ground (by means of the law of attraction and gravitation) Miln 255; opp. na ṭhānaŋ upa° to find no place to rest, to go into nothingness Miln 180, 237, 270. — (b) ṭhānaŋ vijjati there is a reason, it is logically sound, it is possible D I 163, 175; M III.64; Ps II.236 sq.; cp. M Vastu II.448; opp. na etaŋ ṭhānaŋ vijjati it is not possible, feasible, plausible, logically correct Vin II.284; D I.104, 239; M II.10; III.64; Miln 237; Nett 92 sq. — (c) aṭṭhānaŋ an impossibility Sn 54 (aṭṭhāna, with elision of ŋ); aṭṭhāne at the wrong time J I.256; ṭhāna is that one of the gatis which is accessible to human influence, as regards gifts of relief or sacrifice (this is the pettivisaya), whilst aṭṭhāna applied to the other 4 gatis (see gati) PvA 27 sq. In cpd. ṭhānâṭhāna-gata it means referring or leading to good & bad places (gatis): of sabbe khayadhammā (i. e. keci saggûpagā keci apāyûpagā) Nett 94. In combn apucchi nipuṇe pañhe ṭhānâṭhānagate (Miln 1) it may mean either questions concerning possibilities & impossibilities or truths & falsehoods, or questions referring to happy & unhappy states (of existence): ṭhānâṭhāna-ñāṇa is "knowledge of correct & faulty conclusions" Nett 94, cp. Kvu 231 sq.; the same combn occurs with °kusala °kusalatā "accomplished or skilled (& skill) in understanding correct or faulty conclusions" D III.212 (one of the ten powers of the Buddha); M III.64; Dhs 1337, 1338 (trsl. by Mrs. Rh. D. on p. 348 *Dhs. trsl.* as "skill in affirming or negating causal conjuncture"). In the same sense: ṭhānaŋ ṭhānato pajānāti (& aṭṭhānaŋ aṭṭhānato p.) to draw a logical inference from that which is a proper ground for inference (i. e. which is logical) S V.304; M I.69 sq. = A III.417; V.33.

-uppatti arising instantaneously (see ṭhānaso, above III.) VvA 37; J VI.308 (°kāraṇavindana finding a means right on the spot); *-ka* (adj.) on the spot, momentary, spontaneous J VI.304.

Ṭhānīya (adj.) [grd. of tiṭṭhati] standing, having a certain position, founded on or caused by (-°) Vin II.194 (-nīca°); A I.264 (chanda-rāga-dhamma°). See also under tiṭṭhati.

Ṭhāyika (adj.) at Miln 201 "one who gains his living or subsists on" (instr.) is doubtful reading.

Ṭhāyin (adj.-n.) [from tiṭṭhati] standing, being in, being in a state of (-°), staying with, dependent on (with gen.): pariyuṭṭhaṭṭhāyin "being in a state of one to whom it has arisen," i. e. one who has got the idea of . . . or one who imagines S III.3 sq.; arūpa-ṭṭhāyin It 62; Yamassa ṭhāyino being under the rule of Yama Pv I.11⁹.

Ṭhita [pp. of tiṭṭhati = Gr. στατός, Lat. status, Celt. fossad (firm)] standing, i. e. (see ṭhāna I) either upright (opp. nisinna, etc.), or immovable, or being, behaving in general. In the latter function often (with ger.) pleonastic for finite verb (cp. ṭhapita); — resting in, abiding in (-° or with loc.); of time: lasting, enduring; fig. steadfast, firm, controlled: amissīkataṃ ev' assa cittaŋ hoti, ṭhitaŋ ānejjappattaŋ A III.377 = IV.404; tassa ṭhito va kāyo hoti ṭhitaŋ cittaŋ (firm, unshaken) S V.74 = Nd² 475 B²; — D I.135 (khema°); A I.152; Sn 250 (dhamme); It 116 sq. (ṭh. caranto nisinna sayāna); J I.167; 279; III.53. — with ger. nahātvā ṭh. & nivāsetvā ṭh. (after bathing & dressing) J I.265; dārakaŋ gahetvā th. J VI.336. Cp. saṇ°.

-atta self-controlled, composed, steadfast D I.57 (+ gatatta yatatta; expl. at DA I.168 by suppatiṭṭhitacitto); S I.48; III.46; A II.5; IV.93, 428; Sn 370 (+ parinibbuta), 359 (id. expl. at SnA 359 by lokadhammehi akampaneyya-citta); Pug 62; -kappin (adj.) (for kappa-*ṭhitin) standing or waiting a whole kappa Pug 13 (expl. at Pug A 187 by ṭhitakappo assa atthī ti; kappaŋ ṭhapetuŋ samattho ti attho); -citta (adj.) of controlled heart (= °atta) D II.157≈; -dhamma (adj.) everlasting, eternal (of mahāsamudda, the great ocean) Vin II.237 = A IV.198.

Ṭhitaka (adj.) = ṭhita in meaning of standing, standing up, erect Vin II.165; D II.17 = III.143; M II.65; J I.53, 62; VvA 64.

Ṭhitatā (f.) the fact of standing or being founded on (-°) S II.25 = A I.286 (dhamma° + dhamma-niyāmatā).

Ṭhitatta (nt.) standing, being placed; being appointed to, appointment J I.124.

Ṭhiti (f.) [from tiṭṭhati Sk. sthiti, Gr. στάσις, Lat. statio (cp. stationary), Ohg. stat, Ags. stede] state (as opposed to becoming), stability, steadfastness; duration, continuance, immobility; persistence, keeping up (of: c. gen.); condition of (-°) relation S II.11; III.31; IV.14, 104, 228 sq., A V.96; Vism 32 (kāyassa); in jhāna: S III.264, 269 sq., saddhammassa (prolongation of) S II. 225; A I.159; II.148; III.177 (always with asammosa & anantaradhāna), cp. M II.26 sq.; — dhammaṭṭhitiñāṇa (state or condition of) S II.124; Ps I.50 sq. — n' atthi dhuvaŋ ṭhiti: the duration is not for long M II.64 = Dh 147 = Th 1, 769 = VvA 77, cp. Th 2, 343 (= ThA 241); Sn 1114 (viññāṇa°) PvA 198 (position, constellation), 199 (jīvita° as remainder of life, cp. ṭhitakappin); Dhs 11≈(cittassa), 19≈(+ āyu = subsistence).

-bhāgiya connected with duration, enduring, lasting, permanent (only appl. to samādhi) D III.277; A III.427; Nett 77; cp. samādhissa ṭhitikusala "one who is accomplished in lasting concentration" A III.311, 427; IV.34.

Ṭhitika (adj.) [Der. fr. ṭhiti] standing, lasting, enduring; existing, living on (-°), e. g. āhāra° dependent on food Kh III. (see āhāra); nt. adv. ṭhitikaŋ constantly VvA 75.

Ṭhīyati see patiṭṭhīyati.

Ḍ.

Ḍaŋsa [see ḍasati] a yellow fly, gadfly (orig. " the bite ") Nd² 268 (=pingala-makkhika, same at J III.263 & SnA 101); usually in combⁿ with other biting or stinging sensations, as °siriŋsapa Sn 52, & freq. in cpd. ḍaŋsa-makasa-vāt' ātapa-siriŋsapa-samphassa M I.10= A II.117, 143=III.163; A III.388; V.15; Vin I.3; Nd² s. v. (enumᵈ under var. kinds of dukkhā); Vism 31 (here explᵈ as ḍaŋsana-makkhikā or andha-makkhikā).

Ḍaṭṭha [pp. of daŋśati or dasati to bite] bitten PvA 144.

Ḍasati (& ḍaŋsati) [cp. Sk. daśati & daŋśati, Gr. δάκνω, Ohg. zanga, Ags. tonge, E. tong] to bite (esp. of flies, snakes, scorpions, etc.), pres. ḍasati M I.519; pot. ḍaseyya M I.133; A III.101=IV.320 (where ḍaŋs°) & ḍaŋseyya A III.306; ppr. ḍasamāna J I.265 (gīvāya); fut. ḍaŋsayissāmi J VI.193 (v. l. ḍass°); aor. aḍaŋsi Vv 80⁸ (=Sk. adānksīt), ḍaŋsi PvA 62 & ḍasi J I.502; DhA II.258; inf. ḍasituŋ J I.265; ger. ḍasitvā J I.222; II.102; III.52, 538; DhA I.358. — Pp. ḍaṭṭha; cp. also dāṭhā & saṇḍāsa.

Ḍahati (& dahati) [Sk. dahati, pp. dagdha, cp. dāha, nidāgha (summer heat); Gr. τέφρα ashes, Lat. favilla (glowing) cinders, Goth. dags, Ger. tag, E. day=hot time] to burn (trs.) consume, torment M I.365; II.73; A V.110; J II.44 (aor. 3 sg. med. adaḍḍha=Sk. adagdha); Dh 31, 71, 140; Miln 45, 112 (cauterize). Pp. daḍḍha — Pass. ḍayhati S I.188 (kāmarāgena ḍayhāmi cittam me pariḍayhati); ib. (mahārāga: mā ḍayhittho punappunaŋ) M II.73; S III.150 (mahāpaṭhavī ḍayhati vinassati na bhavati) esp. in ppr. ḍayhamāna consumed with or by, burning, glowing Dh 371; It 23 (°ena kāyena & cetasā Pv I.11¹⁰, 12²; II.2³) (of a corpse being cremated); PvA 63, 152 (vippaṭisārena: consumed by remorse). See also similes *J.P.T.S.* 1907, 90. Cp. uḍ°.

Ḍāka (m. nt.) [Sk. sāka (nt.) on ś>ḍ cp. Sk. sākinī> ḍākinī] green food, eatable herbs, vegetable Vin I.246 (°rasa), 248; Th 2, 1; Vv 20⁶ (v. l. sāka); VvA 99 (=taṇḍuleyyakādi-sākavyañjana).

Ḍāha [Sk. dāha, see ḍahati] burning, glow, heat D I.10 (disā° sky-glow=zodiacal light?); M I.244; PvA 62; Miln 325. Sometimes spelt dāha, e. g. A I.178 (aggi°); Sdhp 201 (id.); — dava° a jungle fire Vin II.138; J I.461.

Ḍeti [Sk. *ḍayate=dīyati; ḍayana flying. The Dhtp gives the root as ḍī or ḷī with def. of " ākāsa-gamana "] to fly; only in simile " seyyathā pakkhī sakuṇo yena yen' eva ḍeti . . ." D I.71=M I.180, 269=A II.209= Pug 58; J V.417. Cp. dayati & dīyati, also uḍḍeti.

T.

-T- as composition-consonant (see Müller pp. 62, 63, on euphonic cons.) especially with agge (after, from), in ajja-t-agge, tama-t-agge, dahara-t-agge A V.300; cp. deva ta-t-uttari for tad-uttari A III.287, 314, 316.

Ta° [Vedic tad, etc.; Gr. τόν τήν τό; Lat. is-te, tālis, etc.; Lith. tás tā; Goth. þata; Ohg. etc. daz; E. that] base of demonstr. pron. for nt., in oblique cases of m. & f., & in demonstr. adv. of place & time (see also sa). — I. *Cases: nom.* sg. nt. tad (older) Vin I.83; Sn 1052; Dh 326; Miln 25 & taŋ (cp. yaŋ, kiŋ) Sn 1037, 1050; J III.26; *acc.* m. taŋ J II.158, f. taŋ J VI.368; *gen.* tassa, f. tassā (Sn 22, 110; J I.151); *instr.* tena, f. tāya (J III. 188); *abl.* tasmā (J I.167); tamhā Sn 291, 1138; (J III.26) & tato (usually as adv.) (Sn 390); *loc.* tasmiŋ (J I.278), tamhi (Dh 117); tahiŋ (adv.) (Pv I.5⁷) & tahaŋ (adv.) (J I.384; VvA 36); pl. *nom.* m. te (J II.129), f. tā (J II.127), nt. tāni (Sn 669, 845); *gen.* tesaŋ, f. tāsaŋ (Sn 916); *instr.* tehi, f. tāhi (J II.128); *loc.* tesu, f. tāsu (Sn 670). — In composition (Sandhi) both tad- & taŋ- are used with consecutive phonetic changes (assimilation), viz. (a) tad°: (α) in subst. function: tadagge henceforth D I.93 taduṭṭhāya DhA III.344; tadūpiya (cp. Trenckner, *Notes* 77, 78=tadopya (see discussion under opeti), but cp. Sk. tadrūpa Divy 543 & tatrupāya. It is simply tad-upa-ka, the adj.-positive of upa, of which the compar.-superlative is upama, meaning like this, i. e. of this or the same kind. Also spelt tadūpikā (f.) (at J II.160) agreeing with, agreeable, pleasant Miln 9; tadatthaŋ to such purpose SnA 565. — With assimilation: taccarita; tapparāyaṇa Sn 1114; tappoṇa (=tad-pra-ava-nata) see taccarita; tabbisaya (various) PvA 73; tabbiparīta (different) Vism 290; DhA III.275; tabbiparītatāya in contrast to that Vism 450. — (β) as crude form (not nt.) originally only in acc. (nt.) in adj. function like tad-ahan this day, then felt as euphonic *d*, esp. in forms where similarly the euphonic *t* is used (ajja-t-agge). Hence ta- is abstracted as a crude (adverbial) form used like any other root in composition. Thus: tad-ah-uposathe on this day's fast-day=to-day (or that day) being Sunday D I.47; Sn p. 139 (explᵈ as tam-ah-uposathe, uposatha-divase ti at SnA 502); tadahe on the same day PvA 46; tadahū (id.) J V.215 (=tasmiŋ chaṇa-divase). tad-anga for certain, surely, categorical (orig. concerning this cp. kimanga), in tadanga-nibbuta S III.43; tadanga-samatikkama Nd² 203; tadanga-vikkhambhana-samuccheda Vism 410; tadanga-pahāna DhsA 351; SnA 8; tadangena A IV.411. — (b) tan°: (α) as subst.: tammaya (equal to this, up to this) Sn 846

(=tapparāyana Nd² 206); A I.150. — (β) Derived from acc. use (like a β) as adj. is tankhaṇikā (fr. taŋ khaṇaŋ) Vin III.140 (=muhuttikā). — (γ) a reduced form of taŋ is to be found as ta° in the same origin & application as ta-d- (under a β) in combⁿ ta-y-idaŋ (for taŋ-idaŋ > taŋ-idaŋ > ta-idaŋ > ta-y-idaŋ) where y. takes the place of the euphonic consonant. Cp. in application also Gr. τοῦτο & ταῦτα, used adverbially as therefore (orig. just that) Sn 1077; Pv I.3³; PvA 2, 16 (=taŋ idaŋ), 76. The same ta° is to be seen in tāhaŋ Vv 83¹⁶ (=taŋ-ahaŋ), & not to be confused with tāhaŋ=te ahaŋ (see tvaŋ). — A similar combⁿ is taŋyathā Miln 1 (this is how, thus, as follows) which is the Sk. form for the usual P. seyyathā (instead of ta-(y)-yathā, like ta-y-idaŋ); cp. Trenckner, P.M. p. 75. — A sporadic form for tad is tadaŋ Sn p. 147 (even that, just that; for tathaŋ ?). — II. *Application*: 1. ta° *refers or points* back to somebody or something just mentioned or under discussion (like Gr. αὐτός, Lat. hic, Fr. ci in voici, ect homme-ci, etc.): this, that, just this (or that), even this (or these). In this sense combᵈ with api: te c' āpi (even these) Sn 1058. It is also used to indicate something immediately following the statement of the speaker (cp. Gr. ὅδε, E. thus): this now, esp. in adv. use (see below); taŋ kiŋ maññasi D I.60; yam etaŋ pañhaŋ apucchi Ajita taŋ vadāmi te: Sn 1037; taŋ te pavakkhāmi (this now shall I tell you:) Sn 1050; tesaŋ Buddho vyākāsi (to those just mentioned answered B.) Sn 1127; te tositā (and they, pleased . . .) ib. 1128. — 2. *Correlative use*: (a) in rel. sentences with ya° (preceding ta°): yaŋ ahaŋ jānāmi taŋ tvaŋ jānāsi "what I know (that) you know" D I.88; yo nerayikānaŋ sattānaŋ āhāro tena so yāpeti "he lives on that food which is (characteristic) of the beings in N.; or: whichever is the food of the N. beings, on this he lives" PvA 27. — (b) elliptical (with omission of the verb to be) yaŋ taŋ=that which (there is), what (is), whatever, used like an adj.; ye te those who, i. e. all (these), whatever: ye pana te manussā saddhā . . . te evam ahaŋsu . . . "all those people who were full of faith said" Vin II.195; yena tena upāyena gaṇha "catch him by whatever means (you like)," i. e. by all means J II.159; yaŋ taŋ kayirā "whatever he may do" Dh 42. — 3. *Distributive and iterative use* (cp. Lat. quisquis, etc.): . . . taŋ taŋ this & that, i. e. each one; yaŋ yaŋ passati taŋ taŋ pucchati whomsoever he sees (each one) he asks PvA 38; yaŋ yaŋ manaso piyaŋ taŋ taŋ gahetvā whatever . . . (all) that PvA 77; yo yo yaŋ yaŋ icchati tassa tassa taŋ taŋ adāsi "whatever anybody wished he gave to him" PvA 113. So with adv. of ta°: tattha tattha here & there (freq.); tahaŋ tahaŋ id. J I.384; VvA 36, 187; tato tato Sn 390. — (b) the same in disjunctive-comparative sense: taŋ . . . taŋ is this so & is this so (too)=the same as, viz. taŋ jīvaŋ taŋ sarīraŋ is the soul the same as the body (opp. aññaŋ j. a. s.) A V.193, etc. (see jīva). — 4. *Adverbial use* of some cases (localᵃ, temporalᵇ, & modalᶜ): *acc.* taŋ (a) there (to): tad avasari he withdrew there D. II.126, 156; (b) taŋ enaŋ at once, presently (=tāvad-eva) Vin I.127 (cp. Ved. enā); (c) therefore (cp. kiŋ wherefore, why), that is why, now, then: S II.17; M I.487; Sn 1110; Pv I.2³ (=tasmā PvA 11 & 103); II.7¹⁶; cp. taŋ kissa hetu Nd² on jhāna. — *gen.* tassa (c) therefore A IV.333. — *instr.* tena (a) there (direction=there to), always in correl. with yena: where—there, or in whatever direction, here & there Freq. in formula denoting approach to a place (often unnecessary to translate); e. g. yena Jīvakassa ambavanaŋ tena pāyāsi: where the Mango-grove of J. was, there he went=he went to the M. of J. D I.49; yena Gotamo ten' upasankama go where G. is D I.88; yena āvasathâgāraŋ ten' upasankami D II.85 etc.; yena vā tena vā palāyanti they run here & there A II.33; (c) so then, now then, therefore, thus (often with hi) J I.151, 279; PvA 60; Miln 23; tena hi D II.2; J I.266; III.188; Miln 19. — *abl.* tasmā (c) out of this reason, therefore Sn 1051, 1104; Nd² 279 (=taŋ kāraṇaŋ): PvA 11, 103; tato (a) from there, thence Pv I.12³; (b) then, hereafter PvA 39. — *loc.* tahiŋ (a) there (over there > beyond) Pv I.5⁷; (c) =therefore PvA 25; tahaŋ (a) there; usually repeated: see above II. 3 (a). — See also tattha, tathā, tadā, tādi, etc.

Taka a kind of medicinal gum, enumerated with two varieties, viz. takapattī & takapaṇṇī under jatūni bhesajjāni at Vin I.201.

Takka¹ [Sk. tarka doubt; science of logic (lit. "turning & twisting") *treik, cp. Lat. tricæ, intricare (to "trick," puzzle), & also Sk. tarku bobbin, spindle, Lat. torqueo (torture, turn)] doubt; a doubtful view (often= diṭṭhi, appl. like sammā°, micchā-diṭṭhi), hair-splitting reasoning, sophistry (=itihītihaŋ Nd² 151). Opp. to takka (=micchā-sankappo Vbh 86, 356) is dhamma-takka right thought (:vuccati sammā-sankappo Nd² 318; cp. Dhs 7, 298), D I.16 (°pariyāhata); M I.68 (id.); Sn 209 (°ŋ pahāya na upeti sankhaŋ) 885 (doubt), 886; Dhs 7, 21, 298 (+vitakka, trsl. as "ratiocination" by Mrs. Rh. D.); Vbh 86, 237 (sammā°) 356; Vism 189. See also vitakka.
-āgama the way of (right) thought, the discipline of correct reasoning Dāvs V.22; -âvacara as neg. atakkâ-vacarâ in phrase dhammā gambhīrā duddasā aᵘ nipuṇā (views, etc.) deep, difficult to know, beyond logic (or sophistry; i. e. not accessible to doubt ?), profound Vin I.4=D I.12=S I.136=M I.487. Gogerley trsl. "unattainable by reasoning," Andersen "being beyond the sphere of thought"; -āsaya room for doubt Sn 972; -gahaṇa the thicket of doubt or sophistry J I.97; -vaḍḍhana increasing, furthering doubt or wrong ideas Sn 1084 (see Nd² 269); -hetu ground for doubt (or reasoning ?) A II.193=Nd² 151.

Takka² (nt.) [Should it not belong to the same root as takka¹ ?] buttermilk (with ¼ water), included in the five products from a cow (pañca gorasā) at Vin I.244; made by churning dadhi Miln 173; J I.340; II.363; DhA II.68 (takkâdi-ambila).

Takkaṇa (nt.) thought, representation (of: -°) J I.68 (ussāvabindu°).

Takkara¹ (=tat-kara) a doer thereof D I.235, M I.68; Dh 19.

Takkara² a robber, a thief J IV.432.

Takkaḷa (nt.) a bulbous plant, a tuberose J IV.46, 371 (biḷāli°, expl. at 373 by takkala-kanda)=VI.578.

Takkārī (f.) the tree Sesbania Aegyptiaca (a kind of acacia) Th 2, 297 (=dālika-laṭṭhi ThA 226).

Takkika (adj.) [fr. takka¹] doubting, having wrong views, foolish; m. a sophist, a fool Ud 73; J I.97; Miln 248.

Takkin (adj.-n.) [fr. takka¹] thinking, reasoning, esp. sceptically; a sceptic D I.16≈(takkī vīmaŋsī); M I.520; DA I.106 (=takketvā vitakketvā diṭṭhi-gāhino etaŋ adhivacanaŋ), cp. pp. 114, 115 (takki-vāda).

Takketi [Denom. of tarka] to think, reflect, reason, argue DA I.106; DhsA 142. — attānaŋ t. to have self-confidence, to trust oneself J I.273, 396, 468; III.233.

Takkoṭaka [is reading correct ?] a kind of insect or worm Vism 258. Reading at id. p. KhA 58 is **kakkoṭaka**.

Takkola [Sk. kakkola & takkola] Bdellium, a perfume made from the berry of the kakkola plant J I.291; also as Nɪ at Miln 359 (the Takola of Ptolemy; perhaps= Sk. karkoṭa: Trenckner, *Notes*, p. 59).

Tagara (nt.) the shrub Tabernaemontana coronaria, and a fragrant powder or perfume obtained from it, incense

Vin I.203; It 68 (= Udānavarga p. 112, No. 8); Dh 54, 55, 56 (candana+); J IV.286; VI.100 (the shrub) 173 (id.); Miln 338; Dāvs V.50; DhA I.422 (tagara-mallikā two kinds of gandhā).

Taggaruka = tad + garuka, see taccarita.

Taggha [tad + gha, cp. in-gha & Lat. ce-ce ego-met, Gr. ἐγώ-γε] affirmative particle ("ekaŋsena" DA I.236; ekaŋsa-vacana J V.66; ekaŋse nipāta J V.307): truly, surely, there now! Vin II.126, 297; D I.85; M I.207, 463; III.179; J V.65 (v. l. tagghā); Sn p. 87.

Taca (& taco nt.) [Vedic tvak (f.), gen. tvacaḥ] 1. bark. — 2. skin, hide (similar to camma, denoting the thick, outer skin, as contrasted with chavi, thin skin, see chavi & cp. J I.146). — 1. bark: M I.198, 434, 488; A V.5. — 2. skin: often used together with nahāru & aṭṭhi (tendons & bones), to denote the outer appearance (framework) of the body, or that which is most conspicuous in emaciation: A I.50 = Sdhp. 46; taca-maŋsāvalepana (+ aṭṭhī nahārusaŋyutta) Sn 194 = J I.146 (where °vilepana); SnA 247; aṭṭhi-taca-mattā-vasesasarīra "nothing but skin & bones" PvA 201. — Of the cast-off skin of a snake: urago va jiṇṇaŋ tacaŋ jahāti Sn 1, same simile Pv I.12[1] (= nimmoka PvA 63). — kañcanasannibha-taca (adj.) of golden-coloured skin (a sign of beauty) Sn 551; Vv 30[2] = 32[3]; Miln 75; VvA 9. — valita-tacatā a condition of wrinkled skin (as sign of age) Nd[2] 252≈; Kh III.; KhA 45; Sdhp 102.

-gandha the scent of bark Dhs 625; -pañcaka-kammaṭṭhāna the fivefold "body is skin," etc, subject of kammaṭṭhāna-practice. This refers to the satipaṭṭhānā (kāye kāy' ânupassanā:) see kāya I. (a) of which the first deals with the anupassanā (viewing) of the body as consisting of the five (dermatic) constituents of kesā lomā nakhā dantā, taco (hair of head, other hair, nails, teeth, skin or epidermis: see Kh III.). It occurs in formula (inducing a person to take up the life of a bhikkhu): taca-p-kammaṭṭhānaŋ ācikkhitvā taŋ pabbājesi J I.116; DhA I.243; II.87, 140, 242. Cp. also Vism 353; DhA II.88; SnA 246, 247; -pariyonaddha with wrinkled (shrivelled) skin (of Petas: as sign of thirst) PvA 172; -rasa the taste of bark Dhs 629, -sāra (a) (even) the best (bark, i. e.) tree S I.70 = 90 = It 45; — (b) a (rope of) strong fibre J III.204 (= veṇudaṇḍaka).

Taccarita (adj.) in combn with tabbahula taggaruka tanninna tappoṇa tappabhāra freq. as formula, expressing: converging to this end, bent thereon, striving towards this (aim): Nd[2] under tad. The same combn with Nibbāna-ninna, N.-poṇa, N.-pabhāra freq. (see Nibbāna).

Taccha[1] [Vedic takṣan, cp. taṣṭṛ, to takṣati (see taccheti) Lat. textor, Gr. τέκτων carpenter (cp. architect), τέχνη art] a carpenter, usually as °ka: otherwise only in cpd. °sūkara the carpenter-pig (= a boar, so called from felling trees), title & hero of Jātaka No. 492 (IV.342 sq.). Cp. vaḍḍhakin.

Taccha[2] (adj.) [Der. fr. tathā + ya = tath-ya "as it is," Sk. tathya] true, real, justified, usually in combn w. bhūta. bhūta taccha tatha, D I.190 (paṭipadā: the only true & real path) S V.229 (dhamma; text has tathā, v. l. tathaŋ better); as bhūta t. dhammika (well founded and just) D I.230. bhūta + taccha: A II.100 = Pug 50; VvA 72. — yathā tacchaŋ according to truth Sn 1096 which is interpreted by Nd[2] 270: tacchaŋ vuccati amataŋ Nibbānaŋ, etc. — (nt.) taccha a truth Sn 327. — ataccha false, unreal, unfounded; a lie, a falsehood D I.3 (abhūta+); VvA 72 (= musā).

Tacchaka = taccha[1]. (a) a carpenter Dh 80 (cp. DhA II 147); Miln 413. magga° a road-builder J VI.348. — (b) = taccha-sūkara J IV.350. — (c) a class of Nāgas D II.258. — f. tacchikā a woman of low social standing (= veṇī, bamboo-worker) J V.106.

Tacchati [fr. taccha[1], cp. taccheti] to build, construct; maggaŋ t. to construct or repair a road J VI.348.

Taccheti [probably a denom. fr. taccha[1] = Lat. texo to weave (orig. to plait, work together, work artistically), cp. Sk. taṣṭṛ architect = Lat. textor; Sk. takṣan, etc., Gr. τέχνη craft, handiwork (cp. technique), Ohg. dehsa hatchet. Cp. also orig. meaning of karoti & kamma] to do wood-work, to square, frame, chip J I.201; Miln 372, 383.

Tajja [tad + ya, cp. Sk. tadīya] "this like," belonging to this, founded on this or that; on the ground of this (or these), appropriate, suitable; esp. in combn with vāyāma (a suitable effort as "causa movens") A I.207; Miln 53. Also with reference to sense-impressions, etc. denoting the complemental sensation S IV.215; M I. 190, 191; Dhs 3-6 (cp. *Dhs. trsl.* p. 6 & Com. expl. anucchavika). — PvA 203 (tajjassa pāpassa katattā: by the doing of such evil, v. l. SS tassajjassa, may be a contraction of tādiyassa otherwise tādisassa). *Note.* The expln of Kern, *Toev.* II.87 (tajja = tad + ja "arising from this") is syntactically impossible.

Tajjanā (f.) [from tajjeti] threat, menace J II.169; Vv 50[9]; VvA 212 (bhayasantajjana).

Tajjaniya [grd. of tajjeti] to be blamed or censured Vism 115 (a°); (n.) censure, blame, scorn, rebuke. M 50th Sta; Miln 365. As t. t. °kamma one of the sangha-kammas: Vin I.49, 53, 143 sq., 325; II.3 sq., 226, 230; A I.99.

Tajjita [pp. of tajjeti] threatened, frightened, scared; spurred or moved by (-°) D I.141 (daṇḍa°, bhaya°); Dh 188 (bhaya°); Pug 56. Esp. in combn maraṇa-bhaya° moved by the fear of death J I.150, 223; PvA 216.

Tajjeti [Caus. of tarjati, to frighten. Cp. Gr. τάρβος fright, fear, ταρβέω; Lat. torvus wild, frightful] to frighten, threaten; curse, rail against J I.157, 158; PvA 55. — Pp. tajjita. — Caus. tajjāpeti to cause to threaten, to accuse PvA 23 (= paribhāsāpeti).

Taṭa [*tḷ, see tala & cp. tālu, also Lat. tellus] declivity or side of a hill, precipice; side of a river or well, a bank J I.232, 303; II.315 (udapāna); IV.141; SnA 519, DhA I.73 (papāta°). See also taḷāka.

Taṭataṭāyati [Onomatopoetic, to make a sound like taṭ-taṭ. Root *kḷ (on ṭ for ḷ cp. taṭa for tala) to grind one's teeth, to be in a frenzy. Cp. ciṭiciṭāyati. See note on gala and kiṇakiṇāyati] to rattle, shake, clatter; to grind or gnash one's teeth; to fizz. Usually said of people in frenzy or fury (in ppr. °yanto or °yamāna): J I.347 (rosena) 439 (kodhena); II.277 (of a bhikkhu kodhana "boiling with rage" like a "uddhane pakkhitta-loṇaŋ viya"); the latter trope also at DhA IV.170; DhA I.370 (aggimhi pakkhitta-loṇasakkharā viya rosena t.); III.328 (vātāhata-tālapaṇṇaŋ viya); VvA 47, 121 (of a kodhābhibhūto; v. l. kaṭakaṭāyamāna), 206 (+ akkosati paribhāsati), 256. Cp. also kaṭakaṭāyati & karakarā.

Taṭṭaka [Etym. unknown] a bowl for holding food, a flat bowl, porringer, salver J III.10 (suvaṇṇa°), 97, 121, 538; IV.281. According to Kern, *Toev.* s. v. taken into Tamil as taṭṭaŋ, cp. also Av. tašta. Morris (*J.P.T.S.* 1884, 80) compares Marathi tasta (ewer).

Taṭṭikā (f.) [cp. kaṭaka] a (straw) mat Vin IV.40 (Bdhgh on this: teṭṭikaŋ (sic) nāma tālapaṇṇehi vā vākehi vā katataṭṭikā, p. 357); J I.141 (v. l. taddhika); Vism 97.

Taṇḍula (*Sk. taṇḍula: dialectical] rice-grain, rice husked & ready for boiling; freq. comb^d with tila (q. v.) in mentioning of offerings, presentations, etc.: loṇaŋ telaŋ taṇḍulaŋ khādaniyaŋ sakaṭesu āropetvā Vin I.220, 238, 243, 249; talitaṇḍulâdayo J III.53; PvA 105. — Vin I.244; A I.130; J I.255; III.55, 425 (taṇḍulāni metri causa); VI.365 (mūla° coarse r., majjhima° medium r., kaṇikā the finest grain); Sn 295; Pug 32; DhA I.395 (sāli-taṇḍula husked rice); DA I.93. Cp. ut°.

-ammaṇa a measure (handful ?) of rice J II.436. -doṇa a rice-vat or rice-bowl DhA IV.15; -pāladvārā "doors (i. e. house) of the rice-guard" Npl. M II.185; -muṭṭhi a handful of rice PvA 131; -homa an oblation of rice D I.9.

Taṇḍuleyyaka [cp. Sk. taṇḍulīya] the plant Amaranthus polygonoides VvA 99 (enum^d amongst various kinds of ḍāka).

Taṇhā (f.) [Sk. tṛṣṇā, besides tarśa (m.) & tṛṣ (f.) = Av tarśna thirst, Gr. ταρσία dryness, Goth. þaúrsus, Ohg. durst, E. drought & thirst; to *ters to be, or to make dry in Gr. τέρσομαι, Lat. torreo to roast, Goth. gaþairsan, Ohg. derren.—Another form of t. is tasiṇā] lit. drought, thirst; fig. craving, hunger for, excitement, the fever of unsatisfied longing (c. loc.: kabaḷinkāre āhāre "thirst" for solid food S II.101 sq; cīvare piṇḍapāte taṇhā = greed for Sn 339). Opp^d to peace of mind (upekhā, santi). — A. *Literal meaning*: khudāya taṇhāya ca khajjamānā tormented by hunger & thirst Pv II.1^5 (= pipāsāya PvA 69). — B. *In its secondary meaning*: taṇhā is a state of mind that leads to rebirth. Plato puts a similar idea into the mouth of Socrates (Phædo 458, 9). Neither the Greek nor the Indian thinker has thought it necessary to explain how this effect is produced. In the Chain of Causation (D II. 34) we are told how Taṇhā arises—when the sense organs come into contact with the outside world there follow sensation and feeling, & these (if, as elsewhere stated, there is no mastery over them) result in Taṇhā. In the First Proclamation (S V.420 ff.; Vin I.10) it is said that Taṇhā, the source of sorrow, must be rooted out by the way there laid down, that is by the Aryan Path. Only then can the ideal life be lived. Just as physical thirst arises of itself, and must be assuaged, got rid of, or the body dies; so the mental "thirst," arising from without, becomes a craving that must be rooted out, quite got rid of, or there can be no Nibbāna. The figure is a strong one, and the word Taṇhā is found mainly in poetry, or in prose passages charged with religious emotion. It is rarely used in the philosophy or the psychology. Thus in the long Enumeration of Qualities (Dhs), Taṇhā occurs in one only out of the 1,366 sections (Dhs 1059), & then only as one of many subordinate phases of lobha. Taṇhā binds a man to the chain of Saŋsāra, of being reborn & dying again & again (2^b) until Arahantship or Nibbāna is attained, taṇhā destroyed, & the cause alike of sorrow and of future births removed (2^c). In this sense Nibbāna is identical with "sabbupadhi-paṭinissaggo taṇhakkhayo virāgo nirodho" (see Nibbāna). — 1. *Systematizations*: The 3 aims of t. kāma°, bhava°, vibhava°, that is craving for sensuous pleasure, for rebirth (anywhere, but especially in heaven), or for no rebirth; cp. Vibhava. These three aims are mentioned already in the First Proclamation (S V.420; Vin I.10) and often afterwards D II.61, 308; III.216, 275; S III.26, 158; It 50; Ps I.26, 39; II.147; Vbh 101, 365; Nett 160. Another group of 3 aims of taṇhā is given as kāma°, rūpa° & arūpa° at D III.216; Vbh 395; & yet another as rūpa°, arūpa° & nirodha° at D III.216. — The source of t. is said to be sixfold as founded on & relating to the 6 bāhirāni āyatanāni (see rūpa), objects of sense or sensations, viz. sights, sounds, smells, etc.: D II.58; Ps I.6 sq.; Nd^2 271^I; in threefold aspects (as kāma-taṇhā, bhava° & vibhava°) with relation to the 6 senses discussed at Vism 567 sq.; also under the term cha-taṇha-kāyā (sixfold group, see cpds.) M I.51; III.280; Ps I.26; elsewhere called chadvārika-taṇhā "arising through the 6 doors" DhA III.286. — 18 varieties of t. (comprising worldly objects of enjoyment, ease, comfort & well-living are enum^d at Nd^2 271^{III} (under taṇhā-lepa). 36 kinds: 18 referring to sensations (illusions) of subjective origin (ajjhattikassa upādāya), & 18 to sensations affecting the individnal in objective quality (bāhirassa upādāya) at A II.212; Nett 37; & 108 varieties or specifications of t. are given at Nd^2 271^{II} (under Jappā) = Dhs 1059 = Vbh 361. — Taṇhā as "kusalā pi akusalā pi" (good & bad) occurs at Nett 87; cp. Tālapuṭa's good t. Th I.1091 f. — 2. *Import of the term*: (a) various characterizations of t.: mahā° Sn 114; kāma° S I.131; gedha° S I.15; bhava° D III.274 (+ avijjā); grouped with diṭṭhi (wrong views) Nd^2 271^{III}, 271^{IV}. T. fetters the world & causes misery: "yāya ayaŋ loko uddhasto pariyonaddho tantākulajāto" A II.211 sq.; taṇhāya jāyatī soko taṇhāya jāyatī bhayaŋ taṇhāya vippamuttassa natthi soko kuto bhayaŋ Dh 216; taṇhāya uḍḍito loko S I.40; yaŋ loke piyarūpaŋ sātarūpaŋ etth' esā taṇhā . . . Vbh 103; it is the 4th constituent of Māra's army (M-senā) Sn 436; M's daughter, S I.134. In comparisons: t. + jālinī visattikā S I.107; = bharādānaŋ (t. ponobbhavikā nandirāga-sahagatā) S III.26; V.402; gaṇḍa = kāya, gaṇḍamūlan ti taṇhāy' etaŋ adhivacanaŋ S IV.83; = sota S IV.292 (and a khīṇāsavo = chinnasoto); manujassa pamatta-cārino t. vaḍḍhati māluvā viya Dh 334. — (b) taṇhā as the inciting factor of rebirth & incidental cause of saŋsāra: kammaŋ khettaŋ viññāṇaŋ bījaŋ taṇhā sineho . . . evaŋ āyatiŋ punabbhavâbhinibbatti hoti A I.223; t. ca avasesā ca kilesā: ayaŋ vuccati **dukkha-samudayo** Vbh 107, similarly Nett 23 sq.; as **ponobbhavikā** (causing rebirth) S III.26; Ps II.147, etc.; as a link in the chain of interdependent causation (see paṭiccasamuppāda): vedanā-paccayā taṇhā, taṇhā-paccayā upādānaŋ Vin I.1, 5; D II.31, 33, 56, etc.; t. & upadhi: taṇhāya sati upadhi hoti t. asati up. na hoti S II.108; ye taṇhaŋ vaḍḍhenti te upadhiŋ vaḍḍhenti, etc. S II.109; taṇhāya nīyati loko taṇhāya parikissati S I.39; taṇhā saŋyojanena saŋyuttā sattā dīgharattaŋ sandhāvanti saŋsaranti It 8. See also t.-dutiya. — (c) To have got rid of t. is Arahantship: **vigata-taṇha vigata-pipāsa vigata-pariḷāha** D III.238; S III.8, 107 sq., 190; samūlaŋ taṇhaŋ abbuyha S I.16 = 63, 121 (Godhiko parinibbuto); III.26 (nicchāto parinibbuto); vita° Sn 83, 849, 1041 (+ nibbuta); taṇhāya vippahānena S I.39 ("Nibbānan" iti vuccati). 40 (sabbaŋ chindati bandhanaŋ); taṇhaŋ mā kāsi mā lokaŋ punar āgami Sn 339; taṇhaŋ pariññāya . . . te narā oghatiṇṇā ti Sn 1082; ucchinna-bhava-taṇhā Sn 746; taṇhāya vūpasama S III.231; t.-nirodha S IV.390. — See also M I.51; Dh 154; It 9 (vita° + anādāna), 50 (°ŋ pahantvāna); Sn 495, 496, 916; & cp. °khaya. — 3. *Kindred terms* which in Commentaries are expl^d by one of the taṇhā-formulæ (cp. Nd^2 271^V & 271^{VII}): (a) t. in groups of 5: (α) with kilesa saŋyoga vipāka duccarita; (β) diṭṭhi kilesa duccarita avijjā; (γ) diṭṭhi kil° kamma duccarita. — (b) quasi-synonyms: ādāna, ejā, gedha, jappā, nandī, nivesana, pariḷāha, pipāsā, lepa, loluppa, vāna, visattikā, sibbanī. — In cpds. the form taṇhā is represented by taṇha before double consonants, as taṇhakkhaya, etc.

-âdhipateyya mastery over t. S III.103; -âdhipanna seized by t. S. I.29; Sn 1123; -ādāsa the mirror of t. A II.54; âbhinivesa full of t. PvA 267; -āluka greedy J II.78; -uppādā (pl.) (four) grounds of the rise of craving (viz. cīvara, piṇḍapāta, senâsana, itibhavâbhava) A II.10 = It 109; D III.228; Vbh 375; -kāyā (pl.) (six) groups of t. (see above B 1) S II.3; D III.244, 280; Ps I.26; Vbh 380; -kkhaya the destruction of the excitement of cravings, almost synonymous with Nibbāna (see above B2c): °*rata* Dh 187 (expl^d at DhA III.241: arahatte c' eva nibbāne ca abhirato hoti); — Vv 73^5 (expl^d by Nibbāna VvA 296); therefore in the expositionary formula of Nibbāna as equivalent with N. Vin I.5; S III.133; It 88, etc. (see N.). In the same sense: sabbañjaho taṇhakkhaye vimutto Vin I.8= M I.171=Dh 353; taṇhākkhaya virāga nirodha nibbāna A II.34, expl^d at Vism 293; bhikkhu arahaŋ cha ṭhānāni adhimutto hoti: nekkhammâdhimutto, paviveka°, avyāpajjha°, upādānakkhaya°, taṇhakkhaya°, asammoha° Vin I.183; cp. also Sn 70, 211, 1070, 1137; -gata obsessed with excitement, i. e. a victim of t. Sn 776; -gaddula the leash of t. Nd^2 271^{II}≈; -cchida breaking the cravings Sn 1021, 1101; -jāla the snare of t. M I.271; Th I, 306; Nd^2 271^{II}; -dutiya who has the fever or excitement of t. as his companion A II.10= It 9=109=Sn 740, 741=Nd^2 305; cp. *Dhs. trsl.* p. 278; -nadī the river of t. Nd^2 271^{II}; cp. nadiyā soto ti: taṇhāy' etaŋ adhivacanaŋ It 114; -nighātana the destruction of t. Sn 1085; -pakkha the party of t., all that belongs to t. Nett 53, 69, 88, 160; -paccaya caused by t. Sn p. 144; Vism 568; -mūlaka rooted in t. (dhammā: 9 items) Ps I.26, 130; Vbh 390; -lepa cleaving to t. Nd^1 271^{III}; (+diṭṭhi-lepa); -vasika being in the power of t. J IV.3; -vicarita a thought of t. A II.212; -sankhaya (complete) destruction of t.; °*sutta* M I.251 (cūla°), 256 (mahā°): °*vimutti* salvation through cessation of t. M I.256, 270, & °*vimutta* (adj.) S IV.391; -samudda the ocean of t. Nd 271^{II}; -sambhūta produced by t. (t. ayaŋ kāyo) A II.145 (cp. Sn p. 144; yaŋ kiñci dukkhaŋ sambhoti sabbaŋ taṇhāpaccayā); -saŋyojana the fetter of t. (adj.) fettered, bound by t., in phrase t.-saŋyojanena saŋyuttā sattā dīgharattaŋ sandhāvanti saŋsaranti It 8, & t.-saŋyojanānaŋ sattānaŋ sandhāvataŋ saŋsarataŋ S II.178=III.149= PvA 166; A I.223; -salla the sting or poisoned arrow of t. S I.192 (°assa hantāraŋ vande ādiccabandhunaŋ), the extirpation of which is one of the 12 achievements of a mahesi Nd^2 503 (°assa abbuḷhana; cp. above).

Taṇhīyati [=taṇhāyati, denom. fr. taṇhā, cp. Sk. tṛṣyati to have thirst] to have thirst for S II.13 (for v. l. SS. tuṇhīyati; BB. ṭasati); Vism 544 (+upādiyati ghaṭ-yati); cp. tasati & pp. tasita.

Tata [pp. of tanoti] stretched, extended, spread out S I 357 (jāla); J IV.484 (tantāni jālāni Text, katāni v. l. for tatāni). *Note:* samo tata at J I.183 is to be read as samotata (spread all over).

Tatiya [Sk. tṛtīya, Av. ϑritya, Gr. τρίτος, Lat. tertius, Goth. þridja, E. third] Num. ord. the third. — Sn 97 (parābhavo); 436 (khuppipāsā as the 3rd division in the army of Māra), 1001; J II.353; Dh 309; PvA 69 (tatiyāya jātiya: in her third birth). Tatiyaŋ (nt. adv.) for the 3rd time D II.155; Sn 88, 95, 450; tatiyavāraŋ id. DhA I.183; VvA 47 (=at last); yāva tatiyaŋ id. Vin II.188; J I.279; DhA II.75; PvA 272 (in casting the lot: the third time decides); yāva tatiyakaŋ id. D I.95.

Tato [abl. of pron. base ta° (see ta° II.4)] 1. from this, in this S III.96 (tatoja); J III.281 (tato paraŋ beyond this, after this); Nd^2 664 (id.); DA I.212 (tatonidāna). — 2. thence J I.278; Miln 47. — 3. thereupon, further, afterwards J I.58; Dh 42; Miln 48; PvA 21, etc.

Tatta^1 [pp. of tapati] heated, hot, glowing; of metals: in a melted state (cp. uttatta) A II.122≈(tattena talena osiñcante, as punishment); Dh 308 (ayoguḷa); J II.352 (id.); IV.306 (tattatapo "of red-hot heat," i. e. in severe self-torture); Miln 26, 45 (adv. red-hot); PvA 221 (tatta-lohasecanaŋ the pouring over of glowing copper, one of the punishments in Niraya).

Tatta^2 (nt.) [tad+tva] truth; abl. tattato according to truth; accurately J II.125 (ñatvā); III.276 (ajānitvā not knowing exactly).

Tattaka^1 [tatta pp. of tappati^2+ka] pleasing, agreeable, pleasant Miln 238 (bhojana).

Tattaka^2 (adj.) (=tāvataka) of such size, so large Vism 184 (corresponding with yattaka); tattakaŋ kālaŋ so long, just that time, i. e. the specified time (may be long or short=only so long) DhA I.103 (v. l. ettakaŋ); II.16 (=ettaka).

Tattha [Sk. tatra adv. of place, cp. Goth. þaþro & also Sk. atra, yatra] A. 1. of *place:* (a) place where= there, in that place Sn 1071, 1085; Dh 58; J I.278; Pv I.10^{15}; often with eva: tatth' eva right there, on the (very same) spot S I.116; J II.154; PvA 27. In this sense as introduction to a comment on a passage: in this, here, in this connection (see also tatra) Dhs 584; DhA I.21; PvA 7, etc. (b) direction: there, to this place J II.159 (gantvā); VI.368; PvA 16 (tatthagamanasīla able to go here & there, i. e. wherever you like, of a Yakkha). — 2. as (loc.) case of pron. base ta°= in this, for or about that, etc. Sn 1115 (etam abhiññāya tato tattha vipassati: SnA tatra); tattha yo manku hoti Dh 249 (=tasmiŋ dāne m. DhA III.359); tattha kā paridevanā Pv I.12^3 ("why sorrow for this?"). — 3. of *time:* then, for the time being, interim (=ettha, cp. tattaka^2) in phrase tattha-parinibbāyin, where corresp. phrases have antarā-parinibbāyin (A II.238 e. g.≈I.134; see under parinibbāyin) D I.156; A I.232; II.5; IV.12; S V.357; M II.52, etc. The meaning of this phrase may however be taken in the sense of tatra A 3 (see next). — B. Repeated: tattha tattha here and there, in various places, all over; also corresponding with yattha yattha wherever . . . there It 115; Nett 96 (°gāmini-paṭipadā); VvA 297; PvA 1, 2, 33, 77, etc. — See tatra.

Tatra (Sk. tatra]=tattha in all meanings & applications, viz. A. 1. there: Dh 375; PvA 54. tatrâpi D I.81= It 22≈(tatrâpāsiŋ). tatra pi D I.1 (=DA I.42). tatra kho Vin I.10, 34; A V.5 sq.; 354 sq. (cp. atha kho). — In explanations: PvA 19 (tatrâyaŋ vitthārakathā "here follows the story in detail"). — 2. in this: Sn 595 (tatra kevalino smase); Dh 88 (tatr' abhirati: enjoyment in this). — 3. a special application of tatra (perhaps in the same sense to be explained tattha A 3) is that as first part of a cpd., where it is to be taken as generalizing (=tatra tatra): all kinds of (orig. in this & that), in whatever condition, all-round, complete (cp. yaŋ taŋ under ta° II.2, yena tena upāyena): tatramajjhattatā (complete) equanimity (keeping balance here & there) Vism 466 (cp. tatra-majjhatt' upekkhā 160); DhsA 132, 133 (majjh°+tatra majjh°); Bdhd 157. tatrûpāyaññū (=tatra upāyaññū) having all-round knowledge of the means and ways Sn 321 (correct reading at SnA 330); tatrupāyāya vīmaŋsīya samannāgatā endowed with genius in all kinds of means Vin IV.211 (or may it be taken as "suitable, corresponding, proportionate"? cp. tadūpiya). — B. tatra tatra, in t.-t.-abhinandinī (of taṇhā) finding its delight in this & that, here & there Vin I.10; Ps II.147; Nett 72; Vism 506.

Tatha (adj.) [an adjectivized tathā out of comb^n tathā ti "so it is," cp. taccha] (being) in truth, truthful; true, real D I.190 (+bhūta taccha); M III.69; Th I, 347; Sn 1115 (=Nd^2 275 taccha bhūta, etc.). (nt.) tathaŋ=saccaŋ, in cattāri tathāni the 4 truths S V.430, 435; Ps II.104 sq. (+avitathāni anaññathāni). As ep. of Nibbāna: see derivations & cp. taccha. abl. tathato exactly v. l. B for tattato at J II.125 (see tatta^2). — yathā tathaŋ (cp. yathā tacchaŋ) according

to truth, for certain, in truth Sn 699, 732, 1127. — Cp. vitatha.
-parakkama reaching out to the truth J v.395 (=saccanikkama); -vacana speaking the truth (cp. tathāvādin) Miln 401.

Tathatā (f.) [abstr. fr. tathā > tatha] state of being such, such-likeness, similarity, correspondence Vism 518.

Tathatta (nt.) [*tathātvaŋ] "the state of being so," the truth, Nibbāna; only in foll. phrases: (a) tathattāya paṭipajjati to be on the road to (i. e. attain) Nibbāna D I.175, similarly S II.199; S II.209 (paṭipajjitabba being conducive to N.); Miln 255; Vism 214. — (b) tathattāya upaneti (of a cittaŋ bhāvitaŋ) id. S IV.294 = M I. 301; S V.90, 213 sq. — (c) tathattāya cittaŋ upasaŋharati id. M I.468. — abl. tathattā in truth, really Sn 520 sq. (cp. M Vastu III.397).

Tathā (adv.) [Sk. tathā, cp. also kathaŋ] so, thus (and not otherwise, opp. aññathā), in this way, likewise Sn 1052 (v. l. yathā); J I.137, etc. — Often with eva: tath' eva just so, still the same, not different D III.135 (taŋ tath' eva hoti no aññathā); J I.263, 278; Pv I.8[3]; PvA 55. Corresponding with yathā: tathā-yathā so —that Dh 282; PvA 23 (tathā akāsi yathā he made that . . ., cp. Lat. ut consecutive); yathā-tathā as—so also Sn 504; J I.223; Pv I.12[3] (yath' āgato tathā gato as he has come so he has gone). — In cpds. tath' before vowels.
-ûpama such like (in comparisons, following upon a preceding yathā or seyyathā) Sn 229 (=tathāvidha KhA 185), 233; It 33, 90; -kārin acting so (corresp. w. yathāvādin: acting so as he speaks, cp. tāthāvādin) Sn 357; It 122; -gata see sep.; -bhāva "the being so," such a condition J I.279; -rūpa such a, like this or that, esp. so great, such Vin I.16; Sn p. 107; It 107; DA I.104; PvA 5, 56. nt. adv. thus PvA 14. Cp. evarūpa; -vādin speaking so (cp. °kārin) Sn 430; It 122 (of the Tathāgata); -vidha such like, so (=tathārūpa) Sn 772, 818, 1073, 1113; Nd[2] 277 (=tādisa taŋsaṇṭhita tappakāra).

Tathāgata [Derivation uncertain. Buddhaghosa (DA I.59-67) gives eight explanations showing that there was no fixed tradition on the point, and that he himself was in doubt]. The context shows that the word is an epithet of an Arahant, and that non-Buddhists were supposed to know what it meant. The compilers of the Nikāyas must therefore have considered the expression as pre-Buddhistic; but it has not yet been found in any pre-Buddhistic work. Mrs. Rhys Davids (Dhs. tr. 1099, quoting Chalmers *J.R.A.S.* Jan., 1898) suggests "he who has won through to the truth." Had the early Buddhists invented a word with this meaning it would probably have been tathaŋgata, but not necessarily, for we have upadhī-karoti as well as upadhiŋ karoti. — D I.12, 27, 46, 63; II.68, 103, 108, 115, 140, 142; III.14, 24 sq., 32 sq., 115, 217, 264 sq., 273 sq.; S I.110 sq.; II.222 sq.; III.215; IV.127, 380 sq.; A I.286; II.17, 25, 120; III.35, etc.; Sn 236, 347, 467, 557, 1114; It 121 sq.; KhA 196; Ps I.121 sq.; Dhs 1099, 1117, 1234; Vbh 325 sq., 340, etc., etc.
-balāni (pl.) the supreme intellectual powers of a T. usually enum[d] as a set of ten: in detail at A V.33 sq. = Ps II.174; M I.69; S II.27; Nd[2] 466. Other sets of five at A III.9; of six A III.417 sq. (see bala); -sāvaka a disciple of the T. D II.142; A I.90; II.4; III.326 sq.; It 88; Sn p. 15.

Tathiya (adj.) [Vedic tadā = taccha] true, Sn 882, 883.

Tadanurūpa (adj.) [cp. ta° 1 a] befitting, suitable, going well with J VI.366; DhA IV.15.

Tadā (adv.) [Vedic; cp. kadā] then, as that time (either past or future) D II.157; J II.113, 158; Pv I.10[6]; PvA 42. Also used like an adj.: te tadā-mātāpitaro etarahi m° ahesuŋ "the then mother & father" J I.215 (cp. Lat. quondam); tadā-sotāpanna-upāsaka J II.113.

Tadūpika & Tadūpiya see ta° I. a.

Tanaya & tanuya [at S I.7, v. l. tanaya, cp. BSk. tanuja AvŚ II.200] offspring, son Mhvs VII.28. pl. tanuyā [= Sk. tanayau] son & daughter S I.9.

Tanu [Vedic tanu, f. tanvī; also n. tanu & tanū (f.) body *ten (see tanoti) = Gr. ταυ-, Lat. tenuis, Ohg. dunni, E. thin] 1. (adj.) thin, tender, small, slender Vv 16[2] (vara° graceful = uttamarūpa-dhara VvA 79; perhaps to 2); PvA 46 (of hair: fine + mudhu). — 2. (n. nt.) body (orig. slender part of the body = waist) Vv 53[7] (kañcana°); Pv I.12[1]; Vism 79 (uju+). Cp. tanutara.
-karaṇa making thinner, reducing, diminishing Vin II.316 (Bdhgh on CV. V.9, 2); -bhāva decrease Pug 17; -bhūta decreased, diminished Pug 17; esp. in phrase °*soka* with diminished grief, having one's grief allayed DhA III.176; PvA 38.

Tanuka (adj.) = tanu; little, small Dh 174 (=DhA 175); Sn 994 (soka).

Tanutara the waist (lit. smaller part of body, cp. body and bodice) Vin IV.345 (sundaro tanutaro "her waist is beautiful").

Tanutta (nt.) [n.-abstr. of tanu] diminution, reduction, vanishing, gradual disappearance A I.160 (manussānaŋ khayo hoti tanuttaŋ paññāyati); II.144 (rāga°, dosa°, moha°); esp. in phrase (characterizing a sakadāgāmin) "rāga-d.-mohānaŋ tanutta sakadāgāmī hoti" D I.156; S V.357 sq., 376, 406; A II.238; Pug 16.

Tanoti [*ten; cp. Sk. tanoti, Gr. τείνω, τόνος, τέτανος; Lat. teneo, tenuis, tendo (E. ex-tend); Goth. þanjan; Ohg. denen; cp. also Sk. tanti, tāna, tantra] to stretch, extend; rare as finite verb, usually only in pp. tata. — Pgdp 17.

Tanta (nt.) [Vedic tantra, to tanoti; cp. tantrī f. string] a thread, a string, a loom J I.356 (°vitata-ṭṭhāna the place of weaving); DhA I.424. At J IV.484 tanta is to be corrected to tata (stretched out).
-âkula tangled string, a tangled skein, in phrase tantākalajātā guḷāguṇṭhikajāta "entangled like a ball of string & covered with blight" S II.92; IV.158; A II.211; Dpvs XII.32. See guḷā; -āvuta weaving, weft, web S V.45; A I.286; -bhaṇḍa weaving appliances Vin II.135; -rajjuka "stringing & roping," hanging, execution J IV.87; -vāya a weaver J I.356; Miln 331; Vism 259; DhA I.424.

Tantaka (nt.) "weaving," a weaving-loom Vin II.135.

Tanti (f.) [Vedic tantrī, see tanta] 1. the string or cord of a lute, etc.; thread made of tendon Vin I.182; Th 2, 390 (cp. ThA 257); J IV.389; DhA I.163; PvA 151. — 2. line, lineage (+ paveṇi custom, tradition) J VI.380; DhA I.284. -dhara bearer of tradition Vism 99 (+ vaŋsānurakkhhake & paveṇipolake). — 3. a sacred text; a passage in the Scriptures Vism 351 (bahu-peyyāla°); avimutta-tanti-magga DA I.2; MA I.2.
-ssara string music Vin I.182; J III.178.

Tantu [Vedic tantu, cp. tanta] a string, cord, wire (of a lute) J V.196.

Tandita (adj.) [pp. of tandeti = Sk. tandrayate & tandate to relax. From *ten, see tanoti] weary, lazy, giving way Miln 238 (°kata). Usually a° active, keen, industrious, sedulous Dh 305, 366, 375; Vv 33[22]; Miln 390; VvA 142. Cp. next.

Tandī (f.) [Sk. tanita] weariness, laziness, sloth S V.64; M I.464; A I.3; Sn 926, 942; J V.397 (+ ālasya); Vbh 352 (id.).

Tapa & Tapo [from tapati, cp. Lat. tepor, heat] 1. torment, punishment, penance, esp. religious austerity, self-chastisement, ascetic practice. This was condemned by the Buddha: Gotamo sabbaŋ tapaŋ garahati tapassiŋ lūkhajīviŋ upavadati D I.161=S IV.330; anattha-sañhitaŋ ñatvā yaŋ kiñci aparaŋ tapaŋ S I.103; J IV.306 (tattatapa: see tatta). — 2. mental devotion, self-control, abstinence, practice of morality (often= brahmacariyā & saŋvara); in this sense held up as an ideal by the Buddha. D III.42 sq., 232 (attan & paran°), 239; S I.38, 43; IV.118, 180; M II.155, 199; D II.49= Dh 184 (paramaŋ tapo), 194 (tapo sukho); Sn 77= S I.172 (saddhā bījaŋ tapo vuṭṭhi); Sn 267 (t. ca brahmacariyā ca), 655 (id.), 901; Pv I.3^{2} (instr. tapasā= brahmacariyena PvA 15); J I.293; Nett 121 (+indriyasaŋvara); KhA 151 (pāpake dhamme tapatī ti tapo): VvA 114 (instr. tapasā); PvA 98.
-kamma ascetic practice S I.103; -jigucchā disgust for asceticism D I.174; III.40, 42 sq., 48 sq.; A II.200; -pakkama=°kamma D I.165 sq. (should it be tapopakkama=tapa+ upakkama, or tapo-kamma ?). -vana the ascetic's forest Vism 58, 79, 342.

Tapati [Sk. tapati, *tep, cp. Lat. tepeo to be hot or warm, tepidus=tepid] 1. to shine, to be bright, Dh 387 (divā tapati ādicco, etc.=virocati DhA IV.143); Sn 348 (jotimanto narā tapeyyuŋ), 687 (suriyaŋ tapantaŋ). — ger. tapanīya: see sep. — pp. **tatta**[1].

Tapana (adj.-n.) [to tapati & tapa] burning, heat; fig. torment, torture, austerity. — 1. (as nt.) PvA 98 (kāya °sankhāto tapo). — 2. (as f.) tapanī J V.201 (in metaphorical play of word with aggi & brahmacārin; Com. visīvana-aggiṭṭha-sankhātā-tapanī).

Tapanīya[1] [grd. of tapati] burning: fig. inducing self torture, causing remorse, mortifying A I.49=It 24, A IV.97 (Com. tāpajanaka); V.276; J IV.177; Dhs 1305.

Tapanīya[2] (nt.) also **tapaneyya** (J V.372) & **tapañña** (J VI.218) [orig. grd. of tapati] shining; (n.) the shining, bright metal, i. e. gold (=rattasuvaṇṇa J V.372; ThA 252) Th 2, 374; Vv 84^{16}; VvA 12, 37, 340.

Tapassin (adj.-n.) [tapas+vin; see tapati & tapa] one devoted to religious austerities, an ascetic (non-Buddhist). Fig. one who exercises self-control & attains mastery over his senses Vin I.234=A IV.184 (tapassī samaṇo Gotamo); D III.40, 42 sq., 49; S I.29; IV.330, 337 sq.; M I.77; Sn 284 (isayo pubbakā āsuŋ saññatattā tapassino); Vv 22^{10}; Pv I.3^{2} (°rūpa, under the appearance of a "holy" man: samaṇa-patirūpaka PvA 15); II.6^{14} (=saŋvāraka PvA 98; tapo etesaŋ atthī ti ibid.).

Tappaṇa (nt.) [Sk. tarpaṇa] satiating, refreshing; a restorative, in netta° some sort of eye-wash D I.12 (in comb^{n} w. kaṇṇa-tela & natthu-kamma).

Tappati[1] [Sk. tapyate, Pass. of tapati] to burn, to be tormented: to be consumed (by remorse) Dh 17, 136 (t. sehi kammehi dummedho=paccati DhA III.64).

Tappati[2] [Sk. tṛpyate, caus. tarpayati; *terp=Gr. τέρπω] (instr.) to be satiated, to be pleased, to be satisfied J I.185 (puriso pāyāsassa t.); II.443; V.485=Miln 381 (samuddo na t. nadīhi the ocean never has enough of all the rivers); Vv 84^{13}. — grd. **tappiya** satiable, in atappiya-vatthūni (16) objects of insatiability J III.342 (in full). Also **tappaya** in cpd. dut° hard to be satisfied A I.87; Pug 26. — pp. titta. — *Caus.* tappeti to satisfy, entertain, regale, feed It 67 (annapānena); Pv II.4^{8} (id.) Miln 227; — pp. **tappita.**

Tappara (adj.) [Sk. tatpara] quite given to or intent upon (-°), diligent, devoted ThA 148 (Ap. 57, 66) (mānapūjana° & buddhopaṭṭhāna°).

Tappetar [n. ag. to tappeti] one who satisfies, a giver of good things in comb^{n} titto ca tappetā ca: self-satisfied & satisfying others A I.87; Pug 27 (of a Sammāsambuddha).

Tab° in cpds. tabbisaya, tabbahula, etc.=taŋ°, see under ta° I. a.

Tama (nt.) & tamo [Sk. tamas, **tam** & **tim**, cp. tamisra= Lat. tenebræ; also timira dark & P. tibba, timira; Ohg. dinstar & finstar; Ags. thimm, E. dim] darkness (syn. andhakāra, opp. joti), lit. as well as fig. (mental darkness=ignorance or state of doubt); one of the dark states of life & rebirth; adj. living in one of the dark spheres of life (cp. kaṇhajāta) or in a state of suffering (duggati) Sn 248 (pecca tamaŋ vajanti ye patanti sattā nirayaŋ avaŋsirā), 763 (nivutānaŋ t. hoti andhakāro apassataŋ), 956 (sabbaŋ tamaŋ vinodetvā); Vbh 367 (three tamāni: in past, present & future). adj.: puggalo tamo tama-parāyaṇo D III.233; A II.85= Pug 51; J II.17. — tamā tamaŋ out of one "duggati" into another Sn 278 (vinipātaŋ samāpanno gabbhā gabbhaŋ t. t. . . . dukkaŋ nigacchati), cp. M Vastu II.225, also tamāto tamaŋ ibid. I.27; II.215. — tama-t.-agge beyond the region of darkness (or rebirth in dark spheres), cp. bhavagge (& Sk. tamaḥ pāre) S V. 154, 163.
-andhakāra (complete) darkness (of night) v. l. for samandha° at J III.60 (Kern: tamondhakāra); -nivuta enveloped in d. Sn 348; -nuda (tama° & tamo°), dispelling darkness, freq. as Ep. of the Buddha or other sages Sn 1133, 1136; It 32, 108; Nd^{2} 281; Vv 35^{2} (=VvA 161); Miln 1, 21, etc.; -parāyaṇa (adj.) having a state of darkness or "duggati" for his end or destiny S I.93; A II.85=Pug 51.

Tamāla [Sk. tamāla] N. of a tree (Xanthochymus pictorius) Pv III.10^{5} (+uppala).

Tamba (nt.) [Sk. tāmra, orig. adj.=dark coloured, leaden; cp. Sk. adj. taŋsra id., to tama] copper ("the dark metal"); usually in combinations, signifying colour of or made of (cp. loha bronze), e. g. lākhātamba (adj.) Th 2, 440 (colour of an ox); °akkhin Vv 32^{3} (timira°) Sdhp 286; °nakhin J VI.290; °nettā (f.) ibid.; °bhājana DhA I.395; °**mattika** DhA IV.106; °vammika DhA III.208; °loha PvA 95 (=loha).

Tambūla (nt.) [Sk. tambūla] betel or betel-leaves (to chew after the meal) J I.266, 291; II.320; Vism 314; DhA III.219. -°**pasibbaka** betel bag J VI.367.

Taya (nt.) [Sk. trayaŋ triad, cp. trayī; see also tāvatiŋsa] a triad, in **ratana-ttaya** the triad of gems (the Buddha, the Norm, & the Community) see ratana; e. g. PvA 1, 49, 141. — **piṭaka-ttaya** the triad of the Piṭakas SnA 328.

Tayo [f. tisso, nt. tīṇi; Vedic traya, trī & trīṇi; Gr. τρεῖς, τρία; Lat. trēs, tria; Goth. preis, þrija; Ohg. drī; E. three, etc.] num card. three.
nom.-acc. m. tayo (Sn 311), & tayas (tayas us dhammā Sn 231, see KhA 188) f. tisso (D I.143; A V.210; It 99) nt. tīṇi (A I.138, etc.), also used as absolute form (eka dve tīṇi) Kh III. (cp. KhA 79 & tīṇi lakkhaṇā for lakkhaṇāni Sn 1019); gen. m. nt. tiṇṇaŋ (J III.52, 111, etc.), f. tissannaŋ; instr. tīhi (ṭhānehi Dh 224, vijjāhi It 101); loc. tīsu (janesu J I.307; vidhāsu Sn 842). — In composition & derivation: ti in numerical cpds.: tidasa (30) q. v.; tisata (300) Sn 566 (brāhmaṇā tisatā); 573 (bhikkhavo tisatā); **tisahassa** (3000) Pv II.9^{51} (janā °ā); in numerical derivations: tiŋsa (30), tika (triad), tikkhattuŋ (thrice); tidhā (threefold). — In nominal cpds.: see ti°. te (a) in numerical cpds.: terasa (SnA 489; DhsA 333; VvA 72: terasī the 13th day) & teḷasa (S I.192 Sn pp. 102, 103) (13) [Sk. trayodaśa, Lat. tredecim]; **tevīsa** (23)

VvA 5; tettiṇsa (33) J I.273; DhA I.267; tesaṭṭhi (63) PvA 111 (Jambudīpe tesaṭṭhiyā nagarasahassesu). — (b) in nominal cpds.: see te°.

Tara [see tarati] (n.) crossing, "transit," passing over Sn 1119 (maccu°). — (adj.) to be crossed, passable, in duttara hard to cross S IV.157; Sn 174, 273 (oghaŋ t. duttaraŋ); Th 2, 10; It 57. Also as su-duttara S I. 35; V.24.
-esin wanting to pass over J III.230

Taranga [tara+ga] a wave Vism 157.

Taraccha [Derivation unknown. The Sk. forms are tarakṣu & tarakṣa] hyena Vin III.58; A III.101; Miln 149, 267; DhA 331; Mhbv 154. — f. taracchi J V.71, 406; VI.562.

Taraṇa (nt.) [see tarati] going across, passing over, traversing Vin IV.65 (tiriyaŋ°); Ps I.15; II.99, 119.

Tarati[1] [Vedic tarati, ***ter** (tṛ) to get to the other side, cp. Lat. termen, terminus, Gr. τέρμα, τέρθρον; also Lat. trans=Goth. þairh=Ags. þurh=E. through] (lit.) to go or get through, to cross (a river), pass over, traverse; (fig.) to get beyond, i. e. to surmount, overcome, esp. oghaŋ (the great flood of life, desire, ignorance, etc.) S I.53, 208, 214; V.168, 186; Sn 173, 273, 771, 1069; sangaŋ Sn 791; visattikaŋ Sn 333, 857; ubhayaŋ (both worlds, here & beyond) Pv IV.13[1] (=atikkameti PvA 278); Nd[2] 28- — ppr. taranto Vin I.191 (Aciravatiŋ); grd. taritabba Vin IV.65 (nadī); aor. atari J III.189 (samuddaŋ) & atāri Sn 355, 1047 (jāti-maraṇaŋ), pl. atāruŋ Sn 1045. — See also tāreti (Caus.), tāṇa, tāyate, tiro, tiriyaŋ, tīra, tīreti.

Tarati[2] [tvarate, pp. tvarita; also turati, turayati from ***ter** to turn round, move quickly, perhaps identical with the ***ter** of tarati[1]; cp. Ohg. dweran=E. twirl; Gr. τορύνη=Lat. trua=Ger. quirl twirling-stick, also Lat. torqueo & turba & perhaps Ger. stüren, zerstören; E. storm, see Walde, *Lat. Wtb.* under trua] to be in a hurry, to make haste Th 1, 291; ppr. taramāna in °*rūpa* (adj.) quickly, hurriedly Sn 417; Pv II.6[2]; PvA 181 (=turita) & ataramāna Vin I.248; grd. taraṇiya Th 1, 293. — See also tura, turita, turiya.

Tarahi (adv.) [Vedic tarhi, cp. carahi & etarahi] then, at that time Vin II.189.

Tari (f.) [from tarati] a boat Dāvs IV.53.

Taritatta (nt.) [abstr. of tarita pp. of tarati[1]] the fact of having traversed, crossed, or passed through VvA 284.

Taru [Perhaps dialect. for dāru] tree, PvA 154 (°gaṇā), 251.

Taruṇa (adj.) [Vedic taruṇa, cp. Gr. τέρης, τέρην; Lat. tener & perhaps tardus] 1. tender, of tender age, young; new, newly (°-) fresh. Esp. appl[d] to a young calf: M I.459 (in simile); °vaccha, °vacchaka, °vacchi: Vin I.193; J I.191; DhA II.35; VvA 200.— Vin I.243 (fresh milk); D I.114 (Gotamo t. c' eva t.-paribbājako ca "a young man and only lately become a wanderer"); PvA 3, 46 (°janā), 62 (°putta); Bdhd 93, 121. — 2. (m. & nt.) the shoot of a plant, or a young plant Vin I.189 (tāla°); M I.432; Vism 361 (taruṇa-tāla).

Tala (nt.) [Derivation uncertain. Cp. Sk. tala m. & nt.; cp. Gr. τῆλια (dice-board), Lat. tellus (earth), tabula (=table). Oir. talam (earth), Ags. þel (=deal), Ohg. dili=Ger. diele] (a) flat surface (w. ref. to either top or bottom: cp. Ger. boden), level, ground, base J I.60, 62 (pāsāda° flat roof); III.60 (id.); paṭhavī° (level ground) J II.111, cp. bhūmi° PvA 176; ādāsa° surface of a mirror Vism 450, 456, 489; salila° (surface of pond) PvA 157; VvA 160; heṭṭhima° (the lowest level) J I.202; PvA 281; — J I.233 (base); 266 (khagga° the flat of the sword); II.102 (bheri°). — (b) the palm of the hand or the sole of the foot J II.223; Vism 250; & cpds. — See also taṭa, tāla, tālu.
-ghātaka a slap with the palm of the hand Vin IV.260, 261; -sattika in °ŋ uggirati to lift up the palm of the hand Vin IV.147; DhA III.50; cp. *Vin. Texts* I.51.

Talika (adj.) [from tala] having a sole, in eka-°upāhanā a sandal with one sole. J II.277; III.80, 81 (v. l. BB. paṭilika); cp. Morris, *J.P.T.S.* 1887, 165.

Taluṇa=taruṇa DhsA 333 (cp. Burnouf, *Lotus* 573).

Taḷāka (nt.) [Derivation uncertain. Perhaps from taṭa. The Sk. forms are taṭaka, taṭāka, taḍāga] a pond, pool, reservoir Vin II.256; J I.4, 239; PvA 202; DA I.273; Miln I, 66=81, 246, 296, 359.

Tasa (adj.) [from tasati[2]] 1. trembling, frightened J I.336=344 (vakā, expl. at 342 by tasita); perhaps the derived meaning of: — 2. moving, running (cp. to meaning 1 & 2 Gr. τρέω to flee & to tremble), always in comb[n] tasa-thāvarā (pl.) movable & immovable beings [cp. M Vastu I.207 jangama-sthāvara; II.10 calaŋ sthāvara]. Metaphorically of people who are in fear & trembling, as distinguished from a thāvara, a self-possessed & firm being (=Arahant KhA 245). In this sense t. is interpreted by tasati[1] as well as by tasati[2] (to have thirst or worldly cravings) at KhA 245: tasanti ti tasā, sataṇhānaŋ sabhayānañ c' etaŋ adhivacanaŋ; also at Nd[2] 479: tasa ti yesaŋ tasitā (tasiṇā ?) taṇhā appahīnā, etc., *&* ye te santāsaŋ āpajjanti. — S I.141; IV.117, 351; V.393; Sn 146, 629; Dh 405, Th 1, 876; J V.221; Nd[2] 479; DhA IV.175.

Tasati[1] [Sk. tṛṣyati=Gr. τέρσομαι to dry up, Lat. torreo (=E. torrid, toast), Goth. gaþairsan & gaþaúrsnan, Ohg. derren; see also taṇhā & taṇhīyati] to be thirsty, fig. to crave for S II.13; Miln 254. — pp. tasita[1]. Cp. pari°

Tasati[2] [Vedic trasati=Gr. τρέω, Lat. terreo (=terror); ***ters** fr. ***ter** in Sk. tarala, cp. also Lat. tremo (=tremble) and trepidus] to tremble, shake, to have fear; to be frightened Sn 394 (ye thāvarā ye ca tasanti loke); Nd[2] 479 (=santāsaŋ āpajjati); KhA 245 (may be taken as tasati[1], see tasa). — pp. **tasita**[2], cp. also tasa & uttasati.

Tasara (nt.) [Vedic tasara, cp. tanta, etc.] a shuttle Sn 215, 464, 497; DhA I.424; III.172. Cp. Morris, *J.P.T.S.* 1886, 160.

Tasiṇā (f.) [Diæretic form of taṇhā, cp. dosiṇā>juṇhā, kasiṇa>kṛtsna, etc.] thirst; fig. craving (see taṇhā) S V.54, 58; Nd[2] 479 (to be read for tasitā ?); Dh 342, 343.

Tasita[1] [pp. of tasati[1]] dried up, parched, thirsty S II.110, 118; Sn 980, 1014 (not with Fausböll=tasita[2]); J IV.20; Pv II.9[36] (chāta+), 10[3] (=pipāsita PvA 143); III.6[5] (=pipāsita PvA 127, 202); Miln 318 (kilanta+).

Tasita[2] [pp. of tasati[2]] frightened, full of fear J I.26 (bhīta+), 342, IV.141 (id.): Nd[2] 479 (or=tasiṇā ?). — atasita fearless S III.57.

Tassa-pāpiyyasikā (f.) (viz. kiriyā) N. of one of the adhikaraṇa-samathā: guilt (legal wrong) of such & such a character Vin I.325; in detail expl. M II.249; +tiṇavatthāraka D III.254; A I.99. °**kammaŋ** karoti to carry out proceedings against someone guilty of a certain legal offence Vin II.85, 86; °*kata* one against whom the latter is carried out A IV.347.

Tāṇa (nt.) [from Vedic root **trā**, variation of ***ter** in tarati. Orig. bringing or seeing through] shelter, protection, refuge, esp. as tt. of shelter & peace offered by the Dhamma. Mostly in comb[n] with leṇa & saraṇa (also dīpa & abhaya), in var. contexts, esp. with ref.

to Nibbāna (see Nd^2 s. v.): D I.95 (°ŋ, etc. gavesin seeking refuge); A I.155; S IV.315 (maŋtāṇa, etc. adj. protected by me, in my shelter). — S I.2, 54, 55, 107 (°ŋ karoti); IV.372 (°gāmī maggo); A IV.184; Sn 668 (°ŋ upeti); Dh 288; J I.412 (=protector, expl^d by tāyitā parittāyitā patiṭṭhā); Sdhp 224, 289. Cp. tātar & tāyati.

Tāṇatā (f.) [abstr. of tāṇa] protection, sheltering Dh 288.

Tāta [Vedic tāta, Gr. τάτα & τέττα, Lat. tata, Ger. tate, E. dad(dy); onomat.] father; usually in *voc. sg.* tāta (and pl. tātā) used as term of affectionate, friendly or respectful address to one or more persons, both younger & older than the speaker, superior or inferior. As father (perhaps=tātā, see next) at Th 2, 423, 424 (+ammā). tāta (sg.) in addr. one: J III.54; IV.281 (amma tāta mammy & daddy) DhA II.48 (=father); III.196 (id.); PvA 41 (=father), 73 (a son), 74 (a minister); J I.179 (id.); Miln 15, 16, 17 (a bhikkhu or thera), in addr. several Vin I.249; J II.133; PvA 50. tātā (pl.) J I.166; 263; IV.138.

Tātar [from Vedic **trā**, n. ag. to trāyati to protect] protector, saviour, helper DA I.229. For meaning "father" see tāta & cp. pitā=tāyitā at J I.412.

Tādin (adj. n.) (nom. tādī & tādi, in cpds. tādi°) [Vedic tādṛś from tad-dṛś of such appearance] such, such like, of such (good) qualities, "ecce homo"; in pregnant sense appl. to the Bhagavant & Arahants, characterized as "such" in 5 ways: see Nd^1 114 sq.; SnA 202 & cp. Miln 382. tādī: Sn 712, 803 (& 154 tādī no for tādino, see SnA 201 sq.); tādi Sn 488, 509, 519 sq.; Dh 95; gen. tādino Dh 95, 96; with ref. to the Buddha D II. 157≈(ṭhitacittasa tādino, in BSk. sthiracittasya tāyinaḥ AvŚ II.199); Vv 18^6 (expl^n VvA 95: iṭṭhādisu tādilakkhaṇasampattiyā tādino Satthu: see Nd^1 114 sq.), of Arahant A II.34; Sn 154 (or tādī no); instr. tādinā Sn 697; Miln 382; acc. tādiŋ Sn 86, 219, 957; loc. pl. tādisu Pv II.9^{71} (=iṭṭhādisu tādilakkhaṇappattesu PvA 140, cp. VvA 95). — See tādisa^1.
-**bhāva** "such-ness," high(est) qualification Vism 5, 214. -**lakkhaṇa** the characteristic of such (a being) J III.98 (°yoga, cp. nakkhatta-yoga); SnA 200 (°patta); VvA 95 (°sampatti).

Tādina (adj.) [enlarged form of tādin)=tādin, only in loc. tādine Vv 21^2 (=tādimhi VvA 106).

Tādisa^1 (adj.) [Vedic tādṛśa from tad-dṛśa=tad-rūpa; a reduction of this form in P. tādin] such like, of such quality or character, in such a condition J I.151; III.280; Sn 112, 317, 459; Nd^2 277 (in expl. of tathāvidha); It 68; Pv II.9^4; PvA 69, 72; Miln 382. Also correlative tādisa-tādisa the one—the other VvA 288. — f. tādisī [Sk. tādṛśī] Pv I.5^6 (vaṇijjā).

Tādisa^2 (adj.) [tvaŋ+disa. Cp. Sk. tvādṛśa] like you J I.167; V.107.

Tādisaka (adj.)=tādisa^1, of such character Sn 278; It 68.

Tāpana (nt.) [from tāpeti] burning, scorching, roasting; fig. tormenting, torture, self-mortification VvA 20 (aggimhi t. udake vā temanaŋ). Cp. ā°; upa°; pari°.

Tāpasa [from tapa & tapas] one who practises tapas, an ascetic (brahmin). Eight kinds are enum^d at DA I.270 & SnA 295. — J II.101, 102; V.201; PvA 153; °pabbajjā the life of an a. J III.119; DhA IV.29; DA I.270. — f. tāpasī a female ascetic Mhvs VII.11, 12.

Tāpeti [Sk. tāpayati, Caus. to tapati] to burn out, scorch, torment, fig. root out, quench Sn 451 (attānaŋ); J V. 267 (janapadaŋ); VvA 114 (kilesaŋ t. in expl. of tapassin). Cp. pari°.

Tāma [Sk. tāma] desire, longing, greed in tāmatamadasangha-suppahīna Th I, 310, an epithet of frogs, which perhaps (with Kern, *Toev.* II.88) is to be read as tāma-tamata-suppahita; "horribly greedy" (Kern, gruwelijk vraatzuchtig).

Tāyati [Sk. trāyate & trāte, connected with ***ter** in tarati, orig. to see through, to save, cp. tāṇa, etc.] to shelter, protect, preserve, guard; bring up, nourish S IV.426 (rūpa-balaŋ, bhoga°, ñāti°, putta°); J IV.387; Sn 579 (paralokato na pitā tāyate puttaŋ ñātī vā pana ñātake); PvA 7 (khettaŋ tāyati bījaŋ).

Tāyitar [n. ag. from tāyati] one who protects, shelters or guards J I.412 (in expl. of tāṇa, q. v.).

Tārā (f.) [Sk. tārā=Gr. ἀστήρ, ἄστρον (=Lat. astrum, in E. disaster), Lat. stella, Goth. stairnō, Ohg. sterro (:E. star), perhaps loan word from Semitic sources] a star, a planet Sn 687 (tārāsabha the lord, lit. "the bull" of the stars, i. e. the Sun).
-**gaṇa** (tāra°) the host of stars Pv II.9^{67} (cando va t.-gaṇe atirocati). -**maṇivitāna** "star-jewel-awning"; canopy of jewelled stars Vism 76.

Tārakā (f.) [Sk. tārakā] 1. a star, a planet: osadhī viya tārakā like the morning-star (Venus) Vv 9^2=Pv II.1^{10}; — J I.108; tāraka-rūpa the light (or sparkling) of the stars D III.85, 90; S III.156=It 19; S V.44; VvA 79; Dhs 617. — 2. fig. sparkling, glitter, twinkle; akkhi° the pupil of the eye M I.80; udaka° sparkling of the water ibid.

Tāreti^1 [Caus. of tarati^1] to make cross, to help over, to bring through, save, help, assist Sn 319 (pare tārayetuŋ), 321 (so tāraye tattha bahū pi aññe); It 123 (tiṇṇo tarayataŋ varo: "one who is through is the best of those who can help through"); J I.28 (V.203). aor. atārayi Sn 539, 540 & tāresi Sn 545.

Tāreti^2 [Caus. of tarati^2] to make haste Th I, 293.

Tāla [Sk. tāla, cp. Gr. τᾶλις & τηλεθάω (be green, sprout up) Lat. talea shoot, sprout] 1. the palmyra tree (fan palm), Borassus flabelliformis; freq. in comparisons & similes M I.187; J I.202 (°vana), 273 (°matta as tall as a palm): VvA 162; PvA 100 (chinnamūlo viya tālo). — 2. a strip, stripe, streak J V.372 (=rāji).
-**aṭṭhika** a kernel of the palm fruit DhA II.53, cp. 60 (°aṭṭhi-khaṇḍa); -**kanda** a bulbous plant J IV.46 (=kalamba); -**kkhandha** the trunk of a palm J IV.351; VvA 227 (°parimāṇā mukhatuṇḍā: beaks of vultures in Niraya): PvA 56; -**cchidda** see tāḷa°; -**taruṇa** a young shoot of the p. Vin I.189; -**pakka** palm fruit It 84; -**paṇṇa** a palm-leaf DhA I.391; II.249; III.328; Bdhd 62; also used as a fan (tālapattehi kata-maṇḍala-vijanī VvA 147) Vv 33^{43} (Hardy for °vaṇṭha of Goon. ed. p. 30); VvA 147 (v. l. °vaṇṭa q. v.); Nd^2 562 (+vidhūpana); -**patta** a palm-leaf Vin I.189; VvA 147; -**miñja** the pith of a p. J IV.402; -**vaṇṭa** [Sk. tālavṛnta] a fan A II.130 (+vidhūpana), 137; J I.265; VvA 44, cp. °paṇṇa; -**vatthu** (more correct tālāvatthu=tāla-avatthu) in tālāvatthukata a palm rendered groundless, i. e. uprooted; freq. as simile to denote complete destruction or removal (of passions, faults, etc.). Nearly always in formula pahīna- ucchinna-mūla t° anabhāvaŋ-kata "given up, with roots cut out, like a palm with its base destroyed, rendered unable to sprout again" (Kern, *Toev.* II.88; as een wijnpalm die niet meer geschikt is om weêr uit te schieten). This phrase was misunderstood in BSk.: M Vastu III.360 has kālavastuŋ. — The readings vary: tālāvatthu e. g. at M I.370; S I.69; IV.84; A I.135; II.38; J V.267; tālav° S III.10; V.327; Th 2, 478 (ThA 286: tālassa chinditaṭṭhāna-sadisa); Nd^2 freq. (see under pahīna); tālāvatthukatā at Vin III.3. — In other comb^n tālāvatthu bhavati (to be pulled out by the roots & thrown away)

J v.267 (=chinnamūla-tālo viya niraye nibbattanti p. 273), cp. M I.250; -vāra "palm-time" (?) or is it tāḷa° (gong-turn?) DhA II.49 (note: from tala-pratiṣṭhāyāŋ ?).

Tālīsa (nt.) (also tālissa J IV.286, tālīsaka Miln 338) [cp. Sk. tālī, tālīśa & talāśā] the shrub Flacourtia cataphracta & a powder or ointment obtained from it Vin I.203 (+tagara); J IV.286 (id.); Miln 338.

Tālu [Sk. tālu, see tala] the palate Sn 716; J I.419; Vism 264 (°matthaka top of p.); PvA 260.

Tāḷa[1] [taḍ, cp. Sk. tāla a blow, or musical time; tālīyaka cymbal] beating, striking, the thing beaten or struck, i. e. a musical instrument which is beaten, an instr. of percussion, as a cymbal, gong, or tambourine (for tāḷa= gong cp. thāla): (a) gong, etc. J I.3; VI.60; Th I, 893; DA I.85; DhsA 319 (kaŋsa°). — (b) music in general DhA IV.67.

-âvacara musical time or measure, music, a musician D II.159 (v. l. tāla°); J I.60 (l); IV.41; VvA 257 (°parivuta, of an angel).

Tāḷa[2] (nt.) [Sk. tālaka=tāḍa AvŚ II.56, tāḍaka Divy 577] a key (orig. a "knocker"?) Vin II.148 (3 kinds: loha°, kaṭṭha°, visāṇa°); Bdhd I.

-cchiggala a key-hole S IV.290; V.453; Vism 500. -cchidda id. Vin II.120, 148, 153 (all tāla°); III.118; DhA III.8 (l).

Tāḷī (f.) a strike, a blow, in urattāḷiŋ karoti to strike one's chest (as a sign of grief) PvA 39, etc. (see ura).

Tāḷeti [Sk. tāḍayati, taḍ perhaps=tud] to strike a blow, flog, beat, esp. freq. in phrase kasāhi tāḷeti to flog with whips, etc. (in list of punishments, see kasā) M I.87; A II.122; Nd[2] 604; PvA 4, etc. — ppr. pass. taḍḍamāna (for *tāḍyamāna) J VI.60 (so read for taddamāna; Com poṭhīyamāna). — pp. tāḷita J VI.60 (turiya°); Vv 62[1] (id.); Sdhp 80. Cp. abhi°.

Tāva (adv.) [Sk. tāvat] so much, so long; usually correl. with **yāva** how long, how much; in all meanings to be understood out of elliptical application of this correlation. Thus I. **yāva-tāva** as long as: yāva dve janā avasiṭṭhā ahesuŋ tāva aññamaññaŋ ghātayiŋsu J I. 254; yāva dukkhā nirayā idha tattha pi tāva ciraŋ vasitabbaŋ Sn 678. Neg. na tāva-yāva na not until: M I.428; S V.261; A I.141≈(na t. kālaŋ karoti yāva na taŋ papakammaŋ byantihoti he does not die until his evil kamma is exhausted). II. *Elliptical:* I. temporal: so long as, for the time (tāvakālikaŋ=yāvak°-tāvak°; see below). — 2. comparative: (such-) as, like, so, such, just so, rather, in such a degree; even tāvabahuŋ suvaṇṇaŋ so much gold Vin I.209; t.-mahanto so much J I.207; t. madhuraphala with such sweet fruit J II.105; asītiyā tāva kimi-kulānaŋ sādhāraṇa (of the body) or rather, i. e. Vism 235; vatthāni t. devapātubhūtāni PvA 44; paṭhamaŋ t. (even) at once, right away PvA 113, 132; gilānāya t. ayaŋ etissā rūpasobhā even in sickness she is so beautiful VvA 76; parittakassa kusalakammassa t.=quidem PvA 51; paŋsukūlikangaŋ t. in the first place Vism. 62. — 3. concessive: (a) (absol.) as far as it goes, considering, because: yadi evaŋ pitā tāva purisabhāve na rodati, mātu nāma hadayaŋ mudukaŋ "even if the father as man does not weep, surely," &c., PvA 63. — (b) with imper. in expr. like gaccha tāva go as long as you like (to go) (=gaccha tāva yāva gaccheyyāsi), i. e. if you like, cp. Ger. geh' immer; passa tāva just look=Lat. licet. Therefore sometimes=please or simply an emphatic imper. as "do go," etc. J II.5 (ete t. aguṇā hontu let them be faulty), 133 (ehi t.), 352 (tiṭṭha t. leave off please), III.53 (pāto va t. hotu only let it be to-morrow, i. e. wait til t-m.); IV.2 taŋ t. me detha give me this though); VvA 289 (vīmaŋsatha t. just think); PvA 4 (t. ayyo āgametu yāvâyaŋ puriso pānīyaŋ pivissati may your honour wait till this man shall have drunk the water), 13 (therā t. gacchantu). With prohibitive: mā tāva ito agā please do not go from here Pv II.3[22]. — 4. hortative, with 1st pers. fut. equal to imperative-subjunctive or injunctive, cp. 3 (b): let me, well, now, then (cp. Lat. age in dic age, etc.). J I.62 (puttaŋ t. passissāmi please let me see the son), 263 (vīmaŋsissāmi t. let me think), 265 (nahāyissāmi t. just let me bathe). — III. *In other combinations:* tāva-na although—yet= not even: ajjā pi t. me balaŋ na passasi not even to-day have you yet seen my full strength J I.207; t. mahādhanassāmī na me dātuŋ piyaŋ ahu although lord of wealth yet I did not like to give Pv II.7[6]. na-tāva (or tāva in neg. sentence) not yet, not even, not so much as (=Lat. ne-quidem) Pv II.11[2] (na ca tāva khīyati does not even diminish a bit); PvA 117 (attano kenaci anabhibhavanīyataŋ eva tāva: that he is not to be overpowered, even by anyone). tāva-d-eva just now, instantly, on the spot, at once Sn 30; J I.61, 151; IV.2; Pv II.8[9] (=tadā eva PvA 109); PvA 23, 46, 74, 88, etc. tāvade (=tāva-d-eva) for all times Pv IV.3[38] (=PvA 255).

-kālika (adj.) "as long as the time lasts," i. e. for the time being, temporary, pro tempore Vin II.174; III.66; IV.286; J I.121, 393; Vism 95; ThA 288; PvA 87 (=na sassata).

Tāvataka (adj.) [der. fr. tāva] just so much or just so long (viz. as the situation requires), with (or ellipt. without) a corresp. yāvataka Vin I.83 (yāvatake-t. as many as): D II.18 (yāvatakv' assa kāyo tāvatakv' assa vyāmo as tall as is his body so far can he stretch his arms: the 19th sign of a Mahāpurisa); instr. as adv. tāvatakena after a little time Miln 107; DhA III.61. — See also tattaka (contracted of tāvataka).

Tāvatā (adv.) [from tāva] I. so long (corr. to yāva) Dpvs IV.17. — 2. on that account, thus D I.104 (v. l. ettāvatā); Dh 266.

Tāvatiŋsa [tayo+tiŋsa. Cp. Vedic trayastriŋśat] No. 33, only in cpds. denoting the 33 gods, whose chief is Sakka, while the numeral 33 is always tettiŋsa. This number occurs already in the Vedas with ref. to the gods & is also found in Zend-Avesta (see Haug, *Language & Writings*, etc., pp. 275, 276). The early Buddhists, though they took over the number 33, rejected the superstitious beliefs in the magical influence and mystic meaning of that & other simple numbers. And they altered the tradition. The king of the gods had been Indra, of disreputable character from the Buddhist point of view. Him they deposed, and invented a new god named Sakka, the opposite in every way to Indra (see for details *Dial.* II.294-298). Good Buddhists, after death in this world, are reborn in heaven (sagga), by which is meant the realm of the Thirty-three (D II.209). There they are welcomed by the Thirty-three with a song of triumph (D II.209, 211, 221, 227). The Thirty-three are represented as being quite good Buddhists. Sakka their new chief and Brahmā address them in discourses suitable only for followers of the new movement (D II.213, 221). See further Vin I.12; M I.252; II.78; III.100; A III.287; IV.396=VvA 18 (cp[d] with the people of Jambudīpa); V.59, 331, Vism 225, etc. — See also tidasa.

-devaloka the god-world of the 33; freq. e. g. J I.202; Vism 399; DhA III.8; -bhavana the realm of the 33 gods J I.202; Vism 207 sq., 390, 416, and passim.

Tāvata (nt.) [abstr. fr. tāva] lit. "so-much-ness," i. e. relative extent or sphere, relatively Vism 481, 482.

Tāsa [see tasati[2]] terror, trembling, fear, fright, anxiety S III.57; J I.342; III.177, 202; Miln 24. Cp. san°.

Tāsaniya (adj.) to be dreaded, dreadful, fearful Miln 149.

Tāhaŋ contraction of 1. taŋ ahaŋ: see ta°; 2. te ahaŋ: see tvaŋ.

Ti (adv.) [cp. Sk. iti] the apostrophe form of iti, thus. See iti.

Ti° [Vedic tris, Av. þriś, Gr. τρίς, Lat. ter (fr. ters>*tris, cp. testis>*tristo, trecenti>*tricenti), Icl. þrisvar, Ohg. driror] base of numeral three in compⁿ; consisting of three, threefold; in numerical cpds. also= three (3 times).
-**kaṭuka** threefold spices (kaṭuka-bhaṇḍa) VvA 186; -**gāvuta** a distance of ¾ of a league (i. e. about 2 miles), DhA I.108 (less than yojana, more than usabha), 131, 396; II.43, 61, 64, 69; III.202, 269; VvA 227; B. on S I.52 (sarīra); -**catu** three or four DhA I.173; -**cīvara** (nt.) the 3 robes of a bhikkhu, consisting of: diguṇā sanghāṭi, ekacciya uttarāsanga, ekacciya antaravāsaka Vin I.289, 296; II.302. ticīvarena avippavāsa Vin I.109 sq. — Vism 60, 66; DhA IV.23. -**tālamattaŋ** 3 palm-trees high DhA II.62. -**daṇḍa** 1. a tripod as one of the requisites of a hermit to place the water-pot on (kuṇḍikā) J I.8 (tidaṇḍakuṇḍikādike tāpasa-parikkhārā), 9 (hanging from the kāja); II.317 (see tedaṇḍika). — 2. part of a chariot A IV.191 (v. l. daṇḍa only). -**diva** the 3 heavens (that is the Tāvatiŋsa heaven) D II.167, 272 (tidivûpapanna); S I.96 (°ŋ ṭhānaŋ upeti), 181 (ākankha-māno °ŋ anuttaraŋ). -**pada** [cp. Vedic tripad or tripād, Gr. τρίπους, Lat. tripes: tripod] consisting of 3 feet or (in prosody) of 3 padas Sn 457 (w. ref. to metre Sāvittī); -(**p**)**pala** threefold Vism 339; -**pallattha** "turning in 3 ways," i. e. skilled in all occupations (Kern, *Toev.*: zeer listig) J I.163 (of miga; Com. expl. as lying on 3 sides of its lair); -**piṭaka** the 3 Piṭakas Vism 62, 241; DhA I.382; -**peṭaka**=tepiṭaka Miln 90; tipeṭakin at Vin V.3; -**maṇḍala** (nt.) the 3 circles (viz. the navel & the 2 knees) Vin II.213 (°ŋ paṭicchādento parimaṇḍalaŋ nivāsento); cp. *Vin. Texts* I.155; -**yojana** a distance of 3 leagues, i. e. 20 miles, or fig. a long dist.; Vism 392 (tiyojanika setacchatta); DhA II.41 (°magga); VvA 75 (°mattake vihāraŋ agamāsi); PvA 216 (sā ca pokkharaṇī Vesaliyā °mattake hoti); °*satika* 300 cubits long J II.3; -**loka** the 3 worlds (i. e. kāma, rūpa, arūpa-loka) Sdhp 29, 276, 491 (cp. tebhūmaka); -**vagga** consisting of 3 divisions or books DA I.2 (Dīghāgamo vaggato t. hoti); -(**v**)**angika** having 3 angas (of jhāna) Dhs 161; -**vassika** for the 3 seasons (-gandha-sālibhattaŋ bhuñjantā) DhA II.9; J I.66 (id.); -**vidha** 3 fold, of sacrifice (yañña) D I.128, 134, 143; of aggi (fire) J I.4 & Miln 97; Vism 147 (°kalyāṇatā). -**visākha** a three-forked frown on the forehead S I.118; M I.109; -**sandhi** consisting of 3 spaces J VI.397 (tāya senāya Mithilā t.-parivāritā), explᵈ as an army made up of elephants, chariots, cavalry, and infantry, with a space between each two.

Tiŋsaŋ (tiŋsa°) [Vedic triŋśat, cp. Lat. trīginta, Oir. tricha] the number 30 D I.81≈(tiŋsaŋ pi jātiyo); S II.217 (t.-mattā bhikkhū); dat. instr. tiŋsāya A V.305 (dhammehi samannāgato); Sn p. 87 (pi dadāmi) PvA 281 (vassasahassehi): t.-yojana-maggaŋ (āgato) DhA II.76, 79; III.172; PvA 154; °yojanika kantāra DhA II. 193 (cp. 192); J V.46 (magga); DhA I.26 (vimāna); t.-vassasahassāni āyuppamāṇaŋ (of Konāgamana Buddha) D II.3; t.-mattāni vassāni Miln 15; t.-vassasahassāni PvA 281=DhA II.10. So of an immense crowd: tiŋsa bhikkhu-sahassāni D II.6; tiŋsa-mattā sūkarā J II.417; °sahassa-bhikkhū DhA I.24.

Tika (adj.-n.) [Vedic trika] consisting of 3, a triad S II. 218 (t.-bhojana); DhA IV.89 (-nipāta, the book of the triads, a division of the Jātaka), 108 (t.-catukka-jhāna the 3 & the 4 jhānas); Miln 12 (tika-duka-paṭimaṇḍitā dhammasanganī); Vism 13 sq.; DhsA 39 (-duka triad & pair).

Tikicchaka [fr. tikicchati] a physician, a doctor A V.219; J I.4 (adj. & vejja); IV.361; PvA 233.

Tikicchati [also cikicchati=Sk. cikitsati. Desid. of **cit**, to aim at, think upon, in pregnant sense of endeavouring to heal] to treat medically, to cure Vin I.276; S I.222; Miln 172, 272, 302. Caus. tikicchāpeti J I.4.

Tikicchā (f.) [from last] the art of healing, practice of medicine D I.10 (dāraka° infant healing); Sn 927 (°ŋ māmako na seveyya). — See also tekiccha.

Tikkaŋ at J V.291 in "yāva majjhantikā tikkam āgami yeva" is to be read as "yāva majjhantik' âtikkamm'-āgami yeva."

Tikkha (adj.) [=tikhiṇa] sharp, clever, acute, quick (only fig. of the mind), in tikkh-indriya (opp. mud-indriya) Nd² 235³ᴾ=Ps I.121=II.195; & tikkha-paññatā A I.45.

Tikkhattuŋ (adv.) [Sk. trikṛtvaḥ] three times (cp. tayo II. C 2), esp. in phrase vanditvā t. padakkhiṇaŋ katvā "having performed the reverent parting salutation 3 times" VvA 173, 219; t. sāvesi he announced it 3 times J II.352; DhA II.4; t. paggaṇhāpesi offered 3 times PvA 74. See also J IV.267; V.382; VI.71; DhA II.5, 42, 65, 338; IV.122 & passim.

Tikhiṇa (adj.) [Vedic tikṣṇa of which t. is the diæretic form, whereas the contracted forms are tiṇha (q. v.) & tikkha. Cp. also Sk. tikta pp. of **tij**, tejate. From ***steg** in Gr. στίζω "stitch" & στικτός, Lat. instīgo, Ohg. stehhan, Ger. stecken, E. stick] pointed, sharp, pungent, acrid; fig. "sharp," clever, cunning, acute (in this meaning only in contr. form tikkha) J V.264; DhA II.9; IV.13; PvA 152, 221 (=tippa). (ati-) tikhinatā Miln 278. See also tippa & tibba & cp. tejo.

Tiṭṭha (adj.) [pp. of tasati¹] dry, hard, rough J VI.212 (°sela hard rock).

Tiṭṭhati [Frequentative of Vedic **sthā**, stand (cp. sthāna, Lat. sto: see ṭhāna)=Av. hištaiti, Gr. ἵστημι, Lat. sisto] to stand, etc. — I. *Forms*: pres. ind. tiṭṭhati (Sn 333, 434; Pv I.5¹); imper. 2nd tiṭṭha, 3rd tiṭṭhatu; ppr. tiṭṭhaŋ, tiṭṭhanto, tiṭṭhamāna; pot. tiṭṭhe (Sn 918, 968) & tiṭṭheyya (Sn. 942); fut. ṭhassati (J I.172, 217); aor. aṭṭhāsi (J I.279, pl. aṭṭhaŋsu J II.129) & aṭṭhā (cp. agā, orig. impf.) (Sn 429; J I.188); inf. ṭhātuŋ (PvA 174); ger. ṭhatvā (Sn 887); grd. ṭhānīya (PvA 72). — pp. ṭhita, Caus. ṭhapeti. An apparent Med.-Pass. ṭhīyati, as found in cpd. pati-ṭṭhīyati is to be explᵈ as Med. of paṭi+**sthyā** (see thīna), and should be written paṭi-tthīyati. See under patiṭṭhīyati. See also ṭhāna & ṭhiti. — II. *Meanings*. — 1. to stand, stand up, to be standing (see ṭhāna I. 1ᵃ): ṭhānakappana-vacanaŋ nisajjādi-paṭikkhepato PvA 24; opp. to walking or lying down: tiṭṭhaŋ caraŋ nisinno vā Sn 151, 193; tiṭṭhamānāya eva c' assā gabbhavuṭṭhānaŋ ahosi "she was delivered standing" J I.52; ekamantaŋ aṭṭhāsi PvA 68, etc.; cankamana-koṭiyaŋ ṭhatvā PvA 79. — 2. to stop, stay, abide; to last, endure, be at rest; fig. to remain in, abide by, acquiesce in (see ṭhāna I. 1ᵇ). In imper. tiṭṭhatu it approaches the meanings of ṭhapeti viz. leave it alone, let it be so, all right. yāva kāyo ṭhassati tāva naŋ dakkhinti deva-manussā (as long as the body shall last) D I.46. tiṭṭhe shall he live on (cp. ṭhāna II.ᵈ Sn 1053, 1072 =Nd² 283, tiṭṭheyya saṭṭhikappasahassāni to stay on indefinitely); tiṭṭheyya kappaŋ D II.103. tiṭṭhantī anto vimānasmiŋ "remaining inside the castle" Pv I.10¹; tiṭṭha tāva "stop please" J II.352; tiṭṭhabhadantika one who bids the guest stay (combᵈ w. ehi-bh°) D I.166; M I.342; A I.295; II.206: ovāde ṭhatvā (abiding by) J I.153; VI.367; similarly J VI.336. — Imper. tiṭṭhatu J IV.40; Miln 14; PvA 74. — 3. to live (on=instr.), behave, exist, be (see ṭhāna I. 2); to be in a certain condition [gati, cp. ṭhāna II. (c)]. Often periphrastically for finite verb (with ger.: cp. gata & ṭhita) tiṭṭhantaṃ enaṃ jānāti (he knows their "gati") Sn 1114 (see Nd² 283); āhārena tiṭṭhati PvA 27 (is supported by, cp. ṭhiti); yāvatāyukaṃ ṭhatvā (outliving their lives) PvA 66; karuṇa-ṭhānīya (=*kāruṇayitabba) deserving pity PvA 72; yā tvaṃ tiṭṭhasi (how you are or look!) Vv 44¹, etc. — *with ger.*: pharitvā aṭṭhāsi (pervaded) J VI.367; aṭṭhiṃ āhacca aṭṭhāsi (cut through to the bone) J IV.415; gehaṃ samparivāretvā aṭṭhaṃsu (encircled the house) PvA 22.

Tiṇa (nt.) [Vedic tṛṇa, from *ter (cp. tarati) to pierce, orig. "point" (=blade); Goth. þaúrnus, Ags. þorn=E. thorn, Ger. dorn] grass, herb; weed; straw; thatch; hay, litter S III.137 (tiṇa, kasā, kusa, babbaja, bīraṇa); satiṇakaṭṭhodaka full of grass, wood & water (of an estate) D I.87, 111, etc.; sītaṃ vā uṇhaṃ vā rajo vā tiṇaṃ vā ussāvo vā (dust & weeds) D II.19; A I.145; t.+paṇṇa (grass & leaves!) A I.183; VvA 5. — J I.108 (dabba°), 295; III.53; Pv I.8¹ (harita t.); IV.1⁴⁸; Vism 353 (kuṇṭha°); DA I.77 (alla° fresh grass); PvA 7 (weed), 62 (grass), 112; DhA IV.121; Miln 47 (thatch), 224 (id.).

-aṇḍupaka a roll of grass Vin I.208=II.249; -āgāra a thatched cottage A I.101 (+naḷāgāra); -ukkā a firebrand of dry grass or hay S II.152; III.185; J I.212, 296; Vism 428; DhA I.126; ThA 287; Bdhd 107; -karala a wisp of grass DhA III.38; -kājaka a load of g. DhA IV.121; -gahaṇa a thicket of g., a jungle A I.153; -cuṇṇa crushed & powdered (dry) grass or herbs Vin I.203; VvA 100 (-rajânukiṇṇa); -jāti grass-creeper VvA 162; -dāya a grass-jungle S II.152; -dosa damaged by weeds (khetta) Dh 356; PvA 7; -pupphaka (-roga) sickness caused by the flowering of grass, hay-fever Miln 216; -purisaka a straw-man, a scarecrow Miln 352; Vism 462; DhsA 111; -bhakkha eating grass; of animals M III.167; of ascetics D I.166; Pug 55; A I.241, 295; -bhusa chaff, litter, dry grass VvA 47; -rukkha a shrub; -vatthāraka one of the seven Adhikaraṇasamathas (ways in which litigation may be settled). In case mutual complaints of breach of the rules have been brought before a chapter, then the chapter may decline to go into the details and, with the consent of the litigants, declare all the charges settled. See *Vin. Texts*, III.30-34. This is the "covering over as if with grass" Vin II.87 (in detail, cp. also tassapāpiyyasikā); D III.254; A I.99; M II.250; -santhāraka a mat of grass Vin I.286; II.113, 116; J I.360.

Tiṇava a sort of drum A II.117.

Tiṇḍuka see tinduka.

Tiṇṇa [pp. of tarati] one who has reached the other shore (always fig.) gone through, overcome, one who has attained Nibbāna. Ogha° gone through the great flood S I.3, 142; Sn 178, 823, 1082, 1101, 1145; D III. 54; Sn 21 (+pāragata), 359 (+parinibbuta), 515, 545 (tiṇṇo tāres' imaṃ pajaṃ); It 123 (tiṇṇo tārayataṃ varo); Dh 195 (-sokapariddava); Nd² 282.

-kathankatha (adj.) having overcome doubt, free from doubt Sn 17, 86, 367; -vicikiccha=prec. Vin I.16; D I.110; II.224, 229; Pug 68; DA I.211.

Tiṇha [see tikhiṇa] sharp (of swords, axes, knives, etc.) D I.56 (sattha); S IV.160, 167 (kuṭhārī); A IV.171; Sn 667 (°dhāra), 673 (asipattavana); J I.253; Sdhp 381.

Titikkhati [Sk. titikṣate, Desid. of **tij**, cp. tijo & tikhiṇa to bear, endure, stand S I.221; Sn 623; Dh 321=Nd² 475 B⁷; Dh 399 (titikkhissaṃ=sahissāmi DhA IV.3); J V.81, 368.

Titikkhā (f.) [see last] endurance, forgiveness, long-suffering S I.7; V.4; Dh 184; Nd² 203.

Titta [pp. of tappati²] satisfied (with=instr.) enjoying (c. gen.), happy, contented A I.87=Pug 26 (+tappetar); Miln 249; VvA 86 (=pīnita); PvA 46 (dibbâhārassa), 59 (=suhita), 109 (=pīṇita). —atitta dissatisfied, insatiate J I.440; III.275; Dh 48 (kāmesu).

Tittaka (adj.) [cp. Sk. tiktaka from tij] sharp, bitter (of taste) M I.80 (°alābu), 315 (id.); PvA 47 (id.; so read for tintaka lābu) Dhs 629=Nd² 540 (tittika; enum^d between lavaṇa & kaṭuka); DhsA 320.

Tittakatta (nt.) [abstr. to tittaka] bitterness, enum^d with lavaṇattaṃ & kaṭukattaṃ at Miln 56=63 (cp. Nd² 540).

Titti (f.) [from tappati²] satisfaction (in=loc.) Dh 186 =ThA 287 (na kahāpaṇavassena t. kāmesu vijjati); n' atthi t. kāmānaṃ Th 2, 487; J V.486 (dhammesu); VvA 11; PvA 32 (°ṃ gacchati find s.) 55 (paṭilabhati), 127.

Tittika in sama° at D I.244, Vin I.230, brimful, of a river. Derivation & meaning doubtful. See the note at *Buddhist Suttas*, 178, 9.

Tittimant (adj.) [titti+mant] satisfied, contented, so read at J III.70 & VI.508 for kittimant.

Tittira [Onomat. cp. Vedic tittira & tittiri, Gr. τατύρας pheasant, Lit. teterva heath-cock; Lat. tetrinnio to cackle] partridge J I.218; III.538. -pattikā a kind of boot Vin I.186.

Tittiriya (adj.) [fr. tittira] belonging to a partridge, like a partridge J I.219 (brahmacariya).

Tittha (nt.) [Vedic tīrtha, from *ter, tarate, to pass through, orig. passage (through a river), ford] 1. a fording place, landing place, which made a convenient bathing place D II.89=Vin I.230 (Gotama° the G. ford); J I.339, 340 (titthāraṇa); II.111; III.228 (°nāvika ferryman); 230 (nāvā° a ferry); IV.379; Pv II.1²⁰; III.6⁴; IV.12² (su°); Dāvs. V.59 (harbour). Titthaṃ jānāti to know a "fording place," i. e. a means or a person to help over a difficulty or doubt M I.223=A V.349 (neg.) 2. a sect (always with bad connotation. Promising to lead its votaries over into salvation, it only leads them into error).

-âyatana the sphere or fold of a sect (cp. titthiya) Vin I.60, 69; II.279; M I.483; A I.173; Pug 22; Dhs 381, 1003 (cp. *Dhs. trsl.* p. 101"); DA I.118; Ledi Sadaw in *J.P.T.S.* 1913, 117-118; -kara a "ford-maker," founder of a sect D I.47, 116; M I.198; Sn pp. 90, 92; Miln 4, 6, etc.; -ññutā knowledge of a ford, in fig. sense of titthaṃ jānāti (see above) Nett 29, 80.

Titthika (adj.) [Possible reading in Burmese MSS. for tittika. But the two compound letters (tt and tth) are so difficult to distinguish that it is uncertain which of the two the scribe really meant].

Titthiya [from **tittha** 2, cp. Divy 81⁷; AvŚ I.48; II.20. An adherent of another sect (often as añña°), an heretic Vin I.54, 84, 136, 159 (°samādāna), 306 (°dhaja), 320; S I.65; IV.37, 394; D III.44, 46; Sn 381, 891; Nd² 38; Ps I.160; Pug 49; Vbh 247. añña° e. g. Vin I.101; D I.175 sq.; III.130 sq.; J II.415, 417. -sāvaka a follower of an heretic teacher Vin I.172; J I.95; Vism 17.

Tithi [Sk. tithi] a lunar day DhA I.174; PvA 198.

Tidasa (num.) [Vedic tridaśa] thirty (cp. tiṃsa), esp. the thirty deities (pl.) or belonging to them (adj.). It is the round figure for 33, and is used as equivalent to tāvatiṃsa. Nandanaṃ rammaṃ tidasānaṃ mahāvanaṃ Pv III.1¹⁹=Vv 18¹³; devā tidasā sahindakā Vv 30¹; Sdhp 420.

-âdhipati the Lord of the 30 (viz. Sakka) Vv 47⁸; -inda ruler of the 30 Sdhp 411, 478; -gaṇa the company of the 30 Sn 679 (Com. tettiŋsa); Vv 41[6]; -gatin going to the 30 (as one of the gatis) Vv 35[12] (=tidasabhavanaŋ gata Tāvatiŋsadevanikāyaŋ uppanna VvA 164); -pura the city of the 30, i. e. Heaven Miln 291; -bhavana the state of the 30, i. e. heavenly existence VvA 164 (=Tāvatiŋsabhavana).

Tidhā (adv.) [ti+dhā] in three ways or parts, threefold Miln 282 (-pabhinna nāgarājā).

Tinta (adj.) [=timita from temeti] wet, moist Miln 286; DhA II.40 (°mukha).

Tintaka at PvA 47 (°alābu) is to be read as tittaka°.

Tintiṇa (nt.) greed, desire; (adj.) greedy. Ep. of a pāpabhikkhu A V.149 (Com. tintiṇaŋ vuccati taṇhā, tāya samannāgato āsankābahulo vā); Vbh 351 (tintiṇaŋ tintiṇāyanā, etc.=loluppaŋ).

Tintiṇāti & Tintiṇāyati [either=Sk. timirayati to be obscured, from **tim** in timira, or from **stim** (Sk. *tistimāyati> *stistim° after tiṣṭhati> *stiṣṭhati; =P. titiṇāyati) to become stiff, cp. timi, thīna and in meaning mucchati. The root **tam** occurs in same meaning in cpd. nitammati (q. v.=Sk. nitāmyati) at J IV.284, expl[d] by atikilamati] to become sick, to swoon, to (stiffen out in a) faint J I.243 (tintiṇanto corresp. with mucchita); VI.347 (tintiṇāyamāna, v. l. tiṇāy°).

Tinduka [Sk. tinduka] the tree Diospyros embryopteris D I.178 (v. l. tiṇḍ°; J V.99; tiṇḍukāni food in a hermitage J IV.434; VI.532. —tindukakandarā Npl. the T. cave Vin II.76. — See also timbaru & timbarūsaka.

Tipu [cp. Sk. trapu, non-Aryan ?] lead, tin Vin I.190 (°maya); S V.92; J II.296; Miln 331 (°kāra a worker in lead, tinsmith); Vism 174 (°maṇḍala); DhA IV.104 (°parikhā).

Tipusa (nt.) [Sk. trapusa] a species of cucumber J V.37; VvA 147.

Tippa (adj.) [a variant of tibba=Sk. tīvra, presumably from **tij** (cp. tikhiṇa), but by Bdhgh connected w. **tap** (tapati, burn): tippā ti bahalā tāpana-vasena vā tippā Com. to Anguttara (see M I.526)] piercing, sharp, acute, fierce; always & only with ref. to pains, esp. pains suffered in Niraya. In full comb[ns] sarīrikā vedanā dukkhā tippā kharā M I.10; A II.116, 143, 153; ekantadukkhā t. kaṭukā ved. M I.74; bhayānakā ekantatippa Niraya Pv IV.1[8] (=tikhiṇadukkha° PvA 221); nerayikā sattā dukkhā t. kaṭukā ved° vediyamānā Miln 148.

Tibba (adj.) probably a contamination of two roots of different meaning; viz. **tij** & **tim** (of tamas) or=**stim** to be motionless, cp. styā under thīna] 1. sharp, keen, eager: tibbagārava very devout A II.21; Nett 112 (cp. tīvraprasāda AvŚ I.130); t.-cchanda D III.252, 283.— 2. dense, thick; confused, dark, dim: t.-rāga Dh 349 (=bahalarāga DhA IV.68): A II.149; tibba vanasaṇḍo avijjāya adhivacanaŋ S III.109; tibbasārāga (kāmesu) S III.93=It 90; A II.30; tibbo manussaloko (dark, dense) Miln 7; °andhakāra dense darkness Vism 500 sq.; °kilesu deep blemish (of character) Vism 87.

Timi [Derivation unknown. Sk. timi] a large fish, a leviatban; a fabulous fish of enormous size. It occurs always in comb[n] w. timingala, in formula timi timingala timitimingala, which should probably be reduced to *one* simple timitimingala (see next).

Timingala [timi+gila, **gl**, see note on gala] in comb[n] w. timi, timitimingala. Sk. has timingila & timingilagila: redupl. in 2nd syllable where P. has redupl. in 1st; fish-eater, redupl. as intens.=greedy or monstrous fish-eater, a fabulous fish of enormous size, the largest fish in existence Vin II.238=A IV.200=Nd[2] 235[3a]; Ps II.196; Miln 377. At Ud 54 sq. & Miln 262 we find the reading timi timingala timirapingala, which is evidently faulty. A Sanskritized form of t. is timitimingala at Divy 502. See timiratipingala, & cp. also the similar Sk. cilicima a sort of fish.

Timira (adj.) [Sk. timira fr. **tim**=**tam** (as in tamas), to which also belong tibba 2 & tintiṇāti. This is to be distinguished from **tim** in temeti to (be or) make wet. See tama] dark; nt. darkness Vv 32[3] (t.-tamba); J III.189 (t.-rukkha); vanatimira a flower J IV.285; V.182.

Timiratipingala (nt.) a great ocean fish, DhsA 13, v. timingala.

Timirāyittata (nt.) [abstr. to timirāyita, pp. of timirayati to obscure, denom. to timira] gloom, darkness S III.124 (=Māra).

Timisa (nt.) [Vedic tamisrā=tamas] darkness J III.433 (andhakāra-timissāya); Pug 30 (andh°-timisāya).

Timisikā (f.) [timisa+ka] darkness, a very dark night Vv 9[6]; J IV.98; Miln 283.

Timbaru a certain tree (Strychnos nux vomica or Diospyros) J VI.336; °tthanī (f.) "with breasts like the t. fruit" Sn 110; J VI.457 (SnA 172: taruṇadārikā); VvA 137 (t.-nādasadisa).

Timbarukkha=timbarūsaka J VI.529.

Timbarūsaka=timbaru (Diospyros or Strychnos) Vin III.59; Vv 33[27] (=tindukaphala VvA 147: tipusa sadisā ekā vallijāti timbarūsakan ti ca vadanti); DhA III.315.

Tiraccha (adv.) [Vedic tiryañc, obliquely, from ***ter** (tarati). Goth. þairh, Ohg. durh, E. through, cp. tiriyaŋ] across, obliquely; in °bhūta deviating, going wrong, swerving from the right direction DA I.89 (see under tiracchāna-kathā).

Tiracchāna [for °gata=Sk. tiraścīna (°gata)=tiraśca; "going horizontally," i. e. not erect. Cp. tiraccha, tiriyaŋ, tiro] an animal It 92 (tiracchānaŋ ca yoniyo for tiracchāna-yoniyo); Vbh 339 (°gāminī paṭipadā leading to rebirth among beasts); VvA 23 (manussa-tiracchāna an animal-man, wild man, "werwolf").

-kathā "animal talk"; wrong or childish talk in general Vin I.188; D I.7, 178; III.54; Vism 127; expl[d] at DA I.89 by aniyyānikattā sagga-mokkha-maggānaŋ tiraccha-bhūtā katha; -gata an animal, a beast Vin IV.7; S III.152=DA I.23; (t. pāṇā) M III.167 (t. pāṇā tiṇabhakkhā); Nd[2] on Sn 72 (t.-pāṇā); J I.459 (=vanagocara); Vbh 412 sq.; -yoni the realm of the brute creation, the animals. Among the 5 gatis (niraya t. manussā devā pettivisaya) it counts as an apāyagati, a state of misery D I.228; III.234; S I.34; III.225 sq.; IV. 168, 307; A I.60; II.127, 129; Pv IV.11[1]; Vism 103, 427; PvA 27, 166; -yonika (& yoniya A I.37) belonging to the realm of the animals S V.356; -vijjā a low art, a pseudo-science Vin II.139; D I.9 sq.

Tiriyaŋ (adv.) [Vedic tiryañc (tiryak) to tiras, see tiro & cp. perhaps Ger. quer=E. thwart, all to ***ter** in tarati] transversely, obliquely, horizontally (as opp. to uddhaŋ vertically, above, & adho beneath), slanting, across. In comb[n] uddhaŋ adho tiriyaŋ sabbadhi "in all directions whatever" D I.251=A II.129; similarly uddhaŋ adho t. vāpi majjhe Sn 1055; with uddhaŋ & adho D I.23, 153; Vism 176 (where expl[d]). — A II.48; Sn 150, 537; J I.96; It 120; DhA I.40 (dvāra-majjhe t. across the doorway), 47 (sideways); DA I.312; KhA 248.

-taraṇa ferrying across, adj. °ā nāvā, a vessel crossing over, a traject Vin IV.65.

Tiriyā (f.) a kind of grass or creeper A III.240, 242 (tiriyā nāma tiṇajāti; Com. dabbatiṇa).

Tirivaccha a certain tree J v.46.

Tirīṭa (nt.) the tree Symplocos racemosa, also a garment made of its bark Vin I.306 (°ka); D I.166 = A I.295; M I.343; Pug 51.

Tiro (prep. & adv.) (always °-) [Vedic tiras across, crossways, from *ter of tarati = to go through; cp. Av. tarō, Lat. trans, Cymr. tra] across, beyond, over, outside, afar. See also tiraccha & tiriyaŋ.
-karaṇī (f.) a curtain, a veil (lit. "drawing across") Vin I.276; II.152; -kucchigata having left the womb D II.13; -kuḍḍa outside the fence or wall, over the wall Vin IV.265 (°kuḍḍe uccāraŋ chaḍḍeti); D I.78 = A III.280 (in phrase tirobhāvaŋ t. kuḍḍaŋ t. pākāraŋ t.-pabbataŋ asajjamāno gacchati to denote power of transplacement); Pv I.5^1 (°kuḍḍesu tiṭṭhanti: the Tirokuḍḍa-Sutta, Khp VII.); Vism 176, 394; DhA I.104; PvA 23, 31; -gāma a distant village Vin III.135; -chada "outside the veil," conspicuous J VI.60; -janapada a distant or foreign country D I.116; -pākāra beyond or over a fence (°pākāraŋ or °pākāre) Vin IV.266; see also °kuḍḍa; -bhāva (ŋ) beyond existence, out of existence, magic power of going to a far away place or concealment Vism 393 sq. (= a-pākaṭa-pāṭihāriya), see also under °kuḍḍa. -raṭṭha a foreign kingdom D I.161 (= para-raṭṭha DA I.286).

Tirokkha 1. (adj.) one who is outside, or absent Vin III.185. — 2. (adv.) [= tiras + ka, cp. tiraskāra disdain, abuse] in tirokkha-vāca one who speaks abusively or with disregard J v.78.

Tila (m. nt.) [Vedic tila m.] the sesame plant & its seed (usually the latter, out of which oil is prepared: see tela), Sesamum Indicum. Often comb^d with **taṇḍula**, e. g. A I.130 = Pug 32; J I.67; III.53. — Vin I.212 (navātilā); A IV.108; Sn p. 126; J I.392; II.352; Vism 489 (ucchu°); DhA I.79; PvA 47 (tilāni piḷetvā telavāṇijjaŋ karoti).
-odana rice with sesame J III.425; **-kakka** sesame paste Vin I.205; -tela ses. oil VvA 54 (°ŋ pātukāma); DhA III.29; Bdhd 105; **-piññāka** tila seed-cake, oil-cake VvA 142; **-piṭṭha** sesamum-grinding, crushed s. seed Vin IV.341. -muṭṭhi a handful of ses. J II.278; -rāsi a heap of t. seeds VvA 54; -vāha a cartload of t. seeds A v.173 = Sn p. 126; -saṅgulikā a ses. cake DhA II.75.

Tilaka [tila + ka, from its resemblance to a sesame seed] 1. a spot, stain, mole, freckle M I.88; S I.170; VvA 253; DhA IV.172 (°ŋ vā kāḷakaŋ vā adisvā). — 2. a kind of tree Vv 6^7 (= bandhu-jīvaka-puppha-sadisa-pupphā ekā rukkha-jāti).

Tilañchaka at J. IV.364 acc. to Kern (*Toev.* II.91) to be read as nilañchaka.

Tisata (num.) [ti + sata] three hundred J VI.427 (°mattā nāvā). See also under tayo.

Tīra (nt.) [Vedic tiras from *ṭer, tarati; orig. the opposite bank, the farther side (of a river or ocean), cp. tittha] a shore, bank Vin I.1; D I.222, 244; A II.29, 50; Dh 85; Sn 672; J I.212, 222, 279; II.111, 159; Dhs 597; Vbh 71 sq.; Vism 512 (orima°); PvA 142, 152. — tīra-dassin finding the shore S III.164; A III.368. — a-tīra-dassanī (f.) not seeing the shore (nāvā a ship) J v.75.

Tīraṇa [from tīreti 2] measurement, judgment, recognition, Nd^2 413 (v. l. tir°); Nett 54 (+ vipassanā), 82 (≈ñāṇa), 191; Vism 162. — tīraṇa is one of the 3 pariññās, viz. t°, pahāna°, ñāta-pariññā. See under pariññā.

Tīriya (adj.) [from *tīra] dwelling on the banks of . . . Vin II.287.

Tīreti [Caus. of tarati] 1. to bring through, to finish, to execute (business), to accomplish: karaṇīyaŋ Miln 7, PvA 203; kiccaŋ PvA 278. — 2. to measure, judge, recognize, always in formula tūleti tīreti vibhāveti (Nd^2 tul° tir°, etc.) as interpretation of jānāti; pp. tīrita (Nd^2 tirita) Ps II.200; Nd^2 under ñāta & No. 413.

Tīvarā (pl.) N. of a people in the time of Buddha Kakusandha S II.191.

Tīhaŋ (adv.) [tri + aha] a period of three days, for 3 days; usually as cpd. dvīhatīhaŋ 2 or 3 days (see dvīha) J II.103, etc.

Tu (indecl.) [Vedic tu, belonging to pron. base of 2nd sg. tvaŋ = Lat. tu; Gr. τύ, τοί = indeed, however (orig. ethical dat. of σύ), τοίνυν, τοίγαρ; Goth. þu, etc., cp. tuvaŋ] however, but, yet, now, then (similar in appl. to tāva); kin tu but (= quid nunc). Frequent in late verse: ante tu, *J.P.T.S.* 1884, 5, 31, 37 etc. *J.P.T.S.* 1913, 5^3; Ed's Man. 11^{62} &c. Usually comb^d with eva: tv eva however Sn p. 141; na tv eva not however, but not A v.173.

Tunga (adj.) [Sk. tunga, **tum** to stand out, cp. Gr. τύμβος hillock, Lat. tumeo & tumulus, Mir. tomm hill] high, prominent, long J I.89; III.433 (pabbata, **expl**^{d} however by tikhiṇa, sharp, rough); Davs. IV.30.
-nāsika one with a prominent or long nose S II.284; cp. saṇha-tunga-sadisī-nāsikā Th 2,258; **-vaṇṭaka** having a long stalk; N. of a plant J VI.537.

Tuccha (adj.) [Sk. tuccha, prob. rel. to Lat. tesqua deserted place, see Walde, *Lat. Wtb.* s. v.] empty, vain, deserted; very often comb^d with ritta D I.55; III.53 (°kumbhi); M I.207; J I.209 (°hattha, empty-handed); VI.365; Sn 883; Pug 45, 46; Miln 5 (+ palāpa), 10 (id.), 13; DhA II.43; PvA 202; Sdhp 431.

Tucchaka = tuccha; always comb^d w. rittaka D I.240; S III.141; M I.329.

Tujjati Pass. of tudati.

Tuṭṭha [pp. of tussati to be satisfied] pleased, satisfied; often comb^d w. haṭṭha (q. v.) i. e. tuṭṭha-haṭṭha J I.19 or haṭṭha-tuṭṭha J II.240; cp. tuṭṭha-pahaṭṭha J II.240. — Sn 683; It 103; J I.62 (°mānasa), 87, 266 (°citta), 308 (id.); IV.138. — **tuṭṭhabba** (grd.) to be pleased with Vin IV.259.

Tuṭṭhi (f.) [from tussati] pleasure, joy, enjoyment S I.48; Dh 331 (nom. tuṭṭhī); J I.60, 207.

Tuṇḍa (nt.) [Sk. tuṇḍa, prob. dial. for tunda which belongs to tudati] the beak of birds, the mouth, snout S v.148 (of a monkey); J I.222; IV.210; DhA I.394.

Tuṇḍaka (nt.) = tuṇḍa J I.222; III.126.

Tuṇḍika see ahi°.

Tuṇḍiya (adj.) [from tuṇḍi] having a beak; n. a pecker, fig. a tax-collector J v.102 (= adhamma-bali-sādhaka 103).

Tuṇhikkhaka (adj.) [fr. tūṣṇīŋ, see next] silent J IV.25 (= kiñci avadanto).

Tuṇhī (indecl.) [Sk. tūṣṇīŋ acc. sg. of fem. abstr. tūṣṇī, used adverbially, from tussati] silently, esp. in phrase tuṇhī ahosi he remained silent, as a sign of consent or affirmative answer (i. e. he had nothing to say against it) D II.155; A v.194; Dh 227; Sn 720 (tuṇhī yāti mahodadhi); PvA 117.

-bhāva silence, attitude of consent, usually in form. adhivāsesi tuṇhī-bhāvena he agreed Vin I.17; Sn p. 104, etc. — S II.236, 273 (ariyo t.-bhāvo); M I.161 (id.); A IV.153 (id.).—Miln 15; PvA 17, 20, etc.; -bhūta silent Sn p. 140; Vv 20; DhA 172, etc.

Tuṇhīyati = taṇhāyati, misspelling at S II.13.

Tuṇhīra inorganic form for tūṇīra quiver J V.128, also as v. l. at J V.48.

Tutta (nt.) [Sk tottra, from tudati to prick, push] a pike for guiding elephants, a goad for driving cattle (cp. tomara & patoda) D II.266 (°tomara); J IV.310; V.238; cp. III.5, 2 (t.-vegahata).

Tudati [Vedic tudati; ***steud**, enlarged fr. ***steu**, cp. Lat. tundo, tudes (hammer); Goth. stautan, Ohg. stozan (to push), E. stutter, Nhg. stutzen; Ags. styntan = E. stunt] to strike with an instrument; to prick, peck, pierce; to incite, instigate J III.189 (= vijjhati). Pass. tujjati to be struck Th 1, 780; Vism 503 (cp. vitujjati); Sdhp 279. — pp. **tunna**. See also tuṇḍa (beak = pecker), tutta (goad), tomara (lance = striker) & thūpa (point).

Tudampatī (dual) husband & wife [tu° = dial. for du°, Sk. dve; dampati from dama = domus, Sk. daŋpati = Gr. δεσπότης; cp. also Kern, *Toev.* II.93, who compares tuvantuva for duvanduva]. See under dampati.

Tunna[1] [pp. of tudati] struck Th 2, 192 (vyādhimaraṇa° str. with sickness and death).

Tunna[2] [from tudati] any pointed instrument as a stick, a goad, a bolt, or (usually) a needle Vin I.290 (+ aggaḷa, means of fastening); J I.8 (id.).

-**kamma** "needle-work," tailoring, patching, sewing J IV.40; VI.366; Vism 112. -**kāra** (& °ka) a (mending) tailor J IV.38 (v. l. °ka); VvA 251 (°ka); PvA 120); -**vāya** [Sk. tunnavāya] a "needle-weaver," a tailor Vin II.159; J VI.364, 368 (°vesaŋ gahetvā in the disguise of a tailor); PvA 161 (id.); Pv II.9[14] (= tunnakāra PvA 120); Miln 331, 365.

Tuma (pron.-adj.) [most likely apostrophe form of ātuma = attā, Sk. ātman self; cp. also Sk. tman oneself. See Oldenberg, *KZ.* XXV.319. Less likely = Sk. tva one or the other (Kern, *Toev.* s. v.). Expl[d] by Com. to A III.124 as esa.] oneself, himself, etc.; every or anybody (= quisque) yaŋ tumo karissati tumo va tena paññāyissati (quid quisque faciat) Vin II.186 = A III.124; Sn 890 (cp. ātumānaŋ v.888), 908; Pv III.2[4] (= attānaŋ PvA 181).

Tumula [Sk. tumala; to ***teu**, Lat. tumeo, tumulus, tumultus, etc. E. thumb (swelling), cp. tunga & tūla] tumult, uproar, commotion J VI.247 (by Com expl[d] as "andhakāra," darkness); Dpvs XVII.100.

Tumba (m. nt.) [possibly = Sk. tumra swollen (of shape), same root as tumula] 1. a kind of water vessel (udaka° DA I.202), made of copper, wood or a fruit (like a calabash, cocoanut, etc., cp. kaṭāha, E. skull) Vin I.205 (loha°, kaṭṭha°, phala°); II.114 (°kaṭāha of gourd); J III.430 (udaka°); IV.114; DhA II.193 (udaka°). — 2. a measure of capacity, esp. used for grain J I.233 (mahā°), 467 (= 4 nāḷi p. 468); Miln 102.

Tumhādisa (pron.-adj.) [tumhe + ādisa] like you, of your kind Sn 459; J VI.528; DA I.146.

Tumhe [pl. of pron. 2nd pers., see tuvaŋ].

Tura (adj.) [Vedic tura, cp. tvaraṇa] swift, quick; only in composition with °ga, etc., "going swiftly," denoting the horse; viz. turaga VvA 279; turanga VvA 281; Miln 192 (gaja°, etc.), 352 (id.) 364; turangama Dāvs V.56; turagamana PvA 57.

Turati [= tarati[2]] to be in a hurry, to be quick, hasten J VI.229 (mā turittho, Prohib.). — pp. turita. Cp. also tura, etc.

Turita [pp. of turati] hastening, speedy, quick; hastily, in a hurry Sn 1014; J I.69 (turita-turita); Vv 80[8] (= sambhamanto VvA 311); DA I.319; PvA 181. —aturita leisurely, with leisure, slow J I.87. — See also tuvaṭaŋ.

Turiya (nt.) [Derivation uncertain, probably connected with tuleti, Sk. tūrya] sometimes tūriya (e. g. Vv 5[4]); musical instruments in general, usually referred to as comprising 5 kinds of special instruments (pancangika t. e. g. Vv 5[4]; 39[1]; VvA 181, 183, 210, 257), viz. ātata, vitata, ātata-vitata, ghana, susira (VvA 37). Freq. in phrase nippurisehi turiyehi parivariyamāna (or paricāriyamāna) "surrounded by (or entertained by) heavenly music" Vin I.15; D II.21; A I.145; J I.58. — Vv 38[4]; 41[2]; 50[24], 64[5]; Pv III.8[1]; DhA III.460; VvA 92; PvA 74.

-sadda the sound of music, music Mhvs VII.30.'

Turī a hen Th 2, 381 (= migī ThA· 254) (v. l. korī, cp. Tamil kōḷi hen).

Tula (adj.) [see tuleti] only in negative atula incomparable, not to be measured, beyond compare or description Vv 30[4] (= anupama VvA 126); Pv II.8[9] (= appamāṇa PvA 110); III.3[2] (= asadisarūpa PvA 188); Miln 343.

Tulanā (f.) [see tuleti] weighing, rating; consideration, deliberation M I.480; II.174; Nett 8, 41.

Tulasi [Derivation unknown] basil (common or sweet) J V.46 (°gahana a thicket of b.; v. l. tūlasi); VI.536 (tuḷasi = tuḷasigaccha).

Tulā (f.) [see tuleti. Vedic tulā; Gr. τάλας, τάλαντον (balance, weighing & weight = talentum), τόλμα; Lat. tollo (lift); Goth. þulan (to carry patiently, suffer); Ger. geduld, etc.] 1. a beam or pole for lifting, carrying or supporting, a rafter Vin II.122; VvA 188 (+ gopānasī); DhsA 107. — 2. a weighing pole or stick, scales, balance A I.88; J I.112; Dh 268; Miln 356 (t. nikkhepanāya). — 3. fig. measure ("weighing," cp. tulanā), standard, rate S II.236 (+ pamāṇa).

-**kūṭa** false weighing, false weight (often comb[d] with kaŋsakūṭa & mānakūṭa, false coining & false measuring) D I.5 = A II.209≈; DA I.79; DhA I.239; -**daṇḍa** the beam or lever of a balance J I.113; -**puttaka** a goldsmith (using scales) J V.424 (or should it be tulādhuttaka?).

Tulita [pp. of tuleti] weighed, estimated, compared, gauged, considered Th 2, 153 (yattakaŋ esā t. what she is worth = lakkhaṇaññūhi parichinna ThA 139); Nd[2] under ñāta (as syn. of tirita); PvA 52 (in expl[n] of mita, measured).

Tuliya [Sk. ?] a flying fox J VI.537.

Tuleti [from tulā; Lat. tollo, etc.] to weigh, examine, compare; match, equal M I.480; Th 1, 107; J VI.283; — ger. tulayitvā M I.480. — grd. tuliya & tulya (see sep.). — pp. tulita.

Tulya & Tuliya (also tulla J IV.102) (adj.) [orig. grd. of tuleti] to be weighed, estimated, measured; matched, equal, comparable Sn 377; J III.324; PvA 87 (= samaka). Mostly in the negative atulya incomparable, not having its equal Sn 83, 683; J IV.102 (atulla); Miln 249 (atuliyā guṇā), 343 (id.). — See also tula.

Tuvaŋ & Tvaŋ [Sk. tvaŋ & (Ved.) tuaŋ, cp. also part. tu; Gr. τύ, σύ; Lat. tu; Goth. þu; E. thou, etc.; Oir. tū] pron. of 2nd pers. in foll. forms & applications:— I. *Full forms*: 1. sg.: (a) tv°, tu°, tuyh°: nom. tvaŋ (in prose & verse) Sn 179, 241, 1029, 1058; J I.279; II.159; Pv I.8⁴. Also for nom. pl. at J I.391, 395; VI.576; tuvaŋ (in verse) Sn 1064, 1102, 1121; J III.278, 394; Pv I.3³; II.3²; also for acc. Sn 377; Pv II.8¹; tuyhaŋ (gen. & dat.) [Sk. tubhyaŋ] Sn 983, 1030; J I.279; PvA 3, 60, 73, etc. — (b) ta°, tay°, taŋ (acc.) M I.487; Sn 31, 241, 1043, 1049; J I.222; II.159; Pv I.10¹; II.1⁶; tayā (instr.) Sn 335, 344; J I.222; Pv II.3⁶ (=bhotiyā PvA 86): PvA 71; tayi (loc.) Sn 382; J I.207; tava (gen.) Sn 1102, 1110; J II.153; PvA 106. — 2. pl.: tumh° [Sk. yuṣm°]: tumhe (nom. & acc.) It 31; J I.221 (acc.); Pv I.11². Also as pl. majesticus in addressing one person J II.102; IV.138; tumhaŋ (gen.) PvA 58 (for sg.), 78; tumhākaŋ (gen. dat.) S II.65; It 32; J I.150; II.102; tumhesu (loc.) J I.292 (for sg.); tumhehi (instr.) J II.154; Pv I.5¹². — II. *Enclitic forms* (in function of an ethical dative "in your interest," therefore also as possessive gen. or as instrumental, or any other case of the interested person according to construction). 1. sg. te D II.127 (dat.); Sn 76, 120, 1099 (dat.), 1102 (dat.); J I.151; II.159 (instr.); Pv I.2³ (dat.); II.3² (gen.), 4⁶ (gen.). — 2. pl. vo S III.33 (instr.) Sn 135, 172 (dat.), 331 (dat.); J I. 222 (acc.); II.133; III.395 (gen.).

Tuvaṭaŋ (adv.) [Sk. tvaritaŋ, cp. tūrata] quickly A V.342; J I.91; II.61; VI.519 (as tvātaŋ); Miln 198; Vism 305, 313.

Tuvaṭṭeti (for *Sk. dvandvayati, denom. fr. dvandva] to share (with=loc. or abl.) Vin II.10, 124; IV.288.

Tuvantuva (nt.) [Sk. dvandva, with dialect. t. (cp. tudampati), not (with Müller, *P. Gr.* 38) through confusion with pron. tvaŋ] quarrel, strife M I.110, 410.

Tussati [Sk. tuṣyati to ***teus** to be quiet, contented, happy] to be satisfied, pleased or happy J III.280; IV.138; Miln 210. Cp. tuṭṭha (pp.), tuṭṭhi, tuṇhī, tosa, tosana, toseti.

Tussana (nt.) [Sk. toṣaṇa] satisfying, pleasing, in °kāraṇa cause for satisfaction or delight J III.448.

Tūṇira=tūṇī, Vism 251.

Tūṇī (f.) [Sk. *tūṇa & tūṇī, to ***tḷn**: see under tulā; cp. Lat. tollo. On ṇ>l. cp. cikkaṇa & cikkhala, guṇa> guḷa, kiṇi>kili, etc.] a quiver (lit. "carrier") J II.403 (dhanuŋ tūṇiñ ca nikkhippa); V.47.

Tūla (nt.) [Sk. tūla, to ***ten**, Sk. taviti, to swell or be bushy, cp. Gr. τύλη swelling; Ags. þol peg] a tuft of grass, cotton Vin II.150 (3 kinds: rukkha°, latā°, poṭaki°); Sn 591=J IV.127 (vāto tūlaŋ va dhaŋsaye); DA I.87.

-picu cotton-wool Vism 282, 285, 404; DhA III.202; KhA 173. -puṇṇikā ("stuffed with tuft or cotton") a kind of shoe Vin I.186.

Tūlikā (f.) [der. fr. tūla] a mattress (consisting of layers of grass or wool: tiṇṇaŋ tūlānaŋ aññatara-puṇṇa-tūlikā DA I.87) Vin I.192; II.150; D I.7; A I.181.

Tūlinī (f.) [Sk. tūlinī] the silk-cotton tree M I.128.

Te° [Sk. trai°] secondary base of numeral three (fr. ti) in compⁿ: having a relation to a triad of, three-; in numerical cpds. also=three (see under tayo).

-kaṭula containing 3 spices (of yāgu), viz. tila, taṇḍula, mugga Vin I.210; III.66; -cīvarika wearing three robes (cp. ticīvara) Vin I.253; Ud 42; Pug 69; Vism 60. -daṇḍika carrying the tripod (see tidaṇḍa), Ep. of a brahmin ascetic A III.276; J II.316 (=kuṇḍikaŋ ṭhapanatthāya tidaṇḍaŋ gahetvā caranto); -dhātuka (nt.) the (worlds of the) threefold composition of elements=tiloka Nett 14, 63 (tedhātuke vimutti= sabbadhi vippamutta), 82; cp. Kvu 605; -piṭaka versed in the three piṭakas (see piṭaka), Ep. of theras & bhikkhus J IV.219; Miln 18 sq.; DhA I.7, 384; III.385; Dāvs V.22. Cp. Sk. tripiṭo bhikṣuḥ (AvŚ I.334 & Index to Divy); -bhātika having 3 brothers DhA I.88, 97. -bhūmaka belonging to the 3 stages of being (viz. the kāma, rūpa, arūpa existences; cp. °dhātuka & tiloka) DhA I.305; IV.72; DhsA 50, 214 (°kusala), 291; -māsa (nt.) 3 months, i. e. a season M I.438; Miln 15; DhA II.192; PvA 20; -vācika pronouncing the threefold formula (of the saraṇa-gata) Vin I.18; -vijja (adj.) possessed of the 3 fold knowledge (i. e. either the higher knowledge of the Brahmins, i. e. the 3 Vedas [cp. Sk. trayī vidyā=the knowledge of the Vedas] or of the Buddha & Arahants, as defined at A I.164 sq., viz. (1) remembrance of former births, (2) insight into the (future) destiny of all beings, (3) recognition of the origin of misery & of the way to its removal, i. e. of the Path): 1. brahmanic: D I.238; A I.163; also as tevijjaka (n.) D I.88, 107, 119. — 2. buddhistic: Vin II.161; M I.482; S I.194; A I.167 =It 100; Sn 594=VvA 10; Pug 14; DhA I.138; Sdhp 420. -tevijjatā (abstr.) Vism 5.

Tekiccha (adj.) [der. fr. tikiccha] curable; fig. one who can be helped or pardoned. Only in cpds. a° incurable, unpardonable VvA 322 (of a sick person); DhA I.25 (id.); Miln 322; of Devadatta w. ref. to his rebirth in Niraya Vin II.202=It 85; M I.393; & sa° pardonable Miln 192, 221, 344.

Teja & Tejo [Vedic tejas (nt.) from **tij** to be sharp or to pierce=a (piercing) flame. See tejate; semantically (sharp> light) cp. Ger. strahl (ray of light)=Ags. strael (arrow). — The nt. tejo is the usual form; instr. tejasā (Dh 387; Sn 1097) & tejena (J III.53), cp. tapa & tapo] "sharpness," heat, flame, fire, light; radiance, effulgence, splendour, glory, energy, strength, power D II.259 (personified as deva, among the 4 Elements paṭhavī, āpo, t., vāyo; cp. tejo-dhātu); S IV.215; M I.327; Sn 1097 (glory of the sun compᵈ with that of the Buddha); Dh 387 (sabbaŋ ahorattiŋ Buddho tapati tejasā); J III.53 (sīla°); I.93 (puñña° the power of merit); Vbh 426 (id.); Ps I.103; Vism 350 (def.); VvA 116.

-kasiṇa fire-contemplation for the purpose of kammaṭṭhāna practice (see kasiṇa) D III.268; Dhs 203; Vism 171; DhA II.49; III.214; Bdhd 106; -dhātu the element of flame (or fire), the 3rd of the 6 Elements, viz. paṭhavī āpo t. vāyo ākāsa viññāṇa (cp. *Dhs. trsl.* p. 242) D III.27, 228, 247; M I.188, 422; A I.176; II.165; Dhs 588, 648, 964; Nett 74; Vism 363.

Tejate [Vedic tejate from **tij** (*stij)=Lat. in-stigo (to spur), Gr. στίζω, στικτός, Ohg. stehhan, Nhg. stecken, E. stick] to be sharp or to make sharp, to prick, to incite, etc. — See tikkha, tikhiṇa, tiṇha, titikkhati, tittaka, teja, etc.

Tejana (nt.) [see tejate] the point or shaft of an arrow, an arrow Th I, 29; Dh 80, 145; DhA II.147.

Tejavant (adj.) [tejas+vant] 1. splendid, powerful, majestic DhA I.426. — 2. in flames, heated, burning with (-°) Miln 148.

Tejin (adj.-n.) [see teja] having light or splendour, shining forth, glorious Sn 1097 (=Nd² 286 tejena samannāgata).

Tettiŋsa (num.) [tayo+tiŋsa] thirty-three J I.273; DhA I.267 sq. See also under tayo & tāvatiŋsa.

Temana (nt.) [from temeti] wetting, moistening Vism 338; VvA 20 (aggimhi tāpanaŋ udake vā temanaŋ); DhA III.420.

Temeti [cp. Divy 285 timayati; Caus. of **tim** to moisten. There is an ancient confusion between the roots **tim**, tamas, etc. (to be dark), **tim**, temeti (to be wet), and

stim to be motionless. Cp. tintiṇāyati, tinta, tibba (=tamas), timira] to make wet, to moisten Vin I.47 (temetabba); II.209 (temetvā); DhA I.220, 394 (id.); J I.88≈KhA 164; J II.325 (temento); PvA 46 (sutemitvā for temetvā).

Terasa see under tayo.

Terovassika (adj.) [tiro+ vassa+ ika] lasting over or beyond a year (or season), a year old, dried up or decayed S IV.161 (thero vassiko in text)=185 (of wood) M I.58 (of bones).

Tela (nt.) [from tila] sesamum-oil (prepared from tila seeds), oil in general (tela=tilatelādika DA I.93); used for drinking, anointing & burning purposes Vin I.205, 220, 245, etc.; A I.209, 278 (sappi vā t. vā); II.122≈(tattena pi telena osiñcante; punishment of pouring over with boiling oil); J I.293; II.104; Pv IV.1[48] (tiṇena telaŋ pi na tvaŋ adāsi·: frequent as gift to mendicants); Pug 55; Dhs 646, 740, 815; PvA 80 (kaḷebarānaŋ vasā telañ ca: fat or oil in general). — tila °ŋ pātukāma desire to drink tila-wine VvA 54; pāka-tela oil concoction VvA 68=DhA III.311; J II.397 (sata°); III.372 (sabassa° worth a thousand); V.376 (sata° worth a hundred); pādabbhañjana° oil for rubbing the feet VvA 44; sāsapa° (mustard seed & oil) PvA 198; sappi° (butter & oil) Sn 295; PvA 278 (also + madhu) as var. objects of grocery trade (dhañña).

-koṭṭhāgāra oil store DhA I.220; -ghaṭa oil jar DA I.144; -cāṭi an oil tank DhA I.220; -dhūpita spiced or flavoured with oil (of a cake) Vv 43[6]; -nāḷi a reed used for keeping oil in, an oil tube Vism 99; DhA II.193 (+udakatumba); -pajjota an oil lamp Vin I.16= D I.85=A I.56=Sn p. 15; -padīpa an oil lamp Vin I.15; S III.126; V.319; VvA 198; -pāka an oil decoction, mixed with spirits, oil-wine Vin I.205; -pilotikā (pl.) rags soaked in oil DhA I.221; -makkhana anointing (the body) with oil Miln 11; -miñjaka an oil-cake PvA 51; -vaṇijjā oil trade PvA 47; -homa an oblation of oli D I.9.

Telaka (nt.)=tela Vin I.204 ("a small quantity of oil"); II.107 (sittha-t. oil of beeswax).

Teliya (adj.) oily J III.522.

Tomara (m. nt.) [Sk. tomara from **tud**, see tudati] a pike, spear, lance, esp. the lance of an elephant-driver D II.266 (tutta-t. a driving lance); M III.133 (t. hattha); Vism 235; DA I.147.

Toya (nt.) [Vedic toya from ***tāu** to melt away; Lat. tabeo, tabes (consumption); Ags. þāwan=E. dew, Oir. tām= tabes; also Gr. τήκω, etc.] water (poetical for udaka); only in simile: puṇḍarīkaŋ (or padumaŋ) toyena na upalippati A II.39=Sn 547; Sn 71=213; Th 1, 700; Nd[2] 287 (t. vuccati udakaŋ); — Bdhd 67, 93.

Toraṇa (nt.) [Sk. toraṇa, perhaps related to Gr. τύρσις, τύρρις=Lat. turris (tower), cp. Hor. Od. I.4[7] "regumque turris"=palaces] an arched gateway, portal; Vin II.154; D II.83; Vv 35[1] (=dvārakoṭṭhaka-pāsādassa nāmaŋ VvA 160); J III.428; Dāvs V.48.

Tosana (adj.-n.) [see tosetu] satisfying, pleasing; satisfaction Sn 971.

Tosāpana (adj.) [=tosana, in formation of a 2nd causative tosāpeti] pleasing, giving satisfaction J II.249.

Toseti [Caus. of tussati] to please, satisfy, make happy Sn 1127 (=Nd[2] 288); J IV.274; Sdhp 304. — pp. tosita contented, satisfied Sn 1128. Cp. pari°.

Tya [Sk. tya°, nt. tyad; perhaps to Gr. σήμερον to-day, σῆτες in this year] base of demonstr. pron.=ta°, this, that; loc. sg. tyamhi J VI.292; loc. pl. fem. tyāsu J V.368 (Com. tāsu).

Tvaŋ see tuvaŋ.

Tvātaŋ see tuvataŋ.

Th.

Thakana (nt.) [see next] covering, lid; closing up DhA IV.85 (saŋvara+).

Thaketi [Sk. sthagayati, Caus. to sthagati, from ***steg** to cover; cp. Gr. *στέγω* cover, *τέγη* roof; Lat. tego, tegula (E.=tile), toga; Oir. tech house; Ohg. decchu cover, dah roof. On P. form cp. Trenckner, *Notes*, p. 62] to cover, cover up, close (usually of doors & windows) Vin II.134 (kaṇṇagūthakehi kaṇṇā thakitā honti: the ears were closed up), 148 (kavaṭā na thakīyanti, Pass.), 209 (vātapāna); IV.54; J IV.4 (sabbe apihitā dvārā; api-dhā=Gr. *ἐπι-θη°*, cp. Hom. Od. 9, 243: *ἠλίβατον πέτρην ἐπέθηκε θύρῃσιν* the Cyclops covered the door with a polished rock) V.214; DhA IV.180 (ṭhakesi, v. l. ṭhapesi); VvA 222; PvA 216 (dvārā) Dāvs IV.33; V.25 (chiddaŋ mālāguḷena th.).

Thañña (nt.) [see thana] mother's milk Vin II.255=289 (°ŋ pāyeti); A IV.276; J III.165; VI.3 (madhura°) Th 2, 496.

Thaṇḍila (nt.) [Vedic sthaṇḍila a levelled piece of ground prepared for a sacrifice. Cognate with sthala, level ground] bare, esp. hard, stony ground Pv IV.7^{5} (=kharakaṭhāna bhūmippadesa PvA 265).
-**sāyikā** (f.) the act of lying on the bare ground (as a penance) [BSk. sthaṇḍila-śāyika] S IV.118; Dh 141 (=DhA III.77: bhūmisayana); -**seyyā** (f.) a bed on bare ground D I.167≈(v. l. BB. taṇḍila°) Miln 351; cp. Sk. sthaṇḍilaśayyā.

Thaddha [pp. of thambeti, Sk. stabhnāti to make firm, prop, hold up; cp. Av. stawra firm, Gr. *ἀστεμφής*, *σταφυλή*; Goth. stafs, Ags. staef=E. staff; Ohg. stab. See also khambha & chambheti] 1. lit. hard, rigid, firm J I.293 (opp. muduka); Vism 351 (°lakkhaṇa); PvA 139 (=ujjhangala). — 2. fig. (a) hardened, obdurate, callous, selfish D I.118 (māna°); III.45 (+atimānin); A II.26=It 113 (kuha th. lapa); Sn 104 (see gotta°); J I.88 (māna°) II.136; Sdhp 90. — (b) slow Miln 103 (opp. lahuka; cp. BSk. dhandha, on which Kern, *Toev.* II.90). — See thambha & thūṇa.
-**maccharin** obdurate & selfish, or very selfish DhA III.313; VvA 69; PvA 45; -**hadaya** hard-hearted J III.68.

Thana [Vedic stana; cp. Gr. *στηνιον*=*στῆθος* (Hesychius)] 1. the breast of a woman D II.266; J V.205; VI.483; Sdhp 360. — 2. the udder of a cow M I.343=Pug 56; DhA II.67.
-**mukha** the nipple J IV.37. -**sita-dāraka** [see sita] a child at the breast, a suckling Miln 364=408.

Thanaka, a little breast, the breast of a girl Th 2, 265 (=ThA 212).

Thanita (nt.) [pp. of thaneti cp. Vedic (s)tanayitnu thunder=Lat. tonitrus, Ohg. donar, etc.] thundering, thunder J I.470; Th 1, 1108; Miln 377.

Thanin (adj.) having breasts, -breasted; in timbaru° Sn 110; J VI.457. — pucimanda° J VI.269.

Thaneti [Vedic stanayati & stanati to thunder; cp. Gr. *στένω*, *στενάζω* to moan, groan, *στονος*; Lat. tono; Ags. stunian; Ger. stöhnen] to roar, to thunder D II.262; S I.100, 154 (megho thanayaŋ), 154 (thaneti devo); It 66 (megho thanayitvā). — pp. thanita. See also gajjati & thunati.

Thapati [Vedic sthapati, to **sthā**+pati] 1. a builder, master carpenter M I.396=S IV.223; M III.144. — 2. officer, overseer S V.348.

Thabbha is to be read for °tthambha in para° J IV.313.

Thambha [see etym. under thaddha; occasionally spelt thamba, viz. A I.100; M I.324; PvA 186, 187] 1. a pillar, a post Vin I.276; D I.50 (majjhimaŋ °ŋ nissāya); II.85 (id.); Sn 214; Vv 78^{2} (veḷuriya°, of the pillars of a Vimāna); Pv III.3^{1} (id.); DhA IV.203; VvA 188 (+tulā-gopānasī); PvA 186. — 2. (fig.) in all meanings of thaddha, applied to selfishness, obduracy, hypocrisy & deceit: viz. immobility, hardness, stupor, obstinacy (cp. Ger. "verstockt"): thambho ti thaddha-bhāvo SnA 288, 333; th. thambhanā thambhittaŋ kakkhaliyaŋ phāruliyaŋ ujucittatā (an° ?) amudutā Vbh 350. — Often comb^{d} w. māna (=arrogance), freq. in set sāṭheyyaŋ th. sārambho māno, etc. A I.100, 299=Nd^{2} under rāga=Miln 289; cp. M I.15. — A III.430 (+māna); IV.350, 465 (+sāṭheyya); Sn 245 (+mada), 326, 437 (as one of Māra's combatants: makkho th. te aṭṭhamo); J I.202. — 3. a clump of grass M I.324; cp. thambhaka.

Thambhaka (=thambha 3) a clump of grass-VvA 276 (=gumba).

Thambhati & thambheti, see upa°, pati°.

Thambhanā (f.) [abstr. to thambha] firmness, rigidity, immobility Dhs 636=718; Vbh 350.

Thambhitatta (nt.) [abstr. to thambha]=thambha 2, viz. hardness, rigidity, obduracy, obstinacy Vbh 350. *Note*. Quite a late development of the term, caused by a misinterpretation of chambhitatta, is "fluctuation, unsteadiness, inflation" at Dhs 965 (in def. of vāyodhātu: chambhittattaŋ [?] thambhitattaŋ. See on this Dhs. trsl. p. 242), & at Vbh 168 (in def. of vicikicchā; v.l. chambhitatta), and at Asl. 338 (of vayo). None of these meanings originally belong to the term thambha.

Thambhin (adj.) obstinate Th 1, 952.

Tharaṇa (nt.) [Sk. staraṇa to **stṛ**] strewing, spreading. In cpds. like assa°, bhumma°, ratha°, hattha°, etc. the reading ass-attharaṇa, etc. should be preferred (=ā **stṛ**). See attharaṇa and cpds.

Tharati [Sk. stṛṇoti] only in cpds. ā°, ava°, etc.

Tharu [Sk. tsaru] the hilt or handle of a sword or other weapons, a sword A III.152; J III.221 (=sword); Miln 178; DhA II.249 (°mūla); IV.66 (asi°). — tharusmiŋ sikkhati to learn the use of a sword Vin II.10; Miln 66.
-**ggaha** one who carries a sword-(handle) Miln 331 (dhanuggaha+; not in corresponding list of occupations at D I.51); -**sippā** training in swordsmanship Ud 31.

Thala[1] (nt.) [Vedic sthala, to **sthā**, orig. standing place; cp. Gr. στέλλω, στόλος; Ags. steall (place); also P. thaṇḍila] dry ground, viz. high, raised (opp. low) or solid, firm (opp. water) S IV.179. As plateau opp. to ninna (low lying place) at Sn 30 (SnA 42 = ukkūla); Dh 98; It 66 = S I.100 (megho thalaŋ ninnañ ca pūreti); PvA 29 (= unnatapadesa). As dry land, terra firma opp. to jala at Dh 34; J I.107, 222; Pv IV.1[21]; PvA 260. As firm, even ground or safe place at D I.234; Sn 946. — Cp. J III.53; IV.142; Vism 185.
-**gocara** living on land J II.159; -**ja** sprung from land (opp. vārija Dh 34 or udakarūha Vv 35[6] = water-plant); referring to plants A I.35; J I.51; Vv 35[6] (= yodhikādikā VvA 162); Miln 281; -**ṭṭha** standing on firm ground A II.241; -**patha** a road by land (opp. jala° by water) J I.121; III.188.

Thala[2] (nt.) [prob. dialect. variant of tharu] the haft of a sword, the scabbard J III.221 (reading uncertain).

Thava [see thavati] praise, praising, eulogy Nett 161, 188, 192.

Thavati [Sk. stauti, Av. staviti, cp. Gr. στεῦται] to praise, extol; inf. thutuŋ Sn 217 (= thometuŋ SnA 272). — Caus. thaveti [Sk. stavayati] pp. thavita Miln 361. See thuta, thuti, thoma, thometi.

Thavikā (f.) [derivation uncertain] a knapsack, bag, purse; esp. used for the carrying of the bhikkhu's strainer Vin I.209 (parissāvanāni pi thavikāyo pi pūretvā), 224 (patte + pariss° + th.); J I.55 (pattaŋ thavikāya pakkhipitvā); VI.67 (pattaŋ thavikāya osāretvā); VvA 40 (patta-thavikato parissāvanaŋ nīharitvā). Also for carrying money: **sahassathavikā** a purse of 1,000 pieces J I.54, 195, 506; VvA 33; Anvs 35. See also Vin II.152, 217; Vism. 91.

Thāma (& thāmo nt. in instr. thāmasā M I.498; S II.278 = Th 1, 1165; III.110, see below) [Vedic sthāman & sthāmas nt., **sthā** cp. Gr. στήμων, Lat. stamen (standing structure); Goth. stoma foundation] "standing power," power of resistance, steadfastness, strength, firmness, vigour, instr. thāmena (Miln 4; PvA 193); thāmasā (see above); thāmunā (J VI.22). Often comb[d] with bala J I.63; Sn 68; with bala + java PvA 4; with bala + viriya Nd[2] 289, 651; with java J I.62; VvA 104; with viriya J I.67. — D III.113; S I.78; II.28; V.227; A I.50; II.187 sq.; IV.192. J I.8, 265 (°sampanna); II.158 (id.); Dhs 13, 22; Vism 233 (°mahatta); DhA IV.18; PvA 259. — Instr. used as adv.: thāmena hard, very much PvA 193; thāmasā obstinately, perseveringly M I.257.
-**gataditthika** (adj.) one in whom heresy has become strong J I.83 = VI.220.

Thāmaka (adj.) having strength Sn 1144 (dubbala° with failing strength); Nd[1] 12 (appa° + dubbala).

Thāmavant (adj.) [thāma + vant] strong, steadfast, powerful, persevering S V.197, 225; A II.250; IV.110, 234, 291; V.24; Nd[2] 131; Vv 5[1] (= thira balavā VvA 35).

Thāra see vi°, san°.

Thāla (nt.) [from thala orig. a flat dish] a plate, dish, vessel D I.74; J I.69; Miln 282. Kaŋsa° a gong Miln 62; Vism 283 (in simile). See also thālī.

Thālaka (nt.) [thāla + ka] a small bowl, beaker Pv II.1[7] (thālakassa pāniyaŋ), 1[19] (id.); Nett 79 (for holding oil: dīpakapallika Com.).

Thālikā (f.) = thālaka Vin I.203, 240. See āḷhaka°.

Thālī (f.) (thāli° in cpds.) [Sk. sthālī, cp. thāla] an earthen pot, kettle, large dish; in -**dhovana** washing of the dish A I.161 (+ **sarāva-dhovana**); -**pāka** an offering of barley or rice cooked in milk Vin III.15; D I.97 (= DA I.267); S II.242; V.384; A I.166; J I.186; Miln 249.

Thāvara[1] (adj.) [Vedic sthāvara, from **sthā**, cp. sthavira, Gr. σταυρός post, Lat. re-stauro, Goth. stana judgment & stojan to judge] "standing still," immovable (opp. to tasa) firm, strong (Ep. of an Arahant: KhA 245) DhA IV.176. Always in connection with **tasa**, contrasting or comprising the movable creation (animal world) & the immovable (vegetable world), e. g. Sn 394 ("sabbesu bhūtesu nidhāya daṇḍaŋ ye thāvarā ye ca tasanti loke"); It 52 (tasaŋ vā thāvaraŋ vā). See **tasa** for ref.

Thāvara[2] (nt.) [from thavira = thera, old] old age PvA 149 (thāvari-jiṇṇa in expl. of therī, otherwise jarā-jiṇṇa. Should we read thāvira-jiṇṇa ?).

Thāvariya (nt.) [fr. thāvara] immobility, firmness, security, solidity, an undisturbed state; always in **janapada**° an appeased country, as one of the blessings of the reign of a Cakkavattin. Expl[d] at DA I.250 as "janapadesu dhuvabhāvaŋ thāvarabhāvaŋ vā patto na sakkā kenaci cāletuŋ." D I.88; II.16, 146, 169; S I.100; Sn p. 106; It 15.

Thāvareyya (nt.) [from thāvara[2]] the rank of a Thera. A I.38; II.23. This has nothing to do with seniority. It is quite clear from the context that Thera is to be taken here in the secondary sense explained under Thera. He was a bhikkhu so eminently useful to the community that his fellow bhikkhus called him Thera.

Thāsotu° in thāsotujana-savana at ThA 61 according to Morris, *J.P.T.S.* 1884, 81 it is to be read ṭhānaso tu jana°.

Thika (adj.) [cp. Sk. styāyate to congeal, form a (solid) mass; see cognates under thīna & cp. theva] dropping, forming drops: madhutthika J III.493; VI.529 (= madhuŋ paggharantiyo madhuttheyasadisā p. 530) "dropping honey."

Thiṇṇa pp. of tharati, only in cpds. parivi°, vi°.

Thira (adj.) [Vedic sthira, hard, solid; from **sthā** or Idg. ster (der. of **stā**) to stand out = to be stiff; cp. Gr. στερεός; Lat. sterilis (sterile = hardened, cp. Sk. starī); Ohg. storrēn, Nhg. starr & starren, E. stare; also Lat. strenuus] solid, hard, firm; strenuous, powerful J I.220; IV.106 (= daḷha); Miln 194 (thir-āthira-bhāva strength or weakness); VvA 212 (id.), 35 (= thāmavant); Sdhp 321.

Thiratā (f.) [fr. thira] steadfastness, stability DhA IV.176 (thiratāya thavarā; so read for ṭhira°).

Thī (f.) [Vedic strī, on which see Walde, *Lat. Wtb.* under sero. This form thī is the normal correspondent to Vedic strī; the other, more usual (& dial.) form is itthi] a woman J I.295, 300; V.296 (thī-pura), 397; VI.238.

Thīna (nt.) [Sk. styāna; orig. pp. of styāyate to become hard, to congeal; **steiā** (cp. also thira) = Gr. στέαρ grease, talc; Lat. stīpo to compress; also Sk. stimita (motionless) = P. timi; stīma (slow), Mhg. stīm; Goth. etc. stains = E. stone; Gr. στῖφος (heap); Lat. stipes (pale); Ohg. stīf = E. stiff] stiffness, obduracy, stolidity, indifference (cp. thaddha & tandī, closely related in meaning). Together with middha it is one of the 5 hindrances (nīvaraṇāni) to Arahantship (see below). Def. as cittassa akammaññatā, unwieldiness or impliability of mind (= immobility) at Nd[2] 290 = Dhs 1156, 1236 = Nett 86; as citta-gelaññaŋ morbid state of mind ("psychosis") at DA I.211. — Sn 942 (niddaŋ tandiŋ sahe thīnaŋ pamādena na saŋvase), 1106; Vbh 352 (= Nd[2] 290 as expl[n] of linatta); Vism 262 (°sineha, where p. 361 reads patthinna°).

-middha sloth & drowsiness, stolidity & torpor; two of the 5 nīvaraṇāni (*Dhs. trsl.* pp. 120, 310) Vin II.200 (vigata°); D I.71, 246; III.49, 234, 269, 278: S I.99; III.106; V.277 sq.; A III.69 sq.; 421; Sn 437 (pañcami senā Mārassa); It 27, 120; Ps. I.31, 45, 162; II.12, 169, 179, 228; Pug 68; Dhs 1154, 1486; Vism 469; Sdhp 459.

Thīyati see patiṭṭhīyati.

Thīyanā (f.) & **thīyitatta** (nt.) [abstr. formations from thīna] = thīna, in exegesis at Nd² 290≈(see thīna): Vbh 352.

Thuta [cp. pp. of thavati] praised DhsA 198; J IV.101 (sada° = sadā thuto niccapasattho); Miln 278 (vaṇṇita th. pasattha).

Thuti (f.) [cp. thavati] praise J IV.443 (thutiŋ karoti); VvA 158.

Thunati [see thaneti] 1. to moan, groan, roar S V.148 (thunaŋ ppr.; v. l. thanaŋ); Vv 52¹ (of beings in Niraya, otherwise ghosenti), v.l.SS thananti (better ?). — 2. to proclaim; shout, praise (confused with thavati) Sn 884.

Thulla see thūla.

Thusa (nt.) [Vedic tuṣa (m.)] husk of grain, chaff A I.242 (together w. other qualities of corn); J IV.8; Vism 346.— athusa D III.199.
-aggi a fire of husks Nett 23; -odaka gruel (= sabba-sambhārehi kataŋ sovīrakaŋ Pug A 232) D I.166 = A I.295 = Pug 55; -pacchi a bird stuffed with chaff, a straw-bird J I.242; -piṇḍa a lump of husks Vin II.151; -rāsi a heap of h. DhA I.309; -homa an oblation of h. D I.9 (= DA I.93; v. l. BB kana, for kaṇa; cp. kaṇa-homa D I.9).

Thūṇā (f.) [Vedic sthūṇā from **sthā**, standing fast, as in thambha, thīna, etc. Nearest relation is thāvara (= thūrā, on r: ṇ = l (thūla): n see tūṇī). Cp. Gr. σταυρός (post); Lat. restauro (to prop up again); Gr. στῦλος pillar, "style"; Goth. stojan etc. (see thāvara); Ags. styran = E. steer, Ger. steuer] a pillar, prop, support A II.198; Vv 54¹ (= thambha VvA 245); DA I.124. Esp. the sacrificial post in phrase thūṇûpanīta "lead to sacrifice" (yūpa-sankhātuŋ thūṇaŋ upa° DA I.294): D I.127≈S I.76≈DhA II.7; J III.45. -kumbhathūṇā a sort of drum D I.6 etc. (see kumbha, where also kumbha -thūṇika Vin IV.285). — eka-thūṇaka with *one* support J IV.79.

Thūṇira [der. fr. thūṇā] house-top, gable Th I, 184 (= kaṇṇikā Com.).

Thūpa [Vedic stūpa, crown of the head, top, gable; cp. Gr. στύπος (handle, stalk). Oicel. stūfr (stump), to ***steud** as in tudati] a stupa or tope, a bell-shaped pile of earth, a mound, tumulus, cairn; dome, esp. a monument erected over the ashes of an Arahant (otherwise called dhātugabbha = dāgaba), or on spots consecrated as scenes of his acts. In general as tomb: Vin IV.308; J III.156 (mattika°) = Pv I.8⁴; in special as tope: D II.142, 161, 164 sq.; A I.77; M II.244; J V.39 (rajata°); VvA 156 (Kassapassa bhagavato dvādasayojanikaŋ kanaka°); Ud 8; Pv III.10⁵. Four people are thūpârahā, worthy of a tope, viz. a Tathāgata, a Tathāgata-sāvaka, a Paccekabuddha, a Cakkavattin D II.143 = A II.245. — At Dpvs VI.65 th. is to be corrected into dhūpaŋ.

Thūpika (adj.) [from thūpa. The ika applies to the whole compound] having domed roofs ("house-tops") J VI.116 (of a Vimāna = dvādasayojanika maṇimaya-kañcanathūpika; cp. p. 117: pañcaṭhūpaŋ vimānaŋ, expl^d as pañcahi kūṭāgārehi samannāgataŋ).

Thūpikata (adj.) [thūpa + kata] "made a heap," heaped of an alms-bowl: so full that its contents bulge out over the top Vin IV.191.

Thūla (a) & **Thulla** (b) (the latter usual in cpds.) (adj.) [Vedic sthūla (or sthūra); cp. Lith. storas (thick); Lat. taurus, Goth. stiur, Ags. steor (bull = strong, bulky); Ohg. stūri (strong). From **sthā**: see thīna, cp. thūṇā. To ūl: ull cp. cūḷa: culla] compact, massive: coarse, gross; big, strong, clumsy; common, low, unrefined, rough D I.223; Sn 146 (aṇuka°), 633 (id.); Dh 31, 265, 409; J I.196 (b); Dhs 617; KhA 246; PvA 73, 74 (of a cloak); VvA 103; Sdhp 101, 346. — thullāni gajjati to speak rough words J I.226 (= pharusavacanāni vadati).
-anga (adj.) heavy-limbed J I.420; -accaya a grave offence Vin I.133, 167, 216; II.110, 170 etc.; Vism 22. -kacchā thick scurf Vin I.202; -kumārī (Vin. V.129) & kumārikā a stout, fat girl J III.147; IV.220 (Com. pañcakāmaguṇika-rāgena thūlatāya thullak° ti vuccati); Vism 17. -phusitaka (deva) (the rain-god, probably with reference to the big drops of the rain cp. DA I.45) M I.453; S III.141; V.396; A I.243; II.140 (a); V.114 sq.; DhA III.243; -vajja a grave sin Vin II.87 (a); -vattha a coarse garment J V.383; -sarīra (adj.) fat, corpulent J I.420; IV.220 (opp. kisa thin); -sāṭaka coarse cloth DhA I.393 (a).

Thūlatā (f.) [abstr. to thūla] coarseness, roughness, vileness J IV.220.

Theta (adj.) [Sk. from tiṭṭhita, Müller *P. Gr.* 7 = sthātṛ] firm, reliable, trustworthy, true D I.4 (DA I.73: theto ti thiro; ṭhita-katho ti attho); M I.179; S IV.384; A II.209 = Pug 57; Nd² 623. — abl. thetato in truth S III.112. — attheta J IV.57 (= athira).

Thena [Vedic stena & stāyu, besides which tāyu, the latter prob. original, cp. Gr. τητάω to deprive; Oir. tāid thief, to a root meaning "conceal"] a thief adj. stealing: athenena not stealing, not stealthily, openly D I.4; DA I.72. f. athenī A III.38. Cp. kumbhatthena Vin II.256 (see k.).

Thenaka [= prec.] a thief J VI.115.

Theneti [Denom. fr. thena] to steal, to conceal J IV.114; DhA I.80.

Theyya (nt.) [Vedic steya] theft Vin I.96; A I.129; Sn 119 (theyyā adinnaŋ ādiyati); 242, 967 (°ŋ na kareyya); Vv 15⁸ (: theyyaŋ vuccati thenabhāvo VvA 72); Miln 264, 265; Vism 43 (°paribhoga); DA I.71; Sdhp 55, 61.
-citta intending to steal Vin III.58; -saŋvāsaka one who lives clandestinely with the bhikkhus (always foll. by titthiyapakkantaka) Vin I.86, 135, 168, 320; V.222; Miln 310; -sankhātaŋ (adv.) by means of theft, stealthily D III.65 sq., 133; A III.209; IV.370 sq.; V.264.

Thera [Vedic sthavira. Derivation uncertain. It may come from **sthā** in sense of standing over, lasting (one year or more), cp. thāvara old age, then "old = venerable"; (in meaning to be compared w. Lat. senior, etc. from num. **sem** "one" = one year old, i. e. lasting over one and many more years). Cp. also vetus = Gr. ἔτος, year, E. wether, one year old ram, as cpd. w. veteran, old man. Or it may come from **sthā** in der. *stheuā in sthūra (sthūla: see etym. under thūla) thus, "strong = venerable"] t.t. only used with ref. to the bhikkhus of Gotama Buddha's community. — (a) (adj.) senior, Vin I.47, 290 (th. bhikkhū opp. navā bh.), 159 (th. bhikkhu a senior bh. opp. to navaka bh. a novice), 187; II.16, 212. Therânutherâ bhikkhū seniors & those next to them in age dating not from birth, but from admission to the Order). Three grades are distinguished, thera bh., majjhima bh., nava bh., at D I.78. — See also A II.23, 147, 168; V.201, 348; D III.123 sq., 218; Dh

260, 261. In *Sangha-thera*, used of Bhikkhus not senior in the Order, the word thera means distinguished. Vin II.212, 303. In *Mahāthera* the meaning, as applied to the 80 bhikkhus so called, must also have some similar meaning Dīpv IV.5 *Psalms of the Brethren* xxxvi.; J V.456. At A II.22 it is said that a bhikkhu, however junior, may be called thera on account of his wisdom. It is added that four characteristics make a man a thera —high character, knowing the essential doctrines by heart, practising the four Jhānas, and being conscious of having attained freedom through the destruction of the mental intoxications. It is already clear that at a very early date, before the Anguttara reached its extant shape, a secondary meaning of thera was tending to supplant that of senior—that is, not the senior of the whole Order, but the senior of such a part of the Sangha as live in the same locality, or are carrying out the same function. — *Note*. thera in thero vassiko at S IV.161 is to be read tero-vassiko.

-gāthā hymns of senior bhikkhus, N. of a canonical book, incorporated in the Khuddaka-Nikāya. Theratara, very senior, opp[d] to navatara, novice D II.154. -vāda the doctrine of the Theras, the original Buddhist doctrine M I.164; Dpvs IV.6. 13.

Theraka (adj.) strong (?), of clothes: therakāni vatthāni D II.354 (vv. ll. thevakāni, dhorakāni, corakāni).

Therī & Therikā (f.) [see thera] 1. an old woman (cp. sthavirikā M Vastu III.283) Pv II.11[6] (=thāvarijiṇṇā PvA 149). — 2. a female thera (see cpds.), as therikā at Th 2, 4; Dpvs XVIII. 11.

-gāthā hymns of the theris, following on the Thera-gāthā (q. v.).

Theva (m. ?) [see etym. under thīna, with which cp. in meaning from same root Gr. σταγών & Lat. stiria, both = drop. Cp. also thika. Not with Trenckner (Notes p. 70) fr. **stip**] a drop; stagnant water. In Vin. only in phrase: cīvaraŋ . . . na acchinne theve pakkamitabbaŋ Vin I.50, 53 = II.227, 230; J VI.530 (madhu-ttheva a drop of honey).

Thevati [fr. theva; orig. "to be congealed or thick"] to shine, glitter, shimmer (like a drop) J VI.529 (=virocati p. 530).

Thoka (adj.) [for etymology see under thīna] little, small, short, insignificant; nt. a trifle. A IV.10; J VI.366; PvA 12 (kāla): nt. thokaŋ as adv. = a little J I.220; II.103, 159; V.198; PvA 13. 38. 43. — thokaŋ thokaŋ a little each time, gradually, little by little Dh 121, 239; Miln 9; SnA 18; PvA 168.

Thokaka (adj.) = thoka; fem. thokikā Dh 310.

Thoma [Vedic stoma a hymn of praise] praise.

Thomana (nt.) & thomanā (f.) [see thavati] praising, praise, laudation J I.220 (=pasaŋsa); Pug 53; PvA 27.

Thometi [denom. fr. thoma; cp. thavati] to praise, extol, celebrate (often with vaṇṇeti) D I.240; Sn 679, 1046; Nd[2] 291; J VI.337; SnA 272 (=thutuŋ); VvA 102; PvA 196. — pp. thomita J I.9.

D.

-D- euphonic consonant inserted to avoid hiatus: (a) orig. only sandhi-cons. in forms ending in t & d (like tāvat, kocid, etc.) & thus restored in cpds. where the simplex has lost it; (b) then also transferred to & replacing other sandhi-cons. (like puna-d-eva for punar eva). — (a) dvipa-d-uttama Sn 995; koci-d-eva PvA 153; kinci-d-eva ibid. 70; tāva-d-eva ib. 74; yāva-d-atthaŋ ib. 217; ahu-d-eva Miln 22 etc. — (b) puna-d-eva Pv II.11^3 (v. l. BB); DhA II.76; samma-d-eva Sn p. 16; VvA 148; PvA 66 etc.; cp. SnA 284. bahu-d-eva J I.170.

-Da (adj.) [Suffix of **dā**, see dadāti] giving, bestowing, presenting, only -°, as anna°, bala°, vaṇṇa°, sukha°, Sn 297; vara° Sn 234; kāma° J VI.498; Pv II.13^8; ambu° giving water, i. e. a cloud Dāvs V.32; amatamagga° Sdhp 1; uḷāraphala° ib. 26; maŋsa° Pgdp 49. etc.

Daŋsaka: see vi°.

Daŋseti (for dasseti): see upa°; pavi°, vi°.

Daka (nt.) [=udaka, aphæretic from comb^{ns} like sītodaka which was taken for sīto+daka instead of sīt' odaka] Vin III.112; S III.85; A II.33=Nd^2 420 B^3 (: the latter has udaka, but Nd^1 14 daka).
-āsaya (adj.) (beings) living in water A II.33≈; -ja (adj.) sprung from water, aquatic J I.18 (thalajā d pupphā); -rakkhasa a water-sprite J I.127, 170; VI.469.

Dakkha[1] (adj.) [Vedic dakṣa=Gr. *ἀρι-δείκετος* & *δεξιός*; dakṣati to be able; to please, satisfy, cp. daśasyati to honour, Denom. fr. *dasa=Lat. decus honour, skill. All to ***dek** in Lat. decet to be fit, proper, etc. On var. theories of connections of root see Walde, *Lat. Wtb.* under decet. It may be that ***deks** is an intens. formation fr. ***diś** to point (see disati), then the original meaning would be "pointing," i. e. the hand used for pointing. For further etym. see dakkhiṇa] dexterous, skilled, handy, able, clever D I.45, 74, 78; III.190 (+analasa) M I.119; III.2; S I.65; Nd^2 141 (+analasa & sampajāna); J III.247; DA I.217 (=cheka); Miln 344 (rūpadakkhā those who are of "fit" appearance).

Dakkha[2] (nt.) [dakkha^1+ya, see dakkheyya] dexterity, ability, skill J III.466.

Dakkhati & Dakkhiti see dassati.

Dakkhiṇa (adj.) [Vedic dakṣiṇa, Av. dašinō; adj. formation fr. adv. ***deksi**=*deksinos, cp. purāṇa fr. purā, viṣuṇa fr. viṣu, Lat. bini (=bisni) fr. bis. From same root ***deks** are Lat. dexter (with compar.-antithetic suffix ter=Sk. tara, as in uttara) & Gr. *δεξιτερός*; cp. also Goth. taihswa (right hand), Ohg. zeso & zesawa. See dakkha for further connections] 1. right (opp. vāma left), with a tinge of the auspicious, lucky & prominent: Vin II.195 (hattha); PvA 112, 132 (id.); Ps I.125 hattha, pāda, etc. with ref. to a Tathāgata's body); J I.50 (°passa the right side); PvA 178 (id.), 112 (°bāhu); Sn p. 106 (bāha); PvA 179 (°jāṇumaṇḍalena with the right knee: in veneration). — 2. skilled, well-trained (=dakkha) J VI.512 (Com. susikkhita). — 3. (of that point of the compass which is characterized through "orientation" by facing the rising sun, & then lies on one's right:) southern, usually in comb^n with disā (direction): D III.180 (one of the 6 points, see disā), 188 sq. (id.); M I.487; II.72; S I.145, etc.
-āvattaka (adj.) winding to the right D II.18 (of the hairs of a Mahāpurisa, the 14th of his characteristics or auspicious signs; cp. BSk. dakṣiṇāvarta a precious shell, i. e. a shell the spiral of which turns to the right AvŚ I.205; Divy 51, 67, 116); J V.380; **-janapada** the southern country the "Dekkan" (=dakkhiṇaŋ) D I.96, 153 (expl^d by Bdhgh as "Gangāya dakkhiṇato pākaṭa-janapado" DA I.265); **-samudda** the southern sea J I.202.

Dakkhiṇā (f.) [Vedic dakṣiṇā to **daks** as in daśasyati to honour, to consecrate, but taken as f. of dakkhiṇa & by grammarians expl. as gift by the "giving" (i. e. the right) hand with popular analogy to **dā** to give (dadāti)] a gift, a fee, a donation; a donation given to a "holy" person with ref. to unhappy beings in the Peta existence ("Manes"), intended to induce the alleviation of their sufferings; an intercessional, expiatory offering, "don attributif" (Feer) (see Stede, *Peta Vatthu*, etc. p. 51 sq.; Feer *Index to AvŚ* p. 480) D I.51=III.66 (d.-uddhaggikā), cp. A II.68 (uddhaggā d.); A III.43, 46, 178, 259; IV.64 sq., 394; M III.254 sq. (cuddasa pāṭipuggalikā d. given to 14 kinds of worthy recipients) Sn 482, 485; It 19; J I.228; Pv I.4^4 (=dāna PvA 18), I.5^9 (petānaŋ d °ŋ dajjā), IV.1^{51}; Miln 257; Vism 220; PvA 29, 50, 70, 110 (pūjito dakkhiṇāya). guru-d. teacher's fee VvA 229, 230; dakkhiṇaŋ ādisati (otherwise uddisati) to designate a gift to a particular person (with dat.) Vin I.229=D II.88.
-āraha a worthy recipient of a dedicatory gift Pv II.8^6; -odaka water to wash in (orig. water of dedication, consecrated water) J I.118; IV.370; DhA I.112; PvA 23; -visuddhi. purity of a gift M II.256 sq.=A II.80, sq.=D III.231, cp. Kvu 556 sq.

Dakkhiṇeyya (adj.-n.) [grd.-formation fr. **dakkhiṇā** as from a verb *dakṣiṇāti=pūjeti] one worthy of a dakkhiṇā. The term is expl. at KhA 183, & also (with ref. to brahmanic usage) at Nd^2 291; — S I.142, 168, 220; M I.37, 236 sq.; 446; A I.63, 150; II.44; III.134, 162, 248; IV.13 sq.; D III.5; It 19 (annañ ca datvā bahuno dakkhiṇeyyesu dakkhiṇaŋ . . . saggaŋ gacchanti dāyakā); Sn 227, 448 sq., 504, 529; Nd^2 291 (as one of the 3 constituents of a successful sacrifice, viz. yañña the gift, phala the fruit of the gift, d. the recipient of the gift). Cp. I.10^6 (where also adj. to be given, of dāna). Pv IV.1^{33}; VvA 120, 155 (Ep. of the Sangha=ujubhūta); PvA 25, 125, 128, 262.
-aggi the (holy) fire of a good receiver of gifts; a metaphor taken from the brahmanic rite of sacrifice, as one of the 7 fires (=duties) to be kept up (or discarded) by a follower of the Buddha A IV.41, 45; D III.217; -khetta the fruitful soil of a worthy recipient of a gift PvA 92; -puggala an individual deserving a donation J I.228; there are 7 kinds enum^d at D III.253; 8 kinds at D III.255; -sampatti the blessing of finding a worthy object for a dakkhiṇā PvA 27, 137 sq.

Dakkhiṇeyyatā (f.) [abstr. fr. prec.] the fact of being a dakkhiṇeyya Miln 240 (a°).

Dakkhita [Vedic dīkṣita pp. of **dīkṣ**, Intens to daśayati: see dakkha¹] consecrated, dedicated J v.188. Cp. dikkhita.

Dakkhin (adj.) [fr. dakkhati, see dassati] seeing, perceiving; f. °ī in atīra-dakkhiṇī nāvā a ship out of sight of land D I.222.

Dakkheyya (nt.) [cp. dakkha²] cleverness, skill J II.237 (Com. kusalassa-ñāṇa-sampayuttaŋ viriyaŋ); III.468.

Daṭṭha [pp. of daśati, see ḍasati] bitten J I.7; Miln 302; PvA 144.

Daṭṭhar [n. ag. to dassati] one who sees A II.25.

Daṭṭhā (f.) [cp. dāṭhā] a large tooth, tusk, fang Miln 150 (°visa).

Daḍḍha [Sk. dagdha, pp. of dahati, see ḍahati] burnt, always with aggi° consumed by fire Sn 62; Pv I.7⁴; Miln 47; PvA 56 (indaggi°).
-ṭṭhāna a place burnt by fire J I.212; also a place of cremation (sarīrassa d.) PvA 163 (=āḷāhana).

Daḍḍhi° [not with Trenchner, *Notes* p. 65=Sk. dārḍhya, but with Kern, *Toev.* 113=Sk. dṛḍhī (from dṛḍha, see daḷha), as in compⁿ dṛḍhī karoti & bhavati to make or become strong] making firm, strengthening, in **kayā-daḍḍhi-bahula** strengthened by gymnastics, an athlete J III.310 (v. l. ḍalhi°), IV.219 (v. l. distorted kādaḷi-phahuna).

Daṇḍa [Vedic daṇḍa, dial.=*dal[d]ra; (on ṇ: l cp. guṇa: guḷa etc.) to ***del** as in Sk. dala, dalati. Cp. Lat. dolare to cut, split, work in wood; delere to destroy; Gr. δαίδαλον work of art; Mhg. zelge twig; zol a stick. Possibly also fr. *dan[d]ra (r=l freq., ṇ: l as tulā: tūṇa; veṇu: veḷu, etc. cp. aṇḍa, caṇḍa), then it would equal Gr. δένδρον tree, wood, & be connected with Sk. dāru] 1. stem of a tree, wood, wood worked into something, e. g. a handle, etc. J II.102; 405 (v. l. dabba); Vism 313; PvA 220 (nimbarukkhassa daṇḍena [v. l. dabbena] katasūla). tidaṇḍa a tripod. — 2. a stick, staff, rod, to lean on, & as support in walking; the walking-stick of a Wanderer Vin II.132 (na sakkoti vinā daṇḍena āhiṇḍituŋ), 196; S I.176; A I.138; 206; Sn 688 (suvaṇṇa°); J III.395; V.47 (loha°); Sdhp 399 (eka°, °dvaya, ti°). daṇḍaŋ olubbha leaning on the st. M. I.108; A III.298; Th 2, 27. — 3. a stick as means of punishment, a blow, a thrashing: daṇḍehi aññamaññaŋ upakkamanti "they go for each other with sticks" M I.86=Nd² 199; °ŋ dadāti to give a thrashing J IV.382; V.442; daṇḍena pahāraŋ dadāti to hit with a stick S IV.62; brahma° a certain kind of punishment D II.154, cp. Vin II.290 & Kern, *Manual* p. 87; pañca satāni daṇḍo a fine of 500 pieces Vin I.247; paṇīta° receiving ample p. Pv IV.1⁶⁶; purisa-vadha° J II.417; rāja-daṇḍaŋ karoti (c. loc.) to execute the royal beating PvA 216. See also Dh 129, 131, 310, 405 — 4. a stick as a weapon in general, only in cert. phrases & usually in combⁿ w. sattha, sword. daṇḍaŋ ādiyati to take up the stick, to use violence: attadaṇḍa (atta=ā-dā) violent Sn 935; attadaṇḍesu nibbuta Dh 406=Sn 630; a.+kodhābhibhūta S IV.117: ādinna-daṇḍa ādinna-sattha Vin I.349; opp. daṇḍaŋ nidahati to lay down the stick, to be peaceful: sabbesu bhūtesu nidhāya daṇḍaŋ Sn 35, 394, 629; nihita-d. nihita-sattha using neither stick nor sword, of the Dhamma D I.4, 63; M I.287; A I.211; II.208; IV.249; V.204. daṇḍaŋ nikkhipati id. A I.206. d.-sattha parāmasana Nd² 576. daṇḍa-sattha-abbhukkirana & daṇḍa-sattha-abhinipātana Nd² 576⁴. Cp. paṭidaṇḍa retribution Dh 133. — 5. (fig.) a means of frightening, frightfulness, violence, teasing. In this meaning used as nt. as M I.372; tīṇi daṇḍāni pāpassa kammassa kiriyāya: kāyadaṇḍaŋ vacī°, mano°; in the same sense as m. at Nd² 293 (as explᵈ to Sn 35). — 6. a fine, a penalty, penance in general: daṇḍena nikkiṇāti to redeem w. a penalty J VI.576 (dhanaŋ datvā Com.); daṇḍaŋ dhāreti to inflict a fine Miln 171, 193; daṇḍaŋ paṇeti id. Dh 310 (cp. DhA III.482); DhA II.71; aṭṭha-kahāpaṇo daṇḍo a fine of 8 k. VvA 76. — adaṇḍa without a stick, i. e. without force or violence, usually in phrase adaṇḍena asatthena (see above 4): Vin II.196 (ad. as. nāgo danto mahesinā; thus of a Cakkavattin who rules the world peacefully: paṭhaviŋ ad. as. dhammena abhivijiya ajjhāvasati D I.89=A IV.89, 105, or dhammena-m-anusāsati Sn 1002=S I.236.
-**ābhighata** slaying w. cudgels PvA 58; -**āraha** (adj.) deserving punishment J V.442; VvA 23; -**ādāna** taking up a stick (weapon) (cp. above 4), combᵈ with satth' adāna M I.110, 113, 410; D III.92, 93, 289; A IV.400; Vism 326. -**kaṭhina** k. cloth stretched on a stick (for the purpose of measuring) Vin II.116; -**kathālikā** a large kettle with a handle Vin I.286; -**kamma** punishment by beating, penalty, penance, atonement J III.276, 527; V.89; Miln 8; °ŋ karoti to punish, to inflict a fine Vin I.75, 76, 84; II.262; -**koṭi** the tip of a branch or stick DhA I.60; -**dīpikā** a torch J VI.398; Vism 39; DhA I.220, 399; -**ppatta** liable to punishment Miln 46; -**paduma** N. of a plant (cp. Sk. daṇḍotphala=sahadevā, Halāyudha) J I.51; -**parāyana** supported by or leaning on a stick (of old people) M I.88; A I.138; Miln 282; -**parissāvana** a strainer with a handle Vin II.119; -**pahāra** a blow with a stick D I.144; -**pāṇin** carrying a staff, "staff in hand" M I.108; -**bali** (-ādi) fines & taxes, etc. DhA I.251; -**bhaya** fear of punishment A II.121 sq.=Nd² 470=Miln 196; -(m)**antara** among the sticks D I.166=A I.295=II.206=M I.77, 238, 307, 342=Pug 55; see note at *Dial.* I.228; -**yuddha** a club-fight D I.6; J III.541; -**lakkhaṇa** fortune-telling from sticks D I.9; -**vākarā** a net on a stick, as a snare, M I.153; -**veḷupesikā** a bamboo stick J IV.382; -**sikkā** a rope slung round the walking-staff Vin II.131; -**hattha** with a stick in his hand J I.59.

Daṇḍaka [Demin. of daṇḍa] 1. a (small) stick, a twig; a staff, a rod; a handle D I.7 (a walking stick carried for ornament: see DA I.89); J I.120 (sukkha° a dry twig); II.103; III.26; DhA III.171; Vism 353. — aḍḍha° a (birch) rod, used as a means of beating (tāḷeti) A I.47; II.122=M I.87=Nd² 604=Miln 197; ubhato° two handled (of a saw) M I.129=189; ratha° the flag-staff of a chariot Miln 27; veṇu° a jungle rope J III.204. — See also kudaṇḍaka a twig used for tying J III.204. — 2. the crossbar or bridge of a lute J II.252, 253.
-**dīpikā** a torch J I.31; -**madhu** "honey in a branch," a beehive DhA I.59.

Daṇḍaniya (adj.) [grd. formation from daṇḍa] liable to punishment Miln 186.

Datta¹ [pp. of dadāti] given (-° by; often in Np. as Brahmadatta, Deva-datta=Theo-dor. etc.) Sn 217 (para°) =SnA 272 (v. l. dinna).

Datta² (adj.-n.) [prob.=thaddha, with popular analogy to datta¹, see also dandha & cp. dattu] stupid; a silly fellow M I.383; J VI.192 (Com.: dandha lāḷaka).

Datti (f.) [from dadāti+ti] gift, donation, offering D I.166; M I.78, 342; A I.295; II.206; Pug 55.

Dattika (adj.) [der. fr. datta] given; J III.221 (kula°); IV.146 (id.); nt. a gift D I.103 (=dinnaka DA I.271).

Dattiya=dattika, given as a present J II.119 (kula°); V.281 (sakka°); VI.21 (id.): VvA 185 (mahārāja° by the King).

Dattu (adj. ?) [is it base of n. ag. dātar ? see datta²] stupid, in d°-pannatta a doctrine of fools D I.55=M I.515; J IV.338.

Dada (-°) (adj.-suff.) [Sk.° dad or °dada, cp °da & dadāti base 3] giving, to be given S I.33 (paññā°); Kh VIII.10 (kāma°); Pv II.9[1] (id. = dāyaka PvA 113); II.12[4] (phala° = dāyin PvA 157); VvA 171 (puriŋ°). — **duddada** hard to give S I.19 = IV.65 = J II.86 = VI.571.

Dadāti [Redupl. formation dā as in Lat. do, perf. de-di, Gr. δίδωμι; cp. Lat. dōs dowry, Gr. δώς; Ohg. dati; Lith. dů̄ti to give] to give, etc. I. *Forms*. The foll. bases form the Pāli verb-system: dā, dāy, dadā & di.—1. Bases dā & (reduced) da. — (a) dā°: fut. **dassati** J I.113, 279; III.83; A III.37; 1st sg. dassāmi J I.223; II.160; PvA 17, 35, etc. — dammi interpreted by Com. as fut. is in reality a contraction fr. dātuŋ ihāmi, used as a hortative or dubitative subjunctive (fr. dāhāmi, like kāhami I am willing to do fr. kātuŋ īhāmi) Sn p. 15 ("shall I give"); II.112; IV.10 (varaŋ te dammi); Pv I.10[3]; II.3[24] (kin t' āhaŋ dammi what can I give thee = dassāmi PvA 88). — pret. adā Sn 303; Pv II.2[8] (= adāsi PvA 81); Mhvs VII.14; 2nd sg. ado J IV.10 (= adāsi Com.): Miln 384; 1st. pl. adamha J II.71; Miln 10; 2nd pl. adattha J I.57 (mā ad.); Miln 10, & dattha J II.181; — aor. adāsi J I.150, 279; PvA 73, etc.; pl. adaŋsu Pv I.11[6]. — inf. dātuŋ J III.53; PvA 17, 48 (°kāma), etc. & **dātave** Sn 286. — grd. **dātabba** J III.52; PvA 7, 26, 88, etc. — (b) da°: pp. datta -ger. **datvā** J I.152, 290 (a°); PvA 70, 72, etc. & **datvāna** Pv I.11[3]; also as °dā (for °dāya or °dāna) in prep. cpds., like an-upādā, ādā, etc. Der. fr. 1. are Caus. dāpeti, pp. dāpita; n. ag. dātar; nt. dāna. See also suffix dā,° **datti**, **dattikā**, etc.; and pp. **atta** (= ā-d[a]ta). — 2. Bases dāy & (reduced) day, contracted into de. (a) dāy°: only in der. dāya, dāyaka, dāyin and in prep. cpds. ā-dāye (ger. of ādāti). — (b) de°: pres. ind. deti Sn 130; J II.111, 154; PvA 8; 1st sg. demi J I.228, 307; 2nd desi J I.279; PvA 39. 1st pl. dema J I.263; III.126; PvA 27, 75 (shall we give); 2nd detha J III.127; 3rd denti Sn 244. — imper. **dehi** Vin I.17; J I.223; IV.101; PvA 43, 73; 3rd sg. detu J I.263; II.104; 2nd pl. detha It 66 J III.126; PvA 29, 62, 76. — ppr. **dento** J I.265; PvA 3, 11 etc. — grd. **deyya** Mhvs VII.31. B'Sk. deya. — Other der. fr. base 2 are dayati & dayā (q. v.). — 3. Base dadā: pres. ind. dadāti S I.18; Sn p. 87; 1st. sg. dadāmi J I.207; Sn 421; 3rd. pl. dadanti J III.220; Dh 249. — imper. **dadāhi** Pv II.1[4]. — pot. **dadeyya** PvA 17; Miln 28 & **dade** Pv II.3[22]; Vv 62[5]; 1st. sg. dadeyyaŋ J I.254, 265; 2nd. sg. dadeyyāsi J III.276 Also contracted forms **dajjā** S I.18 (may he give); Dh 224; Pv I.4[1] (= dadeyya PvA 17); II.9[40]; 1st sg. dajjaŋ Vin I.232 (dajjâhaŋ = dajjaŋ ahaŋ). . Cp. I.10[9] (dajjâhaŋ); J IV.101 (= dammi Com.); Pv II.9[45]; 2nd. pl. dajjeyyātha Vin I.232; 3rd y. dajjeyya & 3rd. pl. dajjuŋ in cpd. anupa°. — ppr. **dadanto** Sn p. 87. gen. etc. dadato It. 89; Dh 242; Pv II.9[42]; & **dadaŋ** Sn 187, 487; Pv II.9[42]; Vv 67[6]. — ppr. med. dadamāna J I.228, II.154; PvA 129. — aor. **adadaŋ** Vv 34[11] (= adāsiŋ VvA 151); proh. 2nd. pl. mā dadittha DhA I.396; J III.171. - - ger. **daditvā** Pv II.8[9] (v. l. BB datvā): contr. into dajjā (should be read dajja) Pv II.9[67] (= datvā PvA 139). — Der. **dada** for °da. — 4. (Passive) base **di** (& dī): pp. dinna pres. **dīyati** S I.18; Th 2, 475; PvA 26, & **diyyati** VvA 75; cp. ādiyati; pret. diyittha DhA I.395; — ppr. **dīyamāna** PvA 8, 26, 49, 110, 133, etc. — Der. fr. 4 are Desid. dicchati, diti, etc. — II. *Meanings* 1. (trs.) with acc. to give, to present with: dānaŋ deti (w. dat. & abs.) to be liberal (towards), to be munificent, to make a present S I.18; It 89; Pv I.4[1]; II[3]; PvA 8, 27, etc. — (fig.) okāsaŋ to give opportunity, allow J I.265; ovādaŋ to give advice PvA 11; **jīvitaŋ** to spare one's life J II.154; paṭivacanaŋ to answer J I.279; **sādhukāraŋ** to applaud J I.223; paṭiññaŋ to promise PvA 76; — to offer, to allow: maggaŋ i. e. to make room Vin II.221; J II.4; maggaŋ dehi let me pass J IV.101; — to grant: varaŋ a wish J IV.10; Pv II.9[40]; — to give or deal out: daṇḍaŋ a thrashing J IV.382; pahāraŋ a blow S IV.62. — 2. *with ger.* to give out, to hand over: dārūni āharitvā aggiŋ katvā d. to provide with fire J II.102; sāṭake āharitvā to present w. clothes J I.265; dve koṭṭhāse vibhajitvā d. to deal out J I.226; kuṭikāyo kāretvā adaŋsu had huts built & gave them PvA 42. — 3. (abs.) *with inf.* to permit, to allow: khādituŋ J I.223; nikkhamituŋ J II.154; pavisituŋ J I.263, etc.

Daddabha [onomatop.] a heavy, indistinct noise, a thud J III.76 (of the falling of a large fruit), v. l. duddabhaya-sadda to be regarded as a Sk. gloss = dundubhya-śabda. See also dabhakka.

Daddabhāyati [Denom. fr. prec.] to make a heavy noise, to thud J III.77.

Daddara[1] [onomat. from the noise, cp. next & cakora, with note on gala] partridge J III.541.

Daddara[2] [cp. Sk. dardara] a cert. (grinding, crashing) noise A IV.171; J II.8; III.461; N. of a mountain, expl[d] as named after this noise J II.8; III.16, 461.

Daddaḷhati [Sk. jājvalyati, Intens. of **jval**, see jalati] to blaze, to shine brilliantly; only in pp. med. daddaḷhamāna resplendent, blazing forth S I.127 = J I.469; Vv 17[3]; 34[1]; Pv II.12[6]; III.3[5]; VvA 89 (ativiya vijjotamāna); PvA 157 (at. virocamāna), 189 (at. abhijalanto). — Spelling daddallamāna at J V.402; VI.118.

Daddu (nt.) [Sk. dadru f. & dardru a kind of leprosy, dadruṇa leprous (but given by Halāyudha in the meaning of ringworm, p. 234 Aufrecht); fr. ***der** in Sk. dṛṇāti to tear, chap, split (see dara & dala); cp. Lat. derbiosus; Ohg. zittaroh; Ags. teter] a kind of cutaneous eruption Miln 298; Vism 345.

-bandhana in d.-bandhanādi-bandhana at ThA 241 should be read daṇḍa°.

Daddula[1] a cert. kind of rice D I.166; M I.78, 343; A I.241, 295; II.206; Pug 55.

Daddula[2] (nt.) [Sk. dārdura ?] in nahāru° (v. l. dala & dadalla) both at M I.188 (kukkuṭapattena pi. n-daddulena pi aggiŋ gavesanti) & A IV.47 (kukkuṭapattaŋ vā n-daddulaŋ vā aggimhi pakkhittaŋ paṭilīyati) unexplained; perhaps a muscle.

Dadhi (nt.) [Sk. dadhi, redpl. formation fr. dhayati to suck. Cp. also dhenu cow, dhīta, etc.] sour milk, curds, junket Vin I.244 (in enum[n] of 5-fold cow-produce, cp. gorasa); D I.201 (id.); M I.316; A II.95; J II.102; IV.140; Miln 41, 48, 63; Dhs 646, 740, 875; Vism 264, 362.

-**ghaṭa** a milk bowl J II.102; -**maṇḍaka** whey S II.111; -**māla** "the milk sea," N. of an ocean J IV.140; -**vāraka** a pot of milk-curds J III.52.

Danta[1] [Sk. danta fr. acc. dantaŋ of dan, gen. datah = Lat. dentis. Cp. Av. dantan, Gr. ὀδόντα, Lat. dentem, Oir. dēt; Goth. tunþus, Ohg. zand, Ags. tōot (= tooth) & tusc (= tusk); orig. ppr. to ***ed** in atti to eat = "the biter." Cp. dāṭhā], a tooth, a tusk, fang, esp. an elephant's tusk; ivory Vin II.117 (nāga-d. a pin of ivory); Kh II. (as one of the taca-pañcaka, or 5 dermatic constituents of the body, viz. kesā, lomā nakhā d. taco, see detailed description at KhA 43 sq.); pankadanta rajassira "with sand between his teeth & dust on his head" (of a wayfarer) Sn 980; J IV.362, 371; M I.242; J I.61; II.153; Vism 251; VvA 104 (īsā° long tusks); PvA 90, 152 (fang); Sdhp 360.

-**ajina** ivory M II.71 (gloss: dhanadhaññaŋ); -**aṭṭhika** "teeth-bone," ivory of teeth i. e. the tooth as such Vism 21. -**āvaraṇa** the lip (lit. protector of teeth) J IV.188; VI.590; DhA I.387. -**ullahakaŋ** (M III.167) see ullahaka; -**kaṭṭha** a tooth-pick Vin I.46 = II.223; I.51, 61; II.138; A III.250; J I.232; II.25; VI.75; Miln 15; DhA II.184; VvA 63; -**kāra** an artisan in ivory,

ivory-worker D I.78; J I.320; Miln 331; Vism 336; -kūṭa tooth of a maimed bullock (?) (thus taking kūṭa as kūṭa⁴, and equivalent to kūṭadanta), in phrase asanivicakkaŋ danta-kūṭaŋ D III.44=47, which has also puzzled the translators (cp. *Dial.* III.40: "munching them all up together with that wheel-less thunderbolt of a jawbone," with note: "the sentence is not clear"). -pāḷi row of teeth Vism 251; -poṇa tooth-cleaner, always comb^d with mukh' odaka water for rinsing the teeth Vin III.51; IV.90, 233; J IV.69; Miln 15; SnA 272. The C. on Pārāj. II.4, 17, (Vin III.51) gives 2 kinds of dantapoṇa, viz. chinna & acchinna. -mūla the root of a tooth; the gums J V.172; -vakkalika a kind of ascetics (peeling the bark of trees with their teeth ?) DA I.271; -vaṇṇa ivory-coloured, ivory-white Vv 45¹⁰; -valaya an iv. bangle DhA I.226; -vikati a vessel of iv. D I.78; M II.18; J I.320; Vism 336. -vikhādana biting with teeth, i. e. chewing Dhs 646, 740, 875; -vidaŋsaka (either=vidassaka or to be read °ghaŋsaka) showing one's teeth (or chattering ?) A I.261 (of hasita, laughter); -sampatti splendour of teeth DhA I.390.

Danta² (adj.) [Sk. dānta] made of ivory, or iv.-coloured J VI.223 (yāna=dantamaya).
-kāsāva ivory-white & yellow Vin I.287; -valaya see danta¹.

Danta³ [Sk. dānta, pp. dāmyati to make, or to be tame, cp. Gr. δμητός, Lat. domitus. See dameti] tamed, controlled, restrained Vin II.196; S I.28, 65, 141 (nāgo va danto carati anejo); A I.6 (cittaŋ dantaŋ); It 123 (danto damayataŋ seṭṭho); Sn 370, 463, 513, 624; Dh 35, 142 (=catumagga-niyamena d. DhA III.83), 321 sq.=Nd² 475. — sudanta well-tamed, restrained Sn 23; Dh 159, 323.
-bhūmi a safe place (=Nibbāna), or the condition of one who is tamed S III.84; Nd² 475 (in continuation of Dh 323); DhA IV.6.

Dantaka a pin of tooth or ivory; makara° the tooth of a sword-fish Vin II.113, 117; IV.47. See details under makara.

Dandha (adj.) [Sk. ? Fausböll refers it to Sk. tandra; Trenckner (*Notes* 65) to dṛḍha; see also Müller, *P. Gr.* 22, & Lüders *Z.D.M.G.* 58, 700. A problematic connection is that with thaddha & datta² (q. v.)] slow; slothful, indocile; silly, stupid M I.453; S IV.190; Dh 116; J I.116, 143; II.447; V.158; VI.192 (+ laḷāka); Th 1, 293; Miln 59, 102, 251; DhA I.94, 251; III.4. Vism 105, 257 (with ref. to the liver).
-abhiññā sluggish intuition D III.106; A V.63; Dhs 176; Nett 7, 24, 50, 123 sq., cp. A II.149 sq.; Vism 85.

Dandhatā (f.) stupidity DhA I.250; as dandhattaŋ at D III.106.

Dandhanatā (f.), in a° absence of sluggishness Dhs 42, 43

Dandhāyanā (f.) clumsiness Miln 105.

Dandhāyitatta (nt.) [der. fr. dandheti] stupidity (=dandhatā) D I.249 (opp. vitthāyitatta); S II.54; Miln 105; DA I.252.

Dandheti [Denom. fr. dandha] to be slow, to tarry Th 1, 293 (opp. tāreti). — pp. dandhāyita see in der. °tta.

Dapeti Caus. fr. dā⁴ to clean, see pariyo°; pp. dāta see ava°.

Dappa [Sk. darpa, to dṛpyati] wantonness, arrogance J II.277; Miln 361, 414; Pgdp 50. Cp. ditta². — In def. of root gabb at Dhtm 289.

Dappita (adj.) arrogant, haughty J V.232, 301.

Dabba¹ (adj.-n.) [Sk. dravya, nt. to dravati (dru)] (a) fit for, able, worthy, good, S I.187=Th 1, 1218, cp. *Pss. of the Brethren*, 399, *n.* 4 (=Sk. bhavya, cp. Pāṇini V.3, 104 dravyaŋ ca bhavyaḥ). — (b) material, substance, property; something substantial, a worthy object Pgdp 14.
-jātika of good material, fit for, able M I.114; A I.254 (cp. Sk. pātrabhūta); Vism 196. -saŋhāra collecting something substantial PvA 114 (should prob. be read sambhāra). -sambhāra the collection of something substantial or worth collecting, ; a gift worth giving J IV.311; V.48; VI.427; DhA I.321; II.114.

Dabba² (adj.-n.) [Sk. dravya, of dru wood, see dāru] tree-like, wooden; a tree, shrub, wood J I.108 (d.-tiṇagaccha a jungle of wood & grass); V.46 (d.-gahana a thicket of shrubs & trees); Vism 353 (°tiṇa).

Dabbī (f.) [Sk. darvī=*dāru-ī made of wood, see dāru] a (wooden) spoon, a ladle; (met.) the hood of a snake (dabbimattā phaṇapuṭakā DhA IV.132). — Dh 64; gen. & instr, davyā J III.218; Miln 365. — In cpds. dabbi°.
-kaṇṇa the tip of the ladle DhA I.371; -gāha holding a spoon, viz. for the purposes of offering M II.157 (of a priest); Pv II.9⁵³ (=kaṭacchu-gāhika PvA 135); -mukha a kind of bird J VI.540 (=āṭa); -homa a spoon-oblation D I.9.

Dabbha [Sk. darbha to dṛbhati, to plait, interlace, etc. cp. Lith. darbas plaiting, crating] a bunch of kuśa grass (Poa Cynosuroides) D I.141; M I.344; A II.207.
-puppha "kuśa-flower," Ep. of a jackal J III.334.

Dabhakkaŋ (?) (indecl.)=daddabhaŋ; a certain noise (of a falling fruit) J III.77 (v. l. duddabha=daddabha).

Dama (adj.-n.) (& of a nt. damo the instr. damasā) [Ved. dama; Ags. tam=E. tame, Ohg. zam to *demā in dameti] taming, subduing; self-control, self-command, moderation D I.53 (dānena damena saŋyamena=It 15; expl. at DA I.160 as indriya-damena uposatha-kammena) III.147, 229; S I.4, 29, 168=Sn 463 (saccena danto damasā upeto); S IV.349; A I.151; II.152 sq.; M III.269 (+ upasama); Sn 189, 542 (°ppatta), 655; Dh 9, 25, 261; Nett 77; Miln 24 (sudanto uttame dame). duddama hard to tame or control Dh 159; PvA 280; Sdhp 367. — arindama taming the enemy (q. v.).

Damaka (adj.-n.) [=dama] 1. subduing, taming; converting; one who practises self-control M I.446 (assa°); III.2 (id.) J I.349 (kula° bhikkhu), one who teaches a clan self-mastery 505 (go°, assa°, hatthi°); Th 2, 422 (=kāruññāya paresaŋ cittassa damaka ThA 268). — 2. one who practises self-mortification by living on the remnants of offered food (Childers) Abhp 467.

Damatha [Sk. damatha] taming, subduing, mastery, restraint, control M I.235; D III.54 (+ samatha); Dh 35 (cittassa d.); PvA 265; Dpvs VI.36.

Damana (adj.-nt.) taming, subduing, mastery PvA 251 (arīnaŋ d°-sīla=arindama).

Damaya (adj.) [Sk. damya, see damma] to be tamed: duddamaya difficult to tame Th 1, 5 (better to be read damiya).

Damita [Sk. damāyita=danta³; cp. Gr. α-δάματος; Lat. domitus] subdued, tamed J V.36; PvA 265.

Dameti [Sk. damayati, caus. to dāmyati of *dam to bring into the house, to domesticate; Gr. δαμάω, δμητός; Lat. domare; Oir. dam (ox); Goth. tamjan=Ohg. zemman=Ags. temian=E. tame; to *demā of dama house, see dampati] to make tame, chastise, punish, master, conquer, convert Vin II.196 (daṇḍena); M II.102; Dh 80, 305 (attānaŋ); It 123 (ppr. [danto] damayataŋ seṭṭho [santo] samayataŋ isi); Miln 14, 386; PvA 54 (core d.=converted).

Dametar [n.-ag. to dameti = Sk. damayitṛ, cp. Sk. damitṛ = Gr. (παν)δαμάτωρ δμητήρ; Lat. domitor] one who tames or subdues, a trainer, in phrase adantānaŋ dametā " the tamer of the untamed " (of a Buddha) M II.102; Th 2, 135.

Dampati [Sk. dampati master of the house; dual: husband & wife; cp. also patir han, ***dam**, as in Gr. δῶ, δῶμα & δεσ- in δεσπότης = dampati, short base of ***dama** house = Ved. dama, Gr. δόμος, Lat. domus to ***demā** (as also in dameti to domesticate) to build, cp. Gr. δέμω & δέμας; Goth. timrjan; Ohg. zimbar; E. timber] master of the house, householder, see tudampati & cp. gahapati.

Damma (adj.) [Sk. damya, grd. of dāmyati see dameti & cp. damaya (damiya)] to be tamed or restrained; esp. with ref. to a young bullock M I.225 (balagāvā dammagāvā the bulls & the young steers); It 80; also of other animals: assadamma-sārathi a horse-trainer A II.112; & fig. of unconverted men likened to refractory bullocks in phrase purisa-damma-sārathi (Ep. of the Buddha) " the trainer of the human steer " D I.62 (misprint °dhamma°) = II.93 = III.5; M II.38; A III.112; Vv 17^{13} (nara-vara-d.-sārathi cp. VvA 86.

Dayati^1 = dayati (q. v.) to fly J IV.347 (+ uppatati); VI.145 (dayassu = uyyassu Com.).

Dayati^2 = [Ved. dayate of **day** to divide, share, cp. Gr. δαίομαι, δαίνυμι, δαίτη, etc. to **dā** (see dadāti, base 2), & with p. Gr. δαπάνη, Lat. daps (see Walde, *Lat. Wtb.* s. v.)] to have pity (c. loc.), to sympathize, to be kind J VI.445 (dayitabba), 495 (dayyāsi = dayaŋ kareyyāsi).

Dayā (f.) [Ved. dayā, to dayati^2] sympathy, compassion, kindness M I.78; Sn 117; J I.23; VI.495. Usually as anuddayā; freq. in cpd. dayāpanna showing kindness D I.4 (= dayaŋ metta-cittaŋ āpanno DA I.70); M I.286; A IV.249 sq.; Pug 57; VvA 23.

Dara [Sk. dara; see etym. connection under darī] fear, terror; sorrow, pain Vin II.156 = A I.138 (vineyya hadaye daraŋ); S II.101, 103; IV.186 sq.; Th 2, 32 (= cittakato kilesa patho ThA, 38); J IV.61; Vv 83^8 (= daratha VvA 327); Pv I.8^5 (= citta-daratha PvA 41). — sadara giving pain, fearful, painful M I.464; A II.11, 172; S I.101. Cp. ādara & purindada.

Daratha [Sk. daratha, der. fr. dara] anxiety, care, distress A II.238; M III.287 sq. (kāyikā & cetasikā d.); Sn 15 (darathajā: the Arahant has nought in him born of care C^y explains by pariḷāha fever); J I.61 (sabbakilesa-d.) PvA 230 (id.); DhA II.215; Miln 320; PvA 23, 41; VvA 327.

Darī (f.) [Sk. darī to dṛṇāti to cleave, split, tear, rend, caus. darayati ***der** = Gr. δέρω to skin, δέρμα, δορά skin); Lith. dirù (id.) Goth. ga-tairan = Ags. teran (tear) = Ohg. zeran (Ger. zerren). To this the variant (r : l) ***del** in dalati, daḷa, etc. See also daddara, daddu, dara, avadīyati, ādiṇṇa, uddīyati, purindada (= puraŋ-dara)] a cleavage, cleft; a hole, cave, cavern J I.18 (v. 106), 462 (musikā° mouse-hole); II.418 (= maṇiguhā); SnA 500 (= padara).

-**cara** a cave dweller (of a monkey) J V.70; -**mukha** entrance of a cave Vism 110. -**saya** a lair in a cleft Cp. III.7^1.

Dala (nt.) [Sk. dala, ***del** (var. of ***der**, see dara) in dalati (q. v.) orig. a piece chipped off = a chip, piece of wood, cp. daṇḍa, Mhg. zelge (branch); Oir delb (figure, form), deil (staff, rod)] a blade, leaf, petal (usually -°); akkhi-d. eyelid ThA 259; DA I.194; DhsA 378; uppala° Dhs 311; kamala° (lotus-petal) VvA 35, 38; muttā° (?) DA I.252; rattā-pavāḷa° J I.75.

Dalati [Sk. dalati, **del** to split off, tear; Gr. δαιδάλλω, Lat. dolare & delere. See dala & dara] to burst, split, break. — Caus. dāleti Sn 29 (dalayitvā = chinditvā SnA 40); Miln 398. — Pass. dīyati (Sk. dīryate) see uddīyati.

Dalidda & Daḷidda (adj.-n.) [Sk. daridra, to daridrāti, Intens. to drāti run (see dava), in meaning cp. addhika wayfarer = poor] vagrant, strolling, poor, needy, wretched; a vagabond, beggar — (l:) Vin II.159; S I.96 (opp. aḍḍha); A II.57, 203; III.351; IV.219; V.43; Pug 51; VvA 299 (l:) M II.73; S V.100, 384, 404; Vv20^1 (= duggata VvA 101); DA I.298; PvA 227; Sdhp 89, 528.

Daḷiddatā (f.) [Sk. daridratā] poverty VvA 63.

Daḷiddiya see dāḷiddiya.

Daḷha (adj.) [Sk. dṛḍha to dṛhyati to fasten, hold fast; ***dhergh**, cp. Lat. fortis (strong). Gr. ταρφύς (thick), Lith. diržas (strap). For further relations see Walde, *Lat. Wtb.* under fortis] firm, strong, solid; steady, fast; nt. adv. very much, hard, strongly — D I.245; S I.77; A II.33; Sn 321 (nāvā), 357, 701, 821 (°ŋ karoti to strengthen), 966 (id.); Dh 112; J II.3; IV.106; DhA IV.48; KhA 184; VvA 212 (= thira); PvA 94, 277. — daḷhaŋ (adv.) Dh 61, 313.

-**dhamma** strong in anything, skilled in some art, proficient S II.266 = A II.48 (of an archer); M I.82; J VI.77; Vv 63^1 acc. to Trenckner, *Notes* p. 60 (cp. also VvA 261) = dṛḍha-dhanva, from dhanu = having a strong bow; -**nikkama** of strong exertion Sn 68 (= Nd^2 294); -**parakkama** of strong effort, energetic M II.95; A II.250; Dh 23; Th 2, 160; -**pahāra** a violent blow J III.83; -**pākāra** (etc.) strongly fortified S IV.194; -**bhattin** firmly devoted to somebody DhsA 350.

Daḷhī° [f. of dṛḍha > daḷha in comp^n like dṛḍhī-bhūta, etc.; cp. daḍḍhi] in kāya-daḷhī-bahula strong in body, athletic Vin II.76, cp. Com. on p. 313; J III.310; IV.219. daḷhīkaraṇa steadiness, perseverance SnA 290 (+ ādhāraṇatā), 398 (id). In cpds. also daḷhi° viz. -**kamma** making firm; strengthening Vin I.290; J V.254; Pug 18, 22; Vism 112.

Dava^1 [Sk. dava, to dunoti (q. v.); cp. Gr. δαΐς fire-brand] fire, heat J III.260. — See also dāva & dāya.

-**ḍāha** (= Sk. davāgni) conflagration of a forest, a jungle-fire Vin II.138; M I.306; J I.641; Cp. III.9^3; Miln 189; Vism 36.

Dava^2 [Sk. drava to dravati to run, flow, etc. ***dreu** besides ***drā** (see dalidda) & ***dram** (= Gr. δρόμος); cp. abhiddavati, also dabba = dravyaŋ] running, course, flight; quickness, sporting, exercise, play Vin II.13; M I.273; III.2; A I.114; II.40, 145; IV.167; Pug 21, 25. — davā (abl.) in sport, in fun Vin II.101; davāya (dat.) id. Nd^2 540; Miln 367; Dhs 1347, cp. DhsA 402. — davaŋ karoti to sport, to play J II.359, 363.

-**atthāya** in joke, for fun Vin II.113; -**kamyatā** fondness for joking, Vin IV.11, 354; M I.565.

Dasa^1 [Sk. daśa = Av. dasa, Gr. δέκα, Lat. decem, Goth. taíhun, Oir. deich, Ags. tīen, Ohg. zehan fr. ***dekm̥**, a cpd. of dv + km̥ = " two hands "] the number ten; gen. dasannaŋ (Dh° 137); instr. dasahi (Kh III.) & dasabhi (Vin I.38). In cpds. (-°) also as ḷasa (soḷasa 16) & rasa (terasa 13; pannar° 15; aṭṭhār° 18).

Metaphorical meaning. (A) In the first place 10 is used for measurement (more recent & comprehensive than its base 5); it is the no of a set or comprehensive unity, not in a vague (like 3 or 5), but in a definite sense. (B) There inheres in it the idea of a fixed measure, with which that of an authoritative, solemn & auspicious importance is coupled. This applies to the unit as well as its decimal comb^{ns} (100, 1000). Ethically it denotes a circle, to fulfil all of which constitutes a high achievement or power.

Application (A) (based on natural phenomena): dasa disā (10 points of the compass; see disā): Sn 719, 1122; PvA 71, etc.; d. lokadhātuyo Pv II.9[61] (=10×1000; PvA 138); d. māse (10 months as time of gestation) kucchiyā pariharitvā J I.52; PvA 43, 82. — (B) (fig.) 1. *a set*: (a) *personal* (cp. 10 people would have saved Sodom: Gen. 18, 32; the 10 virgins (2×5) Matt. 25, 1): divase divase dasa dasa putte vijāyitvā (giving birth to 10 sons day by day) Pv I.6. — (b) *impersonal*: 10 commandments (dasa sikkhāpadāni Vin I.83), cp. Exod. 34, 28; 10 attributes of perfection of a Tathāgata or an Arahant: Tathāgata-balāni; with ref. to the Buddha see Vin. I.38 & cp. *Vin Texts* I.141 sq.; dasah' angehi samannāgato arahā ti vuccati (in memorizing of No. 10) Kh III. dasahi asaddhammehi sam° kāko J III.127; — 10 heavenly attributes (ṭhānāni): āyu etc. D III.146; S V.275; PvA 9, opp. 10 afflictions as punishment (cp. 10 plagues Exod. 7-11): dasannaŋ aññataraŋ ṭhānaŋ nigacchati Dh 137 (=das. dukkha-kāraṇānaŋ, enum[d] v. 138, 139) "afflicted with one of the 10 plagues"; cp. DhA III.70. — 10 good gifts to the bhikkhu (see deyyadhamma) Nd[2] 523; PvA 7; 10 rules for the king: PvA 161; — dividing the Empire into 10 parts: PvA 111, etc. vassa-dasa a decade: das' ev' imā vassa-dasā J IV.396 (enum[d] under vassa); dasa-rāja-dhammā J II.367; das' akkosa-vatthūni DhA I.212.— See on similar sets A V.1-310; D III.266-271. — 2. a larger unity, *a crowd*, a vast number (of time & space): (a) *personal*, often meaning "all" (cp. 10 sons of Haman were slain Esth. 9, 10; 10 lepers cleansed at one time Luke 17, 12): dasa bhātaro J I.307; dasa bhātikā PvA 111; dasa-kaññā-sahassa-parivārā PvA 210 etc. — (b) *impersonal* (cp. 10×10=many times, *S.B.E.* 43, 3): dasa-yojanika consisting of a good many miles DhA III.291. dasavassasahassāni dibbāni vatthāni paridahanto ("for ever and aye") PvA 76, etc.

-kkhattuŋ [Sk. °kṛtvah] ten times DhA I.388; **-pada** (nt.) a draught-board (with 10 squares on each side); a pre-Buddhistic game, played with men and dice, on such a board D I.6; Vin II.10=III.180 (°e kīḷanti); DA I.85. **-bala**, [Sk.-daśabala] endowed with 10 (supernormal) powers, Ep. of the Buddhas, esp. of Kassapa Buddha Vin I.38=J I.84; S II.27; Vism 193, 391; DhA I.14; VvA 148, 206, etc. **-vidha** tenfold DhA I.398. **-sata** ten times a hundred Vin I.38 (°parivāro); Sn 179 (yakkhā); DhsA 198 (°nayano). **-sahassa** ten times a thousand (freq.); °ī in dasa-sahassi-lokadhātu Vin I.12 (see lokadhātu).

Dasa[2] (-°) [Sk.-dṛśa; cp. dassa] seeing, to be seen, to be perceived or understood D I.18 (aññadatthu° sure-seeing, all-perceiving=sabbaŋ passāmī ti attho DA I.111); Sn 653 (paṭiccasamuppāda°), 733 (sammad°); J I.506 (yugamatta°; v. l. dassa). —duddasa difficult to be seen or understood D I.12 (dhammā gambhīrā d.; see gambhīra); M I.167, 487; Sn 938; Dh 252; also as sududdasa Dh 36.

Dasaka (nt.) 1. a decad, decade, a decennial J IV.397; DhsA 316. khiḍḍā° the decad of play Vism 619; cakkhu° etc. sense-decads Vism. 553; *Comp.* 164, 250; kāya°, Vism. 588.

Dasana [Sk. daśana to ḍasati] a tooth Dāvs V.3 (d.-dhātu, the tooth relic of the Buddha).

Dasā (f.) & **dasa** (nt.) [Sk. daśā] unwoven thread of a web of cloth, fringe, edge or border of a garment D I.7 (digha° long-fringed, of vatthāni); J V.187; DhA I.180; IV.106 (dasāni). —**sadasa** (nt.) a kind of seat, a rug (lit. with a fringe) Vin IV.171 (=nisīdana); opp. **adasaka** (adj.) without a fringe or border Vin II.301=307 (nisīdana). **-anta** edge of the border of a garment J I.467; DhA I.180 sq., 391.

Dasika[1] (adj.) (-°) [Sk. dṛśika, cp. dassin] to be seen, to behold, being of appearance, only in dud° or frightful app., fierce, ugly S I .94 & id. p. (q. v. under okoṭimaka); J I.504 (kodha, anger); PvA 24, 90 (of Petas). — *Note*. The spelling is sometimes °dassika: A II.85; Pug 51; PvA 90.

Dasika[2] (adj.) [fr. dasā] belonging to a fringe, in dasika -sutta an unwoven or loose thread Vin III.241; DhA IV.206 (°mattam pi not even a thread, i. e. nothing at all, cp. Lat. nihīlum=ne-fīlum not a thread=nothing). See also dasaka under dasā.

Dassa (-°) [Sk. -darśa; cp. dasa[2]] to see or to be seen, perceiving, perceived Sn 1134 (appa° of small sight, not seeing far, knowing little=paritta-dassa thoka-dassa Nd[2] 69). Cp. akkha° a judge Miln 114. -su° easily perceived (opp. duddasa) Dh 252.

***Dassati**[1] [Sk. *darś in dadarśa pref. to dṛś; caus. darśayati. Cp. Gr. δέρκομαι to see; Oir. derc eye; Ags. torht; Goth. ga-tarhjan to make conspicuous. The regular Pāli Pres. is dakkhiti (younger dakkhati), a new formation from the aor. addakkhi=Sk. adrākṣīt. The Sk. Fut. draksyati would correspond formally to dakkhati, but the older dakkhiti points toward derivation from addakkhi. This new Pres. takes the function of the Fut.; whereas the Caus. dasseti implies a hypothetical Pres. *dassati. On dakkhati, etc. see also Kuhn, *Beitr.* p. 116; Trenckner, *Notes* pp. 57, 61; Pischel, *Prk. Gr.* § 554] to see, to perceive.

1. (pres.) base dakkh [Sk. drakṣ]: pres. (a) dakkhati Nd[2] 428 (=passati), 1st dakkhāmi ibid. (=passāmi), 2nd dakkhasi S I.116; Pv II.1[13] (v. l. BB adakkhi); imper. dakkha Nd[2] 428 (=passa). — (b) dakkhiti Sn 909 (v. l. BB dakkhati), 3rd pl. dakkhinti Vin I.16≈Sn p. 15 (v. l. BB dakkhanti); D I.46. — aor. addakkhi (Sk. adrakṣīt) Vin II.195; S I.117; Sn 208 (=addasa SnA 257), 841, 1131; It 47; J III.189; & dakkhi It 47; 1st sg. addakkhiŋ Sn 938. Spelling also adakkhi (v. l. BB at Pv II.1[3]) & adakkhiŋ (Nd[2] 423). — inf. dakkhituŋ Vin I.179. — Caus. p.p. dakkhāpita (shown, exhibited) Miln 119. — Der. dakkhin (q. v.).

2. (pret.) base dass (Sk. darś & draṣ): aor. (a) addasa (Sk. adarśat) Sn 358, 679, 1016; J I.222; V.2; Pv II.3[23] (mā addasa=addakkhiŋ PvA 88); DhA I.26; PvA 73. & (older, cp. agamā) addasā Vin II.192, 195; D I.112; II.16; Sn 409 (v. l. BB addasa), 910 (id.); Miln 24, 1st sg. addasaŋ S I.101; Nd[2] 423 & addasaŋ Sn 837 (=adakkhiŋ Nd[1] 185), 1st pl. addasāma Sn 31, 178, 459. 3rd pl. (mā) addasuŋ Pv II.7[6] (=mā passiŋsu PvA 102). — (b) addasāsi, 1st sg. addasāsiŋ Sn 937, 1145; Vv 35[52] (v. l. addasāmi), 3rd pl. addasāsuŋ Vin II.195; D II.16; M I.153. — (c) shortened forms of aor. are: adda Th 1, 986; addā J VI.125, 126. — inf. daṭṭhuŋ Sn 685 (daṭṭhukāma); J I.290; Pv IV.1[3] (=passituŋ PvA 219); PvA 48, 79; VvA 75. — ger. daṭṭhu (=Sk. dṛṣṭvā) Sn 424 (in phrase nekkhammaŋ daṭṭhu khemato)=1098; 681. Expl. at Nd[2] 292 with expl. of disvā=passitvā, etc. — grd. daṭṭhabba (to be regarded as) D II.154; PvA 8, 9, 10, etc., Vism 464; & dassanīya (see sep.). Also in Caus. (see below) & in daṭṭhar (q. v.).

3. (med.-pass.) base diss (Sk. dṛś): pres. pass. dissati (to be seen, to appear) Vin I.16; Sn 194, 441, 688 (dissare), 956; J I.138; Dh 304; Pv I.8[4]; PvA 61 (dissasi you look, intrs.); ppr. dissamāna (visible) PvA 71, 6 (°rūpa), 162 (id.); VvA 78 (°kāya); Mhvs. VII.35, & der. dissamānatta (nt.) (visibility) PvA 103. — ger. disvā Sn 48, 409, 687 sq. It 76; PvA 67, 68, etc., & disvāna Vin I.15; II.195; Sn 299, 415, 1017; Pv II.8[7], etc., also a ger. form diṭṭhā, q. v. under adiṭṭhā. — pp. diṭṭha (q. v.).

4. *Caus.* (of base 2) dasseti (Sk. darśayati), aor. dassesi & (exceptional) dassayi, only in dassayi tumaŋ showed himself at Pv III.2[4] (=attānaŋ uddisayi PvA 181) & III.2[16] (=attānaŋ dassayi dassesi pākaṭo ahosi PvA 185). 3rd pl. dassesuŋ; ger. dassetvā; inf. dassetuŋ to point out, exhibit, explain, intimate Dh 83; J I.84, 200, 263, 266; II.128, 159; III.53, 82; PvA 4, 8,

16 (ovādaŋ d. give advice), 24, 45, 73 etc. — to point to (acc.) PvA 151 (sunakhaŋ), 257 (dārakaŋ). — to make manifest, to make appear, to show or prove oneself; also intr. to appear J II.154 (dubbalo viya hutvā attānaŋ dassesi: appeared weak); VI.116; Pv III.2[3] (=sammukhībhāvaŋ gacchanti PvA 181); PvA 13 (mitto viya attānaŋ dassetvā: acting like a friend), Miln 271. Esp. in phrase attānaŋ dasseti to come into appearance (of Petas): PvA 32, 47, 68, 79, etc. (cp. above dassayi). — pp. dassita.

Dassati[2] fut. of dadāti, q. v.

Dassana (nt.) [Sk. darśana, see dassati[1]] — 1. *Lit.* seeing, looking; noticing; sight of, appearance, look. Often equivalent to an infinitive "to see," esp. as dat. dassanāya in order to see, for the purpose of seeing (cp. dassana-kāma = daṭṭhu-kāma): [Bhagavantaŋ] dassanāya M II.23, 46; A I.121; III.381; Sn 325. — (a) (nt.) "sight" D II.157 (visūka°, looking on at spectacles); A III.202 (+savana hearing); IV.25 sq. (bhikkhu°); Sn 207 (muni°, may be taken as 2, cp. SnA 256), 266 (=pekkhaṇa KhA 148); Dh 206 (ariyānaŋ d., cp. ariyānaŋ dassāvin), 210 (appiyānaŋ), 274; Vv 34[2]; VvA 138 (sippa° exhibition of art, competition).— (b) adj. as (-°) "of appearance" (cp. °dasa) Sn 548 (cāru° lovely to behold); PvA 24 (bhayānaka° fearful to look at), 68 (bībhaccha°). — 2. *Appld.* (power of) perception, faculty of apperception, insight, view, theory; esp. (a) in combn ñāṇa-dassana either "knowing & seeing," or perhaps "the insight arising from knowledge," perfect knowledge, realization of the truth, wisdom (cp. ñāṇa): S I.52; II.30; V.28, 422; M I.195 sq., 241, 482 (Gotamo sabbaññū sabba-dassāvī aparisesaŋ ñ-d °ŋ paṭijānāti; id. II.31); D III.134; A I.220; II.220; IV.302 sq.; cp. ñ-d-paṭilābha A I.43; II.44 sq.; III.323; ñ-d-visuddhi M I.147 sq. Also with further determination as adhideva-ñ-d° A IV.428; alam-ariya° S III.48; IV.300; V.126 sq.; M I.68, 71, 81, 207, 246, 440 sq., A I.9; III.64, 430; V.88; parisuddha A III.125; maggâmagga° A V.47; yathâbhūta° A III.19, 200; IV.99, 336; V.2 sq., 311 sq.; vimutti° S I.139; V.67; A III.12, 81, 134; IV.99, 336; V.130; It 107, 108; Miln 338. See also vimutti. — (b) *in other contexts*: ariyasaccāna-dassana Sn 267; ujubhūta° S V.384, 404; dhamma° (the right doctrine) S V.204, 344, 404; A III.263; pāpa° (a sinful view) Pv IV.3[88]; viparīta° A III.114; IV.226; V.284 sq. (and a°), 293 sq. sammā° (right view) S III.189; A III.138; IV.290; V.199; sabbalokena d. S IV.127; sahetu d. S V.126 sq.; suvisuddha d. S IV.191. — S III.28, 49; M II.46; III.157; Sn 989 (wisdom: Jinānaŋ eta d. corresponding with ñāṇa in preceding line); Dhs 584, 1002 (insight: cp. *Dhs. trsl.* p. 256). — (adj.) perceiving or having a view (cp. dasseti) S I.181 (visuddha°); Th 1, 422. — (c) *as nt.* from the Caus. dasseti: pointing out, showing; implication, definition, statement (in Com. style) PvA 72; often as °ākāra-dassana: PvA 26 (dātabba°), 27 (thomana°), 35 (kata°) & in dassanatthaŋ in order to point out, meaning by this, etc. PvA 9, 68. — 3. adassana not seeing S I.168 = Sn 459; invisibility J IV.496 (°ŋ vajjati to become invisible); wrong theory or view A V.145 sq.; Sn 206; Pug 21.

-anuttariya (nt.) the pre-eminence or importance of (right or perfect) insight; as one of the 3 anuttariyāni, viz. d°, paṭipadā°, vimutta° at D III.219, 250, 281; A III.284, 325; -kāma (adj.) desirous of seeing A I.150; IV.115; Miln 23; -bhūmi the level or plane of insight Nett 8, 14, 50; -sampanna endowed with right insight S II.43 sq., 58.

Dassanīya (adj.) [Sk. darśanīya; grd. formation of dassana, also as dassaneyya], fair to behold, beautiful, good-looking (=dassituŋ yutta DA I.141), often in formula abhirūpa d. pāsādika paramāya vaṇṇapokkharatāya samannāgata to express matchless physical beauty: D I.114; S II.279; PvA 46 etc. Also with abhirūpa & pāsādika alone of anything fair & beautiful: D I.47. — Vin IV.18; S I.95; J III.394; Pug 52, 66; DA I.281; PvA 44 (=subha), 51 (=rucira). — Comparative dassanīyatara S I.237; Sdhp 325; DhA I.119.

Dassaneyya (adj.) = dassanīya J V.203 (bhusa°).

Dassāvitā (f.) [abstr. to dassāvin] seeing, sight (-°) Miln 140 (guṇavisesa°).

Dassāvin (adj.-n.) [Sk. *darśavant] full of insight, seeing, perceiving, taking notice of. In combn with °ñū (knowing) it plays the part of an additional emphasis to the 1st term = knowing & seeing i. e. having complete or highest knowledge of, gifted with "clear" sight or intuition (see jānāti passati & cp. ñāṇa-dassana). — (a) As adj. -°: seeing, being aware of, realizing; anicca° S III.1; ādīnava° S II.194; IV.332; M I.173; A V.181 sq.; pariyanta° A V.50 sq.; bhaya° S V.187; It 96; esp. in phrase anumattesu vajjesu bhaya° D I.63 = It 118 (cp. bhaya-dassin); lokavajjabhaya° S I.138; sabba° (+sabbaññū) M I.482 (samaṇo Gotamo s° s°); II.31; Miln 74 (Buddho s° s°); cp. M Vastu III.51 sarvadarśāvin; sāra° Vin II.139. — (b) (n.) one who sees or takes notice of, in phrase ariyānaŋ dassāvī (+sappurisānaŋ dassāvī & kovido) M I.8; S III.4; opp. adassāvī one who disregards the Noble Ones S III.3, 113; M III.17; Dhs 1003 (cp. DhsA 350).

Dassika (-°): see dasika[1].

Dassita[1] [Sk. darśita, pp. of dasseti[1]] shown, exhibited, performed Vin IV.365; J I.330. Cp. san°.

Dassita[2] at J VI.579 accord. to Kern (*Toev.* p. 114) = Sk. daŋśita mailed, armed.

Dassin (-°) (adj.) [Sk. °darśin] seeing, finding, realizing, perceiving. Only in cpds., like attha° Sn 385; ananta° S I.143; ādīnava° Sdhp 409; ekanga° Ud 69; jātikkhaya° Sn 209; It 40; ñāṇa° Sn 478 (=sacchikatasabbaññuta-ñāṇa SnA 411; cp. dassāvin); tīra° S III.164 sq.; A III.368, cp. tīra-dakkhin; dīgha° (=sabbadassāvin) PvA 196; bhaya° Dh 31 (°dassivā = dassī vā?), 317; It 40; DA I.181 (=bhaya dassāvin); viveka° Sn 474, 851.

Dassimant see attha°.

Dassu [Sk. dasyu, cp. dāsa] enemy, foe; robber, in **dassukhīla** robber-plague D I.135, 136 (=corakhīla DA I.296).

Dassetar [Sk. darśayitṛ, n. agent to dasseti] one who shows or points out, a guide, instructor, teacher A I.62, 132 = It 110.

Dasseti Caus. of dassati[1] (q. v.).

Dasso n. pl. of dāsī.

Daha [Sk. draha, through metathesis fr. hrada, **hlād**, see hilādate] a lake D I.45 (udaka°); J I.50; II.104; V.412; Miln 259; PvA 152; Dpvs I.44.

Dahati[1] (dahate) [Sk. dadhāti to put down, set up; ***dhe** = Gr. τίθημι, Lat. facio, Ohg. tuon, Ags. dōn = E. to do. See also **dhātu**] to put, place; take for (acc. or abl.), assume, claim, consider D I.92 (okkākaŋ pitāmahaŋ = ṭhapeti DA I.258); S III.113 (mittato daheyya); A IV.239 (cittaŋ d. fix the mind on); Sn 825 (bālaŋ dahanti mithu aññamaññaŋ = passanti dakkhanti, etc. Nd[1] 163). Pass **dhīyati** (q. v.); grd. **dheyya** (q. v.). — *Note.* dahati is more frequent in combn with prefixes & compositions like ā°, upa°, pari°, sad°, san°, samā°, etc.

Dahati[2] = ḍahati to burn; as dahate Pv II.9[8] (=dahati vināseti PvA 116).

Dahana [Sk. dahana, to dahati, orig. "the burner"] fire Vism 338 (°kicca); ThA 256; Dāvs v.6; Sdhp 20.

Dahara (adj.) [Sk. dahara & dahra for dabhra to dabhnoti to be or make short or deficient, to deceive] small, little, delicate, young; a young boy, youth, lad D I.80, 115; S I.131; II.279 (daharo ce pi paññavā); M I.82; II.19, 66; A v.300; Sn 216, 420 (yuvā+), 578 (d. ca mahantā ye bālā ye ca paṇḍitā sabbe maccuvasaŋ yanti); J I.88 (daharadahare dārake ca dārikāyo), 291 (°itthī a young wife); II.160, 353; III.393; Dh 382; Pv IV.1[60] (yuvā); DhA I.397 (sāmaṇera); DA I.197 (bhikkhū), 223 (=taruṇa), 284 (id.); PvA 148; VvA 76; ThA 239, 251. Opposed to mahallaka J IV.482; to vuḍḍha Vism 100. — f. daharā Vv 31[6] (young wife) (+yuvā VvA 129) & daharī J IV.35; v.521; Miln 48 (dārikā).

Daharaka = dahara, young Miln 310. — f. °ikā a young girl Th 2, 464, 483.

Dāṭhā (f.) [Sk. daŋṣṭrā to ḍasati (q. v.), cp. also daṭṭha] a large tooth, fang, tusk; as adj. (-°) having tusks or fangs D II.18 (susukkha°); J I.505 (uddhaṭa-dāṭho viya sappo); IV.245 (nikkhanta°); DhA I.215; PvA 152 (kaṭhina°); Sdhp 286.
-āvudha [Sk. daŋṣṭrāyudha] using a tusk as his weapon J v.172; -danta a canine tooth KhA 44; -balin one whose strength lies in his teeth (of a lion) Sn 72.

Dāṭhikā (f.) [Sk. *dāḍhikā = Prk. for daŋṣṭrikā] beard, whiskers Vin II.134 (na d. ṭhapetabbā, of the bhikkhus); J I.305; v.42 (tamba°), 217 (mahā° having great whiskers); DA I.263 (parūḷha-massu° with beard & whiskers grown long).

Dāṭhin (adj.) [cp. Sk. daŋṣṭrin] having tusks J II.245; IV.348; Th I, p. I; Sdhp 286.

Dātar [Sk. dātṛ, n. ag. of dadāti to give; cp. Gr. δώτωρ & δοτήρ] a giver, a generous person Pgdp 50. — adātā one who does not give, a miser Pv II.8[2]; otherwise as na dātā (hoti) A II.203; It 65.

Dātta (nt.) [Sk. dātra, to dā, Sk. dāti, dyati to cut, divide, deal out; cp. Gr. δατέομαι, δαίομαι & see dāna, dāpeti, dāyati] sickle, scythe Miln 33.

Dāna (nt.) [Ved. dāna, dā as in dadāti to give & in dāti, dyāti to deal out, thus: distribution (scil. of gifts); cp. Gr. δάνος (present), Lat. damnum (E. damages); Gr. δῶρον, Lat. donum; also Ags. tīd (=E. tide, portion, i. e. of time), & tīma (=E. time). See further dadāti, dayati, dātta, dāpeti. Defⁿ at Vism 60: dānaŋ vuccati avakhaṇḍanaŋ] (a) giving, dealing out, gift; almsgiving, liberality, munificence; esp. a charitable gift to a bhikkhu or to the community of bhikkhus, the Sangha (cp. deyyadhamma & yañña). As such it constitutes a meritorious act (puññaŋ) and heads the list of these, as enumerated in order, dānamaya puññaŋ, sīlamaya p., bhāvanāmaya p. viz. acts of merit consisting of munificence, good character & meditation (D III.218 e. g.; cp. cāga, puñña, sīla). Thus in formula dānādini puññāni katvā J I.168; PvA 66, 105; cp. cpds. under °maya. — (b) Special merit & importance is attached to the mahādāna the great gift, i. e. the great offering (of gifts to the Sangha), in character the buddhistic equivalent of the brahmanic mahāyajña the chief sacrifice. On 16 Mahādānas see Wilson *Hindu Caste* 413; on 4 Beal. *Chinese Texts* 88. — A IV.246; J I.50, 74; v.383 (devasikaŋ chasatasahassa-pariccāgaŋ karonto mahādānaŋ pavattesi "he gave the great largesse, spending daily 600,000 pieces"); PvA 19, 22, 75, 127, etc. — (c) Constituents, qualities & characteristics of a dāna: 8 objects suitable for gifts form a standard set (also enumᵈ as 10), viz. anna pāna vattha yāna mālā gandha-vilepana seyyāvasātha padīpeyya (bread, water, clothes, vehicle, garlands, scented ointment, conveniences for lying down & dwelling, lighting facility) A IV.239; cp. Pv II.4[9] & see °vatthu & deyyadhamma. *Eight* ways of giving alms at D III.258 = A IV.236, *five* ways, called sappurisa-dāna (& asapp°) at A III.171 sq.; *eight* sapp° at A IV.243. *Five* manners of almsgiving metaphorically for sīlas 1-5 at A IV.246 = DA I.306. *Five* characteristics of a beneficial gift at A III.172, viz. saddhāya dānaŋ deti, sakkaccaŋ d.d., kālena (cp. kāladāna A III.41), anuggahitacitto, attānañ ca parañ ca anupahacca d.d. — (d) Various passages showing practice & value of dāna: Vin I.236; D I.53 (+dama & saŋyama; cp. It 15; PvA 276); II.356 sq. (sakkaccaŋ & a°); A IV.392 sq. (id.); D III.147 sq., 190 sq., 232; S I.98 (dānaŋ dātabbaŋ yattha cittaŋ pasīdati); A I.91 = It 98 (āmisa° and dhamma°, material & spiritual gifts); A I.161; III.41 (dāne-ānisaŋsā); IV.60, 237 sq. (mahapphala), 392 sq. (°ssa vipāka); v.269 (petānaŋ upakappati); J I.8 (aggaḷa°); II.112 (dinna°), III.52 (id.); Sn 263, 713 (appaŋ dānaŋ samaṇabrāhmaṇānaŋ) PvA 54 (āgantuka° gift for the newcomer); Sdhp 211-213. — adāna withholding a gift, neglect of liberality, stinginess Pv II.9[45]; Miln 279; PvA 25; cp. °sīla under cpds.: atidāna excessive almsgiving Pv II.9[45] (cp. PvA 129); Miln 277.
-agga [Sk. dānāgara, cp. bhattagga, salākagga; see Trenckner, *Notes* p. 56] a house where alms or donations are given, a store-house of gifts, fig. a source or giver of gifts, a horn of plenty J VI.487; DhA I.152, 189; Miln 2; PvA 121, 124, 127, 141. A possible connection w. agga = āgra is suggested by combⁿ dānāni mahādānāni aggaññāni A IV.246; -ādhikāra supervision or charge of alms-distributing PvA 124 (cp. Pv II.9[27]); -ānisaŋsa praise of generosity PvA 9; cp. A III.41; -upakaraṇa means or materials for a gift PvA 105; -upapatti (read uppatti at D III.258) an object suitable for gifts, of which 8 or 10 are mentioned (see above c) A IV.239 = D III.258; -kathā talk or conversation about (the merit & demerit of) almsgiving, one of the anupubbi-kathā Vin I.15, 18; -dhamma the duty or meritorious act of bestowing gifts of mercy (cp. deyyadhamma) PvA 9; -pati "lord of alms," master in liberality, a liberal donor (def. by Bdhgh as: yaŋ dānaŋ deti tassa pati hutvā deti na dāso na sahāyo DA I.298) D I.137 (+saddho & dāyako, as one of the qualifications of a good king); A III.39; IV.79 sq. (+saddho); Sn 487; Pv I.11[4] (+amaccharin); J I.199; Miln 279 sq.; Sdhp 275, 303; -puñña the religious merit of almsgiving or liberality (see above a) PvA 73; -phala the fruit of munificence (as accruing to the donor) A III.39; IV.79; Pv II.8[3] (°ŋ hoti paramhi loke: is rewarded in the life to come, cp. It 19); PvA 8 (cp. Pv I.1); -maya consisting in giving alms or being liberal (see above a) D III.218 (puññakiriya-vatthu); Vbh 135 (kusala-cetanā), 325 (pañña); PvA 8 (puñña), 60 (id.), 9 (kusala-kamma), 51, etc.; -vaṭṭa alms J VI.333; -vatthu that which constitutes a meritorious gift; almsgiving, beneficence, offering, donation D III.258 = A IV.236; PvA 20 (=annapānādika dasavidha dātabbavatthu 7); -veyyāvaṭika services rendered at the distribution of gifts DhA III.19; -saŋvibhāga liberal spending of alms D III.145, 169; A I.150, 226; III.53, 313; v.331; It 19; Vism 306; freq. with °*rata* fond of giving alms S v.351, 392; A IV.6 (vigatamalamaccherena cetasā), 266 (id.); -salā a hall, built for the distribution of alms & donations to the bhikkhus & wanderers J I.231, 262; IV.402 (six); v.383 (id.); -sīla liberal disposition PvA 89; usually as adāna-sīla (adj.) of miserly character, neglecting the duty of giving alms Sn 244; Pv II.8[3] (°ā na saddahanti dānaphalaŋ hoti paramhi loke); PvA 45 (=adāyaka), 59 (+maccharin), 68 (id.).

Dānava [Sk. dānava] a kind of Asuras or Titans, the offspring of Danu J III.527; v.89; Miln 153; Dpvs XVII.98.

Dāni (adv.) [shortened form for idāni, q. v.] now, Vin I.180; II.154; S I.200, 202; II.123; IV.202; J II.246; Miln 11, etc.

Dāpana: see vo°.

Dāpita [Sk. dāpayita pp. of dāpeti[1]] given, sent PvA 6; Mhvs VII.26.

Dāpeti[1] [Sk. dāpayati, **dap** fr. **dā** (see dadāti & dayati) = deal out, spend, etc., cp. Gr. δάπτω, δαπάνη (expenditure), δεῖπνον (meal); Lat. daps (id.), damnum (expense fr. *dapnom). See also dātta & dāna] to induce somebody to give, to order to be given, to deal out, send, grant, dedicate J VI.485; PvA 46; aor. dāpesi J IV.138; DhA I.226, 393 (sent); PvA 5 (id.), 31; fut. dāpessati J II.3; DhA 371. Cp. ava°.

Dāpeti[2] [Sk. drāvayati & drapayati, Caus. to **dru**, see davati] to cause to run J II.404.

Dāma (nt.) [Sk. dāman to dyati to bind (Gr. δίδημι), ***dō**, as in Gr. δέσμα (rope), διάδημα (diadem), ὑπόδημα (sandal)] a bond, fetter, rope; chain, wreath, garland S IV.163 (read dāmena for damena), 282, (id.); A III.393 (dāmena baddho); Sn 28 (= vacchakānaŋ bandhanatthāya katā ganthitā nandhipasayuttā rajjubandhanavisesā); Vism 108. Usually -°, viz. anoja-puppha° J I.9; VI.227; olambaka° VvA 32; kusuma° J III.394; gandha° J I.178; VvA 173, 198; puppha° J I.397; VvA 198; mālā° J II.104; rajata° J I.50; III.184; IV.91; rattapuppha° J III.30; sumana° J IV.455.

Dāya[1] [Sk. dāva, conflagration of a forest; wood = easily inflammable substance; to dunoti (to burn) Caus. dāvayati, cp. Gr. δαίω (to burn) & P. dava[1]] wood; jungle, forest; a grove Vin I.10 (miga°), 15, 350; II.138; S II.152 (tiṇa°); IV.189 (bahukaṇṭaka d. = jungle); A V.337 (tiṇa°); J III.274; VI.278. See also dāva.
-**pāla** a grove keeper Vin I.350; M I.205.

Dāya[2] [Sk. dāya, to dadāti, etc.] a gift, donation; share, fee D I.87≈(in phrase rājadāya brahmadeyya, a king's grant, cp. rājadattiya); J IV.138; V.363; VI.346. Cp. dāyāda & brahmadeyya.

Dāyaka [Sk. dāyaka, **dā** as in dadāti & dāna] (adj.) giving, bestowing, distributing, providing (usually -°); (n.) a donor, benefactor; a munificent person M I.236 sq.; A I.26, 161; II.64, 80; III.32, 336; IV.81; Sn p. 87; It 19 (ito cutā manussattā saggaŋ gacchanti dāyakā); J V.129 (kaṇḍa°); Pv I.1[1] sq.; 1[2]; 4[2]; 5[6]; DA I.298; PvA 113 (= dada); Miln 258 (°ānaŋ dakkhiṇā); Sdhp 276. — f. dāyikā Vin II.216 (bhikkhā°), 289 (khīrassa). — adāyaka a stingy person, one who neglects almsgiving (cp. adānasīla) Pv I.11[9]; f. °ikā Pv I.9[3].

Dāyajja (nt.) [Sk. dāyādya; see dāyāda] inheritance Vin I.82; D III.189; A III.43; J I.91; Vism 43 sq.; dowry J III.8. — (adj.) one who inherits Vin III.66 (pituno of the father).
-**upasampadā**, lit. the Upasampadā by way of inh., a particular form of ordination conferred on Sumana & Sopāka, both novices seven yrs. old DhA IV.137.

Dāyati [Sk. dāti & dyāti (**dā**) to cut, divide, etc.; cp. dayati, dātta, dāna] to cut, mow, reap, caus. dāyāpeti to cause to be cut or mowed DhA III.285.

Dāyana (nt.) [see dayati] cutting; °agga the first of what has been cut (on fields) DhA I.98; °atthaŋ for the purpose of mowing DhA III.285.

Dāyāda [Sk. dāyāda = dāya + ā-da receiving the (son's) portion, same formation on ground of same idea as Lat. heres = *ghero + ē-do receiver of what is left: see Brugmann, *Album Kern* p. 29 sq.] heir M I.86 = Nd[2] 199; S I.69, 90; IV.72; A III.72 sq.; II.181; VI.151; Kh VIII.5. Often fig. with **kamma°** one who inherits his own deeds (see kamma 3 A *b* & cpds.): M I.390 sq.; A V.289; & as dhamma° (spiritual heir) opposed to āmisa° (material h.): M I.12; It 101; also as dhamma° D III.84; as **brahma°** M II.84; D III.83. — **adāyāda** not having an heir S I.69; J V.267. See dāyajja & dāyādaka.

Dāyādaka [= dāyāda] heir M II.73; Th 1, 781, 1142; 1. °ikā Th 2, 327 (= dāyajjarahā ThA 234).

Dāyika (adj.) = dāyaka PvA 157; Sdhp 211, 229.

-Dāyin (adj.) [Sk. dāyin, of dadāti] giving, granting, bestowing PvA 121 (icchit' icchita°). 157 (= [kāma] dada); Sdhp 214 (dānagga°).

Dāra & Dārā (f.) [Sk. dāra (m.) & dārā (f.), more freq. dārā (m.pl.); instr. sg. dārena J IV.7; Pv IV.1[77], etc.; instr. pl. dārehi Sn 108 (sehi d. asantuṭṭho not satisfied with his own wife), loc. pl. dāresu Sn 38 (puttesu dāresu apekkhā), orig. "wives, womenfolk," female members of the household = Gr. δοῦλος (slave; Hesychius: δοῦλος = ἡ οἰκία; cp. also origin of Germ. frauenzimmer & E. womanhood). Remnants of pl. use are seen in above passage. fr. Sn.] a young woman, esp. married woman, wife. As dārā f. at Nd[2] 295 (d. vuccati bhariyā) & It 36; f. also dārī maiden, young girl Pv I.11[5]. Otherwise as dāra (coll-masc.): Dh 345; J I.120; II.248; IV.7; V.104, 288; VvA 299 (°paṭiggaha). — **putta-dārā** (pl.) wife & children Sn 108, 262; J I.262; cp. saputtadāra with w. & ch. Pv IV.3[47]; putta ca dārā ca Sn 38, 123. Freq. in definition of sīla No. 3 (kāmesu micchācārin or abrahmacariyā, adultery) as sakena dārena santuṭṭha A III.348; V.138; Sn 108 (a°); Pv 1[77], etc. — **paradāra** the wife of another M I.404 sq.; Dh 246, 309; Sn 396 (parassa d.) PvA 261.

Dāraka [Sk. dāraka, cp. dāra & Gr. δοῦλος (slave)] a (young) boy, child, youngster; a young man. f. **dārikā** girl (see next) Vin I.83; J I.88 (dārake ca dārikāyo boys & girls); II.127; VI.336; Pv I.12[7] (= bāla° PvA 65); DhA I.99 (yasa° = yasa-kulaputta); Miln 8, 9; PvA 176. — Freq. as gāmadārakā (pl.) the village-boys, street-urchins J II.78, 176; III.275.
-**tikicchā** the art of infant-healing D I.12 (= komārabhacca-vejjakamma DA I.98).

Dārikā (f.) [Sk. dārikā, see dāraka] a young girl, daughter J III.172; VI.364; Miln 48, 151; PvA 16 (daughter), 55, 67, 68.

Dāru (nt.) [Sk. dāru, ***dereṇo** (oak) tree; cp. Av. dāuru (wood) Gr. δόρυ (spear), δρῦς (oak); Lat. larix (fr. *dārix) = larch; Oir. daur (oak); Goth. triu, Ags. treo = tree. Also Sk. dāruṇa, Lat. dūrus (hard) etc., Oir. dru strong. See also dabba[2], dabbī & duma] wood, piece of wood; pl. woodwork, sticks A I.112; It 71; Dh 80; J II.102; III.54; VI.366; DhA I.393; PvA 76 (candana°), 141.
-**kuṭikā** a hut, log-house Vin III.43; -**kkhandha** pile of wood PvA 62; -**gaha** a wood yard Vin III.42 sq.; -**ghaṭika** wooden pitcher ThA 286. -**cīriya** "wood-barked" Np, DhA II.35. -**ja** made of wood S I.77; Dh 345; -**dāha** the burning of wood S I.169; -**dhītalikā** a wooden doll Vin III.36, 126; -**patta** a wooden bowl Vin II.112, 143; **pattika** one who uses a wooden bowl for collecting alms D I.157; III.22; DA I.319; **pādukā** a wooden shoe, a clog Vin II.143; -**bhaṇḍa** wooden articles Vin II.143 (specified), 170, 211; -**maṇḍalika** a wooden disk DhA III.180; -**maya** wooden VvA 8, DhA I.192; -**yanta** a wooden mill Vism 595; -**sanghāta** (-**yāna**) "a vehicle constructed of wood," i. e. a boat J V.194; -**samādahāna** putting pieces of wood together S I.169.

Dāruka (cp. dāru] a log S I.202 = Th 1, 62 = DhA III.460; adj. made of wood Th 2, 390 (°cillaka, a wooden post, see ThA 257).

Dāruṇa (adj.) [Ved. dāruṇa, to dāru ("strong as a tree"), cp. Gr. δροόν = ἰσχυρόν Hesych; Lat. dūrus; Oir. dron (firm), Mir. dūr (hard) Ags. trum] strong, firm, severe; harsh, cruel, pitiless S I.101; II.226; Sn 244; Dh 139; J III.34; Pv IV.3[6] (=ghora PvA 251); Miln 117 (vāta); PvA 24, 52 (=ghora), 159 (sapatha a terrible oath = ghora), 181 (=kurūrin), 221 (°kāraṇa); Sdhp 5, 78, 286.

Dālana [f. dalati] see vi°.

Dālikā & Dālima [Sk. dālika the colocynth & dāḍima the pomegranate tree] in °laṭṭhi a kind of creeper; equivalent to takkāri (?) Th 2, 297 (dālikā) = ThA 226 (dālikā & dālima).

Dāḷiddiya (& daḷiddiya) (nt.) [Sk. *dāridrya] poverty D III.65, 66; A III.351 sq.; J I.228; Dāvs II.60; Sdhp 78.

Dāleti see dalati.

Dāva [Sk. dāva, see dava[1] & daya[1]] in °aggi a jungle-fire J I.213; III.140; Vism 470; DhA I.281.

Dāvika (adj.) in piṇḍa°, a cert. rank in the army (v. l. piṇḍa-dāyika) D I.51 = Miln 331 (DA I.156: sāhasika-mahāyodhā, etc., with popular expl. of the terms piṇḍa & davayati).

Dāsa [Ved. dāsa; orig. adj. meaning "non-Aryan," i. e. slave (cp. Gr. βάρβαρος, Ger. sklave = slave); Av. dāha = a Scythian tribe. Also connected w. dasyu (see dassukhīla)] a slave, often comb[d] w. f. dāsī. Def. by Bdhgh as "antojāto" (DA 1.300), or as "antojāta-dhanakkīta-karamarânīta-sāmaŋ dāsabyaŋ upagatānaŋ aññataro" (ibid. 168). — In phrase dāsā ca kammakarā "slaves & labourers" Vin I.243, 272; II.154; as dāso kammakaro "a slave-servant" D I.60 (cp. d.-kammakara). — Vin I.72, 76 (dāso na pabbājetabbo: the slave cannot become a bhikkhu); D I.72; M II.68 (fig. taṇhā°); J I.200, 223; III.343 (bought for 700 kahāpaṇas), 347; Pug 56; PvA 112.

-**kammakara** (porisa) a slave-servant, an unpaid labourer, a serf Vin I.240; A I 206; D III.189; DhA IV.1; -**gaṇa** a troop of slaves Pv IV.1[41]; -**purisa** a servant J I.385; -**porisa** a servant, slave Sn 769 (cp. Nd[1] 11, where 4 kinds of d. are mentioned); -**lakkhaṇa** fortune-telling from (the condition of) slaves D I.9.

Dāsaka = dāsa in °putta a slave, of the sons of the slaves, mentioned as one of the sipp' āyatanas at D I.51≈ (expl. by Bdhgh as balavasinehā-gharadāsa-yodhā DA I.157). — **sadāsaka** with slaves, followed by slaves Vv 32[4]. — f. dāsikā a female slave (=dāsī) M I.126; J VI.554.

Dāsabyatā (f.) = dāsavya Sdhp 498.

Dāsavya & Dāsabya (nt.) [cp. Sk. dāsya] the condition of a slave, slavery, serfdom D I.73; M I.275 (b); J I.226; DA I.168 (b), 213; DhA III.35; PvA 112, 152.

Dāsitta (nt.) [Sk. dāsītva] the status of a (female) slave Miln 158.

Dāsima a species of tree J VI.536.

Dāsiyā = dāsikā, a female slave J VI.554.

Dāsī (f.) [Sk. dāsī, cp. dāsa. Nom. pl. dasso for dāsiyo J IV.53; in cpds. dāsi°] a female servant, a handmaiden, a slave-girl Vin I.217, 269, 291; II.10 (kula°), 78 = III.161; M I.125; II.62 (ñāti°); Pv II.3[21] (ghara°); PvA 46, 61, 65. — Cp. kumbha°.

-**gaṇa** a troop of slave-girls J II.127; -**dāsā** (pl.) maid- & man-servants DhA I.187; freq. to cpd. d-d-*paṭiggahaṇa* slave-trading D I.5≈(cp. DA I.78); -**putta** the son of a slave, an abusive term (gharadāsiyā va putto Dh I.257; cp. Sk. dāsīsuta) D I.93 (°vāda); -**bhoga** the possessions of a slave Vin III.136.

Dāha see ḍaha.

Di° secondary base of numeral "2," contracted fr. dvi: see under dvi B I.4.

Dikkhita [Sk. dīkṣita "having commenced the preparatory rites for sacrifice"] initiated, consecrated, *cira*° initiated long since S I.226 = J V.138, 139 (where dakkhita, q. v.; Com. cira-pabbājita).

Digucchā (f.) [= jigucchā; Sk. jugupsā] disgust DhsA 210 (asuci°).

Dighacchā (f.) [= jighacchā] hunger A II.117.

Dighañña (adj.) [for jighañña = Sk. jaghanya fr. janghā] inferior, low, last, hindmost (i. e. westward) J V.24 (where the Com. seems to imply a reading jighacchaŋ with meaning of 1st sg. pot. intens. of ghas, but d. is evidently the right reading), 402, 403 (°rattiŋ at the end of the night).

Dicchati [Sk. ditsati, Desid. fr. dadāti, base 4, q. v.] to wish to give, to be desirous of giving S I.18, 20 (dicchare 3rd pl.); J IV.64.

Dija see under dvi B I.4.

Diṭṭha[1] [Sk. dṛṣṭa, pp. of *dassati] 1. seen; a° not seen D I.222 (a° + avedita asacchikata); M I.3 sq. (diṭṭhaŋ diṭṭhato sañjānāti); Sn 147 (diṭṭhā vā ye vā addiṭṭhā), 995 (na me diṭṭho ito pubbe na ssuto . . . Satthā); J II.154; III.278; Pv I.2[3] (sāmaŋ d. = seen by yourself); 3[3] (id.). — nt. diṭṭhaŋ a vision J III.416. — Since sight is the principal sense of perception as well as of apperception (cp. cakkhu), that which is seen is the chief representation of any sense-impression, & diṭṭha comb[d] with suta (heard) and muta (sensed by means of smell, taste & touch), to which viññāta (apperceived by the mind) is often joined, gives a complete analysis of that which comprises all means of cognition & recognition. Thus diṭṭha + suta stands collectively for the whole series Sn 778, 812, 897, 1079; Pv IV.1[3]; diṭṭha suta muta (see Nd[2] 298 for detail & cp. diṭṭhiyā sutiyā ñāṇena) Sn 790, 901, 914, 1082, 1086, 1122 (na tuyhaŋ adiṭṭhaŋ asutaŋ amutaŋ kiñcanaŋ atthi = you are omniscient); d. suta muta viññāta in the same sense as Sn 1122 in "yaŋ sadevakassa lokassa d. s. m. v. sabbaŋ taŋ Tathāgatena abhisambuddhaŋ" of the cognitive powers of the Tathāgata D III.134 = Nd[2] 276 = It 121; D III.232; Sn 1086, 1122. — 2. known, understood M I.486; Sn 761; diṭṭha pañha a problem or question solved J VI.532. See also conclusion of No. 1. — 3. (adj.) visible, determined by sight, in conn. with dhamma meaning the visible order of things, the world of sensation, *this* world (opp. samparāyika dhamma the state after death, the beyond). Usually in cpds. (-°): of this world, in this world. — diṭṭhadhamma Vin II.188; D III.222 sq.; A I.249; II.61; Nd[2] 297 (= ñāta-dhamma); DA I.278; Sdhp 470. — °*abhinibbuta* attained to Nibbāna in this birth A I.142; Sn 1087 (see Nibbāna); °*nibbāna* earthly N. D I.36; DA I.121; °*sukhavihāra* (& °in) happy condition (or faring well) in this world Vin II.188; M I.40, 331, 459; S II.239; Dhs 577, 1283; DhsA 296; °*vedanīya* to be perceived in this condition A I.249, 251; PvA 145. — Freq. in loc. diṭṭhe dhamme (in this world) It 17 (attha, opp. samparāyika attha), or diṭṭhe va dhamme (already or even in the present existence) D I.156, 167, 177, 196; III.108; M I.341 sq., 485; II.94, 103; A II.155, 167; III.429; Sn 141, 343, 1053; It 22, 23, etc. — In the same sense diṭṭhadhammika (adj.) belonging or referring to this world or the present existence, always contrasted with samparāyika belonging to a future state: Vin I.179; III.21; D III.130; A I.47, 98; Nd[2] 26; It 16; VvA 149; PvA 131, etc.

-**ānugati** imitation of what one sees, emulation, competition S II.203; M I.16; A I.126; III.108, 251, 422;

Pug 33; DhA IV.39; -āvikamma making visible or clear, open statement, confession Vin V.183, 187 sq.; -kāla the time of seeing (anybody), opportunity VvA 120; -ppatta one who has obtained (Nibbāna) in this world Nett 190; -padā (pl.) visible signs or characteristics A IV.103; -mangalika (adj.) of puccha, a question asked in order to compare (one's views) on things seen, that is on ordinary worldly matters, with views held by others fond of prying J IV.390; as °ikā (f.) Np at J IV.376 sq.= SnA 185 sq. -saŋsandana Nd² 447=DhsA 55.

Diṭṭha² [Sk. dviṣṭa, pp. of dveṣṭi **dviṣ** to hate] (n.) an enemy J I.280; cp. Sk. dviṣat. — (adj.) poisoned, in diṭṭhagatena sallena with a p. arrow S II.230; misreading for diddh-agadena, q. v. The Cy. has diddhagatena with v. l. dibba-gadena.

Diṭṭhaka (adj.) [=diṭṭha¹] seen, visible, apparent DhA II.53, 90.

Diṭṭhā (indecl.) [Sk. dṛṣṭyā, instr. of diṭṭhi] exclamation of joy, hurrah! D iii.73; J I.362.

Diṭṭhi (f.) [Sk. dṛṣṭi; cp. dassana] view, belief, dogma, theory, speculation, esp. false theory, groundless or unfounded opinion. — (a) The latter is rejected by the Buddha as pāpa° (A IV.172) and pāpikā d. (opp. bhaddikā: A V.212 sq.; It 26): Vin I.98, 323; Dh 164; Pv IV.3⁵⁴; whereas the right, the true, the best doctrine is as sammā d. the first condition to be complied with by anyone entering the Path. As such the sammā d. is opposed to micchā d. wrong views or heresy (see b). Equivalent with micchā d. is kudiṭṭhi (late) Dāvs II.58. — (b) Characterized more especially as: (*a*) sammā diṭṭhi right doctrine, right philosophy Vin I.10; S II.17; V.11, 14, 30 sq., 458 sq., M I.315; II.12, 29, 87; III.72; Nd² 485; Vbh 104s q. See magga. — ujukā d. S V.143, 165; ujugatā d. M I.46 sq. — (*β*) micchā d. wrong theory, false doctrine S I.145; II.153 (caused by avijjā); M III.71; Dh 167, 316; Nd² 271ᴵᴵᴵᵇ; Vbh 361, 389. — The foll. theories are to be considered as varieties of micchā d., viz. (in limited enumⁿ) **akiriyavāda** S III.208; IV.349; **aññaŋ aññena** S III.211; **antaggāhikā** A I.154; II.240; III.130; **antânantikā** D I.22 sq. S III.214, 258 sq.; **assāda°** A III.447; **ahetukavādā** S III.210; **ucchedavādā** D I.34; S II.20; III.99; 110 sq.; **bhava°** S III.93; M I.65; A I.83; **sakkāya°** A III.438; V.144; Sn 231 (cp. KhA 188); Nd² 271ᴵᴵᴵᵇ (20 fold, as diṭṭhilepa); **sassatavādā** D I.13; S II.20; III.98, 213 sq., 258 sq. — (c) Various theories & doctrines are mentioned & discussed at: Vin I.115; S I.133; II.61 sq., 75 sq., 222; III.215 sq., 258 sq.; IV.286; V.448 (=D I.31); D III.13 sq., 45, 246, 267; M I.40; A I.32; II.252 sq.; III.132, 289, 349; Th 2, 184; Ps I.135 sq.; Pug 22; Dhs 392, 1003 (cp. *Dhs. trsl.* pp. 257 sq., 293, 325); Vbh 145, 245, 341, 393 sq.; Sdhp 13, 333. — (d) Miscellaneous: 4 diṭṭhiyo at Vbh 376; also at Vism 511 (sakkāya°, uccheda°, sassata°, akiriya°); 5 Vbh 378; 6 at M I.8; Vbh 382; 7 at Vbh 383; 20 see under sakkāya°; 62 under diṭṭhigata. — In series **diṭṭhi khanti ruci laddhi** characterizing "diṭṭhadhamma" at Nd² 299 & passim. Diṭṭhiyā sutiyā ñāṇena in def. of a theory of cognition at Nd² 300 as complementing taṇhā: see taṇhā B 3. Coupled with vācā & citta in formula (taŋ) vācaŋ appahāya cittaŋ appahāya diṭṭhiŋ appaṭinissajjitvā . . . (nikkhitto evaŋ niraye) at S IV.319= D III.13, 15; combᵈ with (& opposed to) sīla (as pāpaka & bhaddaka) at It 26, 27. — diṭṭhiŋ āsevati to hold a view M I.323; °ŋ bhindati to give up a view J I.273; Dāvs II.58.

-ânugati a sign of speculation Vin II.108; S II.203; Pug 33. **-ânusaya** inclination to speculation D III.254, 282; S V.60; A IV.9; **-āsava** the intoxicant of speculation, the 3rd of four āsavā, viz. kāma°, bhava°, d.°, avijjā° Vin III.5; Nd² 134; Dhs 1099, 1448; Vbh 273; cp. °ogha; **-upadānā** taking up or adhering to false doctrines, the 2nd of the four upādānāni or attachments, viz. kāma°, d.°, sīlabbata°, attavāda° D III.230; Dhs 1215, 1536; **-ogha** the flood of false doctrine, in set of four ogha's as under °āsava D III.230, 276; Nd² 178; **-kantāra** the wilderness of groundless speculation Dhs 381, 1003, 1099, etc.; see °gata; **-ganṭhi** the web or tangle of sophisticism VvA 297; cp. °saṅghāṭa; **-gata** (nt.) "resorting to views," theory, groundless opinion, false doctrine, often followed by series of characterizing epithets: d.-gahana, °kantāra, °visūka, °vipphandita, °saññojana, e. g. M I.8; Nd² 271ᴵᴵᴵᵇ. Of these sophistical speculations 2 are mentioned at It 43, Ps I.129; 6 at Ps I.130; 62 (the usual number, expressing "great and small" sets, cp. dvi A II.) at D I.12-39 (in detail); S IV.286; Ps I.130; Nd² 271ᴵᴵᴵᵇ; Nett 96, 112, 160. — Vin I.49; D I.162, 224, 226; S I.135, 142; II.230; III.109, 258 sq. (anekavihitāni); IV.286 (id.); M I.8, 176, 256 sq. (pāpaka), 326 (id.), 426 sq.; A IV.68; V.72 sq., 194 (pāpaka); Sn 649, 834, 913; Pug 15; Dhs 277, 339, 392, 505; Vism 454. — adj. °*gatika* adhering to (false) doctrine Dpvs VI.25; **-gahana** the thicket of speculation Dhs 381, 1003; see °gata; **-jāla** the net of sophistry D I.46; DA I.129; **-ṭṭhāna** a tenet of speculative philosophy D I.16; M I.136; A V.198; Ps I.138 (eight); Miln 332; DA I.107; **-nijjhānakkhanti** forbearance with wrong views S II.115; IV.139; A I.189 sq.; II.191; Nd² 151; **-nipāta** a glance VvA 279; **-nissaya** the foundation of speculation M I.137; D II.137 sq.; **-pakkha** the side or party of sophists Nett 53, 88, 160; **-paṭilābha** the attainment of speculation M III.46; **-paṭivedha**=prec. D III.253; **-patta** one who has formed (a right or wrong) view D III.105, 254; M I.439; A I.74; 118, IV.10; V.23; **-parāmasa** perversion by false doctrine Dhs 1498; **-maṇḍala** the circle of speculative dogmatics DhsA 109; **-vipatti** failure in theory, the 3rd of the four vipattiyo viz. sīla°, ācāra°, d.°, ājīva°; opp. °sampadā Vin V.98; D III.213; A I.95, 268; Pug 21; Dhs 1362; Vbh 361; **-vipallāsa** contortion of views A II.52; **-visaŋyoga** disconnection with false doctrine D III.230, 276; **-visuddhi** beauty of right theory A I.95; M I.147 sq.; D III.214, 288; **-visūka** (nt.) the discord or disunion (lit. the going into parties) of theories, the (?) puppet-show of opinion M I.8, 486; Sn 55 (=dvāsaṭṭhi diṭṭhigatāni), *K S* II.44; Vv 84²⁶; Pv IV.1³⁷; Nd² 301 (=vīsati-vattukā sakkāya-diṭṭhi); cp. Nd² 25 (attānudiṭṭhi); Dhs 381 (cp. *Dhs. trsl.* p. 101), 1003, 1099. See also °gata; **-vyasana** failing or misfortune in theory (+sīla°, in character) D III.235; Nd² 304; **-saŋyojana** the fetter or bond of empty speculation (cp. °anusaya) D III.254; A IV.7 sq.; **-saṅghāta** the weft or tangle of wrong views (cp. °ganṭhi) Nd¹ 343; Nd² 503; **-samudaya** the origin of wrong views A IV.68; **-sampadā** success in theory, blessing of right views, attainment of truth D III.213, 235 (opp. °vipatti), S V.30 sq.; A I.95, 269; III.438; IV.238; Pug 25; Dhs 1364; VvA 297; **-sampanna** endowed with right views S II.43, 58, 80; V.11; A III.438 sq.; IV.394; Vbh 366; *Dialogues* iii.206, *n.* 10; **-sārin** (adj.) following wrong views Sn 911.

Diṭṭhika (adj.) (-°) seeing, one who regards; one who has a view M III.24 (āgamana° one who views the arrival, i. e. of guests); S II.168 sq. (sammā° & micchā° holding right & wrong theories); D III.96 (vītimissa°). See añña°, micchā°, sammā°.

Diṭṭhitā (f.) [fr. diṭṭhi] the fact of having a (straightforward) view (uju°) Miln 257.

Diṭṭhin (adj.-n.) one who has a view, or theory, a follower of such & such a doctrine Ud 67 (evaŋ°+evaŋ vādin).

Diṇṇa [Sk. dīrṇa, pp. of **dṛ**, dṛṇāti, see darī] broken, split, undone, torn, as neg. adiṇṇa unbroken D I.115 (so read for ādina-khattiya-kula; v. l. BB. abhinna°); S V.74 (so read for ādīna-mānaso, v. l. BB. adinā & SS ādina°). Cp. also ādiṇṇa.

Ditta[1] [Sk. dīpta, dīp; cp. dīpa] blazing. Dāvs v.32. Usually in cpd. āditta.

Ditta[2] [Sk. dṛpta; cp. dappa] proud, arrogant, insolent; wanton Th 1, 198; J II.432; III.256=485; V.17, 232; VI.90, 114.

Diddha [Sk. digdha to dih, see deha] smeared J v.425 sq.; esp. smeared with poison, poisoned J IV.435 (sara, a poisoned arrow); perhaps to be read at It 68 for duṭṭha (scil. sara) and at S II.230 for diṭṭha. Cp. san°.

Dina (nt.) [Sk. dina; Lat. nun-dinae (*noven-dinom); Oir. denus; Goth. sin-teins; cp. divasa] day Sdhp 239. -duddinaŋ darkness Dāvs v.50 (d. sudinaŋ ahosi, cp. I.49, 51); also as f. duddinī Vin I.3.

Dindibha [cp. Sk. ṭiṭṭibha ?] a kind of bird J VI.538.

Dindima (nt.) [Sk. ḍiṇḍima, cp. dundubhi] a musical instrument, a small drum J VI.580; Bu I.32. See also deṇḍima.

Dinna [Sk. dinna, pp. of dadāti] given, granted, presented etc., in all meanings of dadāti q. v.; esp. of giving alms Pv IV.3[26] (=mahādāna PvA 253) & in phrase adinn'-ādāna taking what is not given, i. e. stealing, adj. adinnâdāyin stealing, refraining from which constitutes the 2nd sīla (see under sīla). — dinna: D I.55≈(n' atthi dinnaŋ, the heretic view of the uselessness of alms-giving); J I.291; II.128; Sn 191, 227, 240; Dh 356; PvA 68 (given in marriage). Used as finite tense freq., e. g. J I.151, 152; VI.366. — adinna: M I.39, 404; Sn 119 (theyyā adinnaŋ ādiyati), 156, 395, 400, 633; PvA 33 etc.

-ādāyin taking (only) what is given D I.4; DA I.72; -dāna almsgiving J III.52; DhA I.396; -dāyin giving alms, liberal, munificent D III.191.

Dinnaka an adopted son, in enumⁿ of four kinds of sons (atraja, khettaja, antevāsika, d.) Nd[2] 448; J I.135 (=posāvanatthāya dinna).

Dippati [Sk. dīpyate, see under dīpa[1] & cp. jotati] to shine, to shine forth, to be illustrious Vin II.285. Cp. pa°.

Dibba (adj.) [Ved. divya=P. divya in verse (q. v.), Gr. δῖος (*διFιος), Lat. dius (*divios)—divine. Cp. deva], of the next world, divine, heavenly, celestial, superb, magnificent, fit for exalted beings higher than man (devas, heroes, manes etc.), superhuman, opp. mānusaka human. Freq. qualifying the foll. "summa bona": cakkhu the deva-eye, i. e. the faculty of clairvoyance, attr. in a marked degree to the Buddha & other perfect beings (see cakkhumant) D I.82, 162; II.20 (yena sudaŋ samantā yojanaŋ passati divā c' eva rattiñ ca); III.219; S I.196; II.55 sq.; M II.21; It 52; Th 2, 70; Ps I.114, II.175; Vism 434; Sdhp 482; PvA 5 (of Moggallāna); Tikp 278; Dukp 54. sota the d. ear, matching the d. eye D I.79, 154; J v.456; also as sotadhātu A I.255; M II.19; D III.38, 281; Vism 430. rūpa D I.153. Āyu, vaṇṇa etc. (see dasa ṭhānāni) A I.115; III.33; IV.242; PvA 9, 89. kāmā Sn 361; Dh 187; It 94; also as kāmaguṇā A v.273. Of food, drink, dress & other commodities: A I.182; J I.50, 202; III.189; PvA 23, 50, 70, 76 etc. — Def. as devaloke sambhūta DA I.120; divibhavattā dibba KhA 227; divibhāvaŋ devattabhāva-pariyāpanna PvA 14. — See further e. g. S I.105; D III.146; Sn 176, 641; Dh 236, 417; Pug 60; Vism 407 (defⁿ), 423.

-osadha magical drugs Miln 283; -kāmā (pl.) heavenly joys (see above) J I.138 (opp. mānusakā); -cakkhuka endowed with the superhuman eye S II.156; A I.23, 25; -paṇṇākāra (dasavidha°) the (tenfold) heavenly gift (viz. āyu, vaṇṇa etc.: see ṭhāna) DhA III.292; -bhāva divine condition or state PvA 110; -yoga union with the gods S I.60; -vihāra supreme condition of heart Miln 225; -sampatti heavenly bliss J IV.3; DhA III.292; PvA 16, 30.

Dibbati [Sk. dīvyati, pp. dyūta see jūta] to sport, to amuse oneself VvA 18 (in expl. of devi); to play at dice M II.106 (akkhehi).

Dirasaññu (adj.) [Sk. dara-saŋjña ? See Kern, *Toev.* p. 118] one who has little common-sense J VI.206, 207, 213, 214. Com. explˢ wrongly on p. 209 with "one who possesses two tongues" (of Agni), but has equivalent nippañña on p. 217 (text 214: appapañña+).

Diva [Sk. diva (nt.), weak base diu (div) of strong form diē (see deva) to *deieuo to shine; cp. Sk. dyo heaven, divā adv. by day; Lat. biduum (bi-divom) two days] (a) heaven J IV.134 (°ŋ agā); V.123 (°ŋ patta); PvA 74 (°ŋ gata). — (b) day Sn 507 (rattindivaŋ night & day); VvA 247 (rattindiva one night & one day, i. e. 24 hrs.); DhA II.8 (divā-divassa so early in the day). Also in divaŋ-kara, daymaker, = sun, VvA 307; usually as divākara (q. v.). Cp. devasika; see also ajja.

-santatta heated for a whole day J IV.118 (cp. divasa°).

Divasa (m; nt. only in expression satta divasāni 7 days or a week J IV.139; Miln 15) [Sk. divasa; see diva] a day A I.206 (°ŋ atināmeti); J III.52 (uposatha°); PvA 31 (yāva sattadivasā a week long), 74 (sattamo divaso). Usually in oblique cases adverbially, viz. acc. divasaŋ (during) one day, for one day, one day long A III.304 = IV.317; J I.279; II.2; DhA III.173 (taŋ d. that day); eka° one day J I.58; III.26; PvA 33, 67. — gen. divasassa (day) by day S II.95 (rattiyā ca d. ca); J v.162; DA I.133. — instr. divasā day by day J IV.310; divasena (eka°) on the same day J I.59; sudivasena on a lucky day J IV.210. — loc. divase on a day: eka° J III.391; jāta° on his birth-day J III.391; IV.138; dutiya° the next day PvA 12, 13, 17, 31, 80 etc.; puna° id. J I.278; PvA 19, 38; sattame d. on the 7th day Sn 983; Miln 15; PvA 6; ussava° on the festive d. VvA 109; aparaˇ on another day PvA 81. Also repeated divase divase day after day, every day J I.87; PvA 3. — abl. divasato from the day (-°) J I.50; DA I.140.

-kara the "day-maker," i. e. the sun (cp. divākara) VvA 169, 271; -bhāga the day-part (opp. ratti° the night-part), day-time Miln 18 (°ena); PvA 152 (°ŋ), 206 (°e = divā); -santatta heated the livelong day S I.169; M I.453; A IV.70, cp. Vin I.225; Miln 325; cp. diva°.

Divā (adv.) [Ved. divā, cp. diva] by day S I.183; M I.125; Dh 387; DA I.251; PvA 43, 142, 206 (=divasa-bhāge). Often combᵈ & contrasted with rattiŋ (or ratto) by night; e. g. divārattiŋ by day & by night S I.47; divā c' eva rattiñ ca D II.20; rattim pi divā pi J II.133; divā ca ratto ca S I.33; Sn 223; Dh 296; Vv 31[4]; VvA 128. — divātaraŋ (compar. adv.) later on in the day M I.125; J III.48, 498. — atidivā too late S I.200; A III.117.

-kara (=divaŋ kara) the day-maker, the sun ThA 70 (Ap. v.10); PvA 155; -divassa (adv.) early in the day, at sunrise, at an early hour Vin II.190; S I.89, 91, 97; A v.185; M II.100, 112; J II.1; VI.31; DhA II.8; VvA 239, 242; -vihāra the day-rest, i. e. rest during the heat of the day Vin I.28, S I.129, 132, 146, 193=Th 1, 1241; Sn 679; -saññā consciousness by day, daily c. D III.223=A II.45; -seyyā =°vihāra D I.112.

Divi° an abstraction fr. divya constructed for etym. explⁿ of dibba as divi-bhava (°bhāva) of divine existence or character, a divine being, in "divi-bhavāni divyāni ettha atthi ti divyā" SnA 219; "divi-bhavattā dibbā ti" KhA 227; "divibhāvaŋ devattabhāvapariyāpanno ti dibbo" PvA 14.

Divilla a musical instrument Dpvs XVI.14.

Divya [Sk. divya; the verse-form for the prose-form dibba (q. v.)] (adj.) divine Sn 153 (cp. SnA 219 under divi°), 524 (+ mānusaka); J VI.172. — (nt.) the divinity, a divine being (=devatā) J VI.150; SnA 219.

Disa [Sk. dviṣant & dviṣa (-°); dveṣṭi & dviśati to hate; cp. Gr. δεινός (corynthic δFεινία, hom. δείδFιμεν) fearful; Lat. dīrus=E. dire] an enemy Dh 42, 162; J III.357; IV.217; V.453; Th 1.874-6; cp. *Pss. Breth.*, 323, *n.* 1.

Disatā[1] (f.) [Sk. diśatā, see disā] direction, quarter, region, part of the world J IV.359; Pv II.9[21] (kiŋ disataŋ gato "where in the world has he gone?"); Vv II.3[2] (sādisatā the circle of the 6 directions, cp. VvA 102).

Disatā[2] (f.) [Sk. *dviṣatā, see disa] state of being an enemy, a host of enemies J IV.295 (=disasamūha, v. l. as gloss: verasamoha).

Disati [Ved. diśati, ***deik** to show, point towards; cp. Gr. δείκνυμι (δίκη=diśā), Lat. dico (indico, index=pointer, judex), Goth. gateihan=Ger. zeigen, Ags. taecan=E. token] to point, show; to grant, bestow etc. Usually in comb[n] with pref. ā, or in Caus. deseti (q. v.). As simplex only at S I.217 (varaŋ disā to be read for disaŋ; cp. Sk. adiśat). See also upa°.

Disā (f.) [Ved. diś & diśā, to diśati "pointing out," point; cp. Gr. δίκη=diśā] point of the compass, region, quarter, direction, bearings. The 4 principal points usualy enum[d] are puratthimā (E) pacchimā (W) **dakkhiṇā** (S) uttarā (N), in changing order. Thus at S I.101, 145; II.103; III.84; IV.185, 296; Nd[2] 302; Pv II.12[6] (caturo d.); PvA 52 (catūsu disāsu nirayo catūhi dvārehi yutto), and passim. — To these are often added the two locations "above & below" as **uparimā** & heṭṭhimā disā (also as uddhaŋ adho S III.124 e. g.; also called paṭidisā D III.176), making in all 6 directions: D III.188 sq. As a rule, however, the circle is completed by the 4 anudisā (intermediate points; sometimes as vidisā: S I.224; III.239; D III.176 etc.), making a round of 10 (dasa disā) to denote completeness, wide range & all pervading comprehensiveness of states, activities or other happening: Sn 719, 1122 (disā catasso vidisā catasso uddhaŋ adho: dasa disā imāyo); Th 2, 487; Ps II.131; Nd[2] 239 (see also cātuddisa in this sense); Pv I.11[1]; II.1[10]; Vism 408. sabbā (all) is often substituted for 10: S I.75; D II.15; Pv I.2[1]; VvA 184; PvA 71. —**anudisā** (sg.) is often used collectively for the 4 points in the sense of "in between," so that the circle always implies the 10 points. Thus at S I.122; III.124. In other combinations as 6 abbreviated for 10; four disā plus uddhaŋ & anudisaŋ at D I.222=A III.368; four d.+uddhaŋ adho & anudisaŋ at S I.122; III.124; A IV.167. In phrase "mettāsahagatena cetasā ekaŋ disaŋ pharitvā viharati" (etc. up to 4th) the all-comprehending range of universal goodwill is further denoted by **uddhaŋ adho tiriyaŋ** etc., e. g. D I.250; Vbh 272; see mettā. — As a set of 4 or 8 disā is also used allegorically (" set, circle") for var. combinations, viz. the 8 states of jhāna at M III.222; the 4 satipaṭṭhānā etc. at Nett 121; the 4 āhārā etc. at Nett 117. — See also in other applications Vin I.50 (in meaning of "foreign country"); II.217; S I.33 (abhayā) 234 (puthu°); III.106; V.216; D III.197 sq.; It 103; Th 1, 874; Vv 41[6] (disāsu vissutā). — disaŋ kurute to run away J V.340. diso disaŋ (often spelt disodisaŋ) in all directions (lit. from region to region) D III.200; J III.491; Th 1, 615; Bu II.50; Pv III.1[6]; Miln 398. But at Dh 42 to disa (enemy), cp. DhA I.324=coro coraŋ. See also *J.P.T.S.* 1884, 82 on abl. diso=diśatah. Cp. **vidisā**.

-kāka a compass-crow, i. e. a crow kept on board ship in order to search for land (cp. Fick, *Soc. Gl.* p. 173; E. Hardy, *Buddha* p. 18) J III.126, 267; **-kusala** one who knows the directions Vin II.217; **-cakkhuka** "seeing" (i. e. wise) in all directions J III.344; **-ḍāha** "sky-glow," unusual redness of the horizon as if on fire, polar light (?) or zodiacal light (?) D I.10; J I.374; VI.476; Miln 178; DA I.95; cp. BSk. diśodāha AvŚ II.198; **-pati** (disampati) a king S I.86; J VI.45; **-pāmokkha** world-famed J I.166; **-bhāga** [Sk. digbhāga] direction, quarter Vin II.217; **-mūḷha** [Sk. diṅmūḍha] one who has lost his bearings Dpvs IX.15; **-vāsika** living in a foreign country DhA III.176. **-vāsin**=°vāsika DhA IV.27.

Dissati Pass. of *dassati, q. v.

Dīgha (adj.-n.) [Ved. dīrgha, cp. Caus. drāghayati to lengthen, ***dlāgh** as in Gr. δολιχός (shaft), ἐνδελεχής (lasting etc.; cp. E. entelechy); Lat. indulges; Goth. tulgus (enduring)] 1. (adj.) long D I.17; M I.429; S I.104 (°ŋ addhānaŋ); So 146, 633 (opp. rassa); Dh 60, 409; Pv I.10[11] (°ŋ antaraŋ all the time); II.9[65] (id.); Th 1, 646 (°m-antare); Dhs 617; KhA 245; PvA 27, 28, 33, 46. See def. at Vism 272. — dīghato lengthways J VI.185; dīghaso in length Vin IV.279; atidīgha too long Vin IV.7, 8. — 2. (m.) a snake (cp. M Vastu II.45 dīrghaka) J I.324; II.145; IV.330. — 3. N. of the Dīgha Nikāya ("the long collection") Vism 96.

-angulin having long fingers (the 4th of the marks of a Mahāpurisa) D II.17; III.143, 150; **-antara** corridor J VI.349. **-āyu** long-lived (opp. app' āyu) D I.18; J V.71. Also as °ka D III.150; DA I.135; Sdhp 511; **-āvu**=°āyu in the meaning of āyasmant (q. v.) J V.120; **-jāti** (f.) a being of the snake kind, a snake DhA III.322; also as °*ka* at J II.145; III.250; IV.333; V.449; DA I.252; **-dasa** having long fringes D I.7; **-dassin** [Sk. dīrghadarśin] far-seeing (=sabba-dassāvin) PvA 196; **-nāsika** having a long nose Vism 283. **-bhāṇaka** a repeater or expounder of the Dīgha Nikāya J I.59; Vism 36, 266, 286; DA I.15, 131; **-rattaŋ** (adv.) [Sk. *dīrgharātraŋ, see Indexes to AvŚ; Divy & Lal. V.; otherwise dīrgha-kālaŋ] a long time D I.17, 206; A V.194; Sn 649; It 8; J I.12, 72; Pv I.4[4]; II.13[11] (°rattāya=°rattaŋ PvA 165); Pug 15; DhA IV.24; **-loma** long-haired Vin III.129; also as °ka at J I.484, f. °ikā S II.228; **-sotthiya** (nt.) long welfare or prosperity DhA II.227.

Dīghatta (nt.) [Sk. dīrghatvaŋ] length A I.54.

Dīna (adj.) [Sk. dīna] poor, miserable, wretched; base, mean, low D II.202 (?) (°māna; v. l. ninnamāna); J V.448; VI.375; Pv II.8[2] (=adānajjhāsaya PvA 107); IV.8[1]; Miln 406; PvA 120 (=kapaṇa), 260 (id.), 153; Sdhp 188, 324.

Dīnatta (nt.) [Sk. *dīnatvaŋ] wretchedness, miserable state Sdhp 78.

Dīpa[1] [Ved. dīpa to Ved. **dī**, dīpyate; Idg. *deiā to shine (see dibba, deva); cp. Gr. δέαλος, δῆλος; see also jotati] a lamp J II.104 (°ŋ jāleti to light a l.); DhA II.49 (id.), 94 (id.)

-**acci** the flame of a lamp ThA 154; **-āloka** light of a l. J I.266; VI.391; DhA I.359; VvA 51; — (°ŋ)**kara** making light, shining, illuminating Nd[2] 399 (=pabhaŋ kara Sn 1136; but cp. Dh 236 under dīpa[2]); Vism 203. **-tittira** a decoy partridge (cp. dīpaka°) J III.64; **-rukkha** lit. lamp-tree, the stand of a lamp, candlestick DhA IV.120; **-sikhā** the flame (lit. crest) of a l. Vism 171; DhA II.49.

Dīpa[2] (m. & nt.) [Ved. dvīpa=dvi+ap (*sp.) of āpa water, lit. "double-watered," between (two) waters] an island, continent (mahā°, always as 4); terra firma, solid foundation, resting-place, shelter, refuge (in this sense freq. comb[d] w. tāṇa lena & saraṇa & expl. in Com. by patiṭṭhā) — (a) lit. island: S V.219; J III.187; VvA 19; Mhvs VII.7, 41. — continent: cattāro mahādīpā S V.343; Vv 20[10] (=VvA 104); VvA 19; PvA 74 etc. Opp. the 2000 paritta-dīpā the smaller islands KhA 133. — (b) fig. shelter, salvation etc. (see also tāṇa): S III.42 (atta°+attasaraṇa etc., not with S Index to dīpa[1]); V.154. 162 (id.) IV.315 (maŋ°, not to dīpa[1]), 372; A I.55 sq. (+tāṇa etc.); Sn 501 (atta° self-reliant, self-supported, not with Fausböll to dīpa[1]), 1092, 1094, 1145 (=Satthā); Nd[2] 303; Dh 236 (°ŋ karohi=patiṭṭhā PvA 87); Pv III.1[9] (id. PvA 174); J V.501=VI.375 (dīpañ ca parāyaṇaŋ); Miln 84, 257 (dhamma-dīpa, Arahantship).

-**ālaya** resting place J VI.432; -**gabbhaka** same J VI.459, 460.

Dīpa[3] [cp. Sk. dvīpa tiger's skin] a car covered with a panther's skin J I.259; V.259=VI.48.

Dīpaka[1] (=dīpa[1]) (a) f. dīpikā a lamp, in daṇḍa° a torch DhA I.220, 399. — (b) (°-) an image of, having the appearance of, sham etc.; in -**kakkara** a decoy partridge J II.161; -**tittira** same J III.358; -**pakkhin** a decoy bird J V.376; -**miga** a d. antelope J V.376.

Dīpaka[2] (=dīpa[2]) a (little) island J I.278, 279; II.160.

Dīpaka[3] in vaṇidīpaka PvA 120 for vanibbaka (q. v.).

Dīpana (adj.) illustrating, explaining; f. °ī explanation, commentary, N. of several Commentaries, e. g. the Paramattha -dīpanī of Dhammapāla on Th 2; Pv & Vv. — Cp. jotikā & uddīpanā.

Dīpika [fr. dīpin] a panther J III.480.

Dīpita [pp. of dīpeti] explained Vism 33.

Dīpitar [n. ag. fr. dīpeti] one who illumines Vism 211.

Dīpin [Sk. dvīpin] a panther, leopard, tiger Vin I.186 dīpicamma a leopard skin=Sk. dvīpicarman); A III.101; J I.342; II.44, 110; IV.475; V.408; VI.538. **dīpi-rājā** king of the panthers Vism 270. — f. **dīpinī** Miln 363, 368; DhA I.48.

Dīpeti [Sk. dīpayati, Caus. to **dīp**, see dīpa[1] & cp. dippati] to make light, to kindle, to emit light, to be bright; to illustrate, explain A V.73 sq.; Dh 363; Miln 40; PvA 94, 95, 102, 104 etc.; Sdhp 49, 349. Cp. ā°.

Du°[1] (& before vowels dur°) (indecl.) [Sk. duḥ & duṣ=Gr. δυς-, Oir. du-, Ohg. zur-, zer-; antithetic prefix, generally opposed to su°=Gr. εὐ- etc. Ultimately identical with du[2] in sense of asunder, apart, away from=opposite or wrong] 1. syllable of exclamation (=duḥ) "bad, woe" (beginning the word du (j) -jīvitaŋ) DhA II.6, 10=PvA 280, cp. J III.47; Bdhgh's expl[n] of the syllable see at Vism 494. — 2. prefix, implying perverseness, difficulty, badness (cp. dukkha). Original form *duḥ is preserved at dur- before vowels, but assimilated to a foll. consonant according to the rules of Assimilation, i. e. the cons. is doubled, with changes of v to bb & usual lengthening dū before r (but also du°). For purposes of convenience all cpds. with du° are referred to the simplex, e. g. dukkaṭa is to be looked up under kata, duggati under gati etc.

See: A. dur°. akkhāta, accaya, atikkama, atta, adhiroha, anta, annaya, abhisambhava; āgata, ājāna, āyuta, āsada; itthi; ukkhepa, ubbaha. — B. du°: (k)kata, kara; (g)ga, gata, gati, gandha, gahita; (c)caja, carita, cola; (j)jaha, jāna, jivha, jīvita; (t)tappaya, tara; (d)dama, dasika; (n)naya, nikkhaya, nikkhitta, niggaha, nijjhāpaya, nibbedha, nīta; (p)pañña, paṭiānaya, paṭinissaggin, paṭipadā, paṭivijjha, paṭivedha, pabhajja, pamuñca, pameyya, parihāra, payāta, pasu, peyya, posa; (p)phassa; (bb=b): bala, balika, budha; (bb=v): dubbaca=) vaca, vacana, vaṇṇa, vijāna, vidū, vinivijjha, visodha, vuṭṭhika; (b) bhaga, bhara, bhāsita, bhikkha; (m)mati, mana, manku, mukha, mejjha, medha; (y)yiṭṭha, yuja, yutta; (du+r)=du-ratta, ropaya (dū+r): dū-rakkha; (l)labha; (s)saddhapaya, sassa, saha, sīla; hara.

Du°[2] in cpds. meaning two°; see dvi B II.

Du[3] (-°) (adj.-suff.) [Sk. druha, **druḥ**, see duhana & duhitika] hurting, injuring, acting perfidiously, betraying, only in mitta° deceiving one's friends S I.225; Sn 244 expl. as mitta-dūbhaka SnA 287, v. l. B mitta-dussaka; cp. mitta-dubbhika & mitta-dubbhin.

Duka (nt.) [see dvi B II] a dyad DhsA 36, 343, 347, 406; Vism 11 sq. & in titles of books "in pairs, on pairs," e. g. Dukapaṭṭhāna; or chapters, e. g. J II.1 (°nipāta).

Dukūla [Sk. dukūla] a certain (jute ?) plant; (nt.) [cp. Sk. dukūlaŋ woven silk] very fine cloth, made of the fibre of the d. plant S III.145; A IV.393; J II.21; IV.219; V.400; VI.72; Vism 257, 262; VvA 165; DA I.140; Dāvs V. 27.

Dukkha (adj.-n.) [Sk. duḥkha fr. duḥ-ka, an adj. formation fr. prefix duḥ (see du). According to others an analogy formation after sukha, q. v.; Bdhgh (at Vism 494) expl[s] dukkha as du+kha, where du=du[1] and kha=ākāsa. See also def. at Vism 461.] *A.* (adj.) unpleasant, painful, causing misery (opp. sukha pleasant) Vin I.34; Dh 117. Lit. of vedanā (sensation) M I.59 (°ŋ vedanaŋ vediyamāna, see also below III.1 e); A II.116=M. I.10 (sarīrikāhi vedanāhi dukkhāhi). — Fig. (fraught with pain, entailing sorrow or trouble) of kāmā D I.36 (=paṭipīḷan-aṭṭhena DA I.121); Dh 186 (=bahudukkha DhA III.240); of jāti M I.185 (cp. ariyasacca, below B I.); in comb[n] dukkhā paṭipadā dandhābhiññā D III.106; Dhs 176; Nett 7, 112 sq., cp. A II.149 sq. **ekanta°** very painful, giving much pain S II.173; III.69. **dukkhaŋ** (adv.) with difficulty, hardly J I.215.

B. (nt.; but pl. also dukkhā, e. g. S I.23; Sn 728; Dh 202, 203, 221. Spelling dukha (after sukha) at Dh 83, 203). There is no word in English covering the same ground as Dukkha does in Pali. Our modern words are too specialised, too limited, and usually too strong. Sukha & dukkha are ease and dis-ease (but we use disease in another sense); or wealth and ilth from well & ill (but we have now lost ilth); or well-being and ill-ness (but illness means something else in English). We are forced, therefore, in translation to use half synonyms, no one of which is exact. Dukkha is equally mental & physical. Pain is too predominantly physical, sorrow too exclusively mental, but in some connections they have to be used in default of any more exact rendering. Discomfort, suffering, ill, and trouble can occasionally be used in certain connections. Misery, distress, agony, affliction and woe are never right. They are all much too strong & are only mental (see Mrs. Rh. D. *Bud. Psy.* 83-86, quoting Ledi Sadaw).

I. *Main Points in the Use of the Word.*—The recognition of the fact of Dukkha stands out as essential in early Buddhism. In the very first discourse the four so-called Truths or Facts (see saccāni) deal chiefly with dukkha. The first of the four gives certain universally recognised cases of it, & then sums them up in short. The five groups (of physical & mental qualities which make an individual) are accompanied by ill so far as those groups are fraught with āsavas and grasping. (Pañc' upādānakkhandhā pi dukkhā; cp. S III.47). The second Sacca gives the cause of this dukkha (see Taṇhā). The third enjoins the removal of this taṇhā. And the fourth shows the way, or method, of doing so (see Magga). These ariyasaccāni are found in two places in the older books Vin I.10=S V.421 (with addition of soka-parideva . . . etc. [see below] in some MSS). Comments on this passage, or part of it, occur S III.158, 159; with expl[n] of each term

(+soka) D I.189; III.136, 277; M I.185; A I.107; Sn p. 140; Nd^2 under sankhārā; It 17 (with dukkhassa atikkama for nirodha), 104, 105; Ps I.37; II.204, 147; Pug 15, 68; Vbh 328; Nett 72, 73. It is referred to as dukkha, samudaya, nirodha, magga at Vin I.16, 18, 19; D III.227; Nd^2 304^{IIb}; as āsavānaŋ khaya-ñāṇa at D I.83; Vin III.5; as sacca No. 1 + paṭiccasamuppāda at A I.176 sq. (+soka°); in a slightly diff. version of No. 1 (leaving out appiyehi & piyehi, having soka° instead) at D II.305; and in the formula catunnaŋ ariyasaccānaŋ ananubodhā etc. at D II.90 = Vin I.230.

II. *Characterisation in Detail.*—1. A further specification of the 3rd of the Noble Truths is given in the Paṭicca-samuppāda (q.v.), which analyses the links & stages of the causal chain in their interdependence as building up (anabolic = samudaya) &, after their recognition as causes, breaking down (katabolic = nirodha) the dukkha-synthesis, & thus constitutes the Metabolism of kamma; discussed e. g. at Vin I; D II.32 sq. = S II.2 sq.; S II.17, 20, 65 = Nd^2 680^{I-c}; S III.14; M I.266 sq.; II.38; A I.177; mentioned e. g. at A I.147; M I.192 sq., 460; It 89 (= dukkhassa antakiriyā). — 2. **Dukkha** as one of the 3 *qualifications of the* sankhārā (q. v.), viz. anicca, d., anattā, evanescence, ill, nonsoul: S I.188; II.53 (yad aniccaŋ taŋ dukkhaŋ); III.112 (id.) III.67, 180, 222; IV.28, 48, 129 sq.; 131 sq. — rūpe anicc' ânupassī (etc. with dukkh' & anatt') S III.41. anicca-saññā, dukkha° etc. D III.243; A III.334, cp. IV.52 sq. — sabbe sankhārā aniccā etc. Nd^2 under sankhārā. — 3. *Specification of Dukkha.* The Niddesa gives a characteristic description of all that comes under the term dukkha. It employs one stereotyped explanation (therefore old & founded on scholastic authority) (Nd^2 304^{I}), & one expl^n (304^{III}) peculiar to itself & only applied to Sn 36. The latter defines & illustrates dukkha exclusively as suffering & torment incurred by a person as punishment, inflicted on him either by the king or (after death) by the guardians of purgatory (niraya-pālā; see detail under niraya, & cp. below III. 2 b). — The first expl^n (304^{I}) is similar in kind to the definition of d. as long afterwards given in the Sānkhya system (see Sānkhya-kārikā-bhāṣya of Gauḍapāda to stanza 1) & classifies the various kinds of dukkha in the foll. groups: (a) all suffering caused by the fact of being born, & being through one's kamma tied to the consequent states of transmigration; to this is loosely attached the 3 fold division of d. as dukkha°, sankhāra°, vipariṇāma° (see below III. 1 c); — (b) illnesses & all bodily states of suffering (cp. ādhyātmikaŋ dukkhaŋ of Sānkhya k.); — (c) pain & (bodily) discomfort through outward circumstances, as extreme climates, want of food, gnat-bites etc. (cp. ādhibhautikaŋ & ādhidaivikaŋ d. of Sk.); — (d) (Mental) distress & painful states caused by the death of one's beloved or other misfortunes to friends or personal belongings (cp. domanassa). — This list is concluded by a scholastic characterisation of these var. states as conditioned by kamma, implicitly due to the afflicted person not having found his "refuge," i. e. salvation from these states in the 8 fold Path (see above B I.).

III. *General Application,* & various views regarding dukkha. — 1. As *simple sensation* (: pain) & related to other terms: (a) principally a vedanā, sensation, in particular belonging to the body (kāyika), or physical pain (opp. cetasika dukkha mental ill: see domanassa). Thus defined as kāyikaŋ d. at D II.306 (cp. the distinction between śarīraŋ & mānasaŋ dukkhaŋ in Sānkhya philosophy) M I.302; S V.209 (in def. of dukkhindriya); A II.143 (sarīrikā vedanā dukkhā); Nett 12 (duvidhaŋ d.: kāyikaŋ = dukkhaŋ; cetasikaŋ = domanassaŋ); Vism 165 (twofold), 496 (dukkhā aññaŋ na bādhakaŋ), 499 (seven divisions), 503 (kāyika); SnA 119 (sukhaŋ vā dukkhaŋ vā Sn 67 = kāyikaŋ sātāsātaŋ). Bdhgh. usually paraphrases d. with vaṭṭadukkha, e. g. at SnA 44, 212, 377, 505. — (b) Thus to be understood as physical pain in comb^n **dukkha + domanassa** "pain & grief," where d. can also be taken as the gen. term & dom° as specification, e. g. in cetasikaŋ dukkhaŋ domanassaŋ paṭisaŋvedeti A I.157, 216; IV.406; S II.69; rāgajaŋ d°ŋ dom °ŋ paṭisaŋvedeti A II.149; kāmûpasaŋhitaŋ d °ŋ dom °ŋ A III.207; d °ŋ dom °ŋ paṭisaŋvediyati S IV.343. Also as cpd. dukkhadomanassānaŋ atthangamāya A III.326, & freq. in formula soka-parideva-d°-domanass-upāyāsā (grief & sorrow, afflictions of pain & misery, i. e. all kinds of misery) D I.36 (arising fr. kāmā); M II.64; A V.216 sq.; It 89 etc. (see above B I. 4). Cp. also the comb^n dukkhī dummano "miserable and dejected" S II.282. — (c) dukkha as "feeling of pain" forms one of the three **dukkhatā** or painful states, viz. d.-dukkhatā (painful sensation caused by bodily pain), sankhāra° id. having its origin in the sankhārā, vipariṇāma°, being caused by change S IV.259; V.56; D III.216; Nett 12. (d) Closely related in meaning is ahita "that which is not good or profitable," usually opposed to sukha & hita. It is freq. in the ster. expression "hoti dīgharattaŋ ahitāya dukkhāya" for a long time it is a source of discomfort & pain A I.194 sq.; M I.332 D III.157; Pug 33. Also in phrases anatthāya ahitāya dukkhāya D III.246 & akusalaŋ . . . ahitāya dukkhāya saŋvattati A I.58. — (e) Under **vedanā** as sensation are grouped the 3: **sukhaŋ** (or sukhā ved.) pleasure (pleasant sensation), **dukkhaŋ** pain (painful sens.), **adukkham-asukhaŋ** indifference (indifferent sens.), the last of which is the ideal state of the emotional habitus to be gained by the Arahant (cp. upekhā & **nibbidā**). Their rôle is clearly indicated in the 4th jhāna: sukhassa pahānā dukkhassa pahānā pubbe va somanassadomanassānaŋ atthangamā adukkham-asukhaŋ upekhā parisuddhiŋ catutthaŋ jhānaŋ upasampajja viharati (see jhāna). — As contents of vedanā: sukhaŋ vediyati dukkhaŋ v. adukkham-asukhaŋ v. tasmā vedanā ti S III.86, 87; cp. S II.82 (vedayati). tisso vedanā: sukha, d°, adukkham-asukhā° D III.275; S II.53; IV.114 sq., 207, 223 sq., cp. M I.396; A I.173; IV.442; It 46, 47. yaŋ kiñc' āyaŋ purisa-puggalo paṭisaŋvedeti sukhaŋ vā d °ŋ vā a °ŋ vā sabban taŋ pubbe katabetū ti = one's whole life-experience is caused by one's former kamma A I.173 = M II.217. — The comb^n (as complementary pair) of **sukha + dukkha** is very freq. for expressing the varying fortunes of life & personal experience as pleasure & pain, e. g. n' âlam aññamaññassa sukhāya vā dukkhāya vā sukhadukkhāya vā D I.56 = S III.211. Thus under the 8 "fortunes of the world" (loka dhammā) with lābha (& a°), yasa (a°), pasaŋsā (nindā), sukha (dukkha) at D III.260; Nd^2 55. Regarded as a thing to be avoided in life: puriso jīvitukāmo . . . sukhakāmo dukkha-paṭikkūlo S IV.172, 188. — In similar contexts: D I.81≈; III.51, 109, 187; S II.22, 39; IV.123 sq.; A II.158 etc. (cp. sukha).

2. As *complex state* (suffering) & its valuation in the light of the Doctrine: (a) any worldly sensation, pleasure & experience may be a source of discomfort (see above, I.; cp. esp. kāma & bhava) Ps I.11 sq. (specified as jāti etc.); dukkhaŋ = mahabbhayaŋ S I.37; bhārādānaŋ dukkhaŋ loke bhāra-nikkhepanaŋ sukhaŋ (pain is the great weight) S III.26; kāmānaŋ adhivacanaŋ A III.310; IV.289; cp. A III.410 sq. (with kāmā, vedanā, saññā, āsavā, kamma, dukkhaŋ). — (b) **ekanta°** (extreme pain) refers to the suffering of sinful beings in Niraya, & it is open to conjecture whether this is not the first & orig. meaning of dukkha; e. g. M I.74; A II.231 (vedanaŋ vediyati ekanta-d°ŋ seyyathā pi sattā nerayikā); see ekanta. In the same sense: . . . upenti Roruvaŋ ghoraŋ cirarattaŋ dukkhaŋ anubhavanti S I.30; niraya-dukkha Sn 531; pecca d°ŋ nigacchati Sn 278, 742; anubhonti d°ŋ kaṭuka-pphalāni Pv I.11^{10} (= āpāyikaŋ d°ŋ PvA 60); PvA 67; mahādukkhaŋ anubhavati PvA 43, 68, 107 etc. atidukkhaŋ PvA 65; dukkhato pete mocetvā PvA 8. — (c) to

suffer pain, to experience unpleasantness etc. is expressed in foll. terms: dukkhaŋ anubhavati (only w. ref. to Niraya, see b); anveti Dh 1 (=kāyikaŋ cetasikaŋ vipāka-dukkhaŋ anugacchati DhA 1.24), upeti Sn 728; carati S 1.210; nigacchati M 1.337; Sn 278, 742; paṭisaŋvedeti M 1.313 (see above); passati S 1.132 (jāto dukkhāni passati: whoever is born experiences woe); vaḍḍheti S 11.109; viharati A 1.202; 11.95; 111.3; S IV.78 (passaddhiyā asati d°ŋ v. dukkhino cittaŋ na samādhiyati); vedayati, vediyati, vedeti etc. see above III. 1 e; sayati A 1.137. — (d) More specific reference to the cause of suffering & its removal by means of enlightenment: (α) *Origin* (see also above I. & II. 1): dukkhe loko patiṭṭhito S 1.40; yaŋ kiñci dukkhaŋ sambhoti sabbaŋ sankhāra-paccayā Sn 731; ye dukkhaŋ vaḍḍhenti te na parimuccanti jātiyā etc. S 11.109; d°ŋ ettha bhiyyo Sn 61, 584; yo paṭhavī-dhātuŋ abhinandati dukkhaŋ so abhin° S1 1.174; taṇhā d °ssa samudayo etc. Nett 23 sq.; as result of sakkāyadiṭṭhi S IV.147, of chanda S 1.22 of upadhi S 11.109, cp. upadhīnidānā pabhavanti dukkhā Sn 728; d°ŋ eva hi sambhoti d°ŋ tiṭṭhati veti ca S 1.135. — (β) *Salvation* from Suffering (see above I.): kathaŋ dukkhā pamuccati Sn 170; dukkhā pamuccati S 1.14; 111.41, 150; IV.205; V.451; na hi putto pati vā pi piyo d °ā pamocaye yathā saddhamma-savanaŋ dukkhā moceti pāṇinaŋ S 1,210; na appatvā lokantaŋ dukkhā atthi pamocanaŋ A 11.49. Kammakkhayā . . . sabbaŋ d°ŋ nijjiṇṇaŋ bhavissati M 11.217, cp. 1.93. kāme pahāya . . . d°ŋ na sevetha anatthasaŋhitaŋ S 1.12=31; rūpaŋ (etc.) abhijānaŋ bhabbo d -°kkhayāya S 111.27; IV.89; d°ŋ pariññāya sakhettavatthuŋ Tathāgato arahati pūraḷāsaŋ Sn 473. pajānati d°ŋ Sn 789, 1056. dukkhassa samudayo ca atthangamo ca S 11.72; 111.228 sq.; IV.86, 327. — dukkhass' antakaro hoti M 1.48; A 111.400 sq.; It 18; antakarā bhavāmase Sn 32; antaŋ karissanti Satthu sāsana-kārino A 11.26; d °parikkhīṇaŋ S 11.133; akiñcanaŋ nânupatanti dukkhā S 1.23; sankhārānaŋ nirodhena n' atthi d°assa sambhavo Sn 731. — muniŋ d°assa pārayuŋ S 1.195=Nd² 136ᵛ; antagū 'si pāragū d°assa Sn 539. — sang' ātiko maccujaho nirūpadhi pahāya d°ŋ apunabbhavāya S IV.158; ucchinnaŋ mūlaŋ d°assa, n' atthi dāni punabbhavo Vin 1.231 = D 11.91.

-âdhivāha bringing or entailing pain S IV.70; **-anubhavana** suffering pain or undergoing punishment (in Niraya) J IV.3; **-antagū** one who has conquered suffering Sn 401; **-âbhikiṇṇa** beset with pain, full of distress It 89; **-âsahanatā** non-endurance of ills Vism 325. **-indriya** the faculty of experiencing pain, painful sensation S V.209, 211; Dhs 556, 560; Vbh 15, 54, 71; **-udraya** causing or yielding pain, resulting in ill, yielding distress M 1.415 sq.; A 1.97; IV.43 (+dukkha-vipāka); V.117 (dukh°), 243; J IV.398; of kamma: Ps 1.80; 11.79; Pv 1.11¹⁰ (so read for dukkhandriya, which is also found at PvA 60); DhA 11.40 (°uddaya); **-ûpadhāna** causing pain Dh 291; **-ûpasama** the allayment of pain or alleviation of suffering, only in phrase (aṭṭhangiko maggo) d-ūpasama-gāmino S 111.86; It 106; Sn 724=Dh 191; — **(m)esin** wishing ill, malevolent J IV.26; **-otiṇṇa** fallen into misery S 111.93; M 1.460; 11.10; **-kāraṇa** labour or trials to be undergone as punishment DhA 111.70 (see Dh 138, 139 & cp. dasa¹ B 1 b); **-khandha** the aggregate of suffering, all that is called pain or affliction (see above B II. 1) S 11.134; 111.93; M 1.192 sq.; 200 sq.; etc.; — **khaya** the destruction of pain, the extinction of ill M 1.93; 11.217 (kammakkhayā d-kkhayo); S 111.27; Sn 732. Freq. in phrase (nīyāti or hoti) sammā-d-kkhayāya "leads to the complete extinction of ill," with ref. to the Buddha's teaching or the higher wisdom, e. g. of brahmacariyā S 11.24; of paññā D 111.268; A 111.152 sq.; of ariyā diṭṭhi D 111.264=A 111.132; of sikkhā A 11.243; of dhamma M 1.72; **-dhamma** the principle of pain, a painful object, any kind of suffering (cp. °khandha) D 111.88; S IV.188 (°ānaŋ samudayañ ca atthagamañ ca yathābhūtaŋ pajānāti); It 38 (nirodha °anaŋ); **-nidāna** a source of pain M 11.223; Dhs 1059, 1136; **-nirodha** the destruction of pain, the extinction of suffering (see above B II. 1) M 1.191; 11.10; A 111.410, 416; etc.; **-paṭikkūla** averse to pain, avoiding unpleasantness, in combⁿ sukhakāmo d-p. S IV.172 (spelt °kulo), 188; M 1.341; **-patta** being in pain J VI.336; **-pareta** afflicted by pain or misery S 111.93; It 89=A 1.147; **-bhummi** the soil of distress Dhs 985; **-vāca** hurtful speech Pv 1.3² (should probably be read duṭṭha°); **-vipāka** (adj.) having pain as its fruit, creating misery S 11.128; D 111.57, 229; A 11.172 (kamma); Ps 11.79 (id.); **-vepakka** =°vipāka Sn 537 (kamma); **-saññā** the consciousness of pain Nett 27; **-samudaya** the rise or origin of pain or suffering (opp. °nirodha; see above B II. 1) S IV.37; M 1.191; 11.10; 111.267; Vbh 107 (taṇhā ca avasesā ca kilesā: ayaŋ vuccati d-s.); **-samphassa** contact with pain M 1.507; Dhs 648; f. abstr. °tā Pug 33; **-seyya** an uncomfortable couch DhA IV.8.

Dukkhatā (f.) [cp. Sk. duḥkhatā, abstr. to dukkha] state of pain, painfulness, discomfort, pain (see dukkha B III. 1 c) D 111.216; S IV.259; V.56; Nett 12 (expl.).

Dukkhati [fr. dukkha] to be painful Vism 264.

Dukkhatta (nt.) [Sk. *duhkhatvaŋ]=dukkhatā D 111.106 (+dandhatta).

Dukkhāpana (nt.) [abstr. to dukkhāpeti] bringing sorrow, causing pain Miln 275 sq., 351.

Dukkhāpita [pp. of dukkhāpeti] pained, afflicted Miln 79, 180.

Dukkhāpeti [caus. to dukkha] to cause pain, to afflict J IV.452; Miln 276 sq.; PvA 215. — pp. **dukkhāpita.**

Dukkhita (adj.) [Sk. duḥkhita; pp. of *dukkhāpeti] afflicted, dejected, unhappy, grieved, disappointed; miserable, suffering, ailing (opp. sukhita) D 1.72 (puriso ābādhiko d. bāḷha-gilāno); 11.24; S 1.149; 111.11=IV.180 (sukhitesu sukhito dukkhitesu dukkhito); V.211; M 1.88; 11.66; Vin IV.291; Sn 984, 986; J IV.452; Miln 275; DhA 11.28; VvA 67.

Dukkhin (adj.-n.) [Sk. duḥkhin] 1. afflicted, grieved, miserable S 1.103 sq., 129 sq., 11.282 (+dummano); IV.78; A 111.57. — 2. a loser in the game J 11.160.

Dukkhīyati [Sk. duḥkhīyati & duḥkhāyati Denom. fr. dukkha; cp. vediyati & vedayati] to feel pain, to be distressed DhA 11.28 (=vihaññati).

Dugga [du+ga] a difficult road Dh 327; Pv 11.7⁸. **dugge sankamanāni** passages over difficult roads, usually combᵈ with papā (water-shed) S 1.100; Vv 52²²; Pv 11.9²⁵.

Duṭṭha (adj.-n.) [Sk. duṣṭha, pp. of dussati, q. v.] spoilt, corrupt; bad, malignant, wicked Vin 111.118; S 11.259, 262; IV.339; A 1.124 (°aruka), 127 (id.), 157 sq.; It 68 (saro d., perhaps should be read as diddho); J 1.187, 254 (°brāhmaṇa); IV.391 (°caṇḍāla); PvA 4 (°corā: rogues of thieves); Sdhp 86, 367, 434. — **aduṭṭha** not evil, good Sn 623; It 86; DhA IV.164. Cp. pa°.

-gahaṇika suffering from indigestion Vin 1.206; **-citta** evil-minded Vin 11.192; M 111.65.

Duṭṭhu (adv.) [Sk. duṣṭhu, cp. suṣṭhu] badly, wrong DhsA 384; SnA 396; VvA 337.

Duṭṭhulla (adj.) wicked, lewd Vin IV.128; S 1.187 (°bhāṇin "whose speech is never lewd," cp. Th 1, 1217 padullagāhin, explᵈ as duṭṭhullagāhin *Psalms of Brethren* 399 *n.* 3); M 1.435; 111.159; Vism 313. — (nt.) wickedness Vin 111.21; kāya° unchastity M 111.151; Th 1, 114; Vism 151.

-âduṭṭhulla that which is wicked & that which is not Vin v.130; -āpatti a grave transgression of the Rules of the Order, viz. the 4 Pārājika & the 13 Saṅghādisesa Vin iv.31 (opp. a° Vin iv.32).

Dutiya (num. ord.) [Sk. dvitīya, with reduction of dvi to du, as in compⁿ mentioned under dvi B II. For the meaning "companion" cp. num. ord. for two in Lat. secundus<sequor, i. e. he who follows, & Gr. δεύτερος> δεύομαι he who stays behind, also Sk. davīyas farther] (a) (num.) the second, the following J II.102, 110; dutiyaŋ for the second time (cp. tatiyaŋ in series 1, 2, 3) Vin II.188; D II.155. — (b) (adj. n.) one who follows or is associated with, an associate of; accompanying or accompanied by (-°); a companion, friend, partner Vin IV.225; S I.25 (saddhā dutiyā purisassa hoti=his 2nd self); IV.78 (id.) I.131; It 9; J V.400; Th 2, 230 (a husband); Sn 49 (=Nd² 305, where two kinds of associates or companions are distinguished, viz. taṇhā° & puggalo°). taṇhā-dutiyā either "connected with thirst" or "having thirst as one's companion" (see taṇhā) S IV.37; It 109=A II.10; bilaṅga° kaṇājaka (rice with sour gruel) Vin II.77; S I.90, 91. —adutiya alone, unaccompanied PvA 161.

Dutiyaka (adj.-n.) [Demin. of dutiya] (a) the second, following, next J I.504 (°cittavāre); °ŋ a 2nd time M I.83. — (b) a companion; only in f. dutiyakā a wife or female compⁿ Vin IV.230, 270 (a bhikkhunī as compⁿ of another one); Freq. as purāṇa-dutiyikā one's former wife Vin I.96; III.16; S I.200; M II.63; J I.210; V.152; DhA I.77. Cp. M Vastu II.134 dvitīyā in the same sense.

Dutiyyatā (f.) companionship, friendship, help J III.169.

Duddabha see daddabha.

Duddha (Sk. dugdha, pp. of **duh**, see dohati] milked, drawn Sn 18 (duddha-khīra=gāvo duhitvā gahita-khīra SnA 27); M II.186. — (nt.) milk Dāvs V.26.

Dudrabhi [another form of dundubhi, cp. duddabha & dundubhya] a kettle-drum, in Amata° the drum of Nibbāna Vin I.8=M I.171 (dundubhi at the latter passage); PvA 189 (v. l. for dundubhi).

Dundubhi (m. & f.) [Sk. dundubhi, onomat.; cp. other forms under daddabha, dudrabhi] a kettle-drum, the noise of a drum, a heavy thud, thunder (usually as deva° in the latter meaning) Pv III.3⁴; J VI.465; PvA 40, 189 (v. l. dudrabhi). — Amata° the drum of Nibbāna M I.171=Vin I.8 (: dudrabhi); deva° thunder D II.156; A IV.311.

***Dunoti** to burn, see der, dava, dāva & dāya.

Dupaṭṭo see dvi B II.

Dubbaṇṇa see under vaṇṇa.

Dubbuṭṭhika see under vuṭṭhi.

Dubbha (& dūbha) (adj.) [Sk. dambha, see dubbhati] deceiving, hurting, trying to injure Vin II.203 (=It 68 where dubbhe); Pv II.9³ (mitta°). adubbha one who does not do harm, harmless Pv II.9⁸ (°pāṇin=ahiŋsa-kahattha). As nt. harmlessness, frankness, friendliness, good-will Vin I.347 (adrūbhāya, but cp. vv. ll. p. 395: adubbhaya & adrabbhāvāya); S I.225 (adubbhāya trustily); J I.180 (id. as adūbhāya); spelt wrongly adrūbhaka (for adubbbaka, with v. l. adrabhaka in expl. of adubbha-pāṇin) at J VI.311. *Note:* dabhāya (dat.) is also used in Sk. in sense of an adv. or infinitive, which confirms the etymology of the word. Cp. dobha.

Dubbhaka (adj.) [Sk. dambhaka] perfidious, insidious, treacherous Th I, 214 (citta°). Cp. dubbhaya & dūbhaka.

Dubbhati (& dūbhati) [Sk. dabhnoti cp. *J.P.T.S.* 1889, 204: **dabh** (dambh), pp. dabdha; idg. ***dhebh**, cp. Gr. ἀτέμβω to deceive. Cp. also Sk **druh** (so Kern, *Toev.* p. 11, s. v. padubbhati). See also dahara & dūbha, dūbhaka, dūbhi] to injure, hurt, deceive; to be hostile to, plot or sin against (either w. dat. J V.245; VI.491, or w. loc. J I.267; III:212) S I.85 (ppr. adubbhanto), 225; It 86 (dubbhe=dusseyya Com.)=Vin II.203 (where dubbho); Th I, 1129; J II.125; IV.261; V 487, 503. — ppr. also dūbbato J IV.261; ger. dubbhitvā J IV.79; grd. dubbheyya (v. l. dūbheyya) to be punished J V.71. Cp. pa°.

Dubbhana (nt.) [Sk. *dambhana] hurtfulness, treachery, injury against somebody (c. loc.) PvA 114 (=anattha).

Dubbhaya =dubbhaka, S I.107.

Dubbhika =dubbhaka, Pv III.1¹³ (=mittadubbhika, mittānaŋ bādhaka PvA 175).

Dubbhikkha see bhikkhā.

Dubbhin (adj.-n.) [Sk. dambhin] seeking to injure, deceitful; a deceiver, hypocrite J IV.41; Pv II.9⁸ (mitta°); DhA II.23 (mitta-dūbhin). — f. dubbhinī VvA 68 (so read for dubbinī).

Dubha (num.-adj.) [See dubhaya & cp. dvi B II.] both; only in abl. dubhato from both sides Th I, 1134; Ps I.69; II.35, 181; Vv 46²¹; VvA 281 (for Vv 64¹⁹ duvaddhato).

Dubhaya (num. adj.) [a contaminated form of du(ve) & ubhaya; see dvi B II.] both (see ubhaya) Sn 517, 526, 1007, 1125; J III.442; VI.110.

Duma [Sk. druma=Gr. δρυμός, see dāru] tree A III.43; J I.87, 272; II.75, 270; VI.249, 528; Vv 84¹⁴; Miln 278, 347; VvA 161.

-agga 1. the top of a tree J II.155. — 2. a splendid tree Vv 35⁴. — 3. a tooth-pick J V.156; -inda "king of trees," the Bodhi tree Dpvs I.7; -uttama a magnificent tree Vv 39³; -phala fruit of a tree M II.74; Vism 231 (in comparison).

Duyhati Pass to dohati (q. v.).

Dussa¹ (nt.) [Sk. dūrśa & dūṣya] woven material, cloth, turban cloth; (upper) garment, clothes Vin I.290; II.128, 174; IV.159. D I.103; S V.71; M I.215; II.92; A V.347; Sn 679; Pv I.10³ (=uttariyaŋ sāṭakaŋ PvA 49): II.3¹⁴; Pug 55; PvA 73, 75. — cīvara°, q. v.; chava° a miserable garment D I.166; A I.295; II.206; M I.78, 308.

-karaṇḍaka a clothes-chest S V.75=M I.215; A IV.230; -koṭṭhagāra a store-room for cloth or clothes DhA I.220, 393; -gahaṇa (-maṅgala) (the ceremony of) putting on a garment DhA II.87; -cālanī a cloth sieve Vin I.202; -paṭṭa turban cloth Vin II.266 (=setavattha-paṭṭa Bdhgh.); S II.102; -phala having clothes as fruit (of magic trees, cp. kapparukkha) Vv 46² (cp. VvA 199); -maya consisting in clothes Vv 46⁷ (cp. VvA 199); -yuga a suit of garments Vin I.278; M I.215=S V.71; Miln 31 (cp. M Vastu I.61); DhA IV.11; -ratana "a pearl of a garment," a fine garment Miln 262. -vaṭṭi fringed cotton cloth Vin II.266. -veṇi plaited cotton cloth Vin II.266.

Dussa² at J III.54 is usually taken as =amussa (cp. amuka). C. explˢ as "near" & adds "asammussa." Or is it Sk. dūṣya easily spoilt? See on this passage Andersen *Pali Reader* II.124.

Dussaka =dūsaka (q. v.).

Dussati [Sk. duṣyati, Denom. fr. pref. duḥ (du°); pp. duṣṭha, caus. dūṣayati] to be or become bad or corrupted, to get damaged; to offend against, to do wrong

Vin II.113; S I.13=104; Dh 125=PvA 116; Dh 137; It 84 (dosaneyye na d.) cp. A III.110 (dussanīye d.); J VI.9; Miln 101, 386. — pp. duṭṭha (q. v.). — Caus. dūseti (q. v.). See also dosa¹ & dosaniya; & pa°.

Dussanā (f.) & **Dussana** (nt.) [Sk. dūṣana, cp. dussati] defilement, guilt A II.225; Pug 18, 22; Dhs 418, 1060; DA I.195 (rajjana-d. muyhana).

Dussanīya (adj.) [cp. Sk. dveṣaṇīya, because of doṣa = dveṣa taken to **dus**] able to give offence, hateful, evil (always comb^d with rajanīya, cp. rāga dosa moha) A III.110 (dusanīye dussati, where It 84 has dosaneyye); J VI.9; Miln 386.

Dussassa see sassa.

Dussika a cloth merchant J VI.276; Miln 262, 331 sq.

Dussitatta (nt.) [Sk. *dūṣitatva] = dussanā, Pug 18, 22.

Duha (adj.-°) [Sk. duh & duha; see dohati] milking; yielding, granting, bestowing: kāma° giving pleasures J IV.20; V.33.

Duhati (to milk) see dohati.

Duhana (adj.-n.) [Sk. *druhana, to druh, druhyati to hurt, cp. Oir. droch; Ohg. triogan to deceive, traum = dream; also Sk. dhvarati. For further connections see Walde, *Lat. Wtb.* under fraus] one who injures, hurts or deceives; insidious, infesting; a robber, only in pantha° a dacoit D I.135; DA I.296. — (nt.) waylaying, robbery (pantha°) J II.281 (text dūhana), 388 (text: pantha-dūbhana, vv. ll. duhana & dūhana); DhsA 220. — Cp. maggadūsin.

Duhitika (adj.) [cp. Sk. druha, fr. druhyati] infested with robbers, beset with dangers S IV.195 (magga). — *Note.* This interpretation may have to be abandoned in favour of duhitika being another spelling of dvīhitika = hard to get through (q. v.), to be compared are the vv. ll. of the latter at S IV.323 (S.S. dūhitika & dūhītika).

Dūta¹ [Ved. dūta, prob. to dūra (q. v.) as "one who is sent (far) away," also perhaps Gr. δοῦλος slave. See Walde, *Lat. Wtb.* under dudum] a messenger, envoy Vin I.16; II.32, 277; D I.150; S IV.194; Sn 411 (rāja°), 417. — deva° Yama's envoy, Death's messenger A I.138, 142; M II.75 sq.; J I.138. — °ŋ pāheti to send a messenger Miln 18, PvA 133.

Dūta² (nt.) [Sk. dyūta, see jūta] play, gaming, gambling J IV.248.

Dūteyya (nt.) [Sk. dūtya, but varying in meaning] errand, commission, messages A IV.196; J III.134; DA I.78.— °ŋ gacchati to go on an errand Vin II.202; °ŋ harati to obtain a commission Vin III.87; IV.23.
-kamma doing a messenger's duty Vin I.359; -pahiṇagamana sending & going on messages D I.5 = M III.34; A II.209; M II.180.

Dūbha (adj.) deceiving, see dubbha.

Dūbhaka¹ (adj.) [Sk. dambhaka] deceiving, treacherous, harmful SnA 287 (mitta°); f. °ikā J II.297.

Dūbhaka² [Sk. dambha, cp. dambholi] a diamond J I.263 = III.207.

Dūbhana (nt.) deceiving, pillaging, robbing etc. at J II.388 is to be read as (pantha-) duhana.

Dūbhin (adj.) = dubbhin J II.180 (vv. ll. dūbha & dubbhi), 327; IV.257; DhA II.23.

Dūbhī (f.) [cp. Sk. dambha, see dubbhati] perfidy, treachery, J I.412; IV.57 (v. l. dubhī); VI.59 (= aparādha).

Dūra (adj.) [Sk. dūra, Ved duva (stirring, urging on), compar. davīyān, Av. dūrō (far). ***dāu**; cp. Ohg. zawen, Goth. taujan = E. do. Another form is ***deuā**, far in respect to time, as in Gr. δήν, δηρόν, Lat. dū-dum (cp. dū-rare = en-dure). See also dutiya & dūta] far, distant, remote, *opp.* āsanna (J II.154) or santika (Dhs 677; Vism 402). — PvA 117. Often in cpds. (see below), also as dūri°, e. g. dūri-bhāva distance Vism 71, 377; DhsA 76. — Cases mostly used adverbially, viz. acc. dūraŋ far J II.154; DhA I.192. — abl. dūrato from afar, aloof Vin I.15; II.195; S I.212; Sn 511; Dh 219; J V.78 (dūra-dūrato); Miln 23; PvA 107. dūrato karoti to keep aloof from PvA 17.—loc. dūre at a distance, also as prep. away from, far from (c. abl.), e. g. Sn 468; J II.155, 449 (= ārā); III.189. — Sn 772; Dh 304; J VI.364; Dhs 677. — dūre-pātin one who shoots far [cp. Sk. dūra-pātin] A I.284; II.170, 202. J IV.494. See also akkhaṇavedhin. — atidūre too far Vin II.215.
-kantana at Th I, 1123: the correct reading seems to be the v. l. durākantana, see ākantana; -gata gone far away Pv II.13⁴ (= paralokagata PvA 164); DhA III.377 (durā°). -(ŋ)gama far-going, going here & there Dh 37 (cp. DhA I.304); Pv II.9¹⁰; -ghuṭṭha far-renowned Pv II.8²; -vihāra (-vuttin) living far away Sn 220.

Dūrakkha [du¹ + rakkha] see rakkha & cp. du¹.

Dūratta (adj.) [du¹ + ratta] reddish M I.36 (°vaṇṇa).

Dūsaka (adj.-n.) [Sk. dūṣaka] corrupting, disgracing, one who defiles or defames; a robber, rebel A V.71 (bhikkhunī°); J II.270; IV.495; Sn 89 (kula° one who spoils the reputation of the clan); DhA II.23 (kuṭi° an incendiary); Miln 20 (pantha°). As dussaka at J V.113 (kamma°); Sn A 287 (mitta°, v. l. B. for dūbhaka). — panthadūsaka a highwayman Miln 290. — f. dūsikā J III.179 (also as **dūsiyā** = dosakārikā); a° harmless Sn 312 (see a°).

Dūsana (nt.) [see dūseti] spoiling, defiling J II.270; Sdhp 453.

Dūsita [Sk. dūṣita, pp. of **dūseti**] depraved, sinful, evil PvA 226 (°citta).

Dūsin (adj.-n.) [Sk. dūṣin] = dūsaka, in magga° (cp. pantha-dusaka) a highway robber Sn 84 sq.

Dūseti [Sk. dūṣayati, caus. of dussati (q. v.). Also as dusseti PvA 82] to spoil, ruin; to injure, hurt; to defile, pollute, defame Vin I.79, 85, 86; IV.212 (maŋ so dūsetukāmo, said by a bhikkhunī), 316 (dūsetuŋ); A IV.169 sq.; J I.454; II.270; DhA II.22 (kuṭiŋ, damage, destroy). — aor. **dūsayi** J II.110 (fared ill). — pp. dūsita. Cp. pa°, pari°

Dūhana¹ (nt.) [see duhana] infesting, polluting, defaming; robbing, only in pantha° (with v. l. duhana) waylaying J II.281, 388; Tikp 280.

Dūhana² (nt.) [Sk. dohana, see dohati] milking (-°), in kumbha° filling the pails with milk, i. e. giving much milk (gāvo; cp. Sk. droṇadughā a cow which yields much milk) Sn 309.

Dūhitika see duhitika.

Dejjha (= dvejjha, see dvi B I.5] divided, in a° undividedness J III.7 (com. abhejja), 274 = IV.258 (dhanuŋ a °ŋ karoti to get the bow ready, v. l. BB. sarejjhaŋ; C. expl^d jiyāya ca sarena ca saddhiŋ ekam eva katvā).

Deḍḍubha [Sk. duṇḍubha] a water-snake; salamander J III.16; VI.194; Sdhp 292. See next.

Deḍḍubhaka 1. a sort of snake (see prec.) J I.361. — 2. a kind of girdle (in the form of a snake's head) Vin II.136 (expl^d by udaka-sappi-sira-sadisa).

Deṇḍima (m. nt.) [Sk. diṇḍima, cp. dindima] a kind of kettle-drum D I 79 (v. l. dindima); Nd^2 219 (°ka, v. l. dind°); J I.355; (=paṭaha-bheri); V.322=VI.217; VI.465=580.

Depiccha (adj.) [=dvepiccha, see dvi B I. 5] having two tail-feathers J V.339.

Deyya (adj.) [Sk. deya, grd. of **dā**, see dadāti I. 2, b] (a) to be given (see below). — (b) deserving a gift, worthy of receiving alms J III.12 (a°); Miln 87 (rāja°) *-nt.* a gift, offering Vin I.298 (saddhā°).

-dhamma a gift, lit. that which has the quality of being given; esp. a gift of mercy, meritorious gift S I.175; A I.150, 166; II.264 (saddhā°); Pv I.1^1; II.3^{18}; PvA 5, 7 sq., 26, 92 (°bīja), 103, 129; cp. AvŚ I.308. The deyyadhamma (set of gifts, that which it is or should be a rule to give) to mendicants, consists of 14 items, which are (as enum^d at Nd^2 523 under the old Brahman's term yañña "sacrifice") (1) cīvara, (2) piṇḍapāta, (3) senāsana, (4) gilāna-paccaya-bhesajja-parikkhāra, (5) anna, (6) pāna, (7) vattha, (8) yāna, (9) mālā, (10) gandhā, (11) vilepana, (12) seyya, (13) āvasatha, (14) padīpeyya. A similar enum^n in diff. order is found at Nd^1 373.

Deva [Ved. deva, Idg. ***deịā** to shine (see dibba & diva), orig. adj. *deiṇos belonging to the sky, cp. Av. daēvō (demon.), Lat. deus, Lith. dēvas; Ohg. Zio; Ags. Tīg, gen. Tīwes (=Tuesday); Oir. dia (god). The popular etymology refers it to the root **div** in the sense of playing, sporting or amusing oneself: dibbanti ti devā, pañcahi kāmaguṇehi kīḷanti attano vā siriyā jotantī ti attho KhA 123] a god, a divine being; usually in pl. **devā** the gods. As title attributed to any superhuman being or beings regarded to be in certain respects above the human level. Thus primarily (see 1^a) used of the first of the next-world devas, **Sakka**, then also of subordinate deities, demons & spirits (devaññatarā some kind of deity; snake-demons: nāgas, tree-gods: rukkhadevatā etc.). Also title of the king (3). Always implying splendour (cp. above etym.) & mobility, beauty, goodness & light, & as such opposed to the dark powers of mischief & destruction (asurā: Titans; petā: miserable ghosts; nerayikā sattā: beings in Niraya). A double position (dark & light) is occupied by Yama, the god of the Dead (see Yama & below 1 c). Always implying also a kinship and continuity of life with humanity and other beings; all devas have been man and may again become men (cp. D I.17 sq.; S III.85), hence "gods" is not a coincident term. All devas are themselves in saŋsāra, needing salvation. Many are found worshipping saints (Th I.627-9; Th II 365). — The collective appellations differ; there are var. groups of divine beings, which in their totality (cp. tāvatiŋsa) include some or most of the well-known Vedic deities. Thus some collect. designations are **devā sa-indakā** (the gods, including Indra or with their ruler at their head: D II.208; S III.90, A V.325), **sa-pajāpatikā** (S III.90), **sa-mārakā** (see deva-manussaloka), **sa-brahmakā** (S III.90). See below 1 b. Lists of popular gods are to be found, e. g. at D II.253; III.194. — A current distinction dating from the latest books in the canon is that into 3 *classes*, viz. **sammuti-devā** (conventional gods, gods in the public opinion, i. e. kings & princes J I.132; DA I.174), **visuddhi°** (beings divine by purity, i. e. of great religious merit or attainment like Arahants & Buddhas), & **upapatti°** (being born divine, i. e. in a heavenly state as one of the gatis, like bhumma-devā etc.). This division in detail at Nd^2 307; Vbh 422; KhA 123; VvA 18. Under the 3rd category (upapatti°) *seven groups* are enumerated in the foll. order: Cātummahārājikā devā, Tāvatiŋsā d. (with Sakka as chief), Yāmā d., Tusitā d., Nimmānarati d., Paranimmita-vasavattī d., Brahmakāyikā d. Thus at D I.216 sq.; A I.210, 332 sq.; Nd^2 307; cp. S I 133 & J I.48. See also devatā.

1. good etc. — (a) sg. a god, a deity or divine being, M I.71 (d. vā Māro vā Brahmā vā); S IV.180=A IV.461 (devo vā bhavissāmi devaññataro vā ti: I shall become a god or some one or other of the (subordinate gods, angels); Sn 1024 (ko nu devo vā Brahmā vā Indo vāpi Sujampati); Dh 105 (+gandhabba, Māra, Brahmā); A II.91, 92 (puggalo devo hoti devaparivāro etc.); PvA 16 (yakkho vā devo vā). — (b) pl. devā gods. These inhabit the 26 devalokas one of which is under the rule of Sakka, as is implied by his appellation S. **devānaŋ indo** (his opponent is Vepacitti Asur-indo S I.222) S I.216 sq.; IV.101, 269; A I.144; Sn 346; PvA 22 etc. — Var. kinds are e. g. appamāṇ'-ābhā (opp. paritt' ābhā) M III.147; ābhassarā D I.17; Dh 200; khiḍḍāpadosikā D I.19; gandhabba-kāyikā S III.250 sq.; cattāro mahārājikā S V.409, 423; Jat I.48; Pv IV.11^1; PvA 17, 272; naradevā tidasā S I.5; bhummā PvA 5; manāpa-kāyikā A IV.265 sq.; mano-padosikā D I.20; valāhaka-kāyikā S III.254. — Var. attributes of the Devas are e. g. āyuppamāṇā A I.267; II.126 sq.; IV.252 sq.; dīghāyukā S III.86; A II.33; rūpino manomayā M I.410, etc. etc. — See further in general: D I.54 (satta devā); II.14, 157, 208; S V.475=A I.37; Sn 258 (+manussā), 310 (id.); 404, 679; Dh 30, 56, 94, 230, 366; Ps I.83 sq.; II.149; Vbh 86, 395, 412 sq., Nett 23; Sdhp 240. — (c) **deva=Yama** see deva-dūta (expl^d at J I.139: devo ti maccu). — **atideva** a pre-eminent god, god above gods (Ep. of the Buddha) Nd^2 307; DhsA 2 etc.; see under cpds. — 2. the sky, but *only* in its rainy aspect, i. e. rain-cloud, rainy sky, rain-god (cp. Jupiter Pluvius; *K.S.* I.40, *n.* 2 on Pajjunna, a Catumahārājika), usually in phrase deve vassante (when it rains etc.), or devo vassati (it rains) D I.74 (: devo ti megho DA I.218); S I.6, 154 (cp. It 66 megha); Sn 18, 30; J V.201; DhA II.58, 82; PvA 139. devo ekam ekam phusāyati the cloud rains drop by drop, i. e. lightly S I.104 sq., 154, 184; IV.289. — **thulla-phusitake deve vassante** when the sky was shedding big drops of rain S III.141; V.396; A I.243; II.140; V.114; Vism 259. — **vigata-valāhake deve** when the rain-clouds have passed S I.65; M II.34, 42. — 3. king, usually in voc. deva, king! Vin I.272; III.43; A II.57; J I.150, 307; PvA 4, 74 etc.

devī (f.) 1. goddess, of Petīs, Yakkhiṇīs etc.; see etym. expl. at VvA 18. — Pv II.1^{12}; Vv 1^3 etc. — 2. queen Vin I.82 (Rahulamātā), 272; D II.14; A II.57, 202 (Mallikā) J I.50 (Māyā); III.188; PvA 19, 75.

-accharā a divine Apsarā, a heavenly joy-maiden Vism 531; PvA 46, 279; **-aññatara**, in phrase devo vā d. vā, a god or one of the retinue of a god S IV.180=A IV.461; PvA 16; **-âtideva** god of gods, i. e. divine beyond all divinities, a super-deva, of Buddha Nd^2 307 & on Sn 1134; J IV.158=DhA I.147; Vv 64^{27}; VvA 18; Miln 241, 258, 368, 384 & passim; cp. M Vastu I.106, 257, 283, 291; **-attabhāva** a divine condition, state of a god PvA 14; **-ânubhāva** divine majesty or power D II.12; M III.120; J I.59; **-āsana** a seat in heaven It 76; **-âsura-sangâma** the fight between the Gods & the Titans D II.285; S I.222; IV.201; V.447; M I.253; A IV.432 (at all passages in identical phrase); **-iddhi** divine power Vv 31^3; VvA 7; **-isi** a divine Seer Sn 1116; Nd^2 310; **-ûpapatti** rebirth among the gods PvA 6; **-orohaṇa** descent of the gods DhA III.443; **-kaññā** a celestial maiden, a nymph S I.200; J I.61; VvA 37, 78; **-kāya** a particular group of gods S I.200; It 77; Th 2, 31; **-kuñjara** "elephant of the gods," of Indra J V.158; **-kumāra** son of a god (cp. °putta) J III.391; **-gaṇa** a troop of gods J I.203; DhA III.441; **-gaha** a temple, chapel Vin III.43; **-cārikā** a visit to the gods, journeying in the devaloka VvA 3, 7, 165 etc.; **-ṭṭhāna** heavenly seat J III.55; a temple, sacred place Miln 91, 330; **-dattika** given or granted by a god, extraordinary PvA 145; **-dattiya**=°dattika J III.37; DhA I.278; **-dāruka** a species of pine J V.420; **-dundubhi** the celestial drum, i. e. thunder D I.10; Miln 178; DA I.95; **-dūta**

the god's (i. e. Yama's see above 1ᶜ) messenger A I.138, 142; M II.75; III.179; J I.138; DhA I.85 (tayo d.); Mhbv. 122 (°suttanta); -deva "the god of gods," Ep. of the Buddha (cp. devâtideva) Th 1, 533, 1278 (of Kappāyana); DhsA 1; PvA 140; -dhamma that which is divine or a god A III.277 (°ika); DhA III.74; -dhītā a female deva or angel (cp. devaputta), lit. daughter of a god J II.57; VvA 137, 153 (with ref. to Vimānapetīs); -nagara the city of the Devas, heaven J I.168, 202; DhA I.280; -nikāya a class, community or group of gods, celestial state or condition D II.261 (sixty enumᵈ); S IV.180; M I.102 sq.; A I.63 sq.; II.185; III.249 sq.; IV.55; V.18; -pañha questioning a god, using an oracle D I.11 (=DA I.97: devadāsiyā sarīre devataŋ otāretvā pañha-pucchanaŋ); -parivāra a retinue of gods A II.91; -parisā the assembly of gods A II.185; Tikp 241. -putta "son of a god," a demi-god, a ministering god (cp. f. deva-dhītā), usually of Yakkhas, but also applᵈ to the 4 archangels having charge of the higher world of the Yāmā devā (viz. Suyāma devaputta); the Tusitā d. (Santusita d.); the Nimmānaratī d. (Sunimmita d.); & the Paranimmitavasavattī d. (Vasavattī d.) D I.217 sq.; cp. J I.48. — D II.12, 14; S I.46 sq.; 216 sq.; IV.280; A I.278; It 76; J I.59 (jarā-jajjara); IV.100 (Dhamma d.); VI.239 (fava d.); PvA 6, 9, 55, 92, 113 (Yakkho ti devaputto); Miln 23; -pura the city of the gods, heaven S IV.202; Vv 64³⁰ (=Sudassana-mahānagara VvA 285); J IV.143; -bhava celestial existence PvA 167; -bhoga the wealth of the gods PvA 97; -manussā (pl.) gods & men D I.46, 62≈, 99 (°mānuse); M II.38, 55; Sn 14 (sa°), 236 (°pūjita), 521; It 80 (°seṭṭhā); Kh VIII.10; KhA 196; PvA 17, 31, 117; -°*loka* the world of gods and men. It comprises (1) the world of gods proper (Devas, i. e. Sakka, Māra & Brahmā; corresp. to sammuti-devā, see above); (2) samaṇas & brāhmaṇas (cp. visuddhi-devā); (3) gods & men under the human aspect (gati, cp. upapatti devā): Sn 1047, 1063; expl. at Nd² 309 & (with diff. interpretations) DA I.174 sq.; -yāna leading to the (world of) the gods, i. e. the road to heaven Sn 139, also in °yāniya (magga) D I.215; -rājā king of the devas, viz. Sakka Nd¹ 177; J III.392 (=devinda); DhA III.441; PvA 62; -rūpa divine appearance or form PvA 92; -loka the particular sphere of any devas, the seat of the devas, heaven; there exist 26 such spheres or heavens (see loka); when 2 are mentioned it refers to Sakka's & Brahma's heavens. A seat in a devaloka is in saŋsāra attained by extraordinary merit: Dh 177; J I.202, 203; IV.273; ThA 74; KhA 228; PvA 5, 9, 21, 66, 81, 89; Vism 415, etc.; -vimāna the palace of a deva J I.58; VvA 173; -sankhalikā a magic chain J II.128; V.92, 94; -sadda heavenly sound or talk among the devas It 75 (three such sounds).

Devaka (adj.) (-°) [deva+ka] belonging or peculiar to the devas; only in sa°-loka the world including the gods in general D I.62; Nd² 309; Sn 86, 377, 443, 760 etc.; Miln 234. See also devamanussa-loka.

Devata (adj.) (-°) having such & such a god as one's special divinity, worshipping, a worshipper of, devotee of Miln 234 (Brahma°+Brahma (garuka). — f. devatā in pati° "worshipping the husband," i. e. a devoted wife J III.406; VvA 128.

Devatā (f.) [deva+tā, qualitative-abstr. suffix, like Lat. juventa, senecta, Goth. hauhiþa, Ohg. fullida cp. Sk. pūrṇatā, bandhutā etc.] "condition or state of a deva," divinity; divine being, deity, fairy. The term comprises all beings which are otherwise styled devas, & a list of them given at Nd² 308 & based on the principle that any being who is worshipped (or to whom an offering is made or a gift given: de-vatā=yesaŋ deti, as is expressed in the conclusion "ye yesaŋ dakkhiṇeyyā te tesaŋ devatā") is a devatā, comprises 5 groups of 5 kinds each, viz. (1) ascetics; (2) domestic animals (elephants, horses, cows, cocks, crows); (3) physical forces & elements (fire, stone etc.); (4) lower gods (: bhumma devā) (nāgā, suvaṇṇā, yakkhā, asurā, gandhabbā); (5) higher gods (: inhabitants of the deva-loka proper) Mahārājā, Canda, Suriya, Inda, Brahmā), to which are added the 2 aspects of the sky-god as deva-devatā & disā-devatā). — Another definition at VvA 21 simply states: devatā ti devaputto pi Brahmā pi deva-dhītā pi vuccati. — Among the var. deities the foll. are frequently mentioned: rukkha° tree-gods or dryads M I.306; J I.221; PvA 5; vatthu° earth gods (the four kings) Pv 4¹; PvA 17; vana° wood-nymphs M I.306; samudda° water-sprites J II.112 etc. etc. — D I.180 (mahiddhikā, pl.), 192; II.8, 87, 139, 158; S I. sq.; IV.302; M I.245; II.37; A I.64, 210, 211; II.70 (sapubba°); III.77 (bali-paṭiggāhikā), 287 (saddhāya samannāgatā); 309; IV.302 sq., 390 (vippaṭisāriniyo); V.331; Sn 45, 316, 458, 995, 1043; Dh 99; J I.59, 72, 223, 256; IV.17, 474; Vv 16³; Pv II.1¹⁰; KhA 113, 117; PvA 44.

-ânubhāva divine power or majesty J I.168; -ânussati "remembrance of the gods," one of the 6 ānussati-ṭṭhānāni, or subjects to be kept in mind D III.250, 280, cp. A I.211; Vism 197. -uposatha a day of devotion to the gods A I.211; -paribhoga fit to be enjoyed by gods J II.104; -bali an offering to the gods A II.68; -bhāva at PvA 110 read as devattabhāva (opp. petatta-bhāva).

Devati [div] to lament, etc.; see pari°. Cp. also paridevа etc.

Devatta (nt.) [deva+tta] the state of being a deva, divinity ThA 70; PvA 110 (°bhāva as Yakkha, opp. petatta bhāva; so read for devatā-bhāva).

Devattana (nt.) [=last] state or condition of a deva Th 1, 1127; cp. petattana in the foll. verse.

Devara [Sk. devṛ & devara Gr. δαήρ (*δαιϝήρ), Lat. levir, Ohg. zeihhur, Ags. tācor] husband's brother, brother-in-law J VI.152; Vv 32⁸ (sa°), popularly explᵈ at VvA 135 as "dutiyo varo ti vā devaro, bhattu kaniṭṭha bhātā."

Devasika (adj.) [Der. fr. divasa] daily J V.383; DA I.296 (°bhatta = bhattavetena); DhA I.187 sq., -nt. °ŋ as adv. daily, every day J I.82, J I.149, 186; VvA 67, 75; DhA I.28; II.41.

Desa [Ved. deśa, cp. disā] point, part, place, region, spot, country, Vin I.46; II.211; M I.437; J I.308; DhsA 307 (°bhūta); PvA 78 (°antara prob. to be read des°), 153; KhA 132, 227. —desaŋ karoti to go abroad J V.340 (p. 342 has disaŋ). — kañcid-eva desaŋ pucchati to ask a little point D I.51; M I.229; A V.39, sometimes as kiñcid-eva d. p. S III.101; M III.15; v. l. at D I.51. — desāgata pañha a question propounded, lit. come into the region of some one or having become a point of discussion Miln 262.

Desaka (adj.) [Sk. deśaka] pointing out, teaching, advising Sdhp 217, 519 — (nt.) advice, instruction, lesson M I.438.

Desanā (f.) [Sk. deśanā] 1. discourse, instruction, lesson S V.83, 108; J III.84; Pug 28; Nett 38; Vism 523 sq. (regarding Paṭiccasamuppāda); PvA 1, 2, 9, 11; Sdhp 213. 2. Freq. in dhamma° moral instruction, exposition of the Dhamma, preaching, sermon Vin I.16; A I.53; II.182; IV.337 sq.; It 33; J I.106 etc. (a° gāmini āpatti), a Pārājika or Sanghādisesa offence Vin II.3, 87; V.187. Cp. *Vin. Texts* II.33. — 3. (legal) acknowledgment Miln 344. — Cp. ā°.

-avasāne (loc.) at the end of an instruction discourse or sermon DhA III.175; PvA 54; -pariyosāne = prec. PvA 9, 31 etc. -vilāsa beauty of instruction Vism 524; Tikapaṭṭhāna 21.

Desika (adj.) [Sk. deśika] = desaka, su° one who points out well, a good teacher Miln 195.

Desita [pp. of deseti] expounded, shown, taught etc., given, assigned, conferred Vin III.152 (marked out); V.137; D II.154 (dhamma); Dh 285 (nibbāna); PvA 4 (magga: indicated), 54 (given).

Desetar [n. ag. to deseti] one who instructs or points out; a guide, instructor, teacher M I.221, 249; A I.266; III.441; V.349.

Deseti [Sk. deśayati, Caus. of disati, q. v.] to point out, indicate, show; set forth, preach, teach; confess. Very freq. in phrase dhammaŋ d. to deliver a moral discourse, to preach the Dhamma Vin I.15; II.87, 188; V.125, 136; D I.241, A II.185, V.194; It 111; J I.168; III.394; Pug 57; PvA 6. — aor. adesesi (S I.196 = Th 1 1254) & desesi (PvA 2, 12, 78 etc.) — pp. desita (q. v.).

Dessa & **Dessiya** (adj.) [Sk. dveṣya, to **dvis**, see disa] disagreeable, odious, detestable J I.46; II.285; IV.406; VI.570, ThA 268, Miln 281.

Dessati [Sk. dviṣati & dveṣṭi; see etym. under disa] to hate, dislike, detest SnA 168 (= na piheti, opp. kāmeti).

Dessatā (f.) [Sk. dvesyatā] repulsiveness Miln 281.

Dessin (adj.) [Sk. dveṣin] hating, detesting Sn 93 (dhamma°).

Deha [Sk. deha to ***dheigh** to form, knead, heap up (cp. kāya = heap), see diddha. So also in uddehaka. Cp. Kern, *Toev.* p. 75 s. v. sarīradeha. Cp. Gr. τεῖχος (wall) = Sk. dehī; Lat. fingo & figura; Goth. deigan (knead) = Ohg. teig = E. dough] body A II.18; PvA 10, 122. Usually in foll. phrases: hitvā mānusaŋ dehaŋ S I.60; Pv II.9[66]; pahāya m. d. S I.27, 30; jahati d. M II.73; °ŋ nikkhipati Pv II.6[16]; (muni or khīṇāsavo) antima-deha-dhārin (°dhāro) S I.14, 53; II.278; Sn 471; Th II.7, 10; It 32, 40, 50, 53. °nikkhepana laying down the body Vism 236.

Dehaka (nt.) = deha; pl. limbs Th 2, 392; cp. ThA 258.

Dehin (adj. -n.) that which has a body, a creature Pgdp 12, 16.

Doṇa [Sk. droṇa (nt.) conn. with ***dereuo** tree, wood, wooden, see dabbi & dāru & cp. Sk. druṇī pail] a wooden pail, vat, trough; usually as measure of capacity (4 Āḷhaka generally) Pv IV.3[33] (mitāni sukhadukkhāni donehi piṭakehi). taṇḍula° a doṇa of rice DhA III.264; IV.15. At J II.367 doṇa is used elliptically for doṇamāpaka (see below).

-**pāka** of which a d. full is cooked a doṇa measure of food S I.81; DhA II.8. -**māpaka** (mahāmatta) (a higher official) supervising the measuring of the doṇa-revenue (of rice) J II.367, 378, 381; DhA IV.88; -**mita** a d. measure full D I.54; M I.518.

Doṇika (adj.) [fr. doṇa] measuring a doṇa in capacity Vin I.240 (catu° piṭaka).

Doṇikā (f.) = doṇī[1], viz. a hollow wooden vessel, tub, vat Vin I.286 (rajana° for dyeing); II.120 (mattikā to hold clay) 220 (udaka°), 221 (vacca° used for purposes of defæcation). See also passāva°.

Doṇī[1] (f.) [Sk. droṇī, see doṇa] 1. a (wooden) trough, a vat, tub S II.259; A I.253; V.323; J I.450; Miln 56. — tela° an oil vat A III.58 (āyasā made of iron & used as a sarcophagus). — 2. a trough-shaped canoe (cp. Marāthi ḍon " a long flat-bottomed boat made of uṇḍi wood," & Kanarese ḍoni " a canoe hallowed from a log "] J IV.163 (= gambhīrā mahānāvā p. 164); PvA 189. — 3. a hollow, dug in the ground Miln 397. — 4. the body of a lute, the sounding-board (?) J I.450; Miln 53; VvA 281.

Doṇī[2] (f.) [Sk. droṇi ?] an oil-giving plant (?) (or is it = doṇī[1] meaning a cake made in a tub, but wrongly interpreted by Dhammapāla ?) only in -nimmiñjana oil-cake Pv I.10[10]; as °nimmijjani at Vv 33[38]; expl[d] by telamiñjaka at PvA 51 & by tilapiññāka at VvA 147.

Dobbhagga (nt.) [Sk. daurbhāgya fr. duḥ + bhāga] ill luck, misfortune Vin IV.277; DhA 281 (text: °dobhagga).

Dobha [see dubbha] fraud, cheating D II.243 (v. l. dobbha = dubbha).

Domanassa (nt.) [Sk. daurmanasya, duḥ + manas] distress, dejectedness, melancholy, grief. As mental pain (cetasikaŋ asātaŋ cet. dukkhaŋ S V.209 = Nd[2] 312; cp. D II.306; Nett 12) opp. to dukkha physical pain: see dukkha B III. 1 a). A synonym of domanassaŋ is appaccaya (q. v.). For def[n] of the term see Vism 461, 504. The freq. comb[n] dukkha-domanassa refers to an unpleasant state of mind & body (see dukkha B III. 1 b; e. g. S IV.198; V.141; M II.64; A I.157; It 89 etc.). the contrary of somanassaŋ with which dom° is comb[d] to denote " happiness & unhappiness," joy & dejection, e. g. D III.270; M II.16; A I.163; Sn 67 (see somanassa). — Vin I.34; D II.278, 306; S IV.104, 188; V.349, 451; M I.48, 65, 313, 340; II.51; III.218; A I.39 (abhijjhā° covetousness & dejection, see abhijjhā); II.5, 149 sq.; III.99, 207; V.216 sq.; Sn 592, 1106; Pug 20, 59; Nett 12, 29 (citta-sampīḷanaŋ d.) 53, Dhs 413, 421, 1389; Vbh 15, 54, 71, 138 sq.; Dh I.121.

-**indriya** the faculty or disposition to feel grief D III.239 (+ som°); S V.209 sq.; -**upavicāra** discrimination of that which gives distress of mind D III.245; -**patta** dejected, disappointed J II.155.

Dolā (f.) [Sk. dolā, ***del** as in Ags. tealtian = E. tilt, adj. tealt unstable = Sk. dulā iṣṭakā an unstable woman] a swing J IV.283; VI.341; Vism 280 (in simile).

Dolāyati [Denom. of dolā] to swing, to move to & fro J II.385.

Dovacassa (nt.) [contamination of Sk. *daurvacasya evil speech & *daurvratya disobedience, defiance] unruliness, indocility, bad conduct, fractiousness S II.204 sq. (°karaṇā dhammā); M I.95 (id. specified); A II.147; III.178; Nett 40, 127.

Dovacassatā (f.) [2nd abstr. of dovacassa] unruliness, contumacy, stubbornness, obstinacy A I.83, III.310, 448; V.146 sq.; D III.212, 274; Pug 20; Dhs 1326 (cp. *Dhs. trsl.* p. 344); Vbh 359, 369, 371.

Dovacassiya (nt.) = dovacassa Pug 20; Dhs 1325.

Dovārika [cp. Sk. dauvārika, see dvāra] gatekeeper, janitor Vin I.269; D II.83; III.64 sq., 100; S IV.194; M I.380 sq.; A IV.107, 110; V.194; J II.132; IV.382 (two by name, viz. Upajotiya & Bhaṇḍa-kucchi), 447; VI.367; Miln 234, 332; Vism 281; Sdhp 356.

Dovila (adj.) [Sk. ?] being in the state of fructification, budding J VI.529 (cp. p. 530); Miln 334.

Dosa[1] [Sk. doṣa to an Idg. ***deu(s)** to want, to be inferior etc. (cp. dussati), as in Gr. δέομαι, δεύομαι] corruption, blemish, fault, bad condition, defect; depravity, corrupted state; usually -° as khetta° blight of the field Miln 360; tiṇa° spoilt by weeds Dh 356; PvA 7; visa° ill effect of poison Th 1, 758, 768; sneha° blemish of sensual affection Sn 66. Four kasiṇa-dosā at Vism 123; eighteen making a Vihāra unsuitable at Vism 118 sq. — J II.417; III.104; Miln 330 (sabba-d.-virahita faultless); DA I.37, 141. — pl. dosā the (three) morbid affections, or disorder of the (3) humours Miln 43; adj. with disturbed humours Miln 172, cp. DA I.133.

Dosa[2] [Sk. dveṣa, but very often not distinct in meaning from dosa[1]. On dveṣa see under disa] anger, ill-will, evil intention, wickedness, corruption, malice, hatred. In most freq. combⁿ of either rāga (lust) d. & moha (delusion), or lobha (greed) d. moha (see rāga & lobha), to denote the 3 main blemishes of character. For defⁿ see Vism 295 & 470. Interpreted at Nd[2] 313 as "cittassa āghāto paṭighāto paṭigho . . . kopo . . . kodho . . . vyāpatti." — The distinction between dosa & paṭigha is made at DA I.116 as: dosa=dubbala-kodha; paṭigha=balavakodha. — In combⁿ lobha d. moha e. g. S I.98; M I.47, 489; A I.134, 201; II.191; III.338; It 45 (tīṇi akusalamūlāni). With rāga & moha: Dh 20; It 2=6; with rāga & avijjā; It 57; rāga & māna Sn 270, 631 etc. — See for ref.: Vin I.183; D III.146, 159, 182, 214, 270; S I.13, 15, 70; V.34 sq.; M I.15, 96 sq., 250 sq., 305; A I.187; II.172, 203; III.181; Sn 506; It 2 (dosena duṭṭhāse sattā gacchanti duggatiŋ); Ps I.80 sq., 102; Pug 16, 18; Dhs 418, 982, 1060; Vbh 86, 167, 208, 362; Nett 13, 90; Sdhp 33, 43. — *Variously characterised as:* 8 purisa-dosā Vbh 387; khila, nīgha, mala S V.57; agati (4 agati-gamanāni: chanda, d. moha, bhaya) D III.228, cp. 133, 182; ajjhattaŋ A III.357 sq.; its relation to kamma A I.134; III.338; V.262; to ariyamagga S V.5, 8. —**sadosa** corrupted, depraved, wicked D I.80; A I.112; **adosa** absence of ill-will, adj. kind, friendly, sympathetic A I.135, 195, 203; II.192; Vbh 169, 210; Dhs 33 (cp. *Dhs. trsl.* 21, 99); VvA 14 (+alobha amoha).

-**aggi** the fire of anger or ill-will D III.217; S IV.19 sq.; It 92 (+rāgaggi moh°); J I.61; -**antara** (adj.) bearing anger, intending evil in one's heart Vin II.249; D III.237; M I.123; A I.59; III.196 sq.; V.81 (opp. metta-citta); perhaps at PvA 78 (for des°); -**kkhaya** the fading away, dying out of anger or malice S III.160, 191; IV.250; V.8; Vbh 73, 89; -**gata**=dosa (+paṭigha) S IV.71; -**garu** full of anger S I.24; -**dosa** (: dosa[1]) spoilt by anger Dh 357; -**saññita** connected with ill-will It 78; -**sama** like anger Dh 202; -**hetuka** caused by evil intention or depravity A V.261 (pāṇātipāta).

Dosaniya, Dosanīya & Dosaneyya (adj.) [grd.-formation either to dosa[1] or dosa[2], but more likely=Sk. *dūṣanīya=dūṣya (see dussa[2] & dussati) influenced by dveṣaṇiya] corruptible; polluting, defiling; hateful, sinful S IV.307; A II.120; It 84 (where A III.110 has dussaniya in same context).

Dosā (f.) [Sk. doṣā & doṣas, cp. Gr. δύω, δύομαι to set (of the sun)] evening, dusk. Only in acc. as adv. dosaŋ (=doṣāŋ) at night J VI.386.

Dosin (adj.) [to dosa[2]] angry J V.452, 454.

Dosinā (f.) [Sk. jyotsnā, cp. P. juṇhā] a clear night, moonlight; only in phrase ramaṇiyā vata bho dosinā ratti "lovely is the moonlight night" D I.47≈J I.509; J V.262; Miln 5, 19 etc. Expl[d] in popular fashion by Bdhgh. as "dosāpagatā" ratti DA I.141.

-**puṇṇamāsī** a clear, full moon night Th 1, 306, 1119; -**mukha** the face of a clear night J VI.223.

Doha[1] [Sk. doha & dogha] milking, milk J V.63, 433.

Doha[2] (adj.) [Sk. droha] injuring (-°) DA I.296.

Dohaka [Sk. doha] a milk-pail J V.105.

Dohati [Sk. dogdhi, to which prob. duhitṛ daughter: see under dhītā & cp. dhenu] to milk. — pres. 1 pl. dohāma & duhāma J V.105; pret. 1 pl. duhāmase ibid.; pot. duhe J V.211; ger. duhitvā SnA 27; pp. duddha (q. v.) — Pass. duyhati S I.174 (so read for duhanti); J V.307; ppr. duyhamāna Miln 41. — See also dūhana, doha[1], dohin.

Dohaḷa [Sk. dohada & daurhṛda, of du+hṛd, sick longing, sickness, see hadaya. Lüders *Göttinger Gelehrte Nachrichten* 1898, 1 derives it as dvi+hṛd] (a) the longing of a pregnant woman J III.28, 333; DhA I.350; II.139. — (b) intense longing, strong desire, craving in general J II.159, 433; V.40, 41; VI.263, 308; DhA II.86 (dhammika d.).

Dohaḷāyati [Denom. fr. dohaḷa] to have cravings (of a woman in pregnancy) J VI.263.

Dohaḷinī (adj.-f.) a woman in pregnancy having cravings; a pregnant woman in general J II.395, 435; III.27; IV.334; V.330 (=gabbhinī); VI.270, 326, 484; DhA III.95.

Dohin (adj. n.) one who milks, milking M I.220 sq.=A V.347 sq. (anavasesa° milking out fully).

Drūbha incorrect spelling for dubbha (q. v.) in adrūbhāya Vin I.347.

Dva° in numeral composition, meaning two etc., see under dvi B III.

Dvaya (adj.-n.) [Ved. dvaya; cp. dvi B I. 6] (adj.) (a) twofold Sn 886 (saccaŋ musā ti dvayadhammaŋ); Dh 384; Pv IV.1[28] (dvayaŋ vipākaŋ=duvidhaŋ PvA 228). — **advaya** single A V.46. — (b) false, deceitful Vin III.21. — nt. a duality, a pair, couple S II.17 (°ŋ nissito loko); J III.395 (gātha°); PvA 19 (māsa°); Dha II.93 (pada° two lines, "couplet").

-**kārin** "doing both," i. e. both good & evil deeds (su° & duccaritaŋ) S III.241, cp. 247 sq.; D III.96.

Dvā (cp. dva°) see dvi B III.

Dvāra (nt.) [Ved. dvār (f.) & dvāra (nt.), base ***dhvār**, cp. Av. dvarəm; Gr. θύρα, θυρών; Lat. fores (gate), forum; Goth. daúr, Ohg. turi=Ger. tür, Ags. dor=E. door.] 1. lit. an outer door, a gate, entrance Vin I.15; S I.58, 138, 211; J I.346; II.63; VI.330; Vbh 71 sq.; PvA 4, 67 (village gate), 79; Sdhp 54, 356. — That d. cannot be used for an inner door see Vin II.215; on knocking at a d. see DA I.252; cp. DhA I.145 (dvāraŋ ākoṭeti); to open a door: āvarati; to shut: pidahati; to lock: thaketi. dvāraŋ alabhamāna unable to get out Vin II.220. —**mahā°** the main or city gate J I.63; **culla°** J II.114; **catu°** (adj.) having 4 doors (of niraya) Pv I.10[13]; **cha°** with 6d. (nagaraŋ, w. ref. to the 6 doors of the senses, see below) S IV.194; **pure°** the front d. J II.153; **pacchima°** the back d. J VI.364; **uttara°** the E. gate (PvA 74); **nagara°** the city gate (J I.263; **deva°** DhA I.280); **gāma°** the village g. (Vin III.52; J II.110); **ghara°** (J IV.142; PvA 38) & **geha°** (PvA 61) the house door; **antepura°** the door of the inner chamber M II.100; **kula°** the doors of the clan-people Sn 288. — metaph. of the door leading to Nibbāna: **amata°** S I.137; A V.346. — 2. (fig.) the doors=in- & outlets of the mind, viz. the sense organs; in phrase indriyesu gutta-dvāra (adj.) guarding the doors with respect to the senses or faculties (of the mind): see gutta (e. g. S II.218; IV.103 & cp. *Dhs. trsl.* p. 175). — S IV.117, 194 (with simile of the 6 gates of a city); VvA 72 (kāya-vacī°). The *nine* gates of the body at Vism 346. Thus also in f. abstr. gutta-dvāratā the condition of well protected doors (see gutta).

-**kavāṭa** a door post J I.63; II.334; VI.444; PvA 280, -**koṭṭhaka** [cp. Sk. dvārakoṣṭhaka Sp. AvŚ I.24, 31] gateway; also room over the gate Ud 52, 65; J I.290; III.2; IV.63, 229; VvA 6, 160; DhA I.50; II.27, 46; IV.204; Vism 22; Miln 10. — bahidvārakoṭṭhake or °ā outside the gate M I.382; II.92; A III.31; IV.206; -**gāma** a village outside the city gates, i. e. a suburb (cp. bahidvāragāma J I.361) J III.126 (°gāmaka), 188; IV.225; DhA II.25 (°ka); -**toraṇa** a gateway J III.431. -**pānantara** at J VI.349 should be read °vātapānantara; -**pidahana** shutting the door Vism 78. -**bāhā** a door post S I.146; Pv I.5[1]; DhA III.273; -**bhatta** food scattered before the door Sn 286; -**vātapāna** a door-window Vin II.211; J VI.349; -**sālā** a hall with doors M I.382; II.61.

Dvārika (-°) (adj.) referring or belonging to the door of—; in cha °ā taṇhā, craving or fever, arising through the 6 doors (of the senses) DhA IV.221, & kāya° -saŋvara control over the " bodily " door, i. e. over action (opp. speech) PvA 10 (so read for kāyañ cārika°).

Dvi [Sk. dvi, dva etc. — *Bases :* I. **dvi** = Sk. dvi in dvipad = Lat. bipēs (fr. duipēs). Ags. twiféte ; dvidant = bidens. Reduced to di (see B I.^{4}) as in Gr. δίπους (= dipad), Lat. diennium & pref. dis- (cp. Goth. twis asunder, Ogh. zwisk between). — II. **du** (= dvi in reduced grade, cp. Lat. du-plex, dubius etc.). — III. **dvā** (& dva) = Sk. dvāu, dvā, f. nt. dve (declined as dual, but the P. (plural) inflexion from base I. see B I.^{1}) ; Gr. δύω, Lat. duo ; Oir. dāu, dā, f. dī ; Goth. twai, f. twōs ; Ags. twā (= E. two) ; Ohg. zwēne, zwō zwei. Also in cpd. num. dva-daśa twelve = Gr. δ(F)ώδεκα = Lat. duodecim.] number two.

A. *Meanings*—I. *Two as unit :* 1. with objective foundation : (a) denoting a comb^n (pair, couple) or a repetition (twice). In this conn. frequent both objective & impersonal in mentioning natural pairs as well as psychologically contrasted notions. E. g. dvipad (biped), nāgassa dve dantā (elephants' tusks), cakkhūni (eyes) ; dvija (bird), duvija (tooth), dijivha (snake). See also dutiya & dvaya. — dve : kāmā, khiḍḍā, gatiyo (Sn 1001), dānāni (It 98), piyā, phalāni (Sn 896 ; It 39), mittā, sinehā etc. See Nd^2 under dve, cp. A I.47-100 ; D III.212-214. — (b) denoting a separation (in two, twofold etc.) : see dvidhā & cpds. — 2. with symbolic, sentimental meaning : (a) *only* two (i. e. next to one or " next to nothing "). cp. the two mites of the widow (Mark XII. 42), two sons of Rachel (Gen. 30) : dumāsika not more than 2 months (Vin II.107) ; dvemāsiko gabbho (Pv I.6^7) ; dvevācika : duvangula (see below). — (b) *a few* = more than one, some, a couple (often intermediate between 1 & 3, denoting more than once, or a comparatively long, rather long, but not like 3 a *very* long time) : māsadvayaŋ a couple of months ; dvisahassa dīpā 2000 islands (= a large number) ; diyaḍḍhasata 150 = very long etc. ; dvīhatīha (2 or 3 = a couple of days) q. v. ; dvirattatiratta (id. of nights) ; dvīsu tīsu manussesu to some people (PvA 47) ; dvatikkhattuŋ several times ; cp. dvikkhattuŋ (more than once), dutiyaŋ (for the 2nd time).

II. Two as unit *in connection with* its own & other *decimals* means a complex *plus* a pair, which amounts to the same as a large & a small unit, or so to speak " a year & a day." E. g. 12 (sometimes, but rarely = 10 + 2, see sep.) ; — 32 : rests usually on 4 × 8, but as No. of the Mahāpurisa-lakkhaṇāni it denotes 30 + 2 = the great circle plus the decisive (Invisible) pair ; — 62 : views of heresy : see diṭṭhi ; also as a year of eternity = 60 kappas + 2 ; — 92 : as measure of eternity = 90 + 2 kappas = a year & a day.

III. *Number twelve.* 1. Based on natural phenomena it denotes the solar year (dvādasamāsako saŋvaccharo VvA 247). — 2. Connected with the solar cult it is used with human arrangements to raise them to the level of heavenly ones and to impart to them a superior significance. Thus : (a) as denoting a *set* (cp. 12 months = companions of the Sun) it is the No. of a respectful, holy, venerable group (cp. 12 sons of Jacob Gen. 35. 22 ; cakes as shewbread Lev. 25. 5 ; stones erected Josh. 4. 8 ; apostles Math. 10, 2 ; patriarchs Acts 7. 8 ; companions of Odysseus Hom. Od. 9. 195 ; Knights of Arthur etc.) : of theras, accomp^d by 12 bhikkhus PvA 67, 141, 179 etc. ; dvādasa koṭisatāni Sn 677 ; five groups of 12 musicians VvA 96 (cp. 5 × 12 cromlechs in the outer circle of Stonehenge). — (b) as *measure* of distance in space & time it implies vast extent, great importance, a climax, divine symmetry etc. 12 yojanas wide extends the radiance VvA 16 ; 12 y. as respectful distance PvA 137 (cp. 2000 cubits in same sense at Josh. 3. 4) ; 12 y. in extent (height, breadth & length) are the heavenly palaces of the Vimāna-petas or Yakkhas Vv 55^1 ; J VI.116 ; VvA 6, 217, 244, 291, 298 etc. In the same connection we freq. find the No. 16 : soḷasa-yojanikaŋ kanaka-vimānaŋ Vv 67^1 ; VvA 188, 289 etc. — Of *years :* J III.80 ; VvA 157 (dvādasa-vassikā ; in this sense also 16 instead of 12 : soḷasa-vassuddesika VvA 259 etc. See soḷasa).

B. *Bases & Forms*—I. **dvi** ; main base for numeral & nominal composition & derivation, in :

1. numeral **dve** (& **duve**) two : nom. acc. dve (Sn p. 107 ; It 98 ; J I.150 ; IV.137 etc.) & (in verse) **duve** (Sn 896, 1001) ; gen. dat. **dvinnaŋ** (It 39, 40, 98 ; J II.154) ; instr. **dvīhi** (J I.87 : v. l. dīhi ; 151 ; II.153) ; loc. **dvīsu** (J I.203 ; PvA 47) & **duvesu** (Vv 41^2).

2. as numeral base : **-sahassa** 2000 (see A I. 2^b) J I.57 ; VvA 261 ; PvA 74 ; also in **dvittā** and adv. **dvikkhattuŋ** twice & **dvidhā** in two parts. — (b) as nominal base : — **(r)āvaṭṭa** [Sk. dviḥ cp. Lat. bis] turning twice S I.32 ; **-ja** " twice born," i. e. a bird J I.152 (gaṇā) ; **-jātin** one who is born twice, i. e. a brāhmaṇa Th. 2, 430 (ThA 269 = brahmajātin) ; **-tālamatta** of the size of 2 palms DhA II.62 ; **-pad** [Sk. dvipad, Lat. bipes, Gr. δίπους etc.] a biped, man S I.6 ; **-pala** twofold Vism 339 ; **-pādaka** = dvipad Vin II.110 ; **-bandhu** having two friends J VI.281 ; **-rattatiratta** two or three nights Vin IV.16 ; also in **dvīha** two days (q. v.).

3. as diæretic form **duvi°** : **-ja** (cp. dija) " growing again " i. e. a tooth J V.156.

4. as contracted form **di°** : **-(y)aḍḍha** one and a half (lit. the second half, cp. Ger. anderthalb) Dh 235 ; J I.72 (diyaḍḍha-yojana-satika 150 y. long or high etc.), 202 ; IV.293 (°yāma) ; DhA I.395 ; DA I.17 ; Miln 243, 272 ; DhsA 12 ; **-guṇa** twofold, double Vin I.289 ; Sn 714 ; J V.309 ; Miln 84 ; DhA II.6 ; VvA 63, 120 ; **-ja** (cp. dvija, duvija) (a) " twice-born," a bird S I.224 ; Sn 1134 (d. vuccati pakkhī Nd^2 296) ; J I.152, 203 ; II.205 ; IV.347 ; V.157 ; Pv II.12^3 ; Vv 35^8 (cp. VvA 178) ; Miln 295. — (b) a brahmin ThA. 70, 73 ; **-jivha** " two-tongued," i. e. a snake (cp. du°) J III.347 ; **-pad** (-pada or -pa) a biped (cp. dvi°) A I.22 ; V.21 ; Sn 83 (dipa-d-uttama), 995 (id.) 998 ; Dh 273 ; **-pādaka** = °pad Th I, 453 = Sn 205.

5. as sec. cpd. form (with guṇa) **dve°** (and de°) : **-caturanga** twice fourfold = eightfold Th I, 520 (°gāmin) ; **-patha** a " double " path, a border path, the boundary berween two villages Vv 53^{17} (= sīmantika-patha VvA 241) ; **-piccha** having two tail-feathers J V.341 (cp. de°) ; **-pitika** having two feathers J V.424 ; **-bhāva** doubling kacc. 21 ; **-māsika** two months old Pv I.6^7 ; **-vācika** pronouncing (only) two words, viz. Buddha & Dhamma (cp. tevācika, saying the whole saraṇa-formula). Vin I.4 ; J I.81 ; **-sattaratta** twice seven nights, a fortnight [cp. Sk. dvisapata] J VI.230. — See also der. fr. numer. adv. dvidhā, viz. dvejjha (& dejjha), dvedhā°, dveḷhaka.

6. as noun-derivation dvaya a dyad (q. v.).

II. **du** ; reduced base in numeral and nominal comp^n & der^n :

-(v)addhato from both sides (a distorted form of dubhato q. v.) Vv 64^{19} (= dubhato VvA 281) ; **-(v)angika** consisting of two parts Dhs 163 ; **-(v)angula** & **dvangula** two finger-breadths or depths, two inches long, implying a minimum measure (see above A I.2^a) Vin II.107 ; IV.262 ; usually in cpds. — *kappa* the 2 inch rule, i. e. a rule extending the allotted time for the morning meal to 2 inches of shadow after mid-day Vin II.294, 306 ; *-pannā* wisdom of 2 finger-breadths, i. e. that of a woman S I.129 = Th 2, 60 (dvanguli°, at ThA 66 as °saññā) ; *-buddhika* = °paññā VvA 96 ; **-jivha** two-tongued (cp. di°) ; a snake J IV.330 ; V.82, 425 ; **-paṭṭa** " double cloth " (Hind. dupaṭṭā ; Kanarese dupaṭa, duppaṭa ; Tamil tuppaṭṭā a cloak consisting of two cloths joined together, see Kern, *Toev.* I.179) ; J I.119 ; IV.114, 379 (ratta°) ; DhA I.249 (suratta°) ; III.419 (°cīvarā) ; **-matta** (about) 2 in measure Miln 82 ;

-māsika 2 months old or growing for 2 months (of hair) Vin II.107; -vagga consisting of two Vin I.58; -vassa 2 years old Vin I.59; -vidha twofold, instr. duvidhena M III.45 sq.; etc. — Derivations from du° see sep. under duka (dyad), dutiya (the second), & the contamination forms dubha (to) & dubhaya (for ubha & ubhaya).

III. dvā (& reduced dva), base in numeral compⁿ only: dvatikkhattuŋ two or three times J I.506; DA I.133, 264; DhA IV.38; dvādasa twelve (on meaning of this & foll. numerals see above A II. & III.) J III.80; VI.116; DhA I.88; III.210; VvA 156, 247 etc.; °yojanika J I.125; IV.499; dvāvīsati (22) VvA 139; dvattiŋsa (32) Kh II. (°ākāra the 32 constituents of the body); DhA II.88; VvA 39 etc.; dvācattālīsa (42) Nd² 15; Vism 82; dvāsaṭṭhi (Nd² 271ᴵᴵᴵ· & dvaṭṭhi (62) D I.54; S III.211; DA I.162); dvānavuti (92) PvA 19, 21. — *Note.* A singular case of dva as adv. = twice is in dvâhaŋ Sn 1116.

Dvikkhattuŋ (adv.) [Sk. *dvikṛtvaḥ] twice Nd² on Sn 1116 (= dva); Nd² 296 (jāyati dijo). See dvi B I. 2ᵃ.

Dvittā (pl.) [Sk. dvitrā; see dvi B I. 2ᵃ] two or three S I.117 (perhaps we should read tad vittaŋ: Windisch, *Māra & Buddha* 108).

Dvidhā (num. adv.) [Sk. dvidhā, see dvi B I. 2ᵃ] in two parts, in two M I.114; J I.253 (karoti), 254 (chindati), 298 (id.); III.181; IV.101 (jāta disagreeing); VI.368 (bhindati). See also dvedhā & dveḷhaka.

-gata gone to pieces J V.197; -patha a twofold way, a crossing; only fig. doubt S II.108; M I.142, 144; Ud 90. See also dvedhāpatha.

Dvīha (adv.) [Sk. dvis-ahnah; see dvi B I.2ᵇ] two days; dvīhena in 2 days S II.192; dvīha-mata 2 days dead M I.88; III.91.

-tīha 2 or 3 days (°ŋ adv.) (on meaning cp. dvi A I.2ᵇ) D I.190 (°assa accayena after a few days); J II.316; DhA III.21 (°accayena id., gloss: katipāh'-accayena); DA I.190 (°ŋ) 215; VvA 45.

Dvīhika (adj.) every other day M I.77.

Dvīhitika (adj.) [du-īhitika, of du¹ + īhati] to be gained or procured with difficulty (i. e. a livelihood which is hardly procurable), only in phrase "dubbhikkhā d. setaṭṭhikā salākavuttā," of a famine Vin III.6, 15, 87; IV.23; S IV.323. On the term & its explⁿ by Bdhgh. (at Vin III.268: dujjīvikā īhī tī . . . dukkhena īhitaŋ ettha pavattatī ti) see Kern, *Toev.* I.122. — *Note.* Bdhgh's explⁿ is highly speculative, & leaves the problem still unsolved. The case of du¹ appearing as du- (and not as dur-) before a vowel is most peculiar; there may be a connection with druh (see duhana), which is even suggested by vv. ll. at S IV.223 as dūhitika = duhitika (q. v.).

Dve & **Dve°** see dvi B I & 5.

Dvejjha (adj.) [Sk. dvaidhya; cp. dvi B I. 5] divided, twofold, only in neg. advejjha undivided, certain, doubtless; simple, sincere, uncontradictory A III.403; J IV.77; Nd² 30 (+ adveḷhaka); Miln 141. — Cp. dejjha.

Dvejjhatā (f.) [fr. prec.] in a° undividedness J IV.76.

Dvedhā (adv.) [Sk. dvedhā, cp. dvidhā] in two J V.203, 206 (°sira); DhA II.50 (bhijji: broke in two, broke asunder).

Dvedhāpatha [cp. dvidhā & dvi B I.5] (a) a double, i. e. a branching road; a cross-road DhA II.192; Miln 17. — (b) doubt Dh 282; Dhs 1004, 118; Vism 313.

Dveḷhaka (nt.) [Sk. *dvaidhaka fr. adv. dvidhā, cp. dvi B I. 5] doubt Vin III.309; Dhs 1004, 1161; DA I.68; DhsA 259; °citta uncertain PvA 13; °jāta in doubt Vin III.309; D III.117 sq.; 210. — adveḷhaka (adj.) sure, certain, without doubt Nd² 30 (+ advejjha).

Dh.

Dhaŋsati [Ved. dhvaŋsati to fall to dust, sink down, perish; Idg. **dheṷes** to fly like dust, cp. Sk. dhūsara "dusky"; Ags. dust; Ger. dust & dunst; E. dusk & dust; prob. also Lat. furo] to fall from, to be deprived of (c. abl.), to be gone D III.184 (with abl. asmā lokā dh.) A II.67; V.76, 77; It 11; Th 1, 225, 610; J III.260, 318, 441, 457; IV.611; V.218, 375. — Caus. dhaŋseti [Sk. dhvaŋsayati, but more likely = Sk. dharṣayati (to infest, molest = Lat. infestare. On similar sound-change P. dhaŋs° > Sk. dharṣ cp. P. daŋseti > Sk. darśayati). Caus. of dhṛṣṇoti to be daring, to assault cp. Gr. θάρσος audacious, bold, Lat. festus, Goth. gadars = E. dare; Ohg. gitar] to deprive of, to destroy, assault, importune D I.211; S III.123; Sn 591; J III.353; Miln 227; Sdhp 357, 434. Cp. pa°, pari°.

Dhaŋsana (n.-adj.) [Sk. dharṣana] destroying, bringing to ruin, only in kula° as v. l. to kula-gandhana (q. v.) at It 64, and in **dhaŋsanatā** at DhA III.353 in expl^n of dhaŋsin (q. v.).

Dhaŋsin (adj.-n.) [Sk. dharṣin to dhṛṣṇoti, see dhaŋseti] obtrusive, bold, offensive M I.236; A II.182; Dh 244 (= DhA III.353 paresaŋ guṇaŋ dhaŋsanatāya dh.).

Dhanka [Sk. dhvānkṣa, cp. also dhunkṣā] a crow S I.207; II.258; Sn 271 = Nd^2 420; J II.208; V.107, 270; VI.452; Pv III.5^2 (= kāka PvA 198); VvA 334.

Dhaja [Sk. dhvaja, cp. Ohg. tuoh "cloth" (fr. *dwōko)] a flag, banner; mark, emblem, sign, symbol Vin I.306 (titthiya°: outward signs of); II.22 (gihi°); S I.42; II.280; A II.151; III.84 sq. (panna°); M I.137 (id.); A III.149 (dhamma); J I.52 (+ patākā); VvA 173 (id.); J I.65 (arahad °;) Th 1.961; J V.49 = Miln 221; J V.509; VI.499; Nd^1 170; Vv 36^1, 64^{28} (subhāsita° = dhamma° VvA 284); Dhs 1116, 1233; Vism 469 (+ paṭāka, in comparison); PvA 282; VvA 31, 73; Miln 21; Sdhp 428, 594. Cp. also panna.

-agga the top of a standard S I.219; A III.89 sq.; Pug 67, 68; Vism 414 (°paritta). **-ālu** adorned with flags Th 1, 164 = J II.334 (: dhajasampanna Com.); **-āhaṭa** won under or by the colours, taken as booty, captured Vin III.139, 140; Vism 63. **-baddha** captured (= °āhaṭa) Vin I.74 (cora).

Dhajinī (f.) [Sk. dhvajinī, f. to adj. dhvajin] "bearing a standard," i. e. an army, legion Sn 442 (= senā SnA 392).

Dhañña^1 (nt.) [Ved. dhānya, der. fr. dhana] grain, corn. The usual enum^n comprises 7 sorts of grain, which is however not strictly confined to grain-fruit proper ("corn") but includes, like other enum^{ns}, pulse & seeds. These 7 are sāli & vīhi (rice-sorts), yava (barley), godhuma (wheat), kangu (millet), varaka (beans), kudrūsaka (?) Vin IV.264; Nd^2 314; DA I.78. — Nd^2 314 distinguishes two categories of dhañña: the natural (pubbaṇṇa) & the prepared (aparaṇṇa) kinds. To the first belong the 7 sorts, to the second belongs sūpeyya (curry). See also bīja-bīja. — Six sorts are mentioned at M I.57, viz. sāli, vīhi, mugga, māsa, tila, taṇḍula. — D I.5 (āmaka°, q. v.); A II.209 (id.); M I.429; A II.32 (+ dhana); Th 1, 531; Pug 58; DhA I.173; VvA 99; PvA 29 (dhanaŋ vā dh °ŋ vā), 198 (sāsapa-tela-missitaŋ), 278 (sappi - madhu - tela - dhaññādībi vohāraŋ katvā). — dhaññaŋ ākirati to besprinkle a person with grain (for good luck) Pv III.5^4 (= mangalaŋ karoti PvA 198, see also mangala).

-āgāra a store house for grain Vin I.240; **-piṭaka** a basket full of grain DhA III.370; **-rāsi** a heap of g. A IV.163, 170; **-samavāpaka** grain for sowing, not more & not less than necessary to produce grain M I.451.

Dhañña^2 (adj.) [Sk. dhānya, adj. to dhana or dhānya. Semantically cp. āḷhiya] "rich in corn," rich (see dhana); happy, fortunate, lucky. Often in comb^n dhana-dhañña. — DhA I.171; III.464 (dhaññādika one who is rich in grains etc., i. e. lucky); DhsA 116. — dhañña-puñña-lakkhaṇa a sign of future good fortune & merit PvA 161; as adj. endowed with the mark of . . . J VI.3. See also dhāniya.

Dhata [Sk. dhṛta, pp. of dharati; cp. dhara & dhāreti] 1. firm, prepared, ready, resolved A III.114; Dāvs V.52. — 2. kept in mind, understood, known by heart Vin II.95; A I.36.

Dhana (nt.) [Ved. dhana; usually taken to **dhā** (see dadhāti) as "stake, prize at game, booty," cp. pradhāna & Gr. θέμα; but more likely in orig. meaning "grain, possession of corn, crops etc.," cp. Lith. dūna bread, Sk. dhānā pl. grains & dhañña = dhana-like, i. e. corn, grain] wealth, usually wealth of money, riches, treasures. 1. *Lit.* D I.73 (sa°); M II.180; A III.222; IV.4 sq.; Nd^2 135 (+ yasa, issariya etc.) Th 2, 464 (+ issariya); J I.225 (paṭhavigataŋ karoti: hide in the ground), 262, 289; II.112; IV.2; Sn 60, 185, 302; Pv II.6^{10}; DhA I.238. Often in comb^n aḍḍha mahaddhana mahābhoga to indicate immense wealth (see aḍḍha) PvA 3, 214 etc. (see also below °dhañña). — 2. *fig.* Used in the expression sattavidha-ariya-dhana "the 7 fold noble treasure" of the good qualities or virtues, viz. saddhā, cāga etc. (see enum^d under cāga) D III.163, 164, 251; VvA 113; ThA 240.

-agga the best treasure (i. e. the ariya-dhana) D III.164; **-atthika** wishing for or desiring wealth Sn 987; **-āsā** craving for wealth; **-kkīta** bought for money DhA II.3, **-thaddha** proud of wealth, snobbish Sn 104; **-dhañña**, usually Dvandva-cpd. "money & money's worth," but as adj. (always in phrase pahūta°) it may be taken as Tatpuruṣa "rich in treasures," otherwise "possessing money & money's worth" cp. pahūtadhana-dhaññavā J I.3. As n. Pv I.11^{11}; III.10^4; PvA 60; Miln 2, 280; as adj. freq. "pahūtadhana-dhañña" Vv 63^{13} = Pv II.6^{11}; PvA 97. Thus in ster. formula of aḍḍha mahaddhana etc. D III.163 sq.; S I.71; A II.86; **-parājaya** loss of money, as adj. appl. to kali: the dice marking loss in game Sn 659; **-lobha** "greed of gold" J IV.1; **-lola** = lobha J II.212; **-viriya** wealth & power Sn 422; **-hetu** for the sake of wealth Sn 122.

Dhanatta (nt.) [Sk. *dhanatvaŋ] being bent on having money J V.449.

Dhanavant (adj.) [Sk. dhanavant] wealthy Nd^2 462; J I.3.

Dhanāyati [Denom. to dhana] to desire (like money), to wish for, strive after M I.260 (perhaps better to be read vanāyati, see formula under allīyati, and note M I.552).

Dhanika [Sk. dhanika] a creditor, Th 2, 443, ThA, 271; PvA 276. Cp. dhaniya.

Dhanita [Sk. dhvanita, pp. of **dhvan,** cp. Ags. dyn noise = E. din; Ags. dynnan to sound loud] sounded; as nt. sonant (said of a letter) Miln 344.

Dhaniya = dhanika Vin I.76.

Dhanu (nt.) [Sk. dhanus, to Ohg. tanna fir-tree, also oak, orig. tree in general, cp. dāru] a bow M I.429; J I.50, 150; II.88; IV.327; PvA 285.
-kalāpa bow & quiver Vin II.192; M I.86; II.99; A III.94; PvA 154; -kāra a bow maker Miln 331; -kārika N. of a tree J V.420; -kārin = prec. J V.422 (=°pāṭali); -ggaha an archer D I.51; A II.48; IV.107; J I.58, 356; II.87, 88; III.220 (dhanuggaha) J III.322; V.129 (where 4 kinds are enum^d); Vism 150 (in simile); DA I.156; -takkāri (f.) a plant J VI.535; -pāṭali N. of a tree J V.422; -lakkhaṇa prophesying from marks on a bow D I.9.

Dhanuka (nt.) [Sk. dhanuṣka] a (small) bow Vin II.10; III.180; D I.7; A III.75; V.203; J VI.41; Miln 229; DA I.86.

Dhanta [Sk. dhvānta in meaning of either dhvanita fr. **dhvan** to sound, or dhamita fr. **dhmā** to blow, see dhameti] blown, sounded A I.253; J I.283, 284.

Dhama (-°) (adj.) [Sk. dhama, to dhamati] blowing, n. a blower, player (on a horn: sankha°) D I.251; S IV.322.

Dhamaka (-°) (adj.) one who blows Miln 31; see vaṇsa°, sankh°, singa°.

Dhamati [Ved. dhamati, **dhmā,** pp. dhamita & dhmāta, cp. Ohg. dampf "steam"] to blow, to sound (a drum); to kindle (by blowing), melt, smelt, singe A I.254; IV.169; J I.283, 284; VI.441; Nd^1 478; Miln 262. — ppr. **dhamāna** S I.106; Miln 67. — Caus. **dhameti** to blow (an instrument) J II.110; Miln 31, and **dhamāpeti** to cause to blow or kindle DhA I.442. — pp. **dhanta** & **dhanita** (the latter to **dhvan,** by which dhamati is influenced to a large extent in meaning. Cp. uddhana).

Dhamadhamāyati [cp. Sk. dadhmāti, Intens. to dhamati] to blow frequently, strongly or incessantly Miln 117.

Dhamani (f.) [Sk. dhamani, to dhamati, orig. a tube for blowing, a tubular vessel, pipe] a vein Th I, 408. Usually in cpd.: -santhata strewn with veins, with veins showing, i. e. emaciated (: nimmaṇsa-lohitatāya sirājālehi vitthatagatta PvA 68) Vin III.110, J IV.371; V.69; Dh 395 = Th I, 243 = Pv II.1^{13}; Pv IV.10^1; DhA I.299, 367; IV.157; ThA 80. So also in Jain Sk. "kisa dhamaṇisaṇtata": Weber, *Bhagavati* p. 289; cp. Lal. Vist. 226. — Also as °santhatagatta (adj.) having veins showing all over the body for lack of flesh Vin I.55; III.146; M II.121; J I.346, II.283; ThA 80.

Dhamma^1 (m. & rarely nt.) [Ved. dharma & dharman, the latter a formation like karman (see kamma for expl^n of subj. & obj. meanings); **dhṛ** (see dhāreti) to hold, support: that which forms a foundation and upholds = constitution. Cp. Gr. θρόνος, Lat. firmus & fretus; Lith. derme (treaty), cp. also Sk. dhariman form, constitution, perhaps = Lat. forma, E. form] constitution etc. A. *Definitions by Commentators:* Bdhgh gives a fourfold meaning of the word dhamma (at DA I.99 = DhA I.22), viz. (1) guṇe (saddo), applied to good conduct; (2) desanāyaṇ, to preaching & moral instruction; (3) pariyattiyaṇ, to the 9 fold collection of the Buddh. Scriptures (see navanga); (4) nissatte (-nijjīvate), to cosmic (non-animistic) law. — No. 1 is referred to freq. in expl^n of the term, e. g. dhammiko ti ñāyena samena pavattati ti DA I.249; dhamman ti kāraṇaṇ ñāyaṇ PvA 211; as paṭipatti-dhamma at VvA 84; No. 3 e. g. also at PvA 2. Another and more adequate fourfold definition by Bdhgh is given in DhsA 38, viz. (1) pariyatti, or doctrine as formulated, (2) hetu, or condition, causal antecedent, (3) guṇa, or moral quality or action, (4) nissatta-nijjīvatā, or "the phenomenal" as opposed to "the substantial," "the noumenal," "animistic entity." Here (2) is illustrated by hetumhi ñāṇaṃ dhammapaṭisambhidā: "analytic knowledge in dhamma's means insight into condition, causal antecedent" Vibh 293, and see Niyama (dhamma°). Since, in the former fourfold definition (2) and (3) really constitute but one main implication considered under the two aspects of Doctrine as taught and Doctrine as formulated, we may interpret Dhamma by the fourfold connotation:—doctrine, right, or righteousness, condition, phenomenon. — For other exegetic definitions see the Com^y & the Niddesa, e. g. Nd^1 94; for modern expl^n & analyses see e. g. Rhys Davids, *Buddh. India* pp. 292-4; Mrs. Rh. Davids, *Buddhism* (1912) pp. 32 sq., 107 sq., 235 sq.; *Dhs. trsl.* XXXIII sq.; and most recently the exhaustive monograph by M. & W. Geiger, *Pāli Dhamma,* Abhandlungen der Bayer. Akademie XXXI. 1; München 1920; which reached the editors too late to be made use of for the Dictionary.

B. *Applications and Meaning.*—1. *Psychologically;* "mentality" as the constitutive element of cognition & of its substratum, the world of phenomena. It is that which is presented as "object" to the imagination & as such has an effect of its own:—a presentation (*Vorstellung*), or *idea,* idea, or purely mental phenomenon as distinguished from a psycho-physical phenomenon, or sensation (re-action of sense-organ to sense-stimulus). The mind deals with ideas as the eye deals with forms: it is the abstraction formed by mano, or mind proper, from the objects of sense presented by the sense-organ when reacting to extreme objects. Thus cakkhu "faculty of sight" corresponds to rūpa "relation of form" & mano "faculty of thought" (citta & ceto its organ or instrument or localisation) corresponds to dhamma "mentalized" object or "idea" (Mrs. Rh. D. "mental object in general," also "state of mind") — (a) *subjective:* mental attitude, thought, idea, philosophy, truth, & its recognition (anubodhi) by the Buddha, i. e. the Dhamma or world-wisdom = philosophy of the Buddha as contained & expounded in the Dialogues of the 5 Nikāyas (see below C.) — *Note.* The idea of dhamma as the interpreted Order of the World is carried further in the poetical quasi-personification of the Dh. with the phrase "dhammaja dh-nimmita dh-dāyāda" (born of the Norm, created by the Norm, heir of the Norm; see under cpds. and Dhammatā; also s. v. Niyama). That which the Buddha preached, the Dhamma κατ' ἐξοχήν, was the order of law of the universe, immanent, eternal, uncreated, not as interpreted by him only, much less invented or decreed by him, but intelligible to a mind of his range, and by him made so to mankind as bodhi: revelation, awakening. The Buddha (like every great philosopher & other Buddhas preceding Gotama: ye pi te ahesuṇ atītaṇ addhānaṇ Arahanto Sammāsambuddhā te pi dhammaṇ yeva sakkatvā S I.140) is a discoverer of this order of the Dhamma, this universal logic, philosophy or righteousness ("Norm"), in which the rational & the ethical elements are fused into one. Thus by recognition of the truth the knower becomes the incorporation of the knowable (or the sense of the universe = Dhamma) & therefore a perfect man, one who is "truly enlightened" (sammā-sambuddha): so Bhagavā jānaṇ jānāti passaṇ passati cakkhu-bhūto ñāṇa-bhūto dhamma° brahma° & in this possession of the truth he is not *like* Brahmā, but Brahmā himself & the lord of the world as the "master of the Truth": vattā pavattā atthassa ninnetā Amatassa dātā dhammassāmi S IV.94; & similarly "yo kho Dhammaṇ passati so mam passati; yo mam passati so Dhammaṇ passati" = he who sees the Buddha sees the Truth S III.120. Cp. with this also the dhamma-cakka idea (see cpds.). On equation Dhamma = Brahman see esp. Geiger, *Dhamma* pp. 76-80, where is also discussed the formula Bhagavato putto etc. (with dhammaja for the brahmanic brahmaja). — In later (Abhidhamma) literature the (dogmatic) personification of Dhamma occurs. See e. g. Tikp A 366.

As 6th sense-object "dhamma" is the counterpart of "mano": manasā dhammaŋ viññāya "apperceiving presentations with the mind" S IV.185 etc. (see formula under rūpa); mano-viññeyyā dhammā S IV.73; cp. S III.46; IV.3 sq.; V.74; D III.226, 245, 269. Ranged in the same category under the anupassanā-formula (q. v.) "dhammesu dhamm-ânupassin" realising the mentality of mental objects or ideas, e. g. D II.95, 100, 299; A I.39, 296; II.256; III.450; IV.301. Also as one of the 6 taṇhās "desire for ideas" D III.244, 280. — As spirituality opposed to materiality in contrast of dh. & āmisa: It 98 (°dāna: a mat. & a spir. gift). — (b) *objective:* substratum (of cognition), piece, constituent (= khandha), constitution; phenomenon, thing, "world," cosmic order (as the expression of cosmic sense, as under a & 2). Thus applied to the khandhas: vedanādayo tayo kh. DhA I.35 (see Khandha B 3); to rūpa vedanā saññā sankhārā viññāna S III.39; = sankhārā D III.58, 77, 141. Freq. in formula sabbe dhammā aniccā (+ dukkhā anattā: see nicca) "the whole of the visible world, all phenomena are evanescent etc." S III.132 sq. & passim. diṭṭhe [va] dhamme in the phenomenal world (opp. samparāyika dh. the world beyond): see under diṭṭha (S IV.175, 205 etc.). — ye dhammā hetuppabhavā tesaŋ hetuŋ Tathāgato āha "of all phenomena sprung from a cause the Buddha the cause hath told" Vin I.40 (cp. Īsā Upanishad 14). — **lokadhammā** things of this world (viz. gain, fame, happiness etc., see under lābha) D III.260; Nd² 55. — **uttari-manussa-dh°ā** transcendental, supernormal phenomena D I.211, cp. D III.4; **abbhuta-dh°ā** wonderful signs, portents Miln 8 (tayo acchariyā a. dh. pātura-hesuŋ); PvA 2: hassa-khiḍḍhā-rati-dh.-samāpanna endowed with the qualities or things of mirth, play & enjoyment D I.19; III.31; gāma° things or doings of the village D I.4 (cp. DA I.72).

2. *Ratio-ethically*—(a) *objective:* "rationality," anything that is as it should be according to its reason & logicality (as expressed under No. 1 a), i. e. right property, sound condition, norm, propriety, constitution as conforming to No. 1 in universal application i. e. *Natural or Cosmic Law:* yattha nāmañ ca rūpaŋ cā asesam uparujjhati, taŋ te dhammaŋ idhâññāya acchiduŋ bhavabandhanaŋ (recognising this law) S I.35 cittacetasikā dh° ā a term for the four mental khandhas, and gradually superseding them Dhs 1022 (cf. Compendium of Philosophy, 1); dasadhamma-vidū Vin I.38 (see dasa); with attha, nirutti and paṭibhāna; one of the 4 Paṭisambhidās (branches of analytic knowledge A II.160; Pṭs I.84, 88 etc.; Vibh. 293 f., *Points of Controversy*, p. 380. In this sense freq. -° *as adj.:* being constituted, having the inherent quality (as based on Natural Law or the rational constitution of the Universe), destined to be . . ., of the (natural) property of . . ., like (cp. Gr. -ώδης or E. -able, as in change-able = liable to change, also E. -hood, -ly & P. -gata, -ṭhita), e. g. **khaya-dhamma** liable to decay (+ vaya°, virāga°, nirodha°), with ref. to the Sankhāras S IV.216 sq.; in the Paṭiccasamuppāda S II.60; akkhaya imperishable Pv IV.1⁵² (dānaŋ a-dh. atthu). **cavana°** destined to shift to another state of existence D I.18; III.31; It 76; VvA 54. **jāti-jarā-maraṇa°** under the law of birth, age, & death D III.57; A I.147; III.54; PvA 41 (sabbe sattā . . .); **bhedana°** fragile (of kāya) D I.76; S I.71; PvA 41 (bhijjana° of sankhārā). **vipariṇāma°** changeable A I.258; IV.157; PvA 60 (+ anicca). **a°** unchanging D III.31 sq. **samudaya° & nirodha°**, in formula yaŋ kiñci s-dh°ŋ sabban tan n-dh°ŋ "anything that is destined to come into existence must also cease to exist" D I.110, 180; S IV.47 & passim. Cp. further: anāvatti° avinipāta° D I.156; III.107, 132; A I.232; II.89, 238; IV.12; anuppāda° D III.270. — (b) *subjective:* "morality," right behaviour, righteousness, practice, duty; maxim (cp. ṭhāna), constitution of character as conforming to No. 1 in social application, i. e. *Moral Law.* — Often in *pl.:* tenets, convictions, moral habits; & as *adj.* that which is proper, that which forms the right idea; good, righteous, true; opp. adhamma false, unjust etc.; evil practice — (α) Righteousness etc.: S I.86 (eko dh. one principle of conduct; II.280 (dh. isinaŋ dhajo: righteousness is the banner of the Wise); kusala dh. D I.224; dhamme ṭhita righteous Vv 16⁸; ñāti° duty against relatives PvA 30; deyya° = dāna PvA 9, 70; sad° faith (q. v.) — opp. adhamma unrighteousness, sin A II.19; V.73 sq.; D III.70 (°rāga + visama-lobha & micchā-dhamma); Pv III.9⁶ (°ŋ anuvattisaŋ I practised wrong conduct). — In the same sense: dh. asuddho Vin I.5 = S I.137 (pāturahosi Magadhesu pubbe dh. a.); pāpa° (adj.) of evil conduct Vin I.3; aṭṭhita° unrighteous D III.133; lobha° greedy quality D I.224, 230; methuna dh. fornication D III.133. — (β) (pl.) Tenets, practices etc. — (aa) good: kusalā dh. D II.223, 228; III.49, 56, 82, 102 etc.; S II.206; sappurisa° A V.245, 279; PvA 114; samaṇa° Wanderer's practice or observances DhA II.55. brāhmaṇakaraṇā D I.244; yesaŋ dh°ānaŋ Gotamo vaṇṇavādin D I.206; cp. sīlaŋ samādhi paññā ca vimutti ca anuttarā: anubuddhā ime dhammā Gotamena yasassinā D II.123. dhammānaŋ sukusalo perfect in all (these) qualities D I.180; samāhite citte dhammā pātubhavanti "with composed mind appear true views" S IV.78; dhammesu patiṭṭhito S I.185; ananussutesu dh°esu cakkhuŋ udapādi "he visualized undiscovered ideas" S II.9. — (bb) evil: āvaraṇīyā S IV.104; pāpakā Vin I.8; D I.70; A I.202; akusalā D III.56, 57, 73, 91 etc.; lobha°, dosa°, moha° S I.70 = It 45 = Nd² 420; S I.43; M III.40; dukkhavipākā vodanīyā saŋkilesikā ponobbhavikā D I.195; III.57. — (cc) various: gambhīrā duddasā etc. Vin I.4; D I.12; S I.136; — Cp. S II.15, 26; Nd² 320; It 22, 24; Ps I.5, 22, 28; Vbh 105, 228, 293 sq. etc. etc. — (γ) (adj.) good, pious, virtuous etc.: adhammo nirayaŋ neti dhammo pāpeti suggatiŋ "the sinners go to niraya, the good to heaven" Th 1, 304 = DA I.99 = DhsA 38 = DhA I.22. kalyāṇa° virtuous A I.74, 108; II.81, 91, 224 sq.; PvA 13. Opp. pāpa° Vin III.90; cp. above α. — (δ) (phrases). Very freq. used as adv. is the instr. dhammena with justice, justly, rightly, fitly, properly Vin I.3; D I.122; S IV.331; Vv 34¹⁹ (= kāraṇena ñāyena vā VvA); Pv II.9³⁰ (= yutten' eva kāraṇena PvA 125, as just punishment); IV.16⁹ (= anurūpakāraṇena PvA 286). Esp. in phrase of the cakkavattin, who rules the world according to justice: adaṇḍena asatthena dhammena anusāsati (or ajjhāvasati) D I.89; II.16; S I.236 = Sn 1002; cp. Sn 554 (dhammena cakkaŋ vattemi, of the Buddha). Opp. adhammena unjustly, unfitly, against the rule Vin IV.37; S I.57; IV.331; DA I.236. — **dhamme** (loc.) honourably J II.159. — **dhammaŋ carati** to live righteously Pv II.3³⁴; see also below C 3 & dh.-cariyā.

C. *The* Dhamma, i. e. moral philosophy, wisdom, truth as propounded by Gotama Buddha in his discourses & conversations, collected by the compilers of the 5 Nikāyas (dhamma-vinayaŋ sangāyantehi dhammasangāhakehi ekato katvā VvA 3; cp. mayaŋ dh.°ŋ ca vinayañ ca sangāyāma Vin II.285), resting on the deeper meaning of dhamma as expl^d under B 1 a, & being in short the "doctrinal" portions of the Buddhist Tipiṭaka in contradiction to the Vinaya, the portion expounding the rules of the Order (see piṭaka). Dhamma as doctrine is also opposed to Abhidhamma "what follows on the Dhamma." — (1) *Dhamma and Vinaya,* "wisdom & discipline," as now found in the 2 great Piṭakas of the B. Scriptures, the Vinaya and Suttanta-Piṭaka (but the expression "Piṭako" is later. See

Piṭaka). Thus bhikkhū suttantikā vinaya-dharā dhamma kathikā, i. e. "the bhikkhus who know the Suttantas, remember the Vinaya & preach the Word of the Buddha" Vin II.75 (≈I.169), cp. IV.67. Dhamma & Vinaya comb[d]: yo 'haŋ evaŋ svâkkhāte Dh-vinaye pabbajito S I.119; bhikkhu na evarūpiŋ kathaŋ kattā hoti: na tvaŋ imaŋ Dh-v°ŋ ājānāsi, ahaŋ imaŋ Dh-v°ŋ ājānāmi etc. S III.12; imaŋ Dh-v°ŋ na sakkomi vitthārena ācikkhituŋ S I.9; samanā . . . imasmiŋ Dh-v°e gâdhanti S III.59. — Thus in var. cpds. (see below), as Dh-dhara (+V-dh.) one who knows both by heart; Dh-vādin (+V-v.) one who can recite both, etc. — See e. g. the foll. passages: Vin II.285 (dh. ca v. ca pariyatta), 304; III.19, 90; D I.8, 176, 229; II.124 (ayaŋ Dh. ayaŋ V. idaŋ Satthu-sāsanaŋ); III.9, 12, 28, 118 sq.; S I.9, 119, 157; II.21, 50, (dh-vinaye assāsa); A III.297 (id.); S II.120; III.91; IV.43 sq., 260; A I.34, 121, 185, 266; II.2, 26, 117, 168; III.8, 168 sq.; IV.36, 200 sq.; V.144, 163, 192; It 112; Sn p. 102; Ud 50.— 2. *Dhamma, Buddha, Saṅgha*. On the principle expl[d] in Note on B 1 a rests the separation of the personality of the teacher from that which he taught (the "Doctrine," the "Word," the Wisdom or Truth, cp. Dhamma-kāyo Tathāgatassa adhivacanaŋ D III.84). A person becoming a follower of the B. would conform to his teaching (Dh.) & to the community ("Church"; Sangha) by whom his teaching was handed down. The formula of Initiation or membership is therefore threefold, viz. Buddhaŋ saraṇaŋ upemi (gacchāmi), Dh °ŋ . . ., Sanghaŋ . . . i. e. I put myself into the shelter of the B., the Dh. & the S. (see further ref. under Sangha) S I.34 (Buddhe pasannā Dhamme ca Sanghe tibbagāravā: ete sagge pakāsenti yattha te upapajjare, i. e. those who adore the B. & his Church will shine in Heaven); D II.152 sq., 202 sq., 352; S IV.270 sq. (°saraṇagamana); DhA I.206; PvA 1 (vande taŋ uttamaŋ Dh °ŋ, B °ŋ, S °ŋ). Cp. Satthari, Dhamme, Sanghe kankhati, as 3 of the ceto-khilā A III.248≈. —3. *Character of the Dhamma* in var. attributes, general phraseology. — The praise of the Dh. is expressed in many phrases, of which only a few of the more frequent can be mentioned here. Among the most famous is that of "dhammaŋ deseti ādi-kalyāṇaŋ majjhe-k°, pariyosāna-k°, etc. "beautiful in the beginning, beautiful in the middle & beautiful in the end," e. g. D I.62; S I.105; IV.315; A II.147, 208; III.113 sq., 135, 262; D III.96, 267; Nd[2] 316; It 79; VvA 87. It is welcome as a friend, beautifully told, & its blessings are immediate: sv' akkhāta, sandiṭṭhika, akālika, ehipassika etc. D II.93; III.5, 39, 45, 102; S I.9, 117; II.199; IV.271; A III.285 etc. It is mahā-dh. S IV.128; ariya° S I.30; A V.241, 274; Sn 783; sammā° S I.129. It is likened to a splendid palace on a mountain-top Vin I.5 = It 33, or to a quiet lake with sīla as its banks S I.169 = 183; and it is above age & decay: satañ ca dhammo na jaram upeti S I.71. Whoever worships the Dh. finds in this worship the highest gratification: diyo loke sako putto piyo loke sako pati, tato piyatarā . . . dhammassa magganā S I.210; ye keci ariyadhamme khantiyā upetā . . . devakāyaŋ paripūressanti S I.30. Dh °ŋ garukaroti D III.84. Opp. Dhamme agārava A III.247, 340; IV.84: the slanderers of the Dh. receive the worst punishment after death S I.30 (upenti Roruvaŋ ghoraŋ). — *Var. phrases*: to find the truth (i. e. to realize intuitively the Dh.)=dh°ŋ anubodhati D II.113; S I.137, or vindati D I.110, 148. To expound the Dh., teach the truth, talk about problems of ethics & philosophy: dh°ŋ deseti Vin IV.134; S I.210 etc.; katheti PvA 41; bhāsati Vin I.101; bhaṇati Vin I.169; pakāseti S II.28; IV.121. To hear the Dh., to listen to such an exposition: dh°ŋ suṇāti S I.114, 137, 196, 210; A I.36; III.163; DhA III.81, 113. To attain full knowledge of it: dh °ŋ pariyāpuṇāti A II.103, 185; III.86, cp. 177 & °pariyatti. To remember the Dh.: dhāreti A III.176 (for details of the 5 stages of the Dh.-accomplishment): to ponder over the Dh., to study it: dh °ŋ viciṇāti S I.34 = 55, 214; A IV.3 sq. To enter a relation of discipleship with the Dh.: dh °ŋ saraṇaŋ gacchati (see above 2) Pv IV.3[48]; dhammaŋ saraṇatthaŋ upehi Vv 53[2] (cp. VvA 232). — See further Ps I.34, 78, 131; II.159 sq.; Pug 58, 66; Vbh 293 sq., 329; Nett 11, 15, 31, 83, 112; & cp. cpds. — 4. *Dhamma and anudhamma*. Childers interprets anudhamma with "lesser or inferior dhamma," but the general purport of the Nikāya passages seems to be something like "in conformity with, in logical sequence to the dhamma" i. e. lawfulness, righteousness, reasonableness, truth (see *KS* II.202; Geiger, *Pāli Dhamma* pp. 115-118). It occurs (always with Dh.) in the foll. contexts: dhammassa c' ânudh °ŋ vyākaroti "to explain according to the truth of the Dhamma" D I.161; III.115; Ud 50; dhammassa hoti anudhammacārin "walking in perfect conformity to the Dh." A II.8; dh.-anudh °ŋ ācaranti id. D III.154; dh.-anudh° paṭipanna "one who has reached the complete righteousness of the Dh." D II.224; III.119; S III.40 sq.; It 81; A III.176 (where it forms the highest stage of the Dhamma-knowledge, viz. (1) dh °ŋ suṇāti; (2) pariyāpuṇāti; (3) dhāreti; (4) atthaŋ upaparikkhati; (5) dh-anudh °ŋ paṭipajjati). Further in series bahussuta, dhamma-dhara, dh-anudh°-paṭipanna D II.104; S V.261; A II.8; Ud 63; also in dhamma-kathika, dh-anudh°-paṭipanna, diṭṭha-dhamma-nibbāna-patta S II.18 = 114 = III.163; & in atthaŋ aññāya, dhammaŋ aññāya, dh-anudh°-paṭipanna A I.36; II.97.

-akkhāna discussing or preaching of the Dhamma Nd[1] 91; -atthadesanā interpretation of the Dh. Miln 21; -âdhikaraṇa a point in the Dh. S IV.63 = V.346; -âdhipa Lord of righteousness (+anudhamma-cārin) A I.150; cp. °ssāmi; nt. abstr. °âdhipateyya the dominating influence of the Dh. A I.147 sq.; D III.220; Miln 94; Vism 14. -ânudhamma see above C 4; -anuvattin acting in conformity with the moral law Dh 86, cp. DhA II.161; -ânusārin of righteous living D III.105, 254 (+saddhā°); M I.226, 479; A I.74; IV.215; IV.23; S V.200; Pug 15; Nett 112, 189; -anvaya main drift of the faith, general conclusions of the Dh., D II.83 = III.100; M II.120; -abhisamaya understanding of the Truth, conversion to the Dhamma [cp. dharmâbhisamaya Divy 200] S II.134 (+dh.-cakkhu-paṭilābha); Pug 41; Miln 20; DhA I.27; IV.64; PvA 31 etc.; -âmata the nectar of righteousness or the Dh. Miln 22 (°meghena lokaŋ abhitappayanto), 346; -ādāsa the mirror of the Dhamma D II.93 (name of an aphorism) S V.357 (id.); Th 1, 395; ThA 179; -āyatana the field of objects of ideation S II.72; Dhs 58, 66, 147, 397, 572, 594; Vbh 70, 72 sq.; -ārammaṇa: dh. as an object of ideation Dhs 146, 157, 365; cp. *Dhs. trsl.* 2; -ārāma "one who has the Dh. as his pleasure-ground," one who rejoices in the Dh. A III.431; It 82 (+dh-rata); Sn 327; Dh 364, cp. DhA IV.95; -ālapana using the proper address, a fit mode of addressing a person as followed by the right custom. See *Dial.* I.193-196; J V.418; -āsana "the Dh-seat," i. e. flat piece of stone or a mat on which a priest sat while preaching J I.53; DhA II.31; -ûposatha the fast day prescribed by the Dh. A I.208; -okkā the torch of Righteousness J I.34; -oja the essence or sap of the Dh. S V.162; DhA IV.169; -osadha the medicine of the Dh. Miln 110, 335. -kathā ethical discussion, fit utterance, conversation about the Dh., advice D III.154; J I.217; VvA 6; PvA 50, 66; -kathika (adj.) one who converses about ethical problems, one who recites or preaches the Dh., one who speaks fitly or properly. Often in combn. with *Vinaya-dhara* "one who masters (knows by heart) the Vinaya," & bahussuta "one who has a wide knowledge of tradition": Vin IV.10, 13, 141; A III.78; DhA II.30; also with *suttantika* "one who is versed in the Suttantas" Vin I.169; II.75; IV.67. The ability to preach the Dh. is the first condition of one who wishes to become perfected in righteousness (see dhamm-ânudhamma, above

C 4): S II.18, 114=III.163; M III.40. — A I.25 sq.; II.138; Pug 42; J I.217; IV.2 (°thera). Cp. also AvŚ II.81; -kathikatta (nt.) speaking about the Dh.; preaching M III.40; A I.38 (+vinayadhara-katta); -kamma a legally valid act, or procedure in accordance with the Rules of the Order Vin IV.37, 136, 232; A I.74 (+vinaya°); a° an illegal act Vin IV.232; A I.74; -karaka a proper or regulation (standard) water-pot, i. e. a pot with a filter for straining water as it was used by ascetics Vin II.118, 177, 301; J I.395; VI.331; DhA III.290, 452; VvA 220 (not °karaṇena); PvA 185; Miln 68; -kāma a lover of the Dh. D III.267; A V.24, 27, 90, 201; Sn 92. -kāya having a body according to the Norm (the dhammatā of bodies). See Bdhgh as translated in *Dial.* III. ad loc.; having a normal body (*sic* Bdhgh, esp. of the B. D III.84; -ketu the standard of the Dh., or Dh. as standard A I.109=III.149; -khandha the (4) main portions or articles of the Dh. (sīla, samādhi, paññā, vimutti) D III.229; cp. Sp. AvŚ II.155; -gaṇa a body of followers of the Dh. PvA 194; -gaṇḍikā (better gaṇṭhikā, q v.) a block of justice, i. e. of execution J I.150, 151; II.124; VI.176; V.303; -garu worshipping the Dh. S IV.123; DhA I.17 (°ka); -gariya a kind of acrobatic tumbler, lit. excellent t. (+brahma°) Miln 191; -gu one who knows the Dh. (analogous to vedagu) J V.222; VI.261; -gutta protecting the Dh. or protected by the Dh. (see gutta) S I.222; J V.222 (+dh-pāla); -ghosaka (-kamma) praise of the Dh. DhA III.81; -cakka the perfection or supreme harmony of righteousness (see details under cakkha), always in phrase dh-cakkaŋ pavatteti (of the Buddha) "to proclaim or inaugurate the perfect state or ideal of universal righteousness" Vin I.8=M I.171; Vin I.11; S I.191; III.86; Sn 556, 693; Miln 20, 343; DhA I.4; VvA 165; PvA 2, 67 etc.; besides this also in simile at S I.33 of the car of righteousness; -cakkhu "the eye of wisdom," perception of the law of change. Freq. in the standing formula at the end of a conversation with the Buddha which leads to the "opening of the eyes" or conversion of the interlocutor, viz. "virajaŋ vītamalaŋ dh-cakkhuŋ udapādi" D I.86, 110; II.288; S IV.47; A IV.186; Vin I.11, 16, 40 etc. Expl. at DA I.237: dhammesu vā cakkhuŋ dhammamayaŋ vā cakkhuŋ. Cp. S II.134 (°paṭilābha; +dhammâbhisamaya); *Dial.* I.184; II.176; -cariyā walking in righteousness, righteous living, observance of the Dh., piety (=dānādi-puñña-paṭipatti VvA 282) S I.101 (+samacariyā kusala-kiriyā); A II.5; III.448; V.87, 302; Sn 263 (=kāyasucaritâdi° Sn A 309), 274 (+brahma°). a° evil way of living A I.55 (+visama-cariyā); -cārin virtuous, dutiful M I.289; II.188; Dh 168; Miln 19 (+samacārin); -cetiya a memorial in honour of the Dh. M II.124; -chanda virtuous desire (opp. kāma°) DhsA 370; Vbh 208; -ja born of the Dh. (see above, Note on B I a), in formula "Bhagavato putto oraso dh-jo, dh-nimmito, dh.dāyādo" (the spiritual child of the Buddha) D III.84=S II.221; It 101; -jāla "net of the Dh.," name of a discourse (cp. °ādāsa & pariyāya) D I.46; -jīvin living righteously It 108; Dh 24 (=dhammena samena DhA I.239); -ññū one who knows the Dh. J VI.261; -ṭṭha standing in the Law, just, righteous S I.33 (+sīlasampanna); Sn 749; J III.334; IV.211; ThA 244, -ṭṭhita=°ṭṭha D I.190; -ṭṭhiti° having a footing in the Dh. S II.60, 124, cp. °ṭṭhitatā: establishing of causes and effects S II.25; -takka right reasoning Sn 1107 (=sammā-sankappa Nd² 318); -dāna gift of; -dāyāda heir of the Dh.; spiritual heir (cp. above note on B I a) D III.84; S II.221; M I.12; III.29; It 101; -dīpa the firm ground or footing of the Dh. (usually comb^d with atta-dīpa: having oneself as one's refuge, self-dependent) D II.100; III.58, 77; S V.154; -desanā moral instruction, exposition of the Dh. Vin I.16; D I.110 etc. (see desanā); -dessin a hater of the Dh. Sn 92; -dhaja the banner of the Dh. A I.109=III.149; Nd² 503; Miln 21; -dhara (adj.) one who knows the Dh. (by heart); see above C 4. Comb^d w. Vinaya-dhara Vin I.127, 337; II.8; A I.117, & bahussuta (ibid). Sn 58 (cp. SnA 110). — See also A III.361 sq., IV.310; Nd² 319; -dhātu the mental object considered as irreducible element Dhs 58, 67, 147 etc.; Vbh 87, 89 (see above B I); an ultimate principle of the Dh., the cosmic law D II.8; M I.396; S II.143 sq.; Nett 64 sq.; Vism 486 sq. -dhāraṇa knowledge of the Dh. M II.175; -nāṭaka a class of dancing girls having a certain duty J V.279; -nimmita see °ja; -niyāma belonging to the order of the Norm D I.190; DA on D II.12: dhammatā; (°ka); -niyāmatā, certainty, or orderliness of causes and effects S II.25; *Points of Controversy*, 387; -netti=niyāma Miln 328; DA I.31; cp. Sk. dharmanetrī M Vastu II.357; III.234, 238; -pajjota the lamp of the Dh. Miln 21; -pada (nt.) a line or stanza of the Dhamma, a sentence containing an ethical aphorism; a portion or piece of the Dh. In the latter meaning given as 4 main subjects, viz. anabhijjhā, avyāpāda, sammā-sati, sammā-samādhi D III.229; A II.29 sq. (in detail); Nett 170. — S I.22 (dānā ca kho dh-padaŋ va seyyo). 202 (dh-padesu chando); A II.185; Sn 88 (dh-pade sudesite=nibbāna-dhammassa padattā SnA 164); J III.472 (=nibbāna); DhA III.190 (ekaŋ dh-padaŋ). As Np. title of a canonical book, included in the Khuddaka Nikāya; -pamāṇa measuring by the (teaching of) Dh. Pug 53; DhA III.114 (°ikāni jātisatāni); -pariyatti attainment of or accomplishment in the Dh., the collection of the Dh. in general A III.86 (w. ref. to the 9 angas, see navanga); -pariyāya a short discourse, or a verse, or a poem, with a moral or a text; usually an exposition of a single point of doctrine D I.46; II.93; III.116; M I.445; Vin I.40 (a single verse); A I.65; IV.63 (a poem Sn 190-218, where also it is called a dh°pariyāyo); A V.288, 291. Such a dh°pariyāya had very often a special name. Thus Brahmajāla, the Wondrous Net D I.46; Dhammādāso dh°p°, the Mirror of the Law D II.93=S V.357; Sokasallaharaṇa, Sorrow's dart extractor A III.62; Ādittap° dh°p°, the Red-hot lancet S IV.168; Lomahaŋsana° M I.83; Dhammatā-dhamma° Miln 193, etc. -pāla guardian of the Law or the Dh. J V.222, freq. also as Np.; -pīti (-rasa) the sweetness of drinking in the Dh. (pivaŋ) Sn 257; Dh 79 (=dhamma-pāyako dhammaŋ pivanto ti attho DhsA II.126); -bhaṇḍāgārika treasurer of the Dh., an Ep. of Ānanda Th 1, 1048; J I.382, 501; II.25; DhA III.250; PvA 2. -bhūta having become the Dh.; righteousness incorporated, said of the Buddhas D III.84. Usually in phrase (Bhagavā) cakkhu-bhūta . . . dh-bhūta brahma-bhūta A V.226 sq. (cp. cakkhu); Th I, 491; see also above, note B I a; -bheri the drum of the Dh. Miln 21; -magga the path of righteousness Sn 696; Miln 21; -maya made (built) of the Dh. (pāsāda) S I.137; -yanta the (sugar-) mill of the Dh. (fig.) Miln 166. -yāna the vehicle of the Law (the eightfold Noble Path) S V.5; -rakkhita rightly guarded Sn 288; -rata fond of the Law Sn 327; Dh 364; DhA IV.95; cp. dh.-[gatā]rati Th I.742; Dhp. 354; -rasa taste of Dhp. 354; -rājā king of righteousness, Ep. of the Buddha S I.33=55; D I.88 (of a cakkavatti); A I.109; III.149; Sn 554; J I.262; interpreted by Bdhgh at DA I.249 as "dhammena rajjaŋ labhitvā rājā jāto ti"=a king who gained the throne legitimately; -laddha one who has acquired the Dh., holy, pious S II.21; J III.472; justly acquired (bhogā) Sn p. 87; -vara the best of truths or the most excellent Doctrine Sn 233, 234; -vādin speaking properly, speaking the truth or according to the Doctrine Vin II.285; III.175 (+Vinaya-vādin); D III.135 (id.); D I.4, 95 (of Gotama; DA I.76: nava-lokuttara-dhamma sannissitaŋ katvā vadati); S IV.252; A I.75; II.209; -vicaya investigation of doctrine, religious research Dhs 16, 20, 90, 309, 333, 555; Vbh 106; Vism 132; -vitakka righteous thought A I.254; -vidū one who understands the Dh., an expert in the Dh. J V.222; VI.261; -vinicchaya righteous decision, discrimination of the truth Sn 327; Dh 144; DhA III.86; -vihārin living according to the Dh. A III.86 sq.; -saŋvibhāga sharing out or distribution of the Dh., i. e. spiritual gifts It 98 (opp. āmisa° material gifts); -sangāhaka a compiler of the sacred scriptures, a διασκευαστής VvA 3, 169; -saññā righteous thought, faith, piety PvA 3; -sabhā a hall for the discussion of the Dh., a chapel, meeting-house J VI.333; DhA I.31; II.51; IV.91; PvA 38, 196; -samaya a meeting where the Dh. is preached S I.26; -samādāna acquisition of the Dh., which is fourfold as discussed at M I.305; D III.229; -saraṇa relying on or putting one's faith in the Dh. (see above C 3) D III.58, 77; S V.154; -savana hearing the preaching of the Dh., "going to church" Vin I.101; M II.175; A II.248, 381; IV.361; Sn 265; DhA III.190; -sākaccha conversation about the Dh. Sn 266; -ssāmi Lord of the Truth, Ep. of the Buddha (see above B 1 a note) S IV.94; -sāra the essence of the Dh. S V.402; -sārathi in purisa-dh.-s° at D I.62 misprint for purisa-damma-s°; -sārin a follower of the Dh. S I.170; -sudhammatā excellency of the Dh. S II.199; Th I, 24, 220, 270, 286; -senāpati "captain of the Dhamma," Ep. of Sāriputta Th I, 1083; J I.408, Miln 343; DhA III.305; VvA 64, 65, 158; -soṇḍatā thirst after justice J V.482; -sota the ear of the Dh. S II.43.

Dhamma[2] (adj.) [Sk. *dhārma, cp. dhammika] only in f. -ī in comb[n] with kathā: relating to the Dhamma, viz. conversation on questions of Ethics, speaking about the Dh., preaching, religious discourse, sermon. Either as dhammī kathā Vin II.161; IV.56 & in instr.-abl. dhammiyā kathāya (sandasseti samādapeti samuttejeti saŋpahaŋseti: ster. formula) S I.114, 155, 210, IV.122, PvA 30 etc.; or as cpd. dhammī-kathā D II.1; M I.161; Sn 325; & dhammi-kathā S I.155; PvA 38.

Dhamma[3] (adj.) [Sk. dhanvan] having a bow: see daḷha°; also as dhammin in daḷha° S I.185 (see dhammin).

Dhammatā (f.) [Sk. dharmitā] conformity to the Dhamma-niyāma (see niyāma), fitness, propriety; a general rule, higher law, cosmic law, general practice, regular phenomenon, usual habit; often used in the sense of a finite verb: it is a rule, it is proper, one should expect S I.140 (Buddhānaŋ dh. the law of the B.'s i. e. as one is wont to expect of the B.s), 215 (su°); IV.216 sq. (khaya° etc.); D II.12; A II.36 (kusala°); V.46; Th I, 712; J I.245; II.128; Nett 21, 50, cp. Miln 179; PvA 19; VvA 7. See also AvŚ Index.

Dhammattā (f.) [Sk. *dharmatvaŋ] liability to be judged Vin II.55 (& a°).

Dhammani only found in S I.103, where the Comy. takes it as a locative, and gives, as the equivalent, "in a forest on dry land" (araññe thale). Cp. *Kindred Sayings* I.129, *n.* 2.

Dhammika (adj.) [=Sk. dharmya, cp. dhammiya] lawful, according to the Dh. or the rule; proper, fit, right; permitted, legitimate, justified; righteous, honourable, of good character, just, esp. an attr. of a righteous King (rājā cakkavattī dhammiko'dhammarājā) D I.86; II.16; A I.109=III.149; J I.262, 263; def. by Bdhgh as "dhammaŋ caratī ti dh." (DA I.237) & "dhammena caratī ti dh., ñāyena samena pavattalī ti" (ib. 249). — Vin IV.284; D I.103; S II.280 (dhammikā kathā); III.240 (āhāra); IV.203 (dhammikā devā, adh° asurā); A I.75; III.277; Sn 404; DhA II.86 (dohaḷa); IV.185 (°lābha); PvA 25 .(=suddha, manohara). Also as saha-dh° (esp. in conn. w. pañha, a justified, reasonable, proper question: D I.94; S IV.299 in detail) Vin IV.141; D I.161; III.115; A I.174. — a° unjust, illegal etc. Vin IV.285; S IV,203; A III.243.

Dhammin[1] (adj.) [Sk. dharmin] only -°: having the nature or quality of, liable to, consisting in, practising, acting like, etc. (as °dhamma B 2 a), viz. uppāda-vaya° D II.157; maraṇa° (=maraṇadhamma) A I.147; pāpa° Pv I.11[7] of evil nature.

Dhammin[2] (-°) only in daḷha-dh°, which is customarily taken as a der[n] from dhanu, bow=having a strong bow (see dhamma[3]); although some passages admit interpretation as "of strong character or good practice," e. g. S I.185.

Dhammiya (adj.) [Sk. dharmya; cp. dhammika] in accordance with the Dhamma PvA 242 (also a°); Vism 306 (°lābha).

Dhammilla [Sk. dhammilla] the braided hair of women Dāvs IV.9.

Dhammī in °kathā see dhamma[2].

***Dhayati** to suck: see dhātī. Caus. dhāpayati, pp. dhāta (q. v.).

Dhara (usually -°, except at Miln 420) (adj.) [Sk. dhara, to dhṛ, see dharati] bearing, wearing, keeping; holding in mind, knowing by heart. Freq. in phrase dhamma-dhara (knowing the Dhamma, q. v.), vinaya°, mātikā°, e. g. D II.125. dhamma° also Sn 58; Th I, 187; Nd[2] 319; vinaya° Miln 344; jaṭājina° Sn 1010. See also dhāra.

Dharaṇa (adj.) bearing, holding, comprising VvA 104 (suvaṇṇassa pañcadasa° nikkha holding, i. e. worth or equal to 15 parts of gold). — f. -ī bearing, i. e. pregnant with Sn 26 (of cows: godharaṇiyo paveṇiyo=gabbhiniyo SnA 39). As n. the Earth J V.311; VI.526; Miln 34; dharaṇī-ruha N. of a tree J VI.482, 497; Miln 376.

Dharati [Sk. dharati, dhṛ as in Gr. θρόνος; Lat. firmus & fretus. See also daḷha, dhata, dhamma, dhiti, dhuva] to hold, bear, carry, wear; to hold up, support; to bear in mind, know by heart; to hold out, endure, last, continue, live Sn 385 (take to heart, remember); DhA II.68; — ppr. dharamāṇa living, lasting J I.75 (dh°e yeva suriye while the sun was still up); II.6; Miln 240, 291 (Bhagavato dh°-kāle); — grd. dhareyya, in dh°-divasa the day when a young girl is to be carried (into the house of her husband) ThA, 25; cp. dhāreyya Th 2, 472=vivāha ThA 285. — pp. dhata (q. v.) — Caus. dhāreti (q. v.).

Dhava[1] [Sk. dhava=madhuratvaca, Halāyudha] the shrub Grislea Tomentosa A I.202, 204; J IV.209; VI.528.

Dhava[2] [Sk. dhava, a newly formed word after vidhava, widow, q. v.] a husband ThA 121 (dh. vuccati sāmiko tad abhāvā vidhavā matapatikā ti attho).

Dhavala (adj.) [Sk. dhavala, to dhavati, see dhāvati & dhovati] white, dazzling white VvA 252; Dāvs II.123; V.26.

Dhavalatā (f.) whiteness VvA 197.

Dhāta [Sk. *dhāyita of dhayati to suck, nourish, pp. dhīta] fed, satiated; satisfied, appeased Vin I.222; J I.185; II.247, 446; V.73; VI.555; Pv I.11[8] (so read for dāta)=PvA 59 (: suhita titta); Miln 238, 249. — f. abstr. dhātatā satiation, fulness, satisfaction, in ati° J II.293.

Dhātī (f.) [Sk. dhātrī=Gr. τιθήνη wet nurse, to dhayati suck, suckle; Idg. *dhēi as in Gr. θῆσθαι to milk, θῆλυς feeding, θηλή female breast; cp. Lat. felare, femina ("giving suck"), filius ("suckling"); Oir. dinu lamb; Goth. daddjan; Ohg. tila breast. See also dadhi, dhītā, dhenu] wet nurse, fostermother D II.19; M I.395; II.324; J I.57; III.391; PvA 16, 176. In cpds. dhāti°, viz. -cela swaddling cloth, baby's napkin S I.205=J III.309.

Dhātu (f.) [Sk. dhātu to dadhāti, Idg. *dhē, cp. Gr. τίθημι, ἀνά-θημα, Sk. dhāman, dhātṛ (=Lat. conditor); Goth. gadēds; Ohg. tāt, tuom (in meaning -°=dhātu, cp. E. serf-dom "condition of . . .") tuon=E. to do; & with k-suffix Lat. facio, Gr. (ἔ)θηκ(α), Sk. dhāka; see also dhamma] element. Closely related to dhamma in meaning B 1^b, only implying a closer relation to physical substance. As to its gen. connotation cp. *Dhs. trsl.* p. 198. — 1. a primary element, of which the usual set comprises the four paṭhavī, āpo, tejo, vāyo (earth, water, fire, wind), otherwise termed cattāro mahā-bhūtā(ni): D I.215; II.294; III.228; S I.15; II.169 sq., 224; IV.175, 195; A II.165; III.243; Vbh 14, 72; Nett 73. See discussed at *Cpd.* 254 sq. — A def^n of dhātu is to be found at Vism 485. — Singly or in other comb^{ns} paṭhavī° S II.174; tejo° S I.144; D III.227; the four plus ākāsa S III.227, plus viññāna S II.248; III.231; see below 2 b. — 2. (a) natural condition, property, disposition; factor, item, principle, form. In this meaning in var. comb^{ns} & applications, esp. closely related to khandha. Thus mentioned with khandha & āyatana (sensory element & element of sense-perception) as bodily or physical element, factor (see khandha B 1 d & cp. Nd^2 under dhātu) Th 2, 472. As such (physical substratum) it constitutes one of the lokā or forms of being (khandha° dhātu° āyatana° Nd^2 550). Freq. also in comb^n kāma-dhātu, rūpa° arūpa° "the elements or properties of k. etc." as preceding & conditioning bhava in the respective category (Nd^2 s. v.). See under d. — As "set of conditions or state of being (-°)" in the foll.: loka° a world, of which 10 are usually mentioned (equalling 10,000: PvA 138) S I.26; V.424; Pv II 9^{61}; Vbh 336; PvA 138; *KS* II.101, *n.* 1; — nibbāna° the state of N. S V.8; A II.120; IV.202; J I.55; It 38 (dve: see under Nibbāna); Miln 312. Also in the foll. connections: amata° It 62; bhū° the verbal root bhū DA I.229; ṭhapitāya dhātuyā "while the bodily element, i. e. vitality lasts" Miln 125; vaṇṇa° form, beauty S I.131; Pv I.3^1. In these cases it is so far weakened in meaning, that it simply corresponds to E. abstr. suffix -hood or -ity (cp. °hood = origin. "form": see ketu), so perhaps in Nibbāna° = Nibbāna-dom. Cp. dhātuka. — (b) elements in sense-consciousness: referring to the 6 ajjhattikāni & 6 bāhirāni āyatanāni S II.140 sq. Of these sep. sota° D I.79; III.38; Vbh 334; dibbasota° S II.121, 212; V.265, 304; A I.255; III.17, 280; V.199; cakkhu° Vbh 71 sq.; mano° Vbh 175, 182, 301; mano-viññāṇa° Vbh 87, 89, 175, 182 sq. — (c) various: aneka° A I.22; III.325; V.33; akusala° Vbh 363; avijjā° S II.132; ābhā° S II.150; ārambha° S V.66, 104 sq.; A I.4; II.338; ṭhiti° S II.175; III.231; A III.338; dhamma° S II.56; nekkhamma° S II.151; A III.447; nissāraṇiyā dhātuyo (5) D III.239; A III.245, 290. See further S I.134, 196; II.153, 248 (aniccā); III.231 (nirodha); IV.67; A I.176; II.164; IV.385; Dhs 58, 67, 121; Nett 57, 64 sq.; ThA 20, 49, 285. — (d) Different sets and enumerations: as 3 under kāma°, rūpa°, arūpa A I.223; III.447; Ps I.137; Vbh 86, 363, 404 sq.; under rūpa°, arūpa°, nirodha° It 45. — as 6 (pathavī etc. + ākāsa° & viññāṇa°): D III.247; A I.175 sq.; M III.31, 62, 240; Ps I.136; Vbh 82 sq. — as 7 (ābhā subha etc.): S II.150. — 18: Ps I.101, 137; II.230, Dhs 1333; Vbh 87 sq., 401 sq.; Vism 484 sq. — 3. a humour or affection of the body DA I.253 (dhātusamatā). — 4. the remains of the body after cremation PvA 76; a relic VvA 165 (sarīra°, bodily relic); Dāvs V.3 (dasana° the tooth-relic). — abl. dhātuso according to one's nature S II.154 sq. (sattā sattehi saddhiŋ saŋsandanti etc.); It 70 (id.); S III.65.

-kathā N. of 3rd book of the Abhidhamma Vism 96. -kucchi womb Miln 176; -kusala skilled in the elements M III.62; °kusalatā proficiency in the (18) elements D III.212; Dhs 1333; -ghara "house for a relic," a dagoba SnA 194. -cetiya a shrine over a relic DhA III.29; -nānatta diversity of specific experience D III.289; S II.143; IV.113 sq., 284; -vibhāga distribution of relics VvA 297; PvA 212.

Dhātuka (adj.) (only -°) having the nature, by nature, affected with, -like (cp. °dhamma B 2^a); often simply = first part of cpd. (cp. E. friend-like = friendly = friend) J I.438 (kiliṭṭha° miserable), II.31 (sama°), 63 (badhira° deaf), 102 (paṇḍuroga° having jaundice), 114 (dhuttika°); IV.137 (vāmanaka° deformed), 391 (muddhā°); V.197 (āvāta°); DhA I.89 (anattamana°).

Dhātura (adj. -°) [= *dhātuya] in cha° consisting of six elements (purisa) M III.239 (where āpodhātu omitted by mistake). See dhātu 2 c.

Dhāna (adj.-n.) [Sk. dhāna, to dadhāti; cp. dhātu] (adj.) holding, containing (-°) M I.11 (ahi kaṇṭaka°; cp. ādhāna & kaṇṭaka). — (n.) nt. a receptacle Dh 58 (sankāra° dust-heap = ṭhāna DhA I.445). f. dhānī a seat (= ṭhāna), in rāja° "the king's seat," a royal town. Often in comb with gāma & nigama (see gāma 3 a): Vin III.89; J VI.397; Pv II.13^{18}

Dhāniya (adj.) [Sk. dhānya, cp. dhañña^2] wealthy, rich, abundant in (-°) J III.367 (pahūtadhana°; v. l. BB °dhāritaŋ); (nt.) riches, wealth J V.99, 100.

Dhāra (adj.) (-°) [Sk. dhāra to dhāreti; cp. dhara] bearing, holding, having D I.74 (udaka-rahado sītavāri°); M I.281 (ubhato°) Sn 336 (ukkā°); It 101 (antimadeha°), 108 (ukkā°). See also dhārin.

Dhāraka (adj.-n.) 1. bearing, one who holds or possesses DhA III.93 (sampattiŋ). — 2. one who knows or remembers A II.97 (°jātika); IV.296 sq., 328 (id.).

Dhāraṇa (nt.) [cp. Sk. dhāraṇa, to dhāreti] 1. wearing, in mālā° (etc.) D I.5 = A II.210 = Pug 58; KhA 37; cīvara° A II.104 = Pug 45. — 2. maintaining, sustaining, keeping up Miln 320 (āyu° bhojanā). — 3. bearing in mind, remembrance Vin IV.305; M II.175 (dhamma°).

Dhāraṇaka [der. fr. dhāraṇa] 1. a debtor (see dhāreti 4) J II.203; IV.45. — 2. a mnemonician Miln 79.

Dhāraṇatā (f.) 1. wearing, being dressed with (= dhāraṇa 1) Miln 257. — 2. mindfulness (= dhāraṇa 3) Nd^2 628 = Dhs 14.

Dhāraṇā (f.) [to dhāraṇa] 1. memory Miln 79. — 2. the earth ("the upholder," cp. dharaṇī) J VI.180.

Dhārā^1 (f.) [Sk. dhārā, from dhāvati 1] torrent, stream, flow, shower D I.74 (sammā° an even or seasonable shower; DA I.218 = vuṭṭhi); II.15 (udakassa, streams); J I.31; Ps I.125 (udaka°); Pv II.9^{70} (sammā°); VvA 4 (hingulika°); PvA 139; DhA IV.15 (assu°); Sdhp 595 (vassa°).

Dhārā^2 (f.) [Sk. dhārā, from dhāvati 2.] the edge of a weapon J I.455; VI.449; DhA 317; DA I.37. — (adj.) (-°) having a (sharp) edge J I.414 (khura°) Miln 105 (sukhuma°); ekato°-ubhato° single- & double-edged J I.73 (asi); IV.12 (sattha).

Dhārin (adj. -°) [Sk. dhārin, see dhāreti & cp. °dhara, °dhāra] holding, wearing, keeping; often in phrase antimadeha° "wearing the last body" (of an Arahant) S I.14; Sn 471; It 32, 40. — J I.47 (virūpa-vesa°); Dāvs V.15. — f. °inī Pv I.10^8 (kāsikuttama°).

Dhāretar [n. ag. to dhāreti 3] one who causes others to remember, an instructor, teacher (cp. dhāraṇaka) A IV.196 (sotā sāvetā uggahetā dh.).

Dhāreti [Caus. of dharati, q. v. for etym.] to hold, viz. 1. to carry, bear, wear, possess; to put on, to bring, give D I.166 ≈ (chavadussāni etc.); Vin I.16 = D I.110 ≈ (telapajjotaŋ); D II.19 (chattaŋ to hold a sunshade over a person); PvA 47 (id.); dehaŋ dh. to "wear," i. e. to have a body It 50, 53 (antimaŋ d.); J IV.3 (padumaŋ); VI.136; Pv I.3^1 (vaṇṇaŋ dh. = vahasi PvA 14); tassa kahāpaṇaŋ daṇḍaŋ dh. "to inflict a fine of a k. on him" Miln 171. — 2. to hold back, restrain Vin IV.261 (kathaŋ dhāretha how do you suppress or conceal pregnancy?); Dh 222 (kodhaŋ). — 3. to bear in mind, know by heart, understand: dhammaŋ to know the Dhamma A III.176; tipiṭakaŋ buddhavacanaŋ to know the 3 Piṭakas Miln 18. — D II.2; Pug 41 (suṇāti, bhaṇati, dh. = remember). Cp. upadhāreti. — With double acc.: to receive as, to take = believe, to take for, consider as, call: upāsakaŋ maŋ dhāretu Bhagavā "call me your disciple" Vin I.16 & passim; atthajālan ti pi naŋ dhārehi (call it . . .) D I.46; yathā pañhaŋ Bhagavā vyākaroti tathā naŋ dhāreyyāsi (believe it) D I.222; yathā no (atthaŋ) Gotamo vyākarissati tathā naŋ dhāressāma D I.236; evaŋ maŋ dhārehi adhimutta-cittaŋ (consider as) Sn 1149 (= upalakkhehi Nd[2] 323). — 4. to admit, allow, allow for, take up, support (a cause); to give, to owe D I.125 (may allow), 126; A II.69 (na kassa kiñci dh. pays no tribute); Miln 47 (atthaŋ).

Dhāreyya (nt.) [orig. grd. of dhāreti] the ceremony of being carried away, i. e. the marriage ceremony, marriage (cp. dhareyya under dharati) Th 2, 472 (text has vāreyya, but ThA, 285 explains dhāreyya = vivāha).

Dhāva [Sk. dhāva] running, racing M I.446.

Dhāvati [Sk. dhāvati & dhāvate: 1. to flow, run etc.; cp. Gr. θέω (both meanings); Ags. déaw = E. dew; Ohg. tou = Ger. tau; cp. also dhārā & dhunāti. — 2. to clean (by running water) etc. — P. dhovati, q. v.] 1. to run, run away, run quickly Sn 939 (cp. Nd[1] 419); Dh 344; J I.308; VI.332; Nd[1] 405 = Nd[2] 304[III, C]; Pv IV.16[1] = palāyati PvA 284[1]; DhA I.389 (opp. gacchati); PvA 4; Sdhp 378. — 2. to clean etc.: see dhovati; cp. dhavala & dhārā[2].

Dhāvana (nt.) [Sk. dhāvana] running, galloping J II.431; Miln 351.

Dhāvin: see pa°.

Dhi[1] & **Dhī** (indecl.) [Sk. dhik] an excl[n] of reproach & disgust: fie! shame! woe! (with acc. or gen.) S V.217 (read dhī taŋ for dhitaŋ); Dh 389 (dhī = garahāmi DhA IV.148); J I.507; DhA I.179 (haŋ dhī), 216 (v. l. BB but text has haŋdi). An inorganic r replaces the sandhi-cons. in dhī-r-atthu jīvitaŋ Sn 440; cp. Th 1.1150; dhi-r-atthu jātiyā J I.59.

Dhi[2] (f.) [Sk. dhīḥ to didheti, cp. Av. dī to see, Goth. (ülu-) deisei cunning. See also dhīra] wisdom, only in Com. expl. of paññā: "dhi vuccati paññā" (exegesis of dhīra) at Nd[1] 44 = J II.140 = III.38.

Dhikkita (adj.) [Sk. dhikkṛta, of dhi[1] + kata] reproached, reviled; used also medially: blaming, censuring, condemning J I.155 (= garahitā Com.); also in Com. expl. of dhīra (= dhikkita-pāpa detesting evil) at Nd[1] 44 = J II.140 = III.38 (cp. dhi[2]).

Dhiti (f.) [Sk. dhṛti to **dhṛ**, see dharati] energy, courage, steadfastness, firm character, resolution. S I.122, 215 = Sn 188 (cp. SnA 237); J I.266, 280; III.239; VI.373; Vbh 211; Dhs 13 (+ thāma), 22, 289, 571; Miln 23, 329; Sdhp 574. Equivalent to "wisdom" (cp. juti & jutimant & Sk. dhīti) in expl. of dhīra as "dhitisampanna" Nd[1] 44≈(see dhi[2]); PvA 131.

Dhitimant (adj.) [Sk. dhṛtimant; cp. also dhīmant] courageous, firm, resolute A I.25; Sn 462, 542; Th 1,6; J II.140; VI.286 (wise, cp. dhiti).

Dhītar and **Dhītā** (f.) [Sk. dhitā, orig. pp. of dhayati to suck (cp. Lat. filia): see dhāta & dhātī, influenced in inflection by Sk. duhitṛ, although etymologically different] daughter Th 2, 336 (in faith); J I.152, 253; VI.366; Pv I.11[5]; DhA III.171, 176; PvA 16, 21, 61, 105. deva° a female deva (see deva) VvA 137 etc.; nattu° a granddaughter PvA 17; mātula° a niece PvA 55; rāja° a princess J I.207; PvA 74. In comp[n] dhītu°.

-**kkama** one who is desirous of a daughter J VI.307 (= dhītu atthāya vicarati Com.; v. l. dhītu-kāma); -**dhītā** granddaughter PvA 16.

Dhītalikā (f.) [Demin. of dhītā; cp. dhītikā & potthalikā] a doll Vin III.36, 126 (dāru°); DhsA 321; PvA 16.

Dhītikā (f.) [cp. dhītalikā] a doll Th 2, 374 (= dhītalikā ThA 252).

Dhīna see adhīna.

Dhīyati [Sk. dhīyate, Pass. to dahati[1]] to be contained ThA 13 (so read for dhiyati); PvA 71.

Dhīra (adj.) [combining in meaning 1. Sk. dhīra "firm" fr. dhārayati (see dharati & dhiti); 2. Vedic. dhīra "wise" fr. didheti (see dhi[2]). The fluctuation of connotation is also seen in the expl[s] of Com[y] which always give the foll. three conventional etymologies, viz. dhikkitapāpa, dhiti-sampanna, dhiyā (= paññāya) samannāgata Nd[1] 44≈(see dhi[2])] constant, firm, self-relying, of character; wise, possessing the knowledge of the Dhamma, often paṇḍita & Ep. of an Arahant D II.128; S I.24 (lokapariyāyaŋ aññāya nibbutā dh.), 122, 221; Sn 45, 235 (nibbanti dhīrā), 913 (vippamutto diṭṭhigatehi dh.), 1052; It 68 (°upasevanā, opp. bāla), 122 (dh. sabbaganthapamocano); Dh 23, 28, 177 (opp. bāla); Th 1, 4; 2, 7 (dhammā = tejussadehi ariyamaggadhammehi ThA 13); J III.396; V.116; Pv II.1[6]; II.9[45]; Nd[1] 44, 55, 482; Nd[2] 324 (= jutimant); Miln 342; KhA 104, 224, 230; DhA III.189 (= paṇḍita).

Dhuta (& **Dhūta**) [cp. Sk. dhuta & dhūta, pp. of dhunāti] 1. shaken, moved Dāvs V.49 (vāta°). — 2. lit. "shaken off," but always expl[d] in the commentaries as "one who shakes off" either evil dispositions (kilese), or obstacles to spiritual progress (vāra, nīvaraṇa). The word is rare. In one constantly repeated passage (Vin I.45 = 300 = II.2 = III.21 = IV.213) it is an adj. opposed to kosajja lazy, remiss; and means either scrupulous or punctilious. At D I.5 it is used of a pain. At Sn 385 we are told of a **dhutadhamma**, meaning a scrupulous way of life, first for a bhikkhu, then for a layman. This poem omits all higher doctrine and confines itself to scrupulousness as regards minor, elementary matters. Cp. Vism 61 for a def[n] of dhuta.

-**anga** a set of practices leading to the state of or appropriate to a dhuta, that is to a scrupulous person. First occurs in a title suffixed to a passage in the Parivāra deprecating such practices. The passage occurs twice (Vin V.131, 193), but the title, probably later than the text, is added only to the 2nd of the two. The passage gives a list of 13 such practices, each of them an ascetic practice not enjoined in the Vinaya. The 13 are also discussed at Vism 59 sq. The Milinda devotes a whole book (chap. VI.) to the glorification of these 13 dhutangas, but there is no evidence that they were ever widely adopted. Some are deprecated at M I.282, & examples of one or other of them are given at Vin III.15; Bu 1.59; J III.342; IV.8; Miln 133, 348, 351; Vism 59 (°kathā), 65 (°cora), 72 (id.), 80 (def[n]); SnA 494; DhA I.68; II.32 (dhūtanga); IV.30. Nd[1] 188 says that 8 of them are desirable. -**dhara** mindful of punctiliousness Miln 342 (āraññaka dh. jhāyin). -**vata** the vow to perform the dhutangas DhA VI.165. -**vāda** one who inculcates punctiliousness S II.156; A I.23; Miln 380; Vism 80; ThA 69; DhA II.30. -**vādin** = °vāda J I.130.

Dhutatta (nt.) [Sk. *dhūtatvaŋ] the state of being punctilious Vin I.305 (of going naked).

Dhutta [Sk. dhūrta, from dhūrvati & dhvarati to injure, deceive, cp. Lat. fraus; Idg. ***dhreu**, an enlarged form of which is ***dreugh** in Sk. druhyati, drugdha. Ohg. triogan, troum etc.: see duhana] of abandoned life, wild, fast, cunning, crafty, fraudulent; wicked, bad. (m.) a rogue, cheat, evil-minded person, scoundrel, rascal. There are three sorts of a wild life, viz. **akkha**° in gambling, itthi° with women, **surā**° in drink (Sn 106;

J IV.255). — Vin 277 (robber, bighwayman); A III.38 (a°); IV.288 (itthi°); J I.49 (surā°), 290, 291; II.416; III.287; IV.223, 494 (surā°); ThA 250 (itthi°), 260 (°purisa), 266 (°kilesa); PvA 3, 5 (itthi°, surā°), 151. — f. dhutti (dhuttī) J II.114 (°brāhmaṇī).

Dhuttaka = dhutta S I.131; Th 2, 366 (=itthi-dhutta ThA 250); DhA III.207; Dpvs IX.19. — f. dhuttikā always in combⁿ w. chinnikā (meretrix, q. v.) Vin III.128; J II.114; Miln 122.

Dhunana (nt.) [Sk. dhūnana] shaking, in °ka (adj.) consisting in shaking off, doing away with, giving up (kilesa°) SnA 373.

Dhunāti [Sk. dhunoti (dhūnoti), dhunāti & dhuvati, Caus. dhūnayati. Idg. *dhū to be in turbulent motion; cp. Gr. θύω, θύνω (to be impetuous), θύελλα (storm), θύμος "thyme"; Lat. fūmus (smoke = fume), suffio; Lith. duja (dust); Goth. dauns (smoke & smell); Ohg. toum. Connected also w. dhāvate; see further dhūpa, dhūma, dhūsara, dhona & a secondary root Idg. *dheues in dhaṃsati] to shake, toss; to shake off, remove, destroy S I.156 (maccuno senaŋ); Th I, 256 = Miln 245; dhunāti pāpake dhamme dumapattaŋ va māluto Th I.2; J I.11 (v. 48); III.44 (hatthe dhuniŋsu, wrung their hands); Vv 64⁹ (=VvA 278 misprint dhumanti); aor. adhosi [=Sk. adhauṣīt] Sn 787 (micchādiṭṭhiŋ = pajahi SnA 523). pp. dhuta & dhūta (q. v.). Cp. nis°, o°.

Dhuma in °kaṭacchuka = druma° having a wooden spoon (see duma), cp. Mar. dhumārā ? (Ed. in note) DhA II.59. [Doubtful reading.]

Dhura (m. & nt.) [Sk. dhur f. & dhura m.] 1. a yoke, a pole, the shaft of a carriage J I.192 (purima-sakaṭa°), 196; Cp. II.8, 4. — 2. (fig.) a burden, load, charge, office, responsibility Sn 256 (vahanto porisaŋ dh °ŋ "carrying a human yoke" = purisânucchavikā bhārā SnA 299), 694 (asama° one who has to bear a heavy burden = asamaviriya SnA 489); DhA II.97 (sama°); dve dhurāni two burdens (viz. gantha° & vipassanā, study & contemplation) DhA I.7; IV.37; asamadhura J I.193; VI.330. *Three* dhurā are enumᵈ at J IV.242 as saddhā°, sīla°, and paññā°. — Sdhp 355 (saddhā°), 392 (+ viriya), 413 (paññā°) dh °ŋ nikkhipati to take off the yoke, to put down a burden, to give up a charge or renounce a responsibility (see °nikkhepa): nikkhitta-dhura A I.71; II.148; III.65, 108, 179 sq.; a° S V.197, 225; Nd² 131; SnA 236 (=dhuravant). — 3. the fore-part of anything, head, top, front; fig. chief, leader, leading part. nāvāya dh. the forecastle of a ship J III.127 = IV.142; dh-vāta head wind J I.100; ekaŋ dh °ŋ nīharati to set aside a foremost part DA I.135. — 4. the far end, either as top or beginning J III.216 (yāva dh-sopānā); IV.265 (dh-sopānaŋ katvā making the staircase end); V.458 (magga-dhure ṭhatvā standing on the far end or other side of the road, i. e. opposite; gloss BB maggantare); VvA 44 (dh-gehassa dvāre at the door of the top house of the village, i. e. the first or last house).

-gāma a neighbouring village (lit. the first v. that one meets) J I.8, 237; IV.243; DhA III.414; -dhorayha a yoked ox S I.173 = Sn 79 (viriyam me dh-dh °ŋ); SnA 150. -nikkhepa the putting down of the yoke, the giving up of one's office J III 243; Vism 413. -bhatta a meal where a monk is invited as leader of other monks who likewise take part in it J I.449. v. l. (for dhuva°); III.97 (v. l. dhuva°); Vism 66. -yotta yoke-tie, i. e. the tie fastening the yoke to the neck of the ox J I.192; VI.253; -vahana bearing a burden (cp. dhorayha) DhA III.472; -vihāra a neighbouring monastery (cp. °gāma) J I.23; IV.243; DhA I.126 (Np.); III.224 (id.); -sampaggāha "a solid grip of the burden" (Mrs. Rh.D.) Dhs 13, 22 etc. (opp. nikkhepa); -ssaha enduring one's yoke Th I, 659. Cp. dhuratā.

Dhuratā (f.) [abstr. fr. dhura] in cpd. anikkhitta-dh. "a state of unflinching endurance" Nd² 394, 405 = Dhs 13 etc. = Vbh 350, 370 (+ dhura-sampaggāha); opp. nikkhitta-dh. weakness of character, lack of endurance (=pamāda) ibid.

Dhuravant (adj.) [cp. Sk. dhuradhara] one who has or bears his yoke, patient, enduring S I.214 = Sn 187 (: cetasika-viriya-vasena anikkhittadhura SnA 236).

Dhuva (adj.) [Sk. dhruva, cp. Lith. drúta firm; Goth. triggws = Ohg. triuwi (Ger. treue, trost); Ags. tréowe = E. true, of Idg. *dheru, enlarged form of *dher, see dharati] stable, constant, permanent; fixed, regular, certain, sure D I.18; S I.142; IV.370; A II.33; J I.19; V.121 (°sassataŋ maraṇaŋ); III.325; Bu II.8; Miln 114 (na tā nadiyo dh-salilā), 334 (°phala); Vism 77; DA I.112 (maraṇaŋ apassanto dh.), 150 (=thāvara); DhA III.170 (adhuvaŋ jīvitaŋ dhuvaŋ maraṇaŋ); ThA 241; Sdhp 331. — *nt.* permanence, stability M I.326; Dh 147. Also Ep. of Nibbāna (see °gāmin). — nt as adv. dhuvaŋ continuously, constantly, always J II.24 = Miln 172; PvA 207; certainly J I.18, V.103. — adhuva (adhuva) changing, unstable, impermanent D I.19 (anicca a. appāyuka); M I.326; S IV.302; J I.393; III.19 (ad-dhuva-sīla); VvA 77.

-gāmin leading to permanence, i. e. Nibbāna S IV.370 (magga); -colā (f.) constantly dressed, of a woman Vin III.129; -ṭṭhāniya lasting (of shoes) Vin I.190; -dhamma one who has reached a stable condition DhA III.289; -paññatta (a) permanently appointed (seat) Vin IV.274; -bhatta a constant supply of food Vin I.25, 243; II.15 (°ika); J I.449 (where the v. l. dhura° seems to be preferable instead of dhuva°, see dhurabhatta); cp. niccabhatta; -yāgu constant (distribution of) rice-gruel Vin I.292 sq.; -lohitā (f.) a woman whose blood is stagnant Vin III.129; -ssava always discharging, constantly flowing J I.6, V.35.

Dhūta & **Dhūtanga** see dhuta.

Dhūpa [Sk. dhūpa of Idg. *dhūp, enlarged fr. *dhū in dhunāti (q. v.)] incense J I.51, 64, 290 (gandha°, dvandva, cpd.); III.144; VI.42; PvA 141 (gandhapuppha°). dh°ŋ dadāti to incense (a room) J I.399. Sometimes misspelt dhūma, e. g. VvA 173 (gandhapuppha°).

Dhūpana (nt.) [Sk. dhūpana] incensing, fumigation; perfume, incense, spice J III.144; IV.236; Pv III.5³ (sāsapa°).

Dhūpāyati & **Dhūpayati** [Sk. dhūpayati; caus. fr. dhūpa] to fumigate, make fragrant, perfume Vin I.180; S I.40 (dhūpāyita) = Th I, 448; A II.214 sq.; J I.73; Miln 333 (sīlagandhena lokaŋ dh.); DhA I.370 (aor. dhūpāyi); III.38 (ppr. dhūpayamāna). — pp. dhūpita.

Dhūpita [pp. of dhūpāyati] fumigated, flavoured Vv 43⁶ (tela° flavoured with oil). Cp. pa°.

Dhūma [Vedic dhūma = Lat. fumus; Gr. θυμός (mood, mind), θυμιάω (fumigate); Ohg. toum etc. Idg. *dhu, cp. Gr. θύω (burn incense), θύος (incense). See also dhunāti] smoke, fumes Vin I.204 (aroma of drugs); M I.220 (dh °ŋ kattā); A V.352 (id.); A II.53; IV.72 sq.; V.347 sq.; J III.401, 422 (tumhākaŋ dh-kāle at the time when you will end in smoke, i. e. at your cremation); DhA I.370 (eka° one mass of smoke); VvA 173 (for dhūpa, in gandhapuppha°); PvA 230 (micchā-vitakka° in expl. of vidhūma).

-andha blind with smoke J I.216; -kālika (cp. above dh.-kāle) lasting till a person's cremation Vin II.172, 288; -ketu fire (lit. whose sign is smoke) J IV.26; V.63; -jāla a mass of smoke J V.497; -netta a smoke-tube, i. e. a surgical instrument for sniffing up the smoke of medical drugs Vin I.204; II.120; J IV.363; ThA 14; -sikhā fire (Ep. of Agni; lit. smoke-crested) Vv 35² (sikha) = VvA 161; Vism 416; also as sikhin J VI.206.

Dhūmāyati & **Dhūmayati** [Sk. dhūmayati, Denom. fr. dhūma] to smoke, to smoulder, choke; to be obscured, to cloud over M I.142 (v. l. dhūpāyati); Pv I.6[4] (pariḍayhati+dh. hadayaŋ); DhA I.425 (akkhīni me dh.= I see almost nothing). pp. dhūmāyita.

Dhūmāyanā (f.) smoking, smouldering M I.143; Nett 24 (as v. l. to dhūpāyanā).

Dhūmāyitatta (nt.) [abstr. to dhūmāyati] becoming like smoke, clouding over, obscuration S III.124 (+timirāyitattaŋ).

Dhūsara (adj.) [Sk. dhūsara, Ags. dust=E. dust & dusk, Ger. dust; see dhvaŋsati & dhunoti & cp. Walde, *Lat. Wtb.* under furo] dust-coloured VvA 335.

Dhenu (f.) [Sk. dhenu, to dhayati to give suck, ese dhāti & dhītar] a milch cow, a female animal in general J I.152 (miga° hind); Vv 80[6]; DhA I.170; 396; PvA 112. In simile at Vism 313.

Dhenupa [dhenu+pa from pibati] a suckling calf M I.79; Sn 26.

Dheyya (-°) [Sk. dheya, orig. grd. of **dhā**, see dahati[1]] 1. in the realm of, under the sway or power of: anañña° J IV.110; kamma° A IV.285; maccu° (q. v.) S I.22; Sn 358, 1104; Th 2, 10 (=maccu ettha dhīyati ThA 13); māra° A IV.228. — 2. putting on, assigning, in nāma° Dhs 1307.

Dhota [Sk. dhauta, pp. of dhavati[2], see dhovati] washed, bleached, clean J I.62 (°sankha a bleached shell); II.275; PvA 73 (°vattha), 116 (°hattha with clean hands), 274 (id.); Vism 224 (id.).

Dhona (adj.-n.) [either=dhota, Sk. dhauta, see dhovati or=dhuta, see dhuta & dhunana. Quite a diff. suggestion as regards etym. is given by Kern, *Toev.* 117, who considers it as a possible der° fr. (a)dho, after analogy of poṇa. Very doubtful] 1. purified M I.386; Sn 351, 786, 813, 834 (=dhutakilesa SnA 542); J III.160 (°sākha=patthaṭasākha Com.; v. l. BB vena°); Nd[1] 77=176 (: dhonā vuccati paññā etc., dhuta & dhota used indiscriminately in exegesis following). — 2. (pl.) the four requisites of a bhikkhu DhA III.344 (: dhonā vuccati cattāro paccayā, in Com. on atidhonacārin Dh 240; gloss K dhovanā, cp. Morris, *J.P.T.S.* 1887, 100).

Dhopati [a variant of dhovati, taken as Caus. formation] to wash, cleanse D I.93 (dhopetha, imper.; v. l. B. dhovatha), 124 (dhopeyya; v. l. B. dhoveyya).

Dhopana (nt.) [a variant of dhovana, q. v.] 1. ceremonial washing of the bones of the dead D I.18; **aṭṭhi-dhovana** Bdhgh at DA I.84; A V.216 (see Commentary at 364). — 2. Surgical washing of a wound J II.117. — 3. In vaŋsa-dhopana, apparently a feat by acrobats J IV.390. It is possible that the passage at D I.18 really belongs here. See the note at *Dial.* I.9.

Dhorayha [for *dhor-vayha=Sk. *dhaurvahya, abstr. fr. dhurvaha; may also directly correspond to the latter] "carrying a yoke," a beast of burden S I.28; D III.113 (purisa°); A I.162.

-vata (nt.) the practice of carrying a burden, the state of a beast of burden, drudgery S I.28; **-sīla** accustomed to the yoke, enduring; patient Dh 208 (=dhuravahana-sīlatāya dh. DhA III.272); **-sīlin**= °sīla J II.97 (=dhura-vahanaka-ācārena sampanna Com.).

Dhoreyya (-°) [Sk. dhaureya, der. fr. dhura] "to be yoked," accustomed to the yoke, carrying a burden, in kamma° Miln 288.

Dhova (adj.-n.) [Sk. dhāva, see dhovati] washing, cleansing Bu II.15.

Dhovati [Sk. dhāvati, see dhāvati] to rinse, wash, cleanse, purify Vin II.208, 210, 214; Sn p. 104 (bhājanāni); J I.8; V.297. — **dhovi** J VI.366; DhA III.207. ger. **dhovitvā** J I.266; IV.2; VvA 33 (pattaŋ), 77 (id.); PvA 75, 144. inf. **dhovituŋ** Vin II.120; IV.261. pp. **dhota** (q. v.) & **dhovita** J I.266. — See also **dhopati** (*dhopeti).

Dhovana (nt.) [Sk. dhāvana; see also dhopana] washing Vin IV.262; S IV.316 (bhaṇḍa°); A I.132, 161, 277; It 111 (pādānaŋ); J II.129; VI.365 (hattha°); Miln 11; Vism 343; PvA 241 (hattha-pāda°); DhA II.19 (pāda°); fig. (ariyaŋ) A V.216.

N.

Na[1] [Sk. na (in cana) & nā (in nānā, vi-nā) Idg. pron. base *no, cp. Gr νή, ναί; Lat. nē, nae surely, also encl. in ego-ne & in question utrumne, nam; fuller form *eno, as in Sk. anā (adv.) anena, anayā (instr. pron. 3rd); Gr. ἔνη "that day"; Lat. enim] expletive-emphatic particle, often used in comparative-indefinite sense: just so, like this, as if, as (see cana & canaŋ) J v.339 (Com. cttha na-kāro upamāne). Also as naŋ (cp. cana> canaŋ) Vin II.81, 186 (kathaŋ naŋ=kathaŋ nu); J II.416; v.302; vi.213 (Com. p. 216: ettha eko na-karo pucchanattho hoti); Th 1, 1204; Miln 177. Perhaps at Sn 148 (kattha-ci naŋ, v. l. BB na; but Com. KhA 247= etaŋ). To this na belongs na[3]; see also nu & nanu.

Na[2] [Ved. na=Idg. *nĕ; Lat. ne in n' unquam etc., Goth. ni; Sk. na ca=Lat. neque=Goth. nih. Also Sk. nā= Idg. *nē, cp. Lat. Goth. nē] negative & adversative particle "not" (Nd[2] 326: paṭikkhepa; KhA 170: paṭisedhe) 1. often apostr. n': n' atthi, n' etaŋ etc.; or contracted: nāhaŋ, nāpi etc., or with euphonic consonant y: nayidaŋ (It 29, J iv.3), nayidha (It 36, 37), nayimaŋ (It 15) etc. As double negation implying emphatic affirmation: na kiñci na all, everything J 1.295. — 2. In disjunctive clauses: na . . . na neither—nor, so—or not so. In question: karoti na karoti ("or not") J II.133. Cp. mā in same use. — Often with added pi (api) in second part: na-nāpi neither—nor ("not—but also not") S II.65; M 1.246; Pv 1.11[9]. — 3. In syntactic context mostly emphasized by var. negative & adversative particles, viz. nāpi (see under 2); n' eva indeed not, not for all that J III.55; or not KhA 219; n' eva-na neither—nor D 1.33, 35; M 1.486; A v.193; J 1.207, 279; Vin II.185; DhA 1.328; II.65; DA 1.186, 188; n' eva-na pana id. D 1.24; na kho not indeed J II.134; na ca but not (=this rather than that) J 1.153; na tāva=na kho Vv 37[13]; na nu (in quest.= nonne) is it not? PvA 74, 136; na no surely not Sn 224; na hi [cp. Gr. οὐχί not at all; ναίχι certainly] certainly not Dh 5, 184; Sn 666; Kh vii.6; na hi jātu id. Sn 152. — See also nu, nū, no. — 4. na is also used in the function of the negative prefix a- (an-) in cases where the word-negation was isolated out of a sentence negation or where a negated verb was substantified, e. g. (a) nacira (=acira) short, napparūpa abundant, napuŋsaka neuter, neka (=aneka) several; (b) natthi, natthika etc. (q. v.).

Na[3] [identical with na[1]] base of demonstr. pron. 3rd pers. (=ta°), only in foll. cases: acc. sg. naŋ (mostly enclit.), fuller form enaŋ him, her, that one etc. Sn 139, 201, 385, 418, 980, 1076; It 32; Dh 42, 230; J 1.152, 172, 222; III.281; KhA 220; DhA 1.181; III.173; PvA 3, 68, 73. — nom. acc. pl. ne them It 110 (v. l. te); Sn 223 (=te manusse KhA 169); J II.417; III.204; v.458; DhA 1.8, 13, 61, 101, 390; VvA 299. — gen. dat. pl. nesaŋ D 1.175, 191; It 63; J 1.153; DhA iv.41; VvA 37, 136; PvA 54, 201, 207. See also ena; cp. nava[2].

Nakula [Ved. nakula, cp. nakra crocodile] a mungoose, Viverra Ichneumon A v.289 sq.; J II.53; vi.538; Miln 118, 394.

Nakkhatta (nt.) [Ved. nakṣatra collect. formation from naktiḥ & naktā=Gr. νύξ, Lat. nox, Goth. nahts, E. night=the nightly sky, the heavenly bodies of the night, as opposed to the Sun: ādicco tapataŋ mukhaŋ Vin 1.246] the stars or constellations, a conjunction of the moon with diff. constellations, a lunar mansion or the constellations of the lunar zodiac, figuring also as Names of months & determinant factors of horoscopic and other astrological observation; further a celebration of the beginning of a new month, hence any kind of festival or festivity. — The recognised number of such lunar mansions is 27, the names of which as given in Sk. sources are the same in Pāli, with the exception of 2 variations (Assayuja for Aśvinī, Satabhisaja for Śatatāraka). Enum[d] at Abhp. 58-60 as follows: Assayuja [Sk. Aśvinī] Bharaṇī, Kattikā, Rohiṇī, Magasiraŋ [Sk. Mṛgaśīrṣa], Addā [Sk. Ārdrā], Punabbasu, Phussa [Sk. Puṣya], Asilesā, Maghā, Pubba-phaggunī [Sk. Pūrva-phalgunī] Uttara°, Hattha, Cittā [Sk. Chaitra], Sāti [Svātī], Visākhā, Anurādhā, Jeṭṭhā, Mūlaŋ, Pubb-āsāḷha [°āṣāḍha], Uttar°, Savaṇa, Dhaniṭṭhā, Satabhisaja [Śatatāraka], Pubba-bhaddapadā, Uttara°, Revatī. — It is to be pointed out that the Niddesa speaks of 28 N. instead of 27 (Nd[1] 382: aṭṭhavīsati nakkhattāni), a discrepancy which may be accounted by the fact that one N. (the Orion) bore 2 names, viz. Mṛgaśīrṣa & Agrahayanī (see Plunkett, *Ancient Calendars* etc. p. 227 sq.). — Some of these Ns. are more familiar & important than others, & are mentioned more frequently, e. g. Āsāḷha (Āsāḷhi°) J 1.50 & Uttarāsāḷha J 1.63, 82; Kattikā & Rohiṇī SnA 456. — nakkhattaŋ ādisati to augur from the stars, to set the horoscope Nd[1] 382; oloketi to read the stars, to scan the constellations J 1.108, 253; ghoseti to proclaim (shout out) the new month (cp. Lat. calandae fr. cālāre to call out, scil. mensem), and thereby announce the festivity to be celebrated J 1.250; n. ghuṭṭhaŋ J 1.50, 433; saŋghuṭṭhaŋ PvA 73; ghositaŋ VvA 31; kīḷati to celebrate a (nakkhatta-) festival J 1.50, 250; VvA 63; DhA 1.393 (cp. °kīḷā below). n. ositaŋ the festival at an end J 1.433. — nakkhatta (sg.) a constellation Sn 927; collect. the stars Vv 81[1] (cando n-parivārito). nakkhattāni (pl.) the stars: nakkhattānaŋ mukhaŋ chando (the moon is the most prominent of the lights of night) Th II.143; Vin 1.246=Sn 569 (but cp. expl. at SnA 456: candayogavasena "ajja kattikā, ajja Rohiṇī" ti paññāṇato ālokakāraṇato sommabhāvato ca nakkhattānaŋ mukhaŋ cando ti vutto); D 1.10 (nakkhattānaŋ pathagamanaŋ & uppatha-gamanaŋ a right or wrong course, i. e. a straight ascension or deviation of the stars or planets); II.259; III.85, 90; A iv.86; Th 2, 143 (nakkhattāni namassantā bālā).

-kīḷana=kīḷā DhA III.461; -kīḷā the celebration of a festival, making merry, taking a holiday J 1.50; ThA 137; VvA 109; -ggāha the seizure of a star (by a demon: see gāha), the disappearance of a planet (transit?) D 1.10 (expl. at DA 1.95 as nakkhattasa angārakādi-gahasamāyoga); -patha "the course of the stars," i. e. the nocturnal sky Dh 208; -pada a constellation Vin II.217; -pāṭhaka an astrologer, soothsayer, augur Nd[1] 382; -pīḷana the failing or obscuration of a star (as a sign of death in horoscopy) DhA 1.166; — mālā a garland of stars VvA 167; -yoga a conjunction of the planets, a constellation in its meaning for the horoscope J 1.82

253; DhA I.174 (+ tithi-karaṇa); °ŋ oloketi to set the horoscope DhA I.166, °ŋ uggaṇhāti id. Pv III.5^4. -rājā the king of the nakkhattas (i. e. the moon) J III.348.

Nakha [Ved. nakha, cp. Sk. anghri foot; Gr. ὄνυξ (claw, nail), Lat. unguis = Oir. inga; Ohg. nagal = E. nail] a nail of finger or toe, a claw Vin II.133; Sn 610 (na angulihi nakhehi vā); J v.489 (pañcanakhā sattā five-nailed or -toed beings); Kh II. = Miln 26, cp. taca (pañcatacakaŋ); KhA 43; VvA 7 (dasa-nakhasamodhāna putting the 10 fingers together); PvA 152, 192; Sdhp 104.

Nakhaka (adj.) belonging to, consisting of or resembling a claw, in hatthi° like elephants' claws, Ep. of a castle (pāsāda) Vin II.169 (Bdhgh on p. 323: hatthikumbhe patiṭṭhitaŋ, evaŋ evaŋkatassa kir' etaŋ nāmaŋ) (?).

Nakhin (adj.) having nails J VI.290 (tamba° with copper-coloured nails).

Naga [Sk. naga tree & mountain, referred by Fausböll & Uhlenbeck to na + gacchati, i. e. immovable (= sthāvara), more probably however with Lidén (see Walde under nāvis) to Ohg. nahho, Ags. naca "boat = tree"; semantically mountain = trees, i. e. forest] mountain S I.195 = Nd^2 136^A (nagassa passe āsīna, of the Buddha); Sn 180 (= devapabbata royal mountain SnA 216; or should it mean "forest"?); Th I, 41 (°vivara), 525; Pv II.9^{61} (°muddhani on top of the Mount, i. e. Mt. Sineru PvA 138; the Buddha was thought to reside there); Miln 327 (id.); Vv 16^6 (°antare in between the (5) mountains, see VvA 82).

Nagara (nt.) [Ved. nagara, Non-aryan? Connection with agāra is very problematic] a stronghold, citadel, fortress; a (fortified) town, city. As seat of the government & as important centre of trade contrasted with gāma & nigama (village & market-place or township) Vin III.47 (°bandhana), 184; cp. gāma 3 b. deva° deva-city J I. 3, 168, 202; DhA I.280 etc.; cp. yakkha° J II.127. — Vin I.277, 342, 344; II.155, 184; D II.7; S II.105 sq.; IV.194 (kāyassa adhivacanaŋ); V.160; A I.168, 178; IV.106 sq. (paccantima); V.194 (id.) Dh 150 (aṭṭhīnaŋ); Sn 414, 1013 (Bhoga°); J I.3, 50 (Kapilavatthu°); II.5; III.188; VI.368 etc.; Pug 56; DhA IV.2; PvA 3, 39, 73; Dpvs XIV.51 (+ pura). Cp. nāgara.

-ûpakārikā a town fortified with a wall covered with cement at its base D I.105, cp. DA I.274; -ûpama like a citadel (of citta) Dh 40, cp. DhA I.317 & Nagaropama sūtra Divy 340; -kathā town-gossip D I.7; -guttika superintendent of the city police J III.30, 436; IV.279; Miln 345 (dhammanagare n-g.), DhA IV.55. Cp. Kern, *Toev.* p. 167; -vara the noble town (of Rājagaha) Vv 16^6, cp. VvA 82; -vīthi a city street J II.416; -sobhinī the city belle, a town courtesan J II.367 (°anā); III.435 (Sulasā), 475 (°anī); DhA I.174; II.201; PvA 4 (Sulasā); Miln 350.

Nagaraka (nt.) a small city D I.146 = 169, quoted J I.391.

Nagga (adj.) [Ved. nagna = Lat. nudus (fr. *noguedhos) Goth. naqaps = Ohg. naccot, Ags. nacod = naked; Oir. nocht; perhaps Gr. γυμνός] naked, nude Vin II.121; J I.307; Pv I.6^1 (= niccola PvA 32); II.1^5; 8^1; PvA 68, 106.

-cariyā going naked Dh 141; DhA III.78; cp. Sk nagnacaryā Divy 339; -bhogga one whose goods are nakedness, an ascetic J IV.160; V.75; VI.225.

Naggatta (nt.) [Sk. nagnatva] = naggiya nakedness PvA 106.

Naggiya (nt.) [Sk. *nagnyaŋ] naked state, nudity Vin I.292, 305; S IV.300; Sn 249.

Naggiyā (adj. f.) [Sk. nagnikā] = naggā, naked Pv II.3^{12}.

Nangala (nt.) [Ved. lāngala; nangala by dissimilation through subsequent nasal, cp. Milinda > Menandros. Etym. unknown, prob. dialectical (already in RV IV. 57^4), because unconnected with other Aryan words for plough. Cp. Balūčī nangār] a plough S I.115; III.155; A III.64; Sn 77 (yuga° yoke & plough); Sn p. 13; J I.57; Th 2, 441 (= sīra ThA 270); SnA 146; VvA 63, 65; PvA 133 (dun° hard to plough); DhA I.223 (aya°); III.67 (id.).

-īsā the beam of a plough S I.104 (of an elephant's trunk); -kaṭṭhakaraṇa ploughing S V.146 = J II.59; -phāla [mod. Ind. phār] ploughshare (to be understood as Dvandva) DhA I.395.

Nangalin (adj.-n.) having or using a plough, ploughman, in mukha° "using the mouth as plough" Th I, 101 (maulvergnügt, Neumann) (Mrs. Rh. D. harsh of speech).

Nanguṭṭha (nt.) [dial. for *nangūlya > *nanguḷhya ?] = nangula A II.245; J I.194 (of a bull); II.19 (of an elephant); III.16 (sūci°), 480 (panther); IV.256 (of a deer); DhA I.275 (of a fish); II.64.

Nangula (nt.) [Sk. lāngūla to langa & lagati (q. v.), cp. Gr. λαγγάζω, Lat. langueo] a tail Th I, 113 = 601 (90°).

Nacira (adj.) [Sk. nacira = na + cira] not of long duration, short Sn 694; gen. nacirass' eva after a short time, shortly Sn p. 16; J IV.2, 392; Miln 250.

Nacca (nt.) [Ved. nṛtya = Anglo-Ind. nautch, etym. uncertain, cp. naccati & naṭati] (pantomimic) dancing; usually comb^d with singing (gīta, q. v.) & instrumental music (vādita). — nacca: A I.261; D III.183; J I.61, 207; DA I.77; PvA 231. — nacca-gīta: J I.61; Pv IV.7^2; DhA III.129; VvA 131, 135. — nacca-gīta-vādita (+ visūkadassana): Vin I.83; D I.5, 6; KhA 36; cp. Vv 81^{10} (naccagīte suvādite).

Naccaka [Sk. *nṛtyaka, distinguished from but ultimately identical with naṭaka, q. v.] a dancer, (pantomimic) actor Miln 191, 331, 359 (naṭa°). — f. naccakī Vin II.12.

Naccati [Ved. nṛtyati **nṛt**, cp. nacca & naṭati] to dance, play Vin II.10; J I.292; Vv 50^1 (= naṭati VvA 210); 64^{21}. — pp. naccento D I.135; fut. naccissati Vin II.12; aor. nacci J III.127; inf. naccituŋ J I.207. — Caus. naccāpeti to make play Vism 305 (so read for nacch°).

Naccana (nt.) [Ved. *nṛtyana, cp. naṭana] dance, dancing VvA 282, 315.

Najjuha [Sk. dātyūha] a kind of cock or hen J VI.528, 538.

Naṭa [Sk. naṭa dial. ṭ, cp. Prk. naḍa, of **nṛt**, see naccati] a dancer, player, mimic, actor Vin IV.285; S IV.306 sq.; DhA IV.60 (°dhītā), 65 (°karaka), 224 (°kīḷā); Miln 359 (°naccaka); Sdhp 380. — Cp. naṭaka & nāṭaka

Naṭaka [Sk. naṭaka] = naṭa Vin IV.285; Miln 331; PvA 3. — f. naṭikā DA I.239.

Naṭati [Sk. naṭati, of **nṛt**, with dial. ṭ, cp. naccati] to dance, play VvA 210 (= naccati).

Naṭṭha [Sk. naṣṭha, pp. of nassati (naśyati), q. v.] perished, destroyed; lost A II.249; J I.74; 267.

Naṭṭhana (nt.) [Der. fr. naṭṭha] destruction Miln 180, 237.

Naṭṭhāyika [cp. Sk. naṣṭhārtha, i. e. naṣṭha + artha] bankrupt Miln 131, 201.

Nata [Sk. nata, pp. of namati, q. v.] bent (on) S I.186 (a°); Sn 1143; Nd^2 327.

Nati (f.) [Sk. nati of **nam**] bending, bent, inclination S II.67; IV.59; M I.115.

Natta (nt.) [Sk. nakta, see nakkhatta] night, acc. nattaŋ by night, in nattam-ahaŋ by day & by night Sn 1070 (v. l. BB and Nd[2] rattamahaŋ).

Nattar [Sk. naptṛ, analogy-formation after mātṛ etc. from Ved. napāt; cp. Lat. nepos; Ags. nefa = E. nephew; Ohg. nevo] grandson J I.60 (nattu, gen.), 88; Ud 91, 92; PvA 17 (nattu-dhītā great-grand-daughter), 25 (nattā nom.).

Natthika (adj.-n.) [Sk. nāstika] one who professes the motto of "natthi," a sceptic, nihilist S I.96; usually in cpds.
-diṭṭhi scepticism, nihilistic view, heresy Sn 243 (= micchādiṭṭhi Com.); VvA 342; PvA 244; -vāda one who professes a nihilistic doctrine S III.73; M I.403; A II.31; PvA 215 (+ micchādiṭṭhika).

Natthitā (f.) [Sk. nāstitā, fr. n' atthi] nihilism S II.17; J V.110.

Natthibhāva [n' atthi-bhāva] non-existence DhA III.324.

Natthu [cp. Sk. nas f. & nasta, see etym. under nāsā] 1. the nose J V.166 (= nāsā Com.). — 2. = °kamma, medical treatment through the nose Vin III.83 (deti).
-kamma nose-treatment, consisting in the application of hot oil (DA I.98: telaŋ yojetvā n-karaṇaŋ) D I.12; Vin I.204; M I.511; DhA I.12; -karaṇī a pockethandkerchief Vin I.204.

Nadati [Ved. nadati, **nad** of unknown etym.] to roar, cry, make a noise (nadaŋ nadati freq.) Sn 552 (sīha), 684 (id.), 1015; J I.50, 150; II.110; aor. nadi J III.55 & anādisuŋ J IV.349. Caus. nadāpeti to make roar J II.244. See also nadī & nāda, & cp. onadati.

Nadana (nt.) [cp. Sk. nadanu] roaring J I.19 (sīhanāda° the sound of a lion's roar).

Nadita (nt.) [cp. Sk. nādita, pp. of caus. nadayati] roar, noise J II.110.

Nadī (f.) [Ved. nadī, from nadati = "the roaring," cp. also nandati] a river; often characterised as mahā° in opp. to kun° rivulet; pl. nadiyo also collect. "the waters." — D I.244 (Aciravatī nadī); S II.32, 118, 135; V.390; A I.33, 136, 243 (mahā°); II.55, 140 (mahā°); III.52; IV.101 (m°), 137; Sn 425, 433, 568, 720; Dh 251; J I.296; II.102; III.51; III.91 (Kebukā); V.269 (Vetaraṇī°); VI.518 (Ketumatī); Pv IV.3[54]; Vism 468 (sīghasotā); PvA 256 (m°); Sdhp 21, 194, 574. — gen. sg. nadiyā J I.278; It 113; instr. nadiyā J I.278; PvA 46; pl. nom. nadiyo Miln 114 (na tā n. dhuva-salilā). najjo PvA 29 (mahā°); & najjāyo J VI.278; gen nadīnaŋ Vin I.246 = Sn 569 (n. sāgaro mukhaŋ). — kunnadī a small river S I.109; II.32, 118; V.47, 63; A II.140; IV.100; V.114 sq. — On n. in similes see *J.P.T.S.* 1906, 100.
-kuñja a river glen DA I.209; -kūla the bank of a river cp. III.7[1]; -tīra = °kūla J I.278; -dugga a difficult ford in a river S II.198; -vidugga = °dugga A I.35; III.128.

Naddha [Sk. naddha pp. of **nah**, see nayhati] tied, bound, fastened, put on J I.175 (rathavarattaŋ); Bu 1.31 (camma°, of a drum); Mhvs VII.16 (°pañcāyudha); Miln 117 (yuga°); DhsA 131. Cp. onaddha, vi°, san°.

Nanandar (f.) [Sk. nanāndṛ & nanāndā, to nanā "mother"] husband's sister J V.269 (= sāmikassa bhaginī p. 275).

Nanikāma (adj.) [na + nikāma = anikāma] disagreeable, unpleasant Dh 309 (°seyyā an uncomfortable bed).

Nanu (indecl.) [Ved. nanu] 1. part. of affirmation (cp. na[1]): surely, certainly Pv II.6[7] (so to be read for nanda? v. l. BB nuna); Manor. Pūr. on A V.194 (Andersen P. R. 91). — 2. part. of interrogation (= Lat. nonne) "is it not" (cp. na[2]): J I.151; III.393; DhA I.33.

Nantaka (nt.) [a contamination of namataka (Kern, *Toev.* p. 169), maybe Sk. naktaka "cover for nakedness" (Trenckner, *Notes* 81[1]), unless it be non-Aryan] a shred, rag, worn-out cloth, usually expl[d] by jiṇṇapilotika (J III.22) or khaṇḍabhūtā pilotikā (PvA 185) or pilotika only (VvA 311). — S V.342; A III.187; IV.376 (°vāsin as v. l.; text has nantikavāsin); Vv 80[7] (anantaka); Pv III.2[14]; J III.22 (°vāsin clad in rags).

Nanda at Pv II.6[7] used either as interj. (= nanu, q. v.) or as voc. in the sense of "dear"; the first expl[n] to be preferred & n. probably to be read as nanu (v. l. nuna) or handa (in which case nanu would be gloss).

Nandaka (adj.) [Sk. nandikā] giving pleasure, pleasing, full of joy; f. nandikā J IV.396 (+ khiḍḍā), either as adj. or f. abstr. pleasure, rejoicing (= abhindandanā Com.).

Nandati [Ved. nandati, **nand** = **nad** (cp. vind > vid etc.) orig. to utter sounds of joy] to be glad, to rejoice, find delight in, be proud of (c. instr.) S I.110; A IV.94 sq.; Sn 33; Dh 18. — Caus. nandeti to please, to do a favour J IV.107 (nandaya = tosehi Com.); PvA 139 (= toseti). — ppr. nandayanto J VI.588. — Cp. ānandati.

Nandanā (f.) [Sk. nandanā] rejoicing, delight, pleasure S I.6 = Sn 33.

Nandi[1] & (freq.) Nandī (f.) [Sk. nandi, but cp. BSk. nandī Divy 37] 1. joy, enjoyment, pleasure, delight in (c. loc.) S I.16, 39, 54; II.101 sq. (āhāre); III.14 (= upādāna); IV.36 sq.; A II.10 (kāma°, bhava°, diṭṭhi°), III.246; IV.423 sq. (dhamma°); Sn 1055 (+ nivesana); Nd[2] 330 (= taṇhā); Pug 57; Dhs 1059≈(in def. of taṇhā); Vbh 145, 356, 361; DhsA 363; ThA 65, 167. — For nandī at Miln 289 read tandī. — 2. a musical instrument: joy-drum [Sk. nandī] Vin III.108 (= vijayabheri). Cp. ā°.
-(y)āvatta "turning auspiciously" (i. e. turning to the right: see dakkhiṇāvatta), auspicious, good Neṭṭ 2, 4, 7, 113 (always attr. of naya); -ûpasecana (rāgasalla) sprinkled over with joy, having joy as its sauce Nett 116, 117; cp. maŋsûpasecana (odana) J III.144 = VI.24; -kkhaya the destruction of (finding) delight S III.51; -(ŋ)jaha giving up or abandoning joy Sn 1101 (+ okañjaha & kappañjaha); Nd[2] 331; -bhava existence of joy, being full of joy, in °*parikkhīṇa* one in whom joy is extinct (i. e. an Arahant), expl[d] however by Com. as one who has rid himself of the craving for rebirth (tīsu bhavesu parikkhīnataṇha DhA IV.192 = SnA 469) S I.2, 53; Sn 175, 637 = Dh 413; -mukhī (adj.-f.) "joy-faced," showing a merry face, Ep. of the night (esp. the eve of the uposatha) Vin I.288 (ratti); II.236 (id.); -rāga pleasure & lust, passionate delight S II.227; III.51; IV.142, 174, 180; M I.145; Dhs 1059≈, 1136; esp. as attr. of taṇhā in phrase n-r-sahagata-taṇhā (cp. M Vastu III.332: nandīrāgasahagatā tṛṣṇā) Vin I.10; S III.158; V.425 sq.; Ps III.137; Nett 72; -saŋyojana the fetter of finding delight in anything Sn 1109, 1115; Nd[2] 332; -samudaya the rise or. origin of delight M III.267.

Nandi[2] = nandhi.

Nandin (adj.) [Sk. nandin] finding or giving delight, delighting in, pleasurable, gladdening S II.53 (vedanā); A II.59, 61; It 112.

Nandha see yuga°.

Nandhati [for nayhati, der. fr. naddha after analogy of baddha > bandhati] meaning not so much "to bind" as "to cover": see apiḷandhati, upanandhati, onandhati, pariyonandhati.

Nandhi (f.) (usually spelt nandi) [Sk. naddhrī to naddha, pp. of **nah** to bind] a strap, thong J I.175 (rathassa cammañ ca nandiñ ca); Sn 622 = Dh 398 (+ varatta); SnA 400; DhA I.44, IV.160.

Napuŋsaka (adj.) [Ved. napuŋsaka = na + puŋs "not-male"] of no sex; lit. Vism 548, 553; ThA 260; Vbh 417; in gram. of the neuter gender Kacc. 50; PvA 266 (is reading correct?)

Nabha (nt.) & **Nabhas** (in oblique cases) [Sk. nabhas; Gr. νέφος & νεφέλη, Lat. nebula, Oir. nēl, Ags. nifol (darkness), Ohg. nebul. See also abbha] mist, vapour, clouds, sky A I.242; II.50 (nabhā), III.240, Sn 687 (nabhasi-gama, of the moon); Vv 32^3, 35^2 (= ākāsa VvA 161), 53^4 (id. 236), 63^{27} (id. 268); PvA 65; Mhvs VII.9 (nabhasā instr.).

Nabbho = nābhiyo, nom. pl. of nābhi (q. v.).

Namataka (nt.) [word & etym. doubtful; cp. nantaka & Bdhgh. Vin II.317: matakan (sic) ti satthaka-vedhanakaŋ (= veṭhanakaŋ) pilotikakhaṇḍaŋ] a piece of cloth Vin II.115 (satthaka), 123, 267 (°ŋ dhāreti).

Namati [Ved. namati, Idg. ***nem** to bend; also to share out, cp. Gr. νέμω, Goth. niman = Ger. nehmen. See cognates in Walde loc. cit. under nemus] to bend, bend down (trs. & instr.) direct, apply S I.137 (cittaŋ); Sn 806; J I.61 (aor. nami, cittaŋ). — Caus. nameti (*not* nāmeti, Fsb. to Sn 1143 nāmenti, which is to be corrected to n' âpenti) to bend, to wield Dh 80 = 145 (namayati). As nāmeti at J VI.349. pp. namita (q. v.).

Namana (nt.) [a philosophical term constructed by Bdhgh. from nāma, cp. ruppana—rūpa] naming, giving a name KhA 78; DhsA 52 (see nāma^2); Vism 528.

Namanā (f.) [abstr. to namati, cp. Sk. namana nt.] bent, application, industry Vbh 352.

Namassati [Ved. namasyati, Denom. fr. namo] to pay honour to, to venerate, honour, do homage to (often with pañjalika & añjaliŋ katvā) Sn 236, 485, 598, 1058, 1063; Nd^2 334; J III.83; Pv $II.12^{20}$; KhA 196; pot. namasseyya It 110; Dh 392, 1st pl. namassemu Sn 995; ppr. namassaŋ Sn 344, 934; namassanto SnA 565, & (usually) namassamāna Sn 192, 1142; Nd^1 400; J II.73; VvA 7. — aor. namassiŋsu Sn 287. — ger. **namassitvā** J I.1. — grd. (as adj.) namassaniya (venerable), Miln 278.

Namassana (nt.) (?) veneration J I.1.

Namassiyā (namassā) (f.) [Sk. namasyā] worship, veneration Miln 140.

Namita [pp. nameti] bent on, disposed to (-°), able or capable of J III.392 (pabbajjāya-namita-citta); Miln 308 (phalabhāra°).

Namo (nt.) & **Nama** (nt.) [Ved. namas, cp. Av. nəmo prayer; Gr. νέμος, Lat. nemus (see namati)] homage, veneration, esp. used as an exclamation of adoration at the beginning of a book (namo tassa Bhagavato Arahato Sammāsambuddhassa) Sn 540, 544; PvA 1, 67.

Namuci (Np.) a name of Māra.

Naya (adj.-n.) [from nayati, to lead, see neti] "leading"; usually m: way (fig.), method, plan, manner; inference; sense, meaning (in grammar); behaviour, conduct A II.193 = Nd^2 151 (°hetu through inference); Nett 2 (method), 4 (id.), 7, 113; Miln 316 (nayena = nayahetu); KhA 74; VvA 112 (sense, context, sentence); PvA 1 (ways or conduct), 117 (meaning), 126 (id.), 136, 280. — nayaŋ neti to draw a conclusion, apply an inference, judge, behave S II.58 = Vbh 329; J IV.241 (anayaŋ nayati dummedho: draws a wrong conclusion); PvA 227 (+ anumināti). — With °ādi° N. has the function of continuing or completing the context = "and similarly," e. g. °ādinaya-pavatta dealing with this & the following VvA 2; . . . ti ādinā nayena thus & similarly, & so forth J I.81; PvA 30. — Instr. nayena (-°) as adv. in the way of, as, according(ly): āgata° according to what has been shown or said in . . . J I.59; VvA 3; PvA 280; purima° as before J I.59; IV.140; vutta° as said (above) (cp. vutta-niyāmena) PvA 13, 29, 36, 71, 92 etc. — sunaya a sound judgment J IV.241; **dunnaya** a wrong principle, method or judgment, or as adj.: wrongly inferred, hard to be understood, unintelligible A III.178 = Nett 21; J IV.241.

Nayati see neti.

Nayana (nt.) [Sk. nayana, to nayati = the leader cp. also netra = P. netta] the eye Th 2, 381; Vv 35^3; Dhs 597; Vbh 71 sq.; Miln 365; ThA 255; VvA 161 (= cakkhu); PvA 40 (nettāni nayanāni), 152; Sdhp 448, 621.

Nayhati [Ved. nahyati, Idg. ***nedh** as in Lat. nodus & Ved. nahu] to tie, bind; only in comp. with prep. as upanayhati (cp. upāhanā sandal), pilandhati etc. — pp. naddha (q. v.). See also nandhi, nāha; onayhati, unnahanā, piḷayhati.

Nayhana (nt.) [Sk. nahana] tying, binding; bond, fetter DhA IV.161.

Nara [Ved. nara, cp. nṛtu; Idg. ***ner** to be strong or valiant = Gr. ἀνήρ, ἀγ-ήνωρ (valiant), δρώψ (*νρώψ); Lat. neriosus (muscular), Nero (Sabinian, cp. Oscan ner = Lat. vir); Oir. nert] man (in poetry esp. a brave, strong, heroic man), pl. either "men" or "people" (the latter e. g. at Sn 776, 1082; Pv $I.11^{12}$). — A I.130; II.5; III.53; Sn 39, 96, 116, 329, 591, 676, 865 etc.; Dh 47, 48, 262, 309, 341; J III.295; Nd^1 12 = Nd^2 335 (definition); VvA 42 (popular etymology: narati netī ti naro puriso, i. e. a "leading" man); PvA 116 = Dh 125.
-**ādhama** vilest of men Sn 246; -**āsabha** "man bull," i. e. lord of men Sn 684, 696; -**inda** "man lord," i. e. king Sn 836; J I.151; -**uttama** best of men (Ep. of the Buddha) S I.23; D III.147; Sn 1021; -**deva** god-man or man-god (pl.) gods, also Ep. of the B. "king of men" S I.5; Pv $IV.3^{52}$; -**nārī** (pl.) men & women, appl. to male & female angelic servants (of the Yakkhas) Vv 32^4, 33^7, 53^8; Pv $II.11^2$; -**vīra** a hero (?), a skilled man (?) Th 1, 736 (naravīrakata "by human skill & wit" Mrs. Rh. D.). -**sīha** lion of man J I.89.

Naraka [Sk. naraka; etym. doubtful, problematic whether to Gr. νέρτερος (= inferus), Ags. nord = north as region of the underworld] 1. a pit D I.234; Th 1, 869; J IV.268 (°āvāṭa PvA 225). — 2. a name for Niraya, i. e. purgatory; a place of torment for the deceased (see niraya & cp. list of narakas at Divy 67) S I.209; Sn 706; PvA 52; Sdhp 492 (saŋsāraghora°), 612.
-**angāra** the ashes of purgatory Sdhp 32.

Narada (nt.) [Sk. nalada, Gr. νάρδος, of Semitic origin, cp. Hebr. nird] nard, ointment J VI.537.

Nala & **Naḷa** [Ved. naḍa & Sk. naḷa, with dial. ḍ (ḷ) for *narda, cp. Gr. νάρθηξ] a species of reed; reed in general Vin IV.35; A II.73; Dh 337; Nd^2 680_{II}; J I.223; IV.141, 396 (n. va chinno); Pv $I.11^6$ (id.); DhA III.156; IV.43. See also nāḷa, nāḷī & nāḷikā.
-**āgāra** a house built of reeds S I.156; IV.185 (+ tiṇāgāra); A I.101 (+ tiṇāgāra); Nd^2 40^{II} (id.), Miln 245; cp. AvŚ Index II.228 (naḍāgāra); -**aggi** a fire of reeds J VI.100 (°vaṇṇaŋ pabbataŋ); -**kalāpī** a bundle of r. S II.114; -**kāra** a worker in reeds, basket-maker; D I.51 (+ pesakāra & kumbhakāra); J V.291; ThA 28; PvA 175 (+ vilivakāra); DhA I.177; -**daṇḍaka** a shaft of r. J I.170; -**maya** made of r. Vin II.115; -**vana** a thicket of reeds J IV.140; Miln 342; -**sannibha** reed-coloured J VI.537 (Com.: naḷa-puppha-vaṇṇa rukkha-sunakha); -**setu** a bridge of reeds Sn 4.

Naḷapin a water-animal J VI.537.

Nalāṭa (nt.) [Ved. lalāṭa = rarāṭa; on n > l cp. nangala] the forehead S I.118; J III.393; IV.417 (nalāṭena maccuŋ ādāya: by his forelock); Vism 185; DhA I.253.

-anta the side of the forehead J VI.331; -maṇḍala the round of the f. D I.106; Sn p. 108.

Nalāṭikā (f.) [Sk. lalāṭikā] "belonging to the forehead," a frown Vin II.10 (nalāṭikaŋ deti to give a frown).

Nalinī (f.) [Sk. nalinī] a pond J IV.90; Vism 84, 17.

Nava[1] (num.) [Ved. navan, Idg. *neuṇ, cp. Lat. novem (*noven), Gr. ἐννέα, Goth. niun, Oir. nōin, E. nine. Connection with nava[2] likely because in counting by tetrads (octo = 8 is a dual!) a *new* series begins with No. 9] number nine. gen.-dat. navannaŋ (Sn p. 87); instr.-abl. navahi (VvA 76), loc. navasu.

Meaning and Application: The primitive-Aryan importance of the "mystic" nine is not found in Buddhism and can only be traced in Pali in folkloristic undercurrents (as fairy tales) & stereotype traditions in which 9 appears as a number implying a higher trinity $= 3^2$. 1. navabhūmaka pāsāda (a palace 9 stories high more freq. satta°, 7) J I.58; nava-hiraññakoṭīhi (w. 9 koṭis of gold) VvA 188; nava yojana DhA II.65. — 2. navangabuddhasāsana "the 9 fold teaching of Buddha," i. e. the 9 divisions of the Buddh. Scriptures according to their form or style, viz. suttaŋ geyyaŋ veyyākaraṇaŋ gāthā udānaŋ itivuttakaŋ jātakaŋ abbhutadhammaŋ vedallaŋ M I.133; A II.103, 178; III.86 sq., 177 sq.; Pug 43; Miln 344; Dpvs IV.15; PvA 2. Cp. chaḷanga.—nava sattāvāsā "9 abodes of beings" Kh IV. (in exemplifying No. 9), viz. (see D III.263 = KhA 86, 87 cp. also A IV.39 sq.) (1) manussā, devā, vinipātikā; (2) Brahmakāyikā devā; (3) Ābhassarā; (4) Subhakiṇhā; (5) Asaññasattā; (6) Ākāsanañcāyatana-upagā; (7) Viññāṇanañcāyatana°; (8) Ākiñcaññāyatana°; (9) Nevasaññāsaññāyatana°. — nava sotā (Sn 197) or nava dvārā (VvA 76; v. l. mukhā) 9 openings of the body, viz. (SnA 248) 2 eyes, ears, nostrils, mouth, anus & urethra (cp. *S.B.E.* 39, 180; 40, 259 sq.). — nava vitakkā 9 thoughts Nd[2] 269 (q. v.). — 3. a trace of the week of 9 days is to be found in the expression "navuti-vassasatasahass-āyukā" giving the age of a divinity as 9 million years (= a divine week) VvA 345. — Cp. navuti.

Nava[2] (adj.) [Ved. nava, Idg. *neuṇ (cp. nava[1]) = Lat. novus, Gr. νέος (*νέϜος), Lith. navas; Goth. niujis etc. = E. new; also Sk. navya = Gr. νεῖος, Lat. Novius. May be related to na[3]] 1. new, fresh; unsoiled, clean; of late, lately acquired or practised (opp. pubba & purāṇa). Often syn. with taruṇa. Sn 28, 235 (opp. purāṇaŋ). 944 (id.), 913 (opp. pubba); Pv I.9[2] (of clothes = costly); J IV.201 (opp. purāṇa); Miln 132 (salila fresh water). — 2. young, unexperienced, newly initiated; a novice Vin I.47 (navā bhikkhū the younger bhs., opp. therā); S I.9 (+ acira-pabbajita); II.218; Sn p. 93 (Gotamo navo pabbajjāya "a novice in the Wanderer's life"); DhA I.92 (bhikkhu).

-kamma building new, making repairs, "doing up," mending Vin II.119, 159; III.81; J I.92; IV.378; Nd[2] 385; -kammika an expert in making repairs or in building, a builder (cp. vaḍḍhaki) Vin II.15, IV.211; -ghata fresh ghee J II.433 (v. l. °sappi).

Navaka (adj.-n.) [Sk. navaka] young; a young man, a newly ordained bhikkhu (opp. thera), novice (cp. Divy 404) J I.33 (sangha°); PvA 76 (id.). — Freq. in compar. navakatara a younger one, or the youngest (opp. theratara) D II.154; J I.218; Miln 24.

Navanīta (nt.) & nonīta [cp. Ved. navanīta] fresh butter Vin I.244 (cp. gorasa); D I.201; M III.141; Pv III.5[5] (nonīta); Pug 69, 70; Miln 41, Dhs 646, 740; DhA I.417; PvA 199.

Navama (num. ord.) [Sk. navama = Oir. nōmad; cp. Lat. nonus; Gr. ἔνατος, Goth. niunda with diff. superl. suffixes] the ninth Sn 109; f. °ī VvA 72.

Naviya (adj.) [Sk. navya, either grd. of navate to praise; or = nava, q. v.] praiseworthy Miln 389.

Navuti (num.) [Ved. navati] number ninety VvA 345 & in compⁿ eka° 91 D II.2 (i. e. 92 minus 1; in expr. ekanavuto kappo, v. l. ekanavuti kappe); **dvā°** 92 (see dvi A II. & B III.); PvA 19, 21; aṭṭhā° 98; Sn 311 (diseases sprung fr. orig. 3).

Navutiya (adj.) worth ninety J V.485. Cp. nāvutika.

Nassati (v. intr.) [Ved. naś; naśyati & naśati, cp. Gr. νέκυς, νεκρός (corpse), νέκταρ ("overcoming death" = nec + tṛ, cp. tarati); Lat. neco, noceo, noxius] to perish, to be lost or destroyed, to disappear, come to an end Sn 666 (na hi nassati kassaci kammaŋ); It 90; J I.81, 116, 150; pret. nassaŋ (prohib.) Sn 1120, pl. anassāma M I.177; aor. nassi A III.54 (mā nassi prohib.); J IV.137 (cakkhūni °iṇsu: the eyes failed); fut. nassisati J I.5; cond. nassissa J II.112. — Caus. nāseti (q. v.). See also pa°.

Nassana (nt.) [cp. Sk. naśana] disappearance, loss, destruction A III.54 (°dhamma adj. doomed to perish).

Nahāta [Sk. snāta, see nahāyati] one who has bathed Vin II.221; J I.266; DhA IV.232 (°kilesatā washed off moral stain).

Nahātaka [Ved. snātaka, cp. nahāta & nahāyati] "one who has bathed," a brahmin who has finished the studies M I.280; A IV.144; Dh 422 (expl. at DhA IV.232 with ref. to perfection in the Buddha's teaching: catusaccabuddhatāya buddha); cp. Sn 521 (one who has washed away all sin), 646.

Nahāna (nt.) [Sk. snāna] bathing, a bath Vin I.47, 51 = II.224; I.196 (dhuva° constant bathing), 197; S I.183; V.390 (fig.); J I.265; PvA 50; Vism 27.

-kāla bathing time PvA 46; **-koṭṭhaka** bath-room DhA III.88; -garuka fond of bathing Vin I.196; **-cuṇṇa** bath powder (cp. nahāniya°) DhA I.398; **-tittha** a shallow place for bathing DhA I.3; III.79.

Nahāniya (adj.) belonging to a bath, bath-; in °cuṇṇa bath-powder PvA 46.

Nahāpaka [Sk. snāpaka, fr. Caus. nahāpeti; cp. nahāpita] a barber, bath attendant D I.74; A III.25; DA I.157 (= ye nahāpenti); PvA 127 (= kappaka).

Nahāpana (nt.) bathing, washing (trs.) D I.7, 12; A I.62, 132; II.70; IV.54; It 111 (ucchādana +); VvA 305 (udakadāna +).

Nahāpita [Sk. only snāpaka (see nahāpaka); new formation fr. Caus. nahāpeti as n. ag. with a- theme instead of ar-, cp. sallakatta for sallakattar] a barber, who has also the business of preparing & giving baths (cp. Ger. "bader") a bath-attendant (see kappaka). Barbers ranked as a low class socially, and rebirth in a barber's family was considered unfortunate. Vin I.249 (°pubba who had formerly been a barber); D I.225; J I.137; II.5; III.451; IV.138 (eight kahāpaṇas as a barber's fee); DA I.157 (= kappaka); VvA 207 (°sālā a barber's shop).

Nahāpeti [Sk. snāpayati, Caus. of nahāpeti] to wash, to give a bath, bathe J I.166; PvA 49; VvA 68, 305.

Nahāmin (adj.-n.) [= nahāpaka; Kern, *Toev.* asks: should it be nahāpin?] a barber, a low-class individual Pv III.1[14] (= kappaka-jātika PvA 176).

Nahāyati (rarely nhāyati) [Ved. snāti & snāyati, **snā** = Gr. νήχω (to swim), ναρός, Νηρεύς (Nereid), νῆσος (island); Lat. nare (to swim); cp. also Sk. snauti, Gr. νάω, νέω; Goth. sniwan] to bathe (trs. & intr.), to wash, to perform an ablution (esp. at the end of religious studentship or after the lapse of a lustrative period) Vin II.280;

J I.265; VI.336; PvA 93. ppr. nahāyanto (PvA 83) & nahāyamāna (Vin II.105); inf. nahāyituŋ (Vin I.47; PvA 144); ger. nahāyitvā (J I.50; VI.367; PvA 42) & nahātvā (J I.265; III.277; DhA III.88; PvA 23, 62) (after mourning), 82; grd. nahāyitabba (Vin II.220, 280).

Nahāru & **Nhāru** [Sk. snāyu, Idg. *snē to sew, cp. Gr. νέω, νῆθω, νῆμα (thread); Ohg. nājan; also Gr. νεῦρον (=Lat. nervus); Ags. sinu (=sinew); Ohg. senawa; Goth. neþla=Ags. nǣdl (=needle); Oir. snātha (thread); Ohg. snuor (cord)=Ags. snōd] sinew, tendon, muscle. In the anatomy of the body n. occupies the place between maŋsa (flesh, soft flesh) & aṭṭhi (bone), as is seen from ster. sequence chavi, camma, maŋsa, nahāru, aṭṭhi, aṭṭhi-miñja (e. g. at Vin I. 5; J III.84). See also defⁿ in detail at SnA 246 sq. & KhA 47. — Vin I.25 (nh°); M I.429 (used for bow strings); A I.50; III.324; IV.47 sq. (°daddula), 129; Kh III.; Sn 194 (aṭṭhi°) Nd² 97 (nh°); DhA III.118; ThA 257 (nh°); PvA 68 (aṭṭhi-camma°), 80 (camma-maŋsa°); Sdhp 46, 103.

Nahuta (nt.) [Sk. nayuta (m. pl.) of unknown etym. Is it the same as navuti? The corresponding v>y>h is frequent, as to meaning cp. nava 3] a vast number, a myriad Sn 677; J I.25, 83; Pv IV.1⁷; DhA I.88; PvA 22, 265.

Nāga [Ved. nāga; etym. of 1. perhaps fr. *snagh=Ags. snaca (snake) & snaegl (snail); of 2 uncertain, perhaps a Non-Aryan word distorted by popular analogy to nāga¹] 1. a serpent or Nāga demon, playing a prominent part in Buddh. fairy-tales, gifted with miraculous powers & great strength. They often act as fairies & are classed with other divinities (see devatā), with whom they are sometimes friendly, sometimes at enmity (as with the Garuḷas) D I.54; S III.240 sq.; V.47, 63; Bu. I.30 (dīghāyukā mahiddhikā); Miln 23. Often with supaṇṇā (Garuḷas); J I.64. DhA II.4; PvA 272. Descriptions e. g. at DhA III.231, 242 sq.; see also cpds. — 2. an elephant, esp. a strong, stately animal (thus in combⁿ hatthi-nāga characterising "a Nāga elephant") & freq. as symbol of strength & endurance ("heroic"). Thus Ep. of the Buddha & of Arahants. Popular etymologies of n. are based on the excellency of this animal (āguŋ na karoti=he is faultless, etc.): see Nd¹ 201=Nd² 337; Th I, 593; PvA 57. — (a) the animal D I.49; S I.16; II.217, 222; III.85; V.351; A II.116; III.156 sq.; Sn 543; Vv 5⁵ (=hatthināga VvA 37); Pv I.11³. mahā° A IV.107, 110. — (b) fig.= hero or saint: S II.277; III.83; M I.151, 245; Dh 320; Sn 29, 53, 166, 421, 518. Of the Buddha: Sn 522, 845, 1058, 1101; Miln 346 (Buddha°). — 3. The Naga-tree (now called "iron-wood tree," the P. meaning "fairy tree"), noted for its hard wood & great masses of red flowers (=Sk. nāgakesara, mesua ferrea Lin.): see cpds. °rukkha, °puppha, °latā.

-âpalokita "elephant-look" (turning the whole body), a mark of the Buddhas M I.337; cp. BSk. nāgâvalokita Divy 208; -danta an ivory peg or pin, also used as a hook on a wall Vin II.117 (°ka Vin II.114, 152); J VI.382; -nāṭaka snakes as actors DhA IV.130; -nāsūru (f.) (woman) having thighs like an elephant's trunk J V.297; -puppha iron-wood flower Miln 283; -bala the strength of an elephant J I.265; II.158; -bhavana the world of snakes Nd¹ 448; J III.275; DhA IV.14; -māṇavaka a young serpent J III.276; f. °ikā ib. 275; DhA III.232; -rājā king of the Nāgas, i. e. serpents J II.111; III.275; Sn 379 (Erāvaṇa, see detail SnA 368); DhA I.359; III.231, 242 sq. (Ahicchatta); IV.129 sq. (Paṇṇaka); -rukkha the iron-wood tree J I.35 (cp. M Vastu II.249); -latā=rukkha J I.80 (the Buddha's toothpick made of its wood), 232; DhA II.211 (°dantakaṭṭha toothpick); -vatta habits of serpents Nd¹ 92, also adj. °ika ibid. 89; -vana elephant-grove Dh 324; DhA IV.15; -vanika el. hunter M I.175; III.132; -hata one who strikes the el. (viz. the Buddha) Vin II.195.

Nāgara [Sk. nāgara, see nagara] a citizen J I.150; IV.404; V.385; Dāvs II.85; VvA 31; PvA 19; DhA I.41.

Nāgarika (adj.) [Sk. nāgarika] citizen-like, urbane, polite DA I.282.

Nāṭaka [Sk. nāṭaka; see naccati] 1. (m.) a dancer, actor, player J I.206; V.373; DhA III.88; IV.59, 130; nāṭakitthi a dancing-girl, nautch-girl DhA III.166; VvA 131. — 2. (nt.) a play, pantomime J I.59; V.279, also used coll.=dancing-woman J I.59 (?) II.395.

Nātha [Ved. nātha, nāth, to which Goth. niþan (to support), Ohg. gināda (grace)] protector, refuge, help A V.23, 89; Dh 160 (attā hi attano n.), 380; Sn 1131 (Nd² has nāga); DhA IV.117; PvA 1. lokanātha Saviour of the world (Ep. of the Buddha) Sn 995; PvA 42. — anātha helpless, unprotected, poor J I.6 (nāthânāthā rich & poor); PvA 3 (°sālāp oor house) 65. Cp. nādhati.

Nāda [Sk. nāda, see nadati] loud sound, roaring, roar J I.19 (sīha°), 50 (koñca°), 150 (mahā°). Cp. pa°.

Nādi (f.)=nāda, loud sound, thundering (fig.) Vv 64¹⁰.

Nādhati [Sk. nādhate=nāthate (see nātha), only in nadhamāna, cp. RV X.65, 5: nādhas] to have need of, to be in want of (c. gen.) J V.90 (Com. explˢ by upatappati milāyati; thinking perhaps of nalo va chinno).

Nānatta (nt. m.) [Sk. nānatva; abstr. fr. nānā] diversity, variety, manifoldness, multiformity, distraction; all sorts of (opp. ekatta, cp. M I.364: "the multiformity of sensuous impressions," M.A.). Enumⁿ of diversity as nānattā, viz. dhātu° phassa° vedanā° saññā° sankappa° chanda° pariḷāha° pariyesanā° lābha° D III.289; S II.140 sq., cp. IV.113 sq., 284 sq.; Ps I.87. — A IV.385; Ps I.63 sq., 88 sq.; S II.115 (vedanā°); Ps I.91 (samāpatti° & vihāra°); J II.265. In composition, substituted sometimes for nāna. Cp. *Dialogues* I.14, *n.* 2.

-kathā desultory talk, gossip D I.8; (=niratthakakathā DA I.90); S V.420; -kāya (adj.) having a variety of bodies or bodily states (combᵈ with or opp. to ekatta°, nānatta-saññin, & ekatta-saññin), appl. to manussā, devā, vinipātikā (cp. nava sattâvāsā) A IV.39 sq.=Nd² 570²; D III.253, 263, 282; -saññā consciousness of diversity (Rh. D.: "idea of multiformity," *Dial.* II.119; Mrs. Rh. D. "consciousness of the manifold") M I.3; S IV.113 sq.; D III.224, 262 sq., 282; A I.41, 267; II.184; III.306; Ps II.172; Dhs 265 (cp. trsl. p. 72); Vbh 342, 369; -saññin having a varying consciousness (cp. °kaya), D I.31 (cp. DA I.119) 183; III.263.

Nānattatā (f.) [2nd abstr. to nānā]=nānatta, diversity (of states of mind). Seven sorts at Vbh 425: ārammaṇa° manasikāra° chanda° paṇidhi° adhimokkha° abhinihāra° paññā°.

Nānā (adv.) [Ved. nānā, a redupl. nā (emphatic particle, see na¹) "so and so," i. e. various, of all kinds] variously, differently. 1. (abs.) A I.138 (on different sides, viz. right<left); Sn 878 (=na ekaŋ SnA 554; =vividhaŋ aññoññaŋ puthu na ekaŋ Nd¹ 285), 884 sq. — 2. more frequently in cpds., as first part of adj. or n. where it may be trslᵈ as "different, divers, all kinds of" etc. Before a double cons. the final ā is shortened: nānagga (for nānā+agga), nānappakāra etc. see below.

-agga (-rasa) all the choicest delicacies J I.266 (°bhojana, of food); VI.366; PvA 155 (°dibbabhojana); -âdhimuttikatā diversity of dispositions DA I.44; Nett 98; -āvudhā (pl.) various weapons J I.150; -karaṇa difference, diversity Vin I.339 (sangha°); M II.128; cp. Divy 222; -gotta of all kinds of descent Pv II.9¹⁰; -citta of varying mind J I.295 (itthiyo); -jana all kinds of folk Sn 110[2]; Nd[1] 308 (puthu°); -titthiya of var. sects D III.16 sq.; -pakkāra various, manifold J I.52 (sakuṇā), 127. 278 (phalāni); DAI. 148 (āvudhā); PvA 50, 123, 135; -ratta multi-coloured Sn 287; J VI.230; -rasā (pl.) all kinds of dainties Pv II.9[11]; -vāda difference of opinion D I.236; -vidha divers, various, motley PvA 53, 96, 113, and passim; -saŋvāsaka living in a different part, or living apart Vin I.134 sq. (opp. samāna°), 321; II.162.

Nābhi & Nābhī (f.) [Vedic nābhi, nābhī; Av. nabā; Gr. ὀμφαλός (navel); Lat. umbo & umbilicus; Oir. imbliu (navel); Ags. nafu; Ohg. naba (nave), Ger. nabel=E. nave & navel] 1. the navel A III.240; J I.238; DA I.254 (where it is said that the Vessā (Vaiśyas) have sprung from the navel of Brahmā). — 2. the nave of a wheel Vv 64[4] (pl. nabhyo & nabbho SS=nābhiyo VvA 276); J I.64; IV.277; Miln 115.

Nāma (nt.) [Vedic nāman, cp. Gr. ὄνομα (ἀν-ώνυμος without name); Lat. nomen; Goth. namō; Ags. noma, Ohg. namo] name. — 1. *Literal.* nom. nāmaŋ S I.39; Sn 808; J II.131; Miln 27; acc. nāmaŋ PvA 145 (likhi: he wrote her name). — nāmaŋ karoti to give a name Sn 344; Nd[2] 466 (n' etaŋ nāmaŋ mātarā kataŋ on "Bhagavā"); J I.203, 262 (w. double acc.). — nāmaŋ gaṇhāti to call by name, to enumerate J IV.402; PvA 18 (v. l. BB nāmato g.). Definitions at Vin IV.6 (two kinds: hīna° & ukkaṭṭha°) and at Vism 528 (=namanalakkhaṇa). — 2. *Specified.* nāma as metaphysical term is opposed to rūpa, & comprises the 4 immaterial factors of an individual (arūpino khandhā, viz. vedanā saññā sankhāra viññāṇa; see khandha II. B[a]). These as the noëtic principle comb[d] with the material principle make up the individual as it is distinguished by "name & body" from other individuals. Thus nāmarūpa= individuality, individual being. These two are inseparable (aññamaññûpanissitā ete dhammā, ekato va uppajjanti Miln 49). S I.35 (yattha n. ca rūpañ ca asesaŋ uparujjhati taŋ te dhammaŋ idh' aññāya acchiduŋ bhavabandhanaŋ); Sn 1036, 1100; Nd[1] 435=Nd[2] 339 (nāma=cattāro arūpino khandhā); DhA IV.100 (on Dh 367): vedanādīnaŋ catunnaŋ rūpakkhandhassa cā ti pañcannaŋ khandhānaŋ vasena pavattaŋ nāmarūpaŋ; DhsA 52: nāmarūpa-duke nāmakaraṇaṭṭhena nāmaṭṭhena namanaṭṭhena ca nāmaŋ ruppanaṭṭhena rūpaŋ. Cp. D I.223; II.32, 34, 56, 62; S I.12 (taṇhā n-rūpe), 23 (n-rūpasmiŋ asajjamāna); II.3, 4, 66 (n-rūpassa avakkanti), 101 sq. (id.); M I.53; A I.83, 176; III.400; IV.385 (°ārammaṇa); V.51, 56; Sn 355, 537, 756, 909; Dh 367; It 35; Ps I.193; II.72, 112 sq.; Vbh 294; Nett 15 sq., 28, 69; Miln 46. Nāma+rūpa form an elementary pair D III.212; Kh IV. Also in the Paṭicca-samuppāda (q. v.), where it is said to be caused (conditioned) by viññāṇa & to cause saḷāyatana (the 6 senses), D II.34; Vin I.1 sq.; S II.6 sq.; Sn 872 (nāmañ ca rūpañca paṭicca phassā; see in detail expl[d] at Nd[1] 276). Synonymous with nāmarūpa is **nāmakāya**: Sn 1074; Nd[2] 338; Ps I.183; Nett 27, 41, 69, 77. — In this connection to be mentioned are var. definitions of nāma as the principle or distinguishing mark ("label") of the individual, given by Com[s], e. g. Nd[1] 109, 127; KhA 78; with which cp. Bdhgh's speculation concerning the connotation of nāma mentioned by Mrs. Rh. D. at *Dhs. trsl.* p. 341. — 3. *Use of Cases.* Instr. nāmena by name PvA 1 (Petavatthū ti n.); Mhvs VII.32 (Sirīsavatthu n.). — acc. nāma (the older form, cp. Sk. nāma) by name S I.33, 235 (Anoma°); Sn 153, 177; J I.59 (ko nām' esa "who by name is this one"=what is his name), 149 (nāmena Nigrodhamigarājā n.), 203 (kiŋsaddo nāma esa); II.4; III.187; VI.364 (kā nāma tvaŋ). See also evaŋnāma, kinnāma; & cp. the foll. — 4. nāma (acc.) as *adv.* is used as emphatic particle=just, indeed, for sure, certainly J I.222; II.133, 160, 326; III.90; PvA 6, 13, 63 etc. Therefore freq. in exclamation & exhortation ("please," certainly) J VI.367; DhA III.171; PvA 29 (n. detha *do* give); in comb[n] with interr. pron.=now, then J I.221 (kiŋ n.), 266 (kathaŋ n.); III.55 (kiŋ); Kh IV. (ekaŋ n. kiŋ); with neg.=not at all, certainly not J I.222; II.352; III.126 etc. — Often further emphasised or emphasising other part.; e. g. pi (=api) nāma really, just so Vin I.16 (seyyathā p. n.); Sn p. 15 (id.); VvA 22 (read nāma kāro); PvA 76; app' (=api) eva n. thus indeed, forsooth Vin I.16; It 89=M I.460; J I.168; Pv II.2[6] (=api nāma PvA 80); eva nāma in truth PvA 2; nāma tāva certainly DhA I.392, etc.

-kamma giving a name, naming, denomination Dhs 1306; Bdhd 83; -karaṇa name-giving, "christening" DhA II.87; -gahaṇa receiving a name, "being christened" J I.262 (°divasa) -gotta ancestry, lineage S I.43 (°ŋ na jīrati); Sn 648, Nd[2] 385 (mātāpettikaŋ n.); -dheyya assigning a name, name-giving J III.305; IV.449; V.496; Dhs 1306. -pada see pada. -matta a mere name Miln 25.

Nāmaka (adj.) [fr. nāma] 1. (-°) by name S II.282 (Thera°); PvA 67, 96 (kaṇha°). — 2. consisting of a mere name, i. e. mere talk, nonsense, ridiculous D I.240.

Nāmeti at Sn 1143 (Fsb.) is to be read as nāpenti. Otherwise see under namati.

Nāyaka [BSk. nāyaka (cp. anāyaka without guide AvŚ I.210); fr. neti; cp. naya] a leader, guide, lord, mostly as Ep. of the Buddha (loka° "Lord of the World") Sn 991 (loka°); Mhvs VII.1 (id.); Sdhp 491 (tilokassa); bala-nāyakā gang leaders J I.103.

Nārāca [Sk. nārāca; perhaps for *nāḍāca & conn. with nālika, a kind of arrow, to nāḷa] an iron weapon, an arrow or javelin M I.429; J III.322; Miln 105, 244, 418. -valaya an iron ring or collar (?) Mhvs VII.20 (Com. "vaṭṭita-assanārāca-pasa"=a noose formed by bending the ends of the n. into a circle).

Nārī (f.) [Sk. nārī to nara man, orig. "the one belonging to the man"] woman, wife, female Sn 301, 836; Dh 284; J I.60; III.395; IV.396 (°gaṇa); Vv 6[1], 44[16]; Pv I.9[1] (=itthi PvA 44). pl. nariyo (Sn 299, 304, 703), & nāriyo (Sn 703 v. l. BB; Pv II.9[52]). Comb[d] with nara as naranārī, male & female (angels), e. g. -Vv 53[8]; Pv II.11[2] (see nara).

Nāla & Nāḷa (nt.) [Sk. nāla, see nala] a hollow stalk, esp. that of the water lily A IV.169; J I.392 (°pana v. l. °vana); VvA 43. See also nāḷikā & nāḷī.

Nālaŋ (adv.) [=na alaŋ] not enough, insufficient It 37; J I.190; DA I.167.

Nāḷikā (f.) [Sk. nāḍikā & nālikā] a stalk, shaft; a tube, pipe or cylinder for holding anything; a small measure of capacity Vin II.116 (sūci°, cp. sūcighara, needle-case); D I.7 (=bhesajja° DA I.89); A I.210; J I.123 (taṇḍula° a nāḷi full of rice); VI.366 (aḍḍha-n-matta); Nd[2] 229. Cp. pa°.

-odana a nāḷi measure of boiled rice S I.82; DhA IV.17; -gabbha an (inner) room of tubular shape Vin II.152.

Nāḷikera [Sk. nārikera, nārikela, nalikera, nālikela: dialect, of uncertain etym.] the coconut tree Vv 44[13]; J IV.159; V.384; DA I.83; VvA 162.

Nāḷikerika (adj.) belonging to the coconut tree J V.417.

Nāḷi (f.) & (in cpds.) nāḷi [Sk. nāḍī, see nala] a hollow stalk, tube, pipe; also a measure of capacity Vin I.249; A III.49; J I.98 (suvaṇṇa°), 124 (taṇḍula°), 419; III.220 (kaṇḍa° a quiver); IV.67; DhA II.193 (tela°), 257. Cp. pa°.

-paṭṭa a covering for the head, a cap J VI.370, 444 (text °vaṭṭa); -matta as much as a tube holds A II.199; PvA 283; DhA II.70; J I.419 (of aja-laṇḍikā).

Nāvā (f.) [Ved. nāuḥ & nāvā, Gr. ναῦς, Lat. navis] a boat, ship Vin III.49 (q. v. for definition & description);

S I.106 (eka-rukkhikā); III.155 = V.51 = A IV.127 (sāmuddikā "a liner"); A II.200; III.368; Sn 321, 770, 771; Dh 369 (metaphor of the human body); J I.239; II.112; III.126; 188; IV.2, 21, 138; V.75 (with "500" passengers), 433; VI.160 (= nāvyā canal? or read nālaŋ?); Vv 6[1] (= pota VvA 42, with pop. etym. "satte neti ti nāvā ti vuccati"); Pv III.3[5] (= doṇi PvA 189); Miln 261 (100 cubits long); Dāvs IV.42; PvA 47, 53; Sdhp 321. In simile Vism 690.
-tittha a ferry J III.230; -sañcaraṇa (a place for) the traffic of boats, a port Miln 359.

Nāvāyika [Sk. nāvāja = Gr. ναυηγός, cp. Lat. navigo] a mariner, sailor, skipper Miln 365.

Nāvika [Sk. nāvika] 1. a sailor, mariner J II.103; IV.142; Miln 359; Dāvs IV.43 (captain). — 2. a ferryman J II.111; III.230 (Avariya-pitā.).

Nāvutika (adj.) [fr. navuti] 90 years old J III.395 (°ā itthi); SnA 172.

Nāsa [Sk. nāśa, see nassati] destruction, ruin, death J I.5, 256; Sdhp 58, 319. Usually vi°, also adj. vināsaka. Cp. panassati.

Nāsana (nt.) [Sk. nāśana] destruction, abandoning, expulsion, in °antika (adj.) a bhikkhu who is under the penalty of expulsion Vin I.255.

Nāsā (f.) [Vedic nāsā (du.); Lat. nāris, Ohg. nasa, Ags. nasu] 1. the nose, Sn 198, 608. — 2. the trunk (of an elephant) J V.297 (nāga°-uru); Sdhp 153.
-puṭa "nose-cup"; the outside of the nose, the nostril J VI.74; Vism 195 (nāsa°), 264 (nāsa°, but KhA 67 nāsā°), 283 (nāsa°). -vāta wind, i. e. breath from the nostrils J III.276.

Nāsika (adj.) [cp. Sk. nāsikya] belonging to the nose, nasal, in °sota the nostril or nose (orig. "sense of smell") D I.106; Sn p. 108.

Nāsitaka (adj.) [see nāsa & nāseti] one who is ejected Vin IV.140 (of a bhikkhu).

Nāseti [Sk. nāśayati, Caus of nassati, q. v.] 1. to destroy, spoil, ruin; to kill J I.59; II.105, 150; III.279, 418. — 2. to atone for a fault (with abl.) Vin I.85, 86, 173 etc. — Cp. vi°.

Nāha (nt.) [cp. nayhati, naddha] armour J I.358 (sabba°-sannaddha). Cp. onāha.

Ni° [Sk. ni- & niḥ-, insep. prefixes: (a) ni down = Av. ni, cp. Gr. νειός lowland, νείατος the lowest, hindmost; Lat. nīdus (*ni-zdos: place to sit down = nest); Ags. nēol, niđer = E. nether; Goth. nidar = Ohg. nidar; also Sk. nīca, nīpa etc. — (b) niḥ out, prob. fr. *seni & to Lat. sine without]. Nearly all (ultimately prob. all) words under this heading are cpds. with the pref. ni. — A. *Forms*. 1. Pāli ni° combines the two prefixes ni & nis (nir). They are outwardly to be distinguished inasmuch as ni is usually followed by a single consonant (except in forms where double cons. is usually restored in composition, like ni-kkhipati = ni + kṣip; nissita = ni + śri. Sometimes the double cons. is merely graphic or due to analogy, esp. in words where ni- is contrasted with ud- ("up"), as nikkujja > ukkujja, niggilati > uggilati, ninnamati > unnamati). On the other hand a comp[n] with nis is subject to the rules of assimilation, viz. either *doubling* of cons. (nibbhoga = nir-bhoga) where vv is represented by bb (nibbiṇṇa fr. nir-vindati), or lengthening of ni to nī (nīyādeti as well as niyy°; nīharati = nir + har), or *single* cons. in the special cases of r & v (niroga besides nīroga for nirroga, cp. duratta > dūrakkha; nivethetі = nibbetheti, nivāreti = *nivvāreti = nīvāreti). Before a vowel the sandhi-cons. r is restored: nir-aya, nir-upadhi etc. — 2. Both ni & nis are base-prefixes only, & of stable, well-defined character, i. e. never enter comb[ns] with other prefixes as first (modifying) components in verb-function (like saŋ, vi etc.), although nis occurs in such comb[n] in noun-cpds. negating the *whole* term: nir-upadhi, nis-saŋsaya etc. — 3. ni is freq. emphasised by saŋ as saŋni° (tud, dhā, pat, sad); nis most freq. by abhi as abhinis° (nam, pad, vatt, har).
B. *Meanings*. 1. ni (with secondary derivations like nīca "low") is a verb-pref. only, i. e. it characterises action with respect to its direction, which is that of (a) a *downward* motion (opp. abhi & ud); (b) often implying the aim (= down into, on to, cp. Lat. sub in subire, or pref. ad°); or (c) the reverting of an upward motion = back (identical with b); e. g. (a) ni-dhā (put down), °kkhip (throw d.), °guh (hide d.), °ci (heap up), °pad (fall d.), °sad (sit d.); (b) ni-ratta (*at*-tached to), °mant (speak to); °yuj (ap-point), °ved (ad-dress), °sev (be devoted to) etc.; (c) ni-vatt (turn back). — 2. nis (a) as verb-pref. it denotes the directional "out" with further development to "away from, opposite, without," pointing out the finishing, completion or vanishing of an action & through the latter idea often assuming the meaning of the reverse, disappearance or contrary of an action = "un" (Lat. dis-), e. g. nikkhamati (to go out from) opp. pavisati (to enter into), °ccharati (nis to car to go forth), °ddhamati (throw out), °pajjati (result from), °bbattati (vatt spring out from), nīharati (take out), nirodhati (break up, destroy). — (b) as noun-pref. it denotes "being without" or "not having" = E. *-less*, e. g. niccola without clothes, °ttaṇha (without thirst), °ppurisa (without a man), °pphala (without fruit); niccala motion-less, °kkaruṇa (heartless), °ddosa (fault°), °maŋsa (flesh°), °saŋsaya (doubt°) nirattha (useless), °bbhaya (fear°). — Bdhgh evidently takes ni- in meaning of nis only, when defining: ni-saddo abhāvaŋ dīpeti Vism 495.

Nikacca see nikati.

Nikaṭṭha (adj.) [cp. Sk. nikṛṣṭa, ni + kasati] brought down, debased, low. As one kind of puggala (n-kāya + n-citta) A II.137. loc. nikaṭṭhe (adv.) near J III.438 = ThA 105 (v. 33) (= santike J III.438).

Nikaṇṇika (adj.) under (4) ears, secret, cp. catukkaṇṇa J III.124; nt. adv. secretly Vin IV.270, 271.

Nikata (adj.) [Sk. nikṛta, ni + karoti "done down"] deceived, cheated M I.511 (+ vañcita paladdha); S IV.307 (+ vañcita paluddha).

Nikati (f.) [Sk. nikṛti, see prec.] fraud, deceit, cheating D I.5 (= DA I.80 paṭirūpakena vañcanaŋ); III.176; Sn 242 (= nirāsaŋ-karaṇaŋ SnA 286); J I.223; Pv III.9[6] (+ vañcana); Pug 19, 23, 58; VvA 114; PvA 211 (paṭirūpadassanena paresaŋ vikāro). — instr. nikatiyā (metri causa) J I.223, nikatyā J II.183, nikacca S I.24. Cp. nekatika.

Nikanta (adj.) [Sk. nikṛtta & nikṛntita (cp. Divy 537, 539), ni + kantati[2]] cut, (ab-)razed M I.364 (of a fleshless bone).

Nikantati [Sk. ni-kṛntati, see kantati[2]] to cut down, to cut up, cut off PvA 210 (piṭṭhi-maŋsāni the flesh of the back, v. l. SS for ukkant°); Pgdp 29.

Nikanti (f.) [Sk. nikānti, ni + kamati] desire, craving, longing for, wish Th 1, 20; Ps II.72, 101; Dhs 1059, 1136; Vism 239, 580; DhsA 369; DhA IV.63; DA I.110; Dāvs III.40.

Nikara [Sk. nikara, ni + karoti] a multitude Dāvs V.25 (jātipuppha°).

Nikaraṇā (f. or is it °aŋ?) = nikati (fraud) Pug 19, 23 (as syn. of māyā).

Nikaroti [Sk. nikaroti, ni+ karoti] to bring down, humiliate, to deceive, cheat Sn 138 (nikubbetha Pot. = vañceyya KhA 247). pp. nikata (q. v.).

Nikasa [Sk. nikasa, ni+ kasati] a whetstone Dāvs III.87 (°opala).

Nikasāva (adj.) [Sk. niṣkaṣāya nis+ kasāva see kasāya 2[d]] free from impurity Vin I.3; opp. anikkasāva (q. v.) Dh 9≈.

Nikāma [Vedic nikāma, ni+ kāma] desire, pleasure, longing: only in cpds.; see nanikāma.
-kāra read by Kern (*Toev.* 174) at Th 1, 1271 for na kāmakāra but unjustified (see SnA on Sn 351); -lābhin gaining pleasure S II.278; M I.354; III.110; A II.23, 36; Pug 11, 12; Vbh 332.

Nikāmanā (f.) = nikanti, Dhs 1059.

Nikāmeti [Sk. ni-kāmayati, ni+ kāmeti] to crave, desire, strive after, ppr nikāmayaŋ S I.122, & nikāmayamāna Vin II.108. Cp. nikanta & nikanti.

Nikāya [Sk. nikāya, ni+ kāya] collection (" body ") assemblage, class, group; 1. *generally* (always -°): eka° one class of beings DhsA 66; tiracchāna° the animal kingdom S III.152; deva° the assembly of the gods, the gods D II.261 (60); M I.102; S VI.180; A III.249; IV.461; PvA 136; satta° the world of beings, the animate creation, a class of living beings S II.2, 42, 44; M I.49 (tesaŋ tesaŋ sattānaŋ tamhi tamhi s.—nikāye of all beings in each class); Vbh 137; PvA 134. — 2. *especially* the coll. of Buddhist Suttas, as the 5 sections of the Suttanta Piṭaka, viz. Dīgha°, Majjhima°, Saŋyutta°, Anguttara° (referred to as D.M.S.A. in Dictionary-quotations), Khuddaka°; enum[d] PvA 2; Anvs p. 35; DhA II.95 (dhammāsanaŋ āruyha pañcahi nikāyehi atthañ ca kāraṇañ ca ākaḍḍhitvā). The *five* Nikāyas are enum[d] also at Vism 711; *one* is referred to at SnA 195 (pariyāpuṇāti master by heart). See further details under piṭaka. Cp. nekāyika.

Nikāra [Sk. nikāra in diff. meaning, ni+ kāra] service, humility J III.120 (nikāra-pakāra, prob. to be read nipaccākāra, q. v.).

Nikāsa (n.-adj.) [ni+ kaś] appearance; adj. of appearance, like J v.87 (-°), corresp. to °avakāsa.

Nikāsin (adj.) [cp. Sk. nikāśin; fr. ni+ kāsati] " shining," resembling, like J III.320 (aggi-nikāsinā suriyena).

Nikiṇṇa (adj.) [Sk. *nikīrṇa, pp. ni+ kirati, cp. kiraṇa] " strewn down into," hidden away, sheltered J III.529.

Nikīḷita (adj.) [Sk. *nikrīḍita, pp. of nikrīḍayati, ni+ kīḷati] engrossed in play J VI.31.

Nikīḷitāvin (adj.) [fr. ni-kīḷati] playful, playing or dallying with (c. loc.), finding enjoyment in S I.9 (a° kāmesu); IV.110 (id.).

Nikujja see nikkujja, q. v. also for nikujjita which is more correctly spelt k than kk (cp. Trenckner, Preface to Majjhima Nikāya & see ni° A 1).

Nikujjati [ni+ kujjati, see kujja & cp. nikkujja] to be bent down on, i. e. to attach importance to, to lay weight on D I.53 (as vv. ll. to be preferred to text reading nikkujj°, cp. nikujja); DA I.160 (nikk°).

Nikuñja [Sk. nikuñja, ni+ kuñja] a hollow down, a glen, thicket Dāvs IV.32.

Nikūjati [ni+ kūjati " to sing on "] 1. to chirp, warble, hum Th 1, 1270 (nikūjaŋ): ThA 211 (nikūji). — 2. to twang, jingle, rustle J III.323. — pp. nikūjita. — Cp. abhi°.

Nikūjita [see nikūjati] sung forth, warbled out Th 2, 261.

Nikūṭa [ni+ kūṭa to kūṭa²] a corner, top, climax J I.278 (arahatta°, where usually arahattena kūṭaŋ etc.); DA I.307 (id.).

Niketa [Sk. niketa settlement, ni+ cināti] 1. house, abode Dh 91 (= ālaya DhA II.170). — 2. (fig.) company, association. (In this sense it seems to be interpreted as belonging to ketu " sign, characteristic, mark," and niketa-sārin would have to be taken as " following the banner or flag of . . .," i. e. belonging or attached to, i. e. a follower of, one who is devoted to:) a° not living in company, having no house Sn 207; Miln 244 (+ nirālaya).
-vāsin (a°) not living in a house, not associating with anybody Miln 201; -sayana = °vāsin Miln 361; -sārin (a°) " wandering homeless " or " not living in company," i. e. not associating with, not a follower of . . . S III.9 sq. = Nd¹ 198; Sn 844 = S III.9; SnA 255 = S III.10; Sn 970 (= Nd¹ 494 q. v.).

Niketavant (adj.) [to niketa] parting company with Miln 288 (kamma°).

Niketin (adj.) having an abode, being housed, living in Sn 422 (kosalesu); J III.432 (duma-sākhā-niketinī f.).

Nikkankha (adj.) [Sk. niḥśanka, nis+ kankha, adj. of kankhā, cp. kankhin] not afraid, fearless, not doubting, confident, sure J I.58. Cp. nissaŋsaya.

Nikkankhā (f.) [Sk. niḥśankā, nis+ kankhā] fearlessness, state of confidence, trust (cp. nibbicikicchā) S v.221.

Nikkaḍḍhati [Sk. niṣkarṣati, nis+ kasati, cp. kaḍḍhati] to throw out Vin IV.274 (Caus. nikkaḍḍhāpeti ibid.); J I.116; II.440; SnA 192. pp. nikkaḍḍhita.

Nikkaḍḍhanā (f.) throwing out, ejection J III.22 (a°); v.234. (= niddhamanā).

Nikkaḍḍhita (adj.) [Sk. *niṣkarṣita see nikkaḍḍhati] thrown out J II.103 (gehā); PvA 179 (read ḍḍh for ḍḍ).

Nikkaṇṭaka (adj.) [Sk. niṣkaṇṭaka, nis+ kaṇṭaka] free from thorns or enemies Miln 250; cp. akaṇṭaka.

Nikkaddama (adj.) [nis+ kaddama] unstained, not dirty, free from impunity DA I.226.

Nikkama (n.-adj.) [Sk. niṣkrama; nis+ kama] exertion, strength, endurance. The orig. meaning of " going forth " is quite obliterated by the fig. meaning (cp. nikkhamati & nekkhamma) A I.4; III.214; Vv 18⁷ (= viriya VvA 96); Dhs 13, 22, 219, 571; Vism 132; Miln 244 (+ ārambha). — (adj.) strong in (-°), enduring, exerting oneself S I.194 (tibba°); v.66, 104 sq.; Sn 68 (daḷha°, cp. Nd² under padhānavā), 542 (sacca°).

Nikkamati [Sk. niṣkramati, nis+ kamati, see also nikkhamati & nekkhamma] to go out, to go forth; in fig. meaning: to leave behind lust, evil & the world, to get rid of " kāma " (craving), to show right exertion & strength Miln 245 (+ arabhati) + S I.156 (kkh).

Nikkaya [cp. Sk. niṣkraya, nis+ kaya cp. nikkiṇāti] " buying off," redemption J VI.577.

Nikkaruṇa (adj.) [nis+ karuṇa, adj. of karuṇā] without compassion, heartless Sn 244 (= sattānaŋ anatthakāma); Sdhp 508.

Nikkarunatā (f.) = following Vism 314.

Nikkaruṇā (f.) [Sk. niṣkaruṇatā; nis+ karuṇā] heartlessness PvA 55.

Nikkasāva see nikasāva.

Nikkāma (adj.) [Sk. niṣkāma, nis+kāma] without craving or lust, desireless Sn 1131 (=akāmakāmin Nd² 340; pahīnakāma SnA 605 with v. l.: nikkāma). Cp. next.

Nikkāmin (adj.) [nis+kāmin]=nikkāma Sn 228 (=kata-nikkhamana KhA 184).

Nikkāraṇā (abl.=adv.) [Sk. niṣkāraṇā, nis+kāraṇaŋ] without reason, without cause or purpose Sn 75 (=akāraṇā ahetu Nd² 341).

Nikkāsa is Bdhgh's reading for ikkāsa (q. v.) Vin II.151, with C. on p. 321.

Nikkiṇati [Sk. niṣkriṇāti, nis+kiṇāti] to buy back, to redeem J VI.576, 585; Miln 284.

Nikkiṇṇa (adj.) [Sk. niṣkīrṇa, nis+kiṇṇa, see kiraṇa] spread out, spread before, ready (for eating) J VI.182 (=ṭhapita Com.).

Nikkilesa [nis+kilesa] freedom fr. moral blemish Nd¹ 340=Nd² under pucchā Nd² 185; as adj. pure, unstained DhA IV.192=SnA 469 (=anāvila).

Nikkujja (adj.) [ni+kubja, better spelling is nikujja, see nikkujjati] bent down, i. e. head forward, lying on one's face; upset, thrown over A I.130; S V.48; Pv IV.7⁷ (k); Pug 31. Opp. ukkujja.

Nikkujjati [for nikujjati (q. v.) through analogy with opp. ukkujjati. Etym. perhaps to kujja humpback, Sk. kubja, but better with Kern, *Toev.* I. p. 175= Sk. nyubjati, influenced by kubja with regard to k.] to turn upside down, to upset Vin II.113; A IV.344 (pattaŋ). — pp. nikkujjita.

Nikkujjita (adj.) [pp. of nikkujjati; often (rightly) spelt nikujjita, q. v.] lying face downward, overturned, upset, fallen over, stumbled Vin I.16; D I.85, 110; 147, M I.24 (k.); A I.173; III.238; Th 2, 28, 30 (k.); J III.277; SnA 155 (=adhomukha-ṭhapita); DA I.228.

Nikkuha (adj.) [nis+kuha] without deceit, not false A II.26=It 113; Sn 56; Nd² 342.

Nikkodha (adj.) [nis+kodha] without anger, free from anger J IV.22.

Nikkha (m. & nt.) [Vedic niṣka; cp. Oir. nasc (ring), Ohg. nusca (bracelet)] 1. a golden ornament for neck or breast, a ring J II.444; VI.577. — 2. (already Vedic) a golden coin or a weight of gold (cp. a "pound sterling"), equal to 15 suvaṇṇas (VvA 104=suvaṇṇassa pañcadasa-dharaṇaŋ nikkhan ti vadanti) S II.234 (suvaṇṇa° & singi°); J I.84 (id.); A IV.120 (suvaṇṇa°); Vv 20⁸=43⁸ (v. l. SS nekkha) J VI.180; Miln 284. suvaṇṇa-nikkha-sataŋ (100 gold pieces) J I.376; IV.97; V.58; °sahassaŋ (1000) J V.67; DhA I.393. — See also nekkha.

Nikkhanta (adj.) [pp. of nis+kamati, see nikkhamati] gone out, departed from (c. abl.), gone away; also med. going out, giving up, fig. leaving behind, resigning, renouncing (fusing in meaning with kanta¹ of kāmyati =desireless) S I.185 (agārasmā anagāriyaŋ); Sn 991 (Kapilavatthumhā n. lokanāyako); J I.149; II.153; IV.364 (°bhikkhā, in sense of nikkhāmita°, v. l. nikkhitta°, perhaps preferable, expl^d p. 366 nibaddha°=designed for, given to); SnA 605 (fig.; as v. l. for nikkāma); DhA II.39; PvA 61 (bahi); Nd² under nissita; Nd² 107 (free, unobstructed).

Nikkhama (adj.) [cp. Sk. niṣkrama] going out from PvA 80 (nāsikāya n.-mala). dun° at ThA 72 is to be read dunnikkhaya, as indicated by vv. ll. See the latter.

Nikkhamati [Sk. niṣkramati, nis+kamati] to go forth from, to come out of (c. abl.), to get out, issue forth, depart, fig. to leave the household life behind (agārā n.), to retire from the world (cp. abhinikkhamati etc.), or to give up evil desire. — (a) lit. (often with bahi outside, out; opp. pavisati to enter into: A V.195). D II.14 (mātu kucchismā); J I.52 (mātukucchito). Imper. nikkhama Pv I.10³; ppr. nikkhamanto J I.52; II.153; III.26 (mukhato); PvA 90; aor. nikkhami J II.154; III.188; fut. °issati J II.154; ger. nikkhamma J I.51, 61 (fig.) & nikkhamitvā J I.16, 138 (fig.), 265; III.26; IV.449 (n. pabbajissāmi); PvA 14, 19 (fig.) 67 (gāmato), 74 (id.); inf. nikkhamituŋ J I.61 (fig.); II.104; Pv I.10² (bahi n.); grd. nikkhamitabba Vin I.47. — (b) fig. (see also nikkamati, & cp. nekkhamma & BSk. niṣkramati in same meaning, e. g. Divy 68 etc.) S I.156 (ārabbhati+)=Miln 245 (where nikkamati); J I.51 (agārā), 61 (mahābhinikkhamanaŋ "the great renunciation"), PvA 19 (id.). — pp. nikkhanta; caus. nikkhameti (q. v.).

Nikkhamana [BSk. niṣkramaṇa, to nikkhamati] going out, departing J II.153; VvA 71 (opp. pavesana); fig. renunciation KhA 184 (kata° as adj.=nikkāmin). See also abhi°.

Nikkhameti & **Nikkhāmeti** [Caus. of nikkhamati] to make go out or away, to bring out or forth S II.128; J I.264, II.112. — pp. nikkhāmita J III.99 (+nicchuddha, thrown out, in expl^n of nibbāpita; v. l. BB. nikaḍhāpita).

Nikkhaya (adj.) [Sk. *niḥkṣaya, nis+khaya] liable to destruction, able to be destroyed, in dun° hard to destroy J IV.449 (=dun-nikkaḍḍhiya Com.); also to be read (v. l.) at Th I, 72 for dunnikkhama. Cp. nikhīṇa.

Nikkhitta (adj.) [Sk. nikṣipta, see nikkhipati] laid down, lying; put down into, set in, arranged; in cpds. (°-) having laid down=freed of, rid of D II.14 (maṇi-ratanaŋ vatthe n. set into); It 13 (sagge: put into heaven); J I.53, 266; Pv III.6⁸; Miln 343 (agga° put down as the highest, i. e. of the highest praise; cp. BSk. agra-nikṣipta Lal. V. 167); PvA 148 (dhana n.=collected, v. l. SS. nikkita). nikkhitta-daṇḍa (adj.) not using a weapon (cp. daṇḍa) S I.141 etc.; nikkhitta-dhura unyoked, freed of the yoke A I.71; III.108; cp. DhsA 145; — su° well set, well arranged A II.147 sq. (°assa pada-vyañjanassa attho sunnayo hoti); opp. dun° A I.59; Nett 21.

Nikkhittaka (adj.-n.) [fr. nikkhitta] one to whose charge something has been committed Dpvs IV.5 (agga° thera: original depositary of the Faith).

Nikkhipati [Sk. nikṣipati, ni+khipati] 1. to lay down (carefully), to put down, to lay (an egg) Vin II.114; It 13, 14 (Pot. nikkhipeyya); Pug 34; J I.49 (aṇḍakaŋ). — 2. to lay aside, to put away Vin I.46 (patta-cīvaraŋ); A I.206 (daṇḍaŋ to discard the weapon; see daṇḍa); Mhvs 14, 10 (dhanu-saraŋ). — 3. to eliminate, get rid of, give up Pv II.6¹⁶ (dehaŋ to get rid of the body); DhsA 344 (vitthāra-desanaŋ). — 4. to give in charge, to deposit, entrust, save Pug 26; VvA 33 (sahassa-thavikaŋ). — aor. nikkhipi D II.161 (Bhagavato sarīraŋ) J II.104, 111, 416; fut. °issati D II.157 (samussayaŋ); ger. °itvā M III.156 (cittaŋ); J II.416; VI.366; grd. °itabba Vin I.46. — pp. nikkhitta (q. v.). — Caus. nikkhipāpeti to cause to be laid down, to order to be put down etc. PvA 215 (gosīsaṭṭhiŋ). Cp. abhi°.

Nikkhepa [Sk. nikṣepa, see nikkhipati] putting down, laying down; casting off, discarding, elimination; giving up, renunciation; abstract or summary treatment DhsA 6, 344 (see under mātikā); in grammar: pada° the setting of the verse; i. e. rules of composition (Miln 381). Vin I.16 (pādukānaŋ=footprint, mark, impression); J III.243 (dhura° giving up one's office or charge), I.236 (sarīra °ŋ kāresi had the body laid out); Dpvs XVII.109 (id.). Vism 618 (=cuti); DhA II.98 (sarīra°); DA I.50 (sutta°); DhsA 344; Miln 91.

Nikkhepana (nt.) = nikkhepa S III.26 (bhāra° getting rid of the load, opp. bhārādānaŋ); Miln 356 (= comparison); Vism 236 (deha°).

Nikhanati & **Nikhaṇati** [Sk. nikhanati, ni+ khanai] to dig into, to bury, to erect, to cover up Vin II.116; III.78 (akkhiŋ = cover the eye, as a sign); J V.434 = DhA IV.197 (id.); D II.127 (ŋ); J I.264; SnA 519 (ŋ, to bury). — pp. nikhāta.

Nikhāta [pp. of nikhaṇati] 1. dug, dug out (of a hole), buried (of a body) SnA 519. — 2. dug in, erected (of a post) Sn 28; DhA II.181 (nagara-dvāre n. indakhīla). See also a°.

Nikhādana (nt.) [Sk. *nikhādana, ni+ khādati, cp. khādana] "eating down," a sharp instrument, a spade or (acc. to Morris, *J.P.T.S.* 1884, 83) a chisel Vin III.149; IV.211; J II.405 (so read for khādana); IV.344; V.45.

Nikhila (adj.) [Sk. nikhila cp. khila] all, entire, whole Dāvs V.40 (°loka v. l. sakala°).

Nikhīṇa (adj.) [nis+ khīṇa] having or being lost J VI.499 (°patta without wings, deprived of its wings).

Niga in gavaya-gokaṇṇa-nig-âdīnaŋ DhsA 331 is misprint for miga.

Nigacchati [Sk. nigacchati, ni+ gacchati] to go down to, to "undergo," incur, enter, come to; to suffer esp. with dukkhaŋ & similar expressions of affliction or punishment S IV.70 (dukkhaŋ); M I.337 sq. (id.); A I.251 (bandhanaŋ); Dh 69 (dukkhaŋ = vindati, paṭilabhati DhA II.50), 137; Nd[2] 199[4] (maraṇaŋ+ maraṇamattam pi dukkhaŋ) Pv IV.7[7] (pret. nigacchiṭṭha = pāpuṇi PvA 266).

Nigaṇṭha [BSk. nirgrantha (Divy 143, 262 etc.) "freed from all ties," nis+ gaṇṭhi. This is the customary (correct ?) etym. Prk. niggantha, cp. Weber, *Bhagavati* p. 165] a member of the Jain order (see M I.370-375, 380 & cp. jaṭila) Vin I.233 (Nātaputta, the head of that Order, cp. D I.57; also Sīho senāpati n-sāvako); S I.78, 82 (°bhikkhā); A I.205 sq. (°uposatha), cp. 220; II.196 (°sāvaka); III.276, 383; V.150 (dasahi asaddhammehi samannāgata); Sn 381; Ud 65 (jaṭilā, n., acelā, ekasāṭā, paribbājakā); J II.262 (object to eating flesh); DA I.162; DhA I.440; III.489; VvA 29 (n. nāma samaṇajāti). — f. nigaṇṭhī D I.54 (nigaṇṭhi-gabbha).

Nigati (f.) [ni+ gati, q. v.] destiny, condition, behaviour J VI.238. See also niyati & cp. niggatika.

Nigama [Sk. nigama, fr. nigacchati = a meeting-place or market, cp. E. moot-hall = market hall] a small town, market town (opp. janapada); often comb[d] with gāma (see gāma 2) Vin I.110 (°sīma), 188 (°kathā), 197 (Setakaṇṇika°); D I.7 (°kathā), 101 (°sāmanta), 193, 237; M I.429, 488; Pv II.13[18]; J VI.330; PvA 111 (Asitañjana°, v. l. BB nagara). Cp. negama.

Nigamana (nt.) [Sk. nigamana] quotation, explanation, illustration Vism 427 (°vacana quotation); PvA 255 (perhaps we should read niyamana); conclusion, e. g. Paṭṭh.A 366; VbhA 523.

Nigaḷa [Sk. nigaḍa, ni+ gaḷa, cp. gala[3]] an (iron) chain for the feet J I.394; II.153; VI.64 (here as "bracelet").

Nigāḷhika (better v. l. nigāḷhita) [Sk. nigāḍhita; ni+ gāḍhita, see gāḷha[2]] sunk down into, immersed in Th I, 558 (gūthakūpe).

Nigūḷha [Sk. nigūḍha, but BSk. nirgūḍha (Divy 256); ni+ gūḷha] hidden (down), concealed; (n.) a secret J I.401; Dāvs III.39.

Nigūhati [Sk. nigūhati, ni+ gūhati] to cover up, conceal, hide J I.286; III.392; IV.203; Pv III.4[3] (≈ parigūhāmi, v. l. SS guyhāmi). pp. nigūḷha (q. v.).

Nigūhana (nt.) [Sk. nigūhana, see nigūhati] covering, concealing, hiding VvA 71.

Niggacchati [Sk. nirgacchati, nis+ gacchati] to go out or away, disappear; to proceed from, only in pp. niggata (q. v.); at J VI.504 as ni°.

Nigganthi (adj.) [Sk. nirgranthi, nis+ gaṇṭhi, cp. also nigaṇṭha] free from knots (said of a sword) Miln 105. See also nighaṇḍu.

Niggaṇhāti [Sk. nigṛhṇāti, ni+ gaṇhāti] 1. to hold back, restrain Dh 326; J IV.97; Miln 184; Vism 133. — Opp. paggaṇhāti. — 2. to rebuke, censure (c. instr.) A III.187; J III.222; Miln 9 (musāvādena); DhA I.29. — ger. niggayha, pp. niggahīta (q. v.). Cp. abhi°.

Niggata (adj.) [Sk. nirgata, see niggacchati] 1. going out, proceeding from (abl.): dahato niggatā nadī (a river issuing from a lake) PvA 152. — 2. (= nigata? or = nis+ gata "of ill fate") destined, fateful; miserable, unfortunate PvA 223 (°kamma = punishment in expl[n] of niyassa kamma, v. l. SS. nigaha for niggata; see also niya & niyata); Sdhp 165 (of niraya = miserable), cp. niggatika & niggamana.

Niggatika [Sk. *nirgatika, nis+ gati-ka] having a bad "gati" or fate, ill-fated, bad, unfortunate, miserable J III.538 (v. l. BB as gloss, nikkāruṇika); IV.48 (v. l. BB nikatika).

Niggama (n.) in logic, deduction, conclusion. *Pts. of Controversy* p. 1.

Niggamana [Sk. *nirgamana, of niggacchati] 1. going away DA I.94. — 2. result, fate, consequence, outcome Sdhp 172, 173 (dun°). — 3. (log.) conclusion Kvu 4.

Niggayha-vādin (adj.) [see niggaṇhāti] one who speaks rebukingly, censuring, reproving, resenting Dh 76 (see expl[n] in detail at DhA II.107 & cp. M III.118).

Niggayhati [Sk. nigṛhyate, ni+ gayhati, Pass. of niggaṇhāti] to be seized by (?), to be blamed for DhA I.295 (cittaŋ dukkhena n., in expl[n] of dunniggaha).

Niggaha [Sk. nigraha, ni+ gaha[2]; see niggaṇhāti] 1. restraint, control, rebuke, censure, blame Vin II.196; A I.98, 174; V.70; J V.116 (opp. paggaha); VI.371 (id.); Miln 28, 45, 224. — dun° hard to control (citta) Dh 35 (cp. expl. at DhA I.295). — 2. (log.) refutation Kvu 3.

Niggahaṇa (adj.) [Sk. *nirgahaṇa, cp. nirgṛha homeless; nis+ gahaṇa] without acquisitions, i. e. poor J II.367 (v. l. BB. as gloss nirāhāra).

Niggahaṇatā (f.) [abstr. fr. ni+ gṛh, cp. next] restraint Vism 134 (cittassa). Opp. pagg°.

Niggahīta (adj.) [Sk. nigṛhīta, but cp. Divy 401: nigṛhīta; ni+ gahita] restrained, checked, rebuked, reproved S III.12; A I.175 (aniggahīto dhammo); J VI.493.

Niggāhaka (adj.-n.) [ni+ gāhaka, see niggaṇhāti] one who rebukes, oppresses, oppressor Sn 118 (= bādhaka SnA 178, with v. l. ghātaka); J IV.362 (= balisādhaka Com.).

Niggilati (niggalati) [Sk. nigirati, ni+ gilati] to swallow down (opp. uggilati to spit out, throw up) J IV.392 (sic as v. l.; text niggalati).

Nigguṇa (adj.) [Sk. nirguṇa, nis+ guṇa] devoid of good qualities, bad Miln 180.

Nigguṇḍi (f.) [Sk. nirguṇḍī, of obscure etym.] a shrub (Vitex Negundo) Miln 223 (°phala); Vism 257 (°puppha).

Niggumba (adj.) [Sk. *nirgulma, nis+ gumba] free from bushes, clear J I.187; Miln 3.

Nigghātana (nt.) [Sk. nirghātana, nis+ ghātana, but cp. nighāta] destruction, killing, rooting out Sn 1085 (taṇhā°; SnA 576 = vināsana); Nd[2] 343 (v. l. nighātana).

Nigghosa [Sk. nirghoṣa, nis+ghosa] 1. "shouting out," sound; fame, renown; speech, utterance, proclamation; word of reproach, blame S I.190; A IV.88 (appa° noiseless, lit. of little or no noise); Sn 719, 818 (=nindāvacana SnA 537), 1061 J I.64; VI.83; Vv 5[5]; Nd[1] 150; Nd[2] 344; Dhs 621; VvA 140 (madhura°); 334 (in quotation appa-sadda, appa°); Sdhp 245. — 2. (adj.) noiseless, quiet, still Sn 959 (=appasadda appanigghosa Nd[1] 467).

Nigrodha [Sk. nyagrodha; Non-Aryan ?] the banyan or Indian fig-tree, Ficus Indica, usually as cpd. °rukkha Vin IV.35; D II.4; Sn 272; J III.188 (r.) DhA II.14 (r.); PvA 5 (r.) 112, 244; Sdhp 270; -pakka the fruit of the fig-tree Vism 409. -parimaṇḍala the round or circumference of the banyan D II.18; III.144, 162.

Nigha[1] (nīgha) (adj.-n.) is invented by Com. & scholiasts to explain the comb[n] anigha (anīgha sporadic, e. g. S V.57). But this should be divided an-īgha instead of a-nīgha. — (m.) rage, trembling, confusion, only in formula rāgo n. doso n. moho n. explaining the adj. anīgha. Thus at S IV.292 =Nd[2] 45; S V.57. — (adj.) anīgha not trembling, undisturbed, calm [see etym. under īgha=Sk. ṛgh of ṛghāyati to tremble, rage, rave] S I.54; IV.291; J V.343. Otherwise always comb[d] with nirāsa: S I.12=23, 141; Sn 1048, 1060, 1078. Expl[d] correctly at SnA 590 by rāgādi-īgha-virahita. Spelling anīgha J III.443 (Com. niddukkha); Pv IV.1[34] (+nirāsa; expl[d] by niddukkha PvA 230). anīgha also at It 97 (+chinnasaŋsaya); Ud 76; Dh 295 (v. l. anīggha; expl[d] by niddukkha DhA III.454).

Nigha[2] (nt.) [prob. ni+gha=Sk. °gha of hanati (see also P. °gha), to kill; unless abstracted from anigha as in prec. nigha[1]] killing, destruction Th 2, 491 (=maraṇasampāpana ThA 288).

Nighaŋsa [Sk. nigharṣa] rubbing, chafing DhsA 263, 308.

Nighaŋsati [Sk. nigharṣati, ni+ghaŋsati[1]] 1. to rub, rub against, graze, chafe Vin II.133; Vism 120; DhA I.396. — 2. to polish up, clean J II.418; III.75.

Nighaŋsana (nt.) [Sk. nigharṣana]=nighaŋsa Miln 215.

Nighaṇḍu [Sk. nighaṇṭu, dial. for nirgrantha from grathnāti (see gaṇṭhi & ghaṭṭana), orig. disentanglement, unravelling, i. e. explanation; cp. nigganṭhi, which is a variant of the same word. — BSk. nighaṇṭa (Divy 619; AvŚ II.19), Prk. nighaṇṭu] an explained word or a word expl[n], vocabulary, gloss, usually in ster. formula marking the accomplishments of a learned Brahmin "sanighaṇḍu-keṭubhānaŋ . . . padako" (see detail under keṭubha) D I.88; A I.163, 166; III.223; Sn p. 105; Miln 10. Bdhgh's expl[n] is quoted by Trenckner, *Notes* p. 65.

Nighāta [Sk. nighāta, ni+ghāta] striking down, suppressing, destroying, killing M I.430; Nett 189. Cp. nighāti.

Nighāti [ni+ghāti] "slaying or being slain," defeat, loss (opp. ugghāti) Sn 828. Cp. nighāta.

Nicaya [Sk. nicaya, ni+caya, cp. nicita] heaping up, accumulation; wealth, provisions S I.93, 97; Vin V.172 (°sannidhi). See also necayika.

Nicita (adj.) [Sk. nicita, ni+cita, of nicināti] heaped up, full, thick, massed, dense Th 2, 480 (of hair); PvA 221 (ussanna uparūpari nicita, of Niraya).

Nicula [Sk. nicula] a plant (Barringtonia acutangula) VvA 134.

Nicca (adj.) [Vedic nitya, adj.-formation fr. ni, meaning "downward"=onward, on and on; according to Grassmann (*Wtb. z. Rig Veda*) originally "inwardly, homely"] constant, continuous, permanent D III.31; S I.142; II.109, 198; IV.24 sq., 45, 63; A II.33, 52; V.210; Ps II.80; Vbh 335, 426. In chain of synonyms: nicca dhuva sassata avipariṇāmadhamma D I.21; S III.144, 147; see below anicca. — nt. adv. niccaŋ perpetually, constantly, always (syn. sadā) M I.326; III.271; Sn 69, 220, 336; Dh 23, 109, 206, 293; J I.290; III.26, 190; Nd[2] 345 (=dhuvakālaŋ); PvA 32, 55, 134. — Far more freq. as anicca (adj.; aniccaŋ nt. n.) unstable, impermanent, inconstant; (nt.) evanescence, inconstancy, impermanence. — The emphatic assertion of impermanence (continuous change of condition) is a prominent axiom of the Dhamma, & the realization of the evanescent character of all things mental or material is one of the primary conditions of attaining right knowledge (: anicca-saññaŋ manasikaroti to ponder over the idea of impermanence S II.47; III.155; V.132; Ps II.48 sq., 100; PvA 62 etc. — kāye anicc' ânupassin realizing the impermanence of the body (together with vayânupassin & nirodha°) S IV.211; V.324, 345; Ps II.37, 45 sq., 241 sq. See anupassanā). In this import anicca occurs in many combinations of similar terms, all characterising change, its consequences & its meaning, esp. in the famous triad "aniccaŋ dukkhaŋ anattā" (see dukkha II.2), e. g. S III.41, 67, 180; IV.28 (sabbaŋ), 85 sq., 106 sq.; 133 sq. Thus anicca addhuva appāyuka cavanadhamma D I.21. anicca+dukkha S II.53 (yad aniccaŋ taŋ dukkhaŋ); IV.28, 31, V.345; A IV.52 (anicce dukkhasaññā); M I.500 (+roga etc.); Nd[2] 214 (id. cp. roga). anicca dukkha vipariṇāmadhamma (of kāmā) D I.36. aniccasaññī anattasaññī A IV.353; etc. — Opposed to this ever-fluctuating impermanence is Nibbāna (q. v.), which is therefore marked with the attributes of constancy & stableness (cp. dhuva, sassata amata, vipariṇāma). — See further for ref. S II.244 sq. (saḷāyatanaŋ a.), 248 (dhātuyo); III.102 (rūpa etc.); IV.131, 151; A II.33, 52; V.187 sq., 343 sq.; Sn 805, Ps I.191; II.28 sq., 80, 106; Vbh 12 (rūpa etc.), 70 (dvādasâyatanāni), 319 (viññāṇā), 324 (khandhā), 373; PvA 60 (=ittara).

-kālaŋ (adv.) constantly Nd[2] 345; -dāna a perpetual gift D I.144 (cp. DA I.302); -bhatta a continuous food-supply (for the bhikkhus) J I.178; VvA 92; PvA 54; -bhattika one who enjoys a continuous supply of food (as charity) Vin II.78; III.237 (=dhuva-bhattika); IV.271; -saññā (& adj. saññin) the consciousness or idea of permanence (adj. having etc.) A II.52; III.79, 334; IV.13, 145 sq.; Nett 27; -sīla the uninterrupted observance of good conduct VvA 72; PvA 256.

Niccatā (f.) [abstr. to nicca] continuity, permanence, only as a° changeableness, impermanence S I.61, 204; III.43; IV.142 sq., 216, 325.

Niccatta (nt.)=niccatā Vism 509.

Niccamma [Sk. niścarman, nis+camma] without skin, excoriated, in °ŋ karoti to flog skinless, to beat the skin off J III.281. niccamma-gāvī "a skinless cow," used in a well-known simile at S II.99, referred to at Vism 341 & 463.

Niccala (adj.) [Sk. niścala, nis+cala] motionless J IV.2; PvA 95.

Niccittaka (adj.) [Sk. niścitta, nis+citta (ka)] thoughtless J II.298.

Niccola (adj.) [nis-cola] without dress, naked PvA 32 (=nagga).

Nicchanda (adj.) [nis+chanda] without desire or excitement J I.7.

Nicchaya [Sk. niścaya, nis+caya of cināti] discrimination, conviction, certainty; resolution, determination J I.441 (°mitta a firm friend); DhsA 133 (adhimokkha=its paccupaṭṭhāna): SnA 60 (daḷha° adj. of firm resolution). See vi°.

Niccharaṇa (nt.) [fr. niccharati] emanation, sending out, expansion, efflux Vism 303.

Niccharati [Sk. niścarati, nis+carati] to go out or forth from, to rise, sound forth, come out It 75 (devasadda); Vv 38²; J I.53, 176; DhA I.389; VvA 12, 37 (saddā). — Caus. nicchāreti to make come out from, to let go forth, get rid of, emit, utter, give out D I.53 (anattamanavācaṃ a° not utter a word of discontent); J III.127; V.416 (madhurassaraŋ); Pug 33; Miln 259 (garahaŋ); Dāvs I.28 (vācaŋ).

Nicchāta [Sk. *niḥpsāta, nis+chāta] having no hunger, being without cravings, stilled, satisfied. Ep. of an Arahant always in combⁿ with nibbuta or parinibbuta: S III.26 (taṇhaŋ abbuyha); IV.204 (vedanānaŋ khayā); M I.341; 412, A IV.410; V.65 (sītibhūta); Sn 707 (aniccha), 735, 758; It 48 (esanānaŋ khayā); Th 2, 132 (abbūḷhasalla). — Expl^d at Ps II.243 by nekkhammena kāmacchandato n.; arahattamaggena sabbakilesehi n. muccati.

Nicchādeti see nicchodeti.

Nicchāreti Caus. of niccharati, q. v.

Nicchita (adj.) [Sk. niścita, nis+cita, see nicchināti] determined, convinced Mhvs 7, 19.

Nicchināti [Sk. niścinoti, nis+cināti] to discriminate, consider, investigate, ascertain; pot. **niccheyya** Sn 785 (expl^d by nicchinitvā vinicchinitvā etc. Nd¹ 76); Dh 256 (gloss K vinicchaye). — pp. **nicchita.**

Nicchuddha (adj.) [Sk. niḥkṣubdha, nis+chuddha, see nicchubhati] thrown out J III.99 (=nibbāpita, nikkhāmita); Miln 130.

Nicchubhati [Sk. *niḥkṣubhati, nis+khubhati or chubhati, cp. chuddha & khobha, also nicchodeti & upacchubhati and see Trenckner, Miln pp. 423, 424] to throw out J III.512 (=nīharati Com.; v. l. nicchurāti); Miln 187. — pp. nicchuddha q. v.

Nicchubhana (nt.) [see nicchubhati] throwing out, ejection, being an outcaste Miln 357.

Nicchodeti (& v. l. **nicchādeti**) [shows a confusion of two roots, which are both of Prk. origin, viz. **chaḍḍ** & **choṭ,** the former=P. chaḍḍeti, the latter=Sk. kṣodayati or BSk. chorayati, Apabhraŋśa chollai; with which cp. P. chuddha] to shake or throw about, only in phrase odhunāti nidhunāti nicchodeti at S III.155=M I.230=374=A III.365, where S has correct reading (v. l. °choṭeti); M has °chādeti (v. l. °chodeti); A has °chedeti (v. l. °choreti, °chāreti; gloss nippoṭeti). The C. on A III.365 has: nicchedetī ti bāhāya vā rukkhe vā paharati. — nicchedeti (**chid**) is pardonable because of Prk. chollai "to cut." Cp. also nicchubhati with v. l. BB nicchurāti. For sound change P. ch>Sk. kṣ cp. P. chamā>kṣāra, chārikā>kṣāra, churikā>kṣurikā etc.

Nija (adj.) [Sk. nija, wth dial. j. for nitya=P. nicca] own Dāvs II.68. Cp. niya.

Nijana (nt.) [fr. **nij**] washing, cleansing Vism 342 (v. l. nijj°).

Nijigiŋsati [Sk. nijigīṣati, ni+jigiŋsati] to desire ardently, to covet DA I.92 (=maggeti pariyesati).

Nijigiŋsanatā (f.) [fr. last] covetousness Vism 23 sq. (defined), 29 (id.=magganā), referring to Vbh 353, where T has jigiŋsanatā, with v. l. nijigīsanatā.

Nijigiŋsitar (n. adj.) [n. ag. fr. prec.] one who desires ardently, covetous, rapacious D I.8 (lābhaŋ) A III.111 (id.).

Nijjaṭa (adj.) [Sk. *nirjaṭa, nis+jaṭa, adj. to jaṭā] disentangled J I.187; Miln 3.

Nijjara (adj.) [Sk. nirjara in diff. meaning, P. nis functioning as emphatic pref.; nis+jara] causing to decay, destroying, annihilating; f. °ā decay, destruction, death S IV.339; A I.221; II.198; V.215 sq. (dasa-n-vatthūni); Ps I.5 (id.).

Nijjareti [Sk. nir-jārayati; nis+jarati¹] to destroy, annihilate, cause to cease or exist M I.93; Th 2, 431 (nijjaressāmi=jīrāpassāmi vināpessāmi ThA 269).

Nijjāleti [nis+jāleti] to make an end to a blaze, to extinguish, to put out J VI.495 (aggiŋ).

Nijjiṇṇa (adj.) [Sk. nirjīrṇa, nis+jiṇṇa] destroyed, overcome, exhausted, finished, dead D I.96; M II.217=A I.221 (vedanākkhayā sabbaŋ dukkhaŋ n. bhavissati); M I.93; A V.215 sq.; Nett 51.

Nijjita (adj.) [Sk. nirjita, nis+jita] unvanquished Miln 192 (°kammasūrā), 332 (°vijita-saṅgāma); Sdhp 360

Nijjīvata (adj.) [Sk. nirjīvita, nis+jīva¹] lifeless, soulless DhsA 38; Miln 413.

Nijjhatta (adj.) [pp. of nijjhāpeti, *Sk. nidhyapta or nidhyāpita] satisfied, pacified, appeased J VI.414 (=khamāpita Com.); Vv 63¹⁰ (=nijjhāpita VvA 265); Miln 209. See also paṭi°.

Nijjhatti (f.) [abstr. to nijjhatta, cp. BSk. nidhyapti, formation like P. ñatti>Sk. jñapti] conviction, understanding, realization; favourable disposition, satisfaction M I.320; A IV.223; Ps II.171, 176; Miln 210.

Nijjhāna¹ (nt.) [*Sk. nidhyāna, ni+jhāna¹] understanding, insight, perception, comprehension; favour, indulgence (=nijjhāpana), pleasure, delight J VI.207. Often as °ŋ khamati: to be pleased with, to find pleasure in: S III.225, 228; M I.133, 480; Vv 84¹⁷. Thus also diṭṭhinijjhāna-kkhanti delighting in speculation A I.189 sq.; II.191. Cp. upa°.

Nijjhāna² (nt.) [nis+jhāna²] conflagration, in anto°=nijjhāyana PvA 18 (cittasantāpa+in explⁿ of soka).

Nijjhāpana (nt.) [Sk. *nidhyāpana, ni+jhāpana, Caus. to jhāpeti] favourable disposition, kindness, indulgence J IV.495 (°ŋ karoti=khamāpeti Com.; text reads nijjhapana).

Nijjhāpaya (adj.) [Sk. *ni-dhyāpya, to nijjhāpeti] to be discriminated or understood, in dun° hard to . . . Miln 141 (pañha).

Nijjhāpeti [Sk. nidhāyayati, ni+jhāpeti, Caus. to jhāyati¹; cp. Sk. nididhyāsate] to make favourably disposed, to win somebody's affection, or favour, to gain over Vin II.96; M I.321; J IV.108; 414, 495; VI.516; Miln 264; VvA 265 (nijjhāpita=nijjhatta).

Nijjhāma (adj. n.) [Sk. niḥkṣāma, cp. niḥksīṇa, nis+jhāma of jhāyati²=Sk. kṣāyati] burning away, wasting away, consuming or consumed A I.295; Nett 77, 95 paṭipadā.

-**taṇha** (adj.) of consuming thirst, very thirsty J I.44; -**taṇhika**=°taṇha denoting a class of Petas (q. v.) Miln 294, 303, 357.

Nijjhāyati¹ [Sk. nidhyāyati, ni+jhāyati¹] to meditate, reflect, think S III.140 sq. (+passati, cp. jānāti), 157; M I.334 (jhāyati n. apajjhāyati); III.14 (id.). Cp. upa°.

Nijjhāyati² [ni+jhāyati²] to be consumed (by sorrow), to fret Nd¹ 433.

Nijjhāyana (nt.) [Sk. *niḥkṣāyana, nis+jhāyana of jhāyati²] burning away, consumption; fig. remorse, mortification in anto° J I.168 (cp. nijjhāna²).

Niṭṭha (adj.) [Sk. niṣṭha, ni+ °tha; cp. niṭṭhā¹] dependent on, resting on, intent upon S III.13 (accanta°); Nd¹ 263 (rūpa°).

Niṭṭhā¹ (f.) [Sk. niṣṭhā; ni+ ṭhā, abstr. of adj.-suff. °ṭha] basis, foundation, familiarity with Sn 864 (expl. SnA 551 by samiddhi, but see Nd¹ 263).

Niṭṭhā² (f.) [Vedic niṣṭhā (niḥṣṭhā), nis+ ṭhā from °ṭha] end, conclusion; perfection, height, summit; object, aim Vin I.255; S II.186; A I.279 (object); Ps I.161. niṭṭhaŋ gacchati to come to an end; fig. to reach perfection, be completed in the faith M I.176; J I.201; Miln 310; freq. in pp. niṭṭhaŋ gata (niṭṭhangata) one who has attained perfection (=pabbajitānaŋ arahattaŋ patta) DhA IV.70; S III.99 (a°); A II.175; III.450; V.119 sq.; Dh 351; Ps I.81, 161.

Niṭṭhāti [Sk. niṣṭiṣṭhati,' nis+ tiṭṭhati, the older *sthāti restored in compᵒ] to be at an end, to be finished J I.220; IV.391; DhA I.393.—pp. niṭṭhita, Caus. niṭṭhāpeti (q. v.).

Niṭṭhāna (nt.) [abstr. of niṭṭhāti] being finished, carrying out, execution, performance D I.141; ThA 19 (=avasāya). Cp. san°.

Niṭṭhāpita (& **niṭṭhapita**) [pp. of niṭṭhāpeti] accomplished, performed, carried out J I.86, 172 (°ṭha°), 201.

Niṭṭhāpeti [Caus. to niṭṭhāti] to carry out, perform; prepare, make ready, accomplish J I.86, 290; VI.366; DhA III.172.—pp. niṭṭhāpita Cp. pari°.

Niṭṭhita (adj.) [Sk. niṣṭhita (niḥṣṭhita), nis+ ṭhita, cp. niṭṭhāti] brought or come to an end, finished, accomplished; (made) ready, prepared (i. e. the preparations being finished) Vin I.35; D I.109 (bhattaŋ: the meal is ready); II.127 (id.); J I.255 (id.); J II.48; III.537 (finished); VvA 188; PvA 81; & often at conclusion of books & chapters. aniṭṭhita not completed DhA III.172. —su° well finished, nicely got up, accomplished Sn 48, 240. Cp. pari°.

Niṭṭhubhati (& **nuṭṭhubhati** Vin I.271; J I.459; also **niṭṭhuhati**) [Sk. niṣṭhubhati, but in meaning=Sk. niṣṭhīvati, nis+ *thīv, **stubh** taking the function of **ṣṭhīv**, since **stubh** itself is represented by thavati & thometi] to spit out, to expectorate Vin I.271 (nuṭṭhuhitvā); II.132 (id.); J II.105, 117 (nuṭṭh°); VI.367; DhA II.36 (niṭṭhuhitvā). pp. nuṭṭhubhita Sdhp 121.—Cp. oṭṭhubhati.

Niṭṭhubhana (nt.) [Sk. niṣṭhīvana, see niṭṭhubhati & cp. Prk. niṭṭhuhana] spitting out, spittle J I.47; PvA 80 (=kheḷa, v. l. SS niṭṭhuvana, BB niṭhūna).

Niṭṭhurin (adj.) [Sk. niṣṭhura or niṣṭhūra, ni+ thūra= thūla; cp. Prk. niṭṭhura] rough, hard, cruel, merciless Sn 952 (a°; this reading is mentioned as v. l. by Bdhgh at SnA 569, & the reading anuddharī given; vv. ll. SS anuṭṭhurī, BB anuṭṭharī, explᵈ as anissukī. Nd¹ 440 however has aniṭṭhurī with explⁿ of nitthuriya as under issā at Vbh 357).

Niṭṭhuriya (nt.) [cp. Sk. niṣṭhuratva] hardness, harshness, roughness Nd¹ 440; Nd² 484 (in exegesis of makkha)= Vbh 357.

Niḍḍāyati [Sk. nirdāti, nis+ dāyati, cp. Sk. nirdātar weeder] to cut out, to weed D I.231 (niddāyit°); It 56 (as v. l. niddāta for ninhāta, q. v.); J I.215. Caus. niḍḍāpeti to cause to weed, to have weeds dug up Vin II.180.

Niḍḍha (nt.) [Vedic niḍa resting-place ni+ **sad** "sitting down"] nest, place, seat Dh 148 (v. l. niḷa).

Ninhāta (adj.) [Sk. *niḥsnāta, nis+ nahāta] cleansed, purified It 56 (°pāpaka=sinless; with several vv. ll. amongst which niddāta of niḍḍāyati=cleansed of weeds) =Nd¹ 58 (ninhāta°)=Nd² 514 (ninhāta, v.l. SS ninnahāta).

Nitamba [Sk. nitamba; etym. unknown] the ridge of a mountain or a glen, gully DA I.209.

Nitammati [Sk. nitāmyati, ni+ **tam** as in tama] to become dark, to be exhausted, faint; to be in misery or anxiety J IV.284 (Com.: atikilamati).

Nitāḷeti [Sk. nitāḍayati, ni+ tāḷeti] to knock down, to strike J IV.347.

Nittaṇha (adj.) [BSk. niṣtṛṣṇa (Divy 210 etc.), nis+ taṇhā] free from thirst or desire, desireless PvA 230 (=nirāsa). f. abstr. nitthaṇhatā Nett 38.

Nittaddana (better: **nitthaddhana**) (nt.) [Sk. *niṣṭambhana, abstr. fr. ni+ thaddha=making rigid] paralysing D I.11 (jīvhā°=mantena jivhāya thaddhakaraṇa DA I.96; v. l. (gloss) nibandhana).

Nittāreti see nittharati.

Nittiṇa (adj.) [Sk. niṣṭṛṇa, nis+ tiṇa] free from grass J III.23.

Nittiṇṇa (pp.) [Sk. nistīrṇa, nis+ tiṇṇa] got out of, having crossed or overcome D II.275 (-ogha; v. l. BB nitiṇṇa); Nd¹ 159 (as v. l.; text has nitiṇṇa); Nd² 278 (t.). Cp. nittharati.

Nittudana (nt.) [nis+ tudana, abstr. fr. tudati; cp. Sk. nistodā] pricking, piercing A I.65 (text: nittuddana); III.403 sq.

Nitteja (adj.) [cp. Sk. nistejas only in meaning 1; nis+ teja] 1. without energy Vism 596.—2. "put out," abashed, put to shame, in °ŋ karoti to make blush or put to shame J II.94 (lajjāpeti+).

Nitthanati & **Nitthunati** [Sk. nisstanati "moan out," nis +thaneti & thunati¹] to moan, groan: (a) °thanati: J I.463; II.362; IV.446; V.296; DA I.291.—(b) °thunati Vin II.222; J V.295, 389; Vism 311; VvA 224. Cp. nitthuna.

Nitthanana (nt.) [nis+ thanana, abstr. to thaneti] groaning, moaning DA I.291 (v. l. BB. °thuna). As **nitthunana** Vism 504.

Nittharaṇa¹ (nt.) [Sk. nistaraṇa, nis+ taraṇa, cp. nittharati] getting across, ferrying over, traversing, overcoming S I.193 (oghassa); A II.200 (id.); It 111 (id.); M I.134; J I.48 (loka°); Dāvs II.29 (id.); Vism 32; Sdhp 334 (bhava°), 619 (tiloka°).

Nittharaṇa² (nt.) [Sk. nistaraṇa, ni+ tharaṇa] "strewing or being strewn down," putting down, carrying, bearing S IV.177 (bhārassa, of a load, cp. nikkhepa); VvA 131 (so read for niddharaṇa, in kuṭumba-bhārassa n-samatthā=able to carry the burden of a household).

Nittharati [Sk. nistarati, nis+ tarati¹] to cross over, get out of, leave behind, get over D I.73 (kantāraŋ). pp. nittiṇṇa q. v. Caus. nitthāreti to bring through, help over Nd² 630 (nittāreti).

Nitthāra [Sk. nistāra; nis+ tāra of tarati¹] passing over, rescue, payment, acquittance, in °ŋ vattati to be acquitted, to get off scot-free M I.442 (v. l. netth°, which is the usual form). See netthāra.

Nitthuna [Sk. *nis-stanana & nistava to thunati] (a) (of thunati¹) moan, groan DA I.291 (as v. l. BB for nitthanana)—(b) (of thunati²) blame, censure, curse PvA 76 (°ŋ karoti to revile or curse).

Nitthunati etc., see nitthanati etc.

Nidassana (nt.) [Sk. nidarśana, ni+dassana] "pointing at" evidence, example, comparison, apposition, attribute, characteristic; sign, term D I.223 (a° with no attribute); III.217 (id.); S IV.370 (id.); A IV.305 sq. (nīla°, pīta° etc.); Sn 137; Vbh 13, 64, 70 sq. (sa°, a°); VvA 12, 13; PvA 26, 121 (pucchanākāra°) 226 (paccakkhabhūtaŋ n. "sign, token").

Nidassati v. l. BB at Sn 785 for nirassati (q. v.) Nd^1 76 has nid° in text, nir° as v. l. SS; SnA 522 reads nirassati.

Nidassita (pp.) [see nidasseti] pointed out, defined as, termed Pv I.5^{12}; PvA 30.

Nidasseti [Sk. nidarśayati, ni+dasseti] to point out ("down"), explain, show, define VvA 12, 13 (°etabbavacana the word to be compared or defined, correl. to nidassana-vacana). — pp. nidassita (q. v.).

Nidahati [Sk. nidadhāti, ni+dahati^1] to lay down or aside, deposit; accumulate, hoard, bury (a treasure) Vin I.46 (cīvaraŋ); Miln 271; ger. nidahitvā PvA 97 (dhanadhaññaŋ) & nidhāya Dh 142, 405; Sn 35 (daṇḍaŋ), 394, 629; Nd^2 348; pres. also nidheti KhA 217, 219; fut. nidhessati PvA 132. Pass. nidhīyati KhA 217. Caus. nidhāpeti PvA 130 (bhoge). See also nidāhaka, nidhāna & nidhi; also upanidhāya.

Nidāgha [Sk. nidāgha, fr. nidahati, ni+dahati^2, see ḍahati] heat, summer-heat, summer, drought J I.221 (-samaya dry season); II.80; Vism 259 (°samaya, where KhA 58 reads sarada-samaya); PvA 174 (-kāla summer). fig. J IV.285; V.404; Dāvs II.60.

Nidāna (nt.) [Sk. nidāna, ni+*dāna of **dā**, dyati to bind, cp. Gr. δέσμα, δῆμα (fetter) & see dāma] (a) (n.) tying down to; ground (lit. or fig.), foundation, occasion; source, origin, cause; reason, reference, subject ("sujet") M I.261; A I.134 sq.; 263 sq., 338; II.196; IV.128 sq.; Dhs 1059 (dukkha°, source of pain), 1136; Nett 3, 32; Miln 272 (of disease: pathology, ætiology), 344 (°paṭhanakusala, of lawyers); PvA 132, 253. — (b) (adj.-°) founded on, caused by, originating in, relating to S V.213 sq. (a° & sa°); A I.82 (id.); Sn 271 (ito°), 866 (kuto°), 1050 (upadhi°=hetuka, paccayā, kāraṇā Nd^2 346); 872 (icchā°) etc.; VvA 117 (vimānāni Rājagaha° playing at or referring to R.). — (c) nidānaŋ (acc. as adv.) by means of, in consequence of, through, usually with tato° through this, yato° through which D I.52, 73; M I.112; Pv IV.1^{61} (through whom=yaŋ nimittaŋ PvA 242); PvA 281; ito° by this Nd^2 291^2.

Nidāhaka (adj.) [fr. nidahati] one who puts away, one who has the office of keeper or warder (of robes: cīvara°) Vin I.283.

Nidda (nt.) [nis+dara, see darī] a cave Nd^1 23 (Ep. of kāya).

Niddanta [so read for niddanna, v. l. niddhā=niddā; cp. supinanta]=niddā J VI.294.

Niddaya (adj.) [Sk. nirdaya, nis+dayā (adj.)] merciless, pitiless, cruel Sdhp 143, 159.

Niddara (adj.) [nis+dara] free from fear, pain or anguish Dh 205=Sn 257 (expl^d at DhA III.269 by rāgadarathānaŋ abhāvena n.; at SnA 299 by kilesapariḷāhâbhāvena n.).

Niddasa see niddesa.

Niddā (f.) [Vedic nidrā, ni+**drā** in Sk. drāti, drāyate, Idg. ***dorē**; cp. Gr. (hom.) ἔδραθον, Lat. dormio] sleep A II.48, 50; III.251; Sn 926 (opp. jāgariyā), 942 (see expl^n at Nd^1 423); J I.61, 192; II.128. — niddaŋ okkamati to fall asleep Vin I.15 (niddā ?); J III.538; IV.1; DhA 1.9; VvA 65; PvA 47; °ŋ upagacchati id. PvA 43, 105, 128.

-**ārāma** fond of sleep, slothful, sluggish It 72 (+kammarāma, bhassarata); -**ārāmatā** fondness of sleep, laziness, sluggishness A III.116, 293 sq., 309 sq.; IV.25 (+kamm°, bhass°); V.164; -**sīlin** of drowsy habits, slothful, sleepy Sn 96.

Niddāna (nt.) [Sk. *nirdāna, nis+dāna of dayati^3, Sk. dāti, cp. dātta] cutting off, mowing, destroying Sn 78 (=chedana lunana uppāṭana SnA 148)=S I.172; *K.S.* I.319, cp. niḍḍāyati.

Niddāyati [Denom. fr. niddā] to sleep D I.231; J I.192, 266; II.103; V.68, 382; DhA III.175; SnA 169.

Niddāyitar [n. ag. fr. niddāyati] a sleepy person Dh 325.

Niddiṭṭha (pp.) [see niddisati] expressed, explained, designated Miln 3; DhsA 57; Vism 528; VvA 13.

Niddisati (& **niddissati**) [Sk. nir-diśati, nis+disati, cp. Lat. distinguo] to distinguish, point out, explain, designate, define, express, to mean It 122=Nd^2 276^f; Miln 123, 345; DhsA 57; DhA II.59; PvA 87, 217 (°itvā); aor. niddisi DhsA 57; SnA 61. — grd. niddisitabba DhsA 56; Nett 96. Pass. niddissīyati PvA 163. — pp. niddiṭṭha (q. v.).

Niddukkha (adj.) [nis+dukkha] without fault or evil J III.443 (in expl^n of anīgha); PvA 230 (id.); (in expl^n of mārisa) *K.S.* (S.A.) 1, 2, *n.* 1.

Niddesa [Sk. nirdeśa, fr. niddisati, cp. desa, desaka etc.] 1. description, attribute, distinction PvA 7 (ukkaṭṭha°); °vatthu object of distinction or praise D III.253= A IV.15 (where reading is niddasa, which also as v. l. at D III.253 & Ps 1.5). — 2. descriptive exposition, analytic explanation by way of question & answer, interpretation, exegesis Vin V.114 (sa°); Nett 4, 8, 38 sq.; Vism 26; DhsA 54; VvA 78; PvA 71, 147. — 3. N. of an old commentary (ascribed to Sāriputta) on parts of the Sutta Nipāta (Aṭṭhaka-vagga, interpreted in the Mahā-Niddesa; Pārāyana-vagga and, as a sort of appendix, the Khaggavisāṇa-sutta, interpreted in the Culla-Niddesa); as one of the canonical texts included in the Khuddaka Nikāya; editions in *P.T.S.* Quoted often in the Visuddhimagga, e. g. p. 140, 208 sq. etc.

Niddosa^1 (adj.) [Sk. nirdośa, nis+dosa^1] faultless, pure, undefiled Sn 476; DhsA 2; PvA 189 (=viraja); DhA I.41.

Niddosa^2 (adj.) [Sk. nirdveṣa, nis+dosa^2] free from hatred J IV.10 (su°; Com. "adussanavasena," foll. upon sunikkodha).

Niddhana (adj.) [nis+dhana] without property, poor J V.447.

Niddhanta (adj.) [pp. of niddhamati, nis+dhanta, q. v.] blown off, removed, cleaned, purified A I.254 (jātarūpa "loitered," cp. niddhota); Sn 56 (°kasāva-moha; Com. vijahati); Dh 236 (°mala, malānaŋ nīhaṭatāya DhA III.336); Nd^2 347 (=vanta & pahīna); J VI.218 (of hair; Com. expl^s siniddharutā, v. l. BB siniddha-anta, thus meant for Sk. snigdhānta).

Niddhamati [in form=Sk. nirdhmāti, nis+dhamati, but in meaning the verb, as well as its derivations, are influenced by both meanings of niddhāvati (dhāvati^1 & ^{2}): see niddhāpeti, niddhamana, & niddhovati] to blow away, blow off; to clean, cleanse, purify; to throw out, eject, remove Sn 281=Miln 414 (kāraṇḍavaŋ); Sn 282 (°itvā pāpicche), 962 (malaŋ=pajahati (Nd^1 478); Dh 239 (id.); Miln 43. — pp. niddhanta).

Niddhamana (nt.) [of niddhamati or=*nirdhāvana= °dhovana to dhāvati^2] drainage, drain, canal Vin II.120 (udaka°; dhovituŋ immediately preceding); J I.175, 409, 425; III.415; IV.28; V.21 (udaka°); DhA II.37.

Niddhamanā (f.) [either to niddhamati or to niddhāpeti] throwing out, ejection, expulsion J v.233 (=nikkaḍḍhanā Com.).

Niddharaṇa (nt.) not with Hardy (Index VvA)=Sk nirdhāraṇa (estimation), but to be read as nittharaṇa (see nittharaṇa[2]).

Niddhāpita (adj.) [pp. of niddhāpeti, q. v.] thrown out J III.99 (v. l. for nibbāpita).

Niddhāpeti [Sk. nirdhāvayati, nis+dhāveti (dhāpeti), Caus. of dhāvati[1]; may also stand for niddhamāpeti, Caus. fr. niddhamati, cp. contamination niddhāmase at J IV.48, unless misread for niddhāpaye, as v. l. BB bears out] to throw out, chase away, expel J IV.41 (niddhāpayiŋsu), 48 (? for niddhāmase). pp. niddhāpita.

Niddhāmase at J IV.48 should probably be read niddhāpaye (as v. l. BB), q. v.

Niddhunāti [Sk. nirdhunoti, nis+dhunāti] to shake off S III.155; A III.365 (odhunāti+; spelt nidhunāti); M I.229; Th 1, 416; PvA 256 (=odhunāti).

Niddhuniya (?) (nt.) [=Sk. nihnuvana fr. nihnute with diff. derivation] hypocrisy Pug 18 (=makkha); cp. *J.P.T.S.* 1884, 83.

Niddhūpana (adj.) [nir+dhūpana] unscented J VI.21 (udaka).

Niddhota (adj.) [nis+dhota; pp. of niddhovati] washed, cleansed, purified Dāvs v.63 (°rūpiya; cp. niddhanta).

Niddhovati [Sk. nirdhāvati, nis+dhovati, cp. niddhamati] to wash off, clean, purify A I.253 (jātarūpaŋ, immediately followed by niddhanta). pp. **niddhota.**

Nidhāna (nt.) [Vedic nidhāna, see nidahati] laying down, depositing, keeping; receptacle; accumulation (hidden) treasure J IV.280 (nidhi°); PvA 7 (udaka-dāna-nīharaṇa-n°), 97 (n-gata dhana=hoarded, accumulated), 132 (°ŋ nidhessāmi gather a treasure); DhsA 405 (°kkhama).

Nidhānavant (adj.) forming or having a receptacle, worth treasuring or saving D I.4 (=hadaye nidhātabba-yuttavāca DA I.76).

Nidhāpeti, Nidhāya & Nidhīyati, see nidahati.

Nidhi [Vedic nidhi, ni+**dhā,** see nidahati] 1. "setting down," receptacle; (hidden) treasure Sn 285 (brahma n.); Dh 76; Kh VIII.2 (see KhA 217 sq.: nidhīyatī ti nidhi, def. of n.), 9 (acoràharaṇo nidhi cp. "treasures in heaven, where thieves do not steal" Matt. 6, 20); Sdhp 528, 588. — 2. "putting on," a cloak J VI.79 (expl[d] as vākacira-nivāsanaŋ=a bark dress). Cp. sannidhi.

-kumbhī a treasure-pot, a treasure hidden in a pot =a hidden treasure DhA II.107; IV.208; **-nidhāna** laying up treasures, burying a treasure J IV.280; **-mukha** an excellent treasure A v.346.

Nidhura see nidhura.

Nidheti see nidahati.

Nindati [Sk. nindati, **nid** as in Gr. ὄνειδος (blame), Lith. naids (hatred), Goth. naitjan (to rail or blaspheme), Ohg. neizzan (to plague); cp. Goth. neiþ=Ohg. nīd (envy)] to blame, find fault with, censure A II.3; v.171, 174; Sn 658; J VI.63; Dh 227; inf. ninditun Dh 230; grd. nindanīya SnA 477. pp. nindita (q. v.); cp. also nindiya.

Nindana (nt.) [abstr. fr. nindati] blaming, reviling, finding fault DhA III.328.

Nindā (f.) [cp. Sk. nindā, to nindati] blame, reproach, fault-finding, fault, disgrace S III.73; A II.188; IV.157 sq.; M I.362; Sn 213 (+pasaŋsā blame & praise); Dh 81 (id.); Sn 826, 895, 928; Dh 143, 309; Nd[1] 165, 306, 384; DhA II.148. — In comp[n] nindi° see anindi°.

Nindita (adj.) [pp. of nindati] blamed, reproved, reviled; faulty, blameworthy Dh 228; Pv II.3[34] (a° blameless= agarahita pasaŋsa PvA 89); Sdhp 254, 361. — anindita J IV.106 (°angin).

Nindiya (adj.) [Sk. nindya, orig. grd. of nindati] blameable, faulty, blameworthy Sn 658 (=nindanīya SnA 477); Nett 132. pi nindiyā at PvA 23 is to be read as pīṇitindriyā.

Ninna (adj.-n.) [Vedic nimna, der. fr. ni down, prob. comb[d] with °na of **nam** to bend, thus meaning "bent down," cp. unna & panna] 1. (adj.) bent down (cp. ninnata), low-lying, deep, low, sunken J II.3 (magga); PvA 29 (bhūmibhāga), 132 (ṭhāna); esp. freq. as -°: bent on, inclining to, leading to, aiming at, flowing into etc. Often comb[d] with similar expressions in chain taccarita tabbahula taggaruka tanninna tappoṇa tappabbhāra tadādhimutta (with variation nibbāna°, viveka° etc. for tad°): Nd[2] under tad; J II.15; Ps II.197; — Vin II.237=A IV.198 (samuddo anupubba° etc.); A IV.224 (viveka°); v.175 (id.); M I.493 (Nibbāna°). Similarly: samudda° Gangā M I.493; nekkhamma° J I.45 (v.258); samādhi° Miln 38. — 2. (acc. as adv.) downward: ninnaŋ pavattati to flow downward M I.117; Pv I.5[7]; ninnagata running down Miln 259 (udaka); ninnaga Dāvs IV.28. — 3. (nt.) low land, low ground, plain (opp. thala elevation, plateau): usually with ref. to a raincloud flooding the low country Sn 30 (mahamegho °ŋ pūrayanto); SnA 42 (=pallala); It 66 (megho °ŋ pūreti); Pv II.9[45] (megho °ŋ paripūrayanto). **-unnata** low lying & elevated Miln 349 (desabhāga).

Ninnata (adj.) [ni+nata] bent down, bent upon, in ninnatattā (fem. abstr.) aim, purpose (?) DhsA 39 (is the reading correct ?).

Ninnāda (& **Nināda** Miln, Dāvs) [Sk. ninàda, ni+nāda] sounding forth, sound, tune, melody A II.117 (°sadda); J VI.43; VvA 161; Miln 148; Dāvs v.31.

Ninnādin (adj.) [fr. ninnāda] sounding (loud), resonant (of a beautiful voice) D II.211 (cp. aṭṭhanga brahmassara & bindu).

Ninnāmin (adj.) [fr. ni+**nam**] bending downwards, descending A IV.237.

Ninnāmeti [Caus. of ni+namati] to bend down, put out (the tongue) D I.106 (jivhaŋ=nīharati DA I.276); J I.163, 164; cp. Divy 7, 71 (nirṇāmayati).

Ninnīta (adj.) [pp. of ninneti] lead down, lead away; drained, purified, free from (°-) A I.254 (niṇnīta-kasāva of gold: free fr. dross).

Ninnetar [n. ag. to ni-nayati=Sk. *ninayitṛ, cp. netar] one who leads down to, one who disposes of (c. gen.), bringer of, giver, usually in phrase atthassa n. (bringer of good: "Heilbringer") of the Buddha S IV.94; M I.111; A v.226 sq., 256 sq.; Ps II.194.

Ninneti [Sk. ninayati, ni+nayati] to lead down, lead away; drain, (udakaŋ), desiccate Vin II.180. — pp. ninnīta, q. v.

Ninhāta see niṇhāta.

Nipa at J v.6 read as nīpa.

Nipaka (adj.) [cp. BSk. nipaka chief, fr. Sk. nipa, chief, master] intelligent, clever, prudent, wise S I.13, 52, 187; M I.339; A I.165 (+jhāyin); III.24, 138; Sn 45≈Dh

328 ≈ DhA I.62 ; Sn 283, 962, 1038 ; Nd² 349 (=jatimā) = Nd¹ 478 ; Bu I.49 ; Vbh 426 ; Miln 34, 342, 411 ; Vism 3 (def°).

Nipakka at Vin I.200 read nippakka.

Nipacc-ākāra [nipacca, ger. of nipatati+ ākāra] obedience, humbleness, service S I.178 ; v.233 ; A v.66 ; J I.232 ; IV.133 ; VvA 22, 320 ; PvA 12.

Nipacca-vādin (adj.) [nipacca, ger. of nipāteti+ vādin] speaking hurtfully Sn 217 (=dāyakaŋ nipātetvā appiyavacanāni vattā SnA 272).

Nipajjati [Sk. nipadyate, ni+ pajjati] to lie down (to sleep) D I.246 ; A IV.332 ; J I.150 ; DhA I.40 ; PvA 280 ; aor. nipajji J I.279 ; II.154 ; III.83 ; VvA 75, 76 ; PvA 74, 75, 93 ; ger. nipajja J I.7 (v.44 : °ṭṭhānacankama). — Caus. nipajjāpeti to lay down, deposit J I.50, 253, 267 ; III.26, 168 ; DhA I.50 ; VvA 76 (°etvā rakkhāpetha). Cp. abhi°.

Nipatati [Sk. nipatati, ni+ patati] 1. (instr.) to fall down, fly down, descend, go out Vin II.192 (Bhagavato pādesu sirasā n. bending his head at the feet of Bh.) ; PvA 60 (id.) ; J I.278 ; v.467 (nippatissāmi = nikkhamissāmi Com.) Pv II.8⁹ (v. l. BB parivisayītvā) = nikkhamitva PvA 109 (cp. nippatati). — 2. (trs.) to bring together, to convene, in nipatāmase (pres. subj.) " shall we convene ?" J IV.361. See also nipadāmase. — Cp. abhi°, san°.

Nipadāmase at J III.120 is an old misreading & is to be corrected into nipatāmase (=let us gather, bring together = dedicate), unless it be read as nipphadāmase (=do, set forth, prepare, give), in spite of Com. explⁿ p. 121 : nikārapakārā (=nipaccakārā ?) upasaggā (upasajja ?) dāmase (dā) ti attho ; endorsed by Müller, *P.G.* p. 97 & Kern, *Toev.* p. 175. It cannot be ni+ pa+ dāmase, since ni is *never* used as secondary (modifying) verb-component (see ni° A 2), & Bdhgh's explⁿ is popular etym. Cp. nipatāmase at J IV.361 (see nipatati).

Nipanna (adj.) [pp. of nipajjati] lying down J I.151, 279 ; II.103 ; III.276 (°kāle while he was asleep), IV.167 ; PvA 43, 75, 265 (spelt nippanna, opp. nikujja).

Nipannaka (adj.) = nipanna Ps II.209 ; J I.151.

Nipalāvita (pp.) (Com. reading for vipalāvita text), [Sk. viplāvita, see plavati] made to swim, immersed, thrown into water J I.326.

Nipāka (adj.) [Sk. nipāka, ni+ pāka (pacati)] full grown, fully developed, in full strength J VI.327 (of a tree).

Nipāta [Sk. nipāta, ni+ pāta, of nipatati] 1. falling down Dh 121 (udabindu°) ; VvA 279 (diṭṭhi°, a glance) ; PvA 45 (asa°). — 2. descending M I.453. — 3. a particle, the gram. term for adverbs, conjunctions & interjections J v.243 (assu) ; PvA 11 (mā), 26 (vo), 40 (taŋ), 50 (ca). — 4. a section of a book (see next). Cp. vi°, san°

Nipātaka (adj.) [to nipāta] divided into sections or chapters Dpvs IV.16.

Nipātana (nt.) [to nipatati] 1. falling upon DhA I.295. — 2. going to bed VvA 71 (pacchā° opp. pubbuṭṭhāna). Cp. nipātin.

Nipātin (adj.) [to nipatati] 1. falling or flying down, chancing upon Dh 35, 36 (yatthakāma° cittaŋ = yattha yattha icchati tattha tatth' eva nipatati DhA I.295). — 2. going to bed D I.60 (pacchā° going to bed late). — Cp. abhi°.

Nipāteti [ni+ Caus. of patati] to let fall, throw down into (c. loc.) ; bring to fall, injure ; fig. cast upon, charge with D I.91 ; M I.453 (ayokaṭāhe) ; J III.359 ; SnA 272 ; PvA 152 (bhūmiyaŋ). pp. nipātita corrupt, evil, wicked Vin II.182 (caṇḍa + ; text nippātita, v. l. nipphātita).

Nipuṇa (adj.) [Sk. nipuṇa, dial. for nipṛṇa, to pṛṇoti, pṛ] clever, skilful, accomplished ; fine, subtle, abstruse D I.26≈(n. gambhīra dhamma), 162 (paṇḍita +) ; M I.487 (dhamma) ; S I.33 ; IV.369 ; A III.78 ; Sn 1126 (=gambhīra duddasa etc. Nd² 350) ; Vbh 426 ; Miln 233, 276 ; DA I.117 ; VvA 73 (ariyasaccesu kusala +), 232 ; PvA I, 16. Cp. abhinipuṇa.

Nippakāra (adj.) [nis+ pakāra 2] of no flavour, tasteless, useless J I.340.

Nippakka (adj.) [nis+ pakka] boiled, infused Vin I.200.

Nippajjati & **Nipphajjati** [Sk. niṣpadyate, nis+ pajjati] to be produced, be accomplished, spring forth, ripen, result, happen DhA II.4 (pph) ; PvA 19 (=upakappati), 71 (phalaŋ ijjhati n.), 120 (id.). pp. nipphanna. See also nipphādeti & nipphatti etc. ; cp. also abhi°.

Nippañña (adj.) [nis+ pañña] unwise, foolish PvA 40, 41 (=dummati).

Nippatati & **Nipphatati** [nis+ patati] to fall out ; rush out, come forth, go out from (c. abl.) Vin II.151 (nipphaṭati, v. l. nippaṭati) ; J v.467 (=nikkhamati Com. ; or is it nipatati ?). — ger. nippacca (cp. BSk. nirpatya AvŚ I.209).

Nippatta (adj.) [nis+ patta] 1. without wings, plucked (of a bird) Vin IV.259. — 2. without leaves J III.496 (=patita-pattā) ; SnA 117 (°puppha). — *Note* nippatta at Dhs 1035 is to be read as nibbatta.

Nippatti see nipphatti.

Nippadā (?) at S I.225 read nipphadā (q. v.).

Nippadesa [Sk. *niṣpradesa, nis+ padesa] only in instr. & abl. = separately DhsA 2, 30, 37, 297.

Nippanna see nipanna & nipphanna.

Nippapañca (adj.) [nis+ papañca] free from diffuseness S IV.370 ; Dh 254 (Tathāgata) ; °ārāma not fond of delay M I.65 (Neumann trsl. I.119 : " dem keine Sonderheit behagt ") ; A III.431 ; IV.229 sq. ; Miln 262.

Nippabha (adj.) [nis+ prabhā] without splendour J II.415 ; Miln 102.

Nippariyāya [nis+ pariyāya] 1. without distinction or difference, absence of explanation or demonstration DhsA 317 (°ena not figuratively), 403 (°desanā) ; VvA 320. — 2. unchangeable, not to be turned Miln 113, 123, 212.

Nippalāpa (adj.) [nis+ palāpa] free from prattle or talk, not talking A II.183 (apalāpa+ ; v. l. °palāsa).

Nippalibodha (adj.) [nis+ palibodha] without hindrances unobstructed Miln 11.

Nippādeti see nipphādeti.

Nippāpa (adj.) [nis+ pāpa] free from sin Sn 257 = Dh 205.

Nippitika (adj.) [Sk. *niṣpaitṛka = fatherless or *niṣprītika ?] a bastard J I.133 (v. l. nippītika q. v.).

Nippipāsa (adj.) [nis+ pipāsā] without thirst or desire Sn 56 ; Nd² 351.

Nippītika (adj.) [nis+ pīti+ ka] 1. free from (feelings of) enjoyment (characteristic of 3rd jhāna, q. v.) D I.75 ; A I.81. — 2. being unloved, a foster child etc. (?) see nippitika.

Nippīḷana (nt.) [nis+ pīḷana] squeezing, pressing; a blow J III.160. Cp. abhinippīḷanā.

Nippīḷeti [nis+ pīḷeti] to squeeze, press, clench, urge J I.63, 223. Pass. nippīḷiyati, only in ppr. nippīḷiyamāna being urged Vin II.303; VvA 138; PvA 31, 192. Cp. abhi°.

Nippurisa (adj.) [nis+ purisa] 1. without men PvA 177. — 2. without men, executed by females (female devas) only (of turiyā = a female orchestra) Vin I.15; D II.21; J v.506. Cp. M Vastu III.165 (niṣpuruṣena nāṭakena) & AvŚ I.321 (niṣpuruṣena tūryeṇa; see also note in Index p. 229), whereas Divy 3 (see Index) has niṣparuṣa (soft), with v. l. niṣpuruṣa.

Nippesika [cp. Sk. niṣpeṣa clashing against, bounce, shock, niṣ+ **piṣ**] one who performs jugglery, a juggler D I.8 (= nippeso silaŋ etesan ti DA.I.91); A III.111.

Nippesikatā (f.) [abstr. fr. prec.] jugglery, trickery (cp. Kern, *Toev.* p. 176) Vbh 353 (expl[d] at Vism 29); Miln 383.

Nippothana (nt.) [nis+ pothana of **puth** to crush] crushing, beating, destroying SnA 390.

Nipphajjati see nippajjati.

Nipphajjana (nt.) (or °nā f. ?) [n. abstr. fr. nipp(h)ajjati] resulting, procedure, achievement, plot J IV.83.

Nipphatti (f.) [cp. Sk. niṣpatti] result, accomplishment, effect, end, completion, perfection J I.56, 335 (of dreams), 343, 456; IV.137 (sippe); VI.36; VvA 138 (sippa°); DhA II.6 (import, meaning, of a vision); DhsA 354; PvA 122, 282 (sippe); Nett 54. Cp. abhi°.

Nipphattika (adj.) [fr. nipphatti] having a result J III.166 (evaŋ° of such consequence).

Nipphanna (adj.) [pp. of nippajjati] accomplished, perfected, trained S I.215 (°sobhin, spelt nippanna); J IV.39 (°sippa master of the art, M.A.); DhA III.285 (sasse); DhsA 316; in phil. determined, conditioned Kvu XI.7; XXIII.5; Vism 450; *Pts. of Controversy*, 395. Cp. abhi°, pari°. See also *Cpd.* 156, 157.

Nipphala (adj.) [nis+ phala] without fruit, barren in a° not without fruit, i. e. amply rewarded (dāyaka, the giver of good gifts) Pv I.4[2]; 5[6], PvA 194; Sdhp 504.

Nipphalita (adj.) [Sk. niṣphārita, pp. of nipphaleti, nis + phaleti] broken out, split open J I.493 (lasī = nikkhantā Com.; v. l. nipphalita).

Nipphāṇitatta (nt.) [nis+ phāṇita + tvaŋ] state of being free from sugar or molasses J III.409.

Nipphādaka (adj.) [fr. nipphādeti] producing, accomplishing DhsA 47; PvA 147 (sukha -°ŋ puññaŋ).

Nipphādana (nt.) [Sk. niṣpādana, to nipphādeti] accomplishment Miln 356; DA I.195.

Nipphādar [n. ag. = Sk. niṣpādayitṛ cp. nipphāditar] one who produces or gains S I.225 (atthassa; read nipphādā, nom. for nippadā).

Nipphādita [pp. of nipphādeti] (having) produced, producing (perhaps = nipphāditar) VvA 113.

Nipphāditar [n. ag. to nipphādeti, cp. nipphādar] one who produces or accomplishes PvA 8 (read "so nipphādītā" for sā nipphādikā). Cp. **nipphādita** and nipphādaka.

Nipphādeti [Caus. of nippajjati] to bring forth, produce; accomplish, perform J I.185 (lābhasakkāraŋ); v.81; Miln 299; VvA 32, 72 (grd. nipphādetabba, n. of ablative case); Sdhp 319, 426. — pp. nipphādita. Cp. abhinipphādeti.

Nipphoṭana (nt.) [nis+ pothanā] beating S IV.300 (v. l. ṭh.). Cp. nippothana.

Nipphoṭeti [nis+ potheti] to beat down, smother, crush S I.101, 102.

Nibaddha (adj.) [ni+ baddha] bound down to, i. e. (1) fixed, stable, sure J IV.134 (bhattavetana); Miln 398 (a°, unstable, °sayana). At DA I.243 two kinds of cārikā (wanderings, pilgrimages) are distinguished, viz. nibaddha° definite, regular and anibaddha° indefinite, irregular pilgrimage. — (2) asked, pressed, urged J III.277. — (3) nibaddhaŋ (nt. as adv.) constantly, always, continually J I.100, 150; III.325; V.95, 459; VI.161; PvA 267 (°vasanaka); DhA II.41, 52 sq.

Nibandha [Sk. nibandha, ni+ bandha] binding, bond; attachment, continuance, continuity S II.17; VvA 259, 260 (perseverance). acc. nibandhaŋ (often misspelt for nibaddhaŋ) continually VvA 75. Cp. vi°.

Nibandhati [ni+ bandhati] 1. to bind Miln 79. — 2. to mix, apply, prepare Vin II.151 (anibandhanīya unable to be applied, not binding); J I.201 (yāgubhattaŋ). — 3. to press, urge, importune J III.277.

Nibandhana (nt.) [ni+ bandhana] tying, fastening; binding, bond; (adj.) tied to, fettered Sn 654 (kamma°); Miln 78, 80.

Nibodhati [ni+ bodhati] to attend to, to look out for, to take J III.151 (= gaṇhati). — Caus. nibodheti to waken, at Th 3, 22 is probably to be read as vibodheti.

Nibbatta (pp.) [Sk. nirvṛtta, nis+ vaṭṭa, pp. of nibbattati] existing, having existed, being reborn Vin I.215 (n. bījaŋ phalaŋ fruit with seed); J I.168; II.111; PvA 10 (niraye), 35 (petayoniyaŋ), 100 (pubbe n.-ṭhānato paṭṭhāya); Miln 268 (kamma°, hetu° & utu°).—Cp. abhi°.

Nibbattaka (adj.) [cp. nibbatta] producing, yielding PvA 26 (phala °ŋ kusalakammaŋ), 126 (= sukha° = sukhāvaha).

Nibbattati [nis+ vattati] to come out from (cp. E. turn out), arise, become, be produced, result, come into being, be reborn, ex-ist (= nir-vatt) Dh 338; Pv I.1[1] (nibbattate); ThA 259 (= jāyati); DhA III.173; PvA 8 (= uppajjati) 71 (id.); ger. nibbattitvā J II.158 (kapiyoniyaŋ); PvA 68, 78; aor. nibbatti J I.221; PvA 14 (Avīcimhi), 67 (petesu), 73 (amaccakule). — pp. nibbatta (q. v.). Caus. nibbatteti (q. v.). Cp. abhi°.

Nibbattana (nt.) [abstr. fr. nibbattati] growing, coming forth; (re)birth, existence, life J II.105; PvA 5 (devaloke n-araha deserving rebirth in the world of gods) 9, 67 etc.

Nibbattanaka (adj.) [fr. nibbattana] 1. arising, coming out, growing ThA 259 (akkhidalesu n. pīḷikā) -- 2. one destined to be reborn, a candidate of rebirth J III.304 (sagge).

Nibbattāpana (nt.) [fr. nibbattāpeti, see nibbatteti] reproduction Miln 97.

Nibbatti (f.) [Sk. nirvṛtti, nis+ vatti] constitution, product; rebirth J I.47; Nett 28, 79; Vism 199, 649; VvA 10. Cp. abhi°.

Nibbattita (adj.) [pp. of nibbatteti] done, produced, brought forth PvA 150 (a°kusalakamma = akata).

Nibbattin (adj.) [fr. nibbatti] arising, having rebirth, in neg. anibbattin not to be born again J VI.573.

Nibbatteti [nis+ vatteti, Caus. of nibbattati] to produce, bring forth; practise, perform; to bring to light, find something lost (at Miln 218) Nd[2] = jāneti (s. v.); J I.66, 140; III.396 (jhānābhiññaŋ); PvA 76 (jhānāni),

30; Miln 200; Sdhp 470. — pp. **nibbattita** (q. v.); 2nd Caus. **nibbattāpeti** to cause rebirth DhA III.484; see also nibbattāpana. — Cp. abhi°.

Nibbahati (adj.) [nis+vanka] not crooked, straight DhA I.288.

Nibbajjeti [nis+vajjeti] to throw away, to do without, to avoid Th I, 1105.

Nibbana (adj.) 1. [Sk. nirvana] without forest, woodless J II.358. — 2. [an abstr. fr. nibbāna, see nibbāna I.; cp. vana². Freq. nibbāna as v. l. instead of nibbana] without cravings Sn 1131 (nikkāmo nibbano); Dh 283 (nibbanā pl.) Vv 50[14] (better reading nibbāna, in phrase "vanā nibbānaŋ āgataŋ," as found at A III.346 = Th I, 691, although the latter has nibbanaŋ in text), expl[d] by "nittaṇhabhāvaŋ nibbānam eva upagataŋ" VvA 213.

Nibbanatha (adj.) [nis+vanatha] free from lust or cravings S I.86, 180 (so 'haŋ vane nibbanatho visallo); Th I, 526; Dh 344; Dāvs I.18

Nibbasana (adj.) [nis+vasana] no longer worn, cast off (of cloth) S II.202, 221.

Nibbahati [nis+bahati] to stretch out J III.185 (asiŋ); to pull out J V.269 (jivhaŋ = jivhaŋ balisena n. 275). See also nibbāheti & nibbāhāpeti.

Nibbāti [see nibbuta etym.; influenced in meaning by Sk. nirvāti, nis+vāti to blow, i. e. to *make* cool, see vāyati & nibbāpeti] (instr.) to cool off (lit. & fig.), to get cold, to become passionless Sn 235 (nibbanti dhīrā yathâyaŋ padīpo = vijjhāyanti; yathâyaŋ padīpo nibbuto evaŋ nibbanti KhA 194, 195), 915 (kathaŋ disvā nibbāti bhikkhu = rāgaŋ etc. nibbāpeti Nd¹ 344); J IV.391 (pāyāsaŋ). See also parinibbāti (e. g. Vbh 426).

Nibbāna (nt.). — I. *Etymology* Although nir+**vā** "to blow" (cp. BSk. nirvāṇa) is already in use in the Vedic period (see nibbāpeti), we do not find its distinctive application till later and more commonly in popular use, where **vā** is fused with **vṛ** in this sense, viz. in application to the extinguishing of fire, which is the prevailing *Buddhist* conception of the term. Only in the older texts do we find references to a simile of the *wind* and the flame; but by far the most common metaphor and that which governs the whole idea of **nibbāna** finds expression in the putting out of *fire* by *other* means of extinction than by blowing, which latter process rather tends to incite the fire than to extinguish it. The going out of the fire may be due to covering it up, or to depriving it of further fuel, by not feeding it, or by withdrawing the cause of its production. Thus to the *Pali* etymologist the main reference is to the root **vṛ** (to cover), and *not* to **vā** (to blow). This is still more clearly evident in the case of **nibbuta** (q. v. for further discussion). In verbal compn. nis+**vā** (see vāyati) refers only to the (non-) emittance of an odour, which could never be used for a meaning of "being exhausted"; moreover, one has to bear in mind that native commentators themselves never thought of explaining nibbāna by anything like blowing (vāta), but always by nis+vana (see nibbana). For Bdhgh's def[n] of nibbāna see e. g. Vism 293. — The *meanings* of n. are: 1. the going out of a lamp or fire (popular meaning). — 2. health, the sense of bodily well-being (probably, at first, the passing away of feverishness, restlessness). — 3. The dying out in the heart of the threefold fire of **rāga, dosa** & **moha**: lust, ill-will & stupidity (Buddhistic meaning). — 4. the sense of spiritual well-being, of security, emancipation, victory and peace, salvation, bliss.

II. *Import and Range of the Term.* A. Nibbāna is purely and solely an *ethical* state, to be reached in this birth by ethical practices, contemplation and insight. It is therefore not transcendental. The first and most important way to reach N. is by means of the eightfold Path, and all expressions which deal with the realisation of emancipation from lust, hatred and illusion apply to *practical* habits and not to speculative thought. N. is realised in one's *heart*; to measure it with a speculative measure is to apply a wrong standard. — A very apt and comprehensive discussion of nibbāna is found in F. Heiler, "Die buddhistische Versenkung" (München² 1922), pp. 36-42, where also the main literature on the subject is given. — N. is the untranslatable expression of the Unspeakable, of that for which in the Buddha's own saying there *is* no word, which cannot be grasped in terms of reasoning and cool logic, the Nameless, Undefinable (cp. the simile of extinction of the flame which may be said to pass from a visible state into a state which cannot be defined. Thus the Saint (Arahant) passes into that same state, for which there is "no measure" (i. e. no dimension): "atthangatassa na pamāṇam atthi . . . yena naŋ vajju: taŋ tassa n' atthi" Sn 1076. The simile in v. 1074: "accī yathā vāta-vegena khitto atthaŋ paleti, na upeti sankhaŋ: evaŋ munī nāmakāyā vimutto atthaŋ paleti, na upeti sankhaŋ"). Yet, it *is* a *reality*, and its characteristic features may be described, may be grasped in terms of earthly language, in terms of space (as this is the only means at our disposal to describe abstract notions of time and mentality); e. g. accutaŋ ṭhānaŋ, pāraŋ, amataŋ padaŋ, amata (& nibbāna-) dhātu. — It is the speculative, scholastic view and the dogmatising trend of later times, beginning with the Abhidhamma period, which has more and more developed the simple, spontaneous idea into an exaggerated form either to the positive (i. e. seeing in N. a definite *state* or sphere of existence) or the negative side (i. e. seeing in it a condition of utter annihilation). Yet its sentimental value to the (exuberant optimism of the) early Buddhists (Rh. Davids, *Early Buddhism*, p. 73) is one of peace and rest, perfect passionlessness, and thus supreme happiness. As Heiler in the words of R. Otto (*Das Heilige* etc. 1917; quoted l. c. p. 41) describes it, "only by its concept Nirvāna is something negative, by its sentiment, however, a positive item in most pronounced form." — We may also quote Rh. Davids' words: "One might fill columns with the praises, many of them among the most beautiful passages in Pāli poetry and prose, lavished on this condition of mind, the state of the man made perfect according to the B. faith. Many are the pet names, the poetic epithets, bestowed upon it, each of them—for they are not synonyms—emphasising one or other phase of this many-sided conception—the harbour of refuge, the cool cave, the island amidst the floods, the place of bliss, emancipation, liberation, safety, the supreme, the transcendental, the uncreated, the tranquil, the home of ease, the calm, the end of suffering, the medicine for all evil, the unshaken, the ambrosia, the immaterial, the imperishable, the abiding, the further shore, the unending, the bliss of effort, the supreme joy, the ineffable, the detachment, the holy city, and many others. Perhaps the most frequent in the B. texts is Arahantship, 'the state of him who is worthy'; and the one exclusively used in Europe is Nirvana, the 'dying out,' that is, the dying out in the heart of the fell fire of the three cardinal sins—sensuality, ill-will, and stupidity (Saŋyutta IV.251, 261)." (*Early Buddhism* pp. 72, 73.) And Heiler says (p. 42 l. c.): "Nirvāna is, although it might sound a paradox, in spite of all conceptional negativity nothing but 'eternal salvation,' after which the heart of the religious yearns on the whole earth."

The current simile is that of fire, the consuming fire of passion (rāg-aggi), of craving for rebirth, which has to be extinguished, if a man is to attain a condition of indifference towards everything worldly, and which in the end, in its own good time, may lead to freedom from rebirth altogether, to certain and final extinction (parinibbāna). — Fire may be put out by water, or may go out of itself from lack of fuel. The ethical state called Nibbāna can only rise from within. It is therefore in the older texts compared to the fire going out, rather than to the fire being put out. The latter point of view, though the word nibbāna is not used, occurs in one or two passages in later books. See J I.212; Miln 346, 410; SnA 28; Sdhp 584. For the older view see M I.487 (aggi anāhāro nibbuto, a fire gone out through lack of fuel); Sn 1094 (akiñcanaŋ anādānaŋ etaŋ dīpaŋ anāparaŋ Nibbānaŋ iti); S I.236 (attadaṇḍesu nibbuto sādānesu anādāno); S II.85 (aggikkhandho purimassa upādānassa pariyādānā aññassa ca anupāhārā anāhāro nibbāyeyya, as a fire would go out, bereft of food, because the former supply being finished no additional supply is forthcoming); sa-upādāno devānaŋ indo na parinibbāyati, the king of the gods does not escape rebirth so long as he has within him any grasping S IV.102; pāragū sabbadhammānaŋ anupādāya nibbuto A I.162; pāragato jhāyī anup° nibbuto, a philosopher, freed, without any cause, source, of rebirth A IV.290 (etc., see nibbuta). dāvaggi-nibbānaŋ the going out of the jungle fire J I.212; aggi nibbāyeyya, should the fire go out M I.487; aggikkhandho nibbuto hoti the great fire has died out Miln 304; nibbuto ginī my fire is out Sn 19. The result of quenching the fire (going out) is coolness (sīta); and one who has attained the state of coolness is sītibhūta. sītibhūto 'smi nibbuto Vin I.8; Pv $I.8^{7}$; sītibhūto nirūpadhi, cooled, with no more fuel (to produce heat) Vin II.156; A I.138; nicchāto nibbuto sītibhūto (cp. nicchāta) A II.208; V.65. anupādānā dīpacci viya nibbutā gone out like the flame of a lamp without supply of fuel ThA 154 (Ap. 153). — nibbanti dhīrā yath' āyaŋ padīpo the Wise go out like the flame of this lamp Sn 235. This refers to the pulling out of the wick or to lack of oil, not to a *blowing* out; cp. vaṭṭiŋ paṭicca telapadīpo jāleyya S II.86; Th 2, 116 (padīpass' eva nibbānaŋ vimokkho ahu cetaso). The pulling out of the wick is expressed by vaṭṭiŋ okassayāmi (=dīpavaṭṭiŋ ākaḍḍhemi ThA 117) cp. on this passage Pischel, *Leben & Lehre des Buddha* 71; Mrs. Rh. Davids, *Buddhism* 176; Neumann, *Lieder* 298). pajjotass' eva nibbānaŋ like the going out of a lamp S I.159≈.

B. Since rebirth is the result of wrong desire (kāma, kilesa, āsava, rāga etc.), the dying out of that desire leads to freedom & salvation from rebirth and its cause or substratum. Here references should be given to: (1) the *fuel* in ethical sense (cp. A I: aggi); (2) the aims to be accomplished (for instance, coolness=*peace*); (3) the seat of its realisation (the *heart*); (4) the means of achievement (the Path); (5) the obstacles to be removed. — 1. *Fuel*=cause of rebirth & suffering: āsāva (intoxications). khīṇāsavā jutimanto te loke parinibbutā the wise who are rid of all intoxications are in this world the thoroughly free S V.29; sāvakā āsavānaŋ khayā viharanti A IV.83; kodhaŋ pahatvāna parinibbiŋsu anāsavā (are completely cooled) A IV.98; āsavakhīṇo danto parinibbuto Sn 370; saggaŋ sugatino yanti parinibbanti anāsavā those of happy fate go to heaven, but those not intoxicated die out Dh 126; nibbānaŋ adhimuttānaŋ atthangacchanti āsavā Dh 226; āsavānaŋ khayā bhikkhu nicchāto parinibbuto It 49; vimutti-kusuma-sañchanno parinibbissati anāsavo Th I, 100. — kāmā (cravings) nikkāmo nibbano Nāgo Sn 1131. — kilesa-(nibbāna) vice (only in certain commentaries). kilesa-nibbānass' āpi anupādā parinibbānass' āpi santike DhA I.286; upādānaŋ abhāvena anupādiyitvā kilesa-nibbānena nibbutā DhA IV.194. — nibbidā (disenchantment). Nibbānaŋ ekanta-nibbidāya virāgāya etc. saŋvattati S II.223; nibbijjha sabbaso kāme sikkhe nibbānaŋ attano Sn 940. — rāga virāgo nirodho nibbānaŋ S I.136≈; desento virajaŋ dhammaŋ nibbānaŋ akutobhayaŋ S I.192; yo rāgakkhayo (dosa° . . . moha° . . .): idaŋ vuccati nibbānaŋ S IV.251, & same of Amata S V.8; chandarāga-vinodanaŋ nibbānapadaŋ accutaŋ Sn 1086; kusalo ca jahati pāpakaŋ rāgadosamoha-kkhayā parinibbuto Ud 85; ye 'dha pajahanti kāmarāgaŋ bhavarāgānusayañ ca pahāya parinibbānagatā Vv 53^{24}. — vana sabba-saŋyojan' atītaŋ vanā nibbānaŋ āgataŋ A III.346; nikkhantaŋ vānato ti nibbānaŋ KhA 151; taṇhā-sankhāta-vānābhāvato nibbānaŋ SnA 253.

2. *Aims:* khema (tranquillity). ātāpī bhikkhu nibbānāya bhabbo anuttarassa yogakkhemassa adhigamāya It 27; ajaraŋ amaraŋ khemaŋ pariyessāmi nibbutiŋ J I.3; acala (immovable, not to be disturbed). patto acalaṭṭhānaŋ Vv 51^{4}; accuta (stable) patthayaŋ accutaŋ padaŋ S III.143; chandarāga-vinodanaŋ nibbānapadaŋ accutaŋ Sn 1086. nekkhamma (renunciation, dispassionateness). vanā nibbānaŋ āgataŋ kāmehi nekkhammarataŋ A III.346. — pāragū (victor). pāragū sabbadhammānaŋ anupādāya nibbuto A I.162 (cp. A IV.290 with tiṇṇo pāragato). — santipada (calm, composure). santī ti nibbutiŋ ñatvā Sn 933; santimaggaŋ eva brūhaya nibbānaŋ sugatena desitaŋ Dh 285; s.=acala VvA 219. — samatha (allayment, quietude). sabbasankhārasamatho nibbānaŋ S I.136≈. — sotthi (welfare). saccena suvatthi hotu nibbānaŋ Sn 235.

3. *The Heart:* (a) attā (heart, self). abhinibbut-atto Sn 456; thitatto frequent, e. g. parinibbuto ṭh° Sn 359; danto parinib° ṭh° Sn 370. — (b) citta (heart). apariḍayhamāna-citto SnA 347 (for abhinibbutatto Sn 343). — (c) hadaya (heart) nibbānaŋ hadayasmiŋ opiya S I.199; mātuhadayaŋ nibbāyate J I.61; nibbāpehi me ḥadaya-pariḷāhaŋ (quench the fever of my heart) Miln 318. — (d) mano (mind). mano nibbāyi tāvade J I.27; disvā mano me pasīdi Vv 50^{14}.

4. *The Path:* dhīra. lokapariyāyaŋ aññāya nibbutā dhīrā tiṇṇā etc. S I.24; nibbanti dhīrā . . . Sn 235 sabbābhibhū dhīro sabbagantha-ppamocano It 122 — Recognition of anicca (transitoriness, see nicca). aniccasaññī . . . bhikkhu pāpuṇāti diṭṭh' eva dhamme nibbānaŋ A IV.353. — paññā. nibbānaŋ ev' ajjhagamuŋ sapaññā S I.22; n' abhirato paññā S I.38. — paṇḍita & nipaka. anupubbena n°ŋ adhigacchanti paṇḍitā A I.162; nipakā asesaŋ parinibbanti It 93. — vijjā. bhikkhu paṇihitena cittena avijjaŋ bhecchati vijjaŋ uppādessati n°ŋ sacchikarissati the bhikkhu with devout heart will destroy ignorance, gain right cognition & realise Nibbāna A I.8; idh' aññāya parinibbāti anāsavo A III.41; sabb' āsave pariññāya parinibbanti anāsavā Vbh 426.

5. *The Obstacles:* gantha (fetter). nibbānaŋ adhigantabbaŋ sabba-g°-pamocanaŋ S I.210; It 104; similarly It 122 (see above). gabbhaseyya (rebirth). na te punam upenti gabbhaseyyaŋ, parinibbānagatā hi sītibhūtā Vv 53^{24}. — nīvaraṇa (obstacles). pañca n°. anibbāna-saŋvattanikā S V.97. — punabbhava (rebirth). nibbāpehi mahārāgaŋ mā ḍayhittho punappunaŋ S I.188; vibhavañ ca bhavañ ca vippahāya vusitavā khīṇapunabbhavo sa bhikkhu Sn 514; bhava-nirodha nibbānaŋ S II.117. — sankhārā (elements of life). sabbasankhāra-samatho nibbānaŋ S I.136; N.=sabbasankhārā khayissanti A III.443. — saŋyojanāni (fetters). sabbas-ātītaŋ vanā Nibbānaŋ āgataŋ A III.346; s. pahāya n°ŋ sacchikarissati A III.423; saŋyojanānaŋ parikkhayā antarā-parinibbāyī hoti S V.69.

III. Nibbāna: its ethical importance and general characterisation. 1. *Assurance* of N. (nibbānass' eva santike, near N., sure of N.): S I.33 (yassa etādisaŋ yānaŋ . . . sa etena yānena n. e. s.: with the chariot of the Dhamma sure of reaching N.); IV.75; A II.39 (abhabbo parihānāya n. e. s. impossible to fail in the assurance of final release, of one "catuhi dhammehi samannāgato, viz. sīla, indriyaguttadvāratā, bhojanamattaññutā, jāgariyā"); III.331 (id. with appamādagaru: ever active & keen); II.40=It 40 (id. with appamāda-rato); Sn 822. — 2. *Steps and Means to N.:*

nibbāna-sacchikiriyā, attainment of N., is mangalaŋ uttamaŋ & to be achieved by means of tapo, brahmacariyā and ariyasaccāna-dassanaŋ Sn 267. — brahmacariya (a saintly life) is n.-parāyanā (leading to N.) S III.189. cp. v.218; also called n.-ogadhā (with similar states of mind, as nibbidā, virāgo, vimutti) ibid.; A II.26 = It 28, cp. It 29 (nibbān'-ogadha-gāminaŋ b°ŋ). The stages of sanctification are also discussed under the formula "nibbidā virāgo vimutti . . . vimuttasmiŋ vimuttaŋ iti ñāṇaŋ hoti: khīṇā jāti etc." (i. e. no more possibility of birth) S II.124 = IV.86. — dhamma: Buddha's teaching as the way to N.: "dhammavaraŋ adesayi n.-gāmiŋ paramaŋ hitāya" Sn 233; ahaŋ sāvakānaŋ dhammaŋ desemi sattānaŋ visuddhiyā . . . n°assa sacchikiriyāya A v.194, cp. 141; pubbe dh.-ṭhiti-ñāṇaŋ pacchā nibbāne ñāṇan ti S II.124. — magga: Those practices of a moral & good life embraced in the 8 fold Noble Path (ariyamagga). Sace atthi akammena koci kvaci na jīyati nibbānassa hi so maggo S I.217; ekāyano ayaŋ maggo sattānaŋ visuddhiyā . . . N°assa sacchikiriyāya D II.290; S v.167, 185; bhāvayitvā sucimaggaŋ n° -ogadha-gāminaŋ . . . Vbh 426; ādimhi sīlaŋ dasseyya, majjhe maggaŋ vibhāvaye, pariyosānamhi nibbānaŋ . . . DA I.176. — N.-gamanaŋ maggaŋ: tattha me nirato mano "my heart rejoices in the path to Nibbāna" S I.186; N.-gāminī paṭipadā A IV.83 (the path to salvation). Cp. §§ 4 & 7. — 3. *The Search for N.* or the goal of earnest endeavour. ārogya-paramā lābhā nibbānaŋ paramaŋ sukhaŋ, aṭṭhangiko ca maggānaŋ khemaŋ amata-gāminaŋ "N. is a higher bliss than acquisition of perfect health, the eightfold Path (alone) of all leads to perfect peace, to ambrosia" M I.508, cp. Dh 204 ("the fullest gain is for health etc.; N. is the highest happiness" DhA III.267). Similarly: khantī paramaŋ tapo titikkhā, n°ŋ paramaŋ vadanti buddhā D II.49 = Dh 184; n°ŋ paramaŋ sukhaŋ: Dh 204 = Sn 257 = J III.195; id.: Dh 203; jhānaŋ upasampajja . . . okkamanāya n.°assa A IV.111 sq.; cp. 230 sq.; kaṭuviyakato bhikkhu . . . ārakā hoti N°ā A I.281; n°ŋ ajjhagamuŋ sapaññā S I.22; devalokañ ca te yanti . . . anupubbena n°ŋ adhigacchanti paṇḍitā A I.162; n°ŋ abhikankhati S I.198; abhipassati A I.147; tiṇṇakathankatho visallo n.-âbhirato Sn 86; bhikkhu bhabbo anuttaraŋ sītibhāvaŋ sacchikātuŋ . . . paṇītâdhimutto hoti n.-âbhirato ca A III.435; n.-âbhirato . . . sabbadukkhā pamuccati S I.38; n.-ogadhaŋ brahmacariyaŋ vussati n.-parāyaṇaŋ n.-pariyosānaŋ S III.189 = v.218; n°ŋ gavesanto carāmi (Bodhisat, J I.61). All means of conduct & all ideals of reason & intellect lead to one end only: Nibbāna. This is frequently expressed by var. similes in the phrase n.-ninna, °poṇa, °pabbhāra, e. g. S v.75 = 134 = 137 = 190; v.244; A v.75, 134, 190, 244 = 291; Vv 84[42]. Saddahāno arahataŋ dhammaŋ n.-pattiyā sussūsā labhate paññaŋ appamatto S I.214 = Sn 186, cp. S I.48; Gotamo n.-paṭisaŋyuttāya dhammiyā kathāya bhikkhū sandasseti S I.214 = 192 = 210; Ud 80; n°ŋ pariyesati A II.247; n.-pariyosānā sabbe dhammā A v.107; n.-poṇaŋ me mānasaŋ bhavissati, saŋyojanā pahānaŋ gacchanti A III.443; odhunitvā malaŋ sabbaŋ patvā n.-sampadaŋ muccati sabba-dukkhehi: sā hoti sabbasampadā A IV.239; nibbijjha sabbaso kāme sikkhe n°ŋ attano Sn 940, cp. 1061. — 4. Some *Epithets* of Nibbāna: akutobhayaŋ A II.24 = It 122; accutaŋ padaŋ (careyya āditta-sīso va patthayaŋ a. p.) S III.143; Sn 1086; pattā te acalaṭṭhānaŋ yattha gantvā na socare Vv 51[4]; amataŋ A II.247; M III.224 (Bhagavā atthassa ñāṇanti a °assa dātā); Miln 319; Vv 64[27] (apāpuranto a °assa dvāraŋ); VvA 85 (a-rasa); Vv 50[20] (amatogadha magga = nibb°-gāminī paṭipadā); amosadhammaŋ Sn 758; khemaŋ appaṭibhayaŋ S IV.175; S I.189 = Sn 454; Th 2, 350 (°ṭṭhāne vimuttā te patta te acalaŋ sukhaŋ); M I.508 (+ amatagāminaŋ); A II.247 (yogakkhemaŋ anuttaraŋ); same at A III.294; It 27; Dh 23. — taṇhakkhaya Vv 73[5]; ṭhānaŋ duddasaŋ S I.136 (= sabba-sankhāra-samatho); dhuvaŋ (q. v.); niccaŋ Kvu 121; nekkhammaŋ A I.147 (°ŋ daṭṭhu khemato . . . nibbānaŋ abhipassanto); Vv 84[42]. sabba-gantha-pamocanaŋ (deliverance from all ties) S I.210; II.278 (sabbadukkha°); It 222 = A II.24; yathābhūtaŋ vacanaŋ S IV.195; yathāsukhaŋ (the Auspicious) A IV.415 sq.; (chanda-) rāga vinodanaŋ Sn 1086; rāgakkhayo (dosa°, moha°) S v.8; rāgavinayo (dosa°, moha°) ibid., santi (calm, peace) Vv 50[21] = Sn 204 (chandarāga-viratto bhikkhu paññāṇavā ajjhagā amataŋ santiŋ nibbānapadaŋ accutaŋ); VvA 219 (= acala); santimaggaŋ eva brūhaya n°ŋ Sugatena desitaŋ Dh 285 = Nett 36; sandiṭṭhikaŋ akālikaŋ etc.; A I.158; samo bhūmibhāgo ramaṇīyo S III.109; sassataŋ Kvu 34; suvatthi Sn 235. — 5. N. is *realisable in this world*, i. e. in this life *if it is mature* (diṭṭhe va dhamme): S II.18 = 115 = III.163 = IV.141 (diṭṭha-dh-n-patta); M II.228; A IV.353 = 358, cp. 454. — 6. *Definitions* with regard to the destruction of the causes or substrata of life (cp. above I.): taṇhāya vippahānena n°ŋ iti vuccati S I.39 = Sn 1109; as sabba-sankhāra-samatho (calming down of all vital elements) Vin I.5; S I.136; A II.118 = III.164; IV.423; v.8, 110, 320, 354; akiñcanaŋ anādānaŋ etaŋ dīpaŋ anāparaŋ n°ŋ iti nam brūmi jarāmaccu-parikkhayaŋ Sn 1094; bhavanirodho n°ŋ ti S II.117; A v.9; rāga-kkhayo (dosa°, moha°) S IV.251 = 261; virāgo nirodho n°ŋ in typical & very freq. exposition at Nd[2] = S I.136≈. See also vana & cp. the foll.: taṇhā-sankhāta-vānâbhāvato n°ŋ SnA 253; nikkhantaŋ vānato ti n°ŋ KhA 151; kilesa-n° ass' âpi anupādā parinibbānass' âpi santike yeva DhA I.286 (on Dh 32). — 7. N. as perfect *wisdom* and what is conducive to such a state (saŋvattati). The foll. phrase is one of the oldest stereotype phrases in the Canon & very freq.; it is used of all the highest means & attainments of conduct & meditation & may be said to mark the goal of perfect understanding & a perfect philosophy of life. It is given in 2 variations, viz. in a simple form as "upasamāya abhiññāya sambodhāya nibbānāya saŋvattati," with ref. to majjhimā paṭipadā at Vin I.10 = S IV.331 = v.421; of satta bojjhangā at S v.80; and in a fuller form as "ekanta-nibbidāya virāgāya nirodhāya upasamāya etc. as above" at D I.189 (negative); II.251 (of brahmacariyaŋ), 285; III.130 (sukhallikânuyogā, neg.) 136 (avyākataŋ, neg.); S II.223 (brahmacariya); v.82 (satta bojjhangā), 179 (satipaṭṭhānā), 255 (iddhipādā), 361 (ariyamagga), 438 A III.83, 326 sq.; etc. — Cp. n-saŋvattanika S v.97 (upekhāsambojjhanga); Nd[2] 281 (neg. of tamo). — 8. N. as the *opposite of rāga* (passion, lust). Freq. is the combn of virāga nirodha nibbāna, almost used as three synonyms, thus at S II.18; Vin III.20 = 111; A II.118 = III.164 = IV.423 = v.8 = Nd[2] under Nibbāna; A II.34 = It 88 (dhammānaŋ aggaŋ akkhāyati, madanimmadano pipāsa-vinayo ālaya-samugghāto vaṭṭûpacchedo taṇhakkhayo virāgo nirodha nibbānaŋ), cp. Vin III.20≈. Similarly S I.192 (Sugataŋ payirupāsati desentaŋ virajaŋ dhammaŋ nibbānaŋ akutobhayaŋ). — 9. *Various Characterisations & Similes* (cp. above II. A 4 & 5). sukkâbhijātiko samāno akaṇhaŋ asukkaŋ n°ŋ abhijayati D III.251; A III.384 sq.; aniccā sabbe sankhārā dukkhā 'nattā ca sankhātā: nibbānañ c' eva paññatti anattā iti nicchayā Vin v.86. On anicca & anattā in rel. to N. see also S IV.133 sq.; A IV.353; dukkhato & sukhato n°ŋ samanupassati A III.442. On comparison with a lamp see e. g. S I.159 = D II.157 = Th I, 905 (pajjotass' eva nibbānaŋ vimokkho cetaso ahū), A IV.3 (pajjotass' eva n. vimokkho hoti cetaso); Sn 235 (. . . te khīṇabījā avirūḷhichandā nibbanti dhīrā yathâyaŋ padīpo).

-abhirata fond of N. (cp. III. 3) S I.38; A III.435; Sn 86 (visalla +); -ogadha merging into N. (of brahmacariya) S III.189; v.218; A II.26 = It 28; Vbh 426, cp. amatogadha A v.107; -gamana (magga; cp. III. 2) leading to N. D II.223; S I.186, 217; A IV.83; (dhamma:)

S v.11; Sn 233; -dhātu the sphere or realm of N. always in phrase anupādisesāsaya n.-dhātuyā parinibbāyate Vin ii.239; D iii.135; It 38, 121; Ps i.101; cp. rāga-vinayo n.-dhātuyā adhivacanaŋ S v.8. See parinibbāyin; -ninna (+°poṇa, °pabbhāra; cp. III. 3) converging into N. A iii.443; Vv 84[42] & passim; -paṭisaññuta (dhammikathā; cp. III. 2) relating or referring to N. S i.114=192=210; Ud 80; -patta having attained N. (diṭṭha-dhamma°, see above III. 5) S ii.18=114=iii.163; -patti attainment of N. S i.48, 214=Sn 186; -pada=Nibbāna (see pada 3) Sn 204. -pariyosāna ending in N. having its final goal in N. S iii.189; v.218; A v.107; -saŋvattanika conducive to N.; contributing toward the attainment of N. S v.97; Nd[2] 281 (a°); cp. above III. 7; -sacchikiriyā realisation of N. (identical with ñāṇa and constituting the highest ideal; cp. above III. 2) Sn 267. Cp. also D ii.290; S v.167; A iii.423; v.141; -saññā perception of N. A iii.443; -sampatti successful attainment of N. Kh viii.13; -sampadā the blessing of the attainment of N. A iv.239.

Nibbāpana (nt.) [abstr. fr. nibbāpeti] means of extinguishing, extinction, quenching S i.188 (cittaŋ pariḍayhati: nibbāpanaŋ brūhi=allayment of the glow); A iv.320 (celassa n°āya chandaŋ karoti: try to put out the burning cloth); Miln 302 (jhāyamāno n°ŋ alabhamāno), 318 (pariḷāha°).

Nibbāpita (adj.) [pp. of nibbāpeti] extinguished, put out, quenched J iii.99 (=nicchuddha).

Nibbāpeti [Sk. ni(r)vārayati, Caus. of ni(r)varati, influenced in meaning by nirvāpayati. Caus. of nirvāti=make cool by blowing (e. g. RV x.16[13]). See nibbuta on etym.] 1. to extinguish, put out, quench S i.188 (mahā-rāgaŋ); It 93 (rāg-aggiŋ; & nibbāpetvā aggiŋ nipakā parinibbanti); cp. aggiŋ nijjāleti J vi.495; Pv i.8[5] (vārinā viya osiñcaŋ sabbaŋ daraŋ nibbāpaye); Miln 304 (aggikhandhaŋ mahāmegho abhippavassitvā n.), 318 (nibbāpehi me hadaya-pariḷāhaŋ), 410 (megho uṇhaŋ n.); DhA ii.241 (fire); Sdhp 552 (bhavadukkh' aggiŋ).—2. to cleanse, purify (cittaŋ, one's heart) Vism 305.—pp. nibbāpita. See also nibbāpana.

Nibbāyati [Sk. ni-(or nir-)vriyate, Pass. of ni(r)varati, influenced by nirvāyati intrs. to cease to blow; see on etym. & Pāli derivation nibbuta] 1. to be cooled or refreshed, to be covered up=to be extinguished, go out (of fire), to cease to exist, always used with ref. to fire or heat or (fig.) burning sensations (see nibbāna II. A end): aggikkhandho purimassa ca upādānassa puriyādānā aññassa ca anupāhārā anāhāro nibbāyeyya S ii.85 (opp. jāleyya); do. of telaŋ & vaṭṭiŋ paṭicca telappadīpo n. S ii.86=iii.126=iv.213=v.319; sace te purato so aggi nibbāyeyya jāneyyāsi tvaŋ: ayaŋ . . . aggi nibbuto M i.487; A iv.70 (papaṭikā n.); aggi udake tiṇukkā viya n. J i.212; mātuhadayaŋ n. J i.61; aggi upādāna-sankhayā n. Miln 304.—aor. nibbāyi [Sk. niravāri] J i.27 (mano n.: was refreshed) 212 (aggi udake n.: was extinguished); vi.349 (cooled down).—2. to go out (of light) Vism 430 (dīpā nibbāyiŋsu the lights went out); ThA 154 (dīpacci n. nirāsanā: went out). See also parinibbāyati & cp. nibbuta, nibbāpeti, nibbāpana.

Nibbāyin see pari°.

Nibbāhana (adj.-n.) [fr. nibbāheti] leading out, removing, saving; (nt.) removal, clearance, refuge, way out Miln 119, 198, 295, 309, 326 (°magga). [Miln. the only references!]

Nibbāhati [nis+vahati] to lead out, carry out, save from, remove Miln 188.—2nd Caus. nibbāhāpeti to have brought out, to unload (a waggon) Vin ii.159 (hiraññaŋ); iii.43. See also nibbāhana & nibbuyhati.

Nibbikappa [nis+vikappa] distinction, distinguishing Vism 193.

Nibbikāra (adj.) [nis+vikāra] steady, unchanged, steadfast; persevering J i.66; PvA 178, 253 (+nicca); SnA 189, 497; Vism 311.

Nibbicikicchā (f.) [nis+vicikicchā] surety, reliance, trust S ii.84; v.221 (=nikkankhā); VvA 85 (=ekaŋsikā).

Nibbijjhati [nis+vijjhati, **vyadh**] to pierce, transfix, wound S v.88 (+padāleti); Sdhp 153 (patodehi). ger. nibbijjha Sn 940 (=paṭivijjhitvā Nd[1] 420).—pp. nibbiddha. Cp. abhi°.

Nibbiṭṭha (pp.) [nis+viṭṭha, of nibbisati] gained, earned Vin iv.265; Sn 25; SnA 38.

Nibbiṇṇa (adj.) [Sk. nirviṇṇa, pp. of nibbindati] tired of, wearied of, dissatisfied disgusted with (c. instr. or loc.), wearied of, dissatisfied with, "fed up" J i.347; vi.62; Th 2, 478 (=viratta ThA 286); DhA i.85 (°hadaya); VvA 207 (°rūpa); PvA 159 (tattha-vāsena n-mānaso tired of living there), 272 (°rūpa), 283 (°rūpa, tired of: purohite).

Nibbidā (f.) [Sk. nirvid, f. (also BSk. e. g. Lal. V. 300) & nirveda; to nibbindati] weariness, disgust with worldly life, tedium, aversion, indifference, disenchantment. N. is of the preliminary & conditional states for the attainment of Nibbāna (see nibbāna II B 1) & occurs frequently together with virāga, vimutti & nibbāna in the formula: etaŋ ekanta-nibbidāya virāgāya nirodhāya . . . sambodhāya nibbānāya saŋvattati "this leads to being thoroughly tired (of the world), to dispassionateness, to destruction (of egoism), to perfect wisdom, to Nibbāna," e. g. at D i.189; S v.82, 179, 255, 361; A iii.83; iv.143; v.216.—In other connections: Vin i.15 (nibbidāya cittaŋ saṇṭhāsi); D iii.130 sq.; S ii.30; iii.40; 179, 189; iv.86, 141 (read nibbidāya for nibbindāya?); A i.51, 64; iii.19, 200, 325 sq.; iv.99, 336; v.2 sq., 311 sq.; J i.97; iv.471, 473; Sn 340; Ps i.195; ii.43 sq.; Vbh 330; Nett 27, 29; Vism 650. Cp. abhi°.

Nibbiddha [pp. of nibbijjhati] 1. in phrase °pingala (with) disgustingly red (eyes) (perhaps=nibbiṇṇa?) J v.42 (of a giant).—2. with ref. to a road: broken up, i. e. much frequented, busy street J vi.276 (of vīthi, bazaar, in contrast with a-nibbiddha-raccha carriage-road, which is not a thoroughfare. The reading patatthiyo at J vi.276, for which nibbiddha-vīthiyo is the C. expl°, is to be corrected into pathaddhiyo).

Nibbindati [nis+vindati, **vid**[2]] to get wearied of (c. loc.), to have enough of, be satiated, turn away from, to be disgusted with. In two roots A. **vind**: prs. nibbindati etc. usually in comb[n] with virajjati & vimuccati (cp. nibbāna III. 2). Vin i.35; S ii.94; iv.86, 140; A v.3; Dh 277 sq.; It 33; J i.267; Miln 235, 244; Sdhp 612. ppr. nibbindaŋ S iv.86; PvA 36 (nibbinda-mānasa); ger. nibbindiya J v.121 (°kārin).—B **vid**: Pot. nibbide (v. l. BB nibbije) J v.368 (=nibbindeyya Com.); ger. nibbijjitvā J i.82, & nibbijja Sn 448=S i.124 (nibbijjāpema=nibbijja pakkameyya SnA 393).—pp. nibbiṇṇa. See also nibbidā.

Nibbiriya (adj.) [nis+viriya] lacking in strength, indolent, slothful, weak J iv.131; PvA 175 (=alasa, kusīta].

Nibbivara (adj.) [nis+vivara] without holes or fissures, without omissions J v.429; VvA 275 (=ativa sangata).

Nibbisa [to nibbisati] earning, wages Th 1, 606=1003=Miln 45 (cp. Manu vi.45); SnA 38.

Nibbisanka (adj.) [nis+visanka, Sk. viśankā] fearless, not hesitating, undaunted SnA 61.

Nibbisati [nis+visati] to enter into; to earn, gain, find, enjoy, only in pp. anibbisaŋ not finding Th 2, 159 (=avindanto ThA 142); J i.76=Dh 153.—pp. nibbiṭṭha. See also nibbisa.

Nibbisaya (adj.) [nis+ visaya] having no residence, banished, driven from (-°) J II.401.

Nibbisevana (adj.) [nis+ visevana] not self-indulgent, self-denying, meek, tame, gentle J II.210 (dametvā nibbisevanaŋ katvā), 351; V.34, 381, 456; VI.255; DhA I.288 (cittaŋ ujuŋ akuṭilaŋ n. karoti), 295; VvA 284 (°bhava =jitindriya)

Nibbisesa (adj.) [nis+ visesa] showing no difference, without distinction, equal, similar J II.32; VI.355; Miln 249.

Nibbujjhati [ni+ yujjhati, **yudh.** Pāli form difficult to explain: niy°=niyy°=nivv°=nibb°] to wrestle, to fight with fists Vin III.180. — pp. nibbuddha.

Nibbuta (adj.) [Nibbuta represents Sk. nirvṛta (e. g. AvŚ I.48) as well as nivṛta, both pp. of **vṛ**, which in itself combines two meanings, as exhibited in cognate languages and in Sk. itself: (a) Idg. **ṷer** to cover, cover up (Lat. aperio=*apa-verio to cover up, Sk. varutram upper garment, "cover") and (b) ***ṷel** to resolve, roll, move (Lat. volvo=revolve; Gr. ἕλιξ, ἐλύω; Sk. vāṇa reed=Lat. ulva; Sk. ūrmi wave; P. valli creeper, valita wrinkled). ***ṷer** is represented in P. by e. g. vivarati to open, nivāreti to cover, obstruct, nīvaraṇa, nivāraṇa obstruction; ***ṷel** by āvuta, khandh-āvāra, parivāra, vyāvaṭa (busy with=moving about), samparivāreti. Thus we gain the two meanings comb^d and used promiscuously in the one word because of their semantic affinity: (a) ***nivṛta** covered up, extinguished, quenched, and (b) ***nirvṛta** without movement, with motion finished (cp. niṭṭhita), ceasing, exhaustion, both represented by P. nibbuta. — In derivations we have besides the root-form **vṛ** (=P. bbu°) that with guṇa **vṝ** (cp. Sk. vārayati, vrāyati) or **vrā**=P.* bbā° (with which also cp. paṭivāṇa=*prativāraṇa). The former is in nibbuti (ceasing, extinction, with meaning partly influenced by nibbuṭṭhi=Sk. nirvṛṣṭi pouring of water), the latter in instr. nibbāti and nibbāyati (to cease or to go out) and trs. nibbāpeti (Caus.: to make cease, to stop or cool) and further in nibbāna (nt. instr. abstr.) (the dying out)] (lit.) extinguished (of fire), cooled, quenched (fig.) desireless (often with nicchāta & sītibhūta), appeased, pleased, happy. — (a) (lit.) aggi anāhāro n. M I.487; Sn 19 (ginī n.=magga-salila-sekena n. SnA 28); J IV.391 (anibbute pāyāse); Miln 304 (aggikkhandha), 346 (mahāmeghena n°ŋ pathaviŋ); ThA 154 (anupādānā dīp' accī); KhA 194 (padīpo n.). — (b) (fig.) comb^d with sītibhūta (& nicchāta): Vin I.8; M I.341; A II.208 =D III.233=Pug 56, 61; A IV.410; V.65; Sn 593, 707; Pv I.8^7. — In phrase **anupādāya nibbuta**: S II.279; A I.162; IV.290=Dh 414=Sn 638. — In other connections: attadaṇḍesu n. sādānesu anādāno S I.236= Dh 406=Sn 630; aññāya nibbutā dhīrā S I.24; tadanga-n. S III.43; ejānugo anejassa nibbutassa anibbuto It 91; vītataṇho n. Sn 1041; tiṇṇa-sokapariddavo n. Dh 196; rāg' agginihi n. & n. mātā, pitā, nārī J I.60; n. veyyākaraṇena Miln 347; upādānānaŋ abhāvena . . . kilesanibbānena n. DhA IV.194. — See also **abhinibbuta** and **parinibbuta**.

Nibbuti (f.) [Sk. nirvṛtti, abstr. to nibbuta] allayment, refreshment, cooling, peace, happiness J I.3 (khemaŋ pariyessāmi n°ŋ); Sn 228 (nikkāmino n°ŋ bhuñjamānā), 917, 933 (santī ti n°ŋ ñatvā); Nd^1 399; Pv I.7^4 (n°ŋ n' ādhigacchāmi=quenching of hunger & thirst); KhA 185 (=paṭippassaddha-kilesa-daratha).

Nibbuddha [Sk. niyuddha, pp. of nibbujjhati] wrestling, fist-fight D I.6 (=mallayuddhaŋ DA I.85); DhsA 403.

Nibbuyhati [Sk. niruhyate, nis+ vuyhati, Pass. of vahati, cp. nibbāhati] to be led out to (c. acc.): susānaŋ Th 2, 468 (=upanīyati ThA 284); to be led out of=to be saved S I.1, cp. RV I.117, 14; VI.62, 6.

Nibbusitattā (nibbusitattan ?) [Sk. *nir-vasit-ātman or *nirvasitatvaŋ (nt. abstr.), to nis-vasati, cp. nirvāsana =nibbisaya] a dislocated or disconcerted mind, unrest, uneasiness D I.17.

Nibbecikicchā=nibbicikicchā (certainty, doubtlessness) Nd^2 185 (opp. savicikicchā).

Nibbejaniya at S I.124 should probably be read as nibbeṭhaniya (rejecting, evading).

Nibbeṭhana (nt.) [Sk. nirveṣṭana, nis+ veṭhana] unwinding, fig. explanation Miln 28.

Nibbeṭhita [pp. of nibbeṭheti] explained, unravelled, made clear Miln 123 (su°).

Nibbeṭheti [Sk. nirveṣṭate, nis+ veṭheti, to twist round] 1. to unravel, untwist, unwind; to explain, make clear D I.54 (nibbeṭhiyamāna, v. l. BB nibbedh°); Pv IV.3^{29} (°ento=niveṭhīyamāna PvA 253 v. l. BB nibbedh°); Miln 3; Sdhp 153. — 2. to deny, reject Vin II.79; D I.3 (=apanetabba Com.); S III.12 (v. l. BB °dh°). — 3. to give an evasive answer Vin III.162. — See also nibbejaniya. — pp. **nibbeṭhita**, q. v.

Nibbedha [nis+ vedha, to **vyadh**] penetration, insight; adj.: penetrating, piercing, scrutinising, sharp. Freq. in phrase **nibbedha-bhāgiya** (sharing the quality of penetration), with ref. to samādhi, saññā etc. [cp. BSk. nirvedha° Divy 50; but also nirbheda° AvŚ II.181, of kusalamūlāni; expl^d as lobhakkhandhassa (etc.) nibbijjhanāni at Nett 274] D III.251, 277; A III.427; Vbh 330; Nett 21, 48, 143 sq., 153 sq.; Vism 15, 88; DhsA 162. — Also in nibbedha-gāminī (paññā) It 35; & **dunnibbedha** (hard to penetrate, difficult to solve Miln 155, 233 (pañha); spelt **dunniveṭha** at Miln 90).

Nibbedhaka (adj.) [nis+ vedhaka, to **vyadh**] piercing, sharp, penetrating, discriminating; only in f. **nibbedhikā** (cp. āvedhikā), appl^d to **paññā** (wisdom) D III.237, 268; S V.197, 199; M I.356; A I.45; II.167; III.152; 410 sq., 416; V.15; Ps II.201; Nd^2 235, 3^a (+ tikkha-paññā), 415, 689; J II.9, 297; IV.267.

Nibbematika (adj.) [nis+ vimati+ ka] not disagreeing, of one accord, unanimous Vin II.65; DhA I.34.

Nibbhacceti [Sk. nirbhartsayati, nis+ bhaccheti] to threaten, revile, scorn J III.338.

Nibbhaya (adj.) [nis+ bhaya] free from fear or danger, fearless, unafraid J I.274; III.80; V.287; Vism 512.

Nibbhujati [Sk. ni- or nirbhujati, nis+ bhujati] to twist round, bend, wind, contort oneself Miln 253. Cp. vi°.

Nibbhoga (adj.) [Sk. nirbhoga, nis+ bhoga^1] deprived of enjoyment; deserted, being of no avail, useless J VI.556; Pv I.12. Cp. vi°.

Nibbhoga [ni+ bhoga^2] bending, contortion J II.264 (oṭṭha°).

Nibyaggha see nivyaggha.

Nibha (adj.) [Sk. nibha, to bhāti] shining; like, equal to, resembling (-°) J V.372; Vv 40^9; Pv IV.3^2; VvA 122 (vaṇṇa°=vaṇṇa); Nd^1 608.

Nibhatā (f.) [abstr. to nibha] likeness, appearance VvA 27.

Nibhā (f.) [to nibha] shine, lustre, splendour VvA 179 (nibhāti dippatī ti nibhā).

Nibhāti [ni+ bhāti] to shine VvA 179 (=dippati).

Nimajjhima (adj.) the middle one J V.371.

Nimantaka (adj.-n.) one who invites Miln 205.

Nimantana (nt.) [to nimanteti] invitation Vin I.58 = II.175; D I.166; M I.77; A I.295; J I.116 (n), 412; Pug 55.

Nimantanika (adj.) inviting; (nt.) N. of a Suttanta M I.331; quoted at Vism 393.

Nimantita [pp. of nimanteti] invited Sn p. 104; PvA 22 (bhattena to the meal), 86 (= āmantita), 141.

Nimanteti [Sk. nimantrayati, ni+ manteti] to send a message, to call, summon, invite, coax (to = c. instr.) Sn 981 (nimantayi aor., āsanena asked him to sit down); J VI.365; Nd^2 342; DhA III.171 (°ayiŋsu); DA I.169; VvA 47 (pāniyena invite to a drink); PvA 75, 95. — pp. nimantita, q. v. — Cp. abhi°.

Nimitta (nt.) [cp. Sk. nimitta, to **mā**, although etym. uncertain] 1. sign, omen, portent, prognostication D I.9 (study of omens = n. satthaŋ DA I.92, q. v. for detailed expl^n); J I.11 (caturo nimitte nâddasaŋ); Miln 79, 178. Esp. as pubba° signs preceding an event, portents, warnings, foreshadowings S V.154, 278, 442; It 76 (cp. Divy 193, of the waning of a god); J I.48, 50 (32 signs before birth, some at DA I.61), 59; Miln 298; Vism 577. — 2. outward appearance, mark, characteristic, attribute, phenomenon (opp. essence) D III.249; A I.256; III.319, 375 sq.; IV.33, 418 sq.; J I.420; Ps I.60, 91 sq., 164, 170; II.39, 64; Vbh 193 sq. — Mental reflex, image (with ref. to jhāna) Vism 123, cp. DhsA 167. — Specified e. g. as foll.: oḷārika S V.259; pasādaniya S V.156; paccavekkhana° D III.278; Vbh 334; bahiddhā-sankhārā° Ps I.66 sq.; bāla° (opp. paṇḍita°) M III.163; A I.102; mukha° (= face) D I.80; S III.103; V.121; A V.92, 97 sq., 103; rūpa°, sadda° etc. S III.10; M I.296; Ps I.92, 112; samatha° D III.213; samādhi° etc. A I.256 sq.; subha° (& asubha°) S V.64, 103 sq.; A I.3 sq., 87, 200; V.134; Vism 178 sq. **nimittaŋ gaṇhāti** to make something the object of a thought, to catch up a theme for reflection Vin I.183, cp. S V.150 sq. (°ŋ uggaṇhāti); M I.119 (= five sorts of mental images); Nd^2 659; DhsA 53 (= ākāra). See below n-gāhin & animitta.— nimittaŋ parivajjeti to discard the phenomenal S I.188; Sn 341. — 3. mark, aim: in nimittaŋ karoti to pick out the aim, to mark out J V.436; Nd^2 235. 1^d; Miln 418. — 4. sexual organ (cp. lakkhaṇa) Vin III.129 (n. & a°, as term of abuse); see also kāṭa & koṭacikā. — 5. ground, reason, condition, in nimittena (instr.) and nimittaŋ (acc.) as adv. = by means of, on account of DhA III.175 (instr.) PvA 8, 97 (jāti-nimittaŋ), 106 (kiŋ n°ŋ = kissa hetu), 242 (yaŋ n°ŋ = yato nidānaŋ). gahita-nimittena "by means of being caught" Vism 144 = DhsA 116 (read trsl^n 154 accordingly!). adj. nimitta (-°) caused by, referring to PvA 64 (maraṇa-nimittaŋ rodanaŋ). — **animitta** free from marks or attributes, not contaminated by outward signs or appearance, undefiled, unaffected, unconditioned (opp. sa°) S I.188; IV.225 (phassa), 268, 360 (samādhi); M I.296 (cetovimutti); A I.82; III.292; IV.78; Vin III.129; Th I, 92; D III.219, 249; Dh 92; Sn 342; Ps I.60, 91; II.36, 59 sq. (vimokha), 65 sq., 99; Dhs 530 (read a° [illegible]), Vism 236; DhsA 223 (absence of the 3 lakkhaṇas); Miln 333, 413; DhA II.172; ThA 50. See also *Cpd.* 199, 211^5. sanimitta S V.213 sq.; A I.82.

-ânusārin following outward signs (= °gāhin) A III.292; Nett 25; **-kamma** prognostication, prophecy Vin V.172; Vbh 353; **-karaṇa** = gāhin S IV.297; **-gāhin** "taking signs," enticed or led away by outward signs, entranced with the general appearance, sensuously attracted. D I.70 (cp. *Dialogues* I.80); III.225; S IV.104, 168; A II.16; III.99; V.348; Pug 20, 24, 58; Dhs 1345; Miln 367, 403. Cp. Vism 151, 209.

Nimināti [Sk. niminoti in diff. meaning, the P. meaning being influenced by **mā**; ni+ mināti, **mi** to fix, measure cp. Sk. nimaya barter, change] to turn round, change; to barter, exchange for (c. instr.): pres. imper. niminā J V.343 (= parivattehi Com.); pres. 1st pl. nimimhase J II.369, pot. nimineyya J III.63; fut. nimissati J V.271, 453 (devatāhi nirayaŋ); aor. nimmini J III.63; ger. niminitvā Milo 279.

Nimisa [cp. Vedic nimiṣ f. & nimiṣa nt.] winking, shutting the eyes; animisa not winking Dāvs V.26. See also nimesa.

Nimisatā (f.) [abstr. to nimisati] winking J VI.336 (a°).

Nimisati [Sk. nimiṣati, ni+ misati] to wink D II.20 (animisanto, not winking; v. l. BB animm°; J III.96 (ummisati +). Cp. nimisatā.

Nimīlati (& **Nimmīlati**) [ni+ mīlati] to shut, close (the eyes) J I.279; DhA II.6 (akkhīni nimmīlituŋ nâsakkhi). Caus. nim(m)ī-leti id. M I.120; DhA II.28 (paralokaŋ; opp. ummīleti); J I.279; Vism 292 (akkhīni ni°).

Nimugga (adj.) [cp. Sk. nimagna, pp. of nimujjati] plunged, immersed in, sunk down or fallen into (-°) (c. loc.) Vin III.106 (gūthakūpe sasisakaŋ n.); D I.75; J I.4; III.393 (gūthakalale), 415; Nd^1 26; Pug 71; Miln 262; Sdhp 573.

Nimujjā (nimmujjā) [Sk. *nimajj-yā] diving, immersion, in cpd. ummujja-nimujja(ŋ karoti) D I.78. See ummujjā.

Nimujjati [Sk. nimajjati, ni+ mujjati] to sink down, plunge into (with loc.), dive in, be immersed A IV.11; Pug 74; J I.66, 70; III.163, 393 (kāmakalale); IV.139; aor. nimujji J II.293; PvA 47 (udake). — Caus. nimujjeti (so read for nimujjati J V.268) & **nimujjāpeti** to cause to sink or dive, to drown J III.133; IV.142 (nāvaŋ). — pp. nimugga q. v.

Nimujjana (nt.) [Sk. nimajjana] diving, ducking; bathing PvA 47.

Nimesa [= nimisa, cp. Vedic nimesa] winking Miln 194.

Nimokkha = vimokkha S I.2 (v. l. SS vi°, preferable).

Nimba [Sk. nimba, non-Aryan] the Nimb tree (Azadirachta Indica), bearing a bitter leaf, & noted for its hard wood Vin I.152 (°kosa), 284 (id.), 201 (°kasāva); A I.32; V.212; Vv 33^{38} (°muṭṭhi, a handful of N. leaves); J II.105, 106; DhA I.52 (°kosa); DhsA 320 (°paṇṇa, the leaf of the N. as example of tittaka, bitter taste); VvA 142 (°palāsa); PvA 220 (°rukkhassa daṇḍena katasūla).

Nimmaŋsa (adj.) [nis+ maŋsa] fleshless M I.58, 364; PvA 68.

Nimmakkha (adj.) [nis+ makkha, cp. Sk. nirmatsara without egotism, not false, not slandering Sn 56 (cp. Nd^2 356 makkha = niṭṭhuriya; see also SnA 108: paraguṇa-vināsana-lakkhaṇo makkho).

Nimmakkhika (adj.) [Sk. nirmakṣika] free from flies J I.262; DhA I.59.

Nimmajjana (**Nimmiñjana** ?) [*mṛd-yana ? perhaps non-Aryan] a kind of (oil-)cake Vv 33^{38} (nimmajjani = tilapiññāka VvA 147); Pv 1.10^{10} (°miñjana, v. l. BB °majjani); PvA 47 (doṇi°).

Nimmathana (nt.) [nis+ mathana] crushing J III.252; Vism 234 (sattu°); DhA III.404; VvA 284.

Nimmatheti [nis+ matheti] to crush out, suppress, destroy J I.340. Cp. abhimatthati.

Nimmadana (nt.) [to nimmādeti] touching, touch, crushing, subduing A II.34 (mada-nimmadana, crushing out pride; may, however, be taken as nis+ mada of **mad** = "de-priding," lit. disintoxication); Bu I.81; Vism 293.

Nimmadaya (adj.) [Sk. nirmṛdya, grd. of nimmadeti] suppressible D II.243.

Nimmaddana (nt.) [nis+ **mṛd**] touching, crushing Miln 270 (na vāto hattha-gahaṇaŋ vā nimmaddanaŋ vā upeti: the wind cannot be grasped).

Nimmanussa (nt.) [nis+ manussa+ ya] void of men, absence of men J III.148.

Nimmala (adj.) [nis+ mala] free from impurity, stainless, clean, pure A IV.340; Dh 243; Nd[2] 586; Vism 58; Sdhp 250.

Nimmāta-pitika (adj.) [nis+ māta-pitika] one who has neither mother nor father, an orphan DhA II.72.

Nimmātar [Sk. nirmātṛ, n. ag. of nimmiṇāti] maker, builder, creator D I.18, 56 (in formula: brahmā . . . kattā nimmātā . . .).

Nimmādeti [either = Sk. nirmṛdayati (**mṛd**) or *nirmādayati to nirmada free from pride = nirmāna] to crush, subdue, humiliate; insult D I.92 (v. l. °maddeti; = DA I.257 nimmadati nimmāne karoti), 93, 96.

Nimmāna[1] (nt.) [Sk. nirmāṇa, see nimmiṇāti] measuring; production, creation, work; issara-n-hetu caused by God M II.122; A I.173; Vbh 367. N.-ratī devā a class of devas, e. g. at D I.218; It 94; Vism 225; DA I.114; ThA 169; VvA 149. Cp. (para-) nimmita.

Nimmāna[2] (adj.) [Sk. nirmāna, nis+ māna] free from pride, humble DA I.257.

Nimmāniyati [Pass. to nimmāna, of nis+ māna] to be abased, to be mocked Vin II.183.

Nimmita (adj.-pp.) [pp. of nimmiṇāti] measured out, planned, laid out; created (by supernatural power, iddhi); measured, stately D I.18, 56 (iddhiyā pi DA I.167), 219 (Su° devaputta, Np.), ibid. (Paranimmitavasavattī devā a class of devas, lit. "created by others," but also possessed of great power: VvA 79, 80); also one of the 5, or the 3 spheres (kāmûpapattiyo) in the kāmaloka, viz. paccupaṭṭhita-kāmā, nimmānarati° (or nimmita°), paranimmita°. It 94; Dhs 1280 (cp. kāma); D III.218; J I.59, 146 (kāyo n' eva deva° na brahma°), 232, Nd[2] 202[4], also under pucchā; P II.1[19] (su°, well constructed, i. e. symmetrical); Vism 228 (Mārena nimmitaŋ Buddharūpaŋ); VvA 36 (= mitaŋ gacchati vāraṇo), 79; ThA 69, 70; Miln 1, 242. See also abhinimmita.

Nimmiṇāti [cp. Sk. nirmamāti & nirmāti, nis+ mināti, **mā**; cp. nimiṇāti] to measure out, fashion, build, construct, form; make by miracle, create, compose; produçe, lay out, plan, aor. nimmini J I.232; PvA 245; DhA IV.67; ger **nimminitvā** J I.32; VvA 80, & nimmāya Vv 16[3]. — pp. **nimmita** See also nimmātar and nimmāna. Cp. abhi°.

Nimmileti see nimīlati.

Nimmūla (adj.) [nis+ mūla] without root, rootless J VI.177.

Nimmoka [Sk. nirmoka fr. nis+ moceti] the slough or cast-off skin of a snake PvA 63.

Niya (adj.) [Sk. nija, q. v.] one's own Sn 149 (°putta = orasaputta KhA 248); niyassakamma at A I.99 & Pv IV.1[13] (v. l. Minayeff tiyassa) is to be read as nissayakamma (q. v.).

Niyaka (adj.) [= niya] one's own Th 2, 469; ThA 284; DhsA 169, 337; DA I.183; Vbh 2; Vism 349.

Niyata (adj.) [pp. of ni+ **yam**] restrained, bound to, constrained to, sure (as to the future), fixed (in its consequences), certain, assured, necessary D II.92 (sambodhiparāyanā), 155; III.107; Sn 70 (= ariyamaggena niyāmappatta SnA 124, cp. Nd[2] 357); Dh 142 (= catumagga-niyamena n. DhA III.83); J I.44 (bodhiyā); Pug 13, 16, 63; Kvu 609 sq.; Dhs 1028 sq. (micchatta° etc.; cp. Dhs. trsl. 266, 267), 1414, 1595; Vbh 17, 24, 63, 319, 324; Miln 193; Tikp 168 (°micchādiṭṭhi); DhA III.170; PvA 211. Discussed in *Pts. of Contr.* (see Index). — aniyata see separately.

Niyati (f.) [cp. Sk. niyati, ni+ **yam**] necessity, fate, destiny D I.53; DA I.161; VvA 341; PvA 254.

Niyama [cp. Sk. niyama, ni+ **yam**; often confused with niyāma] 1. restraint, constraint, training, self-control Miln 116 (yama +); PvA 98 (yama +). — 2. definiteness, certainty, limitation DhA III.83 (catumagga°, v. l. niyāma); SnA 124 (niyāma); DhsA 154; PvA 166 (ayaŋ n. saŋsāren' atthi: law, necessity). — **aniyama** indefiniteness, choice, generality DhsA 57; VvA 16 (yaŋ kiñci = aniyame, i. e. in a general sense), 17 (same of ye keci); PvA 175 (vā saddo aniyamattho = indefinite). — **niyamena** (instr.) adv. by necessity, necessarily PvA 287; **niyamato** (abl.) id. DhsA 145, 304 (so read). — 3. natural law, cosmic order; in Commentarial literature this was fivefold: utu-, bīja-, kamma-, citta-, dhamma-DA on D II.11; *Dial.* II.8; DhsA 272; trs. 360.

Niyamana (nt.) [Sk. niyamana, to niyameti] fixing, settling, definition, explanation in detail Miln 352 (lakkha-n° aiming at the target); VvA 22 (visesattha°); 231, PvA 255 (so read for nigamana ?).

Niyameti [cp. Sk. niyamayati, ni+ yamati] to tie down, to fix; explain in detail, exemplify PvA 265; Vism 666. — pp. niyamita see a°.

Niyāteti see niyyādeti.

Niyāma [Sk. niyama & niyāma] way, way to an end or aim, esp. to salvation, right way (sammatta°); method, manner, practice S I.196; III.225 (sammatta°); A I.122; Sn 371 (°dassin = sammatta-niyāmabhūtassa maggassa dassāvin SnA 365); Nd[1] 314 (°avakkanti); Nd[2] 358 (= cattāro maggā); Ps II.236 sq. (sammatta° okkamati); Pug 13, 15; Vbh 342. — **niyāmena** (instr.) adv. in this way, by way of, according to J I.278; IV.139, 414 (suta° as he had heard); DhA I.79; II.9, 21; VvA 4; PvA 260; Kvu trs. 383. — **aniyāmena** (see also aniyāmena) without order, aimlessly, at random J V.337.

Niyāmaka[1] (adj.) [either to niyama or niyāma] sure of or in, founded in, or leading to, completed in D I.190 (dhamma-n. paṭipadā, cp. niyamatā).

Niyāmaka[2] (see niyyāmaka) ship's captain Vism 137 (simile).

Niyāmatā (f.) [abstr. to niyāma, influenced in meaning by niyama] state of being settled, certainty, reliance, surety, being fixed in (-°) S II.25 (dhamma° + dhammaṭṭhitatā); A I.286 (id.), J I.113 (saddhammassa n. assurance of . . .); Kvu 586 (accanta° final assurance).

Niyāmeti [Denom. fr. niyāma or niyama] to restrain, control, govern, guide Miln 378 (nāvaŋ).

Niyujjati [Pass. of niyuñjati] to be fit for, to be adapted to, to succeed, result, ensue PvA 49 (= upakappati).

Niyutta(ka) (adj.) [pp. of niyuñjati] tied to, appointed to (with loc.), commissioned, ordered DhsA 47; PvA 20 (janapade), 124 (dānâdhikāre), 127 (dāne).

Niyoga [ni+ yoga] command, order; necessity, abl. niyogā "strictly speaking" Dhs 1417.

Niyojeti [Caus. of niyuñjati] to urge, incite to (with loc.) Vin II.303; A IV.32; Pv II.1[4]; Miln 229.

Niyyati = **Niyati** (Pass. of nayati).

Niyyatta (nt.) [cp. Sk. niryaṇa] escape J I.215.

Niyyāta (pp.) = niyyādita M I.360.

Niyyātana (nt.) [fr. niyyāti] returning, return to (-°) J v.497 (saka-raṭṭha°); Vism 556; DA I.234.

Niyyātar [n. ag. to niyyāma] a guide, leader M I.523 sq.

Niyyāti [Sk. niryāti, nis + yāti] to go out, get out (esp. of saŋsāra); S v.6 (niyyanti dhīrā lokamhā); SnA 212; aor. niyyāsi D I.49, 108; J I.263; Sn 417; 3rd pl. niyyiŋsu A v.195; fut. niyyassati A v.194. — See also niyyāna & niyyānika.

Niyyādita [pp. of niyyādeti] assigned, presented, given, dedicated PvA 196 (dhana ni°). As niyyātita at Vism 115.

Niyyādeti (niyyāteti, nīyādeti) [cp. Sk. ni- or nir-yātayati, Caus. of ni(r)yatati] to give (back), give into charge, give over, assign, dedicate, to present, denote S I.131 (niyyātayāmi); IV.181 (sāmikānaŋ gāvo), 194; J I.30, 66, 496; II.106, 133; Vv 46[8] niyyādesi = sampaṭicchāpesi, adāsi VvA 199); Pv III.2[11] (niyātayiŋsu = adaŋsu PvA 184); Vism 115 (t); DhA I.70; II.87; VvA 33, 67; PvA 20 (vihāraŋ nīyādetvā), 25 (= uddissati dadāti), 42, 81, 276 (at all PvA passages as ni°). — pp. niyyādita. Cp. similarly paṭiyādeti & paṭiyādita.

Niyyāna (nt.) [nis + yāna, cp. niyyāti] 1. going out, departure D I.9 (= niggamana DA I.94). — 2. way out, release, deliverance Sn 170, 172 ("magga-saccaŋ bhāvento lokamhā niyyāti" SnA 212); Ps I.163, 176; Nett 119. Cp. niyyānika. — aniyyāna DhA II.209.

Niyyānika (adj.) [to niyyāna] leading out (of saŋsāra), leading to salvation, salutary, sanctifying, saving, profitable D I.235, 237; S I.220; v.82, 166, 255, 379 sq.; J I.48 (a°), 106; Dhs 277, 339, 505 (cp. *Dhs. trsl.* pp. 82, 335); Vbh 12, 19, 56, 319, 324; Nett 29, 31, 63, 83; DhA IV.87. — Also found in spelling nīyānika e. g. A III.132 (ariyā diṭṭhi n. nīyāti takkarassa sammā-dukkha-khayāya); DA I.89 (anīyānikattā tiracchānabhūtā kathā).

Niyyāma(ka) [Sk. niyāmaka & niryāma(ka). Cp. also P. niyāmaka] a pilot, helmsman, master mariner, guide J I.107 (thala°); IV.137, 138; Miln 194, 378 sq.; Dāvs IV.42.

Niyyāsa [cp. Sk. niryāsa, Halāyudha 5, 75] any exudation (of plants or trees), as gum, resin, juice, etc. Vism 74 (°rukkha, one of the 8 kinds of trees), 360 (paggharitan.-rukkha). Cp. nivāyāsa.

Niyyūha [Sk. niryūha (& nirvyūha ?), perhaps to vah] a pinnacle, turret, gate M I.253; DA I.284 (pāsāda+).

Nirankaroti (& **nirākaroti**) [Sk. nirākaroti, nis + ā kṛ] to think little of, despise, neglect, disregard, repudiate; throw away, ruin, destroy Th 1, 478; It 83 (nirākare); J III.280 = v.498; IV.302; Pv III.9[6] (= chaḍḍeti pajahati PvA 211); VvA 109. — pp. (a)nirākata It 39.

Niraggala (niraggaḷa) (adj.) [nis + aggala] unobstructed, free, rich in result S I.76 = It 21; A II.43; IV.151; M I.139; Sn 303; Nd[2] 284 C[4]; Vv 64[31] (= VvA 285).

Niraggika (adj.) [nis + aggi + ka] without fire Miln 324 (°okāsa).

Nirajjati [Pass. of nirajati, nis + ajati, Vedic nirajati to drive out cattle] to be thrown out, to be expelled, to lose (with abl.) J VI.502, 503 (raṭṭhā); v. l. BB nirajhati; Com. ni(g)gacchati; Th 2, 93 (aor. nirajji 'haŋ = na jānim ahaŋ ThA. 90. Kern (wrongly) proposes reading virajjhi).

Nirata (adj.) [pp. of niramati] fond of, attached to (-°) S I.133; DA I.250; PvA 5 (duccarita°), 89, 161 (hitakaraṇa°).

Niratta[1] (adj.-nt.) [Sk. *nirātman, nis + attan] soulless; view of soullessness or unsubstantiality; thus interpreted (in preference to niratta[2]) by Com. on Sn 787, 858, 919. See foll.

Niratta[2] (adj.) [Sk. nirasta, pp. of nirasyati, see nirassati] rejected, thrown off, given up Sn 1098; Nd[2] 359. — *Note.* At Sn 787, 858, 919 the interpretation of Nd[1] 82 = 248 = 352 and also Bdhgh assume a cpd. of nis + attan (= nirātman): see niratta[1].

Nirattha (adj.) [nis + attha] useless, groundless, unprofitable, vain (opp. sāttha profitable) Sn 582 (nt. as adv.), 585 (niratthā paridevanā); Dh 41; J III.26; PvA 18 (°bhāva uselessness), 83 (= duḥ).

Niratthaka (adj.) = nirattha; VvA 324; PvA 18, 40, 63, 102 etc. — f. °ikā ThA 258; Miln 20; Sdhp 68.

Nirantara (adj.) [nis + antara] having no interval, continuous, uninterrupted PvA 135. Usually in nt. as adv. nirantaraŋ always, incessantly, constantly; immediately, at once DhsA 168; PvA 52, 80, 107, 110 (= satataŋ), 120; DhA I.13.

Niraparādha (adj.) [nis + aparādha] without offence, guiltless, innocent J I.264.

Nirapekkha (adj.) [nis + apa + īkṣ] not heeding, unsuspecting, disregarding, indifferent, reckless VvA 27, 47 (jīvitaŋ); PvA 62; DA I.177; Miln 343 (jīvitaŋ).

Nirabbuda[1] (m. nt.) [cp. BSk. nirarbuda & abbuda 3] a vast number; also N. of a hell S I.149 = A II.3 = v.171 (expl[d] at 173 as "seyyathā pi vīsati abbudā nirayā evam eko nirabbudo nirayo"); J III.360 (Com.: vīsati abbudāni ekaŋ nirabbudaŋ).

Nirabbuda[2] (adj.) [nis + abbuda[2]] free from boils or tumours, healthy (also fig.) Vin III.18 (of the Sangha).

Niraya [BSk. niraya, nis + aya of i = to go asunder, to go to destruction, to die, cp. in meaning Vedic nirṛti. The popular etym. given by Dhammapāla at PvA 53 is "n' atthi ettha ayo sukhan ti" = there is no good; that given by Bdhgh at Vism 427 "n' atthi ettha assāda-saññito ayo" (no refreshment)] purgatory, hell, a place of punishment & torture, where sin is atoned (i. e. kamma ripens = paccati, is literally boiled) by terrible ordeals (kāraṇāni) similar to & partly identical with those of Hades & Tartarus. There are a great number of hells, of which the most fearful is the Avīci-mahāniraya (see Avīci). Names of other purgatories occur frequently in the *Jātaka* collection, e. g. Kākola VI.247; Khuradhāra v.269 sq.; Dhūma-roruva v.271; Patāpana v.266, 271, 453; Paduma IV.245; Roruva III.299; v.266; VI.237; Sanghāta v.266; Sañjīva ibid.; Sataporisa v.269; Sattisūla v.143. As the principal one n. is often mentioned with the other apāyas (states of suffering), viz. tiracchānayoni (animal world) & pittivisaya (the *manes*), e. g. at Nd[1] 489; Nd[2] 517, 550; Pv IV.11; ThA 282; PvA 27 sq. (see apāya). — There is a great variety of qualifying adjectives connected with niraya, all of which abound in notions of fearful pain, awful misery & continuous suffering, e. g. kaṭuka, ghora, dāruṇa, bhayānaka, mahābhitāpa, sattussada etc. — Descriptions of N. in glowing terms of frightfulness are freq. found from the earliest books down to the late Peta-Vatthu, Pañcagati-dīpana & Saddham-mopāyana. Of these the foll. may be quoted as characteristic: S I.152 (10 nirayas); M III.183; A I.141; Sn p. 126 = A v.173; Nd[1] 404 sq. = Nd[2] 304[III.c]; J IV.4 (Mittavindaka); Vv 52 (Revatī); Pv I.10; III.10; IV.1; 7; DhA I.148. — See on the whole subject, esp. L. Scherman, *Materialen zur indischen Visionsliteratur*, Leipzig 1792; & W. Stede, *Die Gespenstergeschichten des Peta Vatthu*, Leipzig 1914, pp. 33-39. — *References:* Vin I.227 (apāya duggati vinipāta niraya); D I.82, 107 (id.); Vin II.198 (yo kho sanghaŋ bhindati kappaŋ nirayamhi paccati), 204; II.203 = It 86; D I.228 (+ tiracchānayoni), 54 (read nirayasate for niriyasate); III.111; S IV.126; V.356, 450; M I.73, 285, 308, 334; II.86, 149, 186; III.166, 203, 209; A IV.405; V.76, 182, 184; Sn 248 (patanti sattā nirayaŋ avaŋsirā), 333, 660 sq., 677 sq.; Dh 126, 140, 306, 311, 315; Th I, 304 (adhammo nirayaŋ neti dhammo pāpeti suggatiŋ) = DhsA 38 = DA I.99 = DhA I.22; Th 2, 456; It 12; J IV.463; Pug 60; Ps I.83 (Avīci°); Vbh 86, 337; Vism 102; Miln 148; DhA I.22; III.71; Sdhp 7, 285. — See also **nerayika**.

-gāmin (adj.) leading to purgatory (magga) Sn 277; **-dukkha** the pain of H. Sn 531; **-pāla** a guardian of P., a devil A I.138, 141; M III.179; Nd[1] 404; VvA 226. Names of guardians (after their complexion) e. g. Kāḷa (black) & Upakāḷa (blackish) J VI.248. **-bhaya** the fear of P. J I.168; Vism 392; **-saŋvattanika** conducive to P. Nd[1] 489.

Niravasesa (adj.) [nis + avasesa] without remainder, complete, inclusive Nett 14, 15, cp. Miln 91, 182.

Nirasana (adj.) [nis + asana[2]] without food or subsistence, poor J IV.128.

Nirassati [cp. Sk. nirasyati, nis + assati, as to throw] to throw off, despise, neglect Sn 785, 954; Nd[1] 76 (so read for nidassati, v. l. SS nir°), 444; SnA 522. — pp. **niratta**[2].

Nirassāda (adj.) [nis + assāda] without task, insipid, dull Vism 135. Cp. nirāsāda.

Nirākaroti see nirankaroti.

Nirākula (adj.) [nis + ākula] unconfused, clear, calm, undisturbed J I.17 (v. 94).

Nirātanka (adj.) [nis + ātanka] healthy Miln 251 (of paddy).

Nirādīnava (adj.) [nis + ādīnava] not beset with dangers, not in danger, unimperilled Vin III.19.

Nirāma (adj.) [nis + āma, cp. nirāmaya] healthy, undepraved, without sin, virtuous Sn 251, 252 (°gandha = nikkilesayoga SnA 293), 717 (id. = nikkilesa SnA 499).

Nirāmaya (adj.) [nis + āmaya] not ill, healthy, good, without fault PvA 164.

Nirāmisa (adj.) [nis + āmisa] having no meat or prey; free from sensual desires, disinterested, not material S I.35, 60; IV.219, 235; V.68, 332; A III.412; D III.278; Vbh 195; Vism 71; Sdhp 475, 477.

Nirārambha (adj.) [nis + ārambha] without objects (for the purpose of sacrificing), i. e. without the killing of animals (of yañña) S I.76; A II.42 sq.

Nirālamba (adj.) [nis + ālamba] unsupported Miln 295 (ākāsa).

Nirālaya (adj.) [nis + ālaya] houseless, homeless Miln 244 (= aniketa). At DhA IV.31 as expl[n] of appossukka. — f. abstr. **nirālayatā** homelessness Miln 162, 276, 420.

Nirāsa (adj.) [nis + āsā] not hungry, not longing for anything, desireless S I.12, 23, 141; A I.107 sq.; Sn 1048 (anigha +), 1078 (id.); Nd[2] 360; Pug 27; Py IV.1[33] (= nittanha PvA 230). See also amama.

Nirāsaŋsa (adj.) [nis + āsaŋsa, **śaŋs**] without wishes, expectations or desires, desireless Sn 1090 (Nd[2] reading for nirāsaya); Nd[2] 361 (cp. DhA IV.185 nirāsāsa = *nirāsaŋsa, v. l. for nirāsaya).

Nirāsanka (adj.) [nis + āsankā] without apprehension, unsuspicious, not doubting J I.264; Vism 180.

Nirāsankatā (f.) [abstr. fr. nirāsanka] the not hesitating J VI.337.

Nirāsattin (adj.) [adj. to pp. āsatta[1] with nis] not hanging on to, not clinging or attached to (c. loc.) Sn 851 (= nittaṇha SnA 549); Nd[1] 221.

Nirāsaya (adj.) [nis + āsaya, fr. **śri**] without (outward) support, not relying on (outward) things, without (sinful) inclinations Sn 56 (: Nd[2] 360 b reads nirāsasa), 369, 634, 1090 (Nd[2] 361 reads nirāsaŋsa); Dh 410; DhA IV.185 (v. l. BB nirāsāsa; expl[d] by nittaṇha).

Nirāsava (adj.) [nis + āsava] without intoxication, undefiled, sinless ThA 148.

Nirāsāda (adj.) [nis + assāda] tasteless, yielding no enjoyment Th I, 710. Cp. nirassāda.

Nirāhāra (adj.) [nis + āhāra] without food, not eating, fasting J IV.225; Sdhp 389.

Niriñjana (adj.) [nis + iñjanā, fr. iñjati] not moving, stable, unshaken Vism 377 (= acala, āneñja).

Nirindhana (adj.) [nis + indhana] without fuel (of fire), ThA 148 (aggi); DhA I.44 (jātaveda).

Nirīha(ka) (adj.) [nis + īha] inactive, motionless, without impulse ThA 148 (°ka); Miln 413 (+ nijjīvata); Vism 484, 594 sq.

Nirujjhati [Pass. of nirundhati (nirodhati) ni + rundhati] to be broken up, to be dissolved, to be destroyed, to cease, die Vin I.1; D I.180 sq., 215; II.157; S III.93 (aparisesaŋ); IV.36 sq., 60, 98, 184 sq.; 294, 402; V.213 sq.; A III.165 sq. (aparisesaŋ); V.139 sq.; J I.180; Pug 64; Sdhp 606. — pp. **niruddha**. Cp. **nirodha**.

Niruttara (adj.) [nis + uttara] making no reply PvA 117.

Nirutti (f.) [Sk. nirukti, nis + **vac**] one of the Vedāngas (see chaḷanga), expl[n] of words, grammatical analysis, etymological interpretation; pronunciation, dialect, way of speaking, expression Vin II.139 (pabbajitā . . . sakāya niruttiyā Buddhavacanaŋ dūsenti); D I.202 (loka°, expression); M III.237 (janapada°); S III.71 (tayo n-pathā); A II.160 (°paṭisambhidā); III.201; Dh 352 (°padakovida = niruttiyañ ca sesapadesu cā ti catūsu pi paṭisambhidāsu cheko ti attho DhA IV.70; i. e. skilled in the dialect or the original language of the holy Scriptures); Ps I.88 sq.; II.150 (°paṭisambhidā); Nd[2] 563; Dhs 1307; Nett 4, 8, 33, 105; Miln 22; Vism 441; SnA 358; PvA 97.

Nirudaka (adj.) [nis + udaka] without water, waterless M I.543; Nd[2] 630.

Niruddha (pp.) [pp. of nirundhati, cp. nirujjhati] expelled, destroyed; vanished, ceased S III.112; Dhs 1038.

Nirundhati see nirujjhati, niruddha, nirodha & nirodheti. Cp. parirundhati.

Nirupakāra (adj.) [nis + upakāra] useless J II.103.

Nirupaghāta (adj.) [nis + upaghāta] not hurt, not injured or set back Miln 130.

Nirupatāpa (adj.) [nis + upatāpa] not harassed (burnt) or afflicted (by pain or harm) Th 2, 512.

Nirupaddava (adj.) [nis + upaddava] without affliction or mishap, harmless, secure, happy J IV.139; PvA 202 (sotthi).

Nirupadhi (adj.) (in verse always **nirūpadhi**) [nis + upadhi, cp. upadhika] free from passions or attachment, desireless, controlled Vin II.156; S I.194 (vippamutta +);

IV.158; A I.80, 138 (sītibhūta+); Dh 418 (id.); Th 1, 1250; 2, 320 (vippamutta+; expl^d by niddukkha ThA 233); It 46, 50, 58, 62; Sn 33, 34, 642 (sītibhūta+); Pv IV.1^34; DhA IV.225 (=nirupakkilesa); PvA 230.

Nirupama (adj.) [nis+upama] without comparison, incomparable SnA 455 (=atitula).

Nirumbhati [Sk. ? Trenckner, *Notes* p. 59 ni+**rudh** (?)] to suppress, hush, silence J I.62 (text nirumhitvā, v. l. SS nirumbhitvā, cp. san-nirumhitvā VvA 217).

Niruḷha (adj.) [cp. Sk. nirūḍha, pp. of niruhati] grown, risen; usual, customary, common VvA 108.

Nirussāsa (adj.) [cp. Sk. nirucchvāsa, nis+ussāsa] breathless J III.416; IV.121, cp. VI.197; VI.82.

Nirussukka (adj.) [nis+ussukka], careless, unconcerned, indifferent to (c. loc.) ThA 282.

Niroga see nīroga.

Niroja (adj.) [nis+oja] tasteless, insipid J II.304; III.94; VI.561.

Nirodha [BSk. nirodha, to nirundhati, cp. nirujjhati & niruddha] oppression, suppression; destruction, cessation, annihilation (of senses, consciousness, feeling & being in general: sankhārā). Bdhgh's expl^n of the word is: "ni-saddo abhāvaŋ, rodha-saddo ca cārakaŋ dīpeti Vism 495.—N. in many cases is synonymous with nibbāna & parinibbāna; it may be said to be even a stronger expression as far as the *active* destruction of the causes of life is concerned. Therefore frequently comb^d with nibbāna in formula "sabbasankhāra-samatho . . . virāgo nirodho nibbānaŋ," e. g. S I.136; It 88. Nd^2 s. nibbāna (see nibbāna III.6). Also in comb^n with nibbidā, e. g. S III.48, 223; III.163 sq.; V.438.—The opposite of nirodha is samudaya, cp. formula "yaŋ kiñci samudaya-dhammaŋ sabban taŋ nirodha-dhammaŋ" e. g. Nd^2 under sankhārā & passim. (a) Vin I.1, 10; D II.33, 41, 57 sq., 112; III.130 sq., 136 sq., 226 sq.; J I.133; II.9 sq., 223; III.59 sq., 163; V.438; M I.140, 263, 410; A I.299; IV.456 (=āsavānaŋ parikkhaya); Th 2, 6 (=kilesanirodha ThA 13), 158; It 46=Sn 755 (nirodhe ye vimuccanti te janā maccuhāyino); It 62=Sn 754; Sn 731, 1037; Ps I.192; II.44 sq., 221; Pug 68; Vbh 99 sq., 229; Nett 14, 16 sq.; Vism 372; VvA 63; PvA 220 (jīvitassa).—(b) (as-°): anupubba° D III.266; A IV.409, 456; abhisaññā° D I.180; asesavirāga° S II.4, 12; IV.86; V.421 sq.; A I.177; II.158, 161; upādāna° S III.14; kāma° A III.410 sq.; jāti° S IV.86; taṇhā° D III.216; dukkha° D III.136; S III.32, 60; IV.4 sq., 14, 384; A I.177; nandi° S III.14; IV.36; bhava° (=nibbāna) S II.117; III.14; A V.9; Ps I.159; sakkāya° D III.240; S V.410; A II.165 sq.; III.246, 325 sq.; V.238 sq.; saññāvedayita° D III.262, 266; S IV.217, 293 sq.; V.213 sq.; A I.41; III.192; IV.306; V.209.

-dhamma subject to destruction, able to be destroyed, destructible (usually in formula of samudaya-dhamma, see above) Vin I.11; D I.110; S IV.47, 107, 214; M III.280; A V.143 sq.; -dhammatā liability to destruction S IV.217; -dhātu the element or condition of annihilation, one of the 3 dhātus, viz. rūpa, arūpa° n°. D III.215; It 45; Nett 97; -saññā perception or consciousness of annihilation D III.251 sq., 283; A III.334; -samāpatti attainment of annihilation Ps I.97, 100; Miln 300; Vism 702.

Nirodhika (adj.) [fr. nirodha] obstructing, destroying It 82 (paññā°), cp. M I.115.

Nirodheti [Denom. fr. nirodha] to oppress, destroy Vism 288 (in expl^n of passambheti).

Nilaya [fr. ni+**lī**] a dwelling, habitation, lair, nest J III.454.

Nilicchita see nillacchita.

Nilīna (adj.) [pp. of nilāyati] sitting on (c. loc.), perched; hidden, concealed, lying in wait J I.135, 293; III.26; VvA 230.

Nilīyati [ni+līyati] to sit down (esp. for the purpose of hiding), to settle, alight; to keep oneself hidden, to lurk, hide J I.222, 292; Miln 257; PvA 178. aor. nilīyi J I.158; III.26; DhA II.56; PvA 274.—pp. nilīna. Caus. II. nilīyāpeti to conceal, hide (trs.) J I.292.

Nilīyana (nt.) [abstr. fr. nilīyati, cp. Sk. nilayana] hiding J V.103 (°ṭṭhāna hiding-place).

Nilenaka (nt.) [cp. Sk. nilayana, fr. ni+**lī**] settling place, hiding-place, refuge J V.102 (so read for nillenaka; expl^d by nilīyanaṭṭhāna p. 103).

Nillacchita (adj.) [Sk. *nirlāñchita, nis+lacchita of nillaccheti] castrated Th 2, 440; written as nilicchitá at J VI.238 (v. l. BB as gloss niluñcita). expl^d by "vacchakakāla . . . nibbījako kato, uddhaṭabījo" (p. 239).

Nillaccheti [nis+laccheti of **lāñch**, cp. lakkhaṇa] to deprive of the marks or characteristics (of virility), to castrate Th .2, 437 (=purisa-bhāvassa lacchana-bhūtāni bījakāni nillacchesi nīhari ThA 270). See also nillañchaka & nillacchita.

Nillajja (adj.) [nis+lajjā] shameless Sdhp 382.

Ni(l)lañchaka (adj.-n.) [cp. Sk. nirlāñchana, of nirlāñchayati=nis+laccheti] one who marks cattle, i. e. one who castrates or deprives of virility J IV.364 (spelt tilañchaka in text, but right in v. l.), expl^d as "tisūlādi-ankakaraṇena lañchakā ca lakkhaṇakārakā ti attho" (p. 366). cp. nillacchita.

Nillapa (adj.) [nis+lapa] without deceit, free from slander A II.26=It 113.

Nillāḷeti & **Nilloḷeti** [nis+**lul**, cp. Sk. laḍayati & loḍayati] to move (the tongue) up & down S I.118; M I.109; DA I.42 (pp. nillāḷita-jivhā); DhA IV.197 (jivhaŋ nilloḷeti; v. l. nillāleti & lilāḷeti)=J V.434 (v. l. nillelati for °lo°).

Nillekha (adj.) [nis+lekha] without scratches, without edges (?) Vin II.123 (of jantāghara).

Nillokana (adj.-n.) [nis+lokana] watching out; watchful, careful J V.43, 86 (°sīla).

Nilloketi [nis+loketi] to watch out, keep guard, watch, observe Vin II.208.

Nillopa [cp. Sk. nirlopa, nis+**lup**] plundering, plunder D I.52; A I.154; Nd^1 144 (°ŋ harati); Nd^2 199^7; Tikp 167, 280; DA I.159.

Nillobha (adj.) [nis+lobha] free from greed J IV.10.

Nillolup(p)a (adj.) [nis+loluppā] free from greed or desires Sn 56 (=Nd^2 362 nittaṇha); J V.358.

Nivatta (pp.) [pp. of nivattati] returned, turning away from, giving up, being deprived of, being without (°-) Vin II.109 (°bīja); J I.203; VvA 72.

Nivattati [Vedic nivartati, ni+vattati] to turn back, to return (opp. gacchati), to turn away from, to flee, vanish, disappear Vin I.46; D I.118; J I.223; II.153; IV.142; Sn p. 80; Pv II.9^34; IV.10^7; SnA 374; PvA 74, 161. aor. nivatti J II.3; PvA 141. pp. nivatta (q. v.).—Caus. I. nivatteti to lead back, to turn from, to make go back, to convert J I.203; VvA 110; PvA 204 (pāpato from sin). Cp. upa°, paṭi°, vi°.—Caus. II. nivattāpeti to send back, to return PvA 154.

Nivattana (nt.) [fr. nivattati] 1. returning, turning, fig. turning away from, giving up, "conversion" PvA 120 (pāpato). — 2. a bend, curve (of a river), nook J I.324; II.117, 158; IV.256; V.162.

Nivattanīya (adj.) [grd. formation fr. nivattana] only neg. a° not liable to return, not returning DhA I.63.

Nivatti (f.) [fr. ni+vṛt] returning, return PvA 189 (gati° going & coming).

Nivattha (pp.) [pp. of ni+vasati¹] clothed in or with (-° or acc.), dressed, covered S I.115; J I.59 (su°), 307 (sāṭakaŋ); PvA 47, 49 (dibbavattha°), 50.

Nivapati [ni+vapati] to heap up, sow, throw (food) M I.151 sq. (nivāpaŋ). — pp. nivutta (q. v.).

Nivaraṇa see vi°.

Nivarati [ni+varati] only in Caus. nivāreti (q. v.), pp. nivuta.

Nivasati [ni+vasati²] to live, dwell, inhabit, stay Vin II.11. — pp. nivuttha, cp. also nivāsana² & nivāsin.

Nivaha [fr. ni+vah] multitude, quantity, heap Dāvs IV.53; V.14, 24, 62.

Nivāta¹ (adj.) [Sk. nivāta, ni+vāta "wind-down"] with the wind gone down, i. e. without wind, sheltered from the wind, protected, safe, secure Vin I.57, 72; M I.76 = A I.137 (kūṭāgāra); A I.101 (id.); It 92 (rahada); Th 1, 1 (kuṭikā); 2, 376 (pāsāda). — (nt.) a calm (opp. pavāta) Vin II.79.

Nivāta² [identical with nivāta¹, sheltered from the wind = low] lowliness, humbleness, obedience, gentleness M I.125; Sn 265 (= nīcavattana KhA 144); J VI.252; Pv IV.7¹². Cp. M Vastu II.423. Freq. in cpd. nivātavutti (id.) A III.43; Sn 326 (= nīcavutti SnA 333); J III.262; Miln 90, 207; VvA 347.

Nivātaka [fr. nivāta¹] a sheltered place, a place of escape, opportunity (for hiding) J I.289 = V.435; cp. Miln 205 (where reading is nimantaka, with v. l. nivātaka, see note on p. 426). See Com. on this stanza at J V.437.

Nivāpa [cp. Sk. nivāpa, ni+vap, cp. nivapati] food thrown (for feeding), fodder, bait; gift, portion, ration M I.151 sq. (Nivāpa-sutta); J I.150; III.271; DhA I.233 (share); III.303; VvA 63 (diguṇaŋ °ŋ pacitvā cooking a double portion). Cp. nevāpika.

-tiṇa grass to eat J I.150; -puṭṭha fed on grains Dh 325 (= kuṇḍakâdinā sūkara-bhattena puṭṭho DhA IV.16 = Nett 129 = Th 1, 17; -bhojana a meal on food given, a feeding M I.156).

Nivāyāsa (?) oozing of trees, Bdhgh's expl° of ikkāsa at Vin II.321. See niyyāsa.

Nivāraṇa (nt. & adj.) [fr. nivāreti] warding off, keeping back, preventing; refusal Sn 1034, 1035, 1106 (= Nd² 363 āvāraṇa rakkhaṇa gopana); DhsA 259; PvA 102, 278; Sdhp 396.

Nivāraya (adj.) [grd. of nivāreti] in dun° hard to check or keep back Miln 21 (+durāvaraṇa).

Nivārita (adj.) [pp. of nivāreti] unobstructed, open PvA 202 (= anāvaṭa).

Nivāretar [n. agent to nivāreti] one who holds back or refuses (entrance) (opp. pavesetar) D II.83 = S IV.194 = A V.194 (dovāriko aññātānaŋ nivāretā ñātānam pavesetā).

Nivāreti [Caus. of nivarati] to keep back, to hold back from (c. abl.), to restrain; to refuse, obstruct, forbid, warn Vin I.46; II.220; S I.7 (cittaŋ nivāreyya), 14 (yato mano nivāraye); IV.195 (cittaŋ); Dh 77, 116 (pāpā cittaŋ nivāraye); J I.263; Pv III.7⁴; VvA 69; PvA 79, 102; DhA I.41.

Nivāsa [fr. nivasati²] stopping, dwelling, resting-place, abode; living, sheltering J I.115 (°ŋ kappeti to put up); II.110; PvA 76, 78. Usually in phrase pubbe-nivāsaŋ anussarati "to remember one's former abode or place of existence (in a former life)," characterising the faculty of remembering one's former birth D I.13, 15, 16, 81; S I.167, 175, 196; II.122, 213; V.265, 305; A I.25, 164; II.183; III.323, 418 sq.; IV.141 sq.; V.211, 339. Also in pubbenivāsaŋ vedi It 100; Sn 647 = Dh 423; p-n-paṭisaŋyuttā dhammikathā D II.1; p-n-anussatiñāṇa D III.110, 220, 275; A IV.177. Cp. nevāsika.

Nivāsana¹ (adj.-nt.) [fr. nivāseti] dressed, clothed; dressing, clothing, undergarment (opp. pārupana) Vin I.46; II.228; J I.182 (manāpa°), 421; III.82; PvA 50, 74, 76, 173 (pilotikakkhaṇḍa° dressed in rags).

Nivāsana² (nt.) [fr. nivasati²] dwelling, abode PvA 44 (°ṭṭhāna place of abode), 76 (id.).

Nivāsika (adj.) [fr. nivāsa] staying, living, dwelling J II.435 (= nibaddha-vasanaka C.).

Nivāsin (adj.-n.) [to nivasati] dwelling, staying; (n.) an inhabitant Dāvs V.45.

Nivāseti [Caus. of nivasati¹] to dress oneself, to put on (the undergarment), to get clothed or dressed. Freq. in ster. phrase "pubbantasamayaŋ nivāsetvā pattacīvaram ādāya . . .," describing the setting out on his round of the bhikkhu; e. g. D I.109, 178, 205, 226. — Vin I.46; II.137, 194; D II.127; J I.265; Pug 56; Pv I.10³; PvA 49, 61, 75, 127 (nivāsessati + pārupissati), 147 (= pārupāmi). — Caus. II. nivāsāpeti to cause or order to be dressed (with 2 acc.) J I.50; IV.142; DhA I.223.

Nivicikicchā see nibbicikicchā; M I.260.

Nivijjha see vi°.

Niviṭṭha (adj.) [pp. of nivisati] settled, established (in); confirmed, sure; fixed on, bent on, devoted to (loc.) Sn 57 (= satta allina etc. Nd² 364), 756, 774, 781 (ruciyā), 824 (saccesu), 892; Nd¹ 38, 65, 162; It 35, 77; J I.89, 259 (adhammasmiŋ); Miln 361; VvA 97 (°gāma, built, situated); DA I.90 (su° & dun° of a street = well & badly built or situate). Cp. abhi°.

Nivisati [ni+visati] to enter, stop, settle down on (loc.), to resort to, establish oneself Vin I.207; J I.309 = IV.217 (yasmiŋ mano nivisati). — pp. niviṭṭha ger. nivissa (q. v.). Caus. niveseti.

Nivissa-vādin (adj.-n.) [nivissa (ger. of nivisati) + vādin] "speaking in the manner of being settled or sure," a dogmatist Sn 910, 913, expl^d at Nd¹ 326 as "sassato loko idam eva saccaŋ, mogham aññan ti"; at SnA 560. As "jānāmi passāmi tath' eva etan ti."

Nivuta (adj.) [pp. of nivarati (nivāreti) cp. nivārita] surrounded, hemmed in, obstructed, enveloped D I.246; S II.24; IV.127; Sn 348 (tamo°), 1032, 1082; It 8; Nd² 365 (= ophuṭa, paṭicchanna, paṭikujjita); Miln 161; SnA 596 (= pariyonaddha).

Nivutta¹ (pp.) [pp. of ni+vac] called, termed, designated PvA 73 (dasavassa-satāni, vassa-sahassaŋ n. hoti).

Nivutta² (pp.) [Sk. *nyupta, pp. of vapati¹ to shear] shorn, shaved, trimmed Sn 456 (°kesa = apagatakesa, ohāritakesamassu SnA 403).

Nivutta³ (pp.) [Sk. *nyupta, pp. of vapati² to sow] sown, thrown (of food), offered, given M I.152; J III.272.

Nivuttha (pp. of nivasati) inhabited; dwelling, living; see san°.

Niveṭha in pañhe dunniveṭha at Miln 90 see nibbedha.

Niveṭhana see vi°.

Niveṭheti see nibbeṭheti.

Nivedaka (adj.) [to nivedeti] relating, admonishing J vi.21.

Nivedeti [ni+vedeti, Caus. of **vid.**] to communicate, make known, tell, report, announce J i.60, 307; PvA 53, 66 (attānaŋ reveal oneself); Dāvs v.42.

Nivesa [Vedic niveśa, fr. ni+**viś**] 1. entering, stopping, settling down; house, abode Vv 82² (=nivesanāni kacchantarāni VvA 50). — 2. = nivesana², in diṭṭhi° Sn 785 (=idaŋ-sacchâbhinivesa-saṅkhātāni diṭṭhi-nivesanāni SnA 522).

Nivesana (nt.) [Vedic niveśana, fr. nivesati, cp. niviṭṭha] 1. entering, entrance, settling; settlement, abode, house, home D i.205, 226; ii.127; J i.294; ii.160 (°ṭṭhāna); PvA 22, 81, 112. — 2. (fig.) (also nivesanā f.: Nd² 366) settling on, attachment, clinging to (in diṭṭhi° clinging to a view = dogmatism cp. nivissa-vādin) Sn 1055 (nandi+; =taṇhā Nd² 366); Dh 40 (diṭṭhi°); Nd¹ 76, 110. See also nivesa.

Nivesita (adj.) [pp. of nivesati] settled, arranged, designed, built VvA 82 (=sumāpita).

Niveseti [Caus. of nivesati] to cause to enter, to establish; to found, build, fix, settle; (fig.) to establish in, exhort to (c. loc.), plead for, entreat, admonish D i.206; S v.189; Dh 158, 282 (attānaŋ); It 78 (brahmacariye); Th 2, 391 (manaŋ); J v.99; Pv iii.7⁷ (saŋyame nivesayi); DA i.273 (gāmaŋ); PvA 206.

Nivyaggha (adj.) [nis+vyaggha] free from tigers J ii.358 (v. l. nibbyaggha).

Nisagga (& **Nissagga**) [ni or nis+**sṛj**] giving forth, bestowing; natural state, nature S i.54 (°ss°). Cp. nisaṭṭha.

Nisankhiti (f.) [Sk. ni-saŋskṛti, ni+saŋ+**kṛ**] deposit (of merit or demerit), accumulation, effect (of kamma) Sn 953 (=Nd¹ 442 abhisankhārā).

Nisajjā (f.) [Sk. *niṣadyā of **ni sad**] sitting down, opportunity for sitting, seat Pv iv.1² (seyyā+); J i.217; PvA 24 (°ādipaṭikkhepa-ṭṭhāna), 219 (pallankâbhujanādi-lakkhaṇā nisajjā). Cp. nesajjika.

Nisajjeti [sic MSS. for niss°; Sk. niḥsarjayati, nis+sajjeti, Caus. of **sṛj**] to spend, bestow, give, give up PvA 105 (dānûpakaraṇā nisajjesi read better as °karaṇāni sajjesi). See also nissajjati.

Nisaṭṭha (pp.) [nis+saṭṭha of **sṛj**] given up, spent, lost Th 2, 484 (v. l. °ss°); ThA 286 (=pariccatta). Cp. nisajjeti & nisagga.

Nisada & **Nisadā** (f.) [Sk. dṛṣad f.; for n: d cp. P. nijjuha = Sk. dātyūha etc.] a grindstone, esp. the understone of a millstone Vin i.201; (°pota id.); Miln 149; Vism 252 (°pota, where KhA at id. p. reads °putta). Cp. ā°.

Nisanti (f.) [Sk. *niśānti, ni+**śam**] careful attention or observation A ii.97; iii.201; iv.15 (dhamma°), 36 (id.), 296; v.166 (dhamma°); Dpvs i.53 (°kāra). Cp. nisamma & nisāmeti.

Nisabha [Sk. nṛ+ṛṣabha, cp. usabha. On relation of usabha: vasabha: nisabha see SnA 40] "bull among men," i. e. prince, leader; "princeps," best of men; Ep. of the Buddha S i.28, 48, 91; M i.386; J v.70; vi.526; Vv 16⁷ (isi°), cp. VvA 83 for expl°; Vv 63⁷ (isi° = ājānīya VvA 262).

Nisamma (adv.) [orig. ger. of nisāmeti, Sk. niśamya, **śam**] carefully, considerately, observing Sn 54; Nd² 367 = 481 b (=sutvā). Esp. in phrase n.-kārin acting considerately Dh 24 (=DhA i.238); J iii.106; vi.375; Miln 3; cp. n. kiriyāya Miln 59. Cp. nisanti.

Nisā (f.) [Sk. niś & niśā, prob. with niśītha (midnight) to ni+**śi** = lying down] night Vv 35² (loc. nise); VvA 161 (loc. nisati, v. l. nisi = rattiyaŋ); Miln 388 (loc. nisāya); Dāvs ii.6; v.2 (nisāyaŋ). See also nisītha.

Nisātaka in koka° J vi.538, a certain wild animal; the meaning is not clear, etymologically it is to be derived fr. Sk. niśātayati to strike, to fell See Kern, *Toev.* i. p. 152, s. v. koka. The v. l. is °nisādaka, evidently influenced by nisāda.

Nisāda [cp. Sk. niṣāda, a Non-Aryan or barbarian] a robber J iv.364. Cp. nesāda.

Nisādika (adj.) [cp. Sk. niṣādin, ni+**sad**] fit for lying down, suitable for resting Vin i.239 (go°).

Nisādin (adj.) [fr. ni+**sad**] lying down D iii.44, 47.

Nisāna [ni+**śā** to sharpen, to whet, cp. nisita] a hone on which to sharpen a knife Miln 282.

Nisāmaka (adj.) [cp. Sk. niśāmana] observant, listening to, attending to, careful of A v.166, 168 (dhammānaŋ).

Nisāmeti [ni+sāmeti] to attend to, listen to, observe, be careful of, mind J iv.29 (anisāmetvā by not being careful); v.486; DhA i.239 (+upadhāneti); PvA 1 (imper. nisāmayatha). Cp. nisanti, nisamma.

Nisāra (adj.-n.) [ni+sāra] full of sap, excellent, strong (of a tree) Vv 63¹ (=niratisaya-sārassa nisiṭṭhasārassa rukkhassa VvA 261).

Nisiñcati [ni+siñcati] to besprinkle Mhvs vii.8.

Nisita (adj.) [Sk. niśita, ni+pp. of **śā** to whet] sharp M i.281 (āvudhajāta pīta° ?); J iv.118 (su°); VvA 233; PvA 155, 192, 213.

Nisinna (adj.) [Sk. niṣanna, pp. of nisīdati] sitting down, seated J i.50, 255; iii.126; KhA 250; PvA 11, 16, 39 & passim. — Often comb⁴ & contrasted with tiṭṭhaŋ (standing), caraŋ (walking) & sayaŋ (sayāna; lying down), e. g. at Sn 151, 193; It 82.

Nisinnaka (adj.) = nisinna; M i.333; J i.163; DhA iii.175.

Nisītha [Sk. niśītha, see nisā] midnight, night Th 1, 3 (aggi yathā pajjalito nisīthe; v. l. BB nisive), 524 (v. l. nisive); J iv.432; v.330, 331 (v. l. BB nisive), 506 (=rattibhāga Com.).

Nisīdati [Sk. niṣīdati, ni+sīdati] to sit down, to be seated, to sit, to dwell Nd² 433; J iii.392; vi.367; Pv ii.9³ (nisīdeyya Pot.); PvA 74. aor. nisīdi Vin i.1; J ii.153; PvA 5, 23, 44; 3rd pl. nisīdiŋsu (J i.307) & nisīdisuŋ (Mhvs vii.40); ger. nisīditvā (J ii.160; PvA 5, 74), nisajja D ii.127) and nisīditvāna (Sn 1031); grd. nisīditabba Vin i.47. pp. nisinna (q. v.). — Caus. II. nisīdāpeti [cp. Sk. niṣādayati] to cause to sit down, to make one be seated, to invite to a seat J iii.392; vi.367; PvA 17, 35 (there āsane); Miln 20. Cp. abhi°, san°.

Nisīdana (nt.) [Sk. niṣadana, fr. nisīdati] sitting down, occasion or opportunity to sit, a mat to sit on Vin i.295; ii.123 (°ena vippavasati); S v.259 (°ŋ gaṇhāti). °paccattharaṇa a mat for sitting on Vin i.47, 295; ii.209, 218.

Nisumbhati [ni+**sumbh** (subhnāti)] to knock down Th 2, 302 (=pāteti ThA 227).

Nisūdana (nt.) [ni+**sūd**] destroying, slaughtering Miln 242.

Nisedha (adj.-n.) [fr. ni+ **sedh**] holding back, restraining; prevention, prohibition Dh 389; DhA IV.148; hirī° restrained by shame S I.168 = Sn 462; Dh 143.

Nisedhaka (adj.) [fr. nisedha] prohibiting, restraining; one who prohibits, an obstructer J II.220.

Nisedhanatā (f.) [abstr. to nisedheti] refusing, refusal, prohibition Miln 180 (a°).

Nisedheti [Caus. of ni+ **sedh**] to keep off, restrain, prohibit, prevent S I.121 (nisedha, imper.); J III.83, 442; ThA 250; VvA 105 (nirayûpapattiŋ). — Cp. nisedha.

Nisevati [ni+ **sev**] to resort to, practise, pursue, follow, indulge in J II.106; Sn 821 (=Nd[1] 157); Pv II.3[19] (=karoti PvA 87); Miln 359. — pp. **nisevita.**

Nisevana (nt. also -ā f.) [Sk. niṣevana, cp. nisevati] practising, enjoying; pursuit Pug 20, 24; Sdhp 406.

Nisevita (adj.) [pp. of nisevati] frequented, practised, enjoyed, indulged in M I.178; Sdhp 373.

Nissaŋsaya (adj.) [nis+ saŋsaya] having no doubt, free from doubt Miln 237. — acc. as *adv.* without doubt, undoubtedly Pv IV.8[1]; DhA I.106; PvA 95.

Nissakka [fr. nis+ sakkati = **sakk**] "going out from," ttg. a name of the *ablative* case J V.498; VvA 152, 154, 180, 311; PvA 147, 221.

Nissakkana (nt.) [Sk. *niḥsarpana, nis+ **sakk**, confused with **sṛp**, see Trenckner, *Notes* p. 60 & cp. apassakkati, o°, pari°] going out, creeping out; only in biḷāra° at D II.83 (v. l. BB as gloss nikkhamana)+ S IV.194 = A V.195.

Nissaggiya (adj.) [Sk. *niḥsārgya grd. of nis+ sajjeti, not = Sk. naisargika] to be given up, what ought to be rejected or abandoned Vin I.196, 254; III.195 sq.

Nissanga (adj.) [nis+ sanga] unattached, unobstructed, disinterested, unselfish Sdhp 371, 398, 411 etc.; Tikp 10; f. abstr. °tā disinterestedness J I.46.

Nissajjati [nis+ sajjati, **sṛj**. See also nisajjeti] to let loose, give up, hand over, give, pour out Vin II.188; ger. nissajja [Sk. niḥsṛjya] Sn 839 (v. l. nisajja); Nd[1] 189 (id.); SnA 545. pp. nisaṭṭha & nissaṭṭha (q. v.). Cp. nissaggiya & paṭi°.

Nissaṭa (adj.) [pp. of nis+ sarati, **sṛ**] flown or come out from, appeared; let loose, free, escaped from S III.31; IV.11 sq.; A I.260; IV.430 (a°); V.151 sq.; J III.530; VI.269; Nd[2] under nissita; Ps II.10 sq.; Miln 95, 225 (bhava°). See also nissaraṇa. Cp. abhi°.

Nissaṭṭha (adj.) [pp. of nissajjati] dismissed, given up, left, granted, handed over, given Vin III.197 (°cīvara); M I.295; II.203; VvA 341. See also nisaṭṭha & paṭi°.

Nissatta (adj.) [Sk. *nihsattva, nis+ satta] powerless, unsubstantial; f. abstr. °tā absence of essence, unsubstantiality (see dhamma A) DhsA 38, 139, 263; cp. *Dhs. trsl.* pp. XXXIII. & 26.

Nissadda (adj.) [nis+ sadda] noiseless, soundless, silent J I.17 (V.94); DhA III.173.

Nissantāpa (adj.) [nis+ santāpa] without grief or self-mortification PvA 62.

Nissanda [Sk. nisyanda & niṣyanda, ni+ **syand** (syad), see sandati] flowing or trickling down; discharge, dropping, issue; result, outcome, esp. effect of Kamma A III.32; J I.31, 205, 426 (sarīra°); DhA I.395; II.36, 86; VvA 14 (puñña-kammassa n.-phala); PvA 47 (puñña-kammassa), 58 (id.); Miln 20, 117; Pgdp 102.

Nissama [ni+ sama] exertion, endeavour J V.243.

Nissaya [Sk. niśraya, of ni+ **śri**, corresp. in meaning to Sk. āśraya] that on which anything depends, support, help, protection; endowment, resource, requisite, supply; foundation, reliance on (acc. or -°) Vin I.58 (the four resources of bhikkhu, viz. piṇḍiyālopa-bhojanaŋ, paŋsukūla-cīvaraŋ, rukkhamūla-senāsanaŋ, pūtimutta bhesajjaŋ); II.274, 278; D III.137, 141; A I.117; III.271; IV.353; V.73; Sn 753, 877; Nd[1] 108 (two n.: taṇhā° & diṭṭhi°), 190, cp. Nd[2] s. v.; Nd[2] 397[A] (the requisites of a bhikkhu in diff. enumeration); Ps II.49 sq., 58 sq., 73 sq.; II.220; Nett 7, 65; Vism 12, 535. **nissayaŋ karoti** to rely on, to be founded on, to take one's stand in Sn 800. — Cp. nissāya & nissita.

-**kamma** giving assistance or help, an (ecclesiastical) act of help or protection Vin I.49, 143, 325; II.226; A I.99; Pv IV.1[1] (so to be read at the 2 latter passages for niyassa°). -**sampanna** finding one's strength in A IV.353.

Nissayatā (f.) [abstr. to nissaya] dependence, requirement, resource Sn 856; Nd[1] 245.

Nissayati [Sk. niśrayati, but in meaning = āśrayati, ni+ **śri**] to lean on, a foundation on, rely on, trust, pursue, Sn 798 (sīlabbataŋ; SnA 530 = abhinivisati); VvA 83 (katapuññaŋ). Pass. nissīyati VvA 83. pp. **nissita**; ger. nissāya (q. v.).

Nissaraṇa (nt.) [Sk. niḥsaraṇa, to nis+ sarati, cp. BSk. nissaraṇa giving up (?) AvŚ II.193] going out, departure; issue, outcome, result; giving up, leaving behind, being freed, escape (fr. saŋsāra), salvation Vin I.104; D III.240, 248 sq.; S I.128, 142; II.5; III.170 (catunnaŋ dhātūnaŋ); IV.7 sq. (id.); V.121 sq.; A I.258, 260; II.10 (kāmānaŋ etc.); III.245 sq.; IV.76 (uttariŋ); V.188; M I.87 (kāmānaŋ), 326 (uttariŋ); III.25; It 37, 61; Ps II.180, 244; Vbh 247; Vism 116; ThA 233; DhsA 164; Sdhp 579. Cp. nissaṭa & nissaraṇīya.

-**dassin** wise in knowing results, prescient, able to find a way to salvation S IV.205; -**pañña** (adj.) = °dassin D I.245 (a°); III.46; S II.194; IV.332; A V.178 (a°), 181 sq.; Miln 401.

Nissaraṇīya (adj.) [grd. of nissarati, with relation to nissaraṇa] connected with deliverance, leading to salvation, able to be freed. The 3 n. dhātuyo (elements of deliverance) are nekkhamma (escape from cravings), āruppa (from existence with form), nirodha (from all existence), in detail at It 61 (kāmānaŋ n. nekkhammaŋ, rūpānaŋ n. āruppaŋ, yaŋ kiñci bhūtaŋ sankhataŋ n. nirodho). The 5 n-dh. are escape fr. kāma, vyāpāda, vihesā, rūpa, sakkāya: A III.245; cp. A I.99; III.290.

Note. The spelling is often nissāraṇiya, thus at Vin IV.225; D III.239 (the five n-dhātuyo), 247, 275.

Nissarati [nis+ sarati] to depart, escape from, be freed from (c. abl.) A I.260 (yasmā atthi loke nissaraṇaŋ tasmā sattā lokamhā nissaranti). — pp. **nissaṭa**, grd. nissaraṇiya (q. v.); cp. also nissaraṇa & paṭi°.

Nissāya (prep. c. acc.) [ger. of nissayati, Sk. *niśrāya, BSk niśritya, ni+ **śri**] leaning on (in all fig. meanings) Nd[2] 368 (= upanissāya, ārammaṇaŋ ālambanaŋ karitvā). — 1. near, near by, on, at J I.167 (pāsānapiṭṭhaŋ), 221 (padumasaraŋ); PvA 24 (bāhā), 134 (taŋ = with him). — 2. by means of, through, by one's support, by way of J I.140 (rājānaŋ: under the patronage of the k.); IV.137 (id.); II.154 (tumhe); Miln 40 (kāyaŋ), 253 (id.); PvA 27 (ye = yesaŋ hetu), 154 (nadī° alongside of). — 3. because of, on account of, by reason of, for the sake of J I.203 (amhe), 255 (dhanaŋ), 263 (maŋ); PvA 17 (kiŋ), 67 (namaŋ), 130 (taŋ). — Cp. nissaya, nissita.

Nissāra (adj.) [nis+ sāra] sapless, worthless, unsubstantial J I.393; Sdhp 51, 608, 612.

Nissārajja (adj.) [Sk. niḥ+śārada+ya] without diffidence, not diffident, confident J I.274 (+ nibbhaya).

Nissāraṇa (nt.) [fr. nissarati] going or driving out, expulsion Miln 344 (osāraṇa-n.-patisāraṇa). 357.

Nissita (adj.) [Sk. niśrita, pp. of nissayati, corresp. in meaning to Sk. āśrita] hanging on, dependent on, inhabiting; attached to, supported by, living by means of, relying on, being founded or rooted in, bent on. As -° often in sense of a prep. = by means of, on account of, through, esp. with pron. kiŋ° (= why, through what) Sn 458; taŋ° (therefore, on acct. of this) S IV.102. — For comb° with var. synonyms see Nd² s. v. & cp. Nd¹ 75, 106. — S II.17 (dvayaŋ; cp. III.134); IV.59, 365; V.2 sq., 63 sq.; A III.128; Dh 339 (rāga°); Sn 752, 798, 910; J I.145; Nd¹ 283; Pv I.8⁶ (sokaŋ hadaya° lying in); II.6⁶ (paṭhavi° supported by); Vbh 229; Nett 39 (°citta); Miln 314 (inhabiting); PvA 86 (māna°). — anissita unsupported, not attached, free, emancipated Sn 66, 363, 753, 849, 1069 (unaided); J I.158; Miln 320, 351. — Cp. apassita.

Nissitaka (adj.-n.) [fr. prec.] adherent, supporter (orig. one who is supported by), pupil J I.142, 186; DhA I.54.

Nissitatta (nt.) [fr. nissita] dependence on, i. e. interference by, being too near, nearness Vism 118 (pantha°). Cp. san°.

Nissirīka (adj.) [nis+siri] having lost his (or its) splendour or prosperity J VI.225 (ājīvika), 456 (rājabhavana).

Nissīma (adj.) [cp. Sk. niḥsīman with diff. meanings ("boundless"), nis+sīma] outside the boundary Vin I.255 (°ṭṭha), 298 (°ŋ gantuŋ); II.167 (°e ṭhito).

Nissuta (adj.) [fr. nis+**sru**, see savati] flown out or away, vanished, disappeared M I.280.

Nisseṇi (f.) [fr. nis+**śri**, orig. that which leans against, or leads to something, cp. Sk. śreṇi a row] a ladder, a flight of stairs D I.194, 198; J I.53; II.315; III.505; Miln 263; Vism 244, 340 (in simile); DhA I.259.

Nissesa (adj.) [nis+sesa] whole, entire; nt. acc. as adv. nissesaŋ entirely, completely Nd² 533.

Nissoka (adj.) [nis+soka] free from sorrow, without grief, not mourning PvA 62; KhA 153.

Nihata (adj.) [pp. of nihanti, ni+**han**] "slain"; put down, settled; destroyed; dejected, humiliated; humble Vin II.307 (settled); J V.435 (°bhoga one whose fortunes are destroyed).
-māna "with slain pride," humiliated, humble S IV.203; Th 2, 413 (= apanīta-māna ThA 267); J II.300; VI.367.

Niharati see nīharati.

Nihita (adj.) [Sk. nihita, pp. of ni+**dhā**, see dahati] put down, put into, applied, settled; laid down, given up, renounced. As °- often in the sense of a prep. = without, e. g. °daṇḍa °sattha without stick & sword (see daṇḍa . . .) D I.70 (°paccāmitta); Pv IV.3²⁶ (su° well applied); PvA 252 (bhasma-nihita thrown into the ashes); Sdhp 311.

Nihīna (adj.) [Sk. nihīna, pp. of nihīyati or nihāyati] lost; degraded, low, vile, base, inferior, little, insignificant S I.12; Sn 890; Nd¹ 105, 194; PvA 198 (jāti° low-born); Sdhp 86. Opp. to seyya J VI.356 sq.
-attha one who has lost his fortune, poor Pv IV.1⁶; -kamma of low action Sn 661 = It 43; Dh 306; J II.417; -citta low-minded PvA 107 (= dīna); -jātika of inferior birth or caste PvA 175; -pañña of inferior wisdom Sn 890 (= paritta-pañña Nd¹ 299); -sevin of vile pursuit A I.126.

Nihīnatā (f.) [abstr. to nihīna] lowness, inferiority; vileness, baseness D I.98, 99.

Nihīyati [ni+hīyati, Pass. of **hā**, see jahāti] to be left, to come to ruin, to be destroyed A I.126 = J III.324 (= vināsaŋ pāpuṇāti). pp. nihīna (q. v.).

Nihuhunka (adj.) [fr. nī° = nis+huhunka] one who does not confide in the sound huŋ Vin I.3 (cp. *J.P.T.S.* 1901, 42).

Nīka [Sk. nyanku? Doubtful reading] a kind of deer (or pig) J V.406 (vv.ll. nika, ninga).

Nīgha (in anīgha) see nigha¹.

Nīca (adj.) [Vedic nīca, adj.-formation fr. adv. ni°, cp. Sk. nyañc downward] low, inferior, humble (opp. ucca high, fr. adv. ud°) Vin I.46, 47; II.194; D I.109, 179, 194; A V.82; SnA 424 (nīcaŋ karoti to degrade); & passim.
-kula of low clan J I.106; Sn 411; -(°ā) kulīna belonging to low caste Sn 462; -cittatā being humble-hearted Dhs 1340; DhsA 395; -pīṭhaka a low stool DhA IV.177; -mano humble Sn 252 (= nīcacitto SnA 293); -seyya a low bed A I.212 (opp. uccâsayana).

Nīceyya (adj.) [compar. of nīca (for °iya?), in function of °eyya as "of the kind of," sort of, rather] lower, inferior, rather low M I.329; Sn 855, 918; Nd¹ 244, 351.

Nīta (pp.) [pp. of neti] led, guided; ascertained, inferred A I.60 (°attha); J I.262; II.215 (kāma°); Nett 21 (°attha, natural meaning, i. e. the primarily inferred sense, opp. neyyattha); Sdhp 366 (dun°). Cp. vi°.

Nīti (f.) [Sk. nīti, fr. nīta] guidance, practice, conduct, esp. right conduct, propriety; statesmanship, polity PvA 114 (°maṅgala commonsense), 129 (°sattha science of statecraft, or of prudent behaviour), 130 (°cintaka a lawgiver), 131 (°naya polity & law), 132 (°kusala versed in the wisdom of life); Miln 3 (here meaning the Nyāya-philosophy, cp. Trenckner, *Notes* p. 58).

Nīdha = nu idha, see nu.

Nīdhura (?) [Sk. ? Cp. keyura] bracelet, bangle J VI.64, (= valaya; v. l. BB nivara). Also given as nīyura (cp. Prk. neura & P. nūpura).

Nīpa (adj.) [Vedic nīpa, contr. fr. ni+āpa "low water"] lit. lying low, deep, N. of the tree Nauclea cadamba, a species of Asoka tree J I.13 (v. 61) = Bu II.51; J V.6 (so read for nipa).

Nībhata [cp. Sk. nirbhṛta, pp. of nis+**bhṛ**] bought out J III.471.

Nīyati [Sk. nīyati, Pass. of neti] to be led or guided, to go, to be moved S I.39 (cittena nīyati loko); Dh 175; Pv I.11¹ (= vahīyati PvA 56); J I.264 (ppr. nīyamāna); PvA 4 (id.); DhA III.177; Sdhp 292, 302. Also found in spelling niyyati at Sn 851; Nd¹ 223 (= yāyati, vuyhati), 395. — In the sense of a Med. in imper. niyāmase (let us take) Pv II.9¹ (= nayissāma PvA 113).

Nīyāti see niyyāti.

Nīyādita, Nīyādeti see niyy°.

Nīyānika see niyy°.

Nīraja (adj.) [Sk. nīraja, nis+raja] free from passion Sdhp 370.

Nīrava (adj.) [Sk. nīrava, nis+rava] soundless, noiseless, silent DA I.153 (tuṇhī+).

Nīrasa (adj.) [Sk. nirasa, nis+rasa] sapless, dried up, withered, tasteless, insipid J III.111.

Nīruja (adj.) [Sk. niruja, nis+ rujā] = nīroga Sdhp 496.

Nīroga (adj.) [Sk. nīroga, nis + roga] free from disease, healthy, well, unhurt J I.421; III.26; IV.31; PvA 198 (ni°). Cp. nīruja.

Nīla (adj.) [Vedic nīla, perhaps conn. with Lat. nites to shine, see Walde, *Lat. Wtb.* s. v.] dark-blue, blue-black, blue-green. Nīla serves as a general term to designate the "coloured-black," as opposed to the "coloured-white" (pīta yellow), which pairs (nīla-pīta) are both set off against the "pure" colour-sensations of red (lohitaka) & white (odāta), besides the distinct black or dark (see kaṇha). Therefore n. has a fluctuating connotation (cp. Mrs. Rh. D. *Buddh. Psych.* p. 49 & *Dhs. trsl.* p. 62), its only standard comb^{n} being that with pita, e. g. in the enum^{n} of the ten kasiṇa practices (see kasiṇa): nīla pīta lohita odāta; in the description of the 5 colours of the Buddha's eye: nīla pītaka lohitaka kaṇha odāta (Nd² 235, I^{a} under cakkhumā); which goes even so far as to be used simply in the sense of "black & white," e. g. VvA 320. Applied to hair (lomāni) D II.144; M II.136. See further enum° at VvA 111 & under kaṇha. — A III.239; IV.263 sq., 305, 349; V.61; Vism 110, 156, 173; ThA 42 (mahā° great blue lotus); Dhs 617; Pv II.2⁵; PvA 32, 46, 158; Sdhp 246, 270, 360.

-abbha a black cloud Pv IV.3⁹. -abhijāti a dark (unfortunate) birth (cp. kaṇh°) A III.383; -uppala blue lotus J III.394; Vv 45⁴ (= kuvalaya); DhA I.384; -kasiṇa the "blue" kasiṇa (q. v.) D III.248; Dhs 203; (Vam 172 etc.; -gīva "blue neck," a peacock Sn 221 = maṇi-daṇḍa-sadisāya gīvāya n. ti SnA 277); -pupphī N. of plant ("blue-blossom") J VI.53; -bījaka a water-plant ("blue-seed") Bdhgh at Vin III.276; -maṇi a sapphire ("blue-stone") J II.112; IV.140; DhA III.254; -vaṇṇa blue colour, coloured blue or green J IV.140 (of the ocean); Dhs 246.

Nīlaka (adj.) for nīla M II.201; see vi°.

Nīliya [fr. nīlī] an (indigo) hair dye J III.138 (Com. nīliyaka).

Nīlī (f.) [Sk. nīlī] the indigo plant, indigo colour A III.230, 233.

Nīḷa [Vedic nīḍa] a nest (J V.92): see niḍḍha: cp. °pacchi bird cage J II.361; roga° It 37; vadharoga° Th I.1093.

Nīvaraṇa (nt. occasionally m.) [Sk. *nivāraṇa, nis + varaṇa of vṛ (vṛṇoti), see nibbuta & cp. nivāraṇa] an obstacle, hindrance, only as tt. applied to obstacles in an ethical sense & usually enum^{d} or referred to in a set of 5 (as pañca nīvaraṇāni and p. āvaraṇāni), viz. kāmacchanda, (abhijjhā-)vyāpāda, thīna-middha, uddhacca-kukkucca, vicikicchā i. e. sensuality, ill-will, torpor of mind or body, worry, wavering (cp. *Dhs. trsl.* p. 310): D I.73 (°e, acc. pl.), 246; II.83, 300; III.49 sq., 101, 234, 278; S II.23; III.149; V.60, 84 sq., 93 sq., 145, 160, 226, 327, 439; M I.60, 144, 276; III.4, 295; A I.3, 161; III.16, 63, 230 sq.; 386; IV.457; V.16, 195, 322; Sn 17; Nd¹ 13; Nd² 379; Ps I.31, 129, 163; Pug 68; Dhs 1059, 1136, 1495; Vbh 199, 244, 378; Nett 11, 13, 94; Vism 146, 189; DA I.213; Sdhp 459, 493 and passim. — Other enum^{ns} are occasionally found e. g. 10 at S V.110; 8 at M I.360 sq.; 6 at Dhs 1152.

Nīvaraṇiya (adj.) [fr. nīvaraṇa] belonging to an obstacle, forming a hindrance, obstructing Dhs 584, 1164, 1488; Vbh 12, 30, 66, 130 etc.

Nīvāra [Sk. nīvāra, unexplained] raw rice, paddy D I.166; A I.241, 295; II.206; Pug 55; J III.144 (°yāgu).

Nīhaṭa [pp. of nīharati = Sk. nirhṛta] thrown out, removed; in f. abstr. °tā ejection, removal [cp. Sk. nirhṛti] DhA III.336 (malānaŋ n. the extirpation of impurity or removal of stain).

Nīharaṇa (nt.) [fr. nīharati] taking out, carrying away, removing DA I.296; PvA 7.

Nīharati [nis+ hṛ] to take out, to throw out, drive out J I.150, 157; III.52; VI.336; Nd² 199⁷ (ni°); VvA 222, 256; PvA 73, 254; Miln 8, 219. aor. nīhari D I.92; J I.293; II.154; PvA 41, 178 (gehato taŋ n.). grd. nīharitabba DhA I.397 (opp. pavesetabba). — pp. nīhaṭa. — Caus. nīharāpeti to have thrown out, to order to be ejected VvA 141.

Nīhāra [cp. Sk. nirhāra] way, manner Vin I.13; J I.127; DhA IV.7. At Vin I.13 also in nīhāra-bhatta (= nīhāraka).

Nīhāraka (adj.-n.) [fr. nīhāra, cp. nīharaṇa] one who carries away Vin I.13 (nīhāra-bhatta); S V.12, 320, 325 (piṇḍapāta).

Nu (indecl.) [Ved. nu, Idg. *nu, orig. adv. of time = now; cp. Lat. num (to nunc, now), see nūna] affirm.-indef. part. "then, now." — 1. most freq. comb^{d} with interr. pron. and followed by kho, as kin nu kho J II.159; kacci J I.279; kaccin nu (for kaccid nu) J II.133; kathan nu (kho) Vin I.83; kattha PvA 22; etc. — 2. as interr. part. (= Lat. ne, num) in enclitic position Vin I.17; J III.52; Sn 866, 871, 1071; etc. As such also comb^{d} with na = nanu (Lat. nonne), which begins the sentence: Vin II.303 (nanu tvaŋ vuḍḍho vīsativasso 'sī ti?); Pv I.8⁴; PvA 39, 136 etc. — Often comb^{d} with other emphatic or dubitative particles, like api nu Vin II.303; D I.97; nu idha, contr. to nīdha Vv 83⁶ or with sandhi as nu-v-idha D I.108 (v. l. nu khv idha). Cp. na¹, nūna, no.

Nuṭṭhubhati see niṭṭhubhati. (aor. nuṭṭhubhi, e. g. J II.105).

Nuda (-°) (adj.) [Sk. °nud & °nuda, to nudati] expelling, casting out, dispelling; in tamo° dispelling darkness Sn 1133; Vv 35² (= viddhaŋsana VvA 161).

Nudaka or **Nūdaka** (-°) = nuda J V.401 (āsa-nūdaka).

Nudati [Vedic nudati; Idg. *(s)neu to push, cp. Sk. navate, Gr. νεύω & νύσσω, Lat. nuo; Ags. neosian, Low Ger. nucken] to push, impel; expel, drive away, reject Dh 28; J IV.443; DhA I.259. aor. nudi Nd² 281. Cp. apa°, pa°, vi°. — pp. nunna (nuṇṇa).

Nunna (nuṇṇa) [pp. of nudati] thrust, pushed, driven away, removed Nd² 220 (ṇṇ = khitta), cp. panuṇṇa A II.41.

Nūtana (adj.) [Vedic nūtana, adj.-formation fr. adv. nū, cp. nūna. In formation cp. Sk. śvastana (of to-morrow), Lat. crastinus etc.] "of now," i. e. recent, fresh, new Dāvs IV.47.

Nūna (& nūnaŋ DhsA 164) (indecl.) [Ved. nūnaŋ = Gr. νύν, Lat. nunc (cp. num); Goth. nu, Ger. nun, cp. E. now. See also nu] affirmative-dubitative particle with Pot. or Ind., viz. 1. (dubit.-interrog.) is it then, now, shall I etc. (= Lat. subjunctive, hortative & dubitative) D I.155 (= Lat. num, cp. nu). Esp. freq. with rel. pron. yaŋ = yaŋ nūna what if, shall I, let me (Lat. age) Sn p. 80 (yaŋ nūn' âhaŋ puccheyyaŋ let me ask, I will ask); J I.150, 255; III.393; PvA 5 (y. n. âhaŋ imassa avassayo bhaveyyaŋ = let me help him). — 2. (affirm.) surely, certainly, indeed Sn 1058 (api nūna pajaheyyuŋ); A V.194; J I.60; V.90; Pv II.9²⁴ (nuna); Miln 20; DhsA 164; PvA 95 (nuna as v. l.; text reads nanda).

Nūpura [Sk. nūpura; Non-Aryan. Cp. Prk. ṇeura & nīdhura (nīyura)] an ornament for the feet, an anklet Th 2, 268; DA I.50.

Ne, Nesan see na[3].

Neka (adj.) [Sk. naika = na eka, cp. aneka] not one, several, many Sn 308; Vv 53[6] (°citta variegated = nānāvidhacitta VvA 236), 64[1] (id. = anekacitta VvA 275); Tikp 366.

Nekatika (adj.) [fr. nikati] deceitful, fraudulent; a cheat D III.183; Th 1, 940; Miln 290; PvA 209; J IV.184.

Nekāyika (adj.) [fr. nikāya] versed in the 4 (or 5) Nikāyas Miln 22; cp. Cunningham, *Stupa of Bharhut* 142, 52.

Nekkha [Vedic niṣka; cp. nikkha] a golden ornament, a certain coin of gold S I.65; A I.181; II.8, 29; Dh 230 (= DhA III.329 jambonada nikkha); Vism 48; v. l. at Vv 20[8], 43[8].

Nekkhamma (nt.) [formally a derivation fr. nikkhamma (ger. of nikkhamati) = Sk. *naiṣkramya, as shown also by its semantic affinity to nikkhanta, in which the metaphorical sense has entirely superseded the literal one. On the other hand, it may be a bastard derivation fr. nikkāma = Sk. *naiṣkāmya, although the adj. nikkāma does not show the prevailing meaning & the wide range of nikkhanta, moreover formally we should expect nekkamma. In any case the connection with kāma is pre-eminently felt in the connotation of n., as shown by var. passages where a play of word exists between n. & kāma (cp. kāmānaŋ nissaraṇaŋ yad idaŋ nekkhammaŋ It 61, cp. Vin I.104; A III.245; also M I.115). The use of the similar term abhinikkhamana further warrants its derivation fr. nikkhamati] giving up the world & leading a holy life, renunciation of, or emancipation from worldliness, freedom from lust, craving & desires, dispassionateness, self-abnegation, Nibbāna Vin I.18 (°e ānisaŋsa); D I.110 (id.), III.239, 275, 283; M III.129; A I.147 (= khema, i. e. nibbāna); III.245; IV.186 (ānisaŋsa), 439 sq.; Sn 424 (°ŋ daṭṭhu khemato); Dh 181; Ps I.107 sq.; II.169 sq.; Nd[2] 370; Vism 116, 325; J I.19; 137; Vv 84[42] (= nibbāna VvA 348); Nett 53, 87, 106 sq.; Miln 285 (°ŋ abhinikkhanta); DhA III.227; ThA 266.
-ādhimutta bent on self-abnegation (enum[d] with 5 other ideals of Arahantship: paviveka, avyāpajjha, upādānakkhaya, taṇhakkhaya, asammoha) Vin I.183; A III.376; **-ābhirata** fond of renunciation A IV.224; V.175; Ps II.173; **-dhātu** the sphere or element of dispassionateness S II.152; Vbh 86; Nett 97; Vism 487. **-ninna** merging into or bent on a holy life S III.233; **-vitakka** a thought of self-abnegation S II.152; A I.275; II.252; It 82; **-saṅkappa** = prec. S II.152; A III.146; Vbh 104, 235; **-sita** based or bent on a holy life (opp. geha° q. v.) S IV.232; **-sukha** the joy or happiness of Arahantship M III.110; A I.80; Dh 267, 272; DhA III.400.

Negama (adj.-n.) [fr. nigama] the inhabitant of a (small) town; citizen; also collect. = jana, people Vin I.268, 273; D I.136, 139; J IV.121; VI.493; Dāvs III.3; DA I.297. Often comb[d] with °jānapadā (pl.) "townsmen & country-folk" S I.89; D III.148, 172; J 149.

Necayika (adj.) [fr. nicaya] rich, wealthy D I.136, 142 (read nevāsika cp. naivasika M Vastu III.38); A V.149 (v. l. BB nerayika, Com. nevāsiko ti nivāsakaro).

Netar [Vedic netṛ, n. ag. of neti] a leader, guide, forerunner Sn 86, 213; Nd[1] 446.

Neti (nayati) [Vedic nayati, nī] to lead, guide, conduct; to take, carry (away); fig. to draw a conclusion, to understand, to take as Dh 80, 145, 240, 257; J I.228; IV.241 (nayaŋ n. to draw a proper conclusion); VvA 42 (narati = nayati); imper. naya Pv II.11[3], & nehi J II.160; PvA 147; poetic imper. nayāhi see in paṭi°; pot. naye Dh 256 (to lead a cause = vinicchineyya DhA III.381). fut. nessāmi J II.159; Pv II.4[6]; aor. nayi J IV.137. ger. netvā PvA 5, 6, etc. inf. netuŋ PvA 123, 145 (°kāma), & netave J I.79 = Dh 180. grd. neyya (see sep.), pp. nīta. Pass. nīyati (q. v.). Cp. naya, nīti, netta etc.; also ā°, upa°, paṭi°, vi°.

Netta[1] [Sk. netra, fr. neti] a guide J III.111; Nett. 130.

Netta[2] (nt.) [Sk. netra] guidance, anything that guides, a conductor, fig. the eye. S I.26 (sārathī nettāni gahetvā = the reins); Vin I.204 (dhūma° for smoke); J IV.363 (id.); D I.12 (°tappana, set t. & cp. DA I.98); Sn 550 (pasanna°), 1120; Nd[2] 371 (= cakkhu), 669; J VI.290 (tamba° with red eyes); Pv I.8[3] (eyes = nayanāni Com.); Dhs 597; Vbh 71 sq.

Netti (f.) [Vedic netrī, f. to netṛ] a guide, conductor; support (= nettika[2]) It 37 (āhāra°-pabhava), 38 (bhava°), 94 (netticchinna bhikkhu = Arahant). Cp. nettika[2] & dhamma°, bhava°.

Nettiŋsa [cp. Sk. nistriŋśa, Halāyudha 2, 317; very doubtful, whether nis + triŋśa (thirty), prob. a dial. distortion] a sword J II.77 (°vara-dhārin; C. nettiŋsā vuccanti khaggā); IV.118 (C. gives it as adj. = nikkaruṇa, merciless; & says "khaggassa nāmaŋ"); VI.188 (°vara-dhārin).

Nettika (adj.-n.) [netta + ika] 1. having as guide or forerunner, in Bhagavaŋ° dhamma M I.310; A I.199; IV.158, 351; V.355. — 2. a conduit for irrigation; one who makes conduits for watering Dh 80 (= udakaŋ nenti nettikā), 145; fig. that which supplies with food or water, in bhava° ("the roots of existence, clinging to existence") D I.46 (ucchinna° with the roots of existence cut); sanettika clinging to existence, a bad man A II.54. Cp. netti.

Netthar [see nittharati; does any connection exist with Vedic neṣṭṛ ?] only in phrase netthāraŋ vattati to behave in such a way as to get rid of blame or fault Vin II.5; III.183; M I.442. — Bdhgh on Vin II.5 (p. 309) explains: nittharantānaŋ etan ti netthāraŋ yena sakkā nissaraṇā nittharituŋ taŋ aṭṭhārasa-vidhaŋ sammāvattuŋ vattantī ti attho.

Nepakka (nt.) [fr. nipaka] prudence, discrimination, carefulness; usually as sati° S V.197 sq.; M I.356; A III.11; IV.15; Nd[2] 629 B; Vbh 244, 249; Vism 3 (= paññā); DhA IV.29.

Nepuñña (nt.) [fr. nipuna] experience, skill, cleverness Pug 25, 35; Dhs 16, 292; DhsA 147.

Nema [cp. nemi] edge, point; root S V.445; A IV.404; gambhīra° (adj.) with deeply rooted point, firmly established S V.444; A IV.106.

Nemantanika (adj.) [fr. nimantana] one who lives by invitations M I.31.

Nemi (f.) [Vedic nemi, perhaps to namati] the circumference of a wheel, circumference, rim, edge (cp. nema) A I.112; Vv 64[6]; Miln 238, 285; Vism 198 (fig. jarāmaraṇa°, the rim of old age & death, which belongs to the wheel of Saŋsāra of the chariot of existence, bhavaratha); DhA II.124 (°vaṭṭi); VvA 277.

Nemitta [Sk. naimitta, fr. nimitti] a fortune-teller, astrologer D II.16, 19; A III.243.

Nemittaka & Nemittika [Sk. naimittika, fr. nimitta] an astrologer, fortune-teller, soothsayer D I.8 (i) = DA I.91; A III.11; J IV.124; Miln 19 (i), 229; Vism 210 (i); DhA II.241 (a).

Nemittikatā (f.) [abstr. fr. nemittika] = nimitta-kammaŋ, i. e. prognostication; inquisitiveness, insinuation Vbh 352 = Vism 23; expl[d] at Vism 28.

Nemiya (adj.) [=nemika] (-°) having a circumference etc. J VI.252.

Neyya (adj.) [grd. of neti; Sk. neya] to be led, carried etc.; fig. to be instructed; to be inferred, guessed or understood Sn 55, 803, 846, 1113; Nd[1] 114, 206; Nd[2] 372; Pug 41; Nett 9 sq., 125; -attha the meaning which is to be inferred (opp. nītattha) A I.60; Nett 21.

Nerayika (adj.) [fr. niraya, cp. BSk. nairayika Divy 165] belonging to niraya or purgatory, hellish; one doomed to suffering in purgatory (n. satta=inhabitant of n.) Vin II.205 (āpāyiko n. kappaṭṭho); IV.7; D III.6, 9, 12; A I.265; II.231 (vedanaŋ vediyati . . . seyyathā pi sattā nerayikā); III.402 sq.; Sn 664; Nd[1] 97 (gati); Vv 52[1], J IV.3 (sattā); Pug 51; Vbh 412 sq.; Vism 415 (°sattā), 424; Miln 148 (sattā); PvA 27 (id.), 52 (°bhāva), 255; VvA 23; Sdhp 193, 198.

Nerutta (adj.-n.) [fr. nirutti] based on etymology; an etymologist or philologist ThA 153; Nett 8, 9, 32, 33.

Neḷa (& **Nela**) (adj.) [na+eḷa=Sk. anenas, of enas fault, sin. The other negated form, also in meaning "pure, clean," is aneḷa (& aneḷaka), q. v. On ḷ: n. cp. lāngala; nangala; tulā: tūṇa etc.] 1. without fault or sin, blameless, faultless; not hurting, humane, gentle, merciful, innocuous D I.4 (Bdhgh explains: elaŋ vuccati doso; n' assā (i. e. vācāya) elan ti nelā; niddosā ti attho. "Nelango setapacchādo" ti ettha vuttanelaŋ viya; DA I.75); A II.209; V.205; J V.156; Vv 50[18], 63[6] (=niddosa VvA 262); Pug 29, 57; Dhs 1343 (vācā)=niddosa DhsA 397. — 2. (somewhat doubtful) "clean," with ref. to big cats (mahā-biḷārā nelamaṇḍalaŋ vuccati), whereas young ones are called "elephants, cubs" (something like "pigs") (taruṇā bhinka-cchāpamaṇḍalaŋ) J V.418.
-anga of faultless limbs or parts, of a chariot (ratha) =running perfectly S IV.291=Ud 76 (nelagga text, nelanga v. l.)=DA I.75=DhsA 397. -patī (f.)=neḷavatī (of vācā) humane, gentle J VI.558 (na elapati elapāta-rahitā madhurā Com.).

Neva (indecl.) [na+eva] see na[2]. — nevasaññā-nâsañña (being) neither perception nor non-perception, only in cpd. °āyatana & in nevasaññī-nâsaññin: see saññā.

Nevāpika (adj.-n.) [fr. nivāpa] a deer-feeder M I.150 sq.

Nevāsika (adj.) [fr. nivāsa, cp. BSk. naivāsika AvŚ I.286, 287] one who inhabits, an inmate; living in a place, local J I.236 sq.; DhA II.53 sq. Cp. necayika.

Nesajjika (adj.) [fr. nisajjā] being & remaining in a sitting position (as an ascetic practice) A III.220; Th I, 904, 1120; Nd[2] 587; J IV.8; Pug 69; Vism 79; Miln 20, 342. The n-°anga is one of the dhūtanga-precepts, enjoining the sitting posture also for sleeping, see Vin V.193, Vism 61, & dhūtanga.

Nesāda [fr. nisāda; cp. Sk. niṣāda & naiṣāda=one who lies in wait] a hunter; also a low caste Vin IV.7 (+veṇa & rathakāra); S I.93 (°kula); A I.107; II.85; J II.36; III.330; IV.397, 413; V.110, 337; VI.71; Pug 51 (°kula); Miln 311; DhA III.24; PvA 176.

No[1] (indecl.) affirm. & emphatic part.=nu (cp. na[1]): indeed, then, now Sn 457, 875, 1077; J V.343 (api no= api nu), 435 (=nipātamattaŋ p. 437).

No[2] (indecl.) [Sk. no=na+u, a stronger na; cp. na[2]) negative & adversative particle=neither, nor, but not, surely not, indeed not. — (a) in neg. sentences: Sn 852, 855, 1040; It 103 (but not); Pv II.3[13] (but not). as answer: no hi etaŋ "indeed not, no indeed" Vin I.17; D I.3; no hi idaŋ D I.105. — no ca kho "but surely not" D I.34, 36; A V.195. — Often emphasized by na, as no na not at all J I.64; na no Sn 224 (="avadhāraṇe" KhA 170); disjunctively na hi . . . no neither—nor Sn 813; na no . . . na neither—nor (not—nor) Sn 455. — (b) in disjunctive questions: "or not," as evaŋ hoti vā . . . no vā (is it so—or not) D I.61, 227; kacci . . . no (is it so—or not; Lat. ne-annon) D I.107; nu kho . . . no udāhu (is it that—or not; or rather) D I.152. — (c) noce (no ce=Sk. no ced) if not (opp. sace) Sn 348, 691, 840; J I.222; VI.365; VvA 69. Also in sense of "I hope not" J V.378.

No[3] [Sk. naḥ] enclitic form, gen. dat. acc. pl. of pron. 1st (we)=amhākaŋ, see vayaŋ; cp. na[3].

Nodeti [fr. nud] see vi°.

Nonīta see navanīta.

Nhāru see nahāru. Found e. g. at Vin I.25.

THE PALI TEXT SOCIETY'S PALI-ENGLISH DICTIONARY

EDITED BY

T. W. RHYS DAVIDS F.B.A. D.Sc. Ph.D. LL.D. D.Litt.

and WILLIAM STEDE Ph.D.

Part V (P—Ph.)

PUBLISHED BY
THE PALI TEXT SOCIETY
LONDON

First published - - - 1923
Reprinted - - - - 1949
Reprinted - - - - 1952

P.

Pa° (indecl.) [Ved. pra, Idg. *pro, cp. Gr. πρό, Lat. pro, Goth. fra, Lith. pra, prō, Oir. ro-] directional prefix of forward motion, in applied sense often emphasising the action as carried on in a marked degree or even beyond its mark (cp. Ger. ver- in its function of Goth. fra & Ger. vor). Thus the sphere of pa- may be characterised in foll. applications: 1. forth, forward, out: papatati fall forward, i. e. down; °neti bring forth (to); °gaṇhāti hold out; °tharati spread forth; °dhāvati run out; °bajati go forth; °sāreti stretch out; etc. — 2. (intensive) in a marked degree, more than ordinarily (cp. E. up in cut up, heap up, fill up; thus often to be trsl^{d} by "up," or "out," or "about"): pakopeti up-set; °chindati cut up; °bhañjati break up; °cinati heap up; °kiṇṇaka scattered about; °nāda shouting out; °bhāti shine forth; °bhavati grow up, prevail; °dūseti spoil entirely; °jahati give up entirely; °tapeti make shine exceedingly (C. ativiya dīpeti); °jalati blaze up; °jānāti know well. — In this meaning often with adjectives like patanu very thin; °thaddha quite stiff; °dakkhiṇa right in pre-eminence; °bala very strong. — 3. "onward": paṭṭhāya from . . . onward; pavattati move on; fig. "further, later": paputta a later (secondary) son, i. e. grandson. — 4. "in front of," "before": padvāra, before the door. — 5. Sometimes in trs. (reflexive) use, like pakūjin singing out to (each other, cp Ger. besingen, an-rufen).— The most frequent combination with other (modifying) prefixes is sam-ppa; its closest relatives (in meaning 2 especially) are ā and pari. The double (assimilation) p is restored after short vowels, like appadhaṃsiya (a + pa°).

°Pa (adj.) [Cp. Ved. °pa, adj. base of **pā** to drink, as °ga fr. **gam** or °tha fr. **sthā**] drinking; only in foll. cpds.: dhenu° drinking of the cow, suckling calf M I.79; Sn 26 (= dhenuŋ pivanto SnA 39); — pāda° a tree (lit. drinking with its feet, cp. expl^{n} at PvA 251 "pādasadischi mūl' âvayavehi udakassa pivanato pādapo ti") Pv IV.3^{9}; — majja° drinking intoxicants Sn 400; Pv IV.1^{77} (a°).

Paŋsu [cp. Ved. pāŋsu] dust, dirt, soil S V.459; A I.253; Pv II.3^{7}. — paŋsvāgārakā playmates S III.190; saha-paŋsukīḷitā id. (lit. playing together with mud, making mud pies) A II.186; J I.364; PvA 30. Cp. BSk. sahapāŋśukrīḍita MVastu III.450.
-kūla rays from a dust heap (cp. *Vin. Texts* II.156) Vin I.58; M I.78; S II.202; A I.240, 295; II.206; IV.230; It 102 = A II.26; Dh 395; Pug 69; PvA 141, 144. A quâsi definition of p.-k. is to be found at Vism 60. **-kūlika** one who wears clothes made of rags taken from a dust heap M I.30; S II.187; A III.187, 219, 371 sq.; Vin III.15; IV.360; Ud 42; Pug 55; DhA IV.157; °*attan* (nt. abstr.) the habit of wearing rags M I.214; III.41; A I.38; III.108. **-gunṭhita** (vv. ll. °kuṇḍita, °kunṭhita) covered with dust or dirt S I.197; J VI.559; Pv II.3^{6}. — **pisâcaka** a mud sprite (some sort of demon) J III.147; IV.380; DhA II.26. **-muṭṭhi** a handful of soil J VI. 405. **-vappa** sowing on light soil (opp. kalalavappa sowing on heavy soil or mud) SnA 137.

Paŋsuka (adj.) [Epic Sk. pāŋśuka; Ved. pāŋsura] dusty; (m.) a dusty robe KhA 171 (v. l. paŋsukūla).

Pakaṭṭhaka [pa + kaṭṭha + ka; kaṭṭha pp. of **kṛṣ**, cp. Sk. prakarṣaka of same root in same meaning, but cp. also kaṭṭha^{2}] (adj.) troublesome, annoying; (m.) a troubler, worrier S I.174 (v. l. pagaṇḍaka; C. rasagiddha; trsl. "pertinacious").

Pakaṭṭhita see pakk°.

Pakata [pp. of pa + kṛ] done, made; as -° by nature (cp. pakati) Sn 286; J IV.38; Pv I.6^{8}; II.3^{16}; III.10^{5} (pāpaŋ = samācaritaŋ PvA 214); Miln 218; DhA II.11 (pāpaŋ); PvA 31, 35, 103 (t), 124. — icchāpakata covetous by nature A III.119, 219 sq.; Pug 69; Vism 24 (here however taken by Bdhgh as "icchāya apakata" or "upadduta"); issāpakata envious by nature S II.260; PvA 46, cp. macchariyā pakata afflicted with selfishness PvA 124. On pakata at It 89 see apakata. —**pakatatta** (pakata + attan) natural, of a natural self, of good behaviour, incorrupt, "integer" Vin II.6, 33, 204; J I.236 (bhikkhu, + sīlavā, etc.). At Vin II.32 the **pakatatta** bhikkhu as the regular, ordained monk is contrasted with the pārivāsika bh. or probationer.

Pakati (f.) [cp. Ved. prakṛti] 1. original or natural form, natural state or condition (lit. make-up); as °-: primary, original, real Vin. I.189; II.113; J I.146 (°vesena in her usual dress); KhA 173 (°kammakara, °jeṭṭhaputta); VvA 12 (°pabhassara), 109 (°bhaddatā). — instr. pakatiyā by nature, ordinarily, as usual Ps II.208; VvA 78; PvA 215, 263. — 2. occasion, happening, opportunity, (common) occurrence D I.168 (trsl. "common saying"); Pv II.8^{9} (= °pavutti PvA 110). — Der. pakatika & pākatika.
-upanissaya sufficing condition in nature: see *Cpd.* 194 n. 3. — **gamana** natural or usual walk DhA I 389. **-citta** ordinary or normal consciousness Kvu 615 (cp. *Kvu trsl.* 359 n. 5, and BSk. prakṛti-nirvāṇatva Bodhicary. at Poussin 256). **-yānaka** ordinary vehicle DhA I.391. **-sīla** natural or proper virtue DA I.290.

Pakatika (adj.) [fr. pakati] being by nature, of a certain nature J II.30; Miln 220; DA I.198; PvA 242 (= rūpa); DhsA 404.

Pakattheti [pa + kattheti] talk out against, denounce J V.7 (mā °katthāsi; C. akkosi garahi nindi; gloss paccakkhāsi). Should it be 'pakaḍḍhāsi ?

Pakappanā (f.) [fr. pakappeti] fixing one's attention on, planning, designing, scheme, arrangement Sn 945 (cp. Nd^{1} 72 186, where two pakappanā's, viz. taṇhā° & diṭṭhi°; at Nd^{1} 429 it is synonymous with taṇhā; Bdhgh has reading pakampana for °kapp° and expl^{d} by kampa-karaṇa SnA 568).

Pakappita [pp. of pakappeti] arranged, planned, attended to, designed, made Sn 648 (= kata SnA 471), 784, 776 (diṭṭhi "prejudiced view" Fausböll; cp. Nd^{1} 72 and pakappanā), 802, 838 (= kappita abhisankhata saṇṭhapita Nd^{1} 186), 902, 910.

Pakappeti [pra + Caus. of **kḷp**, cp. Ved. prakalpayitar] to arrange, fix, settle, prepare, determine, plan S II.65 (ceteti p. anuseti); Sn 886 (pakappayitvā = takkayitvā vitakkayitvā saŋkappayitvā Nd[1] 295). — pp. **pakappita** (q. v.).

Pakampati [pa + kampati. Cp. BSk. prakampati Jtm 220; Mvyutp. 151 = kampati.] to shake, quake, tremble J I.47 (v. 269); PvA 199. — Caus. pakampeti S I.107.

Pakampana see pakappanā.

Pakampita [pp. of pa + **kamp**] shaken, trembling S I.133 = Th 2, 200.

Pakaraṇa (nt.) [fr. pa + **kṛ**] 1. performance, undertaking paragraph (of the law) D I.98 ("offence"? see *Dial.* I.120); S III.91; Miln 189. — 2. occasion Vin I.44; II.75; III.20. — 3. exposition, arrangement, literary work, composition, book; usually in titles only, viz. Abhidhamma° J I.312; Dpvs V.37; Kathāvatthu° Paṭṭhāna° Miln 12; Netti° one of the Canonical books (see netti).

Pakaroti [pa + **kṛ**, Ved. prakaroti] to effect, perform, prepare, make, do S I.24 (pakubbati); Sn 254 (id.), 781, 790 (ppr. med. pakubbamāna; cp. Nd[1] 65); It 21 (puññaŋ); SnA 169 (pakurute, corresponding with sevati). — pp. **pakata** (q. v.).

Pakāra [pa + **kṛ**, cp. last; but Sk. prakāra "similarity"] 1. make-up, getting up, fixing, arrangement, preparation, mode, way, manner J II.222; DA I.132; PvA 26, 109, 123, 135, 178, 199; Sdhp 94, 466. — 2. ingredient, flavour, way of making (a food) tasty Sn 241 (kathappakāro tava āmagandho); Miln 63. — 3. (-°) of a kind, by way of, in nānā° (adj.) various, manifold J I.52 (sakuṇā), 278 (phalāni); PvA 50; vutta° as said, the said Vism 42, 44; PvA 136.

Pakāraka (-°) (adj.) [fr. pakāra] of that kind S II.81; J VI.259.

Pakāreti [Denom. fr. pakāra] to direct one's thought towards (dat.) J VI.307.

Pakāsati [pa + **kāś**] to shine forth, to be visible, to become known Sn 445, 1032 (= bhāsati tapati virocati Nd[2] 373). — Caus. pakāseti to show up, illustrate, explain, make known, give information about Vin II.189; S I.105; It 111 (brahmacariyaŋ); Dh 304; Sn 578, 1021; Pug 57; J VI.281 (atthaŋ to explain the meaning or matter); DhA II.11 (id.); PvA 1, 12 (ānisaŋsaŋ) 29 (atthaŋ upamāhi), 32 (attānaŋ), 40 (adhippāyaŋ), 42 (saccāni) 72 etc. — grd. **pakāsaniya** to be made known or announced in °kamma explanation, information, annunciation Vin II.189 (cp. *Vin. Texts* III.239). — pp. pakāsita (q. v.).

Pakāsana (nt.) [pa + **kāś**, cp. pakāsati] explaining, making known; information, evidence, explanation, publicity Ps I.104 (dhamma°); Miln 95; SnA 445; PvA 2, 50, 103 (expl^n of āvi).

Pakāsita [pp. of pakāseti] explained, manifested, made known S I.161, 171 sq.; II.107 (su°); PvA 53, 63.

Pakiṇāti [pa + kiṇāti] to deal in Vin II.267 (grd. °kiṇitabba).

Pakiṇṇaka (adj.) [pa + kiṇṇa (pp. of kirati) + ka] scattered about; fig. miscellaneous, particular, opp. to sādhāraṇa KhA 74; cp. *Cpd.* 13, 95[2]; Vism 175 (°kathā); 317 sq. (id.). — As Np. name of the xiv^th book of the Jātakas.

Pakitteti [pa + kitteti] to proclaim J I.17 (v. 85).

Pakirati [pa + kirati] 1. to let down (the hair), scatter, let fall D II.139 = 148 (ger. pakiriya); J V.203 (so read for parikati); VI.207 (aor °kiriŋsu). — ger. pakira (= pakiritvā) J VI.100 (read pakira cārī, cp. C on p. 102), 198 (read p. parī). — Caus. pakireti 1. to throw down, upset Vin IV.308 (thūpaŋ); S I.100; It 90 (v. l. kīrati). — 2. to scatter S I.100 = It 66; Pug 23. — pp. pakiṇṇa (see °ka).

Pakiledeti [Caus of pa + **kliś**, cp. kelideti] to make wet, moisten (with hot water) J VI.109 (= temetvā khipati C.).

Pakujjhati [pa + **krudh**] to be angry S I.221, 223 (°eyyaŋ).

Pakuṭa (?) [v. l. pakuṭṭa] an inner verandah Vin II.153; cp. *Vin. Texts* III.175. — Kern, *Toev.* s. v. expl^d it as miswriting for pakuṭṭha (= Sk. prakoṣṭha an inner court in a building, Prk. paoṭṭha, cp. P. koṭṭha[1] & koṭṭhaka[1]). Spelling pakulla at Nd[2] 485 B (for magga, v. l. makula).

Pakuppati [pa + **kup**] to be angry J IV.241.

Pakubb° see pakaroti.

Pakūjin (adj.) [pa + **kūj**] to sing out to (each other) (aññamaññaŋ) J VI.538.

Pakopa [pa + kopa] agitation, effervescence, anger, fury Dhs 1060; Vism 235, 236.

Pakopana (adj.) [pa + kopana, of **kup**] shaking, upsetting, making turbulent It 84 (moho citta-pakopano).

Pakka (adj.) [Ved. pakva, a pp. formation of **pac** to cook, Idg. *pequ̯o = Lat. coquo "cook," Av. pac-, Obulg. peką, Lith. kepù, Gr. πέσσω, ἀρτοκόπος baker, πέπων ripe; also pp. of pacati pakta = Gr. πεπτός, Lat. coctus] 1. ripe (opp. āma raw, as Vedic, ; and apakka) and also "cooked, boiled, baked" S I.97 (opp. āmaka); IV.324 (°bhikkhā); Sn 576; J V.286. — nt. **pakkaŋ** that which is ripe, i. e. a fruit, ripe fruit Pug 44, 45; often in connection with amba° i. e. a (ripe) mango fruit J II.104, 394; Pv IV.12[3]; DhA III.207; PvA 187. — apakka unripe PugA 225; Sdhp 102. — 2. ripe for destruction, overripe, decaying, in phrase °gatta (adj.) having a decaying body, with putrid body [BSk. pakvagātra Divy 82], comb^d with arugatta at M I.506; S IV.198; Miln 357 (cp. Miln trsl. II.262), 395. — 3. heated, glowing Dpvs I.62.

-**āsaya** receptacle for digested food, i. e. the abdomen (opp. āmāsaya) Vism 260, 358; KhA 59. -**odana** (adj.) having cooked one's rice Sn 18 (= siddhabhatta SnA 27), cp. J III.425. -**jjhāna** "guessing at ripeness," i. e. foretelling the number of years a man has yet to live; in list of forbidden crafts at D I.9, expl^d at DA I.94 as "paripāka-gata-cintā." -**pakka** ripe fruit KhA 59. -**pūva** baked cake J III.10. -**vaṇṇin** of ripe appearance Pug 44, 45, cp. PugA 225. -**sadisa** ripe-like, appearing ripe PugA 225.

Pakkaṭhati [pa + kaṭhati of **kvath**] to cook, boil up; only in Caus. II. pakkaṭṭhāpeti (with unexpl^d ṭṭh for ṭh) to cause to be boiled up J I.472 (v. l. pakkuṭṭh°, cp. *J.P.T.S.* 1884, 84). — pp. pakkaṭhita (q. v.).

Pakkaṭhita (pakkuthita) [also spelt with ṭṭh instead of ṭh or th, perhaps through popular etym. pakka + ṭṭhita for pa + kaṭhita. To **kvath**, P. kuthati & kaṭhati, appearing in pp. as kaṭhita, kuthita, kaṭṭhita and kuṭṭhita, cp. Geiger, *P.Gr.* § 42] cooked up, boiled, boiling hot, hot Thūpavaŋsa 48[33]; J V.268 (pakaṭṭh° vv. ll. pakkudh° & jakankaṭhi); VI.112 (°kaṭṭh°), 114 (id.; v. l. BB °kuthita); DhA I.126 (kaṭṭh°, v. l. pakkanta), 179 (kaṭṭh°, v. l. pakuṭṭh°); II.5 (kaṭṭh°, vv. ll. pakuṭṭh° & pakkuth°); III.310 (1st passage kaṭṭh°, v. l. pakuṭṭh°, pakkuṭṭh°, pakkutbita; = pakkuṭṭhita at id. p. VvA 67; in 2nd passage kaṭṭh°, v. l. pakuṭṭh° & pakkuthita, left out at id. p. VvA 68); ThA 292 (pakkuthita).

Pakkaṭṭhī (f.) [fr. pa+**kvat**, evidently as abstr. to pakkaṭṭhita; reading uncertain] a boiling (-hot) mixture (of oil?) M I.87, expl[d] by C. as katita- (=kaṭh°) gomaya, boiling cow-dung. v. l. chakaṇakā see p. 537. The id. p. at Nd[2] 199 reads chakaṇaṭi, evidently a bona fide reading. The interpretation as "cow-dung" is more likely than "boiling oil."

Pakkanta [pp. of pakkamati] gone, gone away, departed S I.153; Sn p. 124; J I.202 (spelt kkh); PvA 78.

Pakkandati [Ved. prakrandati, pra+**krand**] to cry out, shout out, wail Sn 310 (3rd pret. pakkanduŋ) J VI.55 (id.), 188 (id.), 301 (id.).

Pakkama [fr. pa+**kram**] going to, undertaking, beginning D I.168 (tapo°; trsl. "all kinds of penance").

Pakkamati [Ved. prakramati, pra+**kram**] 1. to step forward, set out, go on, go away, go forth M I.105; Pug 58; DA I.94; PvA 13.—pret. 3 sg. **pakkāmi** S I.92, 120; Sn pp. 93, 124; PvA 5 (uṭṭhāy'āsanā), 19 (id.); 3rd pl. pakkamuŋ Sn 1010, and pakkamiŋsu S I.199.—pp. pakkanta (q. v.).—2nd to go beyond (in archery), to overshoot the mark, miss the aim Miln 250.

Pakkava [etym. ?] a kind of medicinal plant Vin I.201 (cp. paggava).

Pakkula see pākula.

Pakkosati [pa+kosati, **kruś**] to call, summon J I.50; II.69, 252 (=avheti); V.297; VI.420; DhA I.50; PvA 81 (v. l. °āpeti).—Caus. II. pakkosāpeti to call, send for, order to come J I.207; PvA 141, 153; DhA I.185.

Pakkha[1] [Ved. pakṣa in meanings 1 and 3; to Lat. pectus, see Walde, *Lat. Wtb.* s. v.] 1. side of the body, flank, wing, feathers (cp. pakkhin), in cpds. °**biḷāla** a flying fox (sort of bat) Bdhgh on ulūka-camma at Vin I.186 (MV. V.2, 4; cp. *Vin. Texts* II.16 where read ulūka° for lūka?); J VI.538; and °**hata** one who is struck on (one) side, i. e. paralysed on one side, a cripple (cp. Sk. pakṣāghāta) Vin II.90; M III.169; A III.385; Pug 51 (=hatapakkho pīṭhasappi PugA 227); Miln 245, 276 (cp. *Miln trsl.* II.62, 117)—also as wing of a house at DhsA 107; and wing of a bird at S II.231; SnA 465 (in expl[n] of pakkhin).—2. side, party, faction; adj (-°) associated with, a partisan, adherent Vin II.299; Sn 347 (aññāṇa°), 967 (kaṇhassa p.=Māra° etc., see Nd[1] 489; Nett 53 (taṇhā° & diṭṭhi°) 88 (id.), 160 (id.); DA I.281; DhA I.54; PvA 114 (paṭiloma°). pakkhasankanta gone over to a (schismatic) faction Vin I.60; IV.230, 313.—pakkhaŋ dāpeti to give a side, to adhere to (loc.) J I.343.—3. one half of the (lunar) month, a fortnight. The light or moon-lit fortnight is called sukka-pakkha (or juṇha°), the dark or moonless one kāḷa° (or kaṇha°) M I.20 (cātuddasī pañcadasī aṭṭhamī ca pakkhassa 14th, 15th & 8th day of the fortnight) ≈ Sn 402; A I.142 (aṭṭhamī pakkhassa), 144=Vv 15[6] (cātuddasī etc.; cp. VvA 71): A V.123 sq. (kāḷa°, juṇha°); Th 2, 423 (=aḍḍhamāsa-mattaŋ ThA 269); Pv II.95[6] (bahumāse ca pakkhe ca=kaṇha-sukka-bheda p. PvA 135); Vism 101 (dasâhaŋ vā pakkhaŋ vā); VvA 314 (sukka°); PvA 55 (kāḷa°).—4. alternative, statement, loc. pakkhe (-°) with regard or reference to KhA 80 (tassa pañhassa vyākaraṇapakkhe); SnA 168 (id.).

Pakkha[2] (adj.) [cp. Ved. prakhya clear, & Sk. (-°) prakhya like, of pra+**khyā**] visible, clear; -° resembling, like Miln 75 (mātu° and pitu°).

Pakkha[3] [cp. Sk. phakka (?)] a cripple. Cp III.6, 10; J VI.12 (=pīṭha-sappī C.). *Note* BSk. phakka is enum[d] at Mvyut. 271[120] with jātyaṇḍa, kuṇḍa & pangu, reminding of the comb[n] kāṇo vā kuṇi vā khañjo vā pakkhahato vā Vin II.90=S I.94=A II.85; III.385=Pug 51.

Pakkhaka (& °ika) (nt. ?) [fr. pakkha[1]] a dress made of wings or feathers, in cpd. ulūka° of owl's wings (see ulūka°) Vin III.34 (°ŋ nivāsetvā); A II.206 ≈ (°ika).

Pakkhatta (nt.) [fr. pakkha[1]] being a partner of, siding in with Vism 129, 130.

Pakkhanta at DA I.38 read as pakkanta.

Pakkhandaka (adj.)=pakkhandin SnA 164.—f. pakkhandikā [Ved. (?) praskandikā, BR. without refs.] diarrhœa, dysentery D II.127 (lohita°); J III.143; V.441 (lohita°); Miln 134.

Pakkhandati [pa+khandati, of **skand**] to spring forward, to jump on to M I.86; J I.461; Vv 84[12] (ger. pakkhandiyāna=pakkhanditvā anupavisitvā VvA 338); to be after someone in pursuit DhA I.198; usually fig. to rejoice in, find pleasure or satisfaction in (loc.), to take to, in phrases cittaŋ pakkhandati pasīdati santiṭṭhati M I.186; S III.133; cp. Miln 326 (nibbāne); A II.165; III.245 (avyāpāde); IV.442 (adukkha-m-asukhe); It 43 (dhamme); and na me tattha mānasaŋ p. Miln 135.—pp. pakkhanna (q. v.).

Pakkhandana (nt.) [fr. pakkhandati] 1. leaping, springing J II.32; Ps I. 194 (pariccāga- & pakkh°- nissagga).—2. attack, assault, chasing DhA I.198.

Pakkhandin (adj. n.) [fr. pakkhandati] 1. (adj.) bold, braggart, lit. jumping on or forth Dh 244; Sn 89 (=pakkhandaka SnA 164).—2. a military scout, lit. an onrusher, a bravo D I.51 (cp. Dial. I.68); DA I.157; J II.32, 281.

Pakkhanna [pp. of pakkhandati; often wrongly spelt pakkhanta] jumped on, fallen on to or into, chanced upon, acquired M I.39; Th I, 342 (diṭṭhigahanā°); J V.471; Miln 144 (saŋsaya°), 156, 390 (kupatha°).

Pakkhara [cp. Sk. prakṣara & prakhara "ein Panzer für Pferde" BR.] bordering, trimming J VI.223 (of a carriage).

Pakkhalati[1] [pa+**kṣal**] to wash, cleanse J V.71 (ger. pakkhalya=dhovitvā C. p. 74). Caus. pakkhāleti (q. v.).

Pakkhalati[2] [pa+khalati, of **skhal**] to stumble, trip, stagger J III.433; VI.332; DA I.37; DhsA 334.

Pakkhāyati [pa+**khyā**, Ved. prakhyāyate; cp. khāyati & pakkha[2]] to appear, shine forth, to be clearly visible D II.99 (cp. Th I, 1034, where pakkhanti for pakkhāyanti metri causâ); M II.32; S IV.144; V.153, 162; A III.69 sq.

Pakkhāleti [Caus. of pa+**kṣal**, cp. khaleti] to wash, cleanse Vin I.9 (pāde); D II.85 (id.); M I.205; S I.107; J VI.24 (pāde); VvA 261.

Pakkhika (adj.) [for pakkhiya=Ved. pakṣya of pakkha[1] 3] 1. belonging or referring to the (2) lunar fortnights, fortnightly, for a fortnight or in the (specified) fortnight of the month (cp. *Vin. Texts* III.220). As one special provision of food mentioned in enum[n] of five bhojanāni, viz. niccabhatta, salākabhatta, pakkhika, uposathika, pāṭipadika, Vin I.58=II.175; IV.75; J II.210; Vism 66.—2. (cp. pakkha 2 & pakkhin 2) contributing to, leading to, associated with, siding with (-°) Vism 130, in phrase vighāta° anibbāna-saŋvattanika associated with destruction, etc. M I.115; DhsA 382. Also in mūga° leading to deafness J I.45 (V.254).—DhA I.82 (paramattha-sacca°).

Pakkhitta [pp. of pakkhipati] put down into, thrown into (loc.) Sn p. 15 (pāyāso udake p.); PvA 58 (ātave p. naḷo is perhaps better read ātāpe paditto), 153 (pokkharaṇiyaŋ p.).

Pakkhin (adj. n.) [fr. pakkha[1] = pakkhānaŋ atthitāya pakkhī ti vuccati SnA 465; Ved. pakṣin bird] 1. winged, the winged one, a bird D I.71 (+sakuṇa = pakkha-yutto sakuṇo DA I.208) = A II.209 = V.206 = Pug 58; S II.231; Sn 606 (= sakuṇo SnA 465); Pv III.5[3] (°gaṇā = sakuṇagaṇā PvA 198). — 2. (cp. pakkha 2) participating in, contributing to S V.97 (vighāta° for the usual °pakkhika).

Pakkhipati [pa + kṣip, in sense of putting down carefully cp. nikkhipati & BSk. prakṣipati to start a ship Divy 334] 1. to put down into (with loc. of receptacle), place into, enclose in (often used for ceremony of putting a corpse into a shell or mount) D II.162 (tela-doṇiyā Bhagavato sarīraŋ p.); S II.85; J II.210 (mukhe); Miln 247 (Amat' osadhaŋ); PvA 41 (atthikāni thūpe p.); DhA I.71 (the corpse into the fire). — 2. to throw into, hurl into, in Niraya-passage at M III.183 = A I.141 = Nd[2] 304[III]; cp. nikkhipati. — 3. (fig.) to include in, insert, arrange, interpolate Miln 13 (Abhidhamma-piṭakaŋ kusalā dhammā, akusalā dh., avyākatā dh. ti tīsu padesu p.). — Caus. II. pakkhipāpeti J I.467; DA I.136. — pp. pakkhitta (q. v.).

Pakkhima [= pakkhin] a bird Th 1, 139 (read °me for °maŋ); J V.339.

Pakkhiya (adj. n.) [fr. pakkha[1] 2; cp. pakkhikā] siding with, associating with; m. part, side; only in phrase (satta-tiŋsa-) bodhi-pakkhiya-dhammā the 37 parts of enlightenment It 75 (satta only); J I.275; Vism 678 sq.; SnA 164; VvA 95; see *Cpd.* 179 and note 1. — pakkhiya at Th 2, 425 is not clear (expl[d] at ThA 269 by vaccha, v. l. sacca).

Pakkhepa (m.) & °na (nt.) [fr. pa + kṣip] throwing, hurling; being thrown into (loc.) PvA 221 (lohakumbhi° in passage of ordeals in Niraya); DhA I.357 (nadiyaŋ visa-pakkhepana).

Pakhuma [Ved. pakṣman, diaeretic form for the contracted form pamha, the latter prepondering in poetry, while pakhuma is mostly found in prose. Similar doublets are sukhuma & saṇha; as regards etym. cp. Av. pasnəm eyelid, Gr. πέκτω to comb, πόκος fleece, Lat. pecto to comb, pecten comb, Ohg. fahs hair] an eyelash, uusally as adj.: having eyelashes (-°) D II.18 (go°); S I.132 (°antarikāyaŋ between the lashes); J V.216 (visāla° for alārapamha T.); ThA 255 (dīgha° for āyatapamha Th 2, 283); VvA 162, 279.

Pagaṇḍaka see pakaṭṭhaka.

Pagabbha (adj.) [cp. Epic Sk. pragalbha] bold, daring, forward, reckless M I.236; S I.201 (sup°); A III.433; Sn 89, 852 (ap° = na pagabbha KhA 242, cp. also Nd[1] 228); Dh 244 (= kāyapāgabbhiyādihi samannāgata DhA III.354); J II.32, 281, 359; V.448; Miln 389; Dāvs III.26. — apagabbha at Vin. III.3 is used in quite a dif. sense, viz. "one who has no more connection with a womb" (a + pa + *garbha)

Pagabbhatā (f.) [abstr. fr. pagabbha, cp. Sk. pragalbhatā] resoluteness, boldness, decision J VI.273. See also pāgabbhiya.

Pagabbhin (adj.) [= pagabbha] bold J VI.238.

Pagama [fr. pra + gam] going forth from (-°) DhsA 329.

Pagāḷha [pp. of pagāhati] sunk into, immersed in (loc.) Sn 441, 772 (= ogāḷha ajjhogāḷha nimugga Nd[1] 26).

Pagāhati [pa + gāhati] to dive into, sink into Sn 819 (≈ ajjhogāha SnA 537; = ogāhati ajjhogāhati pavisati Nd[1] 152). — pp. pagāḷha.

Pagiddha (adj.) [pa + giddha] greedy after, clinging to, finding delight in (loc.) J V.269 (= gadhita mucchita C. on p. 274).

Paguṇa (adj.) [pa + guṇa cp. Sk. praguṇa straight, der. "kind"] learned, full of knowledge, clever, well-acquainted, familiar D III.170; Vv 53[2] (= nipuṇa VvA 232); J II.243; IV.130; V.399; Vism 95 (Majjhimo me paguṇo: I am well versed in the M.), 242 (dve tayo nikāyā paguṇā); DA I.95; SnA 195; KhA 73. — paguṇaŋ karoti, to make oneself familiar with, to learn by heart, to master thoroughly J II.166; III.537 (tayo vede); Miln 12 (Abhidhamma-piṭakaŋ).

-bhāva familiarly with, acquaintance, efficient state, cleverness in, experience, knowledge (cp. pāguñña) J III.537; Dhs 48, 49.

Paguṇatā (f.) & **Paguṇatta** (nt.) (doubtful) abstr. to paguṇa in expl[n] of pāguññatā at Dhs 48 & 49 (trsl. fitness, competence).

Pagumba [pa + gumba] a thicket, bush, clump of trees Sn 233.

Pageva (adv.) [page = Sk. prage + eva, but BSk. prāgeva] (how) much more or much less, a fortiori, lit. "right at the earliest" J I.354; V.242; Miln 91; Vism 93, 259, 322; VvA 258, PvA 115, 116, 117. — Compar. pagevataraŋ M III.145; atippage too early J III.48; atippago id. M I.84; S II.32; A V.48.

Paggaṇhāti [pa + gaṇhāti] 1. to stretch forth, hold out or up, take up D I.123 (sujaŋ the sacrificial ladle), 125 (añjaliŋ stretch out the hollow hands as a token of respectful greeting); S I.141; II.280; J I.89 (paveṇiŋ); PvA 74 (turiyāni). ger. **paggayha** taking up, raising up, stretching forth Sn 350 (= uttāretvā SnA 349); Dh 268 (tulaŋ); Pv II.9[17] (bāhuŋ); IV.7[4] (uccaŋ p.); VvA 7 (añjaliŋ). Often in phrase **bāhā paggayha** kandati to wail or lament with outstretched arms (a special pose of mourning) J V.267; VI.188; PvA 92 (= pasāreti). — 2. to take up, take care of, favour, support, befriend (opp. niggaṇhāti) J I.511; II.21; V.116, 369; Miln 185, 186; PvA 114 (sappurisa-dhammaŋ). — 3. to put to, exert, strain, apply vigorously (cittaŋ one's mind) S V.9; Ps II.20 (paggaṇhanto viriyena carati). — pp. paggahita (q. v.). — Caus. paggaheti to exert Miln 390 (mānasaŋ). — Caus. II. paggaṇhāpeti to cause to hold up or out, to cause to uphold or support Miln 21 (dhamma-dhajaŋ); J V.248; PvA 74 (turiyāni).

Paggalita [pp. of pa + gal] dripping PvA 56 (v. l. for T. vigalita).

Paggava [etym ?] a medicinal plant with bitter fruit J II.105 (v. l. pakkava).

Paggaha & **Paggāha** [fr. paggaṇhāti] 1. exertion, energy; (*a*) paggaha: D III.213 (v. l. paggāha, also °nimitta); Ps II.8 (°cariyā), 20 (°ṭṭha); DA I.63 (viriy-indriyassa °lakkhaṇa); (*b*) paggāha: A I.83, 256 (°nimitta); Dhs 277 (trsl. "grasp"), 336, 1359 (°nimitta); DhsA 406. — 2. (paggaha) favour, kindness, patronage [same meaning in Ep. Sk.] Vin III.145 = A III.66; J V.116 (opp. niggaha); VI.371 (id.).

Paggahaṇa (nt.) [fr. pa + gṛh, cp. paggaṇhāti] stretching forth, lifting, holding out; of the hands as sign of respectful salutation (cp. añjaliŋ paggaṇhāti) J III.82. — Abstr. °tā = paggaha 1. Vism 134.

Paggahita [pp. of paggaṇhāti, cp. BSk. pragṛhīta lofty Divy 7, 102] holding up, or (being) held up Vin II.131 (chatta° holding up a parasol,) 207 (id.); J VI.235; SnA 175 (= Sn p. 21).

Paggāha see paggaha.

Paggāhika (adj.) [paggāha + ika] belonging to, receiving (or trading ?) in cpd. °sālā a shop Vin II.291 (cp. *Vin. Texts* III.383: "would he set up as a hawker in cloth, or would he open a shop").

Paggharaṇa (adj., n.) [fr. paggharati] trickling, oozing, dripping J I.146; VI.187 (a°); f. °ī D I.74 (=bindu-bindun udakaŋ paggharati DA I.218); the 'mark' of liquid DhsA 332.

Paggharaṇaka (adj.) [fr. paggharati] flowing, trickling, oozing out J VI.187 (app°-velā), 531; DhA I.126 (lohitaŋ); Vism 262.

Paggharati [pa+gharati, which stands for kṣarati, also appearing as jharati, cp. Sk. nirjhara, Prk. pajjharati Mālati-M. p. 51. BSk. pragharati Divy 57, 409; AvŚ I.282] to flow forth or out, to ooze, trickle, drip S I.150; Sn p. 125 (pubbañ ca lohitañ ca. p.); J VI.328; Pv I.6[7] (gabbho pagghari=vissandi PvA 34); II.9[11] (=vissandati PvA 119); II.9[26] (akkhini p.=vissandanti PvA 123, sic lege!); Miln 180; VvA 76 (navahi dvārehi puḷuvakā pagghariŋsu). — pp. paggharita (q. v.).

Paggharita [pp. of paggharati] flowing, trickling S II.179; Th 2, 466; PvA 198 (khīra).

Paghaṇa (nt.) [cp. Sk. praghaṇa] a covered terrace before a house Vin II.153 ("paghanaŋ nāma yaŋ nikkhamantā ca pavisantā ca pādehi hananti. tassa vihāra-dvāre ubhato kuṭṭaŋ niharitvā katapadesass' etaŋ adhivacanaŋ" Bdhgh, quoted *Vin. Texts* III.175).

Paṅka [cp. Epic Sk. paṅka, with k suffix to root *pene for *pele, as in Lat. palus; cp. Goth. fani mire, excrements, Ohg. fenna "fen," bog; also Ital. fango mud, Ohg. fūht wet. See Walde *Lat. Wtb.* under palus. BSk. paṅka, e. g. Jtm 215 paṅka-nimagna] mud, mire; defilement, impurity S I.35, 60; III.118; A III.311; IV.289; Sn 970 (°danta rajassira with dirt between their teeth and dust on their heads, from travelling); III.236 (id.); IV.362 (id.); Sn 535, 845, 945, 1145 (Nd[2] 374: kāma-paṅko kāma-kaddamo etc.); Dh 141, 327; Nd[1] 203; Pv III.3[3]; IV.3[2]; Miln 346; Dhs 1059, 1136.

Paṅga [?] only in cpd. paṅgacīra (nt.) at D I.6 "blowing through toy pipes made of leaves" (*Dial.* I.10, where is cpd. Sinhalese pat-kulal and Marathī pungī after Morris *J.P.T.S.* 1889, 205). Bdhgh expl[ns] as "p. vuccati paṇṇa-nāḷikā; taŋ dhamantā kīḷanti" DA I.86.

Paṅgu (adj.) [Sk. paṅgu; etym. ?] lame, crippled, see pakkha[3] and next.

Paṅgula (adj.) [fr. paṅgu] lame J VI.12; Vism 280.

Pacati [Ved. pacati, Idg. *peqŭō, Av. pac-; Obulg. peką to fry, roast, Lith. kepù bake, Gr. πέσσω cook, πέπων ripe] to cook, boil, roast Vin IV.264; fig. torment in purgatory (trs. and intrs.): Niraye pacitvā after roasting in N. S II.225, PvA 10, 14. — ppr. pacanto tormenting, gen. pacato (+Caus. pācayato) D I.52 (expl[d] at DA I.159, where read pacato for paccato, by pare daṇḍena piḷentassa). — pp. pakka (q. v.). — Caus. pacāpeti & pāceti (q. v.). — Pass. paccati to be roasted or tormented (q. v.).

Pacana (nt.) [fr. pac, su pacati] cooking J III.425 (°thālikā); V.385 (°bhājana); ThA 29 (bhatta°); DA I.270; PvA 135.

Pacarati [pa+carati] to go after, walk in; fig. practise, perform, observe Vv 32[9] (v. l. pavarati, cp. VvA 136).

Pacala [fr. pa+cal] shaking, trembling, wavering DhsA 378.

Pacalati [pa+calati] to dangle VvA 36 (v. l. BB paj°).

Pacalāyati [quasi-denom. or caus. fr. pacala, pa+cal, cp. daṇḍāyati and pacāleti] to make (the eyelid) waver, to wink, to be sleepy, nod, begin to doze A III.343=IV.344; IV.85 (quot. at DhsA 236); J I.384 (°āyituŋ ārabbhi); Vism 300.

Pacalāyikā (f.) [abstr. fr. pacalāyati] nodding, wavering (of the eyelids), blinking, being sleepy Dhs 1157 (=akkhidalādīnaŋ pacalabhāvaŋ karoti DhsA 378).

Pacalita [pp. of pacalati] shaken, wavering, unstable Th I, 260.

Pacāpeti [Caus. of pacati] to cause to be cooked, to cook Vin IV.264; J I.126 (āhāraŋ); II.15 (bhattaŋ), 122.

Pacāreti [pa+cāreti, Caus. of car] to go about in (acc.), to frequent, to visit A I.182, 183 (pacārayāmi, glass sañcarissāmi).

Pacālaka (adj.) [fr. pacāleti] swinging, shaking; nt. acc. as adv. in kāya- (& bāhu°) ppacālakaŋ after the manner or in the style of swaying the body (or swinging the arms) Vin II.213.

Pacāleti [pa+Caus. of cal] to swing, sway, move bout Th I, 200 (mā pacālesi "sway and nod" Trsl[n]).

Pacinati [or °cināti) [pa+cināti, cp, ācināti] 1. to pick, pluck, gather, take up, collect, accumulate S III.89; IV.74 (dukkhaŋ=ācināti p. 73); Dh 47, 48 (pupphāni=ocinati DhA I.366); J III.22; fut. pacinissati DhA I.361. — 2. to pick out (mentally), to discern, distinguish, realise, know Sn 837 (ppr. pacinaŋ=pacinanto vicinanto tulayanto tīrayanto Nd[1] 185; =pavicinati SnA 545); fut. pacessati Dh 44, 45 (sic F.; MSS. vijessati, & vicessati the latter perhaps preferable to pac°; expl[d] at DhA I.334 by vicinissati upaparikkhissati paṭivijjhissati sacchikarissati). — Pass. paciyati to be heaped up, to increase, accumulate S IV.74 (opp. khīyati).

Pacuṭa is doubtful reading at DA I.164 (with vv. ll. pamuṭa, pamuca, papuṭa) for D I.54, T. paṭuva (vv. ll. pamuṭa, samudda) and is expl[d] by gaṇṭhika, i. e. block or knot. The whole passage is corrupt; see discussed under pavuṭā.

Pacura (adj.) [cp. late Sk. pracura] general, various, any; abundant, many J V.40 (=bahu salabha C.); Miln 208 (°jana) Dāvs IV.11, 50; VvA 213 (°jano for yādisakīdiso Vv 50[11]). See also pasura.

Pacessati see pacinati.

Pacca° is contracted form of paṭi before a, like paccakampittha pret. fr. paṭikampati.

Paccakkosati [paṭi+ā+kruś] to curse in return S I.162; A II.215.

Paccakkosana (nt.) [fr. paṭi+ā+kruś] cursing in return DhA IV.148 (a°).

Paccakkha (adj.) [paṭi+akkha[3], cp. Ved. pratyakṣa] "before the eye," perceptible to the senses, evident, clear, present DhsA 254; PvA 125; Sdhp 416. Often in obl. cases, viz. instr. °ena personally J I.377; abl. °ato from personal experience J V.45, 195, 281; appaccakkhāya without seeing or direct perception, in expl[n] of paccaya at Vism 532; also in phrase paccakkhato ñatvā having seen or found out for himself, knowing personally J I.262; III.168.

-kamma making clear, i. e. demonstration, realisation, only neg. a° not realising etc. S III.262; Dhs 390 (trsl. "inability to demonstrate"; cp. DhsA 254).

Paccakkhāta [pp. of paccakkhāti] rejected, given up, abandoned, repudiated Vin II.244, 245 (sikkhā); III.25 (id.); J IV.108; DhA I.12. Cp. *Vin. Texts* I.275.

Paccakkhāti [paṭi+akkhāti=ā+khyā] lit. to speak against, i. e. to reject, refuse, disavow, abandon, give up, usually in connection with Buddhaŋ, dhammaŋ, sikkhaŋ or similar terms of a religious-moral nature Vin III.25; S II.231, 271; A IV.372. — ger. paccakkhāya, in foll. conn^s ācariyaŋ J IV.200; sikkhaŋ Vin III.23, 34 (a°); S II.231; IV.190; Pug 66, 67; sabbaŋ S IV.15; ariyasaccaŋ S V.428. paccakkhāsi at J V.8 is gloss for pakatthāsi. — pp. paccakkhāta (q. v.). — Intens. paccācikkhati (q. v.).

Paccakkhāna (nt.) [fr. paṭi + ā + **khyā**] rejection, refusal J VI.422.

Paccagū (adj.-n.) [a difficult word, composed of pacca + gū, the latter a by-form of °ga, as in paṭṭhagū, vedagū pāragū. pacca may be praṭya, an adv. form^n of prep. prati, and paṭṭha its doublet. It is not certain whether we should read paṭṭhagū here as well (see paṭṭhagū). The form may also be expl^d as a substantivised pl. 3rd pret. of prati + gacchati = paccaguŋ] "one who goes toward," a pupil S I.104 (Mārassa); vv. ll. baddhabhū, paṭṭhagū. Windisch, *Māra & Buddha* trsl^s "unter M's Herrschaft," and refers paṭṭhagu to Sk., pātyagāh. Bdhgh (see *Kindred Sayings*, I, p. 319) reads baddhagū and expl^ns by bandhavara sissa antevāsika.

Paccaggaḷa (adj.) [pratyak + gaḷa] in phrase paccaggaḷe aṭṭhāsi "stuck in his throat" M I.333.

Paccaggha (adj.) [paṭi + aggha, cp. Sk. pratyagra of diff. derivation] recent, new, beautiful, quite costly Vin I.4; J I.80; II.435; Pv II.3^15 (= abhinava mahaggha vā PvA 87); III.10^5 (= abhinava PvA 214); Dāvs V.25; PvA 44.

Paccanga (nt.) [paṭi + anga] lit. "by-limb," small limb, only in comp^d angapaccangāni limbs great and small, all limbs: see anga.

Paccañjana (nt.) [paṭi + añjana] anointing, ointment, unction D I.12 = M I.511; DA I.98 (= bhavanīya-sītala-bhessajj' añjanaŋ).

Paccati [Pass. of pacati, cp. BSk. pacyate Divy 422] to be boiled, fig. to be formented or vexed, to suffer. Nearly always applied to the torture of boiling in Niraya, where it is meant literally. — S I.92; V.344 (kālena paccanti read for kāle na p.); A I.141 (phenuddehakaŋ p. niraye); Sn 670, 671; Dh 69, 119, 120 (pāpaŋ suffer for sin, cp. DhA III.14); J V.268; Pv IV.1^29 (= dukkhaŋ pāpuṇanti PvA 228); IV.3^39 (niraye paccare janā = paccanti PvA 255); DhA III.64 (expl^n for tappati).

Paccatta (adj.) [paṭi + attan] separate, individual; usually acc. °ŋ adv. separately, individually, singly, by himself, in his own heart D I.24 (yeva nibbuti viditā); DA on D II.77 = attano attano abbhantare; M I.251, 337 (°vedaniya N. of a purgatory), 422; S II.199; III.54 sq., IV.23, 41 sq., 168, 539; Sn 611, 906; Dh 165; Pv III.10^6 (°vedanā separate sufferings, = visuŋ visuŋ attanā anubhūyamānā mahādukkhavedanā PvA 214); Dhs 1044 (ajjhatta +; trsl^d "self referable"); Miln 96 (°purisa-kāra); DhsA 169; VvA 9, 13; PvA 232.
-vacana expression of separate relation, i. e. case of reference, or of the direct object, reflexive case, N. of the acc. case SnA 303; VvA 281; PvA 30, 35; KhA 213, 236; in lieu of karaṇa KhA 213. of sāmin SnA 594.

Paccatthata [pp. of gaṭi + ā + **stṛ**] spread out D II.211.

Paccattharaṇa (nt.) [pati + ā + **stṛ**, cp. BSk. pratyāstaraṇa Divy 19] something spread against, i. e. under or over, a cover, spread, rug, cushion or carpet to sit on, bedding of a couch (nisīdana°) Vin I.47, 295, 296; II.208, 218; D I.7 (kadali-miga-pavara°, cp. DA I.87); A I.137 (id.); III.50 (id.); J I.126; IV.353 (uṇṇāmaya); PvA 141, 137.

Paccatthika (adj. n.) [paṭi + attha + ka, lit. opposite to useful, cp. Sk. pratyanīka & pratyarthin] an opponent, adversary, enemy Vin II.94 sq. (atta° personal enemy); A V.71 (id.; T. attha°); D I.50, 70, 137; It 83; PvA 62. Cp. paccāmitta.

Paccana (nt.) [fr. paccati, cp. pacana] being boiled, boiling, torture, torment J V.270; SnA 476 (°okāsa).

Paccanīka, Paccanīya (adj. n.) [cp. Sk. pratyanīka & see paccatthika] 1. contrary, adverse, opposed; (1) m. enemy, adversary, opponent M I.378; S I.179; IV.127 = Sn 761; Ps II.67 sq.; SnA 288. Cp. vi.° — 2. (in method) reverse, negative, opp. to anuloma. Tikp 71 passim; cp. paṭiloma.
-gāthā response, responding verse (cp. paṭigāthā) SnA 39.

Paccanubhāsati [paṭi + anubhāsati, cp. BSk. pratyavabhāṣate to call to Divy 9] to speak out or mention correspondingly, to enumerate KhA 78, 79 sq.

Paccanubhoti [paṭi + anu + **bhu**, BSk. pratyanubhavati Divy 54, 262 etc.] to experience, undergo, realise M I.295; S V.218, 264 sq., 286 sq. 353; A III.425 sq.; It 38; PvA 26, 44, 107 (dukkhaŋ). — fut. paccanubhossati D II.213; S I.133, 227; Pv III.5^6. — Pass. paccanubhavīyati PvA 146 (for upalabbhati). — pp. paccanubhūta M II.32; S II.178; It 15.

Paccanusiṭṭha [paṭi + anusiṭṭha] advised, admonished D II.209 = 225.

Paccanta (adj. n.) [paṭi + anta, cp. Sk. pratyanta] adj. adjoining, bordering on, neighbouring, adjacent Dh 315; J I.11 (V.47, °desa), 377 (°vāsika); PvA 201 (°nagara); DhA III.488 (id.); Sdhp 11 (°visaya). — (m.) the border, outskirts, neighbourhood Vin I.73; J I.126 (vihāra°); II.37; Miln 314 (°e kupite in a border disturbance); DhA I.101 (id.); PvA 20 (id.). °ŋ vūpasāmeti to appease the border PvA 20. — P. in sense of "heathen" at Vism 121.

Paccantima (adj.) [fr. paccanta, cp. BSk. pratyantima frontier Divy 21, 426] bordering, adjoining, next to Vin. II.166; Sdhp 5.

Paccabhiññāṇa (nt.) [paṭi + abhi + ñāṇa] recognition DhsA 110.

Paccaya [fr. paṭi + i, cp. Ved. pratyaya & P. pacceti, paṭicca] lit. resting on, falling back on, foundation; cause, motive etc. See on term as t.t. of philosophy Tikapaṭṭhāna I, *foreword*; *J.P.T.S.* 1916, 21 f.; *Cpd.* 42 sq. & esp. 259 sq. — 1. (lit.) support, requisite, means, stay. Usually with ref. to the 4 necessaries of the bhikkhu's daily life, viz. cīvara, piṇḍapāta, senāsana, (gilānapaccaya-) bhesajja, i. e. clothing, food as alms, a dwelling-place, medicine: see under cīvara. Sn 339 (paccaya = gilāna-paccaya SnA 342); Miln 336; Mhvs 3, 15. — 2. (appl^d) reason, cause, ground, motive, means, condition M I.259 (yaŋ yad eva paccayaŋ paṭicca by whatever cause or by whichever means); S II.65; Nett 78 sq.; DA I.125; PvA 104. The fourfold cause (catubbidho paccayo) of rūpa (material form) consists of kamma, citta, utu, āhāra: Vism 600. Var. paccayas discussed at VbhA 166 sq. (twofold, with ref. to paṭisandhi), 183 (eightfold), 202, 205 sq, 254 (4). sappaccaya founded, having a reason or cause S V.213 sq.; A I.82; Nd^2 mūla; Dhs 1084, 1437. — yathā paccayaŋ karoti do as he likes Nd^2 p. 280 = S III. 33. Often coupled with hetu, e. g. at S IV.68 sq.; A. I.66; IV.151 sq.; D III.284; Nd^2 under mūla; Ps II.116 sq., *paccaya* came to be distinguished from hetu as the genus of which *hetu* was the typical, chief species. I. e. paccaya became synonymous with our "relation," understood in a causal sense, hetu meaning condition, causal antecedent, and 23 other relations being added as special modes of causality. Later still these 24 were held reducible to 4 Tikp 1 f. (and foreword); *Cpd.* 197. Cp. Paṭṭhāna. — Abl. paccayā as adv. by means of, through, by reason of, caused by D I.45 (vedanā °taṇhā etc., see paṭicca-samuppāda); M I.261 (jātippaccayā jarāmaraṇaŋ); Pv I.5² (kamma°); IV.1⁶⁰ (tap°); PvA 147 (kamma°). — 3. ground for, belief, confidence, trust, reliance J I.118, 169; apara° without relying on anyone else S III.83, 135; A IV.186, 210; PvA 226. -ākāra the mode of causes, i. e. the Paṭiccasamuppāda DhsA 2, 3; VbhA 130 sq. (cp. Vism 522 sq.).

Paccayatā (f.) [abstr. fr. paccaya] the fact of having a cause, causation, causal relation, in phrase idappaccayatā (adv.) from an ascertained cause, by way of cause Vin I.5; D I.185; S I.136; II.25.

Paccayika (adj.) [fr. paccaya] trustworthy D I.4; S I.150; A II.209; J VI.384 (paccāyika); Pug 57; DA I.73; SnA 475.

Paccaladdhaŋsu see paṭilabhati.

Paccavidhuŋ & **Paccavyādhiŋ** see paṭivijjhati.

Paccavekkhati [paṭi+avekkhati] to look upon, consider, review, realise, contemplate, see M I.415; S III.103; 151 sq., IV.111, 236 sq.; J V.302; Vbh 193, 194 (cp. A III.323); Miln 16; PvA 62, 277; VvA 6, 48.

Paccavekkhana (nt.) & °nā (f.) [paṭi+avekkhana, cp. late Sk. pratyaveksana & °nā] looking at, consideration, regard, attention, reflection, contemplation, reviewing (cp. *Cpd.* 58) M I.415; D III.278; A III.27; Pug 21 (a°); Dhs 390(a°=dhammānaŋ sabbhāvaŋ pati na apekkhati DhsA 254, trsl. "inability to consider"); Miln 388; Nett 85; VbhA 140; Vism 43 (twofold); Sdhp 413.

Paccavekkhā (f.) [cp. late Sk. pratyavekṣā] imagination Mbhv 27.

Paccasāri see paṭisarati.

Paccassosi see patissuṇāti.

Paccākata [pp. of paṭi+a+kṛ] rejected, disappointed Vin IV.237, 238.

Paccākoṭita [pp. of paṭi+ākoṭeti] flattened or smoothed out, pressed, ironed (ākoṭita+of the robes) M I.385; S II.281; DhA I.37.

Paccāgacchati [paṭi+āgacchati] to fall back on, return again, to go back to (acc.), withdraw, slide back from (° to) Vin I.184; M I.265; III.114; Nd¹ 108, 312; Kvu 624 (spelt wrongly pacchā°); PvA 14, 109, 250. Cp. pacceti.

Paccāgata [pp. of paccāgacchati] gone back, withdrawn J V.120; Miln 125.

Paccāgamana (nt.) [fr. paṭi+ā+gam] return, going back, backsliding Miln 246.

Paccācamati [paṭi+ā+camati; often spelt °vamati, but see Trenckner, Miln 425] to swallow up, resorb S V.48 = A V.337; J I.311; Miln 150; Caus. °camāpeti Miln 150.

Paccācikkhati [Intens. of paccakkhāti, paṭi+ā+cikkhati of **khyā**] to reject, repudiate, disallow D III.3; M I.245; 428; Vin IV.235.

Paccājāta [pp. of paccājāyati] reborn, come to a new existence D I.62; III.264; M I.93; Pug 51.

Paccājāyati [paṭi+ā+jāyati] to be reborn in a new existence M III.169; S II.263; V.466, 474. — pp. paccājāta (q. v.).

Paccāneti [paṭi+ā+neti] to lead back to (acc.) Pv II.11⁶ (=punar āneti C.).

Paccāmitta [paccā=Sk. pratyak, adv.;+mitta, cp. Ep. Sk. pratyamitra] lit. "back-friend," adversary, enemy D I.70; A IV.106; J I.488; DA I.182; PvA 155.

Paccābhaṭṭha [pp. of paccābhāsati] recited, explained J II.48.

Paccābhāsati [paṭi+ābbhāsati] to retort, recite, explain, relate PvA 57 (sic lege for pacchā°). — pp. paccābhaṭṭha.

Paccāropeti [paṭi+āropeti] to show in return, retort, explain M I.96; A IV.193. Cp. paccabhāsati.

Paccāsati [fr. paṭi+āsā or=paccāsaŋsati or °siŋsati ?] to ask, beg, pray Pv IV.5⁶ (°anto for °āsaŋsanto ? C. explnˢ by āsiŋsanto).

Paccāsanne (adv.) [paṭi+āsanne] near by PvA 216=280.

Paccāsā f. [paṭi+āsā, cp. Sk. pratyāśā] expectation Vin IV.286.

Paccāsāreti [paṭi+ā+sāreti, Caus. of sṛ] to make go (or turn) backward M I.124=A III.28 (=paṭinivatteti C.); Vism 308 (sāreti pi p. pi).

Paccāsiŋsati [paṭi+āsiŋsati] to expect, wait for, desire, hope for, ask D II.100; A III.124; J I.346, 483; III.176; V.214; DhA I.14; II.84; DA I.318; VvA 336, 346; PvA 22, 25, 63, 260.

Paccāharati [paṭi+āharati] to bring back, take back Vin II.265; III.140; J IV.304.

Paccukkaḍḍhati [paṭi+ukkaḍḍhati] to draw out again Vin II.99.

Paccukkaḍḍhana (nt.) [fr. preceding] drawing out again Vin V.222.

Paccuggacchati [paṭi+ud+**gam**] to go out, set out, go out to meet Vin II.210; M I.206; Sn 442 (=abhimukho upari gacchati SnA 392).

Paccuggata [pp. of paccuggacchati] illustrious J VI.280.

Paccuggamana (nt.) [fr. preceding] going out to, meeting, receiving J IV.321; PvA 61, 141 (°ŋ karoti).

Paccuṭṭhapanā (f.) [paṭi+ud+Caus. of **sthā**] putting against, resistance, opposition Sn 245 (=paccanīkaṭṭhapanā SnA 228).

Paccuṭṭhāti [paṭi+ud+**sthā**] to rise, reappear, to rise from one's seat as a token of respect; always combᵈ with abhivadati D I.61 (Pot. °uṭṭheyya), 110 (Fut. °uṭṭhassati).

Paccuṭṭhāna (nt.) [fr. preceding] rising from one's seat, reverence D I.125.

Paccuttarati [paṭi+uttarati, but cp. BSk. pratyavatarati to disembark Divy 229] to go out again, to withdraw S I.8; A III.190. Cp. paccupadissati.

Paccudāvattati [paṭi+ud+ā+vattati] to return again to (acc.) S I.224; II.104; A V.337.

Paccudāvattana (nt.) [fr. preceding] coming back, return DhsA 389.

Paccudāharati [paṭi+ud+ā+**hṛ**] recite in reply Th 2, 40.

Paccudeti [paṭi+ud+**i**] go out towards J VI.559.

Paccuddharati [paṭi+uddharati] to wipe off or down (with a cloth, colakena) Vin II.122 (udakapuñchaniŋ; trsl. *Vin. Texts* II.152 "to wear out a robe"), 151 (gerukaŋ; trsl. *Vin. Texts* II.151 "to wipe down").

Paccuddhāra [paṭi+uddhāra] taking up, casting (the lot) again Vin IV.121.

Paccupaṭṭhahati [pati+upa+**sthā**] "to stand up before," to be present; only in pp. paccupaṭṭhita and in Caus. paccupaṭṭhāpeti (q. v.).

Paccupaṭṭhāna (nt.) [fr. paṭi+upa+**sthā**; cp. *Cpd.* 13 & Lakkhaṇa] 1. (re)appearance, happening, coming on, phenomenon J III.524; Nett 28; SnA 509; DhsA 332; ThA 288. 2. tending D III.191. 3. *vv. ll.* gilānupaṭṭhāna.

Paccupaṭṭhāpeti [Caus. of paccupaṭṭhahati] 1. to bring before or about, to arrange, provide, instal, fix S IV.121; J III.45; IV.105; V.211. 2. to minister to, wait upon D III.189 sq.

Paccupaṭṭhita [pp. of paccupaṭṭhahati; cp. BSk. pratyupasthita, Divy Index] (re)presented, offered, at one's disposal, imminent, ready, present D III.218 (°kāmā); It 95 (id.); Sn p. 105; It 111; Kvu 157, 280; Miln 123.

Paccupadissati [reading uncertain; either paṭi+upadissati, or fut. of paṭi+upadisati, cp. upadaŋseti. It is not to be derived fr. °upadadāti] to accept, receive; or: to show, point out J V.221 (v. l. paccuttarissati to go through, perhaps preferable; C. on p. 225 expl^s by sampaṭicchissati).

Paccupalakkhaṇā (f.) [paṭi+upalakkhaṇā] differentiation S III.261 (a°) Dhs 16=Pug 25; Dhs 292, 555, 1057.

Paccupekkhaṇā (f.)=paccavekkhaṇā S III.262 (a°).

Paccupeti [paṭi+upeti] to go up or near to, to approach, serve, beset J III.214. fut. °upessati J IV.362 (gloss upasevati).

Paccuppanna [pp. of paṭi+uppajjati, cp. Sk. pratyutpanna] what has arisen (just now), existing, present (as opposed to atīta past & anāgata future) M I.307, 310; III.188; 190, 196; S I.5; IV.97; A I.264; III.151, 400; D III.100, 220, 275; It 53; Nd¹ 340; Pv IV.6²; Dhs 1040, 1043; VbhA 157 sq.; PvA 100. See also atīta.

Paccuyyāti [paṭi+ud+**yā**] to go out against, to go to meet somebody S I.82, 216.

Paccūsa° [paṭi+Ved. uṣas f.; later Sk. pratyūṣa nt.] "the time towards dawn," morning, dawn; always in comp^n with either **°kāle** (loc.) at morning DhA IV.61; DA I.168; or °velāyaŋ (loc.) id. VvA 105, 118, 165; PvA 61; or °samaye (loc.) id. S I.107; J I.81, 217; SnA 80; PvA 38.

Paccūha [cp. late Sk. pratyūha, prati+**vah**] an impediment, obstacle S I.201 (bahū hi saddā paccūhā, trsl. "Ay there is busy to-and-fro of words." C. expl^s by paṭiloma-saddā); J VI.571.

Pacceka (adj.) [paṭi+eka, cp. BSk. pratyeka Divy 335, 336] each one, single, by oneself, separate, various, several D I.49 (itthi); II.261 (°vasavattin, of the 10 issaras); S I.26 (°gāthā a stanza each), 146 (°brahma an independent Brahma); A II.41 (°sacca); V.29 (id.); Sn 824 (id.), 1009 (°gaṇino each one having followers= visuŋ visuŋ gaṇavanto SnA 583); J IV.114 (°bodhiñāṇa); Nd¹ 58 (°muni); DA I.148 (paccekā itthiyo); SnA 52 (°bodhisatta one destined to become a Paccekabuddha), 67 (id.), 73 (°sambodhi), 476 (niraya a separate or special purgatory); PvA 251 (id.); Sdhp 589 (°bodhi). — paccekaŋ (adv.) singly, individually, to each one VvA 282. See also pāṭekka.

-buddha one enlightened by himself, i. e. one who has attained to the supreme and perfect insight, but dies without proclaiming the truth to the world. M III.86; S I.92 ("Silent Buddha" trsl^n); J III.470; IV.114; Ud 50 (P. Tagarasikhi); Nett 190; KhA 178, 199; SnA 47, 58, 63; DhA I.80, 171, 224, 230; IV.201; PvA 144, 263, 265 (=isi), 272, 283.

Pacceti [paṭi+i] to come on to, come back to, fig. fall back on, realise, find one's hold in D I.186 ("take for granted," cp. note *Dial.* I.252); M I.309 (kaŋ hetuŋ), 445 (id.); S I.182 ("believe in," C. icchati pattheti); Sn 662, 788, 800, 803, 840=908; Dh 125 (=patieti DhA III.34); Nd¹ 85, 108 (=paccāgacchati), 114; Pv II.3²⁰ (=avagacchati PvA 87); Nett 93; Miln 125, 313; PvA 116 (bālaŋ), 241 (agree to=paṭijānāti). — ger. paṭicca (q. v.). Cp. paccāgacchati — pp. paṭīta (q. v.).

Paccoḍḍita [paṭi+oḍḍita] laid in return (of a snare) J II.183 (v. l. paccoṭṭita).

Paccora (adj.) [paṭi+avara, cp. Sk. pratyavara] lower, 1 t. lower part, hindquarter, bottom (?) A IV.130; DhA I.189.

Paccorohaṇī (f.) [fr. paccorohati] the ceremony of coming down again (?), approaching or descending to (acc.), esp. the holy fire A V.234 sq., 249 sq., V. 251. Cp. orohaṇa & Sk. pratyavarohaṇa "descent," N. of a cert. Gṛhya celebration (BR.).

Paccorohati [paṭi+orohati] to come down again, descend D I.50; II.73; A V.65, 234.

Paccosakkati [paṭi+osakkati which is either ava+sakkati (of **ṣvaṣk** Geiger, *P.Gr.* § 28² or **sṛp** Trenckner Notes 60), or apa+sakkati] to withdraw, retreat, go away again D I.230; J I.383; Mhvs 25, 84.

Paccosakkanā (f.) [abstr. fr. paccosakkati] withdrawal retreat, going back, shrinking from DhsA 151.

Pacchaḍḍana (nt.) [pa+chaḍḍana] vomiting, throwing out Sdhp 137.

Pacchato (adv.) [abl. formation fr. *paccha=Ved. paścā & paścāt, fr. Idg. *pos as in Lith. pàs near by, pastaras the last; cp. Av. pasca behind, Lat. post, after] behind, after Dh 348 (=anāgatesu khandhesu DhA IV.63; opp. pure); PvA 56, 74; DhA III.197 (°vatti). Often doubled pacchato pacchato, i. e. always or close behind, J II.123 (opp. purato purato). — Cp. **pacchā** & **pacchima**.

Pacchada [fr. pa+**chad**, cp. Sk. pracchada] a cover, wrapper; girdle Th 2, 378 (=uracchada ThA253); DhsA 397 (v. l. for °cchāda).

Pacchanna [pa+channa, of **chad**] covered, wrapped, hidden Th 1, 299; J III.129.

Pacchā (adv.) [Vedic paścā & paścāt see pacchato] behind, aft, after, afterwards, back; westward D I.205; Sn 645, 773, 949; Nd¹ 33 (=pacchā vuccati anāgataŋ, pure vuccati atītaŋ); Nd² 395; Dh 172, 314, 421; Pv I.11¹, 11⁵ (opp. purato); II.9⁹ (=aparabhāge PvA 116); PvA 4, 50, 88; VvA 71.

-ânutappati [fr. ânutāpa] to feel remorse Pv II.7¹²; J V.117. — **ânutāpa** [cp. Sk. paścattāpa] remorse, repentance Sdhp 288. **-āsa** (nt.) [āsa²] "eating afterwards," i. e. aftermath S I.74 — **gacchati** at *Kvu* 624 see paccā°. **-gataka** going or coming behind J VI.30. **-jāta** (-paccaya), 11th of the 24 paccayas, q. v. causal relation of posteriority in time. **-nipātin** one who retires to rest later than another (opp. pubb' uṭṭhāyin getting up before others) D I.60; III.191; A III.37; IV.265, 267 sq.; DA I.168. — **bāhaŋ** "arm behind," i. e. with arms (tied) behind one's back D I.245; J I.264; DhA II.39. — **bhatta** "after-meal," i. e. after the midday meal, either as °ŋ (acc.-adv.) in the afternoon, after the main meal, usually comb^d with piṇḍapāta. paṭikkanta "returning from the alms-round after dinner" A III.320; PvA 11, 16, 38 and passim (cp. BSk. paścādbhakta-piṇḍapāta-pratikrānta, see Indexes to AvŚ. & Divy), or as °kicca the duties after the midday meal (opp. purebhatta°) DA I.47 (in detail); SnA 133, 134. **-bhattika** one who eats afterwards, i. e. afternoon, when it is improper to eat A III.220 (khalu°, q. v.). **-bhāga** hind or after part J II.91; PvA 114. **-bhāsati** see paccā°. **-bhūma** belonging to the western country S III.5. **-bhūmaka** id. S IV.312=A V.263. **-mukha** looking westward M III.5; D II.207; Th 1, 529;

DhA III.155 (opp. pācīna eastern). — vāmanaka dwarfed in his hind part J IV.137. — samaṇa [BSk. paścācchramaṇa & opp. purahśramaṇa AvŚ II.67, 150; Divy 154, 330, 494] a junior Wanderer or bhikkhu (Thera) who walks behind a senior (Thera) on his rounds. The one accompanying Gotama Buddha is Ānanda Vin I.46; III.10 (Ānanda); IV.78 (id.); Ud 90 (Nāgasamāla); J IV.123; Miln 15 (Nāgasena); PvA 38, 93 (Ānanda).

Pacchāda [pa+chāda] cover, covering, wrapper, in phrase nelango setappacchādo S IV.291 = Ud 76 = DA I.75 = DhsA 397.

Pacchānntappati see under pacchā.

Pacchāyā (f.) [pa+chāyā] a place in the shade, shaded part Vin I.180; II.193; D I.152 (=chāyā DA I.310); II.205; A III.320.

Pacchāḷiyaŋ at A III.76 is of uncertain reading & meaning; in phrase **p.** khipanti: either "throw into the lap" (?) or (better) read pacchiyaŋ, loc. of pacchi "into the basket" (of the girls & women).

Pacchāsa [cp. pacchāli? perhaps fr. pacchā+**aś**] aftermath S I.74.

Pacchi (f.) [etym. doubtful] a basket J I.9, 243; II.68; III.21; VI.369 (paṇṇa°), 560 (phala°); DhA II.3; IV.205 (°pasibbaka).

Pacchijjati [pa+chijjati, Pass. of **chid**] to be cut short, to be interrupted J I.503 (lohitaŋ p.).

Pacchijjana (nt.) [fr. last] stopping, interruption J III.214 (read assu-pacchijjana-divaso? passage corrupt.).

Pacchita [pa+chita, Sk. pracchita, pp. of **chā**, only in comb[n] with prefixes] cut off, skinned J VI.249.

Pacchindati [pa+chindati] 1. to break up, cut short, put an end to Vin IV.272; J I.119 (kathaŋ °itvā), 148 (kathaŋ °ituŋ); IV.59; PvA 78 (dānavidhiŋ °i). — 2. to bring up (food), to vomit DhA I.183 (āhāraŋ).

Pacchima (adj.) [Sk. paścima, superl. formation fr. *paśca, cp. pacchato & pacchā] 1. hindmost, hind-, back-, last (opp. purima), latest D I.239; M I.23 (°yāma the last night watch); DA I.45 sq. (id. °kicca duties or performances in the 3rd watch, corresp. to purima° & majjhima°); Sn 352; J IV.137 (°pāda); VI.364 (°dvāra); PvA 5, 75. — 2. western (opp. purima or puratthima) D I.153 (disā); S I.145. — 3. lowest, meanest Vin II.108; M I.23; S II.203.

Pacchimaka (adj.) [fr. pacchima] 1. last, latest (opp. purimaka) Vin II.9; Nd[2] 284 D. = Th I, 202; DhsA 262; J VI.151. — 2. lowest, meanest J I.285 (pacchimakā itthiyo).

Pacchedana (nt.) [fr. pa+**chid**] breaking, cutting DA I.141.

Pajagghati [pa+jagghati] to laugh out loud J VI.475.

Pajappati [pa+jappeti] to yearn for, crave, to be greedy after S I.5 = J VI.25 (anāgataŋ = pattheti C.).

Pajappā (f.) [pa+jappā] desire, greed for, longing J VI.25 (anāgata°); Sn 592; Dhs 1059, 1136.

Pajappita [pp. of pajappeti] desired, longed for S I.181; J VI.359.

Pajaha (adj.) [pa+jaha, pres. base of jahati] only neg. a° not giving anything up, greedy A III.76.

Pajahati (°jahāti) [pa+jahati of **hā**] to give up, renounce, forsake, abandon, eliminate, let go, get rid of; freq. as synonym of jahati (see Nd[2] under jahati with all forms). Its wide range of application with reference to all evils of Buddhist ethics is seen from exhaustive Index at S VI.57 (Index vol.). — Pres. pajahati S I.187; III.33 = Nd[2] 680, Q 3 (yaŋ na tumhākaŋ taŋ pajahatha); It 32 (kiŋ appahīnaŋ kiŋ pajahāma); 117; A IV.109 sq. (akusalaŋ, sāvajjaŋ); Sn 789 (dukkhaŋ), 1056, 1058; Ps I.63; II.244. ppr. pajahaŋ S III.27; fut. pahāssaŋ (cp. Geiger, *P.Gr.* § 151[1]) M II.100. — aor. pajahi & pahāsi Vin I.36; S I.12 = 23 (sankhaŋ); Sn 1057. — ger. pahāya S I.12 (kāme), 23 (vicikicchaŋ), 188 (nīvaraṇāni), Sn 17, 209, 520 & passim; Nd[2] 430; PvA 16, 122 (=hitvā), 211; pahatvāna Sn 639, and pajahitvā. fut. pajahissati S II.226. — grd. pahātabba M I.7; Sn 558; VvA 73, & pajahitabba — pp. pahīna (q. v.). — Pass. pahīyati (q. v.).

Pajā (f.) [Ved. prajā, pra+**jan**] progeny, offspring, generation, beings, men, world (of men), mankind (cp. use of Bibl. Gr. γέννημα in same meaning) D II.55; S V.346, 362 sq.; A II.75 sq.; IV.290; V.232 sq., 253 sq.; Sn 298, 545, 654, 684, 776, 936, 1104 (=sattā Nd[2] 377); Dh 28, 85, 254, 343 (=sattā DhA IV.49); Nd[1] 47, 292; Pv II.11[7]; IV.3[34]; Pug 57; Vism 223 (=pajāyana-vasena sattā); DhA I.174; PvA 150, 161. — Very freq. in formula sassamaṇa-brāhmaṇī pajā "this world with its samaṇas and brāhmans" D I.250; S I.160, 168, 207; II.170; III.28, 59; IV.158; V.204, 352; A II.130; V.204; Sn p. 15; It 121 etc.

Pajānanā (f.) [fr. pajānāti] knowledge, understanding, discernment; used in exegetical literature as syn. of paññā Nd[2] 380 = Dhs 16, 20, 555; Pug 25; Nett 28, 54. As nt. °a at Vism 436.

Pajānāti [pa+jānāti] to know, find out, come to know, understand, distinguish D I.45 (yathābhūtaŋ really, truly), 79 (ceto paricca), 162, 249; Sn 626, 726 sq., 987; It 12 (ceto paricca); Dh 402; Pv I.11[12] (=jānāti PvA 60); J V.445; Pug 64. — ppr. pajānaŋ Sn 884, 1050, 1104 (see expl[n] at Nd[1] 292 = Nd[2] 378); It 98; Pv IV.1[64]; and pajānanto Sn 1051. — ger. paññāya (q. v.) — Caus. paññāpeti; pp. paññatta; Pass. paññāyati & pp. paññāta (q. v.). Cp. sampajāna.

Pajāpati (°ī) 1. (m.) [Ved. prajāpati, prajā + pati Lord of all created beings, Lord of Creation] Prajāpati (Np.), the supreme Lord of men, only mentioned in one formula together with Inda & Brahmā, viz. devā saindakā sabrahmakā sapajāpatikā in sense of foll. Also at VbhA 497 with Brahmā. — 2. prajāpati (f.) [of Ved. prajāvant, adj.-n. fr. prajā "having (or rich in) progeny," with p for v, as pointed out by Trenckner *Notes* 62[16]] "one who has offspring," a chief wife of a man of the higher class (like a king, in which case = "chief queen") or a gahapati, in which case simply "wife"; cp. BSk. prajāpatī "lady" Divy 2, 98. — Vin I.23; III.25; IV.18, 258; S II.243; A I.137 (catasso °iyo); IV.210, 214; Vv 41[6] (=one of the 16,000 chief queens of Sakka VvA 183); DhA I.73; PvA 21, 31. sapajāpatika (adj.) together with his wife Vin I.23, 342; IV.62; J I.345; PvA 20.

Pajāyati [pa+jāyati] to be born or produced J V.386; VI.14.

Pajāyana (nt.) [fr. pa+**jan**] being born Vism 223.

Pajja[1] [cp. Sk. padya] a path, road Sn 514; DA I.262.

Pajja[2] (nt.) [cp. Sk. padya & pādya belonging to the feet, Lat. acupedius swift-footed; Gr. πεζός foot-soldier, see also pattika[1]] foot-oil, foot-salve Vin I.205; D II.240; J III.120; IV.396; V.376 (=pādabbhañjana C.).

Pajjati [**pad**, Vedic padyate only in meaning "to come to fall," later Sk. also "to go to"] to go, go to; usually not in simplex, but only in comp[n] with prefixes; as āpajjati, uppajjati, nipajjati etc. — Alone only in one doubtful passage, viz. A IV.362 (vv. ll. paccati, pabbati, gacchati.). — pp. panna (q. v.).

Pajjalati [pa + jalati of **jval**] to burn (forth), blaze up, go into flame Vin I.180; Sn 687 (sikhi pajjalanto); J I.215; ThA 62; PvA 38. — pp. pajjalita (q. v.).

Pajjalita [pp. of pajjalati] in flames, burning, blazing S I.133; Sn p. 21 (aggi); Dh 146; PvA 43 (sāṭakā).

Pajjunna [Ved. parjanya, for etym. see Walde, *Lat. Wtb.* under quercus & spargo] rain-cloud J I.332 (p. vuccati megho); IV.253. Otherwise only as Np. of the Rain God D II.260; S I.29; J I.331.

Pajjota [cp. Ved. pradyota, pra + **dyut**] light, lustre, splendour, a lamp S I.15, 47; A II.140; Sn 349; Pug 25; Sdhp 590. — telapajjota an oil lamp Vin I.16 = D I.85 = A I.56 ≈; Sn p. 15. — dhammapajjota the lamp of the Dhamma Miln 21. paññā-pajjota the torch of knowledge Dhs 16, 20, 292, 555; VbhA 115. pajjotassa nibbānaŋ the extinguishing of the lamp D II.157; S I.159; A IV.3.

Pajjhāyati [pa + jhāyati^{2}] to be in flames, to waste, decay, dry up; fig. to be consumed or overcome with grief, disappointment or remorse Vin III.19; IV.5; A II.214, 216; III.57; J III.534 (pajjhāti metri causa; C = anusocati) = Miln 5. — ppr. pajjhāyanto downcast, in formula tuṇhībhūto mankubhūto pattakkhandho adhomukho p. M I.132, 258 and passim.

Pañca (adj.-num.) [Ved. pañca, Idg. ***penque**; cp. Gr. πέντε, Lat. quīnque, Goth. fimf, Lith. penkí, Oir. coic] number 5. — Cases: gen. dat. pañcannaŋ, instr. abl. pañcahi, loc. pañcasu; often used in compositional form pañca° (cp. Ved. pañcāra with 5 spokes I.164^{13}; Gr. πεμπώβολος, Lat. quinqu-ennis etc.). — I. Characteristics of No. 5 in its use, with ref. to lit. & fig. application. "Five" is the number of "comprehensive and yet simple" unity or a set; it is applied in all cases of a natural and handy comprehension of several items into a group, after the 5 fingers of the hand, which latter lies at the bottom of all primitive expressions of No. 5 (see also below pañc' angulika. The word for 5 itself in its original form is identical with the word for hand *prəq, cp. Lat. com°, decem, centum etc.) —

A. No. 5, appl^{d} (a) with ref. to *time:* catupañcāhaŋ 4 or 5 days J II.114 (cp. quinque diebus Horace Sat I.3^{16}); maraṇaŋ tuyhaŋ oraŋ māsehi pañcahi after 5 months Vv 63^{10}, p. māse vasitvā DA I.319 (cp. qu. menses Hor. Sat. II.3^{289}). — (b) of space: °yojanaṭṭhāna J III.504; °yojan-ubbedho gajavaro VvA 33; °bhūmako pāsādo J I.58 (cp. the house of Death as 5 stories high in Grimm, Märchen No. 42 ed. Reclam). — (c) of a group, set, company, etc. (cp. 5 peoples RV III.37^{9}; VI.11^{4}; VIII.9^{2} etc.; gods X.55^{3}; priests II.34^{14}; III.7^{7}; leaders of the Greek ships Hom. Iliad 16, 171; ambassadors Genesis 47^{2}; quinque viri Hor. Sat. II.5^{55}; Epist. II.1^{24}): p. janā J V.230; p. amaccā J V.231; p. hatthino DhA I.164; pañca nāriyo agamiŋsu Vv 32^{2}; p. puttāni khādāmi Pv I.6^{3}. — *Note.* No. 5 in this appl^{n} is not so frequent in Pāli as in older literature (Vedas e. g.); instead of the simple 5 we find more freq. the higher decimals 50 and 500. See also below §§ 3, 4.

B. No. 15 in two forms: pañcadasa (f. °ī the 15th day of the month Vv 15^{6} = A I.144; Sn 402) VvA 67 (°kahāpaṇa-sahassāni dāpesi), and paṇṇarasa (also as f. ī of the 15th or full-moon day Pv III.3^{1}; DhA I.198; III.92; IV.202; VvA 314; SnA 78) Sn 153 (pannaraso uposatho); Vv 64^{2} (paṇṇarase va cando; expl^{d} as paṇṇarasiyaŋ VvA 276); DhA I.388 (of age, 15 or 16 years); DA I.17 (°bhedo Khuddaka-nikāyo); SnA 357 (pannarasahi bhikkhu-satehi = 1500, instead of the usual 500); PvA 154 (°yojana). The appl^{n} is much the same as 5 and 50 (see below), although more rare, e. g. as measure of space: °*yojana* DhA I.17 (next in sequence to paṇṇāsa-yojana); J I.315; PvA 154 (cp. 15 furlongs from Jerusalem to Bethany John 11, 18; 15 cubits above the mountains rose the flood Gen. 7. 20).

C. No. 25 in two forms: **pañcavīsati** (the usual) e. g. DhsA 185 sq.; Miln 289 (citta-dubbalī-karaṇā dhammā); **paṇṇa-vīsati**, e. g. J IV.352 (nāriyo); Th 2, 67, and paṇṇuvīsaŋ (only at J III.138). Similarly to 15 and 25 the number 45 (**pañca-cattāḷīsa**) is favoured in giving distances with °**yojana**, e. g. at J I.147, 348; DhA I.367.—*Application*: of **25**: (1) time: years J III.138; DhA I.4; (2) space: miles high and wide DhA II.64 (ahipeto); VvA 236 (yojanāni pharitvā pabhā).

2. Remarks on the use of 50 and 500 (5000). Both 50 and 500 are found in stereotyped and always recurring combinations (not in Buddhist literature alone, but all over the Ancient World), and applied to any situation indiscriminately. They have thus lost their original numerical significance and their value equals an expression like our "thousands," cp. the use of Lat. mille and 600, also similarly many other high numerals in Pāli literature, as mentioned under respective units (4, 6, 8 e. g. in 14, 16, 18, etc.). Psychologically 500 is to be expl^{d} as "a great hand," i. e. the 5 fingers magnified to the 2nd decade, and is equivalent to an expression like "a lot" (originally "only one," cp. casting the lot, then the one as a mass or collection), or like heaps, tons, a great many, etc. — Thus 50 (and 500) as the numbers of "comm-union" are especially freq. in recording a company of men, a host of servants, animals in a herd, etc., wherever the single constituents form a larger (mostly impressive, important) whole, as an army, the king's retinue, etc. — A. No. 50 (paññāsa; the by-form paṇṇāsa only at DhA III.207), in foll. appl^{ns}: (a) of *time*: does not occur, but see below under 55. — (b) of *space* (cp. 50 cubits the breadth of Noah's ark Gen. 6. 15; the height of the gallows (Esther 5. 14; 7. 9) J I.359 (yojanāni); DhA III.207 (°hattho ubbedhena rukkho); Vism 417 (paripuṇṇa °yojana suriyamaṇḍala); DhA I.17 (°yojana). — (c) of a *company* or group (cp. 50 horses RV II.18^{5}; V.18^{5}; wives VIII.19^{36}; men at the oars Hom. Il. 2. 719; 16. 170, servants Hom. Od. 7, 103, 22, 421) J III.220 (corā); V.161 (pallankā), 421 (dijakaññāyo); Sn p. 87; SnA 57 (bhikkhū). — *Note.* 55 (pañcapaññāsa) is used instead of 50 in *time* expressions (years), e. g. at DhA I.125; II.57; PvA 99, 142; also in *groups*: DhA I.99 (janā). — B. No. 500 (pañcasata°, pañcasatā, pañcasatāni). — (a) *of time*: years (as Peta or Petī) Vv 84^{34}; Pv II.1^{5}; PvA 152 (with additional 50). (b) *of space:* miles high Pv IV.3^{28}; J I.204 (°yojana-satikā); Vism 72 (°dhanu-satika, 500 bows in distance). — (C) of *groups* of men, servants, or a herd, etc. (cp. 500 horses RV X.93^{14}; witnesses of the rising of Christ 1 Cor. 15-6; men armed Vergil Aen. 10. 204; men as representatives Hom. Od. 3. 7; 500 knights or warriors very frequently in Nibelungenlied, where it is only meant to denote a "goodly company, 500 or more") Arahants KhA 98; Bhikkhus very frequent, e. g. D I.1; Vin II.199; J I.116, 227; DhA II.109, 153; III.262, 295; IV.184, 186; Sāvakas J I.95; Upāsakas J II.95; PvA 151; Paccekabuddhas DhA IV.201; PvA 76; Vighāsādā J II.95; DhA II.154; Sons PvA 75; Thieves DhA II.204; PvA 54; Relatives PvA 179; Women-servants (parivārikā itthiyo) Pv II.12^{6}; VvA 69, 78, 187; PvA 152; Oxen A IV.41; Monkeys J III.355; Horses Vin III.6. — Money etc. as present, reward or fine representing a "round-sum" (cp. Nibelungen 314: horses with gold, 317: mark; dollars as reward Grimm No. 7; drachms as pay Hor. Sat. II.7^{43}) kahāpaṇas Sn 980, 982; PvA 273; blows with stick as fine Vin I.247. — *Various*: a caravan usually consists of 500 loaded wagons, e. g. J I.101; DhA II.79; PvA 100, 112; chariots VvA 78; ploughs Sn p. 13. Cp. S I.148 (vyagghī-nisā); Vin II.285 (ūna-pañcasatāni); J II.93 (accharā); V.75 (vāṇijā); DhA I.89 (suvaṇṇasivikā), 352 (rāja-satāni); IV.182 (jāti°) KhA 176 (paritta-dīpā). Also BSk. pañ'opasthāyikā-śatāni Divy 529; pañca-mātrāṇi strī-śatāni Divy 533. — *Note.* When Gotama said that his "religion" would last 500

years he meant that it would last a very long time, practically for ever. The later change of 500 to 5,000 is immaterial to the meaning of the expression, it only indicates a later period (cp. 5,000 in Nibelungeniled for 500, also 5,000 men in ambush Joshua 8. 12; converted by Peter Acts 4. 4; fed by Christ with 5 loaves Matthew 14. 21). Still more impressive than 500 is the expression 5 Koṭis (5 times 100,000 or 10 million), which belongs to a comparatively later period, e. g. at DhA I.62 (ariya-sāvaka-koṭiyo), 256 (°mattā-ariyasāvakā); IV.190 (p. koṭi-mattā ariya-sāvakā).

3. *Typical sets of 5 in the Pali Canon.* °aggaŋ first fruits of 5 (kinds), viz. khett°, rās°, koṭṭh°, kumbhi°, bhojan° i. e. of the standing crop, the threshing floor, the granary, the pottery, the larder SnA 270. °angā 5 gentlemanly qualities (of king or brahmin): sujāta, ajjhāyaka, abhirūpa, sīlavā, paṇḍita (see anga; on another comb^n with anga see below). The phrase pañc' anga-samannāgata & °vippahīna (S I.99; A V.16) refers to the 5 nīvaraṇāni: see expl^d at Vism 146. °angikaturiya 5 kinds of music: ātata, vitata, ātata-vitata, ghana, susira. °abhiññā 5 psychic powers (see *Cpd.* 209). °ānantarika-kammāni 5 acts that have immediate retribution (Miln 25), either 5 of the 6 abhiṭhānas (q. v.) or (usually) murder, theft, impurity, lying, intemperance (the 5 sīlas) cp. *Dhs trsl.* 267. °indriyāni 5 faculties, viz. saddhā, viriya, sati, samādhi, paññā (see indriya B. 15-19). °vidhaŋ (rāja-) kakudhabhaṇḍaŋ, insignia regis viz. vāḷavījanī, uṇhīsa, khagga, chatta, pādukā. °kalyāṇāni, beauty-marks: kesa°, maŋsa°, aṭṭhi°, chavi°, vaya°. °kāmaguṇā pleasures of the 5 senses (= taggocarāni pañc' āyatanāni gahitāni honti SnA 211). °gorasā 5 products of the cow: khīra, dadhi, takka, navanīta, sappi. °cakkhūni, sorts of vision (of a Buddha): maŋsa° dibba° paññā° buddha° samanta°. °taṇhā cravings, specified in 4 sets of 5 each: see Nd^2 271^V. °nikāyā 5 collections (of Suttantas) in the Buddh. Canon, viz. Dīgha° Majjhima° Saŋyutta°, Anguttara° Khuddaka°, e. g. Vin II.287. °nīvaraṇāni or obstacles: kāmacchanda, abhijjhā-vyāpāda, thīna-middha, uddhacca-kukkucca, vicikicchā. °patiṭṭhitaŋ 5 fold prostration or veneration, viz. with forehead, waist, elbows, knees, feet (Childers) in phrase °ena vandati (sometimes °ŋ vandati, e. g. SnA 78, 267) J V.502; SnA 267, 271, 293, 328, 436; VvA 6; DhA I.197; IV.178, etc. °bandhana either 5 ways of binding or pinioning or 5 fold bondage J IV.3 (as "ure pañcangika-bandhanaŋ" cp. kaṇṭhe pañcamehi bandhanehi bandhitvā S IV.201); Nd^1 304$^{III\,B2}$ (rājā bandhāpeti andhu-bandhanena vā rajju°, sankhalika°, latā°, parikkhepa°), with which cp. Śikṣāsamucc. 165: rājñā pañcapāśakena bandhanena baddhaḥ. — There is a diff. kind of bandhana which has nothing to do with binding, but which is the 5 fold ordeal (obligation: pañcavidha-bandhana-kāraṇaŋ) in Niraya, and consists of the piercing of a red hot iron stake through both hands, both feet and the chest; it is a sort of crucifixion. We may conjecture that this "bandhana" is a corruption of "vaddhana" (of **vyadh**, or viddhana?), and that the expression originally was pañcaviddhana-kāraṇa (instead of pañca-vidha-bandhana-k°). See passages under bandhana & cp. M III.182; A I.141; Kvu 597; SnA 479. °balāni 5 forces: saddhā° viriya° sati° samādhi° paññā° D II.120; M II.12; S III.96; A III.12 (see also bala). °bhojanāni 5 kinds of food: odāna, kummāsa, sattu, maccha, maŋsa Vin IV.176. °macchariyāni 5 kinds of selfishness: āvāsa° kula° lābha° vaṇṇa° dhamma°. °rajāni defilements: rūpa°, sadda° etc. (of the 5 senses) Nd^1 505; SnA 574. °vaṇṇā 5 colours (see ref. for colours under pīta and others), viz. nīla, pītaka, lohitaka, kaṇha, odāta (of B's eye) Nd^2 235^{1a}; others with ref. to paduma-puṇḍarīka VvA 41; to paduma DhA III.443; to kusumāni DA I.140; DhA IV.203. °*vaṇṇa* in another meaning (fivefold) in connection with pīti (q. v.). °saŋyojanāni fetters (q. v.). °sangā impurities, viz. rāga, dosa, moha, māna, diṭṭhi (cp. taṇhā) DhA IV.109. °sīla the 5 moral precepts, as sub-division of the 10 (see dasasīla and Nd^2 under sīla on p. 277).

4. *Other (not detailed) passages with* 5: Sn 660 (abbudāni), 677 (nahutāni koṭiyo pañca); Th 2, 503 (°kaṭuka = pañcakāmaguṇa-rasa ThA 291); DhA II.25 (°mahānidhi); SnA 39 (°pakāra-gomaṇḍala-puṇṇa-bhāva). Cp. further: guṇā Miln 249; paṇṇāni Vin I.201 (nimba°, kuṭaja°, paṭola°, sulasi°, kappāsika°); Paṇḍu-rāja-puttā J V.426; pabbagaṇṭhiyo Miln 103; pucchā DhsA 55; mahā-pariccāgā DhA III.441; mahā-vilokanāni DhA I.84; vatthūni Vin II.196 sq.; vāhanāni (of King Pajjota) DhA I.196; suddhāvāsā Dhs A 14. In general see Vin V.128-133 (var. sets of 5).

-anga five (bad) qualities (see anga 3 and above 3), in phrase vippahīna free from the 5 sins D III.269; Nd^2 284 C; cp. BSk. pañcānga-viprahīna. Ep. of the Buddha Divy 95, 264 & °samannāgata endowed with the 5 good qualities A V.15 (of senāsana, expl^d at Vism 122): see also above. -angika consisting of 5 parts, fivefold, in foll. comb^{ns}: °jhāna (viz. vitakka, vicāra, pīti, sukha, cittass' ekaggatā) Dhs 83; °turiya orchestra S I.131; Th 1, 398; 2, 139; Vv 36^4; DhA I.274, 394; °bandhana bond J IV.3. -angula = °angulika J IV.153 (gandha°); SnA 39 (usabhaŋ nahāpetvā bhojetvā °ŋ datvā mālaŋ bandhitvā). -angulika (also °aka) the 5 finger-mark, palm-mark, the magic mark of the spread hand with the fingers extended (made after the hand & 5 fingers have been immersed in some liquid, preferably a solution of sandal wood, gandha; but also blood). See Vogel, the 5 finger-token in Pāli Literature, Amsterdam Akademie 1919 (with plates showing ornaments on Bharhut Tope), cp. also *J.P.T.S.* 1884, 84 sq. It is supposed to provide magical protection (esp. against the Evil Eye). Vin II.123 (cp. *Vin. Texts* II.116); J I.166, 192; II.104 (gandha °ŋ deti), 256 (gandha°, appl^d to a cetiya); III.23, 160 (lohita°); Vv 33^{18} (gandha-°ŋ adāsiŋ Kassapassa thūpasmiŋ); Mhvs 32, 4 (see trsl. p. 220); DhA III.374 (goṇānaŋ gandha-°āni datvā); SnA 137 (setamālāhi sabba-gandha-sugandhehi p°akehi ca alankatā paripuṇṇa-angapaccangā, of oxen). Cp. MVastu I.269 (stūpeṣu pañcangulāni; see note on p. 579). Quotations of similar use in brahmanical literature see at Vogel p. 6 sq. -āvudha (āyudha) set of 5 weapons (sword, spear, bow, battle-axe, shield, after Childers) Miln 339 (see *Miln trsl.* II.227), cp. p° sannaddha J III.436, 467; IV.283, 437; V.431; VI.75; sannaddha-p° J IV.160 (of sailors). They seem to be different ones at diff. passages. -âhaŋ 5 days Vin IV.281; J II.114. -cūḷaka with 5 topknots J V.250 (of a boy). -nakha with 5 claws, N. of a five-toed animal J V.489 (so read for pañca na khā, misunderstood by C.). -paṭṭhika at Vin II.117, 121, 152; is not clear (v. l. paṭika). *Vin. Texts* III.97 trsl. "cupboards" and connect it with Sk. paṭṭikā, as celapattikaŋ Vin II.128 undoubtedly is ("strip of cloth laid down for ceremonial purposes," *trsl.* III.128). It also occurs at Vin IV.47. -patikā (f.) having had 5 husbands J V.424, 427. -mālin of a wild animal J VI.497 (= pancangika-turiya-saddo viya C., not clear). -māsakamattaŋ a sum of 5 māsakas DhA II.29. -vaggiya (or °ika SnA 198) belonging to a group of five. The 5 brahmins who accompanied Gotama when he became an ascetic are called p. bhikkhū. Their names are Aññākondañña, Bhaddiya, Vappa, Assaji, Mahānāma. M I.170; II.94; S III.66; PvA 21 (°e ādiŋ katvā); SnA 351; cp. chabbaggiya. -vidha fivefold J I.204 (°ā abhirakkhā), VI.341 (°paduma), °*bandhana*: see this. -sādhāraṇa-bhāva fivefold connection J IV.7. -seṭṭha (Bhagavā) "the most excellent in the five" Sn 355 (= pañcannaŋ paṭhama-sissānaŋ pañcavaggiyānaŋ seṭṭho, pañcahi vā saddhā-dīhi indriyehi sīlādīhi vā dhamma-khandhehi ativisiṭṭhehi cakkhūhi ca seṭṭho SnA 351). -hattha having 5 hands J V.431.

Pañcaka (adj.) [fr. pañca] fivefold, consisting of five J I.116 (°kammaṭṭhāna); Dhs. chapters 167-175 (°naya fivefold system of jhāna, cp. *Dhs. trslⁿ* 52); SnA 318 (°nipāta of Anguttara). — nt. pañcakaŋ a pentad, five Vin I.255 (the 5 parts of the kaṭhina robe, see *Vin. Texts* II.155), cp. p. 287; pl. **pañcakā** sets of five Vism 242. The 32 ākāras or constituents of the human body are divided into 4 pañcaka's (i. e. sets of 5 more closely related parts), viz. taca° "skin-pentad," the 5 dermatoid constituents: kosā, lomā, nakhā, dantā, taco; vakka° the next five, ending with the kidneys; papphāsa° d. ending with the lungs & comprising the inner organs proper; matthalunga° id. ending with the brain, and 2 *chakka's* (sets of 6), viz. meda° & mutta°. See e. g. VbhA 249, 258.

Pañcakkhattuŋ (adv.) five times.

Pañcadhā (adv.) in five ways, fivefold DhsA 351.

Pañcama (adj.) [compar.-superl. formation fr. pañca, with °ma as in Lat. supremus, for the usual °to as in Gr. πέμπτος, Lat. quintus, also Sk. pañcathaḥ] num. ord. the fifth D I.88; Sn 84, 99, 101; VvA 102; PvA 52 (°e māse in the 5th month the Petī has to die); DhA III.195 (°e sattāhe in the 5th week). — f. pañcamā PvA 78 (ito °āya jātiyā) and pañcamī Sn 437 (senā); PvA 79 (jāti).

Pañcamaka (adj.) = pañcama J I.55.

Pañcaso (adv.) by fives.

Pañja [is it to be puñja?] heap, pile A II.75 (meaning different?); Cp. I.10[16].

Pañjara (m. & nt.) [cp. Epic Sk. pañjara, which probably belongs to Lat. pango, q. v. Walde, *Lat. Wtb.* s. v.] a cage, J I.436; II.141; III.305 (sīha°); IV.213; V.232 (sīha), 365; VI.385 (sīha°), 391; Miln 23 (°antaragata gone into the c.); 27; DhA I.164 (nakha°), where meaning is "frame"; VbhA 238.

Pañjali (adj.) [pa + añjali. Cp. Ep. Sk. prāñjali] with outstretched hands, as token of reverence Sn 1031; in cpd. **pañjali-kata** (cp. añjalikata; añjali + pp. of kṛ) raising one's folded hands Sn 566, 573; Th 1, 460; J VI.501. Cp. BSk. prāñjalikṛta MVastu II.257, 287, 301.

Pañjalika (adj.) [fr. pañjali] holding up the clasped hands as token of respectful salutation S I.226; Sn 485, 598.

Pañjasa (adj.) [pa + añjasa] in the right order, straight A II.15.

Pañña (-°) (adj.) [the adj. form of paññā] of wisdom, endowed with knowledge or insight, possessed of the highest cognition, in foll. cpds.: anissaraṇa° D I.245; S II.194; IV.332; anoma° Sn 343; appa° S I.198; J II.166; III.223, 263; avakujja° A I.130; gambhīra° S I.190; javana° S I.63; Nd² 235; tikkha°; dup° D III.252, 282; S I.78, 191; II.159 sq.; M III.25; A II.187 sq.; Dh 111, 140; Pug 13; DhA II.255; nibbedhika° S I.63; A II.178; Nd² 235; puthu° ibid.; bhāvita° S IV.111; A V.42 sq.; bhūri° S III.143; IV.205; manda° VbhA 239; mahā° S I.63, 121; II.155; A I.23, 25; II.178 sq.; Nd² 235; SnA 347; sap° S I.13, 22, 212; IV.210; A IV.245; Pv I 8[8]; 11[5]; PvA 60 (= paṇḍita), 131 (+ buddhimant); suvimutta° A V.29 sq.; bāsa° S I.63, 191; V.376; Nd² 235. By itself (i. e. not in cpd.) only at Dh 208 (= lokiyalokuttara-paññāya sampanna DhA III.172) and 375 (= paṇḍita DhA IV.111).

Paññatā (f.) [secondary abstract formation fr. paññā, in meaning equal to paññāṇa] having sense, wisdom A III.421 (dup° = foolishness) V.159 (id.); mahā°, puthu°, vipula° A I.45. See also paññattaŋ.

Paññatta[1] [pp. of paññāpeti, cp. BSk. prajñapta] pointed out, made known, ordered, designed, appointed, ordained S II.218; A I.98, 151; IV.16, 19; V.74 sq.; Pv IV.1[35]; DhA I.274; VvA 9 (su° mañca-pīṭha), 92 (niccabhatta); PvA 78. Esp. freq. in ster. formula paññatte āsane nisīdi he sat down on the appointed (i. e. special) chair (seat) D I.109, 125, 148; S I.212; Dh 148; SnA 267; PvA 16, 23, 61.

Paññatta[2] (nt.) [abstr. fr. paññā] wisdom, sense etc. S V.412 (v. l. paññatā). See also paññatā.

Paññatti (f.) [fr. paññāpeti, cp. paññatta[1]] making known, manifestation, description, designation, name, idea, notion, concept. On term see *Cpd.* 3 sq., 198, 199; *Kvu trslⁿ* 1; *Dhs trslⁿ* 340. — M III.68; S III.71; IV.38 (māra°), 39 (satta°, dukkha°, loka°); A II.17; V.190; Ps II.171, 176; Pug 1; Dhs 1.309; Nett 1 sq., 38, 188; KhA 102, 107; DA I.139; SnA 445, 470; PvA 200. The spelling also occurs as paṇṇatti, e. g. at J II.65 (°vahāra); Miln 173 (loka°); KhA 28; adj. paṇṇattika (q. v.).

Paññavant (adj.) [paññā + vant, with reduction of ā to a see Geiger, *P.Gr.* § 23] possessed of insight, wise, intelligent, sensible Vin I.60; D III.237, 252, 265, 282, 287; M I.292; III.23; S I.53, 79; II.159 sq., 207, 279 (daharo ce pi p.); IV.243; V.100, 199, 392, 401; A II.76, 187, 230; III.2 sq., 127, 183; IV.85, 217, 271, 357; V.25, 124 sq.; Sn 174; Nd² 259; Dh 84; J I.116; Pug 13; DhA II.255; KhA 54; VbhA 239, 278; PvA 40. Cp. paññāṇavant.

Paññā (f.) [cp. Vedic prajñā, pa + jñā] intelligence, comprising all the higher faculties of cognition, "intellect as conversant with general truths" (*Dial.* II.68), reason, wisdom, insight, knowledge, recognition. See on term Mrs. Rh. D. "*Buddhism*" (1914) pp. 94, 130, 201; also *Cpd.* 40, 41, 102 and discussion of term at *Dhs. trsl.* 17, 339, cp. scholastic definition with all the synonyms of intellectual attainment at Nd² 380 = Dhs 16 (paññā pajānanā vicayo etc.). As tt. in Buddbist Psych. Ethics it comprises the highest and last stage as 3rd division in the standard "Code of religious practice" which leads to Arabantship or Final Emancipation. These 3 stages are: (1) sīla-kkhandha (or °sampadā), code of moral duties; (2) samādhi-kkhandha (or citta-sampadā) code of emotional duties or practice of con centration & meditation; (3) paññā-kkhandha (or °sampadā) code of intellectual duties or practice of the attainment of highest knowledge. (See also jhāna[1].) They are referred to in almost every Suttanta of Dīgha I (given *in extenso* at D I.62-85) and frequently mentioned elsewhere, cp. D II.81, 84, 91 (see khandha, citta & sīla). — D I.26 = 162 (°gatena caranti diṭṭhigatāni), 174 (°vāda), 195 (°pāripūrin); II.122 (ariyā); III.101, 158, 164, 183, 230, 237, 242, 284 sq.; S I.13 = 165 (sīla, citta, paññā), 17, 34, 55; II.185 (sammā°), 277; V.222 (ariyā); M I.144 (id.); III.99 (id.), 245 (paramā), 272 (sammā°); A I.61, 216; II.1 (ariyā); IV.105 (id.); III.106 (sīla, citta, p.), 352 (kusalesu dhammesu); IV.11 (id.); V.123 sq.; It 35, 40 (°uttara), 51 (sīla-samādhi p. ca), 112 (ariyā°); Sn 77, 329, 432, 881, 1036 and passim; Dh 38, 152, 372; Nd¹ 77; Nd² 380; Ps I.53, 64 sq., 71 sq., 102 sq., 119; II.150 sq., 162, 185 sq.; Pug 25, 35, 54 (°sampadā); Dhs 16, 20, 555; Nett 8, 15, 17, 28, 54, 191; VbhA 140, 396; PvA 40 (paññāya abhāvato for lack of reason); Sdhp 343. On paññāya see sep. article. See also adhipanna (adhisīla, adhicitta +).

-**âdhipateyya** the supremacy of wisdom A II.137. -**indriya** the faculty of reason (with sati° & samādhi°) D III.239, 278; Dhs 16, 20 etc.; Nett. 7, 15 sq; 191. -**obhāsa** the lustre of wisdom Ps I.119; Dhs 16, 20 etc. -**kkhandha** the code of cognition (see above) Vin I.62; D III.229, 279; It 51; Nd¹ 21; Nett 70, 90, 128. It is always combᵈ with sīla° & samādhi-kkhandha. -**cakkhu** the eye of wisdom (one of the 5 kinds of extraordinary sight of a Buddha: see under cakkhumant) D III.219; S V.467; It 52; Nd¹ 354; Nd² 235. -**dada** giving or bestowing wisdom S I.33; Sn 177. -dhana the treasure of perfect knowledge (one of the 7 treasures, see dhana) D III.163, 251; A III.53; VvA 113. -nirodhika tending to the destruction of reason S v.97; It 82. -paṭilābha acquisition of wisdom S v.411; A I.45; Ps II.189. -pāsāda the stronghold of supreme knowledge Dh 28 (=dibba-cakkhuŋ sankhātaŋ °ŋ). -bala the power of reason or insight, one of the 5 powers D III.229, 253; M III.72; A IV.363; Sn 212; Dhs 16, 20 etc.; Nett 54, 191; VvA 7. -bāhulla wealth or plenty of wisdom S v.411; A I.45. -bhūmi ground or stage of wisdom; a name given to the Paṭicca-samuppāda by Bdhgh at Vism XVII, pp. 517 sq. (°niddesa). -ratana the gem of reason or knowledge Dhs 16, 20 etc. -vimutta freed by reason D II.70; III.105, 254; M I.35, 477; A I.61; II.6; IV.452; Sn 847; Nd[1] 207; Kvu 58; Nett 199. -vimutti emancipation through insight or knowledge (always paired with ceto-vimutti) D I.156, 167; III.78, 102, 108, 132, 281; It 75, 91; Sn 725, 727; Nett 7, 40, 81, 127; DA I.313; VbhA 464. -visuddhi purity of insight D III.288. -vuddhi increase of knowledge S v.97, 411; A I.15, 45; II.245. -sampadā the blessing of higher knowledge (see above) A I.62; II.66; III.12 sq., 182 sq.; IV.284, 322. -sīla conduct and (higher) intelligence Dh 229 (°samāhita=lokuttarapaññāya c' eva pārisuddhisīlena ca samannāgata DhA III.329); Vv 34[23] id. =ariyāya diṭṭhiyā ariyena sīlena ca sāmannāgata VvA 155). Often used with yathābhūtaŋ q. v. Cp. paññāya.

Paññāṇa (nt.) [pa+ñāṇa, cp. Vedic prajñāno in both meanings & paññā] 1. wisdom, knowledge, intelligence D I.124 (sīla+); S I.41; A IV.342; Sn 96, 1136; DA I.171, 290. — 2. mark, sign, token J v.195.

Paññāṇavant (adj.) [paññāṇa+vant] reasonable, sensible, wise Sn 202, 1090; J v.222; VI.361; Nd[2] 382.

Paññāta [pp. of pajānāti] known, renowned DA I.143; ap° unknown, defamed Vin IV.231; S IV.46; A III.134 (where also der. appaññātika).

Paññāpaka (adj. n.) [fr. paññāpeti] one who advises, assigns or appoints Vin II.305 (āsana°).

Paññāpana (nt.) [fr. paññāpeti] disclosure, discovering M III.17; S III.59; declaration DhsA 11.

Paññāpetar [n. ag. of paññāpeti] one who imparts knowledge, discloser of truths, discoverer D II.223.

Paññāpeti [Caus. of pajānāti] 1. to make known, declare, point out, appoint, assign, recognise, define D I.119 (brāhmaṇā brāhmaṇaŋ), 180, 185, 237; It 98 (tevijjaŋ brāhmaṇaŋ), Pug 37, 38; PvA 61 (āsanaŋ). — 2. to lay down, fold out, spread PvA 43 (sanghāṭiŋ). — pp. paññatta (q. v.). — Caus. II. paññāpāpeti J III.371.

Paññāya (indecl.) [ger. of pajānāti, in relation °ñāya: ñatvā as uṭṭhāya: ṭhatvā; so expl[d] by P. Commentators, whereas modern interpreters have taken it as instr. of paññā] understanding fully, knowing well, realising, in full recognition, in thorough realisation or understanding. Used most frequently with yathābhūtaŋ (q. v.) S I.13 (bhāveti), 44 (lokasmiŋ pajjoto), 214 (parisujjhati); II.7 sq. (uppajjati), 68 (suppatividdho); III.6 (id.); v.324 (ajjhupekkhati); A I.125 (anuggahissati); III.44 (vaḍḍhati); IV.13 sq. (pariyogāhamāna); v.39 (disvā) Sn 1035 (see Nd[2] 380[a]); It 93 (moh'aggiŋ, v. l. saññāya); PvA 60 (upaparikkhitvā, as expl[n] of ñatvā), 140=viceyya.

Paññāyati [Pass. of pajānāti] to be (well) known, to be clear or evident, to be perceived, seen or taken for, to appear It 89; DhA I.14, 95 (fut. paññāyissatha you will be well known); II.75; PvA 83 (pālito eva), 166 (dissati+); ppr. paññāyamāna DhA I.29; PvA 96 (=perceivable). — aor. paññāyi PvA 172 (paccakkhato).

Pañha [Ved. praśna, for details of etym. see pucchati] mode of asking, inquiry, investigation, question D I.11 (deva°) M I.83; III.30; A I.103, 288; III.81, 191 sq., 419 sq.; v.50 sq.; Sn 512, 957, 1005, 1024, 1148 etc., Nd[1] 464; Miln 28, 340; DA I.97. pañhaŋ pucchati to ask a question Nd[2] under pucchā (q. v.).
-paṭibhāna an answer to a question M I.83; Miln 28. -vīmaŋsaka one who tests a question Sn 827; Nd[1] 166; SnA 538. -vyākaraṇa mode of answering questions, of which there are 4, viz. ekaŋsa "direct," vibbajja "qualified," paṭipucchā "after further questioning," ṭhapanīya "not to be answered or left undecided," thus enum[d] at D III.229; A I.197 sq.; II.46; Miln 339.

Paṭa [cp. Epic Sk. paṭa, etym. unknown, prob. dialectical] cloth; cloak, garment S II.219 (°pilotika); Th I, 1092 (bhinna-paṭan-dhara "wearing the patchwork cloak" trsl.); J IV.494; KhA 45, 58 (°tantu); DA I.198; DhA II.45 (puppha°); III.295 °kañcuka, v. l. kaṭak°); Vism 16 (bhinna-paṭa-dhara in def[n] of bhikkhu); VbhA 327 (id.); DhsA 81 (paṭa-paṭa sadda); VvA 73, 201; PvA 185. Cp. paṭikā & paṭalikā; also kappaṭa.

Paṭaggi [paṭi+aggi] counter-fire Vin II.138; J I.212; kacc. 31.

Paṭanga [cp. *Sk. phaḍingā, but influenced by Sk. pataga a winged animal, bird] a grasshopper Sn 602; J VI.234, 506; Miln 272, 407; DhA IV.58; PvA 67; Pgdp 59.

Paṭaccarin (adj.) [paṭa+carin but cp. Sk. pāṭaccara a shoplifter Halāyudha 2, 185] poor (lit. dressed in old clothes): so read perhaps at J VI.227 (vv. ll paḷaccari & paṭiccari).

Paṭala (nt.) [connected with paṭa, cp. Sk. paṭala in meaning "section" Vedic, in all other meanings later Sk.] 1. a covering, membrane, lining, envelope, skin, film Vism 257 (maŋsa° of the liver, where KhA 54 reads maŋsa-piṇḍa), 359 (phaṇa°); DhsA 307 (7 akkhi° membranes of the eye); KhA 21 (samuppaṭana), 55 (udara° mucous membrane of the stomach), 61 (id.); DhsA 330 (id.); SnA 248 (id.); PvA 186 (eka° upāhanā, single-lined, cp. paṭalika & palāsika & see Morris *J.P.T.S.*1887, 165); Vism 446 (kappāsa° film of cotton seed); Bdhd 66 (id.). — 2. roof, ceiling PvA 52 (ayo° of iron). — 3. a heap, mass (esp. of clouds) J I.73 (megha°); DhsA 239 (abbha°). —madhu° honey comb J I.262; DhA I.59; III.323. — 4. cataract of the eye Dāvs v.27.

Paṭalika (adj.) [fr. paṭala] belonging to a cover or lining, having or forming a cover or lining, as adj. said of sandals (eka° with single lining) J II.277 (v. l. for ekatalika); III.80, 81 (id.). — as n. f. paṭalikā a woven cloth, a woollen coverlet (embroidered with flowers), usually comb[d] with paṭikā Vin I.192; II.162; D I.7 (=ghana-puppho uṇṇāmayo attharako. So āmilākapaṭṭo ti pi vuccati DA I.87); A I.137, 181; III.50, IV.94, 231, 394.

Paṭaha [cp. Epic Sk. paṭaha, dial.] a kettle-drum, war drum, one of the 2 kinds of drums (bheri) mentioned at DhsA 319, viz. mahā-bheri & p.-bheri; J I.355; Dpvs 16, 14; PvA 4.

Paṭāka (nt.) [cp. Sk. paṭāka, connected with paṭa] a flag M I.379; Miln 87; Vism 469; ThA 70.

Paṭāṇi at Vin IV.46 (paṭāṇi dinnā hoti) is not clear, it is expl[d] by Bdhgh as "mañcapidhānaŋ (for °pīṭhānaŋ) pādasikhāsu āṇi dinno hoti." At DA I.77 we find the foll.: "visūkaŋ paṭāni (sic.) -bhūtaŋ dassanan ti visūkadassanaŋ," and at DhsA 393: "paṭāni-gahaṇaŋ gahetvā ekapaden' eva taŋ nissaddaŋ akāsiŋ."

Paṭi (indecl.) [Ven. prati, to Idg. *preti as in Lat. pretium (fr. *pretios) "price" (cp. precious), i. e. equivalent; Gr. πρέs (aeol.), προτί, πρός against] directional *prefix* in well-defined meaning of "back (to), against, towards, in opposition to, opposite." As *preposition* (with acc. and usually postponed) towards, near by, at; usually spelt pati (cp. sampati & sampaṭika) Sn 291 (?), 425 (Nerañjaram (pati); Th 1, 628 (suriyass' uggamanam p.); 2, 258 (abhiyobbanam p.), 306 (Nerañjaram p.); J 1.457 (paṭi suriyaŋ thatvā standing facing the sun); IV.93; VI.491; Pv II.9[11] (suriy' uggamanam p.); Miln 116 (dānam p.); PvA 154 (paṭi Gangaŋ against the G.). — Most freq. combns are: paṭi+ā (paṭiyā°), paṭisaŋ°; vi+paṭi°, sampaṭi°. The composition (assimilation-) form before vowels is pacc° (b. v.).—*Meanings.* I. (lit.) "back," in the sense of: (1) against, in opposition (opp. anu, see below III.), contrary: viz. (a) often with the implication of a hostile attack (anti-, against): °kaṇṭaka, °kosati (re-ject), °kūla, °khipati (re-fuse, op-pose), °gha, °codeti (re-prove), thambhati, °disā, °deseti, °pakkha, °patha, °piŋsati, °pīḷita, °magga, °manteti, °yodha (at-tack), °vacana (re-ply), °vadati, °vedeti, °sattu (enemy), °suṇāti, °hata; — (b) warding off, protecting against (counter-, anti-): °kara (antidote), °sedhati (ward-off). — (c) putting against, setting off in a comparison (counter-, rival): °puggala (one's equal), °purisa (rival), °bala (adequate), °bimba (counterpart), °bhāga (id.); °malla (rival wrestler), °sama, °sāsana, °sūra, °seṭṭha; — (d) close contact (against, be-): °kujjita (covered), °gādha, °channa ("be-deckt") °vijjhana. — (2) in return, in exchange (in revenge) °akkosati, °āneti, °katheti, °karoti, °kūṭa[1], °kkamati, °khamāpeti, °gāti (sing in response), °gīta, °daṇḍa (retribution), °dadāti, °dāna, °nivāsana, °paṇṇa (in reply), °pasaŋsati, °piṇḍa, °pucchati (ask in return), °māreti (kill in revenge), °bhaṇḍa (goods in exchange), °bhaṇḍati (abuse in return) °rodana, °roseti, °vera (revenge), °sammodeti, °sātheyya. — (3) (temporal) again, a second time (re-): °dasseti (re-appear), °nijjhatta, °nivattati, °pavesati, °pākatika (re-stored), °bujjhati, °vinicchinati, °sañjīvita (re-suscitated), °sandhi (re-incarnation), °sammajjati.— (4) away from, back to (esp. in compn paṭivi°): °kuṭati (shrink back), °ghāta (repulsion), °dhāvati, °neti, °paṇāmeti (send away), °bandhati (hold back), °bāhati (id.), °vijacchati, °vineti, °vinodeti (drive out), °virata, °saŋharati, °sallīna, °sutta, °sumbhita. — II. (applied, in reflexive sense): (1) to, on to, up to, towards, at-: °oloketi (look at), °gijjha (hankering after) °ggaha, °jānāti °pūjeti, °peseti (send out to), °baddha (bound to), °bhaya, °yatta, °rūpa, °laddha, °labhati (at-tain), °lābha, °lobheti, °sāmeti, °sevati (go after), °ssata. (2) together (con-, com-), esp. combd with °saŋ°; °saŋyujati; °passaddha, °maṇḍita, °sankharoti, °santhāra. — (3) asunder, apart ("up"): °kopeti (shake up), °viŋsa (part), °vibhatta (divided up). (4) secondary, complementary, by-, sham (developed out of meaning I. 1 c.): °nāsikā (a false nose), °sīsaka (sham top knot); esp. freq. in redupl. (iterative) cpds., like anga-paccanga (limb & by-limb, i. e. all kinds of limbs), vata-paṭivatta (duties & secondary duties, all duties). In the latter application paṭi resembles the use of ā, which is more frequent (see ā[3]). — III. The opposite of paṭi in directional meaning is anu, with which it is freq. combd either (a) in neg. contrast or (b) in positive emphasis, e. g. (a) anuvātaŋ paṭivātaŋ with and against the wind; anuloma+paṭiloma with and against the grain; °sotaŋ w. & against the stream; (b) anumasati paṭimasati to touch cloesly (lit. up & down). — *Note.* The spelling pati for paṭi occurs frequently without discrimination; it is established in the combn with **sthā** (as patiṭṭhāti, patiṭṭhita etc.). All cases are enumd under the respective form of paṭi°, with the exception of patiṭṭh°.

Paṭi-āneti [paṭi+ā+**nī**] to lead or bring back, in duppaṭi-ānaya difficult to bring back J IV.43.

Paṭi-orohati [paṭi+ava+**ruh**] to descend from DA I.251 (°itvā).

Paṭikankhati [paṭi+kānkṣ] to wish for, long for S I.227. adj. °kankhin M I.21. See also pāṭikankhin.

Paṭikacca (indecl.) [so read for °gacca as given at all passages mentioned, see Trenckner Miln p. 421, & Geiger *Pr.* § 38[1]. — ger. fr. paṭikaroti (q.v.), cp. Sk. pratīkāra in same meaning "caution, remedy"] 1. previously (lit. as cautioned) Vin IV.44; Miln 48 (v. l. °kacca) usually as paṭigacc' eva, e.g. Vin I.342; D II.118. — (2) providing for (the future), preparing for, with caution, cautiously Vin II.256; S I.57; V.162; A II.25; D II.144; Th 1, 547; J III.208; IV.166 (in expln of paṭikata & paṭikaroti); V.235.

Paṭikaṇṭaka [paṭi+kantaka[4]] an enemy, adversary, robber, highwayman J I.186; II.239; DhA III.456 (v. l. °kaṇḍaka).

Paṭikata [pp. of paṭikaroti] "done against," i. e. provided or guarded against J IV.166.

Paṭikatheti [paṭi+katheti] to answer, reply J VI.224; DA I.263.

Paṭikampati [paṭi+kampati] to shake; pret. paccakampittha J V.340.

Paṭikamma (nt.) [paṭi+kamma, cp. paṭikaroti] redress, atonement A I.21 (sa° & a° āpatti) Miln 28; DA I.96.

Paṭikara [fr. paṭi+**kṛ**] counteracting; requital, compensation Vin IV.218 (a°); D I.137 (ovāda° giving advice or providing for ? v. l. pari°); III.154.

Paṭikaroti [paṭi+karoti) 1. to redress, repair, make amends for a sin, expiate (āpattiŋ) Vin I.98, 164; II.259; IV.19; S II.128=205; A V.324; DhA I.54. — 2. to act against, provide for, beware, be cautious J IV.166. — 3. to imitate J II.406. — ger. paṭikacca (q. v.). — pp. paṭikata (q. v.).

Paṭikassana (nt.) [paṭi+**kṛṣ**] drawing back, in phrase mūlāya p. "throwing back to the beginning, causing to begin over & over again" Vin II.7, 162; A I.99.

Paṭikassati [paṭi+kassati] to draw back, remove, throw back Vin I.320 (mūlāya); II.7 (id.).

Paṭikā (f.) [Sk. paṭikā dial. fr. paṭa cloth] a (white) woollen cloth (: uṇṇāmayo set' attharako DA I.86) D I.7; A I.137, 181; III.50; IV.94, 231, 394; Dāvs V.36. See also paṭiya.

Paṭikāra [paṭi+**kṛ**] counteraction, remedy, requital Sdhp 201, 498; usually neg. app° adj. not making good or which cannot be made good, which cannot be helped Vin IV.218 (=anosārita p. 219); PvA 274 (maraṇa) Cp. foll.

Paṭikārika (adj.) [fr. preceding] of the nature of an amendment; app° not making amends, not making good J V.418.

Paṭikiṭṭha inferior, low, vile A I.286=Dh I.144; in meaning "miserable" at DhA II.3 is perhaps better to be read with v. l. as pakkiliṭṭha, or should it be **paṭikuṭṭha ?**

Paṭikibbisa (nt.) [paṭi+kibbisa] wrong doing in return, retaliation J III.135.

Paṭikirati [paṭi+kirati] to strew about, to sprawl Pv IV.10[8] (uttānā paṭikirāma=vikirīyamān'angā viya vattāma PvA 271).

Paṭikiliṭṭha (adj.) [paṭi+kiliṭṭha] very miserable PvA 268 (v. l.); and perhaps at DhA II.3 for paṭikiṭṭha (q. v.).

Paṭikujjati[paṭi+**kubj**, see kujja & cp. patikuṭati] to bend over, in or against, to cover over, to enclose D II.162; M I.30; A III.58. Caus. °eti J I.50; 69. — pp. **paṭikujjati** (q. v.).

Paṭikujjana (nt.) [fr. paṭi+**kubj**] covering, in °phalaka covering board, seat KhA 62 (vacca-kuṭiyā).

Paṭikujjita [pp. of paṭikujjeti] covered over, enclosed A I.141; Th I, 681; J I.50, 69; V.266; Pv I.10[13] (=upari pidahita PvA 52); DhsA 349.

Paṭikujjhati [paṭi+**krudh**] to be angry in return S I.162= Th I, 442.

Paṭikuṭati [paṭi+**kuṭ** as in kuṭila, cp. **kuc** & paṭikujjati] to turn in or over, to bend, cramp or get cramped; fig. to shrink from, to refuse A IV.47 sq. (v. l. °kujjati); Miln 297 (pati°; cp. Miln trsl[n] II.156); Vism 347 (v. l. BB; T. °kuṭṭati); DhA I.71; II.42. — Caus. paṭikoṭṭeti (q. v.). — pp. paṭikuṭita (q. v.). See also paṭilīyati.

Paṭikuṭita [pp. of paṭikuṭati] bent back, turned over (?) Vin II.195 (reading uncertain, vv. ll. paṭikuṭṭiya & paṭikuṭiya).

Paṭikuṭṭha [pp. of paṭi+**kruś**, see paṭikkosati & cp. BSk. pratikruṣṭa poor Divy 500] scolded, scorned, defamed, blameworthy, miserable, vile Vin I.317; PvA 268 (v. l. paṭikiliṭṭha); as neg. app° blameless, faultless S III.71-73; A IV.246; Kvu 141, 341. See also paṭikiṭṭha.

Paṭikuṇika (adj.) [for °kuṭita ?] bent, crooked PvA 123 (v. l. kuṇita & kuṇḍita).

Paṭikuṇṭhita [cp. kuṇṭhita]=pariguṇṭhita (q. v.); covered, surrounded J VI.89.

Paṭikuttaka [or uncertain etym.; paṭi+kuttaka ?] a sort of bird J VI.538.

Paṭikubbara [paṭi+kubbara] the part of the carriage-pole nearest to the horse(?) A IV.191.

Paṭikulyatā (f.) [fr. paṭikūla, perhaps better to write paṭikkulyatā] reluctance, loathsomeness M I.30; A V.64. Other forms are paṭikūlatā, pāṭikkūlyatā, & pāṭikulyā (q. v.).

Paṭikūṭa (nt.) [paṭi+kūṭa[1]] cheating in return J II.183.

Paṭikūlatā (f.) [fr. paṭikkūla] disgustiveness Vism 343 sq.

Paṭikelanā see parikelanā; i. e. counter-playing Dh I.286.

Paṭikoṭṭeti [paṭi+koṭṭeti as Caus. of kuṭati] to bend away, to make refrain from M I.115; S II.265 (cp. id. p. A IV.47 with trs. °kuṭati & v. l. °kujjati which may be a legitimate variant). The T. prints pati°.

Paṭikopeti [paṭi+kopeti] to shake, disturb, break (fig.) J V.173 (uposathaŋ).

Paṭikkanta [pp. of paṭikkamati] gone back from (-°), returned (opp. abhi°) D I.70 (abhikkanta+); A II.104, 106 sq., 210; Pv IV.1[43] (cp. PvA 240); DA I.183 (=nivattana); VvA 6 (opp. abhi°) PvA 11 (piṇḍapāta°), 16 (id.). For opp. of paṭikkanta in conn. with piṇḍāya see paviṭṭha.

Paṭikkantaka [fr. last] one who has come or is coming back DhA I.307.

Paṭikkama [fr. paṭi+**kram**] going back Pv IV.1[2] (abhikkama+ "going forward and backward"; cp. PvA 219).

Paṭikkamati [paṭi+**kram**] to step backwards, to return (opp. abhi°) Vin II.110, 208; M I.78; S I.200, 226; II.282; Sn 388 (ger. °kkamma=nivattitvā SnA 374); SnA 53. — Caus. paṭikkamāpeti to cause to retreat J I.214 Miln 121. — pp. paṭikkanta (q. v.).

Paṭikkamana (nt.) [fr. paṭikkamati] returning, retiring, going back Dh I.95; in °sālā meaning "a hall with seats of distinction" SnA 53.

Paṭikkūla (adj.) [paṭi+kūla] lit. against the slope; averse, objectionable, contrary, disagreeable Vin I.58 (°kūla); D III.112, 113; M I.341 (dukkha°); S IV.172 (id.); J I.393; VvA 92 (K.); PvA 77; VbhA 250 sq. —app° without objection, pleasant, agreeable Vv 53[2] (K.); Vism 70 (k). — nt. °ŋ loathsomeness, impurity VvA 232. See also abstr. pāṭikkūlyatā (paṭi°).

-gāhitā as neg. a° "refraining from contradiction" (*Dhs trsl*[n]) Pug 24 (k.); Dhs 1327 (k.). -manasikāra realisation of the impurity of the body DhA II.87 (°kkula); VbhA 251. -saññā (āhāre) the consciousness of the impurity of material food D III.289, 291; S V.132; A IV.49; adj. °saññin S I.227; V.119, 317; A III.169.

Paṭikkosati [paṭi+**kruś**] to blame, reject, revile, scorn Vin I.115; II.93; M III.29; D I.53 (=paṭibāhati DA I.160); S IV.118 (+apavadati); Sn 878; Dh 164; J IV.163; Miln 131, 256; DhA III.194 (opp. abhinandati). — pp. paṭikuṭṭha (q. v.).

Paṭikkosana (nt.) & °ā (f.) [fr. paṭikkosati] protest Vin I.321; II.102 (a°).

Paṭikkhati [paṭi+**īks**] to look forward to, to expect Sn 697 (paṭikkhaŋ sic ppr.=āgamayanā SnA 490).

Paṭikkhitta [pp. of paṭikkhipati] refused, rejected D I.142; M I.78, 93; A I.296; II.206; J II.436; Nett 161, 185 sq.; DhA II.71.

Paṭikkhipati [paṭi+khipati] to reject, refuse, object to, oppose J I.67; IV.105; Miln 295; DA I.290; DhA I.45; II.75; PvA 73, 114, 151, 214 (aor. °khipi=vāresi). —appaṭikkhippa (grd.) not to be rejected J II.370. — Contrasted to samādiyati Vism 62, 64 & passim.

Paṭikkhepa [fr. paṭi+**kṣip**] opposition, negation, contrary SnA 228 for "na"), 502; PvA 189 (°vacana the opp. expression). °to (abl.) in opposition or contrast to PvA 24.

Paṭikhamāpita [pp. of paṭi+khamāpeti, Caus. of khamati] forgiven DhA II.78.

Paṭigacca see paṭikacca.

Paṭigacchati to give up, leave behind J IV.482 (gehaŋ); cp. paccagū.

Paṭigandhiya only as neg. appaṭi° (q. v.).

Paṭigāthā (f.) [paṭi+gāthā] counter-stanza, response SnA 340. Cp. paccanīka-gāthā.

Paṭigādha [paṭi+gādha[2]] a firm stand or foothold A III.297 sq.; Pug 72=Kvu 389.

Paṭigāyati (°gāti) [paṭi+gāyati] to sing in response, to reply by a song J IV.395 (imper. °gāhi).

Paṭigijjha (adj.) [paṭi+gijjha, a doublet of giddha, see gijjha[2]] greedy; hankering after Sn 675 (SnA 482 reads °giddha and expl[ns] by mahāgijjha).

Paṭigīta (nt.) [paṭi+gīta] a song in response, counter song J IV.393.

Paṭiguhati (°gūhati) [paṭi+gūhati] to concert, keep back Cp. I.9[18].

Paṭiggaṇhanaka (adj.-n.) [paṭiggaṇhana (=paṭiggahaṇa) +ka] receiving, receiver PvA 175.

Paṭiggaṇhāti (paṭigaṇhāti) [paṭi+gaṇhāti] to receive, accept, take (up) D I.110 (vatthaŋ), 142; Vin I.200; II.109, 116 (a sewing-needle); S IV.326 (jātarūpa-rajataŋ); Sn 479, 689, 690; Dh 220; J I.56, 65; DA I.236; PvA 47. In special phrase accayaŋ paṭiggaṇhāti to accept (the confession of) a sin, to pardon a sin Vin II.192; D I.85; M I.438; J V.379. — pp. paṭiggahita (q. v.). — Caus. °ggaheti Vin II.213; M I.32.

Paṭiggaha [fr. paṭigganhāti] 1. receiving, acceptance; one who receives, recipient J I.146; II.9; VI.474; Pv III.1[11]. — 2. friendly reception J VI.526. — 3. receptacle (for water etc.) Vin II.115, 213 (udaka°). — 4. a thimble Vin II.116.

Paṭiggahaṇa (nt.) [fr. paṭigganhāti] acceptance, receiving, taking M III.34; S V.472; SnA 341. — accaya° acceptance of a sin, i. e. pardon, absolution J V.380.

Paṭiggahita [pp. of paṭigganhāti] received, got, accepted, appropriated, taken Vin I.206, 214; J VI.231. — As appaṭiggahitaka (nt.) "that which is not received" at Vin IV.90.

Paṭiggahītar [n. ag. of paṭigganhāti] one who receives, recipient D I.89.

Paṭiggāha see patiṭṭhāha.

Paṭiggāhaka (adj.-n.) [fr. paṭigganhāti] receiving, accepting; one who receives, recipient Vin II.213; D I.138; A I.161; II.80 sq.; III.42, 336; J I.56; PvA 7, 128, 175 (opp. dāyaka); VvA 195; Sdhp 268.

Paṭiggāhaṇa (nt.) [fr. paṭigganhāti] reception, taking in J VI.527.

Paṭigha (m. & nt.) [paṭi+gha, adj. suffix of **ghan**=**han**, lit. striking against] 1. (ethically) repulsion, repugnance, anger D I.25, 34; III.254, 282; S I.13; IV.71, 195, 205, 208 sq.; V.315; A I.3, 87, 200; Sn 371, 536; Dhs 1060; Miln 44; DA I.22. — 2. (psychologically) sensory reaction D III.224, 253, 262; S I.165, 186; A I.41, 267; II.184; Dhs 265, 501, 513, 579; VbhA 19. See on term *Dhs trsl*[n] 72, 204, 276 and passim. —appaṭigha see separately s. v. *Note.* How shall we read paṭighaṭṭha nānighaŋso at DhsA 308? (paṭigha-ṭṭhāna-nighaŋso, or paṭighaṭṭana-nighaŋso?)

Paṭighavant (adj.) [fr. paṭigha] full of repugnance, showing anger S IV.208, 209.

Paṭighāta [paṭi+ghāta, of same root as paṭigha] 1. (lit.) warding off, staying, repulsion, beating off D III.130; M I.10; A I.98; IV.106 sq.; J I.344; Vism 31 (=paṭihanana); Miln 121; DhA II.8; PvA 33. — 2. (psych.) resentment Dhs 1060, cp. *Dhs trsl.* 282.

Paṭighosa [paṭi+ghosa] echo Vism 554.

Paṭicamma in °gataŋ sallaŋ at J VI.78 to be expl[d] not with C. as from paṭi+camati (**cam** to wash, cp. ācamati), which does not agree with the actual meaning, but according to Kern, Toev. II.29, s. v. as elliptical for paṭibhinna-camma, i. e. piercing the skin so as to go right through (to the opp. side) which falls in with the C. expl[n] "vāmapassena pavisitvā dakkhiṇapassena viniggatan ti."

Paṭicaya & (paṭiccaya) [paṭi+caya] adding to, heaping up, accumulation, increase Vin II.74; III.158 (pati°); S III.169; A III.376 sq. (v. l. pati°); IV.355; V.336 sq.; Th 1, 642; Ud 35 (pati°); Miln 138.

Paṭicarati [paṭi+carati) 1. to wander about, to deal with Miln 94. — 2. to go about or evade (a question), to obscure a matter of discussion, in phrase aññena aññaŋ p. "to be saved by another in another way," or to from one (thing) to another, i. e. to receive a diff, answer to what is asked D I.94; Vin IV.35; M I.96, 250, 442; A IV.168 (v. l. paṭivadati); expl[d] at DA I.264 by ajjhottharati paṭicchādeti "to cover over," i. e. to conceal (a question). See on expression *Dialogues* I.116.

Paṭicaleti [Caus. of paṭicalati] to nudge J V.434.

Paṭicāra [fr. paṭi+**car**] intercourse, visit, dealing with Miln 94.

Paṭicodana (nt.) [abstr. fr. paṭicodeti] rebuking, scolding (back) DhsA 393.

Paṭicodeti [paṭi+codeti] to blame, reprove M I.72; Vin IV.217; Ud 45.

Paṭicca [ger. of pacceti, paṭi+i; cp. BSk. pratītya] grounded on, on account of, concerning, because (with acc.) M I.265 (etaŋ on these grounds); S III.93=It 89 (atthavasaŋ); J II.386 (=abhisandhāya); Sn 680, 784, 872, 1046; SnA 357; DhA I.4; PvA 64 (maraṇaŋ), 164, 181 (kammaŋ), 207 (anuddayaŋ). See also foll. -vinīta trained to look for causality M III.19.

Paṭicca-samuppanna [p.+samuppana] evolved by reason of the law of causation D III.275; M I.500; S II.26; A V.187; Ps I.51 sq., 76 sq.; Vbh 340, 362. Cp. BSk. pratitya samutpanna MVastu III.61.

Paṭicca-samuppāda [p.+samuppāda, BSk. prātītyasamutpāda, e. g. Divy 300, 547] "arising on the grounds of (a preceding cause)" happening by way of cause, working of cause & effect, causal chain of causation; causal genesis, dependent origination, theory of the twelve causes. — See on this Mrs. Rh. D. in *Buddhism* 90 f., *Ency. Rel. & Ethics*, s. v. & *KS* II., preface. *Cpd.* p. 260 sq. with diagram of the "Wheel of Life"; *Pts. of Controversy*, 390 f. — The *general* formula runs thus: Imasmiŋ sati, idaŋ hoti, imass' uppādā, idaŋ uppajjati; imasmiŋ asati, idaŋ na hoti; imassa nirodhā, idaŋ nirujjhati. This being, that becomes; from the arising of this, that arises; this not becoming, that does not become: from the ceasing of this, that ceases M II.32; S II.28 etc. The term usually occurs applied to dukkha in a famous formula which expresses the Buddhist doctrine of evolution, the respective stages of which are conditioned by a preceding cause & constitute themselves the cause of resulting effect, as working out the next state of the evolving (shall we say) "individual" or "being," in short the bearer of evolution. The respective links in this chain which to study & learn is the first condition for a "Buddhist" to an understanding of life, and the cause of life, and which to know forward and backward (anuloma-paṭilomaŋ manas' âkāsi Vin I.1) is indispensable for the student, are as follows. The root of all, primary cause of all existence, is avijjā ignorance; this produces sankhārā: karma, dimly conscious elements, capacity of impression or predisposition (will, action, Cpd.; synergies Mrs. Rh. D.), which in their turn give rise to viññāṇa thinking substance (consciousness, Cpd.; cognition Mrs. Rh. D.), then follow in succession the foll. stages: nāmarūpa individuality (mind & body, animated organism Cpd.; name & form Mrs. Rh. D.), saḷāyatana the senses (6 organs of sense Cpd.; the sixfold sphere Mrs. Rh. D.), phassa contact, vedanā feeling, taṇhā thirst for life (craving), upādāna clinging to existence or attachment (dominant idea Cpd.; grasping Mrs. Rh. D.), bhava (action or character Cpd.; renewed existence Mrs. Rh. D.), jāti birth (rebirth conception Cpd.), jarāmaraṇa (+soka-parideva-dukkha-domanass' ûpayāsā) old age & death (+tribulation, grief, sorrow, distress & despair). The BSk. form is pratītya-samutpāda, e. g. at Divy 300, 547.

The Paṭicca-samuppāda is also called the Nidāna ("basis," or "ground," i. e. cause) doctrine, or the Paccay' ākāra ("related-condition"), and is referred to in the *Suttas* as Ariya-ñāya ("the noble method or system"). The term paccay' ākāra is late and occurs only in Abhidhamma-literature. — The oldest account is found in the Mahāpadāna Suttanta of the Dīgha Nikāya (D II.30 sq.; cp. *Dial.* II.24 sq.), where 10 items form the constituents of the chain, and are given in backward order, reasoning from the appearance of dukkha in this world of old age and death towards the *original* cause of it in viññāṇa. The same chain occurs again at S II.104 sq. — A later development shows 12 links, viz. avijjā and sankhārā added to precede viññāṇa (as above). Thus at S II.5 sq. — A detailed exposition of the P.-s. in Abhidhamma literature is the exegesis given by Bdhgh at Vism XVII. (pp. 517-586, under the title of Paññā-bhūmi-niddesa), and at VbhA 130-213 under the title of Paccayākāra-vibhanga. — Some passages selected for ref.: Vin I.1 sq.; M I.190, 257; S I.136; II.1 sq., 26 sq., 42 sq., 70, 92 sq., 113 sq.; A I.177; V.184; Sn. 653; Ud 1 sq.; Ps I.50 sq.; 144; Nett 22, 24, 32, 64 sq.; DA I.125, 126.

-kusala skilled in the (knowledge of the) chain of causation M III.63; Nd[1] 171; f. abstr. °kusalatā D III.212.

Paṭicchaka (adj.) [fr. paṭicchati) receiving J VI.287.

Paṭicchati [paṭi + icchati of iṣ²; cp. BSk. pratīcchati Divy 238 and sampaṭicchati] to accept, receive, take A III.243 (udakaŋ); Vin IV.18; Th 2, 421; J I.233; II.432; III.171; IV.137; V.197; DhA III.271. — pp. paṭicchita (q. v.). Caus. II. paṭicchāpeti to entrust, dedicate, give J I.64, 143, 159, 383, 506; II.133; PvA 81.

Paṭicchanna [pp. of paṭicchādeti] covered, concealed, hidden Vin II.40; A I.282; Sn 126, 194; Pv I.10² (kesehi = paṭicchādita PvA 48); II.10² (kesehi); DA I.276, 228; SnA 155; KhA 53; VbhA 94 (°dukkha); PvA 43, 103. -appaṭicchanna unconcealed, open, unrestrained Vin II.38; J I.207.

-kammanta of secret doing, one who acts underhand or conceals his actions A II.239; Sn 127.

Paṭicchavi in appaṭicchavi at Pv II.1¹³ read with v. l. as sampatitacchavi.

Paṭicchāda [fr. paṭi + chad] 1. covering, clothes, clothing Pv II.1¹⁶ (= vattha PvA 76). — 2. deceiving, hiding; concealment, deception Sn 232.

Paṭicchādaka = prec. DhsA 51.

Paṭicchādana (nt.) [fr. paṭicchādeti] covering, hiding, concealment M I.10; A III.352; Vbh 357 = SnA 180.

Paṭicchādaniya (nt.) [fr. paṭicchādeti] the flavour of meat, flavouring, meat broth or gravy Vin I.206, 217; Miln 291.

Paṭicchādita [pp. of paṭicchādeti, cp. paṭicchanna] covered, concealed, hidden J VI.23 (= paṭisanthata) PvA 48.

Paṭicchādī (f.) [fr. paṭicchādeti] 1. covering, protection Vin II.122. — 2. antidote, remedy, medicine (or a cloth to protect the itch) Vin I.296; IV.171.

Paṭicchādeti [paṭi + chādeti, Caus. of chad] 1. to cover over, conceal, hide S I.70, 161; DA I.264; VvA 65 (dhanaŋ); KhA 191; PvA 76, 88, 142 (kesehi), 194 (= parigūhati). — 2. to clothe oneself Vin I.46. — 3. to dress (surgically), to treat (a wound) M I.220. — 4. to conceal or evade (a question) DA I.264. — pp. paṭicchādita & paṭicchanna (q. v.).

Paṭicchita [pp. of paṭicchati] accepted, taken up Sn 803 (pl. °tāse, cp. Nd[1] 113 & SnA 531).

Paṭijaggaka (adj.) [fr. paṭijaggati] fostering, nursing, taking care of J V.111.

Paṭijaggati [paṭi + jaggati, cp. BSk. pratijāgarti Divy 124, 306] lit. to watch over, i. e. to nourish, tend, feed, look after, take care of, nurse Dh 157; J I.235, 375; II.132, 200, 436; Vism 119; DhA I.8, 45, 99, 392; IV.154; PvA 10, 43. — pp. paṭijaggita (q. v.). — Caus. °jaggāpeti.

Paṭijaggana (nt.) [fr. paṭijaggati] rearing, fostering, tending; attention, care J I.148; Miln 366; DhA I.27; II.96.

Paṭijagganaka (adj.) [fr. paṭijaggana] to be reared or brought up J VI.73 (putta).

Paṭijaggāpeti [Caus. II. of paṭijaggati] to make look after or tend Vism 74.

Paṭijaggita [pp. of paṭijaggati] reared, cared for, looked after, brought up J V.274, 331.

Paṭijaggiya (adj.) [grd. of paṭijaggati] to be nursed DhA I.319.

Paṭijānāti [paṭi + jānāti] to acknowledge, agree to, approve, promise, consent D I.3, 192; S I.68, 172; II.170; III.28; V 204, 423; Sn 76, 135, 555, 601, 1148; J I.169; DhA I.21; PvA 223 (pot. paṭiññeyya), 226 (id.), 241; ger. paṭiññāya Vin II.83 (a°). — pp. paṭiññāta (q. v.).

Paṭijīvan (-°) in phrase jīva-paṭijīvaŋ at J II.15 is to be taken as a sort of redupl. cpd. of jīva, the imper. of jīvati "live," as greeting. We might translate "the greeting with 'jīva' and reciprocating it."

Paṭiñña (adj.) [= paṭiññā] acknowledged; making belief, quâsi-; in phrase samaṇa° a quâsi-Samaṇa, pretending to be a Samaṇa A I.126; II.239; cp. Sakyaputtiya° S II.272; sacca° J IV.384, 463; V.499.

Paṭiññā (f.) [fr. paṭi + jñā; cp. later Sk. pratijñā] acknowledgment, agreement, promise, vow, consent, permission D III.254; J I.153; Pv IV.1¹², 1⁴⁴; Miln 7; DhA II.93; PvA 76, 123; SnA 397, 539.—patiññaŋ moceti to keep one's promise DhA I.93.

Paṭiññāta [pp. of patijānāti] agreed, acknowledged, promised Vin II.83, 102; D I.88; A I.99; IV.144; PvA 55.

Paṭita (adj.) satisfied, happy DhA II.269 (°ācāra)

Paṭitiṭṭhati (paṭiṭṭhahati) etc. see pati°.

Paṭititthа (nt.) [paṭi + tittha] opposite bank (of a river) J V.443.

Paṭitthambhati [paṭi + thambhati] to stand firm (against) Miln 372.

Paṭidaṇḍa [paṭi + daṇḍa] retribution Dh 133, cp. DhA III.57, 58.

Paṭidadāti [paṭi + dadāti] to give back, to restore J I.177; IV.411 (°diyyare); PvA 276 (ger. °datvā).

Paṭidasseti [paṭi + dasseti] to show oneself or to appear again, to reappear Pv III.2²⁷.

Paṭidāna (nt.) [paṭi + dāna] reward, restitution, gift PvA 80.

Paṭidisā (f.) [paṭi + disā] an opposite (counter-) point of the compass, opposite quarter D III.176 (disā ca p. ca vidisā ca).

Paṭidissati [paṭi + dissati; usually spelt pati°] to be seen, to appear J III.47 = PvA 281; Sn 123; J IV.139; SnA 172.

Paṭidukkhāpanatā (f.) [paṭi + abstr. of dukkhāpeti, Caus. -Denom. fr. dukkha] the fact of being afflicted again with suffering Miln 180.

Paṭideseti [paṭi + deseti] to confess Vin II.102. See also pāṭidesanīya.

Paṭidhāvati [paṭi + dhāvati] to run back to (acc.) M I.265 ≈ S II.26 (pubbantaŋ; opp. aparantaŋ ādhāvati M, upadhāvati S); Sdhp 167.

Paṭinandati [paṭi + nandati] to accept gladly, to greet in return S I.189.

Paṭinandita [pp. of paṭi + **nand**] rejoicing or rejoiced; greeted, welcomed Sn 452 (pati°); J VI.14, 412.

Paṭināsikā (f.) [paṭi + nāsikā] a false nose J I.455, 457.

Paṭinijjhatta (adj.) [paṭi + nijjhatta] appeased again J VI.414.

Paṭiniddesa [paṭi + niddesa] coming back upon a subject Nett 5.

Paṭinivattati [paṭi + nivattati] to turn back again Vin I.216; J I.225; Miln 120, 152 (of disease), 246; PvA 100, 126. — Caus. °nivatteti to make turn back PvA 141; C. on A III.28 (see paccāsāreti).

Paṭinivāsana (nt.) [paṭi + nivāsana^1] a dress given in return Vin I.46 = II.223.

Paṭinissagga [paṭi + nissagga of nissajjati, nis + **sṛj**, Cp. BSk. pratinisarga AvŚ II.118, pratiniḥsarga ib. II.194; MVastu II.549; pratinissagga MVastu III.314, 322] giving up, forsaking; rejection, renunciation Vin III.173; S III.13; V.311, 421 sq.; A I.100, 299; IV.148, 350; Ps I.194 (two p., viz. pariccāga° and pakkhandana°); Pug 19, 21, 22. — ādāna° S V.24; A V.233, 253 sq.; upadhi° It 46, 62; sabbûpadhi° S I.136; III.133; V.226; A I.49; V.8, 100, 320 sq.; °ânupassanā Ps II.44 sq.; °ânupassin M III.83; S IV.211; V.329; A IV.88, 146 sq.; V.112, 359.

Paṭinissaggin (adj.) [fr. paṭinissagga] giving up, renouncing, or being given up, to be renounced, only in cpd. duppaṭi° (sup°) hard (easy) to renounce D III.45; M I.96; A III.335; V.150.

Paṭinissajjati [paṭi + nissajjati, cp. BSk. pratinisṛjati AvŚ II.190] to give up, renounce, forsake Vin III.173 sq.; IV.294; S II.110; A V.191 sq. — ger. paṭinissajja S I.179; A IV.374 sq.; Sn 745, 946 (cp. Nd^1 430). — pp. paṭinissaṭṭha (q. v.).

Paṭinissaṭṭha [pp. of paṭinissajjati, BSk. pratiniḥsṛṣṭa Divy 44 and °ṇisṛṣṭa Divy 275] given up, forsaken (act. & pass.), renouncing or having renounced Vin III.95; IV.27, 137; M I.37; S II.283; A II.41; It 49; Nd^1 430, 431 (vanta pahīna p.); PvA 256.

Paṭinissarati [paṭi + nissarati] to depart, escape from, to be freed from Nett 113 (= niyyāti vimuccati C.).

Paṭineti [paṭi + neti] to lead back to (acc.) Vv 52^{17}; Th 2, 419; Pv II.12^{21} (imper. °nayāhi); PvA 145, 160.

Paṭipakkha (adj.-n.) [paṭi + pakkha] opposed, opposite; (m.) an enemy, opponent (cp. pratipakṣa obstacle Divy 352) Nd^1 397; J I.4, 224; Nett 3, 112, 124; Vism 4; DhA I.92; SnA 12, 21, 65, 168, 234, 257, 545; PvA 98; DhsA 164; Sdhp 211, 452.

Paṭipakkhika (adj.) [fr. paṭipakkha] opposed, inimical Sdhp 216.

Paṭipajjati [paṭi + **pad**, cp. BSk. pratipadyate] to enter upon (a path), to go along, follow out (a way or plan), to go by; fig. to take a line of action, to follow a method, to be intent on, to regulate one's life D I.70 (saŋvarāya). 175 (tathattāya); S II.98 (kantāramaggaŋ); IV.63 (dhammass' anudhammaŋ); V.346 (id.); IV.194 (maggaŋ); A I.36 (dhammânudhammaŋ); II.4; Sn 317, 323, 706, 815, 1129 (cp. Nd^2 384); Dh 274 (maggaŋ); Pug 20 (saŋvarāya); PvA 43 (maggaŋ), 44 (ummaggaŋ), 196 (dhanaŋ); Sdhp 30. — 3rd sg. aor. paccāpādi J IV.314. — ger. pajjitabba to be followed PvA 126 (vidhi), 131 (id.), 281. — pp. paṭipanna (q. v.). — Caus. paṭipādeti (q. v.).

Paṭipajjana (nt.) [fr. paṭipajjati] a way or plan to be followed, procedure, in °vidhi method, line of action PvA 131 (v. l. BB), 133.

Paṭipaṇāmeti [paṭi + pa + Caus. of **nam**] to make turn back, to send back, ward off, chase away M I.327 (siriŋ); S IV.152 (ābādhaŋ); Miln 17 (sakaṭāni).

Paṭipaṇṇa (nt.) [paṭi + paṇṇa] a letter in return, a written reply J I.409.

Paṭipatti (f.) [fr. paṭi + **pad**] "way," method, conduct, practice, performance, behaviour, example A I.69; V.126 (dhammânudhamma°), 136; Ps II.15; Nd^1 143; Nd^2 s. v.; Miln 131, 242; DhA II.30; DhA IV.34 (sammā° good or proper behaviour); PvA 16 (parahita°), 54, 67; DA I.270; Sdhp 28, 29, 37, 40, 213, 521.

Paṭipatha [paṭi + patha] a confronting road, opposite way Vin II.193 (°ŋ gacchati to go to meet); III.131; IV.268; Miln 9; Vism 92; DhA II.88.

Paṭipadā (f.) [fr. paṭi + **pad**] means of reaching a goal or destination, path, way, means, method, mode of progress (cp. *Dhs. trsl*^{n} 53, 82, 92, 143), course, practice (cp. BSk. pratipad in meaning of pratipatti "line of conduct" AvŚ II.140 with note) D I.54 (dvatti p.), 249 (way to); S II.81 (nirodhasāruppa-gāminī p.); IV.251 (bhaddikā), 330 (majjhimā) V.304 (sabbattha-gāminī), 361 (udaya-gāminī sotāpatti°), 421; D III.288 (ñāṇa-dassana-visuddhi°); A I.113, 168 (puñña°) II.76, 79, 152 (akkhamā); Vbh 99, 104 sq., 211 sq., 229 sq., 331 sq. — In pregnant sense *The* path (of the Buddha), leading to the destruction of all ill & to the bliss of Nibbāna (see specified under magga, ariyamagga, sacca), thus a quâsi synonym of magga with which freq. comb^d (e.g. D I.156) Vin I.10; D I.157; III.219 (anuttariya); M II.11; III.251, 284; S I.24 (daḷhā yāya dhīrā pamuccanti); A I.295 sq. (āgāḷhā nijjhāmā majjhimā); Sn 714 (cp. SnA 497), 921; Ps II.147 (majjhimā); Nett 95 sq.; Pug 15, 68; VvA 84 (°sankhāta ariyamagga). Specified in various ways as follows: āsava-nirodha-gāminī p. D I.84; dukkha-nirodha-g°. D I.84, 189; III.136; S V.426 sq.; A I.177; Ps I.86, 119; Dhs 1057; loka-nirodha-g° A II.23; It 121; with the epithets sammā° anuloma° apaccanīka° anvattha° dhammânudhamma° Nd^1 32, 143, 365; Nd^2 384 etc. (see detail under sammā°). — There are several groups of 4 paṭipadā mentioned, viz. (a) dukkhā dandhâbhiññā, sukhā & khippâbhiññā dandh° & khipp°, i. e. painful practice resulting in knowledge slowly acquired & quickly acquired, pleasant practice resulting in the same way D III.106; A II.149 sq., 154; V.63; SnA 497; (b) akkhamā, khamā, damā & samā p. i. e. want of endurance, endurance, self-control, equanimity.

Paṭipanna [pp. of paṭipajjati] (having) followed or following up, reaching, going along or by (i. e. practising), entering on, obtaining S II.69; IV.252; A I.120 (arahattāya); IV.292 sq. (id.), 372 sq.; It 81 (dhammânudhamma°); Sn 736; Dh 275 (maggaŋ); Vv 34^{23} (= maggaṭṭha one who has entered the path VvA 154) = Pv IV.3^{49}; Pug 63; Miln 17; DA I.26; PvA 78, 112 (maggaŋ), 130, 174 (sammā°), 242; (dhammiyaŋ paṭipadaŋ); DhA I.233 (magga° on the road, wandering).

Paṭipannaka (adj. n.) [fr. paṭipanna] one who has entered upon the Path (ariyamagga) Pug 13 (= maggaṭṭhaka, phalatthāya paṭipannattā p. nāma PugA 186); Miln 342, 344; Nett 50; DhsA 164. See also *Miln trsl.* II.231, 237.

Paṭiparivatteti [paṭi + p.] to turn back or round once more M I.133.

Paṭipaviṭṭha [pp. of paṭipavisati] gone inside again Sn 979.

Paṭipavisati [paṭi + pavisati] to go in(to) again; Caus. °paveseti to make go in again, to put back (inside) again Vin I.276. — pp. paṭipaviṭṭha (q. v.).

Paṭipasaŋsati [paṭi + pasaŋsati] to praise back or in return J II.439.

Paṭipaharati [paṭi + paharati] to strike in return DhA I.51.

Paṭipahiṇati [paṭi + pahiṇati] to send back (in return) DhA I.216.

Paṭipākatika (adj.) [paṭi + pākatika] restored, set right again, safe and sound J III.167 (= pākatika at PvA 66); IV.407; VI.372; PvA 123, 284.

Paṭipāṭi (f.) [paṭi + pāṭi] order, succession Vin I.248 (bhatta°); Vism 411 (khandha°); usually in abl. paṭipāṭiyā adv. successively, in succession, alongside of, in order Vism 343 = J V.253 (ghara° from house to house); ThA 80 (magga°); DhA I.156; II.89; III.361; SnA 23, 506; PvA 54; VvA 76, 137.

Paṭipāṭika (adj.) [fr. last] being in conformity with the (right) order ThA 41.

Paṭipādaka [fr. paṭi + **pad**] the supporter (of a bed) Vin I.48; II.208.

Paṭipādeti [Caus. of paṭipajjati, cp. BSk. pratipādayati in same meaning AvŚ I.262, 315] to impart, bring into, give to, offer, present M I.339; J V.453, 497; Pv II.8[1] (vittaŋ).

Paṭipiṇsati [paṭi + piŋsati] to beat against S II.98 (ure); J VI.87; Vism 504 (urāni).

Paṭipiṇḍa [paṭi + piṇḍa] alms in return J II.307; V.390 (piṇḍa° giving & taking of alms); Miln 370.

Paṭipīta in asuci° at A III.226 is not clear (v. l. °pīḷita perhaps to be preferred).

Paṭipīḷana (nt.) [fr. paṭipīḷeti] oppression Miln 313, 352.

Paṭipīḷita (adj.) [paṭi + pp. of **pīḍ**] pressed against, oppressed, hard pressed Miln 262, 354.

Paṭipuggala [paṭi + puggala] a person equal to another, compeer, match, rival M I.171 = Miln 235; S I.158; Sn 544; It 123 (natthi te paṭipuggala). — appaṭipuggala without a rival, unrivalled, without compare S I.158; III.86; Th 2, 185; J I.40; Miln 239 (cp. *Miln trsl.* II.43).

Paṭipuggalika (adj.) [fr. paṭipuggala] belonging to one's equal, individual Dhs 1044. Perhaps read pāṭi° (q. v.).

Paṭipucchati [paṭi + pucchati] to ask (in return), to put a question to, to inquire D I.60; M I.27; S III.2; Sn p. 92; J I.170; IV.194; PvA 32, 56, 81; A I.197; II.46; also neg. appaṭipucchā (abl. adv.) without inquiry Vin I.325.

Paṭipucchā (f.) [paṭi + pucchā] a question in return, inquiry; only °- (as abl.) by question, by inquiry, by means of question & answer in foll. cpds.: °karaṇīya Vin I.325; °vinīta A I.72; °vyākaraṇīya (pañha) D III.229.

Paṭipurisa [paṭi + purisa] a rival, opponent Nd[1] 172.

Paṭipūjana (nt.) or °ā (f.) [fr. paṭi + **pūj**] worship, reverence, honour Miln 241.

Paṭipūjeti [paṭi + pūjeti] to honour, worship, revere Sn 128; Pv I.1[3]; Miln 241.

Paṭipeseti [paṭi + peseti] to send out to PvA 20.

Paṭippaṇāmeti [paṭi + paṇāmeti] to bend (back), stretch out DhsA 324.

Paṭippassaddha [pp. of paṭippassambhati] allayed, calmed, quieted, subsided S IV.217, 294; V.272; A I.254; II.41; J III.37, 148; IV.430; Ps II.2; Pug 27; KhA 185; PvA 23, 245, 274. *Note.* The BSk. form is pratiprasrabdha Divy 265.

Paṭippassaddhi (f.) [fr. paṭippassaddha] subsidence, calming, allaying, quieting down, repose, complete ease Vin I.331 (kammassa suppression of an act); Ps II.3, 71, 180; Nett 89; Dhs 40, 41, 320; SnA 9. Esp. frequent in the Niddesas in stock phrase expressing the complete calm attained to in emancipation, viz. vūpasama paṭinissagga p. amata nibbāna, e. g. Nd[2] 429.

Paṭippassambhati [paṭi + ppa + sambhati of **śrambh.** Note however that the BSk. is °praśrambhyati as well as °srambhyati, e. g. MVastu I.253, 254; Divy 68, 138, 494, 549, 568] to subside, to be eased, calmed, or abated, to pass away, to be allayed S I.211; V.51; aor. °ssambhi DhA II.86 (dohaḷo); IV.133 (ābādho). — pp. paṭippassaddha (q. v.). — Caus. paṭippassambheti to quiet down, hush up, suppress, bring to a standstill, put to rest, appease Vin I.49 (kammaŋ), 144 (id.), 331 (id.); II.5 (id.), 226 (id.); M I.76; J III.28 (dohaḷaŋ).

Paṭipassambhanā (f.) & **°ppassambhitatta** (nt.) are exegetical (philosophical) synonyms of paṭippassaddhi at Dhs 40, 41, 320.

Paṭippharati [paṭi + pharati] to effulge, shine forth, stream out, emit, fig. splurt out, bring against, object M I.91 sq.; A IV.193 (codakaŋ); J I.123, 163; Nd[1] 196 (vādaŋ start a word-fight); Miln 372; DhA IV.4 (vacanaŋ).

Paṭibaddha (adj.) [paṭi + baddha, pp. of **bandh**] bound to, in fetters or bonds, attracted to or by, dependent on D I.76; Vin IV.302 (kāya°); A V.87 (para°); Dh 284; Miln 102 (āvajjana°); PvA 134 (°jīvika dependent on him for a living). — Freq. in cpd. °citta affected, enamoured, one's heart bound in love Vin III.128; IV.18; Sn 37 (see Nd[2] 385), 65; PvA 46, 145 (°tā f. abstr.), 151, 159 (rañño with the king).

Paṭibandha (adj.) [paṭi + bandha] bound to, connected with, referring to Ps I.172, 184.

Paṭibandhati [paṭi + bandhati] to hold back, refuse J IV.134 (vetanaŋ na p. = aparihāpetvā dadāti).

Paṭibandhu [paṭi + bandhu] a connection, a relation, relative Dhs 1059, 1136, 1230; DhsA 365.

Paṭibala (adj.) [paṭi + bala] able, adequate, competent Vin I.56, 342; II.103, 300; III.158; A V.71; Miln 6.

Paṭibāḷha [pp. of paṭibāhati, though more likely to paṭi + **vah**[2]] (op)pressed, forced, urged Vbh 338 = Miln 301.

Paṭibāhaka [of paṭi + bādh] antidote Miln 335; repelling, preventing J VI.571.

Paṭibāhati [paṭi + ***bāh** of bahis adv. outside] to ward off, keep off, shut out, hold back, refuse, withhold, keep out, evade Vin I.356; II.162, 166 sq., 274; IV.288; J I.64, 217; DhA II.2 (rañño āṇaŋ), 89 (sitaŋ); VvA 68; PvA 96 (maraṇaŋ), 252, 286 (grd. appaṭibāhanīya). Caus. °bāheti in same meaning J IV.194; DhA II.71; PvA 54. — pp. **paṭibāḷha** (q. v.).

Paṭibāhana exclusion, warding off, prevention Miln 81; Vism 244.

Paṭibāhiya (adj.) [grd. of paṭibāhati] to be kept off or averted, neg. ap° J IV.152.

Paṭibāhira (adj.) [paṭi + bāhira] outside, excluded Vin II.168.

Paṭibimba (nt.) [paṭi + bimba] counterpart, image, reflection Vism 190; VvA 50; VbhA 164.

Paṭibujjhati [paṭi + bujjhati] to wake up, to understand, know, A III.105 sq.; ThA 74; PvA 43, 128. — pp. paṭibuddha (q. v.).

Paṭibuddha [pp. of paṭibujjhati] awakened, awake Sn 807.

Paṭibodha [fr. paṭi + **budh**, cp. paṭibujjhati] awaking, waking up Vv 50[24]

Paṭibhajati [paṭi + **bhaj**] to divide M III.91.

Paṭibhaṇḍa [paṭi + bhaṇḍa, cp. BSk. pratipanya Divy 173, 271, 564] merchandise in exchange, barter J I.377; PvA 277.

Paṭibhaṇḍati [paṭi + bhaṇḍati] to abuse in return S I.162 (bhaṇḍantaŋ p.); A II.215 (id.); Nd[1] 397 (id.).

Paṭibhaya [paṭi + bhaya] fear, terror, fright S IV.195; PvA 90; Dāvs IV.35. Freq. in cpd. ap° & sap°, e. g. Vin IV.63; M I.134; III.61.

Paṭibhāga [paṭi + bhāga] 1. counterpart, likeness, resemblance Nd[2] s. v.; Vism 125 (°nimitta, imitative mental reflex, memory-image); SnA 65, 76, 83, 114, 265; PvA 46, 178, 279. — 2. rejoinder J VI.341 (pañha°). — 3. counterpart, opposite, contrary M I. 304. — **appaṭibhāga** (adj.) unequalled, incomparable, matchless Miln 357 (+ appaṭiseṭṭha); DhA I.423 (= anuttara).

Paṭibhāti [paṭi + **bhā**] to appear, to be evident, to come into one's mind, to occur to one, to be clear (cp. *Vin. Texts* II.36) S I.155 (°tu taŋ dhammikathā); V.153 (T. reads patibbāti); Sn 450 (p. maŋ = mama bhāgo pakāsati SnA 399); Nd[1] 234 = Nd[2] 386 (also fut. °bhāyissati); J V.410; VvA 78 = 159 (maŋ p. ekaŋ pañhaŋ pucchituŋ "I should like to ask a question").

Paṭibhāna (nt.) [paṭi + bhāna. Cp. late Sk. pratibhāna, fr. Pali] understanding, illumination, intelligence; readiness or confidence of speech, promptitude, wit (see on term *Vin. Texts* III.13, 172; *Pts. of Controversy*, 378 f.) D I.16, 21, 23; S I.187; A II.135, 177, 230; III.42; IV.163; V.96; Ps II.150, 157; J VI.150; Pug 42; Vbh 293 sq.; VbhA 338, 394, 467; Miln 21; DA I.106. — **appaṭibhāna** (adj.) bewildered, not confident, cowed down Vin II.78 = III.162; M I.258; A III.57; J V.238, 369; VI.362.

Paṭibhānavant (adj.) [fr. paṭibhāna] possessed of intelligence or ready wit A I.24; Sn 58, 853, 1147; Nd[1] 234 = Nd[2] 386; SnA 111 (pariyatti° & paṭivedha°).

Paṭibhāneyyaka (adj.) [ger. formation + ka fr. paṭibhāna] = paṭibhānavant Vin I.249 (cp. *Vin. Texts* II.140); A I.25.

Paṭibhāsati [paṭi + **bhās**] to address in return or in reply S I.134; Sn 1024.

Paṭimaŋsa (adj.) [for paṭimassa = Sk. *pratimṛśya, ger. of prati + **mṛś**, cp. in consonants haŋsa for harṣa etc.] as neg. app° not to be touched, untouched; faultless Vin II.248 (acchidda +); A V.79.

Paṭimagga [paṭi + magga, cp. similarly paṭipatha] the way against, a confronting road; °ŋ gacchati to go to meet somebody J IV.133; VI.127.

Paṭimaṇḍita [pp. of paṭi + **maṇḍ**] decorated, adorned with J I.8, 41, 509; PvA 3, 66, 211.

Paṭimantaka [fr. paṭi + **mant**] one who speaks to or who is spoken to, i. e. (1) an interlocutor J IV.18 (= paṭivacana-dayaka C.); — (2) an amiable person (cp. Lat. affabilis = affable) M I.386.

Paṭimanteti [paṭi + manteti] to discuss in argument, to reply to, answer, refute; as paṭi° at Vin II.1; D I.93 (vacane), 94; Dh I.263; J VI.82, 294.

Paṭimalla [paṭi + malla] a rival wrestler S I.110; Nd[1] 172.

Paṭimasati [paṭi + masati of mṛś, cp. paṭimaŋsa] to touch (at) D I.106; Sn p. 108 (anumasati +). — Caus. paṭimāseti (q. v.).

Paṭimā (f.) [fr. paṭi + **mā**] counterpart, image, figure J VI.125; Dāvs V.27; VvA 168 (= bimba); DhsA 334. — **appaṭima** (adj.) without a counterpart, matchless, incomparable Th 1, 614; Miln 239.

Paṭimānita [pp. of paṭimāneti] honoured, revered, served PvA 18.

Paṭimāneti [paṭi + Caus. of **man**] to wait on, or wait for, look after, honour, serve Vin II.169; IV.112; D I.106; J IV.2, 203; V.314; Miln 7; PvA 12; DA I.280. — pp. paṭimānita (q. v.).

Paṭimāreti [paṭi + Caus. of **mṛ**] to kill in revenge J III.135.

Paṭimāseti [Caus. of patimasati] to hold on to, to restrain, keep under control; imper. paṭimāse (for °māsaya) Dh 379 (opp. codaya; expl[d] by °parivīmaŋse "watch" DhA IV.117).

Paṭimukka (adj.) [pp. of paṭimuñcati; cp. also paṭimutta & ummukka, see Geiger, *P.Gr.* § 197] fastened on, tied to, wound round, clothed in S IV.91; M I.383; It 56; Th 2, 500 (? v. l. paripuṇṇa, cp. ThA 290); J I.384; VI.64; Miln 390; DhA I.394 (sīse); VvA 167 (so read for °mukkha), 296.

Paṭimukha (adj.) [paṭi + mukha] facing, opposite; nt. °ŋ adv. opposite SnA 399 (gacchati).

Paṭimuñcati [paṭi + **muc**] 1. to fasten, to bind (in lit. as well as appl[d] sense), to tie, put on Vin I.46; S I.24 (veraŋ °muñcati for °muccati!); J I.384; II.22, 88, 197; IV. 380 (ger. °mucca, v. l. °muñca), 395; V.25 (attain), 49; VI.525; DhA III.295. — Pass. paṭimuccati to be fastened, aor. °mucci J III.239; VI.176. — 2. to attain, obtain, find J IV.285 = VI.148.

Paṭimutta (& °ka) (adj.) [pp. of paṭimuñcati, cp. paṭimukka] in sup° well purified, cleansed, pure J IV.18 (°kambu = paṭimutta-suvaṇṇ' ālankāra C.); V.400; Pv IV.1[33] (°ka-suṭṭhu paṭimuttabhāṇin PvA 230).

Paṭimokkha [fr. paṭi + **muc**] 1. a sort of remedy, purgative D I.12 osadhīnaŋ p. expl[d] at DA I.98 as "khārâdīni datvā tad-anurūpo khaṇc gate tesaŋ apanayanaŋ." Cp. *Dial.* 26. — 2. binding, obligatory J V.25 (sangaraŋ p. a binding promise). Cp. pātimokkha.

Paṭiya (nt.) [= paṭikā] a white woollen counterpane J IV.352 (= uṇṇāmaya-paccattharaṇāni setakambalāni pi vadanti yeva C.).

Paṭiyatta [pp. of paṭi + **yat**] prepared, got ready, made, dressed Vin IV.18 (alankata°); J IV.380 (C. for pakata), PvA 25 (C. for upaṭṭhita), 75 (alankata°), 135 (id.), 232 (id.), 279 (id.); KhA 118 (alankata°).

Paṭiyāti [paṭi + **yā**, cp. pacceti] to go back to, reach J VI.149 (C. for paṭimuñcati).

Paṭiyādita [pp. of paṭiyādeti] given, prepared, arranged, dedicated Miln 9; DhA II.75.

Paṭiyādeti [for *paṭiyāteti = Sk. pratiyātayati, Caus. of paṭi + **yat**, like P. niyyādeti = Sk. niryātayati] to prepare, arrange, give, dedicate SnA 447. — pp. **paṭiyādita** (q. v.). — Caus.II. **paṭiyādāpeti** to cause to be presented or got ready, to assign, advise, give over Vin I.249 (yāguŋ); Sn p. 110 (bhojaniyaŋ); PvA 22, 141.

Paṭi-y-ālokaŋ gacchati "to go to the South" Vin IV.131, 161.

Paṭiyodha [paṭi + yodha] counterfight J III.3.

Paṭiyoloketi (T. **paṭi-oloketi**) [paṭi + oloketi] to look at, to keep an eye on, observe J II.406.

Paṭirava [paṭi + rava] shouting out, roar Dāvs IV.52.

Paṭirājā [paṭi + rājā] hostile king, royal adversary J VI.472; DhA I.193.

Paṭiruddha [pp. paṭi+**rudh**] obstructed, hindered, held back, caged J IV.4 (oruddha-paṭiruddha sic.).

Paṭirūpa (adj.) [paṭi+rūpa] fit, proper, suitable, befitting, seeming D I.91; Vin II.166 (seyyā); M I.123; S I.214; II.194 (ap°); Th 2, 341; Pv II.12[16]; J V.99; Pug 27; DhA III.142; PvA 26, 122 (=yutta), 124. -°desavāsa living in a suitable region D III.276=A II.32; Nett 29, 50. — Spelt pati° at Dh 158; Sn 89, 187, 667; SnA 390. Cp. pātirūpika.

Paṭirūpaka (adj.) (-°) [fr. paṭirūpa] like, resembling, disguised as, in the appearance of, having the form of S I.230; DhA I.29 (putta°); PvA 15 (samaṇa°). As pati° at SnA 302, 348, 390. — nt. an optical delusion DhA III.56.

Paṭirūpatā (f.) [abstr. fr. paṭirūpa] likeness, semblance, appearance, pretence PvA 268 (=vaṇṇa).

Paṭirodati [paṭi+rodati of **rud**] to cry in return, to reply by crying J III.80; pp. paṭirodita=paṭirodana.

Paṭirodana (nt.) [paṭi+rodana] replying through crying J III.80.

Paṭirodeti [paṭi+Caus. of **rud**] to scold back S I.162.

Paṭirosati [paṭi+rosati] to annoy in return, to tease back S I.162; A II.215; Nd[1] 397.

Paṭiladdha [pp. of paṭilabhati] received, got, obtained PvA 15 (=laddha), 88.

Paṭilabhati [paṭi+labhati] to obtain, receive, get It 77; J I.91; Nd[2] 427 (pariyesati p. paribhuñjati); Pug 57; VvA 115; PvA 6, 7, 16, 50, 60, 67 etc. — pret. 3rd pl. paccaladdhaŋsu S I.48 (so v. l. & C. T. °latthaŋsu), expl[d] by paṭilabhiŋsu cp. *K. S.* 319. — aor. 1st sg. paṭilacchiŋ J V.71. — Caus. paṭilābheti to cause to take or get, to rob J V.76 (paṭilābhayanti naŋ "rob me of him").

Paṭilābha [fr. paṭi+**labh**] obtaining, receiving, taking up, acquisition, assumption, attainment D I.195; M I.50; A II.93, 143; Ps II.182, 189; Nd[1] 262; Dh 333; Pug 57; VvA 113; PvA 50, 73, 74. — attabhāva° obtaining a reincarnation, coming into existence S II.256; III.144; A II.159, 188; III.122 sq. — See also paribhoga.

Paṭilika v. l. BB together with paṭalika for talika at J III.80 (cp. A III 36 ?).

Paṭilīna [pp. of paṭilīyati] having withdrawn, keeping away S I.48 (°nisabha "expert to eliminate"; reading pati°); with reading pati also; A II.41; IV.449; Sn 810, 852; Nd[1] 130, 224 (rāgassa etc. pahīnattā patilīno).

Paṭilīyati [paṭi+līyati of **lī**] to withdraw, draw back, keep away from, not to stick to A IV.47=Miln 297 (+paṭikuṭati paṭivaṭṭati; Miln & id. p. at S II.265 print pati°); Vism 347 (+paṭikuṭṭati pativaṭṭati). — pp. paṭilīna; Caus. paṭileṇeti (q. v.).

Paṭileṇeti [Sec. der[n] fr. pp. paṭilīna in sense of Caus.; cp. Sk. °lāpayati of **lī**] to withdraw, to make keep away, not to touch S II.265 (pati°, as at Miln 297 patilīyati).

Paṭilobheti [paṭi+Caus. of **lubh**] to fill with desire, to entice J V.96.

Paṭiloma (adj.) [paṭi+loma] "against the hair," in reverse order, opposite, contrary, backward; usually comb[d] with **anuloma** i. e. forward & backward Vin I.1; A IV.448; etc (see paṭiccasamuppāda); J II.307. -°pakkha opposition PvA 114 (cp. paṭipakkha).

Paṭivacana (nt.) [paṭi+vacana] answer, reply, rejoinder J IV.18; Miln 120; PvA 83 (opp. vacana); ThA 285.

Paṭivaṭṭati (& °vattati) [paṭi+**vṛt**] (intrs.) to roll or move back, to turn away from A IV.47=Miln 297 (paṭilīyati paṭikutati p.); Caus. paṭivaṭṭeti in same meaning trs. (but cp. Childers s. v. "to knock, strike") S II.265 (T. spells pati°, as also at Miln 297). — grd. paṭivattiya only in neg. ap° (q. v.). — pp. paṭivatta (q. v.).

Paṭivatta (nt.) [pp. of paṭivattati] moving backwards, only in cpd. vatta-paṭivatta-karaṇa "moving forth or backwards," performance of different kinds of duties; doing this, that & the other DhA I.157.

Paṭivattar [paṭi+vattar, n. ag. of **vac**] one who contradicts S I.222.

Paṭivadati [pati+vadati] to answer, reply A IV.168 (v. l. for paṭicarati); Sn 932; Dh 133; Nd[1] 397; PvA 39.

Paṭivasati [paṭi+vasati] to live, dwell (at) D I.129; Vin II.299; S I.177; J I.202; SnA 462; PvA 42, 67.

Paṭivāṇa, Paṭivāṇitā, Paṭivāṇī etc. occur only in neg. form app°, q. v.

Paṭivātaŋ (adv.) [paṭi+vātaŋ, acc.' cp. Sk. prativāta & prativātaŋ] against the wind (opp. anuvātaŋ) Vin II.218; S I.13; Sn 622; Dh 54, 125; PvA 116; Sdhp 425.

Paṭivāda [paṭi+vāda] retort, recrimination Miln 18 (vāda° talk and counter-talk).

Paṭivāpeti [Caus. of paṭi+**vap**] to turn away from, to free from, cleanse M I.435=A IV.423; DhsA 407.

Paṭivāmeti [paṭi+Caus. **vam**] to throw out again Dh I.39.

Paṭiviŋsa [paṭi-aŋsa with euphonic consonant v instead of y (paṭi-y-aŋsa) and assimilation of a to i (paṭiyiŋsa > paṭiviŋsa)] lit. "divided part," sub-part, share, bit, portion, part Vin I.28; III.60 (T. reads paṭivisa); J II.286; DhsA 135; DhA I.189; III.304; VvA 61 (°vīsa), 64 (v. l. °vīsa), 120 (id.).

Paṭiviŋsaka [prec.+ka] part share, portion DhA II.85.

Paṭivigacchati [pati+vi+gacchati] to go apart again, to go away or asunder A III.243; Miln 51.

Paṭivijānāti [paṭi+vi+jānāti] to recognise Vin III.130; Nd[2] 378 (ājānāti vijānāti p. paṭivijjhati); Miln 299.

Paṭivijjha (adj.) [grd. of paṭivijjhati] in cpd. dup° hard to penetrate (lit. & fig.) S V.454.

Paṭivijjhati [paṭi+vijjhati of **vyadh**] to pierce through, penetrate (lit. & fig.), intuit, to acquire, master, comprehend Vin I.183; S II.56; V.119, 278, 387, 454; A IV.228, 469; Nd[2] 378; J I.67, 75; Ps I.180 sq.; Miln 344; DhA I.334. — aor. paṭivijjha Sn 90 (=aññāsi sacchākāsi SnA 166), and paccavyādhi Th 1, 26=1161 (°byādhi); also 3rd pl. paccavidhuŋ A IV.228. — pp. paṭividdha (q. v.). On phrase uttariŋ appaṭivijjhanto. See uttari.

Paṭivijjhanaka (adj.) [paṭi+vijjhana+ka, of **vyadh**] only in neg. ap° impenetrable DhA IV.194.

Paṭividita [pp. of paṭi+**vid**] known, ascertained D I.2; Ps I.188.

Paṭividdha [pp. of paṭivijjhati] being or having penetrated or pierced; having acquired, mastering, knowing M I.438; S II.56 (sup°); Ps II.19, 20; J I.214; VvA 73 (°catusacca=saccānaŋ kovida). — **appaṭividdha** not pierced, not hurt J VI.446.

Paṭivinaya [paṭi+vi+**nī**] repression, subdual, only in cpd. āghāta° D III.262, 289; A III.185 sq. See āghāta.

Paṭivinicchinati [paṭi+vinicchinati] to try or judge a case again, to reconsider J II.187.

Paṭivinīta [pp. of paṭivineti] removed, dispelled, subdued S II.283; V.76, 315.

Paṭivineti paṭi + vi + **nī**] to drive out, keep away, repress, subdue S I.228; M I.13; A III.185 sq.; J VI.551; PvA 104 (pipāsaŋ). Cp. BSk. prativineti MVastu II.121. — pp. paṭivinīta (q. v.).

Paṭivinodana (nt.) [fr. paṭivinodeti] removal, driving out, explusion A II.48, 50; Miln 320.

Paṭivinodaya (adj.-n.) [fr. paṭivinodeti] dispelling, subduing, riddance, removal; dup° hard to dispel A III.184 sq.

Paṭivinodeti [paṭi + vi + Caus. of **nud**, Cp. BSk. prativinudati Divy 34, 371 etc.] to remove, dispel, drive out, get rid of D I.138; M I.48; Pv III.5[8]; Pug 64; VvA 305; PvA 60.

Paṭivibhajati [paṭi + vibhajati] to divide off, to divide into (equal) parts M I.58 (cp. III.91; paṭibhaj° & v. l. vibhaj°).

Paṭivibhatta (adj.) [paṭi + vibhatta] (equally) divided M I.372; A IV.211; VvA 50. On neg. ap° in cpd. °bhogin see **appaṭivibhatta**.

Paṭivirata (adj.) [pp. of paṭiviramati, cp. BSk. prativiramati Divy 11, 302, 585] abstaining from, shrinking from (with abl.) D I.5; M III.23; S V.468; It 63; Pug 39, 58; DA I.70; PvA 28, 260. — **app°** not abstaining from Vin II.296; S V.468; It 64.

Paṭivirati (f.) [fr. paṭivirata] abstinence from Dhs 299; M III.74; PvA 206.

Paṭiviramati [paṭi + viramati] to abstain from M I.152.

Paṭivirujjhati [paṭi + vi + **rudh**] to act hostile, to fall out with somebody, to quarrel (saddhiŋ) J IV.104. — pp. **paṭiviruddha** (q. v.).

Paṭiviruddha [pp. of paṭivirujjhati, cp. BSk. prativiruddha rebellious Divy 445] obstructed or obstructing, an adversary, opponent J VI.12; DA I.51 (°ā satta = pare); Miln 203, 403.

Paṭivirūhati [paṭi + virūhati] to grow again Vism 419.

Paṭivirodha [paṭi + virodha] hostility, enmity, opposition Dhs 418, 1060; Pug 18; Miln 203.

Paṭivisiṭṭha [paṭi + visiṭṭha] peculiar M I.372.

Paṭivisesa [paṭi + visesa] sub-discrimination J II.9.

Paṭivissaka (adj.) [fr. paṭi + *veśman or *veśya] dwelling near, neighbouring M I.126; J I.114, 483; III.163; IV.49; V.434; DhA I.47 (°itthi), 155, 235 (°dārakā).

Paṭivutta (paṭi + vutta, pp. of **vac**] said against, replied Vin III.131, 274.

Paṭivekkhiya see ap°.

Paṭivedeti [paṭi + vedeti, Caus. of **vid**] to make known, declare, announce Vin I.180; S I.101, 234; Sn 415 (aor. °vedayi); DA I.227; PvA 6 (pītisomanassaŋ).

Paṭivedha [fr. paṭi + **vyadh**ī cp. paṭivijjhati & BSk. prativedha MVastu I.86] lit. piercing, i. e. penetration, comprehension, attainment, insight, knowledge A I.22, 44; D III.253; Ps I.105; II.50, 57, 105, 112, 148, 182; Vbh 330; Miln 18; SnA 110, 111; Sdhp 65. — **appaṭivedha** non-intelligence, ignorance Vin I.230; S II.92; III.261; V.431; A II.1; Dhs 390, 1061, 1162; Pug 21. — **duppaṭivedha** (adj.) hard to pierce or penetrate; fig. difficult to master Miln 250. — **maggaphala°** realisation of the fruit of the Path DhA I.110.

Paṭivera [paṭi + vera] revenge DhA I.50.

Paṭivellati [paṭi + vellati] to embrace, cling to J V.449.

Paṭivyāharati [paṭi + vyāharati] to desist from, aor. **paccavyāhāsi** D II.232.

Paṭivyūhati (pati°) [paṭi + vyūhati] to heap up against (?) SnA 554.

Paṭisaŋyamati [paṭi + saŋyamati] to restrain, to exercise self-control J IV.396.

Paṭisaŋyujati [paṭi + saŋ + **yuj**] to connect with, fig. to start, begin (vādaŋ a discussion or argument) S I.221 (bālena paṭisaŋyuje = paṭippharеyya C.; "engage himself to bandy with a fool" *K.S.* 284); Sn 843 (vādaŋ p. = paṭippharеyya kalahaŋ kareyya Nd[1] 196). — pp. paṭisaŋyutta (q. v.).

Paṭisaŋyutta [pp. of paṭisaŋyujati] connected with, coupled, belonging to Vin IV.6; S I.210 (nibbāna °dhammikathā); Th I, 598; It 73; VvA 6, 87; PvA 12.

Paṭisaŋvidita [pp. of paṭi + saŋ + **vid** same (prati) at MVastu III.256] apperceived, known, recognised, in phrase "pubbe appaṭisaŋvidita pañho" S II.54.

Paṭisaŋvedin (adj.) [fr. paṭisaŋvedeti; BSk. pratisaŋvedin Divy 567] experiencing, feeling, enjoying or suffering M I.56; S I.196; II.122; IV.41; V.310 sq.; A I.164 (sukhadukkha°); IV.303 (id.); V.35 (id.); It 99; Ps I.95, 114 (evaŋsukhadukkha°), 184, 186 sq.; Pug 57, 58.

Paṭisaŋvedeti [pati + saŋ + vedeti, Caus. of **vid**] to feel, experience, undergo, perceive D I.43, 45; A I.157 (domanassaŋ); IV.406 (id.); Pug 59; PvA 192 (mahādukkhaŋ). There is also a by-form, viz. **paṭisaŋvediyati** S II.18, 75, 256 (attabhāva-paṭilābhaŋ); It 38 (sukkha-dukkhaŋ; v. l. °vedeti).

Paṭisaŋharaṇa (nt.) [fr. paṭisaŋharati] removing Nett 27, 41.

Paṭisaŋharati [paṭi + saŋ + **hṛ**, cp. BSk. pratisaŋharati MVastu I.82] to draw back, withdraw, remove, take away, give up Vin II.185 (sakavaṇṇaŋ); D I.96; S V.156; PvA 92 (devarūpaŋ).

Paṭisakkati [paṭi + sakkati[2]] to run back Vin II.195; A IV.190.

Paṭisankhayanto is ppr. of paṭi + saŋ + **kṣi**, to be pacified Th I, 371.

Paṭisankharoti [paṭi + saŋ + **kṛ**] to restore, repair, mend Vin II.160; A II.249; J III.159 (nagaraŋ). Caus. II. paṭisankhārāpeti to cause to repair or build up again M III.7; J VI.390 (gehāni).

Paṭisankhā (f.) [paṭi + sankhā of **khyā**] reflection, judgment, consideration Vin I.213; S IV.104 (°yoniso); Ps I.33, 45, 57, 60, 64; Pug 25, 57; Dhs 1349. **appaṭisankhā** (see also °sankhāti) want of judgment, inconsideration Ps I.33, 45; Dhs 1346 = Pug 21. — *Note.* In comb[n] **paṭisankhā yoniso** "carefully, with proper care or intention" p. is to be taken as ger. of paṭisankhāti (q. v.). This connection is frequent, e. g. S IV.104; A II.40; Nd[1] 496; Nd[2] 540.

Paṭisankhāti [paṭi + saŋ + **khyā**] to be careful, to think over, reflect, discriminate, consider; only in ger. **paṭisankhā** (as adv.) carefully, intently, with discrimination Vin I.213; M I.273; III.2; J I.304; Nd[2] 540; Pug 25; cp. paṭisankhā (+ yoniso); also ger. **paṭisankhāya** Sddp 394. — Opp. **appaṭisankhā** inconsiderately, in phrase sahasā app° rashly & without a thought M I.94; S II.110, 219. — Cp. **paṭisañcikkhati.**

Paṭisankhāna (nt.) [fr. paṭisankhāti] carefulness, mindfulness, consideration J I.502; VvA 327; DhsA 402 (°paññā); Sdhp 397. -°bala power of computation A I.52, 94; II.142; D III.213, 244; Ps II.169, 176; Dhs 1354 (cp. *Dhs trslⁿ* 354); Nett 15, 16, 38.

Paṭisankhārika & °ya (adj.) [fr. paṭisankharoti] serving for repair Vin III.43 (dārūni); PvA 141 (id.; °ya).

Paṭisañcikkhati [paṭi+saŋ+cikkhati of **khyā**; cp. paṭisankhati & BSk. pratisañcikṣati MVastu II.314] to think over, to discriminate, consider, reflect Vin I.5; D I.63; M I.267, 469; III.33; S I.137; A I.205; Pug 25; Vism 283.

Paṭisañjīvita [pp. of paṭi+saŋ+**jīv**] revived, resurrected M I.333.

Paṭisatena (adv.) [paṭi+instr. of sataŋ] by the hundred, i. e. in front of a hundred (people) Vin I.269.

Paṭisattu [paṭi+sattu] an enemy (in retaliation) J II.406; Nd[1] 172, 173; Miln 293.

Paṭisanthata [pp. of paṭisantharati] kindly received (covered, concealed? C.) J VI.23 (=paṭicchāditaŋ guttaŋ paripuṇṇaŋ vā C.).

Paṭisantharati [paṭi+saŋ+tharati of **stṛ**] to receive kindly, to welcome, Miln 409; DhsA 397. ger. °santhāya J VI.351. — pp. paṭisanthata (q. v.).

Paṭisanthāra [fr. paṭi+saŋ+**stṛ**] lit. spreading before, i. e. friendly welcome, kind reception, honour, goodwill, favour, friendship D III.213, 244; A I.93; III.303 sq.; IV.28, 120; V.166, 168 (°aka adj. one who welcomes); J II.57; Dh 376 (expl[d] as āmisa° and dhamma° at DhA IV.111, see also DhsA 397 sq. & *Dhs trsl.* 350); Dhs 1344; Vbh 360; Miln 409. paṭisanthāraŋ karoti to make friends, to receive friendly PvA 12, 44, 141, 187.

Paṭisandahati [paṭi+sandahati] to undergo reunion (see next) Miln 32.

Paṭisandhi [fr. paṭi+saŋ+**dhā**] reunion (of vital principle with a body), reincarnation, metempsychosis Ps I.11 sq., 52, 59 sq.; II.72 sq.; Nett 79, 80; Miln 140; DhA II.85; VvA 53; PvA 8, 79, 136, 168. A detailed discussion of p. is to be found at VbhA 155-160. — appaṭisandhika see sep.

Paṭisama (adj.) [paṭi+sama] equal, forming, a counterpart Miln 205 (rāja°); neg. appaṭisama not having one's equal, incomparable J I.94; Miln 331.

Paṭisambhidā (f.) [paṭi+saŋ+**bhid**; the BSk. pratisaŋvid is a new formation resting on confusion between **bhid** & **vid**, favoured by use & meaning of latter root in P. paṭisaŋvidita. In BSk. we find pratisaŋvid in same application as in P., viz. as fourfold artha° dharma° nirukti° pratibhāna° (?) MVastu III.321] lit. "resolving continuous breaking up," i. e. analysis, analytic insight, discriminating knowledge. See full discussion & explⁿ of term at Kvu trslⁿ 377-382. Always referred to as "the four branches of logical analysis" (catasso or catupatisambhidā), viz. attha° analysis of meanings "in extension"; dhamma° of reasons, conditions, or causal relations; nirutti° of [meanings "in intension" as given in] definitions paṭibhāna° or intellect to which things knowable by the foregoing processes are presented (after Kvu trslⁿ). In detail at A II.160; III.113, 120; Ps I.88, 119; II.150, 157, 185, 193; Vbh 293-305; VbhA 386 sq. (cp. Vism 440 sq.), 391 sq. — See further A I.22; IV.31; Nd[2] 386 under paṭibhānavant; Ps I.84, 132, 134; II.32, 56, 116, 189; Miln 22 (attha-dh°-nirutti-paṭibhāna-pāramippatta), 359; VvA 2; DhA IV.70 (catūsu p-° āsu cheka). p°-patta one who has attained mastership in analysis A I.24; III.120; Ps II.202. — Often included in the attainment of Arahantship, in formula "saha paṭisambhidāhi arahattaŋ pāpunāti," viz. Miln 18; DhA II.58, 78, 93.

Paṭisammajjati [paṭi+sammajjati] to sweep over again Miln 15.

Paṭisammodeti [paṭi+saŋ+Caus. of **mud**] to greet friendly in return J VI.224 (=sammodaniya-kathāya paṭikatheti C.).

Paṭisaraṇa (nt.) [paṭi+saraṇa[1]] refuge in (-°), shelter, help, protection M I.295 (mano as p. of the other 5 senses); III.9; S IV.221; V.218; A I.199 (Bhagavaŋ°); II.148 (sa° able to be restored); III.186 (kamma°); IV.158, 351; V.355; J I.213; VI.398. — appaṭisaraṇa (adj.) without shelter, unprotected Vin II.153 (so read for appatiss°). — *Note.* In meaning "restoration" the derivation is prob. fr. paṭi+**sṛ** to move (Sk. saraṇa and not śaraṇa protection). Cp. paṭisāraṇiya.

Paṭisarati[1] [paṭi+**sṛ**] to run back, stay back, lag behind Sn 8 sq. (opp. atisarati; aor. paccasāri expl[d] by ohiyyi SnA 21).

Paṭisarati[2] [paṭi+**smṛ**] to think back upon, to mention DA I.267.

Paṭisallāna (& °āṇa, e. g. S V.320) (nt.) [for *paṭisallayana, fr. paṭi+saŋ+**lī**, cp. paṭilīna & paṭilīyati, also BSk. pratisaŋlayana Divy 156, 194, 494] retirement for the purpose of meditation, solitude, privacy, seclusion D III.252; M I.526; S I.77; III.15; IV.80, 144; V.12, 398, 414; A II.51, 176; III.86 sq., 116 sq., 195; IV.15, 36, 88; V.166, 168; Sn 69 (cp. Nd[2] s. v.); J II.77 (paṭi°); Vbh 244, 252; Miln 138, 412.
-ārāma fond(ness) of solitude or seclusion (also °rata) A III.261 sq.; It 39; Nd[2] 433. -sāruppa very suitable for seclusion Vism 90.

Paṭisallīyati (°līyati) [fr. paṭi+saŋ+**lī**, cp. paṭilīyati] to be in seclusion (for the purpose of meditation) Vin III.39 (inf. °salliyituŋ); D II.237; S V.12 (id.), 320, 325; Miln 139. — pp. paṭisallīna (q. v.).

Paṭisallīna [pp. of paṭisalliyati; cp. BSk. pratisaŋlīna Divy 196, 291.] secluded, retired, gone into solitude, abstracted, plunged in meditation, separated Vin I.101 (rahogata+); D I.134, 151; S I.71, 146 sq. (divāvihāragata+), 225; II.74 (rahogata+); IV.80, 90, 144; V.415; A II.20; SnA 346 (paṭi°); J I.349; Miln 10, 138 sq.; VvA 3; DA I.309 (paṭi°).

Paṭisāṭheyya (nt.) [paṭi+sāṭheyya] a deceit in return (cp. paṭikūṭa) J II.183.

Paṭisāmita [pp. of paṭisāmeti] arranged, got ready Vism 91.

Paṭisāmeti [paṭi+Caus. of **śam**, samati to make ready; cp. BSk. pratiśāmayati Divy passim] to set in order, arrange, get ready Vin II.113, 211, 216; M I.456; J III.72; Miln 15 (pattacīvaraŋ); VvA 118 (v. l. °yāpeti), 157 (v. l. °nameti).

Paṭisāyati [paṭi+sāyati] to taste, eat, partake of food Vin II.177.

Paṭisāra [paṭi+**smṛ**] see vi°.

Paṭisāraṇa (nt.) [fr. paṭi+sāveti] act of protection, expiation, atonement Miln 344 (in law); appl[d] fig. in psychology M I.295=S V.218.

Paṭisāraṇiya (adj. nt.) [a grd. formation fr. paṭi+sāreti, Caus. of **sṛ** to move] only as t.t. in combⁿ with **kamma** (official act, chapter), i. e. a formal proceeding by which a bhikkhu expiates an offence which he has committed against someone, reconciliation (cp. *Vin. Texts* II.364) Vin I.49 (one of the 5 Sangha-kammas, viz. tajjaniya°, nissaya°, pabbājaniya°, p.°, ukkhepaniya°), 143 (id.), 326; II.15-20, 295; A I.99; IV.346; DhA II.75.

Paṭisārin (adj.) [fr. paṭi + **sr**, cp. paṭisāraniya & paṭisaraṇa Note] falling back upon, going back to, trusting in, leaning on (-°) D I.99 (gotta°); S I.153 (id.); II.284 (id.).

Paṭisāsana (nt.) [paṭi + sāsana] counter-message, reply DhA I.392.

Paṭisibbita [pp. of paṭi + sibbati] sewn, embroidered VvA 167 (paṭi°).

Paṭisīsaka [paṭi + sīsaka] a false top-knot, "chignon" (?) J II.197 (°ŋ paṭimuñcitvā); V.49 (id.); Miln 90 (muṇḍaka°).

Paṭisutta [pp. of paṭi + **svap**] sunk into sleep Th I, 203.

Paṭisumbhita [pp. of paṭi + **śumbh**] fallen down Pv III.1[8] (= patita PvA 174).

Paṭisūra [paṭi + sūra] a rival hero or fighter, an opponent in fight Sn 831 (= paṭipurisa paṭisattu paṭimalla Nd[1] 172); Nd[1] 173 (id.).

Paṭiseṭṭha (adj.) [paṭi + seṭṭha] having a superior; neg. app° incomparable, unsurpassed Miln 357 (appaṭibhāga +).

Paṭisedha [fr. paṭi + **sidh**[1], sedhati drive off] warding off, prohibition Miln 314 ("resubjugation"); SnA 402 (with ref. to part "na"); KhA 170 (id.); PvA 11 (°nipāta = "mā"); VvA 224.

Paṭisedhaka (adj. n.) [fr. paṭisedha] warding off, one who prevents or puts a stop to S I.221; Miln 344.

Paṭisedhati & (Caus.) °sedheti [paṭi + sedhati] to ward off, prohibit, prevent, refuse S IV.341; PvA 11.

Paṭisedhana (nt.) [cp. paṭisedha] warding off, refusal, prohibition, stopping S I.221, 223; PvA 11, 25; Sdhp 397.

Paṭisedhitar [n. ag. fr. paṭisedhati] one who prohibits or refuses J II.123. = V.91.

Paṭisena [paṭi + sena, of either **sī** or **śri**, cp. usseneti] repulsion, opposition, enmity, retaliation; only in compn with **kṛ** as °senikaroti to make opposition, to oppose, retaliate Sn 932, cp. Nd[1] 397; -°senikattar (n. ag.), one who repulses, fighter, retaliator, arguer Sn 832, cp. Nd[1] 173.

Paṭiseneti [paṭi + seneti, see usseneti] to repel, push away, be inimical towards, retaliate (opp. usseneti) A II.215 (paṭisseneti); Sn 390 (°seniyati).

Paṭisevati [paṭi + sevati, cp. BSk. pratisevate Divy 258 in same meaning] to follow, pursue, indulge in (acc.), practise Vin II.296 (methunaŋ dhammaŋ); M I.10; A II.54 (methunaŋ); J I.437; VI.73, 505; Dh 67; Nd[1] 496; Pug 62; Miln 224; DhA II.40; PvA 130; Sdhp 396. — *Note.* paṭisevati is spelt pati° at Dh 67, 68; J III.275, 278.

Paṭisevana (nt.) [fr. paṭisevati] going after, indulging in, practice M I.10.

Paṭisevitar [n. ag. of paṭisevati] one who practises, pursues or indulges in (acc.) A III.143 sq. (bhesajjaŋ).

Paṭisotaŋ (adv.) [paṭi + sotaŋ, acc. of sota] against the stream (opp. anusotaŋ) It 114; J I.70; PvA 154. — paṭisotagāmin going against the stream, toiling, doing hard work S I.136; A II.6 (opp. anu°), 214 sq.

Paṭissata [paṭi + sata, pp. of **smṛ**] recollecting, thoughtful, mindful, minding Sn 283 = Miln 411; Dh 144 (t); Vv 21[10]; and with spelling pati° at S III.143; IV.74, 322, 351; A III.24; It 10, 21, 81; Sn 283, 413.

Paṭissati (f.) [paṭi + sati of **smṛ**] mindfulness, remembrance, memory M I.36 sq.; Dhs 23; Pug 25. app° lapse of memory Dhs 1349.

Paṭissatika (adj.) [fr. paṭissati] mindful, thoughtful Th I, 42.

Paṭissava [fr. paṭi + **śru**] assent, promise, obedience J VI.220; VvA 351 (cp. paṭissava VvA 347).

Paṭissavatā (f.) [abstr. fr. paṭissava] obedience; neg. appaṭissavatā want of deference Dhs 1325 = Pug 20.

Paṭissā & **Patissā** (f.) [paṭi + **śru**, cp. paṭissuṇāti & paṭissāvin; in BSk. we find pratīśā which if legitimate would refer the word to a basis different than **śru**. The form occurs in cpd. sapratīśa respectful Divy; also MVastu I.516; II.258; besides as sapratisa MVastu III.345] deference, obedience, only in cpd. sappaṭissa (q. v.) obedient, deferential It 10 (sappatissa); Vv 84[41] (cp. VvA 347), & appaṭissa disobedient, not attached to S I.139; II.224 sq.; A II.20; III.7, 247, 439; J II.352 (°vāsa anarchy; reading t); PvA 89.

Paṭissāvin (adj.) [fr. paṭi + **śru**] assenting, ready, obedient, willing D I.60; S III.113 (kinkāra-paṭi°).

Paṭissuṇāti [paṭi + **śru**] to assent, promise, agree aor. paccassosi Vin I.73; D I.236; S I.147, 155; Sn p. 50, and paṭisuṇi SnA 314; ger. °suṇitvā freq. in formula "sādhū ti paṭissuṇitvā" asserting his agreement, saying yes S I.119; PvA 13, 54, 55; & passim; also paṭissutvā S I.155. — f. abstr. paṭissutavatā SnA 314.

Paṭisseneti see paṭiseneti.

Paṭihaŋsati [for ghaŋsati?] to beat, knock against PvA 271 (for ghaṭṭeti Pv IV.10[8]; v. l. paṭipisati).

Paṭihankhati [fut. of paṭihanti] only in one stock phrase viz. hurānañ ca vedanaŋ paṭihankhāmi navañ ca vedanaŋ na uppādessāmi "I shall destroy any old feeling and not produce any new" S IV.104 = A II.40 = III.388 = IV.167 = Nd[1] 496 = Nd[2] 540[2]; Vism 32, 33.

Paṭihata [pp. of paṭihanti] stricken, smitten, corrupted Pv III.7[9]; PvA 20 (°citta), 207 (id.). — app° unobstructed DhA II.8; VvA 14.

Paṭihanana (nt.) [fr. paṭi + **han**] repulsion, warding off Vism 31.

Paṭihananaka (adj.) [fr. paṭi + **han**] one who offers resistance DhA I.217.

Paṭihanti [paṭi + **han**] to strike against, ward off, keep away, destroy M I.273; Miln 367; ppr. paṭihanamāna meeting, impinging on, striking against Vism 343. — ger. paṭihacca S V.69, 237, 285; fut. paṭihankhati; pp. paṭihata (q. v.). — Pass. paṭihaññati It 103; J I.7; DhsA 72.

Paṭiharati [paṭi + **hṛ**] to strike in return Vin II.265; D I.142; S IV.299. — Caus. paṭihāreti to repel, avoid J VI.266, 295. — Cp. pāṭihāriya etc.

Paṭu (adj.) [cp. Epic. Sk. paṭu] sharp, pungent; fig. keen, wise, clever, skilful Vism 337 (°saññākicca), 338. Cp. paddha[1] & pāṭava.

Paṭuppādana (nt.) [paṭa (?) + upp°] subtraction (opp. sankalana) DA I.95. The word is not clear (cp. *Dial.* I.22).

Paṭuva at D I.54 is read as pacuṭa by Bdhgh. & trsln (see *Dial.* I.72). See under pavuṭā.

Paṭola [dial.?] a kind of cucumber, Trichosanthes Dioeca Vin I.201 (°paṇṇa).

Paṭṭa [cp. late Sk. paṭṭa, doubtful etym.] 1. slab, tablet, plate, in cpds. ayo° iron plate A IV.130, 131; J IV.7 (suvaṇṇa°); PvA 43 (ayomaya°); loha° brass plate PvA 44; silā° stone slab J I.59 etc. When written on, it is placed into a casket (mañjūsā) J II.36; IV.335. — 2. a bandage, strip (of cloth) Vv 33[41] (āyoga°) = VvA 142. — 3. fine cloth, woven silk, cotton cloth, turban (-cloth) Vin II.266 (dussa° = setavattha-paṭṭa Bdhgh, see *Vin. Texts* III.341); S II.102 (id.) J I.62 (sumana° cloth with a jasmine pattern); VI.191 (°sāṭaka), 370 (nāḷi°); KhA 51 (°bandhana); DA I.87 (āmilāka); DhA I.395 (°vattha); II.42 (rajata°). —dupaṭṭa "double" cloth, see under dvi B II

Paṭṭaka (adj. n.) [fr. paṭṭa] made of or forming a strip of cloth; a bandage, strip (of cloth), girdle Vin II.136 (paṭṭikā); A I.254 (= paṭṭikā C.); J V.359 (aya° an iron girdle), VbhA 230 (paṭṭikā).

Paṭṭana (nt.) [*Sk. paṭṭana] a place, city, port J I.121; IV.16, 137, V.75; PvA 53. — °ka a sort of village J VI.456.

Paṭṭikā see paṭṭaka.

Paṭṭoli in yāna° at Vism 328 is doubtful. It might be read as yāna-kaḷopi (on account of comb[n] with kumbhimukha), or (preferably) as putoḷi (with v. l. BB), which is a regular variant for mutoḷi. The trsl° would be "provision bag for a carriage." See further discussed under mutoḷi.

Paṭṭha (adj.) [fr. pa + **sthā**, see paṭṭhahati] "standing out," setting out or forth, undertaking, able (clever ?) Vin III.210 (dhammiŋ kathaŋ kātuŋ); IV.60 (cīvarakammaŋ kātuŋ), 254 (dhammiŋ kathaŋ kātuŋ) 285, 290; Nd[2] p. 46 (for Sn prose part puṭṭha; v. l. seṭṭha); Nd[2] no. 388 (in expl[n] of paṭṭhagū Sn 1095; here it clearly means "being near, attending on, a pupil or follower of"). See also paddha[1] and paddhagu.

Paṭṭhapita [pp. of paṭṭhahati; cp. BSk. prasthapita Divy 514] established, or given PvA 119 (cp. patiṭṭhāpitatta).

Paṭṭhahati [pa + **sthā** = P. tiṭṭhati, with short base *ṭṭha for *tiṭṭha in trs. meaning, see patiṭṭhahati] to put down, set down, provide; ppr. **paṭṭhayamāna** PvA 128 (varamāna + ; v. l. paṭṭhap°); aor. **paṭṭhayi** Pv II.9[34] (dānaŋ; v. l. paṭṭhapayi, expl[d] by paṭṭhapesi PvA 126). ger. **paṭṭhāya** see sep. — Caus. II. **paṭṭhapeti** to put out or up, to furnish, establish, give S II.25; Pv II.9[24] (fut. °ayissati dānaŋ, v. l. paṭṭhayissati; expl[d] by pavattessati PvA 123); J I.117; PvA 54 (bhattaŋ), 126 (dānaŋ). — pp. **paṭṭhapita** (q. v.).

Paṭṭhāna (nt.) [fr. pa + **sthā**, cp. paṭṭhahati] setting forth, putting forward; only in cpd. sati° setting up of mindfulness (q. v. and see discussion of term at *Dial* II.324). Besides in later lit. meaning "origin," starting point, cause, in title of the 7th book of the Abhidhamma, also called Mahāpakaraṇa. See Ledi, *J.P.T.S.* 1915-16, p. 26; Mrs. Rh. D., Tika p. I, vi. — At Sdhp 321 it has the Sk. meaning of "setting out" (?).

Paṭṭhāya (indecl.) [ger. fr. paṭṭhahati] putting down, starting out from, used as prep. (with abl.) from . . . onward, beginning with, henceforth, from the time of, e. g. ajjato p. from to-day VvA 246; ito p. from here, henceforth J I.60, 63, 150; cp. J I.52 (mūlato); VI.336 (sīsato); PvA II (galato), 13 (gihikālato). paṭṭhāya-yāva (with acc.) from—up to Vism 374.

Paṭṭhika in pañca° see under pañca.

Paṭhati [**paṭh** to read, Sk. paṭhati] to read (of a text) VvA 72; PvA 58, 59, 70 etc.; see also pāṭha.

Paṭhana (nt.) [fr. paṭhati] reading (textual) Miln 344.

Paṭhama (adj.) [Ved. prathama, cp. Av. fratəma; also Ved. prataraŋ further, Gr. πρότερος superl. formation fr. prep. *pro, Sk. pra etc. see pa°] num. ord. "the first," in foll. meanings: (1) the first, foremost, former Sn 93, 436, 1031; J II.110; KhA I.192; DhA III.5, 196 (°vaya, contrasted with majjhima & pacchima); PvA 5, 13, 56. nt. acc. **paṭhamaŋ** at first, for the first time Vin I.16; D II.14; Dh 158; J I.222; II.103, 153; often as first part of cpd. °-, meaning either "first" or "recently, newly, just" Vin I.1 (°âbhisambuddha having just attained Buddhaship); D III.253(°âbhinibbatta), Sn 420 (°uppattika "in his first youth"); J III.394 (°uggata newly sprung up). — A second compar. formation is **paṭhamatara**, only as adv. °ŋ at the (very) first, as early as possible, first of all Vin I.30; J VI.510; DhA I.138; VvA 230; PvA 93.

Paṭhavatta (nt.) [abstr. fr. paṭhavī] earthliness M I.329.

Paṭhavant (adj.-n.) [fr. paṭhavī] a wayfarer S I.37.

Paṭhavī (f.) [Ved. pṛthivī, doublets in Pāli pathavī, puthavī, puthuvī, puṭhuvī, see Geiger, *P.Gr.* §§ 12[4], 17°. To ad., pṛthu: see puthu, **prath** to expand, thus lit. the broad one, breadth, expansion. Not (as Bdhgh at Vism 364: patthaṭattā paṭhavī, cp. *Cpd.* 155 even modern linguists!) to be derived fr. pattharati] the earth. Acc. to Nd[2] 389 syn. with jagati. It figures as the first element in enum[n] of the 4 elements (see dhātu I), viz. p., āpo, tejo, vāyo (earth, water, fire, wind or the elements of the extension, cohesion, heat and motion: *Cpd.* 155). At D III.87 sq. ≈ Vism 418 rasa° is opposed to bhūmi-pappaṭaka. Otherwise it is very frequent in representing the earth as solid, firm, spacious ground. See D II.14, 16; M I.327 sq.; S I.113 (p. udrīyati), 119 (id.), 186; II.133, 169 sq.; V.45, 78, 246, 456 sq.; A II.50; IV.89, 374, V.263 sq.; Sn 307, 1097; It 21; Dh 41, 44, 178 (pathavyā); Pv II.6[6]; Miln 418; PvA 57, 75, 174. —mahā° M I.127; S II.179, 263; III.150; J I.25, 74; III.42; Miln 187; aya° iron soil (of Avīci) DhA I.148. In comp° both paṭhavi° & pathavi°.

-**oja** (paṭhavoja) sap or essence of the earth DhA II,154. -**kampa** shaking the earth, an earthquake DA I.130. -**kampana** = kampa J I.47. -**kasiṇa** the earth artifice (see *Dhs trsl* 43) D III.286. -**dhātu** the earth element (see above) D I.215; II.294; III.228, 247; M I.185; 421; S II.170; Dhs 588, 648, 962 (cp. *Dhs. trsl*[n] 241); Nett 73, 74; VbhA 55; -**maṇḍala** the circle of the E. D I.134; S I.101; A IV.90. -**rasa** taste of earth S I.134; SnA 5. -**lekha** writing on (or in) earth A I.283; Pug 32. -**saññā** earth consciousness M. II.105; A IV.312; V.7 sq., 318 sq. 353 sq. -**sama** like the earth M I.127, 423; Dh 95.

Paḍayhati v. l. at PvA 60 for T. pariḍayhati.

Paṇa [in this meaning unknown in Sk; only in one faulty var. lect. as "house"; see BR s. v. paṇa. Usual meaning "wager"] a shop J IV.488 [v. l. pana].

Paṇaka see paṇṇaka. —paṇaka (comb) see phaṇaka.

Paṇati [cp. Sk. paṇati] to sell, barter, bargain, risk, bet J V.24 (= voharati attānaŋ vikkiṇati C.). — See also paṇitaka & paṇiya.

Panamati [pa + **nam**] to bend, to be bent or inclined Ps I.165, 167; — pp. paṇata ibid. — Caus. panāmeti (q. v.).

Paṇaya [classical Sk. praṇaya, fr pra + **nī**] affection J VI.102.

Paṇava [cp. Ep. Sk. paṇava, dial; accord. to BR a corruption of praṇava] a small drum or cymbal D I.79; S II.128; IV.344; A II.117, 241; J III.59 (of an executioner; PvA 4 in id. p. has paṭaha); Th I, 467; Bu I.32; Vv 81[10]; Dhs 621 (°sadda); DhA I.18.

Panāma [fr. pa + **nam**, see paṇamati] bending, salutation, obeisance (cp. paṇāmeti I) VvA 321 (°ŋ karoti = añjaliŋ karoti). — As paṇāmana nt. at J IV.307.

Paṇāmita [pp. of paṇāmeti] 1. (=paṇāmeti 1) raised, bent or stretched out Sn 352 (añjalī sup°). — 2. (=paṇāmeti 3) dismissed, given leave Vin I.54; M I.457 (bhikkhu-sangho); Miln 209 (id.), 187.

Paṇāmeti [Caus. of paṇamati] 1. to bend forth or over, stretch out, raise, in phrase añjaliŋ p. to raise the hands in respectful salutation Vin II.188; D I.118; Sn p. 79. — 2. to bend to or over, to shut, in kavāṭaŋ p. to shut the door Vin I.87; II.114, 207; pattaŋ Vin II.216. — 3. to make go away, to turn someone away, give leave, dismiss Vin I.54; II.303; S I.7; Th I, 511, 557; J V.314; Miln 187 (parisaŋ); Pass. paṇāmīyati (ibid.) — pp. paṇāmita (q. v.).

Paṇitaka (adj. nt.) [fr. paṇita — pp. of paṇati] staked, wagered, bet, wager, stake at play J VI.192 (so read for paṇīta°).

Paṇidahati [pa+ni+**dhā**] to put forth, put down to, apply, direct, intend; aspire to, long for, pray for S V.156 (atthāya cittaŋ paṇidahiŋ). ger. paṇidhāya S I.42=Sn 660 (vācaŋ manañ ca pāpakaŋ); S I.170 (ujuŋ kāyaŋ); A III.249 (deva-nikāyaŋ p.); IV.461 sq. (id.); Vbh 244 (ujuŋ kāyaŋ p.)=DA I.210. Also lit. (as prep. with acc.) "in the direction of, towards" M I.74 (angārā-kāsuŋ). — pp. paṇihita (q. v.).

Paṇidhāna (nt.) [fr. paṇidahati; cp. philosophical literature & BSk. praṇidhāna] aspiration, longing, prayer VvA 270; Sdhp 344.

Paṇidhi (f.) [fr. paṇidahati; cp. BSk. praṇidhi Divy 102, 134, in same meaning. The usual Sk. meaning is "spy"] aspiration, request, prayer, resolve D III.29, 276; S II.99, 154; III.256 (ceto°); IV.303; A II.32; IV.239 sq. (ceto°); V.212 sq.; Sn 801; Vv 47^{12}; Nd^1 109; Dhs 1059, 1126; SnA 132 (=paṇidhāna); DhA II.172; DhsA 222 (rāga-dosa-moha°).

-kamma (in deva cult) payment of a vow D I.12, cp. DA I.97 (which Kern, however, *Toev.* s. v., interprets as "application of an enema," comparing Sk. pranidheya to be injected as a clyster).

Paṇipatati [pa+ni+**pat**] to fall down before Th I, 375.

Paṇipāta [fr. pa+ni+**pat**] prostration, adoration Dāvs V.53.

Paṇipātika (adj.) [fr. paṇipāta] consisting of a football, humbling or humble, devotional SnA 157.

Paṇiya (adj.) [ger. formation fr. **paŋ**, see paṇati & cp. BSk. paṇya in tara-paṇya fare AvŚ I.148] to be sold or bought, vendible, nt. article of trade, ware A II.199; Vv 84^7 (=bhaṇḍa VvA 337); J IV.363 (=bhaṇḍa C. 366).

Paṇihita [pp. of paṇidahati] applied, directed, intent, bent on, well directed, controlled S IV.309 (dup°); A I.8; V.87; Dh 43; (sammā °ŋ cittaŋ); Sn 154 (su° mano= suṭṭhu ṭhapito acalo SnA 200); Ps II.41 (vimokkha); Miln 204, 333; 413. —appaṇihita in connection with samādhi & vimokkha seems to mean "free from all longings," see Vin III.93=IV.25; S IV.295, 309, 360; Ps II.43 sq., 100; Miln 337.

Paṇāma [fr. pa+**nam**, see paṇamati] bowing, bow, obeisance Th 2, 407 (°ŋ karoti).

Paṇīta (adj.) [pp. of pa+neti in same application BSk.; cp. Divy 385] 1. (lit.) brought out or to, applied, executed; used with ref. to punishment (see paṇeti daṇḍaŋ) Pv IV.1^{66} (°daṇḍa receiving punishment= ṭhapita-sarīra-daṇḍa PvA 242). — 2. (appl^d) brought out or forth, (made) high, raised, exalted, lofty, excellent; with ref. to food (very often used in this sense) "heaped up, plentiful, abundant." Synonymous with uttama (DA I.109, 171), uḷāra (PvA 25, 228), atula (PvA 110); opp. hīna (D III.215; A III.349; V.140; Vism 11), lūkha (S II.153; VvA 64). — D I.12 (dhammā gambhīrā . . . paṇītā . . .), 109 (khādaniya); II.127 (id.) III.215 (with hīna & majjhima-dhātu); S I.136 (dhammo gambhīro etc.); II.153 (dhātu), 154 (paṇidhi); III.47; IV.360; V.66 (dhammā), 226 (etaŋ padaŋ), 266 (sattā); A I.284; II.171, 190; IV.10, 332, 423; V.8, 36 and passim; Sn 240, 389; It 44; Pv I.5^3; IV.1^{27}; Pug 28 (°ādhimutta having high aspirations), 30, 60; Dhs 269, 1027, 1411; PvA 12, 35 (āhāra), 42 (id.); DhA II.154 (bhojana). Compar. paṇītatara, often comb^d with abhikkantatara, e. g. D I.62, 74, 216; S I.80; A I.119, 171; V.37, 140, 203 sq.

Paṇītaka [perhaps=Sk. paṇita, or **paŋ** (see paṇa), as P. formation it may be taken as pa+nīta+ka, viz. that which has been produced] a gambler's stake J VI.192. See paṇitaka.

Paṇudati, Paṇunna see panudati etc.

Paṇeti [pa+**nī**] to lead on to, bring out, adduce, apply, fig. decree (a fine or punishment), only used in phrase daṇḍaŋ paṇeti to give a punishment D II.339=Miln 110; M II.88; Dh 310; J II.207; III.441; IV.192; Miln 29; DhA III.482. — pp. paṇīta (q. v.).

Paṇḍa see bhaṇḍati.

Paṇḍaka [cp late (dial.) Sk. paṇḍa & paṇḍaka; for etym. see Walde, *Lat. Wtb.* under pello] a eunuch, weakling Vin I.86, 135, 168, 320; IV.20, 269; A III.128; V.71; Sdhp 79. — With ref. to the female sex as paṇḍikā at Vin II.271 (itthi°).

Paṇḍara (adj) [Ved. pāṇḍara; cp. paṇḍu, q. v. for etym.] white, pale, yellowish J II.365; V. 340; Nd^1 3; Dhs 6= Vbh 88 (*Dhs trsl.* "that which is clear"? in def. of citta & mano) Dhs 17, 293, 597; Miln 226; DhA IV.8; VvA 40; PvA 56 (=seta); Sdhp 430.

Paṇḍicca (nt.) [fr. paṇḍita] erudition, cleverness, skill, wisdom J I.383; Ps II.185; Pug 25; Dhs 16 (=paṇḍitassa bhāvo DhsA 147), 292, 555. As pandicciya J VI.4.

Paṇḍita (adj.) [cp. Ved. paṇḍita] wise, clever, skilled, circumspect, intelligent Vin II.190 (+buddhimanto); D I.12 (°vedaniya comprehensible only by the wise), 120 (opp. duppañña); III.192; M I.423; III.61, 105, 178; S IV.375 (+viyatta medhāvin); V.151 (+vyatta kusala); A I.59, 68, 84, 101 sq., 162 (paṇḍitā nibbānaŋ adhigacchanti); II.3 sq., 118, 178, 228; III.48=It 16; Sn 115, 254, 335, 523, 721, 820, 1007, 1125 (Ep. of Jatukaṇṇī); It 86; Dh 22, 28, 63 (°mānin), 79, 88, 157, 186, 238, 289; J III.52 (sasa°); Nd^1 124; Pv IV.3^{32} (opp. bāla; =sappañña PvA 254); Dhs 1302; Miln 3, 22; DA I.117; DhA IV.111; VvA 257; PvA 39, 41, 60 (=pañña), 93, 99.

Paṇḍitaka (adj.) [paṇḍita+ka] a pedant D I.107.

Paṇḍu (adj.) [cp. Ved. pāṇḍu, palita, pāṭala (pale-red); Gr. πελιτνός, πελλός, πολιός (grey); Lat. palleo (to be pale), pullus (grey); Lith. patvas (pale-yellow), pilkas (grey); Ohg. falo (pale, yellowish, withered); E. pale] pale-red or yellow, reddish, light yellow, grey; only at Th 2, 79 (kisā paṇḍu vivaṇṇā), where paṇḍu represents the usual up-paṇḍ'-uppaṇḍuka-jātā: "thin, pale and colourless" see ThA 80). Otherwise only in cpds., e. g.

-kambala a light red blanket, orange-coloured cloth S I.64 (=ratta-kambala C.); A I.181; Sn 689 (=ratta° SnA 487); also a kind of ornamental stone, Sakka's throne (p.-k.-silā) is made of it J I.330; II.93; II.53. (°silāsana); V.92 (id.); Pv II.9^{60} (°silā=p.-k-nāmaka silāsana PvA 138); VvA 110 (id.); KhA 122 (°varāsana); DhA I.17 (°silāsana). -palāsa a withered leaf Vin I.96=III.47; IV.217; Dh 235; VbhA 244; KhA 62; on °palāsika (DA I.270) see *J.P.T.S.* 1893, 37. -mattikā yellow loam, clay soil KhA 59. -roga jaundice Vin I.206 (°ābādha) 276 (id.); J I.431; II.102; DhA I.25. -rogin suffering from jaundice J II.285; III.401. -vīṇā yellow flute (of Pañcasikha): see beluva. -sīha yellow lion, one of the 4 kinds SnA 125 (cp. Manor.-pūr. on A II.33). -sutta orange-coloured string D I.76.

Paṇḍuka (-roga) perhaps to be read with v. l. at M II.121 for bandhuka°.

Paṇṇa (nt.) [Ved. parṇa, cp. Ags. fearn, E. fern] 1. a leaf (esp. betel leaf) Vin I.201 (5 kinds of leaves recommended for medicinal purposes, viz. nimba° Azadirachta Indica, kuṭaja° Wrightia antidysenterica, paṭola° Trichosanthes dioeca, sulasi° or tulasi° basil, kappāsika° cotton, see *Vin. Texts* II.46) A I.183 (tiṇa+) Sn 811 (p. vuccati paduma-pattaŋ Nd[1] 135); J I.167; II.105 (nimba)°; KhA 46 (khitta-p.-kosa-saṇṭhāna); PvA 115 (=patta) tālapaṇṇa a fan of palm leaves Vv 33[43] (=tālapattebi kata-maṇḍala-vijanī VvA 147); haritapaṇṇa greens, vegetable SnA 283; sūpeyyapaṇṇa curry leaf J I.98. — 2. a leaf for writing upon, written leaf, letter; donation, bequest (see below paṇṇākāra) J I.409 (cp. paṭipaṇṇa); II.104; IV.151 (ucchangato p. °ŋ niharati); DhA I.180; PvA 20 (likhā° written message). paṇṇaŋ āropeti to send a letter J I.227; pahiṇati id. J IV.145; V.458; peseti id. J I.178; IV.169. paṇṇaŋ likhati to write a letter J II. 174; VI.369 (paṇṇe wrote on a leaf), 385 iṇa° a promissory note J I.230; IV.256. — p. as ticket or label at DhsA 110. — 3. a feather, wing see su°.
-ākāra "state or condition of writing" (see ākāra 1), i. e. object of writing; that which is connected or sent with a letter, a special message, donation, present, gift J I.377; II.166; III.10; IV.316, 368; VI.-68, 390; SnA 78; DhA .184 326, 392,339: II.80; III.292 (dasavidha dibba°, viz. āyu etc.: see ṭhāna); IV.11. -kuṭi a hut of leaves D III.94; S I.226; J II.44; Pv III.2[20]; DA I.318. -chatta a fan of leaves J II.277. -chattaka a leaf-awning S I.90, 92. -dhāra a holder made of leaves J V.205. -pacchi leaf-basket, a b. for greens J VI.369. -puṭa a palm-leaf basket PvA 168. -saññā a mark of leaves (tied up to mark the boundary of a field) J I.153. -santhāra a spreading leaf, leaf cover, adj. spread with leaves A I.136; J VI.24. -sālā a hut of leaves, a hermitage J I.6, 7, 138; II.101 sq.; VI.30, 318 (nala-bhittikaŋ °ŋ katvā); VI.24. -susa (& sosa) drying the leaves (said of the wind) KhA 15.

Paṇṇaka [paṇṇa+ka] 1. green leaves (collectively), vegetable, greens J VI.24 (kāra° vegetable as homage or oblation); Pv III.3[3] (panko paṇṇako ca, expl[d] as "kaddamo vā udakacchikkhalo vā" PvA 189, but evidently misunderstood for "withered leaves"); PvA 256 (tiṇakaṭṭha-paṇṇaka-sala, is reading correct?). — 2. N. of a water plant, most likely a kind of fern (see Kern, *Toev.* p. 16 s. v.). Often comb[d] with sevāla (Blyxa Octandra), e. g. at J II.324; V.37. — The spelling is also paṇaka, even more frequent than paṇṇaka and also comb[d] with sevāla, e. g. Vin III.177 (in comb[n] saṇkha -sevāla°, where Bdhgh explains "sankho ti dīghamūlako paṇṇasevālo vuccati, sevālo ti nīlasevālo, avaseso udaka-pappaṭaka-nīla-bījak' ādi sabbo 'ti paṇako ti sankhaŋ gacchati"); S V.122; A III.187, 232, 235; J IV.71 (sevāla°); Miln 35 (sankha-sevāla-p. which the Manor-pūṛ expl[ns] by udaka-pappaṭaka, and also as "nīlamaṇḍūkapiṭṭhivaṇṇena udakapiṭṭhiŋ chādetvā nibattapaṇakaŋ" see Trenckner, Miln 421 and cp. *Miln. trsl[n]* I.302), 210 (suvaṇṇa°), 401 (cakkavāko sevāla paṇaka-bhakkho); KhA 61 (sevāla°; cp. Schubring's kalpasūtra p. 46 sq.). — 3. (see paṇṇa 2) a written leaf, a ticket DhsA 110.

Paṇṇatti see paññatti.

Paṇṇattika (adj.) [fr. paṇṇatti] having a manifestation or name, in a°-bhāva state without designation, state of non-manifestation, indefinite or unknown state (with ref. to the passing nature of the phenomenal world) DhA I.89; II.163.

Paṇṇarasa & **Paṇṇavīsati** see pañca 1. B, & C.

Paṇṇāsa see pañca 2. A.

Paṇṇi (f.) [=paṇṇa] a leaf Vin I.202 (taka°).

Paṇṇika [paṇṇa+ika] one who deals with greens, a florist or greengrocer J I.411; II.180; III.21 (°dhītā); Miln 331.

Paṇṇikā (f.) [to paṇṇaka; cp. Sk. parṇikā; meaning uncertain, cp. Kern, *Toev.* p. 17 s. v.] greens, green leaves, vegetable Vin II.267 (na harītaka °ŋ pakiṇitabbaŋ, trsl. at *Vin. Texts* III.343 by "carry on the business of florist and seedsman," thus taken as paṇṇika, cp. also *Vin. Texts* III.112); J I.445 (paṇṇikāya saññaŋ adāsi is faulty; reading should be saṇṇikāya "with the goad," of saṇ(ṇ)ikā =Sk. sṛṇi elephant-driver's book).

Paṇhi (m. & f.) [Ved. pārṣṇi, Av. paṣṇā, Lat. perna, Gr. πτέρνα. Goth. fairzna, Ohg. fersana =Ger. ferse] the heel Vin II.280 (°samphassa); J II.240; V.145; Sdhp 147, 153. See next.

Paṇhikā (f.) [fr. paṇhi] the heel J I.491; KhA 49 (°aṭṭhi); Vism 253 (id.); PvA 185.

Paṇhin (adj.) [fr. paṇhi] having heels D II.17 (āyata° having projecting heels, the 3rd of the 32 characteristics of a Mahāpurisa).

Patati [Ved. patati, Idg. *pet "to fly" as well as "to fall." Cp. Av. pataiti fly, hurry; Gr. πέτομαι fly, ὠκυπέτης quick, πίπτω fall; Lat. praepes quick, peto to go for, impetus, attack etc.] to fall, jump, fall down on (loc., acc. & instr.), to alight J I.278 (dīpake); Sn 248 (nirayaŋ); Pv IV.10[8] (1st pl. patāmase); Miln 187; PvA 45, ppr. patanto J I.263 (asaniyā); III.188 (nāvāya); fut. patissati J III.277; aor. pati Sn 1027 (sirasā); J III.55; Pv I.7[8]; ger. patitvā J I.291; III.26; PvA 16; DhA III.196 (vv. ll. papāta & papatā the latter aor. of papatati, q. v.); ger. patitvā J I.291; III.26; PvA 16. — pp. patita (q. v.). — Caus. pāteti (q. v.). Pass. (Caus.) patīyati is brought to fall also intrs. rush away J IV.415 (=palāyati C.); Miln 187.

Patatthi at J VI.276 is misprint for pathaddhi (q. v.).

Patana (nt. adj.) [fr. patati] falling, falling out, ruin, destruction J I.293 (akkhīni); II.154; III.188 (geha°); VI.85 (usu° range of his arrow).

Patanaka (adj.) [fr. patana] on the point of falling, going to fall, falling J VI.358.

Patanu (adj.) [pa+tanu] very thin J VI.578 (°kesa); Dhs 362 (°bhāva) =DhsA 238; Kvu 299 (id.).

Patara [Vedic pradara, pa+dṛ, with t. for d.; see Trenckner, *Notes* 62[16]; Geiger, *P.Gr.* § 39, 4] a split, a slit J IV.32.

Patarati [pa+tarati] 1. to go through or forth, to run out, to cross over D I.248; J III.91 (aor. patari). — 2. to overflow, boil over (of water) Miln 260. — Caus. patāreti (q. v.).

Patākā (f.) [cp. later Sk. patākā] a flag, banner (cp. dhaja) J I.52; VvA 31, 173.

Patāpa [fr. pa+tap] splendour, majesty Vv 40[8] (=tejas, ānubhāvo VvA 180).

Patāpavant (adj.) [fr. patāpa] splendid, majestic Sn 550 (=jutimantatāya p. SnA 453); Th 1, 820.

Patāpeti [pa+tāpeti, Caus. of tap] scorch, burn fiercely Vv 79[6] (=ativiya dīpeti VvA 307). Sdhp 573.

Patāyati [in form = pa + tāyati, diff. in meaning; not sufficiently expl[d], see Kern, *Toev.* p. 29 s. v. It is probably a distorted *sphāṭayati: see under pharati, phalaka and phāteti] to be spread out, intrs. to spread (?) A IV.97 (kodho p., as if fr. **pat**); J III.283 (C. nikkhamati, as if fr. **tṛ**, Kern. trsl[n] "to be for sale").

Patāreti [Caus. of patarati] to make go forth, to bring over or through M I.225; A III.432 (v. l. M. pakaroti). — aor. patārayi in meaning "strive" at J III.210 (= patarati vāyamati C. but Rhys Davids, "to get away from"); as "assert" at J V.117.

Pati[1] [Ved. pati, Av. paitis lord, husband; Gr. πόσις husband, Lat. potis, potens, possum, hos-pes; Goth. brūþ-faþs bridegroom, hunda faþs centurion, Lith. pāts husband] lord, master, owner, leader. — 1. in general D III.93 (khettānaŋ p. gloss adhipati). Mostly -°; see under gavam°, gaha°, dāna°, yūtha°, senā°. — 2. husband S I.210; Sn 314; J III.138; PvA 161. See also sapatika (with her husband), patibbatā & patika.
-kula her husband's clan ThA 283; VvA 206; -devatā a devoted wife J III.406; VvA 128.

Pati[2] (indecl.) [Vedic prati etc.] a doublet of paṭi; both often found side by side; pati alone always as prep. (with acc.) and as prefix with **sthā** (patiṭṭhāti, patiṭṭhita etc.). All cases are referred to the form with paṭi°, except in the case of patiṭṭh°. The more frequent cases are the foll.: patikāra, °kuṭati, °caya, °dissati, °nandati, °manteti, °māneti, °ruddha, °rūpa, °līna, °sallāna, etc. °sibbati, °sevati, °ssata, °ssaya, °ssava.

Patika (adj.) [only f. patikā and only as -°] having a husband in mata° "with husband dead," a widow Th 2, 221 (= vidhuva ThA 179); J V.103 (ap° without husband, v. l. for appatīta, C. expl[n] by assāmika). pavuttha° (a woman) whose husband lives abroad Vin II.268; III.83; Miln 205 (pavuttha°). See also pañcapatika & sapatika.

Patika at Vism 28 is to be read pātika (vessel, bowl, dish).

Patiṭṭhahati (& **Patiṭṭhāti**) [paṭi + **sthā**] to stand fast or firmly, to find a support in (loc.), to be established (intrs.), to fix oneself, to be set up, to stay; aor. patiṭṭhahi DhA III.175 (sotāpattiphale), PvA 42 (id.), 66 (id.); VvA 69 (sakadāgāmiphale); and patiṭṭhāsi Miln 16. — fut. °ṭṭhahissati J V.458 (°hessati); DhA III.171. — ger. patiṭṭhāya Sn 506; J II.2 (rajje); III.52; V.458 (rajje); Miln 33; PvA 142. — pp. **patiṭṭhita** (q. v.). — Caus. patiṭṭhāpeti (q. v.).

Patiṭṭhā (f.) [fr. pati + **sthā**. Cp. Ved. pratiṣṭhā support, foundation] support, resting place, stay, ground, help, also (spiritual) helper, support for salvation S I.1 (ap°); II.65; III.53; Sn 173; Dh 332; J I.149; IV.20; Miln 302; DhsA 261; VvA 138; PvA 53, 60 (= dīpa), 87 (= dīpa), 141 (su°), 174 (su° = dīpa).

Patiṭṭhāna (nt.) [fr. paṭi + **sthā** cp. late Sk. pratiṣṭhāna] fixing, setting up, support, help, ground (for salvation) Sn 1011; PvA 123.

Patiṭṭhāpita [pp. of patiṭṭhāpeti] put down, set down, established PvA 139.

Patiṭṭhāpitar [n. ag. of patiṭṭhāpeti] one who establishes A V.66.

Patiṭṭhāpeti [Caus. of patiṭṭhahati, cp. BSk. pratiṣṭhāpayati Jtm 224] to establish, set up, fix, put into, instal D I.206; S I.90; J I.152; 168, 349 (sotāpatti-phale); PvA 22 (id.), 38 (id.) 50 (saraṇesu ca sīlesu ca), 223 (id.), 76 (cetiyaŋ), 78 (upāsakabhāve), 131, 132 (hatthe). — aor. patiṭṭhāpesi J I.138. — pp. patiṭṭhāpita (q. v.).

Patiṭṭhāha [fr. patiṭṭhahati] having one's footing in, hold on, tenacity Dhs 381 = Nd[2] 271[III] = DhsA 253. The v. l. at Nd[2] is paṭiggāha which is also read by Dhs.

Patiṭṭhita [pp. of patiṭṭhahati] established in (loc.), settled, fixed, arrayed, stayed, standing, supported, founded in D III.101 (supatiṭṭhita-citta); M I.448; S I.40, 45, 185 (dhammesu); It 77; Sn 409, 453; J I.51 (kucchimhi), 262 (rajje); Pv I.4[4]; II.9[69] (dussīlesu); Miln 282; VvA 110 (°gabbhā), 259 (°saddha); PvA 34 (jāta +). — nt. °ŋ arrangement, settling, in pañca° the fivefold array, a form of respectful greeting, see under pañca.

Patiṭṭhīyati [only apparently (Pass.) to patiṭṭhahati, of **sthā**, but in reality = Sk. prati-sthyāyate, of **sthyā**, see thīna. Ought to be paṭitthīyati; but was by popular analogy with patiṭṭhāya changed to patiṭṭhīyati] to be obdurate, to offer resistance A I.124; II.203; III.181 sq.; J IV.22 (aor. °ṭṭhiya); Pug 36; KhA 226.

Patita [pp. of patati] fallen Dh 68, 320; J I.167; Miln 187; PvA 31 (read pātita), 56.

Patitaka (adj.) [fr. last] thrown or fallen into (loc.), dropped Vism 62.

Patitiṭṭhati [paṭi + titthati] to stand up again Th 1, 173.

Patittha [pa + tittha] a bank of a river or lake, su° (adj.) with beautiful banks S I.90; Pv II.1[20] (= sundaratittha PvA 77).

Patibbatā (f.) [pati + vatā] a devoted wife (cp. patidevatā) J II.121; VI.533; VvA 56, 110.

Patissata see paṭi°.

Patīta [pp. of pacceti] pleased, delighted Dh 68; Sn 379, 679; Vv 84[10] (= pahaṭṭha VvA 337). — neg. appatīta displeased M I.27; J V.103 (v. l. appatika, C. expl[n] by assāmika, i. e. without husband).

Patīyati see patati.

Pateyya in phrase **alam-pateyya** at D III.71 (kumārikā alam-pateyyā), 75 (id.) means "surely fit to have husbands, ripe for marriage" (?)

Patoda [fr. pa + **tud** cp. Ved. pratoda] a goad, driving stick, prick, spur M I.124; III.97; S IV.176; A II.114; III.28; IV.91; V.324; Th 1, 210; J I.57, 192; Dhs 16, 20, 292; Pug 25; SnA 147; ThA 174; Sdhp 367.
-laṭṭhi a driver's stick, goad-stick [cp. BSk. pratodayaṣṭi Divy 7, 76, 463, 465] D I.105, 126; J VI.249; Miln 27; DhA 1.302; II.38; IV.216; VvA 64. As °yaṭṭhi at Dpvs XI.30.

Patodaka (adj. n.) [fr. pa + **tud**] lit. pushing, spurring; only in phrase **aṅguli°** nudging with one's fingers Vin III.84 = IV.110 (here to be taken as "tickling"); D I.91 (cp. Dial. I.113); A IV.343.

Patta[1] (nt.) [Ved. patra, to ***pet** as in patati (q. v. & see also paṇṇa); cp. Gr. πτερόν wing, πτέρυξ id.; Lat. penna feather = Ger. fittig.; acci-piter; Ohg. fedara = E. feather etc.] 1. the wing of a bird, a feather Vin IV.259; D I.71. kukkuṭa° a hen's quill (for sewing) Vin II.215. — 2. a leaf M I.429; Sn 44 = 64 (sañchinna°, see Nd[2] 625); 625 (pokkhara° lotus l.); Dh 401 (id.); Nd[1] 135 (paduma°); Pv II.9[6] (= paṇṇa PvA 15); VvA 147 (tāla°); ThA 71; PvA 283 (nigrodha°). asi-patta-vana "sword-leaf-forest" (a forest in Niraya) Sn 673; PvA 221. — 3. a small thin strip of metal at the lute Miln 53; VvA 281.
-āḷhalka a toy measure made of palm-leaves Vin II.10; III.180; D I.6 (cp. DA I.86); M I.266; A V.203; Miln 229. -gandha odour of leaves Dhs 625. -nāḷi rib of a feather DhA I.394. -phala leaf-fruit, a leaf and fruit, vegetables Sn 239 (= yaŋ kiñci harita-paṇṇaŋ SnA

283); PvA 86. -yāna having wings as vehicle, "wing-goer," i. e. a bird Sn 606 (=pattehi yantī ti pattayānā SnA 465); J II.443. -rasa taste of leaves Dhs 629; juice of leaves Vin I.246 (+puppharasa & ucchurasa). -salākā leaf-ticket DhA IV.65.

Patta[2] (m. & nt.) [Ved. pātra, fr. Idg. *pōtlom=Lat. poculum beaker, Oir. ōl. See pāna & pibati] a bowl, esp. the alms-bowl of a bhikkhu Vin I.46, 50, 51, 61, 224 (patte pūresuŋ); II.111, 126, 224, 269; S I.112; A IV.344; Sn 413, 443; J I.52, 55 (pattaŋ thavikāya pakkhipati), 69; III.535 (puṇṇa °ŋ deti to give a full bowl, i. e. plenty); V.389 (pl. pattāni); Vism 108 (āṇigaṇṭhik' āhato ayopatto); DhA IV.220 (°ŋ pūreti); PvA 35, 61, 76, 88, 141. — Two kinds of bowls are mentioned at Vin 243, viz. ayo° of iron & mattikā° of clay, dāru° a wooden bowl Vin II.112, 143. uda° a bowl of water or a water-bowl M I.100; S V.121; A III.230 sq. cp. odapattakinī. — pattassa mukhavaṭṭi J V.38. — fut. pātī (q. v.).

-ādhāraka bowl support, bowl-hold Vin II.113. -kaṇḍolikā a wicker-work stand for a bowl Vin II.114 (cp. *Vin. Texts* III.86). -gata gone into the bowl, alms given Th 1, 155; Pv IV.7[3]. -gāhāpaka one who is going to take a bowl, a receiver of a b. Vin II.177 (+sāṭiya° etc.); A III.275. -cīvara bowl and robe (see note in *Dial* II.162) Vin I.46; II.78, 194; S I.76; J III.379; Pv II.13[16]; DA I.45, 186; PvA 61. -tthavikā a bag to carry a bowl in Vin II.114; J III.364; VvA 40, 63; KhA 45. -dhovana "bowl-washing," (the water used for) washing the bowl Vin II.214. -pāṇin hand on bowl, bowl in hand Sn 713; It 89=S III.93≈; *onīta*° removing the hand from the bowl: see onīta. -piṇḍika "eating from one vessel only" A III.220. -maṇḍala a circular artificial bottom of a bowl Vin II.112. -māḷaka a raised parapet (?) on which to put the bowl Vin II.114 (cp. *Vin. Texts* III.86). -mūla the bottom of the bowl Vin II.269. -vaṭṭi the brim of a bowl S IV.168. -saññin paying attention to one's bowl Vin II.214.

Patta[3] [pp. of pāpuṇāti] obtained, attained, got, reached (pass. & med.) Sn 55, 138, 478, 517, 542, 992; Dh 134 (nibbānaŋ) 423; J I.255 (vināsaŋ); IV.139 (samuddaŋ); PvA 4 (anayavyasanaŋ), 5 (sīsacchedaŋ), 71 (manussabhāvaŋ). Very frequent as -° and in meaning equal to finite verb or other phrase, when spelling °ppatta is restored (Sk. prāpta), e. g. ummādappatta out of mind PvA 6; jarā° old J III.394; dukkha° afflicted with pain J VI.336; domanassa° dejected J II.155; patti° attained one's (possible) share It 32; bala° (become) strong D II.157; vaya° (become) old, come of age J II.421 (+soḷasa-vassa-kāle); PvA 68; somanassa° pleased J III.74; haritu° covered with green M I.343; J I.50, 399. Also as °-, but less frequent, meaning often equal to prep. "with," "after," etc., as pattâbhiseka after consecration DhA IV.84; SnA 484; pattuṇṇa with wool SnA 263; °dhamma mastering the Dh. Vin I.16; the same at DhA IV.200 in meaning of patti°, i. e. "merit attained"; °mānasa (?) It 76 (v. l. satta°); °sambodhi It 97 (v. l. satta°). — Opp. appatta not obtained (see also patti 2), i. e. without Dh 272 (cp. DhA III.58); Pug 51 (°pānabhojana, so read for appanna°). — Cp. sam°.

Patta[4] at Dpvs XI.18 for pattin or pattika, foot-man, infantry.

Patta-kkhandha [perhaps patta[1]+khandha, thus "leaf-shouldered," i. e. with shoulders drooping like leaves; the Commentators explain patta as contracted form of patita fallen, thus "with shoulders falling." We may have to deal with an old misspelling for panna (=pa+**nam** bent down, put down), which expl[n] would suit the sense better than any other] downcast, dejected, disappointed Vin II.77=III.162 (trsl[d] "with fallen hearts," expl[d] as patita, see *Vin. Texts* III.13); S I.124; M I.132, 258; III.298; A III.57; J V.17; Miln 5.

Pattaka (nt.) [fr. patta[2]] a (little) bowl Th 2, 28.

Pattatta (nt.) (-°) [abstr. fr. patta[3]] the fact of being furnished or possessed with Vism 524.

Pattabba (adj.) [grd. of pāpuṇāti] to be gained or attained; nt. that which can be attained or won SnA 443. See also pattiya[2].

Pattali (°lī) (f.) [according to Kern, *Toev.* s. v. to be read as either sattali or sattalā] plantain Th 2, 260 (=kadali ThA 211).

Patti[1] [Ved. patti, *pad (of pada)+ti] on foot, one who is on foot, a foot-soldier Vin IV.105 (as one of the 4 constituents of a senā or army, viz. hatthī elephants, assā, horses, rathā chariots, pattī infantry); J IV.494 (hatthī, assā, rathā, pattī); 463 (hatthī assā rathā, pattī senā padissate mahā); Vism 19. Cp. pattika[1].

-kāya a body of foot soldiers, infantry S I.72 (cp. BSk. same, at Jtm 215 with hasty-aśva-ratha°). -kārika (for °kārika, of prec.) a foot soldier, lit. one of a body of infantry J IV.134; V.100; VI.15 (hatthāruhā anīkaṭṭhā rathikā pattikārikā), 21, 463 (hatthī assā rathikā p.).

Patti[2] (f.) [Classical Sk. prāpti fr. pa+āp, cp. patta[3]] 1. (-°) obtaining, acquiring, getting, entering into, state of S I.189=Th 1, 1230 (nibbāna°); Sn 68 (paramattha°), 186 (nibbāna°); PvA 5 (vyasana), 112 (id.); Sdhp 379. — 2. attainment, acquisition S II.29 (aggassa); Sn 425 (yogakkhemassa); Nd[2] 390 (=lābhā paṭilābhā adhigamo phusanaŋ sacchikiriyā); esp. in phrase apattassa patti "att' of the unattained" D III.255=A IV.332; S I.217; II.29; A II.148; III.179; Kvu 581. — 3. gaining, gain, profit, advantage S I.169 (brahma° "best vantage ground"). — 4. merit, profit, in special sense of a gift given for the benefit of someone else (as a "dakkhiṇā"), accrediting, advising, transference of merit, a gift of merit J II.423, 425 (=dakkhiṇā); IV.21; DhA I.270 (opp. to mūla price); II.4; IV.200 sq. (opp. to mūla). See also cpds. °dāna & °dhamma. — 5. that which obtains (as a rule), occasion, happening, state, place, as gram. t. t. loc. pattiyaŋ or pattiyā (-°) in lieu of SnA 310, 317. — See sam°.

-dāna an assigned or accredited gift, giving of merit (as permanent acquisition), transference of merit VvA 188, 190; PvA 9 (°vasena dānadhamma-pariccāgo), 49 (=dakkhiṇā) 88 (id.); Sdhp 229. -dhamma the practice of transferred merit, see *Kvu trsl*[n] 161[1], 170, & cp. pattadhamma. -patta, one who has obtained what can be obtained, or the highest gain (i. e. Nibbāna) Sn 536 (=pattabbaŋ patto pattabbaŋ arahattaŋ patto ti vuttaŋ hoti SnA 433), 537, 540.

Patti[3] (f.) [for patta[1] ?] leaf, leafy part of a plant Vin I.201 (taka, taka-patti, taka-paṇṇi).

Pattika[1] [fr. patti[1] cp. pajja[2]] on foot, a pedestrian or soldier on foot, D I.50, 89, 106, 108; II.73; A II.117 (hatth'-āruha, assāruha, rathika, p.); J VI.145; Vism 396 (manussā pattikā gacchanti); Sn 418; 448 (hatthāruha anīkaṭṭha rathike pattikārika); DhA I.385.

Pattika[2] [fr. patti[2]] having a share, gain or profit; a partner, donor DhA I.270, 271.

Pattika[3] (adj.-n.) [fr. patta[2]] in dāru° (collecting alms) with a wooden bowl, man with a wooden bowl D I.157 (cp. DA I.319).

Pattikā (f.) [fr. patta[1] or patti[3]] a leaf, in tāla° palm-leaf S II.217, 222.

Pattin (adj. n.) [fr. patta[3], Sk. *prāptin] attaining, one who obtains or gains Sn 513 (kiŋ°=kiŋ patta, adhigata SnA 425).

Pattiya[1] (adj. n.) [for *pratyaya = paccaya, cp. Trenckner, *Notes* 7[3], 9] believing, trusting, relying J v.414 (para°); (m.) belief, trust J v.231 (parapattiyena by relying on others), 233 (id.), 414 (id.).

Pattiya[2] (adj.) [grd. of pāpuṇāti; cp. pattabba] to be attained, to be shared or profited Pv II.9[31] (para° profitable to others, see expl° at PvA 125).

Pattiyāyati [denom. fr. pattiya[1]] to believe, trust, rely on J I.426; v.403; DA I.73.

Pattiyāyana (nt.) [fr. pattiyāyati] belief J v.402.

Pattiyati [denom. fr. patti[2]] to gain, to profit from (acc.) Miln 240 (attānaŋ na p. does not profit from himself).

Pattha[1] [fr. pa + sthā. Cp. Epic Sk. prastha plateau] a lonely place, in cpd. vana° D I.71; Pug 59 etc., a wilderness in the forest, expl[d] by Bdhgh as "gāmantaŋ atikkamitvā manussānaŋ anupacāra-ṭṭhānaŋ yattha na kasanti na vapanti" DA I.210; Ud 43 (patthañ ca sayan' āsanaŋ, ed.; but better with id. p. Dh 185 as pantañ, which is expl[d] at DhA III.238 by "vivittaŋ," i. e. separately). Cp. with this Sk. vana-prastha a forest situated on elevated land.

Pattha[2] [cp. late Sk. prastha] a Prastha (certain measure of capacity) = ¼ of an Āḷhaka; a cooking utensil containing one Prastha DhA II.154; SnA 476 (cattāro patthā āḷhakaŋ).

Patthaṭa [pp. of pattharati] stretched, spread out J I.336; Vism 364; DA I.311.

Patthaṇḍila [pa + thandila] hermitage M II.155.

Patthaddha [pa + thaddha] (quite) stiff Vin II.192; Th I, 1074.

Patthanā (f.) [of ap + **arth**, cp. Sk. prārthayati & prārthana nt., prārthanā f.] aiming at, wish, desire, request, aspiration, prayer S II.99, 154; A I.224; III.47; v.212; Nd[1] 316, 337 (p. vuccati taṇhā); Nd[2] 112; Nett 18, 27; Dhs 1059; Miln 3; SnA 47, 50; DhA II.36; PvA 47. — patthanaŋ karoti to make a wish J I.68; DhA I.48; °ŋ ṭhapeti id. DhA I.47; II.83; IV.200.

Patthara [cp. late Sk. prastara. The ord. meaning of Sk. pr. is "stramentum"] 1. stone, rock S I.32. — 2. stoneware Miln 2.

Pattharati [pa + tharati] to spread, spread out, extend J I.62; IV.212; VI.279; DhA I.26; III.61 (so read at J VI.549 in cpd °pāda with spreading feet, v. l. patthaṭa°). — pp. **patthaṭa** (q. v.). — Caus. patthāreti with pp. patthārita probably also to be read at Th I, 842 for padhārita.

Pattharika [fr. patthara] a merchant Vin II.135 (kaŋsa°).

Patthita [pp. of pattheti] wished for, desired, requested, sought after Sn 836; Miln 227, 361; DhA IV.201; PvA 47 (°ākāra of the desired kind, as wished for); Sdhp 79 (a°).

Patthina [pa + thina] stiff D II.335; DhsA 307. Also as **patthinna** at Vin I.286 (= atirajitattā thaddha Bdhgh, on p. 391); Vism 361 (= thīna p. 262); VbhA 67 (°sneha).

Pattheti [pa + **arth**, cp. Sk. prārthayati] to wish for, desire, pray for, request, long for S IV.125; v.145; Sn 114, 899; Th 2, 341; Nd[1] 312, 316; PugA 208 (āsaŋsati +); PvA 148; Sdhp 66, 319; ppr. **patthento** PvA 107; **patthayanto** J I.66 (paramâbhisaŋbodhiŋ); **patthayaŋ** Sn 70 (= icchanto patthayanto abhijappanto Nd[2] 392); **patthayamāna** M I.4; Sn 902; J I.259; DhA III.193; PvA 226 (= āsiŋsamāna); & **patthayāno** Sn 900; It 67, 115. — grd. patthetabba PvA 96, patthayitabba PvA 95, and patthiya which only occurs in neg. form apatthiya what ought not to be wished J IV.61; Pv II.6[7] (= apatthayitabbaŋ PvA 95); DhA I.29; also as na-patthiya (med.) one who does not wish for himself Sn 914 (cp. Nd[2] 337). — pp. patthita (q. v.).

Patvā see pāpuṇāti.

Patha [of **path**, Ved. pathi with the 3 bases pathi, path° aud panth°, of which only the last two have formed independent nouns, viz. patha and pantha (q. v.)] 1. path, road, way D I.63; Sn 176 (loc. pathe), 385, 540, 868; Nd[2] 485 B (+ pantha, in expl[n] of magga); J I.308 (loc. pathe); II.39; VI.525 (abl. pathā); Th I, 64; Pug 22, 57; Mhvs 21, 24 (pathe); 36, 93 (loc. pathi, see Geiger, Gr. § 89); Sdhp 241. — 2. Very frequent as -°, where it is sometimes pleonastic, and acts in the function of an abstract formation in *°tā* or *°ttaŋ* (cp. similar use of anta: see anta[1] 5; and pada: see pada 3), e. g. anila° (air) J IV.119; anupariyāya° A IV.107; ādicca° (path of the sun, sky) DhA III.177; ummagga° S I.193; kamma° DhA I.36; gaṇana° (range of) calculation Miln 20; cakkhu° J IV.403 (= cakkhūnaŋ etaŋ nāmaŋ C.); catummahā° A III.28, 42, 394; dve° Vv 53[17]; nakkhatta° Dh 208; yañña° (= yañña) Nd[2] 524; yogga° A III.122; rajā° S II.219; rāga° (sensuality) S IV.70; vacana° (way of saying, speech) Vv 63[17] (= vacana VvA 262), etc. See also cakkhu°, ñeyya°, dveḷhā°, manussa°, yañña°, vāda°, sagga°, hattha°; der. pātheyya. — See also byappatha. —**apatha** where there is no way or road, wrong way J II.287; ThA 255; VvA 337.

-addhan "the journey or stretch of the path": see under addhan. -addhi (?) so perhaps to be read for patatthi, according to Fausböll J VI.276. Unclear in meaning, expl[d] by nibbiddha vīthi (frequented road ?) -gamana "going on their course," of the stars D I.10 (see *Dial.* I.20: "their usual course").

Pathabya [fr. pathavi = paṭhavi] belonging to the earth, ruler of the earth (?) A IV.90 (reading uncertain).

Pathavi see paṭhavi.

Pathāvin [fr. patha] a traveller Vin IV.108; J VI.65; DA I.298.

Pada (nt.) [Ved. pad, pād (m.) foot, and also pāda; pada (nt.) step. Cp. Gr. πώς (ποὺς) = Lat. pēs, Goth. fōtus = Ohg fuoz = E. foot; further Arm. het track, Gr. πεδά after, πέδον field, πεζός on foot, etc.; Lith. pėdà track; Ags. fetvan = E. fetch. — The decl. in Pāli is vocalic (a), viz. pada; a trace of the consonant (root) decl. is instr. sg. padā (Th I, 457; Sn 768), of cons. (s) decl. instr. padasā with the foot, on foot (D I.107; J III.371; DhA I.391). — Gender is nt., but nom. pl. is frequently found as padā, e. g. at Dh 273; Nett 192 (mūla°)] 1. foot Dh 273 = SnA 366 (? saccānaŋ caturo padā); DA I.85; usually -°, like hatthipadaŋ elephant's foot M I.176, 184; S I.86; v.43, 231; and with numerals dvi° & di°, catup°, aṭṭha° (q. v.). In aṭṭha° also meaning "square of a chessboard." — 2. step, footstep, track Dh 179 (of a Buddha, cp. DhA III.194 & 197) J I.170 (footmark) II.154; in redupl.-iterative formation padāpadaŋ step by step Sn 446 (v. l. padânupadaŋ), and pade padaŋ Sn p. 107 (cp. SnA 451). — 3. (Often synonymous with °patha i. e. way, kind, & sometimes untranslatable) (a) lit. way, path, position, place Vin II.217 (nakkhatta° constellation); J I.315 (assama° = assama); v.75 (id.), 321 (id.); VI.76 (id.); VI.180 (v. l. patha; C. mahāmagga); mantapada = manta D I.104 (cp. DA I.273). See also janapada, saggapada. — (b) in appl[d] meaning (modal): case, lot, principle, part, constituent, characteristic, ingredient, item, thing, element M I.176 (cattāri padāni 4 characteristics);

S I.7 (pade pade "now in this thing, now in that" C. ārammaṇe ārammaṇe), 212 (amataŋ p. = nibbāna); II.280 (id.); A II.51 (id.), It 39 (p. asankhataŋ = nibbāna); Sn 88 (dhammapade sudesite; expl[d] as nibbāna-dhamma SnA 164; dhammapada = Dhamma), ibid. (anavajja-padāni sevamāna = principles), 700 (money-yaŋ uttamaŋ padaŋ, thing; but SnA 491 expl[s] as uttama-paṭipadaŋ), 765; Dh 21, 93, 114 (amataŋ), 254, 368 (santaŋ = nibbānass' etaŋ nāmaŋ, santa-koṭṭhāsaŋ DhA IV.108); Pv IV.3[48] (amataŋ); Nett 2 = 192 (nava padāni kusalāni); SnA 397 (nāmādi p.); Sdhp 47 (accutaŋ santaŋ p.), 615 (paramaŋ). See further dhamma°, nibbāna°, santi°, sikkhā°. — 4. a word, verse (or a quarter of a verse), stanza, line, sentence S II.36 (ekena padena sabbo attho vutto); S IV.379 = A V.320 (agga°); A II.182 (+ vyañjana & desanā); 189 (attha° text, motto); III.356 (id.); Sn 252 (= dhamma-desanā SnA 293), 374; Dh 273; J I.72 (atireka-pada-satena); Nett 4 (akkharaŋ padaŋ vyañjanaŋ, cp. nāmādīhi padehi at SnA 397, which is to be understood as nāma, pada & vyañjana, i. e. word, sentence & letter, cp. Mvyutp. 104, 74-76); Miln 148 (āhacca°); KhA 169; SnA 409 (ubhaya°), 444; VvA 3, 13; PvA 10, 26, 117 (word, term). abl. padaso (adv.) sentence by s[tce] or word by word Vin IV.14 (dhammaŋ vāceti = anupadaŋ C.; cp. KhA 190 p. °dhamma). At MA I.2 pada (sentence or division of a sentence) is contrasted with *akkhara* (word), when it is said that the Majjhima Nikāya consists of 80,523 padas and 740,053 akkharas. — Neg. apada (1) without feet, footless A IV.434 (Māra; v. l. apara); It 87 (sattā, + dvipada etc.). — (2) trackless, leaving no footprint, fig. having no desires (i. e. signs of worldliness) Dh 179 (rāga, etc., as padāni DhA III.197, but cp. also p. 194.)

-attha meaning of a word KhA 81, 84; SnA 91. **-ânupadaŋ** (adv.) on the track DhA II.38. **-ânupadika** following one's footsteps J II.78; DhA II.94 (therānaŋ); nt. adv. °ŋ close behind DhA I.290. **-ānupubbatā** (or °ta) succession of words Nd[1] 140 (in expl[n] of "iti"; cp. SnA 28); Nd[2] 137 (id.; reading °ka). **-uddhāra** synopsis of a verse SnA 237 (atthuddhāra +). **-kusala** clever at following a trail J III.501, 505. **-cārikā** a female (foot-) servant J IV.35. **-cetiya** "step-shrine," a holy footprint, a miraculous footprint left on the ground by a holy man DhA III.194. **-ccheda** separation of words, parsing SnA 150. **-jāta** (nt.) pedal character S I.86. **-ṭṭhāna** [cp. Sk. padasthāna footprint] "proximate cause" (*Cpd.* 13, 23) Nett 1 sq., 27 sq., 40 sq., 104; Vism 84. **-dvaya** twofold part (of a phrase), i. e. antecedent and subsequent DhsA 164. **-parama** one whose highest attainment is the word (of the text, and not the sense of it) A II.135, J VI.131; Pug 41 ("vyañjana-padam eva paramaŋ assā ti" PugA 223. **-pāripūrī** (f.) expletive particle Nd[2] 137; SnA 28. **-pūraṇa** filling out a verse; as tt. g. expletive particle SnA 590 (a), 139 (kho), 137 (kho pana), 378 (tato), 536 (pi), 230 (su), 416 (ha), 377 (hi); KhA 219 (tam), 188 (su); VvA 10 (maya). **-bhājana** dividing of words, i. e. treating each word (of a phrase) separately DhsA 234. **-bhājaniya** division of a phrase DhsA 54 **-bhāṇa** reciting or preaching (the words of the Scrpitures) DhA II.95; III.345; IV.18. **-vaṇṇanā** expl[n] of a pada or single verse SnA 65, 237; KhA 125, 132, 228. **-valañja** a footprint, track J VI.560; DhA II.38; III.194. **-viggaha** separation of words, resolution of a compound into its components VvA 326. **-vibhāga** separation of words, parsing SnA 269; PvA 34. **-saŋsagga** contact of words Nd[1] 139; Nd[2] 137; SnA 28. **-sadda** sound of footsteps Sn p. 80; J IV.409. **-sandhi** euphonic combination of words Nd[1] 445; Nd[2] 137; KhA 155, 224; SnA 28, 40, 157 etc.; PvA 52. **-silā** a stone for stepping on, flag Vin II.121 = 154.

Padaka[1] (adj.) [fr. pada[4]] one who knows the padas (words or lines), versed in the padapāṭha of the Veda (Ep. of an educated Brahmin) D I.88 = Sn p. 105 (where AvŚ II.19 in id. p. has padaśo = P. padaso word by word, but Divy 620 reads padako; ajjheti vedeti cā ti padako); M I.386; A I.163, 166; Sn 595; Miln 10, 236.

Padaka[2] (nt.) = pada 3, viz. basis, principle or pada 4, viz. stanza, line J V.116 (= kāraṇa-padāni C.).

Padaka[3] (nt.) [fr. pada[1]] in cpd. aṭṭha° an "eight-foot," i. e. a small inset square (cp. aṭṭha-pada chess-board), a patch (?) Vin I.297. See also **padika**.

Padakkhiṇa (adj.) [pa + dakkhiṇa] 1. "to the right," in phrase **padakkhiṇaŋ karoti** (with acc. of object) to hold (a person, etc.) to one's right side, i. e. to go round so as to keep the right side turned to a person, a mode of reverential salutation Vin I.17; S I.138; A I.294; II.21, 182; III.198; Sn 1010; J I.50, 60; III.392. — 2. "(prominent) with the right," i. e. skilful, clever, quick in learning J IV.469 (= susikkhita C.). — 3. lucky, auspicious, turning out well or favourable J V.353 (= sukha-nipphattin vuddhi-yutta C.).

-ggāhin "right-handed," i. e. cleverly taking up (what is taught), good at grasping or understanding A III.79, 180, V.24 sq., 90, 338; DhA II.105. — Opp. appadakkhiṇaggāhin "left-handed," unskilled, untrained (cp. Ger. "linkisch") S II.204 sq.; J III.483. **-ggāhitā** skilfulness, quick grasp, cleverness KhA 148.

Padatta (nt.) [abstr. fr. pada] being or constituting a lot, part or element SnA 164.

Padara (nt.) [pa + dara of **dṛ**, cp. dabba, darati, dāru] 1. a cleft, split, fissure, crevice M I.469; S II.32; Sn 720 (= darī SnA 500); comb[d] with kandara at Miln 36, 296, 411; PvA 29. — 2. a board, plank J II 10 91 (°sakaṭa) 112; III.181; V.47 sq.; VI.432 (°cchanna); SnA 330 (dabba° oar), 355; DhA II.55; III.296. — 3. Wrong spelling for badara at J IV.363 (beluvā p°āni ca) & VI.529.

-sañcita filled with clefts (?) Vin IV.46. **-samācāra** refractiousness, disobedience (?) M I.469.

Padahati [pa + **dhā**] 1. to strive, exert D III.221 (cittaŋ paggaṇhāti p.); PvA 31 (yoniso p.). — 2. to confront, take up, fight against, stand J VI.508 (usīraŋ muñja-pubbajaŋ urasā padahessāmi "I shall stand against the grasses with my chest"; C. expl[s] by dvedhā katvā purato gamissāmi, i. e. break and go forward). — *Note.* padahasi at J IV.383 read pade hasi (see Windisch, *Māra & B.* p. 124 & Morris, *J.P.T.S.* 1893, 51. Windisch takes padahasi as pa + **dah** to burn, & translates "du willst das Feuer brennen," i. e. you attempt something impossible, because the fire will burn you). — pp. pahita (q. v.).

Padahana see padhāna.

Padātar [n. ag. of padāti] extravagant, a squanderer Pdgp. 65, 68.

Padāti (padadāti, padeti) [pa + **dā**] 1. to give, bestow Pv I.11[6] (ger. padatvā, perhaps better to read ca datvā, as v. l. BB); J III.279 (fut. padassati); V.394 (id.). — 2. to acquire, take, get J I.190 (inf. padātave, C. gahetuŋ). — Pass padiyati (q. v.).

Padāna (nt.) [fr. pa + **dā**] giving, bestowing; but appears to have also the meaning of "attainment, characteristic, attribute" A I.102 (bāla° & paṇḍita°); J I.97 (sotāpatti-magg' ādi°); PvA 71 (anubala°); ThA 35 (anupatti-dhammatā°). — At Th 1, 47 Kern (*Toev.* II.138) proposes to read tuyhaŋ padāne for T. tuyh' âpadāne, and translates padāna by "footstep, footprint." See also sapadāna & sampadāna.

Padāraṇa (nt.) [pa + **dṛ**] splitting, tearing Th 1, 752.

Padālana (nt.) [fr. padāleti] cleaving, bursting open, breaking Nett 61, 112 (mohajāla°); ThA 34 (mohakkhandha°).

Padālita [pp. of padāleti] broken, pierced, destroyed S I.136; III.83; A V.88 (appadālita-pubbaŋ lobhakkhandhaŋ); Sn 546 (āsavā te p.; quoted at VvA 9); ThA 34 (as A. V.88 with moha°).

Padālitatta (nt.) [abstr. fr. padālita] the fact of having (med.) or being (pass.) pierced or broken, abl. padālitattā on account of baving broken Miln 287.

Padāletar [n. ag. to padāleti] one who pierces or destroys, a destroyer, breaker, in phrase mahato kāyassa padāletā the destroyer of a great body (or bulk) A I.284 sq. (in sequence dūre-pātin, akkhaṇavedhin, m. k. p.); II.170 sq., 202; cp. padāleti^1.

Padāleti [Caus. of pa+**dal**] 1. to cleave, break, pierce, destroy, in comb^n °khandhaŋ padāleti to destroy the great mass of . . ., e. g. tamo° It 8 (padālayuŋ); Th 2, 28 (ger. padāliya = moha° padālitvā ThA 34); lobha° S V.88; avijjā° A I.285. — 2. to break, break down, tear down, burst open J I.73 (pabbata-kūṭāni); IV.173 (matthakaŋ p°etvā uṭṭhita-singā); V.68 (silāya matthakaŋ); Miln 332 (diṭṭhi-jālaŋ); DA I.37 (Sineruŋ). See also sam°. — pp. padālita (q. v.).

Padika (adj.) [fr. pada 1; cp. padaka^3] consisting of feet or parts, -fold; dvādasa° twelve fold J I.75 (paccayākāra).

Paditta [pp. of pa+**dīp**, cp. Sk. pradīpta] kindled, set on fire, blazing S III.93 ≈ (chav' âlataŋ ubhato padittāŋ); J VI.108; Sdhp 208 (°angārakāsuŋ).

Padippati [pa+dippati] to flame forth, to blaze Cp III 9^3 (davaḍāho p.). — pp. paditta (q. v.). — Caus. padīpeti (q. v.).

Padissa (adj.) [grd. of padissati] being seen, to be seen, appearing D II.205 (upasantappa°).

Padissati [pa+dissati, Pass. of **dṛś**] to be seen Sn 108 (doubtful; v. l. padussati; expl^d at SnA 172 by patidissati, v. l. padussati, cp. p. 192); Cp I.10^2; J VI.89; Sdhp 427.

Padīpa [cp. Epic Sk. pradīpa] 1. a light Dh 146; Vv 46^2 (jalati blazes); Tikp 14; Miln 40; VvA 51 (padīpaŋ ujjāletvā lighting a lamp, making a light); PvA 38; Sdhp 250. — 2. a lamp Sn 235 (nibbanti dhīrā yath' âyaŋ p.); DhA II.163 (anupādāno viya p.). °ŋ karoti to make a light, to light up Vin I.118; °ŋ ujjāleti see under 1. Usually as tela-padīpa an oil lamp Vin I.15; S II.86 (telañ ca vaṭṭiñ ca telapadīpo jhāyati) = IV.213; V.319; A I.137; VvA 198. —appadīpa where there is no light, obscure Vin IV.268.
-kāla lighting time Vv 9^6.

Padīpita [pp. of padīpeti] lit, burning, shining Miln 40.

Padīpiya & **Padīpeyya** (nt.) [padīpa+(i) ya] that which is connected with lighting, material for lighting a lamp, lamps & accessories; one of the gifts forming the stock of requisites of a Buddhist mendicant (see Nd^2 523: yañña as deyyadhamma). The form in °eyya is the older and more usual one, thus at A II.85, 203; IV.239; It 65; Pug 51; VvA 51. — The form in °iya at Vv 22^5, 26^6, 37^6; J VI.315; VvA 295.

Padīpeti [Caus. of padippati] to light a light or a lamp Vin I.118 (padīpeyya, padīpetabba); Miln 40; ThA 72 (Ap. V. 46); Sdhp 63, 332, 428. — pp. padīpita (q. v.).

Padīyati [Pass. of padāti] to be given out or presented; Pv II.9^{16}; Sdhp 502, 523.

Paduṭṭha [pp. of padussati] made bad, spoilt, corrupt, wicked, bad (opp. pasanna, e. g. at A I.8; It 12, 13) D III.32 (°citta); M III.49; A II.30; Sn 662; Dh 1; J II.401; DhA I.23 (opp. pasanna); PvA 34, 43 (°manasa). —appaduṭṭha good, not corrupt D I.20; III.32; M III.50; S I.13; Pv IV.7^{10}.

Padubbhati [pa+dubbhati] to do wrong, offend, plot against J I.262 (ger. °dubbhitvā).

Paduma (nt.) [cp. Epic Sk. padma, not in RV.] the lotus Nelumbium speciosum. It is usually mentioned in two varieties, viz. ratta° and seta°, i. e. red and white lotus, so at J V.37; SnA 125; as ratta° at VvA 191; PvA 157. The latter seems to be the more prominent variety; but paduma also includes the 3 other colours (blue, yellow, pink ?), since it frequently has the designation of pañcavaṇṇa-paduma (the 5 colours however are nowhere specified), e. g. at J I.222; V.337; VI.341; VvA 41. It is further classified as satapatta and sahassapatta-p., viz. lotus with 100 & with 1,000 leaves: VvA 191. Compared with other species at J V.37, where 7 kinds are enum^d as uppala (blue, red & white), paduma (red & white), kumuda (white) and kallahāra. See further kamala and kuvalaya. — (1) the lotus or lotus flower M III.93; S I.138, 204; A I.145; II.86 sq.; III.26, 239; Sn 71, 213; J I.51 (daṇḍa° N. of a plant, cp. Sk. daṇḍotphala), 76 (khandha°, latā°, daṇḍaka°, olambaka°); IV.3; VI.564; Dh 458; Nd^1 135; Vv 35^4 (= puṇḍarīka VvA 161); 44^{12} (nānā-paduma-sañchanna); Pv II.1^{20} (id.); II.12^2 (id.); Pug 63; Vism 256 (ratta°); DA I.219; KhA 53; SnA 97; Sdhp 359. — (2) N. of a purgatory (°niraya) S I.151-152; Sn 677; p. 126; SnA 475 sq.
-acchara (heavenly) lotus-maiden SnA 469. -uttara N. of Buddha SnA 341, 455 etc. -kaṇṇikā a peak in the shape of a lotus VvA 181. -kalāpa a bunch of lotuses VvA 191. -gabbha the calyx of a l. ThA 68 (°vaṇṇa). -patta a l. leaf Nd^1 135 (= pokkhara); DhA IV.166 (= pokkhara-patta). -puñja a l. cluster J III.55. -puppha a lotus flower Nd^2 393; SnA 78. -rāga "lotus hued," a ruby VvA 276. -vyūha one of the 3 kinds of fighting, viz. p.°, cakka°, sakaṭa° J II.406 = IV.343 (cp. Sk. p.-vyūha-samādhi a kind of concentration, & see J trsl^n II.275). -sara a lotus pond J I.221; V.337; SnA 141.

Padumaka [fr. paduma] 1. the Paduma purgatory S I.152. — 2. a lotus J II.325.

Padumin (adj.-n.) [cp. Sk. padmin, spotted elephant] having a lotus, belonging to a lotus, lotus-like; N. of (the spotted) elephant Sn 53 (expl^d at SnA 103 as "padumasadisa-gattatāya vā Padumakule uppannatāya vā padumī," cp. Nd^2 p. 164). — f. padumini [cp. Sk. padminī lotus plant] 1. a lotus pond or pool of lotuses D I.75; II.38; M III.93; S I.138; A III.26. — 2. the lotus plant Nelumbium speciosum J I.128 (°paṇṇa); IV.419 (°patta); SnA 369; KhA 67 (°patta); PvA 189.

Padulla [?] in cpd. padulla-gāhin is perhaps misreading; trsl. "clutching at blown straws (of vain opinion)," expl^d by C. as duṭṭhullagāhin; at id. p. S I.187 we find duṭṭhullabhāṇin "whose speech is never lewd" (see *Psalms of Brethren* 399, n. 3).

Padussati [pa+dussati] to do wrong, offend against (with loc.), make bad, corrupt DA I.211 (see padosa); Sn 108 (v. l. for padissati); aor. padussi J II.125, 401. — pp. paduṭṭha; Caus. padūseti (q. v.).

Padūsita [pp. of padūseti] made bad, corrupted, spoilt It 13 (v. l. padussita).

Padūseti & **Padoseti** [Caus. of padussati, but the latter probably Denom. fr. padosa^2] to defile, pollute, spoil, make bad or corrupt [cp. BSk. pradūṣyati cittaŋ Divy 197, 286] D I.20; M I.129; It 86; DA I.211 (see padosa^1);

ThA 72 (Ap. v. 40; to be read for paduse, Pot. = padoseyya): J v.273 (manaŋ p., for upahacca). —padusseti read also at A iv.97 for padasseti (dummanku 'yam padusseti dhūm' aggimhi va pāvako). — As padoseti at PvA 212 (cittāni padosetvā) and in stock phrase manaŋ padosaye (Pot.) in sense of "to set upon anger" (cp. padosa²) S i.149 ("sets his heart at enmity") = A ii.3; v.171, 174 = Sn 659 (= manaŋ padoseyya SnA 477) = Nett 132; S iv.70; SnA 11 (mano padoseyya). — pp. padūsita (q. v.).

Padesa [fr. pa + diś, cp. late Sk. pradeśa] indication, location, range, district; region, spot, place S ii.227, 254; v.201; A ii.167 (cattāro mahā°); Dh 127 (jagati°), 303; J ii.3, 158 (Himavanta°); iii.25 (id.), 191 (jāti-gotta-kula°); SnA 355; PvA 29, 33 (hadaya°), 36 (so read for padase), 43, 47; Sdhp 252.
-kārin effecting a limited extent S v.201. -ñāṇa knowledge within a certain range, limited knowledge S v.457. -bodhisatta a limited Bodhisatta Kvu 283 (cp. *Kvu trsl*ⁿ 139³, 166²). -rajja principality over a district, local government It 15; ThA 26 (Ap. v. 10). -rājā a local or sub-king Vism 301 (cakkavatti +). -lakkhaṇa regional or limited characteristics Kvu 283. -vassin raining or shedding rain only locally or over a (limited) district It 64-66.

Padesika (adj.) (-°) [fr. padesa] belonging to a place of indication, indicating, regional, reaching the index of, only with numerals in reference to age (usually soḷasavassa° at the time of 16 years) J i.259 (id.) 262 (id.); ii.277 (id.). — See also uddesika in same application.

Padosa¹ [pa + dosa¹, Sk. pradoṣa] defect, fault, blemish, badness, corruption, sin D i.71 (= padussati paraŋ vā padūseti vināsetī ti padoso DA i.211); M iii.3; S iv.322 (vyāpāda°); A i.8 (ceto°); iii.92 (vyāpāda); It 12; J v.99; Pug 59, 68; Dhs 1060. — *Note.* At ThA 72 we find reading "apace paduse (padose?) pi ca" as uncertain conjecture for v. l. BB "amacce manase pi ca."

Padosa² [pa + dosa², Sk. pradveṣa, see remarks to dosa²] anger, hatred, ill-will; always as mano° "anger in mind" M i.377; Sn 328 (= khāṇu-kaṇṭak' ādimhi p. SnA 334), 702; J iv.29; Miln 130; Vism 304; SnA 477.

Padosika (adj.) [fr. padosa¹] sinful, spoiling or spoilt, full of fault or corruption, only in 2 phrases, viz. khiḍḍā° "debauched by pleasure" D i.19; and mano° "debauched in mind" D i.20, 21.

Padosin (adj.) [fr. padosa¹] abusing, damaging, spoiling, injuring S i.13 (appaduttha°); Pv iv.7¹⁰.

Padoseti see padūseti.

Paddha¹ (adj.) [cp. Sk. prādhva (?) in diff. meaning "being on a journey," but rather prahva] 1. expert in (loc.) J vi.476 (v. l. patha = paṭṭha; C. cheko paṭibalo). — 2. subject to, serving, attending J iv.35 (p. carāmi, so read for baddha, see Kern, *Toev.* s. v.; C. padacārikā).

Paddha² (adj.) [cp. Sk. prārdha] half (?) J iii.95 (probably = paddha¹, but C. expl^os as aḍḍha upaḍḍha).

Paddhagu (adj. n.) [cp. Sk. prādhvaga] 1. going, walking J iii.95 (T. na p' addhaguŋ, but C. reads paddhaguŋ). — 2. humble, ready to serve, servant, attendant, slave S i.104 (so read for paccagu); Sn 1095 (T. for paṭṭhagu, q. v. — Nd² reads paṭṭhagu but SnA 597 paddhagu and expl^os by paddhacara paricārika); J vi.380 (hadayassa); Th i, 632.

Paddhacara (adj.-n.) [paddha¹ + cara, cp. Sk. prādhva and prahva humble] ready to serve, subject to, ministering; a servant S i.144 (T. baddhacara, v. l. paṭṭha°; trsl. "pupil"); J iv.35 (read paddhacarā 'smi tuyhaŋ for T. baddha carāmi t., as pointed out by Kern, *Toev.* s. v. baddha. The Cy. misunderstood the wrong text reading and expl^d as "tuyhaŋ baddha carāmi," but adds "veyyāvaccakārikā padacārikā"); v.327 (as baddhañcara; C. veyyāvacca-kara); vi.268 (°ā female servant = C. pāda-paricārikā); Nd¹ 464 (+ paricārika); SnA 597 (+ paricāraka, for paddhagū).

Padma see paduma.

Padmaka (m. & nt.) [Sk. padmaka] N. of a tree, Costus speciosus or arabicus J v.405, 420; vi.497 (reading uncertain), 537.

Padvāra (nt.) [pa + dvāra] a place before a door or gate J v.433; vi.327.
-gāma suburb Dāvs v. 3.

Padhaŋsa see appadhaŋsa.

Padhaŋsati [pa + dhaŋsati] to fall from (abl.), to be deprived of Vin ii.205 (yogakkhemā p.; so read for paddh°). — Caus. padhaŋseti to destroy, assault, violate, offend J iv.494. (= jīvitakkhayaŋ pāpeti); PvA 117. — grd. padhaŋsiya in cpds. su° & dup° easily (or with difficulty) overwhelmed or assaulted Vin ii.256 = S ii.264. Also neg. appadhaŋsiya (& °ka) (q. v.). — pp. padhaŋsita (q. v.).

Padhansita [pp. of padhaŋseti] offended, assaulted J ii.422. See also app°.

Padhāna (nt.) [fr. pa + dhā, cp. padahati] exertion, energetic, effort, striving, concentration of mind D iii.30, 77, 104, 108, 214, 238; M ii.174, 218; S i.47; ii.268; iv.360; v.244 sq.; A iii.65-67 (5 samayā and 5 asamayā for padhāna), 249; iv.355; v.17 sq.; Sn 424, 428; It 30; Dh 141; J i.90; Nd² 394 (= viriya); Vbh 218 (citta-samādhi p° etc.); Nett 16; DA i.104; DhA i.85 (mahā-padhānaŋ padahitvā); ThA 174; PvA 134. Padhāna is fourfold, viz. saŋvara°, pahāna°, bhāvana°, anurakkhaṇā° or exertion consisting in the restraint of one's senses, the abandonment of sinful thoughts, practice of meditation & guarding one's character. These 4 are mentioned at D iii.225; A ii.16; Ps i.84; ii.14 sq., 56, 86, 166, 174; Ud 34; Nd¹ 45, 340; Sdhp 594. — Very frequently termed sammappadhāna [cp. BSk. samyak-pradhāna MVastu iii.120; but also samyak-prahāṇa, e. g. Divy 208] or "right exertion," thus at Vin i.22; S i.105; iii.96 (the four); A ii.15 (id.); iii.12; iv.125; Nd¹ 14; Ps i.21, 85, 90, 161; SnA 124; PvA 98. — As padahana at Ps i.17, 21, 181.

Padhānavant (adj.) [fr. padhāna] gifted with energy, full of strength (of meditation etc.), rightly concentrated S i.188, 197; Sn 70 (cp. Nd² 394), 531.

Padhānika (adj.) [fr. padhāna] making efforts, exerting oneself in meditation, practising "padhāna" DA i.251.

Padhāniya (adj.) [fr. padhāna] belonging to or connected with exertion, worthy of being pursued in cpd. °anga (nt.) a quality to be striven after, of which there are 5, expressed in the attributes of one who attains them as saddho, appābādho, asaṭho, āraddha-viriyo, paññavā D iii.237 = M ii.95, 128 = A iii.65; referred to at *Miln trsl*ⁿ i.188. Besides these there is the set called pārisuddhi-padhāniy' angāni and consisting either of 4 qualities (sīla°, citta°, diṭṭhi°, vimutti°) A ii.194, or of 9 (the four + kankhā-vitaraṇa°, maggāmagga-ñāṇa°, paṭipadāñāṇa-dassana°, ñāṇa-dassana°, paññā°) D iii.288; Ps i.28.

Padhārita ("born in mind") read patthārita at Th i, 842 (see pattharati). — padhārehi (v. l. F.) at Sn 1149 read dhārehi. — padhārita in meaning of "considered, understood" in cpd. su° at S iii.6; v.278.

Padhāvati [pa+dhāvati] to run out or forth Pv III.1[7] (ger. °itvā = upadhāvitvā PvA 173).

Padhāvin (adj.) [fr. padhāvati] rushing or running out or forth M II.98.

Padhūpāti (= padhūpāyati) [pa+dhūpāyati] to blow forth smoke or flames Vin I.25 (aor. padhūpāsi); IV.109 (id.); Vism 400 (id.), (so read for padhūmāsi T., v. l. SS padhūpāyi & padhūmāyi). — pp. padhūpita (q. v.).

Padhūpita [pa+dhūpita, latter only in meaning "incensed," cp. dhūpa etc.] fumigated, reeking, smoked out S I.133 (trsl[d] "racked [wrapt] in flames"; C. santāpita); VvA 237 (so read with v. l. SS. for T. pavūsita; meaning: scented, filled with scent).

Padhota (adj.) [pa+dhota] cleansed, in cpd. sup° well cleansed D II.324.

Pana (indecl.) [doublet of Sk. puna(ḥ) with diff. meaning (see puna), cp. Geiger, *P.Gr.* § 34] adversative & interrogative particle, sometimes (originally, cp. puna "again, further") merely connecting & continuing the story. — (1) (adversative) but, on the contrary J I.222; II.159; VvA 79 (correl. with tāva). ca pana "but" J I.152; atha ca pana "and yet" D I.139; J I.279; na kho pana "certainly not" J I.151; vā pana "or else" Vin I.83; Dh 42; Sn 376, 829. — (2) (in questions) then, now J II.4 (kiŋ p.), 159 (kahaŋ p.); VvA 21 (kena p.); PvA 27 (katamaŋ p.). — (3) (conclusive or copulative) and, and now, further, moreover D I.139 (siyā kho p. be it now that . . .); Sn 23, 393, 396, 670; J I.278; PvA 3.

Panaccati [pa+naccati] to dance (forth), to dance ThA 257 (ppr. panaccanto). — pp. panaccita (q. v.).

Panaccita [pp. of panaccati] dancing, made to dance Th 2, 390.

Panasa [cp. late Sk. panasa, Lat. penus stores, Lith. pĕnas fodder, perhaps Goth. fenea] the Jack or bread-fruit tree (Artocarpus integrifolia) and its fruit J I.450; II.160; V.205, 465; Vv 44[13]; KhA 49, 50, 58 (°phala, where Vism 258 reads panasa-taca); SnA 475; VvA 147.

Panassati [pa+nassati, cp. also BSk praṇāśa Divy 626] to be lost, to disappear, to go to ruin, to cease to be M I.177; S II.272 (read panassissati with BB); J V.401; VI.239; Th 1, 143.

Panāda [pa+nāda] shouting out, shrieks of joy J VI.282.

Panādeti [Caus. of pa+**nad**] to shout out, to utter a sound Th 1, 310.

Panāḷikā (f.) [fr. panāḷī] a pipe, tube, channel, water course DA I.244.

Panāḷī (f.) [pa+nāḷī] a tube, pipe A IV.171 (udapāna°).

Panigghosa in cpd. appanigghosa is wrongly registered as such in A Index (for A IV.88); it is to be separated appa + nigghosa (see nigghosa).

Panudati [pa+nudati] to dispel, repel, remove, push away S I,167 sq., 173; Dh 383; Sn 81, 928 (pot. panudeyya or metri causa panūdeyya = pajaheyya etc. Nd[1] 385); J VI.491 (1. pl. panudāmase). — ger. panuditvā SnA 591, & panujja Sn 359, 535, 1055 (expl[d] at Nd[2] 395 as imper. pres. = pajaha, cp. SnA 591 = panudehi); J III.14; V.198 (= pātetvā C.). — Fut. panudahissati Th 1, 27, 233. — Pass. panujjati, ppr. panujjamāna in phrase "api panujjamānena pi" even if repulsed M I.108, cp. A IV.32 & Nett 164 (v. l. to be substituted for T. pamajjamānena). — pp. panunna & panudita (q. v.).

Panudita [pp. of panudati] dispelled, driven out Sn 483 (panūdita metri causa, v. l. panudita). See also panunna.

Panunna (Paṇunna & Panuṇṇa) [pp. of panudati] (med. & pass.) put away, rejected or rejecting, dispelled, driven away, sent A II.29; V.31; Sn 469 (°kodha); J VI.247, 285; Kvu 597 (ito p., trsl[d] "ending here").
-paccekasacca one who has rejected each of the four false truths (the 5th of the 10 noble states, ariyavāsā: see *Vin. Texts* I.141) D III.269, 270; A II.41; V.29 sq.

Panūdana (nt.) [fr. panudati] removal, dispelling, rejection Sn 252 (sabba-dukkhâpanūdana SnA 293 should be read as sabba-dukkha-apanūdana, as at Vin II.148 = J I.94), 1106 (= pahānaŋ etc. Nd[2] 396).

Panta (adj.) [cp. Epic Sk. prānta edge, margin, border, pra+anta; also BSk. prānta in meaning of Pali, e. g. MVastu III.200; Divy 312 (prānta-śayan-āsana-sevin)] distant, remote, solitary, secluded; only in phrase pantaŋ senāsanaŋ (sayanāsanaŋ) or pantāni senāsanāni "solitary bed & chair" M I.17, 30; A I.60; II.137; III.103; V.10, 202; Sn 72 (cp. Nd[2] 93), 338, 960 (°amhi sayanāsane), 969 (sayanamhi pante); Dh 185 (= vivitta DhA III.238); Ud 43 (so read for patthañ); J III.524 (°ambi sayanāsane); Vism 73 (panta-senāsane rata); SnA 263 (v. l. pattha).
-sena (adj.) one who has his resting place far away from men, Ep. of the Buddha M I.386.

Panti (f.) [Ved. paṅkti set or row of five, group in general] a row, range, line Vism 392 (tisso sopāna-pantiyo); DhA III.219 (uddhana°); ThA 72 (satta pantiyo); VvA 198 (amba°).

Pantha [base panthan°, Ved. panthāḥ, with bases path° panth° and pathi. Same as patha (q. v.). For etym. cp. Gr. πόντος sea(-path), πάτος path, Av. pantā°, also Goth. finþan = E. find, of Idg *pent to come or go (by)] a road, roadway, path J I.18 (gen. pl. panthānaŋ = kantāramagga C; "jungle road" trsl.); Sn 121 (loc. panthasmiŋ); Nd[2] 485 B (+patha in expl[n] of magga), Miln 157 (see panthaŋ).
-gū a traveller (lit. going by road) S I.212 (v. l. addhagū, as at id. p. Th 2, 55); J III.95 (v. l.). -ghāta highway robbery J I.253; IV.184. -duhana waylaying, robbery; m. a robber D I.135 (see DA I.296); J II.281, 388; D III.68, and Tikp 280 (°dūhana). -dūbhin a highwayman J II.327. -dūsaka a robber Miln 20. -devatā a way spirit, a spirit presiding over a road, road-goddess J VI.527. -makkaṭaka a (road) spider Miln 364, 407. -sakuṇa a "road-bird," i. e. a bird offered (as a sacrifice) to the goddess presiding over the roads, propitiation; it is here to be understood as a human sacrifice J VI.527 (vv. ll. pattha° & bandha°).

Panthika [fr. pantha, formation panthika: panthan = addhika: addhan] a traveller Miln 20.

Panna [pp. of pajjati but not satisfactorily expl[d] as such, for pajjati & panna never occur by themselves, but only in cpds. like āpajjati, āpanna, upp°, upa°, sam°, etc. Besides, the word is only given in lexic. literature as pp. of pajjati, although a tendency prevails to regard it as pp. of patati. The meaning points more to the latter, but in form it cannot belong to **pat.** A more satisfactory expl[n] (in meaning and form) is to regard panna as pp. of pa+**nam**, with der. fr. short base. Thus panna would stand for panata (paṇata), as unna for unnata, ninna for ninnata, the double nn to be accounted for on analogy. The meaning would thus be "bent down, laid down," as panna-ga = going bent, panna-dhaja = flag bent or laid down, etc. Perhaps patta of patta-kkhandha should belong here as panna°] fallen, gone, gone down; also: creeping, only in foll. cpds.:
-ga a snake Th 1, 429 (°inda chief of snake-demons); J V.166; Miln 23. -gandha with gone down (i. e.

deteriorated) smell, ill-smelling, or having lost its smell J v.198 (=thokaŋ duggandha C.). -dhaja one whose flag gone or is lost, i. e. whose fight is over (Ep. of the Buddha), cp. BSk. prapātito māna-dhvajaḥ Lal. V. 448 (with derivation from **pat** instead of **pad**, cp. papātana) M I.137 sq., 386; A III.84 sq.; in eulogy on the Buddha (see exegesis to mahesi Nd[1] 343; Nd[2] 503) reference is made to mānadhaja (°papātanaŋ) which is opposed to dhamma-dhaja (-ussapana); thus we should explain as "one who has put down the flag of pride." -bhāra one who has put down his burden, one whose load has gone, who is delivered or saved M I.139; A III.84; S I.233; Dh 402 (=ohita-khandha-bhāra DhA IV.168); Sn 626, 914 (cp. Nd[1] 334); Th I, 1021. -bhūmi state of one who has fallen DA I.163 (opp. to jina-bhūmi, one of the 8 purisa-bhūmiyo. — cp. D I.54 & *Dial.* I.72[2]). -loma one whose hairs have fallen or are put down (flat, i. e. do not stand erect in consequence of excitement), subdued, pacified (opp. haṭṭha loma) Vin II.184 (cp. Vin II.5 & Bdhgh on p. 309 lomaŋ pāteti, Bdhgh pādeti; also *Vin. Texts* II.339); III.266; M I.450; J I.377. Another form is palloma (q. v. & cp. *J.P.T.S.* 1889, 206). See also remarks on parada-vutta.

Pannaka (adj.) [fr. panna] silent (?) DA I.163.

Pannarasa (adj. num.) [see pañcadasa & paṇṇarasa under pañca] fifteen (and fifteenth), usually referring to the 15th day of the lunar month, i. e. the full-moon day Sn 153 (pannaraso uposatho); pannarase on the 15th day S I.191=Th I, 1234; M III.20; Sn 502, 1016; f. loc. pannarasāya id. S I.233. See also paṇṇarasa.

Pannarasama (num. ord.) [fr. pannarasa] the 15th SnA 366 (gāthā).

Pannarasika (adj.) [fr. pannarasa] belonging to the 15th day (of the lunar month) Vin IV.315.

Papa (nt.) [see pibati, pānīya etc. of pā] water J I.109 (āpaŋ papaŋ mahodakan ti attho). The word is evidently an etym. construction. See also papā.

Papaccati [Pass. of pa+pacati] to be cooked, to become ripe PvA 55 (°itvā).

Papañca [in its P. meaning uncertain whether identical with Sk. prapañca (pra+pañc to spread out; meaning "expansion, diffuseness, manifoldedness"; cp. papañceti & papañca 3) more likely, as suggested by etym. & meaning of Lat. im-ped-iment-um, connected with pada, thus perhaps originally "pa-pad-ya," i. e. what is in front of (i. e. in the way of) the feet (as an obstacle)] I. obstacle, impediment, a burden which causes delay, hindrance, delay DhA I.18; II.91 (kathā°). °ŋ karoti to delay, to tarry J IV.145; °ŋ akatvā without delay J I.260; VI.392. — atі° too great a delay J I.64; II.92. — 2. illusion, obsession, hindrance to spiritual progress M I.65; S I.100; IV.52, 71; A II.161 sq.; III.393 sq.; Sn 530 (=taṇhā-diṭṭhi-mānabheda-p. SnA 431; and generally in Commentaries so resolved, without verbal analysis); Ud 77 (as f. papañcā); Th I, 519, 902, 989 (cp. *Brethren* 344, 345 & *J.R.A.S.* 1906, 246 sq.; Neumann trsln "Sonderheit," see *Lieder* p. 210, 211 & *Mittlere Sammlung* I.119 in trsl. of M I.65 nippapañca); Dh 195, 254 (°âbhiratā pajā, nippapañcā Tathāgatā: =taṇhâdisu p° esu abhiratā DhA III.378); J I.9; Pv IV.1[34] (=taṇh'-ādi-p. PvA 230); Nett 37, 38; SnA 495 (gihi). — nippapañca (q. v.) without obsession. — 3. diffuseness, copiousness SnA 40.

-sankhā sign or characteristic of obsession Sn 874 (cp. SnA 553; =taṇhā° diṭṭhi° and māna° Nd[1] 280), 916 (=avijjādayo kilesā mūlaŋ SnA 562). -saññā (°sankhā) idea of obsession, idée fixe, illusion D II.277 (cp. *Dial* II.312); M I.109, 112, 271, 383; S IV.71.

Papañcita [pp. of papañceti] obsessed, illusioned SnA 495 (a° gihipapañ-cena). — nt. obsession, vain imagination, illusion S IV.203 ≈ Vbh 390.

Papañceti [Denom. fr. papañca] I. to have illusions, to imagine, to be obsessed M I.112; DhA I.198 (tesaŋ suvaṇṇa-lobhena papañcentānaŋ). — 2. to be profuse, to talk much, to delay on SnA 136. — pp. papañcita.

Papaṭā (papatā) (f.) [fr. papāta? Cp. papaṭikā] a broken-off piece, splinter, fragment; also proclivity, precipice, pit (?) S II.227 (papatā ti kho lābha-sakkāra-silokass' etaŋ adhivacanaŋ: cp. S III.109: sobbho papāto kodh' ûpāyāsass' etaŋ adhivacanaŋ); Sn 665 (=sobbha SnA 479; gloss papada). See also pappaṭaka.

Papaṭikā (f.) [cp. Sk. prapāṭikā (lexic. & gram.) young shoot, sprout; and parpharīka (RV.) one who tears to pieces; also Sk. parpaṭa N. of a plant] I. a splinter, piece, fragment, chip Vin II.193 (read tato pap.°); A IV.70 sq. (of ayophāla); J V.333 (same as Vin passage); Miln 179. — 2. the outer dry bark or crust of a tree, falling off in shreads; also shoots, sprouts M I.78, 192 sq., 488; A I.152; III.19 sq., 44, 200, 360; IV.99, 336; V.4 sq., 314 sq.; J III.491. Cp. pheggu.

Papatati [pa+patati] to fall forward, to fall down, off or from, to fall into (acc.) Vin II.284; M I.79, 80; S I.48 (visame magge), 187 (=Th I, 1220 patanti); 100, II.114; V.47; Dh 336; J V.31; Pv I.10[12] (nirayaŋ papatiss' ahaŋ, cp. PvA 52; v. l. SS niray' ûpapatiss' âhaŋ). — aor. papatā Vin III.17, cp. II.126; J VI.566. See also patati.

Papatana (nt.) [fr. pa+pat] falling down Sn 576=J IV.127 (abl. papatanā papatanato C.).

Papada (or **Papadā**?) [pa+pada] tip of the foot, toes; but in diff. meaning (for papatā or papāta to **pat**) "falling down, abyss, pit" at Sn 665 (gloss for papaṭa; expl[d] at SnA 479 by "mahāniraya").

Papā (f.) [Ved. prapā, pa+pā] a place for supplying water, a shed by the roadside to provide travellers with water, a well, cistern D III.185; S I.33=Kvu 345 (=pānīya-dāna-sālā SA); S I.100 (read papañ ca vivane); J I.109; DhA III.349=J I.302 (=pānīya-cāṭī C.); Vv 52[22] (+udapāna); Pv II.7[8] (n. pl. papāyo=pānīya-sālā PvA 102); II.9[25] (+udapāna).

Papāta [cp. Epic. Sk. prapāta, of pra+**pat**] I. falling down, a fall Vin II.284 (chinna-papātaŋ papatanti); S V.47. — 2. a cliff, precipice, steep rock M I.11; S III.109 (sobbho p. kodh' upāyāsass' etaŋ adhivacanaŋ; cp. papatā); A III.389 (sobbho p.); J III.5; 530; V.70; VI.306, 309; Vism 116; PvA 174; Sdhp 208, 282, 353. — adj. falling off steeply, having an abrupt end Vin II.237=A IV.198, 200 (samuddo na āyatakena p.).

-taṭa a rocky or steep declivity DhA I.73.

Papātin (adj.) [fr. papatati] falling or flying forward, flying up J III.484 (uccā° flying away).

Papitāmaha [pa+pitāmaha] a paternal great-grandfather Dāvs III.29.

Papīyana (nt.) [fr. **pā**, ger. pa-pīya] drinkable, to be drunk, drinking J I.109 (udakaŋ papiyana-bhāvena papā ti).

Papīḷita [pa+pīḷita] worn out, rubbed through (of the sole of sandals) J II.223.

Paputta [pa+putta, cp. Sk. praputra (BR.: "doubtful") Inscr.] a grandson J VI.477.

Papupphaka (adj.) [pa+pupphaka] "with flowers in front," flower-tipped (of the arrows of Māra) Dh 46 (but expl[d] at DhA I.337 as "p.° sankhātāni tebhūmakāni vaṭṭāni," i. e. existence in the 3 stages of being).

Pappaṭaka [etym. uncertain] 1. a broken bit, splinter, small stone (?) (Rh. D. in *Dial.* III.83 "outgrowth") D III.87 (bhūmi °ŋ paribhuñjati); Vism 418 (≈). Nett 227 (Com.) (°ojaŋ khādāpento). —2. a water plant: see pannaka 2; cp. also papaṭikā² & Sk. parpaṭa N. of medicinal plant.

Pappoṭheti [pa+poṭheti; sometimes spelt papphoṭeti] to strike, knock, beat, flap (of wings) Vin I.48; II.208, 217; M I.333 (papph°); J II.153 (pakkhe); III.175 (papoṭh° = sañcuṇṇeti C.); Miln 368 (papph°); DA I.7; Vism 283 (pph).

Pappoti [the contracted form of pāpuṇāti, Sk. prāpnoti] to obtain, get, gain, receive, attain D III.159, 165; Sn 185, 187, 584; Dh 27; DhA I.395. — Pot. 1st pl. pappomu J V.57 (=pāpuṇeyyāma C.). — ger. pappuyya S I.48; Sn 482 (or pot ?), 593, 829 (=pāpuṇitvā Nd¹ 170). — For further ref. see pāpuṇāti.

Papphāsa (nt.) [fr. sound-root* **phu**, not corresponding directly to Sk. pupphusa (cp. Geiger, *P.Gr.* § 34), to which it stands in a similar relation as ***ghur** (P.) to ***ghar** (Sk.) or phurati > pharati. From same root Gr. φυσάω to blow and Lat. pustula bubble, blister; see Walde under pustula] the lungs D II.293; M I.185, 421; III.90; Sn 195 = J I.146; Kh III. (cp. KhA 56); Miln 26.

Pabandha (adj.) (?-) [pa+bandha] continuous Vism 32.

Pabala (adj.) [cp. Sk. prabala] very strong, mighty Sdhp 75.

Pabāḷha¹ [pp. of pabāhati] pulled out, drawn forth D I.77 (T. reads pavāḷha). See pavāḷha.

Pabāḷha² (adj.) [pa+bāḷha] strong, sharp (of pain) D II.128; J V.422, Miln 174.

Pabāhati [pa+bṛh to pull, see abbahati] to pull out, draw forth D I.77 (T. reads pavāhati, v. l. pabbāḷhati, evidently fr. pabāḷha); cp. Śatapatha-brāhmaṇa IV.3, 3, 16. — pp. **pabāḷha**¹ (q. v.).

Pabujjhati [pa+bujjhati] to wake up (intrs.), awake S I.4, 209; Dh 296 sq.; It 41 (suttā p.); J I.61; II.103; IV.431 (opp. niddāyati); DA I.140. — pp. pabuddha (q. v.).

Pabuddha [pp. of pabujjhati] awakened S I.143 (sutta° from sleep awakened), J I.50; VvA 65.

Pabodhati [pa+bodhati] to awake, also trs. awaken, stir up, give rise to (or: to recognise, realise ?); only in *one* phrase (perhaps corrupt), viz. yo nindaŋ appabodhati S I.7 = Dh 143 (= nindaŋ apaharanto bujjhati DhA III.86; trsl. *KS* 13 "forestalleth blame"). — Caus. pabodheti (1) to enlighten, instruct, give a sign J I.142; III.511. — (2) to set going, arouse J I.298; V.390. — (3) to render oneself conspicuous J V.8.

Pabodhana (adj.-nt.) [fr. pabodhati] 1. (nt.) awakening, waking, arising DhA I.232 (°codana-kamma). — 2. (adj.) arousing (or realising ?) Vv 64²² (= kata-pīti-pabodhano VvA 282); awaking Th 1, 893 (samma-tāḷa°).

Pabba (nt.) [Ved. parvan] 1. a knot (of a stalk), joint, section Vin IV.35; M I.80; J I.245 (veḷu°); Vism 358 (id.; but nāḷika p. 260); VbhA 63 (id.); Th 1, 243. — aṅgula° finger joint Vin IV.262, M I.187; DA I.285. — pabba-pabbaŋ knot for knot DhsA 11. — 2. the elbow S IV.171. — 3. section, division, part Vism 240 (14 sections of contemplation of the body or kāyagatā-sati); VbhA 275, 286.

-**gaṇṭhi** a knot Miln 103. -**valli** a species of Dūrvā J V.69; -**vāta** intermittent ague Vin I.205.

Pabbaja [Sk. balbaja, cp. Geiger *P.Gr.* § 39. 6] a species of reed, bulrush Vin I.190 (T. reads babbaja); S I.77; II.92; III.137 (v. l. babbaja), 155 (°lāyaka); Th 1, 27; J II.140, 141; V.202; VI.508. For further refs. see babbaja.

Pabbajati [cp. Sk. pravrajati, pra+**vraj**] to go forth, to leave home and wander about as a mendicant, to give up the world, to take up the ascetic life (as bhikkhu, samaṇa, tapassin, isi etc.). S I.140, 141; Sn 157, 1003; imper. pabbaja DhA I.133. Pot. pabbajeyya J I.56; Pug 57. — Fut. pabbajissati Sn 564; DhA I.133; IV.55. Aor. pabbaji M III.33; S I.196 = Th 1, 1255; Sn 405; Vv 82⁶; PvA 76; ger. pabbajitvā J I.303; PvA 21 and °vāna Sn 407. — (agārasmā) anagāriyaŋ pabbajati to go forth into the homeless state Vin III.12; M III.33; S I.196; A V.204; Pv II.13¹⁸. sāsane p. to become an ascetic in (Buddhas) religion, to embrace the religion (& practice) of the Buddha J I.56; PvA 12. pabbajjaŋ pabbajati to go into the holy life (of an ascetic friar, wanderer etc.): see pabbajjā. — Caus. pabbājeti (q. v.). — pp. pabbajita.

Pabbajana (nt.) [fr. pabbajati] going into an ascetic life J III.393 (a°).

Pabbajita [pp. of pabbajati, cp. BSk. pravrājita Divy 236] one who has gone out from home, one who has given up worldly life & undertaken the life of a bhikkhu recluse or ascetic, (one) ordained (as a Buddhist friar), gone forth (into the holy life or pabbajjā) Vin III.40 (vuḍḍha-pabbajito bhikkhu); IV.159; D I.131 (agārasmā anagāriyaŋ p.), 157; III.31 sq., 147 sq.; M I.200, 267, 345, 459; II.66, 181; III.261; S I.119 (dhamma-vinaye p.); IV.260, 330; V.118 sq., 421; A I.69, 107, 147, 168; II.78, 143; III.33, 78 (vuḍḍha°), 244, 403 (acira°); IV.21 (cira°); V.82, 348 sq.; Sn 43 (see Nd² 397), 274, 385, 423; Dh 74, 174, 388; J I.56; Pv II.8¹ (= samaṇa PvA 106); II.11¹ (bhikkhu = kāmādi-malānaŋ pabbajitattā paramatthato pabbajito PvA 146); II.13¹⁷ (= pabbajjaŋ upagata PvA 167); Miln 11; DA I.270; DhA I.133; PvA 5, 55.

Pabbajjā (f.) [fr. pa+**vraj**, cp. pabbajati, Epic & BSk. pravrajyā] leaving the world, adopting the ascetic life; state of being a Buddhist friar, taking the (yellow) robe, ordination. — (1) ordination or admission into the Buddha's Order in particular: Vin III.13; S I.161 etc. — sāmaṇera° ordination of a Novice, described in full at Vin I.82. — pabbajjaŋ yācati to beg admission Vin IV.129; labhati to gain admission to the Order Vin I.12, 17, 32; D I.176; S IV.181. — (2) ascetic or homeless life in general D III.147 sq.; M III.33 (abbhokāso p.); S V.350 (id.; read pabbajjā); A V.204 (id.); S II.128 (read °jjā for °jā); IV.260; A I.151, 168; IV.274 sq.; Sn 405, 406, 567; It 75 (pabbajjāya ceteti); Miln 19 (dhamma-cariya-samacariy' atthā p.); DhA I.6; SnA 49, 327, 423; ThA 251. — pabbajjaŋ upagata, gone into the homeless state PvA 167 (for pabbajita); agārasmā anagāriyaŋ p. the going forth from home into the homeless state Vin II.253; M II.56; pabbajjaŋ pabbajati to undertake or go into the ascetic life, in foll. varieties: isi° of a Saint or Sage J I.298, 303; DhA IV.55; PvA 162 (of the Buddha); tāpasa° of a Hermit J III.119; DA I.270 (described in detail); DhA IV.29; PvA 21; samaṇa° of a Wanderer PvA 76. — *Note.* The ceremony of admission to the priesthood is called **pabbajjā** (or pabbajana), if viewed as the act of the candidate of orders, and **pabbājana** (q. v.), if viewed as the act of the priest conferring orders; the latter term however does not occur in this meaning in the Canon.

Pabbata [Vedic parvata, fr. parvan, orig. knotty, rugged, massive] (1) a mountain (-range), hill, rock S I.101, 102, 127, 137; II.32, 185, 190; A I.243; II.140; IV.102 (dhūpāyati); Sn 413, 417, 543, 958, 1014; Nd¹ 466; Dh 8, 127 (°ānaŋ vivaro) = PvA 104; Dh 188 (n. pl.

°āni), 304; DA I.209; Miln 346 (dhamma°); PvA 221 (angāra°) Sdhp 352, 545, 574. — The 7 mountains round Veḷuvana are enumᵈ at J V.38. — Names of some (real or fictitious) mountains, as found in the Jātaka literature: Cakkavāḷa J VI.282; Caṇḍoraṇa J IV.90; Canda J IV.283; V.38, 162; Daṇḍaka-hirañña J II.33; Daddara J II.8; III.16; Nemindhara J VI.125; Neru J III.247; V.425; Paṇḍava Sn 417; SnA 382 sq.; Mahāneru J IV.462; Mahindhara Vv 32[10] (cp. VvA 136); Meru J I.25; IV.498; Yugandhara PvA 137; Rajata J I.50; Vipula J VI.518; Sineru S II.139; J I.48 & passim; Suvaṇṇa J I.50; VI.514 (°giritāla). — (2) [cp. Sk. pārvata mountainous] a mountaineer Miln 191.

-utu the time (aspect) of the mountain (in prognostications as to horoscope) DhA I.165 (megha-utu, p.-utu, aruṇa-utu). -kaccha a mountain meadow (opp. nadī-kaccha) SnA 33. -kandara a m. cave S II.32; V.396, 457 sq.; A V.114 sq.; -kūṭa m. peak Vin II.193; J I.73. -gahaṇa m. thicket or jungle PvA 5. -ṭṭha standing on a m. Dh 28. -pāda the foot of a m. J III.51; DhA IV.187; PvA 10. -muddhā mountain top Vin I.5. -raṭṭha m.-kingdom SnA 26. -rājā "king of the mountain," Ep. of Himavā S I.116; II.137 sq., 276; III.149; V.47, 63, 148; A I.152; III.240; IV.102; PvA 143. -sankhepa top of a m. D I.84 (=p. -matthaka DA I.226). -sānu m.-glen Vv 32[10] (cp. VvA 136). -sikhara mountain-crest J V.421.

Pabbataka [fr. pabbata] a mountain J I.303.

Pabbateyya (adj.) [fr. pabbata] belonging to mountains, mountain-born (of a river) A III.64 (nadī p°ā sighasotā hāraharinī); IV.137 (id.); Vism 231 (id.), 285 (nadī).

Pabbaniya (adj.) [fr. pabba] forming a division or section, consisting of, belonging to KhA 114 (khaya°) (?).

Pabbājana (nt.) [fr. pa+Caus. of **vraj**, see pabbajati & pabbājeti] keeping out or away, removing, banishment, exiling D I.135; III.93; Miln 357; Dh I.296 (=nīharaṇa); DhA IV.145.

Pabbājaniya (adj.) [fr. pabbājana] belonging to banishment, deserving to be exiled Miln 186; also in cpd. °kamma excommunication, one of the 5 ecclesiastical acts enumᵈ at Vin I.49, 143. See also A I.79; DhA II.109.

Pabbājita [pp. of pabbājeti] taken into the order, made a bhikkhu M II.62.

Pabbājeti [Caus. of pabbajati] 1. to make go out or away, drive out, banish, exile D I.92 (raṭṭhasmā out of the kingdom; =nīharati DA I.258); M II.122; Dh 388 (attano malaŋ pabbājayaŋ, tasmā pabbajito ti vuccati); DhA IV.145 (explⁿˢ as "attano rāgādimalaŋ pabbājento vinodento") J I.262 (raṭṭhā); III.168 (id.); VI.350, 351; DhA II.41; PvA 54 (core). — 2. to make go forth (into the homeless state), to make somebody take up the life of an ascetic or a bhikkhu, to take into the (Buddha's) order, to ordain Vin I.82 (description of ordination of a novice), 97; III.12; IV.129; DhA I.19, 133. — pp. pabbājita (q. v.).

Pabbedha [pa+vedha of **vyadh**, cp. BSk. pravedha in same phrase at Divy 56, viz. ṣoḍaśa-pravedho] piercing through (measuring) an arrow shot Th 1, 164 = J II.334 (soḷasa° = soḷasa-kaṇḍa pāta-vitthāro C.). — *Note.* pabbedha owes its bb to analogy with ubbedha. It also corresponds to the latter in meaning: whereas ubbedha refers to the height, pabbedha is applied to the breadth or width.

Pabbhamati [pa+bhamati] to roam forth or about J V.106 (=bhamati C.).

Pabbhāra [cp. BSk. prāg-bhāra Divy 80 etc.] 1. (m.) a decline, incline, slope J I.348; adj. (usually -°) bending, inclining, sloping; fig. tending or leading to (cp. E. "bearing on") M I.493 (samudda°); S I.110 (id.); V.38, 216, 219; A IV.198 (anupubba°), 224 (viveka°); Miln 38 (samādhi°). Very frequent in combⁿ with similar expressions, e. g. ninna, poṇa (cp. PvA ninna-poṇa-pabbhāraŋ cittaŋ): see further ref. under ninna; with adhimutta & garuka at Vism 117 (Nibbāna°). — apabbhara (sic.) not slanting or sloping J V.405 (=samatittha C.). — 2. (m. & nt.) a cave in a mountain Miln 151; J V.440; DhA II.59 (nt.), 98.

-ṭṭhāna a slope J I.348; DhsA 261. -dasaka the decade (period) of decline (in life), which in the enum° of the 10 decades (vassadasā) at J IV.397 is given as the seventh.

Pabha is adj. form (-°) of pabhā (q. v.).

Pabhaŋsana (adj.-nt.) [fr. pa+**bhraŋś**, cp. nāva-prabhraŋśana Npl. A.V.] causing to fall or disappear, depriving, taking away, theft, in maṇi° jewel-theft J VI.383. (Rh. D. "polishing"?) Kern in *Toev.* s. v. takes pabhaŋsana as a der. fr. pa+**bhrās** to shine, i. e. making bright, polishing (as Rh. D.).

Pabhagga [pp. of pabhañjati, cp. Sk prabhagna] broken up, destroyed, defeated Vin III.108.

Pabhankara [pabhaŋ, acc. of pabhā, +kara] one who makes light, one who lights up, light-bringer (often as Ep. of the Buddha) S I.51 (quoted at VvA 116), 210; A II.51 sq.; It 80; J III.128; Sn 991, 1136 (=ālokakara obhāsakara etc. Nd² 399); Vv 21⁴ (=ñāṇ' obhāsa-kara VvA 106); 34[25] (=lokassa ñāṇ' āloka-kara VvA 115).

Pabhanga [fr. pa+**bhañj**] destruction, breaking up, brittleness Ps II.238 (calato pabhangato addhuvato); but id. p. at Nd² 214[11] and Miln 418 read "calato pabhanguto addhuvato."

Pabhangu, Pabhanguṇa & °**gura** (adj.) [fr. pa+**bhanj**, cp. BSk. prabhanguṇatā destruction, perishableness MVastu III.338] brittle, easily destroyed, perishable, frail. (a) pabhangu: S III.32; V.92; A I.254, 257 sq.; III.16; DhsA 380; Sdhp 51, 553. — (b) °guṇa: It 37; J I.393 (ittarā addhuvā pabhanguno calitā; reading may be pabhanguṇā); Dh 139 (as n.; = pabhangubhāva, pūtibhāva, DhA III.71), 148 (=pūtikāya ibid. 111). — (c) °gura Dh 148 (v. l.); ThA 95; Sdhp 562, 605. — See also pabhanga.

Pabhañjati [pa+**bhañj**] to break up, destroy J IV.494. — pp. pabhagga (q. v.).

Pabhava (m. & nt.) [fr. pa+**bhu**, cp. Ved. prabhava] production, origin, source, cause M I.67; S I.181; II.12; It 37 (āhāra-netti°); Sn 728, 1050; Nd² under mūla (with syn. of sambhava & samuṭṭhāna etc.); J III.402 = VI.518.

Pabhavati see pahoti.

Pabhassati [pa+**bhraŋś**; cp. Sk. prabhraśyate] to fall down or off, to disappear Vin II.135 (pret. pabhassittha); IV.159 (id.). — Cp. pabhaŋsana.

Pabhassara (adj.) [fr. **bhās**] shining, very bright, resplendent S I.145; V.92, 283; A I.10, 254, 257 sq., III.16; Sn 48 (=parisuddha pariyodāta Nd² 402); J V.202, 170; Vv 17¹ (rucira+); Pv III.3¹ (rucira+); Vism 223; 377; DhA I.28; VvA 12 (pakati° bright by nature).

Pabhā (f.) [fr. pa+**bhā**, cp. Epic Sk. prabhā] light, radiance, shine A II.139; V.22; It 19, 20; PvA 56 (sarīra°), 137 (id.), 71, 176; Sdhp 250. — canda-ppabhā moonshine It 20; DhsA 14. — adj. pabha (-°), radiating, lucid, in cpd. sayam° self-lucid or self-radiant D I.17 (=attano attano va tesaŋ pabhā ti DA I.110); A V.60; Sn 404.

Pabhāṇin at Kern, *Toev.* s. v. is wrongly given with quot. J v.421 (in meaning "speaking") where it should be read manāpa-bhāṇin, and not manā-p°.

Pabhāta [pp. of pabhāti] become clear or light, shining, dawning Sn 178 (sup°); esp. in phrase pabhātāya rattiyā when night had become light, i.e. given way to dawn, at daybreak J 1.81, 500. — (nt.) daybreak, morning S 1.211; SnA 519 (pabhāte); atipabhāte in broad daylight J 1.436.

Pabhāti [pa+**bhā**] to shine forth, to become light, gleam, glitter J v.199 (said of a river; =pavattati C.). — pp. pabhāta.

Pabhāva [fr. pa+bhū] might, power, strength, majesty, dignity J v.36; vi.449.

Pabhāvita [pp. of pabhāveti] increased, furthered, promoted Th 1, 767 (bhava-netti°); expl[d] by samuṭṭhita C.

Pabhāveti [Caus. of pabhavati] to increase, augment, foster Pv ii.9[64] =DhA iii.220 (dakkhiṇeyyaŋ). — pp. pabhāvita.

Pabhāsa [fr. pa+**bhās**] shining, splendour, beauty S 1.67; sap° with beauty S v.263; Miln 223; ap° without beauty Miln 299.

Pabhāsati [pa+**bhas**] to tell, declare, talk Th 1, 582.

Pabhāseti [Caus. of pa+**bhās**] to illumine, pervade with light, enlighten Dh 172 (=obhāseti DhA iii.169), 382 (=obhāseti ekālokaŋ karoti DhA iv.137); J 1.87; Pv 1.10[9] (so read for ca bh°); ii.1[12]; Ps 1.174; Miln 336; PvA 10 (=obhāseti).

Pabhindati [pa+bhindati] to split asunder (trs.), break, destroy Sn 973 (=bhindati sambhindati Nd[1] 503); ger. **pabhijja** S 1.193=Th 1, 1242. — Pass. **pabhijjati** to be broken, to burst (open), to split asunder (intrs.), to open S 1.150 (aor. pabhijjiŋsu); Sn p. 125 (id.); Vv 41[3] (break forth=pabhedaŋ gacchanti VvA 183; gloss pavajjare for pabhijjare); SnA 475 (=bhijjati). Also "to open, to be developed" (like a flower) Miln 93 (buddhi p.). — pp. **pabhinna.**

Pabhinna [pp. of pabhindati] 1. to burst open, broken (like a flower or fruit), flowing with juice; usually appl[d] to an elephant in rut, mad, furious M 1.236 (hatthi°); Dh 326 (hatthi°=mattahatthi DhA iv.24)=Th 1, 77; J iv.494; vi.488; Pv 1.11[3] (read chinna-pabhinna-gatta); Miln 261, 312 (hatthināgaŋ tidhā-pabhinnaŋ); DA 1.37 (°madaŋ caṇḍa-hatthiŋ). — 2. developed, growing Miln 90 (°buddhi).

Pabhuti (adj.) (-°) [Vedic prabhṛti] beginning, in meaning of: since, after, subsequently; tato p. from that time, henceforth VvA 158.

Pabhutika (adj.) [fr. pabhuti] dating from, derived or coming from (abl.) D 1.94 (kuto p.).

Pabhu [fr. pa+**bhū**] lord, master, ruler, owner DA 1.250.

Pabheda [fr. pa+**bhid**, cp. pabhindati] breaking or splitting up, breaking, opening VvA 183; akkhara° breaking up of letters, word-analysis, phonology D 1.88 (=sikkhā ca nirutti ca DA 1.247=SnA 447). — adj. (-°) breaking up into, i. e. consisting of, comprising, of various kinds J 1.84; PvA 8 (paṭisandhi-ādi°), 130 (saviññāṇak' aviññāṇaka°).

Pabhedana (nt.) [cp. pabheda] breaking up, destruction Sn 1105 (avijjāya°=bhedanaŋ pahānaŋ etc. Nd[2] 403).

Pabhoti etc. see pahoti.

Pamajjati[1] [pa+**mad**] 1. to become intoxicated S 1.73. — 2. to be careless, slothful, negligent; to neglect, waste one's time S iv.125, 133; Sn 676, 925, 933; cp. Nd[1] 376 & Nd[2] 70; Dh 168, 172, 259; J iii.264 (with acc.); iv.396 (with gen.); Pv 1.11[12] (dāne na p.); iv.13 (jāgaratha mā p.); Sdhp 16, 620. — aor. 2 pl. pamādattha M 1.46; A iii.87; iv.139. Other noteworthy forms are aor. or precative (mā) pamādo S iv.263; Th 1, 119; Dh 371 (see Geiger *P.Gr.* § 161 b), and cond. or aor. pamādassaŋ M iii.179; A 1.139 (see Geiger l. c. 170 & Trenckner *Notes* 75[2]). — appamajjanto (ppr.) diligent, eager, zealous PvA 7. — pp. pamatta (q. v.).

Pamajjati[2] [pa+**mṛj**] 1. to wipe off, rub off, sweep, scour Vin 1.47; ii.209 (bhūmi itabbā); M 1.383. — 2. to rub along, stroke, grope, feel along (with one's hands) Vin ii.209 (cīvara-rajjuŋ °itvā; cp. *Vin. Texts* iii.279). — *Note.* pamajjamāna in phrase gale pi p° ānena at Nett 164 is after the example of similar passages M 1.108 and A iv.32 and as indicated by v. l. preferably to be read as "api panujjamānena pi" (see panudati).

Pamajjanā (f.) & °itatta (nt.) are abstr. formations fr. pa+**mad**, in the sense of pamāda carelessness etc., & occur as philological synonyms in exegesis of pamāda at Vbh 350=Nd[1] 423; Nd[2] 405. Also at DhA 1.228 (°bhāva=pamāda).

Pamaññā (f.) [abstr. fr. pamāṇa, for *pamānyā, grd. form. of pa+**mā** for the usual pameyya] only neg. ap° immeasurableness Vbh 272 sq. (catasso appamaññāyo, viz. mettā, karuṇā, muditā, upekhā). See appamaññā.

Pamaṭṭa in cpd. luñcita-pamaṭṭā kapotī viya (simile for a woman who has lost all her ḥair) at PvA 47 is doubtful, it should probably be read as luñcita-pakkhikā k. viya i. e. like a pigeon whose feathers have been pulled out (v. l. °patthaka).

Pamatta [pp. of pamajjati] slothful, indolent, indifferent, careless, negligent D iii.190; S 1.61=204; A 1.11, 139; iv.319; v.146; Sn 57, 70, 329 sq., 399, 1121; Dh 19, 21, 29, 292, 309 (=sati-vossaggena samannāgata DhA iii.482), 371; Nd[2] 404; PvA 276 (quot. °ŋ ativattati). appamatta diligent, careful, eager, mindful S 1.4, 140, 157; A v.148; Th 1, 1245; Pv iv.1[38]; PvA 66 (dānaŋ detha etc.), 219, 278. See also appamatta[2].
-cārin acting carelessly Dh 334 (=sati-vossagga-lakkhaṇena pamādena p.-c. DhA iv.43). **-bandhu** friend of the careless (Ep. of Māra) S 1.123, 128; Sn 430; Nd[2] 507.

Pamattaka (adj.)=pamatta, only in neg. form ap° careful, mindful PvA 201.

Pamathita [pp. of pa+mathati to crush] crushed, only in cpd. sam° (q. v.).

Pamadā (f.) [Classical Sk. pramadā, fr. pra+**mad**, cp. pamāda] a young (wanton) woman, a woman Sn 156, 157 (gloss for pamāda cp. SnA 203); J iii.442 (mara-pamadānaŋ issaro; v. l. samuddā), 530 (v. l. pamuda, pamoda).

Pamaddati [pa+**mṛd**] to crush down, destroy, overcome, defeat; pp. pamaddita J vi.189 (mālutena p. corresponding with vāta pahaṭa).

Pamaddana (adj. nt.) [fr. pamaddati] crushing, defeating, overcoming D 1.89 (°parasena°); Sn p. 106 (id.=madditu ŋ samattho SnA 450); Sn 561 (Mārasena°); DA 1.250.

Pamaddin (adj.) [fr. pa+**mṛd**] crushing, able to crush, powerful, mighty J iv.26 (=maddana-samattha C.).

Pamāṇa (nt.) [of pa+**mā**, Vedic pramāṇa] 1. measure, size, amount S ii.235; A 1.88; iii.52, 356 sq.; v.140 sq.; Miln 285 (cp. *trsl.* ii.133, n. 2); SnA 137; VvA 16;

PvA 55 (ghaṭa°), 70 (ekahattha°), 99 (tālakkhandha°), 268 (sīla°). — 2. measure of time, compass, length, duration PvA 136 (jīvitaŋ paricchinna °ŋ); esp. in cpd. āyu° age S I.151; A I.213; II.126 sq. and passim (cp. āyu). — 3. age (often by Com. taken as "worldly characteristic," see below rūpa° and cp. Nd^2 406 on Sn 1076); DhA I.38. — 4. limit PvA 123, 130 (dhanassa). — 5. (appl^d meaning) standard, definition, description, dimension S IV.158 ≈ Sn 1076 (perhaps ("age"). pamāṇaŋ karoti set an example DhA III.300 (maŋ p. katvā). — adj. (-°) of characteristic, of the character of, measuring or measured by, taking the standard of, only in cpd. rūpa° measuring by (appearance or) form, or held in the sphere of form (defined or Pug A 229 as "rūpa-ppamāṇ' ādisu sampattiyuttaŋ rūpaŋ pamāṇaŋ karotī ti") A II.71 = Pug 53; Nd^2 406. — appamāṇa without a measure, unlimited, immeasurable, incomparable D I.31; II.12 (+ uḷāra); M III.145 (ceto-vimutti); A I.183, 192; II.73; III.52; V.299 sq., 344 sq.; Sn 507; PvA 110 (= atula). See also appamāṇa.

-kata taken as standard, set as example, being the measure, in phrase p.-kataŋ kammaŋ D I.251; S IV.322.

Pamāṇavant (adj. n.) [fr. pamāṇa] having a measure, finite; or: to be described, able to be defined Vin II.110; A II.73.

Pamāṇika (adj. n.) [fr. pamāṇa] 1. forming or taking a measure or standard, measuring by (-°) DhA III.113 (rūpa° etc., see A II.71); (n.) one who measures, a critic, judge A III.349 sq.; V.140; Sdhp 441 (as pamāṇaka). — 2. according to measure, by measure Vin III.149; IV.279.

Pamāda [cp. Vedic pramāda, pa + **mad**] carelessness, negligence, indolence, remissness D I.6 (jūta°, see DA I.85); III.42 sq., 236; M I.151; S I.18, 20, 25, 146, 216; II.43, 193; IV.78, 263; V.170, 397; A I.212 (surāmerayamajja°) = S II.69; A I.16 sq.; II.40; III.6, 421, 449; IV.195, 294, 350; V.310, 361; Sn 156, 157 (gloss pamadā, cp. SnA 203), 334, 942, 1033; Dh 21, 30 sq 167 (= sati-ossagga-lakkhaṇa p. DhA III.163), 241, 371; Th 1, 1245 = S I.193; It 86; Nd^1 423 = Nd^2 405; Ps II.8 sq., 169 sq., 197; Pug 11, 12; Nett 13, 41; Miln 289 (māna atimāna mada +); SnA 339 (= sati-vippavāsa); DhA I.228; PvA 16 (pamādena out of carelessness); Sdhp 600. — appamāda earnestness, vigilance, zeal D III.236; S I.158; II.29; Dh 21.

-pāṭha careless reading (in the text) Nett Ṭ. (see introd. xi. n. 1); KhA 207; PvA 25.

Pamādavatā (f.) [abstr. fr. pamāda + vant, adj.] remissness A I.139.

Pamādin (adj.) [fr. pamāda] infatuating, exciting, in phrase citta° Th 2, 357 (trsl^o "leading to ferment of the mind"; vv. ll. °pamaddin & °pamāthin, thus "crushing the heart," cp. ThA 243).

Pamāya^1 [ger. of paminātí i. e. pa + **mā**] having measured, measuring Sn 894 (sayaŋ p. = paminitvā Nd^1 303); J III.114.

Pamāya^2 [ger. of paminātí i. e. pa + **mṛ**, Sk. pramārya of pramṛṇāti] crushing, destroying Sn 209 (bījaŋ; = hiŋsitva vadhitvā SnA 257). See on this passage Morris, *J.P.T.S.* 1885, 45.

Pamāyin (adj.) [fr. pa + **mā**] measuring, estimating, defining S I.148 (appameyyaŋ p. "who to th' illimitable limit lays" trsl.; corresponds with paminanto).

Pamāreti [pa + māreti, Caus. of **mṛ**, marati to die] to strike dead, maltreat, hurt DhA III.172.

Paminātí [pa + minātí to **mā** with pres. formation fr. **mi**, after Sk. minoti; see also anuminātí] to measure, estimate, define A III.349, 351; V.140, 143; Sdhp 537. — ppr. paminanto S I.148; inf. paminituŋ VvA 154; ger. paminitvā Nd^1 303, and pamāya (q. v.); grd. paminitabba VvA 278; aor. 3.^{d} sq. pāmesi J V.299, 3rd pl. pamiŋsu A II.71; Th 1, 469 (pāmiŋsu).

Pamilāta [pp. of pa + **mlā**] faded, withered, languished Miln 303.

Pamukhā^1 (adj.) [pa + mukha, cp. late Sk. pramukha] lit. "in front of the face," fore-part, first, foremost, chief, prominent S I.234, 235; Sn 791 (v. l. BB and Nd^1 92 for pamuñca); J V.5, 169. loc. pamukhe as adv. or prep. "before" S I.227 (asurindassa p.; v. l. sammukhe); Vism 120. As -° having as chief, headed by, with NN at the head D II.97; S I.79 (Pasenadi° rājāno); PvA 74 (setacchatta° rājakakudhabhaṇḍa); freq. in phrase Buddha° bhikkhusangha, e. g. Vin I.213; Sn p. 111; PvA 19, 20. Cp. pāmokkha.

Pamukha^2 (nt.) [identical with pamukha^1, lit. "in front of the face," i. e. frontside, front] 1. eyebrow (?) only in phrase alāra° with thick eyebrows or lashes J VI.503 (but expl^d by C. as "visāl' akkhigaṇḍa); PvA 189 (for aḷāra-pamba Pv III.3^5). Perhaps we should read pakhuma instead.

Pamuccati Pass. of pamuñcati (q. v.).

Pamucchita [pa + mucchita] 1. swooning, in a faint, fainting (with hunger) Pv III.1^8 (= khuppipāsādi-dukkhena sañjāta-mucchā PvA 174); IV.10^8. — 2. infatuated S I.187 (v. l.; T. samucchita) = Th 1, 1219; J III.441.

Pamuñca [fr. pa + **muc**] loosening, setting free or loose, in cpd. °kara deliverer S I.193 = Th 1, 1242 (bandhana°). — adj. dup° difficult to be freed S I.7; Sn 773; Dh 346; J II.140.

Pamuñcati [pa + muñcati of **muc**] 1. to let loose, give out, emit Sn 973 (vācaŋ; = sampamuñcati Nd^1 504); J I.216 (aggiŋ). — 2. to shake off, give up, shed Dh 377 (pupphāni). Perhaps also in phrase saddhaŋ p. to renounce one's faith, although the interpretation is doubtful (see Morris, *J.P.T.S.* 1885, 46 sq. & cp. *Dial.* II.33) Vin I.7 = D II.39 = S I.138 (C. vissajjati, as quoted *KS* p. 174). — 3. to deliver, free Sn 1063 (kathan kathāhi = mocehi uddhara etc. Nd^2 407^a), 1146 (pamuñcassu = okappehi etc. Nd^2 407^b). — Pass. pamuccati to be delivered or freed S I.24, 173; Sn 80, 170 sq. (dukkhā); Dh 189 (sabbadukkhā), 276 (fut. pamokkhati), 291 (dukkha), 361. — pp. pamutta (q. v.). — Caus. pamoceti to remove, liberate, deliver, set free S I.143, 154, 210; Th 2, 157 (dukkhā); cp. II.7^6; III.10^3 sq. Caus. II. pamuñcāpeti to cause to get loose DA I.138.

Pamuṭṭha [pp. of pamussati] being or having forgotten Vin I.213; Ps I.173 (a°); J III.511 (T. spells pamm°); IV.307 (id.); Miln 77. Cp. parimuṭṭha.

Pamutta [pp. of pamuñcati] 1. let loose, hurled J VI.360 (papātasmiŋ). — 2. liberated, set free S I.154; Sn 465, 524 sq.

Pamutti (f.) [fr. pa + **muc**] setting free, release S I.209; Th 2, 248; J IV.478; Nett 131 (= S I.209; but read pamutty' atthi); PvA 103 (dukkhato).

Pamudita (& °**modita**) [pp. of pamodati] greatly delighted, very pleased M I.37; S I.64; A III.21 sq.; Sn 512; J III.55; DA I.217, ThA 71; PvA 77, 132. — Spelt pamodita at Sn 681, J I.75; V.45 (āmodita +).

Pamuyhati [pa + muyhati of **muh**] to become bewildered or infatuated J VI.73. — pp. pamūḷha (q. v.).

Pamussati [pa + **mṛṣ**, Sk. mṛṣyati = P. *mussati] to forget J III.132, 264 (pamajjati +); IV.147, 251. — pamuṭṭha (q. v.).

Pamūḷha [pp. of pamuyhati] bewildered, infatuated Sn 774; Nd^1 36 (= sammūḷha), 193 (+ sammūḷha).

Pameyya (-°) (adj.) [grd. of pamināti, like Epic Sk. prameya] to be measured, measurable, only in foll. cpd.: appameyya not to be measured, illimitable, unfathomable S I.148; V.400; M III.71, 127; A I.266; Vv 34^{19} (= paminituŋ asakkhuṇeyya VvA 154); 37^7 (expl^d as before at VvA 169); duppameyya hard to be gauged or measured A I.266; Pug 35; opp. suppameyya ibid.

Pamokkha [fr. pa + **muc**, see pamuñcati] 1. discharging, launching, letting loose, gushing out; in phrases itivāda° pouring out, gossip M I.133; S V.73; A II.26; DA I.21; and caravāda° id. S III.12; V.419. — 2. release, deliverance S I.2; PvA 103 (pamutti +); abl. pamokkhā for the release of, i. e. instead of (gen.) J V.30 (pituno p. = pamokkha-hetu C.).

Pamocana (adj. n.) [fr. pa + **muc**] loosening, setting free; deliverance, emancipation S I.172 = Sn 78; A II.24, 37, 49 sq.; Sn 166 (maccupāsā, abl. = from), 1064 (pamocanāya dat. = pamocetuŋ Nd^2); It 104 (Nibbānaŋ sabbagantha °ŋ). At Dh 274 we should read pamohanaŋ for pamocanaŋ.

Pamoceti Caus. of pamuñcati (q. v.).

Pamoda [fr. pa + **mud**, cp. Vedic pramoda] joy, delight Sdhp 528, 563. See also pāmojja.

Pamodati [pa + **mud**] to rejoice, enjoy, to be delighted, to be glad or satisfied S I.182; A III.34 (so read for ca modati); Dh 16, 22; Pv I.11^3, 11^5; VvA 278 (= āmodati). — Caus. pamodeti id. Sdhp 248. — pp. pamudita (& pamodita) (q. v.). Cp. abhippamodati.

Pamodanā (f.) [fr. pa + **mud**] delight, joy, satisfaction Dhs 9, 86, 285 (āmodanā +).

Pamoha [pa + **muh**, cp. Epic Sk. pramoha] bewilderment, infatuation, fascination Sn 841 (v. l. Nd^1 sammoha); Nd^1 193 (+ sammoha andhakāra); J VI.358; J VI.358; Pug 21; Dhs 390, 1061.

Pamohana [fr. pa + **muh**] deceiving, deception, delusion Dh 274 (T. reads pamocana; DhA III.403 expl^s by vañcana).

Pampaka [etym ? Cp. Sk. pampā N. of a river (or lake), but cp. ref. in BR. under pampā *varaŋ-ādi*] a loris (Abhp. 618) i. e. an ape; but probably meant for a kind of bird (cp. Kern, *Toev.* s. v.) J VI.538 (C. reads pampuka & expl^s by pampaṭaka).

Pamha (nt.) [the syncope form of pakhuma = Sk. pakṣman used in poetry and always expl^d in C. by pakhuma] eye-lash, usually in cpd. aḷāra° having thick eyelashes, e. g. at J V.215; Vv 35^7; 64^{11}; Pv III.3^5; asāyata° at Th 2, 384.

Pamhayati [pa + **smi**, Sk. prasmayate] to laugh; Caus. pamhāpeti to make somebody laugh J V.297 (= parihaseti C.), where it is syn. with the preceding umhāpeti.

Paya (nt.) [Ved. payas, nt, of **pī**] milk, juice J I.204; VI.572.

Payacchati [pa + yacchati of **yam**] to offer, present, give Dpvs XI.28; Pgdp 63, 72, 77 sq. — pp. payata (q. v.).

Payata [pp. of payacchati] restrained, composed, purified, pure D I.103 (= abhiharitvā dinna); A III.313; Th 1, 348, 359 (°atta); It 101 (°pāṇin) = Miln 215; Sn 240 (= sakkāra-karaṇena p. alankata SnA 284); Vism 224 (°pāṇin — parisuddha-hattha); Sdhp 100.

Payatana (nt.) [cp. Sk. prayatna, of **yat**] striving after, effort, endeavour KhA 108.

Payatta [pp. of pa + **yat**] making effort, taking care, being on one's guard, careful Miln 373.

Payāta [pp. of payāti] gone forth, set out, proceeded Pv IV.5^6 (= gantuŋ āraddha PvA 260); J III.188, 190. Strange is "evaŋ nānappayātamhi" at Th 1, 945 (Mrs. Rh. D. "thus when so much is fallen away"; Neumann "in solcher Drangsal, solcher Not"). — duppayāta going or gone wrong, strayed Vv 84^9 (= duṭṭhu payātha apathe gata VvA 337).

Payāti [pa + **yā**] to go forward, set out, proceed, step out, advance, only aor pāyāsi J I.146, 223, 255; 3rd pl. pāyiŋsu J I.253 and pāyesuŋ J IV.220. — pp. payāta, (q. v.). See also pāyāti.

Payirudāharati [pari + ud + āharati with metathesis payir° for pariy°] to speak out, to proclaim aor payirudāhāsi D II.222 (vaṇṇe); J I.454 (vyañjanaŋ).

Payirupāsati [pari + upa + **ās**, with metathesis as in payirudāharati] 1. "to sit close round," i. e. to attend on (acc.), to honour, pay homage, worship D I.47; II.257; M II.117; S I.146; A I.124, 126, 142; IV.337; Dh 64, 65; Th 1, 1236; J VI.222 (imper. °upāsaya); Pv II.9^{61}; Pug 26, 33; SnA 401; VbhA 457 (here def^d by Bdhgh as "punappunaŋ upasankamati"). — ppr. °upāsanto S V.67 = It 107; PvA 44; and upāsamāna DhA II.32. — aor. °upāsiŋ A IV.213 (Bhagavantaŋ); PvA 50. — ger. °upāsiya D II.287. — 2. to visit Vin I.214 (ger. °upāsitvā); IV.98. — pp. payirupāsita (q. v.).

Payirupāsana (nt.) & °ā (f.) [fr. payirupāsati] attending to, worshipping: worship, homage M II.176; S V.67 = It 107; DA I.142; PvA 138.

Payirupāsika [fr. payirupāsati] a worshipper ThA 200.

Payirupāsita [pp. of payirupāsati] worshipped PvA 116 (= upaṭṭhita), 205 (= purakkhata).

Payuñjati [pa + **yuj**] to harness, yoke, employ, apply; Pass. payujjati to be applied to Sdhp 400 (ppr. °māna). — pp. payutta (q. v.). — Caus. payojeti (q. v.)

Payuta [pp. of pa + **yu**, cp. Sk. pra + yuta united, fastened to, increased] (wrongly) applied, at random, careless: "misdirected" A I.199; Sn 711 (°ŋ vācaŋ = obhāsaparikathā-nimitta-viññatti-payuttaŋ ghāsesana-vācaŋ SnA 497), 930 (= cīvarādīhi sampayutta tadatthaŋ vā payojita SnA 565; Nd^1 389 however reads payutta and expl^s as "cīvarapayutta" etc.).

Payutta [pp. of payuñjati] 1. yoked Sn p. 13 (= yottehi yojita SnA 137). — 2. applied, intent on, devoted to, busy in (acc., loc., or -°) J V.121 (ajjhattaŋ); Pv III.7^{10} (sāsane); SnA 497 (viññatti°). — 3. applicable (either rightly or wrongly); as su° well-behaved, acting well Miln 328; by itself (in bad sense), wrongly applied, wasted (cp. payuta) A II.81 sq.; Sn 930 (see Nd^1 389). — 4. planned, schemed, undertaken Vin II.194 (Deva dattena Bhagavato vadho p.).

Payuttaka (adj. n.) [payutta + ka] one who is applied or put to a (bad) task, as spy, hireling; bribed J I.262 (°cora), 291 (°dhutta).

Payoga [Vedic prayoga, fr. pa + **yuj**, see payuñjati] 1. means, instrument J VI.116 (= karaṇa); SnA 7; DhsA 215 (sa°). — 2. preparation, undertaking, occupation, exercise, business, action, practice Vin IV.278; Ps II.213 (sammā°); Miln 328 (sammā°); KhA 23, 29 sq.; PvA 8 (vapana°), 96 (manta°), 103, 146 (viññatti°; cp. payutta 2), 285 (sakkhara-kkhipana°). payogaŋ karoti to exert oneself, to undertake, to try PvA 184 (= parakkamati).

-karaṇa exertion, pursuit, occupation DhA III.238 -vipatti failure of means, wrong application PvA 117, 136. -sampatti success of means VvA 30, 32. -suddhi excellency of means, purity in application DhsA 165; VvA 60. -hīna deficient in exertion or application Miln 288.

Payogatā (f.) [fr. payoga] application (to) Vism 134 (majjhatta°).

Payojana (nt.) [fr. pa+**yuj**] 1. undertaking, business PvA 201. — 2. appointment J I.143. — 3. prescript, injunction DhsA 403. — 4. purpose, application, use Sdhp 395.

Payojita [pp. of payojeti] 1. connected with, directed to, applied SnA 565. — 2. instigated, directed Miln 3.

Payojeti [Caus. of payuñjati] 1. to undertake, engage in, begin D I.71 (kammante "set a business on foot"); A II.82 (kammantaŋ); Sn 404 (vaṇijjaŋ); J I.61; PvA 130 (kammaŋ). — 2. to prepare, apply, use, put to, employ PvA 46 (bhesajjaŋ cuṇṇena saddhiŋ). — 3. to engage, take into service, set to, hire J I.173; II.417. — 4. to engage with, come to close quarters J II.10. — 5. to put out at interest (vaḍḍhiyā) DA I.270. — pp. payojita (q. v.).

Payyaka [pa+ayyaka] (paternal) great-grandfather J I.2 (ayyaka°); PvA 107 (id.).

Para (adv.-adj.) [fr. Idg. *per, *peri (cp. pari); Ved. para, parā, paraŋ; Lat. per through, Gr. πέρα & πέραν beyond; see Walde, *Lat. Wtb.* under per & also pari, pubba, pura, purāṇa] 1. (adv. & prep.) beyond, on the further side of (with abl. or loc.), over PvA 168 (para Gangāya, v. l. °āyaŋ). See in same meaning & application paraŋ, paro and parā & cp. cpds. like paraloka. — 2. (adj.) para follows the pron. declension; cases: sg. nom. paro Sn 879, acc. paraŋ Sn 132, 185, gen. dat. parassa Sn 634; Pv II.9[19], instr. parena PvA 116, loc. paramhi Sn 634, and pare Pv II.9[43]; pl. nom. pare Dh 6, acc. pare Dh 257; PvA 15, gen. dat. paresaŋ D I.3; Th I, 743; J I.256; Sn 818, instr. parehi Sn 240, 255; PvA 17. — Meanings: (a) beyond, i. e. "higher" in space (like Ved. para as opp. to avara lower), as well as "further" in time (i. e. future, to come, or also remote, past: see loc. pare under c.), freq. in phrase paro loko the world beyond, the world (i. e. life) to come, the beyond or future life (opp. ayaŋ loko) Sn 185 (asmā lokā paraŋ lokaŋ na socati), 634 (asmiŋ loke paramhi ca); Dh 168 (paramhi loke); Pv II.8[3] (id. = paraloke PvA 107); but also in other comb[n], like santi-para (adj.) higher than calm Dh 202. Cp. paraloka, paraŋ and paro. — (b) another, other, adj. as well as n., pl. others Sn 396 (parassa dāraŋ nâtikkameyya), 818 (paresaŋ, cp. Nd[1] 150); Dh 160 (ko paro who else), 257 (pare others); Pv II.9[19] (parassa dānaŋ); II.9[43] (pare, loc. = paramhi parassa PvA 130); DhA IV.182 (gen. pl.); PvA 15, 60 (paresaŋ dat.), 103, 116, 253 (parassa purisassa & paraŋ purisaŋ). Often contrasted with and opposed to attano (one's own, oneself), e. g. at M I.200 (paraŋ vambheti attānaŋ ukkaŋseti); Sn 132 (attānaŋ samukkaŋse paraŋ avajānāti); J I.256 (paresaŋ, opp. attanā); Nd[2] 26 (att-attha opp. par-attha, see cpds. °ajjhāsaya & °attha). — paro . . . paro "the one . . . the other" D I.224 (kiŋ hi paro parassa karissati); paro paraŋ one another Sn 148 (paro paraŋ nikubbetha). — In a special sense we find pare pl. in the meaning of "the others," i. e. outsiders, aliens (to the religion of the Buddha), enemies, opponents (like Vedic pare) D I.2 (= paṭiviruddhā sattā DA I.51); Vin I.349; Dh 6. — (c) some oblique cases in special meaning and used as adv.: paraŋ acc. sg. m. see under cpds., like parantapa; as nt. adv. see sep. In phrase puna ca paraŋ would be better read puna c' aparaŋ (see apara). —parena (instr.) later on, afterwards J III.395 (= aparena samayena C.). —pare (loc.); cp. Gr. παραί at; Lat. prae before; Goth. faúra = E. for, old dat. of *per) in the past, before, yet earlier J II.279 (where it continues ajja and hiyyo, i. e. to-day and yesterday, and refers to the day before yesterday. Similarly at Vin IV.63 pare is contrasted with ajja & hiyyo and may mean "in future," or "the day before yesterday." It is of interest to notice the Ved. use of pare as "in the future" opp. to adya & śvas); J III.423 (the day before yesterday). At DhA I.253 (sve vā pare vā) and IV.170 in the sense of "on the day after tomorrow." —parā (only apparently abl., in reality either para+a° which represents the vocalic beginning of the second part of the cpd., or para+ā which is the directional prefix ā, emphasizing para. The latter expl[n] is more in the spirit of the Pali language): see separately. -paro (old abl. as adv. = Sk. paras) beyond further: see sep. —parato (abl.) in a variety of expressions and shades of meaning, viz. (1) from another, as regards others A III.337 (attano parato ca); Nett 8 (ghosa), 50 (id.). — (2) from the point of view of "otherness," i. e. as strange or something alien, as an enemy M I.435 (in "anicca"-passage); A IV.423; Nd[2] 214[II]; Ps II.238; Kvu 400; Miln 418 and passim; in phrase parato disvā "seen as not myself" Th I, 1160; 2, 101; S I.188 (sankhāre parato passa, dukkhato mā ca attato). — (3) on the other side of, away from, beyond J II.128; PvA 24 (kuḍḍānaŋ). — (4) further, afterwards, later on S I.34; J I.255; IV.139; SnA 119, 482. — *Note.* The compounds with para° are combinations either with para 1 (adv. prep.), or para 2 (adj. n.). Those containing para in form parā and in meaning "further on to" see separately under parā°. See also pāra, pārima etc.

-ajjhāsaya intent on others (opp. att°) SnA 46. -attha (parattha, to be distinguished from adv. parattha, q. v. sep.) the profit or welfare of another (opp. attattha) S II.29; A III.63; Dh 166; Nd[2] 26. -âdhīna dependent on others D I.72 (= paresu adhīno parass' eva ruciyā pavattati DA I.212); J VI.99; ThA 15 (°vuttika); VvA 23 (°vutti, paresaŋ bhāraŋ vahanto). -ûpakkama aggression of an enemy, violence Vin II.194. -ûpaghāta injuring others, cruelty Vv 84[40]. -ûpaghātin killing others Dh 184 (= paraŋ upahananto p. DhA III.237). -ûpavāda reproaching others Sn 389. -kata see parankata. -kamma service of others, *°kārin* serving others Vv 33[22]. -kāra see below under parankāra. -kula clan of another, strange or alien clan Sn 128; Dh 73. -kkanta [para° or parā° *krānta ?] walked (by another ? or gone over ?) J VI.559 (better to be read with v. l. on p. 560 as pada° i. e. walked by feet, footprint). -kkama (parā+**kram**) exertion, endeavour, effort, strife D I.53; III.113; S I.166 (daḷha°); II.28 (purisa°); V.66, 104 sq.; A I.4, 50 (purisa°); IV.190; Sn 293; Dh 313; Nd[1] 487; J I.256; II.153; Dhs 13, 12, 289, 571; Miln 244; DhA IV.139; Sdhp 253; adj. (-°) sacca° one who strives after the truth J IV.383. -kkamati [*parakramati] to advance, go forward, exert oneself, undertake, show courage Sn 966 (ger. parakkamma); Dh 383 (id.); Pv III.2[13] (imper. parakkāma, v. l. parakkama); Pug 19, 23; PvA 184 (= payogaŋ karoti); Sdhp 439. -kkaroti [either for parā+**kṛ** or more likely paras+**kṛ**, cp. paro] lit. "to put on the opposite side," i. e. to remove, do away with J IV.26 (corresponding to apaneti, C. expl[ns] as "parato kāreti," taking parato in the sense of para 2 c 3), 404 (mā parākari = mā pariccaji C.). -gatta alien body, trsl. "limbs that are not thou" Th I, 1150. -gavacaṇḍa violent against the cows of another A II.109 = Pug 47 (opp. sakagavacaṇḍa, cp. PugA 226: yo attano gogaṇaŋ ghaṭṭeti, paragogaṇe pana so rato sukhasīlo hoti etc.). -(n)kata made by something or somebody else, extra-self, extraneous, alien S I.134 (nayidaŋ attakataŋ bimbaŋ nayidaŋ parakataŋ aghaŋ); with ref. to loka & dukkha and opposed to *sayankata* D III.137 sq.; S II.19 sq., 33 sq., 38 sq.;

Ud 69 sq. -(n)kāra condition of otherness, other people, alienity Ud 70 (opp. ahankara selfhood). -citta the mind or heart of others A v.160. -jana a stranger, enemy, demon, fig. devil (cp. Sk. itarajana) M I.153, 210. -tthaddha [parā + tthaddha] propped against, founded on, relying on (with loc.) J VI.181 (= upatthadda C.). -tthabbha is to be read for °tthambha at J IV.313, in meaning = °tthaddha (kismiŋ). -dattûpajīvin living on what is given by others, dependent on another's gift Sn 217; Miln 294. -davutta see sep. under parada -dāra the wife of another, somebody else's wife M I.87; A II.71, 191; Sn 108, 242 (°sevanā); Dh 246, 309 (°upasevin, cp. DhA III.482); J VI.240; DhA III.481 (°kamma). -dārika (better to be read as pāra°) an adulterer S II.188, 259; J III.43. -dhammika "of someone else's norm," one who follows the teaching of another, i. e. of an heretic teacher Sn 965 (Nd^1 485: p° ā vuccanti satta sahadhammika ṭhapetvā ye keci Buddhe appasannā, dhamme appasannā, sanghe appasannā). -niṭṭhita made ready by others S I.236. -nimmita "created by another," in °*vasavattin* having power under control of another, N. of a class of Devas (see deva) D I.216 sq.; A I.210; It 94; Pug 51; DA I.114, 121; KhA 128; VvA 79. -neyya to be led by another, under another's rule Sn 907 Nd^1 321 (= parapattiya parapaccaya). -(n)tapa worrying or molesting another person (opp. attantapa) D III.232; M I.341, 411; II.159; Pug 56. -paccaya resting, relying, or dependent on someone else Nd^1 321; usually neg. a° independent of another Vin I.12, 181 and passim. -pattiya = prec. Nd^1 321. -pāṇa other living beings Sn 220. -puggala other people D III.108. -putta somebody else's son A v.169; Sn 43. -pessa serving others, being a servant Sn 615 (= parçsaŋ veyyāvacca SnA 466). -pessiyā a female servant or messenger, lit. to be sent by others J III.413 (= parehi pesitabbā pesanakārikā C.). -ppavāda [cp. BSk. parapravādin "false teacher" Divy 202] disputation with another, challenge, opposition in teaching (appl^d to Non-Buddhistic systems) S v.261; A II.238; Miln 170, 175. -bhāga outer part, precinct part beyond PvA 24. -bhuta [Sk. parabhṛta] the Indian cuckoo (lit. brought up by another) J v.416 (so read for parābhūta). -bhojana food given by others Sn 366 (= parehi dinnaŋ saddhādeyyaŋ SnA 364). -loka [cpd. either with para 1. or para 2. It is hardly justified to assume a metaphysical sense, or to take para as temporal in the sense of paraŋ (cp. paraŋmaraṇā after death), i. e. the future world or the world to come] the other world, the world beyond (opp. agaŋ loko *this* world or idhaloka the world *here*, see on term Stede, *Peta Vatthu* p. 29 sq.) D I.27, 58, 187; II.319; S I.72, 138; Sn 579, 666, 1117; Nd^1 60; Nd^2 214 (v. l. for paloka in anicca-passage) 410 (= manussalokaŋ ṭhapetvā sabbo paraloko); Ps I.121; Vv 84^5 (= narakaŋ hi sattānaŋ ekantânatthatāya parabhūto paṭisattubhūto loko ti visesato paraloko ti VvA 335); PvA 5, 60 (= pettivisaya parattha), 64, 107, 253 (idhalokato p. natthi); SnA 478 (= parattha); Sdhp 316, 326, 327. -vambhitā contempt of others M I.19 (a°). -vambhin contempting others M I.19, 527. -vasatta power (over others) Dāvs IV.19. -vāda (1) talk of others, public rumour S I.4; Sn 819 (cp. Nd^1 151); SnA 475. (2) opposition Miln 94 sq. -vādin opponent Miln 348. -visaya the other world, realm of the Dead, Hades Pv IV.8^7 (= pettivisaya PvA 268). -vediya to be known by others, i. e. heterodox D II.241; Sn 474 (= parehi ñāpetabba SnA 410). -sattā (pl.) other beings A I.255 = III.17 (+ parapuggalā). -suve on the day after tomorrow DhA IV.170 (v. l. SS for pare, see para 2 c.). -sena a hostile army D I.89 = II.16 = III.59 = Sn p. 106 ≈ (cp. DA I.250 = SnA 450). -hattha the hand of the enemy J I.179. -hiŋsā hurting others Pv III.7^3. -hita the good or welfare of others (opp. attahita) D III.233; PvA 16, 163. -hetu on account of others, through others Sn 122 (attahetu +); Pug 54.

Paraŋ (param°) (adv.) [orig. nt. of para] further, away (from); as prep. (w. abl.) after, beyond; absolute only in phrase ito paraŋ from here, after this, further e. g. KhA 131; SnA 160, 178, 412, 512, 549; PvA 83, 90; also in **tato paraŋ** J III. 281.

-parā (f.) [adv. converted into a noun paraŋ + abl. of para] lit. "after the other," i. e. succession, series Vin II.110; IV.77, 78 (parampara-bhojana "taking food in succession," successive feeding, see under bhojana, and cp. C. at Vin IV.77, 78 and *Vin Texts* I.38); D I.239; M I.520; A II.191 (paramparāya in phrase anussavena p. itikirāya, as at Nd^2 151); Bu I.79; J I.194; IV.35 (expl^d by C. as purisa°, viz. a series of husbands, but probably misunderstood, Kern, *Toev.* s. v. interperts as "defamation, ravishing"); Nett 79 (°parahetu); Miln 191, 276; DhsA 314; SnA 352; DhA I.49 (sīsa°). -maraṇā (adv.) after death; usually in comb^n with kāyassa bhedā p. after the dissolution of the body, i. e. after death S I.231; D I.245; PvA 27, 133; absolutely only in phrase hoti Tathāgato p. D I.188, 192; A v.193. -mukhā (adv.) in one's absence, lit. with face turned away (opp. *sammukhā* in presence, thus at J III.263 where parammukhā corresponds to raho and sam° to āvi; PvA 13) D I.230 (parammukhin ?); DhA II.109.

Parajjhati see parājeti.

Parattha (adv.) [Vedic parastāt beyond] elsewhere, hereafter, in the Beyond, in the other world S I.20; Sn 661 = It 42 = Dh 306; Dh 177; J II.417; Pv I.11^{10} (= paraloke PvA 60); III.1^{20} (= samparāye PvA 177); SnA 478 (= paraloke).

Parada (adj.) [for uparada (?) = uparata, pp. of upa + **ram**] finding pleasure in, fond of, only in two (doubtful) cpds. viz. °**vutta** [unexpl^d, perhaps v for y, as daya > dava through influence of d in parada°; thus = parata + yutta ?] "fond of being prepared," adapted, apt, active, alert; only in one stock phrase (which points to this form as being archaic and probably popular etymology, thus distorting its real derivation), viz. appossukkà pannaloma + Vin II.184 (*Vin. Texts* III.232 trsl. "secure," cp. Vin II.363); M I.450; II.121 (v. l. BB paradatta°), — and °samācāra living a good (active) life M I.469.

Parama (adj.) [Vedic parama; superl. formation of para, lit. "farthest," cp. similarly, although fr. diff. base, Lat. prīmus] highest, most excellent, superior, best; paraphrased by agga seṭṭha visiṭṭha at Nd^2 502 A = Nd^1 84, 102 (the latter reading viseṭṭha for visiṭṭha); by **uttama** at DhA III.237; VvA 78. — D I.124 (ettaka°); M II.120 (°nipacca); S I.166; II.277; v.230; A v 64 (°diṭṭha-dhamma-nibbāna); Sn 138 (yasaŋ paramaŋ patto), 296 (°ā mittā), 788 (suddhaŋ °ŋ arogaŋ), 1071 (saññāvimokhe °e vimutto); Dh 184 (nibbānaŋ °ŋ vadanti Buddhā), 203, 243; Vv 16^1 (°alankata = paramaŋ ativiya visesato VvA 78) Pv II.9^{10} (°iddhi); Pug 15, 16, 60; SnA 453 (°issara); PvA 12 (°nipacca), 15 (°duggandha), 46. — At the end of a cpd. (-°) "at the outmost, at the highest, at most; as a minimum, at least" Vin IV.263 (dvangula-pabba°); esp. freq. in phrase sattakkhattu° one who will be reborn seven times at the outmost, i. e. at the end of the 7 rebirth-interval S II.185 (sa°); v.205; A I.233; IV.381; v.120; It 18; Kvu 469. See pāramī & pāramitā.

-attha [cp. class. Sk. paramārtha] the highest good, ideal; truth in the ultimate sense, philosophical truth (cp. *Kvu trsl.* 180; *J.P.T.S.* 1914, 129 sq.; *Cpd.* 6, 81); Arahantship Sn 68 (= vuccati Amataŋ Nibbānaŋ etc. Nd^2 409), 219 (°dassin); Nd^2 26; Miln 19, 31; °dīpanī Exposition of the Highest Truth, N. of the Commentary on Th, Vv and Pv; mentioned e. g. at PvA 71; °jotikā id., N. of the C. on Kh and Sn, mentioned e. g. at KhA 11. — As °-, in instr. and abl. used adverbially in meaning of "in the highest sense, absolutely, κατ' ἐξοχήν, primarily, ideally, in an absolute sense," like °pāramī Bu I.77 °visuddhi A v.64; °saññita Th 2. 210; °suñña Ps II.184; °suddhi SnA 528; abl. **paramat-thato** Miln 28; VvA 24 (manusso), 30 (bhikkhu), 72 (jīvitindriyaŋ); PvA 146 (pabbajito, corresponding to anavasesato), 253 (na koci kiñci hanati = not at all); instr. paramatthena Miln 71 (vedagū), 268 (sattû-paladdhi). **-gati** the highest or best course of life or future exsitence Vv 35[12] (= anupādisesa-nibbāna VvA 164).

Paramatā (f.) [fr. parama, Vedic paramatā highest position] the highest quantity, measure on the outside, minimum or maximum D I.60 (ghāsa-cchādana-paramatāya santuṭṭho contexted with a minimum of food & clothing; DA I.169 expl^d by uttamatāya); M I.10 (abyabajjha°); S I.82 (nāḷik' odana-paramatāya on a nāḷi of boiled rice at the most); freq. in phrase sattakkhattuŋ p. interval of seven rebirths at the outside (cp. parama), being reborn seven times at the most S II.134 sq.; v.458; Kvu 469 (cp. *Kvu trsl.* 268[3]).

Parasupahāra at S v.441 is to be corrected to pharasu°.

Parā° (prefix) [para + ā, not instr. of para: see para 2 c; in some cases it may also correspond to paraŋ°] prep. meaning "on to," "over" (with the idea of mastering), also "through, throughout." The ā is shortened before double consonant, like parā + **kr** = parakkaroti, parā + **kram** = parakkamati (see under cpds. of para).

Parākaroti see parakkaroti (paraŋ° ? or parā ?).

Parājaya [parā + ji, opp. of jaya] 1. defeat D I.10; J VI.209; VvA 139. — 2. defeat in game, loss, losing at play S I.149 (dhana°) = A v.171 = Sn 659; J VI.234 (°gāha sustainment of a loss).

Parājita [pp. of parājeti] defeated, having suffered a loss Vin IV.5; S I.224; A IV.432; Sn 440, 681; Dh 201 (= parena parājito DhA III.259, where Bdhgh takes it evidently as instr. of para = parā); J I.293; II.160 (sahassaŋ), 403.

Parājeti [parā + jeti of **ji**, cp. jayati] to defeat, conquer; in gambling: to make lose, beat PvA 151 (sahassaŋ p. by 1,000 coins). — aor. parāji in 3rd pl. °jiŋsu, only in one stock phrase referring to the battle of the Gods & Titans, viz. at D II.285 = M I.253 (°jiniŋsu) = S I.221 = 224 (v. l. °jiniŋsu) = A IV.432 (°jiyiŋsu, with v. l. °jiniŋsu), where a Pass. is required ("were defeated, lost") in opp. to jiniŋsu, and the reading °jiyiŋsu as aor. pass. is to be preferred. — Pass. °jiyati to be defeated, to suffer defeat S I.221 (Pot. parājeyya, but form is Active); J I.290; and parajjhati (1st pl. parajjhāma) J II.403; aor. parājiyi: see above parāji. — pp. parājita (q. v.).

Parābhava [fr. parā + **bhu** Vedic parābhava] defeat, destruction, ruin, disgrace S II.241; A II.73; IV.26; Sn 92, 115; J III.331; SnA 167.

Parābhavati [parā + **bhū**] 1. to go to ruin Sn 91 (= parihāyati vinassati). — 2. to win through, to surpass Th 1, 1144 (cp. trsl. 381[4]). — pp. parābhūta (q. v.). See also **parābhetvā**.

Parābhūta [pp. of parābhavati] ruined, fallen into disgrace M II.210 (avabhūta +). — *Note.* parābhūta at J v.416 is to be read parabhuta (q. v.).

Parābhetvā at J v.153 is not clear (C.: hadayaŋ bhinditvā olokento viya . . .); perhaps we have here a reading parābh° for parāg° (as bhenḍuka wrongly for genḍuka), which in its turn stands for parādhetvā (cp. similarly BSk. ārāgeti for ārādheti), thus meaning "propitiating."

Parāmaṭṭha [pp. of parāmasati] touched, grasped, usually in bad sense: succumbing to, defiled, corrupted D I.17; for a different, commentarial interpretation see Parāmāsa (evaŋ° so acquired or taken up; cp. DA I.107: nirāsanka-cittatāya punappuna āmaṭṭha); S II.94; Nd[2] 152 (gahita p. abhiniviṭṭha; cp. gahessasi No. 227); Dhs 584, 1177, 1500; Sdhp 332. —dup° wrongly grasped, misused S I.49. —apparāmaṭṭha [cp. BSk. aparāmṛṣta not affected Mvyutp. p. 84] untarnished, incorrupt D II.80 (cp. *Dial* II.85); III.245; S II.70; A III.36.

Parāmasa [parā + **mṛś**, but see parāmāsa] touching, seizing, taking hold of M I.130 (v. l. °māsa which reading is probably to be preferred, cp. Trenckner on p. 541); S III.46 (v. l. °māsa). — neg. aparāmasa not leading astray, not enticing D I.17 (°to), 202. — Perhaps we should read parāmāsa altogether.

Parāmasati [para + masati of **mṛś**] to touch, hold on to, deal with, take up, to be attached or fall a victim to (acc.) Vin II.47, 195, 209; D I.17; M I.257; S III.110; J IV.138; in comb^n with gaṇhāti & nandati (abhiniveseti) at Nd[2] 227. — ger. parāmassa D II.282; M I.130, 498 (but cp. p. 541); grd. parāmasitabba J I.188. — pp. parāmaṭṭha (q. v.).

Parāmasana (nt.) [fr. parāmasati] touching, seizing, taking up Nd[2] 576 (daṇḍa-sattha°); DhsA 239 (anga-paccanga°); PvA 159 (kiriyā°).

Parāmāsa [parā + **mṛś**, cp. Epic Sk. parāmarśa being affected by; as philos. term "reflection"] touching, contact, being attached to, hanging on, being under the influence of, contagion (*Dhs. trsl.* 316). In Asl. 49, Bdhgh analyses as parato āmasantīti parāmāsā: p. means "they handle dhamma's *as other*" (than what they really are, e. g. they transgress the real meaning of anicca etc. and say nicca). Hence the renderings in Asl. trs. "Reversion," in Dialogues III.28, 43, etc. "perverted" (parāmasāmi parāmaṭṭha) — S III.46, 110; A II.42 (sacca°); III.377 (sīlabbata°), 438 (id.); v.150 (sandiṭṭhi°); D III.48; Th 1, 342; It 48 (itisacca°, cp. idaŋsaccābhinivesa under kāyagantha); Pug 22; Dhs 381, 1003, 1175 (diṭṭhi° contagion of speculative opinion), 1498 (id.). It is almost synonymous with abhinivesa; see kāyagantha (under gantha), and cp. Nd[2] 227 (gāha p. abhinivesa) and Nd[2] under taṇhā III. 1 C. — See also parāmasa.

Parāmāsin (adj.) [fr. parāmāsa] grasping, seizing, perverting D III.48; M I.43, 96 (sandiṭṭhi°).

Parāyana (Parāyaṇa) (nt.) [fr. parā + **i**, cp. Vedic parāyaṇa highest instance, also BSk. parāyaṇa e. g. Divy 57, 327] 1. (n.) final end, i. e. support, rest, relief S I.38; A I.155, 156 (tāṇa lena dīpa etc.); J v.501 = VI.375 (dīpañ ca p.). — 2. (adj. -°) (a) going through to, ending in, aiming at, given to, attached to, having one's end or goal in; also: finding one's support in (as daṇḍa° leaning on a stick M I.88; A I.138), in foll. phrases prevalent: Amata° S v.217 sq.; tama° Pug 51; Nibbāna° S IV.373; v.218; brahmacariya° S I.234; Maccu° S v.217; sambodhi° D I.156; II.155; Pug 16. Cp. also Sn 1114 (tap° = tad°, see Nd[2] 411); Miln 148 (ekanta-soka°); DhA I.28 (rodana, i. e. constantly weeping). — (b) destined to, having one's next birth in., e. g. Avīci° J III.454; IV.159; duggati° PvA 32; devaloka° J I.218; brahmaloka° J III.396; Miln 234; sagga° J VI.329; PvA 42, 160; sugati° PvA 89 similarly nīlamañca° Pv II.2[6]. See also parāyana.

Parāyika see sam°.

Parāyin (adj.) [fr. parāyana] having one's refuge or resort (in), being supported, only neg. aparāyinī (f.) without support J III.386.

Pari° (indecl.) [Idg. *peri to verbal root ***per**, denoting completion of a forward movement (as in Sk. **pṛ²**, piparti. to bring across, promote; cp. Vedic **pṛc** to satisfy, pṛṇāti to fill, fulfill. See also P. para). Cp. Vedic pari, Av. pairi, Gr. πέρι, Lat. per (also in adj. per-magnus very great); Obulg. pariy round about, Lith. per through, Oir er- (intensifying prefix), Goth. faír, Ohg. fir, far = Ger. ver-] prefix, signifying (lit.) around, round about; (fig.) all round, i. e. completely, altogether. The use as *prep.* (with acc. = against, w. abl. = from) has entirely disappeared in Pāli (but see below 1a). As *adv.* "all round" it is only found at J VI.19 (parī metri causa; combd with samantato). — The composition form before vowels is pariy°, which in combn with ud and upa undergoes metathesis, scil. payir°. Frequent combns with other preps. are pari + ā (pariyā°) and pari + ava (pariyo°); sampari°. Close affinities of p. are the preps. adhi (cp. ajjhesati > pariyesati, ajjhogāhati > pariyogāhati) and abhi (cp. abhirādheti > paritoseti, abhitāpa > paritāpa, abhipīḷita > pari°, abhipūreti > pari°, abhirakkhati > pari°), cp. also its relation to ā in var. combns. — *Meanings.* 1. (lit.) (a) away from, off (cp. Vedic pari as prep. c. abl.:) °kaḍḍhati to draw over, seduce, °cheda cutting off, restriction, °puñchati wipe off. — (b) all round, round (expld by samantato, e. g. at Vism 271 in pallanka): °anta surrounded, °esati search round, °kiṇṇa covered all round (i. e. completely, cp. expln as "samantato ākiṇṇa"), °carati move round, °jana surrounding people, °dhāvati run about, °dhovati wash all round, °paleti watch all round, fig. guard carefully, °bhamati roam about, °maṇḍala circular (round), °sā assembly (lit. sitting round, of **sad**). — 2. (fig.) (a) quite, completely, very much, κατ' ἐξοχήν: °ādāna consummation, °āpanna gone completely into, °odāta very pure, °osāna complete end, °gūhati to hide well, °toseti satisfy very much, °pūreti fulfil, °bhutta thoroughly enjoyed, °yañña supreme sacrifice, °suddha extremely clean. — (b) too much, excessively (cp. ati° and adhi°): °tāpeti torment excessively, °pakka over-ripe. — A derivation (adv.) from pari is parito (q. v.). On its relation to Sk. pariṣ see parikkhāra. A frequently occurring dialectical variant of pari° is pali° (q. v.). — *Note.* The expln of P. Commentators as regards pari is "pariggahaṭṭho" Ps 1.176; "paricca" SnA 88; "parito" VvA 316; PvA 33.

Parikaḍḍhati [pari + k°, cp. BSk. parikaḍḍhati MVastu II.255] to draw over or towards oneself, to win over, seduce D II.283 (purisaŋ); Miln 143 (janapadaŋ). Cp. parikassati and samparikaḍḍhati.

Parikaḍḍhana (nt.) [fr. prec.] drawing, dragging along J II.78; Miln 154.

Parikati [*parikṛti of **kṛ** (?)] arrangement, preparation, getting up J V.203.

Parikatta [pp. of pari + kantati²; corresponds to Sk. kṛtta, which is usually represented in P. by kanta²] cut round, cut off Miln 188.

Parikathā (f.) [pari + kathā, cp. BSk. parikathā Divy 225, 235] 1. "round-about tale," exposition, story, esp. religious tale D II.204; Vism 41 (= pariyāya-kathā). — 2. talk about, remark, hint Vin I.254 (cp. *Vin. Texts* II.154); Vbh 353 = Vism 23 (with obhāsa & nimitta); SnA 497. — 3. continuous or excessive talk Vism 29.

Parikanta¹ [pari + kanta² of kantati²] cut open Vin III.89 (kucchi p.). See also parikatta & cp. Kern, *Toev.* s. v. (misreading for °katta ?). — *Note.* Reading parikantaŋ upāhanaŋ at J VI.51 is with v. l. to be changed to pariyantaŋ.

Parikanta² at Vin II.80 (bhāsita°) is probably to be read as pārikata [pp. of parikaroti]. Bdhgh explns as parikkamctvā kata, but it is difficult to derive it fr. parikkamati. *Vin. Texts* III.18 trsl. "as well in speech as in act" and identify it with parikanta¹, hardly justified. Cp. also Kern. *Toev.* s. v. The passage is evidently faulty.

Parikantati¹ [pari + kantati¹] to wind round, twist J III.185 (pāso pādaŋ p.; but taken by C. as parikantati², expld as "cammādīni chindanto samantā kantati").

Parikantati² [pari + kantati²] to cut (round), cut through, pierce M I.244 (vātā kucchiŋ p.); J III.185 (see parikantati¹).

Parikappa [fr. pari + **kalp**] 1. preparation, intention, stratagem Th 1, 940. — 2. assumption, supposition, surmise A I.197; V.271; DhsA 308.

Parikappita [pp. of parikappati] inclined, determined, decided, fixed upon Sdhp. 362, 602.

Parikamma (nt.) [pari + kamma] "doing round," i. e. doing up, viz 1. arrangement, getting up, preparation Vin II.106 (°ŋ kārāpeti), 117 (geruka° plastering with red chalk) 151 (id.). parikammaŋ karoti to make (the necessary) preparation, to set to work Vism 395 and passim (with ref. to iddhi). Usually in form parikammakata arranged, prepared Vin II.175 (bhūmi), as -° "with," viz. geruka° plastered with red chalk Vin I.48; II.209; lākhā° J III.183; IV.256; su° beautifully arranged or prepared, fitful, well worked Miln 62 (dāru), 282 (maṇiratana); VvA 188. In special sense used with ref. to jhāna, as **kasiṇa°** processes whereby jhāna is introduced, preparations for meditation J I.141; IV.306; V.162, 193; DhsA 168; cp. *Cpd.* 54; DhA I.105. — 2. service, attention, attending Vin I.47; II.106, 220; S I.76; Th 2, 376 (= veyyāvacca ThA 253); Pug 56; DhA I.96, 333, chiefly by way of administering ointments etc. to a person, cp. J V.89; DhA I.250. sarīra° attending the body DA I.45, 186; SnA 52.

-kāraka one who ministers to or looks after a person, attendant; one who makes preparations Th 2, 411 (f. -ikā = paricārikā ThA 267), J I.232.

Parikara [fr. pari + **kṛ**; a similar formation belonging to same root, but with fig. meaning is to be found in parikkhāra, which is also expld by parivara cp. parikaroti = parivāreti] "doing round," i. e. girdle, loincloth J IV.149; DhA I.352. — In cpd. ovāda° it is v. l. SS at D I.137 for paṭikara (q. v.).

Parikaroti [pari + **kṛ**] to surround, serve, wait upon, do service for J. IV.405 (= parivāreti C.); V. 353 (id.), 381; VI.592. Cp. parikara & parikkhāra.

Parikassati [pari + **kṛṣ**, cp BSk. parikarṣayati to carry about Divy 475, and parikaḍḍhati] 1. to drag about S I.44, cp. DhsA 68. — 2. sweep away, carry away DhA II.275 (mah' ogho viya parikassamāno, v. l. °kaḍḍhamāno). — Pass. parikissati (q. v.).

Parikiṇṇa [pp. of parikirati] scattered or strewn about, surrounded J IV.400; VI.89, 559; Pv I.6¹ (makkhikā° = samantato ākiṇṇa PvA 32); Miln 168, 285; DA I.45 (spelt parikkhiṇṇa). Cp. sampari°.

Parikittita [pp. of parikutteti] declared, announced, made public Sdhp 601.

Parikitteti [pari + kitteti] to declare, praise, make public Miln 131, 141, 230, 383. — pp. parikittita (q. v.).

Parikirati [pari + kirati] to strew or scatter about, to surround S I.185 = Th 1, 1210; aor. parikiri J VI.592 (v. l. for parikari, see parikaroti). — pp. parikiṇṇa (q. v.).

Parikiraṇa [fr. pari + kirati] strewing about, trsld "consecrating sites" D I.12 (vatthu-kamma + vatthu°; v. l. paṭi°; expld at DA I.98 as "idañ c' idañ ca āharathā ti vatvā tattha balikamma-karaṇaŋ"). The BSk. form appears to be parīkṣā, as seen in phrase vatthuparīkṣā at Divy 3 & 16. See under parikkhā.

Parikilanta [pp. of parikilamati] tired out, exhausted Miln 303.

Parikilamati [pari+kilamati] to get tired out, fatigued or exhausted J v.417, 421. — pp. parikilanta (q. v.).

Parikilissati [pari+kilissati] to get stained or soiled; fig. get into trouble or misery (?) see parikissati. — pp. parikiliṭṭha see parikkiliṭṭha.

Parikilesa [pari+kilesa] misery, calamity, punishment ThA 241 (for °klesa, q. v.).

Parikissati [most likely Pass. of parikassati; maybe Pass. of kisa (=Sk. kṛśa) to become emaciated. Mrs. Rh. D. at *K.S.* 319 takes it as contracted form of kilissati] to be dragged about or worried, to be harassed, to get into trouble S 1.39 (trsl. "plagues itself"); A II.177; IV.186; Sn 820 (v. l. Nd¹ °kilissati; expl^d at Nd¹ 154 as kissati parikissati parikilissati, with vv. ll. kilissati pakirissati).

Parikujati at Sdhp 145, meaning? Cp. palikujjati.

Parikupita [pp. of pari+**kup**] greatly excited, very much agitated A II.75; Miln 253.

Parikeḷanā (f.) [pari+keḷanā] adornment, adorning oneself, being fond of ornaments Nd² 585² (v. l. parilepanā); DA 1.286 has paṭikelanā instead, but Vbh id. p. 351 parikeḷanā with v. l. parikelāsanā.

Parikopeti [Caus. of pari+**kup**] to excite violently Miln 253.

Parikkamana (nt.) [pari+**kram**] walking about M 1.43, 44; adj. sa° having (opportunity for) walking about, i. e. accessible, good for rambling in, pleasant, said of the Dhamma A v.262 (opp. a°).

Parikkita at J v.74 is probably to be read parikkhita (pari+**ukṣ**): see okkhita "sprinkled, strewn," unless it is misreading for parikiṇṇa.

Parikkiliṭṭha [pp. of parikilissati] soiled, stained Vin II.296 (for parikiliṭṭha, cp. Kern, *Toev.* s. v.); id. p., at A II.56 has paṭikiliṭṭha, cp. upakkiliṭṭha Vin II.295.

Parikkha (-°) see parikkhā.

Parikkhaka (adj.) [fr. parikkhati] investigating, examining, experienced, shrewd PvA 131 (lokiya° experienced in the ways of the world, for agarahita).

Parikkhaṇa (nt.) [fr parikkhati; cp. Class. Sk. parīkṣaṇa] putting to the test, trying Sdhp 403 (sarīra°, or should we read parirakkhaṇa? Cp. parirakkhati).

Parikkhata¹ [pp. of pari+**kṣan**] wounded, hurt, grazed J III.431; PvA 272 (a°).

Parikkhata² [pp. of *parikkharoti; cp. Sk. pariṣkṛta] made up, prepared, endowed with, equipped, adorned D II.217; M III.71; Miln 328.

Parikkhatatā (f.) [abstr. fr. parikkhata²] "making up," pretence, posing, sham Pug 19 (23)=Vbh 351 (358).

Parikkhati [pari+**īkṣ**] to look round, to inspect, investigate, examine A I.162 (vaṇṇaŋ parikkhare 3rd pl.). See also parikkhaka, parikkhavant & parikkhā.

Parikkhattiya read pāri° (=parikkhatatā) q. v.

***Parikkharoti** [pariṣ+**kṛ**] lit. to do all round, i. e. to make up, equip, adorn (cp. parikaroti); pp. parikkhata² (q. v.); see also parikkhāra.

Parikkhaya [fr. pari+**kṣi²**, cp. Epic Sk. parikṣaya] exhaustion, waste, diminution, decay, loss, end D 1.156; M 1.453; III.37 sq.; S 1.2, 90, 152; v.461; A 1.100, 299; II.68; III.46 (bhogā °ŋ gacchanti); IV.148, 350; Th 1, 929; Sn 374, 749, 1094 (=pahānaŋ etc. Nd² 412); Dh 139; J 1.290; Pv II.6¹⁵; Pug 16, 17, 63; Miln 102; DhA IV.140 (°ŋ gacchati to come to waste, to disappear= atthaŋ gacchati of Dh 384); ThA 285; PvA 3 (dhanasannicayo °ŋ na gamissati). In the latter phrase freq. comb^d with pariyādāna (q. v.).

Parikkhavant (adj.) [fr. parikkhati] circumspect, clever, experienced J III.114.

Parikkhā (f.) [fr. pari+**īkṣ**, cp. BSk. parīkṣā Divy 3 & 16 in vastu°, ratna° etc. with which cp. P. vatthu-parikiraṇa] examination, investigation, circumspection, prudence J III.115; Nett 3, 4, 126 (cp. Index p. 276); Sdhp. 532 (attba°).

Parikkhāra [fr. *parikkharoti, cp. late Sk. pariṣkāra] "all that belongs to anything," make-up, adornment (so Nd² 585 bāhirā p. of the body). — (a) requisite, accessory, equipment, utensil, apparatus Vin 1.50, 296 (°colaka cloth required for water-strainers & bags, cp. *Vin. Texts* II.229); II.150 (senāsana°-dussa cloth-requirement of seat & bed); IV.249 sq., 284; D 1.128, 137 (yaññassa p. =parivāra DA 1.297); M 1.104 (jīvita°); III.11; S II.29; A IV.62 (citt' ālankāraŋ citta-parikkhār' atthaŋ dānaŋ), 236 (id.); J III.470 (sabba°-sampannaŋ dānaŋ with all that belongs to it); v.232; Sn 307; Nd² 585; Nett 1 sq.; 4, 108; DA 1.294, 299; DhA 1.38, 240 (geha°), 352 (v. l. for parikara); PvA 81 (sabba°). —saparikkhāra together with the (other) requisites, i. e. full of resources; used with reference to the samādhi-parikkhārā (see below) D II.217; M III.71. — (b) In a special sense and in very early use it refers to the "set of necessaries" of a Buddhist monk & comprises the 4 indispensable instruments of a mendicant, enum^d in stock phrase "cīvara-piṇḍapāta-senāsana-gilānapaccaya-bhesajja-p." i. e. robe, alms-bowl, seat & bed, medicine as help in illness. Thus freq. found in Canon, e. g. at Vin III.132; D III.268; S IV.288, 291; Nd² 523 (as 1st part of "yañña"); also unspecified, but to be understood as these 4 (different *Vin Texts* III.343 which take it to mean the 8 requisites: see below) at Vin II.267. — Later we find another set of mendicants' requisites designated as "aṭṭha parikkhārā," the 8 requirements. They are enum^d in verse at J 1.65= DA 1.206, viz. ticīvaraŋ, patto, vāsi, sūci, (kāya-) bandhanaŋ, parissāvana, i. e. the 3 robes, the bowl, a razor, a needle, the girdle, a water-strainer. They are expl^d in detail DA 1.206 sq. Cp. also J IV.342 (aṭṭha-parikkhāra-dhara); v.254 (kāyabandhana-parissāvana-sūci-vāsi-satthakāni; the last-named article being "scissors" instead of a razor); DhA II.61 (°dhara thera). — (c) In other comb^ns: satta nagara° A IV.106 sq. (cp. nagarūpakārikā D 1.105); satta samādhi° D II.216; M III.71; A IV.40; soḷasa° (adj.) of yañña: having sixteen accessories D 1.134 (cp. *Dial.* 1.174, 177). bahu° having a full equipment, i. e. being well-off Vin III.138; J 1.126. — *Note*. A set of 12 requisites (1-8 as under b and 4 additional) see detailed at DA 1.207.

Parikkhārika (-°) (adj.) [fr. parikkhāra] one who has the parikkhāras (of the mendicant). Usually the 8 p. are understood, but occasionally 12 are given as in the detailed enum^n of p. at DA 1.204-207.

Parikkhiṇṇa at DA 1.45 is to be read parikiṇṇa (q. v.).

Parikkhitta [pp. of parikkhipati] thrown round, overspread, overlaid, enclosed, fenced in, encircling, surrounded by (-°) M III.46; A IV.106 (su°); S 1.331 (read valligahana°); Pv IV.3³⁶ (v. l. for pariyanta as in 1.10¹³); Vism 71 (of gāma); ThA 70; DhA 1.42 (pākāra°); PvA 52 (=pariyanta 1.10¹³), 283 (sāṇi-pākāra°); Sdhp 596.

Parikkhipati [pari + **kṣip**] to throw round, encircle, surround Vin II.154; J I.52 (sāṇiŋ), 63, 150, 166; II.104; III.371; DhA I.73. — pp. parikkhitta (q. v.) — Caus. II. **parikkhipāpeti** J I.148 (sāṇiŋ); II.88 (sāṇi-pākāraŋ).

Parikkhīṇa [pp. of parikkhīyati] exhausted, wasted, decayed; extinct Vin IV.258; M III.80; S I.92; II.24; V.145, 461; D III.97, 133 (°bhava-saŋyojana); It 79 (id.); A IV.418, 434 (āsavā); Sn 175, 639, 640; Dh 93; Pug 11, 14; Miln 23 (°āyuka); PvA 112 (°tiṇodak'-āhāra).

Parikkhīṇatta (nt.) [abstr. of parikkhīṇa] the fact of being exhausted, exhaustion, extinction, destruction DA I.128 (jīvitassa); PvA 63 (kammassa), 148 (id.).

Parikkhīyati [pari + khīyati of **kṣi**²] to go to ruin, to be wasted or exhausted Th 2, 347 (=parikkhayaŋ gacchati ThA 242). — pp. parikkhīṇa (q. v.).

Parikkhepa [fr. pari + **kṣip**] 1. closing round, surrounding, neighbourhood, enclosure Vin IV.304; J I.338; IV.266; SnA 29 (°dāru etc.). — 2. circumference J I.89; V.37; Vism 205; KhA 133; SnA 194. — 3. "closing in on," i. e. fight, quarrel It 11, 12.

Pariklesa [pari + klesa] hardship, misery, calamity S I.132 =Th 2, 191; Th 2, 345 (=parikilesa ThA 241).

Parikhā (f.) [fr. pari + **khan**, cp. Epic Sk. parikhā] a ditch, trench, moat Vin II.154; D I.105 (ukkiṇṇa-parikha adj. with trenches dug deep, comb^d with okkhittapaligha; expl^d by khāta-parikha ṭhapita-paligha at DA I.274); M I.139 (sankiṇṇa° adj. with trenches filled, Ep. of an Arahant, comb^d with ukkhittapaligha) = A III.84 sq. = Nd² 284 C (spelt kkh); A IV.106 (nagara°); J I.240, 490; IV.106 (ukkiṇṇ' antaraparikha); VI.276, 432; Cp II.1³ (spelt kkh); Miln 1 (gambhīra°); SnA 519 (°taṭa); PvA 201 (°piṭṭhe), 261 (id.), 278 (id., v. l. °parikkhāṭa-tire).

Pariganhana (nt.) [fr. parigaṇhāti] comprehension J II.7 (°paññā comprehensive wisdom).

Parigaṇhāti (& **Pariggaheti** Caus.) [pari + **grh**] 1. to embrace, seize, take possession of, hold, take up M I.80, 137; J III.189; DA I.45. — 2. to catch, grasp DhA I.68. — 3. to go all round DhA I.91 (sakala-jambudīpaŋ). — Caus. °ggaheti (aor. °esi, ger. °etvā, inf. °etuŋ) 1. to embrace, comprehend, fig. master Vin II.213; J II.28; III.332; SnA 549 (mantāya); DhA III.242; PvA 68 (hattesu), 93; VvA 75. — 2. to explore, examine, find out, search J I.162; II.3; III.85, 268 (°ggahetuŋ), 533; V.93, 101; DhA II.56. — Caus. II. parigaṇhāpeti J I.290. — 3. to comprise, summarise KhA 166, 167. — pp. pariggahita (q. v.).

Parigalati [pari + galati, see gaḷati] to sink down, slip or glide off J IV.229, 250; V.68.

Parigilati [pari + gilati] to swallow J I.346.

Parigūhati [pari + gūhati] to hide, conceal A I.149; IV.10, 31; Pv III.4³ (=paṭicchādeti PvA 194).

Parigūhanā (f.) [fr. patigūhati] hiding, concealment, deception Pug 19, 23.

Pariggaha [fr. pari + **grh**] 1. wrapping round, enclosing Th 1, 419 (? cp. *Brethren* 217 n. 6). — 2. taking up, seizing on, acquiring, acquisition, also in bad sense of "grasping" Sn 779 (=taṇhā and diṭṭhi° Nd¹ 57); Ps I.172; II.182 (nekkhamma° etc.); Nd¹ 11 (itthi° acquiring a wife); J VI.259; Miln 244 (āhara° abstinence in food), 313 (id.). — 3. belongings, property, possessions D II.58; III.289 = A IV.400; M I.137 (quoted at Nd¹ 122); S I.93; Sn 805; J IV.371; VI.259; PvA 76 (°bhūta belonging to, the property of); VvA 213, 321. sa° with all (its) belongings S I.32. — 4. a wife ThA 271; PvA 161 (kata° wedded), 282; ThA 271. sapariggaha > apariggaha married > unmarried (in general, with ref. to the man as well as the woman) D I.247; J IV.190; VI.348, 364. — 5. grace, favour DA I.241 (āmisa° material grace).

Pariggahita [pp. of parigaṇhāti] taken, seized, taken up, haunted, occupied Vin III.51 (manussānaŋ p. by men); IV.31, 278; DhA I.13 (amanussa° by ghosts); PvA 87, 133; Sdhp 64. — f. abstr. °ta being possessed (Vism 121 (amanussa°).

Pariggāhaka (adj.) [fr. pariggaha] including, occupying Nett 79 (=upathambhaka C. as quoted in Index p. 276).

Parigha [Vedic parigha, of which the usual P. representative is paligha (q. v.)] a cross-bar ThA 211 (°daṇḍa).

Parighaŋsati [pari + ghaŋsati¹] to rub (too) hard, scrub, scratch, only in ppr. aparighaŋsanto Vin I.46; II.208.

Paricakkhitar [n. ag. fr. pari + **cakṣ**, cp. akkhi & cakkhu] one who looks round or enquires, neg. a° J V.77.

Paricaya [fr. pari + **ci**] familiarity, acquaintance J VI.337; Vism 153; PvA 74. — adj. (-°) acquainted with, versed in (loc.) J II.249 (jāta°), VvA 24 (kata°); PvA 4 (id.), 129 (id.).

Paricaraṇa (nt.) [fr. pari + **car**] 1. going about, mode of life DhA I.382 (gihīnaŋ °ṭṭhānaŋ, v. l. for vicaraṇa°). — 2. attending to, looking after, worshipping DhA I.199 (aggi-p°-ṭṭhāna fire-place). — 3. enjoyment, pleasure (indriyānaŋ) PvA 16. See also paricāraṇā.

Paricaraṇaka [fr. paricaraṇa] servant, attendant DA I.269.

Paricarati [pari + carati] to move about, in var. senses, viz. 1. to go about, look after A III.94 (upaṭṭhahati +) J V.421; PvA 175. — 2. to worship (only in connection aggin p. to worship the fire) D I.101; S I.166; Dh 107; J I.494; Sn p. 79 (=payirupāsati SnA 401). — 3. to roam about, to feast one's senses, to amuse oneself, play, sport PvA 77 (indriyāni = kīḷāmi Pv II.1²¹). — We often find reading pariharati for paricarati, e. g. at DhA II.232; cp. paricāreti for °hāreti PvA 175; paricaraṇā for °haraṇā PvA 219. — pp. pariciṇṇa; Caus. paricāreti (q. v.).

Paricariyā (f.) [fr. paricarati] going about, service, ministration, worship S I.182; A I.132; DhA II.232 (aggi°). Occurs also as pāricariyā (q. v.), e. g. at J V.154. See also paricārikā.

Paricāra fr. [paricāreti] serving, attendance; (m.) servant, attendant Th 1, 632 (C. on this stanza for paddhagū).

Paricāraka (adj.-n.) [fr. paricāreti] attending, serving honouring; (m.) attendant, worshipper, follower (cp. BSk. paricāraka attendant AvŚ I.170; II.167] D I.101; II.200; Th 1, 475; Sn p. 218 (Nd² reads °cārika); J I.84; IV.302; Pv IV.8⁷ (not °vāraka); DA I.137, 269. See also paricārika.

Paricāraṇā (f.) [fr. paricāreti] care, attention, loking after; pleasure, feasting, satisfaction Pv II.1² (gloss for °cārika); PvA 219.

Paricārika (adj.-n.) = paricāraka (servant, attendant) A V.263 (aggi° fire-worshipper); Pv II.6²⁰ (amacca° minister & attendant); ThA 267; SnA 597. — f. °carikā (1) a maid-servant, handmaiden, nurse, (personal) attendant M I.253; cp. S I.125; J I.204 (pāda°), 291; II.395; IV.35 (veyyāvacca-kārikā p.), 79; V.420; Pv II.12⁶ (=veyyāvacca-kārinī PvA 157); PvA 46. — (2) care, attention; pleasure, pastime (so here, probably another form of paricāriyā) Pv IV.1² (=indriyānaŋ parihāraṇā PvA 219; gloss °cāraṇā).

Paricārita [pp. of paricāreti] served by, delighted by, indulging in M I.504.

Paricārin (adj. n.) [fr. paricāreti] serving, attending, f. a maid-servant J II.395.

Paricāreti [Caus. of paricarati] 1. to serve, wait on, attend upon, honour, worship [cp. BSk. paricārayati Divy 114 sq., 421] S I.124 (pāde): DhA III.196 (id.); J I.81 (°cāritabba-ṭṭhāna place of worship); IV.274; V.9. — Pass. paricāriyati, ppr. °iyamāna M I.46, 504; J I.58. In this sense it may also be taken as "being delighted or entertained by." — 2. to amuse oneself, gratify one's senses, to have recreation, find pleasure [cp. BSk. paricārayati Divy 1, and freq. phrase pañcahi kāmaguṇehi samarpitā samangibhūtā p. e. g. MVastu I.32] Vin II.290; III.72 (pañcahi kamaguṇehi samappitā etc.); D I.36 (id.), 104 (id.); M I.504 (id.); Th 1, 96 (saggesu); Pv I.11[6] (=yathā sukkhaŋ cārenti indriyāni PvA 58); IV.1[29] (read °cārayanti for °vārayanti, cp. PvA 228 indriyāni p.). — pp. paricārita q. v. See also parivāreti.

Paricinna [pari+ciṇṇa, pp. of carati] 1. surrounded, attended J V.90. — 2. worshipped M I.497; S IV.57 (me Satthā p.), cp. Th 1, 178 (Satthā ca p. me) & 891 (p. mayā Satthā). — 3. practised, performed Miln 360.

Paricita[1] [pp. oj pari+ci, cinoti, P. cināti] gathered, accumulated, collected, increased, augmented M III.97; S I.116; II.264; IV.200; A II.67 sq., 185; III.45, 152; IV.282, 300; V.23; Th 1, 647; Ps I.172 (expl[d]); PvA 67; Sdhp 409.

Paricita[2] [pp. of pari+ci, ciketi, P. cināti; but perhaps identical with paricita[1]] known, scrutinized, accustomed, acquainted or familiar with, constantly practised Vin II.95 (vācasā p.), 109 (aggi° etc. read aggiparijita); ThA 52; Miln 140 (iddhipādā p.); Dāvs IV.19. —aparicita unfamiliar DhA I.71.

Paricumbati [pari+cumbati] to kiss (all round, i. e. from all sides), to cover with kisses M II.120; S I.178, 193; A IV.438; DhA I.330.

Paricca (indecl.) [ger. of pari+i, cp. Sk. (Gr.) parītya & P. pariyeti] lit. "going round," i. e. having encircled, grasped, understood; grasping, finding out, perceiving; freq. in phrase cetasā ceto paricca (pajānāti) grasping fully with one's mind, e. g. at D I.79; M I.445; III.12; S II.121, 233; It 12; Vbh 329; Vism 409 (=paricchinditvā).. See pariyeti.

Pariccajati [pari+cajati of tyaj] to give up, abandon, leave behind, reject S I.44; It 94; J II.335; VI.259 (=chaddeti) Miln 207; DhA IV.204; PvA 121, 132, 221 (read jīvitaŋ pariccajati for parivajjati; cp. BSk. jīvitaŋ parityakṣyāmi AvŚ I.210); Sdhp 539. — pp. pariccatta (q. v.).

Pariccajana (nt.) & °nā (f.) [fr. pariccajati] 1. giving up, rejection, leaving It 11, 12. — 2. giving out, bestowing, giving a donation PvA 124.

Pariccajanaka [fr. prec.] one who gives (up) or spends, a giver, donor PvA 7.

Pariccatta [pp. of pariccajati; cp. BSk. parityakta in meaning "given to the poor" AvŚ I.3] given up, abandoned, thrown out, left behind J I.69, 174, 477; Miln 280; PvA 178, 219 (=virādhita); Sdhp 374.

Pariccāga [fr. pariccajati] 1. giving up, abandonment, sacrifice, renunciation A I.92 (āmisa° & dhamma° material & spiritual); Ps II.98; J I.12 (jīvita°); DhA III.441 (pañca mahāpariccāgā the five great sacrifices, i. e. the giving up of the most valuable treasures of wife, of children, of kingdom, of life and limb). — 2. expense DhA II.231 (sahassa° expenditure of a thousand coins). — 3. giving (to the poor), liberality DhsA 157; SnA 295 (mahā°, corresponding to mahādāna); PvA 7 sq.; 27, 120 sq., 124.

Paricchada [fr. pari+chad] a cover, covering J I.341, 466.

Paricchanna [pari+channa, pp. of chad] enveloped, covered, wrapped round Vin IV.17.

Paricchāta [pari+chāta] very much seared, scorched (?) Sdhp 102 (°odara-ttaca).

Paricchādanā (f.) [fr. pari+chad] covering, hiding, concealing Pug 19=23=Vbh 358.

Paricchindati [pari+chindati] 1. to mark out VvA 291 (vasana-ṭṭhānaŋ). — 2. to determine, to fix accurately, to decide J I.170 (padaŋ the track), 194 (nivāsavetanaŋ); III.371; IV.77; Miln 272; Vism 184, 409; SnA 434 (paññāya p.). — 3. to limit, restrict, define Miln 131; DA I.132. — pp. paricchinna (q. v.).

Paricchindana (nt.) [fr. paricchindati] "cutting up," definition, analysis VvA 114.

Paricchindanaka (adj.) [fr. pari+chind] marking out, defining, analysing, DhsA 157 (ñāṇa).

Paricchinna [pp. of paricchindati] 1. restricted, limited, small DhA I.58; PvA 136 (°ppamāṇa). — 2. divided, measured Vism 184; PvA 185 (=mita).

Paricceheda [fr. pari+chid; late Sk. (philos.) in same meaning] 1. exact determination, circumscription, range, definition, connotation, measure J III.371; Vism 184 (as one of the nimittas of the body), 236 (referring to the 5 nimittas of the life-principle); SnA 160, 229, 231, 376, 408, 503; KhA 182 (gaṇana°); VvA 194 (id.); DhsA 3; DhA II.73 (avadhi°); PvA 254 (kāla°), 255 (āyuno p.); VbhA 417 (citta°, for citta-paricce ñāṇa Vbh 330). — 2. limit, boundary Miln 131, 405; J III.504 (°nadī-tīra). — 3. limitation, restriction DhA II.88, 98; PvA 20 (°ŋ karoti to restrict). — 4. division (of time), in ratti° & divā°, night- & day-division Vism 416. — 5. (town)-planning, designing VbhA 331.

Paricchedaka (adj.). [fr. pariccheda] determining, fixing VbhA 346 (uṭṭhāna-velā °ā saññā).

Parijana [pari+jana] "the people round," i. e. attendants, servants, retinue, suite Vin I.15; J I.72, 90; DhA III.188; VvA 63; PvA 58, 62. —saparijana with one's servants Cp II.8[2] (T. saparijjana metri causâ).

Parijapati [pari+japati, cp. BSk. parijapta enchanted Divy 397] to mutter (spells), to practise divination J III.530; Miln 200 (vijjaŋ).

Parijapana (nt.) [fr. parijapati] mumbling, uttering spells Miln 356 (mantaŋ).

Parijānanā (f.) [pari+jānanā=jānana] cognition, recognition, knowledge Nett 20 (as paraphrase of pariññā).

Parijānāti [pari+jānāti] to know accurately or for certain, to comprehend, to recognise, find out M I.293; S I.11, 24; II.45, 99, III.26, 40, 159; IV.50; V.52, 422; A III.400 sq.; Sn 202, 254, 943; Nd[1] 426; J IV.174; Th 1, 226; Miln 69; DhA IV.233 °jānitvā). — ppr. parijānaŋ S III.27; IV.89; It 3 sq. — pp. pariññata (q. v.). ger. pariññāya see under pariññā[1].

Parijiṇṇa [pp. of pari+jar, i. e. decayed; Kern *Toev.* s. v. proposes reading ° jīna of ji, i. e. wasted, see parijīyati] worn out, gone down, decayed, reduced J I.111 (seṭṭhi-kulaŋ p.); V 99, 100 (bhoga°); VI.364; Dh 148; DhA II.272 (°kula).

Parijita [pp. of pari+**ji**, jayati; Kern, *Toev.* s. v. proposes reading parijita, Sk. form of P. parijīna, pp. of pari+jīyati, but hardly necessary, see also *Vin. Texts* III.75] overpowered, injured, damaged Vin II.109 (so read for paricita).

Parijīyati [pari+jīyati] to become worn out, to decay, fade, S I.186; J IV.111. Speit °**jiyyati at Th** ', 1215.— pp. parijīna (see parijiṇṇa).

Parijegucchā (f.) [pari+jegucchā] intense dislike of, disgust with (-°) D I.25, cp. DA I.115.

Parijjanā is doubtful reading at A III.38 (v. l. parivajjanā) =IV.266 (T. reads parijjana, cp. parijana; vv. ll. parivajjanā & parijanā); meaning ?.

Pariñña (-°) [the adj. form of pariññā, cp. abhiñña] knowing, recognising, understanding It 44 (bhūta° so, or should we read bhūtapariññāya ?); also in cpd. pariññacārin (to be exp^d as shortened gr. pariññā ?) Sn 537 (=paññāya paricchinditvā caranto living in full knowledge, i. e. rightly determining); also (abstr.) pariññatthaŋ at It 29 (abhiññatthaŋ+), cp. S IV.253.

Pariññā^1 (f.) [cp. Epic Sk. parijñāna; the form parijñā given by BR only with the one ref. Vyutp. 160; fr. pari+**jñā**] accurate or exact knowledge, comprehension, full understanding M I.66, 84; S III.26 (yo rāgakkhayo dosā° moha° ayaŋ vuccati p.), 159 sq., 191; IV.16, 51, 138, 206, 253 sq.; V.21, 55 sq., 145, 236, 251, 292; A I.277 (kāmānaŋ rūpānaŋ vedanānaŋ), 299; V.64; Pug 37; Nett 19, 20, 31; KhA 87; SnA 251.— In exegetical literature *three* pariññās are distinguished, viz. ñāta°, tīraṇa° pahāna°, which are differently interpreted & applied according to the various contexts. See e. g. the detailed interpretation at Nd^1 52 sq.; Nd^2 413; J VI.259 (where ñāṇa° for ñāta°); DhA II.172 (in ref. to food); mentioned at SnA 517.— adj. pariñña. — The form **pariññāya** is an apparent instr., but in reality (in form & meaning, the ger. of parijānāti (like abhiññāya > abhijānitvā) for the usual parijānitvā. It is freq. found in poetry & in formulas (like yathābhūtaŋ p.); its meaning is "knowing well in right knowledge": S V.182; Sn 455, 737, 778 (=parijānitvā Nd^1 51 sq.), 1082 (corresp. with pahāya, cp. similar phrase pahāya parijānitvā DhA IV.232); It 62; J VI.259.

Pariññā^2 (indecl.) [ger. of parijānāti for *parijñāya, cp. same short forms of ādā & abhiññā] having full knowledge or understanding of Sn 779 (=parijānitvā Nd^1 56 & SnA 518); It 4 (perhaps to be read pariññāya for pariññā so).

Pariññāta [pp. of parijānāti] well understood, thoroughly known Th 2, 106; M I.1 sq.; S II.99; V.182; PvA 1, 287. With ref. to food (°bhojana & °āhāra) it means food understood according to the three pariññās (q. v.); Dh 92 (°bhojano adj. one who lives on recognised food or takes the right view of the food he eats, cp. DhA II.172); Miln 352 (°āhāro); contrasted with bhāvita: consciousness is to be well studied, insight is to be made to grow M I.293.

Pariññātatta (nt.) [abstr. fr. pariññāta] the fact of having full or exact knowledge S V.182.

Pariññātāvin (adj.) [fr. pariññāta] one who has correct knowledge S III.159 sq., 191 (puggala).

Pariññeyya (adj.) [grd. of parijānāti] knowable, perceivable, to be known (accurately) M I.4; S III.26; IV.29; DhA IV.233 (cp. Nd^2 under abhiññeyya).

Pariḍahati [pari+ḍadati] to burn: Pass. pariḍayhati to be burnt or scorched M I.422; S I.188=Th 1, 1224; A I.137; III.95, 98; Sn 63; Ps I.128 (l); Pv I.6^4 (=parito jhāyati PvA 33); Miln 303; PvA 60. Cp. pariḷāha.

Pariṇata [pp. of pariṇamati] 1. bent down, crooked VvA 222 (°dāṭhā fangs, or does it mean "long"?). — 2. changed S III.40. — 3. ripened, matured, hatched, ripe J III.174, 286, 431, VvA 288; DhA I.47 (gabbha).

Pariṇamati [pari+namati] 1. to change (trs. & intrs.), lit. to bend round, to turn (round), to be transformed into (acc.) S III.3 (reading pariṇamati once, at other passages vi°, cp. p. 40); Miln 136 (bhojanaŋ visamaŋ p. food changes, i. e. turns bad), 277 (id.); VvA 13; PvA 144 (for parivattati Pv II.10^5), 194 (id. III.4^4). — 2. to change into a diff. state, to ripen, mature (often said of the fœtus) Miln 93, 358. — pp. pariṇata (q. v.). — Caus. pariṇāmeti (q. v.).

Pariṇāma [fr. pari+**nam**, cp. class Sk. pariṇāma in all meanings] "bending round," i. e. 1. change, alteration, in utu° (sudden) change of season, unseasonable weather, with ref. to illnesses caused by such (°ja ābādhā)=illness arising from the change of season A II.87; III.131; V.110; Nd^2 304^1; Miln 112, 135 sq., 304; Vism 31. — 2. alteration of food, digestion, in phrase sammā-pariṇāmaŋ gacchati M I.188; S I.168; A III.30; cp. MVastu I.211. — 3. ripening Miln 93. — 4. course, development, fulfilment, in special sense: dispensation, destiny J V.171; Pv IV.3^{25}; PvA 252, 254. — Cp. vi°.

Pariṇāmana (nt.) [fr. parinamati] diverting to somebody's use Vin IV.157.

Pariṇāmita [pp. of pariṇāmeti] 1. bent down J VI.269 (of trees, overladen with fruit, C. expl^s as "entangled"). — 2. issued, apportioned, destined J V.171; PvA 254.

Pariṇāmitar [n. ag. of pariṇāmeti] one who destines or makes develop, fate, destiny J VI.189.

Pariṇāmin (adj.) [fr. pariṇāma] ending in, resulting in (-°) M I.11, 526; III.88.

Pariṇāmeti [Caus. of parinamati] to bend to, to change into, to turn to use for somebody, to procure for, obtain, appropriate D I.92; Vin III.259 (puttassa rajjaŋ p. for his son); IV.156; PvA 281. — ppr. °ṇāmayamāna J V.424. See also āvajjeti. — pp. pariṇāmita (q. v.).

Pariṇāyaka [fr. pari+**ni**, cp. pariṇeti] a leader, guide, adviser; one of the 7 treasures (ratanāni) of a great king or Cakkavattin (according to Bdhgh on D II.177; the eldest son; in the Lal. Vist. a general cp. Divy 211, 217; Senart, *Lég. de Buddha* p. 42), i. e. a wonderful Adviser D I.89; II.17, 177; M I.220; II.175; A III.151; Sn p. 106 (cp. SnA 450=DA I.250); J I.155; IV.93; Miln 38, 314. — f. pariṇāyikā. Ep. of wisdom, synonymous with paññā, i. e. insight, cleverness Dhs 1057; Pug 25; Vism 3; DhsA 148.

Pariṇāha [fr. pari+**nah**] compass, circumference, breadth, extent, girth S II.206 (of the moon)=A V.19; J III.192, 277, 370; V.299; Pug 53; Miln 282, 311; SnA 382 (āroha+).

Pariṇeti [pari+neti] to lead round or about S II.128.

Paritajjita [pari+tajjita] scared (exceedingly), frightened Sdhp 147.

Paritatta [pp. of paritappati] tormented, worried, vexed, grieved Miln 313.

Paritappati [Pass. of pari+**tap**] to be vexed, to grieve, worry, sorrow Th 2, 313 (=santappati ThA 233); Miln 313. — pp. paritatta (q. v.).

Paritasita (nt.) [pari+tasita^1 or tasita^2] worry, excitement D I.40 (v. l. °tassita, cp. Dial I.53).

Paritassati (°tasati) [pari+tasati^1, in form clearly=Sk. paritṛṣyati, but freq. confused with tasati^2, cp. tasa.

Sn 924 is the only example of paritasati representing tasati[2]] to be excited, to be tormented, to show a longing after, to be worried D II.68; M I.36, 67, 151; S II.82, 194; III.43, 55; IV.23, 65, 168; A II.27; III.133 sq.; Sn 621 (=taṇhāya na bhāyati SnA 467, thus combining tasati[1] & tasati[2]), 924 (Pot. parittase, interpreted by Nd[1] 373 as taseyya, uttaseyya, bhāyeyya, thus taken as tasati[2]); Miln 253, 400; Dh 397 (=taṇhāya na bhāyati DhA IV.159); Sdhp 476. — ppr. aparitassaŋ D II.68; M I.67; S II.82; III.55; It 94. — pp. paritasita (q. v.).

Paritassanā (f.) [fr. paritassati, q. v. for meaning] trembling, fear; nervousness, worry; excitement, longing D I.17 (=ubbijjanā phandanā etc. DA I.111); M I.136; III.227; S III.15 sq., 133; Miln 253, 400. — neg. a° S III.15; M I.136.

Paritassin (adj.) [fr. paritassati] trembling, excited, worrying, only neg. a° A IV.108, 111, 230 sq.

Paritāpa = foll. Miln 313 (ātāpa+).

Paritāpana (nt.) [pari+tāpana, of **tap**] tormenting, torture, affliction, mortification M I.78, 341-344; A I.151, 296; II.205 sq. (atta° self-mortification, opp. para°); Pug 55, 56, 61; PvA 18 (atta°), 30 (id.). Often comb[d] with ātāpana (q. v.).

Paritāpeti [pari+tapeti] to burn, scorch, molest, trouble, torture, torment M I.341 (ātāpeti+), 506; S IV.337; A III.54, 380; J V.420 (mā paritāpi).

Parituleti [pari+tuleti] to weigh, consider, estimate, think Vism 522. — VbhA 130.

Parito (adv.) [fr. pari, cp. Sk. paritaḥ] round about, around, on every side, everywhere, wholly Vin II.194; SnA 393; VvA 316; PvA 33.

Paritoseti [pari+toseti] to please, appease, satisfy, make happy J I.262; III.386; V.216; PvA 213 (v. l. SS+ āsiñcati).

Paritta[1] (adj.) [BSk. parītta, pari+pp. of **dā** in short form *tta, like ātta for ādatta. The development of meaning however causes difficulties, paridatta meaning given up, transmitted, cp. Divy 388, whereas P. paritta means trifling. The BSk. form parītta (e. g. Divy 204, 498, 504; AvŚ I.329; II.137) may be a re-translation of P. paritta, which may correspond to Sk. prarikta, pp. of pra+**ric**, meaning "that which is exceeded," i. e. left (over or behind)] small, little, inferior, insignificant, limited, of no account, trifling Vin I.270; D I.45; M III.148 (°ābha of limited splendour, opp. appamāṇ'-ābha); S II.98; IV.160 (opp. adhimatta); A IV.241; V.63; It 71; Sn 61, 390 (°pañña of inferior wisdom, cp. Nd[2] 415), 1097 (id.); J I.221; Dhs 181, 584, 1018, 1034 (cp. Dhs trsl. 265, 269); DA I.119; KhA 133 (°dīpā the 2,000 inferior islands), 176 (500 do.); PvA 198; Sdhp 251, 261. Synonyms: appaka, omaka, lāmaka, dukkha Nd[2] 414; catukka Nd[2] 415 (opp. mahā); appaka PvA 48, 60; appamattaka PvA 262; ittara PvA 60; oma SnA 347; oraka SnA 489; lāmaka SnA 347.

Paritta[2] (nt.) & **Parittā** (f.) [fr. pari+**trā**, cp. tāṇa, tāyati & also parittāna] protection, safeguard; (protective) charm, palliative, amulet Vin II.110 (atta° f. personal protection) IV.305 (gutt' atthāya °ŋ pariyāpuṇāti); A II.73 (rakkhā+parittā); J I.200 (manto+parittaŋ+vaḍḍhiŋ), 396 (paccekabuddhehi °ŋ kārāpeti makes them find a safeguard through the P.); IV.31 (osadhaŋ vā °ŋ vā); Miln 150 (f. & nt.). — Var. parittās in the way of Suttantas are mentioned at Vism 414 (Khandha°; Dhajagga°: S I.218 sq.; Āṭānāṭiya°: D III.195 sq.; Mora°: J II.33). Cf. *Dialogues* III.185.

-vālikā sand worn on the head as an amulet J I.396, 399. -suttaka a thread worn round the head as a charm J I.396, 399.

Parittaka [paritta[1]+ka] small, insignificant, little Nd[1] 306 (for appaka etc. as at Nd[2] 414); Pv I.10[11]; II.9[67]; Miln 121 (a°), 253; DA I.170 (for appa); PvA 51; Sdhp 42. — f. parittikā Th 1, 377.

Parittāṇa (nt.) [pari+tāna. Cp. Epic Sk. paritrāna] protection, shelter, refuge, safeguard, safety D I.9 (sara° from an arrow, i. e. a shield); III.189; J VI.455; PvA 284; Sdhp 396.

-kitikā a protecting arrangement Vin II.152, cp. *Vin. Texts* III.174.

Parittāyaka (adj.) [fr. pari+tāyati] safeguarding against, sheltering against, keeping away from Vism 376 (angāra-vassaŋ p. thero).

Parittāsin (adj.) [pari+tāsin, fr. tāsa of tasati[2]] being in dread of (-°) S I.201.

Paridaṇḍa (adj.) [pari+daṇḍa] "with a stick around," i. e. surrounded by a stick; only in one phrase viz. "saparidaṇḍā itthi" a woman protected by a stick, or liable to punishment (?), in stock phrase enumerating 10 kinds of women M I.386 = III.46 = Vin III.139 = A V.264 = VvA 73.

Paridamana (nt.) [pari+damana] controlling, taming Vism 375.

Paridameti [pari+dameti] to control, tame, keep under Vism 376.

Paridahati [pari+dahati, of **dhā**] to put round, put on, clothe Dh 9 (fut. °dahessati); J II.197; V.434 (ger. °dahitvā); VI.500; Pv II.1[18]; PvA 76 (vatthāni), 77, 127 (°dahissati for paridhassati Pv II.9[36], which read for T. parivassati). ger also paridayha J V.400 (= nivāsetvā cp pārupitvā ca C.). — pp. paridahita (q. v.). — Caus. II. paridahāpeti to cause to be clothed PvA 49 (=acchādeti).

Paridahita [pp. of paridahati] put round, put on (of clothing) PvA 43.

Paridīpaka (adj.) [fr. paridīpeti, cp. dīpaka[1]] illuminating, explaining, explanatory SnA 40.

Paridīpana (nt.) [pari+dīpana] illuminating, elucidating, explanation Miln 318; KhA 111; SnA 394 sq.

Paridīpanā (f.) [fr. paridīpeti, cp. paridīpana] explanation, illustration Miln 131.

Paridīpita [pp. of paridīpeti] 1. in flames, set ablaze Th 2, 200 (=punappunaŋ ādīpitatāya p. ThA 170). — 2. explained, made clear, illuminated Vism 58; KhA 8; Sdhp 305.

Paridīpeti [pari+dīpeti] to make bright, to illustrate, to explain Miln 131; Sdhp 491. — pp. paridīpita (q. v.).

Paridūseti [pari+dūseti] to spoil altogether, to ruin, corrupt, defile Sdhp 409.

Parideva [pari+deva of **div**, devati; only in *one* passage of Epic Sk. (Mbhār. VII.3014); otherwise paridevana nt.] lamentation, wailing M I.200; S II.1; III.3 sq.; A I.144; II.195; Sn 328, 592, 811, 923, 969; J I.146; VI.188, 498; Nd[1] 128, 134, 370, 492; Ps I.11 sq., 38, 59, 65; Vbh 100, 137; Nett 29. It is exegetically paraphrased at D II.306 = Nd[2] 416 (under pariddava) with synonyms ādeva p. ādevanā paridevanā ādevitattaŋ paridevitattaŋ; often comb[d] with soka grief, e. g. at D I.36; Sn 862; It 89; PvA 39, 61. — Bdhgh at DA I.121 expl[ns] it as "sokaŋ nissita-lālappana-lakkhaṇo p."

Paridevati [pari+devati, **div**] to wail, lament D II.158 (mā socittha mā paridevittha); Sn 582, 774 = Nd[1] 38 (as °devayati), 166; J VI.188, 498; PvA 18 (socati+); ger.

°devamāna S I.199, 208; J V.106; PvA 38, & °devayamāna Sn 583. — grd. °devaniya Nd^1 492; SnA 573, & °devaneyya Sn 970 (=ādevaneyya Nd^1 493). — pp. paridevita (q. v.).

Paridevanā (f.)=parideva, Sn 585; Nd^2 416 (see under parideva) Pv I.4^3 (=vācā-vippalāpa PvA 18); I.12^3; PvA 41.

Paridevita (nt.) [pp. of paridevati] lamentation, wailing Sn 590; Pv I.12^3 (=rudita, PvA 63); Miln 148 (kandita-p.°-lālappita-mukha).

Paridevitatta (nt.) [abstr. fr. paridevita] lamentation etc.; only exegetical construction in expl^n of parideva at D II.306=Nd^2 416.

Pariddava [according to Trenckner M I.532 (on M I.56, where SS read p., whereas BB have parideva) the metrical substitute for parideva; therefore not=Sk. paridrava, which is only a late re-translation of the P. word]=parideva M I.56 (soka°); A I.221; Th 2, 345 (soka°); Sn 1052, cp. Nd^2 416 (see parideva).

Paridhaŋsaka (adj.) [fr. paridhaŋsati] destructive, ruinous PvA 15 (°vacano speaking destructively, scandalmonger).

Paridhaŋsati [pari+dhaŋsati] to be deprived, to lose, to come to ruin It 90; Miln 249, 265. — Caus. paridhaŋseti in same meaning at Nd^1 5. It is almost synonymous with paripatati & parihāyati.

Paridhāvati [pari+dhāvati] to run about J I.127 (ādhāvati+), 134 (id.), 158 (id.); II.68 (id.)=ThA 54; V.106.

Paridhota [pp. of paridhovati] washed, rinsed, cleansed, purified D I.124.

Paridhovati [pari+dhovati] to wash (all round), cleanse, clean Vin I.302. — pp. paridhota.

Pariniṭṭhāna (nt.) [pari+niṭṭhāna] 1. end PvA 287. — 2. accomplishment J V.400.

Pariniṭṭhāpeti [pari+niṭṭhāpeti] to bring to an end, attain, accomplish DhsA 363.

Pariniṭṭhita (adj.) [pari+niṭṭhita] accomplished M III.53; Th 2, 283; DhA II.78.

Parininna (adj.) [pari+ninna] deeply hollowed, sunken Sdhp 103.

Parinipphanna (adj.) [pari+nipphanna] predetermined Kvu 459 (v. l. °nibbāna), 626 (a°); cp. **Kvu** trsl. 261^6, 368^1.

Parinibbāna (nt.) [pari+nibbāna] "complete Nibbana" in two meanings: 1. complete extinction of khandhalife; i. e. all possibility of such life & its rebirth, final release from (the misery of) rebirth and transmigration, death (after the last life-span of an Arahant). This is the so-called "an-upādi-sesa Parinibbāna," or "extinction with no rebirth-substratum left." — 2. release from cravings & attachment to life, emancipation (in this life) with the assurance of final death; freedom of spirit, calm, perfect well-being or peace of soul. This is the so-called "sa-upādisesa-P.," or "extinction (of passion) with some substratum left." — The two kinds are distinguished by Bdhgh at DhA II.163 as follows: "arahatta-pattito paṭṭhāya kilesa-vaṭṭassa khepitattā sa-upādi-sesena, carima-citta-nirodhena khandhavaṭṭassa khepitattā an-upādi-sesena cā ti dvīhi pi parinibbānehi parinibbutā, an-upādāno viya padipo apaṇṇattika-bhāvaŋ gatā." — 1. D II.72 sq. (the famous Mahā-parinibbāna-suttanta or "Book of the Great Decease"); M III.127, 128; A II.79 (°samaye); III.409 (°dhamma, contrasted with āpāyika nerayika, cp. DhA IV.42); Mhvs 7, 1 (°mañcamhi nipanna); VvA 158; PvA 244. — 2. D III.55; A V.64; Sn 514 (°gata+vitiṇṇa-kankho); Vv 53^{24} (°gata+sītibhūta). This state of final emancipation (during life) has also received the determination of anupādā-parinibbāna, i. e. emancipation without ground for further clinging (lit. without fuel), which corresponds to Bdhgh's term "kilesavaṭṭassa khepitattā sa-upādi-sesa p." (see above); thus at M I.148; S IV.48; V.29; A I.44; V.65 (nicchāto nibbuto sītibhūto etc).; A V.233=253=Dh 89 (+khīṇāsava).

Parinibbānika (adj.) [fr. parinibbāna] one who is destined to or that which leads to complete extinction D III.264; 265 (opasamika+).

Parinibbāpana (nt.) [pari+nibbāpana] refreshing, cooling, quenching; controlling, subduing, training Ps I.174 (atta-damatha, atta-samatha, atta-p.).

Parinibbāpetar [n. ag. fr. parinibbāpeti] one who pacifies, a calmer, trainer M II.102 (dametar sametar p.).

Parinibbāpeti [pari+nibbāpeti] to bring to complete coolness, or training (see next), emancipation or cessation of the life-impulse, to make calm, lead to Nibbāna, to exercise self-control, to extinguish fever of craving, or fire of rāga, dosa, moha. Always coupled with the quâsi synonyms sameti & dameti (cp. damatha samatha parinibbāpana) D III.61=A III.46 (attānaŋ dameti, sameti, p.); M I.45 (fut. °bbapessati); A II.68 (attānaŋ d. s. p.). — pp. parinibbuta (see p. No. 3) & **parinibbāpita** (only in n. ag. °āpetar, q. v.).

Parinibbāyati (& **°nibbāti**) [pari+nibb° cp. BSk. parinirvāti Divy 150 (Buddhā Bhagavantaḥ parinirvānti) & ger. parinirvātavya ibid. 402] 1. to be completed, perfected, in any work or art, e. g. of a trained horse, M I.446. Cp. τελειόω. — 2. to die without being reborn, to reach complete extinction of existence Vin II.194 (Tathāgathā °āyanti); M III.128 (aor °nibbāyi); S V.152 (°nibbāyeyyaŋ), 261 (°nibbāyissāmi); A II.120 (anupādisesāya nibbāna-dhātuyā p.); IV.202 (id.), 313 (id.); Miln 175 (id.); J I.28 (id.), 55 (id.); VvA 158 (fut. °nibbāyissāmi); PvA 21, 283 (of a Paccekabuddha). — 2. to become emancipated from all desire of life D II.68 (cp. *Dial.* II.65 & *Brethren* 417); S IV.102 (diṭṭh' eva dhamme), ibid. (sa-upādāno devānaŋ indo na parinibbāyati), 168; A III.41=Vin II.148, 164 (parinibbāti anāsavo); A IV.98 (aor. °nibbiŋsu anāsavā) Th 1, 100 (fut. °nibbissati anāsavo), 364; It 93 (°nibbanti), cp. 95; Dh 126 (°nibbanti anāsavā perhaps better taken to No. 1!); Vbh 426 (sabbāsave pariññāya parinibbanti anāsavā); Sdhp 584 (°nibbanti mahoghen' eva aggino). — pp. parinibbuto (q. v.). — Caus. parinibbāpeti (q. v.).

Parinibbāyana (nt.) [abstr. fr. parinibbāyin] passing away, see parinibbāyin 2 b.

Parinibbāyin [fr. parinibbāyati] one who attains Parinibbāna. Of the 2 meanings registered under parinibbāna we find No. 1 only in a very restricted use, when taken in both senses of sa- and an- upādisesa parinibbāna; e. g. at A II.155 sq., where the distinction is made between a sa-sankhāra p. and an a-sankhāra p., as these two terms also occur in the fivefold classification of "Never-returners" (i. e. those who are not reborn) viz. antarā-parinibbāyin, upahacca°, sasankhāra°, uddhaŋsota, akaniṭṭhagāmin. Thus at D III.237; S V.201, 237; A I.233; IV.14, 71 sq., 146, 380; V.120; Pug 16, 17. — 2. In the sense of Parinibbāna No. 2 (i. e. sa-upādisesa p.) we find parinibbāyin almost as an equivalent of arahant in two combn^s, viz. (a) **tattha°** (always comb^d with opapātika, i. e. above the ordinary cause of birth) [cp. BSk. tatra-parinirvāyin anāgāmin Divy 533]. It is also invariably comb^d with anāvattidhamma, e. g. at D I.156; III.108, 132; M II.56, 146; A I.232; 245, 290; II.5, 89, 238; IV.12, 399, 423; V.343; S V.346 (cp. 406), 357; Pug 16, 62, 83. See also *Kvu trsl.* 74². — (b) antara° [cp. BSk. antarāparinirvāyin MVastu I.33] one who passes away in the middle of his term of life in a particular heaven; an Anāgāmin (cp. Bdhgh's explⁿ at PugA 198 as "āyu-vemajjhassa antarā yeva parinibbāyanato a. p.") S V.69=A IV.70; S V.201=204, 237, 285, 314, 378; A II.134; Ps I.161; Pug 16; Nett 190 (cp. A IV.380).

Parinibbuta (adj.) [pari+nibbuta] completely calmed, at peace, at rest (as to the distinction of the twofold application see parinibbāna and cp. Mrs. Rh.D. *Buddhism* p. 191; *Cpd.* p. 168), viz. — 1. gone out, or passed away without any remaining cause of rebirth anywhere, completely extinct, finally released (fr. rebirth & trans migration), quite dead or at rest [cp. BSk. parinirvṛta Divy 79]. It is usually applied to the Buddha, or the Tathāgatha, but also to Theras & Arahants who have by means of moral & intellectual perfection destroyed all germs of further existence. With ref. to Gotama Buddha: Vin II.284 (atikkhippaŋ Bhagavā p.), 294 (vassasata° e Bhagavati); V.119, 120; D I.204 (acira-°e Bhagavati); S I.158 (Tathāgato p. II.191); V.172 (°e Tathāgate); Vv III.9⁷ (°e Gotame=anupādisesāya nibbāna-dhātuyā parinibbuto VvA 169); PvA 140 (Satthari p.), 212 (Bhagavati). Of others: S I.121, 122 (Godhika); III.124 (Vakkali); IV.63 (Puṇṇa); Sn p. 59, 60 (a Thera); Miln 390 (Arahant); VvA 158; PvA 76; DhA II.163; IV.42. — 2. emancipated, quite free (from earthly bonds), calm, serene, at peace, perfected Vin II.156=A I.138 "spiritually free" *Vin. Texts* III.182); D II.123 (cp. *Dial.* II.132); III.55; M I.235; II.102; S I.1 (+tiṇṇo loke visattikaŋ), 7=IV.179 (ahetha-yāno+); I.54 (+tiṇṇo loke visattikaŋ); 187 (p. kan-khati kālaŋ); Sn 359 (+ṭhitatta), 370 (id.), 467 (p. udaka-rahado va sito); Th 1, 5 (cp. *Brethren* 11³); J IV.303, 453; Ud 85 (rāga-dosa-moha-kkhayā p.); Miln 50 (°atta). Freq. in combⁿ with kindred terms like sītibhūta (cooled), e. g. Vin II.156=A I.138; Vv 53²⁴; or nicchāta (without hunger), e. g. S III.26; IV.204=It 46; Sn 735 sq.; It 48 (esanānaŋ khayā), 49 (āsavānaŋ khayā). — 3. (to be understood as pp. of parinibbā-peti) calmed, well trained, domesticated M I.446 (of a horse).

Parinimmita at Dhs 1280 read para°.

Paripakka (adj.) [pari+pakka] 1. (quite) ripe, ripened, matured, developed D I.54; S IV.105=DA I.50; A IV.357; Dh 260; J I.91, 231; VI.1 (ap°); Ud 36 (id.); Miln 194, 288; DhA III.338; KhA 56; ThA 273; PvA 274 (su°). — 2. overripe, rotten Miln 223.

Paripakkata [pp. of pari+pakkirati] scattered Th 2, 391 (reading doubtful).

Paripaccati [pari+paccati] to become ripe, to heal (of a wound) Miln 112.

Paripaccana (nt.) [pari+paccana] ripening, healing (of a wound) Miln 112.

Paripañhati [denom. fr. pari+pañha] to question A V.16.

Paripaṭati [doublet of paripatati] to go to ruin, to come to fall, to come to naught Miln 91 (opp. sambhavati); combᵈ with paridhaŋsati at Nd¹ 5; Miln 249, 265.

Paripatati [pari+patati, cp. nipatati] to fall down, to fall off from (abl.) Vin II.152 sq.; J V.417/ 420; Pv IV.5³ (bhūmiyaŋ) DA I.132; PvA 37, 47, 55, 62. — Caus. paripāteti (q. v.). — See also paripaṭati.

Paripantha [pari+pantha] 1. "way round," edge, border; paripanthe in ambush (near a road) M I.87; J III.65. — 2. obstacle, hindrance, danger. It refers esp. to danger arising out of mishaps to or bad conditions of roads in the forests. D I.52; S I.43; A I.153; III.252; V.136; Ps I.162; J I.395; III.268; IV.17; VI.57 (n. pl. °ayo=kilesa-paripanthā C.), 75; DhA I.14 (magga°), 16 (id.), 51, 69; migānaŋ p. danger to the crops from (the nuisance of) deer J I.143, 154.—saparipantha full of danger DhA I.63. See also palipatha.

Paripanthika (adj.) [fr. paripantha] forming or causing an obstacle A I.161. The usual form is pāri° (q. v.).

Paripanna see palipanna.

Paripāka [fr. pari+pac] 1. ripeness, maturity, development, perfection D I.9 (cp. DA I.94); Ud 36 (pañca dhammā paripākāya saŋvattanti); J I.142, 148; VI.236; Miln 288; Vism 116 (bodhi°), 199; DhA I.89 (°gatatta nt. state of perfection); ThA 79; PvA 276. — 2. overripeness, decay, collapse, only in phrase "indriyānaŋ p.," i. e. decay of the (mental) faculties, in formula defining jarā (old age) at D II.305; M I.49; S II.2, 42 sq.; A V.203; Nd² 252; Dhs 644; cp. BSk. indriyaparipāka AvŚ II.110.

Paripācana (nt.) [pari+pācana¹] ripening, maturing, digestion Vims 351, 363, 365.

Paripācaniya (adj.) [fr. paripācana] bringing to maturity, leading to perfection, accomplishing, only in phrase vimuttiparipācaniyā dhammā (5) things achieving emancipation (see Ud 36) S IV.105=DA I.50; ThA 273.

Paripāceti [pari+pāceti, Caus. of pacati] to bring to maturity, to cause to ripen, to develop, prepare J VI.373 (atthaŋ p. °ācayitvā=vaḍḍhetvā C.); Miln 232, 285, 288, 296. — pp. paripācita Vism 365.

Paripātita [pp. of paripāteti] attacked, pursued, brought into difficulty VvA 336.

Paripāteti (or °pāṭeti) [Caus. of paripatati. Cp. BSk. pari-pāṭayati to destroy Divy 417] to cause to fall down, to bring to ruin, to attack, pursue Vin IV.115; J II.208; III.380; Miln 279, 367; KhA 73 (see *App.* II. p. 353 n. 9). — pp. paripātita (q. v.).

Paripālita [pp. of paripāleti] guarded Vism 74.

Paripāleti [pari+pāleti] to watch, guard (carefully) PvA 130 (=rakkhati). — pp.. paripālita (q. v.). — Pass. °pāliyati Nett 105 (=rakkhitaŋ).

Paripīta (adj.) [pari+pīta] very dear, highly valued Sdhp 571.

Paripīḷita (adj.) [pari+pīlita, pp. of pīḍ] oppressed, vexed, injured Miln 97 (aggi-santāpa-pariḷāha°), 303 jighac-chāya).

Paripucchaka (adj.) [fr. pari+prch] asking a question, enquiring Nd¹ 234=Nd² 386; Sdhp 90. — f. abstr. paripucchakatā questioning Vism 132 (one of the 7 constituents of dhamma-vicaya-sambojjhanga).

Paripucchati [pari+pucchati] to ask a question, to interrogate, inquire Vin I.47=224; II.125; S I.98; A V.16; Sn 380, 696 (°iyāna ger.), 1025; Pug 41; Miln 257, 408; SnA 111.

Paripucchā (f.) [pari+pucchā] question, interrogation Vin I.190 (uddesa+); II.219 (id.); A I.285; Nd¹ 234=Nd² 386 (cp. SnA 111). See also uddesa.

Paripuñchati [pari+puñchati] to wipe off, stroke down Vin III.14 (pāṇinā gattāni p.).

Paripuṇṇa (adj.) [pp. of paripūrati] 1. (quite) full, fulfilled, complete, finished, satisfied M I.200 (°sankappa), III.11; S II.283; IV.104; V.315; Ps I.172 (=pariggah' aṭṭhena parivār' aṭṭhena, paripūr' aṭṭhena p., i. e. acquiring, keeping, fulfilling); Sn 889 (°mānin = samatta-mānin Nd[1] 298), 904; It 40 (°sekha); Pv IV.16[3]; Vism 45 (°sankappa): PvA 13, 54 (°vassa whose years are completed, i. e. old enough for ordination), 68 (°gabbha ready to be delivered), 77 (vārinā). — 2. complete, i. e. not defective, perfect, sound, healthy Sn 548 (°kāya = lakkhaṇehi puṇṇatāya ahīn' anga-paccangatāya ca paripuṇṇa-sarīro SnA 452); Miln 249.

Paripuṇṇatā (f.) [abstr. fr. paripuṇṇa] fullness, completeness SnA 452.

Paripūra (adj.) [pari + pṛ] full, complete, perfected, accomplished D I.75; I.133; III.94; S II.32; IV.247; V.269 (f. °ī); A II.77; V.10 sq.; Sn 205, 1017; Ps I.15, 18, 49, 172; II 122; Pug 35, 36. -aparipūra not completed, imperfect, incomplete A II.77; IV.314 sq.; V.10 sq; It 107; Pug 35, 36.
-kāritā completion M I.64, 66 sq. -kārin completing, fulfilling, making complete, doing to the full M I.33 sq., 64; S V.201; A II.136; III.215; IV.380; V.131 sq.; Pug 37; Miln 243.

Paripūraka (adj.((-°) one who fills, filling Vism 300 (niraya°).

Paripūraṇa (nt.) [fr. paripūreti] fulfilment, completion Vism 3 (sīla°). See pāripūraṇa.

Paripūrati [pari + pūrati] to become full or perfect Dh 38; J IV.273 (devaloko p.); Miln 395 (sāmaññaŋ); fut. paripūrissati DhA I.309. — Pass. **paripūriyati** to be fulfilled or perfected DhA I.309. — pp. paripuṇṇa (q. v.). — Caus. paripūreti (q. v.).

Paripūratta (nt.) [abstr. fr. paripūra] fullness, completeness, completion S V.200 sq. (+ samatta).

Paripūrita [pp. of paripūreti] filled (to overflowing), full PvA 216.

Paripūrī (f.) [fr. paripūra, but better spelt pāripūrī, q. v.] fulfilment, completion S I.139.

Paripūreti [Caus. of paripūrati] to fulfil; to fill (up), make more full, supplement, fill out, add to D I.74 (parisandeti p. parippharati; DA I.217 expl[ns] as "vāyunā bhastaŋ viya pūreti"); II.221; M III.92; S I.27 (devakāyaŋ) = 30; II.29, 32; III.93 (sāmaññatthaŋ) = A II.95 = It 90; Pv II.9[46] (ppr. °ayanto); Pug 31, 35; Miln 349 (lekhaŋ); PvA 29 (sāgaraŋ), 30 (ñātidhammo °pūretabbo), 136 (vassasahassāni); Sdhp 371. — ppr. med. °pūramāna D I.103. — pp. **paripūrita** (q. v.).

Paripothita [pp. of paripotheti] beaten, whipped Miln 188 (laguḷehi).

Parippharati [pari + **sphur**] to pervade D I.74 (= samantato phusati DA I.217); M III.92 sq. See also **paripūreti** — pp. paripphuta & °pphuṭṭha (q. v.).

Paripphuṭṭha [pp. of parippharati] filled, pervaded D I.75; M III.94 (spelt here paripphuta). Cp. BSk. parisphuṭa MVastu II.349; III.274; Lal. Vist. 33, 385.

Paripphosakaŋ (adv.) [either with Kern, *Toev*, s. v. ger. of paripphoseti (i. e. paripphosa) + kaŋ or preferably with Trenckner, *Notes* 80 absolutive in °aka (i. e. nt. formation fr. adj. paripphosa, as phenuddeba + kaŋ etc.). Cp. also Geiger *P.Gr.* § 62. 1] sprinkled all round D I.74; M I.276; II.15; III.92; expl[d] as "siñcitvā" at DA I.218.

Paripphosita [pp. of paripphoseti] sprinkled all round J VI.51, 481 (candana sāra°).

Paripphoseti [pari + Caus. of **pruṣ**] to sprinkle over, Vin II.209 (udakena °pphositvā; so read for °ppositvā); A I.257; J VI.566; Pv III.10[2] (°itvā = āsiñcitvā PvA 231). — pp. paripphosita (q. v.).

Pariplava [fr. pari + **plu**] unsteady, wavering, swerving about Dh 38 (= upplavana DhA I.309).

Pariplavati [pari + **plu**] to quiver, roam about, swerve J III.484 (ppr. pariplavanto = upplavamāna C. — pp. paripluta (q. v.).

Paripluta [pp. of pariplavati] immersed, drenched J VI.78 (= nimugga C.); Dāvs III.34.

Pariphandati [pari + **spand**] to tremble, quiver, throb, waver Sn 776 (cp. Nd[1] 46 sq.), 1145; Dh 34 (= saṇṭhātuŋ na sakkoti DhA I.289); J IV.93; Miln 91, 249. — pp. pariphandita (q.v .).

Pariphandita [pp. of pariphandati] wavered, trembled, quivered J III.24.

Paribandha at ThA 242 is C. reading for paripantha at Th 2, 352; also at Vism 147, 152.

Paribādheti [pari + **bādh**] to oppress, attack PvA 193 (= hiŋsati).

Paribāhati [pari + bāhati or preferably bāheti: see bahati[3]] to keep out, keep away from, hinder J I.204 (ger. °bāhiya); PvA 214 (°bāhire).

Paribāhira (adj.) [pari + bāhira] external, alien to; an outsider Vin II.140; IV.283; S I.126; J I.482; III.213; Nd[1] 144; (parimussati p. hoti, in expl[n] of mussati) Vism 54; PvA 131; ThA 209; DA I.30.

Paribbajati [pari + **vraj**] to wander about (as a religious mendicant) Sn 74, 639; It 109; Dh 346, 415; J IV.452.

Paribbaya [pari + vaya, i. e. *vyaya] 1. earned money, earnings, wages J I.156 (°ŋ datvā), 296 (id.), 433; IV.170; DhA IV.196. — 2. expense, expenditure J II.213, (nivāsa° expense for a lodging), 249, 368; III.287 (°ŋ karoti to invest); VI.383; VvA 75; PvA 3 (sahassaŋ sahassaŋ °ŋ karoti), 97 (nicca°); Dāvs V.66.

Paribbasāna (adj.) [ppr. med. of pari + **vas**] abiding, staying by Sn 796 (= vasamāna SnA 529; sakāya diṭṭhiyā vasanti Nd[1] 102), 878, 880, 895.

Paribbāja = paribbājaka S I.49; Sn 134; Dh 313; DhA III.485. °**vata** the vow of a p. ThA 73.

Paribbājaka [fr. pari + **vraj**] a wandering man, a Wanderer, wandering religious mendicant, not necessarily Buddhist (cp. Muir, *J.R.A.S.* 1866, 321; Lassen, *Ind. Alt* II.114, 277, 468; *Vin. Texts* I.41) Vin I.342; IV.285 (bhikkhuñ ca sāmaṇerañ ca ṭhapetvā yo koci paribbājaka-samāpanno); D I.157; III.1 sq., 35 sq., 53 sq., 130 sq.; M I.64, 84; S I.78; II.22, 119, 139; III.257 sq.; IV.230, 251, 391 sq.; A I.115, 157, 185, 215; II.29 sq., 176; IV.35 sq., 338, 378; V.48 sq.; Sn 537, 553; J I.85; Ud 14, 65; DA I.35; PvA 31. — f. **paribbājikā** Vin IV.285; M I.305; S III.238 sq.; Ud 13, 43 sq.

Paribbājana (nt.) [fr. paribbajati] wandering about or practising the customs of a mendicant SnA 434.

Paribbājayitar [n. ag. of paribbajati] one who indulges in the practice of a Wanderer, fig. one who leads a virtuous ascetic life Sn 537 (T. °vajjayitā). Perhaps we should read °bājayitvā for °bājayitā, cp. SnA 434 nikkhamet[v]ā niddhamet[v]ā.

Paribbūḷha (adj.) [pp. of paribrūhati] encompassed, provided with, surrounded A III.34; Sn 301 (= parikiṇṇa SnA 320); J IV.120; V.68, 322, 417; VI.452.

Paribbhamati [pari + bhamati] 1. to walk or roam about PvA 6, 47 (ito c' ito), 63 (saŋsāre), 100, 166 (saŋsare). — 2. to reel about J III.288; IV.407. — Caus. °**bbhameti** to make reel round J VI.155.

Paribyattatā (f.) [pari + vyatta + tā] great distinction, clearness; wide experience, learnedness Miln 349.

Paribrahaṇa (nt.) [to bṛh, see paribrūhati & cp. late Sk. paribarhaṇā] growth, increase, promotion Th 1, p. 2^n. Cp. paribrūhana.

Paribrūhati [pari + brūhati of bṛh^2] to augment, increase, do with zest VvA 115. — Caus. °brūheti [cp. Sk. paribṛnhayati] to make strong, increase J v.361 (aparibrūhayi aor. med. with a° neg., i. e. was weakened, lost his strength; but expl^d by C. as "atibrūhesi mahāsaddaŋ nicchāresi," thus taking it to brū to speak, which is evidently a confusion). — pp. paribbūḷha & paribrūhita (q. v.).

Paribrūhana (nt.) [fr. paribrūhati, cp. upabrūhana] augmentation, increase Nett 79.

Paribrūhita [pp. of paribrūheti] increased, furthered, strengthened ThA 245.

Paribhaṭṭha^1 [pp. of paribhassati of bhraś] fallen, dropped J I.482; Th 1, p. 12^n.

Paribhaṭṭha^2 [pp. of paribhāsati] abused, censured, scolded J VI.187.

Paribhaṇḍa [for paribandha, dialectical, see Kern. *Toev.* I.36, who compares Tamil panda "a surrounding wall" = P. bandha. The meaning is rather uncertain, cp. notes in *Vin. Texts* II.154; III.85, 213] 1. a binding along the back Vin I.254, 297; II.116; J v.254 (v. l. °daṇḍa). — 2. a girdle, belt J VI.125; DhA II.174. — 3. a plastered flooring Vin II.113, 172, 220; J III.384; IV.92; v.437, 440. — 4. slough of a serpent (?) J VI.339. — 5. (°-) adj. encircling, comprehensive, in °ñāṇa Vism 429.

Paribhata [pp. of pari + bhṛ] nurtured, nourished M II.56 (sukha°). Also in expl^n of pāribhaṭyatā (q. v.).

Paribhava [pari + bhū] contempt, disrespect Vin IV.241; A III.191; J v.436; VI.164; Vbh 353 sq.; PvA 257.

Paribhavana (nt.) = paribhava DA I.255.

Paribhavati [pari + bhū], also paribhoti to treat with contempt, to neglect, despise S I.69; A III.174 sq. (°bhoti); J III.16; v.442; Miln 23, 259; PvA 266. — grd. paribhotabba S I.69; Sn p. 93 (= paribhavitabba SnA 424). — Caus. paribhāveti; pp. paribhūta (q. v.).

Paribhāvanā (f.) [fr. paribhāveti] permeation, penetration DhsA 163 (= vāsanā).

Paribhāvita [pp. of paribhāveti] 1. penetrated, supplied, filled with, trained, set D II.81 (saddhā-p. cittaŋ, sīla° etc.: trsl. "set round with," cp. *Dial.* II.86), cp. S v.369; Sn 23 (cittaŋ p.; SnA 37 saŋvāsiya); Miln 361; PvA 139 (°aya bhāvanāya codito). — 2. compounded of, mixed with J I.380, cp. IV.407; PvA 191. — 3. fostered, treated, practised Miln 394 (bhesajjena kāyaŋ); PvA 257. — 4. sat on (said of eggs), being hatched M I.104; S III.153; A IV.125 sq., 176.

Paribhāveti [Caus. of paribhavati] to cause to be pervaded or penetrated, to treat, supply Vin I.279 (uppalahatthāni bhesajjehi p.); J IV.407. — pp. paribhāvita (q. v.).

Paribhāsa [fr. pari + bhāṣ] censure, abuse, blame J v.373; PvA 175.

Paribhāsaka (adj.) [fr. paribhāsa, cp. BSk. paribhāṣaka Divy 38] reviling, abusing, abusive S I.34; A IV.79; Pv I.11^6 (= akkosaka PvA 58); IV.8^4; VvA 69. See also akkosaka.

Paribhāsati [pari + bhāṣ, cp. BSk. paribhāṣate Divy 38] to abuse, scold, revile, censure, defame S I.221; IV.61; Vin IV.265; Sn 134, 663; J I.112, 384 (for °hāsiŋsu) 469; III.421; IV.285 (read paribhāsenti for aribhāsenti); v.294; VI.523; Pv II.10^8; Pug 37; Miln 186; PvA 43. — aor. °bhāsissaŋ Pv IV.8^5, pl. °bhāsimhase Pv III.1^{11}. grd. °bhāsaniya Miln 186. — Very frequently comb^d with akkosati (+ p.), e. g. at Vin II.14, 296; Ud 44; Pv I.9^3; PvA 10. — pp. paribhaṭṭha^2 (q. v.). — Caus. II. °bhāsāpeti id. Pv I.6^7.

Paribhindati [pari + bhid] 1. to break up, split, create dissension, to set at variance J I.439; IV.196; v.229; VI.368; PvA 13. — 2. to break (see °bhinna). — pp. paribhinna.

Paribhinna [pp. of paribhindati] 1. broken, broken up M I.190 (a°); VvA 184 (°vaṇṇa of broken up appearance, i. e. crumbly.). — 2. set at variance, disconcerted, split Vin III.161; J II.193; DhsA 308; PvA 13. — Cp. vi°.

Paribhuñjati [pari + bhuj] 1. to enjoy, to use, to enjoy the use of Vin II.109; M I.153 (nivāpaŋ p.), 207, S II.29; Sn 240, 241, 423; Pv I.1^2; I.9^4; IV.5^2 (= khādituŋ PvA 259); Nd^2 427 (pariyesati paṭilabhati paribhuñjati); Miln 366, 395 (ālopaŋ °bhuñjisaŋ); Pv 3, 5 (modake eat up), 8, 13, 23, 47; Sdhp 394. — grd. °bhuñjiya J I.243 (dup°); & °bhuñjitabba PvA 71 (with nt. abstr. °tabbatta). — Pass. °bhuñjiyati, ppr. °iyamāna S I.90. — 2. [see bhuñjati^2] to purify, clean, cleanse M I.25; J VI.75. — pp. paribhutta (q. v.).

Paribhuñjana (nt.) [fr. paribhuñjati] eating PvA 35.

Paribhutta [pp. of paribhuñjati, cp. BSk. paribhukta Divy 277] used, employed, made use of Vin II.109 (su°); J III.257 (a°); DA I.261 (sayaŋ °bhesajja); SnA 19.

Paribhūta [pp. of paribhavati] treated with contempt, disregarded, despised Vin IV.6; S II.279; Miln 229, 288.

Paribheda [fr. pari + bhid, see paribhindati] 1. breaking, breaking up, falling to pieces Dhs 738, 874. — 2. bursting, breaking open PvA 55.

Paribhedaka (adj.) [fr. paribheda in sense of paribhindati] breaking; a disturber of peace, breedbate J II.173; III.168; v.245; VI.437.

Paribhoga [fr. pari + bhuj] 1. material for enjoyment, food, feeding J I.243; II.432; Miln 156, 403; DhA II.66; SnA 342. — 2. enjoyment, use Vin IV.267; S I.90; Nd^1 262; Vism 33 (with pariyesana & paṭiggahana); DhA I.60; PvA 25, 26, 220. — Four paribhogas are distinguished at J v.253 and at Vism 43. viz. theyya°, iṇa,° dāyajja°, sāmi°. Paribhoga discussed in relation to paṭilābha at Vism 43.

-**cetiya** a tree, shrine etc., used by the Buddha, & consequently sacred KhA 222. -**dhātu** a relic consisting of something used by the dead Saint (opp. sarīradhātu, remains of the body) Mhvs 15, 163. (cp. pāribhogika-dhātu); SnA 579.

Paribhojaniya (or °iya) (nt.) [orig. grd. of paribhunjati 2] that which is used for cleaning, water for washing Vin II.76, 208, 216 (°ghaṭa), 226 (cp. *Vin. Texts* III.8); III.119 (pāniyaŋ); J I.416; VI.75; DhA I.58.

Parima = parama (cp. Geiger *P.Gr.* 19^1) M III.112.

Parimajjaka (adj.) [fr. pari + marj] touching, reaching (up to) Miln 343 (candasuriya°, cp. MVastu II. candramasūrya-parimārjako maharddhiko etc.).

Parimajjati [pari + majjati] 1. to wipe away, wipe off or out M I.78. — 2. to touch, stroke D I.78; M III.12; S II.121; Dh 394; J I.192, 305; II.395 (piṭṭhiŋ). — 3. to rub, polish, groom (a horse) A v.166, 168. — pp. parimaṭṭha (q. v.).

Parimajjana (nt.) [fr. parimajjati] 1. wiping off or out Pug 33 (ukkhali°). — 2. rubbing, grooming (a horse) A v.166, 168 (ājānīya°).

Parimaṭṭha [pp. of parimajjati] rubbed, stroked, polished, in su° well polished S II.102. See also palimaṭṭha.

Parimaṇḍala (adj.) [pari+maṇḍala] 1. round, circular J I.441; II.406 (āvāṭa); VI.42; Pv IV.3[28] (guḷa°); Dhs 617 (expl[d] at DhsA 317 as "egg-shaped," kukkuṭ-aṇḍa-saṇṭhāna). — nt. as adv. in phrase °ŋ nivāseti to dress or cover oneself all round Vin I.46; II.213; IV.185 (= nābhimaṇḍalaŋ jānu-maṇḍalaŋ paṭicchādentena C.; cp. timaṇḍala). — 2. rounded off, i. e. complete, correct, pleasant, in phrase °āni padavyañjanāni well sounding words and letters, correct speech Vin II.316; M I.216; A I.103; DA I.282; SnA 177, 370.

Parimaddati [pari+mṛd] 1. to rub, crush, rub off, treat, shampoo, massage J IV.137 (sarīraŋ examine the body & put it right); Miln 241. — Of leather (i. e. treat) M I.128. — 2. to go together with, to frequent DhA I.90 (samayaŋ p.). — pp. parimaddita (q. v.).

Parimaddana (nt.) [fr. pari+mṛd] rubbing, kneading, shampooing, massage; usually in stock phrase (kāyo) anicc'-ucchādana-parimaddana-bhedana-viddhaŋsana-dhammo D I.76 (cp. DA I.88, but trsl[d] at *Dial.* I.87 as "subject to erasion, *abrasion*, dissolution and disintegration"); M I.500; S IV.83; J I.416. See further D I.7; A I.62; IV.54 (ucchādana-p.-nahāpana-sambāhana); Miln 241 (ucchādana°); Sdhp 578.

Parimaddita [pp. of parimaddati] crushed, rubbed, treated M I.129 (su° well-treated).

Parimaddhita [pp. of pari+maddheti, Caus. of mṛdh to neglect] brought to an end or standstill, destroyed J I.145 (°sankhāra).

Parimasati [pari+mṛś] to touch, stroke, grasp (usually comb[d] with parimajjati), D I.78; II.17; M I,34, 80; III.12; S II.121; IV.173; A III.70. — pp. parimaṭṭha (same as pp. of parimajjati), q. v.

Parimāṇa (nt.) [of pari+mā] measure, extent, limit, as adj. (-°) measuring, extending over, comprising J I.45; SnA I (pariyatti°); PvA 113 (yojana°), 102 (anekabhāra°). — neg. aparimāṇa without limit, immeasurable, very great Vin II.62, 70; S V.430; A II.182; KhA 248; DA I.288 (°vaṇṇa); PvA 110, 129.

Parimārita [pp. of pari+māreti, Caus. of mṛ] mortified, only in phrase °indriya J I.361; III.515; IV.9, 306; V.152; Dāvs I.16.

Parimita [pp. of pariminàti] measured, restricted, limited, only in neg. a° measureless Pv II.8[11]; Miln 287, 343.

Parimitatta (nt.) [fr. parimita] the condition of being measured PvA 254.

Pariminàti [pari+mā] to measure, mete out, estimate, limit, restrict; inf. °metuŋ Miln 192; ThA 26; and °minituŋ Miln 316; grd. °meyya (q. v.). — pp. parimita (q. v.).

Parimeyya (adj.) [grd. of pariminàti] to be measured, neg. a° countless, immeasurable Miln 331, 388; PvA 212.

Parimukha (adj.) [pari+mukha] facing, in front; only as nt. adv. °ŋ in front, before, in phrase parimukhaŋ satiŋ upaṭṭhapeti "set up his memory in front" (i. e. of the object of thought), to set one's mindfulness alert Vin I.24; D II.291; M I.56, 421; S I.170; A III.92; It 80; Ps I.176 (expl[d]); Pug 68; DA I.210. Also in phrase °ŋ kārāpeti (of hair) Vin II.134 "to cut off (?) the hair in front" (i. e. on the breast) *Vin. Texts* III.138, where is quoted Bdhgh's expl[n] "ure loma-saŋharaṇaŋ."

Parimuccati [Pass. of pari+muc] to be released, to be set free, to escape Vin II.87; M I.8; S I.88, 208; II.24, 109; III.40, 150, 179; Miln 213, 335 (jātiyā etc.) aor. °mucci M I.153. — pp. parimutta; Caus. parimoceti (q. v.).

Parimuṭṭha [pari+muṭṭha, pp. of mussati, cp. pamuṭṭha] forgetful, bewildered Vin I.349 = J III.488 (= muṭṭhassati C.); cp. *Vin. Texts* II.307.

Parimutta [pp. of parimuccati] released, set free, delivered S III.31.

Parimutti (f.) [fr. pari+muc] release J I.4 (v. 20); Miln 112, 227; PvA 109.

Parimussati [pari+mussati] to become bewildered or disturbed, to vanish, fall off Nd[1] 144.

Parimoceti [Caus. of parimuccati] to set free, deliver, release D I.96; J I.28 (v. 203); Miln 334; DA I.263; DhA I.39.

Parimohita (adj.) [pp. of pari+Caus. of muh] very confused, muddled, dulled, bewildered, infatuated Sdhp 206.

Pariya [either short form of pariyāya, or ger. of pari+ī substantivised (for the regular form paricca) representing an ending *-ya* instead of *-tya*. — Bdhgh at Vism 409 takes pariya as *nt.*, but seems to mix it with the idea of a ppr. by defining it as "pariyātī ti pariyaŋ, paricchindatī ti attho"] encompassing, fathoming, comprehending (as ger.); penetration, understanding (as n.). Only in phrase ceto-pariya-ñāṇa knowledge encompassing heart or mind (cp. phrase cetasā ceto paricca) D II.82 sq. (v. l. °āya); III.100 (v. l. °āye); DA I.223 (corresp. with pubbe-nivāsa-ñāṇa); with which alternates the phrase indriya-paro-pariya-ñāṇa in same meaning (see indriya cpds. & remark on paropariya) J I.78. — See also pariyatta[1] pariyatti, pariyāya 3, and cpds. of ceto.

Pariyañña [pari+yañña] supreme or extraordinary offering or sacrifice SnA 321, 322.

Pariyatta[1] (nt.) [abstr. fr. pariya (pari+i) but confused with pariyatta[2] & pariyatti fr. pari+āp] learning, understanding, comprehension, only in phrase indriya-paro pariyatta (-ñāṇa) (knowledge of) what goes on in the intentions of others A V.34, 38; Ps I.121 sq.; Vbh 340.

Pariyatta[2] (adj.) [cp. Sk. paryāpta, pp. of pari+āp, see pāpuṇāti] (a) capable of, mastered, kept in mind, learned by heart; only in phrase dhammo ca vinayo ca p. Vin II.285 = KhA 92; D III.241 sq. (yathā sutaŋ yathā p°ŋ dhammaŋ). — (b) sufficient, enough PvA 33 (= alaŋ).

Pariyatti (f.) [fr. pari+āp, cp. Epic Sk. paryāpti & P. pariyāpuṇāti] adequacy, accomplishment, sufficiency, capability, competency; indriya-paro° efficiency in the (knowledge of) thoughts of others S V.205; Nett 101. Three accomplishments are distinguished at DA I.21 sq., viz. alagadd-ûpamā (like a serpent), nissaraṇatthā (on account of salvation) and bhaṇḍâgārika° (of a treasurer), apariyatti-kara bringing no advantage DhA I.71. — 2. accomplishment in the Scriptures, study (learning by heart) of the holy texts Vism 95. Also the Scriptures themselves as a body which is handed down through oral tradition. In this meaning the word is only found in later, dogmatic literature; -tīsu piṭakesu tividho pariyatti-bhedo DA I.21. At SnA 494 it is classed with paccaya dhutanga & adhigama; as a part of paṭibhāna at Nd[1] 234 = Nd[2] 386. pariyattiŋ uggaṇhāti to undertake the learning (of the Scriptures) DhA II.30; cp. KhA 91 (tipiṭaka-sabba-p.-pabheda-dhara); J II.48 (°ŋ ṭhapetvā leaving the learning aside); Miln 115, 215, 345, 411 (āgama°). — *abl.* pariyattito through learning

by heart SnA 195 (opp. to atthato according to the meaning).
-dhamma that which belongs to the holy study, part or contents of the Scriptures, the Tipiṭaka comprising the nine divisions (see navanga Buddha-sāsana) KhA 191, 193; SnA 328; PvA 2; cp. °sāsana. -dhara knowing the Scriptures by heart Miln 21. -dhura (=ganthadhura): see vāsadhura. -paṭibhānavant possessed of intelligence as regards learning the Scriptures SnA 111. -parimāṇa extent of study SnA 1, 6r 8. -bahula clever in the study of the Dhamma A III.86. -bahussuta versed in the Scriptures SnA 110. -sāsana object, instruction of the Scriptures, code of the holy Texts (cp. °dhamma) Nd[1] 143; DhA IV.39.

Pariyanta [pari+anta, cp. Sk. paryanta] 1. limit, end, climax, border S I.80 (manāpa° "limit-point in enjoyment"; cp. C. nipphattikaŋ koṭikaŋ *K.S.* 320); J I.149 (hattha-pāda° hoofs), 221 (udaka°), 223 (sara°); II.200 (angana°); Pv II.13[12]; DhA III.172 (parisa°). — 2. limit, boundary, restriction, limitation Vin II.59, 60 (āpatti°); Nd[1] 483 (distinguishes between 4 pariyantā with ref. to one's character, viz. sīlasaŋvara° indriyasaŋvara°, bhojane mattaññutā°, jāgariyânuyoga°). — 3. (adj.-°) bounded by, limited by, surrounded, ending in Vin IV.31; M III.90; S II.122 (āyu°); A I.164 (id.); Sn 577 (bhedana°); Pv I.10[13] (parikkhitta PvA 52). —apariyanta (adj.) boundless, limitless PvA 58, 166. -kata restricted, limited, bounded Nd[2] taṇhā[m] (with sīmakata & odhikata; v. l. pariyanti°, cp. BSk. paryantīkṛta "finished" Divy 97, 236). -cārin living in self-restriction Sn 964 (cp. Nd[1] 483). -dassāvin seeing the limit A V.50. -rahita without limits DhA III.252.

Pariyantavant (adj.) [fr. pariyanta] having a limit, having a set or well-defined purpose; f. °vatī (vācā) discriminating speech D I.4=M III.49=Pug 58; expl[d] as "paricchedaŋ dassetvā yatha 'ssa paricchedo paññāyati, evaŋ bhāsatī ti attho" DA I.76=PugA 238.

Pariyantika (adj.) (-°) [fr. pariyanta] ending in, bounded or limited by S II.83=A II.198 (kāya-p. °ā & jīvita-p. °ā vedanā); Vism 69 (bhojana°, udaka°, āsana°); Sdhp 440 (kāla° sīla).

Pariyaya [cp. Epic Sk. paryaya, pari+i; the usual P. form is pariyāya, but at the foll. passages the short a is required *metri causa*] revolution, lapse of time, period, term J III.460 (=kālapariyāya C.); V.367 (kāla°).

Pariyā (f.) [fr. pari+yā] winding round, turning round; of a tree, branch J VI.528 (duma°; read °pariyāsu with v. l. instead of T. pariyāyesu; C. expl[s] by sākhā).

Pariyāgata [pari+ā+gata] having come to, reached, attained J VI.237 (phalaŋ; C=upagata), 238 (kusalaŋ; C.=pariyāyena attano vārena āgata).

Pariyāgāra (adj.) [pari+āgāra] having the house all round, entirely surrounded by the house Vin III.119 (of gabbha).

Pariyāti [pari+yā] 1. to go round (acc.) J I.307. — 2. to come near J II.440.

Pariyādāti [pari+ādāti] to take up in an excessive degree, to exhaust. Only in secondary forms of med-pass. ādiyati, pp. °ādinna, ger. ādāya (q. v.).

Pariyādāna (nt.) [pari+ādāna, opp. upādāna] "taking up completely," i. e. using up, consummation, consumption, finishing, end M I.487 (kaṭṭha°, opp. to upādāna); S I.152; III.16 sq. (cetaso p., cp. pariyādāya & °dinna); IV.33 (sabb' upādāna°) A II.139; J V.186. Cp. BSk. paryādāna Divy 4, 55, 100. — Esp. in foll. phrases: āsava° & jīvita° D I.46 (jīvita-pariyādānā abl., expl[d] at Dh I.128 as "jīvitassa sabbaso pariyādinnattā parikkhīṇattā puna appaṭisandhika-bhāvā ti attho"); S II.83=A II.198; S III.126; IV.213; A IV.13, 146; Pug 13; Miln 397; and comb[d] with parikkhaya in °ŋ gacchati to be exhausted or consummated A V.173= Sn p. 126; Miln 102; PvA 147, cp. BSk. parikṣayaŋ paryādānaŋ gacchati Divy 567; AvŚ I.48; II.193.

Pariyādāya (indecl.) [ger. of pariyādati] 1. taking all round, summing up, completely Nd[2] 533 (in expl[n] of ye keci, as synonymous with sabbato, i. e. for completeness, exhaustively). — 2. exhausting, overpowering, enticing, taking hold of, as cittaŋ p. "taking hold of the mind" M I.91; It 19; DhA I.15. — 3. losing control over, giving out (cittaŋ) S III.16; IV.125. In absolute sense perhaps at S V.51=A IV.127 (with vv. ll. pariyenāya & pariyāya).

Pariyādinna [often spelt °diṇṇa, e. g. in vv. ll. at D II.8; M II.172; III.118. — pp. of pariyādiyati] 1. (Pass.) exhausted, finished, put an end to, consummated Vin I.25 (tejo); D II.8=M III.118; S II.133 sq. (dukkhaŋ; parikkhīṇaŋ+); V.461 sq. — neg. apariyādinna not finished, not exhausted M I.79 (muttakarīsaŋ °ādiṇṇaŋ), 83 (dhammadesanā ādiṇṇā); S II.178 sq. — 2. (Med.) having exhausted, lost control over, being overcome (usually °citta adj.) Vin II.185; M II.172; S II.228; Nd[2] 32; PvA 279.

Pariyādinnatta (nt.) [abstr. fr. pariyādinna] exhaustion, consummation DA I.128.

Pariyādiyati [sometimes spelt °diyyati, e. g. Nd[2] s. v.; pari+ādiyati, q. v. for etym. ref.] 1. to put an end to, exhaust, overpower, destroy, master, control S III.155 (rāgaŋ); Nd[2] under parisahati. — Pot. °ādiyeyyaŋ Vin I.25 (tejaŋ). — ger. °adiyitvā Vin I.25 (tejaŋ); IV.109 (id.); S I.84 (trsl. "confiscate"). — 2. to become exhausted, give out J V.186 (udakaŋ); Miln 297 (cittaŋ p.; opp. to parivaḍḍhati). — pp. pariyādinna (q. v.).

Pariyāpajjati [pari+āpajjati] to be finished A IV.339. — pp. pariyāpanna (q. v.). — Caus. pariyāpādeti (q. v.).

Pariyāpadāna (nt.) [pari+apadāna, the latter for ava°, and metrical lengthening of a] good advice, application, trick, artfulness, artifice J V.361, 369. (C. expln[s] as parisuddha after v. l. pariyodāta which was prob. misread for pariyodāna), 370.

Pariyāpanna [pari+āpanna, cp. adhipanna] 1. "gone completely into," included in, belonging to, got into Vin I.46 (patta° that which has been put into the bowl); D I.45 (=ābaddha DA I.127); SnA 397 (milakkhabhāsa° etc.); KhA 136 (vinaya°), 191 (sangha°); DhA I.158 (idhaloka-paraloka°); PvA 14, 33, 59, 129 (devaloka°), 150. — 2. accomplished (i. e. gone into the matter), thorough, mastering (said of vācā) S II.280 =A II.51. — 3. (°ā dhammā) the Included, viz. all that is contained in the threefold cycle of existence (i. e. the worlds of sense, form & formless) Dhs 1268; Vbh 12, 15, 19 & passim; DhsA 50. Opp. apariyāpannā (dhammā) the Unincluded (viz. all that is exempt from this cycle) Ps I.101; Dhs 583 (cp. *Dhs trsl[n]* 165, 254, 329, 332), 992, 1242; Kvu 507.

Pariyāpannatta (nt.) [abstr. fr. pariyāpanna] includedness SnA 174.

Pariyāpādeti [Caus. of pariyāpajjati] to finish off, i. e. put to death completely S IV.308 sq.=A III.94.

Pariyāpuṇana (nt.) [abstr. form[n] fr. pariyāpuṇāti] mastery over, accomplishment in (gen.) Vism 442 (Buddhavacanassa).

Pariyāpuṇāti [pari+āp, cp. BSk. paryavāpnoti Divy 613] 1. to learn (by heart), to master, to gain mastership over, to learn thoroughly Vin IV.305 (parittaŋ a charm); D I.117 (=jānāti DA I.117); A III.86 (dhammaŋ); fut.

pariyāpuṇissati DhA I.382 (dhammaŋ); ger. pariyāpuṇitvā S I.176; II.120; SnA 195 (nikāyaŋ). — 2. (with inf.) to know (to do something), to be able to Vin II.109 (aor. °iŋsu), 121. — pp. pariyāputa and pariyatta (q. v.).

Pariyāputa [pp. of pariyāpuṇāti] 1. learned by heart, known Nd[1] 234 = Nd[2] 386 (Buddhavacana). — 2. learned, accomplished DA I.21. — See also pariyatta[2].

Pariyāya [fr. pari + **i**, cp. Class. Sk. paryāya in all meanings, already Vedic in meaning of "formula," in liturgy, cp. below 4] lit. "going round" analysed by Bdhgh in 3 diff. meanings, viz. vāra (turn, course), desanā (instruction, presentation), and kāraṇa (cause, reason, also case, matter), see DA I.36 and cp. *Kindred Sayings* I.320. — 1. arrangement, disposition, in phrase °ŋ karoti to arrange D I.179 (trsl[n] takes it literally "departure," i. e. going out of one's way, détour; or change of habit, see *Dial* I.245); M I.252, 326; III.7, 62; S I.142 (trsl. "make occasion" [for coming]). — 2. order, succession, turn, course (= vāra) D I.166 ≈ (°bhatta i. e. feeding in turn or at regular intervals; expl[d] as vāra-bhatta PugA 232); M I.78, 206, 481; S II.51 sq.; A II.206; J V.153 (= vāra); PvA 242 (aparā°). — 3. what goes on, way, habit, quality, property S I.146 (ceto° habits of mind, thoughts, but see also pariya); A V.160 (citta°, see ceto). — 4. discussion, instruction, method (of teaching), discourse on (-°), representation of (-°) (= desanā); thus āditta° (of Vin I.34) DhA I.88; esp. in cpd. dhamma° disquisition on the Dhamma D I.46; II.93; M I.83; III.67; S II.74; V.357; A III.62; IV.166, 381; Sn p. 218; also in foll.: vitakka° M I.122; deva° A III.402 sq.; peta° PvA 92; cp. Vism 41 (°kathā). — 5. in Abhidhamma terminology, specifically: pariyāyena, the mode of teaching in the Suttanta, *ad hominem*, discursively, applied method, illustrated discourse, figurative language as opposed to the abstract, general statements of Abhidhamma = nippariyāyena, nippariyāyato, Vism 473, 499; cp. DhsA 317 (figuratively). — 6. mode, manner, reason, cause, way (= kāraṇa) D I.185 (iminā °ena), 186 (id.); II.339 (ayaŋ p. yena °ena); DA I.106 (tena tena °ena in some way or other); DhsA 366 (iminā °ena for this reason); esp. in phrase aneka-pariyāyena in many (or various) ways Vin I.16, 45; D I.1 (cp. DA I.36), 174; M I.24; A I.56; Sn p. 15. — 7. winding round (of a tree: branch), in doubtful reading at J VI.528 (see pariyā). — See also nippariyāya.

Pariyāhata [pari + āhata] struck out, affected with (-°), only in phrase takka° "beaten out by argumentations" D I.16 (cp. DA I.106); M I.520.

Pariyāhanana (nt.) [fr. pari + ā + **han**] striking, beating Vism 142 (āhanana° in exposition of vitakka) = DhsA 114 ("circumimpinging" *Expos.* 151).

Pariyiṭṭha [pp. of pariyesati] sought, desired, looked for S IV.62 (a°); Miln 134; Vism 344 (°āhāra).

Pariyiṭṭhi = pariyeṭṭhi Sn 289 (SnA 316 reads pariyeṭṭhi). Perhaps we should read pariyeṭṭhuŋ (see pariyesati).

Pariyukkhaṇṭhati [pari + ukkaṇṭhati] to have great longing, to be distressed J V.417, 421 (mā °kaṇṭhi).

Pariyuṭṭhati [pari + uṭṭhāti] to arise, pervade; intrs. to become prepossessed, to be pervaded DhsA 366 (cittaŋ p.; corā magge pariyuṭṭhiŋsu). — pp. pariyuṭṭhita (q. v.).

Pariyuṭṭhāna (nt.) [pari + uṭṭhāna, it is doubtful whether this connection is correct, in this case the meaning would be "over-exertion." BSk. paryavasthāna points to another connection, see Divy 185] state of being possessed (or hindered) by (-°), prepossession, bias, outburst M I.18, Kvu XIV.6 (thīnamiddha°), 136; A I.66 (°ajjhosāna); V.198 (adhiṭṭhāna-°samuṭṭhāna); Nd[2] under taṇhā[n] (= Dhs 1059, where trsl[n] is "pervading," based on expl[n] at DhsA 366: uppajjamānā [scil. taṇhā] cittaŋ pariyuṭṭhāti, and allegorical interpretation ibid.: the heart becomes possessed by lust as a road by highwaymen); Pug 21 (avijjā°); Vbh 383 (where 7 pariyuṭṭhānā [sic! pl. m.] are enum[d] in the same set as under headings of anusaya & saŋyojana, thus placing p. into the same category as these two); Dhs 390, 1061 (avijjā°), 1162 (id.); Nett 13, 14, 18, 37, 79 sq.; DhsA 238; ThA 80; Vism 5 (with vītikkama & anusaya). Cp. also adhiṭṭhāna.

Pariyuṭṭhita [pari + uṭṭhita, with v. l. at D II.104 parivuṭṭhita and BSk. rendering paryavasthita: see remarks on pariyuṭṭhāna and *Dial.* II.111] possessed by (the C. expl[n] as given *K.S.* 320 is "abhibhūta"), biassed, taken up by, full of (-°) M I.18; III.14; S IV.240 (maccheramala° ceto); A I.281; II.58; It 43 (diṭṭhigatehi); Kvu I.91 (kāma-rāga°); ThA 78; Sdhp 581.

-citta whose heart is possessed by (-°) D II.104 (Mārena); PvA 142 (maccheramala°), 195 (id.), 279 (kilesasamudācārena). -ṭṭhāyin being rooted in prepossession, affected by bias, S III.3 sq. (so read for pariyuṭṭhaṭṭhāyin ?).

Pariyudāharati [pari + udāharati] to utter solemnly, to proclaim aloud DhsA 1 (aor. °āhāsi).

Pariyeṭṭhi [pari + eṭṭhi of esati, ā + **iṣ**] search for D I.222; A I.93 (āmisa° & dhamma°); III.416; Sn 289 (vijjācaraṇa°) J I.14; Nett 1, 5; DA I.271.

Pariyeti [pari + **i**] to go about, to go round, encircle, encompass; ger. paricca (q. v.). The pp. is represented by pareta, see also pareti which seems to stand for pariyeti.

Pariyena [fr. pari + **i**, cp. Sk. *paryayana] going round, walking round; of a ship: sailing round, tour, voyage S V.51 (pariyenāya, v. l. pariyādāya) = A IV.127 (reads pariyādāya v. l. pariyāya). Reading is doubtful.

Pariyesati [pari + esati, cp. BSk. paryeṣate to investigate AvŚ I.339. The P. word shows confusion between esati & icchati, as shown by double forms °iṭṭhuŋ etc. See also anvesati] to seek for, look, search, desire D I.223 (°esamāna ppr.); Sn 482 (id.); S I.177, 181; IV.62; A II.23, 25, 247; Nd[1] 262; Nd[2] 427 (+ paṭilabhati and paribhuñjati); J I.3, 138; Miln 109, 313; DhA III.263 (ppr. °esanto); PvA 31; Sdhp 506. — grd. °esitabba S II.130; inf. °esituŋ SnA 316; and °eṭṭhuŋ (conj. °iṭṭhuŋ ?) Sn 289 (cp. SnA 316 which gives reading °eṭṭhuŋ as gloss); ger. °esitvā SnA 317, 414; — pp. **pariyesita** & **pariyiṭṭha** (q. v.). Cp. for similar formation & meaning ajjhesati with pp. ajjhesita & ajjhiṭṭha. — Cp. vi°.

Pariyesanā (f.) & °**na** (nt.) [fr. pariyesati] search, quest, inquiry (a) (°nā) D II.58, 61, 280 (twofold, viz. sevitabbā and asevitabbā); III.289; M I.161 (twofold, viz. ariyā & anariyā); A II.247 (id.); S I.143; II.144, 171; III.29; IV.8 sq. (assāda° & ādīnava°); A I.68 (kāma°), 93. — (b) (°na) Nd[1] 262 (°chanda, + paṭilābha° & paribhoga°); DhA III.256 (kāmaguṇe °ussukka). With paṭiggahaṇa & paribhoga at DhA I.75.

Pariyesita [pp. of pariyesati] searched, sought for, desired It 121. See also **pariyiṭṭha**.

Pariyoga [fr. pari + **yuj**] cauldron (see Kern, *Toev.* s. v.) Miln 118.

Pariyogāya at M I.480 is contracted form (ger.) of pariyogāhitvā (so expl[d] by C.).

Pariyogāḷha [pp. of pariyogāhati, see also ogāḍha¹] dived into, penetrated into, immersed in (loc.) Vin I.181; D I.110; M I.380; S II.58; IV.328; Vbh 329; Miln 283. **-dhamma** one who has penetrated into the Dhamma Vin I.16; A IV.186, 210; Ud 49.

Pariyogāha [pari+ogāha] diving into, penetration; only in cpd. dup° hard to penetrate, unfathomable S IV.376; Miln 70.

Pariyogāhati & °**gāheti** [pari+ogāhati] to penetrate, fathom, scrutinise A II.84; IV.13, 145 sq. (paññāya); J I.341; Pug 33 (a°), 48 sq. Cp. ajjhogāhati.

Pariyogāhana (nt.) & **ā** (f.) [pari+ogāhana] plunging into, penetration Ps I.106, 112; II.183; Dhs 390 (a°), 425 (a°); Pug 21 (a°); DhsA 260.

Pariyottharati [pari+ottharati] to spread all over (intrs.) Miln 197.

Pariyodapana (nt.) & **ā** (f.) [fr. pariyodapeti], cleansing, purification A I.207 (cittassa); Dh 183 (=vodāpana DhA III.237); Nett 44. In BSk. distorted to paryadapana MVastu III.12 (= Dh 183).

Pariyodapita [pp. of pariyodapeti] cleansed, purified Nett 44 (cittaŋ).

Pariyodapeti [pari+odapeti, of Caus. of **dā**⁴ to clean] to cleanse, purify M I.25; Dh 68 (=vodapeti parisodheti) DhA II.162; Nett 44; ThA 237 (indriyāni). — pp. **pariyodāta** & **pariyodapita** (q. v.).

Pariyodāta (adj.) [pari+odāta, cp. pariyodapeti] 1. very clean, pure, cleansed, mostly comb^d with parisuddha (+) D I.75, 76 (+); M I.26; S I.198; III.235 (+); V.301; A III.27 (+); IV.120 sq.; J V.369 (+; see pariyāpadāna); Pug 60; DA I.219; DhA IV.72 (+); VvA 138. — 2. very clever, accomplished, excellent [cp. BSk. paryavadāta in same meaning at Divy 100] J III.281 (°sippa); Vism 136 (id.).

Pariyodāpaka (adj.) [fr. pariyodapeti] cleansing, purifying Vism 149 (ñāṇa).

Pariyodha [pari+yodha] defence A I.154.

Pariyonaddha [pp. of pariyonandhati, cp. onaddha & BSk. paryavanaddha "overgrown" Divy, 120, 125] covered over, enveloped D I.246; III.223 (a°); M I.25; S V.263; A II.211 (uddhasta+); IV.86; J I.30; Miln 161; SnA 596 (= nivuta); DhA III.199; PvA 172 (taca°).

Pariyonandhati [pari+avanandhati] to tie down, put over, envelop, cover up Vin II.137; S V.122; J III.398; DhA III.153. — pp. **pariyonaddha** (q. v.).

Pariyonandhana (nt.) [fr. above] covering DA I.135; DhA III.198.

Pariyonāha [pari+onāha] enveloping, covering D I.246 (=nīvaraṇa); Dhs 1157 (cp. *Dhs trsl.* 311); Miln 300.

Pariyosāna (nt.) [pari+osāna of ava+**sā**] 1. end, finish, conclusion J I.106 (sacca° = desanā°); PvA 9 (desanā° and passim), 136 (āyūha°), 162 (id.), 281 (-anta). Often contracted with ādi beginning & majjha middle (see e. g. SnA 327), esp. in phrase ādi-kalyāṇa majjhe kalyāṇa °kalyāṇa with reference to the Dhamma (expl^d as "ekagāthā pi hi samanta-bhaddakattā dhammassa paṭhamapadena ādik° dutiyatatiya-padehi majjhe k° pacchima-padena pariyosānak°" etc. at SnA 444), e. g. D I.62; It 111 & passim. — 2. end, i. e. perfection, ideal, Arahantship (see on these fig. meanings and its appl^n to Nibbāna DA I.175, 176) D I.203 (brahmacariya +); II.283 (cp. *Dial.* II.316); III.55 (brahmacariya+); S V.230; A III.363 (nibbāna°), 376 (brahmacariya°); Vism 5.

Pariyosāpeti [Caus. of pari+ava+**sā**, Sk. syati, of which pp. pariyosita cp. osāpeti] 1. to make fulfil Vin III.155; DA I.241; ThA 159 (for khepeti Th 2, 168). — 2. to bring to an end, to finish Vism 244.

Pariyosita 1. [pp. of pari+ava+**sā**] finished, concluded, satisfied, D II.224; M I.12 (paripuṇṇa+). — 2. [pp. of pari+ava+**śri**, cp. ajjhosita] fixed on, bent on Miln 140 (°sankappa).

Parirakkhaṇa (nt.) [fr. pari+**rakṣ**] guarding, preserving, keeping Miln 356, 402; PvA 130.

Parirakkhati [pari+**rakṣ**, cp. abhirakkhati] to guard, protect; preserve, maintain Sn 678 (pot. °rakkhe); Miln 410; Sdhp 413, 553 (sīlaŋ).

Parirañjita [pari+rañjita] dyed, coloured; fig. marked or distinguished by (instr.) Miln 75.

Pariḷāha [pari+ḍāha of **ḍah**, cp. pariḍahati. On change of ḍ and ḷ see Geiger, *P.Gr.* § 42³] burning, fever; fig. fever of passion, consumption, distress, pain D III.238 (avigata°), 289 (°nānatta); M I.101 (kāme); S II.143 sq. (°nānatta), 151 (kāma°; vyāpāda°, vihiŋsā°); III.7 sq. (taṇhā, pipāsā, p.), 190 (vigata°); IV.387; V.156 (kāyasmiŋ), 451 (jāti°, jarā°); A I.68 (kāma°), 137 (rāgaja, mohaja etc.); II.197 (vighāta); III.3, 245 sq., 388 sq.; IV.461 sq.; Sn 715 (=rāgajo vā dosajo vā appamattako pi p. SnA 498); Dh 90 (cp. DhA II.166: duvidho p. kāyiko cetasiko ca); Nd² 374 (kāma°); J II.220; Miln 97, 165, 318; ThA 41, 292; VvA 44; PvA 230.

Parillaka [cp. Sk. pirilī, pirillī Bṛh. Saŋh. 86, 44] N. of a bird C on Th 1, 49.

Parivaccha (nt.) [formation from ger. of pari+**vṛt**, corresp. to *parivṛtyaŋ (?)] being active, preparation, outfit J V.46; VI.21 (gamana°); DhA I.207 (gloss & v. l. gamana-parisajja), 395 (v. l. parisajja).

Note. According to Kern, *Toev.* s. v. parivaccha is wrong spelling for parivacca which is abstr. from pariyatta (*pariyatya), with va for ya as in pavacchati, pavecchati = Sk. prayacchati.

Parivajjana (nt.) [fr. pari+**vṛj**] avoiding, avoidance M. I.7, 10; A III.387, 389; Miln 408; Vism 33. As f. °ā at Vism 132, and ibid. as abstr. parivajjanatā.

Parivajjeti [pari+vajjeti, Caus. of **vṛj**] to shun, avoid, keep away from (acc.) M I.10; S I.69, 102, 188, 224; Sn 57 (=vivajjeti Nd² 419), 395 sq., 768 (kāme, cp. Nd¹ 6), 771; It 71; Dh 123 (pāpāni), 269; J IV.378 (fut. °essati); Pv IV.1⁴⁶ (nivesanaŋ); IV.1⁷⁷ (loke adinnaŋ °ayassu); Miln 91 (grd. °ajjayitabba), 300, 408; PvA 150 (v. l. °ajjati), 221 (jīvitaŋ, for vijahati, better read with v. l. pariccajati).

Parivaṭuma (?) (adj.) [doubtful spelling & expl^o; perhaps "parivaṭṭin ?] forming a circle, circular D I.22 (trsl^d "a path could be traced round it" *Dial.* I.36). Can it be misspelling for pariyanta? Kern, *Toev.* s. v. equals it to Sk. parivartman, and adds reference °kata "bounded" (syn. paricchinna) Miln 132.

Parivaṭṭa [fr. pari+**vṛt**, cp. parivattana] round, circle, succession, mainly in two phrases, viz. **catu°** fourfold circle M III.67; S III.59 (pañcupādāna-kkhandhe, cp. aṭṭha-parivaṭṭa-adhideva-ñāṇadassana A IV.304); and **ñāti°** circle of relatives D I.61 (=ñāti DA I.170; cp. expl^o ābandhan' atthena ñāti yeva ñāti parivaṭṭo DA I.181 = PugA 236); II.241; M III.33; Pug 57; ThA 68; VvA 87. — See further at DA I.143 (rāja°), 283 (id., but spelt °vatta); SnA 210.

Parivaḍḍhati [pari+**vṛdh**] to increase, to be happy or prosperous Miln 297 (cittaŋ p.; opp. pariyādiyati).

Parivaṇṇita [pp. of parivaṇṇeti] extolled, praised Sdhp 557.

Parivaṇṇeti [pari+vaṇṇeti] to describe, praise, extol J VI.213 (ppr. °vaṇṇayanto). — pp. °vaṇṇita.

Parivatta (adj.) [fr. pari+**vṛt**] changing round, twisting, turning; f. pl. āyo J V.431.

Parivattaka [fr. parivatta] circle (lit. turning round) J I.101; cp. parivattika in phrase paligha° (q. v.).

Parivattati [pari+**vṛt**] 1. to turn round, twist (trs. & intrs.), go about Vin II.220; J V.431 (singaŋ); Pv IV.5[3] (= pariyāti PvA 260); Miln 118; DA I.265. — 2. (intrs.) to change about, move, change, turn to Pv II.10[5] (=pariṇamati PvA 144); III.4[4] (id. 194); III.6[5]; PvA 178. — Caus. parivatteti (q. v.). Cp. vipari°.

Parivattana (nt.) [fr. parivattati] setting going, keeping up, propounding J I.200 (°manta adj. one who knows a charm); Nett 1 sq., 106.

Parivattita [pp. of parivatteti] 1. turned round, twisted J IV.384. — 2. recited Vism 96.

Parivatteti [Caus. of parivattati] 1. to turn round (trs.), to turn over J I.202; II.275 (sarīraŋ); V.217; DA I.244. — 2. to deal with, handle, set going, put forth, recite Vism 96, in phrase mantaŋ p. to recite, practise a charm J I.200, 253; Pv II.6[13] (=sajjhāyati vāceti PvA 97); cp. mantaŋ pavatteti & pavattar; saraŋ p. to make a sound J I.405; adhippāyaŋ speak out, propound, discuss PvA 131. — 3. to change, exchange Vin II.174; J III.437. — pp. parivattita (q. v.).

Parivadentikā (f.) [pari+vadento+ikā; vadento being ppr. Caus. of **vad**] making resound, resounding, in cpd. godhā° "string-resounding," i. e. a string instrument, lute J VI.580 (cp. Sk *parivāda an instrument with which the lute is played). — Another parivadentikā we find at J VI.540 (C. reading for T. °vadantikā, with v. l. °devantikā) denoting a kind of bird (ekā sakuṇajāti).

Parivasati [pari+**vas**[2]] to stay, dwell, to live under probation Vin III.186 (grd. °vatthabba); IV.30, 127; D I.176; M I.391; S II.21; Sn 697 (=pabbajitvā tāpasavesena vasati SnA 490). — ppr. med. paribbasāna; pp. parivuṭṭha & parivuttha (q. v.).

Parivassati at Pv II.9[36] is to be read as paridhassati (see paridahati).

Parivahati [pari+vahati] to carry about Th 2, 439 (dārake).

Parivāta (-°) [pp. of pari+**vā**] blown round or through, i. e. filled with, stirred by Miln 19 (isi-vāta°).

Parivādinī (f.) [fr. pari+**vad**, late Sk. the same] a lute of seven strings Abhp. 138. — See parivadentikā.

Parivāra [fr. pari+**vṛ**] 1. surrounding, suite, retinue, followers, entourage, pomp J I.151; IV.38; VI.75; PvA 21, 30 (°cāga-cetana, read pariccāga-cetana?); usually as *adj.* -° surrounded by, in company of Vin I.38 (dasasata°); A II.91 (deva° & asura°); J I.92 (mahā-bhikkhusangha°); Pug 52 (pheggu sāra°; with expl[n] PugA 229: rukkho sayaŋ-pheggu hoti, parivāra-rukkhā pan' assa sārā honti); Miln 285 (dvisahassa-paritta-dīpa-p° ā, cattāro mahā dīpā); Vism 37; DhA III.262 (pañcasata-bhikkhu°); PvA 53 (accharā-sahassa°), 74 (dvisahassa-dīpa°); sa° with a retinue (of . . .) J I.49 (cattāro dīpe); PvA 20. — 2. followers, accompaniment or possession as a sign of honour, and therefore meaning "respect," attendance, homage, fame (cp. paricāra) A I.38 °sampadā) Ps I.172 (pariggaha, p., paripūra); DhA II.77; ThA 241 (dhana+, riches and fame); VbhA 466; PvA 137 (sampatti=yaso); VvA 122 (=yaso). — 3. ingredient, accessories (pl.), requisite J I.266 (pañca-sugandhika°); Miln 290 (sa° dāna); DA I.297 (=parikkhārā). — 4. as N. it is the name of the last book of the Vinaya Piṭaka ("The Accessory"), the Appendix a sort of résumé and index of the preceding books SnA 97 (sa-parivāraka Vinaya-piṭaka); VbhA 432.

Parivāraka (adj.) [parivāra+ka] accompanying, forming a retinue J V.234. See also parivāra 4 and paricāraka.

Parivāraṇa (nt.) [fr. pari+**vṛ**] 1. covering, drapery (so trsl. at *K.S.* p. 45) S I.33. — 2. (adj.) (-°) surrounded by J V.195 (=parikkhitta C.).

Parivārita [pp. of parivāreti] surrounded, fig. honoured S I.166, 192=Th 1235; J II.48; purakkhata+); DhA IV.49 (=purakkhata Dh 343); DhsA 1 (devānaŋ gaṇena); Dāvs I.16 (v. l. for parimārita).

Parivāreti [Caus. of pari+**vṛ**] to cover, encompass, surround J I.181 (nagaraŋ °ayiŋsu); II.102 (fut. °essati); III.371 (rukkhaŋ); IV.405 (for parikaroti); VI.179. — ger. parivāretvā used as prep. "round" J I.172 (pokkharaṇiŋ). — In meaning "to serve, attend upon," also "to attend upon oneself, to amuse oneself," parivāreti is often erroneously read for paricāreti, e. g. at D II.13; Pv IV.1[29] (v. l. °cāreti); PvA 228; in ppr. med. °vāriyamāna (with v. l. °cāriyamāna) at D II.21; A I.145; J I.58; VvA 92. — See also anuparivāreti. — pp. parivārita (q. v.).

Parivāsa [fr. pari+**vas**[2], cp. Epic Sk. parivāsa only in meaning 1] 1. sojourn, stay, in phrase vipassanā° DhA III.118; DhsA 215. — 2. period under probation, (living under) probation Vin III.186 (°ŋ vasati, cp. parivuttha); IV.30; S II.21 (°ŋ vasati). °ŋ deti to allow probation Vin I.49; II.7; IV.30, 127; °ŋ yācati to ask for probation Vin IV.30, 127. —samodhāna° inclusive probation Vin II.48 sq.; suddhanta° probation of complete purification Vin II.59 sq. — 3. period, time (lit. stay), interval, duration Ud 7 (eka-ratti°).
-dāna the allowance of probation A I.99.

Parivāsika (adj.) [fr. pari+**vas**[2], see parivasati] 1. "staying," i. e. usual, accustomed, common SnA 35 (°bhatta; or is it "fermented," and thus to be taken to No. 3?); ā° unusual, new, uncommon J II.435 (where it is comb[d] with abhinava, which should be substituted for readings accuṇha, abbhuṇha & abhiṇha according to similar expl[n] of paccaggha at PvA 87), with v. l. samparivāsita (well-seasoned?). — 2. a probationer Vin II.162. In this meaning usually spelt pāri° (q. v.). — 3. in comb[n] cira° (with ref. to food) it may be interpreted either as "staying long, being in use for a long time," i. e. stale; or it may be derived fr. vāsa[3] (odour, perfume or seasoning) and translated (so Mrs. Rh. D. in *Expositor* 63, 64) "long-fermented" (better "seasoned"?) DhsA 48 (°vāsika & vāsiya); ThA 29.

Parivāsita (adj.) [pari+pp. of vāseti fr. vāsa[3]] perfumed (all round) J I.51 (v. l °vārita); cp. samparivāsita (well-seasoned?), which is perhaps to be read at J II.435 for aparivāsika.

Parivitakka [pari+vitakka, cp. BSk. parivitarka Divy 291] reflection, meditation, thought, consideration M II.170 (ākāra°), Vin II.74; S II.115 (id.); A II.193 (id.); Miln 13; DhA II.62; DhsA 74; VvA 3; PvA 282 (vutta-°e nipāta in expl[n] of nūna). Usually in phrase cetasā ceto-parivitakka mental reflection, e. g. D I.117; II.218; S I.121, 178; III.96; V.294; A III.374; and cetaso-parivitakka, e. g. D I.134; S I.71, 103, 139; II.273; III.96, 103; IV.105; V.167; A II.20.

Parivitakkita [pp. of parivitakketi] reflected, meditated, thought over M I.32; S I.193. — nt. °ŋ reflection, thinking over PvA 123 (°e with ref. to nūna, i. e. particle of reflection).

Parivitakketi [pari+vitakkcti] to consider, reflect, meditate upon J III.277. — pp. °vitakkita (q. v.).

Parivitthiṇṇa [pari+vitthiṇṇa, Sk. vistīrṇa, pp., of vi+stṛ] spread out wide Miln 99.

Parivisaka (adj.) [fr. parisati] providing, serving food Vism 108.

Parivisati [pari+viś, viveṣṭi; same use of parivise (inf.) in R.V. x.61[10]] to serve (with food=instr.), wait upon, present, offer Vin I.240 (bhattena); II.77 (kaṇājakena bilangadutiyena); D II.127; J I.87, 90; II.277; IV.116; Pv II.8[4] (=bhojeti PvA 107); II.8[8] (id. 109); Vism 108, 150 (sūdo bhattāraŋ p.); VvA 6; PvA 42, 78.

Parivīmaŋsati [pari+vīmaŋsati, Desid. of pari+**man**, cp. vīmaŋsā for mīmāŋsā] to think over, consider thoroughly, examine, search S II.80 sq.; It 42 =Sn 975 (ppr. dhammaŋ °vīmaŋsamāna, cp. Nd[1] 508); DA I.134; DhA IV.117 (attānaŋ).

Parivīmaŋsā (f.) [pari+vīmaŋsā] complete inquiry, thorough search or examination M III.85; S III.331; V.68; SnA 173.

Parivuṭṭha & °**vuttha** [pp. of parivasati] staying (a period), living (for a time), spending (or having spent) one's probation (cp. BSk. paryuṣita-parivāsa AvŚ I.259) Vin III.186 (tth); S II.21 (ṭṭh).

Parivuta [pp. of pari+**vṛ**] surrounded by (-° or instr.) S I.177; J I.152 (miga-gaṇa°), 203 (devagaṇena); II.127 (dāsi-gaṇa°); III.371 (mahā-jana°); VI.75; Vv 16[6] (=samantato p. VvA 81); PvA 3 (dhutta-jana°), 62 (parijana°), 140 (deva-gaṇa°).

Pariveṭhita [pp. of pari+**veṣṭ**] enveloped, covered Miln 22. Opp. **nibbeṭṭhita** (q. v.).

Pariveṇa (nt.) [etym. ?] 1. all that belongs to a castle, a mansion and its constituents Vv 84[53] (expl[d] at VvA 351 as follows: veṇiyato pekkhitabbato pariveṇaŋ pāsāda-kūṭâgāra-ratti-ṭṭhān' ādisampannaŋ pākāra-parikkhittaŋ dvārakoṭṭhaka-yuttaŋ āvāsaŋ); DhA I.260 (pāsāda°). — 2. a cell or private chamber for a bhikkhu (cp. *Vin. Texts* III.109, 203) Vin I.49 =II.210 (p. koṭṭhaka upaṭṭhāna-sālā); I.216 (vihārena vihāraŋ pariveṇena pariveṇaŋ upasankamitvā), 247 (id.); II.167 (vihāra+); III.69, 119 (susammaṭṭhaŋ); IV.52, 252 (°vāsika); J I.126; Miln 15 (°ŋ sammajjati), 19; Vism 90; DhA II.179 (°dvāra); IV.204; VbhA 13.

Pariveṇi (f.) =pariveṇa 2; Vin I.80 (anu pariveṇiyaŋ each in their own cell), 106 (id.).

Parivesaka (adj.) [fr. pari+**viṣ**] waiting, serving up meals Vism 109. — f. °ikā ThA 17.

Parivesanā (f.) [fr. pari+vis] distribution of food, feeding, serving meals Vin I.229; S I.172; Sn p. 13 (=bhatta-vissagga SnA 140); Miln 247, 249; DhA IV.162; PvA 109 (°ṭṭhāna), 135 (id.).

Parivyatta (adj.) [pari+vyatta] quite conspicuous or clear Vism 162.

Parisaŋsibbita [pari+pp. of saŋsibbati] sewn together, entwined DhA III.198 (v. l. for saŋsibbita+).

Parisakkati [pari+sakkati] to go about to (with inf. or dat.), to endeavour, undertake, try Vin II.18 =A IV.345 (alābhāya); J I.173 (vadhāya); II.394; Pv IV.5[2] (=payogaŋ karoti PvA 259).

Parisankati [pari+sankati] to suspect, fear, have apprehension J III.210, 541; DhA I.81. — pp. °sankita (q. v.). Cp. āsankati.

Parisankā (f.) [fr. pari+**śank**] suspicion, misgiving Vin IV.314; D III.218. Cp. āsankā.

Parisankita [pp. of parisankati] suspecting or suspected, having apprehensions, fearing Vin II.243 (diṭṭha-suta°); A III.128; J IV.214; V.80; Miln 372; DhA I.223 (āsankita°). — Cp. āsankita & ussankita.

Parisanku in °patha the region round the path of stakes & sticks, N. of a path leading up to Gijjha-pabbata (see expl[n] at J III.485) J III.484.

Parisangāhāpeti [pari+Caus. of sanganhāti] to induce someone to mention or relate something J VI.328.

Parisaṭha (adj.) [pari+saṭha] very fraudulent or crafty Pug 23 (saṭha+).

Parisaṇṭhāti [pari+saṇṭhāti] to return into the former state, to be restored; aor. °saṇṭhāsi J III.341.

Parisaṇha (adj.) [pari+saṇha] very smooth or soft Miln 198.

Parisandeti [pari+Caus. of **syad**] to make flow round, to make overflow, to fill, in phrase kāyaŋ abhisandeti p. D I.75, 214; M III.92 sq. etc. expl[d] as "samantato sandeti" at DA I.217. — pp. parisanna (q. v.).

Parisanna [pp. of parisandati, cp. parisandeti] surrounded or filled with water, drenched, well-watered D I.75 = M III.94.

Parisappati [pari+**sṛp**] to run about, crawl about, to be frightened Dh 342, 343 (=saŋsappati bhāyati DhA IV.49).

Parisappanā (f.) [fr. parisappati] running about, fear, hesitation, doubt, always comb[d] with āsappanā and only found with ref. to the exegesis of "doubt" (vicikicchā or kankhā) Nd[2] 1; Dhs 425 (cp. Dhs trsl. 116 and DhsA 260); DA I.69.

Parisamantato (adv.) [pari+samantato] from all sides VvA 236.

Parisambāhati [pari+sambāhati] to stroke, to rub from all sides M II.120; S I.178, 194; A V.65.

Parisarati [pari+**smṛ**, but according to Kern, *Toev.* s. v. pari here fr. Prk. paḍi=Sk. prati, thus for pratismarati] to remember, recollect J VI.199 (read parissaraŋ).

Parisahati [pari+sahati] to overcome, conquer, master, get the better of S IV.112; exegetically in formula sahati p. abhibhavati ajjhottharati etc. Nd[1] 12, 361 =Nd[2] 420.

Parisā (f.) [cp. Vedic pariṣad; in R.V. also pariṣad as adj. surrounding, lit. "sitting round," fr. pari+**sad**. — In Pāli the cons. stem has passed into a vocalic ā-stem, with the only preservation of cons. loc. sg. parisati Vin IV.285; A II.180 (i); J V.61; DA I.141 and parisatiŋ M I.68; A II.180 (v. l.); J V.332, besides the regular forms parisāyaŋ (loc. sg.) Vin II.296; A V.70; and parisāsu (loc. pl.) S II.27; It 64] surrounding people, group, collection, company, assembly, association, multitude. Var. typical sets of assemblies are found in the Canon, viz., *eight* assemblies (khattiya°, brāhmaṇa°, gahapati°, samaṇa°, Cātummahārājika°, Tāvatiŋsa°, Māra°, Brahma°, or the assemblies of nobles, brahmins, householders, wanderers, of the angel hosts of the Guardian Kings, of the Great Thirty-Three, of the Māras, and of the Brahmās) D II.109; III.260; M I.72; A IV.307. — *four* assemblies (the first four of the above) at D III.236; Nd[1] 163; other four, representing the Buddha's Order (bhikkhu°, bhikkhunī°, upāsaka°, upāsikā°, or the ass. of bhikkhus, nuns, laymen and female devotees; cp. same enum[n] at Divy 299) S II.218; A V.10; cp. J I.40 (catu-parisa-majjhe), 85 (id.), 148 (id.). — *two* assemblies (viz. Brahma°, Māra°) at D III.260; allegorically two groups of people (viz. sāratta-rattā & asāratta-rattā)

M II.160 = A I.70 sq. — For var. uses of the word see the foll. passages: Vin II.188, 296 (rājaparisā); III.12 (Bhagavā mahatiyā parisāya parivuto surrounded by a great multitude); IV.153 (gen. parisāya); M I.153 (nevāpika°); II.160; III.47; S I.155 (brahma°), 162 sarājikā p.), 177; A I.25 (mahā°), 70 (uttānā p.), 71 (ariya°), 242 (tisso p.); II.19 (°āya mando), 133, 183, 185 (deva°); III.253 (khattiya°); IV.80, 114; It 64 (upāsakā °sāsu virocare); Sn 349, 825 sq.; J I.151, 264; VI.224 (omissaka°); Pv III.9[6]; Miln 187, 249, 359 (38 rāja-parisā, or divisions of the royal retinue); PvA 2, 6, 12, 21, 78 and passim; Sdhp 277. saparisa together with the assembly Vin IV.71; adv. °ŋ ThA 69. — *Note*. The form of parisā as first part of a cpd. is parisa° (= *parisad, which latter is restored in cpd. parisaggata = *parisad-gata). — See also pārisagga.

-antare within the assembly J III.61. **-âvacara** one who moves in the society, i. e. the Brotherhood of the Bhikkhus A IV.314; V.10. **-gata (ggata)** having entered a company Sn 397 (= pūga-majjha-gata SnA 377); Pug 29. **-ññū** knowing the assembly A III.148; IV.113 (+ kālaññū puggalaññū), cp. D III.252. **-dussana** defilement of the Assembly A II.225 (opp. °sobhaṇā). **-pariyanta** the outer circle of the congregation DhA I.67; III.172. **-majjhe** in the midst of the assembly J I.267; II.352; PvA 11. **-sārajja** being afraid of the a. Miln 196 = Nd[2] 470 (so read for parisārajja).

Parisiñcati [pari + siñcati] to sprinkle all over, to bathe M I.161; S I.8 (gattāni); Sdhp 595.

Parisibbita [pp. of pari + sibbati] sewn round, bordered Vin I.186; J V.377.

Parisukkha (adj.) [pari + sukkha] dried up, very dry J I.215 (of fields); Miln 302 (of the heart); PvA 64 (°sarīra).

Parisukkhita [pp. of pari + śukṣ. Intens. of śuṣ] dried up, withered Miln 303 (°hadaya).

Parisujjhati [Pass. of pari + śudh] to become clear or clean, to be purified S I.214; Sn 183, 184. — pp. parisuddha (q. v.).

Parisuddha (adj.) [pari + pp. of śudh] clean, clear, pure, perfect Vin II.237; M I.26; III.11; S II 199 (°dhammadesanā); III.235; V.301, 354; A III.125 (°ñāṇa-dassana); IV.120 sq.; J I.265; Vism 2 (accanta°); Pug 68 (samāhite citte parisuddha); Miln 106; DA I.177, 219; SnA 445 (apanetabbassa abhāvato niddosa-bhāvena p.); PvA 44, 70. Very freq. comb[d] with pariyodāta (q. v.). — aparisuddha unclean Vin II.236, M I.17.

-ājīva (adj.) of pure livelihood D I.63 (see DA I.181); A III.124 (cp. pārisuddhi).

Parisuddhatta (nt.) [abstr. fr. parisuddha] purity, cleanliness, perfection M I.36; Miln 103 sq.; Vism 168. — As f. pari-suddhatā at Vism 30.

Parisuddhi (f.) [fr. pari + śudh] purity, purification S I.169. The usual spelling is pārisuddhi (q. v.).

Parisumbhati [pari + sumbhati] to strike, hit, throw down J III.347 (= paharati C.); VI.370, 376 (id. C.).

Parisumbhana (nt.) [fr. pari + śumbh] throwing down J VI.508 (bhūmiyā p.).

Parisussati [pari + sussati] to dry quite up, waste quite away J II.5, 339, 437. — Caus. parisoseti (q. v.).

Parisussana (nt.) [fr. pari + śuṣ] drying up completely, withering J V.97.

Parisedita [pp. of pari + Caus. of svid, Sk. parisvedita in slightly diff. use] heated, hatched, made ripe M I.104 (bījāni); S III.153; Vin III.3; A IV. 125 (aṇḍāni), 176.

Parisesa [pari + sesa] remnant, remainder, rest; only neg. aparisesa (adj.) without remainder, complete, entire M I.92, 110; A III.166 = Pug 64; A IV.428 (°ñāṇadassana).

Parisoka [pari + soka] great grief, severe mourning Ps I.38 (anto° in def. of soka).

Parisodhana (nt.) [fr. parisodheti] cleansing, purification Miln 215.

Parisodhita [pp. of parisodheti] cleaned, cleansed, purified Miln 415; Sdhp 414.

Parisodheti [pari + Caus. of śudh] to cleanse, clean, purify M III.3, 35 (aor. °sodhesi); Sn 407 (aor. °sodhayi); DhA II.162 (vodapeti +). — Freq. in phrase cittaŋ p. to cleanse one's heart (from = abl.) D III.49; S IV.104; A II.211; III.92; Nd[1] 484; Pug 68. — pp. parisodhita (q. v.).

Parisosa [fr. pari + śuṣ] becoming dried up, dryness, withering away S I.91.

Parisosita [pp. of parisoseti] dried up, withered away Sdhp 9.

Parisoseti [Caus. of parisussati] to make dry up, to exhaust, make evaporate (water) Miln 389. — pp. parisosita (q. v.).

Parissañjati (°ssajati ?) [pari + svaj] to embrace, enfold, J I.466; VI.150 (°itvā, v. l. °ssajitvā & palisajjitvā).

Parissanta [pp. of parissamati] tired, fatigued, exhausted Pv II.9[36]; VvA 305; Sdhp 9, 101.

Parissama [fr. pari + śram] fatigue, toil, exhaustion, VvA 289, 305 (addhāna° from journeying); PvA 3, 43, 113, 127.

Parissaya (m. & nt.) [fr. pari + śri ? Etym. doubtful, cp. Weber, *Ind. Streifen* III.395 and Andersen, *Pāli Reader* II.167, 168] danger, risk, trouble M I.10 (utu°); A III.388 (id.); Sn 42, 45, 770, 921, 960 sq.; Dh 328 (°ayāni = sīha-vyaggh'-ādayo pākaṭa-parissaye, rāga-bhaya-dosa-bhay' ādayo paṭicchanna-parissaye DhA IV.29); Nd[1] 12 = Nd[2] 420 (where same division into pākaṭa° & paṭicchanna°); Nd[1] 360, 365; J I.418; II.405; V.315, 441 (antarāmagga p. cp. paripantha in same use); Vism 34 (utu°); SnA 88 (expl[d] as paricca sayanti ti p.); DhA III.199 (°mocana); PvA 216, DhsA 330.

Parissâvana (nt.) [fr. pari + Caus. of sru] a water strainer, filter (one of the requisites of a bhikkhu) Vin I.209, II.119 and passim; J I.198; III.377; Nd[1] 226; DhA III.260 (udaka°); VvA 40, 63; Sdhp 593.

Parissâvanaka (adj.-n.) [fr. parissâvana] only neg. a°: 1. one who has no strainer Vin II.119; J I.198. — 2. not to be filtered, i. e. so that there is nothing left to be filtered J I.400 (so read for °ssavanaka). Or is it "not overflowing"?

Parissâvita [pp. of parissâveti] strained, filtered J I.198 (udaka).

Parissâveti [Caus. of pari + sru] to strain or filter J I.198 (pāniyaŋ); DA I.206 (udakaŋ); III.207 (pāniyaŋ). — pp. parissāvita (q. v.).

Parissuta [pp. of pari + sru] overflowing J VI.328 (= atipuṇṇattā pagharamāna).

Parihaṭa (°hata) [pp. of pariharati] surrounded by (-°) encircled; only in phrase sukha-parihaṭa (+ sukhe ṭhita) steeped in good fortune Vin III.13 (corr. sukhedhita accordingly!); J II.190 (pariharaka v. l. BB); VI.219 (= sukhe ṭhita).

Parihaṭṭha [pp. of pari + hṛṣ] gladdened, very pleased PvA 13.

Parihāraka (adj. n.) [fr. pari + hṛ] 1. surrounding or surrounded, having on one's hands J II.190 (sukha°, v. l. for °parihaṭa) — 2. an armlet, bracelet VvA 167 (v. l. °haraṇa; expl^d as hatthâlankāra.) See also parihāraka.

Pariharaṇa (nt.) [fr. pari + hṛ] 1. protection, care Vism 500 (gabbha°); KhA 235; DA 1.207 (kāya°); DhA II.179 (kāyassa). — 2. keeping up, preservation, keeping in existence; in phrase khandha° DhA III.261, 405. Cp. foll.

Pariharaṇā (f.) [= pariharaṇa] 1. keeping up, preserving, care, attention, pleasure PvA 219 (with v. l. °caraṇā; for paricārikā Pv IV.1^12). — 2. keeping secret, guarding, hiding, deceiving Vbh 358 = Pug 23.

Pariharati [pari + hṛ] 1. to take care of, to attend to (acc.), shelter, protect, keep up, preserve, look after Vin I.42; II.188; D II.100 (sanghaŋ); D II.14 (gabbhaŋ kucchinā); M I.124, 459; S III.1; A III.123; J I.52 (kucchiyā), 143, 170; Miln 392, 410 (attānaŋ) 418; SnA 78; DhA II.232 (aggiŋ, v. l. paricarati, which is the usual); PvA 63 (kucchiyā), 177. Cp. BSk. pariharati in same meaning e. g. AvŚ I.193, 205. — 2. to carry about D II.19 (ankena); M I.83; Sn 440 (muñjaŋ parihare, 1 sg. pres. med.; SnA 390 takes it as parihareyya); Miln 418 (āḷakaŋ p.). — 3. (intrs.) to move round, go round, circle, revolve M I.328; A I.277 (candima-suriyā p.; cp. A V.59) = Vism 205; J I.395; IV.378; VI.519; DA I.85; PvA 204. — 4. to conceal Vin III.52 (sunkaŋ). — 5. to set out, take up, put forward, propose, only in phrase (Com. style) uttān' atthāni padāni p. to take up the words in more explicit meaning SnA 178, 419, 437, 462. — pp. parihaṭa. Pass. parihīrati (q. v.). — See also anupariharati.

Pariharitabbatta (nt.) [abstr. fr. grd. of pariharati] necessity of guarding Vism 98.

Parihasati [pari + has] to laugh at, mock, deride J I.457. — Caus. parihāseti to make laugh J V.297.

Parihāna (nt.) [fr. pari + hā] diminution, decrease, wasting away, decay S II.206 sq.; A II.40 (abhabbo parihānāya), III.173, 309, 329 sq., 404 sq. (°dhamma); V.103 (id.), 156 sq.; It 71 (°āya saŋvattati); Dh 32 (abhabbo p. °āyo); Pug 12, 14.

Parihāni (f.) [fr. pari + hā] loss, diminution (opp. vuddhi) S II.206; IV.76, 79; V.143, 173; A I.15; III.76 sq.; IV.288; V.19 sq., 96, 124 sq.; J II.233; DhA III.335; IV.185.

Parihāniya (adj.) [parihāna + ya] connected with or causing decay or loss D II.75 sq. (°ā dhammā conditions leading to ruin); A IV.16 sq.; Vbh 381; VbhA 507 sq. — a° S V.85.

Parihāpeti [Caus. of parihāyati] 1. to let fall away, to lose, to waste S II.29; J IV.214 (vegaŋ); Miln 244 (cittaŋ to lose heart, to despair); PvA 78. — 2. to set aside, abandon, neglect, omit Vin I.72 (rājakiccaŋ); J II.438; IV.132 (vaṭṭaŋ); V.46; Miln 404 (mūlakammaŋ). — Neg. ger. aparihāpetvā without omission DhsA 168; ppr. aparihāpento not slackening or neglecting Vism 122.

Parihāyati [pari + hā] to decay, dwindle or waste away, come to ruin; to decrease, fall away from, lack; to be inferior, deteriorate Vin I.5; M III.46 sq. (opp. abhivaḍḍhati); S I.120, 137; III.125; IV.76 sq.; A III.252; Dh 364; Sn 767; J II.197; IV.108; Nd¹ 5 (paridhaŋsati +) Miln 249 (id.); Pug 12 (read °hāyeyya for °hāreyya); SnA 167 (+ vinassati); PugA 181 (nassati +); PvA 5, 76 (v. l.), 125 (°hāyeyyuŋ). — pp. parihīna, Pass. parihiyyati, Caus. parihāpeti (q. v.).

Parihāra [fr. pari + hṛ, cp. pariharati] 1. attention, care (esp. -°), in cpds. like gabbha° care of the fœtus DhA I.4; dāraka° care of the infant J II.20; kumāra° looking after the prince J I.148, II.48; DhA I.346; dup° hard to protect J I.437; Vism 95 (Majjhimo d. hard to study?) — 2. honour, privilege, dignity Vin I.71; J IV.306 (gārava°). — 3. surrounding (lit.), circuit of land J IV.461. — 4. surrounding (fig.), attack; in cpd. visama° being attacked by adversities A II.87; Nd² 304^1c; Miln 112, 135. — 5. avoidance, keeping away from J I.186.

-patha "circle road," i. e. (1) a roundabout way DhA II.192. (2) encircling game D I.6 = Vin II.10 (expl^d as "bhūmiyaŋ nānāpathaŋ maṇḍalaŋ katvā tattha pariharitabbaŋ pariharantānaŋ kīḷanaŋ" DA I.85; trsl^d as "keeping going over diagrams" *Dial.* I.10, with remark "a kind of primitive hop-scotch").

Parihāraka (adj.-n.) [fr. pari + hṛ] surrounding, encircling; a guard A II.180.

Parihārika [fr. parihāra] keeping, preserving, protecting, sustaining D I.71 (kāya° cīvara, kucchi° piṇḍapāta; expl^d as kāya-pariharaṇa-mattakena & kucchi° at DA I.207; correct reading accordingly); M I.180; III.34; Pug 58; Vism 65 (kāya°, of āvara).

Parihārin (adj.) [fr. parihāra] taking care of, (worth) keeping S IV.316 (udaka-maṇika).

Parihāsa [fr. pari + has, cp. parihasati] laughter, laughing at, mockery J I.116 (°keḷi), 377; DhA I.244.

Parihāsiŋsu at J I.384 is to be read ° bhāsiŋsu.

Parihiyyati [Pass. of parihāyati, Sk. °hīyate] to be left, to be deserted, to come to ruin (= dhaŋsati) J III.260.

Parihīna [pp. of parihāyati] fallen away from, decayed; deficient, wanting; dejected, destitute S I.121; A III.123; Sn 827, 881 (°pañña); J I.112, 242; IV.260; Nd¹ 166, 289; Miln 249, 281 (a°); PvA 220 (= nihīna).

Parihīnaka (adj.) [parihīna + ka] one who has fallen short of, neglected in, done out of (abl. or instr.) D I.103.

Parihīrati [Pass. of pariharati, Sk. parihriyate in development °hriyate > *hiriyati > *hiyirati > °hīrati] to be carried about (or better "taken care of," according to Bdhgh's expl^n SnA 253; see also *Brethren* 226) Sn 205 = Th I, 453.

Parīta see vi°.

Parūpa° as para + upa° (in parūpakkama, parūpaghāta etc.) see under para.

Parūḷha (adj.) [pp. of pa + ruh, cp. BSk. prarūḍha (-śmaśru) Jtm 210] grown, grown long, mostly in phrase °kaccha-nakha-loma having long nails, & long hair in the armpit, e. g. at S I.78; Ud 65; J IV.362, 371; VI.488; Miln 163 (so read for p.-kaccha-loma); Sdhp 104. — Kern, *Toev.* II.139 s. v. points out awkwardness of this phrase and suspects a distortion of kaccha either from kesa or kaca, i. e. with long hairs (of the head), nails & other hair. — Further in foll. phrases: mukhaŋ p. bearded face J IV.387; °kesa-nakha-loma J I.303; °kesa-massu with hair & beard grown long J IV.159; °kaccha with long grass J VI.100; °massu-dāṭhika having grown a beard and tooth DA I.263.

Pare (adv.) see para 2 c.

Pareta [pp. of pareti, more likely para + i than pari + i, although BSk. correspondent is parīta, e. g. śoka-parīta Jtm 31^91] gone on to, affected with, overcome by (-°), syn. with abhibhūta (e. g. PvA 41, 80). Very frequent in comb^n with terms of suffering, misadventure and passion, e. g. khudā°, ghamma°, jighacchā°, dukkha°, dosa°, rāga°, soka°, sneha°, Vin I.5; D II.36; M I.13, 114, 364, 460; III.14, 92; S II.110; III.93; IV.28; A I.147 = It 89; A III.25, 96; Sn 449, 736, 818 (= samohita samannāgata pibita Nd¹ 149) 1092, 1123; J III.157; Pv I.8⁶; II.2⁴; Miln 248; PvA 61, 93.

Pareti [in form = parā + i but more likely pari + i, thus = pariyeti] to set out for, go on to, come to (acc.) S II.20; A V.2, 139 sq., 312; J V.401 (= pakkhandati C.). pp. pareta (q. v.).

Paro (adv.) [cp. Vedic paras; to para] beyond, further, above, more than, upwards of; only °- in connection with *numerals* (cp. Vedic use of paras with acc. of numerals), e.g. paropaññāsa more than 50 D II.93; parosataŋ more than 100 J V.203, 497; parosahassaŋ over 1,000 D II.16; S I.192 = Th 1, 1238; Sn p. 106 (= atireka-sahassaŋ SnA 450). See also parakkaroti.

Parokkha (adj.) [paro + akkha = Vedic parokṣa (paraḥ + akṣa)] beyond the eye, out of sight, invisible, imperceptible, Miln 291. — abl. parokkhā (adv.) behind one's back, in the absence of J III.89 (parammukhā C.; opp. sammukhā).

Parodati [pa + **rud**] to cry out (for) J I.166; PvA 16, 257.

Paropariya (°ñāṇa) see under indriya°. The form is paro + pariya, paro here taking the place of para. Yet it would be more reasonable to explain the word as para + apara (upara ?) + ya, i. e. that which belongs to this world & the beyond, or everything that comes within the range of the faculties. Cp. parovara.

Parovara (adj.-n.) [para + avara, sometimes through substitution of apa for ava also paropara. We should expect a form *parora as result of contraction: see Nd² p. 13] high & low, far & near; pl. in sense of "all kinds" (cp. uccâvaca). The word is found only in the Sutta Nipāta, viz. Sn 353 (v. l. BB varāvaraŋ, varovaraŋ; expl^d as "lokuttara-lokiya-vasena sundar' âsundaraŋ dūre-santikaŋ vā" SnA 350), 475 (°ā dhammā; v. l. BB paroparā; expl^d as "parâvarā sundar' âsundarā, parā vā bāhirā aparā ajjhattikā" SnA 410), 704 (kāme parovare; v. l. BB paropare; expl^d as sundare ca asundare ca pañca kāmaguṇe" SnA 493), 1048 (reading paroparāni Nd²; see expl^n Nd² 422^b; expl^d as "parāni ca orāni ca, par' atta-bhāva-sak' attabhāv' ādīni parāni ca orāni ca" SnA 590), 1148 (paroparaŋ Nd²; see Nd² 422^d; expl^d as "hīna-ppaṇītaŋ" SnA 607). — *Note.* Already in RV. we find para contrasted with avara or upara; para denoting the farther, higher or heavenly sphere, avara or upara the lower or earthly sphere: see e. g. RV. I.128, 3; I.164, 12. — On paropara see further Wackernagel, *Altind. Gr.* II.121 d.

Pala (-°) [classical Sk. pala] a certain weight (or measure), spelt also phala (see phala²), only in cpd. sata° a hundred (carat) in weight Th 1, 97 (of kaŋsa); J VI.510 (sata-phala kaŋsa = phalasatena katā kañcana-pātī C.). Also in comb^n catuppala - tippala - dvipala - ekapala - sāḷikā Vism 339.

Palaka [cp. late Sk. pala, flesh, meat] a species of plant J VI.564.

Palagaṇḍa [cp. Sk. palagaṇḍa Halāyudha II.436; BSk. palagaṇḍa AvŚ I.339; Aṣṭas. Pār. 231; Avad. Kalp. II.113] a mason, bricklayer, plasterer M I.119; S III.154 (the reading phala° is authentic, see Geiger, *P.G.* § 40); A V.127.

Palaṇḍuka [cp. Epic Sk. palāṇḍu, pala (white) + aṇḍu (= aṇḍa ? egg)] an onion Vin IV.259.

Paladdha [pp. of pa + **labh**] taken over, "had," overcome, deceived M I.511 (nikata vañcita p. where v. l. and id. p. S IV.307 however reads paluddha); J III.260 (dava° = abhibhūta C.).

Palapati [pa + lapati] to talk nonsense J II.322. Cp. vi°.

Palambati [pa + lambati] to hang down ThA 210; Sdhp 110. — pp. palambita (q. v.). See also abhi°.

Palambita [pp. of palambati] hanging down Th 2, 256, 259; ThA 211.

Palambheti [pa + lambheti] to deceive D I.50, cp. DA I.151.

Palaḷita [pa + laḷita] led astray S IV.197 (v. l. °lāḷita). At A III.5 we read palāḷita, in phrase kāmesu p. ("sporting in pleasures"? Or should we read palolita ?).

Palavati [Vedic plavati, **plu**] to float, swim Vin IV.112; Dh 334; Th 1, 399; J III.190.

Palasata [according to Trenckner, *Notes* p. 59, possibly fr. Sk. parasvant] a rhinoceros J VI.277 (v. l. phalasata; expl^d as "khagga-miga," with gloss "balasata"); as phalasata at J VI.454 (expl^d as phalasata-camma C.). See palāsata.

Palahati [pa + lahati] to lick Pv III.5² = PvA 198.

Palāta [contracted form of palāyita, pp. of palāyati, cp. Prk. palāa (= *palāta) Pischel, *Prk. Gr.* § 567] run away J VI.369; Vism 326; VvA 100; DhA II.21.

Palātatta (nt.) [abstr. fr. palāta] running away, escape J I.72.

Palāpa¹ [Vedic palāva, cp. Lat. palea, Russ pelëva; see also Geiger, *P.Gr.* § 39⁶, where pralāva is to be corr. to palāva] chaff of corn, pollard A IV.169 (yava°); J. I.467, 468; IV.34; SnA 165 (in exegesis of palāpa²; v. l. BB palāsa), 312 (id.); J IV.34, 35 (perhaps better to read kula-palāso & palāsa-bhūta for palāpa).

Palāpa² [Vedic pralāpa, pa + **lap**; taken by P. Com. as identical with palāpa¹, their example followed by Trenckner, *Notes* 63, cp. also *Miln. trsl.* II.363 "chaff as frivolous talk"] prattling, prattle, nonsense; adj. talking idly, chaffing, idle, void M III.80 (a°); S I.166 (not palapaŋ), 192 = Th 1, 1237; A IV.169 (samaṇa° in allegory with yava° of palāpa¹); Sn 89 (māyāvin asaŋyata palāpa = palāpa-sadisattā SnA 165), 282 = Miln 414 (here also expl^d as palāpa¹ by SnA 312); VbhA 104. In phrase tuccha palāpa empty and void at Miln 5, 10.

Palāpin in apalāpin "not neglectful" see palāsin.

Palāpeti¹ [Caus. of palāyati] to cause to run away, to put to flight, drive away J II.433; DhA I.164, 192; III.206.

Palāpeti² [Caus. of pa + **lap**, cp. palāpa to which it may be referred as Denom.] to prattle, talk J I.73, 195.

Palāyati [cp. Vedic palāyati, **palāy**] to run (away) Vin III.145 (ubbijjati uttasati p.); A II.33 (yena vā tena vā palayanti); Sn 120; J II.10; DhA I.193; PvA 253, 284 (= dhāvati). — ppr. palāyanto S I.209 = Th 2, 248 = Pv II.7¹⁷ = Nett 131 = DhA IV.21; aor. palāyi S I.219; J I.208; II.209, 219, 257; IV.420; DhA III.208; DA I.142; PvA 4, 274; ger. palāyitvā J I.174; PvA 154; inf. palāyituŋ J I.202; VI.420. — Contracted forms are: pres. paleti (see also the analogy-form pāleti under pāleti, to guard) D I.54 (spelt phaleti, expl^d DA I.165 by gacchati); Sn 1074, 1144 (= vajati gacchati Nd² 423); Dh 49; Nd¹ 172; J V.173, 241; Vv 84³⁶ (= gacchati VvA 345); Pv I.11¹ (gacchati PvA 56); aor. palittha J V.255; fut. palehiti Th 1, 307; imper. palehi Sn 831 (= gaccha SnA 542) — pp. palāta & palāyita; Caus. palāpeti¹ (q. v.).

Palāyana (nt.) [fr. **palāy**] running away DhA I.164. See also pālana.

Palāyanaka (adj.) [fr. **palāy**] running away J II.210 (°ŋ karoti to put to flight).

Palāyin (adj.) [fr. **palāy**] running away, taking to flight S I.221 = 223. — Usually neg. apalāyin S I.185, and in phrase abhīru anutrāsin apalāyin S I.99; Th I, 864; J IV.296 and passim. See **apalāyin** & **apalāsin.**

Palāla (m. & nt.) [cp. Ved. & Epic Sk. palāla] straw J I.488; DhA I.69.
-channaka a roof of thatch Th I, 208. -piṇḍa a bundle of straw Vism 257 = KhA 56. -pīṭhaka "straw foot-stool," a kind of punishment or torture M I.87 = A II.122 = Miln 197 (see *Miln trsl.* I.277 "Straw Seat," i. e. being so beaten with clubs, that the bones are broken, and the body becomes like a heap of straw); Nd[1] 154; Nd[2] 604; J V.273. -puñja a heap of straw D I.71; M III.3; A I.241; II.210; Pug 68; VbhA 367. -puñjaka same as puñja Miln 342.

Palāḷita see palaḷita.

Palāsa[1] (m. & nt.) [Vedic palāśa] I. the tree Butea frondosa or Judas tree J III.23 (in Palāsa Jātaka). — 2. a leaf; collectively (nt.) foliage, pl. (nt.) leaves S II.178; J I.120 (nt.); III.210, 344; PvA 63 (°antare; so read for pās' antare), 113 (ghana°), 191 (sāli°). puppha° blossoms & leaves DhA I.75; sākhā° branches & leaves M I.111; J I.164; Miln 254; paṇḍu° a sear leaf Vin I.96; III.47; IV.217; bahala° (adj.) thick with leaves J I.57. —palāsāni (pl.) leaves J III.185 (= palāsapaṇṇāni C.); PvA 192 (= bhūsāni).

Palāsa[2] & (more commonly) **Paḷāsa** [according to Trenckner, *Notes* 83, from **ras**, but BSk. pradāśa points to pa + **dāśa** = **dāsa** "enemy" this form evidently a Sanskritisation] unmercifulness, malice, spite. Its nearest synonym is **yuga-ggāha** (so Vbh 357; Pug 18, where yuddhaggāha is read; J III.259; VvA 71); it is often comb[d] with **macchera** (Vv 15[5]) and **makkha** (Miln 289). — M I.15, 36, 488; A I.79; J II.198; Vbh 357; Pug 18 (+ paḷāsāyanā, etc.). —**apaḷāsa** mercifulness M I.44.

Palāsata [so read for **palasata** & **palasada**; cp. Vedic parasvant given by BR. in meaning "a certain large animal, perhaps the wild ass"] a rhinoceros J V.206, 408; VI.277.

Palāsika (adj.) [fr. palāsa[1]] I. in cpd. paṇḍu° one who lives by eating withered leaves DA I.270, 271. —2. in cpd. eka° (upāhanā) (a shoe) with one lining (i. e. of leaves) Vin I.185 (= eka paṭala Bdhgh; see *Vin. Texts* II.13).

Palāsin (paḷāsin) (adj.) [fr. palāsa[2]] spiteful, unmerciful, malicious M I.43 sq., 96; A III.111; comb[d] with makkhin at Vin II.89 (cp. *Vin Texts* III.38); J III.259. apaḷāsin D III.47 (amakkhin +); M I.43; A III.111; Pug 22; see also separately.

Pali° [a variant of pari°, to be referred to the Māgadhī dialect in which it is found most frequently, esp. in the older language, see Pischel, *Prk. Gr.* § 257; Geiger, *P.Gr.* § 44] round, around (= pari) only as prefix in cpds. (q. v.). Often we find both pari° & pali° in the same word.

Palikujjati [pali + kujjati] to bend oneself over, to go crooked M I.387.

Palikuṇṭhita [a var. of paliguṇṭhita, q. v. & cp. Geiger, *P.Gr.* § 39[1]] covered, enveloped, smeared with J II.92 (lohita°).

Palikha [a variant of paligha on kh for gh see Geiger, *P.Gr.* § 39[2]] a bar J VI.276 (with palighā as gloss).

Palikhaṇati [pali + **khaṇ**, cp. parikhā] to dig up, root out S I.123; II.88 (so read for paliŋ° & phali°) = A I.204; ger. palikhañña Sn 968 (= uddharitvā Nd[1] 490); palikhāya S I.123 (cp. KS 320); & palikhaṇitvā S II.88; SnA 573. — pp. palikhata (q. v.).

Palikhata [pp. of palikhaṇati] dug round or out S IV.83 (so read with v. l. for T. palikhita).

Palikhati [pa + **likh**] to scratch, in phrase oṭṭhaŋ p. to bite one's lip J V.434 = DhA IV.197.

Palikhādati [pali + khādati] to bite all round, to gnaw or peck off M I.364 (kukkuro aṭṭhikankalaŋ p.).

Paligijjhati [pali + gijjhati] to be greedy Nd[2] 77 (abhigijjhati +).

Paliguṇṭhita [pali + guṇṭhita, variant palikuṇṭhita, as kuṇṭhita & guṇḍhita are found] entangled, covered, enveloped Sn 131 (mohena; v. l. BB °kuṇṭhita); J II.150 = DhA I.144 (v. l. °kuṇṭh°); IV.56; Miln II. Expl[d] by pariyonaddha J II.150, by paṭicchādita J IV.56. Cp. pāliguṇṭhima.

Paligedha [pali + gedha but acc. to Geiger, *P.Gr.* § 10 = parigṛddha] greed, conceit, selfishness A I.66; Nd[2] taṇhā II (gedha +); Dhs 1059, 1136.

Paligedhin (adj.) [fr. paligedha, but Geiger, *P.Gr.* § 10 takes it as *parigṛddhin, cp. giddhin] conceited, greedy, selfish A III.265.

Paligha [pari + gha of **(g)han**, cp. P. & Sk. parigha] I. a cross-bar Vin II.154; Th 2, 263 (vaṭṭa° = parighadaṇḍa ThA 211); J II.95; VI.276. — 2. an obstacle, hindrance D II.254 = S I.27. — (adj.) (-°) in two phrases: okkhitta° with cross-bars erected or put up D I.105 (= ṭhapita° DA I.274), opp. **ukkhitta°** with cross-bars (i. e. obstacles) withdrawn or removed M I.139 = A III.84 = Nd[2] 284 C.; Sn 622 (= avijjā-palighassa ukkhittattā SnA 467); cp. parikhā.
-parivattika turning round of the bar the "Bar Turn," a kind of punishment or torture (consisting in "a spike being driven from ear to ear he is pinned to the ground" Hardy, *E.M.* 32, cp. *Miln trsl.* I.277) M I.87 = A I.47 = II.122 = Nd[1] 154 = Nd[2] 604 B (reads palingha, v. l. paligha) = Miln 197.

Palita (adj.) [cp. Vedic palita; Gr. πελιτνός, πελιός black-grey; Lith. pilkas grey; Ags. fealu = Ohg. falo, E. fallow, Ger. fahl; also Sk. pāṇḍu whitish; P. paṇḍu, pāṭala pink] grey, in cpd. °kesa with grey (i. e. white) hair M I.88 (f. °kesī); A I.138; J I.59, 79; abs. only at J VI.524. The spelling phalita also occurs (e. g. PvA 153). — Der. pālicca.

Palitta [pp. of palippati] smeared Th 2, 467 (= upalitta ThA 284).

Palipa fr. [pa + **lip**] sloppiness, mud, marsh M I.45; Th I, 89; 2, 291 (= panka ThA 224); J III.241 (read palipo, cp. C. = mahākaddamo ibid.) = IV.480.

Palipatha [for paripatha = °pantha (q. v.), the bases path° & panth° frequently interchanging. Trenckner (*Notes* 80) derives it fr. pa + **lip**] danger, obstacle (or is it "mud, mire" = palipa?) A IV.290; Sn 34 = 638 (= rāga° SnA 469) = Dh 414 (= rāga° DhA IV.194).

Palipadaka see pāli°.

Palipanna [for paripanna, pp. of paripajjati] fallen, got or sunk into (-° or loc.) Vin I.301 (muttakarīse); D II.24 (id.); M I.45 (palipa°) = Nd[2] 651 B; M I.88; J VI.8; Vism 49 (muttakarīse).

Palippati [Med.-Pass. of pa + **lip**; often spelt palimpati] to be smeared; to stick, to adhere to Pv IV.1[5] (°amāna read for palimpamāna). — pp. **palitta** (q. v.).

Palibujjhati see palibuddhati.

Palibujjhana (nt.) [fr. palibujjhati] obstruction DhA III.258.

Palibuddha [pp. of palibujjhati] obstructed, hindered, stopped; being kept back or delayed, tarrying J II.417; Nd² 107 (palivethita+); Miln 388 (ākāso a°) 404; DhA III.198. Often in phrase lagga laggita p. Nd² 88, 107, 332, 596, 597, 657.

Palibuddhati [the etym. offered by Andersen, *Pāli Reader* s. v. palibuddha, viz. dissimilation for pari+ruddhati (**rudh**) is most plausible, other explⁿˢ like Trenckner's (*Notes* 66 for pari+**bādh**, med-pass. bajjhati=*bādhyate, seemingly confirmed by v. l. Nd² 74 & 77 °bajjhati for °bujjhati) and Kern's (*Toev.* s. v.=Ogh. firbiotan, Ger. verbieten) are semantically not satisfactory. Cp. **avaruddhati** & **avaruddha**] 1. to obstruct, refuse, keep back, hinder, withhold Vin II.166; IV.42, 131; J I.217 (cp. paṭibāhati ibid.); III.138 (aor. °buddhi.); IV.159; Miln 263. — 2. to delay Miln 404 (or should we read °bujjhati i. e. sticks, tarries, is prevented ?). — Pass. **palibujjhati** [this word occurs only in Commentary style & late works. In the Niddesa the nearest synonym is **lag**, as seen from the freq. combⁿ palibuddha+lagga, palibodha+laggana: see Nd² p. 188 under nissita] to be obstructed or hindered, to be kept by (instr. or loc.) to stick or adhere to, to trouble about, attend to Nd² 74, 77 (paligijjhati+), 88, 107, 597, 657; Miln 263. — pp. **palibuddha** (q. v.).

Palibodha [see palibuddhati] obstruction, hindrance, obstacle, impediment, drawback J I.148; III.241 (a° non-obstruction), 381 (id.); Nett 80; also in var. phrases, viz. kāma° Nd² 374 (+kāmapariḷāha); kula° cīvara° Nd² 68, cp. Miln 388 (kule p.); ghar'āvāsa°, putta-dāro etc. Nd¹ 136; Nd² 172ᵃ B, 205, cp. J II.95 (ghara°); KhA 39 (enumᵈ as set of dasa **palibodhā** which are also given and explᵈ in detail at Vism 9 sq.); cp. DhsA 168, and in combⁿ **laggana bandhana** p. Nd² 332, 620. *Two* palibodhas are referred to at Vin I.265, viz. āvāsa° and cīvara° (cp. *Vin. Texts* II.157) and *sixteen* at Miln 11. Cp. *Cpd.* 53. — The minor obstacles (to the practice of kammaṭṭhāna) are described as **khuddaka°** at Vism 122 & referred to at DhsA 168. — See also sam°.

Palibhañjana (nt.) [pari+bhañjana] breaking up Nd² 576 (sambhañjana+; v. l. pari°). See also sam° The spelling phali° occurs at ThA 288.

Palimaṭṭha [pp. of pari+**mṛj**] polished J V.4. Cp. **parimaṭṭha**. See also sam°

Palivethana (adj. nt.) [fr. pari+**veṣṭ**] wrapping, surrounding, encircling, encumbrance J IV.436; Pug 34; Vism 353 (°camma); DhsA 366.

Palivethita [pp. of palivetheti] wrapped round, entwined, encircled, fettered Nd² 107 (°veṭṭh°, combᵈ with laggita & palibuddha); J IV.436; VI.89. Cp. sam°.

Palivetheti [pari+**veṣṭ**] to wrap up, cover, entwine, encircle M I.134; J I.192; II.95; DhA I.269; DhsA 366. — Pass. **palivethīyati** Miln 74. — pp. **palivethita** (q. v.). See also sam°

Palisajjati [pari+**sṛj**] to loosen, make loose S II.89 (mūlāni).

Palissajati [pari+**svaj**] to embrace D II.266; J V.158 (aor. palissaji=āliṅgi C), 204, 215; VI.325.

Palissuta [pp. of pari+**sru**] flowing over J VI.328.

Palugga [pp. of palujjati, Sk. *prarugṇa] broken up, crushed, crumbled Bu II.24; Miln 217.

Palujjati [Pass. of palujati=pa+**ruj**] to break (intrs.) to fall down, crumble, to be dissolved Vin II.284; D II.181; M I.488; S II.218; III.137; IV.52=Nd² 550 (in exegesis of "loka"); Miln 8; Vism 416. — pp. **palugga** (q. v.). Cp. BSk. **pralujyati** MVastu II.370.

Palujjana (nt.) [fr. palujjati] breaking up, destruction SnA 506.

Paluddha [pp. of pa+**lubh**] seduced, enticed S IV.307 (where id. p. M I.511 reads paladdha); J I.158; VI.255, 262. See also **palobheti** & **palobhita**.

Palumpati [pa+**lup**] to rob, plunder, deprive of A I.48.

Paleti see palāyati.

Palepa [fr. pa+**lip**] smearing; plaster, mortar Th 2, 270; ThA 213.

Palepana (nt.) [fr. pa+**lip**] smearing, anointing; adj. (-°) smeared or coated with M I.429 (gāḷha° thickly smeared).

Paloka [fr. pa+***luj**=**ruj**, thus standing for *paloga, cp. roga] breaking off or in two, dissolution, decay Vin II.284; M I.435=Miln 418 (in formula aniccato dukkhato rogato etc., with freq. v. l. paralokato; cp. A IV.423; Nd² 214; Ps II.238); S III.167 (id.) IV.53; V. 163.

Palokin (adj.) [fr. paloka] destined for decay or destruction S IV.205=Sn 539 (acc. palokinaŋ=jarā-maraṇehi palujjana-dhamma SnA 506); Th 2, 101 (acc. pl. palokine, see Geiger, *P.Gr.* § 95²).

Palobha [fr. pa+**lubh**] desire, greed PvA 265.

Palobhana (nt.)=palobha J I.196, 210; II.183; Miln 286.

Palobhita [pp. of palobheti] desired PvA 154.

Palobheti [Caus. of pa+**lubh**] to desire, to be greedy Sn 703; J I.79, 157, 298; VI.215; SnA 492; DhA I.123, 125; PvA 55. — pp. **palobhita** (q. v.).

Pallanka [pary+anka, cp. Class Sk. palyanka & Māgadhī paliyanka] 1. sitting cross-legged, in instr. **pallankena** upon the hams S I.124, 144; and in phrase **pallankaŋ ābhujati** "to bend (the legs) in crosswise" D I.71; M I.56; A III.320; J I.17, 71; Ps I.176; Pug 68; Miln 289; DhA II.201. — This phrase is explᵈ at Vism 271 and VbhA 368 as "samantato ūru-baddh' āsanaŋ bandhati." — 2. a divan, sofa, couch Vin II.163, 170 (cp. *Vin. Texts* III.209, which is to be corrected after *Dial.* I.12); D I.7; S I.95; J I.268; IV.396; V.161; Vv 31¹; Pv II.12⁷; III.3²; DhA I.19; PvA 189, 219.

Pallati (pallate), is guarded or kept, contracted (poetical) form of pālayate (so Cy.) J V.242.

Pallattha [Sk. *paryasta, pari+pp. of **as** to throw, cp. Prk pallattha Pischel, *Prk. Gr.* § 285] the posture of sitting or squatting or lolling J I.163 (here in explⁿ of tipallattha: pallatthaŋ vuccati sayanaŋ, ubhohi passehi ujukam eva ca go-nisinnaka-vasenā ti tih'ākārehi pallatthaŋ etc.; see under ti°). Cp. ti°, vi°.

Pallatthikā (f.) [fr. pallattha] same meaning as pallattha Vin II.213; III.162 (cp. *Vin. Texts* I.62; III.141); Vism 79 (dussa°).

Pallatthita [doubtful, perhaps we should read paliyattha, see Kern, *Toev.* s. v.] perverse J V.79.

Pallala (nt.) [cp. Class Sk. palvala=Lat. palus; Ohg. felawa Ger. felber willow; Lith. pélkē moor; BSk. also palvala, e. g. Divy 56] 1. marshy ground M I.117; S III.108 sq. — 2. a small pond or lake Vin I.230=D II.89; J II.129; V.346.

Pallava (nt.) [cp. Class Sk. pallaka] a sprout J I.250; II.161. See also phallava.

Pallavita (adj.) [fr. pallava] having sprouts, burgeoning, budding Miln 151; VvA 288 (sa° full of sprouts).

Pallāsa see vi°.

Palloma [a contraction of pannaloma, see *J.P.T.S.* 1889, 206] security, confidence D I.96; M I.17; cp. DA I.266 "loma-haŋsa-mattam pi 'ssa na bhavissati."

Pavakkhati [fut. of pa+**vac**] only in 1st sq. pavakkhāmi "I will declare or explain" Sn 701, 963=1050 (cp. Nd[1] 482 & Nd[2] under brūmi).

Pavacchati [Sk. prayacchati] see anu°, & cp. pavecchati.

Pavajati [pa+**vraj**] to wander forth, go about, perambulate; ppr. pavajamāna S I.42 (but may be pavajjamāna "being predicated" in play of word with act. pavadanto in same verse).

Pavajjati [Pass. of pavadati] to sound forth, to be played (of music) J I.64 (pavajjayiŋsu, 3rd pl. aor.); VvA 96 (pavajjamāna ppr. med.).

Pavajjana (nt.) [fr. pavajjati, Pass. of pavadati] sounding, playing of music VvA 210.

Pavaḍḍha [pp. of pavaḍḍhati] grown up, increased, big, strong J V.340 (°kāya of huge stature; so read for pavaddha°; expld as vaḍḍhita-kāya).

Pavaḍḍhati [pa+**vṛdh**] to grow up, to increase M I.7; S II.84, 92; Sn 306 (3rd sg. praet. °atha); Dh 282, 335, 349; Pug 64; PvA 8 (puññaŋ). — pp. **pavaḍḍha** & **pavuddha.**

Pavati[1] [pa+**vā**] to blow forth, to yield a scent Th I, 528 (=gandhaŋ vissajjati C.). See **pavāti.**

Pavati[2] [of **plu**, cp. Vedic plavate to swim & Epic Sk. pravate to jump] to hurry on, to rush VvA 42 (but better read with v. l. patati as syn. of gacchati).

Pavatta (adj.) [pp. of pavattati] 1. (adj.) happening, going on, procedure, resulting Th 2, 220 (assu ca pavattaŋ, taken by Mrs. Rh. D. as "tears shed"); ThA 179; PvA 35, 83 (gāthāyo), 120, esp. with ref. to natural products as "that which comes," i. e. normal, natural, raw; °phala ready or natural, wild fruit (gained without exertion of picking), in cpds. °phalika SnA 295 sq.; °bhojana (adj.) J I.6; III.365; Vism 422, and °bhojin one who lives on wild fruit (a certain class of ascetics, tāpasā) D I.101; M I.78, 344; A I.241; II.206; cp. DA I.269 sq. & SnA 295, 296. °maŋsa fresh or raw meat (flesh) Vin I.217 (cp. *Vin. Texts* II.81). — 2. (nt.) "that which goes on," i. e. the circle or whirl of existence Miln 197, 326 (cp. *Miln trsl*n II.200 "starting afresh in innumerable births," quot. fr. C.), opp. appavatta freedom from Saŋsāra, i. e. Nibbāna ibid. — 3. founded on, dealing with, relating to, being in S IV.115 (kuraraghare p. pabbata); DA I.92 (ādinaya°), 217 (°pīti-sukha being in a state of happiness).

Pavattati [pa+vattati, **vṛt**] (intrs.) 1. to move on, go forward, proceed Pv I.5[7]; PvA 8, 131; of water: to flow S II.31; J II.104; PvA 143, 154, 198. — 2. to exist, to be, continue in existence J I.64; PvA 130 (opp. ucchijjati). — 3. to result, to go on PvA 45 (phalaŋ), 60 (vippaṭisār' aggi). — pp. **pavatta**; Caus. **pavatteti** (q. v.).

Pavattana (adj. nt.) [fr. pavattati] 1. moving forward, doing good, beneficial, useful; f. °ī M I.214; Pug 35 (spelt pavattinī in T. as well as Pug A 218). — 2. execution, performance, carrying out Miln 277 (āṇā,° cp. pavatti).

Pavattayitar [n. ag. to pavatteti] one who sets into motion or keeps up DA I.273 (see foll.).

Pavattar [n. ag. of either pa+**vac** or pa+**vṛt**, the latter more probable considering similar use of parivatteti. The P. commentators take it as either] one who keeps up or keeps going, one who hands on (the tradition), an expounder, teacher D I.104 (mantānaŋ p.=pavattayitar DA I.273); S IV.94; Dh 76 (nidhīnaŋ p.=ācikkhitar DhA II.107).

Pavattāpanatta (nt.) [fr. Caus. II. of pavatteti=pavattāpeti] making continue, keeping going, preservation, upkeep Vism 32 (T. °attha).

Pavatti (f.) [fr. pa+**vṛt**] 1. manifestation, wielding, execution, giving, in āṇā° royal authority J III.504; IV.145; ThA 283. — 2. happening, incident, news J I.125, 150; II.416; Vism 91; PvA 6, 17, 29, 35, 92, 152, 242, etc.; DhA I.80 (v. l. pavutti). Cp. **pavutti.**

Pavattita [pp. of pavatteti] set going, inaugurated, established Vin I.11 (dhammacakka); M III.29, 77; S I.191; Sn 556, 557 (dhammacakka); PvA 67 (id.), 140 (sangiti); SnA 454.

Pavattin (adj.) [fr. pa+**vṛt**] 1. advancing, moving forward, proceeding, effective, beneficial; only in phrase dhammā pavattino A I.279; DA I.4=PvA 2; and in suppavattin (good-flowing, i. e. well-recited?) A IV.140 (of pātimokkha; trsld as "thoroughly mastered" *J.P.T.S.* 1909, 199 V.71 (id.). — 2. going on, procedure (in f. °inī) Vin II.271 sq., 277.

Pavatteti [Caus. of pavattati] (trs.) 1. to send forth, set going Vin I.87 (assūni); S II.282 (id.) J I.147 (selagulaŋ pavaṭṭ°); esp. in phrase **dhammacakkaŋ** p. to inaugurate the reign of righteousness Vin I.8, 11; M I.171; S III.86; Sn 693; Miln 20, 343; VvA 165; PvA 21, etc. — 2. to cause, produce, make arise J II.102 (mah' oghaŋ); Miln 219. — 3. to give forth, bestow, give (dānaŋ a gift) Vin IV.5 (spelt ṭṭ); PvA 19, 123, 139. — 4. to continue, keep on, practise, go on with DhA I.257; PvA 29 (attabhāvaŋ). 42 (kammante). — 5. to move about, behave, linger DhA I.14 (ṭṭ). — 6. to display, execute, wield, enforce Miln 189 (āṇaŋ; cp. āṇāpavatti). — pp. **pavattita** (q. v.).

Pavadati [pa+**vad**] to speak out, speak to, talk, dispute; ppr. pavadanto S I.42 (trsl. "predicate"); Nd[1] 293. — aor. pāvādi ThA 71. — Cp. pāvadati.

Pavana[1] (nt.) [cp. Sk. pavana & pāvana, of **pū**] winnowing of grain Miln 201 (read pavanena ṭṭhāyiko who earned his living by winnowing grain).

Pavana[2] (nt.) [cp. Vedic pravaṇa; not with Müller, *P.Gr.* 24=upavana; perhaps=Lat. pronus "prone"] side of a mountain, declivity D II.254; M I.117; S I.26; II.95, 105; Th I, 1092; J I.28; II.180; VI.513; Cp. I.1[5], 10[1]; III.13[1]; Miln 91, 198 sq., 364, 408; Vism 345. Cp. Pavananagara SnA 583 (v. l. BB for Tumbavanagara=Vanasavhaya). *Note*. Kern, *Toev.* s. v. defends Müller's (after Subhūti) interpretation as "wood, woodland," and compares BSk. pavana MVastu II.272, 382.

Pavana[3] at Vin II.136 in cpd. pavan-anta refers to the end of the girdle (kāyabandhana), where it is tied into a loop or knot. Bdhgh on p. 319 (on C.V. V.29, 2) explˢ it by pās' anta.

Pavapati [pa+**vap**] to sow out Th 2, 112.

Pavayha (adv.) [ger. of pavahati] carrying on, pressing, urgently, constantly, always repeated as pavayha pavayha M III.118=DhA II.108; M I.442, 444.

Pavara (adj.) [pa + vara] most excellent, noble, distinguished S III.264; Sn 83, 646, 698 (muni°); Dh 422; Pug 69; Miln 240; PvA 2 (°dhamma-cakka), 67 (id.), 39 (°buddh'āsana); Sdhp 421.

Pavasati [pa + **vas**] to "live forth," i. e. to be away from home, to dwell abroad Sn 899; J II.123 (=pavasaŋ gacchati); V.91. — pp. pavuttha (q. v.). Cp. vi°.

Pavassati [pa + **vṛṣ**] to "rain forth," to begin to rain, shed rain S I.100; Sn 18 sq. (imper. pavassa), 353 (v. l.); J VI.500 ("cry"), 587 (aor. pāvassi). — pp. pavaṭṭha & pavuṭṭha: see abhi°.

Pavassana (nt.) [fr. pa + **vṛṣ**] beginning to rain, raining Miln 120.

Pavāta (nt.) [pa + vāta, cp. Vedic pravāta] a draught of air, breeze Vin II.79 (opp. nivāta).

Pavāti [pa + **vā**] to diffuse a scent Dh 54; Th 1, 528; J V.63 (disā bhāti p. ca). See also pavāyati.

Pavāda [pa + **vad**, cp. Epic Sk. pravāda talk, saying] talk, disputation, discussion D I.26, 162; M I.63; Sn 538.

Pavādaka (adj.) [fr. pavāda] 1. belonging to a discussion, intended for disputation D I.78 (samaya° "debating hall"). — 2. fond of discussing Miln 4 (bhassa° "fond of wordy disputation"). Cp. pavādiya.

Pavādiya (adj.) [fr. pavāda, cp. pavādaka] belonging to a disputation, disputing, arguing, talking Sn .885 (n. pl. °āse, taken by Nd[1] 293 as pavadanti, by SnA 555 as vādino).

Pavāyati [pa + **vā**] to blow forth, to permeate (of a scent), to diffuse J I.18 (dibba-gandho p.); Vism 58 (dasa disā sīla-gandho p.). Cp. pavāti.

Pavāraṇā (f.) [pa + **vṛ**, cp. BSk. pravāraṇā Divy 91, 93; whereas Epic Sk. pravāraṇa, nt., only in sense of "satisfaction"] 1. the Pavāraṇā, a ceremony at the termination of the Vassa Vin I.155, 160 (where 2 kinds: cātuddasikā & pannarasikā), II.32, 167; D II.220; S I.190. pavāraṇaŋ ṭhapeti to fix or determine the (date of) P. Vin II.32, 276. Later two kinds of this ceremony (festival) are distinguished, viz. mahā° the great P. and °saṅgaha, an abridged P. (see DA I.241) J I.29, 82, 193 (mahā°); Vism 391 (id.); SnA 57 (id.); VvA 67 (id.); PvA 140 (id.); — 2. satisfaction Vism 71.

Pavārita [pp. of pavāreti] 1. satisfied M I.12 (+ paripuṇṇa pariyosita); Miln 231; Vism 71. — 2. having come to the end of the rainy season Vin I.175. — Freq. in formula bhuttāvin pavārita having eaten & being satisfied Vin I.213 (cp. *Vin. Texts* I.39); II.300; IV.82; PvA 23.

Pavāreti [Caus. of pa + **vṛ**, cp. BSk. pravārayati Divy 116, 283, etc.] 1. to invite, offer, present, satisfy S I.190; A IV.79; J III.352. — 2. to celebrate the Pavāraṇā (i. e. to come to the end of the Vassa) Vin I.160 sq.; II.255; DhA I.87; J I.29, 215; IV.243 (vuttha-vassa p.); Vism 90; SnA 57. — pp. pavārita (q. v.) See also sam°.

Pavāla & **Pavāḷa** (m. & nt.) [cp. Class Sk. prabāla, pravāḍa & pravāla] 1. coral J I.394 (°ratta-kambala); II.88; IV.142; Miln 267 (with other jewels), 380 (id.); SnA 117; VvA 112 (°ratana). — 2. a sprout, young branch, shoot J III.389, 395 (kāḷa-valli°); V.207; Nett 14 (°aṅkura); SnA 91 (id.).

Pavāḷha [apparently pp. of pavahati (pavāheti), but in reality pp. of pa + **bṛh**[1], corresp. to Sk. prabṛḍha (pravṛdha), cp. abbūḷha & ubbahati (ud + **bṛh**[1]), but cp. also ubbāḷha which is pp. of ud + **bādh**. At D I.77 (where v. l. pabbāḷha = pabūḷha, unexpl[d] by Bdhgh) it is synonymous with uddharati = ubbahati] 1. carried away (?), turned away, distracted, dismissed S III.91 (bhikkhu-sangho p.). — 2. drawn forth, pulled out, taken out D I.77 = Ps II.211 = Vism 406 (muñjamhā isīkā p.); J VI.67 (muñja v'isikā p.).

Pavāsa [fr. pa + **vas**, cp. Vedic pravāsa in same meaning] sojourning abroad, being away from home J II.123; V.434; VI.150; Miln 314. — Cp. vi°.

Pavāsita 1. (perhaps we should read pavārita?) given as present, honoured J V.377 (= pesita C.). — 2. (so perhaps to be read for pavūsita T.) scented, permeated with scent [pp. of pavāseti] VvA 237 (v. l. padhūpita preferable).

Pavāsin (adj.) [fr. pavāsa] living abroad or from home, in cira° long absent Dh 219 (= cirappavuttha DhA III.293).

Pavāhaka (adj.) [fr. pa + **vah**] carrying or driving away Th 1, 758.

Pavāhana (adj. & nt.) [fr. pa + **vah**] 1. carrying off, putting away, Th 1, 751. — 2. wiping off J III.290.

Pavāhitatta (nt.) [abstr. fr. pavāhita, pp. of pavāheti] the fact of being removed or cleansed J V.134.

Pavāhati [Caus. fr. pa + **vah**] 1. to cause to be carried away, to remove; freq. with ref. to water: to wash away, cleanse M I.39; S I.79, 183 (pāpakammaŋ nahānena); II.88; Th 1, 349; J I.24; III.176, 225, 289; IV.367; V.134; VI.197; 588; Miln 247; Dāvs II.59; PvA 256. — 2. to pull out, draw out D I.77 (better to be read as pabāhati).

Pavikatthita [pp. of pa + vi + katthati] boasted J I.359.

Pavicaya [fr. pa + vicinati] investigation Sn 1021; Th 1, 593; Pug 25; Nett 3, 87.

Pavicarati [pa + vicarati] to investigate thoroughly M III.85; S V.68.

Pavicinati [pa + vicinati] to investigate, to examine M III.85; S V.68, 262; Nett 21; SnA 545. grd. paviceyya J IV.164, & pavicetabba Nett 21.

Pavijjhati [pa + **vyadh**] to throw forth or down Vin II.193 (silaŋ cp. J I.173 & V.333); III.82, 178, 415; DA I.138, 154. — pp. paviddha (q. v.).

Pavijjhana (nt.) [fr. pavijjhati] hurling, throwing J V.67 (Devadattassa silā°, cp. Vin II.193); J I.173; V.333.

Paviṭṭha [pp. of pavisati] entered, gone into (acc.), visited S I.197; II.19; Dh 373; DA I.288; PvA 12, 13.

Pavitakka [pa + vitakka] scepticism, speculation, controversy Sn 834; Nd[1] 176.

Pavidaŋseti [pa + vi + Caus. of **dṛś**; daŋseti = dasseti] to make clear, to reveal J V.326 (aor. pavidaŋsayi).

Paviddha [pp. of pavijjhati] thrown down, fig. given up, abandoned Th 1, 350 (°gocara).

Pavineti [pa + vineti] to lead or drive away, expel Sn 507 = J V.148.

Pavibhajati [pa + vi + **bhaj**. Cp. Class Sk. pravibhāga division, distribution] to distribute, to apportion S I.193 (°bhajjaŋ, ppr., with jj metri causa) = Th 1, 1242 (°bhajja ger.).

Pavilīyati [pa + vi + **lī**] to be dissolved, to melt or fade away S IV.289 (pavilīyamānena kāyena with their body melting from heat; so read for paveliyamānena).

Paviloketi [pa + viloketi] to look forward or ahead J VI.559.

Pavivitta [pp. of pa+vi+**vic**] separated, detached, secluded, singled M I.14, 77, 386; II.6; S II.29; Vism 73; PvA 127 DhA II.77. Often in phrase appiccha santuṭṭha pavivitta referring to an ascetic enjoying the satisfaction of seclusion Nd² 225=Nd¹ 342[1a]=Vism 25; J I.107; Miln 244, 358, 371 (with appa-sadda appanigghosa).

Paviveka [fr. pa+vi+**vic**] retirement, solitude, seclusion Vin I.104; II.258 (appicchatā santuṭṭhi+; cp. pavivitta); D I.60; M I.14 sq.; S II.202; V.398; A I.240; Sn 257; Dh 205 (°rasa, cp. DhA III.268); Th 1, 597; J I.9; Ps II.244; Vism 41, 73 (°sukha-rasa); Sdhp 476; DA I.169.

Pavivekatā (f.) [abstr. fr. paviveka]=paviveka Vism 81 (appicchatā etc. in enumⁿ of the 5 dhuta-dhammas).

Pavivekiya (adj.) [fr. paviveka] springing from solitude Th 1, 669.

Pavisati [pa+**viś**] to go in, to enter (acc.) Sn 668, 673; DhA II.72 (opp. nikkhamati); PvA 4, 12, 47 (nagaraŋ). Pot. °vise Sn 387 imper. pavisa M I.383; S I.213; fut. pavisissati Vin I.87; J III.86; pavissati (cp. Geiger *P.Gr.* § 65²) J II.68; Cp. I.9[56], and pavekkhati S IV.199; J VI.76 (nāgo bhūmiyaŋ p.); Dāvs III.26; aor. pāvisi Vin II.79 (vihāraŋ); M I.381; J I.76 (3rd pl. pāvisuŋ), 213; J II.238; Vism 42 (gāmaŋ) PvA 22, 42, 161, 256; and pavisi J II.238; PvA 12, 35; ger. pavisitvā S I.107; J I.9 (araññaŋ); Vism 22; PvA 4, 12, 46, 79 & pavissa S I.200; Dh 127=PvA 104.—pp. paviṭṭha (q. v.).—Caus. paveseti (q. v.).

Pavisana (nt.) [fr. pa+**viś**] going in, entering, entrance J I.294; II.416; VI.383; DhA I.83. Cp. pavesana.

Pavīṇa (adj.) [cp. Class. Sk. pravīṇa] clever, skilful Dāvs V.33; VvA 168 (v. l. kusala).

Pavīnati [pa+**vī** to seek, Sk. veti, but with diff. formation in P. cp. Trenckner *Notes* 78 (who derives it fr. veṇ) & apaviṇāti. The form is doubtful; probably we should read pacināti] to look up to, respect, honour J III.387 (T. reading sure, but v. l. C. pavīrati).

Pavīhi [pa+vīhi] in pl. diff. kinds of rice J V.405 (=nānappakārā vīhayo).

Pavuccati [Pass. of pavacati] to be called, said, or pronounced Sn 436, 513, 611 & passim; Dh 257; Pv IV.3[17]; PvA 102. The form pavuccate also occurs, e. g. at Sn 519 sq.—pp. pavutta¹ (q. v.).

Pavutā at M I.518 is unexplained. The reading of this word is extremely doubtful at all passages. The vv. ll. at M I.518 are pavudhā, pavujā, paṭuvā, *phutā, and the C. explⁿ is pavuṭā=ganṭhikā (knot or block?). The identical passage at D I.54 reads paṭuvā (q. v.), with vv. ll. pamuṭā, pamuvucā, while DA I.164 explˢ pacuṭā =ganṭhikā (vv. ll. pamuṭā, pamucā, papuṭā). *Dial.* I.72 reads pacuṭa, but leaves the word untranslated; Franke, *Dīgha*, p. 58 ditto.

Pavuṭṭha (pavaṭṭha) [pp. of pavassati] see abhi°.

Pavutta¹ [pp. of pa+**vac**, but sometimes confounded with pavatta, pp. of pa+**vṛt**, cp. pavutti] said, declared, pronounced D I.104 (mantapada p.; v.l. °vatta which is more likely; but DA I.273 explˢ by vutta & vācita); S I.52; Sn 383 (su°=sudesita SnA 373), 868 (=ācikkhita desita, etc. Nd¹ 271).

Pavutta² [pp. of pa+**vap**] scattered forth, strewn, sown S I.227.

Pavutti [fr. pa+**vṛt**, cp. Class. Sk. pravṛtti] happening, proceeding, fate, event PvA 31 (v. l. pavatti), 46, 53, 61, 78, 81 and passim (perhaps should be read pavatti at all passages).

Pavuttha [pp. of pavasati] dwelling or living abroad, staying away from home D II.261 (°jāti one who dwells away from his caste, i. e. who no longer belongs to any caste); J V.434; DhA III.293. Freq. in phrase pavutthapatikā itthi a woman whose husband dwells abroad Vin II.268; III.83; Miln 205.

Pavūsita at VvA 237 is misreading either for pavāsita or (more likely) for padhūpita (as v. l. SS.), in meaning "blown" i. e. scented, filled with scent.

Pavekkhati is fut. pavisati.

Pavecchati [most likely (as suggested by Trenckner, *Notes* 61) a distortion of payacchati (pa+**yam**) by way of *payecchati > pavecchati (cp. sa-yathā > seyyathā). Not with Morris, *J.P.T.S.* 1885, 43 fr. pa+**vṛṣ**, nor with Müller *P.Gr.* 120 fr. pa+**viṣ** (who with this derivation follows the P. Commentators, e. g. J III.12 pavesati, deti; SnA 407 (pavesati paṭipādeti); Geiger *P.Gr.* § 152, note 3 suggests (doubtfully) a Fut. stem (of **viś**?)] to give, bestow S I.18; Sn 463 sq., 490 sq.; Th 2, 272; J I.28; III.12 (v. l. pavacchati), 172; IV.303; VI.502, 587 (vuṭṭhi-dhāraŋ pavecchanto devo pāvassi tāvade; v.l. pavattento); Pv II.9[43] (=deti PvA 130); II.9[70] (=pavatteti ibid. 139); II.10⁷(=deti ibid. 144); Miln 375.

Paveṇi (f.) [pa+veṇi; cp. late Sk. praveṇi in meanings 1 & 2] 1. a braid of hair, i. e. the hair twisted & unadorned A III.56—2. a mat, cover D I.7 ≈ (see ajina°).—3. custom, usage, wont, tradition J I.89; II.353; V.285; VI.38((kula-tanti, kula-paveṇi); Dpvs XVIII.1; Miln 134 (°upaccheda break of tradition), 190, 226 (+vaŋsa), 227; DhA I.284 (tanti+); PvA 131.—4. succession, lineage, breed, race Sn 26 (cp. SnA 39); DhA I.174.

-**pālaka** guardian of tradition Vism 99 (tanti-dhara, vaŋsanurakkhaka+); DhA III.386.

Pavedana (nt.) [fr. pa+**vid**] making known, telling, proclamation, announcement only in stanza "nisid' ambavane ramme yāva kālappavedanā," until the announcement of the time (of death) Th 1, 563 (trslⁿ "until the hour should be revealed")—J I.118—Vism 389=DhA I.248.

Pavedita [pp. of pavedeti] made known, declared, taught M I.67 (su° & du°); S I.231; Dh 79, 281; Sn 171, 330, 838; Nd¹ 186.

Pavedeti [Caus. of pa+**vid**] to make known, to declare, communicate, relate S I.24; IV.348; Dh 151; Sn p. 103 (=bodheti ñāpeti SnA 444); PvA 33, 58, 68 (attānaŋ make oneself known), 120.—pp. pavedita (q. v.).

Pavedhati [pa+**vyath**, cp. pavyatheti] to be afflicted, to be frightened, to be agitated, quiver, tremble, fear Sn 928 (=tasati etc. Nd¹ 384); Vism 180 (reads pavedheti) ThA 203 (allavatthaŋ allakesaŋ pavedhanto, misreading for pavesento); DhA II.249.—Freq in ppr. med. pavedhamāna trembling M I.88; Pv III.5⁵ (=pakampamāna PvA 199); J I.58; III.395.—pp. pavedhita & pavyadhita (q. v.).

Pavellati [pa+**vell**] to shake, move to & fro, undulate S IV.289 (paveliyamānena kāyena); J III.395.—pp. pavellita (q. v.).

Pavellita [pp. of pavellati] shaken about, moving to & fro, swinging, trembling J VI.456.

Pavesa (-°) [fr. pa+**viś**] entrance ThA 66 (Rājagaha°); DhA IV.150.

Pavesana (nt.) [fr. paveseti] 1. going in, entering, entrance J I.142; PvA 79 (v. l. for T. °vesa), 217, 221 (asipattavana°).—2. beginning VvA 71 (opp. nikkhamana).—3. putting in, application J II.102 (daṇḍe p.).—4. means of entry, as adj. able to enter J VI.383.

Pavesetar [n. ag. of paveseti] one who lets in or allows to enter, an usher in S IV.194; A V.195.

Paveseti [Caus. of pavisati] 1. to make enter, allow to enter, usher in M I.79; J I.150 (miga-gaṇaŋ uyyānaŋ), 291; VI.179; Vism 39; PvA 38, 44, 61 (gehaŋ), 141 (id.); DhA 1.397. — 2. to furnish, provide, introduce, procure, apply to (acc. or loc.) J III.52 (rajjukaŋ gīvāya); VI.383 (siriŋ); Miln 39 (gehe padīpaŋ), 360 (udakaŋ); DA I.218. Perhaps at ThA 203 for pavedheti. — Caus. II. pavesāpeti J I.294 (mātugāmaŋ aggiŋ).

Pavyatheti [Caus. of pa + **vyath**] to cause to tremble, to shake J V.409. Cp. pavedhati. — pp. pavyadhita (q. v.).

Pavyadhita [pp. of pa + **vyath**; the dh through analogy with pavedhita] afflicted, frightened, afraid J VI.61, 166.

Pasaŋsaka [fr. pasaŋsati] flatterer M I.327; J II.439; Sdhp 565.

Pasaŋsati [pa + **saŋs**] to speak out, praise, commend, agree D I.163; S I.102, 149, 161; J I.143; II.439; V.331; It 16; Sn 47, 163, 390, 658, 906; Dh 30; Pv II.9[43]; DA I.149; PvA 25, 131 (= vaṇṇeti). — pp. pasattha & pasaŋsita (q. v.). Cp. paṭipasaŋsita.

Pasaŋsana (nt.) [fr. pa + **śaŋs**] praising, commendation Pug 53; Sdhp 213; PvA 30.

Pasaŋsā (f.) [fr. pa + **śaŋs**; cp. Vedic praśaŋsā] praise, applause D III.260; S I.202; Th 1, 609; Sn 213, 826, 895; Miln 377; SnA 155. In composition the form is pasaŋsa°, e. g. °āvahana bringing applause Sn 256; °kāma desirous of praise Sn 825, cp. Nd[1] 163; °lābha gain of praise Sn 828. As adj. pasaŋsa "laudable, praiseworthy" it is better taken as grd. of pasaŋsati (= pasaŋsiya); thus at Pv IV.7[13] (pāsaŋsa Minayeff); PvA 8, 89 (= anindita).

Pasaŋsita [pp. of pasaŋsati, cp. pasattha] praised S I.232; Sn 829, 928; Dh 228, 230; Nd[1] 169; PvA 116 (= vaṇṇita) 130.

Pasaŋsiya (adj.) [grd. of pasaŋsati, cp. Vedic praśaŋsia] laudable, praiseworthy S I.149; III.83; A II.19; Sn 658; J I.202; Sdhp 563. Cp. pasaŋsā.

Pasakkati [pa + sakkati] to go forth or out to; ger. pasakkiya S I.199 = Th 1, 119; Th 1, 125.

Pasakkhita at J IV.305 is doubtful; perhaps we should read **pasakkita** (pp. of pasakkati); the C. expl[s] as "lying down" (nipanna acchati, p. 307); Kern, *Toev.* s. v. proposes change to **pamakkhita** on ground of vv. ll. vamakkhita & malakita.

Pasankanta [pp. of pa + sankamati, of **kram**] gone out to, gone forth PvA 22.

Pasankamati [pa + saŋ + **kram**] to go out or forth to (acc.) Sdhp 277. — pp. pasankanta.

Pasanga [fr. pa + **sanj**. Class Sk. prasanga in both meanings] 1. hanging on, inclination, attachment to KhA 18; PvA 130. — 2. occasion, event; loc. **pasange** at the occasion of (-°), instead of KhA 213 (karaṇavacana°, where PvA 30 in id. p. reads karaŋ' atthe).

Pasajati [pa + **sṛj**] to let loose, produce; to be attached to Sn 390 (= allīyati SnA 375).

Pasaṭa [pp. of pa + **sṛj**] let out, produced D III.167; SnA 109 (conj. for pasava in expl[n] of pasuta).

Pasata[1] (adj.) [Vedic pṛṣant, f. pṛṣatī] spotted, only in cpd. °miga spotted antelope J V.418 (v. l. pasada°). The more freq. P. form is **pasada°**, e. g. S II.279 (gloss pasata°); J V.24, 416; VI.537; SnA 82.

Pasata[2] (nt.) [etym. ? Late Sk. pṛṣat or pṛṣad a drop; cp. phusita[1] rain-drop = pṛṣata; BR. under pṛṣant = pasata[1], but probably dialectical & Non-Aryan] a small measure of capacity, a handful (seems to be applied to water only) J I.101 (°mattaŋ udakaŋ); IV.201 (udaka°); V.382 (°mattaŋ pānīyaŋ). Often redupl. pasataŋ pasataŋ "by handfuls" M I.245, J V.164. At DA I.298 it is closely connected with sarāva (cup), as denoting the amount of a small gift.

Pasattha (& **Pasaṭṭha**) [pp. of pasaŋsati] praised, extolled, commended S I.169; J III.234; Vv 44[21]; Miln 212, 361. As pasaṭṭha at Pv II.9[73] (so to be read for paseṭṭha); IV.1[52] (= vaṇṇita PvA 241); DhsA 124.

Pasada. See pasata[1].

Pasanna[1] (adj.) [pp. of pasīdati] 1. clear, bright Sn 550 (°netta); KhA 64 & 65 (°tilatelavaṇṇa, where Vism 262 reads vippasanna°); Vism 409 (id.). — 2. happy, gladdened, reconciled, pleased J I.151, 307; Vism 129 (muddha°). — 3. pleased in one's conscience, reconciled, believing, trusting in (loc.), pious, good, virtuous A III.35 (Satthari, dhamme sanghe); S I.34 (Buddhe); V.374; Vv 5[9]; Sn 698; Dh 368 (Buddha-sāsane); J II.111; DhA 1.60 (Satthari). Often comb[d] with saddha (having faith) Vin II.190; PvA 20, 42 (a°), and in cpd. °citta devotion in one's heart Vin I.16; A VI.209; Sn 316, 403, 690; Pv II.1[8]; SnA 490; PvA 129; or °mānasa Sn 402; VvA 39; PvA 67; cp. pasannena manasā S I.206; Dh 2. See also **abhippasanna** & **vippasanna**.

Pasanna[2] [pp. of pa + **syad**] flowing out, streaming, issuing forth; in assu-pasannaŋ shedding of tears S II.179.

Pasannā (f.) [late Sk. prasannā] a kind of spirituous liquor (made from rice) J I.360.

Pasammati [pa + **śram**] to become allayed, to cease, to fade away Th 1, 702.

Pasayha is ger. of pasahati (q. v.).

Pasaraṇa (nt.) [fr. pa + **sṛ**] stretching, spreading, being stretched out PvA 219 (piṭṭhi°). See also pasāraṇa.

Pasava [fr. pa + **su**] bringing forth, offspring S I.69.

Pasavati [pa + **su**] to bring forth, give birth to, beget, produce; mostly fig. in comb[n] with the foll. nouns: **kibbisaŋ** to commit sin Vin II.204; A V.75; **pāpaŋ** id. Pv IV.1[60]; **puññaŋ** to produce merit S I.182, 213; A V.76; PvA 121; opp. **apuññaŋ** Vin II.26; S I.114; **veraŋ** to beget hatred S II.68; Dh 201. — Caus. **pasaveti** in same meaning J VI.106 (pāpaŋ) — pp. **pasūta** (q. v.).

Pasavana (nt.) [fr. pa + **su**] 1. giving birth PvA 35. — 2. producing, generating, effecting PvA 31 (puñña°).

Pasaha [fr. pa + **sah**] overcoming, mastering, in dup° (adj.) hard to overcome J II.219; Miln 21.

Pasahati [pa + **sah**] to use force, subdue, oppress, overcome M II.99; Sn 443; Dh 7, 128; DhA III.46; J IV.126, 494; V.27. — ger. **pasayha** using force, forcibly, by force D II.74 (okkassa +); A IV.16 (id.); S I.143; Sn 72; J I.143; Pv II.9[2]; II.9[10]; (read appasayha for suppasayha); Miln 210 (okassa + ; for okkassa ?). Also in cpd. **pasayha-kārin** using force J IV.309; V.425.

Pasākha (m. & nt.) [pa + sākhā; Epic Sk. praśākhā branch] 1. a smaller branch J VI.324 (sākha°). — 2. branch-like wood, i. e. hard wood Th 1, 72. — 3. the body where it branches off from the trunk, i. e. abdomen & thighs; the lower part of the body Vin IV.316 (= adho-nābhi ubbha-jānu-maṇḍalaŋ C.). Cp. Suśruta II.31, 10. — 4. the extremities (being the 5th stage in the formation of the embryo) S I.206.

Pasāda [fr. pa+**sad**, cp. Vedic prasāda] 1. clearness, brightness, purity; referring to the colours ("visibility") of the eye J I.319 (akkhīni maṇiguḷa-sadisāni paññāyamāna pañca-ppasādāni ahesuŋ); SnA 453 (pasanna-netto i. e. pañca-vaṇṇa-ppasāda-sampattiyā). In this sense also, in Abhidhamma, with ref. to the eye in function of "sentient organ, sense agency" sensitive surface (so Mrs Rh. D. in Dhs. *trsl.* 174) at DhsA 306, 307. — 2. joy, satisfaction, happy or good mind, virtue, faith M I.64 (Satthari); S I.202; A I.98, 222 (Buddhe etc.); II.84; III.270 (puggala°); IV.346; SnA 155, PvA 5, 35. — 3. repose, composure, allayment, serenity Nett 28, 50; Vism 107, 135; ThA 258. — *Note.* pasāda at Th 2, 411 is to be read pāsaka (see *J.P.T.S.* 1893 pp. 45, 46). Cp. abhi°.

Pasādaka (adj.) [fr. pasāda] 1. making bright Miln 35 (udaka° maṇi). — 2. worthy, good, pious PvA 129 (a°). Cp. pāsādika.

Pasādana (nt.) [fr. pa+**sad**] 1. happy state, reconciliation, purity PvA 132. — 2. granting graces, gratification DhA III.3 (brahmaṇo mama p.°ṭṭhāne pasīdati he is gracious instead of me giving graces). — Cp. sam°.

Pasādaniya (adj.) [fr. pasāda] inspiring confidence, giving faith S V.156; Pug 49, 50; VbhA 282 (°suttanta); Sdhp 543; the 10 pāsādaniyā dhammā at M III.11 sq. Cp. sam°.

Pasādiyā at J VI.530 is doubtful; it is expl[d] in C. together with saŋsādiyā (a certain kind of rice: sūkara-sāli), yet the C. seems to take it as "bhūmiyaŋ patita"; v. l. pasāriya. Kern, *Toev.* s. v. takes it as rice plant & compares Sk. *prasātikā.

Pasādeti [Caus. of pa+**sad**, see pasīdati] to render calm, appease, make peaceful, reconcile, gladden, incline one's heart (cittaŋ) towards (loc.) D I.110, 139; S I.149; A V.71; Pv II.9[42] (cittaŋ); Miln 210; PvA 50, 123 (khamāpento p.). — Cp. vi°.

Pasādhana (nt.) [fr. pa+**sādh**; cp. Class. Sk. prasādhana in same meaning] ornament, decoration, parure J II.186 (rañño sīsa °kappaka King's headdress-maker i. e. barber); III.437; IV.3 (ura-cchada°); DhA I.227 (°peḷikā), 342 (°kappaka), 393; ThA 267; VvA 165, 187; PvA 155.

Pasādhita [pp. of pasādheti] adorned, arrayed with ornaments, embellished, dressed up J I.489 (maṇḍita°); II.48 (id.); IV.219 (id.); V.510 (nahāta°).

Pasādheti [Caus. of pa+**sādh**] to adorn, decorate, array Mhvs VII.38; DhA I.398. — pp. pasādhita (q. v.).

Pasāraṇa (nt.) [fr. pa+**sṛ**, cp. pasaraṇa] stretching out DA I.196 (opp. sammiñjana); DhA I.298 (hattha°).

Pasārita [pp. of pasāreti] 1. stretched out, usually in contrast with sammiñjita, e. g. at D I.222; Vin I.230; M III.35, 90; S I.137; Vism 19; VvA 6. — 2. put forth, laid out, offered for sale Miln I.336.

Pasāreti [Caus. of pa+**sṛ**] 1. to cause to move forwards, to let or make go, to give up J VI.58 (pasāraya, imper.). — Pass. pasāriyati Vism 318; PvA 240 (are turned out of doors). — 2. to stretch out, hold out or forth, usually with ref. to either arm (bāhuŋ, bāhaŋ, bāhā) S I.137 (opp. sammiñjeti); DA I.196; PvA 112, 121; or hand (hatthaŋ) J V.41; VI.282; PvA 113; or feet (pāde, pādaŋ) Th 2, 44, 49, cp. ThA 52; DhsA 324 (=sandhiyo paṭippaṇāmeti). — 3. to lay out, put forth, offer for sale Vin II.291; DhA II.89. — pp. pasārita (q. v.). Cp. abhi°.

Pasāsati [pa+**śās**] 1. to teach, instruct S I.38; J III.367, 443. — 2. to rule, reign, govern D II.257; Cp. III.1[1]; PvA 287.

Pasāsana (nt.) [fr. pa+**śās**] teaching, instruction J III.367.

Pasibbaka (m. nt.) [fr. pa+**siv**, late Sk. prasevaka > P. pasebbaka > pasibbaka, cp. Geiger. *P.Gr.* 15[1]] a sack, Vin III.17; J I.112, 351; II.88, 154; III.10, 116, 343 (camma° leather bag); IV.52, 361; V.46 (pūpa°), 483; VI.432 (spelling pasippaka); DA I.41; DhA IV.205.

Pasibbita [pp. of pa+**siv**] sewn up enveloped by (-°) Th 1, 1150 (maŋsa-nahāru°).

Pasīdati [pa+**sad**] 1. to become bright, to brighten up PvA 132 (mukha-vaṇṇo p.). — 2. to be purified, reconciled or pleased; to be clear & calm, to become of peaceful heart (mano or cittaŋ p.); to find one's satisfaction in (loc.), to have faith D II.202; S I.98; II.199 (sutvā dhammaŋ p.); A III.248; Sn 356, 434, 563; Nd[2] 426 (=saddahati, adhimuccati okappeti); Vv 50[14] (mano me pasīdi, aor.); Vism 129; Miln 9; DhA III.3 (=he is gracious, i. e. good); VvA 6 (better v. l. passitvā); PvA 141. — pp. pasanna (q. v.). See also pasādeti & vippasīdati.

Pasīdana (nt.) [fr. pasīdati] calming, happiness, purification Ps II.121 (SS passādana).

Pasu [Vedic paśu, cp. Lat. pecu & pecunia, Gr. πέκος fleece, Goth. vieh, E. fee] cattle M I.79; J V.105; Pv II.13[12] (°yoni); Miln 100; PvA 166 (°bhāva); n. pl. pasavo S I.69; Sn 858; gen. pl. pasūnaŋ Sn 311; Pv II.2[5]. — dupasu bad cattle Th 1, 446.

Pasuka = pasu Vin II.154 (ajaka+).

Pasuta [pp. of pa+**sā** or **si**, Sk. prasita, on change of i to u see Geiger, *P.Gr.* § 19[3]. In meaning confounded with pasavate of pa+**su**] attached to (acc. or loc.), intent upon (-°), pursuing, doing D I.135 (kamma°); Sn 57 (see Nd[2] 427), 709, 774, 940, Dh 166, 181; Vism 135 (doing a hundred & one things: aneka-kicca°); DhA III.160; PvA 151 (puñña-kammesu), 175 (kīḷanaka°), 195, 228 (pāpa°).

Pasura (adj.) [reading doubtful] many, abundant J VI.134 (=rāsi, heap C.). We should probably read pacura, as at J V.40 (=bahu C.).

Pasūta [pp. of pasavati] produced; having born, delivered PvA 80.

Pasūti (f.) [fr. pa+**su**] bringing forth, birth, in ghara lying-in chamber Nd[1] 120; Vism 235; KhA 58 (where Vism 259 reads sūtighara).

Paseṭṭha at Pv II.9[73] is to be read pasaṭṭha (see pasattha).

Pasodheti [pa+Caus. of **śudh**] to cleanse, clean, purity D I.71 (cittaŋ).

Passa[1] [cp. Sk. paśya, fr. passati] seeing, one who sees Th 1, 61 (see Morris, in *J.P.T.S.* 1885, 48).

Passa[2] (m. & nt.) [Vedic pārśva to parśu & pṛṣṭi rib, perhaps also connected with pārṣṇi side of leg, see under paṇhi] 1. side, flank M I.102; III.3; A V.18; Sn 422; J I.264; III.26. Pleonastic in piṭṭhi° (cp. E. backside) the back, loc. behind J I.292; PvA 55. — 2. (mountain-) slope, in Himavanta° J I.218; V.396 (loc. pasmani = passe C.).

Passati [Vedic paśyati & *spaśati (aor. aspaṣṭa, Caus. spāśayati etc.); cp. Av. spasyeiti, Gr. σκέπτομαι, (E. "scepsis"); Lat. species etc.; Ohg. spehon = Ger. spähen (E. spy). — The paradigm pass°, which in literary Sk. is restricted to the pres. stem (**paś**) interchanges with the paradigm dakkh° & dass° (**dṛś**): see dassati[1]] 1. to see — Pres. passati Vin I.322; S I.69, 132, 198; II.29; Sn 313, 647, 953, 1063, 1142 (cp. Nd[2]

428), Pv I.2²; Miln 218; PvA II. 102; 1st pl. passāma Sn 76, 153, 164; Pv I.10¹ (as future); imper. sg. **passa** Sn 435, 580, 588, 756; J I.223; II.159; Pv II.1¹⁸, 1¹⁹; PvA 38; pl. passatha S II.25; Sn 176 sq., 777, & passavho (cp. Sk. paśyadhvaŋ) Sn 998. — ppr. passaŋ (see Geiger, *P.Gr.* 97²) M II.9; Sn 739, 837, 909; & passanto J III.52; PvA 5, 6; f. passantī S I.199. — grd. passitabba J IV.390 (a°). — fut. passissati Pv II.4⁶; PvA 6. — aor. passi J II.103, 111; III.278, 341. — 2. to recognise, realise, know: only in combⁿ with jānāti (pres. jānāti passati; ppr. jānaŋ passaŋ): see jānāti II. — 3. to find Sn 1118 (=vindati paṭilabhati Nd² 428ᵇ); J III.55; Pv II.9⁸. — Cp. vi°.

Passaddha [pp. of passambhati, cp. BSk. praśrabdha Divy 48] calmed down, allayed, quieted, composed, at ease. Almost exclusively with ref. to the body (kāya), e. g. at Vin I.294; D III.241, 288; M I.37; III.86; S I.126; IV.125; A I.148; V.30; Vism 134; VbhA 283 (°kāya-puggala). — In lit. applⁿ °ratha when the car had slowed down J III.239. See also paṭi°.

Passaddhatā (f.) [abstr. fr. passaddha] calmness, repose Nd² 166.

Passaddhi (f.) [fr. pa+**śrambh**] calmness, tranquillity, repose, serenity M III.86; S II.30; IV.78; V.66; A IV.455 sq.; Ps II.244; Dhs 40 (kāya°), 41 (citta°), cp. *Dhs. trsl.* 23; Vism 129; VbhA 314 (kāya°, citta°); DhsA 150 (=samassāsa-ppatta). Often combᵈ with pāmujja & pīti, e. g. D I.72, 73, 196; Nett 29, 66. Six passaddhis at S IV.217 (with ref. to vācā, vitakka-vicārā, pīti, assāsa-passāsā, saññā-vedanā, rāga-dosa-moha, through the 4 jhānas etc.). Passaddhi is one of the 7 sambojjhangas (constituents of enlightenment): see this & cp. M III.86; Vism 130, 134 = VbhA 282 (where 7 conditions of this state are enumᵈ).

Passanā see anu°, vi°.

Passambhati [pa+**śrambh**] to calm down, to be quiet Vin I.294 (fut °issati); D I.73; M III.86; S V.333; A III.21. — pp. passaddha; Caus. passambheti (q. v.).

Passambhanā (f.) [fr. passambhati] allayment, calmness, composure Dhs 40, 41, 320.

Passambhati [Caus. of passambhati] to calm down, quiet, allay M I.56, 425; S III.125; Vism 288 (=nirodheti). ppr. passambhayaŋ M I.56; III.82, 89.

Passaya [fr. pa+**śri**, cp. Class. Sk. praśraya reverence] refuge Cp. III.10⁴. — *Note*. °passaya in kaṇṭakapassaya J III.74, & kaṇṭakāpassayika D I.167 (kaṇṭh°); J IV.299 (kaṇṭaka°) is to be read as °apassaya (apa+**śri**).

Passavati [pa+**sru**] to flow forth, to pour out Miln 180.

Passasati [pa+**śvas**] to breathe in D II.291; M I.56; III.82; J III.296; V.43; Vism 271; DhA I.215. See also assasati & remarks under ā¹ 3.

Passāva [fr. passavati] urine (lit. flowing out) Vin II.141; IV.266 (p. muttaŋ vuccati); D I.70 (uccāra+); M III.3, 90; J I.164 (uccāra-passāvaŋ vissajjeti), 338; V.164, 389; Vism 235 (uccāra°).
-doṇikā a trough for urine Vin II.221; Vism 235.

Passāsa [fr. pa+**śvas**] inhaled breath, inhalation S I.106, 159; Ps I.95, 164 sq., 182 sq. Usually in combⁿ assāsa-passāsa (q. v.). At Vism 272 passāsa is explᵈ as "ingoing wind" and assāsa as "outgoing wind."

Passāsin (adj.) [fr. passāsa] breathing; in ghuru-ghuru° snoring S I.117.

Passika (adj.) (-°) [fr. imper. passa of passati, + ka] only in cpd. ehipassika (q. v.).

Passupati [pa+**svap**] to sleep, rest, aor. passupi; fut. passupissati J V.70, 71.

Paha¹ (nt.) [?] flight of steps from which to step down into the water, a ghat (=tittha Bdhgh) D I.223. The meaning is uncertain, it is trslᵈ as "accessible" at *Dial.* I.283 (q. v. for further detail). Neumann (*Majjhima trslⁿ* I.513) trslˢ "ganz und gar erloschen" (pabhā ?). It is not at all improbable to take pahaŋ as ppr. of pajahati (as contracted fr. pajahaŋ like pahatvāna for pajahitvāna at Sn 639), thus meaning "giving up entirely." The same form in the latter meaning occurs at ThA 69 (Ap. V.3).

Paha² (adj.) = pahu, i. e. able to (with inf.) J V.198 (C. pahū samattho).

Pahaŋsati¹ [pa+haŋsati¹ = ghaŋsati¹, of **ghṛṣ** to rub, grind] to strike, beat (a metal), rub, sharpen (a cutting instrument, as knife, hatchet, razor etc.) J I.278; II.102 (pharasuŋ); DhA I.253 (khuraŋ pahaŋsi sharpened the razor; corresponds to ghaṭṭeti in preceding context). — pp. pahaṭṭha¹ & pahaŋsita¹ (q. v.).

Pahaŋsati² [pa+haŋsati² = hassati, of **hṛṣ** to be glad, cp. ghaŋsati²] to be pleased, to rejoice; only in pp. pahaṭṭha² & pahaŋsita² (q. v.), and in Pass. pahaŋsīyati to be gladdened, to exult Miln 326 (+kuhīyati). See also sam°.

Pahaŋsita¹ [pp. of pahaŋsati] struck, beaten (of metal), refined J VI.218 (ukkā-mukha°), 574 (id.).

Pahaŋsita² [pp. of pahaŋsati²] gladdened, delighted, happy DhA I.230 (°mukha); VvA 279 (°mukha SS pahasita at Miln 297 is better to be taken as pp. of pahasati, because of combⁿ haṭṭha pahaṭṭha hasita pahasita.

Pahaṭa [pp. of paharati] assailed, struck, beaten (of musical instruments) J II.102, 182; VI.189; VvA 161 (so for pahata); PvA 253. Of a ball: driven, impelled Vism 143 (°citra-genḍuka) = DhsA 116 (so read for pahaṭṭha-citta-bhenḍuka and correct *Expositor* 153 accordingly). The reading pahaṭa at PvA 4 is to be corrected to paṭaha.

Pahaṭṭha¹ [pp. of pahaŋsati¹] struck, beaten (of metal) J VI.217 (suvaṇṇa).

Pahaṭṭha² [pp. of pahaŋsati²] gladdened, happy, cheerful, delighted Vin III.14; J I.278 (twice; once as °mānasa, which is wrongly taken by C. as pahaṭṭha¹), 443; II.240 (tuṭṭha°); Vism 346 (haṭṭha°); DhA I.230 (tuṭṭha°); VvA 337. In its original sense of "bristling" (with excitement or joy), with ref. to ear & hair of an elephant in phrase pahaṭṭha-kaṇṇa-vāla at Vin II.195 = J V.335 (cp. Sk. prahṛṣṭa-roman, N. of an Asura at Kathāsaritsāgara 47, 30).

Pahata [pp. of pa+**han**] killed, overcome M III.46; S II.54; J VI.512.

Paharaṇa (nt.) [fr. paharati] striking, beating SnA 224; PvA 285.

Paharaṇaka (adj.) [fr. paharaṇa] striking, hitting J I.418.

Paharati [pa+**hṛ**] to strike, hit, beat J III.26, 347; VI.376; VvA 65; PvA 4; freq. in phrase accharaŋ p. to snap one's finger, e. g. J II.447; see accharā¹. aor. pahāsi (cp. pariyudāhāsi) Vv 29⁸ (=pahari VvA 123). — pp. pahaṭa (q. v.). Caus. paharāpeti. — 1. to cause to be assailed J IV.150. — 2. to put on or join on to J VI.32 (°hārāpesi).

Pahasati [pa+**has**] to laugh, giggle J V.452 (ūhasati+). See also pahassati & pahāsati. — pp. pahasita (q. v.).

Pahasita [pp. of pahasati or °hassati] laughing, smiling, joyful, pleased Miln 297; J I.411 (nicca° mukha); II.179.

Pahassati [pa + **has**, perhaps pa + **hṛṣ**, Sk. harṣati, cp. pahaŋsati²] to laugh, be joyful or cheerful Sn 887 (= haṭṭha pahaṭṭha Nd¹ 290; cp. SnA 555 hāsajāta). The pp. pahasita (q. v.) is derived fr. pres. pahasati, which makes the equation pahassati = pahaŋsati² all the more likely.

Pahāna (nt.) [fr. pa + **hā**, see pajahati] giving up, leaving, abandoning, rejection M I.60, III.4, 72; S I.13, 132 (dukkha°); II.170; III.53; IV.7 sq.; D III.225, 246; A I.82, 134; II.26, 232 (kaṇhassa kammassa °āya); III.431; Sn 374, 1106 (= vūpasama paṭinissagga etc. Nd² 429); Dh 331; J I.79; Ps I.26; II.98, 156; Pug 16; Dhs 165, 174, 339; Nett 15 sq., 24, 192; Vism 194 (nīvaraṇa-santāpa°); DhsA 166, 345; VvA 73. -°pariññā see pariññā; -°vinaya avoidance consisting in giving up (coupled with saŋvara-vinaya avoidance by protection, prophylaxis), based on the 5 qualities tadanga-pahāna, vikkhambhana°, samuccheda°, paṭippassaddhi°, nissaraṇa° DhsA 351; SnA 8.

Pahāya is ger. of pajahati (q. v.).

Pahāyin (adj.) [fr. pa + **hā**, see pajahati] giving up, abandoning Sn 1113, 1132, cp. Nd² 431; Sdhp 500.

Pahāra [fr. pa + **hṛ**, Class. Sk. prahāra, see paharati] 1. a blow, stroke, hit D I.144 (daṇḍa°); M I.123, 126; Pv IV.16⁷ (sālittaka°); M I.; DhA III.48 (°dāna-sikkhāpada the precepts concerning those guilty of giving blows, cp. Vin IV.146); PvA 4 (ekappahārena with one stroke). 56 (muggara°), 66 (id.) 253. — ekappahārena at Vism 418 as adv. "all at once." pahāraŋ deti to give a blow Vin IV.146; S IV.62; A III.121; Vism 314 (pahāra-satāni); PvA 191 (sīse). — 2. a wound J IV.89; V.459 (°mukha).

Pahāraṇa see abhi°.

Pahārin (adj.) [fr. paharati] striking, assaulting J II.211.

Pahāsa [fr. pa + **has**, cp. Class. Sk. prahāsa] laughing, mirth Dhs 9, 86, 285; VvA 132; Sdhp 223.

Pahāsati in pahāsanto saparisaŋ at ThA 69 should preferably be read as pahāsayanto parisaŋ, thus taken as Caus. of pa + **has**, i. e. making one smile, gladdening.

Pahāsi is 3rd sg. aor. of paharati; found at Vv 29⁸ (musalena = pahari VvA 113); and also 3rd sg. aor of pajahati, e. g. at Sn 1057 (= pajahi Nd² under jahati)

Pahāseti [Caus. of pahasati] to make laugh, to gladden, to make joyful Vism 289 (cittaŋ pamodeti hāseti pahāseti).

Pahiṇa (adj.-n.) [fr. pa + **hi**] sending; being sent; a messenger, in °gamaṇa going as messenger, doing messages D I.5; M I.345; J II.82; Miln 370; DA I.78. See also pahana.

Pahiṇaka (nt.) [fr. pahiṇati ?] a sweetmeat A III.76 (v. l. pahenaka). See also paheṇaka. The (late) Sk. form is prahelaka.

Pahiṇati [pa + **hi**, Sk. hinoti] to send; Pres. pahiṇati Vin III.140 sq.; IV.18; DhA II.243; aor. pahiṇi J I.60 (sāsanaŋ); V.458 (paṇṇāni); VvA 67; DhA I.72; II.56, 243; ger. pahiṇitva VvA 65. — pp. pahita² (q. v.). There is another aor. pāhesi (Sk. prāhaiṣīt) in analogy to which a new pres. pāheti has been formed, so that pāhesi is now felt to be a der. fr. pāheti & accordingly is grouped with the latter. All other forms with he° (pahetuŋ e. g.) are to be found under pāheti.

Pahiṇana (nt.) [fr. pahiṇati] sending, dispatch DhA II.243.

Pahita¹ [pp. of padahati] resolute, intent, energetic; only in cpd. pahitatta of resolute will (cp. BSk. prahitātman Divy 37) M I.114; S I.53 (expl^d by Bdhgh with wrong derivation fr. peseti as "pesit-atta" thus identifying pahita¹ & pahita², see *K.S.* 320); II.21, 239; III.73 sq.; IV.60, 145, V.187, A II.14, III.21, IV.302 sq.; V.84; Sn 425, 432 sq., 961; It 71; Nd¹ 477; Th 2, 161 (expl at ThA 143, with the same mistake as above, as pesita citta); Nd¹ 477 (id.; pesit-atta); Miln 358, 366, 406.

Pahita² [pp. of pahiṇati] sent J I.86 (sāsana); DhA II.242; III.191 (interchanging with pesita).

Pahīna [pp. of pajahati] given up, abandoned, left, eliminated Vin III.97 = IV.27; S II.24; III.33; IV.305; Sn 351 (°jāti-maraṇa), 370, 564, 1132 (°mala-moha); It 32; Nd² s. v.; Ps I.63; II.244; Pug 12, 22.

Pahīyati [Pass. of pajahati] to be abandoned, to pass away, vanish M I.7; S I.219 (fut. °issati); II.196 (ppr. °īyamāna); V.152; Sn 806; Nd¹ 124; VbhA 271. Spelt pahiyyati at S V.150.

Pahū (adj.) [cp. Vedic prabhū, fr. pa + **bhū**] able Sn 98; J V.198; Nd² 615^c.

Pahūta (adj.) [pp. of pa + **bhū**, cp. Vedic prabhūta] sufficient, abundant, much, considerable Sn 428, 862 sq.; Pv I.5² (= anappaka, bahu, yāvadattha C.; Dhp at PvA 25 gives bahuka as inferior variant); I.11⁷ (= apariyanta, uḷāra; v. l. bahū); II.7⁵ (v. l. bahūta); PvA 145 (dhana; v. l. bahuta); SnA 294 (id.), 321 (id.). See also bahūta.

-**jivha** large tongued D II.18; III.144, 173. -**jivhatā** the characteristic of a large tongue Sn p. 107. -**dhañña** having many riches J IV.309. -**dhana** id. Th 2, 406 (C. reading for T. bahuta-ratana). -**pañña** rich in wisdom So 359, 539, 996. -**bhakkha** eating much, said of the fire S I.69. -**vitta** = °dhañña D I.134; Sn 102; PvA 3.

Pahūtika (adj.) = pahuta PvA 135 (v. l. BB bahuta; in expl^n of bahu).

Paheṇaka (nt.) [cp. BSk. praheṇaka in sense of "sweetmeat" at Divy 13, 258; the *Sk. form is prahelaka] a present J VI.369 (so here, whereas the same word as pahiṇaka at A III.76 clearly means "sweetmeat").

Pahena (nt.) [paheṇa ?] same as pahiṇa in °gamana going on errands J II.82.

Pahoti & (in verse) pabhavati [pa + **bhū**, cp. Vedic prabhavati in meaning "to be helpful"] 1. to proceed from (with gen.), rise, originate D II.217; M III.76; S II.184; as pabhavati at Sn 728 = 1050 (cp. Nd² 401); (perf. med.) pahottha it has arisen from (gen.), i. e. it was the fault of J V.102. — 2. to be sufficient, adequate or able (with inf.) D I.240; M I.94; S I.102; Sn 36, 867; J V.305; DA I.192; III.254 (fut. pahossati); VvA 75; Dāvs IV.18. Neg. both with na° & a° viz. nappahoti J VI.204; DhA III.408; nappahosi J I.84; appahoti DhA IV.177; appabhonto PvA 73; in verse appabhavaŋ J III.373 (= appahonto C.). — pp. pahūta (q. v.).

Pahona in °kāla at J III.17 read as pahonaka°.

Pahonaka (adj.) [fr. pahoti] sufficient, enough J I.346; II.122; III.17 (so read for pahona°); IV.277; Vism 404; DhA I.78, 219; VvA 264; PvA 81.

Pāka [Vedic pāka, see pacati] that which is cooked, cooking, quantity cooked J VI.161 (tīhi pākehi pacitvā); VvA 186. Esp. in foll. comb^n tela° "oil cooking," an oil decoction Vin II.105; thāli° a th. full of cooking J I.186; doṇa° a d. full S I.81; DhA II.8; sosāna° Dhātumañjūsā 132 (under kaṭh). On pāka in appl^d meaning of "effect, result" see *Cpd.* 88³. — As nt. in stanza "pākaŋ pākassa paccayo; apākaŋ avipākassa" at VbhA 175. — Cp. vi°.

-tela an oil concoction or mixture; used for rubbing the body; usually given with its price worth 100 or 1,000 pieces, e. g. sata° J II.397; V.376; VvA 68 = DhA III.311; sahassa° J III.372. -vaṭṭa subsistence, livelihood, maintenance Mhvs 35. 120; DhA II.29; VvA 220. -haŋsa a species of water bird J v.356; VI.539; SnA 277.

Pākata (adj.) [=pakata; on ā for a see Geiger, *P.Gr.* § 33[1]. Cp. Sk. prakaṭa Halāyudha. The spelling is sometimes pākaṭa] 1. common, vulgar, uncontrolled, in phrase **pākat-indriya** of uncontrolled mind S I.61 (=saŋvarâbhāvena gihikāle viya vivaṭa-indriya *K.S.* 320), 204; III.93; V.269; A I.70, 266, 280; III.355, 391; Th 1, 109 (C. asaŋvuta, see *Brethren* 99); Pug 35. — At Miln 251 pākatā is to be read pāpakā. — 2. open, common, unconcealed J I.262 (pākaṭo jāto was found out); Sn A 343; PvA 103 (for āvi). — 3. commonly known, familiar Vism 279; PvA 17 (devā), 23, 78 (su°), 128; VvA 109 (+paññāta); °ŋ karoti to make manifest Vism 287; °bhāva being known DhsA 243; PvA 103. — 4. renowned, well-known DA I.143; PvA 107.

Pākatika (adj.) [fr. pakati, cp. BSk. prākṛtaka (loka) Bodhicaryâvatāra v. 3, ed. Poussin] natural, in its original or natural state J V.274; Miln 218 (maṇi-ratana); DhA I.20; VvA 288; PvA 66 (where id. p. J III.167 reads paṭipākatika), 206; pākatikaŋ **karoti** to restore to its former condition, to repair, rebuild J I.354, also fig. to restore a dismissed officer, to reinstate J V.134.

Pākāra [cp. Epic Sk. prākāra, pa+ā+**kṛ**] an encircling wall, put up for obstruction and protection, a fence, rampart Vin II.121 (3 kinds: made of bricks, of stone, or of wood, viz. iṭṭhakā°, silā, dāru°); IV.266 (id.); M III.11; S IV.194 (°toraṇa); A IV.107; V.195; J I.63; II.50; VI.330 (mahā°), 341 (+parikhā & aṭṭāla); Pv I.10[13] (ayo°); Miln 1; Vism 394 (=parikkhepa-pākāra); DhA III.441 (tiṇṇaŋ pākārānaŋ antare); PvA 24, 52; sāṇi° screen-fencing J II.88; PvA 283.
-iṭṭhakā brick or tile of a wall J III.446 (T. iṭṭhikā). -parikkhitta surrounded by a wall DA I.42. -parikkhepa a fencing Vism 74.

Pākāsiya (adj.) [fr. pa+ā+**kāś**, cp. pakāsati & Class. Sk. prākāśya] evident, manifest, open, clear J VI.230 (opp. guyha; C. pākāsika).

Pākula (adj.) [pa+ākula] read at Ud 5 in comb[n] akkula-pakkula (=ākula-pākula) "in great confusion"; read also in gāthā 7 pākula for bakkula. Cp. Morris, *J.P.T.S.* 1886, 94 sq.

Pāgabbhiya (nt.) [fr. pagabbha] boldness, impudence, forwardness Sn 930; Nd[1] 228 sq. (3 kinds, viz. kāyika, vācasika, cetasika), 390 sq.; J II.32; V.449 (pagab-bhiya); SnA 165; KhA 242; DhA III.354 (pa°); VvA 121.

Pāguññatā (f.) [abstr. of pāguñña, which is der. fr. paguna] being familiar with, experience Dhs 48, 49; Vism 463 sq., 466.

Pāgusa [cp. Sk. vāgusa, a sort of large fish Halāyudha 3, 37] a certain kind of fish J IV.70 (as gloss, T. reads pāvusa, SS puṭusa, BB pātusa & pāvuma; C. expl[ns] as mahā-mukha-maccha).

Pācaka (adj.-n.) [fr. **pac**, cp. pāceti] one who cooks, a cook; f. °ikā J I.318.

Pācana[1] (nt.) [fr. **pac**, Caus. pāceti] bringing to boil, cooking J I.318 (yāgu°). Cp pari°.

Pācana[2] (nt.) [for pājana, cp. pāceti[2] & SnA 147] a goad, stick S I.172; Sn p. 13; V.77; J III.281; IV.310.
-yaṭṭhi driving stick, goad stick S I.115.

Pācariya (-°) [pa+ācariya] only as 2nd part of a (redupl.) compound ācariya-pācariya in the nature of comb[ns] mentioned under a[1] 3 b: "teacher upon teacher" (expl[d] by C[s] as "teacher of teachers") D I.90 (cp. DA I.254); II.237, etc. (see ācariya).

Pācittiya (adj.) [most likely prāk+citta+ika, i. e. of the nature of directing one's mind upon, cp. pabbhāra = *prāg+bhāra. So expl[d] also by S. Lévi *J.As.* x.20, p. 506. Geiger, *P.Gr.* § 27, n. 1 inclines to etym. prāyaś+cittaka] requiring expiation, expiatory Vin I.172, 176; II.242, 306 sq.; IV.1 sq., 258 sq.; A II.242 (dhamma); Vism 22. — It is also the name of one of the books of the Vinaya (ed. Oldenberg, vol. IV.). See on term *Vin. Texts* I.18, 32, 245.

Pācīna (adj.) [Vedic prācīna, fr. adv. prāc bent forward] eastern i. e. facing the (rising) sun (opp. pacchā) J I.50 (°sīsaka, of Māyādevī's couch), 212 (°lokadhātu); Miln 6; DA I.311 (°mukha facing east); DhA III.155 (id.); VvA 190; PvA 74, 256. The opposite apācīna (e. g. S III.84) is only apparently a neg. pācīna, in reality a der. fr. apa (apa+**ac**), as pācīna is a der. fr. pra+**ac**. See apācīna.

Pāceti[1] [Caus. of pacati] to cause to boil, fig. to cause to torment D I.52 (ppr. pācayato, gen., also pācento). Cp. vi°.

Pāceti[2] [for pājeti, with c. for j (see Geiger, *P.Gr.* § 39[3]); pra+**aj**: see aja] to drive, urge on Dh 135 (āyuŋ p. = gopālako viya . . . peseti DhA III.60).

Pājana (nt.) [fr. pa+**aj**, cp. pācana[2]] a good SnA 147.

Pājāpeti [Caus. of pājeti] to cause to drive or go on J II.296 (sakaṭāni); III.51 (so read for pajāpeti; BB pāceti & pājeti)

Pājeti [Caus. of pa+**aj**, cp. aja] 1. to drive (cp. pāceti[2]) J II.122, 143, III.51 (BB for T. pājāpeti); V.443 (nāvaŋ); VI.32 (yoggaŋ); SnA 147; DhA IV.160 (gone). — 2. to throw (the dice) J VI.281. — Caus. II. pājāpeti (q. v.).

Pāṭankī (f.) "sedan chair" (?) in phrase sivikaŋ pāṭankiŋ at Vin I.192 (MV v.10, 3) is not clear. The vv. ll. (p. 380) are pāṭangin, pāṭangan pāṭakan. Perhaps pallankaŋ?

Pāṭala (adj.) [cp. Class. Sk. pāṭala, to same root as palita & pāṇḍu: see Walde, *Lat. Wtb.* under palleo & cp. paṇḍu] pale red, pink J IV.114.

Pāṭali (f.) [cp. Class. Sk. pāṭalī, to pāṭala] the trumpet flower, Bignonia Suaveolens D II.4 (Vipassī pāṭaliyā mūle abhisambuddho); Vv 35[9]; J I.41 (°rukkha as the Bodhi tree).; II.162 (pātali-bhaddaka sic. v. l. for phālibhaddaka); IV.440; V.189; VI.537; Miln 338; VvA 42, 164; ThA 211, 226.

Pāṭava (nt.) [cp. late Sk. pāṭava, fr. paṭu] skill KhA 156.

Pāṭikankha (adj.) [grd. of paṭikankhati, Sk. *pratikānkṣya] to be desired or expected M I.25; III.97; S I.88; II.152; A III.143 = Sn p. 140 (=icchitabba SnA 504); Ud 36; DhA IV.2 (gati °ā); PvA 63 (id.).

Pāṭikankhin (-°) (adj.-n.) [fr. paṭi+**kānkṣ**, cp. patikan-khin] hoping for, one who expects or desires D I.4; M III.33; A II.209; J III.409.

Pāṭikā (f.) [etym. unknown; with pāṭiya cp. Sk. pāṣya?] half-moon stone, the semicircular slab under the staircase Vin I.180 (cp. *Vin. Texts* II.3). As pāṭiya at J VI.278 (=piṭṭhi-pāsāṇa C.).

Pāṭikulyā (f.) [fr. paṭi(k)kūla] = pāṭikkūlyatā (perhaps to be read as such) J V.253 (nava, cp. Vism 341 sq.).

Pāṭikkulyatā (f.) [abstr. fr. paṭikkūla] loathsomeness, objectionableness A III.32; IV.47 sq.; V.64. Cp. paṭikulyatā, paṭikūlatā & pāṭikulyā.

Pāṭidesanīya (adj.) [grd. of paṭideseti with pāṭi for pāṭi in der.] belonging to confession, (a sin) which ought to be confessed Vin I.172; II.242; A II.243 (as °desanīyaka).

Pāṭipada[1] (adj.) [the adj. form of paṭipadā] following the (right) Path M I.354 = It 80 (+sikha).

Pāṭipada[2] [fr. paṭi + **pad**, see patipajjati & cp. paṭipadā] lit. "entering, beginning"; the first day of the lunar fortnight Vin I.132; J IV.100; VvA 72 (°sattamī).

Pāṭipadaka (adj.) [fr. pāṭipada[2]] belonging to the 1st day of the lunar fortnight; only with ref. to bhatta (food) & in combn with pakkhika & uposathika, i. e. food given on the half-moon days, on the 7th day of the week & on the first day of the fortnight Vin I.58 = II.175; IV.75, 78.

Pāṭipuggalika (adj.) [fr. paṭipuggala] belonging to one's equal M III.254 sq. (dakkhiṇā).

Pāṭibhoga [for paṭibhoga (?); difficult to explain, we should suspect a ger. formation *prati-bhogya for *bhujya i. e. "counter-enjoyable," i. e. one who has to be made use of in place of someone else; cp. Geiger, *P.Gr.* § 24] a sponsor A II.172; Ud 17; It 1 sq.; J II.93; Vism 555 sq.; DhA I.398; VbhA 165.

Pāṭimokkha (pāti)° (nt.) [with Childers plausibly as paṭi + mokkha, grd. of **muc** (Caus. mokṣ°) with lengthening of paṭi as in other grd. like pāṭidesaniya. Thus in reality the same as paṭimokkha 2 in sense of binding, obligatory, obligation, cp. J V.25. The spelling is freq. pāti° (BB pāṭi°). The Sk. prātimokṣa is a wrong adaptation fr. P. pātimokkha, it should really be pratimokṣya "that which should be made binding." An expln of the word after the style of a popular etym. is to be found at Vism 16] a name given to a collection of various precepts contained in the Vinaya (forming the foundation of the Suttavibhanga, Vin vols. III & IV., ed. Oldenberg), as they were recited on Uposatha days for the purpose of confession. See Geiger, *P. Lit.* c. 7, where literature is given; & cp. *Vin. Texts* I.27 sq.; Franke, *Dighanikāya* p. 66 sq.; —pāṭimokkhaŋ uddisati to recite the P. Vin I.102, 112, 175; II.259; III.8; IV.143; Ud 51; opp. °ŋ ṭhapeti to suspend the (recital of the) P. Vin II.240 sq. — See Vin I.65, 68; II.95, 240 sq. 249; S V.187; Sn 340; Dh 185, 375; Nd[1] 365; Vism 7, 11, 16 sq., 36, 292; DhA III.237 (=jeṭṭhaka-sīla); IV.111 (id.); Sdhp 342, 355, 449. -uddesa recitation of the P. Vin I.102; D II.46; M II.8; SnA 199. -uddesaka one who recites the P. Vin I.115, cp. *Vin. Texts* I.242. -ṭhapana suspension of the P. Vin II.241 sq.; A V.70. -saŋvara "restraint that is binding on a recluse" (*Dial.* I.79), moral control under the P. Vin IV.51; D I.62; II.279; III.77, 266, 285; A III.113, 135, 151; IV.140; V.71, 198; It 96, 118; Ud 36; Vism 16 (where expld in detail); VbhA 323; cp. saŋvuta-pāṭimokkha (adj.) Pv IV.1[32].

Pāṭiyekka see pāṭekka.

Pāṭirūpika (adj.) [fr. paṭirūpa, cp. paṭirūpaka] assuming a disguise, deceitful, false Sn 246.

Pāṭihāra [=pāṭihāra, with pāṭi after analogy of pāṭihāriya] striking, that which strikes (with ref. to marking the time) J I.121, 122 (v. l. SS pāṭihāriya).

Pāṭihārika [=pāṭihāriya or der. fr. pāṭihāra in meaning of °hāriya] special, extraordinary; only in cpd. °pakkha an extra holiday A I.144; Vv 15[6] (cp. VvA 71, 109); ThA 38.

Pāṭihāriya (adj.) [grd. formation fr. paṭi + **hṛ** (paṭihāra) with usual lengthening of pati to pāṭi, as in °desanīya, °mokkha etc. Cp. pāṭihīra; BSk. prātihārya] striking, surprising, extraordinary, special; nt. wonder, miracle. Usually in stock phrase iddhi°, ādesanā°, anusāsanī° as the 3 marvels which characterise a Buddha with regard to his teaching (i. e. superhuman power, mind reading, giving instruction) D I.212; III.3 sq.; S IV.290; A I.170; V.327; Ps II.227. — Further: Vin I.34 (aḍḍhuḍḍha° sahassāni); Vism 378, 390 (yamaka°); VvA 158 (id.); PvA 137 (id.). For yamaka-pāṭihāriya (or °hīra) see yamaka. — Two kinds of p. are given at Vism 393, viz. pākaṭa° and apākaṭa°. —sappāṭihāriya (with ref. to the Dhamma) wonderful, extraordinary, sublime, as opposed to appāṭi° plain, ordinary, stupid M II.9 (where Neumann, *Majjhima Nikāya* II.318 trsls sa° "intelligible" and a° "incomprehensible," referring to Chāndogyopaniṣat I.11, 1); D II.104; cp. also Windisch, *Māra* 71.

-pakkha an extra holiday, an ancient festival, not now kept S I.208 (cp. Th 2, 31); Sn 402 (cp. explo at SnA 378, where var. opinions are given); J IV.320; VI.118. See also Kern's discussion of the term at *Toev.* II.30.

Pāṭihīra (adj.) [contracted form of pāṭihāriya viâ metathesis *pāṭihāriya > *pāṭihēra > paṭihīra] wonderful; nt. a wonderful thing, marvel, miracle Ps I.125 (yamaka°); II.158 (id.); Mhvs 5, 118; Miln 106; Dāvs I.50; DhA III.213. —appāṭihīrakathā stupid talk D I.193, 239; Kvu 561 (diff. Kern. *Toev.* II.30); opp. sa° ibid.

Pāṭī (f.) [?] at VvA 321 in phrase sukka-pakkha-pāṭiyaŋ "in the moonlight half" is doubtful. Hardy in Index registers it as "part, half-," but pakkha already means "half" and is enough by itself. We should probably read paṭipāṭiyaŋ "successively." Note that the similar passage VvA 314 reads sukka-pakkhe pannarasiyaŋ.

Pāṭuka & Pāṭubha only neg. a° (q. v.).

Pāṭukamyatā: see pātu°.

Pāṭekka (Pāṭiyekka) (adj.) [paṭi + eka; the diaeretic form of pacceka: see Geiger, *P.Gr.* § 24] several, distinct, single Vin I.134; IV.15; J I.92 (T. pāṭiekka, SS pāṭiyekka); Vism 249 (pāṭiyekka, SS pāṭiekka), 353, 356, 443, 473; DhA IV.7 (pāṭiy° SS pāṭieka). — nt. °ŋ (adv.) singly, separately, individually Vism 409 (pāṭiy°); VvA 141.

Pāṭeti [Caus. of **paṭ**] to remove; Pass. pāṭiyati Pv IV.1[47] (turned out of doors); v. l. pātayati (bring to fall). Prob. in sense of Med. at Miln 152 in phrase visaŋ pāṭiyamāno (doubtful, cp. Kern, *Toev.* II.139, & Morris, *J.P.T.S.* 1884, 87).

Pāṭha [fr. **paṭh**] reading, text-reading; passage of a text, text. Very freq. in Commentaries with phrase "ti pi pāṭho," i. e. "so is another reading," e. g. KhA 78, 223; SnA 43 (°ŋ vikappeti), 178, 192, 477; PvA 25 (pamāda° careless text), 48, 58, 86 and passim.

Pāṭhaka (-°) [fr. pāṭha] reciter; one who knows, expert Nd[1] 382 (nakkhatta°); J I.455 (asi-lakkhaṇa°); II.21 (angavijjā°), 250 (id.); V.211 (lakkhaṇa° fortune-teller, wise man).

Pāṭhīna [cp. Sk. pāṭhīna Manu 5, 16; Halāyudha 3, 36] the fish Silurus Boalis, a kind of shad J IV.70 (C: pāṭhīna-nāmakaŋ pāsāṇa-macchaŋ); V.405; VI.449.

Pāṇa [fr. pa + **an**, cp. Vedic prāṇa breath of life; P. apāna, etc.] living being, life, creature D III.48, 63, 133; S I.209, 224; V.43, 227, 441 (mahā-samudde); A I.161; II.73, 176, 192; Sn 117, 247, 394, 704; Dh 246; DA I.69, 161; KhA 26; ThA 253; PvA 9, 28, 35; VvA 72; DhA II.19. — pl. also pāṇāni, e. g. Sn 117; Dh 270. —

Bdhgh's def^n of pāṇa is "pāṇanatāya pāṇā; assāsa-passās' āyatta-vuttitāyā ti attho" Vism 310.
-âtipāta destruction of life, murder Vin I.83 (in "dasa sikkhāpadāni," see also sīla), 85, 193; D III.68, 70, 149, 182, 235; M I.361; III.23; Sn 242; It 63; J III.181; Pug 39 sq.; Nett 27; VbhA 383 (var. degrees of murder); DhA II.19; III.355; DA I.69; PvA 27. -âtipātin one who takes the life of a living being, destroying life D III.82; M III.22; S II.167; It 92; DhA II.19. -upeta possessed or endowed with life, alive [cp. BSk. prāṇopeta Divy 72, 462 etc.] S I.173; Sn 157; DA I.236. -ghāta slaying life, killing, murder DA I.69; -ghātin = âtipātin DhA II.19. -bhu a living being J IV.494. -bhūta = °bhu M III.5; A II.210; III.92; IV.249 sq.; J IV.498. -vadha = âtipāta DA I.69. -sama equal to or as dear as life J II.343; Dpvs XI.26; DhA I.5. -hara taking away life, destructive M I.10 = III.97; S IV.206; A II.116, 143, 153; III.163.

Pāṇaka (adj.-n.) (usually -°) [fr. pāṇa] a living being, endowed with (the breath of) life S IV.198 (chap°); DhA I.20 (v. l. BB mata°); sap° with life, containing living creatures J I.198 (udaka); ap° without living beings, lifeless Vin II.216; M I.13, 243; S I.169; Sn p. 15 (udaka); J I.67 (jhāna).

Pāṇana (nt.) [fr. pāṇa] breathing Vism 310 (see pāṇa); Dhātupāṭha 273 ("bala" pāṇane).

Pāṇi [Vedic pāṇi, cp. Av. pərənā hand, with n-suffix, where we find m-suffix in Gr. παλάμη, Lat. palma, Oir lām, Ohg. folma = Ags. folm] the hand Vin III.14 (pāṇinā paripuñchati); M I.78 (pāṇinā parimajjati); S I.178, 194; Sn 713; Dh 124; J I.126 (°ŋ paharati); PugA 249 (id.); PvA 56; Sdhp 147, 238. As *adj.* (-°) "handed," with a hand, e. g. alla° with clean hand Pv II.9^9; payata° with outstretched hand, open-handed, liberal S V.351; A III.287; IV.266 sq.; V.331.
-tala the palm of the hand D II.17. -bhāga hand-share, division by hands VvA 96. -matta of the size of a hand, a handful PvA 70, 116, 119. -ssara hand-sound, hand music, a cert. kind of musical instrument D I.6; III.183; DA I.84 (cp. Dial I.8), 231; J V.390, 506; cp. BSk. pāṇisvara MVastu II.52. Also *adj.* one who plays this instrument J VI.276; cp. BSk. pāṇisvarika MVastu III.113.

Pāṇikā (f.) [fr. pāṇi; Sk. *pāṇikā] a sort of spoon Vin II.151. Cp. puthu-pāṇikā (°pāṇiyā ?) Vin II.106.

Pāṇin (adj.-n.) [fr. pāṇa] having life, a living being S I.210, 226; Sn 220 (acc. pl. pāṇine, cp. Geiger, *P.Gr.* § 95^2), 587 (id.), 201, 575; PvA 287; DhA II.19.

Pāta (-°) [fr. pat] 1. fall DA I.95 (ukkā°); PvA 45 (asani°). The reading "anatthato pātato rakkhito" at PvA 61 is faulty we should prefer to read apagato (apāyato ?) rakkhito. — 2. throwing, a throw Sn 987 (muddha°); PvA 57 (akkhi°). See also piṇḍa.

Pātana (nt.) [fr. pāteti] bringing to fall, destroying, killing, only in gabbha° destroying the fœtus, abortion (q. v.) DhA I.47 and passim.

Pātar (adv.) [Vedic prātar, der. fr. *prō, *prā, cp. Lat. prandium (fr. prām-edịom = pātar-āsa); Gr. πρωί early; Ohg. fruo = Ger. früh] early in the morning, in foll. forms: (1) pātar (before vowels), only in cpd. °āsa morning meal, breakfast [cp. BSk. prātar-aśana Divy 631] D III.94; Sn 387; J I.232; VvA 294, 308; SnA 374 (pāto asitabbo ti pātar-āso piṇḍa-pātass' etaŋ nāmaŋ). — katapātarāsa (adj.) after breakfast J I.227; VI.349 (°bhetta); Vism 391. — (2) pāto (abs.) D III.94; DhA II.60; PvA 54, 126, 128; pāto va right early J I.226; VI.180. — (3) pātaŋ S I.183; II.242; Th 2, 407. — *Note.* Should piṇḍa-pāta belong here, as suggested by Bdhgh at SnA 374 (see above)? See detail under piṇḍa.

Pātavyatā (f.) [fr. pāt, see pāteti] downfall, bringing to fall, felling M I.305; A I.266; Vin IV.34 (°by°); VbhA 499.

Pātāpeti [Caus. II. of pāteti] to cause to fall, to cause an abortus Vin II.108; DA I.134.

Pātāla [cp. Epic Sk. pātāla an underground cave] proclivity, cliff, abyss S I.32, 127, 197; IV.206; Th 1, 1104 (see *Brethren* 418 for fuller expl^n); J III.530 (here expl^d as a cliff in the ocean).

Pāti [Vedic pāti of pā, cp. Gr. πῶυ herd, ποιμήν shepherd, Lat. pāsco to tend sheep] to watch, keep watch, keep J III.95 (to keep the eyes open, C. ummisati; opp. nimisati); Vism 16 (= rakkhati in def. of pātimokkha).

Pātika = pāti, read at Vism 28 for patika.

Pātita [pp. of pāteti] brought to fall, felled, destroyed Sn 631; Dh 407; J III.176; PvA 31 (so read for patita).

Pātin (-°) (adj.) [fr. pāta] throwing, shooting, only in cpd. dūre° throwing far A I.284; II.170. See akkhaṇa-vedhin.

Pātimokkha see pāṭi°.

Pātī & Pāti (f.) [the former of patta, which is Vedic pātra (nt.); to this the f. Ved. pātrī] a bowl, vessel, dish Vin I.157 (avakkāra°), 352 (id.); II.216 (id.); M I.25 (kaŋsa°), 207; S II.233; A IV.393 (suvaṇṇa°, rūpiya°, kaŋsa°); J I.347, 501; II.90; V.377 (suvaṇṇa°) VI.510 (kañcana°); VvA 65; PvA 274.

Pātukamyatā is frequent v. l. for cāṭu-kamyatā, which is probably the correct reading (see this). The meaning (according to Vism 27 = VbhA 483) is "putting oneself low," i. e. flattery, "fawning" (*Vism trsl.* 32). A still more explicit def^n is found at VbhA 338. The diff. spellings are as follows: cāṭukamyatā Vism 17, 27; KhA 236; VbhA 338, 483; cāṭukammatā Miln 370; pāṭukamyatā Vbh 246; pātukamyatā Nd^2 39. See standing phrase under mugga-sūpyatā.

Pātur (-°) (°pātu) (indecl.) [cp. Vedic prāduḥ in prādur + bhū; on t for d see Geiger, *P.Gr.* § 39^4. As regards etym. Monier Williams suggests prā = pra + dur, door, thus "before the door, openly"; cp. dvāra] visible, open, manifest; only in comp^n with kṛ and bhū, and with the rule that pātu° appears before cons., whereas pātur° stands before vowels. (1) with kṛ (to make appear): pres. pātukaroti Sn 316; J IV.7; Pug 30; SnA 423; aor. pātvākāsi S II.254; DhA II.64; pp. pātukata Vv 84^41. — (2) with bhū (to become manifest, to appear): pres. pātubhavati D I.220; D II.12, 15, 20, 226; M I.445; S IV 78; Pv II.9^41 (pot. °bhaveyyuŋ); aor. pāturahosi [cp. BSk. prādurabhūt Jtm. 211] Vin I.5; D I.215; II.20; S I.137; Pv II.8^6; Miln 10, 18; VvA 188; pl. pāturahaŋsu J I.11, & °ahiŋsu J I.54. — pp. pātubhūta S III.39; Dhs 1035; PvA 44.
-kamma making visible, manifestation S II.254; DhA IV.198. -bhāva appearance, coming into manifestation M I.50; S II.3; IV.78; A I.266; II.130; Sn 560, 998; J I.63; Nd^2 s. v.; Vism 437.

Pāteti [Caus. of pat] 1. to make fall, drop, throw off S I.197 (sakuṇo rajaŋ); J I.93 (udakaŋ); Miln 305 (sāraŋ). — 2. to bring to fall J V.198; Miln 187. — 3. to kill, destroy, cut off (the head) J I.393; III.177; PvA 31, 115. — pp. pātita. Caus. II. pātāpeti (q. v.). — Cp. abhi°. *Note.* In meaning 3 it would be better to assume confusion with pāṭeti (for phāṭeti = Sk. sphāṭayati to split [sphuṭ = (s)phal], see phāleti & phāṭeti In the same sense we find the phrase kaṭṭhaŋ pāteti to split firewood M I.21 (MA ereti), besides phāleti.

Pātheyya (nt.) [grd. form. fr. patha] "what is necessary for the road," provisions for a journey, viaticum Vin I.244; S I.44; Dh 235, 237; J V.46, 241; DA I.288; DhA I.180; III.335; PvA 5, 154.

Pātheyyaka (nt.) = patheyya PvA 126.

Pāda [Vedic pāda, see etym. under pada] 1. the foot, usually pl. pādā both feet, e. g. Vin I.9, 34, 188; It 111; Sn 309, 547, 768, 835, 1028; J II.114; IV.137; DhA III.196; PvA 4, 10, 40, 68; VvA 105. In sg. scarce, and then specified as eka° & dutiya°, e. g. at Nd^2 304^{III}; J VI.354. — 2. foot or base of a mountain Vism 399 (Sineru°); DhA I.108 (pabbata°). — 3. the fourth part ("foot") of a verse (cp. pada 4) SnA 239, 273, 343, 363; ThA 23. — 4. a coin Vin III.47; VvA 77 (worth here ¼ of a kahāpaṇa and double the value of māsaka; see also kākaṇikā).

-anguṭṭha a toe M I.337. -anguṭṭhaka same J II.447; Vism 233. -anguli same PvA 125 (opp. to hatth' anguli finger). -aṭṭhika bone of the foot M I.58, 89; III.92; KhA 49. -âpacca offspring fr. the foot (of Brahmā): see bandhu. -ûdara "(using) the belly as feet," i. e. a snake Sn 604. -odaka water for washing the feet Vin I.9. -kathalika (°iya) acc. to Bdhgh either a foot stool or a towel (adhota-pāda-ṭhapanakaŋ pāda-ghaŋsanaŋ vā, see *Vin. Texts* I.92; II.373) Vin I.9, 46; II.22; IV.310; Kvu 440; VvA 8; DhA I.321. -kudārikā holding the feet like an axe (?) Pv IV.1^{47} (expl^d at PvA 240 by pādasankhātā kudārikā; does k. here represent kuṭhārikā? The reading & meaning is uncertain). -khīla a corn in the foot Vin I.188 (as °ālādha, cp. *Vin Texts* II.19). -ghaŋsanī a towel for rubbing the feet (dry) Vin II.130. -cāra moving about on feet J IV.104. -tala the sole of the foot Vin I.179; M III.90; D III.143, 148; PvA 74. -dhovana cleaning or washing one's feet DhA II.9. -pa "drinking with the foot," N. for tree Pv IV.3^9 (cp. PvA 251); Miln 117, 376; Vism 533; VvA 212; Sdhp 270. -paricārikā "serving on one's feet," i. e. a wife (cp. S I.125) J III.95; VI.268; DhA III.194. -pīṭha a foot-stool Vin I.9 (cp. *Vin. Texts* I.92); IV.310; DhA III.120 = 186; VvA 291. -puñchana(ka) wiping one's feet (with a towel) Vism 358 (°rajju-maṇḍalaka, in comparison = VbhA 62); VbhA 285 (°colaka); KhA 144; SnA 333; DhA I.415 (°ka). -puñchanī a towel for the feet Vin II.174. -bbhañjana ointment for the feet, foot-salve Vin I.205; J V.197, 376; PvA 44, 78; anointing the feet VvA 44 (°tela), 295 (id.). -mūla the sole of the foot, the foot J IV.131. Cp. mūla. -mūlika "one who sits at one's feet," a foot-servant, lackey J I.122, 438; II.300 sq. (Gāmaṇicaṇḍa); III.417; V.128; VI.30. -lola loafing about, one who lingers after a thing, a greedy person Sn 63, 972; Nd^1 374; Nd^2 433; abstr. f. °lolatā SnA 36, & °loliya Nd^2 433. -visāṇa "a born on the foot," i. e. an impossibility J VI.340. -sambāhana massaging the feet DhA I.38.

Pâdaka (adj. n.) [fr. pāda] 1. having a foot or basis Vin II.110 (a°); Sn 205; ThA 78. — 2. fundamental; pādakaŋ karoti to take as a base or foundation Vism 667. — 3. (nt.) basis, foundation, base PvA 167. — pādaka-jjhāna meditation forming a basis (for further introspective development) Vism 390, 397, 412 sq., 428, 667. — Cp. āhacca°.

Pâdāsi is aor. of padāti.

Pâduka [= pādaka] a little foot J VI.554.

Pâdukā (f.) [cp. Epic Sk. pāduka & pādukā] a shoe, slipper, clog Vin I.190; II.142, 222; J III.327; IV.129, 379; V.298; VI.23; Miln 330; DA I.136; DhA III.451 (muñja°). — At Vin II.143 (according to Rh. D.) pādukā (dāru°) is a kind of stool or stand in a privy.

Pāna [Vedic pāna, fr. **pā**, pibati = Lat. bibo, pp. pīta, Idg. *po[i], cp. Gr. πίνω to drink, πότος drink; Obulg. piti to drink, pivo drink; Lith. pěnas milk; Lat. potus drink, poculum drinking vessel (= Sk. pātra, P. patta)] drink, including water as well as any other liquid. Often comb^d with anna° (food), e. g. Sn 485, 487; Pv I.5^2; and °bhojana (id.) e. g. Dh 249; J I.204. Two sets of 8 drinks are given in detail at Nd^1 372. — Vin I.245, 249 (yāgu°); S V.375 (majja°); Sn 82, 398, 924; J I.202 (dibba°); Pug 51; PvA 7, 8, 50.

-âgāra a drinking booth, a tavern Vin II.267; III.151; J I.302 (= surā-geha C.); Vbh 247; VbhA 339.

Pānaka (nt.) [fr. pāna] a drink J II.285; IV.30; Dāvs V.2; DhA III.207 (amba°); VvA 99, 291. — Der. pānakatta (abstr. nt.) being provided with drink J V.243 (a°).

Pānada in cpd. pānad' ûpama at J II.223 is faulty. The meaning is "a badly made sandal," and the reading should probably be (with v. l. & C.) "dupāhan' ûpama," i. e. du(h) + upāhanā. The C. expl^s as "dukkat-upāhan' ûpama."

Pānīya (adj. nt.) [Vedic pānīya, fr. pāna] 1. drinkable S II.111. — 2. drink, beverage, usually water for drinking Vin II.207; IV.263; J I.198, 450; III.491; V.106, 382; Pv I.10^7; II.1^{19}, 7^{10}; PvA 4, 5. A reduced form pāniya (cp. Geiger, *P.Gr.* § 23) is also found, e. g. Vin II.153; D I.148; Pv II.10^2.

-ghaṭa a pot for drinking water Vin II.216; J VI.76, 85. -cāṭika drinking vessel DhA IV.129. -cāṭi id. J I.302. -ṭhālika drinking cup Vin II.214; IV.263. -bhājana id. Vin II.153. -maṇḍapa water reservoir (BSk. id. e. g. AvŚ II.86) Vin II.153. -māḷaka (?) J VI.85 (Hardy: Flacourtia cataphracta). -sālā a hall where drinking water is given Vin II.153; PvA 102; cp. papā.

Pānudi see panudati.

Pāpa (adj. nt.) [Vedic pāpa, cp. Lat. patior ≈ E. passion etc.; Gr. πῆμα suffering, evil; ταλαίπωρος suffering evil] 1. (adj.) evil, bad, wicked, sinful A II.222 sq. (and compar. pāpatara); Sn 57; Dh 119 (opp. bhadra). Other compar-superl. forms are pāpiṭṭha S V.96; pāpiṭṭhatara Vin II.5; pāpiyyasika D III.254. See pāpiya. — 2. unfertile (of soil) S IV.315. — 3. (nt) evil, wrong doing, sin Sn 23, 662; Dh 117 (opp. puñña), 183; Pv I.6^6; 11^2; IV.1^{50}; DhA II.11. — pp. pāpāni Sn 399, 452, 674; Dh 119, 265.

-iccha having bad wishes or intentions Vin I.97; D III.246; S I.50; II.156; A III.119, 191, 219 sq.; IV.1, 22, 155; V.123 sq.; Sn 133, 280; It 85; Nd^2 342; Vism 24 (def.); VbhA 476; -icchatā evil intention A IV.160, 165; DhA II.77. -kamma evil doing, wickedness, sin, crime D III.182; It 86; Sn 407; Dh 127; Vism 502; VbhA 440 sq.; PvA 11, 25, 32, 51, 84. -kammanta evil-doer, villain S I.97. -kammin id. M I.39; Dh 126. -kara id. Sn 674. -karin id. Dh 15, 17. -dassana sinful view Pv IV.3^{55}. -dhamma wickedness, evil habit Dh 248, 307; Pug 37; DhA III.4; PvA 98; as adj. at PvA 58. -dhammin one of evil character or habits Pv I.11^7. -parikkhaya decay or destruction of demerit (opp. puñña°) Pv II.6^{16}. -mitta an evil associate, a bad companion (opp. kalyāṇa°) M I.43, 470; D III.182. -mittatā bad company, association with wicked people A I.13 sq., 83; IV.160, 165; D III.212; Dhs 13, 27; Vbh 359, 369, 371. -sankappa evil thought Sn 280. -sīla bad morals Sn 246. -supina an evil dream (opp. bhaddaka) Vism 312; DhA III.4.

Pāpaka (adj.) [fr. pāpa] bad, wicked, wretched, sinful Vin I.8; S I.149, 207; V.418 (p. akusala citta); Sn 127, 215, 664; Dh 66, 78, 211, 242; J I.128; Pv II.7^{16} (= lāmaka C.); II.9^3; Pug 19; Dhs 30, 101; Miln 204 (opp. kalyāṇa); Vism 268 (= lāmaka), 312 (of dreams, opp. bhaddaka). — f. pāpikā Dh 164, 310; a° without sin, innocent, of a young maiden (daharā) Th 2, 370; Vv 31^4; 32^6 (so expl^d by VvA. but ThA expl^{ns} as faultless, i. e. beautiful).

Pāpaṇika (adj. n.) [pa + āpaṇa + ika] belonging to a shop, i. e. 1. a shopkeeper A I.115 sq. — 2. laid out in the shop (of cīvara) Vin I.255; Vism 62 (=āpaṇa-dvāre patitaka). See also *Vin. Texts* II.156.

Pāpika = pāpaka D I.90 (cp. DA I.256); A IV.197.

Pāpita [pp. of pāpeti[1], in meaning = pāpika] one who has done wrong, sinful, evil M II.43 (where D I.90 at id. p. has pāpika); DA I.256 (for pāpika, v. l. vāpita).

Pāpimant (adj. n.) [fr. pāpa, cp. Vedic pāpman] sinful; a sinner, esp. used as Ep. of Māra, i. e. the Evil, the wicked one S I.103; A IV.434; Ud 64; Sn 430; Th I, 1213; Miln 155 sq.; DhA IV.32.

Pāpiyo (adj.) [compar. of pāpa, cp. Sk. pāpīyas] worse, more evil or wicked S I.162, 202; Sn 275; Dh 42, 76; J I.158; IV.303; Miln 155; DhA II.108.

Pāpuṇana (nt.) [fr. pāpuṇāti] attainment J IV.306.

Pāpuṇāti [pa + **āp**; cp. Sk. prāpnoti] to reach, attain, arrive at, obtain, get to learn. — pres. **pāpuṇāti** Vin II.208; J IV.285; VI.149; Pug 70; DA 21; PvA 74, 98, 125, 195; and pappoti S I.25; Dh 27; Vism 501; DhA I.395; pot. pāpuṇe Sn 324; Dh 138; J V.57 (1st pl. pāpuṇeyyāma for T. pappomu); DhA IV.200. aor. apāpuṇi ThA 64, and pāpuṇi J II.229. pret. apattha J V.391 (proh. mā a.). fut. pāpuṇissati J I.260. ger. pāpuṇitvā S II.28; patvā Sn 347, 575, and pappuyya S I.7 (cp. Vin II.56; A I.138), 181, 212. inf. **pappotuŋ** SI. 129 = Th 2, 60, and pāpuṇituŋ VbhA 223. — grd. pattabba S I.129; II.28; SnA 433. — pp. **patta**; Caus. pāpeti[2] (q. v.).

Pāpuraṇa (nt.) [through *pāvuraṇa fr. pra + **vṛ**, cp. Sk. prāvaraṇa] cover, dress, cloak S I.175; Miln 279; DhA III.1. See also pārupana.

Pāpurati [fr. pa + ā + **vṛ**, cp. Vedic pravṛṇoti] to cover, veil; shut, hide; only neg. a° and only in phrase apāpurati Amatassa dvāraŋ to open the door of Nibbāna Vin I.5; Vv 64[27] (= vivarati VvA 284).

Pāpeti[1] [Denom. fr. pāpa] to make bad, bring into disgrace Vin IV.5. — pp. pāpita.

Pāpeti[2] [Caus. of pāpuṇāti] to make attain, to let go to, to cause to reach, to bring to J IV.494; V.205, 260; DA I.136. imper. pāpaya S I.217, and pāpayassu J IV.20. fut. pāpessati J I.260, and pāpayissati J V.8.

Pābhati (nt.) [para + ā + pp. of **bhṛ**] "that which has been brought here," viz. 1. a present, bribe DA I.262. — 2. money, price J I.122; V.401, 452. —**kathā°** "a tale brought," occasion for something to tell, news, story J I.252, 364, 378; SnA 356.

Pāmanga (nt.) [etym. ?] a band or chain Vin II.106; III.48; Mhvs 11, 28; Dpvs XII.1; DhA IV.216. See on this *Vin. Texts* III.69 & *Mhvs trsl.* 79[7].

Pāmujja (nt.) [grd. form. fr. pa + **mud**, see similar forms under pāmokkha] delight, joy, happiness; often comb[d] with pīti. — D I.72, 196; S III.134; IV.78 = 351; V.156, 398; A III.21; V.1 sq., 311 sq., 339, 349; Sn 256; Nett 29; DA I.217; Sdhp 167. See also **pāmojja**.

Pāmokkha (adj.) [a grd. form. fr. pamukha, with lengthening of a as frequently in similar forms like pāṭidesanīya, pāṭimokkha, pāmojja] 1. chief, first, excellent, eminent, (m.) a leader. — A II.168 (sanga sa°); Pug 69, 70; Miln 75 (hatthi° state elephant). disā° world-famed J I.166, 285; II.278; VI.347. — Freq. in series agga seṭṭha pāmokkha uttama, in exegesis of mahā (at Nd[2] 502 A e. g., when A II.95 reads mokkha for p.). See mahā. Def[d] as "pamukhe sādhū ti" at VbhA 332. — 2. facing east Pv IV.3[63] (= pācīna-dis' âbhimukha).

Pāmojja = pāmujja [Cp. BSk. prāmodya Divy 13, 82, 239] D II.214; III.288; M I.37, 98; S I.203; II.30; V.157; Dh 376, 381; Ps I.177; Dhs 9, 86; Miln 84; Vism 2, 107, 177 (T. pa°); DhA IV.111 (°bahula).

Pāya [fr. pa + ā + **yā**] setting out, starting S II.218 (nava° newly setting out); instr. pāyena (adv.) for the most part, commonly, usually J V.490; DA I.275 (so read for pāṭhena).

Pāyaka (-°) [fr. **pā** to drink] drinking J I.252 (vāruṇi°)

Pāyāta [pp. of pāyāti] gone forth, set out, started J I.146.

Pāyāti [pra + ā + **yā**] to set out, start, go forth DhA II.42; aor. 3rd sg. pāyāsi D II.73; J I.64, 223; III.333; VvA 64; PvA 272; 3rd pl. pāyesuŋ J IV.220, and pāyiŋsu D II.96; J I.253; DhA III.257. — pp. pāyāta (q. v.). See also the quasi synonymous abhiyāti.

Pāyāsa [cp. Class. Sk. pāyāsa] rice boiled in milk, milk-rice, rice porridge S I.166; Sn p. 15; J I.50, 68; IV.391; V.211; Vism 41; SnA 151; DhA I.171; II.88; VvA 32.

Pāyin (adj. n.) [fr. **pā**, see pivati] drinking J III.338.

Pāyeti [Caus. fr. **pā**, see pibati] 1. to give to drink, to make drink D II.19; Sn 398 (Pot. pāyaye); Miln 43, 229; DhA I.87 (amataŋ); VvA 75 (yāguŋ); PvA 63; aor. apāyesi S I.143; ger. pāyetvā J I.202 (dibba-pānaŋ); II.115 (lohitaŋ); III.372 (phāṇit' odakaŋ); IV.30 (pānakaŋ); VI.392 (suraŋ). — 2. to irrigate J I.215. — ppr. f. pāyamānā a woman giving suck, a nursing woman D I.166; M I.77; A I.295; II.206; III.227; Pug 55; DhA I.49. — Caus. II. pāyāpeti J V.422.

Pāra (adj.-nt.) [fr. para] 1. as *adv.* (°-) beyond, over, across, used as prep. with abl., e. g. pāra-Gangāya beyond the G. S I.207, 214; SnA 228. See under cpds. — 2. as *nt.* the other side, the opposite shore S I.169, 183; Sn 1059; Nd[1] 20 (= amataŋ nibbānaŋ); Dh 385; DhA IV.141 aparā pāraŋ gacchati to go from this side to the other (used with ref. to this world & the world beyond) S IV.174; A V.4; Sn 1130; pāraŋ gavesino M II.64 = Th I, 771-3. Cases adverbially: acc. pāraŋ see sep.; abl. pārato from the other side Vin II.209. — 3. the guṇa form of para, another: see cpds.:

-**atthika** (pār') wishing to cross beyond D I.244. -**ga** "going beyond," traversing, crossing, surmounting S IV.71 (jātimaraṇassa); Sn 32, 997. -**gata** one who has reached the opposite shore S I.34; II.277; IV.157; A IV.411; Sn 21, 210, 359; Dh 414; Vv 53[1] (cp. VvA 231); one who has gone over to another party Th I, 209. -**gavesin** looking for the other shore Dh 355; DhA IV.80. -**gāmin** = gata S I.123; A V.232 sq., 253 sq.; DhA II.160. -**gū** (a) gone beyond, i. e. passed, transcended, crossed S I.195 = Nd[2] 136[A] (dukkhassa), IV.210 (bhavassa); A II.9 (id.); III.223; It 33 (jarāya); Dh 348. (b) gone to the end of (gen. or. -°), reached perfection in, well-versed in, familiar with, an authority on Sn 992 (sabbadhammānaŋ), 1105 (cp. Nd[2] 435); D I.88 (tiṇṇaŋ vedānaŋ); DhA III.361 (id.). -**dārika** an adulterer, lit. one of another's wife S II.259; J III.43 (so read for para°); DhA II.10.

Pāraŋ (adv.-prep.) [acc. of pāra] beyond, to the other side D I.244; M I.135; Sn 1146 (Maccu-dheyya°, vv. ll. °dheyassa & °dheyya°), expl[d] by Nd[2] 487 as amataŋ nibbānaŋ; VvA 42.

-**gata** (cp. pāragata) gone to the other side, gone beyond, traversed, transcended M I.135; S II.277; Sn 803; Nd[1] 114; Nd[2] 435; Pug 72; Vism 234. -**gamana** crossing over, going beyond S V.24, 81; A V.4, 313; Sn 1130.

Pāramitā (f.) [pāramī + tā] = pāramī Nett 87.

Pāramī (f.) [abstr. fr. parama, cp. BSk. mantrāṇāŋ pāramiŋ gata Divy 637] completeness, perfection, highest state Sn 1018, 1020; Pug 70; DhA I.5; VvA 2 (sāvakañāṇa°); PvA 139; Sdhp 328. In later literature there is mentioned a group of 10 perfections (dasa pāramiyo) as the perfect exercise of the 10 principal virtues by a Bodhisatta, viz. dāna°, sīla°, nekkhamma°, paññā°, viriya°, khanti°, sacca°, adhiṭṭhāna°, mettā°, upekhā° J I.73; DhA I.84.
-ppatta (pārami°) having attained perfection M III.28; Nd² 435; Miln 21, 22; cp. *Miln trsl.* I.34.

Pārājika [etym. doubtful; suggested are parā+aj (Burnouf); para+ji; pārācika (S. Lévi, see Geiger, *P.Gr.* § 38, n. 3; also Childers s. v.)] one who has committed a grave transgression of the rules for bhikkhus; one who merits expulsion (see on term *Vin. Texts* I.3; *Miln trsl*ⁿ I.268; II.78) Vin I.172; II.101, 242; A II.241; III.252; V.70; J VI.70, 112; Miln 255; Vism 22; KhA 97, DhA I.76 (as one of the divisions of the Suttavibhanga, see also Vin III.1 sq.).

Pārāpata [Epic Sk. pārāvata] a dove, pigeon J I.242; V.215; VvA 167 (°akkhi); Pgdp 45. See the doublet pārevata.

Pārāyana (nt.) [late Sk. pārāyaṇa, the metric form of parāyana] the highest (farthest) point, final aim, chief object, ideal; title of the last Vagga of the Sutta Nipāta A III.401; Sn 1130; Nd² 438; SnA 163, 370, 604.

Pārikkhattiya=parikkhattatā, Pug 19=VbhA 358.

Pāricariyā (f.) same as paricariya serving, waiting on, service, ministration, honour (for=loc.) D III.189, 250, 281; M II.177; S IV.239; A II.70; III.284, 325, 328; J III.408; IV.490; V.154, 158 (kilesa°); PvA 7, 58, 128. Cp. BSk. pāricāryā MVastu II.225.

Pāricchatta=pāricchattaka, Sn 64 (°ka Nd² 439; expl[d] as koviḷāra); J V.393.

Pāricchattaka [Epic Sk. pārijāta, but P. fr. pari+chatta+ka, in pop. etym. "shading all round"] the coral tree Erythmia Indica, a tree in Indra's heaven Vin I.30; A IV.117 sq.; Vv 38¹ (expl[d] as Māgadhism at VvA 174 for pārijāta, which is also the BSk. form); J I.40; II.20; KhA I.122; SnA 485; DhA I.273; III.211; DhsA 1; VvA 12, 110; PvA 137.

Pārijāta=pāricchattaka, VvA 174.

Pārijuñña (nt.) [abstr. fr. parijuṇṇa, pp. of pari+jur] 1. decay, loss M II.66; DhA I.238; VvA 101 (bhoga°). — 2. loss of pròperty, poverty PvA 3.

Pāripanthika [fr. paripantha] 1. highwayman, robber S II.188; J V.253. — 2. connected with danger, threatening, dangerous to (-°) Vism 152; PugA 181 (samādhi°, vipassanā°).

Pāripūrī (f.) [abstr. fr. pari+pūr, cp. BSk. pāripūri AvŚ II.107] fulfilment, completion, consummation S I.139; A V.114 sq.; Sn 1016; J VI.298; Nd² 137 (pada°); SnA 28 (id.); Pug 53; Dhs 1367; DhA I.36; PvA 132, 133; VbhA 468 (°mada conceit of perfection).

Pārima (adj.) [superl. form. fr. pāra] yonder, farther, only comb[d] with °tīra the farther shore D I.244; M I.134, 135; S IV.174; Miln 269; DhA II.100. Cp. BSk. pārimaŋ tīraŋ AvŚ I.148.

Pāribhaṭya (nt.) (& der.) [fr. pari+bhṛ] "petting (or spoiling) the children" (*Miln trsl.* II.287) but perhaps more likely "fondness of being petted" or "nurture" (as *Vism trsl.* 32) (being carried about like on the lap or the back of a nurse, as expl° at Vism 28=VbhA 483). The readings are different, thus we find °bhaṭyatā at Vbh 246; VbhA 338, 483; °bhatyatā at Vism 17, 23, 27 (vv. ll. °bhaṭṭatā & °bbhaṭṭatā); °bhaṭṭakatā at Miln 370; °bhaṭṭatā at Vbh 352; KhA 236; Nd² 39. The more det. expl° at VbhA 338 is "alankāra-karaṇ' ādihi dāraka-kiḷāpanaŋ etaŋ adhivacanaŋ." — See stock phrase under mugga-sūpyatā.

Pāribhogika (adj.) [fr. paribhoga] belonging to use or enjoyment, with ref. to relics of personal use J IV.228 (one of the 3 cetiyas, viz. sarīrika, pāribhogika, uddesika); Miln 341 (id.).

Pārivattaka (adj.)=pari°; changing, turning round (of cīvara) Vin IV.59, 60.

Pārivāsika=pari° (a probationer), Vin I.136; II.31 sq., where distinguished from a pakatatta bhikkhu, a regular, ordained bh. to whom a pārivāsika is inferior in rank.

Pārisajja [fr. parisā] belonging to an assembly, pl. the members of an assembly, esp. those who sit in council, councillors (cp. BSk. pāriṣadya councillor Divy 291) Vin I.348; D I.136; III.64, 65; M I.326; S I.145, 222; A I.142; Miln 234; DA I.297.

Pārisuddhi (f.) [fr. parisuddha] purity Vin I.102, 136 (cp. *Vin. Texts* I.242, 280); M III.4; A II.194 sq. (°padhāniy' angāni, the four, viz. sīlapārisuddhi, citta°, diṭṭhi°, vimutti°); Nd¹ 475; Ps I.42 (°sīla); Dhs 165; Miln 336 (ājīva°, and in 4th jhāna); Vism 30 (=parisuddhatā), 46 (°sīla), 278; DhA III.399 (catu° -sīla); IV.111 (ājīva°); Sdhp 342.

Pārihāriya (adj.) [fr. parihāra] connected with preservation or attention, fostering, keeping Vism 3 (°paññā), 98 (°kammaṭṭhāna); SnA 54 (id.).

Pāruta [pp. of pārupati] covered, dressed S I.167, 175; Th I, 153; J I.59, 347; SnA 401; PvA 48, 161. —duppāruta not properly dressed (without the upper robe) Vin I.44; II.212; S II.231, 271. See also abhipāruta. *Note.* The form apāruta is apparently only a neg. pāruta, in reality it is apa+ā+vṛta.

Pārupati [metathesis fr. pāpurati=Sk. prāvṛṇoti, pra+vṛ; see also pāpurati etc.] to cover, dress, hide, veil D I.246; Vin IV.283; M III.94; S II.281; J II.24, 109; Pv II.11² (=nivāseti PvA 147); Mhvs 22, 67; Vism 18; DhA III.325; VvA 44, 127; PvA 73, 74, 77. — pp. pāruta (q. v.).

Pārupana (nt.) [fr. pārupati] covering, clothing; dress J I.126, 378; III.82; Miln 279; DhA I.70, 164; PvA 74, 76.

Pāreti [Denom. fr. pāra; cp. Lat. portare] to make go through, to bore through, pierce, break (?) J III.185 (reading uncertain).

Pārevata [the Prk. form (cp. Māgadhi pārevaya) of the Sk. pārāpata, which appears also as such in P.] 1. a dove, pigeon A I.162 (dove-coloured); Vv 36³ (°akkhi=pārāpat' akkhi VvA 167); J VI.456. — 2. a species of tree, Diospyros embryopteris J VI.529, 539.

Pāroha [fr. pra+ruh, cp. Sk. *prāroha] 1. a small (side) branch, new twig (of a Nigrodha tree) J V.8, 38, 472; VI.199; SnA 304; PvA 113. — 2. a shoot, sprout (from the root of a tree, tillering) S I.69 (see C. expl° at *K.S.* 320); J VI.15; DhA II.70; VbhA 475; 476.

Pāla (-°) [fr. pā, see pāleti] a guard, keeper, guardian, protector S I.185 (vihāra°); J V.222 (dhamma°); VvA 288 (ārāma°); Sdhp 285. See also go°, loka°.

Pālaka (-°) [fr. pā] a guardian, herdsman M I.79; S III.154; A IV.127; J III.444.

Pālana (nt.) (& pālanā ?) [fr. pāleti 2, to all likelihood for palāyana through *pālāna, with false analogy] moving, running, keeping going, living, in phrase vutti pālana **yapana** etc. at Vism 145; DhsA 149, 167; also in defn of bhuñjati[1] as "pālan' ajjhohāresu" by eating & drinking for purposes of living, at Dhtp 379. As pālanā at the Dhs passages of same context as above (see under **yapana**).

Pālanā (f.) [fr. pāleti cp. Ep. Sk. pālana nt.] guarding, keeping J I.158; Dhs 19, 84, 295.

Pāli (Pāḷi) (f.) [cp. Sk. pālī a causeway, bridge Halāyudha III.54] 1. a line, row Dāvs III.61; IV.3; Vism 242 (dvattiŋs' ākāra°), 251 (danta°); SnA 87. — 2. a line, norm, thus the canon of Buddhist writings; the text of the Pāli Canon, i. e. the original text (opp. to the Commentary; thus "pāliyaŋ" is opposed to "aṭṭhakathāyaŋ" at Vism 107, 450, etc). It is the literary language of the early Buddhists, closely related to Māgadhī. See Grierson, *The Home of Lit. Pāli* (Bhandarkar Commemoration vol. p. 117 sq.), and literature given by Winternitz, *Gesch. d. Ind. Litt.*, II.10; III.606, 635. The word is only found in Commentaries, not in the Piṭaka. See also Hardy, *Introd. to Nett*, p. xi. — J IV.447 (°nayena accord. to the Pāli Text); Vism 376 (°nay' anusārena id.), 394, 401, 565 (°anusārato accord. to the text of the Canon); 607, 630, 660 sq., 693, 712; KhA 41; SnA 333, 424, 519, 604; DhsA 157, 168; DhA IV.93; VvA 117, 203 (pālito + aṭṭhuppattito); PvA 83, 87, 92, 287; and freq. elsewhere.

-**vaṇṇanā** is explanation of the text (as regards meaning of words), purely textual criticism, as opposed to vinicchaya-kathā analysis, exegesis, interpretation of sense Vbh 291; Vism 240 (contrasted to bhāvanāniddesa).

Pāliguṇṭhima (adj.) [doubtful, fr. pali + **guṇṭh**, see paliguṇṭhita; hapax legomenon] covered round (of sandals) Vin I.186 (*Vin. Texts* II.15: laced boots); v. l. BB °guṇṭhika.

Pālicca (nt.) [fr. palita] greyness of hair M I.49; S II.2, 42; A III.196; Dhs 644, 736, 869; VbhA 98.

Pālibhaddaka [fr. palibhadda = pari + bhadda, very auspicious] the tree Butea frondosa J IV.205; Nd[2] 680A[II]; Vism 256 (°aṭṭhi); VbhA 239 (id.); KhA 40, 53; DhsA 14; DhA I.383. As phālibhaddaka (-vana) at J II.162 (v. l. pātali°).

Pāleti [cp. (Epic) Sk. pālayati, fr. **pā**] 1. to protect, guard, watch, keep Sn 585; J I.55; IV.127; VI.589; Miln 4 (paṭhavī lokaŋ pāleti, perhaps in meaning "keeps, holds, encircles," similar to meaning 2); Sdhp 33. — 2. (lit. perhaps "to see through safely"; for palāyati by false analogy) to go on, to move, to keep going, in defn of carati as viharati, iriyati, vattati, pāleti, yapeti, yāpeti at Nd[2] 237; Vbh 252; DhsA 167. Cp. pālana. So also in phrase **atthaŋ pāleti** (so read for paleti ?) "to come home" i. e. to disappear Sn 1074 (see expld Nd[2] 28). See other refs. under palāyati. — pp. pālita. See also abhi° & pari°. A contracted (poetical) form is found as **pallate** at J V.242, expld by C. as pālayati (pālayate), used as Med.-Pass.

Pāvaka (adj. n.) [fr. **pu**, Vedic pāvaka] 1. (adj.) pure, bright, clear, shining J V.419. — 2. (m.) the fire S I.69; A IV.97; Dh 71, 140; J IV.26; V.63 (= kaṇha-vattanin) VI.236 (= aggi C.); Pv I.8[5]; Vism 170 (= aggi).

Pāvacana (nt.) [pa + vacana, with lengthening of first a (see Geiger, *P.Gr.* § 33[1])] a word, esp. the word of the Buddha D I,88; S II.259; Th 1, 687; 2, 457.

Pāvadati [= pavadati] to speak out, to tell, show J II.439; Pv IV.1[48]; PvA 118.

Pāvassi see pavassati.

Pāvāra [fr. pa + **vṛ**] 1. a cloak, mantle Vin I.281; J V.409 (expld as pavara-dibba-vattha !). — 2. the mango tree KhA 58 (°puppha; Vism 258 at id. p. has pāvāraka°).

Pāvārika [fr. pāvāra] a cloak-seller (?) Vin IV.250.

Pāvāḷa [see pavāḷa] hair; only in cpd. °nipphoṭanā pulling out one's hair S IV.300.

Pāvisa & **Pāvekkhi** see pavisati.

Pāvuraṇa (nt.) [fr. pa + ā + **vṛ**, see pāpuraṇa & pārupana] cloak, mantle M I.359; Vin IV.255, 289; ThA 22.

Pāvusa [pa + **vṛṣ**, cp. Vedic prāvṛṣa & pravarṣa] 1. rain, the rainy season (its first 2 months) Th 1, 597; J V.202, 206. — 2. a sort of fish J IV.70 (gloss pāgusa, q. v.).

Pāvussaka (adj.) [fr. pāvusa] raining, shedding rain M. I.306; S V.51; A IV.127; J I.95, 96; Miln 114.

Pāsa[1] [Vedic pāśa] a sling, snare, tie, fetter S I.105, 111; A II.182; IV.197; Vin IV.153 (? hattha°); Sn 166; It 36 (Māra°); J III.184; IV.414; PvA 206. On its frequent use in similes see *J.P.T.S.* 1907, 111.

Pāsa[2] [Class. Sk. prāsa fr. pra + **as**] a spear, a throw Sn 303; A IV.171 (kuṭhāri° throw of an axe). —asi° a class of deities Miln 191.

Pāsa[3] (a stone ?) at PvA 63 (pās' antare) is probably a misreading and to be corrected to palāsa (palās' antare, similarly to rukkh' antare, kaṭṭh'- and mūl' antare), foliage.

Pāsaŋsa (adj.) [grd. fr. pasaŋsati with pā for pa as in similar formations (see pāmokkha)] to be praised, praiseworthy M I.5, 404; II.227 (dasa °ṭṭhānāni); A V.129 (id.); J III.493; Pv IV.7[13]; Nett 52.

Pāsaka[1] [fr. pāsa[1]] a bow, for the dress Vin II.136; for the hair Th 2, 411 (if Morris, *J.P.T.S.* 1893, 45, 46, is right to be corr. fr. pasāda).

Pāsaka[2] [fr. pāsa[2]] a throw, a die J VI.281.

Pāsaka[3] lintel Vin II.120 = 148 (see *Vin. Texts* III.144).

Pāsaṇḍa [cp. late Sk. pāṣaṇḍa] heresy, sect S I.133; A II.466; Th 2, 183 Miln 359; ThA 164. -°ika heretic, sectarian Vin IV.74.

Pāsāṇa [Epic Sk. pāṣāṇa] a rock, stone A I.283; Sn 447; J I.109, 199; V.295; Vism 28, 182, 183; VbhA 64 (its size as cpd with pabbata); DhA III.151; DhsA 389; VvA 157; Sdhp 328.

-**guḷa** a ball of (soft) stone, used for washing (pumice stone ?) A II.200 (sāla-laṭṭhiŋ . . . taccheyya . . . likheyya . . . pāsāṇaguḷena dhopeyya . . . nadiŋ patāreyya), cp. M I.233; and Vism 28 "bhājane ṭhapitaŋ guḷapiṇḍaŋ viya pāsāṇaŋ." -**cetiya** a stone Caitya DhA III.253. -**tala** a natural plateau J I.207. -**piṭṭhe** at the back of a rock Vism 116. -**pokkharaṇī** a natural tank Vism 119. -**phalaka** a slab of stone J IV.328. -**macchaka** a kind of fish (stone-fish) J IV.70; VI.450. -**lekha** writing on a stone Pug 32. -**sakkharā** a little stone, fragment of rock S II.137; A IV.237. -**sevāla** stone Vallisneria J V.462. -**vassa** rain of stones SnA 224.

Pāsāṇaka = pāsāṇa Vin II.211.

Pāsāda [pa + ā + **sad**, cp. Class. Sk. prāsāda] a lofty platform, a building on high foundations, a terrace, palace Vin I.58, 96, 107, 239; II.128, 146, 236 (cp. *Vin. Texts* I.174; III.178); D II.21; S I.137; A I.64; Sn 409; It 33; Pv II.12[6]; J II.447; IV.153 (pillars); V.217; Vism 339 (°tala); DhsA 107; SnA 502; ThA 253, 286; VvA 197; PvA 23, 75, 279 (cp. upari°); Sdhp 299. —satta-bhūmaka° a tower with 7 platforms J I.227, 346; IV.323, 378; V.426, 577. The Buddha's 3 castles at D II.21; A I.145; J VI.289. See also *J.P.T.S.* 1907, 112 (p. in similes).

Pāsādika (adj.) [fr. pasāda] 1. pleasing, pleasant, lovely, amiable Vin IV.18; D III.141; S I.95; II.279; A II.104 sq., 203; III.255 sq.; DhA I.119; ThA 266, 281; DA I.141, 281; VvA 6; PvA 46, 186, 187, 261. —samanta° lovely throughout A I.24; V.11. — 2. comfortable Vism 105.

Pāsāvin (adj.) [fr. pasavati] bringing forth S V.170; J I.394.

Pāsuka [for the usual phāsuka] a rib Vin II.266. (loop? Rh.D.).

Pāsuḷa [for phāsuka] a rib Vin III.105.

Pāssati fat. of pibati (for pivissati).

Pāhuna (m. nt.) [fr. pa+ā+hu, see also āhuna & der.] 1. (m.) a guest A III.260; J VI.24, 516. — 2. (nt.) meal for a guest D I.97 = M II.154; Vism 220; DA I.267.

Pāhunaka (m.-nt.) [fr. pāhuna] 1. (m.) a guest J I.197; IV.274; Miln 107; DA I.267, 288; DhA II.17. — 2. (nt.) meal for a guest S I.114.

Pāhuṇeyya (adj.) [fr. pāhuna, see also āhuneyya] worthy of hospitality, deserving to be a guest D III.5; S I.220; II.70; A II.56; III.36, 134, 248, 387; IV.13 sq.; V.67, 198; It 88; Vism 220.

Pāhuṇeyyaka = pāhuṇeyya J III.440.

Pāheti [secondary form. after aor. pāhesi fr. pahiṇati] to send J I.447; Miln 8; PvA 133.

Pi (indecl.) [the enclitic form of api (cp. api 2a); on similarities in Prk. see Pischel, *Prk. Gr.* § 143] emphatic particle, as prefix only in pidahati and pilandhati, where api° also is found (cp. api 1b). — 1. also, and also, even so D I.1; Vin IV.139 (cara pi re get away with you: see re); J I.151, 278. — 2. even, just so; with numbers or num. expressions "altogether, in all, just that many" J I.151; III.275; IV.142. — cattāro pi J III.51; ubho pi J I.223; sabbe pi Sn 52; J I.280. — 3. but, however, on the other hand, now (continuing a story) J I.208; IV.2. — 4. although, even if J II.110 (ciram pi kho . . . ca although for a long time . . . yet). — 5. perhaps, it is time that, probably Sn 43; J I.151; II.103. — 6. pi . . . pi in correlation (like api . . . api): (a) both . . . and; very often untranslatable Sn 681 (yadā pi . . . tadā pi when . . . then), 808 (diṭṭhā pi sutā pi); J I.222 (jale pi thale pi); (b) either . . . or J I.150; II.102.

Piṇsa [pp. of piṇsati²] crushed, ground, pounded DhA III.184 (v. l. piṭṭha, perhaps preferable).

Piṇsati¹ [**piś** or **piṇś**, cp. Vedic piṇśati, with two bases viz. Idg. ***peig**, as in P. piñjara & pingala; Lat. pingo to paint, embroider; and ***peik**, as in Sk. piṇśati, peśaḥ; Av. paes- to embellish; Gr. ποικίλος many-coloured; Goth. fēh, Ags. fāh id. See detail in Walde, *Lat. Wtb.* under pingo] to adorn, form, embellish; orig. to prick, cut. Perhaps piṇsare (3. pl. med.) J V.202 belongs here, in meaning "tinkle, sound" (lit. prick), expl^d in C. by viravati. Other der. see under pingala, piñjara, pesakāra.

Piṇsati² [**piś** or **piṇś**, Vedic pinaṣṭi, cp. Lat. pinso to grind, pīla = pestle, pistillum = pistil; Lith. paisýti to pound barley; Gr. πτίσσω id.; Ohg. fesa = Nhg. fese] 1. to grind, crush, pound J I.452; II.363; IV.3 (matthakaṇ), 440 (akaluñ candanañ ca silāya p.); Miln 43; DhA III.184 (gandhe piṇsissati; BB pisissati). — 2. to knock against each other, make a sound J V.202: see piṇsati¹. — pp. piṇsa & piṭṭha¹. See also pisati and paṭi°.

Pinka [for pinga yellow, brownish, tawny] a young shoot, sprout J III.389 (v. l. singa, which also points to pinga; expl^d by pavāla).

Pinga see pinka.

Pingala (adj.) [see piṇsati¹, cp. Vedic pingala] 1. reddish-yellow, brown, tawny S I.170; J VI.199 (= pingiya). — 2. red-eyed, as sign of ugliness J IV.245 (as Np.; comb^d with nikkhanta-dāṭha); V.42 (tamba-dāṭhika nibbiddha-pingala); Pv II.4[1] (= °locana PvA 90; + kaḷāra-danta).
-kipillaka the red ant DhA III.206. -cakkhutā red-eyedness PvA 250. -makkhikā the gadfly J III.263 (= ḍaṇsa) Nd² 268 = SnA 101 (id.); SnA 33 (where a distinction is made between kāṇa-makkhikā and pingala°), 572 (= ḍaṇsa).

Pingiya (adj.) [fr. Vedic pinga] reddish-brown, yellow J VI.199.

Pingulā (f.) [a var. of Sk. pingalā, a kind of owl] a species of bird J VI.538.

Picu¹ [cp. Class. Sk. picu] cotton Vin I.271; usually in cpds, either as kappāsa° S V.284, 443, or tūla° S V.284, 351 (T. thula°), 443; J V.480 (T. tula°).
-paṭala membrane or film of cotton Vism 445. -manda the Nimb or Neem tree Azadizachta Indica Pv IV.1[6] (cp. PvA 220); the usual P. form is pucimanda (q. v.).

Picu² [etym. unknown, prob. Non-Aryan] a wild animal, said to be a kind of monkey J VI.537.

Piccha (nt.) [cp. Epic Sk. piccha & puccha tail, to Lat. pinna, E. fin. Ger. finne] tail-feather, esp. of the peacock Vin I.186 (mora°). — dve° (& de°) having two tail-feathers J V.339, 341 (perhaps to be taken as "wing" here, cp. Halāyudha 2, 84 = pakṣa). Cp. piñcha & piñja.

Picchita in su° J V.197 is not clear, C. expl^s by suphassita, i. e. pleasing, beautiful, desirable, thus dividing su-p-icch°.

Picchila (adj.) [cp. Class. Sk. picchila] slippery Vism 264; VbhA 247 (lasikā = p-kuṇapaṇ); DhA III.4 (°magga).

Piñcha = piccha, i. e. tail-feather, tail Vin II.130 (mora°). Cp. piñja.

Piñja (nt.) [= piccha] a (peacock's) tail-feather J I 38 (mora° kalāpa), 207 (= pekkhuṇa); III.226 (BB piccha & miccha); DA I.41 (mora°); DhA I.394 (id.); VvA 147 (mayūra°; BB piñcha, SS pakkha); PvA 142 (mora° kalāpa).

Piñjara [cp. Class. Sk. piñjara; for etym. see piṇsati¹] of a reddish colour, tawny J I.93; DA I 245; VvA 165, 288.
-odaka fruit of the esculent water plant Trapa Bispinosa J VI.563 (v. l. ciñcarodaka), expl^d by singhāṭaka.

Piñjita (adj.) [fr. piṇsati, cp. Sk. piñjana] tinged, died Miln 240. On expression see Kern, *Toev.* s. v.

Piññāka (nt.) [to piṇsati², cp. Class. Sk. piṇyāka] ground sesamum, flour of oil-seeds M I.78, 342; Vin IV.341. (p. nāma tilapiṭṭhaṇ vuccati); VvA 142 (tila° seed cake); PvA 48.
-bhakkha feeding on flour of oil-seeds D I.166; A I.241, 295; II.206; Nd¹ 417; Pug 55.

Piṭaka [cp. Epic Sk. piṭaka, etym. not clear. See also P. pelā & peḷikā] 1. basket Vin I 225 (ghaṭa p. uc-changa), 240 (catudoṇika p.); Pv IV.3[33]; Vism 28 (piṭake nikkhitta-loṇa-maccha-phāla-sadisaṇ phaṇaṇ); dhañña° a grain-basket DhA III.370; vīhi° a rice basket DhA III.374. Usually in combⁿ **kuddāla-piṭaka** "hoe and basket," wherever the act of digging is referred to, e. g. Vin III.47; D I.101; M I.127; S II.88; V.53; A I.204; II.199; J I.225, 336; DA I.269. — 2. (fig.) t.t. for the 3 main divisions of the Pāli Canon "the three baskets (basket as container of tradition Winternitz, *Ind. Lit.* II.8; cp. peḷā 2) of oral tradition," viz. Vinaya°, Suttanta°, Abhidhamma°; thus mentioned by name at PvA 2; referred to as "tayo piṭakā" at J I.118; Vism 96 (pañca-nikāya-maṇḍale tīṇi piṭakāni parivatteti), 384 (tiṇṇaŋ Vedānaŋ uggahaṇaŋ, tiṇṇaŋ Piṭakānaŋ uggahaṇaŋ); SnA 110, 403; DhA III.262; IV.38; cp. Divy 18, 253, 488. With ref. to the Vinaya mentioned at Vin V.3. — Piṭaka is a later collective appellation of the Scriptures; the first division of the Canon (based on *oral* tradition entirely) being into *Sutta* and *Vinaya* (i. e. the stock paragraphs learnt by heart, and the rules of the Order). Thus described at D II.124; cp. the expression **bhikkhu suttantika vinayadhara** Vin II.75 (earlier than tepiṭaka or piṭakadhara). Independently of this division we find the designation "Dhamma" applied to the doctrinal portions; and out of *this* developed the 3rd Piṭaka, the Abhidhamma-p. See also Dhamma C. 1. — The Canon as *we* have it comes very near in language and contents to the canon as established at the 3rd Council in the time of King Asoka. The latter was in Māgadhī. — The knowledge of the 3 Piṭakas as an accomplishment of the bhikkhu is stated in the term **tepiṭaka** "one who is familiar with the 3 P." (thus at Miln 18; Dāvs V.22; KhA 41 with v. l. ti°; SnA 306 id.; DhA III.385). **tipetakī** (Vin V.3 Khemanāma t.), **tipeṭaka** (Miln 90), and **tipiṭaka-dhara** KhA 91. See also below °ttaya. In BSk. we find the term **trepiṭaka** in early inscriptions (1st century A.D., see e. g. Vogel, Epigraphical discoveries at Sārnāth, *Epigraphia Indica* VIII. p. 173, 196; Bloch, *J. As. Soc. Bengal* 1898, 274, 280); the term **tripiṭaka** in literary documents (e. g. Divy 54), as also **tripiṭa** (e. g. AvŚ I.334; Divy 261, 505). — On the Piṭakas in general & the origin of the P. Canon see Oldenberg, in ed. of Vin I; and Winternitz, *Gesch. d. Ind. Litt.* 1913, II.1 sq.; III.606, 635. — Cp. **peṭaka**.

-ttaya the triad of the Piṭakas or holy Scriptures SnA 328. **-dhara** one who knows (either one or two or all three) the Piṭaka by heart, as eka°, dvi°, ti° at Vism 62, 99. **-sampadāya** according to the P. tradition or on the ground of the authority of the P. M I.520 (itihītiha etc.); II.169 (id.); and in exegesis of itikirā (hearsay-tradition) at A I.189 = II.191 = Nd[2] 151.

Piṭṭha[1] (nt.) [pp. of piŋsati[2], cp. Sk. piṣṭa] what is ground, grindings, crushed seeds, flour Vin I.201, 203; IV.261, 341 (tila° = piññāka); J II.244 (māsa°). As piṭṭhi at J I.347.

-khādaniya "flour-eatables," i. e. pastry Vin I.248 (cp. *Vin. Texts* II.139). **-dhītalikā** a flour-doll, i. e. made of paste or a lump of flour PvA 16, 19 (cp. uddāna to the 1st vagga p. 67 piṭṭhi & reading piṇḍa° on p. 17). **-piṇḍi** a lump of flour Vism 500 (in comp.). **-madda** flour paste Vin II.151 (expld in C. by piṭṭha-khali; cp. piṭṭhi-madda J III.226, which would correspond to piṣṭi). **-surā** (intoxicating) extract or spirits of flour VvA 73.

Piṭṭha[2] (nt.) [identical in form with piṭṭha[3]] a lintel (of a door) Vin I.47 (kavāṭa°); II.120 (°saṅghāṭa, cp. *Vin. Texts* III.105), 148, 207.

Piṭṭha[3] (nt.) [cp. Vedic pṛṣṭha, expld by Grassmann as pra-stha, i. e. what stands out] back, hind part; also surface, top J I.167 (pāsāṇa° top of a rock). Usually in oblique cases as adv., viz. instr. **piṭṭhena** along, over, beside, by way of, on J II.111 (udaka°); IV.3 (samudda°), loc. **piṭṭhe** by the side of, near, at: parikhā° at a ditch PvA 201; on, on top of, on the back of (animals): ammaṇassa p. J VI.381 (cp. piṭṭhiyaŋ); tiṇa° J IV.444; paṅka° J I.223; samudda° J I.202. — assa° on horseback D I.103; similarly: vāraṇassa p. J I.358; sīha° J II.244; hatthi° J II.244; III.392. See also following.

Piṭṭhi & **Piṭṭhī** (f.) [= piṭṭha[3], of which it has taken over the main function as noun. On relation piṭṭha > piṭṭhi cp. Trenckner, *Notes* 55; Franke, *Bezzenberger's Beiträge* XX.287. Cp. also the Prk. forms piṭṭha, piṭṭhī & piṣṭī, all representing Sk. pṛṣṭha: Pischel, *Prk. Gram.* § 53] 1. the back Vin II.200 (piṭṭhī); M I.354; J I.207; II.159, 279. **piṭṭhiŋ** (paccāmittassa) passati to see the (enemy's) back, i. e. to see the last of somebody J I.296, 488; IV.208. piṭṭhi as opposed to ura (breast) at Vin II.105; Sn 609; as opposed to tala (palm) with ref. to hand & foot: hattha (or pada-) tala & °piṭṭhi: J IV.188; Vism 361. — abl. **piṭṭhito** as adv. (from) behind, at the back of Sn 412 (+ anubandhati to follow closely); VvA 256; PvA 78 (geha°). **piṭṭhito karoti** to leave behind, to turn one's back on J I.71 (cp. pṛṣṭhato-mukha Divy 333). **piṭṭhito piṭṭhito** right on one's heels, very closely Vin I.47; D I.1, 226. — 2. top, upper side (in which meaning usually piṭṭha[3]), only in cpd. °pāsāṇa and loc. **piṭṭhiyaŋ** as adv. on top of J V.297 (ammaṇa°). piṭṭhi at VvA 101 is evidently faulty reading.

-ācariya teacher's understudy, pupil-teacher, tutor J II.100; V.458, 473, 501. **-kaṇṭaka** spina dorsi, backbone M I.58, 80, 89; III.92; Vism 271; VbhA 243; KhA 49 sq.; Sdhp 102. **-koṭṭhaka** an upper room (bath room?) DhA II.19, 20. **-gata** following behind, foll. one's example Vism 47. **-paṇṇasālā** a leaf-hut at the back J VI.545. **-parikamma** treating one's back (by rubbing) Vin II.106. **-passe** (loc.) at the back of, behind J I.292; PvA 55, 83, 106. **-pāda** the back of the foot, lit. foot-back, i. e. the heel Vism 251; KhA 51, (°aṭṭhika); DA I.254. **-pāsāṇa** a flat stone or rock, plateau, ridge J I.278; II.352; VI.279; DhA II.58; VbhA 5, 266. **-bāha** the back of the arm, i. e. elbow (cp. °pāda) KhA 49, 50 (°aṭṭhi): **-maŋsa** the flesh of the back PvA 210; SnA 287. **-maŋsika** backbiting, one who talks behind a person's back Sn 244 (= °maŋsa-khādaka C.); J II.186 (of an unfair judge); V.1; Pv III.9[7] (BB; T. °aka). As °maŋsiya at J V.10. **-maŋsikatā** backbiting Nd[2] 39. **-roga** back-ache SnA 111. **-vaŋsa** back bone, a certain beam in a building DhA I.52.

Piṭṭhika (adj.) (-°) [fr. piṭṭhi] having a back, in dīgha° with a long back or ridge Sn 604; mudu° having a flexible back Vin III.35.

Piṭṭhikā (f.) = piṭṭhi; loc. **piṭṭhikāya** at the back of, behind J I.456 (maṇḍala°).

Piṭṭhimant (adj.) [fr. piṭṭhi] having a back, in f. piṭṭhimatī (senā) (an army) having troops on (horse- or, elephant-) back J VI.396.

Piṭhara (m. & nt.) [cp. Epic Sk. piṭhara] a pot, a pan Miln 107 (spelt pithara). As **piṭharaka** [cp. BSk. piṭharikā Divy 496; so read for T. piparikā] at KhA 54 to be read for T. pivaraka according to App. SnA 869.

Piṇḍa [cp. Vedic piṇḍa; probably connected with **piṣ** i. e. crush, grind, make into a lump; Grassmann compares **pīḍ** to press; on other attempts at etym. see Walde, *Lat. Wtb.* s. v. puls] 1. a lump, ball, thick (& round) mass S I.206 (aṭṭhīyaka°); Pv III.5[5] (nonīta°); VvA 62 (kummāsa°), 65; Sdhp 529 (ayo°). — 2. a lump of food, esp. of alms, alms given as food S I.76; Sn 217, 388, 391; J I.7 (nibbuta° cooled); Miln 243 (para °ŋ ajjhupagata living on food given by others). **piṇḍāya** (dat.) for alms, freq. in combn with carati, paṭikkamati, (gāmaŋ) pavisati, e. g. Vin II.195; III.15; M III.157; Sn 386; SnA 141, 175; PvA 12, 13, 16, 47, 81, 136 and passim. — 3. a conglomeration, accumulation, compressed form, heap, in akkhara° sequence of letters or syllables, context DhA IV.70.

-attha condensed meaning, résumé J I.233, 275, 306; KhA 124, 192. Cp. sampiṇḍanattha. -ukkhepakaŋ in the manner of taking up lumps (of food), a forbidden way of eating Vin II.214 = IV.195, cp. *Vin. Texts* I.64 (= piṇḍaŋ piṇḍaŋ ukkhipitvā C.). -gaṇanā counting in a lump, summing up DA I.95. -cāra alms-round, wandering for alms Sn 414. -cārika one who goes for alms, begging Vin II.215; III.34, 80; IV.79; J I.116; VvA 6. -dāyika (& °dāvika) one who deals out food (as occupation of a certain class of soldiers) D I.51 (°dāvika); A IV.107 (v. l. °dāyaka); Miln 331; cp. DA I.156. See also Geiger, *P.Gr.* 46, 1; Rh. D. *Dial.* I.68 (trsl. "camp-follower"); Franke, *Digha trsl.* 53[1] trsl. "Vorkämpfer" but recommends trsl. "Klossverteiler" as well). -dhītalikā a doll made of a lump of dough, or of pastry PvA 17; cp. piṭṭha°. -paṭipiṇḍa (kamma) giving lump after lump, alms for alms, i. e. reciprocatory begging J II.82 (piṇḍa-paṭipiṇḍena jīvikaŋ kappesuŋ), 307 (piṇḍapāta-paṭipiṇḍena jīvikaŋ kappenti); V.390 (mayaŋ piṇḍa-paṭipiṇḍa-kammaŋ na karoma). -pāta food received in the alms-bowl (of the bhikkhu), alms-gathering (on term see Vism 31 yo hi koci āhāro bhikkhuno piṇḍolyena patte patitattā piṇḍapāto ti vuccati, and cp. BSk. piṇḍapāta-praviṣṭha AvŚ I.359; piṇḍapātra-nirhāraka Divy 239) Vin I.46; II.32 (°ŋ niharāpeti), 77, 198, 223; III.80, 99; IV.66 sq., 77; M III.297; S I.76, 92; A I.240; II.27, 143; III.109, 145 sq.; V.100; Sn 339; J I.7, 149, 212, 233; Pug 59; Vism 31, 60; VbhA 279 (°âpacāyana); SnA 374; PvA 11 sq., 16, 38, 240. -pātika one who eats only food received in the alms-bowl; *°anga* is one of the dhutanga ordinances (see dhutanga) Vin I.253; II.32 (°anga), 299 (+ paŋsukūlika); III.15 (id.); M I.30; III.41; A III.391; Pug 59, 69; SnA 57 (°dhutanga). *-piṇḍapātika bhikkhu* a bh. on his alms-round Vism 246 (in simile); VbhA 229 (id.). Cp. BSk. piṇḍapātika AvŚ I.248. -pātikatta (abstr. to prec.) the state of eating alms-food, a characteristic of the Buddhist bhikkhu M III.41; S II.202, 208 sq.; A I.38; III.109.

Piṇḍaka [fr. piṇḍa] (alms)-food A IV.185 (SS piṇḍapāta); in phrase na piṇḍakena kilamati not go short of food Vin III.15, 87; IV.23, in ukka-piṇḍaka meaning a cluster of insects or vermin Vin I.211 = 239 (v. l. piṇḍuka).

Piṇḍi (f.) [cp. piṇḍa & Sk. piṇḍī] a lump, round mass, ball, cluster D I.74 = A III.25 (nahāniya° ball of fragrant soap; DA I.218: piṇḍa); M III.92; J I.76 (phala°); II.393; III.53 (amba°); Miln 107; Vism 500 (piṭṭha°); DhA III.207 (amba°).

Piṇḍika (-°) in chatta°-vivara is a little doubtful, the phrase prob. means "a crevice in the covering (i. e. the round mass) of the canopy or sunshade" J VI.370. — Dutoit (*J. trsl*[n] VI.457) translates "opening at the back of the sunshade," thus evidently reading "piṭṭhika."

Piṇḍita (adj.) [pp. of piṇḍeti, cp. BSk. piṇḍitamūlya lump-sum Divy 500] 1. made into a lump, massed together, conglomerated, thick Th 2, 395. — 2. "ball-like," close, compact; of sound: J II.439; VI.519.

Piṇḍiyālopa [piṇḍi + ālopa] a morsel of food Vin I.58 (°bhojana), 96 (id.); A II.27; It 102.

Piṇḍeti [Denom. fr. piṇḍa] to ball together, mix, put together Pv II.9[52] (= pisana-vasena yojeti PvA 135). — pp. piṇḍita.

Piṇḍola [etym. unclear] one who seeks alms S III.93 = It 89; cp. Np. °bhāradvāja SnA 346, 514, 570.

Piṇḍolya (nt.) [fr. piṇḍola] asking for alms, alms-round S III.93 = It 89; Vism 31.

Pitar [Vedic pitṛ, pitar-; cp. Gr. πατήρ; Lat. pater, Juppiter, Dies-piter = Ζεὺς πατήρ; Goth. fadar = Ger. vater = E father; Oir. athir etc. to onomat. syllable *pa-pa, cp. tāta & mātā] father. — *Cases*: sg. nom. pitā S I.182; Dh 43; J V.379; SnA 423; acc. pitaraŋ Dh 294; & pituŋ Cp. II.9[3]; instr. pitarā J III.37, pitunā, petyā J V.214; dat. gen. pitu M III.176; J IV.137; VI.365, 589; & pituno Vin I.17 (cp. Prk. piuṇo); abl. pitarā J V.214; loc. pitari. — pl. nom. pitaro Sn 404; J IV.1; PvA 38, 54 (mātā°); acc. pitaro PvA 17, pitare, & pitū Th 2, 433; instr. pitarehi & pitūhi; dat. gen. pitunnaŋ J III.83; (mātā°); VI.389 (id.); Pv II.8[4]; pitūnaŋ It 110; loc. pitusu Th 2, 499; J I.152 (mātā°); and pitūsu PvA 3 (mātā°). *Further*: abl. sg. pitito by the father's side D I.113 (+ mātito); A III.151; J V.214. — A I.62, 132, 138 sq.; Sn 296, 579 (paralokato na pitā tāyate puttaŋ); Nd[2] 441 (= yo so janako); J I.412 (= tāta); V.20; VbhA 108 (where pretty popular etym. is given with "piyāyatī ti pitā"), 154 (in simile). — Of *Brahmā*: D I.18, cp. DA I.112; of *Inda* J V.153. There is sometimes a distinction made between the father as such and the grandfather (or ancestors in gen.) with culla° (cūḷa°), i. e. little and mahā° i. e. grand-father, e. g. at J I.115 (+ ayyaka); PvA 107. The collective term for "parents" is mātāpitaro (pl. *not* dual), e. g. Sn 404; J I.152; III.83; IV.1; PvA 107. On similes of father and son cp. *J.P.T.S.* 1907, 112. In *cpds.* there are the 3 bases pitā, piti° & pitu°. (a) pitā°: °putta father & son J I.253; pl. °puttā fathers & sons, or parents & children J IV 115; VI.84. °mahā grand-father Pv II.8[4]; J II.263; DA I.281; PvA 41; °mahā-yuga age of a grandfather (i. e. a generation of ancestors) D I.113 (see det. expl[n] DA I.281 = SnA 462); Sn p. 115; KhA 141; petti-pitā-mahā great-grandfathers, all kinds of ancestors J II.48 (= pitu-vitā mahā C.). — (b.) piti°: °kicca duty of a father J V.153; °ghāta parricide J IV.45 (BB pitu°); °pakkha father's side DhA I.4; °pitāmahā (pl.) fathers & grandfathers, ancestors J V.383; °vadha parricide DA I.135. — (c) pitu°: °ja originating from the father J VI.589 (+ mātuja); °ghātaka parricide (+ mātughātaka) Vin I.88, 136, 168, 320; °nāma fathers name SnA 423; °pitāmahā (pl.) ancestors (cp. piti°) A IV.61; J I.2; II.48. °rakkhita guarded by a father M III.46. °santaka father's possession J I.2. °hadaya father's heart J I.61.

Pitika (-°) (adj.) [fr. pitā] one who has a father, having a father VvA 68 (sa° together with the f.); PvA 38 (mata° whose f. was dead): cp. dve° with 2 fathers J V.424.

Pitucchā (f.) [pitu + svasā, cp. Sk. pitṛ-ṣvasṛ] father's sister, aunt; decl. similarly to pitā & mātā DhA I.37; acc. sg. pitucchasaŋ [Sk. *svasaŋ instead of *svasāraŋ] J IV.184.

-dhītā aunt's daughter, i. e. (girl) cousin DhA I.85. -putta aunt's son, i. e. (boy) cousin S II.282 (Tisso Bhagavato p.); III.106 (id.); J II.119, 324.

Pitta (nt.) [cp. Vedic pitta] 1. the bile, gall; the bile also as seat of the bilious temperament, excitement or anger. Two kinds are distinguished at KhA 60 = Vism 260, viz. baddha° & abaddha°, bile as organ & bile as fluid. See also in detail Vism 359; VbhA 65, 243. — In enumerations of the parts or affections of the body pitta is as a rule comb[d] with semha (cp. Vin II.137; Kh III; Vism 260, 344; Miln 298). — Vin II.137; M III.90; S IV.230, 231 (+ semha); A II.87; III.101, 131; Sn 198 (+ semha), 434 (id., expl[d] as the two kinds at SnA 388); Nd[1] 370; J I.146 (+ semha); II.114 (pittan te kupitaŋ your bile is upset or out of order, i. e. you are in a bad mood); Miln 112 (vāta-pitta-semha . . .), 304 (roga, + semha), 382 (+ semha); DhsA 190 (as blue-green); DhA III.15 (cittaŋ n' atthi pittaŋ n' atthi has no heart and no bile, i. e. does not feel & get excited; vv. ll. vitta & nimitta). — 2. [according to Morris, *J.P.T.S.* 1893, 4 for *phitta = phīta, Sk. sphīta] swelling, a gathering Vin II.188 (*Vin. Texts* III.237 "a burst gall, i. e. bladder"); S II.242. The passage is not clear, in C. on Ud I.7 we read cittaŋ, see Morris loc. cit. May the meaning be "muzzle"? -kosaka gall-bladder KhA 61; Vism 263; VbhA 246.

Pittika (adj.) [fr. pitta] one who has bile or a bilious humour, bilious Miln 298 (+semhika).

Pittivisaya [Sporadic reading for the usual petti°] the realm of the departed spirits M I.73; J I.51; Nd[1] 489.

Pittivisayika (adj.) [fr. pittivisaya] belonging to the realm of the departed Nd[1] 97 (gati; v. l. petti°).

Pithīyati (pithiyyati) [Pass. of pidahati, cp. api-dahati, Sk. apidhīyate] to be covered, obscured or obstructed; to close, shut M II.104; III.184; Sn 1034, 1035; Nd[2] 442 (BB pidhiyyati; expl[d] by pacchijjati), Th I, 872; Dh 173; J I.279 (akkhīni pithīyiŋsu the eyes shut); II.158 (=paṭicchādiyati); VI.432. The spelling of the BB manuscripts is pidhīyati (cp. Trenckner, *Notes* 62).

Pidalaka [etym.? Kern, *Toev.* s. v. suggests diminutive-formation fr. Sk. bidala split bamboo] a small stick, skewer Vin II.116, cp. Bdhgh on p. 317: "daṇḍa-kathina-ppamāṇena kaṭasārakassa pariyante paṭisaŋharitvā duguṇa-karaṇa." See also *Vin Texts* III.94.

Pidahati [api+**dhā**, cp. apidahati & Prk. piṇidhattae= Sk. apinidhātave] to cover, to close, conceal, shut M I.117, 380 (dvāraŋ); J I.292; III.26; V.389; Miln 139 (vajjaŋ); DhA I.396; II.4, 85; IV.197 (ūruŋ); Sdhp 321; aor. **pidahi** J IV.308 (kaṇṇe); ger. **pidahitvā** Pv II.7[6] (dvāraŋ); Vism 182 (nāsaŋ); DA I.136, **pidhatvā** Th 2, 480, & **pidhāya** J I.150 (dvāraŋ), 243 (id.); ThA 286; DhA II.199 (dvārāni). — Pass. pithīyati; pp. pihita (q. v.). The opp. of p. is **vivarati.**

Pidahana (nt.) [fr. api+**dhā**, cp. apidahana] covering up, shutting, closing Vism 20; DhA IV.85 (=thakana).

Pidhara [fr. api+**dhṛ**] a stick (or rag?) for scraping (or wiping?) Vin II.141 (avalekhana°), 221 (id.). Meaning doubtful.

Pidhāna (nt.) [=pidahana] cover J VI.349. -°phalaka covering board Vism 261 (where KhA in same passage reads paṭikujjana-phalaka)=VbhA 244.

Pināsa [cp. Sk. pīnasa] cold in the head, catarrh, in enum[n] of illnesses under dukkha, at Nd[2] 304[I] ≈ (kāsa, sāsa, pināsa, etc.).

Pipati [dial. form for pibati, pivati, usually restricted to Gāthā Dial., cp. Geiger, *P.Gr.* § 132] to drink, only in imper. pres. **pipa** M I.316; S I.459, and ppr. **pipaŋ** J V.255, gen. pl. pipataŋ Sn 398.

Pipāsā (f.) [Desid. form. fr. **pā**, pibati>pipati, lit. desire to drink] 1. thirst Nd[2] 443 (=udaka-pipāsā); Miln 318; VbhA 196 (in comparison); PvA 23, 33, 67 sq.; Sdhp 288. Often comb[d] with **khudā** (hunger) e. g. Sn 52, 436 (khup°); PvA 67; or **jighacchā** (id.), e. g. M I.10; S I.18; A II.143, 153; Miln 304. — 2. longing (for food), hunger J II.319. — 3. desire, craving, longing D III.238 (avigata°); S III.7, 108, 190; IV.387; A II.34 (pipāsa-vinaya; expl[d] at Vism 293); IV.461 sq.

Pipāsita (adj.) [pp. of pipāsati, Desid. fr. **pā**, cp. pipāsā] thirsty S I.143; II.110 (surā°); J VI.399; Miln 318 (kilanta-tasita-p.); Vism 262; PvA 127; Sdhp 151.

Pipāsin (adj.) [fr. pipāsā] thirsty D II.265.

Pipi (adj.) [fr. **pā**, see pivati] drinking (?) in su° good to drink (?) J VI.326 (v. l. BB sucimant). Or is it "flowing" (cp. Vedic pipiṣvat overflowing)?

Pipīlikā (f.) & **pipillika** [cp. Vedic pipīlikā, pipīlaka & pipīlika; BSk. pipīlaka AvŚ II.130 (kunta°). See also kipillikā] ant J III.276 (BB kipillikā); Sdhp 23; as pipillikā at J I.202.

Pippala [for the usual P. pipphalī, Sk. pippalī] pepper Vin I.201, cp. *Vin. Texts* II.46.

Pipphala [cp. Epic Sk. pippala, on ph for p see pipphalī] the fruit of Ficus religiosa, the holy fig tree J VI.518 (Kern's reading, *Toev.* s. v. for T. maddhu-vipphala, C. reads madhuvipphala & expl[ns] by madhuraphala).

Pipphalaka (nt.?) [etym.? BR give Sk. *pippalaka in meaning "thread for sewing"] scissors (? so ed.) DA I.70.

Pipphalī (f.) [with aspirate ph for p, as in Sk. pippalī, see Geiger, *P.Gr.* § 62. See also pippala. Etym. loan words are Gr. πέπερι=Lat. piper=E. pepper, Ger. pfeffer] long pepper S V.79; J III.85; Vv 43[6]; DhA I.258 (°guhā Npl.); IV.155.

Piya[1] (adj.) [Vedic priya, **prī**, cp. Gr. προπρεών; Goth. frijōn to love, frijonds loving=E. friend; Ger. frei, freund; Ohg. Frīa=Sk. priyā, E. Friday, etc.] dear, in two applications (as stated Nd[1] 133=Nd[2] 444, viz. dve piyā: sattā vā piyā sankhārā vā piyā, with ref. to living beings, to sensations): 1. dear, beloved (as father, mother, husband, etc.) S I.210 (also compar. °tara); Dh 130, 157, 220; Vism 296, 314 sq.; often comb[d] with manāpa (pleasing, also in 2), e. g. D II.19; III.167; J II.155; IV.132. — 2. pleasant, agreeable, liked Sn 452, 863: Dh 77, 211; often comb[d] (contrasted) with appiya, e. g. Sn 363, 450 (see also below). nt. **piyaŋ** a pleasant thing, pleasantry, pleasure S I.189; Sn 450, 811; DhA III.275. —**appiya** unpleasant M I.86; Kh VIII.5. **appiyatā** unpleasantness J IV.32. See also pīti & pema.

-**âpāya** separation from what is dear to one, absence of the beloved A III.57; Dh 211. -**âppiya** pleasant & unpleasant D II.277 (origin of it); Dh 211. -**kamya** friendly disposition Vin IV.12. -**ggāhin** grasping after pleasure Dh 209, cp. DhA III.275. -**cakkhu** a loving eye D III.167. -**dassana** lovely to behold, good-looking D III.167. -**bhāṇin** speaking pleasantly, flattering J V.348. -**manāpatā** belovedness M I.66. -**rūpa** pleasant form, an enticing object of sight D I.152 (cp. DA I.311); S II.109 sq.; A II.54; It 95, 114; Sn 337, 1086 (cp. Nd[2] 445); Vbh 103; Nett 27. -**vacana** term of endearment or esteem, used with ref. to āyasmā Nd[2] 130; SnA 536, etc.; or mārisa SnA 536. — **vācā** pleasant speech S I.189; Sn 452. -**vādin** speaking pleasantly, affable D I.60 (manāpacārin+); A III.37; IV.265 sq. -**vippayoga** separation from the beloved object Sn 41 (cp. Nd[2] 444); PvA 161 (here with ref. to the husband); syn. with appiya-sampayoga, e. g. at Vism 504 sq.

Piya[2] [sporadic for **phiya**, q. v.] oar; usually so in cpd. **piyâritta** (nt.) oar & rudder S I.103; A II.201; J IV.164.

Piyaka [cp. Class. Sk. priyaka] a plant going under various names, viz. Nauclea cadamba; Terminalia tomentosa; Vitex trifolia J V.420 (=setapuppha C.); VI.269.

Piyangu (f.) [cp. Vedic priyangu] 1. panic seed, Panicum Italicum Vv 53[7]; J I.39; PvA 283. Mixed with water and made into a kind of gruel (piyangûdaka) it is used as an emetic J I.419. See also kangu. — 2. a medicinal plant, Priyangu J V.420.

Piyatta (nt.) [abstr. fr. piya[1]] belovedness, pleasantness A V.164 sq.; Sdhp 66.

Piyāyati [Denom. fr. piya[1]] to hold dear, to like, to be fond of (acc.), to be devoted to S I.210; J I.156; II.246; VI.5; VbhA 108 (in etym. of pitā, q. v.); DhA IV.125; SnA 78; VvA 349; PvA 71. — pp. **piyāyita.** *Note.* A ppr. **piyaŋ** is found at SnA 169 for Sn 94 adj. piya, and is expl[d] by pīyamāna tussamāna modamāna.

Piyāyanā (f.) [fr. piyāyati] love, fondness for (loc.) S I.210.

Piyāyita [pp. of piyāyati] held dear, fondled, loved, liked Sn 807; Nd[1] 126.

Piyāla [cp. Class. Sk. priyāla] the Piyal tree, Buchanania latifolia J v.415. — (nt.) the fruit of this tree, used as food J iv.344; v.324.

Pire at Vin iv.139 is to be separated (cara pi re get away with you), both pi and re acting as part. of exclamation. The C. expl^n (p. 362) by "pire (voc. ?) = para, amāmaka" is an artificial construction.

Pilaka [cp. Class. Sk. piḍakā] a boil Sn p. 124 (piḷaka, v. l. pilaka); Vism 35 (pīḷaka); DhA i.319 (v. l. piḷaka).— See also piḷakā.

Pilakkha [cp. Vedic plakṣa] the wave-leaved fig tree, Ficus infectoria Vin iv.35; DA i.81. As pilakkhu [cp. Prk. pilakkhu Pischel, *Prk. Gr.* § 105] at S v.96; J iii.24, 398.

Pilandha (adj.) (-°) [fr. pilandhati] adorning or adorned Miln 336, 337. Cp. apiḷandha.

Pilandhati [see apilandhati, api + **nah**] to adorn, put on, bedeck Miln 337; J v.400. Caus. II. pilandhāpeti J i.386.

Pilandhana & **Piḷandhana** (nt.) [= apilandhana] putting on ornaments, embellishment, ornament, trinkets A i.254, 257; iii.16; Th 2, 74; Vv 64^{17} (ḷ); J i.386 (ḷ); v.205; VbhA 230 (°vikati; ḷ); VvA 157 (ḷ), 167 (ḷ); PvA (ḷ); Sdhp 243.

Pilava & **Plava** [fr. **plu**, cp. Vedic plava boat, Russ. plov ship] 1. swimming, flowing, floating J v.408 (suplav-atthaŋ in order to swim through well = plavana C.). — 2. a kind of duck [so Epic Sk.] Vv 35^8 (cp. VvA 163); J v.420.

Pilavati & **Plavati** [cp. Vedic plavati; **plu**, as in Lat. pluo to rain, pluvius rain, Gr. πλέω swim, πλύνω wash; Ohg. flouwen etc. to rinse = E. flow] to move quickly (of water), to swim, float, sway to & fro Th 1, 104; Miln 377; VvA 163; DhsA 76. As plavati at J i.336 (verse); Dh 334 (v. l. SS; T. palavati). As palavati at Th 1, 399. — See also uppalavati (uppluta), opilāpeti, paripalavati.

Pilavana & **Palavana** (nt.) [fr. **plu**] swimming, plunging J v.409 (pl°).

Pilāpanatā (f.) [fr. **plu**, see pilavati] superficiality Dhs 1349, cp. DhsA 405.

Pilāla at J i.382 (°piṇḍa + mattikā-piṇḍa) is doubtful. Fausböll suggests mistake for palala straw, so also Ed. Müller, *P.Gr.* 6.

Pilotikā (f.) [cp. Class. Sk. plota (BR = prota), Suśr. i.15, 3; 16, 7 & passim] a small piece of cloth, a rag, a bandage Vin i.255, 296 (khoma° cp. *Vin. Texts* ii.156); M i.141 (chinna-°o-dhammo laid bare or open); S ii.28 (id.), 219 (paṭa°); J i.220; ii.145; iii.22 (jiṇṇa°), 511; vi.383; Miln 282; Vism 328; KhA 55; DhA i.221 (tela° rags dipped in oil); VvA 5; PvA 185; — As m. at J iv.365. The BSk. forms vary; we read chinna-pilotika at AvŚ i.198; MVastu iii.63; pilotikā (or °ka) at MVastu iii.50, 54. Besides we have ploti in karmaploti (pūrvikā k.) Divy 150 etc. AvŚ i.421.
-khaṇḍa a piece of rag DhA iv.115; ThA 269; PvA 171.

Pillaka [cp. Sk. *pillaka] the young of an animal, sometimes used as term for a child J ii.406 (sūkara°); DhA iv.134 (as an abusive term; vv. ll. SS kipillaka; gloss K pitucūḷaka, BB cūḷakaniṭṭha); Sdhp 164, 165. — As pillika at J i.487 (godha°, v. l. BB godha-kippillika).

Piḷakā (f.) [cp. Class. Sk. piḍakā] 1. a small boil, pustule, pimple Vin i.202; S i.150; J v.207, 303; Nd^1 370; Miln 298; DA i.138. — 2. knob (of a sword) J vi.218. — Cp. pilaka.

Piḷayhati [api + nayhati, cp. Sk. pinahyate] to fasten on, put on, cover, dress, adorn J v.393 (piḷayhatha 3rd sg. imper. = pilandhatu C.).

Piḷhaka (v. l. miḷhakā) at S ii 228 is to be read as miḷhakā "cesspool" (q. v.). The C. quoted on p. 228 expl^s incorrectly by "kaŋsalak' ādi gūthapāṇakā," which would mean "a low insect breeding in excrements" (thus perhaps = paṭanga ?). The trsl. (*K.S.* ii.155) has "dung-beetle."

Pivati & **Pibati** [Vedic pāti & pibati, redupl. pres. to root Idg. *__poi__ & __pī__, cp. Lat. bibo (for * pibo); Gr. πίνω to drink, πότις drink; Obulg. piti to drink, also Lat. pōtus drink, pōculum beaker (= pātra, P. patta). See also pāyeti to give drink, pāna, pānīya drink, pīta having drunk] to drink. — pres. pivati D i.166; iii.184; J iv.380; v.106; PvA 55. — 1st pl. pivāma Pv i.11^8; 2nd pl. pivatha PvA 78 & pivātha Pv i.11^2; 3rd pl. med. piyyare J iv.380. — imper. piva PvA 39, & pivatu Vin iv.109. — ppr. pivaŋ Sn 257; Dh 205, & pivanto SnA 39. — fut. pivissati J vi.365; PvA 5, 59; pissāmi J iii.432; pāssati J iv.527. — aor. pivi J i.198; apivi Mhvs 6, 21; pivāsiŋ Ud 42; apāyiŋha J i.362 (or °siŋha ?); apaŋsu A i.205. — ger. pivitvā J i.419; iii.491; vi.518; PvA 5, 23; pītvā Sn 257; Dh 205; J i.297; pitvāna J ii.71; pitvā Pv i.11^8. — grd. pātabba Vin ii.208; peyya; see kāka.° — inf. pātuŋ J ii.210; Pv i.6^4. — pp. pīta (q. v.). — Of forms with p for v we mention the foll.: pipati M i.32; DhsA 403 (as v. l.); imper. pipa J i.459; ppr. pipaŋ M i.316, 317. — Caus. pāyeti & pāyāpeti (q. v.).

Pivana (nt.) [fr. pivati] drinking PvA 251.

Pivaraka see piṭharaka.

Pisati [= piŋsati] to grind, crush, destroy; Pass. pisīyati to perish VvA 335 (+ vināseti). — pp. pisita.

Pisana (nt.) [fr. piŋsati ?] grinding, powder, see upa°.

Pisāca [cp. Sk. piśāca & Vedic piśāci; to same root as pisuna = Vedic piśuna, & Lat. piget, Ohg. fēhida enmity = Ags. faehp ("feud"), connected with root of Goth. fijan to hate; thus pisāca = fiend] 1. a demon, goblin, sprite D i.54 (T. pesācā, v. l. pisācā, expl^d at DA i.164 as "pisācā mahanta-mahantā sattā ti vadati"), 93; S i.209; A iii.69; Ud 5; J i.235; iv.495 (yakkha p. peta); Miln 23; VvA 335; PvA 198; Sdhp 313. — f. pisācī J v.442. — 2. [like pisāca-loha referring to the Paiśāca district, hailing from that tribe, cp. the term malla in same meaning and origin] a sort of acrobat, as pl. pisācā "tumblers" Miln 191.
-nagara town of goblins (cp. yakkha-nagara) Vism 531. -loha [connected with the tribe of the Paiśāca's: Mhbh vii.4819; cp. Paiśācī as one of the Prākrit dialects: Pischel, *Prk. Gr.* § 3] a kind of copper VbhA 63 (eight varieties).

Pisācaka = pisāca, only in cpd. paŋsu° mud-sprite J iv.380, 496; DA i.287; DhA ii.26.

Pisācin (adj. n.) [fr. pisāca, lit. having a demon] only f. pisācinī a witch (= pisācī) Th 1, 1151.

Pisācillikā (f.) [fr. pisāca] a tree-goblin Vin i.152; ii.115, 134; SnA 357; cp. *Vin. Texts* i.318.

Pista [pp. of pisati] crushed, ground Vism 260 (= piṭṭha KhA id. p.); VbhA 243.

Pisīyati Pass. of pisati (q. v.).

Pisila (nt.) [Sk. piśāla] a dial. expression for pāti or patta "bowl" M iii 235 (passage quite misunderstood by Neumann in his trsl^n iii.414).

Pisuṇa (adj.) [Vedic piśuna, see etym. under pisāca] backbiting, calumnious, malicious M iii.33, 49; J i.297; Pug 57; PvA 15, 16. Usually comb^d with vācā malicious speech, slander, pisuṇavācā and pisuṇāvācā D i.4, 138; iii.70 sq., 171, 232, 269; M i.362; iii.23; adj. pisuṇāvāca & M iii.22, 48; S ii.167; Pug 39. — Cp. pesuṇa.

Pisodara [pṛṣa, i. e. pṛṣant + udara, see pasata¹] having a spotted belly KhA 107 (ed. compares pṛṣodarādi Pāṇini VI.3, 109).

Pihaka (nt.) [cp. Sk. plihaṇaka & plīhan (also Vedic plāśi?), Av. sparəzan; Gr. σπλήν, σπλάγχνα entrails; Lat. lien spleen] the spleen M III.90; Sn 195; J V.49. In detail at Vism 257; VbhA 240.

Pihana (nt.) & °ā (f.) [fr. piheti] envying Dhs 1059; SnA 459 (°sīla).

Pihayati & **Piheti** [cp. Vedic spṛhayati, **spṛh**] 1. to desire, long for (with acc.) Vin II.187; S II.242 (pihāyittha 2nd pl. aor.); J I.401; IV.198 (pattheti +); Th 2, 454; Vv 84[45] (= piyāyati VvA 349). — 2. to envy (with gen. of person & object), covet M I.504; S I.202, 236; Th 1, 62; Sn 823, 947; It 36; Dh 94 (= pattheti DhA 177), 181 (id. III.227), 365 (ppr. pihayaŋ = labhaŋ patthento DhA IV.97); J I.197 (aor. mā pihayi); Miln 336. — pp. pihayita.

Pihayita [pp. of pihayati] desired, envied, always combd with patthita Miln 182, 351.

Pihā (f.) [fr. **spṛh**, cp. Sk. spṛhā] envy, desire M I.304; J I.197; Vism 392 (Bhagavantaŋ disvā Buddha-bhāvāya pihaŋ anuppādetvā ṭhita-satto nāma n' atthi). — adj. apiha without desire S I.181.

Pihāyanā (f.) = pihanā Nett 18.

Pihālu (adj.) [cp. Sk. spṛhālu, fr. **spṛh**, but perhaps = Ved. piyāru malevolent. On y > h cp. P. paṭṭhayati for paṭṭhahati] covetous, only neg. a° S I.187 = Th 1, 1218; Sn 852; Nd¹ 227.

Pihita [pp. of pidahati] covered, closed, shut, obstructed (opp. vivaṭa) M I.118; III.61; S I.40; A II.104; Nd¹ 149; J I.266; Miln 102 (dvāra), 161; Vism 185; DA I.182 (°dvāra).

Pīṭha (nt.) [cp. Epic Sk. pīṭha] a seat, chair, stool, bench. — 4 kinds are given at Vin IV.40 = 168, viz. masāraka, bundikābaddha, kuḷirapādaka, āhaccapādaka (same categories as given under mañca). — Vin I.47, 180; II.114, 149, 225; A III.51 (mañca°, Dvandva); IV.133 (ayo°); Ps I.176; Vv 1¹ (see discussed in detail at VvA 8); VvA 295 (mañca°). — pāda° footstool J IV.378; VvA 291; bhadda° state-chair, throne J III.410.

-sappin "one who crawls by means of a chair or bench," i. e. one who walks on a sort of crutch or support, a cripple (pīṭha here in sense of "hatthena gahana-yogga" VvA 8; exlpd by Bdhgh as "chinn' iriyāpatha" *Vin. Texts* I.225) J I.76, 418; V.426 (khujja +) VI.4, 10; Miln 205, 245, 276; Vism 596 (& jaccandha, in simile); DhA I.194; II.69; PugA 227; PvA 282.

Pīṭhaka [fr. pīṭha] a chair, stool VvA 8, 124. See also palāla°.

Pīṭhikā (f.) [fr. pīṭha] a bench, stool Vin II.149 ("cushioned chair" Bdhgh; see *Vin. Texts* III.165); J IV.349; DA I.41; VvA 8.

Pīṇana (nt.) [fr. **prī**, cp. pīti] 1. gladdening, thrill, satisfaction Vism 143 = DhsA 115. — 2. embellishment Vism 32 (= maṇḍana).

Pīṇita [pp. of pīṇeti] pleased, gladdened, satisfied Vv 16¹³ (= tuṭṭha VvA 84); Miln 238, 249, 361; usually in phrase pīṇitindriya with satisfied senses, with joyful heart M II.121; PvA 46, 70.

Pīṇeti [cp. Vedic prīṇāti, **prī**, see piya. The meaning in Pāli however has been partly confused with **pī**, pinvati (see pīna), as suggested by Bdhgh in DA I.157: "pīṇentī ti pīṇitaŋ thāma-bal' ûpetaŋ karonti"] to gladden, please, satisfy, cheer; to invigorate, make strong, often in phrase (attānaŋ) sukheti pīṇeti "makes happy and pleases" D I.51; III.130 sq.; S I.90; IV.331; PvA 283; cp. DhsA 403 (sarīraŋ p.). It also occurs in def. of pīti (pīṇayatī ti pīti) at Vism 143 = DhsA 115. — pp. pīṇita.

Pīta¹ [pp. of pivati] 1. having drunk or (pred.) being drunk (as liquid) S I.212 (madhu°); J I.198; PvA 25 (with asita, khāyita & sāyita as fourfold food). — 2. soaked or saturated with (-°), in kasāyarasa° J II.98 (or = pīta²?) and visapīta (of an arrow) J V.36; Vism 303, 381; which may however be read (on acct. of v. l. visappīta) as visappita "poison-applied" (see appita). Does M I.281 pīta-nisita belong here (= visapīta)? — 3. (nt.) drink M I.220 sq. = A V.347 sq.; A V.359; Th 1, 503; Pv II.7¹⁰; Nett 29, 80.

Pīta² (adj.) [Epic Sk. pīta, etym. unclear] yellow, golden-coloured Vin I.217 (virecana); D I.76 (nīla p. lohita odāta); III.268 (°kasiṇa); M I.281 (pīta-nisita, belonging here or under pīta¹?), cp. 385 (below); A III.239; IV.263, 305, 349; V.61; J VI.185 (nīla p. lohita odāta mañjeṭṭhaka), 449 (°alankāra, °vasana °uttara, cp. 503); Dhs 203 (°kasiṇa), 246, 247 (nīla p. lohitaka, odāta); Vism 173 (°kasiṇa). — pīta is prominent (in the sense of golden) in the description of Vimānas or other heavenly abodes. A typical example is Vv 47 (Pītavimāna V.1 & 2), where everything is characterised as pīta, viz. vattha, dhaja, alankāra, candana, uppala, pāsāda, āsana, bhojana, chatta, ratha, assa, bījanī; the C. expln of pīta at this passage is "suvaṇṇa"; cp. Vv 36¹ (= parisuddha, hemamaya VvA 166); 78⁴ (= suvaṇṇamaya C. 304).

-antara a yellow dress or mantle Vv 36 (= pītavaṇṇā uttarīyā C. 166). **-aruṇa** yellowish red Th 2, 479. **-âvalepana** "golden-daubed" M I.385.

Pītaka (adj.) [fr. pīta] yellow Vin IV.159; Th 2, 261; J II.274; Pv III.1³ (= suvaṇṇavaṇṇa PvA 170); Dhs 617 (nīla p. lohitaka odāta kāḷaka mañjeṭṭhaka); ThA 211. **-pītakā** (f.) saffron, turmeric M I.36.

Pīti (f.) [cp. Class. Sk. prīti & Vedic prīta pp. of **prī**, see pīṇeti & piya] emotion of joy, delight, zest, exuberance. On term see *Dhs. trsl.* 11 and *Cpd.* 243. Classed under sankhārakkhandha, not vedanā°. — D I.37, 75; III.241, 265, 288; M I.37; S II.30; IV.236; A III.26, 285 sq.; IV.411, 450; V.1 sq., 135, 311 sq., 333 sq.; Sn 257, 687, 695, 969, 1143 (= Bhagavantaŋ ārabbha p. pāmujjaŋ modanā pamodanā citti-odagyaŋ etc. Nd² 446); Nd¹ 3, 491; Pug 68; Dhs 9, 62, 86, 172, 584, 999; Nett 29; Vism 145 (& sukha in contrasted relation), 212, 287 (in detail); DA I.53 (characterised by ānanda); DhA I.32; Sdhp 247, 461. On relation to jhāna see the latter. In series pīti passaddhi samādhi upekkhā under sambojjhanga (with eleven means of cultivation: see Vism 132 & VbhA 282). — Phrase pītiyā sarīraŋ pharati "to pervade or thrill the body with joy" (aor. phari), at J I.33; V.494; DhA II.118; IV.102; all passages refer to pīti as the fivefold pīti, pañcavaṇṇā pīti, or joy of the 5 grades (see *Dhs. trsl.* 11, 12, and *Cpd.* 56), viz. khuddikā (slight sense of interest), khaṇikā (momentary joy), okkantikā (oscillating interest, flood of joy), ubbegā (ecstasy, thrilling emotion), and pharaṇā pīti (interest amounting to rapture, suffusing joy). Thus given at DhsA 115 & Vism 143, referred to at DhsA 166. — pīti as nirāmisa (pure) and sāmisa (material) at M III.85; S IV.235.

-gamanīya pleasant or enjoyable to walk M I.117. **-pāmojja** joy and gladness A III.181, 307 (°pāmujja); Dh 374; DhA IV.110; KhA 82. **-pharaṇatā** state of being pervaded with joy, joyous rapture, ecstasy D III.277; Ps I.48; Vbh 334; Nett 89. **-bhakkha** feeding on joy (Ep. of the Ābhassara Devas) D I.17; III.28, 84, 90; A V.60; Dh 200; A I.110; DhA III.258; Sdhp 255. **-mana** joyful-hearted, exhilarated, glad of heart or mind M I.37; III.86; S I.181; A III.21; V.3; Sn 766;

Nd¹ 3; J III.411; Vbh 227. **-rasa** taste or emotion of joy VvA 86. **-sambojjhanga** the joy-constituent of enlightenment M III.86; D III.106, 226, 252, 282. Eleven results of such a state are enum^d at DhsA 75, viz. the 6 anussatis, upam' ânussati, lūkhapuggala-parivajjanatā, siniddha-pug.-sevanatā, pasādanīya-suttanta-paccavekkhaṇatā, tadadhimuttatā (cp. Vism 132 & VbhA 282). **-sahagata** followed or accompanied by joy, bringing joy Dhs 1578 (dhammā, various things or states); Vism 86 (samādhi). **-sukha** zest and happiness, intrinsic joy (cp. *Cpd.* 56, 243) S I.203; D III.131, 222; Dhs 160; Vism 158; ThA 160. According to DhsA 166 "rapture and bliss," cp. *Expositor* 222. **-somanassa** joy and satisfaction J V.371; Sn 512; PvA 6, 27, 132.

Pītika (-°) (adj.) [fr. pīti] belonging to joy; only as sappītika & nippītika bringing joy & devoid of joy, with & without exuberance (of sukha) A III.26; IV.300, 441.

Pītin (adj.) [fr. pīta¹] drinking, only at Dh 79 in cpd. dhamma° drinking in the Truth, expl^d as dhammapāyako, dhammaŋ pivanto at DhA II.126.

Pīna (adj.) [cp. Epic Sk. pīna of **pī** to swell up (with fat); to which also Vedic pīvan & pīvara fat, Gr. πιμελή & πίων fat, Lat. opīmus fat, Ger. feist & fett = E. fat] fat, swollen Th 2, 265 (of breasts).

Piḷaka [fr. **pīḍ** ?] a (sort of) boil Vism 35; see pilaka.

Pīḷana (nt.) [fr. **pīḍ**, cp. pīḷā] oppression, injury, suffering (from dukkha) Vism 212 = 494; also in nakkhatta° harm to a constellation, i. e. occultation DhA I.166 sq.

Pīḷā (f.) [cp. Class. Sk. pīḍā fr. **pīḍ**] 1. pain, suffering J I.421; Miln 278; Vism 42. — 2. oppression, damage, injury SnA 353; DA I.259.

Pīlikoḷikā (f.) [reading not quite sure, cp. koḷikā] eye-secretion Th 2, 395 (= akkhigūthaka ThA 259, q. v. for fuller expl°; see also *J.P.T.S.* 1884, 68).

Pīḷita [pp. of pīḷeti] crushed, oppressed, molested, harassed Vin IV.261; Vism 415 (dubbhikkha°); DhA IV.70; ThA 271. Cp. abhi°, pa°.

Pīḷeti [cp. Vedic pīḍayati, **pīḍ**, cp. Gr. πιέζω (*πισεζω ?) to press, oppress (lit. sit upon ?)] 1. to press, press down Vin II.225 (coḷakaŋ). — 2. to weigh down heavily J I.25 (ppr. pīḷiyamāna), 138. — 3. to press, clench Miln 418 (mutthiŋ pīḷayati); DhA IV.69 (anguliyā pīḷiyamānāya). — 4. to crush, keep under, subjugate Miln 277 (janaŋ). — 5. to molest VvA 348 (pīḷanto ppr. for pīḷento ?). — pp. pīḷita.

Puŋ as a term for Purgatory (niraya): see Bdhgh's etym. of puggala Vism 310, as quoted under puggala.

Puŋs [Vedic puŋs (weak base) and pumāŋs (strong base), often opp. to strī (woman, female); cp. putra & potaka]. Of the simplex no forms are found in Pāli proper. The base puŋ occurs in pukusa (?), puggala (?), pungava, pullinga; puŋs in napuŋsaka (cp. Prk. napuŋsaveya Pischel, *Gram.* § 412). The role of puŋs as contrast to itthi has in Pāli been taken over by purisa, except in itthi-pumā at the old passage D III.85. The strong base is in P. puman (q. v.). See also posa¹.

Pukkusa [non-Aryan; cp. Epic Sk. pukkuśa, pukkaśa pulkasa. The "**Paulkāsa**" are mentioned as a mixed caste at Vājasaneya Saŋhitā 30, 17 (cp. Zimmer, *Altind. Leben* 217)] N. of a (Non-Aryan) tribe, hence designation of a low social class, the members of which are said (in the Jātakas) to earn their living by means of refuse-clearing. On the subject see Fick, *Sociale Gliederung* 206, 207. — Found in foll. enumerations: khattiyā brāhmaṇā vessā suddā caṇḍāla-pukkusā A I.162 = III.214; J III.194 (expl^d by C. chava-chaḍḍaka-caṇḍālā ca puppha-chaḍḍaka-pukkusā ca); IV.303; Pv II.6¹²; Miln 5. Further as **pukkusakula** as the last one of the despised clans (caṇḍālakula, nesāda°, veṇa°, rathakāra°, p.°) at M III.169; S I.94; A II.85; Vin IV.6; Pug 51. With nesāda at PvA 176. — Cp. M III.169.

Puggala [cp. Class. Sk. pudgala, etym. connected with puŋs, although the fantastic expl^n of native Commentators refers it to puŋ "a hell" and **gal**; so at Vism 310: "pun ti vuccati nirayo, tasmiŋ galanti ti puggalā"] 1. an individual, as opposed to a group (sangha or parisā), person, man; in later philosophical (Abhidhamma) literature = character, soul (= attan). — D I.176; M III.58; S I.93 sq.; III.25; A I.8, 197; II.126 sq.; Sn 544, 685; Dh 344; Ps I.180 sq.; II.1 sq., 52; Pv II.3²⁵ (cp. PvA 88); II.9⁷; PvA 40, 132. — pl. puggalā people VvA 86 (= sattā), 149. — **para-puggala** another man D I.213; S II.121; V.265; Vism 409. —**purisa-puggala** individual man, being, person S II.206; IV.307; A I.173 = M II.217. Characterised as an individual in var. ways, e. g. as agga° Sdhp 92, 558; abhabba° J I.106; ariya° Vin V.117; asura-parivāra° A II.91; kodhagaru° A II.46; gūtha°, puppha° madhubhāṇī° A I.128; dakkhiṇeyya° VvA 5; diṭṭhisampanna° A I.26 sq.; III.439 sq.; IV.136; nibbiriya kusīta° J IV.131; pāsāṇalekh' ûpama° etc. A I.283; valāhak' ûpama A II.102 sq.; saddha, asaddha Ps I.121; II.33; sivāthik' upama A III.268; suppameyya etc. A I.266 sq. [a]sevitabba A IV.365; V.102, 247, 281; hīna majjhima paṇīta S II.154. — *Groups* of characters: (2) A I.76, 87; (3) gilān' ûpama etc. A I.121 sq.; avuṭṭhika-sama padesa-vassin, sabbatth' âbhivassin It 64 sq.; satthar, sāvaka, sekha It 78; sekha asekha n' eva-sekha-nāsekha D III.218; (4) D III.232, 233; S I.93; J IV.131; (5) Nett 191; (6) rāga-carita, dosa°, moha°, saddhā°, buddha°, vitakka° Vism 102; (7) ubhato-bhāga-vimutta, paññā-vimutta etc. D III.105; (8) A III.212; S V.343 (19) Nett 190; (26) Nett 189, 190. — See also **paṭipuggala**. — 2. (in general) being, creature Miln 310 (including Petas & animals).

-ñū knowing individuals D III.252, 283. **-paññatti** descriptions of persons, classification of individuals D III.105 (cp. *Dial.* III.101); also N. of one of the canonical books of the Abhidhamma-piṭaka. **-vemattatā** difference between individuals S II.21; V.200; Sn p. 102 (= °nānatta SnA 436).

Puggalika (adj.) [fr. puggala] belonging to a single person, individual, separate Vin I.250; II.270. The BSk. paudgalika at Divy 342 is used in a sense similar to the Vin passages. Divy Index gives, not quite correctly, "selfish."

Punkha [cp. Epic Sk. punkha, etym. puŋ (base of puŋs) + kha (of **khan**), thus "man-digging"?] the feathered part of an arrow J II.89. Cp. ponkha.

Pungava [puŋ + gava (see go), cp. Class. Sk. pungava in both meanings] a bull, lit "male-cow," A I.162; II.75 sq.; Sn 690; J III.81, 111; V.222, 242, 259, 433; SnA 323. As -° in meaning "best, chief" Vism 78 (muni°); ThA 69 (Ap V.5) (nara°).

Pucimanda [fr. picumanda] the Nimba tree, Azadirachta Indica J III.34; IV.205; VI.269 (°thanī, of a woman = nimba-phala-saṇṭhāna-thana-yuggalā C.).

Puccaṇḍatā (f.) [pūti + aṇḍa + tā, viâ *pūtyaṇḍatā] state of a rotten egg M I.357.

Puccha (nt.) [cp. Vedic puccha (belonging with punar to Lat. puppis) & P. piccha] a tail DhsA 365 (dog's tail). See **puñcikata**.

Pucchaka (adj.) [fr. **pṛch**] asking, questioning DhsA 2, 3 (pañha°).

Pucchati [**pṛcch**, cp. Vedic pṛcchati = Lat. posco, postulo, with which connected also Lat. precor = Goth. fraihnan;

Ohg. frāgōn; Vedic praśna = P. pañha] 1. to ask, to question S I.207, 214; Vin II.207; Sn 995; Nd[1] 341 etc. — Pres. 1st sg. pucchāmi Sn 83, 241, 682, 1043, 1049; Nd[2] 447; Pv II.1[12]. — 1st pl. pucchāma Sn 1052; Imper. puccha Sn 460; DA I.155; pucchatha D II.154; pucchassu Sn 189, 993; Pot. puccheyyāmi D I.51; puccheyya A I.199; PvA 6; ppr. pucchanto Sn 1126; aor. 1st sg. apucchissaŋ Sn 1116, pucchisaŋ Vv 30[11], apucchiŋ VvA 127; 2nd sg. apucchasi Sn 1050; 3rd sg. apucchi Sn 1037, apucchasi Nd[2] 447; pucchi Sn 981, 1031; PvA 6, 39, 68; 1st pl. apucchatha Sn 1017; 3rd pl. pucchiŋsu J I.221; pucchisuŋ Mhvs 10, 2. Fut. pucchissāmi J VI.364. Inf. pucchituŋ Vin I.93; Sn 510; puṭṭhuŋ Sn 1096, 1110; pucchitāye J V.137. Grd. pucchavho Sn 1030; Pass. pucchiyati DhA I.10. — Caus. II. pucchāpeti Mhvs 10, 75. — pp. puṭṭha & pucchita (q. v.). — 2. to invite to (instr.), to offer, to present to somebody (acc.), lit. to ask with Vin II.208, 210 (pāniyena); III.161 (odanena, sūpena etc.); D II.240. — See also anu°, abhi°, sam°.

Pucchana (nt.) & °ā (f.) [fr. **pṛch**] asking, enquiring, questioning Sn 504 (ā); PvA 121, 223.

Pucchā (f.) [cp. Class. Sk. pṛcchā = Ohg. forsca question] a question Sn 1023; SnA 46, 200, 230. A system of questions ("questionnaire") is given in the Niddesa (and Commentaries), consisting of 12 groups of three questions each. In full at Nd[1] 339, 340 = Nd[2] under pucchā (p. 208). The first group comprises the three adiṭṭha-jotanā pucchā, diṭṭha-saṃsandanā p., vimaticchedanā p. These three with addition of anumati p. and kathetu-kamyatā p. also at DA I.68 = DhsA 55. The complete list is referred to at SnA 159. —**apuccha** (adj.) that which is not a question, i. e. that which should not be asked Miln 316. —**puccha-vissajjanā** question and answer PvA 2. — At Nett 18 p. occurs as quâsi synonym of icchā and patthanā.

Pucchitā [pp. of pucchati] asked Sn 76, 126, 383, 988, 1005; Nd[1] 211; KhA 125 (°kathā); PvA 2, 13, 51. — Cp. **puṭṭha**.

Pucchitar [n. ag. to pucchita] one who asks, a questioner M I.472; S III.6 sq.; Sn p. 140.

Pujja (adj.) [grd. of **pūj**, cp. Sk. pūjya] to be honoured M III.38 sq., 77 sq.; A III.78 (v. l.); Nett 52, 56 (= pūjaniya C.). Compar. pujjatara M I.13; & see pūja.

Puñcikatā is wrong reading at Dhs 1059 in taṇhā paraphrase (pattern I Nd[2] taṇhā) for **mucchañcikatā**. The readings of id. p. are **puñcikatā** Dhs 1136, 1230; Vbh 351, 361 (v. l. pucchañji°); mucchañci° at Nd[1] 8 (v. l. BB mucchañji°, SS suvañci°); Nd[2] p. 152 (v. l. BB pucchiñci°, SS pupañci°); pucchañjikatā VbhA 477. The translation of Dhs gives "agitation" as meaning. The C. (DhsA 365) reads puñcikatā (vv. ll. puñcaŋ vikatā; pucañcikaka; pucchakatā) and connects it with pucchaŋ cāleti (wagging of a dog's tail, hence "agitation"); *Expositor* II.470 gives "fluster." The C. on Vbh (VbhA 477) explⁿ as "lābhan' âlābhanaka-ṭṭhāne vedhanā kampanā nīcavuttatā," thus "agitation."

Puñchati [cp. Sk. *proñchati, but BSk. poñcchate (v. l. puñchati & pocchate) Divy 491: upânahān mūlāc ca p.] to wipe off, clean Vin II.208 (upāhanā), 210; A IV.376 (rajoharaṇaŋ suciŋ p., asuciŋ p. etc.); J I.392 (akkhīni); Vism 63 (gabbha-malaŋ), 415 = KhA 120 = J I.47 (assūni hatthehi p.); KhA 136 (paŋsukaŋ). The reading puñjati occurs at J I.318 (akkhīni); V.182; VI.514, also as v. l. at A IV.376 (v. l. also muñcati: cp. puñcikatā). — Caus. II. **puñchāpeti** Vism 63. Cp. pari°.

Puñchana (adj. nt.) [fr. **proñch**] wiping Vin I.297 (mukha°-colaka); II.208 (upāhana°-colaka), 210. Cp. puñchanī.

Puñchanī (f.) [see puñchana] a cloth for wiping, a towel Vin II.122; Th 1, 560 (pāda° napkin for the feet). See *Vin. Texts* III.114.

Puñja (usually -°) [cp. Epic Sk. puñja] a heap, pile, mass, multitude Vin II.211; J I.146 (sabba-rogānaŋ). As -° in foll. cpds.: aṭṭhi° It 17 (+ aṭṭhikandala); **kaṭṭha°** A III.408; IV.72; J II.327; **gūtha°** J II.211; **tiṇa°** A III.408; **palāla°** D I.71; M III.3; A I.241; II.210; **maŋsa°** D I.52; **vālika°** J VI.560; **sankhāra°** S I.135. -**kata** (& °kita) for **puñjikata**; cf. Sk. puñjīkṛta, with i for a in compⁿ with **kṛ** & **bhū** heaped up, heaped together Vin II.208 (puñjakita); M I.58, 89 (id. but id. p. M III.92 puñjakajāta); A III.324 (puñjakata; v. l. puñjakita & puñjanika); J II.408 (puñjakata, v. l. pancalikata); VI.111 (id., v. l. puñca°).

Puñjaka = puñja M III.92 (°jātāni aṭṭhikāni, where M I.89 at id. p. reads puñjakitāni); Miln 342 (palāla°).

Puñjati is a variant of **puñchati** (q. v.).

Puñña (nt.) [cp. (late) Vedic puṇya favourable, good; etym. not clear, it may be dialectical. The word is explᵈ by Dhammapāla as "santānaŋ punāti visodheti," i. e. cleaning the continuation (of life) VvA 19, thus taken to **pu**. The explⁿ is of course fanciful] merit, meritorious action, virtue. Always represented as foundation and condition of heavenly-rebirth & a future blissful state, the enjoyment of which depends on the amount of merit accumulated in a former existence. With ref. to this life there are esp. 3 qualities contributing to merit, viz., dāna, sīla & bhāvanā or liberality, good conduct & contemplation. These are the puñña-kiriya-vatthūni. (see below). Another set of *ten* consists of these 3 and apaciti, veyyāvacca, patti-anuppadāna, abbhanumodanā, desanā, savana, diṭṭh' ujjuka-kamma. The opp. of puñña is either apuñña (D III.119; S I.114; II.82; A I.154; III.412; Sdhp 54, 75) or pāpa (Sn 520; Dh 39; Nett 96; PvA 5). The true Arahant is above both (Pv II.6[15]). See on term also *Kvu trsl.* 201. — (a) *Passages (selected)*: D III.58, 120; M I.404; II.191, 199; S I.72; II.82; IV.190; IV.190; V.53; A I.151, 155 sq.; III.412; Sn 427 sq., 547, 569, 790; Dh 18, 116 sq., 196, 220, 267, 331, 412; Nd[1] 90; Pv I.[2]; I.5[12]; Pug 55; Vism 541 (puññānaŋ paccayo duvidhā); DhA IV.34; PvA 6, 8, 30, 69 sq.; Sdhp 4, 19 sq. — (b) *Var. phrases & characterisations*: Merit is represented as *great* (uḷāra DA I.110; PvA 5; anappaka Pv I.5[12]) or *little* (paritta DA I.110; appa S II.229); as *adj.* (-°) mahā° S I.191, opp. appa° M II.5. puñña is defined at Nd[1] 90 as follows: "puññaŋ vuccati yaŋ kiñci tedhātukaŋ kusal' âbhisankhāraŋ; apuññaŋ vuccati sabbaŋ akusalaŋ." It is defined as "dāna-sīl'-ādi-pabheda" & "sucaritaŋ kusala-kammaŋ" at VvA 19; considered as leading to future happiness: Vv 1[3]; PvA 58; consisting mainly in dāna (dānamayaŋ p.) PvA 8, 51, 60, 66, 73, but also in vandana PvA 1. To do good = puññaŋ (puññāni) karoti D I.137; S IV.331; A V.177; Pv I.1[9]; or pasavati S I.182, 213; A I.89; II.3 sq.; III.244; V.249, 282; PvA 121, cp. puññaŋ pasutaŋ Pv I.5[12]; VvA 289. Other phrases: °ŋ ākankhati S I.18, 20; pavaḍḍhati S I.33; corehi duharaŋ S I.36; puññānaŋ vipāko A IV.89; āgamo S III.209 IV.349; opadhikaŋ S I.233; It 78; purāṇaŋ & navaŋ S I.92; sayaŋ katāni puññāni S I.37; puññassa dhārā S I.100; V.400.

-**atthika** desirous of merit Sn 487 sq. -**ânubhāva** the majesty of merit PvA 58. -**âbhisankhāra** accumulation of merit D III.217; S II.82; Nd[1] 90, 206, 442; Vism 557 sq., 571; VbhA 142 sq., 166, 184. -**âbhisanda** (+ kusalâbhisanda) meritorious results A II.54 sq.; III.51, 337; IV.245. -**assaya** seat of merit DA I.67. -**iddhi** the magic power of m. PvA 117. -**kata** one who has done a deed of m. A II.32. -**kamma** good works, righteousness, merit S I.97, 143; DA I.10; VvA 32; PvA 54, 87; Sdhp 32. -kāma (adj.) desirous of doing good works S v.462. -kiriyā a good or meritorious action S I.87 (°kriyā), 101; PvA 54; usually as °*kiriya-vatthu* item of m. action (of which 3 are usually enumd: see above) D III.218; A IV.241; It 51; Nett 50, 128. -kkhandha mass of merit (only as mahā°) S v.400; A III.337. -kkhaya decay (or waning of the effect) of merit D I.18 (cp. āyukkhaya & DA I.110). -kkhetta field of m., Ep. of the Sangha or any holy personalities, doing good (lit. planting seeds of merit) to whom is a source of future compensation to the benefactor. Usually with adj. anuttara unsurpassed field of m. (see also sangha) D III.5, 227; M I.446; III.80; S I.167, 220; v.343, 363, 382; A I.244; II.34 sq., 56, 113; III.158, 248, 279 sq., 387; IV.10 sq., 292; It 88; Sn 486; Vv 50[31] (cp. VvA 216); Pv IV.1[33] (of a bhikkhu); Vism 220; VvA 286; PvA 1 (ariyasangha), 5 (Moggallāna), 6 (arahanto), 132, 140, 214 and passim. Cp. BSk. puṇyakṣetra Divy 63, 395 (+udāra). -paṭipadā the meritorious path, path of m. A I.168; Nett 96. -pasavana creation of m. PvA 31. -pekkha looking for merit (i. e. reward), intent upon m. S I.167; Sn 463 sq., 487 sq.; Dh 108 (cp. DhA II.234). -phala the fruit (or result) of m. action S I.217; Pug 51; DhA II.4; PvA 8, 50, 52. -bala the power of m. PvA 195. -bhāga taking part in meritorious action S I.154. -bhāgiya having share in m. M III.72 sq.; Nett 48. -maya = puñña J IV.232 (°iddhi); cp. BSk. puñyamaya AvŚ I.183.

Puññavant (adj.) [fr. puñña] possessing merit, meritorious, virtuous Ps II.213; Vism 382; DhA I.340; PvA 75.

Puṭa [etym. unknown, prob. dialectical, as shown by N. of Pāṭaliputta, where putta = puṭa since unfamiliar in origin] orig. meaning "tube," container, hollow, pocket. — 1. a container, usually made of leaves (cp. J IV.436; V.441; VI.236), to carry fruit or other viands, a pocket, basket: ucchu° basket for sugar J IV.363; paṇṇa° leaf-basket PvA 168; phala° fruit basket J IV.436 = VI.236; phānita(ssa)° basket of molasses, sugar-basket S I.175 (*KS.*: jar); J IV.366; DhA IV.232; mālā° basket for garlands or flowers DhA III.212 (baddha made, lit. bound). In puṭa-baddha-kummāsa VvA 308 perhaps meaning "cup." — 2. a bag or sack, usually referring to food carried for a journey, thus "knapsack" (or directly "provisions," taking the container for what it contains DA I.288 puts puṭaŋsa = pātheyya), in bhatta° bag with provisions J II.82 (with bandhati), 203; III.200; DA I.270. Also at J IV.375 "bag" (tamba-kipillaka°). See below °aŋsa & °bhatta. — 3. a tube, hollow, in nāsā° (nāsa°) nostril J VI.74; Vism 195, 263, 362; KhA 65; hattha° the hollow of the hand Miln 87; vatthi° bladder(-bag) Vism 264; sippi-puṭa oyster shell J V.197, 206. puṭaŋ karoti to form a hollow VbhA 34. — 4. box, container, see °bheda & °bhedana, in pāṭali-puṭa seed box for the P. flower.

-aŋsa "bag-shoulder" (for "shoulder-bag," cp. aŋsapuṭa (assapuṭa) & Ger. rucksack = knapsack. Rightly expld by Bdhgh at DA I.288), a bag carrying provisions on journeys, hence "provision," in phrase **puṭaŋsena** with provisions (v. l. at all places puṭosena) D I.117; M III.80; A II.183; cp. *Dialogues* I.150; see also **mutoḷī**. -pāka something cooked in a bag (like a meal-pudding) Vism 500. -baddha kind of moccasins Vin I.186, see *Vin. Texts* II.15. Spelt *puṭa-bandha* at Vism 251 = VbhA 234. -bhatta "bag-food," viaticum, provisions for journey J II.423; KhA 46. -bheda the breaking of the container (i. e. seed boxes of the Sirīsa plant) VvA 344 (in vatthu where Sirīsa refers to Pāṭaliputta, cp. Vv 84[52, 53]). -bhedana breaking of the (seed-) boxes of the Pāṭali plant, referring primarily to the N. of Pāṭali-putta, where putta represents a secondary Pālisation of Sk. °putra which again represents P. (or Non-Aryan) puṭa (see Pischel, *Prk. Gr.* § 238 & 292). Through popular etym. a wrong conception of the expression arose, which took puṭa in the sense of "wares, provisions, merchandise" (perhaps influenced by puṭaŋsa) and, based on C. on Ud 88 (bhaṇḍakānaŋ mocana-ṭṭhānaŋ vuttaŋ hoti) gave rise to the (wrong) trsln *Dial.* II.92 "a centre for interchange of all kinds of *wares*." See also *Miln trsln* I.2; *Buddh. Suttas* XVI. — Vin I.229 = D II.87 = Ud 88. After the example of Pāṭaliputta applied to the city of Sāgala at Miln 1 (nānā-puṭa-bhedanaŋ S° nagaraŋ). Here clearly meant for "merchandise." — Rh. D. in a note on puṭa-bhedana gives explo "a town at the confluence or bend of a river" (cp. Jaina Sūtras 2, 451).

Puṭaka (nt.) [fr. puṭa] a bag, pocket, knapsack or basket J II.83 (°bhatta = provisions); DA I.263; DhA II.82 (v. l. piṭaka & kutaka); IV.132 (pockets of a serpent's hood). Cp. bhatta.

Puṭṭha[1] [pp. of **pus** (see poseti), Vedic puṣṭa] nourished, fed, strengthened, brought up Sn 831; J III.467.

Puṭṭha[2] [pp. of pucchati, Vedic pṛṣṭa] asked S II.36; Sn 84, 122, 510 sq., 1036; DhA IV.132; PvA 10 (after = acc.) 68, 72 with samāno A I.197. See also **pucchita.**

Puṭṭha[3] see **phuṭṭha** [= Sk. spṛṣṭa, cp. Pischel, *Prk. Gr.* § 311].

Puṭṭhatta (nt.) [abstr. fr. puṭṭha[1]] the fact of being fed or brought up by J II.405 (vaḍḍhakinā °ā).

Puṭṭhavant [fr. puṭṭha[3], cp. same form in Prk. AMg. puṭṭhavaŋ = Sk. spṛṣṭavān: Pischel, *Prk. Gr.* § 569] one who has touched or come in direct contact with ThA 284.

Puṇḍarīka (nt.) [Non-Aryan (?). Cp. Vedic puṇḍarīka] the white lotus D I.75 A III.26 (in sequence uppala, paduma, p.); D II.4 (Sikhī puṇḍarīkassa mūle abhisambuddho); M III.93; S I.138, 204 = J III.309; A I.145 (uppala paduma p.); II.86 sq. (samaṇa° adj.); Sn 547; J V.45, 215 (°ttac' angī ratta-paduma-patta-vaṇṇa-sarīrā); Vv 44[12] (= seta-kamala VvA 191); Pv II.12[2]; III.3[3] (pokkharaṇī bahu °ā); Pug 63; DA I.219, 284 (sankho elo uppalo puṇḍarīko ti cattāro nidhayo). N. of a hell S I.152; Sn p. 126 (here in sq. Uppalaka, Puṇḍ°, Paduma).

Puṇḍarīkinī (f.) [adj. puṇḍarīkin, of puṇḍarīka] a pool or pond of white lotuses D I.75 ≈ (M III.93; S I.138).

Puṇṇa [pp. of **pṛ**, Vedic pṛṇāti, Pass. pūryate, *pele to fill; cp. Sk. prāṇa & pūrṇa = Av. pərəna; Lith. pilnas; Lat. plēnus; Goth fulls = E. full = Ger voll] full, seldom by itself (only passage so far pannarase puṇṇāya puṇṇamāya rattiyā D I.47 = Sn p. 139), nor -° (only Sn 835 muttakarīsa°), usually in cpds., and there mostly restricted to phrases relating to the full moon.

-ghaṭa a full pitcher (for feeding the bhikkhus, as offering on festive days, cp. *J.P.T.S.* 1884) DhA I.147; KhA 118 (v. l. suvaṇṇaghaṭa); DA I.140 (°paṭimaṇḍita ghara). -canda the full moon J I.149, 267; V.215. -patta a full bowl (as gift, °ŋ deti to give an ample gift) J III.535. -baddha at Miln 191 should be read as °bhadda. -bala at DA I.110 read puñña-bala. -bhadda worshipper of Puṇṇabhadda, perhaps a Yakkha (father of the Yakkha Harikesa) Nd[1] 92 (Vāsuvadeva, Baladeva, P. and Maṇibhadda, cp. p. 89); Miln 191 (pisācā maṇibhaddā p.). -mā the full moon (night) D I.47 (komudiyā cātumāsiniyā puṇṇāya puṇṇamāya rattiyā, cp. DA I.140); Sn p. 139 (similar); M III.21; J V.215 (dve p-māyo); Vism 292 (puṇṇa-m-uposatha = puṇṇa-mā-uposatha), 418 (Phagguṇa-puṇṇama-divase); VvA 66 (āsāḷhi p.); PvA 137 (id.); DA I.140; DhA III.461 (komudi). -māsa = °mā only in loc. puṇṇamāse Vv 81[1]

(=puṇṇa-māsiyaŋ sukka-pakkhe pannarasiyaŋ VvA 314; the similar pass. at VvA 321 reads, prob. by mistake, sukka-pakkha-pāṭiyaŋ: see pāṭī); J v.215 (=puṇṇa candāya rattiyā C.). -māsī (f.; fr. °māsa)= mā J 1.86 (Phagguṇi p.); VvA 314; cp. BSk. pūrṇamāsī AvŚ 1.182.

Puṇṇatā (f.) [abstr. to puṇṇa] fulness DA 1.140 (māsa° full-moon).

Puṇṇatta (nt.) [abstr. ro puṇṇa] fulness SnA 502.

Putolī see muṭolī.

Putta [Vedic putra, Idg. *putlo=Lat. pullus (*putslos) young of an animal, fr. pōu, cp. Gr. παῦς, παις child, Lat. puer, pubes, Av. puþra, Lith. putýtis (young animal or bird), Cymr. wyr grandchild; also Sk. pota(ka) young animal and base pu- in pumaŋs, puŋs "man"] 1. a son S 1.210; Sn 35, 38, 60, 557, 858; Dh 62, 84, 228, 345; J IV.309; Vism 645 (simile of 3 sons); PvA 25, 63, 73 sq.; DA 1.157 (dāsaka°). Four kinds of sons are distinguished in the old Cy. viz. atraja p., khettaja, dinnaka, antevāsika, or born of oneself, born on one's land, given to one, i. e. adopted, one living with one as a pupil. Thus at Nd¹ 247; Nd² 448; J 1.135. Good and bad sons in regard to lineage are represented at J VI.380. — Metaph. "sons of the Buddha" S 1.192= Th 1, 1237 (sabbe Bhagavato puttā); It 101 (me tumhe puttā orasā mukhato jātā dhammajā), J III.211. — The parable of a woman eating her sons is given as a punishment in the Peta condition at Pv 1.6 (& 7). — pl. puttāni Pv 1.6³. — aputta-bhāvaŋ karoti to disinherit formally J v.468. — 2. (in general) child, descendant, sometimes pleonastic like E. °man, °son in names: see putta-dāra; so esp. in later literature, like ludda° hunter's son=hunter J II.154; ayya°=ayya, i. e. gentleman, lord J v.94; PvA 66. See also rāja°. — Of a girl Th 2, 464. — mātucchā° & mātula° cousin (from mother's side), pitucchā° id (fr. father's side). On putta in N. Pāṭali° see puṭa. — f. puttī see rāja°.

-jīva N. of a tree: Putranjiva Roxburghii J VI.530. -dāra child & wife (i. e. wife & children, family) D III.66, 189, 192; S 1.92; A II.67; Pv IV.3⁴⁸ (sa° together with his family); J III.467 (kiŋ °ena what shall I do with a family?); v.478. They are hindrances to the development of spiritual life: see Nd². under āsiŋsanti & palibodha. -phala a son as fruit (of the womb) J v.330. -maŋsa the flesh of one's children (sons) a metaphor probably distorted fr. pūta° rotten flesh. The metaphor is often alluded to in the kasiṇa-kammaṭṭhāna, and usually coupled with the akkha-bbhañjana (& vaṇapaticchādana)-simile, e. g. Vism 32, 45; DhA 1.375; SnA 58, 342. Besides at S II.98 (in full); Th 1, 445 (°ūpamā); 2, 221. -mata a woman whose sons (children) are dead M 1.524.

Puttaka [fr. putta] 1. a little son S 1.209, 210. — 2. a little child Th 2, 462 (of a girl). — 3. a young bird (=potaka) J II.154.

Puttatta (nt.) [fr. putta] sonship DhA 1.89.

Puttavant (adj.) [fr. putta] having sons S IV.249. Trenckner, *Notes* 62¹⁶ gives a f. *puttapatī for puttavatī, but without ref.

Puttimant (adj.) [fr. *puttamant] having sons S 1.6; Sn 33.

Puttiya (-°) in Sakya° is compound Sakyaputta+iya "belonging to the son of the Sakyas" (i. e. to the Sakya prince) PvA 43. — asakyaputtiya dhamma Vin II.297.

Puthavī & **Puthuvī** (f.) [doublets of paṭhavī] the earth; as puthavi at S 1.186; J 1.14 (v. l. puthuvi); IV.233, & in cpds. °nābhi the navel of the earth (of the bodhimaṇḍa, the Buddha's seat under the holy fig tree) J IV.232; °maṇḍala the round of the earth Sn 990. — As puthuvī at A II.21, and in cpd. puthuvi-agga SnA 353.

Puthu (adj.) [both Vedic pṛthak & pṛthu, lit. spread out, far & wide, flat, of Idg. *plēt broad, Sk. prath to expand, pṛthaḥ palm of hand Av. fraþah breadth, cp. Gr. πλατύς broad, πλάτανος plane tree, Lith. platùs broad, Lat. planta sole of foot, Ohg. flado pancake, Ags. flet ground, E. flat] 1. (=pṛthak) separated, individual, adv. separated, individual, adv. separately, each (also given as puthag eva Kacc. 29) S 1.75 (puthu attā individual self); Th 1, 86; J IV.346 (=visuŋ visuŋ C.); Miln 4. See further under cpds. — 2. (=pṛthu). The forms (pl.) are both puther & puthū, both as adj. & n.; puthū more freq. found in metre. — numerous, various, several, more, many, most D 1.185 (puthu saññaggā; opp. ekaŋ); S 1.18¹ (puthū), 207 (id.); Sn 769 (puthū kāme=bahū Nd¹ 11); 1043, 1044 (puthū= bahukā Nd² 449ᵇ); Th 2, 344 (puthu=puthu sattā ThA 241); J VI.205 (puthū). nt. adv. puthu & puthuŋ greatly, much, in many ways Sn 580 (=aneka-ppakāraŋ SnA 460); Vv 62⁴ (=mahantaŋ VvA 258).

-gumba experienced in many crafts J VI.448 (=aneka-sippa-ññu C.). -jja (puthu 1, but see remarks on puthujjana) common, ordinary Sn 897, 911 (=puthujjanehi janita Nd¹ 308). -titthakara a common sectarian D 1.116 (thus to puthu 1, but DA 1.287= bahū t.) -ddisā (puthu 1) each separate quarter "all the diverse quarters" S 1.234. -pañña (adj.) of wide wisdom (p. 2) A 1.130; II.67 (v. l. hāsa°). -paññatā wide wisdom A 1.45. -pāṇiya ordinary (p. 1) mode of shampooing with the hand Vin II.106 (Bdhgh on p. 316 explⁿˢ pudhu-pāṇikan ti hattha parikammaŋ vuccati "manual performance," thus not identical with pāṇikā on p. 151). -bhūta (p. 2) widely spread S II.107; but cp. BSk pṛthag bhavati to be peculiar to Divy 58, 100. -mati wide understanding S 1.236. -loma "flat fin," N. of a fish "the finny carp" (Mrs. Rh. D.) Vv 44¹¹ (=dibbha-maccha VvA 191); Th 2, 508 (=so-called fish ThA 292); J IV.466. -vacana "speaking in many (bad) ways," or "people of various speech" (so expl^d Nd¹ 397) Sn 932 (prob. better "speaking ordinary talk"=puthu 1). -sattā (pl.)=puthujjanā, common people, the masses S 1.44; Pv III.7³.

Puthuka [fr. puthu, cp. (late) Vedic pṛthuka "flat corn," also "young of an animal," with which cp. perhaps Gr. παρθένος: see Walde, *Lat. Wtb.* under virgo] rice in the ear DhA 1.98 (°agga as first gift of the field).

Puthujjana [*pṛthag-jana, thus puthu 1+jana, but from the point of Pali identical in form and meaning with puthu 2, as shown by use of puthu in similar cpds. and by C. explⁿˢ. One may even say that puthu 1=pṛthak is not felt at all in the P. word. Trenckner (*Notes* 76) already hinted at this by saying "puthujjana, partly confounded with puthu"; a connection which also underlies its explⁿ as "one-of-the-many-folk" at *Kvu trslⁿ* 80⁷ & 291³. It is felt to belong to puthu 2 in the same sense as Ger. "die *breite* Masse," or Gr. οἱ πολλοί. The explⁿ at Nd¹ 308=328 is puthu-nānā-janā. A long and detailed etym.-speculation explⁿ of the term is found at DA 1.59, trsl^d at *Dhs trslⁿ* 258. The BSk. form is pṛthagjana Divy 133 etc.] an ordinary, average person (4 classes of ordinary people are discussed at *Cpd.* 49, 50), a common worldling, a man of the people, an ordinary man M 1.1, 7, 135, 239, 323; III.64, 227; S 1.148; II.94 sq. (assutavā), 151 (id.); III.46, 108, 162; IV.157, 196, 201 (assutavā), 206 sq.; v.362 (opp. to sotāpanna); A 1.27, 147 (maraṇa-dhammin), 178, 267; II.129, 163; III.54; IV.68, 97, 157, 372; Sn 351, 455, 706, 816, 859; Dh 59, 272; Vv 82⁶ (=anariya VvA 321,+anavabodha); Nd¹ 146, 248; Ps 1.61 sq., 143, 156; II.27; Dhs 1003 (cp. DhsA 248 sq.); Vism 311 (=anariya); VbhA 133 (avijj' ābhikhūta, bhava-taṇh' ābhibhūta), 186 (ummat-

taka, opposed to upabrūhita-ñāṇa-purisa, exemplifying upādāna and kamma); DhA I.5 (opp. ariyasāvaka), 445; Sdhp 363.
-kalyāṇaka (cp. BSk. pṛthagjana-kalyāṇaka Divy 419, 429) an ordinary man striving after his spiritual good Nd[1] 477; Ps I.176; II.190, 193. -bhikkhu a bh. of the common sort DA I.269; VbhA 383. -sukha ordinary happiness M I.454.

Puthujjanatā (f.) [abstr. fr. puthujjana] common-place character S I.187 = Th I, 1217.

Puthujjanika (adj.) [fr. puthujjana] common, ordinary J I.360 (of iddhi).

Puthutta (Puthatta) (nt.) [fr. puthu, cp. Sk. *pṛthutva; not with Kern, *Toev.* s. v. = Sk. pṛthaktva, speciality, peculiarity] being at variance, diversity S II.77 (opp. ekatta; v. l. SS puthatta). At A IV.97 we have to read puth' attānaŋ for puthuttānaŋ which has nothing to do with puthutta, but is puthu + attānaŋ as borne out by v. l. puthujj' attānaŋ, and by AA: puthu nānākāraṇehi attānaŋ hanti.

Puthula (adj.) [fr. puthu] broad, large, flat J III.16 (°sīsa flat-headed); VI.171 (°antaraŋsa flat-chested); Miln 121 (of a river); VvA 301 (°gambhīra). — abl. puthulato (as adv.) across DhA I.396.

Puthuso (adv.) [abl. of puthu] broadly, i. e. diversely, at variance Sn 891, 892 (= puthu-diṭṭhi-gata Nd[1] 301).

Pudava (poddava ?) see gāma° (Vin II.105 with Bdhgh note on p. 315).

Puna (indecl.) [cp. Vedic punar, punaḥ, to base *pū (related to *apo: see apa), as in puccha tail, Lat. puppis, poop, Gr. πύματος the last; orig. meaning "behind"] again. There are several forms of this adv., but puna has to be considered as the orig. Pali form. The form puno is doubtful; if authentic, a Sanskritisation; only found at ThA 71 (Ap. v. 38; v. l. puna) & 72 (Ap. v. 41, v. l. puna). The sandhi r is preserved only in *metre* and in *comp*[n]. That it is out of fashion even in metre is shown by a form punā where ā is the regular metrical lengthening instead of ar (J III.437: na hi dāni punā atthi; v. l. puna). Besides this the r is apparent in the doubling of the first consonants of cpds. (punappunaŋ, punabbhava); it is quite lost in the enclitic form pana. — We find r in punar āgami Sn 339; punar āgato J I.403 (= puna āgato J I.403 (= puna āgato, ra-kāro sandhivasena vutto C.); in cpds.: punar-abhiseka see *J.P.T.S.* 1885, 49; a-punar-āvattitā the fact of not turning back Miln 276 (cp. Prk. apuṇar-avatti Pischel, § 343). Otherwise r stands on the same level as other sandhi (euphonic) consonants (like m. & d., see below), as in puna-r-eva Dh 338; Pv II.8[7]; II.11[6]. We have m in puna-m-upāgamuŋ Sn 306; puna by itself is rarely found, it is usually comb[d] with other emphatic part, like eva and api. The meaning is "again," but in enclitic function (puna still found Sn 677, 876, otherwise pana); it represents "however, but, now" (cp. same relation in Ger. abermals: aber), similar to the development in Prk. puṇo vi & puṇar avi "again": puna "now" (Pischel Gr. § 342). — puna by itself at SnA 597; PvA 3, 45; Mhvs 14, 12. doubled as punappunaŋ S I.174; Th I, 531, 532; Sn 728, 1051; Dh 117, 118, 325, 337; J V.208; SnA 107; PvA 45, 47; punappuna at DhA II.75; as puna-d-eva at D I.60, 142; Pv II.11[3] (v. l.); Vism 163; DhA II.76; puna-m-eva Pv II.11[3]; puna pi once more J I.279; PvA 67, 74; puna-p-pi J V.208. The phrase puna c' aparaŋ "and again something else" stands on the same level as the phrase aparo pi (apare pi), with which one may compare the parallel expressions puna-divase: apara-divase, all of which show the close relation between pi, puna, apara, but we never find para in these connections. Trenckner's (& following him Oldenberg in Vin. and Hardy in A etc.) way of writing puna ca paraŋ (e. g. Miln 201, 388, 418 etc.) is to be corrected to puna c' aparaŋ, cp. punâpara Sn 1004; Cp III.6[1].
-āgamana coming again, return S I.22 (a°). -āvāsa rebirth S I.200. -divase on the following day J I.278; PvA 19, 38. -nivattati to turn back again S I.177. -bbhava renewed existence, new birth D II.15; S I.133; It 62; S IV.201 (āyati°); Sn 162, 273, 502, 514, 733; Nd[2] s. v.; Nett 28, 79 sq.; PvA 63, 200; cp. ponobhavika; a° no more rebirth S I.174, 208; Nd[2] 64; °âbhinibbatti birth in a new existence M I.294; S II.65; A I.223; Vin III.3; PvA 35. -vacana repetition SnA 487. -vāre (loc.) another time J V.21.

Punāti [cp. Vedic pavate, punāti, pū to cleanse, as in Lat. purus clean, purgo, Ohg. fowen to sift also Gr. πῦρ (cp. P. pāvaka) = Ohg. fūir = E. fire, Armen. hur, lit. "cleansing," see also puñña] 1. to clean, cleanse VvA 19 (+ visodheti, in def. of puñña). — 2. to sift J VI.108 (angāraŋ p. = attano sīse angāre p. okirati C.; so read with v. l. for phunati T.); DA I.268 (bhusaŋ pumanto viya like sifting the chaff, winnowing). Cp. puneti.

Puneti [Caus. fr. puna ? or = punāti ?] to experience (over & over) again: in this meaning at It 1 sq. & Nd[1] 202 = Nd[2] 337 (kilese na p. na paeceti etc.); perhaps also at Th I, 533 (sattayugaŋ), although Kern, *Toev.* s. v. takes it = punāti and Mrs. Rh. D. translates "lifts to lustrous purity."

Punnāga [dial. ?] a species of tree J I.9 (°puppha); VI.530; KhA 50 (aggacchinna°-phala), 53 (id.).

Puppha[1] (nt.) [Vedic puṣpa according to Grassmann for *puṣka fr. **puṣ** (?) see poseti] a flower Vin II.123; S I.204 = J III.308; Sn 2, 5; Dh 47 sq.; 377; Vism 430; SnA 78 (paduma°); VvA 73; PvA 127; Sdhp 550. — pupphāni (pl.) VbhA 255 (of 32 colours, in simile), 292 sq. (for Cetiya-worship). — adj. °puppha in ghana° thick with flowers DA I.87. — Cp. pokkharatā.
-âbhikiṇṇa decked with flowers Vv 64[29]; Pv II.11[2]. -ādhāna "a ledge (on a Tope) where offerings of flowers are laid down" (Geiger, Mhvs p. 355; cp. *Mhvs trsl.* p. 202[2]) Mhvs 30, 51, 56, 60; 33, 22 Reading uncertain. -āveḷā flower-garland VvA 125. -āsava wine made from flowers, flower-liquor J IV.117; KhA 26. -gandha odour of flowers Dh 54; Dhs 625. -cumbaṭaka a fl. cushion. -chaḍḍaka a remover of (dead) flowers, a rubbish-remover, a low occupation, including cleaning of privies & bins etc. Vin IV.6; Th I, 620; J V.449 (= vacca-ṭṭhāna-sodhaka C.); Miln 331; Vism 194 (in simile). Cp. *J.P.T.S.* 1884, 89 and *Miln trsl.* II.211. -cchatta a parasol with flowers DhA I.110. -dāna offering of flowers VbhA 336. -dāma a wreath or garland of fls. J I.397; VvA 198. -dhara bearing flowers Pv II.12[4] (so read for T. °dada). -pañjara a cage (ornamented) with flowers J V.365. -paṭa a cloth (embroidered) with flowers J IV.283; DhA II.45. -palāsa a fl. heap DhA I.75. -bhāṇin "speaking flowers," i. e. speaking the truth Pug 29. -mālā garland of fls. SnA 78. -muṭṭhi a handful of fl. Vism 432 (in simile). -rasa (wine-) juice made of fls., flower-liquor Vin I.246; taste of fls. Dhs 629. -rāsi a heap of fls. Dh 53.

Puppha[2] (nt.) [cp. Class. Sk. puṣpa "les fleurs" in strī° the menses Am. Kośa 3, 4, 30, 233 and Mārk. Pur. 51, 42. Similarly phala is used in the sense of "menstruation": see BR s. v. phala 12] blood: see pupphaka & pupphavatī. With ref. to the menses at J V.331.

Pupphaka (nt.) [fr. puppha[2]] blood J III.541 (v. l. pubbaka; C. = lohita); Miln 216 (tiṇa°-roga, a disease, Kern. "hay-fever"). Kern, *Toev.* s. v. trsl[s] the J passage with "vuil, uitwerpsel."

Pupphati [puṣp] to flower J I.76 (aor. °iṇsu); PvA 185 (=phalati). — pp. pupphita.

Pupphavatī (f.) [fr. puppha², but cp. Vedic puṣpavat flowering] a menstruous woman Miln 126.

Pupphita [pp. of pupphati] flowering, in blossom S I.131 = Th 2, 230 (su°); Vv 35⁴; J I.18; Miln 347; ThA 69 (Ap. v. 12); DhA I.280; II.250 (su°).

Pupphin (adj.) [fr. puppha¹ cp. Vedic puṣpin] bearing flowers; in nilapupphī (f.) N. of a plant ("with blue flowers") J VI.53.

Pubba¹ [Vedic pūya > *pūva > *puvva > pubba (Geiger, *P.Gr.* § 46¹); cp. pūyati to smell rotten, Lat. pūs = E. pus, Gr. πύθω to rot, πύον matter; Vedic pūti smelling foul; Goth. fūls = E. foul] pus, matter, corruption M I.57; III.90; S I.150; II.157; A I.34; J II.18; Miln 382; PvA 80. — In detail discussed (as one of the 32 ākāras) at Vism 261, 360; KhA 62; VbhA 244. — Often in combⁿ **pubba-lohita** matter & blood, e. g. Sn p. 125; Sn 671; J V.71; DhA I.319; as food of the Petas Pv I.6⁸; I.9¹ (lohita-pubba); I.11⁸; II.2⁶. **pubba-vaṭṭi** a lump of matter DhA III.117.

Pubba² (adj.) [Vedic pūrva, to Idg. *per, see pari & cp. Goth. fram = from; Gr. πρόμος first, Goth. fruma = As. formo first, Av. pourvō, also Sk. pūrvya = Goth. frauja = Ohg. frō Lord, frouwa = Ger. frau. See also Lat. prandium, provincia] previous, former, before. The adj. never occurs in abs. forms by itself (for which see pubbaka), it is found either as -° or °- or in cases as adv. The phrase pubbam antam anissita Sn 849 is poetical for pubbantam. — 1. (-°) having been before J III.200; na diṭṭha° not seen before Nd¹ 445; māta-bhūta° formerly (been) his mother PvA 79; vuttha° (gāma) formerly inhabited DhA I.15; as adv. bhūta-pubbaŋ before any beings (existed) Vin I.342; DhA I.102 and passim (see bhūta). — 2. (neg.) apubba (nt.) what has not been before, something new VvA 117, 287. acc. as adv. in phrase apubbaŋ acarimaŋ not earlier, not after, i. e. simultaneously M III.65; Pug 13 (=apure apacchā, ekappahāren' evâti attho PugA 186). — 3. (cases adverbially) instr. pubbena in °âpara gradual M III.79; acc. pubbaŋ see 1, 2, with abl. as prep. = before SnA 549 (=purā); loc. pubbe in earlier times (also referring to previous births, cp. pure), in the past, before S IV.307; Sn 831, 949 (with pacchā & majjhe, i. e. future & present); Pv I.3¹; II.2²; SnA 290, 385, 453; PvA 4, 10, 39, 40, 100. With abl. as prep. = before S II.104. In compᵒ with °nivāsa see sep. An old acc. f. *pūrvīŋ (cp. Prk. puvviŋ Pischel, *Gr.* § 103) we find in Cpd. anupubbikathā (q. v.). The compar. pubbatara ("quite early") occurs abs. at S IV. 117 as nom. pl. "ancestors" (cp. Gr. οἱ πρότεροι), as loc. adv. at S I.22.

-**angin** in f. °angī (cāru°) at J V.4 & VI.481 read *sabbangin*. -**aṇṇa** "first grain," a name given to the 7 kinds of grain, as distinguished from *aparaṇṇa*, the 7 sorts of vegetables, with which it is usually combined; Vin III.151; IV.267; Nd¹ 248 (where the 7 are enumᵈ); Nd² 314; J II.185; Miln 106; DA I.78, 270; DhA IV.81 etc. (see aparaṇṇa). See also bīja-bija. -**aṇha** the former part of the day, forenoon, morning (as contrasted with majjhaṇha & sāyaṇha) D I.109, 226; A I.294; III.344; S I.76 (°samayaŋ); SnA 139 (id.); DhA III.98; PvA 61, 216. The spelling pubbanha M I.528 (cp. Trenckner, *Notes* 80). -**anta** (1) the East J I.98 (°ato aparantaŋ aparantato pubbantaŋ gacchati from E. to W. from W. to E.); V.471. — (2) the Past (opp. aparanta the Future) D I.12 sq.; S II.26; Nd¹ 212; Dhs 1004. pubbam antaŋ for pubbantaŋ is poetical at Sn 849. -°*ânudiṭṭhi* theory concerning the past or the beginning of things D I.13 (cp. DA I.103); M II.233; S III.45; Dhs 1320. -**aḷha(ka)** (āḷhaka) at Th 2, 395 is doubtful. T. reads bubbuḷaka, Mrs. Rh. D. translates "bubble of film"; ThA 259 explⁿˢ by "ṭhita-jala-pubbaḷha-sadisa." -**ācariya** (1) an ancient teacher, a scholar of previous times A I.132; II.70; It 110; Vism 523 = VbhA 130; KhA 11, 64, 65. — (2) a former teacher SnA 318. -**āciṇṇa** (-vasena) by way of former practice, from habit SnA 413. -**âpara** (1) what precedes and what follows, what comes first and what last (with ref. to the successive order of syllables and words in the text of the Scriptures) A III.201 (°kusala); Dh 352; Nett 3 (°ânusandhi); cp. BSk. pūrvāpareṇa vyākhyānaŋ karoti "explᵈ in due order" AvŚ II.20. — (2) °*rattaŋ* "as in the former, so in the foll. night," i. e. without ceasing, continuous Th 1, 413. cp. pubbaratt-âparattaŋ DhA IV.129. -**âpariya** former & future, first & last Ud 61 (°vivesa); -**ābhoga** previous reflection ThA 30. -**ārāma** "Eastern Park," N. of a locality east of Sāvatthi A III.344; Sn p. 139 (cp. Sn A 502). -**āsava** former intoxication Sn 913, cp. Nd¹ 331. -**uṭṭhāna** getting up before (someone else) either applied to a servant getting up before the master, or to a wife rising before her husband VvA 71, 136. -**uṭṭhāyin** "getting up earlier" (with complementary Ep. pacchā-nipātin "lying down later"), see above D I.60; III.191; A III.37; IV.265 sq.; DA I.168. — abstr. °*uṭṭhāyitā* J III.406 (°ādīhi pañcahi kalyāṇa dhammehi samannāgatā patidevatā) = V.88; KhA 173. -**uttara** (1) preceding and following Kacc. 44, 47. — (2) "east-northern," i. e. north-eastern J V.38 (°kaṇṇa N.E. corner); VI.519 (id.). -**kamma** a former deed, a deed done in a former existence Cp. III.11³. -**kārin** "doing before," i. e. looking after, obliging, doing a favour A I.87; Pug 26 (=paṭhamaŋ eva kāraka PugA 204); PvA 114. -**kicca** preliminary function Vin V.127 (cattāro pubbakiccā); cp. *Cpd.* 53. -**koṭṭhaka** "Eastern Barn," Npl. A III.345. -(**n**)**gama** (1) going before, preceding A III.108 (okkamane p.); M III.71 sq. — (2) "allowing to go before"; controlled or directed by, giving precedence Dh 2 (mano° dhammā = tena paṭhama-gāminā hutvā samannāgatā DhA I.35); Nd² 318; Pug 15 (paññā° ariyamagga = paññaŋ pure-cārikaŋ katvā PugA 194); Sdhp 547 (paññā°). Cp. BSk. pūrvangama Divy 333 ("obedient" Index). -**carita** former life SnA 382, 385. -**ja** born earlier, i. e. preceding in age PvA 57 (=jeṭṭhaka). -**ñāti** former relative PvA 24. -**deva** a former god, a god of old, pl. the ancient gods (viz. the Asuras) S I.224. -**devatā** an ancient deity A II.70; It 110 (v. l. °deva). -**nimitta** "previous sign," a foregoing sign, prognostic, portent, forecast It 76 (the 5 signs of decay of a god); J I.11 (the 32 signs at the conception of a Buddha, given in detail on p. 51), 48; Miln 298 (of prophetic dreams, cp. *Cpd.* p. 48); VbhA 407 (in dreams); DhA II.85. -**pada** the former, or antecedent, part (of a phrase) DhsA 164. -**parikamma** a former action SnA 284 (opp. to pacchā-parikamma). -**purisa** ancestor D I.93, 94. -**peta** a deceased spirit, a ghost (=peta) D I.8 (°kathā, cp. DA I.90 & *Dial.* I.14). pubbe pete is poetical at Pv I.4¹ for pubbapete. Cp. BSk. pūrvapreta AvŚ I.149 (see Index p. 230); Divy 47, 97. -**bhāga** "former part," i. e. previous PvA 133 (°cetanā opp. apara-bhāga-cetanā. SS omit bhāga). -**bhāsin** speaking obligingly (cp. pubbakārin) D I.116 (trsl. "not backward in conversation"), DA I.287 (bhāsanto va paṭhamataraŋ bhāsati etc.). -**yoga** "former connection," i. e. connection with a former body or deed, former action (and its result) J V.476; VI.480; Miln 2 (pubbayogo ti tesaŋ pubba-kammaŋ). Kern, *Toev.* s. v. remarks that it is frequent in BSk. as pūrvayoga (yoga = yuga; syn. with pūrvakalpa), e. g. Saddh. Puṇḍ. ch. VII.; MVastu II.287; III.175; and refers to *Ind. Studien* 16, 298; *J.R.A.S.* 1875, 5. -**rattâparattaŋ** the past and future time, the whole time, always A III.70; DhA IV.129. -**vāsana** an impression remaining in the mind from former actions Sn 1009;

ThA 31 (Ap. v. 8). -videha Eastern Videha KhA 123, 176; SnA 443. -sadisa an old (former) friend DhA I.57.

Pubbaka (adj.) [fr. pubba²] 1. former, ancient, living in former times D I.104 (isayo), 238 (id.); Sn 284 (id.); S II.105; IV.307 (ācariya-pācariyā); Th 1, 947. — 2. (-°; cp. pubba² 1) having formerly been, previous J I.182 (suvaṇṇakāra° bhikkhu), cp. BSk. °pūrvaka in same use at AvŚ I.259, 296, 322. — 3. (-°) accompanied or preceded by ThA 74 (guṇ' âbhitthavana° udāna); PvA 122 (puññânumodana° maggâcikkhana); cp. āśvāsana-pūrvaka Jtm 210.

Pubbāpeti [Denom. fr. pubba²] occurs only in *one* phrase (gattāni pubbāpayamāno) at M I.161 & A III.345 ≈ 402 in meaning "drying again"; at both A pass. the vv. ll. (glosses) are "sukkhāpayamāno" and "pubba-sadisāni kurumāno"; to the M. pass. cp. Trenckner's notes on p. 543, with the BB expl[n] of the word (=pubba-bhāvaŋ gamayamāno), also Neumann, *Majjh. trsl*[n] I.260. The similar passage at S I.8, 10 has "gattāni sukkhāpayamāno" as T. reading and "pubbāpayamāno" as v. l. BB.

Pubbe (°-) [loc. of pubba², see pubba² 3] in cpds.: "in a former existence": °kata (nt.) deeds done in a past life M II.217 = A I.173 (°hetu); J V.228 (°vādin fatalist); Nett 29 (°punnata). °nivāsa [cp. BSk. pūrve-nivāsa-saŋprayuktaŋ MVastu III.224, otherwise as pūrva-nivāsa Divy 619] abode in a former life, one's former state of existence D II.1, 2; III.31 sq., 50 sq., 108 sq., 230, 281; M I.278; II.21; III.12; S I.167; A I.164 sq.; It 100; Sn 647; Dh 423; Pug 61; Vism 411 (remembered by 6 classes of individuals); ThA 74, 197. — pubbe-nivās' ânussati (-ñāṇa) (knowledge of) remembrance of one's former state of existence, one of the faculties of an Arahant (cp. A I.164 sq., and *Cpd.* 64) D III.110, 220; M I.35, 182, 248, 278, 496; Dhs 1367; Nett 28, 103; Vism 433; VbhA 373 sq., 401, 422; Tikp. 321. — See also under **nivāsa** and cp. Vism ch. XIII, pp. 410 sq.

Pumati [onomat. *pu to blow, cp. Gr. φῦσα blowing, bubble, φυσάω blow, Lat. pustula = pustule, Sk. *pupphusa = P. papphasa lung, phutkaroti blow, etc., see Uhlenbeck *Ai. Wtb.* s. v. pupphusa] to blow, aor. pumi J I.171; ger. pumitvā J I.172. See *J.P.T.S.* 1889, 207 (?).

Puman (Pumā) [see puŋs] a male, a man, nom sg. pumo D II.273; Cp. II.6²; instr. pumunā J VI.550. nom. pl. pumā D III.85 (itthi-pumā men & women; v. l. K. °purisā); J III.459; acc. sg. pumaŋ J V.154 (gata, cp. purisantara-gata). — On decl. cp. Müller, *P.Gr.* p. 79; Greiger, *P.Gr.* § 93⁵.

***Pura** [on etym. see purā, purāṇa, pure] base of adv. & prep. denoting "before"; abl. purato (adv. & prep.) in front of (with gen.), before (only local) Vin I.179; II.32; D II.14 (mātu); S I.137; Pv I.11¹, 11³ (opp. pacchā); II.8⁶ (janâdhipassa); DA I.152; PvA 5 (purisassa), 22, 39 (tassa). Often repeated (distributively) purato purato each time in front, or in front of each, or continuously in front Vin II.213; Vism 18; cp. pacchato pacchato. — Otherwise *pura occurs only in foll. der.: (1) *adverbial:* *puraḥ in purakkharoti, purekkhāra, purohita; purā, pure, puratthaŋ, puratthato. — (2) *adjectival:* purāṇa, puratthima, purima.

Pura (nt.) [Vedic pur. f., later Sk. puraŋ nt. & puri f.] 1. a town, fortress, city Vin I.8 = M I.171 (Kāsinaŋ puraŋ); J I.196, 215; Sn 976, 991, 1012 (°uttama), 1013; J VI.276 (=nagara C); Mhvs 14, 29. —avapure below the fortress M I.68. —devapura city of the Gods S IV.202; Vv 64³⁰ (=Sudassana-mahā-nagara VvA 285). See also purindada. — 2. dwelling, house or (divided) part of a house (=antepura), a meaning restricted to the Jātakas, e. g. V.65 (=nivesana C.); VI.251, 492 (=antepura). Cp. thipura lady's room, harem, also "lady" J V.296, and antepura. — 3. the body [cp. Sk. pura body as given by Halāyudha 2, 355, see Aufrecht p. 273] Th 1, 273, 1150 (so read for pūra, cp. Kern, *Toev.* s. v. & under sarīradeha). — Cp. porin.

Purakkhata [pp. of purakkharoti] honoured, esteemed, preferred D I.50; M I.85; S I.192, 200; Sn 199, 421, 1015; Nd¹ 154; Dh 343 (=parivārita DhA IV.49); J II.48 (°parivārita); Pv III.7¹ (=payirupāsita PvA 205); DA I.152 (=purato nisinna); ThA 170. Cp. purekkhata.

Purakkharoti [fr. puraḥ, cp. Ved. puras-karoti, see pure] to put in front, to revere, follow, honour; only in foll. sporadic forms: ppr. purakkharāna holding before oneself, i. e. looking at S III.9 sq.; aor. 3rd pl. purakkharuŋ Miln 22; ger. purakkhatva M I.28; Sn 969; Nd¹ 491; J V.45 (=purato katvā C.); PvA 21, 141. — purakkhata pp. (q. v.). See also purekkhāra.

Puratthaŋ (adv.) [for Vedic purastāt, fr. puraḥ, see *pura] 1. before S I.141 (na pacchā na puratthaŋ = no after, no before). — 2. east D I.50 (°âbhimukha looking eastward.)

Puratthato (adv.) [fr. puratthaŋ, cp. BSk. purastataḥ MVastu II.198] in front, coram Sn 416 (sic, v. l. BB purakkhato); J VI.242.

Puratthima (adj.) [fr. *pura, cp. Prk. (AMg.) puratthima, acc. to Pischel, Gr. § 602 a der. fr. purastāt (=P. puratthaŋ) as *purastima, like *pratyastima (=paccatthima) fr. *pratyastaŋ] eastern D I.153; S I.144; J I.71 (°âbhimukha: Gotama facing E. under the Bo tree).

Purā (indecl.) [Vedic purā; to Idg. *per, cp. Goth. faúr = Ags. for = E. (be-) fore; also Lat. prae = Gr. παραί = Sk. pare] prep. c. abl. "before" (only temporal) Vin IV.17 (purāruṇā = purā aruṇā before dawn); Sn 849 (purā bhedā before dissolution (of the body), after which the Suttanta is named Purābhedasutta, cp. Nd¹ 210 sq.; expl[d] by sarīra-bhedā pubbaŋ at SnA 549).

Purāṇa (adj.) [Venic purāṇa, fr. *per, cp. Sk. parut in former years, Gr. πέρυσι = Lith. pernai, Goth. fairneis, Ohg. firni = Ger. firn (last year's snow), forn formerly, ferro far] 1. ancient, past Sn 312, 944 (=Nd¹ 428 atītaŋ, opp. nava = paccuppannaŋ); Dh 156 (=pubbe katāni C.); with ref. to former births or previous existences: p. kammaŋ S II.64 = Nd¹ 437 = Nd² 680 Q. 2; puññaŋ S I.92. — 2. old (of age), worn out, used (opp. nava recent) D I.224 (bandhanaŋ, opp. navaŋ); Vin II.123 (udakaŋ p.°ŋ stale water); S II.106 (magga); Sn 1 (tacaŋ); J II.114 (f. purāṇī, of an old bow string, applied jokingly to a former wife); IV.201 (°paṇṇa old leaf, opp. nava); V.202 (a° not old, of years); VI.45 (apurāṇaŋ adv. recently); VbhA 363 (udaka stale water). — 3. former, late, old in cpds. as °dutiyikā the former wife (of a bhikkhu) Vin I.18, 96; IV.263; S I.200; Ud 5; J I.210; °rājorodhā former lady of the harem Vin IV.261; °sālohita former blood-relation Sn p. 91; Ud 7; DhA II.210. Cp. porāṇa.

Purātana (adj.) [fr. purā, cp. sanātana in formation] belonging to the past, former, old Nett A 194.

Purindada [distorted fr. Vedic puraŋ-dara, pura + dṛ to break, see darī, thus "breaker of fortresses," Ep. of Indra (& Agni). The P. Commentator (VvA 171) of course takes it popularly as "pure dānaŋ dadāti ti Purindado ti vuccati," thus pure + dā; see also Trenckner, *Notes* 59⁸; Geiger, *P.Gr.* § 44³] "town-breaker," a name of Sakka (Indra) D II.260; S I.230; Vv 37⁴, 62²; PvA 247.

Purima (adj.) [compar.-superl. formation fr. *pura, cp. Sk. purima] preceding, former, earlier, before (opp. pacchima) D I.179; Sn 773, 791, 1011; Nd^1 91; J I.110; SnA 149 (°dhura); PvA 1, 26. In sequence p. majjhima pacchima; past, present, future (or first, second, last) D I.239 sq.; DA I.45 sq. and passim. — purimatara = purima J I.345 (°divase the day before).

-attabhāva a former existence VvA 78; PvA 83, 103, 119. -jāti a previous birth PvA 45, 62, 79, 90.

Purimaka (adj.) [fr. purima] previous, first Vin II.167 (opp. pacchimaka). f. °ika Vin I.153.

Purisa [according to Geiger, Gr. § 30^3 the base is *pūrṣa, from which the Vedic form puruṣa, and the Prk.-P. form purisa. The further contraction *pussa *possa yielded posa (q. v.). From the Prk. form puliśa (Māgadhī) we get pulla] man (as representative of the male sex, contrasted to itthī woman, e. g. at A III.209; IV.197; J I.90; V.72; PvA 51). Definitions of the C. are "puriso nāma manussa-puriso na yakkho na peto etc." (i. e. man κατ' ἐξοχήν) Vin IV.269 (the same expl^n for purisa-puggala at Vin IV.214); "seṭṭh' aṭṭhena puri seti ti puriso ti satto vuccati" VvA 42. — 1. man D I.61 (p. kassaka "free man"); II.13; S I.225; A I.28, 126; II.115; III.156; Sn 102, 112, 316, 740, 806 and passim; Dh 117, 152, 248; Nd^1 124; PvA 3, 4, 165, 187; VvA 13 (majjhima°, paṭhama°, as t.t. g. ?). uttama° S II.278; III.61, 166; IV.380; It 97; mahā° S V.158; A II.35; III.223; IV.229 (see also under mahā); sappurisa (q. v.). Var. epithets of the Buddha e. g. at S. I.28 sq. — Kāpurisa a contemptible man; kimpurisa a wild man of the woods ("whatever man"), f. kimpurisī J V.215. —purisa as "a man, some one, somebody" as character or hero in var. *similes*, e. g. angārakāsuyaŋ khipanaka° Vism 489; asucimhi patita Vism 465; āgantuka° VbhA 23; dubbala Vism 533; papāte *patanto* VbhA 23 (cannot be a help to others; similarly with *patita* at VbhA 170 = Vism 559); bhikkhusanghaŋ disvā Vism 333; maṇḍapa-lagga Vism 339 sq.; lakuṇṭaka-pāda & dīghapāda VbhA 26; cp. the foll.: of a man pleasing the king VbhA 442 sq.; a man wishing to perform a long journey in *one* day Vism 244; a man breathing when exhausted Vism 274. Frequently elsewhere. — 2. an attendant, servant, waiter Vin II.297; D I.60 (dāsa +), 72 (id.); J I.385 (dāsa°); VI.462. Cp. porisa, posa.

-atthika one who seeks a servant Vin II.297. -anta = purisādhama Sn 664 (anta = Sk. antya; Sn A 479 expl^{ns} by antimapurisa). -antaragatā touched by a man (lit. gone in by . . .), a woman who has sexual intercourse, a woman in intercourse with a man D I.166 (cp. *Dial.* I.228); M I.77; A I.295; II.206; Vin IV.322; Pug 55 (= he does not accept food, lest their intercourse should be broken: rati antarāyo hoti PugA 231); DA I.79 (= itthi, as opp. to kumārikā). Cp. pumaŋ gata, J V.154. -allu (& ālu) N. of certain monstrous beings, living in the wilderness J V.416 (= vaḷavā-mukhayakkhinī, a y. with the face of a mare), 418; VI.537 (°ālu = vaḷavā-m.-pekkhī C.). -ājañña "a noble steed of a man," a thorough-bred or remarkable man S III.91; A V.325 sq., Sn 544; Dh 193; as *-ājāneyya* at DhA I.310; *-ājāniya* at A I.290; II.115; IV.397 sq.; V.324. -āda a bad man ("man-eater") a wild man, cannibal J V.25 (cp. puruṣāda Jtm 31^{41}); °*ādaka* J V.30. -ādhama a wicked man Dh 78; J V.268. -indriya male faculty, masculinity S V.204; A IV.57; Dhs 634, 715, 839, 972; Vism 447, 492. -uttama "the highest of men," an excellent man A V.16, 325 sq.; Sn 544; Dh 78; DhA II.188. -usabha (purisusabha) "a bull of a man," a very strong man Vin III.39. -kathā talk about men D I.8. -kāra manliness D I.53 (cp. DA I.161); Miln 96. -thāma manly strength D I.53; S II.28; A II.118; IV.190. -dammasārathi guide of men who have to be restrained, Ep. of the Buddha [cp. BSk. puruṣa-damya-sārathi Divy 54 and passim] S II.69; A I.168, 207; II.56, 112, 147; Sn p. 103 (= vicitrehi vinayan' ûpāyehi purisadamme sāretī ti SnA 443); It 79; Pug 57; Vism 207; ThA 178. -dosā (pl.) faults or defects in a man; eight are discussed in detail at A IV.190 sq.; Ps I.130; eighteen at J VI.542, 548. -dhorayha a human beast of burden S I.29. -parakkama manly energy D I.53; S II.28. -puggala a man, a human character D III.5, 227 (eight); S I.220 (8); II.69, 82, 206; IV.272 sq. = It 88 (8) (expl^d at Vism 219); A I.32, 130, 173, 189; II.34, 56; III.36, 349; IV.407 (8); V.139, 183 (8), 330 (8); Vin IV.212 sq. (= male); VbhA 497; -bhava state of being a man, manhood, virility J III.124; Dhs 634, 415, 839; PvA 63. -bhūmi man's stage, as "eight stages of a prophet's existence" (*Dial.* I.72) at D I.54, in detail at DA I.162, 163. -medha man-sacrifice, human sacrifice S I.76; A II.42; IV.151; It 21; Sn 303. -yugāni (pl.) (4) pairs of men S IV.272 sq.; A I.208; II.34, 56; III.36; IV.407; V.330; D III.5, 227; It 88; in verse Vv 44^{21}; expl^d Vism 219 (see under yuga). -lakkhaṇa (lucky) marks on a man D I.9. -linga (see also pullinga) a man's characteristic, membrum virile Vin III.35; Dhs 634, 715, 839; Tikp 50; Vism 184. -viriya manly vigour S II.28. -vyañjana the membrum virile (= °linga) Vin II.269.

Purisaka (n.-adj.) [fr. purisa] 1. a (little) man, only in °tiṇa doll effigy made of grass (straw), scarecrow Miln 352; Vism 462; DhsA 111. — 2. (adj.) having a man, f. °ikā in eka° (a woman) having intercourse with only *one* man J I.290.

Purisatta (nt.) [abstr. fr. purisa] manhood, virility Dhs 634, 715, 839.

Purisattana (nt.) [= purisatta, cp. Trenckner, *Notes* 70^{37}] manhood Miln 171.

Pure (indecl.) [is the genuine representative (with Māgadhī e) of Vedic puraḥ, which also appears as *puro in purohita, as *pura in purakkharoti. It belongs to base Idg. *per (cp. pari), as in Gr. πάρος before, earlier, πρέσβυς "preceding in life," i. e. older; Ohg. first] before (both local & temporal), thus either "before, in front" or "before, formerly, earlier." In both meanings the opp. is pacchā—(a) *local* S I.176 (pure hoti to lead); J II.153 (opp. pacchima) — (b) *temporal* S I.200; Sn 289, 311, 541, 645, 773 (= atītaŋ Nd^1 33; opp pacchā); Dh 348 (opp. pacchato); J I.50 (with abl. pure puṇṇamāya). Often meaning "in a former life," e. g. Vv 34^8, 34^{13}; Pv I.2^1 (= pubbe atītajātiyaŋ PvA 10); II.3^2 (cp. purima); II.4^2; II.7^4 (= atītabhāve PvA 101); II.9^{13}. — apure apacchā neither before nor after, i. e. simultaneously PugA 186 (see apubbaŋ). — puretaraŋ (adv.) first, ahead, before any one else DhA I.13, 40. — (c) *modal*, meaning "lest" DA I.4; cp. purā in same sense Jtm. 28.

-cārika going before, guiding, leading, only in phrase °*n katvā* putting before everything else, taking as a guide or ideal J I.176 (mettā-bhāvanaŋ); III.45 (id.), 180 (khantiñ ca mettañ ca); VI.127 (Indaŋ); PugA 194 (paññaŋ). -java [cp. BSk. purojava attendant Divy 211, 214, 379; also Vedic puroyāva preceding] preceding, preceded by, controlled by (= pubbangama) S I.33 (sammādiṭṭhi°); Sn 1107 (dhamma-takka°, cp. Nd^2 318). -jāta happening before, as logical category (°paccaya) "antecedence"; Vism 537 (elevenfold) = Tikp. 17; freq. in Dukp. & Tikp. (as ārammaṇa° & vatthu°), cp. VbhA 403 (°ārammaṇa & °vatthuka). -dvāra front door J II.153. -bhatta the early meal, morning meal, breakfast [cp. BSk. purobhaktakā Divy 307] VvA 120; PvA 109; °ŋ in the morning VvA 51; PvA 78; °*kicca* duties after the morning meal DA I.45 sq.; SnA 131 sq. -bhava "being in front," i. e. superior DA I.75 (in exegesis of porī). -samaṇa one who wanders ahead of someone else Vin II.32 (opp. pacchā°).

Purekkhata = purakkhata Sn 849, 859, (a°); Nd¹ 73, 214.

Purekkharoti [for purakkharoti, pure = Sk. puraḥ] to honour etc. Sn 794 = 803; ppr. purekkharāna Sn 844, 910.

Purekkhāra [for purakkhāra, puraḥ + kṛ, see pure] deference, devotion, honour; usually -° (adj.) devoted to, honouring D I.115; Vin III.130; IV.2, 277; Nd¹ 73, 214; Dh 73 (= parivāra DhA II.77); Vv 34¹⁴ (attha° = hitesin VvA 152); VbhA 466 (°mada); VvA 72.

Purekkhāratā (f.) [abstr. fr. purekkhāra] deference to (-°) DhA IV.181 (attha°).

Purohita [puraḥ + pp. of dhā, ch. Vedic purohita] 1. placed in front, i. e. foremost or at the top, in phrase devā Inda-purohitā the gods with Inda at their head J VI.127 (= Indaŋ pure-cārikaŋ katvā C.). — 2. the king's head-priest (brahmanic), or domestic chaplain, acting at the same time as a sort of Prime Minister D I.138; J I.210; V.127 (his wife as brāhmaṇī); Pug 56 (brāhmaṇa p.); Miln 241, 343 (dhamma-nagare p.); PvA 74.

Pulaka [cp. Sk. pulāka, Halāyudha 5, 43; not Sk. pulaka, as Kern, *Toev.* s. v. for which see also Walde, *Lat. Wtb.* s. v. pilus] shrivelled grain Miln 232 (sukka-yava° of dried barley); DhA II.154 (SS; T. reads mūlakaŋ, which is expl^d by Bdhgh as "nitthusaŋ katvā ussedetvā gahita-yava-taṇḍula vuccanti" ibid). Here belongs pulasa-patta of J III.478 (vv. ll. pulā°, mūlā°, mulā°; expl^d by C. as "saṇhāṇi pulasa-gaccha-paṇṇāni," thus taking pulasa as a kind of shrub, prob. because the word was not properly understood).

Puḷava [etym. ? dial; cp. Class. Sk. pulaka erection of the hairs of the body, also given by lexicographers (Hemachandra 1202) in meaning "vermin"] a worm, maggot M III.168; Sn 672; J III.177; VI.73; Miln 331, 357; Vism 179 (= kimi) DhA III.106, 411. See next.

Puḷavaka (BB puḷuvaka) = puḷava DhA IV.46; VvA 76; PvA 14. One of the (asubha) kammaṭṭhānas is called p. "the contemplation (°saññā idea) of the worm-infested corpse" S V.131; Dhs 264; Vism 110, 179 (puḷu°), 194 (id.; as asubha-lakkhaṇa); DhA IV.47. See also asubha.

Pulasa see pulaka.

Pulina (& **Puḷina**) (nt.) [cp. Epic Sk. pulina, also Halāyudha 3, 48] 1. a sandy bank or mound in the middle of a river J II.366 (vālika°); III.389 (id.); V.414; Miln 297 (l); Dāvs IV.29; Vism 263 (nadi°); VvA 40 (paṇḍara°). — 2. a grain of sand Miln 180 (l).

Pulla [a contracted form of purisa (q. v.)] man, only in cpd. pullinga (= purisa-linga) membrum virile, penis J V.143 (where expl^d by C. as uṇha-chārikā pl. "hot embers": the pass. is evidently misunderstood; v. l. BB phull°).

Pussa° at Nd¹ 90 in cpds. °tila, °tela, dantakaṭṭha, mattikā, etc. is probably to be read with v. l. phussa°; meaning not quite clear ("natural, raw" ?).

Pussaka at A I.188 is to be read as phussaka (see phussa³) cuckoo.

Pussaratha at J VI.39 read phussa° (q. v.).

Pūga¹ (nt.) [etym. ? cp. Vedic pūga in meaning of both pūga¹ & pūga²] heap, quantity; either as n. with gen. or as adj. = many, a lot Sn 1073 (pūgaŋ vassānaŋ = bahūni vassāni Nd² 452); Pv IV.7⁹ (pūgāni vassāni); VbhA 2 (khandhaṭṭha, piṇḍ°, pūg°).

Pūga² (m.) [see preceding] corporation, guild Vin II.109, 212; IV.30, 78, 226, 252; M III.48; A III.300; Ud 71; Pug 29 (= seṇi PugA 210). -āyatana guild's property J VI.108 (= pūga-santaka dhana C.). -gāmaṇika superintendant of a guild, guildmaster A III.76. -majjhagata gone into a guild A I.128 = Pug 29; SnA 377.

Pūga³ [Class. Sk. pūga] the betel-palm, betel nut tree J V.37 (°rukkha-ppamāṇaŋ ucchu-vanaŋ).

Pūja (adj.) [Epic Sk. pūjya, cp. pujja] to be honoured, honourable A III.78 (v. l.; T. pūjja); J III.83 (apūja = apūjaniya C.); pūjaŋ karoti to do homage Vism 312. — See also pūjiya.

Pūjanā (f.) [fr. pūjeti] veneration, worship A II.203 sq.; Dh 106, 107; Pug 19; Dhs 1121; Miln 162.

Pūjaneyya & **Pūjanīya** [grd. of pūjeti] to be honoured, entitled to homage S I.175; SnA 277; -iya J III.83; Sdhp 230, 551.

Pūjā (f.) [fr. pūj, see pūjeti] honour, worship, devotional attention A I.93 (āmisa°, dhamma°); V.347 sq.; Sn 906; Dh 73, 104; Pv I.5⁶; I.5¹²; Dpvs VII.12 (cetiya°); SnA 350; PvA 8; Sdhp 213, 230, 542, 551.
-āraha worthy of veneration, deserving attention Dh 194; DhA III.251. -karaṇa doing service, paying homage PvA 30. -kāra = karaṇa DhA II.44.

Pūjita [pp. of pūjeti] honoured, revered, done a service S I.175, 178; II.119; Th 1, 186; Sn 316; Ud 73 (sakkata mānita p. apacita); Pv I.4² (= paṭimānita C.); II.8¹⁰.

Pūjiya [= pūja, Sk. pūjya] worthy to be honoured Sn 527; J V.405; Sdhp 542.

Pūjetar [n. ag. fr. pūjeti] one who shows attention or care A V.347 sq., 350 sq.

Pūjeti [pūj, occurring in Rigveda only in śacipūjana RV VIII.16, 12] to honour, respect, worship, revere Sn 316 (Pot. pūjayeyya), 485 (imper. pūjetha); Dh 106, 195; DA I.256; PvA 54 (aor. sakkariŋsu garukkariŋsu mānesuŋ pūjesuŋ); Sdhp 538. — pp. pūjita (q. v.).

Pūti (adj.) [cp. Sk. pūti, pūyati to fester; Gr. πύθω, πῦον = pus; Lat. pūtidus putrid; Goth. fūls = Ger. faul, E. foul] putrid, stinking, rotten, fetid D II.353 (khaṇḍāni pūtīni); M I.73, 89 = III.92 (aṭṭhikāni pūtīni); Vin III.236 (anto°); S III.54; Pv I.3²; I.6¹ (= kuṇapa-gandha PvA 32); Vism 261 (= pūtika at KhA 61), 645 (°pajā itthi, in simile); PvA 67; Sdhp 258. — See also puccaṇḍatā.
-kāya foul body, mass of corruption, Ep. of the human body M II.65; S I.131; III.120; Th 2, 466; ThA 283; SnA 40; DhA III.111. -kummāsa rotten junket Vism 343. -gandha bad smell, ill-smelling Pv I.3¹ (= kuṇapa° PvA 15); J V.72. -dadhi rancid curds Vism 362; VbhA 68; cp. pūti-takka Vism 108. -deha = °kāya S I.236. -maccha stinking fish M III.168 (+ °kuṇapa & °kummāsa); in simile at It 68 = J IV.435 = VI.236 = KhA 127. -mukha having a putrid mouth SnA 458 (āsīvisa); PvA 12, 14. -mutta strong-smelling urine, usually urine of cattle used as medicine by the bhikkhu Vin I.58 = 96 (°bhesajja); M I.316; It 103; VvA 5 (°harītaka). -mūla having fetid roots M I.80. -latā "stinking creeper," a sort of creeper or shrub (Coccolus cordifolius, otherwise galoci) Sn 29 = Miln 369; Vism 36, 183; KhA 47 (°saṇṭhāna); DhA III.110, 111 (taruṇā galoci-latā pūtilatā ti vuccati). -lohitaka with putrid blood Pv I.7⁸ (= kuṇapa° PvA 37). -sandeha = °kāya Dh 148.

Pūtika (adj.) = pūti M I.449; S V.51; A I.261; J I.164; II.275; Miln 252; DhA I.321; III.111; VvA 76. —apūtika not rotten, fresh M I.449; A I.261; J V.198; Miln 252.

Pūpa [cp. Epic Sk. pūpa; "a rich cake of wheaten flour" Halāyudha, 2, 164; and BSk. pūpalikā Av.Ś II.116] a special kind of cake, baked or boiled in a bag J v.46 (°pasibbaka cake-bag); DhA I.319 (jāla° net-cake; v. l. pūva). See also **pūva.**

Pūra (adj.) [cp. Class. Sk. pūra; fr. **pṛ,** see pūreti] full; full of (with gen.) D I.244 (nadī); M I.215; III.90, 96; A IV.230; Sn 195, 721; Ud 90 (nadī); J I.146; Pv IV.3[13] (=pānīyena puṇṇa PvA 251); Pug 45, 46; PvA 29. —**dup°** difficult to fill J v.425. —**pūraŋ** (-°) nt. as adv. in kucchi-pūraŋ to his belly's fill J III.268; Vism 108 (udara-pūra-mattaŋ).

Pūraka (adj.) [=pāra+ka] filling (-°) Vism 106 (mukha°).

Pūraṇa (adj. n.) [fr. pūreti] 1. (adj.) filling Sn 312 (? better read purāṇa with SnA 324); PvA 70 (eka-thālaka°), 77 (id.). As Np. in Pūraṇa Kassapa, which however seems to be distorted from Purāṇa K. (D I.47; Sn p. 92, cp. KhA 126, 175; SnA 200, 237, 372). The expl[n] (popular etym.) of the name at DA I.142 refers it to pūreti ("kulassa ekūnaŋ dāsa-sataŋ pūrayamāno jāto" i. e. making the hundred of servants full). — 2. (nt.) an expletive particle (pada° "verse-filler"), so in C. style of "a" SnA 590; "kho" ib. 139; "kho pana" ib. 137; "taŋ" KhA 219; "tato" SnA 378; "pi" ib. 536; "su" ib. 230; "ha" ib. 416; "hi" ib. 377. See pada°.

Pūratta (nt.) [abstr. fr. pūra] getting or being full, fulness Vin II.239 (opp. unattaŋ).

Pūraḷāsa [cp. Vedic puroḍāśa] sacrificial cake (brahmanic), oblation Sn 459 (=carukañ ca pūvañ ca SnA 405), 467, 479 (=havyasesa C.), 486.

Pūrita [pp. of pūreti] filled with (-°), full Pv II.1[20] (=paripuṇṇa PvA 77); PvA 134.

Pūreti [Caus. of **pṛ,** pṛṇāti to fill, intrs. pūryate, cp. Lat. pleo; Gr. πίμ-πλημι, πλήθω, πολύς much, Goth. filu = Ger. viel; Ohg. folc=folk] 1. to fill (with=gen. or instr.) S I.173; Sn 30, 305; J I.50 (pāyāsassa), 347; II.112 (pret. pūrayittha); IV.272 (sagga-padaŋ pūrayiŋsu filled with deva world); DhA II.82 (sakaṭāni ratanehi); IV.200 (pattaŋ); PvA 100 (bhaṇḍassa), 145 (suvaṇṇassa). — 2. to fulfil DhA I.68. — 3. (Caus.) to make fill Vism 137 (lakāraŋ). — pp. puṇṇa. See also pari°. Caus. II. pūrāpeti to cause to fill S II.259; J I.99.

Pūva [cp. Sk. pūpa; with v for p] a cake, baked in a pan (kapalla) A III.76; J I.345 (kapalla° pan-cake), 347; III.10 (pakka°); Vv 13[6]; 29[6] (=kapalla-pūva VvA 123); Pv IV.3[13] (=khajjaka PvA 251); Vism 108 (jāla° net-cake, cp. jāla-pūpa), 359 (pūvaŋ vyāpetvā, in comp.); VbhA 65, 255 (simile of woman going to bake a cake); KhA 56; DA I.142; VvA 67, 73 (°surā, one of the 5 kinds of intoxication liquors, see surā); PvA 244. See also *Vin. Texts* I.39 (sweetmeats, sent as presents).

Pūvika [fr. pūva] a cake-seller, confectioner Miln 331.

Pe is abbreviation of peyyāla (q. v.); cp. **la.**

Pekkha[1] (adj.) (-°) [cp. Sk. prekṣā f. & prekṣaka adj.; fr. pa+**īkṣ**] looking out for, i. e. intent upon, wishing; usually in puñña° desirous of merit S I.167; Dh 108 (=puññaŋ icchanto DhA II.234); Vv 34[21] (=puññaphalaŋ ākankhanto VvA 154); PvA 134.

Pekkha[2] (adj.) [grd. of pekkhati, Sk. prekṣya] to be looked for, to be expected, desirable J VI.213.

Pekkhaka (adj.) (-°) [fr. pekkha[1]] seeing, looking at; wishing to see ThA 73 (Ap. v.59), f. °ikā S I.185 (vihāra°).

Pekkhaṇa (nt.) [fr. pa+**īkṣ**] seeing, sight, look DA I.185, 193; KhA 148 (=dassana).

Pekkhati [pa+**īkṣ**] to behold, regard, observe, look at D II.20; S IV.291; J VI.420. — ppr. pekkhamāna Vin I.180; Sn 36 sq. (=dakkhamāna Nd[2] 453), 1070, 1104; Pv II.3[7]; Vism 19 (disā-vidisaŋ). gen. pl. pekkhataŋ Sn 580 (cp. SnA 460). — Caus. pekkheti to cause one to behold, to make one see or consider Vin II.73≈A v.71. — Cp. anu°.

Pek(k)havant [fr. pekkhā] desirous of (loc.) J v.403.

Pek(k)hā (f.) [fr. pa+**īkṣ**] 1. consideration, view Vbh 325, 328. — 2. desire J v.403 (p. vuccati taṇhā). — 3. (or (pekkhaŋ ?) show at a fair D I.6 (=naṭa-samajjā DA I.84); see *Dial.* I.7, n. 4 and cp. *J.R.A.S.* 1903, 186.

Pekkhin (adj.) [fr. pekkhati] looking (in front), in phrase yugamattaŋ p. "looking only the distance of a plough" Miln 398.

Pekhuṇa (pekkh°) (nt.) [not with Childers fr. *pakṣman, but with Pischel, *Gr.* § 89 fr. Sk. prenkhaṇa a swing, Vedic prenkha, fr. pra+**inkh,** that which swings, through *prenkhuṇa > prekhuṇa > pekhuṇa] 1. a wing Th 1, 211 (su° with beautiful feathers), 1136; J I.207. — 2. a peacock's tail-feathers J VI.218 (=morapiñja C.), 497 (citrapekkhunaŋ moraŋ).

Pecca [ger. of pa+**i**, cp. BSk. pretya Jtm 31[54]] "after having gone past," i. e. after death, having departed S I.182; III.98; A II.174 sq.; III.34, 46, 78; Sn 185, 188, 248, 598, 661; It 111; Dh 15, 131 (=paraloke DhA III.51); J I.169; v.489, Pv I.11[9]; III.7[5] (v. l. pacca). The form peccaŋ under influence of Prk. (AMg.) peccā (see Pischel, *Prk. Gr.* 587) at J VI.360.

Peṭaka (adj.) [fr. piṭaka] "what belongs to the Piṭaka," as title of a non-canonical book for the usual **Peṭak' opadesa** "instruction in the Piṭaka," dating from the beginning of our era (cp. Geiger, *P.Gr.* p. 18), mentioned at Vism 141=DhsA 165. Cp. **tipeṭaka,** see also **piṭaka.**

Peṇāhikā (f.) [dial.; etym. uncertain] a species of bird (crane ?) Miln 364, 402; shortened to **peṇāhi** at Miln 407 (in the uddāna). Cp. *Miln trsl.* II.343.

Peṇṇakata is v. l. for paṇṇakata Npl. at Vv 45[5] sq. (see VvA 197).

Peta [pp of pa+ī, lit. gone past, gone before] dead, departed, the departed spirit. The Buddhistic peta represents the Vedic pitaraḥ (manes, cp. pitṛyajña), as well as the Brāhmaṇic preta. The first are souls of the "fathers," the second ghosts, leading usually a miserable existence as the result (kammaphala) or punishment of some former misdeed (usually avarice). They may be raised in this existence by means of the dakkhiṇā (sacrificial gift) to a higher category of mahiddhikā petā (alias yakkhas), or after their period of expiation shift into another form of existence (manussa, deva, tiracchāna). The punishment in the Nirayas is included in the peta existence. Modes of suffering are given S II.255; cp *K.S.* ii, 170 p. On the whole subject see Stede, *Die Gespenstergeschichten des Peta Vatthu,* Leipzig 1914; in the Peta Vatthu the unhappy ghosts are represented, whereas the Vimāna Vatthu deals with the happy ones. — 1. (souls of the departed, manes) D III.189 (petānaŋ kālakatānaŋ dakkhiṇaŋ anupadassati); A III.43 (id.); I.155 sq.; v.132 (p, ñātisalohita); M I.33; S I.61=204; Sn 585, 590, 807 (petā-kālakatā=matā Nd[1] 126); J v.7 (=mata C.); Pv I.5[7]; I.12[1]; II.6[10]. As **pubba-peta** ("deceased-before") at A II.68; III.45; IV.244; J II.360. — 2. (unhappy ghosts) S II.255 sq.; Vin IV.269 (contrasted with purisa, yakkha & tiracchāna-gata); A v.269 (dānaŋ petānaŋ upakappati); J IV.495 sq. (yakkhā pisācā petā, cp. preta-piśācayoḥ MBhār. 13, 732); Vbh 412 sq.; Sdhp 96 sq. —**manussapeta** a ghost in human form J III.72; v.68; VvA 23. The later tradition on Petas in their var. classes and states is reflected in Miln 294 (4 classes: vantāsikā, khuppipāsā, nijjhāma-taṇhikā, paradatt' ûpajīvino) & 357 (appearance and fate); Vism 501 = VbhA 97 (as state of suffering, with narakā, tiracchā, asurā); VbhA 455 (as nijjhāmataṇhikā, khuppipāsikā, paradatt' upajīvino). — 3. (happy ghosts) mahiddhikā petī Pv I.10[1]; yakkha mahiddhika Pv IV.1[54]; Vimānapeta mahiddhika PvA 145; peta mahiddhika PvA 217. [Cp. BSk. pretamahardhika Divy 14]. — f. petī Vin IV.20; J I.240; Pv I.6[2]; PvA 67 and passim. Vimānapetī PvA 47, 50, 53 and in Vimāna-vatthu passim.

-upapattika born as a peta PvA 119. -katha (pubba°) tales (or talk) about the dead (not considered orthodox) D I.8, cp. DA I.90; A V.128. -kicca duty towards the deceased (i. e. death-rites) J II.5; DhA I.328. -rājā king of the Petas (i. e. Yama) J V.453 (°visayaŋ na muñcati "does not leave behind the realm of the Peta-king"); C. expl[s] by petayoni and divides the realm into petavisaya and kālakañjaka-asura-visaya. -yoni the peta realm PvA 9, 35, 55, 68, 103 and passim. -loka the peta world Sdhp 96. -vatthu a peta or ghost-story; N. of one (perhaps the latest) of the canonical books belonging to the Suttanta-Piṭaka KhA 12; DA I.178 (Ankura°).

Petattana (nt.) [abstr. fr. peta] state or condition of a Peta Th I, 1128.

Pettanika [fr. pitar] one who lives on the fortune or power inherited from his father A III.76 = 300.

Pettāpiya [for pettāviya (Epic Sk. pitṛvya), cp. Trenckner, *Notes* 62[16], 75] father's brother, paternal uncle A III.348; V.138 (gloss pitāmaho).

Pettika (adj.) [fr. pitar, for pētika, cp. Epic Sk. paitṛka & P. petteyya] paternal Vin III.16; IV.223; D II.232; S V.146 = Miln 368 (p. gocara); (sake p. visaye 'your own home-grounds') D III.58; S V.146; J II.59; VI.193 (iṇa). Also in cpd. mātā-pettika maternal & paternal D I.34, 92; J I.146.

Pettivisaya (& **Piṭṭi°**) [Sk. *paitrya-viṣaya & *pitrya-viṣaya, der. fr. pitar, but influenced by peta] the world of the manes, the realm of the petas (synonymous with petavisaya & petayoni) D III.234; It 93; J V.186; Pv II.2[2]; II.7[9]; Miln 310; DhA I.102; IV.226; Vism 427; VbhA 4, 455; PvA 25 sq., 29, 59 sq., 214, 268; Sdhp 9.

Petteyya (adj.) [fr. pitar; cp. Vedic pitrya] father-loving, showing filial piety towards one's father D III.72, 74; S V.467; A I.138; J III.456; V.35; Pv II.7[18]. See also matteyya.

Petteyyatā (f.) [abstr. fr. petteyya] reverence towards one's father D III.70 (a°), 145, 169; Dh 332 (= pitari sammāpaṭipatta DhA IV.34); Nd[2] 294. Cp. matteyyatā.

Petyā (adv.) [fr. pitar, for Sk. pitrā; cp. Trenckner, *Notes* 56[4]] from the father's side J V.214 (= pitito).

Pema (nt.) [fr. **prī**, see pīṇeti & piya & cp. BSk. prema Jtm 221; Vedic preman cons. stem] love, affection D I.50; III.284 sq.; M I.101 sq.; S III.122; IV.72, 329; V.89, 379; A II.213; III.326 sq.; Sn 41; Dh 321; DA I.75. -(a)vigata-pema with(out) love or affection D III.238, 252; S III.7 sq., 107 sq., 170; IV.387; A II.174 sq.; IV.15, 36, 461 sq.

Pemaka (m. or nt.) [fr. pema] = pema J IV.371.

Pemanīya (adj.) [fr. pema as grd. formation, cp. BSk., premaṇīya MVastu III.343] affectionate, kind, loving, amiable, agreeable D I.4 (cp. DA I.75); II.20 (°ssara); A II.209; Pug 57; J IV.470.

Peyya[1] [grd. of pibati] to be drunk, drinkable, only in comp° or neg. apeyya undrinkable A III.188; J IV.205, 213 (apo apeyyo). maṇḍa° to be drunk like cream, i. e. of the best quality S II.29. manāpika° sweet to drink Miln 313. duppeyya difficult to drink Sdhp 158. See also kākapeyya.

Peyya[2] = piya, only in cpds. vajja° [*priya-vadya] kindness of language, kind speech, one of the 4 sangaha-vatthus (grounds of popularity) A II.32, 248; IV.219, 364; D III.190, 192, 232; J V.330. Cp. BSk. priya-vādya MVastu I.3; and °vācā kind language D III.152; Vv 84[36] (= piyavacana VvA 345). — It is doubtful whether vāca-peyya at Sn 303 (Ep. of sacrifice) is the same as °vācā (as adj.), or whether it represents vāja-peyya [Vedic vāja sacrificial food] as Bdhgh expl[s] it at SnA 322 (= vājam ettha pivanti; v. l. vāja°), thus peyya = peyya[1].

Peyyāla (nt. ?) [a Māgadhism for pariyāya, so Kern, *Toev.* s. v. after Trenckner, cp. BSk. piyāla and peyāla MVastu III.202, 219] repetition, succession, formula; way of saying, phrase (= pariyāya 5) Vism 46 (°mukha beginning of discourse), 351 (id. and bahu°-tanti having many discourses or repetitions), 411 (°pāḷi a row of successions or etceteras); VvA 117 (pāḷi° vasena "because of the successive Pāli text"). — Very freq. in abridged form, where we would say "etc.," to indicate that a passage has be to repeated (either from preceding context, or to be supplied from memory, if well known). The literal meaning would be "here (follows) the formula (pariyāya)." We often find pa for pe, e. g. A V.242, 270, 338, 339, 355; sometimes pa + pe comb[d], e. g. S V.466. — As pe is the first syllable of peyyāla so la is the last and is used in the same sense; the variance is according to predilection of certain MSS.; la is found e. g. S V.448, 267 sq.; or as v. l. of pe: A V.242, 243, 354; or la + pe comb[d]: S V.464, 466. — On syllable pe Trenckner, *Notes* 66, says: "The sign of abridgment, pe, or as it is written in Burmese copies, pa, means peyyāla which is not an imperative 'insert, fill up the gap,' but a substantive, peyyālo or peyyālaŋ, signifying a phrase to be repeated over & over again. I consider it a popular corruption of the synonymous pariyāya, passing through *payyāya, with -eyy- for -ayy-, like seyyā, Sk. śayyā." See also *Vin. Texts* I.291; Oldenberg, *K.Z.* 35, 324.

Perita is Kern's (*Toev.* s. v.) proposed reading for what he considered a faulty spelling in bhaya-merita (p for m) J IV.424 = V.359. This, however is bhaya-m-erita with the hiatus-m, and to supplant perita (= Sk. prerita) is unjustified.

Pelaka [etym. ?] a hare J VI.538 (= sasa C.).

Peḷa [a Prk. form for piṇḍa, cp. Pischel, *Prk. Gr.* § 122 peḍhāla] a lump, only in **yaka°** the liver (-lump) Sn 195 (= yakana-piṇḍa SnA 247) = J I.146.

Peḷā [cp. Class. & B. Sk. peṭa, f. peṭī & peṭā, peḍā Divy 251, 365; and the BSk. var. phelā Divy 503; MVastu II.465] 1. a (large) basket J IV.458; VI.185; Cp. II.2[5]; Miln 23, 282; Vism 304; KhA 46 (peḷāghata, wrong reading, see p. 68 App.); ThA 29. — 2. a chest (for holding jewelry etc.) Pv IV.1[42]; Mhvs 36. 20; DhsA 242 (peḷ-opamā, of the 4 treasure-boxes). — Cp. piṭaka.

Peḷikā (f.) [cp. peḷā] a basket DhA I.227 (pasādhana°, v. l. pelakā).

Pesa is spurious spelling for pessa (q. v.).

Pesaka [fr. pa + **iṣ**, cp. Vedic preṣa order, command] employer, controller, one who attends or looks after Vin II.177 (ārāmika° etc.); A III.275 (id.).

Pesakāra [pesa + kāra, epsa = Vedic peśaḥ. fr. **piś**: see piŋsati[1]] weaver D I.52; Vin III.259; IV.7; J IV.475; DhA I.424 (°vīthi); III.170 sq.; VbhA 294 sq. (°dhītā the weaver's daughter; story of -) PvA 42 sq., 67.

Pesana (nt.) [fr. pa + **iṣ**, see peseti] sending out, message; service J IV.362 (pesanāni gacchanti); V.17 (pesane pesiyanto.)
-kāraka a servant J VI.448; VvA 349. -**kārikā** (a girl) doing service, a messenger, servant J III 414; DhA I.227.

Pesanaka (adj.) [fr. pesana] " message sender," employing for service, in °corā robbers making (others) servants J I.253.

Pesanika (°iya) (adj.) [fr. pesana] connected with messages, going messages, only in phrase jangha° messenger on foot Vin III.185; J II.82; Miln 370 (°iya).

Pesala (adj.) [cp. Epic Sk. peśala; Bdhgh's pop. etym. at SnA 475 is " piya-sīla "] lovable, pleasant, well-behaved, amiable S I.149; II.387; A IV.22; V.170; Sn 678; Sn p. 124; Miln 373; Sdhp 621. Often as Ep. of a good bhikkhu, e. g. at S I.187; Vin I.170; II.241; J IV.70; VvA 206; PvA 13, 268.

Pesāca is reading at D I.54 for pisāca (so v. l.).

Pesi (pesī) (f.) [cp. Epic Sk. peśī] 1. a lump, usually a mass of flesh J III.223 = DhA IV.67 (pesi = maŋsapesi C.). Thus at **maŋsapesi** at Vin II.25 ≈ (maŋsapes' ûpamā kāmā); III.105; M I.143, 364; S II.256; IV.193 (in characteristic of lohitaka); Vism 356; PvA 199. — 2. the fœtus in the third stage after conception (between abbuda & ghana) S I.206; J IV.496; Nd[1] 120; Miln 40; Vism 236. — 3. a piece, bit (for pesikā), in veḷu° J IV.205.

Pesikā (f.) (-°) [cp. Sk. *peśikā] rind, shell (of fruit) only in cpds. amba° Vin II.109; vaŋsa° J I.352; veḷu° (a bit of bamboo) D II.324; J II.267, 279; III.276; IV.382.

Pesita [pp. of peseti] 1. sent out or forth Sn 412 (rājadūta p.) Vv 21[7] (= uyyojita VvA 108); DhA III.191. pesit-atta is the C. expl[n] at S I.53 (as given at *K.S.* 320) of pahit-atta (*trsl[n]* " puts forth all his strength "); Bdhgh incorrectly taking pahita as pp. of pahiṇati to send whereas it is pp. of padahati. — 2. ordered, what has been ordered, in pesit-âpesitaŋ order and prohibition Vin II.177.

Pesuṇa (nt.) [fr. pisuṇa, cp. Epic Sk. paiśuna] = pesuñña S I.240; Sn 362, 389, 862 sq., 941; J V.397; Pv I.3[3]; PvA 16; Sdhp 55, 66, 81.
-kāraka one who incites to slander J I.200, 267.

Pesuṇika (adj.) [fr. pesuṇa] slanderous, calumnious PvA 12, 13.

Pesuṇiya & **Pesuṇeyya** (nt.) = pesuñña; 1. (pesuṇiya) Sn 663, 928; Pv I.3[2]. — 2. (pesuṇeyya) S I.228, 230; Sn 852; Nd[1] 232.

Pesuñña (nt.) [abstr. fr. pisuṇa, cp. Epic Sk. paiśunya. The other (diaeretic) forms are pesuṇiya & pesuṇeyya] backbiting, calumny, slander M I.110; D III.69; A IV.401; Vin IV.12; Nd[1] 232, 260; PvA 12, 15.

Peseti [pa + **iṣ** to send] to send forth or out, esp. on a message or to a special purpose, i. e. to employ as a servant or (intrs.) to do service (so in many derivations) 1. to send out J I.86, 178, 253; IV.169 (paṇṇaŋ); V.399; VI.448; Mhvs 14, 29 (rathaŋ); DhA III.190; PvA 4, 20, 53. — 2. to employ or order (cp. pesaka), in Pass. **pesiyati** to be ordered or to be in service Vin II.177 (ppr. pesiyamāna); J V.17 (ppr. pesiyanto). — pp. pesita. See also pessa & derivations.

Pessa [grd. form[n] fr. peseti, Vedic preṣya, f. preṣyā. This is the contracted form, whilst the diaeretic form is pesiya, for which also pesika] a messenger, a servant, often in comb[n] dāsā ti vā pessā ti vā kammakarā ti vā, e. g. D I.141; S I.76, 93 (slightly diff. in verse); A II.208 (spelt pesā); IV.45; DhA II.7. See also A III.37; IV.266, 270; J V.351; Pug 56; DA I.300. At Sn 615 pessa is used in the sense of an abstr. n. = pessitā service (= veyyavacca SnA 466). So also in cpds.
-kamma service J VI.374; -kāra a servant J VI.356.

Pessitā (f.) [abstr. fr. pessa, Sk. *preṣyatā] being a servant, doing service J VI.208 (para° to someone else).

Pessiya & °**ka** [see pessa] servant; m. either pessiya Vv 84[46] (spelt pesiya, expl[d] by pesana-kāraka, veyyāvaccakara VvA 349); J VI.448 (= pesana-kāraka C.), or pessika Sn 615, 651; J VI.552; f. either pessiyā (para°) Vv 18[5] (spelt pesiyā, but v. l. SS pessiyā, expl[d] as pesaniyā paresaŋ veyyāvacca-kārī VvA 94); J III.413 (= parehi pesitabbā pesana-kārikā C. 414), or pessikā J VI.65.

Pehi is imper. 2nd sg. of pa + **i**, " go on," said to a horse A IV.190 sq., cp. S I.123.

Pokkhara (nt.) [cp. Vedic puṣkara, fr. **pus**, though a certain relation to puṣpa seems to exist, cp. Sk. puṣpapattra a kind of arrow (lit. lotus-leaf) Halāyudha 2, 314, and P. pokkhara-patta] 1. a lotus plant, primarily the leaf of it, figuring in poetry and metaphor as not being able to be wetted by water Sn 392, 812 (vuccati paduma-pattaŋ Nd[1] 135); Dh 336; It 84. — 2. the skin of a drum (from its resemblance to the lotus-leaf) S II.267; Miln 261 (bheri°). As Np. of an angel (Gandhabba) " Drum " at Vv 18[9]. — 3. a species of waterbird (crane): see cpd. °sataka.
-ṭṭha standing in water (?) Vin I.215 (vanaṭṭha +), 238 (id.). -patta a lotus leaf Sn 625; Dh 401 (= paduma-patta DhA IV.166); Miln 250. -madhu the honey sap of Costus speciosus (a lotus) J V.39, 466. -vassa " lotus-leaf rain," a portentous shower of rain, serving as special kind of test shower in which certain objects are wetted, but those showing a disinclination towards moisture are left untouched, like a lotus-leaf J I.88; VI.586; KhA 164; DhA III.163. -sataka a species of crane, Ardea Siberica J VI.539 (koṭṭha +); SnA 359. Cp. Np. Pokkharasāti Sn 594; Sn p. 115; SnA 372.

Pokkharaṇī (f.) [fr. *puṣkara lotus; Vedic puṣkariṇī, BSk. has puskiriṇī, e. g. AvŚ I.76; II.201 sq.] a lotus-pond, an artificial pool or small lake for water-plants (see note in *Dial.* II.210) Vin I.140, 268; II.123; D II.178 sq.; S I.123, 204; II.106; V.460; A I.35, 145; III.187, 238; J II.126; V.374 (Khemī), 388 (Doṇa); Pv III.3[3]; IV.12[1]; SnA 354 (here in meaning of a dry pit or dug-out); VvA 160; PvA 23, 77, 152. pokkharaññā gen. Pv II.12[9]; instr. S I.233; loc. Vin II.123. **pokkharaṇiyāyaŋ** loc. A III.309. — pl. **pokkharaṇiyo** Vin I.268; VvA 191; PvA 77; metric **pokkharañño** Vv 44[11]; Pv II.1[19]; II.7[8].

Pokkharatā (f.) [is it fr. pokkhara lotus (cp. Sk. pauṣkara), thus " lotus-ness," or founded on Vedic puṣpa blossom? The BSk. puṣkalatā (AvŚ II.201) is certainly a misconstruction, if it is constructed fr. the Pali] splendidness, " flower-likeness," only in cpd. vaṇṇa-pokkharatā beauty of complexion D I.114; Vin I.268; S I 95; II.279; A I.38, 86; II.203; III.90; DA I.282; KhA 179; VvA 14; PvA 46. The BSk. passage at AvŚ II.202 reads " śobhāŋ varṇaŋ puṣkalatāŋ ca."

Ponkha [increment form of punkha] arrow, only in redupl. (iterative) cpd. **ponkh' ânuponkhaŋ** (adv.) arrow after arrow, shot after shot, i. e. constantly, continuously S V.453, 454; Nd[2] 631 (in def. of sadā); DA I.188; VvAh 351. The expl[n] is problematic.

Poṭa [fr. **sphuṭ**] a bubble J IV.457 (v. l. poṭha). See also phoṭa.

Poṭaki (°ī ?) (m. f. ?) [etym. uncertain, prob. Non-Aryan] a kind of grass, in °tūla a kind of cotton, "grass-tuft," thistle-down (?) Vin II.150 ; IV.170 (id., 3 kinds of cotton, spelt potaki here).

Poṭakila [etym. unknown, cp. poṭaki & (lexic.) Sk. poṭagala a kind of reed ; the variant is poṭagala] a kind of grass, Saccharum spontaneum Th 1, 27=233 ; J VI.508 (=p.°-tiṇaŋ nāma C.).

Poṭṭhabba is spurious reading for phoṭṭhabba (q. v.).

Poṭha [fr. **puth**, cp. poṭhana & poṭheti] is anguli° snapping of one's fingers (as sign of applause) J V.67. Cp. poṭhana & phoṭeti.

Poṭhana (& **Pothana**) (nt.) [fr. poṭheti] 1. striking, beating J II.169 (tajjana°); V.72 (udaka°); VI.41 (kappāsa°-dhanuka). At all J passages th. — 2. (ṭh) snapping one's fingers J I.394 (anguli°, + celukkhepa); ThA 76 (anguli°, for accharā-sanghāta Th 2, 67). Cp. nippothana.

Poṭhita (& **Pothita**) [pp. of poṭheti] beaten, struck Miln 240 (of cloth, see Kern, *Toev.* s. poṭheti); J III.423 (mañca ; v. l. BB pappoṭ°) KhA 173 (°tulapicu cotton beaten seven times, i. e. very soft ; v. l. pothita, see App. p. 877); DhA I.48 (su°); PvA 174. — Cp. paripothita.

Poṭheti (& **Potheti**) [fr. **puth** = **spuṭh**] 1. to beat, strike Sn 682 (bhujāni = appoṭheti SnA 485); J I.188, 483 (th) II.394 ; VI.548 (= ākoṭeti); DhA I.48 ; II.27 (th), 67 (th); VvA 68 (th); PvA 65 (th). — 2. to snap one's fingers as a token of annoyance D II.96 ; or of pleasure J III.285 (anguliyo poṭhesi). — pp. **poṭhita**. — Caus. II. poṭhāpeti (poth°) to cause to be beaten or flogged Miln 221 ; DhA I.399. — Cp. **pappoṭheti**.

Poṇa[1] (nt.) [= poṇa[2] ?] only in cpd. **danta°** a tooth pick Vin IV.90 ; J IV.69 ; Miln 15 ; SnA 272. As dantapoṇaka at Dāvs I.57. — **kūṭa-poṇa** at Vism 268 read °goṇa.

Poṇa[2] (adj.) [fr. pa + ava + **nam**, cp. ninna & Vedic pravaṇa] 1. sloping down, prone, in anupubba° gradually sloping (of the ocean) Vin II.237 = A IV.198 sq. = Ud 53. — 2. (-°) sloping towards, going to, converging or leading to Nibbāna ; besides in var. phrases, in general as tanninna **tappoṇa** tappabbhāra, "leading to that end." As **nibbāna°** e. g. at M I.493 ; S V.38 sq. ; A III.443 ; cp. Vv 84[42] (nekkhamma°-nibbāna-ninna VvA 348); taŋ° Ps II.197 ; **ṭhāne** PvA 190 ; **viveka°** A IV.224, 233 ; V.175 ; **samādhi°** Miln 38 ; **kiŋ°** M I.302.

Poṇika (adj.) [fr. poṇa[2]] that which is prone, going prone ; DA I.23 where the passage is "tiracchāna-gata-pāṇā-poṇika-nikāyo cikkhallika-nikāyo ti," quoted from S III.152, where it runs thus : "tiracchāna-gata pāṇā te pi bhikkhave tiracchānagatā pāṇā citten' eva cittatā." The passage is referred to *with* poṇika at KhA 12, where we read "tiracchāna-gatā pāṇā poṇika-nikāyo cikkhallika-nikāyo ti." Thus we may take poṇika-nikāya as "the kingdom of those which go prone" (i. e. the animals).

Pota[1] [cp. Epic Sk. pota, see putta for etym.] the young of an animal J II.406 (°sūkara); Cp. I.10[2] (udda°); SnA 125 (sīha°).

Pota[2] [Epic Sk. pota ; dial. form for plota (?), of **plu**] a boat Dāvs V.58 ; VvA 42.

Pota[3] [etym. ?] a millstone, grindstone, only as nisada° Vin I.201 ; Vism 252.

Potaka (-°) [fr. pota[1]] 1. the young of an animal M I.104 (kukkuṭa°); J I.202 (supaṇṇa°), 218 (hatthi°); II.288 (assa° colt); III.174 (sakuṇa°); PvA 152 (gaja°). — f. potikā J I.207 (haŋsa°); IV.188 (mūsika°). — 2. a small branch, offshoot, twig ; in amba° young mango sprout DhA III.206 sq. ; araṇi° small firewood Miln 53.

Pottha[1] [?] poor, indigent, miserable J II.432 (= potthaka-pilotikāya nivatthatā pottho C. ; v. l. potha). See also *ponti, with which ultimately identical.

Pottha[2] [later Sk. pusta, etym. uncertain ; loan-word ?] modelling, only in cpd. °kamma plastering (i. e. using a mixture of earth, lime, cowdung & water as mortar) J VI.459 ; carving DhsA 334 ; and °kara a modeller in clay J I.71. Cp. potthaka[1].

Potthaka[1] [cp. Class. Sk. pustaka] 1. a book J I.2 (aya° ledger); III.235, 292 ; IV.299, 487 ; VvA 117. — 2. anything made or modelled in clay (or wood etc.), in rūpa° a modelled figure J VI.342 ; ThA 257 ; DA I.198 ; Sdhp 363, 383. Cp. pottha[2].

Potthaka[2] (nt.) [etym. ?] cloth made of makaci fibre Vin I.306 (cp. *Vin. Texts* II.247); A I.246 sq. ; J IV.251 (= ghana-sāṭaka C. ; v. l. saṇa°); Pug 33.

Potthanikā (f.) [fr. **puth** ?] a dagger (= potthanī) Vin II.190 = DA I.135 (so read here with v. l. for T. °iyā).

Potthanī (f.) [fr. **puth** ?] a butcher's knife J VI.86 (maŋsa-koṭṭhana°), 111 (id.).

Pothujjanika (adj.) [fr. puthujjana] belonging to ordinary man, common, ordinary, in 2 comb[ns] viz. (1) phrase hīna gamma p. anariya Vin I.10 ; S IV.330 ; A V.216 ; (2) with ref. to iddhi Vin II.183 ; J I.360 ; Vism 97. — Cp. *Vin. Texts* III.230. The BSk. forms are either pārthag-janika Lal. Vist 540, or prāthu$_{g}$-janika MVastu III.331.

Pothetvā at J II.404 (ummukkāni p.) is doubtful. The vv. ll. are **yodhetvā** & **sodhetvā** (the latter a preferable reading).

Poddava see gāma°.

Ponobhavika (adj.) [fr. punabbhava, with preservation of the second o (puno > punaḥ) see puna] leading to rebirth M I.48, 299, 464, 532 ; S III.26 ; IV.186 ; D III.57 ; A II.11 sq., 172 ; III.84, 86 ; V.88 ; Nett 72 ; Vism 506 ; VbhA 110.

Ponti (vv. ll. poṭhi, sonti) Th 2, 422, 423 is doubtful ; the expl° at ThA 269 is "pilotikākkaṇḍa," thus "rags (of an ascetic)," cp. *J P.T.S.* 1884. See also pottha[1], with which evidently identical, though misread.

Porāṇa (adj.) [= purāṇa, cp. Epic Sk. paurāṇa] old, ancient, former D I.71, 238 ; S II.267 ; Sn 313 ; Dh 227 (cp. DhA III.328); J II.15 (°kāle in the past); VbhA 1 (°aṭṭhakathā), 523 (id.); KhA 247 (°pāṭha); SnA 131 (id.); DhA I.17 ; PvA 1 (°aṭṭhakathā), 63. — Porāṇā (pl.) the ancients, ancient authorities or writers Vism passim esp. *Note*, 764 ; KhA 123, 158 ; SnA 291, 352, 604 ; VbhA 130, 254, 299, 397, 513.

Porāṇaka (adj.) [fr. porāṇa] 1. ancient, former, of old (cp. purāṇa 1) J III.16 (°paṇḍitā); PvA 93 (id.), 99 (id.); DhA I.346 (kula-santaka). — 2. old, worn, much used (cp. purāṇa 2) J IV.471 (magga).

Porin (adj.) [fr. pora = Epic Sk. paura citizen, see pura. Semantically cp. urbane > urbanus > urbs ; polite = πολίτης > πόλις. For pop. etym. see DA I.73 & 282] belonging to a citizen, i. e. citizenlike, urbane, polite, usually in phrase porī vācā polite speech D I.4, 114 ; S I.189 ; II.280 = A II.51 ; A III.114 ; Pug 57 ; Dhs 1344 ; DA I.75, 282 ; DhsA 397. Cp. BSk. paurī vācā MVastu III.322.

Porisa[1] (adj.-n.) [abstr. fr. purisa, for *pauruṣa or *puruṣya)] 1. (adj.) human, fit for a man Sn 256 (porisa dhura), cp. porisiya & poroseyya. — 2. (m.) = purisa, esp. in sense of purisa 2, i. e. servant, used collectively (abstract form[n] like Ger. dienerschaft, E. service = servants) "servants" esp. in phrase dāsa-kammakara-porisa Vin I.240; A I.145, 206; II.78; III.45, 76, 260; DhA IV.1; dāsa° a servant Sn 769 (three kinds mentioned at Nd[1] 11, viz. bhaṭakā kammakarā upajīvino); rāja° king's service, servant of the king D I.135; A IV.286, 322; sata° a hundred servants Vism 121. For purisa in uttama° (= mahāpurisa) Dh 97 (cp. DhA II.188). Cp. posa.

Porisa[2] (nt.) [abstr. fr. purisa, *pauruṣyaŋ, cp. porisiya and poroseyya] 1. business, doing of a man (or servant, cp. purisa 2), service, occupation; human doing, activity M I.85 (rāja°); Vv 63[11] (= purisa-kicca VvA 263); Pv IV.3[24] (uṭṭhāna° = purisa-viriya, purisa-kāra PvA 252). — 2. height of a man M. I.74, 187, 365.

Porisatā (f.) [abstr. fr. porisa], only in neg. a° inhuman or superhuman state, or: not served by any men (or servants) VvA 275. The reading is uncertain.

Porisāda [fr. purisa + **ad** to eat] man-eater, cannibal J V.34 sq., 471 sq., 486, 488 sq., 499, 510.

Porisādaka = porisāda J V.489. Cp. purisādaka J V.91.

Porisiya (adj.) [fr. purisa, cp. porisa & poroseyya] 1. of human nature, human J IV.213. — 2. Of the height of man Vin II.138.

Poroseyya = porisiya (cp. porisa[1] 1) fit for man, human M I.366. The word is somewhat doubtful, but in all likelihood it is a derivation fr. pura (cp. porin; Sk. *paura), thus to be understood as *paurasya > *porasya > *poraseyya > *poroseyya with assimilation. The meaning is clearly "very fine, urbane, fashionable"; thus *not* derived from purisa, although C. expl[s] by "puris' ânucchavikaŋ yānaŋ" (M. I.561). The passage runs "yānaŋ poroseyyaŋ pavara-maṇi-kuṇḍalaŋ"; with vv. ll. voropeyya & oropeyya. Neumann accepts oropeyya as reading & translates (wrongly) "belüde": see *Mittl. Slg.* [2]1921; vol. II. pp. 45 & 666. The reading poroseyya seems to be established as lectio difficilior. On form see also Trenckner, *Notes* 75.

Porohita = purohita; DhA I.174 (v. l. BB pur°).

Porohacca (nt.) [fr. purohita] the character or office of a family priest D II.243. As porohicca at Sn 618 (= purohita-kamma SnA 466). Cp. Trenckner, *Notes* 75.

Posa[1] [contraction of purisa fr. *pūrṣa > *pussa > *possa > posa. So Geiger, *P.Gr.* 30[3]] = purisa, man (poetical form, only found in verse) Vin I.230; S I.13, 205 = J III.309; A IV.266; Sn 110, 662; Dh 104, 125 (cp. DhA III.34); J V.306; VI.246, 361. — **poso** at J III.331 is gen. sg. of puŋs = Sk. puŋsaḥ.

Posa[2] (adj.) [= *poṣya, grd. of poseti, **puṣ**] to be fed or nourished, only in dup° difficult to nourish S I.61.

Posaka (adj.) [fr. posa[2]] nourishing, feeding A I.62, 132 = It 110 (āpādaka +); f. °ikā a nurse, a female attendant Vin II.289 (āpādikā +).

Posatā (f.) [abstr. fr. posa[2]] only -°, in su° & dup° easy & difficult support Vin II.2.

Posatha = uposatha [cp. BSk. poṣadha Divy 116, 121, and Prk. posaha (posahiya = posathika) Pischel, *Prk. Gr.* § 141] J IV.329; VI.119.

Posathika = uposathika J IV.329. Cp. anuposathika & anvaḍḍhamāsaŋ.

Posana (nt.) [fr. **puṣ**] nourishing, feeding, support VvA 137.

Posāpeti & **Posāveti** [Caus. II. fr. poseti] to have brought up, to give into the care of, to cause to be nourished Vin I.269 (pp. posāpita) ≈ DA I.133 (posāvita, v. l. posāp°).

Posāvanika & °ya (adj.-nt.) [fr. posāvana = posāpana of Caus. posāpeti] 1. (adj.) to be brought up, being reared, fed Vin I.272; J III.134, 432. -°iya DhA III.35; J III.35; J III.429 (&°iyaka). — 2. (nt.) fee for bringing somebody up, allowance, money for food, sustenance J II.289; DhA IV.40; VvA 158 (°mūla). -°iya J I.191.

Posita [pp. of poseti] nourished, fed Cp. III.3[2]; VvA 173 (udaka°).

Posituŋ at Vin II.151 stands for phusituŋ "to sprinkle," cp. *Vin. Texts* III.169. See phusati[2].

Posin (-°) (adj.) [fr. poseti] thriving (on), nourished by Vin I.6; D I.75; S I.138; Sn 65 (anañña° cp. Nd[1] 39), 220 (dāra°); DA I.219.

Poseti [**puṣ**] to nourish, support, look after, bring up, take care of, feed, keep Vin I.269; S I.181; A I.117; J I.134; III.467; Nd[2] 36; Vism 305; VvA 138, 299. — pp. posita. — Caus. posāpeti.

CORRIGENDA

CORRECTIONS AND ADDITIONS

TO PART I.

Page x, *under* 1b *add:* Sammoha-Vinodanī, P.T.S. 1923 (VbhA).
„ xi, „ 3 „ Path of Purity, P.T.S. trsl. 1923, 1st pt, (Vism. Trsl.).
„ xii, „ B, 1 „ VbhA = Sammoha-Vinodanī . . . 1b.
Vism. Trsl. = Path of Purity . . . 3.
„ 17, column 1, *under* **aḍḍha-rattā** *change* J 1.164 *into* 1.264.
„ 27, „ 2, „ **adhikaraṇa** *read under* yatvā°: yato + adhi *for* yat + adhi.
„ 76, „ 1, „ **araṇa**[1] *cross out* No. 1 *before* (adj.).
„ 76, „ 2, „ **araṇi** *read* sadisa-vaṇṇa *for* sadi-savaṇṇa.
„ 91, „ 2, „ **ahaŋ** *read* "The encl. form *in* the sg."

TO PART II.

Page 103, column 2, *under* **ābhata** *add:* see under yathā-bhaṭa.
„ 123, „ 2, „ **isi** *read* Bhāradvāja *for* Bhara°; *and insert* ref. Vin. 1.245.
„ 155, „ 2, „ **ura** *read* urasā *for* urusā.

TO PART III.

Page 12, column 2, *after* **kathāpeti** *insert:* **kathālikā** (f.) [fr. **kuth,** to boil] kettle, cooking pot; in daṇḍa° (a pot with a handle) Vin 1.286 (v. l. kathālaka), and meda° A IV.377; DhA II.179.
„ 31, „ 1, *under* **kāṭa-koṭacikā** *correct* 1889 *to* 89.

TO PART IV.

„ 37-38, *transfer* **kārā**, *bottom of p.* 37 *to p.* 38, *col.* 1, *line* 3, fr. b.
„ 127, *after* **tajjaniya** *insert:* **tajjārī** a linear measure, equal to 36 aṇu's and of which 36 form one rathareṇu Vbh 343; cp. Abhp 194 (tajjarī).
„ 150, column 1, *under* **darī** *read* mūsikā° *for* musikā°.
„ 154, „ 2, „ **dāru** *read* dāru-yanta a wooden *machine* (not *mill*).
„ 156, „ 1, „ **diṭṭha-mangalika** (of pucchā) *put in the simple trsl*[n]: "a question concerning visible omina."
„ 190, „ 1, „ **nikhanati** *read* khanati *for* khanai.

THE PALI TEXT SOCIETY'S PALI-ENGLISH DICTIONARY

EDITED BY

T. W. RHYS DAVIDS F.B.A. D.Sc. Ph.D. LL.D. D.Litt.

and WILLIAM STEDE Ph.D.

Part VI (Ph.—M)

PUBLISHED BY
THE PALI TEXT SOCIETY
LONDON

First published - - - 1924
Reprinted - - - - 1948
Reprinted - - - - 1952

Ph.

Phaggu [in form = Vedic phalgu (small, feeble), but in meaning different] a special period of fasting M I.39 = DA I.139. See also pheggu.

Phagguṇa & Phagguṇī (f.) [cp. Vedic phālguna & °ī] N. of a month (Feb. 15th–March 15th), marking the beginning of Spring; always with ref. to the spring full moon, as phagguṇa-puṇṇamā at Vism 418; phagguṇī° J I.86.

Phaṇa [cp. Epic Sk. phaṇa] the hood of a snake Vin I.91 (°hatthaka, with hands like a snake's hood); J III.347 (patthaṭa°); DhA III.231 (°ŋ ukkhipitvā); IV.133. Freq. as phaṇaŋ katvā (only thus, in ger.) raising or spreading its hood, with spread hood J II.274; VI.6; Vism 399; DhA II.257.

Phaṇaka [fr. phaṇa] an instrument shaped like a snake's hood, used to smooth the hair Vin II.107.

Phaṇijjaka [etym. ?] a kind of plant, which is enum^d at Vin IV.35 = DA I.81 as one of the aggabīja, i. e. plants propagated by slips or cuttings, together with ajjuka & hirivera. At J VI.536 the C. gives bhūtanaka as expl^n. According to Childers it is the plant Samīraṇa.

Phandati [**spand**, cp. Gr. σφαδάζω to twitch, σφοδρός violent; Lat. pendeo "pend" i. e. hang down, cp. pendulum; Ags. finta tail, lit. mover, throbber] 1. to throb, palpitate D I.52 = M I.404, cp. DA I.159; Nd¹ 46. — 2. to twitch, tremble, move, stir J II.234; VI.113 (of fish wriggling when thrown on land). — Caus. II. phandāpeti to make throb D I.52 = M I.404. — pp. phandita (q. v.). Cp. pari°, vi°, sam°. The nearest synonym is calati.

Phandana [fr. phandati, cp. Sk. spandana] 1. (adj.) throbbing, trembling, wavering Dh 33 (phandanaŋ capalaŋ cittaŋ); J VI.528 (°māluvā trembling creeper); DhA I.50 (issa° throbbing with envy). — 2. (m.) N. of a tree Dalbergia (aspen ?) A I.202; J IV.208 sq.; Miln 173. — 3. (nt.) throb, trembling, agitation, quivering J VI.7 (°mattaŋ not even one throb; cp. phandita); Nd¹ 46 (taṇhā etc.).

Phandanā (f.) [fr. phandati] throbbing, agitation, movement, motion SnA 245 (calanā +); DA I.111; Nett 88 C.; cp. iñjanā.

Phandita (nt.) [pp. of phandati] throbbing, flashing; throb M II.24 (°mattā "by his throbbings only"); pl. phanditāni "vapourings," imaginings Vbh 390 (where VbhA 513 only says "phandanato phanditaŋ") cp. *Brethren* 344.

Phanditatta (nt.) [abstr. fr. phandita] = phandanā S V.315 (= iñjitatta).

Pharaṇa (adj.-nt.) [fr. pharati] 1. (adj.) pervading, suffused (with), quite full (of) Miln 345. — 2. (nt.) pervasion, suffusion, thrill J I.82 (°samattha mettacitta); Nett 89 (pīti° etc., as m., cp. pharaṇatā); DhsA 166 (°pīti all-pervading rapture, permeating zest; cp. pīti pharaṇatā). — Cp. anu°.

Pharaṇaka (adj.) [fr. pharaṇa] thrilling, suffusing, pervading, filling with rapture VvA 16 (dvādasa yojanāni °pabho sarīra-vaṇṇo).

Pharaṇatā (f.) [abstr. fr. pharaṇa] suffusion, state of being pervaded (with), only -° in set of 4-fold suffusion, viz. pīti° of rapture, sukha° of restful bliss, ceto° of [telepathic] consciousnss, āloka° of light, D III.277; Ps I.48; Vbh 334; Nett 89.

Pharati [**sphur** & **sphar**, same root as in Gr. σπαίρω to twitch; Lat. sperno "spurn" lit. kick away; Ags. speornan to kick; spurnan = spur] 1. (trs.) to pervade, permeate, fill, suffuse Pv I.10¹⁴ (= vyāpetvā tiṭṭhati PvA 52); J III.371 (sakala-sarīraŋ); V.64 (C. for pavāti); PvA 14 (okāsaŋ), 276 (obhāsaŋ). To excite or stimulate the nerves J V.293 (rasa-haraṇiyo khobhetvā phari: see under rasa). — Often in standard phrase mettā-sahagatena cetasā ekaŋ (dutiyaŋ etc.) disaŋ pharitvā viharati D II.186; S V.115 and passim, where pharitvā at Vism 308 = VbhA 377 is expl^d by phusitvā ārammaṇaŋ katvā. Cp. BSk. ekaŋ disāŋ spharitvopasampadya viharati MVastu III.213. Also in phrase pītiyā sarīraŋ pharati (aor. phari) to thrill the body with rapture, e. g. J I.33; V.494; DhA II.118; IV.102. — 2. [in this meaning better to be derived from **sphar** to spread, expand, cp. pharita & phālita] to spread, make expand J I.82 (metta-cittaŋ phari). — 3. [prob. of quite a diff. origin and only taken to pharati by pop. analogy, perhaps to **phal = sphaṭ** to split; thus kaṭṭh'-atthaŋ pharati = to be split up for fuel] to serve as, only with °atthaŋ in phrases āhāratthaŋ ph. (after next phrase) to serve as food Miln 152; kaṭṭhatthaŋ ph. to serve as fuel A II.95 = S III.93 = It 90 = J I.482; khādaniyatthaŋ & bhojaniyatthaŋ ph. to serve as eatables Vin I.201 (so to be read in preference to °attaŋ). — pp. pharita, phurita & phuṭa; cp. also phuṭṭha; see further anu°, pari°.

Pharasu [cp. Vedic paraśu = Gr. πέλεκυς; on p > ph cp. Prk. pharasu & parasu, Pischel Gr. § 208; Geiger, *Gr.* § 40] hatchet, axe A III.162; J I.199, 399; II.409; V.500; DhA II.204; PvA 277. The spelling parasu occurs at S V.441 & J III.179.

Pharita [pp. of pharati] 1. being pervaded or permeated (by) VvA 68 (mettāya). — 2. spread (out) J VI.284 (kittisaddo sakala-loke ph.). — Cp. phuṭṭha & phālita.

Pharusa (adj.) [cp. Vedic paruṣa, on ph. > p see pharasu, on attempt at etym. cp. Walde, *Lat. Wtb.* s. v. fario] 1. (lit.) rough Pv II.4¹. — 2. (fig.) harsh, unkind, rough (of speech) Vin II.290 (caṇḍa +); Pv II.3⁴; III.5⁷; J V.296; Kvu 619. In comb^n with vācā we find both pharusa-vācā and pharusā-vācā D I.4, 138; III.69 sq., 173, 232; M I.42 (on this and the same uncertainty as regards pisuṇā-vācā see Trenckner, at M I.530). pharusa vacana rough speech PvA 15, 55, 83. — 3. cruel Pv IV.7⁶ (kamma = dāruṇa PvA 265).

Phala[1] (nt.) [cp. Vedic phala, to **phal** [**sphal**] to burst, thus lit. "bursting," i. e. ripe fruit; see phalati] 1. (lit.) fruit (of trees etc.) Vv 84^{14} (dumā nicca-phal' ûpapannā, not to phalu, as Kern, *Toev.* s. v. phalu); Vism 120. —**amba°** mango-fruit PvA 273 sq.; dussa° (adj.) having clothes as their fruit (of magic trees) Vv 46^{2} (cp. VvA 199); **patta°** leaves & fruits, vegetables Sn 239; PvA 86 **pavatta°** wild fruit D 1.101; **puppha°** flower & fruit J III.40. **rukkha°-ûpama** Th 1, 490 (in simile of kāmā, taken fr. M 1.130) lit. "like the fruit of trees" is expl[d] by ThA 288 as "anga-paccangānaŋ p(h)ali-bhañjan' aṭṭhena, and trsl[d] according to this interpretation by Mrs. Rh. D. as "fruit that brings the climber to a fall." — Seven kinds of medicinal fruits are given at Vin 1.201 scil. vilanga, pippala, marica, harītaka, vibhītaka, āmalaka, goṭhaphala. At Miln 333 a set of 7 fruits is used metaphorically in simile of the Buddha's fruit-shop, viz. sotāpatti°, sakadāgāmi°, anāgāmi°, arahatta°, suññata° samāpatti (cp. *Cpd.* 70), animitta° samāpatti, appaṇihita° samāpatti. — 2. a testicle J III.124 (dantehi °ŋ chindati = purisabhāvaŋ nāseti to castrate); VI.237 (uddhita-pphalo, adj., = uddhaṭa-bījo C.), 238 (dantehi phalāni uppāṭeti, like above). — 3. (fig.) fruit, result, consequence, fruition, blessing. As t.t. with ref. to the Path and the progressive attainment (enjoyment, fruition) of Arahantship it is used to denote the realization of having attained each stage of the sotāpatti, sakadāgāmi etc. (see the Miln quot. under 1 and cp. *Cpd.* 45, 116). So freq. in exegetical literature **magga, phala, nibbāna,** e. g. Tikp 155, 158; VbhA 43 & passim. — In general it immediately precedes Nibbāna (see Nd[2] no 645^{b} and under satipaṭṭhāna), and as **agga-phala** it is almost identical with Arahantship. Frequently it is comb[d] with **vipāka** to denote the stringent conception of "consequence," e. g. at D 1.27, 58; III.160. Almost synonymous in the sense of "fruition, benefit, profit" is ānisaŋsā D III.132; phala at Pv 1.12^{5} = ānisaŋsa PvA 64 — Vin 1.293 (anāgāmi°); II.240 (id.); III.73 (arahatta°); D 1.51, 57 sq. (sāmañña°); III.147, 170 (sucaritassa); M 1.477 (appamāda°); S 1.173 (Amata°); Pv 1.11^{10} (kaṭuka°); 11.8^{3} (dāna°); $IV.1^{88}$ (mahap° & agga°); Vism 345 (of food, being digested); PvA 8 (puñña° & dāna°), 22 (sotāpatti°), 24 (issā-macchariya°).

-atthika one who is looking for fruit Vism 120. **-āpaṇa** fruit shop Miln 333. **-âphala** [phala + aphala, see ā[4]; but cp. Geiger, *P.Gr.* § 33[1]] all sorts of fruit, lit. what is not (i. e. unripe), fruit without discrimination; a phrase very freq. in Jātaka style, e. g. J 1.416; II.160; III.127; IV.220; 307, 449, V.313; VI.520; DhA 1.106. **-āsava** extract of fruit VvA 73. **-uppatti** ripening PvA 29. **-esin** yielding fruit J 1.87 = Th 1, 527, cp. phalesin MVastu III.93. **-gaṇḍa** see palagaṇḍa. **-ṭṭha** "stationed in fruition," i. e. enjoying the result or fruition of the Path (cp. *Cpd.* 50) Miln 342. **-dāna** gift of fruit VbhA 337. **-dāyin** giver of fruit Vv 67^{6}. **-pacchi** fruit-basket J VI.560. **-pañcaka** fivefold fruit Vism 580; VbhA 191. **-puṭa** fruit-basket J VI.236. **-bhājana** one who distributes fruit, an official term in the vihāra Vin IV.38, cp. BSk. phalacāraka. **-maya** see sep. **-ruha** fruit tree Mbvs 82. **-sata** see palasata.

Phala[2] is spelling for **pala** (a certain weight) at J VI.510. See pala & cp. Geiger, *P.Gr.* § 40.

Phala[3] [etym. ? Sk. *phala] the point of a spear or sword S II.265 (tiṇha°). Cp. phāla[2].

Phalaka [fr. **phal** = ***sphal** or ***sphaṭ** (see phalati), lit. that which is split or cut off (cp. in same meaning "slab"); cp. Sk. sphaṭika rock-crystal; on Prk. forms see Pischel, *Prk. Gr.* § 206. Ved. phalaka board, phāla ploughshare; Gr. ἄσπαλον, σπολάς, ψαλίς scissors; Lat. pellis & spolium; Ohg. spaltan = split, Goth. spilda writing board, tablet; Oicel. spjald board] 1. a flat piece of wood, a slab, board, plank J 1.451 (a writing board, school slate); V.155 (akkhassa ph. axle board); VI.281 (dice-board). **pidhāna°** covering board VbhA 244 = Vism 261; **sopāna°** staircase, landing J 1.330 (maṇi°); Vism 313; cp. MVastu 1.249; **°āsana** a bench J 1.199; **°kāya** a great mass of planks J II.91. **°atthara-sayana** a bed covered with a board (instead of a mattress) J 1.304, 317; II.68. **°seyya** id. D 1.167 ("plank-bed"). — 2. a shield J III.237, 271; Miln 355; DhA II.2. — 3. a slip of wood or bark, used for making an ascetic's dress (°cīra) D 1.167, cp. Vin 1.305. ditto for a weight to hang on the robe Vin II.136. — 4. a post M III.95 (aggaḷa° doorpost); ThA 70 (Ap. V.17).

Phalagaṇḍa is spurious writing for palagaṇḍa (q. v.).

Phalatā (f.) [abstr. fr. phala] the fact or condition of bearing fruit PvA 139 (appa°).

Phalati [**phal** to split, break open = ***sphal** or ***sphaṭ**, cp. phāṭeti. On etym. see also Lüders, K.Z. XLII, 198 sq.] 1. to split, burst open (intrs.) A 1.77 (asaniyā phalantiyā); usually in phrase "**muddhā sattadhā phaleyya,**" as a formula of threat or warning "your (or my) head shall split into 7 pieces," e. g. D 1.95; S 1.50; Sn 983; J 1.54; IV.320 (me); V.92 (= bhijjetha C.); Miln 157 (satadhā for satta°); DhA 1.41 (m. te phalatu s.); VvA 68; whereas a similar phrase in Sn 988 sq. has adhipāteti (for *adhiphāṭeti = phalati). — Caus. phāleti (& phāṭeti). — pp. phalita & phulla. — 2. to become ripe, to ripen Vin II.108; J III.251; PvA 185.

Phalamaya stands in all probability for **phalika-maya,** made of crystal, as is suggested by context, which gives it in line with kaṭṭha-maya & loha-maya (& aṭṭhi°, danta°, veḷu° etc.). It occurs in same phrase at all passages mentioned, and refers to material of which boxes, vessels, holders etc. are made. Thus at Vin 1.203 (of añjani, box), 205 (tumba, vessel); II.115 (sattha-daṇḍa, scissors-handle), 136 (ganṭhikā, block at dress). The trsl[n] "made of fruits" seems out of place (so Kern, *Toev.* s. v.), one should rather expect "made of crystal" by the side of made of wood, copper, bone, ivory, etc.

Phalavant (adj.) [fr. phala] bearing or having fruit J III.251.

Phalasata see **palasata.**—At J VI.510 it means "gold-bronze" (as material of which a "sovaṇṇa-kaŋsa" is made).

Phalika[1] [fr. phala] a fruit vendor Miln 331.

Phalika[2] & **°kā** (f.) [also spelt with ḷ; cp. Sk. sphaṭika; on change ṭ > ḷ see Geiger, *P.Gr.* § 38^{6}. The Prk. forms are phaḷiha & phāḷiya, see Pischel, *Gr.* § 206] crystal, quartz Vin II.112; J VI.119 (°kā = phaḷika-bhittiyo C.); Vv 35^{1} (= phalika-maṇi-mayā bhittiyo VvA 160); 78^{3} (°kā); Miln 267 (ḷ), 380 (ḷ).

Phalita[1] (adj.) [sporadic spelling for **palita**] grey-haired PvA 153.

Phalita[2] [pp. of **phal** to burst, for the usual **phulla,** after analogy with phalita[3]] broken, only in phrase hadayaŋ phalitaŋ his heart broke DhA 1.173; hadayena phalitena with broken heart J 1.65.

Phalita[3] [pp. of **phal** to bear fruit] fruit bearing, having fruit, covered with fruit (of trees) Vin II.108; J 1 18; Miln 107, 280.

Phalin (adj.) [fr. phala] bearing fruit J V.242.

Phalina (adj.) [fr. phala, phalin ?] at J V.92 is of doubtful meaning. It cannot very well mean "bearing fruit," since it is used as Ep. of a bird (°sakuṇī). The Cy. expl[n] is sakuṇa-potakānaŋ phalinattā (being a source of nourishment ?) phalina-sakuṇī." The v. l. SS is phalīna & palīna.

Phalima (adj.) [fr. phala] bearing fruit, full of fruit J III.493.

Phalu [cp. Vedic paru] a knot or joint in a reed, only in cpd. °bīja (plants) springing (or propagated) from a joint D I.5; Vin IV.34, 35.

Phaleti at D I.54 is spurious reading for paleti (see palāyati), expl[d] by gacchati DA I.165; meaning "runs," not with trsl[n] "spreads out" [to **sphar**].

Phallava is spelling for pallava sprout, at J III.40.

Phassa[1] [cp. Ved. sparśa, of spṛś: see phusati] contact, touch (as sense or sense-impression, for which usually phoṭṭhabbaŋ). It is the fundamental fact in a sense-impression, and consists of a combination of the sense, the object, and perception, as expl[d] at M I.111: tiṇṇaŋ (i. e. cakkhu, rūpā, cakkhu-viññāṇa) sangati phasso; and gives rise to feeling: phassa-paccayā vedanā. (See paṭicca-samuppāda & for expl° Vism 567; VbhA 178 sq.). — Cp. D I.42 sq.; III.228, 272, 276; Vism 463 (phusatī ti phasso); Sn 737, 778 (as fundamental of attachment, cp. SnA 517); J v.441 (rājā dibba-phassena puṭṭho touched by the divine touch, i. e. fascinated by her beauty; puṭṭho = phutto); VbhA 177 sq. (in detail), 193, 265; PvA 86 (dup° of bad touch, bad to the touch, i. e. rough, unpleasant); poet. for trouble Th 1, 783. See on phassa: *Dhs. trsl.* 5 & introd. (lv.) lxiii.; *Cpd.* 12, 14, 94.

-āyatana organ of contact (6, referring to the several senses) PvA 52. -āhāra "touch-food," acquisition by touch, nutriment of contact, one of the 3 āhāras, viz. phass°, mano-sañcetanā° (n. of representative cogitation) and viññāṇ° (of intellection) Dhs 71-73; one of the 4 kinds of āhāra, or "food," with ref. to the 3 vedanās Vism 341. -kāyā (6) groups of touch or contact viz. cakkhu-samphasso, sota°, ghāna°, kāya°, mano° D III.243. -sampanna endowed with (lovely) touch, soft, beautiful to feel J v.441 (cp. phassita).

Phassa[2] (adj.) [grd. fr. phusati, corresp. to Sk. spṛśya] to be felt, esp. as a pleasing sensation; pleasant, beautiful J IV.450 (gandhehi ph.).

Phassati stands for phusati at Vism 527 in def. of phassa ("phassatī ti phasso").

Phassanā (f.) [abstr. fr. phassa] touch, contact with DhsA 167 (jhānassa lābho . . . patti . . . phassanā sacchikiriyā).

Phassita (adj.) [pp. of phasseti = Sk. sparśayati to bring into contact] made to touch, brought into contact, only in cpd. suphassita of pleasant contact, beautiful to the touch, pleasant, perfect, symmetrical J I.220 (cīvara), 394 (dantā); IV.188 (dant' āvaraṇaŋ); v.197 (of the membrum muliebre), 206 (read °phassita for °phussita), 216 (°cheka-karaṇa); VvA 275 (as expl[n] of atīva sangata Vv 64[2]). — *Note.* Another (doubtful) phassita is found at J v.252 (dhammo phassito; touched, attained) where vv. ll. give passita & phussita.

Phasseti [Caus. of phusati[1]] to touch, attain J v.251 (rājā dhammaŋ phassayaŋ = C. phassayanto; vv. ll. pa° & phu°); Miln 338 (amataŋ, cp. phusati), 340 (phassayeyya Pot.). — Pass. phassīyati Vin II.148 (kavāṭā na ph.; v. l. phussiy°). — pp. phassita & phussita[3].

***Phāṭeti** is conjectured reading for pāteti in phrase kaṭṭhaŋ pāteti M I.21, and in adhipāteti to split (see adhipāta & vipāta). The derivation of these expressions from **pat** is out of place, where close relation to phāleti (phalati) is evident, and a derivation from **phaṭ = sphaṭ**, as in Sk. sphāṭayati to split, is the only right expl[n] of meaning. In that case we should put **phal = sphaṭ**, where l = ṭ, as in many Pali words, cp. phalika < sphaṭika (see Geiger, *P.Gr.* § 38[6]). The Prk. correspondent is phāḍei (Pischel, *Gr.* § 208).

Phāṇita (nt.) [cp. Epic Sk. phāṇita] 1. juice of the sugar cane, raw sugar, molasses (ucchu-rasaŋ gahetvā kata-phāṇitaŋ VvA 180) Vin II.177; D I.141; Vv 35[25]; 40[4]; J I.33, 120, 227; Miln 107; DhA II.57. phāṇitassa puṭaŋ a basket of sugar S I.175; J IV.366; DhA IV.232. — 2. (by confusion or rightly?) salt J III.409 (in expl[n] of aloṇika = phāṇita-virahita).

-odaka sugar water J III.372. -puṭa sugar basket J IV.363.

Phāti (f.) [cp. Sk. sphāti, fr. **sphāy**, sphāyate to swell, increase (Idg. *spē(i), as in Lat. spatium, Ohg. spuot, Ags. spēd = E. speed; see Walde, *Lat. Wtb.* s. v. spatium), pp. sphīta = P. phīta] swelling, increase J II.426 (= vaḍḍhi); Vism 271 (vuddhi +). Usually comb[d] with **kṛ**, as phāti-kamma increase, profit, advantage Vin II.174; VbhA 334 & phāti-karoti to make fat, to increase, to use to advantage M I.220 = A v.347; A III.432.

Phāruka (adj.) at VvA 288 is not clear; meaning something like "bitter," comb[d] with kasaṭa; v. l. pāru°. Probably = phārusaka.

Phāruliya at Vbh 350 (in thambha-exegesis) is faulty spelling for phārusiya (nt.) harshness, unkindness, as evidence of id. passage at VbhA 469 shows (with expl[n] "pharusassa puggalassa bhāvo phārusiyaŋ").

Phārusaka [fr. pharusa, cp. Sk. *pāruṣaka Mvyut 103, 143] 1. a certain flower, the (bitter) fruit of which is used for making a drink Vin I.246; Vv 33[31] = DhA III.316. — 2. N. of one of Indra's groves J VI.278, similarly Vism 424; VbhA 439.

Phāla[1] (m. & nt.) [cp. Vedic phāla] ploughshare S I.169; Sn p. 13 & v.77 (expl[d] as "phāletī ti ph." SnA 147); J I.94; IV.118; v.104; Ud 69 (as m.); DhA I.395.

Phāla[2] [to phala[3]] an (iron) board, slab (or ball?), maybe spear or rod. The word is of doubtful origin & meaning, it occurs always in the same context of a heated iron instrument, several times in correlation with an iron ball (ayogula). It has been misunderstood at an early time, as is shown by kapāla A IV.70 for phāla. Kern comments on the word at *Toev.* II.139. See Vin I.225 (phālo divasantatto, so read; v. l. balo corr. to bālo; corresp. with guḷa); A IV.70 (divasa-santatte ayokapāle, gloss ayogule); J v.268; v.109 (phāle ciraratta-tāpite, v. l. pāle, hale, thāle; corresp. with pakaṭṭhita ayogula), id. v.113 (ayomayehi phālehi pīḷeti, v. l. vālehi).

Phāla[3] in loṇa-maccha° a string (?) or cluster of salted fish Vism 28.

Phālaka (adj.) [fr. phāleti] splitting; one who splits Vism 413 (kaṭṭha°).

Phālana (nt.) [fr. phāleti] splitting J I.432 (dāru°); Vism 500 (vijjhana°).

Phālita [= Sk. sphārita, **sphar**] 1. made open, expanded, spread J III.320 (+ vikasita). — 2. split [fr. phāleti **phal**], split open Vism 262 = VbhA 245 (°haliddi-vaṇṇa).

Phāliphulla [either Intensive of phulla, or Der. fr. pariphulla in form phaliphulla] in full blossom M I.218; J I.52.

Phālibhaddaka is spurious spelling for pāli° at J II.162 (v. l. pātali-bhaddaka). Cp. Prk. phālihadda (= pāribhadra Pischel, *Gr.* § 208).

Phālima (adj.) [either fr. Caus. of **phal**[1] (phāleti), or fr. **sphar** (cp. phārita, i. e. expanded), or fr. **sphāy** (swell, increase, cp. sphāra & sphārī bhavati to open, expand)] expanding, opening blossoming in cpd. aggi-nikāsi-phālima paduma J III.320 (where Cy. expl[ns] by phālita vikasita).

Phāleti [Caus. of phalati, **phal**; a variant is phāṭeti fr. **sphaṭ**, which is identical with *(s)phal] to split, break, chop, in phrases 1. **kaṭṭhaŋ phāleti** to chop sticks (for firewood) Vin I.31; J II.144; Pv II.9[51], besides which the phrase **kaṭṭhaŋ *phāṭeti**. 2. **sīsaŋ** (muddhā) sattadhā **phāleti** (cp. adhipāteti & phalati) DhA I.17 (perhaps better with v. l. phal°), 134. — 3. (various:) A I.204 = S II.88; J II.398; Nd[2] 483; Vism 379 (kucchiŋ ; DhA IV.133 (hadayaŋ). — pp. phālita. Caus. II. phālāpeti to cause to split open J III.121; Miln 157 (v. l. phāḷāp°).

Phāsu (adj.) [etym. ? Trenckner, *Notes* 82 (on Miln 14[17]: corr. *J.P.T.S.* 1908, 136 which refers it to Miln 13[15]) suggests connection with Vedic prāśu enjoying, one who enjoys, i.e. a guest, but this etym. is doubtful; cp. phāsuka. A key to its etym. may be found in the fact that it never occurs by itself in form phāsu, but either in composition or as °ka] pleasant, comfortable; only neg. a° in phrase **aphāsu-karoti** to cause discomfort to (dat.) Vin IV.290; and in cpds. °**kāma** anxious for comfort, desirous of (others) welfare D III.164; °**vihāra** comfort, ease Vin II.127; D I.204; Dhs 1348 = Miln 367 (cp. DhsA 404); Miln 14; Vism 33; VbhA 270; PvA 12.

Phāsu at Miln 146 (cp. p. 425) " bhaggā phāsū " is uncertain reading, it is *not* phāsuka; it may represent a pāsa snare, sling. The likeness with phāsukā bhaggā (lit.) of J I.493 is only accidental.

Phāsuka (adj.) [fr. phāsu. Cp. Prk. phāsuya; acc. to Pischel, *Prk. Gr.* § 208 Jain Sk. prāsuka is a distortion of P. phāsuka. Perhaps phāsu is abstracted from phāsuka] pleasant, convenient, comfortable J III.343; IV.30; DhA II.92; PvA 42. —**aphāsuka** unpleasant, uncomfortable, not well J II.275, 395; DhA I.28; II.21. — *Note*. It seems probable that phāsuka represents a Sk. *sparśuka (cp. Pischel § 62), which would be a der. fr. **spṛś** in same meaning as phassa[2] (" lovely "). This would confirm the suggestion of phāsu being a secondary formation.

Phāsukā (f.) [cp. Sk *pārśukā & Ved. pārśva, see passa[2]] a rib, only in pl. phāsukā Vin I.74 (upaḍḍha° bhañjitabbā), in phrase **sabbā te phāsukā bhaggā** J I.493 (lit.), which is fig. applied at Dh 154 (expl[d] as " sabbā avasesa-kilesa-phāsukā bhaggā " at DhA III.128), with which cp. **bhaggā phāsū** at Miln 146; both the latter phrases prob. of diff. origin. — (adj.) (-°) in phrase **mahā°passa** the flank (lit. the side of the great ribs) J I.164, 179; III.273; abs. **mahā°** with great ribs J V.42; **uggata°** with prominent ribs PvA 68 (for upphāsulika adj. Pv II.1[1]). — in *cpds.* as **phāsuka°**, e. g. °**aṭṭhīni** the rib-bones (of which there are 24) Vism 254 (v. l. pāsuka°); VbhA 237; °**dvaya** pair of ribs Vism 252; VbhA 235. — See also pāsuka, pāsuḷa & the foll.

Phāsulikā (f.) [fr. phāsuḷi] rib, only in cpd. **upphāsulika** (adj.) Pv II.1[1].

Phāsuḷā [for phāsukā] rib S II.255 (phāsuḷ-antarikā).

Phāsuḷī [cp. phāsukā & phāsuḷā] a rib M I.80.

Phiya [etym. unknown] oar Sn 321 (+ aritta rudder; expl[d] by dabbi-padara SnA 330); J IV.21 (°ārittaŋ). See also piya[2] which is the more freq. spelling of phiya.

Phīta [pp. of **sphāy**, cp. Sk. sphīta & see phāti] opulent, prosperous, rich; in the older texts only in stock phrase **iddha ph. bahujana** (rich & prosperous & well-populated) D I.211 (of the town Nālandā); II.146 (of Kusāvatī); M I.377; (of Nālandā) II.71 (of country); S II.107 (fig. of brahmacariyaŋ; with bahujañña for °jana); A III.215 (of town). By itself & in other comb[n] in the Jātakas, e. g. J IV.135 (= samiddha); VI.355 (v. l. pīta). With iddha & detailed description of all classes of the population (instead of bahujana) of a town Miln 330.

Phuṭa[1] [pp. of pharati] 1. (cp. pharati[1]) pervaded, permeated, thrilled (cp. pari°) D I.73, 74 (pītisukhena; T. prints phuta; v. l. phuṭa; v. l. at DA I.217 p(h)uṭṭha); M I.276; J I.33 (sarīraŋ pītiyā ph.); DhA II.118 (pītiyā phuṭa-sarīro); SnA 107 (referring to the nerves of taste). — 2. (cp. pharati[2]) expanded, spread out, spread with (instr.) Vin I.182 (lohitena); J V.266 (in nirayapassage T. reads bhūmi yojana-sataŋ phuṭā tiṭṭhanti, i. e. the beings fill or are spread out over such a space; C. 272 expl[ns] by " ettakaŋ ṭhānaŋ anupharitvā tiṭṭhanti." The id. p. at Nd[1] 405 = Nd[2] 304[III D] reads bh. yojana-sataŋ pharitvā (intrs.: expanding, wide) tiṭṭhati, which is the more correct reading). — See also ophuṭa & cp. phuṭa[3].

Phuṭa[2] [pp. of **sphuṭ** to expand, blossom] blossoming out, opened, in full bloom Dāvs IV.49 (°kumuda). Cp. phuṭita.

Phuṭa[3] at M I.377 (sabba-vāri°, in sequence with vārita, yuta, dhuta) is unnecessarily changed by Kern, *Toev.* s. v. into pūta. The meaning is " filled with, spread with," thus = phuṭa[1], cp. sequence under ophuṭa. The v. l. at M I.377 is puṭṭha. On miswriting of phuṭṭa & puṭṭha for phuṭa cp. remark by Trenckner, M I.553. A similar meaning (" full of, occupied by, overflowing with ") is attached to phuṭa in *Avīci* passage A I.159 (Avīci maññe phuṭo ahosi), cp. Anāgata Vaŋsa (*J.P.T.S.* 1886, v.39) & remarks of Morris's *J.P.T.S.* 1887, 165. — The same passage as M I.377 is found at D I.57, where T. reads phuṭṭa (as also at DA I.168), with vv. ll. puṭṭha & phuṭa.

Phuṭita [for phoṭita, pp. of *sphoṭayati, **sphuṭ**] 1. shaken, tossed about, burst, rent asunder, abstr. nt. phutitattaŋ being tossed about Miln 116 (v. l. put °). — 2. cracked open, chapped, torn (of feet) Th 2, 269 (so read for T. phuṭika, ThA 212 expl[ns] by bāhita & has v. l. niphuṭita).

Phuṭṭha [pp. of phusati[1]] touched, affected by, influenced by; in specific sense (cp. phusati[1] 2) " thrilled, permeated " Vin I.200 (ābādhena); A II.174 (rogena); J I.82 (mettacittena, v. l. puṭṭha); V.441 (dibbaphassena); Vism 31 (°samphassa contact by touch), 49 (byādhinā); VvA 6 (in both meanings, scil. pītiyā & rogena). On phuṭṭha at D I.57 see phuṭa[3]. Cp. sam°.

Phunati [?] to shake, sprinkle, of doubtful spelling, at J VI.108 (angārakāsuŋ ph.; v. l. punanti perhaps better; C. expl[os] by vidhunati & okirati). Perhaps we should read **dhunati**.

Phulaka (= pulaka) a kind of gem VvA 111.

Phulla[1] [pp. of phalati, or root formation fr. **phull**, cp. phalita[3]] blossoming, in blossom J V.203. Also as Intensive phāliphulla " one mass of flowers " M I.218; J I.52. *Note*. phulla[1] may stand for phuṭa[2].

Phulla[2] [pp. of phalati, cp. phalita[2]] broken, in phrase akhaṇḍa-phulla unbroken (q. v.), Pv IV.1[76] and passim.

Phullita [pp. of phullati] in flower, blossoming J V.214 (for phīta = rich), 216 (su°-vana).

Phusati[1] [**spṛś**, fr. which sparśa = phassa; cp. also phassati] 1. (lit.) to touch Vism 463 (phusatī ti phasso); DA I.61 (aor. phusī = metri causa for phusi); Miln 157 (grd. aphusa not to be touched). — 2. (fig.) [see on this term of Buddhist ecstatic phraseology *Cpd.* 133[2]. In this meaning it is very closely related to pharati, as appears e. g. from the foll. expl[ns] of Cys.: D I.74 parippharati = samantato phusati DA I.217; D II.186 ≈ pharitvā = phusitvā ārammaṇaŋ katvā Vism 308] to attain, to reach, only in specific sense of attaining to the highest ideal of religious aspiration, in foll. phrases: **ceto-samādhiŋ ph.** D I.13 = III.30, 108 etc.; **nirodhaŋ**

D I.184; samatha-samādhiŋ Vv 16[9] (reads āphusiŋ but should prob. be aphusiŋ as VvA 84, expl[d] by adhigacchiŋ); phalaŋ aphussayi (aor. med.) Pv IV.1[88]; cp. PvA 243; amataŋ padaŋ Pv IV.3[48]; amataŋ Miln 338 (but T. reads khippaŋ *phasseti* a.); in bad sense kappaṭṭhitikaŋ kammaŋ Miln 108 (of Devadatta). — pp. phuṭṭha. Cp. upa°.

Phusati[2] this is a specific Pali form and represents two Sk. roots, which are closely related to each other and go back to the foll. 2 Idg. roots: 1. Idg. ***sp(h)ṛj,** burst out, burst (forth), spring, sprinkle, as in Sk. sphūrjati burst forth, parjanya rain cloud; Gr. σφαραγέω; Ags. spearca = E. spark, E. spring, sprinkle. This is an enlargement of **sphur** (cp. pharati, phuṭṭha, phuta). — 2. Idg. ***spṛk** to sprinkle, speckle, as in Sk. **pruṣ,** pṛśni speckled, pṛṣan, pṛṣati spotted antelope, pṛṣata raindrop; Gr. περκνός of dark (lit. spotted) colour; Lat. spargere = Ger. sprengen. To this root belong P. pasata, phoseti, paripphosaka, phussa, phusita. — Inf. phusituŋ, conjectured reading at Vin I.205 for T. phosituŋ (vv. ll. posituŋ & dhovituŋ), & Vin II.151 for T. posituŋ; *Vin. Texts* III.169 translate "bespatter."

Phusana (nt.) [abstr. fr. phusati[1] 1] touch Vism 463.

Phusanā (f.) [abstr. fr. phusati[1] 2] attainment, gaining, reaching Vism 278 (= phuṭṭha-ṭṭhāna); DhA I.230 (ñāṇa°); VvA 85 (samādhi°).

Phusāyati [Caus. of **pruṣ,** but formed fr. P. phusati[2]] to sprinkle (rain), to rain gently, drizzle S I.104 sq., 154, 184 (devo ekaŋ ekaŋ ph. "drop by drop"). See also anuphusāyati (so read for °phusiyati).

Phusita[1] (nt.) [either pp. of phusati[2] or direct correspondent of Sk. pṛṣata (see pasata[2])] rain-drop M III.300; S II.135; DhA III.243. The Prk. equivalent is phusiya (Pischel, *Gr.* § 208), cp. Ger. sprenkeln > E. sprinkle.

Phusita[2] [pp. of phusati[2] 2. i. e. **pruṣ,** cp. Sk. pruṣita sprinkled, pṛṣatī spotted antelope] spotted, coloured, variegated (with flowers) Sn 233 (°agga = supupphit' agga-sākha KhA 192).

Phus(s)ita[3] [= phassita[2], Kern. *Toev.* s. v. takes it as pp. of ***puŋsayati**] touched, put on, in °aggaḷa with fastened (clinched) bolts (or better: door-wings) M I.76 (reads phassit°; cp. v. l. on p. 535 phussit°); A I.101; Th 1, 385; J VI.510.

Phusitaka (adj.) (-°) [fr. phusita[1]) having raindrops, only in phrase thulla° deva (the sky) shedding big drops of rain S II.32 (reads phulla-phusitaka); III.141; A I.243; II.140; V.114; Vism 259.

Phussa[1] [fr. **puṣ** to blossom, nourish, etc. cp. Ved. puṣya] 1. see phussa[3] 2. — 2. N. of a month (Dec.-Jan.) J I.86. N. of a lunar mansion or constellation Vv 53[4] (= phussa-tārakā VvA 236). — Frequent as Np., cp. Vism 422, and comb[ns] like °deva, °mitta.

Phussa[2] [ger. of phusati[1]] touching, feeling, realising; doubled at D I.45, 54.

Phussa[3] (adj.-n.) [grd. formation fr. phusati[2] 2; scarcely fr. Sk. puṣya (to **puṣ** nourish, cp. poseti), but meaning rather "speckled" in all senses. The Sk. puṣyaratha is Sanskritisation of P. phussa°] 1. speckled, gaily-coloured, °**kokila** the spotted cuckoo [Kern, *Toev.* s. v. phussa however takes it as "male-cuckoo," Sk. puŋs-kokila] J V.419, 423; VvA 57. — As phussaka at A I.188 (so read for pussaka). — 2. in sense of "clear, excellent, exquisite" (or it is puṣya in sense of "substance, essence" of anything, as Geiger, *P. Gr.* § 40 1a?) in °ratha [cp. Sk. puṣpa°, but prob. to be read puṣya°?] a wonderful state carriage running of its own accord J II.39; III.238; IV.34, V.248; VI.39 sq.) v. l. pussa°); PvA 74. -rāga [cp. Sk. puṣpa-rāga] topaz Miln 118; VvA 111. — At Nd[1] 90 as v. l. to be preferred to pussa° in °tila, °tela, °dantakaṭṭha, etc. with ref. to their use by Brahmins.

Pheggu [cp. Vedic phalgu & P. phaggu in form] accessory wood, wood surrounding the pith of a tree, always with ref. to trees (freq. in similes), in sequence mūla, sāra, pheggu, taca, papaṭikā etc. It is represented as next to the pith, but inferior and worthless. At all passages contrasted with sāra (pith, substance). Thus at M I.192 sq., 488; D III.51; S IV.168; A I.152 (pheggu + sāra, v. l. phaggu); II.110 = Pug 52; A III.20; J III.431 (opp. sāra); Miln 267, 413 (tacchako pheggun apaharitvā sāraŋ ādiyati).

Pheggukа (-°) (adj.) [fr. pheggu] having worthless wood, weak, inferior M I.488 (apagata°, where °ka belongs to the whole cpd.); J III.318 (a° + sāramaya).

Phegguta (f.) [abstr. fr. pheggu] state of dry wood; lack of substance, worthlessness Pug A 229.

Pheṇa [cp. Vedic phena, with *ph fr. sp°, connected with Lat. spūma, scum, Ags. fām = Ger. feim = E. foam] scum, foam, froth, only in cpds. viz.:

-**uddehakaŋ** (adv.) (paccamāna, boiling) with scum on top, throwing up foam M III.167; A I.141; Nd[2] 304[III c]; J III.46; Miln 357. -**paṭala** a film of scum Vism 359; VbhA 65. -**piṇḍa** a lump or heap of foam S III.140 sq. = Vism 479 (in simile of rūpa); Nd[2] 680 A[II]; Vism 40 (in comp); VbhA 32 sq. **bubbuḷaka** a bubble of scum Vism 171, 259, 345; VbhA 242. -**mālā** a wreath or garland of scum Miln 117. -**mālin** with a wreath of scum Miln 260. -**missa** mixed with froth Vism 263. -**vaṇṇa** colour of scum Vism 263.

Pheṇaka = pheṇa Vism 254; VbhA 237.

Phoṭa [fr. **sphuṭ,** cp. Sk. sphoṭa] swelling, boil, blister J IV.457; VI.8 (v. l. pota & poṭha); cp. **poṭa** bubble.

Phoṭaka = phoṭa Vism 258; VbhA 242.

Phoṭana "applause," in brahma-pphoṭana at DhA III.210 should be taken as ā + phoṭana (= apphoṭana).

Phoṭeti [Caus. of **sphuṭ,** if correct. Maybe mixed with **sphūrj.** The form apphoṭesi seems to be ā + phoṭeti = Sk. asphoṭayati] to shake, toss (or thunder?) only at two places in similar formula, viz. devatā sādhukāraŋ adaŋsu, brahmāno apphoṭesuŋ (v. l. appoṭh°) Miln 13, 18; Sakko devarājā appoṭhesi (v. l. appoṭesi), Mahābrahmā sādhukāraŋ adāsi J VI.486. Perhaps we should read poṭheti (q. v.), to snap one's fingers (clap hands) as sign of applause. At DhA III.210 we read fut. apphoṭessāmi (i. e. ā + phoṭ).

Phoṭṭhabba (nt.) [grd. of phusati] tangible, touch, contact; it is synonymous with phassa, which it replaces in psychol. terminology. Phoṭṭhabbaŋ is the sense-object of kāya (or taca) touch ("kāyena phoṭṭhabbaŋ phusitvā" D III.226, 250, 269; Nd[2] p. 238 under rūpa). See also āyatana. — D III.102 (in list of ajjhattika-bāhirāni āyatanāni: kāyo c' eva phoṭṭhabbā ca; with pl. like m.); VbhA 79 (°dhātu).

Phosita [pp. of phoseti, cp. Sk. pruṣita] sprinkled J VI.47 (candana°, v. l. pusita).

Phoseti [Caus. of phusati[2], cp. Sk. pruṣāyati = P. phusayati] to sprinkle (over) Vin II.205 (inf. phosituŋ). — pp. phosita. Cp. pari°.

B.

Ba (indecl.) the sound (& letter) *b*, often substituted for or replaced by *p* (& *ph*): so is *e. g.* in Bdhgh's view pahuta the word bahuta, with p for b (KhA 207), cp. bakkula, badara, badālatā, baddhacara, bandhuka 2, bala, balīyati, bahuka, bahūta, billa, bella; also paribandha for paripantha; phāla[2]. Also substituted for *v*, cp. bajjayitvā *v.l.* vajjetvā DAI. 4, and see under Nibb-.

Baka [cp. Epic Sk. baka] 1. a crane, heron Cp. III.10[2]; J I.205 (°suṇikā), 221, 476; II.234; III.252. — 2. N. of a dweller in the Brahma world M I.326; S I.142.

Bakula [cp. Class. Sk. bakula, N. of the tree Mimusops elengi, and its (fragrant) flower] in milāta°-puppha is v. l. KhA 60 (see App. p. 870 Pj.) for °ākuli°, which latter is also read at Vism 260.

Bakkula [=vyākula? Morris, *J.P.T.S.* 1886, 94] a demon, uttering horrible cries, a form assumed by the Yakkha Ajakalāpaka, to terrify the Buddha Ud 5 (see also ākulī, where pākula is proposed for bakkula).

Bajjha see **bandhati.**

Bajjhati Pass. of **bandhati** (q. v.).

Battiṃsa (num. card.) [for dvat-tiṃsa] thirty-two J III.207.

Badara (m. & nt.) [cp. Ved. badara & badarī] the fruit of the jujube tree (Zizyphus jujuba), not unlike a crab-apple in appearance & taste, very astringent, used for medicine A I.130 = Pug 32; A III.76; Vin IV.76; J III.21; DhsA 320 (cited among examples of acrid flavours); VvA 186. Spelling padara for b° ata J IV.363; VI.529.
-aṭṭhi kernel of the j. SnA 247. -paṇḍu light yellow (fresh) jujube-fruit A I.181 (so read for bhadara°). -missa mixture or addition of the juice of jujube-fruits Vin IV.76. -yūsa juice of the j. fruit VvA 185.

Badarī (f.) [cp. Sk. badarī] the jujube tree J II.260.

Badālatā (f.) [etym. uncertain, may it be *padālatā, pa + n. ag. of **dal** Caus., lit. "destroyer"?] a creeper (with thorns Kern, *Toev.* s. v.) D III.87 = Vism 418; Bdhgh says (see *Dial.* III.84) "a beautiful creeper of sweet taste."

Baddha[1] [pp. of bandhati] 1. bound, in bondage M I.275; S I.133; IV.91; Sn 957 (interpreted as "baddhacara" by Nd[1] 464); Dh 324. — 2. snared, trapped J II.153; III.184; IV.251, 414. — 3. made firm, settled, fastened, bound (to a cert. place) KhA 60 (°pitta, opp. abaddha°). — 4. contracted, acquired Vin III.96. — 5. bound to, addicted or attached to Sn 773 (bhavasāta°, cp. Nd[1] 30). — 6. put together, kneaded, made into cakes (of meal) J III.343; V.46; VI.524. — 7. bound together, linked, clustered DhA I.304 kaṇṇika° (of thoughts). — 9. set, made up (of the mind) DhA I.11 (mānasaṃ te b.). — Cp. ati°, anu°, a°, ni°, paṭi°, vini°, sam°.
-añjalika keeping the hands reverently extended Dāvs III.30. -rāva the cry of the bound (or trapped) J IV.279, 415 (v. l. bandhana°). -vera having contracted an enmity, hostile, bearing a grudge DhA I.324.

Baddha[2] (nt.) [fr. bandhati] a leather strap, a thong Vin I.287 (T. bandha perhaps right, cp. ābandhana 3); PvA 127.

Baddhacara see **paddhacara.**

Badhira (adj.) [cp. Vedic badhira, on etym. see Walde, *Lat. Wtb.* s. v. fatuus, comparing Goth. bauþs and M. Irish bodar] deaf Vin I.91, 322; Th 1, 501 = Miln 367; J I.76 (jāti°); V.387; VI.7; DhA I.312. See also **mūga.**
-dhātuka deaf by nature J II.63; IV.146; DhA I.346.

Bandha (adj.) [cp. Vedic bandha, fr. **bandh**] 1. bond, fetter It 56 (abandho Mārassa, not a victim of M.); Nd[1] 328 (taṇhā°, diṭṭhi°); ThA 241. — 2. one who binds or ties together, in assa° horsekeeper, groom J II.98; V.441, 449; DhA I.392. — 3. a sort of binding: maṇḍala° with a circular b. (parasol) Vin IV.338, salāka° with a notched b. ibid. — 4. a halter, tether Dpvs I.76. — Cp. **vinibandha.**

Bandhaka as v. l. of **vaṭṭaka** see **aṃsa°.**

Bandhakī (f.) [fr. bandhaka, cp. Epic Sp. bandhukī a low woman = pāṃśukā & svairinī Halāy 2, 341] an unchaste woman (lit. binder) Vin IV.224 (pl. bandhakiniyo), 265 (id.); J V.425, 431 (va°).

Bandhati [Vedic badhnāti, later Sk. bandhati, Idg. ***bhendh,** cp. Lat. offendimentum i. e. band; Goth. bindan = Ohg. bintan, E. bind; Sk. bandhu relation; Gr. πενθερός father-in-law, πεῖσμα bond, etc.] to bind etc. — I. *Forms:* Imper. bandha D II.350; pl. bandhantu J I.153. Pot. bandheyya S IV.198; Vin III.45; Fut. bandhayissati Mhvs 24. 6; Aor. abandhi J III.232, & bandhi J I.292; DhA I.182. Ger. bandhitvā Vin I.46; S IV.200; J I.253, 428, & bandhiya Th 2, 81. Inf. bandhituṃ Th 2, 299. Caus. bandheti (see above Fut.) & bandhāpeti (see below). — II. *Meanings*—1. to bind S IV.200 (rajjuyā). fig. combine, unite DhA II.189 (gharāvāsena b. to give in marriage). — 2. to tie on, bind or put on to (loc.) Dha I.182 (dasante). fig. to apply to, put to, settle on DhA II.12 (mānasaṃ paradāre). — 3. to fix, prepare, get up, put together J IV.290 (ukkā); also in phrase **cakk' âticakkaṃ mañc' âtimañcaṃ** b. to put wheels upon wheels & couches upon couches J II.331; IV.81; DhA IV.61. fig. to start, undertake, begin, make, in phrases āghātaṃ **b.** to bear malice DhA II.21; and **veraṃ b.** to make enmity against (loc.) J II.352. — 4. to acquire, get J III.232 (atthaṃ b. = nibbatteti C.). — 5. to compose Miln 272 (suttaṃ); J II.33; V.39. — Caus. II. bandhāpeti to cause to be bound (or fettered) Vin IV.224, 316 (opp. mocāpeti); Nd[2] 304[III. 2] (bandhanena); PvA 4, 113. — Pass. bajjhati Nd[2] 74 (for bujjhati, as in palābujjhati to be obstructed: see palibuddhati). I. *Forms* Ind. 3rd pl. bajjhare Th 1, 137; pret. 3rd pl. abajjhare J I.428. Imper. bajjhantu S IV.309; A V.284. Pot. bajjheyya S I.228. Aor. bajjhi J II.37; IV.414. Ger. bajjha J IV.441, 498, & bajjhitvā J II.153; IV.259; V.442. — II. *Meanings.*—1. to be bound, to be imprisoned Sn 508 (cp. SnA 418); J IV.278. — 2. to be caught (in a sling or trap) J III.330; IV.414. — 3. to incur a penalty (with loc., e. g. bahudaṇḍe) J IV.116. — 4. to be captivated by, struck or taken by, either with *loc.* J I.368 (bajjhitvā & bandhitvā in Pass. sense); V.465; or with *instr.* J I.428; IV.259. — pp. baddha (q. v.). — Cp. ati°, anu°, ā, o°, paṭi°, sam°.

Bandhana (nt.) [fr. **bandh**, cp. Vedic bandhana] 1. binding, bond, fetter Vin I.21; D I.226, 245 (pañca kāmaguṇā); III.176; M II.44; S I.8, 24 (Māra°), 35, 40; IV.201 sq. (5 fold) to bind the king of the Devas or Asuras, 291; Sn 532, 948; Th 1, 414; 2, 356 (Māra°) Dh 345 sq.; J II.139, 140; III.59 = PvA 4; V.285; Nd^2 304$^{III.2}$ (var. bonds, andhu°, rajju° etc. cp. Nd^1 433); DA I.121 (with ref. to kāmā). — 2. binding, tying, band, ligature; tie (also fig.) Vin I.204 (°suttaka thread for tying) II.135 (kāya° waistband); II.117 (°rajju for robes); S III.155 (vetta° ligatures of bamboo; cp. V.51); Sn 44 (gihi°, cp. Nd^2 228: puttā ca dāsī ca); DhA I.4 (ghara° tie of the house); KhA 51 (paṭṭa°). — 3. holding together, composition, constitution Vin I.96 (sarīra°), cp. III.28. — fig. composition (of literature) J II.224 (gāthā°). — 4. joining together, union, company DhA II.160 (gaṇa° joining in companies). — 5. handle Vin II.135. — 6. piecing together Vin I.254 (°mattena when it, i. e. the stuff, has only been pieced together, see *Vin. Texts* II.153 n.). — 7. strap (?) doubtful reading in aṇsa° (q. v.) Vv 33^{40}, where we should prefer to read with v. l. °vaṭṭaka. — 8. doubtful in meaning in cpd. pañca-vidha-bandhana "the fivefold fixing," as one of the torments in Niraya. It is a sort of crucifixion (see for detail pañca 3) Nd^2 304$^{III.c}$ = Nd^1 404; J I.174; PvA 221; VbhA 278. In this connection it may mean "set," cp. mūla°. — On use of bandhana in similes see *J.P.T.S.* 1907, 115. Cp. vini°.
-āgāra "fetter-house," prison D I.72; M I.75; Vin III.151; J III.326; DhA II.152; VvA 66; PvA 153. **-āgārika** prison-keeper, head-jailer A II.207.

Bandhanīya (adj.) [grd. of bandhati] 1. to be bound or fettered Miln 186. — 2. apt to bind, binding, constraining D II.337 (cp. *Dial.* II.361); Th 2, 356.

Bandhava [cp. Class. Sk. bāndhava] 1. kinsman, member of a clan or family, relative A III.44; Sn 60 (pl. bandhavāni in poetry; cp. Nd^2 455); Dh 288 (pl. bandhavā); J II.316; V.81; DA I.243. — 2. (-°) one who is connected with or belongs to Sn 140 (manta°, well-acquainted with Mantras; cp. SnA 192; vedabandhū veda-paṭisaraṇā ti vuttaṇ hoti); J V.335 (bodhaneyya°); cp. bandhu 3.

Bandhu [Vedic bandhu, see bandhati & cp. bandhava] 1. a relation, relative, kinsman; pl. bandhū J IV.301; PvA 86 (= ñāti) & bandhavo Nd^2 455 (where Nd^1 11 in id. p. reads bandhū). — **Ādicca°** kinsman of the Sun, an Ep. of the Buddha Vin II.296; A II.17; Sn 54, 915, 1128, cp. Nd^2 152^b; Vv 24^{13}; 78^{10}, cp. VvA 116. — *Four* kinds of relations enum^d at Nd^1 11, viz. ñāti°, gotta°, manta° (where Nd^2 455 reads mitta°), sippa°. — 2. Ep. of Brahmā, as ancestor of the brahmins DA I.254: see below °pāda. — 3. (°-) connected with, related to, dealing with [cp. Vedic amṛta-bandhu RV X.72^5] S I.123 (pamatta°); 128; Sn 241, 315, 430, 911; J IV.525; Miln 65 (kamma°); SnA 192 (veda°). — f. bandhunī J VI.47 (said of the town of Mithilā (rāja°); expl^d by C. as "rāja-ñātakeh'eva puṇṇā").
-pāda the foot of Brahma, from which the Sūdras are said to have originated (cp. Sk. pādaja), in cpd. bandhupād'apacca "offering from the foot of the kinsman," applied as contemptuous epithet to the Samaṇas by a Brahmin D I.90; M I.334; S IV.117.

Bandhuka (adj.) [fr. bandhu] 1. the plant Pentapetes phœnicea J IV.279 (°puppha, evidently only a contraction of bandhu-jīvaka, cp. C. bandhujīvaka-puppha; although Sk. bandhūka is given as syn. of bandhujīva at Halāyudha 2, 53). — 2. in bandhuka-roga M II.121 prob. to be read paṇḍuka°, as v. l. BB; see paṇḍuroga.

Bandhujīvaka [cp. Class. Sk. bandhujīva] the plant Pentapetes phœnicea M II.14 (°puppha): D II.111 (id.); J IV.279; Vism 174; DhsA 14; VvA 43, 161.

Bandhumant (adj.) [fr. bandhu, cp. Vedic bandhumant] having relatives, rich in kinsmen; only as Np. m bandhumā N. of father of the Buddha Vipassin D II.11 = Vism 433; f. bandhumatī N. of mother of the Buddha Vipassin ibid.; also N. of a town D II.12 (capital of king Bandhumā); SnA 190 = J IV.388 (where the latter has Vettavatī), and a river SnA 190 = J IV.388 (: Vettavatī).

Bandhuvant (adj.) [bandhu + vant] having relatives, rich in relatives J VI.357.

Babbaja [cp. Vedic balbaja, doubtful whether it belongs to Lat. bulbus; for the initial b. very often p. is found: see pabbaja] a sort of coarse grass or reed, used to make slippers, etc. Vin I.190; D II.55; S II.92; III.137; IV.158; A II.211; Dh 345; DhA IV.55.
-pādukā a slipper out of b. grass DhA III.451. **-lāyaka** cutter or reaper of grass S III.155; A III.365.

Babbu (& °ka) Epic [Sk. babhruka a kind of ichneumon; Vedic babhru brown, cp. Lat. fiber = beaver, further connection "bear," see Walde, *Lat. Wtb.* s. v. fiber] a cat J I.480 (= biḷāra C.) = DhA II.152.

Babbhara [onomat., cp. Sk. balbalā-karoti to stammer or stutter, barbara = Gr. βάρβαρος stuttering, people of an unknown tongue, balbūtha Np. "stammerer"; also Lat. balbus, Ger. plappern, E. blab; **babbhara** is a redupl. formation fr. *bhara-bhara = barbara, cp. *J.P.T.S.* 1889, 209; Geiger, *P.Gr.* § 20] imitation of a confused rumbling noise M I.128. — Cp. also P. mammana and sarasara.

Barihin [cp. Sk. barhin] a peacock J IV.497.

Barihisa (nt.) [Vedic barhis] the sacrificial grass D I.141; M I.344; A II.207; Pug 56.

Bala^1 (nt.) [Vedic bala, most likely to Lat. de-bilis "without strength" (cp. E. debility, P. dubbala), and Gr. βέλτιστος (superl.) = Sk. baliṣṭha the strongest. The Dhātupāṭha (273) defines b. with pāṇane. At DhsA 124 bala is understood as "na kampati"] 1. strength, power, force D II.73; A I.244; Th 1, 188; Dh 109 (one of the 4 blessings, viz. āyu, vaṇṇa, sukha, bala; cp. DhA II.239); Pv I.5^{12} (= kāya-bala PvA 30); I.7^6; VvA 4 (iddhi°); PvA 71 (id.), 82 (kamma°). — Of cases used as adv. balasā (instr.) is mentioned by Trenckner at Miln 430 (notes), cp. Prk. balasā (Pischel, *Gr.* § 364). yathā balaṇ according to one's power, i. e. as much as possible PvA 1, 54. The comp^n form of bala in conn. with **kṛ** is balī°, e. g. dubbalīkaraṇa making weak M III.4; Pug 59, 68; °karaṇin id. D III.183. — *adj.* bala strong J V.268, abala weak Sn 770, 1120, dubbala id. S I.222; J II.154; Nd^1 12; PvA 55; compar. °tara M I.244, nt. n. abalaṇ weakness S I.222. — 2. an army, military force Mhvs 25, 57; SnA 357. See cpds. below. — Eight balāni or strong points are 1. of young children (ruṇṇa-balaṇ). — 2. of womanhood (kodha°). — 3. of robbers (āvudha°). 4. of kings (issariya°), — 5. of fools (ujjhatti°). — 6. of wise men (nijjhatti°). — 7. of the deeply learned (paṭisankhāna°). — 8. of samaṇas & brāhmaṇas (khanti°) A IV.223 (where used as adj. -° strong in . . .); cp. Sn 212, 623. — Five balāni of women are: rūpabalaṇ, bhoga°, ñāti°, putta°, sīla° S IV.246-8. The five-fold force (balaṇ pañca-vidhaṇ) of a king J V.120, 121 consists of bāhābalaṇ strength of arms, bhoga° of wealth, amacca° of counsellors, abhijacca° of high birth, paññā° the force of wisdom; in the religious sense five balāni or powers are commonly enumd: saddhābalaŋ, viriya°, sati°, samādhi°, paññā° A III.12; D II.120; M II.12, III.296; S III.96, 153; IV.366, V.219, 249; Ps II.56, 86, 166, 174, 223; II.84, 133, 168 etc. They correspond to the 5 indriyāni and are developed with them. S V.219, 220; Nett 31; they are cultivated to destroy the five uddhambhāgiyāni saŋyojanāni S V.251. They are freq. referred to in instructions of the Buddha about the constituents of the "Dhamma," culminating in the eightfold Path, viz. cattāro satipaṭṭhānā, samappadhānā, cattāro iddhipādā, pañcindriyani, p. balāni, sattabojjhangāni, ariyo aṭṭhangiko maggo e. g. S III.96; Ps II.56; Nd[1] 13 = 360 = Nd[2] 420; Nd[2] s. v. satipaṭṭhāna; and passim. [Cp. BSk. catvāra ṛddhipādāh pañc' endriyāni p. balāni, sapta bodhyangāni etc. Divy 208.] Two balāni are specially mentioned A I.52 (paṭisankhānabalaŋ and bhāvanā°), also D III.213, followed here by the other "pair" satibalaŋ and samādhi°. There are four balāni of the ariyasāvaka, by which he overcomes the five fears (pañca bhayāni q. v.); the four are paññābalaŋ, viriya°, anavajja° sangāha° A IV.363 sq., as given at A II.141, also the foll. 3 groups of cattāri balāni:—(1) saddhābalaŋ, viriya°, sati°, samādhi°, cp. D III.229. —(2) sati° samādhi, anavajja°, sangāha°. (3) paṭisankhāna°, bhāvanā°, anavajja°, sangāha°. — For 4 balāni see also D III.229 note, and for paṭisankhānabala (power of computation) see *Dhs. trsl.* 1353. The ten balāni of the Tathāgata consist of his perfect comprehension in ten fields of knowledge A V.32 sq.; M I.69; Nd[2] 466; Miln 105, 285; VbhA 397. — In a similar setting 10 powers are given as consisting iṅ the knowledge of the Paṭiccasamuppāda at S II.27, 28. — The balāni of the sāvaka are distinct from those of the Tathāgatha: Kvu 228 sq. — There are seven balāni D III.253, and seven khīṇāsava-balāni 283 i. e. saddhābalaŋ, viriya° sati°, samādhi°, paññā°, hiri° and ottappa°. The same group is repeated in the Abhidhamma; Dhs 58, 95, 102; DhsA 126. The Ps. also enumerates seven khīṇāsavabalāni I.35; and sixty-eight balāni II.168 sq.

-agga front of an army, troops in array D I.6; Vin IV.107, cp. DA I.85. -ânīka (adj.) with strong array Sn 623; Dh 399 (cp. DhA IV.164). -kāya a body of troops, an army cp. Fick, *Sociale Gliederung* p. 52 note; (also in BSk. e. g. Divy 63, 315) A I.109; IV.107, 110; S I.58; J I.437 (°ŋ saŋharati to draw up troops); II.76; III.319; V.124; VI.224, 451; DhA I.393; PugA 249. -koṭṭhaka fortress, camp J I.179; Mhvs 25, 29. -(k)kāra application of force, violence J I.476; II.421; III.447; instr. °ena by force PvA 68, 113. -gumba a serried troop J II.406. -cakka wheel of power, of sovereignty Dpvs VI.2. -ṭṭha a military official, palace guard, royal messenger Miln 234, 241, 264, 314; Mhvs 34, 17. -da strength-giving S I.32; Sn 297. -dāyin id. A II.64. -deva "God of strength" N. of the elder brother of Kaṇha J IV.82; Nd[1] 89, 92 (Vāsudeva+); Vism 233 (id). -(p)patta grown-strong DhsA 118 (v. l. phala°). -vāhana troops, an army J II.319, IV.170, 433; VI.391, 458. -vīra a hero in strength Vv 53[1], cp. VvA 231. -sata for palāsata, q. v. (cp. *J.P.T.S.* 1908, 108 note).

Bala[2] [cp. *Sk. bala: Halāyudha 5, 23; & P. balākā] a species of carrion crow J V.268; also in cpd. bal'ankapāda having crow's feet, i. e. spreading feet (perhaps for balāka°?) J VI.548 (C. expln by pattharita-pāda, read patthārita°).

Balaka (adj.) [fr. bala] strong; only in kisa° of meagre strength, weakly M I.226; and dub° weak M I.435. Cp. balika.

Balatā (f.) [abstr. fr. bala] strength, lit. strength-quality M I.325.

Balati [fr. **bal**, as in bala] to live KhA 124 (in def. of bālā as "balanti ananti ti bālā").

Balatta (nt.) [abstr. fr. bala, cp. balatā] strength, only in cpd. dubbalatta weakness J II.154.

Balavatā (f.) [abstr. fr. balavant; cp. Epic Sk. balavattā] strength, force (also in military sense) J II.369 (ārakkhassa b.); Miln 101 (kusalassa & akusalassa kammassa b.).

Balavant (adj.) [fr. bala] strong, powerful, sturdy M I.244 (purisa) S I.222; J II.406; DhA II.208; VvA 35; PvA 94. Comparative balavatara Miln 131; f. °a(n)tarī Sdhp 452. In compn balava°, e. g. °gavā sturdy oxen M I.226; °vippaṭisāra deep remorse PvA 14. °balava very strong J II.406. -balavaŋ as nt. adv. "exceedingly," in cpd. balav' âbalavaŋ very (loud and) strong Vin II.1 (= suṭṭhu balavaŋ C.), and °paccūse very early in the morning Vism 93, and °paccūsa-samaye id J I.92; DhA I.26.

Balasata see palasata.

Balākā (f.) [cp. Vedic balākā, perhaps to Lat. fulica, Gr. φαλαρίς a water fowl, Ohg. pelicha = Ger. belche] a crane Th I, 307; J II.363; III.226; Miln 128 (°ānaŋ megha-saddena gabbhâvakkanti hoti); Vism 126 (in simile, megha-mukhe b. viya); DA I.91 (v. l. baka).

Bali [cp. Vedic bali; regarding etym. Grassmann connects it with **bhṛ**] 1. religious offering, oblation D II.74 (dhammika); A IV.17, 19; Sn 223; Mhvs 36, 88 (particularly to subordinate divinities, cp. *Mhvs. trsl*n 263); DhA II.14 (v. l. °kamma). —pañca° the fivefold offering, i. e. ñāti°, atithi°, pubbapeta°, rāja°, devatā°, offering to kinsfolk, guests, the departed, the king, the gods; A II.68; III.45. — 2. tax, revenue (cp. Zimmer, *Altind. Leben* 166 & Fick, *Sociale Gliederung* 75) D I.135, 142; J I.199 (daṇḍa° fines & taxes), 339; DhA I.251 (daṇḍa°). — 3. Np. of an Asura D II.259.

-kamma offering of food to bhūtas, devas & others J I.169, 260; II.149, 215; IV.246 (offering to tutelary genii of a city. In this passage the sacrifice of a human being is recommended); V.99, 473; SnA 138; Mhbv 28. -karaṇa oblation, offering of food PvA 81; VvA 8 (°pīṭha, reading doubtful, v. l. valli°). -kāraka offering oblations J I.384. -°nkatā one who offers (the five) oblations A II.68. -paṭiggāhaka receiving offerings, worthy of oblations J II.17 (yakkha; interpreted by Fick, *Sociale Gliederung* 79 as "tax-collector," hardly justified); f. °ikā A III.77 (devatā), 260 (id.), cp. BSk. balipratigrāhikā devatā Divy 1. -pīḷita crushed with taxes J V.98. -puṭṭha a crow (cp. Sk. balipuṣṭha "fed by oblations") Abhp 638. -vadda (cp. Sk. balivarda, after the Pali?) an ox, esp. an ox yoked to the plough or used in ploughing (on similes with b. see *J.P.T.S.* 1907, 349) S I.115, 170; IV.163 sq., 282 sq.; A II.108 sq.; Sn p. 13 (cp. SnA 137); Dh 152 = Th 1, 1025; J I.57; V.104 (Sāliyo b. phālena pahaṭo); Vism 284 (in simile of their escape from the ploughman); DhA I.24 (dhuraŋ vahanto balivaddassa, v. l. balibaddassa); VvA 258 (vv. ll. °baddha & °bandha). The spelling balibadda occurs at Vin IV.312. -sādhaka tax collector, tax gatherer J IV.366; V.103 sq. -haraṇa taking oblations A V.79 (°vanasaṇḍa).

Balika (adj.) [fr. bala] strong; only in der. balikataraŋ (compar.) adv. in a stronger degree, more intensely, more Miln 84; & dubbalika weak ThA 211. Cp. balaka.

Balin (adj.) [fr. bala] strong Th I, 12 (paññā°); Vv 64[7]; Dh 280; J III.484; VI.147.

Balisa & **Baḷisa** (m. & nt.) [cp. Sk. baḍiśa] a fish-hook S II.226 = IV.158 (āmisa-gataŋ b.); Nd[2] 374 (kāma°,

v. l. palisa); J I.482 sq.; III.283; IV.195; V.273 sq., 389; VI.416; Miln 412; SnA 114 (in expl° of gala Sn 61); ThA 280, 292; VbhA 196 (in comparison); Sdhp 610. On use in similes cp. *J.P.T.S.* 1907, 115.
 -maŋsikā (f.) "flesh-hooking," a kind of torture M I.87; III.164; A I.47; II.122; Nd¹ 154; Nd² 604; Miln 197. -yaṭṭhi angling rod DhA III.397.

Balī° = bala° in comb° with **bhū** & **kṛ**, see bala.

Balīyati [Denom. fr. bala, cp. BSk. balīyati MVastu I.275] to have strength, to grow strong, to gain power, to overpower Sn 770 (=sahati parisahati abhibhavati Nd¹ 12, cp. 361); J IV.84 (vv. ll. khalī° & paliyy°; C. expl° by avattharati) = Pv II.6¹ (=balavanto honti vaḍḍhanti abhibhavanti PvA 94); J VI.224 (3rd pl. balīyare; C. abhibhavati, kuppati, of the border provinces); Nett 6 (vv. ll. bali°, pali°; C. abhibhavati).

Balya¹ (nt.) [der. fr. bala] belonging to strength, only in cpd. dub° weakness M I.364; Pug 60; also spelt **dub-balla** M I.13. — abl. dubbalyā as adv. groundlessly, without strong evidence Vin IV.241 (cp. *J.P.T.S.* 1886, 129).

Balya² [fr. bāla, cp. P. & Sk. bālya] foolishness, stupidity Dh 63 (v. l. bālya); J III.278 (C. bālya); DhA II.30.

Baḷavā (f.) [cp. Vedic vadavā] a mare, only in cpd. °mukha the mare's mouth, i. e. an entrance to Niraya (cp. Vedic vaḍavâgni & vaḍavāmukha) Th 1, 1104 (trsl. "abyss-discharged mouth," cp. *Brethren*, p. 418).

Baḷīyakkha [etym. ?] a species of birds J VI.539.

Bahati¹ [bṛh¹] to pull, see ab°, ub°, nib°, & cp. udabbahe, pavāḷha.

Bahati² [baŋh doublet of bṛh²] to strengthen, increase, see brūhana (upa°); otherwise only in pp. **bāḷha** (q. v.). The Dhtp (344, cp. Dhtm 506) expl°ˢ "baha braha brūha: vuddhiyaŋ."

Bahati³ [a Pali root, to be postulated as der. fr. bahi in sense of "to keep out"] only in Caus. formations: to keep outside, lit. to make stay outside or away. See bāhā 2; bāheti, paribāhati.

Bahala (adj.) [cp. Class. Sk. bahala & Ved. bahula] dense, thick Vin II.112; J I.467 (°palāpa-tumba a measure thickly filled with chaff); II 91; Miln 282; Vism 257 (°pūva, where KhA 56 omits bahala), 263 (opp. tanuka); KhA 62 (°kuthita-lākhā thickly boiled, where in id. p. Vism 261 has accha-lākhā, i. e. clear); DhA IV.68; VvA 162 (=aḷāra). —subahala very thick Miln 258 (rajojalla).

Bahalatta (nt.) [abstr. fr. above] thickness, swollen condition, swelling J I.147.

Bahi (adv.) [cp. Vedic bahis & bahir; the s(ḥ) is restored in doubling of cons. in comp° like bahig-gata Vv 50¹⁵, in bahiddhā and in lengthening of i as bahī J V.65] outside: 1. (adv.) J I.361 (°dvāre-gāma a village outside the city gates); Pv I.10²; DhA III.118; PvA 24, 61. — 2. (prep.) with *acc.* (direction to) J I.298 (°gāmaŋ); with *loc.* (place where) °dvāra-koṭṭhake outside the gate M II.92; A III.31; °nagare outside the city J II.2; PvA 39, 47; °vihāre outside the monastery DhA I.315.
 -gata gone outside (i. e. into worldly affairs, or according to VvA 213 engaged with the bahiddh' ārammaṇāni) Vv 50¹⁵ (abahiggata-mānasa with his mind not gone outside himself). **-nikkhamana** going outside of (abl.), leaving Vism 500 (mātukucchito bahinikkhamanaŋ mūlakaŋ dukkhaŋ).

Bahiddhā (adv.) [fr. bahi, cp. Vedic bahirdhā, formation in °dhā, like ekadhā, sattadhā etc. of numerals] outside (adv. & prep.) D I.16; II.110; S I.169; III.47, 103; IV.205; V.157; Vin III.113 (°rūpa opp. ajjhatta-rūpa); Sn 203; VbhA 260 (kāye); DhA I.211 (c. gen); III.378 (sāsanato b.); DhsA 189. —ajjhatta° inside & outside, personal-external see ajjhatta. — The bahiddh' ārammaṇāni (objects of thought concerning that which is external) are the outward sense-objects in the same meaning as bāhirāni āyatanāni are distinguished fr. ajjhattikāni āyatanāni (see āyatana 3 and ārammaṇa 3). They are discussed at Vism 430 sq.; cp. Dhs 1049. — The phrase "ito bahiddhā" refers to those outside the teaching of the Buddha ("outside this our doctrine"), e. g. at D I.157; S I.133; A IV.25; Dhs 1005.

Bahu (adj.) [Vedic bahu, doubtful whether to Gr. παχύς; fr. bṛh² to strengthen, cp. upabrūhana, paribbūḷha] much, many, large, abundant; plenty; in comp° also: very, greatly (°-) instr. sg. bahunā Dh 166; nom. pl. bahavo Vin III.90; Dh 307, & bahū Dh 53; J IV.366; V.40; VI.472; Bu 2, 47; Pv IV.1⁴; Mhvs 35, 98; PvA 67; nt. pl. **bahūni** Sn 665, 885; gen. dat. **bahunnaŋ** S I.196; Sn 503, 957, & bahūnaŋ J V.446; Kvu 528 (where id. p. M I.447 reads bahunnaŋ); instr. **bahūhi** PvA 241; loc. **bahūsu** PvA 58. — nt. nom. **bahu** Dh 258; **bahuŋ** PvA 166, & **bahud** in comp° bahud-eva (d may be euphonic) J I.170; Bu 20, 32. As nt. n. **bahuŋ** a large quantity A II.183 (opp. appaŋ); abl. **bahumhā** J V.387. As adv. **bahu** so much Pv II.13¹¹. — Compar. bahutara greater, more, in greater number A I.36 (pl. bahutarā, opp. appakā); II.183; S V.457, 466; J II.293; VI.472; Pv II.1¹⁷; Miln 84; PvA 38, 76. — In composition with words beginning with a vowel (in sandhi) bahu as a rule appears as bavh° (for bahv°, see Geiger, *P.Gr.* § 49, 1), but the hiatus form bahu is also found, as in bahu-itthiyo J I.398 (besides bahutthika); bahu-amaccā J I.125; bahu-āyāsa (see below). Besides we have the contracted form bahû as in bahûpakāra, etc.).
 -ābādha (bavh°) great suffering or illness, adj. full of sickness, ailing much M II 94; A I.107; II.75, 85; Miln 65; Sdhp 89 (cp. 77). **-āyāsa** (bahu°) great trouble Th 2, 343. —**(i)tthika** (bahutthika) having many women Vin II.256; S II.264. **-ûdaka** containing much water J III.430 (f. bahūdikā & bahodikā). **-ûpakāra** of great service, very helpful, very useful S IV.295; V.32; M III.253; It 9; Vin V.191; J I.121; Pv IV.1⁵⁶; PvA 114. **-odaka** (bavh°) = °ûdaka Th 1, 390. **-kata** (a.) benevolent, doing service Vin IV.37, 212. (b) much moved or impressed by (instr.), paying much attention to Vin I.247. **-karaṇiya** having much to do, busy D II.76; Vin I.71; S II.215; A III.116; DA I.237. **-kāra** (a) favour Dāvs IV.39 (b) doing much, of great service, very helpful M I.43, 170; A I.123, 132; II.126; S V.67; Pv II.12¹⁹; J IV.422; Miln 264. **-kāratta** service, usefulness KhA 91. **-kicca** having many duties, very busy Vin I.71; D I.106; II.76; S II.215; A III.116; DA I.237. **-khāra** a kind of alkali (product of vegetable ash) J VI.454. **-jañña** see bāhu°. **-jana** a mass of people, a great multitude, a crowd, a great many people D I.4; It 78; J VI.358; Pug 30, 57; Pv II.7⁷; PvA 30. At some passages interpreted by Bdhgh as "the unconverted, the masses," e. g. D I.47, expl^d at DA I.143 by "assutavā andha-bāla puthujjana"; Dh 320 (bahujjana), expl^d at DhA IV.3 by "lokiya-mahājana." **-jāgara** very watchful Dh 29 (=mahante sativepulle jāgariye ṭhita DhA I.262); Sn 972 (cp. Nd¹ 501). **-jāta** growing much, abundant J VI.536. **-ṭhāna** (-cintin) of far-reaching knowledge, whose thoughts embrace many subjects J III.306; IV.467; V.176. **-dhana** with many riches PvA 97. **-patta** having obtained much, loaded with gifts Vin IV.243. **-pada** many-footed, a certain order of creatures, such as centipedes, etc. Vin II.110; III.52; A II.34; It 87. **-(p)phala** rich in fruit Sn 1134, cp. Nd² 456. **-(b)bīhi** t.t g., name of cpds. with adj. sense, indicating possession. **-bhaṇḍa** having an abundance of goods, well-to-do Vin III.138; KhA 241. **-bhāṇika** = °bhāṇin PvA 283. **-bhāṇitā** garrulousness PvA

283. -bhāṇin garrulous A III.254, 257; Dh 227. -bhāva largeness, richness, abundance DhA II.175. -bherava very terrible A II.55. -maccha rich in fish J III.430. -mata much esteemed, venerable Cp. VI.7; PvA 117. -manta very tricky DhA II.4 (v. l. māya). -māna respect, esteem, veneration J I.90; PvA 50, 155, 274. -māya full of deceit, full of tricks J V.357 (cp. °manta). -vacana (tt.g.) the plural number J IV.173; PvA 163. -vāraka the tree Cordia myxa Abhp 558. -vighāta fraught with great pain Th 2, 450. -vidha various, multiform Cp. XV.7; Pgdp 37. -sacca see bāhu°. -(s)suta having great knowledge, very learned, well-taught D I.93, 137; III.252, 282; J I.199; IV.244; A I.24; II.22, 147, 170, 178; III.114; Sn 58 (see Nd² 457); It 60, 80; Th I, 1026; Dh 208; Vin II.95; J I.93; Miln 19; ThA 274, 281; SnA 109, 110. -(s)sutaka of great knowledge (ironical) D I.107 (see *Dial.* I.132).

Bahuka (adj.) [fr. bahu] great, much, many, abundant J III.368 (b. jano most people, the majority of p.); V.388; IV.536; Mhvs 36, 49; PvA 25 (gloss for pahūta Pv I.5²); DhA II.175.—nt. **bahukaŋ** plenty, abundance A II.7 = Pug 63; Vism 403 (opp. thokaŋ). Compar. bahukataraŋ more J II.88 (v. l. bahutaraŋ).

Bahukkhattuŋ (adv.) [bahu + khattuŋ, like sattakkhattuŋ, ti° etc.] many times Miln 215.

Bahutta (nt.) [cp. Sk. bahutvaŋ] multiplicity, manifoldedness VbhA 320 (cetanā°).

Bahudhā (adv.) [fr. bahu, cp. Vedic bahudhā] in many ways or forms S V.264 (hoti he becomes many), 288; M I.34; Sn 966; Pv IV.1⁵² (= bahūhi pakārehi PvA 241); Mhvs 31, 73; Dāvs V.68.

Bahula (adj.) [usually -°, as °- only in cpd. °ājīva] much, abundant, nt. abundance (°-); full of, rich in, fig. given to, intent on, devoted to D II.73; S I.199, 202; A III.86 (pariyatti°), 432 (āloka°); IV.35; It 27, 30; J IV.5 (vināsa°), 22; PvA 80 (chārik' angāra°). —sayana° as much as "particular in one's choice of resting place" Miln 365 nt. **bahulaŋ** (-°) in the fullness of, full of S III.40 (nibbidā°). The compⁿ form with karoti (& kamma) is bahulī° (q. v.). Cp. bāhulla.
-**ājīva** living in abundance (opp. lūkh' ājīvin) D III.44, 47.

Bahula (nt.) [= preceding] N. of a lucky die J VI.281.

Bahulī° [rare in Ep. Sk.; when found, diff. in meaning] in compⁿ with **kar** = bahula (adj.) + **kar**, lit. "to make much of," i. e. to practise, in foll. words: °kata (pp.) practised (frequently), usually combᵈ with bhāvita S II.264; IV.200, 322; V.259; A I.6; Vism 267 (= punappunaŋ kata); °katatta (nt.) practice D II.214; °kamma continuous practice, an act often repeated M I.301; DhsA 406 (= punappuna-karaṇa); °karoti to take up seriously, to practise, devote oneself to (acc.) M I.454; A I.275; III.79; S IV.322; DhA III.356 (sevati +); VbhA 291; °kārā zealous exercise, practice M III.25 sq. (tab-bahulī° to this end).

Bahuso (adv.) [cp. Sk. bahuśaḥ] repeatedly PvA 107.

Bahūta (adj.) [for pahūta = Sk. prabhūta] abundant, much Th 2, 406 (°ratana, so read for bahuta°), 435 (for bahutadhana); J III.425 (bahūtam ajjaŋ "plenty of food"; ajja = Sk. ādya, with Kern, *Toev.* s. v. bahūta for T. bahūtamajjā, which introd. story takes as bahūtaŋ = balaŋ ajja, with ajjā metri causā. C. explˢ however as mataka-bhattaŋ); VI.173 (°tagarā mahī); Pv II.7⁵ (v. l. for pahūta, cp. pahūtika).

Bahūtaso (adv.) [der. fr. bahūta, cp. Sk. prabhūtaśaḥ] in abundance J III.484 (where C. explⁿ with bahūtaso is faulty and should perhaps be read pahūtaso); VI.538.

Bākucī (f.) [cp. *Sk. bākucī] the plant Vernonia anthelminthica Abhp 586.

Bāṇa [cp. Vedic bāṇa] an arrow Mbhv 19.

Bādha [fr. **bādh**] lit. pressing (together), oppression, hindrance, annoyance J VI.224. Cp. sam°.

Bādhaka (adj.) [fr. **bādh**] oppressing, harassing, injurious Vism 496 (dukkhā aññaŋ na °ŋ); VvA 214; PvA 175.

Bādhakatta (nt.) [abstr. fr. bādhaka] the fact of being oppressive or injurious Vism 496.

Bādhati [Vedic bādhate, **bādh**; Idg. ***bheidh** to force, cp. Goth. baidjan, Ohg. beitten. See Walde, *Lat. Wtb.* s. v. fido. In Pali there seems to have taken place a confusion of roots **bādh** and **bandh**, see bādheti & other derivations] to press, weigh on; oppress, hinder, afflict, harm D II.19; J I.211; IV.124; Vism 400; DhA I.24. grd. badhitabba ThA 65; Pass. bādhiyati to be afflicted, to become sore, to suffer SnA 481; ThA 282; ppr. bādhiyamāna PvA 33 (so read for °ayamāna), 69.—Caus. bādheti; pp. **bādhita** (q. v.). Cp. vi°.

Bādhana (nt.) [fr. **bādh**] 1. snaring, catching (of animals etc.) S V.148; J I.211.—2. hindrance DA I.132.—3. affliction, injury, hurting Vism 495; PvA 116.

Bādhita [pp. of bādhati] oppressed, pressed hard, harassed Dh 342 (but taken by C. as "trapped, snared," baddha DhA IV.49); ThA 65.

Bādhin (adj.) (-°) [fr. **bādh**] (lit. oppressing), snaring; as n. a trainer Vin II.26 (Ariṭṭha gaddha°-pubba); IV.218 (id.).

Bādheti [Caus. of bādhati; the confusion with bandhati is even more pronounced in the Caus. According to Kern, *Toev.* s. v. we find bādhayati for bandhayati in Sk. as well] 1. to oppress, afflict, hurt, injure J VI.224; PvA 198 (bādheyya = heṭhayeyya). grd. **bādhanīya** PvA 175. Cp. **paribādheti** in same sense.—2. to bind, catch, snare Th 1, 454; 2, 299; J II.51 (aor. bādhayiŋsu); IV.342; V.295, 445 (pot. bādhaye = bādheyya C. on p. 447; vv. ll. baddh°, bandh°). grd. bādhetabba S IV.298.

Bārāṇaseyyaka (adj.) [fr. Bārāṇasī] of Benares, coming fr. B. (a kind of muslin) D II.110; III.260.

Bāla¹ (adj.) [cp. Sk. bāla (rarely Vedic, more freq. in Ep. & Class. Sk.); its orig. meaning is "young, unable to speak," cp. Lat. infans, hence "like a child, childish, infantile"] 1. ignorant (often with ref. to ignorance in a moral sense, of the common people, the puthujjana), foolish (as contrasted with paṇḍita cp. the Bāla-paṇḍita-sutta M III.163 sq.; D II.305 sq.; Vism 499, and contrasts at Sn 578; Dh 63, 64; Pv IV.3³²; Dhs 1300), lacking in reason, devoid of the power to think & act right. In the latter sense sometimes coupled with andha (spiritually blind), as andhabāla stupid & ignorant, mentally dull, e. g. at DhA I.143; II.89; PvA 254.—A fanciful etym. of b. at KhA 124 is "balanti ananti ti bālā." Other refs.: D I.59, 108; S I.23; A I.59, 68, 84; II.51, 180; Sn 199, 259, 318, 578, 879; It 68; Dh 28, 60 sq., 71 sq., 206 sq., 330; J I.124 (lola° greedy—foolish); V.366 (bālo āmaka-pakkaŋ va); Vv 83⁵; Pv I.8²; IV.1²⁹; Pug 33; Nd¹ 163, 286 sq., 290; SnA 509 (= aviddasu); PvA 193. Compar. bālatara J III.278, 279; VvA 326.—2. young, new; newly risen (of the sun): °ātāpa the morning sun DA I.287; DhA I.164; Mhbv 25; °vasanta "early spring" (= Citramāsa), N. of the first one of the 4 winter months (gimha-māsā) KhA 192; -suriya the newly risen sun J V.284; PvA 137, 211.—3. a child; in wider application meaning a youth under 16 years of age (cp. Abhp 251) DA I.134. Cp. bālaka.

-nakkhatta N. of a certain "feast of fools," i. e. carnival DhA I.256. -saṅgatacārin one who keeps company with a fool Dh 207.

Bāla[2] [for vāla] the hair of the head PvA 285 (°koṭimatta not even one tip of the hair; gloss BB vālagga°).

Bālaka [fr. bāla] 1. boy, child, youth S I.176; ThA 146 (Ap. v.44: spelt °akka); Sdhp 351. — f. bālikā young girl ThA 54 (Ap. v.1). — 2. fool DhsA 51 (°rata fond of fools).

Bālakin (adj.) [fr. bālaka] having fools, consisting of fools; f. °inī M I.373 (parisā).

Bālatā (f.) [abstr. to bāla] foolishness J I.101, 223.

Bālisika [fr. balisa] a fisherman S II.226; IV.158; J I.482; III.52 (cp. Fick. *Sociale Gliederung* p. 194); Miln 364, 412; DhA III.397.

Bālya (nt.) [fr. bāla] 1. childhood, youth S III.1. — 2. ignorance, folly Dh 63; J II.220 (=bāla-bhāva); III.278 (balya); PvA 40. Also used as *adj.* in compar. bālyatara more foolish, extremely foolish Vv 83[6] sq. = DhA I.30 (=bālatara, atisayena bāla VvA 326). — 3. weakness (?) J VI.295 (balya, but C. bālya = dubbala-bhāva).

Bāḷha (adj.) [Vedic bāḍha, orig. pp. of bahati[2]] strong; only as adv. °ŋ and °-, viz. — 1. bāḷhaŋ strongly, very much, excessively, too much, to satiety J II.293; VI.291 (i. e. too often, C. punappunaŋ); Miln 407; PvA 274. Comparative bāḷhataraŋ in a higher degree, even more, too much Vin II.270, 276; Miln 125. — 2. (°-) in bāḷha-gilāna very ill, grievously sick D I.72; A II.144; S V.303; DA I.212.

Bāḷhika (adj.) [fr. bāḷha], only in su° having excess of good things, very prosperous J V.214 (C. expl[s] by suṭṭhu aḍḍha).

Bāvīsati (num.) [bā = dvā, + vīsati] twenty-two Kvu 218; Miln 419; DhsA 2.

Bāhati see bāheti.

Bāhā (f.) [a specific Pali doublet of bāhu, q. v. It is on the whole restricted to certain phrases, but occurs side by side of bāhu in others, like pacchā-bāhaŋ & °bāhuŋ, bāhaŋ & bāhuŋ pasāreti] 1. the arm A II.67 = III.45 (°bala); Vin II.105; J III.62; V.215 (°mudu). pacchā-bāhaŋ arm(s) behind (his back) D I.245 (gāḷha-bandhanaŋ baddha). bāhaŋ pasāreti to stretch out the arm D I.222 = M I.252 ≈. bāhāyaŋ gahetvā taking (him or her) by the arm D I.221 sq.; M I.365 (nānā-bāhāsu g.); PvA 148. bāhā paggayha reaching or stretching out one's arms (as sign of supplication) D II.139; J V.267; PvA 92 and passim. — 2. not quite certain, whether "post" of a door or a "screen" (from bahati[3]), the former more likely. Only -° in ālambana° post to hold on to, a balustrade Vin II.120, 152; dvāra° door-post D II.190; Pv I.5[1]. Cp. bāhitikā.

-aṭṭhi (bāh°) arm-bone KhA 50. -paramparāya arm in arm Vin III.126.

Bāhika (adj.) [=bāhiya] foreign in °raṭṭha-vāsin living in a foreign country J III.432 (or is it N.? Cp. J VII. p. 94).

Bāhitatta (nt.) [abstr. fr. bāhita] keeping out, exclusion Nd[2] 464 (in expl[n] of word brāhmaṇa).

Bāhitikā (f.) [fr. bāhita, pp. of bāheti[1]] a mantle, wrapper (lit. "that which keeps out," i. e. the cold or wind) M II.116, 117.

Bāhiteyya [unclear; grd. of bāheti[1], but formed fr. pp.?] to be kept out (?) M I.328. The reading seems to be corrupt; meaning is very doubtful; Neumann trsl[s] "musst (mir) weichen."

Bāhiya (adj.) [fr. bahi, cp. bāhira and Vedic bāhya] foreign J I.421; III.432.

Bāhira (adj.) [fr. bahi, as Sk. bāhya fr. bahis, cp. also bāhiya] 1. external, outside (opp. abbhantara inside), outer, foreign D II.75; A IV.16; Dh 394 (fig. in meaning of 2); J I.125 (antara° inside & outside); 337 (out of office, out of favour, of ministers); VI.384 (bāhiraŋ karoti to turn out, turn inside out); Pv IV.1[1] (nagarassa b.); Miln 281 (°abbhantara dhana); VvA 68 (°kittibhāva fact of becoming known outside). —santara° (adj.) [=sa-antara] including the inward & outward parts D I.74; A III.25; Th I, 172; J I.125. — 2. external to the individual, objective (opp. ajjhattika subjective) M III.274 (cha āyatanā); J IV.402 (°vatthuŋ ayācitvā ajjhattikassa nāmaŋ gaṇhāti); Dhs 674 (cp. *trsl.* p. 207); Vbh 13; Miln 215; Vism 450. — 3. heretical, outsider in religious sense, non-Buddhist, freq. applied to the Brahmanic religion & their practice (samaya) Kvu 251 (+puthujjana-pakkhe ṭhita); DhA III.378 (=mana, i. e. Bhagavato sāsanato bahiddhā). — Cases as *adv.* bāhirato from outside, from a foreign country J I.121; bāhire outside (the Buddhist order) Dh 254.

-assāda finding his enjoyment in outward things A I.280 (Kern, *Toev.* s. v. suggests "inclined towards heretic views"). -āsa one whose wishes are directed outwards, whose desires are turned to things external Th I, 634. -kathā non-religious discourse, profane story Miln 24 (applied to the introductory chapter, thus "outside story" may be translated). -tittha doctrine of outsiders J III.473. -dāna gift of externals, gift of property as opposed to gift of the person J IV.401; VI.486; Dāvs III.33. -pabbajjā the ascetic life outside the community of the Buddha; Brahmanic saintly life (thus equal to isi-pabbajjā. cp. bāhiraka°). J III.352; IV.305. -bhaṇḍa property, material things, objects J IV.401. -mantā ritualistic texts (or charms) of religions other than the Buddha's J III.27. -rakkhā protection of external means S I.73. -lomi with the fleece outside (of a rug) Vin II.108. -samaya doctrine of the outsiders, i. e. Brahmins DhA III.392.

Bāhiraka (adj.) [=bāhira, but specialised in meaning bāhira 3] outsider, non-religious, non-Buddhist, heretic, profane S II.267; A I.73; III.107; Kvu 172 (isayo); VvA 67 (itthi).

-kathā unreligious discussion, profane story KhA 118 (cp. bāhirakathā). -tapa = foll. J I.390. -pabbajjā the ascetic life as led by disciples of other teachers than the Buddha, esp. Brahmanic (cp. bāhira° and BSk. bāhirako mārgaḥ, e. g. MVastu I.284; II.210; II.223) J III.364; DhA I.311.

Bāhiratta (nt.) [abstr. fr. bāhira] being outside (of the individual), externality Vism 450.

Bāhirima (adj.) [fr. bāhira, compar.-adversative formation] outer, external, outside Vin III.149 (b. māna external measure; opp. abbhantarima); J V.38 (opp. abbhantarima).

Bāhu [cp. Vedic bāhu, prob. to bahati[2]; cp. Gr. πῆχυς in same meaning, Ohg. buoc. It seems that bāhu is more frequent in later literature, whereas the by-form bāhā belongs to the older period] the arm J III.271 (bāhumā bāhuŋ pīḷentā shoulder to shoulder); Vism 192. -°ŋ pasāreti to stretch out the arm (cp. bāhaŋ) PvA 112; pacchā-bāhuŋ (cp. bāhaŋ) PvA 4 (gāḷha-bandhanaŋ bandhāpetvā).

-(p)pacālakaŋ (adv.) after the manner of one who swings his arms about Vin II.213 (see expl[n] at Vin IV.188).

Bāhujañña (adj.) [fr. bahu + jana, cp. sāmañña fr. samaṇa] belonging to the mass of people, property of many people or of the masses D II.106, 219; S II.107 = V.262; J I.29 (V.212). *Note.* The expression occurs only in stock phrase iddha phīta vitthārika bāhujañña.

Bāhulya (nt.) [fr. bahula, the Sk. form for P. bāhulla] abundance Sdhp 77.

Bāhulla (nt.) [fr. bahula] 1. abundance, superfluity, great quantity M I.171; A IV.87 (°kathā) A IV.87; Ps I.197; J I.81. — 2. luxurious living, swaggering, puffed up frame of mind Vin I.9, 59, 209; II.197; III.251. — See also **bāhulya** & **bāhullika.**

Bāhullika (adj.) [fr. bāhulla] living in abundance, swaggering, luxurious, spendthrift Vin I.9 (+padhāna-vibbhanto, as also J I.68, with which Kern, *Toev.* s. v. compares MVastu II.241 & III.329); II.197; III.250; M I.14; III.6; A I.71; III.108, 179 sq.; J I.68; III.363. The reading is often **bāhulika.**

Bāhusacca (nt.) [fr. bahu+sacca, which latter corresponds to a Sk. śrautya fr. **śru,** thus b. is the abstract to bahussuta. See on expl° of word Kern, *Toev.* s. v.] great learning, profound knowledge M I.445; A I.38 (so read for bahu°); II.218; Vin III.10; Dh 271; Vv 63[9].

Bāheti[1] [Caus. of bahati[3] or Denom. fr. bahi] to keep away, to keep outside, to ward off; only with ref. to pāpa (pāpaka) to keep away (from) sin S I.141 (bāhetvā pāpāni); Sn 519 = Nd[2] 464[a] (bāhetvā pāpakāni); Dh 267; a popular etymology of brāhmaṇa (pāpaŋ bahenti) D III.94 (bāhitvā, better bāhetvā, expl[d] by panuditvā DhA III.393; v. l. K vāh°). — pp. **bāhita** (q. v.). See also nib°, pari°.

Bāheti[2] [Caus. of bahati[4], cp. Sk. vāhayati] to carry, see sam° (sambāhana, meaning rubbing, stroking). Whether **atibāheti** belongs here, is doubtful.

Bidala (adj. n.) [cp. Sk. vidala in same meaning, fr. vi+**dal**] 1. a kind of pulse, split pea J IV.353 (=mugga), in °sūpa haricot soup J IV.352. — 2. a split bamboo cane, in °mañcaka a bedstead made of laths of split bamboo, the use of which is given as one of the characteristic features of the ascetic life Vin II.149; J I.9; DhA I.135.

Bindu [cp. Vedic bindu & vindu] 1. a drop, usually a drop of water Sn 392, 812 (uda°); J I.100; Vism 531 (madhu°); ThA 281; PvA 98 (udaka°). — 2. a spot (cp. SBE XVII.155) Vism 222 (°vicitvā gāvī a spotted cow). — 3. (as adj.) one of the eight qualities of perfect sound (brahma-ssara, with ref. to the voice of Brahmā and of Buddha, cp. aṭṭhanga), which are given at D II.211 = 227 as (saro hoti) vissaṭṭho ca viññeyyo ca mañjū ca savanīyo ca bindu [vv. ll. bandu & bhindu] ca avisārī ca gambhīro ca ninnādī ca. We may translate by "full, close, compact" (*Dial.* II.245 "continuous"). See also below °ssara.

-tthanī having breasts round as a bubble J V.215. **-bindu(ŋ)** drop by drop DA I.218. **-matī** (f.) Np. of a courtesan of Pāṭaliputta in the time of Asoka Miln 121 sq. **-matta** measuring a drop, even a drop PvA 100, 104 (eka °ŋ). **-sāra** Np. of king of India, father of Asoka Dpvs V.101; VI.15; Mhvs V.18, 19. **-ssara** a full rounded voice Sn 350 (referred by SnA to a Mahāpurisa); adj. having a full voice (see above bindu 3) Pv III.3[4] (T. vindu°, BB bindu°; PvA expl[ns] by avissaṭṭha-ssara sampiṇḍita-ssara, i. e. "continuous"); J II.439 (=bindhunā avisaṭena piṇḍitena sarena samannāgata C.); V.204, 299 (=sampiṇḍita-ghana-ssara); VI.518 = 581 (=piṇḍita-ssara C.).

Bimba (nt.) [cp. Class. Sk. bimba] 1. shape, image (=paṭimā VvA 168) S I.134 (trsl. "puppet"); V.217 (vimba); J V.452. In phrase **cittakataŋ bimbaŋ** it refers to the human body ("the tricked-out puppet-shape" *Brethren* 303): M II.64 = Th 1, 769 = Dh 147 = VvA 47, cp. DhA III.109 (=attabhāva). — 2. the red fruit of Momordica monadelpha, a species of Amaranth [cp. Sk. bimba & bimbī, a kind of gourd] J III.478; VI.457, 591; Vv 36[8] (kañcana°-vaṇṇa of the colour of the golden Bimba Dhp. at VvA 168 takes it as bimba[1] = paṭimā; DhA I.387 (°phala, with ref. to red lips). **bimboṭṭha** (f. °ī) (having) red lips J III.477; VI.590 (nigrodhapatta-bimb' oṭṭhī) ThA 133 (Ap. V.57). The Sk. vimbī according to Halāyudha 2, 48 is equal to oṣṭhī, a plant (Bryonia grandis ?).

-oṭṭhi see above 2. **-ohana** [second part either = *ūhana vāhana "carrying," or contracted form of odahana fr. ava+dhā, i. e. *odhana *ohana "putting down," or still more likely for ūhana as seen in ūhanati[2] 2 fr. ud+**hṛ** raising, lifting up] a pillow Vin I.47 (bhisi°); II.76, 150, 208, 200, 218; III.90, 119 (bhisi°); IV.279; S II.268; A III.240; VbhA 365; Vism 79. See also bhisi[1]. **-jāla** [BR. bimbajā ?] the Bimba tree, Momordica monadelpha (lit. net of b. fruits) J I.39; VI.497 (cp. p. 498 ratt' ankura-rukkhaŋ probably with v. l. to be read ratta-kuravaka°, see bimbi-jāla); Bu XVI.19.

Bimbaka = bimba 2; VvA 168.

Bimbi (or **bimbī**) [=Sk. bimbī, see bimba] gold, of golden colour DA I.280 = SnA 448 (in Bdhgh's fanciful etym. of king Bimbisāra, viz. bimbī ti suvaṇṇaŋ, sārasuvaṇṇa-sadisa-vaṇṇatāya B.).

-jāla the red amaranth tree, the Bodhi tree of the former Buddha Dhammadassin J I.39; V.155. At J VI.497. 498 the form is bimbajāla. The C. expl[n] gives ratta-kuravaka as a synonym.

Bila[1] (nt.) [Vedic bila, perhaps fr. **bhid** to break, cp. *K.Z.* 12, 123. Thus already expl[d] by Dhtp 489: bila bhedane] a hole, den, cave A II.33 = S III.85; Th 1, 189; Nd[1] 362; J I.480; II.53; VI.574 (=guhā C.); Miln 151; Sdhp 23. —**kaṇṇa°** orifice of the ear Vism 195; **vammīka°** ant's nest J IV.30; sota° = kaṇṇa° DhsA 310.

-āsaya (adj.) living in holes, a cave-dweller, one of the four classes of animals (bil°, dak°, van°, rukkh°) S III.85 = A II.33; Nd[1] 362; Bu II.97; J I.18.

Bila[2] (nt.) [identical with bila[1]] a part, bit J VI.153 (°sataŋ 100 pieces); abl. bilaso (adv.) bit by bit M I.58 = III.91 (v. l. vilaso). At J V.90 in cpd. migābilaŋ (maŋsaŋ) it is doubtful whether we should read mig'ābilaŋ (thus, as we have done, taking ābila = āvila), or migā-bilaŋ with a lengthened metri causā, as the C. seems to take it (migehi khādita-maŋsato atirittaŋ *koṭṭhāsaŋ*).

-kata cut into pieces, made into bits J V.266 (read macchā bilakatā yathā for macchābhīlā katā y.). The C. here (p. 272) expl[s] as *koṭṭhāsa*-kata; at J VI.111 however the same phrase is interpreted as *puñja*-kata, i. e. thrown into a heap (like fish caught by a fisherman in nets). Both passages are applied to fish and refer to tortures in Niraya.

Bila[3] [cp. Sk. viḍa] a kind of salt Vin I.202; M II.178, 181.

Bilanga [etym. doubtful; one compares both Sk. viḍanga the plant Embelia ribes, and vilanga the plant Erycibe paniculata] sour gruel J VI.365 (=kañjiya); usually in stock phrase **kaṇājaka bilanga-dutiya** (seed-cake ?) accompanied by sour gruel Vin II.77, 78; S I.90; A I.145; IV.392; J I.228; III.299; SnA 94; DhA III.10 (v. l. pilanka-°akaŋ); IV.77; VvA 222, 298 (bilanka°).

-thālika a certain torture, called "gruel-pot" (should there be any relation to bila-kata under bila[2] ?) A I.47; II.122; Nd[2] 604 (v. l. khil°); Miln 197, 290, 358 (all passages in standard setting).

Bilangika (adj.) living on sour gruel; N. of a class of brāhmaṇas at Rājagaha S I.164.

Billa [cp. Ved. bilva] fruit of the Bilva tree, Aegle marmelos or Bengal quince, only in *one* stock phrase where its size is compared with sizes of smaller fruits, and where it is preceded by āmalaka S I.150 = A IV.170

(vv. ll. villa, bila, beḷu, bilāla) = Sn p. 125 (vv. ll. pillā billā, billa; T. reading after SS billi). Cp. derivations bella & beluva.

Biḷāra [etym. uncertain, prob. a loan-word; cp. late Sk. biḍāla & see also P. biḷāla. The Prk. forms are birāla & virāla, f. birālī] a cat D II.83; M I.128, 334; S II.270; A III.122 (viḷāra); V.202, 289; Th I, 1138; J I.461 (as representing deceit), 480; V.406, 416, 418; Miln 118; DhA II.152; PugA 225. On biḷāra in similes cp. *J.P.T.S.* 1907, 116.
-**nissakkana** (-matta) (large enough) for a cat to creep through A V.195. -**bhastā** (a bag of) catskin M I.128 (expl^d by Bdhgh as "biḷāra-camma-pasibbako"); Th I, 1138. At both passages in similes.

Biḷārikā (f.) [cp. Sk. biḍālikā] a she-cat J III.265.

Biḷāla[1] [see biḷāra] a cat J I.110; II.244; VI.593. **pakkha**° a flying fox J VI.538.

Biḷāla[2] [see bila[3]] a kind of salt Abhp 461.

Biḷālī (f.) [f. of biḷāla = biḷāra, cp. Sk. biḍālī, also N. of a plant, see on Prk. chira-birālī Sk. kṣīra-biḍālī Pischel *Gr.* § 241] a bulbous plant, a tuber J IV.46 (= °vallī-kanda, cp. gloss latātanta on kalamba), 371 (= °kanda Com. p. 373); VI.578. Cp. takkaḷa.

Biḷibiḷikā (f.) [onomat. cp. E. babble] tittle-tattle S I.260 = Th I, 119. Mrs. Rh. D. (*Brethren* 106 n.) trsl^s "fingle-fangle," noting the commentator's paraphrase "vili-vilikriyā" (lit. sticky-sticky-action ?).

Bīja (nt.) [cp. Vedic bīja] 1. seed, germ, semen, spawn. Used very frequently in figurative sense: see on similes *J.P.T.S.* 1907, 116. — D I.135 (°bhatta seed-corn & food); III.44 (the five kinds: see below under °gāma); M I.457; S I.21, 134, 172, 227; III.54, 91; IV.315; A I.32 (ucchu°), 135, 223, 229, 239; III.404; IV.237; V.213 (ucchu°); Sn 77 (saddhā bījaŋ tapo vuṭṭhi, cp. SnA 142 sq., where a detailed discussion on bīja is found), 209, 235 (khīṇa° adj. fig.); J I.242 (tiṇa°-ādīni grass and other seeds), 281; Pv I.1[1]; Vism 555 (in simile); KhA 194 (on Sn 235, in another comparison); Sdhp 24, 270 sq., 318. **nibbatta**° (or nivatta°) (adj.) that which has dropped its seed (hence a lawful food) Vin I.215, cp. II.109; IV.35. — 2. element, in udaka° whose element is the water J VI.160.
-**gāma** seed-group, seed-kingdom, seed-creation (opp. bhūta-gāma). There are 5 kinds of seeds usually enum^d, e. g. at D I.5 (expl^d at DA I.77, trsl^n at *Dial.* I.6 and passim), viz. mūla°, khandha°, phalu°, agga°, bija°, or plants propagated by roots, cuttings, joints, buddings, shoots, seeds (*Dial.* III.40: tubers, shoots, berries, joints, seeds). The same set occurs at D III.44, 47; Vin IV.34; SnA 144. — Without ref. to the 5 kinds at M III.34; S V.46; Miln 33. -**jāta** species of seed S III.54. -**bīja** one of the 5 groups of edible or useful plants, falling under bījagāma. It is expl^d at Vin IV.35 & DA I.81 by the terms **pubbaṇṇa** (i. e. the seven dhaññāni or grains, sāli, vīhi, yava, godhūma, kangu, varaka, kudrūsa) and **aparaṇṇa** (i. e. beans and other leguminous plants, and gourds such as mugga, māsa, tila, kulattha, alābu, kumbhaṇḍa). -**sakaṭa** a cart (-load) of seeds SnA 137.

Bījaka [fr. bīja] scion, offspring Vin III.18. —**nīla**° a water-plant Vin III.276 (C. on Vin III.177).

Bījati & **Bījanī** are by-forms of **vījati** & **vījanī** (q. v.).

Bījin (-°) (adj.) [fr. bīja] having seed, only in cpd. eka° having one seed (for only *one* future life) left A I.233; S V.205; Nett 189, cp. A. IV.380; Kvu II.471, see also KvuA in *J.P.T.S.* 1889, 137.

Bībhaccha (adj.) [cp. Epic Sk. bibhatsa, bībhatsate to feel disgust. *Not* a des. fr. bādhate: see Walde, *Lat. Wtb.* s. v. fastidium] disgusting, awful, horrible, dreadful J II.276; IV.71 (°vaṇṇa), Sdhp 603. °dassana a disgusting sight, horrible to behold J I.171; PvA 32, 56, 68, 99 (: all with ref. to Petas). — The spelling **bhībhaccha** (after **bhī**) is sometimes found, e. g. at J I.61; IV.491; V.42.

Biraṇa [cp. Sk. vīraṇa & vīraṇī-mūla = uśīra Halāyudha 2, 467] a fragrant grass, Andropogon muricatum S III.137; (here represented as larger than the kusa & babbaja grasses, smaller than a tree).

Bujjhaka (adj.) [fr. **budh**] intelligent, prudent, judicious, in a° Dpvs IX.17, foolish, imprudent, unmindful of their own interest (trsl^n suggested by E. Hardy as preferable to Oldenberg's "unnoticed"). Morris, *J.P.T.S.* 1893, 69 suggests "not fighting," thus making abujjhaka = avujjh° = ayujjh° (of **yudh**).

Bujjhati [**budh**, y-formation, corresp. to Sk. budhyate for the usual bodhate. The sense is that of a Med., but is also used as Act. with acc. of object, e. g. saccāni bujjhi he recognised the truths Vism 209. — The Dhtp (414) and Dhtm (652) explain **budh** by "avagamane" (understanding, see ogamana), Dhtm (242) also by "bodhane" (awakening). Bdhgh's expl^n of the meaning is "kilesa-santāna-niddāya uṭṭhahati cattāri vā ariyasaccāni paṭivijjhati Nibbānam eva vā sacchikaroti" DhsA 217, cp. trsl^n at *Expos.* 294 "to rise from the slumber of the continuum of the lower nature, or a penetrating the Ariyan Truths, or a realizing Nibbāna"] to be awake, to be enlightened in (acc.), to perceive, to know, recognise, understand D II.249; S I.74, 198; Dh 136, 286; Th I, 146; J III.331; IV.49, 425; Miln 165, 348 (pot. bujjheyya); Dpvs I.14 (with gen.) KhA 219 (so attho sukhaŋ b.). 3rd pl. bujjhare Th 2, 453; Bu II.183. imper. **bujjhassu** Bu II.183. — fut. **bujjhissati** Bu II.65; aor. **abujjhi** Bu II.211, and **bujjhi** J IV.425; Vism 209; pret. 3rd sg. **abujjhatha** Bu VII.22. — ppr. **bujjhamāna** Sn 395; Bu VII.22; DhA I.93. — pp. **buddha** (q. v.). — Caus. I. **bodheti** (q. v.). — Caus. II. **bujjhāpeti** to lead to knowledge or recognition J I.407. Two infinitives formed fr. **bodh**, but belonging to **budh** are **bodhuŋ** J V.341, and **boddhuŋ** Th I, 167.

Bujjhana (nt.) [fr. **budh**] awakening, attaining to knowledge, recognition Ps I.18; Miln 194; DA I.51.

Bujjhanaka (adj.) [fr. bujjhana] endowed with knowledge, having the elements of bodhi, being enlightened DhsA 217.

Bujjhitar [n. ag. of bujjhati] one who becomes enlightened or recognises Nd[1] 457 = Ps I.174 = Vism 209 (bujjhitā saccāni, of the Buddha).

Buḍḍha [for vuḍḍha, pp. of **vṛdh**, see vaḍḍhati] aged, old D II.162; J I.164 (°pabbajita one who has become an ascetic in his old age). Compar. **buḍḍhatara** DhA II.239 (v. l. K.B.S. vuḍḍhatara).

Buddha[1] (adj.) [med.-pass. pp. of bujjhati, cp. Epic Sk. buddha] (a) understood S I.35 = 60 (su-dub-buddha very difficult to understand). — (b) having attained enlightenment, wise A IV.449; PvA 16 (buddh' ādayo), 60 (= ariya). Usually appl^d to the Bhagavant (Gotama) M I.386 (one of the adj. describing Gotama to Nigaṇṭha Nāthaputta); Sn 993. The true brāhmaṇa is buddha, e. g. Sn 622, 643, 646.

Buddha[2] [= buddha[1]] A. one who has attained enlightenment; a man superior to all other beings, human & divine, by his knowledge of the truth, a Buddha. At A II.38 the Buddha declares himself to be neither a god (deva) nor a Gandharva, nor a Yakṣa nor a man. — The word Buddha is an appellative, not a proper name (na mātarā kataŋ etc., vimokkh' antikaŋ etaŋ buddhānaŋ Bhagavantānaŋ bodhiyā mūle . . . paññatti) Nd^1 458 & Ps I.174. — There are 2 sorts of B's, viz. Pacceka-buddhas or Buddhas who attain to complete enlightenment, but do not preach the way of deliverance to the world, and Sammāsambuddhas, who are omniscient and endowed with the 10 powers (see bala), and whose mission is to proclaim the saving truth to all beings (cp. Miln 106). In this function the B's are Satthāro or teachers, Masters. In his rôle of a pre-eminent man a Buddha is styled Bhagavā or Lord: Buddho so Bhagavā M I.235; Pv II.9^{60} = DhA III.219. — Besides the 18 dhammā and the 10 balāni they are gifted with the 4 vesārajjāni (A II.9, cp. Miln 106). These teachers appear upon the earth from time to time; the approach of the birth of a B. (buddh'-uppāda) is hailed by the acclamation of the worlds, they live the houseless life and found an Order (Buddha-pamukha bhikkhu-sangha Sn p. 111; Sn 81, 386; Miln 212; DA I.242; PvA 19). The news that a B. has appeared upon earth is a cause of the greatest rejoicing: opportunity to see him is eagerly sought (Vin II.155; S I.210; DA I.248). The B. is always born in a brāhmaṇa or khattiya family. It is impossible here to give all the references for the Buddhas or Buddhahood in general; see e. g. Vin III.24 sq.; Dh 182 sq., 194, 195 (= sammā sambuddhā DhA III.252), 387; J I.51; III.128; Vism 442 (pubba-buddhā); PvA 20. — The remembrance of former births a B. shares with other classes of privileged beings, only in a different (higher) degree. This faculty (in an ascending scale) is possessed by the foll. 6 classes: titthiyā, pakati-sāvakā, mahā-sāvaka, agga-sāvakā, pacceka-buddhā, buddhā (see Vism 411). — B. The word Buddha is specially applied to the Buddha of the present world-age, Gotama by family-name. He is said to be the 25th of the series of former Buddhas (pubbā buddhā) S I.109, 140; IV.52. — *Seven* Buddhas are mentioned in the earlier texts & frequently referred to (cp. the 7 Rishis of the Vedic period, see also under satta, No. 7). They are Vipassī, Sikhī, Vessabhū, Kakusandha, Konāgamana, Kassapa and Gotama (D II.5-7; S II.5-11; cp. Th 1, 491; J II.147). They are also mentioned in an old formula against snake-bites (Vin II.110). The (allegorical) names of the predecessors of these in former ages are Dīpaṅkara, Kondañña, Mangala, Sumana, Revata, Sobhita, Anomadassī, Paduma, Narada, Padumuttara, Sumedha, Sujāta, Piyadassī, Atthadassī, Dhammadassī, Siddhattha, Tissa, Phussa. — The typical career of a Buddha is illustrated in the life of Gotama and the legends connected with his birth, as they appear in later tradition. Before his last existence he practised the 10 perfections (pāramitā, q. v.) for many ages, & finally descended from the Tusita Heaven (see Buddhavaŋsa). He was born in a khattiya family and was distinguished by the 32 signs of a great man (Mahāpurisa-lakkhaṇāni see D II.17 sq. and similar passages; cp. Ud 48). His mother Māyā bore him painlessly and died seven days after his birth M III.118 sq. — The story of each of the 25 Buddhas is given in the Buddhavaŋsa, quoted in the introductory chapters of the Jātak' aṭṭhakathā. — Convinced that asceticism was not the way to enlightenment, he renounced austerities. He became enlightened when seated in meditation under an Assattha tree (Ficus religiosa, hence called Bodhi or Bo tree). At the supreme moment he was tempted by Māra, but vanquished the evil one. He was then ready to depart, but resolved to remain in the world and preach the truth (M I.169; Vin I.6; a rather diff. account A II.20). That day he knew and proclaimed himself to be the Buddha and his career as a teacher began (M I.171; Vin I.9; Sn 558). — Like all the other Sammā-sambuddhas he founded an Order, converting and gladdening men by his discourses. After a long life of teaching he attained Nibbāna (nibbānaŋ adhigacchi), and passed utterly away: S I.210; D II.156; Sn 83, 513, 1133 sq.; Miln 96. — The *Epithets* attributed to all the Buddhas are naturally assigned also to Gotama Buddha. Out of the almost endless series of these we only give a few. He is adored as the highest and holiest of men (S I.47; III.84: loke anuttaro, lokassa aggo; Miln 70). He is the supremely wise, the conqueror of the powers of darkness, the teacher of gods (devas and yakkhas) and men S I.50, 132, 206, 301; A I.142; II.33; III.65; Sn 157 sq. He is the ādicca-bandhu kinsman of the sun S I.186; and compared to a universal monarch (rājā cakkavattī) A I.76; III.150 and to the lion (sīha), the king of the animals A III.122. He is buddha-vīra Th 1, 47; the refuge of all beings M II.305; DA I.233; Miln 95; further appaṭipuggala S I.134; his teaching leads to enlightenment, to self-conquest, to security & deliverance M I.235; Sn 454, 993; DA I.230. He himself is not to be reborn (antima-sarīro with his last body) S I.210; he is vimutto, freed & has come to the end of sorrow A IV.258; S III.65; full of compassion for all beings S I.25, 51; M II.100; he is bhisakko the physician A IV.340; magga-ññu, magga-vidū, magga-kovido S III.66. — Under Buddh' anussati (Vism 198 sq.) we find the *famous formula* Bhagavā Arahaŋ Sammā-sambuddho vijjā-caraṇa-sampanno sugato lokavidū anuttaro purisa-damma-sārathi Satthā devamanussānaŋ buddho Bhagavā (D I.49≈), analysed & exegetically discussed. Here (p. 209) "Buddha" is expl^d with the formula as found at Ps I.174; Nd^1 457. More explicitly with var. epithets at the latter passage. This formula is one of the highest & most comprehensive characterisations of a Buddha, & occurs frequently in the Canon, e. g. M I.179; S II.69; V.343. — A *khattiya* by birth he is called a brāhmaṇa because he carries on the sacred tradition, and because he excels in wisdom, self-control and virtue Miln 225.

-ânubuddha enlightened after the Enlightened one Th 1, 679, 1246 (trsl^d "who next to our Great Waked one was awoke"). -ânubhāva the majestic power of the B. PvA 38, 171. -ânussati mindfulness of the B., one of the 6 anussatis (B.°, dhamma°, sangha°, sīla°, cāga°, devatā°) D III.250, 280; Vism 132 (where followed by upasamânussati and 4 other qualities making up the pīti-sambojjh'anga; see anussati), 197 sq. (the 10, as mentioned under anussati). -ankura a nascent (lit. sprouting) Buddha, one who is destined to be a B. DhA I.83. -antara a Buddha-interval, the period between the appearance of one Buddha & the next Miln 3; DhA I.201 (the 4 last ones); IV.201; PvA 10, 14, 21, 47, 191. -ārammaṇa having its foundation or cause in the B., in °*pīti* joy, caused by contemplation of a B. J III.405; Vism 143 (here as ubbegā-pīti). -ûpaṭṭhāna B.-worship DhA I.101; PvA 93. -uppāda the coming into existence of a Buddha, time or age in which a B. was born (opp. buddh' antara), a Buddha-period J I.59; Mhbv 12; VbhA 50; ThA 28. -kara making a B., bringing about Buddhahood J I.20. -kāraka = °kara Mhbv 9. -kāla the time of a B. Vism 91 (Buddhakālo viya pavattati it is like the time of the B.) -kula Buddha-clan SnA 532 (B.-pitā, °mātā ibid.). -kolāhala the announcement of a Buddha, one of the 5 kolāhalas (q. v.) KhA 121, cp. J I.48. -khetta field or region of (or for the existence of) a Buddha Vism 414 (divided into 3 spheres: jātikkhetta, āṇākkhetta, visayakkhetta, see khetta). -gata directed or referring to the B. S I.211 (sati); Dh 296. -guṇa quality of a B., virtue, character of a Buddha J I.27; II.147; Bu II.177; Mbhv 80; KhA 121 (cp. App.). -cakkhu the eye of a Buddha, i. e. an eye (or the faculty) of complete intuition Vin I.6; ThA 2; see discussed in detail at Nd^1 359 = Nd^2 235^4; cp. cakkhu. -ñāṇa knowledge of a B., which is boundless (cp. Saddh. 73, *J.P.T.S.* 1887, 40) Bu I.64 (appameyya); X.5 (cuddasa). -dhamma Buddhahood Miln 276; pl. condition or attributes of a B. J I.20; referred to as 6 at Nd^1 143 = Nd^2 466 (bhāgī channaŋ °ānan ti Bhagavā), as 18 at

Miln 105, 285. Kern (*Manual & Grundriss* III.8, p. 63) gives (after Lal. Vist. 183, 343) the foll. 18 āveṇika-dharmas ("extraordinary qualities") as such: (1) seeing all things past, (2) present, (3) future, (4) propriety of actions of the body, (5) of speech, (6) of thought, (7) firmness of intuition, (8) of memory, (9) of samādhi, (10) of energy, (11) of emancipation, (12) of wisdom, (13) freedom from fickleness, (14) noisiness, (15) confusedness, (16) hastiness, (17) heedlessness, (18) inconsiderateness. **-pañha** the name given to one question asked by Sāriputta, which the paribbājikā Kuṇḍalakesī was unable to answer DhA II.225. **-pasanna** finding one's happiness, or believing in the B. Vin IV.39. **-putta** son of the B. said of bhikkhus or arahants Miln 143, cp. S III.83: puttā Buddhassa orasā. **-bala** the force of a B. (iddibala & paññā°) Bu I.3. **-bījankura** a future B. Bu II.71. **-bhāva** condition of a B. enlightenment J I.14, 147 (abuddhabhāva un-buddhahood, of Devadatta); MA I.1. **-bhūmi** the ground of Buddhahood Bu II.175. **-manta** mystic verses of a B. DA I.248. **-māmaka** devotedly attached to the B. DhA I.206 (+ Dhamma°, Sangha°). **-rakkhita** saved by the B. (Np.) SnA 534 (+ Dhamma°). **-rasmi** (pl. °iyo) rays shining forth from the person of the Buddha; they are of 6 colours J I.501; SnA 132; Mhbv 6, 15, 38; VvA 207; DhsA 13. **-rūpa** form or figure of the B. Vism 228 (Mārena nimmita, cp. Divy 162, 166: Buddha-nirmāṇa the magic figure of the B.). **-līḷha** (& °līḷhā) deportment, ease, grace of a Buddha J I.54; Mhbv 39; DhA I.33; II.41. **-vacana** the word (teaching) of the Buddha Miln 17; KhA 13; SnA 274, 331. **-visaya** the sphere (of wonder), the range, scope or power of a Buddha (cp. buddha-khetta) DhA I.33; II.199; SnA 154, 228. **-veneyya** one able to be led to enlightenment, accessible to Buddha's teaching SnA 15, 331. **-sāsana** the teaching (instructions) of the B. Dh 368, 381. **-sukumāla** delicate, sensitive (to fatigue), as Buddhas are DhA I.5.

Buddhaka (-°) (adj.) [fr. buddha] in cpd. dvangula-buddhikā (f.) possessing insight as much as 2 finger-breadths VvA 96. — The °ka belongs to the whole cpd.

Buddhatā (f.) [abstr. fr. buddha] enlightenment, wisdom DhA IV.228; ThA 4 (Buddha-subuddhatā). — Cp. buddhatta.

Buddhati to obstruct, withhold etc.: see pali°.

Buddhatta (nt.) [abstr. fr. buddha] state of (perfect) enlightenment, (attainment of) Buddhahood J III 363 (sabbadhammānaŋ b.); Vism 209 (buddhattā Buddho); Mhbv 12. Cp. buddhatā and abhisambuddhatta.

Buddhi (f.) [fr. **budh**; cp. Class. Sk. buddhi] wisdom, intelligence D III.165 (in sequence saddhā sīla suta b. cāga etc.); J III.369; V.257; Miln 349; Sdhp 263. The ref. Vism 439 should be read vuddhi for b°.

-carita one whose behaviour or character is wisdom Vism 104 (= paññavā). **-sampanna** endowed with (highest) wisdom PvA 39.

Buddhika (adj.) (-°) [fr. buddhi] intelligent, in cpds a° unintelligent & sa° possessed of wisdom Miln 76.

Buddhimant (adj.) [fr. buddhi] possessing insight, full of right knowledge Vin II.195; J V.257; Miln 21, 294; PvA 131 (paṇḍita, b., sappañña-jātika).

Bunda [Vedic budhna] the root of a tree Abhp 549.

Bundika in cpd. °ābaddha is of uncertain origin; the whole means a sort of seat or bedstead (fixed up or tied together with slats?) Vin II.149; IV.40, 357.

Bubbuḷa (& **Bubbula**) [cp. Epic Sk. budbuda] a bubble. On similes cp. *J.P.T.S.* 1907, 117. — Usually of a water-bubble **udaka°** S III.141; A IV.137; J V.216; Miln 117; Vism 109; DhA III.209; VbhA 33 (as unsubstantial to which vedanā are likened). In other connection at J I.68 (of cooking gruel).

Bubbuḷaka = bubbuḷa, viz. 1. a bubble DhA III.166; Miln 118. — 2. the iris of the eye Th 2, 395 (cp. Morris, in *J.P.T.S.* 1884, 89, but according to ThA 259 the reading pubbaḷhaka is to be preferred.)

Bubhukkhita [pp. of bubhukkhati, Desid. of bhuñjati] wishing to eat, hungry J II.14; V.70; Miln 66; Dāvs III.32.

Būḷha [for vūḷha, cp. Sk. vyūḍha for the usual vyūha, q. v.] array of troops J I.387.

Būha see vyūha.

Beluva & **Beḷuva** [the guṇa-form of billa, in like meaning. It is the diæretic form of Sk. *bailva or *vailva, of which the contracted form is P. bella] 1. the Vilva tree, Aegle marmelos M I.108; II.6; J IV.363, 368; VI.525, 560. — 2. wood of the Vilva tree S I.22; D II.264; Mhbv 31.

-pakka ripe fruit of the Vilva J V.74. **-paṇḍu(-vīṇā)** a yellow flute made of Vilva wood, representing a kind of magic flute which according to SnA 393 first belonged to Māra, and was then given to Pañcasikha, one of the Heavenly Musicians, by Sakka. See Vism 392 (attributed to Pañcasikha); DhA I.433 (of Māra; v. l. veḷuvadaṇḍa-vīṇā); III.225 (of P.); SnA 393 (v. l. veluva°). **-laṭṭhi** a young sprout of the Vilva tree KhA 118. **-salāṭuka** the unripe fruit of the Vilva, next in size to the smaller **kola**, surpassed in size by the ripe **billa** or billi S I.150 = A IV.170 = Sn p. 125.

Bella (m. & nt.) [= beluva, q. v.] the fruit of the Vilva tree (a kind of citron?) J III.77 (C. beluva); VI.578. Also in doubtful passage at J III.319 (v. l. mella, phella).

Bojjha (nt.) [orig. grd. of bujjhati or bodheti] a matter to be known or understood, subject of knowledge or understanding Nett 20.

Bojjhanga [bodhi + anga; cp. BSk. bodhyanga, e. g. Lal. Vist. 37, where the 7 are given at Divy 208] a factor or constituent of knowledge or wisdom. There are 7 bojjhangas usually referred to or understood from the context. There are enum^d at several places, e. g. at D III.106, where they are mentioned in a list of qualities (dhammā) which contribute to the greatest happiness of gods and man, viz. the 4 satipaṭṭhānā, 4 sammapadhānā, 4 iddhipādā, 5 indriyāni, 5 balāni & the 7 bojjhangas and ariya aṭṭhangika magga, 37 in all. The same list we find at Divy 208. — The 7 b. (frequently also called sambojjhangā) are **sati, dhamma-vicaya, viriya, pīti, passaddhi, samādhi, upekhā** or mindfulness, investigation of the Law, energy, rapture, repose, concentration and equanimity (DhsA 217, cp. *Expositor* II.294). — D II.79, 83, 120, 303; III.101, 128, 284; M I.11, 61; II.12; III.85, 275; S I.54; V.82, 110; A I.14; IV.23; Nd¹ 14, 45, 171 (°kusala), 341; Kvu I.158; Dhs 358, 528, 1354; Vbh 199 sq., 227 sq.; Vism 160; Miln 340; DhA I.230; VbhA 120, 310; ThA 27, 50, 160. They are counted among the 37 constituents of Arahantship, viz. the 30 above-mentioned qualities (counting *magga* as one), with addition of sīlesu paripūrikāritā, indriyesu gutta-dvāratā, bhojane mattaññutā, jāgariy' ânuyoga, sati-sampajaññaŋ (see e. g. Nd¹ 14; Nd² s. v. satipaṭṭhāna & sīla); cp. Th 1, 161, 162; Th 2, 21 (maggā nibbāna-pattiyā); DhsA 217 (bodhāya saŋvattantī ti bojjhangā etc.; also def. as "bodhissa ango ti pi bojjhango sen' angarath' ang' ādayo viya). They are also called the paribhoga-bhaṇḍāni or "insignia" of the Buddha Miln 330.

-kosalla proficiency in the constituents of wisdom Vism 248.

Bodha[1] [fr. **budh**; the usual] form is **sambodha** = bodhi, viz. knowledge, wisdom, enlightenment, Buddhaship D III.54 (v. l. sam°); DhsA 217; in phrase **bodhāya maggo** J I.67; Miln 244, 289; and in **bodha-pakkhiya-dhammā** (for which usually bodhi°) SnA 164 (where given as 37); complementary to santi (arousing, soothing) Th 1, 342. **bodhangama** leading to enlightenment (dhammā) Nett 31, 83 (v. l. bojjh°).

Bodha[2] see pali°.

Bodhana (nt.) [fr. bodheti] 1. knowing Miln 168 (cp. S V.83). — 2. (adj.) enlightening, teaching Bu 26, 22 (pacchima-jana°).

Bodhanīya (adj.) [grd. fr. bodheti] capable of being enlightened, worthy to be taught Bu 5, 31. See also **bodhaneyya.**

Bodhaneyya (adj.) [fr. bodheti, see bodhanīya] capable of being enlightened, to be taught the truth Bu 2, 195 (jana); Miln 169 (yena yogena bodhaneyyā sattā bujjhanti tena y. bodheti); otherwise in combⁿ **bodhaneyya-bandhavo** the (Buddha's) relations (or fellow-men) who are able to be enlightened J I.345 = DhA I.367; J V.335.

Bodhi[1] (f.) [fr. **budh**, cp. Vedic bodhin-manas having an attentive mind; RV V.75, 5; VIII.82, 18] (supreme) knowledge, enlightenment, the knowledge possessed by a Buddha (see also sambodhi & sammā-sambodhi) M I.356; II.95 = D III.237 (saddho hoti, saddahati Tathāgatassa bodhiŋ); D III.159 (anuttaraŋ pappoti bodhiŋ), 165 (id.); S I.103, 196; V.197 sq.; A II.66; VbhA 310 (def.). Bodhi consists of 7 elements called **bojjhangā** or **sambojjhangā,** and is attained by the accomplishment of the perfections called bodhi-pācanā dhammā (see under cpds. & cp. bodhi-pakkhiya-dhammā). The Buddha is said to have found the Path followed by former Buddhas, who "catusu satipaṭṭhānesu supatiṭṭhita-cittā satta-bojjhange yathābhūtaŋ bhāvetvā anuttaraŋ sammā-sambodhiŋ abhisambujjhiŋsu" S V.160. The moment of supreme enlightenment is the moment when the Four Truths (ariya-saccāni) are grasped S V.423. Bodhi is used to express the lofty knowledge of an ascetic (Bodhi-paribbājaka Np. J V.229 sq.), and the stage of enlightenment of the Paccekabuddha (pacceka-bodhi J III.348; pacceka-bodhi-ñāṇa J IV.114; pacceka-sambodhi SnA 73), as distinguished from sammā-sambodhi.

-**ṭṭhāna** the state of Bodhi, state of enlightenment. Dpvs 25. -**pakkhika** = **pakkhiya** (& **pakkhika,** e. g. A III.70 = 300; Th 1, 900; cp. bodha°) belonging to enlightenment, usually referred to as the **37 bodhi-pakkhiyā dhammā** qualities or items constituting or contributing to Bodhi, which are the same as enumᵈ under bojjhanga (q. v.). They are enumᵈ & discussed at Vism 678 sq. and mentioned at many other passages of the Abhidhamma, e. g. Vbh 244, 249; Nett 31, 197, 240, 261; and in the Commentaries, e. g. J I.275; III.290; V.483; DhA I.230. When they are increased to **43** they include the above with the addition of anicca-saññā; dukkha°, anatta°, pahāna°, virāga°, nirodha-saññā, thus at Nett 112, 237. In the older texts we do not find any numbered lists of the b.-p.-dhammā. At A III.70 only indriyesu guttadvāratā, bhojane mattaññutā and jāgariy' ānuyoga are mentioned in connection with bodhipakkhikā dhammā in general. At S V.227, 239 sq. (so read in Vbh preface XIV. for 327, 337!) the term is applied to the 5 indriyas: saddh' indriyaŋ, viriy°, sati°, samādhi°, paññ°. A more detailed discussion of the bodhi-p-dhammā and their mention in the Piṭakas is found in Mrs. Rh. D.'s preface to the Vbh edition, pp. XIV.-XVI. Of BSk. passage may be mentioned Divy 350 (saptatriŋśad-bodhi-pakṣān dharmān-amukhi-kṛtya pratyekāŋ bodhiŋ sākṣāt-kṛtavantah) & 616 (bodhipakṣāŋs tān dharmān Bhagavān saŋprakāśayati sma). -**paripāka** the maturing of enlightenment Vism 116. -**pācana** ripening of knowledge (of a Buddha); adj. leading to enlightenment Bu II. 121 sq.; Cp I.1[1] (cp. J I.22). It is a *late* term. The b. dhammā are the 10 perfections (pāramiyo), i. e. dāna°, sīla°, nekkhamma°, paññā°, viriya°, khanti°, sacca°, adhiṭṭhāna°, mettā°, upekhā°. -**satta** (1) a "bodhi-being," i. e. a being destined to attain fullest enlightenment or Buddhaship. A Bodhisatta passes through many existences & many stages of progress before the last birth in which he fulfils his great destiny. The "ambākaŋ Bodhisatto," or "our Bodhisatta" of the Buddhist Texts (e. g. Vism 419 (imasmiŋ kappe ayam eva Bhagavā Bodhisatta-bhūto); DA I.259) refers to Gotama, whose previous existences are related in the Jātaka collection. These tales illustrate the wisdom & goodness of the future Buddha, whether as an animal, a god, or a human being. In his last existence before attaining Buddhahood he is a man. Reference is made to a Bodhisatta or *the* B. at very many places throughout the Canon. See e. g. M I.17, 163, 240; S II.5; III.27; IV.233; V.263, 281, 317; A II.130; III.240; IV.302, 439; Vism 15, 116, 499; SnA 52 (pacceka°), 67, 72. — (2) N. of the author of a Pali grammar, used by Kaccāyana (not extant): see Windisch, *Proceedings of XIVᵗʰ Or. Congress, Vol.* I.290. -**sambhāra** (pl.) conditions (lit. materials) necessary for the attainment of bodhi J I.1; VI.595; Mbvs 12.

Bodhi[2] [= bohhi[1]] the tree of wisdom, the sacred Bo tree, the fig tree (Assattha, Ficus religiosa) under which Gotama Buddha arrived at perfect knowledge. The tree is near the spot where Buddhagāya is now, about 60 miles fr. Patna. It is regarded by pilgrims as the centre of the world (cp. pathavī-nābhi mahā-bodhi-maṇḍo Mbvs 79). It is also spoken of as Mahābodhi (e. g. J IV.228; Vism 403). — Vism 72, 299, 342; DhA I.105; ThA 62; VbhA 473.

-**angaṇa** the courtyard in which the Bo tree stands DA I.191; Vism 188 (°vatta); VbhA 349. -**tala** "Bodhi-foundation," i. e. the place or ground of the B. tree, otherwise bodhi-maṇḍa J I.105; Mhbv 9; DhA I.117. -**pakka** fruit of the Bo tree J IV.229. -**pādapa** the Bodhi tree Mbhv 1. -**pūjā** veneration of, or offerings to the Bo tree Mhbv 81. -**maṇḍa** (for °maṇḍala) the ground under the Bodhi tree, hence the spot (or "throne"), on which the Buddha was seated at the time of attaining highest enlightenment. The term is only found in very late canonical and post-canonical literature. Bu II.65, 183; Vism 203; J IV.228, 232; Mhbv 79; SnA 2, 30, 225, 258, 281, 340, 391, 441; DhA I.86; II.69; IV.72; ThA 2. Cp. BSk. bodhimaṇḍa Divy 392. -**maha** feast in honour of the Bo tree J IV.229. -**mūla** the root or foot of the Bo tree SnA 32, 391; cp. Bodhiyā mūle Nd[1] 172, 458 = Ps I.174. -**rukkha** the Bodhi tree Vin I.1.

Bodhetar [n. ag. fr. bodheti] awakener, enlightener Nd[1] 457; Ps I.174; Vism 209.

Bodheti [Caus. of bujjhati] 1. to awaken to the truth, to enlighten S I.170; Bu II.195. aor. **bodhesi** Vism 209, abodhayi Bu II.196 & **bodhayi** Bu V.31; XXV.6 inf. **bodhuŋ**: see bujjhati, & **bodhetuŋ** J IV.393. grd. bodhabba D II.246; A IV.136. — 2. to make aware (of), to make known J VI.412; SnA 444.

Bondi [etym. doubtful, one proposed by Morris, *J.P.T.S.* 1889, 207 derives it fr. **bandh** = **bundh** to bind, which is an erroneous comparison; on his hint "probably cognate with E. body" cp. Walde, *Lat. Wtb.* under fidelia. The orig. meaning may have been, as Morris suggests, "trunk." It certainly is a dial. word] body Pv IV.3[32]; J I.503; II.160; III.117; PvA 254.

Bya° etc. (byā°, byu°) words not found under these initials are to be looked up under **vya**° etc.

Byagā 3rd sg. aor. of vi+ **gam**, to depart, to be lost, perish Th 1, 170.

Byaggha [cp. Sk. vyāghra] a tiger J II.110; Sdhp 388. f. **byagghinī** Miln 67.

Byañjana (nt.) [cp. Sk. vyañjana] 1. sign, mark: see vyañjana. — 2. the letter, as compared with attha, the spirit or meaning; thus in phrase atthato byañjanato ca according to the meaning & the letter Miln 18, 345; Nett 23. As **vyañjana** is the more usual (& classical) form, other refs. will be found under vyañjana.

Byatta (adj.) [cp. P. vyatta; Sk. vyakta] experienced, learned Miln 21.

Byattatā (f.) [fr. byatta] experience, learning Miln 349. See also pari°.

Byanti° in °**bhavati, bhāva** etc. see **vyanti**°.

Byapagata [=vy-apa-gata] departed, dispelled Miln 225.

Byappatha [so for byappattha; according to Kern, *Toev.* s. v. the word is a distortion fr. ***vyāpṛta** (for which usually P. **vyāvaṭa**) of vy+ā+pṛ³, pṛṇoti to be busy or active] busy, active. Thus Kern, but the trslⁿ is not satisfactory. It occurs only at 2 passages: Vin IV.2, where combd with vācā, girā, vacībheda, and meaning "mode of speech," and at Sn 961, where it has the same meaning & is referred by Nd¹ 472 to a mode of speech & expld by SnA 572 by **vacana**. Thus the derivation fr. **pṛ** with vyā° can hardly be claimed to be correct for Bdhgh's conception of the word; to him it sounded more likely like vy+ā+patha (cp. cpds. vacana-patha & vāda-patha), thus "way of speaking."

Byamha [cp. vyamha] a celestial mansion, a Vimāna Vv 52³. As **vyamha** at J IV.464.

Byasana see **vyasana**.

Bya (indecl.) [distorted fr. iva=eva, with metathesis & diaeresis ***veyya**>***veyya**>***vyā**>**byā**] intensive particle: just so, certainly, indeed only in phrase "**evaŋ byā kho**" Vin II.26; IV.134=DA 1.27; M 1.130 (evaŋ vyā kho ti evaŋ viya kho C.), 257.

Byādhi [cp. Sk. vyādhi; lit. "upset" fr. vy+ā+**dhā**] sickness, disease A 1.146; Kvu II.457; Miln 351.

Byādhita [pp. fr. byādheti] afflicted with disease Th 1, 73; Miln 168.

Byādheti [Caus. fr. byādhi] to cause to waver, unsettle, agitate, trouble S 1.120; Th 1, 46, 1211. Pass. **byādhiyati** Kvu II.457 (aor. byādhiyiŋsu). — pp. **byādhita.**

Byāpajjha [fr. vy-ā-**pad**] 1. trouble, opp. a° relief M 1.10. — 2. malevolence; neg. a° benevolence Vin 1.3; M 1.38; cp. avyāpajjha S IV.296, 371.

Byāpanna [fr. vyāpajjati] malevolent Sdhp 70; otherwise vy°, e. g. S II.168 (°citta).

Byāpāda [fr. vy+ā+**pad**] ill-will, malevolence, one of the 5 "obstructions" (āvaraṇāni, see e. g. S v.94; Nd² 379); and of the 4 "bonds" (kāya-ganthā see e. g. Nd¹ 98). — M 1.434; S 1.99; It 119; Ps 1.31; II.12; Nd¹ 149, 207, 386.

-**vitakka** a malevolent or angry thought M 1.11; S 1.203; II.151; III.93; V.417; Nd¹ 501; Kvu 113.

Byābādha [vy+ā+**bādh**] evil, wrong, hurt; usually referred to as 3 fold: atta°, para°, ubhaya°, or against oneself, against others, & both — M 1.416; S IV.159 (vyā°), 339.

Byābādheti [Denom. fr. byābādha] to injure, hurt, oppress S V.393 (na kiñci byābādhemi tasaŋ vā thāvaraŋ vā).

Byābhangī (f.) [vy+ā+**bhañj**] 1. a pole for carrying burdens Th 1, 623. — 2. a flail S IV.201.

Byāma [cp. Vedic & P. vyāma cp. Śatap. Br. 1.2, 5, 14 a fathom, measured by both hands being extended to their full length, only in phrase °ppabhā a halo extending for a fathom around the Buddha J 1.12, 90; Bu 1.45; Miln 75; VvA 213.

Byāruddha [pp. of vy+ā+**rundh**; reading by° in Nd¹; vy° in Sn & SnA; v. l. BB] obstructed, opposed, hindered Sn 936 (aññam-aññehi b. in enmity with each other; =paṭiviruddha Nd¹ 408), 938 (412 id.; SnA 566=āhata-citta).

Byāvaṭa [vy+ā+**vṛ**] covered, adorned with VvA 213 (rūpakāya byāvaṭa jana; v. l. byāgata).

Byāsatta [pp. of vy+ā+**sañj**, cp. āsatta¹] attached to, clinging to, in cpd. °mānasa possessed with longing Dh 47 (=sampatte vā asampatte vā lagga-mānasa DhA 1.361), 287 (cp. DhA III.433; lagganatāya sattamānasa).

Byūha [cp. Sk. & P. vyūha fr. vi+**vah**] 1. the array or arrangement of troops in particular positions, order of parade or battle DA 1.85. Three formations of troops are mentioned at J II.404 & 406, viz. paduma-vyūha (lotus formation), cakka° (wheel formⁿ), sakaṭa° (cart formⁿ). — 2. a heap, collection, in **byūhaŋ** karoti to put into a (well-arranged) heap Miln 2 (kacavaraŋ). — 3. a (blind) alley, cul-de-sac Vin IV.271 (byūhan nāma yen' eva pavisanti ten' eva nikkhamanti).

Byūhati [Denom. fr. byūha] to stand in array (like a troop) VvA 104 (byūhanto, v. l. brahmanto).

Brahant (adj.) [cp. Vedic bṛhant, of **bṛh**² to increase, to be great or strong; paribṛdha solid (cp. brūha, paribrahaṇa & paribrūhana), Av. bərəzat high; Arm. barjr high; Oir. brī, Cymr. bre mountain; Goth. baurgs "borough," Ohg. etc. burg "burgh," i. e. fortress; Ger. berg mountain. — The fundamental notion is that of an increase above normal or the ordinary: vuddhi (of **vṛdh**) is used in explns of the term; thus Dhtp 344 (Dhtm 506) baha braha brūha=vuddhiyaŋ; VvA 278 brahā=vuddhā. Its use is almost entirely restricted to poetry] very great, vast, high, lofty, gigantic; nom. sg. **brahā** Sn 410, 550; Th 1, 31; J III.117 (=dīgha C.); IV.111 (su°); 64⁷; Pv IV.3¹⁰ (of a huge tree), acc. sg. **brahantaŋ** A III.346; VvA 182; nom. pl. also **brahantā** Vv 52⁴ (=mahantā VvA 224; of the Yama-dūtā or Death's giant messengers). — f. brahatī J V.215 (=uḷārā C.); also given as N. of a plant Abhp 588. — Superl. brahaṭṭha (=Sk. barhiṣṭha; on inversion bar>bra cp. Sk. paribarhanā>P. paribrahaṇa) in °**puppha** a large or fully developed blossom J V.416.

-**arañña** woodlands, vast forest A 1.187. -**vana** the wild wood, immense forest A 1.152; III.44; Vv 63³; J V.215. -**sukha** (-vivāra-jjhāna-jhāyin) (a thinker enjoying his meditations in) immense happiness Miln 226 (in characterisation of the term "brāhmaṇa").

Brahma & **Brahmā** [fr. **bṛh**, see brahant. Perhaps less with regard to the greatness of the divine principle, than with ref. to the greatness or power of prayer or the ecstatic mind (i. e. holy enthusiasm). On etym. see Osthoff, "*Bezzenberger's Beitrage*" XXIV.142 sq. (=Mir. bricht charm, spell: Oicel. bragr poetry)] — **I. Brahman** (nt.) [cp. Vedic bráhman nt. prayer; nom. sg. bráhma] 1. the supreme good; as a buddhistic term used in a sense different from the brahmanic (save in controversy with Brahmans); a state like that of Brahmā (or Brahman) A II.184 (brahmappatta). In cpds. brahma°. — 2. Vedic text, mystic formula, prayer DA 1.244 (brahmaŋ aṇatī ti brāhmaṇo).

II. Brahmā [cp. Vedic brahmán, m., one who prays or chants hymns, nom. sg. Brahmā] 1. the god Brahmā chief of the gods, often represented as the creator of the Universe (vasavattī issaro kattā nimmātā) D I.18; III.30, also called **Mahābrahmā** (D I.235 sq., 244 sq.; III.30; It 15; Vism 578; DhA II.60); and **Sahampati** (Vin I.5; D II.157; S I.136 sq.; Vism 201; KhA 171; SnA 56) and **Sanaŋkumāra** (D II.226; III.97). The duration of his life is given as being 1 kalpa (see Kvu 207, 208). — nom. **Brahmā** Vin I.5; D II.46; J VI.486; Miln 224; Vism 2 (brahmānaŋ atibrahmā, Ep. of Buddha Bhagavā); SnA 229 (B. mahānubhāvo); gen. abl. **Brahmano** D II.209; Vism 205; SnA 177; instr. **Brahmanā** D I.252; II.239; Dh 105, 230; Vism 48, 405; DhA II.60; acc. **Brahmānaŋ** D II.37; voc. **Brahme** S I.138. — 2. a brahma god, a happy & blameless celestial being, an inhabitant of the higher heavens (brahma-loka; in which to be reborn is a reward of great merit); nom. sq. **brahmā** S I.142 (Baka br.); M I.327 (id.); A IV.83; PvA 138 (°devatā for brahma°?); gen. abl. **brahmuno** S I.142, 155; instr. **brahmunā** D III.147, 150 & **brahmanā** PvA 98; voc. sq. **brahme** M I.328. pl. nom. **brahmāno** Miln 13, 18 (where J VI.486 has Mahā-brahmā in id. p.); DhsA 195; gen. **brahmānaŋ** Vism 2; Mhbv 151. —**paccekabrahmā** a br. by himself S I.149 (of the name of Tudu; cp. pacceka-buddha). —**sabrahmaka** (adj.) including the brahma gods D I.62; A II.70; Vin I.11; DA I.174.

III. **brahma** (adj.-n.) [cp. brahmā II. 2; Vedic brahma° & Sk. brāhma] 1. holy, pious, brahmanic; (m.) a holy person, a brahmin — (adj.) J II.14 (br. vaṇṇa = seṭṭha vaṇṇa C.); KhA 151 (brahma-cariyaŋ = brahmaŋ cariyaŋ). — (m.) acc. **brahmaŋ** Sn 285; voc. **brahme** (frequent) Sn 1065 (= brahmā ti seṭṭha-vacanaŋ SnA 592); J II.346; IV.288; VI.524, 532; Pv I.12⁹ (= brāhmaṇa PvA 66). — 2. divine, as incorporating the highest & best qualities, sublime, ideal, best, very great (see esp. in cpds.), A I.132 (brahmā ti mātāpitaro etc.), 182; IV.76. — 3. holy, sacred, divinely inspired (of the rites, charms, hymns etc.) D I.96 (brahme mante adhiyitvā); Pv II.6¹³ (mantaŋ brahma-cintitaŋ) = brāhmaṇānaŋ atthāya brahmaṇā cintitaŋ) PvA 97, 98). — *Note.* The compⁿ form of all specified bases (I. II. III.) is **brahma°**, and with regard to meaning it is often not to be decided to which of the 3 categories the cpd. in question belongs.

-attabhāva existence as a brahma god DhA III.210. **-ujjugatta** having the most divinely straight limbs (one of the 32 marks of a Great Man) D II.18; III.144, 155. **-uttama** sublime DhsA 192. **-uppatti** birth in the brahma heaven S I.143. **-uposatha** the highest religious observance with meditation on the Buddha & practice of the uposatha abstinence A I.207. **-kappa** like Brahmā Th 1, 909. **-kāya** divine body D III.84; J I.95. **-kāyika** belonging to the company of Brahmā, N of a high order of Devas in the retinue of Br. (cp. Kirfel, *Kosmographie* pp. 191, 193, 197) D I.220; II.69; A III.287, 314; IV.40, 76, 240, 401; Th 1, 1082; Vism 225, 559; KhA 86. **-kutta** a work of Brahmā D III.28, 30 (cp. similarly yaŋ mama, pitrā kṛtaŋ devakṛtaŋ na tu brahmakṛtaŋ tat Divy 22). See also under kutta. **-giriya** (pl.) name of a certain class of beings, possibly those seated on Brahmagiri (or is it a certain class of performers, actors or dancers?) Miln 191. **-ghaṭa** (= ghaṭa²) company or assembly of Brahmans J VI.99. **-cakka** the excellent wheel, i. e. the doctrine of the Buddha M I.69; A II.9, 24; III.417; V.33; It 123; Ps II.174; VbhA 399 (in detail); **-cariya** see separate article. **-cārin** leading a holy or pure life, chaste, pious Vin II.236; III.44; S I.5, 60; II.210; III.13; IV.93, A II.44; M III.117; Sn 695, 973; J V.107, 382; Vv 34¹¹ (acc. pl. brahmacāraye for °cārino); Dh 142; Miln 75; DA I.72 (brahmaŋ seṭṭhaŋ ācāraŋ caratī ti br. c.); DhA III.83; *a°* S IV.181; Pug 27, 36. **-cintita** divinely inspired Pv I.6¹³ = Vv 63¹⁶ (of manta); explⁿ at PvA 97, as given above III.3, differs from that at VvA 265, where it runs: brahmehi Aṭṭhak' ādīhi cintitaŋ paññā-cakkhunā diṭṭhaŋ, i. e. thought out by the divine (seer) Aṭṭhaka and the others (viz. composers of the Vedic hymns: v. s. brāhmaṇa¹, seen with insight). — **ja** sprung from Brahmā (said of the Brāhmaṇas) D III.81, 83; M II.148. Cp. dhammaja. **-jacca** belonging to a brahman family Th 1, 689. **-jāla** divine, excellent net, N. of a Suttanta (D No. 1) Vism 30; VbhA 432, 516; KhA 12, 36, 97; SnA 362, 434. **-daṇḍa** "the highest penalty," a kind of severe punishment (temporary death-sentence?) Vin II.290; D II.154; DhA II.112; cp. Kern, *Manual* p. 87. **-dāyāda** kinsman or heir of Brahmā D III.81, 83. **-deyya** a most excellent gift, a royal gift, a gift given with full powers (said of land granted by the King) D I.87 (= seṭṭha-deyyaŋ DA I.246; cp. *Dial.* I.108 note: the first part of the cpd. (brahma) has always been interpreted by Brahmans as referring to themselves. But *brahma* as the first part of a cpd. never has that meaning in Pali; and the word in our passage means literally "a full gift." — Cp. id. p. Divy 620, where it does *not* need to mean "gift to brahmans," as Index suggests); D I.114; J II.166 = DhA III.125 (here a gift to a br., it is true, but not with that meaning); J VI.486 (sudinnaŋ +); Mhbv 123. We think that both Kern (who at *Toev.* s. v. unjustly remarks of Bdhgh's explⁿ as "unjust") and Fick (who at "*Sociale Gliederung*" p. 126 trslˢ it as "gift to a Brahman") are wrong, at least their (and others') interpretation is doubtful. **-devatā** a deity of the Brahmaloka PvA 138 (so read for brahmā°). **-nimantanika** "addressing an invitation to a brahma-god," title of a Suttanta M I.326 sq., quoted at Vism 393. **-nimmita** created by Brahmā D III.81, 83. **-patta** arrived at the highest state, above the devas, a state like the Br. gods M I.386; A II.184. **-patti** attainment of the highest good S I.169, 181; IV.118. **-patha** the way to the Br. world or the way to the highest good S I.141; A III.346; Th 1, 689. Cp. Geiger, *Dhamma* 77. **-parāyana** devoted to Brahmā Miln 234. **-parisā** an assembly of the Brahma gods D III.260; M I.330; S I.155; A IV.307. **-pārisajja** belonging to the retinue of Br., N. of the gods of the lowest Rūpa-brahmaloka S I.145, 155; M I.330; Kvu 207; cp. Kirfel, *Kosmographie* 191, 194. **-purohita** minister or priest to Mahābrahmā; *°deva* gods inhabiting the next heaven above the Br.-pārisajjā devā (cp. Kirfel loc. cit.) Kvu 207 (read °purohita for °parohita!). **-pphoṭana** [a-pphoṭana; ā + ph.] a Brahma-applause, divine or greatest applause DhA III.210 (cp. Miln 13; J VI.486). **-bandhu** "brahma-kinsman," a brāhmaṇa in descent, or by name; but in reality an unworthy brahman, Th 2, 251; J VI.532; ThA 206; cp. Fick, *Sociale Gliederung* p. 140. **-bhakkha** ideal or divine food S I.141. **-bhatta** a worshipper of Br. J IV.377 sq. **-bhavana** Br.-world or abode of Br. Nd¹ 448. **-bhūta** divine being, most excellent being, said of the Buddha D III.84; M I.111; III.195, 224; S IV.94; A V.226; It 57; said of Arahants A II.206; S III.83. **-yāna** way of the highest good, path of goodness (cp. brahma-patha) S V.5; J VI.57 (C. ariyabhūmi: so read for arāya°). **-yāniya** leading to Brahmā D I.220. **-loka** the Br. world, the highest world, the world of the Celestials (which is like all other creation subject to change & destruction: see e. g. Vism 415 = KhA 121), the abode of the Br. devas; Heaven. — It consists of 20 heavens, *sixteen* being worlds of form (*rūpa*-brahmaloka) and *four*, inhabited by devas who are incorporeal (*arūpa°*). The devas of the Br. l. are free from kāma or sensual desires. Rebirth in this heaven is the reward of great virtue accompanied with meditation (jhāna) A I.227 sq.; V.59 (as included in the sphere called sahassī cūḷanikā lokadhātu). — The brahmās like other gods are not necessarily sotāpannā or on the way to full knowledge (sambodhi-parāyaṇā); their attainments depend on the degree of their faith in the Buddha,

Dhamma, & Sangha, and their observance of the precepts. — See e. g. D III.112; S I.141, 155, 282; A III.332; IV.75, 103; Sn 508, 1117; J II.61; Ps I.84; Pv II.13^{17}; Dhs 1282; Vbh 421; Vism 199, 314, 367, 372, 390, 401, 405, 408, 415 sq., 421, 557; Mhbv 54, 83, 103 sq., 160; VbA 68; PvA 76; VbhA 167, 433, 437, 510. See also *Cpd.* 57, 141 sq.; Kirfel, *Kosmographie* 26, 191, 197, 207, and cp. in BSk. literature Lal. Vist. 171. The Br.-l. is said to be the one place where there are no women: DhA I.270. —yāva Brahmalokā pi even unto Br.'s heaven, expression like "as far as the end of the world" M I.34; S V.265, 288. -°*ūpaga* attaining to the highest heaven D II.196; A V.342; Sn 139; J II.61; Kvu 114. -°*ūpapatti* rebirth in Heaven Sn 139. -°*parāyana* the Br.-loka as ultimate goal J II.61; III.396. -°*sahavyatā* the company of the Br. gods A IV.135 sq. -yāna the best vehicle S V.5 (+ dhammayāna). -vaccasin with a body like that of Mahābrahmā, comb^{d} with -vaṇṇin of most excellent complexion, in ster. passage at D I.114, 115; M II.167, cp. DA I.282: °vaccasī ti Mahābrahmuṇo sarīra-sadisena sarīrena samannāgato; °vaṇṇī ti seṭṭhavaṇṇī. -vāda most excellent speech Vin I.3. -vimāna a palace of Brahmā in the highest heaven D III.28, 29; It 15; Vism 108. -vihāra sublime or divine state of mind, blissful meditation (exercises on *a*, altruistic concepts; *b*, equanimity; see on these meditations *Dial* I.298). There are 4 such "divine states," viz. mettā, karuṇā, muditā, upekkhā (see Vism 111; DhsA 192; and cp. *Expositor* 258; *Dhs trsl.* 65; BSk. same, e. g. Divy 224); D II.196; III.220 (one of the 3 vihāra's: dibba°, brahma°, ariya°); Th I, 649; J I.139 (°vihāre bhāvetvā . . . brahmalok' ūpaga), II.61; Dhs 262; Vism 295 sq. (°niddesa), 319. -veṭhana the head-dress of a brahmin SnA 138 (one of the rare passages where brahma° = brahma III. 1). -sama like Brahmā Sn 508; SnA 318, 325; DhsA 195. -ssara "heavenly sound," a divine voice, a beautiful and deep voice (with 8 fine qualities: see enum^{d} under bindu) D II.211 = 227; J I.96; V.336.

Brahmaka (adj.) only in cpd. sa° with Brahmā (or the Br. world). q. v.

Brahmacariya (nt.) [brahma + cariya] a term (not in the strictly Buddhist sense) for observance of vows of holiness, particularly of chastity: good & moral living (brahmaŋ cariyaŋ brahmānaŋ vā cariyaŋ = brahmacariyaŋ KhA 151); esp. in Buddh. sense the moral life, holy life, religious life, as way to end suffering, Vin I.12, 19, renouncing the world, study of the Dhamma D I.84, 155; II.106; III.122 sq., 211; M I.77, 147, 193, 205, 426, 463, 492, 514; II.38; III.36, 116; S I.38, 43, 87, 105, 154, 209; II.24, 29, 120, 219, 278, 284 (°pariyosāna); III.83, 189; IV.51, 104, 110, 126, 136 sq., 163, 253, V.7 sq., 15 sq., 26 sq., 54 sq., 233, 262, 272, 352; A I.50, 168, 225; II.26, 44, 185; III.250, 346; IV.311; V.18, 71, 136; Sn 267, 274 (vas-uttama), 566, 655, 1128; Th I, 1027, 1079; It 28, 48, 78, 111; Dh 155, 156, 312; J III.396; IV.52; Pv II.9^{13}; DhA IV.42 (vasuttamaŋ); VbhA 504. —brahmacariyaŋ vussati to live the religious life A I.115 (cp. °ŋ vusitaŋ in formula under Arahant II. A); °assa kevalin wholly given up to a good life A I.162; °ŋ santānetuŋ to continue the good life A III.90; DhA I.119; komāra° the religious training of a well-bred youth A III.224; Sn 289. —abrahmacariya unchastity, an immoral life, sinful living M I.514; D I.4; Sn 396; KhA 26.
-antarāya raping DhA II.52. -ânuggaha a help to purity A I.167; IV.167; Dhs 1348. -ûpaddava a disaster to religious life, succumbing to worldly desires M III.116. -vāsa state of chastity, holy & pure life; adj. living a pure life A I.253; J III.393; Kvu 93; DhA I.225.

Brahmacariyaka (adj.) [fr. brahmacariya] only in phrase ādi° leading to the highest purity of life D I.189, 191; III.284; A IV.166.

Brahmacariyavant (adj.) [fr. brahmacariya] leading the religious life, pure, chaste S I.182; Dh 267.

Brahmañña (adj.) [fr. brāhmaṇa] brahman, of the brahman rank; brahmanhood, of higher conduct, leading a pure life D I.115 (at which passage DA I.286 includes Sāriputta, Moggallāna & Mahākassapa in this rank); M II.167; A I.143. — abstr. der. brāhmaññā (nt.) higher or holy state, excellency of a virtuous life D I.166; Vin III.44; J IV.362 (= brāhmaṇa dhamma C.); brahmañña (nt.) D II.248; brahmaññā (f.) D III.72, 74; A I.142; & brahmaññattha (nt.) S III.192; V.25 sq., 195; A I.260 (brāhmaññattha).

Brahmaññatā (& brāh°) [fr. brahma or brāhmaṇa] state of a brahman D III.145, 169; Dh 332, cp. DhA IV.33. — Neg. a° D III.70, 71.

Brahmaññattha see brahmañña.

Brahmatta (nt.) [abstr. fr. brahma] state of a Brahma god, existence in the Br. world Vbh 337; Vism 301; VbhA 437; DhA I.110. brahmattabhāva is to be read as brahm' attabhāva (see under brahma).

Brahmattara at J III.207 (of a castle) is probably to be read brahmuttara "even higher than Brahmā," i. e. unsurpassed, magnificent. C. expl$^{n.}$ by suvaṇṇapāsāda.

Brahmavant (adj.) [fr. brahma] "having Brahmā," possessed or full of Brahmā; f. brahmavatī Np. Vism 434.

Brāhmañña, brāhmaññatā & brāhmaññattha see brahmañ°.

Brāhmaṇa¹ [fr. brahma; cp. Vedic brāhmaṇa, der. fr. brahmàn] a member of the Brahman caste; a Br. teacher. In the Buddhist terminology also used for a man leading a pure, sinless & ascetic life, often even syn. with arahant. — On brāhmaṇas as a caste & their representation in the Jātaka collection see Fick, *Sociale Gliederung;* esp. ch. 8, pp. 117-162. — Var. fanciful etymologies, consisting of a word-play, in P. definitions are e. g. "sattannaŋ dhammānaŋ bāhitattā br." (like def. of bhikkhu) Nd¹ 86 = Nd² 464^{a} (cp. Sn 519); ye keci bho-vādikā Nd¹ 249 = Nd² 464^{b}; brahā-sukhavihāra-jhāna-jhāyin Miln 226; pāpaŋ bāhesuŋ D III.94; bāhita-pāpattā br. DhA III.84; ariyā bāhita-pāpattā br. DA I.244. — pl. brāhmaṇāse Sn 1079 sq. — Var. ref^{s} in the Canon to all meanings of the term: D I.90, 94, 104, 119 sq., 136 (mahāsālā), 150 (°dūta), 247; III.44 sq., 61, 83 sq., 94 sq. (origin of), 147, 170, 258 (°mahāsālā), 270; M I.271 (°karaṇā dhammā), 280; II.84, 148, 177; III.60, 270 (a bhikkhu addressed as br.); S I.47, 54, 94 sq., 99 (°kumāra), 117, 125, 160 sq.; II.77, 259; IV.157; V.194; A I.66, 110, 163 (tevijjā); 166; II.176; III.221 sq. (brāhmaṇa-vagga); It 57 sq., 60, 98, 101; J III.194; IV.9; VI.521 sq.; Vbh 393 sq. For br. with the meaning "arahant" see also: Vin I.3; II.156 (br. parinibbuta); Th I, 140, 221 (brahma-bandhu pure āsiŋ, idāni kho 'mhi brāhmaṇo); Dh 383 sq.; Sn passim (e.g. v. 142 kammanā hoti brāhmaṇo; 284 sq.); J IV.302 sq.; Miln 225. Ten kinds of Br. are pronounced to be apetā brahmaññā degraded fr. brahmanship J IV.361 sq. Diff. schools of br. teachers are enum^{d} at D I.237 sq. (Tevijja Sutta). —brāhmaṇānaŋ pubbakā isayo mantānaŋ kattāro "the ten inspired Seers of old times, who composed the Vedic hymns"; their names are Aṭṭhaka, Vāmaka, Vāmadeva, Vessāmitta, Yamataggi, Angirasa, Bhāradvāja, Vāseṭṭha, Kassapa, Bhagu Vin I.245; D I.104; A III.224; IV.61; cp. VvA 265. — f. brāhmaṇī

(n. or adj.) the wife of a brāhmaṇa D I.193; J V.127 (of a purohita or high priest); DhA I.33; IV.176; PvA 55, 61, 64. Freq. in combⁿ brāhmaṇī pajā this generation of brāhmaṇas, e. g. D I.249; A I.260; II.23 (see pajā). -ibbhā Brahmins & Vaiśyas J VI.228 sq. -kumārikā a brahmin young girl J III.93. -kula a br. clan or family J II.85, 394, 411; III.147, 352; PvA 21, 61. -gahapatikā priests & laymen (".clerk & yeoman" Rh. D. in S.B.E. XI.258) D II.178; III.148, 153, 170 sq.; S I.59, 184; A I.110; Vin I.35; J I.83. -gāma a br. village Vin I.197; D I.87, 127; S I.111; J II.368; III.293; IV.276. -dhamma duty of a br.; see on contrast between Brahmaṇic & Buddhist view J IV.301 sq., cp. also SnA 312-325 (br.-dhammika-suta) & Fick, l. c. 124. -putta son of a br. PvA 62. -bhojana giving food (alms) to brahmans Vin I.44. -māṇava a young brahmin J IV.391. -rūpa (in) form of a br. PvA 63. -vaḍḍhakī a br. carpenter J IV.207. -vaṇṇin having the appearance of a brahmin Cp X.10. -vācanaka a br. disputation, some sort of elocution show J I.318; IV.391. -vāṭaka circle of brahmins DhA IV.177 (v. l. °vādaka). -vāṇija a br. merchant PvA 113. -sacca a brahmanic (i. e. standard, holy) truth A II.176 (where the Buddha sets forth 4 such br. -saccāni, diff. from the usual 4 ariyasaccāni).

Brāhmaṇa[2] (nt.) [for brahmañña] state of a true brahman, "holiness supreme" Th I, 631.

Brūti [**brū**, Sk. bravīti, Med. brūte; cp. Geiger, *P.Gr.* § 141[2]. Expl[d] by Dhtp 366 as "vacane," by Dhtm 593 as "vācāyaŋ, viyattiyaŋ"] to say, tell, call; show, explain D I.95; Sn 308 sq.; Dh 383 sq.; Cp. VI.8; Miln 314, 327. — Constructed with double acc. or with dat. of person & acc. of thing said (cp. Miln 233). — *Forms:* Pres. 1st sg. **brūmi** It 33, 40; S 1033, 1042 sq. (expl[d] as ācikkhāmi desemi paññāpemi etc. by Nd.); Pv I.2[3] (=kathemi PvA 11); Th I, 214; 2nd sg. **brūsi** Sn 457, 1032, 1081; J II.48; Th 2, 58; 3rd sg. **brūti** Sn 122; imper. **brūhi** Th I, 1266; Sn 1018, 1034, 1043; Miln 318. — pret. **abravi** Sn 981; Th I, 1275; J VI.269; Pv II.9[64] (v. l. abruvi); PvA 264; **abruvi** J III.62, and **bravi** J V.204; 3rd sg. med. **bravittha** Vv 53[10] (=kathesi VvA 240); 1st sg. also **abraviŋ** Cp. II.6[8]; 3rd pl. **abravuŋ** J V.112.

Brūmeti [possible Caus. fr. brūti, but as Geiger, *P.Gr.* 141[2], rightly remarks "not critically sound"] to say D I.95 (expl[d] as "brūmetū ti vadatu" DA I.265).

Brūhana (nt.) [fr. brūheti] expansion, increasing, spreading; cultivation, development (trs. & intrs.) Miln 313 (Kern, *Toev.* s. v. "amusement"); DhsA 332; VvA 20 (sukha°). Cp. upa°.

Brūhetar [n. ag. of brūheti] increaser; one who practises, is devoted to; in phrase brūhetā **suññāgārānaŋ** frequenter of solitary places; given up to solitary meditation M I.33, 213.

Brūheti [cp. Sk. bṛŋhayati; fr. **brh**[2] to increase; Dhtp 346 & Dhtm 505: vuddhiyaŋ. Cp. brahant] to cause to grow, increase; hence: to promote, develop, practise, to put or devote oneself to; to look after, to foster, make enjoy; practically syn. with **sevati**; S I.198 (**saddhaŋ**): Sn 324 (kammāni); Dh 285 (imper. brūhaya = vaḍḍhaya DhA III.429); Ud 72; J I.289; Miln 313 (saddena sotaŋ br.); PvA 168 (vaḍḍheti +, for ābhāveti). — Cp. anu°, pari°.

Bh.

Bha (indecl.) the letter or sound (syllable) bh; figuring in Bdhgh's exegesis of the N. Bhagavā as representing *bhava*, whereas ga stands for *gamana*, va for *vanta* KhA 109. — Like ba° we often find bha° mixed up with pa°; — see e. g. bhaṇḍa bhaṇḍati; bh represents b. in bhasta = Sk. basta, bhisa = Sk. bisa, bhusa = Sk. buśa. —**bha-kāra** the sound (or ending) °bha, which at Vin IV.7 is given as implying contempt or abuse, among other low terms (hīnā akkosā). This refers also to the sound (ending) °ya (see ya-kāra). The expl^{n} for this probably is that °bha is abstracted from words ending thus, where the word itself meant something inferior or contemptible, and this shade of meaning was regarded as inhering in the ending, not in the root of the word, as e. g. in ibbha (menial).

Bhakuṭi (f.) [cp. Epic Sk. bhrakuṭi from older bhṛkuti, bhrukuṭi or bhrūkuṭi] superciliousness Sn 485. J III.99; Vism 26 (°karaṇa); SnA 412. Der. bhākuṭika (q. v.). See also bhūkuṭi.

Bhakkha (-°) (adj.) [fr. **bhakṣ**] 1. eating, feeding on D III.41 (sāka° etc.); S I.69 (pahūta° voracious, of fire), 238 (kodha°); Pv I.9[1] (lohita-pubba°); Pug 55 (tiṇa°); Sdhp 388 (tiṇa°). — 2. eatable, to be eaten; nt. °ŋ food, prey, in cpd. appa-bhakkha offering no food Vv 84[3] (appodaka+). — pl. also **bhakkhā** (eatables) J II.14; IV.241 (similar context; = bhojana C.); Pv II.9[41] (= āhārā PvA 129). It is to be pointed out that bhakkhā occurs in poetry, in stock phrase "dibbā bhakkhā pātubhavanti"; cp. Vedic bhakṣa (*m*) feeding, partaking of food, esp. drink (of Soma), thus something extraordinary.

Bhakkhati [**bhakṣ** fr. **bhaj**, cp. Sk. bhakṣati & bhakṣayati; Dhtp 17 & 537 expl^{ns} by "adana"] to eat, to feed upon Pv II.2[5] (pubba-lohitaŋ); DhA II.57 (vātaŋ). — inf. **bhakkhituŋ** J II.14. — Caus. bhakkheti in same meaning J IV.349 (aor. bhakkhesuŋ); cp. BSk. bhakṣayati Divy 276.

Bhaga [Vedic bhaga, **bhaj**, see bhagavant etc.] luck, lot, fortune, only in cpd. dub° (adj.) unhappy, unpleasant, uncomfortable It 90; DA I.96 (°karaṇa). —**bhaga** (in verse "bhagehi ca vibhattavā" in exegesis of word "Bhagava") at DA I.34 read bhava, as read at id. p. Vism 210.

Bhagandala (& ā) [cp. late Sk. bhagandara] an ulcer, fistula Vin I.216, 272; Nd[1] 370. Has expl^{n} at Dhtm 204 "bhaganda secane hoti" ("comes from sprinkling") anything to do with our word?

Bhagalavant [of uncertain origin] N. of a mountain SnA 197 (loc. Bhagalavati pabbate). Occurs also as an assembly-hall under the N. of Bhagalavatī at D III.201. Cp. Kirfel, *Kosmographie* 196.

Bhagavant (adj. n.) [cp. Vedic bhagavant, fr. bhaga] fortunate, illustrious, sublime, as Ep. and title "Lord." Thus applied to the Buddha (amhākaŋ Bh.) and his predecessors. Occurs with extreme frequency; of fanciful exegetic expl^{ns} of the term & its meaning we mention e. g. those at Nd[1] 142 = Nd[2] 466; Vism 210 sq.; DA I.33 sq. Usual trs. Blessed One, Exalted One.

Bhaginī (f.) [Epic Sk. bhaginī] a sister J VI.32. The popular etym. of bh. as given at VbhA 108 is the same as that for bhātar, viz. "bhagatī ti bh." — Cpd. **bhagini-māla** a "sister garland" (?) N. of a tree J VI.270 (= upari-bhaddaka).

Bhagga[1] pp. of **bhañj**, Sk. bhagna] broken, in phrases "sabbā te phāsukā bhaggā" J I.493, which is applied metaphorically at Dh 154 (phāsukā = pāpakā ?), expl^{d} DhA III.128 (artificially) by "avasesa-kilesa-phāsukā bhaggā"; further "bhaggā pāpakā dhammā" Vism 211; bhaggā kilesā Miln 44; and **bhagga-rāga**, °dosa etc. (in def. of Bhagavā) at Nd[1] 142 = Nd[2] 466 B, quoted at Vism 211.

Bhagga[2] (nt.) [fr. bhaga; cp. Sk. & P. bhāgya] fortune, good luck, welfare, happiness Vism 210 (akāsi °ŋ ti garū ti Bhāgyavā etc.).

Bhaggava [cp. Sk. *bhārgava, a der. fr. bhṛgu, & bhargaḥ, of same root as Lat. fulgur lightning; Gr. φλόξ light; Ger. blitzen, blank; Ags. blanca white horse, all of the idea of "shining, bright, radiant." — How the meaning "potter" is connected with this meaning, is still a problem, perhaps we have to take the word merely as an Epithet at the *one* passage where it occurs, which happens to be in the Kumbhakāra-jātaka, v. 6, 7. i. e. the "Jātaka of the potter"] potter (?) J III.381, 382, in voc. **bhaggava** (m.) & **bhaggavī** (f.). The terms are not expl^{d} in C., evidently because somewhat obscure. According to Kern, *Toev.* s. v. the Sk. form in this meaning occurs at MBh. I.190, 47; Saddhp. 191 sq., MVastu III.347.

Bhaggavant (adj. n.) [fr. bhagga[2], cp. Sk. & P. bhāgyavant] having good luck or auspices, fortunate; in def. of "Bhagavā" at Vism 210 = DA I.34 ("bhāgyavā bhaggavā yutto"); with ref. to the 4 qualities implied in the word "bhagavā," which passage is alluded to at VvA 231 by remark "bhāgyavantat' ādīhi catūhi kāraṇehi Bhagavā."

Bhanga[1] (nt.) [cp. Sk. bhanga, which occurs already Atharva-veda XI. 6. 15 (see Zimmer. *Altind. Leben* 68), also Av. baŋha, Polish pienka hemp. On its possible etym. connection with Vedic śaṇa (Ath. Veda II. 4. 5) = P. sana & sāṇa hemp (= Gr. κάνναβις, Ger. hanf, E. hemp) see Walde, *Lat. Wb.* s. v. cannabis] hemp; coarse hempen cloth Vin I.58 (where comb^{d} with sāṇa).

Bhanga[2] (nt.) [cp. Class. Sk. bhanga, fr. **bhañj**: see bhañjati] 1. (lit.) breaking, breaking off, in sākhā° a layer of broken-off branches J III.407. — 2. (fig.) breaking up, dissolution, disruption (see on form *Cpd.* 25. 66) Ps I.57 sq. (°ānupassanā insight into disruption), quoted & expl^{d} at Vism 640 sq.; VbhA 27 (°khaṇa); Sdhp 48, 78 (āsā°). Cp. vi°.

Bhangana & **Bhangaloka** [to bhanga[1] ?] are vv. ll. of Npl. at Nd[1] 155 for Gangaṇa & Angaṇeka respectively. With misspelling bh>g, cp. bheṇḍaka>geṇḍaka.

Bhacca (adj.) [grd. fr. **bhṛ,** cp. Sk. bhṛtya] to be carried, kept or sustained A III.46 (=a dependant) J IV.301 (C. bharitabba). As Kern. *Toev.* s. v. bhacca points out this gāthā "*bhaccā* mātā pitā bandhū, yena jāto sa yeva so" is a distortion of MBh I.74, 110, where it runs "*bhastrā* mātā, pituḥ putro, yena jāto sa eva saḥ" (or is it *bhrastā* ?).

Bhajati [**bhaj** to divide, partake etc.: see Caus. bhājeti & cp. vi°] to associate with (acc.), keep companionship with, follow, resort to; to be attached to (acc.), to love. Freq. syn. of sevati. The Dhtp & Dhtm mark the fig. meaning (bhaj[2]) by sevāyaŋ (Dhtp 61), sevāputhakkare (Dhtm 523) & saŋsevane (ib. 76), whilst the lit. (bhaj[1]) is expressed by vibhājane. — Sn 958 (bhajato rittaŋ āsanaŋ; gen. sq. ppr.=sevato etc. Nd[1] 466); Dh 76, 303; Pug 26, 33; J I.216=III.510 (disā bh.) VI.358; Sdhp 275. — Pot. bhaje Dh 76, 78, and **bhajetha** Dh 78 (=payirupāsetha), 208 in sense of imper.; hence 2nd sg. formed like Caus. as **bhajehi** J III.148 (C. bhajeyyāsi; cp. Geiger, *P.Gr.* 139[2]). — — grd. **bhajitabba** Nd[2] s. v. kāmaguṇā B (sevitabba, bh., bhāvetabba).

Bhajanā (f.) [fer. **bhaj**] resorting to, familiarity with Pug 20=Dhs 1326, cp. saṃ° & *Dhs trsl.* 345.

Bhājin (adj.) [fr. bhajati] loving, attached to, worshipping Nd[1] 142 (in expl[n] of "Bhagavā").

Bhajjati [Vedic bhṛjjati, cp. Gr. φρύγω to roast, φρύγανον dry wood; Lat. frīgo to make dry] to roast, toast Vin IV.264; Dhtp 79 & Dhtm 94, expl[d] by "pāke." — Caus. bhajjāpeti to have, or get roasted Vin IV.264; DhA I.224 (v. l. K. paccāpeti).

Bhañjaka (adj.) [fr. bhañjati] breaking, spoiling, destroying (attha°-visaŋvāda; cp. bhañjanaka) J III.499.

Bhañjati [**bhañj,** cp. Vedic bhañjati & bhanakti, roots with & without r, as Lat. frango=Goth. brikan=Ohg. brehhan, E. break, Sk. giri-bhraj breaking forth from the mountain; and Sk. bhanga, bhañji wave. — The Dhtp. 68 paraphrases by "omaddana," Dhtm 73 by "avamaddana"] 1. (trs. & intrs.) to break Vin I.74 (phāsukā bhañjitabbā ribs to be broken); Dh 337 (mā bhañji=mā bhañjatu C.). Pv II.9[3] (sākhaŋ bhañjeyya =chindeyya PvA 114); PvA 277 (akkho bhañji the axle broke, intrs.). — 2. to fold or furl (the lip): oṭṭhaŋ bh. J II.264. — 3. (fig.) to break up, spoil, destroy, in **atthaŋ** bh. to destroy the good S IV.347 (cp. bhañjanaka). — pp. bhagga[1] (q. v.).

Bhañjana[1] (nt.) [fr. bhañjati] breakage, breaking down, break, only in cpd. akkha° break of the axle Vism 32, 45; DhA I.375; PvA 277.

Bhañjana[2] (nt.) [for byañjana, in composition; maybe graphical mistake] anointing, smearing, oiling, in gatta° and pāda°-bbhañjana-tela oil for rubbing the body and the feet Vism 100; VvA 295.

Bhañjanaka (nt.) [fr. bhañjana[1]] destroying, hurting, spoiling, in phrase attha° destroying the welfare (with ref. to the telling of lies) DhA III.356; VvA 72; cp. bhañjaka.

Bhañjanin (adj.) [fr. **bhañj**] breaking, destroying, in cakka° breaking the wheel, fig. breaking the state of harmony J V.112.

Bhaññam (J V.317) see bhā.

Bhaṭa [cp. Epic & Class. Sk. bhaṭa, fr. dial. **bhaṭ** to hire; originally the same as bhṛtya fr. bhṛta & bhṛti of **bhṛ** Dhtp 94, Dhtm 114. -bhaṭa=bhatyaŋ i. e. bhṛtyaŋ] servant, hireling, soldier Miln 240; VvA 305 (bhattavetana°). As to suggestion of bhaṭa occurring in phrase yathā-bhaṭaŋ (Kern. *Toev.* s. v. yathābhaṭaŋ) see discussion under **yathā bhataŋ.**

-**patha** service, employment, salary Vin IV.265; SnA 542.

Bhaṭṭha[1] [pp. of **bhraŋś,** see bhassati] dropped, fallen down J I.482; IV.222, 382; V.444. Cp. pari°.

Bhaṭṭha[2] [pp. of **bhaṇ,** for bhaṇita] spoken, said Vv 63[19] (su°=subhāsita VvA 265). See also paccā° & pari°; cp. also next.

Bhaṭṭha[3] (?) [perhaps for bhatta ?] wages, tip, donation J IV.261 (by C. expl[d] as kathita, thus same as bhattha[2]). v. l. bhatta. Cp. Sk. bhāṭa & BSk. bhāṭaka MVastu III.37.

Bhaṇati [**bhaṇ;** cp. Sk. bhaṇati; Ohg. ban=E. ban etc. "proclamation." See connections in Walde, *Lat. Wtb.* under fabula. — Expl[d] by Dhtp 111 as "bhaṇana," by Dhtm 162 as "bhāsana"] to speak, tell, proclaim (the nearest synonym is katheti: see Nd[2] s. v. katheti) Dh 264; Pug 33, 56; DhA II.95. — ppr. bhaṇanto Sn 397. Pot. bhaṇe Sn 1131 (=bhaṇeyya Nd[2] 469); Dh 224 (saccaŋ; =dīpeyya vohareyya DhA III.316). Also bhaṇeyya Sn 397. An old subjunctive form is bhaṇāmase S I.209 (cp. Geiger, *P.Gr.* § 126). Prohib. mā **bhāṇi.** A Caus. form is **bhāṇaye** (Pot.) Sn 397.

Bhaṇana (nt.) [fr. bhaṇati] telling, speaking DhA IV.93 (°sīla, adj. wont to speak); Dhtp 111.

Bhaṇe (indecl.) [orig. 1st sg. pres. Med. of bhaṇati] "I say," used as an interjection of emphasis, like "to be sure," "look here." It is a familiar term of address, often used by a king to his subjects Vin I.240 (amhākaŋ kira bhaṇe vijite Bhaddiya-nagare), 241 (gaccha bhaṇe jānāhi . . .) Miln 21 (atthi bhaṇe añño koci paṇḍito . . .).

Bhaṇḍa (nt.) [cp. Epic Sk. bhāṇḍa] 1. stock in trade; collectively goods, wares, property, possessions, also "object" S I.43 (itthi bhaṇḍānaŋ uttamaŋ woman is the highest property), Nd[2] 38; J III.353 (yācita° object asked, =yāca); ThA 288 (id.); Vism 22. —bhaṇḍaŋ kiṇāti to buy goods VbhA 165. —bhaṇḍaŋ **vikkiṇati** to sell goods J I.377 (+paṭibhaṇḍaŋ dāpeti to receive goods in return); vikkiṇiya-bh. goods for sale DhA I.390. —**assāmika°** ownerless goods, unclaimed property J VI.348; **ābharaṇa°** trinkets, jewelry J III.221; **piya°** best goods, treasure J III.279; **bahu°** having many goods, rich in possessions Vin III.138; KhA 241 (of a bhikkhu); **vara°** best property or belongings Vin IV.225. — 2. implement, article, instrument Vin II.142, 143 (where 3 kinds are distinguished: of wood, copper, & of earthenware), 170 (id.); Dāvs IV.50 (turiya°). — In assa(batthi°)-**bhaṇḍa** Vin I.85 sq., the meaning "horse (elephant-) trader (or owner)" does not seem clear; should we read **paṇḍaka ?** Cp. bhaṇḍa=paṇḍa under bhaṇḍati.

-**āgāra** store house, warehouse, only in der. -**āgārika** keeper of stores Vin I.284; II.176; surveyor of the (royal) warehouses, royal treasurer (a higher court office: cp. Fick. *Sociale Gliederung* 101 sq.) J III.293; IV.43; V.117; Miln 37; DA I.21; PvA 2, 20. -**āhāraka** (trader) taking up goods DhA IV.60.

Bhaṇḍaka (adj. in sense of collect. nt.) [fr. bhaṇḍa] 1. article, implement; kīḷā° toys J VI.6. — 2. belongings, property Vin IV.225. — 3. trappings, in assa° horse-trappings J II.113.

Bhaṇḍati [**bhaṇḍ,** cp. "paṇḍa bhaṇḍa paribhāse" Dhtp 568; Dhtm 798] to quarrel, abuse Vin I.76 (saddhiŋ); IV.277; Th I, 933; SnA 357 (aññamaññaŋ).

Bhaṇḍana (nt.) [fr. **bhaṇḍ**, cp. BSk. bhāṇḍana Divy 164] quarrel, quarrelling, strife It 11; J III.149; Nd[1] 196; DhA I.55, 64.

Bhaṇḍi [?] a certain plant or flower J V.420. Reading uncertain.

Bhaṇḍikā (f.) [fr. bhaṇḍaka, in collect. sense] collection of goods, heap, bundle; **bhaṇḍikaŋ karoti** to make into a heap J III.221, 437; or **bhaṇḍikaŋ bandhati** to tie into a bundle DhA II.254; VvA 187. sahassa° a heap of 1,000 kahāpaṇas J II.424; III.60; IV.2. — *Note*. bhaṇḍika is v. l. at J III.41 for gaṇḍikā.

Bhaṇḍu (adj.) [etym. uncertain, dialectical or = paṇḍu ?] bald-headed, close shaven Vin I.71 (°kamma shaving), 76 (kammāra°); J III.22; VI.538 (+ tittira); Miln 11, 128.

Bhata (adj.) [cp. Epic Sk. bhṛta] 1. supported, fed, reared, maintained A III.46 (bhatā bhaccā "maintained are my dependents"); J V.330 (kicchā bh.), given by Kern, *Toev*. s. v. in meaning "full" with wrong ref. J VI.14. Cp. bharita.

Bhataka [cp. Epic Sk. bhṛtaka] a hired servant, hireling, servant Th 1, 606, 685, 1003; J III.446; Miln 379; DhA I,119, 233 (°vīthi servant street). See also Fick, *Sociale Gliederung* 158, 195, 196.

Bhati (f.) [cp. Vedic bhṛti, fr. **bhṛ**] wages, fee, pay J I.475; III.325, 446; DhA I.21, 70; Dhtp 94 (in expl[n] of root **bhaṭ**, see bhaṭa).

Bhatikā (f.) [fr. bhati] fee J IV.184.

Bhatta (nt.) [cp. Epic & Class. Sk. bhakta, orig. pp. of bhajati] feeding, food, nourishment, meal Dh 185; Pug 28, 55; J II.15; V.170 (bhatta-manuñña-rūpaŋ for bhattaŋ-); Vism 66 (where 14 kinds enum[d], i. e. sangha°, uddesa° etc.); Sdhp 118. —ucchiṭṭha° food thrown away PvA 173; uddesa° special food Vin I.58 = 96, cp. II.175; devasika° daily food (as fee or wages) DA I.296 (= bhatta-vetana); dhura° a meal to which a bhikkhu is invited as leader of others, i. e. a responsible meal J I.449; III.97 (v. l. dhuva°); dhuva° constant supply of food Vin I.25, 243.

-agga [cp. BSk. bhaktāgra Divy 335; MVastu II.478] a refectory Vin I.44; M I.28; J V.334. -ammaṇa food trough J VI.381. -âbhihāra gift of food S I.82. -uddesaka (thera) (an elder) who supervises the distribution of food, a superintendent of meals Vism 388, DhA I.244. -kāraka one who prepares the meal or food, a cook, butler J I.150 sq.; V.296; VI.349; DA I.157. -kicca "meal-performance," meal (cp. BSk. bhakta-kṛtya Divy 185) J I.87; Miln 9; Vism 278 (kata° after the meal, cp. kata II.1. a); PvA 76. -kilamatha fatigue after eating SnA 58 (cp. °sammada). -gāma a village giving tribute or service DhA I.398. -dāna gift of a meal PvA 54. -puṭa a bag with food J II.82, 203; III.200; DA I.270. Cp. puṭabhatta. -puṭaka same KhA 44; VbhA 234; Vism 251. -bhoga enjoyment of food S I.92. -randhaka a cook J IV.431. -vissagga serving a meal, meal-function, participation at a meal Vin IV.263; Pv III.2[9] (so read for vissatta; expl[d] at PvA 184 by bhattakicca & bhuñjana); Miln 9; SnA 19, 140. -vetana service for food, food as wages (cp. bhaktā-dāsa a slave working for food Manu VIII.415, see Fick, *Sociale Gliederung* p. 197), in general "hire, wages," also "professional fee" D III.191; Vin III.222 (rañño bh-v.-āhāro "in the King's pay"); J IV.132 sq., Miln 379; DhA I.25 (to a physician); VvA 305. -velā meal-time SnA 111. -sammada drowsiness after a meal S I.7; J VI.57; Vbh 352; Vism 278, 295. -sālā hall for meals, refectory Vism 72.

Bhattar [Vedic bhartṛ to **bhṛ**] a husband; nom. sg. bhattā Th 2, 413; J V.104, 260 (here in meaning "supporter"); VI.492; gen. bhattu J V.169, 170; acc. bhattāraŋ Th 2, 412.

Bhattavant (adj.) [fr. *bhakta, pp. of bhajati] possessing reverence or worship(pers), worshipful, adored; in a (late) verse analysing fancifully the word "Bhagavant," at DA I.34 = Vism 210 sq. Expl[d] at Vism 212 by "bhaji-sevi-bahulaŋ karoti."

Bhatti (f.) [cp. Vedic & Class. Sk. bhakti, fr. **bhaj**; see bhajati] 1. devotion, attachment, fondness Pug 20 = Dhs 1326 (cp. *Dhs trsl*. 345); Pug 65; J V.340 (= sineha C.); VI.349; VvA 353, 354. — 2. in bhatti-kata Th 2, 413 it means "service," thus "doing service" (or "rendered a servant"?). — 3. of uncertain meaning in bhatti-kamma, probably "making lines, decoration, ornamentation" Vin II.113 (°kamma-kata decorated), 151. The reading is uncertain, may be bhati° (? Kern, *Toev*. s. v. trsl[s] "patchwork"?). Cp. vi°.

Bhattika (adj.) (-°) [fr. bhatta] in dhuva° being in constant supply of food, being a regular attendant (servant) or adviser Vin II.15. Also at ThA 267 in meaning "being a servant, working for food" in expl[n] of bhattikatā (= kata-sāmi-bhattikā), said of a toiling housewife.

Bhattimant (adj.) [from bhatti] 1. devoted? 2. discerning, analytical, perspicacious? Th 1, 370; ThA has: yathānusiṭṭhaŋ paṭipattiyā tattha bhattımā nāma.

Bhadanta (Bhaddanta) [a secondary adj. formation from address bhaddaŋ (= bhadraŋ) te "hail to thee," cp. "bhaddaŋ vo" under bhadda 1] venerable, reverend, mostly in *voc*. as address "Sir, holy father" etc., to men of the Order. voc. sg. **bhadante** S I.216 (v. l. bhaddante); voc. pl. **bhadantā** DhA III.414. — A contracted form of bhadante is **bhante** (q. v.). *Note*. In case of bhadanta being the corresp. of Sk. *bhavanta (for bhavān) we would suppose the change v > d and account for dd on grounds of pop. analogy after bhadda. See bhante. The pl. nom. from bhadantā is formed after bhadante, which was felt as a voc. of an a -stem with -e for -a as in Prk. Māgadhi.

Bhadantika (adj.) (-°) [fr. bhadanta] only in cpd. **ehi°**, lit. "one belonging to the (greeting) 'come hail to thee,'" i. e. one who accepts an invitation D III.40, M II.161; A I.295; II.206; Pug 55. See also under ehi.

Bhadara in °paṇḍu at A I.181 is to be read as badara°.

Bhadda[(a)] & **Bhadra**[(b)] (adj.) [cp. Vedic bhadra, on diff. forms see Geiger, *P.Gr*. § 53[2]. Dhtp 143, 589 expl[s] **bhadd** by "kalyāṇe"; whereas Dhtm 205 & 823 gives **bhad (bhadd)** with expl[n] "kalyāṇa kammāni"] 1. auspicious, lucky, high, lofty, august, of good omen, reverend (in address to people of esteem), good, happy, fortunate D II.95[(a)]; S I.117[(b)]; Dh 143 sq.[(b)] (of a good, well-trained horse), 380[(b)] (id.); J VI.281[(b)] (24 bhadrā pāsakā or lucky throws of the dice); DhA I.33[(a)] (voc. bhadde = ayye). — **bhadraŋ** (nt.) something bringing luck, a good state, welfare; a good deed (= kalyāṇaŋ) Dh 120 (= bhadra-kamma, viz. kāya-sucarita etc. DhA III.14); PvA 116 (= iṭṭhaŋ). Also as form of address "hail to thee," bhaddaŋ vo J V.260. — 2. a kind of arrow (cp. Sk. bhalla) J II.275 (v. l. bhadra; so Kern, *Toev*. s. v.; but C. takes it as bhadda lucky, in neg. sense "unlucky, sinister," & expl[s] by bibhaccha awful). — 3. bull (cp. Sk. bhadra, Halāyudha 5, 21) Th 1, 16, 173, 659.

-mukha one whose face brings blessings, a complimentary address, like "my noble &c friend!" cp. BSk. bhadramukha; Divy frequent: see Index] M II.53; S I.74 (cp. *K.S*. I.100[n]) J II.261 (v. l. bhadda°); Vism 92 (v. l. SS bhadda°). -muttaka [cp. Sk. bhadramusta] a kind of fragrant grass (Cyperus rotundus) DA I.81; Abhp 599. -yuga a noble pair DhA I.95 (Kolita & Upatissa). -vāhana the auspicious (royal) vehicle (or carriage) Miln 4.

Bhaddaka[(a)] & **Bhadraka**[(b)] [fr. bhadda] 1. good, of good quality (opp. pāpaka) A IV.169[(a)]. — 2. honoured, of high repute J III.269[(a)] (=sambhāvita C.). — 3. (m. nt.) a good thing, lucky or auspicious possession, a valuable. Appl[d] to the 8 requisites (parikkhārā) of a Samaṇa at J V.254[(b)]. — On upari-bhaddaka (N. of a tree J VI.269; C. = bhagini-mālā) see upari. — At A IV.255 bhaddaka is given as one of the eight ingredients of the sun & moon; it may be gold (? cp. Kirfel, *Kosmographie* 190), or simply a term for a very valuable quality.

Bhanta [pp. of **bham**] swerving, swaying, staggering, deviating; always used of an uncontrolled car (ratha or yāna) Dh 222 (ratha = ativegena dhāvanta DhA III.301); (yāna = adanta akārita aviṇīta Nd[1] 145); DhsA 260 (°yāna). Cp. vi°.

Bhantatta (nt.) [fr. bhanta] turmoil, confusion Dhs 429 (=vibhanti-bhāva DhsA 260, so read for vibhatti°); cp. *Dhs trsl.* 120.

Bhante [would correspond either to Sk. *bhavantaḥ (with ending °e as Māgadhism for °aḥ) = bhavān, or to P. bhadanta. In both cases we have a contraction. The expl[n] bhante = bhadante (bhadantaḥ) is advocated by Pischel, *Prk. Gr.* §§ 165, 366[b], intimated also by Weber, *Bhagavatī* 156 n. 3 (unable to explain -e); the expl[n] bhante = bhavantah (see bhavaŋ) by Geiger, *P.Gr.* 98[3]; hinted at by Weber loc. cit. (bhavantaḥ = bhagavantaḥ)] voc. of polite address: Sir, venerable Sir, used like bhadante. Either abs. as voc.: Vin I.76; D II.154, 283; J II.111; III.46; Miln 19; or with another voc.: Miln 25; or with other oblique cases, as with nom. D I.179; DhA I.62. with gen. D I.179.

Bhabba (adj.) [grd of **bhū**, Sk. bhavya] 1. able, capable, fit for (-° or with dat. or inf.); abhabba unfit, incapable; Vin I.17; S III.27 (dukkha-kkhayāya); IV.89 (id.); Pug 12, 13; Vism 116 (bhikkhu), neg. It 106 (anta-kiriyāya), 117 (phuṭṭhuŋ sambodhiŋ); J I.106 (°puggala a person unfit for the higher truths & salvation). bhabbâbhabba fit & unfit people Nd[2] 235[3] = Vism 205, expl[d] at Vbh 341, 342 by "bhabbā niyāmaŋ okkamituŋ kusalesu dhammesu sammattaŋ." — 2. possible (& abhabba impossible) M III.215 (kammaŋ bhabba-ābhāsa apparently possible). — See also **abhabba**.

Bhabbatā (f.) [abstr. fr. bhabba] possibility; neg. a° impossibility Sn 232; KhA 191; VvA 208.

Bhamati [**bhram**; on etym. see *K.Z.* IV.443; VI.152. Expl[d] at Dhtp 219 by "anavaṭṭhāne," i. e. unsettledness] to spin (of a wheel), to whirl about, to roam Dh 371 (mā te kāmaguṇe bhamassu cittaŋ); J I.414; III.206 = IV.4 (cakkaŋ matthake); IV.6 (kumbha-kāra-cakkaŋ iva bh.); V.478. — pp. **bhanta**. — Caus. **bhameti** to make whirl Vism 142 (cakkaŋ).

Bhamara [cp. Epic & Class. Sk. bhramara; either to **bhram** (semantically quick, unsteady motion = confused noise), cp. Gr. φόρμιγξ zither; or perhaps for *bramara to Ohg. bremo = Ger. bremse gadfly, bremen = brummen to hum; Gr. βρόμος thunder, Lat. fermo to growl, roar: see Walde, *Lat. Wtb.* s. v. fermo] 1. a bee J V.205 (°vaṇṇa bee-coloured, i. e. of *black* colour, in expl[n] of kaṇha); Th II, 252. Usually in similes, e. g. at Dh 49 (cp. DhA I.374 sq.); Vism 142, 152; SnA 139. — 2. in **bhamara-tanti** "the string that sounds," one of the seven strings of the lute J II.253, cp. VvA 140.

Bhamarikā (f.) [fr. bhamara] a humming top J V.478.

Bhamu (f.) [secondary formation after bhamuka] eyebrow J VI.476 (ṭhita°), 482 (nīla°).

Bhamuka (& **Bhamukha**) (f.) [cp. Vedic bhrū; the Pali word is possibly a comp[n] of bhrū + mukha with dissimilation of first u to a] eyebrow Th II, 232 = S I.132 pamukh-; J IV.18 (in expl[n] of su-bbhū = su-bhamukhā in C.; Fausböll puts "bhamuka"? Kern on this passage quotes BSk. bhrūmukha, see *Toev.* s. v.); VI.503 (aḷāra° for pamukha); DhA III.102; IV.90, 197 = J V.434; SnA 285.

Bhaya (nt.) [fr. **bhī**, cp. Vedic bhaya, P. bhāyati] fear, fright, dread A II.15 (jāti-maraṇa°); D III.148, 182; Dh 39, 123, 212 sq., 283; Nd[1] 371, 409; Pug 56; Vism 512; KhA 108; SnA 155; DhA III.23. There are some lengthy enum[n] of objects causing fear (sometimes under term mahabbhaya, mahā-bhaya), e. g. one of 17 at Miln 196, one of 16 (four times four) at A II.121 sq., the same in essence, but in different order at Nd[2] 470, and at VbhA 502; one of 16 (with remark "ādi," and so on) at Vism 645. Shorter comb[ns] are to be found at Sn 964 (5, viz. ḍaŋsā, adhipātā, siriŋsapā, manussa-phassā, catuppādā); Vbh 379 (5, viz. ājīvika°, asiloka°, parisa-sārajja°, maraṇa°, duggati°, expl[d] at VbhA 505 sq.), 376 (4: jāti°, jarā°, vyādhi°, maraṇa°) 367 (3: jāti°, jarā°, maraṇ°); Nd[1] 402 (2: diṭṭha-dhammikaŋ & samparāyikaŋ bh.). —**abhaya** absence of fear, safety Vin I.75 (abhay-ûvara for abhaya-vara?); Dh 317; J I.150; DhA III.491.

-ñāṇa insight into what is to be feared: see *Cpd.* 66. **-dassāvin** seeing or realising an object of fear, i. e. danger Vbh 244, 247 and passim. **-dassin** id. Dh 31, 317. **-bherava** fear & dismay M I.17 (= citt' uttrasassa ca bhayānak' ārammaṇassa adhivacanaŋ MA 113), N. of Suttanta No. 4 in Majjhima (pp. 16 sq.), quoted at Vism 202; SnA 206.

Bhayānaka (adj.) [fr. bhaya, cp. Epic Sk. bhayānaka] frightful, horrible J III.428; MA 113; PvA 24 (as °ika); Sdhp 7, 208. — nt. °ŋ something awful Nd[2] 470 (in def. of bhaya).

Bhara-bhara, a word imitating a confused sound M I.128; otherwise contracted to **babbhara** (q. v.).

Bhara (adj.) (-°) [fr. **bhṛ**] "bearing" in act. & pass. meaning, i. e. supporting or being supported; only in cpd. **dubbhara** hard to support A V.159, 161 (v. l. dubhara), and **subhara** easy to support Th I, 926 (trsl. "of frugal ways").

Bharaṇa (nt.) [fr. **bhṛ**, Epic Sk. bharaṇa] bearing, supporting, maintenance Dhtm 346 (in expl[n] of **bhṛ**); Abhp 1053.

Bharatā (f.) [abstr. fr. bhara] only in cpd. **dub°** difficulty to support, state of being hard to maintain, synonymous with kosajja at A IV.280, and kuhanā at A V.159, 161. — opp. subharatā A IV.280.

Bharati [**bhṛ**, cp. Lat. fero, Gr. φέρω, Av. baraiti, Oir. berim, Goth. bairan = to bear, Ger. gebären. Dhtm expl[s] simply by "bharena"] to bear, support, feed, maintain J V.260 (mama bharatha, ahaŋ bhattā bhavāmi vo; C. expl[ns] as "maŋ icchatha"). — pp. bhata. See also bhaṭa, bhara, bharita, and Der. fr. bhār°. A curious Passive form is anu-bhīramāna (ppr.) M III.123 (chatta: a parasol being spread out), on which see Geiger, *P.Gr.* § 52, 5; 175 n. 3, 191.

Bharita (adj.) [lit. made to bear, i. e. heavy with etc. Cp. formations bhār°, fr. bharati] filled with (-°) J I.2 (suvaṇṇa-rajata° gabbha); IV.489 (udaka°); V.275 (kimi°); SnA 494 (vāta°); ThA 283 (kuṇapa°).

Bhariyā (f.) [fr. **bhṛ**, Vedic bhāryā] a wife (lit. one who is supported) D III.190; It 36; J III.511; DhA I.329.

Bharu [a dial. (inscription) word, cp. Kern, *Toev.* s. v.] sea, in two names for a town and a kingdom viz. **Bharu-kaccha** Nd[1] 155; J II.188; IV.137, and **Bharu-raṭṭha** J II.169 sq., a kingdom which is said to have been swallowed up by the sea. — Also in N. of the King of that country Bharu-rājā J II.171 (v. l. Kuru°). — Der. Bhārukacchaka an inhabitant of Bharukaccha DhsA 305 (so read at *Expos.* II.401).

Bhallaka [lit. from the Bhalla people] a kind of copper, enum^d under the eight pisāca-lohāni, or copper coming from the Pisāca country VbhA 63 (is reading correct ?). It is doubtful whether we should not read mallaka, cp. malla.

Bhallāṭaka [cp. Epic Sk. bhallātaka] the marking nut plant Semicarpus anacardium J VI.578.

Bhava [cp. Sk. bhava, as philosophical term late, but as N. of a deity Vedic; of **bhū**, see bhavati] "becoming," (form of) rebirth, (state of) existence, a "life." There are 3 states of existence conventionally enum^d as **kāma°, rūpa°, arūpa°** or sensual existence, deva-corporeal, & formless existence (cp. rūpa) D II.57; III.216; S II.3; IV.258; A II.223; III.444; Nd^1 48; Nd^2 s. v. dhātu B.; Vism 210 = DA I.34; Vism 529; VbhA 204. — Another view is represented by the division of bhava into kamma° and upapatti° (uppatti°), or the active functioning of a life in relation to the fruitional, or resultant way of the next life (cp. *Cpd.* 43) Vbh 137; Vism 571; VbhA 183; also in def. of bhava at Nd^2 471 (kamma° and paṭisandhika punabbhava). — In the "causal chain" (Paṭicca-samuppāda, q. v.) bhava is represented as condition of birth (jāti), or resultant force for new birth. — See Sn 361, 514, 742, 839, 923, 1055, 1133; Dh 348; Nd^1 274; Vbh 294, 358; Vism 556 sq.; DhA IV.221; Sdhp 33, 333, 335. — On **itibhav'-âbhava** see iti, and add ref. Vbh 375. — A remarkable use of **bhava as nt.** (obstr.) to **bhū** (in cpd.) is to be noted in the def. given by Bdhgh. of divya = divi bhavaŋ (for divi-bhū) KhA 227; SnA 199; and mānasaŋ = manasi bhavaŋ (for manasi-bhū) KhA 248, cp. Pāṇini IV.3, 53. Similarly āroga bhava health DhA I.328 for °bhava. — Cp. anu°, vi°, sam°.

-agga the best (state of) existence, the highest point of existence (among the gods) J III.84; Vbh 426; Miln 132; KhA 179, 249; SnA 17, 41, 507; often as highest, "heaven" as opposed to Avīci, the lowest hell; thus at J IV.182; VI.354; Miln 336. **-anga** constituent of becoming, function of being, functional state of subconsciousness, i. e. subliminal consciousness or subconscious life-continuum, the vital continuum in the absence of any process [of mind, or attention] (thus Mrs Rh. D. in *Expos.* 185 n.), subconscious individual life. See on term *Cpd.* 26 sq., 265-267; & cp. *Dhs trsl.* 134. — J VI.82; Miln 299 sq.; Vism 164, 676; DhsA 72, 140, 269; DhA I.23; VbhA 81, 156 sq., 406. **-antaga** "gone to the ends of existence," past existence, Ep. of the Bhagavan Buddha Vism 210. **-antara** an existence interval, i. e. transition fr. one life to another, a previous or subsequent life Vism 553 sq. **-âbhava** this or that life, any form of existence some sort of existence Sn 1060, 1068; Nd^1 48, 109, 284; Nd^2 472, 664 A; Th I, 784 (ThA mahantāmahanta bh.) ThA 71 (Ap. v. 30); VbhA 501. **-āsava** the intoxicant of existence D III.216; Vbh 364, 373. **-uppatti** coming into (a new) ex. — Four such bh.-uppattis lead to rebirth among the foll. gods: the paritt'-ābhā devā, the appamāṇ'-ābhā d., the sankiliṭṭh'-ābhā d., the parisuddh'-ābhā d. M III.147. **-esanā** longing for rebirth D III.216, 270. **-ogha** the flood of rebirth (see ogha) Nd^1 57, 159; Vism 480. **-cakka** the wheel or round of rebirth, equivalent to the Paṭicca-samuppāda Vism 529, 576 sq.; in the same context at VbhA 138, 194 sq. **-carimakā** the last rebirth Vism 291. **-taṇhā** craving for rebirth D III.212, 216, 274; S V.432; Sn 746; Vbh 101, 358, 365; Th 2, 458; ThA 282; VbhA III.133. **-netti** [cp. BSk. bhava-netrī M.Vastu II.307; °netrika I I.337] leader to renewed ex., guide to ex. Vin I.231; It 38; Dhs 1059 ≈ (cp. DhsA 364 bhava-rajju). **-saŋyojana** the fetter of rebirth: see arahant II. C. **-salla** the sting or dart of rebirth Dh 351 (= sabbāni bhavagāmini sallāni DhA IV.70). **-sāta** (pl. sātāni) the pleasures of ex., variously enum^d in sets of from one to six at Nd^1 30. **-ssita** at J V.371 read with v. l. as ghaṭa-ssita.

Bhavati [**bhū** to become, cp. Sk. bhūmi earth; Gr. φύσις nature (physical), φύομαι to grow; Lat. fui I have been, futurus = future; Oir. buith to be; Ags. būan = Goth. bauan to live, Ger. bauen, also Ags. bŷldan = to build; Lith. bûti to be, būtas house Dhtp I: bhū sattāyaŋ] to become, exist, behave etc. (cp. Nd^2 474 = sambhavati jāyati nibbattati pātu-bhavati). — I. *Forms.* There are two bases used side by side, viz. bhav° and (contracted) ho°, the latter especially in the (later) Gāthā style and poetry in general, also as archaic in prose, whereas bhav° forms are older. On compounds with prepositions, as regards inflection, see Geiger, *P.Gr.* §§ 131^2, 151^3; and cp. anubhavati, abhibhavati, abhisaŋ°, pa° (also pahoti, pahūta), pari°, vi°, saŋ°. — 1. Pres. ind. **bhavāmi** Sn 511 & **homi** J III.260; 2nd **bhavasi** & **hosi** M III.140; Vv 84^{20}; 3rd **bhavati** freq.; Sn 36 (where Nd^2 474 with v. l. BB of Sn reads bhavanti; Divy p. 294 also reads bhavanti snehāḥ as conjecture of Cowell's for MSS. bhavati); Dh 249, 375; & **hoti** freq.; 1st pl. **homa** Pv I.11^8; 2nd **hotha** J I.307; 3rd **bhavanti** & **honti** freq. — imper. 2nd sg. **bhava** Sn 337, 340, 701; Dh 236; Th 2, 8; **bhavāhi** Sn 510; **hohi** Sn 31; M III.134; J I.32; PvA 89. 3rd sg. **hotu** Sn 224; J III.150; PvA 13; Miln 18. pl. 1st med. **bhavāmase** Th I, 1128; Sn 32; 2nd pl. **bhavatha** J II.218, **bhavātha** Sn 692; Dh 144; **hotha** Dh 243; Dh II.141; J II.302; DhA I.57; 3rd pl. **bhavantu** Sn 145; **hontu** J II.4. Pot. 1st sg. **bhaveyyaŋ** J VI.364; 2nd **bhaveyyāsi** Ud 91; PvA 11; 3rd **bhave** Sn 716, **bhaveyya** J II.159; DhA I.329, & **hupeyya** Vin I.8 (for huveyya: see Geiger, *P.Gr.* § 39^6 & 131^2); pl. 1st **bhaveyyāma**; 2nd **bhavetha** Sn 1073, 3rd **bhaveyyuŋ** Sn 906. — ppr. **bhavaŋ** Sn 92, & **bhavanto** Sn 968; f. **hontī** PvA 79. — fut. 1st sg. **bhavissāmi** PvA 49, **hessāmi** Th 2, 460 (ThA 283 reads bhavissāmi), **hessaŋ** Th I, 1100; J III.224; Pv I.10^5; 2nd **bhavissasi** PvA 10, **hohisi** Pv I.3^3; 3rd **bhavissati** Dh 228, 264; DhA II.82, **hessati** J III.279 & med. **hessate** Mhvs 25, 97, **hehiti** Bu II.10 = A I.4; Vv 63^{32}; & **hossati** (in pahossati fr. pahoti DhA III.254); 1st pl. **bhavissāma** Dh 200; 2nd **hessatha** S IV.179; 3rd **bhavissanti** freq. — Cond. 1st sg. **abhavissaŋ** J I.470; 2nd **abhavissa** J II.11; III.30; 3rd **abhavissa** It 37; Vin I.13; D II.57; M III.163; J I.267; II.112 (na bhavissa = nābhavissa ?); 3rd pl. **abhavissaŋsu** Vin I.13. 1st *aor.* (orig. pret. of *huvati, cp. hupeyya Pot.; see Geiger *P.Gr.* 131^2, 162^2): 1st sg. **ahuvā** S I.36, with by-form (see aor.) **ahuvāsiŋ** Vv 82^6; 2nd **ahuvā** ibid., 3rd **ahuvā** Vv 81^{24}; J II.106; III.131; 1st pl. **ahuvāma** M I.93; II.214 & **ahuvamha** ibid.; 2nd **ahuvattha** S IV.112, M I.445; DhA I.57. — 2nd *aor.* (simple aor., with pret. endings): 1st sg. **ahuŋ** Pv II.3^2 (v. l. BB ahu) (= ahosiŋ PvA 83); 2nd **ahu** (sk. abhūḥ) Pv II.3^6; 3rd **ahū** (Sk. abhūt) Sn 139, 312, 504 and passim; Pv I.2^3, & **ahu** Pv I.9^3; I.11^3; & **bhavi** DhA I.329 (pātubhavi); 1st pl. **ahumhā** (Sk. abhūma) Pv I.11^6, & **ahumha** J I.362; DhA I.57. — 3rd *aor.* (see aor.) 1st sg. **ahosiŋ** Th I, 620; J I.106; VvA 321; PvA 10 (= āsiŋ); 2nd **ahosi** J I.107; 3rd **ahosi** Sn 835; Vin I.23; 1st pl. **ahesumha** M I.265; 3rd **ahesuŋ** D II.5; Vv 74^4; J I.149; DhA I.327; & **bhaviŋsu** (Sk. abhāviṣuḥ) DhA IV.15. — Of *medial* forms we mention the 1st pl. pres. **bhavāmahe** Mhvs I.65, and the 3rd sg. pret. **ahuvattha** VvA 103. Inf. **bhavituŋ** Sn 552, & **hetuye** Bu II.10. ger. **bhavitvā** Sn 56, **hutvā** Sn 43, & **hutvāna** Sn 281. — grd. **bhavitabba** J I.440; VI.368; **hotabba** Vin I.46; **bhabba** (Sk. bhavya): see sep.; **bhuyya** see cpd. abhibhuyya. — Caus. **bhāveti** see sep. — pp. **bhūta**. *Note.* In comp° with nouns or adjectives the final vowel of these is changed into ī, as in comb° of the same with the root **kṛ**, e. g. bhasmībhavati to be reduced to ashes, cp. bhasmī-karaṇa s. v. bhasma, etc. — II. *Meanings*. In general the meaning "to become, to get" prevails, but many shades of it are possible according to context & combinations. It is impossible & unnecessary to enumerate all shades of meaning, only a few idiomatic uses may be pointed out. — 1. to happen, to occur, to befall J vi.368. — 2. The fut. bhavissati "is certainly," "must be" DhA iii.171 (sātthikā desanā bh.); Miln 40 (mātā ti pi na bh.). — 3. Imper. **hotu** as adv. "very well" Miln 18 (hotu bhante very well, sir). — 4. aor. in meaning and as substitute of āsiṃ, pret. of **as** to be; etad ahosi this occurred to him DhA i.399 (assā etad ahosi "this thought struck her").

Bhavatta (nt.) [abstr. fr. **bhū**] the fact of being, state, condition KhA 227.

Bhavana (nt.) [fr. **bhū**] dwelling, sphere, world, realm S i.206, Sn 810 (see explⁿ Nd¹ 132 : nerayikānaṃ nirayo bh. etc. & SnA 534 : niray' ādi-bhede bhavane) ; Nd¹ 448 (Inda° the realm of Indra) ; J iii.275 (nāga° the world of the Nāgas).

Bhavant [cp. Sk. (& Vedic) bhavant, used as pron. of the 2nd ; but constructed with 3rd person of the verb. Probably a contraction fr. bhagavant, see Whitney, *Altind. Gr.* 456] pron. of polite address "Sir, Lord," or "venerable, honourable," or simply "you." Cases as follows (after Geiger, *P.Gr.* § 98³) : sg. nom. **bhavaṃ** Sn 486 ; D i.249 ; M i.484. nt. **bhavaṃ** M iii.172. acc. **bhavantaṃ** Sn 597 ; D ii.231 ; instr. **bhotā** D i.93, 110 ; S iv.120. gen. **bhoto** Sn 565 ; M i.486 ; voc. **bhavaṃ** D i.93 & **bho** D i.93 ; M i.484 ; J ii.26. See **bho** also sep. — pl. nom. **bhavanto** Sn p. 107 (only as v. l. ; T. bhagavanto), & **bhonto** ibid. ; M ii.2 ; Miln 25 ; acc. **bhavante** M ii.3 ; instr. **bhavantehi** M iii.13 ; gen. **bhavataṃ** M ii.3 ; voc. **bhonto** Th 1, 832 ; M ii.2 ; — f. **bhotī** : sg. nom. **bhotī** Sn 988 ; J iii.95 ; acc. **bhotiṃ** J vi.523 ; loc. **bhotiyā** ibid. voc. **bhoti** ibid. ; D ii.249. — On form **bhante** see this.

Bhaveyya [cp. Class. Sk. bhavya] a sort of tree, perhaps Averrhoa carambola J vi.529.

Bhasati [cp. Epic Sk. bhaṣate] to bark (of dogs) J iv.182 (aor. bhasi ; so read for T. bhusi). — pp. **bhasitaṃ** (as n.) bark ibid. (mahā-bhasitaṃ bhasi, read for bhusita). See also **bhusati.**

Bhasita 1. see bhasati. — 2. pp. of **bhas** "crumbled to ashes" see bhasma.

Bhasta [cp. Vedic basta] a he-goat J iii.278.

Bhastā (f.) & bhasta (nt.) [cp. Class. Sk. bhastrā (also *one* MBh. passage), orig. n. ag. fr. **bhas** (to bark ?), lit. bellower, blower] 1. a bellows Th 1, 1134 ; J vi.12 (vāta-puṇṇa-bhasta-camma, skin of bellows full of wind) ; SnA 171 (vāta-pūrita-bhastrā viya), 494 (vāta-bharita°) ; DhA i.442 (bhastaṃ dhamāpeti) ; Vism 287. — 2. a sack Th 1, 1151 ; 2, 466 (T. reads gatta, but ThA 283 reads bhasta & expl^s as "camma-pasibbaka") ; J iii.346 (sattu° = sattu pasibbaka flour sack) ; v.45 ; ThA 212 (udaka°). **biḷāra-bhastā** a bag of catskin M i.128 (= biḷāra-camma-pasibbaka Bdhgh) ; Th 1, 1138.

Bhasma(n) (nt.) [cp. Vedic bhasman (adj.) ; Sk. bhasman (n.), originally ppr. of **bhas** to chew & thus n-stem. It has passed into the a-decl. in Pali, except in the loc. **bhasmani** (S i.169). Etymologically & semantically bhasman is either "chewing" or "anything chewed (small)," thus meaning particle, dust, sand, etc. ; and **bhas** is another form of **psā** (cp. Sk. psā morsel of food, psāta hungry = P. chāta). Idg. *bhsā & *bhsam, represented in Gr. ψώχω to grind, ψάμμος & ψῶχος sand ; Lat. sabulum sand. The Dhtp 326 & Dhtm 452 explain **bhas** by bhasmī-karaṇa "reduce to ashes," a pp. of it is bhasita ; it also occurs in Sk. loc. bhasi] ashes S i.169 = Nd² 576 (loc. bhasmani) ; Vv 84⁴⁴ ; J iii.426 ; Vism 469 (in comparison).

-**antāhuti** (bhasm' ant' āhuti) "whose sacrifice ends in ashes" D i.55 (so read for bhassant°, according to DA i.166, & cp. Franke, *Dīgha Nikāya* p. 60) ; M i.515 ; S iii.207. -**acchanna** covered by ashes Dh 71 (= chārikāya paṭichanna DhA ii.68) ; J vi.236 (. . . va pāvaka). -**puṭa** a sack for ashes DA i.267 (as explⁿ for assa-puṭa of D. i.98 ; fanciful ; see assa¹). -**bhāva** "ashy" state, state of being crumbled to dust VvA 348.

Bhassa (nt.) [cp. Class. Sk. bhāṣya, of **bhāṣ**] speech, conversation, way of talking, disputation Sn 328 (v. l. for hassa) ; It 71 ; Miln 90 ; Vism 127 (grouped into fit talk, as the 10 kathā-vatthus, and unfit talk or gossip, as the 32 tiracchāna-kathā).

-**kāraka** one who makes talk, i. e. invites disputation, or one who gossips Vin i.1 ; Nd¹ 142 ; f. °kārikā Vin iv.230. -**pavādaka** one who proposes disputation, one who is fond of debate & discussions M i.161, 227 (°ika) ; Miln 4. -**pavedin** one experienced in debating Miln 90. -**samācāra** (good) conduct in speech, proficiency in disputation D iii.106. -**samussaya** grandiloquence, proud talk Sn 245 (cp. SnA 288 = att'ukkaṃsanatā ti vuttaṃ hoti).

Bhassati [**bhraṅś**, Sk. bhraśyate] to fall down, drop, to droop (Dhtp 455 & Dhtm 695 : adho-patane & adho-pāte) J iv.223 ; vi.530. ppr. **bhassamāna** Miln 82 ; pret. 3rd sg. **bhassittha** J ii.274 (cp. pabhassittha Vin ii.135), & abhassittha S i.122 (so read for abhassatha). — pp. **bhaṭṭha**¹.

Bhassara (adj. n.) [fr. **bhās**] 1. (adj.) shining, resplendent J v.169 (C. pabhassara). — 2. N. of a bird J vi.538 (= sata-haṃsa C.). — Cp. ā°, pa°.

Bhā (f.) [cp. Vedic bhā & bhāḥ nt.] light, splendour ; given as name of a jewel at an extremely doubtful passage J v.317, 318, where T. reads "vara taṃ bhañ ñam icchasi," & C. expl^s. : "bhā ti ratanass' etaṃ nāmaṃ." The v. l. for bhaññaṃ is bhuñjaṃ ; the passage may be corrupt from "varatu bhavaṃ yam icchasi."

Bhākuṭika (adj.) [fr. bhakuṭi] knitting the eyebrows, frowning, only in redupl. cpd. **bhākuṭika-bhākuṭiko** frowning continually, supercilious Vin ii.11 = iii.181 (manda-mando +) ; Nd² 342 (korajika-korajiko +) ; Vism 26 (id.). — f. **bhākuṭikā** a frown, frowning, superciliousness, def. at Vism 26 as "padhāna-parimathita-bhāva-dassanena bhākuṭi [read bhakuṭi] -karaṇaṃ **mukha-sankoco** ti vuttaṃ hoti." It occurs in stock phrase bhākuṭikā bhākuṭiyaṃ kuhanā kuhāyanā in def. of kuhanā at Vbh 352 = Vism 23, 25 (cp. Nd¹ 225), and at Nd² 342 D. See also VbhA 482 (bhākuṭi-karaṇaṃ sīlam assā ti bhākuṭiko). The form **bhākuṭiyaṃ** (nt.) is originally the same as **bhākuṭikā**, only differentiated in C.-style. The def. at Vism 26 is "bhākuṭikassa bhāvo bhākuṭiyaṃ." The v. l. ibid. is bhākuṭitā. —**bhākuṭikaṃ karoti** to make a frowning face, to act superciliously Vism 105 (as a quality of one "dosa-carita").

Bhāga [cp. Vedic bhāga, fr. **bhaj**, bhajati] 1. part, portion, fraction, share Vin i.285 ; Sn 427 (sahassa-bhāgo maraṇassa = sahassaṃ bhāgānaṃ assā ti SnA 387 ; a thousand times a share of death, i. e. very near death, almost quite dead), 702 (v. l. SnA 492 for Sn samāna-bhāva, evenness, proportionate-ness) ; Vv 14⁶ (= kummāsa-koṭṭhāsa VvA 62) ; Pv i.11⁵ (aḍḍhi° one half) ; Vin iv.264. — Cp. vi°. —**bhāgaso** (abl.-adv.) in parts, by parts, by portions, esp. in even portions, i. e. evenly, in proportion S i.193

(according to each one's share; cp. Th 1, 1242); M III.183; Vv 7²; Miln 330, 415 (aneka° hundredfold or more). bhāgaso mita (of cities or dwelling-places etc.) evenly planned, well laid out, i. e. in squares Sn 300, 305 (nivesanāni suvibhattāni bhāgaso); J V.266 (cp. C. on p. 272) = Nd² 304$^{III. D}$; Pv I.10¹³ (= bhāgato mita PvA 52). —bhāgabhatta apportioned food, ration DhA I.134. — Cp. dobbhagga "disproportionateness," i. e. bad luck. — 2. apportioned share (of money), fee, remuneration, always in term ācariya° (ācariyassa) the teacher's fee (usually consisting in 1,000 kahāpaṇas) J I.273; V.457; VI.178; Miln 10; DhA I.253. — 3. division of space, quarter, side, place, region: disā° quarter of the compass Vin II.217; para° outside part KhA 206 = PvA 24 (kuḍḍānaŋ parabhāgā = tiro-kuḍḍā); pacchā-bhāgaŋ (acc. adv.) at the back part, behind PvA 114. — fig. way, respect, in ubhato-bhāga-vimutta "free in both ways" D II.71; M I.477 (see *Dial* II.70; i. e. free both by insight and by the intellectual discipline of the 8 stages of Deliverance, the aṭṭha vimokkhā). — 4. division of time, time, always -°, e. g. pubba° the past, apara° the future PvA 133; obl. cases adverbially: tena divasa-bhāgena (+ratti bhāgena) at that day (& that very night) Miln 18; apara-bhāge (loc.) in future J I.34; PvA 116.

Bhāgavant (adj.) [fr. bhāga, equal to bhāgin] sharing in, partaking of (gen.) Dh 19, 20 (sāmaññassa).

Bhāgin (adj.) [fr. bhāga. Cp. Vedic bhāgin] sharing in, partaking of (with gen.), endowed with; getting, receiving A II.80; III.42 (āyussa vaṇṇassa etc.); J I.87 (rasānaŋ); Miln 18 (sāmaññassa); Vism 150 (lābhassa); DhA II.90; VbhA 418 sq. (paññā as hāna-bhāginī, ṭhiti°, visesa° & nibbedha°). — Also in def. of term Bhagavā at Nd¹ 142 = Nd² 466 = Vism 210. — pl. bhāgino Pv III.1¹² (dukkhassa); PvA 18 (dānaphalassa), 175. — Cp. bhāgavant, bhāgimant, bhāgiya.

Bhāgineyya [fr. bhaginī, Cp. Epic Sk. bhāgineya] sister's son, nephew Sn 695; J I.207; II.237; DhA I.14; PvA 215.

Bhāgimant (adj.) [a double adj. formation bhāgin + mant] partaking in, sharing, possessing (with gen.) Th 2, 204 (dukkhassa); ThA 171 (= bhāgin).

Bhāgiya (adj.) (-°) [fr. bhāga, cp. bhāgin] connected with, conducive to, procuring; in foll. philos. terms: kusala° A I.11; hāna°, visesa° D III.274 sq.; hāna°, ṭhiti°, visesa°, nibbedha° Vism 15 (in verse), 88 = Ps I.35. — Cp. BSk. mokṣa bhāgīya, nirvedha° Divy 50; mokṣa° ibid. 363.

Bhāgya (nt.) [cp. Epic & Class. Sk. bhāgya; fr. bhaga, see also contracted form bhagga²] good luck, fortune J V.484.

Bhāgyavant (adj.) [same as bhaggavant, only differentiated as being the Sk. form and thus distinguished as sep. word by Commentators] having good luck, auspicious, fortunate, in def. of term "Bhagavā" at DA I.34 = Vism 210; also at VvA 231, where the abstr. bhāgyavantatā is formed as expl^{n} of the term. bhāgyavatā (f.) at Vism 211.

Bhājaka (adj.) (-°) [fr. bhajeti] distributing, one who distributes or one charged with the office of distributing clothes, food etc. among the Bhikkhus Vin I.285 (cīvara°); A III.275 (cīvara°, phala°, khajjaka°).

Bhājana¹ (nt.) [cp. Epic Sk. bhājana, fr. **bhāj**] a bowl, vessel, dish, usually earthenware, but also of other metal, e. g. gold (suvaṇṇa°) DA I.295; copper (tamba°) DhA I.395; bronze (kaŋsa°) Vism 142 (in simile). — Vin I.46; Sn 577 (pl. mattika-bhājanā); J II.272 (bhikkhā°); III.366 (id.), 471; V 293 (bhatta°); Miln 107; VvA 40, 292 (v. l. bhojana); PvA 104, 145, 251; Sdhp 571.

-vikati a special bowl J V.292 (so read for T. bhojana°); Vism 376.

Bhājana² (nt.) [fr. **bhāj**] division, dividing up, in pada° dividing of words, treating of words separately DhsA 343; similarly bhājaniyaŋ that which should be classed or divided DhsA 2, also in pada° division of a phrase DhsA 54.

Bhājita [pp. of bhājeti] divided, distributed; nt. that which has been dealt out or allotted, in cpd. bhājit-âbhājita A III.275.

Bhājeti [Caus. of bhajati, but to be taken as root by itself; cp. Dhtm 777 bhāja = puthakkare] to divide, distribute, deal out Vin IV.223 (ppr. bhājiyamāna); J I.265; DhsA 4 (fut. bhājessati) grd. bhājetabba Vin I.285. — pp. bhājita.

Bhāṇa [fr. bhaṇati] reciting or preaching, in pada° reciting the verses of the Scriptures DhA II.95 (v. l. paṭibhāna); III.345; IV.18.

-vāra a section of the Scriptures, divided into such for purposes of recitation, "a recital" Vin I.14; II.247; DA 13; MA 2 (concerning the Bh. of Majjhima Nikāya); SnA 2 (of Sutta Nipāta), 608 (id.); DhsA 6 (of Dhammasangaṇī, cp. *Expos.* 8 n. 3), and frequently in other Commentaries & Expositionary Works.

Bhāṇaka¹ (adj.-n.) [fr. bhaṇati] speaking; (n.) a reciter, repeater, preacher (of sections of the Scriptures), like Anguttara° Vism 74 sq.; Dīgha° DA I.15, 131; J I.59; Vism 36, 266; Jātaka° etc. Miln 341 sq.; Majjhima° Vism 95 (Revatthera), 275, 286, 431; Saŋyutta° Vism 313 (Cūḷa-Sivatthera). Unspecified at SnA 70 (Kalyāṇavihāravāsi-bhāṇaka-dahara-bhikkhu; reading doubtful). — f. bhāṇikā Vin IV.285 (Thullanandā bahussutā bhāṇikā); also in cpd. mañju-bhāṇikā sweet-voiced, uttering sweet words J VI.422.

Bhāṇaka² [cp. Sk. bhāṇḍaka a small box: Kathāsarits. 24, 163; & see Müller, *P.Gr.* p. 48] a jar Vin II.170 (loha°); III.90.

Bhāṇin (adj.) (-°) [fr. bhaṇati] speaking, reciting Sn 850 (manta° a reciter of the Mantras, one who knows the M. and speaks accordingly, i. e. speaking wisely, expl^{d} by SnA 549 as "mantāya pariggahetvā vācaŋ bhāsitā"); Dh 363 (id.; expl^{d} as "mantā vuccati paññā, tāya pana bhaṇana-sīlo" DhA IV.93). —ativela° speaking for an excessively long time, talking in excess J IV.247, 248.

Bhāṇeti Caus. of bhaṇati (q. v.) with 3rd pract. bhāṇi & pot. bhāṇaye.

Bhātar [cp. Vedic bhrātar = Av. bratar, Gr. φράτωρ, Lat. frater, Goth. brōþar = Ohg. bruoder, E. brother] brother, nom. sg. bhātā Sn 296; J I.307; PvA 54, 64; gen. sg. bhātuno ThA 71 (Ap. V.36), & bhātussa Mhvs 8, 9; instr. bhātarā J I.308; acc. bhātaraŋ Sn 125; J I.307; loc. bhātari J III.56. — nom. pl. bhātaro J I.307, & bhātuno Th 2, 408; acc. bhāte Dpvs VI.21. — In cpds. both bhāti° (: bhātisadisa like a brother J V.263), and bhātu° (: bhātu-jāyā brother's wife, sister-in-law J V.288; Vism 95). Cp. bhātika & bhātuka. On pop. etym. see bhaginī.

Bhāti [bhā Dhtp 367, Dhtm 594: dittiyaŋ; Idg. ***bhē**, cp. Sk. bhāḥ nt. splendour, radiance, bhāsati to shine forth; Gr. φάος light, φαίνω to show etc.; Ags. bonian to polish — Ger. bohnen; also Sk. bhāla shine, splendour, = Ags. bael funeral pile] to shine (forth), to appear D II.205; Vv 35²; J II.313. — pp. bhāta: see vi°.

Bhātika (& **Bhātiya**) [fr. bhātar, cp. Class. Sk. bhrātṛka] lit. brotherly, i. e. a brother, often °-: "brother" — (a) bhātika: J I.253 (jeṭṭhaka°); VI.32; DhA I.14 (°thera my Thera-brother or br.-thera), 101, 245; PvA 75.— (b) bhātiya: Vism 292 (dve °therā two Th. brothers). — Cp. bhātuka.

Bhātuka [=bhātika, fr. Sk. bhrātṛka] brother, usually -°, viz. pati° brother-in-law, husband's brother J VI.152; putta° son & brother DhA I.314; sa° with the brother ThA 71 (Ap. v.36).

Bhānu (adj.) [cp. Vedic bhānu (m.) shine, light, ray; Epic Sk. also "sun"] light, bright red J III.62 (of the kaṇavera flower); VvA 175 (°raṇsi).

Bhānumant (adj.) [fr. bhānu, ray of light Vedic bhānumant, Ep. of Agni; also Epic Sk. the sun] luminous, brilliant; mostly of the sun; nom. bhānumā S I.196 = Th I, 1252; Vv 64[17], 78[7] (=ādicca VvA 304); J I.183. acc. bhānumaŋ Sn 1016. — The spelling is sometimes bhāṇumā.

Bhāyati [cp. Sk. bhayate, **bhī**, pres. redupl. bibheti; Idg. ***bhei**, cp. Av. bayente they frighten; Lith. bijótis to be afraid; Ohg. bibēn = Ger. beben. Nearest synonym is **tras**] to be afraid. Pres. Ind. 1st sg. bhāyāmi Th I, 21; Sn p. 48; 2nd sg. bhāyasi Th 2, 248; 1st pl. bhāyāma J II.21; 3rd pl. bhāyanto Dh 129; Imper. 2nd pl. bhāyatha Ud 51; J III.4; Pot. 3rd sg. bhāye Sn 964 & bhāyeyya Miln 208; 3rd pl. bhāyeyyuŋ Miln 208.— Aor. 1st sg. bhāyiŋ DhA III.187; 2nd sg. bhāyi Th I, 764; DhA III.187; & usually in Prohib. mā bhāyi do not be afraid S V.369; J I.222; DhA I.253.— grd. bhāyitabba Nd[2] s.v. kāmaguṇā B; DhA III.23.— Caus. I. bhāyayate to frighten J III.99 (C.: utraseti); Caus. II. bhāyāpeti J III.99, 210. — pp. bhīta.

Bhāyitabbaka (adj.) [grd. of bhāyati+ka] to be feared, dreadful, fearful, Sdhp 95.

Bhāra [fr. **bhṛ**, Vedic bhāra; cp. bhara] 1. anything to carry, a load Vin III.278 (Bdhgh; dāru° a load of wood). bhāraŋ vahati to carry a load A I.84; VvA 23. —garu° a heavy load, as "adj." "carrying a heavy load" J V.439 (of a woman, = pregnant). —bhāratara (adj.-compar.) forming a heavier load Miln 155.— Cp. ati°, sam°.— 2. a load, cartload (as measure of quantity) VvA 12 (saṭṭhi-sakaṭa°-parimāṇa); PvA 102 (aneka°-parimāṇa).— 3. (fig.) a difficult thing, a burden or duty, i. e. a charge, business, office, task, affair Vism. 375; J I.292; II.399; IV.427; VI.413; DhA I.6, 111. Several bhārā or great tasks are mentioned exemplifying the meaning of "gambhīra" & "duddasa" (saccāni) at VbhA 141, viz. mahā-samuddaŋ manthetvā ojāya nīharaṇaŋ; Sineru-pādato vālikāya uddharaṇaŋ; pabbataŋ pīḷetvā rasassa nīharaṇaŋ.— 4. (fig.) in metaphors for the burden of (the factors of renewed) existence (the khandhas and similar agents). Esp. in phrase panna-bhāra "one whose load (or burden) has been laid down," one who has attained Arahantship M I.139; A III.84; S I.233; Dh 402 (=ohita-khandha-bhāra DhA IV.168); Sn 626 (same expl[n] at SnA 467), 914 (expl[d] as patita-bhāra, oropita°, nikkhitta° Nd[1] 334, where 3 bhāras in this sense are distinguished, viz. khandha°, kilesa°, abhisankhāra°); Th I, 1021. So at Vism 512 with ref. to the ariya-saccāni, viz. bhāro = dukkha-saccaŋ, bhār' ādānaŋ = samuda-saccaŋ, bhāra-nikkhepanaŋ = nirodha-s., bhāra-nikkhepan'upāya = magga-s. — On bhāra in similes see *J.P.T.S.* 1907, 118.
-ādāna the taking up of a burden S III.25. **-(m)oropana** "laying down the load," i. e. delivery of a pregnant woman Bu II.115. **-ṭṭha** contained in a load, carried as a burden Vin III.47. **-nikkhepana** the laying down or taking off of a burden S III.25. **-mocana** delivery (of a pregnant woman) J I.19. **-vāhin** "burden-bearer," one who carries an office or has a responsibility A IV.24 (said of a bhikkhu). **-hāra** load-carrier, burden-bearer S III.25 sq.

Bhāraka (-°) [fr. bhāra] a load, only in cpd. gadrabha° a donkey-load (of goods) J II.109; DhA I.123.

Bhārataka [fr. bhara] "the petty descendants of Bhārata" or: load-carrier, porter (?) S IV.117 (indignantly applied to apprentices and other low class young men who honour the Mahā-Kaccāna).

Bhārika (adj.) [fr. bhāra] 1. loaded, heavy J V.84, 477; Miln 261. — 2. full of, loaded down with (-°) VvA 314 (sineha° hadaya). — 3. grievous, serious, sorrowful PvA 82 (hadaya). — 4. important Miln 240, 311. — See bhāriya.

Bhārin (adj.) [fr. **bhṛ**, cp. bhāra] carrying, wearing, only in cpd. mālā° (māla°), wearing a garland (of flowers) J IV.60, 82; V.45; where it interchanges with °dhārin (e. g. Vv.32[3]; v. l. at PvA 211; cp. BSk. °dhārin MVastu I.124). — f. °bhārinī J III.530; VvA 12; and °bhārī Th I, 459 (as v. l.; T. °dhārī). See also under mālā.

Bhāriya (adj.) [fr. bhāra Vedic bhārya to be nourished or supported; bhāryā wife] 1. heavy, weighty, grave, serious; always fig. with ref. to a serious offence, either as bhāriyaŋ pāpaŋ a terrible sin PvA 195, or bh. kammaŋ a grave deed, a sin DhA I.298, 329; II.56; III.120; VvA 68; or bhāriyaŋ alone (as nt.), something grave, a sin DhA I.64. Similarly with ati° as atibhāriyaŋ kammaŋ a very grave deed DhA I.70, or atibhāriyaŋ id. DhA I.186.— 2. bhāriyā (=bhārikā, f. of bhāraka) carrying, fetching, bringing J VI.563 (phala°).

Bhārukacchaka see bharu°.

Bhāva [fr. **bhū**, cp. Vedic bhāva] 1. being, becoming, condition, nature; very rarely by itself (only in later & C. literature, as e. g. J I.295 thīnaŋ bhāvo, perhaps best to be translated as "women's character," taking bhāva = attabhāva); usually -°, denoting state or condition of, and representing an abstr. der. from the first part of the cpd. e. g. gadrabha° 'asininity' J II.109. Thus in connection with (a) ***adjectives:*** atthika° state of need PvA 120; ūna° depletion SnA 463; eki° loneliness Vism 34; sithili° (for sithila° in conn. with **kṛ** & **bhū**) relaxation Vism 502. — (b) ***adverbs.*** upari° high condition M I.45; pātu° appearance Sn 560; vinā° difference Sn 588. (c) ***nouns & noun-derivations:*** atta° individual state, life, character Sn 388 (= citta SnA 374); asaraṇa° state of not remembering DhA III.121; samaṇa° condition of a recluse Sn 551. — (d) forms of ***verbs:*** nibbatta° fact of being reborn DhA III.121; magg' ārūḷha° the condition of having started on one's way VvA 64; baddha° that he was bound; suhita° that they were well J IV.279. The translation can give either a full sentence with "that it was" etc. (VvA 64: "that he had started on his way"), or a phrase like "the fact or state of," or use as an English abstract noun ending in *-ness* (atthika-bhāva needfulness, eki° loneliness), *-ion* (ūna° depletion, pātu° manifestation), *-hood* (atta° selfhood), or *-ship* (samaṇa° recluseship).— Similarly in Com. style: sampayutta-bhāvo (m.) DhA III.94, for *sampayuttattaŋ (abstr.); bhākuṭikassa bhāvo = bhakuṭiyaŋ Vism 26; sovacassassa bhāvo = sovacassatā KhA 148; mittassa bh. = mattaŋ KhA 248. Here sometimes bhava for bhāva. — 2. (in pregnant, specifically ***Buddhistic*** sense) cultivation or production by thought, mental condition, esp. a set mental condition (see der. bhāvanā). Sometimes (restricted to Vin & J) in sense "thinking of someone," i. e. affection, love, sentiment. — (a) in comb[n] khanti, diṭṭhi, ruci, bhāva at Vin II.205; III.93; IV.3, 4. — (b) in Jātaka passages: J V.237; VI.293 (bhāvaŋ karoti, with loc., to love). —abhāva (late, only in C. style) not being, absence, want PvA 25; abl. abhāvato through not being, in want of PvA 9, 17. —sabhāva (sva+bhāva) see sep.

Bhāvanā (f.) [fr. bhāveti, or fr. bhāva in meaning of bhāva 2, cp. Class. Sk. bhāvanā] producing, dwelling on something, putting one's thoughts to, application, developing by means of thought or meditation, cultivation by mind, culture. — See on term *Dhs trsl* 261 (= [2] 240); *Expos.* I.217 (=DhsA 163); *Cpd.* 207 n. 2. — Cp. pari°, vi°, sam°. — Vin I.294 (indriya°); D III.219 (three: kāya°, citta°, paññā°), 221, 225, 285, 291; S I.48; Dh 73, 301; J I.196 (mettā°); III.45 (id.); Nd[1] 143 (saññā°); Nett 91 (samatha-vipassanaŋ); Vbh 12, 16 sq., 199, 325; Vism 130 (karaṇa, bhāvanā, rakkhaṇa; here bh. = bringing out, keeping in existence), 314 (karuṇā°), 317 (upekkhā°); Miln 25 (°ŋ anuyuñjati); Sdhp 15, 216, 233, 451.
-ânuyoga application to meditation Vbh 244, 249. -ārāma joy of or pleasure in self culture A II.28. -bala power to increase the effect of meditation, power of self-culture A I.52; D III.213. -maya accomplished by culture practice; brought into existence by practice (of cultured thought), cp. *Cpd.* 207. D III.218, 219; Nett 8; with *dānamaya & sīlamaya* at It 19, 51; Vbh 135, 325. -vidhāna arrangement of process of culture DhsA 168 = Vism 122.

Bhāvanīya (adj.) [grd. fr. bhāveti, but taken by Bdhgh as grd. formation fr. bhāvanā] "being as ought to be," to be cultivated, to be respected, in a self-composed state (cp. bhāvitatta) M I.33 (garu +; expl[d] by Bdhgh as "addhā 'yam āyasmā jānaŋ jānāti passaŋ passatī ti evaŋ sambhāvanīyo" MA 156); S V.164; A III.110; Miln 373; PvA 9. See also under mano-bhāvanīya.

Bhāvita [pp. of bhāveti] developed, made to become by means of thought, cultured, well-balanced A V.299 (cittaŋ parittaŋ abhāvitaŋ; opp. cittaŋ appamāṇaŋ subhāvitaŋ); Sn 516, 558.

Bhāvitatta[1] (adj.) [bhāvita + attan] one whose attan (ātman) is bhāvita, i. e. well trained or composed. Attan here = citta (as PvA 139), thus "self-composed, well-balanced" A IV.26; Sn 277, 322, 1049; Dh 106, 107; Nd[2] 142; Nd[2] 475 B (indriyāni bh.); J II.112 (°bhāvanāya when the training of thought is perfect); Vism 185 (°bhāvana, adj. one of well-trained character), 267, 400 (+ bahulī-kata); DhA I.122 (a°); ThA 164 (indriya°). See foll.

Bhāvitatta[2] (nt.) [abstr. fr. bhāvita = *bhāvitattvaŋ] only neg. a° the fact of not developing or cultivating S III.153, 475; Pv II.9[66].

Bhāvin (adj.) [fr. bhāva, Epic Sk. bhāvin "imminent"] "having a being," going to be, as -° in avassa° sure to come to pass, inevitable J I.19. — f. bhāvinī future VvA 314 (or is it bhāvanīya? cp. v. l. S bhāvaniyā).

Bhāveti [Caus. of **bhū**, bhavati] to beget, produce, increase, cultivate, develop (by means of thought & meditation). The Buddhist equivalent for mind-work as creative in idea, M I.293; cp. *B.Psy* p. 132. — D II.79; M II.11 (cattāro sammappadhāne & iddhipāde); S I.188 (cittaŋ ekaggaŋ), Th 1, 83, 166 (ppr. bhāvayanto); Sn 341 (cittaŋ ekaggaŋ), 507 (ppr. bhāvayaŋ), 558 (grd. bhāvetabba), 1130 (ppr. bhāvento = āsevanto bahulī-karonto Nd[2] 476); Dh 87, 350, 370; J I.264 (mettaŋ), 415, II.22; Nd[2] s. v. kāmaguṇā (p. 121) (where grd. in sequence "sevitabba, bhajitabba, bhāvetabba, bahulī kātabba"); Pug 15, DhA III.171; Sdhp 48, 495. — Pass. ppr. bhāviyamāna A II.140; KhA 148. — pp. bhāvita.

Bhāsa [cp. Epic Sk. bhāsa] -sakuṇa a bird of prey, a vulture [Abhp. 645, 1049]; as one of the lucky omens enum[d] (under the so-called mangala-kathā) at KhA 118 (with v. l. SS. cāta° & vāca°, BB cāba°) · Nd[1] 87 (on Sn 790) (T. reads vāta°; v. l. SS vāpa°, BB chapa°).

Bhāsaka (adj.) (-°) [fr. **bhāṣ**] speaking DA I.52 (avaṇṇa° uttering words of blame).

Bhāsati[1] [**bhāṣ**; Dhtp 317: vacane; Dhtm 467; vācāya] to speak, to say, to speak to, to call M I.227, Sn 158, 562, 722; Dh 1, 246, 258; also bhāsate Sn 452. — Pot. bhāseyya Vin II.189; Sn 451, 930; SnA 468 (for udīraye Dh 408); bhāse Dh 102; Sn 400; & bhāsaye A II.51 = J V.509 (with gloss katheyya for joteyya = bhāseyya). — Aor. abhāsi Vin IV.54; PvA 6, 17, 23, 69; 1st sg. also abhāsissaŋ (Cond.) Pv I.6[8] (= abhāsiŋ PvA 34); imper. pres. bhāsa Sn 346; ppr. bhāsamāne A II.51 = J V.509; Sn 426; Dh 19; J IV.281 (perhaps better with v. l. as hasamāna); V.63; & bhāsanto Sn 543. — grd. bhāsitabba A IV.115; Vism 127. — Med. ind. pres. 2nd sg. bhāsase Vv 34[2]; imper. pres. 2nd sg. bhāsassu M II.199. — An apparent ger. form abhāsiya It 59, 60 (micchā vācaŋ abhāsiya) is problematic. It may be an old misspelling for ca bhāsiya, as a positive form is required by the sense. The vv. ll. however do not suggest anything else but abhāsiya; the editor of It suggests pa°. — Cp. anu, o°, samanu°.

Bhāsati[2] [**bhās** Dhtm 467: dittiyaŋ] to shine, shine forth, fill with splendour Sn 719 (2nd sg. fut. bhāsihi = bhāsissasi pakāsessasi SnA 499). Usually with prep. prefix pa° (so read at Pv I.10[9] for ca bh.). Cp. o°, vi°.

Bhāsana (nt.) [fr. **bhāṣ**] speaking, speech Dhtm 162; Sdhp 68.

Bhāsā (f.) [cp. Epic Sk. bhāṣā] speech, language, esp. vernacular, dialect J IV.279 (manussa° human speech), 392 (caṇḍāla°); KhA 101 (saka-saka°-anurūpa); SnA 397 (Milakkha°); DA I.176 (Kirātā-Yavanâdi-Millakkhānaŋ bhāsā); MA I.1 (Sīhaḷa°); VbhA 388 (18 dialects, of which 5 are mentioned; besides the Māgadha-bhāsā).

Bhāsita [pp. of bhāsati[1]] spoken, said, uttered A V.194; Miln 28; DhA IV.93. — (nt.) speech, word Dh 363; M I.432. Usually as su° & dub° (both adj. & nt.) well & badly spoken, or good & bad speech Vin I.172; M II.250; A I.102; II.51 (su°; read bhāsita for bāsita); VI.226; Sn 252, 451, 657; J IV.247, 281 (su°, well spoken or good words); Pv II.6[20] (su°); PvA 83 (dub°).

Bhāsitar [n. ag. fr. **bhāṣ**] one who speaks, utters; a speaker S I.156; Pug 56; SnA 549.

Bhāsin (adj.) (-°) [cp. Epic Sk. bhāṣin] speaking A I.102 (dubbhāsita-bhāsin).

Bhāsura (adj.) [cp. Epic Sk. bhāsura fr. **bhas**] bright, shining, resplendent ThA 139, 212; VvA 12.

Bhiŋsa (adj.) [= Vedic bhīṣma, of which there are 4 P. forms, viz. the metathetic **bhiŋsa**, the shortened bhisma, the lengthened bhesma, and the contracted bhīsa (see bhīsana). Cp. also Sk.-P. bhīma; all of **bhī**] terrible; only in cpd. °rūpa (nt. & adj.) an awful sight; (of) terrific appearance, terrible, awful J III.242, 339; IV.271, 494.

Bhiŋsana & °ka (adj.) [the form with °ka is the canonic form, whereas bhiŋsana is younger. See bhiŋsa on connections] horrible, dreadful, awe-inspiring, causing fear. (a) bhiŋsanaka (usually comb[d] with lomahaŋsa) D II.106 = A IV.311; D II.157; Vin III.8; PvA 22; ThA 242 (°sabhāva = bhīmarūpa); J V.43. — (b) **bhiŋsana** Pv IV.3[6] (+ lomahaŋsa).

Bhiŋsā (f.) [fr. bhiŋsa] terror, fright; mahā-bhiŋsa (adj.) inspiring great terror D II.259. Cp. bhismā.

Bhiŋsikā (f.) [fr. bhiŋsa] frightful thing, terror, terrifying omen Mhvs 12, 12 (vividhā bhiŋsikā kari he brought divers terrors topass)

Bhikkhaka [fr. bhikkhu, Cp. Epic Sk. bhikṣuka & f. bhikṣukī] a beggar, mendicant S I.182 (bh. brāhmaṇa); J VI.59 (v. l. BB. °uka); VbhA 327.

Bhikkhati [cp. Vedic bhiksate, old desid. to **bhaj**; def. Dhtp 13 "yācane"] to beg alms, to beg, to ask for S I.176, 182 (so read for T. bhikkhavo); Dh 266; VbhA 327. — ppr. med. bhikkhamāna Th 2, 123.

Bhikkhā (f.) [cp. Epic & Class. Sk. bhaikṣa of **bhikṣ**, adj. & nt.] begged food, alms, alms-begging; food Vin IV.94; Cp I.1[4]; Vv 70[4] (ekāhā bh. food for one day); Miln 16; PvA 3, 75, 131 (kaṭacchu°); bhikkhāya carati to go out begging food [cp. Sk. bhaiksaŋ carati] J III.82; V.75; PvA 51 & passim. —**subhikkha** (nt.) abundance of food D I.11. **dubbhikkha** (nt.) (& °ā f.) scantiness of alms, famine, scarcity of food, adj. famine-stricken (cp. Sk. durbhikṣaŋ) Vin II.175; III.87 (adj.); IV.23 (adj.); S IV.323, 324 (dvīhitikaŋ); A I.160; III.41; J II.149, 367; V.193; VI.487; Cp I.3[3] (adj.); Vism 415 (°piḷita), 512 (f. in simile); KhA 218; DhA I.169; II.153 (f.); III.437 (°bhaya).
-**āhāra** food received by a mendicant J I.237 (=bhikkhu-āhāra?). -**cariyā** going about for alms, begging round Sn 700; PvA 146. -**cāra** =°cariyā Mhbv 28. -**paññatti** declaration of alms, announcement that food is to be given to the Sangha, a dedication of food Vin I.309.

Bhikkhu [cp. later Sk. bhikṣu, fr. **bhikṣ**] an almsman, a mendicant, a Buddhist monk or priest, a bhikkhu. — nom. sg. **bhikkhu** freq. passim; Vin III.40 (vuḍḍhapabbajita); A I.78 (*thera* bh., an elder bh.; and *nava* bh. a young bh.); III.299 (id.); IV.25 (id.); Sn 276, 360, 411 sq., 915 sq., 1041, 1104; Dh 31, 266 sq., 364 sq., 378; Vv 80[1]; acc. **bhikkhuŋ** Vin III.174; Dh 362, & **bhikkhunaŋ** Sn 87, 88, 513; gen. dat. **bhikkhuno** A I.274; Sn 221, 810, 961; Dh 373; Pv I.10[10]; & **bhikkhussa** A I.230; Vin III.175; instr. **bhikkhunā** Sn 389. pl. nom. **bhikkhū** Vin II.150; III.175; D III.123; Vism 152 (in sim.); VbhA 305 (compared with amaccaputtā) & **bhikkhavo** Sn 384, 573; Dh 243, 283; acc. **bhikkhu** Sn p. 78; M I.84; Vv 22[10]; & **bhikkhavo** Sn 384, 573; gen. dat. **bhikkhūnaŋ** Vin III.285; D III.264; Sn 1015; Pv II.1[7]; & **bhikkhunaŋ** S I.190; Th I, 1231; instr. **bhikkhūhi** Vin III.175; loc. **bhikkhūsu** A IV.25, & **bhikkhusu** Th 1, 241, 1207; Dh 73; voc. **bhikkhave** (a Māgadhī form of nom. bhikkhavaḥ) Vin III.175; Sn p. 78; VvA 127; PvA 8, 39, 166; & **bhikkhavo** Sn 280, 385.
There are several allegorical *etymologies* (definitions) of the word bhikkhu, which occur frequently in the commentaries. All are fanciful interpretations of the idea of what a bhikkhu is or should be, and these qualities were sought and found in the word itself. Thus we mention here the foll. (a) bhikkhu = **bhinnakilesa** ("one who has broken the stains" i. e. of bad character) VbhA 328; VvA 29, 114, 310; PvA 51. — (b) Another more explicit expl[n] is "sattannaŋ dhammānaŋ bhinnattā bhikkhu" (because of the breaking or destroying of 7 things, viz. the 7 bad qualities, leading to rebirth, consisting of sakkāyadiṭṭhi, vicikicchā, sīlabbata-parāmāsa, rāga, dosa, moha, māna). This def. at Nd[1] 70 = Nd[2] 477[a]. — (c) Whereas in a & b the first syllable *bhi*(-kkhu) is referred to **bhid**, in this def. it is referred to **bhī** (to fear), with the further reference of (bh-) *ikkh*(u) to **ikṣ** (to see), and bhikkhu defined as "saŋsāre bhayaŋ ikkhati ti bh." Vism 3, 16 (saŋsāre bhayaŋ ikkhaṇatāya vā bhinna-paṭa-dharaditāya vā). — A very comprehensive def. of the term is found at Vbh 245-246, where bhikkhu-ship is established on the ground of 18 qualities (beginning with samaññāya bhikkhu, paṭiññāya bh., bhikkhatī ti bh., bhikkhako ti bh., bhikkhācariyaŋ ajjhupagato ti bh., bhinna-paṭa-dharo ti bh., bhindati pāpake dhamme ti bh., bhinnattā pāpakānaŋ dhammānan ti bh. etc. etc.). — This passage is expl[d] in detail at VbhA 327, 328. — Two *kinds* of bhikkhus are distinguished at Ps I.176; Nd[1] 465 = Nd[2] 477[b], viz. **kalyāṇa[-ka-]puthujjana** (a layman of good character) and **sekkha** (one in training), for which latter the term paṭilīnacara (one who lives in elimination, i. e. in keeping away from the dangers of worldly life) is given at Nd[1] 130 (on Sn 810).
-**gatika** a person who associates with the bhikkhus (in the Vihāra) Vin I.148. -**bhāva** state of being a monk, monkhood, bhikkhuship D I.176; Sn p. 102; -**sangha** the community of bhikkhus, the Order of friars D III.208; Sn 403, 1015; Sn p. 101, 102; Miln 209; PvA 19 sq. & passim.

Bhikkhuka (-°) (adj.) [fr. bhikkhu] belonging to a Buddhist mendicant, a bhikkhu-, a monk's, or of monks, in sa° with monks, inhabited by bhikkhus Vin IV.307, 308; opp. a° without bhikkhus, ibid.

Bhikkhunī (f.) [fr. bhikkhu, cp. BSk. bhiksuṇī, but classical Sk. bhikṣukī] an almswoman, a female mendicant, a Buddhist nun D III.123 sq., 148, 168 sq., 264; Vin IV.224 sq., 258 sq. (°sangha); S I.128; II.215 sq., IV.159 sq.; A I.88, 113, 279; II.132 (°parisā), 144; III.109; IV.75; Miln 28; VbhA 498 (dahara°, story of); VvA 77.

Bhinka [cp. Vedic bhṛnga large bee] the young of an animal, esp. of an elephant, in its property of being dirty (cp. pigs) Vin II.201 = S II.269 (bhinka-cchāpa); J V.418 (with ref. to young cats: "mahā-biḷārā nelamaṇḍalaŋ vuccati taruṇā bhinka-cchāpa-maṇḍalaŋ," T. °cchāca°, vv. ll. bhiñjaka-cchāca; taruṇa-bhiga -cchāpa; bhinga-cchāja).

Bhinkāra[1] (& °gāra) [cp. late Sk. bhṛngāra] a water jar, a (nearly always golden) vase, ceremonial vessel (in donations) Vin I.39 (sovaṇṇa-maya); D II.172; A IV.210 = 214 (T. °gāra, v. l. °kāra); Cp. I.3[5]; J I.85, 93; II.371; III.10 (suvaṇṇa°); Dpvs XI.32; PvA 75; KhA 175 (suvaṇṇa°; v. l. BB °gāra), Sdhp 513 (soṇṇa°).

Bhinkāra[2] [?] cheers, cries of delight (?) Bu I.35 (+ sādhu kāra).

Bhinkāra[3] [cp. Sk. bhṛnga bee, bhṛngaka & bhṛnga-rājā] a bird: Lanius caerulescens J V.416.

Bhijjati [Pass. of bhindati, cp. Sk. bhidyate] to be broken, to be destroyed; to break (instr.); pres. **bhijjati** Dh 148, ppr. **bhijjamāna**; see phrase abhijjamāne udake under abhijj°, with which cp. phrase abhejjantyā pathavyā J VI.508, which is difficult to explain (not breaking? for abhijjantī after abhejja & abhedi, and *abhijjanto for abhijjamāna, intrs.?). imper. **bhijjatu** Th 1, 312. — praet. 2nd pl. **bhijjittha** J I.468; aor. **abhedi** Ud 93 (abhedi kāyo). — fut. **bhijjhissati** DA I.266; grd. **bhijjitabba** J III.56; on grd. °**bhijja** see **pabhindati**; grd. **bhejja** in **abhejja** not to be broken (q. v.).

Bhijjana (nt.) [fr. bhijjati] breaking up, splitting, perishing; destruction J I.392; V.284; VI.11; DhA I.257 (kaṇṇā bhijjan' ākāra-pattā); ThA 43 (bhijjana-sabhāva of perishable nature; expl[n] of bhidura Th 2, 35); PvA 41 (°dhammā destructible, of sankhārā). — Der. **abhijjanaka** see sep.

Bhitti (f.) [fr. **bhid**, cp. *Sk. bhitta fragment, & Class. Sk. bhitti wall] a wall Vin I.48; D II.85; S II.103; IV.183; V.218; J I.491; Vism 354 = VbhA 58 (in comparison); ThA 258; VvA 42, 160, 271, 302; PvA 24.
-**khila** a hin (peg) in the wall Vin II.114, 152. -**pāda** the support or lower part of a wall J IV.318.

Bhittika (adj.) [fr. bhitti] having a wall or walls J IV.318 (naḷa °ā paṇṇasālā); VI.10 (catu° with 4 walls).

Bhidura (adj.) [fr. **bhid**] fragile, perishable, transitory Th 2, 35 (=bhijjana-sabhāva ThA 43).

Bhindati [**bhid**, Sk. bhinatti; cp. Lat. findo to split, Goth. beitan=Ger. beissen. Def. at Dhtp 381, 405 by "vidāraṇe" i. e. splitting] to split, break, sever, destroy, ruin. In two bases: *bhid (with der. *bhed) & *bhind. — (a) ***bhid**: aor. 3rd sg. **abhida** (=Sk. abhidat) D II.107; J III.29 (see also under abhida); abbhidā J I.247; II.163, 164. — fut. **bhecchati** (Sk. bhetsyati) A I.8. — ger. **bhetvā** (Sk. bhittvā) Th 1, 753; Sn 62 (v. l. BB bhitvā). — grd. **bhejja**: only neg. **abhejja** (q. v.). See also der. bheda, bhedana. — pp. **bhinna** & Pass. **bhijjati**. — (b) ***bhind**: pres. **bhindati** Nd¹ 503; DhA I.125 (kathaŋ bh. to break a promise); Sdhp 47. — ppr. **bhindanto** Mhvs 5, 185. — Pot. **bhinde** Vism 36 (sīlasaŋvaran). — fut. **bhindissati** Vin II.198. — aor. **bhindi** J I.467 (mitta-bhāvaŋ), & **abhindi** A IV.312 (atta-sambhavaŋ). — ger. **bhinditvā** J I.425, 490; PvA 12; also in phrase **indriyāni bhinditvā** breaking in one's senses, i. e. mastering, controlling them J II.274; IV.104, 114, 190. — Caus. I. **bhedeti**: see vi°. Caus. II. **bhindāpeti** to cause to be broken J I.290 (sīlaŋ); VI.345 (pokkharaṇiŋ) and **bhedāpeti** Vin III.42. — See also bhindana.

Bhindana (adj.) [fr. bhindati] breaking up, brittle, falling into ruin S I.131 (kāya).

Bhindivāla [Non-Aryan; Epic Sk. bhindipāla spear, but cp. Prk bhiṇḍi-māla & °vāla, Pischel, *Prk. Gr.* § 248; see also Geiger, *P.Gr.* § 38] a sort of spear J VI.105, 248; Abhp 394.

Bhinna [pp. of bhindati] 1. broken, broken up (lit. & fig.) Sn 770 (nāvā); J I.98 (abhinna magga an unbroken path); III.167 (uda-kumbha); PvA 72 (°sarīra-cchavi). — 2. (fig.) split, fallen into dissension, not agreeing D III.117=210, 171. — Usually in cpds., & often to be translated by prep. "without," e.g. **bhinnahirottappa** without shame. — Cp. sam°.
-**ājīva** without subsistence, one who has little means to live on, one who leads a poor mode of living Miln 229 sq. (opp. parisuddh' ājīva); Vism 306. -**nāva** ship-wrecked J IV.159. -**paṭa** a torn cloth, in cpd. *°dhara* "wearing a patchwork cloth," i. e. a bhikkhu (see also s. v. bhikkhu) Th 1, 1092. -**plava** ship-wrecked J III.158. -**manta** disobeying (i. e. breaking) a counsel J VI.437. -**sira** with a broken head J IV.251. -**sīmā** (f.) one who has broken the bounds (of decency) Miln 122. -**sīla** one who has broken the norm of good conduct Vism 56. -**hirottappa** without shame, shameless J I.207.

Bhinnatta (nt.) [fr. bhinna] state of being broken or destroyed, destruction A IV.144.

Bhiyyo (Bhiyo, Bhīyyo) [Vedic bhūyas, compar. form fr. **bhū**, functioning as compar. to bhūri. On relation Sk. bhūyaḥ: P. bhiyyo cp. Sk. jugupsate: P. jigucchati] 1. (adj.) more Sn 61 (dukkhaṁ ettha bhiyyo), 584 (id.), 306 (bh. taṇhā pavaḍḍhatha); Dh 313 (bh. rajan ākirate), 349 (bh. taṇhā pavaḍḍhati). — 2. (adv.) in a higher degree, more, repeatedly, further S I.108 (appaŋ vā bhīyo less or more); Sn 434 (bh. cittaŋ pasīdati); Dh 18 (bh. nandati=ativiya n. C.); Miln 40. — See also bhiyyoso, yebhuyyena.
-**kamyatā** desire for more, greed Vin II.214. -**bhāva** getting more, increase, multiplication D III.221; Vin III.45; S V.9, 198, 244; A I.98; V.70; VbhA 289.

Bhiyyoso (adv.) [abl. formation fr. bhiyyo 1] still more, more and more, only in cpd. °**mattāya** [cp. BSk. bhūyasyā matrāya MVastu II.345; Divy 263 & passim] exceedingly, abundantly A I.124=Pug 30 (expl^d at PugA 212 by "bhiyyoso-mattāya uddhumāyana-bhāvo daṭṭhabbo"); J I.61; PvA 50.

Bhisa (nt.) [cp. Vedic bisa, with bh for b: see Geiger, *P.Gr.* § 40 1a] the sprout (fr. the root) of a lotus, the lotus fibres, lotus plant S I.204; II.268; J I.100; IV.308;
-**puppha** the lotus flower Sn 2 (=paduma-puppha SnA 16). -**muḷāla** fibres & stalk of the lotus J V.39; Vism 361.

Bhisakka [cp. Vedic bhiṣaj physician, P. bhesajja medicine & see Geiger, *P.Gr.* § 63¹] a physician M I.429; A III.238; IV.340; It 101; Miln 169, 215, 229, 247 sq., 302; Vism 598 (in simile); DA I.67, 255.

Bhisi¹ (f.) [cp. Epic Sk. bṛṣī & bṛsī, with bh for b, as in Prk. bhisī, cp. Pischel, *Prk. Gr.* § 209] a bolster, cushion, pad, roll Vin I.287 sq. (cīvara° a robe rolled up); II.150, 170; III.90; IV.279. *Five* kinds are allowed in a Vihāra, viz. uṇṇa-bhisi, cola°, vāka°, tiṇa°, paṇṇa°, i. e. bolsters stuffed with wool, cotton-cloth, bark, grass, or talipot leaves, Vin II.150=VbhA 365 (tiṇa°).
-**bimbohana** bolster & pillow Vin I.47; II.208; DhA I.416; VbhA 365.

Bhisi² [etym. ?] a raft Sn 21. — Andersen, *Pali Reader*, Glossary s. v. identifies it with bhisi¹ and asks: "Could it also mean a sort of cushion, made of twisted grass, used instead of a swimming girdle?"

Bhisikā (f.) [fr. bhisi¹] a small bolster Vin II.148 (vātapāna° a roll to keep out draughts); KhA 50 (tāpasa°, v. l. K^k kapala-bhitti, see Appendix to Indexes on Sutta Nipāta & Pj.).

Bhismā (f.) [=bhiŋsā] terror, fright D II.261 (°kāya adj. terrific).

Bhīta [pp. of bhāyati] frightened, terrified, afraid Dh 310; J I.168 (niraya-bhaya°); II.110 (maraṇa-bhaya°), 129; IV.141 (+tasita); PvA 154, 280 (+tasita). Cp. sam°.

Bhībhaccha see bībhaccha.

Bhīma (adj.) [fr. **bhī**, cp. Vedic bhīma] dreadful, horrible, cruel, awful J IV.26; Miln 275.
-**kāya** of horrible body, terrific J V.165. -**rūpa** of terrifying appearance Th 2, 353. -**sena** having a terrifying army J IV.26; VI.201. Also Np. of one of the 5 sons of King Paṇḍu J V.426; Vism 233.

Bhīmala (adj.) [fr. bhīma] terrifying, horrible, awful J V.43 (T. bhīmūla, but read bhīmala; C. expl^s by bhiŋsanaka-mahāsadda).

Bhīrati Pass. to bharati, only in cpd. ppr. **anubhīramāna** M III.123 (chatta: being brought up or: carried behind). Neumann, M. trsl.² III.248 translates "über ihm schwebt," & proposes reading (on p. 563) anu-hīramāna (fr. **hṛ**). This reading is to be preferred, & is also found at D II.15.

Bhīru (adj. n.) [fr. **bhī**; cp. Vedic bhīru] 1. fearful, i. e. having fear, timid, afraid, shy, cowardly Sdhp 207 (dukkha°); usually in neg. abhīru not afraid, without fear, comb^d with anutrāsin: see utrāsin. — 2. fearful, i. e. causing fear, awful, dreadful, terrible Pv II.4¹ (°dassana terrible to look at). — 3. (m.) fear, cowardice Sn 437 (=utrāsa SnA 390).
-**ttāṇa** refuge for the fearful, adj. one who protects, those who are in fear A II.174; It 25; Sdhp 300.

Bhīruka (adj.) [fr. bhīru] afraid, shy, cowardly, shunning (-°) Vism 7 (pāpa°), 645 (jīvitu-kāma bhīruka-purisa).

Bhīsana (adj.) =bhiŋsana (q. v.) Pv IV.3⁶ (v. l. in PvA 251), expl^d by bhayajanana PvA 251, where C. reading also bhīsana.

Bhukka (adj.) [fr. onomat. root ***bhukk**, dialectical, cp. Prk. bhukkai to bark, bhukkiya barking, bhukkana dog (Pischel, *Prk. Gr.* § 209); the root **bhukk (bukk)** is given by Hemacandra 4, 98 in meaning "garjati" (see P. gajjati), cp. also Prk. bukkaṇa crow] barking, n. a barker, i. e. dog; only in redupl. intens. formation **bho-bhu-kka** (cp. E. bow-wow), lit. bhu-bhu-maker (: kka fr. **kṛ**?) J VI.354 (C.: bhun-karaṇa). See also bhussati.

Bhunkaraṇa (adj.-nt.) [bhu + **kṛ**, see bhukka] making "bhu," i. e. bow-wow, barking J VI.355 (°sunakha); v. l. bhu-bhukka-sadda-karaṇa.

Bhucca (adj.) [ger. of **bhū** in composition, corresponding to *bhūtya > *bhutya, like pecca (*pretya) fr. pra + i. In function equal to **bhūta**] only in cpd. **yathā-bhuccaŋ** (nt. adv.) as it is, that which really is, really (= yathā bhūtaŋ) Th 2, 143. See under yathā.

Bhuja[1] (m. & nt.) [cp. Epic & Class. Sk. bhuja m. & bhujā; **bhuj**, bhujate to bend, lit. "the bender"; the root is expl[d] by **koṭilya** (koṭilla) at Dhtp 470 (Dhtm 521). See also bhuja[3]. Idg. ***bheng**, fr. which also Lat. fugio to flee = Gr. φεύγω, Lat. fuga flight = Sk. bhoga ring, Ohg. bouc; Goth. biugan to bend = Ger. beugen & biegen; Ohg. bogo = E. bow. Semantically cp. Lat. lacertus the arm, i. e. the bend, fr. ***leq** to bend, to which P. laguḷa a club (q. v. for etym.), with which cp. Lat. lacerta = lizard, similar in connotation to P. bhujaga snake] the arm Sn 48 (expl[d] by Nd[2] 478 as hattha, hand); 682 (pl. bhujāni); J V.91, 309; VI.64; Bu I.36; Vv 64[18].

Bhuja[2] [fr. bhuñjati[2]] clean, pure, bright, beautiful J VI.88 (°dassana beautiful to look at; C. expl[ns] by kalyāṇa dassana).

Bhuja[3] (adj.) [fr. **bhuj** to bend] bending, crooked, in **bhuja-laṭṭhi** betel-pepper tree J VI.456 (C.: bhujanga-latā, perhaps identical with bhujaka?), also in cpd. **bhuja-ga** going crooked, i. e. snake Miln 420 (bhujag-inda king of snakes, the cobra); Dāvs. 2, 17; also as **bhujanga** Dāvs 2, 56, & in der. **bhujanga-latā** "snake-creeper," i. e. name of the betel-pepper J VI.457; and **bhujangama** S I.69. — Cp. **bhogin**[2].

Bhujaka [fr. **bhuj**, as in bhuñjati[2]; or does it belong to bhuja[3] and equal to bhuja-laṭṭhi?] a fragrant tree, growing (according to Dhpāla) only in the Gandha-mādana grove of the Devaloka Vv 35[5]; VvA 162.

Bhujissa [cp. BSk. bhujiṣya Divy 302, according to Mhvyut § 84 meaning "clean"; thus fr. **bhuj** (see bhuñjati[2]) to purify, sort out] 1. (n. m.) a freed slave, freeman; a servant as distinguished from a slave Vin I.93; J II.313; PvA 112. —**bhujissaŋ karoti** to grant freedom to a slave J V.313; VI.389, 546; DhA I.19; ThA 200. — f. **bhujissā** Vin II.271 (in same sequence as bhujissa at Vin I.93). — 2. (adj.) freeing fr. slavery, productive of freedom D II.80 (cp. *Dial.* II.80); III.245; S II.70; IV.272; A III.36, 132, 213; Vism 222 (with exegesis). Cp. bhoja & bhojaka.

-bhāva state of being freed fr. slavery, freedom ThA 200.

Bhuñjaka (adj.) [fr. bhuñjati[1]] eating, one who eats or enjoys, in °sammuti definition of "eater," speaking of an eater, declaration or statement of eating VbhA 164.

Bhuñjati[1] [**bhuj** to Lat. fruor, frūx = E. fruit, frugal etc.; Goth. brūkjan = As. brūkan = Ger. brauchen. The Dhtp 379 (& Dhtm 613) expl[ns] **bhuj** by "pālan' ajjhohāresu," i. e. eating & drinking for the purpose of living] to eat (in general), to enjoy, make use of, take advantage of, use Sn 102, 240, 259, 619; Dh 324; Pug 55. Pot. **bhuñjeyya** Sn 400; Dh 308, 2nd pl. **bhuñjetha** Dh 70; Mhvs 25, 113. Imper. 2nd med. **bhuñjassa** S V.53; 3rd act. bhuñjatu S I.141; Sn 479; bhuñjassu Sn 421; ppr. **bhuñjanto** J III.277: **bhuñja-māna** Th I. 12; Sn 240. Fut. 1st sg. **bhokkhaŋ** [Sk. bhoksyāmi] J IV.117. Aor. 1st sg. **bhuñjiŋ** Miln 47; 3rd sg. **bhuñji** J IV.370; 3rd pl. **abhuñjiŋsu** Th I, 922; **abhuñjisuŋ** Mhvs 7, 25. Ger. **bhutvā** J III.53 (= bhuñ jitvā C.); DhA I.182; **bhutvāna** Sn 128. Grd. **bhuñjitabba** Mhvs 5, 127. Inf. **bhottuñ**: see ava°. — pp. **bhutta**. — Caus. **bhojeti** (q. v.). Cp. **bhoga**, bhojana, bhojanīya, bhojja; also Desid. pp. bubbhuk-khita; & ābhuñjati.

Bhuñjati[2] [**bhuj** to purify, cleanse, sift, not given in this meaning by the Dhātupāṭha. Cp. Av. buxti purification **buj** to clean, also Lat. fungor (to get through or rid of, cp. E. function), Goth. us-baugjan to sweep; P. paribhuñjati 2, paribhojaniya & vinibbhujati. See Kern, *Toev.* p. 104, s. v. bhujissa] to clean, purify, cleanse: see bhuja[2] and bhujissa, also bhoja & bhojaka.

Bhuñjana (nt.) [fr. bhuñjati[1]] taking food, act of eating, feasting J IV.371 (°kāraṇa); PvA 184.

-kāla meal-time DhA I.346.

Bhutta [pp. of bhuñjati[1]; Sk. bhukta] 1. (Pass.) eaten, being eaten Sn p. 15; Dh 308; impers. eating Vin IV.82 (bhuttaŋ hoti). Also °geha eating house J V.290, and in phrase **yathā-bhuttaŋ bhuñjatha** "eat according to eating," i. e. as ought to be eaten, eating in moderation D II.173 (where Rh. D., *Dial.* II.203, trsl[s] "ye shall eat as ye have eaten") = III.62, 63 (where Rh. D., *Dial.* III.64 trsl[s] "enjoy your possessions as you have been wont to do"; see note ibid.). We should favour a translation in the first sense. —**dubbhuttaŋ**, indigestible. — 2. (Med. cp. bhuttar) having eaten, one who has eaten Miln 370 (sace bhutto bhaveyy' âhaŋ); also in phrase **bhutta-pātar-āsa** after having eaten breakfast J II.273; DhA IV.226.

-âvasesa the remainder of a meal Vin II.216.

Bhuttar [n. ag. fr. **bhuj**, cp. Sk. bhoktṛ already Vedic & Epic] one who eats or has eaten, or enjoys (cp. bhutta 2) J V.465 (ahaŋ bhuttā bhakkhaŋ ras' uttamaŋ).

Bhuttavant (adj.) [bhutta + vant] having eaten, one who has eaten J V.170 (= kata-bhatta-kicca); VvA 244.

Bhuttāvin (adj.) [bhutta + suffix °āvin, corresponding to Vedic °āyin] having eaten, one who has had a meal; nom. sg. **bhuttāvī** Vin IV.82; Miln 15 (+ onīta-patta-pāṇi); PvA 23 (+ pavārita); SnA 58; instr. **bhuttāvinā** Vin IV.82; gen. dat. **bhuttavissa** D II.195. acc. **bhuttāviŋ** Vin I.213; Sn p. 111 (+ onīta-pattapāṇiŋ); J V.170; nom. pl. **bhuttāvī** Vin IV.81, & **bhuttāvino** S IV.289.

Bhumma (adj.-n.) [fr. bhūmi, Vedic bhūmya] 1. belonging to the earth, earthly, terrestrial; nt. soil, ground, floor Sn 222 (bhūtāni bhummāni earthly creatures, contrasted with creatures in the air, antalikkhe), 236 (id.); Sdhp 420 (sabba-bhummā khattiyā). pl. **bhummā** the earthly ones, i. e. the gods inhabiting the earth, esp. tree gods (Yakkhas) Vv 84[2] (= bhumma-deva VvA 334). — nt. ground: Pv II.10[2] (yāva bhummā down to the ground); v. l. BB bhūm(i). — 2. the locative case KhA 106, 111, 224; SnA 140, 210, 321, 433; PvA 33.

-attharaṇa "earth-spread," a ground covering, mat, carpet Vin I.48; II.208; IV.279. **-antara** "earth-occasion," i. e. (1) sphere of the earth, plane of existence Miln 163; DhsA 296. — (2) in °*pariccheda* discussion concerning the earth, i. e. cosmogony DhsA 3. **-antalikkha** earthly and celestial, over earth & sky (of portents) Miln 178. The form would correspond to Sk. *bhaum-āntarīkṣa. **-jāla** "terrestrial net (of insight) gift of clear sight extending over the globe (perhaps to find hidden treasures) SnA 353 (term of a vijjā, science or magic art). Cp. bhūrikamma & bhūrivijjā. **-ṭṭha** (a) put into the earth, being in the earth, found on or in the earth, earthly Vin III.47.

(b) standing on the earth Dh 28. — (c) resting on the earth Miln 181. Also as °*ka* living on earth, earthly (of gods) J III.87. **-deva** a terrestrial deva or fairy A IV.118; Ps II.149; VbhA 12; DhA I.156; VvA 334; PvA 5, 43, 55, 215, 277. **-devatā** = °deva J IV.287 (= yakkha); KhA 120.

Bhummi[1] (f.) [fr. bhumma] that which belongs to the ground, i. e. a plane (of existence), soil, stage (as t.t. in philosophy) DhsA 277 (°y-āpatti), 339 (id.), 985 (dukkha°), 1368, 1374 sq. (see *Dhs trsl.*[2] 231).

Bhummi[2] [old voc. of bhumma] a voc. of friendly address "my (dear) man" (lit. terrestrial) Vin II.104 (= piyavacanaŋ Bdhgh).

Bhuyya the regular P. representative of Sk. bhūyas (compar.); for which usually bhiyya (q. v.). Only in cpd. yebhuyyena (q. v.).

Bhuvi see bhū.

Bhusa[1] [cp. Vedic busa (nt.) & buśa (m.)] chaff, husks A I.241 (°āgāra chaff-house); Dh 252 (opuṇāti bhusaŋ to sift husks); Ud 78; Pv III.4[1]; III.10[7]; VvA 47 (tiṇa° litter).

Bhusa[2] (adj.) [cp. Vedic bhṛśa] strong, mighty, great Dh 339 (taṇhā = balavā DhA IV.48); J V.361 (daṇḍa; = daḷha, balavā C.). — nt. bhusaŋ (adv.) much, exceedingly, greatly, vehemently. In cpds. bhusaŋ° & bhusa°. — S I.69; J III.441; IV.11; V.203 (bhusa-dassaneyya); VI.192; Vv 6[9]; Pv 3[38]; IV.7[7]; Miln 346; SnA 107 ("verbum intensivum"); Sdhp 289.

Bhusati, Bhussati [perhaps a legitimate form for Sk. bhaṣate (see P. bhasati), with u for a, so that the suggested correction of bhusati to bhasati (see under bhasati) is unfounded] to bark DA I.317 (bhusati; vv. ll. bhussati & bhūsati); DhA I.171, 172. — See also bhasati & bhukka; — pp. bhusita.

Bhusikā (f.) [fr. bhusa[1]] chaff A I.242; Vin II.181.

Bhusita [pp. of bhusati] barking J IV.182 (°sadda, barking, noise). See also bhasita.

Bhuseti [Denom. fr. bhusa[2] = *bhṛśayati; but not certain, may have to be read bhūseti, to endeavour, cp. Sk. bhūṣati] to make strong, to cause to grow (?) J V.218 (C. expl[ns] by "bhusaŋ karoti, vaḍḍheti" p. 224).

Bhū[1] [fr. **bhū**] (adj.) being, (n.) creature, living being in **pāṇa-bhū** a living being (a breathing being) J V.79 (= pāṇa-bhūta C.).

Bhū[2] (f.) [fr. **bhū**, otherwise bhūmi] the earth; loc. bhuvi according to Kaccāyana; otherwise bhuvi is aor. 3rd sg. of **bhū**: see Pischel, *Prk. Gr.* § 516; Geiger, *Pali Gr.* § 86[5].

Bhūkuṭi (f.) [a different spelling of bhakuṭi, q. v. — Cp. Sk. bhṛkuti & bhrukuṭi] frown, anger, superciliousness M I.125 (v. l. bhakuṭi & bhā°); J V.296.

Bhūja [cp. late Sk. bhūrja, with which related Lat. fraxinus ash, Ags. beorc = E. birch, Ger. birke] the Bhūrja-tree, i. e. a kind of willow J V.195, 405 (in both places = ābhuji), 420.

Bhūta [pp. of bhavati, Vedic etc. bhūta] grown, become; born, produced; nature as the result of becoming. — The (exegetical) definition by Bdhgh of the word bhūta is interesting. He (at MA I.31) distinguishes the foll. 7 meanings of the term: (1) animate Nature as principle, or the vital aggregates (the 5 Khandhas), with ref. M I.260; (2) ghosts (amanussā) Sn 222; (3) inanimate Nature as principle, or the Elements (the 4 dhātus) S III.101 (mahābhūtā); (4) all that exists, physical existence in general (vijjamānaŋ) Vin IV.25 (bhūtaŋ); (5) what we should call a simple *predicative* use, is exemplified by a typical dogmatic example, viz. "kālaghaso *bhūto*," where bhūta is given as meaning *khīṇāsava* (Arahant) J II.260; (6) all beings or specified existence, animal kingdom (sattā) D II.157; (7) the vegetable kingdom, plants, vegetation (rukkh' ādayo) Vin IV.34 (as bhūta-gāma). — *Meanings*: 1. bhūtā & bhūtāni (pl.) beings, living beings, animate Nature Sn 35 (expl[d] at Nd[2] 479 as 2 kinds, viz. tasā & thāvarā, movable & immovable; S. II.47 (*K.S.* II.36) mind and body as come-to-be; Dh 131 (bhūtāni), 405; M I.2 sq. (paṭhavī, āpo etc., bhūtā, devā, Pajāpati etc.), 4; MA I.32. The pl. nt. bhūtāni is used as pl. to meaning 2; viz. inanimate Nature, elements, usually enum[d] under term mahā-bhūtāni. — 2. (nt.) nature, creation, world M I.2 (bhūte bhūtato sañjānāti recognises the beings from nature, i. e. from the fact of being nature); DhsA 312 (°pasāda-lakkhaṇa, see *Expos.* 409). See cpds. °gāma, °pubba (?). — 3. (nt. adj.) that which is, i. e. natural, genuine, true; nt. truth; neg. abhūta falsehood, lie Sn 387; PvA 34. See cpds. °bhāva, °vacana, °vāda. — 4. a supernatural being, ghost, demon, Yakkha; pl. bhūtā guardian genii (of a city) J IV.245. See cpds. °vijja, °vejja. — 5. (-°) pp. in *predicative* use (cp. on this meaning Bdhgh's meaning No. 5, above): (a) what has been or happened; viz. mātu-bhūtā having been his mother PvA 78; abhūtapubbaŋ bhūtaŋ what has never happened before happened (now) DA I.43 (in expl[n] of abbhuta); — (b) having become such & such, being like, acting as, being, quâsi (as it were), consisting of, e. g. andha° blind, as it were J VI.139; aru° consisting of wounds DhA III.109; udapāna° being a well, a well so to speak PvA 78; opāna° acting as a spring A IV.185; hetu° as reason, being the reason PvA 58; cp. cakkhu° having become an eye of wisdom. Sometimes bhūta in this use hardly needs to be translated at all.

-kāya body of truth DhA I.11. **-gāma** vegetation, as trees, plants, grass, etc. Under bhūtagāma Bdhgh understands the 5 bīja-jātāni (5 groups of plants springing from a germinative power: see bīja), viz. mūla-bījaŋ, khandha°, phala°, agga°, bīja°. Thus in C. on Vin IV.34 (the so-called bhūtagāma-sikkhāpada, quoted at DhA III.302 & SnA 3); cp. M III.34; J V.46; Miln 3, 244. **-gāha** possession by a demon Miln 168 (cp. Divy 235). **-ṭṭhāna** place of a ghost KhA 170. **-pati** (a) lord of beings J V.113 (of Inda); VI.362 (id.); Vv 64[1] (id.). (b) lord of ghosts, or Yakkhas J VI.269 (of Kuvera). **-pubba** (a) as adj. (-°) having formerly been so & so, as mātā bhūtapubbo satto, pitā etc., in untraced quotation at Vism 305; also at SnA 359 (Bhagavā kuṇāla-rājā bhūtapubbo). — (b) as adv. (bhūtapubbaŋ) meaning: before all happening, before creation, at a very remote stage of the world, in old times, formerly Vin II.201; D I.92; II.167, 285, 337; M I.253; III.176; S I.216, 222, 227; IV.201; V.447; A IV.136 = Vism 237; A IV.432; J I.394; DhA 1.56. **-bhavya** past and future D I.18. **-bhāva** truthful character, neg. a° PvA 14. **-vacana** statement of reality or of the truth SnA 336. **-vādin** truthful, speaking the truth M I.180; D III.175; Pug 58; a° untruthful Dh 306; J II.416. **-vikāra** a natural blemish, fault of growth, deformity SnA 189 (opp. nibbikāra). **-vijjā** knowledge of demons, exorcism D I.9; Dh 1.93, cp. *Dial.* I.17). **-vejja** a healer of harm caused by demons, an exorcist Vin IV.84; J II.215; III.511; Miln 23.

Bhūtatta (nt.) [abstr. fr. bhūta] the fact of having grown, become or being created (i. e. being creatures or part of creation) Vism 310 (in def. of bhūtā); MA I.32 (id.).

Bhūtanaka [cp. *Sk. bhūtṛṇa] a fragrant grass; Andropogon schœnanthus J VI.36 (= phanijjaka); Vism 543 (so v. l. for T. bhūtinaka).

Bhūtika (adj.) (-°) in cpd. câtummahā° belongs to the whole expression, viz. composed of the 4 great elements M I.515.

Bhūnaha [difficult to explⁿ; is it an old misspelling for bhūta+gha? The latter of **han**?] a destroyer of beings Sn 664 (voc. bhūnahu, expl^d by SnA 479 as "bhūti-hanaka vuddhi-nāsaka"; vv. ll. bhūnahaṭa, bhūnahoṭa, bhūhata, all showing the difficulty of the archaic word); J v.266 (pl. bhūnahuno, expl^d by C. 272 as "isīnaŋ ativattāro attano vaḍḍhiyā hatattā bh."). Cp. M I.502 ("puritanical" suggested by Lord Chalmers).

Bhūma (-°) [=bhūmi] 1. (lit.) ground, country, district S III.5 (pacchā° the western district). — 2. (fig.) ground, reason for, occasion; stage, step Sn 896 (avivāda° ground of harmony; according to SnA 557 Ep. of Nibbāna).

Bhūmaka (& °ika) (adj.) (only -°) [from bhūma, or bhūmi] 1. having floors or stories (of buildings) as **dve**° pāsāda DhA I.414; **pañca**° pāsāda a palace with 5 stories J I.58, 89; **satta**° with 7 stories (pāsāda) DhA II.1, 260. The form °ika at DhA I.182 (dve° geha). — 2. belonging to a place or district, as jāti° from the land of (their) birth M I.147; **pacchā**° from the western country S IV.312 (brāhmaṇā). — 3. being on a certain plane or in a certain state, as **paritta**° & **mahā**° Vbh 340 **te**° in 3 planes SnA 4 (of the 5 Khandhas), 510 (°vaṭṭa); DhA I.36 (kusala), 305 (°vaṭṭa); IV.69 (tebhūmaka-vaṭṭa-sankhātaŋ Māra-bandhanaŋ), 72 (dhammā); **catu**° in 4 planes DhsA 296 (kusala); DhA I.35 (citta). The form °**ika** at DhA I.288 (with ref. to citta).

Bhūmi (f.) [cp. Vedic bhūmi, Av. būmiš soil, ground, to **bhū**, as in bhavati, cp. Gr. φύσις etc. See bhavati] 1. (lit.) ground, soil, earth Vin II.175; Sn 418 (yāna° carriage road); Pv I.10[14] ≈; SnA 353 (heṭṭhā-bhūmiyaŋ under the earth); DhA I.414 (id., opp. upari-bhūmiyaŋ). — 2. place, quarter, district, region M I.145 (jāti° district of one's birth); Sn 830 (vighāta°); Nd² 475 (danta°); DhA I.213 (āpāna°); PvA 80 (susāna°). —**uyyāna**° garden (-place or locality) Vv 64[19]; Pv II.12[9]; J I.58. — 3. (fig.) ground, plane, stage, level; state of consciousness, Vin. I.17; Vbh 322 sq.; Vism 126, 442 (with ref. to the 4 Paṭisambhidā, as sekha-bhūmi & asekha-bhūmi), 517 (paññā°-niddesa). Usually -°: indriya° Nett 192; dassana° plane of insight Nett S, 14, 50; sukha° ground for happiness Dhs 984 (cp. DhsA 214). —**bhūmi-ttaya** the 3 stages, viz. kāmâvacara, rūpâvacara, lokuttara Vism 493. — pl. bhūmiyo Ps II.205 = Vism 384 (appl^d to the 4 jhānas); purisa° (aṭṭha p. bh. eight stages of the individual; viz. manda-bhūmi, khiḍḍā°, vīmaŋsana°, ujugata°, sekha°, samaṇa°, jina°, panna°, or as trsl^d by Rh. D. in *Dial.* I.72, under "eight stages of a prophet's existence"; babyhood, playtime, trial time, erect time, learning time, ascetic time, prophet time & prostrate time. Cp. the 10 decades of man's life, as given by Bdhgh at Vism 619). — Bdhgh. when defining the 2 meanings of bhūmi as "mahā-paṭhavī" and as "cittuppāda" (rise of thought) had in view the distinction between its literal & figurative meaning. But this def. (at DhsA 214) is vague & only popular. — An old loc. of bhūmi is **bhumyā**, e. g. J I.507; V.84. Another form of bhūmi at end of cpds. is **bhūma** (q. v.).
-kampa shaking of the ground, earthquake Miln 178. **-gata** "gone into the soil," i. e. hiding, stored away J I.375. **-ghana** thick soil SnA 149, cp. paṭhavi-ghana ibid. 146. **-tala** ground (-surface) PvA 186. **-padesa** place or region upon the earth J VI.95. **-pappaṭaka** outgrowths in the soil D III.87 = Vism 418. **-pothana** beating the ground DhA I.171. **-bhāga** division of the earth, district J I.109; V.200; VvA 125; PvA 29, 154. **-laddh** (uppanna) acquired on a certain stage of existence SnA 4. **-saya** lying or sleeping on the ground DhA II.61.

Bhūri¹ (f.) [cp. late Sk. bhūr] the earth; given as name for the earth (paṭhavi) at Ps II.197; see also def. at DhsA 147. Besides these only in 2 doubtful cpds., both resting on demonology, viz. bhūrikamma D I.12, expl^d as "practices to be observed by one living in a bhūri-ghara or earth-house" (?) DA I.97, but cp. Vedic bhūri-karman "much effecting"; and bhūrivijjā D I.9, expl^d as "knowledge of charms to be pronounced by one living in an earth-house" (?) DA I.93. See *Dial.* I.18, 25. The meaning of the terms is obscure; there may have been (as Kern rightly suggests: see *Toev.* s. v.) quite a diff. popular practice behind them, which was unknown to the later Commentator. Kern suggests that bhūri-vijjā might be a secret science to find gold (digging for it: science of hidden treasures), and °kamma might be "making gold" (alchemistic science). Perhaps the term bhumma-jāla is to be connected with these two.

Bhūri² (adj.) [cp. Vedic bhūri] wide, extensive, much, abundant, DhsA 147 (in def. of the term bhūri¹, i. e. earth); otherwise only in cpds.: °**pañña** (adj.) of extensive wisdom, very wise S IV.205; Sn 346, 792, 1097, 1143; Pv III.5⁵; Ps II.197 ("paṭhavī-samāya vitthatāya vipulāya paññāya samannāgato ti bhūripañño," with other definitions); Nd¹ 95 (same explⁿ as under Ps II.197); Nd² 415 C. (id.). °**paññāṇa** (adj.) same as °pañña Sn 1136 ≈ (cp. Nd² 480). °**medhasa** (adj.) very intelligent S I.42, 174; III.143; A IV.449; Sn 1131, 1136; Th I, 1266; Pv III.7⁷.

Bhūrī (f.) [is it original? Cp. BSk. bhūri in same sense at Lal. V. 444, 541; MVastu III.332] knowledge, understanding, intelligence Dh 282, quoted at DhsA 76 (expl^d as termed so because it is as widespread as the earth; Dhs 16; DhA III.421; same explⁿ at DhsA 148); J VI.415.

Bhūsana (nt.) [fr. **bhūṣ**] ornament, decoration Vism 10 (yatino-sīla-bhūsana-bhūsitā contrasted to rājāno muttāmaṇi-vibhūsitā).

Bhūsā (f.) [fr. **bhūṣ**] ornament, decoration, only in cpd. bhūsa- (read bhūsā-)dassaneyya beautiful as an ornament Pv III.3².

Bhūseti [Caus. of **bhūṣ**, to be busy; in meaning "to adorn" etc. Expl^d at Dhtp. 315, 623 by "alankāra"] to adorn, embellish, beautify. Only in pp. bhūsita adorned with (-°) Pv II.9⁵², 12⁷; III.3⁵; J VI.53. Cp. vi°.

Bheka [cp. Vedic bheka, onomat.] a frog Th I, 310; J III.430; IV.247; VI.208.

Bhecchati is fut. of **bhindati** (q. v.).

Bhejja (adj.) [grd. of bhindati] to be split, only in neg. form abhejja not to be split or sundered Sn 255; J I.263; III.318; Pug 30; Miln 160, 199.

Bhejjanaka (adj.) [fr. bhejja] breakable; like bhejja only in neg. form abhejjanaka indestructible J I.393.

Bheṇḍi [perhaps indentical with & only wrong spelling for bheṇḍu = kaṇḍu²] a kind of missile used as a weapon, arrow Vin III.77 (where enum^d with asi, satti & laguḷa in explⁿ of upanikkhipana).

Bheṇḍu [with v. l. geṇḍu, of uncertain reading & meaning. Pischel, *Prk. Gr.* § 107 gives giṇḍu & remarks that this cannot be derived fr. kaṇḍuka (although kaṇḍu may be considered as gloss of bheṇḍu at Th I, 164: see kaṇḍu²), but belongs with Prk. geṇḍui play & P. geṇḍuka and the originally Sk. words genduka, ginduka, gendu, geṇḍuka to a root **gid, giḍ**, Prk. giṇḍai to play. Morris, *J.P.T.S.* 1884, 90 says: "I am inclined to read geṇḍu in all cases & to compare it with geḍuka & geṇḍuka a ball"] a ball, bead; also a ball-shaped ornament or turret, cupola Th I, 164 (see kaṇḍu²) J I.386 (also °maya ball-shaped); III.184 (v. l. geṇḍu).

Bheṇḍuka[1] [in all probability misreading for geṇḍuka. The v. l. is found at all passages. Besides this occur the vv. ll. keṇḍuka (=kaṇḍuka?) & kuṇḍika] a ball for playing J IV.30, 256; V.196; VI.471; DhsA 116. See also geṇḍuka.

Bheṇḍuka[2] [fr. bheṇḍu, identical with bheṇḍuka[1]] a knob, cupola, round tower J I.2 (mahā-bh°-pamāṇa).

Bhettar [n. ag. fr. **bhid**] a breaker, divider A V.283.

Bheda [fr. **bhid**, cp. Ved. & Class. Sk. bheda in same meanings] 1. breaking, rending, breach, disunion, dissension Vism 64 sq. (contrasted with ānisaṇsa), 572 sq. (with ref. to upādāna & bhava); VbhA 185 (id.); Sdhp 66, 457, 463. —**mithu°** breaking of alliance D II.76; J IV.184; Kvu 314. —**vacī°** breaking of [the rule as to] speech Miln 231. —**sangha°** disunion in the Sangha Vin II.203. —**sīla°** breach of morality J V.163. — abl. bhedā after the destruction or dissolution in phrase kāyassa bhedā param maraṇā, i. e. after the breaking up of the body & after death: see kāya I. e. & cp. D III.52, 146 sq., 258; Dh 140; Pug 51. — 2. (-°) sort, kind, as adj. consisting of, like J II.438; VI.3 (kaṭuk' ādi°); DhA III.14 (kāya-sucarit'-ādi°-bhadra-kammāni); SnA 290 (Avīci-ādi-° niraya).

-**kara** causing division or dissension Vin II.7; III.173; V.93 (cp. Vin I.354 & *Vin. Texts* III.343 for the 18 errors in which the Sangha is brought into division by bhikkhus who are in the wrong); DhsA 29 (aṭṭhārasa bheda-kara-vatthūni the 18 causes of dissension).

Bhedaka (adj. n.) [fr. bheda] breaking, dividing, causing disunion; (m.) divider Vin II.205; J VI.382. — nt. adv. **bhedakaŋ**, as in °nakha in such a way as to break a nail DA I.37.

Bhedana (nt.) [fr. **bhid**, as in Caus. bhedeti] 1. breaking (open), in **puṭa°** breaking of the seed-boxes (of the Pāṭali plant), idiomatic for "merchandise" Miln 1. See under puṭa. — 2. (fig.) breach, division, destruction A IV.247; Dh 138; Bu II.7; J I.467 (mittabhāva°).

-**dhamma** subject to destruction, fragile, perishable A IV.386; J I.146, 392; ThA 254. -**saŋvattanika** leading to division or dissension Vin III.173.

Bhedāpeti & **Bhedeti** are Causatives of bhindati (q. v.).

Bheraṇḍaka [cp. *Sk. bheruṇḍa] a jackal J V.270; the *nom.* probably formed after the *acc.* in phrase bheraṇḍakaŋ nadati to cry after the fashion of, or like a jackal A I.187.

Bherava (adj.) [fr. bhīru, cp. Epic Sk. bhairava] fearful, terrible, frightful Th 1, 189; Sn 959, 965, 984; Nd[1] 370, 467; J VI.520; Dpvs 17, 100; Pgdp 26, 31. —**bahu°** very terrible A III.52; stricken with terror J VI.587. — (n) terror, comb[d] with bhaya fear & dismay M I.17, A IV.291; V.132; Th 1, 367, 1059. —**pahīna-bhaya-bherava** having left behind (i. e. free from) fear & terror S III.83.

-**rāva** cry of terror Miln 254.

Bheri (f.) [cp. Epic Sk. bherī] a kettle-drum (of large size; DhsA 319 distinguishes 2 kinds: mahā° & paṭaha°) D I.79; A II.185; Vv 81[10]; J VI.465; DhA I.396; Sdhp 429. —**issara°** the drum of the ruler or lord J I.283; **paṭaha°** kettle-drum Dpvs 16, 14; DhsA 319; PvA 4; **yāma°** (-velāya) (at the time) when the drum sounds the watch J V.459. —**bheriŋ vādeti** to sound the drum J I.283. —**bheriyo vādentā** (pl.) beating (lit. making sound) the drums J II.110. bheriñ carāpeti to make the drum go round, i. e. to proclaim by beat of drum J V.41; VI.10.

-**caraṇa** the carrying round of the drum (in proclamations), in cpds. °*magga* the proclamation road DhA II.43; & °**vīthi** id. DhA II.45. -**tala** the head of the drum Vism 489 (in comparison); VbhA 80 (id.). -**paṇava** drum & tabor (in battle) A II.117. -**vāda** drum-sound, fig. for a loud voice PvA 89 (bherivādena akkosati rails like drum). -**vādaka** a drummer J I.283. -**saññā** sign of the drum DhA I.396. -**sadda** sound of the drum J I.283.

Bhesajja (nt.) [cp. Vedic bhaiṣajya=bheṣaja, fr. bhiṣaj; see also P. bhisakka] a remedy, medicament, medicine Vin I.278; D II.266; M I.30; SnA 154, 446; Sdhp 393. bhesajjaŋ karoti to treat with a medicine DhA I.25; mūla-bhesajjāni the principal medicines Miln 43; pañca bhesajjāni the 5 remedies (allowed to bhikkhus) DhA I.5.

-**kapālaka** medicine bowl VbhA 361. -**sikkhāpada** the medicine precepts VbhA 69.

Bhesma (adj.) [cp. Vedic bhīṣma of which the regular P. form is bhiŋsa, of **bhī**; bhesma would correspond to a form *bhaiṣma] terrible, awful Vin II.203=It 86 ("bhesmā hi udadhī mahā," so read for *Vin.* bhasmā, with v. l. bhesmā, and for *It* tasmā, with v. l. BB bhesmā, misunderstood by ed. — Bdhgh Vin II.325 on *Vin.* passage expl[d] by bhayānaka); J V.266; VI.133 (v. l. bhasma).

Bho (indecl.) [voc. of bhavant, cp. Sk. bhoḥ which is the shortened voc. bhagoḥ of Vedic bhagavant; cp. as to form P. āvuso > Sk. āyuṣmaḥ of āyuṣmant] a familiar term of address (in speaking to equals or inferiors): sir, friend, you, my dear; pl. sirs D I.88, 90, 93, 111; M I.484; Sn 427, 457, 487; with voc. of noun: **bho purisa** my dear man J I.423; **bho brahmaṇā** oh ye brahmans J II.369. Double **bho bho** DhA IV.158.

-**vādika**=°vādin Nd[1] 249. -**vādin** a brahman, i. e. one who addresses others with the word "bho," implying some superiority of the speaker; name given to the brahman, as proud of his birth, in contrast to brāhmaṇa, the true brahman Sn 620; Dh 396; J VI.211, 214; DhA IV.158.

Bhokkhaŋ is fut. of bhuñjati (q. v.).

Bhokkhi at VbhA 424, in phrase sucikāmo bh. brāhmaṇo is a kind of Desider. formation fr. **bhuj° (bhuñj)**, appearing as *bhukṣ=**bhokkh** (cp. bhokkhaŋ), with ending °in; meaning "wishing to eat." It corresponds to Sk. bhoktu-kāma. Cp. also n. ag. bhoktṛ of *bhukṣ, enjoyer, eater. P. bhokkhi might be Sk. bhoktrī, if it was not for the latter being f. The word is a curiosity.

Bhoga[1] [fr. **bhuñj**: see bhuñjati] 1. enjoyment A IV.392 (kāmaguṇesu bh.). — 2. possession, wealth D III.77; Sn 301, 421; Dh 139, 355; Pug 30, 57; Sdhp 86, 228, 264. —**appa°** little or no possession Sn 114.

-**khandha** a mass of wealth, great possessions D II.86 (one of the 5 profits accruing from virtue). -**gāma** "village of revenue," a tributary village, i. e. a village which has to pay tribute or contributions (in food etc.) to the owner of its ground. The latter is called gāmabhojaka or gāmapati "landlord" J II.135. Cp. Fick, *Sociale Gliederung* 71, 112. -**cāgin** giving riches, liberal A III.128. -**pārijuñña** loss of property or possessions VvA 101. -**mada** pride or conceit of wealth VbhA 466. -**vāsin**, as f. **vāsinī** "living in property," i. e. to be enjoyed or made use of occasionally, one of the 10 kinds of wives: a kept woman Vin III.139, 140; cp. M I.286.

Bhoga[2] [fr. **bhuj** to bend, cp. bhuja[3] & Sk. bhoga id. Halāyudha 3, 20] the coil of a snake J III.58. See also nib°.

Bhogatā (-°) (f.) [abstr. fr. bhoga] condition of prosperity, having wealth or riches, in **uḷāra°** being very rich, M III.38.

Bhogavant (adj.) [fr. bhoga] one who has possessions or supplies, wealthy J V.399; Mhvs 10, 20; Sdhp 511.

Bhogika (-°) (adj.) [fr. bhoga] having wealth or power, in antara° an intermediate aristocrat Vin III.47.

Bhogin[1] (-°) (adj.-n.) [fr. bhoga] enjoying, owning, abounding in, partaking in or devoted to (e. g. to pleasure, kāma°) D II.80; III.124; S I.78; IV.331, 333; A III.289; V.177. — m. owner, wealthy man M I.366.

Bhogin[2] (adj.) [fr. **bhuj**, see bhuja[3]] having coils, of a snake J III.57; VI.317.

Bhogiya is diaeretic form of Sk. bhogya = P. **bhogga**[2] with which identical in meaning 2, similar also to **bhogika**.

Bhogga[1] (adj.) [fr. **bhuj** to bend, pp. corresp. to Sk. bhugna] bent, crooked M I.88; D II.22; A I.138; J III.395.

Bhogga[2] (adj.) [grd. of **bhuñj** to enjoy, thus = Sk. bhogya] 1. to be enjoyed or possessed, n. property, possession, in cpd. **rāja°** (of an elephant) to be possessed by a king, serviceable to a king, royal D I.87; A I.244, 284; II.113, 170; J II.370; DhA I.313 (royal possessions in general); DA I.245. Cp. BSk. rājabhogya MVastu I.287. See in detail under rāja-bhogga. —**nagga-bhogga** one who possesses nothing but nakedness, i. e. an ascetic J IV.160; V.75; VI.225. — 2. (identical with bhogika & bhogiya & similar in meaning to bhoja-rājā) royal, of royal power, entitled to the throne, as a designation of "class" at Vin III.221 in sequence rājā rāja-bhoggā brāhmaṇā, etc., where it takes the place of the usual **khattiya** "royal noble."

Bhoja [lit. grd. of bhuñjati[2], to be sorted out, to be raised from slavery; thus also meaning "dependence," "training," from **bhuj**, to which belongs bhujissa] one who is getting trained, dependent, a freed slave, villager, subject. Only in cpds. like **bhojisiyaŋ** [bhoja + isi + ya = issariya] mastery over dependence, i. e. independence S I.44, 45; **bhojājānīya** a well-trained horse, a thoroughbred J I.178, 179; **bhojaputta** son of a villager J V.165; **bhojarājā** head of a village (-district) a subordinate king Sn 553 = Th 1, 823. — In the latter phrase however it may mean "wealthy" kings, or "titled" kings (khattiyā bh-r., who are next in power to and serve on a rājā cakkavatti). The phrase is best taken as *one*, viz. "the nobles, royal kings." It may be a term for "vice-kings" or substitute-kings, or those who are successors of the king. The expl[n] at SnA 453 takes the three words as three diff. terms and places bhojā = bhogiyā as a designation of a class or rank (= bhogga). Neumann in his trsl[n] of Sn has "Königstämme, kühn und stolz," free but according to the sense. The phrase may in bhoja contain a local designation of the Bhoja princes (N. of a tribe), which was then taken as a special name for "king" (cp. Kaiser > Cæsar, or Gr. βασιλεύς). With the wording "khattiyā bhoja-rājāno anuyuttā bhavanti te" cp. M III.173: "paṭirājāno te rañño cakkavattissa anuyuttā bhavanti," and A V.22: "kuḍḍa-rājāno" in same phrase. — Mrs. Rh. D. at *Brethren*, p. 311, trsl[s] "nobles and wealthy lords."

Bhojan is ppr. of bhojeti, feeding J VI.207.

Bhojaka [fr. **bhuj**, bhojeti] 1. one who provides food, attendant at meals J V.413. — 2. (is this from bhuñjati[2] & bhujissa ?) one who draws the benefit of something, owner, holder, in gāma° landholder, village head man (see *Dial.* I.108 n. & Fick, *Sociale Gliederung* 104 sq.) J I.199, 354, 483; II.135 (= gāmapati, gāmajeṭṭhaka); V.413; DhA I.69. Cp. **bhojanaka**.

Bhojana (nt.) [fr. bhuñjati] food, meal, nourishment in general J II.218; IV.103, 173; J I.178; IV.223; Sn 102, 128, 242, 366, 667; Dh 7, 70; Pug 21, 55; Miln 370; Vism 69, 106; Sdhp 52, 388, 407. Some similes with bhojana see *J.P.T.S.* 1907, 119. —**tika°** food allowed for a triad (of reasons) Vin II.196. dub° having little or bad food J II.368; DhA IV.8. **paṇīta°** choice & plentiful meals Vin IV.88. sabhojane kule in the family in which a bhikkhu has received food Vin IV.94. —**bhojane mattaññu(tā)** knowing proper measure in eating (& abstr.); eating within bounds, one of the 4 restrictions of moral life S II.218; A I.113 sq.; Nd[1] 483. — 5 bhojanāni or meals are given at Vin IV.75, viz. niccabhatta°, salākabhatta°, pakkhikaŋ, uposathikaŋ, pāṭipadikaŋ. — As part of the regulations concerning food, hours of eating etc. in the Sangha there is a distinction ascribed to the Buddha between **gaṇa-bhojanaŋ, parampara-bhojanaŋ, atirittabhojanaŋ, anatirittabhojanaŋ** mentioned at Kvu II.552; see Vin IV.71, 77. All these ways of taking food are forbidden under ordinary circumstances, but allowed in the case of illness (gilāna-samaye), when robes are given to the Bhikkhus (cīvarasamaye) and several other occasions, as enum[d] at Vin IV.74. — The distinction is made as follows: gaṇabhojanaŋ said when 4 bhikkhus are invited to partake together of one of the five foods; or food prepared as a joint meal Vin IV.74; cp. II.196; V.128, 135; **paramparabhojanaŋ** said when a bhikkhu, invited to partake of one of the 5 foods, first takes one and then another Vin IV.78; **atirittabhojanaŋ** is food left over from that provided for a sick person, or too great a quantity offered on one occasion to bhikkhus (in this case permitted to be eaten) Vin IV.82; **anatirittabhojanaŋ** is food that is not left over & is accepted & eaten by a bhikkhu without inquiry Vin IV.84.

-**aggadāna** gift of the best of food SnA 270. -**atthika** in need of food, hungry Pv II.9[29]. -**pariyantika** restricting one's feeding Vism 69. -**vikati** at J V.292 is to be read as **bhājana°** (q. v.).

Bhojanaka = bhojaka, in °gāma owner or headman of the village J II.134.

Bhojaniya, Bhojanīya, Bhojaneyya [grd. of **bhuj**, Caus. bhojeti. Cp. bhuñjitabba] what may be eaten, eatable, food; fit or proper to eat. —**bhojaniya**: food Vin IV.92 (*five* foods: odana rice, kummāsa gruel, sattu meal, flour, maccha fish, maŋsa meat). Soft food, as distinguished from khādaniya hard food J I.90. See also khādaniya. **bhojanīya**: eatable S I.167, cp. pari°. **bhojaneyya**: fit to eat DA I.28; a° unfit to be eaten Sn 81; J V.15.

Bhojin (-°) (adj.) [fr. **bhuj**] feeding on, enjoying A III.43; M I.343; Sn 47; J II.150; Pug 55.

Bhojeti [Caus. of bhuñjati] to cause to eat, to feed, entertain, treat, regale Vin I.243; IV.71; J VI.577; DhA I.101.

Bhojja (adj.) [grd. of bhuñjati] to be eaten, eatable; **khajja°** what can be chewed & eaten DA I.85. °**yāgu** "eatable rice-gruel," i. e. soft gruel, prepared in a certain way Vin I.223, 224.

Bhojjha a good horse, a Sindh horse J I.180.

Bhoti f. of bhavant (q. v.) DhA III.194.

Bhottabba & **Bhottuŋ** are grd. & inf. of bhuñjati (q. v.); **bhottabba** to be eaten J V.252, 253; **bhottuŋ** to eat J II.14.

Bhobhukka [intens-redupl. of **bhukk** = **bukk**, to bark: see bhukka & cp. Sk. bukkati, bukkana] one making a barking sound, barker, i. e. dog J VI.345 (= bhunkaraṇa C.).

M.

-M- euphonic consonant inserted between two vowels to avoid hiatus, as agga-m-agga the best of all Vin IV.232; anga-m-angāni limb by limb Vin III.119; Vv 38[2], etc. See also S III.254 (yena-m-idh' ekacco); Dh 34 (oka-m-okata ubbhato); Sn 765 (aññatra-m-ariyehi); Nd[1] 269 (dvaye-m-eva); J I.29 (asīti-hattha-m-ubbedha, for hatth' ubbedha); III.387 (katattho-m-anubujjhati); V.72 (orena-m-āgama); VI.266 (pacchā-m-anutappati); SnA 309 (rāg' ādi-m-anekappakāraŋ). — On wrong syllable division through Sandhi-m-, and thus origin of specific Pali forms see māsati.

Ma (-kāra) the letter or sound m J III.273 (sandhi-vasena vutta put in for the sake of euphony); V.375 (ma-kāro sandhikaro); KhA 155, 224; SnA 181, 383, 404.

Maŋsa (nt.) [cp. Vedic māŋsa, fr. Idg. *memsro-, as in Gr. μηρός thigh, Lat. membrum limb ("member"); Goth. mims flesh: Oir mīr bite, bit (of flesh)] flesh, meat S II.97 (putta°); Dh 152; J III.184; Pug 55; Vism 258, 357 (in compar.); DhA I.375 (putta°); II.51 (alla° living flesh); VbhA 58, 61 (pilotika-paliveṭhita). Described and defined in detail as one of the 32 ākāras or constituents of the human body at Vism 252, 354; KhA 46; VbhA 235.
-ûpasecana sauce for meat J III.144 = VI.24; DhA I.344. -kalyāṇa beauty of flesh, one of the 5 beauties of a girl (see kalyāṇa) J I.394; DhA I.387. -khādaka flesh-eater J VI.530. -cakkhu the bodily eye, one of the 5 kinds of the sense of sight (see cakkhu III) D III.219; Nd[1] 100, 354. -dhovanī odaka water for washing meat KhA 54. -piṇḍika a meat-ball, lump of flesh Vism 256. -puñja a heap of flesh Vism 361 (in comp.); VbhA 67. -pesi a piece of flesh or meat (see on simile *J.P.T.S.* 1907, 122) Vin II.25; III.105 (°ŋ vehāsaŋ gacchantiŋ addasaŋ); M I.143; A III.97; Miln 280; Vism 195, 252, 468; DhA I.164; VbhA 235; -lohita flesh & blood Dh 150.

Maŋsi (f.) [cp. Sk. māŋsī] a certain plant Nardostychus jatamansi J VI.535.

Maŋsika [fr. maŋsa; cp. *Sk. māŋsika] 1. a dealer in meat, meat-seller Miln 331. — 2. in piṭṭhi° the °ka belongs to the whole cpd., thus: one who is a backbiter, a slanderer Sn 244 (= piṭṭhi-maŋsa-khādaka SnA 287). Similarly piṭṭhi-maŋsikatā (q. v.) Nd[2] 39[1].

Makaci [etym. ?] a kind of cloth, material, fibre DhA III.68 (vākakhaṇḍa).
-pilotikā rough cloth (used for straining) J II.96; DhA II.155. Cp. makkhi-vāla. -vāka m. bark Vism 249 (+ akkavāka); VbhA 232.

Makara [cp. Epic Sk. makara] a mythical fish or sea monster, Leviathan (cp. Zimmer, *Altind. Leben* 97) J II.442; III.188; Miln 131, 377; ThA 204. — f. makarinī Miln 67.
-dantaka the tooth of a sword fish, used as a pin Vin II.113, cp. p. 315. — as a design in painting or carving Vin II.117, 121, 152; IV.47. In these latter passages it occurs comb[d] with latākamma & pañcapaṭṭhika (q. v.). The meaning is not quite clear.

Makaranda [cp. Class. Sk. makaranda] the nectar of a flower J VI.530.

Makasa [fr. Vedic maśaka viâ *masaka > makasa: see Geiger, *P.Gr.* § 47[2]] mosquito Vin II.119; S I.52 (a° free from m.); A II.117; Sn 20; J I.246; Sdhp 50. See also cpd. ḍaŋsa°.
-kuṭikā mosquito net or curtain Vin II.119, 130. -vījanī mosquito fan Vin II.130.

Makuṭa (f.) [cp. BSk. makuṭa Divy 411] a crest Abhp 283 (kirīṭa +, i. e. adornment).

Makula [cp. Sk. makula] 1. a bud (Hardy in Index to VvA gives "Mimusops elengi" after BR) Th 2, 260; Vv 45[26]; J I.273; II.33; IV.333; V.207 (makuḷa), 416; Vism 230 (!); 256 (paduma°); VvA 177 (kaṇavīra°), 194 (makuḷa), 197 (id.); VbhA 228, 239 (where Vism 256 has makulita, & KhA 53 mukulita). — 2. a knob J I.31; II.90; Vism 253 (kandala°). — 3. v. l. at Nd[2] 485 B for pakulla (= pakuṭa).

Makkaṭa [cp. Epic Sk. markaṭa] 1. a monkey J I.385; II.267; DhA II.22; VbhA 408 (°niddā, a m.'s sleep, said to be quickly changing); KhA 73 (in simile); SnA 522 (cp. Sn 791). Names of monkeys famous in Jātaka tales: Sālaka J II.268; Kālabāhu J III.98 sq.; on the monkey as a figure in similes see *J.P.T.S.* 1907, 119, to which add VbhA 228 & 259 (tālavana°), cp. Vism 245. — 2. a spider: see °sutta.
-chāpaka the young of a monkey M I.385; J I.218. -sutta spider's thread J V.47; Vism 136 (in simile); DhA I.304.

Makkaṭaka [cp. Sk. markaṭaka; der. fr. markaṭa = makkaṭa] a spider (see on similes *J.P.T.S* 1907, 119) Dh 347 (cp. DhA IV.58); J II.147 (= uṇṇanābhi); IV.484 (aptly called Uṇṇanābhi); V.47, 469, Miln 364, 407 (pantha° road spider, at both passages). -°sutta spider's thread Vism 285.

Makkaṭiya (nt.) [fr. makkhaṭa + ya] monkey grimace J II.448 (mukha°). The same as mukha-makkaṭika at J II.70.

Makkaṭī (f.) [of makkaṭa] a female monkey Vin III.33, 34; J I.385; DhA I.119.

Makkha[1] [fr. mṛkṣ, lit. smearing over. Cp. BSk. mrakṣa Śikṣ 198, 8, in cpd. māna-mada-mrakṣa-paridāha etc.] hypocrisy; usually comb[d] with paḷāsa (see also palāsa) M I.15; A I.95, 100, 299; IV.148, 456; V.39, 156, 209, 310, 361; It 3; Sn 56, 437, 631, 1132 (cp. Nd[2] 484 = makkhāyanā makkhāyitattaŋ niṭṭhuriya-kammaŋ, i. e. hardness, mercilessness); Dh 150, 407; J V.141; Vbh 357, 380, 389; Pug 18, 22; Miln 289, 380; DhA III.118; VI.181.
-vinaya restraining fr. hypocrisy S II.282; A V.165 sq.

Makkha^2 [probably = makkha^1, but BSk. differentiates with *mrakṣya* Divy 622, trsl. Index "ill-feeling"? Böhtlingk-Roth have: mrakṣya "wohlgefühl"] anger, rage Vin I.25.

Makkhaṇa (nt.) [fr. mṛkṣ, cp. *Sk. mrakṣana] smearing, oil J III.120; Miln 11 (tela°); Dhtp 538.

Makkhāyanā (f.) & **Makkhāyitatta** (nt.) [abstr. fr. makkha] the fact of concealment, hypocrisy: in exegesis of makkha at Nd^2 484; Pug 18, 22.

Makkhikā (f.) [cp. Vedic makṣika & makṣikā] a fly M III.148; Nd^1 484; J II.275 (nīla°); III.263 (pingala° gadfly), 402; SnA 33 (pingala°), 572 (id.); DhA IV.58; Sdhp 396, 529.

Makkhita [pp. of makkheti] smeared with (-°), soiled; anointed M I.364 (lohita°); J I.158 (madhu°); III.226 (piṭṭhi-maddena); V.71 (ruhira°); VI.391.

Makkhin (adj.) [fr. makkha] concealing, hypocritical; harsh, merciless; often comb^d with **palāsin** (e. g. at Vin II.89; J III.259) D III.45, 246. a° (+ apalāsin) D III.47; A III.111; Sn 116; Pug 22.

Makkhi-vāla [cp. makaci-pilotikā] a cloth of hair for straining J II.97.

Makkheti [Caus. of **mṛkṣ**; Dhtp 538: makkhaṇa] to smear, paste, soil, anoint J III.225, 314; Pug 36; Miln 268; Vism 344; DhA II.65. — Pass makkhīyati Miln 74. — Caus. II. **makkhāpeti** to cause to be anointed J I.486; DhA I.400. — pp. makkhita.

Maga [another form of miga = Sk. mṛga, cp. Geiger, *P.Gr.* 12^4] 1. animal for hunting, deer, antelope M I.173 (in simile); S I.199 (id.); A I.70; II.23; Th 1, 958, 989; Sn 275, 763, 880; J V.267. — 2. a stupid person J VI.206, 371.

Magga [cp. Epic Sk. mārga, fr. **mṛg** to track, trace] 1. a road (usually high road), way, foot-path Vism 708 (maggaŋ agata-pubba-purisa, simile of); VbhA 256 (tiyojana°, simile of a man travelling); DhA I.229. — **addhāna°** high road Vin IV.62; M III.158; see under addhāna; **antāra-magge** on the road Miln 16; **ujuka°** a straight way S I.33; DhA I.18; **ummagga** (a) a conduit; (b) a devious way: see ummagga, to which add refs. J V.260; Th 2, 94; **kummagga** a wrong path: see kum°, to which add S IV.195; Th 1, 1174. **passāva°** & **vacca°** place for defecation & urination Vin III.127. **visama°** a bad road S I.48. — 2. the road of moral & good living, the path of righteousness, with ref. to the moral standard (cp. the 10 commandments) & the way to salvation. The exegetic (edifying) etym. of magga in this meaning is "nibbān' atthikehi maggīyati (traced by those who are looking for N.), nibbānaŋ vā maggeti, kilese vā mārento gacchatī ti maggo" (VbhA 114). — Usually designated (a) the "**ariya aṭṭhangika magga**" or the "Noble Eightfold Path" (see **aṭṭhangika**). It is mentioned at many places, & forms the corner-stone of the Buddha's teaching as to the means of escaping "dukkha" or the ills of life. It consists of 8 *constituents*, viz. sammā-diṭṭhi, sammā-sankappa, °vācā, °kammanta, °ājīva, °vāyāma, °sati, °samādhi, or right views, right aspirations, right speech, right conduct, right livelihood, right effort, right mindfulness, right rapture. The 7 first constituents are at D II.216 & M III.71 enum^d as requisites for sammā-samādhi. The name of this table of ethical injunctions is given as "maggam uttamaŋ" at Sn 1130, i. e. the Highest Path. See for ref. e. g. Vin III.93; IV.26; D II.353; III.102, 128, 284, 286; It 18; Nd^1 292; Nd^2 485; Vbh 104 sq. 235 sq., VbhA 114 sq. (its constituents in detail). 121, 216; Vism 509 sq. (where the 8 constituents are discussed). — (b) as **ariya magga**: M III.72; Pug 17; DA I.176 sq., 225 sq., 233; VbhA 373 sq.; ThA 205. — (c) as **pañcangika** or the Path of 5 constituents (the above first 2 and last 3): Dhs 89; Vbh 110 sq., 237 sq. — (d) other expressions of same import: **dhamma°** Miln 21; **magga** alone; S I.191 (Bhagavā maggassa uppādetā etc.) = M III.9 = S III.66; Sn 429, 441, 724 sq., 1130; Dh 57, 273 sq., It 106; VbhA 53, 73. As the first condition & initial stage to the attainment of Arahantship (Nibbāna) it is often found in sequence of either **magga-phala-nirodha** (e. g. Vism 217, cp. Nd^2 under dukkha II. p. 168), or **magga, phala, nibbāna** (e. g. Tikp. 155 sq., 158; VbhA 43, 316, 488). — magga as entrance to Arahantship is the final stage in the recognition (ñāṇa, pariññā, paññā) of the truth of the causal chain, which realises the origin of "ill," the possibility of its removal & the "way" to the removal. These stages are described as **dukkhe ñāṇaŋ, samudaye ñāṇaŋ nirodhe ñāṇaŋ** and **magge ñāṇaŋ** at D III.227, Ps I.118. At the latter passage the foll. chapter (I.49) gives **dukkha-nirodha gāminī paṭipadā** as identical with **magga**. — *Note*. On the term see *Cpd.* 41 sq., 66 sq., 175, 186; *Dhs trsl.*^{2} 58, 299 sq., 362 sq.; *Expos.* 216, 354^n. On passages with **aṭṭhangika magga** & others where magga is used in similes see Mrs. Rh. D. in *J.P.T.S.* 1907, pp. 119, 120. — 3. Stage of righteousness, with ref. to the var. conditions of Arahantship divided into 4 stages, viz. **sotāpatti-magga, sakadāgāmi°, anāgāmi°, arahatta°**, or the stage of entering the stream (of salvation), that of returning once, that of the never-returner, that of Arahantship. — At DhA I.110 **magga-phala** "the fruit of the Path" (i. e. the attainment of the foundation or first step of Arahantship) is identical with **sotāpatti-phala** on p. 113 (a) in general: **arahatta°** S I.78; A III.391; DA I.224. — (b) in particular as the 4 paths: Nd^2 612 A; Vbh 322 sq., 328, 335; Vism 453, 672-678; DhA IV.30; VbhA 301. — 4. In the Tikapaṭṭhāna (under magga-paccaya-niddesa p. 52) 12 constituents of magga are enum^d; viz. paññā, vitakka, sammā-vācā, s-kammanta, s-ājīva, viriya, sati, samādhi, micchā-diṭṭhi, micchā-vācā, m-kammanta, m-ājīva.

-angāni the constituents of the Ariyan Path VbhA 120. **-âmagga** which is the (right) road and which is not M I.147; Vism ch. XX (°ssa kovida) = Sn 627; S III.108 (id.); DhA IV.169 (id.); A V.47 (°ssa ñāṇa-dassana); Dh 403. **-udaka** water found on the road Vism 338 (simile). **-kilanta** wearied by the road J I.129. **-kusala** one who is clever as regards the road, one who knows the road well S III.108; Nd^1 171; VbhA 332 (in simile); KhA 70, 126. **-kovida** = °kusala Nd^1 446. **-kkhāyin** (should be °akkhāyin) one who tells the (right) way M III.5; Nd^1 33. **-jina** Conqueror of the paths Sn 84 sq. **-jivin** who lives in the right path Sn 88. **-jjhāyin** reflecting over the Path Sn 85. **-ñāṇa** knowledge of the Path VbhA 416. **-ññū** knows the Path Nd^1 446. **-ṭṭhāna** one who stands in the Path, attains the P. see *Cpd.* 23, 50. **-ttaya** the triad of the paths (i. e. the first 3 of the 4 Paths as given above under 3) DhA IV.109. **-dūsin** highway robber Sn 84. **-desaka** one who points out the way, a guide Sn 84; J IV.257; as °desika at DhA II.246. **-desin** = °desaka Sn 87. **-dhamma** the rule of the Path, i. e. righteous living Sn 763. **-dhīra** wise as regards the Path Nd^1 45. **-paṭipanna**—1. one on the road, i. e. wandering, tramping DhA I.233. — 2. one who has entered the Path Pv IV.3^{49}. **-parissaya** danger of the road VvA 200. **-bhāvanā** cultivation of the Path (i. e. righteousness) Nd^1 323. **-mūḷha** one who has lost the way VvA 332. **-vaṇṇa** praise of the Path DhA I.115. **-vidū** one who knows the Path Nd^1 446. **-sacca** the truth concerning the Path VbhA 114, 124. **-sira** N. of a month DA I.241.

Maggana (nt.) & **magganā** (f.) [fr. **magg**] tracking, search for, covetousness Vism 29 (syn. for **nijigiŋsanatā** & **gaveṭṭhi**); Dhtp 298 (& gavesana).

Maggika [fr. magga] wayfarer, tramp DhA I.233.

Maggati & (spurious) **mageti** [Denom. fr. magga, cp. Sk. mārgayati. The Dhtp. gives both **mag** & **magg** in meaning "anvesana," i. e. tracking, following up; see Dhtp Nos. 21, 540, 541] to track, hunt for, trace out, follow, seek M I.334 (ppr. magayamāna); S II.270 (pp. maggayamāna); Th 2, 384 (cp. ThA 255=pattheti); J V.102 (where T. reads **maggheyya**, which is expl^d by C. as vijjheyya to pierce, hurt, & which is doubtful in meaning, although Kern, *Toev.* s. v. defends it. The v. l. reads magg°. Same on p. 265 where one ought to read phasseyya in C. instead of passeyya. The form pp. **magga** (?) on p. 102 must belong to the same root); DhsA 162 (=gavesati). — Caus. II. maggāpeti PvA 112. — Pass. maggīyati VbhA 114.

Magghati see maggeti.

Maghavant [cp. Epic Sk. maghavā, on etym. see Walde, *Lat. Wtb.* s. v. Maia] N. of Indra, or another angel (devaputta) S I.221 (voc. maghavā; so read for mathavā), 229; Dh 30. Cp. māgha.

Maghā (f.) [cp. *Sk. maghā] N. of a nakkhatta, in cpd. °deva SnA 352 (cp. M II.74, n. 6, where spelling Makkādeva; we also find Makhadeva at Śatapatha-brāhmaṇa XIV. I. I).

Mankati is given as root **mank** (aor. maki) at Dhtm 13, in meaning maṇḍana, i. e. adornment. It is meant to be an expl^n of mankato ?

Mankato (adv.) [for Sk. mat-kṛte, Cp. E. Müller, *P.Gr.* 12] on my account, for me Miln 384.

Manku (adj.) [cp. Vedic manku; see on meaning Hardy in preface to Anguttara V. p. vi] staggering, confused, troubled, discontented Vin II.118; S V.74; Dh 249; Nd¹ 150; DhA III.41, 359 (with loc.). — f. pl. mankū Vin I.93. —**dummanku** "staggering in a disagreeable manner," evil-minded A I.98; IV.97 (read line as "dummanku' yaŋ padusseti dhūm' aggamhi va pāvako" he, staggering badly, is spoilt like the fire on the crest of smoke); V.70; Vin II.196; III.21; IV.213; S II.218; Nett 50.

-**bhāva** discontent, moral weakness J IV.49; Miln 227; DhA III.359. -**bhūta** discontented, troubled, confused Vin II.19; D II.85; A I.186; Dh 263; J V.211; VI.362; DhA II.76; a° self-possessed A III.40; Miln 21, 339.

Mankuna (& °ṇa) [cp. late Sk. matkuṇa, see Geiger, *P.Gr.* § 6³] an insect, bug or flea J I.10; III.423; Vism 109 (where *kila-mankula* ought to be read as kiṭa-mankuna); DhA II.12.

Mangala (adj.) [cp. Vedic mangala. Expl^d by Dhtp 24 with root **mang**, i. e. lucky; see also mañju] auspicious, prosperous, lucky, festive Nd¹ 87, 88; KhA 118 sq.; SnA 273, 595; Sdhp 551. — nt. **mangalaŋ** good omen, auspices, festivity Sn 258; Vin II.129; PvA 17. A curious popular etymology is put forth by Bdhgh at KhA 123, viz. "maŋ galanti imehi sattā ti" mangalāni. — **mangalaŋ karoti** lit. to make an auspicious ceremony, i. e. to besprinkle with grains etc. for luck (see on this PvA 198), to get married DhA I.182; **mangalaŋ vadati** to bless one J IV.299; DhA I.115. Three (auspicious) wedding-ceremonies at DhA I.115 viz. abhiseka° consecration, geha-ppavesana° entering the house, vivāha° wedding. — Certain other general signs of good luck or omina κατ' ἐξοχήν are given at J IV.72, 73 and KhA 118 sq. (see also mangalika). — Several ceremonious festivities are mentioned at DhA II.87 with regard to the bringing up of a child, viz. nāma-karaṇa-mangala the ceremony of giving a name; āhāra-paribhoga° of taking solid food; kaṇṇa-vijjhana° of piercing the ears; dussa-gahaṇa° of taking up the robe; cūḷā-karaṇa° of making the top-knot. — Cp. abhi°.

-**usabha** an auspicious bull SnA 323. -**chaṇa** a merry time, fair J II.48; DhA I.392. -**kicca** auspicious function, festivity SnA 175, 323. -**kiriyā** festivity, wedding SnA 69; finding good omens J IV.72. -**kolāhala** the lucky, or most auspicious, foreboding, one of the 5 kolāhalas (q. v.) KhA 121. -**pañha** see mangalika. -**divasa** a lucky day J IV.210; DhA III.467. -**vappa** ploughing festival SnA 137. Cp. vappa-mangala. -**sindhava** state horse J I.59. -**silāpaṭṭa** auspicious slab (of stone) J I.59; VI.37; PvA 74. -**supina** lucky dream J VI.330. -**hatthi** state elephant Mhvs 35, 21; DhA I.389.

Mangalika (adj.) (-°) [fr. mangala] 1. one who is feasting in, one whose auspices are such & such; fond of; only in **kotūhala°** fond of excitement J I.372; Miln 94 (apagata°, without passion for excitement). — 2. superstitious, looking out for lucky signs Vin II.129 (gihī), 140 (id.). At J IV.72, 73; three sets of people are exemplified, who believe in omina as either **diṭṭhaŋ** (seen) or **sutaŋ** (heard) or **mutaŋ** (sensed); they are called **diṭṭha-mangalikā, suta°** & **muta°** respectively. The same group is more explicitly dealt with in the Mangala-sutta KhA 118 sq. (cp. Nd¹ 89); **diṭṭha-mangalika pañha** "a question concerning visible omina" J IV.73 (correct meaning given under diṭṭha¹, vol. II.156¹ !), 390 (?). The Np. diṭṭha-mangalikā at J IV.376 sq.

Mangalya (nt.) [fr. mangala] auspiciousness, good luck, fortune Dhtp 24.

Mangura (adj.) [etym. ? or=mangula? See *J.R.A.S.* 1903, 186] golden; in cpd. °cchavi of golden colour, f. cchavi D I.193, 242; M I.246, 429; II.33; Vism 184.

Mangula (adj.) [cp. mangura] sallow; **f. mangulī** woman of sallow complexion S II.260=Vin III.107; Vin III.100.

Macca (adj.-n.) [orig. grd. of marati, **mṛ** corresponding to Sk. martya. A diaeretic form exists in P. mātiya (q. v.)] mortal; (m.) man, a mortal S I.55; Sn 249, 577, 580, 766; J III.154; IV.248; V.393; Dh 53, 141, 182; Vv 63¹²; Kvu 351. — See also refs. under jāta.

Maccu [in form=Vedic mṛtyu, fr. **mṛ**; in meaning differentiated, the Ved.-Sk. meaning "death" only] the God of Death, the Buddhist Māra, or sometimes equivalent to Yama S I.156; Sn 357 (gen. maccuno), 581 (instr. maccunā), 587; Th 1, 411; Dh 21, 47, 128, 135, 150, 287; VbhA 100, SnA 397; DhA III.49; Sdhp 295, 304.

-**tara** one who crosses or overcomes death Sn 119 (=maraṇaŋ tareyya Nd² 486). -**dheyya** the realm of Māra, the sphere of Death S I.4; adj. belonging to death or subject to death (=Māradheyya, maraṇadheyya Nd² 487^b). — Sn 358, 1104 (with expl^n "m. vuccanti kilesā ca khandhā ca abhisankhārā ca" Nd² 487^a), 1146 (°pāra-maccudheyyassa pāraŋ vuccati amataŋ nibbānaŋ Nd² 487); Th 2, 10 (=maccu ettha dhīyati ThA 13); Dh 86; DhA II.161. -**parāyaṇa** surmounting death Sn 578; pareta id. Sn 579. -**pāsa** the sling or snare of Māra Sn 166; J V.367. -**bhaya** the fear of death Mhvs 32, 68. -**maraṇa** dying in death M I.49 (cp. C. on p. 532: maccu-maraṇan ti maccu-sankhātaŋ maraṇaŋ tena samuccheda-maraṇ' ādīni nisedheti. — See also def. of maraṇa s.v.). -**mukha** the mouth of death Sn 776; Nd¹ 48. -**rājā** the king of death Sn 332, 1118 (=Maro pi Maccurājā maraṇaŋ pi Nd² 488); Dh 46, 170; KhA 83. -**vasa** the power of death 3 I.52; Sn 587, 1100 (where *maccu* is expl^d by *maraṇa & Māra*). -**hāyin** leaving death behind, victorious over death It 46=Sn 755; Th 1, 129.

Maccha [cp. Vedic matsya] fish A III.301; Sn 605, 777, 936; J I.210, 211; V.266 (in simile); VI.113 (phandanti macchā, on dry land); Pug 55; Sdhp 610. —maccha is given at Nd² 91 as syn. of ambucārin. —**pūti°** rotten fish M III.168; & in simile at It 68 = J IV.435 = VI.236 = KhA 127. Cp. *J.P.T.S.* 1906, 201. bahu° rich in fish J III.430. loṇa° salt fish Vism 28. rohita° the species Cyprinus rohita J II.433; III.333; DhA II.132. On maccha in simile see *J.P.T.S.* 1907, 121. Of names of fishes several are given in the Jātaka tales; viz. Ānanda (as the king of the fishes or a Leviathan) J I.207; II.352; V.462; Timanda & Timirapingala J V.462; Mitacintin J I.427; Bahucintin J I.427.

-maŋsa the flesh of fishes Sn 249. -bandha one who sets net to catch fish, a fisherman A III.301; Vism 379. -bhatta food for fishes, devoured by fishes J V.75. -vālaka a garment made in a particular fashion (forbidden to bhikkhus) Vin II.137. -sakalika "a bit of fish" (fish-bone?) in description of constitution of the finger nails at Vism 250 = KhA 43 = VbhA 233.

Macchara (adj.) [Vedic matsara & matsarin enjoyable; later period also "envious," cp. maccharin] niggardly, envious, selfish Pgdp II.49. —maccharaŋ (nt.) avarice, envy A IV.285; Sn 811, 862, 954 (vīta-macchara, adj.).

Maccharāyati [Demon. fr. macchariya] to be selfish, greedy or envious J VI.334; DhA II.45, 89.

Maccharāyanā (f.) & **Maccharāyitatta** (nt.) the condition of selfishness, both expressions in defⁿ of macchariya at Dhs 1122; Pug 19, 23; DhsA 375.

Maccharin (adj.) [cp. Vedic matsarin, fr. mat + sṛ, i. e. "reflecting to me"] selfish, envious, greedy (cp. *Dhs trsl.*² p. 320); A II.82; III.139, 258, 265; D III.45, 246; Dh 263; Sn 136, 663; Nd¹ 36; J I.345; V.391; Vv 5₂²⁸; Pug 20; DhsA 394; DhA II.89; Sdhp 89, 97. — a° unselfish D III.47; A IV.2; Sn 852, 860; It 102.

Macchariya & **Macchera** (nt.) [cp. Epic Sk. mātsarya] avarice, stinginess, selfishness, envy; one of the principal evil passions & the main cause of rebirth in the Petaloka. — 1. *macchariya*: A I.95, 299; III.272; Dh III.44 (issā°), 289; Sn 863 (°yutta), 928; Pug 19, 23; Vbh 357, 389, 391. — Five sorts of selfishness are mentioned: āvāsa°, kula°, lābha°, vaṇṇa°, dhamma° D III.234; Nd¹ 118, 227; A IV.456; Dhs 1122 (cp. *Dhs trsl.*² p. 276); Vism 683; DhsA 373, 374. Selfishness is one of the evil conditions which have to be renounced as habits of mind by force of intelligence A V.40, 209; Miln 289; PvA 87, 124. — 2. *macchera* A I.105 (°mala), 281; Dh 242; It 18; Nd¹ 260; Sdhp 313, 510. At A II.58 and elsewhere the state called **vigata-mala-macchera** "with the stain of avarice vanished," is freq. mentioned as a feature of the blameless life and a preparation for Arahantship. — *Note*. The (etym.) explⁿ of macchariya at VbhA 513 is rather interesting: "idaŋ acchariyaŋ mayhaŋ eva hotu, mā aññassa acchariyaŋ hotū ti pavattattā macchariyan ti vuccati" (from the Purāṇas?).

Macchika [fr. maccha] a fish-catcher, fisherman A III.301; J V.270; VI.111; Miln 331.

Macchī (f.) [of maccha] a female fish J II.178.

Macchera see macchariya.

Majja (nt.) [fr. **mad**, cp. Vedic mada & madya] 1. intoxicant, intoxicating drink, wine, spirits Vin I.205; D III.62, 63; Sn 398 (+ pāna = majjapāna); VvA 73 (= surā ca merayañ ca); Sdhp 267. — 2. drinking place J IV.223 (= pān' āgāra).

-pa one who drinks strong drink, a drunkard A IV.261; Sn 400; Pv IV.1⁷⁶ (a°); ThA 38. -pāna drinking of intoxicating liquors Vv 15⁸; VvA 73; Sdhp 87. -pāyaka = majjapa J II.192 (a°). -pāyin = °pāyaka Sdhp 88. -vikkaya sale of spirits J IV.115.

Majjati¹ [**majj** to immerse, submerge, cp. Lat. mergo] is represented in Pali by **mujjati**, as found esp. in cpds. ummujjati & nimujjati.

Majjati² [**mṛj** to clean, polish; connected with either Lat. mergo (cp. Gr. ἀμέργω) or Lat. mulgeo to wipe, stroke, milk (cp. Gr. ἀμέλγω, Mir. mlich = milk etc.) — Dhtp 71 gives root **majj** with meaning "saŋsuddhiyaŋ"] to wipe, polish, clean VvA 165. Cp. sam°. — pp. majjita & maṭṭha.

Majjati³ [**mad** Sk. mādyati; Vedic madati; see mada for etym.] to be intoxicated; to be exultant, to be immensely enjoyed or elated S I.73, 203; A IV.294; Sn 366 (Pot. majje = majjeyya SnA 364), 676 (id., T. reads na ca majje, SnA 482 reads na pamajje); J II.97; III.87 (majjeyya). aor. majji in cpd. pamajji Mhvs 17, 15. — pp. matta.

Majjāra [cp. Epic Sk. mārjāra; dialectical] a cat Miln 23. — f. majjārī (majjāri°) Vin I.186 (°camma cat's skin); DhA I.48; Pgdp 49.

Majjika [fr. majja] a dealer in strong drink, a tavern-keeper Miln 331.

Majjita [pp. of majjati²] cleaned, polished VvA 340 (suṭṭhu m. for sumaṭṭha Vv 84¹⁷). See also maṭṭha.

Majjha (adj.) [Vedic madhya, cp. Lat. medius, Gr. μέσσος, Goth. midjis = Ohg. mitti, E. middle] middle, viz. 1. of *space*: of moderate height D I.243 (contrasted with ucca & nīca). — 2. of *time*: of middle age Sn 216 (contrasted with dahara young & thera old). — 3. often used adv. in loc. majjhe in the middle; i. e. (a) as prep. in between, among (-° or with gen.) Pv I.11¹, 11⁴; J I.207 (sakuṇānaŋ); DhA I.182 (vasana-gāmassa); PvA 11 (parisā°). majjhe chetvā cutting in half J V.387. — (b) in special dogmatic sense "in the present state of existence," contrasted with past & future existences (the latter combᵈ as "ubho antā" at Sn 1040). The explⁿ of majjhe in this sense is at Nd¹ 434: "majjhaŋ vuccati paccuppannā rūpā" etc. (similarly at Nd² 490). — Sn 949 (in sequence pubbe majjhe pacchā), 1099 (id.); Dh 348 (pure majjhe pacchato; i. e. paccuppannesu khandhesu DhA IV.63). — 4. (nt.) majjhaŋ the middle DhA I.184 (tassa ura-majjhaŋ ghaŋsenti).

Majjhaka (adj.) (-°) [fr. majjha] lying or being in the midst of . . ., in pācīna-yava° (dakkhiṇa°, pacchima°, uttara°) nigama, a market-place lying in the midst of the eastern corn-fields (the southern etc.): designation of 4 nigamas situated near Mithilā J VI.330.

Majjhatta (adj.-n.) [for majjha-ṭṭha, which we find in Prk. as majjhattha: Pischel, *Prk. Gr.* § 214; majjha + **sthā**] 1. (adj.) "standing in the middle," umpire, neutral, impartial, indifferent J I.300; II.359 (parama°. + upekkhā-pāramī); VI.8; Miln 403; Vism 230; Mhvs 21, 14. — 2. indifference, balance of mind, equanimity; almost synonymous with **upekkhā**: Vism 134, 296; VbhA 283 (°payogatā); DhA II.214 (°upekkhā); PvA 38 (so read for majjhattha). See also following. — *Note*. A similar term is found in BSk. as **mṛdu-madhyā kṣānti** "state of spiritual calm" Divy 271; see Yoga Sūtra II.34.

Majjhattatā (f.) [abstr. from prec.] impartiality, indifference, balance of mind Nd² 166 (in explⁿ of upekkhā, with syn. passaddhatā); Vbh 230; Vism 134; VbhA 285 (satta° & sankhāra°), 317 (def.); DhsA 133.

Majjhantika [majjha + anta + ika] midday, noon; used either absolutely Vin IV.273; S IV.240; J V.213 (yāva upakaṭṭha-majjhantikā); V.291 (read majjhantik' âtikamm' āgami); Vism 236; Miln 3; or as apposition with *kāla* & *samaya* S I.7 (kāla); Pv IV.3² (id.); Nd² 97⁷ (samaya); DA I.251 (id.).

Majjhāru [etym. doubtful] a certain kind of plant Vin I.196 (v. l. majjaru); doubtful whether designation (like Sk. mārjāra) of Plumbago rosea.

Majjhima (adj.) [Vedic madhyama, with sound change °ama>°ima after Geiger, *P.Gr.* 19¹, or after analogy with pacchima, with which often contrasted] 1. middle, medium, mediocre, secondary, moderate. — Applied almost exclusively in contrast pairs with terms of more or less, in triplets like "small-medium-big," or "first-middle-last" (cp. majjha 3b); viz. (a) of *degree*: hīna-m-paṇīta D III.215 (tisso dhātuyo); Dhs 1025-1027 (dhammā); Vism 11 (sīlaŋ); h. m. ukkaṭṭha Vism 308; omaka m. ukkaṭṭha Vin IV.243; khuddaka m. mahā Vism 100; lāmaka m. paṇīta (i. e. lokuttara) DhsA 45 (dhammā); paritta-m-uḷāra Sdhp 260. — (b) of *time*: paṭhame vāme majjhima° pacchima° J I.75; id. with vaye PvA 5. — 2. (nt.) majjhimaŋ the waist, in cpd. su-majjhimā (f.) a woman with beautiful waist J V.4.

Mañca [cp. Epic Sk. mañca stand, scaffolding, platform] a couch, bed Vin IV.39, 40 (where 4 kinds are mentioned, which also apply to the def° of pīṭha, viz. masāraka, bundikābaddha, kuḷīra-pādaka, āhacca-pādaka; same def° at VbhA 365); Sn 401; J III.423; DhA I.89 (°ŋ bandhati to tie a bed or two together), 130; IV.16; VbhA 20; VvA 291; PvA 93. — heṭṭhā mañce underneath the bed J I.197 (as place where the domestic lies); II.419 (id.); II.275 (where a love-sick youth lies down in the park).

-atimañca bed upon bed, i. e. beds placed on top of each other serving as grand stands at a fair or festival J III.456; VI.277; DhA IV.59. -parāyaṇa ending in bed, kept in bed Pv II.2⁵ (nīla°, fig. for being buried); DhA I.183 (with v. l. maccu°, just as likely, but see maccuparāyaṇa). -pīṭha couch and chair Vin II.270 sq.; A III.51; VvA 9, 220, 295. -vāna stuffing of a couch DhA I.234.

Mañcaka [fr. mañca] bed, couch, bedstead Vin I.271; S I.121=III.123; J I.91; III.423; Th 2, 115; Miln 10; DhA II.53.

Mañjari (f.) [cp. Epic & Class. Sk. mañjarī] a branching flower-stalk, a sprout J V.400, 416.

Mañjarikā (f.)=mañjari, Vin III.180.

Mañjarita (adj.) [fr. mañjari] with (full-grown) pedicles, i. e. in open flower Miln 308 (°patta in full bloom).

Mañjīra [cp. late Sk. mañjīra nt.] an anklet, foot-bangle Abhp 228.

Mañju (adj.) [cp. Class Sk. mañju, also mangala, cp. Gr. μάγγανον means of deceiving, Lat. mango a dealer making up his wares for sale. See further cognates at Walde, *Lat. Wtb.* s. v. mango] pleasant, charming, sweet, lovely (only with ref. to the voice) D II.211, 227 (one of the 8 characteristics of Brahmā's & the Buddha's voice: see bindu & aṭṭhanga); J II.150. — (nt.) a sweet note J VI.591 (of the deer in the forest); VvA 219 (karavīka ruta°).

-bhāṇaka sweet-voiced, speaking sweetly J II.150=DhA I.144; f. bhāṇikā J VI.418, 420. -bhāṇin id. J II.150.

Mañjuka (adj.) [mañju+ka] sweet voiced Vin I.249; J II.350; III.266; VI.412, 496.

Mañjūsaka (-rukkha) [fr. mañjūsa] N. of a celestial tree, famed for its fragrancy Vv 38⁶; SnA 52, 66, 95, 98; VvA 175.

Mañjūsā (f.) [cp. Epic Sk. mañjūṣā] a casket; used for keeping important documents in J II.36 (suvaṇṇapaṭṭaŋ mañjūsāya nikkhipāpesi); IV.335 (suvaṇṇapaṭṭaŋ sāra-mañjūsāyaŋ ṭhapetvā kālam akāsi).

Mañjeṭṭha (adj.) [cp. *Sk. mañjiṣṭhā Indian madder] light (bright) red, crimson, usually enum^d in set of 5 principal colours with nīla, pīta, lohitaka, odāta; e. g. at Vin I.25; S II.101 (f. mañjeṭṭhā); Vv 22¹ (Hardy in T. reads mañjaṭṭha, as twice at VvA 111, with vv. ll. °jiṭṭha & °jeṭṭha, cp. Corrections & Add^ns on p. 372); Miln 61.

Mañjeṭṭhaka (adj.) [fr. mañjeṭṭha, after lohita+ka] crimson, bright red, fig. shining Vv 39¹ (cp. def^n at VvA 177: like the tree Vitex negundo, sindhavāra, or the colour of the Kaṇavīra-bud; same def^n at DhsA 317, with Sinduvāra for Sindha°); usually in sequence nīla, pīta, mañjeṭṭhaka, lohitaka, odāta as the 5 fundamental colours: M I.509 (has °eṭṭhika in T. but v. l. °eṭṭhaka); J VI.185; Dhs 617. — f. mañjeṭṭhikā a disease of sugar cane Vin II.256.

Mañjeṭṭhī (f.) [=Sk. mañjiṣṭhā] Bengal madder DA I.85.

Maññati [man, Vedic manyate & manute, Av. mainyeite; Idg. *men, cp. Gr. μένος mood, anger=Sk. manah mind; μέμονα to think of, wish to, Lat. memini to think of, mens>mind, meneo; Goth. munan to think, muns opinion; Oisl. man, Ags. mon; Ohg. minna love, Ags. myne intention. Dhtp 427: man=ñāṇe, 524=bodhane] 1. to think, to be of opinion, to imagine, to deem Sn 199 (sīsaŋ . . . subhato naŋ maññati bālo), 588 (yena yena hi maññanti, tato taŋ hoti aññathā); J II.258 (maññāmi ciraŋ carissati: I imagine he will have to wander a long time). — With (double) acc.: to take for, to consider as; na taŋ maññāmi mānusiŋ I deem you are not human Pv II.4¹; yassa dāni *kālaŋ maññati* for this now may he think it time (in a phrase of departure), let him do what he thinks fit, we wait the Buddha's pleasure, i. e. let it be time to go [so also BSk. manyate kālaŋ, e. g. Divy 50, 64 etc.] D I.189. — Esp. in phrase taŋ kiŋ maññasi (maññatha 2. pl.) what do you think of this? (the foll.), what is your opinion about this? D I.60; S III.104 & passim. — Pot. 1st sg. maññeyyaŋ I should think PvA 40; 3rd sg. maññeyya S III.103, and maññe Sn 206. The short form 1st sg. maññe is used like an adv. as affirmative particle & is inserted without influencing the grammatical or syntactical construction of the sentence; meaning: methinks, for certain, surely, indeed, I guess, presumably. E. g. D I.137 (patapati m. paccatthike yasasā); S I.181 (m. 'haŋ); IV.289 (paveliyamānena m. kāyena); J II.275; Miln 21; Vism 90, 92 (mato me m. putto); DhA I.107; II.51; PvA 40 (m. goṇo samuṭṭhahe), 65 (tasmā m. sumuttā). —na maññe surely not DhA II.84; PvA 75 (n. m. puññavā rājā). — 2. to know, to be convinced, to be sure Sn 840 (=jānāti Nd¹ 192), 1049, 1142; Nd² 491 (=jānāti); DhA I.29 (maññāmi tuvaŋ marissasi). — 3. to imagine, to be proud (of), to be conceited, to boast Sn 382 (ppr. maññamāna), 806, 813, 855 (maññate); J III.530 (aor. maññi 'haŋ, perhaps maññe 'haŋ? C. expl^d by maññāmi). — pp. mata. — *Note.* Another Present form is munāti (q. v.), of which the pp. is muta.

Maññanā (f.) [fr. man] conceit Nd¹ 124 (taṇhā°, diṭṭhi°, māna°, kilesa° etc.); Dhs 1116 1233; Nett 24; Vism 265 (for mañcanā?).

Maññita (nt.) [pp. of maññati] illusion, imagination M I.486. *Nine* maññitāni (the same list is applied to the phanditāni, the papañcitāni & sankhatāni) at Vbh 390: asmi, ayam aham asmi, bhavissaŋ, na bhavissaŋ, rūpī bhavissaŋ, arūpī bh., saññī bh., asaññī bh., nevasaññī-nāsaññī-bh.

Maññitatta (nt.) [fr. maññita] self-conceit, pride Dhs 1116; DhsA 372.

Maṭaja (nt.) [doubtful] a certain weapon M I.281 (°ŋ nāma āvudhajātaŋ; Neumann trsl^s "Mordwaffe").

Maṭāhaka (adj.) [doubtful spelling & meaning] short (?) Vin II.138 (ati°=atikhuddaka C.).

Maṭṭa & **Maṭṭha** [pp. of **mṛj,** see majjati²] wiped, polished, clean, pure. — (a) maṭṭa: D II.133 (yugaŋ maṭṭaŋ dhāraṇīyaŋ: "pair of robes of burnished cloth of gold and ready for wear" trsl.); Vism 258 (v. l. maṭṭha). Cp. sam.° — (b) maṭṭha: Vv 84¹⁷ (su°); Miln 248; DhA I.25 (°kuṇḍalī having burnished earrings); VvA 6 (°vattha). Cp. vi°.

-sāṭaka a tunic of fine cloth J I.304; II.274; III.498; Vism 284 (ṭṭh).

Maṇi [cp. Vedic maṇi. The connection with Lat. monile (pendant), proposed by Fick & Grassmann, is doubted by Walde, *Lat. Wtb.* s. v. monile, where see other suggestions. For further characterisation of **maṇi** cp. Zimmer, *Altindisches Leben* pp. 53, 263] 1. a gem, jewel. At several places one may interpret as "crystal." — D I.7 (as ornament); Dh 161; J VI.265 (agghiya, precious). In simile at D I.76 (maṇi veḷuriyo). On maṇi in similes see *J.P.T.S.* 1907, 121. —**udaka-pasādaka** maṇi a precious stone (crystal?) having the property of making water clear Miln 35 (cp. below Vism 366 passage); cintā° a "thought-jewel," magic stone (crystal?) J III.504; VvA 32; cūḷā° a jewelled crest or diadem, the crown-jewel J V.441 sq.; jāti° a genuine precious stone J II.417; Vism 216 (in comparison); tārā° (-vitāna) (canopy) of jewelled stars Vism 76; nīla° a dark blue jewel J II.112; IV.140; DhA III.254. The passage "amaṇiŋ udakaŋ maṇiŋ katvā" at Vism 366 (+ asuvaṇṇaŋ leḍḍuŋ suvaṇṇaŋ katvā) refers clearly to meaning "jewel" (that the water is without a jewel or crystal, but is made as clear as crystal; a conjuror's trick, cp. Miln 35). Whether meaning "waterpot" (as given at Abhp 1113 & found in der. maṇika) is referred to here, is not to be decided. — 2. a crystal used as burning-glass Miln 54.

-**kāra** a jeweller Miln 331; DhA II.152. -**kuṇḍala** a jewelled earring, adj. wearing an (ear) ornament of jewels Vin II.156 (āmutta° adorned with ...); Vv 20⁸ (id.); 43⁸ (id.); Pv II.9⁵¹ (id.); Th I.187; Dh 345 (mani-kuṇḍalesu = manīsu ca kuṇḍalesu ca maṇicittesu vā kuṇḍalesu, i. e. with gem-studded earrings DhA IV.56). -**kuṭṭima** at VvA 188 is probably to be read as °kuṇḍala (v. l. °kundima). -**khandha** "jewel-bulk," i. e. a tremendous jewel, large gem, functioning in tales almost like a magic jewel J III.187; V.37 (°vaṇṇaŋ udakaŋ water as clear as a large block of crystal), 183 (°pilandhana). -**guhā** a jewelled cave, cave of crystal J II.417 (where pigs live); SnA 66 (one of three, viz. suvaṇṇa-guhā, m.°, rajata°. At the entrance of it there grows the Mañjūsaka tree). -**canda** "the jewelled moon," i. e. with a crest like the (glittering) moon Vv 64⁶ (= maṇi-maya-maṇḍalânuviddha-canda-maṇḍala-sadisa maṇi VbA 277). -**cchāyā** reflection of a jewel J VI.345. -**thūṇā**, a jewelled pillar, adj. with jewelled pillars Vv 54¹, 67¹. -**pabbata** mountain of gems SnA 358. -**pallanka** a jewelled pallanquin DhA I.274. -**bandha** (place for) binding the jewel(led) bracelet, the wrist Vism 255 = VbhA 238 = KhA 50 (°aṭṭhi). -**bhadda** N. of one of 20 classes of people mentioned Miln 191: trsl^d by Rh. D. *Miln trsl.* I.266 by "tumblers." The term occurs also at Nd¹ 89 & 92. Cp. Sk. Maṇibhadra, N. of a brother of Kuvera & prince of the Yakṣas. -**maya** made of, consisting of, or caused by jewels Pv II.6⁴; VvA 280; DhA I.29. -**ratana** a precious stone or mineral, which is a gem (jewel); i. e. maṇi as a kind of ratana, of which there are seven Vism 189 (in sim.); Miln 218. -**rūpaka** a jewelled image DhA I.370; -**lakkhaṇa** fortune-telling from jewels D I.9; SnA 564.

-**vaṇṇa** the colour or appearance of crystal; i. e. as clear as crystal (of water) J II.304 (pasanna +). -**sappa** a kind of poisonous snake (i. e. a mysterious, magic snake) DA I.197.

Maṇika [cp. Class. Sk. maṇika] a waterpot M II.39. Usually in cpd. udaka° Vin I.277; M I.354; S IV.316; A III.27; Miln 28; DhA I.79. Whether this is an original meaning of the word remains doubtful; the connection with maṇi jewel must have been prevalent at one time.

Maṇikā (f.) [f. of maṇika, adj. fr. maṇi] N. of a charm, the Jewel-charm, by means of which one can read other people's minds D I.214 (m. iddhi-vijjā), cp. *Dial.* I.278, n. 3.).

Maṇila [cp. *Sk. maṇila dewlap ?] a kind of tree Vism 313.

Maṇḍa [later Sk. maṇḍa, perhaps dial. from *mranda, cp. Sk. vi-mradati to soften. Attempts at etym. see Walde, *Lat. Wtb.* s. v. mollis. Cp. also mattikā] the top part, best part of milk or butter, etc. i. e. cream, scum; fig. essence of, the pick of, finest part of anything. parisā° the cream of a gathering, the pick of the congregation, excellent congregation A I.72 (or for °maṇḍala ?); bodhi° essence of enlightenment, highest state of enlightenment; in later literature objectively "the best place of enlightenment, the Throne of Enlightenment or of the Buddha" (does it stand for °maṇḍala in this meaning?) J IV.233 (cp. puthavi-maṇḍa ibid. & puthavi-maṇḍala Sn 990); DhA I.86; II.69; IV.72. sappi° "cream of butter," the finest ghee (cp. AvŚ I.15¹³ sarpimaṇḍa) D I.201; A II.95; Pug 70; Miln 322. —**maṇḍaŋ** karoti to put into the best condition, to make pleasant SnA 81. —manda at DhsA 100 is to be read baddha (v. l. BB). Cp. *Expos.* 132ⁿ.

-**khetta** best soil, fertile ground Miln 255. -**peyya** to be drunk like cream, i. e. of the finest quality, first-class S II.29 (°ŋ idaŋ brahmacariyaŋ).

Maṇḍaka [fr. maṇḍa] 1. the cream of the milk, whey, in dadhi° whey S II.111. — 2. the scum of stagnant water, i. e. anything that floats on the surface & dirties the water, water-weeds, moss etc. J II.304 (gloss sevāla).

Maṇḍana (nt.) [fr. **maṇḍ**] ornament, adornment, finery D I.5, 7; J VI.64; Pug 21, 58; Vbh 351; VbhA 477; Dhtm 13. See under **mada**.

-**ânuyoga** practice of ornamenting, fondness of finery Vin I.190. -**jātika** of an ornament (-loving) nature, fond of dressing D I.80 = Vin II.255 = M II.19, 32.

Maṇḍapa [cp. late Sk. maṇḍapa] a temporary shed or hall erected on special or festive occasions, an awning, tent Vin I.125; Vism 96, 300 (dhamma-savaṇa°), 339 sq. (in simile); DhA I.112; II.45; III.206 (°kāraka); PvA 74, 171, 194; VvA 173.

Maṇḍala [cp. Vedic maṇḍala] 1. circle D I.134 (paṭhavi°, cp. puthavi° Sn 990); Vism 143 (°ŋ karoti to draw a circle, in simile), 174 (tipu° & rajata° lead- & silver circle, in kasiṇa practice); VvA 147 (of a fan = tālapattehi kata°-vijanī). — 2. the disk of the sun or moon; suriya° VvA 224, 271 (divasa-kara°); **canda°** Vism 174; PvA 65. — 3. a round, flat surface, e. g. jāṇu° the disk of the knee, i. e. the knee PvA 179; naḷāta° the (whole of the) forehead D I.106; Sn p. 108. — 4. an enclosed part of space in which something happens, a circus ring; e. g. M I.446 (circus, race-ring); assa° horse-circus, raceground, Vism 308; āpāna° drinking circle, i. e. hall; **kīḷa°** play-circle, i. e. games J VI.332, 333; DhA III.146; **keḷi°** dice board (?) J I.379; gā° Th I.1143, cp. trs. ib. n. 3; go° ox-round Sn 301; **jūta°** dicing table J I.293; **yuddha°** fighting-ring Vism 190; ranga° play-house VvA 139; **vāta°** tornado J I.73. — 5. anything comprised within certain limits or boundaries, a group J V.418 (chāpa° litter of young animals). — 6. border as part of a bhikkhu's dress, hem, gusset Vin I.287; II.177.

-**agga** [cp. Sk. maṇḍal' āgra Halāyudha 2, 317 at Aufrecht p. 301] a circular sword or sabre Miln 339. -**māla** (sometimes māḷa) a circular hall with a peaked roof, a pavilion D I.2, 50 (ḷ); Miln 16 (ḷ); Sn p. 104; SnA 132 (Npl.); VvA 175.

Maṇḍalika (adj.-n.) [fr. maṇḍala, cp. maṇḍalaka-rājā " the king of a small country " Mvyut 94¹ a district officer, king's deputy Vin III.47; f. maṇḍalikā = maṇḍala 4, i. e. circus, ring, round, in assa° race court Vin III.6.

Maṇḍalin (adj.) [fr. maṇḍala] 1. circular Th 1, 863 (maṇḍali-pākāra). — 2. having a disk, orbed (of the sun) S I.51 = VvA 116.

Maṇḍita [pp. of maṇḍeti] adorned, embellished, dressed up Sdhp 244, 540. In cpd. °pasādhita beautifully adorned at J I.489; II.48; VI.219. — Cp. abhi°.

Maṇḍūka [Vedic maṇḍūka] a frog Vv 51²; J IV.247; V.307; VI.164; KhA 46; VvA 217, 218; Sdhp 292. f. maṇḍūkī J I.341. — Maṇḍūka is the name of an angel (devaputta) at Vism 208.

-chāpī a young (female) frog J VI.192. -bhakkha eating frogs, frog eater (i. e. a snake) J III.16.

Maṇḍeti [maṇḍ to adorn, related to Lat. mundus world, cp. in meaning Gr. κόσμος = ornament Dhtp 103: bhūsane, 566: bhūsāyaŋ] to adorn, embellish, beautify J III.138; DhA II.86. — pp. maṇḍita.

Mata¹ [pp. of maññati] thought, understood, considered (as = -°), only late in use Vbh 2 (hīna° paṇīta°, doubtful reading); Sdhp 55; Mhvs 25, 55 (tassā matena according to her opinion); 25, 110 (pasu-samā matā, pl. considered like beasts). Cp. sam°. — *Note.* Does mata-sāyika at Th 1, 501 (= Miln 367) belong under this mata? Then mata would have to be taken as nt. meaning " thought, thinking," but the phrase is not without objection both semantically & syntactically. Mrs. Rh. D. (*Brethren*, p. 240) trsl" " nesting-place of thought."

Mata² [pp. of marati, mṛ] dead M I.88 (ekāha° dead one day); III.159 (matam eyya would go to die); Sn 200, 440, J V.480. Neg. amata see separate article. — *Note.* mata at PvA 110 is to be corrected into cuta.

-kicca duty towards the dead, rites for the dead PvA 274.

Mataka [fr. mata²] dead, one who is dead DhA II.274.

-ākāra condition of one who is dead J I.164 (°ŋ dassati pretends to be dead). -bhatta a meal for the dead, food offered to the manes J IV.151; DhA I.326 (= petakicca p. 328); III.25.

Mati (f.) [Vedic mati, fr. man; cp. Av. maitiš, Lat. mens, mentem (cp. E. mental); Goth. ga-munds, gaminþi, Obg. gi-munt, E. mind] mind, opinion, thought; thinking of, hankering after, love or wish for Vin III.138 (purisa° thought of a man); Mhvs 3, 42 (padīpa lamp of knowledge); 15, 214 (amala° pure-minded); PvA 151 (kāma +). —su° (adj.) wise, clever Mhvs 15, 214; opp. du° (adj.) foolish J III.83 (= duppañña C.); Pv I.8² (= nippañña PvA 40); Sdhp 292.

Matikata (adj.) [cp. Sk. matī-kṛta, fr. matya, nt., harrow = Lat. mateola, Ohg. medela plough] in su° well-harrowed (field) A I.229, 239 (khetta).

Matimant (adj.) [mati + mant] sensible, intelligent, wise, metri causâ as matimā (fr. matimanto, pl.) at Sn 881 (= matimā paṇḍitā Nd¹ 289).

Matta¹ (-°) (adj.) [i. e. mattā used as adj.] " by measure," measured, as far as the measure goes, i. e. — (1) consisting of, measuring (with numerals or similar expressions): appamatto kali Sn 659; pañcamattā sata 500 DA I.35; saṭṭhimatte saṭṭhimatte katvā SnA 510; māsamattaŋ PvA 55; ekādasa° ib. 20; dvādasa° 42; satta° 47; tiŋsamattehi bhikkhūhi saddhiŋ 53. — (2) (negative) as much as, i. e. only, a mere, even as little as, the mere fact (of), not even (one), not any: aṇumattena pi puññena Sn 431; kaṭacchumattaŋ (not) even a spoonful Miln 8; ekapaṇṇa° PvA 115; citta °ŋ pi (not) even as much as one thought ib. 3; nāma° a mere name Miln 25; phandana °ŋ not even *one* throb J VI.7; phandita° the mere fact of . . . M II.24; bindu° only *one* drop PvA 100; rodita° M II.24. — (3) (positive) as much as, so much, some, enough (of); vibhava° riches enough J V.40, kā pi assāsa-mattā laddhā found some relief? PvA 104 (may be = mattā f.). — (4) like, just as, what is called, one may say (often untranslateable): sita°-kāraṇā just because he smiled VvA 68; bhesajja-m attā pītā I have taken medicine D I.205 (= mattā f. ?) okāsa -°ŋ (nt.) permission Sn p. 94; putta° like children A II.124; maraṇa° (almost) dead M I.86; attano nattumatte vandanto DhA IV.178. f. mattī (= mattin ?) see mātu°. — (5) as adv. (usually in oblique cases): even at, as soon as, because of, often with other particles, like api, eva, pi, yeva: vuttamatte eva as soon as said DhA I.330; cintitamatte at the mere thought DhA I.326; naŋ jātamattaŋ yeva as soon as he was born PvA 195; anumodana-mattena because of being pleased PvA 121; upanītamattam eva as soon as it was bought PvA 192; nimujjana-matte yeva as soon as she ducked her head under PvA 47. —na mattena . . . eva not only . . . but even PvA 18 (n. m. nipphalā, attano dānaphalassa bhāgino eva honti).

Matta² [pp. of madati] intoxicated (with), full of joy about (-°), proud of, conceited Sn 889 (mānena m.); J IV.4 (vedanā°, full of pain, perhaps better with v. l. °patta for °matta); VvA 158 (hatthi matto elephant in rut); DhA IV.24 (id.); PvA 47 (surā°), 86 (māna-mada°), 280 (bhoga-mada°).

-kāsinī see matthak' āsinī.

Mattaka (adj.) [fr. matta¹] 1. of the size of Sdhp 238 (pāṇi°). — 2. only as much as, mere D I.12 (appa°, ora°, sīla°); J IV.228 (mana°); DhA IV.178 (pitu-mattakaŋ gabetvā).

Mattatta (nt.) [abstr. fr. matta¹] (the fact of) consisting of, or being only . . . PvA 199 (maŋsa-pesi°).

Mattā (f.) [Vedic mātrā, of mā measure, quantity, right measure, moderation Sn 971 (mattaŋ so jaññā); Dh I.35 (mattā ti pamāṇaŋ vuccati). — Abl. mattaso in °kārin doing in moderation, doing moderately Pug 37 (= pamāṇena padesa-mattam eva karontī ti). — In cpds. shortened to matta°.

-aṭṭhiya (mattaṭṭhiya = °atthika) desirous of moderation, moderate Th 1, 922. -ññu knowing the right measure, moderate, temperate (bhojane or bhojanamhi in eating) A II.40; Sn 338; Pug 25; Dh 8. Cp. jāgariyā. -ññutā moderation (in eating) D III.213; Nd¹ 483; Dh 185; Pug 25; Vbh 249, 360; Dhs 1348; DhA II.238. -sukha (metri causâ: mattā sukha) measured happiness, i. e. small happiness Dh 290 (cp. DhA III.449).

Matti (-sambhava) [for *māti° = mātu° = *mātṛ, after pitti° = pitu° = *pitṛ] born (from a mother) Sn 620 (= mātari sambhūta SnA 466) = Dh 396 (= mātu santike udarasmiŋ sambhūta DhA IV.158).

Mattika (adj.) (°-) [fr. mattikā] made of clay, clay-; only in cpds.:

-kuṇḍala clay earring S I.79 (v. l. mattikā°). -bhājana clay or earthenware vessel Sn 577; Vism 231 (in comparison); DhA I.130. -vāka clay fibre DhsA 321 (v. l. °takka, perhaps gloss = takku spindle, see takka¹).

Mattikā (f.) [cp. Vedic mṛttikā, der. fr. Vedic mṛt (mṛd) soil, earth, clay; with P. maṇḍa, Sk. vimradati, Gr. βλαδαρός soft, Osil. mylsna dust, Goth. mulda, Ags. molde (E. mould, mole = mouldwarp), to same root mṛd as in Sk. mṛdu = Lat. mollis soft, Gr. ἀμαλδύνω to weaken, Sk. mardati & mṛdnāti to crush, powder, Caus. mardayati; also in cognate °mld as appearing in Gr. μέλδω to melt = Ags meltan, Ohg. smëlzan] 1. clay

J VI.372; Mhvs 29, 5 sq. —tamba° red clay DhA IV.106; PvA 191. mattikā pl. kinds of clay (used in cosmetics, like Fuller's earth) J V.89 (nānā-cuṇṇāni+mattikā; see also cuṇṇa). — 2. loam, mud M III.9 (alla° fresh loam or mud); Vism 123 (aruṇa-vaṇṇā); KhA 59 (paṇḍu); VvA 65; PvA 216 (aruṇa-vaṇṇā).
-thāla bowl of clay DhA IV.67. -piṇḍa a lump of clay or loam DA I.289; same trope at PvA 175.

Matteyya (& metteyya) (adj.) [fr. mātā, *mātreyya > *matteyya] reverential towards one's mother, mother-loving D III.74; Pv II.7^{18} (=mātu hita PvA 104; v. l. mett°). Spelling at D III.72 is metteyya. It is difficult to decide about correct spelling, as metteyya is no doubt influenced by the foll. petteyya, with which it is always combined.

Matteyyatā (& mett°) (f.) [abstr. fr. matteyya] filial love towards one's mother; always comb^{d} with petteyyatā D III.145 (v. l. mett°); Nd^{2} 294 (mett°), Dh 332; DhA IV.33.

Mattha [cp. Vedic masta(ka) skull, head, Vedic mastiṣka brains; perhaps to Lat. mentum chin, Cymr. mant jawbone; indirectly also to Lat. mons mountain] the head, etc. Only in cpd. mattha-lunga [cp. Sk. mastu-lunga] the brain Vin I.274; Sn 199; Kh III.; J I.493; KhA 234; Vism 260 (in detail) 264, 359; VbhA 63, 243, 249; DhA II.68; PvA 78, 80. — See also matthaka.

Matthaka [cp. mattha] the head, fig. top, summit J III.206 =IV.4; IV.173, 457; V.478; DA I.226 (pabbata°); Pv IV.16^{3}; DhA I.184. matthaka-matthakena (from end to end) J I,202; III.304. Loc. matthake as adv.: (1) at the head DhA I.109; (2) at the distance of (-°) DhA I.367; (3) on top of (-°) J V.163 (vammīka°); Mhvs 23, 80 (sīsa°); Yugandhara° Miln 6; DhA II.3 (uddhana°).
-āsin sitting on top (of the mountain) J VI.497 (=pabbata-matthake nisinna C.; gloss matta-kāsin i. e. wildly in love, expl^{d} by kāma-mada-matta). The reading is not clear. -tela oil for the head KhA 64 (=muddhani tela Vism 262).

Mathati [Vedic **math, manth** to twirl, shake about, stir etc.; cp. Lat. mamphur part of the lathe=Ger. mandel ("mangle"), E. mandrel; Lith. menturis churning stick, Gr. μόθος tumult μόθουρα shaft of rudder. — The Dhtp (126) gives both roots (math & manth) and expl^{s} by "viḷoḷana," as does Dhtm (183) by "viḷoṭana"] to churn, to shake, disturb, upset. Only in Caus. matheti to agitate, crush, harass, upset (cittaŋ) S IV.210; Sn 50 (=tāseti hāpeti Nd^{2} 492); Pv IV.7^{1} (kammānaŋ vipāko mathaye manaŋ; C 261: abhibhaveyya); Miln 385 (vāyu pādape mathayati; . . . kilesā mathayitabbā). — pp. mathita. See also abhimatthati (sic) & nimmatheti.

Mathana (adj. nt.) [fr. **math**] shaking up, crushing, harassing, confusing Miln 21 (+maddana); DhA I.312; PvA 265.

Mathita [pp. of matheti] 1. (churned) buttermilk Vin II.301 (amathita-kappa). — 2. upset, mentally unbalanced state, disturbance of mind through passion, conceit, etc. M I.486 (maññita+). Neumann trsl^{s} "Vermutung" i. e. speculation, guessing (v. l. matth°).

Mada [Vedic mada, **mad** (see majjati), Idg. ***mad,** as in Av. mata intoxication, drink, mad, to get intoxicated orig. meaning "drip, be full of liquid or fat"; cp. Gr. μαδάω dissolve, μαστός breast (μαζός > Amazone), Lat. madeo to be wet, Ohg. mast fattening, Sk. meda grease, fat, Gr. μέζεα; μεστός full; Goth. mats eatables, Ags. mōs, Ohg. muos=gemüse, etc. Perhaps connected with ***med** in Lat. medeor to heal. For further relations see Walde, *Lat. Wtb.* s. v. madeo. — The Dhtp (412) & Dhtm (642) explain **mad** by "ummāde" Dhtm 210 also by "muda, mada=santose"] 1. intoxication, sensual excess, in formula **davāya madāya maṇḍanāya** (for purposes of sport, excess, personal charm etc.) M I.355=A II.40=Nd^{1} 496=Nd^{2} 540=Pug 21=Dhs 1346, 1348. The commentator's expl^{ns} bearing directly or indirectly on this passage distinguish several kinds of **mada**, viz. **māna-mada & purisa-mada** (at DhsA 403; Vism 293), or **muṭṭhika-mall' ādayo viya madatthaŋ bala-mada-nimittaŋ porisa-mada-nimittañ cā ti vuttaŋ** (at Vism 31). Sn 218 (**mada-pamāda** on which passage SnA 273 comments on mada with jāti-mad' ādi-bhedā madā). — 2. (as mental state or habit) pride, conceit Miln 289 (māna, m., pamāda); Vbh 345 (where 27 such states are given, beginning with jāti°, gotta°, ārogya°, yobbana°, jīvita-mada), 350 (where mada is paraphrased by majjanā majjitattaŋ māno . . . uṇṇati . . . dhajo sampaggāho ketukamyatā cittassa: same formula, as concluding exegesis of **māna** at Nd^{2} 505 & Dhs 1116); sometimes more def. characterised with phrase **mada-matta** elated with the pride or intoxication of . . . (-°). e. g. A I.147 (yobbana°, ārogya°, jīvita°); PvA 86 (māna°), 280 (bhoga°). — The traditional exegesis distinguishes only 3 mada's, viz. **ārogya-mada** the pride of health, **yobbana°** of youth, **jīvita°** of life: D III.220; A I.146.
-nimmadana "disintoxication from intoxication," freedom from pride or conceit A II.34; Bu I.81; Vism 293.

Madana (nt.) [fr. **mad**] lit. making drunk, intoxication Nd^{2} 540 C. (in formula davāya madāya madanāya, instead of maṇḍanāya: see under mada 1); in cpd. °yuta intoxicated, a name for the Yakkhas J I.204. — Cp. **nimmadana.**

Madanīya (adj. nt.) [orig. grd. of madati] 1. intoxicating D II.185 (sadda vaggu rajanīya kāmanīya m.). — 2. intoxication VvA 73.

Madirā (f.) [of adj. Vedic madira intoxicating] intoxicating drink, spirit J V.425; DhsA 48.

Madda 1. [fr. **mṛd,** Sk. marda] crushing etc.; kneading, paste, in piṭṭha paste of flower Vin II.151; J III.226 (piṭṭhi°). — 2. [dialectical, cp. Sk. madra] N. of a country & its inhabitants, in °raṭṭha SnA 68 sq.; °rājakula KhA 73.
-vīṇā a sort of girdle Vin II.136.

Maddati [cp. Vedic **mṛd** to crush: see etym. under mattikā] 1. to tread on, trample on (acc.), crush J III.245, 372 (ppr. maddamāna); DhA II.66. — 2. to defeat, destroy Sn 770 (=abhibhavati Nd^{1} 12); Nd^{2} 85 (madditvā=abhibhuyya); SnA 450; Mhvs I, 41. — fig. to crush a heresy: vādaŋ m. Mhvs 36, 41. — 3. to neglect (an advice), spurn J III.211 (ovādaŋ). — 4. to mix up, knead, jumble together DhA II.155. — 5. to thresh J I.215. — 6. to break down, upset J I.500 (vatiŋ, a fence). — 7. to draw together (a net) J I.208. — Caus. I. **maddeti** to cause to be trampled on Mhvs 29. 4 (aor. maddayi). — Caus. II. **maddāpeti** to cause to be threshed Vin II.180. — pp. **maddita.** See also pari°.

Maddana (nt.) [cp. Epic Sk. mardana, fr. **mṛd**] 1. crushing, grinding, destroying J IV.26; Miln 21 (adj., + mathana); Sdhp 449; Dhtp 156. — 2. threshing Miln 360. — See also **nimmaddana, pamaddana, parimaddana.**

Maddarī (f.) [?] a species of bird, in cpd. **ambaka°** A I.188.

Maddava (adj. nt.) [fr. mṛdu, cp. Epic Sk. mārdava] 1. mild, gentle, soft, suave Dhs 1340; Vbh 359; Miln 229 (cittaŋ mudukaŋ m. siniddhaŋ), 313 (mudu°), 361 (among the 30 best virtues, with siniddha & mudu). — 2. (fr. madda) as Np. name of a king, reigning in Sāgala, the capital of Madda. — 3. withered Dh 377

(=milāta DhA iv.112). — nt. maddavaŋ mildness, softness, gentleness Sn 250 (ajjava+), 292 (id.); J iii.274 (as one of the 10 rāja-dhammā); v.347 (=metta-cittaŋ); DhsA 151.

Maddavatā (f.) [abstr. fr. maddava] gentleness, softness, suavity Dhs 44, 1340; DhsA 151.

Maddālaka [etym. ?] a kind of bird J vi.538.

Maddita [pp. of maddeti, see maddati] 1. kneaded, mixed, in su° Vism 124. — 2. crushed, defeated, in su° Miln 284. — Cp. pa°, pari°.

Maddin (adj.) [fr. **mṛd**, cp. Sk. mardin = mardana] crushing, destroying Sdhp 218. Cp. pamaddin.

Maddhita [of **mṛdh**] see pari°.

Madhu [cp. Vedic madhu, Gr. μέθυ wine, Lith. medùs honey, midùs wine, Ohg. metu=Ger. met wine. Most likely to root *med to be full of juice: see under madati] honey J i.157 sq.; iv.117; Dh 69 (madhū vā read as madhuvā); Mhvs 5, 53; DhsA 320; DhA ii.197 (alla° fresh honey). — pl. madhūni Mhvs 5, 31. — The Abhp (533) also gives "wine from the blossom of Bassia latifolia" as meaning. — On madhu in *similes* see *J.P.T.S.* 1907, 121.

-atthika (madh°) at J iii.493 is with v. l. to be read madhu-tthika (q. v. below). The proposal of Kern's (*Toev.* s. v.) to read madh' aṭṭhika "with sweet kernels" cannot be accepted. The C. explns rightly by "madhura-phalesu pakkhitta madhu viya, madhura-phalo hutvā." -atthika (madhu°) desirous of honey, seeking honey J iv.205; Mhvs 5, 50. -āpaṇa (madhv°) honey shop Mhvs 5, 52. -āsava (madhv°) honey extract, wine from the flower of Bassia latifolia VvA 73 (as one of the 5 kinds of intoxicating liquors). -kara "honey-maker," bee J iv.265; Vism 136 (in simile); DhA i.374. -gaṇḍa honey-comb Mhvs 22, 42; 34, 52. -tthika [madhu+thika, which latter stands for thiya, fr. **styā** to congeal, drip; see thika, thīna, thīya and theva] dripping with honey, full of honey J iii.493 (so read for madh-atthika); vi.529 (=madhuŋ paggharanto C.). Kern, *Toev.* s. v. unnecessarily reads as °*atthika* which he takes=°*aṭṭhika*. -da giving honey, liberal Mhvs 5, 60 (Asoka). -paṭala honey-comb J i.262; DhA i.59; iii.323. -piṇḍikā a ball of honey (to eat), honey-food, a meal with honey Vin i.4; M i.114. -pīta having drunk honey, drunk with honey S i.212. -(b)bata "courting honey," a bee Dāvs iii.65. -bindu a drop of honey Vism 531; VbhA 146 (°giddha, in comparison). -makkhikā smeared with honey J i.158. -madhuka dripping with honey, full of honey J vi.529. -mehika referring to a particular disease madhumeha ("honey-urine," diabetes ?) Vin iv.8. -laṭṭhikā liquorice (no ref. ?); cp. Laṭṭhi-madhuka-vana J i.68. -lāja sweet corn J iv.214, 281. -vāṇija honey seller Mhvs 5, 49. -ssava flowing with honey Pv ii.9[11].

Madhuka (adj. n.) [fr. madhu] connected with honey. 1. (n.) the tree Bassia latifolia (lit. honey tree) Vin i.246; J v.324, 405; vi.529; Miln 165. — 2. the fruit of that tree J iv.434. — 3. (adj.) (-°) full of honey J vi.529 (madhu° containing honey). — 4. connected with an intoxicating drink, given to the drink of (-°) J iv.117 (surā-meraya°).

-aṭṭhika the kernel (of the fruit) of Bassia latifolia Vism 353=KhA 43 (which latter reads madhuka-phal' aṭṭhi; in the description of the finger nails). -puppha the flower of Bassia latifolia from which honey is extracted for liquor Vin i.246 (°rasa liquorice juice); J i.430.

Madhukā (f.) [fr. madhuka] honey drink, sweet drink, liquor Mhvs 5, 52.

Madhura (adj.) [fr. madhu] 1. sweet Sn 50; J iii.493; v.324; Pv ii.67; PvA 119, 147. — 2. of intoxicating sweetness, liquor-like, intoxicating J iv.117. — 3. (nt.) sweetness, sweet drink Dh 363; J i.271 (catu° the 4 sweet drinks, used as cure after poison); Dhs 629; DhsA 320. — 4. (nt.) flattery, praise SnA 287 (opp. avaṇṇa).

-rasa sweet (i. e. honey-) juice, sweet liquor DhA ii.50; PvA 119. -ssara sweet-sounding VvA 57; PvA 151; Mhvs 5, 32.

Madhuraka (adj.) [fr. madhura, cp. similarly madhuka > madhu] full of sweet drink, intoxicated, in phrase madhuraka-jātokāyo **viya** "like an intoxicated body," i. e. without control, weak. The usual translation has been "become languid or weak" ("erschlafft" Ger.). Franke, *Dīgha Übs.* 202 (where more literature) translates: "Ich fühlte mich schwach, wie ein zartes *Pflänzchen*," hardly justifiable. — D ii.99; M i.334; S iii.106, A iii.69. The description refers to a state of swooning, like one in a condition of losing consciousness through intoxication. Rh. D. (*Dial.* ii.107) translates "my body became weak as a *creeper*," hardly correct.

Madhuratā (f.) [abstr. fr. madhura] sweetness J i.68.

Madhuratta (nt.) [abstr. fr. madhura] sweetness Mhvs 2, 13.

Manaŋ (adv.) [cp. Class. Sk. manāk, "a little (of something)" prob. derived from Vedic manā f. a. gold weight =Gr. μνᾶ] "by a certain weight," i. e. a little, somewhat, almost, well-nigh, nearly. Combd with vata in exclamation: M ii.123 (m. v. bho anassāma); DhA iii.147 (m. v. therī nāsitā). Often in phrase man' amhi (with pp.). "I nearly was so & so," e. g. Vin i.109 (vuḷho); J i.405 (upakūḷito); iii.435 (matā), 531 (mārāpito). Cp. BSk. manāsmi khāditā MVastu ii.450.

Manatā (f.) [abstr. fr. mano] mentality DhsA 143 (in expln of attamanatā).

Manasa (adj.) [the -° form of mano, an enlarged form, for which usually either °mana or °mānasa] having a mind, with such & such a mind Sn 942 (nibbāna° "a nibbāna mind," one who is intent upon N., cp. expln at SnA 567); Pv i.6[6] (paduṭṭha-manasā f., maybe °mānasā; but PvA 34 explns "paduṭṭha-cittā paduṭṭhena vā manasā). See also adhimanasa under adhimana.

Manassa (nt.) [*manasyaŋ, abstr. der. fr. mana(s)] of a mind, only in cpds. do° & so° (q. v.).

Maṇāti [cp. Sk. mṛṇāti, mṛ[2]] to crush, destroy; only in Commentator's fanciful etymological analysis of veramaṇi at DhsA 218 (veraŋ maṇāti (sic.) vināsetī ti v.) and KhA 24 (veraŋ maṇātī ti v., veraŋ pajahati vinodeti etc.).

Manāpa (adj.) [cp. BSk. manāpa] pleasing, pleasant, charming Sn 22, 759; Dh 339 (°ssavana); VvA 71; PvA 3, 9. Often in combn piya manāpa, e. g. D ii.19; iii.167; J ii.155; iv.132. — Opp. a°, e. g. Pug 32.

Manāpika = manāpa, Vbh 380; Miln 362.

Manuja [manu+ja, i. e. sprung from Manu, cp. etym. of manussa s. v.] human being; man A iv.159; Sn 458, 661, 1043 sq.; Dh 306, 334. Nd[2] 496 (explns as "manussa" & "satta").

-âdhipa lord of men Mhvs 19, 32. -inda king of men, great king Sn 553; J vi.98.

Manuñña (adj.) [cp. Class. Sk. manojña] pleasing, delightful, beautiful Vv 84[17] (=manorama VvA 340); J i.207; ii.331; Pv ii.12[2]; iv.12[1]; Miln 175, 398; VvA 11, 36; PvA 251; adv. °ŋ pleasantly, delightfully J iv.252. — Opp. a° unpleasant J vi.207.

Manute [Med. form of maññati] to think, discern, understand DhsA 123.

Manussa [fr. manus, cp. Vedic manuṣya. Connected etym. with Goth. manna=man] a human being, man. The popular etym. connects m. with Manu(s), the ancestor of men, e. g. KhA 123: "Manuno apaccā ti manussā, porāṇā pana bhaṇanti 'mana-ussannatāya manussa'; te Jambudīpakā, Aparagoyānikā, Uttarakurukā, Pubbavidehakā ti catubbidhā." Similarly with the other view of connecting it with "mind" VvA 18: "manassa ussannatāya manussā" etc. Cp. also VvA 23, where manussa-nerayika, °peta, °tiracchāna are distinguished. — Sn 75, 307, 333 sq., 611 sq.; Dh 85, 188, 195 sq., 321; Nd[1] 97 (as gati), 340, 484 (°phassa of Sn 964); Vism 312; VbhA 455 (var. clans); DhA I.364. —amanussa not human, a deva, a ghost, a spirit; in cpds. "haunted," ilke °kantāra J I.395, °ṭṭhāna Vv 84[3] (cp. VvA 334 where expl[d]); °sadda DhA I.315. See also separately amanussa.

-attabhāva human existence PvA 71, 87, 122. -itthi a human woman PvA 48, 154. -inda lord of men S I.69; Mhvs 19, 33. -khādaka man eater, cannibal (usually appl[d] to Yakkhas) VbhA 451. -deva (a) "god of men," i. e. king Pv II.8[11]; (b) men & gods (?) VvA 321 (Hardy, in note takes it as "gods of men," i. e. brāhmaṇā). -dhamma condition of man, human state VvA 24. See also uttari-manussa dhamma. -bhūta as a human, in human form Pv I.11[2]; II.1[12]. -loka the world of men Sn 683.

Manussatta (nt.) [abstr. fr. manussa] human existence, state of men It 19; Vv 34[16]; SnA 48, 51; Sdhp 17 sq.

Manussika (adj.) [fr. manussa] see under a°.

Manesikā (f.) [mano+esikā[2]] "mind-searching," i. e. guessing the thoughts of others, mind-reading; a practice forbidden to bhikkhus D I.7 (=m. nāma manasā cintita-jānana-kīḷā DA I.86); Vin II.10.

Mano & **Mana(s)** (nt.) [Vedic manaḥ, see etym. under maññati] I. *Declension.* Like all other nouns of old s-stems mano has partly retained the s forms (cp. cetaḥ > ceto) & partly follows the a-declension. The form mano is found throughout in cpds. as mano°, the other mana at the end of cpds. as °mana. From stem manas an adj. manasa is formed and the der. mānasa & manassa (-°). — nom. mano freq.; & manaŋ Dh 96; acc. mano Sn 270, 388; SnA 11, and freq.; also manaŋ Sn 659=A II.3; V.171=Nett 132; Sn 678; Cp I.8[5]; Vism 466; gen. dat. manaso Sn 470, 967; Dh 390 (manaso piya); Pv II.1[11] (manaso piya=manasā piya PvA 71); instr. manasā Sn 330, 365, 834 (m. cintayanto), 1030; M III.179; Dh 1; Pv II.9[7] (m. pi cetaye); also manena DhA I.42; DhsA 72; abl. manato S IV.65; DhA I.23; Vism 466; loc. manasmiŋ S IV.65; manamhi Vism 466; also mane DhA I.23. & manasi (see this in comp[n] manasi karoti, below). — II. *Meaning:* mind, thought D III.96, 102, 206, 226, 244, 269, 281; S I.16, 172; II.94; M III.55; A III.443; V.171; Sn 77, 424, 829, 873; Dh 116, 300; Sdhp 369. — 1. Mano represents the intellectual functioning of consciousness, while *viññāṇa* represents the field of sense and sense-reaction ("perception"), and *citta* the subjective aspect of consciousness (cp. Mrs. Rh. D. *Buddhist Psychology* p. 19) — The rendering with "*mind*" covers most of the connotation; sometimes it may be translated "thought." As "mind" it embodies the rational faculty of man, which, as the subjective side in our relation to the objective world, may be regarded as a special *sense*, acting on the world, a sense adapted to the rationality (reasonableness, dhamma) of the phenomena, as our eye is adapted to the visibility of the latter. Thus it ranges as the 6th sense in the classification of the senses and their respective spheres (the āyatanāni or relations of subject and object, the ajjhattikāni & the bāhirāni: see āyatana 3). These are: (1) cakkhu (eye) which deals with the sight of form (rūpa); (2) sota (ear) dealing with the hearing of sound (sadda); (3) ghāna (nose) with the smelling of smells (gandha); (4) jivhā (tongue), with the tasting of tastes (rasa); (5) kāya (touch), with the touching of tangible objects (phoṭṭhabba); (6) mano, with the sensing (viññāya) of rational objects or cognisables (dhamma). Thus it is the *sensus communis* (Mrs. Rh. D. *Buddh. Psych.* 140, 163) which recognises the world as a "mundus sensibilis" (dhamma). Both sides are an inseparable unity: the mind fits the world as the eye fits the light, or in other words: mano is the counterpart of dhammā, the subjective dh. Dhamma in this sense is the rationality or lawfulness of the Universe (see dhamma B. 1), Cosmic Order, Natural Law. It may even be taken quite generally as the "*empirical world*" (as Geiger, e. g. interprets it in his *Pali Dhamma* p. 80-82, pointing out the substitution of vatthu for dhamma at Kvu 126 sq. i. e. the *material* world), as the world of "things," of phenomena in general without specification as regards sound, sight, smell, etc. — Dhamma as counterpart of mano is rather an abstract (pluralistic) representation of the world, i. e. the phenomena as such with a certain inherent rationality; manas is the receiver of these phenomena in their abstract meaning, it is the *abstract* sense, so to speak. Of course, to *explain* manas and its function one has to resort to terms of materiality, and thus it happens that the term vijānāti, used of manas, is also used of the 5th sense, that of touch (to which mano is closely related, cp. our E. expressions of touch as denoting rational, abstract processes: *warm* & *cold* used figuratively; to *grasp* anything; terror-*stricken;* deeply *moved feeling* > Lat. palpare to palpitate, etc.). We might say of the mind "sensing," that manas "senses" (as a refined sense of touch) the "sensibility" (dhamma) of the objects, or as *Cpd.* 183 expresses it "cognizable objects." See also kāya II.; and phassa. — 2. In Buddhist Psychological Logic the concept mano is often more definitely circumscribed by the addition of the terms (man-)āyatana, (man-)indriya and (mano-)dhātu, which are practically all the same as mano (and its objective correspondent dhammā). Cp. also below No. 3. The additional terms try to give it the rank of a category of thought. On mano-dhātu and m-āyatana see also the discourse by S. Z. Aung. *Cpd.* 256-59, with Mrs. Rh. D.'s apt remarks on p. 259. — The position of manas among the 6 āyatanas (or indriyas) is one of control over the other 5 (pure and simple senses). This is expressed e. g. at M I.295 (commented on at DhsA 72) and S V.217 (mano nesaŋ gocara-visayaŋ paccanubhoti: mano enjoys the function-spheres of the other senses; cp. Geiger, *Dhamma* 81; as in the Sānkhya: Garbe, *Sānkhya Philosophie* 252 sq.). Cp. Vin I.36; "ettha ca te mano na ramittha rūpesu saddesu atho rasesu." — 3. As regards the relation of manas to citta, it may be stated, that citta is more substantial (as indicated by translation "heart"), more elemental as the seat of *emotion*, whereas manas is the finer element, a subtler feeling or thinking as such. See also citta[2] I., and on rel. to viññāṇa & citta see citta[2] IV. 2[b]. In the more popular opinion and general phraseology however manas is almost synonymous with citta as opposed to body, cittaŋ iti pi mano iti pi S II.94. So in the triad "thought (i. e. intention) speech and action" manas interchanges with citta: see kāya III. — The formula runs kāyena vācāya manasā, e. g. M III.178 (sucaritaŋ caritvā); Dh 391 (natthi dukkaṭaŋ), cp. Dh 96: santaŋ tassa manaŋ, santā vācā ca kamma ca. Besides with citta: kāyena vācāya uda cetasā S I.93, 102; A I.63. rakkhitena k. vācāya cittena S II.231; IV.112. — It is further comb[d] with citta in the scholastic (popular) definition of manas, found in identical words at all Cy. passages:

"mano" is "cittaŋ mano mānasaŋ hadayaŋ, paṇḍaraŋ, man-āyatanaŋ . . . mano-viññāna-dhātu" (mind sensibility). Thus e. g. at Nd^1 3 (for mano), 176 (id.); Nd^2 494 (which however leaves out cittaŋ in exegesis of Sn 1142, 1413, but has it in No. 495 in exegesis of Sn 1039); Dhs 6 (in defⁿ of citta), 17 (of man' indriyaŋ), 65 (of man-āyatanaŋ), 68 (of mano-viññāṇa-dhātu). — The close relation between the two appears further from their combⁿ in the formula of the **ādesanā-pāṭihāriyaŋ** (wonder of manifestation, i. e. the discovery of other peoples' thoughts & intentions), viz. evam pi te **mano** ittham pi te mano iti pi te **cittaŋ**: "so & so is in your mind . . . so & so are your emotions"; D I.213 = III.103 = A I.170. — At S I.53 both are mutually influenced in their state of unsteadiness and fear: niccaŋ utrastaŋ idaŋ **cittaŋ** (heart), niccaŋ ubbiggaŋ idaŋ **mano** (mind). The same relation (citta as instrument or manifestation of mano) is evident from J I.36, where the passage runs: sīho cittaŋ pasādesi. Satthā tassa manaŋ oloketvā vyākāsi . . . At PvA 264 **mano** (of Pv IV.7^1) is expl^d by **cittaŋ**; pīti mano of Sn 766 (glad of heart) expl^d at SnA 512 by santuṭṭha-citto: nibbānamanaso of Sn 942 at SnA 567 by nibbāna-ninna-citto. In the phrase **yathā-manena** "from his heart," i. e. sincerely, voluntarily DhA I.42, mano clearly acts as citta. — 4. *Phrases*: **manaŋ** uppādeti to make up one's mind, to resolve DhA II.140 (cp. citt' uppāda): **manaŋ** karoti: (a) to fix one's mind upon, to give thought to, find pleasure or to delight in (loc.) J IV.223 (rūpe na manaŋ kare = itthi-rūpe nimittaŋ na gaṇheyyāsi C. Cp. the similar & usual manasi-karoti in same sense); VI.45 (Pass. gīte karute mano); (b) to make up one's mind DhA II.87; **manaŋ gaṇhāti** to "take the mind," take the fancy, to please, to win approval J IV.132; DhA II.48. — III. °**mana**: dhamm-uddhacca-viggahita° A II.157 (read °mano for °manā); sankiliṭṭha-manā narā Th 2, 344; atta° pleased; **gedhita°** greedy Pv II.8^2; **dum°** depressed in mind, sad or sick at heart D II.148; S I.103; Vin I.21; A II.59, 61, 198; Th 2, 484; J I.189; opp. **sumana** elated, joyful Pv II.9^{48} (= somanassajāta PvA 132); **pīti°** glad or joyful of heart Sn 766 (expl^d by tuṭṭha-mano, haṭṭha-mano, attamano etc. at Nd^1 3; by santuṭṭha-citto at SnA 512). — IV. **manasi-karoti** (etc.) to fix the mind intently, to bear in mind, take to heart, ponder, think upon, consider, recognise. — 1. (v.) pres. 1st pl. °**karoma** Vin I.103; imper. 2nd sg. °**karohi**, often in formula "suṇāhi sādhukaŋ m.-k." "harken and pay attention" D I.124, 157, 249; cp. M. I.7; A I.227; pl. 2nd °**karotha** A I.171; D I.214 (+ vitakketha); Pot. °**kareyyātha** D I.90 (taŋ atthaŋ sādhukaŋ k.); ppr. °**karonto** DhsA 207; ger. °**katvā** A II.116 (aṭṭhikatvā + . . . ohitasoto suṇāti); Pv III.2^5 (a° = anāvajjetvā PvA 181); VvA 87, 92; PvA 62; grd. °**kātabba** Vism 244, 278; DhsA 205; aor. **manas-ākāti** M II.61; 2nd pl. (Prohib.) (mā) **manasākattha** D I.214; A I.171. Pass. manasi-karīyati Vism 284. — 2. (n.) **manasikāra** attention, pondering, fixed thought (cp. *Cpd.* 12, 28, 40, 282) D III.104, 108 sq., 112, 227 (yoniso), 273 (ayoniso); M I.296; S II.3 (cetanā phasso m.); IV.297 (sabba-nimittānaŋ a° inattention to all outward signs of allurement); Nd^1 501 (ayoniso); Vbh 320, 325, 373 (yoniso), 425; Vism 241 (paṭikūla), VbhA 148 (ayoniso), 248 sq. (as regards the 32 ākāras), 251 (paṭikkūla°), 255 (n'ātisīghato etc.), 270 (ayoniso), 500; DhA II.87 (paṭikkula°); DhsA 133. sammā **manasikāraŋ anvāya** by careful pondering D I.13, 18 ≈. **As adj.** (thoughtful) at ThA 273. — The defⁿ of m. at Vism 466 runs as follows: "kiriyā-kāro, manamhi kāro m. purima-manato visadisaŋ manaŋ karotī ti pi m. Svāyaŋ . ārammaṇa-paṭipādako vīthi-paṭipādako javana-p.° . ti-ppakāro." — Cpds.: *-kusalatā* proficiency in . ention D III.211; *-kosalla* id. VbhA 56 (in detail), 224, 226 sq.; Vism 241 (tenfold), 243 (id., viz. anupubbato, nātisīghato, nātisāṇikato etc.); PvA 63 (yoniso°); *-vidhāna* arrangement of attention VbhA 69, 71; *-vidhi* rule or form of attention Vism 278 (eightfold, viz. gaṇanā, anubandhanā, phusanā, ṭhapanā, sallakhaṇā, vivaṭṭanā, pārisuddhi, tesañ ca paṭipassanā ti). — The composition form of manas is **mano°**, except before vowels, when **man'** takes its place (as man-āyatana VbhA 46 sq.).

-angaṇa (man°) sphere of ideation (*Dhs. trsl.* § 58) D III.243, 280 and passim. **-āvajjana** representative cognition: *Cpd.* 59. **-indriya** (man°) mind-faculty, category of mind, faculty of ideation (cp. *Dhs. trs.* § 17; *Cpd.* pp. 183, 184) D I.70 (with other senses cakkh-undriyaŋ etc.) III.226, and passim. **-kamma** work of the mind, mental action, associated with kāyakamma (bodily action) and vacī° (vocal action) A I.32, 104; Pug 41; Dhs 981 (where omitted in text). **-java** [cp. Vedic manojava] swift as thought Vv 63^{29}; PvA 216 (assājāniya). **-daṇḍa** "mind-punishment" (?) corresponding to kāya° & vacī-daṇḍa, M I.372 sq. (Neumann, trsl^n "Streich in Gedanken"). **-duccarita** sin of the mind or thoughts Dh 233; Nd^1 386; Pug 60. **-dosa** blemish of mind A I.112. **-dvāra** door of the mind, threshold of consciousness VbhA 41; DhsA 425, cp. *Dhs. trsl.* 3 (^{2}p. 2); *Cpd.* 10. **-dhātu** element of apprehension, the ideational faculty (cp. *Dhs. trsl.* 129, ^{2}p. 119, 120; and p. ^{2}lxxxv sq.) Dhs 457 sq.; Vbh 14, 71, 87 sq., 144, 302; Vism 488; VbhA 80, 81, 239 (physiological foundation), 405; DhsA 263, 425; KhA 53. **-padosa** anger in mind, ill-will D III.72; M I.377; Sn 702; J IV.29; Dhs 1060 (cp. DhsA 367: manaŋ padussayamāno uppajjatī ti, i. e. to set one's heart at anger). **-padosika** (adj.) debauched in mind (by envy & ill-will), N. of a class of gods D I.20; VbhA 498, 519. Cp. Kirfel, *Kosmographie*, p. 193 & Kern (*Toev.* I.163), slightly different: from looking at each other too long. **-pasāda** tranquillity of the mind, devotional feeling (towards the Buddha) DhA I.28. **-pubbangama** directed by mind, dominated by thought (see pubba^2) Dh 1, 2; cp. DhA I.21, 35. **-bhāvanīya** of right mind-culture, self-composed S III.1; M III.261; Vv 34^{13} (cp. VvA 152: mana-vaḍḍhanaka); Miln 129. Kern, *Toev.* I.163 trsl^n "to be kept in mind with honour." **-mattaka**, in phrase mana-mattakena (adv.) "by mere mind," consisting of mind only, i. e. memorial, as a matter of mind J IV.228. **-maya** made of mind, consisting of mind, i. e. formed by the magic power of the mind, magically formed, expl^d at Vism 405 as "adhiṭṭhāna-manena nimmitattā m."; at DA I.120 as "jhāna-manena nibbatta"; at DhA I.23 as "mano-nipphanna"; at VvA 10 as "bāhirena paccayena vinā manasā va nibbatta." — Dh 1, 2; J VI.265 (manomayaŋ sindhavaŋ abhiruyha); Sdhp 259; as quality of *iddhi*. Vism 379, 406. — Sometimes a body of this matter can be created by great holiness or knowledge; human beings or gods may be endowed with this power D I.17 (+ pītibhakkha, of the Ābhassaras), 34 (attā dibbo rūpī m. sabbanga-paccangī etc.), 77 (id.), 186 (id.); Vin II.185 (Koliya-putto kālaŋ kato aññataraŋ mano-mayaŋ kāyaŋ upapanno); M I.410 (devā rūpino m.); S IV.71; A I.24; III.122, 192; IV.235; V.60. **-ratha** desired object (lit. what pleases the mind), wish Vism 506 (°vighāta + icchā-vighāta); °ŋ pūreti to fulfil one's wish Mhvs 8, 27 (puṇṇa-sabbamanoratha). **Manoratha-pūraṇī** (f.) "the wish fulfiller" is the name of the Commentary on the Anguttara Nikāya. **-rama** pleasing to the mind, lovely, delightful Sn 50, 337, 1013; Dh 58; Pv II.9^{68} (phoṭṭhabba), Mhvs 18, 48; VvA 340. **-viññāṇa** representative cognition, rationality Vism 489; VbhA 150 (22 fold); DhsA 304, cp. *Dhs. trsl.* 170 (^{2}p. 157); *-dhātu* (element of) representative intellection, mind cognition, the 6th of the viññāṇadhātus or series of cognitional elements corresponding to and based on the 12 simple dhātus, which are the external & internal sense-relations (= āyatanāni) Dhs 58; Vbh 14, 71, 87, 89, 144, 176 and passim. See also above II. 3 and discussions at *Dhs. trsl.* 132 (^{2}p. 122) &

introd., p. 53 sq.; *Cpd.* 123^2, 184. **-viññeyya** to be comprehended by the mind (cp. *Dialogues* II.281^n) D II.281; M III.55, 57; J IV.195. **-vitakka** a thought (of mind) S I.207 = Sn 270 (mano is in C. on this passage expl^d as "kusala-citta" SnA 303). **-sañcetan' āhāra** "nutriment of representative cogitation" (*Dhs. trsl.* 31) S II.11, 13, 99; Dhs 72; Vism 341. **-satta** "with mind attached," N. of certain gods, among whom are reborn those who died with minds absorbed in some attachment M I.376. **-samācāra** conduct, observance, habit of thought or mind (associated with kāya° & vacī°) M II.114; III.45, 49. **-silā** (cp. Sk. manaḥ śila) red arsenic, often used as a powder for dying and other purposes; the red colour is frequently found in later (Cy.) literature, e. g. J V.416 (+ haritāla yellow ointment); Vism 485; DhA IV.113 (id. as cuṇṇa); ThA 70 (Ap. V.20); Mhvs 29, 12; SnA 59 (°piṇḍa in simile); DhA II.43 (°rasa); VvA 288 (°cuṇṇa-piñjara-vaṇṇa, of ripe mango fruit); PvA 274 (°vaṇṇāni ambaphalāni); *-tala* a flat rock, platform (= silātala) SnA 93, 104; as the platform on which the seat of the Buddha is placed & whence he sends forth the lion's roar: J II.219; VI.399; VvA 217; as a district of the **Himavant**: J VI.432; SnA 358. **-hara** charming, captivating, beautiful Mhvs 18, 49; N. of a special gem (the wishing gem ?) Miln 118, 354.

Manta [cp. Vedic mantra, fr. **mantray**] orig. a divine saying or decision, hence a secret plan [cp. def. of **mant** at Dhtp 578 by "gutta-bhāsane"], counsel; hence magic charm, spell. In particular a secret religious code or doctrine, esp. the Brahmanic texts or the Vedas, regarded as such (i. e. as the code of a sect) by the Buddhists. — 1. with ref. to the *Vedas* usually in the pl. mantā (the Scriptures, Hymns, Incantations): D I.96; M II.166 (brahme mante adhiyitvā; mante vāceti); Sn 249 (= devā SnA 291), 302 (mante ganthetvā, criticised by Bdhgh as brahmanic (: heretic) work in contrast with the ancient Vedas as follows: "vede bhinditvā dhammayutte porāṇa-mante nāsetvā adhamma-yutte kūṭa-mante ganthetvā" SnA 320), 1000 (with ref. to the 32 signs of a Mahāpurisa), 1018; Dh 241 (holy studies); J II.100; III.28 (maybe to be classed under 2), 537. — Sometimes in **sg.**: mantaŋ parivattenti brahma-cintitaŋ Pv II.6^{13} (= veda PvA 97) = Vv 63^{16} (= veda VvA 265); — **n.** pl. also mantāni, meaning "Vedas": Miln 10. — 2 (doubtful, perhaps as sub group to No. 3) holy scriptures in general, sacred text, secret doctrine S I.57 (mantā dhīra "firm in doctrine" *K.S.* thus taking mantā as instr.; it may better be taken as **mantar**); Sn 1042 (where Nd^2 497 expl^s as paññā etc.); Mhvs 5, 109 (Buddha° the "mantra" of the B.), 147 (id.). — 3. divine utterance, a word with supernatural power, a charm, spell, magic rat, witchcraft Miln 11 (see about manta in the Jātakas: Fick, *Sociale Gliederung* 152, 153). At PvA 117 m. is combined with **yoga** and ascribed to the devas, while y. is referred to men. — J I.200 (+ paritta); III.511 (°ŋ karoti to utter a charm, cast a spell); DhA IV.227. There are several special charms mentioned at var. places of the Jātakas, e. g. one called Vedabbha, by means of which under a certain constellation one is able to produce a shower of gems from the air J I.253 (nakkhatta-yoge laddhe taŋ mantaŋ *parivattetvā* ākāse ulloki, tato ākāsato satta-ratana-vassaŋ vassati). Others are: paṭhavī-jaya m. (by means of which one conquers the earth) J II.243; sabba-rāva-jānana° (of knowing all sounds, of animals) III.415; nidhi-uddharana° (of finding secret treasures) III.116; catukaṇṇa° (four-cornered) VI.392, etc. — 4. advice, counsel, plan, design Vin IV.308 (°ŋ saŋharati to foil a plan); J VI.438. — 5. (adj.) (-°) parivattana° a charm that can be said, an effective charm J I.200; bahu° knowing many charms, very tricky DhA II.4; bhinna° one who has neglected an advice J VI.437, 438.

-ajjhāyaka one who studies the Mantras or Holy Scriptures (of the Brahmins) J I.167; DhA III.361 (tinnaŋ vedānaŋ pāragū m.-a. brāhmaṇo). **-ajjhena** study of the Vedas SnA 314. **-pada** = manta 1. D I.104 (= veda-sankhāta m. DA I.273. **-pāraga** one who masters the Vedas; in buddh. sense: one who excels in wisdom Sn 997. manta in this sense is by the Cys. always expl^d by *paññā*, e. g., Nd^2 497 (as mantā f.); DhA IV.93 (id.), SnA 549 (mantāya pariggahetvā). **-pāragū** one who is accomplished in the Vedas Sn 251 (= vedapāragū SnA 293), 690 (= vedānaŋ pāragata SnA 488), 976. **-bandhava** one acquainted with the Mantras Sn 140 (= vedabandhū SnA 192); Nd^1 11 (where Nd^2 455 in same connection reads **mitta°** for manta°: see under bandhu). **-bhāṇin** reciter of the Holy Texts (or charms) Th II.281; fig. a clever speaker Sn 850 (but Nd^1 219 reads manta°; see mantar) Dh 363 (cp. DhA IV.93; paññāya bhaṇana-sīla) Th 1, 2. **-yuddka** a weird fight, a bewitched battle Mhvs 25, 49 ("cunningly planned b." trsl. Geiger; "diplomatic stratagem," Turnour).

Mantanaka (adj.) [fr. mantanā] plotting J V.437.

Mantanā f. (& °ṇā) [fr. **mant**] counsel, consultation, deliberation, advice, command D I.104; A I.199; Vin V.164; J VI.437, 438; Miln 3 (ṇ); DA I.273.

Mantar [n. ag. of **mant**, cp. Sk. *mantṛ a thinker] a sage, seer, wise man, usually appositionally nom. mantā "as a sage," "like a thinker," a form which looks like a *fem.* and is mostly expl^d as such by the Commentaries. Mantā has also erroneously been taken as instr. of manta, or as a so-called *ger.* of manteti, in which latter two functions it has been expl^d at "jānitvā." The form has evidently puzzled the old commentators, as early as the Niddesa; through the Abhp (153, 979) it has come down at mantā "*wisdom*" to Childers. Kern, *Toev.* s. v. hesitates and only comes half near the truth. The Index to Pj. marks the word with ? — S I.57 (+ dhīra; trsl^n "firm *in doctrine*"); Sn 159 ("in truth," opp. to musā; SnA 204 expl^{ns} m. = paññā; tāya paricchinditvā bhāsati), 916 (mantā asmī ti, expl^d at SnA 562 by "mantāya"), 1040 = 1042 (= Nd^2 497 mantā vuccati paññā etc.); Vv 63^6 (expl^d as jānitvā paññāya paricchinditvā VvA 262). — Besides this form we have a shortened **manta** (nom.) at Sn 455 (akiñcano +), which is expl^d at SnA 402 as mantā jānitvā. It is to be noted that for manta bhāṇin at Sn 850 the Nd^1 219 reads mantā and expl customarily by "mantāya pariggahetvā vācaŋ bhāsati."

Mantita [pp. of manteti] 1. considered Th 1, 9; Miln 91. — 2. advised, given as counsel J VI.438; DA I.273.

Mantin (adj.-n.) [fr. manta] 1. (adj.) giving or observing counsel S I.236. — 2. (n.) counsellor, minister J VI.437 (paṇḍita m.).

Manteti [cp. Vedic mantrayati; **mant** is given at Dhtp in meaning of gutta-bhāsana, i. e. "secret talk"] to pronounce in an important (because secret) manner (like a mantra), i. e. 1. to take counsel (with = instr. or saddhiŋ) D I.94, 104 (mantanaŋ manteyya to discuss) 122 (2nd pl. imper. **mantavho**, as compared with **mantayavho** J II.107 besides mantavho ibid. Cp. Geiger, *P.Gr.* § 126); II.87, 239; Vin IV.308 (**mantesuŋ** aor.; perhaps "plotted"); Sn p. 107 (= talk privately to); Sn 379; J I.144; VI.525 (**mantayitvāna** ger.); DA I.263 (imper. **mantayatha**); PvA 74 (aor. mantayiŋsu). — 2. to consider, to think over, to be of opinion A I.199 (Pot. mantaye); Miln 91 (grd. **mantayitabba** & inf. **mantayituŋ**). — 3. to announce, advise; pronounce, advise Sn 126; Pv IV.1^{20} (= kathemi kittayāmi PvA 225); SnA 169. — pp. mantita. — Cp. ā°.

Mantha [fr. **math**] a churning stick, a sort of rice-cake (=satthu) Vin I.4. [cp. Vedic mantha "Rührtrank"= homeric κυκεών "Gerstenmehl in Milch verrührt," Zimmer, *Altind. Leben* 268].

Manda (adj.) [cp. late-Vedic & Epic manda] 1. slow, lazy, indolent; mostly with ref. to the intellectual faculties, therefore: dull, stupid, slow of grasp, ignorant, foolish M I.520 (+momuha); Sn 666, 820 (=momūha Nd¹ 153), 1051 (=mohā avidvā etc. Nd² 498); Dh 325 (=amanasikārā manda-pañña DhA IV.7); J IV.221, Pug 65, 69; KhA 53, 54.—2. slow, yielding little result, unprofitable (of udaka, water, with respect to fish; and gocara, feeding on fishes) J I.221.—3. [in this meaning probably=Vedic mandra "pleasant, pleasing," although Halāyudha gives mandākṣa as "bashful"] soft, tender (with ref. to eyes), lovely, in cpds. °akkhin having lovely (soft) eyes J III.190; and °locana id. Th 2, 375 (kinnari-manda°=manda-puthu-vilocana ThA 253); Pv I.11⁵ (miga-manda°=migī viya mand' akkhi PvA 57); Vv 64¹¹ (miga-m°=miga-cchāpikānaŋ viya mudu siniddha-diṭṭhi-nipāta).—4. In cpd. picu (or puci°) manda the Nimb tree, it means "tree" (?) see picu-manda & puci-manda.—5. In composition with **bhū** it assumes the form mandī°, e. g. mandībhūta slowed down, enfeebled, diminished J I.228; VbhA 157.

-**valāhakā** a class of fairies or demi-gods D II.259 ("fragile spirits of the clouds" trsl.).

Mandaka [?] according to Kern, *Toev.* s. v.=*mandra (of sound: deep, bass)+ka; a sort of drum J VI.580.

Mandatā (f.)=mandatta Sdhp 19.

Mandatta (nt.) [fr. manda] stupidity M I.520; Pug 69.

Mandākinī (f.) N. of one of the seven great lakes in the Himavant, enum^d at A IV.101; J V.415; Vism 416; SnA 407; DA I.164. (Halāyudha 3, 51 gives m. as a name for the Ganges.)

Mandāmukhi (f.) [dialectical? reading a little doubtful] a coal-pan, a vessel for holding embers for the sake of heating Vin I.32 (=aggi-bhājana C.); VvA 147 (mandamukhī, stands for angara-kapalla p. 142 in expl^n of hattha-patāpaka Vv 33³²).

Mandārava [cp. Sk. mandāra] the coral tree, Erythrina fulgens (considered also as one of the 5 celestial trees). The blossoms mentioned D II.137 fall from the next world.—D II.137; Vv 22² (cp. VvA 111); J I.13, 39; Miln 13, 18 (dibbāni m.-pupphāni abhippavassiŋsu).

Mandālaka [etym. ?] a water-plant (kind of lotus) J IV.539; VI.47, 279, 564.

Mandiya (nt.) [cp. Sk. māndya] 1. laziness, slackness S I.110.—2. dullness of mind, stupidity J III.38 (=manda-bhāva).

Mandira (nt.) [cp. late Sk. mandira] a house, edifice, palace Sn 996, 1012; J V.480; VI.269, 270; Dāvs II.67 (dhātu° shrine).

Mandī° see manda 5.

Mama gen. dat. of pers. pron. ahaŋ (q. v.) used quasi independently (as substitute for our "self-") in phrase **mama-y-idaŋ** Sn 806 thought of "this is mine," cp. S I.14, i. e. egoism, belief in a real personal entity, expl^d at Nd¹ 124 by **maññanā** conceit, illusion. Also in var. phrases with **kṛ** in form **mamaŋ°**, viz. mamankāra etc.—As adj. "self-like, selfish" only neg. amama unselfish Sn 220 (=mamatta-virahita SnA 276); Pv IV.1³⁴ (=mamankāra-virahita PvA 230); J IV.372; VI.259. See also amama, cp. māmaka.

Mamankāra [mamaŋ (=mama)+kāra, cp. ahaŋ+kāra] selfish attachment, self-interest, selfishness PvA 230. In canonic books only in comb^n with ahankāra & mān' ânusaya (belief in an ego and bias of conceit), e. g. at M III.18, 32; S III.80, 103, 136, 169; IV.41, 197, 202; A I.132 sq.; III.444. See also **maminkāra**.

Mamankāraṇa (nt.) [fr. mamaŋ+**kṛ**] treating with tenderness, solicitude, fondness J V.331.

Mamatta (nt.) [fr. mama] selfishness, self-love, egoism; conceit, pride in (-°), attachment to (-°). Sn 806, 871, 951; Th 1, 717; Nd¹ 49 (two: taṇhā & diṭṭhi°); Nd² 499 (id. but as masc.); SnA 276; DhsA 199; PvA 19.

Mamâyati [Denom. fr. mama, cp. Sk. mamāyate in same meaning (not with Böhtlingk & Roth: envy) at MBh XII.8051 and Aṣṭas Prajñā Pāramitā 254] to be attached to, to be fond of, to cherish, tend, foster, love M I.260; S III.190; Th 1, 1150; Sn 922 (mamāyetha); Nd¹ 125 (Bhagavantaŋ); J IV.359 (=piyāyati C.); Miln 73; VbhA 107 (mamāyatī ti mātā: in pop. etym. of mātā); DhA I.11; SnA 534; Mhvs 20, 4.—pp. **mamāyita**.

Mamāyanā (f.)=mamatta (selfishness) J VI.259 (°taṇhā-rahita in expl^n of amama).

Mamāyita [pp. of mamāyati] cherished, beloved; as n. nt. attachment, fondness of, pride.—(adj. or pp.) S II.94 (etaŋ ajjhositaŋ, m., parāmaṭṭhaŋ); Sn 119; DhA I.11.—(nt.:) Sn 466, 777, 805, 950=Dh 367 (expl^d as: yassa "ahan" ti vā "maman" ti vā gāho n' atthi DhA IV.100); Sn 1056 (cp. Nd² 499).

Maminkaroti [mama(ŋ)+**kṛ** "to make one's own"] to be fond of, to cherish, tend, foster J V.330.

Maminkāra [for maman°, cp. Geiger, *P.Gr.* § 19] self-love, self-interest, egoism M I.486; III.32 (at both places also ahinkāra for ahankāra).

Mamma (nt.) [Vedic marman, fr. **mṛd**] soft spot of the body, a vital spot (in the Vedas chiefly between the ribs near the heart), joint. A popular etym. and expl^n of the word is given at *Expos.* 132^n3 (on DhsA 100).—J II.228; III.209; DhsA 390.

-**ghaṭṭana** hitting a vital spot (of speech, i. e. backbiting. Cp. piṭṭhi-maŋsika) DhA IV.182. -**chedaka** breaking the joints (or ribs), violent (fig. of hard speech) DhA I.75; DhsA 100.

Mammana (adj.) [onomat. cp. babbhara. With Sk. marmara rustling to Lat. fremo to roar=Gr. βρέμω to thud, βροντή thunder, Ger. brummen. Cp. also Sk. murmura=P. mummura & muramurā, Lat. murmur] stammering, stuttering Vin II.90 (one of the properties of bad or faulty speech, comb^d with dubbaca & eḷagalavāca).

Maya (adj.) (-° only) [Vedic maya] made of, consisting of.—An interesting analysis (interesting for judging the views and sense of etymology of an ancient commentator) of maya is given by Dhammapāla at VvA 10, where he distinguishes 6 meanings of the word, viz. 1. asma-d-atthe, i. e. "myself" (as representing mayaŋ!).—2. **paññatti** "regulation" (same as 1. according to example given, but constructed syntactically quite diff. by Dhp.).—3. **nibbatti** "origin" (arising from, with example mano-maya "produced by mind").—4. **manomaya** "spiritually" (same as 3).—5. **vikār' atthe** "alteration" (? more like product, consistency, substance), with example "sabbe-maṭṭikā-maya-kuṭikā."—6. **pada-pūraṇa matte** to make up a foot of the verse (or add a syllable for the sake of completeness, with example "dānamaya, sīlamaya" (=dana; sila).—1. made of: aṭṭhi° of bone Vin II.115; ayo° of iron Sn 669; Pv I.10⁴; J IV.492; udumbara° of Ud. wood Mhvs 23, 87; dāru° of wood, VvA 8; loha° of copper Sn 670; veḷuriya° of jewels Vv 2^1. — 2. consisting in: dāna° giving alms PvA 8, 9; dussa° clothes Vv 46^7; dhamma° righteousness S I.137. — 3. (more as apposition, in the sense as given by Dhp. above under 6) something like, a likeness of, i. e. ingredient, substance, stuff; in āhāra° food-stuff, food J III.523; utu° something like a (change in) season Vism 395; sīla° character, having sīla as substance (or simply-consisting of) It 51 (dāna°, sīla°, bhāvanā°).

Mayaŋ [1st pl. of ahaŋ, for vayaŋ after mayā etc. See ahaŋ] we Vin II.270; Sn 31, 91, 167; Dh 6; KhA 210.

Mayūkha [Vedic mayūkha in diff. meaning, viz. a peg for fastening a weft etc., Zimmer *Altind. Leben* 254] a ray of light Abhp. 64; Dhp. A 426 (old citation, unverified).

Mayūra [Vedic mayūra] a peacock D III.201; S II.279; Th 1, 1113; J II.144, 150 (°gīva) = DhA I.144; J IV.211 (°nacca); V.304; VI.172, 272, 483; Vv 11^1, 35^8 (= sikhaṇḍin VvA 163); VvA 27 (°gīva-vaṇṇa); Sdhp 92. — The form **mayūra** occurs nearly always in the Gāthās and is the older form of the two m. and **mora**. The latter contracted form is found in Prose only and is often used to explain the old form, e, g. at VvA 57. See also **mora**.

Mara (adj.) [fr. **mṛ**] dying; only neg. **amara** not dying, immortal, in phrase **ajarāmara** free from decay & death Th II.512; Pv II.6^{11}. See also **amara**.

Maraṇa (nt.) [fr. **mṛ**] death, as ending *this* (visible) existence, physical death, in a narrower meaning than kālakiriyā; dying, in cpds. death. — The customary stock definition of maraṇa runs; yaŋ tesaŋ tesaŋ sattānaŋ tamhā tamhā satta-nikāyā cuti cavanatā bhedo antaradhānaŋ, maccu maraṇaŋ kālakiriyā, khandhānaŋ bhedo, kaḷebarassa nikkhepo M I.49; Nd^1 123, 124 (adds "jīvit' indriyass' upacchedo"). Cp. similar def^{ns} of birth and old age under jāti and jarā. — S I.121; D III.52, 111 sq., 135 sq., 146 sq., 235, 258 sq.; Sn 32, 318, 426 sq., 575 sq., 742, 806; Nd^2 254 (= maccu); Pug 60; Vbh 99 sq.; VbhA 100 (def^n and exegesis in det., cp. Vism 502), 101 (var. kinds of, cp. Vism 229), 156 (lahuka), 157; DhA III.434; PvA 5, 18, 54, 64, 76, 96; Sdhp 292, 293. —**kāla°** timely death (opp. akāla°); **khaṇika°** sudden death Vism 229.

-anta having death as its end (of jīvita) Dh 148 (cp. DhA II.366: maraṇa-sankhāto antako). **-ânussati** mindfulness of death Vism 197, 230 sq. (under 8 aspects). **-cetanā** intention of death DhA I.20. **-dhamma** subject to death PvA 41. **-pariyosana** ending in death (of jīvita, life) DhA III.111, 170. **-pāra** "the other side of death," Np. at Nd^1 154 (vv. ll. BB purāpuraŋ; SS parammukhaŋ). **-bhaya** the fear of death J I.203; VI.398; Vbh 367. **-bhojana** food given before death, the last meal J I.197; II.420. **-mañca** death-bed Vism 47, 549; °**ka** J IV.132. **-mukha** the mouth of d. PvA 97 (or should we read °dukkha ?). **-sati** the thought (or mindfulness) of death, meditation on death SnA 54; DhA III.171; PvA 61, 66. **-samaya** the time of death VbhA 157-159 (in var. conditions as regards paṭisandhi).

Marati [**mṛ** = Idg. ***mer**, Vedic mriyate & marate; cp. Av. miryeite, Sk. marta = Gr. βροτός mortal, man; māra death; Goth. maurþr = Ags. mort = Ger. mord; Lith. mirti to die; Lat. morior to die, mors death. The root is identical with that of mṛṇāti to crush: see maṇāti, and mṛdnāti (mardati) same: see mattikā. — The Dhtp (No. 245) defines **mṛ** by "pāṇa-cāge," i. e. giving up breathing] to die. — pres. marati Mhvs v. spur. after 5, 27; 36, 83; Pot. **mareyyaŋ** J VI.498; 2nd **mareyyāsi** J III.276. ppr. **maramāna** Mhvs 36, 76. — aor. **amarā** J III.389 (= mata C.; with gloss amari). —**amari** Mhvs 36, 96. — Fut. **marissati** J III.214. — ppr. (= fut.) **marissaŋ** J III.214 (for *mariṣyanta). — Inf. **marituŋ** D II.330 (amaritu-kāma not willing to die); Vism 297 (id.); VvA 207 (positive); and **marituye** Th 2, 426. — The form **miyyati** (mīyati) see separately. — Caus I. **māreti** to kill, murder Mhvs 37, 27; PvA 4. Pass. **māriyati** PvA 5 (ppr. māriyamāna); Sdhp 139 (read mār° for marīy°). — Caus. II. **mārāpeti** to cause to be killed J III.178; Mhvs 37, 28. Cp. **pamāreti.**

Marica (nt.) [cp. scientific Sk. marica] black pepper Vin I.201 (allowed as medicine to the bhikkhus); Miln 63.

-gaccha the M.-shrub J V.12. **-cuṇṇa** powdered pepper, fine pepper J I.455.

Mariyādā (f.) [cp. Vedic maryādā; perhaps related to Lat. mare sea; s. Walde, *Lat. Wb.* under mare] 1. boundary, limit, shore, embankment Vin III.50; A III.227 (brāhmaṇānaŋ); D III.92 = Vism 419; J V.325; VI.536 (tīra°); Mhvs 34, 70; 36, 59 (vāpi°); Miln 416. — 2. strictly defined relation, rule, control J II.215; Vism 15. — adj. keeping to the lines (or boundaries), observing strict rules A III.227 (quoted SnA 318, 325). °**bandha** keeping in control Vin I.287. — Cp. **vimariyādi.**

Marīci (f.) [Vedic marīci; cp. Gr. μαρμαίρω to shimmer, glitter, μαῖρα dog star, ἀμαρύσσω sparkle; Lat. merus clear, pure; perhaps also mariyādā to be taken here] 1. a ray of light VvA 166. — 2. a mirage J VI.209; Vism 496; VbhA 34, 85; often comb^d with māyā (q. v.), e. g. Nd^2 680 A^{II}; J II.330.

-kammaṭṭhāna the "mirage" station of exercise DhA III.165. **-dhamma** like a mirage, unsubstantial J VI.206; Dh 46; DhA I.337.

Marīcikā (f.) = marīci 2; S III.141; Vism 479 (in comp.); Dh 170 (= māyā DhA III.166).

Maru^1 [cp. Epic Sk. maru] a region destitute of water, a desert. Always comb^d with °kantāra: Nd^1 155 (as Name); J I.107; VbhA 6; VvA 332; PvA 99, 112.

Maru^2 [Vedic marut, always in pl. marutaḥ, the gods of the thunder-storm] 1. pl. **marū** the genii, spirits of the air Sn 681, 688; Miln 278 (nāga-yakkha-nara-marū; perhaps in meaning 2); Mhvs 5, 27. — 2. gods in general (°-) Mhvs 15, 211 (°gaṇā hosts of gods); 18, 68 (°narā gods and men). — Cp. **māruta** & **māluta.**

Marumba [etym. ?] a sort of (sweet-scented) earth or sand Vin II.121, 142, 153 (at these passages used for besprinkling a damp living-cell); IV.33 (pāsāṇā, sakkharā, kaṭhalā, marumbā, vālikā); Mhvs 29, 8; Dpvs 19, 2; Miln 197 (pāsāṇa, sakkhara, khara, m.).

Maruvā (f.) [cp. Sk. mūrvā, perhaps connected with Lat. malva] a species of hemp (Sanseveria roxburghiana) M I.429. At J II.115 we find reading marūdvā & marucavāka (C.), of uncertain meaning ?

Mala (nt.) [Vedic mala, see etym. under malina. The Dhtm (395) only knows of one root mal or mall in meaning "dhāraṇa" supporting, thus thinking of mālaka] anything impure, stain (lit. & fig.), dirt. In the Canon mostly fig. of impurities. On mala in similes see *J.P.T.S.*, 1907, 122. — S I.38 (itthi malaŋ brahmacariyassa), 43 (id.); A I.105 (issā°); Sn 378, 469, 962, 1132 (= rāgo malaŋ etc. Nd^2 500); Nd^1 15, 478 sq.; Dh 239 sq.; Vbh 368 (tīṇi malāni), 389 (nava purisa-malāni); Pv II.3^{34} (macchera°); PvA 45 (id.), 80 (id.), 17 (citta°); Sdhp 220. — Compar. **malatara** a greater stain A IV.195 = Dh 243. — See also **māla.**

-âbhibhū overcoming one's sordidness S I.18; J IV.64. **-majjana** "dirt wiper," a barber Vin IV.308 (kasāvaṭa m. nihīnajacca); J III.452; IV.365.

Malina (adj.) [fr. **mal, *mel** to make dirty, to which belongs mala. — Cp. Lat. mulleus reddish, purple; Gr. μέλας black, μολύνω to stain, μίλτος reddish; Lith. mulvas yellowish, mélynas blue; Ohg. māl stain] dirty, stained, impure, usually lit. — J I.467; Miln 324; DhA I.233; VvA 156; PvA 226; VbhA 498.

Malinaka (adj.) [malina+ka] dirty; with ref. to loha, a kind of copper, in the group of copper belonging to Pisāca VbhA 63.

Malya (nt.) [for *mālya, fr. māla] flower, garland of flowers Vv I^1 (-dhara); 2^1; J v.188 (puppha°), 420. — The reading at Pv III.3^3 (pahūta°, adj. having many rows of flowers) is **mālya.**

Malla [cp. Sk. malla, perhaps a local term, cp. Cānura] a wrestler Vin II.105 (°muṭṭhika) J IV.81 (two, named Cānura and Muṭṭhika "fister"); Vism 31 (muṭṭhika+, i. e. boxing & wrestling as amusements: see mada I). Perhaps as "porter" Bdhgh on CV v.29. 5 (see Vin II.319). At Miln 191 the **mallā** are mentioned as a group or company; their designation might here refer to the Mallas, a tribe, as other tribes are given at the same passage (e. g. Atoṇā, Pisācā). Cp. Bhallaka.
 -gaṇa troop of professional wrestlers Miln 331. **-muṭṭhika** boxer Vin II.105. **-yuddha** wrestling contest Miln 232; DhA II.154; DA I.85. **-yuddhaka** a professional wrestler J IV.81.

Mallaka [cp. Sk. mallaka & mallika] I. a bowl, a vessel (?) used in bathing Vin II.106 (mallakena nahāyati; or is it a kind of scrubber? Bdhgh's explⁿ of this passage (CV v. I.4) on p. 315 is not quite clear; mallakaŋ nāma *makara-dantike chinditvā* mūllaka-mūla-saṇṭhānena kata-mallakaŋ vuccati; akata° *danta achinditvā* kataŋ). It may bear some ref. to malla on p. 105 (see malla) & to mallika-makula (see below mallikā). — 2. a cup, drinking vessel A I.250 (udaka°). — 3. a bowl J III.21 (kaŋsa°=taṭṭaka). — 4. in kheḷa° a spittoon Vin I.48; II.175. — *Note.* W. Printz in "*Bhāsa's Prākrit.*" p. 45, compares Śauraseni maḷḷaa, Hindī maḷḷ(a) "cup," maliyā "a small vessel (of wood or cocoanut-shell) for holding the oil used in unction," mālā "cocoanut-shell," and adds: probably a Dravidian word.

Mallikā (f.) [cp. Epic Sk. mallikā, Halāyudha 2, 51; Daṇḍin 2, 214] Arabian jasmine Dh 54 (tagara°); J I.62; III.291; v.420; Miln 333, 338; DhsA 14; KhA 44. **mallika-makula** opening bud of the jasmine Vism 251=VbhA 234 (°saṇṭhāna, in descr. of shape of the 4 canine teeth). — See also **mālikā.**

Maḷorikā (f.) [prob. dialectical for māḷaka: cp. mallaka] a stand, (tripod) for a bowl, formed of sticks Vin II.124 (=daṇḍ' ādhāraka Bdhgh on p. 318).

Masa in line "āsadañ ca masañ jaṭaŋ" at J VI.328 is to be comb^d with ca, and read as camasañ, i. e. a ladle for sacrificing (C.: aggi-dahanaŋ).

Masati [mṛś] to touch: only in cpd. āmasati. The root is expl^d at Dhtp 305 as "āmasana." Another root masu [mṛś ?] is at Dhtm 444 given in meaning "macchera." Does this refer to Sk. mṛṣā (=P. micchā)? Cp. māsati, māsana etc.

Masāṇa (nt.) [etym. ? prob. provincial & local] a coarse cloth of interwoven hemp and other materials D I.166; M I.308, 345; A I.241, 295; Pug 55. At all passages as a dress worn by certain ascetics.

Masāraka [fr. masāra ?] a kind of couch (mañca) or long-chair; enum^d under the 4 kinds of mañcā at Vin IV.40. — See also Vin II.149; IV.357 (where expl^d as: mañca-pāde vijjhitvā tattha aṭṭaniyo pavesetvā kato: made by boring a hole into the feet of the bed & putting through a notched end); VvA 8, 9.

Masāragalla (m. & nt.) [cp. Sk. masāra emerald+galva crystal & musāragalva] a precious stone, cat's eye; also called kabara-maṇi (e. g. VvA 304). It occurs in stereotyped enumⁿ of gems at Vin II.238 (where it is said to be found in the Ocean)=Miln 267; and at Miln 118, where it always stands next to lohitanka. The same combⁿ (with lohit.) is found at Vv 36^3; 78^3=81^3; 84^{15}.

Masi [cp. Class. Sk. maṣi & masi] I. the fine particles of ashes, in angara° charcoal-dust VvA 67=DhA III.309; (agginā) **masiŋ karoti** to reduce to powder (by fire), to burn to ashes, turn to dust S II.88=IV.197=A I.204=II.199. — 2. soot J I.483 (ukkhali° soot on a pot).

Masūraka [connected with masāraka] a bolster J IV.87; VI.185.

Massu [Vedic śmaśru] the beard D II.42; Pug 55; J IV.159. -parūḷha° with long-grown beard DA I.263; bahala° thick-bearded J v.42.
 -kamma beard-dressing J III.114; DhA I.253. **-karaṇa** shaving DhA I.253; DA I.137. **-kutti** [m.+ *kḷpti] beard-trimming J III.314 (C.=°kiriyā).

Massuka (adj.) [fr. massu] bearded; a° beardless (of a woman) J II.185.

Maha (m. & nt.) [fr. **mah,** see mahati & cp. Vedic nt. mahas] I. worthiness, venerableness Miln 357. — 2. a (religious) festival (in honour of a Saint, as an act of worship) Mhvs 33, 26 (vihārassa mahamhi, loc.); VvA 170 (thūpe ca mahe kate), 200 (id.). **mahā°** a great festival Mhvs 5, 94. **bodhi°** festival of the Bo tree J IV.229. **vihāra°** festival held on the building of a monastery J I.94; VvA 188. **hatthi°** a festival called the elephant f. J IV.95.

Mahati [mah; expl^d by Dhtp 331 as "pūjāyaŋ"] to honour, revere Vv 47^{11} (pot. med. I pl. mahemase, cp. Geiger, *P.Gr.* § 129; expl^d as "mahāmase pūjāmase" at VvA 203). Caus. **mahāyati** in same sense: ger. mahāyitvāna (poetical) J IV.236. — Pass. **mahīyati** Vv 62^1 (=pūjiyati VvA 258); 64^{22} (ppr. mahīyamāna= pūjiyamāna VvA 282). pp. mahita.

Mahatta (nt.) [fr. mahat° cp. Sk. mahattva] greatness J v.331 (=seṭṭhatta C.); Vism 132, 232 sq.; VbhA 278 (Satthu°, jāti°, sabrahmacārī°); DA I.35; VvA 191.

Mahant (adj.) [Vedic mahant, which by Grassmann is taken as ppr. to **mah,** but in all probability the n is an original suffix. — cp. Av. mazant, Sk. compar. mahīyān; Gr. μέγας (compar. μείζων), Lat. magnus, Goth. mikils=Ohg. mihhil=E. much] great, extensive, big; important, venerable. — nom. mahā Sn 1008; Mhvs 22, 27. Shortened to maha in cpd. pitāmaha (following a- decl.) (paternal) grandfather PvA 41; & mātāmaha (maternal) grandfather (q. v.). — instr. mahatā Sn 1027. — pl. nom. **mahantā** Sn 578 (opp. daharā). — loc. **mahati** Miln 254. — f. **mahī**— I. one of the 5 great rivers (Np.). — 2. the earth. See separately. — nt. **mahantaŋ** used as adv., meaning "very much, greatly" J v.170; DhA IV.232. Also in cpd. mahantabhāva greatness, loftiness, sublimity DhsA 44. — Compar. **mahantatara** DhA II.63, and with dimin. suffix °ka J III.237. — The regular paraphrase of mahā in the Niddesa is "agga, seṭṭha, visiṭṭha, pāmokkha, uttama, pavara," see Nd^2 502.
 Note on mahā & cpds. — A. In certain cpds. the combⁿ with mahā (mah°) has become so established & customary (often through politeness in using mahā° for the simple term), that the cpd. is felt as an inseparable unity and a sort of "antique" word, in which the 2nd part either does not occur any more by itself or only very rarely, as **mah' aṇṇava,** which is more freq. than aṇṇava; **mah' âbhisakka,** where abhisakka does not occur by itself; cp. **mahânubhāva, mahiddhika,**

mahaggha; or is obscured in its derivation through constant use with mahā, like mahesī [mah + esī, or īsī], mahesakkha [mah + esakkha]; mahallaka [mah + *ariyaka]; mahāmatta. Cp. E. great-coat, Gr. ἀρχ° in ἀρχ-ιατρός = Ger. arzt. Only a limited selection of cpd.-words is given, consisting of more frequent or idiomatic terms. Practically *any* word may be enlarged & emphasized in meaning by prefixing mahā. Sometimes a mahā° lends to special events a standard (historical) significance, so changing the common word into a noun proper, e. g. Mah-âbhinikkhammana, Mahāpavāraṇa. — B. Mahā occurs in cpds. in (a) an elided form mah before a & i; (b) shortened to maha° before g, d, p, b with doubling of these consonants; (c) in the regular form mahā°: usually before consonants, sometimes before vowels. This form is contracted with foll. i to e and foll. u to o. In the foll. list of cpds. we have arranged the material according to these bases.

mah°: -aggha very costly, precious Pug 34; Mhvs 27, 35; PvA 77, 87; Sdhp 18. -agghatā costliness, great value Pug 34, Sdhp 26. -aṇṇava the (great) ocean Mhvs 19, 17. -atthiya (for °atthika) of great importance or use, very useful, profitable J III.368. -andhakāra deep darkness Vism 417. -assāsin fully refreshed, very comfortable S I.81.

maha°: -ggata "become great," enlarged, extensive, fig. lofty, very great M I.263; II.122; A II.63, 184; III.18; VvA 155; J V.113; Dhs 1020 (trsl^n: "having a wider scope") Vbh 16, 24, 62, 74, 126, 270, 326; Tikp. 45; Vism 410, 430 sq. (°ārammaṇa); VbhA 154 (id.), 159 (°citta); DhsA 44. See on term *Cpd.* 4, 12, 55, 101⁴; [cp. BSk. mahadgata Divy 227]. -gghasa eating much, greedy, gluttonous A IV.92; P III.1¹¹ (= bahubhojana PvA 175); Miln 288; Dh 325 (cp. DhA IV.16). -ddhana having great riches (often comb^d with mahābhoga) Dh 123; J IV.15, 22. -pphala much fruit; adj. bearing much fruit, rich in result A IV.60, 237 sq.; Sn 191, 486; Dh 312, 356 sq. -bbala (a) a strong force, a great army Mhvs 10, 68 (v. l., T. has mahā-bala); (b) of great strength, mighty, powerful J III.114; Mhvs 23, 92; 25, 9. -bbhaya great fear, terror S I.37; Sn 753, 1032, 1092, cp. Nd² 501.

mahā°: -anas kitchen Mhvs 5, 27 (spurious stanza). -anasa kitchen J II.361; III.314; V.368; VI.349; DhA III.309; ThA 5. -anila a gale Mhvs 3, 42. -ānisaṇsa deserving great praise (see s. v.), [cp. BSk. mahānuśaṇsa MVastu III.221]. -ānubhāva majesty, adj. wonderful, splendid J I.194; J VI.331; Pv III.3¹; PvA 117, 136, 145, 272. -aparādhika very guilty J I.114. -abhinikkhamana the great renunciation DhA I.85. -abhisakka [abhi + śak] very powerful Th I, 1111. -amacca chief minister Mhvs 19, 12. -araha costly Mhvs 3, 21; 5, 75; 27, 39; PvA 77, 141, 160.

mahā°: -alasa great sloth DhA III.410. -avīci the great Purgatory Avīci, freq. -isi in poetry for mahesi at J V.321. -upaṭṭhāna great state room (of a king) SnA 84. -upāsikā a great female follower (of the Buddha) VvA 5. -karuṇā great compassion DhA I.106, 367. -kāya a great body Miln 16. -gaṇa a great crowd or community DhA I.154. -gaṇḍa a large tumour VbhA 104. -gedha great greed Sn 819; Nd¹ 151. -cāga great liberality, adj. munificent Mhvs 27, 47. As °paricāga at SnA 295 (= mahādāna). -jana a great crowd, collectively for "the people," a multitude PvA 6, 19, 78; Mhvs 3, 13. -taṇha (adj.) very thirsty J II.441. -tala "great surface," the large flat roof on the top of a palace (= upari-pāsāda-tala) J VI.40. -dāna (see under dāna) the great gift (to the bhikkhus) a special great offering of food & presents given by laymen to the Buddha & his followers as a meritorious deed, usually lasting for a week or more Mhvs 27, 46; PvA 111, 112. -dhana (having) great wealth PvA 3, 78. -naraka (a) great Hell, see naraka. -nāga a great elephant Dh 312; DhA IV.4. -nāma N. of a plant Vin I.185; II.267. -niddā deep sleep PvA 47. -nibbāna the great N. DhA IV.110. -niraya (a) great hell SnA 309, 480; PvA 52. See Niraya & cp. Kirfel, *Kosmographie* 199, 200. -nīla sapphire VvA 111. -pañña very wise D III.158; A III.244; Dh 352; DhA IV.71. -patha high road D I.102; Sn 139; Dh 58; Vism 235; DhA I.445. -paduma a great lotus J V.39; also a vast number & hence a name of a purgatory, cp. Divy 67; Kirfel, *Kosmographie* 205. -pitā grandfather PvA 107. -purisa a great man, a hero, a man born to greatness, a man destined by fate to be a Ruler or a Saviour of the World. A being thus favoured by fate possesses (32) marks (lakkhaṇāni) by which people recognise his vocation or prophesy his greatness. A detailed list of these 32 marks (which probably date back to mythological origin & were originally attributed to Devas) is found at D II.17, 19, passim. — D III.287; Sn 1040 sq.; Dh 352; Miln 10; SnA 184, 187 sq., 223, 258, 357, 384 sq.; *°lakkhaṇāni*: D I.88, 105, 116; Sn 549, 1000 sq.; Vism 234; VvA 315; DhA II.41. -bhūta usually in pl. °bhūta(ni) (cattāro & cattā) the 4 great elements (see bhūta), being paṭhavī, āpo, tejo, vāyo, D I.76; Nd¹ 266; Vbh 13, 70 sq.; Vism 366 sq.; Tikp 39, 56 sq., 74 sq., 248 sq.; VbhA 42, 169, 253. — See *Cpd.* 154, 268 sq., & cp. dhātu I. -bhoga great wealth, adj. wealthy PvA 3, 78. -maccha a great fish, sea-monster J I.483. -mati very wise, clever Mhvs 14, 22; 19, 84 (f. °ī); 33, 100 (pl. °ī). -matta [cp. Sk. mahāmātra] a king's chief minister, alias Prime Minister, "who was the highest Officer-of-State and real Head of the Executive" (Banerjea, *Public Administration in Ancient India*, 1916). His position is of such importance, that he even ranges as a rājā or king: Vin III.47 (rājā . . . akkhadassā mahāmattā ye vā pana chejjabhejjaṇ anusāsanti ete rājāno nāma). — *Note.* An acc. sg. mahā-mattānaṇ we find at A I.154 (formed after the prec. rājānaṇ). — Vin I.74 (where two ranks are given: senā-nāyakā m.-mattā the m. of defence, and vohārikā m.-m. those of law); D I.7; III.88; III.64 (here with Ep. khattiya); A I.154, 252, 279; III.128; Vin IV.224; Vism 121; VbhA 312 (in simile of two m.), 340; PvA 169. Cp. Fick. *Sociale Gliederung* 92, 99, 101. -muni great seer Sn 31. -megha a big cloud, thunder cloud M II.117; Sn 30; Vism 417. -yañña the great sacrifice D I.138 sq., 141 (cp. A II.207≈). -yasa great fame Vv 21⁶; Mhvs 5, 22. -ranga [cp. Sk. m.-rajana], safflower, used for dyeing Vin I.185 (sandals); II 267 (cloaks). -rājā great king, king, very freq.: see rājā. -rukkha a great tree Vism 413 (literally); Miln 254 (id.), otherwise the plant euphorbia tortilis (cp. Zimmer, *Altind. Leben* 129). -latā (-pasādhana) a lady's parure called "great creeper" DhA I.392; VvA 165 (-pilandhana); same SnA 520. -vātapāna main window DhA IV.203. -vīṇā a great lute Vism 354; VbhA 58. -vīra (great) hero Sn 543, 562. -satta "the great being" or a Bodhisatta VvA 137 (v. l. SS. bodhisatta). [Cp. BSk. mahāsattva, e. g. Jtm 32]. -samudda the sea, the ocean Mhvs 19, 18; Vism 403; SnA 30, 371; PvA 47. -sara a great lake; usually as satta-mahāsarā the 7 great lakes of the Himavant (see sara), enum^d e. g. at Vism 416. -sāra (of) great sap, i. e. great wealth, adj. very rich J I.463 (°kula, perhaps to be read mahāsāla-kula). -sāla (adj.) having great halls, Ep. of rich people (especially brāhmaṇas) D I.136, 235; III.16, 20; J II.272 (°kula); IV.237 (id.), 325 (id.); V.227 (id.); Pug 56; VbhA 519; DhA III.193. -sāvaka [cp. BSk. mahāśrāvaka Divy 489] a great disciple Vism 98 (asīti °ā); DhA II.93. -senagutta title of a high official (Chancellor of the Exchequer ?) J V.115; VI.2. -hatthi a large elephant M I.184 (°pada elephant's foot, as the largest of all animal feet), referred to as simile (°opama) at Vism 243, 347, 348.

mahi° [mah' i°]: -iccha full of desire, lustful, greedy A IV.229; Th 1, 898; It 91; J I.8; II.441. -icchatā arrogance, ostentatiousness A IV.280; VbhA 472. -iddhika [mahā + iddhi + ka] of great power, always comb[d] with mah-ânubhāva to denote great influence, high position & majesty Vin I.31; II.193; III.101; D I.78, 180 (devatā), 213; S I.145 sq.; II.155, 274 sq., 284 sq.; IV.323; V.265, 271 sq., 288 sq.; A V.129; J VI.483 (said of the Ocean); PvA 6, 136, 145. -inda (ghosa) lit. the roar of the Great Indra, Indra here to be taken in his function as sky (rain) god, thus: the thunder of the rain-god Th 1, 1108. [Cp. BSk. māhendra in °*bhavana* "the abode of the Great Indra," and *varṣa* "the rain of the Gr. I." (here as rain-god), both at AvŚ I.210]. -issāsa [Sk. maheṣvāsa] great in the art of the bow, a great archer S I.185; DhA I.358.

mahe° [mahā+i]: -esakkha [mahā+īsa+khyaŋ; fr. īś] possessing great power or authority A II.204; III.244; Nd[2] 503[2]; Vism 419; Sdhp 511. The BSk. form is maheṣākhya evidently differing in its etymology. The P. etym. rests on the same grounds as esitatta in mahesi DhA IV.232. -esi [mahā+isi; Sk. maharṣi] a great Sage A II.26; Sn 208, 481, 646, 915, 1057, 1061; Th 1, 1132; 2, 149; Dh 422 (expl[d] at DhA IV.232 as "mahantaŋ sīla-kkhandh' ādīnaŋ esitatta m." cp. the similar expl[n] at Nd[2] 503); Nd[1] 343; Vism 505; VbhA 110; PvA 1. -esiyā=mahesī J VI.483. -esī [in P. to be taken as mah+iś, as f. to īsa, but in Sk. (Vedic) as f. of mahiṣa, buffalo] chief queen, king's first wife, king's consort; also the wife of a great personage J II.410; V.45; VI.425; Pug 56; Mhvs 2, 22 (pl. mahesiyo); VvA 184 (sixteen). Usually as agga-mahesī, e. g. J I.262; III.187, 393; V.88. -esitta state of chief consort, queenship J V.443; Pv II.13[10]; ThA 37; VvA 102. -eseyya =°esitta J V.91.

-maho [mahā+u, or+o]: -ogha the great flood (see ogha) Sn 4, 945; Dh 47, 287; DhA III.433. -odadhi the (great) ocean, the sea Sn 720, 1134; Miln 224; Mhvs 18, 8. -odara big belly J VI.358 (addressing a king's minister). -odika full of water, having much water; deep, full (of a river) Sn 319; J II.159; Miln 346. -oraga [m+uraga] a great snake J V.165.

Mahantatā (f.) [fr. mahant°] greatness DhA II.62. At M III.24 the spelling is mahattatā (tt misread for nt?), at M I.184 however mahantatta (nt.).

Mahallaka (adj. n.) [a distorted mah-ariyaka>ayyaka>allaka; cp. ayyaka] old, venerable, of great age; an old man D I.90 (opp. taruṇa), 94, 114, 247; Sn 313, 603; Nd[2] 261 (vuḍḍha m. andhagata etc.) J IV.482 (opp. dahara young); Vv 46[1] (=mahanto VvA 199); DhA I.7, 278; II.4, 55, 91; SnA 313. Compar. mahallakatara DhA II.18. — f. mahallikā an old woman Miln 16; Mhvs 21, 27; VvA 105; PvA 149 (=addhagata). — [The BSk. form is mahalla, e. g. Divy 329, 520.]

Mahikā (f.) [cp. *Sk. mahikā] fog, frost, cold (=himaŋ DhsA 317) Vin II.295=Miln 273; Sn 669; Miln 299; VvA 134 (fog). — As mahiyā at A II.53.

Mahita [pp. of mahati or mahīyati] honoured, revered M II.110; Miln 278; Sdhp 276.

Mahanīya (adj.) [grd. of mahati] praiseworthy VvA 97.

Mahilā (f.) [*Sk. mahilā] woman, female Vin II.281 (°titthe at the women's bathing place); J I.188; Dpvs IX.4; ThA 271.

Mahisa, Mahīsa, Mahiŋsa [cp. Vedic mahiṣa, an enlarged form of mahā; the P. etym. evidently to be connected with mahā+īś, because of mahisa>mahiŋsa] a buffalo. —mahisa: D I.6 (°yuddha b.-fight), 9; J III.26 (vana° wild b.); Mhvs 25, 36 (T. māhisaŋ). —mahīsa J VI.110. —mahiŋsa Vism 191, & in Np. Mahiŋsaka-maṇḍala the Andhra country J I.356, cp. Mahiŋsaka-raṭṭha VbhA 4; as Mahisa-maṇḍala at Mhvs 12, 29. — *Note*. The P. pop. etym. is propounded by Bdhgh as "mahiyaŋ setī ti mahiso" (he lies on the ground, that is why he is a buffalo) DhsA 62.

Mahī (f.) [f. of **mah**, base of mahant, Vedic mahī] the earth (lit. Great One) Mhvs 5, 266; Sdhp 424, 472; loc. mahiyā Miln 128; mahiyaŋ DhsA 62. — *Note*. As mahī is only found in very late P. literature, it must have been re-introduced from Sk. sources, and is *not* a direct correspondent of Vedic mahī.

-tala the ground (of the earth) Mhvs 5, 54. -dhara mountain Miln 343; Mhvs 14, 3; 28, 22 (v. l. mahin°). -pa king (of the earth) Mhvs 14, 22. -pati king Mhvs 5, 48; 33, 32. -pāla king Mhvs 4, 38; 5, 265. -ruha tree ("growing out of the earth") Mhvs 14, 18, 18, 19.

Mā (indecl.) [cp. Vedic mā, Gr. μή] prohibition particle: not, do not, let us hope not, I wish that . . . not [cp. Lat. utinam & ne]. Constructed with various tenses, e. g. 1. with *aor.* (prohibitive tense): mā evaŋ akattha do not thus DhA I.7; mā abhaṇi speak not Pv I.3[3]; mā cintayittha do not worry DhA I.12; mā parihāyi I hope he will not go short (or be deprived) of . . . M I.444; mā bhāyi fear not J II.159; mā mariŋsu I hope they will not die J III.55; mā (te) rucci may it not please (you), i. e. please do not Vin II.198; mā evaŋ ruccittha id. DhA I.13. — 2. with *imper.*: mā gaccha J I.152; mā detha J III.275. mā ghāta do not kill: see māghāta. — 3. with *pot.*: mā anuyuñjetha Dh 27; mā bhuñjetha let him not eat Mhvs 25, 113; mā vadetha J VI.364. — 4. with *indic. pres.*: mā paṭilabhati A V.194. — A peculiar use is found in phrase ānemi mā ānemi shall I bring it *or not?* J VI.334. — 5. mā=na (simple negation) in māsakkhimhā we could not Vin III.23.

-Mā [the short form of māsa, direct der[n] fr. **mā**: see mināti] see puṇṇa-mā.

Māgadha [fr. Magadha] scent-seller, (lit. "from Magadha") Pv II.9[37] (=gandhin PvA 127).

Māgadhaka (nt.) [māgadha+ka, lit. "from Magadha"] garlic Vin IV.259 (lasuṇaŋ nāma māgadhakaŋ vuccati).

Māgavika [guṇa- form to *mṛga=P. miga; Sk. mārgavika] a deerstalker, huntsman A II.207; Pug 56; Miln 364, 412; PvA 207.

Māghāta (nt.) [lit. mā ghāta "kill not"] the injunction not to kill, non-killing order (with ref. to the killing of animals J III.428 (°bheri, the drum announcing this order); IV.115; VI.346 (uposatha°).

Māngalya (adj.) [fr. mangala] auspicious, fortunate, bringing about fulfilment of wishes J VI.179.

Māṇava [cp. *Sk. māṇava] a youth, young man, esp. a young Brahmin Sn 1022, 1027, 1028; J IV.391 (brāhmaṇa°); DA I.36 =satto pi coro pi taruṇo pi; DhA I.89. pl. māṇavā men Th 2, 112. — The spelling māṇava occurs at Sn 456, 589, & Pv I.8[7] (=men Th II.112; kumāra PvA 41).

Māṇavaka [fr. māṇava] a young man, youth a Brahmin Miln 101; in general: young, e. g. nāga° a young serpent J III.276; f. °ikā a Brahmin girl J I.290; Miln 101; nāga° a young female serpent J III.275; DhA III.232.

Mātanga [cp. Epic Sk. mātanga, dial.] an elephant Dh 329, 330 (here as Ep. of nāga); J III.389; VI.47; Vv 43[9]; Miln 368. — 2. a man of a low class [cp. BSk. mātangī Divy 397] SnA 185 sq. (as Np.).

Mātar (f.) [Vedic mātā, stem mātar°, Av. mātar-, Gr. μήτηρ (Doric μάτηρ) Lat. māter, Oir. māthir, Ohg. muoter, Ags. modor=mother; Cp. further Gr. μήτρα uterus, Lat. mātrix id., Sk. mātṛkā mother, grandmother, Ger. mieder corset. From Idg. *ma, onomat. part., cp. "mamma"] mother. — *Cases*: nom. sg.

mātā Sn 296; Dh 43; J IV.463; V.83; VI.117; Nd² 504 (def. as janikā); gen. mātu Th 1, 473; Vin I.17; J I.52; mātuyā J I.53; Mhvs 10, 80; PvA 31; and mātāya J I.62; dat. mātu Mhvs 9, 19; acc. mātaraŋ Sn 60, 124; Dh 294; instr. mātarā Th 2, 212; loc. mātari Dh 284 — pl. does not occur. In combⁿ with pitā father, mātā always precedes the former, thus mātā-pitaro (pl.) "mother & father" (see below). —mātito (abl.-adv.) from the mother's side (cp. pitito) D I.113; A III.151; PvA 29. — On mātā in simile see *J.P.T.S.* 1907, 122; cp. Vism 321 (simile of a mother's solicitude for her children). Similarly the pop. etym. of mātā is given, with "mamāyatī ti mātā" at VbhA 107. — The 4 bases of m. in compⁿ are: mātā°, māti°, mātu°, & matti°. — 1. mātā°: **-pitaro** mother & father D III.66, 188 sq.; Sn 404; Miln 12. See also pitā. **-pitika** having mother & father DhA II.2. **-pitiṭṭhāna** place of m. & f. DhA II.95. **-pettika** having m. & f., of m. & f. Nd² 385 (nāma-gotta). **-petti-bhāra** supporting one's m. & f. S I.228; J I.202; VI.498. **-maha** maternal grandfather J IV.146; DhA I.346. — 2. māti°: **-devatā** protector or guardian of one's mother J III.422 (gloss: mātu-devatā viya). **-pakkha** the mother's side DhA I.4 (+pitipakkha). **-posaka** supporting one's m. J III.422 (v. l. mātu°). — 3. mātu°: **-upaṭṭhāna** (spelt mātupaṭṭh°) reverence towards one's m. DhA IV.14. **-kucchi** m's womb D II.12; Vism 560 (°gata); VbhA 96; DhA I.127. **-gāma** "grex feminarum," womanfolk, women (collectively cp. Ger. frauen-zimmer) A II.126; Vin IV.175; J I.201; III.90; A II.126; Vin IV.175; J I.201; III.90, 530 (pl. °gāmā p. 531); Pug 68; SnA 355; PvA 271; VvA 77. **-ghāta** & (usually) °ka a matricide (+pitu-ghātaka; see abhiṭhāna) Vin I.168, 320; Miln 310; Tikp 167 sq.; VbhA 425. **-ghātikamma** matricide Tikp. 281. **-bhūta** having been his mother PvA 78. **-mattin** (see matta¹ 4) whatever is a mother S IV.110 (°īsu mātucittaŋ upaṭṭhapeti foster the thought of mother towards whatever is a mother, where in sequence with bhaginī-mattin & dhītumattin). **-hadaya** a mother's heart PvA 63. — 4. matti°: see matti-sambhava.

-Mātika (adj.) [fr. mātā, Sk. mātṛka] -mother; in mata° one whose mother is dead, lit. a "dead-mother-ed," J II.131; III.213. Also neg. amātika without a mother J V.251.

Mātikā (f.) [*Sk. mātṛkā] 1. a water course Vism 554 (°ātikkamaka); Mhvs 35, 96; 37, 50; SnA 500 (=sobbha); DhA II.141 (its purpose: "ito c' ito ca udakaŋ haritvā attano sassa-kammaŋ sampādenti"); VvA 301. — 2. tabulation, register, tabulated summary, condensed contents, esp. of philosophical parts of the Canonical books in the Abhidhamma; used in Vinaya in place of Abhidhamma Piṭaka; probably the original form of that (later) Piṭaka Vin I.119, 337; II.8 [cp. semantically in similar sense Lat. mātrix = E. matric, i. e. register. In BSk. mātrikā Divy 18, 333] A I.117 (Dhamma-dhara, Vinaya-dhara, Mātikā-dhara; here equivalent to Abhidhamma); Vism 312 (so pañcavasso hutvā dve mātikā paguṇaŋ katvā pavāretvā); SnA 15; KhA 37, 99, 117.

-nikkhepa putting down of a summary, tabulation Vism 536, 540. The summary itself is sometimes called nikkhepa, e. g. the 4th part of the Atthasālinī (DhsA pp. 343-409) is called **nikkhepa-kaṇḍa** or chapter of the summary; similarly **m.-nikkhepa vāra** at Tikp. 11.

Mātiya (adj. n.) [the diæretic form of macca, used in verse, cp. Sk. martya & Vedic (poetical) martia] (a) mortal J VI.100 (C. macca; gloss māṇava).

Mātu° see mātā.

Mātuka (nt.) [cp. Sk. māṭṛka, fr. mātṛ = mātar] "genetrix," matrix, origin, cause Th 1, 612.

Mātucchā (f.) [Sk. mātṛ-ṣvasā] mother's sister, maternal aunt Vin II.254, 256; J IV.390; Miln 240. **-°putta** aunt's son, male first cousin (from mother's sister's side) S II.281; Ud 24; DhA I.119. Cp. mātula-dhītā.

Mātula [cp. Epic Sk. mātula & semantically Lat. matruus, i. e. one who belongs to the mother] a mother's brother, an uncle J I.225; DhA I.15; PvA 58, 60.

-dhītā (the complement of mātucchā-putta) uncle's daughter, female first cousin (from mother's brother's side) J II.119; DhA III.290; PvA 55.

Mātulaka = mātula DhA I.182.

Mātulānī (f.) [Sk. mātulānī, semantically cp. Lat. matertera] a mother's brother's wife, an aunt J I.387; IV.184; PvA 55, 58.

Mātulunga (nt.) [cp. Class. Sk. mātulunga; dialectical ?] a citron J III.319 (= mella; v. l. bella).

Mādisa (adj.) [Epic & Class. Sk. mādṛś & mādṛśa, maŋ + **dṛś**] one like me Sn 482; Mhvs 5, 193; VvA 207; DhA I.284; PvA 76, 123.

Māna [late Vedic & Epic Sk. māna, fr. **man**, orig. meaning perhaps "high opinions" (i. e. No. 2); hence "pride" (No. 1). Def. of root see partly under māneti, partly under mināti] 1. pride, conceit, arrogance (cittassa uṇṇati Nd¹ 80; Vbh 350). Māna is one of the Saññojanas. It is one of the principle obstacles to Arahantship. A detailed analysis of māna in *tenfold* aspect is given at Nd¹ 80 = Nd² 505; ending with defⁿ "māno maññanā . . . ketukamyatā" etc. (cp. Vbh 350 & see under mada). On term see also Dhs § 1116; *Dhs trsl.* 298 (=² 275) sq. — D III.234; S I.4; Sn 132, 370; 469, 537, 786, 889, 943, Dh 74, 150, 407; Nd¹ 298; Pug 18; Vbh 345 sq., 353 sq., 383 (7 fold), 389 (9 fold); VbhA 486 sq. ("seyyo 'ham asmī ti" etc.); Tikp 166, 278; DhA III.118, 252; Sdhp 500, 539. —**asmi°** pride of self, as real egoism D III.273. — 2. honour, respect J V.331 (+pūjā). Usually in cpd. **bahumāna** great respect Mhvs 20, 46; PvA 50. Also as **māni°** in compⁿ with karoti: see **mānikata.** Cp. vi°, sam°.

-âtimāna pride & conceit, very great (self-) pride, or all kinds of conceit (see 10 fold māna at Nd¹ 80 = Nd² 505) D III.86; Sn 245, 830, 862; Nd¹ 170, 257. **-atthe** at Th 1, 214 read mânatthe = mā anatthe. **-ânusaya** the predisposition or bad tendency of pride M I.486; D III.254, 282; Sn 342. Cp. mamankāra. **-âbhisamaya** full grasp (i. e. understanding) of pride (with sammā°) M I.122 (which Kern. *Toev.* s. v. interprets wrongly as "waanvoorstelling"); S IV.205 sq., 399; Sn 342 (= mānassa abhisamayo khayo vayo pahānaŋ SnA 344). **-jātika** proud by nature J I.88. **-thaddha** stubborn in pride, stiff-necked J I.88, 224. **-da** inspiring respect Mhvs 33, 82. **-mada** (-matta) (drunk with) the intoxicating draught of pride J II.259; PvA 86. **-saññojana** the fetter of pride or arrogance D III.254; Dhs 1116 = 1233. See under saññojana & cp. formulæ under mada 2. **-satta** cleaving to conceit Sn 473. **-salla** the sting or dart of pride Nd¹ 59 (one of the 7 sallāni, viz. rāga, dosa, moha etc., expldᵈ in detail on p. 413. See other series with similar terms & māna at Nd² p. 237 s. v. rāga).

Māna² (nt.) [fr. **mā**: see mināti; Vedic māna has 2 meanings, viz. "measure," and "building" (cp. māpeti)] 1. measure Vin III.149 (abbhantarima inner, bāhirima outer); DA I.140. **-°kūṭa** cheating in measure, false measure Pug 58; PvA 278. — 2. a certain measure, a Māna (cp. mānikā & manaŋ) J I.468 (aḍḍha° half a M., according to C. equal to 8 nāḷis).

Mānatta (nt.) [a doubtful word, prob. corrupted out of something else, maybe omānatta, if taken as der. fr. māna¹. If however taken as belonging to māna² as an abstr. der., it might be expl[d] as "measuring, taking measures," which suits the context letter. The BSk. form is still more puzzling, viz. mānāpya "something pleasant": Mvyut § 265] a sort of penance, attached to the commission of a sanghādisesa offence DhsA 399 (+parivāsa). °ŋ deti to inflict penance on somebody Vin II.7 (+parivāsaŋ deti); IV.225. mānatt' âraha deserving penance Vin II.55.162 (parivāsika+). See on term *Vin. Texts* II.397.

Mānana (nt.) & **Mānanā** (f.) [fr. māna¹] paying honour or respect; reverence, respect S I.66; J II.138; Pug 19, 22; Miln 377 (with sakkāra, vandana, pūjana & apaciti); Dhs 1121; DhsA 373. — Cp. vi°, sam°.

Mānava see **Māṇava.**

Mānavant (adj.) [fr. māna¹] possessed of pride, full of conceit; neg. a° not proud Th I, 1222.

Mānasa (nt.) [a secondary formation fr. manas=mano, already Vedic lit. "belonging to mind"] intention, purpose, mind (as active force), mental action. Almost equivalent to mano Dhs § 6. In later language mānasa is quite synonymous with hadaya. The word, used absolutely, is more a t. t. in philosophy than a living part of the language. It is more frequent as -° in adj. use, where its connection with mano is still more felt. Its absolute use probably originated from the latter use. — DhsA 140 (=mano); Vbh 144 sq. (in definition of viññāṇa as cittaŋ, mano, mānasaŋ, hadayaŋ etc.: see mano II 3); DhA II.12 (paradāre mānasaŋ na bandhissāmi "shall have no intention towards another's wife," i. e. shall not desire another's wife); Mhvs 4, 6 (sabbesaŋ hita-mānasā with the intention of common welfare); 32, 56 (rañño hāsesi mānasaŋ gladdened the heart of the king). — As adj. (-°): being of such & such a mind, having a . . . mind, with a . . . heart; like: **ādīna°** with his mind in danger S V.74 (+apatiṭṭhita-citta); **uggata°** lofty-minded VvA 217; **pasanna°** with settled (peaceful) mind Sn 402 and frequently; **mūḷha°** infatuated Mhvs 5, 239; **rata°** PvA 19; **sañcodita°** urged (in her heart) PvA 68; **soka-santatta°** with a heart burning with grief PvA 38.

Mānasāna (adj.) [fr. mānasa, secondary formation] = mānasa in adj. use Sn 63 (rakkhita°).

Mānassin (adj. n.) [prob. fr. manassin (*manasvin) under influence of māna. Cp. similar formation mānavant] proud Vin II.183 (expl[d] by Bdhgh in a popular way as "mana-ssayino māna-nissitā"). The corresponding passage at J I.88 reads māna-jātikā māna-tthaddhā.

Mānikata [pp. of a verb māni-karoti, which stands for māna-karoti, and is substituted for mānita after analogy of purakkhata, of same meaning] lit. "held in high opinion," i. e. honoured, worshipped S II.119 (garukata m. pūjita).

Mānikā (f.) [cp. māna² 2] a weight, equal to 4 Doṇas SnA 476 (catudoṇaŋ mānikā). Cp. BSk. mānikā, e. g. Divy 293 sq.

Mānita [pp. of māneti] revered, honoured Ud 73 (sakkata m. pūjita apacita). — A rather singular by-form is mānikata (q. v.).

Mānin (adj.) (-°) [fr. mana¹] proud (of) Sn 282 (samaṇa°), 889 (paripuṇṇa°); Dh 63 (paṇḍita° proud of his cleverness, cp. DhA II.30); J I.454 (atireka°); III.357 (paṇḍita°); Sdhp 389, 417. — f. māninī Mhvs 20, 4 (rūpa° proud of her beauty).

Mānusa (adj. n.) [cp. Vedic mānuṣa; fr. same base (manus) as manussa] 1. (adj.) human Sn 301 (bhoga); It 94 (kāmā dibbā ca mānusā); Pv II.9²¹ (m. deha); 9⁵⁶ (id.). —amānusa divine Vv 35⁶; Pv II.12²⁰; ghostly (=superhuman) Pv IV.3⁶; f. amānusī Pv III.7.⁹ — 2. (n. *m.*) a human being, a man Mhvs 15, 64; f. mānusī a (human) woman J IV.231; Pv II.4¹. —amānusa a superhuman being Pv IV.1⁵⁷. — pl. mānusā men Sn 361, 644; Pv II.11⁷. As *nt.* in collective sense=mankind Pv II.11³ (v. l. mānussaŋ; C.=manussaloka).

Mānusaka=mānusa, viz. 1. (adj.) human: A I.213 (sukhaŋ); Sn 524 (brahma-khettaŋ); Dh 417 (yogaŋ= m. kāyaŋ DhA IV.225); Vv 35⁵; J I.138 (kāmā). — f. manusikā Vism 407. — 2. a human being, man Pv IV.1⁵⁷. Also nt. (collectively) pl. mānusakāni human beings, men DhA I.233.

Māneti [Caus. of **man**, cp. Sk. mānayati, Lat. moneo to admonish, Ger. mahnen, Ags. manian. The Dhtp 593 gives root as **mān** in meaning "pūjā"] to honour, revere, think highly of PvA 54 (aor. mānesuŋ, +garu-kariŋsu+pūjesuŋ). — pp. mānita.

Māpaka (-°) (adj. n.) [fr. māpeti] one who measures, only in doṇa° (a minister) measuring the d. revenue (of rice) J II.367, 381; DhA IV.88; and in dhañña° measuring corn or grain J III.542 (°kamma, the process of . . .); Vism 278 (in comparison).

Māpeti [Cuas. of **mā**, see mināti. The simplex mimite has the meaning of "erect, build" already in Vedic Sk.] 1. to build, construct S II.106 (nagaraŋ); Mhvs 6, 35 (id.); Vv 84⁵³; VvA 260. — 2. to create, bring about, make or cause to appear by supernatural power (in folkloristic literature, cp. nimmināti in same sense) J II.111 (sarīraŋ nāvaŋ katvā māpesi transformed into a ship); IV.274; Mhvs 28, 31 (maggaŋ caused a road to appear). — 3. to measure out (?), to declare (?), in a doubtful passage J IV.302, where a misreading is probable, as indicated by v. l. BB (samāpassiŋsu for T. tena amāpayiŋsu). Perhaps we should read tena-m-āsayiŋsu.

Māmaka (adj.) [fr. mama] lit. "mine," one who shows affection (not only for himself), making one's own, i.e. devoted to, loving Sn 806 (=Buddha°, Dhamma°, Sangha° Nd¹ 125; =mamāyamāna SnA 534), 927 (same expl[n] at Nd¹ 382); Miln 184 (ahiŋsayaŋ paraŋ loke piyo hohisi māmako ti). — **Buddha°** devoted to the B. J I.299; DhA I.206. f. °māmikā J III.182. — In voc. f. māmika at Th 2, 207 (cp. ThA 172) "mother," we may perhaps have an allusion to mā "mother" [cp. Sk. māma uncle, Lat. mamma mother, and mātā]. -amāmaka see sep.; this may also be taken as "not loving."

Māyā (f.) [cp. Vedic māyā. Suggestions as to etym. see Walde, *Lat. Wtb.* s. v. manticulor] 1. deceptive appearance, fraud, deceit, hypocrisy Sn 245, 328 (°kata deceit), 469, 537, 786, 941 (: māyā vuccati vañcanikā cariyā Nd¹ 422); Vbh 357, 361, 389; Miln 289; Vism 106 (+sātheyya, māna, pāpicchatā etc.), 479 (māyā viya viññāṇaŋ); VbhA 34 (in detail), 85, 493 (def.). Is not used in Pali Abhidhamma in a philosophical sense. — 2. mystic formula, magic, trick M I.381 (āvaṭṭanī m.). khattiya° the mystic formula of a kh. J VI.375; Miln 190; DhA I.166. In the sense of "illusion" often comb[d] with marīci, e. g. at J II.330; V.367; Nd² 680[A II]. — 3. jugglery, conjuring Miln 3. — On māyā in similes see *J.P.T.S.* 1907, 122; on term in general *Dhs trsl.*² 255 ("illusion"); *Expos.* 333, 468[n]. — As adj. in amāya (q. v.) & in bahu-māye rich in deceit SnA 351. — *Note.* In the word maŋ at KhA 123 (in pop. etym. of man-gala) the ed. of the text sees an acc. of mā which he takes to be a contracted form of māyā (=iddhi).

-**kāra** a conjurer, magician S III.142; Vism 366 (in comparison); VbhA 196.

Māyāvin (adj.) [fr. māyā, cp. Vedic māyāvin] deceitful, hypocritical D III.45, 246; Sn 89, 116, 357; Pug 19, 23; PvA 13. See also amāyāvin.

Māyu [*Sk. māyu] bile, gall Abhp 281.

Māra [fr. **mṛ**, later Vedic, māra killing, destroying, bringing death, pestilence, cp. Lat. mors death, morbus illness, Lith. māras death, pestilence] death; usually personified as Np. Death, the Evil one, the Tempter (the Buddhist Devil or Principle of Destruction). Sometimes the term māra is applied to the whole of the worldly existence, or the realm of rebirth, as opposed to Nibbāna. Thus the defⁿ of m. at Nd² 506 gives "kammâbhisankhāra-vasena paṭisandhiko **khandha-māro, dhātu°, āyatana°**. — Other general epithets of M. (quasi twin-embodiments) are given with **Kaṇha, Adhipati, Antaka, Namuci, Pamattabandhu** at Nd¹ 489 = Nd² 507; the two last ones also at Nd¹ 455. The usual standing epithet is pāpimā "the evil one," e. g. S I.103 sq. (the famous Māra-Saŋyutta: see Windisch, *Māra & Buddha*); Nd¹ 439; DhA IV.71 (Māravatthu) & freq. — See e. g. Sn 32, 422, 429 sq., 1095, 1103; Dh 7, 40, 46, 57, 105, 175, 274; Nd¹ 475; Vism 79, 228, 376; KhA 105; SnA 37, 44 sq., 225, 350 sq., 386 sq.; Sdhp 318, 449, 609. Further refs. & details see under Proper Names.

-âbhibhū overcoming M. or death Sn 545 = 571. **-kāyika** a class of gods Miln 285; KvuA 54. **-dhītaro** the daughters of M. SnA 544. **-dheyya** being under the sway of M.; the realm or kingdom of Māra A IV.228; Sn 764; Dh 34 (= kilesa-vaṭṭa DhA I.289). **-bandhana** the fetter of death Dh 37, 276, 350 (= tebhūmaka-vaṭṭa-sankhātaŋ DhA IV.69). **-senā** the army of M. Sn 561, 563; SnA 528.

Māraka (-°) [fr. māreti] one who kills or destroys, as manussa° man-killer J II.182; hatthi° elephant-killer DhA I.80. — m. in phrase **samāraka** (where the -ka belongs to the whole cpd.) see under **samāraka**.

Māraṇa (nt.) [fr. Caus. māreti] killing, slaughter, death D II.128; Sdhp 295, 569.

Māratta (nt.) [*Māra-tvaŋ] state of, or existence as a Māra god, Māraship Vbh 337.

Mārāpita [pp. of mārāpeti] killed J II.417; III.531.

Mārāpitatta (nt.) [abstr. fr. mārāpita] being incited to kill DhA I.141.

Mārāpeti [Caus. II. of **mṛ**]: see marati. — pp. mārāpita.

Mārita [pp. of māreti] killed S I.66; Vin III.72; J II.417 (aññehi m.-bhāvaŋ jānātha).

Mārisa (adj.) [perhaps identical with mādisa] only in voc. as respectful term of address, something like "Sir," pl. "Sirs." In sg. mārisa M I.327; A III.332; Sn 814, 1036, 1038, 1045 etc.; Nd¹ 140 = Nd² 508 (here expl^d by same formula as āyasmā, viz. piya-vacanaŋ garu-vacanaŋ etc.); J V.140; Pv II.13³; Mhvs I, 27. — pl. mārisā Sn 682; J I.47, 49; Vism 415; PvA 75. Explained by Buddhaghosa to mean niddukkha *K.S.* I.2 *n*.

Māruta [for the usual māluta] the wind S I.127; Mhbv 8.

Māretar [n. ag. to māreti] one who kills, slayer, destroyer S III.189.

Māreti [Caus. of **mṛ**] to kill: see under marati. — pp. mārita.

Māla (māḷa) [?] 1. mud [is it mis-spelling of mala?], in **pakka-m°-kalala** (boiling mud) J VI.400. Kern, *Toev.* s. v. believes to see the same word in phrase **mālā-kaca-vara** at J II.416 (but very doubtful). — 2. perhaps = froth, dirty surface, in pheṇa° Miln 117 (cp. mālin 2), where it may however be māla ("wreaths of foam"). — 3. in asi° the interpretation given under asi (as "dirt" see vol. I. p. 88) is to be changed into "sword-garland," thus taking it as mālā.

Mālaka (**Māḷaka**) [fr. māla or māḷa] a circular (consecrated) enclosure, round, yard (cp. Geiger, *Mhvs. trsl.* 99: "m. is a space marked off and usually terraced, within which sacred functions were carried out. In the Mahāvihāra (Tiss' ārāma) at Anurādhapura there were 32 mālakas; Dpvs XIV.78; Mhvs 15, 192. The sacred Bodhi-tree e. g. was surrounded by a malaka"). — The word is peculiar to the late (Jātaka-) literature, & is not found in the older texts. — J I.449 (vikkama°); IV.306; V.49 (visāla°), 138 (id., spelling maḷaka); Mhvs 15, 36 (Mahā-mucala°); 16, 15; 32, 58 (sanghassa kamma°, encl. for ceremonial acts of the S., cp. 15, 29); DhA IV.115 (°sīmā); Vism 342 (vitakka°).

Mālatī (f.) [fr. mālā] the great-flowered jasmine Abhp 576. Cp. mālikā.

Mālā (f.) [cp. Epic Sk. mālā] garland, wreath, chaplet; collectively = flowers; fig. row, line Sn 401; Pug 56; Vism 265 (in simile); Pv II.3¹⁶ (gandha, m., vilepana, as a "lady's" toilet outfit); II.4⁹ (as one of the 8 or 10 standard gifts to a bhikkhu: see dāna, deyyadhamma & yañña); PvA 4 = J III.59 (ratta-kaṇavera° a wreath of red K. flowers on his head: apparel of a criminal to be executed. Cp. ratta-māla-dhara wearing a red garland J III.179, an ensign of the executioner); PvA 51, 62. —asi°-kamma the sword-garland torture (so correct under asi!) J III.178; Dāvs III.35; **dīpa°** festoons of lamps Mhvs 5, 181; 34, 77 (°samujjota); **nakkhatta°** the garland of stars VvA 167; **puppha°** a garland or wreath of flowers Mhvs 5, 181. — On **mālā** in similes see *J.P.T.S.* 1907, 123. In compⁿ **māla°** sometimes stands for **mālā°**.

-kamma garland-work, garlands, festoons VvA 188. **-kāra** garland-maker, florist, gardener (cp. Fick, *Sociale Gleiderung* 38, 182) J V.292; Miln 331; DhA I.208, 334; VvA 170, 253 (°vīthi). **-kita** adorned with garlands, wreathed Vin I.208. **-guṇa** "garland-string," garlands, a cluster of garlands Dh 53 (= mālā-nikati "make-up" garlands DhA I.419; i. e. a whole line of garlands made as "ekato-vaṇṭika-mālā" and "ubhato-v.-m.," one & two stalked g., cp. Vin III.180). **mālā guṇa-parikkhittā** one adorned with a string of gs., i. e. a marriageable woman or a courtesan M I.286 = A V.264. **-guḷa** a cluster of gs., a bouquet Vin III.139; SnA 224; VvA 32, 111 (v. l. guṇa). **-cumbaṭaka** a cushion of garlands, a chaplet of flowers DhA I.72. **-dāma** a wreath of flowers J II.104. **-dhara** wearing a wreath J III.179 (ratta°, see also above). **-dhārin** wearing a garland or wreath (on the head) Pv III.1¹ (kusuma°; v. l. BB °bhārin); PvA 169 (v. l. °bhārin); f. **dhārinī** Vv 32³ (uppala°, of a Petī. See also bhārin). **-puṭa** a basket for flowers DhA III.212. **-bhārin** wearing a wreath (chaplet) [the reading changes between °bhārin & °dhārin; the BSk. prefers °dhārin, e. g. MVastu I.124 & °dhāra at Divy 218] J IV.60, 82; V.45; PvA 211 (v. l. °dhārin); f. °**bhārinī** J III.530; VvA 12; & **bhārī** Th 1, 459 (as v. l.; T. reads °dhārī). Cp. °dhārin. **-vaccha** [vaccha here = *vṛkṣa] a small flowering tree or plant, an ornamental plant Vin II.12; III.179; Vism 172 (v. l. °gaccha); DhA II.109 (q. v. for explⁿ: taruṇa-rukkha-puppha).

Mālika¹ (nt.) [fr. mālā or mala?] name of a dice J VI.281.

Mālika² [fr. mālā] a gardener, florist Abhp 507.

Mālikā (f.) [fr. mālā] double jasmine Dāvs 5, 49.

Mālin (adj.) [fr. mālā] 1. wearing a garland (or row) of flowers (etc.) Pv III.9¹ (= mālābhārin PvA 211); f. mālinī Vv 36² (nānā-ratana°); Mhvs 18, 30 (vividha-dhaja° mahābodhi). — 2. (perhaps to māla) bearing a stain of, muddy, in pheṇa° with a surface (or is it garland?) of scum Miln 260. — 3. what does it mean in pañca°, said at J VI.497 of a wild animal? (C. not clear with explⁿ "pañcangika-turiya-saddo viya").

Māluka (m. or f. ?) [of uncertain origin] a kind of vessel, only in camma° leather bag (?) J VI.431 (where v. l. reads camma-pasibbakāhi vālukādīhi), 432 (gloss c.-pasibbaka).

Māluta [the proper Pali form for māruta, the a-stem form of maru²=Vedic marut or māruta] wind, air, breeze S IV.218; Th 1.2; II.372; J I.167; IV.222; V.328; VI.189; Miln 319; Vism 172 (=vāyu); VvA 174, 178.
 -īrita (contracted to māluterita) moved by the wind, fanned by the breeze Th I, 754; II.372; Vv 44¹²=81⁶, Pv II.12³. See similar expressions under īrita.

Māluvā (f.) [cp. BSk. mālu] a (long) creeper M I.306; S I.207; A I.202 sq.; Sn 272; Dh 162, 334; J III.389; V.205, 215, 389; V.205, 215, 389; VI.528 (phandana°); DhA III.152; IV.43. — On maluvā in similes see *J.P.T.S.* 1907, 123.

Mālūra [late Sk.] the tree Aegle marmelos Abhp 556.

Mālya see malya.

Māḷa (& **Māla**) [Non-Aryan, cp. Tamil māḍam house, hall] a sort of pavilion, a hall D I.2 (maṇḍala°, same at Sn p. 104, which passage SnA 447 explⁿˢ as "savitānaŋ maṇḍapaŋ"); Vin I.140 (aṭṭa, māla, pāsāda; expl^d at Vin III.201. In the same sequence of Vbh 251 expl^d at VbhA 366 as "bhojana-sālā-sadiso maṇḍala-māḷo; Vinay' aṭṭha-kathāyaŋ pana eka-kūṭa-sangahito caturassa-pāsādo ti vuttaŋ"); Miln 46, 47. — Cp. mālaka. — [The BSk. form is either māla, e. g. MVastu II.274, or māḍa, e. g. Mvyut 226, 43.]

Māḷaka [a Non-Aryan word, although the Dhtm 395 gives roots **mal** & **mall** in meaning "dhāraṇa" (see under mala). Cp. malorika] a stand, viz. for alms-bowl (patta°) Vin II.114, or for drinking vessel (pānīya°) J VI.85.

Māsa¹ [cp. Vedic māsa, & mās; Gr. μήν (Ionic μείς); Av. māh (moon & month); Lat. mensis; Oir. mī; Goth. mēna=moon; Ohg. māno, mānōt month. Fr. ***mē** to measure: see mināti] a month, as the 12ᵗʰ part of the year. The 12 months are (beginning with what chronologically corresponds to our middle of March): Citta (Citra), Vesākha, Jeṭṭha, Āsāḷha, Sāvaṇa, Poṭṭhapāda, Assayuja, Kattika, Māgasira, Phussa, Māgha, Phagguna. As to the names cp. nakkhatta. Usually in acc., used adverbially; nom. rare, e. g. aḍḍha-māso half-month VvA 66; Āsāḷhi-māsa VvA 307 (=gimhānaŋ pacchima māsa); pl. dve māsā PvA 34 (read māse); cattāro gimhāna-māsā KhA 192 (of which the 1ˢᵗ is Citra, otherwise called Paṭhama-gimha "1ˢᵗ winter" and Bāla-vasanta "premature spring"). — Instr. pl. catūhi māsehi Miln. 82; PvA 1.10¹². — *acc. pl.* as adv.: dasamāse 10 months J I.52; bahu-māse PvA 135; also nt. chammāsāni 6 months S III.155. Freq. *acc. sg.* collectively: a period of . . ., e. g. temāsaŋ 3 months DhsA 15; PvA 20; catu° DA I.83; PvA 96; satta° PvA 20; **dasa°** PvA 63; aḍḍha° a fortnight Vin IV.117. — On māsa (& f. māsī), as well as shortened form °ma see puṇṇa.
 -puṇṇatā fullness or completion of the month DA I.140; -mattaŋ (adv.) for the duration of a month PvA 19.

Māsa² [Vedic māṣa, Phaseolus indica, closely related to another species: mudga Phaseolus mungo] a bean (Phaseolus indica or radiata); usually comb^d with mugga, e. g. Vin III.64; Miln 267, 341; DA I.83. Also used as a weight (or measure ?) in dhañña-māsa, which is said to be equal to 7 lice: VbhA 343. — pl. māse Vv 80⁶ (=māsa-sassāni VvA 310).
 -odaka bean-water KhA 237. **-khetta** a field of beans Vv 80⁸; VvA 308. **-bīja** bean-seed DhA III.212. **-vana** plantation J V.37 (+mugga°).

Māsa³ [identical with māsa²] a small coin (=māsaka) J II.425 (satta māsā=s. māsakā C.).

Māsaka [fr. māsa²+ka=māsa³] lit. a small bean, used as a standard of weight & value; hence a small coin of very low value. Of copper, wood & lac (DhsA 318; cp. KhA 37; jatu°, dāru°, loha°); the suvaṇṇa° (golden m.) at J IV.107 reminds of the "gold" in fairy tales. That its worth is next to nothing is seen from the descending progression of coins at DhA III.108=VvA 77, which, beginning with kahāpaṇa, aḍḍha-pāda, places māsaka & kāhaṇikā next to mudhā "gratis." It only "counts" when it amounts to 5 māsakas. — Vin III.47, 67; IV.226 (pañca°); J I.112 (aḍḍha-māsakaŋ na agghati is worth nothing); IV.107; V.135 (first a rain of flowers, then of māsakas, then kahāpaṇas); DhA II.29 (pañca-m.-mattaŋ a sum of 5 m.); PvA 282 (m+aḍḍha° half-pennies & farthings, as children's pocket-money).

Māsakkhimhā at Vin III.23 is for mā asakkhimhā "we could not"; mā here stands for na.

Māsati, Māsana, Māsin [fr. **mṛś**, for massati etc.; see masati] touch, touching, etc. in sense of eating or taking in. So is probably to be read for āsati etc. in the foll. passages, where m precedes this ā in all cases. Otherwise we have to refer them to a root **ās=as** (to eat) and consider the m as partly euphonic. —dumapakkāni-māsita J II.446 (C. reads māsita & explⁿˢ by asita, dhāta); visa-māsita Miln 302 (T. reads visam-āsita) having taken in poison; visa-māsan-ûpatāpa (id.) Vism 166; tiṇa-māsin eating grass J VI.354 (=tiṇa-khādaka C.). — A similar case where Sandhi-m- has led to a wrong partition of syllables and has thus been lost through syncope may be P. eḷaka¹, as comp^d with Sk. methi (cp. Prk. meḍhi), pillar, post.

Māsalu [reading uncertain] only instr. **māsalunā** Miln 292; Trenckner says (note p. 428): "m. is otherwise unknown, it must mean a period shorter than 5 months. Cp. Sk. māsala." — Rh. D. (trsl. II.148) translates "got in a month," following the Sinhalese gloss. — The period seems to be only a *little* shorter than 5 months; there may be a connection with catu in the word.

Māsācita [māsa¹+ācita] filled by the (say 6 or more) month(s), i. e. heavy (alluding to the womb in advanced pregnancy), heaped full M I.332 (kucchi garu-garu viya māsācitaŋ maññe ti; Neumann trslˢ "wie ein Sack voll Bohnen," thus taking m.=māsa², and ācita as "heap" which however is not justified). This passage has given rise to a gloss at Vbh 386, where māsācitaŋ maññe was added to kāyo garuko akammañño, in meaning "heavy, languid." The other enumⁿˢ of the 8 kusīta-vatthūni (A IV.332; D III.255) do not give m. m. It may be that the resemblance between akammañño and maññe has played a part in reminding the Commentator of this phrase. The fact that Bdhgh comments on this passage in the VbhA (p. 510) shows, that the reading of Vbh 386 is a very old one. Bdhgh. takes māsa in the sense of māsa² & explˢ māsācita as "wet bean" (tinta māso), thus omitting explⁿ of ācita. The passage at VbhA 510 runs: "ettha pana māsācitaŋ nāma tintamāso, yathā tintamāso garuko hoti, evaŋ garuko ti adhippāyo."

Māsika (adj.) [fr. māsa¹ 1. of a month, i. e. a month old Miln 302. — 2. of a month, i. e. consisting of months, so many months (old) (-°), as **aḍḍha°** at intervals of half a month D I.166; M I.238, 343; Pug 55; **dve°** two months old Pv I.6⁷. — 3. monthly, i. e. once a month Th I, 283 (bhatta). — Cp. māsiya.

Māsiya (adj.) [=māsika] consisting of months D II.327 (dvādasa° saŋvacchara the year of 12 months).

Miga [Vedic mṛga, to **mṛj,** cp. magga, meaning, when characterised by another attribute "wild animal" in general, animal of the forest; when uncharacterised usually antelope] 1. a wild animal, an animal in its natural state (see cpds.). — 2. a deer, antelope, gazelle. Various kinds are mentioned at J V.416; two are given at Nd[2] 509, viz. eṇi (antelope) & sarabha (red deer): see under eṇi & sarabha. — Sn 39, 72; J I.154; III.270 (called Nandiya); PvA 62, 157. On miga in similes see *J.P.T.S.* 1907, 123, where more refs. are given.

-âdhibhū king of beasts (i. e. the lion) Sn 684. **-inda** king of beasts (id.) Sdhp 593. **-chāpaka** young of a deer VvA 279. **-dāya** deer park J IV.430 (Maddakucchi); VvA 86 (Isipatana). **-dhenu** a hind J I.152; DhA III.148. **-bhūta** (having become) like a wild animal, M I.450 (°bhūtena cetasā). **-mandalocana** the soft eye of the deer Vv 64[11]; Pv I.11[5]. See under manda. **-rājā** king of the beasts (the lion) D III.23 sq. **-luddaka** deer-hunter J I.372; III.49, 184; DhA II.82; VbhA 266 (in simile). **-vadha** deer-slaying J I.149. **-vittaka,** amateur of hunting J IV.267. **-visāna** a deer's horn Pug 56. **-vīthi** deer-road J I.372.

Migavā (f.) [=Sk. mṛgayā, cp. Geiger, *P.Gr.* § 46[1]] hunt, hunting, deer-stalking PvA 154 (°padesa). Usually in devasikaŋ migavaŋ gacchati to go out for a day's hunting J IV.267; or as pp. ekadivasaŋ migavaŋ gata VvA 260; ekāhaŋ m. g. Mhvs 5, 154.

Migī (f.) [f. of miga, cp. Epic Sk. mṛgī] a doe Th 1, 109; J V.215; VI.549; DhA I.48.

Micchatta (nt.) [abstr. fr. micchā] item of wrong, wrongness. There are 8 items of wrong, viz. the 8 wrong qualities as enum[d] under (an-) ariya-magga (see micchā), forming the contrary to the sammatta or righteousness of the Ariyan Path. These 8 at D II.353; III.254; A II.221; IV.237; Vbh 387; Vism 683. Besides these there is a set of 10, consisting of the above 8 plus micchā-ñāṇa and °vimutti wrong knowledge & wrong emancipation: D III.290; Vbh 391; Vism 683 (where °ñāṇa & °viratti for vimutti). — See further D III.217 (°niyata); Pug 22; Dhs 1028 (cp. *Dhs. trsl.* §1028); Vbh 145; Tikp. 32 (°niyata-citta), 325 (°tika), 354 (id.).

Micchā (adv.) [Sk mithyā, cp. Vedic mithaḥ interchanging, separate, opposite, contrary (opp. samyak together: see samma); mithū wrongly; see also mithu] wrongly, in a wrong way, wrong-, false Sn 438 (laddho yaso), 815 (paṭipajjati leads a wrong course of life, almost syn. with anariyaŋ. Illustrated by "pāṇaŋ hanati, adinnaŋ ādiyati, sandhiŋ chindati, nillopaŋ harati, ekāgārikaŋ karoti, paripanthe tiṭṭhati, paradāraŋ gacchati, musā bhaṇati" at Nd[1] 144); VbhA 513 (°ñāṇa, °vimutti). -micchā° often in same comb[ns] as sammā°, with which contrasted, e. g. with the 8 parts of (an-) ariya-magga, viz. °diṭṭhi (wrong) views (D III.52, 70 sq., 76, 111, 246, 269, 287, 290, Dh 167, 316 sq.; Pug 39; Vism 469 (def.) PvA 27, 42, 54, 67; cp. °*ka* one who holds wrong views D III.45, 48, 264; Vism 426); °sankappa aspiration (D III.254, 287, 290 sq., Dh 11); °vācā speech (ibid.); °kammanta conduct (ibid.); °ājīva living (D III.176 sq., 254, 290; A II.53, 240, 270, IV.82); °vāyāma effort (D III.254, 287, 290 sq.); °sati mindfulness (ibid.); °samādhi concentration (ibid.); see magga 2, and cp. the following:

-gahaṇa wrong conception, mistake J III.304. **-cāra** wrong behaviour Pug 39 (& adj. cārin); VbhA 383 (var. degrees). **-paṭipadā** wrong path (of life) Pug 49 (& adj.: °paṭipanna, living wrongly). **-paṇihita** (citta) wrongly directed mind Dh 42 = Ud 39 [cp. BSk. mithyāpraṇidhāna Divy 14]. **-patha** wrong road, wrong course Vbh 145 (lit. & fig.; in exegesis of diṭṭhi, cp. Nd[2] taṇhā III.; Dhs 381; DhsA 253).

Miñja (nt.) & miñjā (f.) [Vedic majjan (fr. **majj** ?); on form see Geiger. *P.Gr.* § 9[1], & cp. Pischel, *Prk. Gr.* §§ 74, 101] marrow, pith, kernel Vin I.25 (in sequence chavi, camma, maŋsa, nahāru, aṭṭhi, miñjā); Vism 235 (id.); Kh III. (aṭṭhi°, f. cp. KhA 52, nt.); J IV.402 (tāla° pith of the palm); Mhvs 28, 28 (panasa°, f., kernels of the seeds of the jak-fruit).

-rāsi heap of marrow Vism 260 (=matthalunga).

Miñjaka=miñja, only in **tela°** inner kernels of tila-seed, made into a cake PvA 51. See **doṇi**[2].

Mita [Vedic mita, pp. of **mā,** mināti, to measure; also in meaning "moderate, measured," cp. in same sense Gr. μέτριος] measured, in measure D I.54 (doṇa° a doṇa measure full); Sn 300 (bhāgaso m. measured in harmonious proportions, i. e. stately); Pv I.10[13] (id.); J III.541. —**amita** unlimited, without measure, boundless, in Ep. amit-ābha of boundless lustre Sdhp 255. Also N. of a Buddha.

-āhāra measured, i. e. limited food Sn 707. **-bhāṇin** speaking measuredly, i. e. in moderation Dh 227; J IV.252.

Mitta (m. nt.) [cp. Vedic mitra, m. & nt., friend; Av. miþro, friend] friend. Usually m., although *nt.* occurs in meaning "friend," in sg. (Nett 164) & pl. (Sn 185, 187); in meaning "friendship" at J VI.375 (=mittabhāva C.). The half-scientific, half-popular etym. of mitta, as given at VbhA 108, is "mettāyantī ti mittā, minantī ti vā m.; sabba-guyhesu anto pakkhipantī ti attho" (the latter: "they enclose in all that is hidden"). — Two kinds of friends are distinguished at Nd[2] 510 (in exegesis of Sn 37 & 75), viz. **āgārika°** (a house- or lay-friend) and **anāgārika°** (a homeless- or clerical-friend). The former is possessed of all ordinary qualities of kindness and love, the latter of special virtues of mind & heart. — A friend who acts as a sort of Mentor, or spiritual adviser, is called a kalyāṇa-mitta (see under kalyāṇa). — Mitta is often comb[d] with similar terms, devoting relationship or friendship, e. g. with amaccā colleagues and ñāti-sālohita° blood-relations, in ster. phrase at Vin II.126; A I.222; Sn p. 104; PvA 28; cp. ñāti-mittā relatives & friends Pv I.5[9]; suhada ("dear heart") D III.187 (four types, cp. m. paṭirūpaka); suhajja one who is dear to one's heart PvA 191; sahāya companion PvA 86. The neut. form occurs for kind things D III.188; S I.37. — Opp. sapatta enemy PvA 13; amitta a sham friend or enemy Sn 561 (=paccatthika SnA 455); D III.185. pāpa-mitta bad friend PvA 5. — For refs. see e. g. Sn 58, 255, 296, 338; Dh 78, 375.

-âbhirādhin one who pleases his friends J IV.274 (=mittesu adubbhamāno C.) **-ddu** [cp. Sk. mitra-druha] one who injures or betrays his friends S I.225; Sn 244; J IV.260; also in foll. forms: °dubbha Pv II.9[8] (same passage at J IV.352; V.240; VI.310, 375); °dūbha J IV.352; VI.310; °dūbhin [cp. Sk. °drohin] J IV.257; V.97 (°kamma); VI.375; DhA II.23. **-paṭirūpaka** a false friend, one pretending to be a friend D III.185 (four types: añña-d-atthu-hara, vacī-parama, anuppiyabhāṇin, apāya-sahāya, i. e. one who takes anything, one who is a great talker, one who flatters, one who is a spendthrift companion.) **-bandhava** a relation in friendship, one who is one's relative as a friend Nd[2] 455 (where Nd[1] 11 has manta-bandhava). **-bheda** see mithu-bheda. **-vaṇṇa** pretence of friendship, a sham friendship Pv IV.8[6] (=mitta-rūpa, m.-paṭirūpatā PvA 268).

Mittatā (f.) -(°) [abstr. fr. **mitta**] state of being a friend, friendship, in **kalyāṇa°** being a good friend, friendship as a helper (see kalyāṇa) D III.274; Vism 107.

Mitti (f.) [a by-form of metti] friendship J I.468 (= metti C.).

Mithu (adv.) [cp. Vedic **mithū** & P. micchā; **mith,** cp. mithaḥ alternately, Av. miϑō wrongly; Goth. misso one another, missa-leiks different; Ger. E. prefix mis- i. e.

wrongly: Ger. missetat wrong doing=misdeed; Lat. mūto to change, mutuus reciprocal; Goth. maiþms present=Ags. maþum; **mith** in Vedic Sk. is "to be opposed to each other," whereas in Vedic mithuna the notion of "pair" prevails. See also methuna] opposite, reciprocally, contrary Sn 825, 882 (taken by Nd¹ 163 & 290, on both passages identically, as n. pl. of adj. instead of adv., & expl^d by "dve janā dve kalaha-kāraka" etc.).
-**bheda** [evidently in meaning of *mitta*-bheda "break of friendship," although *mithu* means "adversary," thus perhaps "breaking, so as to cause opposition"] breaking of alliance, enmity D II.76; J IV.184 (here with v. l. mitta°); Kvu 314.

Middha (nt.) [orig. pp. perhaps to Vedic **mid** (?) to be fat=**medh**, as DhsA 378 gives "medhatī ti middhaŋ." —More likely however connected with Sk. methi (pillar=Lat. meta), cp. Prk. medhi. The meaning is more to the point too, viz. "stiff." Thus semantically identical with thīna. — BSk. also middha; e. g. Divy 555] torpor, stupidity, sluggishness D I.71 (thīna°); Sn 437; A V.18; Dhs 1157; Miln 299, 412 (appa° not slothful, i. e. diligent, alert); Vism 450 (°rūpa; +roga-rūpa, jātirūpa, etc., in def. of rūpa); DA I.211 (expl^d as cetasika gelañña: see on this passage *Dhs trsl.* §1155); Sdhp 459. — See **thīna**.

Middhin (adj.) [fr. middha] torpid, drowsy, sluggish Dh 325 (=thīnamiddh' âbhibhūta DhA IV.16).

Midha [does it refer to **mī²** as in mināti², or to middha?] is given as root in meaning "hiŋsana," to hurt at Dhtm 536 (with var. v.v ll.), not sure.

Minana (nt.) [fr. **mi** to measure, fix, construct] measuring, surveying DA I.79; DhsA 123.

Mināti¹ [roots (Vedic) **mā** & **mi**; pres. minūte & minoti; Idg. ***me**, cp. Sk. mātra measure, māna; Av. mā-, mitiḥ measure; Gr. μάτιον small measure, μῆτις counsel Lat.; metior, mensis, modus; Goth. mēla bushel; Ags. mǣd measure (cp. E. mete, meet=fitting); Lith. mētas year. — The Dhtm 726 gives **mi** in meaning "pamāṇa"] to measure VbhA 108 (see etym. of mitta); Pot. **mine** J V.468 (=mineyya C.); fut. **minissati** Sdhp 585. ger. **minitvā** Vism 72; grd. **minitabba** J V.90. — Pass. **mīyati**: see anu°. — pp. mita. — Cp. anu°, abhi°, ni°, pa°, vi°. Caus. māpeti (q. v.).

Mināti² [Vedic mināti, mī (or mi), to diminish; cp. Gr. μινύω diminish; Lat. minor=E. minor; Goth. mins (little), compar, minniza, superl. minnists=Ger. mindest. — The Dhtp 502 gives **mi** with "hiŋsā," the Dhtm 725 with "hiŋsana." It applies the same interpretation to a root **midh** (Dhtm 536), which is probably abstracted fr. Pass. mīyati] to diminish; also: to hurt, injure. Very rare, only in some prep. comb^ns. — See also **mīyati**.

Miyyati (& **Mīyati**) [corresponding to Vedic mriyate, fr. **mṛ**, viâ *mīryate>miyyati. See marati] to die. — (a) **miyyati**: Sn 804; Nett 23. med. 3rd pl. **miyyare** Sn 575; pot. **miyye** J VI.498; ppr. **miyyamāna** M III.246; Vism 49; fut. **miyyissati** M III.246. — (b) **mīyati** (influenced in form by jīyati & mīyati of mināti²) M III.168 (jāyati jīyati mīyati); J III.189; Dh 21; pot. **mīyetha** D II.63. ppr. **mīyamāna** S I.96. — pp. **mata**.

Milakkha [cp. Ved. Sk. mleccha barbarian, root **mlecch**, onomat. after the strange sounds of a foreign tongue, cp. babbhara & mammana] a barbarian, foreigner, outcaste, hillman S V.466; J VI.207; DA I.176; SnA 236 (°mahātissa-thera Np.), 397 (°bhāsā foreign dialect). The word occurs also in form milakkhu (q. v.).

Milakkhu [the Prk. form (A-Māgadhī, cp. Pischel, *Prk. Gr.* 105, 233) for P. milakkha] a non-Aryan D III.264; Th I, 965 (°rajana "of foreign dye" trsl.; Kern, *Toev.* s. v. translates "vermiljoen kleurig"). As milakkhuka at Vin III.28, where Bdhgh expl^s by "Andha-Damil' ādi."

Milāca [by-form to milakkha, viâ *milaccha>*milacca> milāca: Geiger, *P.Gr.* 62²; Kern, *Toev.* s. v.] a wild man of the woods, non-Aryan, barbarian J IV.291 (not with C.=janapadā), cp. luddā m. ibid., and milāca-puttā J V.165 (where C. also expl^s by bhojaputta, i. e. son of a villager).

Milāta [pp. of milāyati] faded, withered, dried up J I.479; V.473; Vism 254 (°sappa-piṭṭhi, where KhA 49 in same passage reads "milāta-dham(m)ani-piṭṭhi"); DhA I.335; IV.8 (sarīra), 112; SnA 69 (°mālā, in simile); Mhvs 22, 46 (a°); Sdhp 161.

Milātatā (f.) [abstr. fr. milāta] only neg. a° the (fact of) not being withered J V.156.

Milāyati [Vedic **mlā**, to become soft; Idg. ***melā** & ***mlei**, as in Gr. βλάξ, βλακεύω to languish; Lat. flaccus withered (=flaccid); Lith. blakà weak spot; also Gr. βληχρός weak. — Dhtp 440: "milā=gatta-vimāne" (i. e. from the bent limbs); Dhtm 679 id.] to relax, languish, fade, wither S I.126; It 76; J I.329; V.90. — Caus. **milāpeti** [Sk. mlāpayati] to make dry, to cause to wither J I.340 (sassaŋ); fig. to assuage, suppress, stifle J III.414 (taṇhaŋ). — pp. **milāta**.

Millikā at PvA 144 in passage paŋsukūlaŋ dhovitv-âbhisiñcimillikañ ca katvā adāsi is to be read either as "abhisiñci cimillikañ ca k." or "abhisiñcitvā mudukañ ca k."

Miḷhakā at S II.228 is to be read mīḷhakā (q. v.).

Misati [**miṣ**, Vedic miṣati, root given as misa at Dhtm 479, with expl^n "mīlane"] to wink (one's eyes): see ni°.

Missa (adj.) [orig. pp. of **miś**, cp. Vedic miśra. Sk. miśrayati, mekṣayati; Gr. μίγνυμι & μίσγω; Lat. misceo, mixtus; Ags. miscian=mix; Ohg. miskan. — Dhtp 631 "sammissa"] 1. mixed (with: -°); various Vin I.33 (kesa°, jaṭā° etc.=a mixture of, various); Th I, 143; J III.95, 144 (udaka-paṇṇa° yāgu); Pv I.9² (missā kiṭakā). nt. missaŋ as adv. "in a mixed way" Vism 552=VbhA 161 (+dvidhā). — 2. accompanied by (-°), having company or a retinue, a title of honour in names, also as polite address [cp. Sk. miśra & ārya miśra] J V.153 (voc. f. misse), 154 (f. missā). — 3. missa° is changed to missī in comp° with **kṛ** and **bhū** (like Sk.), thus in **missī-bhāva** (sexual) intercourse, lit. mixed state, union J II.330; IV.471; V.86; VbhA 107; and **missī-bhūta** mixed, coupled, united J V.86 (=hatthena hatthaŋ gahetvā kāya-missībhāvaŋ upagata C.). Cp. sam.°
-**kesī** (f.) "mixed hair," Ep. of a heavenly maiden or Apsaras Vv 60¹⁴ (expl^d at VvA 280 as "ratta-mālādihi missita-kesavaṭṭī"). The m. missa-kesa occurs as a term for ascetics (with muṇḍa) at Vism 389.

Missaka (adj. n.) [fr. missa] 1. mixed, combined J II.8 (phalika° rajata-pabbata mountain of silver mixed with crystal); VbhA 16 (lokiya-lokuttara°); usually °-, like **°āhāra** mixed food DhA II.101; **°uppāda** mixed portents, a main chapter of the art of prognosticating (cp. Bṛhat-Saŋhitā ch. 86. miśrak' âdhyāya) Miln 178; **°bhatta**=°āhāra SnA 97; Mhbv 27. — 2. (m.) an attendant, follower; f. missikā DhA I.211 (Sāmāvati°). — 3. (nt.) N. of a pleasure grove in heaven (lit. the grove of bodily union), one of the 3: Nandana, M., Phārusaka J VI.278; Vism 424. — 4. (pl. missakā) a group of devas, mentioned at D II.260 in list of popular gods (cp. missa 2 and missakesī).

Missakatta (nt.) [abstr. fr. missaka] mixing, mixture, combination with (-°) Tikp 291.

Missana (nt.) [fr. misseti] mixing Dhtp 338.

Missita [pp. of misseti] mixed, intermingled Sn 243; J v.460; PvA 198 (dhañña sāsapa-tela°); VvA 280 (see under missa-kesī).

Misseti [Caus. of **miś**, Vedic miśrayati] 1. to mix Miln 126 (mayaŋ missayissāma); PvA 191 (palāse sālīhi saddhiŋ). — 2. to bring together in cohabitation, to couple J v.154 (C.: kilesana misseti). — pp. missita.

Mihati is given as root **mih** in 2 meanings at Dhtp, viz. (1) īsa-hasana (No. 328), i. e. a kind of laugh, for **smi**, as in mihita. (2) secana (No. 342).

Mihita (nt.) [pp. of **smi**; this is the inverted-diæretic (Pāli) form (smita>*hmita>*mhita>mihita) for the other (Sk.) form smita (q. v.). The Dhtp (328) puts root down as **mih**] a smile J III.419; v.452; VI.504. —mihita-pubba with smiles Th 1, 460 (spelt mhita°); J VI.221 (=sita C.). — Cp. vimhaya, vimhāpaka, vimhita.

Mīyati see miyyati (Pass. of marati).

Mīlati [**mil**, given at Dhtp 267 & 614 with "nimīlane"] to wink, only in cpd. nimīlati to close the eyes (opp. um°).

Mīḷha [pp. of **mih**, Vedic mehati to excrete water, i. e. urine, only with ref. to the liquid; Sk. mīḍha=Lat. mictus, pp. of mingo, to urinate. Cp. Av. maēzaiti to urinate, mez urine; Gr. ὀμιχεῖν & ὄμιχμα id.; Ags. mīgan to ur.; in Ohg. mist & Ags. miox the notion refers more to the solid excrement, as in Pāli. — A related root ***meigh** to shed water is found in megha, cloud (watershedder), q. v. for further cognates] excrement M I.454 =III.236 (°sukhaŋ vile pleasure); A III.241, 242; Th 1, 1152; J II.11; VI.112; Vv 52[11] (with ref. to the gūthaniraya); Pv III.4[5] (=gūtha PvA 194); DhA II.53 (°ŋ khāditun).

-**kūpa** pit of excr., cesspool Pgdp 22.

Mīḷhakā (f.) [fr. mīḷha; cp. BSk. mīḍha-ghaṭa] cesspool S II.228 (so read for T. piḷhakā; v. l. BB miḷhakā). See also **piḷhakā**. The trsl. (*K.S.* II.155) gives "dung-beetle."

Mukula [cp. Sk. mukula] a bud; see makula (where also see mukulita). — Abhp 811, 1116.

Mukka [pp. of **muc**, Sk. mukta, for the usual P. mutta; cp. Prk. mukka. Pischel, *Prk. Gr.* § 566] only in um° & paṭi° (q. v.), and as v. l. at M III.61.

Mukkhaka at J I.441 should be read as **mokkhaka**, meaning "first, principal, foremost"; cp. mokkha[2].

Mukha (nt.) [Vedic mukha, fr. Idg. ***mu**, onomat., cp. Lat. mu facere, Gr. μυκάομαι, Mhg. mūgen, Lat. mūgio to moo (of cows), to make the sound "moo"; Ohg. māwen to cry, muckazzen to talk softly; also Gr. μῦθος word, "myth"; Ohg. mūla=Ger. maul; Ags. mule snout, etc. Vedic mūka silent, dumb=Lat. mutus=E. mute] 1. the mouth Sn 608, 1022 (with ref. to the long tongue, pahūta-jivha, of the Buddha or Mahāpurisa); J II.7; DA I.287 (uttāna° clear mouthed, i. e. easy to understand, cp. D I.116); PvA 11, 12 (pūti°), 264 (mukhena). — 2. the face J VI.218 (uṇṇaja m.); PvA 74, 75, 77; °ŋ karoti to make a face (i. e. grimace) Vism 343. —adho° face downward Vin II.78; opp. upari° (q. v.); assu° with tearful face Dh 67; PvA 39; see assu. —dum° (adj.) sad or unfriendly looking J II.393; VI.343; scurrilous J v.78; bhadra° bright-faced PvA 149; ruda° crying Pv I.11[2]. — 3. entrance, mouth (of a river) Mhvs 8, 12; āya° entrance (lit. opening), i. e. cause or means of income DA I.218; ukkā° the opening of a furnace, a goldsmith's smelting pot A I.257; Sn 686; J VI.217; 574. ubhato-mukha having 2 openings M I.57. sandhi° opening of the cleft PvA 4. Hence: — 4. cause, ways, means, reason, by way of J III.55 by way of a gift (dānamukhe); IV.266 (bahūhi mukhehi). —apāya° cause of ruin or loss A II.166; IV.283. — 5. front part, front, top, in isā° of the carriage pole S I.224=J I.203. Hence: — 6. the top of anything, front, head, best part; adj. topmost, foremost Sn 568 (aggihutta-mukhā yaññā), 569 (nakkhattānaŋ mukhaŋ cando; cp. Vin I.246); VbhA 332 (=uttamaŋ, mukha-bhūtaŋ vā). — Der. adj. **mokkha** & **pāmokkha** (q. v.). *Note*. A poetical instr. sg. **mukhasā** is found at Pv 1.2[3] & 1.3[2], as if the nom. were mukho (s-stem). — The abl. **mukhā** is used as adv. "in front of, before," in cpd. sam° & param°, e. g. PvA 13. See each sep.

-**ādhāna** (1) the bit of a bridle M I.446; (2) setting of the mouth, i. e. mouth-enclosure, rim of the m.; in m. siliṭṭhaŋ a well-connected, well-defined mouth-contour DhsA 15 (not with trsl. "opens lightly," but better with note "is well adjusted," see *Expos.* 19, where write °ādhāna for °ādāna). -**āsiya** (? cp. āsita[1]) to be eaten by the mouth DhsA 330 (mukhena asitabba). -**ullokana** looking into a person's face, i. e. cheerful, bright, perhaps also flattering DhA II.193 (as °olokana). -**ullokika** flattering (cp. above) Nd[1] 249 (puthu Satthārānaŋ m. puthujjana); PvA 219. -**odaka** water for rinsing the mouth Nd[2] 39[1]=Miln 370; VvA 65; DhA II.19; IV.28. -**ja** born in (or from) the mouth, i. e. a tooth J VI.219. -**tuṇḍa** a beak VvA 227 [cp. BSk. mukhatuṇḍaka Divy 387]. -**dugga** one whose mouth is a difficult road, i. e. one who uses his mouth (speech) badly Sn 664 (v. l. °dukkha). -**dūsi** blemishes of the face, a rash on the face DA I.223 (m.-dosa ibid.). -**dvāra** mouth opening PvA 180. -**dhovana-ṭṭhāna** place for rinsing the mouth, "lavatory" DhA II.184. -**puñchana** wiping one's mouth Vin I.297. -**pūra** filling the mouth, a mouthful, i. e. as much as to fill the mouth J VI.350. -**pūraka** mouth-filling Vism 106. -**bheri** a musical instrument, "mouth-drum," mouth-organ (?) Nd[2] 219 B; SnA 86. -**makkaṭika** a grimace (like that of a monkey) of the face J II.70, 448 (T. makkaṭiya). -**vaṭṭi** "opening-circumference," i. e. brim, edge, rim DhA II.5 (of the Lohakumbhi purgatory, cp. J III.43 lohakumbha-mukhavaṭṭi); DhA III.58 (of a gong). -**vaṇṇa** the features PvA 122, 124. -**vikāra** contortion of the mouth J II.448. -**vikūṇa** (=vikāra) grimace SnA 30. -**sankocana** distortion or contraction of the mouth, as a sign of displeasure DhA II.270; cp. mukha-sankoca Vism 26. -**saññata** controlling one's mouth (i. e. speech) Dh 363, cp. DhA IV.93.

Mukhara (adj.) [cp. Sk. mukhara; fr. mukha] garrulous, noisy, scurrilous S I.203; V.269; A I.70; III.199, 355; Th 1, 955; Sn 275; J III.103; DhA II.70 (ati°); PvA 11. — opp. amukhara M I.470; Th 1, 926; Pug 35; Miln 414.

Mukharatā (f.) [fr. mukhara] talkativeness, garrulousness, noisiness DhA II.70.

Mugga [Vedic mudga, cp. Zimmer, *Altind. Leben* 240] a kind of kidney-bean, Phaseolus mungo, freq. comb[d] with **māsa**[2] (q. v.). On its size (larger than sāsapa, smaller than kalāya) see A v.170 & cp. kalāya. — D II.293; M 1.57 (+māsa); S I.150; J I.274, 429; III.55; VI.355 (°māsā); Miln 207, 341; SnA 283.

-**sūpa** bean-soup Vism 27. -**sūpyatā** "bean-soup-character," or as *Vism trsl.* 32 has it "bean-curry-talk"; fig. denoting a faulty character, i. e. a man who behaves like bean-soup. The metaphor is not quite transparent; it is expl[d] by Bdhgh as meaning a man speaking half-truths, as in a soup of beans some are only half-boiled. The expl[n] is forced, & is stereotype, as well as is the combⁿ in which it occurs. Its origin remains to be elucidated. Anyhow it refers to an unevenness in character, a flaw of character. The passage (with var. spellings) is always the foll.: **cāṭu-kamyatā** (pātu° Nd²; °kammatā Miln; pāṭu° Vbh) **mugga-sūpyatā** (°sūpatā Nd²; °suppatā Miln & KhA 236; °sūpatā and suppatā Vbh & VbhA 338; supyatā Vism) **pāribhaṭṭatā** (°bhatyatā Vism.; °bhaṭṭakatā Miln; °bhaṭyatā & °bbhaṭṭatā Vbh). At Nd² 39¹ it is used to explain **sāvajja-bhogin**, at Vism 17 & Vbh 246 **anācāra**; at Vbh 352 **lapanā**; at Miln 370 it is used generally (cp. *Miln trsl.* II.287). The C. explⁿ of the Vbh passage, as given at (VbhA 483 &) Vism 17 runs as follows: "mugga-sūpa-samānāya sacc' ālikena jīvita kappanatāy' etaŋ adhivacanaŋ. Yathā hi muggasūpe paccante bahū muggā pākaŋ gacchanti, thokā na gacchanti, evam eva saccālikena jīvitakappake puggale bahuŋ alikaŋ hoti, appakaŋ saccaŋ." The text at VbhA 483 is slightly different, although the sense is the same. Similarly at Vism 27.

Muggatiya (nt.?) [fr. mugga ?] a plant, according to C. a species of bean J VI.536.

Muggara [cp. Sk. mudgara] a club, hammer, mallet J I.113; II.196, 382; V.47; VI.358; Miln 351; Vism 231; DhA I.126; II.21; PvA 4, 55 (ayo°), 56 (°pahāra), 66, 192. The word is specifically peculiar to the so-called Jātaka style.

Mucala occurs as simplex only in Np. Mahā-mucala-mālaka Mhvs 15, 36. It refers to the tree **mucalinda**, of which it may be a short form. On the other hand mucal-inda appears to the speaker of Pāli a cp. noun, viz. king of the mucala(s) (trees). Its (late ?) Sk. correspondent is mucilinda, of which the P. form may be the regular representative (cp. Geiger *P.Gr.* § 34). — 1. the tree Barringtonia acutangula (Nicula*, of which it may be a dialectical distortion: *Abhp 563 nicula > *mucula > *mucala) Vin I.3; J V.405 (°ketakā, Dvandva); VI.269 (id.). — 2. N. of a nāga (serpent) king Vin I.3. — 3. N. of a great lake J VI.534, 535.

Mucchati [**murch,** an enlargement of Vedic **mūr** to get stiff (as in mūra stupid, dull, cp. Gr. μωρός; Sk. mūrakha foolish). Used in 2 senses, viz. (a) to become stiff & (b) (Caus.) to harden, increase in tone, make louder. From (a) a fig. meaning is derived in the sense of to become dulled or stupid, viz. infatuated, possessed. — See also Lüders in *K.Z.* XLII.194 a. How far we are justified to connect Dhtp 216 **mū** & 503 **mu** ("bandhane") with this root is a different question. These 2 roots seem to be without connections. — **mūrch** itself is at Dhtp 50 defined with "mohe"] 1. (spelt **muccati**) to become stiff, congeal, coagulate, curdle Dh 71; DhA II.67. — 2. to become infatuated D III.43 (majjati +). — 3. only in Caus. **muccheti** to make sound, to increase in tone J II.249 (viṇaŋ); III.188 (id.). — pp. **mucchita.**

Mucchanā (f.) [fr. mucchati 2] swelling or rising in tone, increase of sound J II.249 (vīṇaŋ uttama-mucchanāya mucchetvā vādesi).

Mucchañcikatā (°añji°) is probably the correct reading for **puñcikatā**. — We find **puñcikatā** at Dhs 1136, 1230; Vbh 351, 361 (v. l. pucchañji°); DhsA 365; mucchañci° at Nd¹ 8 & Nd² p. 152; pucchañji° at VbhA 477. The meaning is "agitation," as seen from explⁿ of term at DhsA 365 ("wagging of a dog's tail," pucchaŋ cāleti), and VbhA 477 ("lābhan' ālābhanaka-ṭhāne vedhanā kampanā nicavuttatā"). — The etym. explⁿ is difficult; we may take it as a (misunderstood) corruption of ***mucch-angi-kata** i. e. mucchā + anga + **kṛ** "being made stiff-of-limbs," or "swoon." Psychologically we may take "swoon" as the climax of agitation, almost like "hysterics." A similar case of a similar term of swooning being interpreted by Bdhgh as "wavering" (**cal**) is chambhitatta "paralysis," explᵈ as "sakala-sarīra calanaŋ" at DA I.50. — The expression mucchañcikatā reminds us of the term **kaṭukañcukatā.**

Mucchā [fr. **mūrch**] 1. fainting, swoon PvA 174. — 2. infatuation A II.10 (kāma°). Sn 328; Dhs 1059.

Mucchita [pp. of mucchati] 1. fainted, swooning, in a faint J I.243; DhA II.112; PvA 62, 174, 258. — 2. distraught, infatuated S I.61, 204; A I.274; D III.46 (a°); It 92; J III.432; V.274 (C. for pagiddha & gadhita). — Cp. pa°.

Mujjati [The P. form of the Sk. **majj**] to sink, dive, be submerged Dhtp 70 (mujja = mujjana). Only in cpds. um° & ni°.

Muñcati [Vedic muñcati; **muc,** to release, loosen; with orig. meaning "strip off, get rid of," hence also "glide" as in Lith. mūkti to escape, Ags. smūgan to creep, Ger. schmiegen to rub against. See further connections in Walde, *Lat. Wtb.*, s. v. emungo. The Dhtp 376 explˢ by mocane, Dhtm 609 id.; 631: moce; 765: pamocane] I. *Forms.* The 2 bases **muñc°** & **mucc°** are differentiated in such a way, that muñc° is the *active* base, and mucc° the *passive.* There are however cases where the active forms (muñc°) are used for the passive ones (mucc°), which may be due simply to a misspelling, ñc & cc being very similar. — A. *Active.* pres. **muñcati** J I.375; IV.272; V.453; Vv 64¹⁸; pot. **muñcetha** Dh 389; imper. **muñca** Dh 348; ppr. **muñcanto** Sn 791; aor. **muñci** J V.289; Mhvs 19, 44; pl. **muñciŋsu** J IV.142; ger. **muñciya** Mhvs 25, 67; **mutvā** J I.375; & **muñcitvā** ibid.; PvA 43; inf. **muñcituŋ** D I.96. — Caus. II. **muñcāpeti** D I.148. — B. *Passive.* pres. **muccati** Sn 508; ppr. **muccanto** J I.118; imper. sg. **muccassu** Th 2, 2; pl. **muccatha** DhA II.92; pot. **muñceyya** Pv II.2⁸; PvA 104; Dh 127; fut. **muccissati** J I.434 (where also **muñcissati** in same sense); DhA I.105; III.242; PvA 53, 105; also **mokkhasi** Vin I.21 = S I.111; pl. **mokkhanti** Dh 37; aor. **mucci(ŋsu)** S III.132; IV.20; J II.66; inf. **muccituŋ** Th 1, 253; DhA I.297. — Caus. **moceti** & **mocāpeti** (q. v.). — pp. **mutta.** — II. *Meanings.* 1. to release, deliver (from = abl.), set free (opp. bandhati) Sn 508 (sujjhati, m., bajjhati); S III.132 (cittāni mucciŋsu their hearts were cleansed), Th 2, 2 (muccassu); Dh 127 (pāpakammā, quoted at PvA 104); Pv II.2⁸; PvA 53 (niray' ûpapattito muccissati), 105; DhA I.297 (dukkhā muccitu-kāma desirous of being delivered from unpleasantness; v. l. muñc°); II.92 (dukkhā). — 2. to send off, let loose, drop, give J IV.272 (saraŋ an arrow); Vism 313 (dhenu vacchakassa khīra-dhāraŋ m.); Mhvs 25, 63 (phalakaŋ). — 3. to let out of the yoke, to unharness, set free D I.148 (satta usabha-satāni muñcāpeti); PvA 43 (yoggāni muñcitvā). — 4. to let go, emit, send forth (light) J V.289 (obhāsaŋ muñci); Mhvs 19, 44 (rasmiyo). — 5. to send forth (sound); to utter, emit (words etc.) J I.375 (vācaŋ); Vv 64¹⁸ (mālā m. ghosaŋ = vissajjenti VvA 281). — 6. (from 4 & 5 in general) to undertake, to bestow, send forth, let loose on Dh 389: "na brāhmaṇassa paha-reyya nāssa muñcetha brāhmaṇo," where DhA IV.148 supplements *veraŋ* na muñcetha (i. e. kopaŋ na kareyya). In this case veraŋ *muñcati* would be the same as the usual veraŋ *bandhati,* thus opposite notions being used complementarily. The interpretation "give up" (enmity) instead of "undertake" is possible from a mere grammatical point of view. L. v. Schroeder (*Worte der Wahrheit*) trslˢ "noch stürzt der Priester auf den Feind"! — 7. to abandon, give up, leave behind Dh 348 (muñca, viz. taṇhaŋ DhA IV.63); J V.453 (peta-rāja-visayaŋ). — 8. An idiomatic (late) use of the ger. **muñciya** (with acc.) is in the sense of an adv. (or prep.), meaning "except, besides," e. g. maŋ m. Mhvs 25, 67; imaŋ m. (besides this Mhvs 14, 17). — Cp.

pa°, paṭi°, vi°. *Note.* At Dh 71 muccati stands for muccheti (=Sk. mūrchati) to become stiff, coagulate, curdle; cp. DhA II.67.

Muñcana & **Muccana** (nt.) [abstr. fr. **muc**] 1. release, being freed, deliverance J IV.478 (mucc°); °ākāra (muñc°) means of deliverance (dukkhato from ill) DhA I.267; °kāla time of release (dukkhā from suffering) DhA II.11 (mucc°, v. l. muñc°). — 2. letting loose, emitting, giving, bestowing VbhA 249 (speaking, shouting out; Vism reading p. 265 is to be corrected fr. mañcana!); PvA 132 (v. l. dāna).

Muñcanaka (adj.) [fr. muñcana] sending out or forth, emitting VvA 303 (pabhā°).

Muñja [Vedic muñja, cp. Zimmer, *Altind. Leben* 72] 1. a sort of grass (reed) Saccharum munja Roxb. Sn 440. °kesa having a dark mane (like m. grass) D II.174. °pādukā slipper made of m. grass DhA III.451. °maya made of m. grass Sn 28. — The reed itself is called **isīkā** (q. v.). — 2. a sort of fish J IV.70 (+rohita, taken as Dvandva by C.); VI.278 (id.).

Muṭa see mutoḷī. Otherwise occurring in Np. Muṭa-siva at Mhvs 11, 4.

Muṭṭha [pp. of mussati, **mṛṣ**] having forgotten, one who forgets; only in two cpds., viz. °sacca [der. fr. foll.: muṭṭha+sati+ya] forgetfulness, lit. forgotten-mindedness, usually comb^d with asampajañña, D III.213; A V.149; Pug 21; Dhs 1349 (where read: yā asati ananussati . . . adhāraṇatā pilāpanatā sammussanatā); Vbh 360, 373; Vism 21; DhA IV.85; & °sati(n) (adj.) "forgetful in mindfulness," i. e. forgetful, careless, bewildered [cp. BSk. amuṣitasmṛti Lal. V. 562, to all appearance (wrongly) derived from P. musati to rob, **mus**, muṣṇāti] D III.252, 282; S I.61 (+asampajāna); Pug 21, 35 (neither passage expl^d in PugA!); J III.488; VbhA 275. As °satika at Miln 59. — *Note.* muṭṭhasati with var. (unsuccessful) etym. is discussed in detail also by Morris, *J.P.T.S.* 1884, pp. 92-94.

Muṭṭhi (f.) [Vedic muṣṭi, m. f. Does def^n "**muṭ**=maddane" at Dhtm 125 refer to muṭṭhi?] the fist VvA 206. **muṭṭhī katvā** gaṇhāti to take by making a fist, i. e. clutch tightly, clenching one's fist J VI.331. —**muṭṭhiŋ** akāsi he made a fist (as sign) J VI.364. As -° often meaning "handful." —**ācariya-muṭṭhi** close-fistedness in teaching, keeping things back from the pupil D II.100; S V.153; J II.221, 250; VvA 138; SnA 180, 368. **kuṇḍaka°** handful of rice powder VvA 5; DhA I.425. **taṇḍula°** handful of rice PvA 131. **tila°** do. of tila-seeds J II.278. **paŋsu°** do. of soil J VI.405. **ritta°** an empty fist SnA 306=DhA IV.38 (°sadisa alluding to ignorance).

-**yuddha** fist-fight, boxing D I.6. -**sammuñjanī** "fist-broom" a short broom DhA II.184.

Muṭṭhika [fr. muṭṭhi] 1. a fist-fighter, wrestler, boxer Vin II.105 (malla°); J IV.81 (Np.); VI.277; Vism 31 (+malla). — 2. a sort of hammer J V.45.

Muṇḍa (adj.) [cp. BSk. muṇḍa] bald, shaven; a shaven, (bald-headed) ascetic, either a samaṇa, or a bhikkhu or (f.) bhikkhunī S I.175 (m. saṅghāṭi-pāruta); Vin IV.265 (f.); Sn p. 80 (=muṇḍita-sīsa SnA 402). —**kaṇṇa°** with cropped or shorn ears (appl^d to a dog) Pv II.12[10], cp. **muṇḍaka.**

-**pabbataka** a bare mountain J I.303 (Hatthimatta); VvA 302 (v. l. for T. muṇḍika-pabbata). -**vaṭṭin** "shaven hireling" (?), a king's servant, probably porter Vin II.137. The expl^n given by Bdhgh on p. 319 (on CV. v. 29. 5) is twofold, viz. malla-kammakar' ādayo viya kacchaŋ banditvā nivāsenti; and muṇḍa-veṭṭhī (*sic*) ti yathā rañño kuhiñci gacchanto parikkhāra-bhaṇḍa-vahana-manussā ti adhippāyo. Maybe that reading **veṭi** is more correct -**sira** shaven head DhA II.125.

Muṇḍaka=muṇḍa; cp. BSk. muṇḍaka Divy 13. — Sn p. 80; Dh 264 (=sīsa-muṇḍana-matta DhA III.391, qualification of a shaveling); VvA 67 (°samaṇā, Dvandva). —**aḍḍha°** shaven over one half the head (sign of loss of freedom) Mhvs 6, 42. —**kaṇṇa°** "with blunt corners," N. of one of the 7 great lakes: see under kaṇṇa. -**paṭisīsaka** the chignon of a shaveling, in phrase: kāsāyaŋ nivāsetvā **muṇḍaka-paṭisīsakaŋ** sīse paṭimuñcitvā fastening the (imitation) top-knot of a shaveling to his head Miln 90; cp. J II.197 (pacceka-buddha-vesaŋ gaṇhitvā paṭisīsakaŋ paṭimuñcitvā), similarly J V.49.

Muṇḍatta (nt.) [abstr. fr. muṇḍa] the fact of being shaven or shorn PvA 106.

Muṇḍana (nt.) [fr. muṇḍa] shaving, tonsure DhA III.391

Muṇḍika (-pabbata) bare (mountain), uncertain T. reading at VvA 302 for v. l. SS muṇḍa-pabbata (q. v.).

Muṇḍita [pp. of muṇḍeti] shaven SnA 402 (°sīsa).

Muṇḍiya [abstr. fr. muṇḍa] baldness, shaven condition (of ascetics & bhikkhus) M I.515; Sn 249; Kvu I.95; Sdhp 374.

Muṇḍeti [Denom. — Caus. from muṇḍa] to shave Mhbv 103. — pp. **muṇḍita.** — The BSk. has only Caus. II. muṇḍāpayati, at Divy 261. Should Dhtp 106 "muṇḍ=khaṇḍha" be the def^n of muṇḍati? — At J III.368 we find muṇḍati for muṇḍeti (kuṇṭha-satthena muṇḍanto viya), which should prob. be read muṇḍento.

Muta [for mata, cp. Geiger, *P.Gr.* § 18] thought, supposed, imagined (i. e. received by other vaguer sense impressions than by sight & hearing) M I.3; Sn 714 (=phusan' arahaŋ SnA 498), 812; J V.398 (=anumata C.); Vbh 14, 429 sq. — Often in set diṭṭha suta muta what is seen, heard & thought (? more likely "felt," cp. Nd[2] 298: diṭṭha=cakkhunā d., sutaŋ=sotena s., mutaŋ=ghānena ghāyitaŋ, jivhāya sāyitaŋ, kāyena phuṭṭaŋ, *and* viññātaŋ=manasā v.; so that from the interpretation it follows that d. s. m. v. refer to the action (perception) of the 6 senses, where muta covers the 3 of taste, smell & touch, and viññāta the function of the manas) S I.186 (*K.S.* I.237 note); IV.73; Th I.1216. Similarly the psychol. analysis of the senses at Dhs 961: rūp' āyatanaŋ diṭṭhaŋ; sadd-āyat. sutaŋ; gandh°, ras°, phoṭṭhabb° mutaŋ; sabbaŋ rūpaŋ manasā viññātaŋ. See on this passage *Dhs trsl.* § 961 note. In the same sense DhsA 388 (see *Expositor,* II.439). — D III.232; Sn 790 (cp. Nd[1] 87 sq. *in extenso*) 793, 798, 812, 887, 901, 914, 1086, 1122. Thus quite a main tenet of the old (popular) psychology.

-**maṅgalika** one who prophesies from, or derives lucky auspices from impressions (of sense; as comp^d with diṭṭha-maṅgalika visible-omen-hunter, and suta-m. sound-augur) J IV.73 (where C. clearly expl^s by "touch"); KhA 119 (the same expl^n more in detail). -**visuddhika** of great purity, i. e. orthodox, successful, in matters of touch Nd[1] 89, 90. -**suddhi** purity in matter of touch Nd[1] 104, 105.

Muti (f.) [for mati, cp. muta] sense-perception, experience, understanding, intelligence Sn 864; Nd[1] 205 (on Sn 846=hearsay, what is thought); Vbh 325 (diṭṭhi, ruci, muti, where muti is expl^d at VbhA 412 as "*mudati* ti muti"!) 328; Sdhp 221. Cp. sam°.

Mutinga [Sk. mṛdaṅga on d>t. cp. Geiger, *P.Gr.* § 23] a small drum, tabour D I.79; Vin I.15; S II.266 sq (a famous mythological drum, called Ānaka; same also at J II.344); J IV.395 (bheri+); KhA 49. Spelling mudinga at S II.266; J IV.395; Vism 250; VbhA 232; VvA 210 (v. l. SS mutinga), 340 (id.).

-**sadda** sound of the drum J I.3 (one of the 10 sounds, hatthi°, assa° etc.).

Mutimant (adj.) [fr. muti] sensible, intelligent, wise Sn 539; as mutimā at Sn 61, 321, 385; pl. 881; J IV.76 (as mutīmā & mutimā): Nd^2 511 = 259. Cp. matimant.

Mutoḷi [?] a doubtful word occurring only in one stock phrase, viz. "ubhato-mukhā m. pūrā nānā-vihitassa dhaññassa" at M I.57 (vv. ll. putoḷi, mūtoḷī) = III.90 (mūtoḷi) = D II.293 (T. mutoli, v. l. muṭoli; gloss K pūtolī). The *Dial.* II.330 trsl. "sample bag" (see note on this passage; with remark "spelling uncertain"). Neumann, *Mittlere Sammlung* I.101 trsl^n "Sack." — Kern, *Toev.* s. v. mutoḷī tries to connect it with BSk. moṭa (Hindi moṭh), bundle, which (with vv. ll. mūḍha, muṭa, mūṭa) occurs only in one stock phrase "bharaiḥ motaiḥ piṭakaiḥ" at Divy 5, 332, 501, 524. The more likely solution, however, is that mutoḷī is a distortion of puṭosā (puṭosa), which is found as v. l. to puṭaŋsa at all passages concerned (see puṭaŋsa). Thus the meaning is "bag, provision-bag." The BSk. moṭa (muṭa) remains to be elucidated. The same meaning "provision-bag" fits at Vism 328 in cpd. yāna°, where spelling is T. °paṭṭoli, v. l. BB °putoḷi, but which is clearly identical with our term. We should thus prefer to read yāna-puṭosi "carriage-bag for provisions."

Mutta^1 [pp. of muñcati; Sk. mukta] 1. released, set free, freed; as -° free from Sn 687 (abbhā° free from the stain of a cloud); Dh 172 (id.), 382 (id.). — Dh 344; Pv IV.1^{34}; PvA 65 (su°). — 2. given up or out, emitted, sacrificed Vin III.97 = IV.27 (catta, vanta, m.) A III.50 (catta +). Cp. vi°. — 3. unsystematised. *Comp.* 9, 137 (vīthi°).
-ācāra of loose habits D I.166 = III.40 = Pug 55 (where expl^d at PugA 231, as follows: vissatth' ācāro. Uccāra-kamm' ādīsu lokiya-kulaputt' ācārena virahito ṭhitako va uccāraŋ karoti passāvaŋ karoti khādati bhuñjati). -paṭibhāna of loose intelligence, or immoderate promptitude (opp. yutta°), quick-tempered Pug 42 (cp. PugA 223); SnA 110, 111; -saddha given up to faith Sn 1146 (= saddhâdhimutta Nd^2 512). -sirā (pl.) with loose (i. e. confused) heads KhA 120 = Vism 415.

Mutta^2 (nt.) [cp. Vedic mūtra; Idg. ***meud** to be wet, as in Gr. μύζω to suck, μυδάω to be wet; Mhg. smuz (= Ger. schmutz), E. smut & mud, Oir. muad cloud (= Sk. mudira cloud); Av. muþrem impurity, Mir. mūn urine; Gr. μιαίνω to make dirty] urine Vin IV.266 (passāvo muttaŋ vuccati); Pv I.9^1 (gūthañ ca m.); PvA 43, 78. Enum^d under the 32 constituents of the body (the dvattiŋs-ākāraŋ) at Kh III. (cp. KhA 68 in detail on mutta; do. Vism 264, 362; VbhA 68, 225, 248 sq.) = M III.90 = D II.293 etc.
-ācāra see mutta^1. -karaṇa "urine-making," i. e. pudendum muliebre, cunnus Vin IV.260. -karīsa urine & fæces, i. e. excrements Vin I.301; S III.85; A II.33; Sn 835; Nd^1 181; J VI.111; Vism 259, 305, 342, 418 (origin of). -gata what has become urine DhsA 247 (gūtha° +). -vatthi the bladder Vism 345.

Muttaka (adj.) [mutta^1 + ka] only in cpd. antarā° one who is released in the meantime Vin II.167.

Muttakā (f.) = muttā; °maya made of pearls Mhvs 27, 33.

Muttatā (f.) [abstr. fr. mutta^1] state of being liberated, freedom J V.480.

Muttā (f.) [cp. Sk. muktā] a pearl Vv 37^7 (°ācita); Pv II.7^6 (+ veḷuriya); Mhvs 30, 66. Eight sorts of pearls are enum^d at Mhvs. 11, 14, viz. haya-gaja-rath' āmalakā valay'anguli-veṭhakā kakudha-phala-pākatikā, i.e. horse-, elephant-, waggon-, myrobalan-, bracelet-, ring-, kakudha fruit-, and common pearls.
-āhāra a string or necklace of pearls J I.383; VI.489; DhA I.85; SnA 78 (simile); Vism 312. -jāla a string (net) of pearls J IV.120; Mhvs 27, 31; VvA 198. -dāma garland or wreath of p. Mhvs 30, 67 (so T. for v. l. °maya). -vali string of pearls VvA 169. -sikkā string of pearls VvA 244.

Mutti (f.) [fr. **muc**, cp. Sk. mukti] release, freedom, emancipation Sn 344 (muty-apekho); Nd^1 88, 89 (+ vimutti & parimutti); PvA 35, 46; Sdhp 492. — Cp. vi°.

Muttika [fr. muttā] a pearl vendor, dealer in pearls Miln 262.

Mudati [for modati ?] in exegetical expl^n of "muti" at VbhA 412: mudatī ti muti. See muti.

Mudayantī (f.) [cp. Sk. modayantī] a certain plant, perhaps Ptychotis ajowan J VI.536.

Mudā (f.) [fr. **mud**, see modati] joy, pleasure D II.214 (v. l. pamudā); Sdhp 306, 308.

Mudinga see mutinga.

Mudita [pp. of **mud**, modati] pleased, glad, satisfied, only in cpd. °mana (adj.) with gladdened heart, pleased in mind Sn 680 (+ udagga); Vv 83^{16} (+ pasanna-citta). Cp. pa°.

Muditā (f.) [abstr. fr. mudu, for the usual mudutā, which in P. is only used in ord. sense, whilst muditā is in pregnant sense. Its semantic relation to mudita (pp. of **mud**) has led to an etym. relation in the same sense in the opinion of P. Commentators and the feeling of the Buddhist teachers. That is why Childers also derivers it from **mud**, as does Bdhgh. — BSk. after the Pali: muditā Divy 483] soft-heartedness, kindliness, sympathy. Often in triad mettā ("active love" SnA 128), karuṇā ("preventive love," ibid.), muditā ("disinterested love": modanti vata bho sattā modanti sādhu sutthū ti ādinā mayena hita-sukh' âvippayoga-kāmatā muditā SnA 128); e. g. at D I.251; S V.118; A I.196 etc. (see karuṇā). — Cp. also Sn 73; D III.50, 224, 248; Miln 332 (°saññā; + mettā°, karuṇā°); Vism 318 (where defined as "modanti tāya, taŋ-samangino, sayaŋ vā modati etc."); DhsA 192. See on term *Dhs trsl.* §251 (where equalled to συγχαιροσύνη); *Cpd.* 24 (called sympathetic & appreciative), 97 (called "congratulatory & benevolent attitude"); *Expos.* 200 (interpretation here refers to mudutā DhsA 151 "plasticity").

Mudu (adj.) [Vedic mṛdu, fr. **mṛd**; see maddati; cp. Lat. mollis (fr. *molduis); Gr. ἀμαλδύνω to weaken, Cymr. blydd soft] soft, mild, weak, tender D II.17 = III.143 (+ taluṇa); A II.151 (pañcindriyāni mudūni, soft, blunt, weak: opp. tikkha); S II.268 (°taluṇa-hatthapādā); Sn 447 (= muduka SnA 393); Th 1, 460 (= loving); Pv I.9^2; Vism 64; PvA 46, 230. Compar. mudutara S V.201.
-indriya (mud°) weak, slow minded, of dull senses Ps I.121 = II.195; Vism 87. -citta a tender heart PvA 54. -cittatā kind (soft) heartedness DhA I.234. -piṭṭhika having a soft (i. e. pliable) back Vin III.35. -bhūta supple, malleable D I.76 (+ kammaniya); Pug 68. -maddava soft & tender (said of food taken by young women to preserve their good looks) DhsA 403. -hadaya tender-hearted DhA II.5.

Muduka (adj.) [fr. mudu] = mudu. — 1. flexible, pliable, soft S II.221 (sanghāṭi); Vism 66 (giving in easily, cpd. with ukkaṭṭha & majjhima); KhA 49 (°aṭṭhikāni soft bones); Mhvs 25, 102 (sayana); bhūmi Miln 34. — 2. soft, mild, gentle, kindly, tender-hearted J V.83 (m. hadaya), 155; Miln 229 (cittaŋ m.); SnA 84 (°jātika), 393; DhA I.249 (citta); PvA 243. — 3. soft, weak, pampered, spoilt S II.268 (of the Licchavi princes). — See also **maddava**, & cp. ati°.

Mudutā (f.) [cp. Sk. mṛdutā; abstr. fr. mudu. See also muditā] softness, impressibility, plasticity A I.9; D III.153 (trsl^n "loveliness"); Dhs 44 (+ maddavatā); 1340 (id.); Vism 463 sq.; DhsA 151 (= mudubhāva); cp. *Dhs. trsl.* §1340.

Muddā (f.) [cp. (late ?) Sk. mudrā] 1. a seal, stamp, impression; —rāja° the royal seal DhA 1.21. Also with ref. to the State Seal at Miln 280, 281 in cpds. mudda-kāma (amacca) & mudda-paṭilābha. — 2. the art of calculation mentioned as a noble craft (ukkaṭṭhaŋ sippaŋ) at Vin IV.7 (with gaṇanā & lekhā), as the first of the sippāni (with gaṇanā) at M 1.85 = Nd² 199. Further at Miln 3, 59, 78 sq., 178. Cp. BSk. mudrā in same sense (e. g. at Divy 3, 26, 58 in set lipyā, saṅkhyā, gaṇanā, m.). Bdhgh's explⁿ of muddā D 1.11 m. + gaṇanā (see DA 1.95) as "hattha-muddā-gaṇanā" is doubtful; since at Miln 78 sq. muddā & gaṇanā are two quite diff. things. See also Franke, *Dīgha trsl.* p. 18, with note (he marks muddā "Finger-Rechnen" with ?); and cp. Kern, *Toev.* 1.166 s. v. muddā. The *Dial.* 1.21 trsl. "counting on the fingers" (see *Dial.* 1.21, 22 with literature & more refs.). —hattha° is sign-language, gesture (lit. hand-arithmetic), a means of communicating (question & answer) by signs, as clearly evident fr. J VI.364 (hattha-muddāya naŋ pucchissāmi . . . muṭṭhiŋ akāsi, sā "ayaŋ me . . . pucchati" ti ñatvā hatthaŋ vikāsesi, so ñatvā . . .; he then asks by word of mouth). —hattha-muddaŋ karoti to make a sign, to beckon J III.528; cp. Vin V.163: na hattha-vikāro kātabbo, na hattha-muddā dassetabbā.
 -**âdhikaraṇa** the office of the keeper of the Privy Seal, Chancellorship Miln 281.

Muddika (adj. n.) [fr. muddā] one who practises muddā (i. e. knowledge of signs) D 1.51 (in list of occupations, combᵈ with gaṇaka & trslᵈ *Dial.* 1.68 by "accountant"; cp. Franke, *Dīgha* p. 53, "Finger-rechner" ?) Vin IV.8 (m., gaṇaka, lekhaka); S IV.376 (gaṇaka, m., saṅkhāyaka).

Muddikā¹ (f.) [fr. muddā] a seal ring, signet-ring, finger-ring J 1.134; III.416; IV.439; DhA 1.394; II.4 (a ring given by the king to the keeper of the city gates as a sign of authority, and withdrawn when the gates are closed at night); IV.222. anguli° finger-ring, signet-ring Vin II.106; J IV.498; V.467. — Similarly as at DhA II.4 (muddikaŋ āharāpeti) muddikā is fig. used in meaning of "authority," command; in phrase muddikaŋ deti to give the order, to command Miln 379 (with ref. to the captain of a ship).

Muddikā² (f.) [fr. mudu, cp. *Sk. mṛdvīkā] a vine or bunch of grapes, grape, grape wine Vin 1.246 (°pāna); J VI.529; DhA II.155.

Muddha¹ [pp. of **muh,** for the usual mūḷha, corresp. to Sk. mugdha. Not = mṛddha (of **mṛdh** to neglect) which in P. is maddhita: see pari°; nor = mṛdhra disdained] infatuated, bewildered, foolish J V.436.
 -**dhātuka** bewildered in one's nature, foolish(ly) J IV.391 (v. l. luddha°); DhA III.120 (v. l. danta° & mūḷa°).

Muddha² & **Muddhā** [Vedic mūrdhan, the P. word shows a mixture of a- and n- stem] the head; top, summit. — m. sg. muddhā Sn 983, 1026, & muddhaŋ Sn 989; acc muddhaŋ D 1.95; Sn 987 sq., 1004, 1025; Dh 72 (= paññāy' etaŋ nāmaŋ DhA II.73); & muddhānaŋ M 1.243; III.259 = S IV.56; instr. muddhanā Mhvs 19, 30; loc. muddhani Sn 689, 987; M 1.168; Vism 262; Mhvs 36, 66, in meaning "on the top of (a mountain)": Vin 1.5 (here spelt pabbata-muddhini) = S 1.137; J IV.265 (Yugandhara°); Pv II.9⁶¹ (Naga° = Sineru° PvA 138); Vism 304 (vammika° on top of an ant-hill). — Freq. in phrase muddhā (*me,* or *no,* or *te*) sattadhā phaleyya, as an oath or exclamⁿ of desecration or warning: "(your) head shall split into 7 pieces," intrs. spelt both phal° & phāl° at J V.92 (te s. phal°); Miln 157; DhA 1.17 (me . . . phāl°), 41 (te phalatu s.), 42 (ācariyassa m. s. phalissati); IV.125 (no . . . phāleyya); VvA 68 (me s. phal°). — In compⁿ muddha°.
 -(n)aṭṭhi (muddhan-aṭṭhi) bone of the head KhA 51. -**âdhipāta** head-splitting, battering of the head Sn 988 sq., 1004, 1025; -**âdhipātin** head-splitting (adj.) Sn 1026. -**âra** head (top) spoke KhA 172. -**âvasitta** "head-anointed" a properly anointed or crowned king D III.60 sq., 69; Pug 56; Miln 234. -**pāta** = °ādhipāta.

Muddhatā (f.) [fr. muddha¹] foolishness, stupidity, infatuation J V.433 (v. l. muṭhatā, muddatā).

Mudhā (adv.) [Class. Sk. mudhā] for nothing, gratis VvA 77.

Munana (nt.) [fr. munāti, almost equal to mona] fathoming, recognising, knowing; a C. word to explain "muni," used by Dhpāla at VvA 114 (mahā-isibhūtaŋ . . . mahanten' eva ñāṇena munanato paricchindanato mahā muniŋ), & 231 (anavasesassa ñeyyassa munanato muni).

Munāti [= manyate, prob. corresponding to Sk. med. manute, with inversion *munati and analogy formation after jānāti as munāti, may be in allusion to Sk. mṛṇāti of **mṛ** to crush, or also **mā** mināti to measure out or fathom. The Dhtm 589 gives as root **mun** in meaning "ñāṇa." The word is more a Com. word than anything else, formed from muni & in order to explain it] to be a wise man or muni, to think, ponder, to know Dh 269 (yo munāti ubho loke munī tena pavuccati), which is explᵈ at DhA III.396 as follows: "yo puggalo . . . tulaŋ āropetvā minanto viya ime ajjhattikā khandhā ime bāhirā ti ādinā nayena ime ubho pi atthe mināti munī tena pavuccati." *Note.* The word occurs also in Māgadhī (Prk.) as muṇaï which as Pischel (*Prk. Gr.* § 489) remarks, is usually taken to **man,** but against this speaks its meaning "to know" & Pāli munāti. He compares maṇaï with Vedic mūta in kāma-mūta (driven by kāma; mūta = pp. of **mū** = **mīv**) and Sk. muni. Cp. animo movere.

Muni [cp. Vedic muni, originally one who has made the vow of silence. Cp. Chh. Up. VIII.5, 2; *Pss. of the Br.* 132 note. Connected with mūka: see under mukha. This etym. preferred by Aufrecht: Halāyudha p. 311. Another, as favoured by Pischel (see under munāti) is "inspired, moved by the spirit." Pāli explⁿˢ (popular etym.) are given by Dhammapāla at VvA 114 & 231: see munana] a holy man, a sage, wise man. I. The term which was specialised in Brahmanism has acquired a general meaning in Buddhism & is applied by the Buddha to any man attaining perfection in self-restraint and insight. So the word is capable of many-sided application and occurs frequently in the oldest poetic anthologies, e. g. Sn 207-221 (the famous Muni-sutta, mentioned Divy 20, 35; SnA 518; explᵈ SnA 254-277), 414, 462, 523 sq., 708 sq., 811 sq., 838, 844 sq., 912 sq., 946, 1074 & passim (see Pj. Index p. 749); Dh 49, 225, 268 sq., 423. — Cp. general passages & explⁿˢ at Pv II.1¹³; II.13³ (explᵈ at PvA 163 by "attahitañ ca parahitañ ca munāti jānātī ti muni"); Miln 90 (munibhāva "munihood," meditation, self-denial, abrogation); DhA III.521 (munayo = moneyya-paṭipadāya magga-phalaŋ pattā asekha-munayo), 395 (here explᵈ with ref. to orig. meaning tuṇhībhāva "state of silence" = mona). — II. The Com. & Abhidhamma literature have produced several schedules of muni-qualities, esp. based on the 3 fold division of character as revealed in action, speech & thought (kāya°, vacī°, mano°). Just as these 3 are in general exhibited in good or bad ways of living (°sucaritaŋ & °duccaritaŋ), they are applied to a deeper quality of saintship in kāya-moneyya, vacī-moneyya, mano-moneyya; or Muni-hood in action, speech & thought; and the muni himself is characterised as a kāya-muni, vacī° & mano°. Thus runs the long exegesis of muni at Nd² 514ᴬ = Nd¹ 57. Besides this the same chapter (514ᴮ) gives a division of 6 munis, viz. agāra-muni, anagāra° (the bhikkhus), sekha°, asekha° (the Arahants), pacceka° (the Paccekabuddhas), muni° (the Tathāgatas). — The parallel passage to Nd² 514ᴬ at A I.273 gives a muni as kāya-muni, vācā° & ceto° (under the 3 moneyyāni).

Mummura [*Sk. murmura, lit. crackling, rustling; cp. Lat. murmur = E. murmur, Gr. μορμύρω to rustle, Ohg. murmurōn & murmulōn = Ger. murmeln; all to Idg. ***mrem,** to which Sk. marmara: see P. mammara & cp. murumurā] crackling fire, hot ashes, burning chaff J II.134.

Muyhati [Vedic muhyati, **muh;** defⁿ Dhtp 343: mucchāyaŋ; 460: vecitte; cp. moha & momuha] to get bewildered, to be infatuated, to become dull in one's senses, to be stupified. Just as rāga, dosa & moha form a set, so do the verbs rajjati, dussati, muyhati, e. g. Miln 386 (rajjasi rajjanīyesu, dussanīyesu dussasi, muyhase mohanīyesu). Otherwise rare as finite verb; only DhsA 254 (in defⁿ of moha) & Sdhp 282, 605 (so read for mayhạte). — pp. mūḷha & muddha¹.

Muyhana (nt.) [fr. muyhati] bewilderment, stupefaction, infatuation DA I.195 (rajjana-dussana-m.).

Muraja [cp. Epic. & Class. Sk. muraja, Prk. murava: Pischel, *Prk. Gr.* § 254] 1. a small drum, tambourine J V.390; Vv 35³ (= bheri VvA 161); 84¹⁸ (= mudinga VvA 340); SnA 370. — 2. a kind of girdle Vin II.136.

Murumurā (indecl.) [onomat. to sound root **mṛ,** see mammara & mummura] the grinding, crackling sound of the teeth when biting bones, "crack"; in phrase m. ti khādati to eat or bite up to bits J I.342; V.21 (of a Yakkhinī, eating a baby).

Murumurāpeti = murumurāyati J II.127; III.134; V.196 (°etvā khādati).

Murumurāyati [Denom. fr. murumurā] to munch, chew, bite up with a cracking sound J IV.491.

Muḷāla & Muḷālī (f.) [cp. Vedic mulālin. Zimmer, *Altind. Leben* 70 mentions Bisa, Śāluka & Mulālin as edible roots of lotus kinds. — Geiger, *P.Gr.* 12 & 43 puts muḷāla = Sk. mṛṇāla] the stalk of the lotus: **muḷālī** Vin I.215 (bhisa +); muḷāli J VI.530 (= muḷālaka C.); **muḷālikā** Vin I.215 (bhisa +); bhisa-**muḷālaŋ** (nt.) (collective cpd.) fibre & stalks Vin II.201 = S II.269; IV.94; V.39; Vism 361; VbhA 66. —**muḷāli-puppha** a lotus Th 1, 1089.

Musati [in this connection = **mṛṣ** in an active sense, as quasi Denom. fr. musā. Not to **muṣ** to steal, which is given at Dhtp 491 with "theyya"] to betray, beguile, bewilder, dazzle, in cakkhūni m. D II.183 (but trslⁿ "destructive to the eyes"); musati 'va nayanaŋ Vv 35³ (cp. VvA 161).

Musala (m. nt.) [cp. Vedic musala. The etym. is probably to be connected with **mṛd** (see maddati)] 1. a pestle (whilst udukkhala is "mortar," cp. J II.428 & see udukkhala) D I.166 = Pug 55; DhA II.131 (+ suppa). — 2. a club A II.241; VvA 121. — 3. a crowbar J I.199; PvA 258 (°daṇḍa).

Musalaka (nt.) [fr. musala] a little pestle, a toy for little girls DhsA 321.

Musalika only in cpd. **danta°** (an ascetic) who uses his teeth as a pestle J IV.8 (an aggi pakkaŋ khādati, eats food uncooked, only crushed by his teeth).

Musā (adv.) [Vedic mṛṣā, fr. **mṛṣ,** lit. "neglectfully"] falsely, wrongly; usually with verbs **vadati, bhanati, bhāsati** & **brūti** to speak falsely, to tell a lie. — A I.149 (opp. saccaŋ); Sn 122, 158, 397, 400, 757, 883, 967, 1131; Nd¹ 291; Pv I.3³; VvA 72 (= abhūtaŋ atacchaŋ); SnA 19; PvA 16, 152.

-**vāda** lying, a falsehood, a lie D I.4, 25; III.68 sq., 92 sq., 106, 170, 195, 232, 269; M I.414; Sn 129, 242 (cp. D II.174); Dh 246; Pug 57; Nd¹ 268; Vv 15⁸; Pv I.6⁸; VbhA 383 (var. degrees); PvA 16; Sdhp 65; explicitly at Nd¹ 152, 394; Nd² 515. Cp. mosavajja. -**vādin** speaking falsely, lying D I.138; III.15, 82; Dh 176; Pug 29, 38.

Mussati [= **mṛṣ,** mṛṣyati; to which musā "wrongly," quite diff. in origin fr. micchā: mṛṣā > mithyā. Dhtm 437 defines by "sammose," i. e. forgetfulness] v. intrs.: to forget, to pass into oblivion, to become bewildered, to become careless D I.19 (sati m.); J V.369 (id.); Sn 815 (= nassati SnA 536; = parimussati, paribāhiro hoti Nd¹ 144). — pp. muṭṭha. Cpp. pa°, pari°.

Muhutta (m. & nt.) [Vedic muhūrta, fr. muhur suddenly] a moment, a very short period of time, an inkling, as we should say "a second." — Its duration may be seen from descending series of time-connotations at PvA 198 (under jātakamma, prophesy by astrologers at the birth of a child): rāsi, nakkhatta, tithi, m.; and from defⁿ at Nd² 516 by "khaṇaŋ, layaŋ, vassaŋ, atthaŋ." — Usually in oblique cases: **muhuttena** in a short time, in a twinkling of an eye PvA 55; **muhuttaŋ** (acc.) a moment, even a second Sn 1138 (m. api); Dh 65 (id.), 106; PvA 43.

Muhuttika (adj.) [fr. muhutta] only for a moment; °ā (f.) a temporary wife, in enumⁿ of several kinds of wives at Vin III.139 & VvA 73. Syn. tan-khaṇikā.

Mū is given as root as Dhtp 216 in meaning "bandhana."

Mūga (adj.) [Vedic mūka; see etym. under mukha] dumb Vin I.91 (andha, m., badhira); Sn 713; DhA II.102 (andha, m., badhira); SnA 51 (in simile); Sdhp 12. Freq. combᵈ with **eḷa,** deaf (q. v.).

Mūla (nt.) [Vedic mūra & mūla. The root is given as **mūl** in 2 meanings, viz. lit. "rohane" Dhtm 859, and fig. "patiṭṭhāyaŋ" Dhtm 391] 1. (lit.) root A II.200 = M I.233; DhA I.270; IV.200 (opp. patti); Vism 270 (rukkha° = rukkha-samīpaŋ); Pv II.9⁶ (sa° with the root); PvA 43 (rukkhassa mūle at the foot of). — 2. foot, bottom Vin II.269 (patta°); PvA 73 (pāda°), 76 (id.). **rukkha°** foot of a tree: see under rukkha for special meaning. — 3. (applᵈ) ground for, reason, cause, condition, defᵈ as "hetu, nidāna, sambhava" etc. at Nd² s. v.; Sn 14 = 369 (akusalā mūlā n. pl. = ākāra or patiṭṭhā SnA 23); Pv II.3³³ (sa° with its cause); Dukp 272, 297, 312, 320; Miln 12 (& khandha-yamaka, with ref. to the Yamaka). Very freq. in this sense as referring to the three lobha, dosa, moha as conditioning akusala (& absence of them = kusala), e. g. at D III.214, 275; A I.201, 203; Vbh 106 sq., 169, 361; Yam I.1; Vism 454; cp. Nd² 517; VbhA 382. — 4. origin, source, foundation, root (fig.) Vin I.231 = D II.91 (dukkhassa); Vin II.304; Sn 916, 968 (cp. Nd¹ 344, 490); Th 1, 1027 (brahmacariyassa); Dh 247, 337. Freq. in formula (may be taken to no. 1) [pahīna] ucchinna-mūla tālāvatthukata etc. with ref. to the origin of saŋsāra, e. g. at S II.62, 88; III.10, 27, 161, 193; IV.253, 292, 376. See Nd² p. 205 s. v. pahīna, *in extenso*. — 5. beginning, base, in **mūladivasa** the initial day DA I.311; also in phrase **mūlakāraṇato** right from the beginning VvA 132 (cp. BSk. mūlaŋ kramataś ca id. Divy 491). 6. "substance," foundation, i. e. worth, money, capital, price, remuneration Miln 334 (kamma°); DhA I.270 (?); PvA 273; Mhvs 27, 23. **amūla** unpaid Mhvs 30, 17 (kamma labour). —**iṇa°** borrowed capital D I.71.

-**kanda** eatable tuber DhA III.130; IV.78 (mūlaka°). See also kanda. -**kammaṭṭhāna** fundamental k. or k. of causes SnA 54. -**ghacca** radically extirpated Dh 250, 263. -**ṭṭha** one who is the cause of something, an instigator Vin III.75. -**dassāvin** knowing the cause or reason Sn 1043, cp. Nd^2 517. -phala (eatable) fruit, consisting of roots; roots as fruit Sn 239. -bandhana fundamental bond (?) or set of causes (?) Sn 524 sq., 530 sq., cp. SnA 429-431. -bīja having seeds in roots, i. e. propagated by roots, one of the classes of plants enum^d under bījagāma (q. v.). -rasa taste of roots, or juice made fr. roots VbhA 69; see under rasa.

Mūlaka (adj. nt.) [fr. mūla] 1. (adj.) (a) (-°) being caused by, having its reason through or from, conditioned by, originating in Vbh 390 (taṇhā° dhammā); Tikp. 233 sq., 252 sq., 288 sq. & passim; VbhA 200 sq., 207 sq. (sankhāra°, avijjā° etc. with ref. to the constituents of the Paṭicca-samuppāda); PvA 19. — (b) having a certain worth, price, being paid so much, dear Mhvs 27, 23 (a °ŋ kammaŋ unpaid labour); DhA I.398 (nahāna-cuṇṇa °ŋ catu-paṇṇāsa-koṭi dhanaŋ, as price); II.154 (pattha-pattha-mūlakā bhikkhā); III.296 (kiŋ mūlakaŋ how dear?). — 2. (nt.) = mūla, i. e. root, bulb, radish, only in cpd. **mūlaka-kanda** radish (-root) J IV.88, 491; DhA IV.78. — See also **pulaka.**

Mūlika (adj. n.) [fr. mūla] 1. (m.) root-vendor Miln 331. — 2. (adj. -°) belonging to the feet (pāda°), a footman, lackey J I.122, 438; II.300 sq. (N. of the king of Janasandha, Gāmaṇi-caṇḍa); III.417; V.128; VI.30. — 3. in rukkha° one who lives at the foot of a tree: see under rukkha, where also °mūlikatta.

Mūḷha [Vedic mūḍha, pp. of **muh**; cp. also muddha^1 = Vedic mugdha] 1. gone astray, erring, having lost one's way (magga°) D I.85 ≈ (°ssa maggaŋ ācikkhati); Pv IV.1^{48} (id. with pāvadati); PvA 112 (magga°). — 2. confused, infatuated, blinded, erring, foolish D I.59; Pv IV.3^{34} (sa°, better to be written sam°).

-**gabbhā** (f.) a woman whose "fœtus in utero" has gone astray, i. e. cannot be delivered properly, a woman difficult to be delivered J I.407 = DhA IV.192; Miln 169; VbhA 96. -**rūpa** foolish Dh 268; DhA III.395.

Mūsika (m.) & mūsikā (f.) [Vedic mūṣikā, fr. mūṣ] a mouse D II.107 = Pug 43 (f.); Vism 109 (m.), 252 = KhA 46 (m.); Mhvs 5, 30 (m.); VbhA 235.

-**cchinna** (auguries from the marks on cloth (gnawed by mice) D I.9 (mūsikā°; DA I.92 mūsika° = undurakhāyitaŋ; cp. *Dial.* I.17). -**darī** a mouse-hole J I.462 (mūsikā°, so read for musikā°). -**patha** "Mouse-road" N. of a road Nd^1 155, 415 (here mūsikā°). -**potikā** the young of a mouse J IV.188 (mūsika°). -**vijjā** mouse craft D I.9 (cp. DA I.93).

Mūsī (f.) [Vedic mūṣ & mūḥ mouse or rat; cp. Lat. mūs Gr. μῦς, Ohg. mūs = E. mouse. Not to **muṣ** to steal, but to same root as Lat. moveo, to move] a mouse S II.270 (mudu° a tender, little m.).

Me is enclitic form of **ahaŋ** in var. cases of the sg. See under ahaŋ.

Mekhalā (f.) [cp. Vedic mekhalā] a girdle J V.202, 294 (su°, adj.); VI.456; ThA 35; KhA 109; DhA I.39; PvA 46.

Mekhalikā (f.) [fr. mekhalā] a girdle Vin II.185 (ahi°, consisting of a snake).

Megha [Vedic megha; *not* to **mih,** mehati (see mīḷha), but to Idg. ***meigh-**, fog, rain; cp. Sk. mih mist; Av. maēga cloud; Gr. ὀμίχλη fog, Lith. migha fog, Dutch miggelen to drizzle, also Ags. mist = Oicel mistr "mist"] a cloud Pv II.9^{45}; Vism 126; esp. a thunder-cloud, storm, S I.100 (thaneti), 154; Th I.307 (as kāḷa); It 66; J I.332 (pajjunna vuccati megha); DhA I.19; SnA 27 (°thanita-sadda). In this capacity often called **mahā-megha,** e. g. Sn 30; DhA I.165; KhA 21; PvA 132. — On megha in similes see *J.P.T.S.* 1907, 124, 125.

-**nātha** having clouds as protectors (said with ref. to grass-eating animals) J IV.253. -**maṇḍala** cloud-circle, a circle of clouds SnA 27. -**vaṇṇa** cloud-coloured J V.321 (C. for megha-sannibha); *°pāsāṇa* a sort of ornamental building stone Mhvs 30, 59 (v. l., T. meda°; trsl. fat-coloured stones). See meda°.

Mecaka (adj.) [cp. Vedic mecaka] black, dark blue DhsA 13.

Mejjati [cp. Vedic midyati, to **mid,** see meda Dhtp 160, 413 & Dhtm 641 give **mid** with meaning "snehane"] to be fat, to be full of fat; fig. to be in love with or attracted by, to feel affection (this meaning only as a "petitio principii" to explain mettā) DhsA 192 (v. l. mijjati; = siniyhati).

Mejjha (adj.-nt.) [*medhya; fr. medha] 1. (adj.) [to medha^1] fit for sacrifice, pure; neg. **a°** impure Sdhp 363. 2. (nt.) [to medha^2 & medhāvin] in **dum°** foolishness Pug 21 = Dhs 390 (expl^d at DhsA 254 by "yaŋ . . . citta-santānaŋ mejjhaŋ bhaveyya suci-vodānaŋ taŋ duṭṭhaŋ mejjhaŋ iminā ti dummejjhaŋ").

Meṇḍa [dial., cp. Prk. mĕṇṭha & miṇṭha: Pischel, *Prk. Gr.* § 293. The Dhtm (156) gives a root **meṇḍ** (meḍ) in meaning of "koṭilla," i. e. crookedness. The Ved. (Sk.) word for ram is meṣa] 1. a ram D I.9; J IV.250, 353 (°visāṇa-dhanu, a bow consisting of a ram's horn). -°patha Npl. "ram's road" Nd^1 155 = 415. -°**yuddha** ram fight D I.6. — 2. a groom, elephant-driver in cpd. hatthi° elephants' keeper J III.431; V.287; VI.489.

Meṇḍaka (adj.) [fr. meṇḍa] 1. made of ram(s) horn, said of a (very strong) bow J II.88 (°dhanu); V.128 (°singa-dhanu). — 2. belonging to a ram, in **meṇḍaka-pañha** "question about the ram" Miln 90 alluding to the story of a ram in the Ummagga-jātaka (J VI.353-55), which is told in form of a question, so difficult & puzzling that nobody "from hell to heaven" (J VI.354) can answer it except the Bodhisatta. Cp. Trenckner's remark Miln 422.

Metta (adj. nt.) [cp. Vedic maitra "belonging to Mitra"; Epic Sk. maitra "friendly," fr. mitra] friendly, benevolent, kind as adj. at D III.191 (mettena kāya-kammena etc.), 245 (°ŋ vacī-kammaŋ); as nt. for mettā in cpds. of mettā (cp. mettaŋsa) and by itself at D I.227 (mettaŋ + cittaŋ), perhaps also at Sn 507.

Mettā (f.) [abstr. fr. mitra = mitta, cp. Vedic maitraŋ. According to Asl. 192 (cp. *Expos.* 258) derived fr. **mid** to love, to be fat: "mejjati mettā siniyhatī ti attho"] love, amity, sympathy, friendliness, active interest in others. There are var. def^{ns} & expl^{ns} of mettā: the stereotype "metti mettāyanā mettāyitattaŋ mettā cetovimutti" Vbh 86 = 272; occurring as "metti mettāyanā mettāyitattaŋ anudā anudāyana anudāyitattaŋ hitesitā anukampā abyāpādo . . . kusalamūlaŋ" at Nd^1 488 & Dhs 1056 (where T. mettaŋ for metti, but see *Dhs trsl.*^{2} 253). By Bdhgh at SnA 128 expl^d in distinction fr. karuṇā (which is "ahita-dukkh-âpanaya-kāmatā") as "hita-sukh-ûpanaya-kāmatā," i. e. desire of bringing welfare & good to one's fellow-men. Cp. def^n of mettā at Vism 317. — Sn 73 (see Nd^2 p. 232), 967; D III.247 sq., 279; Vism 111, 321 sq.; SnA 54; PvA 66 (khanti, m., anudaya); Sdhp 484, 487. — *Phrases* occurring frequently: **mettā ceto-vimutti** D I.251; S II.265; A IV.150; It 20; Vbh 86 and passim. **mettā-sahagatena cetasā** with a heart full of love D I.250; II.186; III.49 sq., 78, 223 sq.; S V.115; A I.138; II.129; IV.390; V.299, 344; expl^d in detail at Vism 308. **mettaŋ karoti** (loc.) to be friendly or sympathize with Mhvs 12, 23. — In cpds. usually mettā°, but shortened to metta° in metta-cittaŋ kindly thought, a heart full of love D I.167; III.237; Sn 507; Pv II.13^{17}; J VI.71; and metta-jhāna love-meditation, as expl^n of m.-citta at SnA 417; PvA 167.

-**aŋsa** (mettaŋsa) sympathetic, showing love towards It 22 (v. l. °āsa); J IV.71 (=metta-koṭṭhāsa metta-citta C.). -**kammaṭṭhāna** the k. of sympathy DhA IV.108. -**bhāvanā** cultivation or development of friendliness (towards all living beings) J I.176; III.45; Miln 199; Vism 295. -**vihārin** abiding in kindliness Dh 368; DhA IV.108; Nett 25; Vism 324; PvA 230.

Mettāyati [Denom. fr. mettā] to feel friendly, to show love, to be benevolent A IV.151; DhsA 194; VbhA 75. With loc. to show friendship or be affectionate towards J I.365; III.96; Dāvs III.34.

Mettāyanā (f.) & **Mettāyitatta** (nt.) [abstr. formations fr. mettā]: see def^n of mettā.

Metti & **Mettī** (f.) [cp. Epic Sk. maitrī] love, friendship J III.79; V.208; VbhA 75. See also def^n of mettā.

Metteyyatā (f.) is occasional spelling for matteyyatā (q. v.), in analogy to **petteyyatā**; e. g. Nd^2 294.

Methuna (adj.-nt.) [fr. Vedic mithuna pair, der. fr. mithu. Cp. micchā] 1. (adj.) relating to sexual intercourse, sexual, usually with **dhamma**, sex intercourse, in phrase °ŋ **dhammaŋ paṭisevati** to cohabit Vin I.96; D II.133; Sn 291, 704; Nd^1 139; Vism 418; SnA 536. — (m.) an associate J VI.294 (na rājā hoti methuno). — 2. (nt.) sexual intercourse [Vedic maithuna] D I.4; III.9, 88 sq. 133; Sn 400, 609, 814, 835=DhA I.202; Nd^1 139, 145; Pug 67; Vism 51.

Methunaka [fr. methuna] 1. one concerned with (illicit) sexual intercourse, a fornicator Nd^1 139 (in a wider sense). — 2. an associate Vin III.66. — 3. (nt.) coitus J II.360 (=methuna-dhamma C.).

Meda [Vedic medas (nt.) fr. **mid**, see etym. under mada] fat S I.124; Sn 196; J III.484 (ajakaraŋ medaŋ=aja-kara-medaŋ C.); Kh III. (expl^d at Vism 262 as "thīna-sineha" thick or coagulated fluid or gelatine); Vism 361; VbhA 66, 225, 245, 249.

-**kathālika** a cooking pot or saucepan for frying fat A IV.377 (in simile with kāya); DhA II.179 (similar); Vism 195 (in compar.). -**gaṇṭhi** (as medo-gaṇṭhi, Sk. influence!) an abscess of fat, fatty knot or tumour, mentioned as a disease at Miln 149. -**vaṇṇa** fat-coloured; in cpd. °*pāsāṇa* a stone of the (golden) colour of fat found in the Himālaya mountains Sn 447 (=meda-piṇḍa-sadisa SnA 393); Mhvs I, 39; 30, 57 sq., 92; 31, 121; see Geiger's note Mhvs (P.T.S. ed.) p. 355, who puts it beyond doubt, that meda° is the correct reading for the v. l. megha° at all places.

Medaka [meda+ka] in go° a precious stone of light-red (or golden) colour (cp. meda-vaṇṇa-pāsāṇa) VvA 111.

Medinī (f.) [of adj. medin, fr. meda fat, but cp. Vedic medin an associate or companion fr. **mid** in meaning to be friendly] the earth (also later Sk.) Mhvs 5, 185; 15, 47; Vism 125.

Medeti [Denom. fr. meda] to become fat M I.238.

Medha [Vedic medha, in aśva, go°, puruṣa° etc.] sacrifice only in assa° horse-sacrifice & **purisa**° human s. (q. v.), e.g. at A IV.151; Sn 303. — Cp. mejjha.

Medhaga (& °ka) [cp. Sk. methana abusive speech; Vedic methati fr. **mith** to scold] quarrel, strife Vin II.88 (°ka); Th 2, 344; Sn 893, 894 (=kalaha, bhaṇḍana, viggaha vivāda Nd^1 302, 303), 935 (T. °ka; Nd^1 402 & 406 °ga, with v. l. SS °ka); Dh 6; J III.334 (°ka; C.=kalaha), 488 (°ga; C. °ka expl^n kalaha); DhA I.65.

Medhasa (adj.) [=Vedic medhas, as a-base] having wisdom or intelligence, wise, only in cpds. bhūri° of great wisdom Sn 1131; & su° [Ved. sumedhas] very wise Vv 22^2 (=sundara-pañña VvA 111); Pv III.7^7 (both comb^d as bhūri-su-medhasa, hardly correct; v. l. M. bhūrimedhasa PvA 205).

Medhā (f.) [Vedic medhā & medhas, perhaps to Gr. μαθ° in μανθάνω ("mathematics")] wisdom, intelligence, sagacity Nd^1 s. v. (m. vuccati paññā); Pug 25; Dhs 16, DhsA 148; PvA 40 (=paññā). — adj. sumedha wise, clever, intelligent Sn 177; opp. dum° stupid Pv I.8^3. —**khīṇa-medha** one whose intelligence has been impaired, stupefied J VI.295 (=khīṇa-pañña).

Medhāvitā (f.) [abstr. fr. medhāvin] cleverness, intelligence VvA 229.

Medhāvin (adj.) [medhā+in=*medhāyin > medhāvin; already Vedic, cp. medhasa] intelligent, wise, often comb^d with **paṇḍita** & **bahussuta**: D I.120; S IV.375; A IV.244; Vin IV.10, 13, 141; Sn 323 (acc. medhāvinaŋ + bahussutaŋ) 627, 1008 (Ep. of Mogharājā), 1125 (id.); Nd^2 259 (s. v. jātimā, with var. other synonyms); Dh 36; J VI.294; Miln 21; DhA I.257; II.108; IV.169; VvA 131; PvA 41.

Medhi (f.) [Vedic methī pillar, post (to bind cattle to); BSk. medhi Divy 244; Prk. meḍhi Pischel *Gr.* § 221. See for etym. Walde, *Lat. Wtb.* s. v. meta] pillar, part of a stūpa [not in the Canon ?].

Medhin (adj.-n.)=medha in adj. use; only in cpd. **dum-medhin** (=dum-medha) foolish, ignorant Dh 26 (bālā dummedhino janā; =nippaññā DhA I.257).

Meraya (nt.) [Epic Sk. maireya, cp. Halāyudha 2, 175 (Aufrecht p. 314); prob. dial.] a sort of intoxicating liquor, spirits, rum, usually comb^d with surā. D I.146-166; M I.238; Pug 55; Dh 247; J IV.117 (pupph-āsav-ādi, i. e. made fr. flowers, cp. def^n dhātakī-puṣpa-guḍa-dhāny-āmla-sanskṛtaŋ by Mādhava, Halāy. p. 314). *Five* kinds are given by Dhpāla at VvA 73, viz. pupph-āsava, phal' āsava, madhv°, guḷ°, sambhāra-saŋyutta.

Merita in bhayamerita J IV.424=V.359 is to be read as bhaya-m-erita driven by fear; there is no need to change it with Kern, *Toev.* to perita.

Mella [dial. or uncertain reading ?] citron (=mātulunga) J III.319 (gloss bella).

Mokkha^1 [late Vedic & Epic Sk. mokṣa, fr. **muc**, see muñcati. Dhtp 539 mokkha=mocana; Dhtm 751= moca] 1. (lit.) release, freedom from, in bandhanā m. D I.73=M I.276. — 2. (fig.) release, deliverance, salvation Vbh 426 (jarā-maraṇa° from old age & death); DhA I.4 (°magga+sagga-magga, the way to heaven & salvation), 89, 90 (°dhamma=salvation) Mhvs 5, 61. — 3. (lit.) (act.) letting loose, emission, uttering (of speech) J I.375. — 4. it may (& prob. ought to) be taken as adj. (=*mokṣya, grd. of Caus. of **muc**) at Sn 773 (añña°, either=1, as "deliverance for others," or=4, as "to be delivered by others." Bdhgh at SnA 516 gives both expl^{ns}: aññe mocetuŋ (na) sakkonti, *kāraṇa-vacanaŋ* vā etaŋ: aññena mocetabbā (na) honti).

Mokkha^2 (adj.) [fr. mukha 6; Vṛddhi form=*maukhya] the headmost, first, foremost, in series aggo seṭṭho m. uttamo A II.95, where the customary tradition reads **pāmokkha** (see under mahā & cp. Nd^2 502A).

Mokkhaka=mokkha^2; thus we should read at J I.441 for **mukkhaka**.

Mokkhacika (m. or °ā f.) [see on attempt at etym. Morris in *J.P.T.S.* 1885, 49 who takes mokkha as fr. **muc** "tumbling" & cika="turning" fr. **cak=cik**. The word remains obscure, it must be a dialectical expression, distorted by popular analogy & taken perhaps from a designation of a place where these feats or toys had their origin. More probable than Morris' etym. is an analysis of the word (if it *is* Aryan) as mokkha = mokkha², in meaning "head, top," so that it may mean "head over," top-first" & we have to separate *mokkhac-ika the °ika representing °iya "in the manner of, like" & -ac being the adv. of direction as contained in Sk. prāñc = pra-añc.] tumbling, turning somersaults, an acrobatic feat; in list of forbidden amusements at D I.6 (cp. DA I.86; samparivattaka-kīḷanaŋ, i. e. playing with something that rolls along, continuously turning? The foll. sentence however seems to imply turning head over heels: "ākāse vā daṇḍaŋ gahetvā bhūmiyaŋ vā sīsaŋ ṭhapetvā heṭṭh-upariya (so read!) -bhāvena parivattana-kīḷanaŋ"; i. e. trapeze-performing. Cp. *Dial.* I.10 & *Vin. Texts* II.184). The list re-occurs at Vin II.10 (°āya: f.l kīḷanti); III.180; M I.266 ≈ and A V.203 (with important v. l. mokkhaṭika, which would imply mokkha & ending tiya, and not °cika at all. The Cy. on this passage expl^s as: daṇḍakaŋ gahetvā heṭṭh-uppariya (*sic.* as DA I.86; correct to upariya?) -bhāvena parivattana-kīḷanaŋ). The word is found also at Vin I.275, where the boy of a Seṭṭhi in Bārāṇasī contracts injuries to his intestines by "mokkhacikāya kīḷanto," playing (with a) m. — According to its use with kīḷati & in instr. **mokkhacikena** (Nd² 219) may be either a sort of game or an instrument (toy), with which children play.

Mokkhati see under muñcati.

Mogha (adj.) [the Vedic mogha for the later Sk. moha, which is the P. noun moha; fr. **muh.** BSk. mohapuruṣa e. g. at AvŚ II.177; MVastu III.440] empty, vain, useless, stupid, foolish D I.187 (opp. to sacca), 199; Sn 354; Dh 260 (°jiṇṇa grown old in vain; C. expl^s as tuccha-jiṇṇa DhA III.388); DhA I.110 (patthanā a futile wish); PvA 194. — Opp. amogha S I.232; J VI.26; DhA II.34 (°ŋ tassa jīvitaŋ: not in vain). **-purisa** a stupid or dense fellow Vin IV.126, 144.

Moca¹ [cp. *Sk. moca & mocā] the plantain or banana tree' Musa sapientum Vin I.246 (°pāna drink made fr. M. s.; one of the 8 permitted drinks); J IV.181; V.405, 465.

Moca² [root-noun of **moc,** Caus. of **muc**] delivery, setting free Dhtm 631, 751, where Dhtp in same context reads mocana.

Mocana (nt.) [fr. moceti] 1. setting free, delivering DhA III.199 (parissayā°); Dhtp 376, 539; Dhtm 609. Cp. moca². — 2. letting loose, discharging, in assu° shedding tears PvA 18. Cp. vi°.

Mocaya (adj.) [quâsi grd. formation fr. moceti] to be freed, able to escape, in dum° difficult to obtain freedom J VI.234.

Mocāpana (nt.) [fr. Caus. II. mocāpeti] causing one's freedom, deliverance J VI.134.

Mocetar [M. ag. fr. moceti] one who sets free, a deliverer Nd¹ 32.

Moceti [Caus. of muñcati] 1. to deliver, set free, release cause one's release or deliverance from (abl.). imper. praes. **mocehi** Pv II.1⁶ (duggatiyā); PvA 12; aor. **mocesi** PvA 112 (dāsavyato); ger. **mocetvā** PvA 8, 77; inf. **mocetuŋ** PvA 45 (petalokato). — 2. to discharge, emit (semen in coitu) Vin III.36, 39 (as Caus II.), 110. — 3. to let loose, set into motion, stir: **padaŋ** m. to run J III.33. — 4. to discharge, fulfil: **paṭiññaŋ** one's promise DhA I.93. — 5. to unharness DhA I.67. — 6. to detach S I.44. — Caus. II. **mocāpeti** to cause to be freed, to give freedom, to let loose Vin IV.316 (opp. bandhāpeti).

Moṭa [BSk. moṭa, Prk. mrḍa: Pischel § 166, 238] see mutoḷī.

Motar [n. ag. fr. munāti, more likely direct der. fr. muta, pp. of **man,** q. v.] one who feels (or senses) that which can be felt (or sensed), in phrase "mutaŋ na maññati **motabbaŋ** (so read) na maññati motāraŋ" he does not identify what is sensed with that which is not sensed, nor with what is *to be sensed* (**motabba**) nor with him who senses A II.25; where motar & motabba correspond to sotar & sotabba & daṭṭhar & daṭṭhabba. The word does not occur in the similar passage M I.3.

Modaka [cp. Epic. Sk. modaka in meaning 1] 1. a sort of sweetmeat S I.148; A I.130; III.76; Pug 32; PvA 4. — 2. receptacle for a letter, an envelope, wrapper or such like J VI.385 (paṇṇaŋ °assa anto pakkhipitvā). May, however, be same as 1.

Modati [**mud,** cp. Vedic moda joy Dhtp 146: tose] to rejoice, to enjoy oneself, to be happy A III.40; Sn 561; Pv I.5⁴; II.1²¹. — pp. **mudita** (q. v.). For mohayamāna at DhA I.275 the better reading is modayamāna rejoicing, a ppr. med.

Modana (nt.) [fr. **mud**] satisfaction, rejoicing Sdhp 229. Cp. sam°.

Modanā (f.) [fr. **mud**] blending (?); Cy. expl^n at DhsA 143 of term āmodanā.

Modara: In modara at J V.54 (of elephant's teeth) Kern, *Toev.* s. v. sees a miswriting for medura (full of, beset with), which however does not occur in Pali. The C. expl^n is "samantato obhāsento," i. e. shining.

Mona (nt.) [fr. muni, equal to *maunya taken by Nd as root of moneyya] wisdom, character, self-possession Sn 540 (°patha = ñāṇa-patha SnA 435), 718, 723; Nd¹ 57; Nd² 514 A (= ñāṇa & paññā); Th 1, 168 (what is monissaŋ? fut. 1st sg. of ?).

Moneyya (nt.) [fr. muni, cp. Vedic moneya] state of a muni, muni-hood; good character, moral perfection. This is always represented as 3 fold, viz. kāya°, vacī°, mano° (see under muni), e. g. at D III.220; A I.273; Nd¹ 57; Nd² 514 A (where also used as adj.: moneyyā dhammā properties of a perfect character). Cp. also Sn 484, 698, 700 sq. On moneyya-kolāhala (forebodings of the highest wisdom) see the latter.

Momūha (adj.) [intens.-redupl. formation fr. moha & **muh**] dull, silly, stupid, infatuated, bewildered (cp. *Cpd.* 83³) D I.27; A III.164 sq.; Sn 840, 841, 1120; Nd¹ 153 (= manda), 192; Nd² 521 (= avidvā etc.); Pug 65.

Momūhatta (nt.) [abstr. fr. nomūha] silliness, foolishness, bewilderment of the mind M I.520; A III.119, 191, 219 (= mandatta); Pug 69.

Mora [the contracted, regular P. form of *Sk. mayūra, viâ *ma-ūra > mora. See also Geiger, *P.Gr.* § 27 & Pischel, *Prk. Gr.* § 166. — Vedic only mayūrī f. pea-hen] a peacock J II.275 (°upasevin, see C. on this passage); VI.218, 497; PvA 142; DhA I.394. A peacock's tail (sometimes used as a fan) is denoted in var. terms in cpds., as **mora-kalāpa** DhA I.387; **-piccha** Vin I.186; **-piñcha** Vin II.130; **-piñja** PvA 142, 176; VvA 147; **-sikali** (?) KhA 49; **-hattha** Vv 33⁴¹ (= mayūra-piñjehi kataŋ makasa-vījaniŋ); Pv III.1¹⁷. Perhaps also as morakkha "a peacock's eye" at VbhA 63 (morakkhaka loha, a kind of copper, grouped with pisācaloha). It is more likely however that **morakkha** is distorted fr. ***mauryaka,** patronymic of **mura,** a local (tribal) designation (cp. murala), then by pop. etym. connected with mora peacock. With this cp. Sk. **moraka** "a kind of steel" BR.

Moragu [cp. (scientific) Sk. mayūraka] a tender grass (Achyranthes aspera) Vin I.196.

Morinī (f.) [fr. mora] a peahen Miln 67.

Moli (m. & f.) [cp. Epic Sk. mauli, fr. mūla] a chignon; crest, turban J I.64; V.431; Mhvs 11, 28; DA I.136 (v. l. moḷi). Also found (as molin, adj.?) in Np. Yama-moli: see under yakkha 5.
 -galla (?) fat Vin I.85 (expl^d by thūla-sarīra; vv. ll. moḷi° & mukalla). -baddha one who has his hair tied into a top-knot 128, 243, 348.

Mosa (°-) (adj.-nt.) [the guṇa (comp^n) form of musā] belonging to or untruth, false-; only in cpds. -dhamma of a deceitful nature, false, A V.84 (kāma); Sn 739, 757; & -vajja [fr. musā-vāda] false-speaking, lie, untruth S I.169; Sn 819, 866, 943; Nd¹ 152, 265; Nd² 515; Vv 12⁶.

Mosalla (adj.) [fr. musala] worthy of being slain (with clubs), punishable A II.241.

Moha [fr. **muh**, see muyhati; cp. Sk. moha & Vedic mogha] stupidity, dullness of mind & soul, delusion, bewilderment, infatuation D III.146, 175, 182, 214, 270; Vin IV.144, 145; Sn 56, 74, 160, 638, 847; Vbh 208, 341, 391, 402; Pug 16; Tikp 108, 122, 259. — Def^d as "dukkhe aññāṇaŋ etc., moha pamoha, sammoha, avijj' ogha etc.," by Nd² 99 & Vbh 362; as "muyhanti tena, sayaŋ vā muyhati, muyhana-mattaŋ eva vā tan ti moho" and "cittassa andha-bhāva-lakkhaṇo, aññāṇa-lakkhaṇo vā" at Vism 468. — Often coupled with rāga & dosa as one of the 3 cardinal affects of citta, making a man unable to grasp the higher truths and to enter the Path: see under rāga (& Nd² p. 237, s. v. rāga where the wide range of application of this set is to be seen). Cp. the 3 fires: rāg-aggi, dos-aggi, moh-aggi It 92; D III.217 also rāga-kkhaya, dosa°, moha° VbhA 31 sq. — On comb^n with rāga, lobha & dosa see dosa² and lobha. — On term see also *Dhs trsl.* §§ 33, 362, 441; *Cpd* 16, 18, 41, 113, 146. — See further D I.80 (sa-moha-cittaŋ); Nd¹ 15, 16 (with lobha & dosa); VvA 14; PvA 3. —amoha absence of bewilderment Vbh 210 (+ alobha, adosa; as the 3 kusala-mūlāni: cp. mūla 3), 402 (id., as kusala-hetu). — Cp. pa°, sam°.
 -antara (personal) quality of bewilderment (lit. having m. inside) Sn 478 (taken by C. as "*cause* of m.," i. e. °kāraṇa, °paccaya SnA 411; cp. antara = kāraṇa under antara I 2 b.). -ussada quality of dullness Nd¹ 72, 413. -kkhaya destruction of infatuation Vbh 73; VbhA 51. -carita one whose habit is infatuation Nett 90 (+ rāgacarita & dosacarita). -tama the darkness of bewilderment MA I. -dhamma anything that is bewildering or infatuating Sn 276. -pāruta covered or obstructed by delusion Pv IV.3³¹. -magga being on the road of infatuation Sn 347. -salla the sting of bewilderment Nd¹ 59.

Mohatta (nt.) [abstr. fr. moha] infatuation, bewilderment A II.120; III.376.

Mohana (nt.) [fr. **muh** as Caus. form^n] making dull or stupid, infatuation, enticement, allurement Sn 399, 772 (= mohanā vuccanti pañca kāmaguṇā Nd¹ 26). The Sk. meaning is also "sexual intercourse" (cp. Halāyudha p. 315), which may apply to the Sn passages SnA 517 (on Sn 772) expl^s "mohanaŋ vuccati kāmaguṇā, ettha hi deva-manussā muyhanti."

Mohanaka (adj.) [fr. mohana] leading astray, bewildering, leading into error Vin IV.144.

Mohaneyya & **Mohanīya** (adj.) [grd. form^n fr. moha] leading to infatuation A II.120; III.110; J III.499.

Moheti [Caus. fr. **muh**, see muyhati & cp. moha] to deceive, to befool, to take in, surprise, delude, aor. 2nd sg. amohayi Sn 352; 3rd sg. amohayi S IV.158 = It 58 (maccu-rājan; vv. ll. asamohayi & asamohari); reading somewhat doubtful, cp. similar context Sn 1076 with "sabbesu dhammesu samūhatesu" (v. l. samoha°). — 3rd sg. (poet.) also amohayittha Sn 332 (mā vo pamatte viññāya maccurājā amohayittha vasānuge, cp. Sn ed. p. 58). — On mohayamāna DhA I.275 see modati.

ERRATUM.

Part VI, p. 21²: Paṭivāmeti. *For* Dh I.39 *read* DA I.39. Cp. *J.P.T.S.* 1886, p. 160, suggesting paṭivādh°, or paṭibādhayamāno, and referring to Th I, 744.

ADDITIONS AND CORRECTIONS.

VOLUME I.

Page x, *under* 1a *add* Apadāna P.T.S. 1925 (Ap).
,, 1b ,, Manoratha-pūraṇī P.T.S. 1924 (AA); Samanta-pāsādikā P.T.S. 1924 (Sam. Pās. or Vin A).
,, xi, ,, 3 ,, *Human Types*, P.T.S. trsl. 1924 (Pug trsl.) *and insert accordingly on p.* xii *under* B 1.
,, 4, column 2, *under* aggaḷa *insert* 1. (better:) the wing of a door (see phusita^{3}).
,, 17, ,, 1, ,, aḍḍha-telasa *read* $12\frac{1}{2}$ *for* $13\frac{1}{2}$.
,, 102, ,, 1, ,, āpagā *read* Dāvs 1.32 *for* 52.

VOLUME II.

Page 14, column 1, *under* kantita^{2}: at Miln 240 better as kantita^{1}, *i.e.* "spun."
,, 93, ,, 1 ,, camu *last line to be read* camūpati a general Mhvs 10, 65; 23, 4; Dāvs 1.3
,, 100, ,, 1, *insert* Ādissa^{2} (adj.) blameworthy M 1.12; MA = gārayha.
,, 110, ,, 2, *under* jaṭa handle of an *adze* (*instead of* "*razor*").
,, 112, ,, 2, *insert* jalūkā leech DA 1.117.
,, 166, ,, 1, *under* dessin *read* Sn 92 (*for* 93), and: better desin, cp. viddesin
,, 196, ,, 1, ,, nipatati *read* intrs. *for* instr.
,, 209, ,, 1, ,, nivesa *read* nivesana 2 *for* nivesana^{2}.

VOLUME III.

Page 3, column 1, *under* pakkamati *read* 2. *for* 2nd.
,, 12, ,, 1, ,, pañcaka (taca°) *read* kesā *for* kosā.
,, 12, ,, 1, ,, pañjara *add* in comb^{n} sīha° meaning "window."
,, 62, ,, 1, ,, palagaṇḍa *read* A IV.127 *for* V.127.
,, 71, ,, 1, bottom, *read* pahita^{1} *for* pahital.
,, 79, ,, 2, *under* piñjita *read* "dyed" *for* died.
,, 104, ,, 2, line 3 fr. bottom, *read* S II.228 *for* I.228.
,, 115, ,, 1, *read* byā *for* bya.

THE PALI TEXT SOCIETY'S PALI-ENGLISH DICTIONARY

EDITED BY

T. W. RHYS DAVIDS F.B.A D.Sc. Ph.D. LL.D. D.Litt.

and WILLIAM STEDE Ph.D.

Part VII (Y—Vibh)

PUBLISHED BY
THE PALI TEXT SOCIETY
LONDON

First published - - - 1924
Reprinted - - - - 1948
Reprinted - - - - 1952

Y.

-Y- comb^{n} consonant (sandhi), inserted (euphonically) between 2 vowels for the avoidance of hiatus. It has arisen purely phonetically from *i* as a sort of "gliding" or semi-vowel within a word, where the syllable division was in regular speech more openly felt than in the written language, e. g. pari-y-āpanna (Pāli) corresponds to Sk. pary-āpanna, similarly pari-y-osāna = Sk. paryosāna. Thus inserted after *a* before *i* or *e*: cha-y-imā disā D III.188; ta-y-idaŋ Sn 1077; Pv I.3^{3}; tava-y-idaŋ Sn 352; na-y-idaŋ S II.278; mama-y-idaŋ Sn 806; na-y-idha Sn 790; mā-y-idha Vin I.54; yassa-y-etādisī pajā D II.267 (v. l. ss for T yassa-s-etādisī); satiyā-y-etaŋ adhivacanaŋ M II.260; na-y-imassa Pv IV.1^{2}. — After *i* before *a*: pāvisi-y-assamaŋ J V.405; khaṇi-y-asmani J III.433; yā-y-aññaŋ J I.429 (where C. expl^{s}: ya-kāro paṭisandhi-karo). — Cp. yeva for eva. — *Note.* At J VI.106 ya-y-ime jane is to be taken as **ye ime** jane; the spelling **ay** for **e** being found elsewhere as well. Cp. the following ta-y-ime jane.

Ya° [pron. rel. base; Vedic yaḥ = Gr. ὅς who; cp. Goth. jabai if, -ei rel. part. An amplification of the dem. pron. base *i-, *ei- (cp. ayaŋ). See on detail Brugmann, "*Die indogerm. Pronomina*" in Ber. d. sächs. Ges. LX. 41 sq.] I. *Forms.* (See inflection also at Geiger, *P.Gr.* § 110.) The decl. is similar to that of ta°; among the more rarely found forms we only mention the foll.: sg. nom. m. **yo** with by-form (in hiatus) **yv-**, as **yv'āyaŋ** = yo ayaŋ M I.258; **yv'āssa** = yo assa M I.137. Notice the lengthening of the subsequent vowel. — An unsettled ya is to be found at J V.424 (Fausböll remarks "for yassā"?; perhaps to be comb^{d} with preceding pañcapatikā; C. on p. 427 expl^{s} ya-kāro nipātamatto) — abl. **yasmā** in adv. use; **yamhā** Dh 392. — loc. **yamhi** Dh 261, 372, 393. — f. loc. **yassaŋ** A III.151 (see below). See further adv. use of cases (below II.5). — At Pv II.1^{6} yāhi is doubtful (perhaps imper. = yajahi, of yajati; C. leaves it unexpl^{d}).

Special mention must be made of the **nt. n. acc. sg.**, where both **yaŋ** and **yad** are found. The (Vedic) form yad (Ved. yat) has been felt more like ya + expletive (Sandhi-) d, and is principally found in adv. use and certain archaic phrases, whereas yaŋ represents the usual (Pali) form (like **tad** and **taŋ**). See more under II. — A Māgadhized form is **ye** (after se = taŋ), found at D II.278 (see Geiger § 105^{2} & 110^{2}. Cp. Trenckner, *Notes* 75.). The expression **ye-bhuyyena** may belong under this category, if we explain it as **yad + bhuyyena** (bhuyyena equivalent to bhiyyoso). It would then correspond to *seyyathā* (= sad + yathā, cp. sayathā, sace, taŋyathā). See refs. under **yebhuyyena**. — The expression **yevāpanaka** is an adj. form^{n} from the phrase **ye-vā-pana** (= yaŋ vā pana "whatever else there is"). i. e. belonging to something of the same kind, i. e. corresponding, reciprocal, as far as concerned, respective. (See s. v.) — In adv. use it often corresponds to E. *as*; see e. g. yad-icchakaŋ, yad-idaŋ (under II.2 b; II.4 b.).

II. *Meaning:* "which," in correspondence to a following demonstr. pron. (ta°); whichever (generalizing); nt. what, whatever. In immediate comb^{n} with the demonstr. pron. it is qualifying and specifying the person, thing or subject in discussion or question (see below 4).

1. *Regular use* as correl. pron., when ya° (+ noun) is followed by ta° (+ noun). Sometimes (in poetry) the reverse is the case, e. g. at It 84 where ta° (m. sa) is elliptically omitted: atthaŋ na jānāti yaŋ lobho sahate naraŋ "*he* does not know good, *whom* greed overcomes." — Otherwise regular, e. g.: *yassa* jātarūparajataŋ kappati pañca pi *tassa* kāmaguṇā kappanti S IV.326. In a generalizing sense (cp. below II.3): yo vā so vā "der erste beste," some or other, whoever, any J IV.38; V.362; yaŋ vā taŋ vā karotu let her do whatever she likes VvA 208; yasmiŋ vā tasmiŋ vā on every occasion S I.160 na **yo** vā so vā yakkho not *this* or *that* yakkha i. e. not any (ordinary) kind of Yakkha (but Inda) DA I.264. — The same use (ordinary correlative) applies to the nt. forms **yaŋ** & **yad** in correl. to taŋ and tad. (See sep. under II. 2.)

2. *Use of nt. forms.* — (a) nt. **yaŋ** (a) as pronoun: S III.44 (yaŋ dukkhaŋ . . . tad anattā); It 78 (yañ c' aññaŋ whatever else); VbhA 54 (yaŋ labbhati yañ ca na labbhati taŋ sabbaŋ pucchitvā). See also under 3 a (yaŋ kiñci, yaŋ yaŋ). — (b) as adj. adv.: **yaŋ-mukha** facing what, turned where (?) J V.475 (but C. reads & expl^{s} sammukha!); **yaŋ-vipāka** having what or which kind of fruit D II.209. **yaŋ vā** . . . **yaŋ vā** whether . . . or S II.179; **yaŋ no** . . . **na tv' eva** neither . . . nor S II.179-180. — **yaŋ** with pot.: "so that," that (corresp. to Lat. ut *consecutivum*) S III.41 (yaŋ rūpe anatt' ānupassī vihareyya). J V.339 (n' esa dhammo yaŋ taŋ jahe that I should leave you). — In the function of other conjunctions e. g. as *temporal* = when, since, after: J IV.319 (yaŋ maŋ Suruci m-ānayi that, or since, S. married me). As *conditional* or *causal* = if, even if, because: Vin I.276 (yaŋ te sakkā . . . ārogaŋ kātuŋ, taŋ karohi if it is possible . . . do it; or may be taken in sense of "in whatever way you can do it, do"); J III.206 = IV.4 (yaŋ me sirasmiŋ ūhacca cakkaŋ bhamati matthake = because; C.: yena pāpena). — (c) as adv. deictive "so," in comb^{n} with var. other (emphatic) particles as e. g. (yaŋ nūna used in an *exhortative* sense "well, now"; or "rather, let me"; or "so now," always in phrase **yaŋ nūn' āhaŋ** "now then let me" (do this or that) very freq., either with foll. pot., e. g. "y. n. āhaŋ araññaŋ paviseyyaŋ" DhA II.91. "y. n. ā. katakammaŋ puccheyyaŋ" VvA 132; dasseyyaŋ VvA 138; pabbajjeyyaŋ M II.55; āneyyaŋ DhA I.46, vihareyyaŋ ibid. 56; etc. cp. J I.14, 150, 255; III.393; DhA I.91; PvA 5 (avassayo bhaveyyaŋ). — Similarly **yañ hi** "well then, now then" (with Pot.) S II.210, 221 (taŋ vadeyya). Cp. **yagghe. yañ ca** & **yañ ce** [Sk. yac ca, or cet, ca here = ce see ca. & cp. sace = sa + ce] (rather) than that: yañ ca Th 2, 80; J I.210; yañce (with Pot.) S I.176; It 43; Th I, 666. sangāme me mataŋ seyyo yañ ce jīve parājito (than that I live vanquished) Sn 440 (cp. the intricate expl^{n}. at SnA 390); similarly J IV.495: me maraṇaŋ seyyo yañ ce jīve tayā vinā. — (b) nt. **yad**: (a) as pron in

regular relative use e. g. S III.44 (yad aniccaŋ taŋ dukkhaŋ); It 59 (yad eva diṭṭhaŋ tad ev' âhaŋ vadāmi). (b) as adv., e. g. yad-agge (loc.) from what on, i. e. from which time, since what time D I.152 (=mūladivasato paṭṭhāya yaŋ divasaŋ aggaŋ patvā DA I.311); Vv 84^{33} (=yato paṭṭhāya VvA 344). Also as **yad-aggena** (instr.) Vin II.257 (y. Mahāpajāpati-gotamiyā aṭṭha garudhammā paṭiggahitā *tad eva* sā upasampannā); VbhA 387. — **yad-atthaŋ** for what, why Th 2, 163. **yad-atthiya** as much as necessary, as required, sufficient, proper Th 1, 12; 1274 ("which, for the goal desirous, he led" trsl.; refers to brahmacariyaŋ). The same verse occurs at Sn 354. The latter passage is mentioned in P.D. under atthiya with meaning "on account of what" (cp. kim-atthiyaŋ S III.189). The Sn passage is not expl[d] in SnA. — **yad-icchakaŋ** whatever is pleasant, i. e. according to liking, as he pleases A III.28; Pug 11, 12; J I.141 (y. bhutta eaten heartily); Vism 154 (+ya-vadicchaka); VvA 341. Cp. yen' icchakaŋ below II. 5. — **yad-icchita** see under **yathā-icchita**! — **yadidaŋ**: see below II. 4 b.

3. *Generalizing* (or distributive) use of ya: There are two modes of generalization, viz. (a) *by repeating* **ya°**: yassa yass' eva sālassa mūle tiṭṭhasi, so so muñcati pupphāni; "at the foot of whichever tree you stand, he (in all cases concerned) sheds flowers" Vv 39^{3}; yaŋ yaŋ hi manaso piyaŋ "whatever is pleasant to the senses" Pv $II.1^{18}$; yaŋ yaŋ passati taŋ taŋ pucchati "whomsoever he sees, him he asks" J III.155; yassaŋ yassaŋ disāyaŋ viharati, sakasmiŋ yeva vijite viharati" in whichever region he lives, he lives in his own realm" A III.151; yo yo yaŋ yaŋ icchati tassa tassa adāsi "whatever anybody wished he gave to him" PvA 113; yaŋ yaŋ padesaŋ bhajati tattha tatth' eva assa lābhasakkāro nibbattati "whichever region he visits, there (in each) will he have success" DhA II.82. — (b) *by combination* with ko-ci (cp. the identical Lat. qui-cun-que): yassa kassaci rāgo pahīno ayaŋ vuccati . . . "the lust of whosoever is abandoned he is called so & so" It 56. yāni kānici vatthūni . . . sabbāni tāni . . . It 19; ye keci ārabbha "with ref. to whosoever" PvA 17; yaŋ kiñci whatever Pv $I.4^{1}$.

4. *Dependent & elliptic* use of ya (with pron. demonstr.). This represents a sort of deictic (emphatic) use, with ref. to what is coming next or what forms the necessary compliment to what is just being said. Thus it introduces a general truth or definition, as we would say "just this, namely, i. e.," or Ger. "so wie, und zwar." — (a) The usual comb[ns] are those of ya+sa (nt. taŋ) and of ya+ayaŋ (nt. idaŋ), but such with amu (nt. aduŋ) also occur: yaŋ aduŋ khettaŋ aggaŋ evam eva mayhaŋ bhikkhu-bhikkhuniyo "as there is one field which is the best, thus to me the bh. & bhikkhunīs" S IV.315. Cp. the foll.: ya+sa e. g. at M. I.366 (yo so puriso paṭhamaŋ rukkhaŋ ārūḷho sace so na khippam eva oroheyya "just that man, who climbed up the tree first, if he does not come down very quickly"); J II.159 (yena tena upāyena with every possible means); Pv $I.9^{1}$ (yā tā [so read for yā ca!] "just she over there; who as such, i. e. such as she is"); cp. also the foll.: yā sā sīmā . . . taŋ sīmaŋ Vin I.109; ye te dhammā ādikalyāṇā etc. . . . sātthaŋ brahmacariyaŋ abhivadanti tathā rūpā 'ssa dhammā honti . . . M III.11; yāni etāni yānāni (just) these DhA IV.6. —**ya+ayaŋ** e. g. at M I.258 (yv' āyaŋ vado vedeyyo tatra tatra . . . vipākaŋ paṭisaŋvedeti); It 35=93 (nibbāpenti moh'aggiŋ paññāya yā 'yaŋ nibbedha-gāminī: "as it is also penetrating, which as such, or in this quality, or as we know, is penetrating"); Vin IV.134 (ye 'me antarāyikā dhammā vuttā . . . te paṭisevato n' âlaŋ antarāyāya "just those which, or whichever"). Th 1, 124 (panko ti hi naŋ avedayuŋ yâyaŋ vandanapūjanā; here=yā ayaŋ); Dh 56 (appamatto ayaŋ gandho yâyaŋ tagara-candanī; here=yo ayaŋ); M II.220 (yaŋ idaŋ kammaŋ . . . taŋ). — (b) nt. **yad-idaŋ** lit. "as that," which is this (i. e. the following), may be translated by "viz.," that is, "i. e." in other words, so to speak, just this, "I mean"; e. g. kāmānaŋ etaŋ nissaraṇaŋ yad idaŋ nekkhammaŋ "there is an escape from the lusts, viz. lustlessness"; or: "this is the abandoning of lusts, in other words lustlessness" It 61; dvè dānāni āmisa° dhamm°, etad aggaŋ imesaŋ yad idaŋ dhamma° "this is the best of them, I mean dh-d." It 98=100; supaṭipanno sāvaka-sangho, y. i. cattāri purisa-yugāni etc. M I.37. Instead of **yadidaŋ** we also find yāvañ c' **idaŋ**. See also examples given under **yāvatā**.

5. *Cases used adverbially:* Either locally or modally; with regards to the local adverbs it is to be remarked that their connotation is fluctuating, inasmuch as direction and place (where) are not always distinguished (cp. E. where both meanings=where & where-to), but must be guessed from the context. (a) instr. **yena**: (local) where (i. e. at which place) D I.71 (yena yena wherever), 220 (yattha yena yahiŋ=whence, where, whither; *not* with trsl[n] *Dial.* I. 281: where, why, whence!), 238 (id.); yenatena where (he was)—there (he went) D I.88, 106, 112 & passim; cp. D II.85 (yena âvasath' âgāraŋ ten' upasankami); A II.33 (yena vā tena vā here & there or "hither & thither"). —(modal) Dh 326 (yen' icchakaŋ II. 2 b.); Pv $I.11^{2}$ (kiŋ akattha pāpaŋ yena pivātha lohitaŋ: so that).—loc. **yahiŋ** where (or whither) Vv 84^{20} (yahiŋ yahiŋ gacchati tahiŋ tahiŋ modati); & **yasmiŋ**: yasmiŋ vā tasmiŋ vā on every occasion S I.160. — abl. **yasmā** (only modal) because A I.260; It 37 (corresp. to tasmā). On yasmā-t-iha see Geiger, *P.Gr.* 73^{5}.

Yakana (nt.) [fr. gen. yaknaḥ or sec. stem yakan- of Vedic yakṛt; cp. Av. yākars; Gr. ἧπαρ, Lat. jecur. In formation cp. P. chakana fr. Ved. śakṛt.] the liver Kh III.; M I.57, 421; D II.293; A V.109; Miln 26; Vism 257, 356; VbhA 60, 240. The old n-stem is to be seen in cpd. **yaka-peḷa** (q. v.).

Yaka-peḷa [see peḷa] the lump of the liver Sn 195 (=yakana-piṇḍa SnA 247)=J I.146. Dines Andersen suggests: "Could y.-p. possibly be an old error for saka-peḷa, cp. Sk. śaka-piṇḍa & śakṛt-piṇḍa?" Cp. **paṭala** (ref. Vism 257).

Ya-kāra [ya+kāra] 1. the letter (or sound) **y**: J I.430 (padasandhikara); III.433 (vyañjana-sandhi-vasena gahita). — 2. the letter (or syllable) *ya*: J V.427 (nipāta-matta). It is referred to at Vin IV.7 as an ending implying ridiculing or insult, together with the ending °bha. The Cy. means words like dāsiya, gumbiya, bālya etc. where -ya either denotes descendency or property, or stands for -ka as diminutive (i. e. (disparaging) ending. The same applies to °bha. Here at Vin IV.7 this way of calling a person by means of adding -ya- or -bha to his name (cp. E. -y in kid>kiddy etc.) is grouped with a series of other terms of insult (hīnā akkosā).

Yakkha [Vedic yakṣa, quick ray of light, but also "ghost"; fr. **yakṣ** to move quickly; perhaps: swift creatures, changing their abode quickly and at will. — The customary (popular) etym. of Pali Commentators is y. as quâsi grd. of **yaj**, to sacrifice, thus: a being to whom a sacrifice (of expiation or propitiation) is given. See e. g. VvA 224: yajanti tattha baliŋ upaharantī ti yakkhā; or VvA 333: pūjanīya-bhavato yakkho ti vuccati. — The term yakṣa as attendants of Kubera occurs already in the Upanishads.] 1. name of certain non-human beings, as spirits, ogres, dryads, ghosts, spooks. Their usual epithet and category of being is **amanussa**, i. e. not a human being (but not a sublime god either); a being half deified and of great power as regards influencing people (partly helping, partly hurting). They range in appearance immediately above the Petas; many "successful" or happy Petas are in fact Yakkhas (see also below). They correspond to our "genii" or fairies of the fairy-tales and show all their qualities. In many respects they correspond to the Vedic Piśācas, though different in many others, and of diff. origin. Historically they are remnants of an ancient demonology and of considerable folkloristic interest, as in them old animistic beliefs are incorporated and as they represent creatures of the wilds and forests, some of them based on ethnological features. See on term e. g. *Dial.* III.188; on their history and identity Stede, *Gespenstergeschichten des Peta Vatthu* chap. v.; pp. 39-44. — They are sometimes called **devatā**: S I.205; or **devaputtā**: PvA 113, 139. A female Yakkha is called yakkhinī (q. v.).

2. Their usual capacity is one of kindness to men (cp. Ger. Rübezahl). They are also interested in the *spiritual* welfare of those humans with whom they come into contact, and are something like "tutelary genii" or even "angels" (i. e. *messengers* from another world) who will save prospective sinners from doing evil (cp. Pv IV.1). They also act as guides in the "inferno": Pv IV.11, cp. IV.3. A somewhat dangerous "Mentor" is represented at D I.95, where the y. Vajirapāṇī threatens to slay Ambaṭṭha with an iron hammer, if he does not answer the Bhagavā. He is represented as hovering in the air; Bdhgh. (DA I.264) says on this: na yo vā so vā yakkho, Sakko devarājā ti veditabbo: it is to be understood not as this or that y., but as Sakka the king of devas. — Whole cities stand under the protection of, or are inhabited by yakkhas; D II.147 (ākiṇṇa-yakkha full of y.; thus Āḷakamandā may here mean all kinds of supra-mundane beings), cp. Lankā (Ceylon) as inhabited by y.: Mhvs 7, 33. — Often, however, they are cruel and dangerous. The female yakkhas seem on the whole more fearful and evil-natured than the male (see under yakkhinī). They eat flesh and blood: J IV.549; devour even men: D II.346; J II.15-17, or corpses: J I.265; mentioned under the 5 ādīnavā (dangers) at A III.256. A yakkha wants to kill Sāriputta: Ud 4.

3. Var. *classes* of y. are enum[d] at D II.256, 257; in a progressive order they rank between manussa and gandhabba at A II.38; they are mentioned with devas, rakkhasas, dānavas, gandhabbas, kinnaras and mah'-oragas at J V.420. According to VvA 333 Sakka, the 4 great kings (lokapālā), the followers of Vessavaṇa (alias Yama, the yakkhas proper) *and* men (see below 7) go by the name of yakkha. — Sakka, the king of the devas, is often named yakkha: J IV.4; DA I.264. Some are spirits of trees (rukkha-devatā): J III.309 345; Pv I.9; II.9; PvA 5; are also called **bhumma-devā** (earthly deities) PvA 45, 55. Their cult seems to originate primarily from the woods (thus in trees: Pv II.9; IV.3), and secondarily from the legends of sea-faring merchants (cp. the story of the flying-Dutchman). To the latter origin point the original descriptions of a **Vimāna** or fairy-palace, which is due to a sort of mirage. These are usually found in or at the sea, or in the neighbourhood of silent lakes, where the sense of hauntedness has given rise to the fear of demons or supernatural witchcraft. Cp. the entrances to a Vimāna by means of a dried-up river bed (Pv I.9; II.12) and the many descriptions of the Vimānas in the Lake-districts of the Himavant in Vv. (See Stede, *Peta Vatthu* trsl[n] p. 104 sq.)

4. Their *names* too give us a clue as to their origin and function. These are taken from (a) their *bodily appearance*, which possesses many of the attributes of Petas, e. g. **Khara** "Rough-skin" or "Shaggy" Sn p. 48 (= khara-samphassaŋ cammaŋ SnA 302), also as **Khara-loma** "Rough-hair" Vism 208; **Khara-dāṭhika** "Rough-tooth" J I.31. **Citta** "Speckled" Mhvs 9, 22; 10, 4; also as **Citta-rājā** J II.372; Mhvs 10, 84. **Silesa-loma** "Sticky-hair" J I.273. **Sūci-loma** "Needle-hair" Sn p. 47, 48; S I.207; Vism 208; SnA 302. —(b) *places* of inhabitance, attributes of their realm, *animals* and *plants*, e. g. Ajakalāpaka "Goat-bundle" Ud I. **Āḷavaka** "Forest-dweller" J IV.180; VI.329; Mhvs 30, 84; Vism 208. **Uppala** "Lotus" DhA IV.209. **Kakudha** "K.-tree" (Terminalia arjuna) S I.54. **Kumbhīra** "Crocodile" J VI.272. **Gumbiya** either "One of a troop" (soldier of Yama) or "Thicket-er" (fr. gumba thicket) J III.200, 201. **Disāmukha** "Sky-facer" DhA IV.209. **Yamamoli** "Yamachignon" DhA IV.208. **Vajira** "Thunderbolt" DhA IV.209; alias **Vajira-pāṇī** D I.95, or **Vajira-bāhu** DhA IV.209. **Sātāgira** "Pleasant-mount" D II.256; Sn 153; J IV.314; VI.440. **Serīsaka** "Acacia-dweller" VvA 341 (the messenger of Vessavaṇa). —(c) qualities of *character*, e. g. **Adhamma** "Unrighteous" Miln 202 (formerly Devadatta). **Kaṭattha** "Well-wisher" DhA IV.209. **Dhamma** "Righteous" Miln 202 (= Bodhisatta). **Puṇṇaka** "Full(-moon ?)" J VI.255 sq. (a leader of soldiers, nephew of Vessavaṇa). **Māra** the "Tempter" Sn 449; S I.122; M I.338. **Sakaṭa** "Waggon-load" (of riches) DhA IV.209 —(d) *embodiments* of former persons, e. g. **Janavasabha** "Lord of men" D II.205. **Dīgha** M I.210. **Naradeva** J VI.383, 387. **Paṇḍaka** "Eunuch" Mhvs 12, 21. **Sīvaka** S I.241 = Vin II.156. **Serī** "Self-willed" S I.57. — Cp. the similar names of yakkhinīs.

5. They stand in a close relationship to and under the authority of **Vessavaṇa** (Kuvera), one of the 4 lokapālas. They are often the direct servants (messengers) of **Yama** himself, the Lord of the Underworld (and the Peta-realm especially). Cp. D II.257; III.194 sq.; J IV.492 (yakkhinī fetches water for Vessavaṇa); VI.255 sq. (Puṇṇaka, the nephew of V.); VvA 341 (Serīsaka, his messenger). In relation to Yama: dve yakkhā Yamassa dūtā Vv 52[2]; cp. Np. Yamamolī DhA IV.208. — In harmony with tradition they share the rôle of their master **Kuvera** as lord of riches (cp. Pv II.9[22]) and are the keepers (and liberal spenders) of underground riches, hidden treasures etc., with which they delight men: see e. g. the frame story to Pv II.11 (PvA 145), and to IV.12 (PvA 274). They enjoy every kind of splendour & enjoyment, hence their attribute kāma-kāmin Pv I.3[2]. Hence they possess supernatural powers, can transfer themselves to any place *with* their palaces and work miracles; a frequent attribute of theirs is mah' iddhika (Pv II.9[10]; J VI.118). Their appearance is splendid, as a result of former *merit*: cp. Pv I.2; I.9; II.11; IV.3[17]. At the same time they are possessed of odd qualities (as result of former *demerit*); they are shy, and afraid of palmyra leaf & iron: J IV.492; their eyes are red & do not wink: J V. 34; VI.336, 337. — Their abode is their self-created palace (**Vimāna**), which is anywhere in the air, or in trees etc. (see under vimāna). Sometimes we find a communion of yakkhas grouped in a town, e. g. Āḷakamandā D II.147; Sirīsa-vatthu (in Ceylon) Mhvs. 7, 32.

6. Their essential *human* character is evident also from their attitude towards the "Dhamma." In this respect many of them are "fallen angels" and take up the word of the Buddha, thus being converted and able to rise to a higher sphere of existence in saŋsāra. Cp. D III.194, 195; J II.17; VvA 333; Pv II.8[10] (where "yakkha" is expl[d] by Dhpāla as "pet-attabhāvato cuto (so read for mato!) yakkho ataŋ jāto dev-atta-bhāvaŋ patto" PvA 110); SnA 301 (both Sūciloma & Khara converted). — See in general also the foll. passages: Sn 153, 179, 273, 449; S I.206-15; A I.160; Vism 366 (in simile); Miln 23.

7. Exceptionally the term "yakkha" is used as a *philosophical* term denoting the "individual soul" [cp. similar Vedic meaning "das lebendige Ding" (B.R.) at several AV. passages]; hence probably the old phrase: **ettāvatā yakkhassa suddhi** (purification of

heart) Sn 478, quoted VvA 333 (ettāvat' aggaŋ no vadanti h' eke yakkhassa sudhiŋ idha paṇḍitāse). Sn 875 (cp. Nd[1] 282: yakkha=satta, nara, puggala, manussa).

-ānubhāva the potency of a yakkha J I.240. **-āviṭṭha** possessed by a y. J VI.586. **-iddhi** (yakkh°) magic power of a y. PvA 117, 241. **-gaṇa** the multitude of ys. J VI.287. **-gaha**=following DhA III.362. **-gāha** "yakkha-grip," being seized by a y. S I.208; PvA 144. **-ṭṭhāna** the dwelling-place of a y. **-dāsī** "a female temple slave," or perhaps "possessed by a demon" (?) J VI 501 (v. l. BB devatā-paviṭṭhā cp. p. 586: yakkh' āviṭṭhā.) **-nagara** city of ys. J II.127 (=Sirīsavatthu); cp. pisāca-nagara. **-pura** id. Mhvs. 7.32. **-bhavana** the realm or abode of the y. Nd[1] 448. **-bhūta** a yakkha-being, a ghost Pv III.5[2] (=pisāca-bhūta vā yakkha-bh. vā PvA 198); IV.1[35]. **-mahiddhi**=°iddhi; Pv IV.1[54]. **-yoni** the y.-world, realm of the y. SnA 301. **-samāgama** meeting of the y. PvA 55 (where also *devaputtā* join). **-sūkara** a y. in the form of a pig VbhA 494. **-senā** army of ys. D III.194; SnA 209. **-senāpati** chief-commander of the yakkha-army J IV.478; SnA 197.

Yakkhatta (nt.) [fr. yakkha] condition of a higher demon or yakkha D II.57; A II.39; PvA 117.

Yakkhinī (f.) [fr. yakkha, perhaps corresponding directly to Vedic yakṣinī, f. of yakṣin: adj. persecuting, taking vengeance, appl[d] to Varuṇa at RV. VII.88[4]] a female yakkha, a vampire. Their character is usually fierce & full of spite & vengeance, addicted to man- & beast-murder (cp. yakkha 2). They are very much like Petīs in habits. With their names cp. those of the yakkhas, as enum[d] under yakkha 4. — Vin III.37; IV.20 (where sexual intercourse with y. is forbidden to the bhikkhus); S I.209 (Piyankara-mātā); J I.240 (as a goat), 395 sq.; II.127; III.511; V.21 (eating a baby), 209 (eaten by a y.); VI.336 (desirous of eating a child); Vism 121 (singing), 382 (four: Piyankara-mātā, Uttara-mātā, Phussa-mittā, Dhammaguttā), 665 (in simile); Mhvs 7, 11 (Kuvaṇṇā, i. e. bad-coloured); 10, 53 (Cetiyā); 12, 21 (Hāritā "Charming" or fr. harita "green" (?)); DhA I.47; II.35, 36 (a y. in the form of a cow, eating 4 people in successive births). *Note.* A by-form of yakkhinī is **yakkhī**.

-bhāva the state of being a yakkhinī J I.240; II.128 (yakkhini°).

Yakkhī (f.) [direct formation fr. yakkha, like petī fr. peta; form older than yakkhinī (?)]=yakkhinī S I.11; Vin III.121; IV.20; J IV.492; Mhvs 7, 26.

Yagghe (indecl.) [similar in formation & meaning to tagghe (q. v.). It is yaŋ (yad)+gha, the latter in a Māgadhised form ghe, whereas taggha (=tad+gha) only occurs as such] hortative part. used in addressing a (superior) person in the voc., followed by Pot. of jānāti, either 2nd jāneyyāsi, or 3rd sg. jāneyya; to be trsl[d] somewhat like "look here, don't you know," surely, you ought to know; now then; similarly to part. **yaŋ nu, yaŋ nūna** & **yaŋ hi**. The part. is found in the language of the Nikāyas only, thus indicating part of the oldest & original dialect. E. g.: y. bhante jāneyyāsi Vin I.237; *yagghe* deva jāneyyāsi yo te puriso dāso . . . so . . . pabbajito do you know, Oh king D I.60 (trsl.: "*if it please* your majesty, do you know . . ."; DA I.169 expl[s] as "codan' at the nipāto"); y. ayye jāneyyāsi M II.62; mahārāja j. M II.71; id. S I.101; y. bhavaŋ jāneyya S I.180. — The passage M II.157 is somewhat doubtful where we find y. with the *ind.* and in var. forms (see v. l.) of yagghi & taggha: "jānanti pana bhonto yagghe . . .," with reply "na jānāma yagghe . . ." Perhaps the reading taggha would be preferable.

Yajati [**yaj**, cp. Vedic yajati, yajus, Yajur-veda. To Av. yazaitē to sacrifice, Gr. ἅζομαι to revere, worship. On etym. cp. also Walde, *Lat. Wtb.* s. v. aestimo. — The Dhtp (62) defines root by "deva-pūjā, sangati-karaṇa, dānesu," i. e. "said of deva-worship, of assembling, and of gifts." Similarly Dhtm 79] to sacrifice, to make an offering (yaññaŋ); to give alms or gifts — In the P. literature it refers (with yañña, sacrifice) either (when critical) to the Brahmanic rites of sacrificing to the gods according to the rules initiated in the Vedas & Vedic literature; or (when dogmatical) to the giving of alms to the bhikkhu. In the latter sense it implies liberal donation of all the necessities of a bhikkhu (see enum[d] under yañña). The latter use is by far the more frequent. — The construction is with the *acc.* of the deity honoured and the *instr.* of the gift. — Pres. yajati D I.139; A I.168; II.43, 44; Sn 505, 509; DA I.160. — ppr. yajanto D I.52; M I.404; Miln 21; gen. pl. **yajataŋ** Sn 569 (=Vin I.246, where reading is jayataŋ). — ppr. med. **yajamāna** D I.138 (maha-yaññaŋ); Sn 506; S I.233; J VI.502, 505. — imper. 3rd sg. **yajatu** DA I.297; med. yajataŋ D I.138 (=detu bhavaŋ DA I.300). 2nd sg. **yajāhi** J III.519; PvA 280, and perhaps at Pv II.1[6] (for T. yāhi). 2nd med. **yajassu** Sn 302, 506; J V.488 (yaññaŋ), 490 (id.) — Pot. 1st sg. **yajeyyaŋ** D I.134; 3rd pl. **yajeyyuŋ** J VI.211, 215; 3rd sg. med. **yajetha** Dh 106 (māse māse sahassena yo y.=dānaŋ dadeyya DhA II.231), 108; It 98; A II.43; Sn 463. — Fut. 2nd sg. **yajissasi** J III.515; 1st sg. **yajissāmi** J VI.527 (pantha-sakuṇaŋ tuyhaŋ maŋsena); 3rd pl. **yajissanti** J IV.184; 1st pl. **yajissāma** J VI.132. — aor. 1st sg. **yajiŋ** Th 1, 341; 3rd sg. **ayajī** It 102; **yaji** Miln 219, 221. — inf. **yajituŋ** Miln 220; **yiṭṭhuŋ** D I.138 (yiṭṭhu-kāma wishing to sacrifice), and **yaṭṭhuŋ** in °kāma D II.244; Sn 461. — ger. **yajitvā** D I.143; A II.44; Sn 509; J VI.137 (puttehi), 202; Pv II.9[56] (datvā+, i. e. spending liberally; cp. PvA 136); **yajitvāna** Sn 303, 979. — grd. **yajitabba** J VI.133 (sabba-catukkena). — pp. **yajita** & **yiṭṭha**. — Caus. I. **yājeti**; Caus. II. **yajāpeti** (q. v.).

Yajana (nt.) [late formation fr. **yaj**, yajati, for the earlier yañña] the act of sacrificing J III.518; VI.133; Cp. I. 7[2]; Vism 224; PvA 135.

Yajanaka (adj.) [fr. yajana] one who sacrifices J VI.133.

Yajāpeti [Caus. II. of yajati] to cause a sacrifice to be held A I.168 (yajati+).

Yajita [pp. of yajati] sacrificed Miln 219; J IV.19.

Yajubbeda [fr. Vedic yajus the sacrificial formula, +veda] the Yajurveda, the 2nd of the Vedas, dealing with sacrifice Miln 178; DA I.247; SnA 447. As yajuveda at Dpvs V.62, where the 3 Vedas are enum[d] as iruveda, yaju° and sāma°.

Yañña [Vedic yajña, fr. **yaj**: see yajati. The metric reading in the Veda is sometimes yajana, which we are inclined to look upon as *not* being the source of the P. yajana] 1. a brahmanic sacrifice. — 2. almsgiving, charity, a gift to the Sangha or a bhikkhu. The brahmanic ritual of Vedic times has been given a changed and deeper meaning. ' Buddhism has discarded the outward and cruel form and has widened its sphere by changing its participant, its object as well as the means and ways of "offering," so that the yañña now consists entirely in a worthy application of a worthy gift to a worthy applicant. Thus the direct and as it were self-understood definition of yañña is at Nd[2] 523 given with "yañño vuccati deyyadhammo," and as this the 14 constituents of the latter are enum[d]; consisting of the 4 paccayas, *and* of anna, pāna, vattha, yāna, mālā, gandhā, vilepana, seyya, avasatha, padīpeyya. Cp. Nd[1] 373. — The term **parikkhāra**, which refers to the requisites of the bhikkhu as well (see DA 1.204-207), is also used in the meaning of "accessory instrument" concerning the *brahmanic* sacrifice: see D I.129 sq., 137 sq. They are there given as 16 parikkhāras, as follows: (4) cattāro anumati-pakkhā viz. the 4 groups khattiyas, ministers, brahmans and householders, as colleagues by consent; (8) aṭṭhangāni of a king-sacrificer; (4) cattār' angāni of a purohita. — The term mahāyañña refers to the brahmanic ritual (so at M II.204; DhsA 145, cp. *Expositor* 193); its equivalent in Buddhist literature is mahādāna, for which yañña is also used at Pv II.9[50] (cp. PvA 134). — The Jātakas are full of passages referring to the ineffectiveness and cruelty of the Brahmanic sacrifice, e. g. J III.518 sq.; VI.211 sq., & cp. Fick, *Sociale Gliederung*, p. 146 sq. One special kind of sacrifice is the sabba-catukkayañña or the sacrifice of tetrads, where four of each kind of gifts, as elephants, horses, bulls, and even *men* were offered: J I.335; III.44, 45; PvA 280. The number 4 here has the meaning of evenness, completeness, or harmony, as we find it freq., in the notion of the *square* with ref. to Vimānas & lotus ponds (in J., Vv & Pv etc.); often also implying awfulness & magic, as attached e. g. to cross-roads. Cp. the Ep. of niraya (Purgatory) "catu-dvāra" (esp. at Pv I.10). See cpds. of catur. — It may also refer to the 4 quarters of the sky, as belonging to the 4 Guardians of the World (lokapālā) who were specially worth offering to, as their influence was demonic (cp. Pv I.4).

The prevailing meaning of yañña in the Suttapiṭaka is that of "gift, oblation to the bhikkhu, almsgiving." Cp. Sn 295, 461, 484, 1043. At Vv 34[26] the epithets "su-dinna, su-huta, su-yiṭṭha" are attributed to dāna. — The 3 constituents which occur under dāna & deyyadhamma as the gift, the giver and the recipient of the gift (i. e. the Sangha: cp. opening stanza Pv I[1]) are similarly enum[d] under yañña (or yaññapatha) as "ye yaññaŋ (viz. cīvaraŋ etc.) *esanti*" those who wish for a gift, "ye yaññaŋ *abhisankharonti*" those who get it ready, and "ye yaññaŋ *denti*" those who give it, at Nd[2] 70 (under appamatta). Similarly we find the threefold division of "yañña" (=cīvara etc.). "yaññayājaka" (=khattiyā, brāhmaṇā etc., including all 8 classes of men: see Nd[2] p. 129 s. v. khattiya, quoted under jana[b]), and "dakkhiṇeyya" (the recipient of the gift, viz. samaṇa-brāhmaṇā, kapaṇ'addhikā vanibbakā, yācakā) at Nd[2] 449[b] (under puthū). — Cp. the foll. (mixed) passages: D I.97, 128-144 (brahmanic criticised); II.353, 354 (profitable and unprofitable, criticised); M I.82 (brahm.); S I.76, 160; II.42 sq., 63, 207; III.337; IV.41; A I.166; II.43 (nirārambhaŋ yaññaŋ upasankamanti arahanto, cp. DhsA 145); Sn 308 (brahm.), 568 (aggihutta-mukhā yaññā: the sacrifices to Agni are the best; brahm.); Th I, 341; J I.83, 343; III.517 (°ŋ yajati; brahm.); IV.66; V.491, 492; VI.200 (yañña-kāraka-brāhmaṇa), 211 sq.; DA I.267; DhA II.6.

-āgāra a hall for sacrifices Pug 56 (=yañña-sālā PugA 233). **-āvāṭa** the sacrificial pit D I.142, 148; J I.335; III.45, 517; VI.215 (where reading yaññavāṭa, cp. yaññavāṭaka at Cp. I.7[2]). It has been suggested by Kern, *Toev*, s. v., and it seems more to the sense, to read yañña-vāṭa for yaññ' āvāṭa, i. e. enclosed place for sacrifice. Thus at all passages for °āvāṭa. **-kāla** a suitable (or the proper) time for sacrifice D I.137; Sn 458, 482; DA I.297. **-upanīta** one who has been brought to the sacrifice S I.168 (trsl. *K.S.* 211 not quite to the point: "the oblation is brought." Reading is uncertain; v. l. °opanīta which may be read as opavīta "wearing the sacrificial cord": see foll.). **-opavīta** (?) [see upavīta] in phrase yaññ' opavīta-kaṇṭhā "having the (sacrificial, i. e.) alms-cord wound round their necks" SnA 92 (v. l. BB yaññ-opacita-kammā). Cp. yañña-suttaka. **-patha** [cp. patha[2]] (way of) sacrificing, sacrifice Sn 1045; Nd[2] 524 (yañño y' eva vuccati yañña-patho); J VI.212, 215. **-vaṇṇa** praise of sacrifice J VI.200. **-vidhāna** the arrangement or celebration of a sacrifice J VI.202. **-sampadā** success of the sacrifice D I.128 sq. (in its threefold mode), 134, 143, 144; Sn 505, 509. **-sāmin** lord or giver of a sacrifice D I.143. **-suttaka** "sacrificial string," i. e. alms-cord (the sign of a mendicant) DhA II.59. Cp. above: °opavīta.

Yaññatā (f.) [abstr. fr. yañña] "sacrificiality," the function or ceremony of a sacrifice J VI.202 (=yañña-vidhāna C.).

Yaṭṭhi (f.) [cp. Vedic yaṣṭi. Another Pali form is laṭṭhi] 1. a staff, stick, pole M III.133 (tomara° goad); S I.115 (pācana° driving stick, goad); Miln 2; DhA III.140 (kattara° a mendicant's staff); PvA 241; VbhA 241 (yantacakka°); Mhvs 11, 10 (veḷu° a bamboo pole). — 2. a stem, stalk (of a plant), cane in **ucchu°** sugar-stick, sugar-cane DhA III.315 (=ucchu-khaṇḍika at Vv 33[26]); IV.199. — 3. a measure of length (=7 ratanas) VbhA 343.

-koṭi the end of the stick or staff DhA I.15. **-madhukā** ("cane-sweetness") liquorice Mhvs 32, 46. **-luddaka** "stick-hunter" at J IV.392 means a hunter with a *lasso.*

Yata [pp. of **yam**] held, checked, controlled, restrained, careful S II.15, 50; Sn 78, 220, 1079 (=yatta, paṭiyatta, gutta etc. Nd[2] 525); J VI.294 (C. appamatta; Kern, *Toev.* s. v. proposes reading yatta for yata Vism 201 (?). Esp. in two phrases: **yat-atta** (yata+attan) self-controlled, one whose heart is kept down D I.57 (cp. *Dial.* I.75); Sn 216, 490, 723; DA I.168. **—yata-cārin** living in self-restraint, living or behaving carefully Sn 971 (=yatta paṭiyatta gutta etc. Nd[1] 498); Miln 300 (+samāhita-citta, where Kern, *Toev.* s. v. proposes to read yatta-cārin for yata°). A similar passage at Th I, 981 reads *yathā-cārin* (q. v. for further expl[n]). — Cp. saŋyata & see also **yatta.**

Yatati[1] [**yat,** given by Dhtp 121 in meaning "yatana," by Dhtm 175 as "paṭiyatana"] to exert oneself, strive, endeavour, to be cautious or careful; ppr. **yataŋ** It 120 (care, tiṭṭhe, acche etc.; Seidenstücker trsl[s] "gezügelt," thus taking it in meaning of yata). — pp. **yatta.**

Yatati[2] [unidentified, perhaps as expl[n] of yati ?] is given in meaning of "lead ont" (?) at Dhtp 580 ("niyyātane") and Dhtm 813 (id.).

Yatana (nt.) [fr. **yat,** cp. Epic Sk. yatna] endeavour, undertaking J V.346 (C. expl[s] samosaraṇa-ṭṭhāna ?); Dhtp 121 (in expl[n] of yatati[1]).

Yati [fr. **yam,** cp. Vedic yati leader, guide] a Buddhist monk Mhvs 5, 37 (racchāgataŋ yatiŋ); 25, 4; 30, 26 (mattikā-dāyakaŋ yatiŋ); 32, 32 (khīṇāsavassa yatino); Dāvs IV.33 (yatī); Vism 79 (vikampeti Mārassa hadayaŋ yatī); PvA 287 (instr. muni-vara-yatinā).

Yato (adv.) [the abl. case of ya°, used as conjunction, Cp. Vedic yataḥ wherefrom, by which, out of which] 1. (local) from where D I 240 (uggacchanti candima -suriyā; opp. yattha where). — 2. (temporal) whence, since, when, from which time VvA 344 (yato paṭṭhāya). — 3. (modal) from which, out of what cause, because, in as far as D I.36 sq. (yato . . . ettāvatā because . . . therefore); Sn p. 113 (id.) Dh 374, 390 (doubled=from whichever source). — Freq. in two comb[ns]: **yatvâdhi-karaṇaŋ** (yato+adhikaraṇaŋ) because (lit. by reason of which; cp. kim-ādhikaraṇaŋ, see adhik.) D I.70; D I.113; M I.269; Dhs 1346; cp. similarly BSk. yato adhikaraṇaŋ MVastu III.52; *and* **yato-nidānaŋ** on account of which, from which (or what) reason, because M I.109; Sn 273, 869; Pv IV.1[61] (cp. PvA 242). — *Note.* yaticchita at PvA 265 is to be read **yadicchita.**

Yatta [pp. of yatati[1]] strenuous, making an effort, watchful Nd[2] 525 (+paṭiyatta, in exegesis of yata); J IV.222 (+paṭiyatta); VI.294 (Kern's reading for yata; vv. ll. saŋyata & sata, thus warranting yata); Miln 373 (°payatta), 378 (id.=in keen effort). — *Note.* Kern, *Toev.* s. v. would like to equal yatta=Sk. yatna effort.

Yattaka (adj.) [fr. yāvant, a late formation; cp. Trenckner, *Notes,* 80] however much, whatever, as many (in correlation with ta° or **tattaka**) J V.74 (=yāvant); Vism 184 (yattakaŋ ṭhānaŋ gaṇhāti . . . tattakaŋ . . .), 293 (yattakā=yāvatā); DA I.118 (yattaka . . . tattaka as long as); DhA II.50 (°ŋ kālaŋ as long), 128; VbhA 73 (yattakaŋ ṭhānaŋ . . . tattakaŋ), 391 (yattakāni kusala-cittāni . . . tesaŋ *sabbesaŋ*); VvA 175 (yattakāni . . . tāni as many . . . so many, i. e. whatever), 285 (yattakā āhuneyyā nāma . . . tesu *sabbesu* . . .). — instr. **yattakena** as adv. "because, on account of" DhA III.383, 393.

Yattha (adv.) [the regular P. form of Ved. yatra. See also P. yatra] rel. adv. of place "where," at which spot; occasionally "at which time," when; with verbs of motion="whereto." — D I.240 (whither); Sn 79, 170 (here closely resembling *yatra* in meaning="so that"), 191, 313, 445, 995, 1037; Dh 87, 127 (yattha ṭhita, cp. PvA 104) 150, 171, 193, PvA 27. —**yattha vā tattha vā** wherever (or whenever) DhA IV.162; similarly **yattha yattha** wherever (he likes) A II.64. **yattha kāmaŋ** (cp. yathākāmaŋ in same meaning) where to one's liking, i. e. wherever Dh 35 (=yattha katthaci *or* yattha yattha icchati DhA I.295, 299), 326. Similarly we find **yatth-icchakaŋ**, almost identical (originally variant ?) with **yadicchakaŋ** and **yāvadicchakaŋ** at Vism 154.

Yatra (adv.) [the (older ?) reconstituted Sk. form of P. yattha, cp. Vedic yatra in which, where. The P. form is younger than the Vedic, as the P. meaning is doubtful for the V. period. It is merely a differentiation of forms to mark a special meaning in the sense of a causal conjunction, whereas yattha is adv. (of place or time) only] in which, where, since; only in phrase yatra hi nāma (in emphatic exclamations) with Fut.; "as indeed, inasmuch as, that" S II.255 (ñāṇabhūtā vata sāvakā y. h. n. savako ñassati etc.); J I.59 (dhi-r-atthu vata bho jātiyā y. h. n. jātassa jarā paññāyissati "woe to birth that old age is to be noticed in that which is born!"); Miln 13 (acchariyaŋ vata bho . . . y. h. n. me upajjhāyo ceto-parivitakkaŋ jānissati).

Yathā (adv.) [fr. ya°; Vedic yathā; cp. kathā, tathā] as, like, in relation to, after (the manner of). — As *prep.* (with *acc.*): according (to some condition, norm or rule): yathā kāmaŋ (already Vedic) according to his desire, after his liking PvA 113, 136; y. kālaŋ in time, timely PvA 78; matiŋ to his own mind or intention Pv IV.1[67];ruciŋ to his satisfaction, amply, satisfactorily PvA 88, 126, 242; **vibhavaŋ** acc. to their wealth, i. e. plentifully PvA 53; **sukhaŋ** as they liked or pleased PvA 133. Sometimes with *loc.*: yathā padese "according to place," in the right place J III.391. Or *instr.*: y. sattiyā as much as you can DhA I.92; y. manena from his heart, sincerely, voluntarily DhA I.42. — Also with *ger.* yathā haritvā according to his taking (or reward: see under cpd. °bhata) It 14 (y. h. nikkhipeyya, which Seidenstücker, not doing justice to context translates "so wie man etwas nimmt und dann wegwirft"). With foll. adj. expressing something like "as it were" and often untranslateable (see cpds.) — As *conjunction*: "as if," or "so that": yathā mata like dead Dh 21; **yathā na** "in order that not": Vism 31 (y. sarīre ābādhaŋ na uppādeti, evaŋ tassa vinodan' atthaŋ); DhA I.311 (y. assa patitaṭṭhānaŋ na passāmi, tathā naŋ chaḍḍessāmi: so that I shall not see . . ., thus shall I throw him). — As *adv.* just, as, so, even; in comb[n] with other particles: yathā kathaŋ pana how so then, how is it then that S II.283 (cp. yathā tathaŋ under cpds.); yathā **kiŋ viya** somewhat like this Miln 91; yathā pana like as DhA I.158; **yatha-r-iva** (for yathā-iva) just as D I.90; yathā pi . . . evaŋ just as . . . so Dh 51-52. —**yatha-y-idaŋ** (for yathā-idaŋ) positive: "as just this," "so that," "e. g.," "like," "i. e."; after negation "but" It 8, 9 (na aññaŋ . . . yathayidaŋ); Sn 1092 (tvañ ca me dīpam akkhāhi, yathayidaŋ n' âparaŋ siyā "so that there be no further ill"; cp. SnA 597). See also the enlarged forms seyyathā & seyyathīdaŋ. — In correlation with tathā: the same . . . as, like . . . as, as . . . so; Pv I.12[3] (yath' āgato tathā-gato as he has come so has he gone). Often elliptically in direct juxtaposition: yathā tathā in whatever way, in such & such a manner; so and so, according to the occasion; also "correctly, truly, in reality" Sn 504 (tvaŋ h' ettha jānāsi y. t. idaŋ); PvA 199 (y. t. vyākāsi). See yathātathaŋ under cpds. About phrase yathā taŋ see yathātaŋ. — For further refs. on the use of yathā see Indexes to Saŋyutta (S VI.81 s. v. yathābhūtaŋ); Anguttara (A. VI.91 ibid.); Sutta-Nipāta (Index p. 751); & Dhammapada.

-**ânudhammaŋ** according to the rules (leading to enlightenment) Sn 963, cp. Nd[1] 481. -**ânurūpa** suitable, proper Mhvs 28, 42. -**ânusiṭṭhaŋ** in accordance with what has been taught DhA I.158. -**âbhirantaŋ** (adv. nt. of ppr.) to (their) heart's content, as much (or as long) as one likes Vin III.145; Sn 53; DhA I.385; VvA 181. -**āraddha** [=ālabdha] as much as was to be had, sufficient Vin III.160. -**ârahaŋ** (nt. adv.) as is fit or proper, seeming, fitful, appropriately, duly (cp. *Cpd.* 111[1], 118[2]) S I.226; Sn 403; Pv II.9[23]; PvA 78, 132 (yathā codanaŋ v. l. SS), 287; VvA 139. So to be read at all Pv & PvA passages for T. yathā rahaŋ. Very freq. in Mhvs. e. g. 3, 27; 5, 148; 7, 70; 14, 54; 20, 8; 22, 58. -**âlankata** dressed as he was, in full (state-) dress DhA III.79. -**âvajjaŋ** "as if to be blamed," i. e. (imitating) whatever is faulty, mimicry of deformities (as a forbidden pastime) D I.7 (=kāṇa-kuṇi-khañj' ādīnaŋ yaŋ yaŋ vajjaŋ taŋ taŋ payojetvā dassana-kīḷā DA I.86); Vin II.10. -**icchitaŋ** according to one's wish, as he liked, after his heart's content J I.27 (v. 188)=Bu II.179; is preferably to be read as **yad-icchitaŋ** at all PvA passages, e. g. PvA 3 (°ŋ dento), 110 (°ṭhāna whichever place I like), 265 (where T. has yat°). The ed. of Mhvs however reads **yath°** throughout; e. g. 7, 22; 22, 50. -**odhi** as far as the limit, final, utmost M I.37; J III.302. -**odhika** to (its or their) full extent, altogether, only in phrase *yathodhikāni kāmāni* Sn 60 (cp. Nd[2] 526); J III.381 (C. not quite to the point with expl[n] "attano odhivasena ṭhitāni," giving variant *yatodhikāni*, with expl[n] "yato uparato odhi etesan ti yatodhikāni uparata-koṭṭhāsāni"); IV.487 (with better C. expl[n]: "yena yena odhinā ṭhitāni tena tena ṭhitān' eva jahissāmi, na kiñce avasissāmī ti attho"); V.392 (C.: "yathāṭhita-koṭṭhasāni"). -**kamma** (ŋ) according to one's karma or action J I.57, 109; IV.1. Freq. in phrase **yathā-kamm-ûpage satte** (pajānāti) "(he recognises) the beings passing away (or undergoing future retribution) acc. to their deeds" D I.82; M I.482; II.21; III.178; S II.122; A IV.141, 178, 422; V.35; Sn 587; It 99; and **yathā-kamm-ûpaga-ñāṇa** "the knowledge of specific retribution" Vism 433 sq.; Tikp 321; VbhA 373 sq. (°catuttha). -**kāmaŋ** according to wish, at random (see above); ° -*karaṇiya* to be done or dealt with ad lib., i. e. a victim, prey S II.226; IV.91, 159; It 56. -**kārin** as he does It 122 (corresp. to tathā-vādin). -**kālaŋ** according to time, in one time Mhvs 5, 180. -**kkamaŋ** acc. to order, in one order or succession Mhvs 4, 54; Sdhp 269. -**cārin** virtuous (for the usual yatacārin as indicated by C. expl[n] *yata* kāyādihi *sanyatī*: see *Brethren,* p. 342!) Th 1, 981 (trsl. "Whoso according to his powers is virtuous"). -**ṭhita** so-being, such & such, as they are, as they were J V.392; VvA 256.

-tathaŋ according to truth, true & real (corresponding to yathā tathā adv. : see above) It 122 (here as nom. sg. : as he is in one respect, so in the other, i. e. perfect); Sn 1127 (=yathā ācikkhitabbaŋ tathā ācikkhi Nd² 527); Th 1, 708 (diṭṭhe dhamme yathātathe : is reading correct ? perhaps better as yathātathā, cp. trslⁿ *Brethren* 292 : " the truths are seen e'en as they really are "); Dpvs III.2 (so read for yathā-kathaŋ ; v. l. has °tathaŋ); V.64 (pañhaŋ byākarohi yathātathaŋ). -dhamma (used as adj. & adv. °ŋ) " one according to the law," i. e. as the rule prescribes; nt. according to the rule put down. See *Vin. Texts* 1.203 ; Geiger, *Dhamma*, p. 19, 67. — Vin I.135 (yo uddiseyya, yathā-dhammo kāretabbo), 168 (yo pavāreyya, y.-dhammo kāretabbo), 191 (yo māreyya y.-dh. k.); II.67 (ubho pi yathādhammaŋ kārāpetabbā). 132 (yo ajjhohareyya, y.-dhammo kāretabbo); IV.126 (yo jānaŋ (i. e. knowing) yathādhammaŋ nihat' âdhikaraṇaŋ punākammāya ukkoṭeyya, pācittiyan ti i. e. a dispute settled in proper form ; with explⁿ : y.-dhammaŋ nāma dhammena vinayena satthu sāsanena kataŋ), 144 (na tassa . . . mutti atthi yañ ca tattha āpattiŋ āpanno tañ ca yathādhammo kāretabbo, uttari c' assa moho āropetabbo). Cp. the foll. passages; as *adj.* : Vin I.205 ; II.132, 142, 263 ; M III.10 ; Miln 195 ; as *adv.* : with paṭikaroti (to atone, make amends) Vin I.173, 315 ; II.126 ; IV.19 ; D I.85 ; III.55 ; M III.247 ; S II.128, 205 ; A I.103, 238 ; II.146 ; IV.377 ; cp. yathādhammaŋ paṭigaṇhāti S I.239 ; A I.59, 103. At S III.171 yathādhammaŋ is used in the sense of " according to the truth, or reality," where yathā-bhūtaŋ takes its place ; similarly at Th 1, 188. -dhota as if it were washed (so to speak), clean, unsoiled DhA I.196 ; cp. MVastu I.301 yathā-dhauta. -pasādhanaŋ according to a clear state of mind, to one's gratification Dh 249 (=attano pasād' ânurūpaŋ DhA III.359). -puggalaŋ according to the individual, individually Pv III.5¹ (read yathāpu°). -pūrita as full as could be, quite full J I.101. -phāsuka comfortable, pleasant DhA I.8. -balaŋ according to one's power or means DhA I.107 (v. l. °satti) ; Sdhp 97 ; Mhvs 5, 180. -buḍḍha see °vuḍḍha. -bhataŋ is an unexplᵈ ἅπαξ λεγομένον, difficult of analysis because occurring in only one ster. phrase, viz. yathā bhataŋ nikkhitto evaŋ niraye (& sagge) at M I.71 ; S IV.325 (where T. has yathâhataŋ, v. l. bhataŋ) ; A I.8, 105, 292, 297 ; II.71, 83 ; It 12, 14, 26. We have analyzed it as y. bhataŋ in Corr. to pt. 3 ; vol. II.100 (" according to his upbringing "), but we should rather deviate from this explⁿ because the P. usage in this case would prefer the nom. instead of the (adv.) acc. nt. It remains doubtful whether we should separate yathā or yath' ābhataŋ. Suggestions of a trslⁿ are the foll. (1) " as soon as brought or taken " (see Dict. s. v. ābhata) ; (2) " as one has brought " (merit or demerit) ; thus taking ābhataŋ as irregular ger. of â+bhar, trslⁿ suggested by the reading âharitvā (yathâharitvā) in the complementary stanzas at It 12 & 14 ; (3) " according to merit or reward," after Kern's suggestion, *Toev.* s. v. to read yathā bhaṭaŋ, the difficulty being that bhaṭa is nowhere found as v. l. of bhata in this phrase ; nor that bhaṭa occurs in the meaning of " reward." — There is a strong likelihood of (ā)bhata resembling āhata (āhaṭa ?) in meaning " as brought," on account of, cp. It context and reading at S IV.325 ; still the phrase remains not sufficiently cleared up. — Seidenstücker's trslⁿ has been referred to above (under haritvā) as unbefitting. — The suspicion of yathābhataŋ being a veiled (corrupted) yathābhūtaŋ has presented itself to us before (see vol. I. under ābhata). The meaning may suggest something like the latter, in as far as " in truth," " surely " is not far off the point. Anyhow we shall have to settle on a meaning like " according to merit," without being able to elucidate the phrase in all its details. — There is another yathābhataŋ in passage . . . ussavo hoti, yathābhataŋ lasuṇaŋ parikkhayaŋ agamāsi " the garlic diminished as soon as it was brought " Vin IV.258. Here ābhata stands in rel. to harāpeti (to have it fetched & brought) and is clearly pp. of ābharati. -bhucca as is the case, i. e. as one might expect, evident, real, in conformity with the truth D I.12 ; II.222 ; Miln 183, 351 ; Th 2, 159 (=yathābhūtaŋ ThA 142) ; PvA 30, 31 (°guṇā). -bhutta see bhutta. -bhūta(ŋ) in reality, in truth, really, definitely, absolutely ; as ought to be, truthfully, in its real essence. Very freq. in var. combnˢ which see collected & classified as regards Saŋyutta & Anguttara-Nikāyas in Index vols to these texts. E. g. S IV.195 (vacanaŋ, Ep. of Nibbāna) ; V.440 (abhisamaya) ; Sn 194, 202, 653 ; Dh 203 ; PvA 215 (guṇa). *yathābhūtaŋ pajānāti* he knows as an absolute truth or in reality D I.83, 162 ; S IV.188 ; V.304 & passim ; ditto *yathābhūtaŋ jānāti passati* Ps II.62. Similarly with noun : *yathābhūta-ñāṇa* absolute knowledge S V.144 ; Ps II.63 = Vism 605 (+sammādassana) ; Vism 438, 629, 695 ; VbhA 459 (=maggañāṇa) ; also as *°ñāṇa-dassana* in same meaning : A III.19, 200 ; IV.99, 336 ; V.2 sq., 311 sq. ; Ps I.33, 43 sq. ; II.11 sq. ; Nett 29. -mano according to (his) mind Sn 829 ; Nd¹ 170 (explᵈ as nom.=yathācitto, yathāsankappo, yathāviññāṇo). -ruciŋ according to pleasure or liking Mhvs 4, 43 (ruci T. ; ruciŋ v. l. ; thus generally in Mhvs.) ; 5, 230 (°ruci) ; 22, 58 (°ruci). -vādin as speaking, as he speaks (followed by *tathā-kārin* so doing) D II.224, 229 ; Sn 357 ; It 122. -vidhi(ŋ) duly, fitly Mhvs 10, 79. -vihita as appointed or arranged Mhvs 10, 93. -vuḍḍhaŋ according to seniority Vin II.221 ; Mhbv 90 (T. reads °buḍḍhaŋ). -vutta(ŋ) as is said, i. e. as mentioned, aforesaid, of this kind Mhvs 34, 57 ; PvA 45, 116 (°o puggalo). -saka(ŋ) each his own, according to his (or her) own, respective(ly) Vism 525 ; SnA 8, 9 ; VvA 7 ; Mhvs 5, 230 (here simply " their own "). -sata saintly (?), mindful Th 1, 981 (cp. yathā cārin & *Brethren* p. 342). -satti(ŋ) according to one's power S IV.348 (+yathābalaŋ) ; DhA I.107 (v. l. for °balaŋ) ; Sdhp 97. -satthaŋ according to the precepts, as law ordains M III.10 (perhaps an error for yathāsaddha ?). -saddhaŋ acc. to faith, as is one's faith Dh 249. -santhatika accepting whatever seat is offered D I.167 ; A III.220 ; Pug 69 ; Th 1, 854. -°*anga* one of the 13 dhutangas Miln 342, 359 ; Vism 61, 78. -sukhaŋ according to ease, at ease, at will Th 1, 77 ; Dh 326.

Yathātaŋ (adv.) [yathā+taŋ] as it is, as, as if Vin III.5 ; S I.124 ; M I.253. The spelling in our books is yathā taŋ (in *two* words).

Yathāva (adj.) [der. fr. yathā, as yathā+vant, after analogy of yāvant, but following the a-decl., cp. Epic Sk. yathāvat] having the character of being in accordance with (the truth or the occasion), real, true, just It 44 (santaŋ paṇitaŋ yathāvaŋ, nt.) ; Th 1, 188, 422 (°āloka-dassana seeing the real light) ; Miln 171 (°lakkhaṇa true characteristics) ; Vism 588 (as yāthāvasarasa), 639 (id.). — abl. yathāvato (also found as yāthāvato, probably more correctly, being felt as a der. fr. yathā) according to fitness, fitfully, duly, truly, sufficiently PvA 60 (so read for yathā vato), 128 (*all* MSS. yāthāvato !) ; ThA 256 (yā° ; the explⁿ given by Morris, *J.P.T.S.* 1889, 208 is not correct).

Yathāvaka (adj.) [fr. yathāva] being according to reality or sufficiency, essential, true, real, sufficient Th 1, 347 ; VbhA 409 (°vatthu, referring to the " māna "-division of the Khuddaka-vatthu Vbh 353 sq., cp. Nd² 505≈) Should we read yāthāvaka° ?

Yad, Yad-idaŋ etc., see **ya°** 4ᵇ.

Yadā (adv.) [Vedic yadā ; old instr. of ya°] when Sn 200 (y. ca so mato seti), 681, 696 (here as yada, explᵈ as yadā), 923 ; Dh 28, 69, 277 sq., 325, 384, 390 ; It 77 (y. devo devakāyā cavati) ; PvA 54, 67. Cp. kadā & tadā.

Yadi (indecl.) [adv. formation, orig. loc., fr. ya°; cp. Vedic yadi] 1. as conjunction: if; constructed either with *pres. indic.*, as: Sn 189; "yadi bodhiŋ pattuŋ icchasi" J I.24 (v. 167); "yadi dāyako dānaŋ deti . . . etaŋ bījaŋ hoti" PvA 8; or *pot.*; or with a *participle*, as: "yadi evaŋ sante" that being so, if this is so D I.61; "gahito yadi sīho te" if the lion is caught by you Mhvs 6, 27. — With other particles, e. g. **yādi** āsanamattaŋ pi *even if* only a seat VvA 39; **yadi** . . . atha kasmā if . . . how then Miln 4. yadi evaŋ . . . (tu) even if . . . yet (but) PvA 63 (y. e. pitā na rodati, mātu nāma hadayaŋ mudukaŋ). — **yadi va** "or" (cp. Vedic yadi vā "or be it that") Dh 195 (=yadi vā athavā DhA III.252). So **yadi vā** at J I.18 (v. 97: latā vā yadi vā rukkhā etc. Sn 119 (gāme vā yadi vāraññe). — 2. as a strong particle of *exhortation*: **yadi evaŋ** if so, in that case, let it be that, alright, now then PvA 54 (y. e. yaŋ mayhaŋ desitaŋ ekassa bhikkhuno dehi), 217 (y. e. yāvadatthaŋ gaṇhāhi: take as much as you like).

Yanta (nt.) [Vedic yantra, a kind of n. ag. formation fr. **yam** to hold by means of a string or bridle, etc. Idg. ***em** & ***i̯em**, as in Lat. emo to take & red-imio.] a means for holding, contrivance, artifice, instrument, machine, mechanism; fig. instrumentality (as perhaps in. kamma° at *Th* passages). — Referring to the machinery (outfit) of a ship (as oars, helm, etc.) J IV.163 (sabbayant' ûpapanna=piy'-ârittā etc. C.); Miln 379. To mechanism in general (mechanical force) J V.333 (°vegena=with the swiftness of machinery). To a sugar-mill Miln 166; usually as ucchu-yanta J I.25, 339 (°yante gaṇṭhikā), cp. ucchūnaŋ yanta DhA IV.199. —**tela-yanta** (-cakka) (the wheel of) an oil mill J I.25. —**dāru-yanta** a wooden machine (i. e. a mechanical man with hands & feet moved by pulling of strings) DA I.197; Vism 595 (quoted as simile). —**kamma-yanta** the machinery of Kamma Th 1, 419 (i. e. its instrumentality, not, as trsl^n "car"; cp. *Brethren* 217: "it breaks in pieces K's living car," evidently influenced by C. expl^n "attabhāva-yanta"), 754 (similarly: see discussed under yantita). *Note.* yantāni at Nd^2 529 (on Sn 48 sanghaṭṭa-yantāni) is expl^d as "dhuvarāni." The spelling & meaning of the latter is not clear. It must refer to bracelets. — Cp. SnA 96 valayāni.

-**ākaḍḍhana** pulling the machine Vism 258=VbhA 241. -**cakkha-yaṭṭhi** the stick of the wheel of a (sugar-) mill VbhA 60. -**nāḷi** a mechanical tube DhA III.215. -**pāsāṇa** an aerolite (?) J III.258 (read °pāsāṇo). -**phalakāni** the boards of a machine Vism 258. -**yutta** combined by machinery J VI.432. -**sutta** the string of a machine (or mill). Vism 258 (as °ka)=VbhA 241. -**hatthi** a mechanical (automatic) elephant DhA I.192 (of King Caṇḍa-pajjota; cp. the horse of Troy).

Yantaka (nt.) [fr. yanta] a bolt Vin II.148 (vihārā aguttā honti . . . anujānāmi yantakaŋ sūcikan ti), cp. *Vin. Texts* III.162; DA I.200 (kuñcikā+); DhA I.220 (yantakaŋ deti to put the bolt to, to lock up).

Yanti is 3rd pl. pres. of **yā**: see yāti. — *Note.* At D II.269 we should combine yanti with preceding **visamā** & sambādhā, thus forming denom. verbs: **visamāyanti** "become uneven" and **sambādhāyanti** "become oppressed or tight." The trsl^n *Dial* II.305 gives just the opposite by reading incorrectly.

Yantita [pp. of yanteti] made to go, set into motion, impelled Th 1, 574: evâyaŋ vattati kāyo kamma-yantena yantito "impelled by the machinery of Karma"; trsl^n *Brethren* 261 not quite to the point "carried about on Karma's car." Kern, *Toev.* s. v. quite out of place with "fettered, held, restrained," in analogy to his trsl^n of **yanta** id. loc. with "fetter." He may have been misled by Dhtm def^n of **yant** as "sankocana" (see yanteti).

Yanteti [denom. fr. yanta. Dhtm 809 gives a root **yant** in meaning of "sankocane," i. e. contraction] to set into motion, to make go, impel, hurl J I.418 (sakkharaŋ anguliyā yantetvā); pp. yantita.

Yannūna see ya° 2^c.

Yapana see yāpana.

Yapeti see yāpeti.

Yabhati [*one* passage in Atharva Veda; cp. Gr. οἴφω "futuo," Lat. ibex (see Walde, *Lat. Wtb.* s. v.)] to cohabit, futuere, only given as root **yabh** with def^n "methune" at Dhtp 215 & Dhtm 308.

Yama[1] [fr. **yam**] restraint PvA 98 (+niyama).

Yama[2] [Vedic Yama] the ruler of the kingdom of the dead. See details in Dicty. of Names. In cpds. often in general sense of "death" or "manes," or "petā"; e. g.

-**dūta** Death's messenger Sdhp 287; cp. Yamassa dūtā Vv 52^2 (see VvA 224), or deva-dūta A I.138 (see under dūta), alias niraya-pāla A I.138 and passim. -**purisa** (a)=°dūta Dh 235 (cp. DhA III.335); VvA 223; (b) °*purisā* Yama-people, i. e. Petas Pv IV.3^3 (cp. PvA 251). -**loka** the yama-world or world of the Petas Dh 44, 45; PvA 107 & freq. -**visaya**=°loka Pv II.8^3 & passim. -**sādana** Y's kingdom, or the realm of the dead J VI.267, 304; VI.457, 505.

Yama[3] (m. nt.) [Vedic yama=yama^2; fr. **yam** in meaning "to combine," cp. Av. yə̄ma twin, Mir. emuin id.] (nt.) a pair, (m.) a twin Abhp 628. See der. yamaka.

Yamaka [fr. yama^3] 1. (adj.) double, twin; only in foll. comb^{ns}: °**pāṭihāriya** (& °hīra) the miracle of the double appearances, a miracle performed by the Buddha in Sāvatthī to refute the heretical teachers (cp. Vin III.332, Samanta-pāsādika; and in detail DA I.57). It consisted in the appearance of phenomena of opposite character in pairs, as e. g. streaming forth of fire & water. (Cp. *Mhvs trsl^n* 120). The miracle was repeatedly performed by the Buddha & is often referred to, e. g. at Ps I.125 (°hīra); J I.77, 88, 193; Miln 106 (°hīraŋ), 349 (°hāriyaŋ); Mhvs 17, 44, 50; 30, 82; 31, 99; Dāvs I.50 (°hīraŋ); DhA III.213 (id.); SnA 36; Vism 390; PvA 137. -**sālā** the pair of Sal willows in between of which the Buddha passed away VvA 165; PvA 212. — 2. (adj. or m.) a twin, twin child Mhvs 6, 9 (yamake duve puttaŋ ca dhitaraŋ janesi), 37 (solasakkhattuŋ yamake duve putte janayi); DhA I.353 (same, with vijāyi). — 3. (nt.) a pair, couple, N. of one of the Abhidhamma canonical books, also called Yamaka-ppakaraṇa; Tikp 8. — The Yamaka-sutta refers to the conversion of the bhikkhu Yamaka and is given at S III.109 sq.; mentioned at Vism 479 & VbhA 32. The phrase **yamakato sammasana** at Vism 626 may mean "in pairs" (like kalāpato "in a bundle" ibid.), or may refer to the Yamaka-sutta with its discussion of anicca, dukkha, anatta.

Yamataŋ at S I.14 (sa vītivatto yamataŋ sumedho) we should read (with Mrs. Rh. D.'s emendation *K.S.* p. 320) as **yaŋ mataŋ** (Cy.: maññanaŋ; trsl. "he rich in wisdom hath escaped beyond conceits and deemings of the errant mind").

Yamati [**yam**, given in meaning "uparame" i. e. cessation, quieting at Dhtp 226 & Dhtm 322, at the latter with additional "nāse." On etym. see Walde, *Lat. Wtb.* s. v. redimio and emo: cp. yanta] to restrain, suppress, to become tranquil; only in stanza Dh 6=Th I.275=J III.488 as 1st pl. med. yamāmase in imper. sense: "pare ca na vijānanti mayaŋ ettha yamāmase," which is expl^d both at DhA I.65, Th I A, & J III.489 in connection with yama,[2] viz. "yamāmase: uparamāma nassāma satataŋ samitaŋ maccu-santikaŋ gacchāmā ti na jānanti," i. e. let us go continually into the presence of death. A little further at DhA I.66 the expl° of it is "bhaṇḍ'-ādīnaŋ vuddhiyā vāyamāmā ti na vijānanti." The meaning is "to control oneself," cp. saŋyamāmase S I.209. Leop. v. Schroeder however trsls. "Und mancher Mann bedenket nicht: wir alle müssen sterben hier" (*Worte der Wahrheit*, p. 2.). — yameyyātha at S I.217 is wrongly separated from the preceding vā, which ought to be read as **vāyameyyātha** (so *K.S.* I.281).

Yamala [fr. yama[3]] a pair Abhp 628. — yamalī occurs in BSk. only as a kind of dress, at Divy 276; AvŚ I.265.

Yava [Vedic yava, corn; see Zimmer, *Altind. Leben* 239. Cp. Gr. ζεά spelt; Lith. javaĩ corn; Oir. eorna barley] corn (in general), barley (in particular) Vin IV.264; S IV.220; A IV.169.

-**karaṇa** the preparation of corn A IV.169. -**kalāpī** (or °inī) a sheaf of barley S IV.201. -**kāraṇḍava** chaff of corn (or barley) A IV.169. -**kummāsa** barley-gruel VvA 62. -**khetta** corn-field Vin IV.47, 266; VvA 294. -**dūsin** spoiling the corn A IV.169. -**majjhaka** lying in the midst of a corn-field, in *pācina*° of the c.-f. on the E. side (+dakkhiṇa° S.; pacchima° W.; uttara° N.); names of 4 market-places near Mithilā J VI.330. -**sūka** the awn or beard of corn (barley) A I.8; S V.10, 48.

Yavaka (nt.) [yava+collect. ending °ka] in cpd. sāli° (whatever there is of) rice & corn (i. e. rice- and corn-fields C.) J IV.172. Cp. **yāvaka**.

Yavasa (nt.) [fr. yava; Vedic yavasa] grass, hay, fodder J I.338.

Yasassin (adj.) [Vedic yaśasvin] glorious, famous, renowned, having all endowments or comforts of life (as expl[d] at Nd[2] 530: yasappatta, sakkata, lābhī etc.) D I.48 (ñāta+); A II.34; Sn 179, 298, 343, 1117; Pv I.4[1]; III.1[17]; III.3[5]; III.10[8]; Vv 15[9] (=kittimant parivāravant VvA 73); DA I.143; PvA 10; Sdhp 420. — f. **yasassinī** shining, resplendent J V.64.

Yasassimant (adj.) [double adj. ending; yasas+vin+mant] splendid, glorious, full of splendour J V.63 (pāvako yasassimā=teja-sampattiyā yasassinihi accihi yutto C.).

Yasavant (adj.) [cp. Vedic yaśasvat] famous, having renown A II.64 (dīghāyu+).

Yaso & **Yasa** (nt.) [Vedic yaśaḥ (nt.). The word follows the a° declension, but preserves & favours the instr. **yasasā** after the s° decl. (like mano, ceto etc,), e. g. at J I.134. — In the nom. & acc. sg. both forms yaso & **yasa(ŋ)** occur; in cpds. the form **yasa°** is the usual; yaso as *masc.* is found at Sn 438] glory, fame, repute, success, high position. On term as used with ref. to the brahmin see Fick, *Sociale Gliederung* 128, 129 — The prevailing idea of Dhammapāla is that yaso consists of a great retinue, & company of servants, followers etc. This idea is already to be found at D I.118=126 where y. is founded on parisā (cp. DA I.143 on D I.48; DA I.298: yasasā ti āṇā-ṭhapana-samatthatāya). See e. g. VvA 122 (yaso=parivāra); PvA 137 (yasasā=mahati parivāra-sampattiyā); cp. J I.134 (rājā mahantena yasena uppanaŋ gacchati). — D I.137 (as quality of a king); III.260, 286; J IV.275 sq. (dibba y. as one of the 10 qualities of greatness, viz. divine duration of life, complexion, happiness, fame, power, and the 5 sense-objects rūpa, sadda, gandha, rasa, phoṭṭhabba. The same 10 are found at Pv II.9[58, 59]); A I.15; II.32, 66, 188; III.31, 47 sq.; IV.95, 195 sq.; Dh 24, 303 (+bhoga); Thī, 554; Nd[1] 147; Pv III.3[6] (=dev' iddhi PvA 189); Vv 29[1]; J I.134; VI.468; Miln 291 (bhoga+); Vism 393; Sdhp 306, 518. — **yasaŋ deti** to give credit J I.180. mahā-yaso great fame J I.46 (v. 266), cp. **yas-agga** the highest (of) fame J I.51, where coupled with lābh-agga the greatest gain. The latter comb[n] is stereotype in the Niddesa (see e. g. Nd[2] 55), where the 4 worldly ideals are given in sequence lābha, yaso, pasaŋsā, sukha. — With kitti we find yaso at Sn 817 (see def[n] & exegesis at Nd[1] 147). — Opp. ayasa D III.260, 286; A II.188; IV.157 sq.

-**dāyika** giving (or a giver of) repute J VI.285. -**mada** pride of fame VbhA 467. -**mahatta** greatness of fame Vism 233. -**lābha** the gain of fame J III.516 (+dhana-lābha).

Yahiŋ (adv.) [after kuhiŋ] where, wherever Mhvs 15, 209 (corresp. to yattha in v. 210).

Yāga [fr. **yaj**, *Sk. yāga, cp. yañña & yaja] 1. a (*brahmanic*) sacrifice, known otherwise as mahāyāga (or pl. °yāgā), and consisting of the 4: assamedha, purisamedha, sammāpāsa, vāja-peyya. Thus mentioned at S I.76 & Sn 303. — 2. In *Buddhistic* sense: gift, alms-giving, charity; expense or expenditure of giving (almost syn. with cāga) A I.91 (here given in line with dāna & cāga, with distinction of āmisa° & **dhamma°**, i. e. the material sacrifice, as under 1, and the spiritual sacrifice or help); with the same contrast of ā° & dh.° at D III.155; It 98, 102; J V.57, 65; DhA I.27. — J IV.66 (sahassena yāgaŋ yajanto); Miln 21 (dhamma°); VvA 155; PvA 135 (mahā°-saññita yañña), 136 (mahā°). — **suyiṭṭha yāga sampadā** "well-given is the perfection of charity" ThA 40 (Ap. v. 7)=230 (id.).

-**piṇḍa** the sacrificial oblation consisting in a ball of meat or flour (cp. piṇḍa-pitṛ-yajña) J VI.522 (with v. l. yāgu°).

Yāgin (adj.) (-°) [fr. yāga] sacrificing, giving, spending S I.19=J IV.66 (sahassa° giving the worth of a thousand pieces).

Yāgu (f.) [cp. Vedic yavāgū; on form see Geiger, *P.Gr.* § 27[4]] rice-gruel, rice-milk (to drink). See *Vin. Texts* II.89. — Vin I.46=II.223 (sace yāgu hoti, bhājanaŋ dhovitvā yāgu upanametabbā; yāguŋ pītassa udakaŋ datvā . . .), 51 (id.), 61 (id.), 84, 210 (Bhagavato udara-vāt-ābādho tekaṭulāya yāguyā dhuva-yāguŋ dātuŋ; i. e. a constant supply of rice-gruel), 339 (na mayaŋ iminā bhikkhunā saddhiŋ yāgupāne nisīdissāma); IV.311; A III.250 (ānisaŋsā: 5 good qualities: it is good for hunger, for thirst, allays wind, cleans the bladder, helps to digest any undigested food); J I.186; II.128 (for drink); PvA 12, 23, 274. — Often comb[d] (and eaten) with cakes (khajjaka) & other soft food (bhojja), e. g. **yāgu-khajjaka** J I.270; III.20; DhA IV.20; Mhvs 14, 55 (°khajja-bhojja); 36, 100 (+khajja-bhojja).

-**pāna** a drink of rice-milk Vin I.84. -**piṇḍa** see yāga°. -**bhājaka** one who distributes the rice-gruel Vin II.176 (pañcah' angehi samannāgataŋ; together with cīvarabhājaka, phala-bhājaka & khajja-bhājaka); IV.38 (yāgu°, phala°, khajja°), 155 (id.); A III.275.

Yāca (nt.) [fr. **yāc**] anything asked for, donation, alms, begging J III.353; V.233, 234.

-**yoga** (y.+*yogga; perhaps yāja° the original. The variant yājayoga is old & well established: cp. Vism 224) accessible to begging, one ready to comply with another's request, devoted to liberality, open-handed. Freq. in ster. phrase mutta-cāga payata-pāṇī vossagga-rata yāca-yoga dāna-saŋvibhāga-rata to denote great love of liberality, e. g. at A I.226; II.66; III.313. See also A III.53, 313=Vism 223, 224 (where expl[d] as follows: yaŋ yaŋ pare yācanti tassa tassa dānato yāca-nayogo ti attho; yājayogo ti pi pāṭho; yājana-sankhātena yājena yutto ti attho); A IV.6, 266 sq., 271, 284; V.331, 336; Sn p. 87 (cp. expl[n] SnA 414: "yācituŋ yutto, yo hi yācake disvā bhakuṭiŋ katvā pharusa-vacan' ādīni bhaṇati, so na yācayogo hoti" etc.); Sn 487, 488, 489, 509; J III.307 (expl[d] in C. as "yaŋ yaŋ āgantukā yācanti tassa tassa yutto anucchaviko bhavitvā, sabbaŋ tehi yācita-yācitaŋ dadamāno ti attho"); IV.274 ("yācitabba-yuttaka" C.); VI.98 (=yācana-yuttaka or yañña-yuttaka; "ubhayath' āpi dāyakass' ev' etaŋ nāma" C.); Miln 215, 225. — The form **yājayoga** at Sn 1046 (expl[d] at Nd[2] 531 as "yāje yutta"); and mentioned at Vism 224 (see above). — On diff. meaning of **yācayoga** see Kern, *Toev.* s. v. with unidentified ref. Cp. also Mvyut. 140, 4.

Yācaka (adj. n.) [fr. yāca, cp. Epic & later Sk. yācaka] requesting, one who begs, a recipient of alms, a beggar J III.353; Pv II.9[38]; PvA 78, 102 (=yācanaka); Sdhp 324, 331. Freq. in comb[n] with similar terms of wayfaring people in phrase samaṇa-brāhmaṇa-kapaṇ' iddhika-vaṇibbaka-yācakā e. g. at D I.137; It 64. See single terms. — yācaka at Sn 618 (as Fick, *Soc. Gliederung* 144 quotes yācaka) is to be read **yājaka.**

Yācati [Vedic yācati; **yāc,** with which cp. Lat. jocus (dial. juca "prayer"); Ohg. jehan to confess, etc.: see Walde, *Lat. Wtb.* s. v. jocus. — Dhtp (38) only expl[s] yāca= yācane] to beg, ask for, entreat Vin IV.129 (pabbajjaŋ); Sn 566, 980, 983; J III.49, 353; V.233, 404. — aor. 3rd pl. **yāciŋsu** PvA 13, 20, 42; **ayācisuŋ** Mhvs 33, 76 (v. l. ayācayuŋ). — inf. **yācituŋ** PvA 29, 120. — ger. **yāciya** Sn 295; **yācitvā** M I.365; **yācitvāna** Mhvs 17, 58. — pp. **yācita.**

Yācana (dt.) [fr. **yāc**] begging, asking, entreaty J III.353; SnA 161 (inghā ti yācan' atthe nipāto) 551 (id.); PvA 113 (=sādhuka).

-**jīvāna** living by begging J III.353.

Yācanaka [cp. BSk. yācanaka Divy 470, 585]=yācaka A III.136 (ati°); Pv II.7[6]; 9[16]; 9[46]; J III.49; DA I.298.

Yācanā (f.)=yācana; J III.354=Miln 230; J V.233, 404.

Yācita [pp. of yācati] begged, entreated, asked (for) A III.33; Dh 224; J III.307; PvA 39. — Cp. yācitaka.

Yācitaka (adj.) [yācita+diminutive (disparaging) ending °ka] asked, begged, borrowed M I.365 (°ŋ bhogaŋ); J IV.358=VI.127 (°ŋ yānaŋ and °ŋ dhanaŋ, alluding to M I.365-366), with expl[n] J IV.358: "yaŋ parena dinnattā labbhati taŋ yācita-sadisam eva hoti." — (nt.) anything borrowed, borrowed goods: **yācitak' ûpamā kāmā** (in app' assādā kāmā passage) "the pleasures of the senses are like borrowed goods" Vin II.25=M I.130= A III.97=Th 2, 490=Nd[2] 71 (correct yācitan'); expl[d] in detail at M I.365. — See also DhA I.403 (ye y. gahetvā na paṭidenti); ThA 288 (kāmā=yācitaka-bhaṇḍa-sadisā tāvakālik' aṭṭhena).

Yāja [fr. **yaj;** cp. yāja & yājeti] sacrificing, giving alms, liberality (felt as synonymous with cāga, thus influenced by **tyaj,** cp. Sk. tyājana): see yācayoga; — Nd[2] 531 (yāye yutta); Vism 224.

Yājaka (adj.) [fr. **yaj** in its Caus. form yājeti] sacrificing, one who sacrifices, a priest Sn 312, 313 (=yanna-yājino janā SnA 324), 618 (of a purohita; v. l. BB yācaka).

Yājana (nt)=yāja; Vism 224: see yācayoga.

Yājin (adj.) [fr. yāja] sacrificing SnA 324 (yañña°).

Yājetar [n. ag. to yājeti] one who superintends a sacrifice or causes it to be performed D I.143.

Yājeti [Caus. I. of yajati] to cause to sacrifice, to make a priest give an offering (to the gods or otherwise) J VI.211, 215; ppr. **yājento** M I.404; Pot. 2nd sg. **yājeyya** J III.515; 3rd pl. **yājeyyuŋ** J VI.215 (aññaŋ brāhmaṇaŋ); also **yājayeyyuŋ** J VI.211. — ger. **yājetvā** D I.143.

Yāta [pp. of yāti] going, gone, proceeded; habit, custom; only in cpd. **yāt'ânuyāyin** going on according to what (or as it) has gone, i. e. following old habits J VI.309, 310; expl[d] by C. as "pubba-kārinā yātassa puggalassa anuyāyī, paṭhamaŋ karonto yāti nāma pacchā karonto anuyāyati." The usual Sk. phrase is gat-ânugatika. Cp. yātrā, yānikata.

Yāti [Vedic yāti, or **yā,** which represents Idg ***iā,** an amplified ***ĕ** as in eti (q. v.). Cp. Lat. janua door & the Np. Janus (=January); Lith. jóti to ride, Mir. āth ford. — The Dhtp 368 expl[s] **yā** more in appl[d] meaning as "papuṇane," cp. Dhtm 596: pāpuṇe] to go, go on, to proceed, to go away; — pres. 1st **yāmi** Pv II.8[8] (=gacchāmi PvA 107), Mhvs 10, 3; 2nd **yāsi** J I.291; Mhvs 10, 2 (kuhiŋ yāsi?); 3rd **yāti** Sn 720 (tuṇhī y. mahodadhi); Dh 29, 179, 294, 295; J VI.311; Mhvs 5, 47; DhA I.18; 1st pl. **yāma** Mhvs 6, 12 (kiŋ na y., v. l. kiŋ nu· y.); 2nd **yātha**=imper.; 3rd **yanti** Sn 179, 578, 714; Dh 126, 175, 225 (see also note s. v. **yanti**); Pv II.9[16] (=gacchanti PvA 120). — imper. 2nd sg. **yāhi** Pv II.1[6] (read yajāhi?); Mhvs 13, 15; 3rd sg. **yātu** Mhvs 29, 17; 2nd pl. **yātha** Mhvs 14, 29; DhA I.93. — ppr. **yanto** Mhvs 36, 60 (pacchā y. walking behind)· gen. **yantassa** Mhvs 22, 57 (assavegena y.). — inf. **yātave** Sn 834. — Another formation fr. **yā** is **yāyati** (see Geiger, *P.Gr.* § 138), in an intensive meaning of "to drive, to move on quickly or by special means," e. g. in phrase **yānena yāyati** to drive in a carriage Vin I.191 (Pot. yāyeyya); II.276; Sn 654 (ppr.: rathass' āṇī va yāyato) 418 (ger.: yānabhūmiŋ yāyitvā yānā oruyha); J VI.125. As "march" at J VI.449. In special meaning "to drive," i. e. "to be driven or affected by" in expl[n] of the ending of ppr. med kāma-*yamāne* Sn 767 (or kāma-*yāna*) at Nd[1] 4, viz. "taṇhāya yāyati niyyati vuyhati saŋhariyati." Cp. **yāna** as ending. — pp. **yāta.** Caus. **yapeti** & **yāpeti** (q. v.). — See also anupari°, ā°, upa°, uy°, pa° (aor. pāyāsi) paccuy°, pari°; and anuyāyati.

Yātrā (f.) [fr. **yā,** Class. Sk. yātrā, a n. ag. formation like nettī, meaning something like "vehicle," that which keeps going] 1. travel, going on, proceeding, good habit (like yāta; cp. yātrā=anuvṛtti Halāyudha 5, 33) S I.33; S I.16=63 (trsl[n] *K.S.*, perhaps wrongly, "egress": it is more a question of *going on* through life!). Perhaps to be classed under foll. meaning as well. — 2. going on, livelihood, support of life, maintenance in stock phrase occurring at many places of the Canon, viz. "purāṇaŋ vedanaŋ paṭihankhāmi, navañ ca vedanaŋ na uppādessāmi, yātrā ca me bhavissati etc." where DhsA 404 explains **yātrā** by **yāpanā,** as may be inferred also from context. Thus at M I.10 (where Neumann translates: "ein Fortkommen haben," i. e. progress), 355; S IV.104; A II.40; III.388; Nd[1] 496; Nd[2] 540 (correct devanaŋ into vedanaŋ!); Pug 25; Dhs 1348; Miln 367: all passages identical. The whole passage is expl[d] in detail at Vism 31 sq. where **yātrā** is given with "cira-kāla-gamana-sankhātā yātrā," Bdhgh. thus taking it as "keeping going," or "continued subsistence" (longevity trsl[n]). — In one other passage **yātrā** is conjectured for sātrā, viz. at SnA 322 in reading y. -yāga for sātrā yāga, where meaning y. might be taken as "customary." The ed. compares Sk. yātsattra, a certain ceremony.

Yāthāva (adj.) [see yathāva. It is a comb[n] of a guṇader. fr. yathā and an adj.-der. of °vant] sufficient (lit. "just as much"; i. e. such as it is), sufficiently founded, logical, consistent, exact, definite, true Nd[2] 275 (where tatha is expl[d] by taccha, bhūta, yāthāva, aviparīta); DhsA 248 (where micchā-diṭṭhi is expl[d] as incorrect or illogical view. — **yāthāvato** (abl.) exactly, truly, consistently DA I.65; ThA 256; VvA 232. See also yathāvato. — The nearest synonyms of yāthāva are aviparīta (i. e. definite) and yathābhūtaŋ. See also yathāva and yathāvaka.

-nāma having the name of exactitude PvA 231 (+aviparīta-nāma). -māna pride of sufficiency or consistency VbhA 487 sq. (and a°). -lakkhaṇa possessing the characteristic of definiteness or logic Miln 171; Nett 27 (where avijjā is called "sabba dhamma-yāthāva-asampaṭivedha-lakkhaṇā"). -vacana exact, logical or true speech Miln 214 (taccha-vacana, yāthāva-v., aviparīta-v.). -sarasa logical and with its essential (sa+rasa) properties Vism 588, 639.

Yādicchakaŋ at VvA 341 read as yadicchakaŋ (see ya°).

Yādisa (adj.) [Vedic yādṛś & yādṛśa, yad+dṛśa] which like, what like, whichever, how much; in *neg.* sentence: any, whatever little. — Pv. II.1[19] (=yāva mahanto PvA 77). — Often comb[d] with kīdisa in meaning "any one, this or that, whoever," e. g. Vv 50[14] (=yo vā so vā pacura-jano ti attho VvA 213). As adj.: yādisi (sic !=Sk. yādṛśī) -kīdisā jīvikā (no livelihood, whatever little) J VI.584 (V.728; Trenckner, Miln p. 423 gives v. 732 !), expl[d] by C as "yā vā sā vā, lāmakā ti attho"; yādisaŋ kīdisaŋ dānaŋ a gift of whatever kind Miln 278. So also with tādisa: yādisā vā tādisā vā (viz. kāmā) of whichever kind A III.5.

Yādisaka=yādisa; in correlation (generalising sense) yādisaka-tādisaka whatsoever . . . such, any whatsoever A IV.308; S V.96.

Yāna (nt.) [fr. yā, as in yāti. Cp. Vedic yāna and Lat. Janus] 1. going, proceeding J VI.415 (+ayāna, opposed to ṭhāna). — 2. means of motion, carriage, vehicle. Different kinds of carriages are enum[d] at Nd[1] 145 (on Sn 816) with hatthi° (elephant-), go° (cow-), aja° (goat-), meṇḍaka° (ram-), oṭṭha° (camel-?), khara° (donkey-). Cp. Miln 276. — yāna is one of the requisites (carriage or other means of locomotion) of the bhikkhu & as such included in the deyya-dhamma or 14 gifts (see yañña & deyya-dh.). Thus mentioned with anna pāna vattha etc. at S I.94; A II.85; Pug 51. — Cp. the def[n] & application of the term yāna as given below under yāna-sannidhi. — See e. g. the foll. passages: Vin I.191 (bhikkhū yānena yāyanti . . . na bhikkhave yānena yāyitabbaŋ; yo yāyeyya etc.: here a "carriage" is expressly forbidden to the bhikkhu !), 231 (Ambapālī bhadrāni-bhadrāni yānāni yojāpetvā bhadraŋ yānaŋ abhirūhitvā . . .), 242 (same phrase with Meṇḍaka gahapati); D I.7, 89, 106; M I.366 (yānaŋ poroseyyaŋ pavara-maṇi-kuṇḍalaŋ, where vv. ll. on p. 561 read voropeyya and oropeyya, which Neumann (unwarrantedly) adopts in his trsl[n]: *Mittl. Sammlung*[2] 1921, II.666; the C. accepts reading poroseyya with expl[n] "puris-ânucchavikaŋ yānaŋ"); Dh 323 (=hatthiyānādīni DhA IV.6); J III.525 sq.; V.59; VI.223 (=ratha); Kvu 599 (Erāvaṇo hatthināgo sahassa-yuttaŋ dibbaŋ yānaŋ; trsl[d] as "the wondrous elephant E., the thousand-wise yoked celestial *mount*." trsl. p. 347 (lit. vehicle) Pv III.2[28] (=ratha or vayha etc. PvA 186); PvA 113. — iddhi-yāna carriage of magic power Miln 276; deva° godly carriage Miln 276; applied to the 8 fold Aryan Path at Sn 139 (=devalokaŋ yāpetuŋ samatthatā . . . aṭṭha-samāpatti-yānaŋ SnA 184). Similarly of the Path: magg' aṭṭhangika-yāna (-yāyinī) Th 2, 389 (=aṭṭhangika-magga-sankhāta ariya-yāna ThA 257); and brahma-yāna dhamma-yāna "the very best & excellent carriage" as Ep. of magga S V.5, cp. J IV.100. Cp. the later terms mahā and hīna-yāna. See also yānikata.

-ugghata shaking or jolting of the carriage Vin II.276; DhA III.283. -gata having ascended the carriage D I.126. -puṭosā (°puṭoḷī) provision bag on a carriage (provision for the journey?) Vism 328 (so read for paṭṭoli). -bhūmi carriage-ground, i. e. the road as far as accessible to a carriage D I.89; Sn 418. -sannidhi storing up of carriages or means of locomotion D I.6 (with expl[n] at DA I.82 as follows: yānaŋ nāma vayhaŋ ratho sakaṭaŋ sandamānikā patankī ti. Na pan' etaŋ pabbajitassa yānaŋ, upāhanā yānaŋ pana); Sn 924 (=anna-pāna-vattha-yāna-sannidhi Nd[1] 372). -sukha pleasures of riding and driving Kvu 209; cp. *Kvu trsl.* 127.

Yānaka (nt.) [fr. yāna] a (small) cart, carriage, waggon, vehicle J III.49 (°ŋ pūretvā, or a hunter's cart); IV.45; DhA I.325 (sukha°), 391 (pakati°, an ordinary waggon). -°ŋ pājeti to drive a cart J II.112, 143; III.51.

-upatthambha(na) waggon-prop KhA 44 (°ni v. l., see Appendix to Index Pj.); VbhA 234 (°nika; illustrating the shape of the teeth).

Yānika & **Yāniya** (adj.) (-°) [fr. yāna] 1. (lit.) leading to, conducive to, as °yāniya in deva° magga D I.215, & Brahma° magga the way leading to the Brahma-world D I.220. — 2. (in appl[d] meaning, cp. yānikata) °yānika one who has become used to, whose habit it is . . ., in vipassanā° & samatha° at Vism 588.

Yānikata [yāna+kata, with i for a in comp[n] with kṛ, perhaps also in analogy with bahulī-kata] made a habit of, indulged in, acquired, mastered (cp. expl[n] Ps I.172: "yattha yattha ākankhati tattha tattha vasippatto hoti balappatto etc."). The expression is to be compared with yatânuyāgin & yātrā, similarly to which it is used only in *one* stock phrase. It comes very near yātrā in meaning "that which keeps one going," i. e. an acquired & thoroughly mastered habit, an "altera natura." It is not quite to the point when *Dial* II.110 (following Childers ?) translate as "to use as a vehicle." — Occurring with identical phraseology, viz. bahulīkata yāni-kata vatthu-kata anuṭṭhita paricita susamāraddha in application to the 4 iddhipādā at D II.103; A IV.309; S V.260; Miln 140; to mettā at M III.97; S I.116; II.264; IV.200; V.259; A V.342; J II.61; Miln 198. Expl[d] at Ps I.172, cp. II.122, 130.

Yānin (adj.) [fr. yāna] one who drives in a carriage J III.525=IV.223 (where read yānī va for yān iva). At the latter passage the C. somewhat obscurely expl[s] as "sappi-tela-yānena gacchanto viya"; at III.526 the expl[n] is simply "yānena gacchanto viya."

Yāpana (& **yapana**) (nt.) [fr. yāpeti. Cp. Epic & Class. Sk. yāpana] keeping going, sustenance, feeding, nourishment, existence, living. Esp. in one standing comb[n] respecting the feeding and keeping of the body "kāyassa ṭhitiyā yāpanāya etc." (for the maintenance of the body) in yātrā passage: see yatrā 2; in which it is expl[d] at Vism 32 by "pavattiyā avicched' atthaŋ, cira-kāla-ṭṭhit' atthaŋ" i. e. for the preservation of life. — Further at J I.66 (alam me ettakaŋ yāpanāya); V.387 (thokaŋ mama yāpana-mattaŋ eva); DhA IV.210 (yāpana-mattaŋ dhanaŋ); PvA 28. — Used more freq. together with shortened form yapana; in standard phrase vutti pālana, yapana yāpana cāra (cp. yapeti) at Vism 145; DhsA 149, 167. Or similarly as f. with spelling yapanā & yāpanā: yapanā yāpanā iriyanā vattanā pālanā at Dhs 19, 82, 295, 380, 441, 716. At DhsA 404 yāpanā is used as syn. of yātrā.

Yāpanīya (adj.) [grd. formation fr. yāpeti] fit or sufficient for supporting one's life Vin I.59, 212, 253. — Cp. BSk. yāpanīyatara a more healthy state Divy 110.

Yāpeti (& **yapeti**) [Caus. of yāti] 1. (lit.) — (a) in *caus.-intensive* as well as *intrs.* sense; in the latter also with short ă as yapeti and then comb[d] with yāpeti, in stock phrase defining carati "to go," "to be" (or viharati) with synonyms iriyati vattati pāleti yapeti yāpeti at Nd[2] 237; Vbh 252; DhsA 167. Besides singly (yapeti) at DhsA 149. — (b) to cause to go, to make someone go (to), to bring to, lead to (acc.) J vi.458 (sasenāvāhanaŋ yāpesi); SnA 184 (devalokaŋ yāpetuŋ samattha fit to bring one to the d-world). — (c) to get on, move, to be active DhA i.10 (sarīre yāpente); iv.17 (iriyāpathena). — 2. (fig.) to keep going (both *trs.* & *intrs.*), to keep up, esp. to keep oneself going or alive, to live by (instr.) [cp. BSk. yāpayati Divy 93, 150, 196, 292, 293, 471, 488; AvŚ i.209] D i.166 (ekissā dattiyā on only one alms); Pug 56; J ii.204; iii.67; iv.125; vi.532 (uñchena); Pv i.5[7] (ito dinnena yāpenti petā); i.11[7]; iii.2[8] (tava dinnena yāpessanti kurūrino); PvA 27, 29 (=attabhāvaŋ yāpeti=upajīvati).

Yāpya (adj.) [shortened grd.-formation for yāpanīya. *Sk. yāpya in slightly diff. meaning] 1. (lit.) fit for movement or locomotion: in °yāna sedan-chair, palanquin Abhp. 373. — 2. (fig.) concerning the preservation of life, vital, in °rogin one who suffers from a vital disease, lit. a disease concerning the upkeep of the body Vism 33 (trsl[n] *Path of Purity* 39: "patient of long-suffering," from a different point of view, viz. of time only, like Bdhgh.).

Yāma [fr. **yam** in both meanings of yamati & yama[3]] 1. restraint, only as cpd. cātu-yāma 4-fold restraint D i.57; iii.48; S i.66; M i.377; Vism 416. Cp. *Dial.* i.75[1]. — 2. a watch of the night. There are 3 watches, given as paṭhama, majjhima & pacchima (first, middle & last) Nd[1] 377 sq.; or purima, m. & pacchima Nd[2] 631 (under sadā). — A i.114; iv.168; Dh 157 (one of the 3; interpreted as the 3 vayas at DhA iii.138); J i.243 (tīsu yāmesu ekasmiŋ yāme); Mhvs 21, 33; PvA 217, 280. — 3. (usually pl. Yāmā devā) one who belongs to Yama or the ruler of the Underworld; a subject of Yama; the realm of Yama; — pl. inhabitants of Yamaloka A i.210 (yāmā devā); SnA 244 (°bhavana the abode of the Y.); KhA 166 (Yāmato yāva Akaniṭṭhaŋ from the Underworld to the Highest Heaven); Vism 225 (Yāmā); VbhA 519 (Yāmā); VvA 246 (id.); ThA 169 (Y. devā).

-kālika of a restricted time, for a (relatively) short period (lit.) only for one watch of the night, but longer than yāva-kālika temporary. It is one of the three regulation-terms for specified food, viz. y.-k., sattāhakālika & yāvajīvika, or short period, of a week's duration, and life-long food Vin iv.83, 86, 176, 311; to which is added **yāva-kālika**, temporary at Vin i.251 (where mutual relations of the 4 are discussed). **-gaṇḍika(ŋ) koṭṭeti** to beat the block of restraint (?), i. e. exercise self-control (?) (or does it belong to yāma 3?) KhA 233.

Yāyati see yāti.

Yāyin (adj.) (-°) [fr. **yā**, see yāti] going, going on to; in yāna yāyinī (f.) Th 2, 389 (maggaṭṭhangika° having ascended the carriage of the 8-fold Path; expl[d] by "ariya-yāyena nibbāna-puraŋ yāyinī upagatā" ThA 257).

Yāva (abv.) [Vedic yāvat as nt. of yāvant used as adv. in meanings 1 & 2. The final t is lost in Pāli, but restored as d in certain combinations: see below 2. — Cp. tāva & kīva]. 1 (as *prep.*) up to (a point), as far as, how far, so far that (cp. tāva I), both *temporal* and *local*, used either with *absolute* form of noun or adj. (base), or *nom.*, or *abl.* or *acc.* — (a) *absolute*: y. sahassa up to 1000. PvA 21; y. sattama up to the seventh D i.238. — (b) *nom.*: y. deva-bhava-sampatti up to the attainment of a deva existence PvA 167; y. satta divasā up to 7 days, as long as 7 days PvA 31. (c) with *abl.*: y. brahmalokā up to the highest heaven A iii.17; y. mekhalā down to her girdle PvA 46; yāva āyu-pariyosānā up to the end of life PvA 200; y. ajjadivasā till the present day Mhvs 32, 23; y. kapp' āvasānā up to the end of the world Vism 688 (where SnA 5 in same passage reads *acc.* °āvasānaŋ); y. kāla-ppavedanā J i.118+DhA i.248; y. mukhasmā up to the brim Miln 238; yāva bhumm' āvalambare hang down to the ground Pv ii.10[2]. — (d) with *acc.* y. Bodhimaṇḍaŋ as far as the Bodhimaṇḍa Mhvs 30, 88; y. **tatiyakaŋ** for the 3rd time (i. e. the last time; ascending scale!) D i.95; y. tatiyaŋ id. Vin iv.236 samanubhāsitabba); Sn 1116; J iv.126. — Freq. in phrase **yāva jīvaŋ** (see under cpds.). Sattamāsaŋ cha pañca cattāro ti vatvā *yāva* temāsaŋ yāciŋsu "after having said 7, 6, 5, 4, months they begged *down to* 3 months" PvA 20. — With starting-point, *local*: pādatalato . . . yāvakesaggaŋ from the sole of the foot to the tip of the hair ("from tip to toe") DhA i.70; (in modal sense:) paṭhavī-kasiṇato paṭṭhāya yāva odāta-kasiṇaŋ "from the one to the other" Vism 374. Similarly in correlation **yāva-tāva** (see tāva i.) as far—so far, until—so long: y. rājā āgacchati tāva ubho ramissāma J iv.190; heṭṭhā pi yāva Avīci upari yāva Akaniṭṭha-bhavanaŋ, tāva addasa Vism 392; yāva naŋ ānemi tāva idh' eva tiṭṭha DhA iii.194. — 2. (as *adv.*) how, how much, to which or what extent, as great or as much (as) (cp. tāva ii.2), usually in comb[n] **yāva mahā** (mahantaŋ), e. g. yāva mahantaŋ how big PvA 77 (=yādisaŋ of Pv ii.1[19]); VvA 325=DhA i.29 (yāva mahantaŋ). Also in other comb[ns], like **yāva dukkhā** nirayā how (or as) many painful purgatories Sn 678; yāva dukkhā tiracchānayoni M iii.169; yāva pāpo ayaŋ Devadatto alakkhiko . . . "how very wicked is this D." Vin ii.196 Further in comb[n] with attha(ŋ), and eva, in which cases the final d is restored, or may be regarded as euphonic. Thus **yāvad-atthaŋ** as far as need be, as much as you like (with imper.) Pv iv.5[7] (khādassu y.); UbhA 504 (=yattakaŋ icchati tattakaŋ); J v.338; PvA 217 (gaṇhāhi). Cp. Vin iii.37 (yāvadatthaŋ katvā "pleasing herself"). — As adj. sufficient, plenty M i.12 (paripuṇṇa . . . suhita y.); PvA 24 (=pahūta). **yāvad-eva** [cp. the similar tāva-d.-eva] "as much as it is (in extent)" i. e. with limitation as far as is necessary, up to (i. e. not further or more than), ever so much, as much as you like, at least; (then:) as far as, in short, altogether, indeed. — The same idea as our def[n] is conveyed by Bdhgh's at SnA 503 (on Sn p. 140) "paricched' āvadhāraṇa-vacanaŋ," and at DhA ii.73 "avadhiparicchedana": giving a limitation, or saying up to the limit. S ii.276; Sn p. 140; Dh 72; and in stock phrase "n'eva davāya . . . yāvad eva imassa kāyassa ṭhitiyā . . ." ("in short"); see passages under yātrā. The expl[n] of yāvad eva in this phrase as given at DhsA 403 runs: "āhār' āharaṇe payojanassa pariccheda-niyamadassanaŋ," of which the trsl[n] *Expos.* ii.512 is "so as to suffice signifies the limit of the result of taking food." Neumann's trsl[n] at M i.10 is "but only." — *Note.* In the stock phrase of the Buddha's refusal to die until his teaching has been fully proclaimed (Mahāparinibbānasutta) "among gods and men" D ii.106 (=114, 219; iii.122; A iv.311) "yāva-deva-manussehi suppakāsitaŋ" (trsl[n] *Dial.* ii.113: "until, *in a word*, it shall have been well proclaimed among men") we are inclined to consider the reading yāva deva° as original and better than yāvad-eva, although Rhys Davids (*Dial.* ii.236) is in favour of the latter being the original. Cf. *K.S.* ii.75 *n.* The phrase seems to require **yāva** only as continuation of the preceding yāva's; moreover the spirit of the message is for the *whole* of the worlds. Cp. BSk. yāvad-deva manuṣyebhaḥ Divy 201. It is *not a restriction* or special definition of meaning at this passage. But may it not be taken as a summing up= "in short"? It is left doubtful. If it is=yāva, then we should expect yāva **na**, as in the preceding sentence, if it is yāvad eva the meaning "not more than made known by men" seems out of place; in this case the meaning "at least" is preferable. A similar case of insertion of a euphonic consonant m (or is it the a-stem nt in °ŋ instead of °t as in yāvat?) we find in the phrase yāvam pi at J v.508 (with Pot. tiṭṭheyya; see below 3; C. expl[ns] by yattakaŋ kālaŋ). — The form yāvade (for yāvad eva) also occurs (like tāvade for tāvad eva) at M II.207. — For yad-idaŋ we find yāvañ c' idaŋ at A III.34; M III.169. — The latter form (yāvaŋ, as above J v.508) is better to be grouped directly under yāvant, where more & similar cases are given. — 3. (as *conj.*) so long as, whilst, until (cp. tāva II.3, 4; III.); either with Fut. or Pot. or Prohibitive. E.g. S I.202 (ahu pure dhammapadesu chando y. virāgena samāgamimha; trsl[n] "until I met with that Pure thing and Holy"); J VI.266 (y. āmantaye); PvA 4 (*tāva* ayyo āgametu *yāva* ayaŋ puriso . . . pānīyaŋ pivissati or: "you shall wait please, until he shall drink"). Neg. yāva . . . na not until, unless, as long as not D II.106 (na paribbāyissāmi . . . yāva . . . na bhavissati); S I.47 (y. na gādhaŋ labhati); Dh 69 (yattakaŋ kālaŋ na . . . DhA II.50).

-kālika (cp. tāva II.1) "as far as the time or occasion goes," occasional, temporary, at Vin I.251 in foll. context (cp. yāmakālika): "kappati . . . yāvakālikena, yāmakālikaŋ na kappati, kappati yāvakālikena sattāha kālikaŋ na k. etc. with foll. yāvajīvikaŋ & the same with kappati yāma-kālikena, sattāha-kālikena-na k.; kappati satt°, yāvajīv, na k." The reply of the Buddha is: yāvakālikena yāmakālikaŋ tadahu paṭiggahitaŋ kāle kappati vikāle na kappati (same with sattāhakālikaŋ & yāvajīvikaŋ); followed by yāmakālikena . . . sattāhakālikaŋ & yāvajīvikaŋ; sattāhakālikena . . . jāvajīvikaŋ." -jīvaŋ (adv.) for the length of one's life, life-long, all one's life, for life (-time) Vin I.80; II.197; III.23; It 78; Dh 64, 284; Vism 94; DhA I.45; PvA 76, 110 (=satataŋ). Cp. BSk. yāvajīva-sukhya AvŚ II.37. -tajjanī (-vinīta) led only as long as kept under a threat A I.285 (one of the 3 parisā's; so read with v.l. for T. yāvatajjhā°). -tatiyaka "as much as 3 times," name of the last 4 Sanghādisesa offences, because before the punishment is inflicted warning must have been given 3 times: see passage of Vin III.186 under yāva t-ihaŋ. -tihaŋ (read as yāvat-ihaŋ, the latter=aha[2] day) as many days as . . .; in foll. passage: uddiṭṭhā . . . terasa sanghādisesā dhammā, nava paṭham-āpattikā cattāro yāvatatiyakā, yesaŋ bhikkhu aññataraŋ vā aññataraŋ vā āpajjitvā yāvatihaŋ jānaŋ paṭicchādeti tāvatihaŋ tena bhikkhunā akāmā parivatthabbaŋ (for as many days as he knowingly conceals his sin, for so many days . . .), parivuttha-parivāsena bhikkhunā uttariŋ chārattaŋ bhikkhumānattāya paṭipajjitabbaŋ. Vin III.186.

Yāvaka [=yavaka] a dish prepared of barley J VI.373 (=yavataṇḍula-bhatta C.).

Yāvataka (adj.) [fr. yāva, as tāvataka fr. tāva] as much as, as many as, as far as, whatever; usually in correl. with tāvataka e.g. Vin I.83 (yāvataka . . . t.); D II.18 (y. kāyo t. vyāmo); Nd[2] 235[3] (y °ŋ ñeyyaŋ t °ŋ ñāṇaŋ); or similarly M I.397 (y. kathā-sallāpo . . . sabbaŋ taŋ . . .); PvA 103 (yāvatakā=yāvanto). — f. yāvatikā: yāvatikā gati tāvatikaŋ gantvā A I.112; y. nāgassa bhūmi as far as there was ground for the elephant D I.50; similarly: y. yānassa bh. as far as the carriage-road D I.89, 106, 108; y. ñāṇassa bh. Nett 25.

Yāvatā (indecl.) [abl. of yāvant in adv. use cp. tāvatā] as far as, like as, in comparison with, regarding, because Dh 258 (na tena paṇḍito hoti y. bahu bhāsati=yattakena kāraṇena DhA III.383), 259, 266 (similarly, C.=yattakena); Sn 759 (yāvat' atthī ti vuccati; expl[d] at SnA 509 as "yāvatā ete cha ārammaṇā 'atthī' ti vuccanti, vacana-vyattayo veditabbo"); yāvatā ariyaŋ paramaŋ sīlaŋ, nāhaŋ tattha attano sama-samaŋ samanupassāmi kuto bhiyyo "compared with this sīla I do not see anyone quite equal to myself, much less greater." D I.74 yāvatā ariyaŋ āyatanaŋ yavatā vanippatho idaŋ agga-nagaraŋ bhavissati Pāṭaliputtaŋ puṭa-bhedanaŋ Vin I.229=Ud 88=D II.87 (concerning a most splendid site, and a condition for trade, this Pāṭ. will be the greatest town; *trsl[n] Dial.* as far as Aryan people resort, as far as merchants travel . . .). yāvatā satt' āvāsā yāvatā bhavaggaŋ ete aggā ete saṭṭhā [read seṭṭhā] lokasmiŋ yad idam arahanto "as far as the abodes of beings, as far as heaven, these are the highest, these are the best, I mean the Arahants." S III.84. yāvatā dhammā sankhatā vā asankhatā vā virāgo . . . aggam akkhāyati, yad-idaŋ mada-nimmadano . . . A II.34=It 88; "of all the things definite or indefinite: passionlessness deserves the highest praise, I mean the disintoxication of pride etc." The expl[n] at Vism 293 takes yāvatā (grammatically incorrectly) as n. pl.= yattakā. -yāvatā jagato gati as far as (like as) the course of the world It 120.

Yāvant (pron. rel.) [cp. Sk. yāvant; same formation as demonstr. pron. tāvant, of which the P. uses the adv. nt. tāva (t) form more freqnently than the adj. tāvant. The only case so far ascertained where tāvant occurs as adj. is J v.72 (see below)] 1. yāvant as *adj.*: as many (as) Dh 337 (yāvant' ettha samāgatā as many as are assembled here); J v.72 (yāvanto uda-bindūni . . . tāvanto gaṇḍū jāyetha; C. on p. 74 expl[s] by yattakāni; yāvatā pl. as many as Pv II.1[16]; yāvanto Pv II.7[16] (=yāvatakā PvA 103); J v.376 (detha vatthāni . . . yavanto eva icchati as many as he wants). — 2. yāvat (nt.) used *adverbially*. The examples and meanings given here are really to be combined with those given under yāva[2] (yāvad°). It is hardly possible to distinguish clearly between the 2 categories; the t may well have been reduced to d or been replaced by another sandhi consonant. However, the specific Pāli use of yāva (like tāva) justifies a separate treatment of yāva in that form only. — yāvat occurs only in comb[n] with ca (where we may assume either a peculiar nt. form yāvaŋ: see yāva 2; or an assimilation of t to ñ before c. — The form yāva mahantaŋ may originally have been a yāvaŋ m.) as yāvañ ca "and that," "i. e.," how much, however much, so great S I.149 (passa yāvañ ca te idaŋ aparaddhaŋ: see how great a mistake you have made in this); It 91, 92 (passa yāvañ ca ārakā & santike: see how far and near). yāvañ c' idaŋ stands for yad-idaŋ (see ya° 4) in peculiar use of restriction at M. III.169; S II.178; A III.34. — 3. The nt. form yāvat further occurs in foll. cpds.: °āyukaŋ (better as yāvat° than yāvatā°) as long as life lasts, for a lifetime Mhvs 3, 41; VvA 196 (as adj. °āyukā dibba-sampatti); PvA 66, 73, 133; °icchakaŋ as much as is desired, according to one's wishes Pug 12, 25; Vism 154 (here spelt yāvad-icchakaŋ); °ihaŋ see under yāva (cpds.). — instr. yavatā: see sep.

Yāvetaddhi at M II.47 is an obscure expression. The reading is established; otherwise one might think of a corrupted yāv(a) etad ahosi(pi) or yāva-d-ev'-ahosi "was it really so?" or: "did you really have that thought?" Neumann, *Mittl. Sammlung*[2] 1921, II.381, trsl[s] "gar so sehr drängt es dich" (are you in such a hurry?), and proposes reading (on p. 686, note) yāv' etado hi pi, leaving us wondering what etado might be. — Could it be a distorted yāyetar (n. ag. of yāyeti, Caus. yā)?

Yiṭṭha [pp. of yajati with a petrified sandhi y.; Vedic iṣṭa] *med.*: having sacrificed D I.138 (mahā-yaññaŋ y. rājā). — *pass.*: sacrificed, (nt.) sacrifice D I.55 (dinna, y. huta); expl[d] at DA I.165 by "mahāyāga" Vbh 328. (id.); J I.83 (y.+huta); IV.19 (=yajita C.); V.49; VI.527. — duyyiṭṭha not properly sacrificed, a sacrifice not according to rites J VI.522. In specific Buddhistic sense "given, offered as alms, spent as liberal gift" Vin I.36; J I.168=A II.44; M I.82. Dh 108 (yaŋ kiñci yiṭṭhaŋ va hutaŋ va; DhA II.234 = yebhuyyena mangala-kiriya-divasesu dinna-dānaŋ). —suyiṭṭha well given or spent A II.44; ThA 40; Vv 34[26] (in both senses; VvA 155 expl[s] "mahā-yāga-vasena yiṭṭhaŋ").

Yidha in mā yidha at Vin I.54 is to be read mā-y-idha, the y being an euphonic consonant (see y.).

Yuga (nt.) [fr. **yuj**; Vedic yuga (to which also yoga) = Gr. ζυγόν; Lat. jugum = Goth. juk; Ohg. juh; E. yoke; Lith. jùngas] 1. the yoke of a plough (usually) or a carriage DhA I.24 (yugaŋ gīvaŋ bādhati presses on the neck); PvA 127 (ratha°); Sdhp 468 (of a carriage). Also at Sn 834 in phrase **dhonena yugaŋ samāgamā** which Bdhgh. (SnA 542) expl[s] as "dhuta-kilesena buddhena saddhiŋ yugaggāhaŋ samāpanno," i. e. having attained mastery together with the pure Buddha. Neumann, *Sn trsl*[n] not exactly: "weil abgeschüttelt ist das Joch" (but dhona means "pure"). See also below °nangala. —2. (what is yoked or fits under *one* yoke) a pair, couple; appl[d] to objects, as -°: dussa° a pair of robes S v.71.; DhA IV.11; PvA 53; sāṭaka° id. J I.8, 9; PvA 46; vattha° id. J IV.172. —tapassi° a pair of ascetics Vv 22[10]; dūta° a pair of messengers S IV.194; sāvaka° of disciples D II.4; S I.155; II.191; v.164; in general: purisa° (cattāri p.-yugāni) (4) pairs of men S IV.272 sq. = It 88; in verse at Vv 44[21] and 53[8]; expl[d] at Vism 219 as follows: yugaḷa-vasena paṭhama-magga-ṭṭho phala-ṭṭho ti idam ekaŋ yugaḷan ti evaŋ cattāri purisa-yugaḷāni honti. Practically the same as "aṭṭha purisa-puggalā." Referring to "pairs of sins" (so the C.) in a somewhat doubtful passage at J I.374: sa mangala-dosa-vītivatto yuga-yog' âdhigato na jātum eti; where C. expl[s] yugā as kilesā mentioned in pairs (like kodho ca upanāho, or makkho ca paḷāso), and yoga as the 4 yojanas or yogas (oghas ?), viz. kāma°, bhava°, diṭṭhi°, avijjā°. —Also used like an adj. num. in meaning "two," e. g. yugaŋ vā nāvaŋ two boats Dpvs I.76. —3. (connected by descent) generation, an age D I.113 (yāva sattamā pitāmahā-yugā "back through seven generations." Cp. DA I.281: āyuppamāṇa); KhA 141 (id.); J I.345 (purisa°). There are also 5 ages (or stages) in the [life of the] sāsana (see *Brethren*, p. 339): vimutti, samādhi, sīla, suta, dāna.

-anta (-vāta) (storm at) the end of an age (of men or the world), whirlwind J I.26. -ādhāna putting the yoke on, harnessing M I.446. -ggāha "holding the yoke," i. e. control, dominance, domineering, imperiousness; used as syn. for *palāsa* at Vbh 357 = Pug 19 (so read for yuddha°), expl[d] by sama-dhura-ggahaṇaŋ "taking the leadership altogether" at VbhA 492. See further Nd[1] 177; VvA 71 (yugaggāha-lakkhaṇo paḷāso); SnA 542; DhA III.57 (°kathā = sārambha-kathā). -°ŋ *ganhāti* to take the lead, to play the usurper or lord J III.259 (C. for T. palāsin); DhA III.346. -ggāhin trying to outdo somebody else, domineering, imperious VvA 140. -cchidda the hole of a yoke Th 2, 500 (in famous simile of blind turtle). -nangala yoke and plough (so taken by Bdhgh. at SnA 135) Sn 77 = S I.172 ("plough fitted with yoke" Mrs. Rh.D.). -nandha (with v. l. °naddha, e. g. at Ps II.92 sq.; KhA 27 in T.) putting a yoke on, yoking together; as *adj.* congruous, harmonious; as *nt.* congruity, association, common cause Ps II.98 = Vism 682; Ps II.92 sq. (°vagga & °kathā); KhA 27 (nt.); Vism 149 (°dhammā things fitting under one yoke, integral parts, constituents). -mattaŋ (adv.) "only the distance of a plough," i. e. only a little (viz. the most necessary) distance ahead, with expressions of sight: *pekkhati* Sn 410 ("no more than a fathom's length" Rh.D. in *Early Buddhism* 32); *pekkhin* Miln 398; °*dassāvin* Vism 19 (okkhitta-cakkhu +) *pekkhamāna* SnA 116 (as expl[n] of okkhitta-cakkhu). -sāṭaka (= s.-yuga) a pair of robes, two robes Dpvs VI.82.

Yugala & **Yugaḷa** (nt.) [Class. Sk. yugala; in relation to yuga the same as Lat. jugulum ("yoke-bone") to jugum. Cp. also Gr. ζεύγλη yoking strap] a pair, couple J I.12 (yugaḷa-yugaḷa-bhūtā in pairs), 500 (bāhu°); VI.270 (thana° the 2 breasts); Vism 219; VbhA 51 (yugaḷato jointly, in pairs); the six "pairs of adaptabilities" or "words," Yog. 18-23, *Mystic* 30 sq.; cp. Dhs 40 sq. Also used as adj. (like yuga) in phrase yugalaŋ karoti to couple, join, unite Dpvs I.77; VvA 233.

Yugalaka (nt.) [fr. yugala] a pair Tikp 66; VbhA 73.

Yuja (adj.) (-°) [*either* a direct root-derivation fr. **yuj**, corresponding to Sk. yuj (or yuk, cp. Lat. con-jux "conjugal," Gr. ὁμό-ζυξ companion, σύ-ζυξ = conjux; Goth. ga-juka companion); *or* a simplified form of the grd. *yujya > *yujja > yuja] yoked or to be yoked, applicable, to be studied, only in cpd. **duyyuja** hard to be mastered, difficult J v.368 (atthe yuñjati duyyuje he engages in a difficult matter; C. reads **duyyuñja**).

Yujjha (adj.) [grd. cf yujjhati] to be fought; neg. **a**° not to be fought, invincible M II.24 (so read for ayojjha)

Yujjhati [cp. Vedic yudhyate, **yudh**, given in meaning "sampahāra" at Dhtp 415. —Etymologically to Idg. ***ieudh** to shake, fr. which in var. meanings Lat. jubeo to command, juba horse's mane; Gr. ὑσμίνη battle, Lith. jundù, jùdra whirlwind; cp. also Av. yaošti agility] to fight, make war. Rare in older literature; our refs. only from the Mahāvaŋsa; e. g. 22, 82 (fut. yujjhissāma, with instr.: Damiḷehi); 25, 23 (aor. ayujjhi); 25, 58 (ppr. yujjhamāna); 33, 41 (aor. yujjhi). To which add DhA II.154 (mallayuddhaŋ yujjhanto); III.259 (Ajātasattunā saddhiŋ yujjhanto). —pp. **yuddha**. —Caus. **yodheti** (q. v.).

Yujjhana (nt.) [fr. yujjhati] fighting, making war J III.6, 82.

Yujjhāpana (nt.) [fr. yujjhati Caus.] making somebody fight, inciting to war Miln 178.

Yuñjati [Vedic yunakti, yuñjati & yuñkte, **yuj**; cp. Gr. ζεύγνυμι, Lat. jungo to unite, put together (pp. junctus = Sk. yukta, cp. E. junct-ion); Lith. jùngin. The Idg. root ***ieug** is an enlarged form of ***ieue** "to unite," as in Sk. yanti, yuvati, pp. yuta; f. yūti, to which also Lat. jūs = P. yūsa. The Dhtp gives several (lit. & fig.) meanings of **yuj**, viz. "yoge" (No. 378), "samādhimhi" (399), "saŋgamane" (550)] (lit.) to yoke; (fig.) to join with (instr. or loc.), to engage in (loc.), to exert oneself, to endeavour. All our passages show the *applied* meaning, while the lit. meaning is only found in the Caus. yojeti. —Often expl[d] by and coupled with the syn. ghaṭati & vāyamati, e.g. at J IV.131; v.369; DhA IV.137. —*Forms:* pres. **yuñjati** Dh 382; J v.369; 2nd pl. **yuñjatha** Th 2, 346 (kāmesu; = niyojetha ThA 241); ppr. **yuñjanto** J IV.131 (kammaṭṭhāne); imper. **yuñja** S I.52 (sāsane); ThA 12; med. imper. **yuñjassu** Th 2, 5. —Pass. **yujjati** (in grammar or logic) is constructed or applied, fits (in), is meant KhA 168; SnA 148, 403, 456. —Caus. I. **yojeti** & II. **yojāpeti** (q.v.). —pp. **yutta**.

Yuta [pp. of **yu**, yanti to fasten but Dhtp 338: "missane"] fastened to (loc.), attracted by, bent on, engaged in D. I.57 (sabba-vārī°); Sn 842 (pesuṇeyye; Nd[1] 233 reads yutta in exegesis, do. at p. 234, with further expl[n] āyutta, payutta etc.), 853 (atimāne); Dāvs v.18 (dhiti°). —*Note.* yuta is doubtful in phrase **tejasā-yuta** in Niraya passage at A I.142 = M III.183 = Nd[1] 405 = Nd[2] 304[III] = J v.266. The more likely reading is either tejas' **āyuta** (so BSk. M.Vastu 9), or tejasā yutta (so Nd[2] & PvA 52), i. e. endowed with, furnished with, full of heat. —We find a similar confusion between **uyyuta** & **uyyutta**.

Yutta [pp. of yuñjati; Vedic yukta, cp. Lat. junctus, Gr. ζευκτός, Lith. jùnktas] 1. (lit.) yoked, harnessed (to= loc.) Pv 1.11[4] (catubbhi yutta ratha); Mhvs 35, 42 (goṇā rathe yattā); DhA 1.24 (dhure yuttā balivaddā). —2. coupled; connected with; (appl[d]) devoted to, applied to, given to, engaged in (-°, instr. or loc.) Sn 820 (methune), 863 (macchiriya°). 1144 (tena, cp. Nd[2] 532); It 93 (Buddha-sāsane); J VI.206 (yoga°). — 3. furnished; fixed, prepared, in order, ready Sn 442 (Māra; =uyyutta SnA 392); PvA 53. — 4. able, fit (to or for=inf.), suitable, sufficient Sn 826 (cp. Nd[1] 164); J V.219; DA 1.141 (dassituŋ yutta=dassanīya); VvA 191 (=alaŋ); PvA 74. — 5. proper, right PvA 159. — 6. due to (-°, with a grd., apparently superfluous) J III.208 (āsankitabba°); cp. yuttaka. — 7. (nt.) conjunction, i. e. of the moon with one or other constellation Vin II.217. — ayutta not fit, not right, improper PvA 6 (perhaps dele!), 64. — suyutta well fit, right proper, opp. duyutta unbefitting, in phrase suyuttaŋ duyuttaŋ ācikkhati J 1.296 (here perhaps for dur-utta?). du° also lit. "badly fixed, not in proper condition, in a bad state" at J IV.245 (of a gate).
-kāra acting properly PvA 66. -kārin acting rightly Miln 49. -paṭibhāṇa knowledge of fitness Pug 42 (cp. PugA 223). -payutta intent on etc. PvA 150. -rūpa one who is able or fit (to=inf.) J 1.64. -vāha justified VvA 15.

Yuttaka (adj.) (-°) [fr. yutta] proper, fit (for); *nt.* what is proper, fitness: dhamma-yuttakaŋ katheti to speak, righteous speech J IV.356. — Usually comb[d] with a grd., seemingly pleonastically (like yutta), e. g. kātabba° what had to be done PvA 81; DhA 1.13 (as kattabba°); āpucchitabba° fit to be asked DhA 1.6.

Yutti [cp. Vedic yukti connection, fr. **yuj**] "fitting," i. e. 1. application, use Miln 3 (opamma°). — 2. fitness, vāda°, KVA 37; in instr. **yuttiyā** in accordance with Mhvs 10, 66 (vacana°); Sdhp 340 (sutti°); and abl. **yuttito** Sdhp 505. — 3. (logical) fitness, right construction, correctness of meaning; one of the 16 categories (hārā), appl[d] to the exposition of texts, enum[d] in the 1st section of the Netti; e. g. at Nett 1-3, 103; KhA 18; SnA 551, 552. Thus abl. **yuttito** by way of correctness or fitness (contrasted to suttato) VbhA 173=Vism 562; and **yutti-vasena** by means of correctness (of meaning) SnA 103 (contrasted to anussava). — 4. trick, device, practice J VI.215.
-kata combined with; (nt.) union, alloy VvA 13.

Yuddha (nt.) [orig. pp. of yujjhati; cp. Vedic yuddha (pp.) and yudh (f.) the fight] war, battle, fight D 1.6 (daṇḍa° fighting with sticks or weapons); J III.541 (id.); Sn 442 (dat. yuddhāya); J VI.222; Miln 245 (kilesa°, as pp.: one who fights sin); Mhvs 10, 45 (°atthaŋ for the sake of fighting); 10, 69 (yuddhāya in order to fight); 25, 52 (yuddhāy' āgata); 32, 12 (yuddhaŋ yujjhati); 32, 13 (maccu° fight with death); 33, 42; DhA II.154 (malla° fist-fight). — The form **yudhāya** at Sn 831 is to be taken as (archaic) dat. of Vedic yudh (f.), used in sense of an inf. & equal to yuddhāya. Nd[1] 172 expl[s] as "yuddh' atthāya."
-kāla time for the battle Mhvs 10, 63. -ṭṭha engaged in war S 1.100 (so read for °ttha). -maṇḍala fighting-ring, arena J IV.81; Vism 190; VbhA 356 (in comparison).

Yuddhaka [fr. yuddha, for the usual yodha (ka)] a fighter, in malla° fist-fighter, pugilist J IV.81.

Yudhikā (f.) [doubtful] N. of a tree J V.422 (for T. yodhi, which appears as yodhikā in C. reading). The legitimate reading is yūthikā (q. v.), as is also given in vv.ll.

Yuvan [Vedic yuvan; cp. Av. yavan=Lat. juvenis, Lith. jáunas young; Lat. juvencus "calf"; juventus youth; Goth. junda, Ohg. jugund & jung, E. young. — The n.-stem is the usual, but later Pāli shows also decl. after a-stem, e. g. gen. yuvassa Mhvs 18, 28] a youth. — nom. sg. **yuvā** D 1.80=yobbanena samannāgata DA 1.223; Sn 420; Dh 280 (=paṭhama-yobbane ṭhita DhA III.409); Pv III.7[1] (=taruṇa PvA 205). — Cp. yava, **yuvin** & **yobbana**.

Yuvin (adj.-n.) [=yuvan with diff -adj. ending] young J IV.106, 222.

Yūtha (nt.) [Vedic yūtha] a flock, herd of animals Sn 53 (of elephants); J 1.170 (monkeys), 280 (id.); SnA 322 (go°, of oxen).
-pa the leader of a herd Th 2, 437 (elephants). -pati same J III.174 (elephant); DhA 1.81 (id.).

Yūthikā (f.) [cp. later Sk. yūthikā] a kind of jasmine, Jasminum auriculatum J VI.537; Miln 338. So is also to be read at J V.420 (for yodhi) & 422 (yodhikā & yudhikā). See also **yodhikā**.

Yūpa [Vedic yūpa] 1. a sacrificial post D 1.141; A IV.41; J IV.302; VI.211; Miln 21 (dhamma°); SnA 321, 322; DA 1.294. — 2. a pāsāda, or palace Th 1, 163=J II.334.
-ussāpana the erection of the sacr. post DhsA 145 (cp. Miln 21).

Yūsa [Vedic yūṣan, later Sk. yūṣa; fr. base Idg. *i̯ūs, cp. Lat. jūs soup, Gr. ζύμη yeast, ferment, ζωμός soup; Obulg. jucha=Ger. jauche manure; Swedish öst cheese; an enlargement of base ***i̯eu** to mix, as in Sk. **yu** to mix: see yuta, to which further ***i̯eu̯e**, as in yuñjati] 1. juice Vin 1.206 (akaṭa° natural juice); Mhvs 28, 26; VvA 185 (badara° of the jujube); Vism 195 (seda° sweaty fluid). — 2. soup, broth. Four kinds of broths are enum[d] at M 1.245, viz. mugga° bean soup, **kulattha°** of vetch (also at Vism 256), **kaḷāya°** (chick-) pea soup, **hareṇuka°** pea soup; Miln 63 (rañño sūdo yūsaŋ vā rasaŋ vā kareyya).

Yebhuyya (adj.) [ye=yad in Māgadhī form; thus yad bhūya=yad bhiyya "what is more or most(ly)"] abundant, numerous, most. Not found as adj. by itself, except in phrase **yebhuyya-vasena** mostly, as a rule ThA 51 and PvA 136, which is identical with the usual instr. **yebhuyyena** occurring as adv. "as according to most," i. e. (1) almost all, altogether, practically (as in our phrase "practically dead"), mostly D 1.105 (addasā dvattiŋsa lakkhanāni y. ṭhapetvā dve: all except two)=109; Vin III.29 sq.; J 1.246 (gāmako y. andha-bāla-manussehi yeva ussanno the village was peopled by mostly foolish folk); V.335 (y. asīti-mahātherā, altogether). — (2) as it happens (or happened), usually, occasionally, as a rule, ordinarily D 1.17 (saŋvaṭṭamāne loke y. [as a rule] sattā Ābhassara-saŋvaṭṭanikā honti; expl[d] by half allegorical, half popular etym. at DA 1.110 as follows: "ye upari Brahma-lokesu vā Āruppesu vā nibbattanti, tad-avasese sandhāya vuttaŋ"); D II.139: yebhuyyena dasasu loka-dhātusu devatā sannipatitā (as a rule); Sn p. 107 (=bahukāni SnA 451); Miln 6 (y. Himavantam eva gacchanti: usually); DA 1.280 (ordinarily); VvA 234 (occasionally), 246 (pihita-dvāram eva hoti: usually); PvA 2 (Sattari tattha tattha viharante y. tāya tāya atth' uppattiyā), 46 (tassā kesa-sobhaŋ disvā taruṇa-janā y. tattha paṭibaddha-cittā ahesuŋ: invariably). — na **yebhuyyena** not as a rule, usually not (at all): nāpi y. ruditena kāci attha-siddhi PvA 63.

Yebhuyyasikā (f.) [formation fr. yebhuyya like tassa-pāpiyya-sikā. Originally adj., with kiriyā to be understood] lit. "according to the majority," i. e. a vote of majority of the Chapter; name of one of the adhikaraṇa-samathas, or means of settling a dispute. — Vin. II.84 (anujānāmi bh. adhikaraṇaŋ yebhuyyasikāya vūpasametuŋ), 93 (vivād' ádhikaraṇaŋ dvihi samathehi sammati: sammukhā-vinayena ca yebhuyyasi-kāya ca). As one of the 7 methods of settling a dispute mentioned at Vin IV.207=351 (the *seven* are: sammukhā-vinaya, sati-vinaya, amūḷha°, paṭiññā, yebhuyyasikā, tassa-pāpiyyasikā, tiṇ' avatthāraka). Expl[d] in detail at M II.247: if the bhikkhus cannot settle a dispute in their abode, they have to go to a place where there are more bh., in order to come to a vote by majority. Cp. D III.254 (the seven enum[d]); A I.99; IV.144.

Yeva (indecl.) [=eva with accrudescent y from Sandhi. On form and relation between eva & yeva cp. Geiger, *P.Gr.* § 66, I. See also eva 2. — The same form in Prākrit: Pischel, *Prk. Gr.* § 336] emphatic particle, meaning "even, just, also"; occurring most frequently (for eva) after palatal sounds, as ŋ: Sn 580 (pekkhataŋ yeva), 822 (vivekaŋ); DhA II.20 (saddhiŋ); PvA 3 (tasmiŋ), 4 (imasmiŋ), 13 (tumhākaŋ); — further after o: PvA 39 (apanito yeva); — after ā: Sn 1004 (manasā yeva); — after i: S II.206 (vuddhi yena); PvA 11 (ahosi); — after e: J I.82 (vihāre yeva; pubbaṇhe y.); VbhA 135 (na kevalaŋ ete yeva, aññe pi "not only these, but also others"). Cp. Mhvs 22, 56; VvA 222; PvA 47.

Yevāpana(ka) (adj.) [*not* connected with yeva, but an adj. formation from phrase ye vā pana; ye here standing (as Māgadhism) for yaŋ: cp. yebhuyya] corresponding, reciprocal, respective, in corresponding proportion, as far as concerned; lit. "whatever else." The expression is peculiar to exegetical (logical) literature on the Abhidhamma. See e. g. DhsA 152 (yevāpanā, pl. and °kā); Vism 468, 271 sq.; VbhA 63, 70 sq.; cp. *Dhs. trsl.*[1] p. 5 and introd. p. 56. — *Note.* The expression occurring as phrase shows ye as nom. pl., e. g. Dhs 1, 58, 151-161 & passim: ye vā pana tasmiŋ samaye aññe pi dhammā; but cp. in § 1: yaŋ yaŋ vā pan' ārabbha, in same sense.

Yoga [Vedic yoga, see etym. under yuga & yuñjati. Usually m.; pl. nt. yogāni occurs at D II.274 in meaning "bonds"] lit. "yoking, or being yoked," i. e. connection, bond, means; fig. application, endeavour, device. — 1. yoke, yoking (rare?) J VI.206 (meant here the yoke of the churning-sticks; cp. J VI.209). — 2. connection with (-°), application to; (natural) relation (i. e. body, living connection), association; also conjunction (of stars). mānusaka **yoga** the relation to the world of men (the human body), opp. dibba yoga: S I.35=60; Sn 641; Dh 417; expl[d] at DhA IV.225 as "kāya." — association with: D III.176; application: Vism 520 (+uppāda). yogato (abl.) from being connected with, by association with PvA 40 (bālya°), 98 (sammappadhāna°). —**pubba°** connection with a former body, one's former action or life-history J V.476; VI.480; Miln 2. See pubbe[1]. —**aḍḍhayoga** a "half-connected" building, i. e. a half-roofed monastery Vin I.239; Vism 34. —**nakkhatta°** a conjunction of planets, peculiar constellation (in astrology) J I.82, 253 (dhana-vassāpanaka suitable for a shower of wealth); III.98; DhA I.174; DhsA 232 (in simile). — 3. (fig.) bond, tie; attachment (to the world and its lusts), or what yokes to rebirth (*Cpd.* 171[2]). There are 4 **yogas**, which are identical with the 4 **oghas** viz. kāma°, bhava°, diṭṭhi°, avijjā°, or the bonds of craving, existence, false views, and ignorance; enum[d] in detail at A II.10; D III.230, 276; J I.374; cp. Ps I.129 (catūhi yogehi yutto lokasannivāso catu-yoga-yojito); VbhA 35. Mentioned or referred to at S V.59; Dhs 1059 (ogha+, in def[n] of taṇhā), cp. *Dhs trsl*[n] 308; Nett 31 (with ogha), 114 (id.); as **sabba-** (or sabbe) yogā at Th 2, 4; 75; S I.213; DhA III.233; severally at It 95 (bhava-yoga-yutta āgāmī hoti, +kāma°); **ogha+yoga**: Pug 21 (avijjā°); Vism 211, 684; cp. also D II.274 (pāpima-yogāni the ties of the Evil one); It 80 (yogā pamocenti bahujanaŋ). — 4. application, endeavour, undertaking, effort DhA III.233, 234 (=samma-ppadhāna). **yogaŋ karoti** to make an effort, to strive after (dat.) S II.131; A II.93 (āsavānaŋ khayāya y. karaṇīya); Miln 35. **yogaŋ āpajjati** to show (earnest) endeavour, to be active S III.11 sq.; Vbh 356 (attanā). — **dhamma°** one who is devoted to the Dhamma A III.355; **yutta°** (bent on, i. e.) earnest in endeavour J I.65; **yāca°** given to making offerings: see yāca. — 5. pondering (over), concentration, devotion M I.472; Dh 209 (=yoniso manasikāra DhA III.275), 282 (same expl[n] at DhA III.421); Miln 3; Vbh 324 (yoga-vihitesu kamm' & sipp'-āyatanesu; VbhA 410 expl[s]: y. vuccati paññā; — perhaps better to above 4?). — 6. (magic) power, influence, device, scheme J VI.212 (yoga-yogena practice of spells etc. =tāya tāya yuttiyā C.); PvA 117 (comb[d] with manta, ascribed to devas). — 7. means, instrument, remedy J I.380 (vamana° an emetic); VI.74 (ekaŋ yogaŋ datvā; but we better read bhesajjaŋ tassa **datvā** for **vatvā**, and ekaŋ yogaŋ **vatvā** for datvā; taking yoga in meaning of "charm, incantation"); Miln 109 (yena yogena sattānaŋ guṇa-vaḍḍhi . . . tena hitaŋ upadahati).

-âtiga one who has conquered the yoke, i. e. bond of the body or rebirth It 61 (muni), 81 (id.). **-âtigāmin**= °âtiga; A II.12 (same as sabba-yoga-visaŋyutta). **-âvacara** "one at home in endeavour," or in spiritual (esp. jhāna-) exercises; one who practises "yoga"; an earnest student. The term is peculiar to the Abhidhamma literature. — J I.303, 394, 400; III.241 (saŋsāra-sāgaraŋ taranto y.); Ps II.26; Kvu 229; Miln 33 sq., 43, 366, 378 sq.; Vism 245 (as hunter) 246 (as begging bhikkhu), 375 (iddhi-study), 587, 637, 666, 708; DhA II.12 (padhānaŋ padahanto y.); III.241 (°bhikkhu); DhsA 187 (ādhikammika), 246 (°kulayutta); VbhA 115, 220, 228 (as bhikkhu on alms-round), 229 (as hunter), 258, 331; KhA 74; SnA 20, 374. **-kkhema** [already Vedic yoga-kṣema exertion & rest, acquisition & possession] rest from work or exertion, or fig. in scholastic interpretation "peace from bondage," i. e. perfect peace or "uttermost safety" (*K.S.* II.132); a freq. epithet of nibbāna [same in BSk.: yogakṣema, e. g. Divy 98, 123, 303, 498] M I.117 (°kāma), 349, 357, (anuttara); S I.173 (°adhivāhana); II.195 (anuttara), 226; III.112 (°kāma, neg.); IV.125; V.130 sq.; A I.50 (anuttara); II.40, 52 (a°), 87, 247; III.21, 294 sq., 353; D III.123, 125, 164 (°kāma); Vin II.205=It 11 (°ato dhaŋsati, whereas Vin °ā padhaŋsati); It 9, 27 (abhabbo °ssa adhigamāya); Th 2, 6; Sn 79 (°adhivāhana), 425; Dh 23 (anuttara, cp. DhA I.231); Ps I.39; II.81; Vbh 247 (kulāni y-kh-kāmāni, which VbhA 341 expl[s]: catūhi yogehi khemaŋ nibbhayaŋ icchanti); ThA 13. **-kkhemin** finding one's rest, peace, or salvation; emancipated, free, an Arahant S III.13 (accanta°); IV.85; A II.12; IV.310 (patta°); V.326 (accanta°); DhA III.233, 234 (=sabba-yoga-visaŋyutta); neg. **a°** not finding one's salvation A II.52 (in verse)=Ps II.80; It 50. **-ññu** knowing the (right) means Miln 169 sq. **-bahula** strong in exertion A III.432. **-yutta** (Mārassa) one who is tied in the bonds (of Māra) A II.52 (so read for °gutta; the verse also at Ps II.80, 81, and It 50). **-vibhāga** dividing (division) of the relation (in grammar: to yoga 2) SnA 266.

Yoganīya (adj.) [fr. yoga; grd. formation] of the nature of trying, acting as a bond, fetter-ish Dhs 584; DhsA 49 (cp. *Dhs. trsl.* 301). The spelling is also yoganiya, cp. oghaniya.

Yogin (adj.-n.) [fr. yoga, cp. Class. Sk. yogin] 1. (-°) applying oneself (to), working (by means of), using Vism 70 (hattha° & patta° using the hand or the bowl; but trsl[n] p. 80: "hand-ascetic" & "bowl-ascetic"). — 2. one who devotes himself to spiritual things, an earnest student, one who shows effort (in contemplation), a philosopher, wise man. The word does not occur in the four Nikāyas. In the older verses it is nearly synonymous with muni. The oldest ref. is Th 1, 947 (pubbake yogī "Saints of other days" Mrs. Rh. D.). Freq. in Miln, e. g. pp. 2, 356 (yogi-jana); at pp. 366, 393, 404, 417, 418 in old verses. Comb^d with yogâvacara Miln 366, 404. — Further passages are Nett 3, 10, 61; Vism 2, 14, 66, 71 (in verse), 150, 320, 373, 509, 620, 651, 696; DhsA 195, 327.

Yogga¹ (nt.) [Vedic yogya; a grd. formation fr. yoga in meaning of yoga 1] "what may be yoked," i. e. 1. a **coach, carriage**, waggon (usually large & covered, drawn by bullocks) J VI.31 sq. (paṭicchanna), 368 (mahā°); DhA II.151 (mahā° & paṭicchanna). — 2. a draught-bullock, ox Vv 84^8; Pv $II.9^{36}$ (=ratha-yuga-vāhana PvA 127); J VI.221. yoggāni muñcati to unharness the oxen PvA 43, 100.

Yogga² (nt. & adj.) [same as last, in meaning of yoga 7] 1. (nt.) a contrivance J IV.269 (yoggaŋ karoti, may be in meaning "training, practice" here: see yoggā); VvA 8 (gahaṇa°). — 2. (adj.) fit for (=yutta), adapted to, suitable; either -° or with inf.: VvA 291; PvA 25 (here spelt yogya), 135 (bhojana°), 152 (kamma-vipāk' ânubhavana°), 154 (gamana° passable, v. l. yogya), 228 (anubhavana°).

Yoggā (f.) [Vedic and Epic Sk. yogyā; same as yogga², fr. yoga] training, practice J II.165 (yoggaŋ karoti to practise); IV.269 (id.); DhA I.52 (lakkha-yoggaŋ karoti to practise shooting). — adj. (-°) **katayogga** well-practised, trained S I.62, 98 (neg.). Only at these passages, missing at the other daḷha-dhamma-passages, e. g. at S II.266; M I.82; A II.48.
-ācariya a groom, trainer S IV.176=M I.124; M III.97, 222; Th 1, 1140; J I.505.

Yojana (nt.) [Vedic yojana] 1. the yoke of a carriage J VI.38, 42 (=ratha-yuga). — 2. a measure of length: as much as can be travelled with *one* yoke (of oxen), a distance of about 7 miles, which is given by Bdhgh. as equal to 4 gāvutas (DhA II.13). It occurs in descending scale of yojana-tigāvuta-usabha at DhA I.108. — Dh 60; J V.37 (yojana-yojana-vitthatā each a mile square); SnA 194. More favoured comb^ns of yojana with numbers are the foll.: ½ (aḍḍha°): DA I.35; DhsA 142. — 3: DhA II.41. — 4: PvA 113. — 5: VvA 33. — 15: DhA I.17; J I.315; PvA 154. — 18: J I.81, 348. — 20: DhA IV.112 (20 × 110, of a wilderness). — 25: VvA 236. — 45: J I.147, 348; DhA I.367. — 50: Vism 417. — 100: D I.117; It 91; Pv $I.10^{14}$. — 500: J I.204. — 1,000: J I.203. — Cp. yojanika.

Yojanā (f.) [*Sk. yojanā, fr. yojeti] (grammatical) construction; exegesis, interpretation; meaning KhA 156, 218, 243; SnA 20, 90, 122 sq., 131 sq., 148, 166, 177, 248, 255, 313; PvA 45, 50, 69, 73, 139 (attha°). *and passim* in Commentaries.

Yojanika (adj.) [fr. yojana] a yojana in extent J I.92 (vihāra); Dpvs 17, 108 (ārāma); DhA I.274 (maṇi-pallanka).

Yojita [pp. of yojeti] yoked, tied, bound Ps I.129 (catuyoga° fettered by the four bonds); SnA 137 (yottehi y.).

Yojitaka (adj.) [fr. yojita] connected with, mixed; neg. a° not mixed (with poison), unadulterated J I.269.

Yojeti [Caus. of yuñjati] 1. to yoke, harness, tie, bind Pv $II.9^{36}$ (vāhana, the draught-bullock); Mhvs 35, 40 (yojayi aor.; v. l. for yojāpayi); PvA 74 (sindhave). — 2. to furnish (with), combine, unite, mix, apply J I.252 (suraŋ), 269 (id.); Mhvs 22, 4 (ambaŋ visena y. to poison a mango); 36, 71 (visaŋ phalesu poison the fruit). — 3. to prepare, provide, set in order, arrange, fix, fit up Mhvs 30, 39 (pāde upānāhi fitted the feet with slippers); dvāraŋ to put a door right, to fix it properly J I.201; IV. 245 (cp. yojāpeti). — 4. to engage, incite, urge, commission, put up to, admonish Mhvs 17, 38 (manusse); 37, 9 (vihāraŋ nāsetuŋ y. incited to destroy the v.); PvA 69. — 5. to construct, understand, interpret, take a meaning SnA 148 (yojetabba); PvA 98 (id.), 278 (id.). — Caus. II. **yojāpeti** to cause some one to yoke etc.: D II.95 (yānāni, to harness); J I.150 (dvāraŋ, to set right); Mhvs 35, 40 (rathe, to harness). — Pass. yojiyati to become yoked or harnessed J I.57 (nangala-sahassaŋ y.). — pp. **yojita**.

Yojjha in a° M II.24 read **yujjha** (of **yudh**).

Yotta (nt.) [Vedic yoktra, cp. Lat. junctor, Gr. ζευκτῆρες yoke-straps; Epic Sk. yoktṛ one who yokes] the tie of the yoke of a plough or cart S I.172=Sn 77; S IV.163, 282; J I.464; II.247 (camma°); IV.82; V.45 (camma-y.-varatta), 47; Vism 269; DhA I.205; SnA 137. As dhura-yotta at J I.192; VI.253.

Yottaka (nt.) [yatta + ka] a tie, band, halter, rope J VI.252; Miln 53; Vism 254, 255; DhA III.208.

Yodha [cp. Vedic yodha; fr. **yudh**] a warrior, soldier, fighter, champion Vin I.73 (yodhā yuddh' âbhinandino . . . pabbajjaŋ yāciŋsu); J I.180; Miln 293.
-ājīva one who lives by battle or war, a soldier S IV.308=A III.94; A I.284; II.170, 202; III.89 sq. (five kinds); Sn 617, 652; Pug 65, 69. **-hatthin** a war elephant DhA I.168.

Yodhi=yodhikā J V.420.

Yodhikā (f.) [a var. reading of **yūthikā** (q.v.)] a special kind of jasmine Vv 35^4; J IV.440 (yoth°), 442; V.422; VvA 162 (as **thalaja** and a tree).

Yodhin [=yodha] a warrior; camma° a warrior in cuirass, a certain army grade D I.51; A IV.107.

Yodheti [Caus. of yujjhati] to attack, to fight against (acc.) Dh 40 (yodhetha=pahareyya DhA I.317); J V.183.

Yoni (f.) [Vedic yoni] 1. the womb. — 2. **origin**, way of birth, place of birth, realm of existence; nature, matrix. There are *four* yonis or ways of being born or generation, viz. **aṇḍaja** oviparous creation, **jalābuja** viviparous, **saŋsedaja** moisture-sprung, **opapātika** spontaneous: M I.73; D III.230; Miln 146; Vism 552^2, 557 sq.; cp. VbhA 203 sq. — Freq. in foll. comb^ns: tiracchāna° the class of animals, the brute creation A I.37, 60; V.269; It 92; Pv $IV.11^1$; Vism 103, 427; PvA 27, 166; **nāga°** birth among the Nāgas S III.240 sq. (in ref. to which the 4 kinds of birth, as mentioned above, are also applied); Vism 102 (niraya-nāga-yoni); pasu°=tiracchāna° Pv $II.13^{12}$; **pisāca°** world of the Pisācas S I.209; **peta°** the realm of the Petas PvA 68 (cp. peta). —**kamma°** K. as origin A III.186. — yoni upaparikkhitabba (=kiŋ-jātikā etc.) S III.42. —**ayoni** unclean origin Th 1, 219. — 3. thoroughness, knowledge, insight Nett 40. —**ayoni** superficiality in thought S I.203 ("muddled ways" Mrs. Rh. D.). —**yoniso** (abl.) "down to its origin or foundation," i. e. thoroughly, orderly, wisely, properly, judiciously S I.203 ("in ordered governance" *K.S.* I.259); D I.118 (wisely); It 30 (āraddha āsavānaŋ khayāya); Pug 25; Vism 30, 132, 599; PpA 31. Opp. ayoniso disorderly improperly Pug 21; DhA I.327; PvA 113, 278. — Esp. frequent in phrase **yoniso manasikāra** "fixing one's attention with a purpose or thoroughly," proper attention, "having thorough method in one's thought" (*K.S.* I.259) Ps I.85 sq.; It 9; J I.116; Miln 32; Nett 8, 40, 50, 127; Vism 132; PvA

63. See also manasikāra. — Opp. ayoniso manasikāra disorderly or distracted attention D III.273; VbhA 148; ThA 79. In BSk. the same phrase: yoniśo manasikāraḥ Divy 488; AvŚ I.122; II.112 (Speyer: "the right & true insight, as the object of consideration really is"). See further on term *Dial.* III.218 ("systematized attention"); *K.S.* I.131; II.6 ("radical grasp").

-ja born from the womb Sn 620; Dh 396. -pamukha principal sort of birth D I.54; M I.517.

Yobbana (nt.) [cp. late Vedic & Epic Sk. yauvana, fr. yuvan] youth D I.115; A I.68; III.5, 66, 103; Dh 155, 156; Sn 98, 110, 218; Pv I.7[6]; DhA III.409; PvA 3. -mada pride of youth D III.220; A I.146; III.72; VbhA 466.

R.

-R- the letter (or sound) r, used as euphonic consonant to avoid hiatus. The sandhi -r- originates from the final r of nouns in °ir & °ur of the Vedic period. In Pali it is felt as euphonic consonant only, like other sandhi consonants (y for instance) which in the older language were part of the noun itself. Thus r even where it is legitimate in a word may interchange with other sandhi-consonants in the same word, as we find punam-eva and puna-d-eva besides the original puna-r-eva (= Vedic punar eva). At J I.403 we read "punar āgata," where the C. expl[s] "puna āgata, ra-kāro sandhivasena vutto." Similarly: Sn 81 (vutti-r-esā), 214 (thambho-r.-iva), 625 = Dh 401 (āragge-r-iva), 679 (ati-r-iva), 687 (sarada-r-iva), 1134 (haŋsa-r-iva); Vv 64[22] (Vajir' āvudho-r-iva); Pv II.8[7] (puna-r-eva) II.11[6] (id.); PvA 77 (su-r-abhigandha). In the latter cause the r has no historical origin, as little as in the phrase dhir atthu (for *dhig-atthu) Sn 440; J I.59.

Raŋsi & **Rasmi** [Vedic raśmi. The form raŋsi is the proper Pali form, originating fr. raśmi through metathesis like amhi for asmi, tamhā for tasmā etc. Cp. Geiger *P.Gr.* § 50[2]. The form rasmi is a Sanskritism and later] a rein, a ray. — 1. In meaning "rein" only as rasmi, viz. at M I.124; Dh 222; J I.57; IV.149. — 2. In meaning "ray" both raŋsi and rasmi: (a) raŋsi (in poetry) Sn 1016 (vīta° ? perhaps pīta° ? See note in P.T.S. ed.); Vv 53[6] (pl. raŋsī = rasmiyo VvA 236); 63[27] (sahassa° having a thousand rays; = suriya VvA 268); Sdhp 124. Also in cpd. raŋsi-jāla a blaze of rays J I.89; PvA 154; VvA 12 (°sammujjala), 14 (id.), 166 (id.). — (b) rasmi (in prose, late) DhA I.27 (°ŋ vissajjesi); DhsA 13 (nīla-rasmiyo); VvA 125 (candima-suriya°). Also in cpd. buddha-rasmi the ray of enlightenment, the halo around a Buddha, consisting of 6 colours (chabbaṇṇa) J I.444, 501 (°rasmiyo vissajjento); SnA 132; VvA 207, 234, 323; Mhbv 6, 15, 38.

Raŋsika (adj.) [raŋsi + ka] having rays, radiant, in sahassa° having 1000 rays Vv 64[6] (= suriya-maṇḍala viya VvA 277).

Raŋsimant (adj.) [fr. raŋsi] having rays, radiant; n. sg. raŋsimā the sun Vv 81[2] (= suriya VvA 314).

Rakkha (adj.) (-°) [fr. base **rakkh**] guarding or to be guarded; — (a) act.: **dhamma°** guardian of righteousness or truth Miln 344. — (b) pass.: in cpd. dū°, *v. l.* du° hard to guard DhA 1.295. °kathā, s. l. rukkha-°, warding talk ThA I, in *Brethren,* 185, cp. note 416.

Rakkhaka (adj. n.) [fr. rakkha] 1. guarding, protecting, watching, taking care PvA 7; f. °ikā (dāsī) DhA IV.103 (a servant watching the house). — 2. observing, keeping J I.205 (sīla°). — 3. a cultivator J II.110. — 4. a sentry J I.332.

Rakkhati [Vedic raksati, **rakṣ** to Idg. ***ark** (cp. Lat. arceo etc.) in enlarged form ***aleq** = Gr. ἀλέξω to protect (Alexander!); ἀλκή strength; Ags. ealgian to protect, Goth. alhs = Ags. ealh temple. Cp. also base ***areq** in P. aggala. The Dhtp 18 expl[s] **rakkh** by "pālana"] 1. to protect, shelter, save, preserve Sn 220; J IV.255 (maŋ rakkheyyātha); VI.589 (= pāleti); Pv II.9[48] (dhanaŋ); Miln 166 (rukkhaŋ), 280 (attānaŋ rakkheyya save himself); PvA 7. — grd. **rakkhiya** to be protected Mhvs 33, 45. Neg. **arakkhiya** & **arakkheyya** (in meaning 3) see separately. — Pass. ppr. **rakkhiyamāna** J I.140. — 2. to observe, guard, take care of, control (with ref. to **cittaŋ** the heart, and **sīlaŋ** good character or morals) It 67 (sīlaŋ); DhA I.295 (cittaŋ rakkha, equivalent with cittaŋ dama), 397 (ācāraŋ); J IV.255 (vācaŋ); VvA 59 (sīlāni rakkhi); PvA 66 (sīlaŋ rakkhatha, uposathaŋ karotha). — 3. to keep (a) secret, to put away, to guard against (i. e. to keep away from) Sn 702 (mano-padosaŋ rakkheyya); Miln 170 (vacīduccaritaŋ rakkheyya). — pp. **rakkhita.** See also **paripāleti** & parirakkhati.

Rakkhana (nt.) [fr. **rakkh**] 1. keeping, protection, guarding Nett 41; Mhvs 35, 72 (rahassa°-atthāya so that he should keep the secret); PvA 7. — 2. observance, keeping VvA 71 (uposatha-sīla°); PvA 102 (sīla°), 210 (uposatha°).

Rakkhanaka (adj.) [fr. rakkhana] observing, keeping; one who observes J I.228 (pañca-sīla°; so read for rakkhānaka).

Rakkhasa [cp. Vedic rakṣa, either fr. **rakṣ** to injure, or more likely fr. **rakṣ** to protect or ward off (see details at Macdonell, *Vedic Mythology* pp. 162-164)] a kind of harmful (nocturnal) demon, usually making the water its haunt and devouring men Th I, 931; Sn 310 (Asura°); J I.127 (daka° = udaka°), 170 (id.); VI.469 (id.); DhA I.367 (°pariggahita-pokkharaṇī); III.74 (udaka°); Sdhp 189, 313, 366. — f. rakkhasī J III.147 (r. pajā); Mhvs 12, 45 (rudda°, coming out of the ocean).

Rakkhā (f.) [verb-noun fr. **rakkh**] shelter, protection, care A II.73 (+ parittā); Mhvs 25, 3; J I.140 (bahūhi rakkhāhi rakkhiyamāna); PvA 198 (°ŋ saŋvidahati).

Often in comb^n rakkhā + āvaraṇa (+gutti) shelter & defence, e. g. at Vin II.194; D I.61 (dhammikaŋ r.-v.-guttiŋ saŋvidaheyyāma); M II.101; J IV.292. — Cp. gorakkhā. — *Note.* rakkhā at J III.144 is an old misreading for rukkhā.

Rakkhita [pp. of rakkhati] guarded, protected, saved S IV.112 (rakkhitena kāyena, rakkhitāya vācāya etc.); A I.7 (cittaŋ r.); Sn 288 (dhamma°), 315 (gottā°); VvA 72 (mātu°, pitu° etc.); PvA 61, 130. — *Note.* rakkhitaŋ karoti at Mhvs 28, 43 Childers trsl^s "take under protection," but Geiger reads rakkhike and trsl^s "appoint as watchers."
-atta one who guards his character S I.154; J I.412; SnA 324. -indriya guarding one's senses Sn 697. -mānasāna guarding one's mind Sn 63 (=gopitamānasāno-rakkhita-citto Nd^2 535).

Ranga^1 [fr. raj^1, rajati, to be coloured or to have colour] colour, paint Miln 11 (°palibodha).
-kāra dyer Miln 331. -jāta colour M I.385; VbhA 331. -ratta dyed crimson Vin I.185 = 306.

Ranga^2 [fr. raj^2, irajyati, to straighten, order, direct etc.: see uju. The Dhtp (27) only gives one **raj** in meaning "gamana"] a stage, theatre, dancing place, playhouse Vv 33^1; J II.252. —rangaŋ karoti to play theatre DhA IV.62. —rangamajjha the stage, the theatre, usually in loc. °majjhe, on the stage, S IV.306; J IV.495; DhA III.78; same with °maṇḍale J II.253.

Racati [**rac**, later Sk.] to arrange, prepare, compose. The root is defined at Dhtp 546 by "paṭiyattane" (with v. l. **car**), and given at No. 542 as v. l. of **pac** in meaning "vitthāre." — pp. racita.

Racanā (f.) [fr. **rac**] 1. arrangement (of flowers in a garland) VvA 354. — 2. composition (of a book) Sdhp 619.

Racita [pp. of racati] 1. arranged J V.157 (su° in C. for samocita; v. l. sucarita). — 2. strung (of flowers) Mhvs 34, 54. — Cp. vi°.

Racchā (f.) [Sk. rathyā. This the contracted form. The diaeretic forms are rathiyā & rathikā (q.v.)] a carriage road Vin II.194; III.151; IV.271 (=rathiyā); V.205 (raccha-gata); J I.425; V.335; VI.276 (in its relation to vīthi); Dāvs V.48; PvA 24 (koṇa°).

Rajaka [fr. rajati] a dyer (& "washerman" in the same function), more correctly "bleacher." See remarks of Kern's at *Toev.* II.45 on distinction of washerman & dyer. — D I.51 (in list of occupations); Vin III.45; S II.101 = III.152 (in simile; comb^d with cittakāra, here perhaps "painter"?); S III.131; J V.186; VbhA 331 (in simile).

Rajakkha (-°) (adj.) [rajo + ending ka, in comb^n *rajas-ka = rajakkha, like *puras-kata = purakkhata. The °ka belongs to the whole cpd.] only in comb^n with **appa°** and mahā° i. e. having little (or no) and much defilement (or blemish of character) M I.169; S I.137 (here further comb^d with °jātika; cp. BSk. alpa-rajaskajātīya MVastu III.322); Vin I.5 (id.); Ps I.121; II.33, 195; Nd^1 358; Nd^2 235 No. 3 p^2; Vbh 341; Miln 263; Vism 205; VbhA 458.

Rajakkhatā (f.) [abstr. fr. rajakkha] is Kern's (problematic) proposed reading (*Toev.* s. v.) for **rājakhāda** at Sn 831 (rājakhādāya phuṭṭho), which is however unjustified, as the original reading is well-attested and expl^d in the Niddesa as such. The term as proposed would not occur by itself either (like rajakkha, only -°).

Rajata (nt.) [Vedic rajata; see etym. under rajati] silver D I.5 (expl^d at DA I.78 as a general name for all coins except gold: kahāpaṇas etc.); S I.92; Sn 962 (in simile; expl^d at Nd^1 478 as jātarūpa), J V.50; 416 (hema° gold & silver); Vv 35^1 (°hema-jāla); DhA II.42 (°paṭṭa silver tablet or salver); IV.105 (°gabbha silver money box or cabinet for silver, alongside of kahāpaṇa-gabbha and suvaṇṇa°); VbhA 64 (expl^d as "kahāpaṇa"); PvA 95 (for rūpiya).

Rajati [**raj** & **rañj** to shine, to be coloured or light (-red); to Idg. ***areg** to be bright, as in Lat. argus, Gr. ἀργής & ἀργός light; Sk. arjuna (see ajjuna); to which also rajati silver = Lat. argentum, Gr. ἄργυρος; Gallic Argento-ratum (N. of Strassburg); Oir argat.] usually intrs. rajjati (q.v.). As **rajitabba** (grd.) in meaning "to be bleached" (dhovitabba +) only in meaning "bleach" (as compared with **dhovati** clean, & **vijaṭeti** to disentangle, smoothe) Vin III.235 (ppr. fr. pl. dhovantiyo rajantiyo etc.); J I.8 (rajitabba, grd.; dhovitabba +). — Somehow it is difficult to distinguish between the meanings "bleach" and "dye" (cp. rajaka), in some comb^{ns} with dhovati it clearly means "dye," as at Vin I.50 (forms: rajati, rajitabba, rajiyetha 3 sg. Pot. Med.); Vism 65 (forms: rajitvā, rajitabba, rajituŋ). — Another grd. rajanīya in diff. meaning (see sep.). Caus. rajeti to paint, colour Th 1, 1155 (inf. rajetave: (see Geiger, *P.Gr.* § 204, 1. a). Caus. also rañjeti (see under rañjati). Med. Pass. rajjati (q. v.). — Caus. II. rajāpeti to cause to be bleached Vin III.206 (dhovāpeyya rajāpeyya ākoṭāpeyya), 235 (dhovapeti r. vijaṭāpeti); J II.197 (ovaṭṭikaŋ sibbāpetvā rajāpetvā).

Rajana (nt.) [fr. **raj**] colouring, dye D I.110 (suddhaŋ vatthaŋ . . . sammadeva rajanaŋ paṭigaṇheyya); Vin I.50 = 53 II.227; Vin I.286 (6 dyes allowed to the bhikkhus: mūla°, khandha°, taca°, patta°, puppha°, phala°, or made of the root, the trunk, bark, leaf, flower, fruit of trees) Th 1, 965; S II.101 (here either as f. or adj.); J I.220 (washing?).
-**kamma** (the job of) dyeing J I.118; Vism 65. -**pacana** boiling the dye Vism 389 (cp. rajana-pakka *Vin. Texts* II.49). -**bhājana** dye-vessel Vin I.286. -**sālā** colouring-workshop, dyeing-hall Vism 65.

Rajanī (f.) [fr. **raj**, cp. rajanīya 2] the night Dāvs I.39; Abhp 69; PvA 205.

Rajanīya (adj.) [grd. of rajati] of the nature of rajas, i. e. leading to lust, apt to rouse excitement, enticing, lustful. — 1. As Ep. of rūpa (vedanā saññā etc.) S III.79; also at D I.152 sq. (dibbāni *rupāni* passāmi piya-rūpāni kām' ūpasaŋhitāni rajanīyāni; & the same with *saddāni*). In another formula (relating to the 5 kāmaguṇā): rūpā (saddā etc.) iṭṭhā kantā manāpā piyarūpā kām' ūpasaŋhitā rajanīyā D I.245; M I.85. The expl^n of this passage at DA I.311 is: r. = rāgajanaka. — The expression **rajanīyā dhammā** "things (or thoughts) causing excitement" is contrasted with **vimocanīyā dh.** "that which leads to emancipation" at A II.196. The same takes the places of **lobhanīyā** dhammā in comb^n with **dosanīyā** & **mohanīyā** dh. at S IV.307; A II.120; III.169. Another pair is mentioned at Nett 18, viz. r. dhammā and pariyuṭṭhāniyā dh. — 2. In diff. connections it means simply "delightful, lovely" and is e. g. an Ep. of the *night.* So at Pv III.7^1, where the passage runs "yuvā rajanīye kāmaguṇehi sobhasi": youthful thou shinest with the qualities of enjoyment in the enjoyable (night), which at PvA 205 is expl^d in a twofold manner viz. first as "ramaṇīyehi rāguppatti-hetu-bhūtehi" (viz. kāmaguṇehi), referring to a v. l. **rajanīyehi**, and then as "rajanī ti vā rattīsu, ye ti nipātamattaŋ" and "virocasi rattiyaŋ." Thus rajanī is here taken directly as "night" (cp. Abhp 69). — At Pv IV.6^2 the passage runs "pamattā rajanīyesu kām' assād' ābhinandhino" i. e. not heeding the enjoyment of the taste of craving *at nights;* here as m. & not f. — The meaning "lovely" is appl^d to sounds at Th 1, 1233 (sarena rajanīyena); VvA 37 (r. nigghosa).

Rajo (rajas) & **Raja** (nt.) [**raj**, see rajati & rañjati. Vedic rajaḥ meaning: (a) space, as region of mist & cloud, similar to antarīkṣa, (b) a kind of (shiny) metal (cp. rajata); see Zimmer, *Altind. Leben* 55]. A *Forms.* Both rajo & rajaŋ occur as noun & acc. sg., e. g. rajo at D II.19; Sn 207, 334; Dhs 617; rajaŋ at Sn 275; It 83; once (in verse) rajo occurs as m, viz. Sn 662. The other cases are formed from the a-stem only, e. g. rajassa Sn 406; pl. rajāni Sn 517, 974. In compn we find both forms, viz. (1) **rajas** either in visarga form rajaḥ, as (a) **rajo-**, (b) **raja-** and (c) **rajā-** (stressed), or in s-form (d) **rajas-**; (2) raja-, appearing apostrophied as (e) raj-. B *Meanings.* (1) (lit.) dust, dirt; usually wet, staining dust D II.19 (tiṇa+); Sn 662=PvA 116 (sukhumo rajo paṭivātaŋ khitto); It 83; Dhs 617 (dhūmo+). adj. rāja°: in sa° & a° vāta Vin II.209; Vism 31. The meaning "pollen" [Sk. raja, m.] may be seen in "raja-missakaŋ rasaŋ" at DhA I.375.—2. (fig.) stain, dirt, defilement, impurity. Thus taken conventionally by the P. commentators as the 3-fold blemish of man's character: rāga, **dosa**, moha, e. g. Nd[1] 505; SnA 255; DhA III.485; or as kilesa-raja at SnA 479.—Sn 207 (niketā jāyate rajo), 334, 665 (rajaŋ ākirasi, metaph.), 974 (pañca rajāni loke, viz. the excitement caused by the 5 bāhirāni āyatanāni Nd[1] 505. Also in stanza rāgo rajo na ca pana reṇu vuccati (with dosa & moha the same) Nd[1] 505=Nd[2] 590 (slightly diff.)=J I.117=Vism 388, cp. Divy 491 with interesting variation.—adj. raja° in two phrases **apagata°** VvA 236 & **vigata°** Nd[1] 505 ≈ free from defilement.—On raja in similes see *J.P.T.S.* 1907, 126. Cp. **vi°**.—C. *Compounds.* (a) rajo-: °jalla dust and (wet) dirt, muddy dirt D II.18; Vin III.70; J IV.322; V.241; Miln 133, 195, 258, 410; SnA 248, 291. **-jallika** living in dirty mud, designation of a class of ascetics M I.281; J I.390. **-dhātu** "dust-element" (doubtful trsln) D I.54, which DA I.163 explns as "raja-okiṇṇa-ṭṭhānāni," i. e. dusty places. *Dial.* trsl. "places where dust accumulates," Franke, *Dīgha* p. 57 as "Staubiges" but rightly sees a deeper, speculative meaning in the expression (Sānkhya doctrine of rajas?). **-mala** dust & dirt J I.24. **-vajalla** [this expression is difficult to explain. It may simply be a condensed phrase rajo 'va jalla, or a redupl. cpd. rajo+**avajalla**, which was spelt raj-ovajalla for ava° because of rajo, or represents a contamination of **raj-avajalla** and **raj-ojalla**, or it is a metric diaeresis of rajo-jalla] dust and dirt Dh 141 (=kaddama-limpan' ākārena sarīre sannicita-rajo DhA III.77). **-haraṇa** dirt-taking, cleaning; wet rag, floor-cloth, duster Vin II.291; A IV.376; J I.117; DhA I.245.—(b) **raja-**: **-reṇu** dirt and dust J IV.362; **-vaḍḍhana** indulgence in or increase of defilement Th 2, 343 ("fleshly lusts" trsl.); ThA 240 (=rāga-raj' ādi-saŋvaḍḍhana).—(c) **rajā-**: °patha dusty place, dustiness, dust-hole D I.62, 250; S II.219; DA I.180 (here taken metaphorically: rāga-raj' ādīnaŋ uṭṭhāna-ṭṭhānaŋ).—(d) **rajas-**: °sira with dusty head Sn 980; J IV.184, 362, 371. See pankadanta.—(e) **raj-**: -°agga a heap of dust, dirt J V.187 (=raja-kkhandha C.); fig.=kilesa Pug 65, 68 (here perhaps nt. of a distorted rajakkha? So Kern, *Toev.* s. v.). -°upavāhana taking away the dust (or dirt) Sn 391, 392.

Rajja (nt.) [Sk. rājya, fr. **rāj**] kingship, royalty, kingdom, empire; reign, throne; (fig.) sovereignty A III.300 (°ŋ kāreti); Sn 114, 553 (°ŋ kāreti to reign); J I.57; 64 (ekarattena tiṇi rajjāni atikkamma; 3 kingdoms); III.170 (°ŋ amaccānaŋ niyyādetvā), 199 (dukkhaseyyaŋ api rajjaŋ pi kāraye); IV.96, 105, 393 (nava rajja new kingship, newly (or lately) crowned king); VI.4 (rajjato me sussitvā maraṇam eva seyyo: death by withering is better than kingship); VvA 314 (=J I.64 as above); PvA 73 sq.; Mhvs 10, 52 (rājā rajjaŋ akārayi). **—cakkavatti°** rule of a universal king DhA III.191; **deva°** reign amongst gods KhA 227; **padesa°** local sovereignty It 15; Kh VIII.12 (cp. KhA 227).
-siri-dāyikā (devatā) (goddess) giving success to the empire DhA II.17. **-sīma** border of the empire Vism 121.

Rajjati [cp. Sk. rajyati, **raj** or **rañj**, Med. of rajati] to be excited, attached to (loc.), to find pleasure in S IV.74 (na so rajjati rūpesu; =viratta-citta); Sn 160, 813 (contrasted with virajjati); Ps I.58, 77 sq., 130, 178; Nd[1] 138; Miln 386 (rajjasi rajanīyesu etc.: in combn with dosa & moha or derivations, representing rāga or lobha, cp. lobhanīya); VbhA 11.—ppr. **rajjamāna** PvA 3; Pot. **rajjeyya** Miln 280 (kampeyya+); grd. **rajjitabba** Miln 386 (rajanīyesu r.; with dussanīyesu and muyhanīyesu; followed by kampitabba); fut. rajjissati DhsA 194; aor. **arañji** Vin I.36=J I.83 (na yiṭṭhe na hute arañjiŋ).—pp. **ratta.**

Rajjana (nt.) [fr. rajjati] defilement DA I.195. Cp. muyhana.

Rajju (f.) [Vedic rajju, cp. Lat. restis rope, Lith. rēzgis wicker, basket] a cord, line, rope S II.128; Vin II.120, 148 (āviñchana°); Nd[2] 304; J I.464, 483 (fisherman's line); V.173; Mhvs 10, 61; DhA IV.54; VbhA 163; KhA 57; VvA 207; Sdhp 148, 153.
-kāra rope-maker Miln 331. **-gāhaka** "rope-holder," (king's) land-surveyor J II.367=DhA IV.88 (see Fick, *Sociale Gliederung* 97).

Rajjuka [rajju+ka] 1. a rope, line J I.164 (bandhana°); ThA 257.—2.=rajjugāhaka, king's land surveyor J II.367.

Rañjati [**rañj**=**raj**: see rajati & rajjati—Dhtp 66 & 398 defines rañja=rāge] 1. to colour, dye J I.220.—2. (=rajjati) to find delight in, to be excited Sn 424 (ettha me r. mano; v. l. BB rajjati).—Caus. **rañjeti** to delight or make glad D III.93 (in etym. of rājā (q. v.).—pp. **rañjita.**—Caus. II. **rañjāpeti** to cause to be coloured or dyed DhA IV.106 (v. l. raj°).

Rañjana (nt.) [fr. rañjati] delighting, finding pleasure, excitement DhsA 363 (rañjan' aṭṭhena rāgo; v. l. rajano°; perhaps better to be read rajjana°).

Rañjita [pp. of rañjeti] coloured, soiled, in raja° affected with stain, defiled J I.117.—See also **anu°** & **pari°**.

Raṭati [**raṭ**; Dhtp 86: "paribhāsane"] to yell, cry; shout (at), scold, revile: not found in the texts.

Raṭṭha (nt.) [Vedic rāṣṭra] reign, kingdom, empire; country, realm Sn 46 (expld at Nd[2] 536 as "raṭṭhañ ca janapadañ ca koṭṭhāgārañ ca . . . nagarañ ca"), 287, 444, 619; J IV.389 (°ŋ araṭṭhaŋ karoti); PvA 19 (°ŋ kāreti to reign, govern). Pabbata° mountain-kingdom SnA 26; Magadha° the kingdom of Magadha PvA 67.
-piṇḍa the country's alms-food (°ŋ bhuñjati) Dh 308 (saddhāya dinnaŋ); A I.10; S II.221; M III.127; Th 2, 110; It 43, 90. **-vāsin** inhabitant of the realm, subject DhA III.481.

Raṭṭhaka (adj.) [Sk. rāṣṭraka] belonging to the kingdom, royal, sovereign J IV.91 (senāvāhana).—Cp. raṭṭhika.

Raṭṭhavant (adj.) [raṭṭha+vant] possessing a kingdom or kingship Pv II.6[11] (°nto khattiyā).

Raṭṭhika [fr. raṭṭha, cp. Sk. rāṣṭrika] 1. one belonging to a kingdom, subject in general, inhabitant J II.241 (brāhmaṇa-gahapati-r.-dovārik' ādayo).—2. an official of the kingdom [cp. Sk. rāṣṭriya a pretender; also king's brother-in-law] A III.76=300 (r. pettanika senāya senāpatika).

Raṇa [Vedic raṇa, both "enjoyment," and "battle." The Dhtp (115) only knows of **raṇ** as a sound-base saddatthā (=Sk. **raṇ**[2] to tinkle)] 1. fight, battle; only in Th 2, 360 (raṇaŋ karitvā kāmānaŋ): see discussed below; also late at Mhvs 35. 69 (Subharājaŋ raṇe hantvā). — 2. intoxication, desire, sin, fault. This meaning is the Buddhist development of Vedic raṇa = enjoyment. Various influences have played a part in determining the meaning & its expl[n] in the scholastic terms of the dogmatists and exegetics. It is often expl[d] as pāpa or rāga. The Ṭīkā on DhsA 50 (see *Expos.* 67) gives the foll. expl[ns] (late & speculative): (a) = reṇu, dust or mist of lust etc.; (b) fight, war (against the Paths); (c) pain, anguish & distress. — The trsl[n] (*Expos.* 67) takes raṇa as "cause of grief," or "harm," hence araṇa "harmless" and saraṇa "harmful" (the latter trsl[d] as "concomitant with war" by *Dhs. trsl.* of Dhs 1294; and asaraṇa as opp. "not concomitant"; doubtful). At S I.148 (rūpe raṇaŋ disvā) it is almost syn. with raja. Bdhgh. expl[s] this passage (see *K.S.* 320) as "rūpamhi jāti-jarā-bhanga-sankhātaŋ dosaŋ," trsl[n] (*K.S.* 186): "discerning canker in visible objects material."

The term is not sufficiently cleared yet. At Th 2, 358 we read "(kāmā) appassādā **raṇakarā** sukkapakkha-visosana," and v. 360 reads "raṇaŋ karitvā kāmānaŋ." ThA 244 expl[s] v. 358 by "rāg' ādi sambandhanato"; v. 360 by "kāmānaŋ raṇaŋ te ca mayā kātabbaŋ ariyamaggaŋ sampahāraŋ katvā." The first is evidently "grief," the second "fight," but the trsl[n] (*Sisters* 145) gives "stirring strife" for v. 358, and "fight with worldly lusts" for v. 360; whereas Kern, *Toev.* s. v. raṇakara gives "causing sinful desire" as trsl.

The word araṇa (see araṇa[2]) was regarded as neg. of raṇa in both meanings (1 & 2); thus either "freedom fr. passion" or "not fighting." The trsl[n] of DhsA 50 (*Expos.* 67) takes it in a slightly diff. sense as "harmless" (i. e. having no grievous causes). — At M III.235 araṇa is a quâsi summing up of "adukkha an-upaghāta anupāyāsa etc.," and saraṇa of their positives. Here a meaning like "harmfulness" & "harmlessness" seems to be fitting. Other passages of araṇa see under araṇa.

-jaha (raṇañjaha) giving up desires or sin, leaving causes of harmfulness behind. The expression is old and stereotype. It has caused trouble among interpreters: Trenckner would like to read **raṇañjaya** "victorious in battle" (*Notes* 83). It is also BSk., e. g. Lal. Vist. 50; AvŚ II.131 (see Speyer's note 3 on this page. He justifies trsl[n] "pacifier, peace-maker"). At foll. passages: S I.52 (trsl[n] "quitting corruption"); It 108 (Seidenstücker trsl[s]: "dem Kampfgewühl entronnen"); Miln 21; Nett 54; Sdhp 493, 569.

Rata [pp. of ramati] delighting in (loc. or -[n]), intent on, devoted to S IV.117 (dhamme jhāne), 389 sq. (bhava° etc.); Sn 54 (saṅgaṇika°) 212, 250, 327, 330 (dhamme), 461 (yaññe), 737 (upasame); Mhvs. I, 44 (mahākāruṇiko Satthā sabba-loka-hite rato); 32, 84 (rato puññe); PvA 3, 12, 19 (°mānasa).

Ratana[1] (nt.) [cp. Vedic ratna, gift; the BSk. form is **ratna** (Divy 26) as well as ratana (AvŚ II.199)] 1. (lit.) a gem, jewel VvA 321 (not = ratana[2], as Hardy in Index); PvA 53 (nānāvidhāni). — The 7 ratanas are enum[d] under **veḷuriya** (Miln 267). They are (the precious minerals) suvaṇṇa, rajata, muttā, maṇi, veḷuriya, vajira, pavāḷa. (So at Abhp 490.) These 7 are said to be used in the outfit of a ship to give it more splendour: J II.112. The 7 (unspecified) are mentioned at Th 2, 487 (satta ratanāni vasseyya vuṭṭhimā "all seven kinds of gems"); and at DhA I.274, where it is said of a ratana-maṇḍapa that in it there were raised flags "sattaratana-mayā." On ratana in *similes* see *J.P.T.S.* 1909, 127. — 2. (fig.) treasure, gem of (-°) Sn 836 (etādisaŋ r. = dibb' itthi-ratana SnA 544); Miln 262 (dussa° a very fine garment). — Usually as a set of 7 valuables, belonging to the throne (the empire) of a (world-) king. Thus at D II.16 sq.; of Mahā-Sudassana D II.172 sq. They are enum[d] singly as follows: the wheel (cakka) D II.172 sq., the elephant (hatthi, called Uposatha) D II.174, 187, 197; the horse (assa, Valāhaka) ibid.; the gem (maṇi) D II.175, 187; the woman (itthi) ibid.; the treasurer (gahapati) D II.176, 188; the adviser (pariṇāyaka) ibid. The same 7 are enum[d] at D I.89; Sn p. 106; DA I.250; also at J IV.232, where their origins (homes) are given as: cakka° out of Cakkadaha; hatthi from the Upasatha-race; assa° from the clan of Valāhassarāja, maṇi° from Vepulla, and the last 3 without specification. See also remarks on gahapati. Kern, *Toev.* s. v. ratana suspects the latter to be originally "major domus" (cp. his attributes as "wealthy" at MVastu I.108). As to the exact meaning of pariṇāyaka he is doubtful, which mythical tradition has obscured. — The 7 (moral) ratanas at S II.217 & III.83 are probably the same as are given in detail at Miln 336, viz. the 5: sīla°, samādhi°, paññā°, vimutti°, vimutti-ñāṇadassana (also given under the collective name sīla-kkhandha or dhamma-kkhandha), to which are added the 2: paṭisambhidā° & bojjhanga°. These 7 are probably meant at PvA 66, where it is said that Sakka "endowed their house with the 7 jewels" (satta-r.-bharitaŋ katvā). — Very frequent is a *Triad of Gems* (ratana-ttaya), consisting of Dhamma, Sangha, Buddha, or the Doctrine, the Church and the Buddha [cp. BSk. ratna-traya Divy 481], e. g. Mhvs 5, 81; VbhA 284; VvA 123; PvA 1, 49, 141.

-ākara a pearl-mine, a mine of precious metals Th 1, 1049; J II.414; VI.459; Dpvs I.18. **-kūṭa** a jewelled top DhA I.159. **-paliveṭhana** a wrapper for a gem or jewel Pug 34. **-vara** the best of gems Sn 683 (= vara-ratana-bhūta SnA 486). **-sutta** the Suttanta of the (3) Treasures (viz. Dhamma, Sangha, Buddha), representing Sutta Nipāta II.1 (P.T.S. ed. pp. 39-42), mentioned as a parittā at Vism 414 (with 4 others) and at Miln 150 (with 5 others), cp. KhA 63; SnA 201.

Ratana[2] [most likely = Sk. aratni: see ratani] a linear measure (which Abhp p. 23 gives as equal to 12 angula, or 7 ratanas = 1 yaṭṭhi: see Kirfel, *Kosmographie,* p. 335. The same is given by Bdhgh. at VbhA 343: dve vidatthiyo ratanaŋ; satta r. yaṭṭhi) J v.36 (visaŋ-r-sataŋ); VI.401 (°mattaŋ); VvA 321 (so given by Hardy in Index as "measure of length," but to be taken as ratana[1], as indicated clearly by context & C.); Miln 282 (satta-patiṭṭhito aṭṭha-ratan' ubbedho nava-ratan' āyāma-pariṇāho pāsādiko dassaniyo Uposatho nāgarājā: alluding to ratana[1] 2!).

Ratanaka (-°) (adj.) [ratana + ka, the ending belonging to the whole cpd.] characteristic of a gem, or a king's treasure; in phrase **aniggata-ratanake** "When the treasure has not gone out" Vin IV.160, where the chief queen is meant with "treasure."

Ratani [Sk. aratni "elbow" with apocope and diaeresis; given at Halāyudha 2, 381 as "a cubit, or measure from the elbow to the tip of the little finger." The form ratni also occurs in Sk. The etym. is fr. Idg. *ole (to bend), cp. Av. arəþna elbow; Sk. arāla bent; of which enlarged bases *olen in Lat. ulna, ond *oleq in Lat. lacertus, Sk. lakutaḥ = P. laguḷa. See cognates in Walde, *Lat. Wtb.* s. v. lacertus] a cubit Miln 85 (aṭṭha rataniyo).

Ratanika (adj.) [fr. ratana] a ratana in length J I.7 (aḍḍha°); Miln 312 (aṭṭha°).

Rati (f.) [Classic Sk. rati, fr. **ram**] love, attachment, pleasure, liking for (loc.), fondness of S I.133 (°ŋ paccanubhavati), 207; III.256; Sn 41 (= anukkhaṇṭhit' adhivacanaŋ Nd[2] 537), 59 (id.), 270, 642, 956 (= nekkhamma-rati paviveka°, upasama° Nd[1] 457); J III.277 (kilesa°); DhA IV.225; PvA 77. —arati dislike, aversion

S I.7, 54, 128, 180, 197; v.64; Sn 270 (+rati), 642 (id.); Dh 418 (rati+); Th 2, 339; DhsA 193; PvA 64; Sdhp 476. —ratiŋ karoti to delight in, to make love Vism 195 (purisā itthīsu).

Ratin (adj.) (-°) [fr. rati] fond of, devoted to, keen on, fostering; f. ratinī J IV.320 (ahiŋsā°).

Ratta[1] [pp. of rañjati, cp. Sk. rakta] 1. dyed, coloured M I.36 (dūratta-vaṇṇa difficult to dye or badly dyed; MA 167 reads **duratta** and expl[s] as durañjita-vaṇṇa; opp. suratta ibid.); Sn 287 (nānā-rattehi vatthehi); Vism 415 (°vattha-nivattha, as sign of mourning); DhA IV.226 (°vattha). — 2. red. This is used of a high red colour, more like crimson. Sometimes it comes near a meaning like "shiny, shining, glittering" (as in ratta-suvaṇṇa the glittering gold), cp. etym. & meaning of rajati and rajana. It may also be taken as "bleached" in **ratta-kambala**. In **ratta-phalika** (crystal) it approaches the meaning of "white," as also in expl[n] of puṇḍarīka at J v.216 with **ratta-paduma** "white lotus." — It is most commonly found in foll. comb[ns] at foll. passages: Miln 191 (°lohita-candana); Vism 172 (°kambala), 174 (°koraṇḍaka), 191 (°paṭākā); J I.394 (pavāla-ratta-kambala); III.30 (°puppha-dāma); v.37 (°sālivana), 216 (°paduma); 372 (°suvaṇṇa); DhA I.393 (id.), 248 (°kambala); IV.189 (°candana-rukkha red-sandal tree); SnA 125 (where paduma is given as "ratta-set' ādivasena"); VvA 4 (°dupaṭṭa), 65 (°suvaṇṇa), 177 (°phalika); PvA 4 (°virala-mālā; garland of red flowers for the convict to be executed, cp. Fick, *Sociale Gliederung* 104), 157 (°paduma), 191 (°sāli); Mhvs 30, 36 (°kambala); 36, 82 (rattāni akkhīni bloodshot eyes). With the latter cp. cpd. **rattakkha** "with red eyes" (fr. crying) at PvA 39 (v. l. BB.) and Np. **rattakkhin** "Red-eye" (Ep. of a Yakkha). — 3. (fig.) excited, infatuated, impassioned S IV.339; Sn 795 (virāga°); It 92 (maccā rattā); Miln 220. Also in comb[n] **ratta duṭṭha mūḷha**: see Nd[2] s. v. chanda; cp. bhava-rāga-ratta.

Ratta[2] (nt.) & (poet.) rattā (f.) [Epic Sk. rātra; Vedic rātra only in cpd. aho-rātraŋ. Semantically an abstr. formation in collect. meaning "the space of a night's time," hence "interval of time" in general. Otherwise rātri: see under ratti] (rarely) night; (usually) time in general. Occurs only -°, with expressions giving a definite time. Independently (besides cpds. mentioned below) only at one (doubtful) passage, viz. Sn 1071, where BB MSS. read **rattam-ahā** for rattaŋ aho, which corresponds to the Vedic phrase aho-rātraŋ (=P. aho-rattaŋ). The P.T.S. ed. reads nattaŋ; SnA 593 reads nattaŋ, but expl[s] as rattin-divaŋ, whereas Nd[2] 538 reads rattaŋ & expl[s]: "rattaŋ vuccati ratti, ahā (sic lege!) ti divaso, rattiñ ca divañ ca." — Otherwise only in foll. adv. expressions (meaning either "time" or "night"): *instr.* eka-rattena in one night J I.64; satta° after one week (lit. a seven-night) Sn 570. — *acc. sg.* cira-rattaŋ a long time Sn 665; dīgha° id. [cp. BSk. dīrgha-rātraŋ freq.] Sn 22; M I.445; aḍḍha° at "half-night," i. e. midnight A III.407; pubba-ratt' āpara-rattaŋ one night after the other (lit. the last one and the next) DhA IV.129. — *acc. pl.* cira rattāni a long time J v.268. — *loc.* in var. forms, viz. vassa-ratte in the rainy season J v.38 (Kern, *Toev.* s. v. gives wrongly III.37, 143; aḍḍha-**ratte** at midnight PvA 152; aḍḍha-**rattāyaŋ** at midnight Vv 81[16] (=aḍḍharattiyaŋ VvA 315); divā ca **ratto** ca day & night Vv 31[5] (=rattiyaŋ VvA 130); cira-**rattāya** a long time J v.267; Pv I.9[4].

-andhakāra the dark of night, nightly darkness Vin IV.268 (oggate suriye); M I.448. **-ûparata** abstaining from food at night D I.5 (cp. DA I.77). **-ññu** of long standing, recognised D I.48 (in phrase: r. cira-pabbajito addhagato etc.; expl[d] at DA I.143 as "pabbajjato paṭṭhāya atikkantā bahū rattiyo jānātī ti r."); A II.27 (here the pl. rattaññā, as if fr. sg. ratta-ñña); Sn p. 92 (therā r. cira-pabbajitā; the expl[n] at SnA 423 is rather fanciful with the choice of either=ratana-ññu, i. e. knowing the gem of Nibbāna, or=bahu-ratti-vidū, i. e. knowing many nights); ThA 141. A f. abstr. °ññutā "recognition" is found at M I.445 (spelt ratañ-ñūtā, but v. l. °utā). -samaye (loc., adv.) at the time of (night) J I.63 (aḍḍha-ratta° at midnight), 264 (id.); IV.74 (vassa° in the rainy season); PvA 216 (aḍḍha°).

Ratti (f.) [Vedic rātrī & later Sk. rātri. — Idg *lādh as in Gr. λήθω=Lat. lateo to hide; Sk rāhu dark demon; also Gr. Λητώ (=Lat. Latona) Goddess of night; Mhg. luoder insidiousness; cp. further Gr. λανθάνω to be hidden, λήθη oblivion (E. lethargy). — The by-form of ratti is ratta[2]] night D I.47 (dosinā). gen. sg. ratyā (for *rattiyā) Th 1, 517; Sn 710 (vivasane=ratti-samatik-kame SnA 496); J VI.491. abl. sg. rattiyā in phrases abhikkantāya r. at the waning of night D II.220; Vin I.26; S I.16; M I.143; & pabhātāya r. when night grew light, i. e. dawn J I.81, 500. instr. pl. rattīsu Vin I.288 (hemantikāsu r.). A loc. **ratyā** (for *rātryām) and a nom. pl. ratyo (for *rātryaḥ) is given by Geiger, *P.Gr.* § 58[3]. — Very often comb[d] with and opp. to diva in foll. comb[ns]: rattin-diva [cp. BSk. rātrindiva=Gr. νυχθήμερον, AvŚ I.274, 278; II.176; Divy 124] a day & a night (something like our "24 hours"), in phrase dasa rattindivā a decade of n. & d. (i. e. a 10-day week) A v.85 sq.; adverbially satta-rattin-divaŋ a week DhA I.108. As adv. in acc. sg.: rattin-divaŋ night and day A III.57; Sn 507, 1142; It 93; J I.30; or rattiñ ca divañ ca Nd[2] 538, or rattiŋ opposed to adv. divā by night—by day M I.143; PvA 43. — Other *cases as adv.: acc.* eka **rattiŋ** one night J I.62; Pv II.9[7]; PvA 42; taŋ rattiŋ that night Mhvs 4, 38; imaŋ r. this night M I.143; yañ ca r. . . . yañ ca r. . . . etasmiŋ antare in between yon night and yon night It 121; rattiŋ at night Miln 42; rattiŋ rattiŋ night after night Mhvs 30, 16. — *gen.* **rattiyā** ca divasassa ca by n. & by day S II.95. — *loc.* **rattiyañ** by night VvA 130, 315 (aḍḍha° at midnight); PvA 22; and **ratto** in phrase **divā** ca **ratto** ca Sn 223; Th 2, 312; Dh 296; Vv 31[5]; 84[32]; S I.33.

-khaya the wane of night J I.19. **-cāra** (sabba°) all-night wandering S I.201 (trsl. "festival"). **-cheda** interruption of the probationary period (t. t.) Vin II.34 (three such: sahavāsa, vippavāsa, anārocanā). **-dhū-māyanā** smouldering at night Vism 107 (v. l. dhūp°), comb[d] with divā-pajjalanā, cp. M I.143: ayaŋ vammīko rattiŋ dhūmāyati divā pajjalati. **-pariyanta** limitation of the probationary period (t. t.) Vin II.59. **-bhāga** night-time J III.43 (°bhāge); Miln 18 (°bhāgena). **-bhojana** eating at night M I.473; DA I.77. **-samaya** night-time, only in loc. aḍḍha-ratti-samaye at midnight VvA 255; PvA 155.

Ratha[1] [Vedic ratha, Av. raþa, Lat. rota wheel, rotundus ("rotund" & round), Oir. roth=Ohg rad wheel, Lith. rātas id.] a two-wheeled carriage, chariot (for riding, driving or fighting S I.33 (ethically); A IV.191 (horse & cart; diff. parts of a ratha); M I.396; Sn 300, 654; Vism 593 (in its comp[n] of akkha, cakka, pañjara, īsā etc.); J III.239 (passaddha° carriage slowing up); Th 2, 229 (caturassaŋ rathaŋ, i. e. a Vimāna); Mhvs 35, 42 (goṇā rathe yuttā); VvA 78 (500), 104, 267 (=Vimāna), PvA 74. —**assatarī°** a chariot drawn by a she-mule Vv 20[8]=43[8]; Pv I.11[1]; J VI.355. — **Phussa-ratha** state carriage J III.238; VI.30 sq. See under ph. — On ratha in similes see *J.P.T.S.* 1907, 127.

-atthara (rathatthara) a rug for a chariot D I.7; Vin I.192; II.163. **-anīka** array of chariots Vin IV.108. **-īsā** carriage pole A IV.191. **-ûpatthara** chariot or carriage cover D I.103; DA I.273. **-esabha** (ratha+ṛṣabha, Sk. rathar̥ṣabha) lord of charioteers. Ratha here in meaning of "charioteer"; Childers sees rathin in this cpd.; Trenckner, *Notes* 59, suggests distortion from rathe śubha. Dhpāla at PvA 163 clearly understands it as ratha-=charioteer explaining "rathesu usabha-sadiso mahā-ratho ti attho"; as does Bdhgh. at SnA 321 (on Sn 303): "mahā-rathesu khattiyesu akampiy' aṭṭhena usabha-sadiso." — Sn 303-308, 552; Pv II.13[1]; Mhvs 5, 246; 15, 11; 29, 12. -**kāra** carriage-builder, chariot-maker, considered as a class of very low social standing, rebirth in which is a punishment (cp. Fick, *Sociale Gliederung* 56, 207, 209 sq.) S I.93; Vin IV.9 (as term of abuse, enum[d] with other low grades: caṇḍāla veṇa nesāda r. pukkusa), 12 (°jāti); M II.152, 183 f.; as kārin at Pv III.1[13] (expl[d] as cammakārin PvA 175). As Npl. name of one of the 7 Great Lakes in the Himālaya (Rathakāradaha), e. g. at Vism 416; SnA 407. -**cakka** wheel of a chariot or carriage Vism 238 (in simile, concerning its circumference); PvA 65. -**pañjara** the body (lit. "cage" or "frame") of a carriage Vv 83[1] (=rath' ûpattha VvA 326); J II.172; IV.60; DhA I.28. -**yuga** a chariot yoke J VI.42. -**reṇu** "chariot-dust," a very minute quantity (as a measure), a mite. Childers compares Sk. trasareṇu a mote of dust, atom. It is said to consist of 36 tajjāri's, and 36 ratha-reṇu's are equal to one **likkhā**: VbhA 343. -**vinīta** "led by a chariot," a chariot-drive (Neumann, "Eilpost"), name of the 24th Suttanta of Majjhima (M I.145 sq.), quoted at Vism 93, 671 and SnA 446. -**sālā** chariot shed DhA III.121.

Ratha[2] [fr. **ram**, cp. Sk. ratha] pleasure, joy, delight: see mano°.

Rathaka[1] (nt.) [fr. ratha, cp. Sk. rathaka m.] a little carriage, a toy cart D I.6 (cp. DA I.86: khuddaka-rathaŋ); Vin II.10; III.180; M I.226; Miln 229.

Rathaka[2] (adj.) [ratha+ka] having a chariot, neg. a° without a chariot J VI.515.

Rathika [fr. ratha] fighter fr. a chariot, charioteer M I.397 (saññāto kusalo rathassa anga-paccangānaŋ); D I.51 (in list of var. occupations, cp. DA I.156); J VI.15 (+patti-kārika), 463 (id.).

Rathikā & **Rathiyā** (f.) [Vedic rathya belonging to the chariot, later Sk. rathyā road. See also **racchā**] a carriage-road. — (a) rathikā: Vin II.268; Vism 60; PvA 4, 67. — (b) rathiyā: D I.83; Vin I.237, 344; M II.108; III.163; S I.201; II.128; IV.344. In comp[n] rathiya°, e. g. rathiya-coḷa "street-rag" Vism 62 (expl[d] as rathikāya chaḍḍita-coḷaka).

Rada at ThA 257 in cpd. "sannivesa-visiṭṭha-rada-visesa-yutta" is not quite clear ("splitting"?).

Radati [**rad**: see etym. at Walde, *Lat. Wtb.* s. v. rado ("rase"). Given in meaning "vilekhana" at Dhtp 159 & Dhtm 220. Besides this it is given at Dhtm 224 in meaning "bhakkhana"] to scratch Dhtp 159; cp. rada & **radana** tooth Abhp 261.

Randha[1] [for Sk. raddha, pp. of randhati 2] cooked J V.505; VI.24; Miln 107.

Randha[2] [Sk. randhra, fr. randhati 1; the P. form viâ *randdha: see Geiger, *P.Gr.* § 58[1]] opening, cleft, open spot; flaw, defect, weak spot A IV.25; Sn 255, 826 randhamesin looking for somebody's weak spot; cp. Nd[1] 165 ("virandham° aparandham° khalitam° galitam° vivaram-esī ti"); J II.53; III.192; SnA 393 (+vivara); DhA III.376, 377 (°gavesita).

Randhaka (-°) (adj.) [fr. randhati 2] one who cooks, cooking, a cook J IV.431 (bhatta°).

Randhati [**radh** or **randh**, differentiated in Pāli to 2 meanings & 2 verbs according to Dhtm: "hiŋsāyaŋ" (148), and "pāke" (827). In the former sense given as raṇḍ, in the latter **randh**. The root is freq. in the Vedas, in meaning 1. It belongs perhaps to Ags. rendan to rend: see Walde, *Lat. Wtb.* s. v. lumbus] to be or make subject to, (intrs.) to be in one's power; (trs.) to harass, oppress, vex, hurt (mostly Caus. **randheti**=Sk. randhayati). Only in Imper. randhehi J I.332, and in Prohib. mā **randhayi** J V.121, and pl. **mā randhayuŋ** Dh 248 (=mā randhantu mā mathantu DhA III.357). See also randha[2]. — 2. to cook (cp. Sk. randhi & randhana) Miln 107 (bhojanaŋ randheyya). — pp. randha[1].

Rapati [**rap**] to chatter, whisper Dhtp 187 ("vacane"); Dhtm 266 ("akkose"). See also **lapati**.

Rabhasa [**rabh=labh**, which see for etym. Cp. also Lat rabies. — Dhtp 205 expl[s] **rabh** (correctly) by ārambha & Dhtm 301 by rābhassa] wild, terrible, violent D I.91, expl[d] by "bahu-bhāṇin" at DA I.256. There are several vv. ll. at this passage.

Rama (-°) (adj.) [fr. **ram**] delighting, enjoyable; only in cpd. dū° (=duḥ) difficult to enjoy, not fit for pleasures; as nt. absence of enjoyment Dh 87=S V.24; and mano° gladdening the mind (q. v.).

Ramaṇa (adj.) [fr. ramati; cp. Sk. ramaṇa] pleasing, charming, delightful DhA II.202 (°ṭṭhāna).

Ramaṇaka (adj.)=ramaṇa J III.207.

Ramaṇīya (& °nīya) (adj.) [grd. of ramati] delightful, pleasing, charming, pleasant, beautiful D I.47 (°ṇīyā dosinā ratti, cp. DA I.141); Sn 1013; Mhvs 15, 69 (ṇ); PvA 42, 51 (expl[n] for rucira). As ramaṇeyya at S I.233. Cp. rāmaṇeyya(ka).

Ramati [**ram**; def[d] by Dhtp 224 & Dhtm 318 by "kīḷāyaŋ"] 1. to enjoy oneself, to delight in; to sport, find amusement in (loc.) S I.179; Vin 197 (ariyo na r. pāpe); Sn 985 (jhāne); Dh 79 (ariya-ppavedite dhamme sadā r. paṇḍito); subj. 1st pl. **ramāmase** Th 2, 370 (cp. Geiger, *P.Gr.* 126); med. 1st sg. **rame** J V.363; imper. **rama** Pv II.12[20] (r. deva mayā saha; better with v. l. as ramma); — fut. **ramissati** PvA 153. — ger. **ramma** Pv II.12[20] (v. l. for rama). grd. **ramma** & **ramaṇīya** (q. v.). — pp. **rata**. — Caus. I. **rameti** to give pleasure to, to please, to fondle Th 1, 13; J V.204; VI.3 (pp. ramayamāna); Miln 313. — pp. **ramita** (q. v.). — Caus. II. **ramāpeti** to enjoy oneself J VI.114.

Ramita [pp. of rameti] having enjoyed, enjoying, taking delight in, amusing oneself with (loc. or saha) Sn 709 (vanante r. siyā); Dh 305 (id.=abhirata DhA III.472); Pv II.12[21] ('mhi tayā saha).

Rambati (& lambati) [**lamb**] to hang down. Both forms are given with meaning "avasaŋsane" at Dhtp 198 and Dhtm 283.

Rambhā (f.) [Sk. rambhā] a plantain or banana tree Abhp 589.

Ramma (adj.) [grd. of ramati] enjoyable, charming, beautiful Sn 305; ThA 71 (v. 30); Mhvs 1, 73; 14, 47; Sdhp 248, 512.

Rammaka (adj.) [Sk ramyaka] N. of the month Chaitra J V.63.

Raya [fr. **ri**, riṇāti to let loose or flow, which is taken as **ray** at Dhtp 234, def[d] as "gamana," and at Dhtm 336 as "gati." The root **ri** itself is given at Dhtm 351 in meaning "santati," i. e. continuation. — On etym. cp. Vedic retaḥ; Lat. rivus river=Gall, Rēnos "Rhine." See Walde, *Lat. Wtb.* s. v. rivus] speed, lit. current Abhp 40. See **rava**[1].

Rava[1] [for raya, with v. for y as freq. in Pāli, Dhtm 352: ru "gate"] speed, exceeding swiftness, galloping, in comb[n] with **dava** running at Vin II.101; IV.4; M I.446

(better reading here dav' atthe rav' atthe for dhāve ravatthe, cp. vv. ll. on p. 567 & Neumann, *Mittl. Sammlg.* II.672 n. 49). *Note.* At the Vin passages it refers to speaking & making blunders by over-hurrying oneself in speaking. — The Dhtm (No. 871) gives rava as a synonym of **rasa** (with assāda & sneha). It is not clear what the connection is between these two meanings.

Rava[2] [fr. **ru**, cp. Vedic rava] loud sound, roar, shout, cry; any noise uttered by animals J II.110; III.277; DhA I.232 (sabba-rava-ññu knowing all sounds of animals); Miln 357 (kāruñña°). See also **rāva** & **ruta**.

Ravaka=rava, in go° a cow's bellowing M I.225.

Ravaṇa (adj.-nt.) [fr. ravati] roaring, howling, singing, only in cpd. °ghaṭa a certain kind of pitcher, where meaning of ravaṇa is uncertain. Only at identical passages (in illustration) Vism 264=362=KhA 68 (reading peḷā-ghaṭa, but see App. p. 870 ravaṇa°)= VbhA 68 (where v. l. yavana°, with ?).

Ravati [**ru**: Idg. ***re** & ***reu**, cp. Lat. ravus "raw, hoarse," raucus, rūmor "rumour"; Gr. ὠρυόμαι to shout, ὠρυδόν roaring, etc.; Dhtp 240: **ru** "sadde"] to shout, cry, make a (loud) noise Miln 254. — aor. ravi J I.162 (baddha-rāvaŋ ravi); II.110; III.102; PvA 100; **arāvi** Mhvs 10, 69 (mahā-rāvaŋ); and **aravi** Mhvs 32, 79. — pp. ravita & ruta. — Cp. abhi°, vi°.

Ravi [cp. Sk. ravi] the sun J II.375 (taruṇa°-vaṇṇaratha).

-**inda** "king of the sun," N. of the lotus Dāvs III.37. -**haŋsa** "sun-swan," N. of a bird J VI.539.

Ravita [pp. of ravati] shouted, cried, uttered Miln 178 (sakuṇa-ruta°).

Rasa[1] [Vedic rasa; with Lat. ros "dew," Lith. rasā id., and Av Raṅhā N. of a river, to Idg. ***eres** to flow, as in Sk. arṣati, Gr. ὄψορρος (to ῥέω); also Sk. ṛṣabha: see usabha[1]. — Dhtp 325 defines as "assādane" 629 as "**assāda-snehanesu**"; Dhtm 451 as "assāde." — The decl. is usually as regular a-stem, but a secondary instr. fr. an s-stem is to be found in **rasasā** by taste A II.63; J III.328] that which is connected with the sense of taste. The def[n] given at Vism 447 is as follows: "jivhā-paṭihanana-lakkhaṇo raso, jivhā-viññāṇassa visaya-bhāvo raso, tass' eva gocara-paccupaṭṭhāno, mūla-raso khandha-raso ti ādinā nayena anekavidho," i. e. rasa is physiologically & psychologically peculiar to the tongue (sense-object & sense-perception), and also consists as a manifold object in extractions from roots, trunk etc. (see next). — The conventional encyclopædic def[n] of rasa at Nd[1] 240; Nd[2] 540, Dhs 629 gives taste according to: (a) the 6-fold objective source as mūla-rasa, khandha°, **taca°**, **patta°**, **puppha°**, **phala°**, or taste (i. e. juice, liquid) of root, trunk, bark, leaf, flower & fruit; and — (b) the 12-fold subjective (physiological) sense-perception as **ambila**, **madhura**, **tittika**, **kaṭuka** **loṇika**, **khārika**, **lambila** (Miln 56: ambila), **kasāva**; **sādu**, **asādu**, **sīta**, **uṇha**, or sour, sweet, bitter, pungent, salt, alkaline, sour, astringent; pleasant, unpleasant, cold & hot. Miln 56 has the foll.: **ambila**, **lavaṇa**, **tittaka**, **kaṭuka**, **kasāya**, **madhura**. — 1. juice [as applied in the Veda to the Soma juice], e.g. in the foll. comb[ns]: ucchu° of sugar cane, extract of sugar, cane syrup Vin I.246; VvA 180; patta° & puppha° of leaf & flower Vin I.246; **madhura°** of honey PvA 119. — 2. taste as (objective) quality, the sense-object of taste (cp. above def[ns]). In the list of the **āyatanas**, or senses with their complementary sense-objects (sentient and sensed) rasa occupies the 4th place, following upon gandha. It is stated that one tastes (or "senses") taste with the tongue (no reference to palate): **jivhāya rasaŋ sāyitvā** (or **viññeyya**). See also āyatana 3 and rūpa. — M III.55 (jivhā-viññeyya r.), 267; D III.244, 250; Sn 387; Dhs 609; PvA 50 (vaṇṇagandha-rasa-sampanna bhojana: see below 5). — 3. sense of taste, as quality & personal accomplishment. Thus in the list of senses marking superiority (the 10 ādhipateyyas or ṭhāṇas), similar to rasa as special distinction of the Mahāpurisa (see cpd. ras-agga) S IV.275 =Pv II.9[58]; A IV.242. — 4. object or act of enjoyment, sensual stimulus, material enjoyment, pleasure (usually in pl.) Sn 65 (rasesu gedha, see materialistic exegesis at Nd[2] 540), 854 (rase na anugijjhati; perhaps better **rasesu**, as SnA); A III.237 (puriso agga°-parititto: perhaps to No. 2). — 5. flavour and its substance (or substratum), e. g. soup VvA 243 (kakkaṭaka° crabsoup), cp. S V.149, where 8 soup flavours are given (ambila, tittaka, kaṭuka, madhura, khārika, akhārika, loṇika, aloṇika); Pv II.1[16] (aneka-rasa-vyañjana "with exceptionally flavoured sauce"); J V.459, 465. **go-rasa** "flavour of cow, i. e. produce of cow: see under **go**. Also **metaphorically**: "flavour, relish, pleasure": Sn 257 (pariveka°, dhamma-pīti°, cp. SnA 299 "assād' aṭṭhena" i. e. tastiness); PvA 287 (vimutti° relish of salvation). So also as **attha°**, **dhamma°**, **vimutti°** Ps II.89. — 6. (in grammar & style) essential property, elegance, brightness; in dramatic art "sentiment" (flavour) (see Childers s. v. naṭya-rasa) Miln 340 (with opamma and lakkhaṇa: perhaps to No. 7); PvA 122 (°rasa as ending in Np. Angīrasa, expl[d] as jutiyā adhivacanaŋ," i. e. brightness, excellency). — 7. at t. t. in philosophy "essential property" (*Expos.* 84), comb[d] with **lakkhaṇa** etc. (cp. *Cpd.* 13, 213), either **kicca°** function or **sampatti°** property DhsA 63, 249; Vism 8, 448; Miln 148. — 8. fine substance, semi-solid semi-liquid substance, extract, delicacy, fineness, dust. Thus in **paṭhavī°** "essence of earth," humus S I.134 (trsl[n] "taste of earth," rather abstract); or **rasa-paṭhavī** earth as dust or in great fineness, "primitive earth" (before taking solid shape) D III.86 sq. (trsl. "savoury earth," not quite clear), opp. to bhūmipappaṭaka; Vism 418; **pabbata-rasa** mountain extract, rock-substance J III.55; **suvaṇṇa°** gold dust J I.93. — 9. (adj. -°) tasting Vv 16[11] (Amatarasā f.=nibbāna-rasāvinī VvA 85).

-**agga** finest quality (of taste), only in further comp[n] with *°aggita* (ras-agga-s-aggita) most delicate sense trsl[n] *Dial.*) D III.167, and *°aggin* (ras-agga-s-aggin, cp. MVastu II.306: rasa-ras' āgrin) of the best quality (of taste, cp. above 2), said of the Mahāpurisa D II.18= III.144 (cp. trsl[n] *Dial.* II.15 "his taste is supremely acute"). The phrase & its wording are still a little doubtful. Childers gives etym. of rasaggas-aggin as rasa-ggas-aggin, ggas representing **gras** to swallow (not otherwise found in Pāli!), and expl[s] the BSk. ras'-āgrin as a distortion of the P. form. -**añjana** a sort of ointment (among 5 kinds), "vitriol" (Rh. D.) Vin I.203. -**āda** enjoying the objects of taste M III.168. -**āyatana** the sphere of taste D III.243, 290; Dhs 629, 653, 1195 (insert after gandha°, see *Dhs. trsl.* 319). -**ārammaṇa** object of taste Dhs 12, 147, 157. -**āsā** craving for tastes Dhs 1059. -**garuka** bent on enjoyment SnA 107. -**taṇhā** thirst for taste, lust of sensual enjoyment D III.244, 280; J V.293; Dhs 1059; DhA IV.196. -**saññā** perception of tastes D III.244 (where also °sañcetanā). -**haraṇī** (f.) [ph. °haraṇiyo, in comp[n] haraṇi°] taste-conductor, taste-receiver; the salivary canals of the mouth or the nerves of sensation; these are in later literature given as numbering 7000, e. g. at J V.293 (khobhetvā phari); DhA I.134 (anuphari); KhA 51 (only as 7!); SnA 107 (paṭhama-kabaḷe mukhe pakkhitta-matte satta rasa-haraṇi-sahassāni amaten' eva phuṭāni ahesuŋ). Older passages are: Vin II.137; D III.167 (referring to the Mahāpurisa: "sampajjasā r-haraṇī susaṇṭhitā," trsl[n]: erect taste-bearers planted well [in throat]).

Rasa² (-°) is a dial. form of °dasa ten, and occurs in Classic Pāli only in the numerals for 13 (terasa), 15 (paṇṇa-rasa, pannarasa), 17 (sattarasa) & 18 (aṭṭhā-rasa, late). The Prk. has gone further: see Pischel, *Prk. Gr.* § 245.

Rasaka [fr. rasa, cp. Classic Sk. rasaka] a cook J v.460, 461, 507.

Rasati [ras] to shout, howl J II.407 (vv. ll. rayati, vasati; C. explˢ as "nadati")=IV.346 (v. l. sarati).

Rasatta (nt.) [fr. rasa] taste, sweetness SnA 299.

Rasavatī (f.) [rasa+vant] "possessing flavours" i. e. a kitchen Vin I.140.

Rasāvin (adj. [fr. rasa] tasting VvA 85 (nibbāna°).

Rasīyati [Pass.-Demon.-formation fr. rasa] to find taste or satisfaction in (gen.), to delight in, to be pleased A IV.387 (bhāsitassa), 388 (C.: tussati, see p. 470).

Rasmi see **raṇsi**.

Rassa (adj.) [cp. Sk. hrasva: Geiger, *P.Gr.* § 49². The Prk. forms are rahassa & hassa: Pischel § 354] short (opp. dīgha) D I.193 (dīghā vā r. vā majjhimā ti vā), 223 (in contrast with d.); Sn 633; Dh 409; J I.356; Dhs 617; Vism 272 (def.); DhA IV.184. — Cp. **ati°**.
-ādesa reduction of the determination (here of vowel in ending) J III.489. -sarīra (adj.) dwarfish, stunted J I.356.

Rassatta (nt.) [fr. rassa] shortness, reduction (of vowel) DhsA 149.

Rahati [**rah**, defᵈ at Dhtp 339 & 632 by "cāga," giving up, also at Dhtm 490 by "cāgasmiṇ," 876 by cāga *and* gata] to leave, desert: see pp. rahita & der. rahas, **rahassa**.

Rahada [Vedic hrada, with diæresis & metathesis *harada >rahada; the other metathetic form of the same hrada is *draha>daha] a (deep) pond, a lake D I.50 (°ṇ iva vippasannaṇ udānaṇ); S I.169=183 (dhammo rahado sīla-tittho); Sn 721=Miln 414 (rahado pūro va paṇḍito); It 92 (rahado va nivāto), 114 (r. sa-ummi sāvaṭṭo sagaho); DhA II.152. — As **udaka°** at D I.74, 84; A III.25 (ubbhid-odako); Pug 47. — On r. in similes see *J.P.T.S.* 1907, 127.

Rahas & **Raho** (nt.) [Vedic rahas. The Pāli word is restricted to the forms raho and rahā° (=*rahaḥ); a loc. rahasi is mentioned by Childers, but not found in the Canon. — To rahati] lonely place, solitude, loneliness; secrecy, privacy. — 1. raho: occurring only as *adv.* "secretly, lonely, in secret," either *absolutely*, e. g. S I.46; Sn 388; Pv II.7¹⁶ (opp. āvi openly); IV.1⁴⁰ (raho nisinna); Vism 201 (na raho karoti pāpāni: arahaṇ tena vuccati); or in *cpds.* e. g. °gata being in private, being alone D I.134 (+paṭisallīna); Sn p. 60. See also under paṭisallīna; °gama "secret convention, secret intercourse," fig. a secret adviser J VI.369 (after Kern, not found!); °vāda secret talk M III.230. See also anu°. — 2. rahā°, only in cpd. rahā-bhāva secrecy, in def° of arahant at DA I.146=Vism 201 (rahābhāvena ten' esa arahan ti). See also der. rāha-seyyaka. *Note.* Hardy's reading yathā rahaṇ at Pv II.9²³ & PvA 78 is not correct, it should be yath' ārahaṇ (cp. similarly pūj-āraha). In the same sense we would preferably read agg' āsan' ādi-arahānaṇ "of those who merit the first seat etc." at J I.217, although all MSS. have aggāsanādi-rahānaṇ, thus postulating a form raha=araha.

Rahassa (adj. nt.) [Sk. rahasya] secret, private; nt. secrecy, secret Mhvs 35, 64 (vatvā rahassaṇ); instr. rahassena (as adv.) secretly Mhvs 36, 80; acc. rahassaṇ id. Pv IV. 1⁶⁵.
-kathā secret speech, whispered words J I.411; II.6.

Rahassaka (adj.) [fr. rahassa] secret Miln 91 (guyhaṇ na kātabbaṇ na rahassakaṇ).

Rahāyati [Denom. fr. rahas; *not* corresponding to Sk. rahayati, C. of rahati to cause to leave] to be lonely, to wish to be alone M II.119.

Rahita [pp. of **rah**] 1. lonely, forsaken Th 2, 373 (gantum icchasi rahitaṇ bhiṇsanakaṇ mahāvanaṇ). — 2. deprived of, without (-°) J III.369 (buddhiyā rahitā sattā); DA I.36 (avaṇṇa°); PvA 63 (bhoga°), 67 (ācāra°), 77 (gandha°). *Note.* samantarahita is to be divided as **sam-antarahita**.

Rāga [cp. Sk. rāga, fr. **raj**: see rajati] 1. colour, hue; colouring, dye Vin II.107 (anga° "rougeing" the body: bhikkhū angarāgaṇ karonti); ThA 78; SnA 315 (nānā-vidha°) — 2 (as t. t. in philosophy & ethics) excitement, passion; seldom by itself, mostly in combⁿ with dosa, & moha, as the three fundamental blemishes of character: *passion* or lust (uncontrolled excitement), *ill-will* (anger) and *infatuation* (bewilderment); see dosa² & moha; cp. sarāga. — These three again appear in manifold combⁿˢ with similar terms, all giving var. shades of the "craving for existence" or "lust of life" (taṇhā etc.), or all that which is an obstacle to **nibbāna**. Therefore the giving up of rāga is one of the steps towards attaining the desired goal of emancipation (vimutti). — Some of the combⁿˢ are e. g. the 3 (r. d. m.)+kilesa; +kodha; very often fourfold r. d. m. with māna, these again with diṭṭhi: see in full Nd² s. v. rāga (p. 237), cp. below ussada. — Of the many passages illustrating the contrast **rāga>nibbāna** the foll. may be mentioned: chandarāga vinodanaṇ nibbānapadaṇ accutaṇ Sn 1086; yo rāgakkhayo (etc.): idaṇ vuccati amataṇ S v.8; yo rāgakkhayo (etc.): idaṇ vuccati nibbānaṇ S IV.251; ye 'dha pajahanti kāmarāgaṇ bhavararāganu-sayañ ca pahāya . . . parinibbāna-gatā Vv 53²⁴; kusalo jahati pāpakaṇ . . . rāga dosa-moha-kkhayā parinibbuto Ud 85. — Personified, **Rāga** (v. l. Ragā), **Taṇhā** & **Arati** are called the "daughters of Māra" (Māradhītā): Sn 835; DhA III.199; Nd¹ 181. — For further detail of meaning & application see e. g. — (1) with **dosa** & **moha**: D I.79, 156; III.107, 108, 132; S I.184; IV.139, 195, 250, 305; V.84, 357 sq.; M II.138 (rasa° the excitement of taste); A I.52, 156 sq., 230 sq.; II.256; III.169, 451 sq.; IV.144; It 56, 57; Vism 421; VbhA 268, 269 (sa° & vīta°). — (2) in other connection: D III.70, 74, 146, 175, 217, 234 (arūpa°), 249 (cittaṇ pariyādāya tiṭṭhati); S II.231=271 (cittaṇ anuddhaṇseti); III.10; IV.72, 329; V.74 (na rāgaṇ jāneti etc.); A II.149 (tibba-rāga-jātiko rāgajaṇ dukkhaṇ paṭisaṇvedeti); III.233, 371 (kāmesu vīta°); IV.423 (dhamma°); Sn 2, 74, 139, 270=S I.207 (+dosa); Sn 361, 493, 764, 974, 1046; Dh 349 (tibba°= bahala-rāga DhA IV.68); Ps I.80 sq.; II.37 (rūpa°), 95 (id.); Vbh 145 sq. (=taṇhā), 368 (=kiñcana), 390; Tikp 155, 167; DA I.116. — Opp. **virāga**.
-aggi the fire of passion D III.217; S IV.19; It 92 (r. dahati macce ratte kāmesu mucchite; +dosaggi & mohaggi); J I.61 (°imhi nibbute nibbutaṇ nāma hoti). -**ānusaya** latent bias of passion (for=dat.) S IV.205 (the 3 anusayas: rāga°, paṭigha°, avijjā°); It 80 (yo su-bhāya dhātuyā rāgo so padūyati). -**ussada** conceit of lust, one of the 7 ussadas (r. d. m., māna, diṭṭhi, kilesa, kamma) Nd¹ 72. -**kkhaya** the decay (waning) of p. S III.51, 160; IV.142, 250, 261; V.8, 16, 25; VbhA 51 sq. -**carita** one whose habit is passion, of passionate behaviour Miln 92; Vism 105 sq. (in det.), 114 (+dosa°, moha°), 193; KhA 54 (colour of the blood of his heart, cp. Vism 409) -**ṭṭhānīya** founded on passion A I.264; AA 32. -**patha** way of lust, lustfulness, passion, sensuality S IV.70; Sn 370, 476 (with explⁿ "rāgo pi hi duggatīnaṇ pathattā rāgapatho ti vuccati" SnA 410). -**rati** passionate or lustful delight DhA III.112; -**ratta**

affected with passion S I.136; Sn 795 (as °rāgin, cp. Nd^1 100 = kāma-guṇesu ratta).

Rāgin (-°) [fr. rāga] one who shows passion for, possessed of lust, affected with passion Sn 795 (cp. Nd^1 100); S I.136; Vism 193, 194 (with var. characterisations).

Rājaka (adj.) (-°) [rāja+ka, the ending belonging to the whole cpd.] characteristic of the king, king-; in cpds. arājaka without a king J VI.39 (raṭṭhe); sarājaka including the king Tikp 26; f. sarājikā Vin I.209 (parisā). Also in phrase anikkhanta-rājake (loc. abs.) when the king has not gone out Vin IV.160.

Rājañña [fr. rājā, cp. Vedic rājanya] "royalty"; a high courtier, a khattiya (= rājabhogga, cp. Fick, *Sociale Gliederung* 100) D I.103 (Pasenadi rājā . . . uggehi vā rājaniyehi vā kañcid eva mantanaŋ manteyya); DA I.273 (= anabhisittā kumārā, i. e. uncrowned princes); Miln 234; VvA 297 (Pāyāsi r.).

Rājatā (f.) [abstr. fr. rājā] state of being a king, kingship, sovereignty J I.119 (anuttara-dhamma° being a most righteous king).

Rājati [**rāj**, cp. rajati & rañjati] to shine VvA 134 (= vijjotati). Cp. vi°.

Rājā (**Rājan**) [cp. Vedic rājā, n-stem. To root *reg, as in Lat. rego (to lead, di-rect, cp. in meaning Gr. ἡγεμών): see etym. under **uju**. Cp. Oir. rī king, Gallic Catu-rīx battle king, Goth reiks = Ohg. rihhi = rich or Ger. reich. Besides we have ***reig** in Ags. rǣcean = reach; Ger. reichen. — The Dhtp only knows of one root **rāj** in meaning "ditti" i. e. splendour] king, a ruling potentate. The def^n at Vin III.222 is "yo koci rajjaŋ kāreti." The fanciful etym. at D III.93 = Vism 419 is "dhammena pare rañjetī ti rājā" i. e. he gladdens others with his righteousness. — At the latter passage the origin of kingly government is given as the third stage in the constitution of a people, the 2 preceding being mahā-sammata (general consent) and khattiya (the land-aristocrats). — *Cases.* We find 3 systems of cases for the original Sk. forms, viz. the contracted, the diæretic and (in the pl.) a new formation with -ū-. Thus *gen. & dat. sg.* rañño [Sk. rājñaḥ] Vin III.107; IV.157; J II.378; III.5; Vv 74^4; and rājino Sn 299, 415; Th 2, 463; J IV.495; Mhvs 2, 14; *instr. sg.* raññā Vin III.43; J V.444; DhA I.164; PvA 22; VbhA 106; and rājinā [Sk. rajña] Mhvs 6, 2; *acc. sg.* rājānaŋ Vin IV.157; *loc.* raññe PvA 76; *voc.* rāja Sn 422, 423. *pl. nom.* rājāno A I.68; *gen. dat.* raññaŋ [Sk. rājñaŋ] D II.87; Mhvs 18, 32; and rājūnaŋ Vin I.228; Ud 11; J II.104; III.487; SnA 484; PvA 101, 133; *instr.* raññāhi A I.279 rājūhi Ud 41; M II.120; J I.179; III.45; Mhvs 5, 80; 8, 21; and rājubhi D II.258. Cp. Geiger, *P.Gr.* § 92^1. — 1. rājā is a term of sovereignship. The term rājā as used in Buddhist India does not admit of a uniform interpretation and translation. It is primarily an appellative (or title) of a khattiya, and often the two are used promiscuously. Besides, it has a far wider sphere of meaning than we convey by any trsl^n like "king" or even "sovereign," or "prince." We find it used as a designation of "king" in the sense of an elected or successory (crowned) *monarch*, but also in the meaning of a distinguished *nobleman*, or a local *chieftain*, or a *prince* with var. attributes characterizing his position according to special functions. From this we get the foll. scheme: (a) [based on mythological views: the king as representing the deity, cp. deva = king. Note that rājā never takes the place of deva in the meaning king, but that mahārāja is used in voc. equivalent to deva] a world-king, over-lord, a so-called **cakkavatti rājā**. This is an office (as "Universal King") peculiar to the Mahāpurisa or the (mythol.) "Great Man," who may become either the Saviour of men in the religious sense, a Sammā-sambuddha, or a just Ruler of the earth in the worldly sense, a King of Righteousness. These are the 2 gatis of such a being, as described at var. places of the Canon (e. g. Sn p. 106; Sn 1002, 1003; D III.142; A I.76). His power is absolute, and is described in the standard phrase "c. dhammiko dhamma-rājā cāturanto vijitāvī janapadatthāvariya-ppatto satta-ratana-samannāgato," e. g. D III.59. Dhammapāla gives the dignity of a C. as the first "human sovereign powers" (PvA 117). — The four iddhi's of a C. are given (quite crudely) at M III.176: he is beautiful, lives longer than others, is of a healthier constitution than others, he is beloved by the brahmins and householders. Other qualities: how his remains should be treated = D II.141; deserves a thūpa D II.142 sq.; his four qualities D II.145 (the 4 assemblies of khattiyas, brāhmaṇas, gahapatis & samaṇas are pleased with him). See under cakkavatti & ratana. — In a similar sense the term **dhamma-rājā** is used as Ep. of the Buddha Sn 554 (rāj' âham asmi dh-.r. anuttaro); J I.262; and a reflection of the higher sphere is seen in the title of politeness (only used in *voc.*) mahārāja, e. g. Sn 416 (addressed to Bimbisāra) PvA 22 (id.); J VI.515. — (b) [in a larger constitutional state] the crowned (muddhâvasitta) monarch (i. e. khattiya) as the head of the principality or kingdom. The def^n of this (general) rājā at Nd^2 542 is significant of the idea of a king prevalent in early Buddhist times. It is: "khattiyo muddh' âbhisitto vijita-sangāmo nihata-paccāmitto laddh' adhippāyo paripuṇṇa-koṭṭhāgāro," i. e. "a crowned noble, victorious in battle, slaying his foes, fulfilling his desires, having his storehouses full." This king is "the top of men" (mukhaŋ manussānaŋ) Vin I.246 = Sn 568. Cp. D I.7; Sn 46 (raṭṭhaŋ vijitam pahāya); J V.448 and passim. See also below 3, 4 & 6. — In similes: see *J.P.T.S.* 1907, 128; & cp. Vism 152 (r. va saddh' antagato), 336 (wishing to become an artisan). Here belongs the title of the king of the devas (Sakka) "**deva-rājā**," e. g. DhA III.269, 441; PvA 62. — (c) [in an oligarchic sense] member of a kula of khattiyas, e. g. the kumāras of the Sakiyans and Koliyans are all called rājāno of the rājakulānaŋ in J. V.413 sq., or at least the heads of those kulas. Cp. *B. Ind.* p. 19. — (d) [in a smaller, autocratic state] a chieftain, prince, ruler; usually (collectively) as a *group*: rājāno, thus indicating their lesser importance, e. g. A V.22 (kuḍḍa-rājāno rañño cakkavattissa anuyuttā bhavanti: so read for anuyantā); Sn 553 (bhoja° similar to rāja-bhoggā or bhogiyā as given at SnA 453); A II.74 sq. (dhammikā & a°); J IV.495. Similarly at Vin I.228 we find the division into the 3 ranks: mahesakkhā rājāno, majjhimā r., nīcā r. Here also belongs the designation of the 4 **lokapālā** (or Guardians of the World) at cattāro **mahā-rājāno**, the mahā° being added for sake of politeness (cp. Note A on mahā), e. g. A IV.242. See also paṭirājā & cp. below 4 c. — (e) A wider range of meaning is attached to several sub-divisions (with rājā or without): officials and men who occasionally take the place of the king (royal functionaries), but are by public opinion considered almost equal to the king. Here belongs the def^n of what is termed "**rājāno**" (pl. like d) at Vin III.47, viz. rājā, padesa-rājā, maṇḍalikā, antarabhogikā, akkhadassā, mahāmattā, **ye vā pana chejjabhejjaŋ anusāsanti** (i. e. those who have juridical power). See also below 4 b, and °putta, °bhogga [& other cpds.]. — 2. It would fill a separate book, if we were to give a full monograph of kingship in and after the Buddha's time; we therefore content ourselves with a few principal remarks. The office of king was hereditary: kula-santakaŋ rajjaŋ J I.395; II.116; IV.124; but we sometimes read of a king being elected with great pomp: J I.470; PvA 74. He had the political and military power in his hand, also the jurisdiction, although in this he is often represented by the mahāmatta, the *active* head of the state. His 10 duties are mentioned at several places (see below under °dhammā). Others are mentioned e. g. at D I.135, where it is said he gives food and seed-corn to the farmer, capital to the trader, wages to the people in government service. His qualifications are 8 fold (see D I.137): well-born (" gentleman," khattiya), handsome, wealthy, powerful (with his army), a believer, learned, clever, intelligent. — His wealth is proverbial and is characterized in a stock phrase, which is also used of other ranks, like seṭṭhi's & brāhmaṇa's, viz. " aḍḍha mahaddhana mahābhoga pahūta-jātarūpa-rajata pahūta-vitt' ûpakaraṇa pahūta-dhana-dhañña paripuṇṇa-kosa-koṭṭhāgāra," e. g. D I.134. For a late description of a king's quality and distinction see Miln 226, 227. — His disciplinary authority is emphasized;. he spares no tortures in punishing adversaries or malefactors, esp. the cora (see below 4 c). A summary example of these punishments inflicted on criminals is the long passage illustrating dukkha (bodily pain) at Nd^2 304^{III}; cp. M III.163 (here also on a cora). — 3. The king (rājā or khattiya) in the popular opinion, as reflected in language, heads several lists, which have often been taken as enumerating " castes," but which are simply inclusive statements of var. prominent ranks as playing a rôle in the social life of the state, and which were formulated according to diff. occasions. Thus some show a more political, some a more religious aspect. E. g. *khattiya* amacca brāhmaṇa gahapati D I.136; *rājā* brāhmaṇa gahapatika A I.68, where another formula has *khattiya* br. g. A I.66; J I.217; and the foll. with an intermediate " rank " (something like " royalty," " the royal household ") between the king and the brahmins: rājā *rājaputtā* brāhmaṇā gahapatikā negama-jānapadā A II.74 sq.; rājāno *rāja-mahāmattā khattiyā* br., gah., titthiyā D III.44 (trsl^n *Dialogues* too weak " rājas & their officials "); rājā *rājabhogga* br., gah. Vin III.221. — 4. Var. aspects illustrating the position of the king in relation to other prominent groups of the court or populace: (a) rājā & khattiya. All kings *were* khattiyas. The kh. is a noble κατ' ἐξοχήν (cp. Gr. ἡγεμών) as seen fr. def^n jāti-khattiya at SnA 453 and var. contexts. Already in the Rig Veda the kṣatriya is a person belonging to a *royal* family (RV x.109, 3), and rājanya is an Ep. of kṣatriya (see Zimmer, *Altindisches Leben* 213). —rājā khattiyo muddhâvassito " a crowned king " D I.69; III.61 sq.; Vin IV.160; A I.106 sq.; II.207 (contrasted with brāhmaṇa mahāsāla); III.299 (if lazy, he is not liked by the people); M III.172 sq. (how he becomes a cakkavatti through the appearance of the cakka-ratana). — Without muddhâvasitta: rājāno khattiyā Dh 294 = Nett 165. Cp. khattiyā bhoja-rājāno the khattiyas, the (noble or lesser?) kings (as followers of the cakkavatti) Sn 553 (see bhoja). At J VI.515. rājāno corresponds directly to khattiyā on p. 517 (saṭṭhisahassa°); cp. expression khattiya-kula J I.217 as equivalent to rāja-kula. (b) rājā & mahāmatta. The latter occupies the position of " Premier," but is a rank equal to the king, hence often called rājā himself: Vin III.47 where styled " akkhadassa mahāmatta." Otherwise he is always termed rāja-mahāmatta " royal minister," or " H.R.H. the Premier," e. g. Vin I.172; A I.279; Vin I.228 (also as Magadha-mahāmatta), and called himself a *khattiya* D III 44. — (c) rājā & cora. A prominent figure in the affairs of State is the " robber-chief " (mahā-cora). The contrast-pair rajāno (so always pl.) & cora is very frequent, and in this connection we have to think of rājāno as either smaller kings, knights or royals (royalists), i. e. officers of the kings or " the king's Guards." Thus at J III.34 the C. expl^n as rāja-purisā. It is here used as a term of warning or frightening " get up, robber, so that the kings (alias ' policeman ') won't catch you ": uṭṭhehi cora mā taŋ gahesuŋ rājāno. Other passages are e. g.: D I.7 (rāja-kathā & cora-kathā) = Vin I.188; M III.163 (rājāno coraŋ āgucāriŋ gahetvā); A I.68, 154; It 89 (rāj' âbhinīta + cor°); & in sequence rājāno corā dhuttā (as being dangerous to the bhikkhus) at Vin I.150, 161. — 5. On the question of kingship in Ancient India see Zimmer, *Altind. Leben* pp. 162-175, 212 sq.; Macdonell & Keith, *Vedic Index* II.210 sq.; Fick, *Soc. Gl.* 63-90; Foy, *Die Königl. Gewalt nach den altind. Rechtsbüchern* (Leipzig 1895); Rh. Davids, *Buddhist India* pp. 1-16; Hopkins, E. W., *The social and military position of the ruling caste in A. I.* in *J.A.O.S.* 13, 179 sq.; Banerjea, *Public Administration* in A. I. 1916, pp. 63-93. — 6. Kings mentioned by name [a very limited & casual list only, for detailed refs. see Dict'y of Names]: Ajātasattu; Udena (DhA I.185); Okkāka; Dīghī (of Kosala; Vin I.342); Parantapa (of Kosambī; DhA I.164;) Pasenadi (of Kosala; D I.87,103; Vin IV.112, 157); Bimbisāra (of Magadha; Vin IV.116 sq.; Sn 419); Bhaddiya; etc. — 7. (fig.) king as sign of distinction (" princeps "), as the *lion* is called rājā migānaŋ Sn 72; Vism 650; the *Himavant* is pabbata-rājā A I.152; III.44; and Gotama's horse *Kanthaka* is called assa-rājā J I.62 = VvA 314. — *Note*. The comp^n form of rājā is rāja°.

-âgāra a king's (garden- or pleasure-) house D I.7 (°ka); DA I.42. -anga royal mark, characteristic or qualification; king's property Vin I.219 (rājangaŋ hatthī: the elephants belong to the king), cp. A I.244: assājāniyo rañño angan t' eva sankhaŋ gacchati is called king's property. -angana royal court PvA 74. -āṇatti king's permission Tikp 26 (in simile). -āṇā (1) the king's command J III.180; cp. PvA 217 " rañño āṇā "; (2) the king's fine or punishment, i. e. a punishment inflicted by the king (cp. Fick, *Soc. Gl.* 74), synonymous with rāja-daṇḍa: J I.369, 433 (rājāṇaŋ karoti to inflict); II.197; III.18, 232, 351; IV.42; VI.18; PvA 242. -ânubhāva king's power, majesty, authority, pomp J IV.247; PvA 279. -antepura the royal harem A V.81, 82 (the 10 risks which a bhikkhu is running when visiting it for alms). -âbhinīta brought by a king It 89 (+cor-âbhinīta). -âbhirājā " king of kings " Sn 553; DhsA 20. -âmacca royal minister J V.444 (°majjhe). -āyatana N. of a tree: " Kingstead tree," the royal tree (as residence of a king of fairies), Buchanania latifolia Vin I.3 sq. (where MVastu III.303 reads kṣīrikā, i. e. milk-giving tree); J I.80; IV.361 sq.; DhsA 35; VbhA 433 (°cetiya). -iddhi royal power PvA 279. -isi a royal seer, a king who gives up his throne & becomes an ascetic (cp. Sk. rājarṣi, freq. in Mhbhārata & Rāmāyana) Th 1, 1127 (read rāja-d-isi); It 21 (rājīsayo, with var vv. ll. not quite the same meaning); J VI.116, 124, 127, 518; DhA IV.29. Kern, *Toev.* s. v. proposes reading rājīsi. -upaṭṭhāna attendance on the king, royal audience Vin I.269; J I.269, 349; III.119, 299; IV.63. -ûpabhoga fit for use by the king Miln 252. -uyyāna royal garden or pleasure ground J III.143; Mhvs 15, 2. -orodhā a lady from the king's harem, a royal concubine Vin IV.261. -kakudha-bhaṇḍa an ensign of royalty (5: khagga, chatta, uṇhīsa, pādukā, vālavījanī) DhA I.356. See under kakudha. -kathā talk about kings (as tiracchānakathā in disgrace), comb^d with corakathā (see above 4 c) D I.7; III.36, 54; Vin I.188. -kammika a royal official, one employed by the king J I.439; IV.169. -kuṭumba the king's property J I.439. -kuṇḍa a " crook of a king " DhA III.56. -kumāra a (royal) prince (cp. khattiya-kumāra) Vin I.269; J III.122; VbhA 196 (in comparison). -kumbhakāra a " royal potter," i. e. a potter being " purveyor to the king " J V.290. -kula the king's court or palace A I.128; II.205; Vin IV.265; J II.301; DhA II.44, 46; III.124. -khādāya phuṭṭha at Sn 831 is according to Kern, *Toev.* to be read as rajakkhatāya ph. (fr. rajakkha). The old Niddesa, however, reads °khādāya & expl^{ns} the word (Nd^1 171) by rājabhojanīyena, i. e. the king's food, which is alright without being changed. -guṇa " virtue of a king " M I.446 (trick of a circus horse;

+rāja-vaŋsa). -daṇḍa punishment ordered by the king PvA 216, 217. -dāya a royal gift D I.127; DA I.246. -dūta king's messenger Sn 411, 412; in meaning of "message," i. e. calling somebody to court, summons at J II.101, 305. -dhamma "king's rule," i. e. rule of governing, norm of kingship; usually given as a set of 10, which are enum^d at J III.274 as "dāna, sīla, pariccāga, ajjava, maddava, tapo, akkodha, avihiŋsā, khanti, avirodhana," i. e. alms-giving, morality, liberality, straightness, gentleness, self-restriction, non-anger, non-hurtfulness, forbearance, non-opposition. These are referred to as *dasa rājadhammā* at J I.260, 399; II.400; III.320; V.119, 378; usually in phrase "dasa rāja-dhamme akopetvā dhammena rajjan kāresi": he ruled in righteousness, not shaking the tenfold code of the king. Another set of 3 are mentioned at J V.112, viz. "vitathaŋ kodhaŋ hāsaŋ nivāraye" (expl^d as giving up musāvāda, kodha & adhamma-hāsa). -dhānī a royal city (usually comb^d with gāma & nigama) A I.159; II.33; III.108; Vin III.89; J V.453; Pv 13^{18}. **-dhītā** king's daughter, princess J I.207; PvA 74. **-nivesana** the king's abode, i. e. palace DhA IV.92. **-parisā** royal assembly Vin II.296. -pīla (?) DhA I.323. **-putta** lit. "king's son," prince, one belonging to the royal clan (cp. similarly kulaputta), one of royal descent, Rājput Sn 455; Miln 331; VbhA 312, 319 (in simile); PvA 20. f. °puttī princess J IV.108; V.94. **-purisa** "king's man," only in pl. °purisā the men of the king, those in the king's service (as soldiers, body-guard, policeman etc.) J III.34; VbhA 80 (°ânubandha-corā), 109. **-porisa** (m. & nt.) servant of the king, collectively: king's service, those who devote themselves to Govt. service D I.135; M I.85=Nd^2 199; A IV.281, 286. See also porisa. **-bali** royal tax J I.354. **-bhaṭa** king's hireling or soldier Vin I.74, 88; SnA 38 (in simile) **-bhaya** fear of the king('s punishment) Vism 121. **-bhāga** the king's share J II.378. **-bhogga** 1. royal, in the service of the king, in foll. phrases: rāja-bhoggaŋ raññā dinnaŋ rāja-dāyaŋ brahma-deyyaŋ D I.87, of a flourishing place. *Dial.* I.108 trsl^s "with power over it as if he were king," and expl^s with: "where the king has proprietary rights." The C. rather unmeaningly expl^s as "rāja-laddha" (DA I.245). The BSk. has a curious version of this phrase: "rājñā-*agni*-dattena brahmadeyyaŋ dattaŋ" (given by the king in the place of agni?) Divy 620. — Further at Vin III.221 in sequence rājā r-bhogga, brāhmaṇa, gahapatika, where the C. expl^s (on p. 222) as "yo koci rañño bhatta-vetan' āhāro." (We should be inclined to take this as No. 2.) — Thirdly, in stock phrase "rājâraha rājabhogga rañño angan t' eva sankhaŋ gacchati," i. e. worthy of a king, imperial, he justifies the royal qualification, said of a thoroughbred horse at A I.244= II.113; of a soldier (yodh' ājīva) at A I.284; of an elephant at J II.370 (where it is expl^d as "rāja paribhoga"). Also as "royal possessions" in general at DhA I.312. 13. — Fick, *Soc. Gl.* 99 does not help much, he takes it as "king's official." — 2. royal, of royal power, one entitled to the throne. Either as bhogga, bhogiya (SnA 453) or (khattiyā) bhoja-rājāno (Sn 553). Thus at Vin III.221, where it takes the place of the usual khattiya "royal noble" & Sn 553, where it is comb^d (as bhoja rājano) *with* khattiyā. See also bhoja & cp. (antara) bhogika and rājañña. **-mahāmatta** king's prime minister (see above 4 b, to which add:) D III.44; A I.154, 252, 279; III.128; VbhA 312 (simile of 2), 340. **-mālakāra** royal gardener J V.292. **-muddā** the royal seal DhA I.21. **-muddikā** id. SnA 577. **-ratha** the king's chariot DhA III.122. **-rukkha** "royal tree," Cathartocarpus fistula VvA 43. **-vara** the best king, famous king Vv 32^1 (=Sakka VvA 134). **-vallabha** the king's favourite, or overseer Mhvs 37, 10; VbhA 501 (in simile). **-vibhūti** royal splendour or dignity PvA 216, 279. **-haŋsa** "royal swan," a sort of swan or flamingo Vism 650 (suvaṇṇa°, in simile).

Rāji[1] [cp. Sk. rāji] a streak, line, row Sn p. 107 (nīla-vana° =dark line of trees, expl^d as nīla-vana rukkha-panti SnA 451); Vv 64^4 (nabhyo sata-rāji-cittita "coloured with 100 streaks"; VvA=lekhā); 64^6 (veḷuriya°); **pabbata°** a mountain range J II.417; **dīgha°** (adj.) of long lineage PvA 68; **dvangula°** a band 2 inches broad Dāvs V.49; **roma°** a row of hair (on the body) J V.430.

Rāji[2] [fr. rāga ?] dissension, quarrel, in phrase **sangha°** (+sanghabheda) Vin II.203 (quoted at VbhA 428); IV.217.

Rājikā (f.) [cp. Sk. rājikā] a certain (gold) weight (a seed-corn of Sinapis ramosa) Th 1, 97=862 (kaŋsa sata° 100 mustard seeds in weight, i. e. very costly); J VI.510 (kaŋse sovaṇṇe satarājike).

Rājita: see **vi°**.

Rājin (adj.) [fr. rāji] having streaks or stripes, in **ud-dhagga°** having prominent stripes (of a lion) J IV.345.

Rājimant (adj.) [fr. rāji^1] having streaks or stripes; f. rājimatī shining, radiant Vv 32^1 (v. l. rājāputti), expl^d at VvA 134 as follows: "rājati vijjotatī ti rājī: rājī ti matā paññātā rājimatī" (thus connecting °mant with **man**).

Rājula [cp. Sk. rājila] a certain reptile Abhp 651.

Rāti [Sk. **rā** to give, bestow; given at Dhtp 369 & Dhtm 597 in meaning "ādāne," with doublet **lā**] to take up: no refs.

Rādheti[1] [Caus. of **rādh** to succeed, rādhyate. The root is given at Dhtp 420 & Dhtm 656 in meaning "saŋsid-dhiyaŋ," i. e. of success. See etym. at Walde, *Lat. Wtb.* s. v. reor.] to please: see cpds. abhi° apa°, ā°, vi°.

Rādheti[2] [**rādh**? Given at Dhtp 424 & Dhtm 656 in meaning "hiŋsāyaŋ," i. e. of hurting] no refs.

Rāma [fr. **ram**; cp. Vedic rāma] pleasure, sport, amusement; **°kara** having pleasure, sporting, making love J V.448.

Rāmaṇeyyaka (adj. nt.) [orig. grd. of rāmeti, **ram**, cp. Sk. rāmaṇīya. On e for ī see Geiger, *P.Gr.* § 10] pleasant, agreeable, lovely A I.35, 37; Dh 98 (=ramaṇīya DhA III.195); nt. delightfulness, lovely scenery M I.365 (four seen in a dream: ārāma°, vana°, bhūmi° pokkharaṇī°).

Rāva [fr. ravati, cp. rava] crying, howling; shout, noise J I.162 (baddha° the cry of one who is caught); IV.415 (id.); VI.475 (of the cries of animals, known to an expert); Miln 254 (bherava-rāvaŋ abhiravati); Mhvs 10, 69 (mahā-rāvaŋ arāvi).

Rāsi [Vedic rāśi] 1. heap, quantity, mass It 17; usually -°, e. g. **angāra°** heap of cinders J I.107; **kaṇikāra-puppha°** of k. flowers VvA 65; **kahāpaṇa°** of money PvA 162; **tila°** of seeds VvA 54; **dhañña°** of corn A IV.163, 170; etc. —**rāsiŋ karoti** to make a heap, to pile up Mhvs 29, 28; VvA 157. — 2. (store of) wealth, riches; in **°agga-dāna** gift of the best treasures (of one's property), one of the 5 "donations of the best," viz. khett°, rās°, koṭṭh°, kumbhi°, bhojan°: SnA 270. See also **°vaḍḍhaka**. — 3. a sign of the Zodiac (the 12, as given at Abhp 61 are: mesa, usabha, methuna, kakkaṭa, sīha, kaññā, tulā, vicchikā, dhanu, makara, kumbha, mīna; or the ram, bull, twins, crab, lion, virgin, balance, scorpion, bow, capricorn, waterpot, fish) PvA 198. — 4. (fig.) at t. t. in logic: group, aggregate, category, congery; freq. in *Abhidhamma*-literature, where 3 "accumulations" are spoken of, viz. micchatta-niyato rāsi, sammatta-niyato r., aniyato r. or "wrong doing entailing immutable evil results, that of well-doing entailing immutable good results, and that of everything not so determined" (*Dialogues* III.210); D III.217; Kvu 611; Nett 96; cp. *Kvu trsl.* 356 *Dhs trsl.* 26, 253. In the 5 factors of individuality (body and mind) khandhā are explained as meaning rāsi, e. g. Asl. 141; *B. Psy.* 42. In other connections: S V.146 (kusala°, akusala°), 186; A III.65 (akusala°); Tikp 45. — *Note.* In BSk. we find only 2 of the 3 categories mentioned at MVastu I.175, viz. mithyātva-niyato & aniyato rāśih.

-vaḍḍhaka one who increases wealth, i. e. a treasurer D I.61 (trslⁿ: "increases the king's wealth"; DA I.170 simply defines "dhañña-rāsiñ ca dhana-rāsiñ ca vaḍḍheti ti r. v."); J I.2; Mhbv 78.

Rāsika (nt.) [fr. rāsi] revenue, fisc D I.135.

Rāhaseyyaka (adj.) [rahas+seyya+ka or rāha (for rahā°)+seyyaka] "having one's bed in loneliness," living in seclusion or secrecy, in manussa° "fit to lie undisturbed by men" Vin I.39 (+paṭisallāna-sāruppa); M II.118.

Rāhu [Vedic rāhu] N. of an Asura: see under Proper Names. —rāhumukha "mouth of Rāhu," designation of a certain punishment for criminals (M I.87; III.164; Nd¹ 154 (in list of tortures)=Nd² 604=Miln 197.

Riṇāti see under raya.

Riñcati [ric, in Vedic & Sk. riṇakti; cp. Av. irinaxti to leave; Gr. λείπω id., λοιπός left; Lat. linquo id.; Goth. leiḫwan=Ohg. līhan to lend; Ags lǣn=loan, cp. E. leave etc. — The defⁿ of the root at Dhtp is given in two forms, viz. **ric** as "virecane" (No. 396; cp. Dhtm 517 "kharaṇe," i. e. flowing; 610 "recane"), and **riñc** as "riñcane" (No. 44)] to leave, abandon, leave behind, give up, neglect Vin I.190 (also fut. riñcissati); M I.155 (riñcissati), 403; S IV.206; A III.86 sq., 108 sq., 343 sq., 366 sq., 437; Th 1, 1052; Sn 156; Miln 419; J V.403. — ppr. med. with neg.: **ariñcamāna** Sn 69; ger. riñcitvā (for Sk. riktvā) Th 2, 93. — pp. ritta. — Pass. riccati [Sk. ricyate] to be left: see ati°.

Riñcana (nt.) [fr. **riñc**] leaving behind, giving up Dhtp 44.

Ritta [pp. of riñcati; cp. atireka] devoid, empty, free, rid (of) M I.207 (+tuccha), 414; Vin I.157=II.216; Sn 823 (emancipated: ritto muni=vivitta etc. Nd¹ 158), 844 (opp. to aritta); Th 2, 265 (see rindi); J I.29 (v. 222); III.492; Miln 383.

-assāda finding one's taste in empty things A I.280 (+bāhir-assāda. Kern, *Toev.* s. v. reads rittāsa and trslˢ "impure (of food)," not according to the sense at all). -āsana an empty seat Sn 963 (explᵈ at Nd¹ 481 as "opportunity for sitting down which is free from unbefitting sights"). -pesuṇa free fr. slander Sn 941 (explᵈ at Nd¹ 422: "yassa pesuññaŋ pahīnaŋ" etc.). -muṭṭhi an empty fist (°sadisa: comparing someone as regards ignorance) SnA 306=DhA IV.38. -hattha (adj.) empty-handed J V.46; Sdhp 309.

Rittaka (adj.) [ritta+ka] empty, void, without reality Th 1, 41; 2, 394 (=tucchaka anto-sāra-rahita ThA 258); Pv III.6⁶ (of a river=tuccha PvA 202); PvA 139 (=suñña, virahita). Usually in combⁿ with **tucchaka** as a standing phrase denoting absolute emptiness & worthlessness, e. g. at D I.240; M I.329; S III.141.

Rindī at Th 2, 265 is doubtful. The T. reading is "te rindī va lambante 'nodaka,'" said of breasts hanging down in old age. The C. compares them with leather water bottles without water (udaka-bhastā viya). We have to read either with Morris, *J.P.T.S.* 1884, 94 "rittī va" (=rittā iva), "as it were, empty," or (preferably) with ThA 212 "therī ti va" ("like an old woman"). The trslⁿ (*Sisters*, p. 124) takes the C. explⁿ of *udaka-bhastā* as equivalent to T. reading *rindi*, in saying "shrunken as skins without water"; but rindī is altogether doubtful & it is better to read therī which is according to the context. We find the same meaning of therī ("old woman") at Pv II.1⁶.

Rissati [Vedic **riṣ**, riṣyati] to be hurt, to suffer harm M I.85 (ḍaŋsa-makasa-vāt' ātapa-siriŋsapa-samphassehi rissamāno; where Nd² 199 in same passage reads samphassamāna).

Ruka in cpd. aḍḍha° at Vin II.134, referring to the shape of a beard, is doubtful. The v. l. is "**duka**." Could it correspond to Vedic **rukma** (a certain ornament worn on the chest)?

Rukkha [Vedic vṛkṣa. See Geiger, *P.Gr.* § 13, with note. Pischel, *Prk. Gr.* § 320 puts rukkha to Sk. **rukṣa** (shining which as Pischel, following Roth, says has also the meaning "tree" in Ṛgveda). The Prk. form is rukkha. Cp. Wackernagel, *Altind. Gr.* I, § 184 b. We find a by-form **rakkha** at J III.144. Cp. *Brethren*, pp. 185, 416, where the Bⁿ MS. has rukkha kathā the meaning being rakkha°] a tree. In the rukkha-mūlik' aṅga (see below) Bdhgh at Vism 74 gives a list of trees which are not to be selected for the practice of "living at the root of a tree." These are sīmantarika-rukkha, cetiya°, niyyāsa°, phala°, vagguli°, susira°, vihāra-majjhe ṭhita°, or a tree standing right on the border, a sacred tree, a resinous tree, a fruit t., a tree on which bats live, a hollow tree, a tree growing in the middle of a monastery. The only one which is to be chosen is a tree "vihāra-paccante ṭhita," or one standing on the outskirt of the Vihāra. He then gives further advice as to the condition of the tree. — Various kinds of trees are given in the defⁿ of r. at Vism 183, viz. assattha, nigrodha, kacchaka, kapitthaka; ucca, nīca, khuddaka, mahanto; kāḷa, seta. — A very complete list of trees mentioned in the Saŋyutta Nikāya is to be found in the Index to that Nikāya (vol. vi. p. 84, 85). On rukkha in similes see *J.P.T.S.* 1907, pp. 128-130. — See also the foll. refs.: A I.137; II.109, 207; III.19, 200, 360; IV.99, 336; V.4 sq., 314 sq.; Sn 603, 712; J I.35 (nāga°); Vism 688 (in simile: mahārukkhe yāva kapp' âvasānā bīja-paramparāya rukkha-paveṇiŋ santāyamāne ṭhite); VbhA 165=Vism 555 (rukkha phalita); VbhA 196 (in compⁿ: jātassa avassaŋ jarā-maraṇaŋ, uppannassa rukkhassa patanaŋ viya), 334 sq. (as garu-bhaṇḍa); SnA 5 ("pathavi-ras' ādim iva rukkhe": with same simile as at Vism 688, with reading *kappâvasānaŋ* and *santānente*); DhA III.207 (amba°); VvA 43 (rāja°), 198 (amba°); DhA IV.120 (dīpa°); PvA 43.

-antara the inside of a tree PvA 63. -koṭṭaka (-sakuṇa) the wood-pecker J III.327 (=java sakuṇa). -gahana tree-thicket or entanglement A I.154 (so for °gahaṇa). -devatā a tree spirit, dryad, a yakkha inhabiting a tree (rukkhe adhivatthā d. Vin IV.34; J II.385; kakudhe adhivatthā d. Vin I.28) J I.168, 322; II.405, 438 sq. (eraṇḍa°), 445; III.23; IV.308 (vana-jeṭṭhaka-rukkhe nibbatta-devatā); DhA II.16; PvA 5 (in a Nigrodha tree), 43 (in the Vindhya forest). — They live in a Nigrodha tree at the entrance of the village (J I.169), where they receive offerings at the foot of the tree (cp. IV.474), and occasionally one threatens them with discontinuance of the offerings if they do not fulfil one's request. The trees are their **vimānas** (J I.328, 442; IV.154), occasionally they live in hollow trees (J I.405; III.343) or in tree tops (J I.423). They have to rely on the food given to them (ibid.); for which they help the people (J III.24; V.511). They assume various forms when they appear to the people (J I.423; II.357, 439; III.23); they also have children (Vin IV.34; J I.442). -paveṇi lineage of the tree Vism 688. -pāṇikā a wooden spoon Vism 124 (opp. to pāsāṇa°). -mūla the foot of a tree (taken as a dwelling by the ascetics for meditation: D I.71, where several such lonely places are recommended, as araññа, r-m., pabbata, kandara, etc. — DA I.209 specifies as "yaŋ kiñci sanda-cchāyaŋ vivittaŋ rukkha-mūlaŋ"); A II.38; IV.139, 392; S I.199 (°gahana); It 102; Sn 708, 958; Nd^1 466; Pug 68; PvA 100 (v. l. sukkha-nadī), 137 (Gaṇḍamba°, with ref. to the Buddha). -°*gata* one who undertakes living at the foot of a tree (as an ascetic) A III.353; V.109 sq., 207, 323 sq.; Pug 68. -°*senāsana* having one's bed & seat at the foot of a tree for meditative practices as a recluse Vin I.58 (as one of the 4 *nissayas*: piṇḍiy' ālopa-bhojana, paŋsukūla-cīvara, r.-m. s., pūti-mutta bhesajja), 96 (id.); A IV.231. -mūlika (a) one who lives at the foot of a tree, an open air recluse M I.282; III.41; A III.219; J IV.8 (āraññaka, paṇṇasālaŋ akatvā r., abbhokāsika); (b) belonging to the practice of a recluse living under a tree "tree rootman's practice" (*Vism trsl*^{n} 84); as °*anga* one of the (13) dhutanga-practices; i. e. practices for a scrupulous way of living Vism 59, 74, 75 (mentioned between the *āraññik'* anga & the *abbhokāsik'*-anga). -mūlikatta the practice of living (alone) under a tree M III.41 (mentioned with paŋsukūlikatta & piṇḍapātikatta); A III.109 (id.). -sunakha "tree dog," a cert. animal J VI.538 (C. in expl^n of naḷa-sannibha "reed-coloured"). -susira a hollow tree PvA 62.

Ruca (-rukkha) & **Rucā** (f.) [fr. **ruc**] N. of a plant, or tree, alias "mukkhaka" (read mokkhaka) "principal" J I.441, 443 (gloss mangala-rukkha).

Rucaka (nt.) [cp. Sk. rucaka a golden ornament] (gold) sand Vv 35^1; VvA 160 (=suvaṇṇa-vālikā).

Ruci (f.) [fr. **ruc**, cp. Vedic ruc (f.) light, Classic Sk. ruci in meaning "pleasure"] 1. splendour, light, brightness Sn 548 (su° very splendid; SnA 453=sundara-sarīrappabha). — 2. inclination liking, pleasure PvA 59 (°ŋ uppādeti to find pleasure, to be satisfied). —**aruci** aversion, dislike Th 2, 472. —**ruci** object of pleasure J V.371. —**ruciyā** (abl.) in the pleasure (of), by the liking (of) (cp. No. 3), in phrases **attano ruciyā** (attano citta-ruciyā: so read for °ruciyaŋ!); as one pleases, by one's own free will, ad lib. J I.106; IV.281; PvA 59; parassa r. pavattati to live by the pleasure (gratiâ) of somebody else, i. e. to be dependent on others DA I.212. —**yathā ruciŋ** according to liking or satisfaction, fully, amply Mhvs 4, 43; 5, 230; PvA 88, 126, 242. — 3. In dogmatic language used in the sense of "will" or "influence" in comb^n diṭṭhi, khanti, ruci one's views, indulgence & pleasure (=will), i. e. one's intellectual, emotional & volitional sphere, e. g. Vin I.70; Sn 781 (without khanti, but see def^n at Nd^1 65); also with saddhā, anussavo, ākāraparivitakke, diṭṭhinijjhānakhanti M II.170, 218; 234; contrasted with dhamma D III.40; Vbh 245 (in def^n of "idha": cp. same at Ps I.176 and Nd^2 145), 325, 328. **aññatra ruciyā** under the influence of someone else's will S II.115; IV.138. See also bhāva 2^a.

Rucika (-°) (adj.) [fr. ruci 3] belonging to the pleasure (of); only in phrase **añña°** being dependent on someone else's will or under another's influence, together with **añña-diṭṭhika** and **añña-khantika** characterizing the various sides of personality (see ruci 3) with ref. to one's intellect, feeling & will D I.187=M I.487. Rhys Davids (*Dial.* I.254) trsl^s: "holding different views, other things approving themselves to you, setting diff. aims before yourself"; thus differing in interpretation of añña, taking it subjectively. Neumann (*Majjhima Übs.* II.250) quite wrongly: "ohne Deutung, ohne Geduld, ohne Hingabe" (without explanation, patience, devotion).

Rucira (adj.) [fr. **ruc**, cp. Sk. rucira] brilliant, beautiful, pleasant, agreeable Pv I.10^9 (=ramaṇīya dassanīya PvA 51); J I.207; V.299; Vv 40^2 (so read for rurira); Mhvs 11, 11; 18, 68; Dāvs IV.29; Miln 2, 398; DhA I.383 (=sobhana); VvA 12; PvA 156 (=vaggu).

Ruccati [*rucyati Med. of **ruc**: see rocati. Same in Prk. — Originally Caus. formation like Epic Sk. rocyate for rocayate] to find delight or pleasure in (loc.), to please, to indulge in, set one's mind on Sn 565 (etañ ce r. bhoto buddha-sāsanaŋ); with khamati to be pleased and to approve of, M II.132; often used by Bdhgh in C. style: yathā r. tathā paṭhitabbaŋ KhA 78; "yaŋ r. taŋ gahetabbaŋ SnA 23, 43, 136, 378" "to take, whichever one pleases" (in giving the choice of 2 readings or interpretations). — ger. **ruccitvā** VvA 282 (r. pūresi "to find thorough delight in," expl^n for abhirocesi). — pret. 1st pl. **ruccādimhase** Pv I.11^8 (=ruccāmaruciŋ uppādema, taŋ attano ruciyā pivissāmā ti attho PvA 59). — Prohibitive **mā rucci** (pl. **mā rucittha**) as an entreaty not to pursue an aim (=please do not do that, please don't) Vin II.198 (alaŋ Devadatta mā te rucci sangha-bhedo); DhA I.13 (mā vo āvuso evaŋ ruccittha).

Ruccana (& ā° f.) (nt.) [fr. ruccati] choice, pleasure DhA I.387 (tava °ṭṭhāne according to your own liking); DA I.106 (°ā).

Ruccanaka (adj.) [fr. ruccana, cp. Sk. rucya] pleasing, satisfying; nt. satisfaction J I.211 (°maccha the fish you like); II.182 (tava °ŋ karosi you do whatever you like). a° unpleasant, distasteful DhA I.251 (attano aruccanakaŋ kiñci kammaŋ adisvā).

Rujaka [fr. **ruj** ?] a lute-player J VI.51, 52, given by Kern, *Toev.* s. v. as conjecture (vīṇaŋ) va rujaka for **virujaka**. The conjecture is based on C. reading "rujaka=vīṇāvādaka."

Rujati [**ruj**, representing an Idg. ***leug**, as in Gr. λευγαλέος, λυγρός sad, awful; Lat. lugeo to mourn; Lith. lúžti to break; German lücke, loch etc. — A specific Pāli l-form is lujjati. A der. fr. **ruj** is roga illness. — The Dhtp (469) defines **ruj** by "bhanga" i. e. breaking] to break, crush; lit. to (cause) pain, to afflict, hurt (trs. & intrs.) J I.7 (pādā rujanti), 396 (pādā me rujanti my feet ache); IV.208 (khandhena rujantena with hurting back); VI.3 (ūrū rujanti); Mhvs 10, 15 (pādā me r.); Miln 26 (pādā r.); DhA I.10, 21 (akkhīni me rujiṇsu); II.3. — fut. rucchiti [cp. Sk. rokṣyate] J VI.80 (v. l. B.B. rujjati; C. takes wrongly as "rodissati," of rodati). — pp. lugga. — Cp. lujjati & comb^{ns}.

Rujana (nt.) [fr. **ruj**, cp. rujā] hurting, feeling pain J II.437 (roga=rujana-sabhāvattaŋ); J IV.147 (yāva piṭṭhiyā rujana-ppamāṇaŋ until his back ached).

Rujanaka (adj.) [fr. rujana] aching, hurting DhA IV.69 (anguli).

Rujā (f.) [fr. **ruj**, see rujati; cp. Sk. rujā] disease, pain Miln 172 (rujaŋ na karoti); Vism 69; DhA IV.163 (accha° a bad pain).

Rujjhati [Pass. of rundhati] to be broken up, to be destroyed J III.181 (pāṇā rujjhanti; C. expl^s by nirujjhati). Cp. **upa°**, **vi°**.

Ruṭṭha [pp. of **ruṣ**; Sk. ruṣṭa] vexed, cross, enraged J IV.358 (opp. to tuṭṭha v. l. atuṭṭha) V.211 (gloss kuddha); Dāvs III.37.

Ruṭhati see luṭhati & cp. rudda.

Ruṇ a sound-particle, denoting a heavy fall, something like "thud" J I.418.

Ruṇṇa & **Roṇṇa** [pp. of rudati for Sk. rudita, after analogy of other roots in -d, as **tud**>tunna, **pad**>panna, **nud**>nunna. The BSk. forms are both ruṇḍa (MVastu

II.218, 224) and ruṇṇa (MVastu III.116); Prk. ruṇṇa (Pischel § 566). See rudati & cp. āruṇṇa] 1. (pp.) crying, in combⁿ ruṇṇa-mukha with tearful face J VI.525 (C. rudam°); Miln 148. — 2. (nt.) weeping, crying, lamentation Th 1, 554; A I.261; Sn 584 (+soka); Pv I.4[3]; Milo 357. As roṇṇa at A IV.197, 223; Th 1, 555; J III.166.

Ruta (nt.) [pp. of ravati: see rava & ravati] noise, sound-(ing); cry, singing Th 1, 1103; J I.207 (T. reading ruda is expl[d] in C. as ruta with °da for °ta: ta-kārassa da-kāro kato); III.276 (sabba-ruta-jānana-manta: spell of knowing all animal-sounds; T. reads rūta; cp. sabba-rāva-jānana J III.415); VI.475 (rudaññu=ruta-jña C.; same meaning); Miln 178 (sakuṇa-ruta-ravita); VvA (karavīka°).

Rutta in du° & su° at DhsA 396 is to be read as dur- and su(r)-utta (see utta).

Ruda stands for ruta (cry) at 2 Jātaka passages, viz. J I.207; VI.475 (ruda-ññu knowing the cries of all animals, expl[d] as "ruta-jña, sabba-rāvaŋ jānāti" C.).

Rudati & **Rodati** [**rud**, the usual Sk. pres. being rodati, but forms fr. base **rud°** are Vedic and are later found also in Prk. (cp. Pischel *Prk. Gr.* § 495): ruyai besides royai & rodasi. — The Idg. root is ***reud**, being an enlargement of ***reu**, as in ravati (q. v.). Cp. cognates Lat. rudo to cry, shout, bray; Lith. raudà wailing; Ohg. riozan= Ags. reotan. — The Dhtp expl[s] **rud** by "rodane" (144), the Dhtm by "assu-vimocane" (206)] to cry, lament, weep, wail. — *Forms* I. **rud°** (the older form): pres. **rudati** (not yet found); ppr. **rudanto** D I.115; Sn 675, 691; **rudamāna** M I.341; A II.95; Pug 62; Miln 275; Sdhp 281; and **rudaŋ** Pv I.8[4]; also in cpd. **rudam-mukha** with weeping face J VI.518 (assu-netta+); Pv I.11[2]; ger. **ruditvāna** Mhvs 35, 24; fut. **rucchati** J V.366 and **rucchiti** J VI.550 (=rodissati C.; see also rujati). — II. **rod°** (the *younger* form & the one peculiar to *prose*): pres. rodati J I.55; III.169 (socati+); Pv I.8[7] (socati+); I.12[4]; PvA 17, 18; Pot. rode Pv I.8[5] (=rodeyyaŋ PvA 64); ppr. **rodanto** J I.65; f. **rodantī** PvA 16; med. **rodamāna** PvA 6; DA I.284. — aor. **rodi** J I.167; DhA II.17 (+hasi); fut. **rodissati** J VI.550; ger. **roditvā** Mhvs 9, 7; inf. **roditun** J I.55. — Caus. II. **rodāpeti** to make someone cry DhA II.86. — pp. **ruṇṇa**, **rudita** & **rodita**.

Rudita (nt.) [pp. of rudati, equivalent to ruṇṇa] crying, weeping PvA 18 (+assu-mocana, in explⁿ of ruṇṇa), 63 (=paridevita).

Rudda (adj.) [cp. Sk. raudra & Vedic rudra (a fierce demon or storm-deity; "the red one," with Pischel from **rud** to be ruddy. See Macdonell, *Vedic Mythology* 74-77). The usual Pāli form is ludda. At Dhtp 473 & Dhtm 135 a root **ruṭh** (or **luṭh**) is given in meaning "upa-ghāte" i. e. killing, which may represent *this* **rud**: see luṭhati] fierce, awful, terrible J IV.416 (so luddako rudda-rūpo; v. l. ludda°); V.425, 431 (su-ruddho, spelling for su-ruddo, very fierce, expl[d] as su-luddo su-pharuso); Mhvs 12, 45 (rudda-rakkhasī, prob. with ref. to the demon Rudra; trslⁿ "fearsome female demon"; vv. ll. ruda°, ruddha°, dudda°).

Ruddha [pp. of rundhati] 1. obstructed, disturbed Dāvs 4, 46. — 2. at J V.425 & 431 in cpd. su-ruddha it stands for **rudda** (q. v.). — Cp. upa°, ni°, paṭi° paṭivi°, vi°.

Rudhira (nt.) [late Vedic rudhira. Etym. connected with Lat. ruber red; Gr. ἐρυθρός red; Oicel. rodra blood, Goth. rauþs=Ger. rot=E. red] blood DhA I.140; PvA 34 (for lohita; v. l. ruhira). See the more freq. words rohita & lohita; a form ruhira (q. v.) occurs e. g. at Pv I.9[1].

Rundhati [**rundh** or **rudh**, both roots in Vedic Sk. — Dhtp (375, 425) expl[s] by "āvaraṇe"; id. Dhtm (608, 662).] 1. to restrain, hinder, prevent, obstruct, keep out Cp. III.10[7]; Miln 313 (+upa°). — 2. to conceal, hide, cover up Th 2, 238 (ppr. rundhanto); PvA 88 (ppr. rundhamāna). — 3. in phrase nagaraŋ r. to surround or besiege a town J I.409 (aor. rundhi); III.159 (°itvā); IV.230 (°iŋsu). — Pass **rujjhati**; pp. ruddha & **rūḷha**. — See also upa°, paṭi° paṭivā, vi°. *Note.* The roots **rudh** & **rundh** are also found in Prk. (see Pischel § 507); besides we have a by-form **rubh** in Prk. as well as in Pāli: see Pischel, § 266, 507, and P. rumbhati.

Ruppa in ruppa-rūpakaŋ (nt.) Th 2, 394 is not clear. It refers to something which is not rūpa, yet pretends to be rūpa, i. e. a sham performance or show. Thus ruppa may correspond to *rūpya & with rūpaka mean "having the form (i. e. the appearance) of form, i. e. substantiality." The Cy. (ThA 259) interprets as "rūpiya-rūpa-sadisaŋ sāraŋ sāraŋ upaṭṭhabantaŋ asāran ti attho"; and Mrs. Rh. D. (*Sisters*, p. 154) trsl[s]: "deluded by puppet shows (seen in the midst of the crowd)."

Ruppati [**rup**=**lup**, one of the rare cases of P. r. representing a Sk. l., whereas the opposite is frequent. The same sound change Idg., as Lat. rumpo to break corresponds to Sk. lumpati. Besides we find the Sk. form ropayati to break off. — The root has nothing to do with rūpa, although the P. Commentators combine these two. — Cp. also Sk. ropa hole; Ags. rēofan to break, rēaf (theft)= Ger. raub, rauben, and many other cognates (see Walde s. v. rumpo). — The root **rup** is def[d] at Dhtm by **nās**, i. e. to destroy; *another* **rup** is given at Dhtm 837 in meaning "ropana"] to be vexed, oppressed, hurt, molested (always with ref. to an illness or pain) Sn 767 (salla-viddho va r.) 1121; Nd[1] 5 (=kuppati, ghaṭṭiyati, pīḷiyati); Nd[2] 543 (=kuppati pīḷayati ghaṭayati). — ppr. gen. **ruppato** S I.198 (salla-viddhassa r.; expl[d] at *K.S.* 320 by "ghaṭṭan-atthena")= Sn 331 (reads salla-viddhāna ruppataŋ, i. e. pl. instead of sg.); Th 1, 967 (salla-viddhassa ruppato (C. sarīra-vikāraŋ āpajjato, *Brethren*, 338); J II.437 (C. ghaṭṭiya-māna pīḷiyamāna)=Vism 49 (dukkhitassa r.); J III.169 (salla-viddhassa r.=ghaṭṭiyamāna C.). —ruppati to Pāli exegesis with its fondness of allegorical ("orthodox") interpretation, is the etym. base of rūpa, thus at S III.86: "ruppatī ti tasmā rūpan ti vuccati kena r.? sītena, uṇhena etc. (all kinds of material dukkha: dukkha II.3[b]) ruppati." — Or at Sn 1121 (ruppanti rūpena), & at other passages given under rūpa (A). See also **ruppana**.

Ruppana (nt.) [fr. **rup**) molestation, vexation, trouble J III.368 (=ghaṭṭana dūsana kuppana C.). Frequent in allegorical exegesis of rūpa, e. g. at DhsA 52 (naman' aṭṭhena nāmaŋ ruppan' aṭṭhena rūpaŋ), 303 (rūp' ādīhi ruppana-bhāva-dīpana); VbhA 4 (ruppan' aṭṭhena rūpaŋ; in explⁿ of passage S III.86 (mentioned under ruppati); KhA 78, 79 (ruppan' aṭṭhena . . . rūpaŋ rūpaŋ ti vuccati).

Rumbhati [so read for rumhati (Trenckner, *Notes* 59[9]; the root is another form of **rudh** (as in Prk.): see rundhati. The Dhtm (547) defines by "uppīḷana"] to obstruct, surround, besiege (=rundhati 3) J VI.391 (where spelling rumhati; in phrase nagaraŋ r.). See also ni°, sanni°. — pp. **rūḷha**.

Rumma (adj.) [put down (rightly) by Geiger, *P.Gr.* § 53 as *different* fr. Sk. rukma (shining); Morris, *J.P.T.S.* 1893, 12 tried the etym. rumma=Sk. **rumra** "tawny," or rukma (rukmin) shiny. It is still an unsolved problem. It may not be far off to trace a relation (by miswriting, dissimilation or false analogy) to ruppa in sense of ruppati, or to **ruj**, or even **rudda**. The C. explⁿ of *all* the rumma- & rummin passages is anañjita, i. e.

unkempt] miserable, dirty, poorly, in cpds. °rūpin J IV.387 (=lūkhavesa C.), with v. l. duma°; and °vāsin poorly dressed J IV.380.

Rummin=**rumma** (dirty-soiled) J IV.322 (v. l. dummi); VI.194 (do.).

Rumhaniya at M I.480 is doubtful in spelling. The meaning is clearly "furthering growth, making or being prosperous, bringing luck" (comb^d with ojavant), as also indicated by v. l. **ruḷh°**. Thus it *cannot* belong to **rumbh**, but must represent either **rup**, as given under ruppati in meaning "ropana" (Dhtm 837), or **ruh** (see rūhati). Kern, *Toev.* s. v. trsl^s "tot groei geschikt" (i. e. able to grow), Neumann, "erquickend" (i. e. refreshing).

Ruyhati is Med. of rūhati (rohati), q. v.

Rurira at Vv 40² is misprint for rucira.

Ruru [Vedic ruru: RV VI.75, 15] a sort of deer, a stag; usually called **ruru-miga** J IV.256, 261; V.406 (pl. rohitā rurū), 416. Cp. **ruruva**.

Rusita [pp. of **ruṣ** to be vexed. The Dhtp defines by "rose" (306, 450), "pārusiye" (626); Dhtm has 2 roots viz. one with "ālepe" (442), the other with "hiŋsāyaŋ" (443)] annoyed, irritated, offended Sn 932, 971 (expl^d by Nd¹ 498 as "khuŋsita, vambhita, ghaṭṭita" etc.). See rosa, roseti etc.

Russati at SnA 121 for **dussati**.

Ruha¹ (adj.) (-°) [fr. **ruh**: see rūhati] growing, a tree, in cpds.: jagati°, dharaṇi°, mahi°, etc.

Ruha² [poetical for ruhira (rohita)=lohita] blood, in cpd. **ruhaŋghasa** blood-eater, a name for panther J III.481 (=ruhira-bhakkha lohita-pāyin C.).

Ruhira (nt.) [fr. rudhira] blood M III.122; Th I, 568; Vin II.193; Miln 125, 220; Sdhp 38.
-akkhita (ruhir' akkhita) "besmeared with blood" J IV.331, is to be read as ruhir' ukkhita of **ukṣ**).

Rūta at J III.276 read **ruta** (q. v.).

Rūpa (nt.) [cp. Vedic rūpa, connected etymologically with varpa (Grassmann). — The nom. pl. is rūpā & rūpāni] form, figure, appearance, principle of form, etc. — A. *Definitions.* According to P. expositors rūpa takes its designation fr. **ruppati**, e. g. "ruppanato rūpaŋ" Vism 588; "ruppan' aṭṭhena r." VbhA 3; "rūpa-rūpaŋ= ruppana sabhāvena yuttaŋ" *Cpd.* 156⁷ (where ruppati is, not quite correctly, given as "change"). "ruppatī ti: tasmā rūpan ti vuccati" S III.86; other def^ns are "rūpayati ti rūpaŋ" (with cakkhu & the other 10 āyatanas) VbhA 45; and more scientifically: "paresu rūp' ādisu cakkhu-paṭihanana lakkhaṇaŋ rūpaŋ" Vism 446. — Of modern interpretations & discussions see e. g. *Dhs. trsl.* introd. ch. vi. (pp. 41-63, or ²48-71); *Dial.* II.244; *Expos.* 67ⁿ; *Cpd.* 270 sq. (where objections are raised to trsl^n "form," and as better (philosophical) terms "matter," "material quality" are recommended). See also **loka** for similar etym. — B. (lit.) appearance, form, figure Dhs 597 sq. (=form either contrasted with what is unseen, or taken for both seen and unseen), 751; Mhvs 27, 30 (sīha-vyagghādirūpāni representations of lions, tigers etc.); 30, 68 (ravi-canda-tāra-rūpāni id.); 36, 31 (loha° bronze statue); ThA 257. — Esp. beautiful form, beauty S IV.275= Pv II.9⁵⁸ (as one of the 10 attributes, with sadda etc., of distinction: see also below D II.a); Miln 285; Mhvs 20, 4 (rūpa-māninī proud of her beauty); PvA 89. —**surūpa** very beautiful ThA 72; **durūpa** of evil form, ugly A I.203 sq. (dubbaṇṇa+). — In phrase **rūpaŋ sikkhati** Vin I.77=IV.129 the meaning is doubtful; it may be "to study drawing, or arts & craft," or (with Mrs. Rh. D.) "weights & measures," or (w. Hardy) "money changing." It is said that through this occupation the eyes become bad; it is opposed to gaṇanā. — C. (-°) of such & such a form, like, kind, of a certain condition or appearance. In this appl^n very frequent & similar to E. -hood, or Ger. -heit, i. e. an abstract formation. Often untranslatable because of the latter character. It is similar to kāya (cp. expl^n of ātura-rūpa Vv 83¹⁴ by abhitunna-**kāya** VvA 328), but not so much with ref. to life & feeling as to appearance and looks. E. g. aneka° Sn 1079 (=anekavidha Nd² 54); adissamāna° invisible PvA 6 (lit. with invisible form); ummatta° as if mad, under the appearance of madness, like a madman Pv I.8¹; II.6³; eva° in such a condition Pv II.1⁵; tapassī° appearing to be an ascetic Pv I.3²; tāraka° the (shapes of the) stars Dhs 617; deva° as a deva PvA 92. *Pleonastically* e. g. in: anupatta° attaining Pv IV.1⁶⁶; taramāna° quickly Pv II.6²; yutta° fit PvA 157; sucitta° variegated Pv I.10⁹. — Cases *ad verbially:* citta-rūpaŋ *according* to intention Vin III.161; IV.177; cetabba-rūpaŋ fit to be thought upon J IV.157. (=°yuttakaŋ C.). —**atta-rūpena** on my own account S IV.97; godha-rūpena as an iguana Mhvs 28, 9. — D. (as philos. t. t.) principle of (material) form, materiality, visibility. — There are var. groups of psychological and metaphysical systematizations, in which rūpa functions as the *material*, gross factor, by the side of other, more subtle factors. In all these representations of rūpa we find that an element of moral psychology overshadows the purely philosophical & speculative aspect. A detailed (Abhidhammatic) discussion of rūpa in var. aspects is to be found at Dhs § 585-980. — 1. rūpa as āyatana or sense object. It is the object of the activity or sphere of the organ of sight (cakkhu). As such it heads the list of the 6 bāhirāni āyatanāni (see e. g. Nd² p. 238 A-E & āyatana³) with "cakkhunā rūpaŋ disvā" (the others: sota>sadda, ghāna>gandha, jivhā>rasa, kāya>phoṭṭhabba, mano>dhamma), *cp.* cakkhu-viññeyyā rūpā iṭṭhā kantā etc. D I.245; M I.266; cakkhunā rūpaŋ passati iṭṭha-rūpaŋ kanta-rūpaŋ etc. S IV.126; — see further: Vin I.34 (sabbaŋ ādittaŋ: cakkhuŋ ādittaŋ, rūpa ādittā etc. with sequence of other āyatanas); D II.308 sq., 336 sq.; M III.18 (yaŋ kho rūpaŋ paṭicca uppajjati sukhaŋ somanassaŋ, ayaŋ rūpe assādo; cp. Ps II.109 sq.), 291 (ye te cakkhu-viññeyyesu rūpesu avīta-rāgā etc.); Ps I.79; II.38 (rūpī rūpāni passatī ti vimokkho); Dhs 617, 653, 878; Tikp 28. — 2. (metaphysically) as the representative of sensory or material existence: (a) universally as forming the corporeal stratum in the world of appearance or form (**rūpa-bhava**) as compared with the incorporeal (**arūpa-bhava**), being itself above, and yet including the **kāma**-bhava. (The kāmabhava is a subdivision of rūpabhava, which has got raised into a third main division.) This triad is also found in comb^ns with **loka** or **dhātu** (see dhātu 2 a & d), or **avacara**. See e. g. D I.17; III.215 (°dhātu), 216 (°bhava); Kvu 370 sq. (°dhātu); Dhs 499 (°āvacara), 585 (°dhātu); Vbh 17 (°āvacara), 25 (as garu-pariṇāma & dandha-nirodha comp^d with arūpa). A similar sequence **rūpa arūpa** & **nirodha** (i. e. nibbāna) in old verses at Sn 755; It 45, 62 (rūpehi arūpā santatāra, arūpehi nirodho santataro). On indriya-rūpa "faculty as form" see indriya B. — (b) individually in the sphere of saŋsāra as one (i. e. the material quality) of the substrata of sensory individual existence or the khandhas. They are the 5: rūpa-kkhandha, vedanā°, saññā°, sankhārā°, viññāṇa°; otherwise called **rūp' ūpādāna-kkhandha** etc. (e. g. D III.223, 278; Vism 443). See **khandha** II. B. — In this property rūpa consists of 28 subdivisions, viz. the 4 (great) dhātūs (mahābhūtāni or else bhūta-rūpa primary matter) and 24 upādā-rūpāni (i. e. derivative forms or accidentals). These are given *in extenso* in the rūpakkhandha section of the Vism (pp. 443-450), also at Dhs 585; the 24 consist of: cakkhu, sota, ghāna, jivhā, kāya, rūpa, sadda, gandha, rasa, itthindriya, purisindriya, jīvitindriya, hadaya-vatthu, kāya-viññatti, vacī-viññatti, ākāsa-dhātu, (rūpassa) lahutā mudutā kammaññatā, upacaya santati jaratā aniccatā, kabaḷinkār'-āhāra; cp. defⁿ at Nett 73: cātu-mahābhūtikaŋ rūpaŋ catunnaŋ ca mahābhūtānaŋ upādāya rūpassa paññatti. The **rūpakkhandha** shares with the others the qualities of *soullessness, evanescence* and *ill* (anattā, anicca, dukkha); e. g. rūpañ ca h' idaŋ attā abhavissa, na y' idaŋ rūpaŋ ābadhāya saŋvatteyya Vin I.13, cp. similarly M III.282 sq.; S III.66; quoted and expl^d in detail at Vism 610; rūpaŋ aniccaŋ Vin I.14; M I.228; III.18 (also expl^d at Vism 610); S III.48, 66, 88; rūpe anicc' ânupassanā Ps II.186 sq. — See also D II.301; III.233; Ps I.23, 53, 104; II.96, 102, 109 (rūpassa ādīnavo); Vbh 1. sq., 12 sq. (in detail); Kvu 11 sq.; Vism 443 sq.; Tikp 33; VbhA 2, 3, 32 sq.=S III.142 (with var. similes); DhA IV.100. — (c) in the making up of the individuality as such (nāma-rūpa), where in contrast with nāma (as abstract, logical, invisible or mind-factor) rūpa represents the visible (material) factor, resembling kāya (cp. phrase nāma-kāya in same sense). The foll. are current def^ns of nāma-rūpa: nāma-(kāya)=vedanā, saññā, cetanā, phassa, manasikāra (otherwise citta-sankhārā), rūpa(-kāya)=cattāro mahā-bhūtā catunnaŋ m-bhūtānaŋ upādāya rūpaŋ (otherwise kāya-sankhārā) S II.4; III.59 sq.; Ps I.183; with expl^ns at Vism 558 & VbhA 169. Defined at Nett 15: "ye phassa-pañcamakā dhammā: idaŋ nāmaŋ, yāni pañc' indriyāni rūpāni: idaŋ rūpaŋ, tad ubhayaŋ nāmarūpaŋ viññāṇa-sampayuttaŋ." Discussed in detail also at Vism 562 (=VbhA 173, 174), 587-597; cp. DhsA 392 (*Expos.* 500, where "mind-matter" is given as corresp. couple in trslⁿ, do. *Cpd.* 271 sq. "mind and body"). See also under paṭicca-samuppāda. — 3. *various references:* D III.102, 212, 225, 244, 273; M I.84 (Gotamo kāmānaŋ pariññaŋ paññāpeti, rūpānaŋ, vedanānaŋ); S II.198; III.11 (evaŋ-rūpo siyaŋ, evaŋ vedano etc.), 101 (id., & the khandhas); Sn 867, 874, 943, 1037, 1121; Nd¹ 425; Tikp 36, 38, 54, 262; Vism 625 (uppajjanaka°).

-ārammaṇa a visible thing as object Dhs 146, 365; DhsA 310 (cp. *Expos.* 407). -āvacara world of form, sphere of matter (cp. *Expos.* 67, 216ⁿ, 264) PvA 163. -ûpaga (satta) (a being) living in (bodily) form It 62; Sn 754. -ūpajīvinī f. a woman living on her beauty, i. e. a harlot PvA 46, 201. -ññu knowing (var.) bodily forms M I.220=A V.347. -taṇhā craving after form D II.309; III.216, 244, 280; VbhA 179 (in det.). -dakkha one clever in forms, viz. an artist (accountant?) Miln 344 (in the Dhamma-nagara). -dhātu the element of form, material element Vism 486; Nett 32, 97. See above D 2. -nimitta sign of form Ps I.92. -patta beautiful J I.61. -pamānika measuring by form (outward appearance), one of the 4 kinds of measurements which the world takes of the Tathāgata (see A II.71 & Pug 53), viz. rūpa°, ghosa°, lūkha°, dhamma° DhA III.113; the same four similarly at SnA 242. -pātubhāva appearance of form (also as °antara° intermediate form) SnA 245. -bhava material existence: see above D 2. -rāga lust after rebirth in rūpa D III.234 (+arūpa°); Nett 28 (pañc' indriyāni rūpīni rūpa-rāgassa padaṭṭhānaŋ. -rūpa material form (mutable material quality?) *Cpd.* 156, doubtful trslⁿ & expl° -saññā perception of material qualities, notion of form D I.34; II.112 (expl^d in det. at Vism 328); III.224, 244, 253; Nd² 545; DhsA 200 (cp. *Expos.* 269). -saññin perceiving form D III.260; Ps II.38; Sn 1113. -santati duration of material form Vism 431; VbhA 21. -samussaya accumulation of form, complex form ThA 98. -samāpatti attainment of beauty J I.406. -sampatti beauty J III.187. -siri personal splendour J I.60.

Rūpaka (nt.) [fr. rupa] form, figure; likeness of, image (-°); representation Vin II.113 (rūpak' okiṇṇāni pattāni, of painted bowls); Th 2, 394 (see ruppa°); DhA I.370 (maṇi° jewelled image); II.69 (assa° toy horse); Mhvs 25, 26 (rāja°); 27, 30 (devatā° shape of devas); VvA 213. -dūrūpaka of squalid appearance J II.167; cp. durūpa.

Rūpatā (f.) [abstr. fr. rūpa] (being) shape(d), appearance; accordance, conformity, in phrase **bhavya-rūpatāya** "by appearance of likelihood" A II.191 (in hearsay formula, where it is missing in id. passage at Nd² 151).

Rūpatta (nt.) [abstr. fr. rūpa] lit. "form-hood," i. e. shaping (being) shape(d) S III.87 (rūpaŋ rūpattāya sankhātaŋ).

Rūpavant (adj.) [rūpa+vant] 1. having bodily form S III.16 & passim (in formula of sakkāya-diṭṭhi); Dhs 1003. — 2. having the form of (-°) Mhvs 14, 3 (gokaṇṇa°). — 3. beautiful Mhvs 10, 30 (f. rūpavatī).

Rūpika (adj.) [fr. rūpa] having shape; neg. a° formless Sdhp 236 (rūp' ârūpika).

Rūpin (adj.) [fr. rūpa] 1. having material qualities, possessed of form or shape or body or matter, belonging to the realm of form. rūpī is nearly always comb^d & contrasted with **arūpī** formless, incorporeal (see rūpa D 2 a), cp. combⁿ rūpī arūpī saññī asaññī nevasaññināsaññī Nd² 617 and similarly It 87=Miln 217. — D I.34 (attā dibbo rūpī), 77 (kāyo r. manomayo), 186 (attā etc.), 195 (attapaṭilābho r. manomayo); III.111, 139; M II.229; S III.46 (r. arūpī saññī etc.); IV.202, 402; A II.34; Nd¹ 97, 137; Ps II.38 (rūpī rūpāni passati); Dhs 635, 1091, 1444; Vbh 123, 342 (read rūpī); Nett 28 (pañc' indriyāni rūpīni), 69 (five rūpīnī indriyāni & five arūpīni); DA I.119 (attā); DhsA 304 (rūpino dhammā); VbhA 511 sq. (attā). — 2. (-°) having the appearance of, resembling: see **rumma°**.

Rūpiya¹ (nt.) [cp. Sk. rūpya, lit. of splendid appearance, cp. name for gold jātarūpa] silver Vin III.239 (here collectively for any transactions in "specie," as expl^d by C. p. 240: rūpiyaŋ nāma satthu-vaṇṇo kahāpaṇo lohamāsako dārumāsako jatumāsako; i. e. copper, wood & lac); S I.104 (suddhaŋ r.); II.233; Dhs 584.

-maya made of silver Vin II.112; S III.144 (sovaṇṇamaya+); Pv II.6⁴ (where in sequence sovaṇṇa°, maṇi°, loha° r.; expl^d as "rajatamaya" PvA 95); DhA I.29.

Rūpiya² see ruppa.

Rūpeti [Caus. Denom. fr. rūpa] 1. to put into shape, to make appear, to make grow (?) SnA 132, 143 (v. l. ropeti). — 2. to be formed, to appear, to come to notice, in defⁿ of rūpa at VbhA 15: "rūpayatī ti rūpaŋ."

Rūḷa [doubtful spelling; perhaps for rūḷha, evidently identical with **rudda**, as Trenckner suggests in *Notes* 63¹⁰] awful, terrible Miln 275 (synonymous with bhīma).

Rūḷha¹ [pp. of rohati; of **ruh**; Sk. rūḍha] 1. grown Sn 20 (°tiṇa). — 2. (see rūhati) healed up Miln 291 (°vaṇa one whose wound has healed): cp. rūhanā.

Rūḷha² at Miln 217 & 218 is a by-form of ruddha, pp. of rundhati (rumbhati) to obstruct; thus meaning "obstructed, difficult" (of a road, together with lugga palugga). Kern, *Toev.* s. v. trsl^s (as rūḷha¹) by "overgrown."

Rūḷhi (f.) [fr. rūḷha, pp. of rohati, cp. Sk. rūḍhi] lit. ascent, growth see vi°. — fig. what has grown by custom, tradition, popular meaning of a word (°sadda). The fig. meaning is the one usually found in Pāli, esp. in Abhidhamma and Commentary literature; e. g. **rūḷhiyaŋ** by tradition, usually, commonly, VbhA 1 (as category with the 3 other: rāsi, guṇa, paṇṇatti); **rūḷhito** id. VbhA 2; **rūḷhiyā** id. SnA 430; PvA 163; also **rūḷhi-vasena** VvA 42; or with **sadda**: **rūḷhi-sadda** usual meaning Vism 333; DhsA 205; °saddena in popular language, in ordinary speech, customarily, commonly speaking Tikp 253; Vism 310; DA I.239, 294; SnA 135, 400.

Rūhati[1] [the specific P. form of the usual Sk. P. rohati (q. v.). The root **ruh** is given at Dhtp 334 with meaning "janana" i. e. causing, which refers more to the compounds with prefixes] 1. to grow, spread It 67; J IV.408 (akkhīni rūhiŋsu; also ppr. med. **ruyhamāna**); V.368; VI.360. — 2. to heal (of a wound), close up Vin I.206 (vaṇo na rūhati); — 3. to have effect in (loc.), to be effective Vin II.203 = It 87 (vādo tamhi na rūhati). — pp. **rūḷha**[2]. See also **rūhita** (pp. of Caus. rūheti = roheti).

Rūhati[2] [for **rundh** (**rumbh, rudh**) or Pass. **rujjh°**; see also rumbhati & ropeti[2]] to be broken or (fig.) to be suspended Vin II.55 (dhammattā rūhati the liability is cancelled). — pp. **rūḷha**[1].

Rūhanā (f.) [cp. Sk. rohaṇa, fr. **ruh**; rūhati[1]] 1. growth J II.322 (virūhanā C.). — 2. healing (of a wound) Miln 112.

Rūhita (nt.) [fr. rūhati[1]] a boil, a diseased growth (lit. "healed") Vin IV.316 (expl^d as "yaŋ kiñci vaṇo"; v. l. rudhita).

Re (indecl.) [shortened for are, q. v.] a part. of exclamation, mostly implying contempt, or deprecation, (DA I.276) "hīḷanavasena āmantanaŋ" i. e. address of disdain: heigh, go on, get away, hallo. — D I.96, 107; J III.184 (C. = āmantaṇe nipāto); often comb^d with similar particles of exhortation, like cara pi re get away with you! M II.108; Vin IV.139 (so read for cara pire which the C. takes as "para," amamaka); or ehi re come on then! J I.225; ha re look out! here they are! PvA 4; aho vata re wish I would! Pv II.9[46] (re ti ālapanaŋ PvA 131); no ca vata re vattabbe but indeed, good sir . . . (Kvu 1).

Rekhā (f.) [fr. **rikh**, for which the Pāli form is **likh**, cp. Sk. rekhā, Lat. rīma, Ohg. rīga row] line, streak Abhp 539. See lekhā.

Recana (nt.) [fr. **ric**] letting loose, emission Dhtm 610. Cp. **vi°**.

Reṇu [cp. Vedic reṇu] 1. dust; pl. reṇū particles of dust. — Vin I.32 (°hatā bhūmi); Vism 338 = Nd[1] 505 = J I.117 (rāgo rajo na ca pana reṇu vuccati); J IV.362 (okiṇṇā raja-reṇūhi; C. expl^s by "paŋsūhi"); Miln 274 (pl.); SnA 132 (reṇuŋ vūpasāmeti allays). — 2. pollen (in this meaning found only in the so-called Jātaka-style) J I.233 (mahā-tumba-matta), 349 (pupphato reṇuŋ gaṇhāti); III.320; V.39 (puppha°); VI.530 (paduma-kinjakkha°); DhA IV.203 (°vaṭṭhi).

Reruka [etym.? Probably dialectical] "elephant's tooth," ivory J II.230 (= hatthi-danta C.).

Roga [Vedic roga; **ruj** (see rujati), cp. Sk. rujā breakage, illness] illness, disease. — The def^n of roga at J II.437 is "roga rujana-sabhāvattaŋ." There are many diff. enumerations of rogas and sets of standard comb^ns, of which the foll. may be mentioned. At Sn 311 (cp. D III.75) it is said that in old times there were only 3 diseases, viz. icchā, **anasanaŋ**, jarā, which gradually, through slaughtering of animals, increased to 98. Bdhgh at SnA 324 hints at these 98 with "cakkhu-rog' ādinā-bhedena." Beginning with this (cakkhuroga affection of the eye) we have a list of 34 rogas at Nd[1] 13 (under pākaṭa-parissayā or open dangers = Nd[1] 360 = Nd[2] 420) & Nd[2] 304[I] B, viz. cakkhu° & the other 4 senses, sīsa°, kaṇṇa°, mukha°, danta°; kāsa, sāsa, pināsa, ḍāha, jara; kucchiroga, mucchā, pakkhandikā, sūlā, visūcikā; kuṭṭhaŋ, gaṇḍo, kilāso, soso, apamāro; daddu, kaṇḍu, kacchu, rakhasā, vitacchikā, lohitapittaŋ, madhumeho, aŋsā, piḷakā, bhagandalā. This list is followed by list of 10 ābādhas & under "dukkha" goes on with var. other "ills," which however do not make up the number 98. The same list is found at A V.110. The 10 ābādhas (Nd[2] 304[I] C.) occur at A II.87 & Miln 308 (as āgantuka-rogā). The 4 "rogas" of the Sun (Miln 273, cp. Vin II.295) are: abbha, mahikā, megha, Rāhu. — Another mention of roga together with plagues which attack the corn in the field is given at J V.401, viz. visa-vāta; mūsika-salabha-suka-pāṇaka; setaṭṭhika-roga etc., i. e. hurtful winds, mice, moths & parrots, mildew. — The comb^n **roga, gaṇḍa, salla** is sometimes found, e. g. M II.230; Vism 335. Of other single rogas we mention: kucchi° (stomach-ache) J I.243; ahivātaka° Vin I.78; J II.79; IV.200; DhA I.231; paṇḍu° jaundice Vin I.206; J II.102; DhA I.25; tiṇapupphaka° hay-fever Miln 216. — See also **ātanka** & **ābādha**. On roga in similes see *J.P.T.S.* 1907, 130. — D I.11, 73; III.182; S III.32; IV.64; A II.128, 142 sq.; IV.289; Nd[1] 486; Vism 236 (as cause of death), 512 (in simile); VbhA 88 (in sim. of dukkha etc.); ThA 288; VvA 6 (rogena phuṭṭha), 75 (sarīre r. uppajji); PvA 86 (kacchu°), 212 (rogena abhibhūta). — Opp. aroga health: see sep.

-ātanka affliction by illness A II.174 sq.; V.169, 318. **-niḍḍha** the nest or seat of disease Dh 148 (cp. DhA III.110); as °**nīḷa** at It 37. **-mūla** the root of disease Sn 530. **-vyasana** distress or misfortune of disease D III.235 (one of the 5 vyasanāni: ñāti°, bhoga°, roga°, sīla°, diṭṭhi°); Miln 196 (id.).

Rogin (adj.) [fr roga] having a disease, suffering from (-°); one who has a disease Vism 194 (ussanna-vyādhi dukkhassa); Sdhp 86. —**paṇḍu°** one who has the jaundice J II.285; III.401.

Rocati [Vedic rocate, **ruc**, Idg. ***leuq**, as in Lat. luceo to be bright (cp. lūx light, lūmen, lūna etc.); Sk. rocana splendid, ruci light, roka & rukṣa light; Av. raocantshining; Gr. ἀμφι-λύκη twi-light, λευκός white; also with l: Sk. loka world, locate to perceive, locana eye; Lith. láukti to await; Goth. liuhaþ light = Ohg. lioht, E. light; Oir lōche lightning. — The Dhtp (& Dhtm) gives 2 roots **ruc**, viz. the one with meaning "**ditti**" (Dhtp 37), the other as "**rocana**" (Dhtp 395), both signifying "light" or "splendour," but the second probably to be taken in sense of "pleasing"] 1. to please, i. e. it pleases (with dat. of person) Th 2, 415 (rocate); Mhvs 15, 9 (nivāso rocatu). Cp. BSk. rocyate AvŚ II.158. — 2. to find pleasure in (loc.) Miln 338 (bhave). — Caus. **roceti**: 1. to be pleased, to give one's consent DhA I.387 (gloss K rucitha ruceyyātha). — 2. (with acc. of object) to find pleasing, to find delight in, to be attached to, to approve of, to choose S I.41 (vadhaŋ); J I.142 (Devadattassa laddhiŋ r.); V.178 (pabbajjaŋ roc' ahaŋ = rocemi C.), 226 (kammaŋ). — Freq. with **dhammaŋ** to approve of a doctrine or scheme, e. g. at Vin II.199 (Devadattassa dhammaŋ); S I.133; Sn 94 (asataŋ dh.), 398 (dhammaŋ imaŋ rocaye); J IV.53 (dh. asataŋ na rocayāma). — Cp. abhi°, ā°, **vi°**.

Roṇṇa see **ruṇṇa**.

Rodati see **rudati**.

Rodana (nt.) [fr. **rud**] crying, weeping DhA I.28; PvA 63, 64; Dhtp 144.

Rodha[1] [fr. **rudh**] obstruction, stopping, in cpd. **para-pāṇa°** stopping the life of somebody else; life-slaughter, murder Sn 220; J II.450. Cp. **anu°, ni°, vi°**.

Rodha[2] (nt.) [fr. **rudh**] bank, dam A III.128 (where id. p. at A. I.154 reads gedha, cave; v. l. also gedha, cp. v. l. rodhi° for gedhi° at Nd[2] 585).

Rodhana (nt.) [fr. **rudh**] obstructing J V.346; Sdhp 57.

Ropa (-°) [fr. **rop**=Caus. of **ruh**] plantation, in vana° & ārāma° S I.33.

Ropaka [ropa+ka] sapling J II.346 (rukkha°).

Ropana (nt.) & ropanā (f.) [fr. ropeti¹] 1. planting PvA 151 (ārāma°); Mhvs 15, 41. — 2. healing S IV.177 (vaṇa°). — 3. furthering, making grow Ps II.115 (buddhi°). — 4. (f.) accusation Vin IV.36.

Ropaya (adj.) (-°) [for *ropya, fr. ropeti¹] to be healed, only in cpd. du° hard to heal (of a wound) Vin I.216 (vaṇa).

Ropāpeti see ropeti¹.

Ropita [pp. of ropeti¹] 1. planted Pv II.7⁸. — 2. growing up Pv 9⁷⁰ (read "pi ropitaŋ" for viropitaŋ). — 3. furnished with, powdered with (-°) Vv 64¹⁵ (Ed. vosita; VvA 280 expl^s by ullitta, vicchurita). — 4. accused, brought forward (of a charge) Vin IV.36.

Ropima (nt.) [fr. ropeti¹] 1. what has been planted Vin IV.267. — 2. a kind of arrow M I.429 (contrasted with kaccha; Neumann trsl^s ropima by "aus Binsen"). — 3. (adj.) at Vv 44¹³ aropima ("not planted"?) is an attribute of trees. It is not expl^d in VvA.

Ropeti¹ [Caus. of rūhati¹] 1. to plant or sow J I.150 (nivāpatiṇaŋ); Mhvs 15, 42 (amb' aṭṭhikaŋ); 19, 56; DhA II.109. — 2. to put up, fix J I.143 (sūlāni). — 3. to further, increase, make grow Sn 208 (Pot. ropayeyya). — 4. (fig.) to fix, direct towards, bring up against: see ropeti² 2. — pp. ropita. Caus. II. ropāpeti to cause to be planted D II.179; J VI.333; Mhvs 34, 40; DhA II.109. — Cp. abhi°, abhini°, ā°.

Ropeti² [Caus. of rūhati². See lumpati] to cause to break off, to cause to suspend or cancel; to pass off, refuse Vin II.261 (bhikkhūhi bhikkhunīnaŋ kammaŋ ropetvā bhikkhunīnaŋ niyyādetuŋ, i. e. by the bhikkhus is an act of the nuns to be passed off and to be referred to the nuns). — 2. to make confess or accuse of (acc.: āpattiŋ a guilt) Vin II.2 (first codeti, then sāreti, then ropeti & lastly (sanghaŋ) ñāpeti), 85 (id.); IV.36 (aññavādakaŋ ropeti to bring the charge of heresy against someone). No. 2 perhaps better to ropeti¹. Cp. *Vin. Texts* II.334. — To ropeti² belong the cpds. oropeti (cut off) & voropeti (deprive). They are better to be taken here than to ava+**ruh**.

Roma (nt.) [Vedic roman; the usual P. form is loma (q. v.)] the hair of the body J V.430 (where in roma-rājiyā maṇḍita-udarā as expl^n of loma-sundarī); Sdhp 119 (°kūpa).

Romaka (adj.) [fr. roma] feathered (?) J II.383 (C. wrong!).

Romañca (?) [fr. roma, cp. Vedic romaśa] hairy (?) Dāvs V.14 (°kancuka).

Romanthaka (adj.) [fr. romanthati] chewing the cud, ruminating Vin II.132.

Romanthati & **Romantheti** [to romantha; cp. Lat. rumen & ruminare=E. ruminate] to chew the cud, to ruminate Vin II.132 (°ati); J IV.392 (°eti).

Romanthana (nt.) [fr. romanthati] ruminating Vin II.321.

Roruva [fr. **ru**, cp. Sk. raurava, N. of a purgatory] 1. a sort of hart (i. e. ruru) M I.429. — 2. N. of a naraka (purgatory): see Dictionary of Names. E.g. J III.299; Dāvs III.12; Sdhp 195. Cp. BSk. raurava Divy 67.

Rosa [cp. Sk. roṣa, of **ruṣ**] 1. anger, angry feeling M I.360. — 2. quarrel J IV.316.

Rosaka (adj.) [fr. rosa; cp. BSk. roṣaka Divy 38] angry, wrathful S I.85, 96; Sn 133; Vv 52⁸ (=paresaŋ ros' uppādanena r. VvA 226); J II.270.

Rosanā (f.) [abstr. fr. rosati] making angry, causing anger, being angry Vbh 86 (hiŋsanā+), expl^d at VbhA 75 by ghaṭṭanā. Cp. BSk. roṣaṇī AvŚ I.178.

Rosaneyya (adj.) [grd. formation fr. rosa] apt to be angry or cause anger; neg. a° not to be angered, not irritable Sn 216.

Rosita [pp. of **rus**, to smear: Sk. rūṣita; given as root **rus** at Dhtm 442 with meaning "ālepa"] smeared (with), anointed J IV.440 (=vilitta C.).

Roseti [Caus. of rosati, **ruṣ**; see rusita] to make angry, to annoy, to irritate S I.162; A II.215 (so read for rosati); III.38; Sn 125, 130, 216; J I.432; IV.491.

Rohañña (adj.) [fr. roha=rohita] red J V.259 (rohaññā pungav'ūsabhā; C. expl^s by ratta-vaṇṇā) Kern. *Toev.* s. v. proposes rohiñño=*rohiṇyah, (cp. pokkharaṇī for °iṇī) red cows.

Rohati: for the Sk. rohati of **ruh** to grow we find the regular P. correspondent **rūhati**: see rūhati¹. The Caus. of this verb is **ropeti** (to make grow): see ropeti! — Another root, restricted to the Pāli, is seen in **rūhati²** (with pp. rūḷha) and is equal to **rundh** (rudh, rumbh) to break. The Caus. of this root (**ropeti²**) is either an indirect formation from it or (more likely) a direct representative of **rup=lup** as in P. lumpati. To the latter belong the prep. cpds. oropeti & voropeti.

Rohicca [fr. rohita, perhaps directly fr. Vedic rohit a ewe, lit. the red one] a kind of deer J VI.537 (°sarabhā migā).

Rohiṇī (f.) [cp. Vedic rohiṇī red cow or mare] 1. a red cow A I.162=III.214. — 2. N. of a nakkhatta or constellation ("red cow") SnA 456; Mhvs 19, 47. — 3. N. of a river SnA 357.

Rohita (adj.) [Vedic rohita; cp. the usual P. word lohita red & blood. See also rudhira & ruhira] red, as attribute of fishes at J V.405 (i. e. a special kind of fish), and of deer at J V.406 in same passage (i. e. a special kind of deer). Otherwise only in standing term rohita-maccha the "red fish," viz. Cyprinus Rohita, which is freq. mentioned in the "Jātaka" literature, e. g. J II.433; III.333; DhA II 132 (four), 140; KhA 118.

L.

La syllable of abbreviation, corresponding to our "etc.": see peyyāla.

Lak-aṭṭhika at VvA 222 is doubtful; aṭṭhika means "kernel," lak° may be a misspelling for labujak° (?).

Lakanaka (nt. ?) [fr. **lag**, with k for g, as lakuṭa: laguḷa etc. Would correspond to Sk. *lagnaka, cp. Trenckner, *Notes* 62; Geiger, *P.Gr.* § 39[1]] ship's anchor (nāvā°) Miln 377 (v. l. lagganaka), 378.

Lakāra [for alankāra, lit. "fitting up," cp. Hindī & Marāthī langara, Tamil ilankaran] a sail J II.112; Miln 378; Dāvs IV.42; Vism 137 (v. l. BB. lankāra).

Lakuṭa [see laguḷa for etym.] a club, cudgel Miln 255 (in sequence daṇḍa-leḍḍu-lakuṭa-muggara), 301, 367, 368. See also laguḷa.

Lakuṇṭaka [dialectical] a dwarf Mhvs 23, 50 (°sarīratta); VbhA 26 (°pāda-purisa, cpd. with arūpa); PugA 227; C. on S I.237.

Lakuṇṭakatta (nt.) [fr. lakuṇṭaka] dwarfishness J VI.337.

Laketi [for laggeti, see lakanaka] to hold fast (lit. to make adhere) Miln 377.

Lakkha (nt.) [fr. **lakṣ** (see lakkhaṇa), or (after Grassmann) **lag** "to fix," i. e. to mark. Cp. Vedic lakṣa price at gambling (Zimmer, *Altind. Leben* 287)] 1. a mark Miln 102. — 2. a target Miln 418; DhA 1.52 (°yoggā target practice, i. e. shooting). — 3. a stake at gambling J VI.271. — 4. a high numeral, a lac or 100,000 (but cp. PvA 255, where lakkha of Pv IV.3[38] is taken as a "period of time," equal to 100 koṭis); Dāvs V.66.

Lakkhañña (adj.) [fr. lakkhaṇa, cp. BSk. lakṣaṇya diviner Divy 474] connected with auspices, auspicious, in phrase "lakkhaññā vata bho dosinā ratti" (how grand a sign, friends, is the moonlight night! trsl°) D I.47 = J I.509 (expld at DA I.141 as "divasa-mās'-ādīnaŋ lakkhaṇaŋ bhavituŋ yuttā"); J V.370 (°sammata considered auspicious).

Lakkhaṇa (nt.) [Vedic lakṣman nt. sign; adj. lakṣmaṇa; later Sk. lakṣmaṇa nt. In the def° of grammarians syn. with anka brand, e. g. Dhtp 536 "anka lakkhaṇe lakkha dassane," or Dhtm 748 "lakkha = dassanaanke"; cp. J I.451 lakkhaṇena anketi to brand. — The Sk. Np. Lakṣmaṇa appears also in Prk. as Lakkhaṇa: Pischel, *Prk. Gr.* § 312] 1. sign, characteristic, mark; esp. a sign as implying something extraordinary or pointing to the future, therefore a prognosticative mark (cp. talisman), a distinguishing mark or salient feature, property, quality (as Rh. D. in *Dial.* I.19 somewhat lengthily, after Bdhgh, trslˢ lakkhaṇa by "signs of good & bad qualities in the foll. things and of the marks in them denoting the health or luck of their owners") D I.9 (a long list, as forbidden practice of fortune-telling, like maṇi° from jewels, daṇḍa° from sticks, asi° from marks on swords etc.); Sn 360 (pl. lakkhaṇā, here as fortune-telling together with *supina* telling fr. dreams, cp. SnA 362: daṇḍa°, vattha° etc. referring to D I.9), 927 (with Āthabbana, supina & nakkhatta, all kinds of secret sciences; expld at SnA 564 as "maṇi-lakkhaṇâdi") 1018 (gottaŋ brūhi sa° "with its distinguishing marks"); J VI.364 (sign of beauty); Miln 171 (yathāva° just characterization); Mhvs 35, 109 (itthi° auspicious signs in women); PvA 161, 219; SnA 386. A long enum° of all sorts of (perfect) marks (tatha-lakkhaṇāni) is found at DA I.62 sq. Cp. tādi-lakkhaṇa marks of such (a being), with ref. to good luck etc. J III.98; SnA 200; VvA 95. — 2. mark on the body, esp. when serving a def. purpose, e. g. as the branding (of slaves), or the marks of a fortunate being, pointing towards his future greatness: (a) brand J I.451, cp. cpd. °āhata. — (b) the (32) marks of a mahā-purisa or a great being, either destined to be a *rājā cakkavatti*, or a *sammā-sambuddha*. These are given at Sn 1019 (pl. lakkhaṇā), 1021, 1022 as only 3 (viz. mukhaŋ jivhāya chādeti, uṇṇ' assa bhamuk' antare, kos' ohitaŋ vattha-guyhaŋ with ref. to his tongue, the hair between the eyebrows & the sexual organ); more completely as 32 at D II.16 sq.; III.142 sq. (the Lakkhaṇa Suttanta); referred to at D I.88, 105; J I.56; Mhvs 5, 91; cp. paripuṇṇa-kāya Sn 548 (with expl° lakkhaṇehi puṇṇatāya at SnA 452). — 3. (in spec. sense:) pudendum J V.197 (subha°, the male member), 366. — 4. (adj.) (-°) having the marks (of), characterized by, of such & such character A I.102 (kamma°; bāla° & paṇḍita°, together with bāla- & paṇḍitanimitta); Miln 111 (sata-puñña°, of the Buddha); VvA 71 (para-sampatti-usuyyā-lakkhaṇā issā); PvA 17, 120. — 5. (as t. t. in philosophy) specific attribute, characteristic (mark). In contrast to *nimitta* more a substantial attribute or primary characteristic (cp. VbhA 261). Compared with other terms of definition we get the foll.: *rasa* essential property, *paccupaṭṭhāna* recurring phenomenon, *padaṭṭhāna* immediate occasion DhsA 63 (trsl° *Expos.* I.84). cp. *Cpd.* 13 (where *padaṭṭhāna* is trsld as "proximate cause"). — Ps I.54 sq. (khandhānaŋ); II.108 (saccānaŋ). VbhA 85, 136 (with ref. to the Paṭiccasamuppāda, cp. Vism 528), 261 (fourfold, of kesā etc.); Vism 278 (with ref. to kammaṭṭhāna) 351 (4, of the dhātus: thaddha°, ābandhana°, paripācana°, vitthambhana°), 363 sq. (id.), 495 (ariya-saccānaŋ); VvA 38 (compd with ārammaṇa with ref. to jhāna). — The 3 properties (tilakkhaṇaŋ) of existing things or of the phenomenal world are **anicca, dukkha, anatta**, or impermanence, suffering, unreality: thus at J I.48 (dhamma-desanā ti-l-°muttā), 275; III.377 (through contemplating them arises vipassanā & pacceka-bodhi-ñāṇa). — abl. **lakkhaṇato** "by or qua characteristic," "in its essential qualification," often found in exegetical analysis in Commentary style combd with var. similar terms (atthato, kamato, nimittato etc.), e. g. Vism 351, 363, 495, 528; VbhA 46, 76, 83, 131, 261 (where Vism 351 has paripācana for uṇhatta); SnA 343. — Cp. upa°, vi°, sa°.

-āhata affected with a mark (of punishment or disgrace), branded Vin I.76; VvA 66. -kusala clever at interpreting bodily marks or at fortune-telling from signs (cp. nemittaka) M I.220; J I.272. -kusalatā cleverness at (telling people's fortune by) signs VvA 138. -paṭiggāhaka one who reads the signs, a soothsayer, wise man J I.56. -pāṭhaka an expert in (interpreting) signs, fortune-teller J I.455; II.194; V.211. -manta the secret science of (bodily) marks Sn 690 (but expl[d] at SnA 488 as "lakkhaṇāni ca vedā ca," thus taking it as Dvandva); DhA III.194. -sampatti excellency of marks J I.54. -sampanna endowed with (auspicious) signs Sn 409; J I.455.

Lakkhika & °ya (adj.) [fr. lakkhī] belonging to auspices, favoured by good luck Sdhp 105 (°ya); usually neg. alakkhika unlucky, unfortunate, ill-fated; either with appa-puñña of no merit, e. g. S V.146=J II.59; Vv 50[8] (=nissirīka, kālakaṇṇi VvA 212); or pāpa wicked Vin II.192 (of Devadatta).

Lakkhita [pp. of lakkheti] see abhi°.

Lakkhī (f.) [Sk. lakṣmī] 1. luck, good fortune, success, personal welfare J III.443 (comb[d] with sirī splendour; expl[d] by parivāra-sampatti & paññā respectively); IV.281 (expl[d] as "sirī pi puññam pi paññā pi"). — 2. splendour, power Dāvs I.6 (rajja° royal splendour); IV.38 (id.). — 3. prosperity Dāvs V.35 (°nidhāna Anurādhapura).

Lakkheti [Denom. fr. lakkha] to mark, distinguish, characterize Nett 30. — pp. lakkhita. — Cp. upa°.

Lagati & **Laggati** [with variant langati; the spelling with gg is the usual one. Root **lag**, as in Vedic lakṣa etc.; Sk. lagati, pp. lagna (from the pp. lagga the double g has been generalized in P.: but see Geiger, *P.Gr.* § 136); perhaps to Lat. langueo, E. languid, from meaning "to lag," but doubtful; see Walde, *Lat. Wtb.* s. v. langueo. — The Dhtp 23 gives **lag** in meaning "sanga," which is the customary syn. in the commentaries. Cp. langī] to adhere to, stick (fast) to (loc.), to hang from Vin I.202; J III.120; DhA I.131; III.298 (ppr. alaggamāna); DA I.257 (for abhisajjati); aor. laggi PvA 153 (tīre); ger. laggitva J III.19; DhA IV.25; PvA 280 (but better to be read laggetvā making fast; as v.l.). — pp. lagga & laggita. — Caus. laggeti to make stick to, to fasten, tie, hang up Vin I.209; II.117, 152; J III.107; V.164, 175; Mhvs 7, 9 (suttañ ca tesaŋ hatthesu laggetvā); DhA I.138. — Caus. II. laggāpeti to cause to fasten or stick, to make stick, to obstruct J III.241; Mhvs 33, 11; 34, 48 (kalāpaŋ); DhA IV.183. — Cp. ālaggeti.

Lagana & **Laggana** (nt.) [fr. **lag**] 1. adhering J I.46 (*g.*; V.281); with *gg*: J III.202 (=sanga); Nd[2] p. 188 (s. v. nissita, in sequence l., bandhana, palibodha); Miln 105; DhA III.433. — 2. slinging round, making fast VvA 212.

Laguḷa [cp. Sk. laguḍa, Marāthī lākūḍa, Hindī lakuṭa stick. The word is really a dialect word (Prk.) and as such taken into Sk. where it ought to be *lakṛta=lakuṭa. Other etym. connections are Lat. lacertus (arm), Gr. λέκρανα, λάξ; Old Prussian alkunis elbow; and distantly related E. leg. See Walde, *Lat. Wtb.* s. v. lacertus. Cp. P. bhuja[1] & ratana] a club, cudgel Vin III.77 (enum[d] with var. weapons of murder, like asi, satti, bheṇḍi, pāsāṇa etc.); Miln 152, 351 (kodaṇḍa-laguḷa-muggara), 355 (kilesa°); J VI.394; Vism 525 (°abhighāta).

Lagga (adj.) [pp. of lag(g)ati] sticking; stuck, attached; obstructed, hindered Nd[2] 107; Miln 346 (laggaŋ disvā mahiŋ); DhsA 127 (alagga-bhāva); DhA I.361 (°mānasa). Neg. alagga unobstructed (lit. not sticking or being stuck to), in phrase ākāso alaggo asatto apatiṭṭhito apalibuddho Miln 388 and elsewhere. — Cp. olagga.

Laggāpana (nt.) [fr. laggāpeti: see lagati] making stick, causing obstruction J III.241.

Laggita [pp. of lag(g)ati] stuck, adhering; obstructed J IV.11. Often in exegetical style in sequence **lagga, laggita**, palibuddha, e. g. Nd[2] p. 188 (s. v. nissita), cp. No. 107.

Laghima (langhima) in phrase aṇima-laghim' ādikaŋ is doubtful in reading & meaning at KhA 108=Vism 211 (spelt langh° here).

Lankāra see **lakāra**.

Langī (f.) [fr. **lag**] bolt, bar, barrier, obstruction, only metaphorically with ref. to avijjā M I.142, 144; Pug 21; Dhs 390; VbhA 141.

Langula (nt.) [cp. Sk. lāngula & lāngūla; also the ordinary P. forms nangula & nanguṭṭha, to **lag**] the tail of an animal Mhvs 6, 6 (lāḷento langulaŋ; v. l. nangulaŋ). See also **nangula** & (concerning l > n) landhati (=nandhati); nalāṭa (for laḷāta).

Langhaka [fr. **langh**] a jumper, tumbler, acrobat J II.142; Miln 34, 191, 331. f. langhikā Vin IV.285 (with naṭakā & sokajjhāyikā).

Langhati [**langh**, a by-form of **lagh**, as in laghu (see lahu) light, quick; Idg. ***legh** & ***lengh**, with meanings of both "quick" & "light" (or "little") from the movement of jumping. Here belong Gr. ἐλαχύς little, ἐλαφρός quick; Lat. levis (fr. *leghuis), Goth. leihto= E. light; Ohg. lungar quick, Ger. ge-lingen to succeed. Further Lat. limen threshold. Perhaps also the words for "lungs," viz. Ger. lunge, E. lights etc. — The Dhtp 33 defines **lagh** (**langh**) by "gati-sosanesu"] 1. to jump over (acc.), step over, to hop J III.272; V.472 (langhamāno yāti); Miln 85. — 2. to make light of, disregard, neglect, transgress PvA 15; VvA 138. — Cp. abhilanghati, ullanghati. — Caus. langheti (=langhati) to jump over (acc.), lit. to make jump J V.472 (vatiŋ); Th 2, 384 (Meruŋ langhetuŋ icchasi); Miln 85. — ger. langhayitvā ThA 255, & (poet.) langhayitvāna J I.431 (=attānaŋ langhitvā C.); Mhvs 25, 44 (pākāraŋ). — Cp. olangheti.

Langhana (nt.) [fr. **langh**] jumping, hopping J I.430 (°naṭaka a tumbler, jumper, acrobat, cp. Fick, *Soc. Gliederung* 188, 190, 192); II.363, 431. Cp. ullanghanā, olanghanā.

Langhamayā (pl.) at J V.408 is problematic. We should expect something like langhiyo or langhimaya in meaning "deer," as it is comb[d] with eneyyaka. The C. reads langhimayā ("like deer; jumping"?) & expl[s] by nānā-ratana-mayā "made of var. jewels," rather strange.

Langhāpana (nt.) [fr. Caus. of **langh**] making jump, raising, lifting Vism 143 ("launching").

Langhi (**Langhī**) (f.) [fr. **langh**] 1. a kind of deer (?) J VI.537. — 2. doubtful of meaning & origin in phrase langhī-pitāmahā at J II.363=III.226: "whose grandfather was a deer, or a jumper" (?); used in disparagingly addressing a crane. The C. to J II.363 expl[s] rather strangely as follows: **langhī vuccati ākāse langhanato megho** "(a) jumping deer is called the cloud because of its jumping in the air," **balākā ca nāma megha-saddena gabbhaŋ gaṇhantī ti** "the cranes conceive by the sound of the cloud," **meghasaddo balākānaŋ pitā megho pitāmaho ti** "the sound of the cloud is the father of the cranes & the cloud the grandfather."

Lajjati [**lajj**; Dhtp 72: lajjane] 1. to be ashamed or abashed, to be modest or bashful PvA 48 (for harāyati);

ppr. lajjamāna DhA I.188; PvA 88; fut. lajjissati J III.218; inf. lajjituŋ DhA I.72; ger. lajjitvā J I.208; grd. lajjitabba (nt.) what one has to be ashamed of, something disgraceful J VI.395; also (an odd form) lajjitāya (so read: see Geiger, *P.Gr.* § 203 against Trenckner, *Notes*, 66[27]) Dh 316. — 2. to have regard of (gen.), to consider, to respect J IV.128. — Caus. II. lajjāpeti to cause to be ashamed, to put to the blush J III.137; V.296. — pp. lajjita.

Lajjana (nt.) [fr. **lajj**] being ashamed Dhtp 72.

Lajjanaka (nt.) [fr. lajjana] causing shame, humiliating, disgraceful J VI.395.

Lajjava (nt.) [fr. **lajj**] shamefacedness D III.213 (where Dhs 1340 has maddava); cp. A I.94.

Lajjā (f.) [fr. **lajj**] shame, bashfulness, modesty M I.414; DA I.70; DhA II.90; instr. lajjāya out of shame PvA 47, 112, 283. Cp. nillajja.

Lajjāpanikā (f.) [fr. lajjāpeti, Caus. II. of lajjati] making ashamed, putting to shame, disgracing J V.284 (kula° bringing disgrace on the clan).

Lajjita [pp. of lajjati] ashamed, bashful Sdhp 35. — f. lajjitā as n. abstr. "bashfulness" DhA I.188.

Lajjitabbaka (nt.) [grd. of lajjati+ka] something to be ashamed of, a cause of shame, disgrace J VI.395.

Lajjin (adj.) [fr. **lajj**] feeling shame, modest, afraid, shy, conscientious (expl[d] as "one who has *hiri & ottappa*" by C. on S I.73: see *K.S.* 320 & cp. *Dhs. trsl*[n] p. 18) D I.4, 63; III.15; S I.73; A II.208; IV.249 sq.; Pug 57; Pv II.9[15] (expl[d] as one who is afraid of sin); Miln 373; DA I.70. — pl. lajjino Vin I.44.
-dhamma (lajji°) modesty, feeling of shame Vin II.53 sq.

Lacchati fut. of labhati (q. v.).

Lañca [cp. Sk. lañca] a present, a bribe J I.201; II.186; V.184; VI.408 (gahita, bribes received); DhA I.269 (°ŋ adāsi); IV.1; PvA 209. The word is a word peculiar to the "Jātaka" literature.
-khādaka "eater of bribes," one who feeds on bribes J II.196; V.1. -ggāha taking of bribes J V.109. -daṇḍaka a staff given as a present (?) J VI.450 (v. l. volañjanaka°). -dāna gift of bribes, bribery J III.205. -vittaka one who gets rich through bribes J I.339.

Lañcaka: Hardy in ed. of Netti, p. 278 suggests writing lañjaka & trsl[d] "making known," "exposition" (cp. Sk. **lañj** to declare], found only at Miln 137 & 217 in cpd. Saŋyutta-nikāya-vara-lañcaka (trl[n] Rh. D.: "most excellent"); at Miln 242 & 258 in Majjhima-nikāya vara°; at Miln 362 in Ekuttara-nikāya-vara°; and at Nett 2 in cpd. nayalañjaka. Trenckner (Miln ed. p. 424) translates it as "excellent gift (to mankind)."

Lañcana in "kārāpesi tilañcanaŋ" at Dpvs 20, 10 is not clear. We may have to correct reading into lañchanaŋ or lañchakaŋ. Oldenberg in his trsl[n] (p. 211) leaves the word out and remarks: "Probably this passage refers to the three *pupphayāna* mentioned in the Mahāvaŋsa (33, 22, where Geiger reads "pupphādhānāni tīṇi," with trsl[n] "3 stone terraces for offerings of flowers"), though I do not know how to explain or to correct the word used here (*tilañcanaŋ*)."

Lañcha [fr. **lañch**] a mark, an imprint J II.425; VbhA 52.

Lañchaka [fr. lañcha; doubtful] one who makes marks (expl[d] by Cy. as "lakkhaṇa-kāraka") J IV.364, 366 (ti°, so expl[d] by Cy. v. l. ni°). See nillañchaka & cp. lañcana (ti°).

Lañchati [**lañch** Dhtp 54 "lakkhaṇe"] to stamp, to seal DhA I.35 (sāsanaŋ rāja-muddāya lañchanto). — Caus. lañcheti. — 1. to seal J I.452 (spelt lañjetvā); II.326; VI.385; SnA 577 (rāja-muddikāya); DhA I.21. — 2. to mark, paint, smear Vin II.107=266 (mukhaŋ). — Caus. II. lañchāpeti to have marked or sealed (by king's command) Vism 38 ("had his seal put to this order"; trsl.). — Cp. nillaccheti.

Lañchana (nt.) [fr. **lañch**] 1. stamp, mark, imprint VvA 89 (sasa°, of the moon); Dāvs II.23 (pada°). — 2. the seal (of a letter or edict) SnA 172. — Cp. lañcana.

Lañchita [pp. of lañcheti] sealed J I.227 (pihita-lañchitā vā loha-cātiyo).

Lañjaka [see lañcaka] in dīpa° stands as equivalent of dīpavaŋsa thus "story of the island" Dpvs 18, 2. Oldenberg (*trsl*[n] p. 204) translates "the island of *Lankā*."

Lañjeti see lañchati and valañjeti.

Laṭukikā (f.) [Dimin. fr. laṭvāka; dial.] the Indian quail, Perdix chinensis D I.91; M I.449 (l. sakuṇikā); J III.44, 174 sq. (quoted at SnA 358 & DhA I.55); V.121; Miln 202; DA I.257. — Cp. Cunningham, *Bharhut Tope*, p. 58.

Laṭṭhaka (adj.) [Kern, *Toev.* s. v. compares Sk. laṭaha, laḍaha, dialectical] beautiful, auspicious, lovely J III.464, 493; IV.1, 477; DA I.284.

Laṭṭhi (f.) [Sk. yaṣṭi, with l for y; also in Prk. see Pischel, *Prk. Gr.* § 255 & cp. Geiger, *P.Gr.* § 46[3]. The doublet yaṭṭhi also in Pāli] 1. a staff, stick D I.105 (patoda° goad), 126 (id.); VvA 64 (id.); J IV.310 (laṭṭhī hata=laṭṭhiyā hata C.); V.280; Miln 27. — 2. stick of sugar cane (ucchu°) PvA 257. — 3. sprout of a plant, offshoot J III.161 (in simile); usually -°, as in anga° sprout ThA 226; dālika° of the d. creeper Th 2, 297; beḷuva° of the Vilva tree KhA 118; sala° of the Sal tree A II.200. Found also in names of places, as Laṭṭhivana (J I.83 etc.).
-madhu(ka) "cane-honey," i. e. liquorice J IV.537; DhA IV.171 (°ka).

Laṭṭhikā (f.)=laṭṭhi, only in Npl. as -° (cp. laṭṭhi 3), e. g. Amba° the grove of mango sprouts DA I.41.

Laṇḍa (nt.) [cp. Sk. laṇḍa (dial.). The Dhtm under No. 155 gives a root **laḍ** in meaning "jigucchana," i. e. disgust] excrement, dung of animals, dirt; mostly used with ref. to elephants (hatthi°), e. g. at J II.19; DhA I.163, 192; IV.156 (here also as assa° horse dung.) Cp. laṇḍikā.

Laṇḍikā (f.) [fr. laṇḍa], only in aja° goat's dirt, pellet of goat's dung J I.419; PvA 283.

Latā (f.) [cp. Sk. latā, connected with Lat. lentus flexible; Ohg. lindi soft, E. lithe; also Ohg. lintea lime tree; Gr. ἐλάτη fir tree] 1. a slender tree, a creeping plant, creeper A I.202 (māluvā°); Vv 35[5] (=vallī VvA 162); 47[4] (kosātakī l.); J I.464 (rukkha°, here perhaps better "branch"); DhA I.392 (°pasādhana: see under mahā°); Miln 253, 351; VvA 12 (kappa°); PvA 51, 121; Vism 183 (where the foll. kinds are given: lābu, kumbhaṇḍī, sāmā, kāḷavallī, pūtilatā). —nāga° the iron wood tree: see under nāga; pūti° a sort of creeper (q. v.). On latā in similes see *J.P.T.S.* 1907, 130. — 2. (fig.) an epithet of taṇhā (greed), as much as it strangles its victim Dhs 1059, 1136; Nett 24, 121. — 3. (fig.) streak, flash, in vijjul-latā flash of lightning J I.103.
-kamma creeper-work (comb[d] with mālā-kamma) Vin II.117, 152.

Laddha [pp. of labhati] (having) obtained, taken, received Sn 106, 239; J V.171; Mhvs 5, 133 (kiñci laddhaŋ); 10, 37 (kaññā laddhā); PvA 5. —laddhatvaŋ at J IV.406. is to be corrected to uddhatvā. — Cp. upa°, pa°.

-adhippāya one who obtains his wishes Nd^2 542. -assāsa getting one's breath again, coming to (out of a swoon) J IV.126. -upasampada one who has obtained ordination PvA 54. -jaya victorious Mhvs 25, 98. -jīvika revived PvA 40. -nāma so-called ThA 292 (puthulomo laddhanāmo maccho); PvA 33 (yamaloka l-n. petaloka), 52 (niraya l-n. naraka), 57 (kuñjara l-n. hatthi), 107 (sūcikā jighacchā), 119 (Purindada= Sakka), 143 (Himavanto=pabbata-rājā), etc.

Laddhā is ger. and 3rd sg. aor.; laddhāna ger. of *labhati* (q. v.).

Laddhi (f.) [fr. **labh**] religious belief, view, theory, esp. heretical view; a later term for the earlier diṭṭhi (cp. *Kvu trsl.* introd. p. 47) J I.142 (Devadattassa), 425; III.487; V.411; Dāvs II.86 (dulladdhi wrong view); DA I.117; PvA 254; Sdhp 65. Cp. upa°.

Laddhika (-°) [fr. laddhi] having a (wrong) view or belief, schismatic J I.373 (evaŋ°); Dpvs VII.35 (puthu°).

Landhati see nandhati & pilandhana. Concerning l>n cp. langula.

Lapa (adj. n.) [fr. **lap**: see lapati] talkative, talking, prattling; a talker, tattler, prattler, chatterer A II.26; Th 1, 959=It 112; Vism 26 (doubled: lapa-lapa)= Nd^1 226 (as lapaka-lapaka).

Lapaka [fr. **lap**] one who mutters, a droner out (of holy words for pay) D I.8 (cp. *Dial.* I.15); A III.111; J III.349; Miln 228; DA I.91.

Lapati [**lap**, cp. Russ. lépet talk, Cymr. llêf voice. The Dhtp 188 & 599 defines **lap** with "vacana"] to talk, prattle, mutter Sn 776; It 122; Pv I.8^1; II.6^3. — Cp. ullapati, palapati, samullapati. — Caus. lapeti (and lāpeti, metri causâ) to talk to, to accost, beg S I.31 (here meaning "declare"); Sn 929 (janaŋ na lāpayeyya=na lapayeyya lapanaŋ pajaheyya Nd^1 389); DhA II.157. — Infin. lapetave (only in Gāthā language cp. Geiger, *P.Gr.* § 204) Ud 21. — pp. lapita. — Caus. II. lapāpeti DhA II.157.

Lapana (nt.) & **lapanā** (f.) 1. talking, muttering; esp. prattling or uttering indistinct words for the sake of begging, patter D I.8; A II.26; III.430; Nd^1 389; Nett 94; Miln 383. As f. lapanā at Vbh 352; Vism 23 & 27 (def.); VbhA 482. — 2. the mouth, in cpd. lapana-ja "mouth born," i. e. tooth J VI.218 (=mukhaja C.). — Cp. ālapana ālapanatā, ullapana.

Lapāpana (nt.) [fr. Caus. II. lapāpeti of **lap**] causing to speak, speaking ThA 78.

Lapita [pp. of lapati] talked, uttered, muttered It 98.

Lapila see lambila.

Labuja [cp. Sk. labuja] the bread-fruit tree, Artocarpus lacucha or incisa D I.53; J IV.363; V.6, 417; PvA 153 (sa°, read as salaḷa°, like Vv 35^5, expl^d at VvA 162).

Labbhamanatta (nt.) [abstr. fr. ppr. med. of labhati] the fact of being taken PvA 56.

Labbhā (indecl.) [best to be taken, with Pischel, *Prk. Gr.* § 465, as an old Opt. 3rd sg., like sakkā which corresponds to Vedic śakyāt. Thus labbhā=*labhyāt, as in Māgadhī] allowable, possible (with inf.); usually neg. (thus=Prohibitive!) Sn 393 na l. phassetuŋ; SnA p. 376 expl^s by "sakkā"), 590; Pv II.6^{10}; J I.64 (na l. tayā pabbajituŋ), 145 (id.), PvA 96 (=laddhuŋ sakkā).

Labha (-°) (adj.) [a base-formation fr. **labh**] receiving, to be received, to get; only in dul° hard to get Sn 75; S I.101; J I.307; Pug 26; Miln 16; Sdhp 17, 27; and su° easy to obtain Pv II.3^{10}.

Labhati [later Vedic **labh** for older **rabh**, cp. rabhate, rabha, rabhasa. Related are Gr. λαμβάνω to get, λάφυρον booty; Lat. rabies=E. rabies; Lith. lõbis wealth. — The Dhtp (204) simply defines as "lābhe." On the Prk. forms see Pischel, *Prk. Gr.* § 484. — See also rabhasa] 1. (the very freq. & ordinary meaning) to get, to receive, obtain, acquire. — 2. (fig.) to obtain permission, to receive an opportunity, etc., as "pabbajituŋ sace lacchāmi" if I am allowed to receive the pabbajjā Mhvs 18, 5; or "labhamāno niccam pi khāditu-kāmo 'mhi" if I get the chance I should always like to eat J I.478; and passim (cp. Pass. labbhati below). The *paradigma* of labhati shows a great variety of forms owing to its frequent occurrence (cp. E. "get"). We have selected the most interesting ones. *Pres. Ind.* labhati rare (late, e. g. Vism 136); usually med labhate Th 1, 35; Sn 185, 439; 1st sg. labhe Pv I.6^4; 2nd sg. labhase J II.220; 3rd pl. labhare S I.110. — ppr. med. labhamāna S I.122 (otāraŋ a°, cp. IV.178; M I.334); also in Pass. sense "getting taken" PvA 71. — *Opt.* 3rd sg. labhe Sn 458, & (med.) labhetha Sn 45, 46, 217; Pv II.9^7; also (usual form) labheyya PvA 115. 2nd sg. med. labhetho (=Sk. °thāḥ) Sn 833. — *Imper.* 2nd sg. labha It 77; 3rd labhatu PvA 112; med. 2nd sg. labhassu Th 2, 432; 3rd sg. labhataŋ D II.150; 1st pl. (as Hortative) labhāmase Pv I.5^5 (=labhāma PvA 27); & labhāmhase Pv III.2^{24}. — *Fut.* 3rd sg. lacchasi (Sk. lapsyati) S I.114; Pv II.4^8; III.3^7; J II.60 (Māro otāraŋ l.), 258; Miln 126; DhA I.29; SnA 405; ThA 69 (Ap.); 1st sg. lacchāmi M II.71; 2nd sg. lacchasi Vv 83^6; Pv IV.1^{60}; 1st pl. lacchāma J I.54; IV.292; & lacchāmase (med.) Vv 32^9. Also (the Com. form) labhissati PvA 190; VvA 136. — *Cond.* 1st pl. alabhissāma J III.35; med. 3rd sg. alabhissatha D II.63. — *Pret.* (& *aor.*) (a) 3rd sg. alattha D I.176 (alattha pabbajjaŋ); M II.49; S IV.302; J IV.310; VvA 66, 69; 1st sg. alatthaŋ D II.268; Vv 81^{22}; Th 1, 747; DhA III.313; 2nd sg. alattha S I.114; 1st pl. alatthamha M II.63; 3rd pl. alatthuŋ D II.274, & alatthaŋsu S I.48. — (b) (Prohib.) mā laddhā (3rd sg. med.) shall not receive (Sk. alabdha) J III.138. — (c) labhi Sn 994; 1st sg. labhiŋ Th 1, 218; 2, 78; J II.154; VvA 68; & alabhitthaŋ Th 1, 217; 3rd sg. alabhittha Pv I.7^7 (spelt bbh); 1st pl. labhimhā (for labhimha) D II.147. — *Inf.* laddhuŋ J II.352; DhA III.117; PvA 96. — *Ger.* laddhā (poet.) Sn 306, 388, 766, 924; laddhāna (poet.) Sn 67 (=laddhā, labhitvā Nd^2 546); It 65; and (ord.) labhitva J I.150; III.332; PvA 95. — *Grd.* (a): labbhiya (only *neg.* alabbhiya what cannot be got) J IV.86; Pv II.6^9; labbhaneyya (a°) (in Com. style as expl^n of labbhanīya) J IV.86 (°ṭhāna); PvA 65 (°vatthu), 96 (id.); and labbhanīya (as a°-ṭṭhānāni impossible things) A III.54 sq. (*five* such items), 60 sq. (id.); J IV.59. — (b): laddhabba J III.332; PvA 112, 252. — (c): laddheyya Pv IV.3^{26}. — *Caus.* labbheti (for *lābheti, a diff. form^n fr. Sk. lambhayati, which is found in P. pa-lambheti) to make someone get, to procure, in 1st sg. aor. alabbhesi Vin IV.5=J I.193; DhA III.213 (v. l. labh°); and. in pres. 3rd sg. labbheti J III.353 (=adhigameti C.). — *Pass.* labbhati (fig.) to be permitted, to be possible or proper; (or simply:) it is to be Mhvs 30, 43; KhA 192 (vattuŋ), 207 (id.). — pp. laddha. — Cp. upa°, pati°, vi°.

Labhana (nt.) [fr. **labh**] taking, receiving, gift, acquisition DhA III.271 (°bhāva); PvA 73 (°ṭṭhāna), 121 (id.).

Lamba (*adj.*) (-°) [fr. **lamb**] hanging down, drooping, pendulous S IV.341, 342 (°cūḷakā bhaṭa hirelings with large or drooping top-knots); J II.185 (°tthana with hanging breasts); III.265 (°cūla-vihangama); Dāvs II.61. —**alamba** not drooping, thick, short J V.302; VI.3 (°tthaniyo). — Cp. ā°, vi° & **ālambana**.

Lambati [**lamb**; cp. Lat. limbus "limb," which may be also in E. *limp*, lit. "hanging down." — The Dhtp defines the root as "ramba lamba avasaŋsane" (No. 199).

as does Dhtm 284] to hang down, to droop, fall Mhvs 32, 70 (laggāni lambiṇsu), 71 (ākāse lambamānāni). — Fut. lambahīti (poet.) J v.302 (=lambissati). — Caus. lambeti to cause to hang up or to be suspended, to hang up Mhvs 34, 48. — Caus. II. lambāpeti id. Mhvs 21, 15. — pp. lambita. — Cp. abhi°, pa°, vi°.

Lambita [pp. of lambeti] hanging down, suspended Mhvs 27, 38; 30, 67.

Lambin (adj.) [fr. **lamb**] hanging down, able to hang or bend down (with ref. to the membrum virile) Vin III.35 ("tassa bhikkhussa angajātaŋ dīghaŋ hoti lambati, tasmā lambī ti vutto" Sam. Pās. I.278).

Lambila (adj.) [reading not quite certain, cp. ambila] sour, acrid, astringent (of taste) Nd[1] 240; Nd[2] 540; Dhs 629; DhsA 320 (reads lapila, v. l. lampila; expl[d] as "badara-sāḷava-kapiṭṭha-sāḷav' ādi"); Miln 56 (reads ambila).

Lambheti [Caus. of **labh**, for which usually labbheti (q. v. under labhati). The Sk. form is lambhayati. — The Dhtm. (840) puts it down as a special root, although it occurs only in cpd. pa° in this special meaning: "labhi vañcane"] see palambheti (to deceive, dupe). It may be possible that reading lampetvā at A II.77 (v. l. lambitvā) is to be corrected to lambhetvā (comb[d] with hāpetvā). —alambhavissa at S v.146 is to be read alam abhavissa, as at J II.59.

Laya [cp. Sk. laya: see līyati] 1. a brief measure of time, usually comb[d] with other expressions denoting a short moment, esp. frequent as khaṇa laya muhutta Vin I.12; III.92; A IV.137; cp. Dpvs I.16 (khaṇe khaṇe laye Buddho sabbalokaŋ avekkhati). — Vism 136 (īsakam pi layaŋ yantaŋ paggaṇheth' eva mānasaŋ). — 2. time in music, equal time, rhythm Dāvs IV.50; VvA 183 (dvādasannaŋ laya-bhedānaŋ vasena pabheda).

Laḷati [**lal**, onomat;. cp. Lat. lallo "lull"; Sk. lalallā; Gr. λάλος talkative; λαλέω talk; Ger. lallen. The Dhtp distinguishes 2 roots: **lal** (=icchā) & **laḷ** (=vilāsa & upasevā)] to dally, sport, sing J II.121 (ppr. laḷamānā); VvA 41 (laḷantī; with kīḷati), 57 (id.). — Caus. laḷeti J I.362 (ppr. lāḷentā); Vism 365; cp. upa° — pp. laḷita: see pa°.

Lalāṭa see nalāṭa (cp. langula).

Lava [fr. **lū**] a small particle, a drop VvA 253 (lavanka a small mark); Sdhp 105 (°odaka).

Lavaka [fr. **lū**] a cutter, reaper SnA 148 (v. l. lāvaka). See lāvaka.

Lavaṇa (nt.) [cp. late Vedic lavaṇa, cp. Zimmer, *Altind. Leben* 54] salt, lotion Miln 112; Sdhp 158. See loṇa.

Lavana (nt.) [fr. lunāti] cutting, reaping Miln 360.

Lavāpeti Caus. of lunāti (q. v.).

Lasagata (hattha) at A II.165 is to be read (with v. l.) as lepagata, i. e. sticky (opp. suddha).

Lasati [represents **las** to gleam, shine; sport, play; as well as **laṣ** to desire, long for. Cp. Lat. lascivus; Gr. λιλαίομαι; Goth. lustus=E., Ger. lust etc. — The Dhtp 324 defs. **las** as "kanti"] to desire, long; to dance, play, sport; to shine; to sound forth. See lāsana, abhilāsa, upaḷāseti, alasa, vilāsa. — Caus. lāseti to sport, to amuse (oneself) Vin II.10 (with vādeti, gāyati, naccati).

Lasikā (f.) [cp. Sk. *lasikā] the fluid which lubricates the joints, synovic fluid Vin I.202; D II.293; M III.90; S IV.111; Sn 196; J I.146; Miln 382. In detail at Vism 264, 362; VbhA 247.

Lasī (f.) [etym. ?] brains J I.493 (=matthalunga C.)= DhA I.145.

Lasuṇa & **Lasuna** (nt.) [cp. Sk. laśuna] garlic Vin II.140; IV.258; J I.474; Vv 43[6]; VvA 186.

Lahati to lick: see ullahaka, palahati, & lehati.

Lahu (adj.) [Sk. laghu & raghu: see etym. under langhati] light, quick A I.10, 45. —lahuŋ karoti to make light, to be frivolous J II.451. — nt. lahuŋ (adv.) quickly Pv IV.1[60]; Dpvs I.53; Mhvs 4, 17. — Usually as lahuka (q. v.).

-citta light-minded S I.201; J III.73. -ṭṭhāna lightness of body, bodily vigour, good health M I.437, 473; D I.204; Ud 15; Miln 14. [Cp. BSk. laghūtthānatā Divy 156.] -parivatta quickly or easily changing VbhA 408.

Lahukā (adj.) [lahu+ka] 1. light (opp. garuka); trifling Vin I.49; A II.48 (āpatti); IV.137 (jīvitaŋ parittaŋ l.); Miln 344 (āpatti). — 2. light, buoyant Th 1, 104 (kāyo); Dhs 648; Miln 105; PvA 280. atilahukaŋ (adv.) too soon Vin II.215. — 3 (as tt. in grammar) light (of letters or syllables), opp. garuka DA I.177 (with ref. to the 10 fold vyañjana of the dhamma).

Lahutā (f.) [fr. lahu] lightness, buoyancy Dhs 42, 322, 585; Vism 448.

Lahusa (adj.) [fr. lahu] easily offended, touchy D I.90; expl[d] by DA I.256 as follows: "lahusā ti lahukā, appaken' eva tussanti vā russanti vā udaka-piṭṭhe lābukaṭāhaŋ viya appakena pi uppilavanti." Cp. rabhasa.

Lahuso (adv.) [orig. abl. of lahu] quickly A IV.247 (sabba°); Vism 238.

Lākhā (f.) [cp. Sk. lākṣā] lac; lac-dye; enum[d] with other colourings at M I.127=S II.101=A III.230. — SnA 577; Vism 261 (as colour of blood).

-ācariya expert in lac-dyeing SnA 577. -guḷaka a ball of lac SnA 80. -goḷaka id. SnA 577. -tamba copper coloured with lac Th 2, 440 (=lākhā-rasa-rattehi viya tambehi lomehi samannāgata ThA 270). -rasa essence of lac, used for dyeing; lac-colouring J v.215 (°ratta-succhavi); VI.269 (id.); KhA 62, 63; ThA 270.

Lāja & **Lājā** (f.) [cp. Vedic lāja: Zimmer, *Altind. Leben* 269] 1. fried grain, parched corn: occurring only in comb[n] madhu-lāja fried grain with honey, sweet corn J III.538; IV.214, 281. — 2. the flower of Dalbergia arborea, used for scattering in bunches (with other flowers making 5 kinds or colours) as a sign of welcome & greeting, usually in phrase lāja-pañcamāni pupphāni ("a cluster of flowers with lāja as the fifth") DhA I.112; VvA 31; J I.55 (°pañcamakāni p.); cp. J II.240 (vippakiṇṇa-lāja-kusuma-maṇḍita-talā); VI.42 (vippakiṇṇa-lāja-kusuma-vāsa-dhūp' andhakāra); DhA I.140 (vippakiṇṇa-valikaŋ pañcavaṇṇa-kusuma-lāja-puṇṇa-ghaṭa-paṭimaṇḍita).

Lājeti [fr. lāja] to fry or have fried J VI.341 (v. l. lañc°, lañj°), 385 (lañchetvā; v. l. lañci°, lañje°).

Lāpa[1] [fr. **lap**] talk: see cpds. abhi°, pa°, sal°.

Lāpa[2] [also fr. **lap**, lit. "talker," cp. similar semantics of E. quail>Ger. quaken, quicken; E. quack. The P. form rests on pop. etym., as in Sk. we find corresponding name as lāba] a sort of quail, Perdix chinensis S v.146=J II.59. As lāpaka-sakuṇa also at J II.59. — Another name for quail is vaṭṭaka.

Lāpana (nt.) [fr. lāpeti, Caus. of **lap**] muttering, utterance, speech It 98; A I.165 (lapita°). Perhaps also to be read at Th 2, 73. — Cp. upa°.

Lāpin (-°) (adj.) [fr. **lap**] talking (silly) S III.143 (bāla°).

Lāpu (f.) [short for alāpu or alābu, cp. Geiger, *P.Gr.* § 39[6]] a kind of cucumber J I.336, 341. See also lābuka. **-latā** the cucumber creeper or plant Miln 374.

Lāpeti: see lapati & cp. upalāpeti.

Lābu (f.) & **Lābuka**=lāpu (alābu) gourd or pumpkin, often used as receptacle J I.158 (°ka), 411 (°kumbhaṇḍa vessel made of the gourd); V.37 (°ka). 155 (addha-lābu-samā thanā); DhA II.59 (°ka); SnA 227 (lābumhi catumadhuraŋ pūretukāmo). **-kaṭāha** a gourd as receptacle Vism 255, 359; VbhA 63.

Lābha [fr. **labh**] receiving, getting, acquisition, gain, possession; pl. possessions D I.8; II.58, 61; M I.508 (ārogya-paramā lābhā); III.39; A I.74; IV.157 sq., 160 (lābhena abhibhūto pariyādinnacitto Devadatto, cp. J I.185 sq.); Sn 31, 438, 828, 854, 1014, 1046 (cp. Nd[2] 548); It 67 (vitta°); J III.516 (yasa°, dhana°); Vism 93, 136 (°ŋ labhati), 150 (°assa bhāgin getting riches); PvA 113, 280.—A dat. sg. lābhā (for lābhāya) is used adverbially with foll. genitive in meaning of "for my (our) gain," "it is profitable," "good for me that" etc.; e. g. Miln 17 (lābhā no tāta, suladdhaŋ no tāta), 232 (lābhā vata tāsaŋ devatānaŋ); A III.313 (lābhā vata me suladdhaŋ vata me), expl[d] at Vism 223; DhA I.98 (lābhā vata me, elliptically); II.95 (l. vata no ye mayaŋ . . . upaṭṭhahimha). **-agga** highest gain J III.125; Miln 21. **-āsā** desire for gain A I.86. **-kamyā** (abl. out of desire for gain Sn 854, 929 (=lābha-hetu Nd[1] 389). **-taṇhā** craving for possession DhA IV.38. **-macchariya** selfishness in acquisitions A III.273; D III.234; Pug 19, 23; Dhs 1122. **-mada** pride of gain VbhA 466. **-sakkāra** gain and honour, usually comb[d] with °siloka fame; the two first e. g. at Vin II.196; It 73; J I.185, 186; V.75; the three comb[d] e. g. at M I.192; S II.227, 237; A II.73; III.343 sq., 377; Vbh 352 sq.; lābha-siloka alone at Vism 67.

Lābhaka (adj. nt.) [fr. lābha] one who receives; reception; a° not getting, non-receiving Vin III.77.

Lābhā see under lābha.

Lābhin (adj.) (-°) [fr. labha] receiving, getting, having, possessed of M III.39 (as n. "a receiver, recipient"); A I.24; II.85; IV.400; Pug 51; Vbh 332 (nikāma°); J I.140.—2. one who has intuition either in reasoning (or logical argument) or psychically, and who may therefore take certain premises for granted (opp. alābhin a denier) DA I.106, 120.

Lāmaka (adj.) [seems to be a specific Pāli word. It is essentially a C. word & probably of dialectical origin. Has it anything to do with omaka ?] insignificant, poor, inferior, bad, sinful. The usual syn. is pāpa.—Vin II.76; Vism 268 (=pāpaka); DhsA 45; KhA 243 (=khudda); PugA 229 (nīca lāmaka=oṇata); KhA 150 (°desanā, cp. ukkaṭṭha); DhA II.77; IV.44 (°bhāva); VvA 116; PvA 15 (for pāpa); 103 (=pāpaka), 125 (°purisa=kāpurisa); Sdhp 28, 253, 426, 526 (opp. ukkaṭṭha).—f. lāmikā J I.285; II.346 (for itarā); DhA II.61 (pāpikā l. diṭṭhi).—Cp. *Dhs. trsl.*[2] § 1025.

Lāmajjaka (lāmañjaka) (nt.) [cp. Sk. lāmajjaka] the root of Andropogon muricatus Vv 43[6] (v. l. °añc°); VvA 186, (°añj°) 187.

Lāyaka (-°) [fr. lāyati] cutter, reaper A III.365=S III.155 (read babbaja°).

Lāyati [for *lāvati, **lū**, for which the ordinary form is lunāti (q. v.), y for v as freq. in Pāli: see Geiger, *P.Gr.* § 46[2].—The Dhtp. has a root **lā** in meaning "ādāna" (No. 370)] to cut (off), mow, reap; ger. lāyitvā A III.365; J I.215; III.226; Vin III.64; Pv I.8[1] (=lāvitvā PvA 40).—pp. **lāyita**.

Lāyana (nt.) [fr. lāyati] cutting J V.45 (tiṇa-lāyana asi, sickle); DhA III.285 (v. l. for dāyana).

Lāyita [pp. of lāyati, lāyeti] cut, reaped J III.130 (tiṇaŋ na lāyita-pubbaŋ); Vism 419 (°ṭṭhāna place where one has reaped).

Lāla (adj.) [fr. **lal**, see laḷati] talking without sense, silly, foolish J VI.360, 417 (l). Cp. alālā.

Lālaka [lala+ka] a wag, silly person, fool J I.205; IV.210.

Lālapati & **Lālappati** [Intens. of lapati] to talk much, to talk silly, to lament, wail Sn 580; Pv IV.5[2] (=vilapati PvA 260); J III.217; Miln 148, 275; Mhvs 32, 68.—pp. **lālappita**.

Lālappa [fr. lālappati] talking much, excited or empty talk, wailing Vbh 100, 138; Ps I.38; Nett 29; VbhA 104 (=punappunaŋ lapanaŋ).

Lāla(p)pana (nt.) & °**ā** (f.)=lālappa, together with lāla(p)-pitatta (nt.) in exegesis of parideva at Nd[2] 416; Vbh 100, 138; VbhA 104; DA I.121.

Lālappita [pp. of lālappati] 1. talking much, wailing Miln 148 (paridevita-l.-mukha).—2. (nt.) much talk, excited talk, talking J VI.498.

Lālā (f.) [cp. laḷati] saliva J I.61, 248; VI.357; Vism 259; DhA I.307 (mukhato lālā galati).

Lāḷana (nt.) [fr. **lal**] swaying, dalliance, sport DA I.197; Sdhp 387; as lāḷanā at ThA 243.

Lāḷeti see laḷati.

Lāvaka [fr. lāvati] a cutter, reaper Miln 33 (yava°); Mhvs 10, 31; SnA 148 (v. l. BB. for lavaka).

Lāvati & **Lāveti** [the latter the usual form, as Caus. of lunāti. lāvati is the simple Pāli formation fr. **lū**. Another Caus. II. is lavāpati (q. v.). See also **lāyati**] to cut, to mow PvA 40 (lāvitvā). Mhvs 10, 30 (lāvayati).

Lāsa [of **las**] sporting, dancing: see abhi°, vi°.

Lāsikā (f.) [fr. **las**] a dancer, Miln 331.

Lāseti see lasati.

Likkhā (f.) [*Sk. likṣā egg of a louse, as measure equal to 8 trasareṇu (BR.).—Connected with Lat. ricinus a kind of vermin (see Walde, *Lat. Wtb.* s. v.)] a kind of measure VbhA 343 (36 rattareṇus equal to one likkhā, 7 likkhās equal to 1 ūkā); KhA 43 (°matta).

Likhati [**likh**; Vedic likhati, also **rikh** in Ved. ārikhati (R.V. VI.53, 7), cp. with palatal riśati, liśati. Connected with Gr. ἐρείκω to tear; Lith. rėkti to cut bread, to plough; Ohg. rīga=Ags. rāw=E. row.—Dhtp 467 simply expl[s] by "lekhane"] 1. to scratch; to cut, carve; write, inscribe M I.127 (rūpāni); J II.372 (suvaṇṇa-patte); IV.257 (id.), 488, 489 (jāti-hingulakena); DhA I.182; PvA 145 (nāmaŋ likhi wrote his name). —**paṇṇaŋ l.** to write a letter J II.174; VI.369 (paṇṇe on a leaf).—2. to shave (off), plane Vin II.112 (inf. likhituŋ).—pp. **likhita**.—Cp. vi.°—Caus. I. lekheti (q. v.). Caus. II. likhāpeti to cause to be cut or carved [cp. BSk. likhāpayati Divy 547] Vin II.110; SnA 577; to cause to be written Miln 42.

Likhana (nt.) [cp. late Sk. likhana; fr. **likh**] scratching, cutting, writing J V.59 (a golden tablet for writing on). Cp. ullikhana.

Likhā in likhā-paṇṇa at PvA 20 is faulty for **lekhā°** (lekha°) letter, cp. lekha-pattra letter Mālatim 172, 7.

Likhita [pp. of likhati] 1. carved, cut, worked (in ivory etc.), in cpd. sankha° brahmacariya the moral life, like a polished shell D 1.63; S II.219, expl^d at DA 1.181 as "likhita-sankha-sadisa dhota-sankha-sappaṭibhāga."— 2. written, inscribed J IV.7 (likhitāni akkharāni); Miln 42 (lekha l.). — 3. made smooth, shaved J VI.482 (cāpa). — 4. marked, proscribed, made an outlaw Vin I.75. — Cp. **ullikhita.**

Likhitaka (adj.) [likhita + qualifying ending ka] one who has been proscribed, an outlaw Vin I.75 (cora).

Linga (nt.) [fr. **ling**; late Vedic & (pre-eminently) Class. Sk. linga] 1. characteristic, sign, attribute, mark, feature M I.360; S V.278; Sn 601 sq. (= saṇṭhāna SnA 464); Vin IV.7 (two: hīna & ukkaṭṭha); J I.18; IV.114 (gihi°), 130; Miln 133 (sāsana°), 162 (dve samaṇassa lingāni), 405 (lingato ca nimittato ca etc.); Vism 184; DhsA 64 (= saṇṭhāna Ṭikā: *Expos.* 86). — 2. mark of sex, sexual characteristic, pudendum (male as well as female, as neither m. nor f.) Vin III.35 (purisa°); J V.197 (°saṇṭhāna); KhA 110 (itthi°); SnA 48 (°sampatti), 51 (id.), 300 (itthi°); DhsA 321 sq. (itthi°). — 3. (in grammar) mark of sex, (characteristic) ending, gender SnA 397. °vipallāsa change or substitution of gender PvA 7, 33, 58, 87, 157.

Lingāla [cp. Sk. lingālikā a kind of mouse] antelope (?) Pgdp 10.

Lingika (adj.) [fr. linga] having or being a characteristic Vism 210 (of nāma); KhA 107 (id.).

Lingeti [Denom. fr. **ling**] 1. to embrace, in poet. ger. lingiya (as if fr. lingati) Th 2, 398 (= ālingetvā ThA 260). See ā°. — 2. to characterize: see ul°.

Lipi [fr. **lip**; late Sk. lipi] the alphabet; a letter of the alphabet; writing Miln 79.

Limpati [**lip**, cp. repa stain, lepa ointment, stain; Gr. λίπος grease, fat, λιπαρός fat, ἀλείφω to anoint; Lat. lippus; Lith. limpù to stick, Goth. bi-leiban, Ohg. bilīban to stay behind, to stay, E. leave & live, Ger. leben. The Dhtp (385) simply expl^s by "limpana"] to smear, plaster, stain; usually in pass. (or med.) sense "to get soiled, to dirty oneself" Th 2, 388; PvA 215. Doubtful in Sn passages, where both limpati & lippati are found as readings, e. g. Sn 778 in Text lippati, but Niddesa reading limpati (Nd[1] 55); Sn 811 lipp°, Nd[1] 133 limp°; Sn 1040, 1042 lipp°, Nd[2] 549 limp.° — Pass. lippati to be soiled (by), to get stained (in character) Sn 250, 547, 625, 778, 913, 1040; cp. Sn 71 (alippamāna ppr.). — pp. litta: see ava°, ul°, vi.° — Cp. also ālimpeti, palimpeti, vilimpati. — Caus. I. lepeti to cause to be plastered J VI.432. — Caus. II. **limpāpeti** to cause to be plastered or anointed Mhvs 34, 42 (cetiyaŋ °āpetvāna).

Limpana (nt.) [fr. **lip**] soiling, smearing Dhtp 385.

Lisati [cp. dial. Sk. liśate = Vedic riśate] to break off, tear off, pull; only at Dhtp 444 expl^d by "lesa."

Lihati [**lih**, Sk. leḍhi or līḍhe, also lihati. Cp. Lat. lingo, Gr. λείχω; Goth. bilaigōn, Ags. liccian = E. lick, Ger. lecken. — The Dhtp 335 expl^s **lih** by "assādane," i. e. taste] to lick; pres. lehati J II.44; aor. lehayiŋsu PvA 198 (v. l. for palabhiŋsu). Cp. parilehisaŋ Vv 81[21]; VvA 316; ger. **lehitvā** DA 1.136 (sarīraŋ); VvA 314. — pp. **līḷha** (?). Cp. **leyya.**

Līna [pp. of līyati] clinging, sticking; slow, sluggish; shy, reserved, dull, A 1.3; Vism 125. Definitions at Vbh 352, 373; Dhs 1156, 1236; S V.277, 279 (ati°). Often comb^d with **uddhata** as "sluggish or shy" and "unbalanced," e. g. at S V.112; Vism 136; VbhA 310. alīna active, open, sincere Sn 68 (°citta), 717 (id.); J I.22 (v. 148; °viriya sīha).

Līnatā (f.) [abstr. formation fr. līna instead of līy°] = līyanā Vism 469. alīnatā open-mindedness, sincerity J I.366; SnA 122.

Līnatta (nt.) [abstr. fr. līna] sluggishness, shyness; only in phrase cetaso līnattaŋ immobility of mind S V.64, 103; A I.3 = IV.32; V.145 sq.; Nett 86, 108; VbhA 272 (= cittassa līn' ākāra).

Līyati [**lī**, Vedic līyati; ***lei** to stick to or cleave: see Walde, *Lat. Wtb.* s. v. lino, which he separates in meaning fr. ***lei** to smear, polish] to stick. The Dhtp evidently favours the separation when interpreting **lī** by "silesana-dravīkaraṇa," i. e. to make slip or run (Dhtp 441; Dhtm 681)] 1. to stick, adhere, cling to: see cpds. all°, o°, ni°, paṭisal°. — 2. to melt, slip: see cpd. pavi° (to dissolve). — pp. līna.

Līyana (nt.) [fr. līyati] sticking to, adhering, resting Sdhp 190 (°ṭṭhāna resting-place).

Līyanā (f.) = līyana; cleaving to, sluggishness, shyness Dhs 1156.

Līyitatta (nt.) [abstr. formation after similar synonymical chains, like bhāvitatta] = līyanā Dhs 1156.

Līlā (līḷā) (f.) [cp. Epic Sk. līlā or *līḍā] play, sport, dalliance; probably for līḷhā at J V.5 & 157, both times comb^d with vilāsa.

-aravinda a lotus serviceable for sport VvA 43 (līḷ°).

Līḷhā (f.) [abstr. of līḷha, Sk. līḍha, pp. of **lih**, lit. being polished, cp. ullīḍha polished] grace, ease, charm, adroitness; always used with ref. to the *Buddha* (Buddhalīḷhā), e. g. J I.155; DhA I.33; III.79. So in phrase **Buddhalīḷhāya** dhammaŋ deseti "to expound the doctrine with the Buddha's mastery" J I.152, 155; III.289; VvA 217 (spelling wrongly līḷāya). Of the B's gait: J I.93, 149; DhA II.41. The comb^n with vilāsa, as mentioned by Childers, applies to līlā (q. v.), which may stand for līḷhā at the passages mentioned, although not used of the Buddha.

Lugga [pp. of rujati; corresponding to Sk. rugṇa] broken (up), rugged (of a path) Miln 217, 218. Cp. vi°.

Lujjati [Pass. of **ruj**, corresponding to Sk. rujyate. Dhtp 400 gives **luj** as sep. root with meaning vināsa. See rujati] to be broken up, to break (up), to be destroyed; to go asunder, to fall apart A I.283 = Pug 32 (here equal to "be wiped out," but it is unnecessary to assume, as Kern, *Toev.* s. v. lujjati does, a by-form of **luc**, luñcati. The Pug C. 215 expl^s by "nassati"); Vin I.297; II.123; S IV.52 (in etymologizing interpretation of loka: "lujjati kho loko ti vuccati"; quoted at Nd[2] 550 on Sn 1119); Th 1, 929. — Cp. olujjati, palujjati. — pp. lugga.

Lujjana (nt.) [fr. lujjati; a word peculiar to Pali dogmatics] breaking up, crumbling away, dissolution DhsA 47 (in etym. of loka = lujjana-palujjan' aṭṭhena vaṭṭaŋ), 308 (id.); Vism 427 (id.).

Luñcati [Vedic luñcati, **luc** or **luñc**, to Lat. runco to pull up weeds; Gr. ῥυκάνη plane. The Dhtp 43 expl^s by apanayana] to pull out, pluck (a bird), tear, peel J I.244, 476; II.97, 363; III.314; IV.191; V.463; Mhvs 23, 46 (aor. **aluñci**); 28, 26 (ger. **luñcitvā**); Vism 248 (kese). — Caus. II. **luñcāpeti** DhA II.53 (kese), and **loceti** Th 1, 283 (kesamassuŋ alocayiŋ). — pp. luñcita.

Luñcita [pp. of luñcati] plucked, pulled Miln 240 (i. e. combed, of wool; Rh. D. trsl^s "pressed"; Nyānatiloka "cut"); PvA 47 (vilūna-kesa +).

Luṭhati [cp. later Sk. luṭhati to plunder, which is one of the dial. variants luṭh, luṇṭh, loṭh, of **lul** to shake. The Dhtp (474) & Dhtm (136) both give **ruṭh** & **luṭh** with meaning "upaghāte"] to rob, plunder.

Luta seems to be a legitimate spelling representing either lutta or lūna, in meaning "cut, cut off" [cp. **lu** for lū under lunāti]. Thus at S I.5 (nalo va harito luto)= 126=J VI.25; and at Sn 532 (lutāni bandhanāni; vv. ll. lūtāni & lunāni; expl^d as "chinnāni padālitāni" at SnA 432).

Lutta [cp. Epic Sk. lupta; pp. of lumpati] broken, cut off; as t. t. in grammar "elided" VvA 13 (of ca), 111 (of iti), 122 (id.).

Ludda (adj.) [the usual P. form of rudda, corresponding to Sk. raudra] 1. fierce, terrible; cruel, gruesome S I.143; A II.174 (pāpa, l., kibbisa); V.149; Pug 56; Vv 84^5 (=dāruṇā pisāc'-ādino VvA 335); J V.243 (ṭhānaŋ= niraya); Sdhp 286. The spelling ludra occurs at J IV.46=VI.306, which is ludda at J V.146. — 2. a hunter, sportsman Sn 247 (dussīla°; SnA 289: luddā ca kurūra-kammantā lohita-pāṇitāya, macchaghātaka-migabandhaka-sākuṇik'ādayo idha adhippetā); Vv 63^1; J II.154 (°putta=luddaka); III.432 (Bharata by name); Pug 56 (māgavika, sākuṇika, l., macchaghātaka etc.: expl^d by dāruṇa kakkhaḷa at Pug A 233); Vism 245= VbhA 259; VbhA 228.

Luddaka=ludda 2, i. e. hunter Vin I.220; J IV.416; Pv III.7^2 (miga°; expl^d as "dāruṇa" PvA 206); Miln 222; VbhA 266 (miga°, in simile); PvA 34, 168. Cp. Fick, *Sociale Gliederung* 143, 207. *Note*. The expression sunakha-luddako at DhsA 273 is not quite clear ("dog-hunter"?). It applies to a female & Maung Tin (*Expositor* II.361) reads "luḍḍhikā" (sic), with trsl^n "dog-mistress," remarking that Pyī reads luddako "hunter-dog" (?).

Luddha [pp. of lubbhati] greedy, covetous A III.433 (with pharusa-vāca & samphappalāpin); It 84; Miln 92 (duṭṭha, mūḷha, l.); J I.124.

Lunana (nt.) [for lūna(na), cp. lavana] cutting, severing SnA 148 (niddānan ti chedanaŋ lunanaŋ uppāṭanaŋ).

Lunāti [**lū**, given as **lu** at Dhtp 504 ("chedana") & Dhtm 728 ("paccheda"). For etym. cp. Gr. λύω to loosen, Lat. luo to pay a fine, Goth. fraliusan to lose; Ger. los, E. lose & loose] to cut, cut off, mow, reap Miln 33 (yavalāvakā yavaŋ lunanti); DhsA 39. — pp. lūna (& luta). — Caus I. lāvayati Mhvs 10, 30; Caus. II. lavāpeti to cause to mow Vin II.180. — A Pass. lūyati [fr. **lu**] is found at D I.141 (aor. lūyiŋsu) and at corresponding passage Pug 56 (imper. lūyantu, where dubbā is to be corrected to **dabbhā**). — See lava, lavaka, lavana, lāyati, lavati.

Lubbhati [Vedic lubhyate, **lubh**, cp. Lat. lubet & libet it pleases, libido longing; Goth. liufs=Ger. lieb & lob; E. love, etc. — Dhtp 434: lobhe] to be lustful or greedy, to covet, long for, desire It 84 (lobhaneyye na lubbhati); Vism 465, 468. — ger. **lubbha** (?) in olubbha is to be referred to **lamb** rather than **lubh**. A grd. formation in lobhaneyya or **lobhanīya** (q. v.). — pp. luddha.

Lubbhana (nt.) [fr. **lubh**] being greedy, greediness, a scholastic word, only found in exegesis of word **lobha**, e. g. at Dhs 32 (where also the enlarged abstr. formation lubbhitatta) & Vism 465, 468 (lubbhana-mattaŋ lobha).

Lumpati [**lup**, Epic Sk. lumpati, found also as **rup** in Pali: see ruppati. Connected with Lat. lugeo to be sorry (cp. rujati, roga; Gr. λύπη sorrow) and rumpo to break. Def^ns at Dhtp 386 & 433 (chedana) and at Dhtm 618 & 669 (cheda, vināsa)] to break, harm, injure; to attack, plunder; with a strong touch of affection (sympathy or desire) **lubh** in it [cp. **lup**: Gr. λύπη; **ruj**: roga], which is still more evident in Intens. **loluppa** (q. v.). — DhsA 365 (in expl^n of loluppa). — pp. lutta. — Cp. ullumpana, ullopa, lopa, vilumpati, vilopa.

Luḷati & **Luṭati** [cp. Ep. Sk. **loṭh** to move & dial. **luḍ**, loḍayati, to stir, agitate, which is a by-form of **lul**, lolati to move, Caus. lolayati to set in motion. Etym. connected with Slavonic ljuljati to rock, Ags. lǣl a (flexible) rod, rood; root due to onomat. formation. — Another form is luṭhati. The Dhtm (117) expl^s **luṭ** by "loṭane" (cp. viloṭana & viloḷana), and **luḷ** (510) by "manthane"] to stir, shake, agitate, upset; intrs. to be in motion, to be stirred Miln 259 (calati khubbhati l. āvilati). — pp. luḷita.

Luḷita [pp. of luḷati] stirred, moved, disturbed; lively; turbid (of water) S V.123=A III.233; (udapatta āvila l.); D II.128=Ud 83 (udakaŋ parittaŋ luḷitaŋ āvilaŋ); J VI.63; Nd^1 488 (āvila+); Miln 35, 177, 220 (°citta), 383 (a°); DhsA 328 (indriyāni paripakkāni aluḷitāni avisadāni).

Lūka [apocope form of ulūka, arisen through wrong syllable-division] owl J VI.497 (=ulūka C.).

Lūkha (adj.) [Vedic rūkṣa; Prk. lūha & lukkha; BSk. lūha, e. g. Divy 13 (praheṇaka), 81 (°cīvara), 425, 427] 1. rough, coarse, unpleasant; poor, bad (usually appl^d to dress or food); mediocre, meagre, wretched. Opp. paṇīta (e. g. Vin I.212; S II.153; A IV.10; J I.228; VvA 64). — S IV.337 sq.; A IV.232 sq.; Vin I.55; Th I, 923; J I.228 (cittasmiŋ paṇīte . . . dānaŋ lūkhaŋ na hoti); Nd^2 342 (p. 182, in exegesis of **nikkuha**, where practices of ascetics are referred to as "lūkhaŋ cīvaraŋ dhāreti, l. piṇḍapātaŋ bhuñjati, l. senāsanaŋ paṭisevati" etc.); VvA 298, 335 sq.; PvA 180. — 2. (of men) low, wretched, rough, miserable, offensive Vin I.199; III.110 (kisa l. dubbaṇṇa); S I.175 (=jiṇṇa C, see *K.S.* 320; trsl^n "looking worn"); M I.77=J I.390. —**lūkha-puggala** a miserable, offensive character (opp. siniddha-puggala) Vism 132; VbhA 282.
-**ājīvin** leading a hard or rough life D I.161; III.44, 47; S II.200; A V.190. -**cīvara** (adj.) wearing a shabby robe, badly clad Vin III.263; Miln 342 (cp. cīvara-lūkha bad condition of clothes A II.71=Pug 53; lūkha-cīvara-dhara A I.25). -**ppamāṇa** (& °ika) taking unpleasantness or misery as one's standard A II.71= Pug 53 (cp. PugA 229); DhA III.114; SnA 242; cp. rūpa-ppamāṇa. -**ppasanna** believing in shabbiness or mediocrity, having (bodily) wretchedness as one's faith Vin II.197; A II.71=Pug 53. -**pāpuraṇa** miserably clad S I.175; DhA IV.8, 9.

Lūkhatā (f.) [fr. lūkha] unpleasantness, wretchedness, poorness, misery PugA 229.

Lūkhasa (adj.) [fr. lūkha] rough, harsh; miserable, self-mortifying Sn 244 (=nīrasa atta-kilamath' ânuyutta SnA 287).

Lūtā (f.) [*Sk. lūtā] spider Abhp 621.

Lūna [pp. of lunāti] cut, mowed, reaped Th 2, 107 (°kesī); J II.365; Dāvs I.32. Cp. vi°.

Lūyati: Pass. of lunāti (q. v.).

Lekha [fr. **likh**, cp. Sk. lekha & lekhā] 1. writing, inscription, letter, epistle J VI.595 (silā° inscription on rock); Mhvs 5, 177 (lekhe sutvā); 27, 6; 33, 40 (°ŋ vissajjayi); Dāvs 5, 67 (cāritta°); Miln 42; SnA 164 (°vācaka reciting), 577. — 2. chips, shavings Vin II.110 (v. l. likha).

Lekhaka [fr. lekha] one who knows the art of writing, a scribe, secretary Vin IV.8 (as a profession); IV.10 (=muddikā & gaṇakā, pl.); Miln 42.

Lekhaṇī (f.) [fr. **likh**; cp. Epic Sk. lekhaṇī stencil Mbh I, 78] an instrument for scratching lines or writing, a stencil, pencil A II.200; J I.230.

Lekhana (nt.) [fr. **likh**] scratching, drawing, writing Dhtp 467.

Lekhā (f.) [fr. **likh**; Vedic lekhā. See also rekhā & lekha] 1. streak, line VvA 277 (=rāji); canda° crescent moon [cp. Epic candralekhā Mbh 3, 1831] Vism 168; DhsA 151. — 2. a scratch, line A I.283; Pug 32; J VI.56 (lekhaŋ kaḍḍhati). — 3. writing, inscription, letter Vin III.76 (°ŋ chindati destroy the letter); J I.451 (on a phalaka); Miln 349 (°ācariya teacher of writing); PvA 20 (°paṇṇa, letter so read for likhā°). — 4. the art of writing or drawing [=lipi Hemacandra], writing as an art. It is classed as a respectable (ukkaṭṭha) profession (sippa) Vin IV.7; and mentioned by the side of muddā and gaṇanā Vin IV.7, 128=I.77; cp. Vin IV.305.

Lekhita [pp. of lekheti] drawn (of lines), pencilled Th 2, 256.

Lekheti [Caus. of likhati or Denom. of lekha] to (make a) scratch J IV. 402. — pp. lekhita.

Leḍḍu [dial. Sk. leṣṭu > *leṭṭhu > *leṭṭu > leḍḍu; also Prk. leḍu & leṭṭhu: Pischel, § 304; cp. Geiger, *P.Gr.* § 62] a clod of earth S V.146=J II.59 (°ṭṭhāna); J I.19, 175; III.16; VI.405; Miln 255; SnA 222 (ākāse khitta, in simile); Vism 28 (trsl^n^ "stone"), 360 (°khaṇḍ'ādīni), 366 (containing gold), 419; VbhA 66 (°khaṇḍā); VvA 141; PvA 284. — The throwing of clods (stones?) is a standing item in the infliction of punishments, where it is grouped with daṇḍa (stick) and sattha (sword), or as leḍḍu-daṇḍ'ādi, e. g. at M I.123; D II.336, 338 (v. l. leṇḍu); J II.77; III.16; VI.350; Vism 419; DhA I.399 (v. l. leṇḍu); III.41; IV.77; VvA 141. — *Note.* leḍḍūpaka in cuṇṇaŋ vā telaŋ vā leḍḍūpakena etc. at DhsA 115 read as **vālaṇḍupakena**, as at Vism 142.

-**pāta** "throw of a clod," a certain measure of (not too far) a distance Vin IV.40; Vism 72; DhsA 315 (trsl^n^ "a stone's throw").

Leḍḍuka = leḍḍu; Vism 28.

Leṇa (& lena) (nt.) [*Sk. layana, fr. **lī** in meaning "to hide," cp. Prk. leṇa] 1. a cave (in a rock), a mountain cave, used by ascetics (or bhikkhus) as a hermitage or place of shelter, a rock cell. Often enum^d^ with **kuṭi** & **guhā**, e. g. Vin IV.48; Miln 151; Vbh 251 (n.). At Vin II.146 it is given as collective name for 5 kinds of hermitages, viz. vihāra, aḍḍhayoga, pāsāda, hammiya, guhā. The expl^n^ of leṇa at VbhA 366 runs as follows: "pabbataŋ khaṇitvā vā pabbhārassa appahonakaṭṭhāne kuḍḍaŋ uṭṭhāpetvā vā katasenāsanaŋ," i. e. opportunity for sitting & lying made by digging (a cave) in a mountain or by erecting a wall where the cave is insufficient (so as to make the rest of it habitable). Cp. Vin I.206=III.248 (pabbhāraŋ sodhāpeti leṇaŋ kattukāmo) Mhvs 16, 12; 28, 31 sq. (n); Miln 200 (mahā°). — 2. refuge, shelter, (fig.) salvation (sometimes in sense of nibbāna). In this meaning often comb^d^ with tāṇa & saraṇa, e. g. at D I.95; S IV.315 (maŋ-leṇa refuge with me; + maŋtāṇa); IV.372 (=nibbāna); A I.155 sq. (n); J II.253; DA I.232. Cp. Vin III.155. leṇ'atthaŋ for refuge Vin II.164 (n); J I.94. —**aleṇa** without a refuge Ps I.127; II.238; Pv II.2^6^ (=asaraṇa PvA 80).

-**gavesin** seeking shelter or refuge J II.407=IV.346. -**guhā** a mountain cave J III.511. -**dvāra** the door of the (rock) hermitage Vism 38; DhA III.39. -**pabbhāra** "cave-slope," cave in a mountain DhA IV.170.

Lepa [fr. **lip**, see limpati; cp. Classic Sk. lepa stain, dirt] 1. smearing, plastering, coating over Vin IV.303 (bāhira°); J II.25 (mattikā°). — 2. (fig.) plaster, i. e. that which sticks, affection, attachment, etc., in taṇhā° the stain of craving, & diṭṭhi° of speculation Nd^1^ 55; Nd^2^ 271^III^. — *Note.* lasagata at A II.165 read with v. l. as **lepa-gata**, i. e. sticky. — Cp. ā°, pa°

Lepana (nt.) [fr. **lip**] smearing, plastering, anointing Vin II.172 (kuḍḍa°); A IV.107 (vāsana°), 111 (id.); J II.117. Cp. abhi°, ā°, pa°.

Lepeti see limpati.

Leyya (adj. nt.) [grd. of **lih**: see lihati] to be licked or sipped; nt. mucilaginous food (opp. *peyya* liquid) A IV.394 (+peyya); Miln 2 (id.).

Lesa [cp. Sk. leśa particle; as Kern, *Toev.* s. v. points out, it occurs in Sk. also in the P. meaning at Mbh V.33, 5 although this is not given in BR. — As "particle" only at Dhtp 444 in def^n^ of lisati] sham, pretext, trick Vin III.169 (where ten lesas are enum^d^, viz. jāti°, nāma°, gotta°, linga°, āpatti°, patta°, cīvara°, upajjhāya°, ācariya°, senāsana°); J II.11; VI.402. —**lesa-kappa** pretext Vin II.166; Vv 84^43^ (=kappiya-lesa VvA 348); Th 1, 941; DA I.103.

Lehati see lihati.

Loka [cp. Vedic loka in its oldest meaning "space, open space." For etym. see rocati. To the etym. feeling of the Pāli hearer loka is closely related in quality to ruppati (as in pop. etym. of rūpa) and rujati. As regards the latter the etym. runs "lujjati kho loko ti vuccati" S IV.52, cp. Nd^2^ 550, and loka=lujjana DhsA 47, 308: see lujjana. The Dhtp 531 gives root **lok** (**loc**) in sense of dassana] world, primarily "visible world," then in general as "space or sphere of creation," with var. degrees of substantiality. Often (unspecified) in the comprehensive sense of "universe." Sometimes the term is applied collectively to the creatures inhabiting this or var. other worlds, thus, "man, mankind, people, beings." — **Loka** is not a fixed & def. term. It comprises immateriality as well as materiality and emphasizes either one or the other meaning according to the view applied to the object or category in question. Thus a trsl^n^ of "sphere, plane, division, order" interchanges with "world." Whenever the *spatial* element prevails we speak of its "*regional*" meaning as contrasted with "*applied*" meaning. The fundamental notion however is that of substantiality, to which is closely related the specific Buddhist notion of impermanence (loka=lujjati). — 1. *Universe:* the distinctions between the universe (cp. cakkavāḷa) as a larger whole and the world as a smaller unit are fluctuating & not definite. A somewhat wider sphere is perhaps indicated by **sabba-loka** (e. g. S I.12; IV.127, 312; V.132; It 122; Mhvs 1, 44; cp. **sabbāvanta** loka D I.251; III.224), otherwise even the smaller loka comprises var. realms of creation. Another larger division is that of loka as **sadevaka, samāraka, sabrahmaka**, or the world with its devas, its Māra and its Brahmā, e. g. S I.160, 168, 207; II.170; III.28, 59; IV.158; V.204; A I.259 sq.; II.24 sq.; III.341; IV.56, 173; V.50; It 121; Nd^1^ 447 (on Sn 956), to which is usually added sassamaṇa-brāhmaṇī pajā (e. g. D I.250, see loci s. v. pajā). With this cp. Dh 45, where the divisions are **paṭhavī, Yamaloka, sadevaka** (loka), which are expl^d^ at DhA I.334 by paṭhavī=attabhāva; Yamaloka=catubbidha apāyaloka; sadevaka=manussaloka devalokena saddhiŋ. — The universe has its evolutional periods: **saŋvaṭṭati** and **vivaṭṭati** D II.109 sq. The Buddha has mastered it by his enlightenment: loko Tathāgatena abhisambuddho It 121. On loka, lokadhātu (=cosmos) and **cakkavāḷa** cp. Kirfel, *Kosmographie* p. 180, 181. — 2. *Regional meaning.* — (a) in general. Referring to this world, the character of evanescence is inherent in it; referring to the universe in a wider sense, it implies infinity, though not in definite terms. There is mention of the different metaphysical theories as regards cosmogony at many places of the Canon. The antânantikā (contending for the finitude or otherwise of the world) are mentioned as a sect at D I.22 sq. Discussions as to whether loka is sassata or antavā are found e. g. at M I.426, 484; II.233; S III.182, 204; IV.286 sq.; A II.41; V.31, 186 sq.; Ps I.123, 151 sq.; Vbh 340; Dhs 1117. Views on consistency of the world (eternal or finite; created or evolved etc.) at D III.137; cp. S II.19 sq. Cp. also the long and interesting discussion of loka as suñña at S IV.54 sq.; Ps II.177 sq.; Nd^2 680; — as well as M II.68 (upanīyati loko addhuvo, and "attāṇo loko, assako loko" etc.); "lokassa anto" is lit. unattainable: A II.50 = S I.62; IV.93; but the Arahant is "lok'antagū," cp. A IV.430. — As regards their order in space (or "plane") there are var. groupings of var. worlds, the evidently popular one being that the world of the devas is *above* and the nirayas *below* the world of man (which is "tiriyaŋ vâpi majjhe"): Nd^2 550. The world of men is as ayaŋ loko contrasted with the beyond, or paro loko: D III.181; S IV.348 sq.; A I.269; IV.226; Sn 779 (n'āsiŋsati lokaŋ imaŋ parañ ca); or as idha-loka D III.105. The def^n of ayaŋ loko at Nd^1 60 is given as: sak'attabhāva, saka-rūpa-vedanā etc., ajjhatt' āyatanāni, manussa-loka, kāmadhātu; with which is contrasted paro loko as: parattabhāva, para-rūpa-vedanā, bāhir'āyatanāni, devaloka, rūpa- & arūpa-dhātu. — The rise and decay of this world is referred to as samudaya and atthangama at S II.73; III.135; IV.86; A V.107. — Cp. D III.33 (attā ca loko ca); Mhvs I, 5 (lokaŋ dukkhā pamocetuŋ); 28, 4 (loko 'yaŋ pīḷito); PvA I (vijjā-caraṇa-sampannaŋ yena nīyanti lokato). — Other divisions of var. kinds of "planes" are e. g. deva° A I.115, 153; III.414 sq.; Brahma° Vbh 421; Mhvs 19, 45; Yama° Dh 44; S I.34; nara° Mhvs 5, 282. See also each sep. head-word, also peta° & manussa°. — The division at Nd^1 550 is as follows: niraya°, tiracchāna°, pittivisaya°, manussa°, deva° (= material); upon which follow khandha°, dhātu°, āyatana° (= immaterial). Similarly at Nd^1 29, where apāya° takes the place of niraya°, tiracchāna°, pittivisaya°. — Another threefold division is sankhāra°, satta°, okāsa° at Vism 204, with expl^{ns}: "sabbe sattā āhāra-ṭṭhitikā" ti = sankhāraloka; "sassato loko ti vā asassato loko" ti = sattaloka; "yāvatā candima-suriyā pariharanti disā 'bhanti virocamānā" etc. (= M I.328; A I.227; cp. J I.132) = okāsaloka. The same expl^n in detail at SnA 442. — Another as kāma°, rūpa°, arūpa°: see under rūpa; another as kilesa°, bhava°, indriya° at Nett 11, 19. Cp. sankhāra-loka VbhA 456; dasa loka-dhātuyo (see below) S I.26. — 3. *Ordinary & applied meaning.* — (a) division of the world, worldly things S I.1, 24 (loke visattikā attachment to *this* world; opp. sabba-loke anabhirati S V.132). — loke in this world, among men, here D III.196 (ye nibbutā loke); It 78 (loke uppajjati); DA I.173 (id.); Vbh 101 (yaŋ loke piya-rūpaŋ etc.); Pv II.1^{13} (= idaŋ C.); KhA 15, 215. See also the diff. def^{ns} of loke at Nd^2 552. — loka *collectively* "one, man": kicchaŋ loko āpanno jāyati ca jīyati ca, etc. D II.30. Also "people": Lanka-loka people of Ceylon Mhvs 19, 85; cp. jana in similar meaning. Derived from this meaning is the use in cpds. (°-) as "usual, every day, popular, common": see e. g. °āyata, °vajja, °vohāra. — (*b*) "thing of the world," material element, physical or worldly quality, sphere or category (of "materiality"). This category of loka is referred to at Vbh 193, which is expl^d at VbhA 220 as follows: "ettha yo ayaŋ ajjhatt' ādi bhedo kāyo pariggahīto, so eva idha-loko nāma." In this sense 13 groups are classified according to the number of constituents in each group (1-12 and No. 18); they are given at Nd^2 551 (under lokantagū Sn 1133) as follows: (1) bhavaloka; (2) sampatti bhavaloka, vipatti bhavaloka; (3) vedanā; (4) āhārā; (5) upādāna-kkhandhā; (6) ajjhattikāni āyatanāni (their rise & decay as "lokassa samudaya & atthangama" at S IV.87); (7) viññāṇaṭṭhitiyo; (8) loka-dhammā; (9) satt'āvāsā; (10) upakkilesā; (11) kāmabhavā; (12) āyatanāni; (18) dhātuyo. They are repeated at Ps I.122 = 174, with (1) as "sabbe sattā āhāra-ṭṭhitikā; (2) nāmañ ca rūpañ ca; and the remainder the same. Also at Vism 205 and at SnA 442 as at Ps I.122. Cp. the similar view at S IV.95: one perceives the world ("materiality": loka-saññin and loka-mānin, proud of the world) with the six senses. This is called the "loka" in the logic (vinaya) of the ariyā. — A few *similes* with loka see *J.P.T.S.* 1907, 131.

-akkhāyikā (f., scil. kathā) talk or speculation about (origin etc. of) the world, popular philosophy (see lokāyata and cp. *Dialogues* I.14) Vin I.188; D I.8; M I.513; Miln 316; DA I.90. -agga chief of the world, Ep. of the Buddha ThA 69 (Ap. V.11). -anta the end (spatial) of the world A II.49 (na ca appatvā lokantaŋ dukkhā atthi pamocanaŋ). -antagū one who has reached the end of the world (and of all things worldly), Ep. of an Arahant A II.6, 49 sq.; It 115, Sn 1133; Nd^2 551. -antara the space between the single worlds J I.44 (V.253: Avīcimhi na uppajjanti, tathā lokantaresu ca). -antarika (scil. Niraya) a group of Nirayas or Purgatories situated in the lokantara (i. e. cakkavāḷ, antaresu J I.76), 8,000 yojanas in extent, pitch dark, which were filled with light when Gotama became the Buddha J I.76; VbhA 4; Vism 207 (lokantariya°); SnA 59 (°vāsa life in the l. niraya); cp. BSk. lokântarikā Divy 204 (andhās tamaso 'ndhakāra-tamisrā). -âdhipa lord or ruler of the world A I.150. -âdhipateyya "rule of the world," dependence on public opinion, influence of material things on man, one of the 3 ādhipateyyas (atta°, loka°, dhamma°) D III.220; Vism 14. -ânukampā sympathy with the world of men [cp. BSk. lokânugraha Divy 124 sq.] D III.211; It 79. -āmisa worldly gain, bait of the flesh M I.156; II.253; Th 2, 356. -āyata what pertains to the ordinary view (of the world), common or popular philosophy, or as Rhys Davids (*Dial.* I.171) puts it: "name of a branch of Brahman learning, probably *Nature-lore*"; later worked into a quâsi system of "casuistry, sophistry." Franke, *Dīgha trsl^n* 19, trsl^s as "logisch beweisende Naturerklärung" (see the long note on this page, and cp. *Dial.* I.166-172 for detail of lokāyata). It is much the same as lok-akkhāy(ika) or popular philosophy. — D I.11, 88; Vin II.139; Sn p. 105 (= vitaṇḍa-vāda-sattha SnA 447, as at DA I.247); Miln 4, 10, 178; A I.163, 166; III.223. Cp. BSk. lokāyata Divy 630, 633, and lokāyatika ibid. 619. See also Kern's remarks at *Toev.* s. v. -āyatika (brāhmaṇa) one who holds the view of lokāyata or popular philosophy S II.77 (trsl^n *K.S.* 53: a Brahmin "wise in world-lore"); Miln 178; J VI.486 (na seve lokāyatikaŋ; expl^d as "anattha-nissitaŋ . . . vitaṇḍa-sallāpaŋ lokāyatika-vādaŋ na seveyya," thus more like "sophistry" or casuistry). -issara lord of the world Sdhp 348. -uttara see under lokiya. -cintā thinking about the world, world-philosophy or speculation S V.447; A II.80 (as one of the 4 acinteyyāni or thoughts not to be thought out: buddha-visaya, jhāna-visaya, kamma-vipāka, l-c.). Cp. BSk. laukika citta Divy 63, 77 etc. -dhammā (pl.) common practice, things of the world, worldly conditions S III.139 sq.; Sn 268 (expl^n loke dhammā; yāva lokappavatti tāva-anivattikā dhammā ti vuttaŋ hoti KhA 153, cp. J III.468); Miln 146. Usually comprising a set of *eight*, viz. lābha, alābha, yaso, ayaso, nindā, pasaŋsā, sukhaŋ, dukkhaŋ D III.260; A IV.156 sq.; V.53; Nd^2 55; Ps I.22, 122; Vbh 387; Nett 162; DhA II.157. -dhātu constituent or unit of the Universe, "world-element"; a world, sphere; another name for cakkavāla. Dasa-sahassi-lokadhātu the system of the 10,000 worlds Vin I.12; A I.227. — D III.114; Pv II.9^{61}; Kvu 476; Vism 206 sq.; Vbh 336; Nd^1 356 (with the stages from *one* to *fifty* lokadhātu's, upon which follow: sahassī cūḷanikā l-dh.; dvisahassī majjhimikā; tisahassī; mahāsahassī); J I.63, 212; Miln 237; VbhA 430, 436. See also cūḷanikā. -nātha saviour of the world, Ep. of the Buddha Sn 995; Vism 201, 234; VvA 165;

PvA 42, 287. -nāyaka guide or leader of the world (said of the Buddha) Sn 991; Ap 20; Mhvs 7, 1; Miln 222. -nirodha destruction of the world It 121 (opp. °samudaya). -pāla (°devatā) guardian (governor) of the world, which are usually sepcified as *four*, viz. Kuvera (= Vessavaṇa), Dhataraṭṭha, Virūpakkha, Virūḷhaka, alias the 4 mahārājāno Pv I.4²; J I.48 (announce the future birth of a Buddha). -byūha "world-array," pl. byūhā (devā) N. of a class of devas J I.47; Vism 415 (kāmâvacara-deva's). -mariyādā the boundary of the world VvA 72. -vajja common sins Miln 266; KhA 190. -vaṭṭa "world-round," i. e. saŋsāra (opp. vivaṭṭa = nibbāna) Nett 113, 119. See also vaṭṭa. -vidu knowing the universe, Ep. of the Buddha D III.76; S I.62; V.197, 343; A II.48; Sn p. 103; Vv 34²⁶; Pug 57; expl^d in full at SnA 442 and Vism 204 sq. -vivaraṇa unveiling of the universe, apocalypse, revelation Vism 392 (when humans see the devas etc.). -vohāra common or general distinction, popular logic, ordinary way of speaking SnA 383, 466; VbhA 164.

Lokiya (& **lokika**) (adj.) [fr. loka; cp. Vedic laukika in meaning "wòrldly, usual"] 1. (ordinarily) "belonging to the world," i. e. — (a) world-wide, covering the whole world, famed, widely known Th 1, 554; J VI.198. — (b) (-°) belonging to the world of, an inhabitant of (as lokika) Pv I.6² (Yama°). — (c) common, general, worldly Vism 89 (samādhi); DhA IV.3 (°mahājana) PvA 131 (°parikkhaka), 207 (sukha), 220 (°sabhāva). See also below 3. — 2. (special meaning) worldly, mundane, when opposed to **lokuttara**. The term lokuttara has *two* meanings— viz. (a) in ordinary sense: the highest of the world, best, sublime (like lokagga, etc.), often applied to Arahantship, e. g. **lokuttara-dāyajja** inheritance of Arahantship J I.91; DhA I.117; ideal: **lokuttara dhamma** (like parama dhamma) the ideal state, viz. Nibbāna M II.181; pl. **l. dhammā** M III.115. — (b) (in later canonical literature) beyond these worlds, supra-mundane, transcendental, spiritual. In this meaning it is applied to the group of nava lokuttarā dhammā (viz. the 4 stages of the Path: sotāpatti etc., with the 4 phala's, and the addition of nibbāna), e. g. Dhs 1094. Mrs. Rh. D. tries to compromise between the two meanings by giving lokuttara the trsl^n "engaged upon the higher ideal" (*Dhs. tsrl.* Introd. p. 98), since meaning (b) has too much of a one-sided philosophical appearance. On term cp. *Cpd.* 91³. — 3. lokiya (in meaning "mundane") is contrasted with **lokuttara** ("transcendental") at many passages of the Abhidhamma, e. g. at Ps II.166; Dhs. 505, 1093, 1446; Vbh 17 sq., 93, 106, 128, 229 sq., 271, 322; Kvu 222, 515, 602; Pug 62; Tikp 41 sq., 52 sq., 275; Dukp 304, 324; Nett 10, 54, 67, 77, 111, 161 sq., 189 sq.; Miln 236, 294 (*lokika*), 390; Vism 10, 85, 438; DA I.331; DhsA 47 sq., 213; VbhA 128, 373; DhA I.76 (*lokika*); II.150; III.272; IV.35.

Locaka (adj.) [fr. **loc**. Caus. of **luñc**; cp. Sk. luñcaka] one who pulls out D I.167 (kesa-massu°, habit of cert. ascetics); M I.308 (id.).

Locana¹ [fr. **loc** or **lok** to see; Dhtp 532 & Dhtm 766: **loc** = dassana] the eye; adj. (-°) having eyes (of . . .) Pv I.11⁵ (miga-manda°); PvA 57, 90 (pingala°).

Locana² (nt.) [fr. **loc**. Caus. of luñcati] pulling, tearing out D I.167 (kesa-massu°); A I.296; Pug 55.

Loceti see luñcati.

Loḷana (nt.) [**luḷ**, cp. *Sk. lolana & viloḷana] shaking, upsetting Dhtm 117. Cp. vi°.

Loṇa (nt.) [cp. Sk. lavaṇa, for which see also lavaṇa. The Prk. form is loṇa] salt; as adj., salty, of salt, alkaline. — Vin I.202 (loṇāni bhesajjāni alkaline medicine, among which are given sāmuddaŋ kāḷaloṇaŋ sindhavaŋ ubbhidaŋ bilaŋ as var. kinds of salt), 220 = 243 (as flavouring, with tela, taṇḍula & khādaniya); A I.210, 250; IV.108; Miln 63; DhA IV.176 (in simile see below); VvA 98, 100, 184 (aloṇa sukkha-kummāsa, unsalted). On loṇa in similes cp. *J.P.T.S.* 1907, 131.

-ambila acid and salt J I.505; II.171, 394. -odaka salt water J VI.37; VvA 99 (°udaka). -kāra salt-maker Vin I.350 (°gāma); A II.182 (°dāraka); J VI.206 (kara); Miln 331. -ghaṭa a pitcher with salt S II.276. See also App. to KhA 68 (in Sn Index 870, 871) on Vism passage with loṇaghaṭaka. -dhūpana salt-spicing VbhA 311 (viya sabba vyañjanesu; i. e. the strongest among all flavourings). -phala a crystal of (natural) salt [phala for phaṭa = *sphaṭa, cp. phalaka] A I.250 (in simile). -rasa alkaline taste A IV.199, 203. -sakkhara a salt crystal (cp. °phala), a (solid) piece of (natural) salt S II.276 (in simile, cp. A I.250); SnA 222 (aggimhi pakkhitta l-s., in the same simile at DhA IV.176: uddhane pakkhitta-loṇa). -sakkharikā a piece of salt-crystal, used as a caustic for healing wounds Vin I.206. -sovīraka salted sour gruel Vin I.210; VvA 99.

Loṇika & **Loṇiya** (adj.) [fr. loṇa] salty, alkaline Dhs 629. —loṇiya-teliya prepared with salt & oil J III.522; IV.71. —aloṇika unsalted 42⁶ (°aka); VvA 184; J I.228; III.409.

Lodda [cp. *Sk. rodhra; on sound changes see Geiger, *P.Gr.* 44, 62²] N. of a tree J V.405; VI.497.

Lopa [fr. **lup**: see lumpati] taking away, cutting off; as tt. g. apocope, elision (of the final letter) VbhA 164 (sabba-loka-vohāra°); SnA 12, 303, 508; VvA 79; often in anunāsika° dropping of (final) ŋ SnA 410; VvA 154, 275. At S V.342 read piṇḍiy 'ālopena for piṇḍiyā lopena. — Cp. ālopa, nillopa, vilopa, vilopiya.

Lobha [cp. Vedic & Epic Sk. lobha; fr. **lubh**: see lubbhati] covetousness, greed. Defined at Vism 468 as "lubbhanti tena, sayaŋ vā lubbhati, lubbhana-mattam eva vā taŋ," with several comparisons following. — Often found in triad of lobha, dosa, moha (greed, anger, bewilderment, forming the three principles of demerit: see kusala-mūla), e. g. at A IV.96; It 83, 84; Vism 116; Dukp 9, 18 sq. See dosa & moha. — D III.214, 275; S I.16, 43, 63, 123 (bhava°); V.88; A I.64 (°kkhaya), 160 (visama°), cp. D III.70 sq.; II.67; Sn 367, 371, 537 (°kodha), 663, 706, 864, 941 (°pāpa); Nd¹ 15, 16, 261; J IV.11 (kodha, dosa, l.); Dhs 982, 1059; Vbh 208, 341, 381, 402; Nett 13, 27; Vism 103; VbhA 18; PvA 7, 13, 17, 89 (+ dosa), 102; VvA 14; Sdhp 52 (°moha), 266. —alobha disinterestedness D III.214; Dhs 32.

-dhammā (pl.) affection of greed, things belonging to greed; (adj.) (of) greedy character M I.91; III.37; D I.224, 230; S IV.111; A III.350; J IV.11. -mūla the root of greed Vism 454 (eightfold; with dosa-mūla & moha-mūla).

Lobhana (nt.) [fr. lobha] being greedy Th 2, 343 (= lobh' uppāda ThA 240).

Lobhaniya (°iya, °eyya) (adj.) [grd. formation fr. lobha] 1. belonging to greed "of the nature of greed" causing greed It 84 (°eyya). See rajaniya. — 2. desirable Miln 361 (paduma).

Loma (nt.) [cp. Vedic roman. The (restituted) late P. form roma only at J V.430; Abhp 175, 259; Sdhp 119] the hair of the body (whereas kesa is the hair of the head only) D II.18 (ekeka°, uddhagga°, in characteristics of a Mahāpurisa); S II.257 (asi°, usu°, satti° etc.); A II.114; Vin III.106 (usu° etc.); Sn 385; J I.273 (khaggo lomesu alliyi); VbhA 57; DhA I.126; II.17

(°gaṇanā); ThA 199; VvA 324 (sūkara°); PvA 152, 157; Sdhp 104. A detailed description of loma as one of the 32 ākāras of the body (Kh III.; pl. lomā) is found at Vism 250, 353; VbhA 233; KhA 42, 43. —aloma hairless J VI.457; puthu° having broad hair or fins, name of a fish J IV.466; Vv 44^{11}. haṭṭha° with hairs erect, excited Mhvs 15, 33. — On loma in similes see *J.P.T.S.* 1907, 131. —lomaŋ pāteti to let one's hair drop, as a sign of subduedness or modesty, opp. to horripilation [pāteti formed fr. **pat** after wrong etym. of panna in panna-loma "with drooping hairs," which was taken as a by-form of patita: see panna-loma]: Vin II.5 (=pannalomo hoti C.); III.183; M I.442. — Cp. anu°, paṭi°, vi°.

-kūpa a pore of the skin J I.67; KhA 51, 63; SnA 155 (where given as 99,000) Vism 195 (id.). -padmaka a kind of plant J VI.497 (reading uncertain; v. l. lodda°). -sundarī (f.) beautiful with hairs (on her body) J V.424 (Kurangavī l.; expl^d on p. 430 as "roma-rājiyā maṇḍita udarā"). -haŋsa horripilation, excitement with fear or wonder, thrill D I.49; A IV.311 sq. (sa°); Sn 270; Vbh 367; Miln 22; Vism 143; DA I.150. -haŋsana causing horripilation, astounding, stupendous Sn 681; J IV.355 (abbhuta+); Pv III.9^3; IV.3^5; Miln 1; Mhvs 17, 55 (abbhuta+). -haṭṭha having the hair standing on end, horrified, thunderstruck, astounded D I.95; S V.270; Sn p. 15; Miln 23; SnA 155; cp. haṭṭha-loma above.

Lomaka (-°) (adj.) [fr. loma] having hair, in cpd. **caturanga°** having fourfold hair (i. e. on the diff. parts of the body?) Vin IV.173. It may refer to the 5 dermatoid constituents of the body (see pañcaka) & thus be characteristic of outward appearance. We do not exactly see how the term caturanga is used here. — Cp. anulomika.

Lomasa (adj.) [cp. Vedic romaśa] hairy, covered with hair, downy, soft M I.305; Pv I.9^2. At J IV.296 lomasā is expl^d as **pakkhino**, i. e. birds; reading however doubtful (vv. ll. lomahaŋsa & lomassā).

Lomin (-°) (adj.) [fr. loma] having hair, in cpds. **ekanta°** & **uddha°**, of (couch-) covers or (bed) spreads: being made of hair altogether or having hair only on top Vin I.192=II.163; D I.7; cp. DA I.87.

Lola (Loḷa) (adj.) [fr. **luḷ**: see luḷati; cp. Epic & Classic Sk. lola] wavering, unsteady, agitated; longing, eager, greedy S IV.111; Sn 22, 922; J I.49 (Buddha-mātā lolā na hoti), 111, 210, 339 (dhana-loḷa); II.319 (°manussa); III.7; Pug 65; Nd^1 366; Dāvs IV.44; Miln 300. —alola not greedy, not distracted (by desire), self-controlled S V.148; Sn 65.

-bhava greediness, covetousness ThA 16.

Lolatā (f.) [fr. lola] longing, eagerness, greed Miln 93; SnA 35 (āhāra°).

Lolita [pp. of loleti] agitated, shaken Th 2, 373 (=ālolita ThA 252).

Lolupa (adj.) [fr. **lup**, a base of lumpati but influenced by **lubh**, probably also by lola. See lumpati] covetous, greedy, self-indulgent Dāvs II.73. a° not greedy, temperate Sn 165. Cp. nil°. — f. lolupā as N. of a plant at J VI.537.

Loluppa (nt.) [abstr. fr. lolupa] greediness, covetousness, self-indulgence, desire; in the language of the Abhidhamma often syn. with jappā or taṇhā. At DhsA 365 loluppa is treated as an adj. & expl^d at "punappuna visaye lumpati ākaḍḍhatī ti," i. e. one who tears again & again at the object (or as *Expos.* II.470: repeated plundering, hauling along in the fields of sense) — J I.340, 429; DhsA 365; Vism 61; & with exegetical synonyms loluppāyanā & loluppāyitattaŋ at Dhs 1059, 1136.

Loleti [Caus. fr. **luḷ**, see luḷati] to make shake or unsteady A III.188 (khobheti+). — pp. lolita.

Loḷī see āloḷi.

Loha (nt.) [Cp. Vedic loha, of Idg. ***(e)reudh** "red"; see also rohita & lohita] metal, esp. copper, brass or bronze. It is often used as a general term & the individual application is not always sharply defined. Its comprehensiveness is evident from the classification of loha at VbhA 63, where it is said lohan ti jātilohaŋ, vijāti°, kittima°, pisāca° or natural metal, produced metal, artificial (i. e. alloys), & metal from the Pisāca district. Each is subdivided as follows: jāti°=ayo, sajjhaŋ, suvaṇṇaŋ, tipu, sīsaŋ, tambalohaŋ, vekantakalohaŋ; vijāti°=nāga-nāsika°; kittima°=kaŋsalohaŋ, vaṭṭa°, ārakūṭaŋ; pisāca°=morakkhakaŋ, puthukaŋ, malinakaŋ, capalakaŋ, selakaŋ, āṭakaŋ, bhallakaŋ, dūsilohaŋ. The description ends "Tesu pañca jātilohāni pāḷiyaŋ visuŋ vuttān' eva (i. e. the first category are severally spoken of in the Canon). Tambalohaŋ vekantakan ti imehi pana dvīhi jātilohehi saddhiŋ sesaŋ sabbam pi idha lohan ti veditabbaŋ." — On loha in *similes* see *J.P.T.S.* 1907, 131. Cp. A III.16=S V.92 (five alloys of gold: ayo, loha, tipu, sīsaŋ, sajjhaŋ); J V.45 (asi°); Miln 161 (suvaṇṇam pi jātivantaŋ lohena bhijjati); PvA 44, 95 (tamba°=loha), 221 (tatta-loha-secanaŋ pouring out of boiling metal, one of the five ordeals in Niraya).

-kaṭāha a copper (brass) receptacle Vin II.170. -kāra a metal worker, coppersmith, blacksmith Miln 331. -kumbhī an iron cauldron Vin II.170. Also N. of a purgatory J III.22, 43; IV.493; V.268; SnA 59, 480; Sdhp 195. -guḷa an iron (or metal) ball A IV.131; Dh 371 (mā °ŋ gilī pamatto; cp. DhA IV.109). -jāla a copper (i. e. wire) netting PvA 153. -thālaka a copper bowl Nd^1 226. -thāli a bronze kettle DhA I.126. -pāsāda "copper terrace," brazen palace, N. of a famous monastery at Anurādhapura in Ceylon Vism 97; DA I.131; Mhvs passim. -piṇḍa an iron ball SnA 225. -bhaṇḍa copper (brass) ware Vin II.135. -maya made of copper, brazen Sn 670; Pv II.6^4. -māsa a copper bean Nd^1 448 (suvaṇṇa-channa). -māsaka a small copper coin KhA 37 (jatu-māsaka, dāru-māsaka+); DhsA 318. -rūpa a bronze statue Mhvs 36, 31. -salākā a bronze gong-stick Vism 283.

Lohatā (f.) [abstr. fr. loha] being a metal, in (suvaṇṇassa) aggalohatā the fact of gold being the best metal VvA 13.

Lohita (adj.-nt.) [cp. Vedic lohita & rohita; see also P. rohita "red"] 1. (adj.) red: rarely by itself (e. g. M II.17), usually in cpds. e. g. **°abhijāti** the red species (q. v.) A III.383; **°kasiṇa** the artifice of red D III.268; A. I.41; Dhs 203; Vism 173; **°candana** red sandal (unguent) Miln 191. Otherwise rohita. — 2. (nt.) blood; described in detail as one of the 32 ākāras at KhA 54 sq.; Vism 261, 360; VbhA 245. — Vin I.203 (āmaka°), 205 (°ŋ mocetuŋ); A IV.135 (saṭṭhi-mattānaŋ bhikkhūnaŋ uṇhaŋ l. mukhato uggañchi; cp. the similar passage at Miln 165); Sn 433; Pv I.6^7; I.9^1 (expl^d as **ruhira** PvA 44); Vism 261 (two kinds: sannicita° and saŋsaraṇa°), 409 (the colour of the heart-blood in relation to states of mind); VbhA 66; PvA 56, 78, 110.

-akkha having red (blood-shot) eyes (of snakes & yakkhas) Vv 52^2 (cp. VvA 224: ratta-nayanā; yakkhānaŋ hi nettāni ati-lohitāni honti); J VI.180. -uppāda (the crime of) wounding a Tathāgata, one of the anantariya-kammas VbhA 427; cp. Tathāgatassa lohitaŋ uppādeti Miln 214. -uppādaka one who sheds the blood of an Arahant Vin I.89, 136, 320; V.222.

-kumbhi a receptacle for blood Ud 17 (with ref. to the womb). -doṇi a bloody trough Vism 358; VbhA 62. -pakkhandikā (or °pakkhandik' ābādha) bloody diarrhœa, dysentery M I.316; D II.127; Ud 82; J II.213; Miln 134, 175; DhA III.269. -homa a sacrifice of blood D I.9; DA I.93.

Lohitaka (adj.) [fr. lohita] 1. red M II.14; A IV.306, 349; Ap. 1; Dhs 247, 617. -°upadhāna a red pillow D I.7; A I.137; III.50; IV.94, 231, 394; °sāli red rice Miln 252. — 2. bloody Pv I.7^8 (pūti° gabbha); Vism 179, 194.

Lohitanka [lohita+anka] a ruby A IV.199, 203; Ap 2; Vv 36^3; VvA 304. See masāragalla for further refs. — *Note.* The word is not found in Vedic and Class. Sk.: a later term for "ruby" is lohitaka. In the older language lohitānga denotes the planet Mars.

Ḷ.

Ḷiyati is given at Dhtp 361 as a variant of **ḍī** to fly (see ḍeti), and expl^d as "ākāsa-gamana." Similarly at Dhtm 586 as "vehāsa-gamana."

V.

-V- euphonic (sandhi-) consonant, historically justified after u (uv from older v), as in su-v-ānaya easy to bring (S I.124); hence transferred to i, as in ti-v-angika threefold (Dhs 161), and ti-v-angula three inches wide (Vism 152, 408); perhaps also in anu-v-icca (see anuvicca).

Va^1 the syllable "va" KhA 109 (with ref. to ending °vā in Bhagavā, which Bdhgh exp^{ls} as "va-kāraŋ dīghaŋ katvā," i. e. a lengthening of va); SnA 76 (see below va^3).

Va^2 (indecl.) [the enclitic, shortened form of iva after long vowels. Already to be found for iva in RV metri causâ] like, like as, as if; only in *poetry* (as already pointed out by Trenckner, Miln 422): It 84 (tālapakkaŋ va bandhanā), 90 (chavālātaŋ va nassati); Dh 28; Sn 38 (vaŋso visālo va: see C. expl^n under va^3); Pv I.8^1 (ummatta-rūpo va; =viya PvA 39); I.11^6 (naḷo va chinno); Miln 72 (chāyā va anapāyinī); J III.189 (kusamuddo va ghosavā); IV.139 (aggīva suriyo va); DhA III.175.

Va^3 (indecl.) [for eva, after long vowels] even, just (so), only; for sure, certainly Dh 136 (aggi-daḍḍho va tappati); J I.138, 149 (so pi suvaṇṇa-vaṇṇo va ahosi), 207; SnA 76 (vakāro avadhāraṇ' attho eva-kāro vā ayaŋ, sandhi-vasen' ettha e-kāro naṭṭho: wrong at this passage Sn 38 for va^2=iva!); PvA 3 (eko va putto), 4 (ñātamattā va).

Va^4 is (metrically) shortened form of **vā**, as found e. g. Dh 195 (yadi va for yadi vā); or in correlation va-va either-or: Dh 108 (yiṭṭhaŋ va hutaŋ va), 138 (ābādhaŋ va cittakkhepaŋ va pāpuṇe).

Vaŋsa [Vedic vaŋśa reed, bamboo (R.V.)] 1. a bamboo Sn 38 (vaŋso visālo va; vaŋso expl^d at Nd^2 556 as "veḷugumba," at SnA 76 as "veḷu"), ibid. (°kaḷīra); J VI.57; Vism 255 (°kaḷīra); KhA 50 (id.). — 2. race, lineage, family A II.27 (ariya° of noble family); S V.168 (caṇḍāla°); J I.89, 139; IV.390 (caṇḍāla°); V.251 (uju°); Mhvs 4. 5 (pitu-ghātaka-vaŋso a parricidal race). — 3. tradition, hereditary custom, usage, reputation Miln 168 (ācariya°), 190 (Tathāgatānaŋ); KhA 12 (Buddha°); Dpvs 18, 3 (saddhamma°-kovidā therā). —vaŋsaŋ nāseti to break family tradition J V.383; vaŋsaŋ ucchindati id. J V.383; or upacchindati J IV.63; opp. patiṭṭhāpeti to establish the reputation J V.386. — 4. dynasty Mhvs 36, 61 (kassa v. ṭhassati).— 5. a bamboo flute, fife Miln 31; VvA 210. — 6. a certain game, at D I.6 in enum^n of pastimes and tricks (caṇḍālavaŋsa-dhopana), a passage which shows an old corruption. Bdhgh at DA I.84 takes each word separately and expl^s vaŋsa as "veṇuŋ ussāpetvā kīḷanaŋ" (i. e. a game consisting in raising a bamboo; is it *climbing* a pole? Cp. vaŋsa-ghatikā "a kind of game" Divy 475), against *Dial.* I.9 "acrobatic feats by Caṇḍālas." Cp. J IV.390 in same passage. Franke (*Dīgha trsl^n*) has "bamboo-tricks"; his conjecture as "vaŋsa-dhamanaŋ," playing the bamboo pipe (cp. Miln 31: "vaŋsa-dhamaka"), as oldest reading is to be pointed out. — On vaŋsa in similes see *J.P.T.S.* 1907, 134.

-āgata come down fr. father to son, hereditary Mhvs 23, 85. -ânupālaka guarding tradition Sdhp 474 (ariya°). -ânurakkhaka preserving the lineage, carrying on the tradition J IV.444; Vism 99 (+paveṇi-pālaka); DhA III.386. -coraka N. of a certain kind of reed (cp. coraka: plant used for perfume) J V.406 (C. for veḷuka). -ja belonging to a race Mhvs 1, 1 (suddha°). -ñña born of good family A II.27. -dhara upholding tradition Miln 164. -dharaṇa id. Miln 226. -naḷaka bamboo reed KhA 52, 59 (with note Sn Index p. 870: naḷaka). -nāḷa id. Miln 102. -rāga the colour of bamboo, a term for the veḷuriya gem J IV.141. -vaṇṇa the veḷuriya gem Abhp 491.

Vaŋsika (-°) (adj.) [fr. vaŋsa] descended from, belonging to a family (of) S v.168 (caṇḍāla°).

Vaka[1] [Vedic vṛka, Idg. *u̯l̥qu̯o=Lat. lupus, Gr. λύκος, Lith. vilkas, Goth. wulfs=E. wolf etc.] wolf, only in *poetry* Sn 201; J I.336; II.450; v.241, 302.

Vaka[2] (indecl.): a root **vak** is given at Dhtp 7 & Dhtm 8 in meaning "ādāne," i. e. grasping, together with a root **kuk** as synonym. It may refer to vaka[1] wolf, whereas **kuk** would explain koka wolf. The notion of voraciousness is prevalent in the characterization of the wolf (see all passages of vaka[1], e. g. J v.302).

Vakula [cp. *Sk. vakula] a tree (Mimusops elengi) J v.420.

Vakka[1] (adj.) [Vedic vakra; the usual P. form is vanka] crooked J I.216.

Vakka[2] (nt.) [Vedic vṛkka] the kidney Sn 195; Kh III.; Miln 26; DhsA 140. In detail described as one of the 32 *ākāras* at Vism 255, 356; VbhA 60, 239, 356.
-**pañcaka** the series of five (constituents of the body) beginning with the kidney. These are vakka, hadaya, yakana, kilomaka, pihaka: VbhA 249.

Vakkanga [vakkaŋ+ga] a term for bird, poetically for sakuṇa J I.216 (tesaŋ ubhosu passesu pakkhā vankā jātā ti vakkangā C.).

Vakkhati is fut. of **vac**: he will say, e. g. at Vin II.190; IV.238. See vatti.

Vakkala [cp. BSk. valkala (e. g. Jtm 210): see vāka] 1. the bark of a tree J II.13 (°antara); III.522. — 2. a bark garment (worn by ascetics): see **vakkali**.

Vakkalaka ("bark-like," or "tuft"?) is at KhA 50 as the Vism reading, where KhA reads daṇḍa. The P.T.S. ed. of Vism (p. 255) reads wrongly cakkalaka.

Vakkali [in compn for in] wearing a garment of bark, an ascetic, lit. "barker" J II.274 (°sadda the sound of the bark-garment-wearer). See also Np. Vakkali.

Vakkalika (adj.) (-°) [fr. vakkala] in **danta°** peeling bark with one's teeth, designation of a cert. kind of ascetics DA I.271.

Vagga[1] [Vedic varga, fr. **vṛj**; cp. Lat. volgus & vulgus (=E. vulgar) crowd, people] 1. a company, section, group, party Vin I.58 (du°, ti°), 195 (dasa° a chapter of 10 bhikkhus). — 2. a section or chapter of a canonical book DhA I.158 (eka-vagga-dvi-vagga-mattam pi); DhsA 27.
-**uposatha** celebration (of the uposatha) in groups, "incomplete congregation" (trsln Oldenberg) Dpvs 7, 36. More likely to vagga[2]! -**gata** following a (sectarian) party (Bdhgh identifies this with the 62 diṭṭhigatikā SnA 365) S I.187; Sn 371. -**bandha**, in instr. *°ena* group by group Mhvs 32, 11. -**bandhana** banded together, forming groups DhA IV.93, 94. -**vagga** in crowds, confused, heaped up J VI.224; PvA 54. -**vādaka** taking somebody's part Vin III.175. -**sārin** conforming to a (heretic) party Sn 371, 800, 912; Nd[1] 108, 329.

Vagga[2] (adj.-nt.) [vi+agga, Sk. vyagra; opposed to samagga] dissociated, separated; incomplete; at difference, dissentious Vin I.111 sq., 129, 160; IV.53 (sangha); A I.70 (parisā); II.240. — instr. **vaggena** separately, secessionally, sectariously Vin I.161; IV.37, 126.
-**ārāma** fond of dissociation or causing separation M I.286; It 11 (+adhamma-ṭṭha; trsln Seidenstücker not quite to the point: rejoicing in parties, i. e. vagga[1]) =Vin II.205. -**kamma** (ecclesiastical) act of an incomplete chapter of bhikkhus Vin I.315 sq. (opp. samagga-kamma). -**rata**=°ārāma.

Vaggati [**valg**, to which belong Oicel. valka to roll; Ags. wealkan=E. walk] to jump Vv 64[9] (expld at VvA 278 as "kadāci pade padaŋ" [better: padāpadaŋ?] nikkhipantā vagganena gamane [read: vagga-gamanena] gacchanti); J II.335, 404; IV.81, 343; v.473.

Vaggatta (nt.) [abstr. fr. vagga[2]] distraction, dissension, secession, sectarianism Vin I.316 (opp. samaggatta).

Vaggana see **vaggati** (ref. of Vv 64[9]).

Vaggiya (-°) (adj.) [fr. vagga[1]] belonging to a group, forming a company, a party of (-°), e. g. pañcavaggiyā therā J I.57, 82; bhikkhū M I.70; II.94; chabbaggiyā bhikkhū (the group of 6 bh.) Vin I.111 sq., 316 sq. & passim; sattarasa-vaggiyā bhikkhū (group of 17) Vin IV.112.

Vaggu (adj.) [cp. Vedic valgu, fr. **valg**; freq. in combn with vadati "to speak lovely words"] lovely, beautiful, pleasant, usually of sound (sara) D II.20 (°ssara); S I.180, 190; Sn 350, 668; Vv 5[3], 36[1], 36[4] (°rūpa), 50[18] (girā), 63[6], 64[10] (ghoso suvaggu), 64[20], 67[2], 84[17]; Pv I.11[3]; II.12[1]; III.3[4]; J II.439; III.21; v.215; Sdhp 245. The foll. synonyms are frequently given in VvA & PvA as explns of vaggu: abhirūpa, cāru, madhura, rucira, savanīya, siniddha, sundara, sobhaṇa.
-**vada** of lovely speech or enunciation Sn 955 (=madhura-vada, pemaniya-vada, hadayangama°, karavīka-ruda-mañju-ssara Nd[1] 446).

Vagguli & **°ī** (m. & f.) [cp. Sk. valgulī, of **valg** to flutter] a bat Vin II.148; Miln 364, 404; Vism 663 (in simile); DhA III.223.
-**rukkha** a tree on which bats live Vism 74. -**vata** "bat-practice," a certain practice of ascetics J I.493; III.235; IV.299.

Vanka (adj.-n.) [cp. Vedic vanka & vakra bending; also Ved. vanku moving, fluttering, walking slant; vañcati to waver, walk crooked. Cp. Lat. con-vexus "convex," Ags. wōh "wrong," Goth. wāhs; Ohg. wanga cheek, and others. — The Dhtp 5 gives "koṭilya" as meaning of **vank.** Another Pāli form is **vakka** (q. v.). The Prk. forms are both vakka & vanka: Pischel, *Prk. Gr.* § 74]. I. (adj.). — 1. crooked, bent, curved M I.31 (+jimha); S IV.118 (read v-daṇḍā); Vin II.116 (suttā vankā honti); J I.9 (of kāja); IV.362 (°daṇḍa), PvA 51. With ref. to a kind of vīṇā at VvA 281. — 2. (fig.) crooked, deceitful, dishonest J III.313 (of crows: kākānaŋ nāmaŋ C.); VI.524; Pv IV.1[34] (a°); Sn 270 (probably to be read dhanka as SnA 303, =kāka). — 3. doubtful, deceitful, deceptive, i. e. haunted Vv 84[3], cp. VvA 334. — II. (m.) — 1. a bend, nook, curve (of ponds) J II.189; VI.333 (sahassa°). — 2. a hook J v.269. — 3. a fish-hook D II.266; Th 1, 749; J VI.437. — On **vanka** in similes see *J.P.T.S.* 1907, 131.
-**angula** a crooked finger A III.6. -**ātivankin** having curves upon curves (in its horns), with very crooked antlers J I.160 (said of a deer). -**gata** running in bends or crooked (of a river) J I.289. -**ghasta** (a fish) having swallowed the hook D II.266; J VI.113. -**chidda** a crooked hole DA I.112. -**dāṭha** having a bent fang (of a boar) J II.405.

Vankaka (nt.) [fr. vanka] a sort of toy: Rh. D. "toy-plough" (*Dial.* I.10); Kern "miniature fish-hook" (*Toev.* s. v.). Rh. D. derives it fr. Sk. vṛka (see P. vaka[1]). Bdhgh at DA I.86 takes it as "toy-plough." See D I.6; Vin II.10 (v. l. vangaka & vankata); III.180 (v.l. cangaka); A v.203 (T. vanka; v. l. vankaka); Miln 229. At ThA 15 **vankaka** is used in general meaning of "something crooked" (to explain Th 2, 11 khujja), which is specified at Th 1, 43 as sickle, plough and spade.

Vankatā (f.) & **Vankatta** (nt.) [abstr. fr. vanka] crookedness A I 112 (tt); Dhs 1339; VbhA 494.

Vankeyya (adj.) [grd. formation fr. vanka] "of a crooked kind," crooked-like; nt. twisting, crookedness, dishonesty M I.340; A IV.189; V.167.

Vanga at DA I.223 is syn. with kaṇa and means some kind of fault or flaw. It is probably a wrong spelling for vanka.

Vangati [cp. *Sk. vangati, to which belongs vañjula. Idg. *ṇag to bend; cp. Lat. vagor to roam, vagus=vague; Ohg. wankon to waver] to go, walk, waver; found only in Dhtp (No. 29) as root **vang** in meaning "gamana." Perhaps confused with **valg**; see vaggati.

Vaca (nt.) a kind of root Vin I.201=IV.35. Cp. vacattha.

Vacatā (f.) [abstr. fr. vaco] is found only in cpd. dubbacatā surliness J I.159.

***Vacati** [**vac**] see vatti.

Vacattha (nt.) a kind of root Vin I.201=IV.35.

Vacana (nt.) [fr. **vac**; Vedic vacana] 1. speaking, utterance, word, bidding S II.18 (alaŋ vacanāya one says rightly); IV.195 (yathā bhūtaŋ); A II.168; Sn 417, 699, 932, 984, 997; Miln 235; Pv II.2^7; SnA 343, 386. — mama vacanena in my name PvA 53. — dubbacana a bad word Th 2, 418 (=dur-utta-vacana ThA 268). — vacanaŋ karoti to do one's bidding J I.222, 253. — 2. (t. t. g.) what is said with regard to its grammatical, syntactical or semantic relation, way of speech, term, expression, as: āmantana° term of address KhA 167; SnA 435; paccatta° expression of sep. relation, i. e. the accusative case SnA 303; piya° term of endearment Nd^2 130; SnA 536; puna° repetition SnA 487; vattamāna° the present tense SnA 16, 23; visesitabba° qualifying (predicative) expression VvA 13; sampadāna° the dative relation SnA 317. At SnA 397 (comb^d with *linga* and other terms) it refers to the "number," i. e. singular & plural.

-attha word-analysis or meaning of words Vism 364; SnA 24. **-kara** one who does one's bidding, obedient; a servant Vv 16^5; 84^{21}; J II.129; IV.41 (vacanaŋ-kara); V.98; PvA 134. **-khama** gentle in words S II.282; A IV.32. **-paṭivacana** speech and counterspeech (i. e. reply), conversation DhA II.35; PvA 83, 92, 117. **-patha** way of saying, speech M I.126 (*five* ways, by which a person is judged: kālena vā akālena vā, bhūtena & a°, saṇhena & pharusena, attha-saŋhitena & an°, mettacittā & dosantarā); A II.117, 153; III.163; IV.277, cp. D III.236; Vv 63^{17} (=vacana VvA 262); SnA 159, 375. **-bheda** variance in expression, different words, kind of speech SnA 169, cp. vacanamatte bhedo SnA 471. **-vyattaya** distinction or specification of expression SnA 509. **-sampaṭiggaha** "taking up together," summing up (what has been said), résumé KhA 100. **-sesa** the rest of the words PvA 14, 18, 103.

Vacanīya (adj.) [grd. formation fr. vacana] to be spoken to, or to be answered D I.175; Sn p. 140.

Vacasa (adj.) (-°) [the adj. form of vaco=vacas] having speech, speaking, in cpd. **saddheyya°** of credible speech, trustworthy Vin III.188.

Vacī (°-) [the composition form of vaco] speech, words; rare by itself (and in this case re-established from cpds.) and poetical, as at Sn 472 (yassa vacī kharā; expl^d at SnA 409 by "vācā"). 973 (cudito vacīhi=vācāhi SnA 574). Otherwise in cpds, like: **-gutta** controlled in speech Sn 78. **-para** one who excels in words (not in actions), i. e. a man of words J II.390. **-parama** id. D III.185. **-bheda** "kind of words," what is like speech, i. e. talk or language Vin IV.2; Miln 231 (meaning here: break of the vow of speech?); various saying, detailed speech, specification KhA 13; SnA 464, 466. See also vākya-bheda & **vācaŋ bhindati**. **-viññatti** intimation by language Vism 448; Miln 370; Dhs 637. **-vipphāra** dilating in talk Miln 230, 370. **-samācāra** good conduct in speech M II.114; III.45; D III.217. — Often coupled (as triad) with kāya° & mano° (=in deed & in mind; where vācā is used when not compounded), e. g. in (vacī) -kamma (+kāya° & mano°) deed by word M I.373, 417; III.207; D III.191, 245; °duccarita misbehaviour in words (*four* of these, viz. musāvāda, pisuṇā vācā, pharusā vācā, samphappalāpa A II.141 D III.52, 96, 111, 214, 217; Nd^1 386; Pug 60; DhA I.23; III.417; °sankhāra antecedent or requisite for speech M I.301; A III.350; S IV.293; VbhA 167; Vism 531; °sañcetanā intention by word VbhA 144; °sucarita good conduct in speech A II.131 (the 4: sacca-vācā, apisuṇā vācā, saṇhā vācā, mantā bhāsā).

Vaco (& **vaca**) (nt.) [Vedic vacas, of **vac**] speech, words, saying; nom. & acc. vaco Sn 54, 356, 988, 994, 1006, 1057, 1110, 1147; J I.188; Nd^1 553 (=vacana byāpatha desanā anusandhi); Pv I.11^{12}. instr. vacasā Vin II.95 (dhammā bahussutā honti dhatā v. paricitā); III.189; S I.12 (+manasā); Sn 365, 663, 890 (=vacanena Nd^1 299); Vism 241; Mhvs 19, 42. — As adj. (-°) vaca in comb^n with du° as dubbaca having bad speech, using bad language, foul-mouthed M I.95; S II.204; A II.147; III.178; V.152 sq.; J I.159; Pug 20; Sdhp 95, 197. Opp. suvaca of nice speech M I.126; A V.24 sq.; Pv IV.1^{33} (=subbaca PvA 230). — Cp. vacī & vācā.

Vacca (nt.) [cp. BSk. vaccaḥ AvŚ I.254] excrement, fæces Vin II.212; IV.229, 265; Vism 250 (a baby's); VbhA 232 (id.), 243; PvA 268. — **vaccaŋ osajjati**, or **karoti** to ease oneself J I.3; PvA 268.

-kuṭī (& **kuṭi**) a privy Vin II.221; J I.161; II.10; Vism 235, 259, 261; VbhA 242; DhA II.55, 56; PvA 266, 268. **-kūpa** a cesspool Vin II.221; J V.231; Vism 344 sq.; DhA I.180. **-ghaṭa** a pot for excrements, chamber utensil, commode Vin I.157=II.216; M I.207. **-doṇikā** id. Vin II.221. **-magga** "the way of fæces," excrementary canal, opening of the rectum Vin II.221; III.28 sq., 35; J I.502; IV.30. **-sodhaka** a privy-cleaner, night-man Mhvs 10, 91.

Vaccasin (adj.) [cp. Sk. varcasvin & Ved. varcin, having splendour, might or energy, fr. Vedic varcas] energetic, imposing D I.114 (brahma°; *Dial.* I.146 "fine in presence," cp. DA I.282). See also under brahma. — *Note.* The P. root **vacc** is given at Dhtm 59 in meaning of "ditti," i. e. splendour.

Vaccita [pp. of vacceti, Denom. of vacca] wanting to ease oneself, oppressed with vacca Vin II.212, 221.

Vaccha^1 [Vedic vatsa, lit. "one year old, a yearling"; cp. Gr. ἔτος year, Sk. vatsara id., Lat vetus old, vitulus calf; Goth. wiþrus a year old lamb=Ohg. widar=E. wether] a calf Dh 284; J V.101; Vism 163 (in simile), 269 (id.; kūṭa° a maimed calf); DhsA 62 (with popular etym. "vadatī ti vaccho"); VvA 100, 200 (taruṇa°). — On vaccha in *similes* see *J.P.T.S.* 1907, 131.

-giddhinī longing for her calf S IV.181. **-gopālaka** a cow-herd Vism 28. **-danta** "calf-tooth," a kind of arrow or javelin M I.429; J VI.448. **-pālaka** cow-herd Vv 51^2.

Vaccha^2 [=rukkha, fr. vṛkṣa] a tree; only in **mālā°** an ornamental plant Vin II.12; III.179; Vism 172; DhA II.109.

Vacchaka [Demin. fr. vaccha^1] a (little) calf J III.444; V.93, 433; Miln 282 (as go-vacchaka).

-pālaka a cow-herd J III.444. **-sālā** cow-shed, cow-pen J V.93; Miln 282.

Vacchatara [fr. vaccha; the compar. suffix in meaning "sort of, -like." Cp. Sk. vatsatara] a weaned calf, bullock D I.127, 148; S I.75; A II.207; IV.41 sq.; Pug 56; DA I.294. — f. **vacchatarī** D I.127; S I.75; Vin I.191; Pug 56.

Vacchati is fut. of vasati to dwell.

Vacchara [cp. Class. Sk. vatsara] year Sdhp 239. See the usual saŋvacchara.

Vacchala (adj.) [cp. Sk. vatsala] affectionate, lit. "loving her calf" ThA 148 (Ap v.64).

Vaja [Vedic vraja: see vajati] a cattle-fold, cow-pen A III.373; J II.300; III.270, 379; Vism 166, 279; DhA I.126, 396.—**giribbaja** a (cattle or sheep) run on the mountain J III.479; as Npl. at Sn 408.

Vajati [Vedic **vraj**, cp. Ved. vraja (=P. vaja) & vṛjana enclosure=Av. vərəzəna-, with which cp. Gr. εἵργνυμι to enclose, εἱργμός, Lat. vergo to turn; Gaelic fraigh hurdle; Ags. wringan=E. wring=Ger. ringen, E. wrinkle =Ger. renken, and many others, see Walde, *Lat. Wtb.* s. v. vergo. — The Dhtp (59) defines **vaj** (together with **aj**) by "gamana"] to go, proceed, get to (acc.), lit. to turn to (cp. **vṛj**, vṛṇakti, pp. vṛkta, which latter coincides with vṛtta of **vṛt** in P. vatta: see vatta[1] & cp. vajjeti to avoid, vajjita, vajjana etc.) Sn 121, 381, 729 (jāti-maraṇa-saŋsāraŋ), 1143; J III.401; IV.103 (nirayaŋ); Pv IV.1[72] (Pot. vajeyya); Nd[2] 423 (=gacchati kamati); Mhvs 11, 35 (imper. vaja as v. l.; T. reads bhaja). See cpds. anubbajati, upabb°, pabb°, paribb°.

Vajalla see rajo-vajalla.

Vajira[1] [cp. Vedic vajira, Indra's thunderbolt; Idg. *u̯eĝ=Sk. **vaj**, cp. Lat. vegeo to thrive, vigeo>vigour; Av. vazra; Oicel. vakr=Ags. wacor=Ger. wacker; also E. wake etc. See also vājeti] a thunderbolt; usually with ref. to Sakka's (=Indra's) weapon D I.95=M I.231 (ayasa); Th 1, 419; J I.134 (vajira-pūritā viya garukā kucchi "as if filled with Sakka's thunderbolt." Dutoit takes it in meaning vajira[2] and trsl[s] "with diamonds"); SnA 225 (°āvudha the weapon of Sakka).

-**pāṇin** having a thunderbolt in his hand (N. of a yakkha) D I.95=M. I.231.

Vajira[2] (m. & nt.) [cp. Sk. vajra=vajira[1]] a diamond A I.124 (°ūpamacitta)=Pug 30; Dh 161; J IV.234; Miln 118, 267, 278; Mhvs 30, 95; KhA 110 (°sankhāta-kāya); DhA I.387 (°panti row of diamonds), 392 sq.

Vajuḷa [cp. Sk. vañjula. Given as **vañjula** at Abhp 553] N. of several plants, a tree (the ratan: Halāyudha 2, 46) J V.420. See also vangati.

Vajja[1] (nt.) [grd. of vajjati, cp. Sk. varjya] that which should be avoided, a fault, sin D II.38; S I.221; Vin II.87 (thūla° a grave sin); A I.47, 98; IV.140; Ps I.122; Dh 252; VbhA 342 (syn. with dosa and garahitabba); KhA 23 (paṇṇatti° & pakati°), 24 (id.), 190 (loka°); DA I.181 (=akusala-dhamma). Freq. in phrase: aṇumattesu vajjesu bhaya-dassāvin "seeing a source of fear even in the slightest sins" D I.63; S V.187 and passim. -°**dassin** finding fault Dh 76 (expl[d] in detail at DhA II.107). —**anavajja** & **sāvajja**, the relation of which to vajja is doubtful, see separately.

Vajja[2] (adj.-nt.) [cp. Sk. vādya, grd. of **vad**] 1. "to be said," i. e. speaking D I.53 (sacca°=sacca-vacana DA I.160). See also mosa-vajja.—2. "to be sounded," i. e. musical instrument J I.500 (°bheri).

Vajja, vajjā, vajjuŋ: Pot. of **vad**, see vadati.

Vajjati[1] [**vṛj**, Vedic vṛṇakti & varjati to turn; in etym. related to vajati. Dhtp 547: "vajjane"] to turn etc.; only as *Pass.* form **vajjati** [in form=Ved. vṛjyate] to be avoided, to be excluded from (abl.) Miln 227; KhA 160 (°itabba, in pop. etym. of **Vajji**).—Caus. vajjeti (*varjayati) to avoid, to abstain from, renounce Sdhp 10, 11, 200. Cp. pari°, vi°.

Vajjati[2] Pass of **vad**, see vadati.

Vajjana (nt.) [fr. vajjati] avoidance, shunning Vism 5 (opp. sevana); DhA III.417.

Vajjanīya (adj.) [grd. formation fr. vajjati[1]] to be avoided, to be shunned; improper Miln 166 (i. e. bad or uneven parts of the wood), 224.

Vajjavant (adj.) [vajja[1]+vant] sinful S III.194.

Vajjha (adj.) [grd. of vadhati] to be killed, slaughtered or executed; object of execution; meriting death Vin IV.226; Sn 580 (go vajjho viya); J II.402 (cora); VI.483 (=vajjhappatta cora C.); Vism 314; KhA 27. —**avajjha** not to be slain, scathless Sn 288 (brāhmaṇa); Miln 221=J V.49; Miln 257 (°kavaca invulnerable armour).

-**ghātaka** a slaughterer, executioner Th 2, 242 (cp. ThA 204). -**cora** a robber (i. e. criminal) waiting to be executed PvA 153. -**paṭaha-bheri** the execution drum PvA 4. -**bhāvapatta** condemned to death J I.439. -**sūkariyo** (pl.) sows which had no young, barren sows (read vañjha° !) J II.406.

Vajjhaka (adj.) (-°)=vajjha DhsA 239.

Vajjhā (f.) [cp. Sk. vadhyā] execution; only in cpd. (as vajjha°) °ppatta condemned to death, about to be executed Vin IV.226; J II.119, 264; VI.483.

Vajjheti [Denom. fr. vajjha] to destroy, kill J VI.527 (siro vajjhayitvāna). Kern, *Toev.* s. v. vaddh° proposes reading vaddhayitvāna (of a root **vardh** to cut), cutting off is perhaps better. The expression is hapax legomenon.

Vañcati [**vañc**: see etym. under vanka.—The Dhtp distinguishes *two* roots **vañc**, viz. "gamane" (46) and "palambhane" (543), thus giving the lit. & the fig. meanings] 1. to walk about J I.214 (inf. °ituŋ=pāda-cāra-gamanena gantuŋ C.).—2. Caus. **vañceti** to cheat, deceive, delude, elude D I.50; Sn 100, 129, 356; J III.420 (aor. avañci=vañcesi C.); VI.403 (°etu-kāma); Pv III.4[2]; Miln 396; Mhvs 25, 69 (tomaraŋ avañcayi).—pp. vañcita.

Vañcana (nt.) [fr. **vañc**, cp. Epic Sk. vañcana] deception, delusion, cheating, fraud, illusion D I.5; III.176; A II.209; Sn 242; Pv III.9[5]; Pug 19; J IV.435; DhsA 363 (for māyā Dhs 1059); DA I.79; DhA III.403; PvA 193. —vañcana in lit. meaning of vañcati 1 is found in **avañcana** not tottering J I.214.

Vañcanika (adj.) [fr. vañcana] deceiving; a cheat D III.183; Th 1, 940; Miln 290.

Vañcaniya (adj.) [grd. formation fr. vañcana, cp. MVastu II.145: vañcanīya] deceiving, deluding Th 2, 490.

Vañcita [pp. of vañceti] deceived, cheated J I.287 (vañcit' ammi=vañcitā amhi).

Vañjula see vajuḷa.

Vañjha (adj.) [cp. Epic & later Sk. bandhya] barren, sterile D I.14, 56; M I.271; S II.29 (a°); IV.169; V.202 (a°); Pv III.4[5] (a°=anipphala C.); J II.406 (°sūkariyo: so read for vajjha°); Miln 95; Vism 508 (°bhāva); DhA I.45 (°itthi); DA I.105; PvA 31, 82; VvA 149; Sdhp 345 (a°).

Vaṭa [cp. Epic Sk. vaṭa. A root **vaṭ**, not connected with *this* vaṭa is given at Dhtm 106 in meaning "veṭhana": see vaṭaŋsa] the Indian fig tree J I.259 (°rukkha); III.325; Mhvs 6, 16; DhA I.167 (°rukkha); PvA 113.

Vaṭa at Pug 45, 46 (tuccho pi hito pūro pi vaṭo) read ti pihito pūro **vivaṭo**. See **vivaṭa**.

Vaṭaŋsa [for avataŋsa: see Geiger, *P.Gr.* § 66[1]; cp. Sk. avataŋsa with t; Prk. vaaŋsa] a kind of head ornament, perhaps ear-ring or garland worn round the forehead Mhvs 11, 28 (C. expln as "kaṇṇapilandhanaŋ vaṭaŋsakan ti vuttaŋ hoti"). Usually as **vaṭaŋsaka** Vin II.10; III.180; Th 1, 523; Vv 38[5] (expld as "ratanamayā kaṇṇikā" (pl.) at VvA 174); J VI.488; VvA 178, 189, 209. — *Note.* The root **vaṭ** given as "veṭhana" at Dhtm 106 probably refers to vaṭaŋsa.

Vaṭaka [cp. *Sk. vaṭaka, fr. vaṭa rope] a small ball or thickening, bulb, tuber; in muḷāla° the (edible) tuber of the lotus J VI.563 (C. kaṇḍaka).

Vaṭākara [probably distorted by metathesis from Sk. vaṭāraka. Fr. vaṭa rope. On etym. of the latter see Walde, *Lat. Wtb.* s. v. volvo] a rope, cable J III.478 (nāvā sa-vaṭākarā).

Vaṭuma (nt.) [cp. Vedic vartman, fr. **vṛt**] a road, path D II.8; S IV.52 (chinna°); J III.412; Vism 123 (sa° & a°). Cp. **ubbaṭuma** & **parivaṭuma**.

Vaṭṭa[1] (adj.-nt.) [pp. of **vṛt**, Sk. vṛtta in meaning of "round" as well as "happened, become" etc. The two meanings have become differentiated in Pāli: vaṭṭa is *not* found in meaning of "happened." All three Pāli meanings are specialized, just as the pres. vaṭṭati is specialized in meaning "behoves"] 1. round, circular; (nt.) circle PvA 185 (āyata+); KhA 50 (°nāli). See cpd. °anguli. — 2. (fig.) "rolling on," the "round" of existences, cycle of transmigrations, saŋsāra, evolution (=involution) (as forward or ascending circle of existences, without implying a teleological idea, in contrast to **vivaṭṭa** "rolling back" or devolution, i. e. a new (descending) cycle of existence in a new aeon with inverted [vi-] motion, so to speak) S III.63; IV.53 (pariyādiṇṇa°), cp. M III.118; Th 1, 417 (sabba°: "all constant rolling on" trsln); SnA 351 (=upādāna); DhsA 238. — There are 3 vaṭṭas, (te-bhūmaka vaṭṭa, see also tivaṭṭa) embracing existence in the stages of **kamma-vaṭṭa**, **kilesa°** and **vipāka°**, or circle of deed, sin & result (found only in Commentarial literature): KhA 189; SnA 510 (tebhūmaka°); DhA I.289 (kileśa°); IV.69 (tebhūmaka°). See also Māra; and °dukkha, °vivaṭṭa below. — 3. "what has been proffered," expenditure, alms (as t. t.) J VI.333 (dāna° alms-gift); DhA II.29 (pāka° cooked food as alms); VvA 222 (id.); Mhvs 32, 61 (alms-pension); 34, 64 (salāka-vaṭṭabhatta). — Cp. vi°.

-anguli a rounded (i. e. well-formed) finger; adj. having round fingers Vv 64[13] (=anupubbato v., i. e. regularly formed, VvA 280); J V.207, 215. **-angulika** same as last J V.204. **-ânugata** accompanied by (or affected with) saŋsāra J I.91 (dhana). **-ûpaccheda** destruction of the cycle of rebirths A II.34=It 88; A III.35; Vism 293. **-kathā** discussion about saŋsāra Vism 525; DA I.126; VbhA 133. **-kāra** a worker in brass. The meaning of vaṭṭa in this connection is not clear; the same vaṭṭa occurs in °loha ("round" metal ?). Kern, *Toev.* s. v. compares it with Sk. vardhra leather strap, taking vaṭṭa as a corruption of vaḍḍha, but the connection brass>leather seems far-fetched. It is only found at Miln 331. **-dukkha** the "ill" of transmigration (a Commentary expression) Vism 315; DhA IV.149; VvA 116. **-paṭighātaka(ŋ)** (vivaṭṭaŋ) (a devolution) destroying evolution, i. e. salvation from saŋsāra SnA 106. **-bhaya** fear of saŋsāra VbhA 256. **-mūla** the root of saŋsāra DhA III.278. **-vivaṭṭa** (1) evolving and devolving; going round and back again, i. e. all round (a formation after the manner of reduplicative cpds. like cuṇṇa-vicuṇṇa in intensive-iterative meaning), *°vasena* in direct and inverse succession, all round, completely J I.75. Cp. also vatta-paṭivatta. — (2) saŋsāra in ascending and descending lines, evolution ("involution") and devolution, or one round of transmigration and the other. It is dogmatically defined at Nett 113 as "vaṭṭaŋ saŋsāro vivaṭṭaŋ nibbānaŋ" (similarly, opposed to vaṭṭa at DA I.126) which is however not the *general* meaning, the vivaṭṭa not necessarily meaning a nibbāna stage. See SnA 106 (quoted above); VvA 68. We have so far not found any passage where it might be interpreted in the comprehensive sense as meaning "the total round of existences," after the fashion of cpds. like bhavâbhava. **-loha** "round metal" (?), one of the 3 kittima-lohāni mentioned at VbhA 63 (kaŋsa°, vaṭṭa°, ārakūṭa); also at Miln 267 (with kāḷa°, tamba° & kaŋsa°, where in the trsln Rh. D. does not give a def. expln of the word).

Vaṭṭa[2] ("rained"): see abhivaṭṭa and vaṭṭha (vuṭṭha); otherwise only at DhA II.265.

Vaṭṭaka (nt.) [fr. **vṛt**, or P. vaṭṭa] a cart, in haṭṭha° handcart Vin II.276.

Vaṭṭakā (f.) (& **vaṭṭaka°**) [cp. Sk. vartakā & Ved. vartikā] the quail M III.159 sq.; J I.172, 208 (vaṭṭaka-luddaka); III.312; DhA III.175 (inst. pl. vaṭṭakesu). — The Vaṭṭaka-jātaka at J I.208 sq. (cp. J V.414).

Vaṭṭati [Vedic **vṛt**. The representative of vattati (=Sk. vartate) in specialized meaning. The regular meaning of *vartate (with vaṭṭana), viz. "turning round," is attached to vaṭṭati only in later Pāli & sometimes doubtful. It is found also in the Caus. vaṭṭeti. The defn of **vaṭṭ** (literal meaning) at Dhtp 89 is "vaṭṭana," and at Dhtm 107 "āvattana"] 1. to turn round, to move on: doubtful in "kattha vaṭṭaŋ na vaṭṭati" S I.15; preferably with v. l. as **vaḍḍhati**. — Caus. I. **vaṭṭeti** to turn or twist J I.338 (rajjuŋ); to cause to move or go on (in weaving; tasaraŋ v. to speed the shuttle) SnA 265, 266. Should we read vaḍḍheti? Cp. āvaṭṭeti. — Caus. II. **vaṭṭāpeti** to cause to turn J I.422. — 2. to be right or fit or proper, to behove; it ought to (with infin.); with instr. of person who ought to do this or that, e. g. sīlācāra-sampannena bhavituŋ vaṭṭati J I.188; kataññunā bhavituŋ v. J I.122. — See e. g. J I.376; II.352, 406; Miln 9; Vism 184; DhA II.38, 90, 168; SnA 414 (vattuŋ to say); VvA 63, 69, 75; PvA 38 (dātuŋ). The *noun* to vaṭṭati is vatta (not vaṭṭa!).

Vaṭṭana (nt.) [fr. **vṛt**, vaṭṭati] turning round Dhtp 89 (in defn of vaṭṭati). Cp. āvaṭṭana.

Vaṭṭanā (f.) [fr. **vṛt**] in °valī is a line or chain of balls ("rounds," i. e. rings or spindles). Reading somewhat doubtful. It occurs at M I.80, 81 (seyyathā v. evaŋ me piṭṭhi-kaṇṭako unnat' âvanato hoti; Neumann trsls "wie eine Kugelkette wurde mein Rückgrat mit den hervor-und zurücktretenden Wirbeln") and at J V.69 (spelt "vaṭṭhanā-vali-sankāsā piṭṭhi te ninnat' unnatā," with C. expln "piṭṭhika-ṭṭhāne āvuṇitvā ṭhapitā vaṭṭhanā-vali-sadisā"). The J trsln by Dutoit gives "einer Reihe von Spinnwirteln dein Rücken gleicht im Auf und Nieder"; the E. trsln has "Thy back like spindles in a row, a long unequal curve doth show."

Vaṭṭani (f.) [cp. Vedic vartani circumference of a wheel, course] a ring, round, globe, ball Th 2, 395 (vaṭṭani-r-iva; expld at ThA 259 as "lākhāya guḷikā viya," trsln *Sisters* 154: "but a little ball").

Vaṭṭi (f.) [represents both Epic Sk. varti and vṛtti, differentiated derivations from **vṛt**, combining the meanings of "turning, rolling" and "encircling, round"] 1. a wick S II.86=III.126=IV.213; J I.243 (dīpa°); DhA 393; ThA 72 (Ap. V.45: nom. pl. vaṭṭini); Mhvs 32, 37; 34, 35. — 2. enclosure, lining, film, skin Vism 258 (anta° entrails), 262 (udara°); J I.260 (anta°, so read for °vaddhi). — 3. edge, rim, brim, circumference Vin

II.120 (aggala° of the door), 148 (id.); S III.141 (patta° of a vase or bowl); IV.168 (id.); DhA II.124 (nemi°). Often as mukha-vaṭṭi outer rim, border, lining, e. g. cakkavāḷa° J I.64, 72; DhA I.319; III.209, patt° J V.38; pāsāda° DhsA 107. — 4. strip, fringe Vin II.266 (dussa°); J V.73 (camma°); Mhvs 11, 15. — 5. a sheath, bag, pod J III.366 (tiṇa°); Mhvs 26, 17 (marica° red pepper pod); DhA IV.203 (reṇu°). — 6. a lump, ball DhA III.117 (pubba°, of matter). — 7. rolling forth or along, a gush (of water), pour J I.109 (or to **vṛṣ** ?).

Vaṭṭikā (f.) [vaṭṭi+kā, cp. Class. Sk. vartikā] 1. a wick Mhvs 30, 94. — 2. a brim Mhvs 18, 28. — 3. a pod Mhvs 26, 16 (marica°).

Vaṭṭin (-°) (adj.) in muṇḍa° porter (?) is not clear. It is a derⁿ fr. vaṭṭi in one or the other of its meanings. Found only at Vin II.137, where it is expl^d by Bdhgh as "veṭṭhin." It may belong to vaṭaŋsa or vaṭa (rope): cp. Dhtm 106 "veṭhana" for vaṭaŋsa.

Vaṭṭula (adj.) [fr. **vṛt**, cp. late Sk. vartula] circular Abhp 707.

Vaṭṭha [pp. of vassati, for the usual vuṭṭha] rained, in nava° newly rained upon DhA I.19 (bhūmi).

Vaṭhara (adj.) [cp. BSk. vaṭhara MVastu II.65. A root vaṭh is given at Dhtm 133 in meaning "thūlattane bhave" i. e. bulkiness] bulky, gross Abhp 701.

Vaḍḍha (nt.) [fr. **vṛdh**] wealth, riches J III.131 (vaḍḍhaŋ vaḍḍhataŋ, imper.). Or should we read vaṭṭa? — Vaḍḍha is used as Np. at KhA 119, perhaps in meaning "prosperous."

Vaḍḍhaka [fr. vaḍḍheti] 1. augmenting, increasing, i. e. looking after the welfare of somebody or something, one who superintends J I.2 (rāsi° the steward of an estate). — 2. a maker of, in special sense (cīvara° robe-cutter, perhaps fr. **vardh** to cut: see vaddheti) a tailor J I.220.

Vaḍḍhaki (& °ī) [cp. Epic & Class. Sk. vardhaki & vardhakin; perhaps from **vardh** to cut: see vaddheti] a carpenter, builder, architect, mason. On their craft and guilds see Fick, *Sociale Gliederung* 181 sq.; Mrs. Rh. D. *Cambridge Hist. Ind.* I.206. — The word is specially characteristic of the Jātakas and other popular (later) literature J I.32, 201, 247; II.170; VI.332 sq., 432; Ap. 51; DhA I.269; IV.207; Vism 94; PvA 141; Mhbv 154. —**iṭṭha°** a stonemason Mhvs 35, 102; **nagara°** the city architect Miln 331, 345; **brāhmaṇa°** a brahmin carpenter J IV.207; **mahā°** chief carpenter, master builder Vism 463. In metaphor taṇhā the artificer lust DhA III.128.

-**gāma** a carpenter village J II.18, 405; IV.159.

Vaḍḍhati [Vedic vardhati, **vṛdh**, cp. Av. varəδaiti to increase. To this root belongs P. uddha "high up" (=Gr. ὀρθός straight). Def^d at Dhtp 109 simply as "vaḍḍhane"] primary meaning "to increase" (trs. & intrs.); hence: to keep on, to prosper, to multiply, to grow S I.15 (read vaḍḍh° for vaṭṭ°); II.206 (vaṇṇena); IV.73, 250; A V.249 (paññāya); Sn 329 (paññā ca sutañ ca); J III.131 (porāṇaŋ vaḍḍhaŋ vaḍḍhataŋ, imper. med. 3rd sg.); V.66 (sadā so vaḍḍhata rājā sukka-pakkhe va candimā); Pv I.1² (dātā puññena v.); Pug 71; Miln 9; Mhvs 7, 68 (putta-dhītāhi vaḍḍhitvā having numerous sons & daughters); 22, 73 (ubho vaḍḍhiŋsu dārakā, grew up); SnA 319; PvA 94. — ppr. **vaḍḍhamāna** (1) thriving KhA 119 (read as Vaḍḍh°, Np.); — (2) increasing J I.199 (putta-dhītāhi); Mhvs 23, 34 (°chāyāyaŋ as the shadows increased). — See also pari°. — pp. vaḍḍha, vaddha, vuḍḍha, vuddha, buḍḍha. — Caus. I. **vaḍḍheti**, in many shades of meaning, all based upon the notion of progressive motion. Thus to be translated in any of the foll. senses: to increase, to make move on (cp. vv. ll. vaṭṭeti), to bring on to, to further; to take an interest in, to indulge in, practise; to be busy with, cause to prosper; to arrange; to make for; and in a general sense "to make" (cp. derivation vaḍḍhaka "maker," i. e. tailor; vaḍḍhaki id., i. e. carpenter; vaḍḍhana, etc.). The latter development into "make" is late. — 1. to increase, to raise Sn 275 (rajaŋ); DA I.115; Mhvs 29, 66 (mangalaŋ to raise the chant); PvA 168 (+brūheti). — 2. to cultivate (vipassanaŋ insight) J I.117 (aor. °esi); PvA 14. — 3. to rear, to bring up Mhvs 35, 103 (aor. vaḍḍhesi). — 4. (with ref. to food) to get ready, arrange, serve in (loc.) J III.445 (pātiyā on the dish); IV.67 (karoṭiyaŋ), 391. — 5. to exalt J I.338 (akulīne vaḍḍhessati). — 6. to participate in, to practise, attend to, to serve (acc.) S II.109 (taṇhaŋ); A II.54 (kaṭasiŋ to serve the cemetery, i. e. to die again and again: see refs. under kaṭasi); Vism 111 (kasiṇaŋ), 152. — 7. to make move on, to set into motion (for vaṭṭeti ?), in tasaraŋ v. SnA 265, 266. — 8. to take up Mhvs 26, 10 (kuntaŋ). — pp. vaḍḍhita. — Caus. II. **vaḍḍhāpeti**: 1. to cause to be enlarged Mhvs 35, 119. — 2. to cause to be brought up or reared J I.455. — 3. to have attended to Vin II.134 (massuŋ). — 4. to cause to be made up (of food) J IV.68.

Vaḍḍhana (nt. & adj.) [fr. vaḍḍheti; see also vaddhana] 1. increasing, augmenting, fostering; increase, enlargement, prolongation M I.518 (hāyana° decrease & increase); J III.422 (kula°, spelling ddh); Mhvs 35, 73 (āyussa); DhsA 406; PvA 31; Miln 320 (bala° strength-increasing); Dhtp 109; Sdhp 361. — 2. indulgence in, attachment; serving, practising Sn 1084 (takka°); J I.146 (kaṭasi°, q. v. & cp. vaḍḍheti 6); Vism 111 (°āvaḍḍhana), 152, 320. Here belong the phrases raja° & loka°. — 3. arrangement J VI.11 (paṭhavi-vaḍḍhanaka-kamma the act of attending to, i. e. smoothing the ground). — 4. serving for, enhancing, favouring Pv III.3⁶ (rati-nandi°). — 5. potsherd [connected with **vardh** ? See vaddheti] J III.226 (C. kaṭhalika; uncertain). — 6. a kind of garment, as puṇṇa° (full of costliness ? but perhaps not connected with vaḍḍh° at all) Mhvs 23, 33 & 37 (where C. expl^s: anagghāni evaŋnāmikāni vattha-yugāni). Cp. vaḍḍhamāna.

Vaḍḍhanaka (adj.) [fr. vaḍḍhana, cp. vaḍḍheti 4] serving, in f. °ikā a serving (of food), a dish (bhatta°) DhA 188 (so read for vaḍḍhinikā).

Vaḍḍhamāna (nt.) at Dpvs XI.33 is probably equivalent to **vaḍḍhana** (6) in special sense at Mhvs 23, 33, and designates a (pair of) special(ly costly) garment(s). One might think of meaning vaḍḍheti [BSk. vardhate] "to bid higher (at a sale)," as in Divy 403; AvŚ I.36, and explain as "that which causes higher bidding," i. e. very precious. The passage is doubtful. It may simply mean "costly" (belonging to nandiyāvaṭṭaŋ); or is it to be read as **vaṭṭamāna** ?

Vaḍḍhamānaka (adj.) [ppr. of vaḍḍheti+ka] growing, increasing, getting bigger; only in phrase vaḍḍhamānaka-cchāyāya (loc.) with growing shade, as the shadows lengthened, when evening drew near DhA I.96, 416; II.79; Mhvs 19, 40.

Vaḍḍhi (f.) [fr. **vṛdh**, Vedic vṛddhi refreshment etc., which is differentiated in Pāli into vuddhi & vaḍḍhi] 1. increase, growth (cp. *Cpd.* 251 sq.) S IV.250 (ariya°); J II.426 (=phāti); Miln 109 (guṇa°); DhsA 327; DhA III.335 (avaḍḍhi=parihāni). — 2. welfare, good fortune, happiness J V.101; VI.330. — 3. (as t. t.) profit, interest (on money, esp. loans) Th 2, 444 (=iṇa-vaḍḍhi ThA 271); DA I.212, 270; VbhA 256 (in simile); SnA 179 (°gahaṇa).

Vaḍḍhika (adj.) [fr. vaḍḍhi] leading to increase, augmenting, prosperous Miln 351 (ekanta°, equal to aparihāniya).

Vaḍḍhita [pp. of vaḍḍheti] 1. increased, augmented; raised, enlarged; big Th 1, 72 (su-su°); DA I.115; DhsA 188, 364; J V.340 (°kāya). — 2. grown up DhA I.126. — 3. brought up, reared J I.455. — 4. served, indulged, supplied: see kaṭasi° (S II.178 e. g.).

Vaṇa (nt. & m.) [cp. Vedic vraṇa; Serbian rāna; Obulg. vařе, both "wound"] a wound, sore Vin I.205 (m.), 218 (vaṇo rūḷho); III.36 (m; angajāte), 117 (angajāte); S IV.177 (vaṇaŋ ālimpeti); A V.347 sq., 350 sq.; 359; Nd[2] 540; PugA 212 (purāṇa-vaṇa-sadisa-citto); DhA II.165 (°ŋ bandhati to bandage); VvA 77; PvA 80; Sdhp 395. On vaṇa in *similes* see *J.P.T.S.* 1907, 132.
-ālepana putting ointment on a sore SnA 58 (in sim.). -coḷaka a rag for dressing a wound Vism 342; VbhA 361. -paṭikamma restoration or healing of a wound DhA II.164. -paṭicchādana dressing of a wound DhA I.375. -paṭṭa id., bandage SnA 100. -bandhana id. Vin I.205. -mukha the opening of a sore A IV.386 (nava °āni); VvA 77 (id.).

Vaṇi (f.) [fr. van to desire] wish, request Ud 53; J IV.404 (=yācana C.); cp. *J.P.T.S.* 1891, 18. See vana[2] & cp. vaṇeti.

Vaṇijjā (f.) [Vedic vaṇijyā, fr. vaṇij° (vaṇik) merchant, cp. vāṇija & vaṇibbaka] trade, trading M II.198; Sn 404 (payojaye dhammikaŋ so vaṇijjaŋ); A II.81 sq.; Pv I.5[6] (no trade among the Petas); J I.169; PvA 47 (tela°); Sdhp 332, 390. — *Five* trades must not be carried on by lay followers of the Buddha, viz. sattha° trade in swords, satta° in living beings, maŋsa° in meat, majja° in intoxicants, visa° in poisons A III.208, quoted at DA I.235 and SnA 379.

Vaṇita [pp. of *vaṇeti, Denom. fr. vaṇa] wounded, bruised Pv II.2[4]; J I.150; Sdhp 395.

Vaṇippattha [vaṇik+patha, in meaning patha 2] trading, trade Vin I.229=D II.87=Ud 88 (with ref. to Pāṭaliputta).

Vaṇibbaka [vaṇibba+ka. The form *vaṇibba, according to Geiger, *P.Gr.* § 46[1], distorted fr. vaṇiya, thus "travelling merchant, wayfarer." Spelling wavers between vaṇibb° & vanibb°. The BSk. form is vanīpaka, e. g. at AvŚ I.248; II.37; Divy 83; occurring also as vanīyaka at Divy 83] a wayfarer, beggar, pauper Sn 100 (ṇ); J IV.403, 406 (n); V.172 (=bhojaputta C.; n); VI.232 (n); DA I.298 (ṇ); PvA 78 (n), 112 (n); VvA 5 (n). Often combd with similar terms in phrase kapaṇ' addhika [iddhika] vaṇibbaka-yācakā indigents, tramps, wayfarers & beggars, e. g. D I.137 (ṇ); Miln 204 (ṇ); DhA I.105 (ṇ). Other spurious forms are vaṇidīpaka PvA 120; vanīpaka Cp. I.4[9].

Vaṇibbin (adj.-n.) [fr. *vaṇibba] begging, a beggar, tramp J III.312; IV.410 (=yācanto C.). Spelling at both places n. See also vanin.

Vaṇīyati see vanīyati.

Vaṇeti [Caus. of van (see etym. under vana[2]), cp. vaṇi (vani). It may be derived directly fr. vṛ, vṛṇāti=P. vuṇāti, as shown by vaṇimhase. A Denom. fr. vani is vanīyati] to wish, desire, ask, beg J V.27 (spelt vaṇṇeti; C. expl[s] as vāreti icchati); pres. med. 1st pl. vaṇimhase (=Sk. vṛṇimahe) J II.137 (=icchāma C.). As vanayati at KhA 111 (vanayatī ti vanaŋ).

Vaṇṭa (nt.) [Epic Sk. vṛnta] a stalk S III.155=D I.73 (°chinna with its stalk cut); J I.70; Ap 62; Vism 356 (in comparison); SnA 296; VbhA 60; DhA II.42; IV.112; VvA 44. avaṇṭa (of thana, the breast of a woman) not on a stalk (i. e. well-formed, plump) J V.155. So to be trsld here, although vaṇṭa as medical term is given in BR with meaning "nipple." — See also tālavaṇṭa

Vaṇṭaka (adj.) (-°) [vaṇṭa+ka] having a stalk; a° not fastened on stalks J V.203.

Vaṇṭati [dial. Sk. vaṇṭ] to partition, share; is given as root vaṇṭ at Dhtp 92, 561 and Dhtm 787 in meaning "vibhājana." — Another root vaṇṭ is found at Dhtm 108 with unmeaning expln "vaṇṭ' atthe."

Vaṇṭika (adj.) (-°) [vaṇṭa+ika] having a stalk; only in phrase ekato° & ubhato° having a stalk on one or on both sides (of a wreath) Vin II.10; III.180; DhA I.419.

Vaṇṇa [cp. Vedic varṇa, of vṛ: see vuṇāti. Customary definition as "vaṇṇane" at Dhtp 572] appearance etc. (lit. "cover, coating"). There is a considerable fluctuation of meaning, especially between meanings 2, 3, 4. One may group as follows. — 1. colour Sn 447 (meda°); S V.216 (chavi° of the skin); A III.324 (sankha°); Th 1, 13 (nīl'abbha°); Vv 45[10] (danta°=ivory white); Pv IV.3[9]; DhA II.3 (aruṇa°); SnA 319 (chavi°); VvA 2 (vicitta°); PvA 215. *Six* colours are usually enumd as vaṇṇā, viz. nīla pīta lohitaka odāta mañjeṭṭha pabhassara Ps I.126; cp. the 6 colours under rūpa at Dhs 617 (where kāḷaka for pabbassara); J I.12 (chabbaṇṇa-buddha-rasmiyo). Groups of *five* see under pañca 3 (cp. J I.222). —dubbaṇṇa of bad colour, ugly S I.94; A V.61; Ud 76; Sn 426; It 99; Pug 33; VvA 9; PvA 32, 68. Opp. suvaṇṇa of beautiful colour, lovely A V.61; It 99. Also as term for "silver." — As t. t. in descriptions or analyses (perhaps better in meaning "appearance") in abl. vaṇṇato by colour, with saṇṭhānato and others: Vism 184 ("kāḷa vā odāta vā manguracchavi vā"), 243=VbhA 225; Nett 27. — 2. appearance S I.115 (kassaka-vaṇṇaŋ abhinimminitvā); J I.84 (id. with māṇavaka°); Pv II.1[10] (=chavi-vaṇṇa PvA 71); III.3[2] (kanakassa sannibha); VvA 16; cp. °dhātu. — 3. lustre, splendour (cp. next meaning) D III.143 (suvaṇṇa°, or=1); Pv II.9[62] (na koci devo vaṇṇena sambuddhaŋ atirocati); III.9[1] (suriya°); Vv 29[1] (=sarīr' obhāsa VvA 122); PvA 10 (suvaṇṇa°), 44. — 4. beauty (cp. vaṇṇavant) D II.220 (abhikkanta°); M I.142 (id.); D III.68 (āyu+); Pv II.9[10] (=rūpa-sampatti PvA 117). Sometimes combd with other ideals, as (in set of 5): āyu, sukha, yasa, sagga A III.47; or āyu, yasa, sukha, ādhipacca J IV.275, or (4): āyu, sukha, bala A III.63. — 5. expression, look, specified as mukha°, e. g. S III.2, 235; IV.275 sq.; A V.342; Pv III.9[1]; PvA 122. — 6. colour of skin, appearance of body, complexion M II.32 (parama), 84 (seṭṭha); A III.33 (dibba); IV.396 (id.); Sn 610 (doubtful, more likely because of its combn with sara to below 8 1), 686 (anoma°); Vism 422 (evaŋ°=odato vā sāmo vā). Cp. °pokkharatā. — In special sense applied as distinguishing mark of race or species, thus also constituting a mark of class (caste) distinction & translatable as "(social) grade, rank, caste" (see on term *Dial.* I.27, 99 sq.; cp. Vedic ārya varṇa and dāsa varṇa RV II.12, 9; III.34, 9: see Zimmer, *Altind. Leben* 113 and in greater detail Macdonell & Keith, *Vedic Index* II.247 sq.). The customary enumn is of 4 such grades, viz. khattiyā brāhmaṇā vessā suddā Vin II.239; A IV.202; M II.128, but cp. *Dial.* I.99 sq. — See also Vin IV.243 (here applied as general term of "grade" to the alms-bowls: tayo pattassa vaṇṇā, viz. ukkaṭṭha, majjhima, omaka; cp. below 7); D I.13, 91; J VI.334; Miln 225 (khattiya°, brāhmaṇa°). — 7. kind, sort Miln 118 (nānā°), cp. Vin IV.243, as mentioned under 6. — 8. timbre (i. e. appearance) of voice, contrasted to sara intonation, accent; may occasionally be taken as "vowel." See A I.229 (+sara); IV.307 (id.); Sn 610 (id., but may mean "colour of skin": see 6), 1132 (giraŋ vaṇṇ' upasaŋhitaŋ, better than meaning "comment"); Miln 340 (+sara). — 9. constitution, likeness, property; adj. (-°) "like": aggi° like fire Pv III.6[6] (=aggi-sadisa PvA 203). — 10. ("good impression") praise DhA I.115 (magga°);

usually comb^d and contrasted with **avaṇṇa** blame, e. g. D I.1, 117, 174; A I.89; II.3; III.264; IV.179, 345; DA I.37. — II. reason ("outward appearance") S I.206 (= kāraṇa *K.S.* I.320); Vv 84⁶ (= kāraṇa VvA 336); Pv IV.1⁶ (id. PvA 220); IV.1⁴⁸.

-**āroha** (large) extent of beauty Sn 420. -**kasiṇa** the colour circle in the practice of meditation VbhA 251. -**kāraka** (avaṇṇe) one who makes something (unsightly) appear beautiful J v.270. -**da** giving colour, i. e. beauty Sn 297. -**dada** giving beauty A II.64. -**dasaka** the ten (years) of complexion or beauty (the 3rd decade in the life of man) Vism 619; J IV.497. -**dāsī** "slave of beauty," courtezan, prostitute J I.156 sq., 385; II.367, 380; III.463; VI.300; DhA I.395; IV.88. -**dhātu** composition or condition of appearance, specific form, material form, natural beauty S I.13; Pv I.3¹; PvA 137 (= chavivaṇṇa); DhsA 15. -**patha** see vaṇṇu°. -**pokkharatā** beauty of complexion D I.114, 115; A I.38; II.203; Pug 66; VbhA 486 (def^d); DhA III.389; PvA 46. -**bhū** place of praise J I.84 (for °bhūmi: see bhū²). -**bhūta** being of a (natural) species PvA 97. -**vādin** saying praise, praising D I.179, 206; A II.27; V.164 sq.; Vin II.197. -**sampanna** endowed with beauty A I.244 sq., 288; II.250 sq.

Vaṇṇaka (nt.) [fr. vaṇṇa] paint, rouge D II.142; Th I,960; Dpvs VI.70.

Vaṇṇata (f.) [abstr. fr. vaṇṇa] having colour, complexion A I.246 (dubbaṇṇatā bad c.); VvA 9.

Vaṇṇanā (f.) [fr. vaṇṇeti] I. explanation, commentary, exposition KhA II, 145, 227; SnA 65 (pada°); PvA 2. —**pāḷi°** explanation of the text (as regards meaning of words), purely textual analysis (opp. vinicchayakathā) VbhA 291. — 2. praise DhA II.100 (vana°).

Vaṇṇanīya (adj.) [grd. formation fr. vaṇṇeti] to be described; a° indescribable J v.282.

Vaṇṇavant (adj.) [fr. vaṇṇa] beautiful A IV.240 (cātummahārājikā devā dīgh'āyukā vaṇṇavanto; v. l. °vantā); Pug 34; Pv III.2¹² (= rūpasampanna PvA 184); DhA I.383.

Vaṇṇita [pp. of vaṇṇeti] I. explained, commented on SnA 368. — 2. praised, extolled Pug 69; J I.9; Miln 278 (+ thuta & pasattha); PvA 116 (= pasaṇsita), 241; VvA 156 (= pasaṇsita).

Vaṇṇin (-°) (adj.) [fr. vaṇṇa] I. having colour Th I, 1190 (accharā nānattavaṇṇiyo "in divers hues"). — 2. belonging to a caste, in cātu° (suddhi) (purity of) the fourfold castes M II.132. — 3. having beauty Sn 551 (uttama°). — 4. having the appearance of A II.106 = Pug 44 (āma°, pakka°); J v.322 (vijju°).

Vaṇṇiya (nt.) [fr. vaṇṇeti] colouring; having or giving colour, complexion M I.446 (in phrase assaṇ assa-damako vaṇṇiyañ ca valiyañ ca anuppavecchati, trsl^d by Neumann as "lässt der Rossebändiger noch die letzte Strählung und Striegelung angedeihen"; still doubtful); A III.54 (dubbaṇṇiyaṇ bad complexion); It 76 (dub° evil colour).

Vaṇṇu (f.) [cp. late Sk. varṇu, N. of a river(-district)] is given at Abhp 663 in meaning of "sand." Occurs only in cpd. **vaṇṇupatha** a sandy place, quicksand, swamp J I.109; Vv 84³ (= vālu-kantāra VvA 334); Pv IV.3² (= petena nimmitaṇ mudu-bhūmi-magga PvA 250, so read for vaṇṇapatha); shortened to **vaṇṇu** at Vv 84¹¹ (where MSS vaṇṇa).

Vaṇṇeti [Denom. fr. vaṇṇa] I. to describe, explain, comment on J I.2, 222; KhA 168; SnA 23, 160, 368. — 2. to praise, applaud, extol J I.59, 84; PvA 131 (+ pasaṇsati). — pp. **vaṇṇita**.

Vata¹ (indecl.) [Vedic bata, post-Vedic vata] part of exclamation: surely, certainly, indeed, alas! Vin III.39 (puris' usabho vat' āyaṇ "for sure he is a human bull"); Th 2, 316 (abbhutaṇ vata vācaṇ bhāsasi); Sn 178, 191, 358; Vv 47¹³; Pv I.8⁵; J IV.355; PvA 13, 61, 75, 121. Often comb^d with other emphatic particles, like aho vata Pv II.9⁴⁵ (= sādhu vata PvA 131); lābhā vata no it is surely a gain that Sn 31; DhA II.95; vata bho J I.81.

Vata² (m. & nt.) [cp. Vedic vrata vow, fr. **vṛt**, meaning later "milk" (see Macdonell & Keith, *Vedic Index* II.341)] I. a religious duty, observance, rite, practice, custom S I.143, 201; IV.180; A IV.461 (sīla, vata, tapas, brahmacariya); v.18; Sn 792, 898; Vv 84²⁴; J III.75; VvA 9; PvA 60. —**subbata** of good practice Vv 34⁶. Cp. patibbata, sīlabbata. — 2. manner of (behaving like) a certain animal (as a practice of ascetics), e. g. aja° like a goat J IV.318; go° like a cow M I.387; J IV.318; **vagguli°** bat practice J I.493; III.235; IV.299; hatthi° elephant behaviour Nd¹ 92 (here as **vatta**; see under vatta¹).

-**pada** an item of good practice, virtue (otherwise called guṇa at Miln 90) J I.202 (where 7 are enum^d, viz. devotion to one's mother & father, reverence towards elder people, speaking the truth, gentle speech, open speech, unselfishness); Miln 70 (where 8 are given in detail, differing from the above). See also vatta² 2, where other sets of 7 & 8 are quoted. -**samādāna** taking up a (good) practice, observance of a vow J I.157.

Vatavant (adj.) [vata² + vant] observant of religious duties, devout Sn 624 (= dhuta-vatena samannāgata SnA 467); Dh 400 (with same expl^n at DhA IV.165 as as SnA 467).

Vati¹ (f.) [later Sk. vṛti, fr. **vṛ**] a fence J I.153; III.272; v.472; Vism 186 (vatī, v. l. vati); SnA 98 (v. l. for gutti), 148 (v. l. for °vatikā).

Vati² (f.) [fr. **vṛ**, cp. Sk. vṛti] a choice, boon DhA I.190 (pubbe Sāmā nāma vatiyā pana kāritattā Sāmāvatī nāma jātā).

Vatika (adj.) (-°) [vata² + ika] having the habit (of), acting like M I.387 (kukkura°).

Vatikā (f.) [fr. vati¹] a fence SnA 148 (kaṇṭaka° & rukkha°).

Vatta¹ (nt.) [orig. pp. of vattati] I. that which is done, which goes on or is customary, i. e. duty, service, custom, function Vin II.31; Sn 294, 393 (gahaṭṭha°); Vism 188 (cetiy' aṅgaṇa° etc.); DhA I.92 (ācariya°); VbhA 354 (gata-paccāgata°); VvA 47 (gāma°). — 2. (for vata²) observance, vow, virtue D III.9 (the 7 vatta-padāni, diff. from those enum^d under vata-pada); Nd¹ 66 (sīlañ ca vattañ ca), 92 (hatthi° etc.: see vata² 2), 104 (°suddhi), 106 (id.), 188 (giving 8 dhutangas as vattas).

-**paṭivatta** all kinds of practices or duties J I.67; II.103; III.339; IV.298; Miln 416 (sucarita°); DhA I.13 sq.; II.277; IV.28. -**bbata** the usual custom DhA IV.44; C. on S I.36 § 2 and on S II.18 § 4 sq. -**sampanna** one who keeps all observances VbhA 297 (where the foll. vattāni are enum^d: 82 khuddaka-vattāni, 14 mahā°, cetiyaṅgaṇa°, bodhiyaṅgaṇa°, pānīyamāḷa°, uposathāgāra°, āgantuka°, gamika°).

Vatta² (nt.) [cp. Sk. vaktra & P. vattar] the mouth (lit. "speaker") Pgdp 55 (sūci-vatto mah'odaro peto).

Vatta³ [vyatta, Sk. vyātta, of vi + ā + dā] opened wide Vin III.37; J v.268 (vatte mukhe).

Vatta[4] at J v.443 is corrupt for **vaṇṭha** cripple.

Vattaka (adj.) [fr. vatta[1]] doing, exercising, influencing; in vasa° having power, neg. avasa° having no free will, involuntary PvA 64.

Vattati [Vedic vartate; **vṛt.** A differentiated P. form is vaṭṭati. — Cp. Av. varət to turn, Sk. vartana turning, vartulā = Lat. vertellum = E. whorl (Ger. wirtel) & vertil; Gr. ῥατάνη; Goth. waírþan = Ger. werden (to become, E. "turn"); Goth. -waírþs = E. -wards; Obulg. vrěteno spindle; and many others (e. g. Lat. vertex, vortex), q. v. Walde, *Lat. Wtb.* s. v. verto] to move, go on, proceed; to happen, take place, to be; to be in existence; to fare, to do Sn p. 13 (parivesanā vattati distribution of food was in progress); Sn 654 (kammanā vattati loko keeps up, goes on); Pv II.9[44] (vatteyya); Miln 338 (na ciraŋ vattate bhavo). — grd. **vattabba** to be proceeded, or simply "to be" Vin II.8 (so read for vatth°): nissāya te v. "thou must remain under the superintendence of others" (*Vin. Texts*, II.344). — Often equal to atthi or (pl.) santi, i. e. is (are), e. g. J VI.504; SnA 100 (bāḷhā vedanā vattanti); PvA 40. — ppr. med. **vattamāna** see sep. — pp. **vatta.** — Caus. **vatteti** to make go on, to keep up, practise, pursue Sn 404 (etaŋ vattayaŋ pursuing this); freq. in phrases **vasaŋ vatteti** to exercise power, e. g. PvA 89; and **cakkaŋ vatteti** to wield royal power, to govern (cp. expression cakkavattin & see pavatteti) Sn 554, 684 (vattessati), 693 (dhamma-cakkaŋ); J III.412. — grd. **vattitabba** to be practised Vin II.32. — pp. **vattita.**

Vattana (nt.) [fr. vattati] moving on, upkeep, existence, continuance Sn 698 (cakka° continuance of royal power); Mhvs 3, 38.

Vattanī (& °i) (f.) [cp. Sk. vartanī, fr. **vṛt**] a track, a road J I.196, 395, 429; III.200. —**kaṇha°** leaving a black trail, Ep. of the fire J III.140.

Vattamāna (adj.-nt.) [ppr. med. of vattati] being in existence, going on, happening at the time; nt. process, progress, (as °-) in progress SnA 4 (°uppanna); PvA 55. -°**vacana** the present tense SnA 16, 23.

Vattamānaka (adj.) [fr. last] going on, being, existing; °bhave in the present existence or period Miln 291.

Vattar [n. ag. of vatti, **vac**] one who speaks, a sayer, speaker M I.470; S I.63; II.182; VI.94, 198; D I.139; A IV.32; V 79 sq., 226 sq.; Th 1, 334 (read ariya-vattā for ° vatā); J I.134; SnA 272; PvA 15.

Vatti [Vedic vakti, **vac**] to speak, say, call; *pres.* not found (for which vadati); *fut.* 1st sg. **vakkhāmi** J I.346; 3rd **vakkhati** S I.142; J I.356; II.40; VI.352; VbhA 51; 1st pl. **vakkhāma** S IV.72; M III.207; Vism 170, 446; 3rd **vakkhanti** Vin II.1; pte. fut. **vakkhamāna** PvA 18. — *aor.* 1st sg. **avacaŋ** J III.280; DhA III.194, & **avocaŋ** Th 2, 124; Vv 79[7]; S I.10; DhA III.285; 2nd **avaca** Th 2, 415, **avoca** Dh 133, & **avacāsi** Vv 35[7]; 53[9]; 3rd **avaca** J I.294; Pv II.3[19]; PvA 65 (mā a.); **avoca** Th 2, 494; S I.150; Sn p. 78; J II.160; PvA 6, 31, 49, & **avacāsi** J VI.525; 1st pl. **avacumha** & **avocumha** M II.91; III.15; 2nd **avacuttha** Vin I.75 (mā a.); II.297; J II.48; DhA I.73; IV.228, & **avocuttha** J I.176; Miln 9; 3rd pl. **avacuŋ** J V.260, & **avocuŋ** M II.147. — *inf.* **vattuŋ** Sn 431; J VI.351; Vism 522 = VbhA 130 (vattukāma); SnA 414; DA I.109; DhA I.329; II.5. — *ger.* **vatvā** SnA 398; PvA 68, 73, & **vatvāna** Sn p. 78. — *grd.* **vattabba** Miln 276 (kiŋ vattabbaŋ what is there to be said about it? i. e. it goes without saying); SnA 123, 174, 178; PvA 12, 27, 92. — *ppr. med.* **vuccamāna** Vin I.60; III.221; PvA 13. — Pass. **vuccati** D I.168, 245; Dh 63; Mhvs 9, 9; 34, 81 (vuccate, v. l. uccate); J I.129 (vuccare, 3rd pl.); PvA 24, 34, 63, 76; — pp. **vutta** (q. v.). — Caus. **vāceti** to make speak, i. e. to read out; to cause to read; also to teach, to instruct Sn 1018, 1020; J I.452 (read); PvA 97. — pp. **vācita** (q. v.). — Desid. **vavakkhati** (see Geiger, *P.Gr.* § 184 = Sk. vivakṣati) to wish to call D II.256.

Vattika = vatika Nd[1] 89 (having the habit of horses, elephants etc.).

Vattita (nt.) [fr. vatteti] that which goes on, round (of existence), revolution Miln 226.

Vattin (adj.) (-°) [fr. **vṛt**] engaged in, having power over, making, doing; only in cpds. **cakka°** & **vasa°** (q. v.).

Vattha[1] (nt.) [Vedic vastra, fr. **vas**, vaste to clothe; Idg. ***ṷes**, enlargement of ***eu** (: Lat. ex-uo); cp. Lat. vestis "vest(-ment)," Gr. ἕννυμι to clothe, εἷμα dress; Goth. wasjan to clothe; wasti dress] 1. cloth; clothing, garment, raiment; also collectively: clothes; M I.36 sq.; A I.132, 209, 286; II.85, 241; III.27 (odātaŋ), 50 (kāsikaŋ), 386 (kāsāyaŋ); IV.60, 186, 210; V.61 sq. (ubhatobhāga-vimaṭṭhaŋ = M II.13, reading **vimaddha**; with the expression cp. ubhato-bhāga-vimutta); Sn 295, 304; KhA 237 (°ŋ pariyodāyati, simile); PvA 43, 50, 70; Sdhp 217. —**alla°** fresh, clean clothes DhA IV.220; **ahata°** new clothes J I.50; Dāvs II.39; **dibba°** heavenly, i. e. exquisite dresses PvA 23, 46, 53. — pl. **vatthāni** garments, clothes Sn 64, 287, 924; Pug 57 (kāsāyāni); DhA I.219 (their uses, from a new dress down to a bit of rag). — 2. hangings, tapestry J IV.304. — On vattha in *similes* see *J.P.T.S.* 1907, 132.

-guyha "that which is concealed by a cloth," i. e. the pudendum D I.106; Sn 1022; DA I.275 (= angajātaŋ: Bhagavato ti vāraṇass' eva kosohitaŋ vatthaguyhaŋ suvaṇṇavaṇṇaŋ paduma-gabbha-samānaŋ). **-yuga** a pair of garments J IV.172; Dāvs I.34. **-lakkhaṇa** fortune telling from clothes SnA 362. **-sannidhi** storing up of clothes D I.6; Nd[1] 372; DA I.82. **-sutta** the Suttanta on clothes (i. e. with the parable of the clothes: vatth' upama-sutta) M I.36 sq., quoted at Vism 377 and SnA 119.

Vattha[2] as pp. of vasati[1] occurs only in cpd. nivattha. The two passages in PvA where vattha is printed as pp. (vatthāni vattha) are to be read as **vattha-nivattha** (PvA 46, 62).

Vatthabba at Vin II.8 is to be spelt **vattabba** (see vattati).

Vatthi (m. & f.) [Vedic vasti in meaning 1; the other meanings later] 1. the bladder Vin III.117; J I.146; Sn 195; Vism 144 = DhsA 117; Vism 264, 345 (mutta°), 362; DA I.161; VbhA 248. — 2. the pudendum: see °kosa. — 3. a clyster (-bag): see °kamma.

-kamma(ŋ karoti) to use a clyster Vin I.216. **-kosa** a membranous sheath enveloping the sexual organ of a male DA I.275 (°kosena paṭicchanna vatthaguyha: so read for °kesena); VvA 252 (°mukha orifice of the pudendum of an elephant).

Vatthu[1] (nt.) [Class. Sk. vastu, fr. **vas**[1]] lit. "ground," hence 1. (lit.) object, real thing, property, thing, substance (cp. vatthu[2]!) A II.209 (khetta°, where khetta in lit. sense, cp. No. 2). Here belongs the def[n] of kāma as twofold: **vatthu-kāma** and **kilesa-kāma**, or desire for realities, objective kāma, and desire as property of stained character, i. e. subjective kāma, e. g. Nd[1] 1; SnA 99, 112; DhsA 62. — On **vatthu** as general philos. term cp. *Dhs. trsl*[n] [2]§§ 455, 679, 1229, also introd. p. 86; *Cpd.* 15, 31, 174[1]. — 2. (appl[d] meaning) object, item Vin I.121 (antima-vatthuŋ ajjhāpannaka guilty of an extreme offence?); V.138 (the 10 āghāta-vatthūni, as at Vbh 86); D III.252 (*seven* niddesa°), 255 (*eight* kusīta°), 258 (*eight* dāna°); S II.41, 56 sq.; Vbh 71 (cakkhu° etc.), 306 sq., 353; Nett 114 (*ten*); SnA 172; DhA IV.2 (akkosa°); PvA 8, 20 (dāna°), 26 (left out in id. p. KhA 209), 29, 65 (alabbhaneyya°), 96 (id.), 119, 121 (iṭṭha°), 177,

220. Cp. °bhūta. — 3. occasion for, reason, ground A II.158 (+ khetta [in fig. sense!], āyatana & adhikaraṇa); IV.334; D I.13 sq. (aṭṭhādasahi vatthūhi etc.); J II.5 (avatthumhi chandaŋ mâkari do not set your heart on what is unreasonable); vatthunā (instr.) because PvA 118; vatthuto (abl.) on account of PvA 241. — 4. basis, foundation, seat, (objective) substratum, substance, element J I.146 (kāyo paridevānaŋ v.); VbhA 404 (+ ārammaṇa). See most of the cpds. — 5. subject-matter, subject, story, account SnA 4; DhA II.66; PvA 77, 92, 263, 269. Cp. °gāthā & titles like Petavatthu, Vimānavatthu.

-**kata** made a foundation or basis of, practised thoroughly J II.61; V.14 and passim (+ bhāvita etc.). In phrase **tālâvatthukata** (= tāla avatthu kata) vatthu means foundation, basis, ground to feed and live on, thus "a palm deprived of its foundation": see refs. under **tāla**. -**gāthā** the stanzas of the story, the introductory (explanatory, essential to its understanding) stanzas, something like "prologue" SnA 483, 575 (preceding Sn 699 & 976). -**dasaka** tenfold substance or material basis VbhA 22. -**bhūta** being an object, i. e. subject to J V.210. -**rūpa** substance or substratum of matter, material form Vism 561, 564; VbhA 22, 172. -**visadakiriyā** clearing of the foundation or fundamentals, purification of the elements VbhA 283 = DhsA 76 (°kiriyatā; trsl° *Expos.* 101 "cleansing of things or substance"); Vism 128; VbhA 276.

Vatthu[2] [Vedic vāstu; fr. **vas**] site, ground, field, plot Vin III.50 (ārāma° & vihāra°), 90 (id.); Sn 209, 473 (sakhetta°, cp. vatthu[1] 4), 769 (khetta +), 858 (id.); Th I, 957 (khetta + vatthu, cp. *Brethren* p. 337[1] & *Vin. Texts* III.389 sq.); Miln 279 (khetta° a plot of arable land); DA I.78 (contrasted with khetta, see khetta I and cp. vatthu[1] I); PvA 88 (gehassa the back yard of the house); haunted by fairies (pariganhanti) D II.87.

-**kamma** "act concerning sites," i. e. preparing the ground for building D I.12 (trsl°: fixing on lucky sites for dwellings), cp. DA I.98: akata-vatthumhi gehapatiṭṭhāpanaŋ. -**devatā** the gods protecting the grounds, field-gods, house-gods Pv I.4[1] (= ghara-vatthuŋ adhivatthā devatā PvA 17). -**parikiraṇa** offerings over the site of a house ("consecrating sites" trsl°) D I.12 (cp. DA I.98 = balikamma-karaṇaŋ). -**vijjā** the science of (building-) sites, the art of determining a suitable (i. e. lucky) site for a house D I.9 (see expl° at DA I 93); S III.239; Nd[1] 372; Vism 269 (in comparison); KhA 237. See also *Dial* II.92 & Fick, *Sociale Gliederung* 152.

Vatthuka (adj.) (-°) [fr. vatthu[1]] 1. having a site or foundation or ground, in ucca° (high) and nīca° (low) Vin II.117, 120; Mhvs 33, 87. — 2. having its ground in, founded on, being of such & such a nature or composition S IV.67 (vācā°); Ps I.130 (micchādiṭṭhi°, correct in Index *J.P.T.S.* 1908!); Vbh 319 (uppanna°; + ārammaṇa), 392 (micchādiṭṭhi°); VbhA 403 (uppanna° etc.).

Vada (adj.) (-°) [fr. **vad**] speaking, in cpd. vaggu° speaking pleasantly Sn 955 (cp. Nd[1] 446; SnA 571 = sundaravada); suddhiŋ° of clean speech Sn 910.

Vadaññu (adj.) [cp. Sk. vadāniya, which also in P. avadāniya] lit. "(easily) spoken to," addressable, i. e. liberal, bountiful, kind S I.43; A II.59, 61 sq.; IV.271 sq., 285, 289, 322; Sn 487; Pv IV.1[33], 3[42], 10[11], 15[4]; VvA 281.

Vadaññutā (f.) [abstr. fr. vadaññu] bounty, kindness, liberality; neg. a° stinginess A V.146, 148 sq.; Vbh 371.

Vadati [**vad**, Ved. vadati; Dhtp 134 vada = vacana] to speak, say, tell A IV.79; Sn 1037, 1077 sq.; Pug 42; PvA 13, 16, 39; Pot. 1st sg. vade (so read for vado?) M I.258; 3rd sg. vadeyya Pv I 3[3]; aor. 3rd pl. vadiŋsu PvA 4. — Cp. abhi°, upa°, pa°, vi°. — Another form (*not* Caus.: see Geiger, *P.Gr.* § 139[2]) is vadeti D I.36; Vin II.1; Sn 825; Sn p. 140 (kiŋ vadetha); J I.294; imper. vadehi PvA 62; Pot. med. 1st pl. vademase D III.197; fut. vadessati Sn 351; aor. vadesi DhA III.174. — A specific Pāli formation is a Caus. vādiyati in *act.* and *med.* sense (all forms only in *Gāthā* style), e. g. indic. vādiyati Sn 824 = 892, 832; expl[d] as vadati SnA 541, 542, or katheti bhaṇati etc. (the typical Niddesa expl° of vadati: see Nd[2] 555) Nd[1] 161. In contracted (& shortened) form Pot. 2nd sg. **vajjesi** (*vādiyesi) you might tell, i. e. please tell Pv II.11[6] (= vadeyyāsi PvA 149); III.6[7] (same expl° p. 203). The other Pot. forms from the same base are the foll.: 1st sg. **vajjaŋ** Th 2, 308; 2nd sg. vajjāsi Th 2, 307; J III.272; VI.19; and **vajja** Th 2, 323; 3rd sg. vajjā Sn 971 (cp. Nd[1] 498); J VI.526 (= vadeyya C.); 3rd pl. vajjuŋ Sn 859 (= vadeyyuŋ katheyyuŋ etc. Nd[2] 555); J V.221. — Caus. vādeti to make sound, to play (a musical instrument) J I.293; II.110, 254 (vādeyyāma we might play); Ap 31 (aor. vādesuŋ); PvA 151 (vīṇaŋ vādento). — Pass. **vajjati** (*vādiyati) to be played or sounded J I.13 (vajjanti bheriyo); Ap 31 (ppr. vajjamāna & aor. vajjiŋsu). — Another form of ppr. med. (or Pass.) is **vadāna** (being called, so-called) which is found in poetry only (contracted fr. vadamāna) at Vin I.36 = J I.83. — pp. udita[1] & vādita (q. v.). — Caus. II. vādāpeti to cause to be played Mhvs 25, 74 (tūriyaŋ).

Vadana (nt.) [fr. **vad**] speech, utterance VvA 345 (+ kathana).

Vadāna see vadati.

Vadāniya [another form of **vadaññu**] see a°

Vadāpana (nt.) [fr. vādāpeti, Caus. II. of vadati] making somebody speak or something sound DhsA 333 (we should better read vād°).

Vaddalikā (f.) [cp. late Sk. vārdala & BSk. vardalikā MVastu III.301; Divy 500] rainy weather Vin I.3; J VI.52 (loc. vaddalike); DhA III.339; VbhA 109.

Vaddha[1] (adj.-n.) [pp. of vaḍḍhati; see also vaḍḍha, vuḍḍha & vuddha. The root given by Dhtp (166) for **vṛdh** is **vadh** in meaning "vuddhi"] 1. grown, old; an Elder; venerable, respectable; one who has authority. At J I.219 *three* kinds of vaddha are distinguished: one by nature (jāti°), one by age (vayo°), one by virtue (guṇa°); J V.140 (= paññāya vuddha C.). Usually comb[d] with apacāyati to respect the aged, e. g. J I.219; and in cpd. vaddh-apacāyika respecting the elders or those in authority J IV.94; and °apacāyin id. Sn 325 (= vaddhānaŋ apaciti-karaṇa SnA 332); Dh 109; DhA II.239 (= buḍḍhatare guṇavuddhe apacāyamāna). Cp. jeṭṭh' apacāyin. — 2. glad, joyful; in cpd. °bhūta gladdened, cheerful J V.6.

Vaddha[2] (m. & nt.) [cp. Vedic vardhra in meaning "tape"] a (leather) strap, thong J II.154 (vv. ll. baddha, bandhana, bandha, vaṭṭa). Occurs as aŋsa° shoulder strap at Ap 310, where ed. prints baddha (= baddha[2]).

-**maya** consisting of a strap, made of leather J II.153.

Vaddhaka [vaddha + ka] in cpd. aŋsa° "shoulder strap" should be the uniform reading for a series of diff. spellings (°vaṭṭaka, °baddhaka, °bandhaka) at Vin I.204; II.114; IV.170. Cp. Geiger, *Zeitschrift für Buddhismus* IV.107.

Vaddhana (nt.) [fr. **vṛdh**; see the usual vaḍḍhana] increase, furthering J III.422 (kula°); Sdhp 247 (pīti°), 307 (id.).

Vaddhava (nt.) [fr. vaddha[1] 2] joy, pleasure J V.6 (but C. = paṇḍita-bhāva).

Vaddhavya (nt.) [fr. vaddha[1] I] (old) age J II.137 (= vuddhabhāva, mahallakatā C.).

Vaddhi in anta° at J I.260 is to be read as vaṭṭi.

Vaddheti [fr. **vardh** to cut, cp. vaḍḍhaka & vaḍḍhakī] to cut off, is Kern's proposed reading (see *Toev.* s. v.) at J VI.527 (siro vaddhayitvāna) for vajjheti (T. reading vajjhayitvāna).

Vadha [fr. **vadh**] striking, killing; slaughter, destruction, execution D III.176; A II.113; Pug 58; J II.347; Miln 419 (°kata); DhA I.69 (pāṇa°+ pāṇa-ghāta), 80, 296; DhA II.39; VbhA 382. — vadhaŋ dadāti to flog J IV.382. — atta° self-destruction S II.241; piti° parricide DA I.153; miga° hunting J I.149.
-bandhana flogging and binding (imprisoning). In this connection **vadh** is given as a separate root at Dhtp 172 & 384 in meaning "bandhana." See A II.209; V.206; Sn 242 (vadha-cheda-bandhana; v. is expl^d at SnA 285 as "sattānaŋ daṇḍ' ādīhi ākoṭanan" i. e. beating) 623 (=poṭhana SnA 467); J I.435; IV.11; VbhA 97.

Vadhaka [fr. **vadh**] slaying, killing; murderous; a murderer S III.112 (in simile); IV.173 (id.); A IV.92 (id.); Th 2, 347; D III.72 (°citta); KhA 27; VvA 72 (°cetanā murderous intention); Vism 230, 231 (in sim.); Sdhp 58. — f. vadhikā J V.425 (pl. °āyo).

Vadhati [Vedic **vadh**; the root is given at Dhtp 169 in meaning of "hiŋsā"] to strike, punish; kill, slaughter, slay; imper. 2nd pl. vadhetha Vism 314; ger. vadhitvā M I.159; D I.98; J I.12; IV.67; SnA 257 (hiŋsitvā+); fut. vadhissati Mhvs 25, 62; aor. vadhi J I.18 (cp. ud-abbadhi); cond. 1st sg. vadhissaŋ Miln 221. — grd. vajjha: see a°. — Caus. vadheti J I.168; Miln 109. — pp. vadhita.

Vadhita [pp. of vadheti] smitten Th 1, 783=M II.73 (*not* with Kern, *Toev.* s. v.=vyathita).

Vadhukā (f.) [fr. vadhū] a daughter-in-law, a young wife A II.78; DhA III.260.

Vadhū (f.) [Ved. vadhū; to Lith. vedù to lead into one's house] a daughter-in-law VvA 123.

Vana^1 (nt.) [Ved. vana. — The P. (edifying) etymology clearly takes vana as belonging to **van**, and, dogmatically, equals it with vana^2 as an allegorical expression ("jungle") to taṇhā (e. g. DhsA 364 on Dhs 1059; DhA III.424 on Dh 283). — The Dhtp (174) & Dhtm (254) define it "sambhattiyaŋ," i. e. as meaning companionship] the forest; wood; as a place of pleasure & sport ("wood"), as well as of danger & frightfulness ("jungle"), also as resort of ascetics, noted for its loneliness ("forest"). Of (fanciful) def^{ns} of **vana** may be mentioned: SnA 24 (vanute vanotī ti vanaŋ); KhA 111 (vanayatī ti vanaŋ); DhsA 364 (taŋ taŋ ārammaṇaŋ vanati bhajati allīyatī ti vanaŋ, yācati vā ti vanaŋ [i. e. vana^2]. vanatho ti vyañjanena padaŋ vaḍḍhitaŋ . . . balava-taṇhāy'etaŋ nāma); DhA III.424 (mahantā rukkhā vanaŋ nāma, khuddakā tasmiŋ vane ṭhitattā vanathā nāma etc., with further distinguishing detail, concerning the allegorical meanings). — D II.256 (bhikkhūnaŋ samitiŋ vanaŋ); A I.35, 37; Dh 283 (also as vana^2); Sn 272, 562 (sīho nadati vane), 1015 (id.), 684 (Isivhaya v.); Sn p. 18 (Jetavana), p. 115 (Icchānangala); Th 2, 147 (Añjanavana; a wood near Sāketa, with a vihāra); J V.37 (here meaning beds of lotuses); Miln 219 (vanaŋ sodheti to clear a jungle); Dhs 1059 ("jungle"=taṇhā); Pv II.6^6 (arañña°-gocara); Vism 424 (Nandana° etc.); DhA IV.53 (taṇhā° the jungle of lust). Characterized as **amba°** mango grove D II.126 and passim; **ambāṭaka°** plum grove Vin II.17; **udumbara** of figs DhA I.284; **tapo°** forest of ascetics ThA 136; DhA IV.53; **nāga°** elephant forest M I.175; **brahā** wild forest A I.152; III.44; Vv 63^3; J V.215; **mahā°** great forest Th 2, 373 (rahitaŋ & bhiŋsanakaŋ). — **vanataraŋ** (with compar. suffix) thicker jungle, denser forest Miln 269 (vanato vanataraŋ pavisāma). — On *similes* see *J.P.T.S.* 1907, 133. Cp. **vi°**.
-anta the border of the forest, the forest itself Sn 708, 709; Pv II.3^{10} (=vana C.). -**kammika** one who works in the woods J IV.210 (°purisa); V.427, 429. -**gahana** jungle thicket Vism 647 (in simile). -**gumba** a dense cluster of trees Vv 81^7 (cp. VvA 315). -**caraka** a forester SnA 51 (in simile). -**cetya** a shrine in the wood J V.255. -**timira** forest darkness; in metaphor °matt-akkhin at J IV.285=V.284, which Kern (*Toev.* s. v.) changes into °patt-akkhin, i. e. with eyes like the leaves of the forest darkness. Kern compares Sk. vanajapattr'ākṣī Mbh I.171, 43. and vanaja-locanā Avad. Kalp. 3, 137. The Cy. expl^{ns} are "vana-timira-puppha-samān' akkhī," and "giri-kaṇṇika-samāna-nettā"; thus taking it as name of the plant Clitoria ternatea. -**dahaka** (& °dahana) burning the forest (aggi) KhA 21 (in simile). -**devatā** forest deva S IV.302. -**ppagumba** a forest grove VbhA 196. -**ppati** (& vanaspati) [cp. Vedic vanaspati, Prk. vaṇapphai] "lord of the forest," a forest tree; as vanappati only at Vin III.47; otherwise **vanaspati**, e. g. S IV.302 (osadhī+ tiṇa+ v.; opposed to herbs, as in R.V.); A I.152; J I.329; IV.233 (tiṇa-latā-vanaspatiyo); DhA I.3. -**pattha** a forest jungle D I.71; III.38, 49, 195; M I.16, 104; Vin II.146; A I.60; III.138 (arañña°); Pug 59, 68; DA I.210. -**pantha** a jungle road A I.241. -**bhanga** gleanings of the wood, i. e. presents of wild fruit & flowers A IV.197. -**mūla** a wild root D I.166 (+ phala); A I.241 (id.); Miln 278. -**rati** delight in the forest DhA II.100. -**vaṇṇanā** praise of the jungle DhA II.100. -**vāsin** forest-dweller SnA 56 (Mahā-tissa-tthera). -**saṇḍa** jungle-thicket, dense jungle D I.87, 117; S III.109 (tibba v. avijjāya adhivacana); A III.30; J I.82, 170; DhA I.313; II.100.

Vana^2 (nt.) [**van**; vanati & vanoti to desire=Av. vanaiti Lat. venus, Ohg. wini friend (: E. winsome, attractive) wunsc=E. wish, giwon=E. wont; also "to win." The spelling sometimes is **vaṇ**: see **vaṇi**. — The def^n at Dhtp 523 is "yācane" (i. e. from begging), at Dhtm 736 "yācāyaŋ"] lust, desire. In exegetical literature mixed up with **vana**^{1} (see definitions of vana^1). — The word to the Pāli Buddhist forms a connection between **vana** and **nibbāna**, which is felt as a quâsi derivation fr. nibbana= nis+ vana: see nibbana & cp. nibbāna *II.* B I. — S I.180 (so 'haŋ vane nibbanatho visallo); Sn 1131 (nibbana); Dh 334; Th 1, 691 (vanā nibbanaŋ āgataŋ). — A Denom. fr. vana^2 is vanāyati (like vaṇīyati fr. vaṇi).

Vanaka (-) (adj.) [fr. vana^1] belonging to the forest, forest-like; adj. in cpd. ku° (kubbanaka, q. v.) brushwood Sn 1134.

Vanati, Vanute, Vanoti [**van**; Sk. vanoti & vanute. See also vana^2, vaṇi, vaṇeti] to desire, love, wish, aim at, ask for SnA 24 (vanute & vanoti); DhsA 364 (vanati, bhajati, allīyati). Caus. vanayati KhA 111.

Vanatha [vana+ tha; same in BSk. e. g. MVastu I.204] underwood, brushwood, thicket. Does not occur in lit. meaning, except in exegesis of Dh 283 at DhA III.424; q. v. under vana^1. Another def^n is given at SnA 24: "taṇhā pariyuṭṭhāna-vasena vanaŋ tanotī ti vanatho, taṇh' ānusayass' etaŋ adhivacanaŋ." — The fig. meaning is "lust, desire," see e. g. S I.186; Th 1, 338; Dh 344; Sn 16 (°ja); Dhs 1059 (as epithet of taṇhā); J II.205 (vanathaŋ na kayirā); Nett 81, 82. — **nibbanatha** free from desire S I.180; DhsA 364.

Vanāyati [Denom. fr. vana^2, cp. vanāyati] to desire, wish, covet, to hanker after M I.260; S III.190. See also allīyati.

Vanika=vanaka; only in cpd. nāga° one belonging to the elephant forest, i e. an elephant-hunter M I.175; III.132.

Vanin (adj.-n.) [either fr. Sk. vani (=P. vaṇi) in meaning "begging," or poetical abbreviation of vaṇibbin] poor, begging; one who asks (for alms) or begs, a mendicant J VI.232 (=vanibbaka C.).

Vanibbaka see vaṇibbaka.

Vanīyati [Denom. fr. vani = P. vaṇi] to desire J VI.264 C.: (pattheti), 270 (hadayaŋ vanīyati, v. l. dhanīyati: cp. allīyati). — See also **vanati** & **vaṇeti**.

Vaneja [vane (loc. of vana[1]) + ja] born in the woods J II.446.

Vanta [pp. of vamati] 1. vomited, or one who has vomited Miln 214; PvA 80. As nt. vomit at Vin I.303. — 2. (fig.) given up, thrown up, left behind, renounced M I.37 (+ catta, mutta & pahīna). Cp. BSk. vāntī-bhāva, syn. with prahāna AvŚ II.188.
-āda refuse-feeder, crow J II.439. **-āsa** one who has given up all wishes, an Arahant Dh 97 (= sabbā āsā iminā vantā DhA I.187). **-āsika** eating what has been vomited, a certain class of Petas Miln 294. **-kasāva** one who has left behind all fault Dh 10 (= chaḍḍita° DhA I.82). **-gamana** at Vism 210 = DA I.34 read either as v' antagamana or c' anta°. **-mala** stainless Dh 261. **-lokāmisa** renouncing worldly profit Dh 378.

Vandaka (adj.) [fr. **vand**] disposed to veneration; f. °ikā Th 2, 337.

Vandati [**vand**, originally identical with **vad**; the def° at Dhtp (135 & 588) is "abhivādana & thuti"] to greet respectfully, salute, to pay homage, to honour, respect, to revere, venerate, adore Sn 366, 547, 573, 1028; Pv II.1[6]; Mhvs 15, 14 (+ pūjeti); Miln 14; SnA 191; PvA 53 (sirasā with the head, a very respectful way of greeting), 67; VvA 71. imper. **vanda** Vv 21[1] (= abhivādaya VvA 105); pl. **vandantu** Sn 573; ppr. **vandamāna** Sn 598; aor. **vandi** Sn 252; J I.88; PvA 38, 61, 81, 141, 275; inf. **vandituŋ** PvA 77; grd. **vandiya** (neg. a°) Vin II.162. — Caus. II. **vandāpeti** to cause somebody to pay homage J I.88; III.11. — pp. **vandita**.

Vandana (nt.) & **Vandanā** (f.) [fr. **vand**, cp. Vedic vandana] salutation, respect, paying homage; veneration, adoration A I.294 (ā); II.203 (+ pūjā); J I.88; Pug 19, 24; Mhvs 15, 18; Miln 377; PvA I.53; SnA 492; ThA 256; Sdhp 221, 540.

Vandāpana (nt.) [fr. vandāpeti; Caus. of vandati] causing to do homage J I.67.

Vandita [pp. of vandati] saluted, revered, honoured, paid homage to; as nt. homage, respect, veneration Sn 702 (akkuṭṭha +); Th 2, 388 (id.); J I.88.

Vanditar [n. ag. fr. vandita] one who venerates or adores, a worshipper J VI.207 (vandit' assa = vanditā bhaveyya C.).

Vapakassati see vavakassati.

Vapati[1] [**vap**, Vedic vapate. Def° at Dhtp 192: bījanikkhepe] to sow Sn p. 13 (kasati +); J I.150 (nivāpaŋ vapitvā); PvA 139. — Pass. **vappate** S I.227 (yādisaŋ v. bījaŋ tādisaŋ harate phalaŋ), and **vuppati** [Vedic upyate] Th 1, 530. — pp. **vutta**. — Caus. I. **vāpeti**: see pp. **vāpita**[1]. — Caus. II. **vapāpeti** to cause to be sown Vin III.131 (khettaŋ); J IV.276 (sāliŋ).

Vapati[2] [**vap**, probably identical with vapati[1]] to shear, mow, to cut, shave: only in pp. of Caus. **vāpita**[2] (q. v.).

Vapana (nt.) [fr. **vap**] sowing SnA 137; DhA III.220 (°kassaka); PvA 8.

Vapayāti [vi + apa + yā] to go away, to disappear, only at Vin. I.2 = Kvu 186 (kankhā vapayanti sabbā; cp. id. p. MVastu II.416 vyapananti, to be read as vyapayanti).

Vappa[1] (m. or nt.) [orig. grd. fr. **vap** = Sk. vāpya] to be sown, sowing; or soil to be sown on, in paŋsu° sowing on light soil & **kalala**° on heavy soil SnA 137. — *Note*. The def° of a root **vapp** at Dhtm 541 with "vāraṇe" refers to P. vappa bank of a river (Abhp 1133) = Sk. vapra, which is not found in our texts.
-kamma the act or occupation of sowing J I.340 (+ kasi-kamma). **-kāla** sowing time Sn p. 13; S I.172 (= vapanakāla, bīja-nikkhepa-kāla SnA 137). **-mangala** ploughing festival J I.57; DhA II.113; SnA 141.

Vappa[2] [cp. Epic. & Class. Sk. bāṣpa] a tear, tears Vin I.345 (vappaŋ puñchitvā wiping the tears).

Vabbhācitaŋ is a ἅπαξ λεγόμενον at M I.172; read perhaps better as vambhayitaŋ: see p. 545. Neumann trsl° only "thus spoken" (i. e. bhāsitam etaŋ).

Vamati [**vam**, Idg. ***uemo**, cp. Lat. vomo, vomitus = vamathu; Gr. ἐμέω (: E. emetic); Oicel. vaema seasickness. — The def° at Dhtp 221 & Dhtm 315 is "uggiraṇa"] to vomit, eject, throw out, discharge Sn 198 = J I.146; J V.255 (fut. vamissati); Pv IV.3[51] (= uḍḍayati chaḍḍayati PvA 256).—Caus. vameti Miln 169. — pp. **vanta**.

Vamathu [fr. **vam**] vomiting; discharged food PvA 173 (°bhatta; + ucchiṭṭha°).

Vamana (nt.) [fr. **vam**] an emetic D I.12; A V.219; cp. *J.P.T.S.* 1907, 452.

Vamanīya [grd. of vamati; cp. Sk. vāmanīya; ā often interchanges with a before l & m, like Caus. vameti & vāmeti] one who has to take an emetic Miln 169.

Vambhanā (f.) [abstr. fr. vambheti] contempt, despite Vin IV.6; M I.402 (att'ukkaŋsana: para-vambhana), Nd[2] 505; Vism 29; VbhA 484; Pgdp 100. — Spelt **vamhanā** at J I.454 (vamhana-vacana) & at DhsA 396 (khuŋsana°).

Vambhanīya (adj.) [grd. of vambheti] to be despised, wretched, miserable PvA 175, 176.

Vambhayita (nt.) [pp. of vambheti] being despised or reviled M I.172; Sn 905; Nd[1] 319 (= nindita, garahita, upavādita).

Vambhin (adj.) (-°) [fr. **vambh**] despising, treating with contempt, disparaging M I.95 (para°, opp. to att' ukkaŋsaka).

Vambheti (& **Vamheti**) [Caus. of **vambh**, a root of uncertain origin (connected with **vam** ?). There is a form vambha given by Sk. lexicographers as a dial. word for vaŋśa. Could it be a contraction fr. vyambheti = vi + Denom. fr. ambho 2, part. of contempt? — The Dhtp (602) defines **vambh** as "garahāyaŋ"] to treat with contempt, despise, revile, scold; usually either comb[d] with khuŋseti or opposed to **ukkaŋseti**, e. g. Vin II.18; IV.4; M I.200 (= Sn 132 avajānāti), 402 sq.; D I.90; A II.27 sq.; Th 1, 621; DA I.256 (= hīḷeti); DhA IV.38; VvA 348. — pp. **vambhayita**. — **vamheti** is found at J I.191, 356; cp. **vamhana**. — *Note*. The spelling bh interchanges with that of h (vamheti), as ambho shows var. amho. Trenckner (introd. to M I. p. 1) gives vambheti (as BB reading) the preference over vamheti (as SS reading). Morris' note on vambheti in *J.P.T.S.* 1884, 96 does not throw any light on its etymology.

Vamma (nt.) [Vedic varman, fr. **vṛ** to cover, enclose] armour J II.22.

Vammika (adj.) [fr. vamma] = vammin Vin I.342.

Vammita [pp. of vammeti, cp. Sk. varmita] armoured, clad in armour J I.179 (assa); II.315 (hatthi); III.8; V.301, 322; DA I.40.

Vammin (adj.) [fr. vamma; Vedic varmin] wearing armour, armoured J IV.353 (= keṭaka-phalaka-hattha C.); V.259, 373; VI.25; Miln 331.

Vammīka & **vammika** (m. & nt.) [cp. Vedic valmīka; Idg. *ṷorm(āi); cp. Av. maoiris, Sk. vamraḥ, Gr. μύρμηξ, Lat. formica, Cymr. mor; all of same origin & meaning] ant-hill: (a) °īka: M I.142 sq.; J III.85; IV.30 (°bila the ant's hole); V.163. — (b) °ika: J I.432; IV.30; Vism 183 (described), 304 (°muddani), 446; DhA II.51; III.208; IV. 154.

Vammeti [Denom. fr. vamma] to dress in armour, to armour J I.180; II.94 (mangala-hatthiŋ). — pp. vammita.

Vamha [for vambha: see vambheti] bragging, boasting, despising J I.319 (°vacana).

Vaya[1] (& vayo) (nt.) [Vedic vayas vitality, age; to be distinguished from another vayas meaning "fowl." The latter is probably meant at Dhtp 232 (& Dhtm 332) with def[n] "gamane." The etym. of vayo (age) is connected with Sk. vīra = Lat. vir. man, hero, vīs strength; Gr. ἴς sinew, ἴφιος strong; Sk. vīḍayati to make fast, also veśati; whereas vayas (fowl) corresponds with Sk. vayasa (bird) & viḥ to Gr. αἰετός eagle, οἰωνός bird of prey, Lat. avis bird] age, especially young age, prime, youth; meaning "old age" when characterized as such or contrasted to youth (the ord. term for *old* age being jarā). Three "ages" or "periods of life" are usually distinguished, viz. paṭhama° youth, majjhima° middle age, pacchima° old age, e. g. at J I.79; Vism 619; DhA III.133. —**vayo anuppatta** one who has attained old age, old D I.48 (= pacchima-vayaŋ anuppatta DA I.143); Sn pp. 50, 92. — Cp. Dh 260; J I.138 (vayo-harā kesā); Vism 619 (the 3 vayas with subdivisions into dasakas or decades of life); Mhvs 2, 26 (ekūnatiŋso vayasā 29 years of age); PvA 5 (paṭhama-vaye when quite young), 36 (id.; just grown up). In cpds. vaya°.
-**kalyāṇa** charm of youth DhA I.387. -**ppatta** come of age, fit to marry (at 16) VvA 120; PvA 3, 112; ThA 266.

Vaya[2] [Sk. vyaya, vi + **i**; occasionally as vyaya in Pāli as well] 1. loss, want, expense (opp. āya) A IV.282 (bhogānaŋ); Sn 739; PvA 130. —**avyayena** safely D I.72. — 2. decay (opp. uppāda) D II.157 = J I.392 (aniccā vata sankhārā uppāda-vaya-dhammino); S IV.28; A I.152, 299.
-**karaṇa** expense, expenditure J IV.355; Vin II 321 (Sam. Pās on C. V. VI.4, 6, explaining **veyyāsika** or veyyāyika of Vin II.157).

Vayaŋ is the Sk. form of the nom. pl. of pers. pron. ahaŋ, represented in Pāli by mayaŋ (q. v.). The form vayaŋ only in grammarians, mentioned also by Müller, *P.Gr.* p. 87 as occurring in Dh (?). The enclitic form for acc. gen. & dat. is no, found e. g. at Pv I.5[3] (gloss for vo; C. amhākaŋ); J II.153, 352; DhA I.101; PvA 20, 73.

Vayassa [cp. Sk. vayasya] a friend J II.31; III.140; V.157.

Vayha (nt.) & **Vayhā** (f.) [grd. formation fr. **vah**; cp. Sk. vahya (nt.)] a vehicle, portable bed, litter Vin IV.339 (enum[d] under yāna together with ratha sakaṭa sandamānikā sivikā & pāṭankī); J VI.500 (f.), with sivikā & ratha.

Vara[1] (adj.) [fr. **vṛ** to wish; Vedic vara] excellent, splendid, best, noble. As attribute it either *precedes* or *follows* the noun which it characterizes, e. g. °**pañña** of supreme wisdom Sn 391, 1128 (= agga-pañña Nd[2] 557); °**bhatta** excellent food (opp. lāmaka°) J I.123; °**lañcaka** excellent gift (?) (Trenckner, Miln p. 424): see under lañcaka. — **dhamma**° the best norm Sn 233; **nagara**° the noble city Vv 16[6] (= uttama°, Rājagahaŋ sandhāya vuttaŋ VvA 82); **ratana**° the best of gems Sn 683; **rāja**° famous king Vv 32[1] (= Sakka VvA 134); or *inserted* between noun and apposition (or predicate), e. g. **ākiṇṇa-vara-lakkhaṇa** full of the best marks Sn 408; **nari-vara-gaṇa** a crowd of most lovely women Sn 301; esp. frequent in comb[n] with predicate **gata**: "gone on to the best of," i. e. riding the most stately (horse or elephant), or walking on the royal (palace) etc., e. g. upari-pāsāda-vara-gata PvA 105; sindha-piṭṭhi-vara-gata J I.179; hatthi-khandha vara-gata PvA 75, 216, 279. —nt. varaŋ in compar. or superl. function: better than (instr.); the best, the most excellent thing A IV.128 (katamaŋ nu kho varaŋ: yaŋ . . . yaŋ); Dh 178 (ādhipaccena sotāpattiphalaŋ v.), 322 (varaŋ assatarā dantā . . . attadanto tato varaŋ).
-**anganā** a noble or beautiful woman Mhvs 33, 84. -**ādāyin** acquiring the best S IV.250; A III.80. -**āroha** (1) state elephant Vv 5[1] (= varo aggo seṭṭho āroho ti varāroho VvA 35); (2) (f.) a noble lady J VI.562 (Maddī varārohā rājaputtī).

Vara[2] (m. & nt.) [fr. **vṛ** to wish] wish, boon, favour Miln 110, 139. Usually in phrases ilke varaŋ dadāti to grant a wish or a boon J IV.10; VvA 260; PvA 20. varaŋ gaṇhāti to take a wish or a vow J V.382; varaŋ vuṇāti (varati) id. J III.493 (varaŋ varassu, imper.); Pv II.9[10, 42]; Miln 227. —**varaŋ yācati** to ask a favour J III.315 (varāni yācāmi).

Varaka[1] [cp. *Sk. varaka] the bean Phaseolus trilobus J II.75 (where equal to kalāya); Miln 267; DhA I.311.

Varaka[2] (adj.) [fr. **vṛ**] wishing or asking (in marriage) Th 2, 406.

Varaṇa [cp. Sk. varaṇa rampart, causeway, wall] the tree Crataeva roxburghii J I.222, 317 (°rukkha), 319 = DhA III.409 (°kaṭṭhabhañja); J VI.535.

***Varati** [**vṛ**] & der. ("to choose" as well as "to obstruct") see **vuṇāti**.

Varatta (nt.) & **Varattā** (f.) [cp. Vedic varatrā, given also in meaning "elephant's girth" at Halāyudha II.66] a strap, thong, strip of leather S I.63; A II.33; Sn 622; Dh 398 (fig. for taṇhā); J II.153; V.45. As "harness" at J I.175; as straps on a ship's mast (to hold the sails) Miln 378. — Cp. **vārattika.**
-**khaṇḍa** strip of leather, a strap M I.244 = II.193 = III.259 = S IV.56 = A III.380.

Varāka (adj.) [cp. Epic Sk. varāka] wretched, miserable S I.231; J IV.285; Vism 315; VvA 101; PvA 120 (syn. for kapaṇa), 175 (id.).

Varāha [Vedic varāha & varāhu, freq. in Rigveda] a boar, wild hog Dh 325 = Th I, 17; J V.406 = VI.277; Miln 364; Sdhp 378.

Valañja (-°) [see valañjeti] 1. track, line, trace, in **pada**° track, footprint J I.8; II.153 (v. l. lañca & lañcha); IV.221 (valañcha T.), 383; DhA II.38. — 2. that which is spent or secreted, i. e. outflow, fæces, excrement, in **sarīra**° fæces J I.70, 80, 421 (°ŋ muñcati to ease oneself); III.486; DhA II.55. — 2. design, use; only neg. **avalañja** useless, superfluous Vin IV.266; VvA 46 (°ŋ akaŋsu rendered useless); DhA IV.116.

Valañjana (nt.) [fr. valañjeti] 1. resorting, acting as, behaviour VvA 248. — 2. giving off, evacuation, easing the body J I.161 (°vacca-kuṭi privy); DhA III.270 (sarīra°).

Valañjanaka (adj.) (-°) [fr. valañjana] being marked off, being traced, belonging to, behaving, living (anto° in the inner precincts, **bahi**° outside the bounds) J I.382, 385, 398.

Valañjita [pp. of valañjeti; cp. BSk. valañjita used, MVastu III.276] traced, tracked, practised, travelled J III.542 (magga).

Valañjeti [customarily expl[d] as ava + **lañj** (cp. Geiger *P.Gr.* § 66[1]), the root **lañj** being given as a Sk. root in meaning "to fry," "to be strong," and a variety of others (see Mon. Williams s. v. lañj). But the root & its derivations are only found in lexicographical and grammatical works, therefore it is doubtful whether it is genuine. lañja is given as "pada," i. e. track, place, foot, and also "tail." We are inclined to see in **lañj** a by-form of **lañch,** which is a variant of **lakṣ** "to mark" etc. (cp. lañcha, lañchaka, °ana, °ita). Thus the meaning would range from originally "trace," mark off, enclose, to: "being enclosed," assigned or belonging to, i. e. moving (in), frequenting etc., as given in C. expl^{ns}. There seems to be a Singhalese word at the root of it, as it is certainly dialectical. — The Dhtm (522) laconically defines **valañj** as "valañjane"] 1. to trace, track, travel (a road); practise, achieve, resort to Miln 359; VvA 58. — 2. to use, use up, spend J I.102; III.342; VI.369, 382, 521. — ppr. Pass. (a-)valañjiyamāna (not any longer) in use J I 111. — pp. valañjita.

Valaya (m. & nt.) [Epic Sk. valaya, fr. Idg. ***uel** to turn; see Sk. roots **vṛ** to enclose, and **val** to turn, to which belong the foll.: varutra upper robe, ūrmi wave, fold, valita bent, vālayati to make roll, valli creeper, vaṭa rope, vāṇa cane. Cp. also Lat. volvo to roll, Gr. ἐλύω to wind, ἕλιξ round, ἔλυτρον cover; Goth. walwjan to roll on, Obg. welzan & walzan = Ags. wealtan (E. waltz); Ags. wylm wave, and many others, q. v. in Walde, *Lat. Wtb.* s. v. volvo. — The Dhtp (274) gives root **val** in meaning saŋvaraṇa, i. e. obstruct, cover. See further vuṇāti] a bracelet Vin II.106; J II.197 (dantakāre valay'-ādīni karonte disvā); III.377; VI.64, 65; DA I.50; DhA I.226 (danta° ivory bangle); PvA 157 (sankha°); Mhvs 11, 14 (°anguli-veṭhakā).

Valāhaka [valāha + ka; of dial. origin; cp. Epic Sk. balāhaka] 1. a cloud, dark cloud, thundercloud S I.212 = Th 2, 55; A II.102; V.22; Th 1, 760; Pug 42, 43; Vv 68[1]; J III.245; 270 (ghana°); Vism 285 (°paṭala); Miln 274; DhsA 317; VvA 12 (= abbhā). — 2. N. of mythical horses S III.145.

-kāyikā (devā) groups of cloud gods (viz. sita°, uṇha°, abbha°, vāta°, vassa°) S III.254.

Valāhassa [valāha + assa] cloud-horse J II.129 (the Valāhassajātaka, pp. 127 sq.); cp. BSk. Bālāh'āśva (-rājā) Divy 120 sq. (see Index Divy).

Vali & Valī (f.) [cp. Epic Sk. vali; fr **val.** Spelling occasionally with ḷ] a line, fold, wrinkle, a streak, row; Vin II.112 (read valiyo for valiŋ ?); Th 2, 256; J IV.109; Shhp 104. — **muttā-vali** a string of pearls VvA 169. For vaṭṭanā-valī see vaṭṭanā. See also **āvali.**

Valika (adj.) [fr. vali] having folds J I.499.

Valita [pp. of **val:** see valeti] wrinkled A I.138 (acc. khaṇḍadantaŋ palita-kesaŋ vilūnaŋ khalitaŋ siro-valitaŋ tilak'āhata-gattaŋ: cp. valin with passage M I.88 = III.180, one of the two evidently misread); PvA 56, 153. In comp^{n} with taca contracted to valittaca (for valitattaca) "with wrinkled skin" DhA II.190 (phalitakesa +); with abstr. **valittacatā** the fact of having a wrinkled skin M I.49 (pālicca +; cp. MA 215); A II.196 (khaṇḍicca pālicca +).

Valin (adj.) [fr. vali] having wrinkles M I.88 (acc. palitakesiŋ vilūnaŋ khalita-siraŋ valinaŋ) = III.180 (palitakesaŋ vilūnaŋ khalitaŋ-siraŋ valinaŋ etc.) See **valita** for this passage. — In comp^{n} **vali-mukha** "wrinkled face," i. e. monkey J II.298.

Valiya at M I.446 is not clear. It is comb^{d} with **vaṇṇiya** (q. v.). See also note on p. 567; v. l. pāṇiya; C. silent.

Valikaŋ [cp. Sk. vyalikaŋ] read for valikaŋ at Th 2, 403, in meaning "wrong, fault"; ThA 266 expl^{s} as "vyālikaŋ dosaŋ." So Kern, *Toev.* s. v.

Valimant (adj.) [fr. vali] having wrinkles Th 2, 269 (pl. valimatā).

Valeti [cp. Sk. vāleti, Caus. of **val** to turn: see valaya] 1. to twist, turn, in **gīvaŋ** to wring (a fowl's neck) J I.436; III.178 (gīvaŋ valitvā: read °etvā). — 2. to twist or wind round, to put (a garment) on, to dress J I.452 (sāṭake valetuŋ; v. l. valañcetuŋ). — pp. **valita.**

Vallakī (f.) cp. Epic Sk. vallakī, BSk. vallikī Divy 108; MVastu I.227] the Indian lute Abhp 138.

Vallabha [cp. Epic & Class. Sk. vallabha & BSk. vallabhaka a sea monster Divy 231] a favourite J IV.404; VI.38, 371; rāja° a king's favourite, an overseer J I.342; Mhvs 37, 10; VbhA 501. — f. vallabhā (a) beloved (woman), a favourite J III.40; VvA 92, 135, 181.

Vallabhatta (nt.) [abstr. fr. vallabha] being a favourite Dāvs V.7.

Vallarī (f.) [cp. Class. Sk. vallarī, Halāyudha II.30] a branching footstalk, a compound pedicle Abhp 550. The word is found in BSk. in meaning of "musical instrument" at Divy 315 and passim.

Vallikā (f.) [cp. Sk. vālikā ?] 1. an ornament for the ear Vin II.106 (cp. Bdhgh's expl^{n} on p. 316). — 2. a jungle rope Vin II.122.

Vallibha [cp. late Sk. valibha wrinkled] the plant kumbhaṇḍa i. e. a kind of gourd Abhp 597 (no other ref. ?).

Vallī (f.) [cp. Sk. vallī; for etym. see valaya] 1. a climbing plant, a creeper Vin III.144; J V.37; VI.536; VvA 147, 335 (here as a root ?). — **santānaka°** a long, spreading creeper VvA 94, 162. — 2. a reed or rush used as a string or rope for binding or tying (esp. in building), bast (?) M I.190 (Neumann, "Binse"); J III.52 (satta rohita macche uddharitvā valliyā āvuṇitvā netvā etc.), 333 (in similar connection); DhA III.118. — 3. in **kaṇṇa°** the lobe of the ear Mhvs 25, 94. — The comp^{n} form of valli is **valli°.**

-koṭi the tips of a creeper J VI.548. **-pakka** the fruit of a creeper Vv 33[30] **-phala** = °pakka J IV.445. **-santāna** spreadings or shoots of a creeper KhA 48. **-hāraka** carrying a (garland of) creeper Vism 523 = VbhA 131 (in comparison illustrating the paṭicca-samuppāda).

Vallura (nt.) [cp. Cass. Sk. vallūra] dried flesh S II.98; J II.245.

Vaḷa at Vism 312 is to be read vāḷa (snake), in phrase vāḷehi upadduta "molested by snakes."

Vaḷabhā [= vaḷavā ?] is not clear; it occurs only in the expression (is it found in the Canon ?) **vaḷabhā-mukha** a submarine fire or a purgatory Abhp 889. The Epic Sk. form is vaḍavā-mukha (Halāyudha I.70; III.1).

Vaḷabhī (f.) [cp. late (dial.) Sk. vaḍabhī] a roof; only in cpd. °**ratha** a large covered van (cp. yogga[1]) M I.175 (sabba-setena vaḷabhī-rathena Sāvatthiyā niyyāti divā divaŋ); II.208 (id.), but *vaḷavābhi*-rathena); J VI.266 (vaḷabhiyo = bhaṇḍa-sakaṭiyo C.). The expression reminds of **vaḷavā-ratha.**

Vaḷavā (f.) [cp. Vedic vaḍavā] a mare, a common horse D I.5; Pug 58; Mhvs 10, 54; J I.180; VI.343; DhA I.399; IV.4 (assatarā vaḷavāya gadrabhena jātā).

-ratha a carriage drawn by a mare D I.89, 105, 106. The expression reminds of **vaḷabhī-ratha.**

Vaḷīna at J VI.90 is not clear (in phrase jaṭaŋ vaḷinaŋ paṅkagataŋ). The C. reads valinaŋ, paraphrased by ākulaŋ. Fausböll suggests **malinaŋ.** Should we accept reading valinaŋ ? It would then be acc. sg. of valin (q. v.).

Vavakaṭṭha [pp. of vavakassati] drawn away, alienated; withdrawn, secluded DhA II.103 (°kāya).

Vavakassati [v+ava+**kṛṣ**, would correspond to Sk. vyavakṛṣyate, Pass.] to be drawn away, to be distracted or alienated (from); so is to be read at all passages, where it is either comb^d with avakassati or stands by itself. The readings are: Vin II.204 (apakāsanti avapakāsanti) = A V.74 (avakassanti vavakassanti); A III.145 (bhikkhu n' âlaŋ sanghamhā 'vapakāsituŋ: read vavakāsituŋ or °kassituŋ), 393 (vapakassat' eva Satthārā, vapakassati garuṭṭhāniyehi). See also apakāsati, avakassati, avapakāsati. — pp. vavakaṭṭha.

Vavakkhati see vatti.

Vavatthapeti & **°ṭṭhāpeti** [Caus. of vi+ava+**sthā**] to determine, fix, settle, define, designate, point out J IV.17 (disaŋ °tthapetvā getting his bearings); Vbh 193 sq.; Vism 182; SnA 67; KhA 11, 42, 89; VvA 220. — ppr. Pass. vavatthāpiyamāna DhA I.21, 35. — pp. vavatthita & vavatthāpita.

Vavatthāna (nt.) [fr. vi+ava+**sthā**; cp. late Sk. vyavasthāna which occurs in Ep. Sk. in meaning "stay"] determination, resolution, arrangement, fixing, analysis Ps I.53; Vin IV.289; Vism 111, 236 (=nimitta), 347 (def^n); Miln 136; KhA 23.

Vavatthāpita [pp. of vavatthāpeti] arranged, settled, established Miln 345 (su°).

Vavatthita [pp. of vi+ava+**sthā**, cp. vavatthapeti & late Sk. vyavasthita "determination"] 1. entered on, arranged, fixed, determined, settled M III.25; DhsA 36. — 2. separated (opp. sambhinna) Vin II.67 sq.

Vavattheti [unusual pres. (Med.-Pass.) formation fr. vi+ava+**sthā**, formed perhaps after vavatthita] to be determined or analysed Ps I.53, 76, 84.

Vavassagga [vi+ava+**sṛj**; Sk. vyavasarga] "letting go," i. e. starting on something, endeavouring, resolution A I.36; J VI.188 (handā ti vavassagg' atthe nipāto); DA I.237 (here handa is expl^d as vavasāy' atthe nipato). — Kern, *Toev.* s. v. wrongly "consent."

Vasa (m. & nt.) [cp. Vedic vaśa; **vaś** to be eager, to desire] power, authority, control, influence S I.43, 240 (kodho vo vasam āyātu: shall be in your power; vasa=āṇāpavattana *K.S.* I.320); M I.214 (bhikkhu cittaŋ vasaŋ vatteti, no ca cittassa vasena vattati: he brings the heart under his control, but is not under the influence of the heart); Sn 297, 315, 578, 586, 968; Sdhp 264. — The instr. *vasena* is used as an adv. in meaning "on account of, because" e. g. mahaggha-vasena mahâraha "costly on account of its great worth" PvA 77; cp. J I.94; PvA 36 (putta°); Mhvs 33, 92 (paṭisanthāra°). — Freq. in phrase vase (loc.) vattati to be in somebody's power J V.316 (te vase vattati), cp. M I.214 (cittassa *vasena* vattati) & 231 (vatteti te tasmiŋ vaso have you power over that?); trs. vase vatteti to get under control, to get into one's power J IV.415 (attano vase vattetvā); V.316 (rājāno attano v. v.); DhA II.14 (rājānaŋ attano v. v.), cp. M I.214 (*vasan* vatteti) & PvA 89 (*vasaŋ* vattento). — *Note.* The comp^n form in connection with **kṛ** and **bhū** is vasī° (q. v.).

-ânuga being in somebody's power, dependent, subjected, obedient Sn 332, 1095; J III.224 (=vasavattin C.); Th 2, 375 (=kinkāra-paṭissāvin ThA 252); Sdhp 249. **-ânuvattin** id.; f. °inī obedient, obliging (to one's husband) Vv 31³. **-uttama** highest authority, greatest ideal Sn 274. **-gata** being in someone's power J V.453 (narīnaŋ); cp. vasī-kata. **-vattaka** wielding power Sdhp 483 (°ika); a° having no free will PvA 64. **-vattana** wielding power, (having) authority Miln 356. **-vattin** — 1. (act., i. e. vatteti) having highest power, domineering, autocrat, (all-)mighty; fig. having self-mastery, controlling one's senses D I.247; II.261; A II.24; It 122; Th 2. 37; Pv II.3³³; Miln 253; DA I.111, 114, 121; SnA 133 (°bhavana). — 2. (pass.; i. e. vattati) being in one's power, dependent, subject J III.224; V.316; ThA 226 (read vattino for °vattito!).

Vasati¹ [**vas**¹; to Idg. ***u̯es**, cp. Gr. ἕννυμι to clothe, Sk. vasman cover, Goth. wasjan clothe, wasti dress; Lat. vestis = E. vest etc.; Dhtp 628 (& Dhtm 870): acchādane] to clothe. pp. **vuttha**¹. Caus. **vāseti**: see ni°. See also vāsana¹ & vāsana¹.

Vasati² [**vas**²; Idg. ***u̯es** to stay, abide; cp. Av. varəhaiti; Lat. Vesta the goddess of the hearth = Gr. ἑστία hearth; Goth. wisan to stay, remain, be (=Ohg. wesan, E. was, were); Oicel. vist to stay, Oir. foss rest. — Dhtm 470: kanti-nivāsesu] to live, dwell, stay, abide; to spend time (esp. with vassaŋ the rainy season); *trs.* to keep, observe, live, practise Sn 469 sq., 1088 (=saŋvasati āvasati parivasati Nd² 558); PvA 3, 12, 78 (imper. vasatha). — **uposathaŋ vasaŋ** (ppr.) keeping the Sunday J VI.232; **brahmacariyaŋ v.** to live a chaste life M I.515 (cp. same expression Ait. Br. 5, 13; Śat. Br. 12, 2, 2; 13, 8. 22). — ppr. **vasanto** PvA 75, 76; ppr. med. **vasamāna** J I.21, 236, 291; PvA 117; Pot. **vaseyya** M I.515; Pv II.9⁷ (gharc), & vase Miln 372. — aor. **vasi** Sn 977; J IV.317 (piya-saŋvāsaŋ); PvA 111; Mhvs 1, 13 (vasī vasi); 5, 229. — ger. **vasitvā** J I.278; IV.317; PvA 13; grd. **vasitabba** Sn 678; PvA 42; & **vatthabba** Mhvs 3, 12; inf. **vatthuŋ** Th 2, 414, & **vasituŋ** PvA 12, 112. Fut. **vasissati** [=Sk. vasiṣyati] Mhvs 14, 26; PvA 12; and (older) **vacchati** [=Sk. vatsyati] Vin I.60; Th 2, 294; J IV.217; 1st sg. **vacchāmi** J V.467 (na te v. santike); VI.523, 524, & **vacchaŋ** Th 2, 414. — Pass. **vussati** [Sk. uṣyate] M I.147 (brahmacariyaŋ v.). — pp. **vasita, vusita** [=vi+uṣita], **vuttha** [perhaps = vi+uṣṭa], q. v. — Caus. I. **vāseti** to cause to live, stay or dwell; to make live; to preserve (opp. **nāseti** at S IV.248) Vin III.140; S IV.248; Miln 211; PvA 160 (inf. vāsetuŋ); see also **vāseti**². — Caus. II. **vasāpeti** (cp. adhivāsāpeti) to make live or spend, to cause to dwell, to detain J I.290; II.27; PvA 20 (vassaŋ). — pp. **vāsita**. — See also adhi°, ā°, ni°, pari°.

Vasati³ (f.) [fr. **vas**², cp. Vedic vasati] a dwelling, abode, residence J VI.292 (rāja° = rāja-paricariyā C.); Miln 372 (rājavasatiŋ vase); Dāvs IV.27 (saka°).

Vasana¹ (nt.) [fr. vasati¹] clothing, clothes Sn 971; Th 2, 374; D III.118 (odāta°), 124 (id.); Nd¹ 495 (the six cīvarāni); PvA 49. — **vasanāni** clothing Mhvs 22, 30. — **vasana** (-°) as adj. "clothed," e. g. **odāta°** wearing white robes Vin I.187; **kāsāya°** clad in yellow robes Mhvs 18, 10; **pilotika°** in rags J IV.380; **suci°** in bright garments Sn 679; Pv I.10⁸.

Vasana² (nt.) [fr. vasati²] dwelling (-place), abode; usually in cpds. like °**gāma** the village where (he) lived J II.153; °**ṭṭhāna** residence, dwelling place PvA 12, 42, 92; DhA I.323 and passim.

Vasanaka (adj.) (-°) [fr. vasana²] living (in) J II.435 (nibaddha°, i. e. of continuous abode).

Vasanta [Vedic vasanta; Idg. ***u̯ēr**, cp. Av. varehar spring, Gr. ἔαρ, Lat. vēr, Oicel. vār spring, Lith. vasarā summer] spring J I.86; V.206; KhA 192 (bāla° = Citra); DA I.132 (°vana); PvA 135.

Vasabha [the Sanskritic-Pāli form (*vṛṣabha) of the proper Pāli usabha (q. v. for etym.). Only in later (Com.) style under Sk. influence] a bull Miln 115 (rāja°); SnA 40 (relation between usabha, vasabha & nisabha); VvA 83 (id.).

Vasala [Vedic vṛṣala, Dimin. of vṛṣan, lit. "little man"] an outcaste; a low person, wretch; adj. vile, foul Vin

II.221; Sn 116, 136; J IV.388; SnA 183. — f. vasalī outcaste, wretched woman S I.160; J IV.121, 375; DhA I.189; III.119; IV.162; VvA 260.
-ādhama = °dhamma Sn 135. -dhamma vile conduct J II.180. -vāda foul talk Ud 28; SnA 347. -sutta the suttanta on outcasts Sn 116 sq. (p. 21 sq.), commented on at SnA 174 sq., 289.

Vasalaka [vasala + ka in more disparaging sense] = vasala Sn p. 21.

Vasā[1] (f.) [Vedic vaśā; cp. vāśitā; Lat. vacca cow] a cow (neither in calf nor giving suck) Sn 26, 27; SnA 49 (= adamita-vuddha-vacchakā).

Vasā[2] (f.) [cp. Vedic vasā] fat, tallow, grease Sn 196; Kh III.; Pv II.2[3]; J III.356; V.489; PvA 80; VbhA 67. In detail at Vism 263, 361; VbhA 246.

Vasi° is the shortened form of vasī° (= vasa) in combns °ppatta one who has attained power, mastering: only in phrase ceto-vasippatta A II.6; III.340; Miln 82; cp. BSk. vaśiprāpta Divy 210, 546; — and °ppatti mastership, mastery Vism 190 (appanā +).

Vasika (adj.) (-°) [fr. vasa, cp. Sk. vaśika] being in the power of, subject to, as in kodha° a victim of anger J III.135; taṇhā under the influence of craving J IV.3; mātugāma° fond of women J III.277.

Vasita [pp. of vasati[2]] dwelled, lived, spent Mhvs 20, 14.

Vasitar [n. ag. fr. vasita] one who abides, stays or lives (in), a dweller; fig. one who has a (regular) habit A II.107 = Pug 43, cp. PugA 225. — vasitā is given as "habit" at *Cpd.* 58 sq., 207.

Vasin (adj.) [fr. vasa] having power (over), mastering, esp. one's senses; a master (over) Vin III.93; D I.18 (= ciṇṇa-vasitattā vasī DA I.112); III.29; Sn 372; Vism 154 (fivefold); Mhvs I, 13 (vasī vasī); Dāvs I.16.

Vasima = vasin It 32 (acc. vasimaŋ; v. l. vasimaŋ).

Vasī° is the composition form of vasa in combn with roots kṛ and bhū, e. g. °kata made dependent, brought into somebody's power, subject(ed) Th 2, 295 (= vasavattino katvā, pl.); Sn 154; cp. BSk. vaśīkṛta ptm 213. See also vasagata. — °katvā having overcome or subjected Sn 561 (= attano vase vattetvā SnA 455). Metri causā as vasiŋ karitvā at Sn 444. — °bhāva state of having power, mastery Nd[2] 466 (*balesu*); Pug 14 (in same passage, but reading *phalesu*), expld at PugA 189 (with v. l. SS *balesu!*) as "ciṇṇa-vasī-bhāva"; Kvu 608 (implies *balesu*); Miln 170. Cp. BSk. bala-vaśī-bhāva MVastu III.379. See also ciṇṇa. — °bhūta having become a master (over), mastering S I.132; Miln 319; cp. MVastu I.47 & 399 vaśībhūta. — The same change of vasa° to vasī° we find in combn vasippatta (vasī + ppatta), q. v. under vasi°.

Vasu (nt.) [Vedic vasu good, cp. Gr. ἐύς good, Oir. fiu worthy, Goth. iusiza better] wealth; only in cpds. °deva the god of wealth, i. e. Kṛṣṇa (Kaṇha) Miln 191 (as °devā followers of K.); J V.326 (here in T. as ādicco vāsudevo pabhankaro, expld in C. as vasudevo vasujotano, i. e. an Ep. of the sun); Vism 233 (Vāsudevo baladevo). -°dharā (f.) (as vasun-dharā) the bearer of wealth, i. e. the earth S I.100; A III.34; J V.425; Vism 205, 366; DA I.61. -°dhā id. J I.25; Ap 53; Vism 125.

Vasumant (adj.) [fr. vasu] having wealth, rich J VI.192.

Vassa (m. & nt.) [cp. Vedic varṣa (nt.) rain. For etym. see vassati[1]] 1. rain, shower J IV.284; VI.486 (khaṇika sudden rain); Miln 307; Mhvs 21, 31; DhA III.163 (pokkhara° portentous); SnA 224 (mahā° deluge of rain); PvA 55 (vāta° wind & rain). — fig. shower, downpour, fall M I.130 = Vin II.25 (kahāpaṇa°); DhA II.83 (kusuma°). — Esp. the rainy season, lasting roughly from June to October (Āsāḷha-Kattika), often called "Lent," though the term does not strictly correspond. Usually in pl. vassā (A IV.138), also termed vassā-ratta "time of rains" (J IV.74; V.38). Cp. BSk. varṣā, e. g. Divy 401, 509. — Keeping Lent (i. e. spending the rainy season) is expressed by vassaŋ vasati Vin III.10; Mhvs 16, 8; or by vassa-vāsaŋ (vass' āvāsaŋ) vasati (see below), vassaŋ upeti S V.152, vassaŋ upagacchati S V.152; PvA 42. One who has kept Lent or finished the residence of the rains is a vuttha-vassa J I.82; Mhvs 17, 1; or vassaŋ vuttha Vin III.11; S I.199; V.405; PvA 43. Cp. BSk. varṣ' oṣita Divy 92, 489. — Vassa-residence is vassa-vāsa (see below). — vassaŋ vasāpeti (Caus.) to induce someone to spend the rainy season PvA 20. — anto-vassaŋ during Lent; cp. antovass' eka-divasaŋ one day during Lent Mhvs 18, 2; antara-vassaŋ id. S IV.63. — 2. (nt.) a year A IV.252 (mānusakāni paññāsa vassāni); Sn 289, 446, 1073. satta° (adj.) seven years old Mhvs 5, 61; satta-aṭṭha° 7 or 8 years old PvA 67. — See cpd. °sata. — 3. semen virile, virility: see cpds. °kamma & °vara.
-agga shelter from the rain, a shed (agga = agāra) J I.123; DhA III.105 = VvA 75. -āvāsa vassa-residence A III.67. -āvāsika belonging to the spending of the rainy season, said of food (bhatta) given for that purpose J VI.71; DhA I.129 (as one of the 4 kinds: salāka°, pakkhika°, navacanda°, vass'-āvāsika°), 298; IV.129 (°lābha a gift for the r. s.). -upagamana entering on the vassa-residence PvA 42. -upanāyikā (f.) the approach of the rainy season, commencement of Vassa residence [BSk. varṣopanāyikā Divy 18, 489; AvŚ I.182, where Ep. of the full moon of Āsāḷha]. Two such terms for taking up the residence: purimikā & pacchimikā A I.51; i. e. the day after the full moon of Ā. or a month after that date. See upanāyika. — vass' ûpanāyika-divasa the first day of Lent Vism 92; DhA IV.118; °ûpanāyikaŋ khandhakaŋ the section of the Vinaya dealing with the entrance upon Lent (i. e. Vin I.137 sq.) Mhvs 16, 9. -odaka rain-water Vism 260 = VbhA 243. -kamma causing virility D I.12 (= vasso ti puriso, vosso ti paṇḍako iti; vossassa vassa-karaṇaŋ vassa-kammaŋ, vassassa vossa-karaṇaŋ vossa-kammaŋ DA I.97). -kāla time for rain J IV.55. -dasa (& °dasaka) a decade of years: see enumd at J IV.397. -pūgāni innumerable years J VI.532, cp. Sn 1073. -vara a eunuch J VI.502. -valāhaka a rain cloud A III.243 (°devā). -vassana shedding of rain, raining DhA II.83. -vāsa Vassa residence S V.326; PvA 20. -vuṭṭhi rainfall SnA 34, cp. 224. -sata a century Sn 589, 804; A IV.138; Pv II.1[15]; PvA 3, 60, 69. -satika centenarian Miln 301.

Vassati[1] [vṛṣ, varṣati, vṛṣate; Idg. *uers to wet, cp. Vedic vṛṣa bull, varṣa rain, vṛṣabha (P. usabha), Av. varšna virile, Lat. verres boar; Gr. ἀρρην virile, ἐρση dew; with which root is connected *eres to flow: Sk. arṣati, ṛṣabha bull, Lat. ros dew = Sk. rasa essence etc. — Dhtm 471 gives "secana" as defn] to rain (intrs.), fig. to shower, pour(down) Vin I.32 (mahāmegho vassi); S III.141 (deve vassante); V.396 (id.); Sn 30 (devassa vassato, gen. sg. ppr.); PvA 6, 139, 287; Mhvs 21, 33; DhA II.83 (vassatu, imper.; vassi, aor.); 265 (devo vassanto nom. sg.). — Cp. kālena kālaŋ devo vṛṣyate Divy 71. — Caus. II. vassāpeti to cause to rain J V.201 (Sakko devaŋ v. let the sky shed rain). — pp. vaṭṭa, vaṭṭha, vuṭṭha. Another pp. of the Caus. *vasseti is vassita.

Vassati[2] [vāś to bellow, Vedic vāśyate; Dhtm 471: "saddane"] to utter a cry (of animals), to bellow, bark, to bleat, to crow etc. S II.230; J I.436 (of a cock); II.37, 153, 307; III.127; VI.497 (ppr. vassamāna = vāsamāna C.). — pp. vassita[2].

Vassana[1] (nt.) [fr. vassati[1]] raining, shedding (water) DhA II.83 (vassa°).

Vassana[2] (nt.) [fr. vassati[2]] bleating; neg. a° J IV.251.

Vassāna [gen. pl. formation fr. vassa, like gimhāna fr. gimha (q. v.). Kern, *Toev.* s. v. sees in it a contraction of varṣāyaṇa. Cp. Trenckner, Miln p. 428] (belonging to) the rainy season Vin IV.286; A IV.138; J II.445; V.177.

Vassāpanaka (adj.) [fr. vassāpeti; Caus. of vassati[1]] shedding, pouring out J I.253 (dhana°).

Vassika (adj.) [fr. vassa] 1. (cp. vassa[1]) for the rainy season D II.21 (palace); cp. AvŚ I.269 varṣaka (id.). — 2. (-°) of years, in gaṇa° for many years Sn 279; SnA 339; tero° more than one year (old): see under tero; satta° seven years old PvA 53.

Vassikā (f.) & **Vassika** (nt.) = vassikī, i. e. Jasminum Sambac; cp. BSk. varṣika Lal. Vist. 366, 431; Divy 628; AvŚ I.163. (a) f. (the plant) Dh 377 (= sumanā DhA IV.112); Miln 251. (b) nt. (the flower, said to be the most fragrant of all flowers) A V.22; S V.44; DhA IV.112 (°puppha).

Vassikī (f.) the great-flowered jasmine, Jasminum Sambac (cp. vassikā) Dh 55 = J III.291 = Miln 333; Miln 181, 338; DhA I.422.

Vassita[1] [pp. of *vasseti, Caus. of vassati[1]] sprinkled with, wet with, endowed with, i. e. full of J IV.494 (balena vassita).

Vassita[2] (nt.) [pp. of vassati[2]] a cry J I.432; IV.217, 225.

Vassitar [n. ag. fr. vassita[1]] a shedder of rain A II.102 = Pug 42.

Vassin (adj. n.) [fr. vassati[1]] raining; in padesa° shedding local showers It 64.

Vaha (-°) [fr. **vah**] 1. bringing, carrying, leading Pv I.5[8] (vāri° river = mahānadī PvA 29); S I.103; PvA 13 (anattha°). Doubtful in hetu-vahe Pv II.8[5], better with v. l. °**vaco**, expl[d] by sakāraṇa-vacana PvA 109. — 2. a current J IV.260 (Gangā°); V.388 (mahā°). — Cp. vāha.

Vahati [**vah**, Idg. ***u̯eĝh** to drive, lead, cp. Sk. vahitra = Lat. vehiculum = E. vehicle; Gr. ὄχος waggon, Av. vazaiti to lead, Lat. veho to drive etc.; Goth. ga-wigan = Ohg. wegan = Ger. bewegen; Goth. wēgs = Ger. weg, E. way; Ohg. wagan = E. waggon, etc. — Dhtp 333 & Dhtm 498: vaha pāpuṇane] 1. to carry, bear, transport J IV.260; PvA 14 (= dhāreti); Miln 415 (of iron: carry weight). — imper. **vaha** Vv 81[17]; inf. **vahituŋ** PvA 122 (perhaps superfluous); grd. **vahitabba** Mhbs 23, 93. — 2. to proceed, to do one's work M I.444; Mhvs 34, 4 guḷayantaŋ vahitvāna, old var. reading for P.T.S. ed. T. reading guḷayantamhi katvāna. — 3. to work, to be able, to have power A I.282. — Pass. **vuyhati** (Sk. uhyate) to be carried (along) Vin I.106; Th I, 88; ppr. vuyhamāna S IV.179; Th I, 88; J IV.260; PvA 153; pass. also **vahīyati** PvA 56 (= nīyati); ppr. **vahīyamāna** Miln 397. — pp. **ūḷha** (see soḍha), **vuḷha** & **vūḷha** (būḷha). — Caus. **vāheti** to cause to go, to carry, to drive away Vin II.237; Sn 282; J VI.443. — ppr. **vāhiyamāna** (in med. pass. sense) J VI.125. — pp. **vahita** (for vāh°) Miln 346. Cp. **ubbahati**[2].

Vahana (adj. nt.) [fr. **vah**] 1. carrying VvA 316; DhA III.472 (dhura°). — 2. a current J IV.260.

Vahanaka (adj.) (-°) [vahana + ka] carrying, bearing J II.97 (dhura°).

Vā (indecl.) [Ved. vā, Av. vā, Gr. ἠ, Lat. -ve] part. of disjunction: "or"; always enclitic Kh VIII. (itthiyā purisassa vā; mātari pitari vā pi). Usually repeated vā vā (is it so —) or, either — or, e. g. Sn 1024 (Brahmā vā Indo vā pi); Dh 1 (bhāsati vā karoti vā); PvA 74 (putto vā dhītā vā natthi ?). — with *negation* in second place: whether — or not, or not, e. g. hoti vā no vā is there or is there not D I.61; taŋ patthehi vā mā vā VvA 226. — Combined with other emphatic particles: (na) vā pana not even Pv II.6[9] (manussena amanussena vā pana); vā pi or even Sn 382 (ye vā pi ca); Pv II.6[14] (isayo vā pi ye santā etc.); iti vā Nd[2] 420; atha vā Dh 83 (sukhena atha vā dukhena); uda . . . vā Sn 232 (kāyena vācā uda cetasā vā). — In verse vā is sometimes shortened to va, e. g. devo va Brahmā vā Sn 1024: see va[1].

Vāk (°-) [Vedic vāc, for which the usual P. form is vācā] speech, voice, talk; only in cpd. °**karaṇa** talk, speaking, conversation, as **kālyāṇa-vāk-karaṇa** good speech A II.37; III.195, 261; IV.296 sq.; 328; V.155; abstr. °**ta** A I.38. Cp. **vākya**.

Vāka (nt.) [late Sk. valka, cp. P. vakka] the bark of a tree D I.167; Vin III.34; J I.304; II.141; Vism 249 = VbhA 232 (akka° & makaci°); Miln 128. — **avāka** without bark J III.522.

-**cīra** (= cīvara) a bark garment worn by an ascetic Vin III.34; A I.240, 295; J I.8, 304; V.132; Pug 55. -**maya** made of bark Vin II.130.

Vākarā = vāgulā; net, snare M I.153 (daṇḍa°, Dvandva); II.65. — As **vākara** at J III.541; as **vākura** at Th 1, 774.

Vākya (nt.) [fr. **vac**: see vāk & vācā; Vedic vākya] saying, speech, sentence, usually found in poetry only, e. g. D II.166 (suṇantu bhonto mama eka-vākyaŋ); A II.34 (sutvā arahato vākyaŋ); III.40 (katvāna vākyaŋ Asitassa tādino); Sn 1102 (= vacana Nd[2] 559); J IV.5; V.78; Ap 25; KhA 166 (°opādāna resumption of the sentence); DhsA 324 (°bheda "significant sentence" trsl[n]).

Vāgamā at Mhvs 19, 28 (tadahe v. rājā) is to be read (tadah' ev) āgamā, i. e. came on the same day. The passage is corrupt: see trsl[n] p. 130.

Vāgura & °**ā** (f.) [cp. Epic & Class. Sk. vāgurā; to Idg. ***u̯eg** to weave, as in Lat. velum sail, Ags. wecca = E. wick; Ohg. waba = Ger. wabe] a net; as °**a** J VI.170; KhA 47 (sūkara°); ThA 78; as °**ā** J VI.582. Another P. form is vākarā.

Vācaka (adj.) [fr. vācā] reciting, speaking, expressing SnA 164 (lekha°); sotthi° an utterer of blessings, a herald Miln 359. — f. °**ikā** speech Sdhp 55.

Vācanaka (nt.) [fr. vāceti] talk, recitation, disputation; invitation (?), in brāhmaṇa° J I.318 (karoti); III.171; IV.391 (karoti); regarded as a kind of festival. At J III.238 vācanaka is used by itself (two brahmins *receiving* it). It refers to the treating of brāhmaṇas (br. teachers) on special occasions (on behalf of their pupils: a sort of farewell-dinner ?). — It is not quite sure how we have to interpret vācanaka. Under brāhmaṇa (cpds.) we have trsl[d] it as "elocution show" (cp. our "speech day"). The E. trsl[n] gives "brahmin feast"; Prof. Dutoit "Brahmanen-backwerk" (i. e. special cakes for br.). vācana *may* be a distortion of vājana, although the latter is never found as v. l. It is at all events a singular expression. BR give vācanaka as ἅπαξ λεγομένον in meaning of "sweetmeat," with the only ref. Hārāvalī 152 (Calc. ed.), where it is expl[d] as "prahelaka" (see P. paheṇaka). On the subject see also Fick, *Soc. Glied.* 137, 205.

Vācanā (f.) [fr. vāceti] recitation, reading; °**magga** way of recitation, help for reading, division of text (into chapters or paragraphs) Tikp 239; KhA 12, 14, 24.

Vācapeyya (1) amiable speech (vācā + peyya = piya) J VI.575 (= piyavacana C.). — (2) spelling for vājapeyya (q. v.).

Vācasika (adj.) [fr. vācā] connected with speech, verbal (contrasted with kāyika & cetasika) Vin IV.2; Pug 21; Miln 91; Vism 18; DhsA 324. — As nt. noun at Miln 352 in meaning "behaviour in speech."

Vācā (f.) [**vac**, vakti & vivakti; cp. vacaḥ (P. vaco); Vedic vāk (vāc°) voice, word, vākya; Av. vacah & vaxs word; Gr. ἔπος word, ὄψ voice, Lat. vox = voice, voco to call; Ohg. gi-wahan to mention etc. The P. form vācā is a remodelling of the nom. vāc after the oblique cases, thus transforming it from the cons. decl. to a vowel (°ā) decl. Of the old inflexion we only find the *instr.* vācā Sn 130, 232. The compⁿ forms are both vācā° and vaci°] word, saying, speech; also as adj. (-°) vaca speaking, of such a speech (e. g. duṭṭha° Pv I.3², so to be read for dukkha°). — D III.69 sq., 96 sq., 171 sq.; S IV.132 (in triad kāyena vācāya manasā: see **kāya** III., and mano II.3); Sn 232 (kāyena vācā uda cetasā vā), 397, 451 sq., 660, 973, 1061 (= vacana Nd² 560); Nd¹ 504; DhsA 324 (vuccatī ti vācā). — In sequence vācā girā byappatha vacībheda vācasikā viññatti, as a defⁿ of speech Vin IV.2, expl^d at DhsA 324: see byappatha. — **vācaŋ bhindati**: (1) to modify the speech or expression SnA 216 (cp. vākya-bheda DhsA 324). — (2) to use a word, so say something Vin I.157; M I.207 (Neumann, "das Schweigen brechen"); Miln 231 (i. e. to break silence? So Rh. D. trsl°). Cp. the English expression "to *break* the news." — vācā is mostly applied with some moral characterization, as the foll., frequently found: **atthasaŋhitā** A III.244; **kalyāṇa°** A III.195, 261; IV.296; V.155; **pisuṇā & pharusā** A I.128, 174, 268 sq.; III.433; IV.247 sq.; DA I.74, 75; Nd¹ 220, and passim; **rakkhita°** S IV.112; **vikiṇṇa°** S I.61, 204; A I.70; III.199, 391 sq.; **sacca°** A II.141, 228; **saṇhā** A II.141, 228; III.244; IV.172; see also **vacī-sucarita**; **sammā°** Vbh 105, 106, 235; VbhA 119; see also **magga**; **hīnā** etc. S II.54.

-ânurakkhin guarding one's speech Dh 281 (cp. vācāya saŋvara DhA IV.86). **-âbhilāpa** "speech-jabbering," forbidden talk Sn 49 (i. e. the 32 tiracchāna-kathā Nd² 561). **-uggata** with well intoned speech Miln 10. **-yata** restrained in speech Sn 850 (= yatta gutta rakkhita Nd¹ 221). **-vikkhepa** confusion of speech, equivocation D I.24 sq.; DA I.115.

Vācetar [n. ag. fr. vāceti] one who teaches or instructs D I.123.

Vāceti [Caus. of **vac**] to make speak or recite, to teach; see vatti. — pp. vācita.

Vāja [cp. Vedic vāja strength; Idg. *ueg̑, cp. vājeti, vajra (P. vajira); Lat. vegeo to be alert ["vegetation"], vigeo to be strong ["vigour"]; Av. vazra; Oicel. wakr = Ags. wacor = Ger. wacker; E. wake, etc.] 1. strength, a strength-giving drink, Soma SnA 322. — 2. the feather of an arrow J IV.260; V.130.

Vājapeyya [cp. Vedic vājapeya; see Macdonell, *Vedic Mythology* pp. 131 sq., 155, quoting Weber, *Vājapeya*: Banerjea, *Public Administration* etc. 92] the vājapeya sacrifice, a soma offering. Spelling often vāca° (mostly as v. l.); see S I.76; A II.42; IV.151; Sn 303; It 21; Miln 219; J III.518. Cp. peyya².

Vājita (adj.) [pp. of vājeti: see vāja] feathered (of an arrow) M I.429.

Vājin (adj.-n.) [fr. vāja] possessed of strength or swiftness; a horse, stallion Dāvs I.31; V.35 (sita°), 53 (sasi-paṇḍara°); VvA 278.

Vāṭa [cp. Class. Sk. vāṭa; on etym. see Walde, *Lat. Wtb.* s. v. vallus] enclosure, enclosed place Vin II.154. See also yañña°.

Vāṭaka (-°) [fr. vāṭa] enclosure, circle, ring; in **gala°** the throat circle, i. e. the bottom of the throat Vism 258; DhsA 316; DhA I.394; caṇḍāla° circle of Caṇḍālas J VI.156; brāhmaṇa° of Brahmins DhA IV.177.

Vāṇija [fr. vaṇij (vaṇik): see vaṇijjā; lit. son of a merchant; Vedic vāṇija] a merchant, trader Vin III.6 (assa°); Sn 614, 651, 1014; J V.156 (so read for va°); Pv I.10⁶; Dāvs I.58; KhA 224; SnA 251; PvA 47, 48, 100, 191, 215, 271. On similes with v. see *J.P.T.S.* 1907, 134.

Vāṇijaka = vāṇijā S II.215 (sūci°); J III.540.

Vāṇijjā (f.) [fr. vāṇija, cp. vaṇijjā] trade, trading Vin IV.6 (as one of the exalted professions); PvA 111, 201, 273, 277.

Vāta [Vedic vāta, of **vā**; cp. Sk. vāti & vāyati to blow, vāyu wind; Lat. ventus, Goth. winds = wind; Ohg. wājan to blow, Oir. feth air; Gr. ἄημι to blow, ἀήτης wind, Lith. áudra storm etc.] wind. There exists a common distinction of winds into 2 groups: "internal" and "external" winds, or the ajjhattikā vāyo-dhātu (wind category), and the bāhirā. They are discussed at Vbh 84, quoted at MA 30, 31, and expl^d in detail at VbhA 70 sq.; Vism 350. The *bāhirā* also at Nd² 562, and in poetical form at S IV.218. — The *internal* winds (see below 2) comprise the foll.: uddhaŋgamā vātā, adhogamā, kucchisayā, koṭṭhāsasayā, aŋgam-ang'-ânusārino, satthakā, khurakā, uppalakā, assāso, passāso, i. e. all kinds of winds (air) or drawing pains (rheumatic?) in the body, from hiccup, stitch and stomach-ache up to breathing. Their complement are the *external* winds (see below 1), viz. puratthimā vātā, pacchimā, uttarā, dakkhiṇā (from the 4 quarters of the sky), sarajā arajā, sītā uṇhā, parittā adhimattā, kāḷā, verambha°, pakkha°, supaṇṇa°, tālavanta°, vidhūpana.° These are characterized according to direction, dust, temperature, force, height & other causes (like fanning etc.). — 1. wind (of the air) S IV.218 (vātā ākāse vāyanti); Sn 71, 348, 591 (vāto tūlaŋ va dhaŋsaye), 622, 1074; J I.72; Pug 32; Vism 31. adhimatta v. S IV.56; mahā° S II.88; A I.136, 205; II.199; IV.312; **veramba°** (winds blowing in high regions: upari ākāse S II.231) A I.137; Th I, 598; J VI.326. — 2. "winds" of the body, i. e. pains caused by (bad) circulation, sometimes simply (uncontrolled) movements in the body, sometimes rheumatic pains, or sharp & dragging pains in var. parts of the body Nett. 74. Also applied to certain *humours*, supposed to be caused by derangements of the "winds" of the body (cp. Gr. θυμός; or E. slang "get the wind up"), whereas normal "winds" condition normal health: Pv II.6¹ (tassa vātā balīyanti: bad winds become strong, i. e. he is losing his senses, cp. PvA 94: ummāda-vātā). — **anga°** pain in the limbs (or joints), rheumatism Vin I.205; **udara°** belly ache J I.393, 433; DhA IV.129; **kammaja°** birth-pains Vism 500; **kucchi°** pains in the abdomen (stomach) VbhA 5; **piṭṭhi°** pains in the back ibid. — 3. (fig.) atmosphere, condition, state; or as pp. (of vāyati) scented (with), full of, pervaded (by), at Vin I.39 (vijana° pervaded by loneliness, having an atmosphere of loneliness; Kern. *Toev.* s. v. vāta wrongly "troop, crowd." The same passage occurs at D III.38, where Rh. D., *Dial.* III.35, trslⁿ "where the breezes from the pastures blow"; with explⁿ vijana = vrjana [see vajati], hardly justified. In same connection at A IV.88); Miln 19 (isi°-parivāta scented with an atmosphere of Sages; Rh. D. differently: "bringing down the breezes from the heights where the Sages dwell"; forced). — On vāta in similes see *J.P.T.S.* 1907, 135.

-ātapa (*Dvandva*) wind and heat. In this phrase Bdhgh. takes vāta as *wind* (above 1) at Vism 31 (saraja & araja v.), but as (bodily) *pain* (above 2) at VbhA 5. See D III.353; S II.88; III.54; V.379; A I.204; II.117, 143, 199; III.394 sq., 404; V.15, 127; Sn 52; J I.93; Miln 259, 314, 416; DhA III.112. **-ābādha** "wind disease," internal pains (*not* rheumatism) Vin I.205;

Miln 134; Vism 41. -āyana air hole, window Mhvs 5. 37; Dāva v.57. -āhata struck by the wind Vism 63; DhA III.328. -erita moved by the wind (of trees) S v.123; A III.232; VvA 175. -kkhandha "wind bulk," mass of wind, region of the wind J VI.326. -ghāta ("wind-struck") the tree Cassia (or Cathartocarpus) fistula, a syn. of uddāla(ka) J IV.298; VvA 197; also as °ka at J v.199, 407; VvA 43. -java swiftness of the wind J VI.274. -dhuta shaken by the wind, swaying in the w. Vv 38[5], cp. VvA 174. -passa the wind side DhA II.17. -pāna lattice, window Vin I.209; II.148, 211; A I.101, 137; IV.231; J II.325; V.214; VI.349 (read vātapān° for dvārapān°); KhA 54; DhA I.211, 370; VvA 67; PvA 4, 216, 279. -bhakkha living on air DhA II.57. -maṇḍala a whirlwind, gust of wind, storm, tornado [cp. BSk. vāyu-maṇḍala at AvŚ I.256 with note] J I.72; SnA 224. -maṇḍalikā id. Vin II.113; IV. 345; J IV.430. -yoga direction of the wind J II.11. -roga "wind disease," upset of the body, disturbance of the intestines, colic SnA 69; VvA 185. -vassā (pl.) wind and rain PvA 55. -vuṭṭhi id. SnA 34. -vega force of the wind Sn 1074; PvA 47. -sakuṇa a certain kind of bird ("wind-bird") Nd[1] 87, where KhA 118 reads bhāsa°.

Vātaka (adj.) (-°) [fr. vāta 2] belonging to or connected with the winds (of the body) in ahi-vātaka-roga a cert. (intestinal) disease (lit. "snake-pain"), pestilence, plague; dysentery (caused by a famine and attacking men and beasts alike) DhA I.169, 187, 231; III.437.

Vāti see **vāyati** (in meaning "weave," as well as "blow").

Vātika (adj.) [fr. vāta 2, cp. *Sk. vātakin Halāyudha II.451] connected with the winds (humours) of the body, having bad circulation, suffering from internal trouble, rheumatic (?) Miln 135, 298.

Vātingaṇa [cp. *Sk. vātingaṇa] the egg plant, Solanum melongena J v.131; DhsA 320.

Vāda [fr. **vad**: see vadati; Vedic vāda (not in RV!), in meaning of "theory, disputation" only in Class. Sk. — The relation of roots **vac**: **vad** is like E. speak: say; but vāda as t. t. has developed quite distinctly the specified meaning of an *emphatic* or *formulated* speech= assertion or doctrine] 1. speaking, speech, talk, nearly always -°, e. g. iti° hearsay, general talk M. I.133; S v.73; A II.26; **kumāraka°** child-talk or childish talk, i. e. in the manner of talking to a child S II.218 sq.; cori° deceitful talk PvA 89 (so read with v. l. for T. bheri°); **dhammika°** righteous speech A v.230; musā° telling lies, false speech A I.129; II.141; IV.401; PvA 15. See under musā. — adj. (-°) speaking up for, proclaiming, advertising D I.174 (sīla°, paññā° etc.); Sn 913 (nivissa° dogmatist); A I.287 (kamma°, kiriya°, viriya°). —**vādaŋ bhindati** to refute a speech, to make a view discrepant (cp. bhinna-vāda under 4!) SnA 45 (Māra-vādaŋ bh.). — 2. what is said, reputation, attribute, characteristic Sn 859 (but SnA 550=nindā-vacana); J I.2 (jāti° genealogy, cp. D I.137). See also cpd. °patha. — 3. discussion, disputation, argument, controversy, dispute Sn 390, 827 (also as adj. hīna°); DhA III.390= Vin IV.1; Mhvs 4, 42 (sutvā ubhinnaŋ vādaŋ). — 4. doctrine, theory put forth, creed, belief, school, sect SnA 539 sq.; in cpds.: **ācariya°** traditional teaching Miln 148; also "heterodoxy" Mhbv 96, cp. Dpvs v.30; **uccheda°** annihilistic doctrine Nd[1] 282: see under uccheda; **thera°** the tradition of the Theras, i. e. the orthodox doctrine or word of Gotama Buddha Mhvs 5, 2; 33, 97 sq.; Dpvs v.10, 14 (theravādo aggavādo ti vuccati), 51 (17 heretical sects, *one* orthodox, altogether 18 schools); **dhuta°** (adj.) expounding punctiliousness Vism 81 (=aññe dhutangena ovadati anusāsati). See under dhuta; **bhinna°** heretical sect (lit. discrepant talk or view) Dpvs v.39, 51 (opp. abhinnaka vāda); **sassata°** an eternalist Ps I.155.

-**ānuvāda** all kinds of sectarian doctrines or doctrinal theses D I.161; III.115; S III.6; IV.51, 340, 381; V.7; A III.4; Nett 52. -**kāma** desirous of disputation Sn 825. -**khitta** upset in disputation, thrown out of his belief Vin IV.1=DhA III.390. -**patha** "way of speech," i. e. signs of recognition, attribute, definition Sn 1076 (expl[d] dogmatically at Nd[2] 563); A II.9. -**sattha** the science of disputation, true doctrine SnA 540. -**sīla** having the habit of, or used, to disputes Sn 381.

Vādaka (adj. n.) [fr. vāda] doctrinal, sectarian, heretical; vagga° (either vagga[1] or vagga[2]) professing somebody's party, sectarian, schismatic Vin III.175 (anu-vattaka+); vādaka-sammuti doctrinal (sectarian) statement A IV. 347.

Vādana (nt.) [fr. vādeti] playing on a musical instrument, music VvA 276.

Vādika[1] (adj.) (-°) [fr. vāda] speaking, talking (of) Mhvs 5, 60 (pāra° speaking of the farther shore, i. e. wishing him across the sea).

Vādika[2] [?] a species of bird J VI.538 (v. l. vāj°).

Vādita (nt.) [pp. of vādeti] (instrumental) music D I.6; III.183; A I.212; II.209; DhA IV.75; DA I.77.

Vāditar [n. ag. fr. vādeti] a speaker, one who professes or has a doctrine D III.232; A II.246; IV.307.

Vādin (adj.) (-°) [fr. vāda] speaking (of), saying, asserting, talking; professing, holding a view or doctrine; arguing. Abs. only at A II.138 (cattāro vādī four kinds of disputants); Sn 382 (ye vā pi c'aññe vādino professing their view). Otherwise -°, e. g. in **agga°** "teacher of things supreme" Th 1, 1142; **uccheda°** professing the doctrine of annihilation Nett 111 (see uccheda); **kāla°**, **bhūta° attha°** etc. speaking in time, the truth & good etc. D I.4, 165; A I.202; V. 205, 265, 328; **caṇḍāla°** uttering the word C. Mhvs 5, 60; **tathā°** speaking thus, consistent or true speaker D III.135; Sn 430; **dhamma°** professing the true doctrine S III.138; in comb[n] with vinaya-vādin as much as "orthodox" Vin III.175; **mahā°** a great doctrinaire or scholar SnA 540; **yatha°** cp. tathā°-; sacca° speaking the truth A II.212; the Buddha so-called Th II.252 f.; **vaṇṇa°** singing the praises (of) Vin II.197.

Vāna[1] (nt.) [fr. **vā**[2]: see vāyati[1]] sewing, stuffing (of a couch) DA I.86; DhA I.234 (mañca°).

Vāna[2] (nt.) [fr. vana, both in meaning 1 & 2 but lit. meaning overshadowed by fig.] lit. "jungle" (cp. vana[1] etym.), fig. desire, lust (=taṇhā craving) DhsA 409; KhA 151, 152.

Vānaya in comb[n] suvānaya (S I.124, 238) is to be separated su-v-ānaya (see ānaya).

Vānara [fr. vana] monkey, lit. "forester" Th 1, 399= Dh 334; Th 1, 454; J II.78 (Senaka), 199 sq. (Nandiya); III.429; IV.308; V.445; Miln 201; DhA II.22.
-**inda** monkey king J I.279; II.159.

Vāpi (f.) [cp. Epic & Classic Sk. vāpī] a pond; °**jala** water from a pond Mhvs 25, 66.

Vāpita[1] [pp. of vāpeti] sown, J I.6 (+ropita, of dhañña).

Vapita[2] [pp. of vāpeti] mown DhsA 238.

Vāpeti [Caus. fr. **vap**, representing vapati[1] as well as vapati[2]] to cause to sow [cp. Divy 213 vāpayituŋ] or to mow. — pp. **vāpita**.

***Vābhi** [fr. **vā** to weave] appears in P. as **nābhi** in uṇṇa-nābhi (q. v.).

Vāma (adj.) [Vedic vāma] 1. left, the left side (always opposed to dakkhiṇa) J IV.407 (°akkhi); Pv IV.7[8]; Miln 295 (°gāhin left-handed); PvA 178 (°passa left side). As "northern" at J V.416. **vāmaŋ karoti** to upset J IV.101. — instr. vāmena on the left Sn p. 80. — abl. **vāmato** from or on the left J III.340; Pv II.3[20] (as much as "reverse"; PvA 87 = vilomato). — 2. beautiful; only in cpd. vām-ūru having beautiful thighs D II.266; J II.443. So read at both places for **vāmuru**.

Vāmana (adj.) [fr. vāma[1], cp. Ger. linkisch = uncouth] dwarfish; m. dwarf Vin I.91; DA I.148.

Vāmanaka (adj.-n.) [fr. vāmana] dwarfish, crippled J II.226; IV.137; V.424. 427. — f. °ikā N. of certain elephants M I.178.

Vāya [fr. **vā**, vāyati[1]] weaving PvA 112 (tunna°). See tanta°.

Vāyati[1] [Vedic vayati, **vā**, cp. Sk. veman loom, vāṭikā band, Gr. ἴτυς willow, Ohg. wida id.; Lat. vieo to bind or plait] to weave, only in pp. **vāyita**. — Pass. viyyati Vin III.259. pp. also **vīta**. — Caus. II. **vāyāpeti** to cause to be woven Vin III.259 (= vināpeti); VvA 181. — See also **vināti**.

Vāyati[2] [Vedic vāti & vāyati. See etym. under vāta] 1. to blow (only as vāyati) Vin I.48; D II.107 (mahāvātā vāyanti); S IV.218 (vātā ākāse v.); J I.18; VI.530; Mhvs 12, 12. — aor. vāyi S IV.290; J I.51. Cp. abhi°, upa°, pa°. — 2. to breathe forth, to emit an odour, to smell Pv I.6[1]; PvA 14; as vāti (2nd sg. vāsi) at J II.11 (= vāyasi C.). — pp. vāta only as noun "wind" (q. v.).

Vāyana (nt.) [fr. **vā**, vāyati[2]] blowing VbhA 71 (upari°-vāta).

Vāyamati [vi + ā + **yam**] to struggle, strive, endeavour; to exert oneself S IV.308; V.398; A IV.462 sq. (chandaŋ janeti v. viriyaŋ ārabhati cittaŋ paggaṇhāti); Pv IV.5[2]; Vbh 208 sq.; Pug 51; Vism 2; DhA III.336; IV.137; PvA 185.

Vāyasa [cp. Vedic vāyasa a large bird, Epic Sk. vāyasa crow] a crow D I.9 (°vijjā: see DA I.93); S I.124; Sn 447, 675; J I.500; II.440; Miln 373; DhA III.206; VvA 27.

Vāyāma [fr. vi + ā + **yam**] striving, effort, exertion, endeavour S II.168; IV.197; V.440; A I.174 (chando +), 219; II.93; III.307; IV.320; V.93 sq.; J I.72; Vbh 123, 211, 235; VbhA 91; DhA IV.109; PvA 259. On vāyāma as a constituent of the "Path" (sammā°) see magga 2.a. — **vāyāmaŋ karoti** to exert oneself DhA IV.26; PvA 259.

Vāyita [pp. of vāyati[1], cp. Divy 276 vāyita] woven M III.253 (sāma°), where Miln 240 in id. p. reads sayaŋ°; Vin III.259. Cp. **vīta**.

Vāyin (adj.) [fr. vāyati[2]] blowing (forth), emitting an odour, smelling PvA 87.

Vāyima (adj.) [fr. **vā**: vāyati[1]] weaving, woven; a° not woven Vin III.224 (of a rug or cover).

Vāyu [Vedic vāya, fr. **vā**: vāyati[2]] wind Miln 385; PvA 156. See next.

Vāyo (nt.) [for vāyu, in analogy to **āpo** & **tejo**, with which frequently enumerated] wind D III.268 (°kasiṇa); M I.1, 424 = A IV.375; A V.7, 318, 353 sq. (°saññā); S III.207; Vism 172 (°kasiṇa), 350 (def.). On vāyo as t. t. for mobility, mobile principle (one of the 4 elements) see *Cpd.* 3, 270; *Dhs trsl*[n] § 962.
-**dhātu** the wind element, wind as one of the *four* great elements, wind as a general principle (consisting of var. kinds: see enum[d] under vāta) Vbh 84; Vism 363; Nett 74; VbhA 55; VvA 15; DA I.194.

Vāra [fr. **vṛ**, in meaning "turn," cp. vuṇāti] 1. turn, occasion, time, opportunity J I.58 (utu-vārena utu-vārena according to the turn of the seasons), 150; VI.294; Vism 431 (santati° interval); DA I.36; DhA I.47 (dve vāre twice); DhsA 215; VvA 47 (tatiya-vāraŋ for the 3rd & last time); PvA 109, 135. — 2. In pada° "track-occasion," i. e. foot-track, walk(ing), step J I.62, 213 (°vārena) by walking (here spelt pāda°), 506 (pādavāre pādavāre at every step). — 3. In udaka° v. stands for vāraka (i. e. bucket), the phrase udaka-vāraŋ gacchati means "to go for water," to fetch water (in a bucket) J IV.492; DhA I.49. Dutoit (*J. trsl*[n] IV.594) trsl[s] "Wunsch nach Wasser." — 4. bhāṇa° "turn for recitation," i. e. a portion for recital, a chapter SnA 194. See bhāṇa.

Vāraka [cp. Sk. vāra & vāraka] a pot, jar Vin II.122 (*three* kinds: loha°, dāru° and cammakhaṇḍa°); J I.349; II.70; III.52 (dadhi°); Miln 260; DhsA 377 (phāṇita°).

Vāraṇa[1] (nt.) [fr. **vṛ** to obstruct] warding off, obstruction, resistance VbhA 194, 195 (= nivāraṇa). — ātapa° sunshade Dāvs I.28; V.35.

Vāraṇa[2] [cp. Vedic vāraṇa strong] 1. elephant J I.358; IV.137; V.50, 416; DA I.275; DhA I.389 (°līḷhā elephant's grace); VvA 36, 257. — 2. the Hatthilinga bird Th 1, 1064.

Vāraṇa[3] [for vāruṇī ?] spirituous liquor J V.505.

Vāraṇika at Th 1, 1129 read cāraṇika (a little play): see *Brethren* 419 note.

Vārattika (adj.) [fr. varatta] consisting of leather or a strap J III.185.

Vāri (nt.) [Vedic vāri, cp. Av. vār rain, vairi- sea; Lat. ūrīna = urine; Ags. waer sea; Oicel. ūr spray, etc.] water D II.266; M III.300; A III.26 (in lotus simile); Th 1, 1273; Sn 353, 591, 625, 811; Vv 79[10]; J IV.19; Nd[1] 135, 203 (= udaka); Miln 121; PvA 77.
-**gocara** living or life (lit. feeding) in water Sn 605. -**ja** "water-born," i. e. (1) a *lotus* Sn 845, cp. Nd[1] 203; — (2) a *fish* Dh 34 (= maccha DhA I.289); J V.464 (= Ānanda-maccha C.), 507. -**da** "water-giver," i. e. cloud Dāvs III.40. -**dhara** water-holder, water jug J V.4. -**bindu** a drop of water Sn 392. -**vāha** "water-carrier," i. e. cloud A II.56; III.53; S V.400; J VI.26, 543, 569; Kh VII.8. -**vārita**, -**yuta**, -**dhuta**, -**phuṭa** (Jain practice) D I.57; M I.377.

Vārita [pp. of vāreti, Caus. of **vṛ**[1]] obstructed, hindered J IV.264; restrained (sabbavāri) see vāri.
-**vata** (so read for cārita°) "having the habit of self-denial" (trsl[n]) S I.28 (cp. *K.S.* I.39 & 320 with note & Bdhgh's expl[n]: "kilesānaŋ pana chinnattā vataŋ phala-samādhinā samāhitaŋ"), cp. bhāvanā-balena vāritattā dhammā etc. at Tikp. 14.

Vāritta (nt.) [fr. **vṛ**, on the analogy of cāritta. The BSk. is vāritra: Mvyut 84] avoidance, abstinence Th 1, 591; Miln 133 (cārittañ ca vārittañ ca); Vism 11.

Vāruṇī (f.) [cp. Sk. vāruṇī, with only ref. in BR.: Harivaŋśa 8432] 1. spirituous liquor A III.213; J I.251 (°vāṇija spirit merchant), 268; VI.502. — 2. an intoxicated woman; term for a female fortune-teller J VI.500 (Vāruṇī 'va pavedhati; C. devatā-bhūta-paviṭṭhā yakkha-dāsī viya gahitā, i. e. possessed), 587 (vāruṇī 'va pavedhentī; C. yakkh' āviṭṭhā ikkhaṇikā viya).

Vāreti [Caus. of vuṇāti, representing **vṛ**[1] (to enclose, obstruct), as well as **vṛ**[1] (to choose)] 1. to prevent, obstruct, hinder Pv II.7[7] (vārayissaŋ I had the habit of obstructing; = nivāresiŋ PvA 102); VvA 68; Sdhp 364. — 2. to ask in marriage ThA 266; PvA 55. — Caus. II. vārāpeti to induce somebody to choose a wife J IV. 289. — *Note.* vāriyamāna (kālakaṇṇi-salākā) at J IV.2 read cār° (cp. PvA 272 vicāresuŋ id.). — pp. vārita.

Vāreyya (nt.) [grd. of vāreti] marriage, wedding Th 2, 464, 472, 479; SnA 19.

Vāla[1] [Vedic vāla; connected with Lat. adūlāre (ad+ūlāre) to flatter (lit. wag the tail, like a dog), cp. E. adulation; Lith. valaī horse hair] 1. the hair of the tail, horse-hair, tail Vin II.195 = J V.335 (pahaṭṭha-kaṇṇavāla with bristling ears & tail, of an elephant); J V.274 (so read for phāla, cp. p. 268, v. 113); PvA 285 (°koṭi, so read for bāla°); Sdhp 139. —pallankassa vāle bhinditvā destroying the hair (-stuffing) of a couch Vin II.170 = DA I.88; cp. Vin IV.299: pallanko āharimehi vālehi kato. — On v. in *similes* see *J.P.T.S.* 1907, 136. — 2. a hair-sieve [also Vedic] M I.229.

-agga the tip of a hair A III.403; Miln 250 (°vedha hitting the tip of a hair, of an archer); DA I.66. -aṇḍupaka a cert. material, head dress (?) A I.209 (so read for vālanduka); Vism 142; DhsA 115 (reads leḍḍūpaka). -kambala a blanket made of horse-tails D I.167; A I.240, 296; Pug 55. -koṭi the tip of the hair PvA 285. -rajju a cord made of hair S II.238; A IV.129; J II.161. -vījanī a fan made of a Yak's tail, a chowrie D I.7. -vedhin (an archer) who can hit a hair J I.58 (akkhaṇa-vedhin+); Vism 150; Mhvs 23, 86 (sadda-vedhin vijju-vedhin+). The abstr. °vedhā hitting a hair, at Vism 150. — fig. an acute arguer, a hair-splitter; in standing phrase paṇḍitā nipuṇā kata-para-ppavādā vālavedhi-rūpā at D I.26; M I.176; II.122; see explⁿ at DA I.117.

Vāla[2] (adj.) [cp. Sk. vyāla] malicious, troublesome, difficult Vin II.299 (adhikaraṇa).

Vāla[3] (nt.) [= vāri, cp. late Sk. vāla] water; only in cpd. °ja a fish (cp. vārija).

Vālatta (nt.) [abstr. fr. vāla[2]] trouble, difficulty Vin II.86 (in same context as vāla[2]); A I.54.

Vāladhi [cp. Epic Sk. vāladhi] a tail (usually of a large animal) Th 1, 695; J I.63, 149; VI.302; Pv I.8[3]; Mhvs 10, 59; VvA 252, Sdhp 621; Vism 36 quoting Ap.

Vālikā (f.) [a by-form of vālukā] sand (often sprinkled in connection with festivities to make the place look neat) A I.253; J I.210; III.52, 407; VI.64; Vism 420; DhA I.3, 111; VvA 160, 305; PvA 189. —paritta° sand (on the head) as an amulet J I.396, 399. — In cpds. usually vālika°. Cp. vālukā.

-puñja a heap of sand J VI.560. -pulina sand bed or bank J II.366; III.389. -vassa a shower of sand SnA 224.

Vālin (adj.) [fr. vāla[1]] having a hairy tail Vv 64[7], cp. VvA 277.

Vālukantāra at VvA 332 probably for vāluka-kantāra, i. e. sandy desert. See **vaṇṇu.**

Vālukā (f.) [cp. Vedic & Epic Sk. vālukā] sand. In compⁿ usually vāluka°. — S IV.376; Vv 39[1]; 44[1]; Ap. 23; Nd[2] p. 72 (Gangāya v.); J II.258; IV.16; Pv II.12[1]; Mhvs 23, 86; DhA III.243, 445; VvA 31, 177; Sdhp 244. See also vālika.

Vāḷa[1] [cp. late Sk. vyāḍa, see Geiger, *P.Gr.* § 54[8]] 1. a snake Vism 312 (so read for vaḷa). — 2. a beast of prey A III.102 (amanussa); J I.295; III.345 (°macchā predaceous fishes); Miln 23 (°vana forest of wild beasts).

-miga a beast of prey, predaceous animal, like tiger, leopard, etc. J VI.569; DhA I.171 (°ṭṭhāna); III.348 (°rocanā); Vism 180, 239.

Vāḷa[2] [misspelt for vāda ?] music (?) Pgdp 83.

Vāvatteti (vi + ā + vṛt) to turn away (trs.), to do away with, remove M I.12 (aor. vāvattayi saŋyojanaŋ, explᵈ at MA 87 as "parivattayi, nimmūlaŋ akāsi") = 122 (with v. l. vi°, see p. 526); A II.249 (v. l. vi°).

Vāsa[1] [**vas** to clothe, see vasati[1]] clothing; adj. (-°) clothed in J VI.47 (hema-kappana-vāsase).

Vāsa[2] [**vas** to dwell, see vasati[2]] 1. living, sojourn, life Sn 191; Mhvs 17, 2 (anātha-vāsaŋ vasati to lead a helpless life); PvA 12 (samagga-vāsaŋ v. live a life of concord); SnA 59 (lokantarika°). Cp. pari°, saŋ°. — 2. home, house, habitation Sn 40. vāsaŋ kappeti to live (at a place), to make one's home J I.242; PvA 47, 100. vāsaŋ upagacchati to enter a habitation (for spending the rainy season) PvA 32. In special sense "bed": see cpd. °ūpagata. — 2. state, condition (-°), in ariya° holy state A V.29 sq.; brahmacariya° chastity PvA 61. — 4. (adj.) (-°) staying, living, abiding, spending time Sn 19 (ekaratti°), 414 (ettha°). vassa° spending Lent PvA 20; vuttha° having spent Lent J I.183. Cp. ante-vāsika-vāsa.

-attha home success, luck in the house, prosperity A II.59, 61 sq. -āgāra bedroom J III.317. -ūpagata (a) having entered one's hut or abode (for the rainy season) Sn 415. — (b) gone to bed Pv II.12[8]; PvA 280. -ghara living room, bedroom SnA 28 (= kuṭi). -dhura ordinary duty (lit. burden) or responsibility of living, or the elementary stages of saintliness SnA 194, 195 (contrasted to pariyatta-dhura), 306 (: ganthadhura).

Vāsa[3] [cp. Class. Sk. vāsa, e. g. Mālatīm. 148, 4; fr. **vā**: see vāta] perfume J I.242; VI.42.

Vāsaka, vāsika (adj.) (-°) [fr. vāsa[2]] living, dwelling; **vāsaka**: see saŋ°. **vāsika**: gāma° villager Mhvs 28, 15; Bārāṇasi° living in Benares J III.49. See also ante°.

Vāsati [**vāś**, see vassati[2]] to cry (of animals) J VI.497.

Vāsana[1] (adj.-nt.) [= vasana[1]] clothing, clothed in (-°) PvA 173

Vāsana[2] (adj.-nt.) [= vasana[2]] dwelling Dpvs V.18.

Vāsanā (f.) [fr. vasati[2] = vāsa[2], but by Rh. D., following the P. Com̄. connected with vāseti & vāsa[3]] that which remains in the mind, recollection of the past, impression, usually as pubba° former impression (Sn 1009; Miln 10, 263). — Cp. Nett 4, 21, 48, 128, 133 sq., 153, 158 sq., 189 sq. — Cp. BSk. vāsanā, e. g. MVastu I.345.

Vāsara [cp. Vedic vāsara matutinal, vasaḥ early] day (opp. night), a day Dāvs I.55; V.66.

Vāsi (f.) [cp. Sk. vāśī] 1. a sharp knife, axe, hatchet, adze (often combᵈ with pharasu) J I.32, 199; II.274; III.281; IV.344; Miln 383; 413; DhA I.178 (tikhiṇā vāsiyā khaṇḍākhaṇḍikaŋ chinditvā: cutting him up piecemeal with a sharp knife); KhA 49. -°jaṭa handle of a mason's adze Vin IV.168; S III.154; A IV.127. — 2. a razor J I.65; II.103; III.186, 377.

Vāsita [fr. vāseti[2]] 1. scented J I.65; II.235 (su°); III.299; V.89; Vism 345. — 2. [preferably fr. vāseti[1] = vasati[2]] established, made to be or live, preserved Mhvs 8, 2. So also in phrase vāsita-vāsana (adj.) or **vāsana-vāsita** one who is impressed with (or has retained) a former impression Sn 1009 (pubba°, = vāsanāya vāsita-citta SnA 583); Miln 263 (id.); Vism 185 (+ bhāvita-bhāvana). If taken as vāseti[2], then to be trslᵈ as "scented, filled, permeated," but preferably as vāseti[1]. — Cp. pari°.

Vāsitaka (adj.) [fr. vāsita] scented, perfumed Vin IV.341 (vāsitakena piññākena nhāyeyya: should bathe with perfumed soap). — f. **vāsitikā** (scil. mattikā) scented clay Vin II.280 (id.).

Vāsin[1] (adj.) (-°) [fr. **vas**[1]] clothed in, clad Sn 456 (sanghāṭi°), 487 (kāsāya°); Pv III.1[6] (sāhunda°); J III.22 (nantaka°); IV.380 (rumma°); f. **vāsinī** Vin III.139 (chanda°, paṭa° etc.) = VvA 73.

Vāsin[2] (adj.) (-°) [fr. **vas**[2]] liking, dwelling (in) Sn 682 (Meru-muddha°), 754 (āruppa°); PvA 1 (Mahāvihāra°), 22 (Anga-Magadha°), 47 (Sāvatthi°), 73 (Bārāṇasi°).

Vāseti[1]: Caus. of vasati[2] (q. v.).

Vāseti[2] [Denom. fr. vāsa perfume] to perfume, to clean or preserve by means of perfumes, to disinfect (?) Vin I.211 (here in the sense of "preserve, cure," probably as vāseti of vasati[2]); II.120; J IV.52 (aṭṭhīni, for the sake of preservation); V.33 (saso avāsesi sake sarīre, expl[d] as "sake sarīre attano sarīraŋ dātuŋ avāsesi vāsāpesī ti attho, sarīrañ c' assa bhakkh' atthāya adāsi." In this passage **vāseti** is by Kern, *Toev.* s. v. taken as Caus. of **vas** to eat, thus "he made eat, feasted, entertained by or on his own body"), 321 (kusumehi vāsetvā: perfume). See also **vasati**[2] (Caus.). — pp. vāsita. — Caus. II. vāsāpeti J V.33.

Vāha (adj.-n.) [fr. **vah**] 1. carrying, leading; a leader, as in sattha° a caravan leader, merchant J I.271; Vv 84[7]; 84[20]; VvA 337. — 2. a cart, vehicle; also cartload Sn p. 126 (tila°= tila-sakaṭa SnA 476); J IV.236 (saṭṭhi°-sahassāni 60,000 cartloads); Miln 80 (°sataŋ).

Vāhaka [fr. vāheti] that which carries (or causes to carry) away, i. e. a current, torrent, flow; only in comp[n] with udaka° a flood of water A I.178; Vin I.32; Miln 176.

Vāhana [fr. vāheti] 1. (adj.) carrying, pulling, drawing Vin II.122 (udaka°-rajju); J I.136 (kaṭṭha° gathering fire-wood); PvA 127 (ratha-yuga°). — 2. (nt.) conveyance, beast of burden, monture Vin I.277 (°āgāra stable, garage); Sn 442 (Māra sa° with his elephant); Pv II.9[28]; DhA I.192 (hatthi°, elephant-mount; cp. p. 196, where five. vāhanāni, belonging to King Pajjota, are enum[d], viz. kaṇeru, dāsa, dve assā, hatthi). — **bala**° army & elephants, i. e. army in general, forces J I.262.

Vāhanaka = vāha 1; VvA 337.

Vāhasā (indecl.) [an instr. of vāha, formed after the manner of balasā, thāmasā, used adverbially] owing to, by dint of, on account of, through Vin IV.158; Th 1, 218, 1127; Miln 379; VvA 100.

Vāhin (adj.-n.) [fr. vāha] carrying, conveying J VI.125 (haya° running by means of horses, i. e. drawn by horses); also as poetical expression for "horse" J VI.252 (= sindhava C.). The reading vāhin at Mhvs 22, 52 is given as v. l. for T. vājin in *P.T.S.* ed. — f. **vāhinī**, an army J III.77 (miga°; expl[d] as "aneka-sahassa-sankhā migasenā"); VI.581.

Vāheti is Caus. of vahati (q. v.).

Vi (indecl.) [prefix, resting on Idg. ***ui** "two," as connotation of duality or separation (Ger. "ent-zwei"), which is contained in viŋsati, num. for "twenty" (see vīsati), cp. Sk. viṣu apart, Gr. ἴδιος private (lit. separate); also Sk. u-bhau both; and ***uidh**, as in Lat. dīvido = divide. A secondary (compar.) formation in Sk. vitara further, farther, Goth. wiþra against, Ger. wider] 1. (a) inseparable prefix of separation and expansion, in original meaning of "asunder," semantically closely related to Lat. dis- & Ger ver-. Often as base-prefix in var. meanings (see below 1-4), also very frequent as modifying prefix (in comb[n] with other primary prefixes like ā, ni, pa, paṭi, saŋ), where its prevailing character is one of emphasis. — (*b*) The native grammarians define **vi**- either as "**vividha**" (i. e. our meaning 2): see Bdhgh. at SnA 136 (viharati = vividhaŋ hitaŋ harati); and Vism 179 vividhaŋ khittaŋ = vikkhittaŋ; see also under vigganhati; or "**prātilomya**" (i. e. meaning 3): Nirukta (ed. Roth) I.3; or paraphrase it by **su**° or **suṭṭhu** (i. e. meaning 4): see under vimāna & vippasanna. The latter meaning also in Hemacandra's Anek' ārtha-sangraha (ed. Calc.) 7, 15: "śreṣṭhe 'tīte nānārthe" (i. e. Nos. 4 & 2). — (c) vi° occurs also as *distributive* (repetitional) prefix in reduplication compounds (here closely resembling paṭi° and the negative a°), like cuṇṇa-vicuṇṇa piecemeal, chidda-vicchidda holes upon holes, vaṭṭa-vivaṭṭa, etc. — Contracted forms are **vy**° (= viy° before vowels) and **vo**° (= vi + ava); the guṇa & vriddhi form is **ve**°. — II. *Meanings.* — 1. denoting *expansion*, spreading out; fig. variety or detail, to be trsl[d] by expressions with *over* or *about* (cp. Lat. e-), as: °kampati shake *about*, °kāseti open *out*, °kirati scatter about, °kūjati sing out (= *upa*-nadati C), °carati move about (= ā-hiṇḍati), °churita sprinkled about, °jāyati bring forth, °tāna "spread out," °tthāra *ex*-tension, *de*-tail, °dāleti break open, °dhammati whirl about, °dhāyaka providing, °pakirati strew all over, °pphāra pervading, °pphārika *ef*-fulgence, °bhajati *ex*-plain, °bhatta *dis*-tributed, °bhāga division, distribution, °ravati shout out, °rūhana growing up, °rocati shine out, °ssajjati give out, °ssaṭṭha sent out, °ssara shouting out, °ssuta far-famed. — 2. denoting *disturbance*, separation, mixing up (opp. saŋ°), as given with "away" or "down," or the prefixes *de-* and *dis-*, e. g. °kasita burst asunder, °kubbana change, i. e. miracle (meta-morphosis), °kkaya sell ("ver-kaufen"), °kkhambhati *de*-stroy, °kkhāleti wash *off* (= ācameti), °kkhepa *de*-rangement, °gata *dis*-appeared (used as def[n] of vi° at ThA 80), °galita dripping down, °ggaha separation, °cinati *dis*-criminate, °jahati *dis*-miss, °desa foreign country (cp. verajjaka), °naṭṭha destroyed, °nata bending down, °nāsa *de*-struction, °nicchaya dis-crimination, °nodaka driving out, °pāteti to be destroyed, °ppalapati to talk confusedly, °rājeti discard as rāga, °rodha destruction, °lumpati break up, °vitta separated, °vidha mixed, °veka separation, °vāha carrying away, i. e. wedding. — 3. denoting the *reverse* of the simple verb, or loss, difference, opposite, reverse, as expressed by *un-* or *dis-*, e. g. °asana *mis*-fortune, °kaṭika unclean, °kappa change round, °kāra per-turbation, *dis*-tortion, °kāla wrong time, °tatha *un*-truth, °dhūma smoke-*less*, °patti corruption, °parīta dubious, °ppaṭipanna on the wrong track, °bhava non-existence (or as 4 "more" bhava, i. e. wealth), °mati doubt, °mānana *dis*-respect, °yoga separation, °raja fault-*less*, °rata *abs*-taining, °rūpa *un*-sightly, °vaṭa unveiled, °vaṇṇeti defame, °vāda dis-pute, °sama uneven, °ssandati overflow, °ssarita *for*-gotten, °siṭṭha distinguished, °sesa difference, distinction. — 4. in *intensifying* sense (developed fr. 1 & 2), mostly with terms expressing *per se* one or the other of shades of meanings given under 1-3; to be trsl[d] by "away," out, all over, "up," or similarly (completely), e. g. °ākula quite confused, °katta cut up, °kopeti shake up, °garahati scold intensely, °chindati cut off, °jita conquered altogether, °jjotita resplendent, °tarati come quite through, °niyoga close connection, °nivatteti turn off completely, °pariṇāma intense change, °ppamutta quite released, °ppasanna quite purified, °pphalita crumpled up, °bandhana (close) fetter, °ramati cease altogether, °sahati have sufficient strength, °sukkha dried up, °suddha very bright, °ssamati rest fully (Ger. aus-ruhen), °haññati to get slain.

Vikaca (adj.) blossoming DA I.40.

Vikaṭa [vi + kata, of **kṛ**] changed, altered, distorted; disgusting, foul, filthy Pgdp 63 (°ānana with filthy mouth). — nt. filth, dirt; four mahā-vikaṭāni applied against snake-bite, viz., gūtha, mutta, chārikā, mattikā Vin I.206. — Cp. **vekaṭika**.

-**bhojana** filthy food D I.167; M I.79.

Vikaṇṇa (adj.) [vi + kaṇṇa] having deranged or bent corners, frayed Vin I.297; II.116.

Vikaṇṇaka [fr. vikaṇṇa] a kind of arrow (barbed ?) J II.227, 228.

Vikata changed, altered Vin I.194 (gihi-vikata changed by the g.).

Vikati (f.) [fr. vi + **kṛ**] "what is made of something," make, i. e. 1. sort, kind J I.59 (ābharaṇa° kind of ornament), 243 (maccha-maŋsa°); Miln 403 (bhojana° all kinds of material things); Vism 376 (bhājana° special bowl); VbhA 230 (pilandhana°); DhA II.10 (khajja°). — 2. product, make; vessel: danta° "ivory make," i. e. vessels of ivory M II.18; D I.78; J I.320. — 3. arrangement, get up, assortment; form, shape J V.292 (mālā° garland-arrangement).
-phala an assortment of fruit J V.417.

Vikatika (f.) [fr. vikati] a woollen coverlet (embroidered with figures of lions, tigers etc.) D I.7 (cp. DA I.87); A I.181; Vin I.192; ThA 55 (Ap V.10: tulikā°).

Vikatta (adj.) [pp. of vi + kantati²] cut open J VI.111 (v. l. °kanta).

Vikattana (nt.) [fr. vi + kantati²] cutter, knife Vin III.89 (tiṇha go°) M I.449; J VI.441.

Vikatthati [vi + katthati] to boast, show off S II.229; J I.454 (= vañcana-vacanaŋ vadati C.). — pp. vikatthita.

Vikatthana (nt.) [fr. vi + **katth**] boasting SnA 549.

Vikatthita (nt.) [fr. vikatthati] boasting J I.359.

Vikatthin (adj.) [fr. vi + **katth**] boasting; only neg. a° not boasting, modest A V.157; Sn 850; Miln 414.

Vikanta = vikatta; cut open, cut into pieces J II.420.

Vikantati [vi + kantati²] to cut J V.368 (= chindati C.). — pp. vikatta & vikanta.

Vikantana (nt.) [fr. vikantati] knife M I.244. Cp. vikattana.

Vikappa [vi + kappa] 1. thinking over, considering, thought, intention Nd 97, 351. — 2. doubtfulness, indecision, alternative, appl[d] to the part. vā SnA 202, 266; KhA 166; DA I.51; PvA 18. —attha° consideration or application of meaning, exposition, statement, sentence J III.521; SnA 433, 591. — Cp. nibbikappa.

Vikappana (nt.) & °**ā** (f.) [fr. vikappeti] 1. assignment, apportioning Vin IV.60 = 123 = 283. At Vin IV.122 two ways of assigning a gift are distinguished: sammukhā-vikappanā & parammukhā°. All these passages refer to the cīvara. — 2. alternative, indecision, indefiniteness (= vikappa), as t. t. g. applied to part. ca and vā, e. g. SnA 179 ("ca"); KhA 166 ("vā").

Vikappita [pp. of vikappeti] prepared, put in order, arranged, made; in comb[n] su° well prepared, beautifully set Sn 7; VvA 188 (manohara +). — Bdhgh. at SnA 21 interprets °kappita as chinna "cut," saying it has that meaning from "kappita-kesa-massu" (with trimmed hair & beard), which he interprets *ad sensum*, but not etymologically correctly. Cp. vikappeti 5.

Vikappin (adj.) [fr. vikappa] having intentions upon (-°), designing A III.136 (an-issara° intentioning unruliness).

Vikappiya (adj.) [grd. of vikappeti] to be designed or intended Sdhp 358.

Vikappeti [vi + kappeti] 1. to distinguish, design, intend, to have intentions or preferences, to fix one's mind on (loc. or acc.) Sn 793 = 802 (= vikappaŋ āpajjati Nd¹ 97), 918 (id. Nd¹ 351). — 2. to detail, describe, state KhA 166; SnA 43. — 3. to assign, apportion, give Vin I.289 (cīvaraŋ); IV.121 (id.). — 4. to arrange, put on, get ready Vin I.297. — 5. to change, alter, shape, form J V.4 (ambapakkaŋ satthena v.; C. not quite correctly = vicchindati). — pp. vikappita.

Vikampati [vi + **kamp**] to shake; fig. to be unsettled, to waver, to be in doubt S IV.71 (cittaŋ na vikampate); Th 1, 1076 (vidhāsu na v.; trsl[n] *Brethren* p. 366: "who is not exercised about himself in this way or in that"); Nd¹ 195 (tīsu vidhāsu, as at Th 1, 1076; as comment on Sn 843); J VI.488. — ppr. med. vikampamāna, only neg. a° not hesitating, settled, well balanced, resolved Sn 842; J IV.310; V.495 (C. anolīyamāna); VI.175 (C. nirāsanka). — pp. vikampita.

Vikampin (adj.) [fr. vikampati] shaking; only neg. a° not shaking, steadfast, steady, settled Sn 952; Vv 50²².

Vikaroti [vi + **kṛ**] to alter, change, disturb; aor. vyakāsi J II.166 (= vikāraŋ akāsi parivattayi C.); so read for T. vyākāsi. — Imper. Pass. 3 sg. vikiriyyatu "let him be disturbed" J III.368 (after Kern, *Toev.* s. v. One may take it to vikirati, q. v.). — pp. vikaṭa & vikata. See also vikubbati, etc.

Vikala (adj.) [Sk. vikala] defective, in want of, deprived, (being) without Th 2, 391; Pv IV.1 (bhoga°); J IV.278; VI.232; Miln 106, 307 (udakena); DA I.222; PvA 4 (hattha°). Cp. vekalla.

Vikalaka (adj.) [vikala + ka] being short of, wanting Vin I.285.

Vikasati¹ [vi + **kas**] to open (out), to expand, to blossom fully (of flowers). — pp. vikasita. Caus. vikāseti to open J VI.364 (hatthaŋ).

Vikasati² [vi + **kāś**, cp. okāsa] to shine; Caus. vikāseti to illuminate Davs V.47 (mukh' ambuja-vanāni vikāsayanto).

Vikasita [pp. of vikasati¹] burst asunder, blossoming, opened (wide), expanded, usually appl[d] to flowers J III.320 (= phālita C.); IV.407; VvA 40, 206 (of eyes); SnA 139; DA I.40

Vikāra [fr. vi + **kṛ**] 1. change, alteration, in mahā° great change Vism 366, 367 (of two kinds: anupādiṇṇa & upādiṇṇa, or primary & secondary, i. e. the first caused by kappa-vuṭṭhāna, the second by dhātu-kkhobha); KhA 107 (vaṇṇa°). — 2. distortion, reversion, contortion, in var. connections, as kucchi° stomach-ache Vin I.301; bhamuka° frowning DhA IV.90; mukha° grimace, contortion of the face, J II.448; PvA 123; hattha° hand-figuring, signs with the hand, gesture Vin I.157 (+ hattha-vilanghaka) = M I.207 (reads vilangaka); Vin V.163 (with other similar gestures); J IV.491; V.287; VI.400, 489. — Kern. *Toev.* s. v. vikāra is hardly correct in translating hattha-vikārena at Vin I.157 by "eigenhandig," i. e. with his own hand. It has to be comb[d] with hattha-vilanghakena. — 3. perturbation, disturbance, inconvenience, deformity Vin I.271, 272 (°ŋ sallakkheti observe the uneasiness); Miln 224 (tāvataka v. temporary inconvenience), 254 (°vipphāra disturbing influence); SnA 189 (bhūta° natural blemish). — 4. constitution, property, quality (cp. *Cpd.* 157², 168¹) Vism 449 (rūpa° material quality); VvA 10 (so correct under maya in *P.D.* vol. III. p. 147). — 5. deception, fraud PvA 211 (= nikati). — Cp. nibbikāra.

Vikāla [vi + kāla] "wrong time," i. e. not the proper time, which usually means "afternoon" or "evening," and therefore often "too late." — Vin IV.274 (= time from sunset to sunrise); J V.131 (ajja vikālo to-day it is too late); VvA 230 (id.). — loc. vikāle (opp. kāle) as adv., meaning: (1) at the wrong time Vin I.200; Sn 386; PvA 12. — (2) too late Vv 84 (= akāle VvA 337); DhA I.356; IV.69. — (3) very late (at night) J V.458.
-bhojana taking a meal at the wrong time, i, e. in the afternoon Vin I.83; D I.5; A I.212; II.209; Sn 400; DA I.77.

Vikāsa [vi+kas: see vikasati¹] opening, expansion J VI.497 (vana° opening of the forest); Dhtp 265.

Vikāsika [fr. vi+kṛṣ: see kasati] a linen bandage (Kern: "pluksel") Vin I.206 (for wound-dressing). May be a derⁿ fr. kāsika, i. e. Benares cloth, the vi° denoting as much as "a kind of."

Vikāsitar [fr. vi+kṛṣ, kasati] one who plucks or pulls, bender of a bow, archer J VI.201.

Vikāsin (adj.) (-°) [fr. vi+kāś: see vikasati²] illumining, delighting Mhvs 18, 68.

Vikāseti see vikasati.

Vikiṇṇa [pp. of vikirati] scattered about, strewn all over, loose Vin I.209 (undurehi okiṇṇa°; overrun); J V.82. -kesa with dishevelled hair J I.47; Vism 415. -vāca (adj.) of loose talk S I.61 (= asaññata-vacana *K.S.* I.320); Pug 35 (same explⁿ PugA 217): J V.77 (= patthaṭa-vacana C.).

Vikitteti [vi+kitteti] to slander Miln 276 (opp. pakitteti).

Vikiraṇa (nt. & adj.) [fr. vikirati] 1. scattering, dispersing; being scattered or dispersed D I.11 (cp. DA I.96).—Vbh 358 (T. reads viki°; v. l. vikāraṇa & vikkir°) = Pug 23 (which reads nikaraṇā; trsl. "guilefulness"). In this connection VbhA 493 interprets vikirana (or °ā) as "denial, abnegation" (pretext?), by saying "nâhaŋ eva karomi ti pāpānaŋ vikkhipanato vikiraṇā." — With ref. to Arahantship (the dissolution of the body) at DhA III.109 in formula bhedana-vikiraṇa-viddhaŋsana-dhamma i. e. "of the nature of total destruction." Cp. BSk. formula śatana-patana-vikiraṇa-vidhvaŋsana (-dharmatā) AvŚ I.96 (where S. Speyer in Index considers vikaraṇa the correct form) = Divy 299 (reading cyavanapatana°) = Lal. V. 242. See also S III.190 (under vikirati). — 2. (adj.) scattering, spending, squandering, f. °ī Sn. 112.

Vikirati [vi+kirati] to scatter about, sprinkle, spread, mix up (trs. & intrs.) M I.127; S III.190 (in simile of playing children: paŋsv' āgārakāni hatthehi ca pādehi ca vikiranti [mix up] vidhamanti [fall about] viddhaŋsenti [tumble over] vikīḷanikaŋ karonti, describing the scrambling and crowding about. In quite a diff. interpretation applᵈ to Arahantship: see under vikiraṇa, as also in the same chapter (S III.190 § 11 sq.) in phrase rūpaŋ vikirati vidhamati etc. where it is meant in trs. sense of "destroy"; thus vi° in the same verb in meaning (vi° 1 & 2); S IV.41 (kāyo vikiri [came to pieces] seyyathâpi bhusa-muṭṭhi); J I.226; Pv II.3⁸ (vikiri, v. l. for okiri); Miln 101, 237 (lokadhātu vikireyya, would fall to pieces; combᵈ with vidhameyya & viddhaŋseyya "drop & tumble," denoting total confusion and destruction. Similarly on p. 250 = 337 "vāri pokkhara-patte vikirati vidhamati viddhaŋsati": the water scatters, drops & falls off; applᵈ figuratively to bad qualities at same passage); SnA 172. — Pass. vikiriyyati & vikirīyati may be taken either to vikirati or vikaroti (cp. kiriyati); DhsA 19 (suttena sangahitāni pupphāni na vikirīyanti na viddhaŋsiyanti: get scattered and fall off); ppr. vikirīyamāna PvA 271 (with sprawling or confused limbs); imper. vikiriyyatu J III.368. — pp. vikiṇṇa.

Vikīḷanika (adj. & nt.) [fr. vi+kīḷana] playing about; in phrase vikīḷanikaŋ karoti (intrs.) to play all over or excitedly (lit. to make play: vi° in meaning vi° 1) S III.190; as trs. to put out of play, to discard (vi° 3) ibid. (rūpaŋ etc. v. karoti).

Vikujjhita [vi+pp. of kujjheti] made angry, angered, annoyed, vexed M II.24 (so read for vikujjita).

Vikuṇita (adj.) [vi+kuṇita] distorted, deformed Vism 346 (°mukha); PvA 123 (id.). Cp. vikūṇa.

Vikuddha (adj.) [vi+kuddha] free fr. anger J V.308.

Vikubbati [vi+kubbati, med. of karoti] to change round, transform, do magic J III.114 (= parivatteti); Dpvs I.40 (vikubbeyya); also in phrase iddhi-vikubbati to work transformation by magic (psychic) potency Kvu 55. — ppr. f. vikubbantī Vv 11² (iddhiŋ working magic, = vikubban' iddhiyo vaḷañjentī VvA 58), and vikubbamānā (iddhi°) Vv 31¹. — pp. *vikubbita miracle: see vikubbana.

Vikubbana (nt.) & °ā (f.) [fr. vikubbati] miraculous transformation, change; assuming a diff. form by supernatural power; miracle Th 1, 1183; Ps II.174, 210; Dpvs VIII.6 (°esu kovida); Mhvs 19, 19; Miln 343; Vism 309, 316 sq. More specific as iddhi-vikubbana (or °ā), i. e. by psychic powers, e. g. D II.213; Vism 373 sq.; or vikubbanā iddhi Vism 378, 406; VvA 58; DhsA 91 (the var. forms of iddhi). Cp. *Kvu trsl.* 50; *Cpd.* 61. — The BSk. form is represented by the pp. of vikubbati, i. e. vikurvita, e. g. AvŚ I.258; Divy 269 etc.

Vikulāva(ka) (adj.) [vi+kulāva] having no nest, without a nest S I.224 (ka); J I.203.

Vikūjati [vi+kūjati] to sing (like a bird), warble, chirp, coo PvA 189 (= upanadati). — ppr. med. vikūjamāna Vin IV.15; J V.12.

Vikūṇa [cp. vikuṇita & vikāra] distortion, grimace (mukha°) SnA 30.

Vikūla (adj.) [vi+kūla] sloping down, low-lying A I.35 (contrasted with ukkūla). We should expect ni° for vi°, as in BSk. (see ukkūla).

Vikūlaka (adj.) [fr. vikūla] contrary, disgusting ThA 2, 467 (= paṭikūla ThA 284).

Vikesikā (adj. -f.) [vi+kesa+ika] with loose or dishevelled hair Vin I.15.

Vikoṭṭita [vi+koṭṭita] beaten, cut, slain, killed Miln 304 (koṭṭita+).

Vikopana (nt.) [fr. vi+kup] upsetting, injuring, doing harm J II.330 = IV.471; Miln 185, 266; DhsA 145.

Vikopin (adj.) [vi+kup] shaking, disturbed; neg. a° J VI.226.

Vikopeti [vi+kopeti] 1. to shake up PvA 253. — 2. to upset, spoil, to do harm Vin III.47; Miln 276 (vikitteti+). — 3. to destroy J VI.68 (padaŋ a track).

Vikkanta [pp. of vi+kram] heroic J I.119; II.211; IV.271; Miln 400 (°cārin, of a lion).

Vikkandati [vi+kandati] to cry out, lament, wail J VI.525.

Vikkaya [vi+kaya] selling, sale A II.209; Sn 929 (kaya+); J I.121; II.200; IV.115 (majja°); Miln 194 (°bhaṇḍa goods for sale, merchandise); PvA 29, 113 (°bhaṇḍa).

Vikkayika & **kāyika** (adj.-n.) [fr. vikiṇāti] 1. a salesman, vendor DhA IV.50 (ā). — 2. for sale J I.201 (ā); DhA I.269 (ā).

Vikkama [fr. vi+kram] 1. walking about, stepping; in °malaka walking-enclosure, "περιπατεῖον," corridor J I.449. — 2. strength, heroism J II.211, 398; III.386 (°porisa).

Vikkamati [vi+kamati] to have or show strength, to exert oneself J III.184 (= parakkamati); Miln 400. — pp. vikkanta.

Vikkiṇāti [vi+kiṇāti] to sell J I.227, 377 (ger. vikkiṇitvā); PvA 100 (id.), 191 (aor. vikkiṇi). — inf. vikketuŋ J III.283. — grd. vikkiṇiya = for sale DhA I.390 (°bhaṇḍa merchandise).

Vikkīḷita (nt.) [vi + kīḷita] sporting, amusement, pastime Nett 124 (in appl^d meaning).

Vikkuthita (adj.) [vi + kuthita] boiled, °duddha boiled milk KhA 60 (T. reads vikkuthita-duṭṭha-vaṇṇa, but App. SnA Index p. 870: vikkuṭṭhita-duddha°). The corresp. passage at Vism 260 has duṭṭha-khīra-vaṇṇa, which seems faulty.

Vikkhaṇḍati [vi + khaṇḍati] to break (up), destroy, spoil Sdhp 450 (ger. °iya). — pp. vikkhaṇḍita.

Vikkhaṇḍita [pp. of vikkhaṇḍati] broken, ruined, spoilt Sdhp 436.

Vikkhambha [vi + khambha 1] diameter (lit. support) J v.268, 271; Mhvs 18, 27

Vikkhambhati [fr. vi + khambha 2] (intrs.) to become stiff (with fear), to be scared or frightened Ap. 50.

Vikkhambhana (nt.) [vi + khambha + na] withdrawal of support, stopping (the nīvaraṇas or any evil influences or corruptions: kilesa°), arresting, paralysing; elimination, discarding Ps II.179; Nd¹ 6; Nd² 338, 606ᵇ; J III.15 (kilesa° + metta-bhāvana-jhān' uppatti); IV.17; Vism 320; Sdhp 455. — Usually in foll. cpds.: °pahāna elimination (of character-blemishes) by discarding J II.230; Nd² 203; Vism 5; DhsA 352; SnA 19; °vimutti emancipation by elimination J II.35; °viveka arrest by aloofness DhsA 12, 164; Vism 140, 141.

Vikkhambhanatā (f.) [vikkhambhana + tā] state of having undone or discarded, removal, destruction, paralysis Nett 15, 16.

Vikkhambhika (adj.) [fr. vikkhambheti] leading to arrest (of passions), conducive to discarding (the blemishes of character) Vism 114.

Vikkhambhita [pp. of vikkhambheti] arrested, stopped, paralysed, destroyed Ps II.179; Tikp 155, 320 sq.; Dukp 10.

Vikkhambhiya (adj.) [grd. of vikkhambheti] in neg. a° not to be obstructed or overcome D III.146.

Vikkhambheti [vi + khambheti] (trs.) to "unprop," unsettle, discard; to destroy, extirpate, paralyse (cp. khambha 2 and chambheti), give up, reject Sn 969 (= abhibhavati etc. Nd¹ 492); Vism 268; J I.303 (jhānabalena kilese v.); Miln 34 (nīvaraṇe); DhA IV.119 (pītiŋ vikkhambhetvā: here in meaning "set up, establish"? Or to produce such pīti as to be called pharaṇā pīti, thus vikkhambheti = pharati 2? Or as Denom. fr. vikkhambha "diameter" = to establish etc.?); VvA 156 (read °etvā.) — pp. vikkhambhita.

Vikkhalita (nt.) [vi + khalita²] stumbling, fault, faux pas A I.199.

Vikkhāyitaka (adj.-nt.) [vi + khāyati (= khādita) + ka] "pertaining (or: of the nature of) to being eaten up," i. e. a (mental) representation obtained by contemplation of a corpse gnawed by animals, one of the asubha-kammaṭṭhānas Vism 110 = Miln 332 (°saññā); Vism 179, 194.

Vikkhālita [pp. of vikkhāleti] washed off, cleansed Vin II.201; Vism 59.

Vikkhāleti [vi + khāleti] to wash off, to wash one's face (mukhaŋ) Vin II.201; S II.269; J I.266, 459; PvA 75, 209, 241 (= ācameti). — pp. vikkhālita.

Vikkhitta (adj.) [vi + khitta] 1. upset, perplexed, mentally upset, confused S II.122 (°citta); V.157, 263 sq.; A III.174 (°citta); V.147 (id.); Vism 410 (= uddhacc' ānugata). — a° undisturbed, composed, collected A V.149; It 94; PvA 26.

Vikkhittaka (adj.) [vi + khitta + ka] 1. scattered all over, deranged, dismembered; of a dead body with respect to its limbs (as one of the asubha-kammaṭṭhāna's: cp. vikkhāyika & vicchiddaka) Vism 110 (°saññā) = Miln 332; Vism 179 (with defⁿ vividhaŋ khittaŋ vikkhittaŋ; aññena hatthaŋ aññena pādaŋ aññena sīsan ti evaŋ tato tato khittassa chava-sarīrassa adhivacanaŋ), 194. —hata° killed & cut up Vism 179.—2. citta° of unbalanced or deranged mind Miln 308.

Vikkhipana (nt.) [cp. BSk. vikṣepa refusal AvŚ I.94] refusal, denial VbhA 493 (see vikiraṇa 1).

Vikkhipatti [Pass. of vikkhipati] to be disturbed J I.400 (gocare, in . . .); Miln 337 (cittaŋ). — pp. vikkhitta.

Vikkhīṇa [vi + khīṇa] totally destroyed, finished, gone Th 2, 22.

Vikkhīyati [vi + khīyati] to go to ruin, to be destroyed, to be lost J V.392 (fut. °īyissati). — pp. vikkhīṇa.

Vikkhepa [vi + khepa] 1. disturbance, derangement J VI.139. — 2. perplexity, confusion D I.59. —vācā° equivocation, senseless talk D I.24. — 3. in citta° & cetaso v. upset of mind, unbalanced mind, mental derangement: citta° S I.126; Pug 69; cetaso A III.448; Dhs 429; Vbh 373. —avikkhepa equanimity, balance D III.213; A I.83; Ps I.94; Dhs 160, 430; Vbh 178 sq., 231 sq., 266 sq., 279 sq., 285 sq.

-paṭibāhana exclusion or warding off of confusion (of mind) or disturbance Vism 244; VbhA 227.

Vikkhepika (adj.) [fr. vikkhepa], in phrase amarā°: see under amarā; another suggestion as to explanation may be: khipa = eel-basket, thus vikhep-ika one who upsets the eel-basket, i. e. causes confusion.

Vikkheḷikā (adj.-f.) [vi + kheḷa + ikā] having saliva dropping from the mouth (of sleeping women), slobbering Vin I.15.

Vikkhobhita [pp. of vikkhobheti: see khobha] thoroughly shaken up or disturbed Miln 377.

Vikhādana (nt.) [vi + khādana] biting, chewing Dhs 646, 740, 875; DhsA 330.

Vigacchati [vi + gacchati] to depart, disappear; to decrease D I.138 (bhogakkhandha vigacchissati); Sdhp 523. — pp. vigata.

Vigata (°-) [pp. of vigacchati, in act. (reflexive) & med-pass. function] gone away, disappeared, ceased; having lost or foregone (for-gone = vi-gata), deprived of, being without; often to be trsl^d simply as prep. "without." It nearly always occurs in compⁿ, where it precedes the noun. By itself rare, e. g. Sn 483 (sārambhā yassa vigatā); VvA 33 (padumā mā vigatā hotu). Otherwise as follows: °āsa Pug 27; °āsava SnA 51; °icchā Dh 359; °khila Sn 19; °cāpalla D I.115; DA I.286; °chavivaṇṇa ThA 80 (= vivaṇṇa); °jīvita PvA 40; °paccaya Vism 541; Tikp 7, 21, 59; °paṭighāta DhA IV.176; °mada Mhvs 34, 94; °raja Sn 517; J I.117; °valita PvA 153. Cp. vīta° in similar application and meaning.

Vigama (-°) [fr. vi + gam] going away, disappearance, departing, departure Dāvs V.68 (sabb' āsava°); DhsA 166; Sdhp 388 (jighacchā°), 503 (sandeha°).

Vigayha see vigāhati.

Vigarahati [vi + garahati] to scold (intensely), to abuse Vin II.161 (dhammiŋ kathaŋ); III.46; S I.30 (ariyadhammaŋ); Miln 227.

Vigaḷati [vi + galati] to drop Miln 250. — pp. vigaḷita. Cp. vinigaḷati.

Vigaḷita [pp. of vigaḷati] dropping, dripping (down) PvA 56.

Vigāhati [vi + gāhati] to plunge into, to enter S I.180 (ger. vigāhiya); J v.381 (°gāhisuŋ, aor.); Mhvs 19, 29 (here as *°gāhetvā*). The ger. is also vigayha at Sn 2, 825; cp. Nd[1] 163 (= ogayha pavisitvā). At Vin II.106 we should prefer to read **viggayha** for **vigayha**.

Vigganhati [vi + ganhati] 1. to take hold of, to quarrel, to be in disharmony with; only in ger. viggayha disputing, quarrelling, fighting Vin II.106 (read gg for g! Bdhgh on p. 315: rubbing against each other); Ud 69; Sn 844, 878; Nd[1] 285 (= uggahetvā parāmasitvā). — 2. to stretch out, disperse, divide, spread; ger. **viggayha** Vv 50[1] (hattha-pāde v.; expl[d] as "vividhehi ākārehi gahetvā" VvA 209).

Viggaha [fr. vi + gah: see ganhati 3] 1. dispute, quarrel J I.208 (ñātakānaŋ aññamaññaŋ viggaho); Miln 90; often comb[d] with **kalaha**, e. g. Vin II.88; A IV.401; Nd[1] 302; Miln 383. — 2. taking up form (lit. seizing on), "incorporation," form, body D II.210 = 226 (sovanno viggaho mānusaŋ viggahaŋ atirocati); Vin I.97 (manussa°); II.286 (id.); IV.215 (tiracchānagata-manussa°), 269 (id.); J V.398 = 405 (= sarīra C); VI.188 (rucira°); Dāvs I.42 (uju-somma°). — 3. (t.t.g.) resolution of words into their elements, analysis, separation of words Miln 381; VvA 226 (pada°); SnA 168; ThA 202 (pada°).

Viggahita [pp. of vigganhati] taken hold of, seized; prejudiced against, seduced by (-), in phrase **dhamm' uddhacca-viggahita-mānasa** A II.157; Ps II.101. Cp. BSk. vigrāhita, e. g. AvŚ I.83 = 308 (Ajātaśatru Devadatta°); Divy 419, 557, 571; Jtm 143, 146.

Viggāhika (adj.) [fr. viggaha] of the nature of dispute or quarrel; only in cpd. °kathā quarrelsome speech, dispute D I.8; S V.419; Sn 930; DA I.91.

Vighattita [vi + ghattita] struck, knocked, beaten J V.203 (a°).

Vighātana (adj.) [fr. vighāteti] unfastening, breaking up, overthrowing Th 1, 419.

Vighātita [pp. of vighāteti, Denom. fr. vi + ghāta, cp. gantheti] overthrown, destroyed Sdhp 314.

Vighāta [vi + ghata] 1. destruction, killing, slaughter PvA 150 (vighātaŋ āpajjati = vihaññati). — as adj. slain, beaten Pv IV.5[3] (= vighātavā vihata-bala). — 2. distress, annoyance, upset of mind, trouble, vexation D III.249; M I.510; A II.197 sq.; IV.161 (°pariḷāha); Sn 814 (= ugghāta pīḷana ghaṭṭana upaddava Nd[1] 140 = 170); Th 2, 450 (bahu° full of annoyance). —sa° connected with, or bringing vexation, with opp. a° free of annoyance: S III.8; V.97; A I.202 sq.; III.3, 429; Th 2, 352; ThA 242. — 3. opposition M I.499.

-**pakkhika** having its part in adversity, associated with trouble M I.115; S V.97; DhsA 382. -**bhūmi** ground for vexation Sn 830 (cp. Nd[1] 170 with expl[n] as above).

Vighātavant (adj.) [vighāta + vant] full of annoyance or vexation S III.16 sq.; A II.143 (= discontented); Th 1, 899 (in same connection, neg.); PvA 260 (= distressed).

Vighāsa (& °ghasa) [fr. vi + ghasati] remains of food, broken meat, scraps Vin IV.265, 266; J II.288; III.113, 191, 311 (read °ghasa for metre); V.268 (do.); Sdhp 389. -**āda** one who eats the remains of food Vin I.200 (panca°-satāni) J I.348; II.96; III.191; DhA II.128. Also N. of an animal J VI.538.

Vicakka (adj.) [vi + cakka] without wheels J I.378 (sakata). Doubtful in phrase **asani°**, where used as a noun, probably in diff. meaning altogether (= asani-pāta?): see S II.229 (= "falling of a thunderbolt" *K.S.* II.155); D III.44, 47.

Vicakkhana (adj.-nt.) [vi + cakkhana, of **caks** to see, attentive, watchful, sensible, skilful; (nt.) application, attention, wit S I.214 = Sn 186 (appamatta +; trsl° *K.S.* I.277 "discerning wit"); Sn 583; J IV.58; VI.286; Miln 216; Vism 43; SnA 238; Sdhp 200, 293.

Vicakkhu (adj.) [vi + cakkhu] eyeless, blind, in phrase °kamma making blind or perplexed S I.111, 118 ("darkening their intelligence" trsl[n]) [cp. BSk. vicakṣu-karma MVastu III.416; Lal V. 490].

Vicakkhuka (adj.) [vicakkhu + ka] not seeing, blinded, dulled in sight, half-blind Miln 295 (Rh. D. "squinting").

Vicaya [fr. **vi + ci**: see vicinati] search, investigation, examination S III.96 (vicayaso, i. e. thoroughly); Pug 25; Miln 340 (dhamma°); Nett 1, 2, 10; DhsA 147; Sdhp 466. For dhamma° see sambojjhanga.

Vicarana (adj.-nt.) [fr. vicarati] going about, circulating, moving, travelling J V.484 (°bhanda travelling merchandise).

Vicarati [vi + carati] to go or move about in (loc.), to walk (a road = acc.), to wander Sn 444 (raṭṭhā raṭṭhaŋ vicarissaŋ, fut.), 696 (dhamma-maggaŋ); Nd[1] 201, 263; Pv III.7[3] (aor. vicari); DhA I.66; PvA 4, 22, 33, 69, 120, 185 (= āhindati); Sdhp 133. — In Sn often with loke (in this world), e. g. Sn 466, 501, 845, 846, 864. — Caus. vicāreti; pp. vicarita, vicārita & vicinna. Cp. anu°.

Vicarita [pp. of vicarati] occupied by (-°), haunted, frequented VvA 163.

Vicāra [vi + cāra] investigation, examination, consideration, deliberation. — Def[d] as "vicaranaŋ vicāro, anusañcaranan ti vuttaŋ hoti" Vism 142 (see in def. under vitakka). — Hardly ever by itself (as at Th 1, 1117 mano°), usually in close connection or direct comb[n] with **vitakka** (q. v.).

Vicāraka (adj.) [fr. vicāreti] 1. looking after something; watching J I.364 (ghara°). — 2. investigating; (n.) a judge Mhvs 35, 18.

Vicāranā (f.) & a° (nt.) [fr. vicāreti] 1. investigation, search, attention Sn 1108, 1109 (f. & nt.); J III.73 (°paññā). — 2. arranging, planning, looking after; scheme J I.220; II.404 (yuddha°); VI.333 sq.

Vicārita [pp. of vicāreti] thought out, considered; thought D I.37 (vitakkita +, like vitakka-vicāra, cp. DA I.122), 213 (id.).; SnA 385.

Vicāreti [Caus. of vicarati] 1. to make go round, to pass round, to distribute PvA 272 (salākaŋ). — 2. to think (over) S V.156 (vitakketi +). — 3. to investigate, examine, test J II.413; III.258; VvA 336 (a° to omit examining). — 4. to plan, consider, construct J II.404; VI.333. — 5. to go about (some business), to look after, administer, provide J II.287; III.378; Mhvs 35, 19 (rajjaŋ); PvA 93 (kammante). — pp. **vicārita** & **vicinna**.

Vicāliya (adj.) [grd. of vi + cāleti] in neg. a° not to be shaken, not wavering Sdhp 444.

Vicikicchati [vi + cikicchati] lit. "dis-reflect," to be distracted in thought, i. e. to doubt, hesitate D I.106; S II.17, 50, 54; III.122, 135; J IV.272 (2 sg. vicikicchase); SnA 451; DA I.275; — pp. **vicikicchita**.

Vicikicchā (f.) [fr. vicikicchati] doubt, perplexity, uncertainty (one of the nivaranas) D I.246; III.49, 216, 234, 269; S I.99; III.106 sq. (dhammesu v. doubt about the precepts); IV.350; A III.292, 438; IV.68, 144 sq.; V.144; Sn 343, 437, 540; Vv 81 (= solasa-vatthuka-vicikicchā VvA 317); J II.266; Pug 59; Vbh 168, 341, 364; Dhs 425; Nett 11; Tikp 108, 122, 152 sq., 171, 255, 275;

Dukp 170 sq., 265 sq., 289 sq.; Vism 471 (= vigatā cikicchā ti v. etc.), 599 sq.; VbhA 209; VvA 156; MA 116; Sdhp 459. — As adj. (-°) vicikiccha, e. g. tiṇṇa° one who has overcome all doubt D I.71, 110; M I.18; A II.211; III.92; 297 sq.; IV.186; 210. — See also *Cpd.* 242; *Dhs. trsl.* § 425 n. 1; and cp. kathankathā, kicchati, vecikicchin.

Vicikicchita (nt.) [pp. of vicikicchati] doubt Pv IV.1^{37}.

Vicikicchin see ve°.

Viciṇṇa [pp. of vicāreti] thought out; in neg. a° not thought out; reading however doubtful, better to be taken as adhiciṇṇa, i. e. procedure, method D I.8 = M II.3 = S III.12 (vi° as v. l.). — DA I.91 reads āciṇṇa (cp. M I.372).

Vicita [pp. of vi + ci to gather] in phrase °kāḷaka bhatta rice from which the black grains have been separated D I.105; M II.8; DA I.274; as vicita-bhatta in same sense at J IV.371.

Vicitta (& °citra) (adj.) [vi + citta^{1}] various, variegated, coloured, ornamented, etc. J I.18, 83; Pv II.1^{9}; Vv 64^{10} (citra); Miln 338, 349; VvA 2, 77; Sdhp 92, 245. — vicitra-kathika eloquent Miln 196.

Vicinati (°cināti) [vi + cināti] 1. to investigate, examine, discriminate S I.34 (yoniso vicine dhammaŋ); A IV.3 sq. (id.); Sn 658, 933; Ap 42; J VI.373; Nd^{1} 398; Nett 10, 22 (grd. vicetabba), 25 sq.; Miln 298; Dpvs IV.2; DhsA 147; PvA 140; Sdhp 344. — ger. viceyya discriminating; with discrimination D II.21 (doubled: with careful discrim^{n}); III.167 (°pekkhitar); Sn 524 sq.; usually in phrase viceyya-dāna a gift given with discrimination S I.21; A IV.244; J IV.361; V.395; Pv II.9^{72}; DhA III.221; Mhvs 5, 35. — 2. to look for, to seek, to linger, to choose Pv III.6^{4} (aor. vicini = gavesi C.); IV.1^{42} (ger. viceyya = vicinitvā PvA 240); J I.419. — See also pacinati.

Vicinana (nt.) [fr. vicinati] discrimination Vism 162.

Vicinteti [vi + cinteti] to think, consider Sn 1023; Mhvs 4, 28 (vicintiya, ger.); 17, 38.

Vicuṇṇa [vi + cuṇṇa] crushed up, only in redupl.-iter. formation cuṇṇa-vicuṇṇa crushed to bits, piecemeal J I.26; III.438 etc. See under cuṇṇa.

Vicuṇṇita [pp. of vi + cuṇṇeti] crushed up J I.203 (vid-dhasta +).

Viccuta [vi + cuta] fallen down J V.403 (expl^{d} as viyutta C.); Dh I.140.

Vicchaḍḍeti [vi + chaḍḍeti] to throw out, to vomit; in late (Sanskritic) Pāli at Sdhp 121 (pp. vicchaḍḍita) and 136 (nt. vicchaḍḍana throwing out).

Vicchandanika (& °ya) (adj.) [vi + chanda + na + ika] fit to disinterest, "disengrossing," in °kathā sermon to rid of the desire for the body Vin III.271 (Sam. Pās. on Pār. III.3, 1); & °sutta the Suttanta having disillusionment for its subject (another name given by Bdhgh to the Vijayasutta Sn 193-206) SnA 241 sq. (°ya). Cp. vicchindati.

Vicchādanā (f.) [vi + chādanā] concealment Pug 19, 23.

Vicchika [cp. Vedic vṛścīka: Zimmer, *Altind. Leben* 98] a scorpion D I.9 (°vijjā scorpion craft); Vin II.110; A II.73; III.101, 306; IV.320; V.289 sq.; J II.146; Miln 272, 394; Vism 235; DA I.93.

Vicchita in phrase **balavicchita-kārin** at Miln 110 is to be read balav' icchita-kārin "a man strong to do what he likes," i. e. a man of influence.

Vicchidda (adj.) [vi + chidda] only in (redupl.) combin. chidda° full of little holes, perforated all over J I.419.

Vicchiddaka [vi + chidda + ka] "having holes all over," referring to one of the asubha-kammaṭṭhānas, obtained by the contemplation of a corpse fissured from decay A II.17 (°saññā); V.106, 310; Miln 332; Vism 110, 178, 194.

Vicchinda [fr. vi + **chind** as in vicchindati] breaking off, cutting off J II.436, 438 (kāya°). Kern, *Toev.* s. v. considers it as a corruption of vicchanda. See vicchandanika.

Vicchindati [vi + chindati] to cut off, to interrupt, to prevent PvA 129 (°itu-kāma). The BSk. form is vicchandayati [= vi + Denom. of chando] e. g. Divy 10, 11, 383, 590. — pp. vicchinna.

Vicchinna [pp. of vicchindati] cut off, destroyed Sdhp 34, 117, 370, 585.

Vicchurita [vi + churita] besprinkled, sprinkled about VvA 4, 280 (= ullitta).

Viccheda [vi + cheda] cutting off, destruction J IV.284 (santati°). a° uninterruptedness VvA 16.

Vijaṭana (nt.) [fr. vijaṭeti] disentangling Miln 11.

Vijaṭita [pp. of vijaṭeti] disentangled S I.165.

Vijaṭeti [vi + Caus. of **jaṭ**: see jaṭita] 1. to disentangle, to comb out; fig. to unravel, explain Vin II.150 (bimbo-hanaŋ kātuŋ tūlāni v.); Miln 3; Vism 1, 2. — 2. to plunder J III.523. — pp. vijaṭita.

Vijana (adj.) [vi + jana] deserted of people, lonely S I.180; ThA 252. -°vāta: see vāta.

Vijambhati [vi + jambhati] to rouse oneself, to display activity, often appl^{d} to the awakening of a lion S III.84; A II.33; J I.12, 493; V.215 (°amāna, ppr., getting roused), 433, 487; VI.173; Vism 311.

Vijambhanā (f.) [vi + jambhanā] arousing, activity, energy J VI.457.

Vijambhikā (f.) [fr. vijambhati] yawning (before rising) i. e. drowsiness, laziness, in ster. comb^{n} with arati & tandī S I.7 (trsl^{n} "the lanquid frame"); A I.3; Vbh 352; Vism 33. As vijambhitā at S V.64; J I.506 (here in meaning "activity, alertness," but sarcastically as sīha°); VbhA 272 (= kāya-vināmanā).

Vijaya [fr. vi + ji] victory; conquering, mastering; triumph over (-°) D I.46; A IV.272 (idha-loka°); SnA 241 sq. (°sutta, another name for the Kāya-vicchandanika-sutta).

Vijayati (& vijinati) [vi + jayati] to conquer, master, triumph over DA I.250 (vijeti); fut. vijessati J IV.102. — ger. vijeyya Sn 524, 1002; and vijetvā J III.523. — pp. vijita. Cp. abhi°.

Vijahati [vi + jahati] to abandon, forsake, leave; to give up, dismiss Pv III.6^{15} (sarīraŋ); VvA 119; Pot. vijaheyya Pv IV.1^{10}; fut. vijahissati S II.220; Pv II.6^{7} (jīvitaŋ). — ger. vihāya Mhvs 12, 55; & vijahitvā Vin IV.269; J I.117; III.361 (iddh' ânubhāvena attabhāvaŋ). — grd. vihātabba A III.307 sq.; Miln 371. — Pass. vihīyati J VI.499 (eko v. = kilamissati C.). — pp. vijahita & vihīna.

Vijahana (nt.) [fr. vijahati] abandoning, relinquishing DA I.197.

Vijahita [pp. of vijahati] left, given up, relinquished; only in neg. a° J I.71, 76, 94, 178.

Vijātā (f.) [pp. of vijāhati] (a woman) having borne J II.140; Pv II.2^{3} (= pasūtā PvA 80).

-**kāla** time of birth J II.140. -**ghara** birth-chamber Miln 301.

Vijāti in °loha a kind of copper VbhA 63.

Vijāna (nt.-adj.) [fr. vijānāti] understanding; as adj. (-°) in cpds. du° (dubbijāna) hard to understand S I.60; J IV.217; and su° easy to perceive Sn 92; J IV.217.

Vijānana (nt.) [the diæretic form of Sk. vijñāna: cp. jānana = ñāṇa] recognition, knowing, knowledge, discrimination Vism 452; DhsA 141.

Vijānāti [vi + jñā] to have discriminative (dis = vi°) knowledge, to recognize, apprehend, ascertain, to become aware of, to understand, notice, perceive, distinguish, learn, know Sn 93 sq., 763; Dh 64, 65; Nd^{1} 442. See also viññāṇa 2^{a}. — imper. 2nd sg. vijāna Sn 1091 (= ājāna Nd^{2} 565^{b}); Pv IV.5^{5} (= vijānāhi PvA 260); ppr. vijānanto Sn 656, 953; Pv IV.1^{88}; PvA 41; *and* vijānaŋ neg. a° ignorant Dh 38, 60; It 103. Pot. 1st sg. (poet.) vijaññaŋ J III.360 (= vijāneyyaŋ C.); Sn 1065, 1090, 1097 (= jāneyyaŋ Nd^{2} 565^{a}); & vijāniyaŋ Vv 41^{5} (paṭivijjhiŋ C.); 3rd sg. vijaññā Sn 253, 316, 967 (cp. Nd^{1} 489). — ger. vijāniya Mhvs 8, 16; viññāya Sn 232; & viññitvā Vin IV.264. — aor. (3rd pl.) vijāniŋsu Mhvs 10, 18. — Pass. viññāyati PvA 197; fut. viññissati Th 1, 703. — inf. viññātuŋ S III.134. — grd. viññātabba (to be understood) VbhA 46; & viññeyya (q. v.). — pp. viññāta. — Caus. II. viññāpeti (q. v.).

Vijāyana (nt.) [fr. vijāyati] bringing forth, birth, delivery A I.78; J III.342; VI.333; Vism 500; VbhA 97.

Vijāyati [vi + jāyati] to bring forth, to bear, to give birth to Sdhp 133; aor. vijāyi VvA 220; PvA 82 (puttaŋ); ger. vijāyitvā Mhvs 5, 43 (puttaŋ); and vijāyitvāna Pv I.6^{3}. — pp. vijāta. — Caus. II. vijāyāpeti to cause to bring forth J VI.340.

Vijāyin (adj.-n.) [fr. vijāyati] in f. °inī able to bear a child, fertile J IV.77 (opp. vañjhā); DhA I.46 (id.).

Vijigucchati [vi + j.] to loathe Sn 41 (°amāna = aṭṭiyamāna harāyamāna Nd^{2} 566), 253, 958 (°ato = aṭṭiyato harāyato Nd^{1} 466), 963; Nd^{1} 479.

Vijita [pp. of vijayati] 1. conquered, subdued, gained, won Sn 46; SnA 352; DA I.160; PvA 75, 76, 161. — Cp. nijjita. — 2. (nt.) conquered land, realm, territory, kingdom J I.262; Vv 81^{20} (= desa VvA 316); DhA I.386. -anga at Pv III.1^{17} (PvA 176) read vijit.° -indriya one who has conquered his senses Sn 250. -sangāma by whom the battle has been won, victorious D II.39; It 76; Nd^{2} 542; Pug 68.

Vijitāvin (adj.) [vijita + āvin; see Geiger, *P.Gr.* 198^{3}] victorious D I.88 (caturanta +); II.146; S III.83; Sn 552, 646; DA I.249; DhA IV.232; SnA 162.

Vijina [doubtful] distress (?), in stock phrase at A V.156, 158, 160, 162 (v. l. at all pass. vicina).

Vijīyati at J III.374 is to be read as vījiyati (Pass. of vījati).

Vijja (adj.) (-°) [= vijjā] having vijjā, possessed of wisdom; in vatthu°, tiracchāna°, nakkhatta° etc. (referring to the lower arts condemned as heretic: vijjā c.) S III.239. te° possessed of threefold wisdom: see vijjā b.

Vijjaṭipatti (f.) [? doubtful spelling] adultery PvA 151.

Vijjati, vijjamāna etc.: see vindati.

Vijjantarikā (f.) is not clear; according to Kern, *Toev.* s. v. = vīthi + antarikā [a very bold assumption: vīthy° contracted to vijj° !], i. e. space in between two streets or midstreet M I.448; A I.124. Neumann (*Mittl. Slg.* II.182) translates "Rinnstein" (i. e. gutter). Under antarikā we have given the trslⁿ "interval of lightning," thus taking it as vijju + antarikā. Quoted DA I.34.

Vijjā (f.) [cp. Vedic vidyā knowledge: etym. see under vindati] one of the dogmatic terms of Buddhist teaching, varying in meaning in diff. sections of the Canon. It is not always the positive to avijjā (which has quite a well-defined meaning from its first appearance in Buddhist psych. ethics), but has been taken into the terminology of Buddhism from Brahmanic and popular philosophy. The opposite of avijjā is usually ñāṇa (but cp. S III.162 f., 171; V.429). Although certain vijjās pertain to the recognition of the "truth" and the destruction of avijjā, yet they are only secondary factors in achieving "vimutti" (cp. abhiññā, ñāṇa-dassana & paññā). That vijjā at M I.22 is contrasted with avijjā is to be expl^{d} as a word-play in a stereotype phrase. — A diff. side of "knowledge" again is given by "bodhi." — (a) Vijjā is a general, popular term for lore in the old sense, science, study, esp. study as a practice of some art (something like the secret science of the medicine man: cp. vejja !); hence appl^{d} in special, "dogmatic" sense as "secret science," revelation (put into a sort of magic formula), higher knowledge (of the learned man), knowledge which may be applied and used as an art (cp. magister artium !), practical knowledge; but also *mysterious* knowledge: "charm." — (b) vijjā, having a varying content in its connotation, is applied to a series of diff. achievements. A rather old tabulation of the stages leading by degrees to the attainment of the highest knowledge is given in the Sāmañña-phala-sutta (D I.63-86), repeated in nearly every Suttanta of D I. It is composed of the 3 *sampadās*, viz. sīla°, citta° & paññā°. Under the first group belong sīla(-kkhandha), indriya-saŋvara, sati-sampajañña, santuṭṭhi; the second is composed (1) of the overcoming of the *nīvaraṇas*, (2) of the 4 *jhānas*; the third consists of 8 items, viz. (1) ñāṇa-dassana, (2) manomaya-kāya, (3) iddhi, (4) dibba-sota, (5) ceto-pariyañāṇa, (6) pubbe-nivās' ânussatiñāṇa, (7) cut' ûpapatti-ñāṇa, (8) āsavānaŋ khaya-ñāṇa. Other terms used are: for the 2nd sampadā: caraṇa (D. I.100), and for the 3rd: vijjā (ibid.). — The discussion at D I.100 is represented as contradicting the (brahmaṇic) opinion of Ambaṭṭha, who thought that "vijjā nāma tayo Vedā, caraṇaŋ pañca sīlāni" (DA I.267 sq.). — In the enumⁿ of 3 vijjās at M I.22 sq. only Nos. 6-8 of the 3rd sampadā (said to have been attained by the Buddha in the 3 night watches) with the verbs anussarati (No. 6), pajānāti (7), abhijānāti (8), each signifying a higher stage of ("saving") knowledge, yet all called "vijjā." Quoted at Vism 202, where all 8 stages are given as "aṭṭha vijjā," and caraṇa with 15 qualities (sīla-saŋvara, indriyesu guttadvāra etc.). The same 3 vijjās (No. 6, 7, 8) are given at D III.220, 275, and poetically at A II.165 as the characteristics of a proper (ariya, *Buddhist*) monk (or brāhmaṇa): "etāhi tīhi vijjāhi tevijjo hoti brāhmaṇo," opposing the three-Veda-knowledge of the Brahmins. — Tevijja (adj.) in same meaning at S I.146 (where it refers to Nos. 3, 5, 8 of above enumⁿ), 192, 194. In *brahmanic* sense at Sn 594 (= tiveda SnA 463). Both meanings compared & contrasted at A I.163 (aññathā brāhmaṇā brāhmaṇaŋ tevijjaŋ paññāpenti, aññathā ca pana ariyassa vinaye tevijjo hoti "different in the Brahmanic and diff. in the Buddhist sense"). — Tisso vijjā (without specification, but referring to above 6, 7, 8) further at Vin II.183; Sn 656; Ps I.34; II.56; Pv IV.1^{34}; Miln 359 (+ chaḷabhiññā); DhA IV.30 (id.). It is doubtful whether the defⁿ of ñāṇa as "tisso vijjā" at Vin III.91 is genuine. — On vijjā-caraṇa see also D III.97, 98, 237; S I.153, 166; II.284; V.197; A II.163; IV.238; V.327; Sn 163, 289, 442. — On vijjā in the doctrinal applⁿ see: D III.156, 214, 274; S II.7 sq. (cakkhu, ñāṇa, paññā, vijjā, āloka); III.47; 163; 171; IV.31, 49 sq. A I.83; II.247; Sn 334 (simply meaning "wisdom," craft, care, but Bdhgh SnA 339 takes it as "āsavānaŋ-khaya-ñāṇa"), 1026 (opposed to avijjā); Pug 14, 57; Vbh 324; Nett 76, 191. — (c) *popular* meanings & usage of vijjā: science, craft, art, charm, spell D I.213 (Gandhārī nāma v., also mentioned at J IV.498 as practised by physicians), 214 (Maṇika n. v.); J III.504 (Cintāmaṇi v.); IV.323 (vatthu°: see under vatthu), 498 (ghora°); V.458 (anga° palmistry); Miln 200; Dh I.259 (bhūmicala n. v. "earthquake" charm), 265 (dhanu-agamanīyaŋ Ambaṭṭha n. v.); KhA 237 (vatthu°, khetta°, anga°); and see the list of forbidden crafts at D I.9 (anga°, vatthu°, khetta° etc.; cp. *Dial.* I.18, 19).

-gata having attained wisdom Sn 730 (opp. avijjā; the playful explⁿ at SnA 505 is "ye arahatta-magga-vijjāya kilese *vijjhitvā* gatā khīṇāsava-sattā"). -caraṇa (-sampanna) (endowed with) special craft (wisdom) & virtue: see above, b. -ṭṭhāna branch of study; there are 18 vijja-ṭṭhānāni or "arts & sciences," subjects of study, referred to at J I.259. -dhara a knower of charms, a sorcerer J III.303, 529; IV.496; V.94; Miln 153, 200, 267. -bhāgiyā (dhammā) (states) conducive to wisdom (6 kinds of saññā) A III.334; cp. D III.243; S V.395; A IV.52 sq. -mayā (iddhi) (potency) accomplished by art or knowledge (*Expos.* I.122) Vism 383; see iddhi. -vimutti wisdom (higher knowledge) as salvation S V.28, 335 sq.; Ps II.243 (in detail).

Vijju & **vijjutā** (f.) [cp. Vedic vidyut; fr. vi+**dyut**: see juti] lightning.—(a) **vijju**: S I.100 (°māli); A I.124 (°ūpamacitta); J V.322 (°vaṇṇin); Pug 30; Miln 22 (°jāla); VvA 12; Sdhp 244, 598.—(b) **vijjutā**: Th 1, 1167; J II.217.—On similes with v. see *J.P.T.S.* 1907, 136.—Cp. next.

Vijjullatā (f.) [vijju(t)+latā] a flash or streak of lightning, forked lightning S I.106; J I.103, 279, 501.

Vijjotati [vi+jotati] to shine (forth) PvA 56; Caus. °eti to illumine PvA 10.—pp. **vijjotita.**

Vijjotalati [Freq. of vijjotati? Or= vijjotayati= vijjoteti?] to flicker Vin II.131; M I.86.

Vijjotita [pp. of vijjotati] resplendent PvA 154.

Vijjhati [**vyadh**] to pierce, perforate; to shoot with an arrow; to strike, hit, split; fut. °issati J IV.272; inf. °ituŋ ibid.; ger. °itvā Vin II.150; J I.201 (boring through timber); SnA 505 (kilese); PvA 155; & **viddhā** J VI.77.—Pass. vijjhati: ger. °itvā having been hit J III.323; ppr. vijjhamāna PvA 107; grd. viddheyya J VI.77.—pp. viddha.—Caus. vijjheti J I.45 (sūlehi vijjhayanto); and vedheti to cause to be pierced J VI.453 (fut. vedhayissati).—pp. **vedhita.**

Vijjhana (nt.) [fr. vijjhati] piercing or getting pierced DA I.75; II.87 (kaṇṇa°-mangala, ear-piercing ceremony); PvA 107.

Vijjhāpeti [vi+jhāpeti] to extinguish Vin I.31; II.219, 221; J IV.292; Miln 42.

Vijjhāyati [vi+jhāyati²] to be extinguished, to go out (of fire) Vin I.31 (imper. °āyatu & fut. °āyissati); DhA I.21 (akkhīni dīpa-sikhā viya vijjhāyiŋsu).

Viññatti (f.) [fr. viññāpeti] intimation, giving to understand, information; begging or asking by intimation or hinting (a practice forbidden to the bhikkhu) Vin I.72 (°bahula, intent on . . .); III.144 sq. (id.); IV.290; J III.72 (v. nāma na vaṭṭati, is improper); Vbh 13; Vism 41 (threefold: nimitta°, obhāsa°, parikathā; as t. t., cp. *Cpd.* 120¹: medium of communication); Miln 343, 370; DhA II.21 (viññattiŋ katvā bhuñjituŋ na vaṭṭati); PvA 146.—*Two* kinds of viññatti are generally distinguished, viz. **kāya°** and **vacī°**, or intimation by body (gesture) and by voice: Dhs 665, 718; Miln 229 sq.; Vism 448, 530, 531. Cp. *Cpd.* 22, 264.

Viññāṇa (nt.) [fr. vi+**jñā**; cp. Vedic vijñāna cognition] (as special term in Buddhist metaphysics) a mental quality as a constituent of individuality, the bearer of (individual) life, life-force (as extending also over rebirths), principle of conscious life, general consciousness (as function of mind *and* matter), regenerative force, animation, mind as transmigrant, as transforming (according to individual kamma) one individual life (after death) into the next. (See also below, c & d). In this (fundamental) application it may be characterized as the sensory and perceptive activity commonly expressed by "mind." It is difficult to give any one word for v., because there is much difference between the old Buddhist and our modern points of view, and there is a varying use of the term in the Canon itself. In what may be a very old Sutta S II.95 v. is given as a synonym of citta (q. v.) and mano (q. v.), in opposition to kāya used to mean body. This simpler unecclesiastical, unscholastic popular meaning is met with in other suttas. E. g. the body (kāya) is when animated called sa-viññāṇaka (q. v. and cp. viññāṇatta). Again, v. was supposed, at the body's death, to pass over into another body (S I.122; III.124) and so find a support or platform (patiṭṭhā). It was also held to be an immutable, persistent substance, a view strongly condemned (M I.258). Since, nowever, the persistence of v. from life to life is declared (D II.68; S III.54), we must judge that it is only the immutable persistence that is condemned. V. was justly conceived more as "minding" than as "mind." Its form is participial. For later variants of the foregoing cp. Miln 86; PvA 63, 219.

Ecclesiastical scholastic dogmatic considers v. under the categories of (a) khandha; (b) dhātu; (c) paṭicca-samuppāda; (d) āhāra; (e) kāya. (a) V. as fifth of the five khandhas (q. v.) is never properly described or defined. It is an ultimate. But as a factor of animate existence it is said to be the discriminating (vijānāti) of e. g. tastes or sapid things (S III.87), or, again, of pleasant or painful feeling (M I.292). It is in no wise considered as a condition, or a climax of the other incorporeal khandhās. It is just one phase among others of mental life. In mediæval dogmatic it appears rather as the bare phenomenon of aroused attention, the other khandhās having been reduced to adjuncts or concomitants brought to pass by the arousing of v. (*Cpd.* 13), and as such classed under cetasikā, the older sankhārakkhandha.—(b) as dhātu, v. occurs only in the category of the four elements with space as a sixth element, and also where dhātu is substituted for khandha (S III.10).—(c) In the chain of causation (**Paṭicca-samuppāda**) v. is conditioned by the sankhāras and is itself a necessary condition of **nāma-rūpa** (individuality). See e. g. S II.4, 6, 8, 12 etc.; Vin I.1; Vism 545 sq.= VbhA 150; Vism 558 sq.; VbhA 169 sq.; 192.—At S II.4= III.61 viññāṇa (in the Paṭicca-samuppāda) is defined in a similar way to the defⁿ under v.-ṭṭhiti (see c), viz. as a quality peculiar to (& underlying) each of the 6 senses: "katamaŋ viññāṇaŋ? cha-y-ime viññāṇa-kāyā (groups of v.), viz. cakkhu° sota° etc.," which means that viññāṇa is the apperceptional or energizing principle, so to speak the soul or life (substratum, animator, life-potency) of the sensory side of individuality. It arises through the mutual relation of sense and sense-object (M III.281, where also the 6 v.-kāyā). As such it forms a factor of rebirth, as it is grouped under upadhi (q. v.). Translations of S II.4: Mrs. Rh. D. (*K.S.* II.4) "consciousness"; Geiger (in Z. f. B. IV.62) "Erkennen."—(d) As one of the four āhāras (q. v.) v. is considered as the material, food or cause, through which comes rebirth (S II.13; cp. *B.Psy.* p. 62). As such it is likened to seed in the field of action (kamma) A I.223, and as entering (a body) at rebirth the phrase viññāṇassa avakkanti is used (D II.63; S II.91). In this connection the expression paṭisandhi-viññāṇa first appears in Ps I.52, and then in the Commentaries (VbhA 192; cf. Vism 548, 659 paṭisandhicitta); in Vism 554= VbhA 163, the v., here said to be located in the heart, is made out, at bodily death, "to quit its former 'support' and proceed (pavattati) to another by way of its mental object and other conditions." Another scholastic expression, both early and late, is abhisankhāra-v., or "endowment consciousness," viz. the individual transmigrant or transmitted function (viññāṇa) which supplies the next life with the accumulation of individual merit or demerit or indifference, as it is expressed at Nd^2 569^a in def^n of v. (on Sn 1055: yaŋ kiñci sampajānāsi . . . panujja viññāṇaŋ bhave na tiṭṭhe): puññ' ābhisankhāra-sahagata-viññāṇaŋ, apuññ' . . ., ānejj' . . . — Under the same heading at Nd^2 569^b we find abhisankhāra v. with ref. to the sotāpatti-stage, i. e. the beginning of salvation, where it is said that by the gradual disappearance of abhis.-v. there are still 7 existences left before nāma-rūpa (individuality) entirely disappears. The climax of this development is "anupādi-sesa nibbāna-dhatu," or the nibbāna stage without a remainder (parinibbāna), which is characterized not by an abhisankhāra-v., but by the carimaka-v., or the *final* vital spark, which is now going to be extinct. This passage is referred to at DhsA 357, where the first half is quoted literally.—(e) As kāya i. e. group, v. is considered psycho-physically, as a factor in sense-perception (D III.243, M III.281, etc.), namely, the contact between sense-organ and object (medium, μεταξύ was not taken into account) produces v. of sight, hearing etc. The three factors constitute the v.-kāya of the given sense. And the v. is thus bound to bodily process as a catseye is threaded on a string (D II.76). Cp. above c.

Other applications of the term v., both Canonical and mediæval: on details as to attributes and functions, see Vin I.13 (as one of the khandhas in its quality of anattā, cp. S IV.166 sq.); D III.223 (as khandha); S II.101 sq. (°assa avakkanti); III.53 sq. (°assa gati, āgati, cuti etc.); A I.223 sq.; III.40; Sn 734 (yaŋ kiñci dukkhaŋ sambhoti, sabbaŋ viññāṇa-paccayā), 1037 (nāma-rūpa destroyed in consequence of v. destruction), 1073 (cavetha v. [so read for bhavetha]; v. at this passage expl^d as "punappaṭisandhi-v." at Nd^2 569^c); 1110 (uparujjhati); Ps I.53 sq., 153 sq.; II.102; Vbh 9 sq., 53 sq., 86; Nett 15 (nāma-rūpa v.-sampayutta), 16 (v.-hetuka n.-r.), 17 (nirodha), 28, 79, 116 (as khandha); Vism 529 (as simple, twofold, fourfold etc.), 545 = VbhA 150 sq. (in detail as product of sankhāras & in 32 groups); VbhA 172 (twofold: vipāka & avipāka); DhA IV.100.

-ānañc'āyatana infinitude (-sphere) of life-force or mind-matter D I.35, 184, 223; III.224, 262, 265; Nett 26, 39. It is the second of the Āruppa-jhānas; see jhāna. **-āhāra** consciousness (i. e. vital principle) sustenance: see above *d* and cp. Dhs 70, 126; Nett 114 sq.; Vism 341. **-kāya**: see above *e*. **-khandha** life-force as one of the aggregates of physical life D III.233; Tikp 61; DhsA 141; VbhA 21, 42. **-ṭṭhiti** viññāṇa-duration, phase of mental life. The emphasis is on duration or *continuation* rather than place, which would be ṭṭhāna. There are (*a*) 4 v.-durations with regard to their "storing" (abhisankhāra) quality, viz. combinations of v. (as the governing, mind-principle) with each of the 4 other khandhas or aggregates of material life (rūpa, vedanā, saññā, sankhārā), v. animating or bringing them to consciousness in any kind of life-appearance; and (*β*) 7 v.-durations with regard to their "regenerating" (new-life comb^n or rebirth = paṭisandhi) quality, viz. the 4 planes of var. beings (from men to devas), followed by the 3 super-dimensional stages (the ānañc' āyatanas) of ākāsa-infinitude, viññāṇa-infin. & ākiñ-cañña-infin. — Passages in the Canon: (*a*) as 4: D I I.262 sq.; S III.53 sq. ("standing for consciousness" & "platform," °patiṭṭhā S III.54; *K.S.* III.45) — (*β*) the 7: D II.68 sq.; III.253 (trsl^n "station of consciousness"), 282; = A IV.39. Both the 4 and the 7 at Nd^2 570. Cp. under a slightly diff. view S II.65 (yaŋ ceteti . . . ārammaṇaŋ . . . hoti viññāṇassa ṭhitiyā). — See also Ps I.22, 122; Sn 1114; Nett 31, 83 sq.; Vism 552; VbhA 169. **-dhātu** mind-element, which is the 6th dhātu after the 4 great elements (the mahābhūtāni) and ākāsa-dhātu as fifth (this expl^d as "asamphuṭṭha-dhātu" at VbhA 55, whereas v.-dhātu as "vijānana-dhātu") D III.247; Vbh 85, 87; VbhA 55; cp. A I.176; M III.31, 62, 240; S II.248. **-vīthi** the road of mind (fig.), a mediæval t. t. for process in sense-perception KhA 102.

Viññāṇaka (adj.) [viññāṇa + ka] having life or consciousness or sense, endowed with vitality. Found in the four Nikāyas only in *one* standard passage in the same connection, viz. sa-viññāṇaka kāya "the body with its viññāṇa" (i. e. life-force or mind): S II.253; III.80, 169; V.311; A I.132; IV.53. Thus (sa°) should be read at all passages. — Later in contrast pair sa° and a°, i. e. with life & without, alive & lifeless, animate & inanimate, e. g. J I.466, 468; DhA I.6; PvA 130.

Viññāṇatta (nt.) [abstr. formation fr. viññāṇa] the fact of being endowed with viññāṇa S III.87; PvA 63.

Viññāta [pp. of vijānāti] apperceived, (re)cognized, understood, cogitated (*Cpd.* 37), learned Sn 323 (°dhamma, one who has recognized or understood the Dhamma); Vv 44^{18} (= viññāta-sāsana-dhamma VvA 192); J I.2; Sdhp 429. — Often in sequence diṭṭha suta muta viññāta to denote the whole range of the cognitional & apperceptional faculties (see muta), e. g. D III.232; Sn 1086, 1122.

Viññātar [n. ag. of viññāta] a perceiver, one who apperceives or takes to heart, a learner D I.56; A III.169; IV.196 (sotar, uggahetar, v.).

Viññāpaka (adj.) [fr. viññāpeti] clever in instruction, able to instruct S V.162 = Miln 373; It 107.

Viññāpana (adj.) [fr. viññāpeti] instructing, informing A II.51, 97. — f. **viññāpanī** instructive, making clear (of speech) D I.114 (atthassa viññāpaniyā = viññāpana-samatthāya DA I.282); A III.114; Dh 408 (= attha° DhA IV.182); Sn 632.

Viññāpaya (adj.) [grd. of viññāpeti, = *viññāpya] accessible to instruction; only in cpds du° & su° indocile & docile S I.138; D II.38; Nd^2 235^3; Ps I.121; II.195; Vbh 341.

Viññāpita [pp. of viññāpeti] instructed, informed; su° well taught Miln 101.

Viññāpetar [n. ag. of viññāpita] an instructor, teacher D I.56; A IV.196.

Viññāpeti [Caus. II. of vijānāti] to address, inform, teach, instruct; to give to understand; to appeal to, to beg Vin I.54; IV.264; D I.251; J III.72 (to intimate); Miln 229; VvA 72, 181. — pp. viññāpita.

Viññāya & **viññāyati** see vijānāti.

Viññutā & **viññūtā** (f.) [fr. viññu] discretion; in phrase viññutaŋ pāpuṇāti to reach the years of discretion or puberty Vin I.269; II.278; J I.231; III.437; PvA 3.

Viññupasaṭṭha [vi + ni + upassaṭṭha, pp. of sṛj (?)] unattacked, not deficient, unmolested, undisturbed: is Kern's (*Toev.* s. v.) proposed reading for viññū-pasattha ("extolled by the wise") at S II.70 (reads ṭṭh); V.343; D II.80; III.245: all identical passages. We consider Kern's change unnecessary: anupasaṭṭha would have been the most natural expression if it had been meant in the sense suggested by Kern.

Viññū (adj.) [cp. Sk. vijña] intelligent, learned, wise D I.163; S I.9; III.134; IV.41 sq., 93, 339; A II.228; V.15; It 98; Sn 39, 294, 313, 396, 403; Ps II.19, 21; Miln 21; DA I.18; VvA 87; PvA 130, 226; Sdhp 45. — a° DhA III.395.

Viññeyya (adj.) [grd. of vijānāti] to be recognized or apperceived (of the sense objects: cakkhu-viññeyya rūpa, etc.) D I.245; M III.291; A III.377; IV.404 sq., 415, 430; Nd[1] 24. — su° easily understood VvA 258.

Viṭapa [cp. Epic Sk. viṭapa] the fork of a tree, a branch J I.169, 215, 222; III.28; VI.177 (nigrodha°).

Viṭapin [viṭapa+in] a tree, lit. "having branches" J VI.178.

Viṭabhī (f.) [=Sk. viṭapin] the fork of a tree M I.306; J II.107; III.203.

Vitakka [vi+takka] reflection, thought, thinking; "initial application" (*Cpd.* 282). — Def[d] as "vitakkanaŋ vitakko, ūhanan ti vuttaŋ hoti" at Vism 142 (with simile on p. 143, comparing vitakka with vicāra: kumbhakārassa daṇḍa-ppahārena cakkaŋ bhamayitvā, bhājanaŋ karontassa uppīḷana-hattho viya vitakko (like the hand holding the wheel tight), ito c' ito sañcaraṇa-hattho viya vicāro: giving **vitakka** the characteristic of fixity & steadiness, **vicāra** that of movement & display). — D II.277 ("pre-occupation" trsl[n]: see note *Dial.* II.311); III.104, 222, 287 (eight Mahāpurisa°); M I.114 (dvidhā-kato v.), 377; S I.39, 126, 186, 203; II.153; IV.69, 216; A II.36; III.87 (dhamma°); IV.229 (Mahāpurisa°), 353 (°upaccheda); Sn 7, 270 sq., 970, 1109; J I.407 (Buddha°, Sangha°, Nibbāna°); Nd[1] 386, 493, 501 (*nine*); Nd[2] s. v. takka; Ps I.36, 136, 178; Pv III.5[8]; Pug 59, 68; Vbh 86, 104 (rūpa°, sadda° etc.), 228 (sa°), 362 (akusala°); Dhs 7, 160, 1268; Tikp 61, 333, 353; Vism 291 (°upaccheda); Miln 82, 309; DhsA 142; DhA IV.68; VbhA 490; PvA 226, 230. —**kāma°**, vihiŋsā°, **vyāpāda°** (sensual, malign, cruel thought): D III.226; S II.151 sq.; III.93; A I.148, 274 sq.; II.16, 117, 252; III.390, 428. Opp. nekkhamma°, **avyāpāda°**, avihiŋsā° A I.275; II.76; III.429. —vitakka is often comb[d] with vicāra or "initial & sustained application" Mrs. Rh. D.; *Cpd.* 282; "reflection & investigation" Rh. D.; to denote the whole of the mental process of thinking (viz. fixing one's attention and reasoning out, or as *Cpd.* 17 expl[s] it "vitakka is the directing of concomitant properties towards the object; vicāra is the continued exercise of the mind on that object." See also above def[n] at Vism 142). Both are properties of the *first* jhāna (called sa-vitakka sa-vicāra) but are discarded in the *second* jhāna (called a°). See e. g. D. I.37; S IV.360 sq.; A IV.300; Vin III.4; Vism 85; and formula of jhāna. The same of pīti & samādhi at Vbh 228, of paññā at Vbh 323. The same comb[n] (vitakka+vicāra) at foll. passages: D III.219 (of samādhi which is either sa°, or a°, or avitakka vicāra-matta); S IV.193; V.111; A IV.409 sq., 450; Nett 16; Miln 60, 62; Vism 453. Cp. rūpa- (sadda- etc.) vitakka+rūpa- (sadda- etc.) vicāra A IV.147; V.360; Vbh 103. — On term (also with vicāra) see further: *Cpd.* 40, 56, 98, 238 sq., 282 (on difference between v. & manasikāra); *Expos.* I.188[n]; *Kvu trsl[n]* 238[1]. — Cp. pa°, pari°.

Note. Looking at the comb[n] **vitakka+vicāra** in earlier and later works one comes to the conclusion that they were once used to denote one & the same thing: just thought, thinking, only in an emphatic way (as they are also semantically synonymous), and that one has to take them as *one* expression, like jānāti passati, without being able to state their difference. With the advance in the Sangha of intensive study of terminology they became distinguished mutually. Vitakka became the inception of mind, or attending, and was no longer applied, as in the Suttas, to thinking in general. The expl[ns] of Commentators are mostly of an edifying nature and based more on popular etymology than on natural psychological grounds.

Vitakkana (nt.)= vitakka Vism 142.

Vitakkita [pp. of vitakketi] reflected, reasoned, argued DA I.121. Cp. pari°.

Vitakketi [Denom. fr. vitakka] to reflect, reason, consider S I.197, 202; IV.169; V.156; A II.36; Miln 311. — pp. vitakkita.

Vitacchika at S II.99= IV.188 read vitaccika (q. v.).

Vitacchikā (f.) [cp. *Sk. (medical) vicarcikā] scabies Nd[2] 304[I] (as roga).

Vitacchita [pp. of vitaccheti] planed, smoothed; su° well carded (of a cīvara) Vin III.259.

Vitaccheti [vi+taccheti] 1. tear, pluck, pick to pieces; in simile M I.364 (+virājeti)= S II.255 (reads vibhajeti for virājeti)= Vin III.105 (id.). — 2. to smoothe: see pp. vitacchita.

Vitaṇḍā (f.) [cp. Epic Sk. vitaṇḍā, e. g. Mbh 2, 1310; 7, 3022] tricky disputation, frivolous or captious discussion; in cpds. vitaṇḍa°: °vāda sophistry SnA 447; DA I.247; °vādin a sophist, arguer DhsA 3 (so read for vidaḍḍha); VbhA 9, 51, 319, 459. See **lokāyata.**

Vitata [pp. of vitanoti] stretched, extended, diffused S I.207; Sn 272, 669 (v. l. vitthata); J I.356 (tanta° where the strings were stretched); Miln 102, 307; Mhvs 17, 31 (vallīhi v.) — nt. **vitata** a drum (with leather on both sides) VvA 37.

Vitatha (adj.) [vi+tatha; cp. Epic & Class. Sk. vitatha] untrue; nt. untruth D II.73 (na hi Tathāgatā vitathaŋ bhaṇanti); Sn 9 sq.; Vv 53[15] (=atatha, musā ti attho VvA 240); J V.112; VI.207; Ps 104; DA I.62. —**avitatha** true S II.26; V.430; Miln 184; Sdhp 530; DA I.65.

Vitanoti (*vitanati) [vi+tanoti] to stretch out, spread out; poet. ger. **vitanitvāna** J VI.453. — Pass. **vitaniyyati** ibid. — pp. **vitata.** Cp. **vitāna.**

Vitaraṇa (nt.) [fr. vitarati] overcoming, getting through M I.147 (kankhā°); Miln 233 (id.), 351; Sdhp 569.

Vitarati [vi+tarati] 1. to go through, come through, overcome Sn 495, 779 (ger. °eyya, taken as Pot. at Nd[1] 57: oghaŋ samatikkameyya), 941, 1052; Pv III.2[4] (vitaritvā = vitiṇṇo hutvā PvA 181, q. v. for detail). — 2. to perform J II.14 (bubhukkhito no vitarāsi bhottuŋ; v. l. visahāmi). — pp. vitiṇṇa.

Vitāna (m. & nt.) [fr. vi+**tan**] spread-out, canopy, awning Vin IV.279; J I.40, 62, 83; DhA II.42; SnA 447; VvA 32, 173; PvA 154. See also cela°.

Vitiṇṇa [pp. of vitarati] 1. overcome or having overcome, gone through, conquered Dh 141 (°kankha); Sn 514 (id.), 746; PvA 181. — 2. given up, rejected, abandoned Dh 176 (°paraloka); J IV.447 (=pariccatta C.).

Vitudati [vi+tudati] to strike, prick, nudge, knock, push, attack D I.105; S IV.225; A III.366; Sn 675; Ud 67; J II.163, 185. — Pass. **vitujjati** Vism 505; VbhA 104, 108. — pp. **vitunna.**

Vitunna [pp. of vitudati] struck, pricked, pushed J III.380.

Vitureyyati at J V.47 is not clear. The v. l. is vitariyati; the C. expl[s] by tuleti tīreti, i. e. contemplates, examines. Kern, *Toev.* s. v. discusses it in detail & proposes writing **vituriyata** (3rd sg. praet. med.), & expl[s] at "get over" [cp. Vedic tūryati overcome, fr. **tur** or **tvar**= P. tarati[2]]. Dutoit trsl[s] "überstieg."

Vitta[1] [orig. pp. of vindati= Av. vista, Gr. ἄιστος, Lat. vīsus; lit. one who has found, acquired or recognized; but already in Vedic meaning (as nt.) "acquired possessions"] property, wealth, possessions, luxuries S I.42; Sn 181 sq., 302; J V.350, 445; VI.308; Pv II.8[1] (= vittiyā upakaraṇa-bhūtaŋ vittaŋ PvA 106). — Often in phrase °**ūpakaraṇa** possessions & means, i. e. wealth,

e. g. D I.134; S I.71; IV.324; Pug 52; Dh I.295; PvA 3, 71. Vittaŋ is probably the right reading S I.126 (15) for cittaŋ. Cf. p. 123 (3); *K.S.* I.153, n. 3.

Vitta[2] (adj.) [identical with vitta[1]] gladdened, joyful, happy J III.413 (= tuṭṭha); IV.103; Vv 41[4] (= tuṭṭha C.); 44[14] (id.), 49[5] (id.).

Vitta[3] [pp. of **vic** to sift, cp. Sk. vikta] see **vi°**.

Vittaka (adj.) [fr. vitta[1]] possessing riches, becoming rich by (-°) J I.339 (lañca°); IV.267 (miga°), VI.256 (jūta°).

Vittakatā (f.) [vittaka + tā] in suta° "the fact of getting rich through learning" as an expl[n] of the name Sutasoma J V.457 (for auspiciousness). Dutoit trsl[s] quite differently: "weil er am Keltern des Somatrankes seine Freude hatte," hardly correct.

Vitti (f.) [cp. Sk. vitti, fr. **vid**] prosperity, happiness, joy, felicity A III.78; J IV.103; VI.117; Kvu 484; Th 1, 609; Dhs 9 (cp. DhsA 143); PvA 106.

Vittha (nt.) [vi + **sthā** ?] a bowl, in surā° for drinking spirits J V.427; DhA III.66.

Vitthaka (nt.) [fr. vittha] a small bowl, as receptacle (āvesana°) for needles, scissors & thimbles Vin II.117.

Vitthata[1] [pp. of vi + **stṛ**] 1. extended, spread out, wide M. I.178; Vin I.297; J V.319; Miln 311; SnA 214; PvA 68 (doubtful !). — 2. wide, spacious (of a robe) Vin III.259. — 3. flat SnA 301.

Vitthata[2] [pp. of vitthāyati (?). A difficult form !] perplexed, confused, hesitating Miln 36 (bhīta +). Ed. Müller, *P.Gr.* 102 considers it as pp. of vi + **tras** to tremble, together with vitthāyati & vitthāyi.

Vitthambhana (nt.) [fr. vi + thambhati] making firm, strengthening, supporting Vism 351 (cp. DhsA 335).

Vitthambheti [vi + thambheti] to make firm, strengthen DhsA 335.

Vitthāyati [vi + **styā**: see under thīna] to be embarrassed or confused (lit. to become quite stiff), to be at a loss, to hesitate Vin I.94 = II.272; aor. vitthāsi (vitthāyi ?) ibid. [the latter taken as aor. of **tras** by Geiger, *P.Gr.* § 166]. — pp. vitthata[2] & vitthāyita.

Vitthāyitatta (nt.) [abstr. fr. vitthāyita, pp. of vitthāyati] perplexity, hesitation D I.249.

Vitthāra [fr. vi + **stṛ**] 1. expansion, breadth; instr. vitthārena in breadth Miln 17; same abl. vitthārato J I.49. — 2. extension, detail; often in C. style, introducing & detailed explanation of the subject in question, either with simple statement "vitthāro" (i. e. here the foll. detail; opp. sankhepa), e. g. DA I.65, 229; SnA 325 [cp. same in BSk. "vistaraḥ," e. g. Divy 428], or with cpds. °kathā SnA 464; PvA 19; °desanā SnA 163; °vacana SnA 416. Thus in general often in instr. or abl. as adv. "in detail," in extenso (opp. sankhittena in short): vitthārena D III.241; S IV.93; A II.77, 177, 189; III.177; Pug 41; PvA 53, 113; vitthārato Vism 351, 479; PvA 71, 77, 81. Cp. similarly BSk. vistarena kāryaŋ Divy 377.

Vitthāratā (f.) [fr. vitthāra] explicitness, detail Nett 2. As vitthāraṇā at Nett 9.

Vitthārika (adj.) [vitthāra + ika] 1. wide-spread Miln 272. — 2. widely famed, renowned Sn 693; J IV.262. See also bahujañña.

Vitthārita [pp. of vitthāreti] detailed, told in full Vism 351; Mhvs 1, 2 (ati° with too much detail; opp. sankhitta).

Vitthāriyati [Denom. fr. vitthāra] to expand, to go into detail Nett 9.

Vitthāreti [fr. vitthāra] 1. to spread out A III.187. — 2. to expand, detail, give in full Vism 351; SnA 94, 117, 127, 274 and passim. — pp. vitthārita; f.pp. vithāretabba.

Vitthiṇṇa [vi + thiṇṇa] "spread out," wide, large, extensive, roomy J II.159 (so read for vittiṇṇa); Miln 102, 283, 311, 382; DhsA 307; SnA 76; VvA 88; Sdhp 391, 617. Cp. pari°.

Vidaŋsaka (ad.) [fr. vidaŋseti] showing; **danta°** showing one's teeth (referring to laughter) A I.261; J III.222.

Vidaŋseti [vi + daŋseti = dasseti] to make appear, to show A I.261; Th 2, 74; J V.196; Miln 39. Cp. pa°.

Vidaḍḍha [vi + daḍḍha] in redupl.-iter. cpd. daḍḍhavidaḍḍha-gatta "with limbs all on fire" Miln 303.

***Vidati** see vindati.

Vidatthi (f.) [cp. Vedic vitasti; see Geiger, *P.Gr.* 38[3]] a span (of 12 angulas or finger-breadths) Vin III.149 (dīghaso dvādasa vidatthiyo sugata-vidatthiyā); IV.279; J I.337; III.318; Miln 85; Vism 65, 124, 171, 175, 408; DhA III.172; IV.220; VbhA 343 (dvādas' angulāni vidatthi; dve vidatthiyo ratanaŋ, etc.).

Vidahati [vi + dahati; **dhā**] to arrange, appoint, assign; to provide; to practise. — Pres. vidahati: see saŋ°; vidadhāti J VI.537; vidheti J V.107. Pot. vidahe Sn 927 (= vidaheyya Nd[1] 382); aor. vidahi J V.347. — Perf. 3rd pl. vidadhu [Sk. vidadhuḥ] J VI.284. — inf. vidhātuŋ Vin I.303 (bhesajjaŋ); ger. vidhāya Mhvs 26, 12 (ārakkhaŋ, posting a guard). — grd. vidheyya in meaning "obedient," tractable J VI.291. — pp. vihita.

Vidāraṇa (nt.) [fr. vidāreti] splitting, rending Dhtp 247 (in expl[n] of **dar**), 381 (do of **bhid**).

Vidārita [pp. of vidāreti] split, rent Sdhp 381.

Vidāreti [vi + dāreti: see under darī] to split, rend J I.340. — pp. vidārita.

Vidālana (nt.) [fr. vidāleti] breaking open, bursting, splitting Miln 1.

Vidālita [pp. of vidāleti] split, broken, burst J I.493; PvA 220.

Vidāleti [vi + dāleti; see dalati] to break open, split, burst Th 1, 184; PvA 135, 185. — pp. vidālita.

Vidita [pp. of vindati] known, found (out) D III.100; S V.180; Sn 436, 1052; Mhvs 17, 4; DA I.135 (a°).

Viditatta (nt.) [abstr. fr. vidita] the fact of having found or known, experience J II.53.

Vidisā (f.) [vi + disā] an intermediate point of the compass S I.224; III.239; Sn 1122; J I.20, 101; VI.6, 531.

Vidugga (adj.-n.) [vi + dugga] hard to walk; troublesome, difficult, painful. — (m.) difficult passage; difficulty, distress D III.27; A III.128; J III.269; IV.271.

Vidura (adj.) [fr. **vid**, cp. Sk. vidura] wise, clever J V.399 (= paṇḍita C.). Cp. vidhura 2.

Vidū (adj.) [Vedic vidu] clever, wise, knowing, skilled in (-°) S I.62 (loka°); V.197; Vin II.241 (pl. paracittaviduno); Sn 677 (vidūhi), 996; J V.222 (dhamma°); Vv 30[11] (= sappañña VvA 127); Miln 276; Mhvs 15, 51 (ṭhān' āṭhāṇa° knowing right & wrong sites). — In Pass. sense in dubbidū hard to know J V.446. — For vidū (vidu) "they knew" see vindati.

Vidūpita at Ud 71 (vitakkā vidūpitā) is to be read as vidhūpita.

Vidūra (adj.) [vi+dūra] far, remote, distant A II.50 (su°). Mostly neg. a° not far, i. e. near Sn 147; PvA 14, 31, 78, 81.

Vidūsita (adj.) [vi+dūsita] corrupted, depraved PvA 178 (°citta).

Videsa [vi+desa; cp. disā at Vin I.50] foreign country Miln 326; VvA 338.

Vidomanassā (f.) [vi+domanassa] absence of dejection Vism 504=VbhA 105.

Viddasu (adj.) [another form of vidvā=Sk. vidvān: see under vindati] skilled, wise M I.65 (gen. sg. & nom. pl. viddasuno), 310 (id.). Usually in neg. form aviddasu foolish Vin II.296=A II.56 (pl. aviddasū); S v.1; Th 2, 164 (pl. aviddasū); Sn 762 (=bāla C.); Dh 268=Nd² 514 (=aviññū DhA III.395); PvA 18.

Viddesa [fr. vi+disa] enmity, hatred J III.353; ThA 268.

Viddesanā (f.) [abstr. formation fr. viddesa, cp. disatā²] enmity Th 2, 446; J III.353.

Viddesin (adj.-n.) [vi+desin; see dessin] hating; an enemy Th 1, 547.

Viddessati [vi+dessati] to hate Th 2, 418. — grd. viddesanīya to be hated, hateful Sdhp 82.

Viddha¹ [pp. of vijjhati] pierced, perforated; hit, struck, hurt Sn 331; Nd¹ 414 (sallena); Miln 251 (eaten through by worms); Sdhp 201 (kaṇṭakena).

Viddha² (adj.) [cp. *Sk. vīdhra clear sky] clear; only in phrase viddha vigata-valāhaka deva a clear sky without a cloud Vin I.3; M I.317=S I.65=III.156=v.44=It 20.

Viddhaŋsa [fr. vidhaŋsati] demolition, destruction J IV.58 (°kārin).

Viddhaŋsati [vi+dhaŋsati] to fall down, to be shattered, to be ruined Miln 237; PvA 125 (Pot. °eyya). —Caus. viddhaŋseti to shatter, to destroy S III.190 (both trs. & intrs., the latter for °ati); J II.298; III.431; v.100; DA I.265; Nd¹ 5 (vikirati vidhameti viddhaŋseti: see also under vikirati). — pp. viddhasta & viddhaŋsita.— Pass. viddhaŋsīyati to drop or to be destroyed, to come to ruin DA I.18=DhsA 19 (suttena sangahitāni pupphāni na vikiriyanti na v.).

Viddhaŋsana (adj.-nt.) [fr. viddhaŋseti; cp. BSk. vidhvaŋsana Divy 180] shattering, destruction (trs. & intrs.), undoing, making disappear; adj. destroying S IV.83; Miln 351 (kosajja°); J I.322; v.267 (adj.); Vism 85 (vikkhepa+); VvA 58, 161 (adj.). — Often in phrase (denoting complete destruction): anicc-ucchādana-parimaddana-bhedana-viddhaŋsana-dhamma, e. g. D I.76; M I.500; A IV.386; J I.146 [cp. Divy 180: śatana-patana-vikiraṇa-vidhvaŋsana-dharmatā; see also under vikiraṇa].

Viddhaŋsaka (adj.) [fr. viddhaŋsana] destroying DhsA 165.

Viddhaŋsanatā (f.) [abstr. formation fr. viddhaŋsana] quality of destruction, ability to destroy Vism 8.

Viddhaŋsita [pp. of viddhaŋseti] shattered, destroyed DhA III.129.

Viddhasta [pp. of viddhaŋsati] fallen to pieces, broken, destroyed M I.227; A II.50; Sn 542; J I.203; v.69, 401; Vv 63¹⁴ (=vinaṭṭha VvA 265).

Viddhā poet. ger. of vijjhati J VI.77.

Vidvā see under vindati.

Vidha¹ (adj. (-°) [=vidhā] of a kind, consisting of, -fold, e. g. aneka° manifold DA I.103; tathā° of such-kind, such-like Sn 772; ti° threefold D I.136; Sn 509; nānā° various PvA 53, 96, 113; bahu° manifold ThA 197; etc.

Vidha² [=vidha¹ as noun] form, kind Th 1, 428 (māna°). — There are several other meanings of vidha, which are, however, uncertain & rest on doubtful readings. Thus it occurs at Vin II.136 in meaning of "buckle" (v. l. pītha; C. silent); at Vin IV.168 in meaning "little box" (?); at DA I.269 as "carrying pole" (=kāca², but text D I.101 has "vividha").

Vidhamaka (adj.) [fr. vidhamati] one who throws away or does away with; destroying, clearing away Miln 344 (kilesa-mala-duggandha°).

Vidhamati & °**eti** [vi+**dhmā** in particular meaning of blowing i. e. driving asunder, cp. dhamati] (trs.) to destroy, ruin; do away with, scatter. — (intrs.) to drop off, fall away, to be scattered, to roll or whirl about. — Both vidhamati & °eti are used indiscriminately, although the Caus. °eti occurs mostly in meaning of "destroy." (1) vidhamati: S III.190; J I.284 (in play of words with dhamati to blow; aor. vidhami=viddhaŋsesi C.); VI.490 (vidhamaŋ te raṭṭhaŋ, is ruined); Miln 91, 226 (Mārasenaŋ), 237, 337 (intrs., with vikirati & viddhaŋsati). — (2) vidhameti: Nd¹ 5; J III.261 (poet. vidhamemasi [write °se!]=vidhamema, nāsema C.); v.309; Miln 39; PvA 168. — pp. vidhamita.

Vidhamana (nt.) [fr. vidhamati] destroying, scattering, dispersing Miln 244 (Maccu-sena°).

Vidhamita [pp. of vidhamati] destroyed Nd² 576ᴬ.

Vidhavā (f.) [Vedic vidhavā widow, vidhu lonely, vidhura separated, Av. vidavā=Goth. widuwō=Ohg. wituwa (Ger. Witwe=E. widow); Gr. ἠίθεος unmarried; Lat. vidua widow, etc., in all Idg. languages] a widow S I.170; A III.128; J VI.33; Miln 288; Vism 17; PvA 65, 161; VbhA 339.

Vidhā (f.) [cp. Sk. vidhā] 1. mode, manner, sort, kind; proportion, form, variety D III.103 (ādesana°); Th 2, 395 (cakkhu° "shape of an eye" trslⁿ); VbhA 496 (in explⁿ of kathaŋ-vidha: "ākāra-saṇṭhānaŋ vidhā nāma"); DA I.222 (iddhi°), 294 (in explⁿ of tividha-yañña: "ettha vidhā vuccati ṭhapanā" i. e. performance, arrangement), 299 (similarly tisso vidhā=tīṇi ṭhapanāni; of yañña). — Used as (abl.) adv. vidhā in meaning "variously" at Pv II.9⁵² (C. explⁿ=vidhātabba, not quite correctly; PvA 135). Perhaps the phrase vidhā-samatikkanta is to be explained in this way, viz. "excelling in a variety of ways, higher than a variety (of things)" or perhaps better: "going beyond all distinctions" (i. e. of personality); free from prejudice [i. e. No. 2] S II.253; III.80, 136, 170; A IV.53. — 2. (ethically) in special sense: a distinctive feature (of a person as diff. from others), a "mode" of *pride* or delusion, a "form" of *conceit*. As such specified as *three* kinds of conceit (tisso vidhā), viz. "seyyo 'ham asmi," "sadiso 'ham asmi," & "hīno 'ham asmi" (i. e. I am better than somebody else, equal to, & worse than somebody else). See e. g. D III.216; S I.12; III.48, 80, 127; v.56, 98; Nd¹ 195; Vbh 367; Sn 842; VbhA 496 (māno va vidhā nāma). — The adj. form is vidha: see sep.

Vidhātar [n. ag. of vidahati] provider, disposer J v.221 (dhātā vidhātā, as of Viśvakarman: cp. Macdonell, *Vedic Mythology* p. 118).

Vidhāna (nt.) [fr. vi+**dhā**; Vedic vidhāna] 1. arrangement, get up, performance, process J III.178 (attano vidhānena "in his robes of office"); Vism 66 sq.; DhsA 168=Vism 122 (bhāvanā°); VbhA 69, 71 (manasikāra°); ThA 273 (id.). — 2. ceremony, rite J VI.202 (yañña°); Miln 3. — 3. assignment, disposition, provision J II.208

(vidhi-vidhāna-ññū ; C. expl^d v. as " koṭṭnāso vā saŋvidahanaŋ vā ") ; PvA 30. — 4. succession (as much as " supplement ") KhA 216 ; SnA 23 (note 2). — Cp. saŋvidahana & saŋvidhāna.

Vidhānavant (adj.) [vidhāna + vant] making dispositions, careful in providing, circumspect, considerable J VI.287.

Vidhāyaka [fr. vi + dhā] providing PvA 60.

Vidhāvati [vi + dhāvati] to run about, roam, cover space (acc.), stray S I.37 ; Sn 411, 939 ; Nd¹ 414 ; DA I.39.

Vidhi (f.) [fr. vi + dhā, cp. Ved. vidhi] 1. form, way ; rule, direction, disposition, method, motto Vism 278 (manasikāra°, eightfold) ; PvA 78 (dāna° = dāna), 126 ; VvA 82. — instr. vidhinā in due form Mhvs 14, 52 ; PvA 130 ; Sdhp 336. — 2. luck, destiny J II.243 (°rahita unlucky).

Vidhutika [etym. ?] a wreath Vin II.10 ; III.180.

Vidhunāti [vi + dhunāti] to shake S I.197 ; Miln 399 ; Vism 71. — 2. to remove, to skin (an animal) Vin I.193.

Vidhura (adj.) [Vedic vidhura : see vidhavā] 1. destitute, lonely ; miserable, wretched J V.399 (so read for vidura ; according to Kern, *Toev.* s. v., but doubtful). — 2. [vi + dhura] " burdenless," unequalled Sn 996 (= vigata-dhura, appaṭima SnA 583) ; A I.116 (here in meaning " clever," perhaps = vidura ; spelt vidhūra). Cp. Np. Vidhura KhA 128 ; SnA 201 (as Vidhūra at J IV.361).

Vidhūpana (adj.-nt.) [fr. vidhūpeti] fanning, a fan Vin II.130 ; IV.263 ; A II.130 ; Nd² 562 ; Vv 33⁴² (= caturassa vījani) VvA 147 ; VbhA 71.

Vidhūpita [pp. of vidhūpeti] scattered, destroyed Sn 472 (= daḍḍha SnA 409) ; Ud 71 (so read for vidūpita).

Vidhūpeti (°dhūpayati) [vi + dhūpayati] 1. to fumigate, perfume, diffuse Miln 252. — 2. to scatter, destroy Vin I.2 (vidhūpayaŋ Māra-senaŋ) ; S I.14 ; III.90 = A V.325 ; S IV.210 ; Ps II.167. — pp. vidhūpita.

Vidhūma (& vidhuma) (adj.) [vi + dhūma] " without smoke," i. e. passionless, quiet, emancipated S I.141 (*K.S.* : " no fume of vice is his ") ; Sn 460 (= kodhadhūma-vigamena v. SnA 405), 1048 (cp. Nd² 576 with long exegesis) ; Pv IV.1³⁴ (= vigata-micchā-vitakkadhūma PvA 230).

Vinaṭṭha [pp. of vinassati] destroyed VvA 265 ; PvA 55.

Vinata [pp. of vi + nam] bent, bending PvA 154 (°sākhā).

Vinadati [vi + nadati] to cry or shout out, to scold J III.147 (kāmaŋ vinadantu let them shout !). Cp. BSk. vinādita " reviled " Divy 540.

Vinaddha [pp. of vinandhati] covered, bound, intertwined Vin I.194 (camma°, onaddha +) ; J V.416 ; VI.589 (kañcanalatā° bheri) ; Vism 1 (= jaṭita saŋsibbita).

Vinandhati [vi + nandhati] to close, encircle, cover Mhvs 19, 48 ; Vism 253 (ppr. vinandhamāna : so read for vinaddh°). — pp. vinaddha.

Vinandhana (nt.) [fr. vi + nandhati] tying, binding Vin II.116 (°rajju rope for binding).

Vinaya [fr. vi + nī, cp. vineti] 1. driving out, abolishing destruction, removal Vin I.3 (asmi-mānassa), 235 = III.3 (akusalānaŋ dhammānaŋ vinayāya dhammaŋ desemi) ; S I.40 ; Sn 921 ; A I.91 (kodha°, upanāha°) ; II.34 (pipāsa°) ; IV.15 (icchā°) ; V.165 (id.) ; SnA 12 ; PvA 114 (atthassa mūlaŋ nikati°). Often in phrase rāga°, dosa°, moha°, e. g. S IV.7 sq. ; V.137 sq., 241 ; A IV.175 ; Nett 22. — 2. rule (in logic), way of saying or judging, sense, terminology (cp. iminā nayena) S IV.95 (ariyassa vinaye vuccati loko) ; A I.163 (ariyassa vinaye tevijjo one called a threefold wise in the nomenclature of the Buddhist) ; II.166 (ariyassa v.) ; SnA 403. — 3. norm of conduct, ethics, morality, good behaviour Sn 916, 974 ; J IV.241 (= ācāra-vinaya C.) ; A II.112 ; III.353 sq. (ariya-vinaye saddhā yassa patiṭṭhitā etc. faith established in Buddhist ethics). — 4. code of ethics, monastic discipline, rule, rules of morality or of canon law. In this sense applied to the large collection of rules which grew up in the monastic life and habits of the bhikkhus and which form the ecclesiastical introduction to the " Dhamma," the " doctrine," or theoretical, philosophical part of the Buddhist Canon. The history & importance of the Vinaya Piṭaka will be dealt with under the title " Vinaya " in the Dictionary of Names. Only a few refs. must suffice here to give a general idea. See also under Dhamma C., and in detail Geiger, *Dhamma* pp. 55-58. — Often comb^d with dhamma : dhammato vinayato ca on the ground of Dh. and V. Vin I.337 ; cp. II.247. — dhammo ca vinayo ca Vin I.356 ; II.285, 302 ; or (as (Dvandva) dhammavinaya (i. e. the teaching of the Buddha in its completeness) D I.229 ; Vin II.237 sq. ; M I.284 ; II.181 sq. ; A I.283 ; III.297, 327 ; S I.9 ; III.65 ; Ud 53 ; VvA 3. Often approaches the meaning of " Buddhist order," e. g. Vin I.69 ; D I.176 ; M I.68, 459, 480 ; III.127 ; S II.120 ; A I.185 ; II.123 ; V.122. — *See further* Vin II.96 (vinaye cheko hoti) ; A II.168 (ayaŋ dhammo, ayaŋ v., idaŋ Satthu-sāsanaŋ) ; Vism 522 ; VbhA 273 ; KhA 106, 151 ; SnA 4, 195, 310. —a-vinaya one who sins against the V. (like a-dhamma one who neglects the Dh.) Vin II.295 sq. ; III.174 ; A I.18 ; V.73 sq. — The division of the books of the Vinaya is given at DhsA 18. Its character (as shown by its name) is given in the foll. verse at DhsA 19 : " (vividha-visesa-) nayattā vinayanato c' eva kāya-vācānaŋ vinayy' attha-vidūhi ayaŋ vinayo Vinayo ti akkhāto," i. e. " Because it shows precepts & principles, and governs both deed and word, therefore men call this scripture V., for so is V. interpreted " (*Expos.* I. 23).

-aṭṭhakathā the (old) commentary on the Vinaya Vism 72, 272 ; VbhA 334 ; KhA 97. -ânuggaha taking up (i. e. following the rules) of the Vinaya Vin III.21 ; A I.98, 100 ; V.70. -kathā exposition of the Vinaya Vin IV.142. -dhara one who knows or masters the V. by heart, an expert in the V. Vin I.169 ; II.299 (with dhamma-dhara & mātikā-dhara) ; A I.25 ; II.147 ; III.78 sq., 179, 361 ; IV.140 sq. ; V.10 sq. ; J III.486 ; IV.219 ; Vism 41, 72 ; KhA 151 ; DhA II.30 (with dhamma-kathika & dhuta-vāda) [cp. BSk. vinayadhara Divy 21]. -piṭaka the V. Piṭaka KhA I 2, 97 ; VbhA 431. -vatthu chapter of the V. Vin II.307. -vādin one who professes the V. (or " speaking in accordance with the rules of conduct "), a V.-follower D I.4 (here expl^d by Bdhgh as " saŋvara-vinaya-pahāna-vinaya sannissitaŋ katvā vadatī ti " v. DA I.76, thus taking it as vinaya 3) = M III.49 = Pug 58 (trsl^n here : " speaking according to self-control ") ; D III.135, 175.

Vinayati see vineti.

Vinayana (nt.) [fr. vi + nī] 1. removing, removal Miln 318 (pipāsā°) ; PvA 39 (soka°). — 2. instruction, discipline, setting an example J V.457 (conversion) ; Miln 220.

Vinaḷīkata (adj.) [vi + naḷa + kata, with naḷī for naḷa in comb^n with kṛ] lit. " having the reed or stem removed," rendered useless, destroyed M I.227 ; A II.39 ; Sn 542 (= ucchinna SnA 435) ; Th 1, 216 ; J VI.60 (viddhasta +, as at Sn 542).

Vinassati [vi + nassati] to be lost ; to perish, to be destroyed S IV.309 ; M II.108 (imper. vinassa " away with you ") ; J III.351 ; V.468 ; Pv III.4⁵ ; Vism 427. — pp. vinaṭṭha. Caus. vināseti.

Vinā (indecl.) [Vedic vinā = vi-nā (i. e. " not so "), of pron. base Idg. **no* (cp. nānā " so & so "), as in Sk. ca-na, Lat. ego-ne, pō-ne behind, etc. See na[1]] without, used as prep. (or post-position) with (usually) *instr.*, e. g. Vin II.132 (vinā daṇḍena without a support); PvA 152 (purisehi vinā without men); or *abl.*, e. g. Sn 589 (ñāti sanghā vinā hoti is separated from his relatives; cp. BSk. vinābhavati MVastu I.243); or *acc.*, e. g. Mhvs 3, 10 (na sakkā hi taŋ vinā). In comp[n] vinā-bhāva separation [cp. BSk. vinābhāva MVastu II.141] Sn 588, 805; Nd[1] 122; J III.95; IV.155; V.180; VI.482 (= viyoga C.).

Vināti [vi, by-form of vā to weave: see vāyati[1]] to weave J II.302; DhA I.428 (tantaŋ); inf. vetuŋ Vin II.150.—Pass. viyyati. Cp. upavīyati.—Caus. II. vināpeti to order to be woven Vin III.259 (= vāyāpeti).

Vināma (m.) & **Vināmana** (nt.) [fr. vināmeti] bending Miln 352 (°na); VbhA 272 (kāya-vināmanā, bending the body for the purpose of getting up; in expl[n] of vijambhikā); Dhtp 208.

Vināmeti [vi + nāmeti; Caus. of namati] to bend, twist Miln 107, 118.

Vināyaka [fr. vi + nī] 1. a leader, guide, instructor M II.94; Vv 16[7] (= veneyya-satte vineti VvA 83); ThA 69.—2. a judge J III.336.

Vināsa [vi + nāsa, of naś] destruction, ruin, loss D I.34 (+ uccheda & vibhava), 55; Pv II.7[10]; Vism 427 (so read for vinasa); DA I.120; PvA 102 (dhana°), 133.

Vināsaka (°ika) (adj.) [fr. vināsa] causing ruin; only neg. a° not causing destruction A III.38; IV.266, 270; J V.116.

Vināsana (adj.) [fr. vināsa], only neg. a° imperishable Dpvs IV.16.

Vināseti [Caus. of vinassati] 1. to cause destruction, to destroy, ruin, spoil Th 1, 1027; Sn 106; Pv II.7[8]; DA I.211; PvA 3 (dhanaŋ), 116; Sdhp 59, 314, 546.—2. to drive out of the country, to expel, banish J IV.200.

Vinigaḷati [vi + nigaḷati] to drop down Miln 349.

Viniggata [vi + niggata] coming (out) from J VI.78; DA I.140; DhA IV.46; Sdhp 23.

Viniggaha [vi + niggaha] checking, restraint Ps I.16; II.119.

Viniggilati [vi + niggilati] to throw out, to emit KhA 95.

Vinighātin (adj.) [fr. vi + nighāta] afraid of defeat, anxious about the outcome (of a disputation), in phrase vinighāti-hoti (for °ī-hoti) Sn 826, cp. Nd[1] 164.

Vinicchaya [vi + nicchaya; cp. Vedic viniścaya] 1. discrimination, distinction, thought, (firm) opinion; thorough knowledge of (-°) A III.354 (pāpakamma°); Sn 327 (dhamma°), 838 (= dvāsaṭṭhi diṭṭhi-vinicchayā Nd[1] 186), 867 (°ŋ kūrute; cp. Nd[1] 265); J III.205 (attha°); PvA 1, 112, 210 (kūṭa°), 287.—2. decision; (as t. t. in law:) investigation, trial, judgment (given by the king or his ministers) D II.58 (with ref. to lābha, expl[d] as deciding what to do with one's gains) = III.289 = A IV.400 = Vbh 390 (expl[d] at VbhA 512, where vinicchaya is said to be *fourfold*, viz. ñāṇa°, taṇhā°, diṭṭhi°, vitakka°); J II.2.—3. court house, hall of judgment J I.176; III.105; IV.122, 370; VI.333; Miln 332 (vinaya°, i. e. having the Vinaya as the law court in the City of Righteousness).—4. (as t. t. in logic & psychology:) (process of) judgment, detailed analysis, deliberation, consideration, ascertainment J V.60 (°ŋ vicāreti); VbhA 46 sq. (according to attha, lakkhaṇa, etc.), 83 sq. (id.); KhA 23, 75.
-kathā analytical discussion, exegesis, interpretation Vism 16; VbhA 291 (opp. pāḷi-vaṇṇanā). -ññū clever in deciding or giving judgment J III.205; V.367 (a°). -ṭṭhāna place of judgment, law court J V.229; DhA III.141; IV.215. -dhamma law practice J. V.125; DhA III.141. -vīthi process of judgment (in logic): see *Cpd.* 241. -sālā the law court(s) J IV.120; DhA III.380.

Viniccharati [vi + niccharati] to go out (in all directions) J IV.181.

Vinicchita [pp. of vinicchināti] discerned, decided, distinguished, detailed Vin I.65 (su°); J V.65 (a°); SnA 477; Sdhp 508.

Vinicchin (adj.) [fr. vinicchināti] discerning Th 1, 551.

Vinicchinana (nt.) [fr. vinicchināti] giving judgment J V.229.

Vinicchināti (°inati) & vinicchati [vi + nicchināti] to investigate, try; to judge, determine, decide J V.229; fut. vinicchissati Vin III.159; ger. vinicchinitvā Nd[1] 76; aor. vinicchini J II.2; inf. vinicchituŋ J I.148; DhA IV.215.—pp. vinicchita.

Vinijjita (adj.) [vi + nijjita] unvanquished Sdhp 318.

Vinidhāya (indecl.) [vi + nidhāya, ger. of vinidahati] lit. " misplacing," i. e. asserting or representing wrongly, giving a false notion of (acc.) Vin II.205, expl[d] at Vin IV.2; SnA 204.

Vinindati [vi + nindati] to censure, blame, reproach J II.346; VI.200.

Vinipāta [fr. vi + nipāteti] ruin, destruction; a place of suffering, state of punishment, syn. with apāya & duggati (with which often comb[d], plus niraya, e. g. Vin I.227; D I.82, 162; M I.73; A III.211; It 58; Pug 60): A V.169; Sn 278; J III.32; Miln 108; Vism 427 (where expl[d] as " vināsā nipatanti tattha dukkaṭakārino," together with duggati & niraya). The sotāpanna is called " avinipāta-dhammo," i. e. not liable to be punished in purgatory; see under sotāpanna, & cp. sym. term khīṇa-niraya A III.211.

Vinipātika (adj.) [fr. vinipāta] destined to suffer in purgatory, liable to punishment after death D II.69; III.253; M I.13, 390; A I.123; II.232 sq.; IV.39, 401; J V.117, 119.

Vinipāteti [vi + nipāteti] to bring to ruin, to destroy, to frustrate Vin I.298; J VI.71; VvA 208.

Vinibaddha (adj.) [vi + nibaddha] bound (to) S I.20; III.9; A III.311 (chanda-rāga°); IV.289 (id.); Nd[1] 30 (+ lagga etc.).

Vinibandha [vi + nibandha] bondage S II.17; III.135, 186; A I.66 (+ vinivesa); Sn 16.—The *five* cetaso vinibandhā (bondages of the mind) are: kāmesu rāgo, kāye rāgo, rūpe rāgo, yāvadatthaŋ udar' āvadehakaŋ bhuñjitvā seyya-sukhaŋ anuyogo, aññataraŋ deva-nikāyaŋ paṇidhāya brahmacariyaŋ; thus at D III.238; M I.103; A III.249; IV.461, 463 sq.; V.17; Vbh 377.

Vinibbhujati (or °bhuñjati) [vi + ni + bhujati] 1. [to **bhuj**, to bend, as in bhuja[1] & nibbhujati] to turn inside out Th 2, 471.—2. [to **bhuj** or **bhuñj** as in bhuñjati[2] and paribhuñjati[2]] to separate, cut off, remove M I.233; S III.141; IV.168 (spells wrongly jj).—3. [id.] to cleanse; fig. to sift out thoroughly, to distinguish, discriminate M I.292; J V.121 (avinibbhujaŋ, ppr.); Miln 63 (dòubled); Vism 438 (spelling wrongly jj); DhsA 311.—pp. **vinibbhutta**.

Vinibbhujana (nt.) [fr. vinibbhujati] turning inside out ThA 284.

Vinibbhutta [pp. of vinibbhujati] separated, distinguished, discriminated Vism 368.

Vinibbhoga[1] (adj.) [vi+nibbhoga] lacking, deprived of (-°), deficient ThA 248 (viññāṇa°).

Vinibbhoga[2] [fr. vinibbhujati 3] sifting out, distinction, discrimination Vism 306 (dhātu°), 368 (id.); neg. a° absence of discrimination, indistinction DhsA 47; used as adj. in sense of "not to be distinguished," indistinct at J III.428 (°sadda).

Vinibhindati [vi+ni+**bhid**] to break (right) through M I.233.

Vinimaya [fr. vi+nimināti] reciprocity, barter, exchange J II.369.

Vinimīleti [vi+nimīleti] to shut one's eyes Sdhp 189.

Vinimutta (Vinimmutta) [vi+nis+mutta] 1. released, free from J I.375 (mm); Sdhp 1, 4, 16, 225. — 2. discharged (of an arrow) DhA III.132 (mm).

Vinimoceti [vi+nis+moceti, cp. nimmoka] to free (oneself) from, to get rid of A III.92; Pug 68.

Viniyujjati [vi+niyujjati] to be connected with, to ensue, accrue PvA 29 (= upakappati).

Viniyoga [vi+niyoga] possession, application, use DhsA 151; VvA 157; PvA 171, 175.

Vinivaṭṭeti (& °vatteti) [vi+nivatteti] 1. to turn over, to repeat J I.25 (ṭṭ), 153 (ṭṭ), 190 (ṭṭ). — 2. to turn (somebody) away from, to distract Pv I.8[8] (read °vattayi for °vattanti); II.6[19] (°vattayi; aor.); J III.290 (ṭṭ). — 3. to roll over, to glide off J III.344 (ṭṭ); DhA II.51 (ṭṭ).

Vinivijjha (adj.) [grd. of vinivijjhati] to be pierced; in dubbinivijjha difficult to pierce, hard to penetrate J V.46.

Vinivijjhati [vi+ni+vijjhati] to pierce through & through J II.91; Miln 339; DhsA 253.

Vinivijjhana (nt.) [fr. vinivijjhati] piercing, perforating, penetrating DhsA 253; ThA 197 (in expl[n] of bahuvidha).

Vinividdha [pp. of vinivijjhati] pierced (all through), perforated J V.269; VI.105; Vism 222.

Viniveṭhana (& °nibbeṭhana) (nt.) [vi+nibbeṭhana] unwrapping, unravelling; fig. explaining, making clear, explanation, refutation Nd[2] 503 (diṭṭhi-saṅghātassa vinibbeṭhana; where id. p. at Nd[1] 343 reads vinivedhana, cp. nibbedha); Miln 96; VvA 297 (diṭṭhi-gaṇṭhi-viniveṭhana).

Viniveṭheti [vi+nibbeṭheti] 1. to disentangle, to unwrap Vin I.3, 276 (anta-gaṇṭhiŋ, the intestines); J II.283 (sarīraŋ); V.47. — 2. to disentangle oneself, to free oneself (from) A III.92; Pug 68.

Vinivesa [vi+nivesa] tie, bond, attachment A I.66 (+vinibandha).

Vinīta [pp. of vineti] led, trained, educated S V.261; A IV.310 (viyatta+); DhA II.66 (°vatthu); PvA 38. — avinīta not trained S IV.287; Vv 29[7]; Dhs 1003, 1217; suvinīta well trained S IV.287; opp. **dubbinīta** badly trained J V.284, 287. — **ratha-vinīta** (nt.) a relay M I.149.

Vinīlaka (adj.) [vi+nīlaka] of a bluish-black (purple) colour, discoloured J II.39 (of a cygnet, bastard of a swan & a crow, "resembling neither father nor mother," i. e. "black & white"). Usually applied to the colour of a corpse (purple, discoloured), the contemplation of which forms one of the 10 asubha-saññās: M I.88 (uddhumātaka+); Sn 200 (id.). — A. I.42; II.17; S V.129 sq.; Dhs 264; Nett 27; Miln 332; Vism 110, 178, 193.

Vinīvaraṇa (adj.) [vi+nīvaraṇa] unobstructed, unbiassed, unprejudiced A II.71; Sdhp 458. Usually in phrase °citta of an unbiassed mind, comb[d] with mudu-citta & udagga-citta: Vin I.16, 181; D I.110, 148; A IV.186. — Same in BSk., e.g. MVastu III.225; Divy 616 sq.

Vinudati is only found in Caus. form vinodeti.

Vinetar [n. ag. fr. vineti] teacher, instructor, guide Sn 484; Ps II.194 (netar, vinetar, anunetar); J IV.320.

Vineti [vi+neti; cp. vinaya] 1. to remove, put away, give up. — ppr. vinayaŋ J VI.499; Pot. 3rd sg. vinayetha Sn 361, & vineyya Sn 590; imper. vinaya Sn 1098, & vinayassu Sn 559. — ger. vineyya Sn 58 (but taken as Pot. at Nd[2] 577[b]); Pv II.3[34] (macchera-malaŋ); vinetvā J V.403 (chandaŋ); vinayitvā VvA 156, & vinayitvāna Sn 485 (bhakuṭiŋ). — 2. to lead, guide, instruct, train, educate A III.106 (inf. vinetuŋ); S IV.105 (Pot. vineyyaŋ & fut. vinessati); aor. vinesi Miln 13 (Abhidhamme); ger. vinayitvāna ThA 69 (Ap. v. 10); grd. vinetabba SnA 464, & vineyya Miln 12; cp. veneyya. — pp. **vinīta.**

Vinodaka (adj.) [fr. vinodeti, cp. nudaka & nūdaka] driving out, dispelling, allaying PvA 114 (parissama°).

Vinodana (adj.-nt.) [fr. vinodeti] dispelling, removal A III.387, 390; Sn 1086 (chanda-rāga°, = pahāna etc. Nd[2] 578); Miln 285; DA I.140 (niddā°); DhA I.41 (tama°, adj.); PvA 38 (soka°).

Vinodeti [Caus. of vi+nudati] to drive out, dispel, remove, put away S IV.70, 76, 190; A II.13, 117; Sn 273, 956, (tamaŋ); 967; Nd[1] 454, 489; J I.183; II.63, 283 (sinehaŋ); Vv 84[26]; Miln 259 (imper. vinodehi, +apanehi, nicchārehi); Mhvs 5, 245 (vimatiŋ); 31, 10 (kankhaŋ); DhA IV.145; PvA 38 (sokaŋ).

Vindati [**vid**, both in meaning "to know" & "to find"; cp. Gr. *εἶδον* I saw, *οἶδα* I know = Sk. veda "Veda," *εἴδωλον* "idol"; Vedic vindati to find, vetti to know, vidyā knowledge; Goth. witan to observe & know = Ger. wissen; Goth. weis = E. wise, etc., for which see Walde, *Lat. Wtb.* s. v. video] the Vedic differentiations vetti "to know" and vindati "to find" are both in Pāli, but only in sporadic forms, some of which are archaic and therefore only found in poetry. Of **vid** are more frequent the Pass. **vijjati** and derivations fr. the Caus. **ved°**. The root **vind** occurs only in the present tense and its derivations. — A. **vid** to know, to ascertain: The old Vedic pres. vetti only at Th 1, 497 (spelt veti). Another old aor. is vedi [Sk. avedit] Dh. 419, 423; J III.420 (= aññāsi); IV.35 (here perhaps as aor. to Caus. vedeti: to cause to know or feel). Remnants of the old *perfect* tense 3rd pl. [Sk. viduḥ] are vidū & viduŋ (appears as vidu in verse), e. g. at Th 1, 497; Sn 758; Pv II.7[4] (= jānanti PvA 102); J V.62 (= vijānanti C.); Mhvs 23, 78. The old participle of the same tense is vidvā [= Sk. vidvān; cp. Geiger *P.Gr.* 100[2]] in meaning "wise" Sn 792, 897, 1056, 1060; expl[d] as vijjāgato ñāṇī vibhāvī medhāvī at Nd[1] 93, 308; Nd[2] 575. Opp. avidvā Sn 535; M I.311. — Younger forms are a reconstructed (grammatical) pres. vidati DA I.139; ger. viditvā S V.193; Sn 353, 365, 581, 1053, 1068 and pp. vidita (q. v.). — Pass. vijjati to be found, to be known, to exist; very frequent, e. g. Sn 20 (pl. vijjare), 21, 431, 611, 856, 1001, 1026; Th 1, 132; D I.18; Pv I.5[6]; II.3[18] (spelt vijjite!) II.9[14] (= atthi C.); 3rd sg. pret. vijjittha Sn 1098 (mā v. = saŋvijjittha Nd[2] 568). ppr. vijjamāna existing J I.214; III.127; PvA 25, 87, 103; Miln 216 (gen. pl. vijjamānataŋ). — Caus. vedeti; Pass. Caus. **vediyati**; grd. **vedanīya**: see separately, with other derivations. — B. **vind** to find, possess, enjoy (cp. vitta[1], vitta[2], vitti) Sn 187 (vindate dhanaŋ), 658; Th 1, 551; 2, 79 (aor. vindi); J VI.508 (vindate, med. = look for, try to find for oneself); Mhvs

1, 13 (ppr. vindaŋ); DhA III.128 (ppr. vindanto), 410. PvA 60, 77. — inf. vindituŋ Miln 122; J 18; grd; vindiya Vism 526 (as avindiya in expl[n] of avijjā). — Cp. nibbindati. — pp. vitta[1] (for which adhigata in lit. meaning).

Vindussara is v. l. of bindu° (q. v.).

Vipakka (adj.) [vi + pakka] fully ripe J I.136.

Vipakkha (adj.) [vi + pakkha[1] 2] opposite, hostile; enemy; only in foll. cpds.:
-sevaka siding in or consorting with the enemy, keeping bad company, a traitor J I.186; III.321; DhA IV.95. -sevin id. J I.487; II.98.

Vipakkhika (adj.) [vipakkha + ika] 1. [vi + pakkha[1] 1] without wings J I.429. — 2. [vi + pakkha[1] 2] opposite, hostile Sdhp 71.

Vipakkhin (adj.) [vi + pakkhin] having no wings, without wings J V.255.

Vipaccatā (f.) at Vin II.88 is perhaps a der. fr. vi + **vac**, and not **pac**, thus representing a Sk. *vivācyatā, meaning "challenging in disputation," quarrelsomeness, provocation. See also **vipāceti**. If fr. vi + **pac**, the meaning would be something like "heatedness, exasperation."

Vipaccati [vi + paccati] 1. to be cooked, i. e. to ripen J V.121; PvA 104. — 2. to bear fruit D II.266; S I.144; M I.388; Nett 37; VvA 171.

Vipaccanaka (adj.) [fr. vipaccati, cp. paccana] bearing fruit, ripening (fully) Miln 421 (Notes); PvA 190.

Vipaccanīka (adj.) [vi + paccanīka] hostile M I.402; A IV.95; J IV.108; Pug 20; Vbh 351, 359, 371; VbhA 478; PvA 87.

Vipajjati [vi + pajjati] to go wrong, to fail, to perish (opp. sampajjati) DhA III.357; PvA 34. — pp. **vipanna**.

Vipañcanā & **Vipañciyati**: see under **vipañcita**.

Vipañcita [fr. vi + **pañc**, cp. papañcita] only in phrase °ññū either: *knowing* diffuseness or detail, or: of unillusioned understanding, clear-minded, unprejudiced, comb[d] with ugghaṭita-ññū at A II.135 = Pug 41 (trsl[d] by B. C. Law as "learning by exposition"; PugA 223 expl[s] as "vitthāritaŋ atthaŋ jānāti," i. e. one who knows a matter expl[d] in detail. The spelling at A II.135 is vipacita°: at Pug 41 vipaccita° & at PugA vipaccita°, with v. l. vipañcita°); Nett 7 sq., 125; SnA 163 (where ugghaṭita-ññū is applied to those who understand by condensed instruction, sankhepa-desanāya, and vipañcita-ññū to those who need a detailed one, vitthāra-desanā; thus "*learning by diffuseness*"). — At Nett 9 we have the var. terms **vipañcanā**, **vipañcayati** & **vipañciyati** (Denom.) used in the description of var. ways of parsing and grammatical analysis. Here vipañcanā (resting clearly on Sk. papañca expansion) means "expanding" (by letters & vowels) and stands midway between ugghaṭanā & **vitthāraṇā** "condensing & detailing." The term **vipañcayati** (= vipañciyati) is used in the same way. — *Note*. The term is not sufficiently cleared up. It occurs in BSk. as **vipañcika** (e. g. Divy 319, 391, 475, where it is appl[d] to "brāhmaṇā naimittikā" & trsl[d] by Cowell as "sooth-sayer"), and vipañcanaka (Divy 548 ?), with which cp. vipañcitājña at Lal. Vist. 520.

Vipaṇeti [vi + Caus. of paṇati] to sell, to trade (with) J IV.363 (= vikkiṇati C.).

Vipatati see vipāṭeti 2.

Vipatti (f.) [vi + patti[2]] wrong state, false manifestation, failure, misfortune (opp. **sampatti**) Vin I.171 (ācāra° failure of morality); A I.270 (ājīva°); IV.26, 160 (atta°, para°); Ps I.122; J VI.292; Nett 126 (the 3 vipattiyo: sīla°, diṭṭhi°, ācāra°); DhA I.16 (sīla°) DA I.235. — Often in pair **diṭṭhi°** wrong view, heresy, & sīla° moral failure: D II.213; A I.95, 268, 270; Vin V.98; Vbh 361; Dhs 1361. —**payoga°** wrong application PvA 117, 136 (opp. °sampatti).

Vipatha [vi + patha] wrong way or course Vv 50[10] (= apatha VvA 212).

Vipanna [pp. of vipajjati] gone wrong, having lost, failing in (-°), opp. sampanna: A III.19 (rukkho sākhā-palāsa° a tree which has lost branches and leaves); Sn 116 (°diṭṭhi one who has wrong views, heretic; expl[d] as "vinaṭṭha-sammādiṭṭhi" SnA 177); Miln 258 (su° thoroughly fallen). -sīla° gone wrong in morals, lacking morality Vin I.63 (+ ācāra°, diṭṭhi°); II.4 (id.); J III.138 (vipanna-sīla).

Vipannatta (nt.) [fr. vipanna] failure, misfortune Dhs A 367.

Viparakkamma (indecl.) [ger. of vi + parakkamati] endeavouring strongly, with all one's might Sn 425

Viparāmosa (Viparāmāsa) [vi + parāmāsa, the form °mosa probably a distortion of °māsa] highway robbery D I.5 (expl[d] as twofold at DA I.80, viz. hima° & gumba°, or hidden by the snow & a thicket; the pop. etym. given here is "janaŋ musanti," i. e. they steal, or beguile people); III.176 (v. l. °māsa); A II.209; V.206; S V.473; Pug 58.

Viparāvatta [pp. of vi + parā + **vṛt**] reversed, changed D I.8; M II.3; S III.12; V.419; DA I.91.

Vipariṇata [vi + pariṇata] changed, perverted Dhs 1038; Vbh 1, 3, 5 sq.; Miln 50.

Vipariṇāma [vi + pariṇāma] change (for the worse), reverse, vicissitude D III.216 (°dukkhatā); M I.457 (also as "disappointment"); S II.274; III.8; IV.7 sq., 67 sq.; A II.177 (°dhamma subject to change); III.32; V.59 sq.; Vbh 379 (°dhamma); Vism 499 (°dukkha), 629 sq.; VbhA 93 (id.); PvA 60. — a° absence of change, steadfastness D I.18; III.31, 33; DhA I.121.

Vipariṇāmeti [Denom. fr. vipariṇāma] to change, alter D I.56 (T. °ṇamati; but DA I.167 °ṇāmeti: sic for °ṇāmati!) = S III.211; PvA 199.

Viparibhinna [vi + paribhinna] (entirely) broken up M I.296; S IV.294.

Vipariyattha in verse at J V.372 is the poet. form of vipallattha (so the C. expl[n]).

Vipariyaya & **Vipariyāya** [vi + pariyaya] change, reversal DA I.148 (ā); SnA 499; DhsA 253 (ā); Sdhp 124, 333. Cp. **vipariyesa** & **vipallāsa**.

Vipariyādikata (adj.) [vipariyāya + kata, with sound change y>d, viz. °āyi>°ādi] thrown out of its course, upset, destroyed Th 1, 184 (cittaŋ; cp. similar phrase vipariyatthaŋ cittaŋ J V.372 — The v. l. at Th passage is vimariyādi°).

Vipariyesa [a contamination form between °pariyaya & °pallāsa] reversal, contrariness, wrong state Kvu 306 (*three* reversals: saññā°, citta°, diṭṭhi°; or of perception, consciousness & views, cp. *Kvu trsl[n]* 176); Vbh 376 (id.). — °gāha inverted grasp i. e. holding opposite views or "holding the contrary aim" (B. C. Law) Pug 22; DhsA 253 (= vipallattha-gāha).

Viparivatta [vi + parivatta] changing or turning round, upset J I.344 (lokassa °kāle).

Viparivattati [vi + parivattati] to turn round, to upset J IV.224 (nāvā °amānā capsizing); Miln 117; ThA 255.

Viparivattana (nt.) [fr. viparivattati] changing, change, reverse DhsA 367.

Viparīta (adj.) [pp. of vi+pari+i] reversed, changed; equivocal; wrong, upset A III.114 (°dassana); IV.226 (id.); V.284; Th 2, 393; J I.334; Kvu 307; Miln 285, 324; Nett 85 (°gāha), 126 (°saññā); PvA 244. —aviparīta unequivocal, certain, distinct, definite A V.268 (°dassana); Miln 214 (°vacana); PvA 231 (=sacca & yāthāva).

Viparītatā (f.) [abstr. fr. viparīta] contradistinction Vism 450 (tabbiparītatā).

Vipalāvita [vi+palāvita, pp. of Caus. of **plu**] made to float, floating, thrown out (into water) J IV.259 (reads viplāvitaŋ)=I.326 (reads vipalāvitaŋ, with reading nipalāvitaŋ in C.). The C. at J IV.259 expl^s as "uttārita," so at J I 326 as "brought *out* of water," fished out=thale ṭhapita, evidently incorrect.

Vipallattha (adj.) [=Sk. viparyasta, pp. of vi+pari+**as**: see vipallāsa] changed, reversed, upset, deranged, corrupt, perverted. Occurs in two forms: vipariyattha J V.372 (°cittaŋ: in poetry); and **vipallattha** Vism 20 (°citta: trsl^o "with corrupt thought"; T. spells vipallatta, v. l. °attha); DhsA 253 (°gāha); PvA 212.

Vipallāsa [cp. Sk. viparyāsa, vi+pari+**as** (to throw). The diaeretic P. form (founded on Sk. is **vipariyāsa**; another bastard form is **vipariyesa** (q. v.)] reversal, change (esp. in a bad sense), inversion, perversion, derangement, corruption, distortion. — The form **vipariyāsa** occurs at Vin II.80 (citta-°kata, with deranged mind or wrong thoughts): J I.344 (where it is expl^d by vipallāsa). Otherwise **vipallāsa**, e. g. Sn 299; Ps II.80; Vism 214 (attha°); Nett 4, 27, 31, 85 sq., 115 sq.; DhA II.228; PvA 7, 70. — There are 3 kinds of **vipallāsas**, viz. saññā° perversion of perception, citta° of thought, diṭṭhi° of views; A II.52; Nett 85; Vism 683. See the same under **vipariyesa**!

Vipallāsayati [Denom. fr. vipallāsa] to be deceived (about), to distort, to have or give a wrong notion (of) Nett 85.

Vipassaka (adj.) [fr. vipassati] qualified to win insight, contemplating, gifted with introspection S II.232; Ps I.167; Miln 342, 369; 393, VbhA 297.

Vipassati [vi+passati] to see clearly; to have intuition, to obtain spiritual insight D III.196 (ye nibbutā loke yathābhūtaŋ vipassisuŋ, aor.); Th I, 471; 2, 271 (vipassi for °passasi); Sn 1115; J III.183 (pabbajitvā vipassitvā arahattaŋ pāpuniŋsu).

Vipassanā (f.) [fr. vi+passati; BSk. vipaśyanā, e. g. Divy 44, 95, 264 etc.] inward vision, insight, intuition, introspection D III.213, 273; S IV.195, 360; V.52 (samatha+); A I.61 (id.), 95; II.140, 157 (samatha+); IV.360; V.99, 131; Ps I.28, 57 sq., 181; II.92 sq.; Pug 25; J I.106; Dhs 55.1356; Nett 7, 42 sq., 50, 82, 88 sq., 125 sq., 160, 191; Miln 16; Vism 2 (with jhāna etc.), 289 (+samādhi), 628 sq. (the 18 mahā°); PvA 14 (samāhita-citta°), 167; VvA 77; Sdhp 457, 466.

-**anga** constituent of intuition SnA 8 (given as "nāmarūpa-paricched etc."). -**upekkhā** indifference by introspection Vism 162. -**kammaṭṭhāna** exercise for intuition DhA IV.46. -**ñāṇa** ability or method of attaining insight Vism 629; DhA IV.30; cp. *Cpd.* 65 sq., where 10 such modes. -**dhura** obligation of introspection DhA I.8; IV.37 sq.

Vipassin (adj.) [fr. vipassati] gifted with insight, wise A IV.244; Sn 349; It 2=7.

Vipāka [fr. vi+**pac**] fruit, fruition, product; always in pregnant meaning of "result, effect, consequence (of one's action)," either as good & meritorious (kusala) or bad & detrimental (akusala). Hence "retribution" (**kamma°**), reward or punishment. See on term e. g. *Dhs. trsl^n* introd.^{2} XCIII; *Cpd.* 43. 249. — D III.150, 160, 176 sq.; S I.34, 57, 92 (kammassa); II.128 (compar. vipākatara), 255 (id.); IV.186 sq., 348 sq.; A I.48, 97 (sukha°, dukkha°), 134 (kamma°), 263; II.34 (agga), 80, 112; III.35, 172 (dānassa), 410 sq. (kāmānaŋ etc.), 436; IV. 303 (kamma°); V.251; Sn 653 (kamma°); Ps II.79 (dukkha°); Pv I.9^1; I.10^7 & passim; Pug 13, 21; Dhs 431, 497, 987; Vbb 16 sq., 73, 319, 326 sq., 334 (sukha°); Kvu 353 sq., 464 (kamma & vipāka); Nett 99, 161, 180 sq.; Tikp 27 (fourfold), 44, 48, 50, 292 (a° & sa°), 328 sq. (°tika), 350 sq.; Dukp 17; Vism 177, 454 (fourfold), 456 (°viññāṇa), 538 (°paccaya), 545 sq.; VbhA 17, 150 sq. (kusala° & akusala), 144, 177, 391; PvA 50, 73, 77; Sdhp 12, 73, 197, 235.

Vipākatta (nt.) [abstr. fr. vipāka] state of being ripe PvA 52.

Vipāceti [Caus. of vi+**pac**, or distorted fr. **vivāceti** ?] to become annoyed, to get angry (lit. to get heated): this meaning as trsl^o of vi+**pac**, although not quite correct, as **pac** means to "ripen" and is not ordinarily used of *heated* conditions. Since the word is not sufficiently cleared up, we refrain from a detailed discussion concerning *possible* explanations. It may suffice to point out that it occurs only in *Vinaya* (and in one sporadic passage S I.232) in standing comb^n ujjhāyati khīyati vipāceti, expressing annoyance or irritation about something; e. g. Vin I.191; II.85, 291; IV.64. The corresponding BSk. phrase is avadhyāyati dhriyati [to resist, **dhṛ**] vivācayati, e. g. Divy 492. It is not quite clear *which* of the two versions is the older one. There may be underlying a misunderstood (dial.) phrase which was changed by popular analogy. The BSk. phrase seems *a priori* the more intelligible one; if we take **vipāceti**=**vivāceti**, we should translate it as "to speak disparagingly." Mrs. Rh. D. at *K.S.* I.296 trsl^s as "were vexed and fretted and consumed with indignation." — See remarks under **khīyati** & cp. **vipaccatā**.

Vipāṭeti [vi+pāṭeti] 1. to rip or tear open Vin II.115. — 2. to be destroyed, to fall to pieces (cp. pāṭeti & Pass. pāṭiyati in sense of "destroy") Pv IV.1^{46} (sanghāṭiyo vipātayanti T.; vv. ll. vināsayati & vidālayati; PvA 240 expl^s as Pass. **vipāḷiyati** [=vipaṭiyati ?] with v. l. vidāliyati); J V.33 (reads: muddhā vipphaleyya sattadhā: perhaps the best reading), 493 (muddhā vipateyya [*sic*] sattadhā). See **vipphalati**.

Vipāḷiyati see vipāṭeti 2.

Vipiṭṭhi [vi+piṭṭhi] in phrase **vipiṭṭhi-katva(na)** Sn 67 & 362, to turn one's back on (acc.), to leave behind, to abandon; cp. **piṭṭhito karoti**. The expl^o at Nd^2 580 is pahāna etc.; at SnA 119 piṭṭhito katvā.

Vipina (nt.) [cp. *Sk. vipina, Halāyudha 2, 55] wood, grove D I.248 (doubtful; vv. ll. vijina, vivada, vivana); Ap 51 (vv. ll. vivana, vicina; C. vivana & vipina); Dāvs IV.39; PvA 81 (read **vicitta**!).

Viputta (adj.) [vi+putta] without a son, bereft of his son J V.106.

Vipubbaka (adj.) [fr. vi+pubba^1] full of corruption or matter, festering (said of a dead body). The contemplation (saññā) of a festering corpse is one of the asubhakammaṭṭhānas. — M I.58, 88; III.91; A III.324. — As °saññā: A II.17; V.310; Dhs 264; Nett 27; Miln 102, 332; Vism 110, 178, 193.

Vipula (adj.) [cp. Sk. vipula] large, extensive, great, abundant. The word is *poetical*. — D III.150; A I.45 (°paññatā); Sn 41, 675, 687, 978, 994; Th I, 588; Nd^1 581 (=adhimatta); Vv 67^6 (=mahanta VvA 290); Ap 40; Pv II.1^{18}; II.4^9; II.9^{69} (=ulāra PvA 139); Miln 164, 311, 404; PvA 7, 76; Sdhp 271.

Vippakata [pp. of vippakaroti; vi+pakata] 1. imperfectly executed, left unfinished, interrupted D I.2 (cp. Dh I.49); Vin II.172, 243, 304; IV.279; A II.196; J I.120. — 2. done wrongly J V.214. — At Vin IV.358 (in Bdhgh's remarks on Pāc. 26, 1) we find vippagatamedhuna as inaccurate spelling for vippakata-methuna ("interrupted intercourse").

Vippakaroti [vi+pa+kṛ] to ill-treat, abuse Vin II.133. — pp. vippakata.

Vippakāra [vi+pakāra] change, mutation, alteration J VI.370; DhA I.28; VvA 46.

Vippakiṇṇa [pp. of vippakirati] strewn all over, beset with, sprinkled (with) J II.240; VI.42; DhA I.140; DA I.40; VvA 36.

Vippakiṇṇatā (f.) [abstr. fr. vippakiṇṇa] the fact of being beset or endowed (with) Vism 8.

Vippakirati [vi+pakirati] 1. to strew all over PvA 92. — 2. to confound, destroy J II.398. — pp. vippakiṇṇa.

Vippakkamati [vi+pakkamati] to part company, to go away Vin IV.284.

Vippajahati [vi+pajahati] to give up, to abandon Sn 817 (inf. °pahātave), 926 (Pot. °pajahe); ger. °pahāya Sn 367, 499, 514; J I.87. — pp. vippahīna.

Vippaṭikkula (adj.) [vi+paṭikkūla] contrary, antagonistic Dhs 1325=Pug 20.

Vippaṭipajjati [vi+paṭipajjati. Cp. BSk. vipratipadyate Divy 293] to go astray; fig. to err, fail; to commit sin Vin III.166; S I.73; J I.438. — pp. vippaṭipanná. — Caus. vippaṭipādeti.

Vippaṭipatti (f.) [vi+paṭipatti] wrong way, error, sin Vism 511.

Vippaṭipanna [pp. of vippaṭipajjati] "on the wrong track," going or gone astray, committing sin Pv IV.1^{59} (°citta=adhammiyaŋ paṭipadaŋ paṭipanna PvA 242).

Vippaṭipādeti [Caus. of vippaṭipajjati] to cause to commit sin (esp. adultery) Vin III.40.

Vippaṭisāra [vi+paṭisāra] bad conscience, remorse, regret, repentance Vin II.250; D I.138; S III.120, 125; IV.46; A III.166, 197, 353; IV.69; J IV.12; V.88; Pug 62; DhA IV.42; VvA 116; PvA 14, 60, 105, 152. — a° no regret, no remorse A III.46.

Vippaṭisārin (adj.) [fr. vippaṭisāra; cp. BSk. vipratisārin Divy 322, 638] remorseful, regretful, repentant S III.125; IV.133, 320 sq., 359 sq.; A III.165 sq.; IV.244, 390; J I.200; Miln 10, 285; Tikp 321, 346.

Vippataccheti [vi+pa+taccheti] to scratch open or apart M I.506.

Vippanaṭṭha [vi+pp. of panassati] strayed, lost, perished Vv 84^{9}=84^{44} (=magga-sammūḷha VvA 337); J IV.139; V.70; VI.525; Miln 326.

Vippamutta [vi+pamutta] released, set free, saved S I.4, 29, 50; III.31, 83; IV.11; A I.10; II.34; Sn 176, 218, 363, 472, 492, 501, 913; J I.84; Vv 20^{4}≈29^{10}; Nd^{1} 331, 336.

Vippamokkha [vi+pamokkha] release, deliverance S I.154; J V.27.

Vippayutta [vi+payutta] separated S II.173 (visaŋyutta+); Sn 914 (or °mutta). -°paccaya the relation of dissociation Tikp 6, 53 sq., 65; Vism 539.

Vippayoga [vi+payoga] separation Sn 41; PvA 161 (piya°).

Vippalapati [vi+palapati] to talk confusedly (as in one's sleep), to chatter, wail, lament Vin I.15; S IV.303; J I.61; III.217; IV.167; DhA II.100; PvA 40, 93.

Vippalambheti [vi+palambheti] to deceive, mock DA I.151; ThA 78.

Vippalāpa [vi+palāpa] confused talk, wailing Ps I.38; PvA 18.

Vippalujjati [vi+palujjati] to be broken up, to be destroyed Nd^{1} 5.

Vippavadati [vi+pavadati] to dispute, disagree J IV.163; VI.267.

Vippavasati [vi+pavasati] to go from home, to be away from (abl.), to be absent Sn 1138 (=apeti apagacchati vinā hoti Nd^{2} 582); J IV.51, 439. — pp. vippavuttha.

Vippavāsa [vi+pavāsa] absence; in sati° absence of mind, neglect, absentmindedness, thoughtlessness J I.410; SnA 339; a° thoughtfulness, mindfulness Vin V.216; Sn 1142; J IV.92.

Vippaviddha [pp. of vippavijjhati, vi+pa+vyadh] pierced through and through J I.61.

Vippavuttha [pp. of vippavasati] absent; °sati neglectful DhA I.239.

Vippasanna (adj.) [vi+pasanna] (quite) purified, clear; happy, bright, pure, sinless Vin III.88 (°chavivaṇṇa); S I.32 (cetas); III.2, 235; IV.118, 294; V.301; A III.41, 236; Sn 637; Dh 82, 413 (=pasanna-citta DhA IV.192); Pv I.10^{10} (=suṭṭhu pasanna); II.9^{35}; Vism 262 (where KhA reads pasanna only); DhA II.127; DA I.221.

Vippasādeti [Caus. of vippasīdati] to purify, cleanse Sn 506.

Vippasīdati [vi+pasīdati] to become bright; fig. to be reconciled or pleased, to be satisfied or happy Dh 82; J I.51; PvA 122 (mukha-vaṇṇa). Caus. vippasādeti.

Vippasukkhati [vi+pa+sukkhati] to dry up entirely J V.106.

Vippahāna (nt.) [vi+pahāna] leaving, abandoning, giving up S I.39=Sn 1109; Sn 1097; J VI.260; Miln 181.

Vippahita (nt.) [vi+pahita^{2}] sending out in all directions, message J III.386 (dūta°).

Vippahīna [pp. of vippajahati] given up, abandoned S I.99; A V.16, 29 sq.; Sn 360, 362.

Vippita at J VI.185 is to be read cipiṭa ("flat").

Vipphandati [vi+phandati; cp. BSk. vispandati Jtm 11 to twitch, writhe, struggle Vv 52^{16} (52^{14} Ha.); J IV.495 — pp. vipphandita.

Vipphandita (nt.) [pp. of vipphandati] "writhing," twitching, struggle M I.446; S II.62; — (fig.) in diṭṭhi° comb^{d} with visūkāyita) "scuffling of opinion" (Mrs. Rh. D.), sceptical agitation, worry & writhing (cp. *Dial.* I.53) M I.8, 486; S I.123 (here without diṭṭhi°; the C. expl^{n} is "hatthirājavaṇṇa sappavaṇṇ' ādidassanāni" *K.S.* I.320); Dhs 381; Pug 22.

Vipphala (or is it pipphala ?)=phala at J VI.518.

Vipphalati [vi+phalati] (intrs.) to split open, to burst asunder: so read at J V.33, 493 (for vipatati); Pv IV.1^{46} (for vipāteti); see detail under vipāṭeti.

Vipphāra [fr. vi+pharati 1 or 2] diffusion, pervasion, (adj.) pervading, spreading out A I.171 (vitakka-vipphāra-sadda, cp. *Kvu trsl^{n}* 241), 206 (mahājutika mahā vipphāra); IV.252; Ps I.112 sq.; II.174; J III.12 (mahā° + mahājutika); V.150 (id.); Miln 230 & 270 (vaci°

dilating in talk), 130, 346; Vism 42; DA I.192; VvA 103 (mahā°+mahājutika); PvA 178 (karuṇā°).

Vipphāravant (adj.) [fr. vipphāra, cp. pharati 1 & vipphurati] possessing vibration DhsA 115=Vism 142.

Vipphārika (adj.) [fr. vi+pharati 2] spreading out (in effulgence) VvA 5 (mahā°).

Vipphārita [pp. of Caus. vi+pharati] expanded Dāvs V.34 (°akkhi-yugala, both eyes wide open).

Vipphālita (adj.) [vi+phālita 2] split open, cut to pieces PvA 152 (su°; so read for vipphalita); Sdhp 188 (°anga).

Vipphāleti [vi+**sphar**: cp. phālita 1. It is *not*=vi+phāleti] to expand, to bend or draw the bow J VI.580.

Vipphuraṇa (nt.) [vi+phuraṇa=pharaṇa] spreading out, effulgence, pervasion VvA 277.

Vipphurati [vi+phurati: see pharati] to vibrate, tremble, quiver, fly asunder, diffuse J I.51; SnA 225; VvA 12 (vijjotamāna vipphurato).

Vipphoṭita (adj.) [vi+phoṭita: see phoṭa, cp. BSk. visphoṭa open Divy 603] burst open (of a boil) Th 1, 306.

Viphala (adj.) [vi+phala] fruitless, useless Sdhp 527.

Vibandha [vi+bandha] fetter PvA 207.

Vibandhana (nt.) [vi+bandhana]=vibandha ThA 243.

Vibādhaka (adj.) [fr. vibādha] doing harm to (-°), injuring, preventing Dāvs II.88.

Vibādhati [vi+bādhati] to oppress, harm Miln 135 (so read for °bhādati); DhsA 42. — Pass. vibādhiyati to be oppressed PvA 239.

Vibbedha [fr. vi+**vyadh** after analogy of ubbedha; *not* vi+bheda] circumference J I.212.

Vibbhanta [pp. of vibbhamati] 1. roaming, straying; strayed, confused M I.171 (padhāna° giving up exertion), 247 (id.). Usually in phrase °citta with wandering (or confused) mind S I.61 (see expl^n of C. at *K.S.* I.321), 204; III.93; V.269; A I.70; II.30; III.391; It 90; J IV.459 (+kupit' indriya); Miln 324. — At DhsA 260 we find the cpd. vibbhanti-bhāva [vibbhanta in comp^n with **bhu**!] of citta, in meaning "wavering, roaming" (of mind): so read for vibhatti-bhāva.

Vibbhantaka (adj.) [vibbhanta+ka] 1. straying away from (-°), confused Vism 187 (jhāna°), 429. — 2. (a bhikkhu) who has forsaken the Order, apostate Vin II.60.

Vibbhamati [vi+bhamati] to wander about, to go astray, to forsake the Order Vin I.72; II.14; III.40 (may be taken in the sense of enjoying oneself or sporting, i. e. cohabiting, at this passage), IV.216; J I.117; III.462 (of a bhikkhu enticed by his former wife), 496. — pp. vibbhanta.

Vibhanga [vi+bhanga, of **bhaj**[1]] distribution, division, distinction, classification Vin I.359; Sn 600 (jāti° classification of species; expl^d as jāti-vitthāra at SnA 464); J IV.361 (+vicaya; C. expl^s as **vibhāga**); Mhvs 30, 87 (dhātu° distribution of relics); SnA 422 (contrasted with uddesa). — Vibhanga is the title of the second book of the Abhidhamma Piṭaka (see Pāli Name Dictionary). Cp. Sutta-vibhanga.

Vibhajati [vi+bhajati, i. e. **bhaj**[1], as in bhājeti] (lit.) to distribute, divide; (fig.) to distinguish, dissect, divide up, classify; to deal with something in detail, to go into details M III.223; S II.2, 255 (vibhājeti)=M I.364 (reads virājeti); S IV.93 (atthaŋ); V.261 (dhammaŋ vivarati vibhajati uttāni-karoti); Sn 87; Pug 41; Vbh 259; Miln 145; SnA 237; DA I.104; PvA 81, 111. ger. vibhajja (q. v.). — pp. vibhatta.

Vibhajana (nt.) & °ā (f.) [fr. vibhajati] distinction, division, going into detail Nett 5, 8 sq., 38 (+vivaraṇā & uttāni-kammatā); Tikp 10; SnA 445 (vivaraṇa, v., uttāni-karaṇa); DhsA 343, 344. Cp. vibhājana.

Vibhajja (adv.) [ger. of vibhajati] dividing, analysing, detailing; in detail (°-) D III.229 (°vyākaraṇīya pañha "discriminating reply" trsl^n); A II.46 (°vacana analysis). — °vāda the Vibhajja doctrine, i. e. the doctrine which analyses, or the "religion of logic or reason"; a term identical with theravāda, the doctrine of the Elders, i. e. the original teaching of the Buddhist church. -°vādin one who teaches the V. doctrine, Ep. of the Buddha Mhvs 5, 271; Tikp 366; VbhA 130; cp. *Kvu trsl^n* introd. p. 38.

Vibhatta (adj.) [pp. of vibhajati] 1. (lit.) divided, distributed; parted, partitioned, having divisions, portioned off Sn 300; Pv I.10[13] (of niraya); J V.266 (id.); Miln 316 (a° samudda). — su° well divided, well planned, proportioned, regular Sn 305; Pv III.2[21]; Miln 330, 345; Vism 108. — 2. (fig.) detailed, explained, analysed Vism 187; SnA 288; PvA 104.

Vibhattavant (adj.) [fr. vibhatta] full of details, giving all detail Vism 212; DA I.34.

Vibhatti (f.) [fr. vibhajati] 1. division, distinction, classification, detail, variety J VI.432 (of paintings); Nett 1 sq., 105; Miln 102, 381; Vism 352 (contrasted with sankhepa); PvA 199, 282 (rūpa° various forms, patterns). — 2. (t. t. g.) inflection of nouns & verbs, declensions, conjugation SnA 397; VvA 78, 199. -°**lopa** omission of inflection VvA 174, 192; PvA 147. — *Note.* vibhatti-bhāva at DhsA 260 is to be read as **vibbhanti°** (see under vibbhanta).

Vibhattika (adj.) [fr. vibhatti] having divisions; (fig.) detailed. Neg. a° not giving details VvA 164.

Vibhava [vi+bhava] 1. power, wealth, prosperity DA I.147; J I.56; V.285; Mhvs 26, 6; DhA I.6; II.9, 84; IV.7; VvA 5, 302 (°sampanna rich); PvA 122, 130, 176, 196. Great wealth is expressed by **asīti-koṭi-vibhava,** consisting in 80 koṭis, e. g. DhA I.367; II.25. — **bahu°** very rich J I.145; **mahā°** id. PvA 97, 107. — **yathā vibhavaŋ** according to one's means or power PvA 54; vibhav' ânurūpaŋ id. VvA 254. — 2. non-existence, cessation of life, annihilation D I.34; Sn 514 (+bhava), 867 (id.); Nd[1] 274, 282; J III.402 (°ŋ gata=vināsaŋ patta C.); V.267 (id.); DhsA 392; DA I.120; VbhA 505 (=bhava-vigama). See also **taṇhā** B 1.
-**taṇhā** "craving for life to end" (*Dial.* III.208), desire for non-existence D III.216, 275; Vin I.10; Ud 33; It 50; VbhA 111. -**diṭṭhi** the theory of non-becoming D III.212; A I.83; Nd[1] 245, 274.

Vibhavati [vi+bhavati] to cease to exist S III.56 (fut. °issati); Sn 873 (vibhoti); Nd[1] 279 (id.). — pp. **vibhūta.**

Vibhassikata (nt.) [vi+bhassa+kata] gossip, lit. "made into talk" Vin IV.241.

Vibhāga [fr. vibhajati, cp. vibhanga & vibhajana] distribution, division; detailing, classification J IV.361; Vism 494; VbhA 83; ThA 100; VvA 37; PvA 122. — **attha°** detailing of meaning Vism 569; **dhātu°** distribution of relics VvA 297; PvA 212; **pada°** division of words SnA 269; PvA 34. — Cp. saŋ°.

Vibhājana (nt.) [vi+bhājana[2]] distribution, division Dhtp 92, 561; Dhtm 776, 787.

Vibhāta [pp. of vibhāti] shining, turned to light, bright; in phrase **vibhātāya rattiyā** when night had become light, i. e. at daybreak or dawn (DhA IV.105; PvA 13, 22). — (nt.) daybreak, dawn DhA II.5 (°khaṇe).

Vibhāti [vi+bhāti] to shine forth, to be or become light (said of the night turning into day); pres. also vibhāyati Vin I.78; fut. **vibhāyissati** D II.148; aor. **vibhāyi** J V.354. — pp. **vibhāta.**

Vibhādati at Miln 135 should be read at vibādhati.

Vibhāyana (nt.) [fr. vibhāti] shining forth, brightening VvA 148.

Vibhāvana (nt.) & °ā (f.) [fr. vibhāveti] 1. making clear, ascertainment, explanation, exposition J III.389; Vbh 342, 343 (ā); Sn A 13, 261 sq., 318; VbhA 409 (ā); ThA 76 (ā), 230; PvA 137, 140 (so read for vibhavanā in attha°). — 2. annihilation, disappearance, making non-existing (cp. vibhava 2) DhsA 163 (vibhāvanā nāma antara-dhāpanā ti attho).

Vibhāvaniya (adj.) [fr. vibhāvana] pertaining to ascertainment, making clear, explaining PvA 244 (paramattha°).

Vibhāvita [pp. of vibhāveti] made non-existing, annihilated Nd[2] 584.

Vibhāvin (adj.) [fr. vibhāveti] intelligent, wise Sn 317; J VI.304; Nd[2] 259 (=medhāvin); Miln 21, 276, 346; Sdhp 382.

Vibhāveti [vi+bhāveti] 1. to understand clearly (lit. "to produce intensively or well") Sn 318 (ger. a-vibhāvayitvā). — 2. to make clear, to explain KhA 89; SnA 406, 472; PvA 1, 70, 92, 135. — 3. to put out of existence, to annihilate [as Caus. of vibhava 2] DhsA 163. — pp. **vibhāvita.**

Vibhāsita [pp. Caus. of vi+bhāsati[2]] illuminated, made bright, shining forth Sdhp 591.

Vibhinna (adj.) [vi+bhinna] scattered; divided, at variance Sn 314 (=aññam-aññaŋ bhinna SnA 324).

Vibhītaka (& °ṭaka) [cp. *Sk. vibhīta & °ka] the plant Terminalia belerica; beleric myrobolan. Dice were made from its fruits, which are also used as medicine (intoxicant); its flowers smell vilely. — Vin I.201; J III.161; V.363; VI.529.

Vibhūta (adj.) [pp. of vibhavati, or vi+bhūta] 1. [cp. bhūta 1, & vibhava 2] destroyed, annihilated, being without Th 1, 715; Sn 871 sq., 1113 (=vibhāvita atikkanta vītivatta Nd[2] 584). — 2. [cp. bhūta 3] false Sn 664. — 3. [cp. vibhāveti 2] clear, distinct A V.325; Miln 311; Abdhs 16 (a° unclear); Vism 112 (& a°). -°ŋ **karoti** to explain Miln 308.

Vibhūti (f.) [fr. vi+bhavati] 1. [cp. vibhūta 2] destruction, ruin Th 1, 1018 (°mandin=malign). — 2. [cp. vibhava 1] splendour, majesty, glory J V.305; PvA 133 (dāna°), 216 (rāja°).

Vibhūsana (nt.) [vi+bhūsana] adornment A I.212; II.40, 145, 209; Sn 59 (cp. Nd[2] 585); Pug 21, 58; J I.8; Dhs 1348; Miln 382.

Vibhūsā (f.) [vi+bhūsā] ornament, decoration, distinction, pride Sn 926; Nd[1] 380; Nd[2] 585; Miln 224 (Rh. D. trsl[n] "dexterity," hardly correct. Should we read "vibhūti"?).

Vibhūsita [pp. of vibhūseti] adorned, decorated Mhvs 25, 102; Vism 10; PvA 46, 157.

Vibhūseti [vi+bhūseti] to adorn, embellish, beautify Th 2, 411; Mhvs 19, 25; DhA I.77. — pp. **vibhūsita.**

Vibheti [vi+bhāyati] to be afraid, to stand in awe of J V.509 (=bhāyati C.). Should we read bibheti?

Vibhedaka [vi+bhedaka] one who disturbs friendship, a slanderer J III.260.

Vibhedika (f.) [fr. vi+**bhid**] the palmyra tree J VI.529.

Vibhedeti [vi+bhedeti] to cause disruption, to slander A V.345 sq.

THE PALI TEXT SOCIETY'S PALI-ENGLISH DICTIONARY

EDITED BY

T. W. RHYS DAVIDS F.B.A D.Sc. Ph.D. LL.D. D.Litt

and WILLIAM STEDE Ph.D.

Part VIII (Vim—H)

PUBLISHED BY
THE PALI TEXT SOCIETY
LONDON

First published - - - 1925
Reprinted - - - - 1949
Reprinted - - - - 1952

Vimajjana (nt.) [fr. vi+majjati[2]] making smooth, polishing M I. 385.

Vimaṭṭha (adj.) [vi+maṭṭha] smoothed, soft, smooth, polished J V.96 (°ābharaṇa), (C. expln as "visāla"), 204, 400 (of ornaments). —ubhato-bhāga° polished or smooth on both sides M I. 385; A V.61=M II.13 (has °maddha).

Vimata (adj.) [fr. vi+**man**] perplexed, in doubt J V.340.

Vimati (f.) [vi+mati] doubt, perplexity, consternation D I.105; S IV.327; A II.79, 185; Ap 29; Dhs 425; J III.522; Miln 119, 144, 339; DA I.274.

Vimada (adj.) [vi+mada] disintoxicated, without conceit J V.158 (taken as "unconscious" by C.).

Vimaddana (nt.) [vi+maddana] crushing, destroying VvA 232.

Vimana (adj.) [vi+mano] 1. perplexed, consternated Miln 23, 118; PvA 274.—2. infatuate Th 2, 380.—3. distracted, distressed Th I, 1051; J VI.523.

Vimariyādikata (adj.) [vi+mariyādā+kata] lit. made unrestricted, i. e. delivered, set free S II.173; III.31 (vippamutto °ena cetasā viharati); VI.11; A V.151 sq. —At Th I, 184 v. l. for vipariyādi°.

Vimala (adj.) [vi+mala] without stains, spotless, unstained, clean, pure A IV.340; Sn 378, 476, 519, 637, 1131 (cp. Nd[2] 586); J I.18; Miln 324; DhA IV.192.

Vimalayaka [cp. Sk. vimalaka] a certain precious stone of dark-blue colour VvA 111.

Vimāna[1] (nt.) [in the Pāli meaning *not* Vedic. Found in meaning "palace-chariot" in the Mbhārata and elsewhere in Epic Sk.] lit. covering a certain space, measuring; the defns given by Dhpāla refer it to "without measure," i. e. immeasurable. Thus=vigata-māne appamāṇe mahanta vara-pāsāda VvA 131; =visiṭṭhamānaŋ, pamāṇato mahantaŋ VvA 160.—Appld meaning: heavenly (magic) palace, a kind of paradise, elysium.—1. *General remarks*: (*a*) The notion of the vimāna is peculiar to the later, fantastic parts of the Canon, based on popular superstition (Vimāna & Peta Vatthu, Apadāna, Jātaka and similar fairy tales). It shows distinct traces of foreign (Hellenic-Babylonian) influence and rests partly on tales of sea-faring merchants (cp. location of V. in mid-ocean). On the other hand it represents the old (Vedic) ratha as chariot of the gods, to be driven at will (cp. below 5, 7, 8). Thus at Vv 16 (here as 500 chariots!), 36, 63, 64; J I.59 (deva-vimāna-sadisa ratha).—(*b*) The vimānas are in remote parts of the world (cp. the island of the blessed), similar to the elysium in Homer's Odyssey, e. g. IV.563 sq.: *σ' ἐς Ἠλύσιον πεδίον καὶ πείρατα γαίης ἀθάνατοι πέμψουσιν* etc. (trsln G. Chapman: "the immortal *ends of all the earth*, the fields Elysian Fate to thee will give; where Rhadamanthus rules, and where men live a never-troubled life, where snow, nor show'rs, nor irksome winter spends his fruitless pow'rs, but *from the ocean* zephyr still resumes a constant breath, that all the fields perfume"). Cp. Ehni, *Yama* p. 206 sq.—(*c*) In popular religion the influence of this eschatological literature has been very great, so great in fact as to make the Vimāna and Peta-vatthus & the Jātaka-stories, exemplifying the theory of retribution as appealing to an ordinary mind by vivid examples of mythology, greater favourites than any other canonical book. From this point of view we have to judge Mhvs 14, 58: Petavatthuŋ Vimānañ ca sacca-saŋyuttaŋ eva ca desesi thero . . .—2. The *descriptions* of the Vimānas are in the most exuberant terms. The palaces (kingdoms in miniature) are of gold, crystal or exquisite jewels, their pillars are studded with gems, their glittering roofs are peaked with 700 pinnacled turrets (VvA 244, 289; also as "innumerable" VvA 188, or 18,000 Ap. 63). Surrounded are these towering (ucca) mansions by lovely, well-planned gardens, the paths of which are sprinkled with gold dust; they are full of wishing-trees, granting every desire. There is a variety of stately trees, bearing heavenly flowers & fruit, swaying gently in delicious breezes. Lotus ponds with cool waters invite to refreshing baths; a host of birds mix their songs with the strains of cymbals and lutes, played by heavenly musicians. Angelic maidens perform their dances, filling the atmosphere with a radiant light which shines from their bodies. Peace and happiness reign everywhere, the joys of such a vimāna cannot be expressed in words. This elysium lasts for aeons (cira-ṭṭhitika Vv 80[1]; kappa-ṭṭhāyin Th I, 1190); in short it is the most heavenly paradise which can be imagined.—For a monograph of vimāna the Vimāna Vatthu and its Commentary should in the first place be consulted.—3. The *inhabitants* of the Vimānas are usually happy persons (or *yakkhas*: see Stede, *P. V. trsl.* 39-41), called devatā, who have attained to such an exalted state through their own merit (*puñña* see foll. 4).—Departed souls who have gone through the Peta-stage are frequently such devas (at Vv 17[2] called pubba-devatā). That these are liable to semi-punishment and semi-enjoyment is often emphasized, and is founded on the character of their respective kamma: J I.240 (vimāna-petiyo sattāhaŋ sukhaŋ anubhavanti, sattāhaŋ dukkhaŋ); J V.2 (vemānika-peta-bhavena-kammassa sarikkhako vipāko ahosi; i. e. by night pleasures, by day tortures); cp. Pv II. 12 (see Stede, *Gespenstergeschichten des Peta Vatthu* p. 106), III. 7[8]; PvA 204, 210, & Divy p. 9. Expressions for these "mixed" devatās who are partly blessed, partly cursed are e. g.: **vimāna-peta** PvA 145, 148, 271, 275; f. **vimāna-petī** PvA 152, 160, 186, 190; **vimāna devatā** PvA 190; **vemānika-peta** J V.2; PvA 244; DhA III.192 (as powerful, by the side of nāgas & supaṇṇas).—In their appearance they are like beautiful human beings, dressed in yellowish (pīta, expld as "golden" robes (cp. the angels in the oldest Christian apocalyptic literature: on their relation to Hellenic ideas see e. g. A. Dieterich, *Nekyia*, Leipzig 1903, pp. 10-18, 29: red & white the colours of the land of the blessed), with gold and silver as complementary outfit in person and surroundings. Thus throughout the Vimāna Vatthu, esp. Nos. 36 & 47 (pīta-vimāna). Their splendour is often likened to that of the moon or of the morning star.—4. *Origin* of Vimānas. A vimāna *arises* in the "other world" (paraloka) at the instant of somebody doing good (even during the lifetime of the doer) and waits for the entry of the owner: DhA III.291 sq. In the description of the vimāna of the nāga-king (J VI.315=Vv 84[22]) it is said on this subject: a vimāna is obtained neither without a cause (adhicca), nor has it arisen in the change of the seasons, nor is it self-made (sayankata), nor given by the gods, but "sakehi kammehi apāpakehi puññehi laddha" (i. e. won by one's own sinless & meritorious deeds).—Entering the Vimāna-paradise is, analogous to all semi-lethal passing over into enchanted conditions in fairy tales, compared with the awakening from sleep (as in a state of trance): sutta-ppabuddha DhA III.7. Of the Vimāna itself it is said that it *appears* (pātur ahosi), e. g. VvA 188; DhA I.131; or *arises* (uggañchi) DhA III.291; VvA 221.—5. *Location* of the Vimānas. The "vimāna" is an individual paradisiacal state. Therefore vimānas are not definitely *located* "Elysian Fields." They are anywhere (in *this* world as well as in the *Beyond*), but certain places are more favourable for their establishment than others. Thus we may state that *κατ' ἐξοχήν* they are found in the neighbourhood of *water*. Thus either in the *Ocean* (majjhe sāgarasmiŋ Th I, 1190; samudda-majjhe PvA 47), where access is possible only through adventures after shipwreck or similar causes (J. IV.1 sq.; Pv IV.11); or at one or the other of the great *lakes* of the Himavant (Pv II.12). They are in out-of-the-way places ("end of the world"); they are also found in the *wilderness*: Vv 84; Pv IV.3[2]. As *tree*-vimānas with rukkha-devatā as inhabitants they occur e. g. at J III.310; V.502; Pv I.9; II.9; PvA 244. Very often they are phantasmagorical castles in the *air*. By special power of their inhabitants they may be transported to any place at will. This faculty of transference is combined with the ability of extremely swift motion (compared to the speed of thought: manojava). Thus a golden palanquin is suspended in mid-air above a palace at VvA 6 (ākāsa-cārin, sīgha-java). They are said to be ākāsaṭṭhānāni J VI.117; SnA 222, 370 (but the palace of the Yakkha Āḷavaka is bhumma-ṭṭha, i. e. stands on the ground, and is described as fortified: SnA 222). The place of a (flying) vimāna may be taken by various conveyances: a chair, an elephant, ship, bed, litter etc. Or the location of it in the other world is in the Cittalatāvana (Vv 37), or the Pāricchattaka tree (Vv 38), or in the Cātummahārājika-bhavana (VvA 331). — Later on, when the theory of meritorious deities (or departed souls raised to special rank) as vemānikā devā was established, their abode was *with* their vimānas settled among the *Tāvatiŋsa* (e. g. VvA 188, 217, 221, 244, 289; DhA III.291), or in the *Tusita* heaven. Thus Tusita-pura interchanges with Tusita-vimāna at DhA II. 208. The latter occurs e. g. at DhA III.173, 219. — 6. The *dimensions* of the Vimānas are of course enormous, but harmonious (being "divine"), i. e. either of equal extent in all directions, or specially proportioned with significant *numbers*. Of these the foll. may be mentioned. The typical numbers of greatest frequency are 12, 16, 30, 700, in connection with yojana. The dimensions, with ref. to which 12 & 16 are used, are length, width, height, & girth, whereas 700 applies usually to the height (DhA III.291 e. g., where it is said to be "*over* 700"), and the number of turrets (see above 2). At VvA 267 (satta-yojana-pamāṇo ratho) No. 7 is used for 700; No. 30 (extent) is found e. g. at DhA III.7; ThA 55; No. 12 e. g. at J VI.116; DhA III.291; VvA 6, 217, 221, 244, 246, 291 sq.; No. 16 at VvA 188, 289. — 7. Vimānas of *sun* and *moon*. A peculiar (late ?) idea is that sun and moon have their vimānas (cp. Vedic ratha = sun). There are only very few passages in the post-canonical books mentioning these. The idea that the celestial bodies *are* vimānas ("immense chariots in the shape of open hemispheres" Kirfel, *Kosmographie der Inder* p. 282) is essentially Jainistic. See on Jain Vimānas in general Kirfel, l. c. pp. 7-9, 292-300. — In the Pāli Com. we find SnA 187, 188 (canda-vimānaŋ bhinditvā = breaking up the moon's palace, i. e. the moon itself); and DhA III.99 (candima-suriyā vimānāni gahetvā aṭṭhaŋsu). — 8. Other terms for vimāna, and *specifications*. Var. other expressions are used more frequently for vimāna in general. Among these are ratha (see above 1 a); nagara (Pv II.12[5]); pura (see above 5, as tusita°); pāsāda, either as dibba° (DhA III.291), or vara° (VvA 130), or vimāna° (Vv 31[10]). — The vimānas are specified as deva-vimāna "heavenly palace," e. g. J I.59; Vism 342; VvA 173; or (in a still more superlative expression) brahma-vimāna, i. e. best or most excellent magic palace, highest paradise, e. g. D I.17 (here perhaps "palace of Brahmā"); III.28 ("abode of brahmās" Rh. D.); It 15; Vism 108. The latter expression is abbreviated to brahma (nt.) "highest, best thing of all," "summum bonum," paradise, magic palace: ThA 47 (Ap. v. 6) & 55 (Ap. v. 8), at both places as sukataŋ, i. e. well made. —A rather odd expression for the paradisiacal state (in concrete form) is attabhāva (existence, cp. Gr. βιοτή Hom. Od. IV.365 ?) instead of vimāna, e. g. DhA I.131 (tigāvuta-ppamāṇa); III.7 (id.). — 9. *Various.* Of innumerable passages in the books mentioned above (under 1) only the foll. may be given for ref.: J III.310, 398, 405; V.165, 171; VI.117 sq., 120 sq.; Ap 35, 55, 59; Dāvs IV.54 (acalaŋ v. antalikkhamhi nāvaŋ gati-virahitaŋ ambhorāsi-majjhamhi disvā); and Vimāna Vatthu throughout. Of passages in the 4 older Nikāyas we have only A II.33 (ye devā dīgh' āyukā uccesu vimānesu cira-ṭṭhitikā). At S I.12 = 23 we should read "na ca mānaŋ" for "na vimānaŋ" (*K.S.* I.18).

Vimāna[2] [vi + māna] disrespect, contempt Sn 887 (°dassin showing contempt).

Vimānana (nt.) [vi + mānana] disrespect, contempt D III. 190 (a°); Miln 377, 386.

Vimānita [pp. of vimāneti] treated with contempt A III.158, 160.

Vimāneti [vi + māneti] to disrespect, to treat with contempt Vin II.260; Sn 888; Nd[1] 297. — pp. **vimānita.**

Vimukha (adj.) [vi + mukha] turning away from, averted, neglectful Mhvs 22, 80; PvA 3 (dhamma-saññā°), 269 (carita°).

Vimuccati [vi + muccati, Pass. of muñcati] to be released, to be free (of passion), to be emancipated M I.352; S II.94, 124; III.46, 189; IV.86; V.218; A IV.126 sq., 135, 179; Sn 755; Pug 61, 68; Sdhp 613. — aor. 3rd pl. vimucciŋsu Sn p. 149. — pp. **vimutta.** See also (an)upādā & (an)upādāya. — Caus. **vimoceti** to cause to be released or emancipated, to set free A II.196 (cittaŋ); Vin III.70 (id.). — grd. **vimocanīya** A II.196.

Vimutta [pp. of vimuñcati] freed, released, intellectually emancipated Vin I.8; A IV.75, 179, 340; V.29; D III.97, 100, 133, 258; S I.23, 35; III.13, 53, 137; Sn 354, 475, 522, 877, 1071 sq., 1101, 1114; Nd[1] 283; Nd[2] 587; Pv IV.1[32] (arahā +); Vism 410. — Often as cittaŋ v. an emancipated heart, e. g. D I.80; A III.21; S I.46, 141; III.90; IV.164; V.157 (here taken by Mrs. Rh. D. at S VI.93, Index, as "unregulated, distrait"); Sn 975; Nd[1] 284; Vbh 197. **ubhatobhāga°** emancipated in both ways (see *Dial* II. 70) D II.71; III.105, 253; S I.191; A I.73; IV.10, 77, 453; V.23; M I.439, 477 sq. — **paññā°**, emancipated by insight, freed by reason (see *Dial.* II.68) S I.191; II.123; D II.70; III.105, 254; M I.439, 477. —**saddhā°** freed by faith A I.73; IV.10, 77; V.23; Ps II.52; M I.439, 477. —**anupādā vimutta** freed without any further clinging to the world M I.486; S II.18; III.59; IV.83 and passim.

-**atta** having an emancipated self S III.46, 55, 58; A IV.428. -**āyatana** point or occasion of emancipation, of which there are 5, viz. hearing the Dhamma taught by the Master, teaching it oneself, reciting it, pondering over it, understanding it A III.21 sq.; D III.241, 279; Ps I.5.

Vimutti (f.) [fr. vimuccati] release, deliverance, emancipation D I.174; III.288; S V.206 sq. (abhijānāti), 222 (ariya°), 266, 356; A II.247, III.165 (yathābhūtaŋ pajānāti), 242; Sn 54, 73, 725 sq.; J I.77, 78, 80; Ps I.22; II.143 sq.; Nd[1] 21; Pug 27, 54 sq.; Vbh 86, 272 sq., 392 (micchā°) Nett 29; Vism 410; Sdhp 614. — **ceto°** (& **paññā°**) emancipation of heart (and reason) D I.156; III.78, 108, 247 sq., 273; S I.120; II.214; IV.119 sq.; V.118 sq., 289 sq.; A I.123 sq., 220 sq.; 243; II.36, 87, 214; III.20, 131, 400; IV.83, 314 sq.; V.10 sq.; Vbh 344; Nett 40, 43, 81 sq., 127. —**sammā°** right or true emancipation A II.222 sq.; V.327; Ps I.107; II.173. — See also arahatta, upekkhā, khandha II.A, dassana, phala, mettā.

-**rasa** the essence of emancipation A I.36; IV.203; PvA 287. -**sāra** substance or essence of emancipation A II.141, 243; IV.385.

Vimokkha (& **Vimokha**) [fr. vi + **muc**, cp. mokkha[1]] deliverance, release, emancipation, dissociation *from* the things of the world, Arahantship D II.70, 111); III.34, 35, 230, 288; M I.196 (samaya° & asamaya°); S I.159 (cetaso v.); II.53, 123; III.121; IV.33; A II.87; IV.316; V.11; Vin V.164 (cittassa); Sn 1071 (which Nd² 588 expl^s as "agga" etc., thus strangely taking it in meaning of mokkha², perhaps as edifying etym.); Nd² 466 (in expl^n of Bhagavā); Ps I.22; II.35 (as 68!), 243; Pug 11 sq.; Vbh 342; Dhs 248; Nett 90, 100, 119, 126; Vism 13, 668 sq.; Miln 159; PvA 98; Sdhp 34, 264. — The *three* vimokkhas are: suññato v., animitto v., appaṇihito v. Ps II.35; Vism 658. The *eight* vimokkhas or stages of emancipation, are: the condition of rūpī, arūpa-saññī, recognition of subha, realization of ākāsânañc'āyatana, of viññāṇ'ânañc'āyatana, ākiñcaññ'āyatana, neva-saññā-n'âsaññ'āyatana, saññā-vedayita-nirodha D III.262 (cp. *Dial.* III.242), A I.40; IV.306; Vbh 342; expl^d in detail at Ps II.38-40. [cp. BSk. aṣṭau vimokṣāḥ, e. g. AvŚ II.69, 153.] — In sequence jhāna vimokkha samādhi samāpatti (magga phala) at Vin I.97, 104; III.91; IV.25; A III.417, 419; V.34, 38; Vbh 342. — See also jhāna.

Vimocana (nt.) [vi+mocana] 1. letting loose, discharging Dhtm 216 (assu°). — 2. release from, doing away with Mhvs 35, 73 (antarāya°).

Vimoceti see vimuccati.

Vimohita [pp. of vi+moheti] deluded, bewildered Sdhp 363.

Vimba is another spelling for bimba at S V.217. Cp. BSk. vimbaka (form of face) Divy 172, 525.

Vimhaya [cp. Sk. vismaya, vi+smi] astonishment, surprise, disappointment J V.69 (in expl^n of vyamhita); Mhvs 5, 92; SnA 42 (explaining "vata"), 256 (do. for "ve" = aho); DA I.43; VvA 234, 329.

Vimhāpaka (adj.) [fr. vimhāpati] deceiving, dismaying SnA 549 (=kuhaka).

Vimhāpana (nt.) [fr. vimhāpeti] dismaying, deceiving, disappointing Vism 24 (in expl^n of kuhana); Dhtp 633 (id.).

Vimhāpeti [Caus. of *vimhayati=vi+smi] to astonish, to cause dismay to, to deceive Mhvs 17, 44; DA I.91 (in expl^n of kuhaka).

Vimhita (adj.) [pp. of vi+smi, cp. mihita] astonished, discouraged, dismayed J VI.270 (su° very dismayed); Miln 122; Mhvs 6, 19; Dāvs II.80.

Viya (indecl.) [another form of iva, viâ *via (so some Prākrits: Pischel *Prk. Gr.*, § 143, 336)>viya. Pischel, *Prk. Gr.* § 336, 337 derives it fr. viva=v' iva] 1. part of comparison: like, as; stands for iva (usually in *verse*) after ā: Sn 420 (jātimā v.); Pv I.8⁵ (vārinā v.); or o: Sn 580 (vajjho v.), 818 (kapaṇo v.); or ŋ: Sn 381 (vajantaŋ v.), 689 (nekkhaŋ v.). — 2. dubitative particle: na viya maññe I suppose not M II.121. — Cp. byā.

Viya° the diaeretic form (for sake of metre) of vya° [=vi+a°], which see generally. Cp. the identical veyya°.

Viyatta (adj.) [cp. Sk. vyakta, vi+pp. of añj] determined, of settled opinion, learned, accomplished; only in stock phrase sāvakā viyattā vinītā visāradā (which Rh. D. trsl^s "true hearers, *wise* and well-trained, ready etc." *Dial.* II. 114) at D II.104=A IV.310=S V.260=Ud 63. The BSk. (at Divy 202) has śrāvakāḥ (for bhikkhū!) paṇḍitā bhaviṣyanti vyaktā vinītā viśāradāḥ. — 2. separated, split, dissenting, heretic Sn 800 (=*vavatthita* bhinna dvejjhāpanna etc. Nd² 108; =bhinna SnA 530). Cp. the *two* meanings of *vavatthita* (=*vyakta), which quasi-correspond to viyatta 1 & 2 At this passage the v. l. (all SS of the Commentary) viyutta is perhaps to be perferred to viyatta.

Note. It is to be noted that viyatta in § 1 does not occur in poetry, but seems to have spelling viy° because of the foll. vinita and visārada. Cp. vyatta & veyyatta.

Viyatti (f.) [cp. Sk. vyakti] distinctness Dhtp 366 & Dhtm 593 (in def^n of brū). Cp. veyyatti.

Viyākāra [vi+ākāra] preparation, display, distinction, splendour, majesty Sn 299 (=sampatti SnA 319).

Viyācikkhati in verse at Sn 1090 for vyācikkhati, i. e. vi+ācikkhati, to tell, relate, explain.

Viyāpanna [vi+āpanna, pp. of vi+āpajjati cp. vyāpajjati] gone down, lost, destroyed Sn 314 (in verse; gloss viyāvatta. The former expl^d as "naṭṭha," the latter as "viparivattitvā aññathā-bhūta" at SnA 324).

Viyāyata [vi+āyata] stretched out or across J III.373 (in verse).

Viyārambha [vi+ārambha] striving, endeavour, undertaking Sn 953 (expl^d as the 3 abhisankhāras, viz. puñña°, apuñña° & āneñja° at Nd¹ 442).

Viyūḷha [apparently vi+ūḷha, pp. of viyūhati, but mixed in meaning with vi+ūha (of vah)=vyūha] massed, heaped; thick, dense (of fighting) M I.86=Nd² 199⁵ (ubhato viyūḷhaŋ sangāmaŋ massed battle on both sides); A III.94, 99 (sangāma, cp. S IV.308); J VI.275 (balaggāni viyūḷhāni; C.=pabbūḷha-vasena ṭhitāni where pabbūḷha evidently in meaning "sambādha." — 2. put in array, prepared, imminent J II.336 (maraṇe viyūḷhe=paccupaṭṭhite C.). Cp. saŋyūḷha.

Viyūhati [vi+ūh, a differentiated form of vah] to take away, carry off, remove Vin III.48 (paŋsuŋ vyūhati); J I.177, 199 (paŋsuŋ), 238, 331 (kaddamaŋ dvidhā viyūhitvā); III.52 (vālikaŋ); IV.265 (paŋsuŋ); VI.448 (vālukaŋ); DhsA 315; DhA II.38; III.207 (paŋsuŋ). — pp. viyūḷha. Cp. saŋyūhati.

Viyūhana (nt.) [fr. viyūhati] removing, removal Vism 302 (paŋsu°).

Viyoga [vi+yoga 2] sèparation J VI.482; Mhvs 19, 16 (Mahābodhi°); PvA 160, 161 (pati° from her husband); Sdhp 77, 164.

Viyyati [Pass. of vāyati¹ or vināti. The Vedic is ūyate] to be woven Vin III.259. — pp. vīta².

Viracita [vi+racita] 1. put together, composed, made VvA 14, 183. — 2. ornamented ThA 257; VvA 188.

Viraja (adj.) [vi+rajo] free from defilement or passion, stainless, faultless Vin I.294 (āgamma maggaŋ virajaŋ); Sn 139, 520, 636, 1105 (see exegesis at Nd² 590); Pv III.3⁶ (=vigata-raja, niddosa PvA 189); DhA IV.142, 187; DA I.237. Often in phrase virajaŋ vītamalaŋ dhamma-cakkhuŋ udapādi "there arose in him the stainless eye of the Arahant," e. g. Vin I.16; S IV.47. —virajaŋ (+asokaŋ) padaŋ "the stainless (+painless) element" is another expression for Nibbāna, e. g. S IV.210; A IV.157, 160; It 37, 46; Vv 16⁹; similarly ṭhānaŋ (for padaŋ) Pv II.3³³ (=sagga PvA 89).

Virajjaka (adj.) [vi+rajja+ka] separated from one's kingdom, living in a foreign country VvA 336.

Virajjati [vi+rajjati] to detach oneself, to free oneself of passion, to show lack of interest in (loc.). S II.94, 125 (nibbindaŋ [ppr.] virajjati); III.46, 189; IV.2, 86; A V.3; Sn 739=S IV.205 (tattha); Th 1, 247; Sn 813 (na rajjati na virajjati), 853; Nd¹ 138, 237; Miln 245; Sdhp 613. — pp. viratta. — Caus. virājeti to put away.

to estrange (acc.) from (loc.), to cleanse (oneself) of passion (loc.), to purify, to discard as *rāga* D II.51; S I.16=Sn 171 (ettha chandaŋ v.=vinetvā viddhaŋsetvā SnA 213); S IV.17=Kvu 178; A II.196 (rajanīyesu dhammesu cittaŋ v.); Sn 139, 203; Th I, 282; Pv II.13[19] (itthi-cittaŋ=viratta-citta PvA 168); ThA 49; DhA I.327 (itthi-bhāve chandaŋ v. to give up desire for femininity). — pp. virājita.

Virajjana (nt.) [fr. virajjati; cp. rajjana] discolouring J III.148 (rajjana+).

Virajjhati [vi+rādh; cp. Sk. virādhyati: see rādheti[1]] to fail, miss, lose S IV.117; J I.17, 490 (aor. virajjhi); II.432 (id.); PvA 59. — pp. viraddha. — Caus. virādheti (q. v.).

Viraṇa (adj. nt.) [vi+raṇa] without fight or harm, peace Sdhp 579.

Virata [pp. of viramati] abstaining from (abl.) Sn 59, 531, 704, 900, 1070; Nd[1] 314; Nd[2] 591; VvA 72; Sdhp 338.

Virati (f.) [vi+rati] abstinence Mhvs 20, 58. The three viratis given at DA I.305 (=veramaṇī) are sampatta°, samādāna°, setughāta° (q. v.). Cp. DhsA 154 (tisso viratiyo), 218; Sdhp 215, 341 & *Cpd.* 244, n. 2.

Viratta [pp. of virajjati] dispassioned, free from passion, detached, unattached to, displeased with (loc.) S III.45 (rūpadhātuyā cittaŋ virattaŋ vimuttaŋ); Sn 204 (chandarāga°), 235 (°citta āyatike bhavasmiŋ); A V.3, 313; J V.233 (mayi); Sdhp 613.

Viraddha [pp. of virajjhati] failed, missed, neglected S V.23 (ariyo maggo v.), 179 (satipaṭṭhānā viraddhā), 254, 294; Nd[1] 512; J I.174, 490; II.384; IV.71, 497; Nett 132.

Viraddhi (f.) (missing, failure ?) at Vin I.359 is uncertain reading. The vv. ll. are visuddhi, visandi & visandhi, with expl[ns] "viddhaṭṭhāna" & "viraddhaṭṭhāna": see p. 395.

Virandha [vi+randha[2]] opening; defect, flaw Nd[1] 165

Viramaṇa (nt.) (-°) [fr. viramati] abstinence, abstaining from (-°) Mhvs 14, 48 (uccā-seyyā°).

Viramati [vi+ramati] to stop, cease; to desist (abl.), abstain, refrain Sn 400 (Pot. °meyya), 828 (Pot. °me), 925; Nd[1] 168, 376; Th 2, 397 (aor. viramāsi, cp. Geiger, *P.Gr.* § 165[1]); Pv IV.3[55] (pāpadassanaŋ, acc.); Miln 85; PvA 204.

Virala (& **Viraḷa**) (adj.) [connected with Vedic ṛte excluding, without, & nirṛti perishing; cp. also Gr. ἐρημος lonely; Lat. rarus=rare] I. sparse, rare, thin Th 2, 254 (of hair, expl[d] as vilūna-kesa ThA 210, i. e. almost bald; spelling l); DhsA 238 (ḷ); DhA I.122 (°cchanna thinly covered); PvA 4 (in ratta-vaṇṇa-virala-mālā read better with v. l. as ratta-kaṇavīra-mālā, cp. J III.59).

Viralita [pp. of Denom. of virala=viraleti, cp. Sk. viralāyate to be rare] thin, sparse, rare Dāvs IV.24 (a°), with v. l. viraḷita.

Virava (& **°rāva**) [vi+rava & rāva; cp. Vedic virava] shouting out, roaring; crying (of animals) J I.25, 74 (ā), 203 (of elephants); V.9 (ā, of swans).

Viravati [vi+ravati] I. to shout (out), to cry aloud; to utter a cry or sound (of animals) J II.350 (kikī sakuṇo viravi); V.206; Mhvs 12, 49 (mahārāvaŋ viraviŋsu mahājanā); PvA 154, 217, 245 (vissaraŋ), 279 (id.); Sdhp 179, 188, 291. — 2. to rattle J I.51. — Caus. virāveti to sound Mhvs 21, 15 (ghaṇṭaŋ to ring a bell):

Viraha (adj.) [vi+raho] empty, rid of, bar, without PvA 137, 139 (sīla°).

Virahita (adj.) [vi+rahita] empty, exempt from, rid of, without Miln 330 (dosa°); PvA 139.

Virāga [vi+rāga] I. absence of rāga, dispassionateness, indifference towards (abl. or loc.) disgust, absence of desire, destruction of passions; waning, fading away, cleansing, purifying; emancipation, Arahantship. — D III.130 sq., 136 sq., 222, 243, 251, 290; S I.136; III.19 sq., 59 sq., 163, 189; IV.33 sq., 47, 226, 365; V.226, 255, 361; A I.100, 299; II.26; III.35, 85, 325 sq.; IV.146 sq., 423 sq.; V.112, 359; Th I, 599; Sn 795; Ps II.220 sq.; Nd[1] 100; Kvu 600=Dh 273=Nett 188 (virāgo seṭṭho dhammānaŋ); Dhs 163; Nett 16, 29; Vism 290 (khaya° & accanta°) 293. — Often nearly synonymous with nibbāna, in the description of which it occurs frequently in foll. formula: taṇhakkhaya virāga nirodha nibbāna, e. g. S I.136; Vin I.5; A II.118; It 88; — or comb[d] with nibbidā virāga nirodha upasama . . . nibbāna, e. g. M I.431; S II.223; cp. nibbāna II.B[1] & III.8. — In other connection (more objectively as "destruction"): aniccatā sankhārānaŋ etc., vipariṇāma virāga nirodha, e. g. S III.43; (as "ceasing, fading away":) khaya(-dhamma liable to), vaya°, virāga°, nirodha° M I.500; S II.26. — 2. colouring, diversity or display of colour, dye, hue (=rāga I) J I.89 (nānā°-samujjala blazing forth different colours); 395 (nānā° variously dyed); PvA 50 (nānā°-vaṇṇa-samujjala).

Virāgatā (f.) [abstr. fr. rāga] disinterestedness, absence of lust Kvu 212=Ud 10.

Virāgita (adj.) [fr. vi+*rāgeti, Denom. of rāga ?] at J V.96 is not clear. It is said of beautiful women & expl[d] by C. as vilagga-sarīrā, tanumajjhā, i. e. "having slender waists." Could it be "excited with passion" or "exciting passion"? Or could it be an old misreading for virājita[2]? It may also be a distorted vilāka (q. v.) or vilaggita.

Virāgin (adj.) [fr. virāga 2, cp. rāgin] I. discoloured, fading in colour J III.88 (fig. saddhā avirāginī), 148 (rāga° fading in the original dye, of citta). — 2. changing, reversing A III.416 (of dukkha: dandha° & khippa° of slow & quick change; v. l. M_6 is viparāgi, which may represent a vipariyāyi, i. e. changing).

Virāguṇa in meaning "fading away, waning" in verse at It 69 (of viññāṇa) is doubtful reading. It corresponds to virāgadhamma of the prose part (virāgudh° vv. ll.). The v. l. is pabhanguṇa (which might be preferable, unless we regard it as an explanation of virāgin, if we should write it thus).

Virāgeti [for virādheti, as in BSk. virāgayati (e. g. Divy 131, 133) to displease, estrange, the fig. meaning of virāgeti like BSk. ārāgeti for Pāli ārādheti in lit & fig. meanings] to fail, miss; only at M I.327 (puriso narakapapāte papatanto hatthehi ca pādehi ca paṭhaviŋ virāgeyya "would miss the earth"; differently Neumann: "Boden zu fassen suchte," i. e. tried to touch ground). — Perhaps also in virāgāya (either as ger. to virāgeti or as instr. to virāga in sense of virādha(na)) Pv I.11[7] (sukhaŋ virāgāya, with gloss virāgena, i. e. spurning one's good fortune; expl[d] as virajjhitvā virādhetvā at PvA 59). Cp. virāye (=virāge ?) at Th I, 1113 (see virādheti).

Virājati [vi+rājati] to shine PvA 189 (=virocati).

Virājita[1] [pp. of virājeti] cleansed, discarded as *rāga*, given up S IV.158 (dosa); J III.404 (=pahīna C.).

Virājita[2] [pp. of Caus. of virājati] shining out, resplendent J II.33 (mora . . . suratta-rāji-virājita here perhaps =streaked ?). Cp. virāgita.

Virājeti see **virajjati**.

Virādhanā (f.) [fr. virādheti] failing, failure D II.287; A V.211 sq.

Virādhita [pp. of virādheti] failed, missed, lost J V.400; Pv IV.1^3 (=pariccatta C.).

Virādheti [vi+rādheti^1, or Caus. of virajjhati] to miss, omit, fail, transgress, sin Sn 899; Th 1. 37. 1113 virāye for virādhaya C., may be virāge, cp. *Brethren* 375^2 & see virāgeti); Nd^1 312; J I.113; Ap. 47; PvA 59. — Cp. virāgeti. — pp. virādhita.

Virāva see virava.

Viriccati [Pass. of vi+riñcati] to get purged D II.128 (ppr. viriccamāna). — pp. viritta. — Cp. vireka.

Viritta [pp. of viriccati] purged Miln 214.

Viriya (nt.) [fr. vīra; cp. Vedic vīrya & vīria] lit. "state of a strong man," i. e. vigour, energy, effort, exertion. On term see also *Dhs. trsl*^{n} § 13; *Cpd.* 242. — D III.113, 120 sq., 255 sq.; S II.132, 206 sq.; Sn 79, 184, 353, 422, 531, 966, 1026 (chanda°); Nd^1 476, 487; Nd^2 394; J I.178 (viriyaŋ karoti, with *loc.*); Pug 71; Vbh 10; Nett 16, 28; Tikp 60, 63; Miln 36; Vism 160 (°upekkhā), 462; KhA 96; SnA 489; DhA IV.231; DA I.63; DhsA 120; VvA 14; PvA 98, 129; Sdhp 343, 517. — accāraddha° too much exertion M III.159; A III.375; opp. atilīna° too little ibid; uṭṭhāna° initiative or rousing energy S I.21, 217; A III.76; IV.282; ThA 267; PvA 129; nara° manly strength J IV.478, 487. -viriyaŋ āra(m)bhati to put forth energy, to make an effort S II.28; IV.125; V.9, 244 sq.; A I.39, 282, 296; II.15 = IV.462. — As adj. (-°) in alīna° alert, energetic J I.22; āraddha° full of energy, putting forth energy, strenuous S I.53, 166, 198; II.29, 207 sq.; IV.224; V.225; A I.4, 12; II.76, 228 sq.; III.65, 127; IV.85, 229, 291, 357; V.93, 95, 153, 335; J I.110; ossaṭṭha° one who has given up effort J I.110; hīna° lacking in energy It 34 (here as vīriya, in metre). — **v.** is one of the indriyas, the balas & the sambojjhangas (q. v.).

-ārambha "putting forth of energy," application of exertion, will, energy, resolution D III.252; S II.202; IV.175; A I.12; III.117; IV.15 sq., 280; V.123 sq.; Ps I.103 sq.; Vbh 107, 194, 208; DhsA 145, 146. **-indriya** the faculty of energy D III.239, 278; S V.196 sq.; Dhs 13; Vbh 123; Nett 7, 15, 19; VbhA 276. **-bala** the power of energy D III.229, 253; A IV.363; J I.109. **-saŋvara** restraint by will Vism 7; SnA 8; DhsA 351.

Viriyatā (f.) [abstr. fr. viriya] manliness, energy, strength M I.19; VvA 284.

Viriyavant (adj.) [viriya+vant] energetic A I.236; Sn 528, 531 (four-syllabic), 548 (three-syllabic); Vism 3 (=ātāpin); Sdhp 475.

Virujaka (vīṇā°) lute-player J VI.51 (=vīṇā-vādaka C.). See **rujaka**.

Virujjhati [vi+rujjhati] to be obstructed Sn 73 (avirujjhamāna unobstructed); J VI.12.

Virujjhana (nt.) [fr. virujjhati] obstructing or being obstructed, obstruction, J VI.448.

Viruta (nt.) [vi+ruta] noise, sound (of animals), cry Sn 927; expl^d as "virudaŋ [spelling with d, like ruda for ruta] vuccati-miga-cakkaŋ; miga-cakka-pāthakā [i. e. experts in the ways of animals; knowers of auspices] migacakkaŋ ādisanti" at Nd^1 382; and as "mig' ādinaŋ vassitaŋ" at SnA 564. The passage is a little doubtful, when we compare the expression **virutañ ca gabbhakaraṇaŋ** at Sn 927 with the passage **viruddha-gabbhakaraṇaŋ** at D I.11 (cp. DA I.96), which seems more original.

Viruddha [pp. of virundhati] hindered, obstructed, disturbed S I.236; Sn 248, 630; Nd^1 239; Miln 99, 310; J I.97. — Often neg. a° unobstructed, free S I.236; IV.71; A III.276 (°ka); Dh 406; Sn 365, 704, 854; VbhA 148 = Vism 543.

-gabbha-karaṇa (using charms for) procuring abortion D I.11; DA I.96 (expl^d here as first trying to destroy the fœtus and afterwards giving medicine for its preservation). See also **viruta**.

***Virundhati** [vi+rundhati] to obstruct etc. Pass. virujjhati (q. v.). — pp. **viruddha**. — Caus. virodheti. (q. v.).

Virūpa (adj.) [vi+rūpa] deformed, unsightly, ugly Sn 50; J I.47; IV.379; VI.31, 114; PvA 24, 32, 47; Sdhp 85.

Virūḷha [pp. of virūhati] having grown, growing S II.65 (viññāṇe virūḷhe āyatiŋ punnabbhav' âbhinibbatti hoti).

Virūḷhi (f.) [vi+rūḷhi, of **ruh**] growth M I.250; S III.53; A III.8, 404 sq.; V.152 sq., 161, 350 sq.; It 113; Miln 33; Mhvs 15, 42; VbhA 196. —avirūḷhi-dhamma not liable to growth Sn 235; DhA I.245.

Virūhati [vi+rūhati^1] to grow, sprout It 113; Miln 386; DA I.120. — Cp. paṭi°. — pp. virūḷha. — Caus II. virūhāpeti to make grow, to foster Miln 386.

Virūhanā (f.) & °a (nt.) [vi+rūhanā] growing, growth J II.323 (f.); Miln 354; Vism 220; DA I.161; PvA 7.

Vireka = virecana; Miln 134 (cp. Vin I.279).

Virecana (nt.) [vi+recana, ric] purging, a purgative Vin I.206 (°ŋ pātuŋ to drink a p.), 279 (id.); D I.12; A V.218; J III.48 (sineha° an oily or softening purgative); DA I.98.

Virecaniya (adj.) [grd. formation fr. virecana] (one who is) to be treated with a purgative Miln 169.

Vireceti [vi+Caus. of riñcati] to purge Miln 229, 335.

Virocati [vi+rocati] to shine (forth), to be brilliant Vin II. 296 (tapati, bhāsati, v.); Sn 378, 550; It 64 (virocare); J I.18, 89; IV.233; Pv I.11^4; II.9^{62}; III.3^5 (=virājati PvA 189); DhA I.446; IV.143; DhsA 14; PvA 110 (°amāna = sobhamāna), 136 sq., 157. Cp. **verocana**. — Caus. viroceti to illumine Miln 336.

Virodha [vi+rodha^1] obstruction, hindrance, opposition, enmity S I.111; IV.71, 210; Sn 362; Pug 18, 22; Kvu 485; Miln 394; DhsA 39. —avirodha absence of obstruction, gentleness M II.105 = Th 1, 875; Pv III.7^3.

Virodhana (adj. nt.) [fr. virodheti] opposing, obstruction, opposition, contradiction, only neg. a° absence of opposition, J III.274, 320, 412; V.378.

Virodhita [pp. of virodheti] obstructed, rendered hostile Pgdp 90 (or is it virādhita?).

Virodheti [Caus. of virundhati] to cause obstruction, to render hostile, to be in disharmony, to exasperate S IV.379 = A V.320 (which latter passage reads viggaṇhati instead); Sdhp 45, 496. — pp. **virodhita**.

Virosanā (f.) [vi+rosanā] causing anger Vbh 86; VbhA 75.

Vilakkhaṇa (adj.-nt.) [vi+lakkhaṇa] wrong or false characteristic; (adj.) discharacteristic, i. e. inconsistent with characteristics, discrepant (opp. sa° in accordance with ch.) Miln 405; Nett 78; VbhA 250 sq.

Vilagga (adj.) [vi+lagga] 1. stuck Vin I.138; M I.393. — 2. slender (of waist) J V.96 (see virāgita), 216 (see **vilāka**).

Vilaggita (adj.) [vi+laggita] stretched or bending (?), slender J IV.20 (see under **vilāka**).

Vilanga (nt.) [*Sk. viḍanga] the plant Erycibe paniculata Vin I.201 (v. l. vil°). — °thālikā at Nd^1 154 read as **bilanga°** (q. v.).

Vilanghaka [fr. vilangheti] in **hattha°** jerking of the hand, beckoning (as a mode of making signs) Vin I.157 = M I.207 (has g for gh, cp. p. 547). — Cp. hattha-vikāra.

Vilanghati [vi + langhati] to jump about, to leap (over) Sdhp 168.

Vilajjati [vi + lajjati] to be ashamed, to be bashful, to pretend bashfulness J v.433.

Vilapati [vi + lapati] 1. to talk idly J I.496. — 2. to lament, wail Th 1, 705; J II.156; v.179; Miln 275; ThA 148 (Ap. v. 66).

Vilamba (adj.) [vi + lamba] hanging down; only in redupl.-iter. cpd. **olamba-vilamba** dropping or falling off all round J IV.380.

Vilambati [vi + lambati] to loiter, to tarry, lit. "hang about" J I.413; DhA I.81.

Vilambin (adj.) [vi + lambin] hanging down, drooping M I.306 (f. °inī, of a creeper, i. e. growing tendrils all over).

Vilaya [vi + laya, cp. līyati] dissolution; °ŋ gacchati, as much as: "to be digested," to be dissolved Miln 67. — adj. dissolved, dispersed Dpvs I.65.

Vilasati [vi + lasati] to play, dally, sport; to shine forth, to unfold splendour J v.38 (of a tree "stand herrlich da" Dutoit), 433 (of woman); VI.44 (of a tree, vilāsamāna T.). — pp. **vilasita**.

Vilasita (adj.) [pp. of vilasati] shining; gay, playful, coquettish J v.420.

Vilāka (adj.) [perhaps = vilagga (Geiger, *P.Gr.* § 612), although difficult to connect in meaning] only in f. °a: slender (of waist); the expln with **vilagga** may refer to a comparison with a creeper (cp. vilambin & J v.215) as "hanging" ("climbing") i. e. slim, but seems forced. See also **virāgita** which is expld in the same way. The word is peculiar to the "Jātaka" style. — J IV.19 (= suṭṭhu-vilaggita-tanu-majjhā); v.155 (+ mudukā; C. expls as sankhitta-majjhā), 215 (°majjhā = vilagga-sarīrā C.), 506 (velli-vilāka-majjhā = vilagga-majjhā, tanu-dīgha-majjhā C.); VvA 280 (°majjhā for sumajjhimā of Vv 64[13]; T. reads vilāta°).

Vilāpa [vi + lāpa] idle talk J I.496; v.24. Cp. saŋ°.

Vilāpanatā (f.) = vilāpa Pug 21.

Vilāsa [fr. vilasati] 1. charm, grace, beauty J I.470; VI.43; Miln 201; ThA 78; PvA 3. — **desanā°** beauty of instruction DA I.67; Vism 524, 541; Tikp 21. — 2. dalliance, sporting, coquetry J III.408; v.436. vilāsa is often coupled with līlā (q. v.).

Vilāsavant (adj.) [fr. vilāsa] having splendour, grace or beauty Mhvs 29, 25.

Vilāsin (adj.) [fr. vilāsa] shining forth, unfolding splendour, possessing charm or grace, charming DA I.40 (vyāmapabhā parikkhepa-vilāsinī splendour shining over a radius of a vyāma).

Vilikhati [vi + likhati] 1. to scrape, scratch S I.124 (bhūmiŋ); IV.198; DhsA 260 (fig. manaŋ v.; in expln of vilekha). — 2. to scratch open Vin II.175. — pp. **vilikhita**.

Vilikhita [pp. of vilikhati] scraped off SnA 207.

Vilitta [pp. of vilimpati] anointed D I.104 (su-nahāta su-vilitta kappita-kesa-massu); J III.91; IV.442.

Vilimpati [vi + limpati] to smear, anoint A III.57; J I.265 (ger. °itvā); III.277 (ppr. °anto); Pv I.10[6] (ger. °itvāna); PvA 62 (°itvā). — pp. **vilitta**. — Caus. II. **vilimpāpeti** to cause to be anointed J I.50 (gandhehi), 254 (id.).

Vilivili (-kriyā) see **biḷibiḷikā**.

Vilīna (adj.) [vi + līna, pp. of vilīyati] 1. clinging, sticking [cp. līyati 1] Vin I.209 (olīna° sticking all over). — 2. matured ("digested"? cp. vilaya) J IV.72 (nava°-gosappi freshly matured ghee); Miln 301 (phalāni ripe-fruit). — 3. [cp. līyati 2] molten, i. e. refined, purified J IV.118 (tamba-loha° molten or liquid-hot copper); v. 269 (tamba-loha°, id.; cp. C. on p. 274: vilīnaŋ tambālohaŋ viya pakkaṭṭhitaŋ lohitaŋ pāyenti); DhsA 14 (°suvaṇṇa). — Cp. **uttatta** in same sense and the expln of velli as "uttatta-ghana-suvaṇṇa-rāsi-ppabbā" at J v.506 C.

Vilīyati [vi + līyati 2] to melt (intrs.), to be dissolved, to perish J IV.498; Vism 420 (pabbata, spelling here with l; Warren wrong "are hidden from view," i. e. nilīyati); DhsA 336 (phānita-piṇḍa; trsln not to the point: "reduced or *pounded*"); Sdhp 383; Pgdp 21. — pp. **vilīna**. — Cp. pa°.

Vilīyana (nt.) [fr. vilīyati] melting, dissolution Sdhp 201.

Vilīva & Viliva (adj.) [Kern, *Toev.* s. v. compares Sk. bilma slip, chip. Phonetically viliva = Sk. bilva: see **billa**] 1. made of split bamboo Vin II.266 (i). — 2. (ī) a chip of bamboo or any other reed, a slip of reed M I.566 (Bdhgh on M I.429); Vism 310 (°maya).

Vilīvakāra [vilīva + kāra] a worker in bamboo, a basket-maker Vin III.82; Miln 331; VbhA 222 (°ka in simile); PvA 175.

Vilugga (adj.) [vi + lugga] broken; only in redupl.-iter. cpd. **olugga-vilugga** all broken up, tumbling to pieces M I.80, 450.

Vilutta [pp. of vilumpati] plundered, stripped, robbed, ruined S I.85 = J II.239; J v.99; VI.44; Miln 303; Mhvs 33, 71 (corehi).

Vilumpaka (adj.) [fr. vi + **lup**] (act. or pass.) plundering or being plundered J I.370 (°cora); II.239 (pass.).

Vilumpati [vi + lumpati] to plunder, rob, steal, ruin S I.85 = J II.239; v.99; Miln 193; VvA 100; DhA III.23. — Pass. **viluppati** J v.254 (gloss for °lump° of p. 253). — pp. **vilutta**. — Caus. II. **vilumpāpeti** to incite to plunder Miln 193; J I.263.

Vilumpana (nt.) [fr. vilumpati] plundering DhA III.23.

Vilumpamāna(ka) [orig. ppr. med. of vilumpati] plundering, robbing J v.254; PvA 4 (°ka cora).

Vilulita (adj.) [vi + luḷita; cp. BSk. vilulita Jtm 210] stirred, agitated, shaken, disturbed Dāvs IV.54 (bhaya°-citta). Cp. viloḷeti.

Vilūna (adj.) [vi + lūna] cut off (always with ref. to the hair) M III.180 = A I.138; Miln 11; PvA 47.

Vilekha [vi + lekha] perplexity, lit. "scratching" Vin IV.143 (here as f. °ā); Dhs 1256 (mano°); DhsA 260. — The more common word for "perplexity" is **vikkhepa**.

Vilepana (nt.) [vi + lepana] ointment, cosmetic, toilet perfume A I.107, 212; II.209; Th 1, 616 (sīlaŋ v. seṭṭhaŋ. Cp. J III.290); Pug 51, 58; Pv II.3[16]; DA I.77, 88.

Vilokana (nt.) [vi + lok (**loc** = **roc**), see loka & rocati] looking, reflection, investigation, prognostication; usually as 5 objects of reflection as to when & where & how one shall be reborn (pañca-mahā-°āni), consisting in kāla, desa, dīpa, kula, mātā (the latter as janetti-āyu i. e. mother and her time of delivery at J I.48) or time (right or wrong), continent, sky (orientation), family (or clan) and one's (future) mother: J I.48, 49; DhA I.84; as 8 at Miln 193, viz. kāla, dīpa, desa, kula, janetti, āyu, māsa, nekkhamma (i. e. the 5 + period of gestation, month of his birthday, and his renunciation). Without special meaning at DA I.194 (ālokana +). Cp. volokana.

Vilokita (nt.) [pp. of viloketi] a look A II.104, 106 sq., 210; Pug 44, 45; DA I.193; VvA 6 (ālokita+).

Viloketar [n. ag. fr. viloketi] one who looks or inspects DA I.194 (āloketar+).

Viloketi [vi+loketi, of **lok,** as in loka] to examine, study, inspect, scrutinize, reflect on Th 2, 282; J I.48, 49; DhA I.84; Miln 193; Mhvs 22, 18. — pp. vilokita. — Cp. pa° & vo°.

Vilocana (nt.) [vi+locana] the eye Dāvs I.41; ThA 253.

Vilopa [vi+lopa] plunder, pillage M I.456 (maccha° fish-haul); J I.7; III.8; VI.409; Dpvs IX.7 (°kamma). — **vilopaŋ** khādati to live by plunder J VI.131.

Vilopaka (adj.) [fr. vilopa] plundering, living by plundering J I.5; Miln 122 (f. °ikā).

Vilopiya (adj.) [grd. formation fr. vilopa] to be plundered; neg. a° Sdhp 311.

Vilomatā (f.) [abstr. fr. viloma] unseemliness, repugnance SnA 106.

Viloma (adj.) [vi+loma] against the grain (lit. against the hair), discrepant, reversed, wrong, unnatural Vin II. 115 (of cīvara: unsightly); J III.113; Dpvs VII.55; DhA I.379; PvA 87

Vilomana (nt.) [fr. viloma] discrepancy, disagreement, reverse DhsA 253.

Vilometi [Denom. fr. viloma] to dispute, disagree with, to find fault Nett 22; Miln 29, 295; DhsA 253.

Vilolana (nt.) [fr. vi+**lul**] & Viloṭana [fr. vi+**luḍ**; cp. Whitney, *Sanskrit Roots*, 1885, p. 149, where themes & their forms are given by **luṭh**[1] to roll, **luṭh**[2] & **luṇṭh** to rob, **luḍ** to stir up (some forms of it having meaning of **luṇṭh**)=**lul** to be lively] shaking, stirring; only found in lexicogr. literature as def^n of several roots, viz. of **gāh** Dhtp 349; Dhtm 504; **math** & **manth** (see mathati) Dhtp 126; Dhtm 183. See also luḷati.

Viloḷeti [vi+loḷeti or loleti, cp. vilulita] to stir, to move about J I.26; Dpvs VI.52.

Viḷayhati [vi+dayhati] to burn (intrs.) J II.220.

Viḷāra at A III.122 read as biḷāra (sasa-biḷārā rabbits & cats).

Vivajjita [pp. of vivajjeti] 1. abandoning, abstaining from VvA 75 (°kiliṭṭha-kamma). — 2. avoided Th 2, 459. — 3. distant from (abl.) Miln 131.

Vivajjeti [vi+vajjeti] to avoid, abandon, forsake S I.43; A V.17; Sn 53 (=parivajj° abhivajj° Nd² 592), 399 (°jjaya), 407 (praet. °jjayi); Vv 84^38 (°jjayātha=parivajjetha VvA 346); J I.473; III.263, 481 (°jjayi); V.233 (Pot. °jjaye); Miln 129; Sdhp 210, 353, 395. — pp. vivajjita. — Pass. vivajjati J I.27.

Vivaṭa [vi+vaṭa, pp. of **vṛ**: see vuṇāti] uncovered, open (lit. & fig.), laid bare, unveiled Sn 19 (lit.), 374 (fig.= anāvaṭa SnA 366), 763, 793 (=open-minded); Nd¹ 96; Pug 45, 46 (read vivaṭa for pi vaṭa; opp. pihita); Vism 185 (opp. pihita); J V.434; DhA III.79; VvA 27; PvA 283 (mukha unveiled). —**vivaṭena cetasā** "with mind awake & clear" D III.223; A IV.86; S V.263; cp. ceto-vivaraṇa. —**vivaṭa** is freq. v. l. for **vivatta** (-cchada), e. g. at A II.44; Sn 372; DhA III.195; SnA 265 (in expl^n of term); sometimes the *only* reading in this phrase (q. v.), e. g. at Nd² 593. — instr. **vivaṭena** as adv. "openly" Vin II.99; IV.21.

-cakkhu open-minded, clear-sighted Sn 921; Nd¹ 354. **-dvāra** (having) an open door, an open house J V.293 (aḍḍha° half open); DhA II.74. **-nakkhatta** a yearly festival, "Public Day," called after the fashion of the people going uncovered (appaṭicchannena sarīrena) & bare-footed to the river DhA I.388.

Vivaṭaka (adj.) [vivaṭa+ka] open (i. e. not secret) Vin II.99.

Vivaṭṭa (m. & nt.) [vi+vaṭṭa¹] 1. "rolling back," with ref. to the development of the world (or the aeons, kappa) used to denote a *devolving* cycle ("devolution"), whereas vaṭṭa alone or **saŋvaṭṭa** denote the *involving* cycle (both either with or without kappa). Thus as "periods" of the world they practically mean the same thing & may both be interpreted in the sense of a *new* beginning. As redupl.-inter. cpds. they express only the idea of constant change. We sometimes find vivaṭṭa in the sense of "renewal" & saŋvaṭṭa in the sense of "destruction," where we should expect the opposite meaning for each. See also **vaṭṭa** & **saŋvaṭṭa.** Dogmatically **vivaṭṭa** is used as "absence of vaṭṭa," i. e. nibbāna or salvation from saŋsāra (see vaṭṭa & cp. citta-vivaṭṭa, ceto°, ñāṇa°, vimokkha° at Ps I.108 & II.70). — Fig. in **kamma°** "the rolling back of k.," i. e. devolution or course of kamma at S I.85. — Abs. & comb^d with saŋvaṭṭa (i. e. devolution comb^d with evolution) e. g. at D I.14, 16 sq.; III.109; A II.142 (where read vivaṭṭe for vivaṭṭo); Pug 60; Vism 419 (here as m. vivaṭṭo, compared with saŋvaṭṭo), 420 (°ṭṭhāyin). In cpd. °kappa (i. e. descending aeon) at D III.51; Pug 60; It 15. — 2. (nt.) part of a bhikkhu's dress (rolling up of the binding ?), comb^d with anu-vivaṭṭa at Vin I.287.

Vivaṭṭati [vi+vaṭṭati] 1. to move back, to go back, to revolve, to begin again (of a new world-cycle), contrasted with **saŋvaṭṭati** to move in an ascending line (cp. vivaṭṭa) D I.17; III.84, 109; Vism 327. — 2. to be distracted or diverted from (abl.), to turn away; to turn over, to be upset Nett 131; Pug 32 (so read for vivattati); Ps II.98 (ppr.). — pp. **vivaṭṭa.**

Vivaṭṭana (nt.) & °ā (f.) [fr. vivaṭṭati] turning away, moving on, moving back Ps I.66; II.98; Vism 278 (f.; expl^d as "magga").

Vivaṭṭeti [vi+vaṭṭeti] to turn down or away (perhaps in dogmatic sense to turn away from saŋsāra), to divert, destroy: only in phrase **vivaṭṭayi saŋyojanaŋ** (in standard setting with acchecchi **taṇhaŋ**), where the usual v. l. is vāvattayi (see vāvatteti). Thus at M I.12, 122; S I.127; IV.105, 205, 207, 399; A I.134; III.246, 444 sq.; IV.8 sq.; It 47 (T. vivattayi).

Vivaṇṇa (adj.) [vi+vaṇṇa] discoloured, pale, wan Sn 585; Th 2, 79; J II.418.

Vivaṇṇaka (nt.) [fr. vivaṇṇeti] dispraise, reviling Vin IV.143.

Vivaṇṇeti [vi+vaṇṇeti] to dispraise, defame Pv III.10^6 (thūpa-pūjaŋ); PvA 212.

Vivatta-cchada (adj.) having the cover removed, with the veil lifted; one who draws away the veil (cp. vivaraṇa) or reveals (the Universe etc.); or one who is freed of all (mental & spiritual) coverings (thus Bdhgh), Ep. of the Buddha. — Spelling sometimes **chadda°** (see chada). — D I.89; II.16; III.142 (dd; sammā-sambuddha loke vivatta-chadda; trsl^n "rolling back the veil from the world"), 177 (dd); A II.44 (v. l. dd); Sn 372 (expl^d as "vivaṭa-rāga-dosa-moha-chadana SnA 365), 378, 1003 (ed. Sn prefers dd as T. reading); Nd² 593 (with allegorical interpretation); J I.51; III.349; IV.271 (dd); DhA I.201 (v. l. dd); III.195; DA I.250. — It occurs either as **vivatta°** or **vivaṭa°.** In the first case (**vivatta°**) the expl^n presents difficulties, as it is neither the opp. of **vatta** ("duty"), nor the same as **vivaṭṭa** ("moving back" intrs.), nor a direct pp. of **vivattati** (like Sk. vivṛtta) in which meaning it would come nearer to "stopped, reverted, ceased." vivattati has not been found in Pāli. The only plausible expl^n would be taking it as an abs. pp. formation fr. vṛt in Caus. sense (vatteti), thus "moved hack, stopped, discarded" [cp. BSk. vivartayati to cast off a garment, Divy 39). In the second case (vivaṭa°) it is pp. of vivarati [vi + vṛ: see vuṇāti], in meaning "uncovered, lifted, off," referring to the covering (chada) as uncovered instead of the uncovered object. See vivaṭa. It is difficult to decide between the two meanings. On the principle of the "lectio difficilior" vivatta would have the preference, whereas from a natural & simple point of view vivaṭa seems more intelligible & more fitting. It is evidently an *old* phrase. *Note.* -vivatta-kkhandha at S I.121 is a curious expression ("with his shoulders twisted round"?). Is it an old misreading for patta-kkhandha? Cp. however, S.A. quoted *K.S.* I.151, n. 5, explaining it as a dying monk's effort to gain an orthodox posture.

Vivattati at Pug 32 is to be read as vivaṭṭati.

Vivadati [vi + vadati] 1. to dispute, quarrel Sn 842, 884; J I.209; Miln 47. — 2. (intrs.) to be quarrelled with S III.138.

Vivadana (nt.) [fr. vivadati] causing separation, making discord D I.11; DA I.96.

Vivadha (carrying yoke) see khārī-vidha and vividha².

Vivana (nt.) [vi + vana] wilderness, barren land S I.100; Vv 77⁶ (=arañña VvA 302); J II.191, 317.

Vivara (nt.) [fr. vi + vṛ] 1. opening (lit. dis-covering), pore, cleft, leak, fissure Dh 127 (pabbatānaŋ; cp Divy 532; Miln 150; PvA 104); Vism 192, 262; J IV.16; V.87; DhA IV.46 (mukha°); SnA 355; PvA 152, 283. — 2. interval, interstice D I.56 (quoted at Pv IV.3²⁷); Vism 185. — 3. fault, flaw, defect A III.186 sq.; J V.376.

Vivaraṇa (nt.) [fr. vivarati] 1. uncovering, unveiling, making open, revelation, in loka° laying open the worlds, unveiling of the Universe; referred to as a great miracle at Vism 392; Miln 350; Dāvs II.120; J IV.266. — 2. opening, unfolding, making accessible, purifying (fig.), in ceto° A III.117, 121; IV.352; V.67. — 3. explanation, making clear (cp. vibhajana) Nett 8 (as f.); SnA 445.

Vivarati [vi + varati, vṛ; see vuṇāti] 1. to uncover, to open Vin II.219 (windows, opp. thaketi); D I.85 (paticchannaŋ v.); J I.63 (dvāraŋ), 69; IV.133 (nagaraŋ); DhA I.328 (vātapānaŋ); DA I.228; PvA 74 (mukhaŋ); VvA 157, 284. — 2. (fig.) to open, make clear, reveal S IV.166; V.261; KhA 12 (+ vibhajati etc.). — pp. vivaṭa.

Vivasati [vi + vasati²] to live away from home, to be separated, to be distant J IV.217. — Cp. vippavasati.

Vivasana (nt.) [vi + vas (uṣ) to shine, cp. vibhāti] (gradually) getting light; turning into dawn (said of the night), only in phrase ratyā vivasane at the end of night, comb^d in stock phrase with suriy' uggamanaŋ pati "towards sunrise" (evidently an old phrase) at Th I, 517; J IV.241; V.381, 461; VI.491; Pv III.8². Also at Sn 710.

Vivaseti [Caus. of vi + vas to shine] lit. to make [it] get light; rattiŋ v. to spend the night (till it gets light) Sn 1142; Nd² 594 (=atināmeti) — vivasati is Kern's proposed reading for vijahati (rattiŋ) at Th I, 451. He founds his conjecture on a v. l. vivasate & the C. expl° "atināmeti khepeti." Mrs. Rh. D. trsl^s "waste" (i. e. vijahati).

Vivāda [fr. vi + vad] dispute, quarrel, contention D I.236; III.246; A IV.401; Sn 596, 863, 877, 912; Nd¹ 103, 167, 173, 260, 307; Pug 19, 22; Ud 67; J I.165; Miln 413; VvA 131. There are 6 vivāda-mūlāni (roots of contention), viz. kodha, makkha, issā, sāṭheyya, pāpicchatā, sandiṭṭhi-parāmāsa or anger, selfishness, envy, fraudulence, evil intention, worldliness: D III.246; A III.334 sq.; Vbh 380; referred to at Ps I.130. There is another list of 10 at A V.78 consisting in wrong representations regarding dhamma & vinaya.

Vivādaka [fr. vivāda] a quarreller J I.209.

Vivādiyati (vivādeti) [Denom. fr. vivāda] to quarrel Sn 832 (=kalahaŋ karoti Nd¹ 173), 879, 895. Pot. 3rd sg. vivādiyetha (=kolahaŋ kareyya Nd¹ 307), & vivādayetha Sn 830 (id. expl° Nd¹ 170).

Vivāha [fr. vi + vah] "carrying or sending away," i. e. marriage, wedding D I.99; Sn p. 105; PvA 144; SnA 448 (where distinction āvāha = kaññā-gahaṇaŋ, vivāha = kaññā-dānaŋ). — As *nt.* at Vin III.135. Cp. āvāha & vevāhika.

Vivāhana (nt.) [fr. vi + vah] giving in marriage or getting a husband for a girl (cp. āvāhana) D I.11; DA I.96. Cp. Vin III.135.

Vivicca (indecl.) [ger. of viviccati] separating oneself from (instr.), aloof from D I.37; A III.25; J VI.388; Dhs 160; Pug 68; Vism 139, 140 (expl^d in detail). — Doubtful reading at Pv I.11⁹ (for viricca?). — As viviccaŋ (& a°) at J V.434 in meaning "secretly" (=raho paticchannaŋ C.).

Viviccati [vi + vic] to separate oneself, to depart from, to be alone, to separate (intrs.) Vin IV.241; ger. viviccitvā DhsA 165, & vivicca (see sep.). — pp. vivitta. — Cp. viveceti.

Vivicchati [Desid. of vindati] to desire, long for, want Nett 11.

Vivicchā (f.) [Desid. of vid, cp. Sk. vivitsā] manifold desire, greediness, avarice DhsA 375; Nett 11 (where expl^n "vivicchā nāma vuccati vicikicchā"). See also veviccha.

Vivitta (adj.) [pp. of viviccati; vi + vitta³] separated, secluded, aloof, solitary, separate, alone D I.71; S I.110; A II.210; III.92; IV.436; V.207, 270; Sn 221, 338, 810, 845; Nd¹ 201; Kvu 605; Miln 205; DA I.208; DhsA 166; DhA III.238; IV.157 (so read for vivivitta!); VbhA 365; PvA 28, 141, 283. Cp. pa°.

Vivittaka (adj.) [vivitta + ka] solitary J IV.242 (°āvāsa).

Vivittatā (f.) [abstr. fr. vivitta] seclusion (=viveka) VbhA 316, cp. *K.S.* I.321.

Vivitti (f.) [fr. viviccati] separation DhsA 166. — Cp. viveka.

Vividha¹ (adj.) [vi + vidha¹] divers, manifold, mixed; full of, gay with (-°) D II.354; Pv II.4⁹; Vv 35⁹; Miln 319; Mhvs 25, 30; SnA 136 (in expl° of vi°: "viharati = vividhaŋ hitaŋ harati").

Vividha² [for Sk. vivadha; vi + vah] carrying-yoke D I.101; S I.78 (as v. l. khāri-vividhaŋ, see khāri); J III.116 (parikkhāraŋ vividhaŋ ādāya, where v. l. reads khāriŋ vividhaŋ).

Viveka [fr. vi + vic] detachment, loneliness, separation, seclusion; "singleness" (of heart), discrimination (of thought) D I.37, 182; III.222, 226, 283 = S IV.191 (°ninna citta); S I.2, 194; IV.365 sq.; V.6, 240 sq.; A I.53; III.329; IV.224; Vin IV.241; Sn 474, 772, 822, 851, 915, 1065; Nd¹ 158, 222; J I.79; III.31; Dhs 160; Pug 59, 68; Nett 16, 50; DhsA 164, 166; ThA 64; PvA 43; Sdhp 471. —viveka is given as *fivefold* at Ps II.220 sq. and VbhA 316, cp. *K.S.* I.321 (Bdhgh on S III.2, 8), viz. tadanga°, vikkhambhana°, samuccheda°

paṭippassaddhi°, nissaraṇa°; as *threefold* at Vism 140, viz. kāya°, citta°, vikkhambhana°, i. e. physically, mentally, ethically; which division amounts to the same as that given at Nd¹ 26 with kāya°, citta°, upadhi°, the latter equivalent to "nibbāna." Cp. on term *Dial.* 1.84. See also jhāna. Cp. pa°.

Vivekattā = vivittatā VbhA 316.

Vivecitatta (nt.) [abstr. fr. vivecita, pp. of viveceti] discrimination, specification DhsA 388.

Viveceti [Caus. of viviccati] to cause separation, to separate, to keep back, dissuade Vin I.64; D I.226; S III.110; M. I.256; Pv III.10⁷ (= paribāheti PvA 214); Miln 339; DhsA 311; Nett 113, 164 (°iyamāna).

Viveṭhiyati [vi + veṭhīyati] to get entangled Vin II.117.

Vivesa [?] distinction D I.229, 233. We should read visesa, as printed on p. 233.

Visa (nt.) [cp. Vedic viṣa; Av. viš poison, Gr. ἰός, Lat. vīrus, Oir. fī: all meaning "poison"] poison, virus, venom M I.316 = S II.110; Th 1, 418; 768; Sn 1 (sappa° snake venom); A II.110; J I.271 (halāhala° deadly p.); III.201; IV.222; Pug 48; Miln 302; PvA 62, 256; ThA 489. — On visa in similes see *J.P.T.S.* 1907, 137. Cp. āsi°.

-uggāra vomiting of poison SnA 176. **-kaṇṭaka** a poisoned thorn or arrow, also name of a sort of sugar DhsA 203. **-kumbha** a vessel filled with p. It 86. -pānaka a drink of p. DhA II.15. -pīta (an arrow) dipped into poison (lit. which has drunk poison). At another place (see pīta¹) we have suggested reading **visappita** (visa + appita), i. e. "poison-applied," which was based on reading at Vism 303. See e. g. J V.36; Miln 198; Vism 303, 381; DhA I.216. **-rukkha** "poison tree," a cert. tree Vism 512; VbhA 89; DA I.39. -vaṇijjā trading with poison A III.208. -vijjā science of poison DA I.93. —vejja a physician who cures poison (ous snake-bites) J I.310. **-salla** a poisoned arrow Vism 503.

Visaŋ is P. prefix corresponding to Sk. **viṣu** (or visva° [see vi°] in meaning "diverging, on opposite sides,") apart, against; only in cpd. °vādeti and derivations, lit. to speak wrong, i. e. to deceive.

Visaŋyutta (& **visaññutta**) (adj.) [vi + saŋyutta] 1. (lit.) unharnessed, unyoked Th 1, 1021 (half-fig.). — 2. detached from the world A I.262 = III.214; S II.279 (ññ); Th 1, 1022; Sn 621, 626, 634; DhA III.233 (sabba-yoga°); IV.141, 159, 185.

Visaŋyoga (& **visaññoga**) [vi + saŋyoga] disconnection, separation from (-°), dissociation Vin II.259 (ññ) = A IV.280; D III.230 (kāma-yoga°, bhava°, diṭṭhi°, avijjā°; cp. the 4 oghas), 276; A II.11; III.156.

Visaŋvāda [visaŋ + vāda] deceiving; neg. a° Miln 354.

Visaŋvādaka (adj.) [visaŋ + vādaka] deceiving, untrustworthy Vism 496; f. °ikā J V.401, 410. — a° not deceiving D III.170; A IV.249; M III.33; Pug 57.

Visaŋvādana (nt.) & °ā (f.) & °atā (f.) [fr. visaŋvādeti] deceiving, disappointing A V.136 (°ā); Vin IV.2. — a° honesty D III.190 (°atā).

Visaŋvādayitar [n. ag. fr visaŋvādeti] one who deceives another D III.171.

Visaŋvādeti [visaŋ + vādeti; cp. BSk. visaŋvādayati AvŚ I.262, after the Pāli] to deceive with words, to break one's word, to lie, deceive Vin III.143; IV.1; Nett 91. — Neg. a° J V.124.

Visaŋsaṭṭha (adj.) [vi + saŋsaṭṭha] separated, unconnected with (instr.) M I.480; DA I.59.

Visaŋhata [vi + saŋhata²] removed, destroyed Th 1, 89.

Visakkiya [vi + sakkiya ?] in °dūta is a special kind of messenger Vin III.74.

Visaggatā see a°.

Visanka (adj.) [vi + sanka; Sk. viśanka] fearless, secure; a° Sdhp 176.

Visankita (adj.) [pp. of vi + śank] suspicious, anxious ThA 134 (Ap. v. 78). — neg. a° not perturbed, trusting, secure Sdhp 128.

Visankhāra [vi + sankhāra] divestment of all material things Dh 154 (= nibbāna DhA III.129). See sankhāra 3.

Visankhita [vi + sankhata] destroyed, annihilated Dh 154; J I.493 (= viddhaŋsita DhA III.129).

Visajjati [vi + sajjati, Pass. of **sañj**; the regular Act. would be visajati] to hang on, cling to, stick to, adhere (fig.); only in pp. visatta (q. v.). — The apparent ger. form visajja belongs to vissajjati.

Visajjana & **visajjeti**: see viss°.

Visañña (adj.) [vi + sañña = saññā] 1. having wrong perceptions Sn 874. — 2. unconscious J V.159. In composition with **bhū** as visaññī-bhūta at J I.67.

Visaññin (adj.) [vi + saññin] unconscious, one who has lost consciousness; also in meaning "of unsound mind" (= ummattaka Nd¹ 279) A II.52 (khitta-citta +); Miln 220; Sdhp 117.

Visaṭa & **visata** [pp. of vi + **sṛ**, Sk. visṛta] spread, diffused, wide, broad D III.167 (!); Sn 1 (T. reads t, v. l. BB has ṭ); J II.439; IV.499 (t); Miln 221, 354 (!; + vitthata), 357. Cp. anu°.

Visaṭā & **visatā** (f.) [abrh. formation fr. vi + **sañj**, spelling t for tt: see **visatta**. The writing of MSS. concerning t in these words is very confused] "hanging on," clinging, attachment. The word seems to be a quasi-short form of visattikā. Thus at Sn 715 (= taṇhā C.; spelling t); Dhs 1059 (trsl⁰ "diffusion," i. e. fr. vi + **sṛ**; spelling ṭ) = Nd² s. v. *taṇhā* (spelt with t).

Visaṭṭha see **vissaṭṭha**.

Visaṭṭhi (f.) [for vissaṭṭhi, fr. vi + **sṛj**] 1. emission; in sukka° emission of semen Vin II.38; III.112; Kvu 163. — 2. visaṭṭhi at S III.133 and A IV.52 (T. visaṭṭhi) probably stands for visatti in meaning "longing," clinging to (cp. BSk. viṣakti AvŚ II.191), or "love for" (loc.).

Visati [**viś**, cp. viś dwelling-place, veśa; Gr. οἶκος house, οἰκέω to dwell; Lat. vīcus, Goth. weihs = E. °wick in Warwick, etc.] to enter, only in comb⁰ with prefixes, like upa°, pa°, pari°, saŋ°, abhisaŋ°, etc. . . . See also vesma (house).

Visatta [pp. of visajjati] hanging on (fig.), sticking or clinging to, entangled in (loc.) A II.25; Sn 38, 272; Nd² 597; J II.146; III.241.

Visattikā (f.) [visatta + ikā, abstr. formation] clinging to, adhering, attachment (to — loc.), sinful bent, lust, desire. — It is almost invariably found as a syn. of taṇhā. P. Commentators explain it with ref. either to visaṭa (diffused), or to visa (poison). These are of course only exegetical edifying etymologies. Cp. *Dhs. trsl*ⁿ § 1059; *Expositor* II.468; *Brethren* 213 n. 3, *K.S.* 1.2, n. 6, and the varied exegesis of the term in the Niddesas. — S I.1, 24, 35, 107, 110; A II.211; IV.434; Sn 333, 768, 857, 1053 sq.; Th 1, 519; Nd¹ 8 sq., 247; Nd² 598; DhA III.198; IV.43; DhsA 364; Nett 24; Dhs 1059.

Visada (adj.) [cp. Sk. viśada] 1. clean, pure, white D II.14; Miln 93, 247; Dāvs V. 28. — 2. clear, manifest Miln 93; DhsA 321, 328 (a°); VbhA 388 sq.
-kiriyā making clear: see under **vatthu**[1]. -bhāva clearness Vism 128; Tikp 59.

Visadatā (f.) [abstr. fr. visada] purity, clearness Vism 134 (vatthu°).

Visanna [pp. of visīdati] sunk into (loc.), immersed J IV.399. The poetical form is **vyasanna**.

Visappana in °rasa at Vism 470 is not clear. Is it "spreading" [vi + **sṛp**], or misprint for visa-pāna ?

Visabhāga (adj.) [vi + sabhāga] different, unusual, extraordinary, uncommon Miln 78 sq.; DA I.212; Vism 180 (purisassa itthisarīraŋ, itthiyā purisa-sarīraŋ visabhāgaŋ), 516; DhA IV.52; PvA 118. -°ārammaṇa pudendum muliebre J II.274 ≈ III.498.

Visama (adj.) [vi + sama[3]] 1. uneven, unequal, disharmonious, contrary A I.74; PvA 47 (vāta), 131 (a° = sama of the "middle" path). — 2. (morally) discrepant, lawless, wrong A III.285; V.329; Sn 57 (cp. Nd[2] 599); Miln 250 (°diṭṭhi). — 3. odd, peculiar, petty, disagreeable A II.87; Miln 112, 304, 357; J I.391 (nagaraka). — As nt. an uneven or dangerous or inaccessible place, rough road; (fig.) unevenness, badness, misconduct, disagreeableness A I.35 (pabbata°); S IV.117; Vbh 368 (two sets of 3 visamāni: rāga, etc.); Miln 136, 157, 277, 351; J V.70; VvA 301. —**visamena** (instr.) in a wrong way Pv IV.14.

Visamāyati [Denom. fr. visama] to be uneven D II.269 (so read for visamā yanti).

Visaya [cp. Sk. viṣaya, fr. vi + **śī**] 1. locality, spot, region; world, realm, province, neighbourhood Sn 977. Often in foll. comb[ns]: petti° (or pitti°) and pettika (*a*) the world of the manes or petas M I.73; S III.224; V.342, 356 sq.; A I.37, 267; II.126 sq.; III.211, 339, 414 sq.; IV.405 sq.; V.182 sq.; Pv II.2[2]; II.7[9]; J I.51; PvA 25 sq., 59 sq., 214. (*b*) the way of the fathers, native or proper beat or range D III.58; S V.146 sq.; A III.67; J II.59. **Yama°** the realm of Yama or the Dead Pv II.8[2] (= petaloka PvA 107). — 2. reach, sphere (of the senses), range, scope; object, characteristic, attribute (cp. *Cpd.* 143 n. 2) S V.218 (gocara°); Nett 23 (iddhi°); Miln 186, 215, 316; Vism 216 (visayī-bhūta), 570 = VbhA 182 (mahā° & appa°); KhA 17; SnA 22, 154 (buddha°), 228 (id.); PvA 72, 89. —**avisaya** not forming an object, a wrong object, indefinable A V.50; J V.117 (so read for °ara); PvA 122, 197. — 3. object of sense, sensual pleasure SnA 100.

Visayha (adj.) [ger. of visahati] possible Pv IV.1[12] (yathā °ŋ as far as possible); a° impossible M I.207 = Vin I.157.

Visara [vi + sara] a multitude DA I.40.

Visalla (adj.) [vi + salla] free from pain or grief S I.180; Sn 17, 86 = 367.

Visaritā (f.) at D II.213 in phrase iddhi° is doubtful reading. The gloss (K) has "**visevitā**." Trsl[n] (*Dial.* II.246): "proficiency." It is comb[d] with iddhi-pahutā & iddhi-vikubbanatā. Bdhgh's expl[n] is "**visavanā**" [fr. vi + **sru** ?].

Visahati [vi + sahati] to be able, to dare, to venture Sn 1069 (= ussahati sakkoti Nd[2] 600); J I.152. — ppr. neg. avisahanto unable VvA 69, 112; and avisahamāna J I.91. — ger. visayha (q. v.).

Visākha (adj.) [visākhā as adj.] having branches, forked; in ti° three-branched S I.118 = M I.109.

Visākhā (f.) [vi + sākhā, Sk. viśākhā] N. of a lunar mansion (nakkhatta) or month (see vesākha), usually as visākha° (-puṇṇamā), e. g. SnA 391; VvA 165.

Visāṭita [pp. of vi + sāṭeti] cut in pieces, smashed, broken J II.163 (= bhinna C.).

Visāṇa (nt.) [cp. Sk. viṣāṇa] 1. the horn of an animal (as cow, ox, deer, rhinoceros) Vin I.191; A II.207; IV.376; Sn 35 (khagga°, q. v.), 309; Pug 56 (miga°); Ap 50 (usabha°); J I.505; Miln 103. — 2. (also as m.) the tusks of an elephant J III.184; V.41, 48.
-maya made of horn Vin II.115.

Visāta (adj.) [fr. vi + **śat**, cp. sāṭeti] crushed to pieces, destroyed M II. 102 (°gabbba, with mūḷha-gabbha; v. l. vighāta).

Visāda [fr. vi + **sad**] depression, dejection D I.248; DA I.121; Sdhp 117. Cp. visīdati.

Visāra [fr. vi + **sṛ**] spreading, diffusion, scattering DhsA 118.

Visāraka (adj.) [vi + sāraka, of **sṛ**] spreading, extending, expanding Vin III.97 (vattu° T.; vatthu° MSS.).

Visārada (adj.) [cp. BSk. viśārada, e. g. AvŚ I.180. On etym. see sārada] self-possessed, confident; knowing how to conduct oneself, skilled, wise D I.175; II.86; S I.181; IV.246; V.261; A II.8 (vyatta +); III.183, 203; IV.310, 314 sq.; V.10 sq.; M I.386; Ap 23; J III.342; V.41; Miln 21; Sdhp 277. —**avisārada** diffident Miln 20, 105.

Visāla (adj.) [cp. Sk. viśāla] wide, broad, extensive Sn 38; J V.49, 215 (°pakhuma); Miln 102, 311.
-akkhī (f.) having large eyes J V.40; Vv 37[1] (+ vipulalocanā; or a petī).

Visālatā (f.) [abstr. fr. visāla] breadth, extensiveness VvA 104.

Visāhaṭa (adj.) [visa + āhaṭa] only neg. **a°** imperturbed, balanced Dhs 11, 15, 24 etc.

Visāhāra [visa + āhāra, or vi + saŋ + āhāra] distractedness, perturbation; neg. **a°** balance Dhs 11, 15.

Visikhā (f.) [cp. *Sk. (lexicogr.) viśikhā] a street, road Vin IV.312; J I.338; IV.310; V.16, 434.
-kathā gossip at street corners D I.179; M I.513; Dh I.90.

Visiṭṭha (adj.) [pp. of visissati] distinguished, prominent, superior, eminent D III.159; Vv 32[4]; J I.441; Miln 203, 239; DhA II.15; VvA 1 (°māna = vimāna), 85, 261; Sdhp 260, 269, 332, 489. — compar. °tara Vism 207 (= anuttara). — As visiṭṭhaka at Sdhp 334. — See also abhi°, paṭi°, and **vissaṭṭha**.

Visiṇṇa [pp. of viseyyati] broken, crushed, fallen to pieces J I.174.

Visineti see usseneti.

Visibbita (adj.) [pp. of vi + sibbeti, **sīv** to sew] entwined, entangled Miln 102 (saŋsibbita° as redupl. — iter. cpd.).

Visibbeti [vi + sibbeti, **sīv**] to unsew, to undo the stitches Vin IV.280. — Caus. II. visibbāpeti ibid. — Another visibbeti see under **visīveti**.

Visissati [Pass. of vi + **śiṣ**] to differ, to be distinguished or eminent Nett 188. — pp. **visiṭṭha**. — Caus. **viseseti** (q. v.).

Visīdati [vi + **sad**; cp. visāda & pp. BSk. viṣaṇṇa Divy 44] 1. to sink down J IV.223. — 2. to falter, to be dejected or displeased S I.7; A III.158; Pug 65. — pp. **visanna**.

Visīyati [vi + sīyati; cp. Sk. śīyate, Pass. of **śyā** to coagulate] to be dissolved; 3rd pl. imper. med. **visīyaruŋ** Th 1, 312 (cp. Geiger, *P.Gr.* § 126).

Visīvana (nt.) [fr. visīveti] warming oneself J I.326; v.202. As visibbana at Vin IV.115.

Visīveti [vi+sīveti, which corresponds to Sk. vi-śyāpayati (lexicogr.!), Caus. of **śyā**, śyāyati to coagulate; lit. to dissolve, thaw. The **v** stands for **p**; **śyā** is contracted to sī] to warm oneself Miln 47; J II.68; DhA I.225, 261; II.89. As **visibbeti** (in analogy to visibbeti to sew) at Vin IV.115. — Caus. II. visīvāpeti J II.69.

Visuŋ (indecl.) [cp. Sk. viṣu, a derivation fr. vi°] separately, individually; separate, apart DhA II.26 (mātā-pitaro visuŋ honti). Usually repeated (distributively) visuŋ visuŋ each on his own, one by one, separately, e. g. Vism 250; Mhvs 6, 44; SnA 583; VvA 38; PvA 214. —**visukaraṇa** separation ThA 257.

Visukkha (adj.) [vi+sukkha] dried out or up PvA 58.

Visukkhita (adj.) [vi+sukkhita] dried up Miln 303.

Visujjhati [vi+sujjhati] to be cleaned, to be cleansed, to be pure Vin II.137; J I.75; III.472. — pp. **visuddha**. — Caus. visodheti (q. v.).

Visuddha (adj.) [pp. of visujjhati] clean, pure, bright; in appl^d meaning: purified, stainless, sanctified Vin I.105; D III.52 (cakkhu); S II.122 (id.); IV.47 (sīla); A IV.304 (su°); Sn 67, 517, 687; Nd^2 601; Pug 60; PvA 1 (su°); Sdhp 269, 383.

Visuddhatta (nt.) [abstr. fr. visuddha] purity, purification A II.239.

Visuddhi (f.) [vi+suddhi] brightness, splendour, excellency; (ethically) purity, holiness, sanctification; virtue, rectitude Vin I.105 (visuddho paramāya visuddhiyā); D I.53; III.214 (diṭṭhi°, sīla°), 288; M I.147; S III.69; A I.95 (sīla° & diṭṭhi°); II.80 (catasso dakkhiṇā°), 195; III.315; V.64 (paramattha°); Sn 813, 824, 840, 892; Dh 16 (kamma°); Ps I.21 (sīla°, citta°, diṭṭhi°); II.85 (id.); Nd^1 138, 162; Vism 2; SnA 188 (°divasa), PvA 13 (°cittatā); Sdhp 447. A class of divine beings (dogmatically the highest in the stages of development, viz. gods by sanctification) is called **visuddhi-devā** Nd^2 307; J I.139; VvA 18. See under **deva**.

Visūka (nt.) [perhaps to **sūc**, sūcayati] restless motion, wriggling, twisting, twitching (better than "show," although connection with **sūc** would give meaning "indication, show"), almost synonymous with vipphandita. Usually in cpd. diṭṭhi° scuffling or wriggling of opinion, wrong views, heresy M I.8, 486; Sn 55 (cp. Nd^2 301); Pv IV.1^{37}.

-**dassana** visiting shows (as fairs) D I.5 (cp. DA I.77: "visūkaŋ paṭani-bhūtaŋ dassanaŋ," reading not clear); A I.212; II.209; Pug 58.

Visūkāyita (nt.) [pp. of visūkāyeti, denom. fr. visūka] 1. restlessness, impatience M I.446. — 2. disorder, twisting, distortion (of views); usually in phrase diṭṭhi° with °visevita & °vipphandita e. g. M I.234; S I.123 (Bdhgh's expl^n at *K.S.* I.321 is "vinivijjhan' aṭṭhena viloman' aṭṭhena"); II.62 (in same comb^n; Bdhgh at *K.S.* II.203: "sabbaŋ micchādiṭṭhi-vevacanaŋ"); Dhs 381 ("disorder of opinion" trsl^n); Nd^2 271^{III}; Vbh 145; DhsA 253. Cp. v. l. S I.123^{17} (*K.S.* I.155 "disorders"; n. p. 321).

Visūcikā (f.) [cp. *Sk. visūcikā] cholera Miln 153, 167.

Viseni° [vi+sena in comb^n with **kṛ** and **bhū**; cp. paṭisena] "without an enemy," in °katvā making armyless, i. e. disarming Sn 833, 1078. Expl^d in the Niddesa as "keep away as enemies, conquering" Nd^1 174 = Nd^2 602 (where Nd^1 reads paṭisenikarā kilesā for visenikatvā kilesā). -°**bhūta** disarmed, not acting as an enemy Sn 793 = 914, where Nd^1 96 = 334 has the same expl^n as for °katvā; S I.141 (+upasanta-citta; trsl^n "by all the hosts of evil *unassailed*" *K.S.* I.178). Kern, *Toev.* s. v. differently "not opposing" for both expressions.

Viseneti to discard, dislike, get rid of (opp. usseneti) S III.89; Ps II.167. See **usseneti**.

Viseyyati [vi+seyyati, cp. Sk. śīryati, of **śṛ** to crush] to be broken, to fall to pieces J I.174. — pp. **visiṇṇa**.

Visevita (nt.) [vi+sevita] 1. restlessness, trick, capers M I.446 (of a horse; comb^d with visūkāyita). — 2. disagreement S I.123 (= viruddha-sevita *K.S.* I.320). Bdhgh at *K.S.* II.203 reads °sedhita. Cp. **visūkāyita**.

Visesa [fr. vi+**śiṣ**, cp. Epic Sk. viśeṣa] 1. (mark of) distinction, characteristic, discrimination A I.267; S IV.210; J II.9; Miln 29; VvA 58, 131; PvA 50, 60. — 2. elegance, splendour, excellence J V.151; DhA I.399. — 3. distinction, peculiar merit or advantage, eminence, excellence, extraordinary state D I.233 (so for **vivesa** all through?); A III.349 (opp. hāna); J I.435; VvA 157 (puñña°); PvA 71 (id.), 147 (sukha°). — 4. difference, variety SnA 477, 504; VvA 2; PvA 37, 81, 135 (pl. = items). abl. **visesato**, distinctively, altogether PvA 1, 259. — 5. specific idea (in meditation), attainment J VI.69: see & cp. *Brethren* 24, n. 1; 110. — Cp. paṭi°.

-**âdhigama** specific attainment A IV.22; M II.96; Nett 92; Miln 412; DhA I.100. [Cp. BSk. viśeṣadhigama Divy 174]. -**gāmin** reaching distinction, gaining merit A II.185; III.349 sq.; S V.108. -**gū** reaching a higher state or attainment J VI.573. -**paccaya** ground for distinction VvA 20. -**bhāgiya** participating in, or leading to distinction or progress (spiritually) D III.272 sq., 277, 282; Nett 77; Vism 11, 88 (abstr. °bhāgiyatā).

Visesaka (m. or nt.) [fr. visesa] 1. a (distinguishing) mark (on the forehead) Vin II.267 (with apanga). — 2. leading to distinction VvA 85.

Visesatā = visesa Sdhp 265.

Visesana (nt.) [fr. viseseti] distinguishing, distinction, qualification, attribute Vv 16^{10}; J III.11; VI.63; SnA 181, 365, 399; VvA 13. — instr. **avisesena** (adv.) without distinction, at all events, anyhow PvA 116.

Visesikā (f.) [fr. visesa] the Vaiśeṣika philosophy Miln 3.

Visesita [pp. of viseseti] distinguished, differentiated Mhvs 11, 32; KhA 18; PvA 56.

Visesin (adj.) [fr. visesa] possessing distinction, distinguished from, better than others Sn 799, 842, 855, 905; Nd^1 244.

Visesiya (adj.) [grd. of viseseti] distinguished Vv 16^{10} (= visesaŋ patvā VvA 85); v. l. visesin (= visesavant C.).

Viseseti [Caus. of visissati] to make a distinction, to distinguish, define, specify J V.120, 451; SnA 343; grd. **visesitabba** (-vacana) qualifying (predicative) expression VvA 13. — pp. **visesita**.

Visoka (adj.) [vi+soka] freed from grief Dh 90; DhA II.166.

Visodha [fr. vi+**śudh**] cleaning, cleansing, in cpd. **dubbisodha** hard to clean Sn 279.

Visodhana (nt.) [fr. visodheti] cleansing, purifying, emending Ps II.21, 23; PvA 130.

Visodheti [Caus. of visujjhati] to clean, cleanse, purify, sanctify Kvu 551; Pv IV.3^{25}; DhA III.158; Sdhp 321.

Visoseti [Caus. of vissussati] to cause to dry up, to make wither, to destroy A I.204; Sn 949 = 1099; Nd^1 434 (= sukkhāpeti); Nd^2 603 (id.).

Vissa[1] (adj.) [Vedic viśva, to vi°] all, every, entire; only in Np. Vissakamma. The word is *antiquated* in Pāli (for it sabba); a few cases in poetry are doubtful. Thus at Dh 266 (dhamma), where DhA III.393 expl[s] as "visama, vissagandha"; and at It 32 (vissantaraŋ "among all beings"? v. l. vessantaraŋ).

Vissa[2] (nt.) [cp. Sk. visra] a smell like raw flesh, as °gandha at Dhs 625; DhsA 319; SnA 286; DhA III.393.

Vissaka [of **viś**] dwelling: see paṭi°.

Vissagga [vi+sagga, vi+**sṛj**, cp. Sk. visarga] dispensing, serving, donation, giving out, holding (a meal), only in phrases **bhatta°** the function of a meal Vin II.153; IV.263; Pv III.2[9] (so read for vissatta); Miln 9; SnA 19, 140; and **dāna°** bestowing a gift Pv II.9[27] (=pariccāga-ṭṭhāne dān'agge PvA 124).

Vissajjaka [fr. vissajjati] 1. giving out, distributing Vin II.177. — 2. one who answers (a question) Miln 295.

Vissajjati [vi+sajjati, of **sṛj**. The ss after analogy of ussajjati & nissajjati, cp. ossajjati for osajjati]. A. The pres. vissajjati is not in use. The only forms of the simple verb system are the foll.: ger. **vissajja**, usually written **visajja**, in meaning "setting free," giving up, leaving behind Sn 522, 794, 912, 1060; Nd[1] 98; Nd[2] 596. — grd. **vissajjaniya** [perhaps better to vissajjeti[1]] to be answered, answerable; nt. a reply Nett 161, 175 sq., 191; and **vissajjiya** to be given away: see under a°. — pp. **vissaṭṭha**. — B. Very frequent is the Caus. **vissajjeti** (also occasionally as **visajj°**) in var. meanings, based on the idea of sending forth or away, viz. to emit, discharge J I.164 (uccāra-passāvaŋ). — to send Mhvs 8, 3 (lekaŋ visajjayi). — to dismiss PvA 81 (there). — to let loose PvA 74 (rathaŋ). — to spend, give away, bestow, hand over Pug 26 (visajj°); Nd[1] 262 (dhanaŋ); Miln 41 (dhaññaŋ); PvA 111, 119. — to get rid of J I.134 (muddikaŋ). — to answer (questions), to reply, retort Sn 1005 (°essati, fut.); VvA 71; PvA 15, 59, 87. — pp. **vissajjita**. — Caus. II. **vissajjāpeti** (in meanings of vissajjeti) J IV.2 (hatthaŋ=to push away); Miln 143; Mhvs 6, 43.

Vissajjana (nt.) & °ā (f.) [fr. vissajjeti] 1. giving out, bestowing Nd[1] 262 (dhana°). — 2. sending off, discharging J I.239 (nāvā° putting off to sea). — 3. answer, reply Vism 6, 84; often in comb[n] pucchā° question and answer, e. g. Mhvs 4, 54; PvA 2.

Vissajjanaka (adj.) (-°) [fr. vissajjana] 1. giving out, bestowing PvA 121. — 2. answering J I.166 (pañha°).

Vissajjāpetar [n. ag. fr. vissajjāpeti] one who replies or causes to reply DhA IV.199. Cp. **vissajjetar**.

Vissajjita [pp. of vissajjeti] 1. spent, given away Sn 982 — 2. let loose, sent off, discharged Mhvs 23, 88.

Vissajjetar [n. ag. fr. vissajjeti] one who answers (a question) A I.103 (pañhaŋ). Cp. **vissajjāpetar**.

Vissaṭṭha [pp. of vissajjati] 1. let loose; sent (out); released, dismissed; thrown; given out Mhvs 10, 68; J I.370; III.373; PvA 46, 64, 123, 174. — 2. (of the *voice*:) distinct, well enunciated D I.114 (=apalibuddha, i. e. unobstructed; sandiddha-vilambit' ādi dosa-rahita DA I.282); II.211; A II.51; III.114; S I.189; J VI.16 (here as **vissattha-vacana**). — 3. vissaṭṭha at J IV.219 in phrase °indriya means something like "strong," distinguished. The v. l. **visatta°** suggests a probable **visaṭa°**; it may on the other hand be a corruption of **visiṭṭha°**.

Vissaṭṭhi see visaṭṭhi.

Vissattha [pp. of vissasati] trusting or trusted; confident; being confided in or demanding confidence, intimate, friendly A III.114; Vin I.87 (so read for ṭṭh); IV.21; J II.305; III.343; Miln 109 (bahu° enjoying great confidence); SnA 188 (°bhāva state of confidence); Sdhp 168, 593. —**vissatthena** (instr.) in confidence Vin II.99. — Cp. abhi°.

Vissandaka (adj.) [fr. vissandati] overflowing PvA 119.

Vissandati [vi+sandati, of **syand**] to flow out, to stream, overflow J I.51; V.274; PvA 34 (aor. °sandi=paggbari), 51 (ppr. °amāna), 80 (ger. °itvā), 119 (°anto=paggharanto), 123 (for paggharati; T. °eti).

Vissamati [vi+samati, of **śram**] to rest, repose; to recover from fatigue J I.485; II.70; 128, 133; III.208; IV.93, 293; V.73; PvA 43, 151. — Caus. **vissameti** to give a rest, to make repose J III.36.

Vissamana (nt.) [fr. vissamati] resting, reposing J III.435.

Vissametar [n. ag. fr. vissameti] one who provides a rest, giver of repose, remover of fatigue J VI.526.

Vissara [fr. vi+sarati, of **svar**] 1. outcry, shout, cry of distress, scream Vin I.87; II.152, 207; IV.316; PvA 22, 245 (s), 279, 284 (°ŋ karoti); Sdhp 188. — 2. distress Vin IV.212, 229.

Vissarati [vi+sarati, of **smṛ**] to forget Vin I.207; IV.261; Mhvs 26, 16. — pp. **vissarita**.

Vissarita [opp. of vissarati] forgotten PvA 202.

Vissavati [vi+savati, of **sru**] to flow, ooze Th I, 453= Sn 205 (v. l. SS vissasati).

Vissasati & **vissāseti** [vi+sasati, of **śvas**] to confide in, to put one's trust in (loc. or gen.), to be friendly with S I.79 (vissase); J I.461 (vissāsayitvā); III.148=525 (vissāsaye); IV.56; VI.292. — pp. **vissattha**.

Vissāsa [vi+sāsa, of **śvas**] trust, confidence, intimacy, mutual agreement Vin I.296; 308, A II.78; J I.189, 487; Miln 126; Vism 190; VvA 66; PvA 13, 265. —**dubbissāsa** difficult to be trusted J IV.462.

Vissāsaka (& °ika) (adj.) [vissāsa] intimate, confidential; trustworthy A I.26; Miln 146; DA I.289.

Vissāsaniya (adj.) [grd. of vissāseti] to be trusted, trustworthy PvA 9; Sdhp 306, 441; neg. a° J III.474; cp. **dubbissāsaniya** hard to trust J IV.462.

Vissāsin (adj.) [fr. vissāsa] intimate, confidential A III.136 (asanthava° intimate, although not acquainted).

Vissuta (adj.) [vi+suta, of **śru**] widely famed, renowned, famous Sn 137, 597, 998, 1009; Pv II.7[4]; Mhvs 5, 19; PvA 107 (=dūra-ghuṭṭha).

Vissussati [vi+**śuṣ**] to dry up, to wither S I.126 (in comb[n] ussussati vissussati, with ss from uss°). Spelling here visuss°, but ss at S III.149. — Caus. **visoseti** (q. v.).

Vissota (adj.) [vi+sota, of **sru**] flown away, wasted Miln 294.

Vihaga [viha, sky, +ga] a bird (lit. going through the sky) DA I.46. -°pati lord of birds, a garuḷa Dāvs IV.33, 38, 55.

Vihanga=vihaga, J V.416; PvA 154, 157; Sdhp 241.

Vihangama (adj.) [viha+**gam**] going through the air, flying; (m.) a bird A II.39; III.43; Sn 221, 606; Th I, 1108; J I.216; III.255; DA I.125=DhsA 141.

Vihaññati [Pass. of vihanati] to be struck or slain; to be vexed or grieved, to get enraged, to be annoyed, suffer hardship; to be cast down Sn 168 sq.; Pv II.11[7] (=vighātaŋ āpajjati PvA 150); IV.5[2] (with same expl[n]); J I.73, 359; II.442; V.330; DA I.289. — ppr. **vihaññamāna** Sn 1121 (with long and detailed exegesis at Nd[2] 604); S I.28 (a°); PvA 150. pp. vihata DA I.231.

Vihata[1] [pp. of vihanati] struck, killed, destroyed, impaired It 100 (where A I.164 reads vigata); J VI.171; Sdhp 313, 425.

Vihata[2] (adj.) [cp. Sk. vihṛti] broad, wide J VI.171 (=puthula C.).

Vihanati [vi+hanati] to strike, kill, put an end to, remove A III.248 (kankhaŋ; v. l. vitarati perhaps to be preferred); Sn 673; Pot. 3rd sg. vihane Sn 975 (cp. Nd[1] 509); & vihāne Sn 348 =Th 1, 1268. — ger. vihacca: see abhi°. — Pass. vihaññati (q. v.). — pp. vihata.

Viharaṇa (nt.) [fr. viharati] abiding, dwelling DhsA 164, 168.

Viharati [vi+harati] to stay, abide, dwell, sojourn (in a certain place); *in general:* to be, to live; *appl^d:* to behave, lead a life (as such expl^d with "iriyati" at Vism 16). Synonyms are given at Vbh 194 with iriyati, vattati, pāleti, yapeti, yāpeti, carati; cp. VbhA 262. — See e. g. D I.251; Sn 136, 301, 925; Pug 68; DhsA 168; DA I.70, 132; PvA 22, 67, 78. — *Special Forms:* aor. 3rd sg. vihāsi Sn p. 16; Pv II.9[60]; Mhvs 5, 233; PvA 54, 121; 3rd pl. vihiŋsu Th 1, 925, & vihaŋsu A II.21; fut. viharissati A III.70; vihessati Th 1, 257; vihissati Th 2, 181; and vihāhisi J I.298 (doubtful reading!), where C. expl^s as "vijahissati, paribhāyissati"; with phrase sukhaŋ vihāhisi cp. dukkhaŋ viharati at A I.95, and see also vihāhesi. — pp. not found.

Vihaviha [for vihaga] a sort of bird Th 1, 49 (v. l. cihaciha). The C. expl^s by "parillaka."

Vihāmi at J VI.78 (lohitaŋ) is poetical for vijahāmi; C. expl^s as niṭṭhubhāmi, i. e. I spit out.

Vihāya is ger. of vijahati (q. v.).

Vihāyasa [cp. Sk. viha & vihāyasa] the air, sky PvA 14. Cases adverbially: °yasā through the air Mhvs 12, 10, & °yasaŋ id. J IV.47. Cp. vehāyasa & vehāsa.

Vihāra [fr. viharati] 1. (as m. & adj.) spending one's time (sojourning or walking about), staying in a place, living; place of living, stay, abode (in general) VvA 50 (jala°); PvA 22, 79; eka° living by oneself S II.282 sq.; janghā° wandering on foot PvA 73; divā° passing the time of day Sn 679; PvA 142. See also below 3 a. — 2. (appl^d meaning) state of life, condition, mode of life (in this meaning almost identical with that of vāsa[2]), e. g. ariya° best condition S v.326; SnA 136; dibba° supreme condition (of heart) Miln 225; brahma° divine state S v.326; SnA 136; Vism 295 sq. (ch. IX.); phāsu° comfort A III.119, 132; sukha° happiness S III.8; v.326; A I.43; II.23; III.131 sq.; IV.111 sq., 230 sq.; v.10 sq. *See further* D I.145, 196; III.220 (dibba, brahma, ariya), 250 (cha satata°), 281; S II.273 (jhāna°); III.235 (id.); A III.294 (°ŋ kappeti to live one's life); Ps II.20; Nett 119 sq. — 3. (a) a habitation for a Buddhist mendicant, an abode in the forest (arañña°), or a hut; a dwelling, habitation, lodging (for a bhikkhu), a single room Vin II.207 sq.; D II.7; A III.51, 299 (yathāvihāraŋ each to his apartment); Sn 220 (dūra° a remote shelter for a bhikkhu), 391; Vism 118 (different kinds; may be taken as c.). — (b) place for convention of the bhikkhus, meeting place; place for rest & recreation (in garden or park) DA I.133. — (c) (later) a larger building for housing bhikkhus, an organized monastery, a Vihāra Vin I.58; III.47; S I.185 (°pāla the guard of the monastery); J I.126; Miln 212; Vism 292; DhA I.19 (°cārikā visit to the monastery), 49 (°pokkharaṇī), 416; Mhvs 19, 77; PvA 12, 20, 54, 67, 141, 151; and passim. See also *Dictionary of Names.* The modern province Behar bears its name from the vihāras.

Vihāraka = vihāra (room, hut) Th 2, 94 (=vasanakaovaraka ThA 90).

Vihārika (adj.)=vihārin; in saddhi° co-resident A III.70.

Vihārin (adj.) (-°) [fr. vihāra] dwelling, living; being in such & such a state or condition D I.162 (appa-dukkha°), 251 (evaŋ°); A I.24 (araṇa°), 26 (mettā); It 74 (appamāda°); Sn 45 (sādhu°), 375; Pv IV.1[33] (araṇa°); PvA 77, 230 (mettā°); VvA 71. — eka° living alone S II.282 sq.; IV.35; opp. saddhi° together with another; a co-resident, brother-bhikkhu S II.204; IV.103; A II.239.

Vihāhesi "he banished" at J IV.471 is 3rd sg. aor. Caus. of vijahati (hā); expl^d in C. by pabbājesi. — Another form vihāhisi see under viharati & cp. viheti[2].

Vihiŋsati [vi+hiŋsati] to hurt, injure, harass, annoy S I.165; It 86; Sn 117, 451; PvA 123, 198.

Vihiŋsanā (f.) a Commentary word for vihiŋsā VbhA 75. A similar vihiŋsakā occurs at PvA 123.

Vihiŋsā (f.) (& adj. °a) [abstr. fr. vi+hiŋs, to injure] hurting, injuring, cruelty, injury D III.215; 226 (°vitakka); S I.202; II.151 (°dhātu); A III.448; Sn 292; Nd[1] 207 (°saññā), 386, 501 (°vitakka); Vbh 86, 363 (°vitakka); Dhs 1348; Pug 25; Nett 97; Miln 337, 367, 390; DhsA 403; VbhA 74 (°dhātu), 118 (°vitakka); Sdhp 510. Neg. avihiŋsā see sep. — See also vihesā.

Vihita (adj.) [pp. of vidahati] arranged, prepared, disposed, appointed; furnished, equipped J VI.201 (loka); Miln 345 (nagara); D I.45, S III.46; Pug 55 (aneka°); Mhvs 10, 93; PvA 51 (suṭṭhu°). añña° engaged upon something else Vin IV.269.

Vihitaka (adj.)=vihita; D III.28 sq. (kathaŋ v. aggaññaŋ how as the beginning of things appointed?); — añña° engaged upon something else J IV.389 (or does it belong to āhāra, in sense of "prepared by somebody else"?).

Vihitatā (f.) [abstr. fr. vihita] in añña° being engaged upon something else DhA I.181.

Vihīna (adj.) [pp. of vijahati] left, given up, abandoned Sdhp 579.

Viheṭhaka (adj.) [fr. viheṭheti] harassing, oppressing, annoying J I.504; v.143; Sdhp 89. Neg. a° see sep.

Viheṭhana (nt.) [fr. viheṭheti] harassing, hurting; oppression VbhA 74; VvA 68; PvA 232.

Viheṭhanaka (adj.) [fr. viheṭhana] oppressing, hurting, doing harm J II.123.

Viheṭheti [vi+heṭheti, of hīḍ or heḷ to be hostile. Same in BSk., e. g. MVastu III.360; Divy 42, 145 etc.] to oppress, to bring into difficulties, to vex, annoy, plague, hurt D I.116, 135; II.12; Sn 35; J I.187; II.267; IV.375; Miln 6, 14; DhA 191; VvA 69 (Pass. °iyamāna).

Viheti[1] [for bibheti?] to be afraid (of) J v.154 (=bhāyati C.). Cp. vibheti.

Viheti[2] [contracted Pass. of vijahāti=vihāyati, cp. vibāhesi] to be given up, to disappear, to go away J IV.216. Kern, *Toev.* s. v. wrongly=vi+eti.

Vihesaka (adj.) [fr. viheseti] annoying, vexing, troubling Vin IV.36; Dpvs I.47. — f. °ikā Vin IV.239, 241.

Vihesā (f.) [for vihiŋsā] vexation, annoyance, injury; worry M I.510; II.241 sq.; S I.136; III.132; IV.73; v.357; D III.240 (a°); Vin IV.143 (+vilekhā); A III.245, 291; Sn 247, 275, 277; Vbh 369; Nett 25; Miln 295; DhA I.55.

Vihesikā (f.) [probably for Sk. *vibhīṣikā, fr. bhī, Epic Sk. bhīṣā, cp. bhīṣma=P. bhiŋsa (q. v.)] fright J III.147. (C. says "an expression of fearlessness").

Viheseti [vi+**hiŋs**, or Denom. fr. vihesā, cp. Geiger, *P.Gr.* § 10²] to harass, vex, annoy, insult S IV.63; V.346; A III.194; Vin IV.36 sq.; Ud 44; Sn 277; Pv IV.1⁴⁷ (vihesaŋ, aor.); IV.1⁴⁹ (vihesayi, aor.).

Vīci (m. & f.) [cp. late Sk. vīci wave; Vedic vīci only in meaning "deceit"; perhaps connected with Lat. vicis, Ags. wīce=E. week, lit. "change," cp. tide] 1. a wave J I.509; Miln 117 (jala°), 319 (°puppha wave-flower, fig.); Vism 63 (samudda°); Dāvs IV.46; DhsA 116=Vism 143.—2. interval, period of time (cp. "tide"=time interval) J V.271 (°antara, in **Avīci** definition as "uninterrupted state of suffering"). In contrast pair avīci (adj.) uninterrupted, without an interval, & savīci with periods, in defⁿ of jarā at VbhA 99 & DhsA 328, where avīci means "not changing quickly," and savīci "changing quickly." Also in defⁿ of sadā (continuously) as "avīci-santati" at Nd² 631. Cp. avīci.

Vījati [**vīj**] to fan J I.165; SnA 487; VvA 6 (T. bījati).—Caus. vījeti DhA IV.213; Mhvs 5, 161.—Pass. **vījiyati**: ppr. vījiyamāna getting fanned J III.374 (so read for vijīy°); PvA 176 (so for vijjamāna!).—pp. **vījita**.

Vījana (nt.) [fr. **vīj**, cp. Class. Sk. vījana] a fan, fanning; in vījana-vāta a fanning wind, a breeze SnA 174.

Vījanī (f.) [fr. vījana, of **vīj**] a fan Vv 47² (T. bījanī, v. l. vīj°); J I.46; Vism 310; DhA IV.39; VvA 147; PvA 176; KhA 95. There are 3 kinds of fans mentioned at Vin II.130, viz. **vākamaya°**, **usira°**, **mora-piñcha°**, or fans made of bark, of a root (?), and of a peacock's tail.

Vījita [pp. of vījati] fanned Pv III.1¹⁷ (°anga).

***Viṇati** (?), doubtful: see **apa°** & **pa°**. Kern, *Toev.* s. v. wrong in treating it as a verb "to see."

Vīṇā (f.) [cp. Vedic vīṇā] the Indian lute, mandoline S I.122=Sn 449 (kacchā bhassati "let the lyre slide down from hollow of his arm" *K.S.* I.153); Th 1, 467; S IV.196 (six parts); A III.375; J III.91; V.196, 281 (named Kokanada "wolf's howl"); VI.465=580; Vv.64¹⁹; 81¹⁰; Miln 53 (all its var. parts); VvA 138, 161, 210; PvA 151.—**vīṇaŋ vādeti** to play the lute Mhvs 31, 82; ThA 203.

-**daṇḍaka** the neck of a lute J II.225. -**doṇikā** the sounding board of a lute (cp. doṇi¹ 4) Vism 251; VbhA 234; KhA 45.

Vīta¹ (adj.) [vi+ita, pp. of **i**] deprived of, free from, (being) without. In meaning and use cp. vigata°. Very frequent as first part of a cpd., as e. g. the foll.:

-**accika** without a flame, i. e. glowing, aglow (of cinders), usually combᵈ with °dhūma "without smoke" M I.365; S II.99 (so read for vītacchika)=IV.188=M I.74; D II.134; J I.15, 153; III.447; V.135; DhA II.68; Vism 301. -**iccha** free from desire J II.258. -**gedha** without greed Sn 210, 860, 1100; Nd¹ 250; Nd² 606. -**taṇha** without craving Sn 83, 741, 849, 1041, 1060; Nd¹ 211; Nd² 607. -**tapo** without heat J II.450. -(**d**)**dara** fearless Th 1, 525; Dh 385. -**dosa** without anger Sn 12. -**macchara** without envy, unselfish Sn 954; Nd¹ 444; J V.398; Pv III.1¹⁵. -**mada** not conceited Sn 328, cp. A II.120. -**mala** stainless (cp. vimala) S IV.47, 107; DA I.237; Miln 16. -**moha** without bewilderment Sn 13. -**raŋsi** rayless (?) Sn 1016 (said of the sun; the expression is not clear. One MS. of Nd² at this passage reads **pīta°**, i. e. with yellow, i. e. golden, rays; which is to be preferred). Cp. note in Index to SnA. -**rāga** passionless Sn 11, 507, 1071; Pug 32; Pv II.4⁷; Miln 76, and frequently elsewhere. -**lobha** without greed Sn 10, 469, 494. -**vaṇṇa** colourless Sn 1120. -**salla** without a sting S IV.64. -**sārada** not fresh, not unexperienced, i. e. wise It 123.

Vīta² [pp. of vāyati¹, or vināti] woven Vin III.259 (su°).

Vītaŋsa [fr. vi+**tan**, according to BR. The word is found in late Sk. (lexicogr.) as **vītaŋsa**. BR compare Sk. avataŋsa (garland: see P. vaṭaŋsa) & uttaŋsa. The etym. is not clear] a bird-snare (BR.: "jedes zum Fangen von Wild & Vögeln dienende Gerät"), a decoy bird Th 1, 139. Kern, *Toev.* s. v. "vogelstrik."

Vīti° is the contracted prepositional combⁿ **vi+ati**, representing an emphatic ati, e. g. in the foll.:

-(**k**)**kama** (1) going beyond, transgression, sin Vin III.112; IV.290; J I.412; IV.376; Pug 21; Miln 380; Vism 11, 17; DhA IV.3.—(2) going on, course (of time) PvA 137 (°ena by and by; v. l. anukkamena). -**kiṇṇa** sprinkled, speckled, gay with J V.188. -**nāmeti** to make pass (time), to spend the time, to live, pass, wait J III.63, 381; DhA II.57; VvA 158; PvA 12, 21, 47, 76. -**patati** to fly past, to flit by, to fly up & down Sn 688; A V.88=Miln 392. -**missa** mingled, mixed (with) M I.318; D III.96; J VI.151. -**vatta** having passed or overcome, gone through; passed, spent S I.14, 145; III.225; IV.52; A II.44; Sn 6, 395, 796; J I.374; ThA 170; PvA 21, 55, 83. -**sāreti** [fr. vi+ati+**sṛ**; not with Childers fr. **smṛ**; cp. BSk. vyatisārayati] to make pass (between), to exchange (greeting), to address, converse (kathaŋ), greet. Often in phrase **sārāṇīyaŋ sammodanīyaŋ kathaŋ vītisāreti** [for which BSk. sammodanīŋ saŋrañjanīŋ vividhāŋ kathāŋ vyatisārayati, e. g. AvŚ II.140] D I.52, 90, 118, 152; Sn 419; cp. Miln 19; J IV.98 (shortened to sārāṇīyaŋ vītisārimha; explᵈ with sārayimha); V.264. -**haraṇa** passing (mutually), carrying in between J VI.355 (bhojanānaŋ). -**harati** to associate with (at a meal) S I.162. -**hāra**, in pada° "taking over or exchange of steps," a stride S I.211; A IV.429; J VI.354. Same in BSk., e. g. MVastu I.35; III.162.

Vīthi (f.) [cp. Epic Sk. vīthi, to Idg. ***u̯eiā-** to aim at, as in Lat. via way, Sk. veti to pursue; Lat. venor to hunt; Gr. εἴσατο he went] 1. street, way, road, path, track A V.347, 350 sq.; Vv 83⁶; J I.158 (garden path); V.350 (dve vīthiyo gahetvā tiṭṭhati, of a house); VI.276 (v. and raccha); DhA I.14; VvA 31; PvA 54. -**antara-vīthiyaŋ** (loc.) in the middle of the road J I.373; PvA 96. -°**sabhāga** share of road J I.422; -°**singhāṭaka** cross-road DhA IV.4.—Of the path of the stars and heavenly bodies J I.23; VvA 326.—Various streets (roads, paths) are named either after the *professions* carried on in them, e. g. **dantakāra°** street of ivory-workers J I.320; **pesakāra°** weaver st. DhA I.424; **bhatakāra°** soldier st. DhA I.233;—or after the main kind of *traffic* frequenting these, e. g. **nāga°** elephant road VvA 316; **miga°** animal rd. J I.372;—or after *special occasions* (like distinguished people passing by this or that road), e. g. **buddha°** the road of the Buddha DhA II.80; **rāja°** King st. ThA 52; Mhvs 20, 38.—2. (t.t. in psychology) course, process (of judgment, sense-perception or cognition, cp. *Cpd.* 25, 124, 241 (vinicchaya°), 266.—Vism 187 (kammaṭṭhāna°); KhA 102 (viññāṇa°). -°**citta** process of cognition (lit. processed cognition) Vism 22; DhsA 269.

Vīthika (adj.) (-°) [fr. vīthi] having (as) a road Miln 322 (satipaṭṭhāna°, in the city of Righteousness).

Vīmaŋsaka (adj.) [fr. vīmaŋsā] testing, investigating, examining S III.6 sq.; Sn 827; Nd¹ 166; J I.369.

Vīmaŋsati (& °eti) [Vedic mīmāŋsate, Desid. of **man**. The P. form arose through dissimilation m>v, cp. Geiger, *P.Gr.* 46, 4] "to try to think," to consider, examine, find out, investigate, test, trace, think over Sn 215 (°amāna), 405; J I.128, 147, 200; VI.334; Miln 143; PvA 145, 215, 272; Sdhp 91.—ger. °itvā J VI.368; Mhvs 5, 36; PvA 155; inf. °ituŋ Mhvs 37, 234; PvA 30, 155, 283 (sippaŋ).—Caus. II. vīmaŋsāpeti to cause to investigate J V.110.—Cp. pari°.

Vīmaŋsana (nt.) & °ā (f.) [fr. vīmaŋsati] trying, testing; finding out, experiment Vin III.79; J III.55; Mhvs 22, 78; PvA 153.

Vīmaŋsā (f.) [fr. vīmaŋsati] consideration, examination, test, investigation, the fourth of the Iddhipādas, q. v.; D III.77 (°samādhi), 222; S v.280; A I.39, 297; III.37, 346; v.24, 90, 338; Ps I.19; II.123; Kvu 508; Dhs 269; Vbh 219 (°samādhi), 222, 227; Tikp 2; Nett 16 (°samādhi), 42; DA I.106; SnA 349 (vīmaŋsa-kāra = sankheyya-kāra). — Cp. pari°.

Vīmaŋsin = vīmaŋsaka Sn 877; Nd[1] 283; DA I.106.

Vīra [Vedic vīra; cp. Av. vīra, Lat. vir, virtus "virtue"; Gotu. wair, Obg. Ags wer; to vayas strength etc.; cp. viriya] manly, mighty, heroic; a hero S I.137; Sn 44, 165 (*not* dhīra), 642, 1096, 1102; Th 1, 736 (nara° hero); Nd[2] 609; DhA IV.225. —mahā° a hero S I.110, 193; III.83 (of the Arahant). —vīra is often an Ep. of the Buddha.

-angarūpa built like a hero, heroic, divine D I.89; II.16; III.59, 142, 145; S I.89; Sn p. 106; expl[d] as "devaputta-sadisa-kāya" at DA I.250 & SnA 450. — The BSk. equivalent is var-anga-rūpin (distorted fr. vīr°), e. g. MVastu I.49; II.158; III.197.

Vīyati [Pass. of vināti] see **viyyati**.

Vīvadāta (adj.) [vi + avadāta, the metric form of **vodāta**] clean, pure Sn 784, 881.

Vīsati & **vīsaŋ** (indecl.) [both for Vedic viŋśati; cp. Av. vīsaiti, Gr. εἴκοσι, Lat. viginti, Oir. fiche, etc.; fr. Idg. ***ṷi + komt** (decad), thus "two decads." Cp. vi°] number 20. — Both forms are used indiscriminately. — (1) **vīsati**, e. g. Vin II.271 (°vassa, as minimum age of ordination); Sn 457 (catu-vīsat'akkharaŋ); J I.89 (°sahassa bhikkhū); III.360; VbhA 191 sq.; DhA I.4 (ekūna°, 19); II.9, 54; III.62 (°sahassa bhikkhū, as followers); as vīsatiŋ at DhA II.61 (vassa-sahassāni). — (2) **vīsaŋ**; e. g. Sn 1019 (°vassa-sata); It 99 (jātiyo); J I.395 (°yojana-sata); v.36 (°ratana-sata); DhA I.8; II.91 (°yojana-sataŋ).

Vīhi [cp. Vedic vrīhi] rice, paddy Vin IV.264 (as one of the 7 kinds of āmaka-dhañña); J I.429; III.356; Miln 102, 267; Vism 383 (°tumba); DhA I.125; III.374 (°piṭaka).

Vuccati [Pass. of **vac**] to be called D I.168, 245; Sn 436, 759, 848, 861, 946; Nd[1] 431; Nd[2] s. v. katheti; SnA 204; DhA II.35. See also **vatti**. — pp. **vutta**.

Vuṭṭha [pp. of vassati[1]] (water) shed, rained Pv I.5[6]; PvA 29 See also **vaṭṭa** & **vaṭṭha**.

Vuṭṭhavant = vusitavant, Nd[2] 179, 284, 611.

Vuṭṭhahati & **vuṭṭhāti** [the sandhi form of uṭṭhahati (q. v.), with euphonic **v**, which however appears in BSk. as vyut° (i. e. vi + ud°); **vyuttisṭhate** "to come back from sea" Divy 35, and freq. in AvŚ, e. g. I.242] 1. to rise, arise; to be produced Vin II.278 (gabbha). — 2. to rise out of (abl.), to emerge from, to come back S IV.294; Vism 661 (vuṭṭhāti). — pp. **vuṭṭhita**. — Caus. **vuṭṭhāpeti** (1) to ordain, rehabilitate Vin IV.226, 317 sq. (= upasampādeti). (2) to rouse out of (abl.), to turn away from A III.115.

Vuṭṭhāna (nt.) [the sandhi form of uṭṭhāna] 1. rise, origin J I.114 (gabbha°). — 2. ordination, rehabilitation (in the Order) Vin IV.320; Miln 344. — 3. (cp. uṭṭhāna 3) rousing, rising out, emerging, emergence; appl[d] as a religious term to revival from jhāna-abstraction (cp. *Cpd.* 67, 215 n. 4; *Dhs. trl*[n], § 1332) M I.302; S III.270; IV.294; A III.311, 418, 427 sq.; Vism 661 (in detail), 681 sq. (id.); Dhs 1332; Nett 100; Tikp 272, 346. -°gāmini (-vipassanā-ñāṇa) "insight of discernment leading to uprising" (*Cpd.* 67) Vism 661, 681 sq.

Vuṭṭhānatā (f.) [fr. vuṭṭhāna] rehabilitation; in āpatti° forgiveness of an offence Vin II.250.

Vuṭṭhānima [?] is an expression for a certain punishment (pain) in purgatory M I.337 (vuṭṭhānimaŋ nāma vedanaŋ vediyamāna).

Vuṭṭhi (f.) [fr. **vṛṣ**, see vassati[1] & cp. Vedic vṛṣṭi] rain S I.172 = Sn 77 (fig. = saddhā bījaŋ tapo vuṭṭhi); A III.370, 378 (vāta°); It 83; Dh 14; J VI.587 (°dhārā); Ap 38 (fig.), 52 (amata°); Miln 416; Vism 37, 234 (salila°); Mhvs 1, 24; SnA 34, 224; PvA 139 (°dhārā shower of rain). —**dubbuṭṭhi** lack of rain, drought (opp. suvuṭṭhi) J II.367 = VI.487; Vism 512.

Vuṭṭhikā (f.) = **vuṭṭhi**; only in cpd. dubbuṭṭhikā time of drought, lack of rain D I.11; DA I.95; It 64 sq. (as avuṭṭhika-sama resembling a drought); DhA I.52.

Vuṭṭhita [pp. of vuṭṭhahati; cp. uṭṭhita] risen (out of), aroused, having come back from (abl.) D II.9 (paṭisallāṇā); Sn p. 59; S IV.294.

Vuṭṭhimant (adj.) [fr. vuṭṭhi, cp. Vedic vṛṣṭimant in same meaning] containing rain, full of rain; the rainy sky Th 2, 487 (= deva, i. e. rain-god or sky ThA 287). Kern, *Toev.* s. v. wrongly = *vyuṣṭi°, i. e. fr. vi + **uṣ** (**vas**) to shine, "luisterrijk," i. e. lustrous, resplendent.

Vuḍḍha & **vuddha** [pp. of vaḍḍhati] old (fig. venerable) — 1. vuḍḍha Pv II.11[6]; Mhvs 13, 2. — 2. vuddha M II.168; J v.140; Sn p. 108 (+ mahallaka); DA I.283.

Vuḍḍhaka (adj.) [vuḍḍha + ka] old; f. °ikā old woman Th 2, 16.

Vuḍḍhi & **vuddhi** (f.) [a by-form of **vaḍḍhi**] increase, growth, furtherance, prosperity. — 1. **vuḍḍhi** PvA 22. Often in phrase vuḍḍhi **virūḷhi** vepulla (all three almost tautological) Miln 51; Vism 129. — 2. vuddhi M I.117 (+ virūḷhi etc.); S II.205 sq.; III.53; v.94, 97; A III.76 (opp. parihāni), 404 (+ virūḷhi), 434 (kusalesu dhammesu); v.123 sq.; It 108; J v.37 (°ppatta grown up); Vism 271, 439 (so read for buddhi); DhA II.82, 87; Sdhp 537.

***Vuṇāti** [we are giving this base as such only from analogy with the Sk. form **vṛṇāti** (vṛṇoti); from the point of view of *Pāli* grammar we must consider a present tense varati as legitimate (cp. saŋ°). There are *no* forms from the base **vuṇāti** found in the present tense; the Caus. vāreti points directly to varati]. The two meanings of the root **vṛ** as existing in Sk. are also found in Pāli, but only peculiar to the Caus. vāreti (the form aor. avari as given by Childers should be read avāriŋsu Mhvs 36, 78). The present tense varati is only found in meaning "to wish" (except in prep. cpds. like saŋvarati to restrain). — Def[ns] of **vṛ**: Dhtp 255 **var** = varaṇa-sambhattisu; 274 **val** = saŋvaraṇe (see valaya); 606 **var** = āvaraṇ'icchāsu. — 1. to hinder, obstruct; to conceal, protect (on meanings "hinder" and "conceal" cp. **rundhati**); Idg. ***ṷer** and ***ṷel**, cp. Gr. ἔλυτρον, Sk. varutra, Lat. volvo, aperio etc. See vivarati. The pp. ***vuta** only in comb[n] with prefixes, like pari°, saŋ°. It also appears as ***vaṭa** in vivaṭa. — 2. to wish, desire; Idg. ***ṷel**, cp. Sk. varaṇa, varīyān "better," Gr. ἔλδομαι to long for, Lat. volo to intend, Goth. wiljan to "will," wilja = E. will. — Pres. **varati** (cp. vaṇeti): imper. varassu J III.493 (varaŋ take a wish; Pot. vare Pv II.9[40] (= vareyyāsi C.); ppr. varamāna Pv II.9[40] (= patthayamāna PvA 128). — pp. does not occur.

Vuṇhi° (& instr. vuṇhinā) at Pgdp 13, 15, 19, 35 must be meant for v-uṇha° (& v'uṇhena), i. e. heat (see uṇha).

Vutta[1] [pp. of vatti, **vac**; cp. utta] said DA I.17 (°ŋ hoti that is to say); DhA II.21, 75, 80; SnA 174. -**vādin** one who speaks what is said (correctly), telling the truth M I.369; S II.33; III.6.

Vutta[2] [pp. of vapati[1]] sown S I.134 (khetta); J I.340; III.12; VI.14; Miln 375 (khetta); PvA 7, 137, 139.

Vutta[3] [pp. of vapati[2]] shaven M II.168 (°siro). Cp. nivutta[2].

Vutta-velā at J IV.45 (tena vutta-velāyaŋ & ittarāya vutta-velāya) is by Kern, *Toev.* s. v. vutta[2] fancifully & wrongly taken as *vyuṣṭa (=vi+uṣṭa, pp. of **vas** to shine), i. e. dawned; it is however simply vutta[1]=at the time *said* by him (or her).

Vuttaka (nt.) [vutta[1]+ka. The P. connection seems to be **vac**, although formally it may be derived fr. **vṛt** "to happen" etc. (cp. vuttin & vattin, both fr. **vṛt**, & vutti). The BSk. equivalent is vṛttaka "tale" (lit. happening), e. g. Divy 439] what has been said, saying; only in title of a canonical book "iti-vuttakaŋ" ("logia"): see under **iti.**

Vûttamāna at S I.129 read as **vattamāna.**

Vuttari of Dh 370 is **pañca-v-uttari(ŋ)**, cp. DhA IV.109.

Vutti (f.) [fr. **vṛt**, cp. vattati; Sk. vṛtti] mode of being or acting, conduct, practice, usage, livelihood, habit S I.100 (ariya°; cp. ariya-vāsa); Sn 81=Miln 228 (=jīvitavutti SnA 152); Sn 68, 220, 326, 676; J VI.224 (=jīvita-vutti C.); Pv II.9[14] (=jīvita PvA 120); IV.1[21] (=jīvikā PvA 229); Miln 224, 253; VvA 23.

Vuttika (adj.) (-°) [vutti+ka] living, behaving, acting A III.383 (kaṇḍaka°); PvA 120 (dukkha°); sabhāga° living in mutual courtesy or properly, always comb^d with sappatissa, e. g. Vin I.187; II.162; A III.14 sq.

Vuttitā (f.) (-°) [abstr. formation fr. vutti] condition Vism 310 (āyatta°).

Vuttin (adj.) [cp. Sk. vṛttin]=vuttika; in sabhāga° Vin I.45; J I.219. Cp. **vattin.**

Vuttha[1] [pp. of vasati[1]] clothed: not found. More usual nivattha.

Vuttha[2] [pp. of vasati[2]] having dwelt, lived or spent (time), only in connection with vassa (rainy season) or vāsa (id.: see vāsa[2]). See e. g. DhA I.7; PvA 32, 43; J I.183 (°vāsa). With ref. to vassa "year" at J IV.317. — At DhA I.327 **vuttha** stands most likely for **vuddha** (arisen, grown), as also in abstr. **vutthattaŋ** at DhA I.330. — See also **parivuttha, pavuttha** & **vusita.**

Vutthaka (adj.) (-°) [vuttha[2]+ka] dwelt, lived, only in pubba° where he had lived before Mhvs I, 53 (so for °vuttaka).

Vuddha & **Vuddhi**: see **vuḍḍha** & **vuḍḍhi.**

Vuppati is Pass. of vapati.

Vuyhati to be carried away: Pass. of vahati, q. v. and add refs.: Miln 69; Vism 603 (vuyhare). — ppr. **vuyhamāna**: — 1. being drawn M I.225 (of a calf following its mother's voice). — 2. being carried away (by the current of a river), in danger of drowning Sn 319. — pp. **vuḷha** & **vūḷha.**

Vuyhamānaka (adj.) [vuyhamāna with disparaging suffix °ka] one who is getting drowned, "drownedling" J III.507.

Vuḷha & **Vūḷha** [pp. of vahati, Pass. vuyhati; but *may* be vi+ūḷha] carried away. — 1. **vuḷha**: Vin I.32, 109. — 2. **vūḷha**: A III.69; J I.193; DhA II.265 (udakena). See also **būḷha.**

Vuvahyamāna at A IV.170 read with C. at **opuniyamāna** "sifting" (fr. **opunāti**): see remark at A IV.476.

Vusita [Kern, *Toev.* s. v. vasati takes it as **vi+uṣita** (of **vas**[2]), against which speaks meaning of vivasati "to live from home." Geiger, *P.Gr.* § 66[1] & 195 expl^d it as uṣita with prothetic v, as by-form of **vuttha.** Best fitting in meaning is assumption of vusita being a variant of vosita, with change of **o** to **u** in analogy to vuttha; thus=vi+osita "fulfilled, come to an end or to perfection"; cp. pariyosita. Geiger's expl^n is supported by phrase **brahmacariyaŋ vasati**] fulfilled, accomplished; (or:) lived, spent (=vuttha); only in phrase **vusitaŋ** brahmacariyaŋ (trsl^n *Dial.* I.93; "the higher life has been fulfilled") D I.84 (cp. Dh I.225= vutthaŋ parivutthaŋ); It 115 (ed. vūsita°); Sn 463, 493; Pug 61. — Also at D I.90 neg. a°, with ref. to avusitavā, where Rh. D. (*Dial.* I.112) trsl^s "ill-bred" and "rude," hardly just. See also **arahant** II.A.

Vusitatta (nt.) [abstr. fr. vusita] state of perfection D I.90 (vusitavā-mānin kiŋ aññatra avusitattā=he is proud of his perfection rather from imperfection).

Vusitavant (adj.) [vusita+vant] one who has reached perfection (in chaste living), Ep. of the arahant D II.223 (trsl^n "who has lived 'the life'"); M I.4; S III.61; A V.16; Sn 514; Nd[1] 611; Miln 104. On D I.90 see vusita (end). See also **arahant** II.C.

Vusīmant (adj.) [difficult to explain; perhaps for vasīmant (see vasīvasa) in sense of **vasavattin**]=vusitavant A IV.340; Sn 1115 (cp. Nd[2] 611=vuṭṭhavā ciṇṇa-caraṇo etc., thus "perfected," cp. ciṇṇavasin in same meaning).

Vussati is Pass. of vasati[2] (q. v.).

Vūpakaṭṭha [doubtful, whether **vi+upakaṭṭha** (since the latter is only used of *time*), or =**vavakaṭṭha**, with which it is identical in meaning. Cp. also BSk. vyapakṛṣṭa AvŚ I.233; II.194; of which it might be a re-translation] alienated, withdrawn, drawn away (from), secluded; often in phrase **eko vūpakaṭṭho appamatto ātāpī** etc. (see arahant II.B.), e. g. D III.76; S I.117; II.21, 244; III.35, 73 sq.; IV.72; A IV.299. Cp. also A IV.435 (gaṇasmā v.).

Vūpakāsa [formed fr. vūpakāseti] estrangement, alienation, separation, seclusion; always as *twofold*: **kāya°** & **citta°** (of body & of mind), e. g. D III.285 (*Dial.* III.260 not correctly "serenity"); S V.67; A IV.152.

Vūpakāseti [Caus. of vavakassati] to draw away, alienate, distract, exclude Vin IV.326; A V.72 sq. — Caus. II. **vūpakāsāpeti** to cause to distract or draw away Vin I.49; IV.326. — pp. **vūpakaṭṭha.**

Vūparati [vi+uparati]=uparati cessation DhsA 403.

Vūpasanta [pp. of vūpasammati] appeased, allayed, calmed S IV.217, 294; A I.4 (°citta); III.205; Sn 82; Pug 61 (°citta); PvA 113.

Vūpasama [fr. vi+upa+**śam**; cp. BSk. vyupaśama Divy 578] 1. allaying, relief, suppression, mastery, cessation, calmness S III.32; IV.217; V.65 (cetaso); D II.157 (sankhārā); A I.4 (id.); II.162 (papañca°); V.72; Pug 69; J I.392; DhsA 403. — 2. quenching (of thirst) PvA 104.

Vūpasamana (nt.) [fr. vi+upa+**śam**; cp. BSk. vyupaśamana AvŚ II.114] allayment, cessation J I.393; Miln 320; PvA 37, 98.

Vūpasammati [vi+upasammati] 1. to be assuaged or quieted S IV.215. — 2. to be suppressed or removed J III.334. — 3. to be subdued or extinguished, to go out (of light) Ap. 35. — pp. **vūpasanta.** — Caus. **vūpasāmeti** to appease, allay, quiet, suppress, relieve S V.50; SnA 132 (reṇuŋ); PvA 20, 38 (sokaŋ), 200.

Vūḷha see **vuḷha.**

Ve[1] (indecl.) [cp. Vedic vē, vai] part. of affirmation, emphasizing the preceding word: indeed, truly Vin I.3 (etaŋ ve sukhaŋ); Dh 63 (sa ve bālo ti vuccati), 83 (sabbattha ve), 163 (yaŋ ve . . . taŋ ve); Sn 1050, 1075, 1082; DhA III.155 (=yeva). See also **have.**

Ve[2] may be enclitic form of **tumhe,** for the usual **vo** at Sn 333 (=tumhākaŋ SnA 339). See P.T.S. ed. of Sn; cp. v. l. **ve** for **vo** at Sn 560 (here as particle!).

Ve° is the *guṇa* (increment) form of **vi°**, found in many secondary (mostly f. & nt. abstr.) derivations from words with **vi°**, e. g. vekalla, vecikicchin, veneyya, vepulla, vematta, vevicchā, veramaṇī, which Bdhgh expl[s] simply as "vi-kārassa ve-kāraŋ katvā veramaṇī" KhA 24. — Cp. **veyy°.**

Vekaṭika (adj.) [fr. vikaṭa] one addicted to dirt, living on dirty food D I.167; Miln 259 (doubled).

Vekaṇḍa [perhaps connected with vikaṇṇaka] a kind of arrow M I.429.

Vekata (adj.) [=vikata] changed VvA 10.

Vekantaka (VbhA 63) is a kind of copper: see **loha.**

Vekalla (nt.) [fr. vikala] deficiency J V.400; Miln 107; Dhs 223; DhA II.26 (anga° deformity), 79; III.22; VvA 193; Sdhp 5, 17. — As **vekalya** at KhA 187 (where contrasted to sākalya). —**jaṇṇū avekallaŋ karoti** to keep one's knees straight Miln 418 (Kern, *Toev.* s. v. trsl[s] "presses tightly together"). See also **avekalla.**

Vekallatā & vekalyatā (f.) [abstr. fr. vekalla] deficiency A III.441 (a°); Vism 350 (indriya°); J I.45 (v. 254) (°lya°).

Vekkhiya is *poetical* for avekkhiya (=avekkhitvā: see avekkhati) in **appaṭivekkhiya** not considering J IV.4. See the usual paccavekkhati.

Vega [cp. Vedic vega, fr. **vij** to tremble] quick motion, impulse, force; speed, velocity S IV.157; A III.158 (sara°); Sn 1074; Miln 202, 258, 391; PvA 11, 47 (vāta°), 62 (visa°), 67, 284 (kamma°); Sdhp 295. — instr. **vegena** (adv.) quickly DhA I.49; another form in same meaning is **vegasā,** after analogy of thāmasā, balasā etc., e. g. J III.6; V. 117. — Cp. **saŋ°.**

Vegha at D II.110 (°missakena, trsl[n] Rh. D. "with the help of things")=S V.153 (T. reads vedha°), & Th 1, 143 (°missena, trsl[n] "violence") may with Kern, *Toev.* s. v. be taken as **veggha**=viggha (Sk. vighna), i. e. obstacle, hindrance; cp. uparundhati Th 1, 143. It remains obscure & Kern's expl[n] problematic. Cp. *Dial.* II.108.

Vecikicchin (adj.) [fr. vicikicchā] doubting, doubtful A II.174 (kankhin+); S III.99 (id.); M I.18; Sn 510.

Vecitta (nt.) [fr. vi+citta[2]] confusion, disturbed state of mind Dhtp 460 (in def[n] of root **muh**)

Vejja [fr. **vid,** *Sk. vaidya, but to Pāli etym. feeling fr. vijjā] a physician, doctor, medical man, surgeon J I.455; III.142; KhA 21; SnA 274 (in simile); VvA 185, 322; DhA I.8; PvA 36, 86; Sdhp 279, 351. —hatthi° elephant-doctor J VI.490; Mhvs 25, 34; visa° a physician who cures poison(ous bites) J I.310; IV.498.

-**kamma** medical practice or treatment J II.421; V.253; Vism 384; DhA III.257, 351; IV.172.

Vejjikā (f.) [fr. vejja ?] medicine (?) Vin III.185.

Veṭha [fr. **viṣṭ, veṣṭ**] wrap, in sīsa° head-wrap, turban M I.244; S IV.56.

Veṭhaka (adj.) [fr. veṭheti] surrounding, enveloping D I.105 ("furbelow" see *Dial.* I.130); Mhvs 11, 14 (valay-anguli°).

Veṭhana (nt.) [fr. veṭheti, cp. Epic & Class. Sk. veṣṭhana] 1. surrounding, enveloping J VI.489. — 2. a turban, head-dress D I.126; A I.145; III.380 (sīsa°); J V.187; DhA IV.213; PvA 161. — 3. wrapping, clothing, wrap, shawl J VI.12. — Cp. **pali°.**

Veṭhita [pp. of veṭheti] enveloped, enclosed, surrounded, wrapped Sdhp 362. Cp. **ni°, pari°.**

Veṭheti [Vedic veṣṭate, **viṣṭ** or **veṣṭ,** to Lat. virga, branch, lit. twisting] to twist round, envelope, wrap, surround J I.5, 422; Miln 282. — Pass. **veṭhiyati**: see vi°. — pp. **veṭhita.** — Cp. **pali°.**

Veṇa [cp. *Sk. vaiṇa, dial.] 1. a worker in bamboo PvA 175. — 2. a member of a low & despised class (cp. pukkusa) Vin IV.6; S I.93 (°kula); A II.85 (id.); III.385; Pug 51; f. **veṇī** J V.306 (=tacchikā C.); Pv III.1[13] (read veṇī for veṇiŋ).

Veṇi (f.) [cp. Sk. veṇi] a braid of hair, plaited hair, hair twisted into a single braid A III.295; Vin II.266 (dussa°); Th 2, 255; Vv 38[4] (=kesa-veṇi C.). fig. of a "string" of people D I.239 (andha°). -°**kata** plaited, having the hair plaited J II.185; V.431.

Veṇu [cp. Vedic veṇu. Another P. form is **veḷu** (q. v.)] bamboo; occurs only in cpds., e. g. -°**gumba** thicket of bamboo DhA I.177; -°**tinduka** the tree Diospyros J V.405 (=timbaru C.); -°**daṇḍaka** jungle-rope J III.204; -°**bali** a tax to be paid in bamboo (by bamboo workers) DhA I.177; °-**vana** bamboo forest J V.38.

Vetaṇḍin (adj.) [fr. vitaṇḍā] full of sophistry, skilled in vitaṇḍā Miln 90 (said of King Milinda).

Vetana (nt.) [cp. Epic & Class. Sk. vetana] wages, hire; payment, fee, remuneration; tip J I.194 (nivāsa° rent); Sn 24; VvA 141; DhA I.25; PvA 112. Most frequently comb[d] with **bhatta°** (q. v.). As **vedana** at J III.349.

Vetabba is grd. of *veti [**vi**]=**vināti** to weave (q. v.), thus "to be woven," or what is left to be woven J VI.26. — inf. **vetuŋ** Vin II.150.

Vetasa [Vedic vetasa] the ratan reed, Calamus rotang J V.167; SnA 451.

Vetāla at D I.6 (in the lists of forbidden crafts) refers to some magic art. The proper meaning of the word was already unknown when Bdhgh at DA I.84 explained it as "ghana-tāḷaŋ" (cymbal beating) with remark "mantena mata-sarīr' uṭṭhāpanan ti eke" (some take it to be raising the dead by magic charms). Rh. D. at *Dial.* I.8 translates "chanting of bards" (cp. vetālika). It is of dialectical origin.

Vetālika [dial.; cp. Epic & Class. Sk. vaitālika] a certain office or occupation at court connected with music or other entertainment, a bard. With other terms in list at Miln 331, some of them obscure and regional. Also at J VI.277, where expl[d] as "vetālā [read vettāya ?] uṭṭhāpake," i. e. those whose duty it is [by vetāla or vetta] to make (people) rise. The expl[n] is obscure, the **uṭṭhāpaka** reminds of Bdhgh's **uṭṭhāpana** (under vetāla). Kern misunderstands the phrase by translating "chasing bards away."

Veti [vi+eti, of **i**; Sk. vyeti] to go away, disappear, wane S III.135; A II.51; J III.154; DhsA 329. Cp. **vyavayāti.**

Vetulla (& vetulya) [cp. *Sk. vaitulya; also called vaipulya, fr. **vipula.** The P. form is not clear; it probably rests on dial. trsl[n] of a later term] a certain dissenting sect (see *Mhvs. trsl*[n] 259, n. 2) in °**vāda** heretic doctrine Mhvs 36, 41; Dpvs 22, 45; -°**vādin** an adherent of this doctrine.

Vetta (nt.) [cp. Epic Sk. vetra] twig, rod; creeper; jungle-rope (cp. veṇu-daṇḍa); cane (calamus). By itself only in standard list of punishments (tortures): **vettehi tāḷeti** to flog with canes, e. g. A I.47; II.122; Miln 196. Otherwise freq. in cpds.:

-agga cane-top, sprout of bamboo (cp. kaḷīra) Vism 255 (where KhA in id. p. reads °ankura); VbhA 60, 239, 252. **-ankura** a shoot of bamboo KhA 52, 67. **-āsana** cane chair VvA 8. **-cāra** (vettācāra) "stick-wandering" (?) J III.541 (+sankupatha; C.: vettehi sañcaritabba); Vv 84^{11} (vettācāraŋ sankupathañ ca maggaŋ, expl^d as vettalatā bandhitvā ācaritabba magga VvA 338); better as "jungle-path." **-patha** "a jungle full of sticks" (trsl^n Rh. D.) Miln 280 (+sankupatha), jungle-path. **-bandhana** binding with twigs (rope?), creeper-bands S III.155; V.51=A IV.127. **-latā** cane creeper J I.342; VvA 8, 338. **-valli** garland of creeper Dāvs III.40.

Veda [fr. **vid**, or more specifically **ved** as P. root] 1. (cp. vediyati & vedanā) (joyful) feeling, religious feeling, enthusiasm, awe, emotion, excitement (something like saŋvega) D II.210 (°paṭilābha+somanassa-paṭilābha); M I.465 (uḷāra); Sn 1029 (=pīti SnA 585); J II.336; III.266. **attha-veda + dhamma-veda** enthusiasm for the truth (for the letter & the spirit) of Buddha's teaching M I.37; A V.329 sq., 333, 349, 352; veda here interpreted as "somanassaŋ" at MA I.173. — See also cpd. °jāta. — 2. (cp. vedeti & vijjā) (higher) knowledge (as "Buddhist" antithesis to the authority of the "Veda"), insight, revelation, wisdom: that which Bdhgh at MA I.173 defines with "ñāṇa," and illustrates with vedagū of Sn 1059; or refers to at DA I.139 with def^n "vidanti etenā ti vedo." Thus at Sn 529 & 792 (=vedā vuccanti catūsu maggesu ñāṇaŋ paññā Nd^1 93), cp. SnA 403. — As adj. veda Ep. of the Buddha "the knower" or the possessor of revelation, at M I.386. See also **vedagū**. — 3. the Veda(s), the *brahmanic* canon of authorized religious teaching (revelation) & practice; otherwise given as "**gantha**" i. e. "text" at MA I.173, & illustrated with "**tiṇṇaŋ vedānaŋ pāragū**." The latter formula is frequent in stock phrase describing the accomplishments of a Brahmin, e. g. at D I.88; M II.133; Sn 1019; A I.163; DhA III.361. In the older texts only the 3 Vedas (irubheda=Rg; yaju° & sāma°) are referred to, whereas later (in the Commentaries) we find the 4 mentioned (athabbana added), e. g. the *three* at S IV.118; J I.168; II.47; III.537; Miln 10; Vism 384; the *four* at DA I.247; Miln 178. — Unspecified (sg.): SnA 462. As adj veda "knowing the Vedas" SnA 463 (ti°), cp. tevijja. — The Vedas in this connection are not often mentioned, they are almost identical with the Mantras (see **manta**) and are often (in Com.) mentioned either jointly with manta or promiscuously, e. g. Pv II.6^{13} (the Vedas with the 6 angas, i. e. vedāngas, called manta); SnA 293 (manta-pāragū+veda-pāragū), 322, 448.

-antagu "one who has reached the end of knowledge," i. e. one who has obtained perfection in wisdom Vin I.3; Sn 463. **-gū** one who has attained to highest knowledge (said of the Buddha). Thus different from "tiṇṇaŋ vedānaŋ pāragū," which is brahmanic. The expl^n of vedagū is "catūsu maggesu ñāṇaŋ" Nd^2 612, & see above 2. — S I.141, 168; IV.83, 206; A II.6; IV.340; Sn 322, 458, 529, 749, 846, 947, 1049, 1060; Nd^1 93, 204, 299, 431. A peculiar meaning of vedagū is that of "soul" (lit. attainer of wisdom) at Miln 54 & 71. **-jāta** thrilled, filled with enthusiasm, overcome with awe, excited A II.63; Sn 995, 1023; Kvu 554=Vv 34^{27} (=jāta-somanassa VvA 156); J I.11; Miln 297. **-pāragū** one who excels in the knowledge of the Vedas, perfected in the Veda SnA 293; cp. above 3. **-bandhu** one who is familiar with the Vedas SnA 192.

Vedaka (adj.) [fr. veda 3] knowing or studying the Vedas SnA 462 (brāhmaṇa).

Vedanaka (adj.) [fr. vedanā] having feeling, endowed with sensation Vbh 419 (a°+asaññaka).

Vedanā (f.) [fr. **ved°**: see vedeti; cp. Epic Sk. vedanā] feeling, sensation (see on term, e. g. *Cpd.* 14 Mrs. Rh. D. *B. Psy.*, ch. iv.) D I.45; II.58 (cp. *Dial.* II.54), 66; III.58, 77, 221, 228, 238 (°upādāna); S III.86 sq.; A I.39, 122, 141; II.79, 198, 256; III.245 sq., 450; IV.301, 385; Kh III. (tisso v.); Sn 435, 529, 739, 1111; Nd^1 109; Nd^2 551 (tisso v.); Ps I.6, 50 sq., 145 sq., 153 sq.; II.109 sq., 181 sq.; Vbh 135 sq., 294, 401, 403 sq.; Dhs 3, 1348; Nett 27, 65 sq.; 83, 123, 126; Tikp 246, 317 sq., 345 sq.; Vism 460 sq.; DA I.125; VbhA 13 sq., 39 sq., 80, 178, 193, 221 (°ānupassanā, in detail), 263 sq., 382 (various). — *Three* modes of feeling (usually understood whenever mention is made of "tisso vedanā"): **sukhā** (pleasant), **dukkhā** (painful) **adukkha-m-asukhā** (indifferent) D III.275; S II.53, 82; IV.207; A III.400; It 46; Tikp 317 sq. — *or:* **kusalā, akusalā, avyākatā** Vism 460. — *Five* vedanās: **sukhaŋ, dukkhaŋ, somanassaŋ, domanassaŋ, upekkhā** Vism 461. Categories of 2 to 108 modes of Vedanā, S IV.223 sq. —vedanā is one of the 5 **khandhas** (see khandha II.B). — On relation of *old* and *new* sensations (purāṇa°>nava°) see e. g. A II.40; III.388; IV.167; Vism 33; and see formula under **yātrā**. — In the Paṭiccasamuppāda (q. v.) vedanā stands between **phassa** as condition and **taṇhā** as result; see e. g. Vism 567 sq. — 2. (in special application) painful sensation, suffering, pain (i. e. dukkha-vedanā) M I.59; A I.153 (sārīrikā bodily pain); II.116 (id.); III.143 (id.); Pv I.10^{15}; Miln 253 (kāyikā & cetasikā); VbhA 101 (maraṇ' antikā v. agonies of death). —**vedan' aṭṭa** afflicted by pain Vin II.61; III.100; J I.293. — As adj. **vedana** suffering or to be suffered Pv III.10^{6} (=anubhūyamāna PvA 214). —**vedana** at J III.349 is to be read as **vetana**.

Vedayita [pp. of vedeti] felt, experienced S I.112; II.65; III.46; A II.198; IV.415; Vism 460.

Vedalla (nt.) [may be dialectical, obscure as to origin; Bdhgh refers it to Veda 1] Name of one of the 9 angas (see **nava**) or divisions of the Canon according to matter A II.7, 103, 178; III.88, 107, 361 sq.; IV.113; Vin III 8; Pug 43; DhsA 26; DA I.24; PvA 22. The DhsA comprises under this anga the 2 suttas so-called in M. (43, 44), the Sammādiṭṭhi, Sakkapañha, Sankhārābhājaniya, Mahāpuṇṇama etc. Suttas, as catechetical DhsA 26=DA I.24. — *Note.* The 2nd part of the word looks like a distortion fr. ariya (cp. mahalla>mah' ariya). Or might it be=vedanga?

Vedi & Vedī (f.) [Vedic vedi sacrificial bench] ledge, cornice, rail Mhvs 32, 5; 35, 2; 36, 52 (pāsāṇa°); 36, 103; Vv 84^{16} (=vedikā VvA 346). — See on term *Dial.* II.210; *Mhvs. tsrl^n* 220, 296. Cp. vedikā & velli.

Vedikā (f.) (& vediyā) [fr. vedi] cornice, ledge, railing D II.179; Vin II.120; J IV.229, 266; Vv 78^{6} (vediyā=vedikā VvA 304); 84^{16} (=vedikā VvA 340); VvA 275.

Vedita [pp. of vedeti] experienced, felt S IV.205 (sukha & dukkha)=Sn 738.

Vedisa [fr. vidisā ?] N. of a tree J V.405; VI.550.

Vedeti [Vedic vedayati; Denom. or Caus. fr. **vid** to know or feel] "to sense," usually in Denom. function (only *one* Caus. meaning: see aor. avedi); meaning twofold: either intellectually "to know" (cp. veda), or with ref. to general feeling "to experience" (cp. **vedanā**). — For the *present* tense *two* bases are to be distinguished, viz. **ved°**, used in both meanings; and **vediy°** (=*vedy°), a specific Pāli formation after the manner of the 4th (y) class of Sk. verbs, used only in meaning of "experience." Thus vedeti: (a) to *know* (as=acc., equal to "to call") Sn 211 sq. (taŋ muniŋ vedayanti); (b) to *feel*, to experience S IV.68 (phuṭṭho vedeti, ceteti, sañjānāti); M I.37; Pv IV.1[50] (dukkhaŋ = anubhavati PvA 241). —vediyati: to feel, to experience a sensation or feeling (usually with vedanaŋ or pl. vedanā) M I.59; II.70 (also Pot. vediyeyya); S II.82; III.86 sq.; IV.207; A I.141; II.198 (also ppr. vediyamāna); J II.241; Miln 253. — aor. avedi he *knew*, recognized J III.420 (= aññāsi C.); he *made known*, i. e. informed J IV.35 (= jānāpesi C.); vedi (recognized, knew) Sn 643, 647, 1148 (= aññāsi aphusi paṭivijjhi Nd[2] 613); & vedayi Sn 251 (= aññāsi SnA 293). — Fut. vedissati (shall *experience*) Pv I.10[15] (dukkhaŋ vedanaŋ v.). — grd. **vediya** (to be *known*) Sn 474 (para° diṭṭhi held as view by others; expl[d] as "ñāpetabba" SnA 410); **vedanīya**: (a) to be *known*, intelligible, comprehensible D I.12; (dhammā nipuṇā . . . paṇḍita-vedanīyā); II.36; M I.487; II.220; (b) to be *experienced* S IV.114 (sukha° & dukkha°); A I.249 (diṭṭhadhamma°); IV.382; Pv II.11[7] (sukha°-kamma = sukha-vipāka PvA 150); III.3[7] (kamma); IV.1[29] (of kamma-vipāka = anubhavana-yogga PvA 228); PvA 145 (kamma); & **veditabba** to be *understood* or *known* D I.186; PvA 71, 92, 104. — pp. **vedita** & **vedayita**.

Vedeha [= Npl. Vedeha] lit. from the Videha country; wise (see connection between Vedeha & **ved**, vedeti at DA I.139, resting on popular etymology) S II.215 sq. (°muni, of Ānanda; expl[d] as "vedeha-muni = paṇḍita-muni," cp. *K.S.* I.321; trsl[n] *K.S.* II.145 "the learned sage"); Mhvs 3, 36 (same phrase; trsl[n] "the sage of the Videha country"); Ap 7 (id.).

Vedha [adj.-n.) [fr. **vidh** = **vyadh**, cp. vyādha] 1. piercing, pricking, hitting A II.114 sq. (where it is said of a horse receiving pricks on var. parts, viz. on its hair: loma°; its flesh: maŋsa°; its bone: aṭṭhi°). —**avedha** [to **vyath**!] not to be shaken or disturbed, imperturbable Sn 322 (= akampana-sabhāva SnA 331). — 2. a wound J II.274 sq. — 3. a flaw Miln 119. — Cp. **ubbedha**.

Vedhati [for *vethati = vyathati, of **vyath**] to tremble, quiver, quake, shake S V.402; Th 1, 651; 2, 237 (°amāna); Sn 899, 902 (Pot. vedheyya); Nd[1] 312, 467; J II.191 (kampati +); Miln 254 (+ calati); VvA 76 (vedhamānena sarīrena); DhA II.249 (Pass. vedhiyamāna trembling; v. l. pa°). Cp. **vyadhati, ubbedhati** & **pavedhati**.

Vedhana (nt.) [fr. **vidh** to pierce] piercing J IV.29; DA I.221.

Vedhabba (nt.) [abstr. fr. vidhavā, = Epic Sk. vaidhavya] widowhood J VI.508.

Vedhavera [for *Sk. vaidhaveya, fr. vidhavā] son of a widow; in two diff. passages of the Jātaka, both times characterized as sukka-cchavī vedhaverā "sons of widows, *with white skins*," and at both places misunderstood (or unintelligibly expl[d]) by the Cy., viz. J IV.184 (+ thulla-bāhū; C.: vidhavā apatikā tehi vidhavā sarantī ti [ti]vidha-verā ca vedhaverā); VI.508 (C.: vidhav' itthakā; v. l. vidhav-ittikāmā purisā).

Vedhitā (f.) [pp. of vedheti, Caus. of vijjhati] shooting, hitting J VI.448.

Vedhin (adj.) [fr. **vidh** = **vyadh**] piercing, shooting, hitting: see **akkhaṇa°**.

Venateyya [fr. vinata] descended from Vinatā, Ep. of a garuḷa Ps II.196; J VI.260; Dāvs IV.45.

Venayika[1] [fr. vi 3 + naya] a nihilist. The Buddha was accused of being a v. M I.140.

Venayika[2] (adj.) [fr. vinaya] versed in the Vinaya Vin I.235; III.3 (cp. Vin A I.135); M I.140; A IV.175, 182 sq.; V.190; Miln 341.

Veneyya (adj.) [= vineyya, grd. of vineti; cp. BSk. vaineya Divy 36, 202 & passim] to be instructed, accessible to instruction, tractable, ready to receive the teaching (of the Buddha). The term is *late* (Jātaka style & Com.) J I.182 (Buddha°), 504; SnA 169, 510; DhA I.26; VbhA 79; VvA 217; ThA 69 (Ap. v. 10). Cp. **buddha°**.

Veneyyatta (nt.) [fr. veneyya] tractableness Nett 99.

Vepakka (nt.) [fr. vipakka] ripening, ripeness, maturity. — (adj.) yielding fruit, resulting in (-°) A I.223 (kāmadhātu° kamma); III.416 (sammoha° dukkha); Sn 537 (dukkha° kamma).

Vepurisikā (f.) [vi + purisa + aka] a woman resembling a man (sexually), a man-like woman, androgyn Vin II.271; III.129.

Vepulla (nt.) [fr. vipula] full development, abundance, plenty, fullness D III.70, 221, 285; S III.53; A I.94 (āmisa°, dhamma°); III.8, 404; V.152 sq., 350 sq.; Miln 33, 251; Vism 212 (saddhā°, sati°, paññā°, puñña°), 619; DhA I.262 (sati°); VbhA 290. — Often in phrase vuḍḍhi virūḷhi vepulla (see vuḍḍhi), e. g. Vin I.60; It 113. Cp. **vetulla**.

Vepullatā (f.) [abstr. formation fr. vepulla] = vepulla; A II.144 (rāga°, dosa°, moha°); Ap 26, 39; Miln 252. As vepullataŋ (nt.) at A III.432.

Vebhanga [fr. vibhanga] futility, failure J IV.451 (opp. sampatti; expl[d] as vipatti C.).

Vebhangika (& °iya) (adj.) see a°.

Vebhavya (& °ā) (nt. & f.) [fr. vibhāvin] thinking over, criticism Dhs 16; Ps I.119; Pug 25; Nett 76.

Vebhassi (f.) vibhassikatā, i. e. gossiping Vin IV.241.

Vebhūtika (& °ya) (adj.-nt.) [fr. vibhūti 1] causing disaster or ruin; nt. calumnious speech, bad language D III.106 (°ya); Sn 158 (°ya); Vv 84[40] (°ka; expl[d] as "sahitānaŋ vinābhāva-karaṇato vebhūtikaŋ," i. e. pisuṇaŋ VvA 347).

Vema (nt.) [fr. vāyati[2], cp. Sk. veman (nt.); Lat. vimen] loom or shuttle DhA III.175; SnA 268.

Vemaka (nt.) = vema Vin II.135.

Vemajjha (nt.) [fr. vi + majjha] middle, centre J IV.250; VI.485; Pug 16, 17; Vism 182 (°bhāga central part); VvA 241, 277. — loc. vemajjhe: (a) in the present, or central interval of saŋsāra Sn 849 (cp. Nd[1] 213 and majjha 3 b); (b) in two, asunder Vism 178.

Vematika (adj.) [fr. vimati] in doubt, uncertain, doubtful Vin I.126; II.65; IV.220, 259; Vism 14 (°sīla). Opp. nibbematika.

Vematta (nt.) [fr. vi + matta[1]] difference, distinction Miln 410; Vism 195.

Vemattatā (f.) [abstr. formation fr. vematta] difference, distinction, discrepancy, disproportion(ateness) M I.453, 494; S II.21; III.101; V.200; A III.410 sq.; Sn p.102 (puggala°); Nett 4, 72 sq., 107 sq.; Miln 284, 285. — The 8 differences of the var. Buddhas are given at SnA 407 sq. as addhāna°, āyu°, kula°, pamāṇa°, nekkhamma°, padhāna°, bodhi°, raŋsi°.

Vemātika (adj.) [vi + °mātika] having a different mother J IV.105 (°bhāginī); VI.134 (°bhātaro); PvA 19.

Vemānika (adj.) [fr. vimāna[1]] having a fairy palace (see vimāna 3) J V.2; DhA III.192.

Veyy° is a (purely phonetic) diaeretic form of vy°, for which viy° & veyy° are used indiscriminately. There is as little difference bewteen viy° & veyy° as between vi° & ve° in those cases where (double, as it were) abstract nouns are formed from words with ve° (vepullatā, vemattatā, etc.), which shows that ve° was simply felt as vi°. Cp. the use of e for i (esp. before y) in cases like alabbhaneyya>°iya; addhaneyya>°iya; pesuṇeyya>°iya, without any difference in meaning.

Veyyaggha (adj.) [fr. vyaggha] belonging to a tiger Dh 295 (here simply=vyaggha. i. e. with a tiger as fifth; veyya°=vya° metri causâ; Bdhgh's expl[n] at DhA III.455 is forced). — (m). a car covered with a tiger's skin J V.259, cp. 377.

Veyyagghin=veyyaggha (adj.) J IV.347.

Veyyañjanika [=vyañjanika] one who knows the signs, a fortune-teller, soothsayer J V.233, 235. — The BSk. equivalent is **vaipañcanika** (MVastu I.207) etc.: see under **vipañcita**, which *may* have to be derived (as viyañcita=viyañjita) from vi+**añj**=vyañjana. See also Kern, *Toev.* p. 19.

Veyyatta=viyatta, i. e. accomplished, clever J V.258.

Veyyatti (f.) [=viyatti] distinction, cleverness, accomplishment J V.258; VI.305.

Veyyattiya (nt.) [abstr. form (°ya=°ka) fr. veyyatti=viyatti] distinction, lucidity; accomplishment D III.38 (paññā° in wisdom); M I.82, 175; II.209.

Veyyākaraṇa (m. nt.) [=vyākaraṇa] 1. (nt.) answer, explanation, exposition D I.46, 51, 105, 223; II.202; A III.125; V.50 sq.; Sn 352, 510, 1127; Pug 43, 50; Miln 347; DA I.247. — 2. (m.) one who is expert in explanation or answer, a grammarian D I.88; A III.125; Sn 595; Miln 236; SnA 447.

Veyyābādhika (adj.) [=vyābādhika] causing injury or oppression, oppressive, annoying (of pains) M I.10; A III.388; Vism 35 (expl[d] diff. by Bdhgh as "vyābādhato uppannattā veyyābādhikā").

Veyyāyika (nt.) [fr. vyaya] money to defray expenses, means Vin II.157.

Veyyāvacca (nt.) [corresponds to (although doubtful in what relation) Sk. *vaiyā-pṛtya, abstr. fr. **vyāpṛta** active, busy (to **pṛ**, pṛṇoti)=P. vyāvaṭa; it was later retranslated into BSk. as **vaiyāvṛtya** (as if vi+ā+**vṛt**); e. g. Divy 54, 347; MVastu I.298] service, attention, rendering a service; work, labour, commission, duty Vin I.23; A III.41; J I.12 (kāya°); VI.154; SnA 466; VvA 94; ThA 253. -°**kamma** doing service, work J III.422; -°**kara** servant, agent, (f.) housekeeper J III.327; VvA 349; °-kārikā (f.) id. PvA 65. — Cp. vyappatha.

Veyyāvaṭika (nt.) [doublet of veyyāvacca; °ka=°ya] service, waiting on, attention Sn p. 104 (kāya°); J IV.463; VI.154, 418, 503 (dāna°); DhA I.27 (kāya°); III.19 (dāna°); Dpvs VI.61.

Vera (nt.) [cp. Sk. vaira, der. fr. vīra] hatred, revenge, hostile action, sin A IV.247; Dh 5; J IV.71; DhA I.50; PvA 13. —**avera** absence of enmity, friendliness; (adj.) friendly, peaceable, kind D I.167, 247 (sa° & a°), 251; S IV.296; A IV.246; Sn 150. The **pañca bhayāni verāni** (or **vera-bhayā**) or **pañca verā** (Vbh 378) "the fivefold guilty dread" are the fears connected with sins against the 5 first commandments (sīlāni): see S II.68; A III.204 sq.; IV.405 sq.; V.182; It 57=Sn 167 (vera-bhay'atīta).

Veraka=vera; a° Pv IV.1[58]. See also **verika**.

Verajja (nt.) [fr. vi+rajja] a variety of kingdoms or provinces S III.6 (nānā°-gata bhikkhu a bh. who has travelled much).

Verajjaka (adj.) [fr. verajja] belonging to var. kingdoms or provinces, coming from various countries (nānā°); living in a different country, foreign, alien D I.113; M II.165 (brāhmaṇā); A III.263 (bhikkhū); Th I, 1037; Vv 84[12] (=videsa-vasika VvA 336); Miln 359.

Veramaṇī (f.) [fr. viramaṇa; cp. the odd form BSk. **vīramaṇī**, e. g. Jtm. 213] abstaining from (-°), abstinence A II.217, 253; V.252 sq., 304 sq.; Sn 291; Pug 39, 43; Vism 11; KhA 24; DhA I.235, 305.

Veramba (& °bha) (adj.) [etym.? Probably dialectical, i. e. regional] attribute of the wind (vāta or pl. vātā), a wind blowing in high altitudes [cp. BSk. vairambhaka Divy 90] S II.231; A I.137; Th I.597; J III.255, 484; VI.326; Nd[2] 562; VbhA 71.

Verika=vera i. e, inimical; enemy (cp. **veraka**) J V.229, 505; Vism 48.

Verin (adj.) [fr. vera] bearing hostility, inimical, revengeful J III.177; Pv IV.3[26] (=veravanto PvA 252); Miln 196; Vism 296 (°puggala), 326 (°purisa, in simile), 512 (in sim.); VbhA 89. — Neg. **averin** Dh 197, 258.

Verocana [=virocana, fr virocati] the sun (lit. "shining forth") S I.51; A II.50.

Velā (f.) [Vedic velā in meaning 1; Ep. Sk. in meanings 2 & 3] — 1. time, point of time (often equal to kāla) Pug 13 (uḍḍahana°); J IV.294; Miln 87; KhA 181; PugA 187; SnA 111 (bhatta° meal-time); DhsA 219; PvA 61, 104, 109 (aruṇ' uggamana°), 129, 155; VvA 165 (paccūsa° in the early morning). — 2. shore, sea-shore Vin II.237=A IV.198; J I.212; Mhvs 19, 30. — 3. limit, boundary A V.250 (between v. & agyāgāra); Th I, 762; Miln 358; DhsA 219; in spec. sense as "measure," restriction, control (of character, **sīla-velā**) at Dhs 299 ("not to trespass" trsl[n]), and in dogmatic exegesis of **ativelaŋ** at Nd[1] 504; cp. Nd[2] 462 & DhsA 219. — 4. heap, multitude (?) DhsA 219 (in Npl. Uruvelā which is however *Uruvilvā).

Velāmika (adj.) [velāma+ika, the word velāma probably a district word] "belonging to Velāma," at D II.198 used as a clan-name (f. Velāmikānī), with vv. ll. Vessinī & Vessāyinī (cp. Velāma Np. comb[d] with Vessantara at VbhA 414), and at D II.333 classed with **khujjā, vāmanikā & komārikā** (trsl[n] "maidens"; Bdhgh: "very young & childish": see *Dial.* II.359); v. l. celāvikā. They are some sort of servants, esp. in demand for a noble's retinue. See also Np. **Velāma** (the V.-sutta at J I.228 sq.).

Velāyati [Denom. fr. velā] to destroy (?) DhsA 219 (cp. *Expos.* II.297); expl[d] by viddhaŋseti. More appropriate would be a meaning like "control," bound, restrict.

Vellāḷin (adj.) [Is it a corruption fr.*veyyāyin=*vyāyin ?] flashing (of swords) J VI.449.

Velli [dial. ?] is a word peculiar to the *Jātaka*. At one passage it is expl[d] by the Commentary as "vedi" (i. e. rail, cornice), where it is applied to the slender waist of a woman (cp. **vilāka & vilaggita**): J VI.456. At most of the other passages it is expl[d] as "a heap of gold": thus at J V.506 (verse: velli-vilāka-majjhā; C: "ettha vellī ti rāsi vilākamajjhā ti vilagga-majjhā uttatta-ghana-suvaṇṇa-rāsi-ppabhā c' eva tanu-dīgha-majjhā ca"), and VI.269 (verse: kañcana-velli-viggaha; C.: "suvaṇṇa-rāsi-sassirīka-sarīrā"). At V.398 in the same passage as VI.269 expl[d] in C. as "kañcana-rūpaka-sadisa-sarīrā"). The idea of "*golden*" is connected with it throughout.

Vellita (adj.) [pp. of vellati, **vell** to stagger, cp. paṭivellati] crooked, bent; (of hair:) curly PvA 189. It is only used with ref. to *hair*.

-agga with bending (or crooked) tip (of hair), i. e. curled Th 2, 252 (cp. ThA 209); J v.203 (=kuñcit' agga C.); vi.86 (sun-agga-vellita); PvA 46, 142. — Cp. kuñcita-kesa J i.89.

Veḷu [=veṇu, cp. Geiger, *P.Gr.* § 43[3] & Prk. veḷu: Pischel, *Prk. Gr.* § 243] a bamboo A ii.73; Vin iv.35; J iv.382 (daṇḍa°); v.71; Vism 1, 17; SnA 76 (=vaŋsa); VbhA 334.

-agga (veḷagga) the top of a bamboo Vin ii.110. -gumba a bamboo thicket SnA 49, 75. -daṇḍa a bamboo stick SnA 330. -dāna a gift of bamboo Vbh 246; Miln 369; SnA 311; KhA 236; VbhA 333. -nāḷi (°nalaka, °nāḷika) a stalk or shaft of bamboo Vism 260; KhA 52; ThA 212. -pabba a stalk or section of the b. J i.245; Vism 358 = VbhA 63.

Veḷuka [fr. veḷu] a kind of tree J v.405 (=vaŋsa-coraka).

Veḷuriya (nt.) [cp. dial. Sk. vaiḍūrya] a precious stone, lapis lazuli; cp. the same word "beryl" (with metathesis r>l; *not* fr. the Sk. form), which the Greeks brought to Europe from India. — D i.76; Vin ii.112; S i.64; A i.215; iv.199, 203 sq.; J iii.437; Pv ii.7[5]; Mhvs 11, 16; DhA ii.220. Often in descriptions of Vimānas, e. g. Vv 2[1]; 12[1]; 17[1]; cp. VvA 27, 60. — Probably through a word-play with veḷu (bamboo; popular etymology) it is said to have the colour of bamboo: see vaŋsa-rāga & vaŋsa-vaṇṇa. At J i.207 a peacock's neck is described as having the colour of the veḷuriya. At Miln 267 (in inventory of "loka") we have the foll. enumeration of precious stones: pavāḷa coral, lohitanka ruby, masāragalla cat's eye, veḷuriya lapis lazuli, vajira diamond. See also under ratana[1].

Veḷuva [cp. Vedic vaiṇava (made of cane)?] probably not to veḷu, but another spelling for beḷuva, in °laṭṭhikā S iii.91, as sometimes v. l. veḷuva for beḷuva (q. v.).

Vevacana (nt.) [fr. vivacana] attribute, epithet; synonym Nett 1 sq., 24, 53 sq., 82, 106; Vism 427; SnA 24, 447. Cp. adhivacana.

Vevaṇṇa (nt.) [fr. vivaṇṇa] discolouring ThA 85 (Ap. v. 42).

Vevaṇṇiya (nt.) [abstr. fr. vivaṇṇa] 1. state of having no caste, life of an outcast A v.87 ≈ 200. [Cp. BSk. vaivarṇika outcast Divy 424]. — 2. discolouring, fading, waning J iii.394.

Vevāhika [fr. vivāha] wedding-guest J ii.420.

Veviccha (nt.) [abstr. formation fr. vivicchā] "multifarious wants," greediness, selfishness, avarice Sn 941 (=pañca macchariyāni Nd[1] 422, as at Nd[2] 614), 1033 (where Nett 11 reads vivicchā); Pug 19, 23; Dhs 1059, 1122; Nd[2] s. v. taṇhā; DhsA 366, 375.

Vesa [cp. Sk. veṣa, fr. viṣ to be active] dress, apparel; (more frequently:) disguise, (assumed) appearance J i.146 (pakati° usual dress), 230 (āyuttaka°); iii.418 (andha°); Miln 12; DhA ii.4; PvA 62, 93 (ummattaka°), 161 (tunnavāya°); Sdhp 384; purisa° (of women) DA i.147.

Vesama = visama VvA 10.

Vesākha [cp. Vedic vaiśākha] N. of a month (April-May) Mhvs 1, 73; 29, 1.

Vesārajja (nt.) [abstr. formation fr. visārada, i. e. *vaiśāradya] (the Buddha's or an Arahant's) perfect self-confidence (which is of 4 kinds), self-satisfaction, subject of confidence. The four are given in full at M i.71 sq., viz. highest knowledge, khīṇāsava state, recognition of the obstacles, recognition & preaching of the way to salvation. See also D i.110; J ii.27; A ii.13; iii.297 sq.; iv.83, 210, 213; M i.380; Ps ii.194; Nd[2] 466[a]; DhA i 86; DA i.278; KhA 104; VvA 213; Sdhp 593.

Vesiyāna [=vessa, with °na as in gimhāna, vassāna etc.] a Vaiśya (Vessa) J vi.15, 21, 328, 490, 492. As vessāyana at Sn 455 (where vesiyāna is required).

Vesī & Vesiyā (f.) [the f. of vessa] a woman of low caste, a harlot, prostitute. — (*a*) vesī: Vin iii.138; J v.425; in cpd. vesi-dvāra a pleasure house Th 2, 73. — (*b*) vesiyā: Vin iv.278; Sn 108; Vbh 247; in cpd. vesiyā-gocara asking alms from a prostitute's house DhA iii.275; DhsA 151; VbhA 339.

Vesma (nt.) [Vedic veśman, fr. viś to enter: see visati] a house J v.84. A trace of the n-stem in loc. vesmani J v.60.

Vessa [cp. Vedic vaiśya, a dial. (local) word] a Vaiśya, i. e. a member of the third social (i. e. lower) grade (see vaṇṇa 6), a man of the people D iii.81, 95 (origin); S i.102, 166; iv.219; v.51; A i.162; ii.194; iii.214, 242; Vbh 394; DA i.254 (origin). — f. vesī (q. v.); vessī (as a member of that caste) D i.193; A iii.226, 229.

Vessikā (f.) [fr. vessa] a Vaiśya woman Sn 314.

Vehāyasa = vihāyasa, i. e. air, sky; only used in *acc.* vehāyasaŋ in function of a *loc.* (cp. VvA 182: vehāyasaŋ = vehāyasa-bhūte hatthi-piṭṭhe), comb[d] with ṭhita (standing in the air) Vv 41; Mhvs 1, 24; PvA 14.

Vehāsa [contraction of vehāyasa] the air, sky, heaven; only in the two cases (both used as *loc.* "in the air"): acc. vehāsaŋ D iii.27; S v.283; Vin iii.105; VvA 78; & loc. vehāse Vin i.320.

-kuṭī "air hut" i. e. airy room, "a hut in which a middle-sized man can stand without knocking his head against the ceiling" (expl[n]) Vin iv.46. -gamana going through the air Vism 382; Dhtm 586. -ṭṭha standing in the air D i.115; DA i.284. -ṭṭhita id. D i.95.

Vehāsaya [=vehāyasa with metathesis y>s] occurs only in acc. (=loc.) vehāsayaŋ, equal to vihāyasaŋ at J iv.471.

Vo[1] (indecl.) a particle of emphasis, perhaps = eva, or = vo[2] (as dative of interest). The Commentaries explain it as "nipāta," i. e. particle. Thus at Sn 560, 760.

Vo[2] [cp. Vedic vaḥ, Av. vō, Lat. vos, Gr. ὔμμε] is enclitic form of tumhe (see under tuvaŋ), i. e. to you, of you; but it is generally interpreted by the C. as "nipāta," i. e. particle (of emphasis or exclamation; i. e. vo[1]). Thus e. g. at Pv i.5[3] (cp. PvA 26).

Vo° is commonly regarded as the prefix comb[n] vi+ava° (i. e. vi+o°), but in many cases it simply represents ava° (=o°) with v as euphonic ("vorschlag"), as in vonata (=onata), voloketi, vokkanti, vokiṇṇa, voropeti, vosāpeti, vosāna, vossagga. In a few cases it corresponds to vi+ud°, as in vokkamati, vocchijjati, voyoga.

Vokāra [v(i)+okāra; cp. vikāra] 1. difference Sn 611. — 2. constituent of being (i. e. the khandhas), usually as eka°, catu° & pañca°-bhava, e. g. Kvu 261; Vbh 137; Tikp 32, 36 sq.; Vism 572; KhA 245; SnA 19, 158. In this meaning vokāra is peculiar to the *Abhidhamma* and is almost synonymous with vikāra 4, and in the Yamaka with khandha, e. g. pañca v., catu v. etc. — 3. worthless thing, trifle S ii.29. — 4. inconvenience, disadvantage (cp. vikāra 3) PvA 12 (line 1 read: anek' ākāra-vokāraŋ).

Vokiṇṇa (adj.) [v(i)+okiṇṇa] covered with, drenched (with); mixed up, full of (instr.) M i.390; S ii.29; A i.123, 148; ii.232; J i.110; DhsA 69. — Cp. abbokiṇṇa.

Vokiṇṇaka (adj.) [vokiṇṇa+ ka] mixed up Miln 300 (kapiniddā-pareto vokiṇṇakaŋ jaggati a person with light sleep, so-called "monkey-doze," lies confusedly awake, i. e. is half asleep, half awake). Rh. D. not quite to the point: "a man still guards his scattered thoughts."

Vokkanta [pp. of vokkamati] deviated from (abl.) It 36.

Vokkanti (f.) [v(i)+ akkanti] descent (into the womb), conception Th 1, 790.

Vokkamati [vi+ ukkamati] to turn aside, deviate from (abl.); mostly in ger. **vokkamma** Vin II.213; D I.230; M III.117; S IV.117; Sn 946; J I.23; Vism 18.—pp. **vokkanta**.

Vokkamana (nt.) [fr. vokkamati] turning aside, deviation fr. (abl.) M I.14; A I.243.

Vokkha (adj.) [? doubtful reading] is at J III.21 given as syn. of **vaggu** (q. v.).

Vocarita [pp. of vi+ ocarati] penetrated (into consciousness), investigated, apperceived M I.478; A IV.363 (=manodvāre samudācāra-ppatta).

Vocchādanā (f.) [fr. vi+ ava+ **chad**] covering up (entirely) VbhA 493.

Vocchijjati [vi+ ud+ chijjati, Pass. of **chid**] to be cut off S III.53 (so read).—pp. neg. **abbocchinna**: see **abbhocchinna** (=*avyucch°).

Votthapana (& °ṭṭhapana) (nt.) [=vavatth°] establishing, synthesis, determination, a momentary stage in the unit called percept (cp. *Cpd.* 29), always with °**kicca** (or °kiriyā) "accomplishing the function of determination" Vism 21; DhsA 401; DA I.194 (v. l. voṭṭhabb°); Tikp 276 (°kiriyā).

Votthāpeti [=vavatthāpeti] to establish, put up, arrange J VI.583.

Vodaka (adj.) [vi+ odaka=udaka] free from water Vin II.113.

Vodapeti (or °dāpeti) [Caus. of vodāyati] to cleanse, purify DhA II.162.

Vodāta (adj.) [vi+ odāta, cp. vīvadāta] clean, pure M I.319.

Vodāna (nt.) [fr. vi+ ava+ **dā**[4] to clean, cp. BSk. vyavadāna Divy 616; AvŚ II.188] 1. cleansing, getting bright (of sun & moon) D I.10 (=visuddhatā DA I.95).—2. purity (from the *kilesas*, or stains of sin), purification, sanctification M I.115 (opp. sankilesa); S III.151 (citta°, adj.; opp. citta-sankilesa); A III.418 sq.; V.34; Ps I.166; Vbh 343; Nett 96, 100, 125 sq.; Vism 51 sq., 89; VbhA 401; DhA III.405.

Vodāniya (adj.) [grd. formⁿ from vodāna] apt to purify, purifying D I.195; III.57. Opp. sankilesika.

Vodāpana (nt.) [fr. vodapeti] cleansing, purification DhA III.237 (=pariyodapana).

Vodāya at J IV.184 appears to be a misreading for codāya (ger. from codeti) in meaning iṇaŋ codeti to undertake a loan, to lend money at interest (=vaḍḍhiyā iṇaŋ payojetvā C.), to demand payment for a loan. The v. l. at all places is **codāya** (=codetvā). See **codeti**.

Vodāyati [vi+ ava+ **dā**[4] to clean] to become clean or clear, to be purified or cleansed A V.169 (fig. saddhammassa), 317 (id.; expl[d] by C. as "vodānaŋ gacchati"); J II.418 (of a precious stone).

Vodāsa [?] only at D III.43 in phrase °ŋ āpajjati in meaning of "making a distinction," being particular (about food: bhojanesu), having a dainty appetite; expl[d] by "dve bhāge karoti" Bdhgh. It seems to stand for vokāra, unless we take it to be a misspelling for **vodāya** "cutting off," fr. vi+ ava+ **dā**, thus "separating the food" (?). Suggestive also is the likeness with vosānaŋ āpajjati.

Vodiṭṭha [pp. of vi+ ava+ **diś**, cp. odissa & the BSk. vyapadeśa pretext Divy 435] defined, fully understood, recognized M I.478; A IV.363 (=suṭṭhu diṭṭha C.).

Vonata (adj.) [v(i)+ onata] bent down Th 1, 662.

Vopeti at DA I.277 (avopetvā) is to be read with v. l. as copeti, i. e. shake, move, disturb, violate (a rule).

Vobhindati [vi+ ava+ bhindati] to split; ppr. °**anto** (fig.) hair-splitting D I.162; M I.176; aor. **vobhindi** (lit.) to break, split (one's head, sīsaŋ) M I.336.

Vomādapeti at DA I.300 is to be read as vodāpeti (cleanse, purify); v. l. BB vodāpeti; SS cāmā[dā]peti, i. e. to cause to be rinsed, cleanse.

Vomissa(ka) (adj.) [v(i)+ omissa(ka)] miscellaneous, various Vism 87 (°katā), 88 (°ka), 104 (°carita).

Voyoga [vi+ uyyoga in sense of uyyutta ?] effort (?), application KhA 243. Reading doubtful.

Voropana (nt.) [abstr. fr. voropeti] depriving (jīvita° of life) J I.99.

Voropeti [=oropeti] to deprive of (abl.), to take away; only in phrase jīvitā voropeti [which shows that **-v-** is purely euphonic] to deprive of life, to kill D I.85; J IV.454; DA I.236; DhA IV.68; PvA 67, 105, 274.

Volokana (nt.) [v(i)+ olokana, but cp. BSk. vyavalokana "inspection" Divy 435] looking at, examination J IV.237 (v. l. vi°).

Voloketi [v(i)+ oloketi; in meaning equal to viloketi & oloketi] to examine, study, scrutinize M I.213 (with gen.); Vin I.6 (lokaŋ); Kvu 591; DhA I.319 (lokaŋ); II.96 (v. l. oloketi).

Vosāṭitaka (nt.) [wrong spelling for *vossaṭṭhika=v(i)+ ossaṭṭha+ ika] (food) put down (on cemeteries etc.) for (the spirits of) the departed Vin IV.89.

Vosāna (nt.) [v(i)+ osāna] 1. (relative) achievement, perfection (in this world), accomplishment M II.211 (diṭṭhadhamm' âbhiññāvosāna-pārami-ppatta); Dh 423 (cp. DhA IV.233); Th 1, 784 (°ŋ adhigacchati to reach perfection).—2. stopping, ceasing; in phrase °ŋ **āpajjati** (almost equal to **pamāda**) to come to an end (with), to stop, to become careless, to flag M I.193; J III.5; PvA 29; antarā °ŋ āpajjati to produce half-way achievement, to stop half-way A V.157, 164; It 85. Kern, *Toev.* s. v. quite wrong "to arrive at a conclusion, to be convinced."

Vosāpeti [v(i)+ osāpeti] to make end, to bring to an end or a finish SnA 46 (desanaŋ).

Vosāraṇiya (adj. nt.) [fr. v(i)+ osāraṇā] belonging to reinstatement A I.99.

Vosita [vi+ osita, pp. of ava+ **sā**. See also **vusita** & **vyosita**] one who has attained (relative) achievement, perfected, accomplished, mastering, in phrase **abhiññā°** one who masters special knowledge S I.167; Dh 423; It 47=61=81; A I.165; cp. DhA IV.233: "niṭṭhānaŋ patto vusita-vosānaŋ vā patto etc."

Vossa (-kamma) (nt.) making impotent (see under vassakamma) D I.12; DA I.97.

Vossagga [=ossagga; ava+ **sṛj**] relinquishing, relaxation; handing over, donation, gift (see on term as ethical Bdhgh at *K.S.* I.321) D III.190 (issariya° handing over of authority), 226; S IV.365 sq.; V.63 sq., 351 (°rata fond of giving); A II.66 (id.); III.53 (id.); Ps I.109; II.24, 117; J VI.213 (kamma°); Nett 16; Vbh 229, 350; Vism 224; VbhA 317. **-sati-vossagga** relaxation of attention, inattention, indifference DhA I.228; III.163, 482; IV.43. **-pariṇāmi,** maturity of surrender S I.88.

Vossajjati [=ossaj(j)ati] to give up, relinquish; to hand over, resign Sn 751 (ger. **vossajja;** SnA 508 reads oss°); J V.124 (issariyaŋ vossajjanto; cp. D III.190).

Voharati [vi+oharati] 1. to express, define, decide M I.499; D I.202; Miln 218. — 2. to decide, govern over (a kingdom), give justice, administrate J IV.134 (Bārāṇasiŋ maŋsa-sur-odakaŋ, i. e. provide with; double acc.), 192 (inf. **vohātuŋ**=voharituŋ C.). — Pass. **vohariyati** to be called SnA 26; PvA 94; ThA 24.

Vohāra [vi+avahāra] 1. trade, business M II.360; Sn 614 (°ŋ upajīvati); J I.495; II.133, 202; V.471; PvA 111, 278. — 2. current appellation, common use (of language), popular logic, common way of defining, usage, designation, term, cognomen; (adj.) (-°) so called SnA 383, 466, 483 (laddha° so-called); DA I.70; PvA 56, 231 (laddha° padesa, with the name) VvA 8, 72 (pāṇo ti vohārato satto), 108 (loka nirūḷhāya samaññāya v.). —**ariya-vohāra** proper (i. e. Buddhist) mode of speech (opp. anariya° unbuddhist or vulgar, common speech) D III.232; A II.246; IV.307; Vin IV.2; Vbh 376, 387. **lokiya-vohāra** common definition, general way of speech SnA 382. On term see also *Dhs. trslⁿ* § 1306. — 3. lawsuit, law, lawful obligation; juridical practice, jurisprudence (cp. vohārika) Sn 246 (°kūṭa fraudulent lawyer); J II.423 (°ŋ sādheti to claim a debt by way of law, or a lawful debt); VI.229; DhA III.12 (°ūpajīvin a lawyer); SnA 289. — 4. name of a sea-monster, which gets hold of ships J V.259.

Vohārika [fr. vohāra] "decider," one connected with a law-suit or with the law, magistrate, a higher official (mahāmatta) in the law-courts, a judge or justice. At Vin I.74 two classes of mahāmattā (ministers) are given: senānāyakā those of defence, and vohārikā of justice; cp. Vin II.158; III.45 (purāṇa-vohāriko mahāmatto); IV.223.

Vy° is the semi-vowel (i. e. half-consonantic) form of vi° before following a & ā (vya°, vyā), very rarely ū & o. The prefix vi° is very unstable, and a variety of forms are also attached to vy°, which, after the manner of all consonant-combⁿˢ in Pāli, may apart from its regular form vy° appear either as *contracted* to vv° (written v°), like vagga (for vyagga), vaya (for vyaya), vosita (=vyosita), *vvūha (=vyūha, appearing as °bbūha), or *diaeretic* as **viy°** (in poetry) or **veyy°** (popular), e. g. viyañjana, viyārambha, viyāyata; or veyyañjanika, veyyākaraṇa, veyyāyika. It further appears as **by°** (like byaggha, byañjana, byappatha, byamha, byāpanna, byābādha etc.). In a few cases **vya°** represents (a diaeretic) vi°, as in vyamhita & vyasanna; and **vyā°**=vi° in vyārosa.

Vyakkhissaŋ at Sn 600 is fut. of vyācikkhati (see viyā°).

Vyagga (adj.) [vi+agga, of which the contracted form is **vagga²**] distracted, confused, bewildered; neg. **a°** S I.96 (°mānasa); V.66, 107.

Vyaggha [cp. Vedic vyāghra] a tiger D III.25; A III.101; Sn 416 (°usabha); Ap 68 (°rājā); J I.357; III.192 (Subāhu); V.14 (giri-sānuja). — f. viyagghinī (biy°) Miln 67. See also **byaggha.**

Vyagghīnasa [?] a hawk S I.148 (as °nisa); J VI.538. Another word for "hawk" is sakuṇagghi.

Vyañjana (nt.) [fr. vi+**añj,** cp. añjati² & abbhañjati] 1. (accompanying) attribute, distinctive mark, sign, characteristic (cp. anu°) Sn 549, 1017; Th 1, 819 (metric: viyañjana); J V.86 (**viyañjanena** under the pretext); Dhs 1306. **gihi°** characteristic of a layman Sn 44 (cp. SnA 91); Miln 11; **purisa°** membrum virile Vin II.269. — 2. letter (of a word) as opposed to attha (meaning, sense, spirit), e, g. D III.127; S IV.281, 296; V.430; A II.139 (Cp. **savyañjana**); or **pada** (word), e. g. M I.399; A I.59; II.147, 168, 182; III.178 sq.; Vin II.316; Nett 4; SnA 177. —**vyañjanato** according to the letter Miln 18 (opp. atthato). — 3. condiment, curry Vin II.214; A III.49 (odano anekasūpo aneka-vyañjano); Pv II.1¹⁵ (bhatta° rice with curry); PvA 50. — Cp. **byañjana.**

Vyañjanaka (adj.) [fr. vyañjana] see **ubhato°** & **veyyañjanika.**

Vyañjayati [vi+añjati, or añjeti] to characterise, denote, express, indicate SnA 91; Nett 209 (Cy.).

Vyatireka [vi+atireka] what is left over, addition, surplus PvA 18 (of "ca"), 228 (°to).

Vyatta (adj.) [cp. viyatta, veyyatta & byatta] 1. experienced, accomplished, learned, wise, prudent, clever S IV.174 (paṇḍita+), 375; A III.117, 258; J VI.368; VvA 131 (paṇḍita+); PvA 39 (id.). —**a°** unskilled, foolish (+bāla) S IV.380; A III.258; J I.98. — 2. evident, manifest PvA 266 (°pākaṭa-bhāva).

Vyattatā (f.) [abstr. fr. vyatta] experience, learning, cleverness Miln 349 (as **by°**); DhA II.38 (**avyattatā** foolishness: so correct under avyattatā *P.D.* I.86).

Vyattaya [vi+ati+aya] opposition, reversal; in **purisa°** change of person (gram.) SnA 545; **vacana°** reversal of number (i. e. sg. & pl.) DA I.141; SnA 509.

Vyathana (nt.) [fr. **vyath**] shaking, wavering Dhtp 465 (as defⁿ of **tud**).

Vyadhati [in poetry for the usual vedhati of **vyath,** cp. Goth. wiþōn] to tremble, shake, waver; to be frightened Vin II.202 (so for **vyādhati**); J III.398 (vyadhase; C. vyadhasi=kampasi). — Caus. **vyadheti** (& **vyādheti**) to frighten, confuse J IV.166 (=vyādheti bādheti C.). — Fut. **vyādhayissati** S I.120=Th I, 46 (by°). Under **byādheti** we had given a different derivation (viz. Caus. fr. vyādhi).

Vyanta (adj. nt.) [vi+anta] removed, remote; nt. end, finish; only as **vyanti°** in combⁿ with **kṛ** and **bhū.** The spelling is often **byanti°.** — (1) **vyantikaroti** to abolish, remove, get rid of, destroy M I.115 (byant' eva ekāsiŋ), 453 (by°); D I.71 (°kareyya); S IV.76, 190; A IV.195; DA I.125, 212. — Fut. **vyantikāhiti** Miln 391 (by°); DhA IV.69. — pp. **vyantikata** Th 1, 526. — (2) **vyantibhavati** to cease, stop; to come to an end, to be destroyed Kvu 597 (by°); or °hoti A I.141; III.74; Ps I.171 (by°); Miln 67 (by°). **vyantibhāva** destruction, annihilation M I.93; A V.292, 297 sq.; Pv IV.1⁷³; Kvu 544 (by°). vyantibhuta come to an end J V.4.

Vyapagacchati [vi+apagacchati] to depart, to be dispelled J II.407 (ger. °gamma). — pp. °**gata.**

Vyapagata [pp. of vyapagacchati] departed J I.17; Miln 133, 225.

Vyapanudati [vi+apanudati] to drive away, expel; ger °nujja Sn 66. aor. vyapānudi Th 2, 318.

Vyapahaññati [vi+apa+haññati] to be removed or destroyed J VI.565.

Vyappatha (nt.) [perhaps a distortion of *vyāpṛta, for which the usual P. (der.) **veyyāvacca** (q. v.) in meaning "duty"] 1. duty, occupation, activity Sn 158 (khiṇa°

of the Arahant: having no more duties, cp. vyappathi). —2. way of speaking, speech, utterance Sn 163, 164 (contrasted to citta & kamma; cp. kāya, vācā, mano in same use), expl[d] at SnA 206 by vacīkamma; & in def[n] of "speech" at Vin IV.2 (see under **byappatha**); DhsA 324 (expl[d] as vākya-bheda).

Vyappathi (f.) [cp. Sk. vyāpṛti] activity, occupation, duty (?) Sn 961. See remarks on **byappatha**.

Vyappanā (f.) [vi+appanā] application (of mind), focussing (of attention) Dhs 7.

Vyamha (nt.) [etym. ?] palace; a celestial mansion, a vimāna, abode for fairies etc. J III.454; VI.119, 251 (=pura & rāja-nivesa C.); Vv 35[1] (=bhavana VvA 160). Cp. **byamha**.

Vyamhita (adj.) [metric for **vimhita**] astounded, shocked, awed; dismayed, frightened J V.69 (=bhīta C.); VI.243, 314.

Vyaya [vi+aya, of **i**; the assimilation form is vaya[2]] expense, loss, decay S IV.68, 140; Miln 393 (as abbaya). **avyayena** (instr.) safely D I.72. Cp. **veyyāyika** & **vyāyika**.

Vyavayāti [vi+ava(=apa)+**i**, cp. **apeti** & **veti**] to go away, disappear J V.82.

Vyavasāna (nt.) [somewhat doubtful. It has to be compared with **vavassagga**, although it should be derived fr. **sā** (cp. pp. vyavasita; or **śri** ?), thus mixture of **sṛj** & **sā**. Cp. a similar difficulty of **sā** under osāpeti] decision, resolution; only used to explain part. handa (exhortation) at SnA 200, 491 (v. l. vyavasāya: cp. vavasāya at DA I.237), for which otherwise **vavassagga**.

Vyavasita (adj.) [pp. of vi+ava+**sā** (or **śri** ?), cp. vyavasāna] decided, resolute SnA 200.

Vyasana (nt.) [fr. vy+**as**] misfortune, misery, ruin, destruction, loss D I.248; S III.137 (anaya°); IV.159; A I.33; V.156 sq., 317 (several); Sn 694 (°gata ruined); Pv I.6[4] (=dukkha PvA 33); III.5[6] (=anattha PvA 199); Vbh 99 sq., 137; VbhA 102 (several); PvA 4, 103, 112; Sdhp 499. —The 5 vyasanas are: ñāti°, bhoga°, roga°, sīla°, diṭṭhi° or misfortune concerning one's relations, wealth, health, character, views. Thus at D III.235; A III.147; Vin IV.277.

Vyasanin (adj.) [fr. vyasana] having misfortune, unlucky, faring ill J V.259.

Vyasanna [metric (diaeretic) for visanna] sunk into (loc.), immersed J IV.399; V.16 (here doubtful; *not*, as C., vyasanāpanna; gloss **visanna**; vv. ll. in C.: vyaccanna, viphanna, visatta).

Vyākata [pp. of vyākaroti] 1. answered, explained, declared, decided M I.431 (by°); A I.119; S II.51, 223; IV.59, 194; V.177; Sn 1023. —**avyākata** unexplained, undecided, not declared, indeterminate M I.431 (by°); D I.187, 189; S II.222; IV.375 sq., 384 sq., 391 sq.; Ps II.108 sq.; Dhs 431, 576. —2. predicted J I.26. —3. settled, determined J III.529 (asinā v. brought to a decision by the sword).

Vyākatatta (nt.) [abstr. fr. vyākata] explanation, definiteness PvA 27.

Vyakattar [n. ag. of vyākaroti; cp. BSk. vyākartṛ Divy 620] expounder A III.81.

Vyākaraṇa (nt.) [fr. vyākaroti; see also veyyākaraṇa] 1. answer (pañha°), explanation, exposition A I.197; II.46; III.119; SnA 63, 99; KhA 75, 76. —2. grammar (as one of the 6 angas) SnA 447; PvA 97. —3. prediction J I.34, 44; DhA IV.120.

Vyākaroti [vi+ā+**kṛ**] 1. to explain, answer (in comb[n] with **puṭṭha**, asked) D I.25, 58, 175, 200; Sn 510, 513 sq., 1102, 1116; Miln 318 (byākareyya); VvA 71. Fut. °karissati D I.236; Sn 993; PvA 281. For vyākarissati we have **vyakkhissati** (of viyācikkhati) at Sn 600. —aor. sg. **vyākāsi** Sn 541, 1116, 1127; PvA 212; pl. **vyākaṃsu** Sn 1084; Pv II.13[5]. —grd. **vyākātabba** D I.94, 118. —2. to prophesy, predict [cp. BSk. vyākaroti in same sense Divy 65, 131] J I.140; Pv III.5[5] (aor. °ākari); Mhvs 6, 2 (aor. °ākaruṃ); DhA IV.120 (°ākāsi); PvA 196, 199 (°ākāsi). —pp. **vyākata**.

Vyākāra see viy°.

Vyākhyāta [pp. of v(i)yācikkhati] told, announced, set forth, enumerated Sn 1,000.

Vyākula (adj.) [vi+ākula] perplexed J I.301; PvA 160; VvA 30; Sdhp 403.

Vyādinna [for vyādiṇṇa, vi+ādiṇṇa ?] at A III.64 (soto vikkhitto visaṭo+) is doubtful in reading & meaning ("split" ?). It must mean something like "interrupted, diverted." The vv. ll. are **vicchinna** & **jiṇṇa**.

Vyādha [fr. **vyadh**: see vedha & vijjhati] a huntsman, deer-hunter Mhvs 10, 89 (read either **vyādha-deva** god of the h.; or **vyādhi°** demon of maladies); 10, 95.

Vyādhi[1] [see byādhi] sickness, malady, illness, disease A I.139 (as devadūta), 146, 155 sq.; III.66; Ps I.59 sq.; II.147; J VI.224; Vism 236. Often in sequence jāti jarā **vyādhi** maraṇa, e. g. A II.172; III.74 sq.; Vism 232.

Vyādhi[2] (camel) see **oṭṭhi°**.

Vyādhita [pp. of vyādheti] 1. affected with an illness, ill J V.497; Miln 168. See **byādhita**. —2. shaken, f. °ā as abstr, shakiness, trembling VbhA 479.

Vyādhiyaka (nt.) [fr. vyādheti] shaking up Vbh 352; VbhA 479 (uppannavyādhitā; i. e. kāya-pphandana).

Vyādheti see **vyadhati**. —pp. **vyādhita**.

Vyāpaka (adj.) [fr. **vyāpeti**] filling or summing up, combining, completing PvA 71 (in expl[n] of "ye keci": anavasesa° niddesa).

Vyāpajjati [vi+āpajjati] (instr.) to go wrong, to fail, disagree; to be troubled; also (trs.) to do harm, to injure S III.119, 184=Nd[2] 40 (by°); A III.101 (bhattaṃ me vyāpajjeyya disagrees with me, makes me ill); Sn 1065 (ākāso avyāpajjamāno not troubled, not getting upset); Nd[2] 74 (by°). —pp. **vyāpanna**. —Caus. **vyāpādeti**.

Vyāpajjanā (f.) [fr. vyāpajjati] injuring, doing harm, ill-will Pug 18; Dhs 418 ("getting upset" *trsl[n]*).

Vyāpajjha (adj.-nt.) [perhaps grd. of vyāpajjati; but see also avyāpajjha] to be troubled or troubling, doing harm, injuring; only neg. **avyāpajjha** (& **abyābajjha**) (adj.) not hurting, peaceful, friendly; (nt.) kindness of heart Vin I.183; M I.90 (abyābajjhaṃ vedanaṃ vedeti), 526; D I.167, 247, 251; S IV.296, 371; A I.98; II.231 sq.; III.285, 329 sq., 376 sq. Cp. **byāpajjha** & **vyābādha** etc.

Vyāpatti (f.) [fr. vyāpajjati] injury, harm; doing harm, malevolence A V.292 sq.; Pug 18; J IV.137; Dhs 418 ("disordered temper" *trsl[n]*).

Vyāpanna (adj.) [pp. of vyāpajjati] spoilt, disagreeing, gone wrong; corrupt; only with **citta**, i. e. a corrupted heart, or a malevolent intention; adj. malevolent D I.139; III.82; A I.262, 299; opp. avyāpanna (q. v.). See also **byāpanna** & **viyāpanna**.

Vyāpāda [fr. vyāpajjati. See also byāpāda] making bad, doing harm; desire to injure, malevolence, ill-will D I.71, 246; III.70 sq., 226, 234; S I.99; II.151; IV.343; A I.194, 280; II.14, 210; III.92, 231, 245; IV.437; Vbh 86, 363 sq., 391; Pug 17 sq.; Dhs 1137; Vism 7; DA I.211; VbhA 74, 118, 369. °anusaya M I.433. °dosa M III.3. °dhātu M III.62. °nīvaraṇa M II.203. See under each affix. — Cp. avyāpāda.

Vyāpādeti [Caus. of vyāpajjati] to spoil Miln 92.

Vyāpāra [vi+ā+pṛ] occupation, business, service, work J I.341; V.60; Vism 595. Cp. veyyāvacca, vyappatha (by°), vyāvaṭa.

Vyāpāritar one occupied with M III.126.

Vyāpin (adj.) [fr. vi+**āp**] pervading, diffused DhsA 311.

Vyāpeti [vi+Caus. of **āp**] to make full, pervade, fill, comprise DhsA 307; VvA 17; ThA 287; PvA 52 (=pharati), 71 (in expl[n] of "ye keci").

Vyābādha (& **byābādha**) [fr. vi+ā+**bādh**, but semantically connected with vi+ā+**pad**, as in vyāpāda & vyāpajjha] oppression, injury, harm, hurting; usually in phrase atta° & para° (disturbing the peace of others & of oneself) M I.89; S IV.339; A I.114, 157, 216; II.179. — Also at S IV.159 (pāṇinaŋ vyābādhāya, with v. l. vadhāya). See also **byābādha**. The corresponding adjectives are (a)**vyāpajjha** & veyyābādhika (q. v.).

Vyābādheti (& **bya°**) [Caus. of vi+ā+**badh**, or distortion fr. vyāpadeti, with which identical in meaning] to do harm, hurt, injure Vin II.77/78; S IV.351 sq.; DA I.167. The BSk. is **vyābādhayate** (e. g. Divy 105).

Vyābāheti [vi+ā+**bah**: see bahati[3]] lit. "to make an outsider," to keep or to be kept out or away Vin II.140 (°bāhiŋsu in Pass. sense; so that they may not be kept away). Oldenberg (on p. 320) suggests reading **vyābādhiŋsu**, which may be better, viz. "may not be offended" (?). The form is difficult to explain.

Vyābhangī (f.) [see byā°] 1. a carrying pole (or flail?) Th I, 623; comb[d] with **asita** (see asita[4] in corr. to pt. 2) "sickle & pole" M II.180; A III.5. — 2. a flail S IV.201.

Vyāma see **byāma** & add ref. D II.18 ≈ Vism 136 (catu°-pamāṇa).

Vyāyata [vi+āyata] stretched; only neg. a° senseless, confused (should it be **vyāyatta**?) J I.496 (=avyatta C.). See also **viyāyata**.

Vyāyāma = **vāyāma** DhsA 146.

Vyāyika (adj.) [fr. vyaya] belonging to decay; only neg. a° not decaying, imperishable A II.51; J V.508.

Vyārambha see **viy°**.

Vyāruddha (adj.) [pp. of vi+ā+**rundh**] opposed, hostile Th I, 344; Sn 936. See **byāruddha**.

Vyārosa [vi+ā+rosa, cp. virosanā] anger M III.78; S III.73.

Vyālika (nt.) [for vy+alika] fault ThA 266.

Vyāvaṭa (adj.) [=Sk. vyāpṛta, cp. vyāpāra, byappatha. & veyyāvacca] doing service, active, busy; eager, keen, intent on (loc.), busy with A IV.195 (mayi = worrying about me); J III.315 (su°); IV.371 (kiccākiccesu v. = uyyatta C.); V.395 (=ussukka); VI.229 (=kāya-veyyāvacca-dān' ādi-kamma-karaṇena vyāvaṭa C.). —**dassana°** keen on a sight, eager to see J I.89; VvA 213 (preferred to T. reading!). —**dāna°** serving in connection with a gift, busy with giving, a "commissioner of gifts," i. e. a superintendent installed by a higher (rich) person (as a king or seṭṭhi) to look after the distribution of all kinds of gifts in connection with a mahādāna. Rh. Davids at *Dial.* II.372 (following Childers) has quite misunderstood the term in referring it to a **vyāvaṭa** in meaning of "hindered," and by translating it as "hindered at the largesse" or "objecting to the largesse." At none of the passages quoted by him has it that meaning. See e. g. D II.354; J III.129; Pv II.9[50] (dāne v. = ussukkaŋ āpanna PvA 135); PvA 112 (dāne), 124 (id.); DA I.296 (? not found). **avyāvaṭa** not busy, not bothering about (loc.), unconcerned with, not worrying D II.141 (Tathāgatassa sarīre; trsl[n] not to the point "hinder not yourselves"); Vin III.136. See also separately. — *Note.* **vyāvaṭa** (& a°) only occur in the meaning given above, and *not* in the sense of "*covered, obstructed*" [wrongly fr. **vṛ**] as given by Childers. Correct the trsl[n] given under byāvaṭa accordingly!

Vyāviddha (adj.) [vi+āviddha] whirling about, flitting (here & there), moving about, pell-mell J VI.530.

Vyāsa [fr. vi+**ās** to sit] separation, division; always contrasted with samāsa, e. g. Vism 82 (vyāsato separately, distributively; opp. samāsato); KhA 187.

Vyāsatta see **byāsatta**.

Vyāsiñcati [vi+āsiñcati] to defile, corrupt, tarnish S IV.78 (cittaŋ). — pp. **vyāsitta** ibid.

Vyāseka [fr. vi+ā+**sic**] mixed; only neg. a° unmixed, untarnished, undefiled D I.70; DA I.183; Pug 59; Th I, 926.

Vyāharati [vi+āharati] to utter, talk, speak Vin II.214; J II.177; IV.225 (puṭṭho vyāhāsi, perhaps with v. l. as vyākāsi). See also **avyāharati**. — Cp. **paṭi°**.

Vyūha [fr. vi+**vah**; see byūha] 1. heap, mass; massing or array, grouping of troops S V.369 (sambādha° a dense crowd, or massed with troops (?); in phrase iddha phīta etc., as given under bāhujañña); J II.406 (battle array: paduma°, cakka°, sakaṭa°). — 2. a side street (?), in sandhibbūha J VI.276.

Vyūhati at VvA 104 is not clear (see byūhati). It looks more like a present tense to **viyūḷha** in sense "to be bulky," than a Denom. fr. vyūha as "stand in array." For the regular verb vi+**vah** see **viyūhati**. Cp. paṭi° & **saŋyūhati**.

Vyosita (adj.) [=vosita] perfected; neg. a° not perfected, imperfect Th I, 784 (aby°).

S.

-S- a *euphonic* -s- seems to occur in comb^{n} ras-agga-s-aggin (see rasa[1]). An apparent hiatus -s in ye s-idha Sn 1083, and evaŋ s-ahaŋ Sn 1134 (v. l.) may be an abbreviated su° (see su[2]), unless we take it as a misspelling for p.

Sa[1] the letter s (sa-kāra) SnA 23; or the syllable sa DhA II.6; PvA 280.

Sa[2] [Idg. *so- (m.), *sā- (f.); nom. sg. to base *to- of the oblique cases; cp. Sk. sa (saḥ), sā; Av. hō, hā; Gr. ὁ, ἡ; Goth. sa, sō; Ags. sē "the" (=that one); þe-s=E. thi-s] base of the nom. of the demonstr. pron. that, he, she. The form sg. m. sa is rare (e. g. Dh 142; Sn 89). According to Geiger (*P.Gr.* § 105) sa occurs in Sn 40 times, but so 124 times. In later Pāli sa is almost extinct. The final o of so is often changed into v before vowels, and a short vowel is lengthened after this v: svājja Sn 998=so ajja; svāhaŋ J I.167=so ahaŋ; svāyaŋ Vin I.2=so ayaŋ. The foll. vowel is dropped in so maŋ It 57=so imaŋ. — A form se is Māgadhism for nt. acc. sg. taŋ, found e. g. at D II.278, 279; M II.254, 255, and in comb^{n} seyyathā, seyyathīdaŋ (for which taŋyathā Miln 1). An idiomatic use is that of so in meaning of "that (he or somebody)," e. g. "so vata . . . palipanno paraŋ palipannaŋ uddharissatī ti: n' etaŋ ṭhānaŋ vijjati" M I.45; cp. "sā 'haŋ dhammaŋ nâssosiŋ" that I did not hear the Dh. Vv 40[5]. Or in the sense of a cond. (or causal) part. "if," or "once," e. g. sa kho so bhikkhu . . . upakkileso ti iti viditvā . . . upakkilesaŋ pajahati "once he has recognised . . ." M I.37. Cp. ya° II.2 b. On correl. use with ya° (yo so etc.) see ya° II.1.

Sa[3] [identical with saŋ°] prefix, used as first pt. of compounds, is the sense of "with," possessed of, having, same as; e. g. sadevaka with the devas Vin I.8; sadhammika having common faith D II.273; sajāti having the same origin J II.108. Often opposed to a- and other neg. prefixes (like nir°). Sometimes almost pleonastical (like sa-antara). — Of combinations we only mention a few of those in which a vocalic initial of the 2nd pt. remains uncontracted. Other examples see under their heading in alph. order. E. g. sa-antara inside DhA III.788 (for santara Dh 315); sa-Inda together with Indra D II.261, 274; A V.325 sq.; °-uttara having something beyond, inferior (opp. an°) D I.80; II.299=M I.59; Dhs 1292, 1596; DhsA 50; °-uttaracchada (& °chadana) a carpet with awnings above it D I.7≈; II.187 (°ava); A I.181; Vin I.192; DA I.87; -°udaka with water, wet Vin I.46; -°udariya born from the same womb, a brother J IV.417, cp. sodariya; -°uddesa with explanation It 99; Vism 423 (nāma-gotta-vasena sa-udd.; vaṇṇ'ādi-vasena sākāra); -°upanisa together with its cause, causally associated S II.30; -°upavajja having a helper M III.266; -°upādāna showing attachment M II.265; -°upādisesa having the substratum of life remaining Sn 354; It 38; Nett 92. Opp. anupādisesa; -°ummi roaring of the billows It 57, 114. — *Note.* sa[2] & sa[3] are differentiations of one and the same sa, which is originally the deictic pronoun in the function of identity & close connection. See etym. under saŋ°.

Sa[4] (reflex. pron.) [Vedic sva & svayaŋ (=P. sayaŋ); Idg. *seu̯o, *su̯e; cp. Av. hava & hva own; Gr. ἑός & ὅς his own; Lat. sui, suus; Goth. swēs own, sik=Ger. sich himself; etc.] own M I.366; D II.209; Sn 905; J II.7; III.164, 323 (loc. samhi lohite), 402 (acc. saŋ his own, viz. kinsman; C=sakaŋ janaŋ); IV.249 (saŋ bhātaraŋ); Pv II.12[1]=DhA III.277 (acc. san tanuŋ); instr. sena on one's own, by oneself J V.24 (C. not quite to the point: mama santakena). Often in composition, like sadesa one's own country Dāvs I.10. Cp. saka.

Saŋ° (indecl.) [prefix; Idg. *sem one; one & the same, cp. Gr. ὁμαλός even, ἅμα at one, ὁμός together; Sk. sama even, the same; samā in the same way; Av. hama same=Goth. sama, samaþ together; Lat. simul (=simultaneous), similis "re-sembling." Also Sk. sa (=sa[2]) together=Gr. ἀ-, ἁ- (e. g. ἄκοιτις); Av. ha-; and samyak towards *one* point=P. sammā. — Analogously to Lat. semel "once," simul, we find sa° as *numeral* base for "one" in Vedic sakṛt "once"=P. sakid (& sakad), sahasra 1000=P. sahassa, and in adv. sadā "always," lit. "in one"] prefix, implying conjunction & completeness. saŋ° is after vi° (19%) the most frequent (16%) of all Pāli prefixes. Its primary meaning is "together" (cp. Lat. con°); hence arises that of a closer connection or a more accentuated action than that expressed by the simple verb (intensifying=thoroughly, quite), or noun. Very often merely pleonastic, esp. in comb^{n} with other prefixes (e. g. sam-anu°, sam-ā°, sam-pa°). In meaning of "near by, together" it is opposed to para°; as modifying prefix it is contrary to abhi° and (more frequently) to vi° (e. g. saŋvadati>vivadati), whereas it often equals pa° (e. g. pamodati>sammodati), with which it is often comb^{d} as sampa°; and also abhi° (e. g. abhivaḍḍhati>saŋvaḍḍhati), with which often comb^{d} as abhisaŋ°. — Bdhgh & Dhpāla explain saŋ° by sammā (SnA 151; KhA 209: so read for samā āgatā), suṭṭhu (see e. g. santasita, santusita), or samantā (=altogether; SnA 152, 154), or (dogmatically) sakena santena samena (KhA 240), or as "saŋyoga" Vism 495. — In comb^{n} with y we find both saŋy° and saññ°. The usual contracted form before r is sā°.

Saŋyata (& saññata) [pp. of saŋyamati] lit. drawn together; fig. restrained, self-controlled D II.88; S I.79; Sn 88, 156, 716; J I.188; Vv 34[11]; Miln 213.

-atta having one's self restrained, self-controlled S I.14 (for saya°); Sn 216, 284 (ññ), 723; Pv II.6[14] (ññ;=saññata-citta PvA 98). -ūru having the thighs pressed together, having firm thighs J V.89, 107 (ññ). 155 (ññ). -cārin living in self-control Dh 104 (ññ). -pakhuma having the eyelashes close together VvA 162.

Saŋyama (& saññama) [fr. saŋ+**yam**] 1. restraint, self-control, abstinence S I.21, 169; D I.53; Vin I.3; A I.155 sq. (kāyena, vācāya, manasā); D III.147; It 15 (ññ); Sn 264, 655; M II.101 (sīla°); Dh 25 (saññama dama); DA

I.160; DhA II.255 (=catu-pārisuddhi-sīla); VbhA 332. — 2. restraint in giving alms, saving (of money etc.), stinginess Vin I.272; Pv II.7[11] (=sankoca PvA 102).

Saŋyamati [saŋ+yamati] to practise self-control S I.209 (pāṇesu ca saŋyamāmase, trsl[n] "if we can keep our hands off living things"). — pp. **saŋyata**. — Caus. saññāmeti to restrain M I.365, 507; Dh 37, 380. Cp. paṭi°.

Saŋyamana (nt.) [fr. saŋ+**yam**] fastening J V.202, 207.

Saŋyamanī (f.) [fr. last] a kind of ornament J V.202 (=maṇisuvaṇṇa-pavāḷa-rajata-mayāni pilandhanāni C.).

Saŋyācikā (f.) [collect. abstr. fr. saŋ+**yāc**] begging, what is begged; only in instr. °āya (adv.) by begging together, by collecting voluntary offerings Vin III.144 (so read for °āyo), 149 (expl[d] incorrectly as "sayaŋ yācitvā"); J II.282 (so read for °āyo).

Saŋyuga (nt.) [fr. saŋ+**yuj**] harness Th I, 659.

Saŋyuñjati [saŋ+yuñjati] to connect, join with (instr.), unite S I.72. Pass. saŋyujjati S III.70. — pp. **saŋyutta**. — Caus. **saŋyojeti** (1) to put together, to endow with D II.355; S V.354; J I.277. — (2) to couple, to wed someone to (instr.) J III.512 (dārena); IV.7 (id.). — pp. saŋyojita.

Saŋyuta (adj.) [saŋ+yuta, of **yu**] connected, combined Sn 574 (ññ), 1026.

Saŋyutta [pp. of saŋyuñjati] 1. tied, bound, fettered M III.275 (cammena); S IV.163; A IV.216 (saŋyojanena s. by bonds to this world); Sn 194 (ññ), 300, 304; It 8; Sdhp 211. — 2. connected with, mixed with (-°) J I.269 (visa°). — Cp. **paṭi°**, **vi°**.

Saŋyūḷha [pp. of saŋyūhati, cp. in similar meaning **viyūḷha**] massed, collected, put together, composed or gathered (like a bunch of flowers D II.267 (gāthā); M I.386; DA I.38 (spelt saŋvūḷha, i. e. saŋvyūḷha; v. l. sañaḷha, i. e. sannaddha).

Saŋyūhati [saŋ+vyūhati] to form into a mass, to ball together, to conglomerate A IV.137 (kheḷapiṇḍaŋ). — pp. saŋyūḷha.

Saŋyoga [fr. saŋ+**yuj**] 1. bond, fetter M I.498; S I.226; III.70; IV.36; A IV.280=Vin II.259 (opp. vi°); Sn 522, 733; Dh 384 (=kāmayog'ādayo saŋyogā DhA IV.140). — 2. union, association J III.12 (ññ); Vism 495. — 3. connection (within the sentence), construction PvA 73 (accanta°), 135 (id.).

Saŋyojana (nt.) [fr. saŋyuñjati] bond, fetter S IV.163 etc.; especially the fetters that bind man to the wheel of transmigration Vin I.183; S I.23; V.241, 251; A I.264; III.443; IV.7 sq. (diṭṭhi°); M I.483; Dh 370; It 8 (taṇhā); Sn 62, 74, 621; J I.275; II.22; Nett 49; DhA III.298; IV.49.

The ten fetters are (1) sakkāyadiṭṭhi; (2) vicikicchā; (3) sīlabbataparāmāso; (4) kāmacchando; (5) vyāpādo; (6) rūparāgo; (7) arūparāgo; (8) māno; (9) uddhaccaŋ; (10) avijjā. The first three are the tīṇi saŋyojanāni — e. g. M I.9; A I.231, 233; D I.156; II.92 sq., 252; III.107, 132, 216; S V.357, 376, 406; Pug 12, 15; Nett 14; Dhs 1002; DA I.312. The seven last are the satta saŋyojanāni, Nett. 14. The first five are called orambhāgiyāni — e. g. A I.232 sq.; II.5, 133; V.17; D I.156; II.92, 252; M I.432; S V.61, 69; Th 2, 165; Pug 17. The last five are called **uddhambhāgiyāni** — e. g. A V.17; S V.61, 69; Th 2, 167; ThA 159; Pug 22; Nett 14, 49.

A different enumeration of the ten saŋyojanas, at Nd[2] 657=Dhs 1113, 1463 (kāmarāga, paṭigha, māna, diṭṭhi, vicikicchā, sīlabbataparāmāsa, bhavarāga, issā, macchariya, avijjā); compare, however, Dhs 1002.

A diff. enum[n] of *seven* saŋyojanas at D III.254 & A IV.7, viz. anunaya°, paṭigha°, diṭṭhi°, vicikicchā°, māna°, bhavarāga°, avijjā°. A list of *eight* is found at M I.361 sq. Cp. also **ajjhatta-saŋyojano** & **bahiddhā-saŋyojano puggalo** A I.63 sq.; Pug 22; **kiŋ-su-s°** S I.39=Sn 1108.

Saŋyojaniya (sañña°) (adj.) [fr. saŋyojana] connected with the saŋyojanas, favourable to the saŋyojanas, A I.50; S II.86; III.166 sq.; IV.89, 107; Dhs 584, 1125, 1462; DhsA 49. Used as a noun, with *dhammā* understood, Sn 363, 375.

Saŋyojita [pp. of saŋyojeti, Caus. of saŋyuñjati] combined, connected with, mixed with J I.269 (bhesajja°).

Saŋrakkhati [saŋ+rakkhati] to guard, ward off Sdhp 364.

Saŋrambha [saŋ+*rambha, fr. **rabh**, as in rabhasa (q. v.)] impetuosity, rage Dāvs IV.34. This is the Sanskritic form for the usual P. sārambha.

Saŋrāga [saŋ+rāga] passion J IV.22. Cp. sārāga.

Saŋrūḷha [pp. of saŋrūhati] grown together, healed J III.216; V.344.

Saŋrūhati [saŋ+rūhati] to grow J IV.429 (=vaḍḍhati).

Saŋroceti [saŋ+roceti] to find pleasure in, only in aor. (*poetical*) samarocayi Sn 290, 306, 405; J IV.471.

Saŋvacana (nt.) [saŋ+vacana] sentence DhsA 52.

Saŋvacchara [saŋ+vacchara; cp. Vedic saŋvatsara] a year D II.327; A II.75; IV.139, 252 sq.; Dh 108; J II.80; Sdhp 239; nom. pl. saŋvaccharāni J II.128.

Saŋvaṭṭa (m. & nt.) [saŋ+vaṭṭa[1]] 1. "rolling on or forward" (opp. vivaṭṭa "rolling back"), with ref. to the development of the Universe & time (kappa) the *ascending* aeon (vivaṭṭa the *descending* cycle), evolution It 99; Pug 60; Vism 419; Sdhp 484, 485. -°vivaṭṭa a period within which evolution & dissolution of the world takes place, a complete world-cycle (see also **vivaṭṭa**) D I.14; A II.142; It 15, 99; Pug 60.

Saŋvaṭṭati [saŋ+vaṭṭati] 1. to be evolved, to be in a process of *evolution* (opp. vivaṭṭati in *devolution*) D I.17; III.84, 109; A II.142; DA I.110. — 2. to fall to pieces, to come to an end (like the world's destruction), to pass away, perish, dissolve (intrs.) J III.75 (paṭhavī s.; v. l. saŋvaddh°); Miln 287 (ākāso °eyya). For saŋvaṭṭ° at J I.189 read saŋvaddh°.

Saŋvaṭṭanika (adj.) [fr. saŋvaṭṭa(na)] turning to, being reborn D I.17.

Saŋvaḍḍha [pp. of saŋvaḍḍhati] grown up, brought up D I.75; II.38; PvA 66.

Saŋvaḍḍhati [saŋ+vaḍḍhati] to grow up; ppr. °amāna (ddh.) growing up, subsisting J I.189 (so far °vaṭṭ°). — Caus. °vaḍḍheti to rear, nourish, bring up J I.231 (ppr. pass. °vaḍḍhiyamāna).

Saŋvaṇṇana (nt.) [saŋ+vaṇṇana] praising, praise J I.234.

Saŋvaṇṇita [pp. of saŋvaṇṇeti] praised, comb[d] with sambhāvita honoured M I.110; III.194, 223.

Saŋvaṇṇeti [saŋ+vaṇṇeti] to praise Vin III.73 sq.; J V.292 (aor. 3rd pl. °vaṇṇayuŋ). Cp. BSk. saŋvarṇayati Divy 115. — **pp.** saŋvaṇṇita.

Saŋvattati [saŋ+vattati] to lead (to), to be useful (for) A I.54, 58 (ahitāya dukkhāya); Vin I.10=S V.421; It 71 sq.; J I.97; Pot. saŋvatteyya Vin I.13. — Often in phrase nibbidāya, virāgāya . . . nibbānāya saŋvattati e. g. D I.189; II.251; III.130; S V.80, 255; A III.83, 326.

Saŋvattanika (adj.) [fr. saŋvattati] conducive to, involving A II.54, 65; It 82; Kvu 618; J I.275; Nett 134=S V.371. As °iya at PvA 205.

Saŋvadati [saŋ+vadati] to agree M I.500 (opp. vivadati).

Saŋvadana (nt.) [fr. saŋvadati] a certain magic act performed in order to procure harmony D I.11; DA I.96; cp. *Dial.* I.23.

Saŋvaddhana (nt.) [fr. saŋ+vṛdh] increasing, causing to grow J IV.16.

Saŋvara [fr. saŋ+vṛ] restraint D I.57, 70, 89; II.281 (indriya°); III.130, 225; A II.26; S IV.189 sq.; It 28, 96, 118; Pug 59; Sn 1034; Vin II.126, 192 (āyatiŋ saŋvarāya "for restraint in the future," in confession formula), Dh 185; Nett 192; Vism 11, 44; DhA III.238; IV.86 (°dvārāni). The *fivefold* saŋvara: sīla°, sati°, ñāṇa°, khanti°, viriya°, i. e. by virtue, mindfulness, insight, patience, effort DhsA 351; as pātimokkha° etc. at Vism 7; VbhA 330 sq. -°vinaya norm of self-control, good conduct SnA 8. cātuyāma°, Jain discipline M I.377.

Saŋvaraṇa (nt.) [fr. saŋ+vṛ] covering; obstruction Dhtp 274 (as def. of root **val**, i. e. **vṛ**).

Saŋvarati [saŋ+varati=vuṇāti I] to restrain, hold; to restrain oneself Vin II.102 (Pot. °vareyyāsi); Miln 152 (pāso na saŋvarati). — pp. saŋvuta.

Saŋvarī (f.) [Vedic śarvarī fr. śarvara speckled; the P. form viâ sabbarī>sāvarī>saŋvarī] the night (*poetical*) D III.196; J IV.441; V.14, 269; VI.243.

Saŋvasati [saŋ+vasati[2]] to live, to associate, cohabitate A II.57; Vin II.237; Nd[2] 423; Pug 65; Dh 167; Dpvs X.8; Miln 250. — Caus. °vāseti same meaning Vin IV.137. — Cp. upa°.

Saŋvāti [saŋ+vāyati[2]] to be fragrant J V.206 (cp. vv. ll. on p. 203).

Saŋvāsa [saŋ+vāsa[2]] 1. living with, co-residence Vin I.97; II.237; III.28; A II.57 sq., 187; III.164 sq.; IV.172; J I.236; IV.317 (piya-saŋvāsaŋ vasi lived together in harmony); Sn 283, 290, 335; Dh 207, 302; Sdhp 435. — 2. intimacy J II.39. — 3. cohabitation, sexual intercourse D I.97; J I.134; II.108; SnA 355.

Saŋvāsaka (adj.) [fr. saŋvāsa] living together Vin II.162; III.173.

Saŋvāsiya [fr. saŋvāsa] one who lives with somebody Sn 22; a°-bhāva impossibility to co-reside Miln 249.

Saŋvigga [pp. of saŋvijjati[1]] agitated, moved by fear or awe, excited, stirred D I.50; II.240; A II.115; S IV.290; V.270; J I.59; Miln 236; PvA 31 (°hadaya).

Saŋvijita [pp. of saŋvejeti] (med.) filled with fear or awe, made to tremble; (pass.) felt, realized Sn 935 (=saŋvejita ubbejita Nd[1] 406).

Saŋvijjati[1] [Vedic vijate, **vij**; not as simple verb in P.] to be agitated or moved, to be stirred A II.114; It 30. — pp. saŋvigga. — Caus. saŋvejeti M I.253; S I.141; Vin I.32; imper. °vejehi S V.270; aor. °vejesi Miln 236; inf. °vejetuŋ S I.197; ger °vejetvā J I.327; grd. °vejanīya that which should cause awe, in *°āni ṭhānāni* places of pilgrimage D II.140; A I.36; II.120; It 30. — pp. saŋvijita & °vejita.

Saŋvijjati[2] [Pass. of saŋvindati] to be found, to exist, to be D I.3; Vin II.122; J I.214 (°amāna); PvA 153.

Saŋvidati [saŋ+vidati: see vindati] to know; ger. °viditvā J III.114; V.172. — pp. saŋvidita.

Saŋvidahati [saŋ+vidahati] to arrange, appoint, fix, settle, provide, prepare D I.61 (Pot. °eyyāma); aor. °vidahi PvA 198; inf. °vidhātuŋ A II.35, & °vidahituŋ Vin I.287; ger. °vidhāya Vin IV.62 sq., 133; Mhvs 17, 37, & °vidahitvā Vin I.287; III.53, 64; J I.59; V.46; also as Caus. form[n] °vidahetvāna J VI.301. — pp. saŋvidahita & saŋvihita.

Saŋvidahana (nt.) [for the usual °vidhāna] arrangement, appointment, provision J II.209; DA I.148; DhsA 111. The word is peculiar to the Commentary style.

Saŋvidahita [pp. of saŋvidahati] arranged Vin IV.64; DhA I.397.

Saŋvidita [pp. of saŋvidati] known Sn 935.

Saŋvidhātar [n. ag. fr. saŋvidahati] one who arranges or provides (cp. vidhātar) D III.148.

Saŋvidhāna (nt.) [fr. saŋvidahati] arranging, providing, arrangement D I.135; J I.140 (rakkhā°).

Saŋvidhāyaka (adj.) [saŋ+vidhāyaka] providing, managing; f. °ikā J I.155.

Saŋvidhāvahāra [saŋvidhā (short ger. form)+avahāra] taking by arrangement, i. e. theft committed in agreement with others Vin III.53.

Saŋvindati [saŋ+vindati] to find; ppr. (a)saŋvindaŋ Th 1, 717. — Pass. saŋvijjati (q. v.).

Saŋvibhajati [saŋ+vibhajati] to divide, to share, to communicate D II.233; Miln 94, 344; inf. °vibhajituŋ Miln 295; Dāvs V.54. — pp. saŋvibhatta. — Caus. °vibhājeti. It 65.

Saŋvibhatta [pp. of saŋvibhajati] divided, shared Th 1, 9.

Saŋvibhāga [saŋ+vibhāga] distribution, sharing out D III.191; A I.92, 150; It 18 sq., 98, 102; Vv 37[5]; Miln 94. —dāna° (of gifts) J V.331; Vism 306.

Saŋvibhāgin (adj.) [fr. saŋvibhāga] generous, open-handed S I.43=J IV.110; V.397 (a°); Miln 207.

Saŋvirūḷha (adj.) [pp. of saŋvirūhati] fully grown, healed up J II.117.

Saŋvirūhati [saŋ+virūhati] to germinate, to sprout Miln 99, 125, 130, 375. — pp. saŋvirūḷha. — Caus. °virūheti to cause to grow, to nourish J IV.429.

Saŋvilāpa [saŋ+vilāpa] noisy talk; fig. for thundering S IV.289 (abbha°).

Saŋvisati [saŋ+visati] to enter; Caus. saŋveseti (q. v.). Cp. abhisaŋvisati.

Saŋvissajjetar [saŋ+vissajjetar] one who appoints or assigns DA I.112.

Saŋvissandati [saŋ+vissandati] to overflow M II.117; Miln 36.

Saŋvihita [pp. of saŋvidahati] arranged, prepared, provided J I.133 (°ārakkha i. e. protected); in cpd. su° well arranged or appointed, fully provided D II.75; M II.75; DA I.147, 182; a° unappointed Vin I.175; Vism 37.

Saŋvījita [saŋ+vījita] fanned Dāvs V.18.

Saŋvuta [pp. of saŋvarati] 1. closed D I.81. — 2. tied up J IV.361. — 3. restrained, governed, (self-)controlled, guarded D I.250; III.48, 97; S II.231; IV.351 sq.; A I.7 (cittaŋ); II.25; III.387; It 96, 118; Sn 340 (indriyesu); Dh 340; DA I.181. **asaŋvuta** unrestrained S IV.70; A III.387; Pug 20, 24; in phrase **asaŋvutā lokantarikā** andhakārā (the world-spaces which are dark &) ungoverned, orderless, not supported, baseless D II.12.

—su° well controlled Vin II.213; IV.186; S IV.70; Sn 413; Dh 8.
-atta self-controlled S I.66. -indriya having the senses under control It 91; Pug 35. -kārin M II.260.

Saŋvūḷha see saŋyūḷha.

Saŋvega [fr. saŋ+**vij**] agitation, fear, anxiety; thrill, religious emotion (caused by contemplation of the miseries of this world) D III.214; A I.43; II.33, 114; S I.197; III.85; V.130, 133; It 30; Sn 935; J I.138; Nd[1] 406; Vism 135=KhA 235 (eight objects inducing emotion: birth, old age, illness, death, misery in the apāyas, and the misery caused by saŋsāra in past, present & future stages); Mhvs I, 4; 23, 62; PvA I, 22, 32, 39, 76.

Saŋvejana (adj.) [fr. saŋ+**vij**] agitating, moving It 30.

Saŋvejaniya (adj.) [fr. saŋvejana] apt to cause emotion A II.120; Vism 238. See also saŋvijjati[1].

Saŋvejita [pp. of saŋvejeti] stirred, moved, agitated S I.197; Nd[1] 406.

Saŋvejeti Caus. of saŋvijjati[1] (q. v.).

Saŋveṭheti [saŋ+veṭheti] to wrap, stuff, tuck in Vin IV.40.

Saŋvedhita [saŋ+vyathita: see vyadhati] shaken up, confused, trembling Sn 902.

Saŋvelli (f.) [saŋ+velli, cp. vellita] "that which is wound round," a loin cloth J V.306. As saŋvelliya at Vin II.137, 271.

Saŋvelleti [fr. saŋ+**vell**] to gather up, bundle together, fold up Vism 327.

Saŋvesanā (f.) [fr. saŋveseti] lying down, being in bed, sleeping J VI.551 sq., 557.

Saŋveseti [Caus. of saŋvisati] to lead, conduct A I.141; Pass. saŋvesiyati to be put to bed (applied to a sick person) M I.88=III. 181; D II.24. Cp. abhi°.

Saŋvossajjati see samavossajjati.

Saŋvohāra [saŋ+vohāra] business, traffic Vin III.239; A II.187=S I.78; A III.77; SnA 471.

Saŋvohārati [Denom. fr. saŋvohāra] to trade (with); ppr. °vohāramāna [cp. BSk. saŋvyavahāramāna Divy 259] A II.188.

Saŋsagga [fr. saŋ+**sṛj**] contact, connection, association Vin III.120; A III.293 sq. (°ārāmatā); IV.87 sq., 331; It 70; J I.376; IV.57; Miln 386; Nd[2] 137; VbhA 340 (an-anulomika°); PvA 5 (pāpamitta°). — Two kinds of contact at Nd[2] 659: by sight (dassana°) and by hearing (savaṇa°). — pada° contact of two words, "sandhi" Nd[1] 139; Nd[2] 137 (for iti); SnA 28. —a° S II.202; Miln 344. -°jāta one who has come into contact Sn 36.

Saŋsaṭṭha [pp. of saŋ+**sṛj**] 1. mixed with (instr.), associating with, joined M I.480 (opp. vi°); A III.109, 116, 258 sq., 393; PvA 47. — 2. living in society Vin I.200; II.4; IV.239, 294; D II.214; Kvu 337=DhsA 42; Dhs 1193; J II.105; DhsA 49, 72. —a° not given to society M I.214; S I.63; Miln 244; Vism 73.

Saŋsati [Vedic śaŋsati, cp. Av. saŋhaiti to proclaim, Lat. censeo=censure; Obulg. θom to say] to proclaim, point out J V.77; VI.533; Pot. saŋse J VI.181; aor. asaŋsi J III.420; IV.395; V.66; & asāsī (Sk. aśaŋsīt) J III.484. Cp. abhi°.

Saŋsatta [pp. of saŋ+**sañj**] adhering, clinging D I.239 (paramparā°).

Saŋsad (f.) [fr. saŋ+**sad**] session, assembly; loc. saŋsati J III.493 (=parisamajjhe C.), 495

Saŋsaddati [saŋ+**śabd**] to sound, in def. of root **kitt** at Dhtp 579; Dhtm 812.

Saŋsandati [saŋ+**syand**, cp. BSk. saŋsyandati AvŚ II.142 sq., 188] to run together, to associate D I.248; II.223; S II.158=It 70; S IV.379; Pug 32. — Caus. saŋsandeti to put together; unite, combine J I.403; V.216; Miln 131; DhA II.12; IV.51.

Saŋsandanā (f.) [fr. saŋsandati] 1. (lit.) coming together J VI.414 (v. l. for T. saŋsandita). — 2. (fig.) import, application, reference, conclusion (lit. "flowing together") Tikp 264. opamma° application of a simile, "tertium comparationis" Vism 326; DA I.127. diṭṭha° (pucchā) a question with reference to observation Nd[2] s. v. pucchā; DhsA 55.

Saŋsanna [pp. of saŋsīdati or saŋsandati] depressed, exhausted Dh 280 (=osanna DhA III.410: see ossanna).

Saŋsappa (adj.) [fr. saŋ+**sṛp**] creeping A V.289.

Saŋsappati [saŋ+sappati] to creep along, to crawl, move A V.289; VvA 278; DhA IV.49.

Saŋsappaniyapariyāya, the creeping exposition, a discussion of the consequences of certain kinds of kamma, A V.288 sq.

Saŋsappin (adj.)=saŋsappa A IV.172.

Saŋsaya [cp. Vedic saŋśaya] doubt A II.24; Nd[2] 660 (=vicikicchā etc.); Miln 94; Dhs 425.

Saŋsayita (nt.) [pp. of saŋsayati=saŋ+seti of **śi**; in meaning=saŋsaya] doubt Dāvs I.50.

Saŋsarati [saŋ+sarati, of **sṛ**] to move about continuously, to come again and again J I.335. — 2. to go through one life after the other, to transmigrate D I.14; DA I.105; ppr. saŋsaranto (& saŋsaraŋ) S III.149; IV.439; It 109; PvA 166; med. saŋsaramāna Vv 19[7]; ger. °saritvā S III.212; Pug 16. — pp. saŋsarita & saŋsita.

Saŋsaraṇa (nt.) [fr. saŋ+**sṛ**] 1. moving about, running; °lohita blood in circulation (opp. sannicita°) Vism 261; KhA 62; VbhA 245. — 2. a movable curtain, a blind that can be drawn aside Vin II.153.

Saŋsarita [pp. of saŋsarati] transmigrated D II.90; A II.1; Th 2, 496. a° M I.82.

Saŋsava [fr. saŋ+**sru**] flowing VvA 227.

Saŋsavaka [fr. saŋsava] N. of a purgatory Vv 52[12], cp. VvA 226 sq.

Saŋsāveti [fr. saŋ+**sru**] to cause to flow together, to pour into (loc.), to put in J V.268 (=pakkhipati C.).

Saŋsādiyā (f.) [cp. *Sk. syavaŋ-sātikā, on which see Kern, *Toev.* II.62, s. v.] a kind of inferior rice J VI.530.

Saŋsādeti Caus. of saŋsīdati (q. v.).

Saŋsāmeti [Caus. of saŋ+**śam**] lit. "to smoothe," to fold up (one's sleeping mat), to leave (one's bed), in phrase senāsanaŋ saŋsāmetvā Vin II.185; IV.24; M I.457; S III.95, 133; IV.288.

Saŋsāyati [saŋ+sāyati, which stands for sādati (of **svad** to sweeten). On y>d cp. khāyita>khādita & sankhāyita] to taste, enjoy J III.201 (aor. samasāyisuŋ: so read for samāsāsisuŋ).

Saŋsāra [fr. saŋsarati] 1. transmigration, lit. faring on D I.54; II.206 (here=existence); M I.81 (saŋsārena suddhi); S II.178 sq.; A I.10; II.12=52; Sn 32; Dh 60; J I.115; Pv II.13[11]; Vism 544 (in detail), 578, 603 (°assa kāraka); PvA 63, 243. For description of saŋsāra (its endlessness & inevitableness) see e. g. S II.178,

184 sq., 263; III.149 sq.; VbhA 134 (anta-virahita) & anamatagga (to which add refs. VbhA 45, 182, 259, 260). — 2. moving on, circulation: vacī° exchange of words A I.79.
-cakka [cp. BSk. saŋsāra-cakra] the wheel of tr. Vism 198, 201; VvA 105 = PvA 7. -dukkha the ill of tr. Vism 531; VbhA 145, 149. -bhaya fear of tr. VbhA 199. -sāgara the ocean of tr. J III.241.

Saŋsijjhati [saŋ + sidh] to be fulfilled Sdhp 451.

Saŋsita[1] = saŋsarita J v.56 (cira-ratta° = carita anuciṇṇa C.).

Saŋsita[2] [pp. of saŋ + śri] dependent Sdhp 306.

Saŋsiddhi (f.) [saŋ + siddhi] success Dhtp 420.

Saŋsibbita [pp. of saŋ + sibbati] entwined Vism 1; Miln 102, 148; DhA III.198.

Saŋsīda [fr. saŋsīdati] sinking (down) S IV.180 (v. l. saŋsāda).

Saŋsīdati [saŋ + sad] 1. to sink down, to lose heart D I.248; A III.89 = Pug 65; Th 1, 681; J II.330. — 2. to be at an end (said of a path, magga) Vin III.131; S I.1. — Caus. saŋsādeti: 1. to get tired, give out M I.214; A I.288. — 2. to drop, fail in A IV.398 (pañhaŋ, i. e. not answer). — 3. to place DA I.49.

Saŋsīdana (nt.) [fr. saŋsīdati] = saŋsīda Th 1, 572 (ogha°).

Saŋsīna [saŋ + sīna, pp. of śṛ to crush, Sk. śīrṇa] fallen off, destroyed Sn 44 (°patta without leaves = patita-patta C.).

Saŋsuddha (adj.) [saŋ + suddha] pure D I.113; Sn 372, 1107; Nd[1] 289; Nd[2] 661; J I.2.
-gahaṇika of pure descent D I.113; DA I.281.

Saŋsuddhi (f.) [saŋ + suddhi) purification Sn 788; Nd[1] 84.

Saŋsumbhati [saŋ + sumbhati] to beat J VI.53, 88 (°amāna).

Saŋsūcaka (adj.) [fr. saŋsūceti] indicating VvA 244, 302.

Saŋsūceti [saŋ + sūcay°, Denom. fr. sūci] to indicate, show, betray Dāvs v.50; DA I.311.

Saŋseda [saŋ + seda] sweat, moisture M I.73; ThA 185.
-ja [cp. BSk saŋsvedaja Divy 627] born or arisen from moisture D III.230; Miln 128; KhA 247; VbhA 161.

Saŋseva (adj.) [fr. saŋ + sev] associating A II.245; v.113 sq. (sappurisa° & asappurisa°); Miln 93.

Saŋsevanā (f.) [fr. saŋsevati] associating Dhs 1326 = Pug 20.

Saŋsevā (f.) [fr. saŋseva] worshipping, attending Miln 93 (sneha°).

Saŋsevita [saŋ + sevita] frequented, inhabited J VI.539.

Saŋsevin (adj.) = saŋseva J I.488.

Saŋhata[1] [pp. of saŋ + han] firm, compact Miln 416; Sdhp 388.

Saŋhata[2] [pp. of saŋ + hṛ] DA I.280; see vi°.

Saŋhanati & **saŋhanti** [saŋ + han] 1. to join together, reach to J v.372. — 2. to suppress, allay, destroy A IV.437 (kaṇḍuŋ). — pp. saŋhata.

Saŋhanana (nt.) [fr. saŋhanati] joining together, closing D I.11; J VI.65.

Saŋhara [fr. saŋ + hṛ] collecting; dus° hard to collect Vin III.148; J IV.36 (here as dussanghara, on which see Kern, *Toev.* I.121).

Saŋharaṇa (nt.) [fr. saŋharati] collecting, gathering Dāvs v.33. Cp. upa° & sangharaṇa.

Saŋharati [saŋ + harati] 1. to collect, fold up Vin I.46; II.117, 150; M III.169; J I.66, 422; Dāvs IV.12; PvA 73. — 2. to draw together Vin II.217. — 3. to gather up, take up SnA 369 (rūpaŋ). — 4. to heap up Pv IV.14 (saŋharimha = sañcinimha PvA 279). — asaŋhāriya (grd.) which cannot be destroyed (see also saŋhīra) S v.219. — Caus. II. °harāpeti to cause to collect, to make gather or grow Vin IV.259 (lomāni), 260 (id.). — Pass. saŋhīrati (q. v.). — pp. saŋhata. Cp. upa°.

Saŋhasati [san + hasati] to laugh with M II.223.

Saŋhāni (f.) [saŋ + hāni] shrinking, decrease, dwindling away D II.305 = M I.49 = S II.2 = Dhs 644; DhsA 328. Cp. parihāni.

Saŋhāra [fr. saŋ + hṛ] abridgment, compilation PvA 114. Cp. upa°.

Saŋhāraka [saŋ + hāra + ka] drawing together, a collector S II.185 = It 17. sabba° a kind of mixed perfume J VI.336.

Saŋhārima (adj.) [fr. saŋ + hṛ] movable Vism 124; Sn 28, 321. a° Vin IV.272.

Saŋhita [pp. of sandahati] connected, equipped with, possessed of D I.5; M II.202; S I.103; Dh 101 (gāthā anattha-pada°). Often as attha° endowed with profit, bringing advantage, profitable D I.189; S II.223; IV.330; v.417; A III.196 sq.; v.81; Sn 722. Cp. upa°.

Saŋhīyati see sandhīyati.

Saŋhīra (& saŋhāriya) [grd. of saŋharati] that which can be restrained, conquerable Th 1, 1248; J v.81. a° immovable, unconquerable S I.193; Vin II.96; A IV.141 sq.; Th 1, 649; Sn 1149; J IV.283. See also asaŋhāriya.

Saŋhīrati [Pass. of saŋharati] to be drawn away or caught in (loc.) M III.188 sq. (paccuppannesu dhammesu); DhsA 420 (id.); J III.333.

Saka (adj.) [sa[4] + ka] own D I.106, 119, 231; II.173 (sakaŋ te "all be your own," as greeting to the king); M I.79; Vin I.3, 249 (ācariyaka); S v.261 (id.); Sn 861; It 76; Nd[1] 252; Pv I.5[1] (ghara); II.6[1] (bhātā). — Opp. assaka[2]. — appassaka having little or nothing as one's own (= daḷidda) A I.261; II.203; kamma-ssaka possessing one's own kamma M III.203 sq.; A v.288; Miln 65; Dhs 1366.
-gavacaṇḍa violent towards one's own cows, harassing one's own Pug 47.

Sakaṭa[1] (m. & nt.) [cp. Sk. śakaṭa; Vedic śakaṭī] a cart, waggon; a cartload D II.110; Vin III.114; J I.191; Miln 238; PvA 102; VbhA 435 (simile of two carts); SnA 58 (udaka-bharita°), 137 (bīja°). sakaṭāni pajāpeti to cause the carts to go on J II.296.
-gopaka the guardian of the waggon DhA IV.60. -bhāra a cart-load VvA 79. -mukha the front or opening of the waggon, used as adj. "facing the waggon or the cart" (?) at D II.234, of the earth — that is, India as then known — and at D II.235 (comp. Mahāvastu III.208), of six kingdoms in Northern India. At the second passage B. explains that the six kingdoms all debouched alike on the central kingdom, which was hexagonal in shape. This explanation does not fit the other passage. Could sakaṭa there be used of the constellation Rohiṇī, which in mediæval times was called the Cart? Cp. *Dial.* II.269. -vāha a cart-load Pv II.7[5]. -vyūha "the waggon array," a wedge-shaped phalanx J II.404; IV.343; Vism 384.

Sakaṭa[2] see kasaṭa.

Sakaṇika (adj.) [sa + kaṇa + ika] having a mole D I.80; DA I.223.

Sakaṇṭaka (adj.) [sa + kaṇṭaka] thorny, dangerous D I.135; Th 2, 352; DA I.296.

Sakaṇṇajappaka [sa + kaṇṇa + jappa + ka] whispering in the ear, a method of (secretly) taking votes Vin II.98 sq. (salāka-gāha).

Sakatā (f.) (-°) [abstr. fr. saka] one's own nature, identity, peculiarity: see kamma-ssakatā & adj. °ssakata. It may also be considered as an abstr. formation fr. kamma-ssaka.

Sakadāgāmin [sakad = sakid, + āgāmin] "returning once," one who will not be reborn on earth more than once; one who has attained the second grade of saving wisdom Vin I.293; D I.156, 229; III.107; M I.34; S III.168; A I.120, 232 sq.; II.89, 134; III.348; IV.292 sq., 380; V.138 sq., 372 sq.; DhA IV.66.

Sakadāgāmitā (f.) [abstr. fr. last] the state of a "once-returner" D II.206.

Sakabala (adj.) [sa + kabala] containing a mouthful Vin IV.195.

Sakamana [saka + mana] is Bdhgh's explⁿ of attamana (q. v.), e. g. DA I.129, 255.

Sakamma (nt.) [sa⁴ + kamma] one's own occupation D I.135.

Sakaraṇīya (adj.) [sa³ + karaṇīya] one who still has something to do (in order to attain perfection) D II.143; Th I, 1045; Miln 138.

Sakaruṇa-bhāva [sa³ + karuṇa + bhāva] being full of compassion SnA 318.

Sakala (adj.) [cp. Sk. sakala] all, whole, entire Vin II.109; Vism 321; SnA 132; PvA 93, 97, 111. Cp. sākalya.

Sakalikā (f.) [fr. sakala = Sk. śakala potsherd] a potsherd; a splinter, bit D II.341; A II.199 = S IV.197; S I.27 = Miln 179; M I.259; A V.9 (°aggi); J IV.430; Miln 134; KhA 43 (maccha°); Nett 23; DhsA 319. — sakalikaŋ sakalikaŋ in little pieces Vin II.112. — sakalika-hīra a skewer J IV.29, 30.

Sakasaṭa (adj.) [sa³ + k.] faulty, wrong (lit. bitter) Miln 119 (vacana).

Sakāsa [sa³ + k. = Sk. kāśa] presence; acc. sakāsaŋ towards, to Sn 326; J V.480; PvA 237; loc. sakāse in the presence of, before J III.24; IV.281; V.394; VI.282.

Sakicca (nt.) [sa⁴ + kicca] one's own duty or business Vism 321 (°pasuta).

Sakiccaya (nt.) [sa⁴ + kiccaya = kṛtya] = sakicca Miln 42; DhsA 196 (°pasuta).

Sakiñcana (adj.) [sa³ + kiñcana] having something; (applᵈ) with attachment, full of worldly attachment Sn 620 = Dh I.246; Dh 396 (= rāg'ādīhi kiñcanehi sakiñcana DhA IV.158).

Sakid & **Sakiŋ** (adv.) [fr. sa° = saŋ] once. (1) sakiŋ: D II.188; J I.397; DhA III.116 (sakiŋvijātā itthi = primipara); once more: Miln 238; once for all: Th 2, 466; DhA II.44; Th 2, 283. — (2) sakid (in composition; see also sakad-āgāmin): in sakid eva once only A II.238; IV.380; Pug 16; PvA 243; at once Vin I.31.

Sakiya (adj.) [fr. saka, cp. Sk. svakīya] own J II.177; III.48, 49; IV.177.

Sakuṇa [Vedic śakuna] a bird (esp. with ref. to augury) D I.71 (pakkhin +); Vin III.147; S I.197; A II.209; III.241 sq., 368; J II.111, 162 (Kandagala); KhA 241. pantha° see under pantha. — f. sakuṇī S I.44. adj. sakuṇa J V.503 (maŋsa).
-kulāvaka a bird's nest KhA 56. -patha bird-course, Npl. Nd¹ 155. -pāda bird foot KhA 47. -ruta the cry of birds Miln 178. -vatta the habit (i. e. life) of a bird J V.254. -vijjā bird craft, augury (i. e. understanding the cries of birds) D I.9; DA I.93.

Sakuṇaka = sakuṇa SnA 27. — f. sakuṇikā D I.91; Miln 202; J I.171; IV.290.

Sakuṇagghi (f.) [sakuṇa + °ghi, f. of °gha] a kind of hawk (lit. "bird-killer") S V.146; J II.59; Miln 365. Cp. vyagghīnasa.

Sakuṇita at PvA 123 read sankucita.

Sakunta [cp. Sk. śakunta] a bird; a kind of vulture Sn 241; Dh 92, 174; J IV.225; VI.272.

Sakuntaka = sakunta Vin I.137.

Sakumāra (adj.) [sa² + kumāra] of the same age; a playmate J V.360, 366.

Sakula [cp. Epic Sk. śakula] a kind of fish J V.405.

Sakka (adj.) [fr. **śak**, cp. Sk. śakya] able, possible Sn 143. sasakkaŋ (= sa³ + s.) as much as possible, as much as one is able to M I.415, 514.

Sakkacca(ŋ) (adv.) [orig. ger. of sakkaroti] respectfully, carefully, duly, thoroughly; often with upaṭṭhahati to attend, serve with due honour. — Vv 12⁶; Miln 305; J IV.310. The form sakkaccaŋ is the older and more usual, e. g. at D II.356 sq.; S IV.314; A II.147; IV.392; Vin IV.190, 275; Th I, 1054; J I.480; Dh 392; PvA 26, 121. The BSk. form is satkṛtya, e. g. MVastu I.10.
-kārin zealous S III.267; Miln 94. -dāna M III.24.

Sakkata [pp. of sakkaroti] honoured, duly attended D I.114, 116; II.167; Nd 73; J I.334; Miln 21; SnA 43. Usually combᵈ with garukata, pūjita, mānita.

Sakkati [**ṣvaṣk**; Dhtp 9: gamana] to go; see osakkati & cp. Pischel, *Prk. Gr.* § 302. Other P. cpds. are ussakkati & paṭisakkati.

Sakkatta (nt.) [fr. Sakka = Indra] Śakraship, the position as the ruler of the devas M III. 65; J I.315; Vism 301 (brahmatta +). °rajja a kingdom rivalling Sakka's J I.315.

Sakkaroti [sat + **kṛ**] to honour, esteem, treat with respect, receive hospitably; often combᵈ with garukaroti, māneti, pūjeti, e. g. D I.91, 117; III.84; M I.126. ppr. °karonto D II.159; Pot. °kareyya It 110; aor. °kari PvA 54; ger. °katvā Pug 35; J VI.14, & °kacca (q. v.). — pp. sakkata. — Caus. sakkāreti = sakkaroti; Mhvs 32, 44; grd. sakkāreyya Th I, 186 (so read for °kareyya).

Sakkā (indecl.) [originally Pot. of sakkoti = Vedic śakyāt; cp. Prk. sakkā with Pischel's explⁿ in *Prk. Gr.* § 465. A corresponding formation, similar in meaning, is labbhā (q. v.)] possible (lit. one might be able to); in the older language still used as a Pot., but later reduced to an adv. with infin. E. g. *sakkā sāmaññaphalaŋ paññāpetuŋ* would one be able to point out a result of samaṇaship, D I.51; *khādituŋ na sakkā*, one could not eat, J II.16; *na sakkā maggo akkhātuŋ*, the way cannot be shown, Mil 269; *sakkā etaŋ mayā ñātuŋ?* can I ascertain this? D I.187; *sakkā honti imāni aṭṭha sukhāni vinditum*, these eight advantages are able to be enjoyed, J I.8; *sakkā etaŋ abhavissa kātuŋ*, this would be possible to do, D I.168; *imaŋ sakkā gaṇhituŋ*, this one we can take J IV.219. See also SnA 338, 376 (= labbhā); PvA 12, 69, 96.

Sakkāya [sat + kāya, cp. BSk. satkāya Divy 46; AvŚ I.85. See on explⁿ of term Mrs. Rh. D. in *J.R.A.S.* 1894, 324; Franke *Digha trslⁿ* p. 45; Geiger *P.Gr.* § 24¹; Kern. *Toev.* II.52] the body in being, the existing body or group (= -nikāya q. v.); as a t.t. in P. psychology almost equal to *individuality*; identified with the five khandhas M I.299; S III.159; IV.259; A II.34; Th 2, 170, 239; DhsA 348. See also D III.216 (cp. *Dial.* III.216[1]); A III.293, 401; Nd[1] 109.

-diṭṭhi theory of soul, heresy of individuality, speculation as to the eternity or otherwise of one's own individuality M I.300 = III.17 = DhS 1003, S III.16 sq. In these passages this is explained as the belief that in one or other of the khandhas there is a permanent entity, an attā. The same explanation, at greater length, in the Diṭṭhigata Sutta (Ps I.143-151). As delusions about the soul or ghost can arise out of four sorts of bias (see **abhinivesa**) concerning each of the five khandhas, we have *twenty* kinds of s° diṭṭhi: fifteen of these are kinds of sakkāya-vatthukā sassata-diṭṭhi, and five are kinds of s°-vatthukā uccheda-diṭṭhi (ibid. 149, 150). Gods as well as men are s° pariyāpannā S III.85; and so is the eye, DhsA 308. When the word diṭṭhi is not expressed it is often implied, Th 2, 199, 339; Sn 231. S° diṭṭhi is the first Bond to be broken on entering the Path (see saŋyojana); it is identical with the fourth kind of Grasping (see upādāna); it is opposed to Nibbāna, S IV.175; is extinguished by the Path, M I.299; S III.159; IV.260; and is to be put away by insight DhsA 346. — See further: D III.234; A III.438; IV.144 sq.; Kvu 81; Sn 950; Dhs 1003; and on term *Dhs. trsl*ⁿ § 1003; *K.S.* III.86, *n.* 3. -nirodha the destruction of the existing body or of individuality A II.165 sq.; III.246; D III.216. -samudaya the rise of individuality D III.216; Nd[1] 109.

Sakkāra [fr. sat + kṛ] hospitality, honour, worship Vin I.27, 183; A II.203; J I.63; II.9, 104; Dh 75; Miln 386; Dhs 1121; Vism 270; SnA 284; VbhA 466. °ŋ karoti to pay reverence, to say goodbye DhA I.398. Cp. **lābha**.

Sakkāreti is Caus. of sakkaroti (q. v.).

Sakkuṇeyyatta (nt.) [abstr. fr. sakkuṇeyya, grd. of sakkoti] possibility; a° impossibility PvA 48.

Sakkoti [śak; def. Dhtp 508 etc. as "sattiyaŋ": see satti] to be able. Pres. sakkoti D I.246; Vin I.31; Miln 4; DhA I.200; sakkati [= Class. Sk. śakyate] Nett 23. Pot. sakkuṇeyya J I.361; PvA 106; archaic 1st pl. sakkuṇemu J V.24; Pv II.8[1]. ppr. sakkonto Miln 27. — Fut. sakkhati Sn 319; sakkhīti [= Sk. śakṣyati] M I.393; pl. 3rd sakkhinti Sn 28; 2nd sg. sagghasi Sn 834; 3rd sg. sakkhissati DhA IV.87. — Aor. asakkhi D I.96, 236; PvA 38; sakkhi Miln 5; J V.116; 1st pl. asakkhimha PvA 262, & asakkhimhā Vin III.23; 3rd sg. also sakkuṇi Mhvs 7, 13. — grd. sakkuṇeyya (neg. a°) (im)possible J I.55; PvA 122. — sakka & sakkā see sep.

Sakkharā (f.) [cp. Vedic śarkarā gravel] 1. gravel, grit Vin III.147 = J II.284; J I.192; A I.253; D I.84; Pv III.2[28]; DhA IV.87. — 2. potsherd VvA 157; PvA 282, 285. — 3. grain, granule, crystal, in loṇa° a salt crystal S II.276; DhA I.370; SnA 222. — 4. (granulated) sugar J I.50.

Sakkharikā (f.) [fr. sakkharā] in **loṇa°** a piece of salt crystal Vin I.206; II.237.

Sakkharilla (adj.) [= sakkharika, fr. sakkharā] containing gravel, pebbly, stony A IV.237.

Sakkhali (& °ikā) (f.) [cp. Sk. śaṣkulī] 1. the orifice of the ear: see kaṇṇa°. — 2. a sort of cake or sweetmeat (cp. saṅguḷikā) A III.76 (T. sakkhalakā; v. l. °likā & sankulikā); Vin III.59; J II.281.

Sakkhi[1] [sa[3] + akkhin; cp. Sk. sākṣin] an eyewitness D II.237 (nom. sg. sakkhī = with his own eyes, as an eyewitness); Sn 479, 921, 934 (sakkhi dhammaŋ adassi, where the corresp. Sk. form would be sākṣād); J I.74. — **kāya-sakkhī** a bodily witness, i. e. one who has bodily experienced the 8 vimokkhas A IV.451; Vism 93, 387, 659. — **sakkhiŋ karoti** [Sk. sākṣī karoti] (1) to see with one's own eyes; S II.255; (2) to call upon as a witness (with gen. of person) J VI.280 (rājāno); DhA II.69 (Moggallānassa sakkhiŋ katvā); PvA 217 (but at 241 as "friendship"). *Note.* The P. form is rather to be taken as an adv. ("as present") than adj.: sakkhiŋ & sakkhī, with reduced sakkhi° (cp. sakid & sakiŋ). See also sacchi°.

-diṭṭha seen face to face M I.369; D I.238; J VI.233. -puṭṭha asked as a witness Sn 84, 122; Pug 29. -bhabbatā the state of becoming an eyewitness, of experiencing M I.494; DhsA 141. -sāvaka a contemporaneous or personal disciple D II.153.

Sakkhī (f.) or sakkhi[2] (nt.) [cp. Sk. sākhya] friendship (with somebody = instr.) S I.123 = A V.46 (janena karoti sakkhiŋ make friends with people); Pv IV.1[57]; IV.1[65]; J III.493; IV.478. Cp. **sakhya**.

Sakya: see Dictionary of Names. In cpd. °puttiya (belonging to the Sakya son) in general meaning of "a (true) follower of the Buddha," A IV.202; Vin I.44; Ud 44; a° not a follower of the B. Vin III.25.

Sakhi [Vedic sakhi m. & f.] a companion, friend; nom. sakhā J II.29; 348; acc. sakhāraŋ J II.348; V.509; & sakhaŋ J II.299; instr. sakhinā J IV.41; abl. sakhārasmā J III.534; gen. sakhino J VI.478; voc. sakhā J III.295; nom. pl. sakhā J III.323; & sakhāro J III.492; gen. sakhīnaŋ J III.492; IV.42; & sakhānaŋ J II.228. In compⁿ with **bhū** as sakhi° & sakhī°, e. g. sakhibhāva friendship J VI.424; PvA 241; & **sakhībhāva** J III.493.

Sakhikā (f.) [fr. sakhi] a female friend J III.533.

Sakhitā (f.) [abstr. fr. sakhi] friendship Th 1, 1018, 1019.

Sakhila (adj.) [fr. sakhi] kindly in speech, congenial D I.116; Vin II.11; J I.202, 376; Miln 207; Pv IV.1[33] (= mudu PvA 230). Cp. sākhalya.

-vācatā use of friendly speech Dhs 1343.

Sakhī (f.) [to sakhi] a female friend J II. 27, 348.

Sakhura (adj.) [sa[3] + khura] with the hoofs J I.9; Bdhgh on M. I.78 (see M I.536).

Sakhya (nt.) [Sk. sākhya; cp. sakkhī] friendship J II.409; VI.353 sq.

Sagandhaka (adj.) [sa[3] + gandha + ka] fragment Dh 52.

Sagabbha (adj.) [sa[3] + gabbha] with a fœtus, pregnant Mhvs 33, 46.

Sagaha (adj.) [sa[3] + gaha[2]] full of crocodiles It 57, 114. As sagāha at S IV.157.

Sagāmeyya (adj.) [grd. formation fr. gāma, + sa[2] = saŋ°) hailing from the same village S I.36, 60.

Sagārava (adj.) [sa[3] + gārava] respectful, usually combᵈ with sappatissa & other syn., e. g. Vin I.45; It 10; Vism 19, 221.

Sagāravatā (f.) [fr. sagārava] respect Th 1, 589.

Saguṇa (adj.) [either sa[3] + guṇa[1] 1, as given under guṇa[1]; or sa° = saŋ° once, as in sakṛt, + guṇa[1] 2] either "with the string," or "in one"; Vin I.46 (saguṇaŋ karoti to put together, to fold up; C ekato katvā). This interpretation (as "put together") is much to be preferred to the one given under guṇa[1] 1; saguṇaŋ katvā belongs to sanghāṭiyo, and not to kāyabandhanaŋ, thus: "the upper robes are to be given putting them into one (bundle)."

Saguḷa [sa[3] + guḷa[2]] a cake with sugar J VI.524. Cp. **saṅguḷikā**.

Sagocara [sa² = saŋ. + gocara] companion, mate (lit. having the same activity) J II.31.

Sagotta [sa² = saŋ, + gotta] a kinsman J V.411; cp. VI.500.

Sagga [Vedic svarga, svar + ga] 1. heaven, the next world, popularly conceived as a place of happiness and long life (cp. the pop. etym. of "suṭṭhu-aggattā sagga" PvA 9; "rūpādīhi visayehi suṭṭhu aggo ti saggo" Vism 427); usually the **kām'āvacara-devaloka**, sometimes also the 26 heavens (ThA 74). Sometimes as sagga ṭhāna (cp. °loka), e. g. J VI.210. — Vin I.223; D II.86; III.52, 146 sq.; M I.22, 483; S I.12; A I.55 sq., 292 sq.; II.83 sq.; III.244, 253 sq.; IV.81; V.135 sq.; Sn 224 (loc. pl. saggesu); It 14; Pv I.1³; Vism 103, 199.
-āpāya heaven and hell Th 2, 63; Sn 647. **-ārohaṇa** (-sopāna) (the stairs) leading to heaven (something like Jacob's ladder) Vism 10. **-kathā** discourse or talk about heaven Vin I.15 (cp. anupubbikathā) **-kāya** the heavenly assembly (of the gods) J VI.573. **-dvāra** heaven's gate Vism 57. **-patha** = sagga J I.256. **-pada** heavenly region, heaven J II.5; IV.272 (= saggaloka). **-magga** the way to heaven J IV.287; DhA I.4. **-loka** the heaven-world M I.73; J IV.272. **-saŋvattanika** leading to heaven D III.66.

Sagguṇa [sat + guṇa] good quality, virtue Sdhp 313.

Saggh° see sakkoti.

Saghaccā (f.) [sat + ghaccā] just or true killing J I.177.

Sankacchā (f.) [saŋ + kacchā¹] part of a woman's dress, bodice, girdle (?) J V.96 (suvaṇṇa°).

Sankacchika (nt.) [fr. sankacchā] a part of clothing, belt, waist-cloth Vin II.272; IV.345. The C. explⁿ is incorrect.

Sankaṭīra (nt.) [unexplained] a dust heap D II.160; S II.270; M I.334. Expl^d as "sankāra-ṭṭhāna" *K.S.* II.203.

Sankaḍḍhati [saŋ + kaḍḍhati] 1. to collect M I.135; J I.254; IV.224; Dh I.49; Pass. °khaḍḍiyati Vism 251 (ppr. °iyamāna being collected, comprising). — 2. to examine, scrutinize J VI.351 (cintetvā °kaḍḍhituŋ).

Sankati [**śank**, Vedic śankate, cp. Lat. cunctor to hesitate; Goth. hāhan = Ags. hangon "to hang"; Oicel. hāetta danger] to doubt, hesitate, to be uncertain about; pres. (med.) 1st sg. sanke S I.111; J III.253 (= āsankāmi C.); VI.312 (na sanke maraṇ'āgamāya); Pot. sanketha J II.53 = V.85. Pass. sankīyati S III.71 = Kvu 141; A IV.246.

Sankathati [saŋ + kathati] to name, explain. Pass. sankathīyati DhsA 390.

Sankanta [pp. of sankamati] gone together with (-°), gone over to, joined Vin I.60; IV.217.

Sankantati [saŋ + kantati] to cut all round, M III.275.

Sankanti (f.) [fr. sankamati] transition, passage Kvu 569; Vism 374 sq.

Sankantika [fr. sankanta] a school of thought (lit. gone over to a faction), a subdivision of the Sabbatthivādins S V.14; Vism 374 sq.; Mhvs 5, 6; Dpvs 5, 48; Mhbv 97.

Sankappa [saŋ + **kḷp**, cp. kappeti fig. meaning] thought, intention, purpose, plan D III.215; S II.143 sq.; A I.281; II.36; Dh 74; Sn 154, 1144; Nd¹ 616 (= vitakka ñāṇa paññā buddhi); Dhs 21; DhA II.78. As equivalent of vitakka also at D III.215; A IV.385; Dhs 7. —**kāma°** a lustful thought A III.259; V.31. **paripuṇṇa°** having one's intentions fulfilled M I.192; III.276; D III.42; A V.92, 97 sq.; sara° memories & hopes M I.453; S IV.76; vyāpāda°, vihiŋsa°, malicious, cruel purposes, M II.27 sq.; sammā° right thoughts or intentions, one of the angas of the 8-fold Path (ariya-magga) Vin I.10; D II.312; A III.140; VbhA 117. Sankappa is def^d at DhsA 124 as (cetaso) abhiniropanā, i. e. application of the mind. See on term also *Cpd.* 238.

Sankappeti [Den. fr. sankappa] 1. to imagine; wish A II.36; M I.402; Pug 19. — 2. to determine, to think about, strive after J III.449 sq.

Sankamati [saŋ + kamati] 1. to go on, to pass over to (acc.), to join D I.55 (ākāsaŋ indriyāni s.); Vin I.54; II.138 (bhikkhū rukkhā rukkhaŋ s., climb fr. tree to tree); Kvu 565 sq. (jhānā jhānaŋ). — 2. to transmigrate Miln 71 sq. (+ paṭisandahati). — grd. sankamanīya to be passed on or transferred Vin I.190; **cīvara°** a dress that should be handed over, which does not belong to one Vin IV.282. — pp. sankanta. — Caus. sankāmeti (1) to pass over, to cause to go, to move, to shift Vin III.49, 58, 59. — 2. to come in together (sensations to the heart) DhsA 264. — Cp. upa°.

Sankama [fr. saŋ + **kram**] a passage, bridge M I.439; Vin III.127; J III.373 (attānaŋ °ŋ katvā yo sotthiŋ samatārayi); Miln 91, 229.

Sankamana (nt.) [fr. sankamati] lit. "going over," i e. step; hence "bridge," passage, path S I.110; Vv 52²²; 77⁵; Pv II.7⁸; II.9²⁵; J VI.120 (papā°). Cp. upa°.

Sankampati [saŋ + kampati] to tremble, shake Vin I.12; D II.12, 108; J I.25. — Caus. sankampeti id. D II.108.

Sankara¹ (fight confusion) wrongly for sangara Nett 149, in quot. fr. M III.187.

Sankara² (adj.) [cp. Sk. śankara] blissful Mhbv 4 (sabba°).

Sankalana (nt.) [fr. saŋ + **kal** to produce] addition DA I.95; MA 1.2.

Sankalaha [saŋ + kalaha] inciting words, quarrel J V.393.

Sankasāyati [fr. saŋ + **kṛṣ**, kasati? Or has it anything to do with kasāya?] to become weak, to fail S I.202; II.277; IV.178; A I.68.

Sankassara (adj.) [doubtful, if Vedic sankasuka] doubtful; wicked Vin II.236 (cp. *Vin. Texts* III.300); S I.49 = Dh 312 (expl^d as "sankāhi saritabba, āsankāhi sarita, ussankita, parisankita" DhA III.485, thus taken as sankā + **sṛ** by Bdhgh; of course not cogent); A II.239; IV.128, 201; S I.66 (°ācāra = "suspecting all" trslⁿ); IV.180; Th 1, 277; Pug 27.

Sankā (f.) [fr. **śank**; see sankati] doubt, uncertainty, fear (cp. visanka) J VI.158; DhA III.485.

Sankāpeti [fr. saŋ + **kḷp**] to prepare, get ready, undertake Vin I.137 (vass'āvāsaŋ); S IV.312.

Sankāyati [Denom. fr. sankā; Dhtp 4 defines **sank** as "sankāyaŋ"] to be uncertain about Vin II.274. Cp. pari°.

Sankāra [fr. saŋ + **kṛ**] rubbish Vin I.48; IV.265; J I.315; II.196.
-kūṭa rubbish heap, dust heap M II.7; Pug 33; Miln 365; DhA I.174. Cp. kacavara & kattara. **-cola** a rag picked up from a rubbish heap J IV.380. **-ṭhāna** dust heap Th 1, 1175, J I.244; Vism 250; DhA II.27. **-dhāna** id. Dh 58. **-yakkha** a rubbish heap demon J IV.379.

Sankāsa [saŋ + kāsa, of **kāś**, cp. okāsa] appearance; (-°) having the appearance of, like, similar J II.150; V.71, 155, 370 (puñña° = sadisa C.); Bu 17, 21; Miln 2.

Sankāsana (nt.) & °ā (f.) [fr. saŋ + **kāś**] explanation, illustration S V.430; Nett 5, 8, 38; SnA 445 (+ pakāsana).

Sankiṇṇa [pp. of sankirati] mixed; impure S III.71; A IV.246.
-parikha having the trenches filled; said of one who is free of *saŋsāra* M I.139; A III.84; Nd² p. 161.

Sankita [fr. **śank**] anxious, doubtful J v.85; Mhvs 7, 15; SnA 60. Cp. pari°, vi°.

Sankittana (nt) [saŋ + kittana] proclaiming, making known PvA 164.

Sankitti (f.) [perhaps saŋ + kitti] derivation & meaning very doubtful; Bdhgh's expl^n at PugA 231 is not to be taken as reliable, viz. "sankittetvā katabhattesu hoti. dubbhikkha-samaye kira acela-kāsâvakā acelakānaŋ atthāya tato tato taṇḍul'ādīni samādapetvā bhattaŋ pacanti, ukkaṭṭhâcelako tato na paṭigaṇhāti." D I.166 (trsl^n *Dial.* I.229 "he will not accept food collected, i. e. by the faithful in time of drought"; Neumann "not from the dirty"; Franke "nichts von Mahlzeiten, für die die Mittel durch Aufruf beschafft sind" ?); M I.77; A II.206; Pug 55. It may be something like "convocation."

Sankin (adj.) [fr. **śank**] anxious Mhvs 35, 101.

Sankiya (adj.) [grd. fr. śankati] 1. apt to be suspected It 67. — 2. anxious J I.334.

Sankiraṇa (nt.) [fr. saŋ + kirati] an astrological t.t., denoting the act of or time for collecting or calling in of debts (Bdhgh; doubtful) D I.11; DA I.96; cp. *Dial.* I.23.

Sankirati [saŋ + kirati] to mix together; Pass. sankīyati (q. v.); pp. **sankiṇṇa.**

Sankiliṭṭha [pp. of sankilissati] stained, tarnished, impure, corrupt, foul D I.247; S II.271; A III.124; V.169; Dh 244; J II.418; Dhs 993, 1243; Pv IV.1^{23} (kāyena vācāya ca); DhsA 319.

Sankilissati [saŋ + kilissati, cp. BSk. sankliśyati Divy 57] to become soiled or impure D I.53; S III.70; Dh 165; J II.33, 271. — pp. **sankiliṭṭha.** — Caus. **sankileseti.**

Sankilissana (nt.) [fr. sankilissati] staining, defiling; getting defiled VvA 329.

Sankilesa [saŋ + kilesa] impurity, defilement, corruption, sinfulness Vin I.15; D I.10, 53, 247 (opp. visuddhi); M I.402; S III.69; A II.11; III.418 sq.; V.34; J I.302; Dhs 993, 1229; Nett 100; Vism 6, 51, 89; DhsA 165.

Sankilesika (adj.) [fr. sankilesa] baneful, sinful D I.195; III.57; A II.172; Dhs 993 (cp. DhsA 345); Tikp 333, 353.

Sankīyati [Pass. of sankirati, saŋ + **kir**; Sk. °kīryate > *kiyyati > P. °kīyati] to become confused or impure S III.71; A II.29; IV.246.

Sankiḷati [saŋ + kiḷati] to play or sport D I.91; A IV.55, 343; DA I.256.

Sanku [cp. Vedic śanku] a stake, spike; javelin M I.337; S IV.168; J VI.112; DhA I.69. —**ayo°** an iron stake A IV.131.

-**patha** a path full of stakes & sticks Vv 84^{11}; J III.485, 541; Miln 280; Vism 305. -**sata** a hundred sticks, hundreds of sticks J VI.112; Vism 153 (both passages same simile with the beating of an ox-hide). -**samāhata** set with iron spikes, N. of a purgatory M I.337; J VI.453.

Sankuka [fr. sanku] a stake VvA 338. Cp. khāṇuka.

Sankucati [saŋ + kucati: see kuñcita] to become contracted, to shrink DhsA 376. — pp. °kucita. — Caus. °koceti.

Sankucita [pp. of sankucati] shrunk, contracted, clenched (of the first: °hattha) J I.275; VI.468 (°hattha, opposed to pasārita-hattha); DA I.287; PvA 123, 124.

Sankuṭika [fr. saŋ + ***kuṭ** = **kuc**, cp. kuṭila] doubled up J II.68; cp. *J.P.T.S.* 1884, 102.

Sankuṭita [= last] doubled up, shrivelled, shrunk; J II.225; Miln 251, 362; DhsA 376; Vism 255 (where KhA reads bahala); VbhA 238.

Sankuṭila (adj.) [saŋ + kuṭila] curved, winding Miln 297.

Sankuṇḍita [pp. of saŋ + **kuṇḍ**: see kuṇḍa] contorted, distorted PvA 123.

Sankuddha [saŋ + kuddha] angry D II.262.

Sankupita [saŋ + kupita] shaken, enraged S I.222.

Sankuppa (adj.) [saŋ + kuppa] to be shaken, movable; a° immovable Th I, 649; Sn 1149.

Sankula (adj.) [saŋ + kula] crowded, full Sdhp 603.

Sankuli [cp. sakkhali 2 & saṅguḷikā] a kind of cake J VI.580.

Sankulya (nt.) = sankuli J VI.524.

Sankusaka (adj.) [cp. Sk. sankasuka crumbling up] contrary; neg. a° J VI.297 (= appaṭiloma C.).

Sankusumita (adj.) [saŋ + kusumita] flowering, in blossom J V.420; Miln 319.

Sanketa [saŋ + keta: see ketu] intimation, agreement, engagement, appointed place, rendezvous Vin I.298; Miln 212; Nett 15, 18; cp. *Cpd.* 6, 33. **sanketaŋ gacchati** to keep an appointment, to come to the rendezvous Vin II.265. **asanketena** without appointing a place Vin I.107. **vassika°** the appointed time for keeping the rainy season Vin I.298.

-**kamma** agreement Vin III.47, 53, 78.

Sanketana (nt.) = sanketa, **°ṭṭhāna** place of rendezvous DhA II.261.

Sankeḷāyati [saŋ + keḷāyati] to amuse oneself (with) A IV.55.

Sankoca [saŋ + koca, of **kuñc**: see kuñcita] contraction (as a sign of anger or annoyance), grimace (mukha°) PvA 103; also as **hattha°**, etc. at PvA 124.

Sankocana (nt.) = sankoca J III.57 (mukha°); DhA III.270; Dhtp 809.

Sankoceti [Caus. of sankucati] to contract J I.228; DhsA 324.

Sankopa see sankhepa.

Sankha[1] [cp. Vedic śankha; Gr. κόγχος shell, measure of capacity, & κόχλος; Lat. congius a measure] a shell, couch; mother-of-pearl; a chank, commonly used as a trumpet D I.79; II.297 = M I.58; A II.117; IV.199; Vv 81^{10}; J I.72; II.110; VI.465, 580; Miln 21 (dhamma°); DhA I 18. Combined with paṇava (small drum) Vism 408; J VI.21; or with **bheri** (large drum) Miln 21; Vism 408.

-**ûpama** like a shell, i. e. white J V.396, cp. VI.572. -**kuṭṭhin** a kind of leper; whose body becomes as white as mother-of-pearl DhA I.194, 195. -**thāla** mother of-pearl, (shell-) plate Vism 126 (sudhota°), 255. -**dhama** a trumpeter D I.259 = M II.19; M II.207 = S IV.322. -**dhamaka** a conch blower, trumpeter J I.284; VI.7. -**nābhi** a kind of shell Vin I.203; II.117. -**patta** mother-of-pearl DhA I.387. -**muṇḍika** the shell-tonsure, a kind of torture M I.87; A I.47; II.122. -**mutta** mother-of-pearl J V.380 (C expl^s as "shell-jewel & pearl-jewel"); VI.211, 230. -**likhita** polished like mother-of-pearl; bright, perfect D I.63, 250; S II.219; A V.204; Vin I.181; Pug 57; DA I.181; DhA IV.195. See also under likhita, & cp. Franke, *Wiener Zeitschrift* 1893, 357. -**vaṇṇa** pearl-white J III.477; M I.58 = A III.324. -**sadda** the sound of a chank A II.186; Vism 408; Dhs 621. -**silā** "shell-stone," a precious stone, mother-of-pearl (?) Ud 54; J IV.85; Pv II.6^4. Frequent in BSk., e. g. AvŚ I.184, 201, 205; Divy 291.

Sankha[2] [etym. ?] a water plant (comb[d] with sevāla) Miln 35. See detail under paṇṇaka 2.

Sankhata [pp. of sankharoti; Sk. saŋskṛta] 1. put together, compound; conditioned, produced by a combination of causes, "created," brought about as effect of actions in former births S II.26; III.56; Vin II.284; It 37, 88; J II.38; Nett 14; Dhs 1085; DhsA 47. As *nt.* that which is produced from a cause, i. e. the sankhāras S I.112; A I.83, 152; Nett 22. asankhata not put together, not proceeding from a cause Dhs 983 (so read for sankhata), 1086; Ep. of nibbāna "the Unconditioned" (& therefore unproductive of further life) A I.152; S IV.359 sq.; Kvu 317 sq.; Pv III.7[10] (= laddhanāma amataŋ PvA 207); Miln 270; Dhs 583 (see *trsl*[n] ibid.), 1439. The discernment of higher jhāna-states as sankhata is a preliminary to the attainment of Arahantship M III.244. Cp. abhi°; visankhita; visankhāra. — 2. cooked, dressed Mhvs 32, 39. — 3. embellished Mhvs 22, 29.
-lakkhaṇa properties of the sankhata, i. e. production, decay and change A I.152; VvA 29.

Sankhati (f.) [cp. Sk. saŋskṛti] cookery M I.448.

Sankhaya [saŋ+khaya] destruction, consumption, loss, end Vin I.42; D II.283; M I.152; S I.2, 124; IV.391; It 38; Dh 282 (= vināsa DhA III.421), 331; J II.52; V.405; Miln 205, 304.

Sankharoti [saŋ+kṛ] to put together, prepare, work PvA 287. a-sankhārāna S I.126. Ger. sankharitvā S II.269 (v. l. sankhāditvā, as is read at id. p. Vin II.201). Cp. abhi°. — pp. sankhata.

Sankhalā (f.) [cp. Sk. śṛnkhalā] a chain Th 2, 509. aṭṭhi° a chain of bones, skeleton A III.97. As °kankalā at Th 2, 488.

Sankhalikā (f.) [fr. sankhalā] a chain S I.76; J III.168; VI.3; Nd[2] 304[III]; Miln 149, 279; DhA IV.54; PvA 152. Sometimes sankhalika (esp. in composition), e. g. J III.125 (°bandhana); VI.3; Miln 279. —aṭṭhi° a chain of bones, a skeleton [cp. BSk. asthi-sankhalikā MVastu I.21] D II.296 = M I.58; Vin III.105; J I.433; Pv II.12[11]; DhA III.479. —deva° a magic chain J II.128; V.92.

Sankhā (f.) & **Sankhyā** (f.) [fr. saŋ+**khyā**] 1. enumeration, calculation, estimating D II.277; M I.109; Miln 58. — 2. number Dāvs I.25. — 3. denomination, definition, word, name (cp. on term *K.S.* I.321) S III.71 sq.; IV.376 sq.; Nd[2] 617 (= uddesa gaṇanā paññatti); Dhs 1306; Miln 25. —sankhaŋ gacchati to be styled, called or defined; to be put into words D I.199, 201; Vin II.239; M I.190, 487; A I.68, 244 = II.113; Pug 42; Nett 66 sq.; Vism 212, 225, 235, 294 (khy); SnA 167 (khy); DhsA 11 (khy). sankhaŋ gata (cp. sankhāta) is called DA I.41 (uyyānaŋ Ambalaṭṭhikā t'eva s. g.). sankhaŋ na upeti (nopeti) cannot be called by a name, does not count, cannot be defined It 54; Sn 209, 749, 911, 1074; Nd[1] 327; Nd[2] 617.

Sankhāta [pp. of sankhāyati] agreed on, reckoned; (-°) so-called, named D I.163 (akusala° dhammā); III.65, 133 = Vin III.46 (theyya° what is called theft); DA I.313 (the sambodhi, by which is meant that of the three higher stages); DhsA 378 (khandha-ttaya° kāya, cp. *Expos.* II.485); PvA 40 (medha° paññā), 56 (hattha° pāni), 131 (pariccāga° atidāna), 163 (caraṇa° guṇa).
-dhamma one who has examined or recognized the *dhamma* ("they who have mastered well the truth of things" *K.S.* II.36), an Ep. of the *arahant* S II.47; IV.210; Sn 70 (°dhammo, with expl[n] Nd[2] 618[II]: "vuccati ñāṇaŋ" etc.; "sankhāta-dh. = ñāta-dhammo," of the paccekabuddha), 1038 (°dhammā = vuccanti arahanto khīṇāsavā Nd[2] 618[I]), Dh 70 (T. sankhata°, but DhA II.63 sankhāta°).

Sankhādati [saŋ+khādati] to masticate Vin II.201 = S II.269 (reads °kharitvā); A III.304 sq.; J I.507. — pp. °khādita.

Sankhādita [pp. of sankhādati] chewed, masticated KhA 56, 257, VbhA 241 (where Vism 257 reads °khāyita).

Sankhāna[1] (nt.) & **Sankhyāna** (nt.) [fr. saŋ+**khyā**, cp. sankhā] calculation, counting D I.11; M I.85; DA I.95; Dhtp 613 (khy).

Sankhāna[2] (nt.) [?] a strong leash ThA 292 (where Th 2, 509 reads sankhalā).

Sankhāyaka [fr. saŋ+**khyā**] a calculator S IV.376.

Sankhāyati & **Sankhāti** [saŋ+**khyā**] 1. to appear J V.203 (°āti). — 2. to calculate Sn p. 126 (inf. °khātuŋ); Dh 196. ger. sankhāya having considered, discriminately, carefully, with open mind D II.227; III.224 (paṭisevati etc.: with ref. to the 4 apassenāni); S I.182; Sn 209, 391, 749, 1048 (= jānitvā etc. Nd[2] 619); Nd[1] 327; Dh 267 (= ñāṇena DhA III.393); It 54. sankhā pi deliberately M I.105 sq.

Sankhāyita = sankhādita; Vism 257.

Sankhāra [fr. saŋ+**kṛ**, *not* Vedic, but as saŋskāra Epic & Class. Sk. meaning "preparation" and "sacrament," also in philosophical literature "former impression, disposition," cp. vāsanā] one of the most difficult terms in Buddhist metaphysics, in which the blending of the subjective-objective view of the world and of happening, peculiar to the East, is so complete, that it is almost impossible for Occidental terminology to get at the root of its meaning in a translation. We can only convey an idea of its import by representing several sides of its application, without attempting to give a "word" as a def. trsl[n]. — An exhaustive discussion of the term is given by Franke in his *Dīgha* translation (pp. 307 sq., esp. 311 sq.); see also the analysis in *Cpd.* 273-276. — Lit. "preparation, get up"; appl[d]: coefficient (of consciousness *as well as* of physical life, cp. viññāṇa), constituent, constituent potentiality; (pl.) synergies, cause-combination, as in S III.87; discussed, *B. Psy.*, p. 50 sq. (cp. DhsA 156, where paraphrased in def[n] of sa-sankhāra with "ussāha, payoga, upāya, paccaya-gahaṇa"); composition, aggregate. 1. Aggregate of the conditions or essential properties for a given process or result — e. g. (i.) the sum of the conditions or properties making up or resulting in life or existence; the essentials or "element" of anything (-°), e. g. āyusankhāra, life-element D II.106; S II.266; PvA 210; bhavasankhāra, jīvitasankhāra, D II.99, 107. (ii.) Essential conditions, antecedents or synergy (co-ordinated activity), mental coefficients, requisite for act, speech, thought: kāya°, vacī°, citta°, or mano°, described respectively as "respiration," "attention and consideration," "percepts and feelings," "because *these* are (respectively) bound up with," or "precede" *those* M I.301 (cp. 56); S IV.293; Kvu 395 (cp. *trsl*[n] 227); Vism 530 sq.; DhsA 8; VbhA 142 sq. — 2. One of the five khandhas, or constitutional elements of physical life (see khandha), comprising all the citta-sampayutta-cetasikā dhammā — i. e. the mental concomitants, or adjuncts which come, or tend to come, into consciousness at the uprising of a citta, or unit of cognition Dhs 1 (cp. M III.25). As thus classified, the sankhāra's form the mental factor corresponding to the bodily aggregate or rūpakkhandha, and are in contrast to the three khandhas which represent a single mental function only. But just as kāya stands for both body and action, so do the concrete mental syntheses called sankhārā tend to take on the implication of synergies, of purposive intellection, connoted by the term abhisankhāra, q. v. — e. g. M III.99, where sankhārā are a purposive, aspiring state of mind to induce a specific rebirth; S II.82, where puññaŋ, opuññaŋ, āṇeñjaŋ s. abhisankharoti, is, in D III.217 & Vbh 135, catalogued as the three classes of abhisankhāra; S II.39, 360; A II.157, where s. is tantamount to sañcetanā; Miln 61, where s., as khandha, is replaced by cetanā (purposive conception). Thus, too, the ss. in the Paṭiccasamuppāda formula are considered as the aggregate of mental conditions which, under the law of kamma, bring about the inception of the paṭisandhiviññāṇa, or first stirring of mental life in a newly begun individual. Lists of the psychologically, or logically distinguisbable factors making up the composite saṅkhārakkhandha, with constants and variants, are given for each class of citta in Dhs 62, etc. (N.B.—Read cetanā for vedanā. § 338.) Phassa and cetanā are the two constant factors in the s-kkhandha. These lists may be compared with the later elaboration of the saṅkhāra-elements given at Vism 462 sq. — 3. sankhārā (pl.) in *popular* meaning. In the famous formula (and in many other connections, as e. g. sabbe sankhārā) "aniccā vata sankhārā uppādavaya-dhammino" (D II.157; S I.6, 158, 200; II.193; Th I, 1159; J I.392, cp. Vism 527), which is rendered by Mrs. Rh. D. (*Brethren*, p 385 e. g.) as "O, transient are our *life's experiences!* Their nature 'tis to rise and pass away," we have the use of s. in quite a general & popular sense of "life, physical or material life"; and sabbe sankhārā means "everything, all physical and visible life, all creation." Taken with caution the term "*creation*" may be applied as t.t. in the Paṭiccasamuppāda, when we regard avijjā as creating, i. e. producing by spontaneous causality the sankhāras, and sankhārā as "natura genita atque genitura" (the latter with ref. to the foll. viññāṇa). If we render it by "formations" (cp. Oldenberg's "Gestaltungen," *Buddha* [7]1920, p. 254), we imply the mental "constitutional" element as well as the physical, although the latter in customary materialistic popular philosophy is the predominant factor (cp. the discrepancies of "life eternal" and "life is extinct" in one & the same European term). None of the "links" in the Paṭicca-samuppāda meant to the people that which it meant or was supposed to mean in the subtle and schematic philosophy (dhammā duddasā nipunā!) of the dogmatists. — Thus sankhārā are in the widest sense the "world of phenomena" (cp. below °loka) all things which have been made up by pre-existing causes. — At PvA 71 we find sankhārā in *lit.* meaning as "things" (preparations) in defn of ye keci (bhogā) "whatever." The sabbe s. at S II.178 (trsln "all the things of this world") denote all 5 aggregates exhausting all conditioned things; cp. Kvu 226 (trsln "things"); Mhvs IV.66 (: the material and transitory world); Dh 154 (vi-sankhāragataŋ cittaŋ = mind divested of all material things); DhsA 304 (trsln "kamma activities," in connection avijjā-paccaya-s°); *Cpd.* 211, n. 3. — The defn of sankhārā at Vism 526 (as result of avijjā & cause of viññāṇa in the P.-S.) is: sankhataŋ abhisankharonti ti sankhārā. Api ca: avijjā-paccayā sankhārā sankhāra-saddena āgata-sankhārā ti duvidhā sankhārā; etc. with further def. of the 4 sankhāras. — 4. Var. passages for sankhāra in general: D II. 213; III.221 sq., M II.223 (imassa dukkha-nidānassa sankhāraŋ padahato sankhāra-ppadhānā virāgo hoti); S III.69 (ekanta-dukkhā sankhārā); IV.216 sq. (sankhārāṇaŋ khaya-dhammatā; id. with vaya°, virāga°, nirodha° etc.); Sn 731 (yaŋ kiñci dukkhaŋ sambhoti sabbaŋ sankhāra-paccayā; sankhārānaŋ nirodhena n'atthi dukkhassa sambhavo); Vism 453, 462 sq. (the 51), 529 sq.; DhA III.264, 379; VbhA 134 (4 fold), 149 (3 fold), 192 (āyūhanā); PvA 41 (bhijjana-dhammā). — Of passages dealing with the sankhāras as aniccā, vayadhammā, anattā, dukkhā etc. the foll. may be mentioned: Vin I.13; S I.200; III.24; IV.216, 259; V.56, 345; M III.64, 108; A I.286; II.150 sq.; III.83, 143; IV.13, 100; It 38; Dh 277, 383; Ps I.37, 132; II.48; 109 sq.; Nd² 414, 450; also Nd² p. 259 (s. v. sankhārā).

-upekkhā equanimity among "things" Vism 161, 162. -ûpasama allayment of the constituents of life Dh 368, 381; cp. DhA IV.108. -khandha the aggregate of (mental) coefficients D III.233; Kvu 578; Tikp 61; DhsA 345; VbhA 20, 42. -dukkha the evil of material life, constitutional or inherent ill VbhA 93 (in the classification of the sevenfold *sukkha*). -paccayā (viññāṇaŋ) conditioned by the synergies (is vital consciousness), the second linkage in the Paṭicca-samuppāda (q. v.) Vism 577; VbhA 152 sq. -padhāna concentration on the sankhāras M II.223. -majjhattatā = °upekkhā VbhA 283. -loka the material world, the world of formation (or phenomena), creation, loka "per se," as contrasted to satta-loka, the world of (morally responsible) beings, loka "per hominem" Vism 205; VbhA 456; SnA 442.

Sankhāravant (adj.) [fr. sankhāra] having sankbāras A II.214 = Dhs 1003.

Sankhitta [pp. of sankhipati] 1. concise, brief Miln 227; DhsA 344; instr. sankhittena in short, concisely (opp. vitthārena) Vin I.10; D II.305; S V.421; Pug 41. Cp. BSk. sankṣiptena Divy 37 etc. — 2. concentrated, attentive D I.80 (which at Vism 410 however is expld as "thīna-middh' ânugata"); S II.122; V.263; D II.299 = M I.59. — 3. contracted, thin, slender: °majjhā of slender waist J V.155. — Cp. abhi°.

Sankhipati [saŋ + khipati] 1. to collect, heap together Mhvs 1, 31. — 2. to withdraw, put off Dāvs IV.35. — 3. to concentrate J I.82. — 4. to abridge, shorten. — pp. sankhitta.

Sankhippa (adj.) [saŋ + khippa] quick J VI.323.

Sankhiyā-dhamma form of talk, the trend of talk D I.2; DA I.43. Cp. sankhyā.

Sankhubhati [saŋ + khubbati] to be shaken, to be agitated, to stir J I.446 (ger. °khubhitvā); DhA II.43, 57; aor. °khubhi PvA 93. — pp. sankhubhita. — Caus. sankhobheti to shake, stir up, agitate J I.119, 350; II.119.

Sankhubhita [pp. of sankhubhati] shaken, stirred J III.443.

Sankhepa [saŋ + khepa] 1. abridgment, abstract, condensed account (opp. vitthāra), e. g. Vism 532, 479; Dh I.125; KhA 183; DhsA 344; SnA 150, 160, 314; VbhA 47. Cp. ati°. — 2. the sum of, quintessence of; instr. °ena (adv.) by way of, as if, e. g. rāja° as if he were king DA I.246; bhūmi-ghara° in the shape of an earth house DA I.260. — 3. group, heaping up, amassing, collection: pabbata-sankhepe in a mountain glen (lit. in the midst of a group of mountains) D I.84; A III.396. bhava° amassing of existences J I.165 sq., 366, 463; II.137. — 4. aṭavi° at A I.178; III.66 is probably a wrong reading for °sankopa "inroad of savage tribes."

Sankheyya[1] (adj.) [grd. of sankhāyati] calculable; only neg. a° incalculable S V.400; A III.366; PvA 212. -°kāra acting with a set purpose Sn 351. — As grd. of sankharoti: see upa°.

Sankheyya[2] (nt.) a hermitage, the residence of Thera Āyupāla Miln 19, 22 etc.

Sankhobha [san + khobha] shaking, commotion, upsetting, disturbance J I.64; Sdhp 471.

Sankhobheti see sankhubhati.

Sanga [fr. sañj: see sajjati[1]] cleaving, clinging, attachment, bond S I.25, 117 sq.; A III.311; IV.289; Dh 170, 342, etc.; Sn 61, 212, 386, 390, 475, etc.; Dhs 1059; DhsA 363; J III.201; the five sangas are rāga, dosa, moha, māna, and diṭṭhi, Thag. 633 = Dhp. 370; DhA IV.187; seven sangas, It. 94; Nd¹ 91, 432; Nd² 620.

-âtiga one who has overcome attachment, free from attachment, an Arahant M I.386; S I.3, 23; IV.158 = It 58; Sn 250, 473, 621; DhA IV.159.

Sangacchati [saŋ+gacchati] to come together, to meet with; ger. °gamma It 123; & °gantva Sn 290. — pp. sangata.

Sangaṇa (adj.) [sa+angaṇa] sinful Sn 279. Cp. sāngana.

Sangaṇikā (f.) [saŋ+gaṇa+ikā, cp. BSk. sangaṇikā MVastu II.355; Divy 464] communication, association, society Vin I.45; A III.256; J I.106.
-ārāma delighting in society D II.78; M III.110; VbhA 474. -ārāmatā delight in company D II.78; M III.110; A III.116, 293 sq., 310, 422. -rata fond of society D II.78; Sn 54; cp. sangaṇike rata Th 1, 84. -vihāra (sangaṇika°) living in society A III.104; IV.342.

Sangaṇha (adj.) [fr. saŋ+**grah**] showing kindness, helping VvA 59 (°sīla).

Sangaṇhāti [saŋ+gaṇhāti] 1. to comprise PvA 80, 117; SnA 200 (ger. °gahetvā), 347 (°gaṇhitvā). — 2. to collect Mhvs 10, 24. — 3. to contain, include Miln 40. — 4. to compile, abridge Mhvs 37, 244. — 5. to take up; to treat kindly, sympathize with, favour, help, protect Vin I.50; J II.6; IV.132; V.426 (aor. °gaṇhi), 438 (to favour with one's love), 510; Miln 234; KhA 160. — aor. sangahesi Mhvs 38, 31; fut. °gahissati J VI.392; ger. °gahetvā Mhvs 37, 244; grd. °gahetabba Vin I.50; ppr. Pass. °gayhamāna DhsA 18. — pp. sangahita. — Caus. II. sangaṇhāpeti: see pari° (e. g. J VI.328).

Sangata [pp. of sangacchati] 1. come together, met Sn 807, 1102 (=samāgata samohita sannipātita Nd² 621); nt. sangataŋ association Dh 207. — 2. compact, tightly fastened or closed, well-joined Vv 64² (=nibbivara VvA 275).

Sangati (f.) [fr. sangacchati] 1. meeting, intercourse J IV.98; V.78, 483. In defⁿ of yajati (=service?) at Dhtp 62 & Dhtm 79. — 2. union, combination M I.111; S II.72; IV.32 sq., 68 sq.; Vbh 138 (=VbhA 188). — 3. accidental occurrence D I.53; DA I.161.

Sangatika [adj.] kalyāṇa°, pāpa°, united with, M II.222, 227.

Sangama [fr. saŋ+**gam**] 1. meeting, intercourse, association Sn 681; J II.42; III.488; V.483. — 2. sexual intercourse M I.407; J IV.106.

Sangara [fr. saŋ+**gṛ**¹ to sing, proclaim, cp. gāyati & gīta] 1. a promise, agreement J IV.105, 111, 473; V.25, 479; sangaraŋ karoti to make a compact Vin I.247; J IV.105; V.479. — 2. (also nt.) a fight M III.187=Nett 149; S V.109.

Sangaha¹ [fr. saŋ+**grah**] 1. collecting, gathering, accumulation Vin I.253; Mhvs 35, 28. — 2. comprising, collection, inclusion, classification Kvu 335 sq. (°kathā), cp. *Kvu. trslⁿ* 388 sq.; Vism 191, 368 (eka°); °ŋ gacchati to be comprised, included, or classified SnA 7, 24, 291. — 3. inclusion, i. e. constitution of consciousness, phase Miln 40. — 4. recension, collection of the Scriptures Mhvs 4, 61; 5, 95; 38, 44; DA I.131. — 5. (applᵈ) kind disposition, kindliness, sympathy, friendliness, help, assistance, protection, favour D III.245; Sn 262, 263; A I.92; J I.86 sq.; III.471; VI.574; DA I.318; VvA 63, 64; PvA 196 (°ŋ karoti). The 4 sangaha-vatthūni or objects (characteristics) of sympathy are: dāna, peyyavajja, atthacariyā, samānattatā, or liberality, kindly speech, a life of usefulness (Rh. D. at *Dial.* III.145: sagacious conduct; 223: justice), impartiality (? better as state of equality, i. e. sensus communis or feeling of common good). The BSk. equivalents (as sangrahavastūni) are dāna, priyavākya, tathārthacaryā, samānasukha-duḥkatā MVastu I.3; and d., p., arthakriyā, samānārthatā (=samāna+artha+tā) Lal. Vist. 30. Cp. Divy 95, 124, 264. The P. refs. are D III.152, 232; A II.32, 248; IV.219, 364; J V.330; SnA 236, 240. See also Kern, *Toev.* II.67 s. v.

Sangaha² (nt.) [fr. saŋ+**grah**] restraining, hindrance, bond It 73 (both reading & meaning very doubtful).

Sangahaṇa (adj.) [fr. sangaṇhāti] firm, well-supported J V.484.

Sangahita (& °**gahīta**) [pp. of sangaṇhāti] 1. comprised, included Miln 40 (eka°); PvA 80. — 2. collected Mhvs 10, 24. — 3. grouped Kvu 335 sq. — 4. restrained Sn 388 (°attabhāva); SnA 291 (°atta). — 5. kindly disposed Vv 11⁶=Pv IV.1⁶⁰ (°attabhāva=paresaŋ sangaṇha-sīla VvA 59, i. e. of sympathetic nature).

Sangāma [fr. saŋ+***gam**: see grāma; lit. "collection"] a fight, battle D I.46; II.285; M I.86, 253; S I.98; IV.308 sq.; A I.106; II.116; III.94; Vin I.6; It 75; Sn 440; Nd² 199; Pug 68; J I.358; II.11; Miln 332; Vism 401. Cp. vijita°.
-âvacara whose sphere is the battle, quite at home on the battlefield J II.94, 95; Vin V.163 sq., 183 (here said fig. of the bhikkhu). -ji (sangāma-j-uttama) victorious in battle Dh 103 (cp. DhA II.227=sangāma-sīsa-yodha). -bheri battle drum DhA III.298; IV.25. -yodha a warrior J I.358.

Sangāmeti [Denom. fr. sangāma; given as special root **sangām**° at Dhtp 605 with defⁿ "yuddha"] to fight, to come into conflict with Vin II.195; III.108; It 75; J II.11, 212. aor. °gāmesi J V.417, 420 (C.=samāgami, cp. sangacchati).

Sangāyati [saŋ+gāyati] to chant, proclaim (cp. sangara), to rehearse, to establish the text of the B. scriptures Vin II.285; DA I.25 (Buddha-vacanaŋ). — pp. **sangīta.**

Sangāyika (adj.) [fr. sangāyati] connected with the proclamation; dhamma°-therā the Elders gathered in the council for proclaiming the Doctrine J V.56.

Sangāha (adj.-n.) [fr. saŋ+**grah**] 1. collecting, collection, Mhvs 10, 24. — 2. restraining, self-restraint A II.142.

Sangāhaka (adj.-n.) [fr. sangāha] 1. compiling, collection, making a recension J I.1; Miln 369; VvA 169 (dhamma°). — 2. treating kindly, compassionate, kind (cp. sangaha 5) A IV.90; J I.203; III.262. — 3. (m.) a charioteer D II.268; J I.203; II.257; IV.63.

Sangāhika (adj.) [=last] 1. comprising, including J I.160; Vism 6; DA I.94. — 2. holding together M I.322=A III.10. — 3. comprehensive, concise J II.236.

Sangīta [pp. of sangāyati] sung; uttered, proclaimed, established as the text Vin II.290; J I.1; DA I.25 (of the Canon, said to have been rehearsed in *seven* months). — (nt.) a song, chant, chorus D II.138; J VI.529.

Sangīti (f.) [fr. saŋgāyati; BSk. sangīti Divy 61] 1. a song, chorus, music J I.32 (dibba°); VI.528 (of birds). — 2. proclamation (cp. sangara), rehearsal, general convocation of the Buddhist clergy in order to settle questions of doctrine and to fix the text of the Scriptures. The *first* Council is alleged to have been held at Rājagaha, Vin II.284 sq.; Dpvs IV.; Mhvs III.; DA I.2 sq.; SnA 67, 483. The *second* Council at Vesāli Vin II.294 sq.; Dpvs IV.27 sq.; Mhvs IV.; the *third* at Pāṭaliputta, Dpvs VII.34 sq.; Mhvs V.268 sq. A Council of heretics, the so-called Mahāsaṅgīti, is mentioned Dpvs V.31 sq. — 3. text rehearsed, recension Vin II.290; DA I.17; Miln 175 (dhamma°); text, formula Vin I.95; II.274, 278. On the question of the Councils see especially Franke *J.P.T.S.* 1908, 1 sq.
-kāra editor of a redaction of the Holy Scriptures SnA 42 sq., 292, 394, 413 sq., 504 and passim; PvA 49, 70, etc. -kāraka id J I.345 -kāla the time of the

redaction of the Pāli Canon, or of (one of them, probably the last) the Council Tikp 241; SnA 580; VvA 270. -pariyāya the discourse on the Holy Text D III.271 (Rh. D. "scheme of chanting together").

Sanguḷikā (f.) [either = Sk. śaṣkulikā, cp. sakkhali 2, or fr. saguḷa = sanguḷa] a cake Vin II.17; DhA II.75; cp. sankulikā A III.78.

Sangopeti [saŋ + gopeti] to guard; to keep, preserve; to hold on to (acc.) J IV.351 (dhanaŋ).

Sangha [fr. saŋ + hṛ; lit. "comprising." The quâsi pop. etym. at VvA 233 is "diṭṭhi-sīla-sāmaññena sanghāṭa-bhāvena sangha"] 1. multitude, assemblage Miln 403 (kāka°); J I.52 (sakuṇa°); Sn 589 (ñāti°); 680 (deva°); D III.23 (miga°); Vv 5[5] (accharā° = samūha VvA 37). bhikkhu° an assembly of Buddhist priests A I.56, etc.; D I.1, etc.; S I.236; Sum I.230, 280; Vin I.16; II.147; bhikkhunī° an assembly of nuns S v.360; Vin I.140; sāvaka° an assembly of disciples A I.208; D II.93; S I.220; PvA 195, etc.; samaṇa° an assembly of ascetics Sn 550. — 2. the Order, the priesthood, the clergy, the Buddhist church A I.68, 123, etc.; D I.2, etc.; III.102, 126, 193, 246; S IV.270 sq.; Sn 227, etc.; J II.147, etc.; Dhs 1004; It 11, 12, 88; Vin I.102, 326; II.164, etc. — 3. a larger assemblage, a community A II.55 = Sv.400; M I.231 (cp. gaṇa). — On the formula Buddha, Dhamma, Sangha see dhamma C 2.

-ânussati meditation on the Order (a *kammaṭṭhāna*) D III.250, 280; A I.30; J I.97. -ārāma a residence for members of the Order J I.94; VbhA 13. -kamma an act or ceremony performed by a chapter of bhikkhus assembled in solemn conclave Vin I.123 (cp. I.53, 143 & expl[n] at *S.B.E.* XXII.7); III.38 sq.; J I.341. -gata gone into the sangha, joining the community M I.469. -thera senior of the congregation Vin II.212, 303. -bhatta food given to the community of bhikkhus Vin I.58; II.109, 212. -bhinna schismatic Vin V.216. -bheda causing dissension among the Order Vin I.150; II.180 sq.; A II.239 sq.; It 11; Tikp 167, 171; J VI.129; VbhA 425 sq. -bhedaka causing dissension or divisions, schismatic Vin I.89, 136, 168; It 11. -māmaka devoted to the Sangha DhA I.206. -rāji [= rāji[1]] dissension in the Order Vin I.339; II.203 = VbhA 428; Vin IV.37.

Sanghaŋsati [saŋ + ghaŋsati] to rub together, to rub against Vin II.315 (Bdhgh).

Sanghaṭita [saŋ + ghaṭita, for °ghaṭṭita, pp. of ghaṭṭeti] 1. struck, sounded, resounding with (-°) J v.9 (v. l. ṭṭ); Miln 2. — 2. pierced together, pegged together, constructed Miln 161 (nāvā nānā-dāru°).

Sanghaṭṭa[1] (adj.) [fr. saŋ + ghaṭṭ] knocking against, offending, provoking, making angry J VI.295.

Sanghaṭṭa[2] (?) bangle Sn 48 (°yanta): thus Nd[2] reading for °māna (ppr. med. of sanghaṭṭeti).

Sanghaṭṭana (nt.) & °ā (f.) [fr. sanghaṭṭeti] 1. rubbing or striking together, close contact, impact S IV.215; V.212; J VI.65; Vism 112; DA I.256 (anguli°). — 2. bracelet (?) SnA 96 (on Sn 48).

Sanghaṭṭeti [saŋ + ghaṭṭeti] 1. to knock against Vin II.208. — 2. to sound, to ring Mhvs 21, 29 (°aghaṭṭayi). — 3 to knock together, to rub against each other J IV.98 (aŋsena aŋsaŋ samaghaṭṭayimha); Dāvs III.87. — 4. to provoke by scoffing, to make angry J VI.295 (paraŋ asanghaṭṭento, C. on asanghaṭṭa); VvA 139 (pres. pass. °ghaṭṭiyati). — pp. sanghaṭ(ṭ)ita.

Sanghara = saghara [sa[4] + ghara] one's own house J V.222.

Sangharaṇa (nt.) [= saŋharaṇa] accumulation J III.319 (dhana°).

Sangharati [= saŋharati] 1. to bring together, collect, accumulate J III.261; IV.36 (dhanaŋ), 371; V.383. — 2. to crush, to pound J I.493.

Sanghāṭa [fr. saŋ + ghaṭeti, lit. "binding together"; on etym. see Kern, *Toev.* II.68] 1. a raft J II.20, 332 (nāvā°); III.362 (id.), 371. Miln 376. dāru° (= nāvā°) J V.194, 195. — 2. junction, union VvA 233. — 3. collection, aggregate J IV.15 (upāhana°); Th I. 519 (papañca°). Freq. as aṭṭhi° (cp. sankhalā etc.) a string of bones, i. e. a skeleton Th I, 570; DhA III.112; J V.256. — 4. a weft, tangle, mass (almost = "robe," i. e. sanghāṭī), in taṇhā°-paṭimukka M I.271; vāda°-paṭimukka M I.383 (Neumann "defeat"); diṭṭhi°-paṭimukka Miln 390. — 5. a post, in piṭṭha° door-post, lintel Vin II.120.

Sanghāṭika (adj.) [fr. sanghāṭi] wearing a sanghāṭi M I.281.

Sanghāṭī (f.) [fr. sanghaṭeti; cp. BSk. sanghāṭī Divy 154, 159, 494] one of the three robes of a Buddhist Vin I.46, 289; II.78, 135, 213; D I.70; II.65; M I.281; II.45; S I.175; A II.104, 106 sq., 210; IV.169 sq.; V.123; Pv IV.1[46]; VbhA 359 (°cīvara); PvA 43.

-cāra wandering about in a sanghāṭī, having deposited the cīvara Vin IV.281. -vāsin dressed in a s. Sn 456.

Sanghāṇi (f.) a loin-cloth Vin IV.339 sq.

Sanghāta [saŋ + ghāta] 1. striking, killing, murder Vin I.137; D I.141; II.354; M I.78; A II.42 sq. — 2. knocking together (cp. sanghaṭṭeti), snapping of the fingers (acchara°) A I.34, 38; J VI.64. — 3. accumulation, aggregate, multitude PvA 206 (aṭṭhi° mass of bones, for the usual °sanghāṭa); Nett 28. — 4. N. of one of the 8 principle purgatories J V.266, 270.

Sanghātanika (adj.) [fr. sanghāta or sanghāṭa] holding or binding together M I.322 (+ agga-sangāhika); A III.10 (id.); Vin I.70 ("the decisive moment" *Vin. Texts* I.190).

Sanghâdisesa [unexplained as regards etym.; Geiger, *P.Gr.* § 38[3], after S. Lévi, = sangh'ātisesa; but atisesa does not occur in Pāli] requiring suspension from the Order; a class of offences which can be decided only by a formal sangha-kamma Vin II.38 sq.; III.112, 186; IV.110 sq., 225 (where explained); A II.242; Vism 22; DhA III.5.

Sanghika (adj.) [fr. sangha] belonging to, or connected with the Order Vin I.250.

Sanghin (adj.) [fr. sangha] having a crowd (of followers), the head of an order D I.47, 116; S I.68; Miln 4; DA I 143. —sanghâsanghī (pl.) in crowds, with crowds (redupl. cpd.!), with gaṇi-bhūtā "crowd upon crowd" at D I.112, 128; II.317; DA I.280.

Sanghuṭṭha (adj.) [saŋ + ghuṭṭha] 1. resounding (with) J VI.60, 277 (turiya-tāḷita°); Mhvs 15, 196; 29, 25 (turiya°); Sdhp 298. — 2. proclaimed, announced PvA 73.

Sacāca (conj.) if indeed Vin I.88; see **sace**.

Sacitta[1] (nt.) [sa[4] + citta] one's own mind or heart D II.120; Dh 183, 327 = Miln 379.

Sacitta[2] (adj.) [sa[2] + citta] of the same mind J V.360.

Sacittaka (adj.) [sa[3] + citta + ka] endowed with mind, intelligent DhsA 295.

Sace (conj.) [sa[2] + ce; cp. sacāca] if D I.8, 51; Vin I.7; Dh 134; J I.311. — sace . . . noce if . . . if not J VI.365.

Sacetana (adj.) [sa[3] + cetana] animate, conscious, rational J I.74; Mhvs 38, 97.

Sacetasa (adj.) [sa[3] + cetasa] attentive, thoughtful A I.254 (= citta-sampanna C.).

Sacca (adj.) [cp. Sk. satya] real, true D I.182; M II.169; III.207; Dh 408; nt. saccaŋ truly, verily, certainly Miln 120; saccaŋ kira is it really true? D I.113; Vin I.45, 60; J I.107; saccato truly S III.112. — (nt. as noun) saccaŋ the truth A II.25, 115 (parama°); Dh 393; also: a solemn asseveration Mhvs 25, 18. Sacce patiṭṭhāya keeping to fact, M I.376. — pl. (cattāri) saccāni the (four) truths M II.199; A II.41, 176; Sn 883 sq.; Dhs 358. — The 4 ariya-saccāni are the truth about dukkha, dukkha-samudaya, dukkha-nirodha, *and* dukkha-nirodha-gāmini-paṭipadā. Thus e. g. at Vin I.230; D II.304 sq.; III.277; A I.175 sq.; Vism 494 sq.; VbhA 116 sq., 141 sq. A shortened statement as dukkha, samudaya, nirodha, magga is freq. found, e. g. Vin I.16; see under dukkha B. I. — See also ariyasacca & asacca. — iminā saccena in consequence of this truth, i. e. if this be true J I.294.

-avhaya deserving his name, Cp. of the Buddha Sn 1133, cp. Nd² 624. **-âdhitthāna** determined on truth M III.245; D III.229. **-ânupatti** realization of truth M II.173 sq. **-ânubodha** awakening to truth M II.171 sq. **-ânurakkhaṇa** warding of truth, M II.176. **-âbhinivesa** inclination to dogmatize, one of the kāya-ganthas S V.59; Dhs 1139; DhsA 377. **-âbhisamaya** comprehension of the truth Sn 758; Th I, 338; ThA 239. **-kāra** ratification, pledge, payment in advance as guarantee J I.121. **-kiriyā** a solemn declaration, a declaration on oath J I.214, 294; IV.31, 142; V.94; Miln 120; Mhvs 18, 39 (see *trsl*ⁿ p. 125 on term). **-ñāṇa** knowledge of the truth Vism 510; DhA IV.152. **-nāma** doing justice to one's name, bearing a true name, Ep. of the Buddha A III.346; IV.285, 289; PvA 231. **-nikkhama** truthful Sn 542. **-paṭivedha** penetration of the truth Ps II.57. **-vanka** a certain kind of fish J V.405 (the Copenhagen MS. has [sa]sacca-vanka, which has been given by Fausböll as sata-vanka). **-vacana** (1) veracity M I.403; Dh I.160; (2) = sacca-kiriyā KhA 169, 180. **-vajja** truthfulness D I.53; S IV.349; J IV.320. **-vācā** id. A II.228; III.244; J I.201. **-vādin** truthful, speaking the truth D I.4; III.170; A II.209; IV.249, 389; S I.66; Sn 59; Dh 217; Miln 120; Nd² 623; DhA III.288. **-vivaṭṭa** revelation of truth Ps I.11. **-sandha** truthful, reliable D I.4; III.170; A II.209; IV.249; DA I.73. **-sammatā** popular truth, maxim S IV.230.

Saccāpeti at A IV.346 = Vin II.19 is probably misreading or an old misspelling for sajjāpeti fr. sajjeti, the confusion sac : saj being frequent. *Meaning*: to undertake, fulfil, realize.

Saccika (adj.) [cp. Sk. satyaka] real, true Miln 226 (the same passage at Ps I.174 & Nd¹ 458 spells **sacchika**). — saccik' aṭṭha truth, reality, the highest truth Kvu I sq.; DhsA 4 (nearly = paramaṭṭha); KhA 102. Kern in a phantastic interpretation (*Toev.* II.49, 50) takes it as sacci-kaṭṭha (= Sk. sīci-kṛṣta) "pulled sideways," i. e. "misunderstood."

Sacceti in fut. saccessati at A IV.343 is most likely an old mistake for ghaṭṭessati is the same passage at A III.343; the meaning is "to touch," or to approach, disturb. It is hardly = **saśc** "to accompany."

Sacchanda (adj.) [sa⁴ + chanda] self-willed, headstrong J I.421; as sacchandin ibid.

Sacchavini (mūlāni) at A III.371 (opp. ummūla) means "roots taking to the soil again." It is doubtful whether it belongs to chavi "skin."

Sacchikata [pp. of sacchikaroti cp. BSk. sākṣātkṛtaḥ AvŚ I.210] seen with one's own eyes, realized, experienced D I.250; S V.422 = Vin I.11; DhA IV.117.

Sacchikaraṇīya (adj.) [grd. of sacchikaroti] (able) to be realized S III.223 sq.; D III.230 = A II.182 (in four ways: by kāya, sati, cakkhu, paññā).

Sacchikaroti [cp. Sk. sākṣāt kṛ; the P. form being *saccha° (= sa³ + akṣ, as in akkhi), with change of °a to °i before **kṛ**. See also sakkhiŋ karoti] to see with one's eyes, to realize, to experience for oneself. Pres. °karoti D I.229; S IV.337; V.11, 49. — Fut. °karissati S V.10; M II.201 (as sacchi vā k.). — Aor. sacch'ākāsi S IV.63; SnA 166. — Grd. °kātabba Vin I.11; S V.422; & °karaṇīya (q. v.). — pp. sacchikata.

Sacchikiriyā (f.) [fr. sacchikaroti] realization, experiencing D I.100; III.255; S IV.254; A I.22; II.148; III.101; IV.332 sq.; Sn 267; Vism 696 sq.; Dhs 296; DhA IV.63.

Sajati¹ [**sṛj**, cp. Av. hərəzaiti to let loose; Sk. sarga pouring out, sṛṣṭi emanation, creation] to let loose, send forth; dismiss, give up Sn 386, 390; J I.359; V.218 (imper. sajāhi); VI.185, 205. — infin. saṭṭhuŋ (q. v.); pp. saṭṭha (see vissaṭṭha). — Caus. sajjeti (q. v.). — For sajj° (Caus.) we find sañj° in sañjitar.

Sajati² [**svaj**; Dhtp 74, 549 = ajjana (?) or = sajati¹ ?] to embrace D II.266 (imper. saja). udakaŋ sajati to embrace the water, poet. for "to descend into the water" J IV.448 (T. sajāti); VI.198 (C. = abhisiñcati), 205 (C. = attano upari sajati [i. e. sajati¹] abbhukkirati). On C. readings cp. Kern, *Toev* II.51.

Sajana [sa⁴ + jana] a kinsman J IV.11 (read °parijanaŋ).

Sajala (adj.-n.) [sa³ + jala] watery, wet; nt. water.
-da giving water, bringing rain (of wind) Vism 10. -dhara holding water, i, e. a cloud VvA 223.

Sajāti (f.) [sa² + jāti] (being of) the same class or caste Vin I.87; J II.108 (°putta).

Sajitar see sañjitar.

Sajīva¹ (adj.) [sa³ + jīva] endowed with life Mhvs 11, 13.

jīva² [for saciva ?] a minister J VI.307, 318 (= amacca C.).

jīvāna (nt.) at S I.44 is *metric* spelling for sa-jīvana [sa² = saŋ, + jīvana] "same livelihood," in phrase kiŋsu kamme s. "what is (of) the same livelihood in work, i. e. occupation?" The form is the same as jīvāna at J III.353. Taken wrongly as *gen. pl.* by Mrs. Rh. D. in trslⁿ (*K.S.* I.63): "who in their work is *mate to sons of men?*" following Bdhgh's wrong interpretation (see *K.S.* I.321) as "kammena saha *jīvantānan*; kamma-dutiyakā nāma honti."

Sajotibhūta (adj.) [sa³ + joti + bhūta; same BSk., e. g. MVastu I.5] flaming, ablaze, aglow D I.95; Vin I.25; A I.141; J I.232; DA I.264.

Sajja (adj.) [grd. formation fr. sajj = sañj Caus.; cp. the exact likeness of Ger. "fertig"] prepared, ready J I.98; II.325; III.271; Miln 351; PvA 156, 256. Of a bow furnished with a bow-string A III.75.

Sajjaka (adj.) = sajja; J IV.45 (gamana° ready for going, "fertig").

Sajjati [Pass. of **sañj** or **saj** to hang. Cp. sanga] I. to cling, to, to be attached S I.38, 111 (aor. 2 sg. sajjittho); II.228; A II.165; J I.376 (id. asajjittho); Sn 522, 536. ppr. (a)sajjamāna (un)-attached Sn 28, 466; J III.352. — 2. to hesitate J I.376 (asajjitvā without hesitation). — pp. satta¹. — Cp. abhi° & vi°.

Sajjana¹ (nt.) [fr. sṛj] decking, equipping ThA 241.

Sajjana² [sat (= sant) + jana] a good man Miln 321.

Sajjā (f.) [orig. grd. of **sad**] seat, couch Pv II.12⁸ (explⁿ at PvA 157 doubtful).

Sajjita [pp. of sajjeti] issued, sent off; offered, prepared S II.186; Vin III.137 (here in sense of "happy" =

sukhita); Miln 244 (of an arrow: sent); Mhvs 17, 7; 27, 16. — nt. offering (=upakkhaṭa) DA 1.294; PvA 107.

Sajju (adv.) [Sk. sadyaṭ, sa+dyaḥ, lit. one the same day] 1. instantly, speedily, quickly Dāvs III.37. — 2. newly, recently Dh 71 (°khīra; cp. DhA II.67).

Sajjukaŋ = **sajju**: 1. quickly Mhvs 7, 6; 14, 62. — 2. newly VvA 197.

Sajjulasa [cp. Sk. sarjarasa; see Geiger, *P.Gr.* § 19²] resin Vin I.202.

Sajjeti [Caus. of **sṛj** (sajati¹), Sk. sarjayati] to send out, prepare, give, equip; to fit up, decorate: dānaŋ to give a donation DhA II.88; pātheyyaŋ to prepare provisions J III.343; gehe to construct houses J I.18; **nāṭakāni** to arrange ballets J I.59; **yaññaŋ** to set up a sacrifice J I.336; dhammasabhaŋ to equip a hall for a religious meeting J III.342; nagaraŋ to decorate the town J V.212; paṇṇākāraŋ to send a present J III.10. — Caus. II. sajjāpeti to cause to be given or prepared J I.446; PvA 81. Cp. vissajjeti.

Sajjha (nt.) [cp. Sk. sādhya] silver D II.351 (v. l.); S V., (v. l.); A III.16. Cp. sajjhu.
 -kāra silversmith Miln 331.

Sajjhāya [cp. Sk. svādhyāya, sva+adhyāya, i. e. sa⁴+ajjhaya, cp. ajjhayana & ajjhāyaka] repetition, rehearsal, study D III.241; Vin I.133; II.194; A IV.136; S V.121; J I.116, 436; II.48; Miln 12, KhA 24; VbhA 250 sq. — °ŋ karoti to study D III.241; A III.22; J V.54.

Sajjhāyati [Denom. fr. sajjhāya, cp. BSk. svādhyāyita AvŚ I.287; II.23] to rehearse, to repeat (aloud or silently), to study J I.435; II.273; III.216; IV.64; Miln 10. — ppr. °āyanto DhA III.347; ger. sajjhāya S I.202, & sajjhāyitvā J IV.477; V.450; KhA 97. — Caus. sajjhāpeti to cause to learn, to teach J III.28 (of teacher, with adhīyati, of pupil). Caus. II. sajjhāyāpeti id. Miln 10.

Sajjhu (nt.) [cp. sajjha] silver D II.351; S V.92; J VI.48; Mhvs 19, 4; 27, 26; 28, 33.

Sañcaya [fr. saŋ+**ci**] accumulation, quantity Sn 697; It 17 (aṭṭhi°); Miln 220.

Sañcara [fr. saŋ+**car**] passage, way, medium DA I.289.

Sañcaraṇa (nt.) [fr. saŋ+**car**] wandering about, meeting, meeting-place J I.163; IV.335; Miln 359. a° impassable Miln 217.

Sañcarati [saŋ+carati] 1. to go about, to wander D I.83. — 2. to meet, unite, come together J II.36 (of the noose of a snare). — 3. to move, to rock J I.265. — 4. to pass J I.491. — Caus. °cāreti to cause to move about Miln 377, 385. — Caus. II. °carāpeti to cause to go, to emit J I.164; to make one's mind dwell on Vism 187.

Sañcaritta (nt.) [fr. saŋ+caritar] 1. going backwards & forwards, acting as go-between Vin III.137. — 2. intercourse Miln 266.

Sañcāra [saŋ+cāra] 1. going, movement, passing through Sdhp 244. — 2. passages entrance, road J I.409; II.70, 122.

Sañcalati [saŋ+calati] to be unsteady or agitated Miln 117. Caus. °cāleti to shake Vin III.127; J V.434. — pp. °calita.

Sañcalita [pp. of sañcalati] shaken Miln 224 (a°).

Sañcicca (adv.) [ger. of saŋ+cinteti; cp. BSk. sañcintya Divy 494] discriminately, purposely, with intention Vin II.76; III.71, 112; IV.149, 290; D III.133; Kvu 593; Miln 380; PvA 103.

Sañcita [pp. of sañcināti] accumulated, filled (with) J VI.249; ThA 282; Sdhp 319.

Sañcināti (& saŋcayati) [saŋ+cināti] to accumulate; ppr. °cayanto Mhvs 21, 4; aor. cini° PvA 202 (puññaŋ), 279 (pl. °cinimha). — pp. **sañcita**. — Cp. abhi°.

Sañcinteti (& °ceteti) [saŋ+cinteti] to think, find out, plan, devise means D II.180, 245 (aor. samacintesuŋ); Th I, 1103 (Pot. °cintaye); J III.438 (aor. samacetayi).

Sañcuṇṇa [saŋ+cuṇṇa] crushed, shattered Bu II.170 = J I.26.

Sañcuṇṇita [pp. of sañcuṇṇeti] crushed J II.41; Miln 188; Vism 259.

Sañcuṇṇeti [saŋ+cuṇṇeti] to crush J II.210, 387 (aor. °esi); III.175 (Pot. °cyya), 176 (ger. °etvā). — pp. °**cuṇṇita**.

Sañcetanā (f.) [saŋ+cetanā] thought, cogitation, perception, intention A II.159 (atta°, para°); D III.231 (id.); S II.11, 40, 99 (mano°); II.39 sq., 247; III.60, 227 sq.; Vbh 285; Dhs 70, 126. Sixfold (i. e. the 6 fold sensory perception, rūpa°, sadda°, etc.): D II.309; III.244; Ps I.136. Threefold (viz. kāya°, vacī°, mano°): Vism 341, 530; VbhA 144, 145.

Sañcetanika (adj.) [fr. sañcetanā] intentional Vin III.112; M III.207; A V.292 sq.; a° M I.377.

Sañcetayitatta (nt.) reflection Dhs 5, 72.

Sañceteti see °cinteti.

Sañcodita [saŋ+codita] instigated, excited PvA 5, 68, 171, 213; ThA 207.

Sañcopati [cp. Sk. copati, as ἅπαξ in Mhbh. We should expect copeti in Pāli, fr. **cup** to stir] to move, to stir; a misunderstood term. Found in aor. samacopi (so read for T. samadhosi & v. l. samañcopi) mañcake "he stirred fr. his bed" S III.120, 125; and sañcopa (pret.) J V.340 (v. l. for T. sañcesuŋ āsanā; C. explᵈ as "caliŋsu").

Sañcopana (nt.) & °ā (f.) [saŋ+copana] touching, handling Vin III.121 (ā); IV.214 (a) (= parāmasanan nāma ito c' ito ca).

Sañchanna [saŋ+channa¹] covered (with = -°) M I.124; Th I, 13; J I.201; SnA 91 (°patta full of leaves; puppha° of flowers). Often in cpd. paduma° covered with lotuses (of ponds) Pv II.1²⁰; II.12²; Vv 44¹; J I.222; V.337.

Sañchavin, M II.217, 259.

Sañchādita [pp. of sañchādeti] covered PvA 157.

Sañchindati [saŋ+chindati] to cut, destroy M III.275 (Pot. °chindeyya); A II.33 = S III.85 (ger. °chinditvā). — pp. sañchinna.

Sañchinna [pp. of sañchindati] Vin I.255 (of the kaṭhina, with samaṇḍalikata "hemmed"). Also in cpd. °patta "with leaves destroyed" is Nd² reading at Sn 44 (where T. ed. & SnA 91 read saŋsīna), as well as at Sn 64 (in similar context, where T. ed. reads sañchinna). The latter passage is explᵈ (Nd² 625) as "bahula-patta-palāsa saṇḍa-cchāya," i. e. having thick & dense foliage. The same meaning is attached to sañchinna-patta at VvA 288 (with v. l. saŋsīna!), thus evidently in sense of sañchanna. The C. on Sn 64 (viz. SnA 117) takes it as sañchanna in introductory story.

Sañjagghati [saŋ+jagghati] to joke, to jest D I.91; A IV.55, 343; DA I.256.

Sañjati is the P. correspondent of sajati¹ (**sṛj**), but Sk. **sañj** = sajjati (to hang on, cling), which at Dhtp 67 & 397 defᵈ as sanga. The Dhtp (64) & Dhtm (82) take sañj in all meanings of āliṅgana (=sajati[2]), vissagga (=sajati[1]), & nimmāna (=sajjeti).

Sañjanati [saŋ+janati] to be born; only in Caus. °janeti to cause, produce; realize Pug 16; Sdhp 564 (ger. °janayitvāna). — pp. sañjāta. See also Pass. saŋjāyati.

Sañjanana (nt.?) producing; f. °ī progenetrix (identical with taṇhā) Dhs 1059; DhsA 363.

Sañjanetar [n. ag. fr. sañjaneti] one who produces S I.191; III.66.

Sañjambhari in °ŋ karoti is not clear in derⁿ & meaning; perhaps "to tease, abuse," see D I.189 (°riyaŋ); A I.187; S II.282. Probably fr. bhṛ (Intensive jarbhṛta Vedic!) as *jarbhari. See on derⁿ Konow, *J.P.T.S.* 1909, 42; Kern, *Toev.* II.69. The C. on S II.282 (*K.S.* II.203) expl[s] as "sambharitaŋ nirantaraŋ phuṭaŋ akaŋsu, upari vijjhiŋsū ti," i. e. continually touching (or nudging) (phuṭa=phuṭṭha or phoṭita).

Sañjāta [pp. of sañjanati] having become, produced, arisen Dhs 1035 (+bhūta & other syn.). °— full of, grown into, being in a state of Sn 53 (°khandha=susaṇṭhita° SnA 103); VvA 312, 318 (°gārava full of respect), 324 (°pasāda).

Sañjāta[2] (adj.) [sa[2]+jāta] of the same origin (con-gener) J IV.134. Cp. sajāti.

Sañjāti (f.) [saŋ+jāti] birth, origin; outcome; produce D I.227; II.305.

Sañjādiya a grove, wood J V.417, 421 (v. l sañcāriya).

Sañjānana (nt.) & °ā (f.) [fr. sañjānāti] knowing, perceiving, recognition Miln 61; DA I.211; characteristic, that by which one is distinguished DhsA 321. As f. at Dhs 4; DhsA 110, 140 (trslⁿ *Expos.* 185: "the act of perceiving by noting").

Sañjānāti [saŋ+jānāti] 1. to recognize, perceive, know to be aware of Vin III.112; D II.12; M I.111, 473; S III.87; A V.46, 60, 63; J I.135; IV.194; ThA 110. — 2. to think, to suppose J II.98. — 3. to call, name, nickname D I.93; J I.148. — Aor sañjāni DA I.261; ger. saññāya J I.187; II.98; saññatvā M I.1; and sañjānitvā J I.352. — Caus. saññapeti (q. v.). — pp. saññāta.

Sañjānitatta (nt.) [fr. sañjānita, pp. Caus. of sañjānāti] the state of having perceived Dhs 4.

Sañjānetar at S III.66 read sañjanetā.

Sañjāyati [saŋ+jāyati, cp. sañjanati] to be born or produced D I.220; J II.97; aor. sañjāyi D II.209; Vin I.32; ppr. °jāyamāna J V.384.

Sañjiṇṇa [saŋ+jiṇṇa] decayed J I.503 (v. l.).

Sañjitar [n. ag. fr. sajati[1], cp. sañjati] creator, one who assigns to each his station D I.18, 221; M I.327; DA I.111 (v. l. sajjitar, cp. Sk. sraṣṭar).

Sañjīvana (adj.) [fr. saŋ+jīv] reviving ThA 181 (Ap. v. 23: putta°).

Sañjhā (f.) [cp. Sk. sandhyā] evening; only in cpds. °ātapa evening sun VvA 4, 12; °ghana evening cloud ThA 146 (Ap. v.44); Dāvs V.60.

Saññ° is frequent spelling for saŋy° (in saŋyojana=saññojana e. g.), q. v.

Saññatta[1] (nt.) [abstr. formation fr. saññā] the state of being a saññā, perceptibility S III.87.

Saññatta[2] [pp. of saññāpeti] induced, talked over Sn 303, 308.

Saññatti (f.) [fr. saññāpeti] 1. informing, convincing A I.75; S I.199; Vin II.98, 199, 307; J III.402. — 2. appeasing, pacification M I.320.

Saññā (f.) [fr. saŋ+ñā] (pl. saññāyo and saññā — e. g. M I.108) 1. sense, consciousness, perception, being the third khandha Vin I.13; M I.300; S III.3 sq.; Dhs 40, 58, 61, 113; VbhA 42. — 2. sense, perception, discernment, recognition, assimilation of sensations, awareness M I.293; A III.443 (nibbāna°); S III.87; Sn 732 (saññāya uparodhanā dukkhakkhayo hoti; expl[d] as "kāmasaññā" SnA); Miln 61; Dhs 4; DhsA 110, 200 (rūpa° perception of material qualities). — 3. consciousness D I.180 sq.; M I.108; Vbh 369 (nānatta° c. of diversity: see nānatta); Miln 159; J IV.391; is previous to ñāṇa D I.185; a constituent part of nāma S II.3, cp. Sn 779; according to later teaching differs from viññāṇa and paññā only as a child's perceiving differs from (*a*) an adult's, (*b*) an expert's Vism 436 sq.; *Dhs. trslⁿ* 7 n. 2, 17 n. 2. —nevasaññā-nâsaññā neither consciousness nor unconsciousness D III.224, 262 sq.; M I.41, 160; II.255; III.28, 44; Ps I.36; Dhs 268, 582, 1417; Kvu 202; Nett 26, 29; Vism 571. — 4. conception, idea, notion D I.28; III.289 (cp. *Dial.* III.263: "concept rather than percept"); M III.104; S I.107; Sn 802, 841; J I.368 (ambaphala saññāya in the notion or imagining of mango fruit); Vism 112 (rūpa° & aṭṭhika°). saññaŋ karoti to imagine, to think J II.71; to take notice, to mind J I.117. — 5. sign, gesture, token, mark J I.287; II.18; paṇṇa° a mark of leaves J I.153; rajjusaññā a rope used as a mark, a guiding rope, J I.287; rukkha-saññaŋ pabbata-saññaŋ karonto, using trees and hills as guiding marks J IV.91; saññaŋ dadāti to give the sign (with the whip, for the horse to start) J VI.302. — 6. saññā is *twofold*, paṭighasamphassajā and adhivacanasamphassajā i. e. sense impression and recognition (impression of something similar, "association by similarity," as when a seen person calls up some one we know), Vbh 6; VbhA 19 sq.; *threefold*, rūpasaññā, paṭighasaññā, and nānattasaññā A II.184; S II.211; cp. Sn 535; *or* kāma°, vyāpāda°, vihiŋsā° (as nānatta°) Vbh 369, cp. VbhA 499; *fivefold* (pañca vimutti-paripācaniyā saññā); anicca°, anicce dukkha°, dukkhe anatta°, pahāna°, virāga° D III.243, cp. A III.334; there are *six* perceptions of rūpa, sadda, gandha, rasa, phoṭṭhabba, and dhamma, D II.309; S III.60; the *sevenfold* perception, anicca-, anatta-, asubha-, ādīnava-, pahāna-, virāga-, and nirodha-saññā, D II.79; cp. A III.79; the *tenfold* perception, asubha-, maraṇa-, āhāre paṭikkūla-, sabbaloke anabhirata-, anicca-, anicce dukkha-, dukkhe anatta-, pahāna-, virāga-, nirodha-saññā A V.105; the *one* perception, āhāre paṭikkūlasaññā, *Cpd.* 21. — 7. *See further* (unclassified refs.): D I.180; II.277 (papañca°); III.33, 223; S II.143; A II.17; IV.312; Nd[1] 193, 207; Nett 27; Vism 111, 437, 461 sq. (in detail); VbhA 20 (pañca-dvārikā), 34; VvA 110; and on term *Cpd.* 40, 42.

-gata perceptible, the world of sense M I.38. -bhava conscious existence Vism 572; VbhA 183. -maya= arūpin M I.410 (opp. manomaya=rūpin). -vedayitanirodha cessation of consciousness and sensation M I.160, 301; III.45; A I.41; Kvu 202; S II.212. -viratta free from consciousness, an Arahant, Sn 847. -vimokkha emancipation from consciousness Sn 1071 sq.; Miln 159=Vin V.116.

Saññāṇa (nt.) [Vedic sañjñāna] 1. perception, knowledge VvA 110. — 2. token, mark J IV.301; DA I.46; Vism 244. — 3. monument Mhvs 19, 35.

Saññāta [pp. of sañjānāti] skilled M I.396.

Saññāpana (nt.) [fr. saññāpeti] convincing J V.462.

Saññāpeti [Caus. of sañjānāti] 1. to make known, to teach J I.344; Miln 45. — 2 to remonstrate with, gain over, convince D I.236; M I.397; A I.75; S IV.313; Vin I.10; II.197; Miln 316. — 3. to appease, conciliate J I.479; PvA 16. Also saññapeti J I.26, etc. — inf. saññattuŋ Sn 597. — pp. saññatta. — At J I.408 read saññāpāpetvā (instead of saññaŋ pāpetvā), or simply saññāpetvā, like the parallel text at Ud 17.

Saññāvant (adj.) [fr. saññā] having perception A II.215 = Dhs 1003.

Saññita [= saññāta; pp. of sañjānāti] so-called, named, so-to-speak Mhvs 7, 45; PvA 135; Sdhp 72, 461. See also aya under niraya.

Saññin (adj.) [fr. saññā] (f. saññinī) conscious, being aware of (-°), perceiving, having perception D I.31, 180; III.49, 111, 140, 260; S I.62; A II.34, 48, 50; III.35; IV.427; Dh 253; Nd[1] 97, 138. — ālokasaññin having a clear perception D I.71; A II.211; V.207; Sum I.211; nānatta° conscious of diversity A IV.39 sq.; paṭhavīsaññin conscious of the earth (kasiṇa), in samādhi A V.8 sq.; paṭhavisaññiniyo (fem. plur.), having a worldly mind D II.139; asubhasaññin perceiving the corruption of the world It 93; vihiŋsasaññin conscious of the trouble Vin I.7; nevasaññī-nâsaññin neither conscious nor unconscious D III.111; A II.34; Nd[1] 97, 138; It 90; DA I.119. Cp. vi°. — In composition saññi°, e. g. °gabbha animate production D I.54; DA I.163.

Saññīvāda [saññin + vāda] name of a school maintaining conscious existence after death D I.31; DA I.119; Mhbv 110.

Saṭa [most likely = Sk. śada (fall), fr. **śad** to fall; Kern *Toev.* s. v. equals it to Sk. sūta (or sṛta) of **sṛ** (or **su**) to run (to impel), as in ussaṭa and visaṭa. The Dhtm (789) gives a root **saṭ** in meaning of "visaraṇa," i. e. profusion, diffusion (cp. visaṭa)] a fall, a heap of things fallen; only in cpd. **paṇṇa°** a heap of fallen leaves M I.21 (= paṇṇa-kacavara MA I.120); J II.271.

Saṭṭha [pp. of sajati[1]] dismissed; in cpd. **-°esana** one who has abandoned all longing or research D III.269 (cp. *Dial.* III.247 "has utterly given up quests"); A II.41 (so read for saṭh°). — saṭṭha at S III.84 is to be read seṭṭha, and at S IV.298 saṭha.

Saṭṭhi (num. ord.) [cp. Sk. ṣaṣṭi: see cha] sixty D I.45; II.261; Sn 538; DhA III.412 (ekūna°). It is found mostly in the same application as cha (group-number), e. g. at J I.64 (°turiya-sahassāni); VvA 92 (id.); J I.87 (°yojana); VI.512 (°sahassa); DhA I.8, 17, 26, 131 (°sakaṭa). **-°hāyana** 60 years old (of elephant) M I.229; J II.343.

Saṭṭhuŋ at J VI.185 (taŋ asakkhi saṭṭhuŋ) is inf. of sajati[1] (**sṛj** = Sk. srasṭuŋ) to dismiss, let loose. The form has caused trouble, since the Com. explains it with gaṇhituŋ "to take." This has induced Kern (*Toev.* s. v.) to see in it a very old (even *pre*-Vedic!) form with *sāḍhuŋ as original. Evidently he derives it fr. **sah** (Epic Sk. soḍhuŋ!), as he trsl[s] it as "to master, overpower."

Saṭha (adj.) [cp. Sk. śaṭha] crafty, treacherous, fraudulent D II.258; III.246; M I.32, 153; S IV.299; A II.41; III.35; V.157; Dh 252; Vin II.89; Nd[1] 395; Miln 250; Dāvs II.88; DhA III.375; Dhtp 100 (= keṭave). — f. saṭhī Pv II.3[4]. See also **kerāṭika, samaya°, sāṭheyya.**

Saṭhatā (f.) [abstr. fr. saṭha] craft, wickedness Pug 19.

Saṭhila (adj.) [Sk. śṛthila, which also appears as sithila, e. g. Th I, 277] loose, inattentive Dh 312.

Saṭhesana see **saṭṭha.**

Saṇa (nt.) [Vedic śana; Gr. κάνναβις = Lat. cannabis; Ags haenep = E. hemp; Ger. hanf.] a kind of hemp D II.350 (v. l.); S I.115 (do.); cp. sāṇ & sāṇī.

-dhovika [perhaps (Kern's suggestion) sāṇa° (v. l.) = visāṇa°?] name of a particular kind of gambol of elephants in water M I.229, 375. Bdhgh at DA I.84 uses the obscure term sāṇa-dhovana-kiḷā to denote a trick of Caṇḍālas. But see **sandhovika.**

Saṇati [**svan**; Idg. *suenō = Lat. sono, Ags. swin music, swinsian to sing; Ohg. swan = swan] to sound, to make a noise Sn 721 (T. sanati) = Miln 414; sanate S I.7 = 203; J VI 507; ppr. saṇanto Sn 720 (T. n).

Saṇiŋ (adv.) [cp. Sk. śanaiḥ] softly, gradually Sn 350; Mhvs 25, 84.

Saṇikaŋ (adv.) [fr. last] slowly, gently, gradually D II.333; M I.120; S I.82, 203; J I.9, 292; II.103; Miln 117; DA I.197; DhA I.60, 389; VvA 36, 178.

Saṇṭha a reed (used for bow-strings) M I.429.

Saṇṭhapeti & **°ṭhāpeti** [Caus. of santiṭṭhati] 1. to settle, to establish A II.94 (cittaŋ); S IV.263; J I.225; PvA 196. — 2. to call to order D I.179 (°āp°). — 3. to adjust, fold up J I.304.

Saṇṭhahana (nt.) [fr. santiṭṭhati] recreation Vism 420 sq.

Saṇṭhāti see santiṭṭhati.

Saṇṭhāna (nt.) [fr. saŋ + **sthā**] 1. configuration, position; composition, nature, shape, form Vin II.76; M I.120 (spelt °nth°); A I.50; IV.190 (C. osakkana); Miln 270, 316, 405; J I.71, 291, 368; II.108; Vism 184, 225, 243; DhsA 321; DA I.88 (nth); SnA 464 (= linga). su° well formed Sn 28. — adj. (-°) having the appearance of megha-vaṇṇa° PvA 251; **chavi°** appearance of the skin J I.489; **vaṇṇa°** outward semblance Nett 27; J I.271; sarīra° the (material) body Vism 193. — 2. fuel J II.330 = IV.471. — 3. (usually spelt °nth°) a resting place, meeting place, public place (market) (cp. Sk. sansthāna in this meaning). At S I.201 in phrase **nadī-tīresu saṇṭhāne sabhāsu rathiyāsu** (i. e. at all public places). S I.201 reads saṇṭhāne (v. l. santhāne); cp. *K.S.* I.256 from C.: "a resting place (vissamana-ṭṭhāne) near the city gate, when market-wares had been brought down," trsl[n] "resting by the gates." This stanza is quoted at SnA 20, where the ed. prefers reading **panthāne** as correct reading (v. l. saṇṭhāne). At M I.481 (°nth°) = S II.28 (2 fr. b.), it seems to be used in the sense of "end, stopping, cessation" = A IV.190 (the editions of S and A have saṇṭhāna). At J VI.113 it is translated by "market place," the comp. **saṇṭhāna-gata** being explained by the Comm. by saṇṭhāna-mariyādaŋ gatā, but at J VI.360 **saṇṭhāna-gata** is by the English translator translated "a wealthy man" (vinicchaye **ṭhito**, Com.), which, however, ought to be "in the court house" (cp. vinicchaya-ṭṭhāna), i. e. publicly. In both places there is also v. l. santhāna-°.

Saṇṭhita [pp. of santiṭṭhati] 1. established in (-°), settled, composed Sn 330 (santi-soracca-samādhi°); Sdhp 458; su° firmly or well established Sn 755; Miln 383; in a good position, well situated DhsA 65. — 2. being composed (as), being of the nature of (-°), ullumpana-sabhāva° of a helping disposition DA I.177; PvA 35.

Saṇṭhiti (f.) [fr. santiṭṭhati] 1. stability, firmness S V.228; Dhs 11; Vism 206; DhsA 143; Sdhp 460. — 2. fixing, settling Miln 144.

Saṇḍa [dial.; Dhtm 157: gumb' attha-m-īraṇe; cp. Sk. ṣaṇḍa] a heap, cluster, multitude; a grove (vana°) D I.87; S III.108; Vin I.23; J I.134 (vana°); **satta°** teeming with beings It 21. — **Jambu°** N. of Jambudīpa Sn 352 Th I, 822 (v. l. °maṇḍa, which Kern considers to be the correct reading; see *Toev.* II.67). — **saṇḍa°-cārin** swarming D I.166 = M I.77 = A II 206.

Saṇḍāsa [saŋ+ḍaŋsa, fr. ḍasati] (long) pincers, tweezers A I.210; J I.223; III.138; used to pull out hair M II.75; Vin II.134.

Saṇṇikā (saṇikā) [cp. saṇi—Sk. sṛṇi] an elephant-driver's hook J I.445 (so read for paṇṇ°).

Saṇha (adj.) [cp. Sk. ślakṣṇa] 1. smooth, soft Vin I.202; II.151; Vv 50[18] (=mudu VvA 213); Vism 260 = KhA 59. saṇhena softly Th 1, 460. — 2. gentle, mild D II.259; Sn 853; J I.202, 376; Nd[1] 234; PvA 56, 215. Of speech (opp. pharusa harsh) M I.126; A III.196; Dhs 1343. — 3. delicate, exquisite Th 2, 258, 262, 264, 268. Cp. pari°.
-karaṇī "a wooden instrument for smoothing the ground, or a sort of trowel." Abhp 1007; J IV.250 (loc. °iyaŋ piŋsito); IV.4 (°ī viya tilāni piŋsamānā); V.271; VI.114 (asani viya viravanto °iyaŋ viya piŋsanto); cp. KhA 59; thus it seems to mean also a sort of instrument for oil-pressing, or a mortar.

Saṇhaka, at J III.394 (of hair growing white "saṇhaka-sadisā") according to Kern, *Toev*. II.69 (coarse) hempen cloth (=sāṇavāka), as indicated by v. l. sāṇalāka. Thus a der. fr. saṇa=sāṇa. Kern compares P. tuṇhīra—tūṇīra; Sk. śaṇa=śāṇaka. According to Andersen, Pāli Glossary "betelnut" (=saṇha).

Saṇheti [Caus. fr. saṇha] to brush down, smooth (kese): only as cpd. o° at Vin II.107; J IV.219.

Sata[1] (num. card.) [Vedic śataŋ; cp. Av. satəm, Gr. ἑ-κατόν, Lat. centum; Goth. hund=hundred; Idg. *kmtóm fr. dkmtóm (=decem), thus ultimately the same as dasa, i. e. decad (of tens)] a hundred, used as nt. (collect.), either -° or as apposition, viz. gāma-sataŋ a hundred(ship of) villages DhA I.180; jaṭila-satāni 100 ascetics Vin I.24; jāti° D I.13; or gāthā sataŋ 100 stanzas Dh 102.—Often in sense of "many" or "innumerable," e. g. °kaku, °raŋsi, etc.; cp. °satāni=bahūni J IV.310, 311.
-kaku having a hundred corners, epithet of a cloud A III.34=S I.100 (v. l. sattakatu) see *J.P.T.S.* 1891-93 p. 5. -patta the Indian crane (or woodpecker ?) J II.153; 388; Miln 404. -padī a centipede A II.73; III.101, 306; IV.320; V.290; Vin II.110, 148; Miln 272. -pala (Th 1, 97) see pala. -pāka (-tela) oil mixture, worth 100 pieces J IV.281; DhA II.48; III.311; see also pāka. -puñña 100, i. e. innumerable merits Vism 211. -pupphā Anethum sowa, a sort of dill or fennel J VI.537. -porisa of the height of a hundred men, extremely high, attribute of a hell Vv 52, 12 sq.; name of a hell J V.269. -mūlī Asparagus racemosus Abhp 585. -raŋsi "having 100 rays," the sun Sdhp 590; J I.44. -rasabhojana food of 100 flavours DhA III.96 (v. l. all pass. satta°) -vanka a kind of fish Abhp 672. -vallikā an under-garment, arranged like a row of jewelry Vin II.137. -sahassa one hundred thousand J II.20; Miln 88; 136; DhA II.86. -sahassima id. S II.133.

Sata[2] [pp. of sarati, of **smṛ**, cp. BSk. smṛta AvŚ I.228; II.197] remembering, mindful, conscious D I.37; II.94; III.49, 107, 222, 269; M I.520 (su-ssata & dus-sata); S IV.211; A III.169 (+sampajāna), 325; IV.311; Sn 741; Dhs 163; DA I.211. — satokārin cultivator of sati Ps I.175.

Sataka (nt.) [cp. BSk. śataka] a hundred, collection of 100 J I.74.

Satakkhattuŋ (adv.) [cp. dvi-kkhattuŋ, ti-kkhattuŋ etc.] a hundred times.

Satata (adj.) [with satrā "completely" & sadā "always" to sa° "one"; see saŋ°; lit. "in one (continuous) stretch"] continual, chronic. Only in nt. satataŋ (adv.) continually A IV.14; It 116; Sn 507; Miln 70; Pv II.8[11] (=nirantaraŋ PvA 110); III.7[10] (=sabbakālaŋ PvA 207); PvA 177; and as °- in °vihāra a chronic state of life, i. e. a behaviour remaining even & the same A II.198=D III.250, 281. Cp. sātacca.

Satadhā (adv.) [sata+dhā, cp. ekadhā, dvidhā etc.] in 100 ways, into 100 pieces D II.341.

Sati (f.) [Vedic smṛti: see etym. under sarati[2]] memory, recognition, consciousness, D I.180; II.292; Miln 77-80; intentness of mind, wakefulness of mind, mindfulness, alertness, lucidity of mind, self-possession, conscience, self-consciousness D I.19; III.31, 49, 213, 230, 270 sq.; A I.95; Dhs 14; Nd[1] 7; Tikp 61; VbhA 91; DhsA 121; Miln 37; upaṭṭhitā sati presence of mind D III.252, 282, 287; S II.231; A II.6, 218; III.199; IV.232; It 120; parimukhaŋ satiŋ upaṭṭhāpetuŋ to surround oneself with watchfulness of mind M III.89; Vin I.24; satiŋ paccupaṭṭhāpetuŋ to preserve self-possession J I.112; IV.215; kāyagatā sati intentness of mind on the body, realization of the impermanency of all things M III.89; A I.43; S I.188; Miln 248; 336; muṭṭhasati forgetful, careless D III.252, 282; maraṇasati mindfulness as to death A IV.317 sq.; J IV.216; SnA 54; PvA 61, 66. asati not thinking of, forgetfulness DhsA 241; instr. asatiyā through forgetfulness, without thinking of it, not intentionally Vin II.289[2]. sati (sammā°) is one of the constituents of the 8-fold Ariyan Path (e. g. A III.141 sq.; VbhA 120): see magga 2.
-âdhipateyya (sat°) dominant mindfulness A II.243 sq.; It 40. -indriya the sense, faculty, of mindfulness A II.149; Dhs 14. -uppāda arising, production of recollection J I.98; A II.185; M I.124. -ullapakāyika, a class of devas S I.16 sq. -paṭṭhāna [BSk. smṛty'upasthāna Divy 126, 182, 208] intent contemplation and mindfulness, earnest thought, application of mindfulness; there are *four* satipaṭṭhānas, referring to the body, the sensations, the mind, and phenomena respectively, D II.83, 290 sq.; III.101 sq., 127, 221; M I.56, 339; II.11 etc.; A II.218; III.12; IV.125 sq.; 457 sq.; V.175; S III.96, 153; V.9, 166; Dhs 358; Kvu 155 (cp. *Kvu. trsl*[n] 104 sq.); Nd[1] 14, 45, 325, 340; Vism 3; VbhA 57, 214 sq., 417. — See on term e. g. *Cpd.* 179; and in greater detail *Dial.* II.322 sq. -vinaya disciplinary proceeding under appeal to the accused monk's own conscience Vin I.325; II.79 etc.; M II.247; A I.99. -vepullappatta having attained a clear conscience Vin II.79. -saŋvara restraint in mindfulness Vism 7; DhsA 351; SnA 8. -sampajañña mindfulness and self-possession D I.70; A II.210; DA I.183 sq. -sambojjhanga (e. g. S V.90) see (sam)bojjhanga. -sammosa loss of mindfulness or memory, lack of concentration or attention D I.19; Vin II.114; DA I.113; Pug 32; Vism 63; Miln 260.

Satika (adj.) (-°) [fr. sata[1]] consisting of a hundred, belonging to a hundred; yojanasatika extending one hundred yojanas Vin II.238; vīsaŋvassasatika of hundred and twenty years' standing Vin II.303.

Satitā (f.) [abstr. formation fr. sati] mindfulness, memory DhsA 405 (-°).

Satima (adj.) [superl. form[n] fr. sata[1]] the hundredth S II.133; J I.167 (pañca°).

Satimant (adj.) [fr. sati] mindful, thoughtful, contemplative, pensive; nom. sg. satimā D I.37; S I.126; Sn 174; A II.35; Dhs 163; DhA IV.117; Pv IV.3[44]; satīmā (in verse) Sn 45; nt. satīmaŋ Sn 211; gen. satimato S I.208; satimato S I.81; Dh 24; nom. pl. satimanto D II.120; Dh 91; DhA II.170; gen. satimataŋ Dh 181; It 35; satimantānaŋ A I.24. — See also D III.77, 141, 221 sq.; A IV.4, 38, 300 sq., 457 sq.; Nd[1] 506; Nd[2] 629.

Satī (f.) [fr. sant, ppr. of as] 1. being J III.251. — 2. a good or chaste woman Abhp 237; asatī an unchaste woman Miln 122=J III.350; J V.418; VI.310.

Satekiccha (adj.) [sa³+tekiccha] curable, pardonable Miln 192, 221; Vism 425. See tekiccha.

Saterată (f.) [cp. Sk. śatahradā, śata+hrada] lightning J v.14, 203. Also as sateritā Vv 33³; 64⁴; VvA 161 (=vijjulatā), 277. As saderitā at Th 1, 260.

Satta¹ [pp. of **sañj:** sajjati] hanging, clinging or attached to Vin I.185; D II.246; Nd¹ 23, 24; Dh 342; J I.376. Cp. āsatta¹ & byāsatta.

Satta² [cp. Vedic sattva living being, satvan "strong man, warrior," fr. sant] 1. (m.) a living being, creature, a sentient & rational being, person D I.17, 34, 53, 56, 82; II.68; A I.35 sq., 55 sq.; S I.135; V.41; Vin I.5; Miln 273; Vism 310 (defⁿ: "rūp'ādisu khandhesu chandarāgena sattā visattā ti sattā," thus=satta¹); Nett 161; DA I.51, 161; VbhA 144. —naraka° a being in purgatory (cp. niraya°) Vism 500. — 2. (nt.) soul (=jīvita or viññāṇa) Pv I.8¹ (gata°=vigata-jivita PvA 40). — 3. (nt.) substance Vin I.287. nissatta non-substantial, phenomenal DhsA 38.
-āvāsa abode of sentient beings (see nava¹ 2) D III.263, 268; A V.53; Vism 552; VbhA 168. -ussada (see ussada 4) teeming with life, full of people D I.87, 111, 131. -loka the world of living creatures SnA 263, 442; Vism 205. See also sankhāra-loka. -vaṇijjā slave trade DA I.235=A III.208 (C.: manussa-vikkaya)

Satta³ [pp. of sapati to curse; Sk. śapta] cursed, sworn J III.460; V.445.

Satta⁴ (num.) [cp. Vedic sapta, Gr. ἑπτά; Av. hapta; Lat. septem, Goth. sibun=E. seven etc.] number *seven*. It is a collective and concluding (serial) number; its application has spread from the *week* of 7 days (or nights), and is based on *astronomical* conception (Babylon!), this science being regarded as *mystic*, it invests the number with a peculiar *magic* nimbus. From time-expressions it was transferred to space, esp. when originally connected with time (like satta-bhūmaka the 7-storied palace; the Vimānas with 700 towers: see vimāna 2 & 6; or the 7 great lakes: see sara³; °yojana 7 miles, cp. the 7 league-boots!). Extremely frequent in folklore and fairy tales (cp. 7 years of famine in Egypt, 7 days' festivals, dragon with 7 heads, 7 ravens, 7 dwarfs, 7 little goats, 7 years enchantment, etc. etc.). — For *time* expressions see in cpds.: °āha, °māsa, °ratta, °vassa. Cp. Sn 446 (vassāni); J II.91 (kāyā, thick masses); DA I.25 (of the Buddh. Scriptures: sattahi māsehi sangītaŋ); DhA II.34 (dhanāni), 101 (mangalā); the collective expression 7 years, 7 months, 7 days at J V.48; the 7×70 ñāṇavatthūni S II.59; and the curious enumeration of heptads at D I.54. — *Cases:* instr. sattahi D I.34; gen. sattannaŋ D I.56; loc. sattasu D II.303=M I.61.
-anga a couch with 7 members (i. e. four legs, head support, foot support, side) Vin II.149. -aṭṭha seven or eight J II.101. -āgārika a "seven-houser," one who turns back from his round, as soon as he has received alms at 7 houses D I.166. -ālopika a "seven-mouthful," one who does not eat more than 7 bits D I.166. -āha (nt.) seven days, a week of 7 days [cp. BSk. saptaka Divy 99] D II.248; Vin I.1, 139; J I.78; II.85; IV.360; V.472; VI.37; DhA I.109; VvA 63. *satta°* 7 weeks DhA I.86; cp. satta-satta-divasā J V.443. -ussada (see ussada 2) having 7 prominences or protuberances (on the body), a sign of a Mahāpurisa D III.18; III.144, 151 (i. e. on both hands, on both feet, on both shoulders, on the back). -guṇa sevenfold Mhvs 25, 36. -jaṭa with seven plaits (of hair) J V.91 (of a hunter). -tanti having 7 strings, a lute VvA 139. -tāla (-matta) (as big as) 7 palm trees DhA II.62, 100. -tiŋsa 37 (see bodhipakkhiya-dhammā). -dina a week Mhvs 11, 23. -pakaraṇika mastering the 7 books of the *Abhidhamma* J I.312; DhA III.223. -patiṭṭha sevenfold firm D II.174; Miln 282. -padaŋ for 7 steps J VI.351 (Kern, *Toev.* s. v. "unfailing"). -bhūmaka (pāsāda) (a palace) with 7 stories Mhvs 37, 11; J I.58; IV.378; DhA I.180, 239; IV.209. -māsaŋ (for) seven months PvA 20. -yojanika 7 miles in extent J V.484. -ratana the 7 royal treasures D I.88; It 15; J V.484. -ratta a week J VI.230 (dve°= a fortnight), 304; Sn 570. -vassika 7 years old Miln 9, 310; DhA II.87, 89 (sāmaṇera), 139; PvA 53 (Sankicca arahattaŋ patvā); DhA III.98 (kumāro arahattaŋ patto); J V.249. On the age of seven as that of child arahants see Mrs. Rh. D. in *Brethren* introd. xxx. -vīsati twenty seven DhA I.4.

Sattakkhattuŋ (adv.) [cp. tikkhattuŋ etc.] seven times Vin I.3; It 18; sattakkhattuparamaŋ seven times at the utmost; °parama one who will not be reborn more than seven times S II.134 sq.; A I.233, 235; IV.381; Kvu 104; Pug 15 sq.; Nett 189; KhA 187; J I.239; DhA III.61, 63.

Sattati [cp. Sk. saptati] seventy D II.256; Ap 118, 126 & passim. As sattari at S II.59; Ap 248 & passim.

Sattatta (nt.) [abstr. fr. satta²] state of having existence D I.29.

Sattadhā (adv.) [fr. satta⁴, cp. dvidhā] in seven pieces D I.94; II.235; Sn 783; J V.33, 493; DhA I.17, 41. Cp. phalati.

Sattapaṇṇi-rukkha N. of a tree Mhvs 30, 47; cp. sattapaṇṇi-guhā N. of a cave KhA 95.

Sattama¹ (adj.) [superl. fr. sant] best, excellent Sn 356; J I.233.

Sattama² (num. ord.) [fr. satta⁴] the seventh D I.89; Sn 103. — f. °mī Sn 437. Often in loc. °divase on the 7th day Sn 983; J I.395; Miln 15; PvA 6, 74. -°bhavika one who has reached the 7ᵗʰ existence (or rebirth) Kvu 475 (cp. *trslⁿ* 271⁴).

Sattarasa (num. card.) [satta⁴+rasa²=dasa] seventeen Vin I.77; IV.112 (°vaggiyā bhikkhū, group of 17).

Sattari=sattati, at S II.59 sq.

Sattali (f.) [cp. Sk. saptalā, name of var. plants, e. g. jasmine, or many-flowered nykkanthes, Halāy. 2, 52] the plantain, and its flower J IV.440 (=kadali-puppha C.; so read for kandala°); and perhaps at Th 2, 260 for pattali (q. v.), which is explᵈ as kadali(-makula) at ThA 211.

Sattava=satta² [a diaeretic sattva] J V.351. Cp. Lal. Vist. 520.

Satti¹ (f.) [fr. **śak**, cp. Vedic śakti] ability, power Dhtp 508 Usually in phrase yathā satti as much as one can do, according to one's ability Cp I.10⁶; DhA I.399; or yathā **sattiŋ** D I.102, or **y. sattiyā** DhA I.92.

Satti² (f.) [cp. Vedic śakti, orig. identical with satti¹] 1. knife, dagger, sword A IV.130; J II.153; Vism 313 (dīgha-daṇḍa° with a long handle); DhA I.189; II.134 (tikhiṇa° a sharp knife). **mukha°** piercing words J I.341. — 2. a spear, javelin S I.13; A II.117; J I.150.
-pañjara lattice work of spears D II.164. -langhana javelin dance J I.430. -simbali-vana the forest of swords (in purgatory) J V.453. -sūla a sword stake, often in simile °*ūpamā kāmā* S I.128; A III.97; Vism 341. Also N. of a purgatory J V.143 sq.

Sattika see tala°.

Sattu¹ [Vedic śatru] an enemy J V.94 (acc. pl. sattavo); Vism 234 (°nimmathana).

Sattu² [cp. Sk. śaktu] barley-meal, flour Vin II.116 (satthu); Nd¹ 372; J III.343 sq.; Pv III.1³; Dhs 646.
-āpaṇa baker's shop J VI.365. -pasibbaka flour sack; °bhasta id. J III.346.

Sattuka [fr. sattu[1]] an enemy J III.154; Mhvs 32, 18.

Sattha[1] (nt.) [cp. Vedic śastra, fr. śas to cut] a weapon, sword, knife; coll. "arms" D I.4, 56; Sn 309, 819 (expld as 3: kāya°, vacī°, mano°, referring to A IV.42, at Nd[1] 151); J I.72, 504; Pv III.10[2]; SnA 458 (°mukhena); PvA 253. Often in combn daṇḍa+sattha (cp. daṇḍa 4), coll. for "arms," Vin I.349; D I.63; A IV.249; Nd[2] 576. —satthaŋ āharati to stab oneself S I.121; III.123; IV.57 sq.
-kamma application of the knife, incision, operation Vin I.205; SnA 100. -kāraka an assassin Vin III.73. -vaṇijjā trade in arms A III.208. -hāraka an assassin Vin III.73; S IV.62.

Sattha[2] (nt.) [cp. Vedic śāstra, fr. śās to teach] a science, art, lore Miln 3; SnA 327, 447. —vāda° science of right belief SnA 540; sadda° grammar SnA 266; supina° dream-telling SnA 564.

Sattha[3] [sa[3]+attha; Sk. sārtha] a caravan D II.130, 339; Vin I.152, 292; Nd[1] 446; Dh 123 (appa° with a small c.), Miln 351.
-gamanīya (magga) a caravan road Vin IV.63. -vāsa encampment D II.340, 344. -vāsika & °vāsin caravan people J I.333. -vāha a caravan leader, a merchant D II.342; Vv 84[7] (cp. VvA 337); leader of a band, teacher; used as Ep. of the Buddha S I.192; It 80, 108; Vin I.6. In exegesis of term *Satthā* at Nd[1] 446=Nd[2] 630=Vism 208.

Sattha[4] [pp. of sāsati; śās] told, taught J II.298 (v. l. siṭṭha).

Sattha[5] (adj.) [wrong for satta=śakta] able, competent J III.173 (=samattha C.).

Sattha[6] [cp. Sk. śvasta, śvas] breathed: see vissattha.

Satthaka[1] (nt.) [fr. sattha[1]] a knife, scissors Vin II.115 (daṇḍa°, with a handle); J V.254 (as one of the 8 parikkhāras); Miln 282. aya° at J V.338 read °paṭṭaka.
-nisādana [cp. Sk. niśātana] knife-sharpening DhA I.308, cp. Miln 282 °nisāna [=Sk. niśāna]. -vāta a cutting pain A I.101=307; J III.445.

Satthaka[2] (adj.) [fr. sattha[3]] belonging to a caravan, caravan people, merchant PvA 274.

Satthar [Vedic śāstṛ, n. ag. fr. śās] teacher, master. — nom. satthā D I.49; Sn 179; acc. satthāraŋ D I.163; Sn 153, 343; instr. satthārā D I.163; instr. satthunā Mhvs 32, 19; gen. satthu D I.110; It 79; Vin I.12; gen. satthuno D II.128; Sn 547, 573. loc. satthari Dhs 1004; nom. and acc. pl. satthāro D I.230; A I.277; Miln 4; gen. pl. satthārānaŋ J I.509. — See e. g. D I.230; A I.277; Vin I.8; Th 2, 387. — The 6 teachers (as in detail at D I.52-59 & var. places) are Pūraṇa Kassapa, Makkhali Gosāla, Nigaṇṭha Nāthaputta, Sañjaya Belaṭṭhiputta, Ajita-Kesakambalī. — 5 teachers at Vin II.186; A III.123. — 3 at D I.230; A I.277. — The Master *par excellence* is the Buddha D I.110; II.128; III.119 sq.; A III.248; IV.120, 460; Sn 153, 545, 955 (see exegesis in detail at Nd[1] 446 Nd[2] 630), 1148; Vism 389, 401, 604. — gaṇa-satthar leader of a company J II.41, 72; satthāra-dassana sight of the Master SnA 49; satthu-d-anvaya successor of the M. Sn 556.

Satthi[1] (nt. & f.) [cp. Sk. sakthi] the thigh Vin II.161; Th I, 151; Vv 81[17]; J II.408; III.83; VI.528; antarā° between the thighs A II.245.

Satthika (adj.) [fr. sattha[3]] belonging to a caravan D II.344.

Satthu see sattu[2]; satthu° see satthar.

Satthuka "having a teacher," in atīta° [belonging to the *whole* cpd.] whose teacher is dead D II.154.

Satthuna [?] a friend J I.365.

Satthuvaṇṇa [satthar°+vaṇṇa] gold (lit. the colour of the Master) Vin III.238, 240.

Sathera (adj.) [sa[3]+thera] including the Theras A II.169

Sadattha [sat (=sant)+attha] the highest good, ideal D II.141; M I.4; A V.207 sq.; Dh 166; Mhvs 3, 24. It *may* be taken as sa[4]+attha (with euphonic-d-), i. e. one's own good, as it is expld by Bdhgh at DhA III.160 ("sake atthe"), & adopted in trsln at *Dial.* II.154.

Sadatthuta (adj.) [sadā+thuta] always praised J IV.101 (=nicca-pasattha C.).

Sadara (adj.) [sa[3]+dara] fearful, unhappy A II.172; M I.280, 465=D III.57 (reads dd).

Sadasa [sa+dasā] a squatting mat with a fringe Vin IV.171.

Sadassa [sat(=sant)+assa] a horse of good breed A I.289.

Sadā (adv.) [fr. saŋ°] always Sn 1041, 1087, 1119; Nd[2] 631 (where long stereotype definition); Dh 79; Pv II.8[11] (=sabbakālaŋ yāvajīvaŋ PvA 110); II.9[37] (=sabbakālaŋ divase divase sāyañ ca pāto ca PvA 127); IV.1[50].
-matta "always revelling," N. of a palace J I.363 sq (cp. Divy 603); a class of devas D II.260.

Sadisa (adj.) [sa[2]+disa=dṛśa] similar, like, equal D II.261; S III.48 sq.; A I.125=Pug 35; Vin I.8; J I.191; Dhs 116; Vism 543=VbhA 148. Cp. sādisa.

Saderita see saterita.

Sadevaka (adj.) [sa[3]+deva+ka] together with the devas, with the deva world D I.62; III.76, 135; Sn 86; Vin I.8, 11; Dh 44; DA I.174. At J I.14 sadevake (loc.) is used in the sense of "in the world of men & gods."

Sadevika (adj.) [sa[3]+devī+ka] together with his queen Mhvs 33, 70.

Sadda [cp. late Vedic śabda; BSk. śabda as *nt.* at AvŚ I.3] 1. sound, noise D I.79, 152; III. 102 sq., 146, 234, 244 sq., 269, 281; M III.56, 267; A III.30 sq.; IV.91, 248; J I.3 (*ten* sounds); Sn 71; Vism 408 (var. kinds); Dhs 621 (udaka°); DhA II.7 (udriyana°); defd at Vism 446 ("sota-paṭihanana-lakkhaṇa," etc.) & at VbhA 45 ("sappati ti saddo, udāhariyatī ti attho"). — 2. voice J II.108. — 3. word Vin I.11; It 114; DhA I.15 (itthi°); VbhA 387 (in nirutti); SnA 261, 318, 335.
-kovida a grammarian or phonetician SnA 321. -dhātu element of sound Dhs 707. -naya science of grammar, etymology KhA 107. -bheda word analysis Vism 519 sq. -vidū a grammarian SnA 169. -vedhin shooting by sound Mhvs 23, 85. -sattha science of words, grammar SnA 266. -siddhi analysis or correct formation of a word, grammatical explanation SnA 304, 551.

Saddana (nt.) [fr. śabd: see saddāyati] making a noise Dhtm 401.

Saddala (adj.) [cp. Sk. śādvala] grassy Th I, 211; J I.87; VI. 518; Miln 286; Pv II.12[10] (=taruṇa-tiṇa PvA 158).

Saddahati [Vedic śrad-dhā, only in impers. forms grd. śrad-dadhāna; pp. śrad-dhita; inf. śrad-dhā; cp. Av. zraz-dā id.; Lat. cred-(d)o (cp. "creed"); Oir. cretim to believe. Fr. Idg. *kred (=cord° heart)+*dhe, lit. to put one's heart on] to believe, to have faith D II.115; 244; S III.225; Pv II.8[3]; J V.480; DhA II.27. ppr saddahanto DA I.81; PvA 148 (a°), 151 (a°), 285; & saddahāna S I.20, 211; Sn 186; It 112. Pot. saddheyya J II.446 (=saddaheyya C.); 2nd pl. saddahetha J III 192; 3rd pl. saddheyyuŋ S II.255. At J VI.575 (Pot.) saddahe seems to be used as an exclamation in the sense of "I wonder" (cp. maññe). —saddahase at Pv IV.8[1] is to be read saddāyase (see saddāyati). — grd. saddhātabba J II.37; V.480; PvA 217; saddahātabba D II.346; saddahitabba Miln 310; saddheyya Vin III.188; *and* saddhāyitabba (*Caus.!*) PvA 109. A *Caus.* aor. 2 sg. is (mā) . . . saddahesi J VI.136[140] — ger. saddhāya J V.176 (=saddahitvā C.); inf. saddhātuŋ J V.445. — pp. (*Caus.*) saddhāyita. — Caus. II. saddahāpeti to make believe, to convince; Pot. °dahāpeyya J VI.575; Pv IV.1[25]; fut. °dahāpessati J I.294.

Saddahanā (f.) [fr. sad + dhā] believing, trusting, having faith Nd² 632; Dhs 12, 25; Nett 15, 19; DhA I.76.

Saddāyati [Denom. fr. sadda; i. e. **śabd**] cp. Epic Sk. śab dayati & śabdāyati] 1. to make a sound Miln 258; Pv IV.8[1] (saddāyase read for saddahase); IV.16[1] (id.); Ud 61 (°āyamāna noisy).— 2. to call, summon (with acc.) J III.288.

Saddita [pp. of **śabd**; cp. saddāyati] sounded, called Sdhp 100.

Saddūla [cp. Sk. śārdūla] a leopard Miln 23.

Saddha[1] (adj.) [orig. adj. of saddha², but felt to be adj. of saddhā; cp. BSk. śrāddha AvŚ I.83, 383] 1. believing faithful D I.171; S I.43; II.159 sq.; A I.150; II.164, 227 sq.; III.3 sq., 34, 182; IV.38, 145, 314 sq.; V.10 sq., 124 sq.; Sn 188, 371; Dh 8; Pv I.10[1]; IV.1[86]; DhA II.82. —as(s)addha unbelieving PvA 42, 54, 67, 243 & passim (see a°). — 2. credulous Sn 853; Dh 97.

Saddha[2] [cp. Epic Sk. & Sūtra literature śrāddha, fr. śrad-dhā] *a funeral rite* in honour of departed relatives connected with meals and gifts to the brahmins D I.97; A I.166; V.269, 273; DA I.267; saddhaŋ pamuñcati to give up offerings, to abandon Brahmanism Vin I.7; D II.39; Sn 1146. The word is n. according to Abhp and A V.269-273; loc. °e, D I.97; J II.360; kaŋ saddhaŋ (acc. in a gāthā), seems to be f.; Com. ib. 360 has saddhā-bhattaŋ, a funeral repast (v. l. saddha-°). Thus it seems to be confused with saddhā.

Saddhamma [sad(=sant) + dhamma, cp. BSk. saddharma, e. g. Jtm 224] the true *dhamma*, the best religion, good practice, the "doctrine of the good" (so Geiger, *Pali Dhamma* pp. 53, 54, q. v. for detailed discussion of the term) M I.46; S V.172 sq.; A I.69; III.7 sq., 174 sq., 435 sq.; V.169, 317; Sn 1020; Dh 38; J V.483; DhA IV.95. *Seven* saddhammas: M I.354, 356; D III.252, 282; A IV.208 sq. — Opp. a-saddhamma (q. v.); *four* a°: A II.47; eight: Vin II.202.

-garu paying homage to the true religion S I.140. -savana hearing the (preaching of the) true dhamma D III.227, 274; A I.279; II.245; IV.25 sq., 221; V.115 sq.

Saddhā (f.) [cp. Vedic śraddhā: see saddahati] faith (on term cp. Geiger, *Saŋyutta trsl*[n] II.45²) D I.63; III.164 sq.; S I.172 = Sn 76; S V.196; Dh 144; A I.150, 210; III.4 sq., 352; IV.23; V.96; Dhs 12; Miln 34 sq.; Tikp 61, 166, 277, 282. — instr. saddhāya (used as adv.) in faith, by faith in (acc. or gen.) Vin II.289 (āyasmantānaŋ), J V.176 (pabbajita); PvA 49 (kammaphalaŋ s.); or shortened to saddhā (-pabbajita) M I.123; A I.24; J I.130. The same phrase as saddhāya pabbajita at S I.120 is expl[d] as "saddahitvā" by Bdhgh (see *K.S.* I.321), thus taking it as ger.

-ânusārin walking according to faith M I.479; A I.74; Pug 15; Nett 112, 189. -indriya (saddh°) the faculty, i. e. the moral sense, of faith D III.239, 278; A II.149; S V.193, 377; Dhs 12, 62, 75; Nett 19. -cariyā living in faith Vism 101. -deyya a gift in faith D I.5; Vin I.298; IV.30; DA I.81. -vimutta emancipated through faith M I.478; A I.74, 118 sq.; Pug 15; Nett 190. -vimutti emancipation through faith Pug 15.

Saddhātar [n. ag. fr. saddahati, i. e. sad + dhātar] a believer Sdhp 39.

Saddhāyika (adj.) [fr. saddhāya, ger. of saddahati] trustworthy D II.320; A IV.109 (so read for °sika); Th 2, 43, 69.

Saddhāyita [pp. of saddahati; BSk. śraddhayita] one who is trusted; nt. that which is believed, faith Pv II.8[5]. May be misspelling for saddhāyika.

Saddhiŋ (& saddhi°) (adv.) [in form = Vedic sadhriŋ "towards *one* aim," but in meaning = Vedic sadhryak (opp. viṣvak, cp. P. visuŋ) "together." Cp. also Vedic saŋyak = P. sammā. The BSk. is sârdhaŋ, e. g. s. vihārin AvŚ II.139] together; as prep. (following the noun): in company with (*instr.*) D I.31; Vin I.32; III.188 (expl[d] as "ekato"); J I.189; II.273; DA I.35; Miln 23; also with *loc.* DA I.15; or *gen.* Vin II.154; J I.420. As adv. saddhiŋ agamāsi J I.154, cp. saddhiŋ-kīḷita J II.20.

-cara companion Sn 45, 46 (=ekato cara Nd² 633); Dh 328. -vihārika (saddhi°) co-resident, fellow-bhikkhu; pupil Vin I.45 sq.; A III.70; J I.182, 224; Vism 94; DhA II.19. -vihārin id. A II.239; III.69; J I.1; f. °vihārinī Vin IV.291.

Saddhiya (nt.) [abstr. fr. *śraddhya] only in neg. a° (q. v.).

Sadhana (adj.) [sa³ + dhana] wealthy, rich D I.73; J I.334.

Sadhamma [sa¹ + dhamma] one's own religion or faith M I.523; Sn 1020; Bu II.6 = J I.3.

Sadhammika [sa² + dhamma + ika] co-religionist D II.273.

San[1] [cp. Vedic śvā, gen. śunaḥ; Av. spā, Gr. κύων; Lat. canis, Oir. cū, Goth. hunds = hound] a dog; nom. sg. sā D I.166 = M I.77; S I.176; III.150; Kvu 336. For other forms of the same base see **suvāṇa**.

San[2] (= saŋ) acc. of sa⁴.

Sanacca (nt.) [sa³ + nacca] dancing (-party) Vin II.267.

Sanati see saṇati.

Sanantana (adj.) [for sanātana (cp. purātana); Idg. *seno = Gr. ἕνος old; Sk. sanaḥ in old times; Av. hana old, Lat. seneo, senex ("senile"), senatus; Goth. sineigs old; Oir. sen old] primeval, of old; for ever, eternal D II.240, 244; S I.189 (cp. *K.S.* I.321: porāṇaka, santānaŋ vā paṇḍitānaŋ dhamma); DhA I.51.

Sanābhika (adj.) [sa³ + nābhi + ka] having a nave (of a wheel) D II.17, 172; A II.37; at both places comb[d] with sa-nemika "with a felly" (i. e. complete).

Sanāmika (adj.) [sa³ + nāma + ika] having a name, called Bu II.194 = J I.28.

Sanidassana (adj.) [sa³ + nidassana] visible D III.217; Dhs 1087.

Sant [ppr. of atthi] 1. being, existing D I.61, 152; A I.176; It 62 sq.; Sn 98, 124. — 2. good, true S I.17; Dh 151. — *Cases*: nom. sg. m. santo Sn 98; Miln 32; Nd² 635 (=samāna); f. satī (q. v.); nt. santaŋ A V.8; PvA 192; acc. santaŋ D II.65; & sataŋ J IV.435 (opp. asaŋ); instr. satā D II.55; loc. sati D II.32; A I.176; III.338; Sn 81; Dh 146; It 85; & sante D I.61; abl. santato Nett 88; DhsA 206 sq. — pl. nom. santo M I.24; S I.71; Sn 450; It 62; Dh 151; nt. santāni D I.152; acc. sante Sn 94, 665; gen. sataŋ M I.24; S I.17; Sn 227; instr. sabbhi D II.246; S I.17, 56; Miln 221 = J V.49; Dh 151; loc. santesu. — Compar. santatara It 62; superl. sattama (q. v.).

Santa[1] [pp. of sammati] calmed, tranquil, peaceful, pure D I.12; Vin I.4; S I.5; A II.18; Sn 746; Pv IV.1[34]

(= upasanta-kilesa PvA 230); Miln 232, 409; Vism 155 (°anga; opp. oḷārik'anga); DhA II.13; III.83. — nt. peace, bliss, nibbāna S IV.370.

-indriya one whose senses are tranquil A II.38; Sn 144; Vin I.195; J I.506; **-kāya** of calmed body Dh 378; DhA IV.114. **-dhamma** peaceful condition, quietude J I.506; **-bhāva** id. Miln 265. **-mānasa** of tranquil mind Vin I.195; J I.506. **-vāsa** peaceful state DhA IV.114. **-vutti** living a peaceful life It 30, 121.

Santa[2] [pp. of sammati[2]] tired, wearied, exhausted Dh 60; J I.498; Pv II.9[36] (=parissama-patta PvA 127).

Santaka[1] (adj.) [fr. sant; cp. BSk. santaka Divy 280 etc.] 1. belonging to J I.122; nt. property J I.91, 494; DhA I.346. — 2. due to (gen.) J III.408; IV.37. — 3. (being) in the power of J IV.260 (bhaya°).

Santaka[2] (adj.) [sa[3]+antaka] limited (opp. anantika) S V.272.

Santacā (f.) [?] bark J V.202 (sattacaŋ ?).

Santajjeti [saŋ+tajjeti] to frighten, scold, menace J I.479; V.94; ThA 65; PvA 123, 195.

Santataŋ (adv.) [=satataŋ, or fr. saŋ+tan] continually, only in cpds.: °**kārin** consistent A II.187; °**vutti** of consistent behaviour A II.187; M I.339; °**sīla** steady in character M I.339.

Santatara see sant.

Santati (f.) [fr. saŋ+**tan**, lit. stretch] 1. continuity, duration, subsistence Dhs 643; Nett 79; Miln 72, 185; VbhA 8, 170, 173; VvA 25; Vism 431, 449. **citta°** continuity of consciousness Kvu 458; cp. *Cpd.* 6, 153[1], 252 sq.; **dhamma°** continuity of states Miln 40; **rūpa°** of form VbhA 21; **sankhāra°** causal connection of material things Th 1, 716. — 2. lineage Miln 160.

Santatta[1] [pp. of santappati] heated, glowing D II.335; M I.453; S I.169 (divasa°); J IV.118; Miln 325; PvA 38 (soka°).

Santatta[2] [pp. of santasati] frightened, disturbed J III.77 (= santrasta C.).

Santaneti (& °tāneti) [Caus. of saŋ+**tan**] to continue A III.96 sq.; S IV.104; Pug 66 sq.; SnA 5 (see santāyati).

Santappati [saŋ+tappati[1]] to be heated or chafed; fig. to grieve, sorrow M I.188; J III.153. — pp. **santatta**[1] — Caus. °**tāpeti** to burn, scorch, torment M I.128; S IV.56 sq. — pp. **santāpita**.

Santappita [pp. of santappeti] satisfied, pleased J II.44; Pv II.8[11] (= pīṇita PvA 110).

Santappeti [Caus. of saŋ+tappati[2]] to satisfy, please D I.109; Vin I.18; J I.50, 272. — pp. **santappita**.

Santara (adj.) [sa[3]+antara, cp. E. with-in] inside; in comp[n] °**uttara** inner & outer Vin III.214; IV.281; °**uttarena** with an inner & outer garment Vin I.298; ThA 171; °**bāhira** within & without D I.74; Dh 315; J I.125; DA I.218; DhA III.488.

Santarati [saŋ+tarati[2]] to be in haste, to be agitated; ppr. °**amāna** (°rūpa) J III.156, 172; VI.12, 451.

Santavant (adj.) [fr. santa[1]] tranquil Dh 378.

Santasati [saŋ+tasati[2]] to be frightened or terrified, to fear, to be disturbed Miln 92. ppr. **santasaŋ** J VI.306 (a°), & **santasanto** J IV.101 (a°); Pot. **santase** J III.147; V.378; ger. **santasitvā** J II.398. — pp. **santasita** & **santatta**.

Santasita [pp. of santasati] frightened Miln 92; PvA 260 (=suṭṭhu tasita).

Santāna (nt.) [fr. saŋ+**tan**] 1. spreading, ramification, tendril (valli°) KhA 48. — 2. one of the 5 celestial trees J VI.239 (°maya made of its flowers). — 3. (also m.) continuity, succession; lineage S III.143; DA I.46; DhsA 63, 217, 297; Vism 555; VbhA 164. Cp. **citta°** continuity of consciousness *Cpd.* 167[7].

Santānaka [santanā+ka] 1. (nt.) = santāna 1; VvA 94, 162 (°valli a sort of long creeper). **mūla°** a spreading root S III.155; J I.277. — 2. = santāna 2 VvA 12. — 3. (nt.) a cobweb Vin I.48. — 4. offspring S I.8.

Santāpa (adj.-n.) [fr. saŋ+**tap**] burning; heat, fire; fig. torment, torture Sn 1123 (cp. Nd[2] 636); J I.502; Miln 97, 324; VbhA 70 (various), 245 (aggi°, suriya°); Sdhp 9, 572.

Santāpita [pp. of santāpeti] heated, aglow Th 2, 504.

Santāpeti see santappati.

Santāyati [saŋ+tāyati] to preserve (connect ?) Vism 688 (better °dhāyati)=SnA 5 (reads °tāneti).

Santāraṇa (nt.) & °ī (f.) [fr. saŋ+tāreti[1]] conveying to the other shore S IV.174; M I.134. — f. santāraṇī Ap 234 (scil. nāvā).

Santāsa [saŋ+tāsa] trembling, fear, shock A II.33; S III.85; J I.274; Miln 146, 207; PvA 22.

Santāsaniya (adj.) [fr. saŋ+tāsana] making frightened, inspiring terror Miln 387.

Santāsin (adj.) [fr. santāsa] trembling, frightened Dh 351.

Santi (f.) [fr. **śam**, cp. Sk. °śānti] tranquillity, peace Sn 204; D II.157; A II.24; Dh 202.

-**kamma** act of appeasing (the gods), pacification D I.12; DA I.97. -**pada** "the place of tranquillity"; tranquil state, i. e. Nibbāna A II.18; VvA 219. -**vāda** an advocate of mental calm Sn 845 (°vada in verse); Nd[1] 203.

Santika (nt.) [sa[3]+antika] vicinity, presence; santikaŋ into the presence of, towards J I.91, 185; santikā from the presence of, from J I.43, 83, 189; santike in the presence of, before, with D I.79, 144; Dh 32; Miln 408; Sn 379; Vin I.12; S I.33; J V.467; with acc. S IV.74; with abl. Mhvs 205; nibbānasantike Dh 372; instr. santikena = by, along with J II.301 (if not a mistake instead of santikaŋ or santike ?).

-**āvacara** keeping or being near D I.206; II.139; J I.67.

Santikā (f.) [unclear in origin & meaning] a kind of game, "spellicans" (Rh. D.); (Kern: knibbelspel) D I.6; Vin II.10; III.180; DA I.85.

Santiṭṭhati [saŋ+tiṭṭhati] 1. to stand, stand still, remain, continue A IV.101 (udakaŋ = stands still), 282, 302 sq.; Pug 31; J I.26. — 2. to be established, to be put into order Vin II.11. — 3. to stick to, to be fixed or settled, to be composed D II.206; III.239 (citta); S V.321; Vin I.9, 15; It 43. — 4. to restrain oneself J I.438. — 5. to wait for (acc.) DhA I.50. — *Forms*: pres. santiṭṭhati D II.206; S III.133; saṇṭhahati J VI.160; & saṇṭhāti Pug 31; J IV.469. ppr. saṇṭhahanto Vin I.9; Pot. saṇṭhaheyya Vin II.11; S V.321. aor. saṇṭhāsi Vin I.15; saṇṭhahiŋsu (3rd pl.) S II.224. Inf. saṇṭhātuŋ J I.438; DhA I.50. — pp. **saṇṭhita** — Caus. II. **saṇṭhapeti** (& °ṭhāpeti).

Santīraṇa (nt.) [saŋ+tīraṇa] investigation, decision; as t.t. denoting a stage in the act of sense-cognition, judging an impression (see *Cpd.* 28, 40, 238) DA I.194; DhsA 264, 269, 272; Vism 459. As °ā (f.) at Nett 82, 191. -**kicca** function of judging Tikp 33; Vism 21, 454.

Santuṭṭha [pp. of santussati] pleased, happy D I.60, 71; M II.6; A II.209; IV.232 sq.; V.25, 67, 130, 154. mahā°, the greatly contented one, the Arahant DhsA 407.

Santuṭṭhi (f.) [saŋ+tuṭṭhi] satisfaction, contentment D I.71; M I.13; Sn 265; Dh 204; A II.27, 31; III.219 sq., 432 (a°); DhA IV.111.

Santuṭṭhitā (f.) [abstr. formation fr. last] state of contentment D III.115; A I.12; Pug 25; Vism 53; Dhs 1367 (a°).

Santuleyya (adj.) [metric for °tulya, grd. of saŋ+tuleti] commeasurable; neg. a° J VI.283.

Santus(s)ita [pp. of santussati] contented, pleased, happy S III.45 (°tussit' attā); Sn 1040; Dh 362 (=suṭṭhu tusita DhA IV.90); Mhbv 31 (ss).

Santussaka (adj.) [fr. santussati] content Sn 144.

Santussati [saŋ+tussati] to be contented, or pleased, or happy; ppr. °amāna Sn 42. — pp. santuṭṭha & °tusita.

Santosa [fr. saŋ+tuṣ] contentment DA I.204.

Santhata [pp. of santharati] 1. spread, strewn with (-°), covered D II.160; Vin III.32; Sn 401, 668. —dhamani°-gatta having the body strewn with veins, emaciated Vin III.146=J II.283; J I.346, 350 & passim (see dhamani). Kern, *Toev.* s. v. considers santata the right spelling. — 2. (nt.) a rug or mat Vin III.224; Vv 63[5] (=tiṇa-santharaka VvA 262).

Santhatika (adj.) [fr. santhata 2] sleeping on a rug Miln 342, 359.

Santhana (nt.) [fr. śam, cp. Sk. śāntvana] 1. appeasing Dh 275. — 2. satisfaction Vv 18[8].

Santhamati at J I.122 is to be read saṇḍhamati "to blow."

Santhambhati [saŋ+thambhati] to restrain oneself, to keep firm Sn 701 (imper. med. 2nd sg. °thambhassu); Pug 65; J I.255; III.95. — Caus. °thambheti to make stiff or rigid, to numb J I.10.

Santhambhanā (f.) & **°thambhitatta** (nt.) [abstr. fr. santhambhati] stiffening, stiffness, rigidity Dhs 636; DhsA 324; J I 10 (a-santhambhana-bhāva).

Santhara [fr. saŋ+stṛ] a couch or mat Vin II.162; A I.277; Ap 97 (tiṇa°).

Santharaka = santhara; only as tiṇa° made of grass Vin I.24; M I.501; J I.360; VvA 262.

Santharaṇaka (adj.) [fr. santharati] spreading, strewing; °vāta a wind which strews things about SnA 67.

Santharati [saŋ+tharati] to spread, strew D II.84. — pp. santhata. — Caus. santhāreti Mhvs 29, 12. — Caus. II. santharāpeti to cause to be spread Vin IV.39; Mhvs 29, 9.

Santhariŋ (adv.) [fr. santhara] by way of spreading; in sabba° so that all is spread, prepared D II.84; cp. Vin I.227, 384.

Santhava [fr. saŋ+stu, cp. santhuta] acquaintance, intimacy S I.17; Sn 37, 168, 207, 245; J I.158; II.27, 42, 180; Dhs 1059; DhsA 364; DhA I.235. nom. pl. santhavāni Sn 844=S III.9; J IV.98. -°jāta having become acquainted, an acquaintance Nd[1] 198. —a°-vissāsin intimate without being acquainted A III.136.

Santhavana (nt.) [fr. saŋ+thavati] acquaintance DhsA 364.

Santhāgāra [Sk. sansthāgāra] a council hall, a mote hall D I.91; II.147; A II.207; M I.228, 353, 457; III.207; DA I.256; J IV.72, 147; Vin I.233; VvA 298; DhA I.347. Cp. saṇṭhāna 3.

Santhāna see saṇṭhāna.

Santhāra [saŋ+thāra] spreading, covering, floor(ing) S I 170; Vin II.120 (3 kinds of floors: iṭṭhakā°, silā°, dāru°, i. e. of tiles, flags, wood); A I.136 (paṇṇa°); J VI.24 (id.); J I.92; Ps I.176. — 2. (cp. paṭi°) friendly welcome A I.93 (āmisa° & dhamma°).

Santhāraka [santhāra+ka cp. BSk. sanstāraka MVastu III.272] a spread, cover, mat Vin II.113 (tiṇa°), 116.

Santhuta (adj.) [saŋ+thuta] acquainted, familiar J I.365; III.63 (cira°); V.448 (so read for santhata); Sdhp 31 Neg. a° J III.63, 221; VI.310. Cp. santhava.

Santhutika (adj.) [fr. santhuta] acquainted Vism 78.

Sanda[1] [cp. Sk. sāndra] 1. (adj.) thick, dense; in -°cchāya giving dense shade S IV.194; J I.57, 249; DA I.209 — (2) (thick) wood, forest; in -°vihāra dwelling in the wood, life as a hermit Th 1, 688.

Sandati [syand; Dhtp 149: passavane] to flow D II.128, 129 (aor. sanditthha); J I.18; VI.534 (v. l. sikandati = siyandati ?); Pv II.10[4] (=pavatteti PvA 143). — Caus. sandāpeti to cause to flow Miln 122. — pp. sanna. — Cp. vissandati & vissandaka.

Sandana[1] (nt.) trappings D II.188 (read sandāna ?).

Sandana[2] [cp. Vedic syandana] a chariot Mhvs 21, 25; Dpvs 14, 56; Vv 64[2]; J IV.103; V.264; VI.22.

Sandamānikā (f.) [fr. syand] a chariot Vin III.49; IV.339; DA I.82; KhA 50; Vism 255.

Sandambhita [fr. Sk. sandarbhati] is Kern's proposed reading for santhambhita at J VI.207.

Sandassaka [fr. sandassati, Caus. of sandissati] instructing M I.145; A II.97; IV.296; S V.162; It 107; Miln 373.

Sandassana showing J I.67.

Sandahati [saŋ+dahati[1]] to put together, to connect, to fit, to arrange J IV.336; Mhvs VII.18; ppr. med. sandahamāna DhsA 113; ger. sandahitvā J IV.336; & sandhāya lit. after putting on J IV.258 (the arrow on to the bow); fig. with reference to, concerning M I.503; J I.203, 274; II.177; PvA 87, 89, 110; towards J I.491; III.295. pp. sandhīyate [& sandhiyyate] to be put together, to be self-contained Pug 32; to be connected SnA 376, 572; to reflect upon, to resent Sn 366; to be reconciled J II.114. — pp. saŋhita.

Sandahana (nt.) [fr. saŋ+dhā] applying, placing (an arrow) on the string Miln 352.

Sandāna (nt.) [saŋ+dāna, fr. dā to bind: see dāma], a cord, tether, fetter D II.274; Th 1, 290; Dhp 398; Sn 622; J II.32; Ud 77 (text sandhāna); DhA IV.161.

Sandāleti [saŋ+dāleti] to break; ger. sandālayitvāna Sn 62.

Sandiṭṭha [pp. of sandissati] seen together, a friend J I.106, 442; Vin III.42; yathāsandiṭṭhaŋ, where one's friends live D II.98; S V.152.

Sandiṭṭhi (f.) [fr. saŋ+dṛś] the visible world, worldly gain D III.45, 247; M I.43; Sn 891; Vin II.89; Nd[1] 288, 300 · °parāmāsin infected with worldliness M I.97.

Sandiṭṭhika [cp. BSk. sandṛṣṭika Divy 426] visible; belonging to, of advantage to, this life, actual D I.51; II.93, 217; III.5; M I.85, 474; A I.156 sq.; II.56, 198; S I.9, 117, IV.41, 339; Sn 567, 1137; Vism 215 sq. — As sandiṭṭhiyā (f) at J VI.213

Sandita [fr. saŋ + **dā**: see sandāna] bound, tied, Th 1, 290 (diṭṭhi-sandāna°).

Sandiddha [saŋ + diddha] smeared, indistinct, husky Vin II.202; DA I.282.

Sandiyyati & **sandīyati** [saŋ + diyyati(= dīyati) = Sk. dīyate of dyati, i. e. **dā**[2] to cut: see dātta] to be vexed, to resent S II.200 sq.; J VI.570 (spelt wrongly sandhiyati; C. expl[s] as "manku hoti").

Sandissati [saŋ + dissati] to be seen together with, to be engaged in, or to tally, agree with, to live conformably to (loc., e. g. dhamme) D I.102; II.75; S V.177; Sn 50; D II.127; Nett 23; ppr. a-saŋdissamāna invisible Dāvs IV.30; Caus. saŋdasseti to teach, instruct D I.126; II.95; Vin I.18; to compare, verify, D II.124; ppr. sandassiyamāna D II.124; J VI.217 (sunakhesu sandissanti, i. e. they are of no more value).

Sandīpeti [saŋ + dīpeti] to kindle J V.32.

Sandesa [Sk. sandeśa] news, message Mhvs 18, 13.

Sandeha [saŋ + deha] 1. accumulation; the human body Dh 148. — 2. doubt Miln 295.

Sandosa [saŋ + dosa] pollution, defilement M I.17; A III.106, 358; V.292; Sn 327.

Sandhana (nt.) [saŋ + dhana] property, belongings M II.180.

Sandhanta [pp. of sandhamati] blown, smelted (of gold), A I.253.

Sandhamati [saŋ + dhamati] to blow, to fan J I.122. — pp. sandhanta.

Sandhātar [saŋ + dhātar] one who puts together, a conciliator D I.4; III.171; M I.345; A II.209; Pug 57.

Sandhāna (nt.) [fr. saŋ + **dhā**] 1. uniting, conciliation, friendship DA I.74; DhsA 113. — 2. bond, fetter Ud 77 (read sandāna ?).

Sandhāpana (nt.) [fr. sandhāpeti, Caus. of sandahati] combination VvA 349.

Sandhāya see sandahati.

Sandhāraka (adj.) [fr. sandhāreti] checking, restraining Vism 205.

Sandhāraṇa (nt.) [fr. sandhāreti] checking Miln 352.

Sandhāreti [saŋ + dhāreti] 1. to hold, bear, carry J III.184. — 2. to hold up, support J IV.167. — 3. to curb, restrain, check Vin II.212; J II.26, 59. —dussandhāriya difficult to keep back J III.340.

Sandhāvati [saŋ + dhāvati] to run through, to transmigrate D I.14; A II.1; S III.149; J I.503; aor. sandhāvissaŋ Dh 153 = J I.76 (= apar' âparaŋ anuvicariŋ DhA III.128).

Sandhi (m. & f.) [fr. saŋ + **dhā**] 1. union, junction Miln 330 (of 2 roads); Bdhgh on S II.270 (between 2 houses). — 2. breach, break, hole, chasm D II.83 = A V.195; Th 1, 786; J V.459. āloka° a window Vin II.172; sandhiŋ chindati to make a break, to break into a house D I.52; DA I.159. — 3. joint, piece, link J II.88; Vism 277 (the 5, of kammaṭṭhāna); Mhvs 33, 11; 34, 47; applied to the joints of the body Vism 185 (the 14 mahā°); DhsA 324. — 4. connection, combination VbhA 191 (hetuphala° & phalahetu° etc.). — 5. euphonic junction, euphony, "sandhi" SnA 76. See pada°. — 6. agreement Mhvs 9, 16.

-cheda (1) housebreaking J I.187 sq.; II.388. — (2) one who has brought rebirths (= paṭisandhi) to an end Dh 97; DhA II.187; III.257. -chedaka one who can cut a break, an underminer J VI.458. -bheda(ka) causing discord J III.151. -mukha opening of a break (made by burglars) into a house Th 1, 786; PvA 4. -samala (-sankaṭīva) refuse heap of a house-sewer (cp. *K.S.* II.181, 203) D II.160; M I.334 = S II.270.

Sandhika (adj.) (-°), in pañca° having 5 links or pieces Vism 277.

Sandhīyati see sandahati.

Sandhunāti [saŋ + dhunāti] to shake D II.336.

Sandhūpeti [saŋ + dhūpeti] to fumigate S III.89; Ps II.167. As sandhūpāyati to cause thick smoke or steam thickly, at Vin I.225; Sn p. 15 (= samantā dhūpāyati SnA 154).

Sandhovati [saŋ + dhovati] to clean A I.253.

Sandhovika [fr. sandhovati] washing; kaṇṇa-sandhovikā khiḍḍā ear-washing sport or gambol (of elephants, with piṭṭhi° etc.) A V.202. So probably for saṇadhovika at M I.229, 375. Cp. sāṇadhovana (?).

Sanna[1] [pp. of sīdati] sunk Dh 327.

Sanna[2] [pp. of sandati] flown J VI.203 (dadhi°).

Sannakaddu [lexicogr. Sk. sannakadru] the tree Buchanania latifolia Abhp 556.

Sannata [pp. of saŋ + **nam**, cp. sannāmeti] 1. bent down, low J VI.58 (opp. unnata). — 2. bent, prepared J V.215 (C. suphassita).

Sannaddha [pp. of sannayhati] 1. fastened, bound, D II.350 (susannaddha); Miln 339. — 2. put on, clothed (with) Pv IV.1[36] (°dussa). — 3. armed, accoutred S II.284; J I.179; Dh 387; DhA IV.144; PvA 154 (°dhanu-kalāpa).

Sannayhati [saŋ + nayhati] to tie, bind, fasten, to arm oneself J I.129; to array, arm D II.175; Vin I. 342; to arrange, fit D I.96; J I.273; aor. sannayhi D I.96; inf. sannayhituŋ J I.179; ger. sannayhitvā D II.175; J II.77; & sannahitvā J I.273.

Sannāmeti [Caus. of saŋ + **nam**] to bend M I.365, 439, 450, 507 = S IV.188 (kāyaŋ sannāmeyya—i. e. to writhe). Cp. *Cpd.* 162 n. 5 ("strengthen" ?).

Sannāha [fr. sannayhati] 1. dressing, fastening together PvA 231. — 2. armour, mail S V.6; J II.443; Th. 1, 543; J I.179.

Sannikāsa (adj.) [saŋ + nikāsa] resembling, looking like J III.522; V.87 = VI.306; V.169 (C. dassana); VI.240, 279.

Sannikkhepana (nt.) [saŋ + nikkhepana] elimination VbhA 355.

Sanniggaṇhāti [saŋ + niggaṇhāti] to restrain S I.238.

Sannighāta [saŋ + nighāta] concussion, knocking against each other Dhs 621.

Sannicaya [saŋ + nicaya] accumulation, hoarding A I.94; II.23; Dh 92; Vin II.95; IV.243; DhA II.171; A IV.108; KhA 62 (lohita).

Sannicita [saŋ + nicita] accumulated, hoarded Miln 120.

Sanniṭṭhāna (nt.) [saŋ + niṭṭhāna] 1. conclusion, consummation, J II.166. — 2. resolve J I.19; 69; 187; IV.167; Vin I.255 sq. — 3. ascertainment, definite conclusion, conviction, J VI.324; Vism 43.

Sannitāḷeti [saŋ + nitāḷeti] to strike J V.71.

Sannitodaka (nt.) [fr. saŋ + ni + **tud**] "pricking," instigating, jeering D I.189; A I.187; S II.282.

Sannidhāna (nt.) [saŋ + nidhāna) lit. "putting down together," proximity Dāvs v.39.

Sannidhi [saŋ + nidhi] putting together, storing up D I.6; Sn 306, 924; Nd[1] 372; -kāra storing D I.6; -kāraka, storing up, store M I.523; Vin I.209; IV.87; D III.235; A III.109; IV.370. -kata stored up Vin II.270; put by, postponed Vin I.254.

Sannipatati [saŋ + nipatati] to assemble, come together J I.167; pp. °ita. Caus. sannipāteti to bring together, convoke D II.76; Miln 6; Caus. II. sannipātāpeti to cause to be convoked or called together J I.58, 153, 271; III.376; Vin I.44; III.71.

Sannipatita [pp. of °nipatati] come together D I.2; II.76.

Sannipāta [fr. sannipatati] 1. union, coincidence S IV.68 sq.; Miln 60, 123 sq.; Nett 28. — 2. assemblage, assembly, congregation D II.5; Miln 7. — 3. union of the humours of the body Miln 303. — 4. collocation Dh 352.

Sannipātika (adj.) [fr. last] resulting from the union of the humours of the body A II.87; V.110; S IV.230; Miln 135, 137, 302, 304.

Sannibha (adj.) [saŋ + nibha] resembling D II.17; Sn 551; J I.319.

Sanniyojeti [saŋ + niyojeti] to appoint, command Mhvs 5, 34.

Sanniyyātana (nt.) [saŋ + niyyātana] handing over, resignation DA I.232.

Sannirata (adj.) [saŋ + nirata] being (quite) happy together J V.405.

Sannirumbhati (°rundhati) [saŋ + nirumbhati] to restrain, block, impede; ger. sannirumhitvā J I.109, 164; II.6; VvA 217. sannirumbhitvā J I.62; II.341. sannirujjhitvā Vism 143; Pot. sannirundheyya M I.115. — pp. sanniruddha Vism 278.

Sannirumhana (nt.) [fr. last] restraining, checking, suppression J I.163; DA I.193; as °bhana at VbhA 355.

Sannivaṭṭa [=saŋ + nivatta] returning, return Vin I.139 sq.

Sannivasati [saŋ + nivasati] to live together, to associate A I.78; pp. sannivuttha.

Sannivāreti [saŋ + nivāreti] to restrain, check; to keep together M I.115; Th 2, 366.

Sannivāsa [saŋ + nivāsa] association, living with; community A I.78; II.57; D III.271; Dh 206; J IV.403; loka-sannivāsa the society of men, all the world J I.366; II.205.

Sannivuttha [pp. of sannivasati] living together (with), associating A IV.303 sq.

Sannivesa [saŋ + nivesa] preparation, encampment, settlement ThA 257.

Sannivesana (nt.) [saŋ + nivesana] position, settlement; pāṭiekka-° private, separate J I.92.

Sannisajjā (f.) [saŋ + nissajjā] meeting-place Vin I.188; II.174 = III.66; sannisajja-ṭṭhāna (n.) the same Vin III.287.

Sannisinna [pp. of sannisīdati] 1. sitting down together D I.2; II.109; Vin II.296; J I.120. — 2. (having become) settled, established Vin II.278 (°gabbhā pregnant).

Sannisīdati [saŋ + nisīdati] 1. (lit.) to sink down, to settle Miln 35. — 2. (fig.) to subside, to become quiet M I.121; S IV.196; A II.157. — Caus. sannisādeti to make quiet, to calm M I.116; A II.94. — Caus. II. sannisīdāpeti to cause to halt J IV.258. — pp. sannisinna.

Sannissayatā (f.) [saŋ + nissayatā] dependency, connection Nett 80.

Sannissita [saŋ + nissita, cp. BSk. sanniśrita] based on, connected with, attached to Vism 43, 118, 120, 554 (viññāṇa is "hadaya-vatthu°"; cp. VbhA 163).

Sannihita [saŋ + nihita; cp. sannidhi] 1. put down, placed Miln 326. — 2. stored up Th 2, 409; ThA 267.

Sannīta [pp. fr. sanneti] mixed, put together, kneaded Mhvs 29, 11 & 12.

Sanneti [fr. saŋ + neti] to mix, knead D I.74 (Pot. sanneyya); III.29; Vin I.47 (grd. °netabba); M I.276; S II.58 sq.; J VI.432. — pp. sannīta.

Sapajāpatika (adj.) 1. with Pajāpati. The passage under pajāpati 1 was distorted through copyist's default. It should read: "only in one formula, with Inda & Brahmā, viz. devā sa-indakā sa-brahmakā sa-pajāpatikā D II.274 (without sa-brahmakā); S III.90 = A V.325. Otherwise sapajāpatika in sense of foll. Also at VbhA 497 with Brahmā." — 2. with one's wife Vin I.23; IV.62; J I.345.

Sapati [śap, cp. Dhtp 184 "akkose"] to swear, curse S I.225; J V.104, 397; Mhvs 25, 113; VvA 336. — pp. satta[3].

Sapatikā (adj.) having a husband, a woman whose husband is alive J VI.158; PvA 86.

Sapatī (f.) having the same husband; a rival wife, a co-wife Pv I.6[6]; II.3[2].

Sapatta [Sk. sapatna] hostile, rival Th 2, 347; ThA 242; sapattarājā a rival king J I.358; II.94; III.416; asapatta without enmity Sn 150; sapatta (m) a rival, foe, It 83; A IV.94 sq.; J I.297.

Sapattaka (adj.) [fr. last] hostile, full of enmity D I.227.

Sapattabhāra [sa[3] + patta[1] + bhāra] with the weight of the wings, carrying one's wings with oneself D I.71; M I.180, 268; A II.210; Pug. 58.

Sapattika (nt.) the state of a co-wife Th 2, 216; ThA 178. — Kern, *Toev.* s.v. proposes reading sā°.

Sapattī (f.) [Sk. sapatnī] a co-wife D II.330; J I.398; IV.316, 491; Th 2, 224; DhA I.47. asapatti without any co-wife S IV.249.

Sapatha [fr. śap] an oath Vin I.347; J I.180, 267; III.138; SnA 418.

Sapadānaŋ (adv.) [fr. phrase sa-padānaŋ-cārikā; i. e. sa[2] + *gen. pl.* of pada (cp. gimhāna). Weber (*Ind. Str.* III.398) suggests sapadā + naŋ, sapadā being an instr. by-form of sapadā, and naŋ an enclitic. Trenckner (*Miln.* p. 428) says sapadi + ayana. Kern (*Toev.* II.73) agrees on the whole, but expl[s] padānaŋ as pad'āyanaŋ] "with the same steps," i. e. without interruption, constant, successive (cp. Lat. stante pede & Sk. adv. sapadi at once). (1) lit. (perhaps a later use) of a *bird* at J V.358 (s. sāliŋ khādanto, without a stop); of a *lion* at Miln 400 (sapadāna-bhakkha). (2) appl[d] in phrase sapadānaŋ carati to go on uninterrupted alms-begging Vin IV.191; S III.238; Sn 413; J I.66; Pv IV.3[44]; VvA 121; and in phrases sapadāna-cārikā J I.89; °cārika (adj.) Vin III.15; °cārin M I.30; II.7; Sn 65; Nd[2] 646. Also as adj. sapadāna (piṇḍapāta) Vin II.214.

Sapadi (adv.) [sa[2] + adv. form[n] fr. pada] instantly, at once Dāvs I.62.

Sapariggaha (adj.) [sa³+pariggaha] 1. provided with possessions D I.247; Sn 393. — 2. having a wife, married J VI.369.

Saparidaṇḍā (f.) a cert. class of women, the use of whom renders a person liable to punishment Vin III.139 = A V.264 = M I.286.

Sapallava (adj.) [sa³+pallava] with the sprouts VvA 173.

Sapāka [san+pāka; cp. Sk. śvapāka] "dog-cooker," an outcast or Caṇḍāla J IV.380. Cp. sopāka.

Sappa [cp. Sk. sarpa, fr. sṛp; "serpent"] a snake M I.130; A III.97, 260 sq.; Sn 768; J I.46, 259, 310, 372; V.447 (kaṇha°); Nd¹ 7; DA I.197; SnA 13. Often in *similes*, e. g. Vism 161, 587; KhA 144; SnA 226, 333. -°potaka a young snake Vism 500; -°phaṇa the hood of a snake KhA 50. — Cp. **sappin.**

Sappaccaya (adj.) [sa³+paccaya] correlated, having a cause, conditioned D I.180; A I.82; Dhs 1083.

Sappañña (adj.) [sa³+pañña] wise M I.225; Sn 591; often as sapañña It 36; Sn 90; J II.65.

Sappaṭigha (adj.) [sa³+paṭigha] producing reaction, reacting D III.217; Dhs 597, 617, 648, 1089; DhsA 317; Vism 451.

Sappaṭipuggala [sa³+paṭipuggala] having an equal, comparable, a friend M I.27.

Sappaṭibhāga (adj.) [sa³+paṭibhāga] 1. resembling, like D II.215; J I.303; Pug 30 sq.; Miln 37. — 2. having as (equal) counterparts, evenly mixed with M I.320 (kaṇhasukka°); Miln 379 (id.).

Sappaṭissa (adj.) [sa+paṭissā, cp. BSk. sapratīśa Divy 333, 484] reverential, deferential It 10; Vin I.45; Vv 84⁴¹ (cp. VvA 347). See also **gārava.**

Sappaṭissava (adj.) [sa+paṭissava] deferential, respectful DhsA 125, 127 = J I.129, 131; -tā deference, reverence Dhs 1327 = Pug 24.

Sappati [sṛp, cp. Vedic sarpati, Gr. ἕρπω, Lat. serpo; Dhtp 191 "gamana"] to creep, crawl: see saŋ°.

Sappadesa (adj.) [sa³+padesa] in all places, all round M I.153.

Sappana (nt.) [fr. sappati] gliding on DhsA 133.

Sappāṭihāriya (adj.) [sa³+pāṭihāriya] accompanied by wonders D I.198; S V.261; Ud 63.

Sappāṭihīrakata (adj.) [sa³+pāṭihīra+kata] made with wonders, substantiated by wonders, substantiated, well founded D I.198; III.121 ("has been made a thing of saving grace" *Dial.* III.115, q. v.).

Sappāṇaka (adj.) [sa³+pāṇa+ka] containing animate beings Vin III.125; J I.198.

Sappāya (adj.) [saŋ+pā (=pra+ā)+i, cp. pāya. The corresponding BSk. form is sāmpreya (=saŋ+pra+i, with guṇa), e. g. AvŚ I.255; III.110] likely, beneficial, fit, suitable A I.120; S III.268; IV 23 sq., 133 sq. (Nibbāna° paṭipadā); J I.182, 195; II.436 (kiñci sappāyaŋ something that did him good, a remedy); Vin I 292, 302; Miln 215 (sappāyakiriyā, giving a drug). nt something beneficial, benefit, help Vism 34, 87 (°sevin); VbhA 265 (various), 271 (°kathā). — Ten sappāyas & 10 asappāyas at DhsA 168. — **sappāyâsappāyaŋ** what is suitable, and what not J I.215, 471; used as the last part of a compound, meaning what is suitable with reference to: senāsanasappāya (nt.) suitable lodgings J 215.

Sappāyatā (f.) [abstr. fr. sappāya] agreeableness, suitability, convenience Vism 79, 121 (a°), 127.

Sappi (nt.) [Vedic sarpis] clarified butter, ghee D I.9, 141, 201; A I.278; A II.95, 207 (°tela); III.219; IV.103; Sn 295 (°tela). Dhs 646; J I.184; II.43; IV.223 (°tela); Vin I.58, etc. -°maṇḍa [cp. BSk. sarpimaṇḍa Divy 3 etc.] the scum, froth, cream of clarified butter, the best of ghee D I.201; A II.95; VvA 172; Pug 70; its tayo guṇā Miln 322.

Sappin (adj.-n.) [fr. sappati] crawling, creeping; moving along: see pīṭha°. — (f.) sappinī a female snake J VI.339 (where the differences between a male and a female snake are discussed).

Sappītika (adj.) [sa³+pīti+ka] accompanied by the feeling of joy, joyful A I.81; J I.10; Vism 86 (opp. nippītika).

Sappurisa [sat (=sant)+purisa] a good, worthy man M III.21, 37; D III.252 (the 7 s°-dhammā), 274, 276, 283; A II.217 sq., 239; Dhs 259 = 1003; Vin I.56; Dh 54; Pv II.9⁸; II.9⁴⁵; IV.1⁸⁷; J I.202; equal to **ariya** M I.8; S III.4; asappurisa = anariya SnA 479. **sappurisatara** a better man S V.20.

Saphala (adj.) [sa³+phala] bearing fruit, having its reward Dh 52.

Saphalaka (adj.) [sa³+phalaka] together with his shield Mhvs 25, 63.

Sabala [Vedic śabala (e. g. A.V. 8, 1, 9) = κέρβερος, Weber, *Ind. Stud.* II.297] spotted, variegated Sn 675; Vism 51; VvA 253; name of one of the dogs in the Lokantara hell J VI.106, 247 (Sabalo ca Sāmo ca). asabala, unspotted D II.80.

-**kārin** acting inconsistently A II.187.

Sabba (adj.) [Vedic sarva = Av. haurva (complete); Gr. ὅλος ("holo-caust") whole; Lat. solidus & soldus "solid," perhaps also Lat. salvus safe] whole, entire; all, every D I.4; S IV.15; Vin I.5; It 3; Nd² s. v., nom. pl. sabbe Sn 66; gen. pl. sabbesaŋ Sn 1030. — nt. **sabbaŋ** the (whole) world of sense-experience S IV.15, cp. M I.3. — At Vism 310 "**sabbe**" is defined as "anavasesa-pariyādānaŋ." In compⁿ with *superlative* expressions sabba° has the meaning of "(best) of all," quite, very, nothing but, all round; entirely: °**bāla** the greatest fool D I.59; °**paṭhama** the very first, right in front PvA 56; °**sovaṇṇa** nothing but gold Pv I.2¹; II.9¹¹; °**kaniṭṭha** the very youngest PvA 111; °**atthaka** in every way useful; °**sangāhika** thoroughly comprehensive SnA 304. — In connection with *numerals* **sabba°** has the *distributive* sense of "of each," i. e. so & so many things of each kind, like °**catukka** (with *four* of each, said of a gift or sacrifice) J III.44; DhA III.3; °**aṭṭhaka** (dāna) (a gift consisting of 8 × 8 things) Miln 291. See detail under **aṭṭha** B 1. a. — °**soḷasaka** (of 16 each) DhA III.3; °**sata** (of 100 each) DhA II.6. — *Cases adverbially:* instr. **sabbena** sabbaŋ altogether all, i. e. with everything [cp. BSk. sarvena sarvaŋ Divy 39, 144, 270; 502] D II.57; PvA 130; 131. — abl. **sabbato** "all round," in every respect Pv I.11¹; J VI.76; & **sabbaso** altogether, throughout D I.34; Sn 288; Dh 265; PvA 119; Nd¹ 421; DhA IV.100. — *Derivations*: 1. **sabbattha** everywhere, under all circumstances S I.134; Dh 83; Sn 269; Nd 133; PvA 1, 18, 107; VbhA 372 sq. °**kaŋ** everywhere J I.15, 176, 172; Dāṭh V.57. — 2. **sabbathā** in every way; sabbathā sabbaŋ completely D II.57; S IV.167. — 3. **sabbadā** always Sn 174, 197, 536; Dh 202; Pv I.9¹ (= sabbakālaŋ C.); I.10¹⁴ (id.). sabbadā-cana always It 36. — 4. **sabbadhi** (fr. Sk. *sarvadha = viçvadha, Weber, *Ind. Str.* III.392) everywhere, in every respect D I.251; II.186; Sn 176; Dh 90; also sabbadhi Sn 952, 1034; Vin I.38; VbhA 377; Vism 308 (= sabbattha); Nd¹ 441, 443.

-atthaka concerned with everything, a do-all J II.30; 74; DhA II.151 (mahāmatta). — profitable to all Miln 373 (T. ṭṭh). of kammaṭṭhāna SnA II.54; Vism 97. **-atthika** always useful Miln 153. **-âbhibhū** conquering all Sn 211; Vin I.8. **-otuka** corresponding to all the seasons D II.179; Pv IV.12²; Sdhp 248. **-kammika** (amacca) (a minister) doing all work Vism 130. **-kālaŋ** always: see **sadā**. **-ghasa** all-devouring J I.288. **-ji** all-conquering S IV.83. **-(ñ)jaha** abandoning everything S II.284; Sn 211; Dh 353 = Vin I.8. **-ññu** omniscient M I.482; II.31, 126; A I.214; Miln 74; VbhA 50; SnA 229, 424, 585; J I.214; 335; °tā (f.) omniscience Pug 61; 103; J I.2, 14; Nett 61, 103; also written **sabbaññūtā**; **sabbaññutā-ñāna** (nt.) omniscience Nett 103; DA I.99; VbhA 197. Also written **sabbaññū°**, thus J I.75; **-dassāvin** one who sees (i.e. knows) everything M I.92. **-byohāra** business, intercourse Ud 65; see **saŋvohāra**. **-bhumma** universal monarch J VI.45. **-vidū** all wise Sn 177, 211; Vin I.8; Dh 353. **-saŋharaka** a kind of perfume "eau de mille fleurs" J VI.336. **-sādhāraṇa** common to all J I.301 sq.

Sabbatthatā the state of being everywhere; **sabbatthatāya** on the whole D I.251; II.187; M I.38; S IV.296; A III.225; V.299, 344. Expl^d at Vism 308 (with tt).

Sabbassa (nt.) [sarvasva] the whole of one's property J III.105; V.100 (read: sabbasaŋ vā pan'assa haranti); °-haraṇa (nt.) confiscation of one's property J III.105; V.246 (v. l.); sabbassaharaṇadaṇḍa (m.) the same J IV.204 (so read instead of sabbappaharaṇa). At some passages sabba (nt.) "all," seems to be used in the same sense, esp. gen. sabbassa—e. g. J III.50; IV.19; V.324.

Sabbāvant (adj.) [cp. BSk. sarvāvant Divy 294, 298, 352] all, entire D I.73, 251; III.224; A III.27; V.299 sq., 344 sq.

Sabbha see a°.

Sabbhin see a°.

Sabrahmaka (adj.) [sa³ + brahma + ka] including the Brahma world D I.62; III.76, 135; A I.260; II.70; S V.423; Vin I.11; DA I.174.

Sabrahmacarin (adj.-n.) [sa³ + brahmacārin] a fellow student D II.77; III.241 sq., 245 sq., 101; A II.97; Sn 973; VbhA 281.

Sabhaggata (adj.) [sabhā + gata] gone to the hall of assembly A I.128; Sn 397; Pug 29.

Sabhā (f.) [Vedic sabhā, cp. *K.Z.* IV.370] 1. a hall, assembly-room D II.274; A I.143; S I.176; J I.119; 157, 204. — 2. a public rest-house, hostelry J I.302. dhamma° chapel J VI.333.
 -gata = sabhaggata S V.394; M I.286.

Sabhāga (adj.) [sa² + bhāga] common, being of the same division Vin II.75; like, equal, similar Miln 79; s. āpatti a common offence, shared by all Vin I.126 sq.; vīthisabhāgena in street company, the whole street in common J II.45; opp. visabhāga unusual J I.303; different Vism 516; Miln 79.
 -ṭṭhāna a common room, a suitable or convenient place J I.426; III.49; V.235. **-vuttin** living in mutual courtesy, properly, suitably Vin I.45; J I.219; a-sabhāgavuttin J I.218; sabhāgavuttika Vin II.162; A III.14 sq.; a-sabhāgavuttika ibid.

Sabhājana [Dhtp 553: pīti-dassanesu] honouring, salutation Miln 2.

Sabhāya (nt.) = sabhā Vin III.200.

Sabhāva [sa⁴ + bhāva] 1. state (of mind), nature, condition Miln 90, 212, 360; PvA 39 (ummattaka°), 98 (santa°), 219. — 2. character, disposition, behaviour PvA 13, 35 (ullumpana°), 220 (lokiya°). — 3. truth, reality, sincerity Miln 164; J V.459; V.198 (opp. musā vāda); J VI.469; **sabhāvaŋ** sincerely, devotedly J VI.486.
 -dhamma principle of nature J I.214; **-dhammatta** = °dhamma Vism 238. **-bhūta** true J III.20.

Sabhoga¹ (adj.) [sa³ + bhoga] wealthy D I.73.

Sabhoga² [sa⁴ + bhoga] property, possession Miln 139.

Sabhojana (adj.-nt.) [sa³ + bhojana] sharing food (?) Vin IV.95; Sn 102.

Sama¹ [fr. *śam*: see sammati¹] calmness, tranquillity, mental quiet Sn 896. **samaŋ carati** to become calm, quiescent J IV.172. Cp. °cariyā & °cārin.

Sama² [fr. *śram*: see sammati²] fatigue J VI.565.

Sama³ (adj.) [Vedic sama, fr. sa²; see etym. under saŋ°] 1. even, level J I.315; III.172; Mhvs 23, 51. **samaŋ** karoti to level Dh 178; SnA 66. Opp. **visama**. — 2. like, equal, the same D I.123, 174; S I.12; Sn 90, 226, 799, 842; It 17, 64; Dh 306; Miln 4. The compared noun is put in the *instr.*; or precedes as first part of cpd. — 3. impartial, upright, of even mind, just A I.74, 293 sq.; Sn 215, 468, 952. — 4. sama°, foll. by *numerals*, means "altogether," e. g. °tiŋsa thirty altogether Bu 18, 18. — 5. Cases as *adv.*: instr. samena with justice, impartially (= dhammena *K.S.* I.321) Dh 257; J I.180; acc. **samaŋ** equally D II.166; together with, at, D II.288; Mhvs 11, 12.
 -cāga equally liberal A II.62. **-jana** an ordinary man, common people M III.154 = Vin I.349. **-jātika** of the same caste J I.68. **-jīvitā** regular life, living economically A IV.281 sq. **-tala** level, even J I.7; Pv IV.12¹ (of a pond). **-dhāraṇa** equal support or sustenance SnA 95. **-dhura** carrying an equal burden, equal J I.191; **asamadhura** incomparable Sn 694 sq.; J I.193. But **sama-dhura-ggahaṇa** "complete imperiousness" VbhA 492 (see yugaggāha). **-vāhita** evenly borne along (of equanimity) DhsA 133. **-vibhatta** in equal shares J I.266. **-sama** exactly the same D I.123; II.136; Pug 64; Miln 410; DA I.290. **-sīsin** a kind of puggala, lit. "equal-headed," i. e. one who simultaneously attains an end of craving and of life (cp. PugA 186. The expl^n in *J.P.T.S.* 1891, 5 is wrong) Pug 13; Nett 190. **-sūpaka** with equal curry (when the curry is in quantity of one-fourth of the rice) Vin IV.190.

Samaka (adj.) [cp. BSk. samaka Divy 585] equal, like, same Miln 122, 410; of the same height (of a seat) Vin II.169. samakaŋ (adv.) equally Miln 82.

Samakkhāta [saŋ + akkhāta] counted, known Sdhp 70, 458.

Samagga (adj.) [saŋ + agga] being in unity, harmonious M II.239; D III.172; A II.240; V.74 sq.; plur. = all unitedly, in common Vin I.105; J VI.273¹. A I.70 = 243; Sn 281, 283; Dh 194; Th 2, 161; ThA 143; J I.198, 209; samaggakaraṇa making for peace D I.4 = A II.209 = Pug 57; DA I.74; samagganandin, samaggarata, and samaggārāma, rejoicing in peace, delighting in peace, impassioned for peace D I.4 = A II.209 = Pug 57; DA I.74; samaggavāsa dwelling in concord J I.362; II.27. — **samaggi-karoti** to harmonize, to conciliate D III.161. — Cp. **sāmaggī** etc.

Samaggatta (nt.) [abstr. fr. samagga] agreement, consent Vin I.316.

Samangitā (f.) [abstr. fr. foll.] the fact of being endowed or connected with (-°) J III.95 (paraloka°); VbhA 438 (fivefold: āyūhana° etc.).

Samangin (adj.) [saŋ + angin] endowed with, possessing Pug 13, 14; J I.303; Miln 342; VbhA 438. — samangibhūta, possessed of, provided with D I.36; A II.125; Sn 321; Vin I.15; DA I.121; **samangi-karoti** to provide with J VI.266, 289, 290 (cp. VI.323: akarī samangiŋ).

Samacariyā [sama[1] + cariyā] (f.) living in spiritual calm, quietism A I.55; S I.96, 101 sq.; It 16, 52; Dh 388; Miln 19; J VI.128; DhA IV.145.

Samacāga [sama[3] + cāga] equally liberal A II.62.

Samacārin (śama-) living in peace M I.289.

Samacitta possessed of equanimity A I.65; IV.215; SnA 174 (°paṭipadā-sutta).

Samacchati [saŋ + acchati] to sit down together J II.67 (samacchare); IV.356; VI.104, 127.

Samacchidagatta (adj.) [sam + ā + chida + gatta] with mangled limbs Sn 673.

Samajja (nt.) [cp. Epic Sk. samāja (fr. saŋ + aj) congregation, gathering, company] a festive gathering, fair; a show, theatrical display. Originally a mountain cult, as it was esp. held on the mountains near Rājagaha. — J II.13; III.541; VI.277, 559; S V.170; DA I.84; DhA IV.59; DhsA 255. — On character and history of the festival see Hardy, *Album Kern* pp. 61-66. — gir-agga-samajjaŋ mountain fair Vin II.107, 150; IV.85, 267, 360; DhA I.89, 113. samajjaŋ karoti or kāreti to hold high revel J VI.383.
-âbhicaraṇa visiting fairs D III.183. **-ṭṭhāna** the place of the festival, the arena, Vin II.150; J I.394; **-dāna** giving festivals Miln 278; **-majjhe** on the arena S IV.306 sq.; J III.541; **-maṇḍala** the circle of the assembly J I.283 sq.

Samajjhagaŋ (B °-guŋ) aor. from sam-adhi-gā. (See samadhigacchati.)

Samañcati [sam + añc] to bend together Vin IV.171, 363.

Samañcara [sama[1] + cara] pacified, calm S I.236.

Samañcinteti to think S I.124; see sañcinteti.

Samaññā (f.) [saŋ + aññā] designation, name D I.202; II.20; M III.68; S II.191; Sn 611, 648; J II.65; Dhs § 1306; loka° a common appellation, a popular expression D I.202.

Samaññāta [saŋ + aññāta] designated, known, notorious S I.65; Sn 118, 820; Nd[1] 153; Vin II.203.

Samaṇa [BSk. śramaṇa, fr. **śram**, but mixed in meaning with **śam**] a wanderer, recluse, religieux A I.67; D III.16, 95 sq., 130 sq.; S I.45; Dh 184; of a non-Buddhist (tāpasa) J III.390; an edifying etymology of the word DhA III.84: "samita-pāpattā s.," cp. Dh 265 "samitattā pāpānaŋ 'samaṇo' ti pavuccati"; four grades mentioned D II.151; M I.63; compare Sn 84 sq.; the state of a Samaṇa is attended by eight sukhas J I.7; the Buddha is often mentioned and addressed by non-Buddhists as Samaṇa: thus D I.4, 87; Sn p. 91, 99; Vin I.8, 350; Samaṇas often opposed to **Brāhmaṇas**: thus, D I.13; It 58, 60; Sn, p. 90; Vin I.12; II.110; **samaṇabrāhmaṇā**, Samaṇas and Brāhmaṇas quite generally: "leaders in religious life" (cp. *Dial.* II.165) D I.5; II.150; A I.110, 173 sq.; It 64; Sn 189; Vin II.295; samaṇadhammaŋ the duties of a samaṇa A III.371; J I.106, 107, 138; pure-samaṇa a junior who walks before a Bhikkhu Vin II.32; pacchāsamaṇa one who walks behind Vin I.186; II.32; A III.137. — **samaṇī** a female recluse S I.333; ThA 18; J V.424, 427; Vin IV.235. — **assamaṇa** not a true samaṇa Vin I.96.
-uddesa a novice, a sāmaṇera D I.151; M III.128; S V.161; Vin IV.139; A II.78; III.343. Cp. BSk. śramaṇoddeśa Divy 160. **-kuttaka** (m.) who wears the dress of a Samaṇa Vin III.68 sq. (= samaṇa-vesa-dhārako, Bdhgh ib. p. 271).

Samaṇaka [samaṇa + ka] a contemptible (little) ascetic, "some sort of samaṇa" D I.90; M II.47, 210; Sn p. 21; Miln 222; DA I.254. At A II.48 samaṇaka is a slip for sasanaka. Cp. muṇḍaka in form & meaning.

Samaṇḍalīkata [sa + maṇḍala + kata] hemmed Vin I.255 (kaṭhina).

Samatā [fr. sama[3]] equality, evenness, normal state Vin I.183; A III.375 sq.; Miln 351.

Samatikkama (adj.) [saŋ + atikamma] passing beyond, overcoming D I.34; II.290; M I.41, 455; Vin I.3; J V.454; Vism 111.

Samatikkamati [saŋ + atikkamati] to cross over, to transcend D I.35; to elapse Mhvs 13. 5; ger. samatikkamma D I.35; M 41; pp. samatikkanta crossed over, or escaped from S III.80; Dh 195.

Samatigganhāti [saŋ + ati + grh] to stretch over, rise above, to reach beyond J IV.411 (ger. samatiggayha).

Samatittha (adj.) [sama[3] + tittha] with even banks (of a pond) J V.407.

Samatitthika (adj.) [sama[3] + tittha + ika] even or level with the border or bank, i. e. quite full, brimful D I.244; II.89; M I.435; II.7 = Miln 213; S II.134; V.170; J I.400; J I.235, 393; Miln 121; Vism 170 (pattaŋ °tittikaŋ pūretvā; v. l. °titthikaŋ); A III.403; Vin I.230; IV.190; often written °tittika and °tittiya. [The form is probably connected with samaicchia—i. e. samaitthia (*samatisthita) in the Deśināmamālā VIII.20 (Konow). Compare, however, Rhys Davids' *Buddhist Suttas*, p. 178[1]; °-aŋ buñjāmi Miln 213; "I eat (only just) to the full" (opp. to bhiyyo bhuñjāmi) suggests the etymology: sama-titti + ka. Kern, *Toev.* s. v. as above.]

Samatimaññati [saŋ + atimaññati] to despise (aor.) samatimaññi Th 2, 72.

Samativattati [saŋ + ativattati] to transcend, overcome Sn 168, cp. Nd[1] 10.

Samativijjhati [saŋ + ativijjhati] to penetrate Dh 13 = Th 1, 133.

Samatta[1] (nt.) [abstr. fr. sama[3]] equality A III.359; Mhvs 3, 7; equanimity, justice A I.75.

Samatta[2] [cp. Sk. samāpta, pp. of saŋ + āp] 1. accomplished, brought to an end A II.193; Sn 781 = paripuṇṇa Nd[1] 65. — 2. [cp. Sk. samasta, pp. of saŋ + as to throw, cp. BSk. samasta, e. g. Jtm XXXI.90] complete, entire, perfect Miln 349; Sn 881; 1000; Nd[1] 289, 298. samattaŋ completely S V.175; accomplished, full Sn 889.

Samattha (adj.) [cp. Sk. samartha, saŋ + artha] able, strong J I.179; 187; SnA 143.

Samatthita (adj.) [cp. Sk. samarthita, saŋ + pp. of arthayati] unravelling Miln 1.

Samatthiya (adj.) [fr. samattha] able Sdhp 619.

Samatha [fr. **śam**, cp. BSk. śamatha] 1. calm, quietude of heart M I.33; A I.61, 95; II.140; III 86 sq. (ceto°), 116 sq., 449; IV.360; V.99; D III.54, 213, 273; DhA II.177; S IV.362; Dhs 11, 15, 54; cessation of the Saŋkhāras S I.136; III.133; A I.133; Sn 732; Vin I.5. — 2. settlement of legal questions (adhikaraṇa) Vin II.93; IV.207; cp. DhsA 144; s. paṭivijjhati Pts I.180
-yānika who makes quietude his vehicle, devoted to quietude, a kind of Arahant; cp. Geiger, *Saŋyutta trsl.* II.172. **-vipassanā** introspection ("auto-hypnosis" *Cpd.* 202) for promoting calm [cp. śamatha-vipaśyanā Divy 95] S V.52; A II.157; DhA IV.140; also separately "calm & intuition," e. g. M I.494.

Samadhigacchati [saŋ + adhigacchati] to attain Th 1, 4; aor. samajjhagā It 83; 3rd pl. samajjhagaŋ S 1.103.

Samadhigaṇhāti [saŋ + adhigaṇhāti] 1. to reach, to get, obtain; ger. samadhiggayha M 1.506; II.25; S 1.86 = It 16. — 2. to exceed, surpass, to overcome, to master J VI.261 (pañhaŋ samadhiggahetvā). Often confounded with samatigaṇhāti.

Samadhosi various reading S III.120 sq.; IV.46; the form is aor. of saŋdhū. See sañcopati.

Samana (nt.) [fr. **śam**] suppression Mhvs 4, 35.

Samanaka (adj.) [sa^3 + mana + ka] endowed with mind A II.48 (text, samaṇaka); S 1.62.

Samanantara (adj.) [saŋ + anantara] immediate; usually in abl. (as adv.); samanantarā immediately, after, just after D II.156; Vin 1.56; rattibhāga-samanantare at midnight J 1.101.

-paccaya the relation of immediate contiguity Tikp 3, 61 sq.; Dukp 26; Vism 534.

Samanukkamati [saŋ + anukkamati] to walk along together J III.373.

Samanugāhati [saŋ + anugāhati] to ask for reasons, to question closely D 1.26; M 1.130; A V.156 sq.; ppr. med. samanuggāhiyamāna being pressed M 1.130; A V.156; Vin III.91.

Samanujānāti [saŋ + anujānāti] to approve; samanujānissanti (fut. 3 pl.) M 1.398; S IV.225; pp. samanuññāta approved, allowed Mhvs 8, 11; aor. 1 sg. samanuññāsin J IV.117 (= samanuñño āsiŋ Com. ib. 117^{15}).

Samanuñña (adj.) [= next] approving D III.271; A II.253; III.359; V.305; S 1.1, 153; IV.187; J IV.117.

Samanuññā (f.) [fr. samanujānāti] approval S 1.1; M 1.359.

Samanupassati [saŋ + anupassati] to see, perceive, regard D 1.69, 73; II.198; M 1.435 sq.; II.205; Pot. Vin II.89; ppr. °passanto J 1.140; ppr. med. °passamāno D II.66; inf. °passituŋ Vin 1.14; rūpaŋ attato samanupassati to regard form as self S III.42.

Samanupassanā (f.) [fr. last] considering S III.44; Nett 27.

Samanubandhati [saŋ + anubandhati] to pursue Mhvs 10, 5.

Samanubhāsati [saŋ + anubhāsati] to converse or study together D 1.26, 163; M 1.130; A 1.138; V.156 sq; Vin III.173 sq.; IV.236 sq; DA 1.117.

Samanubhāsanā (f.) [fr. last] conversation, repeating together Vin III.174 sq.; IV.236 sq.

Samanumaññati [saŋ + anumaññati] to approve; fut. 3 pl. °maññissanti M 1.398; S IV.225; aor. 3 pl. °maññiŋsu J IV.134.

Samanumodati [saŋ + anumodati] to rejoice at, to approve M 1.398; S IV.225; Miln 89.

Samanuyuñjati [saŋ + anuyuñjati] to cross-question D 1.26, 163; M 1.130; A 1.138; V.156; DA 1.117.

Samanussarati (saŋ + anussarati] to recollect, call to mind S IV.196; Vin II.183.

Samanta (adj.) [saŋ + anta "of complete ends"] all, entire Sn 672; Miln 3. occurs usually in oblique cases, used adverbially, e. g. acc. samantaŋ completely Sn 442; abl. samantā (D 1.222; J II.106; Vin 1.32) & samantato (M 1.168 — Vin 1.5; Mhvs 1, 29; Vism 185; and in definitions of prefix pari° DA 1.217; VvA 236; PvA 32); instr. samantena (Th 2, 487) on all sides, everywhere, anywhere; also used as prepositions; thus, samantā Vesāliŋ, everywhere in Vesāli D II.98; samantato nagarassa all round the city Mhvs 34, 39; samāsamantato everywhere DA 1.61.

-cakkhu all-seeing, an epithet of the Buddha M 1.168 = Vin 1.5; Sn 345, etc.; Miln 111; Nd^1 360. -pāsādika all-pleasing, quite serene A 1.24; °kā Buddhaghosa's commentary on the Vinaya Piṭaka DA 1.84; -bhaddakatta complete auspiciousness, perfect loveliness SnA 444; VbhA 132. -rahita entirely gone J 1.29. -veda one whose knowledge (of the Veda) is complete J VI.213.

Samandhakāra [saŋ + andhakāra] the dark of night Vin IV.54; DhA II.94; S III.60.

Samannāgata (adj.) [saŋ + anvāgata] followed by, possessed of, endowed with (instr.) D 1.50; 88 Vin 1.54; Sn p. 78, 102, 104. SnA 177 (in expl^n of ending "-in"), 216 (of "-mant"); PvA 46, 73. — nt. abstr. °annāgatatta PvA 49.

Samannāneti [samanvā + nī] to lead, conduct properly, control, pres. sam-anv-āneti M III.188; ppr. °annānayamāna M 1.477.

Samannāhata [saŋ + anvāhata] struck (together), played upon D II.171.

Samannāharati [saŋ + anu + āharati; cp. BSk. samanvāharati] 1. to concentrate the mind on, to consider, reflect D II.204; M 1.445; A III.162 sq., 402 sq.; S 1.114. — 2. to pay respect to, to honour M II.169; Vin 1.180.

Samannāhāra [saŋ + anu + āhāra] concentration, bringing together M 1.190 sq.; DA 1.123; Miln 189.

Samannesati [saŋ + anvesati] to seek, to look for, to examine D 1.105; S III.124; IV.197; Miln 37; DA 1.274. pres. also samanvesati S 1.122.

Samannesanā (f.) [fr. last] search, examination M 1.317.

Samapekkhaṇa (nt.) considering; a° S III.261.

Samapekkhati [saŋ + apekkhati] to consider, ger. ekkhiya Sdhp 536; cp. samavekkh°.

Samappita [pp. of samappeti] 1. made over, consigned Dh 315; Sn 333; Th 2, 451. — 2. endowed with (-°), affected with, possessed of J V.102 (kaṇṭakena); Pv IV.1^6 (= allīna PvA 265); PvA 162 (soka-salla°-hadaya); Vism 303 (sallena). — yasabhoga° possessed of fame & wealth Dh 303; dukkhena afflicted with pain Vv 52^3; pañcehi kāmaguṇehi s. endowed with the 5 pleasures of the senses D 1.36, 60; Vin 1.15; DA 1.121.

Samappeti [saŋ + appeti] to hand over, consign, commit, deposit, give Mhvs 7, 72; 19, 30; 21, 21; 34, 21; Dāvs II.64. — pp. samappita.

Samabbhāhata [saŋ + abbhāhata] struck, beaten (thoroughly) Vism 153; DA 1.140.

Samabhijānāti [saŋ + abhijānati] to recollect, to know J VI.126.

Samabhisāta joyful Th 2, 461.

Samabhisiñcati [saŋ + abhisiñcati] to inaugurate as a king Mhvs 4, 6; V.14.

Samaya [cp. Sk. samaya, fr. saŋ = i. See also samiti] congregation; time, condition, etc. — At DhsA 57 sq we find a detailed expl^n of the word samaya (s-sadda), with meanings given as follows: (1) samavāya ("harmony in antecedents" trsl^n), (2) khaṇa (opportunity), (3) kāla (season), (4) samūha (crowd, assembly), (5) hetu (condition), (6) diṭṭhi (opinion), (7) paṭilābha (acquisition), (8) pahāna (elimination), (9) paṭivedha (penetration). Bdhgh illustrates each one with fitting examples; cp. DhsA 61. — We may group as follows: 1. coming together, gathering; a crowd, multitude D I.178 (°pavādaka debating hall); II.254 sq.; Miln 257; J I.373; PvA 86 (=samāgama). samayā in a crowd Pv III.3[4] (so read for samayyā; PvA 189 "sangamma"). — 2. consorting with, intercourse Miln 163; DhA I.90; sabba° consorting with everybody J IV.317. — 3. time, point of time, season D I.1; Sn 291, 1015; Vin I.15; VbhA 157 (maraṇa°); Vism 473 (def.); — samayā samayaŋ upādāya from time to time It 75. Cases adverbially: ekaŋ samayaŋ at one time D I.47, 87, 111; tena samayena at that time D I.179; DhA I.90. aparena s. in course of time, later PvA 31, 68; yasmiŋ samaye at which time D I.199; DhsA 61. ekasmiŋ samaye some time, once J I.306. paccūsa° at daybreak PvA 38; aḍḍharatti° at midnight PvA 155; cp. ratta°. — 4. proper time, due season, opportunity, occasion Sn 388; Vin IV.77; Bu II.181; Mhvs 22, 59; VbhA 283 sq.; aññatra samayā except at due season Vin III.212; IV.77; samaye at the right time J I.27. — asamaya inopportune, unseasonable D III.263, 287. — 5. coincidence, circumstance M I.438. akkhara° spelling DhA I.181. — 6. condition, state; extent, sphere (cp. def[n] of Bdhgh, above 9); taken dogmatically as "diṭṭhi," doctrine, view (equal to above def[n] 6) It 14 (imamhi samaye); DhA I.90 (jānana°); Dāvs VI.4 (°antara var. views). bāhira° state of an outsider, doctrine of outsiders, i. e. brahmanic DhA III.392, cp. brāhmaṇānaŋ samaye DA I.291; ariyānaŋ samaye Miln 229. — 7. end, conclusion, annihilation Sn 876; °vimutta finally emancipated A III.173; V.336 (a°); Pug 11; cp. DhsA 57. — Pp. abhi°.

-vasaṭha at A II.41 is to be read as samavasaṭṭha, i. e. thoroughly given up. Thus Kern, *Toev.* The same passage occurs at D III.269 as samavaya-saṭhesana (see under saṭha).

Samara [sa+mara] battle Dāvs IV.1

Samala (adj.) [BSk. samala] impure, contaminated Vin I.5; samalā (f.) dustbin S II.270 (=gāmato gūthanikkhamana-magga, i. e sewer *K.S.* II.203); see sandhi°.

Samalankaroti [saŋ+alankaroti] to decorate, adorn Mhvs 7, 56; °kata pp. Dāvs V.36; °karitvā J VI.577.

Samavaṭṭhita ready Sn 345 (°-ā savanāya sotā)

Samavattakkhandha (adj.) [sama+vatta+kh., but BSk. sasaŋvṛtta°] having the shoulders round, one of the lakkhaṇas of a Buddha D II.18; III.144, 164; *Dial.* II.15: "his bust is equally rounded."

Samavattasaŋvāsa [sama+vatta[1]+saŋvāsa] living together with the same duties, on terms of equality J I.236.

Samavadhāna (nt.) concurrence, co-existence Nett 79.

Samavaya annihilation, termination (?) see samaya (cpd.) & saṭha.

Samavasarati of a goad or spur Th 2, 210. See samosarati.

Samavāpaka (nt.) [sama+vāpaka, cp. vapati[1]] a storeroom M I.451.

Samavāya (m.) coming together, combination S IV.68; Miln 376; DhsA 57, 196; PvA 104; VvA 20, 55. samavāyena in common VvA 336; khaṇa-s° a momentary meeting J I.381.

Samavekkhati [saŋ+avekkhati] to consider, examine M I.225; A II.32; It 30.

Samavekkhitar [fr. last] one who considers It 120.

Samavepākin (adj.) [sama+vepākin, cp. vepakka] promoting a good digestion D II.177; III.166; M II.67; A III.65 sq., 103, 153; V.15.

Samavossajjati [read saŋvossajjati!] to transfer, entrust D II.231.

Samavhaya [saŋ+avhaya] a name Dāvs V.67.

Samasāyisuŋ (aor.) J III.201 (text, samāsāsisuŋ, cp. *J.P.T.S.* 1885, 60; read taŋ asāyisuŋ).

Samassattha [saŋ+assattha[2]] refreshed, relieved J III.189

Samassasati [saŋ+assasati] to be refreshed J I.176; Caus. samassāseti to relieve, refresh J I.175.

Samassāsa [saŋ+assāsa] refreshing, relief DhsA 150 (expl[n] of passaddhi).

Samassita [saŋ+assita] leaning towards Th I, 525.

Samā (f.) [Vedic samā] 1. a year Dh 106; Mhvs 7, 78. — 2. in agginisamā a pyre Sn 668, 670.

Samākaḍḍhati [saŋ+ākaḍḍhati] to pull along; to entice; ger. °iya Mhvs 37, 145.

Samākiṇṇa [saŋ+ākiṇṇa] covered, filled S I.6; Miln 342.

Samākula (adj.) [saŋ+ākula] 1. filled, crowded B II.4 = J I.3; Miln 331, 342. — 2. crowded together Vin II.117. — 3. confused, jumbled together J V.302.

Samāgacchati [saŋ+āgacchati] to meet together, to assemble Bu II.171; Sn 222; to associate with, to enter with, to meet, D II.354; Sn 834; J II.82; to go to see Vin I.308; to arrive, come Sn 698; aor. 1 sg. °gañchiŋ D II.354; 3rd °gacchi Dh 210; J II.62; aor. 2 sg. °gamā Sn 834; ger. °gamma B II.171 = J I.26; ger. °gantvā Vin I.308; pp. samāgata.

Samāgata [pp. of samāgacchati] met, assembled Dh 337; Sn 222.

Samāgama [saŋ+āgama] meeting, meeting with, intercourse A II.51; III.31; Miln 204; cohabitation D II.268; meeting, assembly J II.107; Miln 349; DhA III.443 (three: yamaka-pāṭihāriya°; dev'orohaṇa°; Gangārohana°).

Samācarati [saŋ+ācarati] to behave, act, practise M II.113.

Samācāra [saŋ+ācāra] conduct, behaviour D II.279; III.106, 217; M II.113; A II.200, 239; IV.82; Sn 279; Vin II.248; III.184.

Samātapa [saŋ+ātapa] ardour, zeal A III.346.

Samādapaka [fr. samādapeti; cp. BSk. samādāpaka Divy 142] instructing, arousing M I.145; A II.97; IV.296, 328; V.155; S V.162; Miln 373; It 107; DhA II.129.

Samādapana (nt.) instructing, instigating M III.132.

Samādapetar adviser, instigator M I.16.

Samādapeti [saŋ+ādapeti, cp. BSk. samādāpayati Divy 51] to cause to take, to incite, rouse Pug 39, 55; Vin I.250; III.73; DA I.293, 300; aor. °dapesi D II.42, 95, 206; Miln 195; Sn 695; ger. °dapetvā D I.126; Vin I.18; ger. samādetvā (sic) Mhvs 37, 201; ppr. pass. °dapiyamāna D II.42.

Samādahati [saŋ+ādahati[1]] to put together S I.169; jotiŋ s. to kindle a fire Vin IV.115; cittaŋ s. to compose the mind, concentrate M I.116; pres. samādheti Th 2, 50; pr. part. samādahaŋ S V.312; ppr. med. samādahāna S I.169; aor 3rd pl. samādahaŋsu D II.254. Pass. samādhiyati to be stayed, composed D I.73; M I.37; Miln 289; Caus. II. samādahāpeti Vin IV.115. — pp. samāhita.

Samādāna 1. taking, bringing; asamādānacāra (m.) going for alms without taking with one (the usual set of three robes) Vin I.254. — 2. taking upon oneself, undertaking, acquiring M I.305 sq.; A I.229 sq.; II.52; J I.157, 219; Vin IV.319; KhA 16, 142. kammasamādāna acquiring for oneself of Karma D I.82; A III.417; V.33; S V.266, 304; It 58 sq., 99 sq.; VbhA 443 sq. — 3. resolution, vow Vin II.268; J I.233; Miln 352.

Samādinna [pp. of samādiyati] taken up, undertaken A II.193.

Samādiyati [saŋ+ādiyati[1]] to take with oneself, to take upon oneself, to undertake D I.146; imper. samādiya Bu II.118 = J I.20; aor. samādiyi S I.232; J I.219; ger. samādiyitvā S I.232; & samādāya having taken up, i. e. with D I.71; Pug 58; DA I.207; Mhvs I, 47; having taken upon himself, conforming to D I.163; II.74; Dh 266; Sn 792, 898, 962; samādāya sikkhati sikkhāpadesu, he adopts and trains himself in the precepts D I.63; S V.187; It 118; Sn 962 (cp. Nd[1] 478). — pp. samādinna.

Samādisati [saŋ+ādisati] to indicate, to command D I.211; Mhvs 38, 59.

Samādhāna (nt.) [saŋ+ā+**dhā**] putting together, fixing; concentration Vism 84 (=sammā ādhānaŋ ṭhapanaŋ) in defn of samādhi as "samādhān' aṭṭhena."

Samādhi [fr. saŋ+ā+**dhā**] 1. concentration; a concentrated, self-collected, intent state of mind and meditation, which, concomitant with right living, is a necessary condition to the attainment of higher wisdom and emancipation. In the *Subha-suttanta* of the Digha (D I.209 sq.) samādhi-khandha ("section on concentration") is the title otherwise given to the citta-sampadā, which, in the ascending order of merit accruing from the life of a samaṇa (see *Sāmaññaphala-suttanta*, and cp. *Dial.* I.57 sq.) stands between the sīla-sampadā and the paññā-sampadā. In the *Ambaṭṭha-sutta* the corresponding terms are sīla, caraṇa, vijjā (D. I.100). Thus samādhi would comprise (a) the guarding of the senses (indriyesu gutta-dvāratā), (b) self-possession (sati-sampajañña), (c) contentment (santuṭṭhi), (d) emancipation from the 5 hindrances (nīvaraṇāni), (e) the 4 jhānas. In the same way we find samādhi grouped as one of the sampadās at A III.12 (sīla°, samādhi°, paññā°, vimutti°), and as samādhi-khandha (with sīla° & paññā°) at D III.229 (+vimutti°); A I.125; II.20; III.15; V.326; Nd[1] 21; Nd[2] p. 277 (s. v. sīla). It is defined as cittassa ekaggatā M I.301; Dhs 15; DhsA 118; cp. *Cpd.* 89 n. 4; identified with avikkhepa Dhs 57, and with samatha Dhs 54. — sammā° is one the constituents of the eightfold ariya-magga, e. g. D III.277; VbhA 120 sq. — See further D II.123 (ariya); Vin I.97, 104; S I.28; Nd[1] 365; Miln 337; Vism 84 sq. (with definition), 289 (+vipassanā), 380 (°vipphārā iddhi); VbhA 91; DhA I.427; and on term in general Heiler, *Buddhistische Versenkung* 104 sq. — 2. Description & characterization of samādhi: Its four nimittas or signs are the four satipaṭṭhānas M I.301; six conditions and six hindrances A III.427; other hindrances M III.158. The second jhāna is born from samādhi D II.186; it is a condition for attaining kusalā dhammā A I.115; Miln 38; conducive to insight A III.19, 24 sq., 200; S IV.80; to seeing heavenly sights etc. D I.173; to removing mountains etc. A III.311; removes the delusions of self A I.132 sq.; leads to Arahantship A II.45; the ānantarika s. Sn 226; cetosamādhi (rapture of mind) D I.13; A II.54; III.51; S IV.297; citta° id. Nett 16. dhammasamādhi almost identical with samatha S IV.350 sq. — Two grades of samādhi distinguished, viz. upacāra-s. (preparatory concentration) and appanā-s. (attainment concentration) DA I.217; Vism 126; *Cpd.* 54, 56 sq.; only the latter results in jhāna; to these a 3rd (preliminary) grade is added as khaṇika° (momentary) at Vism 144. — Three kinds of s. are distinguished, suññata or empty, appaṇihita or aimless, and animitta or signless A I.299; S IV.360; cp. IV.296; Vin III.93; Miln 337; cp. 333 sq.; DhsA 179 sq., 222 sq., 290 sq.; see *Yogāvacara's Manual* p. xxvii; samādhi (tayo samādhī) is savitakka savicāra, avitakka vicāramatta or avitakka avicāra D III.219; Kvu 570; cp. 413; Miln 337; DhsA 179 sq.; it is *fourfold* chanda-, viriya-, citta-, and vīmaŋsā-samādhi D II.213; S V.268. — Another fourfold division is that into hāna-bhāgiya, ṭhiti°, visesa°, nibbedha° D III.277 (as "dhammā duppaṭivijjhā").

-indriya the faculty of concentration A II.149; Dhs 15. -khandha the section on s. see above 1. -ja produced by concentration D I.74; III.13; Vism 158. -parikkhāra requisite to the attainment of samādhi: either 4 (the sammappadhānas) M I.301; or 7: D II.216; III.252; A IV.40. -bala the power of concentration A I.94; II.252; D III.213, 253; Dhs 28. -bhāvanā cultivation, attainment of samādhi M I.301; A II.44 sq. (four different kinds mentioned); III.25 sq.; D III.222; Vism 371. -saŋvattanika conducive to concentration A II.57; S IV.272 sq.; D III.245; Dhs 1344. -sambojjhanga the s. constituent of enlightment D III.106, 226, 252; Vism 134=VbhA 283 (with the eleven means of cultivating it).

Samādhika (adj.) [sama+adhika] excessive, abundant D II.251; J II.383; IV.31.

Samādhiyati is Passive of samādahati.

Samāna[1] (adj.) [Vedic samāna, fr. sama[3]] similar, equal, even, same Sn 18, 309; J II.108. Cp. sāmañña[1].

Samāna[2] [ppr. fr. **as** to be] 1. being, existing D I.18, 60; J I.218; PvA 129 (=santo), 167 (id.). — 2. a kind of gods D II.260.

-āsanika entitled to a seat of the same height Vin II. 169. -gatika identical Tikp 35. -bhāva equanimity Sn 702. -vassika having spent the rainy season together Vin I.168 sq. -saŋvāsa living together with equals Dh 302 (a°), cp. DhA III.462. -saŋvāsaka belonging to the same communion Vin I.321. -sīmā the same boundary, parish Vin I.321; °ma belonging to the same parish Vin II.300.

Samānatta (adj.) [samāna+attan] equanimous, of even mind A IV.364.

Samānattatā (f.) [abstr. fr. last] equanimity, impartiality A II.32=248; IV.219, 364; D III.152, 190 sq., 232.

Samāniyā [instr. fem. of samāna, used adverbially, Vedic samānyā] (all) equally, in common Sn 24.

Samānīta [pp. of samāneti] brought home, settled Miln 349.

Samāneti [saŋ+āneti] 1. to bring together J I.68. — 2. to bring, produce J I.433. — 3. to put together, cp. J I.120, 148. — 4. to collect, enumerate J I.429. — 5. to calculate (the time) J I.120, 148; aor. samānayi DA I.275. — pp. samānīta.

Samāpajjati [saŋ+āpajjati] 1. to come into, enter upon, attain D I.215 (samādhiŋ samāpajji); Vin III.241 (Pot. °pajjeyya); samāpattiŋ J I.77; arahattamaggaŋ A II.42 sq.; Vin I.32; saññāvedayitanirodhaŋ to attain the trance of cessation S IV.293; kayavikkayaŋ to engage in buying and selling Vin III.241; sākacchaŋ to engage in conversation D II.109; tejodhātuŋ to convert one's body into fire Vin I.25; II.76. — 2. to become S III.86 (aor. 3rd pl. samāpaduŋ). — pp. samāpajjita & samāpanna.

Samāpajjana (nt.) [fr. last] entering upon, passing through (?) Miln 176.

Samāpajjita [pp. of °āpajjati] attained, reached, got into D II.109 (parisā °pubbā).

Samāpaṭipatti misprint for sammā° A I.69.

Samāpatti (f.) [fr. saŋ+ā+**pad**] attainment A III.5; S II.150 sq.; IV.293 (saññā-vedayita-nirodha°); Dhs 30=101; a stage of meditation A I.94; Dhs 1331; J I.343, 473; PvA 61 (mahā-karuṇā°); Nd¹ 100, 106, 139, 143; the Buddha acquired anekakoṭisata-sahassā s. J I.77. The *eight* attainments comprise the four Jhānas, the realm of the infinity of space, realm of the infinity of consciousness, realm of nothingness, realm of neither consciousness nor unconsciousness Ps I.8, 20 sq.; Nd¹ 108, 328; Bu 192=J I.28, 54; necessary for becoming a Buddha J I.14; acquired by the Buddha J I.66; the *nine* attainments, the preceding and the trance of cessation of perception and sensation S II.216, 222; described M I.159 sq. etc.; otherwise called anupubba-vihārā D II.156; A IV.410, 448 & passim [cp. Divy 95 etc.]. — In collocation with jhāna, vimokkha, and samādhi Vin I.97; A III.417 sq.; cp. *Cpd.* 59, 133 n. 3. -°bhāvanā realizing the attainments J I.67; °kusalatā success in attainment D III.212; Dhs 1331 sq.

Samāpattila [fr. last] one who has acquired J I.406.

Samāpattesiya (adj.) [samāpatti+esiya, adj. to esikā] longing for attainment Kvu 502 sq.

Samāpanna [pp. of samāpajjati] having attained, got to, entered, reached S IV.293 (saññā-nirodhaŋ); A II.42 (arahatta-maggaŋ entered the Path); Dh 264 (icchā-lobha° given to desire); Kvu 572 (in special sense=attaining the samāpattis).

Samāpannaka (adj.) [last+ka] possessed of the samāpattis DA I.119.

Samāpeti [saŋ+āpeti] to complete, conclude Mhvs 5, 273; 30, 55; DA I.307 (desanaŋ). — pp. samatta².

Samāyāti [saŋ+āyāti] to come together, to be united J III.38.

Samāyuta [saŋ+āyuta] combined, united Miln 274.

Samāyoga [saŋ+āyoga] combination, conjunction DA I.95; Sdhp 45, 469.

Samāraka (adj.) [sa³+māra+ka] including Māra Vin I.11=S V.423; D I.250; III.76, 135 & passim.

Samāraddha [pp. of samārabhati] undertaken S IV.197; Dh 293; J II.61.

Samārambha [saŋ+ārambha] I. undertaking, effort, endeavour, activity A II.197 sq. (kāya°, vacī°, mano°); Vin IV.67. — 2. injuring, killing, slaughter Sn 311; D I.5; DA I.77; A II.197; S V.470; Pug 58; DhsA 146. —appasamārambha (written °rabbha) connected with little (or no) injury (to life) D I.143. Cp. ārabhati¹.

Samārabhati [saŋ+ārabhati²] to begin, undertake M I.227; Mhvs 5, 79. — pp. samāraddha.

Samāruhati [saŋ+āruhati] to climb up, to ascend, enter; pres. samārohati J VI.209 (cp. samorohati p. 206, read samārohatī); aor. samārūhi Mhvs 14, 38. — pp. samārūḷha. — Caus. samāropeti to raise, cause to enter Miln 85; to put down, enter Nett 4, 206.

Samārūḷha [pp. of samāruhati] ascended, entered M I.74.

Samāropana [fr. samāropeti] one of the Hāras Nett I, 2, 4, 108, 205 sq., 256 sq.

Samālapati [saŋ+ālapati] to speak to, address J I.478. At J I.51 it seems to mean "to recover the power of speech."

Samāvaya=samavāya, closely united J VI.475 (in verse).

Samāsa [fr. saŋ+**ās**] I. compound, combination Vism 82; SnA 303; KhA 228. Cp. vyāsa. — 2. an abridgment Mhvs 37, 244.

Samāsati [saŋ+āsati] to sit together, associate; Pot. 3 sg. samāsetha S I.17, 56 sq.; J II.112; V.483, 494; Th I, 4.

Samāsana (nt.) [saŋ+āsana] sitting together with, company Sn 977.

Samāsama "exactly the same" at Ud 85 (=D II.135) read sama°.

Samāsādeti [saŋ+āsādeti] to obtain, get; ger. samāsajja J III.218.

Samāhata [saŋ+āhata] hit, struck Sn 153 (ayosanku°); Miln 181, 254, 304. Sankusamāhata name of a purgatory M I.337.

Samāhita [pp. of samādahati] I. put down, fitted J IV.337; — 2. collected (of mind), settled, composed, firm, attentive D I.13; S I.169; A II.6 (°indriya); III.312, 343 sq.; V.3, 93 sq., 329 sq.; Sn 212, 225, 972 etc.; Dh 362; It 119; Pug 35; Vin III.4; Miln 300; Vism 410; Nd¹ 501. — 3. having attained S I.48 (cp. *K.S.* I.321 & Miln 352).

Samijjhati [saŋ+ijjhati] to succeed, prosper, take effect D I.71; Sn 766 (cp. Nd¹ 2=labhati etc.); Bu II.59=J I.14, 267; Pot. samijjheyyuŋ D I.71; aor. samijjhi J I.68; Fut. samijjhissati J I.15. — pp. samiddha. — Caus. II. °ijjhāpeti to endow or invest with (acc.) J VI.484.

Samijjhana (nt.) [fr. samijjhati] fulfilment, success DhA I.112.

Samijjhiṭṭha [saŋ+ajjhiṭṭha] ordered, requested J VI.12 (=āṇatta C.).

Samiñjati [saŋ+iñjati of **r̥ñj** or **r̥j** to stretch] I. to double up M I.326. — 2. (intrs.) to be moved or shaken Dh 81 (=calati kampati DhA II.149). See also sammiñjati.

Samiñjana (nt.) [fr. samiñjati] doubling up, bending back (orig. stretching!) Vism 500 (opp. pasāraṇa). See also sammiñjana.

Samita¹ [saŋ+ita, pp. of sameti] gathered, assembled Vv 64¹⁰; VvA 277. — nt. as adv. samitaŋ continuously M I.93; A IV.13; It 116; Miln 70, 116.

Samita² [sa+mita, of **mā**] equal (in measure), like S I.6.

Samita³ [pp. of sammati¹] quiet, appeased DhA III.84.

Samita⁴ [pp. of saŋ+**śam** to labour] arranged, put in order J V.201 (=saŋvidahita C.).

Samitatta (nt.) [fr. samita³] state of being quieted Dh 265.

Samitāvin [samita³+āvin, cp. vijitāvin] one who has quieted himself, calm, Sn 449, 520; S I.62, 188; A II.49, 50. Cp. BSk. śamitāvin & samitāvin.

Samiti (f.) [fr. saŋ+**i**] assembly D II.256; Dh 321; J IV.351; Pv II.3¹³ (=sannipāta PvA 86); DhA IV.13.

Samiddha [pp. of samijjhati] I. succeeded, successful Vin I.37; Bu II.4=J I.3; Miln 331. — 2. rich, magnificent J VI.393; J III.14; samiddhena (adv.) successfully J VI.314.

Samiddhi (f.) [fr. samijjhati] success, prosperity Dh 84; S I.200.

Samiddhika (adj.) [samiddhi+ka] rich in, abounding in Sdhp 421.

Samiddhin (adj.) [fr. samiddhi] richly endowed with ThA 18 (Ap V.23); fem. -inī J V.90.

Samidhā (f.) [fr. saŋ+**idh**; see indhana] fuel, firewood SnA 174.

Samihita [=saŋhita] collected, composed Vin I.245=D I.104=238; A III.224=229=DA I.273; D I.241, 272.

Samīcī D II.94: see sāmīcī.

Samītar [=sametar] one who meets, assembles; pl. samītāro J V.324.

Samīpa (adj.) [cp. Epic & Class. Sk. samīpa] near, close (to) SnA 43 (bhumma-vacana), 174, 437; KhA 111; PvA 47 (dvāra° magga) (nt.) proximity D I.118. Cases adverbially: acc. °aŋ near to PvA 107; loc. °-e near (with gen.) SnA 23, 256; PvA 10, 17, 67, 120.
-ga approaching Mhvs 4, 27; 25, 74. -cara being near DhsA 193. -cārin being near D I.206; II.139. -ṭṭha standing near Mhvs 37, 164.

Samīpaka (adj.) [samīpa+ka] being near Mhvs 33, 52.

Samīra [fr. saŋ+**īr**] air, wind Dāvs IV.40.

Samīrati [saŋ+īrati] to be moved Vin I.185; Db 81; DhA II.149. — pp. samīrita J I.393.

Samīrita [saŋ+īrita] stirred, moved J I.393.

Samīhati [saŋ+īhati] to move, stir; to be active; to long for, strive after Sn 1064 (cp. Nd² 651); Vv 5¹; VvA 35; J V.388. — pp. samīhita.

Samīhita (nt.) [pp. of samīhati] endeavour, striving after, pursuit J V.388.

Samukkaŋsati [saŋ+ukkaŋsati] to extol, to praise Sn 132, 438; M I.498. — pp. samukkaṭṭha.

Samukkaṭṭha [saŋ+ukkaṭṭha] exalted A IV.293; Th I, 632.

Samukkācanā=ukkācanā Vbh 352; Vism 23.

Samukkheṭita [saŋ+ukkheṭita] despised, rejected Vin III.95; IV.27.

Samugga [Class. Sk. samudga] a box, basket J I.265, 372, 383; Miln 153, 247; Sdhp 360 (read samuggābhaŋ). Samugga-jātaka the 436th Jātaka J III.527 sq. (called Karaṇḍaka-Jātaka ibid.; V.455).

Samuggaṇhāti [saŋ+uggaṇhati] to seize, grasp, embrace; ger. samuggahāya Sn 797; Nd¹ 105. — pp. samuggahīta.

Samuggata [saŋ+uggata] arisen VvA 280; J IV.403 (text samuggagata).

Samuggama [saŋ+uggama] rise, origin VbhA 21 (twofold, of the khandhas).

Samuggahīta [pp. of samuggaṇhāti] seized, taken up Sn 352, 785, 801, 837, 907; Nd¹ 76, 100, 193.

Samuggirati [saŋ+uggirati] to throw out, eject VvA 199; to cry aloud Dāvs V.29.

Samugghāta [saŋ+ugghāta; BSk. samudghāṭa Lal. Vist. 36, 571] uprooting, abolishing, removal D I.135; M I.136; A II.34; III.407; V.198; S II.263; III.131; IV.31; Vin I.107, 110; J III.397.

Samugghātaka (adj.) [fr. last] removing Miln 278.

Samugghātita [pp. of samugghāteti, see samūhanati] abolished, completely removed; nt. abstr. °tta Miln 101.

Samucita [saŋ+ucita, pp. of **uc** to be pleased] suitable Vin IV.147 (must mean something else here, perhaps "hurt," or "frightened") Dāvs V.55.

Samuccaya [saŋ+uccaya] collection, accumulation J II.235 (the signification of the particle vā); SnA 266 (id.). — samuccaya-kkhandhaka the third section of Cullavagga Vin II.38-72.

Samucchaka see samuñchaka.

Samucchati [derivation and meaning uncertain; Windisch, *Buddha's Geburt*, p. 39, n. 1 derives it fr. saŋ+mucchati. Cp. Geiger, *P.Gr.* § 157] to be consolidated, to arise; samucchissatha (Conditional) D II.63.

Samucchita [saŋ+mucchita] infatuated S I.187; IV.71; Th I, 1219. It is better to read pamucchita at all passages.

Samucchindati [saŋ+ucchindati] to extirpate, abolish, spoil, give up D I.34; II.74; M I.101 sq., 360; J IV.63. — pp. samucchinna.

Samucchinna [saŋ+ucchinna] cut off, extirpated D I.34.

Samuccheda [saŋ+uccheda] cutting off, abolishing, giving up M I.360; KhA 142; sammā s. Ps I.101; °pahāna relinquishing by extirpation Vism 5; SnA 9; °maraṇa dying by extirpation (of saŋsāra) Vism 229; °visuddhi Ps II.3; °suññaŋ Ps ii.180.

Samujjala (adj.) [saŋ+ujjala] resplendent J I.89, 92 (pañca-vaṇṇa-vattha°). raŋsi-jāla° resplendent with the blaze of rays VvA 12, 14, 166.

Samujju (adj.) [saŋ+uju] straightforward, perfect Sn 352; S IV.196 (text saŋmuju).

Samuñchaka (adj.) [saŋ+uncha+ka] only as nt. adv. °ŋ gleaning, (living) by gleaning S I.19; J IV.466 (°ŋ carati).

Samuṭṭhahati [saŋ+uṭṭhahati] to rise up, to originate; pres. samuṭṭhāti Vin V.1; aor. samuṭṭhahi Mhvs 28, 16. — pp. samuṭṭhita. — Caus. samuṭṭhāpeti to raise, to originate, set on foot J I.144, 191, 318.

Samuṭṭhāna (nt.) [saŋ+uṭṭhāna] rising, origination, cause; as adj. (-°) arising from A II.87; Dhs 766 sq., 981, 1175; Miln 134, 302, 304; J I.207; IV.171; KhA 23, 31, 123; Vism 366.

Samuṭṭhānika (adj.) [fr. last] originating DhsA 263.

Samuṭṭhāpaka (f. °ikā) [fr. samuṭṭhāpeti] occasioning, causing DhsA 344; VvA 72.

Samuṭṭhita [pp. of samuṭṭhahati] arisen, originated, happened, occurred J II.196; Dhs 1035.

Samuttarati [saŋ+uttarati] to pass over Miln 372.

Samuttejaka (adj.) [fr. samuttejeti] instigating, inciting, gladdening M I.146; A II.97; IV.296, 328; V.155; S V.162; It 107.

Samuttejeti [saŋ+ud+**tij**] to excite, gladden, to fill with enthusiasm Vin I.18; D I.126. Cp. BSk. samuttejayati, e. g. Divy 80.

Samudaya [saŋ+udaya] 1. rise, origin D I.17; II.33, 308; III.227; A I.263 (kamma°); Vin I.10; Sn p. 135; It 16 (samuddaya metri causa) etc. dukkha° the origin of ill, the second ariya-sacca, e. g. D III.136; A I 177; Vism 495 (where samudaya is expl^d in its parts as sam+u+aya); VbhA 124. — 2. bursting forth, effulgence (pabhā°) J I.83. — 3. produce, revenue D I.227.

Samudāgacchati [saŋ+udāgacchati] to result, rise; to be got, to be at hand D I.116; M I.104. — pp. samudāgata.

Samudāgata [pp. of last] arisen, resulted; received S II.24; Sn 648 (=āgata C.).

Samudāgama [saŋ+ud+āgama] beginning J I.2.

Samudācarati [saŋ+ud+ācarati] 1. to be current, to be in use M I.40 (=kāya-vacī-dvāraŋ sampatta s. MA 182). — 2. to occur to, to befall, beset, assail M I.109, 112, 453; S II.273; It 31; Vism 343. — 3. to behave towards, to converse with (instr.), to address Vin I.9; D II.154, 192; A III.124, 131; IV.415, 440; V.103; J I.192. — 4. to practise J II.33 (aor. °ācariŋsu). — 5. to claim, to boast of Vin III.91. — pp. samudāciṇṇa.

Samudācaritatta (nt.) [abstr. fr. samudācarita, pp. of samudācarati] practice Miln 59.

Samudācāra [saŋ+ud+ācāra] behaviour, practice, habit, familiarity J IV.22; SnA 6; DhsA 392; PvA 279.

Samudāciṇṇa [pp. of samudācarati] practised, indulged in J II.33; Tikp 320.

Samudānaya (adj.) [grd. of samudāneti] to be procured or attained J III.313 (su°).

Samudānīta [pp. of samudāneti, cp. BSk. samudānīta MVastu I.231] collected, procured J IV.177.

Samudāneti [saŋ+ud+āneti; cp. BSk. samudānayati Divy 26, 50, 490; AvŚ I.199] to collect, procure, attain, get M I.104; Sn 295. — pp. °ānīta.

Samudāya [fr. saŋ+ud+ā+i] multitude, quantity VvA 175; the whole VvA 276.

Samudāvaṭa [saŋ+ud+āvaṭa? Better read as saŋ+udāvatta] restrained DhsA 75.

Samudāhāra [saŋ+udāhāra, cp. BSk. samudāhāra Divy 143] talk, conversation Miln 344; piya° A V.24, 27, 90, 201, 339; ThA 226.

Samudikkhati [saŋ+udikkhati] to behold ThA 147 (Ap. V.52).

Samudita [saŋ+udita[1]] 1. arisen Dāvs V.4. — 2. excited S I.136. — 3. united VvA 321.

Samudīraṇa (nt.) [saŋ+udīraṇa in meaning udīreti 1] moving M I.119; D I.76; Vism 365; DhsA 307.

Samudīrita [saŋ+udīrita] uttered J VI.17.

Samudeti [saŋ+udeti] to arise; pres. samudayati (v. l. samudiyati) S II.78; samudeti A III.338; pp. samudita.

Samudda [cp. Vedic samudra, fr. saŋ+udra, water] a (large) quantity of water, e. g. the Ganges; the sea, the ocean D I.222; M I.493; A I.243; II.48 sq.; III.240; D III.196, 198; S I.6, 32, 67; J I.230; IV.167, 172; Dh 127; Nd[1] 353; SnA 30; PvA 47, 104, 133, 271; explained by adding sāgara, S II.32; four oceans S II.180, 187; ThA 111. Often characterized as mahā° the great ocean, e. g. Vin II.237; A I.227; II.55; III.52; IV.101; SnA 371; DhA III.44. *Eight* qualities: A IV.198, 206; popular etymology Miln 85 sq. (viz. "yattakaŋ udakaŋ tattakaŋ loṇaŋ," and vice versa); the eye etc. (the senses) an ocean which engulfs all beings S IV.157 (samudda=mahā udakarāsi). — Cp. sāmuddika.
-akkhāyikā (f.) tales about the origin of the sea, cosmogony Vin I.188; M I.513 sq.; D I.8; DA I.91. **-ṭṭhaka** situated in the ocean J VI.158. **-vīci** a wave of the ocean Vism 63.

Samuddaya metri causâ instead of samudaya It 16, 52.

Samuddhaṭa [saŋ+uddhaṭa] pulled out, eradicated Mhvs 59, 15; J VI.309; Sdhp 143.

Samuddharaṇa (nt.) [saŋ+uddharaṇa] pulling out, salvation Miln 232.

Samuddharati [saŋ+uddharati] to take out or away; to lift up, carry away, save from; aor. samuddhari J VI.271; samuddhāsi (aor. thus read instead of samuṭṭhāsi) J V.70.

Samunna [saŋ+unna] moistened, wet, immersed S IV.158; cp. the similar passage A II.211 with ref. to taṇhā as a snare (pariyonaddha).

Samunnameti [saŋ+unnameti] to raise, elevate, Th 1, 29.

Samupagacchati [saŋ+upagacchati] to approach Miln 209.

Samupajaneti [saŋ+upa+janeti] to produce; °janiyamāna (ppr. pass.) Nett 195.

Samupaṭṭhahati [saŋ+upaṭṭhahati] to serve, help; pres. samupaṭṭhāti Sdhp 283; aor. samupaṭṭhahi Mhvs 33, 95.

Samupabbūḷha [saŋ+upa+viyūḷha] set up; heaped, massed, in full swing (of a battle), crowded M I.253; D II.285; S I.98; Miln 292; J I.89.

Samupama [saŋ+upama] resembling Mhvs 37, 68; also samūpama J I.146; V.155; VI.534.

Samuparūḷha [saŋ+uparūḷha] ascended Dāvs IV.42.

Samupasobhita [saŋ+upasobhita] adorned Miln 2.

Samupāgacchati [saŋ+upāgacchati] to come to; aor. samupāgami Mhvs 36, 91; pp. samupāgata.

Samupāgata [saŋ+upāgata] come to, arrived at Mhvs 37, 115; 38, 12; J VI.282; Sdhp 324.

Samupādika being on a level with the water Miln 237 (Trenckner conjectures samupodika). The better reading, however, is samupp°, sama=peace, quiet, thus "producing quiet," calm.

Samupeta [saŋ+upeta] endowed with, Miln 352.

Samuppajjati [saŋ+uppajjati] to arise, to be produced S IV.218; pp. samuppanna.

Samuppatti (f.) origin, arising S IV.218.

Samuppanna [saŋ+uppanna] arisen, produced, come about Sn 168, 599; Dhs 1035.

Samuppāda [saŋ+uppāda] origin, arising, genesis, coming to be, production Vin II.96; S III.16 sq.; It 17; A III.406 (dhamma°); J VI.223 (anilūpana-samuppāda, v. read. °-samuppāta, "swift as the wind"); Vism 521 (sammā & saha uppajjati=samuppāda). Cp. paṭicca°.

Samuppilava (adj.) [fr. saŋ+uppilavati] jumping or bubbling up Sn 670 (°āso nom. pl.).

Samupphosita [saŋ+ud+phosita] sprinkled J VI.481.

Samubbahati [saŋ+ubbahati[2]] to carry Dāvs III.3; V.35; ppr. samubbahanto J VI.21 (making display of).

Samubbhūta [saŋ+ud+bhūta] borne from, produced from Dāvs II.25.

Samuyyuta [saŋ+uyyuta] energetic, devoted Vv 63[33]; VvA 269.

Samullapati [saŋ+ullapati] to talk, converse Vin III.187; PvA 237; ppr. samullapanto J III.49.

Samullapana (nt.) [saŋ+ullapana] talking (with), conversation SnA 71.

Samullāpa [=last] conversation, talk Miln 351.

Samussaya [saŋ+ud+śri, cp. BSk. samucchraya "body," Divy 70=AvŚ I.162] 1. accumulation, complex A II.42=

It 48; It 34; bhassasamuccaya, grandiloquence Sn 245; — 2. complex form, the body D II.157 = S I.148; Vv35[12] (= sarīra VvA 164); Dh 351; Th 1, 202 ("confluence," i. e. of the 5 factors, trsl[n]); Th 2, 22, 270; DhA IV.70; ThA 98, 212; rūpasamussaya the same Th 2, 102; cp. samuccaya.

Samussāpita [saŋ+ussāpita] lifted, raised J III.408.

Samussāhita [saŋ+ussāhita] instigated VvA 105.

Samussita [saŋ+ussita] 1. elevated, erected J III.497. — 2. arrogant, proud, haughty Dh 147 (interpreted at DhA III.109 as "compounded," i. e. the body made up of 300 bones); A I.199; SnA 288 (°ŋ bhassaŋ high and mighty talk).

Samusseti [saŋ+ud+śri] to raise, lift up; Pot. samusseyya A I.199 (here = to be grandiloquent). — pp. samussita.

Samūpasanta [saŋ+upasanta] is v. l. for su-vūpasanta (?) "calmed," at KhA 21.

Samūlaka (adj.) [sa[3]+mūla+ka] including the root Th 2 385; ThA 256.

Samūha [fr. saŋ+**vah, uh**] multitude, mass, aggregation Nett 195; PvA 49, 127, 157 (= gaṇa), 200 (id.).

Samūhata [pp. of samūhanati] taken out, removed D I.136; S III.131; Th 1, 223; Dh 250; Sn 14, 360; It 83; J IV.345 (Kern, wrongly "combined").

Samūhatatta (nt.) [abstr. fr. samūhata] abolition M III.151.

Samūhanati [saŋ+ūhanati[2]] to remove, to abolish Vin I.110; D I.135 sq. (°hanissati); II.91 = S V.432; M I.47; II.193; S V.76; J I.374 = Sn 360; Sn 14, 369, 1076; sikkhāpadaŋ Vin III.23; D II.154; uposathāgāraŋ to discontinue using a Vihāra as an Uposathāgāra Vin I.107; sīmaŋ to remove the boundary Vin I.110. Pres. also samūhanti S III.156; Pot. samūhaneyya Vin I.110; imper. samūhantu D II.154; & °ūhanatu Miln 143; ger. samūhanitvā M I.47; Vin I.107; a° M III.285; inf. samugghātuŋ Mhvs 37, 32; grd. samūhantabba Vin I.107. — Caus. II. samugghātāpeti to cause to be removed, i. e. to put to death Miln 193; samūhanāpeti Miln 142. — pp. samūhata & (Caus.) samugghātita.

Samūheti [Caus. of saŋ+**uh** = **vah**] to gather, collect Mhvs 37, 245.

Samekkhati [saŋ+ikkhati] to consider, to seek, look for; Pot. samekkhe J IV.5; ppr. samekkhamāna Th 1, 547; & samekkhaŋ J II.65; ger. samekkhiya Mhvs 37, 237.

Sameta [pp. of sameti] associating with Miln 396; connected with, provided with Mhvs 19, 69; combined, constituted Sn 873, 874.

Sameti [saŋ+eti] 1. to come together, to meet, to assemble Bu II.199 = J I.29. — 2. to associate with, to go to D II.273; J IV.93. — 3. to correspond to, to agree D I.162, 247; J I.358; III.278. — 4. to know, consider S I.186; Nd[1] 284. — 5. to fit in J VI.334. — imper. sametu J IV.93[20]; fut. samessati S IV.379; It 70; aor. samiŋsu Bu II.199; S II.158 = It 70; & samesuŋ J II.30[16]; ger. samecca (1) (coming) together with D II.273; J VI.211, 318. — (2) having acquired or learnt, knowing S I.186; Sn 361, 793; A II.6. — pp. samita & sameta [= saŋ+ā+ita].

Sametikā Sn 285; read samāhitā.

Samerita [saŋ+erita] moved, set in motion; filled with (-°), pervaded by Sn 937; Nd[1] 410; J VI.529; Vism 172.

Samokiṇṇa [pp. of samokirati] besprinkled, covered (with) J I.233.

Samokirati [saŋ+okirati] to sprinkle Bu II.178 = J I.27. — pp. samokiṇṇa.

Samocita [saŋ+ocita] gathered, arranged J V.156 (= surocita C.).

Samotata [saŋ+otata] strewn all over, spread Vv 81[6] (vv. ll. samogata and samohata); J I.183; Ap 191.

Samotarati [saŋ+otarati] to descend Mhvs 10, 57.

Samodakaŋ (adv.) [saŋ+odakaŋ] at the water's edge Vin I.6 = M I.169 = D II.38.

Samodahati [saŋ+odahati] to put together, supply, apply S I.7; IV.178 sq.; to fix Nett 165, 178; ppr. samodahaŋ S I.7 = IV.179; ger. samodahitvā S IV.178; & samodhāya Vism 105; Sdhp 588. — pp. samohita.

Samodita united VvA 186 (so read for samm°), 320; cp. samudita.

Samodhāna (nt.) [saŋ+odhāna, cp. odahana] collocation, combination Bu II.59 = J I.14; S IV.215 = V.212; application (of a story) J II.381. samodhānaŋ gacchati to come together, to combine, to be contained in Vin I.62; M I.184 = S I.86; V.43, 231 = A V.21 (Com. odhānapakkhepaŋ) A III.364; SnA 2; Vism 7; VbhA 107; samodhānagata wrapped together Miln 362; samodhānaparivāsa a combined, inclusive probation Vin II.48 sq.

Samodhānatā (f.) [abstr. fr. samodhāna] combination, application, pursuance, in vutti° J III.541 (so read for vatti°).

Samodhāneti [Denom. fr. samodhāna] to combine, put together, connect J I.9, 14; DA I.18; SnA 167, 193, 400; especially jātakaŋ s. to apply a Jātaka to the incident J I.106, 171; II.381 & passim.

Samorodha [saŋ+orodha] barricading, torpor Dhs 1157; DhsA 379.

Samorohati [saŋ+orohati] to descend; ger. samoruyha Mhvs 10, 35.

Samosaraṇa (nt.) [saŋ+osaraṇa] coming together, meeting, union, junction D I.237; II.61; S III.156; V.42 sq., 91; A III.364; Miln 38.

Samosarati [saŋ+osarati] 1. to flow down together Miln 349. — 2. to come together, gather J I.178 (see on this Kern, *Toev.* II.60).

Samoha infatuated Pug 61.

Samohita [pp. of samodahati] 1. put together, joined J VI.261 (su°). — 2. connected with, covered with Nd[1] 149 (for pareta); Miln 346 (raja-panka°).

Sampakampati [saŋ+pakampati] to tremble, to be shaken Vin I.12; D II.12, 108; M I.227; III.120. — Caus. sampakampeti to shake D II.108.

Sampakopa [saŋ+pakopa] indignation Dhs 1060.

Sampakkhandati [saŋ+pakkhandati, cp. BSk. praskandati MVastu II.157] to aspire to, to enter into Miln 35.

Sampakkhandana (nt.) [saŋ+pakkhandana] aspiration Miln 34 sq.

Sampaggaṇhāti [saŋ+paggaṇhāti] 1. to exert, strain DhsA 372. — 2. to show a liking for, to favour, befriend J VI.294. — pp. sampaggahīta.

Sampaggaha [saŋ+paggaha] support, patronage Mhvs 4, 44.

Sampaggahīta [saŋ+paggahīta] uplifted Miln 309.

Sampaggāha assumption, arrogance Dhs 1116.

Sampaghosa sound, noise Mhbv 45.

Sampacura (adj.) [saŋ+pacura] abundant, very many A II.59, 61; S I.110.

Sampajañña (nt.) [fr. sampajāna, i. e. *sampajānya] attention, consideration, discrimination, comprehension, circumspection A I.13 sq.; II.93; III.307; IV.320; V.98 sq.; S III.169; D III.213 (sati+samp. opp. to muṭṭha-sacca+asampajañña), 273. Description of it in detail at DA I.183 sq.=VbhA 347 sq., where given as *fourfold*, viz. sātthaka°, sappāya°, gocara°, asammoha°, with examples. Often combined with sati, with which almost synonymous, e. g. at D I.63; A I.43; II.44 sq.; V.115, 118.

Sampajāna (adj.) [saŋ+pajāna, cp. pajānāti; BSk. samprajāna, MVastu I.206; II.360] thoughtful, mindful, attentive, deliberate, almost syn. with sata, mindful D I.37; II.94 sq.; Sn 413, 931; It 10, 42; Pug 25; D III.49, 58, 221, 224 sq.; A IV.47 sq., 300 sq., 457 sq.; Nd[1] 395; Nd[2] 141. sampajānakārin acting with consideration or full attention D I.70; II.95, 292; A II.210; V.206; VbhA 347 sq.; DA I.184 sq.; sampājanamusāvāda deliberate lie Vin IV.2; It 18; D III.45; A I.128; IV.370; V.265; J I.23.

Sampajānāti [saŋ+pajānati] to know S V.154; Sn 1055; Nd[2] 655.

Sampajjati [saŋ+pajjati] 1. to come to, to fall to; to succeed, prosper J I.7; II.105. — 2. to turn out, to happen, become D I.91, 101, 193, 239; PvA 192. aor. sampādi D II.266, 269. — pp. sampanna. — Caus. sampādeti.

Sampajjalita (adj.) [saŋ+pajjalita] in flames, ablaze A IV.131; Vin I.25; D I.95; II.335; J I.232; Miln 84.

Sampaṭike (adv.) [loc. fr. saŋ+paṭi+ka] now J IV.432 (=sampati, idāni C.).

Sampaṭiggaha [saŋ+paṭiggaha] summing up, agreement KhA 100.

Sampaṭicchati [saŋ+paṭicchati] to receive, accept J I.69; III.351; Mhvs 6, 34; ovādaŋ s. to comply with an admonition J III.52; sādhū ti s. to say "well" and agree J II.31; Miln 8. — Caus. II. sampaṭicchāpeti J VI.336.

Sampaṭicchana (nt.) [fr. last] acceptance, agreement DhsA 332; SnA 176 ("sādhu"); Vism 21; Sdhp 59, 62.

Sampaṭinipajjā (f.) [saŋ+paṭi+nipajjā] squatting down, lying down ThA 111.

Sampaṭivijjhati [saŋ+paṭivijjhati] to penetrate; Pass. sampaṭivijjhiyati Nett 220.

Sampaṭivedha [saŋ+paṭivedha] penetration Nett 27, 41, 42, 220.

Sampaṭisaŋkhā deliberately S II.111; contracted from ger. °-saŋkhāya.

Sampatati [saŋ+patati] to jump about, to fly along or about J VI.528 (dumā dumaŋ); imper. sampatantu, ib. VI.448 (itarītaraŋ); ppr. sampatanto flying to J III.491. pp. sampatita.

Sampati [saŋ+paṭi; cp. Sk. samprati] now Miln 87; sampatijāta, just born D II.15=M III.123. Cp. sampaṭike.

Sampatita [pp. of sampatati] jumping about J VI.507.

Sampatta [pp. of sampāpuṇāti] reached, arrived, come to, present J IV.142; Miln 9, 66; PvA 12; KhA 142; SnA 295; Sdhp 56.

Sampattakajāta merged in, given to Ud 75 [read sammattaka (?)].

Sampatti (f.) [saŋ+patti[2]] 1. success, attainment; happiness, bliss, fortune (opp. vipatti) A IV.26, 160; Vism 58, 232; J IV.3 (dibba°); DA I.126; *three* attainments J I.105; Miln 96; DhA III.183 (manussa°, devaloka°, nibbāna°); Nett 126 (sīla°, samādhi°, paññā°; cp. sampadā); *four* VbhA 439 sq. (gati°, upadhi°, kāla°, payoga°); *six* J I.105; *nine* Miln 341. — 2. excellency, magnificence SnA 397; rūpasampatti beauty J III.187; IV.333. — 3. honour Mhvs 22, 48. — 4. prosperity, splendour J IV.455; Mhvs 38, 92; s. bhavaloko Ps I.122. Cp. samāpatti & sampadā.

Sampatthanā (f.) [saŋ+patthanā] entreating, imploring Dhs 1059.

Sampadā (f.) [fr. saŋ+pad, cp. BSk. sampadā Divy 401 (devamanuṣya°), also sampatti] 1. attainment, success, accomplishment; happiness, good fortune; blessing, bliss A I.38; Pv II.9[47] (=sampatti PvA 132). — Sampadā in its pregnant meaning is applied to the accomplishments of the individual in the course of his religious development. Thus it is used with sīla, citta, & paññā at D I.171 sq. and many other passages in an almost encyclopedic sense. Here with sīla° the whole of the sīlakkhandha (D I.63 sq.) is understood; citta° means the cultivation of the heart & attainments of the mind relating to composure, concentration and religious meditation, otherwise called samādhikkhandha. It includes those stages of meditation which are enum[d] under samādhi. With paññā° are meant the attainments of higher wisdom and spiritual emancipation, connected with supernormal faculties, culminating in Arahantship and extinction of all causes of rebirth, otherwise called vijjā (see the 8 items of this under vijjā b.). The same ground as by this 3 fold division is covered by the enumeration of 5 sampadās as sīla°, samādhi°, paññā°, vimutti°, vimutti-ñāṇadassana° M I.145; Pug 54; cp. S I.139; A III.12.

The term sampadā is not restricted to a definite *set* of accomplishments. It is applied to various such sets besides the one mentioned above. Thus we find a set of 3 sampadās called sīla°, citta° & diṭṭhi° at A I.269, where under sīla the Nos. 1-7 of the 10 sīlas are understood (see sīla 2 a), under citta Nos. 8 & 9, under diṭṭhi No. 10. — sīla & diṭṭhi° also at D III.213. — A set of 8 sampadās is given at A IV.322 with uṭṭhāna°, ārakkha°, kalyāṇamittatā, sammājīvitā, saddhā°, sīla°, cāga°, paññā°; of which the first 4 are expl[d] in detail at A IV.281=322 as bringing worldly happiness, viz. alertness, wariness, association with good friends, right livelihood; and the last 4 as leading to future bliss (viz. faith in the Buddha, keeping the 5 sīlas, liberality, higher wisdom) at A IV.284=324. Another set of 5 frequently mentioned is: ñāti°, bhoga°, ārogya°, sīla°, diṭṭhi° (or the blessings, i. e. good fortune, of having relatives, possessions, health, good conduct, right views) representing the "summa bona" of popular choice, to which is opposed deficiency (vyasana, reverse) of the same items. Thus e. g. at A III.147; D III.235. — *Three* sampadās; kammanta°, ājīva°, diṭṭhi,° i. e. the 7 sīlas, right living (sammā-ājīva), right views A I.271. — Another *three* as saddhā°, sīla°, paññā° at A I.287. — Bdhgh at DhA III.93, 94 speaks of *four* sampadās, viz. vatthu°, paccaya°, cetanā°, guṇâtireka°; of the blessings of a foundation (for merit), of means (for salvation), of good intentions, of virtue (& merit). — A (later) set of *seven* sampadās is given at J IV.96 with āgama°, adhigama°, pubbahetu°, attattha-paripucchā°, titthavāsa°, yoniso-manasikāra°, buddh'ūpanissaya°. — Cp. the following: atta° S V.30 sq.; ākappa° A I.38; ājīva° A I.271; DA I.235; kamma° A IV.238 sq.; dassana° Sn 231; nibbāna° Vism 58; bhoga° (+parivāra°) DhA I.78; yāga° ThA 40 (Ap. V.7); vijjācaraṇa° D I.99.

2. execution, performance; result, consequence; thus yañña° successful performance of a sacrifice D I.128; Sn 505, 509; piṭaka-sampadāya "on the authority of the Piṭaka tradition," according to the P.; in exegesis of iti-kira (hearsay) A I.189 = II.191 = Nd² 151; and of itihītiha M I.520 = II.169.

Sampadāti [saŋ+padāti] to hand on, give over J IV.204 (aor. °padāsi).

Sampadāna (nt.) [saŋ+padāna] the dative relation J V.214 (upayogatthe), 237 (karaṇatthe); SnA 499 (°vacana).

Sampadāleti [saŋ+padāleti] to tear, to cut M I.450; A II.33 = S III.85; S III.155; Mhvs 23, 10. — Act. intrs. sampadālati to burst J VI.559 (= phalati, C.).

Sampaditta [saŋ+paditta] kindled Sdhp 33.

Sampaduṭṭha [saŋ+paduṭṭha] corrupted, wicked J VI.317 (a°); Sdhp 70.

Sampadussati [saŋ+padussati] to be corrupted, to trespass Vin IV.260; J II.193; pp. sampaduṭṭha.

Sampadosa [saŋ+padosa¹] wickedness Dhs 1060; a-sampadosa innocence J VI.317 = VI.321.

Sampaddavati [saŋ+pa+**dru**] to run away; aor. sampaddavi J VI.53. — pp. sampadduta.

Sampadduta [pp. of sampaddavati] run away J VI.53.

Sampadhūpeti (°dhūpāyati, °dhūpāti) [saŋ+padhūpāti] to send forth (thick) smoke, to fill with smoke or incense, to pervade, permeate S I.169; Vin I.225; Sn p. 15; Miln 333. Cp. sandhūpāyati.

Sampanna [pp. of sampajjati] 1. successful, complete, perfect Vin II.256; sampannaveyyākaraṇa a full explanation Sn 352. — 2. endowed with, possessed of, abounding in Vin I.17; Sn 152, 727 (ceto-vimutti°); J I.421; vijjācaraṇasampanna full of wisdom and goodness D I.49; Sn 164; often used as first part of a compound, e. g. sampannavijjācaraṇa Dh 144; DhA III.86; sampannasīla virtuous It 118; Dh 57; sampannodaka abounding in water J IV.125. — 3. sweet, well cooked Vin II.196; Miln 395.

Sampaphulla (adj.) [saŋ+pa+phulla] blooming, blossoming Sdhp 245.

Sampabhāsa [saŋ+pa+**bhāṣ**] frivolous talk S V.355.

Sampabhāsati [saŋ+pa+bhās] to shine Miln 338.

Sampamathita [saŋ+pamathita] altogether crushed or overwhelmed J VI.189.

Sampamaddati [saŋ+pamaddati] to crush out Miln 403.

Sampamūḷha (adj.) [saŋ+pamūḷha] confounded Sn 762.

Sampamodati [saŋ+pamodati] to rejoice Vv 36⁸. — pp. sampamodita.

Sampamodita [saŋ+pamodita] delighted, rejoicing Sdhp 301.

Sampayāta [saŋ+payāta] gone forth, proceeded Dh 237.

Sampayāti [saŋ+payāti] to proceed, to go on; inf. sampayātave Sn 834; pp. sampayāta.

Sampayutta [saŋ+payutta] associated with, connected Dhs 1; Kvu 337; DhsA 42. -°paccaya the relation of association (opp. vippayutta°) Vism 539; VbhA 206; Tikp 6, 20, 53, 65, 152 sq.; Dukp 1 sq.

Sampayoga [saŋ+payoga] union, association Vin I.10; S V.421; DA I.96, 260.

Sampayojeti [saŋ+payojeti] 1. to associate (with) Vin II.262; M II.5. — 2. to quarrel Vin II.5; S I.239. — pp. sampayutta.

Samparāya [fr. saŋ+parā+i] future state, the next world Vin II.162; A III.154; IV.284 sq.; D II.240; S I.108; Sn 141, 864, J I.219; III.195; Miln 357; DhA II.50.

Samparāyika (adj.) [fr. last] belonging to the next world Vin I.179; III.21; D II.240; III.130; A III.49, 364; IV.285; M I.87; It 17, 39; J II.74.

Samparikaḍḍhati [saŋ+parikaḍḍhati] to pull about, drag along M I.228.

Samparikantati [saŋ+parikantati] to cut all round M III.275. (Trenckner reads sampakantati.)

Samparikiṇṇa [saŋ+parikiṇṇa] surrounded by Vin III.86; Miln 155.

Samparitāpeti [saŋ+paritāpeti] to make warm, heat, scourge M I.128, 244 = S IV.57.

Samparibhinna (adj.) [saŋ+paribhinna] broken up J VI.113 (°gatta).

Samparivajjeti [saŋ+parivajjeti] to avoid, shun Sdhp 52, 208.

Samparivatta (adj.) [saŋ+parivatta] rolling about Dh 325.

Samparivattaka (adj.) [saŋ+parivattaka] rolling about grovelling J II.142 (turning somersaults); DhA II.5, 12; Miln 253, 357; samparivattakaŋ (adv.) in a rolling about manner M II.138; samparivattakaŋ-samparivattakaŋ continually turning (it) Vin I.50.

Samparivattati [saŋ+parivattati] to turn, to roll about; ppr. samparivattamāna J I.140; pp. samparivatta. — Caus. samparivatteti [cp. BSk. °parivartayati to wring one's hands Divy 263] to turn over in one's mind, to ponder over S V.89.

Samparivāreti [saŋ+parivāreti] to surround, wait upon, attend on J I.61; aor. 3rd pl. samparivāresuŋ J I.164; ger. samparivārayitvā J I.61; °etvā (do.) J VI.43, 108. Cp. sampavāreti.

Samparivāsita see parivāsita.

Sampareta (adj.) [saŋ+pareta] surrounded, beset with J II.317; III.360 = S I.143.

Sampalibodha [saŋ+palibodha] hindrance, obstruction Nett 79.

Sampalibhagga [pp. of next] broken up S I.123.

Sampalibhañjati [saŋ+pari+**bhañj**] to break, to crack M I.234; S I.123; pp. sampalibhagga.

Sampalimaṭṭha [saŋ+palimaṭṭha] touched, handled, blotted out, destroyed S IV.168 sq. = J III.532 = Vism 36.

Sampaliveṭhita (adj.) [saŋ+paliveṭhita] wrapped up, enveloped M I.281.

Sampaliveṭheti [saŋ+paliveṭheti] to wrap up, envelop; °eyya A IV.131 (kāyaŋ).

Sampavanka (adj.) [perhaps saŋ+pari+anka², contracted to *payyanka > *pavanka] intimate, friend D II.78; S I.83, 87; Pug 36.

Sampavankatā (f.) [fr. last] connection, friendliness, intimacy S I.87; A III.422 (pāpa° & kalyāṇa°); IV.283 sq.; V.24, 199; Dhs 1326; Pug 20, 24; DhsA 394. Cp. anu° Vin II.88.

Sampavaṇṇita (adj.) [saŋ+pa+vaṇṇita] described, praised J VI.398.

Sampavattar [saŋ + pavattar] an instigator A III.133.

Sampavatteti [saŋ + pavatteti] to produce, set going A III.222 (saŋvāsaŋ); Mhvs 23, 75.

Sampavāti [saŋ + pavāti] to blow, to be fragrant M I.212; J VI.534; VvA 343 (= Vv 84[32]).

Sampavāyati [saŋ + pavāyati] to make fragrant, Vv 81[6], 84[32]; VvA 344.

Sampavāyana (nt.) [fr. last] making fragrant VvA 344.

Sampavāreti [saŋ + pavāreti; cp. BSk. saŋpravārayati Divy 285, 310, etc.; AvŚ I.90; MVastu III.142] to cause to accept, to offer, to regale, serve with; ger. sampavāretvā Vin I.18; II.128; D I.109; aor. sampavāresi D II.97.

Sampavedhati [saŋ + pavedhati] to be shaken violently, to be highly affected Vin I.12; D II.12, 108; M I.227; Th 2, 231; J I.25; S IV.71. — Caus. sampavedheti to shake violently D II.108; M I.253; Nd[1] 316, 371 (pp. °pavedhita).

Sampavedhin to be shaken Sn 28; Miln 386.

Sampasāda [saŋ + pasāda] serenity, pleasure D II.211, 222; A II.199; M II.262.

Sampasādana [saŋ + pasādana] (nt.) tranquillizing D I.37; Dhs 161; Miln 34; Vism 156; DhsA 170 (in the description of the second Jhāna); happiness, joy Bu I.35.

Sampasādaniya (adj.) [saŋ + pasādaniya] leading to serenity, inspiring faith D III.99 sq. (the S. Suttanta), 116.

Sampasāreti [saŋ + pasāreti] to stretch out, to distract Vism 365. — Pass. sampasāriyati A IV 17; Miln 297; DhsA 376.

Sampasīdati [saŋ + pasīdati] to be tranquillized, reassured D I.106; M I.101; DA I.275.

Sampasīdana (nt.) [fr. last] becoming tranquillized Nett 28.

Sampassati [saŋ + passati] to see, behold; to look to, to consider; ppr sampassanto Vin I.42; D II.285; sampassaŋ Dh 290.

Sampahaŋsaka (adj.) [fr. next] gladdening M I.146; A II.97; IV.296, 328; V.155; It 107; Miln 373.

Sampahaŋsati [saŋ + pahaŋsati[2]] to be glad; pp. sampahaṭṭha. — Caus. sampahaŋseti to gladden, delight Vin I.18; D I.126.

Sampahaŋsana (nt.) [fr. sampahaŋsati] being glad, pleasure; approval Ps I.167; Vism 148 (°ā); KhA 100 ("evaŋ"); SnA 176 ("sādhu"); Sdhp 568.

Sampahaṭṭha[1] (adj.) [saŋ + pahaṭṭha[1]] beaten, struck (of metal), refined, wrought S I.65 (sakusala°; Bdhgh: ukkāmukhe pacitvā s.; *K.S.* I.321); Sn 686 (sukusala°; SnA 486: "kusalena suvaṇṇakārena sanghaṭṭitaŋ sanghaṭṭentena tāpitaŋ").

Sampahaṭṭha[2] [saŋ + pahaṭṭha[2]] gladdened, joyful Sdhp 301.

Sampahāra [saŋ + pahāra] clashing, beating together, impact, striking; battle, strife D II.166; Pug 66 sq.; DA I.150; Miln 161 (ūmi-vega°), 179 (of two rocks), 224.

Sampāka [saŋ + pāka] 1. what is cooked, a cooked preparation, concoction Vin II.259 (maŋsa° etc.); Vv 43[6] (kola°); VvA 186. — 2 ripeness, development J VI.236.

Sampāta [saŋ + pāta] falling together, concurrence, collision It 68; kukkuṭasampāta neighbouring, closely adjoining (yasmā gāmā nikkhamitvā kukkuṭo padasā va aññaŋ gāmaŋ gacchati, ayaŋ kukkuṭasampāto ti vuccati) Vin IV.63, 358; kukkuṭasampātaka lying close together (lit. like a flock of poultry) A I.159. Cp. the similar sannipāta.

Sampādaka [fr. sampādeti] one who obtains Miln 349.

Sampādana (nt.) [fr. sampādeti] effecting, accomplishment Nett 44; preparing, obtaining J I.80.

Sampādeti [Caus. of sampajjati] 1. to procure, obtain Vin I.217; II.214; ekavacanaŋ s. to be able to utter a single word J II.164; kathaŋ s. to be able to talk J II.165; dohaḷe s. to satisfy the longing Mhvs 22, 51. — 2. to strive, to try to accomplish one's aim D II.120; S II.29

Sampāpaka (adj.) [fr. sampāpeti] causing to obtain, leading to, bringing J III.348; VI.235.

Sampāpana (nt.) [fr. sampāpuṇāti] reaching, getting to Miln 355, 536 (tīra°).

Sampāpuṇāti [saŋ + pāpuṇāti] to reach, attain; to come to, meet with; aor. sampāpuṇi J I.67; II.20; pp. sampatta. — Caus. sampāpeti to bring, to make attain Vism 303.

Sampāyati [der° not clear; Kern, *Toev*, I.62 = sampādayati; but more likely = sampāyāti, i. e. sam + pa + ā + **yā**] to be able to explain (DA I.117: sampādetvā kathetuŋ sakkuṇoti), to agree, to come to terms, succeed D I.26; II.284; M I.85, 96, 472; II.157; A V.50; S IV.15, 67; V.109; Vin II.249 (cp. p. 364); aor. sampāyāsi M I.239. Cp. sampayāti.

Sampāruta [saŋ + pāruta] (quite) covered M I.281.

Sampāleti [saŋ + pāleti] to protect J IV.127.

Sampiṇḍana (nt.) [fr. saŋ + piṇḍ°] combining, connection, addition Vism 159 (of "ca"); KhA 228 (id.); DhsA 171.

Sampiṇḍita [pp. of sampiṇḍeti] brought together, restored J I.230; compact, firm J V.89.

Sampiṇḍeti [saŋ + piṇḍeti] to knead or ball together, combine, unite Vism 159; KhA 125, 221, 230; DhsA 177; pp. sampiṇḍita.

Sampiya (adj.) [saŋ + piya] friendly; sampiyena by mutual consent, in mutual love Sn 123, 290.

Sampiyāyati [saŋ + piyāyati] to receive with joy, to treat kindly, address with love J III.482; ppr. sampiyāyanto J I.135; sampiyāyamāna (do.) fondling, being fond of D II.223; J I.191, 297, 361; II.85; DhA II.65. aor. 3rd pl. sampiyāyiŋsu J VI.127.

Sampiyāyanā (f.) [saŋ + piyāyanā] intimate relation, great fondness J III.492.

Sampīṇeti [saŋ + pīṇeti] to satisfy, gladden, please; aor. 2nd sg. sampesi J III.253; ger. sampīṇayitvā Dāvs IV.11.

Sampīḷa (nt.) [saŋ + pīḷa, cp. pīḷā] trouble, pain; asampīḷaŋ free from trouble Miln 351.

Sampīḷita [pp. of sampīḷeti] troubled; as nt., worry, trouble Miln 368.

Sampīḷeti [saŋ + pīḷeti] to press, to pinch, to worry Vin III.126; pp. sampīlita.

Sampucchati [saŋ + pucchati] to ask D I.116; ger. sampuccha having made an appointment with S I.176.

Samputa [cp. saŋ + puṭa (lexicogr. Sk. sampuṭa "round box") & BSk. sampuṭa in meaning "añjali" at Divy 380, in phrase kṛta-kara-sampuṭaḥ] the hollow of the hand (in posture of veneration), in pāṇi° Mhvs 37, 192 i. e. Cūḷavaŋsa (ed. Geiger) p. 15.

Samputita [saŋ + puṭita = phuṭita, cp. BSk. samputaka MVastu II.127] shrunk, shrivelled M I.80.

Sampuṇṇa (sampūrṇa) filled, full Sn 279; Bu II.119 = J I.20; Mhvs 22, 60.

Sampupphita [saŋ + pupphita] in full bloom Pv IV.12 (= niccaŋ pupphita PvA 275).

Sampurekkharoti [saŋ + purakkharoti] to honour M II.169.

Sampūjeti [saŋ + pūjeti] to venerate Mhvs 30, 100.

Sampūreti [saŋ + pūreti] Pass. pūriyati° to be filled, ended; aor. sampūri (māso, "it was a full month since . . .") J IV.458.

Sampha (adj.-n.) [not clear, if & how connected with Sk. śaṣpa, grass. The BSk. has sambhinna-pralāpa for sampha-ppalāpa] frivolous; nt. frivolity, foolishness; only in connection with expressions of talking, as samphaŋ bhāsati to speak frivolously A II.23; Sn 158; samphaŋ giraŋ bh. J VI.295; samphaŋ palapati Tikp 167 sq. — Also in cpds. °palāpa frivolous talk D I.4; III.69. 82, 175, 269; A I.269 sq., 298; II.60, 84, 209; III.254, 433; IV. 248; V.251 sq., 261 sq.; Tikp 168, 281; DA I.76; °palāpin talking frivolously D I.138; III.82; A I.298; Pug 39, 58.

Samphala (adj.) [saŋ + phala] abounding in fruits S I.70; 90 = It 45.

Samphassa [saŋ + phassa] contact, reaction Vin I.3; A II.117; D II.62; M I.85; J I.502; kāya-s. the touch of the skin D II.75; cakkhu-, sota-, ghāna-, jivhā-, kāya-, and mano-s. D II.58, 308; S IV.68 sq.; VbhA 19.

Samphuṭṭha [pp. of samphassati] touched S IV.97; Av.103; It 68.

Samphulla (adj.) [saŋ + phulla] full-blown J VI.188.

Samphusati [saŋ + phusati] to touch, to come in contact with; ppr. samphussaŋ It 68; ppr. med. samphusamāna Sn 671; Nd² 199 (reads samphassamāna, where id. p. at M I.85 has rissamāna); aor. samphusi D II.128; inf. samphusituŋ Sn 835; D II.355; pp. samphuṭṭha.

Samphusanā (f.) [saŋ + phusanā] touch, contact Th 2, 367; Dhs 2, 71.

Samphusitatta (nt.) [abstr. fr. samphusita] the state of having been brought into touch with Dhs 2, 71.

Sambaddha [saŋ + baddha] bound together Sdhp 81.

Sambandha [saŋ + bandha] connection, tie D II.296 = M I.58; SnA 108, 166, 249, 273, 343, 516. °-kula related family J III.362; a-sambandha (adj.) incompatible (C. on asaññuta J III.266).

Sambandhati [saŋ + bandhati] to bind together, to unite Vin II.116; pass. sambajjhati is united, attached to J III.7; ger. sambandhitvā Vin I.274; II.116. — pp. sambaddha.

Sambandhana (nt.) [saŋ + bandhana] binding together, connection J I.328.

Sambarimāyā (f.) [sambarī + māyā] the art of Sambari, jugglery S I.239 (trslⁿ "Sambara's magic art"). Sambara is a king of the Asuras.

Sambala (nt.) [cp. *Sk. śambala] provision S II.98; J V.71, 240; VI.531.

Sambahula (adj.) [saŋ + bahula] many Vin I.32; D I.2; J I.126, 329; Sn 19; sambahulaŋ karoti to take a plurality vote J II.45.

Sambahulatā (f.) [fr. sambahula] a plurality vote J II.45.

Sambahulika (adj.) in °ŋ karoti = sambahulaŋ karoti J II.197.

Sambādha [cp. Sk. sambādha] 1. crowding, pressure, inconvenience from crowding, obstruction Vism 119. janasambādharahita free from crowding Miln 409; kiṭṭhasambādha crowding of corn, the time when the corn is growing thick M I.115; J I.143, 388. — yassa sambādho bhavissati he who finds it too crowded Vin IV.43; asambādha unobstructed Sn 150; atisambādhatā (q. v.) the state of being too narrow J I.7; puttadāra-sambādhasayana a bed encumbered with child and wife Miln 243; cp. S I.78; (in fig. sense) difficulty, trouble S I.7, 48; J IV.488; sambādhapaṭipanna of the eclipsed moon S I.50. As *adjective* "crowded, dense" sambādho gharavāso life in the family is confined, i. e. a narrow life, full of hindrances D I.63, 250; S II.219; V.350; DA I.180; s. magga a crowded path J I.104; nijana° vana Vism 342; s. vyūha S V.369. — atisambādha too confined DhA I.310 (cakkavāḷa). — compar. sambādhatara S V.350; asambādhaŋ comfortably J I.80. — 2. pudendum masculinum Vin I.216; II.134; pudendum muliebre Vin IV.259; Sn 609; sambādhaṭṭhāna (nt.) pudendum muliebre J I.61; IV.260.

Sambādheti [saŋ + bādheti] to be crowded D II.269 (read °bādhāyanti).

Sambāhati [saŋ + bāhati; Kern, *Toev.* s. v. disputes relation to **vah**, but connects it with **bāh** "press"] 1. to rub, shampoo J I.293; II.16; IV.431; V.126; also sambāheti Miln 241; Caus. sambāhāpeti to cause to shampoo Vin IV.342; ppr. sambāhanta J VI.77; aor. sambāhi J I.293. Cp. pari°.

Sambāhana (nt.) [fr. last] rubbing, shampooing D I.7 (as a kind of exercise for wrestlers DA I.88); A I.62; IV.54; Miln 241; J I.286.

Sambuka [cp. Sk. śambuka] a shell D I.84 = A I.9; III.395 (sippi°); J II.100.

Sambujjhati [saŋ + bujjhati] to understand, achieve, know DhsA 218; inf. sambuddhuŋ Sn 765 (v. l. sambuddhaŋ); Caus. sambodheti to teach, instruct J I.142. Cp. sammā°.

Sambuddha [saŋ + buddha] 1. well understood Sn 765 (various reading, sambuddhuŋ = to know); J V.77 (sam° & a°, taken by C. as ppr. "jānanto" & "ajānanto"); susambuddha easily understood Sn 764. — 2. one who has thoroughly understood, being enlightened, a Buddha Sn 178 etc., 559; A II.4; Dh 181; S I.4; It 35 etc.

Sambuddhi (f.) [saŋ + buddhi] complete understanding; adj. °vant wise J III.361 (= buddhisampanna).

Sambojjhanga [saŋ + bojjhanga] constituent of Sambodhi (enlightenment), of which there are seven: sati, self-possession; dhammavicaya, investigation of doctrine; viriya, energy; pīti, joy; passaddhi, tranquillity; samādhi, concentration; upekhā, equanimity D II.79, 303 sq.; III.106, 226; M I.61 sq.; A IV.23; S V.110 sq.; Nd² s. v. Miln 340; VbhA 135, 310. The characteristics of the several constitutents together with var. means of cultivation are given at Vism 132 sq. = VbhA 275 sq.

Sambodha [saŋ + bodha] enlightenment, highest wisdom, awakening; the insight belonging to the three higher stages of the Path, Vin I.10; D III.130 sq., 136 sq.; S II 223; V.214; M I.16, 241; A I.258; II.200, 240 sq., 325 sq.; V.238 sq.; It 27; pubbe sambodhā, before attaining insight M I.17, 163; II.211; III.157; S II.5, 10; IV.6, 8, 97, 233; V.281; A I.258; III.82, 240. abhabba sambodhāya, incapable of insight M I.200, 241 = A II 200. (Cp. *Dial.* I.190-192.)

-gāmin leading to enlightenment D III.264; Sn p. 140. -pakkhika belonging to enlightenment A IV.357. -sukha the bliss of enlightenment A IV.341 sq.

Sambodhana (nt.) [saŋ+bodhana] the vocative case VvA 12, 18.

Sambodhi (f.) [saŋ+bodhi[1]] the same as sambodha, the highest enlightenment D I.156; II.155; Dh 89=S V.29; Sn 478; S I.68, 181; A II.14; It 28, 42, 117; SnA 73. See also sammā°.
-agga [°yagga] the summit of enlightenment Sn 693; -gāmin leading to enlightenment S V.234; -patta having attained enlightenment, an Arahant Sn 503, 696; -parāyana that which has enlightenment as its aim, proceeding towards enlightenment, frequently of the *Sotāpanna* D I.156 (discussed in *Dialogues* I.190 sq.); III.131 sq.; A I.232; II.80, 238; III.211; IV.12, 405; S V.343, 346; DA I.313. -sukha the bliss of enlightenment Kvu 209.

Sambodhiyanga the same as sambojjhanga A V.253 sq.; S V.24; cp. spelling sambodhi-anga at Dh 89; DhA II.162.

Sambodheti see sambujjhati.

Sambhagga [saŋ+bhagga] broken S I.123; M I.237. Cp. sampali°.

Sambhajati [saŋ+bhajati] to consort with, love, to be attached, devoted J III.495; ppr. sambhajanto J III.108; Pot. sambhajeyya ibid. (C. samāgaccheyya). — pp. sambhatta.

Sambhajanā (f.) [saŋ+bhajanā] consorting with Dhs 1326; Pug 20.

Sambhañjati [saŋ+bhañjati] to split, break J V.32; Caus. sambhañjeti to break M I.237; S I.123; pass. aor. samabhajjisaŋ J V.70. — pp. sambhagga. — Cp. sampali°.

Sambhata [saŋ+bhata] brought together, stored up; (nt.) store, provisions M I.116; D III.190; A III.38=IV.266; S I.35; II.185=It 17; J I.338; ThA 11.

Sambhati [**śrambh**, given as **sambh** at Dhtp 214 in meaning "vissāsa"] to subside, to be calmed; only in prep. comb[n] paṭippassambhati (q. v.).

Sambhatta [pp. of sambhajati] devoted, a friend J I.106, 221; Nd[1] 226=Vism 25. — yathāsambhattaŋ according to where each one's companions live D II.98; S V.152.

Sambhatti (f.) [saŋ+bhatti] joining, consorting with Dhs 1326; Pug 20.

Sambhama [saŋ+bhama, fr. **bhram**] confusion, excitement; °-patta overwhelmed with excitement J IV.433.

Sambhamati [saŋ+bhamati] to revolve DhsA 307.

Sambhava [saŋ+bhava] 1. origin, birth, production D II.107; S III.86; A II.10, 18; Sn 724, 741 etc.; Dh 161; J I.168; mātāpettikas° born from father and mother D I.34; DhsA 306; natthi sambhavaŋ has not arisen Sn 235. — 2. semen virile J V.152; VI.160; Miln 124.
-esin seeking birth M I.48; S II.11; Sn 147.

Sambhavati, sambhuṇāti & sambhoti [saŋ+bhavati] 1. to be produced, to arise D I.45, 76; S I.135; IV.67; Sn 734; Dāvs V.6; Miln 210. — 2. to be adequate, competent D II.287; na s. is of no use or avail Miln 152. — 3. to be present, to witness J I.56. — 4. to be together with J II.205 (C. on sambhaj-°). — Pres. °-bhunati or °-bhuṇāti (like abhi-sam-bhuṇāti) in the sense of "to reach" or "to be able to," capable of Vin I.256 (°-bhuṇāti); Sn 396 (part. a-sambhuṇanto=asakkonto, C.); also sambhoti Sn 734; D II.287; fut. sambhossāma Mhvs 5, 99. — aor. sambhavi D I.96; 3rd pl. samabhavuŋ Dāvs V.6; ger. sambhuyya having come together with VvA 232. — pp. sambhūta. — Caus. sambhāveti (q. v.).

Sambhavana (nt.) [fr. sambhavati] coming into existence Nett 28.

Sambhāra [fr. saŋ+**bhṛ**] "what is carried together," viz. 1. accumulation, product, preparation; sambhāraseda bringing on sweating by artificial means Vin I.205. — 2. materials, requisite ingredients (of food) Miln 258; J I.481; V.13, 506; J I.9; II.18; IV.492; dabba° an effective requisite DhA I.321; II.114; bodhis° the necessary conditions for obtaining enlightening J I.1; vimokkhas° ThA 214. — 3. constituent part, element S IV.197; DhsA 306.—4. bringing together, collocation S I.135; Miln 28.

Sambhāvana (nt.) [fr. sambhāveti] supposition, assumption, the meaning of the particle sace Vin I.372[19]; cp. J II.29; DhA II.77.

Sambhāvanā (f.) [fr. sambhāveti] honour, reverence, intention, confidence Mhvs 29, 55; DhsA 163 (=okappanā); Sdhp 224.

Sambhāvita [pp. of sambhāveti] honoured, esteemed M I.110, 145; ThA 200; J III.269 (=bhaddaka); VbhA 109.

Sambhāveti [Caus. of sambhavati. The Dhtp (512) gives a special root **sambhu** in meaning "pāpuṇana"] 1. to undertake, achieve, to be intent on (acc.) Vin I.253; DhsA 163. — 2. to reach, catch up to (acc.) Vin I.277; II.300. — 3. to produce, effect Miln 49. — 4. to consider J III.220. — 5. to honour, esteem; grd. °bhāvanīya to be honoured or respected, honourable VvA 152; MA 156. — pp. sambhāvita.

Sambhāsā (f.) [saŋ+bhāsā] conversation, talk; sukha-° J VI.296 (v. l.); mudu-° J II.326=IV.471=V.451.

Sambhindati [saŋ+bhindati] to mix Vin I.111 (sīmāya sīmaŋ s. to mix a new boundary with an old one, i. e. to run on a boundary unduly); DA I.134 (udakena). — pp. sambhinna. — Cp. sambhejja.

Sambhinna [pp. of sambhindati] 1. mixed, mixed up Vin I.210; II.67, 68 (cp. *Vin. Texts* II.431); J I.55; Sn 9, 319 (°mariyāda-bhāva confusing the dividing lines, indistinctness), 325 (id.). Said of a woman (i. e. of indistinct sexuality) Vin II.271=III.129. — 2. broken up (?), exhausted J I.503 (°sarīra). — asambhinna: 1. unmixed, unadulterated Vism 41 (°khīra-pāyāsa); J V.257 (°khattiyavaŋsa); DhA II.85 (id.). — 2. (of the voice) unmixed, i. e. distinct, clear Miln 360. — 3. name of a kind of ointment Vin IV.117.

Sambhīta (adj.) [saŋ+bhīta] terrified Miln 339; a-sambhīta, fearless Miln 105; J IV.92; V.34; VI.302.

Sambhuñjati [saŋ+bhuñjati] 1. to eat together with Vin IV.137. — 2. to associate with S I.162.

Sambhuṇāti see sambhavati.

Sambhūta [pp. of sambhavati] arisen from, produced Sn 272 (atta° self-; cp. SnA 304: attabhāva-pariyāye attani s.); S I.134.

Sambhejja [grd. of sambhindati] belonging to the confluence of rivers (said of the water of the ocean), united S II.135; V.461 (various reading sambhojja).

Sambheda [saŋ+bheda] mixing up, confusion, contamination D III.72; A I.51=It 36; DA I.260 (jāti° mixing of caste); Vism 123 (of colours).

Sambhoga [saŋ+bhoga] eating, living together with Vin I.97; II.21; IV.137; A I.92; SnA 71; J IV.127; Sdhp 435.

Sambhoti see sambhavati.

Samma[1] [as to etym. Andersen, *P. Reader* II.263 quite plausibly connects it with Vedic śam (indecl.) "hail," which is often used in a vocative sense, esp. in combn śam ca yos ca "hail & blessing!", but also suggests relation to sammā. Other suggestions see Andersen, s. v.] a term of familiar address D I.49, 225; DA I.151; Vin II.161; J I.59; PvA 204; plur. sammā Vin II.161.

Samma[2] [samyak] see sammā.

Samma[3] a cymbal Miln 60; Dhs 621; J I.3; DhsA 319. — Otherwise as °tāḷa a kind of cymbal Th 1, 893, 911; Vv 35[3]; VvA 161; J VI.60; 277 (-l-).

Sammakkhana (nt.) [saŋ+makkhana] smearing Vism 346.

Sammakkhita [saŋ+makkhita] smeared J V.16; abstr. °tta (nt.) Vism 346.

Sammakkheti [saŋ+makkheti] to smear Vism 346.

Sammaggata see under sammā°.

Sammajjati [saŋ+majjati[2]] 1. to sweep Vin I.46; II.209; J II.25; DhA I.58; II.184; III.168. — 2. to rub, polish J I.338. — pp. sammaṭṭha. — Caus. II. sammajjāpeti Vin I.240.

Sammajjana (adj.-nt.) [fr. last] sweeping J I.67; SnA 66 (°ka); VvA 319 (T. sammajja).

Sammajjanī (f.) [fr. last] a broom Vin II.129; A IV.170; Vism 105; DhA III.7; cp. sammujjanī.

Sammaññati see sammannati.

Sammaṭṭha [pp. of sammajjati] swept, cleaned, polished, smooth Vin III.119 (su°); J I.10; III.395 (smooth). Spelt °maṭṭa at Miln 15.

Sammata [pp. of sammannati] 1. considered as M I.39; S II.15; IV.127; D III.89 (dhamma°); Vin IV.161, 295. — 2. honoured, revered M II.213; J I.49; V.79; sādhu-sammata considered, revered, as good D I.47; S IV.398. — 3. authorized, selected, agreed upon D III.93 (mahā-jana°) Vin I.111; III.150.

Sammati[1] [śam; Dhtp 436=upasama] 1. to be appeased, calmed; to cease Dh 5; Pot 3rd pl. sammeyyuŋ S I.24. — 2. to rest, to dwell D I.92; S I.226; J V.396; DA I.262 (=vasati); pp. santa. — Caus. sāmeti to appease, suppress, stop, A II.24; It 82, 83, 117, 183; Dh 265.

Sammati[2] [śram; Vedic śrāmyati Dhtp 220=parissama, 436=kheda] to be weary or fatigued.

Sammati[3] [śam to labour; pres. śamyati; pp. Vedic śamita] to work; to be satisfactory Vin II.119 (paris-sāvanaŋ na s.), 278 (navakammaŋ etc. na s.).

Sammatta[1] [saŋ+matta[2]] intoxicated, maddened, delighted D II.266; Dh 287; J III.188; doting on J V.443; rogasam-matta tormented by illness J V.90 (=°piḷita C.; v. l. °patta, as under matta[2]).

Sammatta[2] (nt.) [abstr. fr. sammā] correctness, righteousness A I.121; III.441; Pug 13; Dhs 1029; Nett 44; 96, 112; Kvu 609; DhsA 45; KvA 141; °kārin, attained to proficiency in Miln 191; sammatta-kāritā *ibid.* — The 8 sammattā are the 8 angas of the ariya-magga (see magga 2 a) D III.255; the 10 are the above with the addition of sammā-ñāṇa and °vimutti A V.240.

Sammad° see sammā.

Sammada [saŋ+mada] drowsiness after a meal D II.195; A I.3; V.83; J II.63; bhatta-° S I.7; J VI.57.

Sammaddati [saŋ+maddati] to trample down Vin I.137; 286 (cīvaraŋ, to soak, steep); ppr. sammaddanto Vin I.137 (to crush).

Sammanteti [saŋ+manteti] to consult together D I.142; J I.269, 399; DA I.135.

Sammannati [saŋ+**man**, fr. Vedic manute, manvate, for the usual manyate: see maññati] 1. to assent, to consent to Mhvs 3, 10; DA I.11. — 2. to agree to, to authorize, select Vin III.150, 158, 238; IV.50; Mhvs 3, 9; sīmaŋ s. to determine, to fix the boundary Vin I.106 sq. — 3. to esteem, honour; inf. sammannituŋ Vin IV.50. samman-nesi D I.105 is misprint for samannesi. — ppr. sammata.

Sammasati [saŋ+masati] to touch, seize, grasp, know thoroughly, master S II.107; Dh 374; Miln 325; to think, meditate on (acc.) J VI.379; ppr. sammasaŋ II.107 & sammasanto Miln 379; J I.74, 75; fem. samma-santī ThA 62; sammasamāna Miln 219, 325, 398; pp. sammasita.

Sammasana [(nt.) fr. last] grasping, mastering Miln 178; Vism 287, 629 sq.; cp. *Cpd.* 65, 210.

Sammasita [pp. of sammasati] grasped, understood, mastered J I.78.

Sammasitar one who grasps, sees clearly Sn 69.

Sammā[1] [cp. Sk. śamyā] a pin of the yoke Abhp 449; a kind of sacrificial instrument SnA 321 (sammaŋ ettha pāsantī ti sammāpāso; *and* sātrā-yāgass' etaŋ adhiva-canaŋ). Cp. Weber *Indische Streifen* I.36, and sammā-pāsa, below.

Sammā[2] (indecl.) [Vedic samyac (=samyak) & samīś "connected, in one"; see under saŋ°] thoroughly, properly, rightly; in the right way, as it ought to be, best, perfectly (opp. micchā) D I.12; Vin I.12; Sn 359; 947; Dh 89, 373. Usually as °-, like sammā-dhārā even or proper showers (i. e. at the right time) Pv II.9[70]; especially in connection with constituents of the eight-fold Aryan Path, where it is contrasted with micchā; see magga 2 a. (e. g. VbhA 114 sq., 121, 320 sq.). — The form sammā is reduced to samma° before *short* vowels (with the insertion of a sandhi *-d-*, cp. puna-d-eva), like samma-d-eva properly, in harmony or completeness D I.110; Vin I.9; PvA 139, 157; samma-d-aññā & °akkhāta (see below); and before *double* consonants arisen from assimilation, like sammag-gata (=samyak+gata). The cpds. we shall divide into two groups, viz. (*A*) cpds. with samma°, (*B*) with sammā°.

A. -akkhāta well preached Dh 86. -aññā perfect knowledge Vin I.183; S I.4; IV.128; Dh 57 (°vimutta, cp. DhA I.434); It 38, 79, 93, 95, 108. -attha a proper or good thing or cause J VI.16. -ddasa having right views A II.18; S IV.205, 207; Sn 733; It 47, 61, 81; Kvu 339. -ggata [cp. BSk. samyaggata Divy 399] who has wandered rightly, perfect M I.66; who has attained the highest point, an Arahant D I.55; S I.76; A I.269; IV.226; V.265; J III.305; It 87; Ap 218. Also sammāgata Vin II.203[17]. -ppajāna having right knowledge Dh 20; It 115. -ppaññā right knowledge, true wisdom Vin I.14; Dh 57, 190; Sn 143; It 17; Miln 39. -ppadhāna [cp. BSk. samyakprahāṇa Divy 208] right exertion Vin I.22; Dhs 358; Dpvs 18, 5; they are four D II.120; M III.296; explained M II.11 (anuppan-nānaŋ pāpakānaŋ akusalānaŋ dhammānaŋ anuppādā-ya; uppannānaŋ pahānāya; anuppannānaŋ kusalānaŋ dhammānaŋ uppādāya; uppannānaŋ ṭhitiyā).

B. -ājīva right living, right means of livelihood, right occupation Vin I.10; S V.421, etc.; formula D II.312; (adj.) living in the right way M I.42; A II.89. -kam-manta right conduct, right behaviour Vin I.10; S V.421 etc.; definition D II.312; Dhs 300; adj. behaving in the right way M I.42; A II.89. -ñāṇa right knowledge, enlightenment, results from right concentration D II.217; A I.292; adj. M I.42. -ñāṇin possessing the right insight A II.89, 222. -dassana right views Vism 605. -diṭṭhi right views, right belief, the first stage of the noble eightfold path, consists in the knowledge of the four truths D II.311; its essence is knowledge Dhs 20, 297, 317; cp. Vism 509; comprises the knowledge of the absence of all permanent Being and the reality of universal conditioned Becoming S II.17; III.135; and of the impermanence of the 5 Khandhas S III.51 = IV.142; and of Sīla, of causation and of the destruction of the Āsavas M I.46-55; how obtained M I.294; two degrees of M III.72; supremely important A I.30-2 292 sq.; (adj.) Miln I.47. -diṭṭhika having the right belief D I.139; A II.89; 220 sq.; III.115, 138; IV.290; V.124 sq.; S IV.322. -dvayatānupassin duly considering both—i. e. misery with its origin, the destruction of misery with the path, respectively Sn p. 140. -dhārā a heavy shower S V.379. -paṭipatti right mental disposition A I.69; Nett 27; Miln 97; sammāpaṭipadā Pug 49 sq.; DhA IV.127; sammāpaṭipanna rightly disposed, having the right view D I.8, 55; Pug 49 sq. -passaŋ viewing the matter in the right way S III.51; IV.142. -pāsa [Sk. śamyāprāsa, but BSk. śamyaprāśa Divy 634] a kind of sacrifice Sn 303; A II.42; IV.151; S I.76; It 21; J IV.302; SnA 321. Cp. sammā¹. -manasikāra right, careful, thought D I.13; DA I.104. -vattanā strict, proper, conduct Vin I.46, 50; II.5. -vācā right speech Vin I.10; DA I.314; definition D II.312; Dhs 299; (adj.) speaking properly M I.42; A II.89. -vāyāma right effort Vin I.10; Dhs 13, 22, 302; definition D II.312; adj. M I.42; A II.89. -vimutta right emancipation A I.292; °vimutti the same D II.217; A II.196, 222; (adj.) M I.42; A II.89. -sankappa right resolve, right intention Dh 12; Vin I.10; Dhs 21, 298; definition D II.312; (adj.) M I.42; A II.89. -sati right memory, right mindfulness, self-possession Vin I.10; Dhs 23, 303; definition D II.313; (adj.) M I.42; A II.89. -samādhi right concentration, the last stage of the noble eightfold path Vin I.10; Dhs 24, 304; definition D II.313; adj. M I.12; A II.89. -sampassaŋ having the right view S IV.142. -sambuddha perfectly enlightened, a universal Buddha Vin I.5; D I.49; Dh 187; J I.44; DhA I.445; III.241; VbhA 436, etc. -sambodhi perfect enlightenment, supreme Buddhaship Vin I.11; D II.83; S I.68, etc.

Sammāna (nt.) [fr. saŋ + **man**] honour J I.182; VI.390; Sdhp 355.

Sammānanā (f.) [saŋ + mānanā] honouring, veneration D III.190; Miln 162, 375, 386.

Sammiñjati (& °eti) [saŋ + iñjati, see also samiñjati; cp. BSk. sammiñjayati Divy 473. See also Leumann, *Album Kern*, p. 393] to bend back, to double up (opp. pasārati or sampasāreti) Vin I.5; M I.57, 168; D I.70; J I.321; Vism 365 (v. l. samiñjeti); DA I.196. — pp. sammiñjita.

Sammiñjana (nt.) [fr. sammiñjati] bending DA I.196 (opp. pasāraṇa); VbhA 358.

Sammiñjita [pp. of sammiñjati] bent back M I.326 (spelt samiñjita); A II.104, 106 sq., 210.

Sammita [saŋ + mita] measured, i. e. just so much, no more or less; °-bhānin Th I, 209.

Sammilāta [saŋ + milāta] withered, shrunk M I.80.

Sammillabhāsinī (f.) [saŋ + milla = mihita, + bhāsin] speaking with smiles J IV.24; name of a girl in Benares J III.93 sq.

Sammissatā (f.) [fr. saŋ + missa] the state of being mixed, confusion DhsA 311.

Sammukha (adj.) [saŋ + mukha] face to face with, in presence; sammukhaciṇṇa a deed done in a person's presence J III.27; sammukhā (abl.) 1. face to face, before, from before D II.155; Sn p. 79; J I.115; III.89 (opp. parokkhā); with acc. Bu II.73 = J I.17; with gen. D I.222; II.220; M I.146.—2. in a full assembly of qualified persons Vin II.3; loc. sammukhe D II.206; J V.461. In composition sammukha°, sammukhā° & sammukhī° (before **bhū**): °bhāva (°a°) presence, confrontation Miln 126; (°ī°) being face to face with, coming into one's presence D I.103; M I.438; A I.150; °bhūta (°ī°) being face to face with, confronted D II.155; S IV.94; Vin II.73; A III.404 sq.; V.226; one who has realized the *saŋyojanas* Kvu 483; °vinaya (°ā°) proceeding in presence, requiring the presence of a chapter of priests and of the party accused Vin II.74, 93 sq.; IV.207; A I.99; DhsA 144. See also yebhuyyasikā.

Sammukhatā (f.) [abstr. fr. sammukha] presence, confrontation Vin II.93 (sangha°).

Sammucchita see samucchita.

Sammujjanī (f.) [= sammajjanī] a broom J I.161; sammuñjanī the same Miln 2.

Sammuṭṭha [saŋ + muṭṭha] confused M I.21; S IV.125; V.331; one who has forgotten Vin IV.4⁵ (= na ssarati); III.165¹³; °ssati id. A I.280.

Sammuti (f.) [fr. saŋ + **man**] 1. consent, permission Vin III.199. — 2. choice, selection, delegation Vin III.159. — 3. fixing, determination (of boundary) Vin I.106. — 4. common consent, general opinion, convention, that which is generally accepted; as °- conventional, e. g. °sacca conventional truth (as opposed to paramattha° the absolute truth) Miln 160; °ñāṇa common knowledge D III.226; °deva what is called a *deva* J I.132; DA I.174; see under **deva**; °maraṇa what is commonly called "death" Vism 229. — sammuccā (instr.) by convention or common consent Sn 648 (v. l. sammacca = ger. of sammannati). — 5. opinion, doctrine Sn 897 (= dvāsaṭṭhī diṭṭhigatāni Nd¹ 308), 904, 911. — 6. definition, declaration, statement Vin I.123 (ummattaka°); A IV.347 (vādaka°); VbhA 164 (bhuñjaka°). — 7. a popular expression, a mere name or word Miln 28. — 8. tradition, lore; combᵈ with suti at Miln 3.

Sammudita [pp. of sammodati] delighted, delighting in Vin I.4; M I.503; S IV.390.

Sammuyhati [saŋ + muyhati] to be bewildered, infatuated, muddle-headed J IV.385; Miln 42. — pp. sammūḷha D II.85; M I.250; A I.165; Sn 583; Caus. sammoheti to befool Miln 224.

Sammuyhana (nt.) [saŋ + muyhana] bewilderment DA I.193

Sammusā M II.202, read sammuccā (from sammuti).

Sammussanatā (f.) [fr. saŋ + mussati] forgetfulness Dhs 14 1349; Pug 21.

Sammūḷha [saŋ + mūḷha] infatuated, bewildered D II.85; M I.250; A I.165; Sn 583; J V.294; Tikp 366.

Sammegha [saŋ + megha] rainy or cloudy weather J VI.51, 52.

Sammoda [fr. saŋ + **mud**] odour, fragrance; ekagandha°, filled with fragrance J VI.9.

Sammodaka (adj.) [fr. sammodati] polite D I.116; DA I.287; a-sammodaka (f. °-ikā) Vin I.341¹⁴.

Sammodati [saŋ + modati] 1. to rejoice, delight; pp. sammudita (q. v.). — 2. to agree with, to exchange friendly greeting with; aor. sammodi Vin I.2; D I.52; Sn 419; J VI.224; ppr. sammodamāna in agreement, on friendly terms J I.209; II.6; ger. sammoditvā J II.107; grd sammodanīya [cp. BSk. sammodanī saŋrañjanī kathā Divy 70, 156 & passim] pleasant, friendly A v.193; cp. Sn 419; Vin I.2; D I.52. — sammodita at VvA 186 read samodita.

Sammodana (nt.) [saŋ+modana] satisfaction, compliment; °ŋ karoti to exchange politeness, to welcome VvA 141, 259.

Sammosa [for *sam-mṛṣa, of **mṛṣ**: see mussati. sammosa after moha & musā>mosa] bewilderment, confusion D I.19; A I.58; II.147; S II.224; IV.190; Vin II.114; Miln 266, 289; Vism 63 (sati° lapse of memory).

Sammoha [saŋ+moha] bewilderment, infatuation, delusion M I.86, 136; Vin I.183; Nd[1] 193; A II.174; III.54 sq., 416; S I.24; IV.206; Dhs 390.

Sammoheti see sammuyhati.

Saya=saka (?) one's own J VI.414 (=saka-raṭṭha C.).

Sayaŋ (adv.) [see etym. under sa[4]] self, by oneself Vin I.8; D I.12; DA I.175; Sn 57, 320, etc.; p. 57, 100, etc.; Mhvs 7, 63 (for f.). Also with ref. to several people, e. g. DhA I.13.

-kata made by itself, spontaneous D III.137 (loka); S II.19 sq. (dukkha); Ud 69 sq. -jāta born from oneself, sprung up spontaneously J I.325; II.129. -pabha radiating light from oneself, a kind of devas D I.17; III.28 sq., 84 sq.; Sn 404; DA I.110 -bhū self-dependent, an epithet of a Buddha Bu XIV.1 = J I.39; Miln 214, 227, 236; Vism 234; SnA 106 (f. abstr. sayambhutā), 135. -vara self-choice J V.426. -vasin self-controlled, independent Bu II.20=J I.5; Dāvs I.22.

Sayatatta at S I.14 read saŋyatatta.

Sayati[1] [śī] to lie down: see seti. Caus. II. sayāpeti ibid.

Sayati[2] [śri which is given in meaning sevā at Dhtp 289] to lean on; to be supported etc.: only in pp. sita, and in prep. cpd. nissayati.

Sayathā (adv.) [cp. Sk. sayathā or tadyathā; see sa[2]. The usual P. form is seyyathā] like as Th 1, 412.

Sayana (nt.) [fr. śī] 1. lying down, sleeping Vism 26; PvA 80 (mañca°). — 2. bed, couch Vin I.57, 72; II.123; D I.5, 7; A I.132; J II.88; V.110 (°ŋ attharāpeti to spread out a bed); Miln 243, 348; Nd[1] 372 (°sannidhi); Pv I.11[7] (kis°=kiŋ°); PvA 78. — sayanakalaha a quarrel in the bedroom, a curtain-lecture J III.20; sayanāsana bed & seat It 112; Dh 185, etc.: see senāsana.

Sayanighara (nt.) a sleeping-room Vin I.140 sq.; IV.160; J I.433; III.275, 276.

Sayāna is ppr. of sayati lying down (e. g. A II.13 sq.): see seti.

Sayāpita [pp. of sayāpeti] made to lie down VbhA 11.

Sayita [pp. of seti] lying down J I.338; V.438. sukha° lying in a good position, sleeping well, well-embedded (of seeds) A III.404=D II.354; Miln 255. sukha-sayita-bhāva "having had a good sleep," being well J V.127.

Sayha see sahati.

Sara[1] [cp. Vedic śara] 1. the reed Saccharum sara Miln 342. — 2. an arrow (orig. made of that reed) D I.9; Dh 304; Miln 396; DhA 216 (visa-pīta).

-tuṇḍa a beak as sharp as an arrow DhA III.32. -daṇḍaka shaft of an arrow DhA II.141. -bhanga arrow-breaking Vism 411 (in comp.).

Sara[2] (adj.-n.) [fr. sarati[1] 1. going, moving, following Sn 3, 901 — 2. fluid, flow J I.359 (pūti°).

Sara[3] (m.-nt.) [Vedic saras] a lake J I.221; II.10; VI.518 (Mucalinda); there are seven great lakes (mahā-sarā, viz. Anotatta, Sīhapapāta, Rathakāra, Kaṇṇamuṇḍa, Kuṇāla, Chaddanta, Mandākini) A IV.101; D I.54; J II.92; DA I.164, 283; aṇṇava° the ocean D II.89; cp. A II.55; loc. sare J II.80; sarasmiŋ Sn 1092; & sarasi Mhvs 10, 7; jātassara a natural lake J I.472 sq.

Sara[4] (adj.) [fr. sarati[2]] remembering M I.453; A II.21; DA I.106. °sankappa mindfulness and aspiration M I.453; III.132; S IV.76, 137, 190; Nett 16.

Sara[5] [Vedic svara, **svar**, cp. Lat. su-surrus, Ger. surren] sound, voice, intonation, accent Vin II.108; D II.24 sq.; A I.227; Pv II.12[4] (of birds' singing=abhiruda C.); J II.109; Sn 610 (+vaṇṇa, which is doubtful here, whether "complexion" or "speech," preferably the former); DhsA 17; eight qualities D II.211, 227; gītassara song Vin II.108; bindussara a sweet voice Sn 350; adj. J II.439; sīhassara with a voice like a lion's J V.296, 311 (said of a prince). Cp. **vissara**. — In comb[n] with vaṇṇa (vowel) at A IV.307; Miln 340.

-kutti [=klpti; can we compare BSk. svaragupti "depth of voice" Divy 222 ?] intonation, resonance, timbre, melodiousness of voice Vin II.108=A III.251; J VI.293 (Kern, "enamoured behaviour" [?]); DhsA 16. Cp. *Vin. Texts* III.72. -bhañña intoning, a particular mode of reciting Vin I.196; II.108, 316; J II.109; DhA I.154. -bhāṇa=°bhañña DhA II.95 (v. l. °bhañña). -bhāṇaka an intoner, one who intones or recites the sacred texts in the Sarabhañña manner Vin II.300. -sara an imitative word; sarasaraŋ karoti to make the noise sarasara M I.128.

Saraŋsā (f.) [fr. sa[3]+raŋsi] the sun (lit. having rays) Mhvs 18, 68.

Saraka a vessel, a drinking vessel J I.157, 266; IV.384; DA I.134, 136; Mhvs 32, 32; DhA II.85; III.7.

Saraja (adj.) [sa+rajo] dusty Vin I.48; A II.54.

Saraṇa[1] (nt.) [cp. Vedic śaraṇa protection, shelter, house, śarman id.; śālā hall; to Idj. ***kel** to hide, as in Lat. celo, Gr. καλύπτω to conceal, Oir. celim, Ohg. Ags. helan, Goth. huljan to envelop; Ohg. hella=E. hell; also E. hall, and others] shelter, house Sn 591; refuge, protection D III.187; Sn 503; J II.28; DA I.229; especially the three refuges—the Buddha, the Dhamma, and the Brotherhood— A I.56; D I.145; J I.28; usually combined with verbs like upeti Vv 53[2]; Sn 31; gacchati D I.116; A III.242; Vin I.4; Dh 190; Sn p. 15, 25; It 63; or yāti Sn 179; Dh 188; asaraṇa, asaraṇībhūta without help and refuge Miln 148. See **leṇa** 2.

-āgamana=°gamana D I.146; SnA 42, 157. -gamana (nt.) taking refuge in the three Saraṇas Vin III.24; S IV.270.

Saraṇa[2] (adj.) [sa+raṇa] concomitant with war Dhs 1294; DhsA 50.

Saraṇa[3] [fr. **smṛ**; i. e. sarati[2]] (nt.) remembrance; -tā (f.) remembering Dhs 14, 23; Pug 21, 25.

Saraṇīya (nt.) [grd. formation fr. saraṇa[3]] something to be remembered A I.106.

Sarati[1] [**sṛ** given by Dhtp 248 as "gati"] to go, flow, run, move along J III.95 (=parihāyati nassati C.); Pot. sare J IV.284. — aor. asarā J VI.199. — pp. sarita[1]. — Caus. sāreti (1) to make go A I.141; III.28=M I.124=S IV.176 J IV.99; Miln 378; Vism 207. — (2) to rub, to mix Vin II.116. Also sarāpeti. A Desid. form[n] is siŋsare (3rd pl. med.) at Vv 64[7] (=Sk. sisīrṣati), cp. Geiger, *P.Gr.* § 184.

Sarati[2] [**smṛ**, cp. smṛti=sati; Dhtp 248 "cintā"; Lat memor, memoria=memory; Gr. μέριμνα care, μάρτυ witness, martyr; Goth. maúrnan = E. mourn to care, etc.] to remember D II.234; Vin I.28; II.79; J II.29. A diæretic form is sumarati Dh 324; ger. sumariya Mhvs 4, 65. — 1st pl. saremhase Th 2, 383; med. sare J VI.227; imper. sara Th 1, 445; & sarāhi Miln 79; 3rd sg. saratu Vin I.273. — ppr. saraŋ Mhvs 3, 6; & saramāna Vin I.103. — aor. sari J I.330; fut. sarissati J VI.496. — ger. saritvā J I.214. — pp. sata[2] & sarita[2]. — Caus. sāreti to remind Vin II.3 sq., 276; III.221; sārayamāna, reminding J I.50; ppr. pass. sāriyamāna Vin III.221; w. acc. D II.234; w. gen. Dh 324; J VI.496; with foll. fut. II. (in °tā) Vin II.125, 4; III.44, 9, etc. — Caus. II. sarāpeti Vin III.44; Miln 37 (with double acc.), 79.

Sarati[3] [śṛ; Dhtp 248: hiŋsā] to crush: see seyyati. Caus. sāreti Vin II.116 (madhu-sitthakena, to pound up, or mix with beeswax). Cp. saritaka.

Sarada [Vedic śarad (f.) traces of the cons. decl. only in acc. pl. sarado sataŋ "100 autumns" J II.16] autumn, the season following on the rains Sn 687; Vv 35[2]. °-samaya the autumn season D II.183; M I.115; A IV.102; V.22; It 20; S I.65; III.141, 155; V.44; VvA 134, 161.

Sarabha [Vedic śarabha a sort of deer J IV.267; VI.537] (rohiccasarabhā migā = rohitā sarabhamigā, C. ibid. 538); Sarabhamigajātaka the 483rd Jātaka J I.193, 406 (text Sarabhanga); IV.263 sq.
-pallanka "antelope-couch," a high seat, from which the Bodhisat preaches J III.342 (cp. vara-pallanka J III.364). -pādaka having legs like those of a gazelle J I.267.

Sarabhasaŋ (adv.) [sa[2] + rabhasaŋ] eagerly, quickly Dāvs IV.22, 34 sq., 43.

Sarabhū (f.) [cp. Sk. saraṭa] a lizard Vin II.110; A II.73; J II.135, 147; SnA 439.

Sarala the tree Pinus longifolia J V.420 (thus read with B instead of salaḷa [?]).

Saravant (adj.) [sara[5] + vant] 1. having or making a sound, well-sounding Vin I.182; A III.375. — 2. with a noise Mhvs 25, 38.

Sarasa (adj.) [sa[3] + rasa] with its essential properties (see rasa) Nd[1] 43; sarasabhāva a method of exposition DhsA 71.

Sarasī (f.) [Vedic sarasī] a large pond Vin II.201 = S II.269; J V.46.

Sarāga (adj.) [sa[3] + rāga] connected with lust, passionate D I.79; II.299; M I.59; Vism 410.

Sarājaka (adj.) [sa[3] + rāja + ka] including the king J I.126; fem. -ikā Vin II.188; S I.162; J II.113, 114 (sarājika at J III.453); with the king's participation Tikp 26 (sassāmika-sarājaka geha).

Sarājita denomination of a purgatory and its inhabitants S IV.309 sq. Various readings Parājita and Sarañjita.

Sarāpana (nt.) [fr. sarāpeti Caus. of sarati[2]] causing somebody to remember Miln 79.

Sarāva [Sk. śarāva] a cup, saucer A I.161; J I.8; M III.235 for patta); Miln 282; DA I.298; PvA 244, 251.

Sarāvaka = sarāva Vin I.203; II.142, 153, 222.

Sari according to Payogasiddhi = sarisa (sadisa) cp. sarīvaṇṇa J II.439 (= samāna-vaṇṇa, C.).

Sarikkha (adj.) [cp. Sk. sadṛkṣa, fr. sadṛś = P. sadisa] like, resembling S I.66; J I.443; III.262.

Sarikkhaka (adj.) [= sarikkha] in accordance with, like J IV.215; PvA 206, 284. See also kamma°.

Sarikkhatā (f.) [fr. sarikkha] resemblance, likeness J III.241 (taŋ° being like that); VvA 6 (cp. kamma°).

Sarikkhatta (nt.) [fr. sarikkha] likeness DhsA 63; as sarikkhakatta (kamma°) at DhsA 347.

Sarita[1] [pp. of sarati[1]] gone, set into motion Dh 341 (= anusaṭa, payāta DhA IV.49).

Sarita[2] [pp. of sarati[2]] remembered Vin II.85.

Saritaka (nt.) powdered stone (pāsāna-cuṇṇa) Vin II.116; saritasipāṭika powder mixed with gum Vin II.116.

Saritar [n. ag. fr. sarati[2]] one who remembers D III.268, 286; A II.35; S V.197, 225.

Saritā (f.) [cp. Vedic sarit, fr. sarati[1]] a river Dhs 1059; saritaŋ acc. Sn 3; gen. pl. J II.442; nom. pl. saritā Miln 125.

Sarisa (adj.) [= sadisa] like, resembling J V.159.

Sarisapa various reading of siriŋsapa M I.10 etc.

Sarīra (nt.) [Vedic śarīsa] 1. the (physical) body D I.157; M I.157; S IV.286; A I.50; II.41; III.57 sq., 323 sq.; IV.190. Sn 478, 584; Dh 151; Nd[1] 181; J I.394 (six blemishes); II.31; antimasarīra one who wears his last body, an Anāgāmin Sn 624; S I.210; Dh 400. — 2. a dead body, a corpse D II.141, 164; M III.91. — 3. the bones D II.164. — 4. relics Vv 63, 32; VvA 269.
-aṭṭhaka the bony framework of the body DhsA 338. -ābhā radiation of light proceeding from the body, lustre SnA 16 (°ŋ muñcati to send forth), 41 (id.), 140 (id.). -kicca (1) funeral ceremonies, obsequies J I.180; II.5; VvA 76, 257; PvA 74, 76, 162. — (2) "bodily function," satisfying the body's wants J II.77; IV.37. -davya (= dabba[1]) fitness of body, good body, beauty J II.137. -dhātu a body relic (of the Buddha) Mhvs 13, 167; VvA 165, 269. -pabhā lustre of the body DhA I.106. -parikamma attending the body SnA 52. -maŋsa the flesh of the body J III.53. -vaṇṇa the (outward) appearance of the body Vism 193. -valañja discharge from the body, fæces DhA II.55; IV.46 (°ṭhāna). See valañja. -sanghāta perfection of body Vism 194. -saṇṭhāna constitution of the body, bodily form Vism 193.

Sarīravant (adj.) [sarīra + vant] having a body S II.279.

Sarīvaṇṇa resembling J II.439 (v. l. sarīra°). Cp. sari.

Sarūpa (adj.) [sa[2] + rūpa] 1. of the same form A I.162; Pug 56. — 2. [sa[3] + rūpa] having a body A I.83.

Saroja (nt.) [Sk. saroja, saras + ja] "lake-born," a lotus Dāvs III.13.

Sarojayoni [fr. last] a Brahmā, an archangel Dāvs I.34.

Saroruha (nt.) [saras + ruha] a lotus Dāvs III.83.

Salakkhaṇa[1] (adj.) [sa[3] + lakkhaṇa] together with the characteristics Sn 1018.

Salakkhaṇa[2] (nt.) [sa[1] + lakkhaṇa] own characteristic, that which is consistent with one's own nature Miln 205; Nett 20. Opp. vilakkhaṇa.

Salana (nt.) [fr. śal] moving, shaking VvA 169; DhsA 62 (in def[n] of *kusala* as "kucchitānaŋ salan'ādīhi atthehi kusalaŋ").

Salabha [cp. Sk. śalabha] a moth J V.401; Ud 72 (C.); VbhA 146.

Salayati [Caus. of śal to leap] to shake DhsA 39.

Salaḷa a kind of sweet-scented tree J V.420; Bu II.51 = J I.13; Vv 35[5]; VvA 162; Miln 338; M II.184.

Salākā (f.) [cp. Vedic śalākā] 1. an arrow, a dart A IV.107 (T. has it as nt.). — 2. a small stick, peg, thin bar S IV.168; Dāvs IV.51. — 3. blade of a grass M I.79; J I.439. — 4. ribs of a parasol Vin IV.338; SnA 487; Miln 226. — 5. a pencil, small stick (used in painting the eyes with collyrium) Vin I.204; J III.419 (añjana°). — 6. a kind of needle Vin II.116. — 7. a kind of surgical instrument, a stick of caustic Miln 112, 149. — 8. a gong stick (of bronze, loha°) J II.342; Vism 283. — 9. membrum virile J II.359. — 10. a ticket consisting of slips of wood used in voting and distributing food, vote, lot Vin II.99, 176, 306; J I.123; PvA 272 (kāḷakaṇṇi°); salākaŋ gaṇhāti to take tickets (in order to vote or to be counted) Vin I.117; II.199; paṭhaman salākaŋ gaṇhanto taking the first vote, first rate A I.24; salākaŋ gāheti to issue tickets, to take a vote Vin II.205; salākaŋ dadāti to issue tickets J I.123; salākaŋ vāreti to throw lots J I.239 (kāḷakaṇṇi°).

-agga room for distributing food by tickets J I.123; Mhvs 15, 205. -odhāniya a case for the ointment-stick Vin I.204. -gāha taking of votes, voting Vin II.85, 98 sq. (3 kinds). -gāhāpaka ticket-issuer, taker of voting tickets Vin II.84. -bhatta food to be distributed by tickets Vin I.58, 96; II.175; J I.123; DhA I.53 (eight kinds). -vātapāna a window made with slips of wood Vin II.148. -vutta "subsisting on blades of grass" (or "by means of food tickets"?) Vin III.6, 67; IV.23; A I.160; S IV.323. Cp. BSk. śalākāvṛtti Divy 131 -hattha brush-hand, a kind of play, where the hand is dipped in lac or dye and used as a brush (?) D I.85; DA I.85.

Salāṭuka (adj.) [cp. *Sk. śalāṭu] fresh, unripe S I.150 = Sn p. 125; Miln 334; VvA 288.

Salābha [sa[4] + lābha] one's own advantage Dh 365.

Salila (nt.) [cp. Sk. salila, to sarati[1]] water Sn 62, 319, 672; J I.8; V.169; VvA 41; PvA 157; Nd[2] 665 ("vuccati udakaŋ"); Miln 132 (written saliḷa); Sdhp 168. It is also adj. salilaŋ āpo flowing water J VI.534; cp. Miln 114: na tā nadiyo dhuva-salilā.

-dhārā shower of water Miln 117. -vuṭṭhi id. Vism 234.

Salla (nt.) [Vedic śalya, cp. śalākā] an arrow, dart M I.429 (°ŋ āharati to remove the a); II.216; S IV.206; J I.180; V.49; Sn 331, 767; Miln 112; Vism 503 (visa° sting of poison; cp. VbhA 104 sallaŋ viya vitujjati); often metaphorically of the piercing sting of craving, evil, sorrow etc., e. g. antodosa° Miln 323; taṇhā° S I.40, 192; bhava° Dh 351; rāga° DhA III.404; PvA 230; soka° Sn 985; Pv I.86; KhA 153. Cp. also D II.283; Sn 51, 334, 938; J I.155; III.157; DhA IV.70. At Nd[1] 59 *seven* such stings are given with rāga°, dosa°, moha°, māna°, diṭṭhi°, soka°, kathankathā°. —abhūḷha° one whose sting of craving or attachment is pulled out D II.283; Sn 593; J III.390; Pv I.8[7] etc. (see abbūḷha). — Cp. vi°.

-katta [*kartṛ cp. Geiger *P.Gr.* § 90, 4] "one who works on the (poisoned) arrow," i. e. a surgeon M I.429; II.216; Sn 562; It 101; Miln 110, 169; Vism 136 (in simile); KhA 21 (id.). The Buddha is the best surgeon: Sn 560; Miln 215. -kattiya surgery D I.12 (T. °ka); DA I.98. -bandhana at Th 2, 347 take as salla + bandhana "arrow & prison bond" (ThA 242 different). -viddha pierced by an arrow Th 1, 967; Sn 331; cp. ruppati. -santhana removal of the sting Dh 275 (= nimmathana abbāhana DhA III.404).

Sallaka [cp. *Sk. śalala & śallaka] a porcupine J V.489.

Sallakī (f.) [cp. Class. Sk. śallakī] the tree Boswellia thurifera (incense tree) J IV.92; pl. °-iyo J VI.535; bahukuṭaja-sallakika Th 1, 115 (= indasālarukkha [?]).

Sallakkhaṇā (f.) [fr. sallakkheti] discernment, testing Dhs 16, 292, 555; Pug 25; Vism 278; VbhA 254; DhsA 147; asallakkaṇa non-discernment S III.261.

Sallakkhita [pp. of sallakkheti] realized, thought DhA I.89.

Sallakkheti [saŋ + lakkheti] to observe, consider Vin I.48, 271; J I.123; II.8; Vism 150; to examine J V.13; to bear in mind DhsA 110; J VI.566; to understand, realize, conclude, think over J IV.146; VvA 185; VbhA 53; asallakkhetvā without deliberation Vin II.215; inadvertently J I.209. — Caus. II. sallakkhāpeti to cause to be noted Mhvs 9, 24; DhsA 121; to persuade, bring to reason J VI.393.

Sallapati [saŋ + lapati] to talk (with) D I.90; II.109; Miln 4; sallapeti the same Vin IV.1[4].

Sallalīkata pierced, perforated J I.180. Trenckner suggests that this form may have arisen from *sallakīkata (from sallaka, porcupine).

Sallahuka (adj.) [saŋ + lahuka] light J I.277; II.26; Vism 65; DhA IV.17; sallahukena nakkhattena on lucky nights J II.278; sallahukavuttin whose wants are easily met, frugal Sn 144; DA I.207.

Sallāpa [saŋ + lāpa] conversation D I.89; A II.182; J I.112, 189; Miln 94. Often in cpd. kathā & allāpa°.

Sallitta [saŋ + litta] smeared (with) Th 1, 1175 (mīḷha°).

Sallīna [saŋ + līna] sluggish, cowering D II.255; asallīna active, upright, unshaken D II.157; S I.159; IV.125; Cp. V.68. paṭi°.

Sallīyanā (f.) stolidity Dhs 1156, 1236.

Sallekha [fr. saŋ + likh] austere penance, the higher life M I.13, 40; Vin I.305; Ps I.102, 103; Pug 69 sq.; DA I.82; Vism 69; Miln 360, 380; adj. Vin I.45; sallekhitācāra practising austere penance Miln 230, 244, 348 sq.; °vutti Vin II.197; Vism 65 (°vuttitā). Cp. abhi°.

Sallekhatā (f.) = sallekha D III.115; Vism 53.

Saḷāyatana (nt.) [ṣaḍ° for which ordinarily chaḷ°: see cha] the six organs of sense and the six objects—viz., eye, ear, nose, tongue, body, and mind; forms, sounds, odours, tastes, tangible things, ideas; occupying the fourth place in the Paṭiccasamuppāda D II.32; M I.52; A I.176; S II.3; Vin I.1; Vism 529, 562 sq., 671; VbhA 174, 176 sq., 319.

Sava (adj.) [fr. sru, savati] dripping, flowing with (-°) Pv II.9[11] (madhu°, with honey).

Savaka see °saŋ.

Savanka a sort of fish J V.405. Cp. satavanka & saccavanka.

Savacanīya [sa[3] + vacanīya] (the subject of a) conversation Vin II.5, 32, 276.

Savati [sru; cp. Sk. srotas stream; Gr. ῥεῦμα, ῥέω to flow; Ags. strēam = stream; Oir. sruth] to flow Sn 197, 1034; J VI.278; Dh 370. — ppr. fr. savantī ThA 109.

Savana[1] (nt.) [fr. śru: see suṇāti] 1. the ear Sn 1120; Miln 258. — 2. hearing D I.153, 179; A I.121; S I.24; Vin I.26; Sn 265, 345; Dh 182; J I.160, 250; Miln 257; Nd[1] 188. sussavanaŋ sāvesi she made me hear a good hearing, she taught me a good thing J I.61; savanaṭṭhāne within hearing J IV.378. dhamma° hearing the preaching of the Dhamma Vin I.101 etc.

Savana[2] (nt.) [fr. savati] flowing Dh 339; J IV.288; V.257; savana-gandha of the body, having a tainted odour Th 2, 466.

Savanīya (adj.) [grd. of suṇāti] pleasant to hear D II.211; J I.96 (-ṇ-); J VI.120 = 122 (savaneyya).

Savantī (f.) [cp. Vedic sravat, orig. ppr. of sru, sravati] a river Vin II.238; Bu II.86 = J I.18; J VI.485; Miln 319.

Savara [Epic Sk. śabara, cp. śabala = P. sabala] an aboriginal tribe, a savage Vin I.168; Miln 191.

Savasa [sa[4] + vasa] one's own will DhsA 61 (°vattitā; cp. *Expos.* 81).

Savighāta (adj.) [sa[3] + vighāta] bringing vexation Th 2, 352; ThA 242.

Savicāra accompanied by investigation D I.37 etc., in the description of the first Jhāna. See vicāra.

Savijjuka (adj.) [sa[3] + vijju + ka] accompanied by lightning D II.262.

Saviññāṇa possessed of consciousness, conscious, animate A I.83; -ka the same A I.132; DhA I.6. — See viññāṇaka.

Savitakka accompanied by reasoning D I.37 etc., in the formula of the first Jhāna. See vitakka.

Savidha (adj.) [Sk. savidha] near; (nt.) neighbourhood Dāvs IV.32; V.9.

Savibhattika (adj.) [sa[3] + vibhatti + ka] (able) to be classified DhsA 134.

Savupādāna = sa-upādāna (A II.163): see upādāna.

Savera (adj.) [sa[3] + vera] angry D I.247.

Savyañjana (adj.) [sa[3] + vyañjana] with the letters Vin I.21; D I.62; DA I.176; Sn. p. 103; Vism 214.

Savhaya (adj.) [sa[3] + avhaya] called, named Dpvs 4, 7; Ap 109.

Sasa [Vedic śaśa, with Ohg. haso = E. hare to Lat. canus grey, greyish-brown; cp. Ags. hasu] a hare, rabbit Dh 342; J IV.85; of the hare in the moon J IV.84 sq.; sasôlūkā (= sasā ca ulūkā ca) J VI.564.
-lakkhaṇa the sign of a hare J I.172; III.55. -lañjana id. VvA 314 (°vant = sasin, the moon). -visāṇa a hare's horn (an impossibility) J III.477.

Sasaka = sasa J II.26; IV.85; Cp I.10[1].

Sasakkaŋ [sa + sakkaŋ] as much as one can M I.415, 514 sq.

Sasati[1] [śas. cp. Dhtp 301: gati-hiŋsā-pāṇanesu] to slay, slaughter; sassamāna ppr. pass. J V.24 (C. = hiŋsamāna). inf. sasituŋ J VI.291 (read sāsituŋ from sāsati?). pp. sattha.

Sasati[2] [śvas] to breathe (cp. Dhtp 301: pāṇana): see vissasati.

Sasattha [sa[3] + sattha] with swords J IV.222; DhsA 62.

Sasambhama (adj.) [sa + sambhama] with great confusion Mhvs 5, 139.

Sasambhāra (adj.) [sa[3] + sambhāra] with the ingredients or constituents Vism 20, 352, 353.

Sasin [Sk. śaśin, fr. śaśa] the moon Dāvs IV.29; J III 141; V.33; Vv 81[1] (= canda VvA 314), 82[3].

Sasīsa (adj.) [sa[3] + sīsa] together with the head; sasīsaŋ up to the head D I.76, 246; J I.298; sasīsaka head and all D II.324; Sn, p. 80.

Sasura [Vedic śvaśura, f. śvaśrū (see P. sassū), Idg. *suekuros, *suekrū; cp. Gr. ἑκυρός & ἑκυρά; Lat. socer & socrus; Goth. swaihra & swaihrō, Ags. swēor & sweger; Ohg. swehur & swigar] father-in-law Vin III.137; M I.168; A II.78; VvA 69, 121; Th 2, 407 (sassura); J I.337; sassu-sasurā mother- and father-in-law J II.347; III.182; IV.38; VI.510; the form sassura Th 2, 407 has probably arisen through analogy with sassu. — f. sasurī VvA 69.

Sasenaka (adj.) [sa[3] + sena + ka] accompanied by an army Mhvs 19, 27.

Sassa (nt.) [cp. Vedic sasya] corn, crop M I.116; J I.86, 143, 152; II.135; Miln 2; DhA I.97; SnA 48; sassasamaya crop time J I.143; susassa abounding in corn Vin I.238; pl. m. sassā J I.340. °-kamma agriculture J VI.101; °-kāla harvest time Vin IV.264; °-ṭṭhāna = °-khetta J VI.297; dussassa (having) bad crops Vin I.238; A I.160; KhA 218 (= dubbhikkhā).
-uddharaṇa lifting the corn Miln 307. -ghāta destroying property S II.218 sq.

Sassata (adj.) [Vedic śaśvat] eternal, perpetual D I.13; III.31 sq., 137 sq.; M I.8, 426; A I.41; Dh 255; Dhs 1099; J I.468; Miln 413; DA I.112; dhuvasassata sure and certain Bu II.111 sq. = J I.19; sassatiyā for ever, Sn 1075; a-sassata J V.176; VI.315; sassatāyaŋ adv. (dat.) for ever (?) J I.468; V.172; Fausböll takes it = sassatā ayam (following the C.), and writes sassat'āyaŋ.
-diṭṭhi eternalism, the doctrine that soul and world are eternal Dhs 1315; S II.20; III.98; Nett 40, 127. -mūla eternalist Dpvs 6, 25. -vāda an eternalist, eternalism D I.13; III.108; S II.20; III.99, 182; IV.400; Pug 38; DA I.104 sq.; Ps I.155; VbhA 509. -vādin eternalist Nett 111; Mhbv 110.

Sassatika [fr. sassata] eternalist D I.17; Mhbv 110 (ekacca° partial eternalist); Vin III.312; °-ika J V.18, 19.

Sassatisamaŋ (adv.) [cp. Sk. śaśvatīḥ samāḥ] for ever and ever D I.14; M I.8; S III.143; also sassati samā J III.255; Vv 63[14] (explained by sassatīhi samāna, like the eternal things—viz., earth, sun, moon, etc., VvA 265); J III.256; DA I.105.

Sassamāṇabrāhmaṇa (fem. -ī) together, with samaṇas and brahmins Vin I.11; D I.62; III.76, 135; S V.423; Sn p. 100; DA I.174.

Sassara imitative of the sound sarasara; chinnasassara giving out a broken or irregular sound of sarasara M I.128; see *J.P.T.S.*, 1889, p. 209.

Sassāmika (adj.) [sa + sāmin + ka] 1. having a master, belonging to somebody D II.176. — 2. having a husband, married J I.177, 397; IV.190.

Sassirīka (adj.) [sa[3] + sirī + ka] glorious, resplendent J I.95; II.1; IV.189; VI.270.

Sassū and **Sassu** (f.) [Vedic śvaśrū: see sasura] mother-in-law Vin III.137; A II.78; Th 2, 407; Sn 125; J I.337; III.425 sq.; V.286 (gen. sassuyā); DhA I.307; VvA 110, 121; PvA 89. sassu-sasure, see sasura; sassudeva worshipping one's mother-in-law as a god S I.86; J IV.322.

Saha[1] (indecl.) [fr. sa[3]; cp. Vedic saha] prep. & prefix, meaning: in conjunction with, together, accompanied by; immediately after (with instr.) Vin I.38; Sn 49, 928; Th 2, 414 = 425; sahā Sn 231.
-anukkama = sahānukkama with the bridle Dh 398; DhA IV.161. -āmacca together with the ministers Mhvs 5, 182. -āvudha together with one's weapons J IV.416. -indaka together with Indra D II.208, 221; Vv 30[1]. -ūdaka together with water J V.407. -oḍha together with the stolen goods; coraŋ °-aŋ gahetvā Vism 180; Mhvs 23, 11 (thena); 35, 11. See oḍḍha. -odaka containing water Mhvs 4, 13. -orodha with his harem Mhvs 5, 182; -kathin conversing with (instr.) M I.489. -kāra a sort of fragrant mango KhA 53. -gata accompanying, connected with, concomitant Vin I.10; D II.186; S V.421; Kvu 337; DhsA 157. -ggaṇa together with his companions Dpvs 14, 58. -cetiya containing a Cetiya Mhvs 33, 10. -ja born at the same time Vv 81[16]. -jāta 1. born at the same time, of equal age J I.54; VI.512. — 2. arisen at the same time,

coinciding with (instr.) Kvu 337, 620; VbhA 127. — 3. (in °paccaya) the relation of co-nascence, coincidence Dukp 17 sq., 52 sq., 113 sq., 129 sq., 145 sq., 225 sq., 334 sq. and passim; Tikp 36 sq., 62 sq., 107 sq., 243 sq.; Vism 535. **-jīvin** (fem. -ī) living together with Vin IV.291, 325 sq. **-dhammika** having the same Dhamma, co-religionist M 1.64; Nd[1] 485 (opp. para°); regarding the Dhamma D 1.94, 161; M 1.368; Vin 1.134; Nett 52; DA 1.263 (=sahetuka, sakāraṇa); that which is in accordance with the dhamma Dhs 1327; M 1.482; °ŋ adv. in accordance with the dhamma Vin 1.60, 69; III.178; IV.141. **-dhammiya** co-religionist Nett 169. **-dhenuka** accompanied by a cow Mhvs 21, 18. **-nandin** rejoicing with It 73. **-paŋsukiḷita** a companion in play, a playfellow A II.186: J 1.364; IV.77; PvA 30. **-pesuṇa** together with slander Sn 862 f.; Nd[1] 257. **-bhāvin** being at one's service J III.181 (amacca). **-bhū** arising together with Dhs 1197; Nett 16; a class of devas D II.260. **-macchara** with envy Sn 862. **-yoga**=karaṇa-vacana SnA 44. **-vatthu** living together with Th 2, 414=425; ThA 269. **-vāsa** living together, associating Vin II.34; It 68. **-vāsin** living together J V.352. **-sangha** together with the Order Mhvs 1, 71. **-seyyā** sharing the same couch, living together Vin IV.16; KhA 190. **-sevaka** together with the servants Mhvs 36, 43. **-sokin** sorrowful (?) S IV.180.

Saha[2] (adj.) [fr. **sah**] submitting to, enduring M 1.33; Th 1, 659; J VI.379; sabbasaha J V.425, 431. — dussaha hard to endure Sdhp 95, 118, 196

Sahati [**sah** to prevail] 1. to conquer, defeat, overcome M 1.33; S IV.157; Sn 942; Dh 335; It 84; J 1.74; II.386 (avamānaŋ); III.423 (id.). — 2. to bear, endure Sn 20; Pug 68. — 3. to be able D II.342 (sayhāmi); Pot. sahe Sn 942; Pot. saheyya M 1.33; saha (imper. excuse, forgive, beg your pardon!) J III.109; grd. sayha that which can be endured, able to be done Sn 253; Dāvs II.29; a-sayha Miln 1148.

Sahattha [sa[4]+hattha] one's own hand J 1.68; usually sahatthā (abl.) with one's own hand Vin 1.18; A 1.274; D 1.109; Sn p. 107; J 1.286; Pv II.9[8]; II.9[54]; Miln 15. instr. sahatthena id. PvA 110, 124, 135; J III.267; VI.305. Cp. sāhatthika.

Sahatthin (adj.) [sa[3]+hatthin] together with the elephant Mhvs 25, 70.

Sahavya (nt.) [fr. sahāya, cp. Sk. sāhāyya] companionship Vv 47[7] (=sahabhāva VvA 202). -°ūpaga· coming into union with D 1.245.

Sahavyatā (f.) [abstr. fr. sahavya] companionship D 1.18, 235; II.206; M II.195; III.99; S IV.306; A III.192.

Sahasā (adv.) [instr. of sahas (Vedic), force] forcibly, hastily, suddenly Sn 123; DhA III.381; PvA 40, 279; inconsiderately J 1.173; III.441. -°**kāra** violence D 1.5; III.176; A II.209; Pug 58; J IV.11; DA 1.80.

Sahassa [Sk. sahasra, see etym. under saŋ°] a thousand, used as a singular with a *noun* in the *plural*, sahassaŋ vācā Dh 100; satasahassaŋ vassāni J 1.29; also in the plural after other numerals cattāri satasahassāni chaḷabhiññā Bu II.204=J 1.29; also with the thing counted in the *genitive*, accharānaŋ sahassaŋ Mhvs 17, 13; A 1.227; or °-, as sahassa-yakkha-parivāra SnA 209. In combination with other numerals, sahassa is sometimes inflected like an *adjective*, saṭṭhisahassā amaccā sixty thousand ministers J VI.484; satasahassiyo gāvo 100,000 cows Sn 308; the thing counted then precedes in a compound jāti-sahassaŋ 1,000 births D 1.13; It 99; ghaṭa-sahassam pi udakaŋ Miln 189; sindhava-sahasso ratho J VI.103; sahassaŋ sahassena a thousand times a thousand Dh 103; sahassass' eva in thousands D II.87. —sahassaŋ (nt.) 1,000 gold pieces Dh 106; J VI.484; Miln 10; satasahassaŋ a hundred thousand J 1.28; sahassa (adj.) (fem. ī) worth a thousand J V.484, 485; ThA 72 (Ap V.45, read sahassayo for °aso); epithet of Brahmā, the B. of a thousand world systems M III.101. Gr. dasa-sahassī.

-akkha thousand-eyed, the god Sakka S 1.229; J VI.203; sahassacakkhu the same J V.394, 407. **-aggha** worth a thousand Miln 284. **-āra** having 1,000 spokes D II.172. **-ṭṭhavikā** a purse with 1,000 pieces (of money) Vism 383; J 1.506; DhA II.37; VvA 33. **-netta** thousand-eyed, the god Sakka S 1.226; Sn 346; J III.426; IV.313; V.408; VI.174; Vv 30[10]; DhA 1.17. **-bāhu** having a thousand arms, said of Ajjuna J V.119, 135, 145 (°-rājā); 267, 273; VI.201. **-bhaṇḍikā** a heap of 1,000 pieces J II.424; III.60; IV.2. **-raŋsi** the sun J 1.183.

Sahassadhā (adv.) [cp. satadhā etc.] in a thousand ways A 1.227; Th 1, 909.

Sahassika (adj.) [fr. sahassa] thousandfold J 1.17; IV.175 (so for °iyo).

Sahassī-lokadhātu (f.) a thousandfold world, a world system D 1.46; A 1.228; DA 1.130; dasasahassī-lokadhātu ten world systems J 1.51, 63; cp. dasasahassī and lokadhātu.

Sahājanetta [sahāja+netta] at Sn 1096 is of doubtful meaning ("all-seeing"?), it is expl[d] as "spontaneously arisen omniscience" at Nd[2] 669 (where spelling is sahajānetta); lit. "coinciding eye"; SnA 598 expl[s] as "sahajāta-sabbaññuta-ñāṇa-cakkhu."

Sahāya [cp. Epic Sk. sahāya, fr. saha+i] companion, friend D II.78; M 1.86; S IV.288; Pug 36; Sn 35, 45 sq.; J II.29; °-kicca assistance (?) J V.339; °-matta companion J IV.76; °-sampadā the good luck of having companions Sn 47; adiṭṭha-° a friend who has not yet been seen personally J 1.377; III.364; bahu-° having many friends Vin II.158; nāhaŋ ettha sahāyo bhavis-sāmi I am not a party to that J III.46; asahāya Miln 225.

Sahāyaka (adj.) [fr. last] f. °yikā companion, ally, friend Vin 1.18; D II.155; A II.79, 186; J 1.165; II.29; V.159; VI.256 (gihī sahāyakā, read gihisahāyakā [?]).

Sahāyatā (f.) [abstr. fr. sahāya] companionship Dh 61; sahāyatta (nt.) the same Mhvs 30, 21.

Sahita [pp. of saŋ+**dhā**, cp. Sk. sahita=saŋhita] 1. accompanied with Mhvs 7, 27. — 2. united, keeping together D 1.4; J IV.347; Pug 57. — 3. consistent, sensible, to the point D 1.8; A II.138; IV.196; S III.12; Dh 19 (at DhA 1.157 expl[d] as a name for the Tipiṭaka, thus equalling Sk. saŋhita); Pug 42. — 4. close together, thick Th 2, 254. — araṇisahita (nt.) firewood and appurtenances Vin II.217; D II.340 sq.; J 1.212; DhA II.246. — sahitaŋvata (adj.) having a consistent or perpetual vow, i.e. living the holy life J V.320 (=sīlācāra-sampanna C.); VI.525 (T. sahitabbata; C. expl[s] as samādinna-vata gahita-tāpasa-vesa). Kern, *Toev.* II.51 takes it as a corrupted Sk. śaŋsita-vrata.

Sahitar [n. ag. fr. sahati] one who endures Sn 42.

Sahirañña (adj.) [sa+hirañña] possessing gold Sn 102.

Sahetu (adj.) [sa+hetu] having a cause, together with the cause Vin 1.2; D 1.180; DA 1.263. See hetu.

Sahetuka having a cause, accompanied by a cause (especially of good or bad karma) A 1.82; Dhs 1073.

Sahoḍha see under saha[1].

Sāka (nt.) [Epic Sk. śāka] 1. vegetable, potherb D 1.166; M 1.78, 156; A 1.241, 295; II.206; Pug 55; Vism 70; Vv 33[33]; J III.225; IV.445; V.103. — 2. (m.) name of a tree (Tectona grandis) D I.92; DA I.250; Vism 250. °-vatthu ground for cultivation of vegetables J IV.446; sāka-paṇṇavaṇṇa "like the colour of vegetable leaf" (said of teeth) J V.206 (cp. 203).

Sākacchā (f.) conversation, talking over, discussing D I.103; II.109; M I.72; S I.79; A II.140, 187 sq.; III.81; Sn 266; Miln 19, 24; DhA I.90 (°aŋ karoti); J VI.414.

Sākaccheti [Denom. fr. sākacchā] to converse with, talk over with, discuss D II.237 (+sallapati); ppr. sākacchanto Vin I.169; fut. sākacchissanti Vin II.75; III.159; grd. sākacchātabba Vin V.123, 196; ppr. med. sākacchāyamāna A II.189.

Sākaṭika [fr. sakaṭa¹] a carter S I.57; Th 2, 443 (ThA 271 = senaka); J III.104; Miln 66, 164.

Sākalya (nt.) [fr. sakala] totality; KhA 187 (opp. vekalya); sākalya A I.94 is misprint for sākhalya.

Sākāra (adj.) [sa³+ākāra] with its characteristics D I.13; III.111; M I.35; Pug 60; Vism 423 (+sa-uddesa).

Sākuṇika [fr. sakuṇa] a fowler S II.256; A III.303; Pug 56; J I.208. Combᵈ with miga-bandhaka & maccha-ghātaka at SnA 289; with māgavika & maccha-ghātaka at Pug 56.

Sākuntika [fr. sakunta] a fowler, bird-catcher A II.207; Th 2, 299; ThA 227; DA I.162.

Sākkharappabheda [sa³+akkhara+pabheda] together with the distinction of letters, with the phonology D I.88; A I.163; Sn, p. 101; Miln 10; DA I.247 (akkharappabhedo ti sikkhā ca nirutti ca).

Sākhapurāṇasanthuta [fr. sakhi+purāṇa°] one with whom one has formerly been friendly J V.448.

Sākhalya & Sakhalla (nt.) [abstr. from sakhila] friendship M I.446 (=tameness); A I.94; D III.213; Dhs 1343; DA I.287; DhsA 396; J IV.57, 58 (=maṭṭhavacana "smooth words").

Sākhavant (adj.) [sākhā+vant] having branches J III.493.

Sākhā [Vedic śākhā, cp. also śanku stick, & Goth. hōha plough] a branch Vin I.28; M I.135; A I.152; II.165, 200 sq.; III.19, 43 sq., 200; IV 99, 336; V.314 sq.; Sn 791; J V.393; J II.44; a spur of a hill A I.243; II.140; Miln 36; also sākha (nt.) Mhvs I, 55; J I.52; IV.350; J I.164 (? yāva aggasākhā). — the rib of a parasol Sn 688. — adj. sīla-sākha-pasākha whose branches and boughs are like the virtues J VI.324. In cpds. sākha° & sākhā°.
-nagaraka "little town in the branches," i. e. a suburb, a small town D II.146; J I.391. -patta-palāsa branches and foliage A III.44; -patta-phal'upeta with branches, leaves & fruit A III.43. -palāsa id. M I.488; A II.200. -bhanga faggots J I.158; III.407; DhA II.204; III.375. -miga a monkey J II.73; -ssita living upon branches (i. e. monkey) J V.233.

Sāgataŋ (indecl.) [su+āgata, orij. nt. = wel-come] "greeting of welcome," hail! D I.179 = M I.481 (sāgataŋ bhante Bhagavato); D II.173; M I.514 (°aŋ bhoto Ānandassa); DA I.287; DhA III.293.

Sāgara [cp. Epic Sk. sāgara] the ocean D I.89; A II.56, 140; III.52; V.116 sq.; Vin I.246; Sn 568; PvA 29; sāgara-ūmi a wave of the ocean, a flood J IV.165; °-vāri the ocean J IV.165; sāgaranta or sāgarapariyanta bounded or surrounded by the ocean (said of the earth) J VI.203; °-kuṇḍala the same J III.32; VI.278.

Sāgāra (adj.) [sa³+agāra] living in a house, It 111; sleeping under the same roof Vin II.279.

Sāngaṇa (adj.) [sa+angaṇa] full of lust, impure M I.24 (var. read sangaṇa; this is also the reading at Sn 279, see above).

Sācakka (nt.) [sā = śvan, dog; +cakka; cp. sopāka & suva] name of a science ("the interpretation of omens to be drawn from dogs") Miln 178.

Sācariyaka (adj.) [sa³+ācariya+ka] together with one's teacher D I.102.

Sāciyoga [sāci+yoga; cp. Sk. sāci crooked] crooked ways, insincerity D I.5; III.176; M I.180; A II.209; V.206; Pug 58; DA I.80.

Sājīva (nt.) rule of life, precept governing the monastic life of the Buddhist bhikkhus Vin III.24¹⁶; adj. °-samāpanna ibid.; adj. °-kara one who supports J IV.42 (=sa-ājīvakara, C.).

Sāṭa [cp. Sk. śāṭa] a garment, cloth Th 2, 245; sāṭī (f.) the same S I.115; Dh 394; J I.230 (udaka° bathing mantle), 481.

Sāṭaka [sāṭa+ka] an outer garment, cloak; cloth ThA 246; J I.89, 138, 195, 373, 426; Vism 54 (sāṇa°), 275 (alla°); DhA I.393 (thūla°). Cp. antara°, alaŋ°.
-lakkhaṇa prognostication drawn from pieces of cloth J I.371.

Sāṭikā (f.) = sāṭaka Vin I.292 sq.; II.31; 272, 279 (udaka° bathing mantle) J I.330; Vism 339 (in simile); Miln 240 (cp. M III.253). sāṭiya the same Vin II.177 (°gāhāpaka receiver of undergarments).

Sāṭetar [n. ag. fr. sāṭeti] one who dispels, drives away M I.220; A V.347 sq., 351, 359.

Sāṭeti [śat to cut, destroy] to cut open, to destroy; fig. to torment: Kern's proposed reading (see *Toev.* s. v. sāveti) for sāveti at J III.198 (amba-pakkāni); IV.402 (attānaŋ sāṭetvā dāsakammaŋ karissāni); VI.486 (kāyaŋ s.). He compares MVastu III.385: śāṭeti gātrāni. Cp. **visāṭita** & **visāta.**

Sāṭheyya (nt.) [abstr. fr. saṭha = *śāṭhya] craft, treachery M I.15, 36, 281, 340; A I.95, 100; Nd¹ 395; Pug 19, 23; Miln 289. Cp paṭi°.

Sāṇa¹ (nt.) [cp. Sk. śāṇa hempen, fr. śaṇa = P. saṇa; cp. bhanga¹] hemp D II.350; Miln 267; a coarse hempen cloth Vin I.58; D I.166; III.41; M I.78; A I.240; S II.202, 221; Pug 55; Vism 54 (°sāṭaka). — sāṇavāka the same Th 2, 252; J III.394 (var. read).

Sāṇa² [sa+iṇa] having a debt, indebted, fig. subjected to the kilesas, imperfect M III.127 = S II.221 (=sakilesa, sa-iṇa *K.S.* II.203); ThA 8; cp. anaṇa under aṇa.

Sāṇadhovana (nt.) a kind of play DA I.84 = saṇadhovikā.

Sāṇikā (f.) [fr. sāṇī] a curtain J III.462.

Sāṇī (f.) [fr. saṇa] hemp-cloth D II.350; Vin III.17; a screen, curtain, tent J I.58, 148 sq., 178, 419; DhA I.194; II.49. °-pākāra a screen-wall Vin IV.269, 279; J II.88; DhA II.68, 71, 186; VvA 173; PvA 283; Mhvs 7, 27; sāṇipasibbaka a sack or bag of hemp-cloth Vin III.17¹⁰. — **paṭṭa-sāṇī** a screen of fine cloth J I.395.

Sāta (adj.) [cp. *Sk. śāta] pleasant, agreeable It 114; Nett 27. Often combᵈ with piya, e. g. It 114; Vbh 103; DA I.311. — Opp. kaṭuka. — **sāta** (nt.) pleasure, joy M I.508; A I.81 sq.; S II.220; J I.410; Dh 341 (°sita = sāta-nissita DhA IV.49); Sn 867 sq.; Nd¹ 30 (three, of bhava); Pv II.11³; IV.5⁴ (+sukha); Dhs 3. **asāta** disagreeable, unpleasant Dhs 1343; J I.410; J I.288; II.105; Sn 867 sq.; sātabhakkha Pug 55, read haṭabhakkha.

-odaka with pleasant water D II.129; M I.76; Vin III.108. -kumbha gold VvA 13. See also v. l. under hāṭaka. -putta a noble son J VI.238 (=amacca-putta C.).

Sātaka name of a kind of bird J VI.539 (koṭṭhapokkhara-°, cp. 540); SnA 359 (id.).

Sātacca (nt.) [fr. satata] perseverance M I.101; S II.132; A III.249 sq.; IV.460 sq.; V.17 sq.; Th 1, 585; Vism 4; VbhA 346. °-kārin persevering S III.268, 271, 277 sq.; Dh 293; °-kiriyatā persevering performance Dhs 1367.

Sātataŋ (adv.) [fr. satata] continually S I.17=57.

Sātatā (f.) [abstr. fr. sāta] happiness S I.17.

Sātatika (adj.) [fr. last] persevering Dh 23; S II.232; It 74; DhA I.230.

Sātatta (nt.) [abstr. fr. sāta] tastiness, sweetness A I.32.

Sātava (nt.) sweet result (of good words) (kalyāṇakamma, Com.) J VI.235, 237. Is it misspelling for sādhava (fr. sādhu)?

Sātiya (adj.) [fr. sāta] pleasant Sn 853.

Sātireka (adj.) [sa+atireka, cp. BSk. sātirikta Divy 27] having something in excess D II.93.

Sātisāra (adj.) [sa+atisāra] trespassing Vin I.55.

Sāttha [sa[3]+attha] with the meaning, in spirit D I.62; II.48; It 79, 111; Sn p. 100; Vin I.21; DA I.176; Vism 214.

Sātthaka (adj.) [sa+atthaka] (fem. -ikā) useful PvA 12.

Sāthalika (adj.) [**śrath**, cp. saṭhila & sithila] lethargic, lax M I.14, 200 sq.; III.6; A I.71; II.148; III.108, 179 sq.

Sātrā-yāga identical with sammāpāsa (Sn 303) SnA 322 (? conjecture yātrā°).

Sādana (nt.) [cp. Vedic sādana, fr. **sad**] place, house J IV.405; Yama-sādanaŋ sampatto come to Yama's abode: dead J IV.405; V.267, 304; VI.457, 505 (do., the MSS. always read °-sādhana).

Sādara (adj.) [sa+ādara] reverential Mhvs 5, 239; 15, 2; 28, 25; 33, 82; sādariya (nt.) and sādariyatā (f.) showing regard and consideration Pug 24; cp. Dhs 1327.

Sādāna (adj.) [sa+ādāna] attached to the world, passionate Dh 406=Sn 630; DhA IV.180.

Säditar [n. ag. fr. sādiyati] one who accepts, appropriates M III.126.

Sādiyati [cp. BSk. svādiyati: MVastu II.145; Med.-Pass fr. *sādeti, Caus. of **svad**] lit. to enjoy for oneself, to agree to, permit, let take place D I.166; Vin II.294; A IV.54, 347; S I.78; IV.226 sq.; Pug 55; Miln 95 sq.; aor. sādiyi Vin III.38 sq.; fut. sādiyissati J VI.158.

Sādiyanā (f.) [fr. sādiyati] appropriating, accepting Miln 95.

Sādisa [fr. sadisa] (fem. -sī) like, similar D II.239; Sn 595; Th 2, 252 (so far sa°); Ap 239; J IV.97; Miln 217 (with instr.).

Sādu (adj.) [Vedic svādu, f. svādvī; fr. **svad**, cp. Gr. ἡδύς, Lat. suavis, Goth. sūts=E. sweet; also Sk. sūda cook; Gr. ἥδομαι to enjoy, ἡδονή pleasure] sweet, nice, pleasant Vin II.196; M I.114; Th 2, 273; Sn 102; J IV.168; V.5; Dhs 629; asādu (ka) J III.145; IV.509 (text, asādhuka, com. on kaṭuka); sādu-karoti makes sweet J III.319; Pot. a-sādu-kiyirā makes bitter, ibid. 319; sādu sweet things Vin II.196; sādu-phala see sādhuphala; for °kamyatā see the latter.

Sādutā (f.) [fr. sādu] sweetness Dāvs I.40.

Sādeti[1] [Caus. of **sad**: see sīdati] to cause to sink, to throw down DhA I.75 (+vināseti; v. l. pāteti).

Sādeti[2] [Caus. of **svad**; given as root in meaning "assādane" at Dhtp 147] to enjoy: see ucchādeti (where better referred to **svad**) and **chādeti**[2].

Sādhaka (adj.) [fr. **sādh**] accomplishing, effecting J I.86; SnA 394, 415; Sdhp 161; iṇa° debt-collector Miln 365; bali° tax-collector J IV.366; V.103, 105, 106.

Sādhakatā (f.) [abstr. fr. sādhaka] effectiveness, efficiency Sdhp 329.

Sādhana (adj.-nt.) [fr. **sādh**] 1. enforcing, proving J I.307; DA I.105. — 2. settling, clearing (a debt) J II.341 (uddhāra°). In this meaning mixed with sodheti; it is impossible to decide which of the two is to be preferred. See iṇa & uddhāra. — 3. yielding, effecting, producing, resulting in (-°) A III.156 (laṇḍa° dung-producing); DA I.273; VvA 194; PvA 278 (hita°). — 4. materials, instrument VvA 349; PvA 199.

Sādhāraṇa (adj.) general, common, joint Vin II.258; III.35; Th 2, 505; J I.202, 302; IV.7 (pañca°-bhāva 5 fold connection); Nett 49 sq.; PvA 122, 194, 265. a° J I.78; DA I.71.

Sādhika (adj.) [sa+adhika; cp. BSk. sādhika Divy 44] having something beyond D II.93; Vv 53[5] (°vīsati). °-porisa exceeding a man's height M I.74, 365; A III.403.

Sādhiya (adj.) [fr. **sādh**] that which can be accomplished Sdhp 258 etc.

Sādhu (adj.) [Vedic sādhu, fr. **sādh**] 1. good, virtuous, pious Sn 376, 393; J I.1; Mhvs 37, 119; PvA 116, 132; asādhu bad, wicked Dh 163, 223; DhA III.313. — 2. good, profitable, proficient, meritorious Dh 35, 206 (=sundara, bhaddaka DhA III.271); D I.88; Pv II.9[7]; nt. adv. well, thoroughly Dh 67; J I.1; Mhvs 36, 97; 37, 73. Very frequent as interjection, denoting (*a*) *request* (adhortative, with imper.: sādhu gaccha please go! Miln 18; gacchatha VvA 305), to be translated with "come on, welcome, please," or similar adverbs. Thus e. g. at Pv IV.1[40] (=āyācane PvA 232); J I.92; PvA 6, 35, 272; VvA 69; — (*b*) *assent & approval* in replies to a question "alright, yes" or similarly; usually with the verbs (in ger.) paṭisuṇitvā, vatvā, sampaṭicchitvā etc. Thus e. g. at J V.297; Vin I.56; Miln 7; DhA III.13; VvA 149; DA I.171; SnA 176 (=sampahaŋsane); PvA 55, 78 and passim.

-kamyatā desire for proficiency VbhA 477. -kāra saying "well," approval, cheering, applause J I.223; Miln 13, 16, 18; VvA 132; DhA I.390; III.385. -kīḷana a festive play, a sacred festivity Mhvs 3, 11; sādhukīḷita the same Mhvs 20, 36; °-*divasa* Vin III.285; sādhu-kīḷā J III.434; V.127; sādhu-kīḷikā J III.433. -jīvin leading a virtuous life It 71. -phala having wholesome fruits J I.272 (read sādu°). -rūpa good, respectable Dh 262. -sammata highly honoured D I.48; S IV.398; Sn p. 90 sq.; Miln 4, 21; DA I.143. -sīliya good character J II.137.

Sādhukaŋ (adv.) [fr. sādhu] well, thoroughly Vin I.46; II.208; D I.62. — instr. sādhukena (as adv.) willingly (opp. with force) Pv II.9[8].

Sādheti [Caus. of **sādh** to succeed. Dhtp 421=saŋsiddhiyaŋ] 1. to accomplish, further, effect J II.236 (Pot. sādhayemase). — 2. to make prosperous PvA 113, 125. — 3. to arrange, prepare Mhvs 7, 24. — 4. to perform, execute J I.38 (ārāmika-kiccaŋ); DA I.194; Mhvs 36, 62; Vism 344 (see udukkhala). — 5. to make clear, bring to a (logical) conclusion, to prove J II.306; SnA 192 (atthaŋ), 459; Tikp 58; PvA 30 (here as much as "is any good "). — 6. to collect or clear a debt, to recover (money). In this sense sādheti is mixed up with sodheti, which is regularly found as v. l., is it almost better to substitute sodheti at all passages for sādheti (cp. iṇa, uddhāra), e. g. J I.230; II.341, 423; III.106; IV.45; DhA III.12. — Cp. abhi°.

Sānu (m. and nt.) [Vedic sānu] ridge Vv 32^{10}; J III.172. The commentary on the former passage (VvA 136), translates vana wood, that on the latter paŋsupabbata; sānupabbata a forest-hill J IV.277; VI.415, 540; pabbatasānu-° J III.175; girisānu-° J III.301; IV.195.

Sānucara (adj.) [sa^3+anucara] together with followers Dh 294; J VI.172.

Sānuvajja (adj.) [sa+anuvajja] blameable A II.3.

Sānuseti [sa (=saŋ)+anuseti] to fill (the mind) completely A II.10.

Sāpa [fr. sap, cp. Sk. śāpa] a curse VvA 336; DhA I.41.

Sāpateyya (nt.) [sā (=guṇa of sva)+pateyya (abstr. fr. pati lord), cp. ādhi-pateyya] property, wealth D I.142; II.180; III.190; Vin I.72, 274; III.66; J I.439, 466; Th 2, 340; ThA 240; J V.117 (sāpateya, var. read. sāpatiyya); DhA I.67.

Sāpattika (adj.) [sa^3+āpatti+ka] one who has committed a sin (see āpatti) Vin I.125; II.240; Nd^1 102.

Sāpada (nt.) [cp. Sk. śvāpada] a beast of prey J II.126; VI.79.

Sāpadesa (adj.) [sa+apadesa] with reasons D I.4; A II.22; M I.180; III.34, 49; Pug 58; DA I.76. Opp. anapadesa M I.287.

Sāpānadoṇī M II.183=152 (C.=sunakhānaŋ pivanadoṇi a dog's trough).

Sāpekha [sa+apekhā] longing for D II.77; III.43.

Sāma^1 [cp. Vedic śyāma black & śyāva brown; Av. syāva; Ags. hǣven blue (=E. heaven); Gr. σκοιός, σκιά (shadow)=Sk. chāyā; Goth. skeinan=shine, etc.] 1. black, dark (something like deep brown) Vin IV.120 (kāḷasāma dark blue [?]); D I.193; M I.246 (different from kāḷa); J VI.187 (°aŋ mukhaŋ dark, i. e. on account of bad spirits); Vism 422 (opp. to odāta in colour of skin). — 2. yellow, of a golden colour, beautiful J II.44, 45 (migī); V.215 (suvaṇṇa-sāmā), 366 (suvaṇṇa-vaṇṇa). — f. sāmā, q. v. — See sabala.

Sāma^2 (nt.) [perhaps=Vedic sāman] song, sacred song, devotion, worship, propitiation D II.288.

Sāmaŋ [on etymology, see Andersen *Pāli Gloss.*, p. 268 (contracted from sayamaŋ, Trenckner), cp. Michelson, *Indog. Forsch.*, vol. xxiii, p. 235, n. 3 (=avest., hāmō; slav., samz)] self, of oneself Vin I.16, 33, 211 (s. pāka); IV.121; D I.165; M I.383; II.211; III.253 (sāmaŋ kantaŋ sāmaŋ vāyitaŋ dussayugaŋ); S II.40; IV.230 sq.; V.390; Sn 270 (asāma-pāka not cooking for oneself), 889; J I.150; sāmaññeva, i. e. sāmaŋ yeva Sn p. 101.

Sāmaggiya (nt.) [fr. samagga] completeness, concord Sn 810; sāmaggiya-rasa J III.21 (" the sweets of concord "); adj. asāmaggiya, unpleasant J VI.517 (C. on asammodiya).

Sāmaggī (f.) [abstr. fr. samagga] completeness, a quorum Vin I.105, 106; meeting, communion Vin I.132 sq.; II.243; unanimity, concord Vin I.97, 136, 357; II.204; D III.245 sq.; A III.289; Nd^1 131; J I.328; It 12.

Sāmacca (adj.) [sa^3+amacca] together with the ministers D I.110.

Sāmañña^1 (nt.) [abstr. fr. samāna] generality; equality, conformity; unity, company Miln 163; SnA 449 (jāti° identity of descent), 449 (generality, contrasted to visesa detail), 548 (id.); VvA 233 (diṭṭhi°, sīla°, equality). °-gata united D II.80; °-nāma a name given by general assent DhsA 390.

Sāmañña^2 (nt.) [abstr. fr. samaṇa] Samaṇaship D I.51 sq.; III.72, 245; M I.281 sq.; S V.25; A II.27=It 103; Dh 19 sq., 311; DA I.158; Vism 132; adj., in accordance with true Samaṇaship, striving to be a samaṇa Miln 18; Samaṇaship A I.142 sq.; Pv II.7^{18} (expl^d at PvA 104 as " honouring the samaṇas ").
-attha the aim of Samaṇaship D I.230; A IV.366; M I.271; S II.15; III.93; J I.482; -phala advantage resulting from Samaṇaship, fruit of the life of the recluse D I.51 sq.; Vism 215, 512; VvA 71; VbhA 317; more especially the fruition of the four stages of the Path, sotāpatti-, sakadāgāmi-, anāgāmi-, and arahatta-phala S V.25; D III.227, 277; Dhs 1016; DhsA 423; Miln 344, 358; DA I.158; three samaññaphalas Kvu 112.

Sāmaññatā^1=sāmañña^1 (identity, congruity etc.) J VI.371 (vaṇṇa°); Vism 234 (maraṇa°).

Sāmaññatā^2=sāmañña^2 D III.145, 169; Dh 332; DhA III.484; IV.33.

Sāmaṇaka (adj.) [fr. samaṇa] worthy of or needful for a Samaṇa Mhvs 4, 26; 30, 37; assāmaṇaka unworthy of a Samaṇa Vin I.45.

Sāmaṇera [fr. samaṇa; cp. BSk. śrāmaṇeraka Divy 342] fem. °-rī a novice Vin I.62 sq.; IV.121; S II.261; Miln 2; VbhA 383; are not present at the recital of the Pātimokkha Vin I.135; °pabbajjā ordination of a novice Vin I.82. °pēsaka superintendent of Sāmaṇeras Vin II.177; A III.275. — f., also -°ā A III.276; as -°ī at Vin I.141.

Sāmattha (adj.) [=samattha] able J II.29.

Sāmatthiya [abstr. fr. samattha] (nt.) ability Mhvs 37, 243

Sāmanta (adj.) [fr. samanta] neighbouring, bordering D I.101; Vin I.46 (āpatti° bordering on a transgression); J II.21; IV.124; connected with M I.95; °jappā (or °jappana) roundabout talk Vbh 353; Vism 28; Nd^1 226; VbhA 484. abl. sāmantā in the neighbourhood of Vin III.36; D II.339; loc. sāmante the same J IV.152 (Kapila-vatthu-°).

Sāmayika (adj.) [fr. samaya] temporary Sn 54; Miln 302 (so read); see sāmāyika.

Sāmalatā (f.) [sāma^1+latā; Sk. śyāmalatā] the creeper Ichnocarpus J I.60.

Sāmā (f.) [Sk. śyāmā Halāyudha 2, 38; see sāma^1, sāmalatā, and sāmāka] a medicinal plant J IV.92 (bhisasāmā, C. bhisāni ca sāmākā ca); the Priyangu creeper J I.500; V.405.

Sāmāka [cp. Vedic śyāmāka] a kind of millet (Panicum frumentaceum) D I.166; M I.78, 156, 343; A I.295; II.206; Sn 239; Pug 55; J III.144, 371; Nett 141; DhA IV.81.

Sāmājika [fr. Sk. samāja: see samajja] a member of an assembly Dāvs III.27.

Sāmādhika (adj.) [fr. samādhi] consisting in concentration S I.120.

Sāmāmigī (f.) a black hind J II.44.

Sāmāyika (adj.) [fr. samaya] 1. on a friendly footing, in agreement M III.110; Miln 22. — 2. occurring in due season, timely Miln 302 sq., 305. — 3. temporary A III.349 sq.; cp. sāmayika.

Sāmi J V.489, read sāvi.

Sāmika [fr. sāmin] 1. owner M I.27; J I.194; Vism 63. — 2. husband Vin III.137; J I.307; II.128; A II.58 sq.; Pv II.3[7].

Sāmin [cp. Sk. svāmin, fr. sva = sa[4]] 1. owner, ruler, lord, master Vin I.303, 307; Sn 83; Mhvs 37, 241; J V.253 (°paribhoga, q. v.); Pv IV.6[6]; Vism 63; DA I.261; PvA 43, 65. voc. sāmi "Sir" J VI.300; DhA I.20. f. sāminī J V.297; VvA 225. See also suvāmin. — assāmin not ruling Miln 253; Pv IV.6[6]. —2. husband PvA 31 (sāmi, voc. = "my lord"), 82. — f. sāminī wife Mhvs 5, 43; PvA 82, 276.

-vacana (sāmi°) the genitive case J I.185; III.98 (upayog'atthe); V.42 (karaṇ'atthe), 444; VvA 304; SnA 210 (for upayoga), 310 (id.).

Sāmiya husband J I.352; see sāmika.

Sāmisa (adj.) [sa + āmisa] 1. holding food Vin II.214 = IV.198. — 2. fleshly, carnal D II.298 = M I.59; A I.81; Ps II.41. Opp. to nirāmisa spiritual (e. g. Ps I.59).

Sāmīcī & **sāmīci°** (f.) [fr. sammā[2] = Vedic samyac, of which pl. nom. f. samīcīḥ freq. in R. V.] right, proper course Vin III.246; D II.104; A II.56, 65; S V.261, 343; Miln 8; DhA I.57.

-kamma proper act, homage Vin II.22, 162, 255; A I.123; II.180; D III.83; J I.218, 219; Miln 8. -paṭipadā right course of life M I.281; A II.65. -paṭipanna correct in life D II.104; S I.220; A II.56; IV.310.

Sāmukkaṇsika (adj.) [fr. samukkaṇsati, cp. ukkaṇsaka. The BSk. is sāmutkarṣikī dharmadeśanā Divy 617] exalting, praising (i. e. the 4 truths), as much as "standard." Kern, *Toev.* II.64, takes it to mean "condensed, given in brief." Usually in phrase °ikā dhammadesanā (thus as f. of °aka!) e. g. Vin I.16, 18; II.156; D I.110; M I.380; A IV.186; V.194; DA I.277 (expl[d]); ThA 137; PvA 38, 195; VvA 50. Only once with ñāṇa at DhsA 9.

Sāmudda (nt.) [fr. samudda] sea salt Vin I.202; Abhp 461.

Sāmuddika (adj.) [fr. samudda] seafaring D I.222; S III.155; A III.368 (vāṇijā); IV.127 (nāvā); Vism 63; DhsA 320. At J VI.581 s.-mahāsankha denotes a kind of trumpet.

Sāmeti see sammati[1].

Sāya [cp. Sk. sāyaṇ, on which Aufrecht, *Halāyudha* p. 380, remarks: "this word seems to be the gerund of **sā**, and to have signified originally 'having finished.' A masc. sāya does not exist." Cp. Vedic °sāya] evening, only adverbially sāyaṇ, at night Vin III.147; J II.83; DhA I.234; usually opposed to pāto (pātaṇ) in the morning, early e. g. sāya-pātaṇ D II.188; Miln 419; J I.432, 460; V.462; sāyaṇ-pātaṇ Vin II.185; DhA II.66; sāyañ ca pāto ca Pv I.6[3]; II.9[37]; PvA 127; sāya-tatiyaka for the third time in the evening D I.167; A II.206; V.263, 266, 268; M I.343; sāyamāsa supper J I.297; V.461; DhA I.204. sāyaṇ as quâsi-nominative: sāyaṇ ahosi J VI.505; atisāyaṇ too late Th I, 231; J II.362; V.94; sāyataraṇ later in the evening (compar.) J VI.366.

Sāyaṇha [sāyaṇ + aṇha, cp. Sk. sāyāhna] evening D II.9; J I.144; -°samayaṇ at evening time D II.205; M I.147; Vin I.21; sāyaṇhasamaye J I.148, 279; PvA 33, 43, 100; °-**kāle** the same J IV.120; sāyaṇhe (loc.) J I.144, 237; atisāyaṇha late evening J VI.540.

Sāyati [**svad**, Sk. svādate, cp. sādiyati] to taste, eat; pres. sāyati Vin II.121; ppr. sāyanto D III.85; grd. sāyanīya savoury Vin I.44; S I.162; ger. sāyitvā S IV.176; A III.163. Cp. saṇsāyati.

Sāyana[1] (nt.) [fr. sāyati] tasting, taste Dhtp 229.

Sāyana[2] the Nāga tree (cp. nāga 3) J VI.535 (vāraṇā sāyanā = nāgarukkhā, C., ibid. 535, var. read. vāyana). Kern, *Toev.* II.77 conjectures sāsanā "with Asana's Terminalia's."

Sāyika (adj.) [fr. **śī**] lying, sleeping, resting in (-°) Dh 141; M I.328 (vatthu°); Th I, 501 = Miln 367.

Sāyita [pp. of sāyati, cp. sāditar] (having) tasted, tasting D I.70; II.95, 292; M I.188, 461; Miln 378; Vism 258 (khāyita +).

Sāyin (adj.) [fr. **śī**] lying Dh 325.

Sāra [Vedic sāra nt.] 1. essential, most excellent, strong A II.110; Vin IV.214; J III.368; Pug 53. — 2. (m.) the innermost, hardest part of anything, the heart or pith of a tree (see also pheggu) M I.111; J I.331; Miln 413; most excellent kind of wood Vin II.110; D II.182, 187; sattasārā the elect, the salt of the earth M III.69. — 3. substance, essence, choicest part (generally at the end of comp.) Vin I.184; A II.141; S III.83, 140; Sn 5, 330, 364; Dh 11 sq.; PvA 132, 211 (candana°). sāre patiṭṭhito established, based, on what is essential M I.31; A II.183. — 4. value Miln 10; appasāra of small value D II.346. — asāra worthless Sn 937; nissāra the same J II.163 (pithless); mahāsāra of high value J I.384, 463.

-ādāyin acquiring what is essential S IV.250. -**gandha** the odour of the heart of a tree Dhs 625. -**gabbha** a treasury J III.408; V.331. -**gavesin** searching for hard wood M I.111, 233; sārapariyesana the same ibid. -**dāru** strong, durable wood J II.68. -**bhaṇḍa(ka)** a bundle of one's best things J II.225. -**bhūmi** good soil J II.188. -**mañjūsā** a box made of choice wood J IV.335. -**maya** being of hard or solid wood J III.318 (C. sāramkkhamaya, "of sāra wood" *trsl*[n]). -**suvaṇṇa** sterling gold SnA 448 (in expl[n] of name Bimbisāra). -**sūci** a needle made of hard wood J I.9.

Sāraka[1] (-°) (adj.) [fr. sāra] having as most essential Miln 133; a-sāraka rotten (said of wood) J II.163.

Sāraka[2] [fr. sarati[1]] a messenger.

Sāraka[3] in the comp. kaṭa-sāraka a mat J IV.248 (v. l.); IV.474; V.97 (cp. osāraka),

Sārakkhati = saṇrakkhati Th I, 729.

Sārakkhā (f.) [fr. sa[3] + rakkha] "standing under protection" (?), a category of married women Vin III.139 (cp. M I.287).

Sārajja (nt.) [abstr. fr. sārada = *sāradya] timidity A III.127, 203; IV.359, 364; Miln 24, 72, 196 (parisa°, cp. Nd[2] 470); J I.334; II.66; nissārajja undaunted J I.274.

Sārajjati [saṇ + **raj**, cp. BSk. sārajyati, Sk. saṇrajyate, cp. sārāga] to be pleased with, to be attached to A I.260; S II.172; III.69 sq.; IV.10 sq.

Sārajjanā (f.) [fr. sārajjati] infatuation, feeling infatuated Dhs 389; J V.446.

Sārajjāyati [Denom. of sārajja] to be embarrassed, perplexed, ashamed S III.92; A IV.359.

Sārajjitatta (nt.) [= sārajjanā] infatuation, the state of being infatuated Dhs 389.

Sāraṇā (f.) [fr. sāreti[2]] reminding, remonstrating with Vin V.158, 164.

Sāratta [= saṇratta, pp. of sārajjati] impassioned, enamoured, passionately devoted Vin III.118; M II.160, 223; S I.74, 77; Dh 345; J I.288; II.140; Mhvs 10, 34 (°mānaso). asāratta unattached Sn 704.

Sārathi [fr. sa-ratha; Vedic sārathi] charioteer, coachman D II.178, 254; S I.33; V.6; A II.112; IV.190 sq.; Sn 83; J I.59, 180; Pv IV.3[3]. assadammasārathi a coachman by whom horses are driven, a trainer of horses M I.124; S IV.176; purisadammasārathi a coachman of the driving animal called man, a man-trainer Vin I.35;

D I.49; Sn p. 103; It 79. — In similes: Vism 466; KhA 21.

Sārada (adj.) [Vedic sārada, fr. śarad autumn (of Babyl. origin? cp. Assyr. šabātu corn month)] autumnal, of the latest harvest, this year's, fresh A III.404=D III.354 (bījāni fresh seeds); A I.135, 181 (badara-paṇḍu); S III.54; V.380; Miln 255; Dh 149 (but at this passage expl^d as "scattered by the autumn winds" DhA III.112). — **asārada** stale, old D II.353; S V.379. Fig. sārada unripe, not experienced, immature (see sārajja shyness), opp. visārada (der. vesārajja) experienced, wise, self-confident; vīta-sārada id. (e. g. A II.24; It 123). — *Note:* At *K.S.* III.46 (=S III.54) s. is wrongly taken as sāra+da, i. e. "giving sāra"; but seeds do not *give* sāra: they *contain* sāra (cp. sāravant). The C expl^n as sār-ādāyin is nearer the truth, but of course not literal; °da is not ā+°da. Moreover, the fig. meaning cannot be reconciled with this expl^n.

Sāradika (adj.) [fr. sārada] autumnal Vin I.199; II.41; Dh 285=J I.183; Vv 64[17]; DhA III.428.

Sāraddha [=saŋraddha] violent, angry A I.148, 282; S IV.125; M I.21; Vism 134 (opp. passaddha-kāya), 282 (°kāya); VbhA 283 (id.).

Sārana [fr. sarati[1]] going DhsA 133.

Sārameya [Vedic sārameya] a dog (lit. "son of Saramā") Mhbv 111.

Sārambha[1] [=saŋrambha] 1. impetuosity, anger A I.100, 299; II.193; M I.16; Dh 133; J IV.26; Miln 289 (sa-saŋrambha). — 2. quarrel Sn 483; J II.223; V.141. — 3. pride Th I, 759; VvA 139.
-kathā angry or haughty talk, imperiousness Dh 133; M I.16; DhA III.57.

Sārambha[2] [sa+ārambha] involving killing or danger to living creatures Vin III.149; A II.42 sq. Cp. samārambha.

Sārambhin (adj.) [fr. sārambha] impetuous J III.259.

Sāravant (adj.) [fr. sāra] valuable, having kernel or pith (said of grain or trees) A IV.170 (synom. daḷha, opp. palāpa); S V.163; M I.111=233.

Sārasa [cp. Epic Sk. sārasa] a water bird, Ardea sibirica VvA 57, 163; at both pass.=koñca.

Sārāga [=saŋrāga, fr. saŋ+raj] affection, infatuation Vin II.258; M I.17, 498; A I.264; S III.69 sq., 93; Dhs 1059, 1230; cp. saŋrāga. — Neg. a° Dhs 32, 312, 315.

Sārāgin (adj.) [fr. last] attached to M I.239 (sukha-°); sukha-sārāgita ibid. impassioned.

Sārāṇīya (adj.) [the question of derivation is still unsettled. According to Trenckner (*Notes* 75) fr. saraṇa (i. e. saraṇa[1] or saraṇa[2]?) with double vṛddhi. Kern (*Toev.* II.74) considers the (B) Sk. saŋrañjanīya as the original and derives it fr. saŋ+raj to rejoice, to gladden: see rañjati. The BSk. is divided: MVastu III.47, 60, 206 etc. has sārāyaṇiya, whereas AvŚ I.229 & Divy 404 read saŋrañjanī and saŋrañjanīya (see below). — The C. at J IV.99 derives it fr. saraṇa[3] in explaining sārāṇīyā kathā as "sāritabba-yuttakā kathā"] courteous, polite, friendly (making happy, pleasing, gladdening?), only in comb^n with kathā, dhamma, or dhammakathā, e. g. s. kathā polite speech, either in phrase *sammodanīyaŋ kathaŋ sārāṇīyaŋ vītisāreti* to exchange greetings of friendliness & courtesy D I.52; M I.16 (expl^d *inter alia* as "anussariyamānasukhato s." at MA 110); A I.55, 281; II.42; cp. BSk. *sammodanīŋ saŋrañjanīŋ vividhāŋ k. vyatisārya* AvŚ I.229. — *sārāṇiyaŋ kathaŋ katheti* DhA I.107; IV.87; sārāṇīyā dhammā states of conciliation, fraternal living (*Dial.* III.231) D III. 245; M I.322; II.250; A III.288; V.89; DhsA 294; J V.382; cp. BSk. *saŋranjañīyan dharmaŋ samādāya* Divy 404. — sārāṇīyaŋ dhammakathaŋ suṇāti DhA IV.168.

Sāri [cp. *Sk. śāri] cheesman DA I.85.

Sārin (adj.) [fr. sāreti] wandering, going after, following, conforming to (loc.) J V.15; aniketasārin wandering about houseless Sn 844, 970; anokasārin wandering homeless Dh 404; Sn 628; diṭṭhisārin a partisan of certain views Sn 911; vaggasārin conforming to a party, a partisan Sn 371, 800, 912.

Sārīrika (adj.) [fr. sarīra] connected with the body, bodily M I.10; A I.168 sq.; II.153; (nt.) bodily relics Miln 341; °ŋ cetiyaŋ one of the 3 kinds: paribhogika, s., uddesika J IV.228.

Sāruppa (nt.) [abstr. fr. sarūpa, BSk. sārūpya & sāropya] equal state; as adj. fit, suitable, proper Vin I.39, 287; D II.277; S IV.21 sq.; J I.65, 362; DhsA 294; Sn 368; p. 79, 97, 104; J IV.404. (a°) (nt.) Vism 24; PvA 269. paribbājaka-s°, as befits a Wanderer J V.228.

Sāreti is Caus. of sarati[1] as well as sarati[2]. Cp. vīti°.

Sāropin (adj.) [saŋ+ropin, cp. ropeti[1] & rūhati[1]] healing, curative M II.257 (vaṇa-°).

Sāla [cp. Sk. śāla & sāla] a Sal tree (Shorea robusta) M I.488; D II.134; A I.202; III.49, 214; Dh 162.
-māḷaka an enclosure of Sal trees J I.316. **-rukkha** Sal tree VvA 176. **-laṭṭhi** Sal sprout A II.200. **-vana** Sal grove D II.134; M I.124; S I.157; Vv 39[2].

Sālaka [Sk. syāla+ka] a brother-in-law J II.268.

Sālakakimi a kind of worm Miln 312.

Sālaya (adj.) [sa[3]+ālaya] having intentions (on), being attached (to=loc.) J III.332.

Sālā (f.) [cv. Vedic śālā, cp. Gr. καλία hut, Lat. cella cell, Ohg. halla, E. hall] a large (covered & enclosed) hall, large room, house; shed, stable etc., as seen fr. foll. examples: **aggi°** a hall with a fire Vin I.25, 49=II.210; **āsana°** hall with seats DhA II.65; **udapāna°** a shed over the well Vin I.139; II.122; **upaṭṭhāna°** a service hall Vin I.49, 139; II.153, 208, 210; S II.280; V.321; J I.160; **kaṭhina°** a hall for the kaṭhina Vin II.117. **kīḷa°** play-house J VI.332; **kutūhala°** a common room D I.179=S IV.398. **kumbhakāra°** potter's hall DhA I.39; **gilāna°** sick room, hospital S IV.210; Vism 259; **jantāghāra°** (large) bath room Vin I.140; II.122; **dāna°** a hall for donations J I.262; **dvāra°** hall with doors M I.382; II.66; **pāniya°** a water-room Vin II.153; **bhatta°** refectory Vism 72; **yañña°** hall of sacrifice PugA 233; **rajana°** dyeing workshop Vism 65; **ratha°** car shed DhA III.121; **hatthi°** an elephant stable Vin I.277, 345; II.194; J I.187.

Sālākiya (nt.) [cp. Sk. śālākya in Suśruta] ophthalmology D I.12, 69; DA I.98.

Sāli [cp. Sk. śali] rice D I.105, 230; II.293; Vin IV.264; M I.57; A I.32, 145; III.49; IV.108 (+yavaka), 231; S V.10, 48; J I.66, 178; IV.276; V.37; VI.531; Miln 251; Sn 240 sq.; Vism 418; pl. °-iyo J I.325; gen. pl. °-inaŋ J VI.510. — **lohitaka°** red rice Miln 252.
-khetta a rice-field A I.241; IV.278; Vin II.256; DhA I.97; III.6. **-gabbha** ripening (young) rice DhA I.97. **-bīja** rice seed A I.32; V.213. **-bhatta** a meal of rice Vism 191. **-bhojana** rice food J I.178.

Sālika (adj.) [fr. sāli] belonging to rice DhA III.33.

Sālikā (f.) [cp. Epic Sk. sārikā crow, usually comb^d with śuka parrot] a kind of bird S I.190=Th I, 1232; J V.110. See sāliya & sāḷikā.

Sālittaka (nt.) [fr. Sk. saŋlepa?] a sling, catapult (?); slinging stones, throwing potsherds etc. Pv IV.16[7]; PvA 285; J I.418, 420; DhA II.69.

Sālin excellent Dāvs I.9.

Sāliya or **sāliyā** the maina bird (=sālikā) J III.203; sāliya-chāpa (a young bird of that kind), and sāliyacchāpa (i. e. sāliyā which is probably the right form) J III.202. — madhu-sāliyā J v.8 (=suvaṇṇa-sālika-sakunā C. p. 9[11]); J VI.199 (suva-sāliya-°), 425 (Sāliya-vacana the story of the maina bird, var. read. suva-khaṇḍa; a section of the 546th Jātaka, but sāḷiyā, sālikā, sāliyā is *not* a parrot.

Sālīna (adj.) [fr. sāli] fine (rice) Miln 16 (°ŋ odanaŋ; cp. śālīnaŋ odanaŋ Divy 559).

Sāluka (& °ūka) (nt.) [cp. Sk. śālūka] the edible root of the water-lily Vin I.246; J VI.563; VvA 142 (°muṭṭhi).

Sālūra [but cp. Sk. śālūra a frog] a dog J IV.438 (°-saŋgha =sunakhagaṇa, C.; spelling l).

Sāloka [sa²+āloka] sight, view; sāloke tiṭṭhati to expose oneself to view in an open door Vin II.267.

Sālohita [fr. sa²+lohita] a kinsman, a blood relation, usually together with ñāti Vin I.4; D II.26, 345; A I.139, 222; II.115; Sn p. 91; PvA 28; VbhA 108.

Sāḷava [cp. Sk. ṣāḍava, which is given in diff. meaning, viz. "comfits with fruits"] a certain dish, perhaps a kind of salad, given as "lambila," i. e. bitter or astringent at DhsA 320 (made of badara or kapiṭṭha); cp. Vin IV.259.

Sāḷika a bird; f. °ā the Maina bird J I.429; VI.421. Spelt sāḷiyā at J VI.425. See sālikā & sāliya.

Sāva [fr. sru] juice VvA 186.

Sāvaka [fr. śru] a hearer, disciple (never an Arahant) D I.164; II.104; III.47, 52, 120 sq., 133; A I.88; M I.234; S II.26; It 75 sq., 79; J I.229; Vism 214, 411. — fem. sāvikā D II.105; III.123; Th 2, 335; S IV.379; A I.25, 88. (Cp. ariya-°, agga-°, mahā).
-sangha the congregation of the eight Aryas M II.120; S I.220 (cattāri purisayugāni aṭṭha purisapuggalā); II.79 sq.; It 88.

Sāvakatta (nt.) [abstr. fr. last] the state of a disciple M I.379 sq.

Sāvajja (adj.) [sa+avajja] blameable, faulty D I.163; II.215; M I.119; S V.66, 104 sq.; Sn 534; Pug 30, 41; (nt.) what is censurable, sin J I.130; Miln 392; VbhA 382 (mahā° or appa°, with ref. to var. crimes).

Sāvajjatā (f.) [fr. last] guilt Miln 293.

Sāvaṭa (nt.) name of a certain throw in playing at dice J VI.281 (v. l. sāvaṭṭa).

Sāvaṭṭa (adj.) [sa³+āvaṭṭa] containing whirlpools It 114.

Sāvaṇa (nt.) [fr. sāveti] shouting out, announcement, sound, word J II.352; Sdhp 67.

Sāvasesa (adj.) [sa³+avasesa] with a remainder, incomplete, of an offence which can be done away Vin I.354; II.88; V.153; A I.88. — Of a text (pāṭha) KhA 238; SnA 96.

Sāvi [Sk. śvāvidh, see Lüder's *Z.D.M.G.* 61, 643] a porcupine J V.489 (MSS. sāmi and sāsi, cp. Manu V.18).

Sāvittī (f.) the Vedic verse Sāvitrī Sn 457, 568=Vin I.246 (Sāvitthī); J IV.184.

Sāvetar [n. ag. fr. sāveti] one who makes others hear, who tells D I.56; A IV.196.

Sāveti is Caus. of suṇāti.

Sāsa [Sk. śvāsa, fr. śvas] asthma A V.110; J VI.295.

Sāsanka (adj.) [fr. sa³+āsankā] dangerous, fearful, suspicious S IV.175 (opp. khema); Th 2, 343; ThA 241; Vism 107; J I.154; PvA 13; Miln 351.

Sāsati [śās, Dhtp 300=anusiṭṭhi] to instruct, teach, command; tell J VI.472 (dūtāni, =pesesi C.); inf. sāsituŋ J VI.291 (=anusāsituŋ C.).

Sāsana (nt.) [cp. Vedic śāsana] order, message, teaching J I.60, 328; II.21; Pv IV.3⁵⁴ (Buddhānaŋ); KhA 11 sq.; the doctrine of the Buddha Vin I.12; D I.110; II.206; A I.294; Dh 381; Sn 482 etc.; J I.116. sāsanaŋ āroceti to give a message (dūtassa to the messenger) Vin III.76.
-antaradhāna the disappearance or decline of the teaching of the Buddha. Said of the doctrine of Kassapa Bhagavā SnA 156 (cp. sāsane parihāyamāne SnA 223), and with ref. to the Pāli Tipiṭaka VbhA 432 sq., where 3 periods of the development of the Buddhist doctrine are discussed, viz. sāsana-ṭhita-kāla, °osakkana-kāla, °antaradhāna. -kara complying with one's order and teaching M I.129; -kāraka the same Sn 445; -kārin the same A II.26; susāsanaŋ dussānaŋ J I.239 (English transl.: "true and false doctrine," "good and bad news"). -hara (+°jotaka) taking up (& explaining) an order SnA 164.

Sāsapa [cp. Sk. sarṣapa] a mustard seed S II.137; V.464; A V.170; J VI.174 (comp. with mt. Meru); Sn 625, 631, p. 122; Dh 401; DA I.93; DhA I.107; II.51; IV.166; Vism 306 (ār'agge), 633; PvA 198 (°tela). -°kuṭṭa mustard powder Vin I.205; II.151.

Sāsava (adj.) [sa³=āsava] connected with the *āsavas* D III.112; A I.81; Dhs 990, 1103; Nett 80.

Sāha six days (cp. chāha) J VI.80 (=chadivasa, C.).

Sāhatthika (adj.) [fr. sahattha] with one's own hand J I.168; DhsA 97; SnA 493; KhA 29.

Sāhaŋ contraction of so ahaŋ.

Sāhasa [fr. sahas power] violent, hasty Sn 329; (nt.) violence, arbitrary action, acts of violence Sn 943; J VI.284; Mhvs 6, 39; sāhasena arbitrarily A V.177; opp. a° ibid.; Dh 257; J VI.280. sāhasaŋ id. J VI.358 (=sāhasena sāhasikaŋ kammaŋ katvā ibid. 359); adv. asāhasaŋ=asāhasena J III.319 (C. sāhasiyataṇhāya ibid. 320, if we do not have to read sāhasiyā taṇhāya, from sāhasī).
-kiriyā violence J III.321.

Sāhasika (adj.) [fr. sāhasa] brutal, violent, savage J I.187, 504; II.11; PvA 209; DhA I.17.

Sāhasiyakamma (nt.) a brutal act J I.412, 438.

Sāhāra (adj.) [sa+āhāra] with its food S III.54 (viññāṇa s.); D II.96 (Vesālī s.; trsl^n "with its subject territory").

Sāhin (-°) (adj.) [fr. sah] enduring It 32. See asayha°.

Sāhu (adj.) [=sādhu] good, well Vin I.45; S I.8; Pug 71 sq.; Th 1, 43; VvA 284.

Sāhuḷacīvara (nt.) a coarse cloth M I.509 (cp. Deśīnāmamālā VIII.52; Karpūramañjarī p. 19; *J.P.T.S.* 1891, 5, and Prākrit sāhulī, *Z.D.M.G.*, xxviii., p. 415).

Sāhuneyyaka see āhuneyya.

Sāhunna [=sāhuḷa] a strip of ragged cloth Pv III.1⁶; PvA 173; *J.P.T.S.* 1891, 5; var. read. sāhunda.

Si (-°) [=svid, for which ordinarily °su] part. of interrogation; e. g. kaŋ-si DhA I.91.

Siŋsaka (nt.) [Sk. śirṣaka ?] name of a water plant J VI.536 (C. not correct).

Siŋsati[1] [śaŋs] to hope for Dhtp 296 (def. as "icchā"); only in cpd. ā° (q. v.).

Siŋsati[2] is Desiderative of sarati[1]. —Siŋsati "to neigh" at J v.304 is to be read hiŋsati (for hesati, q. v.).

Siŋsapā (f.) [cp. Vedic śiŋśapā] the tree Dalbergia sisu (a strong & large tree) S v.437; Siŋsapā-groves (s.-vanā) are mentioned near Āḷavi A I.136; near Setavyā D II.316 sq.; DhA I.71; VvA 297; and near Kosambi S v.437.

Sikatā (f.) [cp. Sk. sikatā] sand, gravel; suvaṇṇa° gold dust A I.253.

Sikāyasa-maya (adj.) made of tempered steel (said of swords) J VI.449 (cp. Note of the *trsl*ⁿ p. 546).

Sikkā (f.) [cp. Sk. śikyā] string, string of a balance Vin II.110; 131, J I.9; II.399; III.13 (text sikkhā); VI.242; VvA 244 (muttā° string of pearls); Kvu 336 sq.

Sikkhati [Vedic śikṣati; Desid. to **śak**: see sakkoti. — The Dhtp (12) gives "vijj' opādāna" as meaning] 1. to learn, to train oneself (=ghaṭati vāyamati Vism 274); usually combined with the locative, thus sikkhā-padesu s. to train oneself in the Sikkhāpadas D I.63, 250; Vin I.84; It 96, 118; also with the dative, indicating the purpose; thus vinayāya s. to train oneself to give up Sn 974; the thing acquired by training is also put in the accusative; thus nibbānaŋ s. to learn, to train oneself towards Nibbāna Sn 940, 1061; Miln 10; Pot. sikkheyyāsi Miln 10; sikkheyyāma D II.245; sikkhema Sn 898; sikkhe Sn 974; sikkheyya Sn 930. Fut. sikkhissāmi Vin IV.141; sikkhissāmase Sn 814; ppr. sikkhanto Sn 657; ppr. med. sikkhamāna training oneself Vin IV.141; D II.241; It 104, 121; sikkhamānā (f.) a young woman undergoing a probationary course of training in order to become a nun Vin I.135, 139, 145, 147, 167; IV.121; A III.276; S II.261; grd. sikkhitabba Vin I.83; J VI.296; M I.123; D II.138; Miln 10; & sikkha that ought to be learnt Miln 10; inf. sikkhituŋ Vin I.84, 270; ger. sikkhitvā Miln 219. — 2. to want to overcome, to try, tempt D II.245. — pp. sikkhita. — Caus. II. sikkhāpeti to teach, to train J I.162, 187, 257; DA I.261; Miln 32; PvA 3, 4.

Sikkhana (nt.) [fr. **śikṣ**] training, study J I.58.

Sikkhā (f.) [Vedic śikṣā] 1. study, training, discipline Vin III.23; D I.181; A I.238; S II.50, 131; v.378; Dhs 1004; VbhA 344 (various). — sikkhaŋ paccakkhātaka one who has abandoned the precepts Vin I.135, 167; II.244 sq. (cp. sikkhā-paccakkhāna Vin II.279, and sikkhaŋ apaccakkhāya Vin III.24; S IV.190; sikkhā apaccakkhātā, ibid.); tisso sikkhā S III.83; Ps I.46 sq.; Miln 133, 237; Nd[1] 39; explained as adhisīla-, adhicitta-, and adhipaññā-sikkhā A I.234 sq.; Nett 126; with the synonyms saŋvara, samādhi & paññā at Vism 274. — 2. (as one of the 6 Vedāngas) phonology or phonetics, comb^d with nirutti (interpretation, etymology) DA I.247=SnA 447.

-**ānisaŋsa** whose virtue is training, praise of discipline A II.243; It 40. -**ānusantatavutti** whose behaviour is thoroughly in accordance with the discipline Nett 112. -**kāma** anxious for training Vin I.44; D II.101; S v.154, 163; A I.24, 238; °-*tā* anxiety for training J I.161. -**samādāna** taking the precepts upon oneself Vin I.146; Miln 162; A I.238 sq.; IV.15; v.165. -**sājīva** system of training Vin III.23 sq.; Pug 57.

Sikkhāpada (nt.) [sikkhā+pada, the latter in sense of pada 3. Cp. BSk. śikṣāpada] set of precepts, "preceptorial," code of training; instruction, precept, rule. — 1. in general: D I.63, 146, 250; M I.33; A I.63, 235 sq.; II.14, 250 sq.; III.113, 262; IV.152, 290 sq.; S II.224; v.187; Vin I.102; II.95, 258; III.177; IV.141 (saha-dhammika), 143 (khudd' ânukhuddakāni); It 96, 118; VbhA 69 (bhesajja°); DhA III.16. — 2. in special: the 5 (or 10) rules of morality, or the precepts to be adopted in particular by one who is entering the Buddhist community either as a layman or an initiate. There seem to have been only 5 rules at first, which are the same as the first 5 sīlas (see sīla 2 b): S II.167; Vbh 285 (expl^d in detail at VbhA 381 sq.); DhA I.32 and passim. To these were added another 5, so as to make the whole list (the dasasikkhāpadaŋ or °padāni) one of 10 (which are *not* the 10 sīlas!). These are (6) **vikāla-bhojanā** (-veramaṇī) not eating at the wrong hour; (7) **nacca-gīta-vādita-visūka-dassanā**° to avoid worldly amusements; (8) **mālā-gandha-vilepana-dhāraṇa-maṇḍana-vibhūsana-ṭṭhānā**° to use neither unguents nor ornaments; (9) **uccā-sayana-mahā-sayanā**° not to sleep on a high, big bed; (10) **jātarūpa rajata-paṭiggahaṇā**° not to accept any gold or silver: Vin I.83=Kh II.; A I.211, and frequently. — **dasa-sikkhāpadikā** (f.) conforming to the 10 obligations (of a nun) Vin IV.343 (=sāmaṇerī). There is nowhere any mention of the 8 sikkhāpadas *as such*, but they are called **aṭṭhangika uposatha** (see sīla 2b), e. g. Mhvs 37, 202. — **diyaḍḍha-sikkhāpada-sata** the 150 precepts, i. e. the Pāṭimokkha A I.230, 234; Miln 243.

Sikkhāpaka (adj.) [fr. sikkhāpeti] teaching PvA 252; Miln 164.

Sikkhāpana (nt.) [fr. sikkhāpeti] teaching Miln 163.

Sikkhāpanaka teaching J I.432.

Sikkhita [pp. of sikkhati] trained, taught Vin IV.343 (°sikkha, adj., trained in . . .; chasu dhammesu); Miln 40; PvA 263 (°sippa).

Sikhaṇḍin (adj.-n.) [Sk. śikhaṇḍin] 1. tufted, crested (as birds); J v.406; VI.539; Th 1, 1103 (mayūra); with tonsured hair (as ascetics) J III.311. — 2. a peacock J v.406; VvA 163.

Sikhara [cp. Sk. śikhara] the top, summit of a mountain J VI.519; Miln 2; a peak DhA III.364 (°thūpiyo or °thūpikāyo peaked domes); the point or edge of a sword M I.243; S IV.56; crest, tuft J II.99; (this is a very difficult reading; it is explained by the C. by sundara (elegant); Trenckner suggests singāra, cp. II.98); a bud Th 2, 382.

Sikhariṇī (f.) [fr. last] a kind of woman (with certain defects of the pudendum Vin II.271; III.129 (text, °aṇī).

Sikhā (f.) [Vedic śikhā] point, edge M I.104; crest, top-knot DA I.89; J v.406; of a flame Dh 308; DhsA 124; of fire (aggi°) Sn 703; J v.213; (dhūma°) J VI.206; of a ray of light J I.88; in the corn trade, the pyramid of corn at the top of the measuring vessel DA I.79; °-bandha top-knot D I.7; vātasikhā (tikkhā a raging blast) J III.484; susikha (adj.) with a beautiful crest Th 1, 211 (mora), 1136.

Sikkhitar [n. ag. fr. sikkhati] a master, adept; proficient, professional J VI.449, 450.

Sikhin (adj.) [fr. sikhā] crested, tufted Th 1, 22 (mora); J II.363 (f. °inī). Also name of (a) the fire J I.215, 288; (b) the peacock Sn 221, 687.

Sigāla (śṛ°) [cp. Vedic sṛgāla; as loan-word in English = jackal] a jackal D II.295; III.24 sq.; A I.187; S II.230, 271; IV.177 sq. (text singāla); IV.199; J I.502; III.532 (Pūtimaŋsa by name). — sigālī (f.) a female jackal J I.336; II.108; III.333 (called Māyāvī); Miln 365. — See also singāla.

Sigālika (adj.) [fr. sigāla] belonging to a jackal J II.108; III.113 (°aŋ nādaŋ, cp. segalikaŋ A I.187, where the Copenhagen MS. has sigālakaŋ corrected to segālakaŋ). — (nt.) a jackal's roar (*sigālakaŋ nadati*) D III.25. Cp. segālaka.

Siggu (nt.) [cp. Vedic śigru, N. of a tribe; as a tree in Suśruta] name of a tree (Hyperanthera moringa) J III.161; V.406.

Singa[1] (nt.) [Vedic śṛnga, cp. Gr. κάρνον, κραγγών; Lat. cornu = E. horn] a horn J I.57, 149, 194; IV.173 (of a cow); Vism 106; VvhA 476.
-**dhanu** horn-bow DhA I.216. -**dhamaka** blowing a horn Miln 31.

Singa[2] the young of an animal, calf J V.92; cp. Deśīnāmamālā VIII.31.

Singāra [cp. Sk. śṛngāra] erotic sentiment; singāratā (f.) fondness of decorations J I.184; an elegant dress, finery Miln 2; (adj.) elegant, graceful (thus read) J II.99; singāra-bhāva being elegant or graceful (said of a horse) J II.98.

Singāla various reading instead of sigāla S II.231 etc.; Vism 196; Pv III.5[2].

Singika (adj.) [fr. singa[1]] having horns J VI.354 (āvelita-° having twisted horns).

Singin (adj.) [Vedic śṛngin] having a horn Vin II.300; J IV.173 (= cow); clever, sharp-witted, false Th 1, 959; A II.26; It 112; cp. *J.P.T.S.* 1885, 53.

Singila a kind of horned bird J III.73; DhA III.22 (v. l. singala).

Singivera (nt.) [Sk. śṛnga + Tamil vera "root," as E. loan word = ginger] ginger Vin I.201; IV.35; J I.244; III.225 (alla-°); Miln 63; Mhvs 28, 21; DhsA 320; DA I.81.

Singī & **singi** (f.) [cp. Sk. śṛngī] 1. gold Vin I.38; S II.234; J I.84. — 2. "ginger" in sense of "dainties, sweets" J IV.352 (= singiver' ādika uttaribhanga C.; cp. Tamil iñji ginger).
-**nada** gold Vv 64[28]; VvA 284. -**loṇa** (-**kappa**) license as to ginger & salt Vin II.300, 306. -**vaṇṇa** gold-coloured D II.133. -**suvaṇṇa** gold VvA 167.

Singu (f.) (?) a kind of fish J V.406; plur. singū J VI.537. According to Abhp. singū is *m*, and Payogasiddhi gives it as *nt*.

Singhati [**singh**, given as "ghāyana" at Dhtp 34] to sniff, to get scent of S I.204 = J III.308; DA I.38. Cp. upa°.

Singhāṭaka [cp. Sk. śṛngāṭaka; fr. śṛnga] (m. and n.) 1. a square, a place where four roads meet Vin I.237, 287, 344; IV.271; D I.83; A II.241; IV.187, 376; S I.212; II.128; IV.194; Miln 62, 330, 365; DhA I.317. aya-s° perhaps an iron ring (in the shape of a square or triangle) M I.393; J V.45. — 2. a water plant (Trapa bispinosa ?) J VI.530, 563.

Singhāṇikā (f.) [Sk. singhāṇaka] mucus of the nose, snot D II.293; M I.187; Sn 196-198 = J I.148 (all MSS. of both books -n- instead of -ṇ-); Miln 154, 382; Pv II.2[3]; Vism 264 & 362 (in detail); DhA I.50; VbhA 68, 247.

Sijjati [**svid**, Epic Sk. svidyate] to boil (intr.), to sweat; ppr. sijjamāna boiling J I.503; Caus. sedeti (q. v.). The Dhtp 162 gives "pāka" as meaning of **sid**. — pp. sinna (wet) & siddha[1] (cooked).

Sijjhati [**sidh**; Epic Sk. sidhyate. The Dhtp gives 2 roots **sidh**, viz. one as "gamana" (170), the other as "saṇsiddhi" (419)] to succeed, to be accomplished, to avail, suit SnA 310; PvA 58, 113, 254 (inf. sijjhituṇ). — pp. siddha.

Siñcaka [fr. siñcati] watering, one who waters Vv 79[7] (amba°).

Siñcati [sic, cp. Av. hinčaiti to pour; Lat. siat "urinate," Ags. sēon; Ohg. sīhan, Ger. ver-siegen; Gr. ἰκμάς wet; Goth saiws = E. sea. — Dhtp 377: kkharaṇe] 1. to sprinkle J III.144; V.26; Mhvs 37, 203; SnA 66. — 2. to bale out a ship Sn 771; Dh 369. inf. siñcituṇ J VI.583; pass. siccati Th 1, 50 (all MSS. siñcati); imper. siñca Dh 369; ppr. med. siñcamāna Mhvs 37, 203; ger. sitvā Sn 771 = Nett 6; pp. sitta. — Caus. seceti to cause to sprinkle Mhvs 34, 45; Caus. II. siñcāpeti J II.20, 104. — Cp. pari°.

Siñcanaka (adj.) [fr. siñcati] sprinkling (water) SnA 66 (vāta).

Siṭṭha [pp. of **śiṣ**; Sk. śiṣṭha] see **vi**°.

Siṇāti see seyyati.

Sita[1] (adj.) [pp. of **śā**; Sk. śita] sharp Dāvs I.32.

Sita[2] [pp. of sayati[2]] 1. (lit.) stuck in or to: hadaya° salla Sn 938; Nd[1] 412. — 2. (fig.) reclining, resting, depending on, attached, clinging to D I.45, 76; II.255; M I.364; Cp. 100; J V.453; Sn 229, 333, 791, 944, 1044. See also asita[2].

Sita[3] [pp. of sinoti] bound; sātu-° Dh 341 (bound to pleasure); taṇhā-° Miln 248. Perhaps as sita[2].

Sita[4] (adj.) [Sk. sita] white Dāvs III.4.

Sita[5] (nt.) [pp. of **smi**, cp. vimhāpeti. The other P. form is mihita] a smile Vin III.105; IV.159; S I.24; II.254; M II.45; Th 1, 630; Ap 21 (pātukari), 22 (°kamma) DhA II.64 (°ṇ pātvakāsi); III.479; VvA 68. -°**kāra** smiling J I.351 (as °ākāra).

Sitta [pp. of siñcati] sprinkled Dh 369; J III.144; Vism 109

Sittha (nt.) [cp. *Sk. siktha] a lump of boiled rice Vin II.165, 214; J I.189, 235; V.387; VI.358 (odana°), 365 (yāgu°); PvA 99; sitthatelaka oil of beeswax Vin II.107, 151.
-**âvakārakaṇ** (adv.) scattering the lumps of boiled rice Vin IV.196.

Sitthaka (nt.) [cp. Sk. sikthaka] beeswax Vin II.116 (madhu°).

Sithila (adj.) [Vedic śithira, later śithila] loose, lax, bending, yielding S I.49, 77 = Dh 346 = J II.140; J I.179; II.249; Miln 144; DhA IV.52, 56; PvA 13. In compn with **bhū** as sithilī°, e. g. °bhāva lax state Vism 502 = VbhA 100; °bhūta hanging loose PvA 47 (so read for sithila°). -°**hanu** a kind of bird M I.429. — Cp. saṭhila.

Siddha[1] [a specific Pali formation fr. sijjati (**svid**) in meaning "to cook," in analogy to siddha[2]] boiled, cooked J II.435 (= pakka); V.201 (°bhojana); Miln 272; SnA 27 (°bhatta = pakk'odana of Sn 18).

Siddha[2] [pp. of sijjhati] ended, accomplished Mhvs 23, 45, 78; successful Miln 247. — (m.) a kind of semi-divine beings possessed of supernatural faculties, a magician Miln 120, 267 [cp. Sk. siddha Halāyudha 1, 87; Yogasūtra 3, 33; Aufrecht remarks: "This is a post-vedic mythological fiction formed on the analogy of sādhya"].
-**attha** one who has completed his task Miln 214.

Siddhatthaka [Sk. siddhārthaka] white mustard ThA 181 (Ap. V.24); J III.225; VI.537; DhA II.273 (in Kisāgotamī story).

Siddhi (f.) [fr. **sidh**, Vedic siddhi] accomplishment, success, prosperity Mhvs 29, 70; Sdhp 14, 17, 325, 469; PvA 63 (attha° advantage); padasiddhi substantiation of the meaning of the word DA I.66; cp. sadda°.

Siddhika (adj.) (-°) [fr. siddhi] connected with success; nāmasiddhika who thinks luck goes by names J I.401; appasiddhika unprofitable, fatal, etc. J IV.4, 5 (sāgara); VI.34 (samudda).

Sināta [pp. of sināti] bathed, bathing M I.39; S I.169=183; J V.330.

Sināti[1] (to bind): see sinoti.

Sināti[2] [Vedic snāti, **snā**. For detail see nahāyati. The Dhtp 426 gives root **sinā** in meaning "soceyya," i. e. cleaning] to bathe; imper. sinähi M I.39; inf. sināyituŋ M I.39; aor. sināyi Ap 204. — pp. sināta.

Sināna (nt.) [fr. **snā**] bathing M I.39; S I.38, 43; IV.118; Nd[2] 39; Vism 17; VbhA 337.

Sināni (f.) bath-powder (?) M II.46, 151, 182.

Siniddha [pp. of siniyhati; cp. Epic Sk. snigdha] 1. wet, moist Vism 171. — 2. oily, greasy, fatty J I.463, 481; SnA 100 (°āhāra fattening food). — 3. smooth, glossy J I.89; IV.350 (of leaves); Miln 133. — 4. resplendent, charming ThA 139. — 5. pliable Vin I.279 (kāya, a body with good movement of bowels). — 6. affectionate, attached, fond, loving J I.10; Miln 229, 361; VbhA 282 (°puggala-sevanatā).

Siniyhati [Vedic snihyate, **snih**; cp. Av. snaēžaiti it snows=Lat. ninguit, Gr. νείφει; Oir. snigid it rains; Lat. nix snow=Gr. νίφα=Goth. snaiws, Ohg. sneo=snow; Oir. snige rain; etc. — The Dhtp 463 gives the 2 forms sinih & snih in meaning piṇana. Cp. sineha] (to be moist or sticky, fig.) to feel love, to be attached Vism 317=DhsA 192 (in def[n] of mettā). Caus. sineheti (sneheti, snehayati) to lubricate, make oily or tender (through purgatives etc.) Vin I.279 (kāyaŋ); Miln 172; DA I.217 (temeti+); to make pliable, to soften Miln 139 (mānasaŋ). — pp. siniddha.

Sineha & **sneha** [fr. **snih**] Both forms occur without distinction; sneha more frequently (as *archaic*) in poetry. — A. sineha: 1. viscous liquid, unctuous moisture, sap S I.134; A I.223 sq.; J I.108; Dhs 652 (=sinehana DhsA 335); Vism 262 (thīna°=meda; vilīna°=vasā). — 2. fat J II.44 (bahu°); VbhA 67. — 3. affection, love, desire, lust J I.190; II.27; PvA 82. — B. sneha: 1. (oily liquid) D I.74; Pv III.5[2] (anguṭṭha°, something like milk; expl[d] as khīra PvA 198). — 2. (affection) A II.10; S IV.188 (kāma°); Sn 36, 209, 943 (=chanda, pema, rāga, Nd[1] 426); J IV.11.
-anvaya following an affection Sn 36. -gata anything moist or oily A III.394 sq.; DhsA 335. -ja sprung from affection Sn 272; S I.207. -bindu a drop of oil Vism 263. -virecana an oily purgative J III.48.

Sinehaka a friend Mhvs 36, 44.

Sinehana (nt.) oiling, softening Miln 229; DhsA 335. — Cp. senehika.

Sinehaniya (adj.) [grd. formation fr. sinehana] softening, oily; **°āni bhesajjāni** softening medicines Miln 172 (opp. lekhaniyāni).

Sinehita [pp. of sineheti] lustful, covetous Dh 341; DhA IV.49.

Sinoti [sā or si; Vedic syati & sināti; the Dhtp 505 gives si in meaning "bandhana"] to bind DhsA 219 (sinoti bandhatī ti setu) pp. sita[3].

Sindī (f.) [etym. ?] N. of a tree Vism 183, where KhA 49 in id. passage reads khajjūrikā. See also Abhp 603; Deśīn VIII.29.

Sinduvāra [Sk. sinduvāra] the tree Vitex negundo DA I.252; DhsA 14, 317; also spelt sindhavāra VvA 177; sinduvārikā J VI.269; sindhuvāritā (i. e. sinduvārikā ?) J VI.550=553; sinduvārita J IV.440, 442 (v. l. °vārakā).

Sindhava [Sk. saindhava] belonging to the Sindh, a Sindh horse J I.175; II.96; III.278; V.259; DhA IV.4 (=Sindhava-raṭṭhe jatā assā); (nt.) rock salt Vin I.202; Sindhavaraṭṭha the Sindh country ThA 270; J V.260.

Sindhavāra see sinduvāra.

Sinna [pp. of sijjati; Vedic svinna] 1. wet with perspiration Vin I.46, 51; II.223. — 2. boiled (cp. siddha[1]) esp. in the comp. **udaka-sinna-paṇṇa**; it occurs in a series of passages J III.142, 144; IV.236, 238, where Fausböll reads sitta, although the var. readings give also sinna. The English translation, p. 149, says "sprinkled with water," but the text, 238, speaks of leaves which are "sodden" (sedetvā).

Sipāṭikā (f.) [cp. Sk. sṛpāṭikā, beak, BR.] 1. pericarp M I.306; Vv 84[33]; VvA 344; hingu° a s. yielding gum Vin I.201. Also written sipātikā; thus ādiṇṇasipātikā with burst pod or fruit skin S IV.193. — 2. a small case, receptable; khura° a razor case Vin II.134. On s. at Pv III.2[29] the C. has ekapaṭalā upānahā PvA 186.

Sippa (nt.) [cp. Sk. śilpa] art, branch of knowledge, craft Sn 261; A III.225; IV.281 sq., 322; D III.156, 189; J I.239, 478; Miln 315; excludes the Vedas Miln 10; sabbasippāni J I.356, 463; II.53; eight various kinds enumerated M I.85; twelve crafts Ud 31, cp. dvādasavidha s. J I.58; eighteen sippas mentioned J II.243; some sippas are hīna, others ukkaṭṭha Vin IV.6 sq.; VbhA 410. asippa untaught, unqualified J IV.177; VI.228=asippin Miln 250. — sippaŋ uggaṇhāti to learn a craft VvA 138
-āyatana object or branch of study, art D I.51; Miln 78; VbhA 490 (pāpaka). -uggahaṇa taking up, i. e. learning, a craft J IV.7; PvA 3. -ṭṭhāna a craft M I.85; cp. BSk. śilpasthāna Divy 58, 100, 212. -phala result of one's craft D I.51. -mada conceit regarding one's accomplishment VbhA 468.

Sippaka=sippa J I.420.

Sippavant [fr. sippa] one who masters a craft J VI.296.

Sippika [fr. sippa] an artisan Sn 613, 651; Miln 78; Vism 336. Also sippiya J VI.396, 397.

Sippikā[1] (f.) [fr. sippī] a pearl oyster J I.426; II.100 (sippikasambukaŋ); Vism 362 (in comp.)=VbhA 68.

Sippikā[2] at Th 1, 49 is difficult to understand. It must mean a kind of bird (°abhiruta), and may be (so Kern) a misread pippikā (cp. Sk. pippaka & pippīka). See also *Brethren* p. 53[3].

Sippī [cp. Prākrit sippī] (f.) a pearl oyster J II.100; sippipuṭa oyster shell J V.197, 206. sippi-sambuka oysters and shells D I.84; M I.279; A I.9; III.395.

Sibala N. of a tree J VI.535.

Sibba (nt.) [fr. **sīv**] a suture of the skull; plur. °-āni J VI.339; sibbinī (f.) the same Vin I.274.

Sibbati [**sīv**, Vedic sīvyati. The root is sometimes given as **siv**, e. g. Dhtp 390, with def[n] "tantu-santāna"] to sew J IV.25; VvA 251. Pres. also sibbeti Vin II.116; IV.61, 280; ger. sibbetvā J I.316; grd. sibbitabba J I.9; aor. sibbi J IV.25; & sibbesi Vin II.289; inf. sibbetuŋ, Vin I.203. — pp. sibbita. — Caus. II. sibbāpeti J II.197; Vin IV.61.

Sibbana (nt.) [fr. sīv] sewing Sn 304=J IV.395; J I.220; VI.218. sibbanī (f.) "seamstress"=greed, lust Dhs 1059; A III.399; DhsA 363; Sn 1040 (see lobha). -°magga suture Vism 260; KhA 60 (id.).

Sibbāpana (nt.) [fr. sibbāpeti] causing to be sewn Vin IV.280.

Sibbita [pp. of sibbati] sewn Vin IV.279 (dus°); J IV.20 (su°); VbhA 252 (°rajjukā). Cp. vi° & pari°.

Sibbitar [n. ag. fr. **sīv**] one who sews M III.126

Sibbinī Dhs 1059, read sibbanī. Cp. sibba.

Simbali (f.) [cp. Vedic śimbala flower of the B., cp. Pischel, *Prk. Gr.* § 109] the silk-cotton tree Bombax heptaphyllum J I.203; III.397; Vism 206; DhA I.279. °-vana a forest of simbali trees J I.202; II.162 (s. °-pālibhaddaka-vana); IV.277. sattisimbalivana the sword forest, in purgatory J V.453.

Siyyati see seyyati.

Sira (nt. and m.) [cp. Vedic śiras, śīrṣan; Av. sarō, Gr. *καράρα* head, *κέρας* horn, *κρανίον*; Lat. cerebrum; Ohg. hirni brain] head, nom. siraŋ Th 2, 255, acc. siraŋ A I.141; siro Sn 768; sirasaŋ J V.434; instr. sirasā Vin I.4; D I.126; Sn 1027; loc. sirasmiŋ M I.32; sire DA I.97; in compounds siro- A I.138. — sirasā paṭigganhāti to accept with reverence J I.65; pādesu sirasā nipatati to bow one's head to another's feet, to salute respectfully Vin I.4, 34; Sn p. 15, p. 101. siraŋ muñcati to loosen the hair J V.434; cp. I.47; mutta° with loose hair KhA 120=Vism 415; adho-siraŋ with bowed head, head down A I.141; IV.133; J VI.298; cp. avaŋ°; dvedhā° with broken head J V.206; muṇḍa° a shaven head DhA II.125.

Sirā [Sk. sirā] (f.) a bloodvessel, vein Mhvs 37, 136; nerve, tendon, gut J V.344, 364; °-jāla the network of veins J V.69; PvA 68.

Siriŋsapa [Sk. sarīsṛpa] a (long) creeping animal, serpent, a reptile Vin I.3; II.110; D II.57; M I.10; S I.154; A II.73, 117, 143; V.15; Sn 52, 964; J I.93; Pv III.5^2; Nd^1 484; VbhA 6. -tta (nt.) the state of being a creeping thing D II.57.

Sirimant (adj.) [siri + mant] glorious D II.240.

Sirī (siri) (f.) [Vedic śrī] 1. splendour, beauty Sn 686 (instr. siriyā); J VI.348 (siriŋ dhāreti). — 2. luck, glory, majesty, prosperity S I.44 (nom. siri); J II.410 (siriŋ), 466; DA I.148; VvA 323 (instr. buddha-siriyā). rajjasirī-dāyikā devatā the goddess which gives prosperity to the kingdom DhA II.17; sirī + lakkhī splendour & luck J III.443. — 3. the goddess of luck D I.11 (see Rh. D. *Buddhist India* 216-222); DA I.97; J V.112; Miln 191 (°devatā). — 4. the royal bed-chamber (= sirigabbha) J VI.383. — assirī unfortunate Nett 62 = Ud 79 (reads sassar'iva). sassirīka (q. v.) resplendent SnA 91; sassirika J V.177 (puṇṇa-canda°); opp. nissirīka (a) without splendour J VI.225, 456; (b) unlucky VvA 212 (for alakkhika). — The composition form is siri°.

-**gabbha** bedroom J I.228, 266; III. 125; V.214. -**corabrāhmaṇa** "a brahmin who stole good luck" J II.409 (cp. sirilakkhaṇa-°). -**devatā** goddess(es) of luck Miln 191 (+ kalidevatā). -**dhara** glorious Mhvs 5, 13. -**nigguṇḍi** a kind of tree J VI.535. -**vilāsa** pomp and splendour J IV.232. -**vivāda** a bedchamber quarrel J III.20 (sayanakalaho ti pi vadanti yeva, C.). -**sayana** a state couch, royal bed J I.398; III.264; VI.10; DhA II.86; PvA 280.

Sirīsa (nt.) [cp. Class. Sk. śirṣa] the tree Acacia sirissa D II.4; S IV.193; Vv 84^{32}; VvA 331, 344; °-puppha a kind of gem Miln 118. Cp. serīsaka.

Siroruha [Sk. śiras + ruha] the hair of the head Mhvs 1, 34; Sdhp 286.

Silā (f.) [cp. Sk. śilā] a stone, rock Vin I.28; S IV.312 sq.; Vin 445; DA I.154; J V.68; Vism 230 (in comparison); VbhA 64 (var. kinds); a precious stone, quartz Vin II.238; Miln 267, 380; Vv 84^{15} (= phalika° VvA 339); pada-silā a flag-stone Vin II.121, 154. Cp. sela.

-**uccaya** a mountain A III.346; Th 1, 692; J I.29; VI.272, 278; Dāvs V.63. -**guḷa** a ball of stone, a round stone M III.94. -**tthambha** (sila°) stone pillar Mhvs 15, 173. -**paṭimā** stone image J IV.95. -**paṭṭa** a slab of stone, a stone bench J I.59; VI.37 (mangala°); SnA 80, 117. -**pākāra** stone wall Vin II.153. -**maya** made of stone J VI.269, 270; Mhvs 33, 22; 36, 104. -**yūpa** a stone column S V.445; A IV.404; Mhvs 28, 2. -**santhāra** stone floor Vin II.120.

Silāghati [Epic Sk. **ślāgh**] to extol, only in Dhtp 30 as root **silāgh**, with def^n "katthana," i. e. boasting.

Silābhu (nt.) a whip snake J VI.194 (= nīlapaṇṇavaṇṇasappa).

Siliṭṭha [cp. Sk. śliṣṭa, pp. of **śliṣ** to clasp, to which śleṣman slime = P. silesuma & semha. The Dhtp (443) expl^s **silis** by "ālingana"] adhering, connected A I.103; DA I.91; J III.154; DhsA 15; Sdhp 489 (a°).

Siliṭṭhatā (f.) [abstr. fr. siliṭṭha] adherence, adhesion, junction Nd^2 137 (byañjana°, of "iti").

Silutta a rat snake J VI.194 (= gharasappa).

Silesa [fr. **śliṣ**] junction, embrace; a rhetoric figure, riddle, puzzle, pun J V.445 (silesūpamā said of women = purisānaŋ cittabandhanena silesasadisā, ibid. 447).

Silesuma (nt.) [Sk. śleṣman, fr. **śliṣ**. This the diæretic form for the usual contracted form semha] phlegm Pv II.2^3 (= semha PvA 80).

Siloka [Vedic śloka Dhtp 8: **silok** = sanghāta] fame D II.223, 255; M I.192; S II.226 (lābha-sakkāra°); A II.26, 143; Sn 438; Vin I.183; J IV. 223 (= kitti-vaṇṇa); Miln 325; SnA 86 (°bhaṇana, i. e. recitation); pāpasiloka having a bad reputation Vin IV.239; asiloka blame A IV.364 (°bhaya); J VI.491. — 2. a verse Miln 71; J V.387.

Silokavant (adj.) [siloka + vant] famous M I.200.

Siva (adj.-n.) [Vedic śiva] auspicious, happy, fortunate, blest S I.181; J I.5; II.126; Miln 248; Pv IV.3^3; Vv 18^7. — 2. a worshipper of the god Siva Miln 191; the same as Sivi J III.468. — 3. nt. happiness, bliss Sn 115, 478; S IV.370.

-**vijjā** knowledge of auspicious charms D I.9; DA I.93 (alternatively explained as knowledge of the cries of jackals); cp. Divy 630 śivāvidyā.

Sivā (f.) [Sk. śivā] a jackal DA I.93.

Sivāṭikā various reading instead of sipāṭikā, which see.

Sivikā (f.) [Epic Sk. śibikā] a palanquin, litter Bu 17, 16 (text savakā); Pv I.11^1; Vin I.192; °-gabbha a room in shape like a palanquin, an alcove Vin II.152; mañca-° J V.136, 262 (a throne palanquin ?). suvaṇṇa° a golden litter J I.52, 89; DhA I.89; Vism 316.

Siveyyaka (adj.) hailing from the Sivi country, a kind of cloth (very valuable) Vin I.278, 280; J IV.401; DA I.133. The two latter passages read siveyyaka.

Sisira (adj.) [Sk. śiśira] cool, cold Dāvs V.33; VvA 132. (m.) cold, cold season Vin II.47 = J I.93.

Sissa [cp. Sk. śiṣya, grd. of **śiṣ** or **śās** to instruct: see sāsati etc.] a pupil; Sn 997, 1028; DhsA 32 (°ānusissā).

Sissati [Pass. of **śiṣ** to leave; Dhtp 630: visesana] to be left, to remain VvA 344. Cp. visissati. — Caus. seseti to leave (over) D II.344 (aor. sesesi); J I.399; V.107; DhA I.398 (asesetvā without a remainder). — pp. siṭṭha: see visiṭṭha.

Sīgha (adj.) [cp. Epic Sk. śīghra] quick, rapid, swift M I.120; A I.45; Dh 29; Pug 42; °-gāmin walking quickly Sn 381; sīghasota swiftly running D II.132; A II.199; Sn 319; °-vāhana swift (as horses) J VI.22; cp. adv.

sīghataraŋ Miln 82; sīghaŋ (adv.) quickly Miln 147; VvA 6; VbhA 256; usually redupl. sīgha-sīghaŋ very quickly J I.103; PvA 4.

Sīta (adj.) [Vedic śīta] cold, cool D I.74, 148; II.129; A II.117, 143; Sn 467, 1014; Vin I.31, 288. (nt.) cold Vin I.3; J I.165; Mhvs 1, 28; Sn 52, 966. In compⁿ with **kṛ** & **bhū** the form is sīti°, e. g. sīti-kata made cool Vin II.122; sīti-bhavati to become cooled, tranquillized S II.83; III.126; IV.213; V.319; Sn 1073 (sīti-siyā, Pot. of bhavati); It 38; °-bhūta, tranquillized Vin I.8; II.156; S I.141, 178; Sn 542, 642; A I.138; V.65; D III.233; Vv 53[24]; Pv I.8[7]; IV.1[32]. sīti-bhāva coolness, dispassionateness, calm A III.435; Th 2, 360; Ps II.43; Vism 248; VbhA 230; PvA 230; ThA 244. — At J II.163 & V.70 read sīna ("fallen") for sīta.
-**āluka** susceptible of cold Vin I.288 (synon. sītabhīruka). -**uṇha** cold and heat J I.10. -**odaka** with cool water (pokkharaṇī) M I.76; Pv II.10[4]; sītodika (°iya) the same J IV.438. -**bhīruka** being a chilly fellow Vin I.288[16] (cp. sītāluka).

Sita (nt.) sail J IV.21. So also in BSk.: Jtm 94.

Sītaka = **sīta** S IV.289 (vāta).

Sītala (adj.) [cp. Vedic śītala] cold, cool J II.128; DA I.1; Miln 246; tranquil J I.3; (nt.) coolness Miln 76, 323; VvA 44, 68, 100; PvA 77, 244. sītalībhāva becoming cool Sdhp 33.

Sītā (f.) a furrow Vin I.240 (satta sītāyo); gambhīrasīta with deep mould (khetta) A IV.237, 238 (text, °-sita).
-**āloḷī** mud from the furrow adhering to the plough Vin I.206.

Sīti° see sīta. The word sītisiyāvimokkha Ps II.43, must be artificial, arisen from the pāda, sīti-siyā vimutto Sn 1073 (on which see explⁿ at Nd² 678).

Sīdati [**sad**, Idg. *si-sd-ō, redupl. formation like tiṭṭhati; cp. Lat. sīdo, Gr. ἵζω; Av. hiđaiti. — The Dhtp (50) gives the 3 meanings of "visaraṇa-gaty-avasādanesu"] to subside, sink; to yield, give way S I.53; Sn 939 (=saŋsīdati osīdati Nd² 420); It 71; Mhvs 35, 35; 3rd pl. sīdare J II.393; Pot. sīde It 71; fut. sīdissati: see ni°. — pp. sanna. — Caus. sādeti (q. v.); Caus. II. sīdāpeti to cause to sink Sdhp 43. — Cp. ni°, vi°.

Sīdana (nt.) [fr. sīdati] sinking Mhvs 30, 54.

Sīna[1] [pp. of śṛ to crush; Sk. śīrṇa] fallen off, destroyed Miln 117 (°patta leafless); J II.163 (°patta, so read for sīta°). See also saŋsīna.

Sīna[2] [pp. of sīyati; Sk. śīna] congealed; cold, frosty M I.79.

Sīpada (nt.) [Sk. slīpada] the Beri disease (elephantiasis) morbid enlargement of the legs; hence **sīpadin** and **sīpadika** suffering from that disease Vin I.91, 322.

Sīmantinī (f.) a woman J IV.310; VI.142.

Sīmā (f.) [cp. Sk. sīmā] boundary, limit, parish Vin I.106 sq., 309, 340; Nd¹ 99 (four); DhA IV.115 (mālaka°); antosīmaŋ within the boundary Vin I.132, 167; ekasīmāya within one boundary, in the same parish J I.425; nissīmaŋ outside the boundary Vin I.122, 132; bahisīmagata gone outside the boundary Vin I.255. bhinnasīma transgressing the bounds (of decency) Miln 122. — In compⁿ **sīma°** & **sīmā°**.
-**anta** a boundary Mhvs 25, 87; sin Sn 484; J IV.311. -**antarikā** the interval between the boundaries J I.265; Vism 74. -**âtiga** transgressing the limits of sin, conquering sin Sn 795; Nd¹ 99. -**kata** bounded, restricted Nd² p. 153 (cp. pariyanta). -**ṭṭha** dwelling within the boundary Vin I.255. -**samugghāta** removal, abolishing, of a boundary Mhvs 37, 33. -**sambheda** mixing up of the boundary lines Vism 193, 307, 315.

Sīyati [for Sk. śyāyati] to congeal or freeze: see visīyati & visīveti. — pp. sīna[2].

Sīra [Vedic sīra] plough ThA 270 (=nangala).

Sīla (nt.) [cp. Sk. śīla. It is interesting to note that the Dhtp puts down a root **sīl** in meaning of samādhi (No. 268) and upadhāraṇa (615)] 1. nature, character, habit, behaviour; usually as -° in adj. function "being of such a nature," like, having the character of . . ., e. g. adāna° of stingy character, illiberal Sn 244; PvA 68 (+maccharin); kiŋ° of what behaviour? Pv II.9[13]; keḷi° tricky PvA 241; damana° one who conquers PvA 251; parisuddha° of excellent character A III.124; pāpa° wicked Sn 246; bhaṇana° wont to speak DhA IV.93; vāda° quarrelsome Sn 381 sq. — dussīla (of) bad character D III.235; Dhs 1327; Pug 20, 53; Pv II.8[2] (noun); II.9[69] (adj.); DhA II.252; IV.3; Sdhp 338; Miln 257; opp. susīla S I.141. — 2. moral practice, good character, Buddhist ethics, code of morality. (a) The dasa-sīla or 10 items of good character (*not* "commandments") are (1) pāṇâtipātā veramaṇī, i. e. abstinence from taking life; (2) adinn'ādānā (from) taking what is not given to one; (3) abrahmacariyā adultery (otherwise called kāmesu micchā-cārā); (4) musāvādā telling lies; (5) pisuna-vācāya slander; (6) pharusa-vācāya harsh or impolite speech; (7) samphappalāpā frivolous and senseless talk; (8) abhijjhāya covetousness; (9) byāpādā malevolence; (10) micchādiṭṭhiyā heretic views. — Of these 10 we sometimes find only the first 7 designated as "sīla" per se, or good character generally. See e. g. A I.269 (where called sīla-sampadā); II.83 sq. (*not* called "sīla"), & sampadā. — (*b*) The **pañca-sīla** or 5 items of good behaviour are Nos. 1-4 of dasa-sīla, and (5) abstaining from any state of indolence arising from (the use of) intoxicants, viz. surā-meraya-majja-pamāda-ṭṭhānā veramaṇī. These five also from the first half of the 10 sikkha-padāni. They are a sort of preliminary condition to any higher development after conforming to the teaching of the Buddha (saraṇaŋ-gamana) and as such often mentioned when a new follower is "officially" installed, e. g. Bu II.190: saraṇāgamane kañci nivesesi Tathāgato kañci pañcasu sīlesu sīle dasavidhe paraŋ. From Pv IV.1[76] sq. (as also fr. Kh II. as following upon Kh I.) it is evident that the sikkhāpadāni are meant in this connection (either 5 or 10), and *not* the sīlaŋ, cp. also Pv IV.3[50] sq., although at the above passage of Bu and at J I.28 as well as at Mhvs 18, 10 the expression dasa-sīla is used: evidently a later development of the term as regards dasa-sīla (cp. *Mhvs trslⁿ* 122, n. 3), which through the identity of the 5 sīlas & sikkhāpadas was transferred to the 10 sikkhāpadas. These 5 are often simply called **pañca dhammā**, e. g. at A III.203 sq., 208 sq. Without a special title they are mentioned in connection with the "saraṇaŋ gata" formula e. g. at A IV.266. Similarly the 10 sīlas (as above a) are only called dhammā at A II.253 sq.; V.260; nor are they designated as sīla at A II.221. — pañcasu sīlesu samādapeti to instruct in the 5 sīlas (alias sikkhāpadāni) Vin II.162. — (*c*) The only standard enumerations of the 5 or 10 sīlas are found at two places in the Saŋyutta and correspond with those given in the Niddesa. See on the 10 (as given under a) S IV.342 & Nd² s. v. sīla; on the 5 (also as under b) S II.68 & Nd² s. v. The so-called 10 sīlas (Childers) as found at Kh II. (under the name of dasa-sikkhāpada) are of late origin & served as memorial verses for the use of novices. Strictly speaking they should not be called dasa-sīla. — The *eightfold* sīla or the eight pledges which are recommended to the Buddhist layman (cp. Miln 333 mentioned below) are the sikkhāpadas Nos. 1-8 (see sikkhāpada), which in the Canon however do not occur under the name of sīla nor sikkhāpada, but as aṭṭhanga-samannāgata uposatha (or aṭṭhangika u.) "the fast-day with its 8 constituents." They are discussed in detail at A IV.248 sq., with a poetical setting of the eight at A IV.254 = Sn 400, 401 — (*d*) Three special tracts on morality are found in the Canon. The Culla-sīla (D I.3 sq.) consists first of the items (dasa) sīla 1-7; then follow specific injunctions as to practices of daily living & special conduct, of which the first 5 (omitting the introductory item of bījagāma-bhūtagāma-samārambha) form the second 5 sikkhāpadāni. Upon the Culla° follows the Majjhima° (D I.5 sq.) & then the Mahā-sīla D I.9 sq. The whole of these 3 sīlas is called sīlakkhandha and is (in the Sāmaññaphala sutta e. g.) grouped with samādhi- and paññākkhandha: D I.206 sq.; at A V.205, 206 sīla-kkhandha refers to the Culla-sīla only. The three (s., samādhi & paññā) are often mentioned together, e. g. D II.81, 84; It 51; DA I.57. — The characteristic of a kalyāṇa-mitta is endowment with saddhā, sīla, cāga, paññā A IV.282. These four are counted as constituents of future bliss A IV.282, and form the 4 sampadās ibid. 322. In another connection at M III.99; Vism 19. They are, with suta (foll. after sīla) characteristic of the merit of the devatās A I.210 sq. (under devat'ānussati). — At Miln 333 sīla is classed as: saraṇa°, pañca°, aṭṭhanga°, dasanga°, pātimokkha-saŋvara°, all of which expressions refer to the sikkhāpadas and not to the sīlas. — At Miln 336 sq. sīla functions as one of the 7 ratanas (the 5 as given under sampadā up to vimuttiñāṇadassana; *plus* paṭisambhidā and bojjhanga). — **cattāro sīlakkhandhā** "4 sections of morality" Miln 243; Vism 15 & DhsA 168 (here as pātimokkha-saŋvara, indriya-saŋvara, ājīva-pārisuddhi, paccaya-sannissita. The same with ref. to catubbidha sīla at J III.195). See also under cpds. — At Ps I.46 sq. we find the fivefold grouping as (1) pāṇâtipatassa pahānaŋ, (2) veramaṇī, (3) cetanā, (4) saŋvara, (5) avītikkama, which is commented on at Vism 49. — A *fourfold* sīla (referring to the sikkhāpada) is given at Vism 15 as bhikkhu°, bhikkhunī°, anupasampanna° gahaṭṭha°. — On sīla and adhisīla see e. g. A I.229 sq.; VbhA 413 sq. — The division of sīla at J III.195 is a distinction of a simple sīla as "saŋvara," of twofold sīla as "caritta-vāritta," threefold as "kāyika, vācasika, mānasika," and fourfold as above under cattāro sīlakkhandhā. — See further generally: Ps I.42 sq.; Vism 3 sq.; Tikp 154, 165 sq., 269, 277; Nd[1] 14, 188 (expl[d] as "pātimokkha-saŋvara"); Nd[2] p. 277; VbhA 143.

-**anga** constituent of morality (applied to the pañca-sikkhāpadaŋ) VbhA 381. -**ācāra** practice of morality J I.187; II.3. -**kathā** exposition of the duties of morality Vin I.15; A I.125; J I.188. -**kkhandha** all that belongs to moral practices, body of morality as forming the first constituent of the 5 khandhas or groups (+samādhi°, paññā°, vimutti°, ñāṇadassana-kkhandha), which make up the 5 *sampadās* or whole range of religious development; see e. g. Nd[1] 21, 39; Nd[2] p. 277. — Vin. 162 sq.; III.164; A I.124, 291; II.20; S I.99 sq.; It 51, 107; Nett 90 sq., 128; Miln 243; DhA III.417. -**gandha** the fragrance of good works Dh 55; Vism 58. -**caraṇa** moral life J IV.328, 332. -**tittha** having good behaviour as its banks S I.169, 183 (*trsl*[n] Mrs. Rh. D. "with virtue's strand for bathing"). -**bbata** [= vata[2]] good works and ceremonial observances Dh 271; A I.225; S IV.118; Ud 71; Sn 231, etc.; sīlavata the same Sn 212, 782, 790, 797, 803, 899; It 79 sq.; °-*parāmāsa* the contagion of mere rule and ritual, the infatuation of good works, the delusion that they suffice Vin I.184; M I.433; Dhs 1005; A III.377; IV.144 sq.; Nd[1] 98; Dukp 245, 282 sq.; DhsA 348; see also expl[n] at *Cpd.* 171, n. 4. — **sīlabbatupādāna** grasping after works and rites D II.58; Dhs 1005, 1216; Vism 569; VbhA 181 sq. — The old form sīlavata still preserves the original good sense, as much as "observing the rules of good conduct," "being of virtuous behaviour." Thus at Th I, 12; Sn 212, 782 (expl[d] in detail at Nd[1] 66), 790, 797, 803; It 79; J VI.491 (ariya°). -**bheda** a breach of morality J I.296. -**mattaka** a matter of mere morality D I.3; DA I.55. -**maya** consisting in morality It 51; VvA 10 (see maya, def[n] 6). -**vatta** morality, virtue S I.143; cp. J III.360. -**vipatti** moral transgression Vin I.171 sq.; D II.85; A I.95; 268 sq.; III.252; Pug 21; Vism 54, 57. -**vipanna** trespassing D II.85; Pug 21; Vin I.227. -**vīmaŋsaka** testing one's reputation J I.369; II.429; III.100, 193. -**saŋvara** self-restraint in conduct D I.69; Dhs 1342; DA I.182. -**saŋvuta** living under moral self-restraint Dh 281. -**sampatti** accomplishment or attainment by moral living Vism 57. -**sampadā** practice of morality Vin I.227; D II.86; M I.194, 201 sq.; A I.95, 269 sq., II.66; Pug. 25, 54. -**sampanna** practising morality, virtuous Vin I.228; D I.63; II.86; M I.354; Th 2, 196; ThA 168; DA I.182.

Sīlatā (f.) (-°) [abstr. fr. sīla] character(istic), nature, capacity DhA III.272.

Sīlavant (adj.) [sīla + vant] virtuous, observing the moral precepts D III.77, 259 sq., 285; A I.150; II.58, 76; III.206 sq., 262 sq.; IV.290 sq., 314 sq.; V.10 sq., 71 sq.; Vism 58; DA I.286; Tikp 279. — nom. sg. sīlavā D I.114; S I.166; It 63; Pug 26, 53; J I.187; acc. -vantaŋ Vin III.133; Sn 624; instr. -vatā S III.167; gen. -vato S IV.303; nom. pl. -vanto Pug 13; Dhs 1328; Nett 191; acc. pl. -vante J I.187; instr. -vantehi D II.80; gen. pl. -vantānaŋ M I.334; gen. pl. -vataŋ Dh 56; J I.144; f. -vatī D II.12; Th 2, 449. compar. -vantatara J II.3.

Sīlika (adj.) (-°) [fr. sīla] = sīlin J VI.64.

Sīlin (adj.) [fr. sīla] having a disposition or character; ariyasīlin having the virtue of an Ārya D I.115; DA I.286; niddāsīlin drowsy, Sn 96; vuddhasīlin increased in virtue D I.114; sabhāsīlin fond of society Sn 96.

Sīliya (nt.) [abstr. fr. sīla, Sk. śīlya for śailya] conduct, behaviour, character; said of bad behaviour, e. g. J III.74 = IV.71; emphasized as dussīlya, e. g. S V.384; A I.105; V.145 sq.; opp. sādhu-sīliya J II.137 (= sundara-sīla-bhāva C.).

Sīvathikā (f.) [etym. doubtful; perhaps = *Sk. śivālaya; Kern derives it as śivan "lying" + atthi "bone," problematic] a cemetery, place where dead bodies are thrown to rot away Vin III.36; D II.295 sq.; A III.268, 323; J I.146; Pv III.5[2] (= susāna PvA 198); Vism 181, 240; PvA 195.

Sīvana & **sīveti**: see vi°.

Sīsa[1] (nt.) [cp. Sk. sīsa] lead D II.351; S V.92; Miln 331; VbhA 63 (= kāḷa-tipu); a leaden coin J I.7; °-**kāra** a worker in lead Miln 331; °-**maya** leaden Vin I.190.

Sīsa[2] (nt.) [Vedic śīrṣa: see under sira] 1. the head (of the body) Vin I.8; A I.207; Sn 199, 208, p. 80; J I.74; II.103; sīsaŋ nahāta, one who has performed an ablution of the head D II.172; PvA 82; āditta-sīsa, one whose turban has caught fire S I.108; III.143; V.440; A II.93; sīsato towards the head Mhvs 25, 93; **adho-sīsa**, head first J I.233. — 2. highest part, top, front: **bhūmi**° hill, place of vantage Dpvs 15, 26; J II.406; **cankamana**° head of the cloister Vism 121; **sangāma**° front of the battle Pug 69; J I.387; **megha**° head of the cloud J I.103. In this sense also opposed to pāda (foot), e. g. **sopāṇa**° head (& foot) of the stairs DhA I.115. Contrasted with sama (plain) Ps I.101 sq. — 3. chief point Ps I.102. — 4. panicle, ear (of rice or crops) A IV.169; DA I.118. — 5. head, heading (as subdivision of a subject), as "chanda-sīsa citta-sīsa" grouped under chanda & citta Vism 376. Usually instr °sīsena "under

the heading (or category) of," e. g. citta° Vism 3; paribhoga° J II.24; saññā° DhsA 200; kammaṭṭhāna° DhA III.159.
-ânulokin looking ahead, looking attentively after something M I.147. -ābādha disease of the head Vin I.270 sq.; J VI.331. -âbhitāpa heat in the head, headache Vin I.204. -kaṭāha a skull D II.297=M I.58; Vism 260=KhA 60; KhA 49. -kalanda Miln 272. [Signification unknown; cp. kalanda a squirrel and kalandaka J VI.227; a blanket [cushion ?] or kerchief.] -cchavi the skin of the head Vin I.277. -cola a head-cloth, turban Mhvs 35, 53. -cchejja resulting in decapitation A II.241. -ccheda decapitation, death J I.167; Miln 358. -ppacālakaŋ swaying the head about Vin IV.188. -paramparāya with heads close together DhA I.49. -virecana purging to relieve the head D I.12; DA I.98. -veṭha head wrap S IV.56. -veṭhana head-cloth, turban M II.193; sīsaveṭha id. M I.244=S IV.56. -vedanā headache M I.243; II.193.

Sīsaka (nt.) [=sīsa] head, as adj. -° heading, with the head towards; uttarasīsaka head northwards D II.137; pācīna° (of Māyā's couch: eastward) J I.50. heṭṭhā-sīsaka head downwards J III.13; dhammasīsaka worshipping righteousness beyond everything Miln 47, 117.

Sīha [Vedic siŋha] I. a lion D II.255; S I.16; A II.33. 245; III.121; Sn 72; J I.165; Miln 400; Nd² 679 (=migarājā); VbhA 256, 398 (with pop. etym. " sahanato ca hananato ca sīho ti vuccati "); J V.425 (women like the lion); KhA 140; often used as an epithet of the Buddha A II.24; III.122; S I.28; It 123; fem. sīhī lioness J II.27; III.149, and sīhinī Miln 67.
-āsana a throne Mhvs 5, 62; 25, 98. -kuṇḍala "lion's ear-ring," a very precious ear-ring J V.348; SnA 138; also as °mukha-kuṇḍala at J V.438. -camma lion's hide A IV.393. -tela "lion-oil," a precious oil KhA 198. -nāda a lion's roar, the Buddha's preaching, a song of ecstasy, a shout of exultation "halleluiah" A II.33; M I.71; D I.161, 175; S II.27, 55; J 119; Miln 22; DhA II.43, 178; VbhA 398; (=seṭṭha-nāda abhīta-nāda); SnA 163, 203. -nādika one who utters a lion's roar, a song of ecstasy A I.23. -pañjara a window J I.304; II.31; DhA I.191. -papātaka "lion's cliff," N. of one of the great lakes in the Himavā SnA 407 and passim. -piṭṭhe on top of the lion J II.244. -potaka a young lion J III.149. -mukha "lion's mouth," an ornament at the side of the nave of the king's chariot KhA 172. See also °kuṇḍala. -ratha a chariot drawn by lions Miln 121. -vikkīḷita the lion's play, the attitude of the Buddhas and Arahants Nett 2, 4, 7, 124. -seyyā lying like a lion, on the right side D II.134; A I.114; II.40, 244; J I.119, 330; VbhA 345; DhA I.357. -ssara having a voice like a lion J V.284, 296 etc. (said of a prince). -hanu having a jaw like a lion, of a Buddha D III.144, 175; Bu XIII.1=J I.38.

Sīhaḷa Ceylon; (adj.) Singhalese Mhvs 7, 44 sq.; 37, 62; 37, 175; Dhvs 9, 1; KhA 47, 50, 78; SnA 30, 53 sq., 397. -°kuddāla a Singhalese hoe Vism 255; VbhA 238; -°dīpa Ceylon J VI.30; DhsA 103; DA I.1; KhA 132; -°bhāsā Singhalese (language) DA I.1; Tikp 259. See Dict. of Names.

Sīhaḷaka (adj.) [fr. last] Singhalese SnA 397.

Su[1] (indecl.) [onomat.] a part. of exclamation "shoo!"; usually repeated su su J II.250; VI.165 (of the hissing of a snake); ThA 110 (scaring somebody away), 305 (sound of puffing). Sometimes as sū sū, e. g. Tikp 280 (of a snake), cp. sūkara. — Denom susumāyati (q. v.).

Su-[2] (indecl.) [Vedic su°, cp. Gr. εὐ-] a particle, combd with adj., nouns, and certain verb forms, to express the notion of "well, happily, thorough" (cp. E. well-bred, wel-come, wel-fare); opp. du°. It often acts as simple *intensive* prefix (cp. saŋ°) in the sense of "very," and is thus also combd with concepts which in themselves denote a deficiency or bad quality (cp. su-pāpika "very wicked") and the prefix du° (e. g. su-duj-jaya, su-duddasa, su-dub-bala). — Our usual practice is to register words with su° under the simple word, whenever the character of the composition is evident at first sight (cp. du°). For convenience of the student however we give in the foll. a few compds as illustrating the use of su°.
-kaṭa well done, good, virtuous D I.55; Miln 5; sukata the same D I.27; (nt.) a good deed, virtue Dh 314; A III.245. -kara feasible, easy D I.250; Dh 163; Sn p. 123; na sukaro so Bhagavā amhehi upasaŋkamituŋ S I.9. -kiccha great trouble, pain J IV.451. -kittika well expounded Sn 1057. -kumāra delicate, lovely Mhvs 59, 29; see sukhumāla. -kumālatta loveliness DA I.282. -kusala very skilful J I.220; -khara very hard (-hearted) J VI.508. (=suṭṭhu khara C.). -khetta a good field D II.353; A I.135; S I.21. -gajjin shrieking beautifully (of peacocks) Th I, 211. -gandha fragrant J II.20; pleasant odour Dhs 625. -gandhi=sugandha J 100. -gandhika fragrant Mhvs 7, 27; J I.266. -gahana a good grip, tight seizing J I.223. -gahita and suggahīta, grasped tightly, attentive A II.148, 169; III.179; J I.163, 222. -ggava virtuous J IV.53 (probably misspelling for suggata). -ghara having a nice house J VI.418, 420. -carita well conducted, right, good Dh 168 sq. (nt.) good conduct, virtue, merit A I.49 sq., 57, 102; D III.52, 96, 152 sq., 169; Dh 231; It 55, 59 sq.; Ps I.115; Vism 199. -citta much variegated Dh 151; DhA III.122. -cchanna well covered Dh 14. -cchavi having a lovely skin, pleasant to the skin D III.159; J V.215; VI.269. -jana a good man Mhvs I, 85. -jāta well born, of noble birth D I.93; Sn 548 sq. -jāti of noble family Mhvs 24, 50. -jīva easy to live Dh 244. -tanu having a slender waist Vv 64[12] (=sundara-sarīra VvA 280). -danta well subdued, tamed D II.254; Dh 94; A IV.376. -dassa easily seen Dh 252; (m.) a kind of gods, found in the fourteenth rūpa-brahmaloka D II.52; Pug 17; Kvu 207. -diṭṭha well seen Sn 178; p. 143. -divasa a lucky day J IV.209. -dujjaya difficult to win Mhvs 26, 3. -duttara very difficult to escape from A V.232 sq., 253 sq.; Dh 86; Sn 358. -dukkara very difficult to do J V.31. -duccaja very hard to give up J VI.473. -duddasa very difficult to see Vin I.5; Th I, 1098; Dh 36; DhA I.300; used as an epithet of Nibbāna S IV.369. -duppadhaŋsiya very difficult to overwhelm D III.176. -dubbala very weak Sn 4. -dullabha very difficult to obtain Sn 138; Vv 44[19]; Vism 2; VvA 20. -desika a good guide Miln 354; DhsA 123; Vism 465. -desita well preached Dh 44; Sn 88, 230. -ddiṭṭha [=su+uddiṭṭha] well set out Vin I.129; J IV.192. -ddhanta well blown M III.243; DhsA 326; =saŋdhanta A I.253; Vin II.59. -dhammatā good nature, good character, goodness, virtue J II.159; V.357; VI.527. -dhota well washed, thoroughly clean J I.331. -nandī (scil. *vedanā*) pleasing, pleasurable S I.53. -naya easily deducted, clearly understood A III.179=*sunnaya* A II.148; III. 179 (v. l.). -nahāta well bathed, well groomed D I.104; as *sunhāta* at S I.79. -nimmadaya easily overcome D 243 and sq. -nisita well whetted or sharpened J IV.118; as °*nissita* at J VI.248. -nisit-agga with a very sharp point VvA 227. -nīta well understood A I.59. -pakka thoroughly ripe Mhvs 15, 38. -paṇṇasālā a beautiful hut J I.7. -patittha having beautiful banks D II.129; Ud 83=sūpatittha M I.76. See also under sūpatittha. -parikammakata well prepared, well polished D I.76; A II.201; DA I.221. -pariccaja easy to give away J III.68. -parimaṇḍala well rounded, complete Mhvs 37, 225. -parihīna thoroughly bereft, quite done for It 35. -pāpa-kammin very wicked J V.143. -pāpa-dhamma very wicked Vv 52[1]. -pāpika very sinful, wicked A II.203. -pāyita well saturated, i. e. hardened (of a sword) J IV.118. Cp. suthita. -pāsiya easily threaded (of a needle)

J III.282. -picchita well polished, shiny, slippery J v.197 (cp. Sk. picchala ?). Dutoit "fest gepresst" (pīḍ ?), so also Kern, *Toev.* II.85. C. expl^s as suphassita. -pipi good to drink J VI.526. -pīta see suthita. -pubbaṇha a good morning A I.294. -posatā good nature Vin I.45. -ppaṭikāra easy requital A I.123. -ppaṭipanna well conducted A II.56; Pug 48; -tā, good conduct Nett 50. -ppaṭippatāḷita well played on D II.171; A IV.263. -ppaṭividdha thoroughly understood A II.185. -ppatiṭṭhita firmly established It 77; Sn 444. -ppatīta well pleased Mhvs 24, 64. -ppadhaŋsiya easily assaulted or overwhelmed D III.176; S II.264. Cp. °duppadhaŋsiya. -ppadhota thoroughly cleansed D II.324. -ppabhāta a good daybreak Sn 178. -ppameyya easily fathomed D I.266; Pug 35. -ppavādita (music) well played Vv 39. -ppavāyita well woven, evenly woven Vin III.259. -ppavedita well preached It 78; Th 2, 341; ThA 240. -ppasanna thoroughly full of faith Mhvs 34, 74. -ppahāra a good blow J III.83. -phassita agreeable to touch, very soft J I.220; V.197 (C. for supicchita); smooth VvA 275. -bahu very much, very many Mhvs 20, 9; 30, 18; 34, 15; 37, 48. -bāḷhika see bāḷhika. -bbata virtuous, devout D I.52; S I.236; Sn 220; Dh 95; J VI.493; DhA II.177; III.99; PvA 226; VvA 151. -bbināya easy to understand Nd 326. -bbuṭṭhi abundant rainfall Mhvs 15, 97; DhA I.52; -kā the same D I.11. -brahā very big J IV.111. -bhara easily supported, frugal; *-tā* frugality Vin I.45; II.2; M I.13. -bhikkha having plenty of food (nt.) plenty D I.11. *-°vāca* called plenty, renowned for great liberality It 66. -bhūmi good soil M I.124. -majja well polished J III.282. -majjhantika a good noon A I.294. -mati wise Mhvs 15, 214. -matikata well harrowed A I.239. -mada very joyful J v.328. -mana, glad, happy D I.3; III.269; A II.198; Sn 222, 1028; Dh 68; Vism 174. kind, friendly J IV.217 (opp. disa). -manohara very charming Mhvs 26, 17. -manta well-advised, careful Miln 318. -mānasa joyful Vin I.25; Mhvs I, 76. -māpita well built J I.7. -mutta happily released D II.162. -medha wise Vin I.5; M I.142; A II.49 and sq.; Dh 208; Sn 117, 211 etc.; It 33; Nd[1] 453. -medhasa wise D II.267; A II.70; Dh 29. -yiṭṭha well sacrificed A II.44. -yutta well suited, suitable J I.296. -ratta very red J I.119; DhA I.249. -rabhi fragrant S IV.71; Vv 84[32]; J I.119; A III.238; Vv 44[12], 53[8], 71[6]; Pv II.12[3]; Vism 195 (°vilepana); VvA 237; PvA 77; Davs IV.40; Miln 358. *-°karaṇḍaka* fragrance box, a fragrant box Th 2, 253; ThA 209. -ruci resplendent Sn 548. -ruddha very fierce J V.425, 431 (read °rudda). -rūpin handsome Mhvs 22, 20. -rosita nicely anointed J V.173. -laddha well taken; (nt.) a good gain, bliss Vin I.17; It 77. -labha easy to be obtained It 102; J I.66; VI.125; PvA 87. -vaca of nice speech, compliant M I.43, 126; Sn 143; A III.78; J I.224. Often with padakkhiṇaggāhin (q. v.). See also subbaca & abstr. der. sovacassa. -vatthi [i. e. su+asti] hail, well-being Cp. 100=J IV.31; cp. sotthi. -vammita well harnessed J I.179. -vavatthāpita well known, ascertained J I.279; Miln 10. -vānaya [i. e. su-v-ānaya] easily brought, easy to catch J I.80, 124, 238. -viggaha of a fine figure, handsome Mhvs 19, 28. -vijāna easily known Sn 92; J IV.217. -viññāpaya easy to instruct Vin I.6. -vidūravidūra very far off A II.50. -vibhatta well divided and arranged Sn 305. -vilitta well perfumed D I.104. -vimhita very dismayed J VI.270. -visada very clean or clear SnA 195. -visama very uneven, dangerous Th II.352; ThA II.242. -vihīna thoroughly bereft J I.144. -vuṭṭhikā abundance of rain J II.80; SnA 27; DA I.95; see subbuṭṭhikā. -vositaŋ happily ended J IV.314. -sankhata well prepared A II.63. -saññā (f.) having a good understanding J V.304; VI.49, 52, 503 (for °soññā ? C. sussoṇiya, i. e. having beautiful hips); Ap 307 (id.). -saññata thoroughly restrained J I.188. -saṇṭhāna having a good consistence, well made Sn 28. -sattha well trained J III.4. -sandhi having a lovely opening J V.204. -samāgata thoroughly applied to A IV.271 (aṭṭhanga°, i. e. uposatha). -samāraddha thoroughly undertaken D II.103; S II.264 sq.; Dh 293; DhA III.452. -samāhita well grounded, steadfast D II.120; Dh 10; DhA IV.114; It 113; *-atta* of steadfast mind S I.4, 29. -samucchinna thoroughly eradicated M I.102. -samuṭṭhāpaya easily raised S V.113. -samudānaya easy to accomplish J III.313. -sambuddha easy to understand Vin I.5; Sn 764; S I.136. -sāyaṇha a good, blissful evening A I.294. -sikkhita well learnt, thoroughly acquired Sn 261; easily trained, docile J I.444; II.43. -sikkhāpita well taught, trained J I.444. -sippika a skilful workman Mhvs 34, 72. -sīla moral, virtuous S I.141. -sukka very white, resplendent D II.18; III.144; Sn 548. -seyya lying on soft beds S II.268. -ssata well remembered M I.520. -ssara melodious Vv 36[4]; SnA 355. -ssavana good news J I.61. -ssoṇi having beautiful hips J IV.19; V.7, 294; cp. sussoṇiya J VI.503, & see °saññā. -hajja friend S IV.59; Dh 219; Sn 37; J I.274; A IV.96; DhA III.293. -hada friendly, good-hearted a friend D III.187 (=sundara-hadaya C.) J IV.76; VI.382; *suhadā* a woman with child J V.330. -hanna modesty J I.421. See hanna. -huṭṭhita [su+uṭṭhita] well risen Sn 178. -huta well offered, burnt as a sacrifical offering A II.44.

Su[3] (indecl.) (-°) [*ssu, fr. Vedic svid, interrog. part., of which other forms are si and sudaŋ. It also stands for Vedic sma, deictic part. of emphasis, for which also sa & assa] a particle of interrogation, often added to interrogative pronouns; thus kaŋ su S I.45; kena ssu S I.39; kissa ssu S I.39, 161 (so read for kissassa); ko su Sn 173, 181; kiŋ su Sn 1108; kathaŋ su Sn 183, 185, 1077; it is often also used as a *pleonastic particle in narration;* thus tadā su then D II.212; hatthe su sati when the hand is there S IV.171. It often takes the forms ssu and assu; thus tyassu=te assu D II.287; yassāhaŋ=ye assu ahaŋ D II.284 n. 5; api ssu Vin I.5; II.7, 76; tad-assu=tadā su then J I.196; tay'assu three Sn 231; āditt'assu kindled D II.264; nāssu not Sn 291, 295, 297, 309; sv-assu=so su J I.196. Euphonic ŋ is sometimes added yehi-ŋ-su J VI.564 n. 3; kacciŋ-su Sn 1045, 1079.

Suŋsumāra [cp. Sk. śiśumāra, lit. child-killing] a crocodile S IV.198; Th 2, 241; ThA 204; J II.158 sq.; Vism 446; SnA 207 (°kucchi); DhA III.194. —°rī (f.) a female crocodile J II.159; suŋsamārīni (f.) Miln 67; suŋsumārapatitena vandeti to fall down in salutation DA I.291.

Suka [Vedic śuka, fr. **śuc**] a parrot J I.458; II.132; instead of suka read sūka S V.10. See suva.

Sukka[1] [Videc śukra; fr. **śuc**] planet, star Ud. 9=Nett 150; (nt.) semen, sukkavisaṭṭhi emission of semen Vin II.38; III.112; IV.30; Kvu 163.

Sukka[2] (adj.) [Vedic śukla] white, bright; bright, pure, good S II.240; V.66, 104; Dh 87; Dhs 1303; It 36; J I.129; Miln 200; sukkadhamma J I.129; kaṇhāsukkaŋ evil and good Sn 526; Sukkā a class of gods D II.260.

-aŋsa bright lot, fortune Dh 72; DhA II.73. -chavi having a white skin J IV.184; VI.508; at both pass. said of the sons of widows. -pakkha [cp. BSk. śukla-pakṣa Divy 38] the bright fortnight of a month A II.19; Miln 388; J IV.26 (opp. kāḷa-pakkha); the bright half, the good opportunity Th 2, 358; ThA 244.

Sukkha (adj.) [Vedic śuṣka, fr. **śuṣ**] dry, dried up D II.347; J I.228, 326; III.435; V.106; Miln 261, 407. Cp. pari°, vi°.

-kaddama dried mud Mhvs 17, 35. -kantāra desert J V.70. -vipassaka "dry-visioned" *Cpd.* 55, 75; with diff. explⁿ Geiger, *Saŋyutta tsrl*ⁿ II.172 n. 1.

Sukkhati [fr. śuṣka dry; śuṣ] to be dried up Miln 152; J v.472; ppr. sukkhanto getting dry J I.498; ppr. med. sukkhamāna wasting away J I.104; Caus. II. sukkhāpeti S I.8; Vin IV.86; J I.201, 380; II.56; DA I.262; see also pubbāpeti. — pp. sukkhita.

Sukkhana (nt.) [fr. sukkha] drying up J III.390 (assu-°).

Sukkhāpana (nt.) [fr. sukkhāpeti] drying, making dry J VI.420.

Sukkhita [pp. of sukkhati] dried up, emaciated Miln 303. Cp. pari°.

Sukha (adj.-n.) [Vedic sukha; in R. V. only of ratha; later generally] agreeable, pleasant, blest Vin I.3; Dh 118, 194, 331; Sn 383; paṭipadā, pleasant path, easy progress A II.149 sq.; Dhs 178; kaṇṇa-s. pleasant to the ear D I.4; happy, pleased D II.233. — nt. sukhaŋ well-being, happiness, ease; ideal, success Vin I.294; D I.73 sq.; M I.37; S I.5; A III.355 (deva-manussānaŋ); It 47; Dh 2; Sn 67; Dhs 10; DhsA 117; PvA 207 (lokiya° worldly happiness). — kāyika sukkha bodily welfare Tikp 283; cp. *Cpd.* 112[1]; sāmisaŋ s. material happiness A I.81; III.412; VbhA 268. On relation to pīti (joy) see Vism 145 (sankhāra-kkhandha-sangahitā pīti, vedanā-kkhandha-sangahitaŋ sukhaŋ) and *Cpd.* 56, 243. — Defined further at Vism 145 & 461 (iṭṭha-phoṭṭhabb-ânubhavana-lakkhaṇaŋ; i. e. of the kind of experiencing pleasant contacts). — *Two* kinds, viz. kāyika & cetasika at Ps I.188; several other pairs at A I.80; *three* (praise, wealth, heaven) It 67; another *three* (manussa°, dibba°, nibbāna°) DhA III.51; *four* (possessing, making good use of possessions, having no debts, living a blameless life) A II.69. — gātha-bandhana-sukh'atthaŋ for the beauty of the verse J II.224. — Opp. asukha D III.222, 246; Sn 738; or dukkha, with which often comb[d] (e. g. Sn 67, 873, with spelling dukha at both pass.). — *Cases:* instr. sukhena with comfort, happily, through happiness Th 1, 220; DhsA 406; acc. sukhaŋ comfortably, in happiness; yathā s. according to liking PvA 133; sukhaŋ seti to rest in ease, to lie well S I.41; A I.136; Dh 19, 201; J I.141. Cp. sukha-sayita. — s. edhati to thrive, proper S I.217; Dh 193; Sn 298; cp. sukham-edha Vin III.137 (with Kern's remarks *Toev.* II.83). s. viharati to live happily, A I.96; III.3; Dh 379. — Der. sokhya.

-atthin fem. -nī longing for happiness Mhvs 6, 4. -āvaha bringing happiness, conducive to ease S I.2 sq., 55; Dh 35; J II.42. -indriya the faculty of ease S V.209 sq.; Dhs 452; It 15, 52. -udraya (sometimes spelt °undriya) having a happy result A I.97; Ps I.80; Pv IV.1[78] (=sukha-vipāka PvA 243); Vv 31[8]. -ūpaharaṇa happy offering, luxury J I.231. -edhita read as sukhe ṭhita (i. e. being happy) at Vin III.13 & S V.351 (v. l. sukhe ṭhita); also at DhA I.165; cp. J VI.219. -esin looking for pleasure Dh 341. -kāma longing for happiness M I.341; S IV.172, 188. -da giving pleasure Sn 297. -dhamma a good state M I.447. -nisinna comfortably seated J IV.125. -paṭisaŋvedin experiencing happiness Pug 61. -ppatta come to well-being, happy J III.112. -pharaṇatā diffusion of well-being, ease Nett 89 (among the constituents of samādhi). -bhāgiya participating in happiness Nett 120 sq., 125 sq., 239 (the four s. dhammā are indriyasaŋvara, tapasaŋkhāta puññadhamma, bojjhangabhāvanā and sabbūpadhipaṭinissaggasankhāta nibbāna). -bhūmi a soil of ease, source of ease Dhs 984; DhsA 346. -yānaka an easy-going cart DhA 325. -vinicchaya discernment of happiness M III.230 sq. -vipāka resulting in happiness, ease D I.51; A I.98; DA I.158. -vihāra dwelling at ease S V.326. -vihārin dwelling at ease, well at ease D I.75; Dhs 163; J I.140. -saŋvāsa pleasant to associate with Dh 207. -saññin conceiving happiness, considering as happiness A II.52. -samuddaya origin of bliss It 16, 52. -samphassa pleasant to touch Dhs 648. -sammata deemed a pleasure Sn 760. -sayita well embedded (in soil), of seeds A III.404=D II.354.

Sukhallikânuyoga [same in BSk.] luxurious living Vin I.10[12] (kāma-°). See under kāma°.

Sukhāyati [Denom. fr. sukha] to be pleased J II.31 (asukhāyamāna being displeased with).

Sukhita [pp. of sukheti] happy, blest, glad S I.52; III.11 (sukhitesu sukhito dukkhitesu dukkhito); IV.180; Sn 1029; Pv II.8[11]; healthy Mhvs 37, 128; °-atta [ātman] happy, easy Sn 972.

Sukhin (adj.) [fr. sukha] happy, at ease D I.31, 73, 108; A II.185; S I.20, 170; III.83; Dh 177; Sn 145; being well, unhurt J III.541; fem. -nī D II.13; M II.126.

Sukhuma (adj.) [Epic Sk. sūkṣma] subtle, minute Vin I.14; D I.182; S IV.202; A II.171; Dhs 676; Th 2, 266; Dh 125=Sn 662; Vism 274, 488 (°rūpā). fine, exquisite D II.17, 188; Miln 313; susukhuma, very subtle Th 1, 71=210 (°-nipuṇattha-dassin); cp. sokhumma; khoma-°, kappāsa-°, kambala-° (n. ?) the finest sorts of linen, cotton stuff, woolwork (resp.) Miln 105. — Der. sokhumma.

-acchika fine-meshed D I.45; DA I.127; Ap 21 (jāla). -diṭṭhi subtle view It 75. -dhāra with fine edge Miln 105.

Sukhumaka=sukhuma Ps I.185.

Sukhumatta (nt.) [abstr. fr. sukhuma] fineness, delicacy D II.17 sq.

Sukhumāla (adj.) [cp. Sk. su-kumāra] tender, delicate, refined, delicately nurtured A I.145; II.86 sq.; III.130; Vin I.15, 179; II.180; beautifully young, graceful J I.397; Sn 298; samaṇa-° a soft, graceful Samaṇa A II.87; fem. sukhumālinī Th 2, 217; Miln 68, & sukhumālī J VI.514.

Sukhumālatā (f.) [abstr. fr. sukhumāla] delicate constitution J V.295; DhA III.283 (ati°).

Sukheti [Caus. fr. sukha] to make happy D I.51; S IV.331; DA I.157; also sukhayati DhsA 117; Caus. II. sukhāpeti D II.202; Miln 79. — pp. sukhita.

Sugata [su+gata] faring well, happy, having a happy life after death (gati): see under gata; cp. Vism 424 (s.= sugati-gata). Freq. Ep. of the Buddha (see Dict. of Names).

-angula a Buddha-inch, an inch according to the standard accepted by Buddhists Vin IV.168. -ālaya imitation of the Buddha J I.490, 491; II.38, 148, 162; III.112. -ovāda a discourse of the Blessed one J I.119, 349; II.9, 13, 46; III.368. -vidatthi a Buddha-span, a span of the accepted length Vin III.149; IV.173. -vinaya the discipline of the Buddha A II.147.

Sugati (f.) [su+gati] happiness, bliss, a happy fate (see detail under gati) Vin II.162, 195; D I.143; II.141; Pug 60; It 24, 77, 112; A III.5, 205; V.268; Vism 427 (where def[d] as "sundarā gati" & distinguished fr. sagga as including "manussagati," whereas sagga is "devagati"); VbhA 158; DhA I.153. — suggati (in verses), Dh 18; D II.202 (printed as prose); J IV.436 (=sagga C.); VI.224. Kern, *Toev.* II.83 expl[d] suggati as svargati, analogous to svar-ga (=sagga); doubtful. Cp. duggati.

Sugatin (adj.) [fr. sugati] righteous Dh 126; J I.219= Vin II.162 (suggati).

Sunka (m. and nt.) [cp Vedic śulka, nt.] 1. toll, tax, customs Vin III.52; IV.131; A I.54 sq.; DhA II.2; J IV.132; VI.347; PvA III. — 2. gain, profit Th 2, 25; ThA 32. — 3. purchase-price of a wife Th 2, 420;

J VI.266; Miln 47 sq. — odhisunka stake J VI.279; °-gahana J V.254; a-suŋkâraha J V.254.

-ghāta customs' frontier Vin III.47, 52. -ṭṭhāna taxing place, customs' house Vin III.62; Miln 359. -sāyika (?) customs' officer Miln 365 (read perhaps °sādhaka or °sālika ?).

Sunkika [sunka+ika] a receiver of customs J V.254.

Sunkiya (nt.) [abstr. fr. sunka] price paid for a wife J VI.266.

Suci (adj.) [Vedic śuci] pure, clean, white D I.4; A I.293; Sn 226, 410. — opp. asuci impure A III.226; V.109, 266. — (nt.) purity, pure things J I.22; goodness, merit Dp 245; a tree used for making foot-boards VvA 8.

-kamma whose actions are pure Dh 24. -gandha having a sweet perfume Dh 58; DhA I.445. -gavesin longing for purity S I.205; DhA III.354. -ghaṭika read sūcighaṭikā at Vin II.237. -ghara Vin II.301 sq.; see sūcighara. -jātika of clean descent J II.11. -bhojana pure food Sn 128. -mhita having a pleasant, serene smile Vv 18^{10}; 50^{25}; 64^{12}; VvA 96, 280 (also explained as a name); J IV.107. -vasana wearing clean, bright clothes Sn 679.

Sucimant (adj.) [suci+mant] pure, an epithet of the Buddha A IV.340.

Sujā (f.) [Vedic sruc, f.] a sacrificial ladle D I.120, 138; S I.169; DA I.289, 299.

Sujjhati [**śudh** which the Dhtp (417) defines as "soceyye," i. e. from cleansing] to become clean or pure M I.39; S I.34, 166; Nd[1] 85; Vism 3; cp. pari°. — pp. suddha. — Caus. sodheti (q. v.).

Sujjhana (nt.) [fr. sujjhati] purification Vism 44.

Suñña (adj.) [cp. Sk. śūnya, fr. Vedic śūna, nt., void] 1. empty, uninhabited D I.17; II.202; S I.180; IV.173; DA I.110; Miln 5. — 2. empty, devoid of reality, unsubstantial, phenomenal M I.435; S III.167; IV.54, 296; Sn 1119; Nd[1] 439 (loka). — 3. empty, void, useless M I.483; S IV.54, 297; Dāvs V.17; Miln 96; Vism 594 sq. (of nāmarūpa, in simile with suñña dāruyanta). suññasuñña empty of permanent substance Ps II.178; asuñña not empty Miln 130. — nt. suññaŋ emptiness, annihilation, Nibbāna Vism 513 (three nirodha-suññāni); abl. °to from the point of view of the "Empty" Nd[2] 680 (long exegesis of suññato at Sn 119); Vism 512; VbhA 89, 261; KhA 74.

-āgāra an empty place, an uninhabited spot, solitude Vin I.97, 228; II.158, 183; III.70, 91 sq.; D I.175; II.86; 291, M I.33; S IV.133, 359 sq.; A III.353; IV.139, 392, 437; V.109, 207, 323 sq.; It 39; J III.191; Miln 344; Vism 270; Nd[2] 94. -gāma an empty (deserted) village (in similes) Vism 484; VbhA 48; Dhs 597; DhsA 309; °*ṭṭhāna* Vism 353; VbhA 57.

Suññata (adj.) [i. e. the abl. suññato used as adj. nom.] void, empty, devoid of lusts, evil dispositions, and karma, but especially of soul, ego Th 2, 46; ThA 50; Dhs 344; Mhvs 37, 7; **nibbāna** DhsA 221; **phassa** S IV.295; **vimokkha** Dh 92; DhA II.172; Miln 413; **vimokkha samādhi**, and **samāpatti** Vin III.92 sq.; IV.25 sq.; **samādhi** (contemplation of emptiness, see *Cpd.* 216) D III.219 (one of *three* samādhis); S IV.360, 363; Miln 337; **anupassanā** Ps II.43 sq.

Suññatā (f.) [abstr. fr. suñña] emptiness, "void," unsubstantiality, phenomenality; freedom from lust, ill-will, and dullness, Nibbāna M III.111; Kvu 232; DhsA 221; Nett 118 sq., 123 sq., 126; Miln 16; Vism 333 (n'atthi; suñña; vivitta; i. e. abhāva, suññatā, vivitt'-ākāra), 578 (12 fold, relating to the Paṭiccasamuppāda), 653 sq.; VbhA 262 (atta°, attaniya°, niccabhāva°).

-pakāsana the gospel of emptiness DA I.99, 123; -paṭisaŋyutta relating to the Void, connected with Nibbāna A I.72 = III.107 = S II.267; DA I.100 sq.; Miln 16; -vihāra dwelling in the concept of emptiness Vin II.304; M III.104, 294. See on term e. g. *Cpd.* 69; *Kvu trsl*[n] 142, n. 4.

Suññatta (nt.) [abstr. fr. suñña] emptiness, the state of being devoid DhsA 221.

Suṭṭhu (indecl.) [cp. Sk. suṣṭhu, fr. su°] well; the usual C. expl[n] of the prefix su[2] PvA 19, 51, 52, 58, 77, 103 etc.; s. tāta well, father J I.170; s. kataŋ you have done well J I.287; DA I.297; suṭṭhutaraŋ still more J I.220; SnA 418.

Suṭṭhutā (f.) [abstr. fr. suṭṭhu] excellence A I.98 sq.; Nett 50.

Suṇa "dog," preferable spelling for suna, cp. Geiger, *P.Gr.* § 93[1].

Suṇāti (suṇoti) [**śru**, Vedic śṛṇoti; cp. Gr. κλέω to praise; Lat. clueo to be called; Oir. clunim to hear; Goth. hliuþ attention, hliuma hearing, and many others] to hear. Pres. suṇāti D I.62, 152; S V.265; Sn 696; It 98; Miln 5. — suṇoti J IV.443; Pot. suṇeyya Vin I.7; D I.79; suṇe J IV.240; Imper. suṇa S III.121; suṇāhi Sn p. 21; suṇobi D I.62; Sn 997; 3rd sg. suṇātu Vin I.56; 1st pl. suṇāma Sn 354; suṇoma Sn 350, 988, 1110; Pv IV.1[31]. — 2nd pl. suṇātha D I.131; II.76; It 41; Sn 385; PvA 13. suṇotha Sn 997; Miln 1. — 3rd pl. suṇantu Vin I.5; — ppr. sunanto Sn 1023; DA I.261; savaŋ J III.277. — inf. sotuŋ D II.2; Sn 384; suṇitum Miln 91. — Fut. sossati D II.131, 265; J II.107; J II.63; Ap 156; VvA 187; 1st sg. sussaŋ Sn 694. — 2nd sg. sossi J VI.423. — aor. 1st sg. assuŋ J III.572. — 2nd sg. assu J III.541. — 3rd sg. suṇi J IV.336; assosi D I.87, 152; Sn p. 103; 1st pl. assumha J II.79. — 2nd pl. assuttha S I.157; II.230. 3rd pl. assosuŋ Vin I.18; D I.111. — ger. sutvā Vin I.12; D I.4; Sn 30. sutvāna Vin I.19; D II.30; Sn 202. suṇitvā J V.96; Mhvs 23, 80. suṇiya Mhvs 23, 101. — Pass. sūyati M I.30; J I.72, 86; Miln 152. suyyati J IV.141; J IV.160; V.459. 3rd pl. sūyare J VI.528. — Grd. savanīya what should be heard, agreeable to the ear D II.211. sotabba D I.175; II.346. — pp. suta: see separately. — Caus. sāveti to cause to hear, to tell, declare, announce J I.344; Mhvs 5, 238; PvA 200; VvA 66. nāmaŋ s. to shout out one's name Vin I.36; DA I.262; maŋ dāsī ti sāvaya announce me to be your slave J III.437; cp. J IV.402 (but see on this passage and on J III.198; VI.486 Kern's proposed reading sāṭeti); to cause to be heard, to play D II.265. Caus. also suṇāpeti DhA I.206. — Desiderative sussūsati (often written sussūyati) D I.230; M III.133 (text sussūsanti), A IV.393 (do.). — ppr. sussusaŋ Sn 189 (var. read., text sussussā); sussūsamāna Sn 383; aor. sussūsiŋsu Vin I.10; fut. sussūsissanti Vin I.150; S II.267 (text sussu-).

Suṇisā (f.) [Vedic snuṣā; cp. Gr. νυός; Obg. snur; Ags. snoru; Lat. nurus] a daughter-in-law Vin I.240; III.136; D II.148; M I.186, 253; J VI.498; Vv 13^{5} (=puttassa bhariyā VvA 61); DhA I.355; IV.8; Pv II.46 (pl. suṇisāyo, so read for sūtisāye). — suṇhā the same Vin II.10; A IV.91; Th 2, 406; J II.347; VI.506; Pv IV.3.[43]

Suta[1] [pp. of suṇāti; cp. Vedic śruta] 1. heard; in special sense "received through inspiration or revelation"; learned; taught A 97 sq.; D III.164 sq., 241 sq.; freq. in phrase "iti me sutaŋ" thus have I heard, I have received this on (religious) authority, e. g. It 22 sq. — (nt.) sacred lore, inspired tradition, revelation; learning, religious knowledge M III.99; A I.210 sq.; II.6 sq.; S IV.250; J II.42; V.450, 485; Miln 248. — appa-ssuta one who has little learning A II.6 sq., 218; III.181; V.40, 152; **bahu-ssuta** one who has much learning, famous for inspired knowledge A II.6 sq.; III.113 sq., 182 sq., 261 sq.; S II.159. See bahu. asuta not heard Vin I.238; Pv IV.1[61]; J III.233; also as assuta J I.390 (°pubba never heard before); III.233.— na suta pubbaŋ a thing never heard of before J III.285. dussuta M I.228; sussuta M III.104. — 2. renowned J II.442.

-ādhāra holding (i. e. keeping in mind, preserving) the sacred learning J III.193; VI.287. -kavi a Vedic poet, a poet of sacred songs A II.230. -dhana the treasure of revelation D III.163, 251; A III.53; IV.4 sq.; VvA 113. -dhara remembering what has been heard (or taught in the Scriptures) A II.23 (+°sannicaya); III.152, 261 sq. -maya consisting in learning (or resting on sacred tradition), one of the 3 kinds of knowledge (paññā), viz. cintā-mayā, s.-m., bhāvanā-mayā paññā D III.219; Vbh 324 (expl[d] at Vism 439); as °mayī at Ps I.4, 22 sq.; Nett 8, 50, 60. -ssava far-renowned (Ep. of the Buddha) Sn 353.

Suta² [Sk. suta, pp. of sū (or su) to generate] son Mhvs I, 47; fem. sutā daughter, Th 2, 384.

Sutatta (nt.) [abstr. fr. suta¹] the fact of having heard or learnt SnA 166.

Sutappaya (adj.) [su+grd. of tappati²] easily contented A I.87; Pug 26 (opp. dut°).

Sutavant (adj.) [suta¹+vant] one who is learned in religious knowledge Vin I.14; A II.178; III.55; IV.68, 157; S III.57; Tikp 279; Sn 70 (=āgama-sampanna SnA 124), 90, 371; sutavanta-nimmita founded by learned, pious men Miln 1; assutavant, unlearned M I.1 (°vā puthujjano laymen); Dhs 1003; A III.54; IV.157.

Suti (f.) [cp. śruti revelation as opp. to smṛti tradition] 1. hearing, tradition, inspiration, knowledge of the Vedas Sn 839, 1078; Miln 3 (+sammuti); Mhvs 1, 3. — 2. rumour; sutivasena by hearsay, as a story, through tradition J III.285, 476; VI.100. — 3. a sound, tone VvA 139 (dvāvīsati suti-bhedā 22 kinds of sound).

Sutitikkha (adj.) [fr. su+titikkhā] easy to endure J 524.

Sutta¹ [pp. of supati] asleep Vin III.117; V.205; D I.70; II.130; Dh 47; It 41; J V.328. — (nt.) sleep D II.95; M I.448; S IV.169. In phrase °-pabuddha "awakened from sleep" referring to the awakening (entrance) in the deva-world, e. g. Vism 314 (brahmalokaŋ uppajjati); DhA I.28 (kanaka-vimāne nibbatti); III.7 (id.); cp. S I.143.

Sutta² (nt.) [Vedic sūtra, fr. sīv to sew] 1. a thread, string D I.76; II.13; Vin II.150; Pv II.11¹ (=kappāsiyā sutta PvA 146); J I.52. — fig. for taṇhā at Dhs 1059; DhsA 364. — kāḷa° a carpenter's measuring line J II.405; Miln 413; dīgha° with long thread J V.389; makkaṭa° spider's thread Vism 136; yantā° string of a machine VbhA 241. — Mentioned with *kappāsa* as barter for cīvara at Vin III.216. — 2. the (discursive, narrational) part of the Buddhist Scriptures containing the *suttas* or dialogues, later called Sutta-piṭaka (cp. Suttanta). As such complementary to the Vinaya. The fanciful expl[n] of the word at DhsA 19 is: "atthānaŋ sūcanto suvuttato savanato 'tha sūdanato suttāṇā-sutta-sabhāgato ca suttaŋ Suttan ti akkhātaŋ." — D II.124; Vin II.97; VbhA 130 (+vinaya); SnA 159, 310 (compared with Vinaya & Abhidhamma). — 3. one of the divisions of the Scriptures (see navanga) A II.103, 178; III.177, 361 sq.; Miln 263. — 4. a rule, a clause (of the Pātimokkha) Vin I.65, 68; II.68, 95; III.327. — 5. a chapter, division, dialogue (of a Buddh. text), text, discourse (see also suttanta) S III.221 (pl. suttā), 253; V.46; Nett 118; DhsA 28. suttaso chapter by chapter A V.72, 81; suttato according to the suttas Vism 562=VbhA 173. — 6. an ancient verse, quotation J I.288, 307, 314. — 7. book of rules, lore, text book J I.194 (go° lore of cows); II.46 (hatthi' elephant trainer's handbook).

-anta 1. a chapter of the Scriptures, a text, a discourse, a sutta, dialogue Vin I.140 sq., 169; II.75; III.159; IV.344; A I.60, 69, 72; II.147; S II.267=A III.107 (suttantā kavi-katā kāveyyā citt'akkharā citta-vyañjanā bāhirakā sāvaka-bhāsitā); Vism 246 sq. (three suttantas helpful for kāyagatā sati). — 2. the Suttanta-piṭaka, opp. to the Vinaya Vism 272 (°aṭṭhakathā opp. to Vinay'aṭṭhakathā). As °piṭaka e. g. at KbA 12; VbhA 431. See Proper Names. -kantikā (scil. itthi) a woman spinner PvA 75; as °kantī at J II.79. -kāra a cotton-spinner Miln 331. -guḷa a ball of string D I.54; M III.95; Pv IV.3[29]; PvA 145. -jāla a web of thread, a spider's web Nd² 260. -bhikkhā begging for thread PvA 145. -maya made of threads, i. e. a net SnA 115, 263. -rajjuka a string of threads Vism 253; VbhA 236. -lūkha roughly sewn together Vin I.287, 297. -vāda a division of the Sabbatthavādins Dpvs 5, 48; Mhvs 5, 6; Mhbv 97. -vibhanga classification of rules Vin II.97. Also title of a portion of the Vinaya Piṭaka.

Suttaka (nt.) [fr. sutta] a string Vin II.271; PvA 145; a string of jewels or beads Vin II.106; III.48; DhsA 321; a term for lust DhsA 364.

Suttantika versed in the Suttantas. A suttantika bhikkhu is one who knows the Suttas (contrasted with vinaya-dhara, who knows the rules of the Vinaya) Vin II.75. Cp. dhamma C 1 & piṭaka. — Vin I.169; II.75, 161; III.159; J I.218; Miln 341; Vism 41, 72, 93; KhA 151. -duka the Suttanta pairs, the pairs of terms occurring in the Suttantas Dhs 1296 sq.; -vatthūni the physical bases of spiritual exercise in the Suttantas Ps I.186.

Sutti¹ (f.) [cp. Sk. śukti, given as pearl-shell (Suśruta), and as a perfume] in kuruvindakasutti a *powder for rubbing* the body Vin II.107; see sotti.

Sutti² (f.) [Sk. sūkti] a good saying Sdhp 340, 617.

Suthita (?) beaten out, Miln 415 (with vv. ll. suthiketa, suphita & supita). Should we read su-poṭhita? Kern, *Toev.* II.85 proposes su-pīta "well saturated" (with which cp. supāyita J IV.118, said of a sword).

Sudaŋ (indecl.) [=Vedic svid, influenced by sma: see su³] a deictic (seemingly pleonastic) particle in comb[n] with demonstr. pronouns and adverbs; untranslatable, unless by "even, just," e. g. tapassī sudaŋ homi, lūkha ssudaŋ [sic] homi etc. M I.77=J I.390; cp. itthaŋ sudaŋ thus Sn p. 59; tatra sudaŋ there Vin I.4, 34; IV.108; D I.87; II.91; It 15; api ssudaŋ D II.264; S I.119; api sudaŋ S I.113; sā ssudam S II.255.

Sudda [cp. Vedic śūdra] (see detail under vaṇṇa 6) a Sūdra Vin II.239; D I.104; III.81, 95 sq. (origin); M I.384; A I.162; II.194; S I.102; Pug 60; Sn 314; fem. suddī D I.241; A III.226, 229; Vin III.133.

Suddha [pp. of sujjhati] 1. clean, pure, Vin I.16; II.152; D I.110; Sn 476. — 2. purified, pure of heart M I.39; Dh 125, 412; Sn 90 — 3. simple, mere, unmixed, nothing but S I.135; DhsA 72; J II.252 (°daṇḍaka just the stick).

-antaparivāsa a probation of complete purification Vin II.59 sq. -ājīva clean livelihood VbhA 116; DhA IV.111. -ājīvin living a pure life Dp 366. -ânupassin considering what is pure Sn 788; Nd¹ 85. -āvāsa pure abode, name of a heaven and of the devas inhabiting it D II.50; Vism 392. *Five* are enum[d] at D III.237, viz. Avihā, Atappā, Sudassā, Sudassī, Akaniṭṭhā; cp. M III.103. -āvāsakāyika belonging to the pure abode, epithet of the Suddhāvāsa devas Vin II.302; D II.253; S I.26. -pīti whose joy is pure Mhvs 29, 49. -buddhi of pure intellect J I.1. -vaŋsatā purity of lineage Mhvs 59, 25. -vasana wearing pure clothes Th 2, 338; ThA 239. -vālukā white sand Mhvs 19, 37. -sankhārapuñja a mere heap of sankhāras S I.135.

Suddhaka (nt.) [suddha+ka] a trifle, a minor offence, less than a Sanghādisesa Vin II.67.

Suddhatā (f.) [abstr. fr. suddha] purity Sn 435.

Suddhatta (nt.) [abstr. fr. suddha] purity D II.14; Vism 44.

Suddhi (f.) [fr. **śudh**] purity, purification, genuineness, sterling quality D I.54; M I.80; II.132, 147; S I.166, 169, 182; IV.372; Th 2, 293; DhA III.158 (v. l. visuddhi); VvA 60 (payoga°); Vism 43 (fourfold: desanā°, saŋvara°, pariyeṭṭhi°, paccavekkhaṇa°); Dhs 1005; Sn 478; suddhiŋvada stating purity, Sn 910; Nd[1] 326; suddhināya leading to purity Sn 910. Cp. pari°, vi°.
-magga the path of purification (cp. visuddhi°) S I.103.

Suddhika (adj.) [suddhi+ka] 1. connected with purification Dhs 519-522; udaka-s. pure by use of water S I.182; Vin I.196; udakasuddhikā (f.) cleaning by water Vin IV.362; susāna-s. fastidious in the matter of cemeteries J II.54.—2. pure, simple; orthodox, schematized; justified Nd[1] 89 (vatta°); Vism 63 (ekato & ubhato), 64 (id.); DhsA 185 (jhāna).

Sudhā (f.) [cp. Sk. sudhā] 1. the food of the gods, ambrosia J V.396; Vism 258=KhA 56 (sakkhara°).—2. lime, plaster, whitewash, cement Vin II.154; °-kamma whitewashing, coating of cement J VI.432; Mhvs 38, 74.

Suna[1] [Sk. śūna, pp. of **śū** to swell] swollen Vin II.253; A IV.275, 470.

Suna[2] [Sk. śuna; see suvāṇa] a dog, also written suṇa J VI.353, 357 (cp. sunakha).

Sunakha [cp. Sk. śunaka; the BSk. form is also sunakha, e. g. MVastu III.361, 369] a dog A I.48; II.122; Th 2, 509; J I.175, 189; II.128, 246; PvA 151, 206.—**rukkha°** some sort of animal J VI.538. fem. sunakhī a bitch J IV.400.—Names of some dogs in the Jātakas are Kaṇha (or Mahā°) J IV.183; Caturakkha III.535; Jambuka, Pingiya ibid.; Bhattabhuñjana II.246. Cp. suvāṇa.

Sunaggavellita [su+agga+vellita, perhaps originally su-v-agga°] beautifully curled at the ends (of hair) J VI.86.

Sundara (adj.) [cp. Epic & Class. Sk sundara] beautiful, good, nice, well J II.11, 98; SnA 410, 493 (cp. parovara). It is very frequent as Commentary word, e. g. for prefix su° PvA 57, 77; VvA 111; for subha PvA 14, 44; for sādhu SnA 176; for sobhana PvA 49; for seyyo PvA 130.

Supaṇṇa [Vedic suparṇa] "Fairwing" a kind of fairy bird, a mythical creature (cp. garuḷa), imagined as winged, considered as foe to the nāgas D II.259; S I.148; J I.202; II.13, 107; III.91, 187, 188; VI.256, 257; Vism 155 (°rājā), 400; Nd[1] 92, 448; DhA I.280; PvA 272; DA I.51; Mhvs 14, 40; 19, 20. Four kinds S III.246.

Supati (suppati, soppati) [**svap**; Vedic svapiti & svapati; svapna sleep or dream (see supina), with which cp. Gr. ὕπνος sleep=Av. xvafna, Lat. somnus, Ags. swefn.—Dhtp 481 "saye"] to sleep; supati Sn 110; J II.61 (sukhaŋ supati he sleeps well); V.215; Pv II.9[38]; suppati S I.107; soppati S I.107, 110; Pot. supe S I.111; ppr. supanto Vin I.15; ppr. med. suppamāna J III.404; aor. supi Miln 89[4]; Vin II.78; PvA 195 (sukhaŋ); inf. sottuŋ S I.111; pp. supita; also sutta[1] & sotta.

Supāṇa [=suvāṇa] a dog D II.295=M I.58, 88; Sn 201; Miln 147. Spelt supāna at J IV.400.

Supāyika J IV.118 (read: supāyita). See under su°.

Supita [pp. of supati] sleeping; (nt.) sleep S I.198 (ko attho supitena)=Sn 331; SnA 338; Pv II.6[1] (so read for supina?).

Supina (m. & nt.) [Vedic svapna; the contracted P. form is soppa] a dream, vision D I.9, 54; S I.198; IV.117 (supine in a dream; v. l. supinena); Sn 360, 807, 927; Nd[1] 126; J I.334 sq., 374; V.42; DA I.92, 164; Vv 44[14]; VbhA 407 (by 4 reasons), 408 (who has dreams); DhA I.215. The *five* dreams of the Buddha A III.240; J I.69. dussupina an unpleasant dream J I.335; PvA 105 (of Ajātasattu); mangala° a lucky dream J VI.330; **mahā°ŋ** passati to have (lit. see) a great vision J I.336 sq. (the 16 great visions); °ŋ ādisati to tell a dream Nd[1] 381.—Supina at Pv II.6[1] read supita.
-anta [anta pleonastic, cp. ThA 258 "supinam eva supinantaŋ"] a dream; abl. °ante in a dream Th 2, 394; J V.328 (spelt suppante; C. sopp°; expl[d] as "supinena"); instr. °antena id. Vin II.125; III.112; J V.40; VI.131; ThA 258; KhA 175; SnA 80. -pāṭhaka a dream-teller, astrologer Nd[1] 381. -sattha science of dream-telling, oneiromantics SnA 564.

Supinaka [supina+ka] a dream Vin II.25; D II.333; M I.365; J V.354; DA I.92.

Supita read Miln 415 for suthita (Kern's suggestion). See under su°.

Supoṭhita [su+poṭhita] well beaten; perhaps at Miln 415 for suthita (said of iron); (nt.) a good thrashing DhA I.48.

Suppa [cp. Vedic śūrpa] a winnowing basket Ud 68; J I.502; II.428; Vism 109 (+sarāva), 123; Miln 282; DhA I.174 (kattara°); II.131; Mhvs 30, 9. **°-ka** a toy basket, little sieve DhsA 321 (+musalaka).

Suppatā (f.) [fr. sūpa] in mugga-s. pea-soup talk, sugared words Miln 370. See under **mugga**.

Suppanta see under soppa.

Suplavattha at J V.408 is doubtful in spelling & meaning. Perhaps to be read "suplavantaŋ" gliding along beautifully; C. expl[d] as "sukhena plavan'atthaŋ."

Subbaca (adj.) [su+vaca] compliant, meek A III.180. See also **suvaca** (under su°). Der. sovacassa.

Subbhū (adj.) [su+bhū, Sk. bhrū, see bhūkuṭi] having beautiful eyebrows J IV.18 (=subhamukhā C.).

Subha (adj.) [Vedic śubhas fr. **subh**; cp. sobhati] shining, bright, beautiful D I.76=II.13=M III.102; Dhs 250; DA I.221; auspicious, lucky, pleasant Sn 341; It 80; good Sn 824, 910; subhato maññati to consider as a good thing Sn 199; J I.146; cp. S IV.111; (nt.) welfare, good, pleasantness, cleanliness, beauty, pleasure; -vasena for pleasure's sake J I.303, 304; asubha anything repulsive, disgusting or unpleasant S I.188; V.320; subhāsubha pleasant and unpleasant Miln 136; J III.243 (niraya=subhānaŋ asubhaŋ unpleasant for the good, C.); cp. below subhāsubha.
-angana with beautiful courts J VI.272. **-âsubha** good and bad, pleasant & unpleasant Dh 409=Sn 633. **-kiṇṇa** the lustrous devas, a class of devas D II 69; M I 2, 329, 390; III.102; A I.122; J III.358; Kvu 207; also written °kiṇha A II.231, 233; IV.40, 401; Vism 414, 420 sq.; VbhA 520; KhA 86. -gati going to bliss, to heaven Mhvs 25, 115. -ṭṭhāyin existing or remaining, continuing, in glory D I.17; DA I.110; A V.60. -dhātu the element of splendour S II.150. -nimitta auspicious sign, auspiciousness as an object of one's thought M I 26; A I.3, 87, 200; S V.64, 103; Vism 20. -saññā perception or notion of what is pleasant or beautiful Nett 27. Opp. asubhasaññā concept of repulsiveness A I.42; II.17; III.79; IV.46; V.106. See **asubha**. **-saññin** considering as beautiful A II.52.

Subhaga (adj.) [su+bhaga] lucky; °karaṇa making happy or beloved (by charms) D I.11; DA I.96.—Der. sobhagga

Sumanā the great-flowered jasmine J I.62; IV.455; DhA IV.12. In composition sumana°.
-dāma a wreath of jasmine J IV.455. -paṭṭa cloth with jasmine pattern J I.62. -puppha j. flower Miln 291; VvA 147. -makula a j. bud DhA III.371. -mālā garland of j. VvA 142.

Sumarati see sarati[2].

Sumbhati (& sumhati) [sumbh (?), cp. Geiger, *P.Gr.* 60, 128. The Dhtm (306 & 548) only says "saṇsumbhane." The BSk. form is subhati MVastu I.14] to push, throw over, strike J III.185 (sumh°); VI.549. — pp. sumbhita. — Cp. ā°, pari°.

Sumbhita [pp. of sumbhati] knocked over, fallen (over) PvA 174.

Suyyati is Passive of suṇāti.

Sura [cp. Epic Sk. sura probably after asura] god Sn 681 (=deva SnA 484); name of a Bodhisatta J V.12, 13; surakaññā a goddess, a heavenly maid J V.407 (=devadhītā, C.); surinda the king of gods Mhbv 28. Opp. asura.

Surata (adj.) [su+rata] (in good sense:) well-loving, devoted: see soracca; (in bad sense:) sexual intercourse, thus wrongly for soracca at J III.442 C., with expl[n] as "dussīlya." Cp. sūrata.

Surā (f.) [Vedic surā] spirituous (intoxicating) liquor ("drink") Vin II.295, 301; IV.110; D I.146; A I.212, 295; It 63; J I.199, 252 (tikhiṇaṇ suraṇ yojetvā mixing a sharp drink); DhA II.9; Dh 247; as *nt.* at J VI.23 (v. l. surā as gloss). — *Five* kinds of surā are mentioned, viz. piṭṭha°, pūva°, odana° (odaniya°), kiṇṇapakkhitta°, sambhāra-saṇyutta° VvA 73; VbhA 381.
-**ādhiṭṭhaka** addicted to drink J V.427. -geha a drinking house J I.302. -ghaṭa a pitcher of liquor J III.477. -ghara=°geha J V.367. -chaṇa a drinking festival J I.489; DhA III.100. -dhutta a drunkard Sn 106; J I.268; III.260. -nakkhatta a drinking festival J 362; SnA 185. -pāna drinking strong liquor J I.50; IV.23; VbhA 383. -pāyikā a woman drinking liquor J V.11. -pipāsita thirsty after strong drink S II.110. -pīta one who has drunk liquor J I.426. -mada tipsiness, intoxication A IV.213; J I.352, 362. -meraya (-pāna) (drinking) rum & spirits A I.261; II.53. See also (pañca-) sikkhāpada. -vitthaka bowl for drinking spirits J V.427; DhA III.66. -soṇḍa a drunkard DhA III.129. -soṇḍaka id. J V.433.

Suriya [Vedic sūrya cp. suvar light, heaven; Idg. *sāuel, as in Gr. ἥλιος, Lat. sōl., Goth. sauil sun; Oir. sūil "eye"; cp. also Gr. σέλας splendour, σελήνη moon, & many others, for which see Walde, *Lat. Wtb.* s. v. sōl] 1. the sun Vin I.2; D II.319; Sn 687; A I.227; S V.29 sq.; J II.73; Vism 231 (in simile), 416 (the seventh sun), 417 (myth of pop. etym.), 690 (in sim.); Miln 299; KhA 21 (bāla°, in simile); PvA 137, 211; VbhA 519; size of the sun DhsA 318; suriyaṇ uṭṭhāpeti to go on till sunrise J I.318. — 2. the sun as a god D II.259; S I.51; J IV.63, etc.; VI.89, 90, 201, 247, 263, etc.
-atthangamana sunset VvA 295. -uggamana sunrise Mhvs 23, 22; J I.107. -kanta the sun-gem, a kind of gem Miln 118. -ggāha eclipse of the sun D I.10; J I.374. -maṇḍala the orb of the sun A I.283; Dhs 617. -rasmi a sunbeam J I.502. -vattika a sun-worshipper Nd[1] 89.

Suru (indecl.) [onamat.] a hissing sound ("suru"); **surusuru-kārakaṇ** (adv.) after the manner of making hissing sounds (when eating) Vin II.214; IV.197.

Surunga [a corruption of σύριγξ] a subterranean passage Mhvs 7, 14 sq.

Sulasī (f.) [cp. Sk. surasī, "basilienkraut" BR; fr. surasa] a medicinal plant Vin I.201; cp. Deśīnāmamālā VIII.40.

Sulopī (f.) a kind of small deer J VI.437, 438.

Suva [cp. Sk. śuka] a parrot J I.324; IV.277 sq.; VI.421; 431 sq. (the two: Pupphaka & Sattigumba); DhA I.284 (°rājā). fem. suvī J VI.421.

Suvaṇṇa [Sk. suvarṇa] of good colour, good, favoured, beautiful D I.82; Dhs 223; It 99; A IV.255; Pug 60; J I.226; suvaṇṇa (nt.) gold S IV.325 sq.; Sn 48, 686; Nd[2] 687 (=jātarūpa); KhA 240; VvA 104; often together with hirañña Vin III.16, 48; D II.179; °-āni pl. precious things J I.206. — Cp. soṇṇa.
-iṭṭhakā gilt tiles DhA III.29, 61; VvA 157. -kāra goldsmith D I.78; M II.18; III.243; A I.253 sq.; J I.182; V.438 sq.; Nd[1] 478; Vism 376 (in sim.); DhA III.340; SnA 15; VbhA 222 (in sim.). -gabbha a safe (-room) for gold DhA IV.105. -guhā "golden cave," N. of a cave SnA 66. -toraṇa gilt spire VbhA 112. -paṭṭa a golden (writing) slab J IV.7; SnA 228, 578; DhA IV.89. -paṇaka a golden diadem Miln 210. -pabbata N. of a mountain SnA 358. -passa id. SnA 66. -pādukā golden slippers Vin I.15. -maya made of gold J I.146. -mālā golden garland DhA I.388. -meṇḍaka a golden ram DhA III.364; IV.217; -bhinkāra a g. vase Mhbv 154 -bhūmi "gold-land," N. of Cambodia Nd[1] 155. -rājahaṇsa golden-coloured royal mallard J I.342. -vaṇṇa gold-coloured (of the body of the Yathāgata) D III.143, 159; J II.104; IV.333; DhA III.113. -vīthi golden street (in Indra's town) J V.386. -sivikā a g. litter DhA III.164. -haṇsa golden swan J I.207; II.353; SnA 277, 349.

Suvaṇṇatā (f.) [abstr. fr. suvaṇṇa] beauty of colour or complexion Pug 34.

Suvāṇa (& suvāna) [cp. Sk. śvan, also śvāna (f. śvānī): fr. Vedic acc. śuvānaṇ, of śvan. For etym. cp. Gr. κύων, Av. spā, Lat. canis, Oir. cū, Goth. hunds] a dog M III.91 (=supāṇa M I.58); J VI.247 (the 2 dogs of hell: Sabala & Sāma); Vism 259 (=supāṇa KhA 58). As suvā° at Sdhp 379, 408. — See also the var. forms san, suṇa, suna, sunakha, supāṇa, soṇa.
-doṇi a dog's (feeding) trough Vism 344, 358; VbhA 62. -piṇḍa a dog biscuit Vism 344. -vamathu dog's vomit Vism 344 (=suvā-vanta Sdhp 379).

Suvanaya [su-v-ānaya] easy to bring S I.124=J I.80.

Suvāmin [metric for sāmin] a master Sn 666.

Suve see sve.

Susāna (nt.) [cp. Vedic śmaśāna] a cemetery Vin I.15, 50; II.146; D I.71; A I.241; II.210; Pug 59; J I.175; Nd[1] 466; Nd[2] 342; Vism 76, 180; PvA 80, 92, 163, 195 sq. āmaka-s. a place where the corpses are left to rot J I.61, 372; VI.10; DhA I.176. Cp. sosānika.
-aggi a cemetery fire Vism 54. -gopaka the cemetery keeper DhA I.69. -vaḍḍhana augmenting the cemetery, fit to be thrown into the cemetery Th 2, 380. Cp. kaṭasi°.

Susānaka (adj.) [fr. last] employed in a cemetery Mhvs 10, 91.

Susira (adj.-nt.) [Sk. śuṣira] perforated, full of holes, hollow J I.146; Sn 199; J I.172, 442; DA I.261; Miln 112; Vism 194=DhsA 199; KhA 172; asusira DhA II.148 (Bdhgh for eka-ghana). (nt.) a hole; PvA 62.

Susu[1] [cp. Sk. śiśu] a boy, youngster, lad Vin III.147=J II.284; Vv 64[14] (=dahara C.); Sn 420; D I.115; M I.82; A II.22; J II.57; ājānīya-susūpama M I.445, read ājānīy-ass-ūpama (cp. Th I, 72). — In phrase susukāḷa the susu is a *double* su°, in meaning "very, very black" (see under kāḷa-kesa), e. g. D I.115=M I.82=

A II.22 = III.66 = J II.57; expl^d as suṭṭhu-kāḷa DA I.284. — susunāga a young elephant D II.254.

Susu[2] the sound susu, hissing J III.347 (cp. su and sū); ThA 189.

Susu[3] the name of a sort of water animal (alligator or sea-cow?) J VI.537 (plur. susū) = V.255 (kumbhīlā makasā susū).

Susukā (f.) an alligator Vin I.200; A II.123 (where id. p. at Nd² 470 has suṇsumāra); M I.459; Miln 196.

Sussati [Vedic śuṣyati; śuṣ (= sosana Dhtp 457)] to be dried, to wither Sn 434; J I.503; II.424; VI.5 (being thirsty); ppr. med. sussamāna J I.498; Sn 434; fut. sussissati J I.48; ger. sussitvā J II.5, 339; PvA 152. Cp. vissussati & sukkhati. — Caus. soseti (q. v.).

Sussūsa (adj.) wishing to hear or learn, obedient S I.6; J IV.134.

Sussūsati [Desid. fr. suṇāti; Sk. śuśrūṣati] to wish to hear, to listen, attend D I.230; A I.72; IV.393; aor. sussūsimsu Vin I.10; ppr. med. sussūsamāna Sn 383.

Sussūsā (f.) [Class. Sk. śuśrūṣā] wish to hear, obedience, attendance D III.189; A V.136; Th I, 588; Sn 186; J III.526; Miln 115.

Sussūsin (adj.) [cp. Epic Sk. śuśrūṣin] obedient, trusting J III.525.

Suhatā (f.) [sukha + tā] happiness J III.158.

Suhita (adj.) [su + hita] satiated M I.30; J I.266, 361; V.384; Miln 249.

Sū (indecl.) an onomat. part. "shoo," applied to hissing sounds: see su¹. Also doubled: sū sū DhA I.171; III.352. Cp. sūkara & sūsūyati.

Sūka [cp. Sk. śūka] the awn of barley etc. S V.10, 48; A I.8.

Sūkara [Sk. sūkara, perhaps as sū + kara; cp. Av. hū pig, Gr. ὗς; Lat. sūs; Ags. sū = E. sow] a hog, pig Vin I.200; D I.5; A II.42 (kukkuṭa +), 209; It 36; J I.197 (Muṇika); II.419 (Sālūka); III.287 (Cullatuṇḍila & Mahā-tuṇḍila); Miln 118, 267; VbhA 11 (vara-sayane sayāpita). — f. sūkarī J II.406 (read vañjha°).

-antaka a kind of girdle Vin II.136. **-maṇsa** pork A III.49 (sampanna-kolaka). -maddava is with Franke (*Dīgha trsl*ⁿ 222 sq.) to be interpreted as "soft (tender) boar's flesh." So also Oldenberg (*Reden des B.* 1922, 100) & Fleet (*J.R.A.S.* 1906, 656 & 881). Scarcely with Rh. D. (*Dial.* II.137, with note) as "quantity of truffles" D II.127; Ud 81 sq.; Miln 175. -potaka the young of a pig J V.19. -sāli a kind of wild rice J VI.531 (v. l. sukasāli).

Sūkarika [fr. sūkara; BSk. saukarika Divy 505] a pig-killer, pork-butcher S II.257; A II.207; III.303; Pug 56; Th 2, 242; J VI.111; ThA 204.

Sūcaka [fr. **sūc** to point out] an informer, slanderer S II.257 (= pesuñña-kāraka C.); Sn 246. Cp. saṇ°.

Sūcana (nt.) indicating, exhibiting Dhtp 592 (for **gandh**).

Sūci (f.) [cp. Sk. sūci; doubtful whether to **sīv**] a needle Vin II.115, 117, 177; S II.215 sq., 257; J I.111, 248; Vism 284 (in simile); a hairpin Th 2, 254; J I.9; a small door-bolt, a pin to secure the bolt M I.126; Th 2, 116; J I.360; V.294 (so for suci); ThA 117; cross-bar of a rail, railing [cp. BSk. sūcī Divy 221] D II.179.

-kāra a needle-maker S II.216. **-ghaṭikā** a small bolt to a door. Vin II.237; Ud 52; A IV.206; J I.346; VI.444; Vism 394. -ghara a needle case Vin II.301 sq.; IV.123, 167; S II.231; J I.170. **-nāḷikā** a needle-case made of bamboo Vin II.116 **-mukha** "needle-mouthed," a mosquito Abhp 646; a sort of intestinal worm; °ā pāṇā (in the Gūthaniraya purgatory) M III.185. -loma needle-haired, having hair like needles S II.257; name of a Yakkha at Gayā S I.207; Sn p. 48; SnA 551; Vism 208. -vatta needle-faced, having a mouth like a needle Pgdp 55. -vāṇijaka a needle-seller S II.215.

Sūcikā (f.) [fr. sūci] 1. a needle; (fig.) hunger Pv II.8³; PvA 107. — 2. a small bolt to a door Vin II.120, 148. — sūcik'aṭṭha whose bones are like needles (?) Pv III.2⁸; PvA 180 (sūcigātā ti vā pāṭho. Vijjhanatthena sūcikā ti laddhanāmāya khuppipāsāya ajjhāpīḷitā. Sūcikaṇṭhā ti keci paṭhanti. Sūcichiddasadisā mukhadvārā ti attho).

Sūju (adj.) [su + uju] upright Sn 143 = Kh IX.1 (= suṭṭhu uju KhA 236).

Sūṇā (f.) a slaughter-house J VI.62; see sūnā.

Sūta [Sk. sūta] a charioteer J IV.408; a bard, panegyrist J I.60; V.258.

Sūtighara (nt.) [sūti + ghara] a lying-in-chamber J IV.188; VI.485; Vism 259 (KhA pasūti°); VbhA 33, 242.

Sūda [Sk. sūda; for etym. see sādu] a cook D I.51; S V.149 sq.; J V.292; DA I.157; Vism 150 (in simile); Pv II.9³⁷, 9⁵⁰.

Sūdaka = sūda (cook) J V.507.

Sūna [Sk. śūna] swollen Miln 357¹⁹; J VI.555; often wrongly spelt suna (q. v.) Vin II.253 = A IV.275 (cp. Leumann, *Gött. Anz.*, 1899, p. 595); DhsA 197 (suna-bhāva).

Sūnā (f.) [Sk. sūnā] a slaughter-house Vin I.202; II.267; asisūnā the same Vin II.26; M I.130, 143; also sūna J VI.111; and sūṇā J V.303; sūnāpaṇa J VI.111; sūna-ghara Vin III.59; sūna-nissita Vin III.151; sūnakāra-ghara VbhA 252.

Sūnu [Vedic sūnu, fr. **sū**, cp. sūti] a son, child Mhvs 38, 87.

Sūpa [Vedic sūpa, cp. Ags. sūpan = Ger. saufen; Ohg. sūf = soup] broth, soup, curry Vin II.77, 214 sq.; IV.192; D I.105; S V.129 sq. (their var. flavours); A III.49 (aneka°); J II.66; Vism 343. samasūpaka with equal curry Vin IV.192. Also nt. Vin I.239²¹ (-āni) and f. sūpi J IV.352 (bidalasūpiyo); sūpavyañjanaka a vessel for curry and sauce Vin I.240.

-vyañjana curry J I.197.

Sūpatittha (adj.) [su + upatittha, the latter = tittha, cp. upavana: vana] with beautiful banks. Usually spelt su°, as if su + patittha (see patittha), e. g. Vin III.108; J VI.518, 555 (= sobhana°); D II.129; Ud 83; Pv II.1²⁰ (= sundara-tittha PvA 77). But sū° at M I.76, 283; Ap 333.

Sūpadhārita = su + upadhārita well-known Miln 10.

Sūpika [sūpa + ika] a cook DA I.157; J VI.62 (v. l.), 277.

Sūpin (adj.) [fr. sūpa] having curry, together with curry J III.328.

Sūpeyya (nt.) [fr. sūpa = Sk. sūpya] 1. belonging to soup, broth, soup M I.448; S III.146. — 2. curry D II.198; Nd² 314; DhA IV.209.

-paṇṇa curry leaf, curry stuff Vism 250 = VbhA 233; J I.98, 99; -sāka a potherb for making curry J IV.445.

Sūyati is passive of suṇāti.

Sūra[1] [Vedic śūra, fr. śū] valiant, courageous S I.21; J I.262, 320; II.119; (m.) a hero, a valiant man D I.51, 89; III.59, 142, 145 sq.; A IV.107, 110; Sn 831; DA 157, 250; (nt.) valour S V.227, read sūriya.
-kathā a tale about heroes D I.8; DA I.90 -kāka the valiant crow DhA III.352. -bhāva strength, valour J I.130; Vism 417 (in def. of suriya).

Sūra[2] [Vedic sūra] the sun ThA 150 (Ap V.90); J V.56.

Sūrata [=surata] soft, mild J VI.286; Mhbv 75; kindly disposed S IV.305. Cp. surata & sorata.

Sūrin (adj.) [fr. sūra[1]] wise Mhvs 26, 23.

Sūriya (nt.) [abstr. fr. sūra[1]] valour S V.227 (text, sūra); J I.282; Miln 3.

Sūla [cp. Vedic śūla] (m. and nt.) 1. a sharp-pointed instrument, a stake Th 2, 488; S V.411; Pv IV.1[6]; Vism 489 (in compar.), 646 (khadira°, ayo°, suvaṇṇa°); ThA 288; J I.143, 326; sūle uttāseti to impale A I.48; J I.326; II.443; IV.29; appeti the same J III.34; VI.17, or āropeti PvA 220. ayasūla an iron stake J IV.29; Sn 667; cp. asi° & satti°. — 2. a spit J I.211; roasted on a spit, roasted meat J III.220; maŋsa° the same, or perhaps a spit with roasted meat J III.52, 220. — 3. an acute, sharp pain DhsA 397; sūlā (f.) the same A V.110[5]. Cp. def^n of sūl as "rujā" at Dhtp 272.
-āropana impaling, execution Miln 197, 290. -koṭi the point of the stake DhA II.240.

Sūḷāra (adj.) [su+uḷāra] magnificent Mhvs 28, 1.

Sūsūyati [Denom. fr. sū] to make a hissing sound "sū sū" (of a snake) DhA II.257 (v. l. susumāyati).

Se (pron.)=taŋ: see under sa[2].

Seka [fr. sic, see siñcati] sprinkling J I.93 (suvaṇṇa-rasa-s.-piñjara).

Sekata (nt.) [Sk. saikata] a sandbank Dāvs I.32.

Sekadhārī (f.) (?) J VI.536 (nīlapupphi-°, C. nīlapupphiti ādikā pupphavalliyo).

Sekha (& sekkha) [cp. Sk. śaikṣa; fr. siks, sikkhati] belonging to training, in want of training, imperfect Vin I.17, 248; III.24; Dhs 1016; one who has still to learn, denotes one who has not yet attained Arahantship D II.143; M I.4, 144; A I.63; Pug 14; It 9 sq., 53, 71; Sn 970, 1038=S II.47; definition A I.231; S V.14, 145, 175, 229 sq., 298, 327; Nd[1] 493 (sikkhatī ti sekkho, etc.) =Nd[2] 689; VbhA 328. s. pāṭipadā the path of the student M I.354; III.76, 300; s. sīla the moral practice of the student A I.219 sq.; II.6, 86 sq.; asekha not to be trained, adept, perfect Vin I.62 sq.; III.24; Pug 14 (=arahant). See asekha.
-bala the strength of the disciple, of five kinds A II.150. -sammata esteemed to be under discipline, educated Vin IV.179.

Sekhavant (?) quick J VI.199 (v. l. sīghavant).

Sekhiya [fr. sekha] connected with training; s. dhamma rule of good breeding Vin IV.185 sq.

Segālaka (nt.) [fr. sigāla] a jackal's cry A I.187 sq. (°ŋ nadati); cp. sigālika.

Secanaka [fr. seceti] sprinkling J VI.69; neg. asecanaka (q. v.).

Seceti see siñcati.

Secchā=sa-icchā, Sdhp 249.

Seṭṭha best, excellent D I.18, 98; S III.13; Sn 47, 181, 822, 907; Dh 1, 26; J I.443; Nd[1] 84=Nd[2] 502 (with syn.); J I.88; cp. seṭṭhatara J V.148.
-kamma excellent, pious deeds Mhvs 59, 9. -sammata considered the best J III.111.

Seṭṭhi [fr. seṭṭha, Sk. śreṣṭhin] foreman of a guild, treasurer, banker, "City man", wealthy merchant Vin I.15 sq., 271 sq.; II.110 sq., 157; S I.89; J I.122; II.367 etc.; Rājagaha° the merchant of Rājagaha Vin II.154; J IV.37; Bārāṇasi° the merchant of Benares J I.242, 269; jana-pada-seṭṭhi a commercial man of the country J IV.37; seṭṭhi gahapati Vin I.273; S I.92; there were families of seṭṭhis Vin I.18; J IV.62; °-ṭṭhāna the position of a seṭṭhi J II.122, 231; hereditary J I.231, 243; II.64; III.475; IV.62 etc.; seṭṭhânuseṭṭhī treasurers and under-treasurers Vin I.18; see *Vinaya Texts* I.102.

Seṭṭhitta (nt.) [abstr. fr. seṭṭhi] the office of treasurer or (wholesale) merchant S I.92.

Seṇi (f.) [Class. Sk. śreṇi in meaning "guild"; Vedic= row] 1. a guild Vin IV.226; J I.267, 314; IV.43; Dāvs II.124; their number was *eighteen* J VI.22, 427; VbhA 466. °-pamukha the head of a guild J II.12 (text seni-). — 2. a division of an army J VI.583; ratha-° J VI.81, 49; seṇimokkha the chief of an army J VI.371 (cp. senā and seniya).

Seta (adj.) [Vedic śveta & śvitra; cp. Av. spaēta white; Lith. szaitýti to make light; Ohg. hwīz=E. white] white D II.297=M I.58; Sn 689; A III.241; VbhA 63 (opp. kāḷa); J I.175; PvA 157, 215. name of a mountain in the Himālayas S I.67=Miln 242; an elephant of King Pasenadi A III.345.
-anga white bodied Mhvs 10, 54. -aṭṭhika lit. (having) white bones, (suffering from) famine [cp. BSk. śvetāsthi Divy 131] Vin III.6; IV.23; S IV.323; A I.160; IV.279. — f. mildew Vin II.256; J V.401. -odaka clear (transparent) water Pv II.1[20]. -kambala white blanket J IV.353. -kamma whitewashing J VI.432. -kuṭṭha white leprosy J V.69; VI.196. -geru N. of a plant J VI.535. -cchatta a white parasol, an emblem of royalty D II.19; A I.145; J I.177, 267; PvA 74; DhA I.167; III.120. -pacchāda with white covering S IV.292=Ud 76=DhsA 397. -puppha "white-flowered," N. of a tree (Vitex trifolia ?) J V.422 (=piyaka). -vārī (& °vārisa) names of plants or trees J VI.535, 536.

Setaka (adj.) [seta+ka] white, transparent D II.129; M I.76, 167, 283.

Setaccha a tree J VI.535; setacchakūṭa adj. J VI.539 (sakuṇa).

Setapaṇṇi (f. [?]) a tree J VI.335.

Seti & **sayati** [śī, Vedic śete & śayate; cp. Av. saēte=Gr. κεῖται to lie, ὠ-κεανός ("ocean")=Sk. ā-śayānah, κοιμάω to put to sleep; Ags. hǣman to marry; also Lat. cīvis=citizen. — The Dhtp simply defines as saya (374)] to lie down, to sleep; (applied) to be in a condition, to dwell, behave etc. — Pres. seti S I.41, 47, 198 (kiŋ sesi why do you lie asleep? Cp. Pv II.6[1]); J I.141; Dh 79, 168; Sn 200; VvA 42; sayati Vin I.57; J II.53; DA I.261. Pot. sayeyya Pv II.3,[9] & saye It 120. ppr. sayaŋ It 82, 117; Sn 193; sayāna (med.) D I.90; II.292; M I.57; It 117; Sn 1145; & semāna D II.24; M I.88; S I.121; J I.180; also sayamāna Th 1, 95. — Fut. sessati S I.83; Sn 970; DhA I.320. — Aor. sesi J V.70; settha Sn 970; sayi J VI.197, asayittha J I.335. — Inf. sayituŋ PvA 157; ger. sayitvā J II.77. — pp. sayita (q. v.). — Caus. II. sayāpeti to make lie down, to bed on a couch etc. J I.245; V.461; Mhvs 31, 35; PvA 104. — pp. sayāpita. — sukhaŋ seti to be at ease or happy S I.212; J V.242 (raṭṭhaŋ i. e. is prosperous); opp. dukkhaŋ s. to be miserable A I.137.

Setu [Vedic setu, to si or sā (see sinoti); cp. Av. haētu dam; Lat. sacta; Ags. sāda rope; etc.] a causeway, bridge Vin I.230=D II.89; J I.199; Vism 412 (simile);

DhA I.83; SnA 357; PvA 102, 151, 215. uttāra°- a bridge for crossing over M I.134; S IV.174; Miln 194; naḷa-° a bamboo bridge Th I, 7.
-kāraka a bridge-maker, one who paves the way S I.33; Kv 345. -ghāta pulling down of the bridge (leading to something) Vin I.59; III.6; A I.220, 261; II.145 sq.; Dhs 299; DhsA 219; DA I.305; Nd² 462; DhA IV.36.

Seda [Vedic sveda, fr. **svid**, cp. Av. xvaēda, Gr. ἱδρώς, Lat. sudor, Ags. svāt=E. sweat] sweat D II.293; A II.67 sq.; It 76; Sn 196; J I.118, 138, 146, 243; in detail (physiologically) at Vism 262, 360; VbhA 66, 245; sweating for medicinal purposes, mahā° a great steam-bath; sambhāra° bringing about sweating by the use of herbs, etc.; seda-kamma sweating Vin I.205. — pl. sedā drops of perspiration DhA I.253.
-âvakkhitta earned in the sweat of the brow A II.67 sq., III.45, 76; IV.95, 282. **-gata** sweat-covered, sweating VvA 305. **-mala** the stain of sweat J III.290; VbhA 276. **-yūsa** sweat Vism 195.

Sedaka (adj.) [fr. seda] sweating, transpiring D II.265.

Sedita [pp. of sedeti] moistened J I.52 (su°). Cp. pari°.

Sedeti [Caus. of sijjati] to cause to transpire, to heat, to steam J IV.238; V.271; KhA 52, 67; Vin III.82 (aor. sedesi); ger. sedetvā J I.324; II.74; pp. sedita. Caus II. sedāpeti J III.122.

Sena¹ [=sayana] lying, sleeping; couch, bed J V.96 (=sayana).

Sena² [Sk. śyena] a hawk J I.273; II.51, 60; DhA II.267.

Senaka¹ a carter ThA 271 (=sākaṭika of Th 2, 443).

Senaka²=sena² J IV.58, 291; VI.246.

Senā [Vedic senā² perhaps fr. **si** to bind] an army Vin I.241; IV.104 sq. (where described as consisting of hatthī, assā, rathā, pattī), 160; S I.112; A III.397; V.82; J II.94; Miln 4; Nd¹ 95 (Māra°), 174 (id.).
-gutta [sena°] a high official, a minister of war, only in cpd. mahā-° J VI.2, 54; mahāsenaguttaṭṭhāna the position of a generalissimo J V.115. **-nāyaka** a general Vin I.73. **-pacca** the position as general Mhvs 38, 81. **-pati** a general Vin I.233 sq.; Sn 556; A III.38; IV.79; J I.133; IV.43; dhamma-° a general of the Dhamma Miln 343; DhA III.305. **-patika** a general A III.76, 78, 300. **-byūha** massing of troops, grouping & fitting up an army Vin IV.107; D I.6; Ps II.213; DA I.85 (-vyūha).

Senānī a general; only in cpd. **°-kuṭilatā** strategy (lit. crookedness of a general) DhsA 151.

Senāsana (nt.) [sayana+āsana] sleeping and sitting, bed & chair, dwelling, lodging Vin I.196, 294, 356; II.146, 150 (°parikkhāra-dussa); III.88 etc.; D II.77; A I.60; It 103, 109; DA I.208; J I.217; VbhA 365 (=seti c'eva āsati ca etthā ti senāsanaŋ). See also panta.
-gāha allotment of lodging-places Vin II.167. **-gāhāpaka** house-steward Vin II.167. **-cārikā** a wandering from lodging to lodging Vin I.182, 203; III.21; J 126. **-paññāpaka** regulator of lodging-places Vin II.75, 176; III.158 sq.; IV.38. **-paṭibāhana** keeping out of the lodging J I.217. **-paviveka** secluson in respect of lodging A I.240 sq. **-vatta** rule of conduct in respect of dwelling Vin II.220.

Seniya [fr. senā] belonging to an army, soldier J I.314.

Senesika at Vin I.200 is to be read senehika (fr. sineha), i. e. greasy.

Sepaṇṇī (f.) [Sk. śrīparṇī, lit. having lucky leaves] name of a tree, Gmelina arborea J I.173, 174; DhA I.145.

Semānaka [semāna+ka; ppr. of seti] lying Th I,14; DhA I.16.

Semha (nt.) [=silesuma] phlegm Vin II.137; D II.14, 293; A II.87; III.101; IV.320; Sn 198, 434; Miln 112, 303. Physiologically in detail at Vism 359; VbhA 65, 244.

Semhāra some sort of animal (monkey ?) (explained by makkaṭa) M I.429.

Semhika (adj.) [fr. semha] a man of phlegmatic humour Miln 298.

Seyya (adj.) [Sk. śreyas, compar. formⁿ] better, excellent; nom. masc. seyyo S III.48 sq.; Sn 918; Dh 308; Dhs 1116; J I.180; nom. fem. seyyasi J V.393; nom. neut. seyyo often used as a noun, meaning good, happiness, well-being Vin I.33; D I.184; II.330; Sn 427, 440; Dh 76, 100; J II.44; VI.4 (maraṇaŋ eva seyyo, with abl. of compar. rajjato); Pv II.9⁴³ (dhanaŋ); IV.1⁶ (jīvitaŋ); nom. fem. seyyā J V.94; nom. acc. neutr. seyyaŋ J II.402; III.237; abl. as adv. seyyaso "still better" Dh 43; J II.402; IV.241. Superl. seṭṭha.

Seyyaka (adj.) [fr. seyyā] lying M I.433, see uttānaseyyaka and gabbhaseyyaka.

Seyyati [śṛ, Vedic śṛṇāti & śīryate] to crush J I.174. See also sarati³ & vi°. — pp. sinna: see vi°.

Seyyathā (adv.) [=taŋ yathā, with Māgadhī se° for ta°; cp. sayathā & taŋyathā] as, just as, s. pi Vin I.5; D I.45; It 90, 113; J I.339; seyyathīdaŋ as follows "i. e." or "viz." Vin I.10; D I.89; II.91; S V.421; It 99.

Seyyā (f.) [Sk. śayyā; fr. śī] a bed, couch M I.502; A I.296; Vin II.167 (°aggena by the surplus in beds); Sn 29, 152, 535; Dh 305, 309; Pv II.3¹¹; IV.1²; J VI.197 (gilāna° sick-bed). Four kinds A II.224; VbhA 345. seyyaŋ kappeti to lie down Vin IV.15, 18 sq. — Combᵈ with āvasatha, e. g. at A II.85, 203; III.385; IV.60; V.271 sq. — As -° used in adj. sense of "lying down, resting," viz. ussūra° sleeping beyond sunrise D III.184=DhA II.227; divā° noon-day rest D I.112, 167; sīha° like a lion D II.134; A IV.87; dukkha° sleeping uncomfortably DhA IV.8.

Seritā (f.) [fr. serin] independence, freedom Sn 39 sq.

Serin (adj.) [cp. Sk. svairin] self-willed, independent, according to one's liking M I.506; Th I, 1144; Pv IV.1⁸⁷; J I.5.

Serivihāra (adj.) [serin+vihāra] lodging at one's own choice M I.469 sq.; Vism 66 (°sukhaŋ).

Serīsaka (adj.) [fr. sirīsa] made of Sirīsa wood, name of a hall D II.356 sq.; Vv 84⁵³; VvA 331, 351.

Serīsamaha a festival in honour of the Serīsaka Vimāna Vv 84³⁷· ⁵³.

Sereyyaka name of a tree (Barleria cristata) J III.253.

Sela [fr. silā] rocky Dh 8; (m.) rock, stone, crystal S I.127; D II.39; A III.346; Dh 81; J II.14; Vin I.4 sq.; III.147=J II.284.
-guḷa a rocky ball J I.147. **-maya** made of rock (crystal ?), of the bowl of the Buddha SnA 139, 159.

Selaka [sela+ka] "rocky," a kind of copper (cp. pisāca) VbhA 63.

Seḷita (selita) [pp. of seḷeti] shouting, noise, row J II.218. To this belongs the doubtful der. selissaka (nt.) noise, row, mad pranks at S IV.117 (v. l. seleyyaka).

Seḷeti [according to Kern, *Toev.* II.78 for sveḷayati, cp. Oir. fét whistle, music etc. Idg. ***sveizd**] to make a noise, shout, cry exultantly Sn 682; J V.67; Bu I.36. — pp. seḷita. — Other. diff. explⁿˢ of the word see in *J.P.T.S.* 1885, p. 54.

Sevaka serving, following; a servant, dependent J II.12, 125, 420; SnA 453. See vipakkha°.

Sevati [sev] 1. to serve, associate with, resort to Vin II.203; A I.124 sq.; Sn 57, 75; Pug 33; It 107; J III.525; SnA 169. — 2. to practice, embrace, make use of Vin I.10=S V.421; D III.157; S I.12; M III.45; Dh 167, 293, 310; Sn 72, 391, 927; Nd[1] 383, 481; J I.152, 361; aor. asevissaŋ J IV.178. — pp. sevita: see ā°, vi°.

Sevanatā (-°) (f.) [abstr, fr. sevati]=sevanā VbhA 282 sq.

Sevanā (f.) [fr. sevati] following, associating with Sn 259; Dhs 1326; Pug 20; Dhtp 285 (as nt.); cohabiting Vin III.29.

Sevā (f.) [fr. sev] service, resorting to S I.110; ThA 179.

Sevāla [cp. Epic Sk. śaivala & saivāla] the plant Blyxa octandra moss, A III.187, 232, 235; J II.150=DhA I.144; J III.520; IV.71; V.462; Miln 35; DhA III.199; Tikp 12 (in sim.). (m. and nt.) J V.37; -mālaka (or -mālika) who makes garlands of Blyxa octandra A V.263; S IV.312. — Often comb[d] with another water-plant, paṇaka (see under paṇṇaka), e. g. A III.187; Vism 261 (simile); VbhA 244 (id.); KhA 61 (cp. Schubring, *Kalpasūtra* p. 46 sq.).

Sevin (adj.) [fr. sev] serving, practising Sn 749; It 54. See vipakkha°.

Seveti to cause to fall, to throw down J III.198 (doubtful; C-expl[s] as pāteti & gives saveti [=sāveti, Caus. of sru to make glide] as gloss; v. l. also sādeti).

Sesa [fr. śiṣ] remaining, left D II.48; Sn 217, 354; J II.128; (nt.) remainder PvA 14, 70; °-ka the same Mhvs 10, 36; 22, 42; 25, 19.

Seseti: see sissati.

Sessaŋ, sessati see seti.

Sehi is instr. pl. of sa[4] (his own): Dh 136; DhA III.64.

Soka [fr. śuc, to gleam (which to the Dhtp however is known only in meaning "soka": Dhtp 39); cp. Vedic śoka the flame of fire, later in sense of "burning grief"] grief, sorrow, mourning; def[d] as "socanā socitattaŋ anto-soko . . . cetaso parijjhāyanā domanassaŋ" at Ps I.38=Nd[1] 128=Nd[2] 694; shorter as "ñāti-vyasan'-ādīhi phuṭṭhassa citta-santāpo" at Vism 503=VbhA. Cp. the foll.: Vin I.6; D I.6; II.305, 103; S I.110, 123, 137; A I.51, 144; II.21; V.141; Sn 584, 586; J I.189; SnA 155; DhA II.166; KhA 153 (abbūḷha°); Pv I.4[8] (=citta-santāpa PvA 18); PvA 6, 14, 38, 42, 61. — asoka without grief: see viraja. See also dukkha B III.1 b.
-aggi the fire of sorrow PvA 41. pl. -divasā the days of mourning (at the king's court after the death of the queen) SnA 89. -parideva sorrow and lamenting A III.32, 326 sq.; V.216 sq.; Vism 503; Nd[1] 128. -pariddava id. Vv 84[30]. -pareta overcome with grief Pv I.8[6]. -vinaya dispelling of grief PvA 39. -vinodana id. PvA 61. -salla the dart or sting of sorrow A III.54, 58; Nd[1] 59, 414; Pv I.8[8]; PvA 93, 162.

Sokajjhāyikā (f.) [soka+ajjhāyaka; *this* soka perhaps *sūka, as in visūka?] a woman who plays the fool, a comedian Vin IV.285; J VI.580 (where C. expl[s] as "grief-dispellers").

Sokavant (adj.) [soka+vant] sorrowful Mhvs 19, 15.

Sokika (adj.) [soka+ika] sorrowful; a-° free from sorrow ThA 229.

Sokin (adj.) [fr. soka] (fem. °nī) sorrowful Dh 28.

Sokhya (nt.) [abstr. der. fr. sukha] happiness Sn 61; J V.205.

Sokhumma (nt.) [abstr. fr. sukhuma] fineness, minuteness A II.17; Th 1, 437. At A II.18 with double suffix °tā.

Sogandhika (nt.) [Sk. saugandhika; fr. sugandha] the white water-lily (Nymphæa lotus) J V.419; VI.518, 537 (seta-sogandhiyehi). — As m. designation of a purgatory A V.173; S I.152; Sn p. 126.

Socati [Vedic śocati, śuc, said of the gleaming of a fire] 1. to mourn, grieve Sn 34; Dh 15; J I.168; Pv I.8[7] (+rodati); I.10[15]; I.12[2]; Miln 11; pres 3rd pl. socare Sn 445; Dh 225; ppr. socamāna J II.75; ppr. asocaŋ not grieving S I.116; mā soci do not sorrow D II.144; J VI.190; plur. mā socayittha do not grieve D II.158; Caus. socayati to cause to grieve D I.52; S I.116; Th 1, 743 (ger. °ayitvā); Miln 226; soceti J II.8. — pp. socita. — Caus. II. socāpayati the same S I.116.

Socana (nt.) [fr. śuc] sorrow, mourning PvA 18, 62; -nā (f.) the same D II.306; S I.108=Sn 34; Nd[2] 694.

Socita (nt.) [fr. socati] grief Th 2, 462.

Socitatta (nt.) sorrowfulness D II.306; Ps I.38=Nd[2] 694.

Socin [fr. socati] grieving A IV.294 (socī ca=socicca).

Sociya [=Sk. śocya] deplorable Sdhp 262.

Soceyya (nt.) [abstr. fr. śuc, *śaucya] purity S I.78; A I.94; II.188; V.263; Vism 8; J I.214; Miln 115, 207; is threefold A I.271; It 55; D III.219; further subdivided A V.264, 266 sq. In meaning of "cleaning, washing" given in the Dhtp as def. of roots for washing, bathing etc. (khal, nahā, sinā, sudh).

Sojacca (nt.) [abstr. fr. sujāta] nobility, high birth J II.137.

Soṇa[1] [see suvāṇa] a dog J I.146; VI.107 (=sunakha); Sn 675; Vism 191; DhA III.255 (+sigāla); soṇī (f.) a bitch Mhvs 7, 8=sona It 36.

Soṇa[2] [cp. śyonāka] a kind of tree; the Bodhi trees of the Buddhas Paduma and Nārada Bu IX.22; X.24; J I.36, 37.

Soṇita (nt.) [Sk. śoṇita, fr. śoṇa red] blood Th 2, 467; DA I.120; Vism 259.

Soṇī (f.) [cp. Sk. śroṇī] 1. the buttock Sn 609; J V.155, 216, 302. — 2. a bitch, see soṇa[1].

Soṇḍa [cp. Sk. śauṇḍa] addicted to drink, intoxicated, a drunkard D II.172; J V.436, 499; Miln 345; Vism 316. a-soṇḍa A III.38; IV.266; J V.166; (fem. -ī) itthisoṇḍī a woman addicted to drink Sn 112 (? better "one who is addicted to women"; SnA 172 expl[s] to that effect, cp. J II.431 itthi-surā-maŋsa-soṇḍa); yuddha-soṇḍa J I.204; dāsi-soṇḍa a libertine J V.436 (+surā°); dhamma-soṇḍatā affectionate attachment to the law J V.482.

Soṇḍaka [soṇḍa+ka] in cpd. surā° a drunkard J V.433; VI.30.

Soṇḍā (f.) [Sk. śuṇḍā] an elephant's trunk Vin II.201;= S II.269; M I.415; A IV.87 (uccā° fig. of a bhikkhu] J I.50, 187; IV.91; V.37; DhA I.58; Miln 368; soṇḍa (m.) the same S I.104.

Soṇḍika [fr. soṇḍa] 1. a distiller and seller of spirituous liquors; M I.228=374. — 2. a drunkard Miln 93.

Soṇḍikā (f.) 1. tendril of a creeper S I.106; Miln 374. — 2. peppered meat S II.98 (cp. Sanskrit śauṇḍī long pepper). — 3. in udaka° KhA 65 (=soṇḍī[1]) a tank.

Soṇḍī[1] (f.) a natural tank in a rock J I.462; DhA II.56 (soṇḍi); udaka-° J IV.333; Vism 119; KhA 65 (soṇḍikā).

Soṇḍi² (f.) the neck of a tortoise S IV.177 (soṇḍi-pañcamāni angāni); Miln 371; the hood of a snake J VI.166 (nāgā soṇḍi-katā).

Soṇṇa (nt.) [the contracted form of suvaṇṇa, cp. sovaṇṇa] gold; (adj.) golden Mhvs 5, 87; Vv 5⁴, 36⁷.
-**âlankāra** with golden ornaments J II.48. -**dhaja** with golden flags J II.48. -**bhinkāra** a golden vase Sdhp 513. -**maya** golden, made of gold J VI.203. -**vālukā** gold dust J VI.278.

Sota¹ (nt.) [Vedic śrotas & śrotra; fr. **śru**; see suṇāti] ear, the organ of hearing Vin I.9, 34; D I.21; Sn 345 (nom. pl. sotā); Vism 444 (defined); Dhs 601; DhsA 310; — dibba-sota the divine ear (cp. dibba-cakkhu) D I.79, 154; III.38, 281; dhamma° the ear of the Dhamma A III.285 sq., 350; V.140; S II.43; sotaŋ odahati to listen (carefully) D I.230; ohita-s. with open ears A IV.115; V.154; J I.129.
-**añjana** a kind of ointment made with antimony Vin I.203. -**ânugata** following on hearing, acquired by hearing A II.185. -**āyatana** the sense of hearing Dhs 601 sq.; D II.243, 280, 290. -**âvadhāna** giving ear, attention M II.175. -**indriya** the faculty of hearing Dhs 604; D III.239. -**dvāra** "door of the ear," auditory sensation VbhA 41. -**dhātu** the ear element, the ear Vin II.299; D I.79; S II.121; A I.255 (dibba°); III.17 (id.); V.199; Vbh 334; Vism 407 (defᵈ); Dhs 601, 604; Miln 6. -**viññāṇa** auditory cognition, perception through the ear Dhs 443. -**viññeyya** cognizable by hearing D II.281; Dhs 467; KhA 101.

Sota² (m. & nt.) [Vedic srotas, nt., fr. **sru**; see savati] 1. stream, flood, torrent Sn 433; It 144; J I.323; sīgha-s. having a quick current D II.132; Sn 319; metaphorically, the stream of cravings Sn 715 (chinna°; cp. MVastu III.88 chinna-srota), 1034; S IV.292; M I.226 (sotaŋ chetvā); It 114; denotes *noble eightfold path* S V.347; bhava-s. torrent of rebirth S I.15; IV.128; viññāṇa-s. flux of mind, D III.105; nom. sing. soto S IV.291 sq.; V.347; nom. plur. sotā Sn 1034; acc. plur. sotāni Sn 433; plur. sotāyo (f. [?], or wrong reading instead of sotāso, sotāse [?]) J IV.287, 288. — 2. passage, aperture (of body, as eyes, ears, etc.), in kaṇṇa° orifice of the ear, and nāsa° nostril, e. g. D I.106; Sn p. 108; J I.163, 164 (heṭṭhā-nāsika-s.); Vism 400 (dakkhiṇa° & vāma-kaṇṇa-s.).
-**āpatti** entering upon the stream, i. e. the noble eightfold path (S V.347), conversion Vin II.93 etc. By it the first three Saŋyojanas are broken S V.357, 376. It has four phases (angas): faith in the Buddha, the Dhamma, and the Order, and, further, the noble Sīlas S II.68 sq.; V.362 sq.; A III.12; IV.405; D III.227 (in detail). Another set of four angas consists of sappurisa-saŋsevā, saddhammasavana, yonisomanasikāra, and dhammânudhammapaṭipatti S V.347, 404. *-phala* the effect of having entered upon the stream, the fruit of conversion Vin I.293; II.183; M I.325; A I.44; III.441; IV.292 sq., 372 sq.; D I.229; III.227; S III.168, 225; V.410 sq.; Pug 13; DhA III.192; IV.5; PvA 22, 38, 66, 142. *-magga* the way to conversion, the lower stage of conversion DA I.237; J I.97; VbhA 307; see magga. -**āpanna** one who has entered the stream, a convert Vin II.161, 240; III.10; D I.156; III.107 sq., 132, 227; A II.89; S II.68; III.203 sq., 225 sq.; V.193 sq.; DA I.313; Vism 6, 709; PvA 5, 153. The converted is endowed with āyu, vaṇṇa, sukha, and ādhipateyya S V.390; he is called wealthy and glorious S V.402; conversion excludes rebirth in purgatory, among animals and petas, as well as in other places of misery; he is a-vinipāta-dhamma: D I.156; II.200; S V.193 sq., 343; A I.232; II.238; III.331 sq.; IV.405 sq., V.182; M III.81; or khīṇa-niraya: A III.211; IV.405 sq. (+khīṇa-tiracchānayoni etc.). The converted man is sure to attain the sambodhi (niyato sambodhipārāyano D I.156, discussed in *Dial.* I.190-192).

Sotatta scorched J I.390=M I.79, read so tatto (cp. M I.536). See sosīta.

Sotar [n. ag. fr. suṇāti] a hearer D I.56; A II.116; III.161 sq. — **sotā** used as a feminine noun ThA 200 (Ap V.3).

Sotavant [sota¹+vant] having ears, nom. pl. sotavanto S I.138; Vin I.7; D II.39.

Sotukāma [sotuŋ (=inf. of suṇāti)+kāma] wish or wishing to hear A I.150; IV.115; Vism 444; f. abstr. °**kamyatā** desire to listen A V.145 sq., SnA 135.

Sotta [pp. of supati, for sutta] asleep S I.170.

Sotti (f.) [Sk. śukti] a shell (?) filled with chunam and lac, used for scratching the back, a back-scratcher acting as a sponge M II.46; A I.208; see sutti e. g. Vin II.107.

Sottiya [=*śrotriya] well versed in sacred learning, a learned man M I.280; Sn 533 sq. See sotthiya.

Sottun see supati

Sotthāna (nt.) [cp. Sk. svastyayana] blessing, well-fare Sn 258; A IV.271, 285; J V.29 (where the metre requires sotthayanaŋ, as at IV.75); VI.139.

Sotthi (f.) [Sk. svasti=su+asti] well-being, safety, blessing A III.38=IV.266 ("brings future happiness"); J I.335; s. hotu hail! D I.96; **sotthiŋ** in safety, safely Dh 219 (=anupaddavena DhA III.293); Pv IV.6⁴ (=nirupaddava PvA 262); Sn 269; **sotthinā** safely, prosperously D I.72, 96; II.346; M I.135; J II.87; III.201. suvatthi the same J IV.32. See **sotthika** & **sovatthika**.
-**kamma** a blessing J I.343. -**kāra** an utterer of blessings, a herald J VI.43. -**gata** safe wandering, prosperous journey Mhvs 8, 10; sotthigamana the same J I.272. -**bhāva** well-being, prosperity, safety J I.209; III.44; DbA II.58; PvA 250. -**vācaka** utterer of blessings, a herald Miln 359. -**sālā** a hospital Mhvs 10, 101.

Sotthika (& °iya) (adj.) [fr. sotthi] happy, auspicious, blessed, safe VvA 95; DhA II.227 (°iya; in phrase dīgha° one who is happy for long [?]).

Sotthiya¹=sottiya a learned man, a brahmin Dh 295; ThA 200 (Ap V.6); J IV.301, 303; V.466.

Sotthiya² (nt.) [der. ?] a childbirth rag Vism 63.

Sotthivant (adj.) [sotthi+vant] lucky, happy, safe Vv 84⁵².

Sodaka (adj.) [sa+udaka] containing water Mhvs 30, 38; 37, 200.

Sodariya (adj.) [sa+udariya] having a common origin (in the same mother's womb), born of the same mother, a brother J I.308; IV.434; PvA 94 (bhātā).

Sodhaka [fr. sodheti] one who cleanses Mhvs 10, 90; PvA 7.

Sodhana (nt.) [fr. sodheti] cleansing Vism 276 (as f. °nā); examining J I.292; payment (see **uddhāra**) J I.321.

Sodheti [Caus. of sujjhati] to make clean, to purify Vin I.47; M I.39; Dh 141; DA I.261, 13⁵; to examine, search J I.200, 291; II.123; III.528; to search for, to seek J II.135; to clean away, to remove J IV.404; to correct J II.48; to clear a debt: in this meaning mixed with sādheti (q. v.) in phrases iṇaŋ s. and uddhāraŋ s.; we read **iṇaŋ sodheti** at PvA 276; **uddhāraŋ sodheti** at J IV.45; otherwise sādheti. — Caus. II. **sodhāpeti** to cause to clean, to clean Vin III.208, 248=I.206; J I.305; II.19; Pass. **sodhīyati** to be cleansed, to be adorned Bu II.40 sq.=J I.12.

Sona dog It 36; see soṇa.

Sopadhīka=sa+upadhika.

Sopavāhana = sa + upavāhana.

Sopāka [= sapāka; śva + pāka] a man of a very low caste, an outcast Sn 137. See also sapāka.

Sopāna (m. and nt.) [cp. Sk. sopāna; Aufrecht "sa + upāyana"] stairs, staircase Vin II.117, 152; D II.178; J I.330, 348; IV.265; Vism 10; VvA 188; PvA 156, 275; Vv 78⁵; dhura-sopāna the highest step of a staircase (?) J I.330.
-kalingara flight of steps Vin II.128 (v. l. sopāṇa-kaḷevara as at M II.92). -panti a flight or row of steps, a ladder Vism 392 (three). -pāda the foot of the steps (opp. °sīsa) DhA I.115. -phalaka a step of a staircase J I.330.

Soppa (nt.) [= supina] sleep, dream S I.110; A I.261 (i. e. laziness). °ante in a dream J V.329 (C. reading for T. suppante).

Soppati see supati.

Sobbha [cp. Sk. śvabhra] a hole, (deep) pit D II.127; M I.11; A I.243; II.140; III.389 (see papāta); V.114 sq.; J VI.166; Th I, 229; SnA 355, 479; a water-pool S II.32; Sn 720; Vism 186; as adj. at S III.109 (+ papāta), i. e. "deep"; kussobbha a small collection of water S II.32, 118; Sn 720; mahāsobbha the ocean S II.32, 118.

Sobhagga (nt.) [abstr. fr. subhaga] prosperity, beauty Th 2, 72; J I.51, 475; II.158; IV.133. As sobhagyatā at DA I.161.

Sobhañjana the tree Hyperanthica moringa J V.405; sobhañjanaka the same J III.161 (= siggurukkha, C.); VI.535.

Sobhaṇa[1] (nt.) [fr. **śubh**] 1. a kind of edging on a girdle Vin II.136. — 2. beauty, ornament Miln 356.

Sobhaṇa[2] (adj.) [fr. **śubh**] 1. adorning, shining, embellishing A II.8, 225; very often spelt sobhana J I.257; ThA 247; nagara-sobhaṇā (or °iṇī) a courtesan J II.367; III.435, 475; Miln 350; PvA 4. — 2. good Miln 46 (text °na); *Cpd.* 96; 101; 106.

Sobhati [**śubh**, Vedic śobhate] 1. to shine, to be splendid, look beautiful J I.89; II.93; sobhetha let your light shine (with foll. yaŋ "in that . . .") Vin I.187, 349 = II.162 = J III.487 = S I.217; ppr. °māna Vism 58. aor. sobhi J I.143; Caus. sobheti to make resplendent, adorn, grace A II.7; Sn 421; J I.43; Miln 1; Vism 79 (ppr. sobhayanto); to make clear D II.105.

Sobhanagaraka (nt.) a kind of game, fairy scenes D I.6, 13; DA I.84.

Sobhā (f.) [fr. **śubh**; Sk. śobhā] splendour, radiance, beauty Mhvs 33, 30; J IV.333; ThA 226; Miln 356.

Sobhiya [cp. Sk. śaubhika; BSk. śobhika MVastu III.113] a sort of magician or trickster, clown J VI.277 (sobhiyā ti nagarasobhanā sampannarūpā purisā; not correct; C.).

Somanassa (nt.) [fr. su + mano; cp. domanassa] mental ease, happiness, joy D I.3; II.278; III.270; M I.85, 313; S IV.232; A II.69; III.207, 238; Dh 341; Sn 67; Pug 59; VbhA 73; PvA 6, 14, 133; DA I.53; it is more than sukha D II.214; defined at Vism 461 (iṭṭh'ārammaṇ'-ānubbhavana-lakkhaṇaŋ, etc.). A syn. of it is veda 1. On term see also *Cpd.* 277.
-indriya the faculty of pleasure D III.224; S V.209 sq.; Dhs 18.

Somanassita (adj.) [Caus. pp. formation fr. somanassa] satisfied, pleased, contented VvA 351.

Somarukkha [soma + rukkha] a certain species of tree J VI.530.

Sombhā (f.) a puppet, doll Th 2, 390; explained as sombhakā ThA 257.

Somma (adj.) [Sk. saumya, fr. soma] pleasing, agreeable, gentle Dāvs I.42; DA I.247; DhsA 127; VvA 205; SnA 456; Vism 168.

Soracca (nt.) [fr. sorata] gentleness, restraint, meekness A II.68, 113; III.248; S I.100, 172, 222; Sn 78, 292; Dhs 1342; J III.442; IV.302; Miln 162; VvA 347. Often comb[d] with khanti forbearance (q. v.). — soracciya (nt.) the same J III.453.

Sorata (adj.) [= su + rata, with so° for sū°, which latter is customary for su° before r (cp. dūr° for dur°). See du[1] 2 and Geiger, *P.Gr.* § 11. — The (B)Sk. is sūrata] gentle, kind, humble, self-restrained M I.125; S I.65; IV.305 (text, sūrata); A II.43; III.349, 393 sq.; Sn 309, 515, 540; J IV.303; DhA I.56.

Soḷasa (num. card.) [Sk. ṣoḍaśa] sixteen D I.128; Sn 1006; J I.78 (lekhā); II.87; III.342 (atappiya-vatthūni); V.175; VI.37; Miln 11 (palibodhā); DhA I.129 (°salākā); IV.208 (°karīsa-matta). instr. soḷasahi D I.31, & soḷasehi D I.139; gen. soḷasannaŋ J IV.124. Very frequent in measures of time & space. -°vassa° (16 years . . .) J I.231, 285; II.43; IV.7; VI.10, 486; DhA I.25 and passim. The fem. °-sī acts as num. ord. "sixteenth," in phrase kalaŋ nagghati soḷasiŋ he is not worth a sixteenth particle of A IV.252; S III.156; V.44, 343; Dh 70; It 19.

Soḷasakkhattuŋ sixteen times DA I.261; DhA I.353 = Mhvs 6, 37.

Soḷasama sixteenth Mhvs 2, 29; Vism 292.

Sovaggika (adj.) [fr. sagga = *svarga; cp. the similar formation dovārika = dvāra] connected with heaven Vin I.294; D I.51; A II.54, 68; III.46, 51, 259; IV.245; S I.90; DA I.158.

Sovacassa (nt.) [fr. suvaca, in analogy to dovacassa] gentleness, suavity D III.267; A II.148; III.180; Nett 40; 127; °-karaṇa making for gentleness M I.96; A II.148 = III.180.

Sovacassatā (f.) = sovacassa M I.126; D III.212, 274; A I.83; III.310, 423 sq., 449; IV.29; Sn 266; Dhs 1327; Pug 24. Sovaccasāya & sovacassiya the same (Dhs 1327; Pug 24).

Sovaṇṇa (adj.) [fr. suvaṇṇa] golden D II.210; A IV.393; PvA II.12[1]; J I.226; °-maya golden Vin I.39; II.116; D II.170 etc.; J II.112.

Sovaṇṇaya (adj.) [= sovaṇṇaka] golden J I.226.

Sovatthika (adj.) [either fr. sotthi with diæresis, or fr. su + atthi + ka = Sk. svastika] safe M I.117; Vv 18⁷ (= sotthika VvA 95); J VI.339 (in the shape of a svastika ?); Pv IV.3³ (= sotthi-bhāva-vāha PvA 250). -**ālankāra** a kind of auspicious mark J VI.488.

Sovīraka (nt.) [dialectical ?] sour gruel Vin I.210; S II.111; Vv 19⁸; PugA 232.

Sosa [fr. **śuṣ**] drying up, consumption Vin I.71; Vism 345.

Sosana (nt.) [fr. soseti] causing to dry (in surgery) Miln 353.

Sosānika (adj.) [fr. susāna] connected with a cemetery, bier-like Vin II.149; m., one who lives in or near a cemetery A III.220; Pug 69 sq.; Miln 342; Vism 61 sq.; DhA I.69.

Sosārita (adj.) [su + osārita] well reinstated (opp. dosārita) Vin I.322.

Sosika (adj.) [fr. sosa] afflicted with pulmonary consumption Vin I.93; IV.8.

Sosīta at J I.390 means either "thoroughly chilled" or "well wetted." It is expl^d as "him'odakena su-sīto suṭṭhu tinto." Perhaps we have to read **so sīta**, or **sīna** (cp. sīna^2), or **sinna**. The corresponding **sotatta** (expl^d as "suriya-santāpena su-tatto") should then be **so tatto**.

Soseti [Caus. of sussati] to cause to dry or wither Mhvs 21, 28; Vi n 120. See vi°.

Sossati is Fut. of suṇāti.

Sohada [Sk. sauhṛda, fr. su + hṛd] a friend Mhvs 38, 98. See also **suhada**.

Sneha see **sineha**.

Svākāra [su + ākāra] being of good disposition Vin I.6.

Svākkhāta [su + akkhāta; on the long ā cp. Geiger, *P.Gr.* § 7; BSk. svākhyāta] well preached Vin I.12, 187; II.199; M I.67; A I.34; II.56; Sn 567. Opp. durakkhāta Vism 213 (in detail).

Svāgata [su + āgata] 1. welcome Vin II.11; Th 2, 337; ThA 236. — 2. learnt by heart Vin II.95, 249; A IV.140 (pātimokkhāni). See sāgata.

Svātana [cp. Sk. śvastana; Geiger, *P.Gr.* § 6, 54] relating to the morrow; dat. °-nāya for the following day Vin I.27; D I.125; J I.11; DhA I.314; IV.12.

Svātivatta [su + ativatta] easily overcome Sn 785; Nd^1 76.

Svāssu = so assu J I.196.

Svāhaŋ = so ahaŋ.

Sve (adv.) [cp. Sk. śvas] to-morrow Vin II.77; D I.108, 205; J I.32, 243; II.47; VvA 230; svedivasa DhA I.103. The diæretic form is **suve**, e. g. Pv IV.1^5; Mhvs 29, 17; and doubled **suve suve** day after day Dh 229; DhA III.329; J V.507.

H.

Ha [freq. in Rigveda, as gha or ha, Idg. *gho, *ghe; cp. Lat. hi-c, Sk. hi] an emphatic particle "hey, oh, hallo, I say" Vin II.109; Sn 666; iti ha, thus Vin I.5, 12; D I.1; a common beginning to traditional instruction Sn 1053; itihītihaŋ (saying), "thus and thus" Sn 1084; SnA 416 (ha-kāra); PvA 4 (ha re), 58 (gloss for su).

Haŋ (indecl.) [cp. Sk. haŋ] an exclamation "I say, hey, hallo, look here!" Vv 50^8 (= nipāta VvA 212); J V.422; VvA 77. Sometimes as han ti, e. g. J V.203; DhA III.108. See also **handa** & **hambho**. In comb^n iti haŋ (= iti) Sn 783; Nd^1 71; or with other part. like haŋ dhī DhA I.179 216 (here as haŋ di).

Haŋsa^1 [fr. haŋsati] bristling: see lomahaŋsa Sn 270 etc

Haŋsa^2 [cp. Sk. haŋsa = Lat. (h)anser "goose," Gr. χήν = Ags. gōs = E. goose, Ger. gans] 1. a water-bird, swan S I.148; Sn 221, 350, 1134; Dh 91, 175; DhA II.170; J II.176 sq.; SnA 277; Pv II.12^3; III.3^4. Considered as (suvaṇṇa-) rāja-haŋsa ("golden royal swan") to be king of the birds: J I.207; II.353; Vism 650. — At SnA 277 Bdhgh gives various kinds of haŋsa's, viz. harita°, tamba°, khīra°, kāḷa°, pāka°, suvaṇṇa°. — **pāka°** a species of water bird J V.356; VI.539; SnA 277. — f. **haŋsī** Dāvs V.24 (rāja°). — 2. a kind of building J I.92. **-potaka** a young swan Vism 153 (in simile). **-rāja** the king of swans Vv 35^8; Vin IV.259.

Haŋsati [cp. Vedic harṣate Idg. ***ĝher** to bristle (of hair), as in Lat. horreo ("horrid, horripilation"), ēr hedgehog ("bristler") = Gr. χήρ id.; Lat. hirtus, hispidus "rough"; Ags. gorst = gorse; Ger. granne & many others, for which see Walde, *Lat. Wtb.* s. v. ēr. — The Dhtp (309) defines as "tuṭṭhi." See also ghaŋsati^2, pahaŋsati^2, pahaṭṭha^2, pahaŋsita^2] to bristle, stand on end (said of the hair) Vin III.8; M I.79; Caus. **haŋseti** to cause to bristle J V.154. — pp. **haṭṭha.**

Haŋsana (adj.-nt.) [fr. **hṛṣ**] bristling, see lomahaŋsa Sn 270 etc.

Haŋsi (indecl.) [?] = hañci if, in case that J VI.343.

Hankhati see paṭi°.

Hacca (adj.) [fr. **han**] killing in bhūnahacca killing an embryo A IV.98; J VI.579 = 587; Miln 314 (text bhūta-).

Hañci (indecl.) [haŋ + ci] if Kvu 1.

Haññati & hañchati see hanti.

Haṭa^1 [pp. of harati] taken, carried off Vin IV.23; J I.498. **haṭa-haṭa-kesa** with dishevelled hair S I.115.

Haṭa^2 [cp. Sk. haṭha & haṭa] a kind of water-plant, Pistia stratiotes D I.166; M I.78, 156; Pug 55 (text sāta-); A I.241, 295 (v. l. sāta; cp. hāṭaka).

Haṭṭha [pp. of haŋsati] 1. bristling, standing on end M I.83; Dāvs V.64; lomahaṭṭhajāta (cp. °loma) with bristling hairs, excited D II.240; Sn p. 14. — 2. joyful, happy Vin I.15; Sn 1017; J I.31, 335; II.32; often comb^d with either **tuṭṭha** (e. g. J VI.427; PvA 113), or **pahaṭṭha** (DhA III.292).

Haṭha [only as lexicogr. word; Dhtp 101 = balakkāra] violence.

Hata [pp. of hanti] struck, killed D II.131; destroyed, spoilt, injured Vin I.25; Dhs 264; J II.175; **reṇuhata** struck with dust, covered with dust Vin I.32; **hatatta** (nt.) the state of being destroyed Dh 390; **hatâvakāsa** who has cut off every occasion (for good and evil) Dh 97; DhA II.188; **hatâvasesaka** surviving D I.135; pakkha° a cripple (q. v.); °vikkhittaka slain & cut up, killed & dismembered Vism 179, 194. — **hata** is also used in sense of med., i. e. one who has destroyed or killed.

e. g. nāga° slayer of a *nāga* Vin II.195; °antarāya one who removes an obstacle PvA I. — ahata unsoiled, clean, new D II.160; J I.50; Dāvs II.39.

Hati (f.) [fr. **han**] destruction Dāvs IV.17.

Hattha [fr. **hr**, cp. Vedic hasta] 1. hand D I.124; A I.47; Sn 610; J VI.40. — forearm Vin IV.221; of animals S V.148; J I.149; °pāda hand and foot M I.523; A I.47; J II.117; PvA 241; DhA IV.7. sahassa° thousand-armed Mhvs 30, 75; pañca° having five hands J V.425; J V.431 (mukhassa ceva catunnaŋ ca caranānaŋ vasena etaŋ vuttaŋ); kata° a practised hand, practised (of an archer) S I.62; A II.48; J IV.211. — hatthe karoti to bring under one's hand, to take possession of, to subdue J VI.490; hatthaŋ gacchati to come under somebody's hand, to come under the sway of J I.179; hatthaga being in the power of; hatthagata fallen into the hand or possession of, hatthappatta what one can put one's hand on, i. e. "before his very eyes" Vin I.15. As °hattha in hand, -handed; e. g. daṇḍa° stick in hand J I.59; ritta° empty-handed Sdhp 309; vīṇā° lute in hand Mhvs 30, 75. Cp. sa° with one's own hand. — 2. the hand as measure, a cubit J I.34, 233 (asīti°, q. v.); Mhvs 38, 52; Vism 92 (nava° sāṭaka). — 3. a handful, a tuft (of hair) VvA 197.

-anguli finger PvA 124 (+pādanguli toe). -aṭṭhika hand-bone KhA 49. -antara a cubit Vism 124. -âpalekhana licking the hands (to clean them after eating — cp. the 52nd Sekhiya Vin IV.198) D I.166; III.40; M I.77, 238, 307; A I.295 (v. l. °āva°); Pug 55. -ābharaṇa bracelet Vin II.106. -âbhijappana (nt.) incantations to make a man throw up his hands D I.11; DA I.97. -âlankāra a (wrist) bracelet, wristlet VvA 167. -kacchapaka making a hollow hand J III.505. -kamma manual work, craft, workmanship, labour J I.220; DhA I.98, 395; IV.64. -gata received, come into the possession of J I.446; II.94, 105; VvA 149; (nt.) possession J VI.392. -gahana seizing by the hand Vin IV.220. -cchinna whose hand is cut off M I.523; Miln 5. -ccheda cutting off the hand J I.155 (read sugatiyā va hatthacchedādi). -cchedana = °cheda J IV.192; DhA III.482. -tala palm of the hand VvA 7. -ttha [cp. Sk. hasta-stha, of **sthā**] lit. standing in the hand of somebody, being in somebody's power (cp. hattha-gata); used as abstr. hatthattha (nt.) power, captivity, °ŋ gacchati & āgacchati to come into the power of (gen.), to be at the mercy of [cp. hattha-gata & hatthaŋ gacchati] J II.383 (āyanti hatthatthaŋ); IV.420, 459; V.346 (°ŋ āgata). As pp. hatth-attha-gata in somebody's power J I.244; III.204; VI.582. An abstr. is further formed fr. hatthattha as hatthatthatā J V.349 (°taŋ gata). The BSk. equivalent is hastatvaŋ MVastu II.182. -pajjotikā hand-illumination, scorching of the hand (by holding it in a torch), a kind of punishment M I.87; A I.47; II.122; Miln 197; Nd^1 154. -patāpaka a coal-pan, heating of the hand Vv 33^{32}; VvA 147; see mandāmukhi. -pasāraṇa stretching out one's hand Vism 569. -pāsa the side of the hand, vicinity Vin IV.221, 230. -bandha a bracelet D I.7; DA I.89. -vaṭṭaka hand-cart Vin II.276. -vikāra motion of the hand J IV.491. -sāra hand-wealth, movable property DhA I.240; J I.114; DA I.216.

Hatthaka [hattha+ka] a handful, a quantity (lit. a little hand) Vv 45^5 (=kalāpa VvA 197).

Hatthin [Vedic hastin, lit. endowed with a hand, i. e. having a trunk] an elephant Vin I.218, 352; II.194 sq. (Nālāgiri) = J V.335 (nom. sg. hatthī; gen. hatthissa); D I.5; A II.209; J I.358; II.102; DhA I.59 (correct haṭṭhi l), 80 (acc. pl. hatthī); size of an elephant Miln 312; one of the seven treasures D I.89; II.174; often mentioned together with *horses* (°ass'ādayo), e. g. A IV.107; M III.104; Vism 269; DhA I.392. ekacārika-h., an elephant who wanders alone, a royal elephant J III.175; caṇḍa h. rogue elephant M I.519; DA I.37. — hatthinī (f.) a she-elephant Dh 105. hatthinikā (f.) the same Vin I.277; D I.49; DA I.147.

-atthara elephant rug Vin I.192; D I.7; A I.181. -âcariya elephant trainer Vin I.345; J II.94, 221, 411; IV.91; Miln 201. -āroha mounted on an elephant, an elephant-driver D I.51; S IV.310. -âlankāra elephant's trappings J II.46. -kanta = manta el. charm DhA I.163. -kantavīṇā lute enticing an elephant DhA I.163. -kalabha the young of an elephant A IV.435. -kumbha the frontal globe of an elephant J II.245. -kula elephant species, *ten* enum^d at VbhA 397. -kkhandha the shoulder or back of an elephant J I.313; Mhvs VI.24. PvA 75, 178. -gopaka an elephant's groom or keeper J I.187. -damaka elephant tamer M III.132, 136; SnA 161. -damma an elephant in training M III.222. -nakha a sort of turrent projecting over the approach to a gate; °*ka* provided with such turrets, or supported on pillars with capitals of elephant heads Vin II.169. -pada an elephant's foot M I.176, 184; S V.43; J I.94. -pākāra "elephant-wall," wall of the upper storey with figures of elephants in relief Mhvs 35, 5. See Geiger, *Mhvs trsl*^{n} 228, n. 2. -ppabhinna a furious elephant Dh 326; M I.236. -bandha J I.135 = hatthibhaṇḍa. -bhaṇḍa an elephant-keeper Vin I.85; II.194. -magga elephant track J II.102. -mangala an elephant festival J II.46. -matta only as big as an elephant J I.303. -māraka elephant hunter DhA I.80. -meṇḍa an elephant's groom J III.431; V.287; VI.498. -yāna an elephant carriage, a riding elephant D I.49; DA I.147; PvA 55. -yuddha combat of elephant's (as a theatrical show) D I.6. -rūpaka elephant image or picture, toy elephant (+assa°) DhA II.69. -laṇḍa elephant dung DhA IV.156. -lingasakuṇa a vulture with a bill like an elephant's trunk DhA I.164. -vatta elephant habit Nd 92. -sālā elephant stable Vin I.277; II.194; DhA I.393. -sippa the elephant lore, the professional knowledge of elephant-training J II.221 sq. -sutta an elephant-trainer's manual J II.46 (cp. Mallinātha on Raghuv. VI.27). -soṇḍaka "elephant trunk," an under-garment arranged with appendages like elephant trunks Vin II.137.

Hadaya [Vedic hṛdaya, hṛd = Av. zǝrǝdā, *not* the same as Lat. cor(dem), but perhaps = Lat. haru entrails (haruspex). See *K.Z.* XL.419] the heart. — 1. the physical organ D II.293; S I.207 (ettha uro hadayan ti vuttaŋ DhsA 140); in detail: Vism 256, 356; VbhA 60, 239. — 2. the heart as seat of thought and feeling, esp. of strong emotion (as in Vedas!), which shows itself in the action of the heart S I.199. Thus defined as "cintā" at Dhtm 535 (as **had**), or as "hadayaŋ vuccati cittaŋ," with ster. expl^n "mano mānasa paṇḍara" etc. Dhs 17; Nd^1 412. Cp. DhsA 140 (cittaŋ abbhantar' aṭṭhena hadayan ti vuttaŋ). — With citta at Sn p. 32 (hadayaŋ te phalessāmi "I shall break your heart"); hadayaŋ phalitaŋ a broken heart J I.65; DhA I.173. chinna h. id. J V.180. hadayassa santi calmness of h. A V.64 sq.; hadayā hadayaŋ aññāya tacchati M I.32. h. nibbāyi the heart (i. e. anger) cooled down J VI.349; h. me avakaḍḍhati my heart is distraught J IV.415. — duhadaya bad-hearted J VI.469.

-aṭṭhi a bone of the heart KhA 49, 50 (so read for pādaṭṭhi, see App. to Pj I.); Vism 255; SnA 116. -gata [°ngata] gone to the heart, learnt by heart Miln 10. -gama [°ngama] heart-stirring, pleasant, agreeable D I.4; III.173; M I.345; A II.209; V.205; Vin III.77; Nd^1 446; Dhs 1343; DA I.75. -pariḷāha heart-glow Miln 318. -phālana bursting of the heart J I.282. -maŋsa the flesh of the heart, the heart J I.278, 347; II.159 etc. (very frequent in the Jātakas); DhA I.5; II.90. -bheda "heart-break," a certain trick in cheating with measures DA I.79. -vañcana deluding the heart SnA 183 (cp. J VI.388 hadaya-tthena). -vatthu (1) the substance of the heart Miln 281; DhsA 140.

(2) "heart-basis," the heart as basis of mind, sensorium commune Tikp 17, 26, 53 sq., 62, 256; Vism 447; SnA 228; DhsA 257, 264. See the discussion at *Dhs. trsl*[n] lxxxvi. and *Cpd.* 277 sq. -santāpa heart-burn, i. e. grief, sorrow Vism 54. -ssita stuck in the heart (of salla, dart) Sn 938; Nd[1] 411.

Han (indecl.) see haŋ.

Hanati[1] (& hanti) [**han** or **ghan** to smite, Idg. ***guhen,** as in Av. jainti to kill; Gr. θείνω to strike, φόνος murder; Lat. de-fendo "defend" & of-fendo; Ohg. gundea = Ags. gūð "battle." The Dhtp (363 & 429) gives "hiŋsā" as meaning of **han**] 1. to strike, to thresh S IV.201; J IV.102. — 2. to kill D I.123; A IV.97 (asinā hanti attānaŋ); Sn 125; Dh 405; maggaŋ° to slay travellers on the road J I.274; III.220. — 3. to destroy, to remove Sn 118; Dh 72. — *Forms:* Pres. 1st sg. hanāmi J II.273; 2nd sg. hanāsi J III.199; V.460; 3rd sg. hanti Sn 118; A IV.97; DhA II.73 (= vināseti); Dh 72; hanāti J V.461; hanati J I.432; 1st pl. hanāma J I.200; 3rd pl. hananti Sn 669. Imper. hana J III.185; hanassu J V.311; hanantu J IV.42; Dh 355; J I.368. Pot. hane Sn 394, 400; haneyya D I.123; Sn 705. ppr. a-hanaŋ not killing D I.116; hananto J I.274. fut. hanissati J IV.102; hañchati J IV.102; hañchema J II.418. aor. hani Mhvs 25, 64; 3rd pl. haniŋsu Sn 295; J I.256; ger. hantvā Sn 121; Dh 294 sq.; hanitvāna J III.185. — Pass. haññati D II.352; S IV.175; Sn 312; J I.371; IV.102; DhA II.28. ppr. haññamāna S IV.201. grd. hantabba D II.173. aor. pass. haññiŋsu D I.141. fut. haññissati DA I.134. — Caus. hanāpeti to cause to slay, destroy J I.262; DA I.159; ghātāpeti Vin I.277; ghāteti to cause to slay Dh 405; Sn 629; a-ghātayaŋ, not causing to kill S I.116; Pot. ghātaye Sn 705; ghātayeyya Sn 394; aor. aghātayi Sn 308; ghātayi Sn 309; pass. ghātīyati Miln 186. See also ghāteti. Cp. upahanati, vihanati; °gha, ghāta etc., paligha.

Hanati[2] [***han** for **had,** probably from pp. hanna. The Dhtm (535) gives **had** in meaning of "uccāra ussagga"] to empty the bowels Pv IV.8[8] (= vaccaŋ osajjate PvA 268). — pp. hanna. Cp. ūhanati[2] & ohanati.

Hanana (nt.) [fr. hanati] killing, striking, injuring Mhvs 3. 42.

Hanu (f.) [Vedic hanu; cp. Lat. gena jaw, Gr. γένυς chin, Goth. kinnus = Ger. kinn = E. chin, Oir. gin mouth] the jaw D I.11; J I.28 (mahā°), 498; SnA 30 (°sañcalana); VbhA 145 (°sañcopana). °-saŋhanana jaw-binding, incantations to bring on dumbness D I.11; DA I.97.

Hanukā (f.) [fr. hanu] the jaw J I.498; DA I.97; Miln 229; also nt. Vin II.266; J I.461; II.127; IV.188; **-°aṭṭhika** the jaw bone J I.265 sq.; Vism 251; VbhA 58; KhA 49; SnA 116.

Hantar [n. ag. fr. hanati] a striker, one who kills D I.56; A II.116 sq.; III.161 sq.; S I.85; Dh 389.

Handa (indecl.) [cp. Sk. hanta, haŋ + ta] an exhortative-emphatic particle used like Gr. ἄγε δή or French allons, voilà: well then, now, come along, alas! It is constructed with 1st pres. & fut., or imper. 2nd person D I.106, 142; II.288; Sn 153, 701, 1132; J I.88, 221, 233; III.135; DA I.237 (= vavasāy'atthe nipāto); Nd[2] 697 (= padasandhi); Pv I.10[3] (= gaṇha PvA 49); II.3[21] (= upasagg'atthe nipāta PvA 88); DhA I.16, 410 (handa je); SnA 200 (vyavasāne), 491 (id.); VvA 230 (hand'-âhaŋ gamissāmi).

Hanna (nt.) [pp. of hanati[2]] easing oneself, emptying of the bowels; su° a good (i. e. modest) performance of bodily evacuation, i. e. modesty J I.421.

Hambho (indecl.) [haŋ + bho] a particle expressing surprise or haughtiness J I.184, 494. See also **ambho.**

Hammiya (nt.) [cp. Vedic harmya house & BSk. harmikā "summer-house" (?) Divy 244] customarily given as "a long, storied mansion which has an upper chamber placed on the top," a larger building, pāsāda, (store-) house Vin I.58, 96, 239; II.146 (with vihāra, aḍḍhayoga, pāsāda, guhā, as the 5 lenāni), 152, 195; Miln 393; Nd[1] 226 = Vism 25. °-gabbha a chamber on the upper storey Vin II.152.

Haya [cp. Vedic haya, fr. **hi** to impel. A diff. etym. see Walde, *Lat. Wtb.* s. v. haedus] 1. a horse Vv 64[1]; J II.98; Miln 2. — 2. speed M I.446. -°vāhin drawn by horses J VI.125.

Hara (adj.) (-°) [fr. **hṛ**] taking, fetching; vayo° bringing age (said of grey hairs) J I.138; du° S I.36.

Haraṇa (nt.) [fr. **hṛ**] taking, seizing, removing J I.117, 118, 232; DA I.71. kucchi° n. filling of the belly J I.277. °bhatta a meal to take along DhA II.144.

Haraṇaka (nt.) [fr. haraṇa] goods in transit, movable goods Vin III.51.

Haraṇī (f.) [fr. haraṇa] 1. a nerve conveying a stimulus (lit. "carrier"); only used with rasa° nerve of taste Vin II.137; usually given as "a hundred thousand" in number, e. g. J V.4, 293, 458; DhA I.134. — 2. in kaṇṇamala°, an instrument to remove the wax from the ear Vin II.135. Cp. hāraka.

Harati [Idg. ***ĝher;** in meaning "take" cp. Gr. χείρ hand; in meaning "comprise" cp. Lat. cohors, Gr. χόρτος; Ags. geard = yard. — The Dhtm expl[s] **har** laconically by "haraṇa"] 1. to carry J II.176; Dh 124; to take with one D I.8, 142; opposed to paccāharati VbhA 349-354; SnA 52-58. — 2. to bring J I.208; to offer J I.238; Sn 223. — 3. to take, gather (fruits) Miln 263. — 4. to fetch, buy J I.291 (mama santikā). — 5. to carry away, to remove D II.160, 166; J I.282; Sn 469; Mhvs 1, 26; to do away with, to abolish J I.345. — 6. to take away by force, to plunder, steal D I.52; J I.187; V.254. — 7. to take off, to destroy J I.222 (jīvitaŋ), 310 (visaŋ); to kill J I.281. — *Forms:* aor. ahāsi Sn 469 sq.; Dh 3; J IV.308; cp. upasaŋhāsi S V.214; pahāsi, pariyuḍāhāsi, ajjhupāhari; ger. haritvā D II.160; **hātūna** J IV.280 (= haritvā C.); inf. harituŋ J I.187; hātave Th 1, 186; hātuŋ: see voharati; hattuŋ: see āharati; Fut. hāhiti J VI.500 (= harissati). — Pass. harīyati M I.33; hīrati J V.254; pret. ahīratha J V.253; grd. haritabba J I.187, 281. — pp. haṭa. — Caus. hāreti to cause to take Sn 395; to cause to be removed, to remove J I.345; II.176; III.431 (somebody out of office); hāretabba that which should be taken out of the way J I.298; Caus. II. harāpeti to cause to be brought, to offer Vin I.245; J II.38; to cause to be taken (as a fine) Miln 193.

Harāyati [Denom. fr. hiri (= hrī), cp. Vedic **hrī** to be ashamed, Pres. jihreti. — The Dhtp (438) gives roots **hiri & hara** in meaning "lajjā"] 1. to be ashamed Vin I.88; II.292; D I.213; M I.120; S IV.62; It 43; Pv I.10[2]; ppr. harāyanto Nd[1] 466, & harāyamāna J IV.171; Nd[2] 566. Often comb[d] with **aṭṭiyati** (q. v.). See also hiriyati. — 2. [in this meaning = Vedic **hṛ** to be angry. Pres. hṛṇīte] to be depressed or vexed, to be cross, to worry (cp. hiriyati) J V.366 (ppr. hariyyamāna); Th 1, 1173 (mā hari "don't worry").

Hari (adj.) [Idg. ***ĝhel,** as in Lat. helvus yellow, holus cabbage; Sk. harita, hariṇa pale (yellow or green), hiri (yellow); Av. zairi; Gr. χλόος green, χλόη "greens"; Ags. geolo = E. yellow. Also the words for "gold": hāṭaka & hiraññya] green, tawny Dhs 617; DhsA 317; °-ssavaṇṇa gold-coloured J II.33 (= hari-samāna-vaṇṇa suvaṇṇa° C.).

-candana yellow sandal Vv 83[1]; DhA I.28; -tāla yellow orpiment Th 2, 393; DhA III.29; IV.113; -ttaca gold-coloured Th 2, 333; ThA 235; -pada gold foot, yellow leg, a deer J III.184.

Hariṇa [fr. hari] a deer J II.26.

Harita (adj.) [see hari for etym.] 1. green, pale(-green), yellowish. It is expl[d] by Dhpāla as nīla (e. g. VvA 197; PvA 158), and its connotation is not fixed. — Vin I.137; D I.148; S I.5; J I.86, 87; II.26, 110; Pv II.12[10] (bank of a pond); Vv 45[7] (°patta, with green leaves, of a lotus); J II.110 (of wheat); SnA 277 (°haŋsa yellow, i. e. golden swan). — 2. green, fresh Vin III.16; A V.234 (kusa); nt. (collectively) vegetables, greens Vin 266 (here applied to a field of fresh (i. e. green) wheat or cereal in general, as indicated by expl[n] "haritaŋ nāma pubbaṇṇaŋ aparaṇṇaŋ" etc.); cp. haritapaṇṇa vegetables SnA 283. — 3. haritā (f.) gold Th 1, 164=J II.334 (°maya made of gold; but expl[d] as "harita-maṇi parikkhata" by C.). — 4. Two cpds., rather odd in form, are haritāmātar "son of a green frog" J II.238 (in verse); and haritupattā (bhūmi) "covered with green" M I.343; J I.50, 399.

Haritaka (nt.) [harita+ka] a pot-herb D II.342.

Haritatta (nt.) [abstr. fr. harita] greenness Vin I.96.

Harītaka [cp. Epic Sk. harītaka] yellow myrobalan (Terminalia citrina or chebula) Vin I.201, 206; J I.80; IV.363; Miln 11; DhsA 320 (T. harīṭaka); VvA 5 (ṭ); °-kī (f.) the myrobalan tree Vin I.30; M III.127. pūtiharītakī Vism 40; °paṇṇika all kinds of greens Vin II.267.

Hareṇukā (f.) [cp. Sk. hareṇukā] a pea M I.245; J V.405 (=aparaṇṇajā ti 406); VI.537; hareṇuka-yūsa pea-soup M I.245 (one of the 4 kinds of soup).

Halaŋ=hi alaŋ (q. v.); "halaŋ dāni pakāsituŋ" why should I preach? Vin I.5=D II.36=M I.168=S I.136.

Halāhala[1] [onomat.; cp. Sk. halāhala] a kind of deadly poison, usually as °visa J I.271, 273, 380; III.103; V.465; Miln 256; Vism 57; ThA 287.

Halāhala[2] (nt.) [onomat.] uproar, tumult J I.47 sq.; Miln 122. Cp. kolāhala.

Haliddā & **Haliddī** (f.) [cp. Sk. haridrā] turmeric. — 1. haliddā: Vin I.201; J V.89. — 2. haliddī (haliddi°) M I.127; A III.230, 233; S II.101; KhA 64; °rāga like the colour of turmeric, or like the t. dye, i. e not fast, quickly changing & fading J III.148 (of citta), cp. J III.524 sq.

Hava [cp. Vedc hava; **hū** or **hvā** to call] calling, challenge Dāvs II.14.

Have (indecl.) [ha+ve] indeed, certainly Vin I.2; D II.168; S I.169; Sn 120, 181, 323, 462; Dh 104, 151, 177, 382; J I.31, 365; DhA II.228.

Havya (nt.) [Vedic havya; fr. **hū** to sacrifice] an oblation, offering S I.169; Sn 473 sq.; 490.

Hasati & **Hassati** [owing to similarity of meaning the two roots **has** to laugh (Sk. hasati, pp. hasita) & **hṛṣ** to be excited (Sk. hṛṣyati, pp. hṛṣita & hṛṣṭa) have become mixed in Pāli (see also hāsa). — The usual (differentiated) correspondent of Sk. hṛṣyati is haŋsati. The Dhtp (309) gives haŋsa (=harṣa) with tuṭṭhi, and (310) hasa with hasana] 1. to laugh, to be merry; pres. hasati Bu I.28; Mhvs 35, 59; hassati Sn 823, 829; ppr. hasamāna is preferable v. l. at J IV.281 for bhāsamāna; aor. hasi J II.103; DhA II.17.— Caus. hāseti [i. e. both fr. **has** & **hṛṣ**] to cause to laugh; to please, to gladden Mhvs 32, 46; J VI.217, 304; DhA II.85; aor. hāsesi Vin III.84; ppr. hāsayamāna making merry J I.163, 209 210; ger. hāsayitvāna Miln 1. — Caus. II. hāsāpeti SnA 401; J VI.311. Cp. pari°, pa°. — 2. to neigh (of horses) J I.62; VI.581 (strange aor. hasissiŋsu, expl[d] as hasiŋsu by C.). — pp. hasita (& haṭṭha).

Hasana (nt.) [fr. hasati] laughter Dhtp 31.

Hasamānaka (adj.) [ppr. of hasati+ka] laughing, merry Mhvs 35, 55; (nt.) as adv. °ŋ jokingly, for fun Vin I.185.

Hasita [pp. of hasati, representing both Sk. hasita & hṛṣita] laughing, merry; (nt.) laughter, mirth A I.261; Pv III.3[5] (=hasitavant hasita-mukhin C.); Miln 297; Bu I.28; J I.62 (? read hesita); III.223; Vism 20.
-uppāda "genesis of mirth," æsthetic faculty Tikp 276; see *Cpd.* 20 sq.

Hasula (adj.) [fr. **has**] is rather doubtful ("of charming speech"? or "smiling"?). It occurs in (corrupted) verse at J VI.503=Ap 40 (& 307), which is to be read as "aḷāra-bhamukhā (or °pamhā) hasulā susoññā tanu-majjhimā." See Kern's remarks at *Toev.* s. v. hasula.

Hassa (adj.-nt.) [fr. **has**, cp. Sk. hāsya] ridiculous Sn 328; (nt.) 1. laughter, mirth D I.19; Sn 926; DA I.72; PvA 226; DhA III.258; Miln 266. — 2. a joke, jest hassā pi, even in fun M I.415; hassena pi the same J V.481; Miln 220; °vasena in jest J I.439.

Hā (indecl.) an exclamation of grief, alas! ThA 154 (Ap V.154); VvA 323, 324.

Hāṭaka (nt.) [cp. Sk. hāṭaka, connected with hari; cp. Goth. gulþ=E. gold] gold A I.215; IV.255, 258, 262 (where T reads haṭaka, with sātaka as v. l. at all passages); Th 2, 382; J V.90.

Hātabba at Nett 7, 32 may be interpreted as grd. of **hā** to go (pres. jihīte). The C. expl[s] it as "gametabba, netabba" (i. e. to be understood). Doubtful.

Hātūna see harati.

Hāna (nt.) [fr. **hā**, cp. Sk. hāna] relinquishing, giving up, falling off; decrease, diminution, degradation A II.167; III.349 sq. (opp. visesa), 427; Vism 11.
-gāmin going into disgrace or insignificance A III.49 sq. -bhāgiya conducive to relinquishing (of perversity and ignorance) D III.272 sq.; A II.167; Nett 77; Vism 85.

Hāni (f.) [cp. Sk. hāni] 1. decrease, loss A II.434; V.123 sq.; S I.111; II.206, 242; J I.338, 346. — 2. falling off, waste Mhvs 33, 103. Cp. saŋ°, pari°.

Hāpana at J V.433 is with Kern. *Toev.* I.132 (giving the passage without ref.) to be read as hāpaka "neglectful" [i. e. fr. hāpeti[1]].

Hāpita [pp. of hāpeti[2]] cultivated, attended, worshipped J IV.221; V.158 (aggihuttaŋ ahāpitaŋ; C. wrongly=hāpita); V.201=VI.565. On all passages & their relation to Com. & BSk. see Kern, *Toev.* I.132, 133.

Hāpeti[1] [Caus. of **hā** to leave: see jahati; to which add *fut.* 2nd sg. hāhasi J III.172; and *aor.* jahi J IV.314; V.469] 1. to neglect, omit A III.44 (ahāpayaŋ); IV.25; Dh 166; J II.437; IV.182; ahāpetvā without omitting anything, i. e. fully A II.77; J IV.132; DA I.99. atthaŋ hāpeti to lose one's advantage, to fail Sn 37; J I.251. — 2. to postpone, delay (the performance of . . .) J III.448; Vism 129. — 3. to cause to reduce, to beat down J I.124; II.31. — 4. to be lost Sn 90 (? read hāyati).

Hāpeti[2] [in form=Sk. (Sūtras) hāvayati, Caus. of juhoti (see juhati), but in meaning=juhoti] to sacrifice to, worship, keep up, cultivate J V.195 (aggiŋ;=juhati C.). See Kern, *Toev.* I.133. — pp. hāpita.

Hāyati is Pass. of jahati [**hā**], in sense of "to be left behind," as well as "to diminish, dwindle or waste away, disappear," e. g. Nd[1] 147 (+pari°, antaradhāyati); Miln 297 (+khīyati); ppr. hāyamāna Nd[2] 543. Cp. hāyana.

Hāyana[1] (nt.) [fr. **hā**] diminution, decay, decrease D I.54; DA I.165. Opposed to vaḍḍhana (increase) at M I.518.

Hāyana[2] (nt.) [Vedic hāyana] year; in saṭṭhi° 60 years old (of an elephant) M I.229; J II.343; VI.448, 581.

Hāyin (adj.) [fr. **hā**] abandoning, leaving behind Sn 755 = It 62 (maccu°).

Hāra [fr. harati] 1. that which may be taken; grasping, taking; grasp, handful, booty. In cpd. °hārin taking all that can be taken, rapacious, ravaging J VI.581 (of an *army*; Kern, *Toev.* I.133 wrong in trsl[n] "magnificent, or something like it"). Of a *river*: tearing, rapid A III.64; IV.137; Vism 231. — 2. category; name of the first sections of the Netti Pakaraṇa Nett 1 sq., 195.

Hāraka (adj.) [fr. hāra] carrying, taking, getting; removing (f. hārikā) M I.385; J I.134, 479; Pv II.9[1] (dhana°); SnA 259 (maŋsa°). — mala° an instrument for removing ear-wax Ap 303; cp. haraṇī. sattha° a dagger carrier, assassin Vin III.73; S IV.62. See also vallī.

Hāri (adj.) [fr. **hṛ**; cp. Sk. hāri] attractive, charming S IV.316; J I.204 (°sadda).

Hārika (adj.) [fr. hāra] carrying D II.348.

Hārin (adj.) [fr. hāra] 1. taking, carrying (f. hārinī) J I.133; Pv II.3[10] (nom. pl. f. hārī); PvA 113. — 2. robbing J I.204. — Cp. hāra°.

Hāriya (adj.) [fr. hāra] carrying Vv 50[9]; ThA 200; VvA 212.

Hālidda (adj.) [fr. haliddā] dyed with turmeric; a° undyed, i. e. not changing colour J III.88; cp. III.148.

Hāsa [fr. **has**, cp. Sk. hāsa & harṣa] laughter; mirth, joy Dh 146; DA I.228 = SnA 155 ("āmeṇḍita"); J I.33; II.82; V.112; Miln 390. See also ahāsa.
 -kara giving pleasure, causing joy Miln 252. -kkhaya ceasing of laughter Dhtp 439 (in def[n] of gilāna, illness). -dhamma merriment, sporting Vin IV.112.

Hāsaniya (adj.) [fr. **has** or **hṛṣ**; cp. Sk. harṣaniya] giving joy or pleasure Miln 149.

Hāsu° (of uncertain origin) occurs with hāsa° in comb[n] with °pañña and is customarily taken in meaning "of bright knowledge" (i. e. hāsa + paññā), wise, clever. The syn. javana-pañña points to a meaning like "quick-witted," thus implying "quick" also in hāsu. Kern, *Toev.* I.134 puts forth the ingenious expl[n] that hāsu is a "cockneyism" for āsu = Sk. āśu "quick," which does not otherwise occur in Pāli. Thus his expl[n] remains problematic. — See e. g. M III.25; S I.63; V.376; J IV.136; VI.255, 329. — Abstr. °tā wisdom S V.412; A I.45.

Hāseti see hasati.

Hāhasi is 2nd sg. fut. of jahati (e. g. J III.172); in cpd. also °hāhisi: see vijahati.

Hāhiti is fut. of harati.

Hi (indecl.) [cp. Sk. hi] for, because; indeed, surely Vin I.13; D I.4; Dh 5; Sn 21; Pv II.1[18]; II.7[10] (= hi saddo avadhāraṇe PvA 103); SnA 377 (= hi kāro nipāto pada-pūraṇa-matto); PvA 70, 76. In verse J IV.495. h'etaŋ = hi etaŋ; no h'etaŋ not so D I.3. hevaŋ = hi evaŋ.

Hiŋsati [**hiŋs**, Vedic hinasti & hiŋsanti] 1. to hurt, injure D II.243; S I.70; Sn 515; Dh 132; Pv II.9[9] (= bādheti C.); III.4[2] (= paribādheti C.); SnA 460. — 2. to kill M I.39; Dh 270. Caus. II. hiŋsāpeti PvA 123. — Cp. vi°.

Hiŋsana (nt.) [fr. **hiŋs**] striking, hurting, killing Mhvs 15, 28.

Hiŋsā (f.) [Vedic hiŋsā] injury, killing J I.445; Dhtp 387. hiŋsa-mano wish to destroy Dh 390. Opp. a°.

Hiŋsitar [n. ag. fr. hiŋsati] one who hurts D II.243; J IV.121.

Hikkā (f.) [cp. Epic Sk. hikkā, fr. **hikk** to sob; onomat.] hiccup Sdhp 279.

Hikkāra [hik + kāra] = hikkā, VbhA 70.

Hinkāra (indecl.) [hiŋ = hi, + kāra, i. e. the syllable "hiŋ"] an exclamation of surprise or wonder J VI.529 (C. hin ti kāraṇaŋ).

Hingu (nt.) [Sk. hingu] the plant asafetida Vin I.201; VvA 186.
 -cuṇṇa powder of asafetida DhA IV.171. -rāja a sort of bird J VI.539.

Hingulaka [cp. Sk. hingula, nt.] vermilion; as jāti° J V.67, 416; VvA[4], 168. Also as °ikā (f.) VvA 324.

Hinguli [Sk. hinguli] vermilion Mhvs 27, 18.

Hiṇḍati [*Sk. **hiṇḍ**] to roam Dhtp 108 (= āhiṇḍana). See ā°.

Hita (adj.) [pp. of dahati[1]] useful, suitable, beneficial, friendly A I.58, 155 sq.; II.191; D III.211 sq.; Dh 163. — (m.) a friend, benefactor Mhvs 3, 37. — (nt.) benefit, blessing, good Vin I.4; Sn 233; A II.96 sq., 176; It 78; SnA 500. — Opp. ahita A I.194; M I.332.
 -ânukampin friendly & compassionate D I.4, 227; Sn 693; J I.241, 244. -ûpacāra beneficial conduct, saving goodness J I.172. -esin desiring another's welfare, well-wishing M II.238; S IV.359; V.157; °*tā* seeking another's welfare, solicitude Dhs 1056; DhsA 362; VvA 260. -kara a benefactor Mhvs 4, 65.

Hinati [**hi**, hinoti] to send; only in cpd. pahiṇati.

Hintāla [hiŋ + tāla] a kind of palm, Phœnix paludosa Vin I.190; DhA III.451.

Hindagu [probably for indagu, inda + gu (= °ga), i. e. sprung from Indra. The h perhaps fr. **hindu**. The spelling h° is a corrupt one] man, only found in the Niddesa in stock def[n] of jantu or nara; both spellings (with & without h) occur; see Nd[1] 3 = Nd[2] 249.

Hima (adj.-n.) [cp. Vedic hima; Gr. χεῖμα & χειμών winter, χιών snow; Av. zaya winter; Lat. hiems etc.] cold, frosty DhsA 317. — (nt.) ice, snow J III.55.
 -pāta-samaya the season of snow-fall Vin I.31, 288; M I.79; J I.390; Miln 396. -vāta a snow or ice wind J I.390.

Himavant (adj.) [hima + vant] snowy J V.63 (= hima-yutta C.). (m.) Himavā the Himālaya: see Dict. of Names.

Hiyyo (adv.) [Vedic hyaḥ, Gr. χθές, Lat. heri; Goth. gistradagis "to-morrow," E. yester-day, Ger. gestern etc.] yesterday Vin I.28; II.77; J I.70, 237; V.461; VI.352, 386; Miln 9. In sequence ajja hiyyo pare it seems to mean "to-morrow"; thus at Vin IV.63, 69; J IV.481 (= sve C.). See para 2. c.

Hirañña (nt.) [Vedic hiraṇya; see etym. under hari & cp. Av. zaranya gold] gold Vin I.245, 276; II.159; A IV.393; Sn 285, 307, 769; Nd[2] 11; gold-piece S I.89; J I.92. Often together with suvaṇṇa Vin I.150; D II.170; h°-suvaṇṇaŋ gold & money M III.175; J I.341. °olokana (-kamma) valuation of gold J II.272.

Hiri & **hirī** (f.) [cp. Vedic hrī] sense of shame, bashfulness, shyness S I.33; D III.212; A I.51, 95; III.4 sq., 331, 352; IV.11, 29; Sn 77, 253, 719; Pug 71; Pv IV.7[3]; J I.129, 207; Nett 50, 82; Vism 8. Expl[d] Pug 23 sq.; is one of the cāga-dhana's: see cāga (cp. Jtm 31[1]). — Often contrasted to & combined with ottappa (cp. below) fear of sin: A I.51; D III.284; S II.206; It 36; Nett 39; their difference is expl[d] at Vism 464 ("kāya-duccarit' ādīhi hiriyatī ti hiri; lajjāy' etaŋ adhivacanaŋ; tehi yeva ottappatī ti ottappaŋ; pāpato ubbegass' etaŋ adhivacanaŋ"); J I.129 sq.; DhsA 124.

-ottappa shame & fear of sin M I.271; S II.220; It 34; A II.78; J I.127, 206; Tikp 61; Vism 221; DhA III.73. Frequently spelt otappa, e. g. J I.129; It 36. -kopīna a loin cloth M I.10; Vism 31, 195. -nisedha restrained by conscience S I.7, 168 = Sn 462; Dh 143; DhA III.86. -bala the power of conscientiousness A II.150; Dhs 30, 101. -mana modest in heart, conscientious D II.78; M I.43; S II.159.

Hirika (& hirīka) (adj.) [fr. hiri] having shame, only as -° in neg. ahirika shameless, unscrupulous A I.51, 85; II.219; Pug 19; It 27 (°īka); J I.258 (chinna° id.); nt. °ŋ unscrupulousness Pug 19.

Hirimant (& hirīmant) (adj.) [fr. hiri] bashful, modest, shy D III.252, 282; S II.207 sq.; IV.243 sq.; A II.218, 227; III.2 sq., 7 sq., 112; IV.2 sq., 38, 109; V.124, 148; It 97; Pug 23.

Hiriya (m. & nt.) [fr. hiri] shame, conscientiousness VvA 194.

Hiriyati (hirīyati) [see harāyati] to blush, to be shy; to feel conscientious scruple, to be ashamed Pug 20, 24; Miln 171; Vism 464 (hirīyati); DhsA 149.

Hirivera (nt.) [cp. Sk. hrīvera] a kind of Andropogon (sort of perfume) J VI.537; DA I.81.

Hilādati [hlād] to refresh oneself, to be glad Dhtp 152 (= sukha), 591 (id.).

Hīna [pp. of jahati] 1. inferior, low; poor, miserable; vile, base, abject, contemptible, despicable Vin I.10; D I.82, 98; S II.154 (hīnaŋ dhātuŋ paṭicca uppajjati hīnā saññā); III.47; IV.88, 309 (citta h. duggata); D III.106, 111 sq., 215 (dhātu); A II.154; III.349 sq.; V.59 sq.; Sn 799, 903 sq.; Nd[1] 48, 103, 107, 146; J II.6; Pv IV.1[27] (opp. paṇita); Vv 24[13] (= lāmaka VvA 116); Dhs 1025; DhsA 45; Miln 288; Vism 13; DhA III.163. — Often opposed to ukkaṭṭha (exalted, decent, noble), e. g. Vin IV.6; J I.20, 22; III.218; VbhA 410; or in graduated sequence hīna (> majjhima) > paṇīta (i. e. low, medium, excellent), e. g. Vism 11, 85 sq., 424, 473. See majjhima. — 2. deprived of, wanting, lacking Sn 725 = It 106 (ceto-vimutti°); Pug 35. — hīnāya āvattati to turn to the lower, to give up orders, return to secular life Vin I.17; S II.231; IV.191; Ud 21; A III.393 sq.; M I.460; Sn p. 92; Pug 66; hīnāya vattati id. J I.276; hīnāy'āvatta one who returns to the world M I.460, 462; S II.50; IV.103; Nd[1] 147.

-âdhimutta having low inclinations J III.87; Pug 26; °ika id. S II.157; It 70. -kāya inferior assembly VvA 298 (here meaning Yamaloka); PvA 5. -jacca low-born, low-caste J II.5; III.452; V.19, 257. -vāda one whose doctrine is defective Sn 827; Nd[1] 167. -viriya lacking in energy It 116; DhA I.75; II.260.

Hīyati is Pass. of jahati.

Hīra [cp. late Sk. hīra] 1. a necklace (?) VvA 176. — 2. a small piece, splinter J IV.30 (sakalika°); hīrahīraŋ karoti to cut to pieces, to chop up J I.9; DhA I.224 (+ khaṇḍâkhaṇḍaŋ).

Hīraka [hīra + ka, cp. lexic. Sk. hīraka "diamond"] a splinter; tāla° "palm-splinter," a name for a class of worms Vism 258.

Hīrati is Pass. of harati.

Hīḷana (nt.) & °ā (f.) [fr. hīḍ] scorn(ing), disdain, contempt Miln 357; DA I.276 (of part. "re": hīlana-vasena āmantanaŋ); as °ā at Vbh 353 (+ ohīḷanā); VbbA 486.

Hīḷita [pp. of hīḷeti] despised, looked down upon, scorned Vin IV.6; Miln 227, 251; Vism 424 (+ ohīḷita oññāta etc.); DA I.256.

Hīḷeti [Vedic hīḍ or hel to be hostile; cp. Av. zēaša awful; Goth. us-geisnan to be terrified. Connected also with hiŋsati. — The Dhtp (637) defines by "nindā"] 1. to be vexed, to grieve S I.308; to vex, grieve Vv 84[46]. — 2. to scorn, disdain, to feel contempt for, despise D II.275; Sn 713 (appaŋ dānaŋ na hīḷeyya); J II.258; DA I.256 (= vambheti); DhA IV.97; Miln 169 (+ garahati). — pp. hīḷita.

Huŋ (indecl.) the sound "huŋ" an utterance of discontent or refusal DhA III.108 = VvA 77; Vism 96. Cp. haŋ. hunkāra growling, grumbling Vism 105. hunkaroti to grumble DhA I.173. hunkaraṇa = °kāra DhA I.173 sq. See also huhunka.

Hukku the sound uttered by a jackal J III.113.

Huta [pp. of juhati] sacrificed, worshipped, offered Vin I.36 = J I.83; D I.55; J I.83 (nt. "oblation"); Vv 34[26] (su°, + sudinna, suyiṭṭha); Pug 21; Dhs 1215; DA I.165; DhA II.234.

-āsana [cp. Sk. hutāśana] the fire, lit. "oblation-eater" Dāvs II.43; Vism 171 (= aggi).

Hutta (nt.) [cp. Vedic hotra] sacrifice: see aggi°.

Hunitabba is grd. of juhati "to be sacrificed," or "venerable" Vism 219 (= āhuneyya).

Hupeyya "it may be" Vin I.8; = huveyya M I.171. See bhavati.

Huraŋ (adv.) [of uncertain origin] there, in the other world, in another existence. As prep. with acc. "on the other side of," i. e. before Sn 1084; Nd[1] 109; usually in connection idha vā huraŋ vā in this world or the other S I.12; Dh 20; Sn 224 = J I.96; hurāhuraŋ from existence to existence Dh 334; Th 1, 399; Vism 107; DhA IV.43. — The expl[n] by Morris *J.P.T.S.* 1884, 105 may be discarded as improbable.

Huhunka (adj.) [fr. huŋ] saying "huŋ, huŋ," i. e. grumbly, rough; °jātika one who has a grumbly nature, said of the brahmins Vin I.2; Ud 3 ("proud of his caste" Seidenstücker). nihuhunka (= nis + h.) not grumbly (or proud), gentle Vin I.3; Ud 3. Thus also Kern, *Toev.* I.137; differently Hardy in *J.P.T.S.* 1901, 42 ("uttering & putting confidence into the word huŋ") Bdhgh (Vin I.362) says: "diṭṭha-mangaliko mānavasena kodhavasena ca huhun ti karonto vicarati."

Hūti (f.) [fr. hū, hvā "to call," cp. avhayati] calling, challenging S I.208.

He (indecl.) a vocative (exclam.) particle "eh," "here," hey M I.125, 126 (+ je); DhA I.176 (double).

Heṭṭhato (adv.) [fr. heṭṭhā] below, from below Ps I.84; Dhs 1282, 1284, Mhvs 5, 64.

Heṭṭhā (indecl.) [cp. Vedic adhastāt = adhaḥ + abl. suff. °tāt] down, below, underneath Vin I.15; D I.198; It 114; J I.71; VvA 78; PvA 113. As prep. with gen. (abl.) or cpd. "under" J I.176; II.103; lower in the manuscript, i. e. before, above J I.137, 206, 350; VvA 203; lower, farther on J I.235.

-āsana a lower seat J I.176. -nāsika-(sota) the lower nostril J I.164. -bhāga lower part J I.209, 484. -mañce underneath the bed J I.197 (°mañcato from under the bed); II.275, 419; IV.365. -vāta the wind below, a wind blowing underneath J I.481. -sīsaka head downwards J III.13.

Heṭṭhima (adj.) [compar.-superl. formation fr. heṭṭhā] lower, lowest Vin IV.168; Dhs 1016; Tikp 41; PvA 281; Sdhp 238, 240, 256. °tala the lowest level J I.202.

Heṭhaka (adj.-n.) [fr. heṭheti] one who harasses, a robber J IV.495, 498. Cp. vi°.

Heṭhanā (f.) [fr. heṭheti] harassing D II.243; VbhA 75.

Heṭheti [Vedic **heḍ** = **hel** or **hīḍ** (see hīḷeti)] to harass, worry, injure J IV.446, 471; Pv III.5[2] (= bādheti PvA 198); ppr. a-heṭhayaŋ Dh 49; S I.21. med. a-heṭhayāna S I.7; IV.179; ger. heṭhayitvāna J III.480. — pp. heṭhayita J IV.447.

Hetaŋ = hi etaŋ.

Hetu [Vedic hetu, fr. **hi** to impel] 1. cause, reason, condition S I.134; A III.440 sq.; Dhs 595, 1053; Vism 450; Tikp 11, 233, 239. In the older use paccaya and hetu are almost identical as synonyms, e. g. n'atthi hetu n'atthi paccayo D I.53; aṭṭha hetū aṭṭha paccayā D III.284 sq.; cp. S III.69 sq.; D II.107; M I.407; A I.55 sq., 66, 200; IV.151 sq.; but later they were differentiated (see Mrs. Rh. D., Tikp introd. p. xi. sq.). The diff. between the two is expl[d] e. g. at Nett 78 sq.; DhsA 303. — There are a number of other terms, with which hetu is often comb[d], apparently without distinction in meaning, e. g. hetu paccaya kāraṇa Nd[2] 617 (s. v. sankhā); mūla h. nidāna sambhava pabhava samuṭṭhāna āhāra ārammaṇa paccaya samudaya; frequent in the Niddesa (see Nd[2] p. 231, s. v. mūla). — In the *Abhidhamma* we find hetu as " moral condition " referring to the 6 mūlas or bases of good & bad kamma, viz. **lobha, dosa, moha** and their opposites · Dhs 1053 sq.; Kvu 532 sq. — *Four* kinds of hetu are distinguished at DhsA 303 = VbhA 402, viz. hetu°, paccaya°, uttama°, sādhāraṇa°. Another 4 at Tikp 27, viz. kusala°, akusala°, vipāka°, kiriya°, and 9 at Tikp 252, viz. kusala°, akusala°, avyākata°, in 3 × 3 constellations (cp DhsA 303). — On term in detail see *Cpd.* 279 sq.; *Dhs. trsl*[n] §§ 1053, 1075. — abl. hetuso from or by way of (its) cause S V.304; A III.417. — acc. hetu (-°) (elliptically as adv.) on account of, for the sake of (with gen.); e. g. dāsa-kammakara-porisassa hetu M II.187; kissa hetu why? A III.303; IV.393; Sn 1131; Pv II.8[1] (= kiŋ nimittaŋ PvA 106); pubbe kata° by reason (or in consequence) of what was formerly done A I.173 sq.; dhana° for the sake of gain Sn 122. — 2. suitability for the attainment of Arahantship, one of the 8 conditions precedent to becoming a Buddha Bu II.59 = J I.14, 44. — 3. logic Miln 3.

-paccaya the moral-causal relation, the first of the 24 Paccayas in the **Paṭṭhāna** Tikp 1 sq, 23 sq., 60 sq., 287, 320; Dukp 8, 41 sq.; Vism 532; VbhA 174. -pabhava arising from a cause, conditioned Vin 1.40; DhA 1.92. -vāda the theory of cause, as adj. " proclaimer of a cause," name of a sect M I.409; opp. ahetu-vāda " denier of a cause," (also a sect) M I.408; ahetu-vādin id. J V.228, 241 (= Jtm 149).

Hetuka (adj.) (-°) [fr. hetu] connected with a cause, causing or caused, conditioned by, consisting in Mhvs I, 45 (maṇi-pallanka°); Dhs 1009 (pahātabba°); VbhA 17 (du°, ti°). Usually as sa° and a° (with & without a moral condition) A I.82; Vism 454 sq.; Dukp 24 sq. sa° Dhs 1073 (trsl[n] " having root-conditions as concomitants "); Kvu 533 (" accompanied by moral conditions "); a° S III.210 (°vāda, as a " diṭṭhi "); Vism 450.

Hetutta (nt.) [abstr. formation fr. hetu] reason, consequence; abl. in consequence of (-°) Vism 424 (diṭṭhi-visuddhi°).

Hetuye see bhavati.

Hema (nt.) [cp. Epic Sk. heman] gold D II.187; J VI.574. -jāla golden netting (as cover of chariots etc.) A IV.393; Vv 35[1], 36[2] (°ka). -vaṇṇa golden-coloured D II.134; Th 2, 333; ThA 235; DhsA 317.

Hemanta [hema(= hima) + anta] winter A IV.138; J I.86; Miln 274.

Hemantika (adj.) [fr. hemanta] destined for the winter, wintry, icy cold Vin I.15, 31 (rattiyo), 288; M I.79; S V.51; A IV.127; Vism 73.

Hemavataka (adj.) [fr. himavant] belonging to, living in the Himālaya J I.506; IV.374, 437; °vatika id. Dpvs V.54.

Heraññika (& °**aka**) [fr. hirañña, cp. BSk. hairaṇyika Divy 501; MVastu III.443] goldsmith (? for which suvaṇṇakāra!), banker, money-changer Vism 515 = VbhA 91; J I.369; III.193; DA I.315; Miln 331 (goldsmith ?).

-phalaka the bench (i. e. table, counter) of a money changer or banker Vism 437 = VbhA 115; J II.429; III.193 sq.

Hevaŋ see hi.

Hesati [both **heṣ** (Vedic) & **hreṣ** (Epic Sk.); in Pāli confused with **hṛṣ** (hasati): see hasati[2]] to neigh J I.51, 62 (here hasati); V.304 (T. siŋsati for hiŋsati; C. expl[s] hiŋsati as " hessati," cp. abbihiŋsanā for °hesanā). — pp. hesita.

Hesā (f.) [fr. hesati] neighing, neigh Dāvs V.56.

Hesita (nt.) [pp. of hesati] neighing J I.62 (here as hasita); Mhvs 23, 72.

Hessati is: 1. Fut. of bhavati, e. g. J III.279. — 2. Fut. of jahati, e. g. J IV.415; VI.441.

Hehiti is Fut. 3rd sg. of bhavati, e. g. Bu II.10 = J I.4 (v. 20).

Hoti, hotabba etc. see bhavati.

Hotta (nt.) [Vedic hotra] (function of) offering; aggi° the sacrificial fire SnA 436 (v. l. BB °hutta).

Homa (m. & nt.) [fr. **hu**, juhati] oblation D I.9; DA I.93 (lohita°).

Horāpāṭhaka [late Sk. horā " hour " (in astrol. literature, fr. Gr. ὥρα: cp. Winternitz, *Gesch. d. Ind. Lit.* III.569 sq.) + pāṭhaka, i. e. expert] an astrologer Mhvs 35, 71.

ADDITIONS AND CORRECTIONS.

Note.—A great many suggested additions (esp. to Vol. I.) I have to leave over for a second edition, as a complete enumeration would greatly augment the inconvenience of the following list, "additions" being a nuisance in any case. I have picked out the most important ones only.

VOLUME I.

Page x, *before* Mahāvaŋsa . . ., Khuddhasikkhā, *J.T.P.S.* 1883 (Khus).
,, x, ,, Netti . . ., Mūlasikkhā, *J.P.T.S.* 1883 (Mūls).
,, x, *under* 1a *add* Apadāna P.T.S. 1925 (Ap).
,, x, ,, 1a ,, **Dukapaṭṭhāna**, P.T.S. 1906 (Dukp).
,, x, ,, 1a ,, **Tikapaṭṭhāna**, 3 vols. P.T.S. 1921-23 (Tikp).
,, x, ,, 1b ,, Manoratha-pūraṇī P.T.S. 1924 (AA); Samanta-pāsādikā P.T.S. 1924 (Sam. Pās. or Vin A).
,, x, ,, 1b ,, **Papañca Sūdanī**, pt. I., P.T.S. 1922 (MA).
,, x, ,, 1b ,, Sammoha-Vinodanī, P.T.S. 1923 (VbhA).
,, xi, *after* Visuddhi . . ., Yogāvacara's Manual, P.T.S. 1896 (Yog).
,, xi, *for* Ilaward *read* Harvard.
,, xi, *to* Mahāvastu . . . *add* (Mvst).
,, xi, *under* 2 : The ed. of *Lalitavistara* which I have used, and from which I quote, is the *Calcutta* ed. (1877), by Rājendralāla Mitra (*Bibl. Indica*), and not Lefmann's.
,, xi, ,, 3 *add* Neumann, Die Reden Gotamo Buddha's (Mittlere Sammlung), Vols. I. to III.[2] 1921.
,, xi, ,, 3 *for* Anug *read* S.Z. Aung.
,, xi, ,, 3 *to* Questions of . . . *add* (Miln).
,, xi, ,, 3 *to* Vinaya Texts . . . *add* (Vin T.).
,, xi, ,, 3 *add* *Human Types*, P.T.S. trsl. 1924 (Pug trsl.) *and insert accordingly on p.* xii *under* B 1.
,, xi, ,, 3 ,, Path of Purity, P.T.S. trsl. 1923. 1st pt. (Vism. Trsl.).
,, xi, ,, 4 ,, Brāhmaṇa (Br.).
,, xi, ,, 4 ,, Dhātupāṭha & Dhātumañjūsā. ed. Andersen & Smith, Copenhagen 1921 (Dhtp, Dhtm).
,, xi, ,, 4 ,, Śatapatha-Brāhmaṇa (trsl. J. Eggeling) (Śat. Br.).
,, xii, ,, B, 1 ,, BR. Boehtlingk and Roth.
,, xii, ,, B, 1 ,, Dhtm Dhātumañjūsa . . . 4.
,, xii, ,, B 1 ,, Dhtp Dhātupāṭha . . . 4.
,, xii, ,, B, 1 ,, Dukp = Dukapaṭṭhāna . . . 1a.
,, xii, ,, B, 1 ,, Paṭṭh = Paṭṭhāna : see Duka° & Tika° . . . 1a.
,, xii, ,, B, 1 ,, Tikp = Tikapaṭṭhāna . . . 1a.
,, xii, ,, B, 1 ,, VbhA = Sammoha-Vinodanī . . . 1b.
,, xii, ,, B, 1 ,, Vism. Trsl. = Path of Purity . . . 3.
,, xii, ,, 4 ,, Kirfel, W. Kosmographie der Inder, Bonn & Leipzig 1920.
,, xiii, ,, 2 ,, cond conditional.
,, 1, column 1. l. 25, *read* ā[4] *for* ā[2].
,, 1, ,, 2, *under* akkamana in [ ] *read* Jtm *for* Itm.
,, 4, ,, 2, ,, aggaḷa *insert* 1. (better :) the wing of a door (see phusita[3]).
,, 5, ,, 2, *read* aghamiga *for* aggha°.
,, 6, ,, 2, l. 22, *read* " part or interest (opp. bāhiraŋ the interest in the outside world) "
,, 8, ,, 1, *read* accasārin *for* accasarin.
,, 8, ,, 1, *put* accāvadati *before* accāsanna.
,, 9, ,, 2, *under* aja : aja-pada refers to a stick cloven like a goat's hoof ; so also at Vism 161.
,, 11, ,, 2, ,, ajjhāvuttha *read* osita *for* anosita.
,, 11, ,, 2, l. 3, *read* excessive *for* ecc°.
,, 14, ,, 2, l. 28, ,, believes *for* belives.
,, 15, ,, 2, to p. 17, column 1 headlines *read* Aṭṭha, Aḍḍha *for* Attha, Addha.
,, 15, ,, 2, l. 21 from bottom, *read* symmetry *for* summetry.
,, 17, ,, 1, *under* aḍḍha-rattā *change* J 1.164 *into* 1.264.
,, 17, ,, 1, ,, aḍḍha-telasa *read* 12½ *for* 13½.
,, 19, ,, 1, l. 6, *read* adulteress *for* adultress.
,, 19, ,, 2, l. 9 from top, *read* atidūra *for* atidura.
,, 21, ,, 1, l. 26, *read* late *for* exete.
,, 22, ,, 2, *transfer* atta-kāma *to* attha°.
,, 23, ,, 1, *under* attaniya *read* soul-like *for* soul-lika.
,, 24, ,, 1, *transfer* °kāma *to* precede kāmin.
,, 24, ,, 2, l. 25, *read* phraseology *for* phraselogy.
,, 26, ,, 1, *under* adda[3] *correct* Nd[2] 99[6] *to* Nd[2] 199[6], *and add* : The reading allāvalepana occurs at Nd[2] 40 (= S IV. 187), and is perhaps to be perferred. The meaning is better to be given as " newly plastered."
,, 26, ,, 2, l. 41, *read* period *for* geriod.

Page 27, column 2, *under* adhikaraṇa *read under* yatva° : yato + adhi *for* yat + adhi.
,, 30, ,, 2, *after* anajjhiṭṭha *insert :* **Anati** [An, Vedic aniti & anati] to breathe KhA 1.124 (in def. of bāla); DA 1.244 (*read* ananti *for* aṇanti). Cp. pāṇa.
,, 32, ,, 2, l. 10, *read* unlucky *for* unluckly.
,, 33, ,, 2, l. 11 from bottom, *read* supplementary *for* supplementy.
,, 35, ,, 1, l. 5 ,, ,, ,, move *for* more.
,, 35, ,, 1, *under* anuggaṇhāti *read* D 1.53 *for* T 1.53.
,, 38, ,, 1, l. 30, *read* worldly *for* wordly *and* 67 *for* 97.
,, 38, ,, 2, l. 24, ,, supreme *for* suppreme.
,, 39, ,, 1, *under* anupāta *add* (vāda°) *after* A 1.161.
,, 41, ,, 2, ,, anurakkhaṇa *read* Pug *for* Rug.
,, 42, ,, 1, l. 1 from bottom, *delete* "*in.*"
,, 42, ,, 2, l. 36, *read* facing *the* wind.
,, 42, ,, 2, *read* Anuvāda *for* Anuvada.
,, 43, ,, 2, l. 46, *read* connected *for* nonnected.
,, 44, ,, 1, l. 2, ,, quarrelling *for* quarelling.
,, 44, ,, 1, l. 39, ,, residuum *for* residium.
,, 44, ,, 1, *under* anusaya, l. 11 of article, *read* is *for* il.
,, 45, ,, 2, *read* anūpaghāta *for* anūpghāta.
,, 47, ,, 2, l. 11 from bottom, *read* Trenckner *for* Trenckener.
,, 48, ,, 1, *under* Antarā *read* -gacchati *for* -gattchati.
,, 52, ,, 1, ,, Apapibati *read* J II.126 *for* III.126.
,, 52, ,, 1, l. 16 from bottom, *read* continuous *for* continuou.
,, 54, ,, 2, *under* api l. 6 from bottom, *read* Yasaŋ *for* yasaŋ.
,, 56, ,, 2, l. 8 from bottom, *read* impulsive *for* in°.
,, 57, ,, 1, l. 19 ,, ,, ,, indestructible *for* °able.
,, 59, ,, 1, l. 14, *read* achievements *for* acch°.
,, 69, ,, 1, *read* abhilakkhita *for* ahhilakkhita.
,, 70, ,, 1, l. 19 from bottom, *read* heathenish *for* °isch.
,, 71, ,, 1, l. 2 ,, ,, ,, possessing *for* posess°.
,, 72, ,, 1, l. 11, *read* Abhisambhū *for* Absambhū.
,, 73, ,, 2, *under* Amassuka *read* J II.185 *for* 175.
,, 76, ,, 1, ,, araṇa[1] *cross out* No. 1 *before* (adj.).
,, 76, ,, 2, ,, araṇi *read* sadisa-vaṇṇa *for* sadi-savaṇṇa.
,, 77, ,, 2, Aribhāseti *correct to* Pari° according to Fausböll (J V. corr.)
,, 77, ,, 2, l. 9, *read* spirituous *for* spiritous.
,, 77, ,, 2, l. 11 from bottom, *read* M 1.7, 300 *for* M 1.7, 1.
,, 79, ,, 2, *under* alla 2 *insert* allâvalepana, *see* adda[3].
,, 81, ,, 2, l. 3 from bottom, *read* experiences.
,, 82, ,, 2, *under* Avadāta *read* metri *for* matri.
,, 83, ,, 1, ,, avanata *read* oṇata *for* avaṇata.
,, 86, ,, 1, ,, Avyāpajjha[1] *read* It 31 (abyābajjh') *for* abyābojjh'.
,, 88, ,, 2, ,, Asi *read* (*under* cpds.) : -māla (-kamma) sword-garland (-torture) J III.178; Dāvs III.35. Preferable to interpretation "sword dirt"; see māla (mālā).
,, 89, ,, 1, *after* Asita[3] *put in new article* Asita[4] (m. nt.) [fr. asi] a sickle J III.129; V.46.
,, 89, ,, 1, l. 35, *read* intuiting *for* intuitising.
,, 91, ,, 1, l. 16, ,, intoxicated *for* intoricated.
,, 91, ,, 2, *under* ahaŋ *read* "The encl. form *in* the sg."
,, 93 should have heading Ā at top of page.
,, 98, column 1, *under* āṇi, last line, *read* five *for* fire.
,, 102, ,, 1, ,, āpagā *read* Dāvs 1.32 *for* 52.
,, 102, ,, 2, ,, āpaṇa *read* ā + **paṇ**.
,, 102, ,, 2, ,, āpatti *add* cpd. °vuṭṭhānatā forgiveness of an offence Vin II.250.
,, 103, ,, 2, ,, ābhata *add :* see under yathā-bhaṭa.
,, 103, ,, 1, ,, āpiyati *read* **ṛ** *for* **ṇ**.
,, 103, ,, 2, ,, ābhata *delete* "for yathābhūtaŋ," *and insert ref.* A II.71; It 12, 14 *with phrase* "yathā-bhataŋ as he has been reared (cp. J V.330 evaŋ kicchā bhaṭo)." Cp. yathābhata.
,, 103, ,, 2, ,, ābhāsa *delete* ref. M II.215.
,, 110, ,, 2, ,, ālupa *add :* the form āluva occurs at Ap 237.
,, 111, ,, 2, ,, āvaṭṭa *read* M 1.461 *for* 460.
,, 115, ,, 1, *after* Āsana *insert* Āsana[2] (?) eating Vism 116 (visam°, cp. visam-āsita Miln 302). See, however, māsana.
,, 117, ,, 1, *under* āhanati *add :* 1st sg. fut. āhañhi Vin 1.8; D II.72, where probably to be read as āhañh' (= āhañhaŋ). See Geiger, *P.Gr.* § 153, 2.
,, 123, ,, 2, ,, isi *read* Bhāradvāja *for* Bhara°; *and insert* ref. Vin. 1.245.
,, 125, ,, 2, *invert* ukkāsikā *and next.*
,, 130, ,, 2, *under* uṇha first word in [ ] *read* "Vedic" *instead of* "adj."
,, 133, ,, 2, *cross out* art. udakanti (which is, of course, udakan ti).
,, 139, ,, 2, *under* upakārin *transfer* ref. M 1.86 (= Nd[2] 199[6]) *to* art. upakārikā *in meaning* "fortification."
,, 149, ,, 1, ,, upahata: The formula at D 1.86 (khata + upahata) is doubtful as to its exact meaning. According to Bdhgh it means "one who has destroyed his foundation of salvation," i. e. one who cannot be saved. Thus at DA 1.237: "bhinna-patiṭṭho jāto," i. e. without a basis. Cp. remarks under khata. The trsl[n] at *Dial.* 1.95 gives it as "deeply affected and touched in heart": doubtful. The phrase **upahacca-parinibbāyin** may receive light from **upahata**.

Page 151, top and bottom of column 1, *read* uppajjati *for* upajjati.
,, 155, column 2, *under* ura *read* urasā *for* urusā.
,, 155, ,, 2, ,, uyyutta *read* zealous *for* zeolaus.
,, 157, ,, 1, ,, ussakkati[1] *read* [ud + sakkati] *for* [ud + sṛp].
,, 159, ,, 1, ,, ūkā *add:* is also used as a linear measure (cp. Sk. yūkālikṣaŋ) VbhA 343 (where 7 likkhā are said to equal 1 ūkā).
,, 170, ,, 2, ,, ora *read* M II.142 *for* III.142, *and add* "doubtful reading."
,, 172, ,, 1, ,, osarati *read* [o + sṛ] to *flow*, to go away, . . .
,, 172, ,, 2, *for* ossajati *read* ossajjati, *and for* osajjana *read* ossajjana.

VOLUME II.

,, 8, ,, 1, line 8 fr. bottom, *read* Sn p. 108 *for* Sn 108.
,, 9, ,, 1, half-way down, *under* kat-atta *read* J. VI.296 *for* IV.291.
,, 12, ,, 1, *under* kathalika: the meaning "bowl" seems to be preferable to Bdhgh's forced interpretation as "towel."
,, 12, ,, 2, *after* kathāpeti *insert:* **kathālikā** (f.) [fr. **kuth**, to boil] kettle, cooking pot; in daṇḍa° (a pot with a handle) Vin I.286 (v. l. kathālaka), and meda° A IV.377; DhA II.179.
,, 14, ,, 1, *under* kantita[2]: at Miln 240 better as kantita[1], i. e. "spun."
,, 17, ,, 1, *exchange respective position of articles* Kamati *and* Kamaṇḍalu; *also write* Kamana *as* Kamaṇa.
,, 24, ,, 1, *under* Karaṇa, in Note, *read passage as follows:* Karaṇa here . . . as by J VI.270, where it expls. kappitakesa-massu and J V.309 & DhA I.253, where massukamma takes the place of °karaṇa; and J III.314, where it is represented by massu-kutti (C.: massukiriya). Cp. also DA I.137.
,, 27, ,, 1, ,, kali, line 4, *read* Dh 252 *for* Dh 1.252.
,, 27, ,, 2, ,, Kalyāṇa *read* 5 kalyāṇāni *for* kalyāni.
,, 31, ,, 1, ,, kāṭa-koṭacikā *correct* 1889 *to* 89.
,, 37-38, *transfer* kārā, bottom of p. 37 *to* p. 38, column 1, line 3 from bottom.
,, 58, column 1, *under* kovilāra *delete* "a sort of ebony."
,, 66, ,, 2, ,, khura[1] *add:* khura-kāse M I.446, *read* (with Neumann) *for* khura-kāye, "in the manner of dragging (**kṛṣ**) the hoofs."
,, 67, ,, 1, *after* khura[2] *insert:* **Khulukhulu-karakaŋ** (nt. adv.) "so as to make the sound khulu, khulu," i. e. clattering or bumping about M II.138. Cp. ghuru-ghuru.
,, 67, ,, 2, bottom, *for* kheḷākapa *read* kheḷāpaka . . . cp. āpaka. ? spittle-dribbler; cp. our "wind-bag."
,, 73, ,, 2, *under* gandha *add* as No. 5: occurs as v. l. *for* gantha (book).
,, 81, ,, 2, ,, guṇa[1] 1 *correct* (a) saguṇa according to expl[n] *under* saguṇa.
,, 83, ,, 1, ,, gūtha: °gata is preferably to be trsl[d] as "covered with dung." See id. p. *under* chavālāta *and add* DhsA 247.
,, 84, ,, 2, ,, go-vatika *read* M I.387 *for* 837.
,, 86, ,, 1, ,, ghaŋsati[2] *put* haŋsati *for* hassati.
,, 90, ,, 1, ,, cakkhu, l. 4, *read* M III.134 *for* 136.
,, 93, ,, 1, ,, camu *last line to be read* camūpati a general Mhvs 10, 65; 23, 4; Dāvs 1.3.
,, 100, ,, 1, *insert* **Ādissa**[2] (adj.) blameworthy M I.12; MA = gārayha.
,, 105, ,, 2, in top line *read* J VI.538 *for* 358.
,, 110, ,, 2, *under* jaṭa handle of an *adze* (*instead of* "*razor*").
,, 112, ,, 2, *insert* jalūkā leech DA I.117.
,, 113, ,, 2, *after* jahati *insert:* **Jahita** [pp. of jahati] left, abandoned Sn 231; J I.311.
,, 118, ,, 2, ,, juhati *add:* Caus. hāpeti[2].
,, 120, ,, 2, ,, jhāpeti, ger. jhatvā *add* ref. S I.161 (*reads* chetvā) = Nett 145 (*reads* jhitvā, with v. l. chetvā).
,, 120, ,, 2, ,, jhāyin *insert:* Jhitvā is reading at Nett 145 for jhatvā (see jhāpeti).
,, 127, *after* tajjaniya *insert:* tajjārī a linear measure, equal to 36 anu's and of which 36 form one rathareṇu Vbh 343; cp. Abhp 194 (tajjarī).
,, 134, column 1, *after* tālīsa *insert:* **Tālīsa**[2] (No. 40) is short for cattālīsa, e. g. Ap 103, 234 and passim.
,, 144, ,, 2, *under* thūla *delete* M I.453.
,, 146, ,, 2, ,, dakkhiṇā, in ref. *under* cpd. °visuddhi *read* M III.256 *for* II.256.
,, 147, ,, 2, ,, daṇḍ'ādāna *read:* "comb[d] with satth'ādāna."
,, 149/150 *reverse order* dameti *and* dametar.
,, 150, column 1, *under* darī *read* mūsikā° *for* musikā°.
,, 150, ,, 2, *after* dava[2] *insert:* **Davya** [for *dravya] = dabba[1], in sarīra° fitness of body, a beautiful body J II.137.
,, 152, ,, 2, *under* dahati[1] *add:* pp. hita.
,, 154, ,, 2, ,, dāru *read* dāru yanta a wooden *machine* (not *mill*).
,, 156, ,, 1, ,, diṭṭha-mangalika (of pucchā) *put in the simple trsl[n]:* "a question concerning visible omina."
,, 166, ,, 1, ,, dessin *read* Sn 92 (*for* 93), *and:* better desfn, cp. viddesin.
,, 170, ,, 1, ,, dhaja, l. 4, *read* M I.139 *for* 137.
,, 170, ,, 1, ,, dhañña, l. 3 from bottom, *read* M I.180, 268, *for* 429.
,, 175, ,, 2, *after* dhāta *insert:* **Dhātar** [n. ag. fr. **dhṛ**] upholder J V.225.
,, 189, ,, 2, *under* nikkhepa *read* ref. Vin I.16 as: (pādukānaŋ = the putting down of the slippers, i. e. the slippers as they were put down).
,, 190, ,, 1, ,, nikhanati *read* khanati *for* khanai.
,, 196, ,, 1, ,, nipatati *read* intrs. *for* instr.
,, 209, ,, 1, ,, nivesa *read* nivesana 2 *for* nivesana[3].
,, 209, ,, 2, *after* nisāda *insert:* **Nisādana** [= ni + śātana] grinding DhA I.308.

VOLUME III.

Page 1, column 1, *under* paṇsu in cpd. °kūla *read* " rags " *for* " rays."
" 3, " 1, " pakkamati *read* 2. *for* 2nd.
" 4, " 2, " paguṇa in cpd. °bhāva *read* " familiarity " *for* " familiarly."
" 8, " 1, " pacceka-buddha *read* M III.68 *for* 86.
" 9, " 2, " pajāpati 1, a line was left out (through copyist's error) ; *read as given correctly under* sapajāpatika.
" 12, " 1, " pañcaka (taca°) *read* kesā *for* kosā.
" 12, " 1, " pañjara *add* in comb^{n} sīha° meaning " window."
" 21, " 2, " Paṭivāmeti ; *For* Dh I.39 *read* DA I.39. Cp. *J.P.T.S.* 1886, p. 160, suggesting paṭivādh°, or paṭibādhayamāno, and referring to Th 1, 744.
" 22, " 2, " paṭisakkati *read* [paṭi + sakkati].
" 23, " 1, " paṭisañcikkhati *read* M I.499 *for* 469.
" 23, " 2, " paṭisāraṇa *delete remainder after* " appl^{d}."
" 25, " 2, " paṭhavī, in cpds., *read* °ojā *for* °oja.
" 26, " 2, " paṇḍita *cross out* refs. M I.423 & III.105.
" 27, " 1, *the ref. under* paṇṇaka *is to be read* Kern, *Toev.* II.16.
" 27, " 2, *under* patati *correct* Milo *to* Miln.
" 29, " 2, " pattika^{1} *cross out all refs. after* Sn 418, *and add :* a form **pattikārika** is found, e. g. at J IV.134 ; V.100 ; VI.15, 463 ; Ap 316.
" 31, " 2, " padāna *delete* sapadāna on last line.
" 34, " 2, *after* pantha *insert :* **Panthāna** (*for* saṇṭhāna) at SnA 20 : see saṇṭhāna 3.
" 35, " 1, *under* panna *read* M I.139 *for* 137.
" 36, " 1, " pappaṭaka 2, *read* paṇṇaka *for* pannaka.
" 37, " 1, *after* pabbhāra *insert :* **Pabrūti** [pa + brūti] to speak out, proclaim, declare (publicly) Sn 131, 649, 870, 952 and passim (cp. Nd^{1} 211, 273 ; Nd^{2} 398, 465).
" 38, " 1, *under* pabhāsati *read* [pa + bhāṣ].
" 43, " 1, *at end of* parama *add :* **paramajja-dhamma** [cp. Vedic parama-jyā] the most influential or ruling doctrine M III.7.
" 49, " 2, *under* paridaṇḍa *read* M I.286 *for* 386.
" 51, " 2, " paripuṇṇa *read* M III.276 *for* III.11.
" 62, " 1, " palagaṇḍa *read* A IV.127 *for* V.127.
" 65, " 1, " pavatta *read* M I.344 *as* 243.
" 67, " 2, " pavecchati: another der^{n} suggested by Dr. Barnett in *J.R.A.S.* 1924, 186 is = Sk. pra-vṛścati.
" 71, " 1, " pahara *read* M I. ; *as* M I.123 ;
" 71, " 1, bottom, *read* pahita^{1} *for* pahital.
" 73, " 1, *under* pāṭipadaka *insert after* Vin IV.75 : (f. °ikā), 78.
" 76, " 1, *after* pāpeti *insert :* **Pābhata** [pa + ābhata] brought, conveyed DA I.262 ; SnA 356 (kathā°).
" 76, " 1, *under* pābhati *read* [pa + ā + pp. of **bhṛ**], and *delete* ref. SnA 356 at end.
" 78, " 2, *after* pāsaṇḍa *insert :* **Pāsati** (?) only in " sammaṇ pāsanti " at SnA 321 as expl^{n} of sammāpāsa (q. v.).
" 78, " 2, *under* pāsaṇsa *read* M I.15 *for* M I.5.
" 79, " 2, " piñjita *read* " dyed " *for* died.
" 86, " 1, *on* line 11 fr. top, *after* PvA 68 *delete* 1st. pl. ; *and insert after* apucchatha Sn 1017 ; 1st. pl. apucchimha Sn 1052.
" 96, " 2, *under* pokkhara (cpds.) *read* °sātaka *for* °sataka.
" 97, " 1, " potheti in [ ] *read* **puth = sphuṭ.**
" 98, " 2, " posin *read* Nd^{2} 36 *for* Nd^{1} 39.
" 102, " 2, " phuta^{2} *read* **sphuṭ** *for* **spuṭh**, as under phuṭita.
" 104, " 2, l. 3 from bottom, *read* S II.228 *for* I.228.
" 115, " 1, *read* **byā** *for* **bya**.
" 115, " 2, *under* byāvata: the meaning (wrongly given as " adorned ") is to be deleted. The reading at VvA 213 is doubtful. It may be kāyavyāvaṭa, but dassana-vyāvaṭa is to be preferred (see under vyāvaṭa).
" 122, " 1, " bhamara *read* Lat. fremo *for* " fermo."
" 137, " 2, " mangura *add in* [ ] " the corresponding passage to M I.246 in Lal. V.320 has madgura."
" 139, " 1, " mañca *after* J I.197 *read* " where the domestic pig lies " *for* " where the domestic lies."
" 142, " 1, " maddava *add :* see also sūkara°.
" 143, " 2, " madhuraka *add :* taken as *noun* also by Winternitz (*Rel. gesch. Lesebuch* 301) : " wohl eine zarte Pflanze mit schwachem Stengel." Mr. F. L. Woodward follows me in discarding trsl^{n} " creeper " and assuming one like " intoxicated " (so also UdA, Sinh. ed. p. 165) : see his note on S III.106 trsl^{n} (*K.S.* III.90).
" 155, " 1, " māsa, l. 14 of article, *read* " summer " *instead of* " winter."

VOLUME IV.

" 36, " 1, " lakāra in [ ] *add after* ilankaran " in meaning anchor."
" 36, " 2, " lakkhaṇa 2 b *add :* the 3 lakkhaṇas at Sn 1022 refer to the brahmin Bāvari.
" 51, " 1, " vajja^{1} last word, *read* avajja *instead of* " separately."
" 66, " 2, line 1 fr. top, *under* vādânuvāda *add:* the trsl^{n} of this phrase (used as adj.) at S III.6 (see *K.S.* III.7) is " one who is of his way of thinking."

Page	71, column	2,	*put*	vikkama & vikkamati before vikkaya.
,,	82, ,,	2,	*under*	vinipātika *read* M 1.73 *for* M 1.13.
,,	84, ,,	1,	,,	vipañcita *add at end :* see remark on veyyañjanika.
,,	91, ,,	1,	,,	vimhita *add :* see also vyamhita.
,,	91, ,,	2,	,,	viyācikkhati *add :* pp. vyākhyāta.
,,	93, ,,	2,	,,	virūpa : at Sn 50 virūpa is taken as " various " by Bdhgh (SnA 99), and virūpa-rūpa expl[d] as vividha-rūpa, i. e. diversity, variety. So also the Niddesa.
,,	102, ,,	1,	*on*	vītaraṇsi I have to remark that the reading vīta° seems to be well established. It occurs very frequently in the Apadāna. Should we take it in meaning of " excessive " ? And are we confronted with an attribute of osadhi, the morning star, which points to Babylonian influence (star of the East) ? As it occurs in the Vatthugāthās of the Pārāyanavagga, this does not seem improbable.

AFTERWORD.

1. Dictionary Work.

It had been my intention at the end of the work to give a full account of Pāli lexicography, its history and aims, but as the Dictionary itself has already been protracted more than others and I have wished, I have, in order to save time and to bring the work to a finish, to reserve a detailed discussion of the method of dictionary work for another occasion, and outline here only the essentials of what seems to me worth mentioning at all events.

When Rhys Davids in 1916 entrusted me with the work, he was still hopeful and optimistic about it, in spite of the failure of the first Dictionary scheme, and thought it would take only a few years to get it done. He seemed to think that the material which was at hand (and the value of which he greatly overrated) could be got ready for press with very little trouble. Alas! it was not so. For it was not merely and not principally a rearrangement and editing of ready material: it was creative and re-creative work from beginning to end, building an intellectual (so to say *manomaya*) edifice on newly sunk foundations and fitting all the larger and smaller (*khuddakânukhuddakāni*) accessories into their places. This was not to be done in a hurry, nor in a leisurely way. It was a path which often led through jungle and thicket, over stones and sticks: "vettācāro sankupatho pi ciṇṇo" (J III.541).

On the road many allurements beset me in the shape of *problems* which cropped up, whether they referred to questions of grammar, syntax, phonology, or etymology; or literature, philosophy, and Buddhist psychology. I had to state them merely as problems and collect them, but I dared not stand still and familiarize with them. Thus much material has been left over as "chips from the dictionary workshop." These I hope I shall some day find an opportunity of working out.

For the first part of the way I had to a great extent the help and guidance of my teacher and friend Rhys Davids; but the second half I had to go quite alone,—Fate did not spare him to see the work right through. I am sure he would not have been less glad than myself to-day to see the task finished.

It happens that with the completion of the P.T.S. Dictionary, the *second* dictionary of Pāli, we celebrate the fiftieth anniversary of the appearance of the *first* Pāli Dictionary by R. C. Childers. That work was a masterpiece of its time, and still retains some of its merits. Our dictionary will not altogether replace Childers, it will supplement him. The character of Childers' Dictionary is so different from ours, there is such an enormous discrepancy between the material which he had for his work and which we had for ours, that it would almost be a farce to recast Childers. We needed something entirely different and original. Childers has now only historical value. Considering that Childers has no references to any of the P.T.S. publications, and that the Pāli Dictionary embraces all the material of these publications as well as of others, we may well speak of an entirely new dictionary, which is essential for the study of Pāli Buddhism from its *sources*, a task which can never be accomplished with Childers alone.[1]

Yet it may be interesting to compare merely on the surface the two dictionaries. The "new" Pāli Dictionary contains 146,000 authentic references against some 38,500 of Childers (of which only half are authentic); the number of head-words treated amounts to 17,920 against 11,420, after omitting in ours about 900 words which Childers gives with an Abhp reference only. Anybody will admit that substantial progress is evidenced by these figures.

[1] In this connection I may quote a remark by a competent critic (Mr. E. J. Thomas), who says: "Rhys Davids wanted to make the Pāli Dictionary 'twice as good as Childers,' but it is far more than that."

2. History of the Dictionary Scheme.

The idea of the Pāli Dictionary, as now published, was first put forth by Rhys Davids in September 1902 (on the thirteenth *International Oriental Congress* at Hamburg). It was to be compiled on the basis of the texts issued by the P.T.S. since its foundation in 1882, and it was conceived on an international plan, according to which some seven or eight famous Sanskrit scholars of Europe should each contribute to the work. Every one of them was enthusiastic about it. In 1903 Rhys Davids announced that the Dictionary would be published in 1905, or at latest in 1906. When I was studying Pāli with Ernst Windisch in 1904 I was undecided, whether I should buy a "Childers" then, or wait until the "International Dictionary" should be out in 1905. Little did I dream that I should have had to wait till I myself finished the International Dictionary in 1925! By 1909 only one-eighth of the work had been done. Gradually the co-workers sent back the materials which Rhys Davids had supplied to them. Some had done nothing at all, nor even opened the packets. Only Messrs. Duroiselle, Konow, and Mrs. Bode had carried out what they had undertaken to do. After Rhys Davids had again conferred with his colleagues at the Copenhagen Congress in 1908, he published the full scheme of the Dictionary in *J.P.T.S.* for 1909. Then the War came and stopped the plans for good.

The failure of the original scheme teaches us that dictionary work cannot be done *en passant* and in one's spare time; it requires one's whole time. At any rate, they were very disappointing years for my friend, and he had almost despaired of the vitality of his pet plan, when, in 1916, he asked me, under the auspices of the P.T.S. and with his assistance, to do the Dictionary on a uniform plan. So he left the compiling to me, and I set to work, conferring with him at frequent intervals. He revised my work. This had become more exhaustive than was planned, because double the amount of texts had been published by 1922 than in 1902. This was a gain for the Dictionary, but meant much more work for the editor.

3. My Material.

The Pāli Dictionary is in a certain respect the result of the work of many. It is a résumé of all the indexes to the texts, so that every indexer has his or her share in the work. But the indexes do not give translations, and thus the main work was often left to me: to find the most correct and adequate English term for the Pāli word. It needs careful and often intricate study to accomplish this task, for even the most skilled and well-read translators have either shirked the most difficult words, or translated them wrongly or with a term which does not and cannot cover the idea adequately. Thus many a crux retarded the work, not to speak of thousands of incorrectnesses in the text of the printed editions.

A few contributors gave more (like Mrs. Bode and Professor Duroiselle), but only from scanty material and texts up to 1909. Rhys Davids' material, copied from his copy of Childers (which was bequeathed him by Childers, interleaved by the binder and filled in from 1878 to 1916), was partly old, and mostly without the English translation, which was only to be found here and there in his translated texts.

Mrs. Rhys Davids has shown her constant sympathy with the work, and I am indebted to her for many suggestions, especially concerning psychological termini. She also condensed and revised my articles on *viññāṇa* and *saṅkhāra*.

To summarize what actual help I have received by using materials other than my own, I have to state that I found the following contributions of use:

(1) For the *whole* alphabet:

All the indexes to the P.T.S. publications.[1] Rhys Davids' annotations to his Childers, representing about 10 per cent. of all important references. Kern's additions to Childers' (Tœvœgselen); to be taken with caution in translations and explanations, but at least equal to Rhys Davids' in extent and importance.[2] Hardy's occasional slips and references (5 per cent. of the whole).

(2) For *single* letters:

Mrs. Bode's collection of **B** and **Bh**. Professor Konow's collection of **S** (*J.P.T.S.* 1909) and **H** (ibid. 1907), which I have used very extensively, after correcting them and bringing them up to date. Professor Duroiselle's collection of one-half of **K** and Mr. E. J. Thomas' **Ñ**.

[1] Many of these are very faulty (the *Kvu trsl*ⁿ word index contains 60 per cent. of error). The only index with which I have no fault to find is that to Sn and SnA by Helmer Smith.

[2] It is to be regretted that this valuable collection is marred by any amount of errors and misprints (see also below, 4 end).

4. How to Judge the Dictionary.

(*a*) I have already given a fairly exhaustive list of abbreviations. To these might be added a good many more if we were writing a dictionary for inexperienced people. The less explanations necessary in a dictionary, the better: it should explain itself; and if there are any little things not intelligible at first, they will become so with gradual use. A dictionary is like a friend with whom you have to get thoroughly acquainted before you come to know his peculiarities.

A dictionary can be too explicit: it will then lose its charm and become tedious. It must contain a certain amount of hints, instead of ready solutions; the more it arouses the curiosity (and sometimes the anger !) of its user, the better it is for the latter. The main purpose of the dictionary is to explain; it is a means of education as well as of information. To this category belong the (sometimes objected to) grammatical and etymological hints. I am fully aware that they are incomplete and sometimes perhaps problematic, but that does not matter so much in a *provisional* dictionary. It does our students good to get a little etymology thrown in once in a while. It makes them interested in the psychology of language, and teaches them the wide range of sound changes, besides making them aware of their study as a thing that has been alive and through a process of *werden*. We are still at a stage of Pāli philology, where we can hardly get enough of that kind of thing.

(*b*) The following are a few additional explanations concerning the use of the Dictionary.—In the Jataka quotations I have not distinguished between the *text* and the *commentary* (J and JA). That is rather a pity; but it was my colleague's wish. We might also have kept the index figures of lines, as it is sometimes very difficult to find a word in the small-print C. portions of the J. books.—Difficult forms, although belonging to some one verb in question, I have given separately, as a help for the student.—The Causatives have undergone a mixed treatment: sometimes they are given under the simple verb, especially when their form was not very different, sometimes separately, when their form was unusual.—The problem of the derivation of Pāli words is not cleared yet. We have interchanged between the Pāli and the Sanskrit derivations.—An asterisk with Sanskrit words (*Sk.) means that the word is late and found only in technical literature, i. e. either gram.-lexic. (like **Amarakośa**), or professional (like **Suśruta**).—For convenience' sake we have identified the guttural **ṅ** with the dental **n**.—The cerebral **ḷ** follows upon **l**.—P.D. refers to Pāli Dictionary.

(*c*) Many of the Dictionary's faults are to be excused by the fact that its composition covers a number of years, and that printing was going on all the time (a great drawback for the unity of the work !), so that changes could not be made in earlier parts, which were found advisable later. Here belong: 1. Roots and compounds cropped up which are not foreseen in the beginning.— 2. Cross-references are not always exact. — 3. There exists a certain inaccuracy in the relation between words beginning with **ava°** and **o°**. At first these were treated jointly, but later separated.—4. Several mistakes were found in Rhys Davids' excerpts later and are, like others which I have corrected (see e. g. **veyyāvacca**), to be explained by lack of material, or by Rhys Davids being misled through Childers.—5. Many explanations are only tentative. I would change them now, but refrain from discussing them in the "Addenda," since too many of these confuse rather than enlighten the student. To these belong e. g. **nibbedha** and **vipañcita** (which ought to be **viyañjita**).— 6. It could hardly be avoided that, in the course of the work, a problem has presented itself with different solutions at different times, so that discrepancies have arisen with one and the same word. These cases, however, are rare.

(*d*) Now, after all this, what is the Dictionary, and what does it claim to be ? First of all, it is meant to be a dictionary of Classical and Literary Pāli. Words only found in native vocabularies (the **Abhp** e. g.) are left out, as they are only Pāli adaptations of Sanskrit words (mostly lexicographical: **sannakaddu=sannakadru**, Am.K. only). Nor are we concerned with Inscriptions. Thus it is intended as a general stock-taking of the Pāli Canon, and a revision of all former suggestions of translations. It is essentially a working basis for further study and improvement. The main object has been to bring as much material as possible to serve future work, and this in a clear and attractive form. Many words remain doubtful. We have given them with **Buddhaghosa's** interpretation, which may be right and which may be wrong. There are some words of which we shall never know the exact meaning, just as it is difficult even in modern times to know the exact meaning of, say, an English or German dialect word.[1]

[1] Other specific terms with a "doctrinal" import are best left untranslated, since we are unable to translate them adequately with our Western Christian terminology. See remarks under **sankhāra** and cp. Mrs. Rhys Davids in *K.S.* III., preface p. v.

(*e*) What are the critics to remember? To find fault with the interpretation of one or the other word is alright, but it must be remembered that, within a few years—which are nothing compared with the life-study required for this purpose—not a few score or a few hundreds of words had to be examined in every detail, but many thousands. Any criticism shows just what the editor himself has felt all along: how much is to be done yet, and how important for Indological studies is the study of Pāli.

Many mistakes and misprints have to be taken with good grace: they are unavoidable; and I may add as an example that Professor Konow's S, in spite of very careful work, contain *one* mistake (or misprint) on almost every page, while the proportion of them in Kern's 315 pages of Tœvœgselen is *four* on every page! We are all human. The discovery of faults teaches us one thing: to try to do better.

5. Issues Involved in the Pāli Dictionary.

It would easily fill a separate volume, if I were to discuss fully all the issues dependent on the new Dictionary, and its bearing on all parts of Buddhist studies. I confine myself to mentioning only a few that are outstanding.

(*a*) Through a full list of references to nearly every word we are now able to establish **better readings** than has been possible up to now. The Pāli Dictionary is indispensable to any editor of new texts.

(*b*) Through sifting the vocabulary we can distinguish several **strata of tradition**, in place as well as in time.

(*c*) The relation of Classical Pāli to **Vedic** and other stages of **Sanskrit** is becoming clearer, as also is the position of Epic Pāli to **Singhalese** and **Tamil**. A good example of the former is offered by the relation of **ava°** to o°. With regard to the term "Vedic" a word of warning has to be uttered. There is an *older* **stratum** of direct Vedic connection in the four Nikāyas; nevertheless in the majority of cases the term is misleading, as we here have to deal with *late* Pāli words which have been reintroduced from Classical Sanskrit à la Renaissance.

It was Rhys Davids' wish, however, that I should use the term "Vedic," whenever a word dated back to that period. — On the subject in general and the linguistic character of Pāli see Childers, Introduction, pp. xiv, xv (with note 1); R. O. Franke, *Pāli and Sanskrit*, Strassburg 1902, especially chapters VII. to XII.[1]

(*d*) The peculiar interrelation between Buddhist Pāli and **Buddhist Sanskrit** can now be stated with greater accuracy.

(*e*) Through a tabulation of all **parallel passages**, given in the Pāli Dictionary, we are now able to compose a complete concordance.

(*f*) From many characteristics, as pointed out in the Pāli Dictionary, we can state with certainty that Pāli was a natural **dialect**, i. e. the language of the people. We can now group the canonical books according to their literary value and origin.[2]

(*g*) It will now be possible to write the history of terms.[3]

(*h*) We cannot always equate Pāli: Classical Sanskrit. It is a wrong method to give the Sanskrit form of a Pāli word as its ultimate reduction and explanation. Sometimes Pāli formation and meaning are different from the **Sanskrit**. Popular language and "Volksetymologie" are concerned here.[4]

[1] Thus some very old (Vedic) words are not found in Classical Pāli, but occur later in the Epics (the Vaŋsas), e. g. sārameya "dog," although Vedic, is only found in Mhbv; sūnu, as frequent as *putra* in Rigveda, occurs only in Mhvs, whereas putta is the regular Pāli word. These examples may be increased by hundreds from the Vaŋsas. There are many more than Rhys Davids assumed on p. vi of preface to Pāli Dictionary.

[2] Therefore we can never have a "standardized" Pāli in the sense in which we are used to "Sanskrit." Among the many signs of popular language (mentioned elsewhere, e. g. Childers introduction) I may also point to the many onomatopœtic words (see note on gala), and the widespread habit of the reduplicative compounds (see my article "Reduplikationskomposita im Pāli," *Zeitschr. f. Buddhismus* vi., 1925, pp. 89-94).

[3] We have material enough to treat philosophical terms (like citta, dhamma, mano, viññāṇa, sankhāra) historically, as well as others of folkloristic importance (e. g. deva, yakkha, vimāna). Light will be thrown on the question of the Mahāpurisalakkhaṇas, which it is interesting to note are in Sn 1022 attributed to Bāvari (i. e. the "Babylonian"), and clearly point to the late origin of the Vatthugāthās as well as to Babylonian influence.

[4] Pāli alla means "clean" as well as "wet" (in spite of *J.R.A.S.* 1924, 186), whereas Sanskrit ārdra means "wet"; Pāli sālūra means "dog," but Sanskrit śālūra "frog"; the root svid has the specific Pāli meaning "boil" or "cook." Many others in the Pāli Dictionary; cp. Childers, p. xv.

(*i*) The Pāli Dictionary affords an interesting comparison of our own interpretation of terms with the fanciful etymological play of words given by the Commentators, which throws a light both on their dogmatic bias and their limited linguistic knowledge. It is quite evident that Bdhgh did not know Sanskrit. — In matters of *grammar* I place Dhammapāla higher than Buddhaghosa.[1]

(*k*) In short, the Pāli Dictionary gives clues to a variety of problems, which it was hitherto almost impossible to approach; the proper study of Pāli Buddhism is aided greatly by it, and an endless field of work lies open to future scholars. On the other hand, nobody realizes more than I do after ten years of intimate study, how far behind the "Classics" we are, both in analysis and synthesis, in explanation, interpretation, and application. And also: that it will be worth the trouble to explore more thoroughly that range of civilization which lies enshrined in the Pāli Canon.[2]

6. Conclusion.

That my share in the actual working out of the Dictionary preponderates over his own, I am sure Rhys Davids would not mind: on the contrary, it was his wish from the beginning that it should be so, and he would repudiate any attempt which would put the faults to my blame and the merits to his credit. His mind was more bent on other aims than dictionary work, which was not his strongest point. But without him there would not have been this Pāli Dictionary.

I cannot conclude without extending my sincere thanks to all those who have made it possible for me to complete the work, and have helped me directly or indirectly with encouragements of various kinds. Among the former are the subscribers to the Dictionary Fund (especially generous Japanese donors); those who have unselfishly handed over to me material collected by themselves, or have assisted me with the copying of indexes, or suggested corrections and given valuable reviews. Above all the Founder of the Pāli Text Society and Mrs. Rhys Davids, who helped me with many suggestions *re* details and with reading the proofs; and last not least my wife, who has been untiring in copying the whole MS. for the printer.

For all deficiencies I sincerely apologize. Had I had another twenty years' experience of Pāli, I would have made a better job of it; but our motto was "Better now and imperfect than perfect and perhaps never!" By no means do I leave the work with a feeling of self-satisfaction. I realize now that I am only at the beginning of the "Perfect" Dictionary. May I, within the next twenty years, see a second edition of the Pāli Dictionary which will come nearer to the ideal. But then the ideal will have moved farther away accordingly! Until then I hope that the "Provisional" Dictionary will do its service and will prove a help to students and scholars of Pāli alike!

W. STEDE.

227, Valley Road,
Streatham,
London, S.W. 16.

April, 1925.

[1] There are more than a score of instances which prove this point, but the following is especially interesting. The word for "whole, entire" vissa is extremely frequent in Vedic and Sanskrit (= viśva), but unknown in Pāli (where sabba takes its place), except for *one* passage in the Dh. (266). Had Bdhgh known Sanskrit, he would have explained it as "sabba," but instead of that he takes it as *visra (musty), which (as a lexic. word) was current in late Pāli, but does not fit the passage mentioned. — Among other errors B explains "stiffness" (swoon) by "calati" (see under chambhita and mucchañcikatā); in parājita he takes parā as instr. of para (= parena DhA III.259); he connects Pāli piṇeti with pinvati (DA I.157, cp. Vism 32 piṇana), and he explains attamana as "saka-mana" (DA I.255), thus equalling atta = ātman.

[2] In connection with this I may point out that one of the greatest needs of Pāli scholarship is a Dictionary of Names. To insert names into this dictionary was not our intention, although more than once I was tempted, and doubtful as to the category of "names," e. g. whether to regard names of trees and months, or titles of books as "names" or "words." Thus the Name Dictionary will be an indispensable supplement to the Word Dictionary. I hope that I shall be placed in a position which will make it possible to edit this supplement, for which Rhys Davids and myself have already collected a large amount of material.